Webster's New World™ Encyclopedia

Webster's New World™ Encyclopedia

Prentice Hall

New York London Toronto Sydney Tokyo Singapore

PRENTICE HALL GENERAL REFERENCE
15 Columbus Circle
New York, New York, 10023

Library of Congress Cataloging-in-Publication Data
Webster's new world encyclopedia.
p. cm.
Rev. ed. of: *The Hutchinson Encyclopedia*. Ninth Edition 1990.
ISBN 0-13-947482-X
1. Encyclopedias and dictionaries. I. Prentice-Hall, inc. II. Hutchinson Encyclopedia.
AG5.W386 1992
032—dc20 91-43020
CIP

First published (as *Hutchinson's Twentieth Century Encyclopedia*) 1948, Second edition 1951, Third edition 1956, Fourth edition (as *Hutchinson's New 20th Century Encyclopedia*) 1964, Fifth edition 1970, Sixth edition (as *The New Hutchinson 20th Century Encyclopedia*) 1977, Seventh edition 1981, Revised impressions 1978 (twice), 1982, 1984, 1986, 1987, Eighth edition (*The Hutchinson Encyclopedia*) 1988, Revised and updated 1989, Ninth edition 1990.

Set in Century Old Style

Pagination and typesetting by Intype, London
Printed and bound in the United States of America

10 9 8 7 6 5 4 3 2 1

First Prentice Hall Edition

Acknowledgments

For permission to reproduce illustrations and copyright material we are grateful to the following:

Ace Photo Library
Alinari-Giraudon
All Souls' College, Oxford
Allsport Photographic
Heather Angel
Arcaid
Ardea
G Ronald Austing
Australian Information Service
Austrian State Tourist Department
Baltimore Museum of Art
Clive Barda
Barnaby's Picture Library
BBC Hulton Picture Library
Belgian National Tourist Office
Boehm
Bridgeman Art Library
British Antarctic Survey
British Museum, London
British Nuclear Fuels
British Petroleum Company
British Tourist Authority
Bubbles Photo Library
Syndics of Cambridge University
Camera Press
Canadian National Railways
J Allan Cash
Cavendish Laboratory, University of Cambridge
Central Electricity Generating Board
Central Office of Information
Central Press Photos Ltd
Christie's, London
Michael Clark
Bruce Coleman
Commissioners of Public Works in Ireland
Commonwealth Secretariat
Courtauld Institute Galleries
Crown Copyright
Daily Telegraph
Danish Tourist Board
Douglas Dickens
Duckwork & Co Ltd
Dulwich Picture Gallery
Esso Petroleum Company
E-T Archive
Thomas Fall Ltd
Feature-Pix
Financial Times
Fox Photos
Foxboro Co.
Peter Fraenkel
Frank Spooner Pictures
French Railways
Friends of the Earth
Galerie otto Stangli, Munich
GeoScience Features Picture Library
Geoslides Photo Library
Gernsheim Collection
Sally and Richard Greenhill
Susan Griggs Agency
Hale Observatories
Hewlett Packard
John Hillelson Agency Ltd
Historical Museum, Vienna
Michael Holford
Eric Hosking
Paul Howard
Hutton-Deutsch Collection
Humber Bridge Board
Hutchinson Picture Library
Ikon
Image Bank
Imperial Chemical Industries
Imperial War Museum, London
India Information Service
Indian Tourist Office
Information Service of the European Communities
Italian State Tourist Office
Japan National Tourist Organization
Japan Information and Cultural Centre
John Soane Museum, London
Keystone Photos
Lacock Abbey Collection
Anthony Lambert
Lambeth Palace Library
Lauros-Giraudon
Lebanese National Tourist Council
Lefevre Gallery (Alex Reid & Lefevre Ltd)
Gary C Lewis
Lewis Walpole Library, Yale University
Library of Congress
London Corporation
London Transport Executive
Lufthansa
Mansell Collection
Marconi Communication Systems
Marineland, Florida
Marlborough Fine Art (London) Ltd
Mary Evans Picture Library
Maxim
Godfrey MacDominic
Angus McBean
McCill University
Merseyside County Art Galleries
Meteorological Office
Michael Nicholson
Military Archive and Research Services
David Munro
John Murray
Musèe du Louvre
Museum of London
Museum of Modern Art, New York
NASA
National Army Museum
National Film Archive, London
National Galleries of Scotland
National Gallery, London
National Library of Australia
National Portrait Gallery, London
National Travel Association of Denmark
National Trust
Peter Newark's Western Americana
Norwegian Embassy
Novosty Press Agency
Philadelphia Museum of Art
Photo Source
Photographers Photo Library
Axel Poignant
Popperfoto
Beatrix Potter Trust
Punch Publications
QA Photos Ltd
RAF Museum
The Registrar General
REX Features
Fulvio Roiter
Romanian National Tourist Office
Ann Ronan Picture Library
Royal Astronomical Society
Royal Collection, Windsor
Royal College of Music
Royal Danish Ministry of Foreign Affairs
Royal Doulton
Royal Greenwich Observatory
Royal Observatory, Edinburgh
Royal Norwegian Agency
RTHPL
Sachem Publishing Associates
Science Museum, London
Science Photo Library
Society for Anglo-Chinese Understanding
Sotheby Parke Bernet & Co
Spanish National Tourist Authority
Christian Steiner
Sugar Bureau
Survival Anglia
Sutcliffe Gallery
Swiss National Tourist Office
Tate Gallery, London
Thai National Tourist Office
Thames Water
The Times
John Topham Picture Library
US Department of the Interior
USIS
Michael Upshall
Mireille Vautier
Vautier-De Nanxe
Victoria and Albert Museum, London
Virago Press
Virgin Group
Walker Art Gallery, Liverpool
Penelope Wallace
Wallace Collection
Western American Picture Library
Witt Library
Prof. H. Wright Baker
Yerkes Regional Primate Center
Zoological Society of London

Editors

Editors
Stephen P Elliott
Martha Goldstein
Michael Upshall

Project Editors
Suzanne Stone Burke
Valerie Buckingham
Helen Varley

Database Editors
Denise Dresner
Claire Jenkins
Sara Jenkins-Jones
Frances Lass

Text Editors
Richard Shaw
Christine Lindberg Stevens

Chief Proofreader
Eileen M Gaffney

Proofreaders
Carol O Behrman
Donald M Lefebvre
Rebecca Lyon
Laurie Romanik
David Travers

Editorial Assistants
Stephen P Elliott, Jr
David Leviton

Office Administration
Anne von Broen
Diane Bell Surprenant

Design
Terry Caven
Edna A Moore, Tek Art

Cartography
Swanston Graphics
Cedric Robson
Eric Smith
Malcolm Ward

Database Software
BRS Software Products

Picture Research
Jane Lewis

Contributors

David Armstrong PhD
Christine Avery MA, PhD
John Ayto MA
Lionel Bender BSc, ChBiol, MIBiol
David Benest
Malcolm Bradbury BA, MA, PhD, Hon D Litt, FRSL
Brendan Bradley MA, MSc, PhD
Roy Brigden BA, FMA
John O E Clark BSc
Mike Corbishley BA, FSA, MIFA
David Cotton BA, PhD
Nigel Davis MSc
Ian D Derbyshire MA, PhD
J Denis Derbyshire BSc, PhD, FBIM
Peter Dews PhD
Dougal Dixon BSc, MSc
Professor George du Boulay FRCR, FRCP, Hon FACR
Robin Dunbar BA, PhD
Suzanne Duke
Jane Farron BA
Peter Fleming BA, PhD
Linda Gamlin BSc, MSc
Derek Gjertsen BA
Lawrence Garner BA
Robert Halasz
Michael Hitchcock PhD
Jane Insley MSc
H G Jerrard PhD
Brian Jones
Roz Kaveney BA
Robin Kerrod FRAS
Charles Kidd
Stephen Kite B Arch, RIBA
Peter Lafferty
Chris Lawn BA, MA
Judith Lewis LLB
Mike Lewis MBC
Graham Ley BA, MPhil
Carol Lister BSc, PhD
Graham Littler BSC, MSc, FSS
Robin Maconie MA
Morven MacKilop
Tom McArthur PhD
Karin Mogg BSc, MSc, PhD
Bob Moore BA, PhD
Ian Morrison
David Munro BSc, PhD
Daniel O'Brien MA
Robert Paisley PhD
Carol Place BSc, PhD
Michael Pudlo MSc, PhD
Ian Ridpath FRAS
Adrian Room MA
John Rowlinson BSc, MSc, CChem, FRSC
Walter Saxon
Jack Schofield BA, MA
William Shapiro
Mark Slade MA
Angela Smith Ba
Imogen Stooke Wheeler, Director of Choreography
Glyn Stone
Ingrid von Essen
Stephen Webster BSc, MPhil
Liz Whitelegg BSc

Introduction

The true measure of an encyclopedia's worth must be how useful it is to the general reader at whom it is aimed, not to the expert. Any prospective reader consulting the *Webster's New World Encyclopedia* is therefore asked to look, not only at a subject they are familiar with but also at a topic about which they know little or nothing. Does the entry inform? Does it include up-to-date facts and figures? Is it accurate? Does it provide a useful introduction to the subject? Is it easy to understand? If relevant, is there a helpful illustration? If the answer to all these questions is yes, then the encyclopedia can be judged a success. This 1st edition of *Webster's New World Encyclopedia* has been written, edited, and illustrated with these aims in mind.

Arrangement of entries

Entries are ordered alphabetically, as if there were no spaces between words. Thus entries for words beginning "federal" follow the order:

Federal Bureau of Investigation
Federalism
Federal Reserve System

However, we have avoided a purely mechanical alphabetization in cases where a different order corresponds more with human logic. For example, sovereigns with the same name are grouped according to country and then by number, so that King George II of England is placed before George III of England, and not next to King George II of Greece. Words beginning "Mc" and "Mac" are treated as if they begin "Mac"; and "St" and "Saint" are both treated as if they were spelled "Saint."

Cross references

These are shown by a ◊ symbol immediately preceding the reference. Cross referencing is selective; a cross reference is shown when another entry contains material directly relevant to the subject matter of any entry, and where the reader may not otherwise think of looking. We do not believe that the existence of a cross reference alone is sufficient for the reader; the encyclopedia should be an aid, not an obstacle course. We have therefore avoided as far as possible entries that consist only of a cross reference; even the shortest cross reference gives some indication of the subject involved.

Foreign names and titles

Names of foreign sovereigns and places are usually shown in their English form, except where the foreign name is more familiar; thus, there are entries for Charles V of Spain, but Juan Carlos (not John Charles), and for Florence, not Firenze. Entries for titled people are under the name by which they are best known to the general reader: thus Anthony Eden, not Lord Avon. Cross references have been provided in cases where confusion is possible.

Units

Measurements of distances, temperatures, sizes, and so on show the English unit first, followed by the metric equivalent. SI (metric) units are used throughout for scientific entries. Entries are also included for many weights and measures no longer in common use.

Science and technology

It would be needlessly pedantic to insist on formally correct terminology for every scientific entry in cases where another name is at present far more familiar. Technical terms and current terminology must of course be included. However, many of these terms are not in common use. Entries are therefore generally placed under the name by which they are better known, with the technical term given as a cross reference. To make it easier for the non-specialist to understand, technical terms are frequently explained when used within the text of an entry, even though they may have their own entry elsewhere.

Systems of government

Individual countries are identified as one of the following systems: liberal democracy, emergent democracy, communism, nationalistic socialism, authoritarian nationalism, military authoritarianism, and absolutism.

Chinese names

Pinyin, the preferred system for transcribing Chinese names of people and places, is generally used: thus there is an entry at Mao Zedong, not Mao Tse-tung. An exception is made for a few names that are more familiar in their former (Wade-Giles) form, such as Sun Yat-sen and Chiang Kai-Shek. Where confusion is likely, Wade-Giles forms are given as cross references.

Webster's New World™ Encyclopedia

A in music, the concert pitch or "concert A" to which instruments of the orchestra are tuned. Today concert A is usually standardized at 440 cycles per second (Hz), although orchestras in Europe are known to favor 442 or 448 cycles per second. Concert pitch has risen from about 424 since the Baroque period.

A in physics, symbol for ◊ampere, a unit of electrical current.

A1 abbreviation for first class (of ships).

Aachen (French *Aix-la-Chapelle*) German cathedral city and spa in the *Land* of North Rhine–Westphalia, 45 mi/72 km SW of Cologne; population (1988) 239,000.

It has thriving electronics, glass, and rubber industries, and is one of Germany's principal railroad junctions. Aachen was the Roman Aquisgranum, and from the time of Charlemagne until 1531 the German emperors were crowned there. Charlemagne, born and buried in Aachen, founded the cathedral 796.

In World War II, Aachen was the first major German town captured by the Allies (Oct 20, 1944).

Aalborg (Danish *Ålborg*) port in Denmark 20 mi/32 km inland from the Kattegat, on the S shore of the Limfjord; population (1988) 155,000. One of Denmark's oldest towns, it has a castle and the fine Budolfi church.

Aalst (French *Alost*) industrial town (brewing, textiles) in East Flanders, Belgium, on the river Dender 15 mi/24 km NW of Brussels; population (1982) 78,700.

Aalto Alvar 1898–1976. Finnish architect and designer. One of Finland's first Modernists, his architectural style was unique, characterized by asymmetry, curved walls, and contrast of natural materials. Among his buildings are the Hall of Residence at the Massachusetts Institute of Technology, Cambridge, Massachusetts 1947–49; Technical High School, Otaniemi 1962–65; and Finlandia Hall, Helsinki 1972. He designed a new form of laminated bent plywood furniture in 1932 and won many design awards for household and industrial items.

Aaltonen Wäinö 1894–1966. Finnish sculptor best known for his monumental figures and busts portraying citizens of Finland, following the country's independence in 1917. He was one of the early 20th-century pioneers of direct carving and favored granite as his medium.

The bronze monument to the athlete Nurmi (1925, Helsinki Stadium) and the bust of the composer Sibelius (1928) are examples of his work. He also developed a more somber style of modern classicism, well suited to his public commissions, such as the allegorical figures in the Finnish Parliament House (1930–32).

aardvark (Afrikaans, "earth-pig") nocturnal mammal *Orycteropus afer*, order Tubulidentata, found in central and S Africa. A timid, defenseless animal about the size of a pig, it has a long head, piglike snout, and large asinine ears. It feeds on termites, which it licks up with its long sticky tongue.

aardwolf nocturnal mammal (*Proteles cristatus*) of the ◊hyena family, Hyaenidae. It is found in E and S Africa, usually in the burrows of the aardvark, and feeds on termites.

Aarhus (Danish *Århus*) second-largest city of Denmark, on the E coast overlooking the Kattegat; population (1988) 258,000. It is the capital of Aarhus county in Jylland (Jutland) and a shipping and commercial center.

Aaron c. 13th century BC. In the Old Testament, the elder brother of Moses and coleader of the ◊Hebrews in their march from Egypt to the Promised Land of Canaan. He made the Golden Calf for the Hebrews to worship when they despaired of Moses' return from Mount Sinai, but he was allowed to continue as high priest. All his descendants are hereditary high priests, called the *cohanim*, or cohens, and maintain a special place in worship and ceremony in the synagogue. See also ◊Levite.

Aaron Hank (Henry Louis) 1934– . US baseball player and all-time home-run leader. In the course of his career, primarily with the Milwaukee and Atlanta Braves, he won the National League batting title twice, 1955 and 1959. In 1957, as a member of the World Championship team, he was named the National League's most valuable player. His greatest achievement was breaking Babe Ruth's lifetime record of 714 home runs; by the time of his retirement in 1976, Aaron had hit a total of 755 home runs. He was elected to the Baseball Hall of Fame in 1982.

Born in Mobile, Alabama, he played with the Indianapolis team of the Negro National League before joining the Milwaukee Braves 1954.

Aasen Ivar Andreas 1813–1896. Norwegian philologist, poet, and playwright. Through a study of rural dialects he evolved by 1853 a native "country language," which he called *Landsmaal*, to take the place of literary Dano-Norwegian.

abacus method of calculating with a handful of stones on "a flat surface" (Latin *abacus*), familiar to the Greeks and Romans, and used by earlier peoples, possibly even in ancient Babylon; it still survives in the more sophisticated Chinese bead-frame form, the Russian *schoty* and the Japanese *soroban*. The abacus has been superseded by the electronic calculator.

Abadan Iranian oil port on the E side of the Shatt-al-Arab; population (1986) 294,000. Abadan is the chief refinery and shipping center for Iran's oil industry, nationalized 1951. This measure was the beginning of the worldwide movement by oil-producing countries to assume control of profits from their own resources.

Abakan coal-mining city and capital of Khakass

abacus *The ancient counting method of the abacus shares many mathematical principles with today's electronic calculator. Still widely used in the East, the abacus is used here at work in China's Logan commune.*

Autonomous Region, Krasnoyarsk Territory, in S USSR; population (1987) 181,000.

abalone edible marine snail of the worldwide genus *Haliotis*, family Haliotidae. They have flattened, oval, spiralled shells, which have holes around the outer edge and a bluish mother-of-pearl lining. This lining is used in ornamental work.

abb. abbreviation for abbreviation.

Abbadid dynasty 11th century. Muslim dynasty based in Seville which lasted from 1023 until 1091. The dynasty was founded by Abu-el-Kasim Mohammed who led the townspeople against the Berbers when the Spanish caliphate fell. The dynasty continued under Motadid (1042–1069) and Motamid (1069–1091) when the city was taken by the ◊Almoravids.

Abbado Claudio 1933– . Italian conductor, long associated with La Scala, Milan. Principal conductor of London Symphony Orchestra from 1979, he also worked with the European Community Youth Orchestra from 1977.

Abbas I the Great c. 1557–1629. Shah of Persia from 1588. He expanded Persian territory by conquest, defeating the Uzbeks near Herat in 1597 and also the Turks. The port of Bandar-Abbas is named after him. At his death his empire reached

Abbas King of
Persia

Abbas I *Called the Great, Abbas I was Shah of Persia 1588–1629. He fought a long war against the Ottoman Turks, regaining lost territory, including Baghdad. He introduced reforms, and encouraged European trade and the flowering of Persian arts. This is an engraving from Herbett's* Travels *1638.*

from the river Tigris to the Indus. He was a patron of the arts.

Abbas II Hilmi 1874–1944. Last ◊khedive (viceroy) of Egypt, 1892–1914. On the outbreak of war between Britain and Turkey in 1914, he sided with Turkey and was deposed following the establishment of a British protectorate over Egypt.

Abbasid dynasty dynasty of the Islamic empire, whose ◊*caliphs* reigned in Baghdad 750–1258. They were descended from Abbas, the prophet Mohammed's uncle, and some of them, such as Harun al-Rashid and Mamun (reigned 813–33), were outstanding patrons of cultural development. Later their power dwindled, and in 1258 Baghdad was burned by the Tatars.

From then until 1517 the Abbasids retained limited power as caliphs of Egypt.

Abbeville town in N France in the Somme *département*, 12 mi/19 km inland from the mouth of the Somme; population (1982) 26,000.

abbey in the Christian church, a monastery (of monks) or a nunnery or convent (of nuns), all dedicated to a life of celibacy and religious seclusion, governed by an abbot or abbess respectively. The word is also applied to a building that was once the church of an abbey, for example, Westminster Abbey, London.

The first abbeys, as established in Syria or Egypt, were mere collections of huts, but later massive and extensive building complexes were constructed throughout Europe. St Benedict's Abbey at Monte Cassino in Italy and Citeaux and Cluny in France set the pattern. In England many abbeys were closed by Henry VIII, who turned from the Roman Catholic Church. In other countries many were closed in the 18th and 19th centuries as a result of political revolutions.

Abbey Edwin Austin 1852–1911. US artist and illustrator. Born in Philadelphia, Abbey was educated by private tutors and later studied at the Pennsylvania Academy of Fine Arts. His illustrations, first published in *Harper's Weekly*, earned him a national reputation and commissions to illustrate many popular books. Living much of his later life in England, he was elected to the Royal Academy and the US National Academy of Design and received the French Legion of Honor. Among his works are the murals he painted for the Boston Public Library depicting the quest for the Holy Grail.

Abbey Theatre playhouse in Dublin associated with the Irish literary revival of the early 1900s. The theater, opened in 1904, staged the works of a number of Irish dramatists, including Lady Gregory, Yeats, J M Synge, and Sean O'Casey. Burned down in 1951, the Abbey Theatre was rebuilt 1966.

Abbott and Costello Adopted names of William Abbott (1895–1974) and Louis Cristillo (1906–1959) US comedy team. They moved to films from vaudeville, and most, including *Buck Privates* 1941 and *Lost in a Harem* 1944, were showcases for their routines. They also appeared on radio and television.

Abd Allah the Sudanese dervish leader Abdullah el Taaisha 1846–1899. Successor to the Mahdi as Sudanese ruler from 1885, he was defeated by the UK general ◊Kitchener at Omdurman 1898 and later killed in Kordofan.

Abd al-Malik Caliph who reigned 685–705. Based in Damascus, he waged military campaigns to unite Muslim groups and battled against the Greeks. He instituted a purely Arab coinage and introduced Arabic as the language for his lands. His reign was turbulent but succeeded in extending and strengthening Omayed power. He was also a patron of the arts.

Abd el-Kader c. 1807–1873. Algerian nationalist. Emir (Islamic chieftain) of Mascara from 1832, he led a struggle against the French until his surrender in 1847.

Abd el-Krim el-Khettabi 1881–1963. Moroccan chief known as the "Wolf of the ◊Riff." With his brother Mohammed, he led the Riff revolt against the French and Spanish invaders, inflicting disastrous defeat on the Spanish at Anual in 1921, but surrendered to a large French army under Pétain in 1926. Banished to the island of Réunion, he was released in 1947 and died in voluntary exile in Cairo.

abdication renunciation of an office or dignity, usually the throne, by a ruler or sovereign.

abdication crisis in British history, the constitutional upheaval of the period Nov 16, 1936 to Dec 10, 1936, brought about by the English king Edward VIII's decision to marry Wallis Simpson, an American divorcee. The marriage of the "Supreme Governor" of the Church of England to a divorced person was considered unsuitable and the king was finally forced to abdicate on Dec 10, leaving for voluntary exile in France. He was created Duke of Windsor and married Mrs Simpson on June 3, 1937.

abdomen in invertebrates, the part of the body below the ◊thorax, containing the digestive organs; in insects and other arthropods, it is the hind part of the body. In mammals, the abdomen is separated from the thorax by the diaphragm, a sheet of muscular tissue; in arthropods, commonly by a narrow constriction. In insects and spiders, the abdomen is characterized by the absence of limbs.

Abdul-Hamid II 1842–1918. Last sultan of Turkey 1876–1909. In 1908 the ◊Young Turks under Enver Pasha forced Abdul-Hamid to restore the constitution of 1876 and in 1909 insisted on his deposition. He died in confinement. For his part in the ◊Armenian massacres suppressing the revolt of 1894–96 he was known as "the Great Assassin"; his actions still motivate Armenian violence against the Turks.

Abdullah ibn Hussein 1882–1951. King of Jordan from 1946. He worked with the British guerrilla leader T E ◊Lawrence in the Arab revolt of World War I. Abdullah became king of Transjordan 1946; on the incorporation of Arab Palestine (after the 1948–49 Arab-Israeli War) he renamed the country the Hashemite Kingdom of Jordan. He was assassinated.

Abdullah Sheik Mohammed 1905–1982. Indian politician, known as the "Lion of Kashmir." He headed the struggle for constitutional government against the Maharajah of Kashmir, and in 1948, following a coup, became prime minister. He agreed to the accession of the state to India, but was dismissed and imprisoned from 1953 (with brief intervals) until 1966, when he called for Kashmiri self-determination. He became chief minister of Jammu and Kashmir 1975, accepting the sovereignty of India.

Abdul Mejid I 1823–1861. Sultan of Turkey from 1839. During his reign the Ottoman Empire was increasingly weakened by internal nationalist movements and the incursions of the great European powers.

Abel in the Old Testament, second son of Adam and Eve; as a shepherd, he made burned offerings of meat to God which were more acceptable than the fruits offered by his brother Cain; he was killed by the jealous Cain.

Abel John Jacob 1857–1938. US biochemist, discoverer of ◊adrenaline. He studied the chemical composition of body tissues, and this led, in 1898, to the discovery of adrenaline, the first hormone to be identified, which Abel called epinephrine. He later became the first to isolate ◊amino acids from blood.

Abel Niels Henrik 1802–1829. Norwegian mathematician. He demonstrated that the general quintic equation

$ax^5 + bx^4 + cx^3 + dx^2 + ex + f = 0$

could not be solved algebraically. Subsequent work covered elliptic functions, integral equations, infinite series, and the binomial theorem.

He lived a life of poverty and ill health, dying of tuberculosis shortly before the arrival of an offer of a position at the University of Berlin.

Abelard Peter 1079–1142. French scholastic philosopher who worked on logic and theology. His romantic liaison with his pupil, ◊Héloïse, caused a medieval scandal. Details of his controversial life are contained in the autobiographical *Historia Calamitatum Mearum/The History of My Misfortunes*.

Abelard, born near Nantes, became canon of Notre Dame in Paris and master of the cathedral school 1115. When his seduction of, and secret marriage to, Héloïse became known, she entered a convent and he was castrated at the instigation of her uncle, Canon Fulbert, and became a monk. Resuming teaching a year later, he was cited for heresy and became a hermit at Nogent, where he built the oratory of the Paraclete, and later abbot of a monastery in Brittany. He died at Châlon-sur-Saône on his way to defend himself against a new charge of heresy. Héloïse was buried beside him at the Paraclete 1164; their remains were taken to Père Lachaise cemetery, Paris, 1817.

He opposed realism in the debate over universals, and propounded "conceptualism" whereby universal terms have an existence only in the mind of the thinker. His love letters from Héloïse survive.

Abeokuta agricultural trade center in Nigeria, W Africa, on the Ogun River, 64 mi/103 km N of Lagos; population (1983) 309,000.

Aberdeen city and seaport on the E coast of Scotland, administrative headquarters of Grampian region; population (1986) 214,082. Shore-based maintenance and service depots for the North Sea oil rigs. It is Scotland's third-largest city.

Aberdeen George Hamilton Gordon, 4th Earl of Aberdeen 1784–1860. British Tory politician, prime minister 1852–55; he resigned because of the Crimean War losses.

aberration of starlight

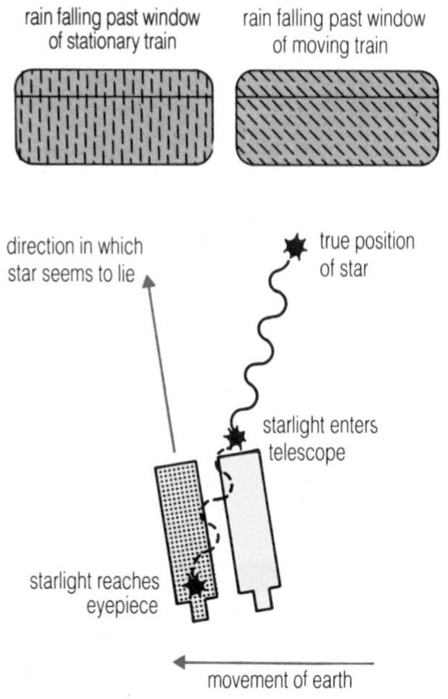
rain falling past window of stationary train
rain falling past window of moving train
direction in which star seems to lie
true position of star
starlight enters telescope
starlight reaches eyepiece
movement of earth

aberration of starlight the apparent displacement of a star from its true position, due to the combined effects of the speed of light and the speed of the Earth in orbit around the Sun (about 18.5 mps/30 kps).

Aberration, discovered in 1728 by James ◊Bradley, was the first observational proof that the Earth orbits the Sun.

aberration, optical any of a number of defects that impair the image in an optical instrument. Aberration occurs because of minute variations in lenses and mirrors, and because different parts of the light ◊spectrum are reflected or refracted

aberration, optical

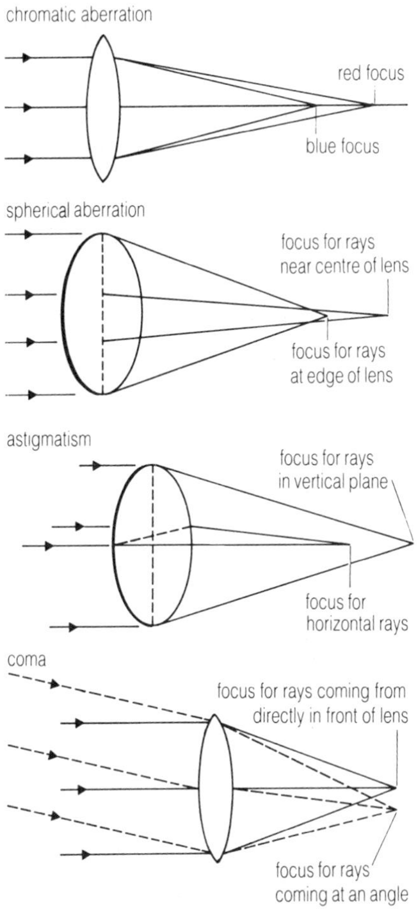
chromatic aberration
red focus
blue focus
spherical aberration
focus for rays
near centre of lens
focus for rays
at edge of lens
astigmatism
focus for rays
in vertical plane
focus for
horizontal rays
coma
focus for rays coming from
directly in front of lens
focus for rays
coming at an angle

by varying amounts. In chromatic aberration the image is surrounded by colored fringes, because light of different colors is brought to different focal points by a lens. In spherical aberration the image is blurred because different parts of a spherical lens or mirror have different focal lengths. In astigmatism the image appears elliptical or cross-shaped because of an irregularity in the curvature of the lens. In coma the images appear progressively elongated toward the edge of the field of view.

Abidja'n port and capital of the Republic of Ivory Coast, W Africa; population (1982) 1,850,000. Products include coffee, palm oil, cocoa, and timber (mahogany). To be replaced as capital by Yamoussoukro.

Abilene city in central Texas; SW of Fort Worth; seat of Taylor county. It is a center for oil-drilling equipment; population (1990) 106,654. Abilene was founded 1881 as the terminus for the Texas and Pacific Railroad.

Abilene town in Kansas, on the Smoky Hill River; population (1990) 6,242. In the 1860s Abilene was the northern terminus of the Chisholm Trail cattle drive and the point from which the herds were shipped east by rail. Its economy includes the manufacture of aircraft and missile components and oil-field equipment. President Eisenhower lived here as a boy and is buried here; the Eisenhower Center, also here, includes a museum and library.

ab init. abbreviation for *ab initio* (Latin "from the beginning").

abiotic factor a nonorganic variable within the ecosystem, affecting the life of organisms. Examples include temperature, light, and soil structure. Abiotic factors can be harmful to the environment, as when sulfur dioxide emissions from power stations produce acid rain.

Abkhazia autonomous Soviet Socialist Republic within Georgia, USSR, situated on the Black Sea; area 3,320 sq mi/8,600 sq km; population (1989) 526,000. Abkhazia, a Georgian kingdom from the 4th century, was inhabited traditionally by Abkhazis, an ethnic group converted from Christianity to Islam in the 17th century. By the 1980s some 17% of the population were Muslims and two-thirds were of Georgian origin. In Mar-Apr and July 1989, Abkhazis demanded secession from Georgia and reinstatement as a full Union republic; violent inter-ethnic clashes erupted in which at least 20 people died. Georgian nationalists, however, want the republic to be incorporated as part of Georgia. The dispute triggered nationalist demonstrations throughout Georgia.

ablative in the grammar of certain inflected languages, such as Latin, the ablative case is the form of a noun, pronoun, or adjective used to indicate the agent in passive sentences or the instrument, manner, or place of the action described by the verb.

ABM abbreviation for antiballistic missile; see ◊nuclear warfare.

Åbo Swedish name for ◊Turku in Finland.

abolitionism in US history, a movement culminating in the late 18th and early 19th centuries, first to end the slave trade, and then to abolish the institution of ◊slavery and emancipate slaves. In the US, Benjamin ◊Franklin had argued against slavery as early as 1775. It was officially abolished by the Emancipation Proclamation 1863 of President Abraham ◊Lincoln, but it could not be enforced until 1865 after the Union victory in the civil war. The question of whether newly admitted states would allow slavery was a major issue in the breakup of the Union.

Abomey port city of ◊Benin, W Africa; population (1982) 54,500. It was once the capital of the kingdom of Dahomey, which flourished in the 17th–19th centuries, and had a mud-built defense wall 6 mi/10 km in circumference.

abominable snowman legendary creature, said to resemble a human, with long arms and a thick-set body covered with reddish-gray hair. Reports of its existence in the Himalayas, where it is known as the yeti, have been made since 1832, but they gained substance from a published photograph of a huge footprint in the snow in 1951. No further "evidence" has been found.

aborigine (Latin *ab origine*, "from the beginning") any indigenous inhabitant of a region or country. The word often refers to the original peoples of areas colonized by Europeans, and especially to ◊Australian Aborigines.

abortion the ending of a pregnancy before the fetus is developed sufficiently to survive outside the womb. Loss of a fetus at a later gestational age is termed premature stillbirth. Abortion may be accidental (miscarriage) or deliberate (termination of pregnancy).

Methods of deliberate abortion vary according to the gestational age of the fetus. Up to 12 weeks, the cervix is dilated and a suction curette passed into the uterus to remove its contents (D and C). Over 12 weeks, a prostaglandin pessary is introduced into the vagina, which induces labor, producing a miscarriage. In 1989 an antiprogesterone pill was introduced in France, under the name RU 486. This also leads to the expulsion of the fetus from the womb, and can be used at an earlier stage in pregnancy. Trials showed that RU486 was effective in 94% of 600 patients up to 10 weeks pregnant.

Abortion as a means of birth control has long been the subject of controversy. The argument centers largely upon whether a woman should legally be permitted to have an abortion and, that being so, under what circumstances. Another aspect is whether, and to what extent, the law should protect the fetus. Those who oppose abortion generally believe that human life begins at the moment of conception, when a sperm fertilizes an egg. This is the view held, for example, by the Roman Catholic Church. Those who support unrestricted legal abortion may believe in a woman's right to choose whether she wants a child, and may take into account the large numbers of deaths and injuries from back-street abortions that are thus avoided. Others approve abortion for specific reasons. For example, if a woman's life or health is jeopardized, abortion may be recommended; and if there is a strong likelihood that the child will be born with severe mental or physical handicap. Other grounds for abortion include pregnancy resulting from sexual assault such as rape or incest.

In the US in 1989, a Supreme Court decision gave state legislatures the right to introduce some restrictions on the unconditional right, established by the Supreme Court in an earlier decision (Roe v. Wade), for any woman to decide to have an abortion.

Aboukir Bay, Battle of also known as the Battle of the Nile: naval battle between the UK and France, in which Admiral Nelson defeated Napoleon's fleet at the Egyptian seaport of Aboukir on Aug 1, 1798.

abracadabra magic word first recorded in a Latin poem of 2nd century AD by the Gnostic poet Serenus Sammonicus. When written in the form of an inverted pyramid, so as to be read across the top and up the right side, it was worn as a health amulet, to ward off illnesses.

Abraham c. 2300 BC. In the Old Testament, founder of the Jewish nation. Jehovah promised him heirs and land for his people in Canaan, (Israel), renamed him Abraham ("father of many nations") and tested his faith by a command (later retracted) to sacrifice his son Isaac.

Abraham was born in Ur, in ◊Sumeria, the son of Terah. With his father, wife Sarah, and nephew Lot, he migrated to Haran, N Mesopotamia, then to Canaan where he received Jehovah's promise of land. After visiting Egypt he separated from Lot at Bethel and settled in Hebron (now in Israel). He was still childless at the age of 76, subsequently had a son (Ishmael) with his wife's maidservant Hagar, and then, at the age of 100, a son Isaac with his wife Sarah. Abraham was buried in Machpelah Cave, Hebron.

Abraham, Plains of plateau near Québec, Canada, where the British commander ◊Wolfe defeated the French under ◊Montcalm, Sept 13, 1759, during the French and Indian War (1754–63).

Abrams v US a US Supreme Court decision 1919 dealing with First Amendment rights in instances of sedition or espionage. Abrams, convicted of publishing pamphlets criticizing the US role in World War I and encouraging resistance to the war, appealed to the Supreme Court for protection under the right to free speech. The Court upheld the 1918 Sedition Law, ruling that Congress had the right to restrict speech that had a "tendency" toward harmful results. A famous dissent was filed by Justices Holmes and Brandeis.

abrasive substance used for cutting and polishing or for removing small amounts of the surface of hard materials. There are two types: natural and artificial abrasives, and their hardness is measured using the ◊Mohs' scale. Natural abrasives include quartz, sandstone, pumice, diamond, and corundum; artificial abrasives include rouge, whiting, and carborundum.

Abruzzi mountainous region of S central Italy, comprising the provinces of L'Aquila, Chieti, Pescara, and Teramo; area 4,169 sq mi/10,800 sq km; population (1988) 1,258,000; capital L'Aquila. Gran Sasso d'Italia, 9,564 ft/2,914 m, is the highest point of the ◊Apennines.

Absalom in the Old Testament, favorite son of King David; when defeated in a revolt against his father he fled on a mule, but caught his hair in a tree branch and was killed by Joab, one of David's officers.

abscess collection of ◊pus in the tissues forming in response to infection. Its presence is signaled by pain and inflammation.

abscissa in coordinate geometry, the horizontal or x coordinate—that is, the distance of a point from the vertical or y-axis. For example, a point with the coordinates (3,4) has an abscissa of 3.

abscission in botany, the controlled separation of part of a plant from the main plant body—most commonly, the falling of leaves or the dropping of fruit. In ◊deciduous plants the leaves are shed before the winter or dry season, whereas ◊evergreen plants drop their leaves continually throughout the year. Fruit drop, the abscission of fruit while still immature, is a naturally occurring process.

Abscission occurs after the formation of an abscission zone at the point of separation. Within this, a thin layer of cells, the abscission layer, becomes weakened and breaks down through the conversion of pectic acid to pectin. Consequently the leaf, fruit, or other part can easily be dislodged by wind or rain. The process is thought to be controlled by the amount of ◊auxin present. Fruit drop is particularly common in fruit trees such as apples, and orchards are often sprayed with artificial auxin as a preventive measure.

absinthe green liqueur containing 60–80% alcohol and made with anise. It was originally flavored with oil of wormwood, which, because it attacks the nervous system is widely banned, so substitutes are now used.

absolute value or modulus in mathematics, the value, or magnitude, of a number irrespective of its sign (denoted $|n|$), and defined as the positive square root of n^2.

For example, 5 and –5 have the same absolute value: $|5| = |-5| = 5$. For a ◊complex number, the absolute value is its distance to the origin when it is plotted on an Argand diagram, and can be calculated (without plotting) by applying the ◊Pythagorean theorem. By definition, the absolute value of any complex number $a + bi$ is given by the expression $|a + bi| = \sqrt{(a^2 + b^2)}$.

absolute zero the lowest temperature theoretically possible, zero degrees kelvin, equivalent to –459.67°F/–273.16°C, at which molecules are motionless. Although the third law of ◊thermodynamics indicates the impossibility of reaching absolute zero exactly, a temperature within 3×10^{-8} kelvin of it was produced in 1984 by Finnish scientists. Near absolute zero, the physical properties of some materials change substantially; for example, some metals lose their electrical resistance and become superconductive. See ◊cryogenics.

absolutism or ***absolute monarchy*** system of government in which the ruler or rulers have unlimited power. The principle of an absolute monarch, given a right to rule by God (see ◊divine right of kings), was extensively used in Europe during the 17th and 18th centuries. Absolute monarchy is contrasted with limited or constitutional monarchy, in which the sovereign's powers are defined or limited.

absorption in science, the taking up of one substance by another, such as a liquid by a solid (ink by blotting-paper) or a gas by a liquid (ammonia by water). In biology, absorption describes the passing of nutrients or medication into and through tissues such as intestinal walls and blood vessels. In physics, absorption is the phenomenon by which a substance retains radiation of particular wavelengths; for example, a piece of blue glass absorbs all visible light except the wavelengths in the blue part of the spectrum; it also refers to the partial loss of energy resulting from light and other electromagnetic waves passing through a medium. In nuclear physics, absorption is the capture by elements, such as boron, of neutrons produced by fission in a reactor.

abstract art nonrepresentational art. Ornamental art without figurative representation occurs in most cultures. The modern abstract movement in sculpture and painting emerged in Europe and North America between 1910 and 1920. Two approaches produce different abstract styles: images that have been "abstracted" from nature to the point where they no longer reflect a conventional reality and nonobjective, or "pure," art forms, supposedly without reference to reality.

Abstract art began in the avant-garde movements of the late 19th century, in Impressionism, Neo-Impressionism, and Post-Impressionism. These styles of painting reduced the importance of the original subject matter and emphasized the creative process of painting itself. In the first decade of the 20th century, some painters in Western Europe began to abandon the established Western convention of imitating nature and storytelling in pictures and developed a new artistic form and expression. Kandinsky is generally regarded as the first abstract artist. His highly colored canvases influenced many younger European artists. In France, the Cubists Picasso and Braque also developed, around 1907, an abstract style; their pictures, some partly collage, were composed mainly of fragmented natural images.

Many variations of abstract art developed in Europe, as shown in the work of Mondrian, Malevich, the Futurists, the Vorticists, and the Dadaists. Sculptors, including Brancusi and Epstein, were inspired by the new freedom in form and content, and Brancusi's ***The Kiss*** 1910 is one of the earliest abstract sculptures.

Two exhibitions of European art, one in New York in 1913 (the Armory Show), the other in San Francisco in 1917, opened the way for abstraction in US art. Many painters, including the young Georgia O'Keeffe, experimented with new styles. Morgan Russell (1886–1953) and Stanton Macdonald-Wright (1890–1973) invented their own school, Synchronism, a rival to Orphism, a similar style developed in France by Robert Delaunay.

Abstract art has dominated Western art from 1920 and has continued to produce many variations. In the 1940s it gained renewed vigor in the works of the Abstract Expressionists. From the 1950s Minimal art provoked more outraged reactions from critics and the general public alike.

Abstract Expressionism US movement in abstract art that emphasized the act of painting, the expression inherent in paint itself, and the interaction of artist, paint, and canvas. Abstract Expressionism emerged in New York in the early 1940s. Arshile Gorky, Franz Kline, Jackson Pollock, and Mark Rothko are associated with the movement.

Abstract Expressionism may have been inspired by Hans Hofmann and Gorky, who were both working in the US in the 1940s. Hofmann, who emigrated from Germany in the 1930s, had started to use dribbles and blobs of paint to create expressive abstract patterns, while Gorky, a Turkish Armenian refugee, was developing his highly colored abstracts with wild organic forms. Abstract Expressionism was not a distinct school but rather a convergence of artistic personalities, each revolting against restricting conventions in US art. The styles of the movement's exponents varied widely: Pollock's huge dripped and splashed work, Willem de Kooning's grotesque figures, Kline's strong calligraphic style, and Robert Motherwell and Rothko's calmer large abstract canvases. The movement made a strong impression on European painting in the late 1950s.

Absurd, Theater of the avant-garde drama originating with a group of playwrights in the 1950s, including Beckett, Ionesco, Genet, and Pinter. Their work expressed the belief that in a godless universe human existence has no meaning or purpose and therefore all communication breaks down. Logical construction and argument gives way to irrational and illogical speech and to its ultimate conclusion, silence, as in Beckett's play *Breath* 1970.

Abu Bakr or ***Abu-Bekr*** 573–634. "Father of the virgin," name used by Abd-el-Ka'aba from about 618 when the prophet Mohammed married his daughter Ayesha. He was a close adviser to Mohammed in the period 622–32. On the prophet's death, he became the first ◊caliph adding Mesopotamia to the Muslim world and instigating expansion into Iraq and Syria.

Traditionally he is supposed to have encouraged some of those who had known Mohammed to memorize his teachings; these words were later written down to form the Koran.

Abu Dhabi sheikdom in SW Asia, on the Arabian Gulf, capital of the ◊United Arab Emirates. Formerly under British protection, it has been ruled since 1971 by Sheik Zayed Bin al-Nahayan, who is also president of the Supreme Council of Rulers of the United Arab Emirates.

Abuja city in Nigeria under construction from 1976 intended to replace Lagos as capital. Shaped like a crescent, it was designed by the Japanese architect Kenzo Tange.

Abu Musa a small island in the Persian Gulf. Formerly owned by the ruler of Sharjah, it was forcibly occupied by Iran in 1971.

Abú Nuwás Hasan ibn Háni 762–c. 815. Arab poet celebrated for the freedom, eroticism and ironic lightness of touch he brought to traditional forms.

Abu Simbel former site of two ancient temples cut into the rock on the banks of the Nile in S Egypt, during the reign of Ramses II and commemorating him and his wife Nefertari. Before the site was flooded by the Aswan High Dam, the temples were moved, in sections, 1966–67.

abutilon any of several ornamental plants of the genus *Abutilon*, family Malvaceae, of which one of the most common is *A. theophrastus*, the Indian mallow or velvet leaf. This has bell-shaped yellow flowers and is the source of a jutelike fiber.

Abydos ancient city in Upper Egypt; the Great Temple of Seti I dates from about 1300 BC.

abyssal plain the broad expanse of sea floor lying 2–4 mi/3–6 km below sea level. Abyssal plains are found in all the major oceans, and they extend from bordering continental rises to midoceanic ridges.

Underlain by outward-spreading, new oceanic crust extruded from ridges, abyssal plains are covered in deep-sea sediments derived from continental slopes and floating microscopic marine organisms. The plains often are interrupted by chains of volcanic islands where plates ride over hot spots in the mantle, and by sea mounts originally formed in midoceanic ridge areas. In the Atlantic Ocean, for example, the abyssal plain extends about 930 mi/1,500 km off the E coast of the US.

abyssal zone dark ocean area 6,500–19,500 ft/2,000–6,000 m deep; temperature 39°F/4°C. Three-quarters of the area of the deep ocean floor lies in the abyssal zone. It is too far from the surface for photosynthesis to take place. Some fish and crustaceans living there are blind or have their own light sources. The region above is the bathyal zone; the region below, the hadyal zone.

Abyssinia former name of ◊Ethiopia.

AC in physics, abbreviation for ◊alternating current.

acacia any of a large group of shrubs and trees of the genus *Acacia* of the legume family Leguminosae. Acacias include the thorn trees of the African savanna and the gum arabic tree *A. senegal* of N Africa, and several North American species of the SW US and Mexico. Acacias are found in warm regions of the world, particularly Australia.

Academy originally, the school of philosophy founded by ◊Plato in the gardens of Academe, NW of Athens; it was closed by the Byzantine Emperor ◊Justinian, with the other pagan schools, in AD 529. The first academy, in the present-day sense of a recognized society established for the promotion of one or more of the arts and sciences, was the Museum of Alexandria, founded by Ptolemy Soter in the 3rd century BC.

Academy Award annual motion-picture awards in

Academy Awards: recent winners

1971	**Best Picture:** *The French Connection*; **Best Director:** William Friedkin *The French Connection*; **Best Actor:** Gene Hackman *The French Connection*; **Best Actress:** Jane Fonda *Klute*
1972	**Best Picture:** *The Godfather*; **Best Director:** Bob Fosse *Cabaret*; **Best Actor:** Marlon Brando *The Godfather*; **Best Actress:** Liza Minnelli *Cabaret*
1973	**Best Picture:** *The Sting*; **Best Director:** George Roy Hill *The Sting*; **Best Actor:** Jack Lemmon *Save the Tiger*; **Best Actress:** Glenda Jackson *A Touch of Class*
1974	**Best Picture:** *The Godfather II*; **Best Director:** Francis Ford Coppola *The Godfather II*; **Best Actor:** Art Carney *Harry and Tonto*; **Best Actress:** Ellen Burstyn *Alice Doesn't Live Here Any More*
1975	**Best Picture:** *One Flew Over the Cuckoo's Nest*; **Best Director:** Milos Forman *One Flew Over the Cuckoo's Nest*; **Best Actor:** Jack Nicholson *One Flew Over the Cuckoo's Nest*; **Best Actress:** Louise Fletcher *One Flew Over the Cuckoo's Nest*
1976	**Best Picture:** *Rocky* **Best Director:** John G Avildsen *Rocky*; **Best Actor:** Peter Finch *Network*; **Best Actress:** Faye Dunaway *Network*
1977	**Best Picture:** *Annie Hall*; **Best Director:** Woody Allen *Annie Hall*; **Best Actor:** Richard Dreyfuss *The Goodbye Girl*; **Best Actress:** Diane Keaton *Annie Hall*
1978	**Best Picture:** *The Deerhunter*; **Best Director:** Michael Cimino *The Deerhunter*; **Best Actor:** John Voight *Coming Home*; **Best Actress:** Jane Fonda *Coming Home*
1979	**Best Picture:** *Kramer vs Kramer*; **Best Director:** Robert Beaton *Kramer vs Kramer*; **Best Actor:** Dustin Hoffman *Kramer vs Kramer*; **Best Actress:** Sally Field *Norma Rae*
1980	**Best Picture:** *Ordinary People*; **Best Director:** Robert Redford *Ordinary People*; **Best Actor:** Robert de Niro *Raging Bull*; **Best Actress:** Sissy Spacek *Coalminer's Daughter*
1981	**Best Picture:** *Chariots of Fire*; **Best Director:** Warren Beatty *Reds*; **Best Actor:** Henry Fonda *On Golden Pond*; **Best Actress:** Katharine Hepburn *On Golden Pond*
1982	**Best Picture:** *Gandhi*; **Best Director:** Richard Attenborough *Gandhi*; **Best Actor:** Ben Kingsley *Gandhi*; **Best Actress:** Meryl Streep *Sophie's Choice*
1983	**Best Picture:** *Terms of Endearment*; **Best Director:** James L Brooks *Terms of Endearment*; **Best Actor:** Robert Duvall *Tender Mercies*; **Best Actress:** Shirley MacLaine *Terms of Endearment*
1984	**Best Picture:** *Amadeus*; **Best Director:** Milos Forman *Amadeus*; **Best Actor:** F Murrav Abraham *Amadeus*; **Best Actress:** Sally Field *Places in the Heart*
1985	**Best Picture:** *Out of Africa*; **Best Director:** Sidney Pollack *Out of Africa*; **Best Actor:** William Hurt *Kiss of the Spiderwoman*; **Best Actress:** Geraldine Page *The Trip to Bountiful*
1986	**Best Picture:** *Platoon*; **Best Director:** Oliver Stone *Platoon*; **Best Actor:** Paul Newman *The Color of Money*; **Best Actress:** Marlee Matlin *Children of a Lesser God*
1987	**Best Picture:** *The Last Emperor*; **Best Director:** Bernardo Bertolucci *The Last Emperor*; **Best Actor:** Michael Douglas *Wall Street*; **Best Actress:** Cher *Moonstruck*
1988	**Best Picture:** *Rain Man*; **Best Director:** Barry Levinson *Rain Man*; **Best Actor:** Dustin Hoffman *Rain Man*; **Best Actress:** Jodie Foster *The Accused*
1989	**Best Picture:** *Driving Miss Daisy*; **Best Director:** Oliver Stone *Born on the 4th of July*; **Best Actor:** Daniel Day-Lewis *My Left Foot*; Best Actress: Jessica Tandy *Driving Miss Daisy*
1990	**Best Picture:** *Dances with Wolves*; **Best Director:** Kevin Costner *Dances With Wolves*; **Best Actor:** Jeremy Irons *Reversal of Fortune*; **Best Actress:** Kathy Bates *Misery*

many categories, given since 1927 by the Academy of Motion Picture Arts and Sciences (founded by Louis B Mayer of Metro-Goldwyn-Mayer 1927). Arguably the film community's most prestigious accolade, the award is a gold-plated statuette, which has been nicknamed "Oscar" since 1931.

Major awards include Best Picture, Best Director, Best Actor and Actress, Best Supporting Actor and Actress, Best Cinematography, Best Visual Effects, Best Screenplay, and Best Music.

Academy, French or *Académie Française* literary society founded by ◊Richelieu in 1635 concerned with maintaining the purity of the French language; membership is limited to 40 "immortals" at a time.

Academy of Sciences, Soviet society founded 1725 by Catherine the Great in St Petersburg. The academy has been responsible for such achievements as the ◊Sputnik satellite, and has branches in the Ukraine (welding, cybernetics), Armenia (astrophysics), and Georgia (mechanical engineering).

Acadia (French *Acadie*) name given to ◊Nova Scotia by French settlers 1604, from which the term ◊Cajun derives.

acanthus any herbaceous plant of the genus *Acanthus* with handsome lobed leaves. Twenty species are found in the Mediterranean region and the Old World tropics, including bear's breech *A. mollis*, whose leaves were used as a motif in Classical architecture, especially on Corinthian columns.

a cappella (Italian "in the style of the chapel") choral music sung without instrumental accompaniment.

Acapulco or *Acapulco de Juarez* port and vacation resort in S Mexico; population (1985) 638,000. Sometimes called the Riviera of Mexico, it attracts many tourists to its beaches, luxury hotels, and gambling casinos. There is deep-sea fishing, and tropical products are exported. Acapulco was founded 1550 and was Mexico's major Pacific coast port until about 1815.

Accad alternate form of ◊Akkad, ancient city of Mesopotamia.

accelerated freeze drying see ◊AFD.

acceleration the rate of change of the velocity of a moving body. Acceleration due to gravity is the acceleration of a body falling freely under the influence of gravity; it varies slightly at different latitudes and altitudes. Retardation (deceleration) is negative acceleration; for example, as a rising rocket slows down, it is being negatively accelerated toward the center of the Earth. Acceleration is expressed in meters per second per second (ms^{-2}) or feet per second per second (ft s^{-2}).

The value adopted internationally for gravitational acceleration on Earth is 32.174 ft s^{-2}/ 9.806 m s^{-2}.

acceleration, secular in astronomy, the continuous and nonperiodic change in orbital velocity of one body around another, or the axial rotation period of a body.

An example is the axial rotation of the Earth. This is gradually slowing down owing to the gravitational effects of the Moon and the resulting production of tides, which have a frictional effect on the Earth. However, the angular ◊momentum of the Earth–Moon system is maintained because the momentum lost by the Earth is passed to the Moon. This results in an increase in the Moon's orbital period and a consequential moving away from the Earth. The overall effect is that the Earth's axial rotation period is increasing by about 15-millionths of a second a year, and the Moon is receding from the Earth at about 1.5 in/4 cm a year.

accelerator

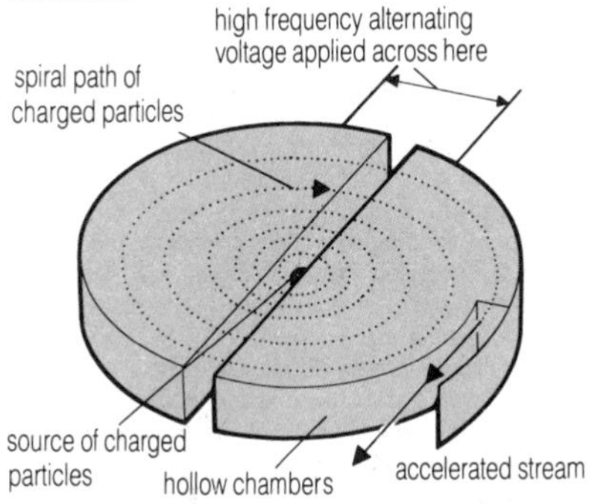
high frequency alternating voltage applied across here
spiral path of charged particles
source of charged particles
hollow chambers
accelerated stream

accelerator in physics, a device to bring charged particles (such as ◊protons) up to high speeds and energies, at which they can be of use in industry, medicine, and pure physics: when high energy particles collide with other particles, the fragments formed reveal the nature of the ◊fundamental forces of nature. For particles to achieve the energies required, successive applications of a high voltage are given to electrodes placed in the path of the particles.

During acceleration, the particles are confined within a circular or linear track using a magnetic field.

The first circular accelerator, the cyclotron, was built in the early 1930s. The early cyclotrons had circumferences of about 4 in/10 cm, whereas the ◊Large Electron–Positron Collider (LEP) at ◊CERN near Geneva, which came into operation 1989, has a circumference of 16.8 mi/27 km, around which ◊electrons and ◊positrons are accelerated before being allowed to collide. In 1988 the US announced the Ronald Reagan Center for High Energy Physics, in Waxahachie, Texas, which will house the Superconducting Super Collider (SSC), an accelerator with a circumference of 53 mi/85 km, to be completed by 1996. The world's largest linear accelerator is the Stanford Linear Collider, in which electrons and positrons are accelerated along a straight track, 2 mi/ 3.2 km long, and then steered into a head-on collision.

accelerometer apparatus, either mechanical or electromechanical, for measuring ◊acceleration or deceleration—that is, the rate of increase or decrease in the ◊velocity of a moving object.

Accelerometers are used to measure the efficiency of the braking systems on road and rail vehicles; those used in aircraft and spacecraft can determine accelerations in several directions simultaneously. There are also accelerometers for detecting vibrations in machinery.

accent a way of speaking that identifies a person with a particular country, region, language, social class, linguistic style, or some mixture of these.

People often describe only those who belong to groups other than their own as having accents and use them as a means of establishing a broader identity; for example, an Irish brogue, a Southern accent.

See also ◊English language.

accessory in law, accessories are criminal accomplices who aid in commission of a crime as a subordinate or in a secondary way. An accomplice may be either "before the fact" (assisting, ordering, or procuring another to commit a crime) or "after the fact" (giving assistance after the crime). An accomplice present when the crime is committed is an "abettor."

access time in computing, the "reaction time": the time required by a computer to read from, or write to, ◊memory after being given an instruction.

acclimation or ***acclimatization*** the physiological changes induced in an organism by exposure to new environmental conditions. When humans move to higher altitudes, for example, the number of red blood cells rises to increase the oxygen-carrying capacity of the blood in order to compensate for the lower levels of oxygen in the air.

accommodation the ability of the vertebrate ◊eye to focus on near or far objects by changing the shape of the lens.

For something to be viewed clearly the image must be precisely focused on the retina, the light-sensitive sheet of cells at the rear of the eye. Close objects can be seen when the lens takes up a more spherical shape, far objects when the lens is stretched and made thinner. These changes in shape are directed by the brain and by a ring of ciliary muscles lying beneath the iris.

accomplice a person who is engaged with another in the commission or attempted commission of a crime.

accordion a musical instrument of the reed organ type comprising left and right wind-chests connected by a flexible bellows. The right hand plays melody on a piano-style keyboard while the left hand has a system of push-buttons for selecting single notes or chord harmonies.

accounting the principles and practice of systematically recording, presenting, and interpreting financial accounts; financial record keeping and management of businesses and other organizations, from balance sheets to policy decisions, for tax or operating purposes. Forms of inflation accounting, such as CCA (current cost accounting) and CCP (current purchasing power) are aimed at providing valid financial comparisons over a period in which money values change.

In the 20th century, especially in the US, the role of accounting has expanded into the realm of decision making, traditionally reserved to the economist. The accountant's role had been one of recording economic events for the purposes of stewardship. The increasing complexity of business organizations has led accountants into the areas of providing information to decision makers and even to prediction and analysis, both historically the function of economists.

accusative in the grammar of some inflected languages, such as Latin, Greek, and Russian, the accusative case is the form of a noun, pronoun, or adjective used for the direct object of a verb. It is also used for the object of certain prepositions.

Acer genus of trees and shrubs of northern temperate regions with over 115 species. *Acer* includes ◊sycamore and ◊maple.

acetaminophenol see ◊paracetamol

acetaldehyde common name for ◊ethanol.

acetate common name for ethanoate.

acetic acid common name for ethanoic acid.

acetone common name for ◊propanone.

acetylene common name for ◊ethyne.

acetylsalicylic acid chemical name for the painkilling drug ◊aspirin.

Achaea in ancient Greece, and also today, an area of the N Peloponnese; the Achaeans were the predominant society during the Mycenean period and are said by Homer to have taken part in the siege of Troy.

Achaean League union in 275 BC of most of the cities of the N Peloponnese, which defeated ◊Sparta, but was then defeated by the Romans 146 BC.

Achaemenid dynasty family ruling the Persian Empire 550–330 BC, and named after Achemenes, ancestor of Cyrus the Great, founder of the empire. His successors included Cambyses, Darius I, Xerxes, and Darius III, who, as the last Achaemenid ruler, was killed after defeat in battle against Alexander the Great in 330 BC.

Achates a character in the *Aeneid*, an epic poem by the Roman poet Virgil from the 1st century BC. Achates was the friend of the hero Aeneas. The name is proverbial for a faithful companion.

Achebe Chinua 1930– . Nigerian novelist whose themes include the social and political impact of European colonialism on African people, and the

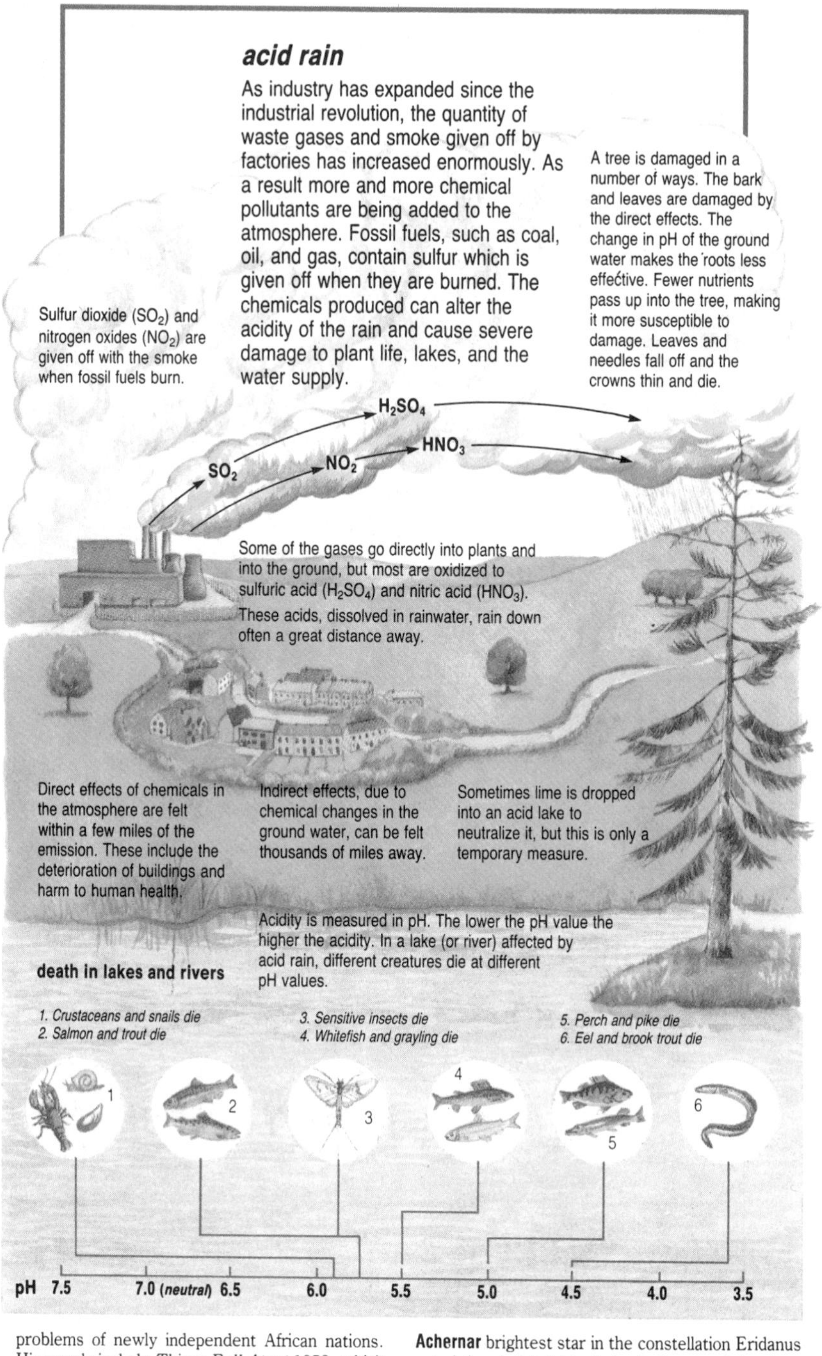
acid rain
As industry has expanded since the industrial revolution, the quantity of waste gases and smoke given off by factories has increased enormously. As a result more and more chemical pollutants are being added to the atmosphere. Fossil fuels, such as coal, oil, and gas, contain sulfur which is given off when they are burned. The chemicals produced can alter the acidity of the rain and cause severe damage to plant life, lakes, and the water supply.
Sulfur dioxide (SO_2) and nitrogen oxides (NO_2) are given off with the smoke when fossil fuels burn.
A tree is damaged in a number of ways. The bark and leaves are damaged by the direct effects. The change in pH of the ground water makes the roots less effective. Fewer nutrients pass up into the tree, making it more susceptible to damage. Leaves and needles fall off and the crowns thin and die.
H_2SO_4
HNO_3
SO_2
NO_2
Some of the gases go directly into plants and into the ground, but most are oxidized to sulfuric acid (H_2SO_4) and nitric acid (HNO_3). These acids, dissolved in rainwater, rain down often a great distance away.
Direct effects of chemicals in the atmosphere are felt within a few miles of the emission. These include the deterioration of buildings and harm to human health.
Indirect effects, due to chemical changes in the ground water, can be felt thousands of miles away.
Sometimes lime is dropped into an acid lake to neutralize it, but this is only a temporary measure.
death in lakes and rivers
Acidity is measured in pH. The lower the pH value the higher the acidity. In a lake (or river) affected by acid rain, different creatures die at different pH values.
1. Crustaceans and snails die
2. Salmon and trout die
3. Sensitive insects die
4. Whitefish and grayling die
5. Perch and pike die
6. Eel and brook trout die
1
2
3
4
5
6
pH 7.5
7.0 (neutral) 6.5
6.0
5.5
5.0
4.5
4.0
3.5

problems of newly independent African nations. His novels include *Things Fall Apart* 1958, which was widely acclaimed, and *Anthills of the Savannah* 1987.

achene a dry, one-seeded ◊fruit that develops from a single ◊ovary and does not split open to disperse the seed. Achenes commonly occur in groups, for example, the fruiting heads of buttercup *Ranunculus* and clematis. The outer surface may be smooth, spiny, ribbed, or tuberculate, depending on the species.

An achene with part of the fruit wall extended to form a membranous wing is called a samara; an example is the pendulous fruit of the elm *Ulmus*. During the development of a ◊caryopsis, the ◊carpel wall becomes fused to the seed coat; this type of fruit is typical of grasses and cereals. A cypsela is derived from an inferior ovary and is characteristic of the daisy family (Compositae). It often has a ◊pappus of hairs attached, which aids its dispersal by the wind, as in the dandelion.

Achernar brightest star in the constellation Eridanus and the ninth brightest star in the sky. It is a hot, luminous blue giant with a true luminosity 650 times that of the Sun. It is 120 light-years away.

Acheron in Greek mythology, one of the rivers of the lower world. The name was taken from a river in S Epirus that flowed through a deep gorge into the Ionian Sea.

Acheson Dean (Gooderham) 1893–1971. US politician; as undersecretary of state 1945–47 in ◊Truman's Democratic administration, he was associated with George C ◊Marshall in preparing the ◊Marshall Plan, and succeeded him as secretary of state 1949–53.

Acheson's foreign policy was widely criticized by Republican members of Congress, especially Senator ◊McCarthy, for an alleged weak response to Communist advances in SE Asia, especially after the outbreak of the Korean war. He advocated containment of the Soviet Union. He survived a vote calling for his resignation, but left the

State Department in 1952 following the election of ◊Eisenhower.

His books include *Power and Diplomacy* 1958 and *Present at the Creation* 1969, which won the Pulitzer prize for history.

Achilles Greek hero of Homer's *Iliad*. He was the son of Peleus, king of the Myrmidons in Thessaly, and the sea nymph Thetis, who rendered him invulnerable, except for the heel by which she held him, by dipping him in the river Styx. Achilles killed Hector in the Trojan War and was himself killed by Paris who shot a poisoned arrow into Achilles' heel.

Achilles tendon the tendon pinning the calf muscle to the heel bone. It is one of the largest in the human body.

Achill Island or ***Eagle Island*** largest of the Irish islands, off County Mayo; area 57 sq mi/ 148 sq km.

achromatic lens combination of lenses made from materials of different refractive indexes, constructed in such a way as to minimize chromatic aberration (which in a single lens causes colored fringes around images because the lens diffracts the different wavelengths in white light to slightly different extents).

acid substance that, in solution in an ionizing solvent (usually water), gives rise to hydrogen ions (H^+ or protons). In modern chemistry, acids are defined as substances that are proton donors and accept electrons from a base to form ◊ionic bonds. Acids react with bases to form salts, and they act as solvents. Strong acids are corrosive; dilute acids have a sour or sharp taste, although in some organic acids this may be partially masked by other flavor characteristics. Acids are classified as monobasic, dibasic, tribasic, and so forth, according to the number of hydrogen atoms, replaceable by bases, in a molecule.

Acids can be detected by using colored indicators such as ◊litmus and methyl orange. The strength of an acid is measured by its hydrogen-ion concentration, indicated by the ◊pH value. The first known acid was vinegar (ethanoic or acetic acid). Inorganic acids include boric, carbonic, hydrochloric, hydrofluoric, nitric, phosphoric, and sulfuric. Organic acids include acetic, benzoic, citric, formic, lactic, oxalic, and salicylic, as well as complex substances such as ◊nucleic acids and ◊amino acids.

acid house a type of ◊house music.

acid rain acidic rainfall, thought to be caused principally by the release into the atmosphere of sulfur dioxide (SO_2) and oxides of nitrogen. Sulfur dioxide is formed from the burning of fossil fuels such as coal that contain high quantities of sulfur, and nitrogen oxides are contributed from industrial activities and automobile exhaust fumes.

Acid rain is linked with damage to and death of forests and lake organisms in Scandinavia, Europe, and eastern North America. It also results in damage to buildings, artworks such as statues, and archeological remains.

aclinic line

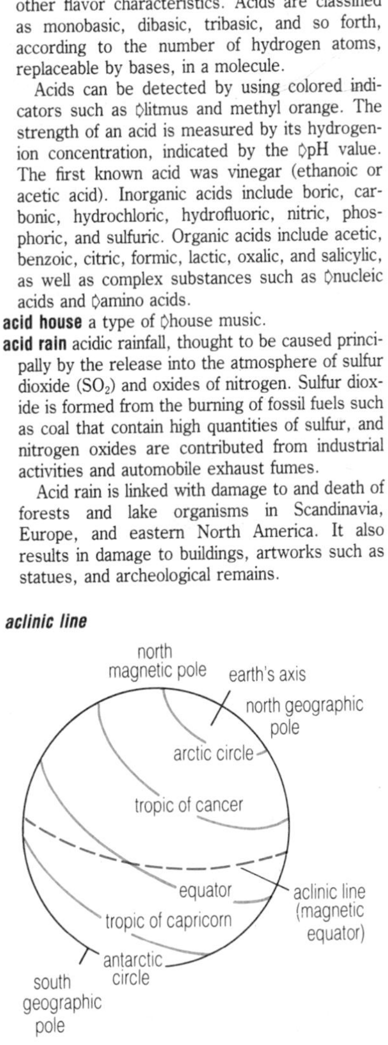
north magnetic pole
earth's axis
north geographic pole
arctic circle
tropic of cancer
equator
aclinic line (magnetic equator)
tropic of capricorn
antarctic circle
south geographic pole

It has become a critical environmental problem that needs to be solved by the industrial nations that produce the causative pollutants.

aclinic line the magnetic equator, an imaginary line near the equator, where the compass needle balances horizontally, where the attraction of the north and south magnetic poles is equal.

acne skin eruption, mainly occurring among adolescents and young adults, caused by inflammation of the sebaceous glands which secrete an oily substance (sebum), the natural lubricant of the skin. Sometimes their openings become stopped and they swell; the contents decompose and pimples form on the face, back, and chest.

Aconcagua an extinct volcano in the Argentine Andes, the highest peak in the Americas. Height 22,834 ft/6,960 m. It was first climbed by Vines and Zeebruggen in 1897.

aconite or ***monkshood*** herbaceous Eurasian plant *Aconitum napellus* of the buttercup family Ranunculaceae, with hooded blue-mauve flowers. It produces aconitine, a powerful alkaloid with narcotic and analgesic properties.

There are about 100 species of the genus *Aconitum* throughout the northern temperate regions, all of which contain poison. Summer aconite *A. uncinatum* is a common North American flower. Winter aconite *Eranthus hyemalis* belongs to another genus of the the buttercup family; it has yellow buttercuplike flowers with six petals and a ruff of leaves below.

acorn fruit of the oak tree, a ◊nut growing in a shallow cup.

acouchi any of several small S American rodents, genus *Myoprocta*. They have white-tipped tails, and are smaller relatives of the ◊agouti.

acoustic in music, a performance or instrument sounding without electrical amplification or assistance. In architecture, the sound-reflecting character of a room.

acoustic ohm unit of acoustic impedance (the ratio of the sound pressure on a surface to the sound flux through the surface). It is analogous to the ohm as the unit of electrical ◊impedance.

acoustics in general, the experimental and theoretical science of sound and its transmission; in particular, that branch of the science that has to do with the phenomena of sound in a particular space such as a room or theater.

Acquaviva Claudius 1543–1615. Neapolitan general of the Jesuits from 1581 and one of their most able organizers and educators.

acquired character a feature of the body that develops during the lifetime of an individual, usually as a result of repeated use or disuse, such as the enlarged muscles of a weight-lifter. ◊Lamarck's theory of evolution assumed that acquired characters were passed from parent to offspring.

Modern evolutionary theory does not recognize the inheritance of acquired characters because there is no reliable scientific evidence that it occurs, and because no mechanism is known whereby bodily changes can influence the genetic material. See also ◊central dogma.

acquired immune deficiency syndrome full name for the disease ◊AIDS.

acquittal in law, the setting free of someone charged with a crime after a trial.

It follows a verdict of "not guilty" and prevents retrial of a defendant on the same charges under the US Constitution (see ◊double jeopardy).

acre traditional English land measure equal to 4,840 square yards (4,047 sq m/0.405 ha). Originally meaning a field, it was the size that a yoke of oxen could plow in a day. It may be subdivided into 160 square rods (one square rod equaling 30.25 sq yd/25.29 sq m).

Acre or ***Akko*** seaport in Israel; population (1983) 37,000. Taken by the Crusaders 1104, it was captured by ◊Saladin 1187 and retaken by ◊Richard I (the Lion-Hearted) 1191. Napoleon failed in a siege 1799; Gen ◊Allenby captured it 1918; and it was part of British mandated Palestine, which became part of Israel 1948.

acre-foot unit sometimes used to measure large volumes of water, such as the capacity of a reservoir (equal to its area in acres multiplied by its average depth in feet). One acre-foot equals 43,560 cu ft/1,233.5 cu m or the amount of water covering one acre to a depth of one foot.

acridine $C_{13}H_9N$ organic compound that occurs in coal tar; it is extracted by dilute acids. It is also obtained synthetically. It is used to make dyes and drugs.

acromegaly rare condition in which enlargement of prominent parts of the body, for example hands, feet, heart, and, conspicuously, the eyebrow ridges and lower jaw, is caused by excessive output of growth hormone in adult life by a nonmalignant tumor of the ◊pituitary gland.

acronym word formed from the initial letters and/or syllables of other words, intended as a pronounceable abbreviation, for example *NATO* (*N*orth *A*tlantic *T*reaty *O*rganization).

acrophobia a ◊phobia involving fear of heights.

acropolis (Greek "high city") citadel of an ancient Greek city. The Acropolis of Athens contains the ruins of the Parthenon and surrounding complexes, built there during the days of the Athenian empire. The term is also used for analogous structures, as in the massive granite-built ruins of Great ◊Zimbabwe.

acrostic (Greek "at the extremity of a line or row") a number of lines of writing, usually verse, whose initial letters (read downward) form a word, phrase, or sentence. A single acrostic is formed by the initial letters of lines only, while a double acrostic is formed by both initial and final letters.

acrylic acid common name for ◊propenoic acid.

Actaeon in Greek mythology, a hunter, son of Aristaeus and Autonöe. He surprised ◊Artemis bathing; she changed him into a stag and he was torn to pieces by his own hounds.

ACTH (adrenocorticotropic hormone) a ◊hormone, secreted by the anterior lobe of the ◊pituitary gland, that controls the production of corticosteroid hormones by the ◊adrenal gland. It is commonly produced as a response to stress.

actinide any of a series of 15 radioactive metallic chemical elements with atomic numbers 89 (actinium) to 103 (lawrencium). Elements 89 to 95 occur in nature; the rest of the series are synthesized elements only. Actinides are grouped together because of their chemical similarities (for example, they are all bivalent), the properties differing only slightly with atomic number. The series is set out in a band in the ◊periodic table of the elements, as are the ◊lanthanides.

actinium (Greek *aktis* "ray") white, radioactive, metallic element, the first of the actinide series, symbol Ac, atomic number 89, atomic weight 227. It is a weak emitter of high-energy alpha particles and occurs with uranium and radium in ◊pitchblende and other ores. It can be synthesized by bombarding radium with neutrons. The longest-lived isotope, Ac-227, has a half-life of 21.8 years (all the other isotopes have very short half-lives). Actinium was discovered in 1899 by the French chemist André Debierne.

action in law, one of the proceedings whereby a person or agency seeks to enforce rights in a law court.

Actions fall into three principal categories, namely civil (such as the enforcement of a debt), criminal (in which a government agency prosecutes a defendant accused of violation of a criminal law), and penal (violation of a law enacted to preserve public order).

action and reaction in physical mechanics, equal and opposite effects produced by a force acting on an object. For example, the pressure of expanding gases from the burning of fuel in a rocket engine (a force) produces an equal and opposite reaction, which causes the rocket to move.

Action Française French extreme nationalist political movement founded 1899, first led by Charles

Maurras (1868–1952); it stressed the essential unity of all French people in contrast to the Socialist doctrines of class warfare. Its influence peaked in the 1920s.

Initially nationalist and republican it was opposed to capitalism and parliamentarism, but from 1914 it became predominantly nationalist. In the 1920s the movement obtained a degree of respectability through an alliance with the former prime minister Clemenceau and seats in the chamber of deputies. By the 1930s, Action Française had been superseded by more radical right-wing movements such as the Jeunesses Patriotes and the Croix de Feu.

action painting or ***gesture painting*** in US art, a dynamic school of Abstract Expressionism. It emphasized the importance of the physical act of painting, sometimes expressed with both inventiveness and aggression, and on occasion performed for the camera. Jackson Pollock was the leading exponent.

Pollock was known to place his canvas on the floor, attacking it with knives and trowels, throwing paint at it, and bicycling over it. The term "action painting" was coined by the US art critic Harold Rosenberg in 1952.

action potential in biology, a change in the potential difference (voltage) across the membrane of a nerve cell when an impulse passes along it. A change in potential (from about –60 to +45 millivolts) accompanies the passage of sodium and potassium ions across the membrane.

Actium, Battle of a naval battle in which ◊Augustus defeated the combined fleets of ◊Mark Antony and ◊Cleopatra in 31 BC. The site is at Akri, a promontory in W Greece.

activity series alternate name for ◊reactivity series.

act of Congress in the US, a bill or resolution passed by both houses of Congress, the Senate and the House of Representatives, which becomes law with the signature of the president. If vetoed by the president, it may still become law if it returns to Congress and is passed by two-thirds of each house.

act of God legal term meaning some sudden and irresistible act of nature that could not reasonably have been foreseen or prevented, such as storms, earthquakes, or sudden death.

Acton Eliza 1799–1859. English cooking writer and poet, whose *Modern Cookery for Private Families* 1845 influenced Mrs Beeton.

Acton John Emerich Edward Dalberg-Acton, 1st Baron Acton 1834–1902. British historian and Liberal politician. Elected to Parliament in 1859, he was a friend and adviser of Prime Minister Gladstone. Appointed professor of modern history at Cambridge in 1895, he planned and edited the *Cambridge Modern History* but did not live to complete more than the first two volumes.

Actors Studio theater workshop in New York City, established 1947 by Cheryl Crawford and Elia Kazan. Under Lee Strasberg, who became artistic director 1948, it became known for the study of Stanislavsky's ◊Method acting.

Acts of the Apostles book of the New Testament, attributed to ◊Luke, which describes the history of the early Christian church.

actuary a mathematician who makes statistical calculations concerning human life expectancy and other risks, on which insurance premiums are based.

The professional body in the US is the Society of Actuaries, formed 1949 by a merger of two earlier bodies.

acupuncture system of inserting long, thin metal needles into the body at predetermined points to relieve pain, as an anesthetic in surgery, and to assist healing. The needles are rotated manually or electrically. The method, developed in ancient China and increasingly popular in the West, is thought to work by somehow stimulating the brain's own painkillers, the endorphins.

acute in medicine, pertaining to a condition that develops and resolves quickly; for example, the common cold and meningitis. In contrast, a chronic condition develops and remains over a long period.

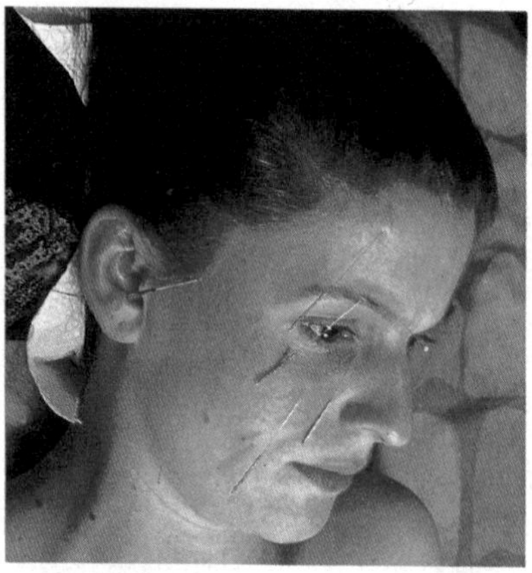

acupuncture *A patient being treated for persistent headaches by acupuncture.*

acute angle an ◊angle whose measure is between 0° and 90°.

AD in the Christian calendar, abbreviation for *Anno Domini* (Latin "in the year of the Lord"); used with dates.

ADA computer-programming language, developed and owned by the US Department of Defense, designed for use in situations in which a computer directly controls a process or machine, such as a military aircraft. The language took more than five years to specify, and became commercially available only in the late 1980s. It is named after Ada Augusta ◊Byron, regarded as the world's first computer programmer.

Adam family of Scottish architects and designers. William Adam (1689–1748) was the leading Scottish architect of his day, and his son Robert Adam (1728–1792) is considered one of the greatest British architects of the late 18th century, who transformed the prevailing Palladian fashion in architecture to a Neo-Classical style. He designed interiors for many great country houses and earned a considerable reputation as a furniture designer. He was associated with one or more of his brothers John, James and William on many projects, including the development of the area known as the Adelphi (Greek "brothers") in London.

Adam (Hebrew *adham* "man") in the Old Testament, founder of the human race. Formed by God from dust and given the breath of life, Adam was placed in the Garden of Eden, where ◊Eve was created from his rib and given to him as a companion. Because she tempted him, he tasted the forbidden fruit of the Tree of Knowledge of Good and Evil, for which trespass they were expelled from the Garden.

Adam Adolphe Charles 1803–1856. French composer of light operas. Some 50 of his works were staged, including the classic ballet *Giselle*.

Adam de la Halle c. 1240–c. 1290. French poet and composer. His *Jeu de Robin et Marion*, written in Italy about 1282, is a theatrical work with dialogue and songs set to what were apparently popular tunes of the day. It is sometimes called the forerunner of comic opera.

Adams Abigail Smith 1744–1818. First lady to US president John Adams and public figure. She married lawyer John Adams of Boston 1764; one of their children, John Quincy Adams, would become the sixth US president. A strong supporter of the cause of American independence, she joined her husband on diplomatic missions to Paris and London after the Revolutionary War. As wife of the US vice-president 1789–97 and later president 1797–1801, she was widely respected.

Born in Weymouth, Massachusetts, she showed an early interest in public affairs. In detailed letters to her husband, she chronicled the events of her day and was an advocate of women's rights.

Adams *US photographer Ansel Adams.*

Adams Ansel 1902–1984. US photographer particularly known for his superbly printed images of dramatic landscapes and organic forms of the American West. He was associated with the ◊Zone System of exposure estimation.

In 1916 Adams made his first trip to Yosemite National Park, and for the rest of his life the High Sierras were a major focus of his work. Although he first became a professional musician, in the late 1920s he turned to professional photography. Light and texture were important elements in his photographs. Adams worked to establish photography as a fine art. He founded the first museum collection of photography, at New York City's Museum of Modern Art 1937. His love of nature also carried over into his work as a conservationist and director of the Sierra Club from 1936.

Adams Charles Francis 1807–1886. US political leader, journalist, and diplomat. Adams was born in Boston, the son of John Quincy Adams. After graduation from Harvard, he studied law with Daniel Webster. As a respected historian and abolitionist, he established the *Boston Whig* and accepted the vice-presidential nomination of the Free Soil party 1848. He later joined the Republican party. After service in the US House of Representatives 1858–61, he was appointed US minister to England by Lincoln. He unsuccessfully sought the 1872 Republican nomination for president.

Adams Franklin Pierce, popularly known as F P A 1881–1960. US humorist and social critic. He gained his greatest fame as a columnist for the New York *Evening Mail*, *Tribune*, *World*, and *Post*. In addition to publishing several books of light verse and collections of his syndicated newspaper columns, he served as a panelist on the popular radio game show "Information Please."

Born in Chicago, Adams studied briefly at the University of Michigan, worked at a succession of odd jobs, and finally joined the *Chicago Journal* as a feature writer 1903.

Adams Henry Brooks 1838–1918. US historian and novelist, a grandson of President John Quincy Adams. He published the acclaimed nine-volume *A History of the United States During the Administrations of Jefferson and Madison* 1889–91, a study of the evolution of democracy in the US.

Born in Boston, he graduated 1858 from Harvard University and later taught medieval history there 1870–77. He also was editor of the *North American Review* 1870–76. His works include a

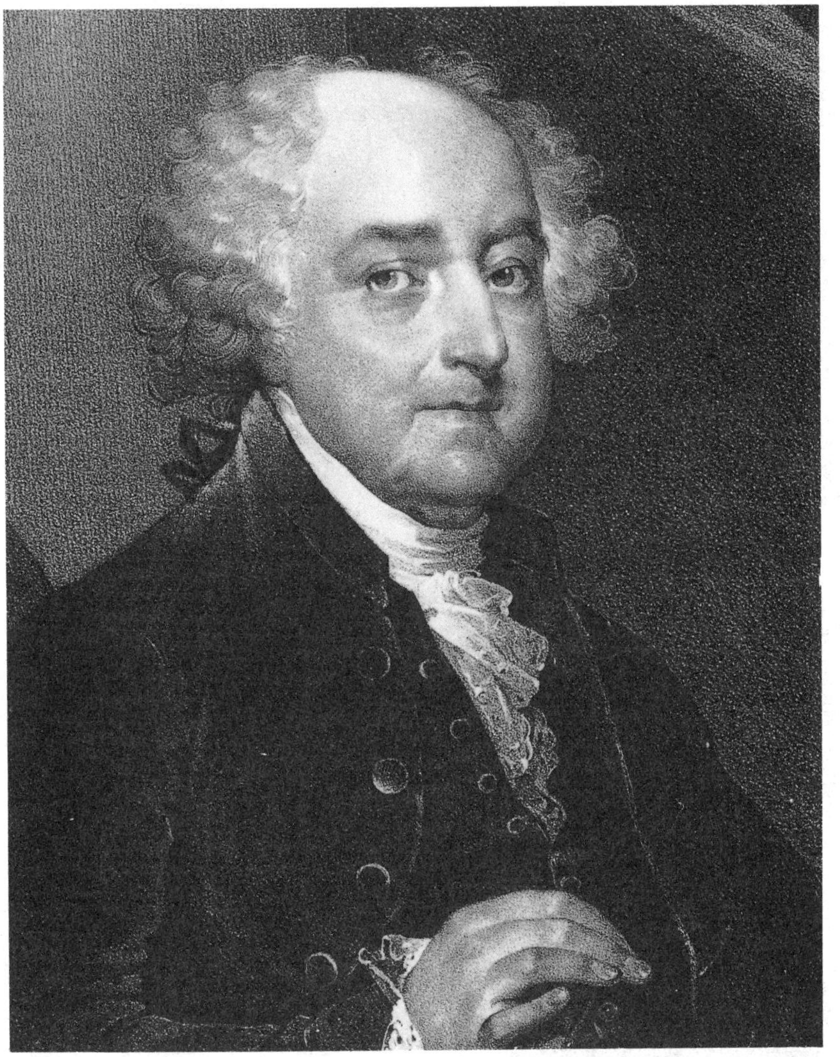

Adams *The 2nd president of the United States of America, John Adams, a Federalist. 1797–1801.*

study of the medieval world *Mont-Saint-Michel and Chartres* 1904, and a classic autobiography *The Education of Henry Adams* 1907, as well as the novels *Democracy, an American Novel* 1880, which reflects his disillusionment with the US political system, and *Esther* 1884, published under a pseudonym, about the conflict between religion and science.

Adams John 1735–1826. The 2nd president of the US 1797–1801, and vice-president 1789–97. Born at Quincy, Massachusetts. He was a member of the Continental Congress 1774–78, and signed the Declaration of Independence. In 1779 he went to France and negotiated the treaties that ended the American Revolution. He was suspicious of the French Revolution, but resisted calls for war with France. In 1785 he became the first US ambassador in London.

Adams John Couch 1819–1892. English astronomer who deduced the existence of the planet Neptune 1845, although it was not found until 1846 by Galle. He also studied the Moon's motion, the Leonid meteors, and terrestrial magnetism.

Adams John Quincy 1767–1848. The 6th president of the US 1825–29. Eldest son of President John ◊Adams, he was born at Quincy, Massachusetts, and became US minister in The Hague, Berlin, St Petersburg, and London. He negotiated the Treaty of Ghent to end the ◊War of 1812 (fought between Britain and the US) on generous terms for the US. In 1817 he became ◊Monroe's secretary of state, formulated the ◊Monroe doctrine 1823, and was elected president by the house of representatives, despite receiving fewer votes than his main rival, Andrew ◊Jackson. As president, Adams was an advocate of strong federal government.

Adams Richard 1920– . English novelist. A civil servant 1948–72, he wrote *Watership Down* 1972, a tale of a rabbit community, which is read by adults and children. Later novels include *Shardik* 1974, *The Plague Dogs* 1977, and *Girl on a Swing* 1980.

Adams Roger 1889–1971. US organic chemist, known for his painstaking analytical work to determine the composition of naturally occurring substances such as complex vegetable oils and plant ◊alkaloids.

Adams Samuel 1722–1803. US politician, second cousin of President John Adams; he was the chief prompter of the Boston Tea Party (see ◊American Revolution). He was also a signatory to the Declaration of Independence, served in the ◊Continental Congress and anticipated the French emperor Napoleon in calling the British a "nation of shopkeepers."

Adamson Joy 1910–1985. German-born naturalist whose work with wildlife in Kenya, including the lioness Elsa, is described in *Born Free* 1960. She was murdered at her home in Kenya. She worked with her third husband, British game warden George Adamson (1906–1989), who was murdered by bandits.

Adana capital of Adana (Seyhan) province, S Turkey; population (1985) 776,000. It is a major cotton-growing center and Turkey's fourth-largest city.

adaptation in biology, any change in the structure or function of an organism that allows it to survive and reproduce more effectively in its environment. In ◊evolution, adaptation is thought to occur as a result of random variation in the genetic make-up of organisms (produced by ◊mutation and ◊recombination) coupled with ◊natural selection.

adaptive radiation in evolution, the formation of several species, with ◊adaptations to different ways of life, from a single ancestral type. Adaptive radiation is likely to occur whenever members of a species migrate to a new habitat with unoccupied ecological niches. It is thought that the lack of competition in such niches allows sections of the migrant population to develop new adaptations, and eventually to become new species.

The colonization of newly formed volcanic islands has led to the development of many unique species. The 13 species of Darwin's finch on the Galápagos Islands, for example, are probably descended from a single species from the South American mainland. The parent stock evolved into different species that now occupy a range of diverse niches.

ADB abbreviation for ◊Asian Development Bank.

Addams Charles 1912–1988. US cartoonist, creator of the ghoulish family published in the *New Yorker* magazine. A successful television comedy series was based on the cartoon in the 1960s.

Addams Jane 1860–1935. US social reformer and feminist who in 1889 cofounded and led Hull House, a settlement house in the slums of Chicago. It was one of the earliest community centers and served as a model for others throughout the US. Innovative services such as day care were provided. She was vice-president of the National American Women Suffrage Association 1911–14, led the Woman's Peace Party and the first Women's Peace Congress 1915, and was president of the Women's International League for Peace and Freedom 1919. She was a US leader in attempts to reform child-labor laws.

Her publications include *Democracy and Social Ethics*, *Newer Ideals of Peace* 1907, and *Twenty Years at Hull House* 1910. She was a cowinner of the Nobel Prize 1931 with Nicholas Murray Butler.

addax light-colored ◊antelope *Addax nasomaculatus* of the family Bovidae. It lives in the Sahara desert, where it exists on scanty vegetation without drinking. It is about 3.5 ft/1.1 m at the shoulder, and both sexes have spirally twisted horns.

adder European venomous snake, the common ◊viper, *Vipera berus*. Growing to about 24 in/60 cm in length, it has a thick body, triangular head, a characteristic V-shaped mark on its head, and, often, zig-zag markings along the back. A shy animal, it feeds on small mammals and lizards. The puff adder, *Bitis arietans*, is a large, yellowish, thick-bodied viper up to 5 ft/1.6 m long, living in Africa and Arabia.

addiction state of dependence on drugs, alcohol, or other substances. Symptoms include uncontrolled craving, tolerance, and symptoms of withdrawal

adder

puff adder

Adams *The 6th president of the United States of America, John Quincy Adams, a Democratic-Republican. 1825–1829.*

when access is denied. Habitual use produces changes in chemical processes in the brain; when the substance is withheld, severe neurological manifestations, even death, may follow. These are reversed by the administration of the addictive substance, and mitigated by a gradual reduction in dosage.

Initially, only opium and its derivatives (morphine, heroin, codeine) were recognized as addictive, but many other drugs, whether therapeutic (for example, tranquilizers or ergotamine) or recreational (such as cocaine and alcohol), are now known to be addictive.

Research points to a genetic predisposition to addiction; environment and psychological make-up are other factors. Although physical addiction always has a psychological element, not all psychological dependence is accompanied by physical dependence. A carefully controlled withdrawal program can reverse the chemical changes of habituation. Cure is difficult because of the many other factors contributing to addiction.

adding machine device for adding (and usually subtracting, multiplying, and dividing) numbers, operated mechanically or electromechanically; now largely superseded by electronic ◊calculators.

Addis Ababa or ***Adis Abeba*** capital of Ethiopia; population (1984) 1,413,000. It was founded 1887 by Menelik, chief of Shoa, who ascended the throne of Ethiopia 1889. His former residence, Menelik Palace, is now occupied by the government. The city is the headquarters of the Organization of African Unity.

Addison Joseph 1672–1719. English writer. In 1704 he celebrated ◊Marlborough's victory at Blenheim in a poem, "The Campaign," and subsequently held political appointments, including under-secretary of state and secretary to the Lord-Lieutenant of Ireland 1708. In 1709 he contributed to the *Tatler*, begun by Richard ◊Steele, with whom he was cofounder in 1711 of the *Spectator*.

Addison Thomas 1793–1863. British physician who first recognized the condition known as ◊Addison's disease in 1855.

Addison's disease rare deficiency or failure of the ◊adrenal glands to produce corticosteroid hormones; it is treated with hormones. The condition, formerly fatal, is characterized by anemia, weakness, low blood pressure, and brownish pigmentation of the skin.

additive in food, any natural or artificial chemical added to prolong the shelf life of processed foods (salt or nitrates), alter the color or flavor of food, or improve its food value (vitamins or minerals). Many chemical additives are used and they are subject to regulation, since individuals may be affected by exposure even to traces of certain additives and may suffer side effects ranging from headaches and hyperactivity to cancer.

They must be listed on labels of prepared foods sold in the US so consumers may be aware of those they cannot tolerate. The natural food movement has grown enormously in the 1970s and 1980s, as increasing awareness of the dangers of additives sent consumers looking for additive-free foods.

artificial sweeteners are used in a range of products for diabetics and for weight loss or weight control.

nutrients may be added to enhance food value. Minerals and vitamins are the most common, especially where the diet would otherwise be deficient, leading to deficiency diseases such as beriberi and pellagra.

preservatives are primarily antioxidants and antimicrobials that control natural oxidation and the action of microorganisms (some of which produce ◊toxins). See ◊food technology.

emulsifiers and surfactants regulate the consistency of fats in prepared food and on the surface of the food in contact with the air.

thickeners, primarily vegetable gums, regulate the consistency of prepared food. Pectin acts in this way on fruit and dairy products.

leavening agents lighten the texture of baked goods without the use of yeasts. Sodium bicarbonate is an example.

acidulants sharpen the taste of foods but may also perform a buffering function in the control of acidity.

bleaching agents assist in the aging and whitening of flours.

anticaking agents prevent powdered products coagulating into solid lumps.

humectants control the humidity of the product by absorbing and retaining moisture.

clarifying agents are used in fruit juices, vinegars, and other fermented liquids. Gelatin is the most common.

firming agents restore the texture of vegetables that may be damaged during processing.

foam regulators are used in beer to provide a controlled "head" on top of the poured product.

Addyston Pipe and Steel Co v US a US Supreme Court decision 1899 that granted the federal government certain regulatory powers over private businesses. The case resulted from a number of convictions of pipe-manufacturing firms

Addison *Kneller's portrait of the English essayist and poet Joseph Addison.*

for price fixing, a violation of the Sherman Antitrust Act. The pipe companies argued that manufacturing was not under federal regulation. The Court ruled that price fixing was a clear impingement on interstate commerce and was therefore under federal regulatory jurisdiction.

Adelaide capital and industrial city of South Australia; population (1986) 993,100. Industries include oil refining, shipbuilding, and the manufacture of electrical goods and automobiles. Grain, wool, fruit, and wine are exported. Founded in 1836, Adelaide was named after William IV's queen.

Adélie Land (French *Terre Adélie*) region of Antarctica which is about 87 mi/140 km long, mountainous, covered in snow and ice, and inhabited only by a research team. It was claimed for France 1840.

Aden (Arabic *'Adan*) capital of South Yemen, on a rocky peninsula at the SW corner of Arabia, commanding the entrance to the Red Sea; population (1984) 318,000. It comprises the new administrative center Madinet al-Sha'ab; the commercial and business quarters of Crater and Tawahi, and the harbor area of Ma'alla. The city's economy is based on oil refining, fishing, and shipping. A British territory from 1839, Aden became part of independent South Yemen 1967.

history After annexation by Britain, Aden and its immediately surrounding area (47 sq mi/121 sq km) were developed as a ship-refueling station following the opening of the Suez Canal 1869.

It was a colony 1937–63 and then, after a period of transitional violence among rival nationalist groups and British forces, was combined with the former Aden protectorate (112,000 sq mi/290,000 sq km) to create the Southern Yemen People's Republic 1967, later renamed the People's Democratic Republic of Yemen.

Adenauer Konrad 1876–1967. German Christian Democrat politician, chancellor of West Germany 1949–63. With the French president de Gaulle he achieved the postwar reconciliation of France and Germany and strongly supported all measures designed to strengthen the Western bloc in Europe.

Adenauer was mayor of his native city of Cologne from 1917 until his imprisonment by Hitler in 1933 for opposition to the Nazi regime. After the war he headed the Christian Democratic Union and became chancellor.

adenoids masses of lymphoid tissue, similar to ◊tonsils, located in the upper part of the throat, behind the nose. They are part of a child's natural defenses against the entry of germs but usually shrink and disappear by the age of ten.

Adenoids may swell and grow, particularly if infected, and block the breathing passages. If they become repeatedly infected, they may be removed surgically (adenoidectomy).

Ader Clément 1841–1925. French aviation pioneer and inventor. He demonstrated stereophonic sound transmission by telephone at the 1881 Paris Exhibition of Electricity. His steam-driven airplane, the *Éole*, made the first powered takeoff in history (1890), but it could not fly. In 1897, with his *Avion III*, he failed completely, despite false claims made later.

adhesion in medicine, the abnormal binding of two tissues as a result of inflammation. The moving surfaces of joints or internal organs may merge together if they have been inflamed.

adhesive substance that sticks two surfaces together. Natural adhesives include gelatin in its crude industrial form (made from bones, hide fragments, and fish offal) and vegetable gums. Synthetic adhesives include thermoplastic and thermosetting resins, which are often stronger than the substances they join; mixtures of ◊epoxy resin and hardener that set by chemical reaction; and elastomeric (stretching) adhesives for flexible joints.

Adige the second-longest river (after the Po) in

adaptation

The beaks of birds are adapted to suit their diet
toucan
long beak to pick berries from thin twigs
hummingbird
long, pointed beak to reach nectar deep inside flowers
eagle
sharp, hooked beak to tear flesh from prey
nightjar
wide gape and bristles around beak to trap flying insects
spoonbill
swings long, wide beak from side to side underwater to capture fish and aquatic insects
oystercatcher
long, straight beak to prise open shells of bivalve molluscs, such as mussels
skimmer
scoops up fish and traps them in its scissor-like beak

Italy, 255 mi/410 km in length. It crosses the Lombardy Plain and enters the Adriatic just N of the Po delta.

Adi Granth or ***Guru Granth Sahib*** the holy book of Sikhism.

ad infinitum (Latin) to infinity, endlessly.

adipose tissue type of ◊connective tissue of vertebrates that serves as an energy reserve, and also pads some organs. It is commonly called fat tissue, and consists of large spherical cells filled with fat. In mammals, major layers are in the inner layer of skin and around the kidneys and heart.

Fatty acids are transported to and from it via the blood system.

Adirondacks mountainous area in NE New York, rising to 5,344 ft/1,629 m at Mount Marcy; the source of the Hudson and Ausable rivers; named after an Indian tribe. The Adirondacks area occupies about 25% of the state of New York, and a state park occupies more than 500 million acres/200 million hectares. Thickly wooded, the region is noted for scenery, health resorts such as Saranac Lake, and sports facilities such as those at Lake Placid, where the 1932 and 1980 winter Olympic Games were held.

adit in mining, a horizontal shaft from the surface to reach the mineral seam. It was a common method of mining in hilly districts and was used to drain water.

adj. in grammar, abbreviation for ◊adjective.

Adjani Isabelle 1955– . French film actress of Algerian-German descent. She played the title role in Truffaut's *L'Histoire d'Adèle H/The Story of Adèle H* 1975 and has since appeared in international productions including *Le Locataire/The Tenant*; *Nosferatu Phantom der Nacht* 1979; and *Ishtar* 1987.

adjective the grammatical ◊part of speech for words that describe nouns (for example, *new* and *enormous*, as in "a new hat" and "an enormous dog"). Adjectives generally have three degrees (grades or levels for the description of relationships): the positive degree (*new, enormous*) the comparative degree (*newer, more enormous*), and the superlative degree (*newest, most enormous*).

Some adjectives do not normally need comparative and superlative forms; one person cannot be "more asleep" than someone else, a lone action is unlikely to be "the most single-handed action ever seen," and many people dislike the expression "most unique" or "almost unique," because something unique is supposed to be the only one that exists. For purposes of emphasis or style these conventions may be set aside ("I don't know who is more unique; they are both remarkable people"). Double comparatives such as "more bigger" are not grammatical in Standard English, but Shakespeare used a double superlative ("the most unkindest cut of all"). Some adjectives may have both the comparative and superlative forms (*commoner* and *more common*; *commonest* and *most common*), usually shorter words take on the suffix *-er/-est* but occasionally they may be given the more/most forms for emphasis or other reasons ("Which of them is the *most clear*?").

When an adjective comes before a noun it is attributive; a predicate adjective comes after noun and verb (for example, "It looks *good*"). Some adjectives can only be used in the predicate ("The child was asleep," but not "the asleep child"). The participles of verbs are regularly used adjectivally ("a *sleeping* child," "*boiled* milk") and often in compound forms ("a *quick-acting* medicine," "a *glass-making* factory"; "a *hard-boiled* egg," "*well-trained* teachers"). Adjectives are often formed by adding suffixes to nouns (sand: sandy; nation: nation*al*).

Adler Alfred 1870–1937. Austrian psychologist. Adler saw the "will to power" as more influential in accounting for human behavior than the sexual drive theory. A dispute over this theory led to the dissolution of his ten-year collaboration with ◊Freud.

Born in Vienna, he was a general practitioner and nerve specialist there 1897–1927, serving as an army doctor in World War I. He joined the circle of Freudian doctors in Vienna about 1900. The concepts of inferiority complex and overcompensation originated with Adler, for example in his books *Organic Inferiority and Psychic Compensation* 1907 and *Understanding Human Nature* 1927.

Adler Cyrus 1863–1940. US educator and public figure. In 1892 he was appointed curator at the Smithsonian Institution and later served as its librarian and assistant secretary. From 1908 until his death, he was president of Dropsie College and a leader of the American Jewish Committee. His appeal for protection of the rights of religious ethnic minorities was adopted in the final text of the Treaty of Versailles after World War I.

Born in Van Buren, Arkansas, Adler studied Semitic languages at the University of Pennsylvania and at Johns Hopkins University, where he received a PhD 1887.

administrative law law concerning the powers and control of government agencies or those agencies granted statutory powers of administration. These powers include those necessary to operate the agency or to implement its purposes, and making quasi-judicial decisions (such as determining tax liability, granting licenses or permits, or hearing complaints against the agency or its officers). The vast increase in these powers in the 20th century in many countries has been widely criticized.

Depending on legislative mandates, administrative law may be actionable in civil or criminal court or subject to review by executive branch agencies.

admiral highest-ranking naval officer.

In the US Navy, in descending order, the ranks of admiral are: fleet admiral, admiral, vice admiral, and rear admiral.

admiral several species of butterfly in the same family (Nymphalidae) as the tortoiseshells. The red admiral *Vanessa atalanta*, wingspan 2.5 in/6 cm, is found worldwide in the N hemisphere. It migrates S each year from N areas to subtropical zones.

Admiralty Islands a group of small islands in the SW Pacific, part of Papua New Guinea; population (1980) 25,000. The main island is Manus. The islands became a German protectorate 1884 and an Australian mandate 1920.

ad nauseam (Latin) to the point of disgust.

Adonis in Greek mythology, a beautiful youth beloved by the goddess ◊Aphrodite. He was killed while boar-hunting but was allowed to return from the lower world for six months every year to rejoin her. The anemone sprang from his blood.

Worshiped as a god of vegetation, he was known as Tammuz in Babylonia, Assyria, and Phoenicia (where it was his sister, ◊Ishtar, who brought him from the lower world). He seems also to have been identified with ◊Osiris, the Egyptian god of the underworld.

adoption the permanent legal transfer of parental rights and duties in respect of a child from one person or institution to another.

State laws determine processes for adoption, rights of adoptees (such as access to information about natural parents), and inheritance rights.

Adowa alternate form of ◊Aduwa, former capital of Ethiopia.

ADP abbreviation for adenosine diphosphate, a raw material in the manufacture of ◊ATP, the molecule used by all cells to drive their chemical reactions.

Adrastus in Greek mythology, king of Argos, and leader of the expedition of the ◊Seven against Thebes, undertaken to place his son-in-law ◊Polynices on the throne of Thebes.

adrenal gland or ***suprarenal gland*** gland situated on top of the kidney. The adrenals are soft and yellow, and consist of two parts: the cortex and medulla. The cortex (outer part) secretes various steroid hormones, controls salt and water metabolism, and regulates the use of carbohydrates, proteins, and fats. The medulla (inner part) secretes the hormones adrenaline and noradrenaline which, during times of stress, cause the heart to beat faster and harder; increase blood flow to the heart and muscle cells; dilate airways in the lungs, thereby delivering more oxygen to cells throughout the body; and in general prepare the body for "fight or flight."

adrenaline or epinephrine hormone secreted by the medulla of the ◊adrenal glands. Adrenaline's action on the ◊liver raises blood-sugar levels by stimulating glucose production; it also increases the heart rate, raises blood fatty-acid levels by its action on adipose tissue, and constricts and dilates blood vessels selectively.

adrenocorticotropic hormone see ◊ACTH.

Adrian Edgar, 1st Baron Adrian 1889–1977. British physiologist who received the Nobel Prize for Medicine in 1932 for his work with Charles Sherrington in the field of nerve impulses and the function of the neuron.

Adrian IV (Nicholas Breakspear) c. 1100–1159. Pope 1154–59, the only British pope. He secured the execution of Arnold of Brescia; crowned Frederick I Barbarossa as German emperor; refused Henry II's request that Ireland should be granted to the English crown in absolute ownership; and was at the height of a quarrel with the emperor when he died.

Adrianople older name of the Turkish town ◊Edirne, after the Emperor Hadrian, who rebuilt it about AD 125.

Adriatic Sea large arm of the Mediterranean Sea, lying NW to SE between the Italian and the Balkan peninsulas. The W shore is Italian; the E is Yugoslav and Albanian. The sea is about 500 mi/805 km long, and its area is 135,250 sq km/52,220 sq mi.

adsorption the taking up of a gas or liquid at the surface of another substance, usually a solid (for example, activated charcoal adsorbs gases). It involves molecular attraction at the surface, and should be distinguished from ◊absorption (in which a uniform solution results from a gas or liquid being incorporated into the bulk structure of a liquid or solid).

Adullam a biblical city with nearby caves in which David and those who had some grievance took refuge (1 Samuel 22). An Adullamite is a person who is disaffected or who secedes from a political party; the term was used to describe about 40 British Liberal MPs who voted against their leaders to defeat the 1866 Reform Bill.

adultery voluntary sexual intercourse by a married person with someone other than his or her legal partner.

It is almost universally recognized as grounds for ◊divorce in the US and is a punishable offense in some states.

Aduwa or ***Adwa***, or ***Adowa*** former capital of Ethiopia, about 110 mi/180 km SW of Massawa at an altitude of 6,270 ft/1,910 m; population (1982) 27,000.

Aduwa, Battle of defeat of the Italians by the Ethiopians at Aduwa in 1896 under Emperor ◊Menelik II. It marked the end of Italian ambitions in this part of Africa until Mussolini's reconquest in 1935.

adv. in grammar, abbreviation for ◊adverb.

advanced gas-cooled reactor type of nuclear power generator; see ◊AGR.

Advent in the Christian calendar, the preparatory season for Christmas, including the four Sundays preceding it, beginning with the Sunday that falls nearest (before or after) St Andrew's Day (30 Nov).

Adventist a person who believes that Christ will return to make a second appearance on the Earth. Expectation of the Second Coming of Christ is found in New Testament writings generally.

Adventist views are held in particular by the ◊Seventh-Day Adventist church (with 1.5 million members in 200 countries), Christadelphians, the Jehovah's Witnesses, the Four Square Gospel Alliance, the Advent Christian church, and the Evangelical Adventist church.

Most American adventists trace their origins to the Millerites of the 1840s, who accepted the calculation of William Miller, a Baptist farmer in New York State, that the Second Coming of Christ would occur on Oct 22, 1844. When it failed to occur, Miller admitted his deductions had been mistaken, but he and his remaining followers continued to expect the imminent return of Christ, and they formed churches that evolved into the contemporary adventist groups.

adventitious root a root developing in an unusual position, as in the ivy, where roots grow sideways out of the stem and cling to trees or walls.

adverb the grammatical ◊part of speech for words that modify or describe verbs ("She ran *quickly*"), adjectives ("a *beautifully* clear day"), and adverbs ("They did it *really* well"). Most adverbs are formed from adjectives or past participles by adding *-ly* (*quick: quickly*) or *-ally* (*automatic: automatically*).

Sometimes adverbs are formed by adding *-wise* (*likewise* and *clockwise*, as in "moving *clockwise*"; in "a *clockwise* direction," *clockwise* is an adjective). Some adverbs have a distinct form from their partnering adjective; for example, *good/well* ("It was *good* work; they did it *well*"). Others do not derive from adjectives (*very*, in "*very* nice"; *tomorrow*, in "I'll do it *tomorrow*"); and some are unadapted adjectives (*pretty*, as in "It's *pretty* good"). Sentence adverbs modify whole sentences or phrases: "*Generally*, it rains a lot here"; "*Usually*, the town is busy at this time of year." Sometimes there is controversy in such matters. *Hopefully* is universally accepted in sentences like "He looked at them *hopefully*" (= in a hopeful way), but some people dislike it in "*Hopefully*, we'll see you again next year" (= We hope that we'll see you again next year).

advertising any of various methods used by a company to increase the sales of its products or to promote a brand name. Advertising can be seen by economists as either beneficial (since it conveys information about a product and so brings the market closer to a state of ◊perfect competition) or as a hindrance to perfect competition, since it attempts to make illusory distinctions (such as greater sex appeal) between essentially similar products.

advocate (Latin *advocatus*, one summoned to one's aid, especially in a court of justice) a professional pleader in a court of justice. More common terms are attorney, ◊lawyer or counsel, but advocate is retained in such countries as Scotland and France, whose legal systems are based on Roman law.

Aegean civilization the cultures of Bronze Age Greece, including the ◊Minoan civilization of Crete and the ◊Mycenean civilization of the E Peloponnese.

Aegean Islands the islands of the Aegean Sea, but more specifically a region of Greece comprising the Dodecanese islands, the Cyclades islands, Lesvos, Samos, and Chios; population (1981) 428,500; area 3,523 sq mi/9,122 sq km.

Aegean Sea branch of the Mediterranean between Greece and Turkey; the Dardanelles connect it with the Sea of Marmara. The numerous islands in the Aegean Sea include Crete, the Cyclades, the Sporades, and the Dodecanese. There is political tension between Greece and Turkey over sea limits claimed by Greece around such islands as Lesvos, Chios, Samos, and Kos.

The Aegean Sea is named after the legendary Aegeus, who drowned himself in the belief that Theseus, his son, had been killed.

Aegeus in Greek mythology, king of Athens, and father of ◊Theseus. On his return from Crete, Theseus forgot to substitute white sails for black to indicate his success in killing the ◊Minotaur. Believing his son dead, Aegeus leapt into the Aegean Sea.

Aegina (Greek *Aíyna* or *Aíyina*) Greek island in the Gulf of Aegina about 20 mi/32 km SW of Piraeus; area 32 sq mi/83 sq km; population (1981) 11,100. In 1811 remarkable sculptures were recovered from a Doric temple in the northeast, restored by Thorwaldsen, and taken to Munich.

Aegir in Scandinavian mythology, the god of the sea.

Aegis in Greek mythology, the shield of Zeus, symbolic of the storm cloud associated with him. In representations of deities it is commonly shown as a protective animal skin.

Aehrenthal Count Aloys von 1854–1912. Foreign minister of Austria-Hungary during the ◊Bosnian crisis of 1908.

Aelfric c. 955–1020. Anglo-Saxon writer and abbot, author of two collections of *Catholic Homilies* 990–92, sermons, and the *Lives of the Saints* 996–97, written in vernacular Old English prose.

Aeneas in Classical legend, a Trojan prince who became the ancestral hero of the Romans. According to Homer, he was the son of Anchises and the goddess Aphrodite. During the Trojan War he owed his life to the frequent intervention of the gods. The legend on which Virgil's epic poem the ◊*Aeneid* is based describes his escape from Troy and his eventual settlement in Laetium, on the Italian peninsula.

Aeneid epic poem by Virgil, written in Latin in 12 books of hexameters and composed during the last 11 years of his life (30–19 BC). It celebrates the founding of Rome through the legend of Aeneas. After the fall of Troy, Aeneas wanders the Mediterranean for seven years and becomes shipwrecked off North Africa. He is received by Dido, queen of Carthage, and they fall in love. Aeneas, however, renounces their love and sails on to Italy where he settles as the founder of Latium and the Roman state.

Aeolian harp a wind-blown instrument, consisting of a shallow soundbox supporting gut strings at low tension and tuned to the same pitch. It produces an eerie harmony that rises and falls with the changing pressure of the wind. It was common in parts of central Europe during the 19th century.

Aeolian Islands another name for the ◊Lipari Islands.

Aeolus in Greek mythology, the god of the winds, who kept them imprisoned in a cave on the ◊Lipari Islands.

Aepyornis genus of large, extinct, flightless birds living in Madagascar until a few thousand years ago. Some stood 10 ft/3 m high and laid eggs with a volume of 2 gallons/9 liters.

Aequi an Italian people, originating around the river Velino, who were turned back from their advance on Rome in 431 BC and were conquered in 304 BC, during the Samnite Wars. Like many other peoples conquered by the Romans, they adopted Roman customs and culture.

aerated water water that has had air (oxygen) blown through it. Such water supports aquatic life and prevents growth of bacteria.

aerenchyma plant tissue with numerous air-filled spaces between the cells. It occurs in the stems and roots of many aquatic plants where it aids buoyancy and facilitates transport of oxygen around the plant.

aerial or ***antenna*** in radio and television broadcasting, a conducting device that radiates or receives electromagnetic waves. The design of an aerial depends principally on the wavelength of the signal. Long waves (hundreds of yards in wavelength) may employ long wire aerials; short waves (several inches in wavelength) may employ rods and dipoles; microwaves may also use dipoles—often with reflectors arranged like a toast rack—or highly directional parabolic dish aerials. Because microwaves travel in straight lines, giving line-of-sight communication, microwave aerials are usually located at the tops of tall masts or towers.

aerial bombardment another name for ◊blitzkrieg.

aerobic in biology, a description of those living organisms that require oxygen (usually dissolved in water) for the efficient release of energy contained in food molecules, such as glucose.

They include almost all living organisms (plants as well as animals) with the exception of certain bacteria. Oxygen is used to convert glucose to carbon dioxide and water, thereby releasing energy. Most aerobic organisms die in the absence of oxygen, but certain organisms and cells, such as muscle cells, can function for short periods ◊anaerobically (without oxygen).

aerobics (Greek "air" and "life") exercises for cardiovascular fitness. A strenuous application of movement to raise the heart rate to 120 beats a minute or more for sessions of 5–20 minutes' duration, 3–5 times per week. For interest and pleasure, often a combination of dance, stretching exercises, and running aim to improve the performance of the heart and lungs system, but swimming, cycling and race-walking are preferred because they are less punishing to the joints and cause fewer sports-related injuries. Aerobics became a health and fitness pursuit in the 1980s.

aerodynamics branch of fluid physics that studies the forces exerted by air or other gases in motion, particularly the airflow around bodies (such as land vehicles, bullets, rockets, and aircraft) moving at speed through the atmosphere. For maximum efficiency, the aim is usually to design the shape of an object to produce a streamlined flow, with a minimum of turbulence in the moving air.

aeronautics the science of travel through the Earth's atmosphere, including ◊aerodynamics, aircraft structures, jet and rocket propulsion, and aerial navigation.

In subsonic aeronautics (below the speed of sound), aerodynamic forces increase at the rate of the square of the speed. Transsonic aeronautics covers the speed range from just below to just above the speed of sound and is crucial to aircraft design. Ordinary sound waves move at about 760 mph/1,225 kph at sea level, and air in front of an aircraft moving slower than this is "warned" by the waves so that it can move aside. However, as the flying speed approaches that of the sound waves, the warning is too late for the air to escape, and the aircraft pushes the air aside, creating shock waves, which absorb much power and create design problems. On the ground the shock waves give rise to a ◊sonic boom. It was once thought that the speed of sound was a speed limit to aircraft, and the term ◊sound barrier came into use. Supersonic aeronautics concerns speeds above that of sound and in one sense may be considered a much older study than aeronautics itself, since the study of the flight of bullets, known as ◊ballistics, was undertaken soon after the introduction of firearms. Hypersonics is the study of airflows and forces at speeds above five times that of sound (Mach 5); for example, for guided missiles, space rockets, and advanced concepts such as ◊HOTOL (horizontal takeoff and landing). For all flight speeds streamlining is necessary to reduce the effects of air resistance.

Aeronautics is distinguished from astronautics, which is the science of travel through space. Astronavigation (navigation by reference to the stars) is used in aircraft as well as in ships and is a part of aeronautics.

aerosol particles of liquid or solid suspended in a gas. Fog is a common natural example. Aerosol cans, which contain pressurized gas mixed with a propellant, are used to spray liquid in the form of tiny drops of products such as insecticides. Many commercial aerosols use chlorofluorocarbons (CFCs) as propellants, and these are now known to cause destruction of the ◊ozone layer in the Earth's atmosphere. As a consequence, the international community has agreed to phase out the use of CFCs as propellants. Unfortunately, so-called "ozone-friendly" aerosols have the disadvantage of using flammable butane or propane as propellants.

aerosol

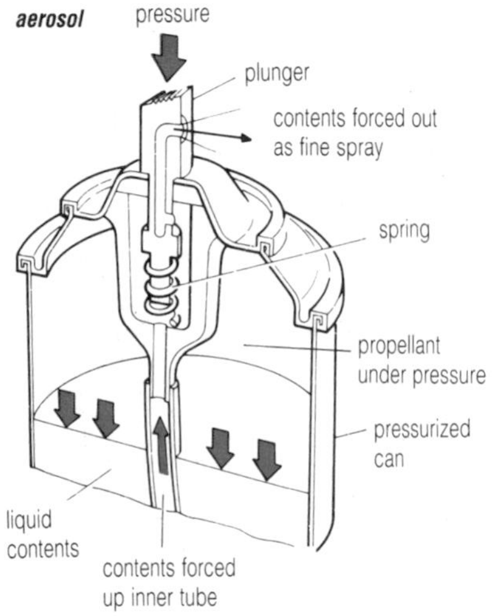
pressure
plunger
contents forced out
as fine spray
spring
propellant
under pressure
pressurized
can
liquid
contents
contents forced
up inner tube

Aeschines lived 4th century BC. Orator of ancient Athens, a rival of ◊Demosthenes.

Aeschylus c. 525–c. 456 BC. Greek dramatist, widely regarded as the founder of Greek tragedy (see ◊Euripides; ◊Sophocles). By the introduction of a second actor he made true dialogue and dramatic action possible. Aeschylus wrote some 90 plays between 499 and 458 BC, of which seven survive. These are *The Suppliant Women* performed about 490 BC, *The Persians* 472 BC, *Seven against Thebes* 467 BC, *Prometheus Bound* (c. 460 BC) and the ◊*Oresteia* trilogy 458 BC.

Aeschylus was born at Eleusis, near Athens, of a noble family. He took part in the Persian Wars and fought at Marathon 490 BC. He twice visited the court of Hieron I, king of Syracuse, and died at Gela in Sicily.

Aesculapius in Greek and Roman mythology, the god of medicine; his emblem was a staff with a snake coiled around it, since snakes seemed to renew life by shedding their skin.

Aesir principal gods of Norse mythology—Odin, Thor, Balder, Loki, Freya, and Tyr—whose dwelling place was Asgard.

Aesop traditional writer of Greek fables. According to Herodotus he lived in the reign of Amasis of Egypt (mid-6th century BC) and was a slave of Iadmon, a Thracian. The fables, for which no evidence of his authorship exists, are anecdotal stories using animal characters to illustrate moral or satirical points.

Aesthetic movement English artistic movement of the late 19th century, dedicated to the doctrine "art for art's sake" – that is, art as self-sufficient, not needing to justify its existence by serving any particular use. Artists associated with the movement include Beardsley and Whistler. The writer Oscar Wilde was in his twenties an exemplary aesthete.

Aetolia district of ancient Greece on the NW of the gulf of Corinth. The Aetolian League was a confederation of the cities of Aetolia which, following the death of Alexander the Great, became the chief rival of Macedonian power and the Achaean League.

Afars and the Issas, French Territory of the former French territory that became the Republic of ◊Djibouti 1977.

AFD abbreviation for accelerated freeze drying, a common method of food preservation. See ◊food technology.

affidavit a legal document, used in court applications and proceedings, in which a person swears that certain facts are true.

affine geometry a geometry that preserves parallelism and the ratios between intervals on any line segment.

affinity in chemistry, the force of attraction (see ◊bond) between chemical elements, which helps to keep them in combination in a molecule.

A given element may have a greater affinity for one particular element than for another (for example, hydrogen has a great affinity for chlorine, with which it easily and rapidly combines to form hydrochloric acid, but has little or no affinity for argon).

affirmation a solemn declaration made instead of taking the oath by a person who has no religious belief or objects to taking an oath on religious grounds.

affirmative action in the US, a government-endorsed policy of positive discrimination that favors members of minority ethnic groups and women in such areas as employment and education, designed to counter the effects of long-term discrimination against them. The policy has been controversial, and has prompted lawsuits by white males who have been denied jobs or education as a result.

The Equal Opportunities Act 1972 set up a commission to enforce the policy in organizations receiving public funds, so many private institutions and employers adopted voluntary affirmative action programs at the same time. In the 1980s the policy was sometimes not rigorously enforced.

Positive discrimination in favor of ethnic-minority construction companies by local government was outlawed Jan 1989.

affluent society a society in which most people have money left over after satisfying their basic needs such as food and shelter. They are then able to decide how to spend their excess ("disposable") income, and become "consumers." The term was popularized by the US economist John Kenneth ◊Galbraith.

Galbraith used the term to describe the Western industrialized nations, particularly the US, in his book *The Affluent Society* 1958, in which he advocated using more of the nation's wealth for public spending and less for private consumption.

Afghan native to or an inhabitant of Afghanistan. The dominant group, particularly in Kabul, are the Pathans. The Tadzhiks, a smaller ethnic group, are predominantly traders and farmers in the province of Herat and around Kabul. The Hazaras, another farming group, are found in the southern mountain ranges of the Hindu Kush. The Uzbeks and Turkomen are farmers, and speak Altaic-family languages. The smallest Altaic minority are the Kirghiz, who live in the Pamir. Baluchi nomads live in the south, and Nuristani farmers live in the mountains of the northeast.

The Pathans, Tadzhiks, and Hazaras are traditionally nomadic horse breeders and speak languages belonging to the Iranian branch of the Indo-European family. The majority of the population are Sunni Muslims, the most recent converts being the Nuristanis.

Afghan hound breed of fast hunting dog resembling the ◊saluki, though more thickly coated, first introduced to the W by British army officers serving on India's North-West Frontier along the Afghanistan border in the late 19th century. The Afghan hound is about 28 in/70 cm tall and has a long, silky coat.

It has an aloof, aristocratic expression, and has become increasingly fashionable since the 1970s.

Afghanistan mountainous, landlocked country in S central Asia, bounded N by the USSR, W by Iran, and S and E by Pakistan.

government The 1977 constitution was abolished after a coup 1978, and legislative and executive authority was assumed by a 57-member revolutionary council, controlled by a smaller presidium of leaders from the only political party,

Afghanistan
Republic of
(Jamhuria Afghanistan)

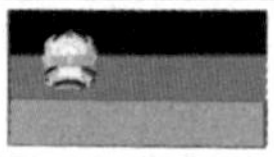

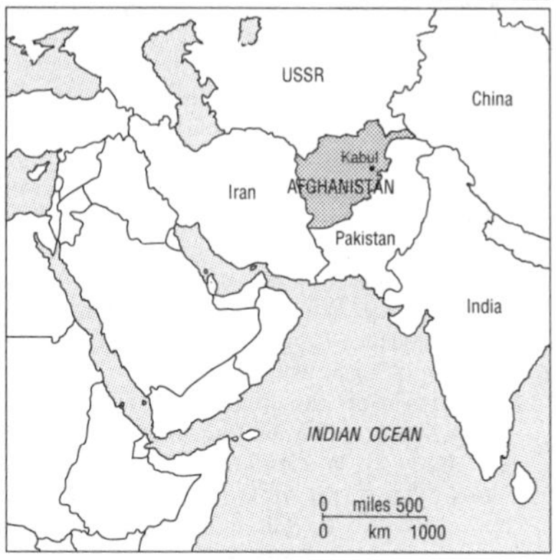
USSR
China
Kabul
AFGHANISTAN
Iran
Pakistan
India
INDIAN OCEAN
0 miles 500
0 km 1000

area 251,707 sq mi/652,090 sq km
capital Kābul
cities Kandahār, Herāt, Mazar-i-Sharif
physical mountainous in center and NE, plains in N and SW
features Hindu Kush mountain range (Khyber and Salang passes, Wakhan salient and Panjshir Valley), Amu Darya (Oxus) River, Helmand River, Lake Saberi
head of state Najibullah Ahmadzai (president) from 1986
head of government Fazl Haq Khaleqiar (prime minister) from 1990
political system military emergency republic
political parties Homeland Party (formerly People's Democratic Party of Afghanistan (PDPA)) Marxist-Leninist; Hesb-i-Islami and Jamiat-i-Islami, Islamic fundamentalist mujaheddin; National Liberation Front, moderate mujaheddin
exports dried fruit, natural gas (piped to USSR), fresh fruits, carpets; small amounts of rare minerals, karakul lamb skins, and Afghan coats
currency afghāni
population (1989) 15,590,000 (more than 5 million became refugees after 1979); growth rate 0.6% p.a.
life expectancy (1986) men 43, women 41
languages Pushtu, Persian (Dari)
religion Muslim: 80% Sunni, 20% Shiite
literacy men 39%/women 8% (1985 est)
GNP $3.3 bn (1985); $275 per head
GDP $1,858 mn; $111 per head
chronology
1747 Afghanistan became an independent emirate.
1838–1919 Afghan Wars waged between Afghanistan and Britain to counter the threat to British India from expanding Russian influence in Afghanistan.
1919 Afghanistan recovered full independence following Third Afghan War.
1953 Lt Gen Daud Khan became prime minister and introduced reform program.
1963 Daud Khan forced to resign and constitutional monarchy established.
1973 Monarchy overthrown in coup by Daud Khan.
1978 Daud Khan ousted by Taraki and the PDPA.
1979 Taraki replaced by Hafizullah Amin; Soviet Union entered country to prop up government; they installed Babrak Karmal in power. Amin executed.
1986 Replacement of Karmal as leader by Dr Najibullah Ahmadzai. Partial Soviet troop withdrawal.
1988 New non-Marxist constitution adopted.
1989 Withdrawal of Soviet troops; state of emergency imposed in response to intensification of civil war.
1990 PDPA renamed the Homeland Party; President Najibullah elected its president.
1991 Peace plan accepted by President Najibullah and Mujaheddin.

the Communist People's Democratic Party of Afghanistan (PDPA). In Nov 1987 a grand national assembly (*Loya Jirgah*) of indirectly elected elders from various ethnic groups approved a new permanent constitution, establishing Islam as the state religion and creating a multi-party, presidential system of government. Under the terms of this constitution, the president, who is elected for a seven-year term by the *Loya Jirgah*, appoints the prime minister and is empowered to approve the laws and resolutions of the elected two-chamber national assembly (*Meli Shura*). The constitution was suspended following the withdrawal of Soviet troops in Feb 1989 and an emergency military-PDPA regime was established. At its head is President Najibullah, who chairs the Supreme Council for the Defence of the Homeland (SCDH).

history Part of the ancient Persian Empire, Darius I and Alexander the Great used the region as a path to India; Islamic conquerors arrived in the 7th century, then Genghis Khan and Tamerlane in the 13th and 14th, respectively. Afghanistan first became an independent emirate 1747. During the 19th century three ◊Afghan Wars were fought between imperial Britain and tsarist Russia for control of Central Asia. The Anglo-Russian treaty 1907 gave autonomy to Afghanistan, with independence achieved by the Treaty of Rawalpindi 1919. The kingdom was founded 1926 by Emir Amanullah.

During the 1950s, Lt-Gen Sardar Mohammad Daud Khan, cousin of King Mohammad Zahir Shah (ruled 1933–73), governed as prime minister and introduced a program of social and economic modernization with Soviet aid. Opposition to his authoritarian rule forced Daud's resignation 1963; the king was made a constitutional monarch, but political parties were outlawed.

After a famine 1972, General Daud Khan overthrew the monarchy in a Soviet-backed military coup 1973. The King fled to exile, and a republic was declared. Daud introduced moderate policies, built up support among minority ethnic groups, and reduced Afghanistan's dependence on the Soviet Union by drawing closer to the nonaligned and Middle East oil states (where many Afghans were employed). A new presidential constitution was adopted 1977, although undermined by fundamentalist Muslim insurgents funded by Libya, Iran, and Pakistan.

In 1978 President Daud was assassinated in a military coup, and Nur Mohammad Taraki, the imprisoned leader of the radical Khalq (masses) faction of the banned PDPA, took charge as president of a revolutionary council. A one-party constitution was adopted, a Treaty of Friendship and Mutual Defense signed with the USSR, and major reforms introduced. Conservative Muslims opposed these initiatives, thousands of refugees fled to Iran and Pakistan, and there was an uprising in the Herat region. Taraki was replaced 1979 by foreign minister Hafizullah Amin.

Internal unrest continued, and the USSR organized a further coup Dec 1979. Hafizullah Amin was executed and Babrak Karmal (1929–), the exiled leader of the gradualist Parcham (banner) faction of the PDPA, was installed as leader. The numbers of Soviet forces in Afghanistan grew to over 120,000 by 1985 as Muslim guerrilla resistance by the "mujaheddin" ("holy warriors") continued. A war of attrition developed, with the USSR failing to gain control of rural areas.

Faced with high troop casualties and a drain of economic resources, the new Soviet administration of ◊Gorbachev moved toward a compromise settlement 1986. In May 1986 Karmal was replaced (ostensibly for health reasons) as PDPA leader by the Pushtun (Pathan) former secret police chief Dr Najibullah Ahmadzai (1947–), and several non-Communist politicians joined the new government. In Oct 1986, 8,000 Soviet troops were withdrawn as a goodwill gesture, and in Jan 1987 the Afghan government announced a six-month unilateral ceasefire. The mujaheddin rejected this initiative, however, insisting on a full Soviet withdrawal and replacement of the communist government. The Najibullah government extended the ceasefire, and in Nov 1987 a new multiparty Islamic constitution was ratified in an attempt to promote "national reconciliation." In Feb 1988 the USSR announced that it would withdraw its forces in a phased manner between May 1988 and Feb 1989, and in April 1988 the Afghan and Pakistan governments signed an agreement providing for noninterference in each other's internal affairs and the voluntary return of refugees, with the US and the USSR acting as guarantors.

On the completion of Soviet troop withdrawal in Feb 1989 a "state of emergency" was imposed by the Najibullah government, which was faced with a mounting military onslaught by the mujaheddin. The guerrillas, whose commanders by now controlled a number of regions outside

Africa

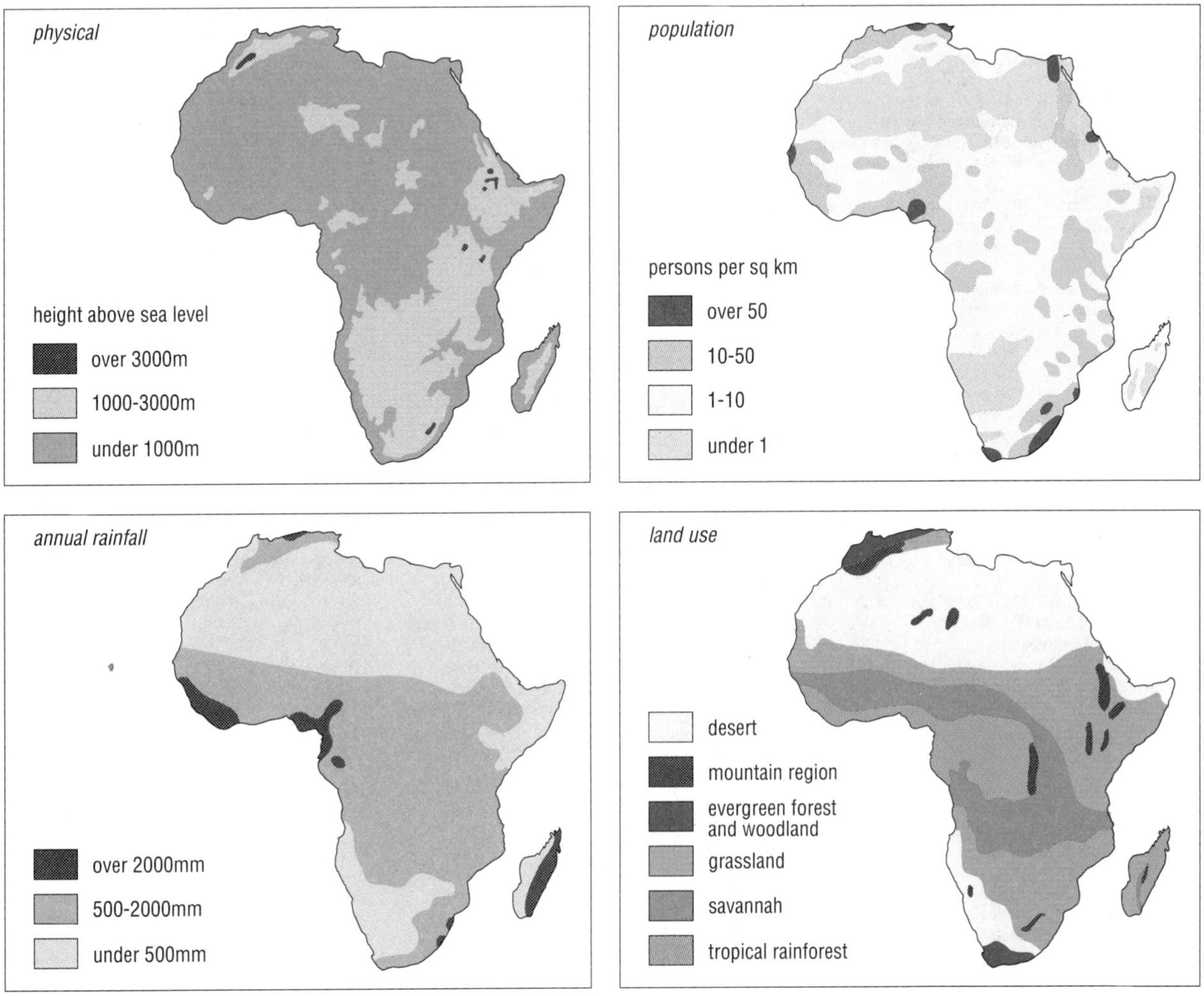
physical
height above sea level
over 3000m
1000-3000m
under 1000m
population
persons per sq km
over 50
10-50
1-10
under 1
annual rainfall
over 2000mm
500-2000mm
under 500mm
land use
desert
mountain region
evergreen forest
and woodland
grassland
savannah
tropical rainforest

Kabul, including the Panjshir Valley and Hindu Kush to the NE, continued to resist the PDPA-regime's "power-sharing" entreaties, demanding that Najibullah should first resign.

The mujaheddin met in Peshawar (Pakistan) in Feb 1989 to try to elect a government in exile. The meeting was riven with factional disputes, but ended on Feb 22 with the election of a prominent moderate, Prof Sibghatullah Mojadidi (head of the Afghan National Liberation Front), as its new president, and the fundamentalist Prof Abdul Rasul Sayyaf as prime minister. By the end of Feb 1989 the mujaheddin claimed control over 85% of Afghanistan, but had no main population center. The government in exile had not been accorded international recognition.

Between 1980 and 1990 the civil war cost the lives of 15,000 Soviet troops, 70,000 Afghan security-force personnel and more than 1 million Afghan civilians (more than 5 million fled as refugees to Iran and Pakistan).

The ruling PDPA was renamed the Homeland Party (*Hezb-e Watan*) in June 1990, and President Najibullah was elected its chair.

In May 1991 the Najibullah government accepted the outline of a comprehensive five-point peace plan fro Afghanistan, set out by the UN Secretary-General Javier Perez de Cuellar, under whose terms, initially, a broad-based interim government would be formed before Afghans would be allowed to choose their own government free of outside interference. In September 1991 the US Secretary of State, James Baker, and Soveit foreign minister, Boris Pankin, agreed to halt all supplies of weapons to the contending parties of Afghanistan by the end of the year.

Afghan Wars three wars waged between Britain and Afghanistan to counter the threat to British India from expanding Russian influence in Afghanistan.

First Afghan War 1838–42, when the British garrison at Kabul was wiped out.

Second Afghan War 1878–80, when Gen ◊Roberts captured Kabul and relieved Kandahar.

Third Afghan War 1919, when peace followed the dispatch by the UK of the first airplane ever seen in Kabul.

AFL-CIO abbreviation for ◊American Federation of Labor and Congress of Industrial Organizations.

Africa second largest of the continents, three times the area of Europe

area 11,620,451 sq mi/30,097,000 sq km

largest cities Cairo, Algiers, Lagos, Kinshasa, Abidjan, Tunis, Cape Town, Nairobi

physical dominated by a central plateau, which includes the world's largest desert, the ◊Sahara; Nile and Zaïre rivers, but generally there is a lack of navigable inlets or rivers, so that Africa has proportionately the shortest coastline of all the continents; comparatively few offshore islands; 75% is within the tropics

features Great Rift Valley; immensely rich fauna and flora; rainforests

products has 30% of the world's minerals; coffee (Kenya), cocoa (Ghana, Nigeria), cotton (Egypt, Uganda)

population (1987) 601,000,000; annual growth rate 3%, leading to 900 million by AD 2000

language Hamito-Semitic in the N; Bantu below the Sahara; Khosan languages with "click" consonants in the far S

religion Islam in the N; animism below the Sahara, which survives alongside Christianity (both Catholic and Protestant) in many central and S areas.

Africa, Horn of the projection constituted by Somalia and adjacent territories.

African native to or an inhabitant of the continent of Africa, especially of sub-Saharan Africa. The region is culturally heterogenous with numerous distinctive ethnic and sociolinguistic groups. There are three major language families: Niger-Congo, Afro-Asiatic (Hamito-Semitic), and Chari-Nile (Sudanic).

African art the art of sub-Saharan Africa, from prehistory onward, ranging from the art of ancient civilizations to the new styles of post-imperialist African nations. Among the best-known examples of historic African art are bronze figures from Benin and Ife (in Nigeria) dating from about 1500 and, also on the west coast, in the same period, bronze or brass figures for weighing gold, made by the Ashanti.

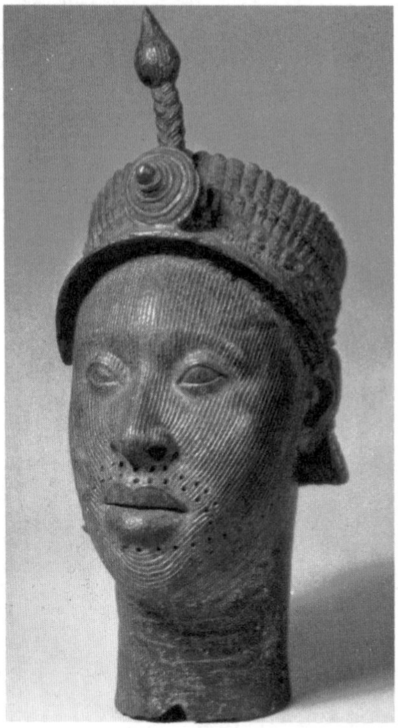

***African art** Bronze head Nigeria (undated), from the Museum of Mankind, London. Sophisticated bronze sculpture was produced by precolonial western African societies. Pieces taken or purchased by Europeans form the basis for many museum collections in the West.*

prehistoric art Rock paintings are found in various regions, notably in the western Sahara, Zimbabwe, South Africa, and, from the end of the period, East Africa. Some of the earliest pictures are of elephants. The images tend to be linear and heavily stylized and sometimes show a geometric style. Terracotta figures from Nigeria, dating from several centuries BC, have stylized features similar to Oceanic art forms and some early South American styles.

Zimbabwe Ruins of ancient stone buildings from before AD 300 suggest a time of outstanding craft skill in the country's history; sculptures have also been found in the ruins.

Benin and Ife The bronze sculptures from the 13th–16th-century realms of Benin and Ife on the west coast of Africa (examples in the British Museum, London) are distinctive in style and demonstrate technical refinement in casting by the lost-wax method (see ◊sculpture). The Ife heads are naturalistic, while those of Benin are more stylized. The art of Benin includes high-relief bronze plaques with figurative scenes, and ivory carvings. Some of these appear to have been designed for the Portuguese trade.

Ashanti Metalworkers of the Ashanti people (in present-day Ghana) made weights, highly inventive forms with comically exaggerated figures.

general Over the centuries, much artistic effort was invested in religious objects and masks, with wooden sculpture playing a large role. Many everyday items, such as bowls, stools, drums, and combs, also display fine craft and a vitality of artistic invention.

Since much of Africa's history up to the late 19th century has not been researched, African art has occupied a meager place in Western art-historical studies. Nevertheless, in the early 20th century West African art had a profound influence on the work of many European painters and sculptors, including Picasso.

African violet

African National Congress (ANC) multiracial nationalist organization formed in South Africa 1912 to extend the franchise to the whole population and end all racial discrimination there. Its president is Oliver ◊Tambo and vice president from 1990 Nelson ◊Mandela. Although originally nonviolent, the ANC was banned by the government from 1960 to Jan 1990, and in exile in Mozambique developed a military wing, Umkhonto we Sizwe, which engaged in sabotage and guerrilla training. The armed struggle was suspended Aug 1990 when the organization's headquarters were moved to Johannesburg.

The ANC is supported by the Organization of African Unity as a movement aimed at introducing majority rule in South Africa. Former ANC leaders include Albert Luthuli and Solomon Plaatje. Several imprisoned leaders were released Oct 1989; Mandela in Feb 1990.

African violet herbaceous plant *Saintpaulia ionantha* from tropical central and E Africa, with velvety green leaves and scentless purple flowers. Different colors and double varieties have been bred.

Afrikaans language an official language of the Republic of South Africa (the other is English). Spoken mainly by the Afrikaners—descendants of Dutch and other 17th-century colonists—it is a variety of the Dutch language, modified by circumstance and the influence of German, French, and other immigrant as well as local languages. It became a standardized written language about 1875.

Afrika Korps the German army in the western desert of North Africa 1941–43 in World War II, commanded by Field Marshal Erwin Rommel. They were driven out of North Africa by May 1943.

Afrikaner (formerly known as Boer) inhabitant of South Africa descended from the original Dutch and ◊Huguenot settlers of the 17th century. Comprising approximately 60% of the white population in South Africa, they were originally farmers but have now become mainly urbanized. Their language is Afrikaans.

Afro-Caribbean West Indian person of African descent. Afro-Caribbeans are the descendants of W Africans captured or obtained in trade from African procurers. European slave traders then shipped them to the West Indies to English, French, Dutch, Spanish, and Portuguese colonies founded from the 16th century. Since World War II many Afro-Caribbeans have migrated to North America and to Europe, especially to the US, Britain, and the Netherlands.

afterbirth the placenta and other material, including blood and membranes, expelled from the mammalian uterus soon after birth. In the natural world it is often eaten.

afterburning method of increasing the thrust of a gas turbine (jet) airplane engine by spraying additional fuel into the hot exhaust duct between the turbojet and the the tailpipe where it ignites. Used for short term increase of power during takeoff, or during combat in military aircraft.

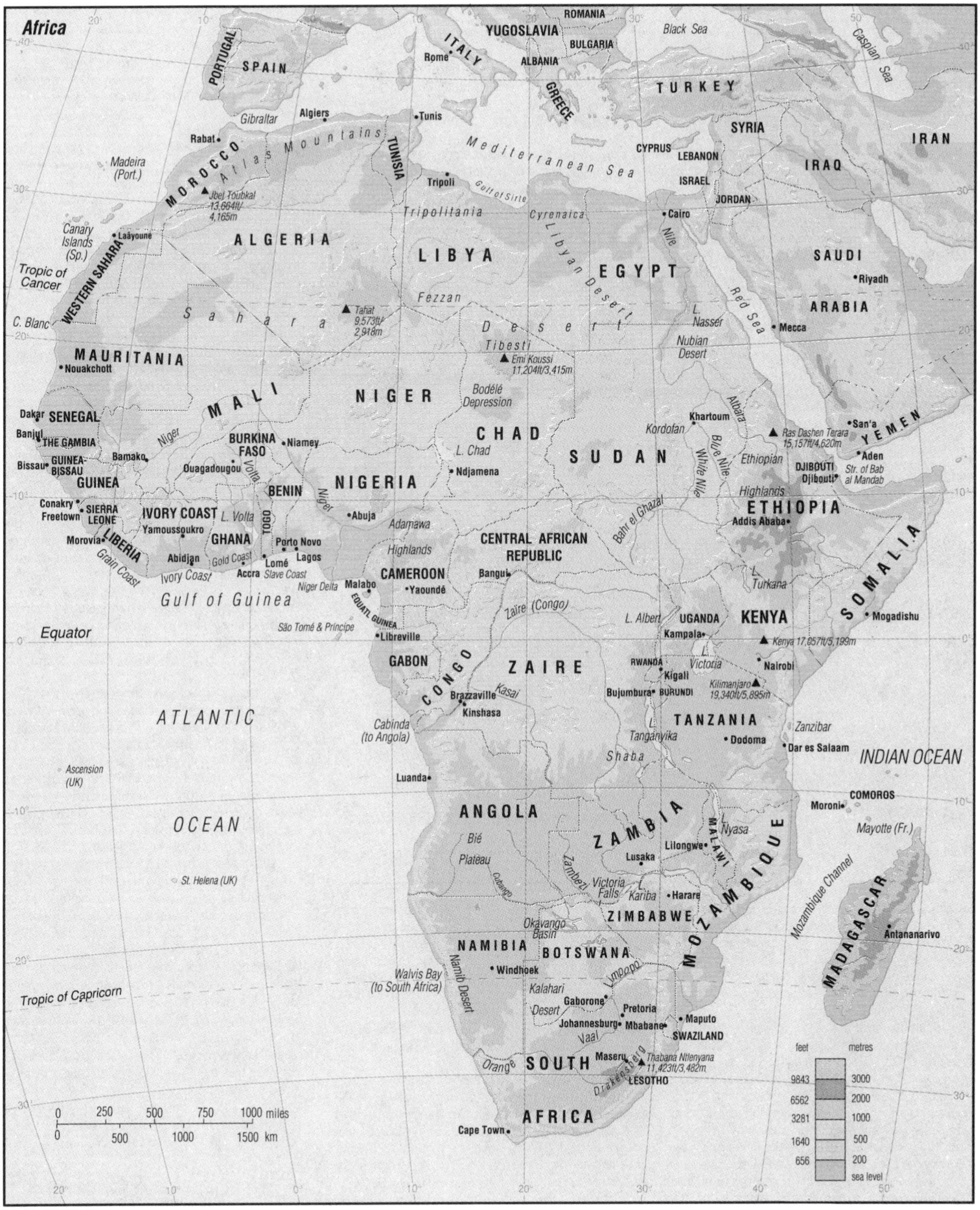
Africa
PORTUGAL
SPAIN
ROMANIA
YUGOSLAVIA
BULGARIA
ITALY
Rome
ALBANIA
GREECE
Black Sea
Caspian Sea
TURKEY
Gibraltar
Algiers
Tunis
Rabat
MOROCCO
Atlas Mountains
TUNISIA
Mediterranean Sea
CYPRUS
SYRIA
LEBANON
ISRAEL
JORDAN
IRAQ
IRAN
Madeira (Port.)
Jbel Toubkal 13,664ft/4,165m
Tripoli
Gulf of Sirte
Tripolitania
Cyrenaica
Cairo
Canary Islands (Sp.)
Laâyoune
ALGERIA
LIBYA
EGYPT
Libyan Desert
Nile
SAUDI
Riyadh
Tropic of Cancer
WESTERN SAHARA
Fezzan
Red Sea
ARABIA
Mecca
C. Blanc
Sahara
Tahat 9,573ft/2,918m
Desert
L. Nasser
Nubian Desert
Tibesti
Emi Koussi 11,204ft/3,415m
MAURITANIA
Nouakchott
MALI
NIGER
Bodélé Depression
Atbara
Dakar
SENEGAL
Banjul
THE GAMBIA
Bissau
GUINEA-BISSAU
GUINEA
Bamako
Niger
BURKINA FASO
Niamey
Ouagadougou
Volta
CHAD
L. Chad
Ndjamena
SUDAN
Khartoum
Kordofan
Blue Nile
White Nile
Ras Dashen Terara 15,157ft/4,620m
San'a
YEMEN
Aden
DJIBOUTI
Djibouti
Str. of Bab al Mandab
Ethiopian Highlands
ETHIOPIA
Addis Ababa
BENIN
NIGERIA
Niger
Conakry
SIERRA LEONE
Freetown
IVORY COAST
L. Volta
TOGO
Abuja
Yamoussoukro
GHANA
Morovia
LIBERIA
Abidjan
Gold Coast
Porto Novo
Lomé
Lagos
Accra
Slave Coast
Grain Coast
Ivory Coast
Adamawa Highlands
CENTRAL AFRICAN REPUBLIC
Bahr el Ghazal
Bangui
CAMEROON
Yaoundé
Niger Delta
Malabo
Gulf of Guinea
EQUATL. GUINEA
Zaïre (Congo)
Turkana
SOMALIA
Equator
São Tomé & Príncipe
Libreville
L. Albert
UGANDA
Kampala
KENYA
Mogadishu
Kenya 17,057ft/5,199m
GABON
CONGO
ZAIRE
RWANDA
Kigali
L. Victoria
Nairobi
Kasai
Brazzaville
Kinshasa
Bujumbura
BURUNDI
Kilimanjaro 19,340ft/5,895m
ATLANTIC
Cabinda (to Angola)
L. Tanganyika
TANZANIA
Dodoma
Zanzibar
Dar es Salaam
Shaba
INDIAN OCEAN
Ascension (UK)
Luanda
COMOROS
Moroni
Mayotte (Fr.)
OCEAN
ANGOLA
Bié Plateau
ZAMBIA
MALAWI
L. Nyasa
Lilongwe
Lusaka
MOZAMBIQUE
Mozambique Channel
St. Helena (UK)
Cubango
Zambezi
Victoria Falls
L. Kariba
Harare
ZIMBABWE
MADAGASCAR
Antananarivo
Okavango Basin
NAMIBIA
BOTSWANA
Windhoek
Walvis Bay (to South Africa)
Namib Desert
Limpopo
Kalahari Desert
Gaborone
Pretoria
Tropic of Capricorn
Maputo
Johannesburg
Mbabane
SWAZILAND
Vaal
feet
metres
Orange
SOUTH
Maseru
Thabana Ntlenyana 11,423ft/3,482m
Drakensberg
LESOTHO
AFRICA
Cape Town
0 250 500 750 1000 miles
0 500 1000 1500 km
9843 3000
6562 2000
3281 1000
1640 500
656 200
sea level

Africa: history

14 million BC	Africa, which is considered the "cradle continent," probably produced the first hominids, or humanlike creatures.
3–5 million	Direct line of descent of modern humans (hominids) was established in E Africa.
10,000–2000	The fertile Sahara became a barrier desert between north and south.
5450–2500	Era of Saharan rock and cave paintings.
3000	Egyptian civilization established; based on political consolidation of Neolithic farming villages.
7th century BC–6th century AD	Assyria, Persia, Greece, Rome, and Byzantium in turn made conquests in North Africa. Meroe: the Egyptian and Negro tradition met in the Nubian kingdom of Kush.
320 BC–AD 50	The kingdom of Axum flourished in Ethiopia and gave rise to the later legend of Prester John.
640	Islamic expansion began in N, E, and Central Africa.
300–1500	Period of the great medieval states: Ghana, Mali, Songhai, Benin, Ife, and the culture of Great Zimbabwe.
12th–15th centuries	Era of the Arab travelers: for example, Ibn Batuta; and of trade, for example, Kilwa.
1488	Diaz rounded the Cape of Good Hope.
15th–16th centuries	European sea trade in gold, ivory, timber, and pepper.
17th–19th centuries	Height of the Atlantic and Indian Ocean slave trade.
18th–19th centuries	European travelers in Africa: Park, Livingstone, Stanley, Speke, Mary Kingsley.
19th century	Colonial wars against well-organized native states: Ashanti, Dahomey, Zululand.
1880–90	Peak of European colonization in the "scramble for Africa."
1899–1902	South African War, the first large-scale war between whites in Africa.
1920	League of Nations mandate system introduced the idea of European trusteeship.
1936	Italy's conquest of Ethiopia.
1942	World War II reached its turning point in the Battles of Alamein.
1951	Libya became the first independent state to be declared by the United Nations.
1954–65	The fight for independence in Algeria precipitated the end of the French Fourth Republic 1958.
1957	Ghana became independent, the first of the revived black nation states.
1952–60	Mau-Mau movement in Kenya began the ousting of white settlers south of the Sahara.
1963	Organization of African Unity founded.
1967–70	Revolt of Biafra within the federation of Nigeria constituted the first civil war in a modern black state.
1975	Mozambique's independence led to the end of dictatorship in Portugal.
1979	Zimbabwe's achievement of independence left South Africa as the last white-ruled state in Africa.
1980	Future of the OAU doubtful due to division over Western Sahara and Libyan aggression toward Chad. Extensive food shortages in many parts of Central and East Africa.
1984	Increasing internal unrest in South Africa leading to violence between black population and minority white groups.
1988	Peace treaty between Angola, South Africa, and Cuba leading to Namibia's independence.
1990	Namibia declared independent. South Africa's African National Congress (ANC) party leader Nelson Mandela freed.
1991	North African states oppose Iraq on Kuwait invasion. Ethiopia's Communist regime collapses.

afterimage persistence of an image on the retina of the eye after the object producing it has been removed. This leads to persistence of vision, a necessary phenomenon for the illusion of continuous movement in films and television. The term is also used for the persistence of sensations other than vision.

after-ripening the process undergone by the seeds of some plants before germination can occur. The length of the after-ripening period in different species may vary from a few weeks to many months. It helps seeds to germinate at a time when conditions are most favorable for growth. In some cases the embryo is not fully mature at the time of dispersal and must develop further before germination can take place. Other seeds do not germinate even when the embryo is mature, probably owing to growth inhibitors within the seed that must be leached out or broken down before germination can begin.

AG abbreviation for *Aktiengesellschaft* (German "limited company").

aga (Turkish "lord") title of nobility, applied by the Turks to military commanders and, in general, to men of high station in some Muslim countries.

Agadir resort and seaport in S Morocco, near the mouth of the river Sus. Population (1984) 110,500. It was rebuilt after being destroyed by an earthquake in 1960.

Agadir Incident international crisis provoked by Kaiser Wilhelm II of Germany. By sending the gunboat *Panther* to demand territorial concessions from the French, he hoped to drive a wedge into the Anglo-French entente. In fact, German aggression during the second Moroccan crisis merely served to reinforce Anglo-French fears of Germany's intentions. The crisis gave rise to the term "gunboat diplomacy."

Aga Khan IV 1936– . Spiritual head (*imam*) of the Ismaili Muslim sect (see ◊Islam). He succeeded his grandfather in 1957.

agama lizard of the Old World family Agamidae, especially the genus *Agama*. There are about 280 species, found throughout the warmer regions of the Old World. Many are brilliantly colored and all are capable of changing the color of their skin.

Agamemnon in Greek mythology, a Greek hero, son of Atreus, king of Mycenae. He married Clytemnestra, and their children included ◊Electra, ◊Iphigenia, and ◊Orestes. He led the capture of Troy, received Priam's daughter Cassandra as a prize, and was murdered by Clytemnestra and her lover, Aegisthus, on his return home. His children Orestes and Electra later killed the guilty couple.

Agana capital of Guam in the W Pacific; population (1980) 896. It is the administrative center of the island, bordered by residential Agana Heights.

agar jellylike substance, obtained from seaweeds. It is used mainly in microbiological experiments as a culture medium for growing bacteria and other microorganisms. The agar is resistant to breakdown by microbes, remaining a solid jelly throughout the course of the experiment. It is also used as a laxative and in preserved foods.

agaric fungus of typical mushroom shape. Agarics include the field mushroom *Agaricus campestris* and the cultivated edible mushroom *Agaricus brunnesiens*. Closely related is the ◊*Amanita* genus, including the fly agaric *Amanita puscaria*.

Agassiz Louis 1807–1873. Swiss-born US paleontologist and geologist. His interests were comparative zoology and Ice Age geology. In 1832 he accepted a professorship at the University of Neuchâtel; coming to the US 1846, he became a member of the faculty of Harvard. Agassiz, known as a conservative in his opposition to Darwin, conducted many expeditions to the American West. His massive *Contributions to the Natural History of the United States* was published 1857–62.

He earned a PhD at the University of Erlangen 1829 and an MD at Munich 1830.

agate a banded or cloudy type of ◊chalcedony, a silica, SiO_2, that forms in rock cavities. Agates are used as ornamental stones and for art objects.

Agate stones, being hard, are also used to burnish and polish gold applied to glass and ceramics.

agave any of several related plants with stiff sword-shaped spiny leaves arranged in a rosette. All species of the genus *Agave* come from the warmer parts of the New World. They include *A. sisalina*, whose fibers are used for rope making, and the Mexican century plant *A. americana*. Alcoholic drinks such as ◊tequila and pulque are made from the sap of agave plants.

Agee James 1909–1955. US journalist, screenwriter, and author. Agee rose to national prominence as the result of his investigation of the plight of sharecroppers in the South during the Depression. In collaboration with photographer Walker Evans, he published the photo and text essay *Let Us Now Praise Famous Men* 1941. His screenwriting credits include *The African Queen* 1951 and *The Night of the Hunter* 1955. His novel *A Death in the Family* won a Pulitzer prize 1958.

Born in Knoxville, Tennessee, Agee graduated from Harvard 1932 and embarked on a career as a magazine reporter and feature writer.

ageism discrimination against older people in housing, employment, pensions, and health care. To combat it the American Association of Retired Persons (AARP) has 30 million members, and the Gray Panthers were formed. They have been responsible for legislation forbidding employers to discriminate; for example, it is illegal in the US to fail to employ, to dismiss, or to reduce working conditions or wages of people aged 40–69.

Agent Orange a selective ◊weedkiller, which contains highly poisonous ◊dioxin. It became notorious in the late 1970s and 1980s. It had been used in the 1960s and 1970s during the Vietnam war by US forces to eliminate ground cover which obscured the enemy. Thousands of US troops who had handled it later developed cancer or fathered deformed babies.

Agent Orange, named after the distinctive orange stripe on its packaging, combines equal parts of 2,4-D (2,4-trichlorophenoxyacetic acid)

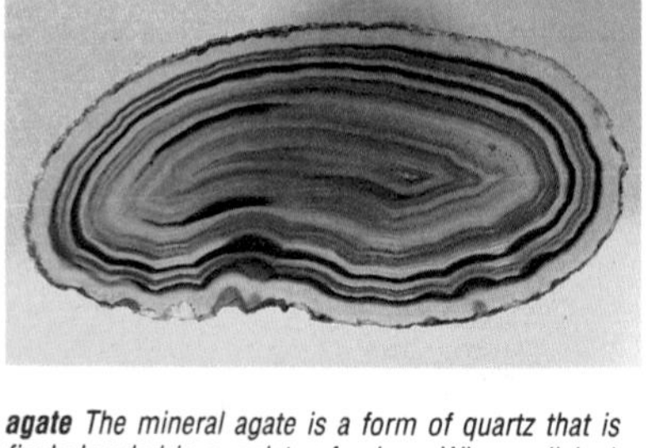

agate *The mineral agate is a form of quartz that is finely banded in a variety of colors. When polished it is considered a semiprecious stone.*

and 2,4,5-T (2,4,5-trichlorophenoxyacetic acid), both now banned in the US. Companies that had manufactured the chemicals faced an increasing number of lawsuits in the 1970s. All the suits were settled out of court in a single ◊class action, resulting in the largest ever payment of its kind ($180 million) to claimants.

agglutination in medicine, the clumping together of ◊antigens, such as blood cells or bacteria, to form larger, visible masses, under the influence of ◊antibodies. As each antigen clumps only in response to its particular antibody, agglutination provides a way of determining ◊blood groups and the identity of unknown bacteria.

aggression in politics, an unprovoked attack often involving an escalating series of threats aimed at intimidating an opponent. The actions of Nazi Germany, under Adolf Hitler in the 1930s, leading to World War II were considered to be aggressive. The invasion of Kuwait by Iraq in 1990 was labeled an act of aggression.

aggression in biology, behavior used to intimidate or injure another organism (of the same or of a different species), usually for the purposes of gaining a territory, a mate, or food. Aggression often involves an escalating series of threats aimed at intimidating an opponent without having to engage in potentially dangerous physical contact. Aggressive signals include roaring by wapiti (American elk), snarling by dogs, the fluffing up of feathers by birds, and the raising of fins by some species of fish.

Agincourt, Battle of battle of the Hundred Years' War in which Henry V of England defeated the French on Oct 24, 1415, mainly through the overwhelming superiority of the English longbow. The French lost more than 6,000 men to about 1,600 English casualties. As a result of the battle, Henry gained France and the French princess, Catherine of Valois, as his wife. The village of Agincourt (modern Azincourt) is south of Calais, in N France.

aging in common usage, the period of deterioration of the physical condition of a living organism that leads to death; in biological terms, the entire life process.

Three current theories attempt to account for aging. The first suggests that the process is genetically determined, to remove individuals that can no longer reproduce. The second suggests that it is due to the accumulation of mistakes during the replication of ◊DNA at cell division. The third suggests that it is actively induced by pieces of DNA that move between cells, or by cancer-causing viruses; these may become abundant in old cells and induce them to produce unwanted ◊proteins or interfere with the control functions of their DNA.

Agnew Spiro 1918– US vice-president 1969–73. A Republican, he was governor of Maryland 1966–69, and vice-president under ◊Nixon. He took the lead in a campaign against the press and opponents of the ◊Vietnam war. Although he was one of the few administration officials not to be implicated in the ◊Watergate affair, he resigned in 1973, shortly before pleading "no contest" to a charge of income-tax evasion.

Agni in Hindu mythology, the god of fire, the guardian of homes, and the protector of humans against the powers of darkness.

Agnon Shmuel Yosef 1888–1970. Israeli novelist. Born in Buczacz, Galicia (now in the USSR), he made it the setting of his most famous book, *A Guest for the Night*. He shared a Nobel Prize 1966.

agnosticism the belief that the existence of God cannot be proven; that in the nature of things the individual cannot know anything of what lies behind or beyond the world of natural phenomena. The term was coined 1869 by T H ◊Huxley.

Whereas an atheist (see ◊atheism) denies the existence of God or gods, an agnostic asserts that God or a First Cause is one of those concepts—others include the Absolute, infinity, eternity, and immortality—that lie beyond the reach of human intelligence, and therefore can be neither confirmed or denied.

agoraphobia a ◊phobia involving fear of open spaces and crowded places. The anxiety produced can be so severe that some sufferers confine themselves to their homes for many years.

agouti small rodent of the genus *Dasyprocta*, family Dasyproctidae. It is found in the forests of Central and South America. The agouti is herbivorous, swift-running, and about the size of a rabbit.

AGR (abbreviation for advanced gas-cooled reactor) type of ◊nuclear reactor widely used in W Europe, especially Britain. The AGR uses a fuel of enriched uranium dioxide in stainless-steel cladding and a moderator of graphite. Carbon dioxide gas is pumped through the reactor core to extract the heat produced by the ◊fission of the uranium. The heat is transferred to water in a steam generator, and the steam drives a turbogenerator to produce electricity.

Agra city of Uttar Pradesh, India, on the river Jumna, 100 mi/160 km SE of Delhi; population (1981) 747,318. A commercial and university center, it was the capital of the Mogul empire 1527–1628, from which period dates the Taj Mahal.

history ◊Zahir ud-din Mohammed (known as "Babur"), the first great Mogul ruler, made Agra his capital in 1527. His grandson Akbar rebuilt the Red Fort of Salim Shah (1566), and is buried outside the city in the tomb at Sikandra. In the 17th century the buildings of ◊Shah-Jehan made Agra one of the most beautiful cities in the world. The Taj Mahal, erected as a tomb for the emperor's wife Mumtaz Mahal, was completed in 1650. Agra's political importance dwindled from 1658, when Aurangzeb moved the capital back to Delhi. It was taken from the Mahrattas by Lord Lake in 1803.

Agricola Gnaeus Julius AD 37–93. Roman general and politician. Born in Provence, he became Consul of the Roman Republic AD 77, and then governor of Britain AD 78–85. He extended Roman rule to the Firth of Forth in Scotland and won the battle of Mons Graupius. His fleet sailed round the N of Scotland and proved Britain an island.

agriculture the practice of farming, including the cultivation of the soil (for raising crops) and the raising of livestock. Crops are for human nourishment, animal fodder, or commodities such as cotton and sisal. Animals are raised for wool, milk, leather, dung (as fertilizer or fuel), or meat. The units for managing agricultural production vary from small holdings and individually owned farms to corporate-run farms and collective farms run by entire communities.

Agriculture developed in the near East and Egypt at least 10,000 years ago. Soon, farming communities became the base for society in China, India, Europe, Mexico, and Peru, then spread throughout the world. Reorganization along more scientific and productive lines took place in Europe in the 18th century in response to dramatic population growth.

Mechanization made considerable progress in the US and Europe during the 19th century. After World War II, there was an explosive growth in the use of agricultural chemicals: herbicides, insecticides, fungicides, and fertilizers. In the 1960s there was development of high-yielding species, especially for the ◊green revolution of the Third World, and the industrialized countries began intensive farming of cattle, poultry, and pigs. In the 1980s, hybridization by genetic engineering methods and pest control by the use of chemicals plus ◊pheromones were developed.

plants For plant products, the land must be prepared (plowing, cultivating, harrowing, and rolling). Seed must be planted and the growing plant nurtured. This may involve fertilizers, irrigation, pest control by chemicals, and monitoring of acidity or nutrients. When the crop has grown, it must be harvested and, depending on the crop, processed in a variety of ways before it is stored or sold.

Greenhouses allow cultivation of plants that would otherwise find the climate too harsh. ◊Hydroponics allows commercial cultivation of crops using nutrient-enriched solutions instead of soil. Special methods, such as terracing, may be adopted to allow cultivation in hostile terrain and to retain topsoil in mountainous areas with heavy rainfall.

livestock Animals may be semidomesticated, such as reindeer, or fully domesticated but nomadic (particularly where naturally growing or cultivated food supplies are sparse), or kept in one location. Animal farming involves accommodation (buildings, fencing, or pasture), feeding, breeding, gathering the produce (eggs, milk, or wool), slaughtering, and further processing (such as meat-processing or tanning).

organic farming From the 1970s there has been a movement toward natural methods, without chemical pesticide sprays or fertilizers. These methods are desirable because nitrates have been seeping into the ground water, insecticides are found in lethal concentrations at the top of the ◊food chain, some herbicides are associated with human birth defects, and hormones fed to animals to promote fast growth have damaging effects on humans.

overproduction The greater efficiency in agriculture achieved since the 19th century, coupled with post–World War II government subsidies for domestic production in the US and the European Community (EC), have led to the development of high stocks, nicknamed "lakes" (wine, milk) and "mountains" (butter, beef, grain). There is no simple solution to this problem, as any large-scale dumping onto the market displaces regular merchandise. Increasing concern about the starving and the cost of storage has led the US and the EC to develop measures for limiting production, such as letting arable land lie fallow to reduce grain crops. The US has had some success at selling surplus wheat to the USSR when the Soviet crop is poor, but the overall cost of bulk transport and the potential destabilization of other economies acts against the high producers exporting their excess on a regular basis to needy countries. Intensive farming methods also contribute to soil ◊erosion and water pollution.

Agrigento town in Sicily, known for Greek temples; population (1981) 51,300.

agrimony herbaceous plant *Agrimonia eupatoria* of the rose family Rosaceae, with small yellow flowers on a slender spike. It grows along hedges and in fields.

Agrippa Marcus Vipsanius 63–12 BC. Roman general. He commanded the victorious fleet at ◊Actium and married Julia, daughter of ◊Augustus.

agronomy study of crops and soils, a branch of agricultural science. Agronomy includes such topics as selective breeding (of plants and animals), irrigation, pest control, and soil analysis and modification.

Aguascalientes city in central Mexico, and capital of a state of the same name; population (1980) 359,454. It has hot mineral springs.

AH with reference to the Muslim calendar, abbreviation for *anno hegirae* (Latin "year of the flight"—of ◊Muhammad, from Mecca to Medina).

Ahab c. 875–854 BC. King of Israel. His empire included the suzerainty of Moab, and Judah was his subordinate ally, but his kingdom was weakened by constant wars with Syria. By his marriage with Jezebel, princess of Sidon, Ahab introduced into Israel the worship of the Phoenician god Baal, thus provoking the hostility of Elijah and other prophets. Ahab died in battle against the Syrians at Ramoth Gilead.

Ahaggar or Hoggar mountainous plateau of the central Sahara, Algeria, whose highest point, Tahat, at 9,576 ft/2,918 m, lies between Algiers and the mouth of the Niger. It is the home of the formerly nomadic Tuaregs.

Ahasuerus (Latinized Hebrew form of the Persian *Khshayarsha*, Greek *Xerxes*). Name of several Persian kings in the Bible, notably the husband of ◊Esther. Traditionally it was also the name of the ◊Wandering Jew.

ahimsa in Hinduism, Buddhism, and Jainism, the doctrine of respect for all life (including the lowest forms and even the elements themselves) and consequently an extreme form of nonviolence. It arises in part from the concept of *karma*, which holds that a person's actions (and thus any injury caused to any form of life) are carried forward from one life to the next, determining each stage of reincarnation.

Ahmadiyya Islamic religious movement founded by Mirza Ghulam Ahmad (1839–1908). His followers reject the doctrine that Mohammed was the last of the prophets and accept Ahmad's claim to be the Mahdi and Promised Messiah. In 1974 the Ahmadis were denounced by their coreligionists as non-Muslims.

Ahmadnagar city in Maharashtra, India, 120 mi/ 195 km E of Bombay, on the left bank of the river Sina; population (1981) 181,000. It is a center of cotton trade and manufacture.

Ahmad Shah Durrani 1724–1773. Founder and first ruler of Afghanistan. Elected shah in 1747, he had conquered the Punjab by 1751.

Ahmedabad or Ahmadabad capital of Gujarat, India; population (1981) 2,515,195. It is a cotton-manufacturing center, and has many sacred buildings of the Hindu, Muslim, and Jain faiths.

Ahmedabad was founded in the reign of Ahmad Shah 1412, and came under the control of the East India Company 1818. In 1930 ◊Gandhi marched to the sea from here to protest against the government salt monopoly.

Ahriman in Zoroastrianism, the supreme evil spirit, lord of the darkness and death, waging war with his counterpart Ahura Mazda (Ormuzd) until a time when human beings choose to lead good lives and Ahriman is finally destroyed.

Ahura Mazda or ***Ormuzd*** in Zoroastrianism, the spirit of supreme good. As god of life and light he will finally prevail over his enemy, Ahriman.

Ahváz industrial capital of the province of Khuzestan, W Iran; population (1986) 590,000.

Ahvenanmaa Island island in the Gulf of Bothnia, Finland; largest of the ◊Åland Islands.

Aidan, St c. 600–651. Irish monk who converted Northumbria to Christianity and founded Lindisfarne monastery on Holy Island off the NE coast of England. His feast day is Aug 31.

aid, foreign financial and other assistance given by richer, usually industrialized, countries to war-damaged or developing states.

In the US it has become an increasingly contentious domestic issue. With severe budget deficits and a large part of the foreign aid budget allocated by treaty to a very few countries, calls have grown for reform. Aid can be bilateral, by agreement with another country, or through international agencies such as the ◊International Development Association. Aid is given for political, commercial, or humanitarian reasons or a combination of all three.

Aidoo Ama Ata 1940– . Ghanaian writer of plays (*Dilemma of a Ghost* 1965), novels (*Our Sister Killjoy* 1977), and short stories.

AIDS abbreviation for acquired immune deficiency syndrome, the newest and gravest of sexually transmitted diseases or ◊STDs. It is caused by the human immunodeficiency virus (HIV), now known to be a ◊retrovirus, an organism first identified 1983. HIV is transmitted in body fluids, mainly blood and sexual secretions.

Sexual transmission of the AIDS virus endangers heterosexual men and women as well as high-risk groups, such as homosexual and bisexual men, prostitutes, intravenous drug-users sharing needles, and hemophiliacs and surgical patients treated with contaminated blood products. The virus itself is not selective, and infection is spreading to the population at large. The virus has a short life outside the body, which makes transmission of the infection by methods other than sexual contact, blood transfusion, and shared syringes extremely unlikely.

Infection with HIV is not synonymous with having AIDS; many people who have the virus in their blood are not ill, and only about half of those infected will develop AIDS within ten years. Some suffer AIDS-related illnesses but not the full-blown disease. However, there is no firm evidence to suggest that the proportion of those developing AIDS from being HIV-positive is less than 100%. Recent evidence indicates that the presence of other diseases, especially syphilis, is linked to the full-blown development of AIDS.

The effect of the virus in those who become ill is the devastation of the immune system, leaving the victim susceptible to (opportunistic) diseases, those that would not otherwise develop. In fact, diagnosis of AIDS is based on the appearance of rare tumors or opportunistic infections in unexpected candidates. Pneumocystis pneumonia, for instance, normally seen only in the malnourished or those whose immune systems have been deliberately suppressed, is common among AIDS victims and, for them, a leading cause of death.

The estimated incubation period for AIDS is 9.8 years. Some victims die within a few months of the outbreak of symptoms, some survive for several years; roughly 50% are dead within three years. There is no cure for the disease, although the drug zidovudine (also known as ◊AZT) is claimed to delay the onset of AIDS and diminish its effects until the balance point, when the medication becomes toxic to the liver and thus compromises the immune system. The search continues for an effective vaccine.

The HIV virus originated in Africa. In the US, 90,990 cases were reported up to April 1989, with 52,435 deaths; 58% of all cases. One million Americans are thought to be infected with the virus.

AIDS

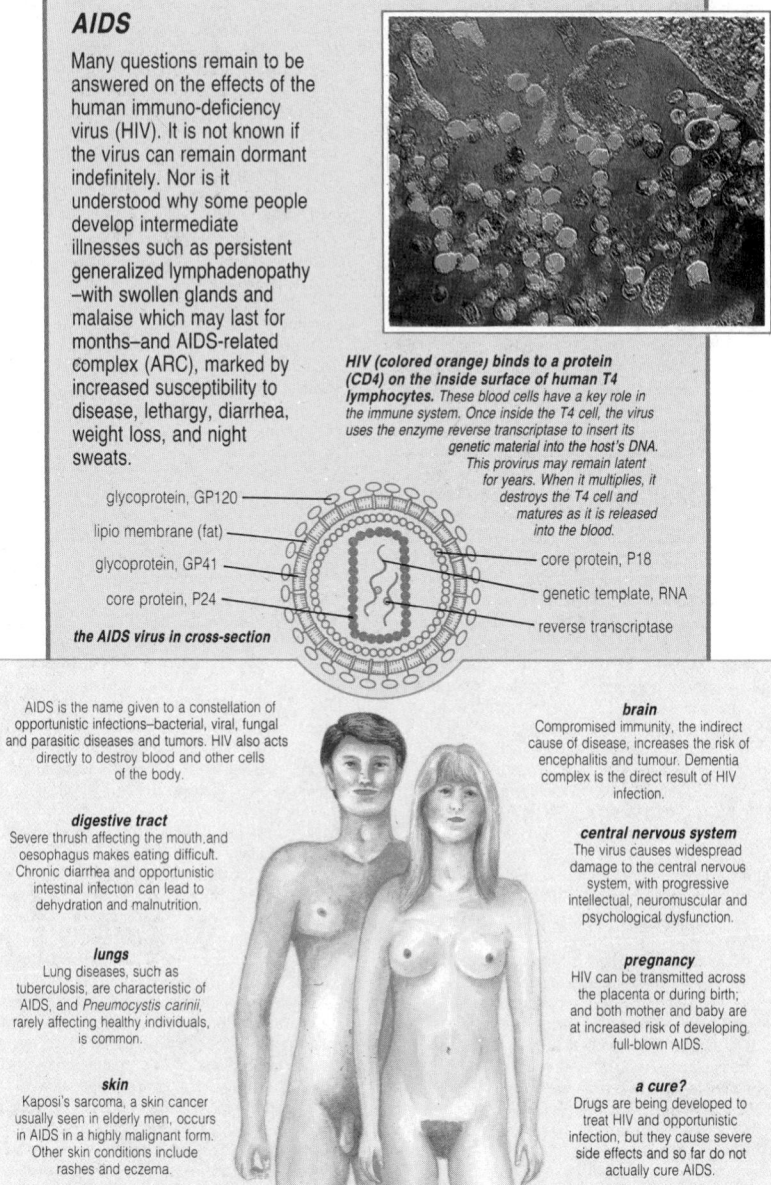

Many questions remain to be answered on the effects of the human immuno-deficiency virus (HIV). It is not known if the virus can remain dormant indefinitely. Nor is it understood why some people develop intermediate illnesses such as persistent generalized lymphadenopathy–with swollen glands and malaise which may last for months–and AIDS-related complex (ARC), marked by increased susceptibility to disease, lethargy, diarrhea, weight loss, and night sweats.

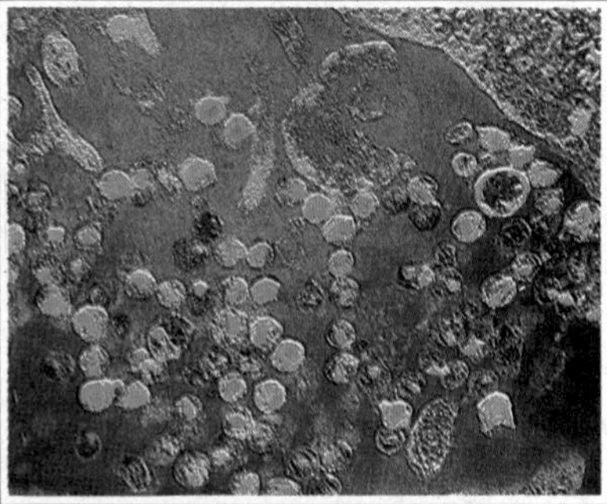

HIV (colored orange) binds to a protein (CD4) on the inside surface of human T4 lymphocytes. *These blood cells have a key role in the immune system. Once inside the T4 cell, the virus uses the enzyme reverse transcriptase to insert its genetic material into the host's DNA. This provirus may remain latent for years. When it multiplies, it destroys the T4 cell and matures as it is released into the blood.*

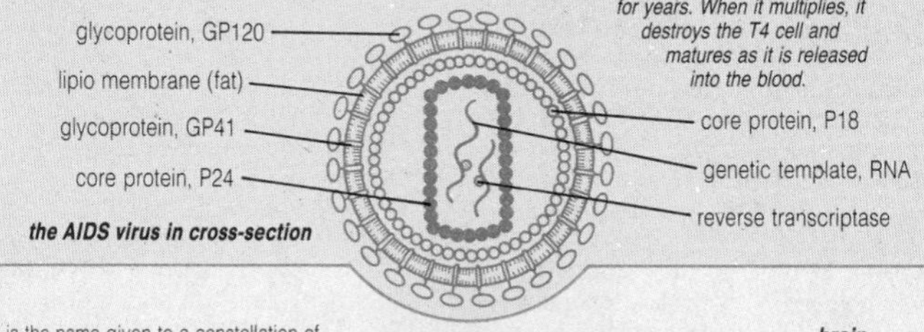
glycoprotein, GP120
lipio membrane (fat)
glycoprotein, GP41
core protein, P24
core protein, P18
genetic template, RNA
reverse transcriptase

the AIDS virus in cross-section

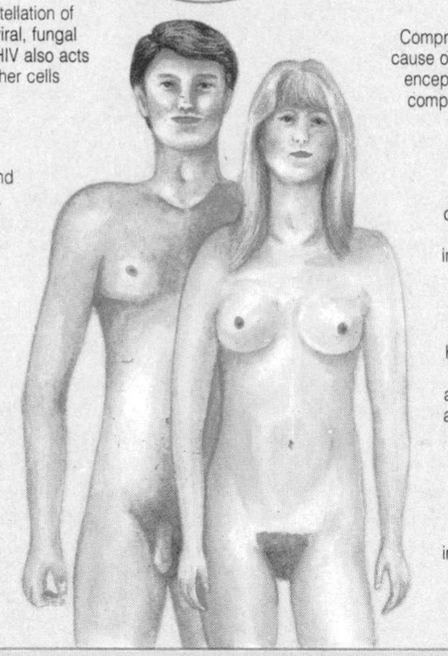
AIDS is the name given to a constellation of opportunistic infections–bacterial, viral, fungal and parasitic diseases and tumors. HIV also acts directly to destroy blood and other cells of the body.
digestive tract
Severe thrush affecting the mouth and oesophagus makes eating difficult. Chronic diarrhea and opportunistic intestinal infection can lead to dehydration and malnutrition.
lungs
Lung diseases, such as tuberculosis, are characteristic of AIDS, and *Pneumocystis carinii*, rarely affecting healthy individuals, is common.
skin
Kaposi's sarcoma, a skin cancer usually seen in elderly men, occurs in AIDS in a highly malignant form. Other skin conditions include rashes and eczema.
brain
Compromised immunity, the indirect cause of disease, increases the risk of encephalitis and tumour. Dementia complex is the direct result of HIV infection.
central nervous system
The virus causes widespread damage to the central nervous system, with progressive intellectual, neuromuscular and psychological dysfunction.
pregnancy
HIV can be transmitted across the placenta or during birth; and both mother and baby are at increased risk of developing full-blown AIDS.
a cure?
Drugs are being developed to treat HIV and opportunistic infection, but they cause severe side effects and so far do not actually cure AIDS.

Aigun, Treaty of treaty between Russia and China signed in 1858 at the port of Aigun in China on the Amur River. The left bank was ceded to Russia, but this has since been repudiated by China.

Aiken Conrad (Potter) 1899–1973. US poet, novelist, and short-story writer whose *Selected Poems* 1929 won the Pulitzer prize. His works were influenced by early psychoanalytic theory and the use of the stream-of-consciousness technique.

Born in Savannah, Georgia, Aiken grew up in New England with relatives after his father, a doctor, killed his mother and then committed suicide. In his autobiography *Ushant* 1952, he confronts this traumatic experience. He graduated from Harvard University 1911 and began to write poetry. Some of Aiken's poetry is in the form of "symphonies," works that attempt to imitate music in its ability to convey meaning on several levels at once. His poetic works include *The House of Dust* 1920, *Senlin* 1925, *Brownstone Eclogues and Other Poems* 1942, *Collected Poems* 1953, *A Letter from Li Po, and Other Poems* 1955, *Sheepford Hills* 1957, and *A Seizure of Limericks* 1964. His novels include *Great Circle* 1933 and *Conversation* 1940. *The Collected Short Stories of Conrad Aiken* appeared 1960.

Aiken Howard 1900– US mathematician. In 1939, in conjunction with engineers from IBM, he started work on the design of an automatic calculator using standard business machine components. In 1944 the team completed one of the first computers, the Automatic Sequence Controlled Calculator (known as the Mark 1), a programmable computer controlled by punched paper tape and using ◊punched cards.

aikido Japanese art of self-defense; one of the ◊martial arts. Two main systems of aikido are tomiki and uyeshiba.

ailanthus any tree or shrub of the genus *Ailanthus* of the quassia family. All have compound leaves made up of pointed leaflets and clusters of small greenish flowers with an unpleasant smell. The tree-of-heaven *Ailanthus altissima*, native to E Asia, is grown worldwide as an ornamental. It can grow to 100 ft/30 m in height and 3 ft/1 m in diameter.

aileron pilot-controlled airfoil attached to, in, or near the trailing edge of an airplane wing, to control the rolling movements of the aircraft. It was invented by US aviation pioneer Glenn ◊Curtiss 1911.

Ain French river giving its name to a *département* (administrative region): length 118 mi/190 km; it is a right-bank tributary of the Rhône.

Aintab Syrian name of ◊Gaziantep, city in Turkey.

Ainu aboriginal people of Japan, with Caucasoid facial features and face and body hair, whose language is unrelated to any other. In the 4th century AD, they were driven north by ancestors of the Japanese; some 16,000 still inhabit the northern

aircraft *Under construction is a Boeing 767, at a Boeing plant in Seattle, Washington.*

09

aircraft carrier *Aerial photograph showing aircraft positioned on the deck of the* USS Saratoga.

Japanese island of Hokkaido. Others settled in Sakhalin in the Kuril Islands, which were divided between Russia and Japan in the 18th century. Sakhalin was occupied by Soviet troops in 1945 and became part of the USSR in 1947.

air see ◊atmosphere.

airbrush small fine spray-gun used by artists and photographic retouchers. Driven by air pressure from a compressor or pressurized can, it can apply a very even layer of ink or paint.

air conditioning system that controls the state of the air inside a building or vehicle. A complete air-conditioning unit controls the temperature and humidity of the air, removes dust and odors from it, and circulates it by means of a fan. US inventor W H Carrier developed the first effective air-conditioning unit in 1902 for a New York printing plant.

The air in an air conditioner is cooled by a type of ◊refrigeration unit comprising a compressor and a condenser. The air is cleaned by means of filters and activated charcoal. Moisture is extracted by condensation on cool metal plates.

A specialized air-conditioning system is installed in spacecraft as part of the life-support system. This includes the provision of oxygen to breathe and the removal of exhaled carbon dioxide.

aircraft any aeronautical vehicle, which may be lighter than air (supported by buoyancy) or heavier than air (supported by the dynamic action of air on its surfaces). ◊Balloons and ◊airships are lighter-than-air craft. Heavier-than-air craft include the ◊airplane, glider, autogyro, and helicopter.

aircraft carrier oceangoing naval vessel with a broad, flat-topped deck for launching and landing military aircraft; an effort to provide a floating military base for warplanes too far from home for refueling, repairing, reconnaissance, escorting, and various attack and defense operations. Although the first flight from the deck of a ship was in 1910, the first true carrier, the British *Argus* 1918, did not see service in World War I. By World War II, carriers were used extensively, especially in the Pacific, by both the Allies and the Japanese. They were used again in both the Korean and Vietnam wars. The USS *Enterprise* was the first nuclear-powered carrier 1961; it could go for almost 300,000 mi/480,000 km before refueling. Since aircraft are now capable of long-range flight, and with the possible use of sophisticated missiles, few carriers were built from the 1970s; their enormous cost, low speed, and vulnerability seem to preclude future construction.

air-cushion vehicle (ACV) craft that is supported by a layer, or cushion, of high-pressure air. The ◊hovercraft is the best-known form of ACV

Airedale terrier breed of large ◊terrier dog, about 2 ft/60 cm tall, with a rough red-brown coat. It originated about 1850 in England, as a cross of the otter hound and Irish and Welsh terriers.

air force a nation's fighting aircraft and the organization that maintains them.

history The emergence of the airplane at first brought only limited recognition of its potential value as a means of waging war. Like the balloon, used since the American Civil War, it was considered a way of extending the vision of ground forces. A unified air force was established in the UK 1918, Italy 1923, France 1928, Germany 1935 (after repudiating the arms limitations of the Versailles treaty), and the US 1947 (it began as the Aeronautical Division of the Army Signal Corps in 1907, and evolved into the Army's Air Service Division by 1918; by 1926 it was the Army Air Corps and in World War II the Army Air Forces). The main specialized groupings formed during World War I—such as combat, bombing (see ◊bomb), reconnaissance, and transport—were adapted and modified in World War II; activity was extended, with self-contained tactical air forces to meet the needs of ground commanders in the main theaters of land operations and for the attack on and defense of shipping over narrow seas.

From 1945–60 piston-engine aircraft were superseded by jet aircraft; computerized guidance systems lessened the difference between missile and aircraft; and flights of unlimited duration became possible with air-to-air refueling. For example, the Strategic Air Command's bombers can patrol 24 hours a day armed with thermonuclear weapons. For some years it was anticipated that the pilot might become obsolete, but the continuation of conventional warfare and the evolution of tactical nuclear weapons have led in the 1970s and 1980s to the development of advanced combat aircraft able to fly supersonically beneath an enemy's radar on strike and reconnaissance missions, as well as stealth aircraft that cannot be detected by radar.

airglow a faint and variable light in the Earth's atmosphere produced by chemical reactions in the ionosphere.

air lock airtight chamber that allows people to pass between areas of different pressure; also an air bubble in a pipe that impedes fluid flow. An air lock may connect an environment at ordinary pressure and an environment that has high air pressure (such as a submerged caisson used for tunneling or building dams or bridge foundations).

An air lock may also permit someone wearing breathing apparatus to pass into an airless environment (into water from a submerged submarine or into the vacuum of space from a spacecraft).

airplane powered heavier-than-air craft supported in flight by fixed wings. Airplanes can be propelled by the thrust of a jet engine, a rocket engine, or airscrew (propeller), as well as combinations of these. They must be designed aerodynamically, as streamlining ensures maximum flight efficiency. The shape of a plane depends on its use and operating speed—aircraft operating at well below the speed of sound need not be as streamlined as supersonic aircraft. The Wright brothers flew the first powered plane (a biplane) in Kitty Hawk, North Carolina, 1903. For the history of aircraft and aviation, see ◊flight.

Efficient streamlining prevents the formation of shock waves over the body surface and wings, which would cause instability and power loss. The wings of an airplane have the cross-sectional

airplane

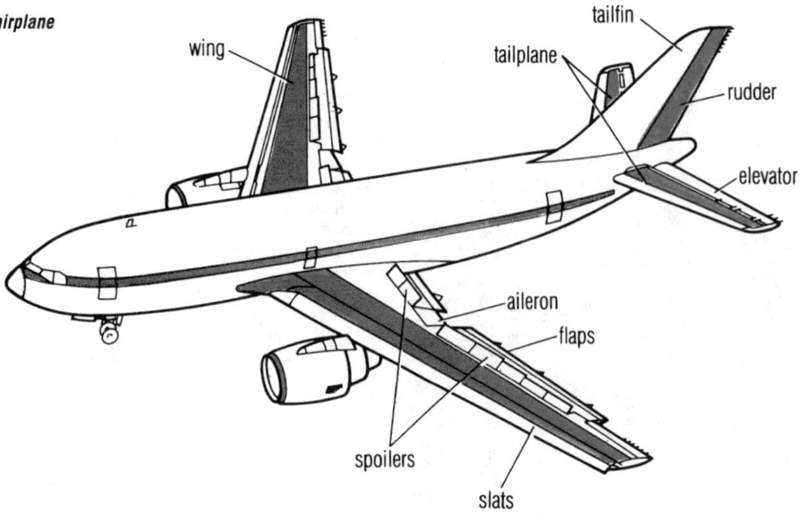
wing
tailfin
tailplane
rudder
elevator
aileron
flaps
spoilers
slats

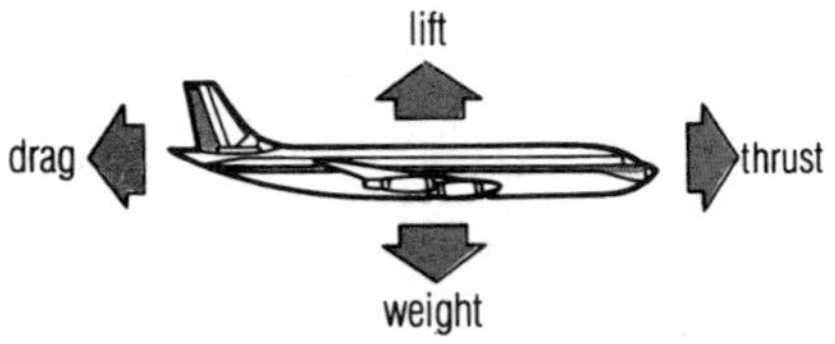
lift
drag
thrust
weight

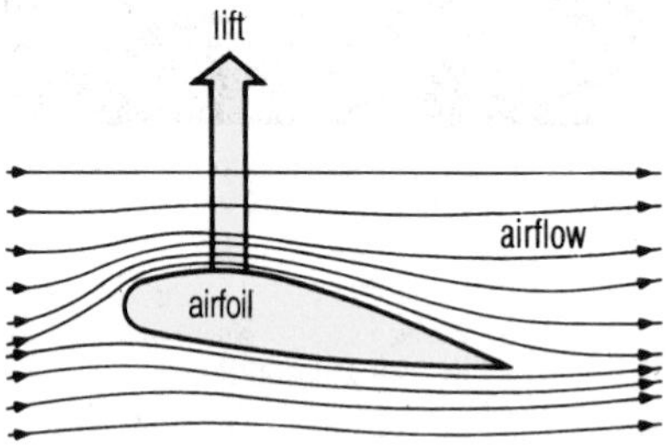
lift
airflow
airfoil

shape of an airfoil: broad and curved at the front, flat underneath, curved on top, and tapering to a sharp point at the rear. It is so shaped that air passing above it is speeded up, reducing pressure below atmospheric pressure. This follows from the ◊Bernoulli effect and results in a force acting vertically upward, called lift, which counters the plane's weight. In level flights, lift equals weight. The wings develop sufficient lift to support the plane when they move quickly through the air. The thrust that causes propulsion comes from the reaction to the air stream accelerated backward by the propeller or the gases shooting backward from the jet exhaust. In flight the engine thrust must overcome the air resistance, or ◊drag. Drag depends on frontal area (for example, large, airliner; small, fighter plane) and shape (drag coefficient); in level flight, drag equals thrust. The drag is reduced by streamlining the plane, resulting in higher speed and reduced fuel consumption for a given power. Less fuel need be carried for a given distance of travel, so a larger payload (cargo or passengers) can be carried.

The shape of a plane is dictated principally by the speed at which it will operate (see ◊aeronautics). A low-speed plane operating at well below the speed of sound (about 600 mph/965 kph) need not be particularly well streamlined, and it can have its wings broad and projecting at right angles from the fuselage. An aircraft operating close to the speed of sound must be well streamlined and have swept-back wings. This prevents the formation of shock waves over the body surface and wings, which would result in instability and high power loss. Supersonic planes (faster than sound) need to be highly streamlined, and require a needle nose, highly swept-back wings, and what is often termed a "Coke-bottle" (narrow-waisted) fuselage, in order to pass through the sound barrier without suffering undue disturbance. To give great flexibility of operation at low as well as high speeds, some supersonic planes are designed with variable geometry, or ◊swing-wings. For low-speed flight the wings are outstretched; for high-speed flight they are swung close to the fuselage to form an efficient ◊delta-wing configuration. Aircraft designers experiment with different designs in ◊wind tunnel tests, which indicate how their designs will behave in flight. Fighter jets in the 1990s are being deliberately designed to be aerodynamically unstable for greater agility. This is achieved by a main wing of continuously modifiable shape, the airflow over which is controlled by a smaller tilting foreplane. New aircraft are being made lighter and faster (to Mach 3) by the use of heat-resistant materials, some of which are also radar-absorbing, making the aircraft "invisible" to enemy defenses.

Planes are constructed using light but strong aluminum alloys such as duralumin (with copper, magnesium, and so on). For supersonic planes special stainless steel and titanium may be used in areas subjected to high heat loads. The structure of the plane, or the airframe (wings, fuselage, and so on) consists of a surface skin of alloy sheets supported at intervals by struts known as ribs and stringers. The structure is bonded together by riveting or by powerful adhesives such as ◊epoxy resins. In certain critical areas, which have to withstand very high stresses (such as the wing roots), body panels are machined from solid metal for extra strength.

On the ground a plane rests on wheels, usually in a tricycle arrangement, with a nose wheel and two wheels behind, one under each wing. For all except some light planes, the landing gear, or undercarriage, is retracted in flight to reduce drag. Seaplanes, which take off and land on water, are fitted with nonretractable hydrofoils.

Wings by themselves are unstable in flight, and a plane requires a tail to provide stability. The tail consists of a horizontal tail plane and vertical tail fin, called the horizontal and vertical stabilizer respectively. The tail plane has hinged flaps at the rear called elevators to control pitch (attitude). Raising the elevators depresses the tail and inclines the wings upward (increases the angle of attack). This speeds the airflow above the wings until lift exceeds weight and the plane climbs. However, the steeper attitude increases drag, so more power is needed to maintain speed and the engine throttle must be opened up. Moving the elevators in the opposite direction produces the reverse effect. The angle of attack is reduced, and the plane descends. Speed builds up rapidly if the engine is not throttled back. Turning (changing direction) is effected by moving the rudder hinged to the rear of the tail fin, and by banking (rolling) the plane. It is banked by moving the ailerons, interconnected flaps at the rear of the wings that move in opposite directions, one up, the other down.

In planes with a delta wing, such as the ◊Concorde, the ailerons and elevators are combined. Other movable control surfaces, called flaps, are fitted at the rear of the wings closer to the fuselage. They are extended to increase the width and camber (curve) of the wings during takeoff and landing, thereby creating extra lift, while movable sections at the front, or leading edges, of the wing, called slats, are also extended at these times to improve the airflow. To land, the nose of the plane is brought up so that the angle of attack of the wings exceeds a critical point and the airflow around them breaks down; lift is lost (a condition known as stalling), and the plane drops to the runway. A few planes (for example, the Harrier) have a novel method of takeoff and landing, rising and dropping vertically by swiveling nozzles to direct the exhaust of their jet engines downward. The ◊helicopter uses rotating propellers (rotors) to obtain lift to take off vertically.

The control surfaces of a plane are operated by the pilot on the flight deck, by means of a control stick, or wheel, and by foot pedals (for the rudder). The controls are brought into action by hydraulic power systems. Advanced experimental high-speed craft known as control-configured vehicles use a sophisticated computer-controlled system. The pilot instructs the computer which maneuver the plane must perform, and the computer, informed by a series of sensors around the craft about the attitude, speed, and turning rate of the plane, sends signals to the control surface and throttle to enable the maneuver to be executed.

air pollution contamination of the atmosphere caused by the discharge, accidental or deliberate, of a wide range of toxic airborne substances. The amount of the released substance may be relatively high in a certain locality, so the harmful effects become more noticeable. The cost of preventing any discharge of pollutants into the air is prohibitive, so attempts are being made to reduce gradually the amount of discharge and to disperse this as quickly as possible by using a very tall chimney, or by intermittent release.

air raid aerial attack, usually on a civilian target such as a factory, rail line, or communications center. In World War II (1939–45), raids were usually made by bomber aircraft, but many thousands were killed in London in 1944 by German V1 and V2 rockets. The air raids on Britain 1940–41 became known as the Blitz. The Allies made retaliatory air raids over European cities, and, during the ◊Gulf War 1991 the UN coalition forces made thousands of air raids on Baghdad, Iraq, to destroy the Iraqi infrastructure and communications network (some 250,000 civilians were killed).

air sac in birds, a thin-walled extension of the lungs. There are nine of these and they extend into the abdomen and bones, effectively increasing lung capacity. In mammals, it is another name for the alveoli in the lungs, and in some insects, for widenings of the trachea.

airship or ***dirigible*** any aircraft that is lighter than air and power-driven, consisting of an elliptical balloon that forms the streamlined envelope or hull and has below it the propulsion system (propellers), steering mechanism, and commodious space for crew, passengers, and/or cargo. The balloon section is filled with lighter-than-air gas, either the nonflammable helium or, before helium was industrially available in large enough quantities, the easily ignited and flammable hydrogen. The envelope's form is maintained by internal air pollution

pollutant	sources	effects
sulfur dioxide SO_2	oil, coal combustion in power stations	acid rain formed, damaging plants, trees, buildings, lakes
oxides of nitrogen NO	high-temperature combustion in automobiles, and to some extent power stations	acid rain formed
lead compounds	from leaded gasoline used by cars	nerve poison
carbon dioxide CO_2	oil, coal, gasoline, diesel combustion	greenhouse effect
carbon monoxide CO	limited combustion of oil, coal gasoline, diesel fuels	poisonous, leads to photochemical smog in some areas
nuclear waste	nuclear power plants, nuclear weapon testing, war	radioactivity, contamination of locality, cancers, mutations, death

pressure in the nonrigid (blimp) and semirigid types (in which the nose and tail sections have a metal framework connected by a rigid keel). The rigid type (zeppelin) maintains its form using an internal metal framework. Airships have been used for luxury travel, polar exploration, warfare, and advertising. Rigid airships predominated from about 1900 until 1940. As the technology developed, the size of the envelope was increased from about 150 ft/45 m to more than 800 ft/244 m for the last two zeppelins built. In 1852 the first successful airship was designed and flown by Henri ◊Giffard of France. In 1900 the first successful rigid type was designed by Count (Graf) Ferdinand von ◊Zeppelin of Germany. In 1919 the first nonstop transatlantic roundtrip flight was completed by a rigid airship, the British R34. In the early 1920s a large source of helium was discovered in the US and was substituted for hydrogen, reducing the danger of fire. The US military attempted to use zeppelins but abandoned the effort early on. In the 1920s and 1930s luxury zeppelin services took passengers across the Atlantic faster and in greater comfort than the great ocean liners. The successful German airship *Graf Zeppelin*, completed in 1927, was used for transatlantic, cruise, and around-the-world trips. In 1929 it traveled 20,000 mi/32,000 km around the world. It was retired and dismantled after years of trouble-free service, replaced by the *Hindenburg* in 1936.

Several airship accidents were caused by structural break-up, during storms, and by fire. The last and best known was the *Hindenberg*, which had been forced to return to the use of flammable hydrogen by a US embargo on helium; it exploded and burned at the mooring mast at Lakehurst, New Jersey, in 1937. The last and largest rigid airship was the German *Graf Zeppelin II*, completed just before World War II; it never saw commercial service but was used as a reconnaissance station off the English coast early in the war (it was the only zeppelin used in the war) but was soon retired and dismantled. Rigid airships, predominant from World War I until the early years of World War II, are no longer in use but blimps continued in use for coastal and antisubmarine patrol until the 1960s, and advertising blimps can be seen until this day. Recent interest in all types of airship has surfaced (including some with experimental and nontraditional shapes for the envelopes), since they are fuel-efficient, quiet, and capable of lifting enormous loads over great distances.

Airy George Biddell 1801–1892. English astronomer. He installed a transit telescope at the Cambridge University Observatory at Greenwich, England, and accurately measured ◊Greenwich Mean Time by the stars along the line of zero longitude defined by the position of the observatory.

Aisne river of N France, giving its name to a *département*; length 175 mi/282 km.

Aix-en-Provence town in the *département* of Bouches-du-Rhône, France, 18 mi/29 km N of Marseille; population (1982) 127,000. It is the capital of Provence and dates from Roman times.

Aix-la-Chapelle French name of ◊Aachen, ancient city in Germany.

Aix-les-Bains spa with hot springs in the *département* of Savoie, France, near Lake Bourget, 8 mi/13 km N of Chambéry; population (1982) 22,534.

air sac

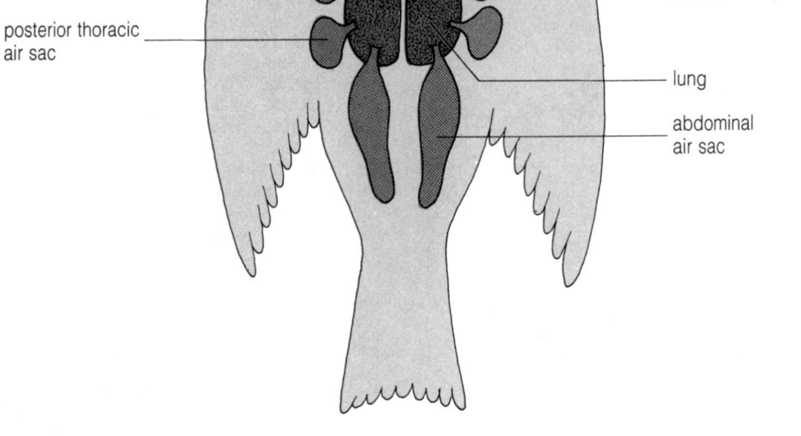
trachea
cervical air sac
interclavicular air sac
anterior thoracic air sac
posterior thoracic air sac
lung
abdominal air sac

Ajaccio capital and second-largest port of Corsica; population (1982) 55,279. Founded by the Genoese in 1492, it was the birthplace of Napoleon; it has been French since 1768.

Ajax Greek hero in Homer's ◊*Iliad*. Son of Telamon, king of Salamis, he was second only to Achilles among the Greek heroes in the Trojan War. When ◊Agamemnon awarded the armor of the dead Achilles to ◊Odysseus, Ajax is said to have gone mad with jealousy, and then committed suicide in shame.

Ajman smallest of the seven states that make up the ◊United Arab Emirates; area 96 sq mi/250 sq km; population (1980) 36,000.

Ajmer city in Rajasthan, India; population (1981) 376,000. Situated in a deep valley in the Aravalli mountains, it is a commercial and industrial center, notably of cotton manufacture. It has many ancient remains, including a Jain temple.

ajolote Mexican reptile of the genus *Bipes*. It and several other tropical burrowing species are placed in the Amphisbaenia, a group separate from lizards and snakes among the Squamata. Unlike the others, however, which have no legs, it has a pair of short but well-developed front legs. In line with its burrowing habits, the skull is very solid, the eyes small, and external ears absent. The scales are arranged in rings, giving the body a wormlike appearance.

AK abbreviation for ◊Alaska.

Akaba alternative transliteration of ◊Aqaba, gulf of the Red Sea.

Akbar Jalal ud-Din Mohammed 1542–1605. Mogul emperor of N India from 1556, when he succeeded his father. He gradually established his rule throughout N India. He is considered the greatest of the Mogul emperors, and the firmness and wisdom of his rule won him the title "Guardian of Mankind"; he was a patron of the arts.

À Kempis Thomas see religious writer, ◊Thomas à Kempis.

Ake v Oklahoma a US Supreme Court decision 1985 dealing with the right of indigent defendants to the "raw materials" needed for an adequate defense. The case was an appeal of the conviction of Glen Ake, a diagnosed paranoid schizophrenic, who had been denied psychiatric assistance by the court during his trial. The Supreme Court ruled that Ake had not been granted due process because his unstable condition, which could have been remedied by treatment, had helped to determine his sentence. The case used the same constitutional grounds to require court-appointed psychiatrists for indigent defendants as an earlier decision had to guarantee court-appointed attorneys.

Akhenaton another name for ◊Ikhnaton, pharaoh of Egypt.

Akhetaton capital of ancient Egypt established by the monotheistic pharaoh ◊Ikhnaton as the center for his cult of the Aten, the sun's disk; it is the modern Tell el Amarna 190 mi/300 km S of Cairo. Ikhnaton's palace had formal enclosed gardens. After his death it was abandoned, and the ◊Amarna tablets, found in the ruins, were probably discarded by his officials.

Akhmatova Anna. Adopted name of Anna Andreevna Gorenko 1889–1966. Russian poet. Among her works are the cycle *Requiem* 1963 (written in the 1930s), which deals with the Stalinist terror, and *Poem Without a Hero* 1962 (begun 1940).

In the 1920s she published several collections of poetry in the realist style of ◊Mandelshtam, but her lack of sympathy with the post-revolutionary regimes inhibited her writing, and her work was banned 1922–40 and again from 1946. From the mid-1950s her work was gradually rehabilitated in the USSR. In 1989 an Akhmatova Museum was opened in Leningrad.

Akihito 1933– . Emperor of Japan from 1989, succeeding his father Hirohito (Showa). His reign is called the Heisei ("achievement of universal peace") era.

Unlike previous crown princes, Akihito was

Akihito *Emperor Akihito and his wife on their wedding day, 1959.*

educated alongside commoners at the elite Gakushuin school and in 1959 he married Michiko Shoda (1934–), the daughter of a flour-company president. Their three children, the Oxford university-educated Crown Prince Hiro, Prince Aya, and Princess Nori, were raised at Akihito's home instead of being reared by tutors and chamberlains in a separate imperial dormitory.

Akins Zoe 1886–1958. US writer. Born in Missouri, she wrote poems, literary criticism, and plays, including *The Greeks Had a Word for It* 1930.

Akkad northern Semitic people who conquered the Sumerians in 2350 BC and ruled Mesopotamia. The ancient city of Akkad in central Mesopotamia, founded by ◊Sargon I, was an imperial center in the 3rd millennium BC; the site is unidentified, but it was on the Euphrates.

Akkaia alternate form of ◊Achaea.

'Akko Israeli name for the port of ◊Acre.

Akron (Greek "summit") city in Ohio, on the Cuyahoga River, 35 mi/56 km SE of Cleveland; population (1990) 223,019. Known as the "Rubber Capital of the World," it is home to the headquarters of several major tire and rubber companies, although production there ended by 1982. The city is also a major trucking center and the site of the University of Akron.

Akron was first settled 1807. Dr B F Goodrich established a rubber factory 1870, and the industry grew immensely with the rising demand for tires from about 1910.

Aksai Chin part of Himalayan Kashmir lying to the east of the Karakoram range. It is occupied by China but claimed by India.

Aksakov Sergei Timofeyevich 1791–1859. Russian writer, born at Ufa, in the Urals. Under the influence of ◊Gogol, he wrote autobiographical novels, including *Chronicles of a Russian Family* 1856, and *Years of Childhood* 1858.

Aksum ancient Greek-influenced Semitic kingdom that flourished 1st–6th centuries AD and covered a large part of modern Ethiopia as well as the Sudan. The ruins of its capital, also called Aksum, lie NW of Aduwa, but the site has been developed as a modern city.

Aktyubinsk industrial city in the republic of Kazakh, USSR; population (1987) 248,000. Established 1869, it expanded after the opening of the Trans-Caspian railroad 1905.

al- for Arabic names beginning *al-*, see rest of name; for example, for "al-Fatah," see ◊Fatah, al-.

AL abbreviation for ◊Alabama.

Alabama Confederate warship cruiser (1,040 tons) in the American ◊Civil War. Built in the UK, it was allowed to leave port by the British, and sank 68 Union merchant ships before it was itself sunk by a Union warship off the coast of France in 1864. In 1871 the international court awarded damages of $15.5 million to the US, a legal precedent.

The court's ruling requires a neutral country to exercise "due diligence" to prevent the arming within its jurisdiction of a vessel intending to carry out a war against a country with which the neutral is at peace.

Alabama state in S US; nickname Heart of Dixie/ Cotton State

area 51,994 sq mi/134,700 sq km

capital Montgomery

cities Birmingham, Mobile, Huntsville, Tuscaloosa

physical the state comprises the Cumberland Plateau in the N; the Black Belt, or Canebrake (excellent cotton-growing country), in the center; S of this, the coastal plain of Piney Woods

features rivers: Alabama, Tennessee; Appalachian mountains, George Washington Carver Museum at the Tuskegee Institute (a college founded for blacks by Booker T Washington); White House of the Confederacy at Montgomery; George C Marshall Space Flight Center at Huntsville; annual Mardi Gras celebration at Mobile, Helen Keller's birthplace at Tuscumbia

products cotton (no longer the prime crop, but still important), soybeans, peanuts, wood products, coal, livestock, poultry, iron, chemicals, textiles, paper

population (1990) 4,040,587.

famous people Hank Aaron, Tallulah Bankhead, Nat King Cole, W C Handy, Helen Keller, Joe Louis, Willie Mays, Jesse Owens, Leroy "Satchel" Paige, George C Wallace, Booker T Washington, Hank Williams

history first settled by the French in the early 18th century; ceded to Britain 1763; passed to the US 1783 and became a state 1819. It was one of the ◊Confederate States in the American Civil War, and Montgomery was the first capital of the Confederacy. Birmingham became the South's leading industrial center in the late 19th century. Alabama was in the forefront of the civil rights movement in the 1950s and 1960s: Martin Luther ◊King, Jr, led a successful boycott of segregated Montgomery buses in 1955; school integration began in the early 1960s despite the opposition of Governor George C Wallace; the 1965 Selma march resulted in federal voting-rights legislation.

alabaster a naturally occurring fine-grained white or light-colored translucent form of ◊gypsum, often streaked or mottled. It is a soft material, used for carvings, and ranks second on the ◊Mohs' scale of hardness.

Aladdin in the ◊*Arabian Nights*, a poor boy who obtains a magic lamp: when the lamp is rubbed, a jinn (genie, or spirit) appears and fulfills its owner's wishes.

Alain-Fournier Adopted name of Henri-Alban Fournier 1886–1914. French novelist. His haunting semiautobiographical fantasy *Le Grand Meaulnes/ The Lost Domain* 1913 was a cult novel of the 1920s and 1930s. His life is intimately recorded in his correspondence with his brother-in-law Jacques Rivière.

Alamein, El, Battles of in World War II, two decisive battles in the western desert, N Egypt. In the First Battle of El Alamein July 1–27, 1942, the British 8th Army under Auchinleck held the German and Italian forces under Rommel. In the Second Battle of El Alamein Oct 23–Nov 4 1942 ◊Montgomery defeated Rommel.

Alamo, the mission fortress in San Antonio, Texas. It was besieged Feb 23–Mar 6, 1836 by ◊Santa Anna and 4,000 Mexicans; they killed the garrison of about 180, including Davy ◊Crockett and Jim ◊Bowie.

The struggle against such overwhelming odds made the battle of the Alamo a rallying point for the settlers in the Texas War of Independence from Mexico.

Alabama

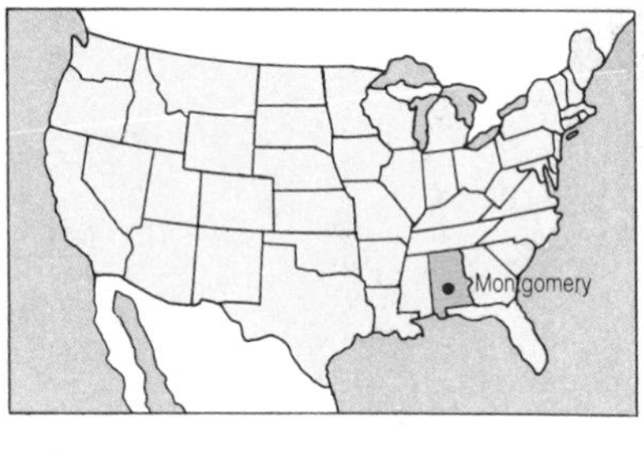
Montgomery

Alaska

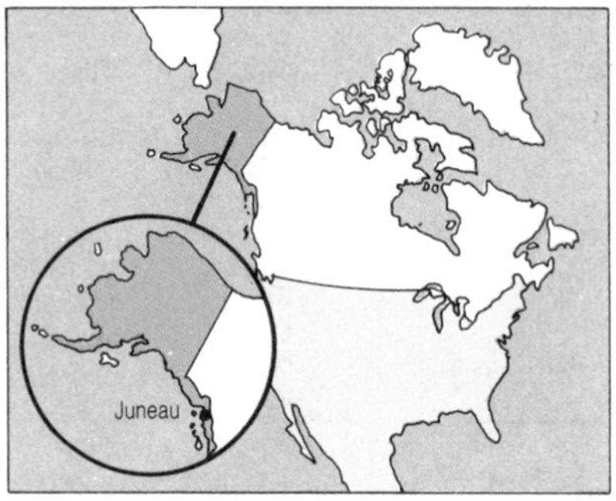
Juneau

Alanbrooke Alan Francis Brooke, 1st Viscount Alanbrooke 1883–1963. British army officer, chief of staff in World War II and largely responsible for the strategy that led to the German defeat.

Åland Islands (Finnish *Ahvenanmaa* "land of waters") group of some 6,000 islands in the Baltic Sea, at the southern extremity of the Gulf of Bothnia; area 572 sq mi/1,481 sq km; population (1988) 23,900. Only 80 are inhabited; the largest island has a small town, Mariehamn. When Finland became independent 1917, the Swedish-speaking islanders claimed the right of self-determination, and were granted autonomous status 1920. The main sectors of the island economy are tourism, agriculture and shipping.

Alarcón Pedro Antonio de 1833–1891. Spanish journalist and writer. The acclaimed *Diario/Diary* was based upon his experiences as a soldier in Morocco. His *El Sombrero de tres picos/The Three-Cornered Hat* 1874 was the basis of Manuel de Falla's ballet.

Alaric c. 370–410. King of the Visigoths. In 396 he invaded Greece and retired with much booty to Illyria. In 400 and 408 he invaded Italy, and in 410 captured and sacked Rome, but he died the same year on his way to invade Sicily.

The river Busento was diverted by his soldiers so that he could be buried in its course with his treasures; the laborers were killed to keep the secret.

Alaska largest state of the US, on the NW extremity of North America, separated from the lower 48 states by British Columbia; nickname Last Frontier

area 591,000 sq mi/1,531,000 sq km

capital Juneau

cities Anchorage, Fairbanks, Fort Yukon, Holy Cross, Nome

physical much of Alaska is mountainous and includes Mount McKinley (Denali), 20,322 ft/ 6,194 m, the highest peak in North America, surrounded by Denali National Park. Caribou thrive in the Arctic tundra, and elsewhere there are extensive forests

features Yukon river; Rocky Mountains, including Mount McKinley and Mount Katmai, a volcano that erupted 1912 and formed the Valley of Ten Thousand Smokes (from which smoke and steam still escape and which is now a national monument); Arctic Wild Life Range, with the only large herd of North American caribou; Little Diomede Island, which is only 2.5 mi/4 km from Big Diomede/Ratmanov Island in the USSR; caribou herds on the tundra. A Congressional act 1980 gave environmental protection to 104 million acres/42 million ha. The chief railroad line runs from Seward to Fairbanks, which is linked by highway (via Canada) with Seattle. Near Fairbanks is the University of Alaska

products oil, natural gas, coal, copper, iron, gold, tin, fur, salmon fisheries and canneries, lumber

population (1990) 550,043; including 9% American Indians, Aleuts, and Eskimos

history Various groups of Indians crossed the Bering land bridge 60,000–15,000 years ago; the Eskimo began to settle the Arctic coast from Siberia about 2000 BC; the Aleuts settled the Aleutian archipelago about 1000 BC. The first European to visit Alaska was Vitus Bering 1741. Alaska was a Russian colony from 1744 until purchased by the US 1867 for $7,200,000; it became a state 1959. Exploited from 1968, especially in the Prudhoe Bay area to the SE of Point Barrow, are the most valuable mineral resources. An oil pipeline (1977) runs from Prudhoe Bay to the port of Valdez. Oilspill from a tanker in Prince William Sound caused great environmental damage in 1989. Under construction is an underground natural-gas pipeline to Chicago and San Francisco.

Alaska Highway road that runs from Dawson Creek, British Columbia, to Fairbanks, Alaska (1,522 mi/2,450 km). It was built 1942 as a supply route for US military forces in Alaska. The highway, which runs along the E edge of the Rocky Mountains, is paved in Alaska but mostly gravel-surfaced in Canada.

Alba Celtic name for Scotland; also an alternate spelling for ◊Alva, Ferdinand Alvarez de Toledo, duke of Alva, Spanish politician and general.

Albacete market town in the province of the same name, SE Spain; population (1986) 127,000. Once famous for cutlery, it now produces clothes and footwear.

albacore name loosely applied to several species of fishes found in warm regions of the Atlantic and Pacific oceans, in particular to a large tuna, *Thunnus alalunga*, and to several other species of the mackerel family.

Alba Iulia (German *Karlsburg*) a city on the river Mures, W central Romania, founded by the Romans in the 2nd century AD. The Romanian kings were crowned here. Population (1985) 64,300.

Albania country in SE Europe, bounded W and SW by the Adriatic Sea, N and E by Yugoslavia, and SE by Greece.

government Under the 1946 constitution (amended 1950), Albania's sole and supreme legislative organ is the 250-member People's Assembly, elected every four years by universal suffrage. This assembly meets twice a year and elects a permanent 15-member presidium, with a chair who acts as state president, to take over its functions in its absence. The People's Assembly also elects a council of ministers, headed by a chair or prime minister, to act as the day-to-day executive government. The Communist Party (Albanian Party of Labor), controlled by its political bureau, is the only political party and is the leading force in the Democratic Front of Albania.

history In the ancient world the area was occupied by the Illyrians, later becoming a Roman province until the end of the 4th century AD. Albania then came under Byzantine rule, which lasted until 1347. There followed about 100 years of invasions by Bulgarians, Serbs, Venetians, and finally Turks, who arrived in 1385 and, after the death of the nationalist leader Skanderbeg (George Castriota) (1403–1468), eventually made Albania part of the ◊Ottoman empire 1468.

Albania became independent 1912 and a republic 1925. In 1928 President Ahmed Beg Zogu was proclaimed King Zog. Overrun by Italy and Germany 1939–44, Albania became a republic with a communist government 1946 after a guerrilla struggle led by Enver ◊Hoxha (1908–1985).

At first closely allied with Yugoslavia, Albania backed ◊Stalin in his 1948 dispute with ◊Tito and developed close links with the USSR 1949–55, entering ◊Comecon 1949. Hoxha imposed a Stalinist system with rural collectivization, industrial nationalization, central planning, and one-party control. Mosques and churches were closed in an effort to create the "first atheist state." Hoxha remained a committed Stalinist and, rejecting ◊Khrushchev's denunciations of the Stalin era, broke off diplomatic relations with the USSR 1961 and withdrew from Comecon. Albania also severed diplomatic relations with China 1978, after the post-Mao accommodation with the US, choosing isolation and neutrality.

The "Hoxha experiment" left Albania with the lowest per capita income in Europe. Since his death 1985, there have been policy adjustments and a widening of external economic contacts. Economic incentives in the form of wage differentials for skilled tasks are gradually being introduced, and the number of countries with which Albania has formal diplomatic relations increased from 74 in 1978 to 111 in 1988. In Feb 1988 Albania attended the conference of Balkan states for the first time since the 1930s.

Tensions have simmered among the ethnic groups in the region, and in Feb 1989 strikes by ethnic Albanians in Yugoslavia brought government denunciation of "second-class citizen" treatment by Yugoslavia of its Albanian residents. A proposal for release of some political prisoners gave the first indication that the reforms spreading in E Europe were having an impact in Albania. Opposition to the regime began to mount during 1990 around the NW border town of Shkoder. In July diplomatic relations with the Soviet Union, which had been broken off in 1961, were restored and embassies reestablished. In Dec 1990 amid continuing protests in Tirana and economic collapse, the Communist Party leadership announced that, as part of a fundamental revision of the Stalinist constitution, the existence of opposition parties had finally been authorized and the ban on religion lifted. Five hardline Politburo members were dismissed. Albania held elections (secret ballot) to the People's Assembly in Feb 1991.

In March 1991 diplomatic relations with the US, suspended since 1946, were restored; relations were reestablished with the UK in May 1991.

In Albania's first free multiparty elections, held in March-April 1991, the ruling Albanian Party of Labor (PLA) captured 169 of the 250 seats in the new People's Assembly. It secured sufficient seats for a two-thirds majority to make constitutional changes.

A new interim constitution, replacing the 1976 one, was adopted in April 1991, and the country was renamed the Republic of Albania, the PLA's leading role was abandoned, and private property was endorsed. The new People's Assembly elected Ramiz Alia as the new executive President of the Republic, replacing the collective presidium, and Commander-in-Chief of the armed forces.

As Albania's economy deteriorated and unemployment rose, Ylli Bufi replaced Fatos Nano as prime minister in June 1991.

On June 13, 1991 the PLA renamed itself the Socialist Party of Albania and elected Fatos Nano its chairman.

Albania
Republic of

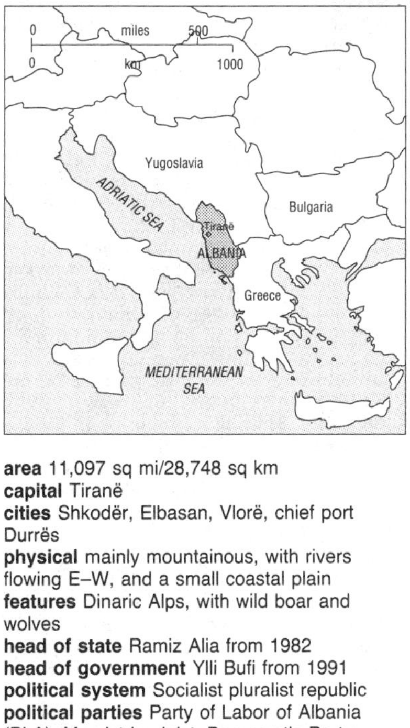
0 miles 500
0 km 1000
Yugoslavia
ADRIATIC SEA
Tiranë
ALBANIA
Bulgaria
Greece
MEDITERRANEAN SEA

area 11,097 sq mi/28,748 sq km
capital Tiranë
cities Shkodër, Elbasan, Vlorë, chief port Durrës
physical mainly mountainous, with rivers flowing E–W, and a small coastal plain
features Dinaric Alps, with wild boar and wolves
head of state Ramiz Alia from 1982
head of government Ylli Bufi from 1991
political system Socialist pluralist republic
political parties Party of Labor of Albania (PLA), Marxist-Leninist; Democratic Party; Amonia (Greek minority party)
exports crude oil, bitumen, chrome, iron ore, nickel, coal, copper wire, tobacco, fruit, vegetables
currency lek
population (1990 est) 3,270,000; growth rate 1.9% p.a.
life expectancy men 69, women 73
language Albanian, Greek
religion Muslim 70%, although all religion banned 1967–90
literacy 75% (1986)
GNP $2.8 bn (1986 est); $900 per head
GDP $1,313 mn; $543 per head
chronology
1468 Albania made part of the Ottoman Empire.
1912 Independence achieved from Turkey.
1925 Republic proclaimed.
1928–39 Monarchy of King Zog.
1939–44 Under Italian and then German rule.
1946 Communist republic proclaimed under the leadership of Enver Hoxha.
1949 Admitted into Comecon.
1961 Break with Khrushchev's USSR.
1967 Albania declared itself the "first atheist state in the world."
1978 Break with "revisionist" China.
1985 Death of Hoxha.
1987 Normal diplomatic relations restored with Canada, Greece, and West Germany.
1988 Attendance of conference of Balkan states for the first time since the 1930s.
1990 One-party system abandoned; first opposition party formed.
1991 Civil unrest; thousands fled to neighboring countries. Albanian Party of Labor (PLA) won a working majority in first free, multiparty assembly elections and PLA leader, Ramiz Alia, reelected president. April: new interim constitution adopted, country renamed the Republic of Albania. PLA government collapsed after widespread strikes and a coalition "national salvation" government was formed. June: prime minister Nano resigned, replaced by Ylli Bufi who formed new interim government including opposition party members.

Alban, St died AD 303. First Christian martyr in England. In 793 King Offa founded a monastery on the site of Alban's martyrdom, around which the city of St Albans grew up.

Albany city on the Flint River, Georgia, SE of Columbus; seat of Dougherty county. It is a commercial center for the production of pecans and peanuts, chemicals, lumber, and other industrial products; population (1990) 78,122.

Albany capital of New York, situated on the W bank of the Hudson River, about 140 mi/225 km N of New York City; population (1990) 101,082. With Schenectady and Troy it forms a metropolitan area, population (1980) 794,298. First reached by Henry Hudson during his 1609 voyage up the river since named for him, Albany, a deepwater port, began as the Dutch trading post Fort Nassau 1614. It was renamed Albany 1664 when the English took control and incorporated 1686. After the

Alberta

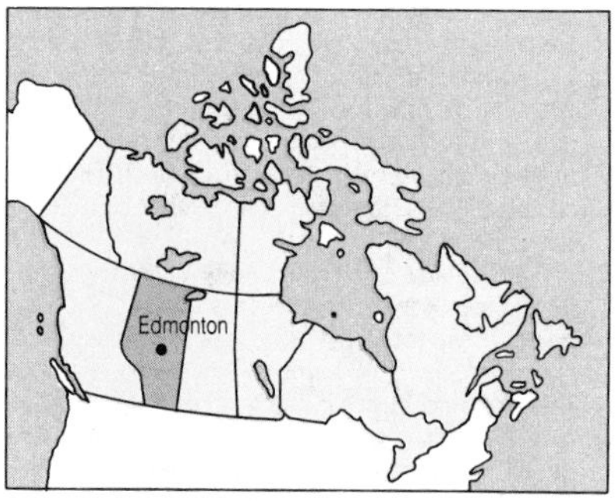
Edmonton

Revolutionary War, in 1797, the state capital was moved there from New York City. The completion of the Erie Canal 1825 fostered its economic development. A massive government complex, the Empire State Plaza, was built in the 1960s.

albatross large seabird, genus *Diomedea*, with long narrow wings adapted for gliding and a wingspan of up to 10 ft/3 m, mainly found in the S hemisphere. It belongs to the order Procellariiformes, the same group as petrels and shearwaters.

Albatrosses cover enormous distances, flying as far as 10,000 miles in 33 days, or up to 600 miles in one day. They continue flying even after dark, at speeds of up to 50 mph, though they may stop for an hour's rest and to feed during the night. They are sometimes called "gooney birds," probably because of their clumsy way of landing. Albatrosses are becoming increasingly rare, and are in danger of extinction.

albedo the fraction of the incoming light reflected by a body such as a planet. A body with a high albedo, near 1, is very bright, while a body with a low albedo, near 0, is dark. The Moon has an average albedo of 0.07, Venus 0.76, Earth 0.37.

Albee Edward 1928– . US playwright. His internationally performed plays are associated with the Theater of the ◊Absurd and include *The Zoo Story* 1960, *The American Dream* 1961, *Who's Afraid of Virginia Woolf?* 1962 (his most successful play, was also filmed with Elizabeth Taylor and Richard Burton as the quarrelling, alcoholic, academic couple in 1966), and *Tiny Alice* 1965. *A Delicate Balance* 1966 and *Seascape* 1975 both won Pulitzer prizes.

Albéniz Isaac 1860–1909. Spanish composer and pianist, born in Catalonia. He composed the suite *Iberia* and other piano pieces, making use of traditional Spanish melodies.

Alberoni Giulio 1664–1752. Spanish-Italian priest and politician, born in Piacenza, Italy. Philip V made him prime minister of Spain in 1715. In 1717 he became a cardinal. He introduced many domestic reforms, but was forced to flee to Italy in 1719, when his foreign policies failed.

Albert Prince Consort 1819–1861. Husband of British Queen ◊Victoria from 1840; a patron of the arts, science, and industry. Albert was the second son of the Duke of Saxe-Coburg-Gotha and first cousin to Queen Victoria, whose chief adviser he became. He planned the Great Exhibition of 1851; the profit was used to buy the sites in London of all the South Kensington museums and colleges and the Royal Albert Hall, built 1871. He died of typhoid.

Albert I 1875–1934. King of the Belgians from 1909, the younger son of Philip, Count of Flanders, and the nephew of Leopold II. In 1900 he married Duchess Elisabeth of Bavaria. In World War I he commanded the Allied army that retook the Belgian coast in 1918.

Alberta province of W Canada

area 255,223 sq mi/661,200 sq km

capital Edmonton

cities Calgary, Lethbridge, Medicine Hat, Red Deer

physical the Rocky Mountains; dry, treeless prairie in the center and S; toward the N this merges into a zone of poplar, then mixed forest. The valley of the Peace river is the northernmost farming land in Canada (except for Eskimo pastures), and good grazing lands lie in the foothills of the Rockies.

features Banff, Elk Island, Jasper, Waterton Lake, and Wood Buffalo national parks; annual Calgary stampede; extensive dinosaur finds near Drumheller

products coal; wheat, barley, oats, sugar beet in the S; cattle; oil and natural gas

population (1986) 2,375,000

history in the 17th century much of its area was part of a grant to the ◊Hudson's Bay Company for the fur trade, and the first trading posts were established in the late 18th century. The grant was bought by Canada 1869, and Alberta became a province 1905.

After an oil strike in 1947, Alberta became a major oil and gas producer.

Albert Canal canal designed as part of Belgium's frontier defenses; it also links the industrial basin of Liège with the port of Antwerp. It was built 1930–39 and named after King Albert I.

Alberti Leon Battista 1404–1472. Italian ◊Renaissance architect and theorist who recognized the principles of Classical architecture and their modification for Renaissance practice in *On Architecture* 1452.

Albert, Lake former name of Lake ◊Mobutu in central Africa.

Albertus Magnus, St 1206–1280. German scholar of Christian theology, philosophy (especially Aristotle), natural science, chemistry, and physics. He was known as "doctor universalis" because of the breadth of his knowledge and tried to reconcile Aristotelian thought with Christian teachings. Feast day Nov 15.

Albi chief town in Tarn *département*, Midi-Pyrénées, SW France, on the river Tarn, 45 mi/72 km NE of Toulouse; population (1983) 45,000. It was the center of the Albigensian heresy (see ◊Albigenses) and the birthplace of the artist Toulouse-Lautrec. It has a 13th-century cathedral.

Albigenses heretical sect of Christians (associated with the ◊Cathars) who flourished in S France near Albi and Toulouse during the 11th–13th centuries. They adopted the Manichean belief in the duality of good and evil and pictured Jesus as being a rebel against the cruelty of an omnipotent God.

The Albigensians showed a consistently anti-Catholic attitude with distinctive sacraments, especially the *consolamentum*, or baptism of the spirit. An inquisition was initiated against the Albigensians in 1184 by Pope Lucius III (although the ◊Inquisition as we know it was not established until 1233); it was, however, ineffective, and in 1208 a crusade (1208–29) was launched against them under the elder Simon de Montfort. Thousands were killed before the movement was crushed in 1244.

albinism rare hereditary condition in which the body has no tyrosinase, one of the enzymes that form the pigment melanin, normally found in the skin, hair, and eyes. As a result, the hair is white and the skin and eyes are pink. The skin and eyes are abnormally sensitive to light, and vision is often impaired. The condition occurs among all human and animal groups.

Albinoni Tomaso 1671–1751. Italian Baroque composer and violinist, whose work was studied and adapted by ◊Bach. He composed over 40 operas. The popular *Adagio*, often described as being by Albinoni, was actually composed by his biographer Remo Giazotto (1910–).

Albion ancient name for Britain used by the Greeks and Romans. It was mentioned by Pytheas of Massilia (4th century BC), and is probably of Celtic origin, but the Romans, having in mind the white cliffs of Dover, assumed it to be derived from *albus* (white).

Alboin 6th century. King of the ◊Lombards about 561–573. At that time the Lombards were settled north of the Alps. Early in his reign he attacked the Gepidae, a Germanic tribe occupying present-day Romania, killing their king and taking his daughter Rosamund to be his wife. About 568 he crossed the Alps to invade Italy, conquering the country as far S as Rome. He was murdered at the instigation of his wife, after he forced her to drink wine from a cup made from her father's skull.

Albone Dan 1860–1906. English inventor of one of the first commercially available farm tractors, the Ivel, in 1902. It was a three-wheeled vehicle with a midmounted twin-cylinder gasoline engine which could plow an acre in 1.5 hours.

Ålborg alternate form of ◊Aalborg, Denmark.

Albufeira fishing village and resort on the Algarve coast of S Portugal, 27 mi/43 km W of Faro.

albumin any of a group of sulfur-containing ◊proteins. The best known is in the form of egg white; others occur in milk, and as a major component of serum. Many vegetables and fluids also contain albumins. They are soluble in water and dilute salt solutions, and are coagulated by heat.

The presence of albumin in the urine, termed albuminuria or proteinuria, may be a symptom of a kidney disorder.

Albuquerque largest city of New Mexico, situated E of the Rio Grande, in the Pueblo district; population (1990) 384,736. Founded 1706, it was named after Alfonso de Albuquerque. It is a resort and industrial center, specializing in electronic products and aerospace equipment.

Sandia Laboratories here is engaged in high-technology defense- and space-related projects. The University of New Mexico was founded here 1889. Kirkland Air Force Base is nearby.

Albuquerque Afonso de 1453–1515. Viceroy and founder of the Portuguese East Indies with strongholds in Ceylon, Goa and Malacca 1508–15, when the king of Portugal replaced him by his worst enemy. He died at sea on the way home when his ship *Flor del Mar* was lost between Malaysia and India.

Alcaeus c. 611–c. 580 BC. Greek lyric poet. Born at Mytilene in Lesvos, he was a member of the aristocratic party and went into exile when the popular party triumphed. He wrote odes, and the Alcaic stanza is named after him.

Alcatraz small island in San Francisco Bay, California. Its fortress was a military prison 1886–1934 and then a federal penitentiary until closed 1963. The dangerous tides allowed few successful escapes. Inmates included the gangster Al Capone and the "Birdman of Alcatraz," a prisoner who used his time in solitary confinement to become an authority on caged birds. American Indian "nationalists" briefly took over the island 1970 as a symbol of their lost heritage.

alcázar (Arabic "fortress") Moorish palace in Spain; one of five in Toledo was defended by the Nationalists against the Republicans for 71 days in 1936 during the Spanish ◊Civil War.

Alcazarquivir, Battle of battle on Aug 4, 1578 between the forces of Sebastian, king of Portugal (1554–1578), and those of the Berber kingdom of Fez. Sebastian's death on the field of battle paved the way for the incorporation of Portugal into the Spanish kingdom of Philip II.

Alcestis in Greek mythology, the wife of Admetus, king of Thessaly. At their wedding, the god Apollo secured a promise from the ◊Fates that Admetus might postpone his death if he could persuade someone else to die for him. Only his wife proved willing, but she was restored to life by ◊Heracles.

alchemy (Arabic *al-Kimya*) the search for the technique of transmuting base metals, such as lead and mercury, into silver and gold by the philosopher's stone, a hypothetical substance, to which was also attributed the power to give eternal life.

This aspect of alchemy constituted much of the chemistry of the Middle Ages. More broadly, however, alchemy was a system of philosophy that dealt both with the mystery of life and the

alcohol

The systematic naming of simple straight-chain organic molecules

Alkane	Alcohol	Aldehyde	Ketone	Carboxylic acid	Alkene
CH_4 methane	CH_3OH methanol	HCHO methanal	–	HCO_2H methanoic acid	–
CH_3CH_3 ethane	CH_3CH_2OH ethanol	CH_3CHO ethanal	–	CH_3CO_2H ethanoic acid	CH_2CH_2 ethene
$CH_3CH_2CH_3$ propane	$CH_3CH_2CH_2OH$ propanol	CH_3CH_2CHO propanal	CH_3COCH_3 propanone	$CH_3CH_2CO_2H$ propanoic acid	CH_2CHCH_3 propene

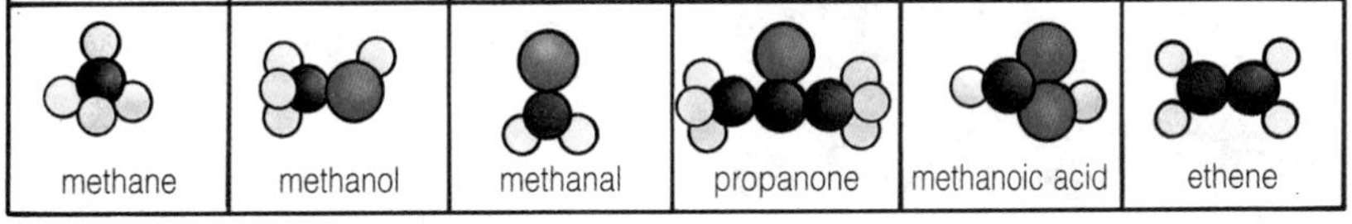
methane
methanol
methanal
propanone
methanoic acid
ethene

formation of inanimate substances. Alchemy was a complex and indefinite conglomeration of chemistry, astrology, occultism, and magic, blended with obscure and abstruse ideas derived from various religious systems and other sources. It was practiced in Europe from ancient times to the Middle Ages but later fell into disrepute when ◊chemistry and ◊physics developed.

Alcibiades 450–404 BC. Athenian general. Handsome and dissolute, he became the archetype of capricious treachery for his military intrigues against his native state with Sparta and Persia; the Persians eventually had him assassinated. He was brought up by ◊Pericles and was a friend of ◊Socrates, whose reputation as a teacher suffered from the association.

Alcmaeonidae a noble family of ancient Athens; its members included ◊Pericles and ◊Alcibiades.

Alcmene in Greek mythology, the wife of Amphitryon, and mother of Heracles (the father was Zeus, king of the gods, who visited Alcmene in the form of her husband).

Alcock John William 1892–1919. British aviator. On June 14, 1919, he and Arthur Whitten Brown (1886–1948) made the first nonstop transatlantic flight, from Newfoundland to Ireland.

Alcoforado Marianna 1640–1723. Portuguese nun. The *Letters of a Portuguese Nun* 1699, supposedly written by her to a young French nobleman (who abandoned her when their relationship became known), is no longer accepted as authentic.

alcohol any member of a group of organic chemical compounds characterized by the presence of one or more OH (hydroxyl) groups in the molecule, and which form ◊esters with ◊acids. The main uses of alcohols are as solvents for gums, resins, lacquers, and varnishes; in the making of dyes; for essential oils in perfumery; and for medical substances in pharmacy. Alcohol (ethanol) is produced naturally in the ◊fermentation process and is consumed as part of alcoholic beverages.

Alcohols may be liquids or solids, according to the size and complexity of the molecule. The five simplest alcohols form a series in which the number of carbon and hydrogen atoms increases progressively, each one having an extra CH_2 (methylene) group in the molecule: methanol or wood spirit (methyl alcohol, CH_3OH); ethanol (ethyl alcohol, C_2H_5OH); propanol (propyl alcohol, C_3H_7OH); butanol (butyl alcohol, C_4H_9OH); and pentanol (amyl alcohol, $C_5H_{11}OH$). The lower alcohols are liquids that mix with water; the higher alcohols, such as pentanol, are oily liquids not miscible with water, and the highest are waxy solids—for example, hexadecanol (cetyl alcohol, $C_{16}H_{33}OH$) and melissyl alcohol ($C_{30}H_{61}OH$), which occur in sperm-whale oil and beeswax respectively.

alcoholic beverage any drink containing alcohol, often used for its intoxicating effects. Ethyl alcohol, a colorless liquid (C_2H_5OH) is the basis of all common intoxicants. Foods rich in sugars, such as grapes, produce this alcohol as a natural product of decay, called fermentation.

malt liquors are beers, ales, and stouts, in which the starch of the grain is converted to sugar by malting, and the sugar then fermented into alcohol by yeasts. Fermented drinks contain less than 20% alcohol.

liquors are distilled from malt liquors or ◊wines and can contain up to 55% alcohol. Examples are whiskey, rum, and brandy.

A concentration of 0.15% alcohol in the blood causes mild intoxication; 0.3% definite drunkenness and partial loss of consciousness; 0.6% endangers life. Alcohol is more rapidly absorbed at higher altitudes, as in, for example, the slightly reduced pressure of an aircraft cabin.

Alcoholics Anonymous voluntary self-help organization established 1934 in the US to combat alcoholism; branches now exist in many other countries.

alcoholism dependence on alcoholic liquor. It is characterized as an illness when consumption of alcohol interferes with normal physical or emotional health. Excessive alcohol consumption may produce physical and psychological addiction and lead to nutritional and emotional disorders. The direct effect is cirrhosis of the liver, nerve damage, and heart disease, and the condition is now showing genetic predisposition.

Support groups include Alcoholics Anonymous.

alcohol strength a measure of the amount of alcohol in an alcoholic beverage. Wine is measured as the percentage volume of alcohol at 68°F/20°C; liquors as a percentage of a mixture of alcohol and water containing by volume 50% ethyl alcohol at 60°F (called ◊proof spirit). Thus a whiskey labeled 100 proof contains 50% alcohol.

Alcott Louisa May 1832–1888. US author. Her children's classic *Little Women* 1869 drew on her own home circumstances, the heroine Jo being a partial self-portrait.

Born in Germantown, Pennsylvania, she spent most of her life in Concord, Massachusetts, the daughter of transcendentalist and educator Amos Bronson Alcott (1799–1888). She was educated in her home by her father and, occasionally, by family friends Ralph Waldo Emerson and Henry David Thoreau. Alcott began writing to help earn money for the family. Her first book was *Flower Fables* 1848; her first success was *Hospital Sketches* 1863. The publication of *Little Women* was followed by *Little Men* 1871. She also wrote *Eight Cousins* 1875, *Under the Lilacs* 1879, and *A Garland for Girls* 1888.

Alcuin 735–804. English scholar. Born in York, he went to Rome in 780, and in 782 took up residence at Charlemagne's court in Aachen. From 796 he was abbot of Tours. He disseminated Anglo-Saxon scholarship, organized education and learning in the Frankish empire, gave a strong impulse to the Carolingian Renaissance, and was a prominent member of Charlemagne's academy.

Aldabra high limestone island group in the ◊Seychelles, some 260 mi/420 km NW of Madagascar; area 59 sq mi/154 sq km. A nature preserve since 1976, it has rare plants and animals, including the giant tortoise.

Aldebaran or ***Alpha Tauri*** brightest star in the constellation Taurus and the 13th brightest star in the sky; it marks the eye of the "bull." Aldebaran is a red giant 68 light-years away, shining with a true luminosity about 100 times that of the Sun.

aldehyde any of a group of organic chemical compounds prepared by oxidation of primary alcohols, so that the OH (hydroxyl) group loses its hydrogen to give an oxygen joined by a double bond to a carbon atom (the aldehyde group, with the formula CHO).

The name is made up from alcohol dehydrogenatum, that is, alcohol from which hydrogen has been removed. Aldehydes are usually liquids and include methanal, ethanal, benzaldehyde, formaldehyde, and citral.

alder any tree or shrub of the genus *Alnus*, in the birch family Betulaceae, found mainly in cooler parts of the northern hemisphere and characterized by toothed leaves and catkins.

Sitka alder *A. sinuata* and red alder *A. rubra* are common to W North America.

alderman (Old English *ealdorman* "older man") Anglo-Saxon term for the noble governor of a shire. After the Norman Conquest 1066, this office was replaced with that of sheriff.

Alderney third largest of the ◊Channel Islands, with its capital at St Anne's; area 3 sq mi/8 sq km; population (1980) 2,000. It gives its name to a breed of cattle, better known as the Guernsey.

Aldiss Brian 1925– . English science-fiction writer, anthologist, and critic. His novels include *Non-Stop* 1958, *The Malacia Tapestry* 1976, and the "Helliconia" trilogy. *Trillion Year Spree* 1986 is a history of science fiction.

aleatory music (Latin *alea* "dice") method of composition (pioneered by John ◊Cage) dating from about 1945 in which the elements are assembled by chance by using, for example, dice or computer.

Aleixandre Vicente 1898–1984. Spanish lyric poet, born in Seville. His verse, which influenced younger Spanish writers, had ◊Republican sympathies, and his work was for a time banned by Franco's government. Nobel Prize for Literature 1977.

Alembert Jean le Rond d' 1717–1783. French mathematician and encyclopedist. He was associated with ◊Diderot in planning the great *Encyclopédie*.

Born in Paris, he was educated by the Jansenist Catholic sect. He studied law and medicine before devoting himself to mathematics.

Alençon capital of the Orne *département* of France, situated in a rich agricultural plain to the SE of Caen; population (1983) 33,000. Lace, now a declining industry, was once a major product.

Alentejo a region of E central Portugal divided into the districts of Alto Alentejo and Baixo Alentejo. The chief towns are Evora, Neja, and Portalegre.

Aleppo (Syrian *Halab*) ancient city in NW Syria; population (1981) 977,000. There has been a settlement on the site for at least 4,000 years.

Alessandria town in N Italy on the river Tanaro; population (1981) 100,500. It was founded 1168 by Pope Alexander III as a defense against Frederick Barbarossa.

Aletsch most extensive glacier in Europe, 14.7 mi/23.6 km long, beginning on the southern slopes of the Jungfrau in the Bernese Alps, Switzerland.

Aleutian Islands volcanic island chain in the N Pacific, stretching 1,200 mi/1,900 km SW of Alaska, of which it forms part. Population 6,000 Aleuts, most of whom belong to the Orthodox

Church, plus a large US defense establishment. There are 14 large and more than 100 small islands running along the Aleutian Trench. The islands are mountainous, barren, and treeless; they are ice-free all year but are often foggy, with only about 25 days of sunshine recorded annually. The islands were settled by the Aleuts c. 1000 BC and discovered by a Russian expedition 1741; they passed to the US with the purchase of Alaska 1867. The Japanese occupied Attu and Kiska islands 1942–43; Attu was retaken in the only ground fighting on North American soil during World War II.

alewife fish *Alosa pseudoharengus* of the ◊herring group, up to 1 ft/30 cm long, found in the NW Atlantic and in the Great Lakes of North America.

Alexander Harold Rupert Leofric George, 1st Earl Alexander of Tunis 1891–1969. British field marshal, a commander in World War II in Burma, N Africa, and the Mediterranean. He was governor general of Canada 1946–52 and minister of defense 1952–54.

Alexander Samuel 1859–1938. Australian philosopher who originated the theory of emergent evolution: that the space-time matrix evolved matter; matter evolved life; life evolved mind; and finally God emerged from mind.

His books include *Space, Time and Deity* 1920. He was professor at Manchester University, England, 1893–1924.

Alexander eight popes, including:

Alexander III (Orlando Barninelli) died 1181. Pope 1159–81. His authority was opposed by Frederick I Barbarossa, but Alexander eventually compelled him to render homage 1178. He supported Henry II of England in his invasion of Ireland, but imposed penance on him after the murder of Thomas à ◊Becket.

Alexander VI (Rodrigo Borgia) 1431–1503. Pope 1492–1503. Of Spanish origin, he bribed his way to the papacy, where he furthered the advancement of his illegitimate children, who included Cesare and Lucrezia ◊Borgia. When ◊Savonarola preached against his corrupt practices Alexander had him executed. Alexander was a great patron of the arts in Italy, as were his children. He is said to have died of poison he had prepared for his cardinals.

Alexander three tsars of Russia:

Alexander I 1777–1825. Tsar from 1801. Defeated by Napoleon at Austerlitz 1805, he made peace at Tilsit 1807, but economic crisis led to a break with Napoleon's ◊continental system and the opening of Russian ports to British trade; this led to Napoleon's ill-fated invasion of Russia. After the Congress of Vienna in 1815, Alexander hoped through the Holy Alliance with Austria and Prussia to establish a new Christian order in Europe.

After Napoleon's defeat Russia controlled the Congress Kingdom of Poland, for which a constitution was provided.

Alexander II 1818–1881. Tsar from 1855. He embarked on reforms of the army, the government, and education, and is remembered as "the Liberator" for his emancipation of the serfs 1861, but he lacked the personnel to implement his reforms. However, the revolutionary element remained unsatisfied, and Alexander became increasingly autocratic and reactionary. He was assassinated by ◊Nihilists.

Alexander III 1845–1894. Tsar from 1881, when he succeeded his father, Alexander II. He pursued a reactionary policy, promoting Russification and persecuting the Jews. He married Dagmar (1847–1928), daughter of Christian IX of Denmark and sister of Queen Alexandra of Britain, in 1866.

Alexander three kings of Scotland:

Alexander I c. 1078–1124. King of Scotland from 1107, known as the Fierce. He was succeeded by his brother David I.

Alexander II 1198–1249. King of Scotland from 1214, when he succeeded his father William the Lion. Alexander supported the English barons in their struggle with King John after Magna Carta.

Alexander II *Despite his nickname "the Liberator," for freeing the serfs, Tsar Alexander II of Russia became increasingly autocratic. He was assassinated, after several attempts, by a bomb tossed into his coach by Nihilists in 1881.*

Alexander III 1241–1285. King of Scotland from 1249, son of Alexander II. In 1263, by military defeat of Norwegian forces, he extended his authority over the Western Isles, which had been dependent on Norway. He strengthened the power of the central Scottish government.

Alexander I Karageorgevich 1888–1934. Regent of Serbia 1912–21 and king of Yugoslavia 1921–34, as dictator from 1929. Second son of ◊Peter I, king of Serbia, he was declared regent for his father in 1912 and on his father's death became king of the state of South Slavs—Yugoslavia—that had come into being in 1918. Rivalries with neighboring powers and among the Croats, Serbs, and Slovenes within the country led Alexander to establish a personal dictatorship. He was assassinated on a state visit to France, and Mussolini's government was later declared to have instigated the crime.

Alexander Nevski, St 1220–1263. Russian military leader, son of the grand duke of Novgorod; in 1240 he defeated the Swedes on the banks of the Neva (hence Nevski), and in 1242 defeated the Teutonic Knights on the frozen Lake Peipus.

Alexander Obrenovich 1876–1903. King of Serbia from 1889 while still a minor, on the abdication of his father, King Milan. He took power into his own hands in 1893 and in 1900 married a widow, Draga Mashin. In 1903 Alexander and his queen were murdered, and ◊Peter I Karageorgevich was placed on the throne.

Alexander Severus AD 208–235. Roman emperor from 222, when he succeeded his cousin Heliogabalus. He was born in Palestine. His campaign against the Persians in 232 achieved some success, but in 235, on his way to defend Gaul against German invaders, he was killed in a mutiny.

Alexander the Great 356–323 BC. King of Macedonia and conqueror of the large Persian empire. As commander of the vast Macedonian army he conquered Greece 336. He defeated the Persian king Darius in Asia Minor 333, then moved on to Egypt, where he founded Alexandria. He defeated the Persians again in Assyria 331, then advanced further east to reach the Indus. He conquered the Punjab before diminished troops forced his retreat.

The son of King Philip of Macedonia and Queen Olympias, Alexander was educated by the philosopher Aristotle. He first saw fighting in 340, and at the battle of Chaeronea 338 contributed to the victory by a cavalry charge. At the age of 20, when his father was murdered, he assumed command of the throne and the army. He secured his northern frontier, suppressed an attempted rising in Greece by his capture of Thebes, and in 334 crossed the Dardanelles for the campaign against the vast Persian empire; at the river Granicus near the Dardanelles he won his first victory. In 333 he routed the Darius at Issus, and then set out for Egypt, where he was greeted as Pharaoh. Meanwhile, Darius assembled half a million men for a final battle but at Arbela on the Tigris in 331 Alexander, with 47,000 men, drove the Persians into retreat. After the victory he stayed a month in Babylon, then marched to Susa and Persepolis and in 330 to Ecbatana (now Hamadán, Iran). Soon after he learned that Darius was dead. In Afghanistan he founded colonies at Herat and Kandahar, and in 328 reached the plains of Sogdiana, where he married Roxana, daughter of King Oxyartes. India now lay before him, and he pressed on to the Indus. Near the river Hydaspes (now Jhelum) he fought one of his fiercest battles against the rajah Porus. At the river Hyphasis (now Beas) his men refused to go farther, and reluctantly he turned back down the Indus and along the coast. They reached Susa in 324, where Alexander made Darius's daughter his second wife. He died in Babylon of a malarial fever.

Alexandra 1872–1918. Last tsarina of Russia 1894–1917. She was the former Princess Alix of Hessen and granddaughter of Britain's Queen Victoria. She married ◊Nicholas II and, from 1907, fell under the spell of ◊Rasputin, a "holy man" brought to the palace to try to cure her son of hemophilia. She was shot with the rest of her family by the Bolsheviks in the Russian Revolution.

Alexandretta former name of ◊Iskenderun, a port in S Turkey.

Alexandria city in central Louisiana, on the Red river, NW of Baton Rouge; seat of Rapides parish. It is a livestock and meatpacking center; population (1990) 49,188.

Alexandria (Arabic *El Iskandariya*) city, chief port, and second-largest city of Egypt, situated between the Mediterranean and Lake Maryut; population (1986) 5,000,000. It is linked by canal with the Nile and is an industrial city (oil refining, gas processing, and cotton and grain trading). Founded 331 BC by Alexander the Great, Alexandria was for over 1,000 years the capital of Egypt.

history The principal center of Hellenistic culture, Alexandria has since the 4th century AD been the seat of a Christian patriarch. In 641 it was captured by the Muslim Arabs, and after the opening of the Cape route its trade rapidly declined. Early in the 19th century it began to recover its prosperity, and its growth was encouraged by its use as the main British naval base in the Mediterranean during both world wars. Of the large European community, most were expelled after the Suez Crisis 1956 and their property confiscated.

Few relics of antiquity remain. The Pharos, the first lighthouse and one of the seven wonders of the ancient world, has long since disappeared. The library, said to have contained 700,000 volumes, was destroyed by the caliph ◊Omar in 640. Pompey's Pillar is a column erected, as a landmark from the sea, by the emperor Diocletian. Two obelisks that once stood before the Caesarum temple are now in London (Cleopatra's Needle) and New York respectively.

Alexandria, Library of library in Alexandria, Egypt, founded 330 BC by ◊Ptolemy I Soter. It was the world's first state-funded scientific institution, and comprised a museum, teaching facilities, and a library that contained 700,000 scrolls, including much ancient Greek literature. It was used by ◊Euclid and ◊Eratosthenes, and after initial depradations was finally burned down in AD 640 at the time of the Arab conquest. In 1989 the Egyptian government planned a new library to be the most

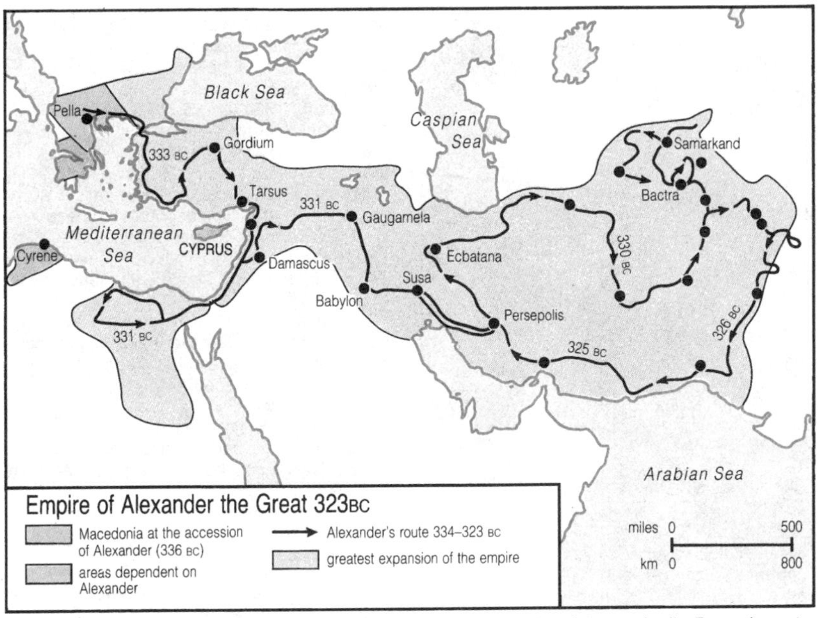
Black Sea
Caspian Sea
Pella
Gordium
333 BC
Tarsus
331 BC
Gaugamela
Samarkand
Bactra
Mediterranean Sea
CYPRUS
Cyrene
Damascus
Babylon
Susa
Ecbatana
330 BC
Persepolis
325 BC
326 BC
331 BC
Arabian Sea
Empire of Alexander the Great 323BC
Macedonia at the accession of Alexander (336 BC)
areas dependent on Alexander
Alexander's route 334–323 BC
greatest expansion of the empire
miles 0 500
km 0 800

important Middle Eastern center for the study of regional civilizations.

Alexandria, School of the writers and scholars of Alexandria, who made the city the chief center of culture in the Western world from about 331 BC to AD 642. They include the poets Callimachus, Apollonius Rhodius, and Theocritus; Euclid, pioneer of geometry; Eratosthenes, the geographer; Hipparchus, who developed a system of trigonometry; the astronomer Ptolemy, who gave his name to the Ptolemaic system of astronomy that endured for over 1,000 years; and the Jewish philosopher Philo. The Gnostics and Neoplatonists also flourished in Alexandria.

alexandrite rare gemstone variety of the mineral chrysoberyl (beryllium aluminum oxide $BeAl_2O_4$), which is green in daylight but appears red in artificial light.

Alexandros an alternate name for ◊Paris in Greek mythology.

Alexandrovsk older name of ◊Zaporozhya, city in the USSR.

Alexeev Vasiliy 1942– . Soviet weight-lifter who broke 80 world records 1970–77, a record for any sport.

He was Olympic super-heavyweight champion twice, world champion seven times. He retired after the 1980 Olympics.

CAREER HIGHLIGHTS

Olympic champion: 1972, 1976
World champion: 1970–71, 1973–75, 1977
European champion: 1970–78.

Alexius five emperors of Byzantium, including:

Alexius I (Comnenus) 1048–1118. Byzantine emperor 1081–1118. The Latin (W European) Crusaders helped him repel Norman and Turkish invasions, and he devoted great skill to buttressing the threatened empire. His daughter ◊Anna Comnena chronicled his reign.

Alexius III (Angelos) died c. 1210. Byzantine emperor 1195–1203. He gained power by deposing and blinding his brother Isaac II, but Isaac's Venetian allies enabled him and his son Alexius IV to regain power as co-emperors.

Alexius IV (Angelos) 1182–1204. Byzantine emperor from 1203, when, with the aid of the army of the Fourth Crusade, he deposed his uncle Alexius III. He soon lost the support of the Crusaders (by that time occupying Constantinople), and he was overthrown and murdered by another Alexius, Alexius Mourtzouphlus (son-in-law of Alexius III) in 1204, an act which the Crusaders used as a pretext to sack the city the same year.

alfalfa or ***lucerne*** perennial tall herbaceous plant *Medicago sativa* of the pea family (Leguminosae). It is native to Eurasia and bears spikes of small purple flowers in late summer. It is now an important fodder crop, generally processed into hay, meal, or silage. Alfalfa sprouts, the sprouted seed, has become a popular salad green.

al-Fatah see ◊Fatah, al.

Alfonsín Foulkes Raúl Ricardo 1927– Argentine politician, president 1983–89, leader of the Radical Union Party (UCR). As president from the country's return to civilian government, he set up an investigation of the army's human-rights violations. Economic problems forced him to seek help from the International Monetary Fund and introduce austerity measures.

Educated at a military academy and a university law school, Alfonsín joined the UCR at the age of 18 and eventually went on to lead it. He was active in local politics 1951–62, being imprisoned 1953 by the right-wing Perón regime, and was a member of the national congress 1963–66. With the return to civilian government in 1983 and the legalization of political activity, Alfonsín and the UCR won convincing victories and he became president. He stepped down in 1989 several months before the end of his term to allow his successor, the Peronist Carlos Menem, to institute emergency economic measures.

Alfonso six kings of Portugal, including:

Alfonso I 1094–1185. King of Portugal from 1112. He made Portugal independent from León.

Alfonso 13 kings of León, Castile, and Spain, including:

Alfonso VII c. 1107–1157. King of León and Castile from 1126, who attempted to unite Spain. Although he protected the Moors, he was killed trying to check a Moorish rising.

Alfonso X called *el Sabio* ("the Wise") 1221–1284. King of Castile from 1252. His reign was politically unsuccessful but he contributed to learning: he made Castilian the official language of the country and commissioned a history of Spain and an encyclopedia, as well as several translations from Arabic concerning, among other subjects, astronomy and games.

Alfonso XI the Avenger 1311–1350. King of Castile from 1312. He ruled cruelly, repressed a rebellion by his nobles, and defeated the last Moorish invasion 1340.

Alfonso XII 1857–1885. King of Spain from 1875, son of ◊Isabella II. He assumed the throne after a period of republican government following his mother's flight and effective abdication 1868.

Alfonso XIII 1886–1941. King of Spain 1886–1931. He assumed power 1906 and married Princess

ÆLFRED REX

Alfred *The profile of Alfred the Great featured on a coin of about 887. He defended England against the Danish invasions.*

Ena, granddaughter of Queen Victoria of the United Kingdom, in the same year. He abdicated 1931 soon after the fall of the Primo de Rivera dictatorship 1923–30 (which he supported), and Spain became a republic. His assassination was attempted several times.

Alfred the Great c. 848–c. 900. King of Wessex from 871. He defended England against Danish invasion, founded the first English navy, and put into operation a legal code. He encouraged the translation of works from Latin (some of which he translated himself), and promoted the development of the ◊Anglo-Saxon Chronicle.

algae (singular alga) diverse group of plants (including those commonly called seaweeds) that shows great variety of form, ranging from single-celled forms to multicellular seaweeds of considerable size and complexity.

Because of their diversity, botanists have established seven separate algae groupings or divisions, belonging to three different kingdoms: Cyanobacteria (blue-green algae) of the kingdom Monerans; Chrysophyta (golden algae ◊diatoms), Englenophyta (plidosynthetic ◊flagellates) and Pyrrophyta (◊dinoflagellates) of the kingdom Protists; and Rhodophyta (red algae), Phaeophyta (brown algae), and Chlorophyta (green algae) of the kingdom Plants.

Algardi Alessandro c. 1595–1654. Italian Baroque sculptor, active in Rome and at the papal court. His major work, on which he was intermittently

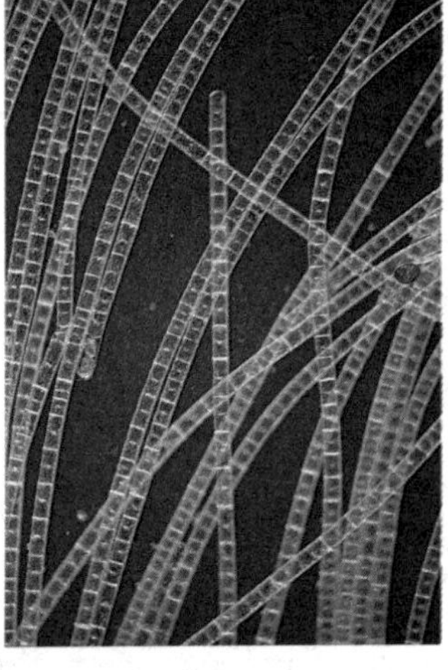

algae *Microscopic view of green filamentary algae. Algae form the basis of marine and freshwater food chains.*

occupied from 1634 to 1652, is the tomb of Pope Leo XI (Medici), in St Peter's, Rome.

Although Algardi's work is more restrained in expression than that of his contemporary and rival Bernini, it is Baroque in style, with figures often violently contorted and full of movement. His portrait busts include *St Philip Neri* 1640 (Sta Maria Vallicella, Rome).

Algarve (Arabic *al-gharb* "the west") ancient kingdom in S Portugal, the modern district of Faro, a popular vacation resort; population (1981) 323,500.

The Algarve began to be wrested from the ◊Moors in the 12th century and was united with Portugal as a kingdom in 1253. It includes the SW extremity of Europe, Cape St Vincent, where the British fleet defeated the Spanish in 1797.

algebra system of arithmetic applying to any set of nonnumerical symbols, and the axioms and rules by which they are combined or operated upon.

It is sometimes known as generalized arithmetic. The basics of algebra were familiar in Babylon 2000 BC, and were practiced by the Arabs in the Middle Ages. In the 9th century, the Arab mathematician Mohammed ibn-Musa al-◊Khwarizmi first used the words *hisāb al-jabr* ("calculus of reduction") as part of the title of a treatise. Algebra is used in many branches of mathematics, such as matrix algebra and Boolean algebra, the method of algebraic reasoning first devised in the 19th century by the British mathematician George Boole and used in working out the logic for computers.

Algeciras port in S Spain, to the W of Gibraltar across the Bay of Algeciras; population (1986) 97,000. Founded by the ◊Moors 713, it was taken from them by Alfonso XI of Castile 1344.

Algeciras Conference a conference held Jan 1906 when France, Germany, Britain, Russia, and Austria-Hungary, together with the US, Spain, the Low Countries, Portugal, and Sweden, met to settle the question of Morocco. The conference was prompted by increased German demands in what had traditionally been seen as a French area of influence, but it resulted in a reassertion of Anglo-French friendship and the increased isolation of Germany.

Alger Horatio 1834–1899. US writer of children's books. He wrote over 100 didactic moral tales in which the heroes rise from poverty to riches through hard work, luck, and good deeds, including the series "Ragged Dick" from 1867 and "Tattered Tom" from 1871.

It is estimated that his books sold more than 20 million copies. A "Horatio Alger tale" has now come to mean any rags-to-riches story, often an implausible one.

Algeria

Democratic and Popular Republic of
(*al-Jumhuriya al-Jazairiya ad-Dimuqratiya ash-Shabiya*)

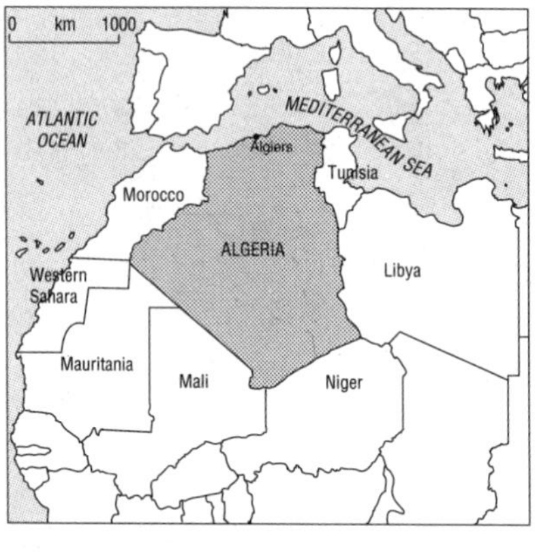
0 km 1000
ATLANTIC OCEAN
MEDITERRANEAN SEA
Algiers
Tunisia
Morocco
ALGERIA
Libya
Western Sahara
Mauritania
Mali
Niger

area 919,352 sq mi/2,381,741 sq km
capital al-Jazair (Algiers)
cities Qacentina/Constantine; ports are Ouahran/Oran, Annaba/Bône
physical coastal plains backed by mountains in N; Sahara desert in S
features Atlas mountains, Barbary Coast, Chott Melrhir depression, Hoggar mountains
head of state Benjedid Chadli from 1979
head of government Sid Ahmed Ghozali
political system one-party Socialist republic
political parties National Liberation Front (FLN), nationalist Socialist
exports oil, natural gas, iron, wine, olive oil
currency dinar
population (1990 est) 25,715,000 (83% Arab, 17% Berber); growth rate 3.0% p.a.
life expectancy men 59, women 62
language Arabic (official); Berber, French
religion Sunni Muslim (state religion)
literacy men 63%/women 37% (1985 est)
GDP $64.6 bn; $2,796 per head
chronology
1954 War for independence from France led by the FLN
1962 Independence achieved from France, Republic declared. Ben Bella elected president.
1965 Ben Bella deposed by military, led by Colonel Houari Boumédienne.
1976 New constitution approved.
1978 Death of Boumédienne.
1979 Bendjedid Chadli elected president. Ben Bella released from house arrest. FLN adopted new party structure.
1983 Chadli reelected.
1988 Riots in protest at government policies; 170 killed. Reform program introduced. Diplomatic relations with Egypt restored.
1989 Constitutional changes proposed, leading to limited political pluralism.
1990 Fundamentalist Islamic Salvation Front won Algerian municipal and provincial elections.
1991 President Chadli Bendjedid promised multiparty elections. Islamic fundamentalists show strength in first elections.
1992 Chadli resigns; military takes over government; elections cancelled.

Algeria country in N Africa, bounded E by Tunisia and Libya, SE by Niger, SW by Mali, NW by Morocco, and N by the Mediterranean Sea.

government The 1976 constitution, amended 1979, created a Socialist republic with Islam as the state religion and Arabic the official language. Algeria is a one-party state with ultimate power held by the National Liberation Front (FLN). The FLN nominates the president, who is elected by universal suffrage for a five-year term. The president chooses the prime minister and the council of ministers and is the effective head of government. There is a single-chamber national people's assembly of 295 deputies, all nominees of FLN, elected for a five-year term.

history From the 9th century the area now known as Algeria was ruled by ◊Carthage, and subsequently by Rome 2nd century BC–5th century AD. In the early Christian era, St ◊Augustine was bishop of Hippo (now called Annaba) 396–430. The area was invaded by the ◊Vandals after the decline of Roman rule and was ruled by ◊Byzantium from the 6th–8th centuries, after which the ◊Arabs invaded the region, introducing ◊Islam and ◊Arabic. Islamic influence continued to dominate, despite Spain's attempts to take control in the 15th–16th centuries; from the 16th century Algeria was under ◊Ottoman rule and flourished as a center for the slave trade. However, the Sultan's rule was often nominal, and in the 18th century Algeria became a pirate state, preying on Mediterranean shipping. European intervention became inevitable, and in 1816 an Anglo-Dutch force bombarded Algiers. In 1830 a French army landed and seized Algiers; by 1847 the north had been brought under French control, and in 1848 was formed into the *départements* of Algiers, Oran, and Constantine. Many French colonists settled in these *départements*, which in 1881 were made part of Metropolitan France. The mountainous region inland, inhabited by the Kabyles, was occupied 1850–70, and the Sahara region, subdued 1900–09, remained under military rule.

After the defeat of France 1940, Algeria came under the control of the ◊Vichy government until the Allies landed in North Africa 1942. Postwar hopes of integrating Algeria more closely with France were frustrated by opposition in Algeria from those of both non-French and French origin. An embittered struggle for independence from France continued 1954–62, when referenda in both Algeria and France resulted in 1963 in the recognition of Algeria as an independent one-party republic with ◊Ben Bella as its first president. In 1965 Colonel Houari ◊Boumédienne deposed Ben Bella in a military coup, suspended the constitution, and ruled through a revolutionary council.

In 1976 a new constitution confirmed Algeria as an Islamic, Socialist, one-party state. Boumédienne died 1978, and power was transferred to Bendjedid ◊Chadli, secretary general of FLN. In 1979 Chadli released Ben Bella from the house arrest imposed on him in the 1965 coup. In the same year FLN adopted a new structure, with a central committee nominating a party leader who automatically becomes president. Chadli was reelected under this system 1983.

During Chadli's presidency, relations with France and the US improved, and there was some progress in achieving greater cooperation with neighboring states, such as Tunisia. In 1981 Algeria acted as an intermediary in securing the release of the US hostages in ◊Iran. In 1987 a proposal by Colonel ◊Khaddhafi for political union with Libya received a cool response. Following public unrest in 1988, Chadli promised to make the government more responsive to public opinion. In Feb 1989 a referendum approved a new constitution, deleting any reference to socialism, and opened the way for a multiparty system. The reforms followed riots and protests of economic austerity measures Oct 1988. The political reforms were designed, in part, to stem the growing Islamic fundamentalist movement. In Jan 1992, as fundamentalists were on the verge of winning political control, Chadli resigned, and the military took control of the government.

Algiers (Arabic *al-Jazair*; French *Alger*) capital of Algeria, situated on the narrow coastal plain between the Atlas mountains and the Mediterranean; population (1984) 2,442,300.

Founded by the Arabs AD 935, Algiers was taken by the Turks 1518 and by the French 1830. The old town is dominated by the Kasbah, the palace and prison of the Turkish rulers. The new town, constructed under French rule, is in European style.

Algiers, Battle of the bitter conflict in Algiers 1954–62 between the Algerian nationalist population and the French colonial army and French settlers. The conflict ended with Algerian independence 1962.

alginate salt of alginic acid $(C_6H_8O)_n$, obtained from brown seaweeds and used in textiles, paper, food products, and pharmaceuticals.

Algoa Bay broad and shallow inlet in Cape Province, South Africa, where Diaz landed after rounding the Cape 1488.

ALGOL (acronym from algorithmic language) in computing, an early high-level programming language, developed in the 1950s and 1960s for scientific applications. A general-purpose language, ALGOL is best suited to mathematical work and has an algebraic style. Although no longer in common use, it has greatly influenced more recent languages, such as ADA and PASCAL.

Algol or ***Beta Persei*** an ◊eclipsing binary, a pair of rotating stars in the constellation Perseus, one of which eclipses the other every 69 hours, causing its brightness to drop by two-thirds. The brightness changes were first explained in 1782 by amateur astronomer John Goodricke (1764–1786).

Algonquian a group of languages spoken by North American Indians of the Eastern Woodland zone S and E of Hudson Bay. Algonquian includes over 20 languages spoken by American Indians of the NE coast as well as by the Cree, Arapaho, Blackfoot, Cheyenne, Ójibwa, and Fox.

Algonquin a member of the Algonquian-speaking hunting-and-fishing people formerly living around the Ottawa River in E Canada. Many now live on reservations in NE USA, E Ontario, and W Québec; others have chosen to live among the general populations of Canada and the US.

algorithm procedure or series of steps that can be used to solve a problem. The word derives from the name of the 9th-century Arab mathematician, ibn-Masa al-◊Khwarizmi. In computer science, where the term is most often used, algorithm describes the logical sequence of operations to be performed by a program. A ◊flow chart is a visual representation of an algorithm.

Alhambra fortified palace in Granada, Spain, built by Moorish kings mainly between 1248 and 1354. The finest example of Moorish architecture, it stands on a rocky hill.

Alhazen Ibn al Haytham c. 965–1038. Arabian scientist, author of the *Kitab al Manazir/Book of Optics*, translated into Latin as *Perspectiva*. For centuries it remained the most comprehensive and authoritative treatment of optics in both East and West.

Ali c. 600–661. 4th caliph of Islam. He was born in Mecca, the son of Abu Talib, uncle to the prophet Mohammed, who gave him his daughter Fatima in marriage. On Mohammed's death 632, Ali had a claim to succeed him, but this was not conceded until 656. After a stormy reign, he was assassinated. Around Ali's name the controversy has raged between the Sunni and the Shi'ites (see ◊Islam), the former denying his right to the caliphate and the latter supporting it.

Ali (Ali Pasha) 1741–1822. Turkish politician, known as Arslan ("the Lion"). An Albanian, he was appointed pasha (governor) of the Janina region in 1788 (now Ioánnina, Greece). His court was visited by the British poet Byron. He was assassinated on the sultan's order.

Ali Muhammad. Born Cassius Marcellus Clay, Jr. 1942– . US boxer. Olympic light-heavyweight champion 1960, he went on to become world professional heavyweight champion 1964, and was the only man to regain the title twice. He was known for his fast footwork and extroverted nature.

He had his title stripped from him 1967 for refusing to be drafted into the US Army. He regained his title 1974, lost it Feb 1978, and regained it seven months later.

He had the last of his 61 professional fights 1982 against Trevor Berbick.

CAREER HIGHLIGHTS

fights: 61
wins: 56 (37 knockouts)
draws: 0
defeats: 5
first professional fight: Oct 29, 1960 v. Tunny Hunsaker *(USA)*
last professional fight:
Dec 11, 1981 v. Trevor Berbick *(Canada)*

Alia Ramiz 1925– Albanian communist politician, head of state from 1982 and party leader from 1985. He slightly relaxed the isolationist policies of his predecessor Enver Hoxha and introduced economic reforms following public unrest, thus earning the description of the Albanian Gorbachev.

Born in Shkodër in NW Albania, the son of poor Muslim peasants, Alia joined the National Liberation Army 1944, actively opposing Nazi control. After a period in charge of agitation and propaganda, Alia was inducted into the secretariat and Politburo of the ruling Party of Labor of Albania (APL) 1960–61. On the death of Hoxha he became party leader.

alibi (Latin "elsewhere") in law, a provable assertion that the accused was at some other place when a crime was committed.

Alice's Adventures in Wonderland a children's story by Lewis Carroll, published 1865. Alice dreams she follows the White Rabbit down a rabbit-hole and meets fantastic characters such as the Cheshire Cat, the Mad Hatter, and the King and Queen of Hearts.

An Alice-in-Wonderland situation has come to mean an absurd or irrational situation, because of the dreamlike logic of Alice's adventures in the book. With its companion volume *Through the Looking-Glass* 1872, it is one of the most quoted works in the English language.

alien in law, a person who is not a citizen of a particular nation.

Federal legislation determines which aliens may legally enter a country or reside in it; their rights at law, both civil and criminal; and the processes and conditions by which they may become citizens.

Alien and Sedition Acts laws passed by the US Congress 1798, when war with France seemed likely. The acts lengthened the period of residency required for US citizenship, gave the president the power to expel "dangerous" aliens, and severely restricted criticism of the government. They were controversial because of the degree of power exercised by central government; they are now also seen as an early manifestation of US xenophobia (fear of foreigners).

alienation a sense of isolation, powerlessness, and therefore frustration; a feeling of loss of control over one's life; a sense of estrangement from society or even from oneself. As a concept it was developed by the German philosophers Hegel and Marx; the latter used it as a description and criticism of the condition that developed among workers in capitalist society.

The term has also been used by non-Marxist writers and sociologists, in particular Durkheim in his work *Suicide* 1897. They use it in discussing unrest in factories and the sense of powerlessness felt by groups such as young people, black people, and women in Western industrial society.

alimentary canal in animals, the tube through which food passes; it extends from the mouth to the anus. It is a complex organ, adapted for ◊digestion. In human adults, it is about 30 ft/9 m long, consisting of the mouth cavity, pharynx, esophagus, stomach, and the small and large intestines.

alimony in the US, monetary allowance given by court order to a former spouse after separation or ◊divorce.

The right has been extended to relationships outside marriage and is colloquially termed "palimony."

Alimony is separate and distinct from court orders for child support.

Ali Pasha Mehmed Emin 1815–1871. Grand vizier (chief minister) of the Ottoman empire 1855–56, 1858–59, 1861, and 1867–71, noted for his attempts to westernize the Ottoman Empire.

After a career as ambassador to the UK, minister of foreign affairs 1846, delegate to the Congress of ◊Vienna 1855 and of Paris 1856, he was grand vizier a total of five times. While promoting friendship with Britain and France, he defended the vizier's powers against those of the sultan.

aliphatic compound any organic chemical compound that is made up of chains of carbon atoms, rather than rings, as in cyclic compounds. The chains may be linear, as in hexane (C_6H_{14}), or branched, as in 2-propanol (isopropanol) $(CH_3)_2CHOH$.

alkali (Arabic *al-qualīy* "ashes") chemical compound classed as a base that is soluble in water. Alkalis neutralize acids and are soapy to the touch.

The hydroxides of metals are alkalis, those of sodium (sodium hydroxide, NaOH) and of potassium being chemically powerful; both were derived from the ashes of plants.

alkali metals any of a group of six metallic elements with similar chemical bonding properties: lithium, sodium, potassium, rubidium, cesium, and francium. They form a linked group in the ◊periodic table of the elements. They are univalent and of very low density (lithium, sodium, and potassium float on water); in general they are reactive, soft, low-melting-point metals.

Because of their reactivity they only occur as compounds in nature; they are used as chemical reactants rather than as structural metals.

alkaline-earth metals any of a group of six metallic elements with similar chemical bonding properties: beryllium, magnesium, calcium, strontium, barium, and radium. They form a linked group in the ◊periodic table of the elements. They are strongly basic, bivalent, and occur in nature only in compounds.

alkaloid any of numerous physiologically active and frequently poisonous substances contained in some plants. They are usually bases and contain nitrogen. They form salts with acids and, when soluble, give alkaline solutions.

Substances in this group are included by custom rather than by scientific rules. Examples include morphine, cocaine, quinine, caffeine, strychnine, nicotine, and atropine.

alkane member of the group of ◊hydrocarbons having the general formula C_nH_{2n+2} (common name paraffins). Lighter alkanes are colorless gases (for example, methane, ethane, propane, butane); in nature they are found dissolved in petroleum. heavier ones are liquids or solids. As they contain only single ◊covalent bonds, they are said to be saturated.

alkene member of the group of ◊hydrocarbons having the general formula C_nH_{2n}, commonly known as olefins. Lighter alkenes, such as ethene ($CH_2{=}CH_2$) and propene ($CH_3CH{=}CH_2$), are gases, obtained from the ◊cracking of oil fractions. They are unsaturated compounds, characterized by one or more double bonds between adjacent carbon atoms. They react by addition, and many useful compounds (such as poly(ethene) and bromoethane) are made from them.

al-Khalil Arabic name for ◊Hebron in the Israeli-occupied West Bank.

al Kūt alternative term for ◊Kūt al Imāra.

alkyne member of the group of ◊hydrocarbons with the general formula C_nH_{2n-2}, commonly known as acetylenes. They are unsaturated compounds, characterized by one or more triple bonds between adjacent carbon atoms. Lighter alkynes are gases (for example, ◊ethyne); heavier ones are liquids or solids.

Allah (Arabic *al-Ilah* "the God") Islamic name for God.

Allahabad ("city of god") historic city in Uttar Pradesh state, NE India, 360 mi/580 km SE of Delhi, on the Yamuna River where it meets the Ganges and the mythical Seraswati River; population (1981) 642,000. A Hindu religious festival is held here every 12 years with the participants washing away sin and sickness by bathing in the rivers.

Allbutt Thomas Clifford 1836–1925. British physician who invented a compact medical thermometer, proved that angina is caused by narrowing of the coronary artery, and studied hydrophobia and tetanus.

Allegheny Mountains range over 500 mi/800 km long extending from Pennsylvania to Virginia, rising to more than 4,900 ft/1,500 m and averaging 2,500 ft/750 m. The mountains are a major source of timber, coal, iron, and limestone. They initially hindered western migration, the first settlement to the W being Marietta 1788.

allegory in literature, the description or illustration of one thing in terms of another; a work of poetry or prose in the form of an extended metaphor or parable that makes use of symbolic fictional characters.

An example of the use of symbolic fictional character in allegory is the romantic epic *The Faerie Queene* 1590–96 by Edmund Spenser in homage to Queen Elizabeth I. Allegory is often used for moral purposes, as in John Bunyan's *Pilgrim's Progress* 1678. Medieval allegory often used animals as characters; this tradition survives in such works as *Animal Farm* 1945 by George Orwell.

allele one of two or more alternate forms of a ◊gene at a given locus on a chromosome, caused by a difference in the ◊DNA. Blue and brown eyes in humans are determined by different alleles of the gene for eye color.

Organisms with two sets of chromosomes (diploids) will have two copies of each gene. If the two alleles are identical the individual is said to be ◊homozygous at that ◊locus; if different, the individual is ◊heterozygous at that locus. Some alleles show ◊dominance over others.

Allen, Bog of morasses E of the river Shannon in the Republic of Ireland, comprising some 240,000 acres/96,000 ha of the counties of Offaly, Leix, and Kildare; the country's main source of peat fuel.

Allen Ethan 1738–1789. American Revolutionary War leader. Born in Litchfield, Connecticut, Allen served in the French and Indian War and later obtained large tracts of land in Vermont. A supporter of independence for Vermont (then claimed by both New Hampshire and New York), he organized the "Green Mountain Boys." At the outbreak of the American Revolution, they joined with Benedict Arnold to capture Fort Ticonderoga, the first victory for the American side, but Allen was captured by the British in the subsequent invasion of Canada. Released by the British 1778, Allen continued to campaign for Vermont's autonomy but died before it achieved statehood in 1791.

Allen Hervey 1889–1949. US novelist, poet, and biographer, known for his historical novel *Anthony Adverse* 1933 set in the Napoleonic era. He also wrote a biography of Edgar Allen Poe, *Israfel* 1926.

Allen Woody. Adopted name of Allen Stewart Konigsberg. 1935– . US film writer, director, and actor, known for his cynical, witty, often self-deprecating parody and offbeat humor.

His film career began with *What's New Pussycat?* 1965, which he wrote and in which he acted. Other films include *Take the Money and Run* 1969, *Bananas* 1971, *Play It Again, Sam* 1972, *Sleeper* 1973, *Love and Death* 1975, *Annie Hall* (for which he won three Academy Awards) 1975, *Interiors* 1978, *Manhattan* 1979, *Stardust Memories* 1982 and *Midsummer Night's Sex Comedy* 1982, *Zelig* 1983, *Broadway Danny Rose* 1984, *Purple Rose of Cairo* 1985, *Hannah and Her Sisters* 1986, and *Radio Days* 1987, and *Alice* 1990. His play *Don't Drink the Water* appeared on Broadway 1966.

Allenby Henry Hynman, 1st Viscount 1861–1936. British field marshal. In World War I he served in France before taking command in 1917–19 of the British forces in the Middle East.

His defeat of the Turkish forces at Megiddo in Palestine in Sept 1918 was followed almost at once by the capitulation of Turkey. He was high commissioner in Egypt 1919–35.

Allende Gossens Salvador 1908–1973. Chilean Marxist politician, president from 1970 until his death during a military coup in 1973.

Allende, born in Valparaiso, became a Marxist activist in the 1930s. He ran unsuccessfully for the presidency in 1952, 1958, and 1964 but won in 1970, becoming the first Marxist to be elected president of an independent country in the W hemisphere. As president, Allende nationalized the banking and copper industries and instituted land reform, provoking the conservative elements in the country. As Chile's economy declined and strikes and disturbances supported by the US Central Intelligence Agency spread, the military staged a coup, during which Allende either was killed or committed suicide.

Allentown city in E Pennsylvania, on the Lehigh river, just NW of Philadelphia. It is an industrial center for textiles, machinery, and electronic equipment; population (1990) 105,090. Center of munitions production during the American Revolution.

allergy special sensitivity of the body that makes it react, with an exaggerated response of the natural immune defense mechanism, especially with ◊histamines, to the introduction of an otherwise harmless foreign substance termed an allergen.

The person subject to hay fever in summer is allergic to one or more kinds of pollen. Many asthmatics are allergic to certain kinds of dust or to microorganisms in animal fur or feathers. Others react severely to poison ivy or are violently sick if they eat shellfish or eggs. Drugs such as antihistamines and corticosteroids are used.

Alliance for Progress a program of US assistance to Latin American countries, initiated by President Kennedy in 1961 under the auspices of the ◊Organization of American States.

It called for expenditure of $20 billion over ten years, but economic conditions continued to worsen in Latin America and President Nixon effectively dismantled the program.

Allier river in central France, a tributary of the Loire; it is 350 mi/565 km long and gives its name to a *département*. Vichy is the chief town on it.

Allies, the in World War I, the 23 countries allied against the Central Powers (Germany, Austria-Hungary, Turkey, and Bulgaria), including France, Italy, Russia, the UK and Commonwealth, and, in the latter part of the war, the US; and in World War II, the 49 countries allied against the ◊Axis powers (Germany, Italy and Japan), including France, the UK and Commonwealth, the US, and the USSR after being attacked by its former ally, Germany).

alligator reptile of the genus *Alligator*, related to the crocodile. There are two species: *A. mississippiensis*, the Mississippi alligator of the S states of the US, and *A. sinensis* from the swamps of the lower Chang Jiang river in China. The former grows to about 12 ft/4 m, but the latter only to 5 ft/1.5 m. Alligators swim well with lashing movements of the tail; they feed on fish and mammals but seldom attack people.

The eggs are laid in sand. The skin is of value for fancy leather, and alligator farms have been established in the US. Closely related are the caymans of South America; these belong to the genus *Caiman*.

alliteration in poetry and prose, the use, within a line or phrase, of words beginning with the same sound, as in "Two tired toads trotting to Tewkesbury." It was a common device in Old English poetry, and its use survives in many traditional English phrases, such as *kith and kin, hearth and home*.

Allium genus of plants belonging to the lily family Liliaceae. Members of the genus are usually strong-smelling with a sharp taste, but form bulbs in which sugar is stored. Cultivated species include onion, garlic, shallot, chives, and leek.

allometry in biology, a regular relationship between a given feature (for example, the size of an organ) and the size of the body as a whole, when this relationship is not a simple proportion of body size. Thus, an organ may increase in size proportionately faster, or slower, than body size does.

allopathy the usual contemporary method of treating disease, using therapies designed to counteract the manifestations of the disease. In strict usage, allopathy is the opposite of ◊homeopathy.

allopurinol drug prescribed for the treatment of ◊gout; it is an isomer of hypexanthine $C_5H_4N_4O$, and acts by reducing levels of ◊uric acid in the blood.

Discovered accidentally in the early 1960s in the search for new immunosuppressives, it has no effects on acute gout attacks, and may even provoke them in the initial stages of therapy. In the long term, it prevents the deposit of urate in the joints and the formation of uric-acid kidney stones.

allotropy the property whereby certain elements exist in different forms (allotropes) in the same physical state. The allotropes of carbon are diamond and graphite.

The allotropes of ◊sulfur are rhombic and monoclinic. These have different crystal structures when solid, as do the the white and gray forms of tin. Oxygen also exists in two different forms: "normal" oxygen (O_2) and ozone (O_3), which have different molecular configurations.

alloy metal blended with some other metallic or nonmetallic substance to give it special qualities, such as resistance to corrosion, greater hardness, or tensile strength. Useful alloys include bronze, brass, cupronickel, duralumin, German silver, gunmetal, pewter, solder, steel, and stainless steel. The most recent alloys include the superplastics, alloys that can stretch 100% at specific temperatures, permitting, for example, their injection into molds as easily as plastic.

Among the oldest alloys is bronze, whose widespread use ushered in the Bronze Age. Complex alloys are now widespread, for example in dentistry, where a cheaper alternative to gold is made of chromium, cobalt, molybdenum, and titanium.

All Saints' Day festival on Nov 1 for all Christian saints and martyrs who have no special day of their own. It is also known as All-Hallows or Hallowmas.

All Souls' Day festival in the Catholic church, held on Nov 2 (following All Saints' Day) in the conviction that through prayer and self-denial the faithful can hasten the deliverance of souls expiating their sins in purgatory.

allspice spice prepared from dried berries of the pimento tree *Pimenta dioica*, cultivated chiefly in Jamaica. It has an aroma similar to a mixture of cinnamon, cloves, and nutmeg.

Allston Washington 1779–1843. US painter of sea- and landscapes, a pioneer of the Romantic movement in the US. His handling of light and color earned him the title "the American Titian." He also painted Classical, religious, and historical subjects.

Allston was born in South Carolina and educated at Harvard. He traveled widely in Europe, making contact and sharing ideals with the Romantic set in Britain, including the poets Wordsworth and Coleridge. He apprenticed himself to Benjamin ◊West and labored over historical paintings in West's manner without much success. Once settled in the US, he produced poetic, moody and visionary scenes, such as *The Moonlight Landscape* 1819 (Museum of Fine Arts, Boston).

alluvial deposit a layer of broken rocky matter, or sediment, formed from material that has been carried in suspension by a river or stream and dropped as the velocity of the current changes. River plains and deltas are made entirely of alluvial deposits, but smaller pockets can be found in the beds of upland torrents.

Alluvial deposits can consist of a whole range of particle sizes, from boulders down through cobbles, pebbles, gravel, sand, silt, and clay. The raw materials are the rocks and soils of upland areas that are loosened by erosion and washed away by mountain streams. Much of the world's richest farmland lies on alluvial deposits. These deposits can also provide an economic source of minerals. River currents produce a sorting action, with particles of heavy material deposited first while lighter materials are washed downstream. Hence heavy minerals such as gold and tin, present in the original rocks in small amounts, can be

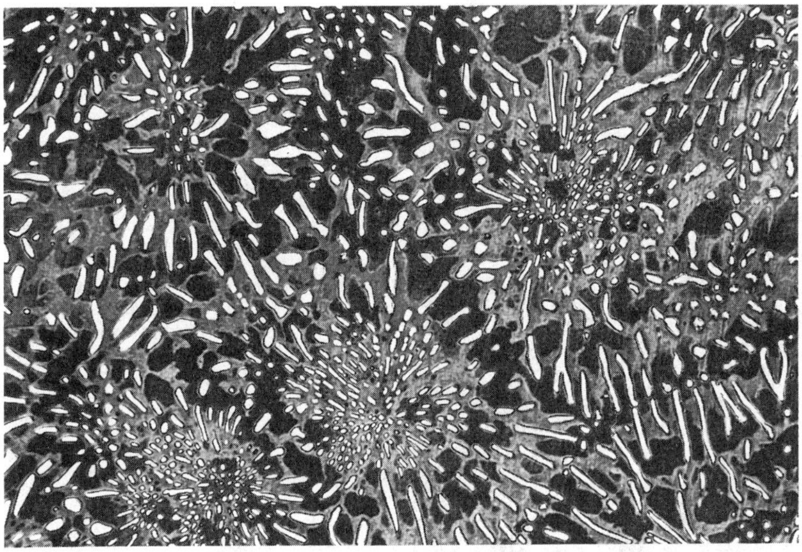

alloy *Ternary eutectic microstructure of a silver-copper-cadmium alloy (x 600). An alloy is prepared by adding other substances to a basic metal to secure desirable properties. Eutectic alloys consist of solid solutions having the lowest melting point. They are used in fuses and safety mechanisms.*

concentrated and deposited on stream beds in commercial quantities. Such deposits are called "placer ores."

alluvial fan a roughly triangular sedimentary formation found at the base of slopes. An alluvial fan results when a sediment-laden stream or river rapidly deposits its load of gravel and silt as its speed is reduced on entering a plain.

The surface of such a fan slopes outward in a wide arc from an apex at the mouth of the steep valley. A small stream carrying a load of coarse particles builds a shorter, steeper fan than a large stream carrying a load of fine particles. Over time, the fan tends to become destroyed piecemeal by the continuing headward and downward erosion leveling the slope.

Allyson June. Adopted name of Ella Geisman 1917– . US film actress, popular in musicals and straight drama in the 1940s and 1950s. Her work includes *Music for Millions* 1945, *The Three Musketeers* 1948, and *The Glenn Miller Story* 1954.

Alma-Ata formerly (to 1921) Vernyi capital of the Republic of Kazakh, USSR; population (1987) 1,108,000. Industries include engineering, printing, tobacco processing, textile manufacturing, and leather products.

Established 1854 as a military fortress and trading center, the town was destroyed by an earthquake 1887.

Almadan mining town in Ciudad Real province, Castilla-La Mancha, central Spain. It has the world's largest supply of mercury, worked since the 4th century BC. Population (1981) 9,700.

Almagest (Arabic *al* "the" and Greek *majisti* "greatest") book compiled by the Greek astronomer ◊Ptolemy during the 2nd century AD, which included the idea of an Earth-centered universe. It survived in an Arabic translation. Some medieval books on astronomy, astrology, and alchemy were given the same title.

Each section of the book deals with a different branch of astronomy. The introduction describes the universe as spherical and contains arguments for the Earth being stationary at the center. From this mistaken assumption, it goes on to describe the motions of the Sun, Moon, and planets; eclipses; and the positions, brightness, and precession of the "fixed stars." The book drew on the work of earlier astronomers such as ◊Hipparchus.

Almeida Francisco de c. 1450–1510. First viceroy of Portuguese India 1505–08. He consolidated rule there and sent expeditions out into the Indian Ocean and as far as Madagascar.

He was killed in a skirmish with the Hottentots at Table Bay, S Africa.

Almería Spanish city, chief town of a province of the same name on the Mediterranean; population (1986) 157,000. The province is famous for its white grapes, and in the Sierra Nevada are rich mineral deposits.

Almohad a Berber dynasty 1130–1269 founded by the Berber prophet Mohammed ibn Tumart (c. 1080–1130). They ruled much of Morocco and Spain, which they took by defeating the ◊Almoravids; they later took the area that today forms Algeria and Tunisia. Their policy of religious "purity" involved the forced conversion and massacre of the Jewish population of Spain. They were themselves defeated by the Christian kings of Spain in 1212, and in Morocco in 1269.

almond tree *Prunus amygdalus*, family Rosaceae, related to the peach and apricot. Dessert almonds are the kernels of the fruit of the sweet variety *P. amygdalus dulcis*, which is also the source of a low-cholesterol culinary oil. Oil of bitter almonds, from the variety *P. amygdalus amara*, is used in flavoring. Almond oil is also used for cosmetics, perfumes, and fine lubricants.

Almoravid a Berber dynasty 1056–1147 founded by the prophet Abdullah ibn Tashfin, ruling much of Morocco and Spain in the 11th–12th centuries. The Almoravids came from the Sahara and in the 11th century began laying the foundations of an empire covering the whole of Morocco and parts of Algeria; their capital was the newly founded Marrakesh. In 1086 they defeated Alfonso VI of Castile to gain much of Spain. They were later overthrown by the ◊Almohads.

Aloe genus of African plants of the family Liliaceae, distinguished by their long, fleshy, spiny-edged leaves. The drug usually referred to as "bitter aloes" is a powerful cathartic prepared from the juice of the leaves of several of the species.

Alost French name for the Belgian town of ◊Aalst.

Aloysius, St 1568–1591. Italian Jesuit who died while nursing plague victims. He is the patron saint of youth. Feast day June 21.

alpaca domesticated South American hoofed mammal, *Lama pacos*, of the camel family, found in Chile, Peru, and Bolivia, and herded at high elevations in the Andes. About 3 ft/1 m tall at the shoulder with neck and head another 2 ft/60 cm, it is bred mainly for its long, fine, silky wool, and like the llama was probably bred from the wild ◊guanaco.

alpha and omega first (α) and last (ω) letters of

alpaca

the Greek alphabet, a phrase hence meaning the beginning and end, or sum total, of anything.

alphabet set of conventional symbols for the purpose of writing, so called from *alpha* (α) and *beta* (β), the names of the first two letters of the Classical Greek alphabet.

The earliest known alphabet is from Palestine, about 1700 BC. Alphabetic writing now takes many forms, for example the Hebrew *aleph-beth* and the Arabic script, both written from right to left; the Devanagari script of the Hindus, in which the symbols "hang" from a line common to all the symbols; and the Greek alphabet, with the first clearly delineated vowel symbols. Each letter of the alphabets descended from Greek represents a particular sound or sounds, usually grouped into vowels (*a, e, i, o, u,* in the English version of the Roman alphabet), consonants (*b, p, d, t*) and semivowels (*w, y*). Letters may be combined to produce distinct sounds (for example *a* and *e* together in words like *tale* and *take*, or *o* and *i* together to produce a "wa" sound in the French *loi*), or may have no sound whatsoever (for example the silent letters *gh* in *high* and *through*).

Alpha Centauri or ***Rigil Kent*** the brightest star in the constellation Centaurus and the third brightest star in the sky. It is actually a triple star (see ◊binary star); the two brighter stars orbit each other every 80 years, and the third, Proxima Centauri, is the closest star to the Sun, 4.3 light-years away.

alpha decay the spontaneous alteration of the nucleus of a radioactive atom, which transmutes the atom from one atomic number to another through the emission of a helium nucleus (known as an alpha particle). As a result, the atomic number decreases by two and the atomic weight decreases by four.

alpha particle positively charged particle emitted from the nucleus of a radioactive ◊atom. It is one of the products of the spontaneous disintegration of radioactive elements such as radium and thorium, and is identical with the nucleus of a helium atom—that is, it consists of two protons and two neutrons. The process of emission, alpha decay, transmutes one element into another, decreasing the atomic number by two, and the atomic mass by four. See ◊radioactivity.

Alps mountain chain, the barrier between N Italy and France, West Germany and Austria.

Famous peaks include Mont Blanc, the highest at 15,777 ft/4,809 m, first climbed by Jacques Balmat and Michel Paccard 1786; Matterhorn in the Pennine Alps, 14,694 ft/4,479 m, first climbed by Edward Whymper 1865 (four of the party of seven were killed when the rope broke during their descent); Eiger in the Bernese Alps/Oberland, 13,030 ft/3,970 m, with a near-vertical rock wall on the N face, first climbed 1858; Jungfrau, 13,673 ft/4,166 m; and Finsteraarhorn 14,027 ft/4,275 m.

Famous passes include Brenner, the lowest,

Alps *The French Alps, showing left to right, Aiguille du Chardonnet, Aiguille Verte, and Aiguille du Dru.*

Austria/Italy; Great St Bernard, the highest, 8,113 ft/2,472 m, Italy/Switzerland (by which Napoleon marched into Italy 1800); Little St Bernard, Italy/France (which Hannibal is thought to have used); and St Gotthard, S Switzerland, which Suvorov used when ordered by the tsar to withdraw his troops from Italy. All have been superseded by all-weather road/rail tunnels. The Alps extend into Yugoslavia with the Julian and Dinaric Alps.

Alps, Australian highest area of the E Highlands in Victoria/New South Wales, Australia, noted for winter sports. They include the Snowy mountains and Mt Kosciusko, Australia's highest mountain, 7,316 ft/2,229 m, first noted by Polish-born Paul Strzelecki 1829 and named after a Polish hero.

Alps, Lunar mountain range on the Moon, NE of the Sea of Showers, cut by a valley 93 mi/150 km long.

Alps, Southern range of mountains running the entire length of South Island, New Zealand. They are forested to the W, with scanty scrub to the E. The highest point is Mt Cook 12,349 ft/3,764 m. Scenic features include gorges, glaciers, lakes and waterfalls. Among its lakes are those at the southern end of the range: Manapori, Te Anau, and the largest, Wakatipu, 52 mi/83 km long, which lies about 1,000 ft/300 m above sea level and has a depth of 1,242 ft/378 m.

Alsace region of France; area 3,204 sq mi/ 8,300 sq km; population (1986) 1,600,000. It consists of the *départements* of Bas-Rhin and Haut-Rhin, and its capital is Strasbourg.

Alsace-Lorraine area of NE France, lying west of the river Rhine. It forms the French regions of ◊Alsace and ◊Lorraine. The former iron and steel industries are being replaced by electronics, chemicals, and precision engineering. The German dialect spoken does not have equal rights with French, and there is autonomist sentiment. Alsace-Lorraine formed part of Celtic Gaul in Caesar's time, was invaded by the Alemanni and other Germanic tribes in the 4th century, and remained part of the German Empire until the 17th century. In 1648 part of the territory was ceded to France; in 1681 Louis XIV seized Strasbourg. The few remaining districts were seized by France after the French Revolution. Conquered by Germany 1870–71 (chiefly for its iron ores), it was regained by France 1919, then again annexed by Germany 1940–44, when it was liberated by the Allies.

Alsatia the old name for ◊Alsace, formerly part of Germany.

alsatian breed of dog known officially from 1977 as the German shepherd. It is about 26 in/63 cm tall, and has a wolflike appearance, a thick coat with many varieties of coloring, and a distinctive gait. They are used as police dogs because of their high intelligence. Alsatians were introduced from Germany into Britain and the US after World War I.

Altai territory of the Russian Soviet Federal Socialist Republic in SW Siberia; area 101,043 sq mi/ 261,700 sq km; population (1985) 2,744,000. The capital is Barnaul.

Altai Mountains mountain system of W Siberia and Mongolia. It is divided into two parts, the Russian Altai, which includes the highest peak, Mount Belukha, 14,783 ft/4,506 m, and the Mongolian or Great Altai.

Altair or ***Alpha Aquilae*** brightest star in the constellation Aquila and the 12th brightest star in the sky. It is a white star 16 light-years away and forms the so-called Summer Triangle with the stars Deneb (in the constellation Cygnus) and Vega (in Lyra).

Altamira caves decorated with Paleolithic wall paintings, the first such to be discovered, in 1879. The paintings are realistic depictions of bison, deer, and horses in polychrome (several colors). The caves are near the village of Santillana del Mar in Santander province, north Spain; other well-known Paleolithic cave paintings are in ◊Lascaux.

Altamira an Amazonian town in the state of Pará, NE Brazil, situated at the junction of the Trans-Amazonian Highway with the Xingu river, 400 mi/ 700 km SW of Belem. In 1989 a protest by Brazilian Indians and environmentalists against the building of six dams, focused world attention on the devastation of the Amazon rainforest.

Altdorf capital of the Swiss canton Uri at the head of Lake Lucerne, Switzerland; population 9,000. It was the scene of the legendary exploits of William ◊Tell.

Altdorfer Albrecht c. 1480–1538. German painter and printmaker, active in Regensburg, Bavaria. Altdorfer's work, inspired by the linear, Classical style of the Italian Renaissance, often depicts dramatic landscapes that are out of scale with the figures in the paintings. His use of light creates tension and effects of movement. Many of his works are of religious subjects.

With Dürer and Cranach, Altdorfer is regarded as one of the leaders of the German Renaissance. *St George and the Dragon* 1510 (Alte Pinakothek, Munich) is an example of his landscape style; *The Battle of Issus* 1529 (also Munich) is a dramatic panorama.

alternate angle in geometry, one of a pair of angles that lie on opposite sides of a transversal (a line that intersects two or more lines in the same plane). The alternate angles formed by a transversal of two parallel lines are equal.

alternating current (AC) electric current that flows for an interval of time in one direction and then in the opposite direction, that is, a current that flows in alternately reversed directions through or around a circuit. Electric energy is usually generated as alternating current in a power station, and alternating currents may be used for both power and lighting.

The advantage of alternating current over direct current (DC), as from a battery, is that its voltage can be raised or lowered economically by a transformer: high voltage for generation and transmission, and low voltage for safe utilization. Railways, factories, and domestic appliances, for example, use alternating current.

alternation of generations the typical life cycle of terrestrial plants and some seaweeds, in which there are two distinct forms occurring alternately: *diploid* (having two sets of chromosomes) and *haploid* (one set of chromosomes). The diploid generation produces haploid spores by ◊meiosis, and is called the sporophyte, while the haploid generation produces gametes (sex cells), and is called the gametophyte. The gametes fuse to form a diploid ◊zygote which develops into a new sporophyte; thus the sporophyte and gametophyte alternate.

alternative energy energy from sources that are renewable and ecologically safe, as opposed to sources that are nonrenewable with toxic byproducts, such as coal, oil, or gas (fossil fuels), and uranium (for nuclear power). The most important alternative energy source is flowing water, harnessed as ◊hydroelectric power. Other sources include the ocean's tides and waves (see ◊tidal power station and ◊wave power), wind (harnessed by windmills and wind turbines), the sun (◊solar energy), and the heat trapped in the Earth's crust (◊geothermal energy).

alternative medicine see ◊medicine, alternative.

alternator an electricity ◊generator that produces an alternating current.

Altgeld John Peter 1847–1902. US political and social reformer. Born in Prussia, he was taken in infancy to the US. During the Civil War he served in the Union army. He was a judge of the Supreme Court in Chicago 1886–91, and as governor of Illinois 1893–97 was a champion of the worker against the government-backed power of big business.

Althing the parliament of Iceland, established about AD 930 and the oldest in the world.

Althusser Louis 1918– . French philosopher and Marxist, born in Algeria, who argued that the idea that economic systems determine family and political systems is too simple. He attempted to show how the ruling class ideology of a particular era is a crucial form of class control.

Althusser divides each mode of production into four key elements—the economic, political, ideological, and theoretical—all of which interact. His structuralist analysis of capitalism sees individuals and groups as agents or bearers of the structures of social relations, rather than as independent influences on history. His works include *For Marx* 1965, *Lenin and Philosophy* 1969, and *Essays in Self-Criticism* 1976.

altimeter instrument used in aircraft that measures altitude, or height above sea level. The common type is a form of aneroid ◊barometer, which works by sensing the differences in air pressure at different altitudes. This must continually be recalibrated because of the change in air pressure with changing weather conditions. The ◊radar altimeter measures the height of the aircraft above the ground, measuring the time it takes for radio pulses emitted by the aircraft to be reflected. Radar altimeters are essential features of automatic and blind-landing systems.

Altiplano densely populated upland plateau of the Andes of South America, stretching from S Peru to NW Argentina. Height 10,000–13,000 ft/ 3,000–4,000 m.

altitude in geometry, the perpendicular distance from a ◊vertex (corner) of a figure (such as a triangle) to the base (the side opposite the vertex); also the perpendicular line that goes through the vertex to the base.

Altman Robert 1922– . US film director. His antiwar comedy *M.A.S.H.* 1970 was a critical and commercial success; subsequent films include *McCabe and Mrs Miller* 1971, *Nashville* 1975, and *Popeye* 1980.

Alton city in W Illinois, on the Mississippi river, just NE of St Louis, Missouri. It is an industrial center with flour mills and oil refineries; population (1990) 32,905. Site of the Lincoln-Douglas debates 1858.

Altoona city in S central Pennsylvania, in the Allegheny Mountains, NW of Harrisburg. There is coal mining, and it is a railroad manufacturing and repair center; population (1990) 51,881. First steel railroad tracks in the US were laid from Pittsburgh to Altoona.

altruism in biology, helping another individual of the same species to reproduce more effectively, as a direct result of which the altruist may leave fewer offspring itself. Female honey bees (workers) behave altruistically by rearing sisters in order to help their mother, the queen bee, reproduce, and forgo any possibility of reproducing themselves.

ALU (abbreviation of arithmetic and logic unit) in a computer, the part of the ◊central processing unit (CPU) that performs the basic arithmetic and logic operations on data.

alum any double sulfate of a monovalent metal or radical (such as sodium, potassium, or ammonium) with a trivalent metal (such as aluminum or iron). The commonest alum is the double sulfate of potassium and aluminum, $KAl(SO_4)_2.12H_2O$, a white crystalline powder that is readily soluble in water. Alums are used in papermaking and to fix dye in textiles.

alumina Al_2O_3 oxide of aluminum, also called corundum, which is very hard (9 on Mohs' scale) and widely distributed in clays, slates, and shales. It is formed by the decomposition of the feldspars in granite and used as an abrasive.

Typically it is a white powder, soluble in most strong acids or caustic alkalis, but not in water. Impure alumina is called "emery." Rubies and sapphires are corundum gemstones.

aluminum lightweight, silver-white, ductile and malleable, metallic element, symbol Al, atomic number 13, atomic weight 26.9815. It is the third most abundant element (and the most abundant metal) in the Earth's crust, of which it makes up about 8.1% by mass. It oxidizes rapidly, the layer of oxide on its surface making it highly resistant to tarnish, and is an excellent conductor of electricity. In its pure state it is a weak metal, but when combined with elements such as copper, silicon, or magnesium it forms alloys of great strength. In nature it is found only in the combined state in many minerals, and it is prepared commercially from the ore bauxite.

The pure metal was not readily obtained until the middle of the 19th century. Because of its light weight (specific gravity 2.70) it is widely used in the shipbuilding and aircraft industries. Consumer uses include food and beverage packaging, foil, outdoor furniture, and homebuilding materials.

The name comes from the Latin for ◊alumina, illustration size?.

aluminum ore raw material from which aluminum is extracted. The main ore is bauxite, a mixture of minerals, found in economic quantities in Australia, Guinea, West Indies, and several other countries.

Alva or ***Alba*** Ferdinand Alvarez de Toledo, duke of 1508–1582. Spanish politician and general. He successfully commanded the Spanish armies of the Holy Roman emperor Charles V and his son Philip II of Spain. In 1567 he was appointed governor of the Netherlands, where he set up a reign of terror to suppress Protestantism and the revolt of the Netherlands. In 1573 he was recalled by his own wish. He later led a successful expedition against Portugal 1580–81.

Alvarado Pedro de c. 485–1541. Spanish conquistador. In 1519 he accompanied Hernándo Cortés in the conquest of Mexico. In 1523–24 he conquered Guatemala.

Alvarez Luis Walter 1911–1988. US physicist who led the research team that discovered the Xi-zero atomic particle 1959. He had worked on the US atomic bomb project for two years, at Chicago and Los Alamos, New Mexico, during World War II. He was awarded a Nobel Prize 1968.

Alvarez was professor of physics at the University of California from 1945 and an associate director of the Lawrence Livermore Radiation Laboratory 1954–59. In 1980 he was responsible for the theory (not generally accepted), based on the discovery of a layer of iridium dated 70 million years ago, that dinosaurs disappeared because a meteorite crashed into Earth 70 million years ago, producing a dust cloud that blocked out the sun for several years, and causing dinosaurs and plants to die.

Alvarez Quintero Serafin 1871–1938 and Joaquin 1873–1945. Spanish dramatists. The brothers, born near Seville, always worked together and from 1897 produced some 200 plays, principally dealing with Andalusia. Among them are *Papá Juan: Centenario* 1909 and *Los Mosquitos* 1928.

alveolus one of the many thousands of tiny air sacs in the ◊lungs in which exchange of oxygen and carbon dioxide takes place between air and the bloodstream.

Alwar city in Rajasthan, India, chief town of the district (formerly princely state) of the same name; population (1981) 146,000. It has fine palaces, temples, and tombs. Flour milling and trade in cotton goods and millet are major occupations.

Alzheimer's disease common manifestation of ◊dementia, thought to afflict one in 20 people over 65. Attacking the brain's "gray matter," it is a disease of mental processes rather than physical function, characterized by memory loss and progressive intellectual impairment.

It was first described by Alois Alzheimer 1906. The cause is unknown, although a link with high levels of aluminum in drinking water was discovered 1989. It has also been suggested that the disease may result from a defective protein circulating in the blood. There is no treatment, but recent insights into the molecular basis of the disease may aid the search for a drug to counter its effects.

AM in physics, abbreviation for amplitude ◊modulation, one way in which radio waves are altered for the transmission of broadcasting signals. AM is constant in frequency, and varies the amplitude of the transmitting wave in accordance with the signal being broadcast.

a.m. or ***A.M.*** abbreviation for ***ante meridiem*** (Latin "before noon").

Amagasaki industrial city on the NW outskirts of Osaka, Honshu island, Japan; population (1987) 500,000.

Amal a radical Lebanese ◊Shiite military force, established by Musa Sadr in the 1970s; its headquarters are at Borj al-Barajneh. The movement split into extremist and moderate groups 1982, but both sides agreed on the aim of increasing Shi'ite political representation in Lebanon. The Amal militia under Nabi Berri fought several bloody battles against the Hezbollah (Party of God) in 1988.

Amal guerrillas were responsible for many of the attacks and kidnappings in Lebanon during the 1980s, although subsequently the group came to be considered one of the more mainstream elements on the Lebanese political scene.

Amalekite in the Old Testament, a member of an ancient Semitic people of SW Palestine and the Sinai peninsula. According to Exodus 17 they harried the rear of the Israelites after their crossing of the Red Sea, were defeated by Saul and David, and were destroyed in the reign of Hezekiah.

Amalfi port 24 mi/39 km SE of Naples, Italy, situated at the foot of Monte Cerrato, on the Gulf of Salerno; population 7,000. For 700 years it was an independent republic. It is an ancient archiepiscopal see (seat of an archbishop) and has a Romanesque cathedral.

amalgam any alloy of mercury with other metals. Most metals will form amalgams, except iron and platinum. Amalgam is used in dentistry for filling teeth, and usually contains copper, silver, and zinc as the main alloying ingredients. This amalgam is pliable when first mixed and then sets hard, but the mercury leaches out and causes a type of heavy-metal poisoning.

Amalgamation, the process of forming an amalgam, is a technique sometimes used to extract gold and silver from their ores. The ores are treated with mercury, which combines with the precious metals.

Amalia Anna 1739–1807. Duchess of Saxe-Weimar-Eisenach. As widow of Duke Ernest, she reigned 1758–75,when her son Karl August succeeded her with prudence and skill, making the court of Weimar a literary center of Germany. She was a friend of the writers Wieland, Goethe, and Herder.

Amanita genus of fungi (see ◊fungus), distinguished by a ring, or *volva*, around the stem, warty patches on the cap, and a clear white color of the gills. Many of the species are brightly colored and highly poisonous.

The fly agaric *A. muscaria* is a dangerous, poisonous toadstool with a white-spotted red cap, which grows under birch or pine. The buff-colored ◊death cap *A. phalloides* is deadly.

Amanullah Khan 1892–1960. Emir (ruler) of Afghanistan 1919–29. Third son of Habibullah Khan, he seized the throne on his father's assassination and concluded a treaty with the British, but his policy of westernization led to rebellion 1928. Amanullah had to flee, abdicated 1929, and settled in Rome, Italy.

Amar Das 1495–1574. Indian religious leader, third guru (teacher) of Sikhism 1552–74. He laid emphasis on equality and opposed the caste system. He initiated the custom of the *langar* (communal meal).

Amarillo town in the Texas panhandle; population (1990) 157,615. The center of the world's largest cattle-producing area, it processes the live animal into frozen supermarket packets in a single con-

Amazon River

Amazon

ameba

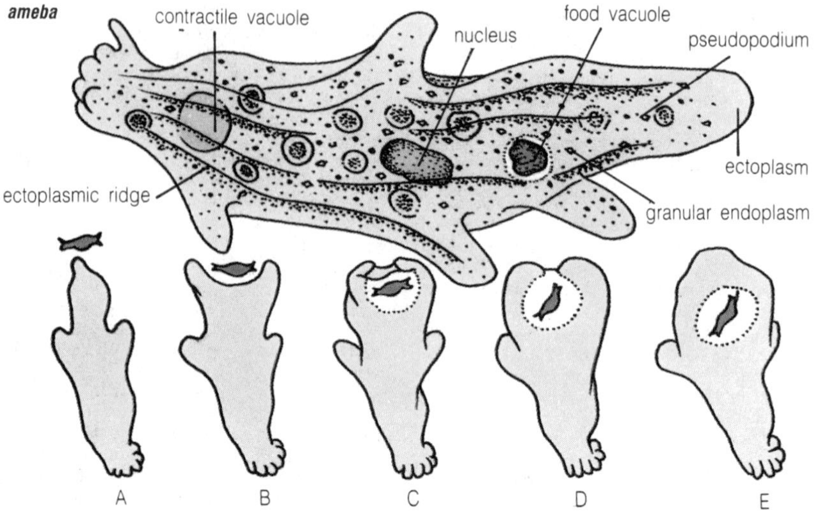
contractile vacuole
nucleus
food vacuole
pseudopodium
ectoplasm
ectoplasmic ridge
granular endoplasm
A
B
C
D
E

tinuous operation on an assembly line. It is also a center for assembly of nuclear warheads.

Amarna tablets collection of Egyptian clay tablets with cuneiform inscriptions, found in the ruins of the ancient city of ◊Akhetaton on the east bank of the Nile. The majority of the tablets, which comprise royal archives and letters of 1411–1375 BC, are in the British Museum.

Amaterasu in Japanese mythology, the sun-goddess, grandmother of Jimmu Tenno, first ruler of Japan, from whom the emperors claimed to be descended.

Amati Italian family of violin-makers, who worked in Cremona, about 1550–1740. Niccolo Amati (1596–1684) taught Andrea ◊Guarneri and Antonio ◊Stradivari.

Nicolo's grandfather Andrea (c. 1500–c. 1580) brought the violin to its classic form.

amatol explosive consisting of ammonium nitrate and TNT (trinitrotoluene) in almost any proportions.

Amazon in Greek mythology, a member of a group of legendary female warriors living near the Black Sea, who cut off their right breasts to use the bow more easily. Their queen, Penthesilea, was killed by Achilles at the siege of Troy. The Amazons attacked Theseus and besieged him at Athens, but were defeated, and Theseus took the Amazon Hippolyta captive; she later gave birth to ◊Hippolytus. The term Amazon has come to mean a large, strong woman.

Amazonian Indian indigenous inhabitant of the Amazon River Basin in South America. The majority of the societies are kin-based; traditional livelihood includes hunting and gathering, fishing, and shifting cultivation. A wide range of indigenous languages are spoken. Their rainforests are being destroyed for mining and ranching, and Indians are being killed, transported, or assimilated.

Amazon River (Indian *Amossona* "destroyer of boats") South American river, the world's second longest, 4,080 mi/6,570 km, and the largest in volume of water. Its main headstreams, the Marañón and the Ucayali, rise in central Peru and unite to flow E across Brazil for about 2,500 mi/4,000 km. It has 30,000 mi/48,280 km of navigable waterways, draining 2,750,000 sq mi/7,000,000 sq km, nearly half the South American land mass. It reaches the Atlantic on the equator, its estuary 50 mi/80 km wide, discharging a volume of water so immense that 40 mi/64 km out to sea, fresh water remains at the surface.

The opening up of the Amazon river basin to settlers from the overpopulated E coast has resulted in a massive burning of tropical forest to create both arable and pasture land. Brazil, with one third of the world's remaining tropical rainforest, has 55,000 species of flowering plant, half of which are only found in Brazilian Amazonia. The problems of massive soil erosion, the disappearance of potentially useful plant and animal species, and the possible impact of large-scale forest clearance on global warming of the atmosphere have become environmental issues of international concern.

Ambala or Umballa city in N India; population (1981) 121,200. It is a railroad junction situated 110 mi/176 km NW of Delhi. Food processing, flour milling, and cotton ginning are the foremost industries. It is an archeological site with prehistoric artifacts.

ambassador officer of the highest rank in the diplomatic service, who represents the head of one sovereign state at the court or capital of another.

amber fossilized resin from coniferous trees of the Middle Tertiary period. It is often washed ashore on the Baltic coast with plant and animal specimens preserved in it; many extinct species have been found preserved in this way. It ranges in color from red brown to yellow, from clear to opaque, and is used to make jewelry.

ambergris fatty substance, resembling wax, found in the stomach and intestines of the sperm ◊whale. It is found floating in warm seas, and was used in perfumery as a fixative.

Basically intestinal matter, ambergris is not the result of disease, but the product of an otherwise normal intestine. The name derives from the French *ambre gris* (gray amber).

Ambler Eric 1909–1986. English novelist. He used Balkan/Levant settings in the thrillers *The Mask of Dimitrios* 1939 and *Journey into Fear* 1940.

amblyopia reduced vision without apparent eye disorder.

Amboina or ***Ambon*** small island in the Moluccas, republic of Indonesia; population (1980) 209,000. The town of Amboina, formerly an historic center of Dutch influence, has shipyards.

Ambrose, St c. 340–397. One of the early Christian leaders and theologians known as the Fathers of the Church. Feast day Dec 7.

ambrosia (Greek "immortal") the food of the gods, which was supposed to confer eternal life upon all who ate it.

ameba any of a number of one-celled organisms, especially of the genus *Amoeba*, that move and feed by extensions of their colorless gelatinous protoplasm. They reproduce by ◊binary fission. Some members of the genus *Entamoeba* are harmful parasites. See also ◊amebiasis.

amebiasis ongoing infection of the intestines, caused by the ◊ameba *Entamoeba histolytica*, resulting in chronic dysentery and consequent weakness and dehydration. Endemic in the Third World, it is now occurring in North America and Europe.

amen Hebrew word signifying affirmation ("so be it"), commonly used at the close of a Jewish or Christian prayer or hymn. As used by Jesus in the New Testament it was traditionally translated "verily."

Amenhotep four Egyptian pharaohs, including:

Amenhotep III c. 1400 BC. King of Egypt who built great monuments at Thebes, including the temples at Luxor. Two portrait statues at his tomb were known to the Greeks as the colossi of Memnon; one was cracked, and when the temperature changed at dawn it gave out an eerie sound, then thought supernatural. His son Amenhotep IV changed his name to ◊Ikhnaton.

America the W hemisphere of the Earth, containing the continents of North America and South America. This great land mass extends from the Arctic to the Antarctic, from beyond 75° N to past 55° S. The area is about 16 million sq mi/42 million sq km, and the estimated population is over 500 million. Politically, it consists of 36 nations and US, British, French, and Dutch dependencies.

The name America is derived from Amerigo Vespucci, the Florentine navigator who was erroneously credited with being the first European to reach the (South) American mainland 1497. The name is also popularly used worldwide to refer to the United States of America, a usage that many Canadians, South Americans, and other non-US Americans dislike.

American Ballet Theater founded 1939 as "Ballet Theater" with codirectors Lucia Chase and Richard Pleasant, then from 1945 Oliver Smith. Aiming to present established and new ballets with frequent celebrity guest appearances, they established a repertoire of exemplary range and quality.

American Civil War 1861–65; see ◊Civil War, American.

American Federation of Labor and Congress of Industrial Organizations AFL-CIO federation of North American labor unions. The AFL was founded 1886, superseding the Federation of Organized Trades and Labor Unions of the US and Canada, and was initially a union of skilled craftworkers. The CIO was known in 1935 as the Committee on Industrial Organization (it adopted its present title 1937 after expulsion from the AFL for its opposition to the AFL policy of including only skilled workers). A merger reunited them 1955, bringing most unions into the national federation, currently representing about 20% of the workforce in North America.

American Indian any of the aboriginal peoples of the Americas; the Arctic peoples (Eskimos and Aleuts) are often included, especially by the Bureau of Indian Affairs (BIA) of the Department of the Interior, responsible for overseeing policy on US Indian life, their reservations, education, and social welfare.

American Indians: major tribes

Area	*Tribe*
North America	
Arctic	Eskimo, Aleut
Sub-Arctic	Algonquin, Cree, Ottawa
NE Woodlands	Huron, Iroquois, Mohican, Shawnee
SE Woodlands	Cherokee, Choctaw, Creek, Hopewell, Natchez, Seminole
Great Plains	Blackfoot, Cheyenne, Comanche, Pawnee, Sioux
NW Coast	Chinook, Tlingit, Tsimshian
Desert West	Apache, Navaho, Pueblo, Hopi, Mohave, Shoshone
Central America	Maya, Aztec, Olmec
South America	
Eastern	Carib, Xingu
Central	Guaraní, Miskito
Western	Araucanian, Aymara, Chimú, Inca, Jivaro, Quechua

Columbus named them Indians in 1492, because he thought he had reached the East Indies. Instead, he had reached the West Indies, inhabited by peoples whose Asian ancestors had migrated, hunting their way from the Old World into the New World on the geologic land bridge exposed by lowered sea level between Siberia and Alaska, during the glaciation of the last ◊Ice Age, some 65,000 to 30,000 years ago. Several migrations occurred after that time, during emergences of the land bridge, with the last being the Eskimo and Aleut of about 3,000 to 1,000 years ago.

Hunting, fishing, and moving camp throughout the Americas, the migrants inhabited both continents, and their nearby islands, and settled all the ecological zones, from the most tropical to the most frozen, including the woodlands, deserts, plains, mountains, and river valleys, from the west coast to the east, and from the Arctic to the Antarctic. As they specialized, many kinds of societies evolved, speaking many languages: hunters and fishers (the Eskimo, the Athabaskans); specialized fishers (along the Northwest Coast); specialized hunters and gatherers (the Iroquois Nation, the Sioux of the Great Plains); specialized collectors (near the Great Lakes and in the Amazonian rainforests); farmers (the Hopi of the Southwest); and ancient civilizations (in Mexico—the Olmec, the Maya, the Aztec; in Peru—the Chimú, the Inca). Some of the specialized collectors of plants evolved into farmers, domesticating corn, beans, and squash in Mexico and Central America; potatoes, tomatoes, peppers, lima beans, avocados, peanuts, manioc, sweet potatoes, and tobacco in South America. Farming surpluses led to trade and taxation, which became the basis for the rise of civilizations, where the rulers and the priesthood prized jade, cacao (chocolate), and vanilla beans for ritual purposes; the arts and sciences were pursued—as was writing, astronomy, mathematics, engineering, architecture, and medicine; and crafts flourished—such as pottery, basketry, weaving, and the working of metals, wood, and leather. Militarism became a fact of life in many areas of North, Central, and South America, but political balances were disrupted and destroyed by the Spanish Conquest and subsequent European colonization.

***distribution*:**

Canada 300,000, including the Eskimos; the largest group is the Six Nations (Iroquois), with a reserve near Brantford, Ontario, for 7,000; they are members of the National Indian Brotherhood of Canada.

United States 1.6 million, almost 900,000 (including Eskimos and Aleuts) living on or near reservations, mainly in Arizona, New Mexico, Utah (where the Navaho have the largest of all reservations), Oklahoma, Texas, Montana, Washington, North and South Dakota, and Wyoming. The rest (700,000) live among the general population. The population level is thought to be about the same as at the time of Columbus, but now includes many people who are of mixed ancestry. Although treaties exist between the US and many Indian nations, Indians were made citizens of the US in 1924. There is an organized American Indian Movement (AIM).

Latin America many mestizo (mixed Indian–Spanish descent), among them half the 12 million in Bolivia and Peru. Since the 1960s they increasingly stress their Indian inheritance in terms of language and culture. The few Indian groups formerly beyond white contact are being transported and killed while their environment is destroyed with the clearing and industrial development of the Amazon Basin.

American Legion community organization in the US, originally for ex-servicemen of World War I, founded 1919. It has approximately 2.7 million members, and has admitted veterans of World War II, the Korean war, and the Vietnam war.

It has a strong national voice on issues concerning US veterans, and sponsors local welfare programs and essay contests.

American literature see ◊United States literature.

American Revolution, the the revolt 1775–83 of the British North American colonies that resulted in the establishment of the United States of America. It was caused by colonial resentment at the contemporary attitude that commercial or industrial interests of any colony should be subordinate to those of the mother country, and the unwillingness of the colonists to pay for a permanent army. It was also fueled by the colonists' antimonarchist sentiment and by a desire to have a voice in those policies affecting them.

It was preceded by:

1773 A government tax on tea led Massachusetts citizens disguised as North American Indians to board the ships carrying the tea and throw it into the harbor, the Boston Tea Party.

1774–75 The First Continental Congress was held in Philadelphia to call for civil disobedience in reply to British measures, including the Intolerable Acts which closed the port of Boston and called for the forced quartering of British troops in private homes.

The War:

1775 Apr 19 hostilities began at Lexington and Concord, Massachusetts, the first shots were fired when British troops, sent to seize illegal military stores (and arrest rebel leaders John ◊Hancock and Samuel ◊Adams) were attacked by the local militia and minutemen (see Paul ◊Revere). May 10 Fort Ticonderoga, New York, was captured from the British. The first battle was at Breed's Hill (see ◊Bunker Hill, Massachusetts, June 17, in which the colonists were defeated; George ◊Washington was appointed commander in chief of the American forces soon afterwards.

1775–76 The Second Continental Congress on Jul 4 1776 issued the ◊Declaration of Independence which specified some of their grievances and called for a new form of government.

1776 Aug 27 at Long Island Washington was defeated, forced to evacuate New York and retire to Pennsylvania but recrossed the Delaware River to win successes at Trenton Dec 26 and Princeton Jan 3, 1777.

1777 A British plan for Sir William Howe (advancing from New York) and Gen Burgoyne (from Canada) to link up, miscarried. Burgoyne surrendered at Saratoga in New York State Oct 17, (the turning point for the Americans); but Howe invaded Pennsylvania, defeating Washington at Brandywine Sept 11 and Germantown Oct 4, and occupying Philadelphia; Washington wintered at ◊Valley Forge 1777–78, enduring harsh conditions and seeing many of his troops leave to return to their families.

1778 France, with the support of its ally Spain, entered the war on the American side (John Paul ◊Jones led a French-sponsored naval unit).

1780 May 12 capture of Charleston, South Carolina, the most notable of a series of British victories in the south, but they alienated support by attempting to enforce conscription.

1781 Oct 19 Cornwallis, besieged in Yorktown, Virginia (Chesapeake Bay), by Washington and the French fleet, surrendered.

1782 Peace negotiations opened.

1783 Sept 3 Treaty of Paris: US independence recognized.

American Samoa see ◊Samoa, American.

American System, the in US history, a federal legislative program following the ◊War of 1812 that was designed to promote an integrated national economy. It introduced tariffs to protect US industry from foreign competition, internal improvements to the transport network, and a national bank to facilitate economic growth.

America's Cup international yacht-racing trophy named after the US schooner *America*, owned by J L Stevens, who won a race around the Isle of Wight 1851.

Offered for a challenge in 1870, it is now contested every three or four years, and is a seven-race series. The US has dominated the race, only twice losing possession, in 1983 to Australia and in 1989 to New Zealand, then regaining it after a court battle. All races were held at Newport, Rhode Island, until 1987 when the Perth Yacht Club, Australia, hosted the series. Yachts are very expensive to produce and only syndicates can afford to provide a yacht capable of winning the trophy.

1962	*Weatherly*
1964	*Constellation*
1967	*Intrepid*
1970	*Intrepid*
1974	*Courageous*
1977	*Courageous*
1980	*Freedom*
1983	*Australia II*
1987	*Stars and Stripes*
1989	*Stars and Stripes*

americium radioactive metallic element of the ◊actinide series, symbol Am, atomic number 95, atomic weight 243.13. It occurs in nature in extraordinarily minute quantities in ◊pitchblende and other uranium ores, where it is produced from the decay of neutron-bombarded plutonium in these ores. It is the element with the highest atomic number that occurs in nature. It is synthesized in quantity only in nuclear reactors by the bombardment of plutonium with neutrons. Its longest-lived isotope is Am-243, with a half-life of 7,650 years.

The element was named by G T Seaborg, one of the team who first synthesized it in 1944, for the United States of *America*, where transuranics were first produced, by analogy with europium, the corresponding ◊lanthanide.

Amerindian a contraction of ◊American Indian.

Amersfoort town in the Netherlands, 12 mi/19 km NE of Utrecht; population (1984) 86,896. Industries include brewing, chemicals, and light engineering.

Ames Adelbert 1880–1955. US scientist, who studied optics and the psychology of visual perception.

He concluded that much of what a person sees depends on what he or she expects to see, based (consciously or unconsciously) on previous experience. The Ames Room is often used to conduct experiments and tests on such viewing.

amethyst a variety of ◊quartz, SiO_2, colored violet by the presence of small quantities of manganese; used as a semiprecious stone.

Amethysts are found chiefly in the USSR, India, the US, Uruguay, and Brazil.

Amhara person of the Amhara culture of the central Ethiopian plateau. They comprise approximately 25% of Ethiopia's population and speak Amharic,

amethyst *Quartz crystals incorporate manganese during their growth, which colors them violet.*

a language of the Semitic branch of the Afro-Asiatic family.

amicus curiae (Latin "friend of the court") in law, a lawyer advising the court in a legal case as a neutral person, not representing either side.

Amida Buddha the "Buddha of immeasurable light." Japanese name for *Amitābha*, the Buddha venerated in Pure Land Buddhism. He presides over the Western Paradise (the Buddha-land of his own creation), and through his unlimited compassion and power to save, true believers can achieve enlightenment and be reborn.

Amiens ancient city of NE France at the confluence of the rivers Somme and Avre; capital of Somme *département* and center of a market-gardening region irrigated by canals; population (1982) 154,500. It has a magnificent Gothic cathedral with a spire 370 ft/113 m high and gave its name to the battles of Aug 1918, when ◊Haig launched his victorious offensive in World War I.

Amies Hardy 1909– . British couturier, one of Queen Elizabeth II's dressmakers. Noted from 1934 for his tailored clothes for women, he also designed for men from 1959.

Amin Dada Idi 1925– . Ugandan politician, president 1971–79. He led the coup that deposed Milton Obote 1971, expelled the Asian community 1972, and exercised a reign of terror over his people. He fled when insurgent Ugandan and Tanzanian troops invaded the country 1979.

amines class of organic chemical compounds in which one or more of the hydrogen atoms of ammonia have been replaced by other groups of atoms.

Methyl amines have unpleasant ammonia odors and occur in decomposing fish. They are all gases at ordinary temperature. Amino acids contain both amine and carboxyl groups. Aromatic amine compounds include aniline, used in dyeing.

amino acid water-soluble organic ◊molecule, mainly composed of carbon, oxygen, hydrogen, and nitrogen, containing both a basic amine group ($-NH_2$) and an acidic carboxyl ($-COOH$) group. When two or more amino acids are joined together, they are known as ◊peptides; ◊proteins are made up of interacting polypeptides (peptide chains consisting of more than three amino acids) and are folded or twisted in characteristic shapes.

Many different proteins are found in the cells of living organisms, but they are all made up of the same 20 amino acids, joined together in varying combinations, (although other types of amino acid do occur infrequently in nature). Eight of these, the essential amino acids, cannot be synthesized by humans and for nutritive purposes must be obtained from the diet. Children need a further two amino acids that are not essential for adults. Other animals also need some preformed amino acids in their diet, but green plants can manufacture all the amino acids they need from simpler molecules, relying on energy from the sun and minerals (including nitrates) from the soil.

Amis Kingsley 1922– English novelist and poet. His works include *Lucky Jim* 1954, a comic portrayal of life in a provincial university, and *Take a Girl Like You* 1960. He won Britain's Booker Prize 1986 for *The Old Devils*. He is the father of Martin Amis.

Amin Dada *Idi Amin, Ugandan president from 1971 until his overthrow in 1979, surrounded by his bodyguard. He is being asked to explain to reporters how the archbishop of Uganda and two cabinet ministers met a violent death while they were in custody in 1977.*

Amis Martin 1949– . English novelist. His works are characterized by their savage wit and include *The Rachel Papers* 1974, *Money* 1984, and *London Fields* 1989.

Amman capital and chief industrial center of Jordan; population (1980) 1,232,600. It is a major communications center, linking historic trade routes across the Middle East.

Amman is built on the site of the Old Testament Rabbath-Ammon (Philadelphia), capital of the Ammonites.

ammeter an instrument that measures electric current, usually in ◊amperes.

Ammon in Egyptian mythology, the king of the gods, the equivalent of ◊Zeus or ◊Jupiter. The name is also spelled Amen/Amun, as in the name of the pharaoh Tutankh*amen*. In art, he is represented as a ram, as a man with a ram's head, or as a man crowned with feathers. He had temples at Siwa oasis, Libya, and Thebes, Egypt.

ammonia NH_3 a colorless pungent-smelling gas, lighter than air and very soluble in water. It is made on an industrial scale by the ◊Haber process, and used mainly to produce nitrogenous fertilizers, some explosives, and nitric acid.

In aquatic organisms and some insects, nitrogenous waste (from breakdown of amino acids and so on) is excreted in the form of ammonia, rather than urea as in mammals.

Ammonite member of an ancient Semitic people, mentioned in the Old Testament or Jewish Bible, who lived NW of the Dead Sea. Their capital was Amman, in present-day Jordan. Worshipers of Moloch, to whom they offered human sacrifices, they were frequently at war with the Israelites.

ammonite extinct marine ◊cephalopod mollusk of the order Ammonoidea, related to the modern nautilus. The shell was curled in a plane spiral and made up of numerous gas-filled chambers, the outermost containing the body of the animal. Many species flourished between 200 million and 65 million years ago, ranging in size from that of a small coin to 6 ft/2 m across.

ammonium chloride or ***sal ammoniac*** NH_4Cl a volatile salt that forms white crystals around volcanic craters. It is prepared synthetically for use in "dry-cell" batteries, fertilizers, and dyes.

amnesia loss or impairment of memory. As a clinical condition it may be caused by disease or injury to the brain, or by shock; in some cases it may be a symptom of an emotional disorder.

Amnesty International human-rights organization established in the UK 1961 to campaign for the release of political prisoners worldwide. It has 700,000 members, and section offices in 43 countries. Amnesty International is politically unaligned. The organization was awarded the Nobel Peace Prize 1977.

amniocentesis sampling the amniotic fluid surrounding a fetus in the womb for diagnostic purposes. It is used to detect Down's syndrome and other genetic abnormalities.

amnion innermost of three membranes that enclose the embryo within the egg (reptiles and birds) or within the uterus (mammals). It contains the amniotic fluid which helps to cushion the embryo.

Amorites ancient people of Semitic or Indo-European origin, who were among the inhabitants of ◊Canaan at the time of the Israelite invasion. They provided a number of Babylonian kings.

amortization in finance, the ending of a debt by paying it off gradually, over a period of time. The term is used to describe either the paying off of a cash debt or the accounting procedure by which the value of an asset is progressively reduced ("depreciated") over a number of years.

Amos book of the Old Testament written c. 750 BC. One of the ◊prophets, Amos was a shepherd who

amino acid

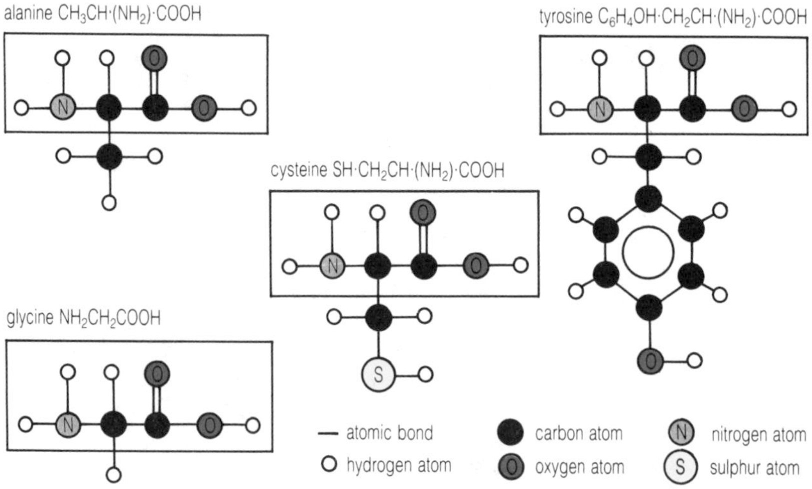
alanine $CH_3CH{\cdot}(NH_2){\cdot}COOH$
tyrosine $C_6H_4OH{\cdot}CH_2CH{\cdot}(NH_2){\cdot}COOH$
cysteine $SH{\cdot}CH_2CH{\cdot}(NH_2){\cdot}COOH$
glycine NH_2CH_2COOH
N
O
S
— atomic bond
hydrogen atom
carbon atom
oxygen atom
nitrogen atom
sulphur atom

foretold the destruction of Israel because of the people's abandonment of their faith.

Amoy ancient name for ◊Xiamen, a port in SE China.

amp in physics, abbreviation for ◊ampere, a unit of electrical current.

ampere SI unit (abbreviation amp or A) of electrical current. Electrical current is measured in a similar way to water current, in terms of an amount per unit time; one ampere represents a flow of about 6.28×10^{18} ◊electrons per second, or a rate of flow of charge of one coulomb per second.

The ampere is defined as the current that produces a specific magnetic force between two long, straight, parallel conductors placed one meter apart in a vacuum. It is named after the French scientist André Ampère.

Ampère André Marie 1775–1836. French physicist and mathematician who made many discoveries in electromagnetism and electrodynamics. He followed up the work of Hans ◊Oersted on the interaction between magnets and electric currents, developing a rule for determining the direction of the magnetic field associated with an electric current. The ammeter and ampere are named after him.

Ampère's rule rule developed by André Ampère connecting the direction of an electric current and its associated magnetic currents. Traveling along a current-carrying wire in the direction of the current (from the positive to the negative terminal of a battery), and facing a magnetic needle, the north pole of the needle is deflected to the left-hand side.

amphetamine synthetic ◊stimulant, known as speed. Used since World War II to help soldiers overcome fatigue, and until the 1970s prescribed by doctors as an appetite suppressant for weight loss; as an antidepressant, to induce euphoria; and as a stimulant, to increase alertness. Indications for its use today are very restricted because of severe side effects, including addiction and distorted behavior. It is a sulfate or phosphate form of $C_9H_{13}N$.

amphibian member of the vertebrate class Amphibia (Greek "double life"), which generally spend their larval (tadpole) stage in fresh water, transferring to land at maturity and generally returning to water to breed. Like fish and reptiles, they continue to grow throughout life, and cannot maintain a temperature greatly differing from that of their environment. The class includes caecilians, wormlike in appearance; salamanders, frogs, and toads.

amphibole any one of a large group of rock-forming silicate minerals with an internal structure based on double chains of silicon and oxygen, and with a general formula $X_2Y_5Si_8O_{22}(OH)_2$; closely related to ◊pyroxene. Amphiboles form orthorhombic, monoclinic, and triclinic ◊crystals.

Amphiboles occur in a wide range of igneous and metamorphic rocks. Common examples are ◊hornblende(X=Ca, Y=Mg, F, A) and tremolite (X=Ca, Y=Mg).

Amphion in Greek mythology, one of the two sons of ◊Zeus and Antiope. He built the walls of Thebes by drawing the stones into place with the music from his lyre, a gift from the god ◊Hermes.

amphioxus or ***lancelet*** filter-feeding animal about 2.5 in/6 cm long with a fishlike shape and a notochord, or flexible rod which forms the supporting structure of its body. It lacks organs such as heart or eyes, and lives half-buried on the sea bottom. It is a primitive relative of the vertebrates.

amphitheater large oval or circular building used for lectures, plays, demonstrations, and by the Romans for gladiatorial contests, fights of wild animals, and other similar events; it is a structure with an open space surrounded by rising rows of seats, hence the name (Greek *amphi*, "around"). The Romans built many amphitheaters. The ◊Colosseum in Rome, completed AD 80, is an example. It held 50,000 spectators.

Amphitrite in Greek mythology, one of the daughters of Nereus and wife of the god ◊Poseidon.

Amphitryon in Greek mythology, the husband of ◊Alcmene, the mother of ◊Heracles.

amphora large pottery storage jar in the Graeco-Roman world used for wine, oil, and dry goods.

amplifier an electronic device that magnifies the strength of a signal, such as a radio signal. The ratio of output signal strength to input signal strength is called the gain of an amplifier. As well as achieving high gain, an amplifier should be free from distortion and able to operate over a range of frequencies. Practical amplifiers are usually complex circuits, although simple amplifiers can be built from single transistors or valves.

amplitude maximum displacement of an oscillation from the equilibrium position. For a wave motion, it is the height of a crest (or the depth of a trough). With a sound wave, for example, amplitude corresponds to the intensity (loudness) of the sound. In AM (amplitude modulation) radio broadcasting, the required audio-frequency signal is made to modulate (vary slightly) the amplitude of a continuously transmitted radio carrier wave.

amplitude or ***argument*** in mathematics, the angle θ between the position vector of a ◊complex number and the real axis. For the complex number z, the amplitude of $z = r(\cos \theta + i \sin \theta)$, in which r is the radius and $i = \sqrt{-1}$. ***The expression*** $r(\cos \theta + i \sin \theta)$ is often abbreviated to r cis θ.

ampulla small vessel with a round body and narrow neck, used for holding oil, perfumes, and so on by the ancient Greeks and Romans.

ampulla in the ◊ear, the slight swelling at the end of each semicircular canal, able to sense the motion of the head. The sense of balance largely depends on sensitive hairs within the ampulla responding to movements of fluid within the inner ear.

amputation loss of part or all of a limb or other body appendage through surgery or accident.

Amritsar industrial city in the Punjab, India; population (1981) 595,000. It is the holy city of ◊Sikhism, with the Guru Nanak University (named after the first Sikh guru) and the Golden Temple from which armed demonstrators were evicted by the Indian army under General Dayal in 1984, 325 being killed. Subsequently, Indian prime minister Indira Gandhi was assassinated in reprisal. In 1919 it was the scene of the Amritsar Massacre.

Amritsar Massacre also called ***Jallianwallah Bagh massacre*** the killing of 379 Indians (and wounding of 1,200) in Amritsar in the Punjab 1919, when British troops under General Edward Dyer (1864–1927) opened fire without warning on a crowd of some 10,000, assembled to protest against the arrest of two Indian National Congress leaders (see ◊Congress Party).

Amsterdam capital of the Netherlands; population (1988) 1,031,000. Canals cut through the city link it with the North Sea and the Rhine, and as a Dutch port it is second only to Rotterdam. There is shipbuilding, printing, food processing, banking, and insurance.

Art galleries include Rijksmuseum, Stedelijk, Vincent Van Gogh Museum, and the Rembrandt house. Notable also are the Royal Palace (1655) and the Anne Frank house.

Amu Darya river formerly called Oxus in Soviet central Asia, flowing 1,580 mi/2,530 km from the ◊Pamirs to the ◊Aral Sea.

Amundsen Roald 1872–1928. Norwegian explorer who in 1903–06 was the first person to navigate the ◊Northwest Passage. Beaten to the North Pole by ◊Peary 1910, he reached the South Pole ahead of ◊Scott 1911.

In 1918, Amundsen made an unsuccessful attempt to drift across the North Pole in the airship *Maud* and in 1925 tried unsuccessfully to fly from Spitsbergen, in the Arctic Ocean N of Norway, to the Pole by airplane. The following year he joined the Italian explorer Umberto Nobile in the airship *Norge*, which circled the North Pole twice and landed in Alaska. Amundsen was killed in a plane crash over the Arctic Ocean while searching for Nobile and his airship *Italia*.

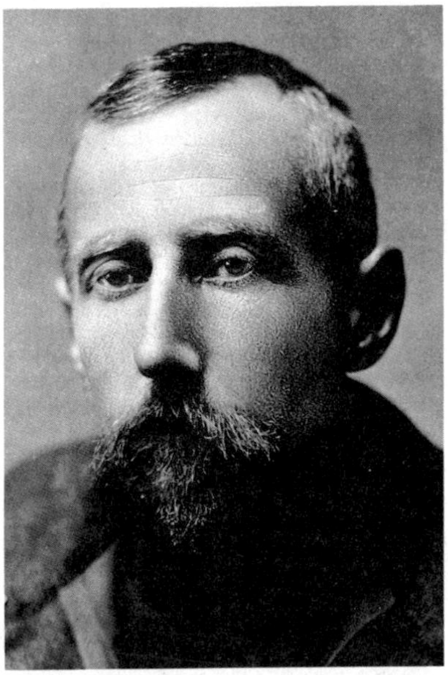

Amundsen Norwegian explorer Roald Amundsen. He devoted his life to polar exploration and in 1911 became the first person to reach the South Pole.

Amur river in E Asia. Formed by the Argun and Shilka rivers, the Amur enters the Sea of Okhotsk. At its mouth at Nikolevsk it is 10 mi/16 km wide. For much of its course of over 2,730 mi/4,400 km it forms, together with its tributary, the Ussuri, the boundary between the USSR and China.

Under the treaties of Aigun (1858) and Peking (1860), 380,000 sq mi/984,200 sq km of territory N and E of the two rivers were ceded by China to the tsarist government. From 1963 China raised the question of its return and there have been border clashes.

amylase one of a group of ◊enzymes that breaks down ◊starches into their component molecules (sugars) for use in the body. It occurs widely in both plants and animals. In humans, it is found in saliva and in pancreatic juices.

Anabaptist (Greek "baptize again") a member of any of various 16th-century radical Protestant sects. They believed in adult rather than child baptism, and sought to establish utopian communities. Anabaptist groups spread rapidly in N Europe, particularly in Germany, and were widely persecuted.

Notable Anabaptists included those in Moravia (the Hutterites) and Thomas Müntzer (1489–1525), a peasant leader who was executed for fomenting an uprising in Mühlhausen (now Mulhouse in E France). In Münster, Germany, Anabaptists controlled the city 1534–35. A number of Anabaptist groups, such as the Mennonites, Amish, and Hutterites, emigrated to N America, where they became known for their simple way of life and pacifism.

anabolic steroid any ◊hormone of the ◊steroid group of organic compounds that stimulates tissue growth. Its use in medicine is limited to the treatment of some anemias and breast cancers; it may help to break up blood clots. Side effects include aggressive behavior, masculinization in women, and, in children, reduced height.

It is used in sports, such as weight lifting and track and field, to increase muscle bulk for greater strength and stamina but it is widely condemned because of dangerous side effects. In 1988 the Canadian sprinter Ben Johnson was stripped of an Olympic gold medal for taking anabolic steroids.

anabolism the process of building up body tissue,

promoted by the influence of certain hormones. It is the constructive side of ◊metabolism, as opposed to catabolism.

anabranch (Greek *ana* "again") stream that branches from a main river, then reunites with it. For example, the Great Anabranch in New South Wales, Australia, leaves the Darling near Menindee, and joins the Murray below the Darling-Murray confluence.

Anaconda town in Montana, which had the world's largest copper smelter (closed 1980); population (1990) 10,278. The city was founded as Copperopolis 1883 by the Anaconda Copper Mining Company, and was incorporated as Anaconda 1888. The town is 5,300 ft/1,615 m above sea level and 26 mi/42 km NW of Butte.

anaconda South American snake *Eunectes murinus*, a member of the python and boa family, the Boidae. One of the largest snakes, growing to 30 ft/9 m or more, it is found in and near water, where it lies in wait for the birds and animals on which it feeds. The anaconda is not venomous, but kills its prey by coiling round it and squeezing until the creature suffocates.

anaerobic in biology, a description of those living organisms that do not require oxygen for the release of energy from food molecules such as glucose. Anaerobic organisms include many bacteria, yeasts, and internal parasites.

Obligate anaerobes such as archaebacteria cannot function in the presence of oxygen; but facultative anaerobes, like the fermenting yeasts and some bacteria, can function with or without oxygen. Anaerobic organisms release 19 times less of the available energy from their food than do ◊aerobic organisms.

In some bacteria, instead of oxygen, an inorganic compound, such as sulfate (SO_4), is the final acceptor of electrons stripped from food molecules during their breakdown. In ◊fermentation (as practiced by yeasts) the final acceptor is an intermediate product of the glucose molecule being degraded.

Anaheim city in SW California, SE of Los Angeles. Its industries produce electronic and farm equipment and processed foods. Disneyland amusement park is here; population (1990) 266,406. Settled by German immigrants 1858 as a wine-producing community.

Analects the most important of the four books that contain the teachings and ideas of ◊Confucianism.

analog computer computing device that performs calculations through the interaction of continuously varying physical quantities, such as voltages (as distinct from the more common ◊digital computer, which works with discrete quantities). An analog computer is said to operate in ◊real time (corresponding to time in the real world), and can therefore be used to monitor and control other events as they happen.

Although common in engineering since the 1920s, analog computers are not general-purpose computers, but specialize in solving ◊differential equations and similar mathematical problems. The earliest analog computing device is thought to be the flat, or planispheric, astrolabe, which originated in about the 8th century.

analysis branch of mathematics concerned with limiting processes on axiomatic number systems; ◊calculus of variations and infinitesimal calculus is now called analysis.

analytic in philosophy, a term derived from ◊Kant: the converse of ◊synthetic. In an analytic judgment, the judgment provides no new knowledge; for example: "All bachelors are unmarried."

analytical chemistry branch of chemistry that deals with the determination of the chemical composition of substances.

Qualitative analysis determines the elements or compounds in a given sample, without necessarily finding their concentrations, using methods such as ◊chromatography and ◊spectroscopy.

Quantitative analysis determines exact composition in terms of concentration, using such techniques as titration (volumetric analysis) and weighing (gravimetric analysis).

analytical engine programmable computing device designed by Charles ◊Babbage in the 1830s. It introduced many of the concepts of the digital computer but, because of limitations in manufacturing processes, was never built.

Among the concepts introduced were input and output, an arithmetic unit, memory, sequential operation, and the ability to make decisions based on data. The design was largely forgotten until some of Babbage's writings were rediscovered in 1937.

analytic geometry another name for ◊coordinate geometry.

Ananda 5th century BC. Favorite disciple of the Buddha. At his plea, a separate order was established for women. He played a major part in collecting the teachings of the Buddha after his death.

anaphylaxis in medicine, a severe allergic response. Typically, the air passages become constricted, the blood pressure falls rapidly, and the victim collapses. A rare condition, anaphylaxis can occur following wasp or bee stings or treatment with some drugs.

anarchism (Greek *anarkhos* "without ruler") political belief that society should have no government, laws, police, or other authority, but should be a free association of all its members. It does not mean "without order"; most theories of anarchism imply an order of a very strict and symmetrical kind, but they maintain that such order can be achieved by cooperation. Anarchism must not be confused with nihilism (a purely negative and destructive activity directed against society); anarchism is essentially a pacifist movement.

Religious anarchism, claimed by many anarchists to be exemplified in the early organization of the Christian church, has found expression in the social philosophy of the Russian writer Tolstoy and the Indian nationalist Gandhi. The growth of political anarchism may be traced through the British Romantic writers William Godwin and Shelley to the 1848 revolutionaries P J ◊Proudhon in France and the Russian ◊Bakunin, who had a strong following in Europe.

The theory of anarchism is expressed in the works of the Russian revolutionary ◊Kropotkin.

Anastasia 1901–1918. Russian Grand Duchess, youngest daughter of ◊Nicholas II. During the Russian Revolution she was presumed shot with her parents by the Bolsheviks after the Revolution of 1917, but it has been alleged that Anastasia escaped. Those who claimed her identity included Anna Anderson (1902–1984). Alleged by some detractors to be a Pole, Franziska Schanzkowski, she was rescued from a Berlin canal 1920. The German Federal Supreme Court found no proof of her claim 1970.

anastomosis in medicine, a connection between two vessels (usually blood vessels) in the body. Surgical anastomosis involves the deliberate joining of two vessels or hollow parts of an organ; for example, when part of the intestine has been removed and the remaining free ends are brought together and stitched.

Anatolia (Turkish *Anadolu*) alternate name for Turkey-in-Asia.

anatomy the study of the structure of the body and its component parts, especially the ◊human body, as distinguished from physiology, which is the study of bodily functions.

Herophilus of Chalcedon (about 300 BC) is regarded as the founder of anatomy. In the 2nd century AD, the Graeco-Roman physician Galen produced an account of anatomy that was the only source of anatomical knowledge until *On the Working of the Human Body* 1543 by Andreas Vesalius. In 1628, William Harvey published his demonstration of the circulation of the blood. Following the invention of the microscope, the Italian Malpighi and the Dutch Leeuwenhoek were able to found the study of ◊histology. In 1747, Albinus (1697–1770), with the help of the artist Wandelaar (1691–1759), produced the most exact account of the bones and muscles, and in 1757–65 Albrecht von Haller gave the most complete and exact description of the organs that had yet appeared. Among the anatomical writers of the early 19th century are the surgeon Charles Bell (1774–1842), Jonas Quain (1796–1865), and Henry Gray (1825–1861). Later in the century came stain techniques for microscopic examination, and the method of mechanically cutting very thin sections of stained tissues (using X rays; see ◊radiography). Radiographic anatomy has been one of the triumphs of the 20th century, which has also been marked by immense activity in embryological investigation.

Anaximander 610–c. 547 BC. Greek astronomer and philosopher. He is thought to have been the first to determine solstices and equinoxes, to have invented the sundial, and to have produced the first geographical map. He believed that the universe originated as a formless mass (*apeiron*, "indefinite") containing within itself the contraries of hot and cold, and wet and dry, from which land, sea, and air were formed out of the union and separation of these opposites.

ancestor worship religious rituals and beliefs oriented toward deceased members of a family or group. Adherents believe that the souls of the dead remain involved in this world and are capable of influencing current events.

Anchises in Classical mythology, a member of the Trojan royal family, loved by the goddess ◊Aphrodite. Their son ◊Aeneas rescued his father on the fall of ◊Troy and carried him from the burning city on his shoulders. The story forms an episode in ◊Virgil's *Aeneid*.

Anchorage port and largest city of Alaska, at the head of Cook Inlet; population (1990) 226,338. Established 1918, Anchorage is an important center of administration, communication, and commerce. Oil and gas extraction and fish canning are also important to the local economy, as are two nearby US military bases, Fort Richardson and Elmendorf Air Force Base. Alaska Pacific University and a branch of the University of Alaska are here. The Fur Rendezvous winter carnival is an annual event. The 1964 earthquake that killed 114 people was the most powerful in North American recorded history—8.4 on the Richter scale.

anchovy small fish *Engraulis encrasicholus* of the ◊herring family. It is fished extensively, being abundant in the Mediterranean, and is also found on the Atlantic coast of Europe and in the Black Sea. It grows to 8in/20 cm.

Pungently flavored, it is processed into fish pastes and essences, and used as a garnish, rather than eaten fresh.

ancien régime the old order; the feudal, absolute monarchy in France before the French Revolution 1789.

ancient art art of prehistoric cultures and the ancient civilizations around the Mediterranean that predate the Classical world of Greece and Rome: for example, Sumerian and Aegean art.

Artifacts range from simple relics of the Paleolithic period, such as pebbles carved with symbolic figures, to the sophisticated art forms of ancient Egypt and Assyria: for example, mural paintings, sculpture, and jewelry.

Paleolithic art The earliest surviving artifacts that qualify as art are mainly from Europe, dating from approximately 30,000 to 10,000 BC. This was a period of hunter-gatherer cultures. Items that survive are small sculptures, such as the *Willendorf Venus* (Kunsthistorisches Museum, Vienna) carved from a small stone and simply painted, and symbolic sculptures carved in ivory. The later cave paintings of Lascaux in France and Altamira in Spain depict realistic animals – bison, bulls, horses, and deer—and a few human figures. The animals are highly colored and painted in profile, sometimes with lively and sinuous outlines.

Neolithic art The Neolithic began in the Near East c. 10,000 BC and the earliest art includes ceramic vessels, human and animal figures, and beads used for necklaces. In Europe the period 4,000–2,400 BC produced great megaliths, such as Carnac in France and Stonehenge in Britain, and decorated ceramics, including pots and figurines—the pots sometimes covered in geometric ornament, heralding the later ornamental art of the Celts. The Near Eastern tradition developed into three related circummediterraneum traditions: Egyptian, Sumerian, and Anatolian/S European, which became Aegean.

Ancient Mariner, The Rime of the a poem by Samuel Taylor Coleridge, published 1798, describing the curse that falls upon a mariner and his ship when he shoots an albatross.

Ancona Italian town and naval base on the Adriatic Sea, capital of Marche region; population (1988) 104,000. It has a Romanesque cathedral and a former palace of the popes.

Andalusia (Spanish *Andalucía*) fertile autonomous region of S Spain, including the provinces of Almería, Cádiz, Córdoba, Granada, Huelva, Jaén, Málaga, and Seville; area 33,698 sq mi/87,300 sq km; population (1986) 6,876,000. Málaga, Cádiz, and Algeciras are the chief ports and industrial centers. The Costa del Sol on the S coast has many tourist resorts, including Marbella and Torremolinos.

Andalusia has Moorish architecture, having been under Muslim rule 8th–15th centuries.

andalusite aluminum silicate, Al_2SiO_5, a white to pinkish mineral crystallizing as square-or rhomb-based prisms. It is common in metamorphic rocks formed from clay sediments under low pressure conditions. Andalusite, kyanite, and sillimanite are all polymorphs of Al_2SiO_5.

Andaman and Nicobar Islands two groups of islands in the Bay of Bengal, between India and Myanmar, forming a Union Territory of the Republic of India; area 3,204 sq mi/8,300 sq km; population (1981) 188,000. The economy is based on fishing, timber, rubber, fruit, and rice.

Andean Group (Spanish *Grupo Andino*) South American organization aimed at economic and social cooperation between member states. It was established under the Treaty of Cartagena 1969, by Bolivia, Chile, Colombia, Ecuador, and Peru; Venezuela joined 1973, but Chile withdrew 1976. The organization is based in Lima, Peru.

Andean Indian any indigenous inhabitant of the Andes range in South America, stretching from Ecuador to Peru to Chile, and including both the coast and the highlands. Many Andean civilizations developed in this region from local fishing–hunting–farming societies—all of which predated the ◊Inca, who consolidated the entire region, and ruled from about 1200 to the 1530s, when the Spanish arrived and conquered. The earliest pan-Andean civilization was the Chavin, about 1200–800 BC, which was followed by large and important coastal city-states, such as the Mochica, the Chimú, the Nazca, and the Paracas. The region was dominated by the Tiahuanaco when the Inca started to expand, took them and outlying peoples into their empire, and imposed the Quechua language on all. It is now spoken by over 10 million people and is a member of the Andean-Equatorial family.

Andersen Hans Christian 1805–1875. Danish writer. His fairy tales such as "The Ugly Duckling," "The Emperor's New Clothes," and "The Snow Queen," gained him international fame and have been translated into many languages.

Andersen was born the son of a shoemaker in Odense, Fyn. His first children's stories were published in 1835. Some are based on folklore; others are original. His other works include the novel *The Improvisatore* 1845, romances, and an autobiography *Mit livs eventyr*/*The Tale of My Life*.

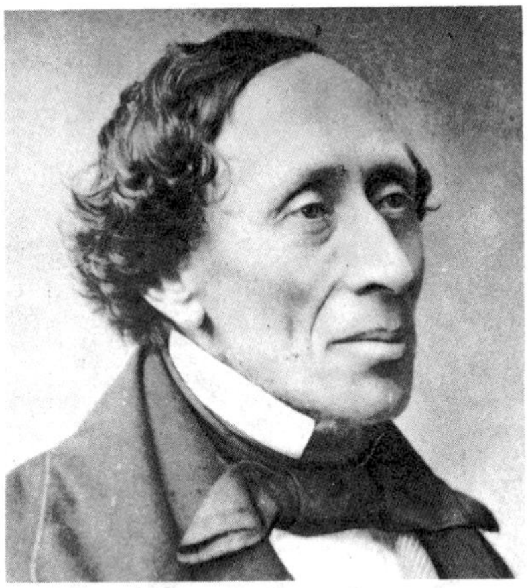

Andersen *The Danish writer Hans Christian Andersen. He was admired by Charles Dickens, whom he visited in 1857.*

Anderson city in E central Indiana, NE of Indianapolis; seat of Madison county. The city's industries produce automobile accessories and paper products; population (1990) 59,459.

Anderson Carl David 1905– . US physicist who discovered the positron (the electron's antiparticle) 1932; he shared a Nobel Prize 1936.

Anderson Marian 1902– . US contralto, whose voice was remarkable for its range and richness.

She toured Europe 1930, but in 1939 she was barred from singing at Constitution Hall, Washington, DC, because she was black. In 1955 she sang at the Metropolitan Opera, the first black singer to appear there. In 1958 she was appointed an alternate delegate to the United Nations.

Following her bar from Constitution Hall, Eleanor Roosevelt and others organized a concert at the Lincoln Memorial; it was attended by 75,000 people.

Anderson Maxwell 1888–1959 US playwright, noted for *What Price Glory?* 1924, written with Laurence Stallings, a realistic portrayal of the American soldier in action during World War I. Anderson followed this with numerous other plays, many in the form of verse tragedies, including *Elizabeth the Queen* 1930, *Winterset* 1935, and *Anne of the Thousand Days* 1948. He won a Pulitzer prize for his comedic prose satire *Both Your Houses*. Most of his plays had moral and social problems as themes..

Anderson Sherwood 1876–1941. US writer, a member of the Chicago Group, who was encouraged by Theodore Dreiser and Carl Sandburg. He was best known for his sensitive, experimental, and poetic novels of the desperation of small-town Midwestern life, such as in his most noted work, *Winesburg, Ohio* 1919.

Born in Camden, Ohio, Anderson joined the army at age 17 and then worked in a factory before leaving his wife and job and going to Chicago. His works include *Windy McPherson's Son* 1916, *Poor White* 1920, *Dark Laughter* 1925, *Hello Towns* 1929, and *Puzzled America* 1935. He also is known for his short-story collections and autobiographical works.

Andes the great mountain system or *cordillera* that forms the western fringe of South America, extending through some 67° of latitude and the republics of Colombia, Venezuela, Ecuador, Peru, Bolivia, Chile, and Argentina. The mountains exceed 12,000 ft/3,600 m for half their length of 4,000 mi/6,500 km.

Geologically speaking, the Andes are new mountains, having attained their present height by vertical upheaval of the entire strip of the Earth's crust as recently as the latter part of the Tertiary era and the Quaternary. But they have been greatly affected by weathering. Rivers have cut profound gorges, and glaciers have produced characteristic valleys. The majority of the individual mountains are volcanic; some are still active. The whole system may be divided into two almost parallel ranges. The southernmost extremity is Cape Horn, but the range extends into the sea and forms islands. Among the highest peaks are Cotopaxi and Chimborazo in Ecuador, Cerro de Pasco and Misti in Peru, Illampu and Illimani in Bolivia, Aconcagua (the highest mountain in the New World) in Argentina, and Ojos del Salado in Chile. Andean mineral resources include gold, silver, tin, tungsten, bismuth, vanadium, copper, and lead. Difficult communications make mining expensive. Transport for a long time was

Andorra
Principality of
(Principat d'Andorra)

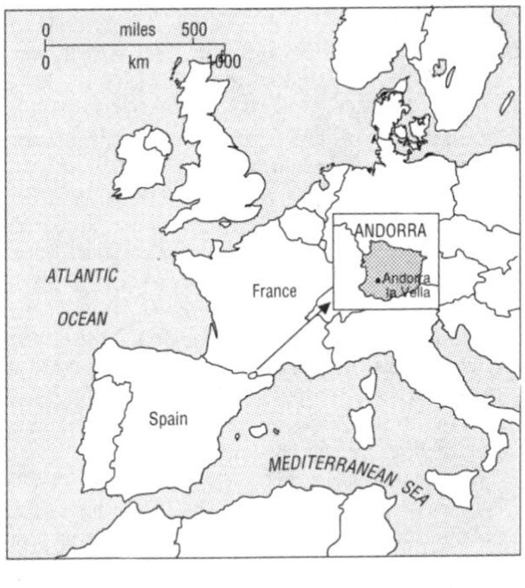

0 miles 500
0 km 1000
ANDORRA
Andorra la Vella
ATLANTIC OCEAN
France
Spain
MEDITERRANEAN SEA

area 181 sq mi/468 sq km
capital Andorra-la-Vella
cities Les Escaldes
physical mountainous, with narrow valleys
features the E Pyrenees, Valira River
heads of state Joan Marti y Alanis (bishop of Seo de Urgel, Spain) and François Mitterrand (president of France)
head of government Josep Pintat Solens from 1986
political system feudal coprincipality
political parties Andorran Democratic Party
exports main industries tourism and smuggling; tobacco
currency French franc
population (1990) 51,000 (30% Andorrans, 61% Spanish, 6% French)
language Catalan (official); Spanish, French
religion Roman Catholic
literacy 100% (1987)
GDP $300 mn (1985)
chronology
1278 Treaty signed making Spanish bishop and French count joint rulers of Andorra (through marriage the king of France later inherited the count's right).
1970 Extension of franchise to third-generation women and second-generation men.
1976 First political organization (Democratic Party of Andorra) formed
1977 Franchise extended to first-generation Andorrans.
1981 First prime minister appointed by General Council.
1982 With the appointment of an Executive Council, executive and legislative powers were separated.
1991 Representatives of the ruling co-princes set timetable for writing the state's first constitution.

chiefly by pack animals, but air transport has greatly reduced difficulties of communications. Three railroads cross the Andes from Valparaiso to Buenos Aires, Antofagasta to Salta, and Antofagasta via Uyuni to Asunción. New roads are being built, including the ◊Pan-American Highway. The majority of the sparse population is dependent on agriculture, the nature and products of which vary with the natural environment. Newcomers to the Andean plateau, which includes Lake ◊Titicaca, suffer from *puna*, mountain sickness, but indigenous peoples have hearts and lungs adapted to altitude.

andesite a volcanic igneous rock, intermediate in silica content between rhyolite and basalt. It is characterized by a large quantity of the feldspar ◊minerals, giving it a light color. Andesite erupts from volcanoes at destructive plate margins (where one plate of the earth's surface moves beneath another; see ◊plate tectonics), including the Andes, from which it gets its name.

Andhra Pradesh state in E central India
area 106,845 sq mi/276,700 sq km
capital Hyderabad
cities Secunderabad
products rice, sugar cane, tobacco, groundnuts, cotton
population (1981) 53,404,000
language Telugu, Urdu, Tamil
history formed 1953 from the Telegu-speaking areas of Madras, and enlarged 1956 from the former Hyderabad state.

Andorra landlocked country in the E Pyrenees, bounded N by France and S by Spain.
government Andorra has no formal constitution and the government is based on its feudal origins. Although administratively independent, it has no individual international status, its joint heads of state being the bishop of Urgel in Spain and the president of France. They are represented by permanent delegates, the vicar general of the Urgel diocese, and the prefect of the French *département* of Pyrenées-Orientales. There is a general council of the villages, consisting of four people from each of the seven parishes, elected by Andorran citizens for a four-year term. The council submits motions and proposals to the permanent delegates for approval.

Until 1982 the general council elected an official called the First Syndic to act as its chief executive, but in that year an executive council was appointed, headed by a prime minister. This introduced a separation between legislative and executive powers and was an important step toward a more constitutional form of government. For the time being, reforms are dependent on the two Co-princes, through their representatives.
history Co-princes have ruled Andorra since 1278. Until 1970 only third-generation Andorran males had the vote. Now the franchise extends to all first-generation Andorrans of foreign parentage aged 28 or over. The electorate is small in relation to the total population, up to 70% of which consists of foreign residents who are demanding political and nationality rights. Immigration, controlled by a quota system, is restricted to French and Spanish nationals intending to work in Andorra. Since 1980 there have been signs of a fragile, but growing, democracy. There are loose political groupings but no direct party representation on the General Council. A technically illegal political organization, the Democratic Party of Andorra, may provide the basis for a future democratic system.

Representatives of the ruling coprinces set a timetable in April 1991 for writing the state's first constitution.

Andrássy Gyula, Count Andrássy 1823–1890. Hungarian revolutionary and statesman who supported the Dual Monarchy of Austro-Hungary 1867 and was Hungary's first constitutional prime minister 1867–71. He became foreign minister of the Austro-Hungarian Empire 1871–79 and tried to halt Russian expansion into the Balkans.

Andrea del Sarto *Draped kneeling figure in red chalk, attributed to Andrea del Sarto.*

André Carl 1935– . US sculptor, a Minimalist, who uses industrial materials to affirm basic formal and esthetic principles. His *Equivalent VIII* 1976, an arrangement of bricks in Palladian proportion (Tate Gallery, London) was much criticized.

André John 1751–1780. British army major in the American Revolution, with whom Benedict ◊Arnold plotted the surrender of ◊West Point. André was caught by Washington's army, tried, and hanged as a spy.

Andrea del Sarto (Andrea d'Agnola) 1486–1531. Italian Renaissance painter active in Florence, one of the finest portraitists and religious painters of his time. His style is serene and noble, characteristic of High Renaissance art.

He trained under Piero de Cosimo and others but was chiefly influenced by ◊Masaccio and ◊Michelangelo. In 1518 he went to work for Francis I in France and returned to Italy in 1519 with funds to enlarge the royal French art collection; he spent it on a house for himself and never went back. His pupils included Pontormo and Vasari. Del Sarto was the foremost painter in Florence after about 1510, along with Fra Bartolommeo, although he was gradually superseded by the emerging Mannerists during the 1520s. Apart from portraits, such as *A Young Man* (National Gallery, London), he painted many religious works, including the *Madonna of the Harpies* (Uffizi, Florence), an example of Classical beauty reminiscent of Raphael. He painted frescoes at Sta Annunziata and the Chiostro dello Scalzo, both in Florence.

Andreas Capellanus Latin name for André le Chapelain.

André le Chapelain 12th century. French priest and author. He wrote *De Arte Honest Amandi/The Art of Virtuous Love*, a seminal work in ◊courtly love literature, at the request of ◊Marie de France, while he was chaplain at her court in Troyes, E France.

Andress Ursula 1936– . Swiss-born US actress specializing in glamour leads. Her international career started with *Dr No* 1962. Other films include *She* 1965, *Casino Royale* 1967, *Red Sun* 1971, and *Clash of the Titans* 1981.

Andrew (full name Andrew Albert Christian Edward) 1960– . Prince of the United Kingdom, Duke of York, second son of Queen Elizabeth II. He married Sarah Ferguson 1986; their daughter, Princess Beatrice, was born in 1988, and their second daughter, Princess Eugenie, was born in 1990. Prince Andrew is a naval helicopter pilot.

Andrews Julie. Adopted name of Julia Elizabeth Wells 1935– . British-born US singer and actress. A child performer with her mother and stepfather in British music halls, she first appeared in the US in the Broadway production *The Boy Friend* 1954. She was the original Eliza Doolittle in *My Fair Lady* 1956. In 1960 she appeared in Lerner and Loewe's *Camelot* on Broadway. Her films include *The Americanization of Emily* 1963, *Mary Poppins* 1964, *The Sound of Music* 1965, *'10'* 1980, and *Victor/Victoria* 1982.

Andrew, St New Testament apostle, martyred on an X-shaped cross (St Andrew's cross). He is the patron saint of Scotland. Feast day Nov 30.

A native of Bethsaida, he was Simon Peter's brother. With Peter, James, and John, who worked with him as fishermen at Capernaum, he formed the inner circle of Jesus' 12 disciples. According to tradition, he went with John to Ephesus, preached in Scythia, and was crucified at Patras.

Andreyev Leonid Nicolaievich 1871–1919. Russian author. Many of his works show an obsession with death and madness, including the symbolic drama *Life of Man* 1907, the melodrama *He Who Gets Slapped* 1915, and the novels *Red Laugh* 1904 and *S.O.S.* 1919 published in Finland, where he fled after the Russian Revolution.

Andrić Ivo 1892–1974. Yugoslavian novelist and nationalist. He became a diplomat, and was ambassador to Berlin 1940. *Na Drini Ćuprija/The Bridge on the Drina* 1945 is an epic history of a small Bosnian town. Nobel Prize 1961.

He was a member of the Young Bosnia organization (another member of which shot the heir to the Austrian throne 1914), and spent World War I in an internment camp because of his political views.

Androcles traditionally, a Roman slave who fled from a cruel master into the African desert, where he encountered and withdrew a thorn from the paw of a crippled lion. Recaptured and sentenced to combat a lion in the arena, he found his adversary was his old friend. The emperor Tiberius was said to have freed them both.

androecium the male part of a flower, comprising a number of ◊stamens.

androgen general name for any male sex hormone, of which ◊testosterone is the most important. They are all ◊steroids and are principally involved in the production of male ◊secondary sexual characters (such as facial hair in humans).

Andromache in Greek mythology, the faithful wife of Hector and mother of Astyanax. After the fall of Troy she was awarded to Neoptolemus, Achilles' son; she later married a Trojan seer called Helenus. Andromache is the heroine of Homer's ◊*Iliad* and the subject of a play by Euripides.

Andromache tragedy by Euripides, first produced about 426 BC. Hermione, wife of Neoptolemus, seeks revenge on Andromache, her husband's lover, whom she blames for her own childlessness, but fails in her attempt to kill Andromache and her son. Neoptolemus is murdered by Orestes, a former suitor of Hermione.

Andromeda in Greek mythology, an Ethiopian princess chained to a rock as a sacrifice to a sea monster. She was rescued by ◊Perseus, who married her.

Andromeda a major constellation of the northern hemisphere, visible in autumn. Its main feature is the Andromeda galaxy. The star Alpha Andromedae forms one corner of the Square of Pegasus. It is named after the princess of Greek mythology.

Andromeda galaxy galaxy 2.2 million light-years away from Earth in the constellation Andromeda and the most distant object visible to the naked eye. It is the largest member of the ◊Local Group of galaxies. Like the Milky Way, it is a spiral orbited by several companion galaxies but contains about twice as many stars. It is about 200,000 light-years across.

Andropov Yuri 1914–1984. Soviet communist politician, president of the USSR 1983–84. As chief of the KGB 1967–82, he established a reputation for efficiently suppressing dissent.

Andropov was politically active from the 1930s.

anechoic chamber *The anechoic room at the Building Research Centre of the UK Department of the Environment at Watford.*

His part in quelling the Hungarian national uprising 1956, when he was Soviet ambassador, brought him into the Communist Party secretariat 1962 as a specialist on E European affairs. He became a member of the Politburo 1973 and succeeded Brezhnev as party general secretary 1982. Elected president in 1983, he instituted economic reforms.

anechoic chamber a room designed to be of high sound absorbency. All surfaces inside the chamber are covered by sound-absorbent materials such as rubber.

The walls are often covered with inward-facing pyramids of rubber, to minimize reflections. It is used for experiments in ◊acoustics and for testing audio equipment.

anemia condition caused by a shortage of hemoglobin, the oxygen-carrying component of red blood cells. The main symptoms are fatigue, pallor, breathlessness, palpitations, and poor resistance to infection. Treatment depends on the cause.

Anemia arises either from abnormal loss or defective production of hemoglobin. Excessive loss occurs, for instance, with chronic slow bleeding or with accelerated destruction or ◊hemolysis, of red blood cells. Defective production may be due to iron deficiency or malnutrition, certain blood diseases (sickle-cell disease and thalassemia), chronic infection, kidney disease, or certain kinds of poisoning. Untreated anemia taxes the heart and may prove fatal.

anemone any plant of the genus *Anemone* of the buttercup family Ranunculaceae. The function of petals is performed by its sepals. The garden anemone *A. coronaria* is white, blue, red, or purple.

The white or lavender-tinged wood anemone *A. quinquefolia* grows in open woods, flowering in spring.

anemophily a type of ◊pollination in which the pollen is carried on the wind. Anemophilous flowers are usually unscented, have either very reduced petals and sepals or lack them altogether, and do not produce nectar. In some species they are borne in ◊catkins. Male and female reproductive structures are commonly found in separate flowers. The male flowers have numerous exposed stamens, often on long filaments; the female flowers have long, often branched, feathery stigmas.

Many wind-pollinated plants, such as hazel *Corylus americana*, bear their flowers before the leaves to facilitate the free transport of pollen. Since air movements are random, vast amounts of pollen are needed: a single birch catkin, for example, may produce over 5 million pollen grains.

anemometer a device for measuring wind speed and liquid flow. A cup-type anemometer consists of cups at the ends of arms, which rotate when the wind blows. The speed of rotation indicates the wind speed. Vane-type anemometers have vanes, like a small windmill or propeller, that rotate when the wind blows. Pressure-tube anemometers use the pressure generated by the wind to indicate speed. The wind blowing into or across a tube develops a pressure, proportional to the wind speed, that is measured by a manometer or pressure gauge. Hot-wire anemometers work on the principle that the rate at which heat is transferred from a hot wire to the surrounding air is a measure of the air speed. Wind speed is determined by measuring either the electric current required to maintain a hot wire at a constant temperature, or the variation of resistance while a constant current is maintained.

aneroid a kind of ◊barometer.

anesthetic drug that produces loss of sensation or consciousness; the resulting state is anesthesia, in which the patient is insensitive to stimuli. Anesthesia may also happen as a result of nerve disorder.

Ever since the first successful operation in 1846 on a patient rendered unconscious by ether, advances have been aimed at increasing safety and control. Sedatives may be given before the anesthetic to make the process easier. Level and duration of unconsciousness are managed precisely. Where general anesthesia may be inappropriate (for example, in childbirth, for a small procedure, or in the elderly), many other techniques are available. A topical substance may be applied to the skin or tissue surface; a local agent may be injected into the tissues under the skin in the area to be treated; or a regional block of sensation may be achieved by injection into a nerve. Spinal anesthetic, such as epidural, is injected into the tissues surrounding the spinal cord, producing loss of feeling in the lower part of the body.

Less than one in 5,000 patients aged 20–40 may become sensitized to anesthetics as a result of previously having undergone operations. Provided this is noticed promptly by the anesthetist, no ill effects should ensue.

Aneto, Pico highest peak of the Pyrenees mountains, rising to 11,052 ft/3,400 m in the Spanish province of Huesca.

aneurysm a weakening in the wall of an artery, causing it to balloon outward, with the risk of rupture and serious, often fatal, blood loss. If detected in time and accessible, some aneurysms can be excised.

Angad 1504–1552. Indian religious leader, second guru (teacher) of Sikhism 1539–52, succeeding Nanak. He popularized the alphabet known as Gurmukhi, in which the Sikh scriptures are written.

angel (Greek *angelos*, messenger) in Jewish, Christian, and Muslim belief, a supernatural being intermediate between God and humans. The Christian hierarchy has nine orders: Seraphim, Cherubim, Thrones (who contemplate God and reflect his glory), Dominations, Virtues, Powers (who regulate the stars and the universe), Principalities, Archangels, and Angels (who minister to humanity). In traditional Catholic belief every human being has a guardian angel. The existence of angels was reasserted by the Pope in 1986.

angel dust popular name for the anesthetic ◊phencyclidine.

Angel Falls highest waterfalls in the New World, on the river Caroní in the tropical rainforest of Bolívar Region, Venezuela; total height 3,210 ft/978 m. Named after the aviator and prospector James Angel who flew over the falls and crash-landed nearby 1935.

angelfish name for a number of unrelated fishes. The freshwater angelfish, genus *Pterophyllum*, of South America, is a tall, side-to-side flattened fish with a striped body, up to 10 in/26 cm long, but usually smaller in captivity. The angelfish or

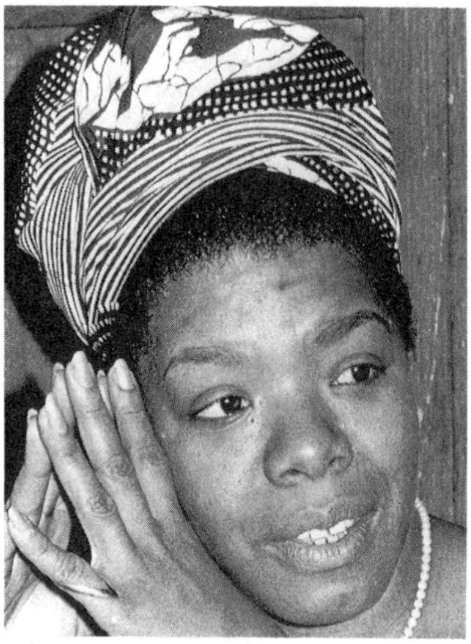

Angelou *US writer Maya Angelou.*

monkfish, of the genus *Squatina* is a bottom-living shark up to 6 ft/1.8 m long with a body flattened from top to bottom. The marine angelfishes, *Pomacanthus* and others, are long narrow-bodied fish with spiny fins, often brilliantly colored, up to 2 ft/60 cm long, living around coral reefs in the tropics.

angelica any plant of the genus *Angelica* of the carrot family Umbelliferae. Mostly Eurasian in distribution, they are tall, perennial herbs with divided leaves and clusters of white or greenish flowers. The roots and fruits have long been used in cooking and for medicinal purposes.

Angelico Fra (Guido di Pietro) c. 1400–1455. Italian painter of religious scenes, active in Florence. He was a monk and painted a series of frescoes at the monastery of San Marco, Florence, begun after 1436. He also produced several altarpieces in a simple style.

Fra Angelico joined the Dominican order about 1420. After his novitiate, he resumed a career as a painter of religious images and altarpieces, many of which have small predella scenes beneath them, depicting events in the life of a saint. The central images of the paintings are highly decorated with pastel colors and gold-leaf designs, while the predella scenes are often lively and relatively unsophisticated. There is a similar simplicity to his frescoes in the cells at San Marco, which are principally devotional works.

Fra Angelico's later fresco sequences, *Scenes from the Life of Christ* (Orvieto Cathedral) and *Scenes from the Lives of SS Stephen and Lawrence* 1440s (chapel of Nicholas V, Vatican Palace), are more elaborate.

Angell Norman 1872–1967. British writer on politics and economics. In 1910 he acquired an international reputation with his book *The Great Illusion*, in which he maintained that any war must prove ruinous to the victors as well as to the vanquished. Nobel Peace Prize 1933.

Angelou Maya (born Marguerite Johnson) 1928– US novelist, poet, playwright, and short-story writer. Her powerful autobiographical works, *I Know Why the Caged Bird Sings* 1970 and its three sequels, tell of the struggles toward physical and spiritual liberation of a black woman growing up in the South.

Anger Kenneth 1932– . US avant-garde filmmaker, brought up in Hollywood. His films, which dispense with conventional narrative, often use homosexual iconography and a personal form of mysticism. They include *Fireworks* 1947, *Scorpio Rising* 1964, and *Lucifer Rising* 1973.

Angers ancient French town, capital of Maine-et-Loire *département*, on the river Maine; population (1982) 196,000. Products include electrical machinery and Cointreau liqueur. It has a 12th–13th century cathedral and castle and was formerly the capital of the duchy and province of Anjou.

Angevin relating to the reigns of the English kings Henry II, and Richard I (also known, with the later English kings up to Richard III, as the Plantagenets). Angevin derives from Anjou, the region in France controlled by English kings at this time. The Angevin Empire comprised the territories (including England) that belonged to the Anjou dynasty.

angina or ***angina pectoris*** severe pain in the chest due to impaired blood supply to the heart muscle because a coronary artery is narrowed.

angiography technique for X-raying major blood vessels. A radiopaque dye is injected into the bloodstream so that the suspect vessel is clearly silhouetted on the X-ray film.

angiosperm flowering plant in which the seeds are enclosed within an ovary, which ripens to a fruit. Angiosperms are divided into ◊monocotyledons (single seed leaf in the embryo) and ◊dicotyledons (two seed leaves in the embryo). They include the majority of flowers, herbs, grasses, and trees except conifers.

Angkor the site of the ancient capital of the Khmer Empire in NW Cambodia, N of Tonle Sap. The remains date mainly from the 10th–12th centuries AD, and comprise temples originally dedicated to the Hindu gods, shrines associated with Theravāda Buddhism, and royal palaces. Many are grouped within the enclosure called Angkor Thom, but the great temple of Angkor Wat (early 12th century) lies outside. Angkor was abandoned in the 15th century, and the ruins were overgrown by jungle and not adequately described until 1863. Buildings on the site suffered damage during the civil war 1970–75.

Angle member of Germanic tribe that invaded Britain in the 5th century; see ◊Anglo-Saxon.

angle in geometry, an amount of rotation. By definition, an angle is a pair of rays (half-lines) that share a common endpoint but do not lie on the same line. Angles are measured in ◊degrees (°) or ◊radians, and are classified generally by their degree measures. Acute angles are less than 90°; right angles are exactly 90°; obtuse angles are greater than 90° but less than 180°; reflex angles are greater than 180° but less than 360°.

No angle is classified as having a measure of 180°, as by definition such an "angle" is actually a straight line.

angler any of an order of fishes Lophiiformes, with flattened body and broad head and jaws. Many species have small, plantlike tufts on their skin. These act as camouflage for the fish as it waits, either floating among seaweed or lying on the sea bottom, twitching the enlarged tip of the thread-like first ray of its dorsal fin to entice prey.

There are over 200 species of angler fish, living in both deep and shallow water in temperate and tropical seas. The males of some species have become so small that they live as parasites on the females.

Anglesey (Welsh *Ynys Môn*) island off the NW coast of Wales; area 278 sq mi/720 sq km; population (1981) 67,000. It is separated from the mainland by the Menai Straits, which are crossed by the Britannia tubular railroad bridge and Telford's suspension bridge, built 1819–26 but since rebuilt. It is a vacation resort with rich fauna (notably bird life) and flora, and many buildings and relics of historic interest. The ancient granary of Wales, Anglesey now has industries such as toy-making, electrical goods, and bromine extraction from the sea. Holyhead is the principal port city; Beaumaris was the county town until the county of Anglesey was merged into Gwynedd 1974.

Anglo- a combining language form with several related meanings. In *Anglo-Saxon* it refers to the Angles, a Germanic people who invaded Britain in the 5th to 7th centuries. In *Anglo-Welsh* it refers to England or the English. In *Anglo-American* it may refer either to England and the English or, commonly but less accurately, to Britain and the British (as in "*Anglo-American* relations"); it may also refer to the English language (as in "*Anglo-American* speech"); or to the Anglo-Saxon heritage in US society (as in WASP, white *Anglo-Saxon* Protestant).

Anglo-Irish Agreement or ***Hillsborough Agreement*** concord reached 1985 between the UK and Irish premiers, Margaret Thatcher and Garret FitzGerald. One sign of the improved relations between the two countries was increased cooperation between police and security forces across the border with Northern Ireland. The pact also gave the Irish Republic a greater voice in the conduct of Northern Ireland's affairs. However, the agreement was rejected by Northern Ireland Unionists as a step toward renunciation of British sovereignty. In March 1988 talks led to further strengthening of the agreement.

Anglo-Irish relations the political relations between England and Ireland. See ◊Ireland, Northern and ◊Ireland, Republic of.

Anglo-Saxon one of the several Germanic invaders (Angles, Saxons, and Jutes) who conquered much of Britain between the 5th and 7th centuries. After the conquest a number of kingdoms were set up, commonly referred to as the Heptarchy; these were united in the early 9th century under the overlordship of Wessex. The Norman invasion 1066 brought Anglo-Saxon rule to an end.

The Jutes probably came from the Rhineland and not, as was formerly believed, from Jutland. The Angles and Saxons came from Schleswig-Holstein, and may have united before invading. There was probably considerable intermarriage with the Romanized Celts of ancient Britain, although the latter's language and civilization almost disappeared. The English-speaking peoples of Britain, Canada, Australia, New Zealand, and the US are often referred to today as Anglo-Saxons, but the term is inaccurate, since the Welsh, Scots, and Irish are mainly of Celtic or Norse descent, and by the 1980s fewer than 15% of Americans were of British descent.

Anglo-Saxon art the painting and sculpture of England from the 7th century to 1066. Sculpted crosses and ivories, manuscript painting, and gold and enamel jewelry survive. The relics of the Sutton Hoo ship burial, 7th century, and the *Lindisfarne Gospels*, about 690 (both British Museum, London), have typical Celtic ornamental patterns, but in manuscripts of southern England a different style emerged in the 9th century, with delicate, lively pen-and-ink figures and heavily decorative foliage borders.

Anglo-Saxon Chronicle a history of England from the Roman invasion to the 11th century, in the form of a series of chronicles written in Old English by monks, begun in the 9th century (during the reign of King Alfred), and continuing to the 12th century.

The Chronicle, comprising seven different manuscripts, forms a unique record of early English history and of the development of Old English prose up to its final stages in the year 1154, by which date it had been superseded by Middle English.

Anglo-Saxon language group of dialects spoken by the Anglo-Saxon peoples who, in the 5th to 7th centuries, invaded and settled in Britain (in what became England and Lowland Scotland). Anglo-Saxon is traditionally known as Old English. See ◊English language.

Angola country in SW Africa, bounded W by the Atlantic ocean, N and NE by Zaïre, E by Zambia, and S by Namibia.

government The 1975 constitution, amended 1976 and 1980, created a one-party "People's Republic," with political power held by the People's Movement for the Liberation of Angola–Workers' Party (MPLA-PT). The president, elected by the congress of MPLA-PT, chooses

Angola
People's Republic of
(República Popular de Angola)

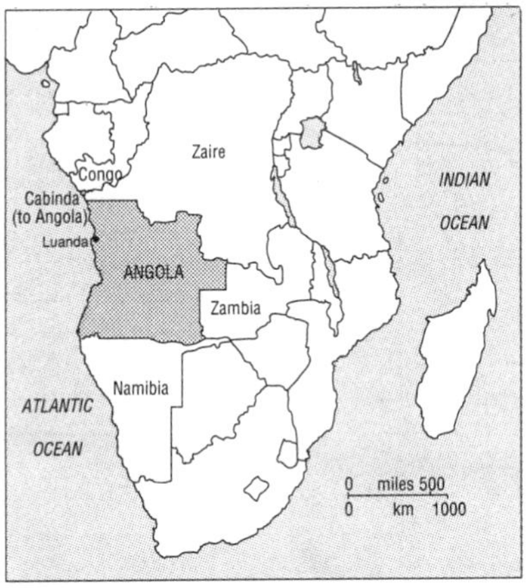
Zaire
Congo
Cabinda
(to Angola)
Luanda
ANGOLA
Zambia
Namibia
INDIAN
OCEAN
ATLANTIC
OCEAN
0 miles 500
0 km 1000

area 481,226 sq mi/1,246,700 sq km
capital (and chief port) Luanda
cities Lobito and Benguela, also ports; Huambo, Lubango
physical narrow coastal plain rises to vast interior plateau with rainforest in NW; desert in S
features Cuanza, Cuito, Cubango, and Cunene rivers; Cabinda exclave
head of state and government José Eduardo dos Santos from 1979
political system Socialist republic
political parties People's Movement for the Liberation of Angola–Workers' Party (MPLA–PT), Marxist-Leninist; National Union for the Total Independence of Angola (UNITA)
exports oil, coffee, diamonds, palm oil, sisal, iron ore, fish
currency kwanza
population (1989 est) 9,733,000 (largest ethnic group Ovimbundu); growth rate 2.5% p.a.
life expectancy men 40, women 44
language Portuguese (official); Bantu dialects
religion Roman Catholic 68%, Protestant 20%, animist 12%
literacy 20%
GDP $2.7 bn; $432 per head

chronology
1951 Angola became an overseas territory of Portugal.
1956 First independence movement formed, the People's Movement for the Liberation of Angola (MPLA).
1961 Unsuccessful independence rebellion.
1962 Second nationalist movement formed, the National Front for the Liberation of Angola (FNLA).
1966 Third nationalist movement formed, the National Union for the Total Independence of Angola (UNITA).
1975 Independence achieved from Portugal. Transitional government of independence formed from representatives of MPLA, FNLA, UNITA, and Portuguese government. MPLA supported by USSR and Cuba, FNLA by "nonleft" power groups of southern Africa, and UNITA by Western powers. MPLA proclaimed People's Republic under the presidency of Dr Agostinho Neto. FNLA and UNITA proclaimed People's Democratic Republic of Angola.
1976 MPLA gained control of most of the country. South African troops withdrawn, but Cuban units remained.
1977 MPLA restructured to become the People's Movement for the Liberation of Angola–Workers' Party (MPLA–PT).
1979 Death of Neto, succeeded by José Eduardo dos Santos.
1980 Constitution amended to provide for an elected people's assembly. UNITA guerrillas, aided by South Africa, continued raids against the Luanda government and bases of the South West Africa People's Organization (SWAPO) bases in Angola.
1984 The Lusaka Agreement.
1985 South African forces officially withdrawn.
1986 Further South African raids into Angola. UNITA continuing to receive South African support.
1988 Peace treaty, providing for the withdrawal of all foreign troops, signed with South Africa and Cuba.
1989 Cease-fire agreed with UNITA broke down and guerrilla activity restarted.
1990 Peace offer by rebels. Return to multiparty politics promised.
1991 Peace agreement signed, civil war between MPLA–PT and UNITA officially ended. Amnesty for all political prisoners.

and chairs the council of ministers and is commander-in-chief of the armed forces. There is a 223-member people's assembly, 20 of whom are nominated by MPLA-PT and the rest elected by electoral colleges of "loyal" citizens.

history Angola became a Portuguese colony in 1491 and an Overseas Territory of Portugal in 1951. In 1956 a movement for complete independence was established, the MPLA, based originally in the Congo. This was followed by the formation of two other nationalist movements, the National Front for the Liberation of Angola (FNLA) and the National Union for the Total Independence of Angola (UNITA). War for independence from Portugal broke out in 1961, involving all the factions, with MPLA supported by Socialist and communist states, UNITA helped by the Western powers and FNLA backed by the "nonleft" power groups of southern Africa.

Three months of civil war followed the granting of full independence in 1975, with MPLA and UNITA the main contestants and foreign mercenaries and South African forces helping FNLA. By 1975 MPLA, with the help of mainly Cuban forces, controlled most of the country and had established the People's Republic of Angola in Luanda. Agostinho Neto, the MPLA leader, became its first president. FNLA and UNITA had, in the meantime, proclaimed their own People's Democratic Republic of Angola, based in Nova Lisboa, renamed Huambo.

President Neto died in 1979 and was succeeded by José Eduardo dos Santos, who maintained Neto's links with the Soviet bloc. UNITA guerrillas, supported by South Africa, continued to operate and in 1980–81 South African forces raided Angola to attack bases of the ◊South-West Africa People's Organization (SWAPO), who were fighting for Namibia's independence. Angola supported Namibia's claim but South Africa and the US called for the withdrawal of Cuban troops from Angola as a precondition for South Africa's departure from Namibia.

In 1983 South Africa proposed a complete withdrawal of its forces if Angola could guarantee that the areas vacated would not be filled by Cuban or SWAPO units. In 1984 Angola accepted South Africa's proposals, and a settlement was made (the Lusaka Agreement), whereby a Joint Monitoring Commission (JMC) was set up to oversee South Africa's withdrawal. In 1985 South Africa announced that this was complete and the mandate for the JMC was ended. In 1986 relations between the two countries deteriorated when further South African raids into Angola occurred. UNITA also continued to receive South African support. Despite the securing of a peace treaty with South Africa and Cuba in 1988, guerrilla activity by the UNITA rebels began again in 1989.

In June 1989 a ceasefire was negotiated between the Luanda government and UNITA's Jonas ◊Savimbi. The accord broke down quickly over Savimbi's future role, but he agreed in Sept to adhere to the agreement, reaffirming his commitment in Dec.

In July 1990 rebel forces announced their willingness to sign a peace treaty, and in Oct President dos Santos promised a return to multiparty politics.

In July 1991 the government proclaimed an amnesty for all political prisoners.

Angora earlier form of ◊Ankara, Turkey, which gave its name to the Angora goat (see ◊mohair), and hence to other species of long-haired animal, such as the Angora rabbit (the source of Angora "wool") and the Angora cat.

Angostura former name of ◊Ciudad Bolívar; port in Venezuela.

angostura flavoring prepared from oil distilled from the bitter, aromatic bark of either of two South American trees *Galipea officinalis* or *Cusparia trifoliata* of the rue family.

It is blended with herbs and other flavorings to give angostura bitters, which was first used as a stomach remedy and is now used to season food and fruit, to make a "pink gin," and to prepare other alcoholic drinks.

Angoulême French town, capital of the *département* of Charente, on the Charente river; population (1982) 104,000. It has a cathedral, and a castle and paper mills dating from the 16th century.

Angry Young Men a group of British writers who emerged about 1950 after the creative hiatus that followed World War II. They included Kingsley Amis, John Wain, John Osborne, and Colin Wilson. Also linked to the group were Iris Murdoch and Kenneth Tynan.

angst (German "anxiety") an emotional state of anxiety without a specific cause. In ◊Existentialism, the term refers to general human anxiety at having free will, that is, of being responsible for one's actions.

ångström unit (abbreviation Å) of length equal to 10^{-10} meter or one-hundred-millionth of a centimeter, used for atomic measurements and the wavelengths of ◊electromagnetic radiation. It is named after the Swedish scientist A J Ångström.

Ångström Anders Jonas 1814–1874. Swedish physicist who worked in spectroscopy and solar physics.

Anguilla island in the E Caribbean
area 62 sq mi/160 sq km
capital The Valley
features white coral-sand beaches
exports lobster, salt
population (1988) 7,000
language English, Creole
government from 1982, governor, executive council, and legislative house of assembly (chief minister Emile Gumbs from 1984)
history a British colony from 1650, Anguilla was long associated with ◊St Christopher-Nevis but revolted against alleged domination by the larger island and in 1969 declared itself a republic. A small British force restored order, and Anguilla retained a special position at its own request, since 1980 a separate dependency of the UK.

angular momentum see ◊momentum.

Angus former county and modern district on the E coast of Scotland, merged in 1975 in Tayside region.

Anhui or Anhwei province of E China, watered by the Chang Jiang (Yangtze river)
area 54,000 sq mi/139,900 sq km
capital Hefei
products cereals in the N; cotton, rice, tea in the S
population (1986) 52,170,000.

Anhwei alternate spelling of ◊Anhui.

anhydrous in chemistry, the total absence of water in a chemical compound.

If the water of crystallization is removed from blue crystals of copper (cupric) sulfate ($CuSO^4$), a

Anguilla

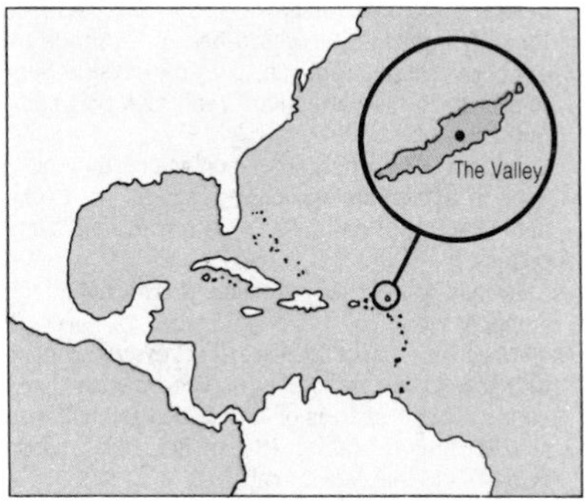
The Valley

animal kingdom

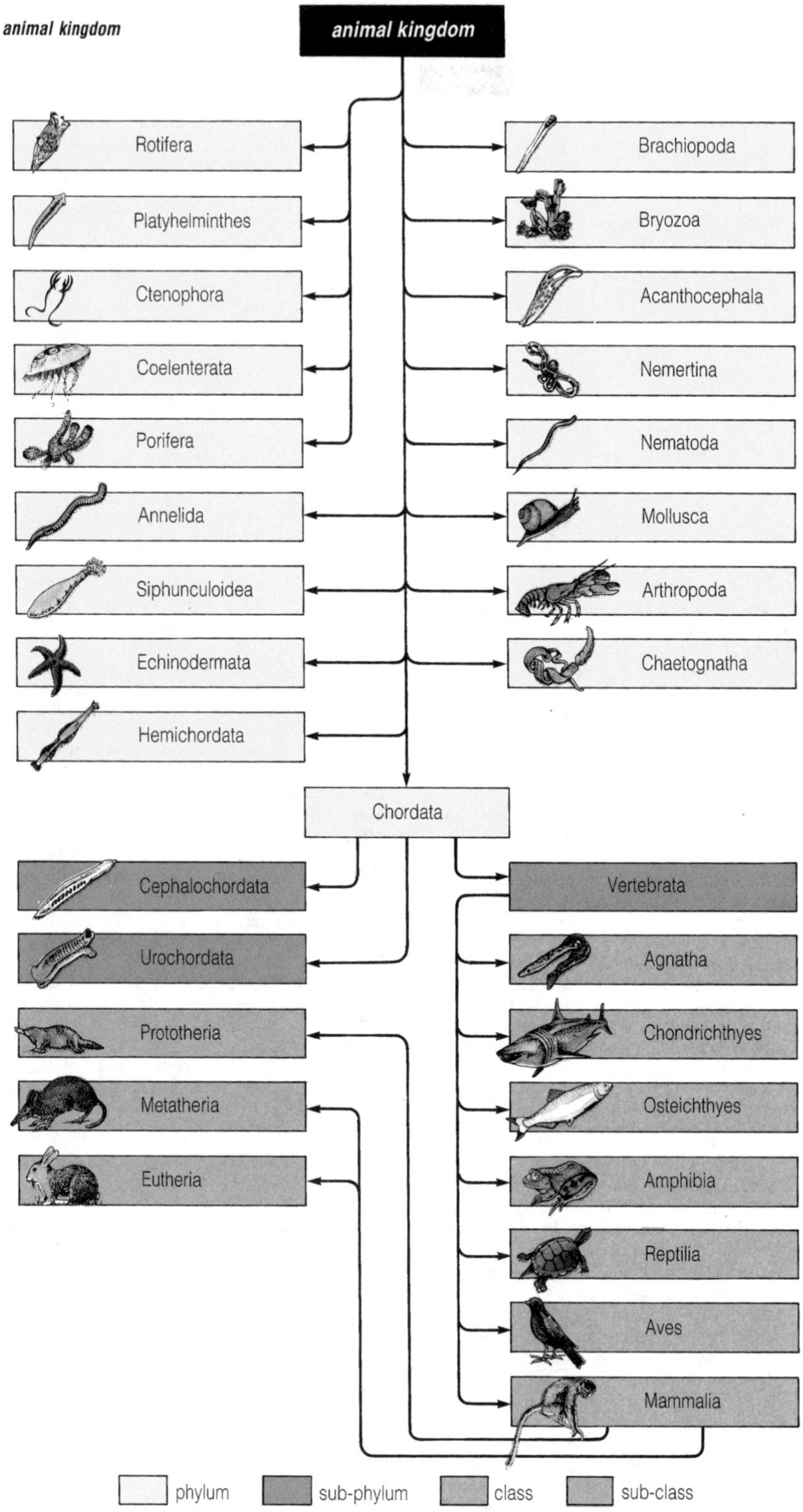
animal kingdom
Rotifera
Platyhelminthes
Ctenophora
Coelenterata
Porifera
Annelida
Siphunculoidea
Echinodermata
Hemichordata
Brachiopoda
Bryozoa
Acanthocephala
Nemertina
Nematoda
Mollusca
Arthropoda
Chaetognatha
Chordata
Cephalochordata
Urochordata
Prototheria
Metatheria
Eutheria
Vertebrata
Agnatha
Chondrichthyes
Osteichthyes
Amphibia
Reptilia
Aves
Mammalia
phylum
sub-phylum
class
sub-class

white powder (anhydrous copper) sulfate results. Liquids from which all traces of water have been removed are also described as being anhydrous.

aniline (Portugese *anil* "indigo") $C_6H_5NH_2$ or phenylamine one of the simplest aromatic chemicals (a substance related to benzene, with its carbon atoms joined in a ring.) When pure, it is a colorless oily liquid; it has a characteristic odor, and turns brown in contact with air. It occurs in coal tar, and is used in the rubber industry and to make drugs and dyes. It is highly poisonous.

It was discovered in 1826, and was originally prepared by the dry distillation of ◊indigo, hence its name.

animal or ***metazoan*** member of the kingdom Animalia, one of the major categories of living things, the science of which is zoology. Animals are all ◊heterotrophs (they obtain their energy from organic substances produced by other organisms); they have ◊eukaryotic cells (the genetic material is contained within a distinct nucleus) bounded by a thin cell membrane rather than the thick cell wall of plants. In the past, it was common to include the single-celled ◊protozoa with the animals, but these are now classified as protists, together with single-celled plants. Thus all animals are multicellular. Most are capable of moving around for at least part of their life cyle.

animal behavior the scientific study of the behavior of animals, either by comparative psychologists (with an interest mainly in the psychological processes involved in the control of behavior) or by ethologists (with an interest in the biological context and relevance of behavior).

animal, domestic or ***domesticated animal*** in general, a tame animal. In agriculture, an animal brought under human control for exploitation of their labor; use of their feathers, hides, or skins; or consumption of their eggs, milk, or meat. Common domestic animals include poultry, cattle (including buffalo), sheep, goats, and pigs. Starting about 10,000 years ago, the domestication of animals has only since World War II led to intensive ◊factory farming.

Increasing numbers of formerly wild species have been domesticated, with stress on scientific breeding for desired characteristics. At least 60% of the world's livestock is in developing countries, but the Third World consumes only 20% of all meat and milk produced. Most domestic animals graze plants that are not edible to humans, although 40% of the world's cereal production becomes animal feed; in the US it is 90%.

animism in psychology and physiology, the view of human personality that attributes human life and behavior to a force distinct from matter.

In religious theory, the conception of a spiritual reality behind the material one: for example, beliefs in the soul as a shadowy duplicate of the body capable of independent activity, both in life and death. In anthropology, the concept of spirits residing in all natural phenomena and objects.

Linked with this last concept is the worship of natural objects such as stones and trees, thought to harbor spirits (naturism); fetishism; and ancestor worship.

anion ion carrying a negative charge, the opposite of cation. During electrolysis, anions in the electrolyte move to the anode (positive electrode).

anise plant *Pimpinella anisum*, of the carrot family Umbelliferae, whose fragrant seeds are used to flavor foods. Aniseed oil is used in cough medicines.

Anjou an old countship and former province in northern France; capital Angers. In 1154 the count of Anjou became king of England as Henry II, but the territory was lost by King John 1204. In 1480 the countship was annexed to the French crown. The *départements* of Maine-et-Loire and part of Indre-et-Loire, Mayenne, and Sarthe cover the area. The people are called Angevins—a name also applied by the English to the ◊Plantagenet kings.

Ankara formerly Angora capital of Turkey; population (1985) 2,252,000. Industries include cement, textiles, and leather products. It replaced Istanbul (then in Allied occupation) as capital 1923.

It has the presidential palace and Grand National Assembly buildings; three universities, including a technical university to serve the whole Middle East; the Atatürk mausoleum on a nearby hilltop; and the largest mosque in Turkey at Kocatepe.

ankh ancient Egyptian symbol (derived from the simplest form of sandal), meaning "eternal life," as in Tut*ankh*amen. It consists of a T-shape surmounted by an oval.

Annaba formerly Bône seaport in Algeria; population (1983) 348,000. The name means "city of jujube trees." There are metallurgical industries, and iron ore and phosphates are exported.

Anna Comnena 1083–after 1148. Byzantine historian, daughter of the emperor ◊Alexius I, who was the historian of her father's reign. After a number of abortive attempts to alter the imperial succession in favor of her husband, Nicephorus Bryennius (c. 1062–1137), she retired to a convent to write her major work, the *Alexiad*. It describes the Byzantine view of public office, as well as the religious and intellectual life of the period.

Anna Karenina a novel by Leo Tolstoy, published 1873–77. It describes a married woman's love affair with Vronski, a young officer, which ends with her suicide.

Annam former country of SE Asia, incorporated in ◊Vietnam 1946 as Central Vietnam. A Bronze Age civilization was flourishing in the area when China conquered it about 214 BC. The Chinese named their conquest An-Nam, "peaceful south." Independent from 1428, Annam signed a treaty with France 1787 and became a French protectorate, part of Indochina 1884. During World War II, Annam was occupied by Japan.

Annapolis seaport and capital of Maryland; population (1990) 33,187. It was named after Princess (later Queen) Anne 1695. The State House, built 1772–80, is the oldest US state capitol in continuous legislative use. It was in session here Nov 1783–June 1784 that ◊Congress received George ◊Washington's resignation as commander-in-chief 1783 and ratified the peace treaty that ended the Revolutionary War. The US Naval Academy is here, and John Paul ◊Jones is buried in the chapel crypt.

Annapurna mountain 26,502 ft/8,075 m in the Himalayas, Nepal. The N face was first climbed by a French expedition (Maurice Herzog) 1950 and the S by a British team 1970.

Ann Arbor city in SE Michigan, W of Dearborn and Detroit, on the Huron river; seat of Washtenaw county. It is a center for medical, aeronautical, nuclear, and chemical research. Site of the University of Michigan 1837; (1990) 109,592.

Anne 1665–1714. Queen of Great Britain and Ireland 1702–14. Second daughter of James, Duke of York, who became James II, and Anne Hyde. She succeeded William III in 1702. Events of her reign include the War of the Spanish Succession, Marlborough's victories at Blenheim, Ramillies, Oudenarde, and Malplaquet, and the union of the English and Scottish parliaments 1707. She was succeeded by George I.

She received a Protestant upbringing, and in 1683 married Prince George of Denmark (1653–1708). Of their many children only one survived infancy, William, Duke of Gloucester (1689–1700). For the greater part of her life Anne was a close friend of Sarah Churchill (1650–1744), wife of John Churchill (1650–1722), afterwards Duke of Marlborough; the Churchills' influence helped lead her to desert her father for her brother-in-law, William of Orange, during the Revolution of 1688, and later to engage in Jacobite intrigues. Her replacement of the Tories by a Whig government 1703–04 was her own act, not due to Churchilian influence. Anne finally broke with the Marlboroughs 1710, when Mrs Masham succeeded the duchess as her favorite, and supported the Tory government of the same year.

Anne (full name Anne Elizabeth Alice Louise) 1950– . Princess of the UK, second child of Queen Elizabeth II, declared Princess Royal 1987. She is an excellent horsewoman, winning a gold medal at the 1976 Olympics, and is actively involved in global charity work, especially for children. In 1973 she married Captain Mark Phillips (1949–), of the Queen's Dragoon Guards; they separated in 1989. Their son Peter (1977–) was the first direct descendant of the Queen not to bear a title. They also have a daughter, Zara (1981–).

annealing process of heating a material (usually glass or metal) for a given time at a given temperature, followed by slow cooling, to increase ductility and strength. It is a common form of ◊heat treatment.

Ductile metals hardened by cold working may be softened by annealing. Thus thick wire may be annealed before being drawn into fine wire. Owing to internal stresses, glass objects made at high temperature can break spontaneously as they cool unless they are annealed. Annealing releases the stresses in a controlled way and, for glass for optical purposes, also improves the optical properties of the glass.

Annecy capital of the *département* of Haute-Savoie, SE France, at the northern end of Lake Annecy; population (1982) 112,600 (conurbation). It has some light industry, including precision instruments, and is a tourist resort.

annelid any segmented worm of the phylum Annelida. Annelids include earthworms, leeches, and marine worms such as lugworms.

They have a distinct head and soft body, which is divided into a number of similar segments shut off from one another internally by membranous partitions, but there are no jointed appendages.

Anne of Austria 1601–1666. Queen of France from 1615 and regent 1643–61. Daughter of Philip III of Spain, she married Louis XIII of France (whose chief minister, Cardinal Richelieu, worked against her). On her husband's death she became regent for their son, Louis XIV, until his majority.

She chose her lover ◊Mazarin as her chief minister.

Anne of Cleves 1515–1557. Fourth wife of ◊Henry VIII of England 1540. She was the daughter of the Duke of Cleves, and was recommended to Henry as a wife by Thomas ◊Cromwell, who wanted an alliance with German Protestantism against the Holy Roman Empire. Henry did not like her looks, had the marriage declared void after six months, pensioned her, and had Cromwell beheaded.

Anne of Denmark 1574–1619. Queen consort of James VI of Scotland (later James I of Great Britain 1603). She was the daughter of Frederick II of Denmark and Norway, and married James 1589. Anne was suspected of Catholic leanings and was notably extravagant.

Annigoni Pietro 1910–1988. Italian portrait painter whose style is influenced by Italian Renaissance portraiture. His sitters included John F. Kennedy and Queen Elizabeth II, 1969 (National Portrait Gallery, London).

annihilation in nuclear physics, a process in which a particle and its ◊antiparticle upon collision create a burst of energy, converting to photons and/or other particles. The energy created is equivalent to the mass of the colliding particles in accordance with the ◊mass–energy equation. For example, an electron and a positron annihilate to produce photons; protons and antiprotons annihilate to produce mesons and photons.

Not all particle–antiparticle interactions result in annihilation; the exception concerns the group called mesons, which are composed of ◊quarks and their antiquarks.

Anniston city in E Alabama, NE of Birmingham; seat of Calhoun county. The site of iron mines, its industries include iron products as well as textiles and chemicals; population (1990) 26,623.

Annobón island in Equatorial Guinea; former name (1973–79) Pagalu; area 7 sq mi/17 sq km. Its inhabitants are descended from slaves of the Portuguese and still speak a form of that language.

anno domini (Latin "in the year of our Lord") in the Christian chronological system, refers to dates since the birth of Jesus, denoted by the letters AD. There is no year 0, so AD 1 follows immediately after the year 1 BC (before Christ). The system became the standard reckoning in the Western world after being adopted by the English historian Bede in the 8th century. The abbreviations CE (Common Era) and BCE (before Common Era) are often used instead by scholars and writers as objective, rather than religious, terms.

The system is based on the calculations made 525 by Dionysius Exiguus, a Scythian monk, but the birth of Jesus should more correctly be placed about 4 BC.

annual plant a plant that completes its life cycle within one year, during which time it germinates, grows to maturity, bears flowers, produces seed and then dies. Examples include the field poppy *Papaver rhoeas* and golden ragwort *Senecio aureus vulgaris*. Among garden plants, some that are described as "annuals" are actually perennials, although usually cultivated as annuals because they cannot survive winter frosts. See also ◊ephemeral, ◊biennial.

annual rings or ***growth rings*** concentric rings visible on the wood of a cut tree trunk or other woody stem. Each ring represents a period of growth when new ◊xylem is laid down to replace tissue being converted into wood (secondary xylem). The wood formed from xylem produced in the spring and early summer has larger and more numerous vessels than the wood formed from xylem produced in autumn when growth is slowing down. The result is a clear boundary between the pale spring wood and the denser, darker autumn wood. Annual rings may be used to estimate the age of the plant (see ◊dendrochronology), although occasionally more than one growth ring is produced in a given year.

Annunciation in the New Testament, the announcement to Mary by the angel Gabriel that she was to be the mother of Christ; the feast of the Annunciation is March 25 (also known as Lady Day).

anode the positive electrode toward which negative particles (anions, electrons) move within a device such as the cells of a battery, electrolytic cells, and diodes.

anodizing process that increases the resistance to ◊corrosion of a metal, such as aluminum, by building up a protective oxide layer on the surface. The natural corrosion resistance of aluminum is provided by a thin film of aluminum oxide; anodizing increases the thickness of this film and thus the corrosion protection.

It is so called because the metal becomes the ◊anode in an electrolytic bath containing a solution of, for example, sulfuric or chromic acid as the ◊electrolyte. During ◊electrolysis oxygen is produced at the anode, where it combines with the metal to form an oxide film.

anomie in the social sciences, a state of "normlessness" created by the breakdown of commonly agreed standards of behavior and morality; the term often refers to situations where the social order appears to have collapsed. The concept was developed by the French sociologist Emile Durkheim.

Durkheim used "anomie" to describe societies in transition during industrialization. The term was adapted by the US sociologist Robert Merton to explain deviance and crime in the US as a result of the disparity between high goals and limited opportunities.

anorexia lack of desire to eat, especially the pathological condition of anorexia nervosa, usually found in adolescent girls and young women, who may be obsessed with the desire to lose weight. Compulsive eating, or ◊bulimia, often accompanies anorexia.

In anorexia nervosa, the patient refuses to eat and finally becomes unable to do so. The result is severe emaciation and, in rare cases, death.

Anouilh Jean 1910–1987. French playwright. His plays, influenced by the Neo-Classical tradition, include *Antigone* 1942, *L'Invitation au château/Ring Round the Moon* 1947, *Colombe* 1950, and *Becket* 1959, about St Thomas à Becket and Henry II.

anoxemia shortage of oxygen in the lungs and tissues. It may be due to breathing air deficient in oxygen (for instance, at high altitude or where there are noxious fumes), disease of the lungs, or some disorder where the oxygen-carrying capacity of the blood is impaired.

anoxia total deprivation of oxygen, a condition that rapidly leads to collapse or death, unless immediately reversed.

Anschluss (German "union") the annexation of Austria with Germany, accomplished by the German chancellor Adolf Hitler March 12, 1938, who had been born an Austrian.

Austria was occupied jointly by the Allies until 1955, when it declared independence as a republic.

Anselm, St c. 1033–1109. Medieval priest and philosopher. Born in Piedmont, he was educated at the abbey of Bec in Normandy, which as an abbot (from 1078) he made a center of scholarship in Europe. He was appointed archbishop of Canterbury by William II of England 1093, but was later forced into exile. He holds an important place in the development of ◊Scholasticism.

Anselm was canonized 1494. In his *Proslogion* he developed the ontological proof of theism, which infers God's existence from our capacity to conceive of a perfect Being. His major work, *Cur deus homo*, treats the subject of the Atonement.

Ansermet Ernest 1883–1969. Swiss conductor with Diaghilev's Russian Ballet 1915–23. In 1918 he founded the Swiss Romande Orchestra, conducting many first performances of works by ◊Stravinsky.

Anshan Chinese city in Liaoning province, 55 mi/89 km SE of Shenyang (Mukden); population (1986) 1,280,000. The iron and steel center started here 1918 was expanded by the Japanese, dismantled by the Russians, and restored by the Communist government of China. It produces 6 million tons of steel annually.

ANSI abbreviation for American National Standards Institution, the US national standards body. It sets official procedures in (among other areas) computing and electronics.

ant insect belonging to the family Formicidae, and to the same order (Hymenoptera) as bees and

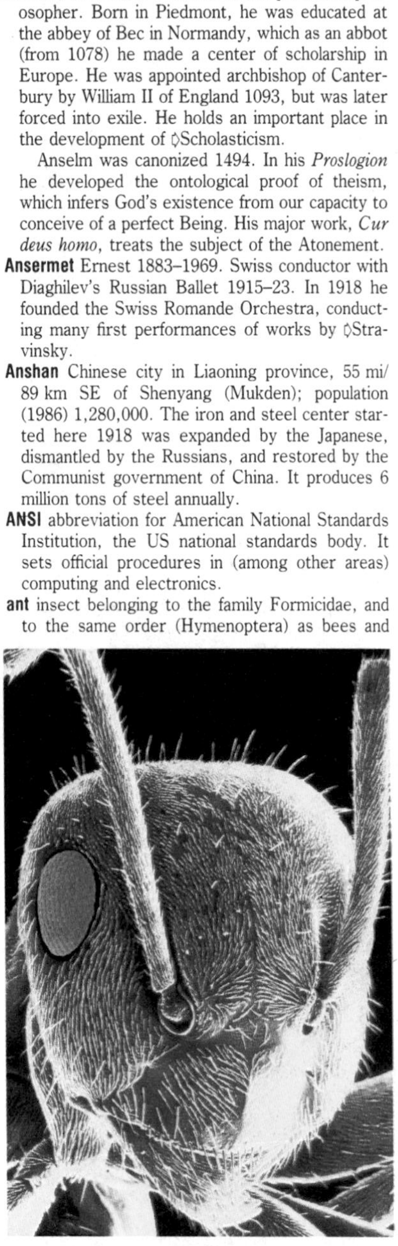

ant Electron-microscope picture of the head of a black garden ant (× 46).

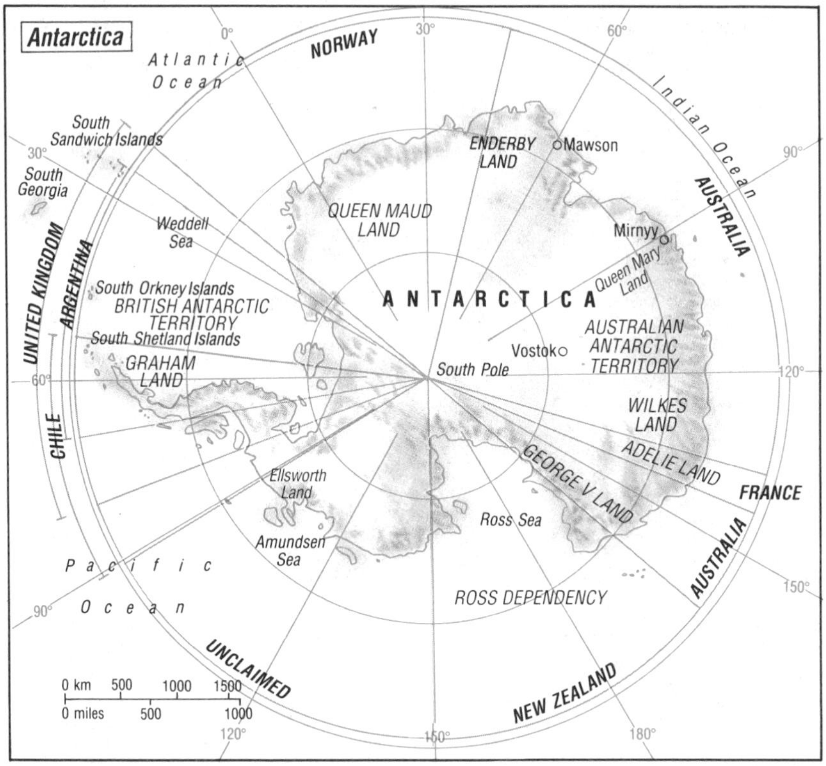

Antarctica
Atlantic Ocean
NORWAY
South Sandwich Islands
South Georgia
Weddell Sea
UNITED KINGDOM
ARGENTINA
South Orkney Islands
BRITISH ANTARCTIC TERRITORY
South Shetland Islands
GRAHAM LAND
CHILE
ENDERBY LAND
Mawson
QUEEN MAUD LAND
Indian Ocean
AUSTRALIA
Mirnyy
Queen Mary Land
A N T A R C T I C A
AUSTRALIAN ANTARCTIC TERRITORY
Vostok
South Pole
WILKES LAND
ADELIE LAND
FRANCE
GEORGE V LAND
Ellsworth Land
Ross Sea
Amundsen Sea
Pacific Ocean
ROSS DEPENDENCY
AUSTRALIA
UNCLAIMED
NEW ZEALAND
0 km 500 1000 1500
0 miles 500 1000
0°
30°
60°
90°
120°
150°
180°

wasps. Ants are characterized by a conspicuous "waist" and elbowed antennae. About 10,000 different species are known; all are social in habit, and all construct nests of various kinds. Ants are found in all parts of the world, except the polar regions. It is estimated that there are about 10 million billion ants.

Ant behavior is complex, but it serves the colony rather than the individual. Ants find their way by light patterns, gravity (special sense organs are located in the joints of their legs), and chemical trails between food areas and the nest.

Communities include workers, sterile wingless females, often all alike, although in some species large-headed "soldiers" are differentiated; fertile females, fewer in number and usually winged; and males, also winged and smaller than their consorts, with whom they leave the nest on a nuptial flight at certain times of the year. After aerial mating, the males die, and the fertilized queens lose their wings when they settle, laying eggs to found their own new colonies. The eggs hatch into wormlike larvae, which then pupate in silk cocoons before emerging as adults. Remarkable species include army (South American) and driver (African) ants, which march nomadically in huge columns, devouring even tethered animals in their path; leaf-cutter ants, genus *Atta*, which use pieces of leaf to grow edible fungus in underground "gardens"; weaver ants, genus *Oecophylla*, which use their silk-producing larvae as living shuttles to bind the edges of leaves together to form the nest; Eurasian robber ants, *Formica sanguinea*, which raid nests of another ant, *Formica fusca*, for pupae, then use the adults as "slaves" when they hatch; and honey ants, in which some workers serve as distended honey stores. In some species, "warfare" is conducted. Others are pastoralists, tending herds of ◊aphids and collecting a sweet secretion ("honeydew") from them.

Antabuse proprietary name for disulfiram, a synthetic chemical used in the treatment of alcoholism. When taken, it produces unpleasant side effects with alcohol, such as nausea, headache, palpitations, and collapse. The "Antabuse effect" is produced coincidentally by certain antibiotics.

antacid any substance that neutralizes stomach acid, such as sodium bicarbonate or magnesium hydroxide ("milk of magnesia"). Antacids are weak ◊bases, swallowed as solids or emulsions. They may be taken between meals to relieve symptoms of hyperacidity, such as pain, bloating, nausea, and "heartburn." Excessive or prolonged need for antacids should be investigated medically.

antagonistic muscles pair of muscles allowing coordinated movement of the skeletal joints.

The extension of the arm, for example, requires one set of muscles to relax, while another set contracts. The individual components of antagonistic pairs can be classified into ◊extensors and ◊flexors.

Antakya or Hatay city in SE Turkey, site of the ancient ◊Antioch; population (1985) 109,200.

Antalya Mediterranean port on the W coast of Turkey and capital of a province of the same name; population (1985) 258,000. The port trades in agricultural and forest produce.

Antananarivo formerly Tananarive capital of Madagascar, on the interior plateau, with a rail link to Tamatave; population (1986) 703,000.

Antarctica the continent covering the South Pole

area 5,300,000 sq mi/13,727,000 sq km

physical the continent, once part of ◊Gondwanaland, is a vast plateau, of which the highest point is the Vinson Massif in the Ellsworth mountains, 16,866 ft/5,139 m high. The Ross Ice Shelf is formed by several glaciers coalescing in the Ross Sea, and Mount Erebus on Ross Island is the world's southernmost active volcano. There is less than 2 in/50 mm of rainfall a year (less than in the Sahara). Little more than 1% of the land is ice-free, the temperature falling to −100°F/−70°C and below, and in places the ice is 16,000 ft/5,000 m deep, comprising over two-thirds of the world's fresh water. Each annual layer of snow preserves a record of global conditions, and where no melting at the surface of the bedrock has occurred the ice can be a million years old. It covers extensive mineral resources, including iron, coal, and uranium and other strategic metals, as well as oil.

features there are only two species of flowering plants, plus a number of mosses, algae, and fungi. Animal life is restricted to visiting whales, seals,

Antarctic exploration

1773–7	James Cook first sailed in Antarctic seas, but exploration was difficult before the development of iron ships able to withstand ice pressure.
1819–21	Antarctica circumnavigated by Bellingshausen.
1823	James Weddell sailed into the sea named after him.
1841–42	James Ross sighted the Great Ice Barrier named after him.
1895	Borchgrevink was one of the first landing party on the continent.
1898	Borchgrevink's British expedition first wintered in Antarctica.
1901–04	Robert Scott first penetrated the interior of the continent.
1907–08	Ernest Shackleton came within 113 mi/182 km of the Pole.
1911	Roald Amundsen reached the Pole, Dec 14, overland with dogs.
1912	Scott reached the Pole, Jan 18, initially aided by ponies.
1928–29	Richard Byrd made the first flight to the Pole.
1935	Ellsworth first flew across Antarctica.
1957–58	Vivian Fuchs made the first overland crossing.
1959	Soviet expedition from the West Ice Shelf to the Pole.
1959	International Antarctic Treaty suspended all territorial claims, reserving an area south of 60° S latitude for peaceful purposes.
1961–62	Bentley Trench discovered, which suggested that there may be an Atlantic-Pacific link beneath the Continent.
1966–67	Specially protected areas established internationally for animals and plants.
1979	Fossils of apelike humenoids resembling E Africa's Proconsul found 300 mi/500 km from the Pole.
1980	International Convention on the exploitation of resources—oil, gas, fish, and krill.
1982	First circumnavigation of Earth (Sept 2, 1979– Aug 29, 1982) via the Poles by Ranulph Fiennes and Charles Burton (UK).
1990	Longest unmechanized crossing (3,182 mi/6,100 km) completed by a 6-person international team, using only skis and dogs.

and penguins, and other seabirds. Fossils of apes resembling humans have been found.

population settlement limited to scientific research stations with changing personnel.

history in 1988, 33 countries signed the Antarctic Minerals Convention, laying Antarctica open to commercial exploitation. Guidelines on environmental protection were included but regarded as inadequate by environmental pressure groups.

Antarctic Circle an imaginary line that encircles the South Pole at latitude 66° 32′ S. The line encompasses the continent of Antarctica and the Antarctic Ocean.

The region south of this line experiences at least one night during the southern summer during which the sun never sets, and at least one day during the southern winter during which the sun never rises.

Antarctic Ocean popular name for the reaches of the Atlantic, Indian, and Pacific oceans extending S of the Antarctic Circle (66° 32′ S). The term is not used by the International Hydrographic Bureau.

Antarctic Peninsula mountainous peninsula of W Antarctica extending 1,200 mi/1,930 km N toward South America. Originally named *Palmer Land* after a US navigator, Captain Nathaniel Palmer, who was the first to explore the region in 1820. It was claimed by Britain 1832, Argentina 1940, and Chile 1942. Its name was changed to the Antarctic Peninsula in 1964.

Antarctic Treaty agreement signed 1959 between 12 nations with an interest in Antarctica (including Britain); 35 countries were party to it by 1990. It came into force in 1961 for a 30-year period. Its provisions (covering the area south of latitude 60° S) neither accepted nor rejected any nation's territorial claims, but barred any new ones; imposed a ban on military operations and large-scale mineral extraction; and allowed for free exchange of scientific data from bases. Since 1980 the treaty has been extended to conserve marine resources within the larger area bordered by the Antarctic Convergence.

Antares or ***Alpha Scorpii*** brightest star in the constellation Scorpius and the 15th brightest star in the sky. It is a red supergiant several hundred times larger than the Sun, lies about 400 light-years away, and fluctuates slightly in brightness.

anteater mammal of the family Myrmecophagidae, order Edentata, native to Mexico, Central America, and tropical South America. An anteater lives almost entirely on ants and termites. It has toothless jaws, an extensile tongue, and claws for breaking into the nests of its prey.

Species include the giant anteater *Myrmecophaga tridactyla*, about 6 ft/1.8 m long including the tail, the tamandua or collared anteater *Tamandua tetradactyla*, about 3.5 ft/90 cm long, and the silky anteater *Cyclopes didactyla*, about 14 in/35 cm long. The name is also incorrectly applied to the aardvark, the echidna and the pangolin.

antebellum (Latin *ante bellum*, "before the war") in US usage, an adjective referring to the period just before the Civil War (1861–65).

The term "prewar" is used when describing the period before any other war.

antelope any of numerous kinds of even-toed hoofed mammals belonging to the cow family, Bovidae. Most antelopes are lightly built and good runners. They are grazers or browsers, and chew the cud. They range in size from the dik-diks and duikers, only 1 ft/30 cm high, to the eland, which can be 6 ft/1.8 m at the shoulder.

The majority of antelopes are African, including the eland, gnu, kudu, springbok, and waterbuck, although other species live in Asia, including the deserts of Arabia and the Middle East. The pronghorn antelope *Antilocapra americana* of North America belongs to a different family, the Antilocapridae.

antenna in zoology, an appendage ("feeler") on the head. Insects, centipedes, and millipedes each have one pair of antennae but there are two pairs in crustaceans, such as shrimps. In insects the antennae are usually involved with the senses of smell and touch. They are frequently complex structures with large surface areas that increase the ability to detect scents.

antenna in radio and television, another name for ◊aerial.

anterior the front of an organism, usually the part that goes forward first when the animal is moving. The anterior end of the nervous system, over the course of evolution, has developed into a brain with associated receptor organs able to detect stimuli including light and chemicals.

anthelion (Greek "antisun") a kind of solar halo, caused by a reflection from the atmosphere, snow or ice, sometimes appearing at the same altitude as the Sun, but opposite to it.

anteater

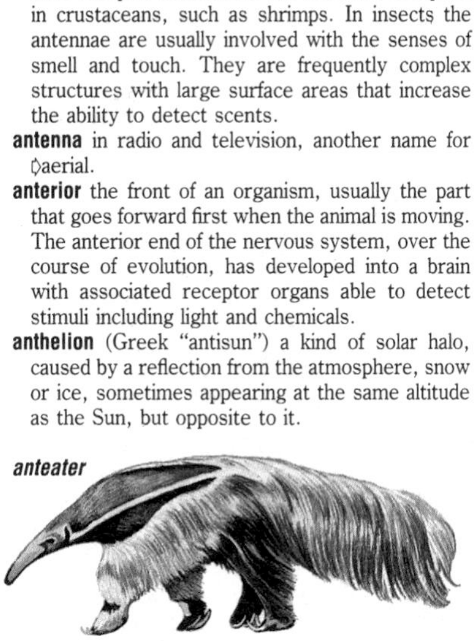

Anthony *American feminist leader Susan B Anthony, who founded the National Woman Suffrage Association in 1869, has been honored with her portrait on a one-dollar US coin.*

anthelmintic a class of drugs effective against a range of intestinal worms.

anther in a flower, the terminal part of a stamen in which the ◊pollen grains are produced. It is usually borne on a slender stalk or filament, and has two lobes, each containing two chambers or pollen sacs within which the pollen is formed.

antheridium an organ producing the male gametes, ◊antherozoids, in algae, bryophytes (mosses and liverworts), and pteridophytes (ferns, club mosses, and horsetails). It may be either single-celled, as in most algae, or multicellular, as in bryophytes and pteridophytes.

antherozoid a motile (or independently moving) male gamete produced by algae, bryophytes (mosses and liverworts), pteridophytes (ferns, club mosses, and horsetails), and some gymnosperms (notably the cycads). Antherozoids are formed in an ◊antheridium and, after being released, swim by means of one or more ◊flagella, to the female gametes. Higher plants have nonmotile male gametes contained within ◊pollen grains.

Anthony Susan B(rownell) 1820–1906. US pioneering campaigner for women's rights who also worked for the antislavery and temperance movements. Her causes included equality of pay for women teachers, married women's property rights, and women's suffrage. In 1869, with Elizabeth Cady ◊Stanton, she founded the National Woman Suffrage Association.

She edited and published a radical women's newspaper, *The Revolution* 1868–70, and worked on the *History of Woman Suffrage* 1881–86. She organized the International Council of Women and founded the International Woman Suffrage Alliance in Berlin 1904. Her profile appears on the 1979 US dollar coin.

Anthony of Padua, St 1195–1231. Portuguese Franciscan preacher who opposed the relaxations introduced into the order. Born in Lisbon, the son of a nobleman, he became an Augustinian monk, but in 1220 joined the Franciscans. Like St Francis, he is said to have preached to animals. He died in Padua, Italy and was canonized in 1232.

Anthony, St c. 251–356. Also known as Anthony of Thebes. Founder of Christian monasticism. Born in Egypt, at the age of 20 he renounced all his possessions and began a hermetic life of study and prayer, later seeking further solitude in a cave in the desert, where he remained for the rest of his life.

In 305 Anthony founded the first cenobitic order, or community of Christians following a rule of life under a superior. Late in his life he went to Alexandria and preached against ◊Arianism. He lived to over 100, and a good deal is known about his life since a biography (by St Athanasius) has survived. Anthony's temptations in the desert were a popular subject in art; he is also often depicted with a pig and a bell.

anthracite (from Greek *anthrax*, "coal") a hard, dense, glossy variety of ◊coal, containing over 90% of fixed carbon and a low percentage of ash and volatile matter, which causes it to burn without flame, smoke, or smell.

Anthracite gives intense heat, but is slow-burning and slow to light; it is therefore unsuitable for use in open fires. Its characteristic composition is thought to be due to the action of bacteria in disintegrating the coal-forming material when it was laid down during the ◊Carboniferous period.

Among the chief sources of anthracite coal are Pennsylvania in the US; S Wales, UK; the Donbas, USSR; and Shanxi province, China.

anthrax cattle and sheep disease occasionally transmitted to humans, usually via infected hides and fleeces. It may develop as black skin pustules or severe pneumonia. Treatment is with antibiotics.

The causative agent is a bacillus (*Bacillus anthracis*).

anthropic principle in science, the idea that "the universe is the way it is because if it were different we would not be here to observe it." The principle arises from the observation that if the laws of science were even slightly different, it would have been impossible for intelligent life to evolve. For example, if the electric charge on the electron were only slightly different, stars would have been unable to burn hydrogen and produce the chemical elements that make up our bodies. Scientists are undecided whether the principle is an insight into the nature of the universe or a piece of circular reasoning.

anthropoid any primate belonging to the suborder Anthropoidea, including monkeys, apes, and humans.

anthropology (Greek *anthropos* "man" and *logos* "discourse") the study of humankind, which developed following 19th-century evolutionary theory to investigate the human species, past and present, physically, socially, and culturally.

The four subdisciplines are physical anthropology, linguistics, cultural anthropology, and archeology.

anthropometry science dealing with the measurement of the human body, particularly stature, body weight, cranial capacity, and length of limbs, in samplings of the populations of living peoples, as well as the remains of buried and fossilized humans.

anthropomorphism the attribution of human characteristics to animals, inanimate objects, or deities. It appears in the mythologies of many cultures and as a literary device in fables and allegories.

anthroposophy system of mystical philosophy developed by Rudolf ◊Steiner, who claimed to possess a power of intuition giving him access to knowledge not attainable by scientific means.

Antibes resort, which includes Juan les Pins, on the French Riviera, in the *département* of Alpes Maritimes; population (1982) 63,248. There is a Picasso collection in the 17th-century castle museum.

antibiotic drug that kills or inhibits the growth of bacteria and fungi. It is derived from living organisms such as fungi or other bacteria, which distinguishes it from other antibacterials.

The earliest antibiotics, the ◊penicillins, came into use from 1941 and were quickly joined by ◊chloramphenicol, the ◊cephalosporins, erythromycins, tetracyclines, and aminoglycosides. A range of broad-spectrum antibiotics, the 4-quinolones, was developed 1989, of which ciprofloxacin was the first. Each class and individual antibiotic acts in a different way and may be effective against either a broad spectrum or a specific type of disease-causing agent. Use of antibiotics has become more selective as side effects, such as toxicity, allergy, and resistance, have become better understood. Bacteria have the ability to develop immunity following repeated or subclinical (insufficient) doses, so more advanced and synthetic antibiotics are continually required to overcome them.

antibody protein molecule produced in the blood by B-lymphocytes (see ◊lymphocyte). Antibodies bind specific foreign agents that invade the body, tagging them for destruction by phagocytes (white blood cells that engulf and destroy invaders) or activating a chemical system that renders them harmless. Each antibody is specific for a particular ◊antigen (the molecular pattern unique to a foreign substance).

anticholinergic any drug that blocks the passage of certain nerve impulses in the ◊central nervous system by inhibiting the production of acetylcholine, a neurotransmitter.

Its wide range of effects makes it an effective component of ◊premedication; it may be put in the eyes before examination or treatment to dilate the pupil and paralyze the muscles of accommodation, or inhaled to relieve constriction of the airways in bronchitis. Tremor and rigidity can be reduced in mild ◊Parkinson's disease. Bladder muscle tone may also be improved in the treatment of urinary frequency. Its usefulness as an ◊antispasmodic is limited by side effects, such as dry mouth, visual disturbances, and urinary retention.

Antichrist in Christian theology, the opponent of Christ, by whom he is finally to be conquered. The idea of conflict between Light and Darkness is present in Persian, Babylonian, and Jewish literature, and it influenced early Christian thought. The Antichrist may be a false messiah, or be connected with false teaching, or be identified with an individual, for example Nero at the time of the persecution of Christians, and the pope and Napoleon in later Christian history.

anticline in geology, a fold in the rocks of the Earth's crust in which the layers or beds bulge upward to form an arch (seldom preserved intact).

The fold of anticline may be undulating or steeply curved. A steplike bend in otherwise gently dipping or horizontal beds is a monocline. The opposite of an anticline is a syncline.

anticoagulant substance that suppresses the formation of ◊blood clots. Common anticoagulants are heparin, produced by the liver and lungs, and derivatives of coumarin. Anticoagulants are used medically in treating heart attacks, for example. They are also produced by blood-feeding animals, such as mosquitoes, leeches, and vampire bats, to keep the victim's blood flowing.

Most anticoagulants prevent the production of thrombin, an enzyme that induces the formation from blood plasma of fibrinogen, to which blood platelets adhere and form clots.

Anti-Comintern Pact (Anti-Communist Pact) agreement signed between Germany and Japan Nov 25, 1936, opposing communism as a menace to peace and order. The pact was signed by Italy 1937 and by Hungary, Spain, and the Japanese puppet state of Manchukuo in 1939. While directed against the USSR, the agreement also had the effect of giving international recognition to Japanese rule in Manchuria.

anticommunism fierce antagonism toward communism linked particularly with right-wing politician Joseph ◊McCarthy's activities in the US during the 1950s. He made numerous unsubstantiated claims that the State Department had been infiltrated by Communist activity, thus triggering a wave of anticommunist hysteria. He did not succeed in identifying any Communists employed by the government.

anticonvulsant any drug used to prevent epileptic seizures (convulsions or fits); see ◊epilepsy.

In many cases, epilepsy can be controlled completely by careful therapy with one agent. Patients should stop or change treatment only under medical supervision.

Anti-Corn Law League in UK history, an extraparliamentary pressure group formed 1838, led by the Liberals ◊Cobden and ◊Bright, which argued for free trade and campaigned successfully against duties on the import of foreign corn to Britain imposed by the ◊Corn Laws, which were repealed 1846.

Formed in Sept 1838 by Manchester industrialists and campaigning on a single issue, the league initiated strategies for popular mobilization and agitation including mass meetings, lecture tours, pamphleteering, opinion polls, and parliamentary lobbying. Reaction by the conservative landed interests was organized with the establishment of the Central Agricultural Protection Society, nicknamed the Anti-League. In June 1846 political pressure, the state of the economy, and the Irish situation prompted Prime Minister ◊Peel to repeal the Corn Laws.

anticyclone an area of high atmospheric pressure caused by descending air, which becomes warm and dry. Winds radiate from a calm center, taking a clockwise direction in the northern hemisphere and an counterclockwise direction in the southern hemisphere. Anticyclones are characterized by clear weather and the absence of rain and violent winds. In summer they bring hot, sunny days and in winter they bring fine, frosty spells, although fog and low cloud are not uncommon. Blocking anticyclones, which prevent the normal air circulation of an area, can cause summer droughts and severe winters.

antidepressant any drug used to relieve symptoms in depressive illness. The two main groups are the tricyclic antidepressants (TCADs) and the monoamine oxidase inhibitors (MAOIs), which act by altering chemicals available to the central nervous system. Both may produce serious side effects and are restricted.

antidiarrheal any substance that controls diarrhea.

Choice of treatment depends on the underlying cause. One group, including opiates, codeine, and atropine, produces constipation by slowing down motility (muscle activity of the intestine wall). Bulking agents, such as vegetable fibers (for example, methylcellulose), absorb fluid. Antibiotics may be appropriate for certain systemic bacterial infections, such as typhoid, salmonella, and enteritis (caused by *Campylobacter* species). Current therapy of acute diarrhea is based on fluid and ◊electrolyte replacement. Chronic diarrhea, a feature of some bowel disorders (for example, Crohn's disease, colitis, celiac disease) may respond to antispasmodics, special diet, and corticosteroids.

antiemetic any substance that counteracts nausea or vomiting.

Antietam, Battle of bloody but indecisive battle of the American Civil War Sept 17, 1862 at Antietam Creek, off the Potomac River. Gen McClellan of the Union blocked the advance of the Confederates under Robert E Lee on Maryland and Washington, DC. This battle persuaded the British not to recognize the Confederacy.

antifreeze substance added to a water-cooling system (for example, that of a car) to prevent it freezing in cold weather. The most common types of antifreeze contain the chemical ethylene ◊glycol, or ($HOCH_2CH_2OH$), an organic alcohol with a freezing point of about 5°F/–15°C.

The addition of this chemical depresses the freezing point of water significantly. A solution containing 33.5% by volume of ethylene glycol will not freeze until about –4°F/–20°C. A 50% solution will not freeze until –31°F/–35°C.

antifungal any drug that acts against fungal infection, such as ringworm and athlete's foot.

antigen any of various specific molecular patterns on the surface of invading foreign agents (such as bacteria, viruses, or pollen grains) that trigger defense responses by the body's ◊immune system. Antibodies (see ◊antibody) bind to antigens. The proteins of incompatible blood groups or tissues also act as antigens, which has to be taken into account in medical procedures such as blood transfusions and organ transplants.

Antigua and Barbuda
State of

USA
ATLANTIC
OCEAN
BARBUDA
St. John's
ANTIGUA
Mexico
Cuba
St Kitts-
Nevis
Montserrat
CARIBBEAN
SEA
Venezuela
PACIFIC
OCEAN
0 miles 500
0 km 1000

area Antigua 108 sq mi/280 sq km, Barbuda 62 sq mi/161 sq km, plus Redonda 0.4 sq mi/1 sq km
capital (and chief port) St John's
cities Codrington (on Barbuda)
physical low-lying tropical islands of limestone and coral with some higher volcanic outcrops; no rivers and low rainfall result in frequent droughts and deforestation
features Antigua is the largest of the Leeward Islands; Redonda is an uninhabited island of volcanic rock rising to 1,000 ft/305 m
head of state Elizabeth II from 1981 represented by governor-general
head of government Vere C Bird from 1981
political system liberal democracy
political parties Antigua Labor Party (ALP), moderate, left-of-center; Progressive Labor Movement (PLM), left-of-center
exports sea-island cotton, rum, lobsters
currency Eastern Caribbean dollar
population (1989) 83,500; growth rate 1.3% p.a.
life expectancy 70 years
language English
religion Christian (mostly Anglican)
literacy 90% (1985)
GDP $173 million (1985); $2,200 per head
chronology
1493 Antigua visited by Christopher Columbus.
1632 Antigua colonized by English settlers.
1667 Treaty of Breda formally ceded Antigua to Britain.
1871–1956 Antigua and Barbuda administered as part of the Leeward Islands Federation.
1967 Antigua and Barbuda became an associated state within the Commonwealth, with full internal independence.
1971 PLM won the general election by defeating the ALP.
1976 PLM called for early independence, but ALP urged caution. ALP won the general election.
1981 Independence from Britain achieved.
1983 Assisted US invasion of Grenada.
1984 ALP won a decisive victory in the general election.
1985 ALP reelected.
1989 Another sweeping general election victory for the ALP.

Antigone in Greek legend, a daughter of Jocasta, by her son ◊Oedipus. She is also the subject of a tragedy by Sophocles.

Antigone tragedy by Sophocles, written about 411 BC. Antigone buries her brother Polyneices, in defiance of the Theban king Creon, but in accordance with the wishes of the gods. Creon imprisons Antigone in a cave, but after a warning that he has defied the gods, he goes to the cave and finds that Antigone has hanged herself.

Antigonus 382–301 BC. A general of Alexander the Great, after whose death in 323 he made himself master of Asia Minor. He was defeated and slain by ◊Seleucus I at the battle of Ipsus.

Antigua and Barbuda country comprising three islands in the eastern Caribbean (Antigua, Barbuda, and uninhabited Redonda).

government Antigua and Barbuda constitute an independent sovereign nation within the ◊Commonwealth, with the British monarch as head of state. The constitution came into effect with independence in 1981. The governor general, representing the British monarch, is appointed on the advice of the Antiguan prime minister, who is chosen by the governor general as the person most likely to have the support of the legislature. The parliament is similar to Britain's, with a prime minister and cabinet answerable to it. It consists of a senate and a house of representatives, each having 17 members. Senators are appointed for a five-year term by the governor general, 11 of them on the advice of the prime minister, four on the advice of the leader of the opposition, one at the governor general's own discretion, and one on the advice of the Barbuda Council, the main instrument for local government. Members of the house of representatives are elected by universal suffrage for a similar term. There are several political parties, the most significant being the Antigua Labor Party (ALP).

history The original inhabitants of Antigua and Barbuda were Carib Indians. The first Europeans to visit Antigua were with Christopher ◊Columbus 1493; although they didn't actually go ashore. He named the island after the church of Santa Maria de la Antigua at Seville. Antigua was first colonized by Britain 1632. In 1685 Charles II leased Barbuda to the Codrington family, who ran a sugar plantation on Antigua. Barbuda was a source of stock and provisions for the plantation and was inhabited almost entirely by black slaves, who used the relatively barren land cooperatively. The Codringtons finally surrendered the lease 1870. Barbuda reverted to the crown in the later 19th century. The Antiguan slaves were freed 1834 but remained poor, totally dependent on the sugar crop market. Between 1860 and 1959 the islands were administered by Britain within a federal system known as the ◊Leeward Islands.

In 1967 Antigua and Barbuda was made an Associated State of the UK and given full internal independence, with Britain retaining responsibility for defense and foreign affairs. Barbuda, with a population of about 1,200 people, started a separatist movement 1969, fearing that Antigua would sell Barbudan land to foreign developers. Projects approved by the central government against the wishes of Barbudans include sand mining and a plan for a toxic-waste disposal site. In the 1971 general election, the Progressive Labor Movement (PLM) won a decisive victory, and its leader, George Walter, replaced Vere Bird, leader of the ALP, as prime minister. The PLM fought the 1976 election on a call for early independence while the ALP urged caution until a firm economic foundation had been laid. The ALP won and in 1978 declared that the country was ready for independence. Opposition from the inhabitants of Barbuda delayed the start of constitutional talks, and the territory eventually became independent as Antigua and Barbuda 1981.

Despite its policy of ◊nonalignment, the ALP government actively assisted the US invasion of ◊Grenada 1983 and went on to win 16 of the 17 seats in the 1984 general election. In the 1989 general election Bird and the ALP won a sweeping victory, but in 1990 his regime was tarnished by the accusation that his son, a cabinet minister, was involved in illegal arms deals.

antihistamine any substance that counteracts the effects of ◊histamine. Antihistamines may be nat-

Antilles

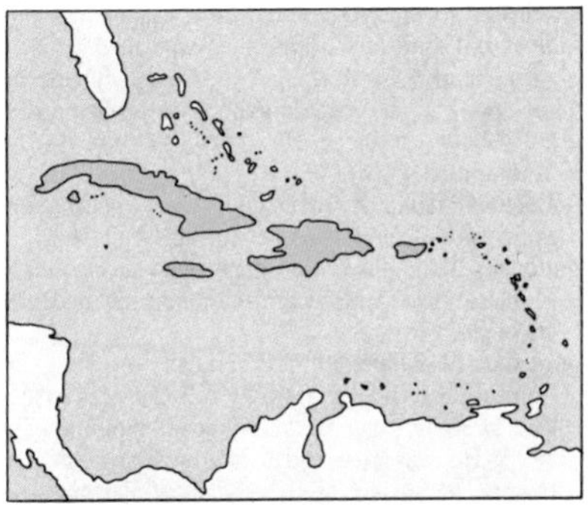

urally produced (such as vitamin C and epinephrin) or synthesized (pseudepinephrin).

H_1 antihistamines are used to relieve allergies, alleviating symptoms such as runny nose, itching, swelling, or asthma. H_2 antihistamines suppress acid production by the stomach, providing treatment for peptic ulcers that often makes surgery unnecessary.

antihypertensive therapy any treatment that controls ◊hypertension. The first step is usually exercise and a change in diet to reduce salt and, if necessary, caloric intake. If further measures are required, a drug regimen may be prescribed.

The regimen may consist of one or a number of substances: a ◊diuretic; a ◊beta-or calcium-channel blocker; a vasodilator (which causes blood vessel walls to expand); and an ACE (angiotensin-converting enzyme) inhibitor, which interrupts a biochemical cycle that increases blood pressure and has a vasodilating effect. Treatment and regular monitoring are continued throughout life.

anti-inflammatory a substance that reduces swelling in soft tissues. Antihistamines relieve allergic reactions; aspirin and ◊NSAIDs are effective in joint and musculoskeletal conditions; rubefacients (counterirritant liniments) ease painful joints, tendons, and muscles; steroids, because of the severe side effects, are only prescribed if other therapy is ineffective, or if a condition is life-threatening. A ◊corticosteroid injection into the affected joint usually gives long-term relief from inflammation.

Anti-Lebanon or ***Antilibanus*** mountain range on the Lebanese-Syrian border, including Mt Hermon, 9,200 ft/2,800 m. It is separated from the Lebanon mountains by the Bekaa valley.

Antilles the whole group of West Indian islands, divided N–S into the Greater Antilles (Cuba, Jamaica, Haiti–Dominican Republic, Puerto Rico) and Lesser Antilles, subdivided into the Leeward Islands (Virgin Islands, St Kitts–Nevis, Antigua and Barbuda, Anguilla, Montserrat, and Guadeloupe) and the Windward Islands (Dominica, Martinique, St Lucia, St Vincent and the Grenadines, Barbados, and Grenada).

antilogarithm or antilog the inverse of ◊logarithm, or the number of which a given number is the logarithm. If $y = \log_a x$, then $x = \text{antilog}_a y$.

antimatter in physics, a form of matter in which all the attributes of elementary particles, such as electrical charge, magnetic moment, and spin, are reversed.

antimony silver-white, brittle, semimetallic element (◊metalloid), symbol Sb (from Latin *stibium*), atomic number 51, atomic weight 121.75. It occurs chiefly in the ore stibnite, and is used to make alloys harder; it is also used in photosensitive substances in color photography, optical electronics, fireproofing, pigment, and medicine. It was used by the ancient Egyptians in a mixture to protect the eyes from flies.

Antioch ancient capital of the Greek kingdom of Syria, founded 300 BC by Seleucus Nicator in memory of his father Antiochus, and famed for its splendor and luxury. Under the Romans it was an early center of Christianity. The site is now occupied by the Turkish town of ◊Antakya.

Antiochus four kings of Commagene (69 BC–AD 72), affiliated to the Seleucid dynasty, including:

Antiochus I king of Commagene, who made peace with Pompey 64 BC, fought on Pompey's side in the civil war, and repelled an attack on Samosata by Mark Antony. He was succeeded by Mithidrates I.

Antiochus II king of Commagene, who succeeded Mithidrates I, and was executed by Augustus.

Antiochus III king of Commagene, who succeeded a Mithidrates. On his death, Commagene became a Roman province.

Antiochus IV Epiphanes 1st century AD. King of Commagene, son of Antiochus III. He was made king in 38 by Caligula, who deposed him immediately. He was restored in 41 by Claudius, and reigned as an ally of Rome against Parthia. He was deposed on suspicion of treason in 72.

Antiochus 13 kings of Syria of the Seléucid dynasty, including:

Antiochus I c. 324–c. 261 BC. King of Syria from 281 BC, son of Seleucus I, one of the generals of Alexander the Great. He earned the title of Antiochus Soter, or Savior, by his defeat of the Gauls in Galatia 278 BC.

Antiochus II c. 286–c. 246 BC. King of Syria 261–246 BC, son of Antiochus I. He was known as Antiochus Theos, the Divine. During his reign the eastern provinces broke away from the Graeco-Macedonian rule and set up native princes. He made peace with Egypt by marrying the daughter of Ptolemy Philadelphus, but was a tyrant among his own people.

Antiochus III the Great c. 241–187 BC. King of Syria from 223 BC, nephew of Antiochus II. He secured a loose suzerainty over Armenia and Parthia 209, overcame Bactria, received the homage of the Indian king of the Kabul valley, and returned by way of the Persian Gulf 204. He took possession of Palestine, entering Jerusalem 198. He crossed into NW Greece, but was decisively defeated by the Romans at Thermopylae 191 and at Magnesia 190. He had to abandon his domains in Anatolia, and was killed by the people of Elymais.

Antiochus IV c. 215–164 BC. King of Syria from 175 BC, known as Antiochus Epiphanes, the Illustrious; second son of Antiochus III. He occupied Jerusalem in about 170 BC, seizing much of the Temple treasure, and instituted worship of the Greek type in the Temple in an attempt to eradicate Judaism. This produced the revolt of the Hebrews under the Maccabees; Antiochus died before he could suppress it.

Antiochus VII Sidetes King of Syria from 138 BC. The last strong ruler of the Seleucid dynasty, he took Jerusalem 134 BC, reducing the Maccabees to subjection, and fought successfully against the Parthians.

Antiochus XIII Asiaticus 1st century BC. King of Syria 69–65 BC, the last of the Seleucid dynasty. During his reign Syria was made a Roman province by Pompey the Great.

antioxidants food ◊additives that prevent oxidation of the unsaturated fats in foods when exposed to air.

Fatty foods, cakes and cookies containing a high proportion of fat or oil can go rancid in storage; fat-soluble vitamins are also destroyed by oxidation. Natural antioxidants such as vitamin E can prevent spoilage, but antioxidants are usually added during food processing as preservatives or to prevent discoloration of cut fruits.

They are limited to 0.02% of the total content by FDA standards.

antiparticle in nuclear physics, a particle corresponding in mass and properties to a given ◊elementary particle but with the opposite electrical charge, magnetic properties, or coupling to other fundamental forces. For example, an electron carries a negative charge whereas its antiparticle, the positron, carries a positive one. When a particle and its antiparticle collide, they destroy each other, in the process called "annihilation," their total energy being converted to lighter particles and/or photons. A substance consisting entirely of antiparticles is known as ◊antimatter.

antiphony in music, a form of composition using widely spaced choirs or groups of instruments to create perspectives in sound. It was developed in 17th-century Venice by Giovanni ◊Gabrieli and his pupil Heinrich ◊Schütz.

antipodes (Greek "opposite feet") places at opposite points on the globe.

The North Pole is antipodal to the South Pole.

antipope a rival claimant to the elected pope for the leadership of the Roman Catholic church, for instance in the Great Schism 1378–1417 when there were rival popes in Rome and Avignon.

antipruritic any skin preparation or drug administered to relieve itching.

antipsychotic or ***neuroleptic*** any drug used to treat the symptoms of severe mental disorder.

antipyretic any drug, such as aspirin, used to reduce fever.

antiracism and antisexism active opposition to ◊racism and ◊sexism; positive action or a set of policies, such as "equal opportunity" can be designed to counteract racism and sexism, often on the part of an official body or an institution, such as a school, a business, or a government agency.

Positive ◊discrimination is used in some government programs to give preference to those groups who have been victims of long-term sexual or racial prejudice.

antirrhinum or ***snapdragon*** any of several plants, genus *Antirrhinum*, in the figwort family Scrophulariaceae. Foxglove and toadflax are relatives. It is native to the Mediterranean region and W North America.

Antirrhinum majus is a common garden flower, native to the Mediterranean.

anti-Semitism literally, prejudice against Semitic people (see ◊Semite), but in practice it has meant prejudice or discrimination against, and persecution of, the Jews as an ethnic group. Historically this was practiced for almost 2,000 years by European Christians. Anti-Semitism was a tenet of Hitler's Germany, and in the Holocaust of 1933–45 about 6 million Jews died in concentration camps and in local extermination ◊pogroms, such as the siege of the Warsaw ghetto. In the USSR and the Eastern bloc, as well as in Islamic nations, anti-Semitism exists and is promulgated by neofascist groups. It is a form of ◊racism.

The destruction of Jerusalem AD 70 led many Jews to settle in Europe and throughout the Roman Empire. In the 4th century Christianity was adopted as the official religion of the Empire, which reinforced existing prejudice against Jews who refused to convert. Anti-Semitism increased in the Middle Ages because of the Crusades and the Inquisition, and legislation was passed forbidding Jews to own land or be members of a craft guild; to earn a living they had to become moneylenders and traders (and were then resented when they prospered). From the 16th century they were forced by law in many cities to live in a separate area, or ghetto.

Late 18th-and early 19th-century liberal thought improved the position of Jews in European society (in the Austro-Hungarian Empire they were allowed to own land) – for example, after the French Revolution the "rights of man" were extended to French Jews 1790 until 19th-century nationalism and the rise of unscientific theories of race instigated new resentments. Anti-Semitism became strong in Austria, France (see ◊Dreyfus), and Germany, and from 1881 pogroms in Poland and Russia caused refugees to flee to the US, where freedom of religion was enshrined in the Constitution, to the UK and other European countries, and to Palestine (see ◊Zionism).

In the 20th century, fascism and the Nazi party's application of racial theories led to organized persecution and genocide. After World War II, the creation of Israel 1948 provoked Palestinian anti-Zionism, backed by the Arab world. Anti-Semitism is still fostered by extreme right-wing groups, such as the National Front in the UK and France, the Neo-Nazis in the US and Germany, and the Palestine Liberation Organization in the Arab nations.

antiseptic any substance that kills or inhibits the growth of microorganisms. The use of antiseptics was pioneered by Joseph ◊Lister. He used carbolic acid (◊phenol), which is a weak antiseptic; substances such as TCP are derived from this.

antispasmodic any drug that reduces motility, the spontaneous action of the muscle walls. Anticholinergics act indirectly by way of the autonomic nervous system, which controls involuntary movement. Other drugs act directly on the smooth muscle to relieve spasm (contraction).

antitrust laws in economics, regulations preventing or restraining trusts, monopolies, or any business practice considered to be unfair or uncompetitive. In the US, antitrust laws prevent mergers and acquisitions that might create a monopoly situation or ones in which restrictive practices might be stimulated.

antitussive any substance administered to suppress a cough. Coughing, however, is an important reflex in clearing secretions from the airways; its suppression is usually unnecessary and possibly harmful, unless damage is being done to tissue during excessive cough spasms.

antiviral any drug that acts against viruses, usually preventing them from multiplying. Most viral infections are not susceptible to antibiotics. Antivirals have been difficult drugs to develop, and do not necessarily cure viral diseases.

antivivisection opposition to vivisection, that is, experiments on living animals, which is practiced in the pharmaceutical and cosmetics industries on the grounds that it may result in discoveries of importance to medical science. Antivivisectionists argue that it is immoral to inflict pain on helpless creatures, and that it is unscientific because results achieved with animals may not be paralleled with human beings.

Antivivisectionist groups, now joined by animal rights activists, sometimes take illegal action to draw attention to their cause.

antler the "horn" of a deer, often branched, and made of bone rather than horn. Antlers, unlike true horns, are shed and regrown each year. Reindeer of both sexes grow them, but in all other types of deer, only the males have antlers.

ant lion larva of one of the insects of the family Myrmeleontidae, order Neuroptera, which traps ants by waiting at the bottom of a pit dug in loose, sandy soil. Ant lions are mainly tropical, but also occur in parts of Europe. They are also found in the US, where they are called doodlebugs.

Antofagasta port of N Chile, capital of a region of the same name. The area of the region is 48,366 sq mi/125,300 sq km; its population (1982) 341,000. The population of the city of Antofagasta is 175,000. Nitrates from the Atacama desert are exported.

Antonello da Messina c. 1430–1479. Italian painter, born in Messina, Sicily, a pioneer of the technique of oil painting, which he is said to have introduced to Italy from N Europe. Flemish influence is reflected in his technique, his use of light, and sometimes in his imagery. Surviving works include bust-length portraits and somber religious paintings.

He visited Venice in the 1470s where his work inspired, among other Venetian painters, the young Giovanni Bellini. *St Jerome in His Study* about 1460 (National Gallery, London) and *A Young Man* 1478 (Staatliche Museen, Berlin) are examples of his work.

Antonescu Ion 1882–1946. Romanian general and politician who headed a pro-German government during World War II and was executed for war crimes in 1946.

Antonine Wall Roman line of fortification built

AD 142–200. The Roman Empire's NW frontier, between the Clyde and Forth rivers, Scotland.

Antoninus Pius 86–AD 161. Roman emperor who had been adopted 138 as Hadrian's heir, and succeeded him later that year. He enjoyed a prosperous reign, during which he built the ◊Antonine Wall. His daughter married ◊Marcus Aurelius Antoninus.

Antonioni Michelangelo 1912– . Italian film director, famous for his subtle presentations of neuroses and personal relationships among the leisured classes. His work includes *L'Avventura* 1960, *Blow Up* 1966, and *The Passenger* 1975.

Antony and Cleopatra a tragedy by William Shakespeare, written and first performed 1607–08. Mark Antony falls in love with the Egyptian queen Cleopatra in Alexandria, but returns to Rome when his wife, Fulvia, dies. He then marries Octavia to heal the rift between her brother Augustus Caesar and himself. Antony returns to Egypt and Cleopatra, but is finally defeated by Augustus. Believing Cleopatra dead, Antony kills himself, and Cleopatra takes her own life rather than surrender to Augustus.

antonymy near or precise oppositeness between or among words. *Good* and *evil* are antonyms, *good* and *bad* are also antonyms, and therefore *evil* and *bad* are synonyms in this context. Antonymy may vary with context and situation: in discussing a color, *dull* and *bright* are antonymous, but when talking about knives and blades, the opposite of *dull* is *sharp* (when it comes to intellect, *bright* and *sharp* are equally used).

Antrim county of Northern Ireland
area 1,092 sq mi/2,830 sq km
cities Belfast (county town), Larne (port)
features Giant's Causeway of natural hexagonal basalt columns, which, in legend, was built to enable the giants to cross between Ireland and Scotland; Antrim borders Lough Neagh, and is separated from Scotland by the 20 mi/32 km wide North Channel
products potatoes, oats, linen, synthetic textiles
population (1981) 642,000.

Antwerp (Flemish *Antwerpen*, French *Anvers*) port in Belgium on the river Scheldt, capital of the province of Antwerp; population (1988) 476,000. One of the world's busiest ports, it has shipbuilding, oil-refining, petrochemical, textile, and diamond-cutting industries. The home of the artist Rubens is preserved, and many of his works are in the Gothic cathedral. The province of Antwerp has an area of 1,119 sq mi/2,900 sq km; population (1987) 1,588,000.

It was not until the 15th century that Antwerp rose to prosperity; from 1500 to 1560 it was the richest port in N Europe. After this Antwerp was beset by religious troubles and the Netherlands revolt against Spain. In 1648 the Treaty of Westphalia gave both shores of the Scheldt estuary to the United Provinces, which closed it to Antwerp trade. The Treaty of Paris 1814 opened the estuary to all nations on payment of a small toll to the Dutch, abandoned 1863. During World War I Antwerp was occupied by Germany Oct 1914–Nov 1918; during World War II, May 1940–Sept 1944.

Anu a Mesopotamian sky-god, commonly joined in a trinity with Enlil and Ea.

Anubis in Egyptian mythology, the jackal-headed god of the dead.

Anuradhapura ancient holy city in Sri Lanka; population (1981) 36,000. It was the capital of the Sinhalese kings of Sri Lanka 5th century BC–8th century AD; rediscovered in the mid-19th century. Sacred in Buddhism it claims a ◊Bo tree descended from the one under which Buddha became enlightened.

anus opening at the end of the alimentary canal that allows undigested food and associated materials to pass out of the animal. It is found in all types of multicellular animal except the coelentorates (sponges) and the platyhelminthes (flat worms), which have a mouth only.

Anvers French form of ◊Antwerp.

anxiety an emotional state of fear or apprehension. Anxiety is a normal response to potentially dangerous situations. Abnormal anxiety can either be free-floating, experienced in a wide range of situations, or it may be phobic, when the sufferer is excessively afraid of an object or situation.

anxiolytic any drug that reduces an anxiety state.

Anyang city in Henan province, E China; population (1980) 430,000. It was the capital of the Shang dynasty (13th–12th centuries BC). Rich archeological remains have been uncovered since the 1930s.

ANZAC acronym from the initials of the Australian and New Zealand Army Corps, applied in general to all troops of both countries serving in World War I and to some extent those in World War II.

Anzhero-Sudzhensk town in W Siberia, USSR, 50 mi/80 km N of Kemerovo in the Kuznetsk basin; population (1985) 110,000. Its chief industry is coal mining.

Anzio, Battle of in World War II, the beachhead invasion of Italy Jan 22–May 23 1944 by Allied troops; failure to use information gained by deciphering German codes (see ◊Ultra) led to Allied troops being stranded temporarily after German attacks. Anzio is a seaport and resort on the W coast of Italy, 33 mi/53 km SE of Rome; population (1984) 25,000. It is the site of the Roman town of Antium and the birthplace of Emperor Nero.

ANZUS acronym for Australia, New Zealand, and the United States (Pacific Security Treaty), a military alliance established 1951. It was replaced 1954 by the ◊Southeast Asia Treaty Organization, (SEATO).

Aomori port at the head of Mutsu Bay, on the N coast of Honshu Island, Japan; 25 mi/40 km NE of Hirosaki; population (1980) 288,000.

aorta the chief ◊artery, the dorsal blood vessel carrying oxygenated blood from the left ventricle of the heart in birds and mammals. It branches to form smaller arteries, which in turn supply all body organs except the lungs. Loss of elasticity in the aorta provides evidence of ◊atherosclerosis, which may lead to heart disease.

In fish a ventral aorta carries deoxygenated blood from the heart to the ◊gills, and the dorsal aorta carries oxygenated blood from the gills to other parts of the body.

Aosta Italian city, 49 mi/79 km NW of Turin; population (1981) 37,200. It is the capital of Valle d'Aosta (French-speaking) autonomous region, and has extensive Roman remains.

Aoun Michel 1935– . Lebanese soldier and Maronite Christian politician, president 1988–90. As commander of the Lebanese army, he was made president without Muslim support, his appointment precipitating a civil war between Christians and Muslims. His unwillingness to accept a 1989 Arab League–sponsored peace agreement increased his isolation until the following year he surrendered to military pressure.

Born in Beirut, he joined the Lebanese army and rose to become, in 1984, its youngest commander. When, in 1988, the Christian and Muslim communities failed to agree on a Maronite successor to the outgoing president Amin Gemayel (as required by the constitution), Gemayel unilaterally appointed Aoun. This precipitated the creation of a rival Muslim government, and, eventually, a civil war. Aoun, dedicated to freeing his country from Syrian domination, became isolated in the presidential palace and staunchly opposed the 1989 peace plan worked out by parliamentarians under the auspices of the Arab League. After defying the government led by Prime Minister Selim al-Hoss in the face of strong military opposition, in Oct 1990 Aoun sought political asylum in the French embassy, and in 1991 he left Lebanon for exile in France.

Aouzu Strip disputed territory 60 mi/100 km wide on the Chad–Libya frontier, occupied by Libya 1973. Lying to the N of the Tibesti massif, the area is rich in uranium and other minerals.

a.p. in physics, abbreviation for atmospheric pressure.

Apache a member of a group of North ◊American Indian peoples, who lived as hunters in the Southwest. They are related to the Navaho, and now number about 10,000, living in reservations in Arizona, SW Oklahoma, and New Mexico. They were known as fierce raiders and horse warriors in the 18th and 19th centuries. Apache also refers to any of several southern Athabaskan languages and dialects spoken by these people.

apartheid (Afrikaans "apartness") the racial-segregation policy of the government of South Africa, which was legislated 1948, when the Afrikaner National Party gained power. Nonwhites (Bantu, colored or mixed, or Indian) do not share full rights of citizenship with the 4.5 million whites (for example, the 23 million black people cannot vote in parliamentary elections), and many public facilities and institutions were until 1990 and, in some cases, remain restricted to the use of one race only; the establishment of ◊Black National States is another manifestation of apartheid.

The term has also been applied to similar movements and other forms of racial separation, for example social or educational, in other parts of the world.

The term "apartheid" was coined in the late 1930s by the South African Bureau for Racial Affairs (Sabra), which called for a policy of "separate development" of the races.

Internally, organizations opposed to apartheid were banned, for example the African National Congress and the United Democratic Front, and leading campaigners for its abolition have been, like Steve Biko, killed or, like Archbishop Tutu, harassed. Anger at the policy has sparked off many uprisings, from ◊Sharpeville 1960 and ◊Soweto 1976 to the Crossroads squatter camps 1986.

Abroad, there are antiapartheid movements in many countries. In 1961 South Africa was forced to withdraw from the Commonwealth because of apartheid; during the 1960s and 1970s there were calls for international ◊sanctions, especially boycotts of sporting and cultural links; and in the 1980s advocates of sanctions extended them into trade and finance.

The South African government's reaction to internal and international pressure was twofold: it abolished some of the more hated apartheid laws (the ban on interracial marriages was lifted 1985 and the pass laws, which restricted the movement of nonwhites, were repealed 1986); and it sought to replace the term "apartheid" with "plural democracy." Under states of emergency 1985 and 1986 it used force to quell internal opposition, and from 1986 there was an official ban on the reporting of it in the media. In Oct 1989 President F W de Klerk permitted antiapartheid demonstrations; the Separate Amenities Act was abolished 1990 and a new constitution promised. In 1990 Nelson Mandela, a leading figure in the African National Congress, was finally released. In 1991 legislation supported by de Klerk dismantled the apartheid system.

apastron in astronomy, the point at which an object traveling in an elliptical orbit around a star is at its furthest from the star. The term is usually applied to the position of the minor component of a ◊binary star in relation to the primary. Its opposite is ◊periastron.

apatite a common calcium phosphate mineral, $Ca_5(PO_4CO_3)_3(F,OH,Cl)$. Apatite has a hexagonal structure and occurs widely in igneous rocks, for example pegmatite, and in contact metamorphic rocks, such as marbles. It is used in the manufacture of fertilizer and as a source of phosphorus. Apatite is the chief constituent of tooth enamel, and it ranks 5 on the ◊Mohs' scale of hardness.

Apatosaurus large plant-eating dinosaur, formerly called *Brontosaurus*, which flourished about 145

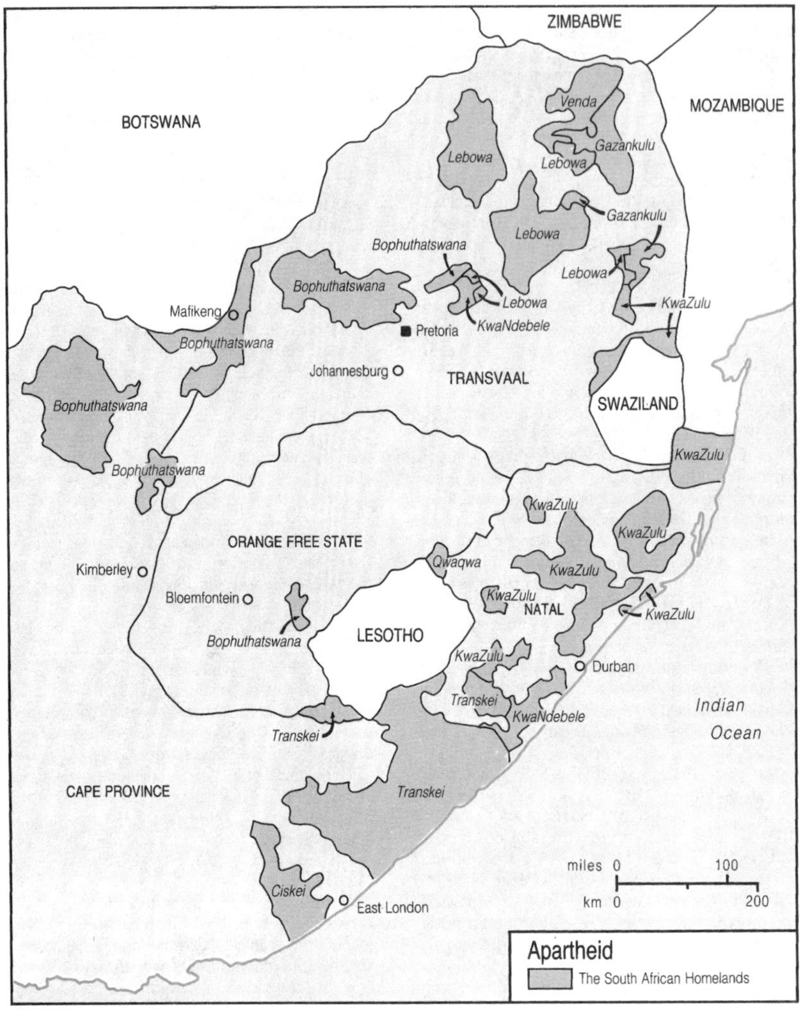
ZIMBABWE
MOZAMBIQUE
BOTSWANA
Venda
Gazankulu
Lebowa
Lebowa
Lebowa
Gazankulu
Lebowa
Bophuthatswana
Bophuthatswana
Lebowa
KwaZulu
Mafikeng
Pretoria
KwaNdebele
Bophuthatswana
Johannesburg
TRANSVAAL
SWAZILAND
Bophuthatswana
KwaZulu
Bophuthatswana
KwaZulu
KwaZulu
ORANGE FREE STATE
Qwaqwa
KwaZulu
Kimberley
Bloemfontein
KwaZulu
NATAL
KwaZulu
Bophuthatswana
LESOTHO
KwaZulu
Durban
Transkei
KwaNdebele
Indian Ocean
Transkei
CAPE PROVINCE
Transkei
Ciskei
East London
miles 0 100
km 0 200
Apartheid
The South African Homelands

million years ago. Up to 69 ft/21 m long and 30 tons in weight, it stood on four elephantlike legs and had a long tail, long neck, and small head. It probably snipped off low-growing vegetation with peglike front teeth, and swallowed it whole to be ground by pebbles in the stomach.

ape ◊primate of the family Pongidae, closely related to humans, including the SE Asian gibbon and orangutan, and the African chimpanzee, and gorilla.

Ape City Yerkes Regional Primate Center, Atlanta, Georgia, where large numbers of primates are kept for physiological and psychological experiment. A major area of research at Ape City is language.

Apeldoorn commercial city in Gelderland province, E central Netherlands. Population (1982) 142,400. Het Loo, which is situated nearby, has been the summer residence of the Dutch royal family since the time of William of Orange.

Apelles 4th century BC. Greek painter, said to have been the greatest in antiquity. He was court painter to Philip of Macedonia and his son Alexander the Great. None of his work survives, only descriptions of his portraits and nude Venuses.

Apennines chain of mountains stretching the length of the Italian peninsula. A continuation of the Maritime Alps, from Genoa it swings across the peninsula to Ancona on the E coast, and then back to the W coast and into the "toe" of Italy. The system is continued over the Strait of Messina along the N Sicilian coast, then across the Mediterranean Sea in a series of islands to the Atlas mountains of N Africa. The highest peak is Gran Sasso d'Italia at 9,560 ft/2,914 m.

Apennines, Lunar mountain range on the Moon, SE of the Sea of Showers.

aperture in photography, an opening in the camera that allows light to pass through the lens to strike the film. Controlled by shutter speed and the iris diaphragm, it can be set mechanically or electronically at various diameters.

aphasia difficulty in speaking, writing, and reading, usually caused by damage to the brain.

aphelion the point at which an object, traveling in an elliptical orbit around the Sun, is at its furthest from the Sun.

aphid any of the family of small insects, Aphididae, in the order Homoptera, that live by sucking sap from plants. There are many species, often adapted to particular plants.

In some stages of their life cycle, wingless females rapidly produce large numbers of live young by ◊parthenogenesis, leading to enormous infestations, and numbers can approach 1 billion per acre/2.5 billion per hectare. They can also cause damage by transmitting viral diseases. Some research suggests, however, that they may help promote fertility in the soil through the waste they secrete, termed "honeydew." Aphids are also known as plant lice, greenflies, or blackflies.

aphrodisiac (from Aphrodite, the Greek goddess of love) any substance that arouses or increases sexual desire.

Sexual activity can be stimulated in humans and animals by drugs affecting the pituitary gland. Preparations commonly sold for the purpose can be dangerous (cantharidin) or useless (rhinoceros horn), and alcohol and marijuana, popularly thought to be effective because they lessen inhibition, often have the opposite effect.

Aphrodite in Greek mythology, the goddess of love (Roman Venus, Phoenician Astarte, Babylonian

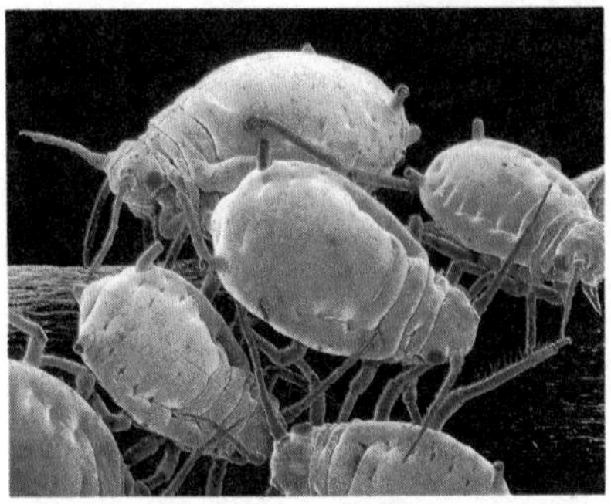

aphid *Electron-microscope picture of a group of wingless aphids (greenflies) feeding on a plant stem (× 32).*

Ishtar); said to be either a daughter of Zeus (in Homer) or sprung from the foam of the sea (in Hesiod). She was the unfaithful wife of Hephaestus, the god of fire, and the mother of Eros.

Apia capital and port of Western ◊Samoa, on the N coast of Upolu island, in the W Pacific; population (1981) 33,000. It was the final home of the writer Robert Louis Stevenson.

Apis ancient Egyptian god with a human body and a bull's head, linked with Osiris (and later merged with him into the Ptolemaic god Serapis); his cult centers were Memphis and Heliopolis, where sacred bulls were mummified.

Apocrypha an appendix to the Old Testament of the Bible, not included in the final Hebrew canon but recognized by Roman Catholics. There are also disputed New Testament texts known as Apocrypha.

apogee the point at which an object, traveling in an elliptical orbit around the Earth, is at its furthest from the Earth.

Apollinaire Guillaume. Adopted name of Guillaume Apollinaire de Kostrowitsky 1880–1918. French poet of aristocratic Polish descent. He was a leader of the avant garde in Parisian literary and artistic circles. His novel *Le Poète assassiné/The Poet Assassinated* 1916, followed by the experimental poems *Alcools/Alcohols* 1913 and *Calligrammes/Word Pictures* 1918, show him as a representative of the Cubist and Futurist movements.

Born in Rome and educated in Monaco, Apollinaire went to Paris in 1898. His work greatly influenced younger French writers, such as Louis ◊Aragon. He coined the word *surrealism* to describe his play *Les Mamelles de Tirésias/The Breasts of Tiresias* 1917.

Aphrodite *An 18th-century cast of the Medici Venus, Greek, 2nd century BC.*

Apollo Marble statue of Apollo (Pergamon Museum, Berlin.) It exemplifies the idealized Greek concept of the beauty of the male form.

Apollinarius of Laodicea Bishop of Laodicea, whose views on the nature of Christ were condemned by the Council of Constantine 381, but who nonetheless laid the foundations for the later ◊Nestorian controversy. Rather than seeing the nature of Jesus as a human and divine soul somehow joined in the person of Christ, he saw Christ as having a divine mind only, and not a human one.

Apollo in Greek and Roman mythology, the god of sun, music, poetry, prophecy, agriculture, and pastoral life, and leader of the Muses. He was the twin child (with Artemis) of Zeus and Leto. Ancient statues show Apollo as the embodiment of the Greek ideal of male beauty.

His chief cult centers were his supposed birthplace on the island of Delos, in the Cyclades, and Delphi.

Apollo asteroid a member of a group of ◊asteroids whose orbits cross that of the Earth. They are named after the first of their kind, Apollo, discovered 1932, and then lost until 1973. Apollo asteroids are so small and faint that they are difficult to see except when close to Earth (Apollo is about 1.2 mi/2 km across).

Apollo asteroids can collide with the Earth from time to time. In 1937 the Apollo asteroid Hermes passed 500,000 mi/800,000 km from Earth, the closest observed approach of any asteroid. A collision with an Apollo asteroid 65 million years ago has been postulated as one of the causes of the extinction of the dinosaurs. A closely related group, the Amor asteroids, come close to Earth but do not cross its orbit.

Apollonius of Perga c. 260–c. 190 BC. Greek mathematician, called "the Great Geometer." In his work *Conic Sections* he showed that a plane intersecting a cone will generate an ellipse, a parabola, or a hyperbola, depending on the angle of intersection. In astronomy, he used a system of circles called epicycles and deferents to explain the motion of the planets; this system, as refined by Ptolemy, was used until the Renaissance.

Apollonius of Rhodes c. 220–180 BC. Greek poet, author of the epic *Argonautica*, which tells the story of Jason and the Argonauts and their quest for the Golden Fleece.

Apollonius of Tyana early 1st century AD. Greek ascetic philosopher of the Neo-Pythagorean school. He traveled in Babylonia and India, where he acquired a wide knowledge of oriental religions and philosophies, and taught at Ephesus. He was said to have had miraculous powers but claimed only that he could see the future.

Apollo of Rhodes the Greek statue of Apollo generally known as the ◊Colossus of Rhodes.

Apollo project US space project to land a person on the Moon, achieved July 20, 1969 when Neil Armstrong was the first to set foot there. He was accompanied on the Moon surface by Col Edwin E Aldrin Jr; Michael Collins remained at the orbiting command controls.

The program was announced 1961 by President Kennedy. The world's most powerful rocket, *Saturn V*, was built to launch the Apollo spacecraft, which carried three astronauts. When the spacecraft was in orbit around the Moon, two astronauts would descend to the surface in a lunar module to take samples of rock and set up experiments that would send data back to Earth. The first Apollo mission carrying a crew, *Apollo 7*, Oct 1968, was a test flight in orbit around the Earth. After three other preparatory flights *Apollo 11* made the first lunar landing. Five more crewed landings followed, the last 1972. The total cost of the program was over $24 billion.

Apollo project Edwin Aldrin landed on the Moon on July 20, 1969, with Neil Armstrong. The two took samples of lunar rocks and brought them back to Earth in Apollo II, *which had been controlled by Michael Collins during the first human landing on the Moon. The project had been eight years in the making by the US National Aeronautics and Space Administration (NASA).*

Apollo–Soyuz test project joint US–Soviet mission begun 1972 to link a Soviet and a US spacecraft in space. The project culminated in the docking of an *Apollo 18* and *Soyuz 15* craft, both of which were launched 15 July 1975.

In the Apollo craft were Thomas Patten Stafford (commander), Vance DeVoe Brand, and Donald Kent Slayton; the Soyuz vehicle carried Alexei Archipovich Leonov (commander) and Valeri Nikolayevich Kubasov. The project began with the signing of an agreement May 1972 by US president Nixon and Soviet premier Kosygin.

Two days later, high over Europe, the two craft docked, allowing the crews access to each other. The original intention was to link an Apollo craft with a Salyut space station.

apologetics philosophical writings that attempt to refute attacks on the Christian faith. Apologists include Justin Martyr, Origen, St Augustine, Thomas Aquinas, Blaise Pascal, and Joseph Butler. The questions raised by scientific, historical, and archeological discoveries have widened the field of apologetics.

Apo, Mount active volcano and highest peak in the Philippines, rising to 9,692 ft/2,954 m on the island of Mindanao.

apoplectic fit alternate name for ◊cerebral hemorrhage.

apoplexy alternate name for ◊stroke.

aposematic coloration in biology, the technical name for ◊warning coloration markings that make a dangerous, poisonous, or foul-tasting animal particularly conspicuous and recognizable to a predator. Examples include the yellow and black stripes of bees and wasps, and the bright red or yellow colors of many poisonous frogs. See also ◊mimicry.

a posteriori (Latin "from the latter") in logic, an argument that deduces causes from their effects; inductive reasoning; the converse of ◊a priori.

apostle (Greek "messenger") in the New Testament, any of the chosen 12 ◊disciples sent out by Jesus after his resurrection to preach the Gospel. In the earliest days of Christianity the term was extended to include some who had never known Jesus in the flesh, notably St Paul.

Apostles' Creed one of the three ancient ◊creeds of the Christian church.

Apostolic Age early period in the Christian church dominated by those personally known to Jesus or his disciples.

apostolic succession the doctrine in the Christian church that certain spiritual powers were received by the first apostles directly from Jesus, and have been handed down in the ceremony of "laying on of hands" from generation to generation of bishops.

apostrophe a punctuation mark ('). In English it either denotes a missing letter (*mustn't* for *must not*) or number (*'47* for *1947*), or indicates possession ("*John's* camera," "the *girl's* dress"). Its correct usage has been disputed by grammarians for many centuries. It is often omitted in names (Actors Studio).

apothecaries' weights obsolete units of mass, formerly used in pharmacy: 20 grains equal one scruple; three scruples equal one dram; eight drams equal an apothecary's ounce (oz apoth.), and 12 such ounces equal an apothecary's pound (lb apoth.). There are 7,000 grains in one pound avoirdupois (0.454 kg).

apothecary a person who prepares and dispenses medicines; a pharmacist.

Appalachians mountain system of E North America, stretching about 1,500 mi/2,400 km from Alabama to Québec, composed of ancient eroded rocks and rounded peaks. The chain separates the Mississippi-Missouri lowlands from the Atlantic coastal plain and includes the Allegheny, Catskill, White, and Blue Ridge mountains, the last having the highest peak, Mount Mitchell, 6,712 ft/2,045 m. The E edge has a fall line to the coastal plain where Philadelphia, Baltimore, and Washington stand. The Appalachians are heavily forested and have deposits of coal and other minerals.

appeasement historically, the conciliatory policy adopted by the British government, in particular under Neville Chamberlain, toward the Nazi and Fascist dictators in Europe in the 1930s in an effort to maintain peace. It was strongly opposed by Winston Churchill, but the ◊Munich Agreement 1938 was almost universally hailed as its justification. Appeasement ended when Germany occupied Bohemia–Moravia March 1939.

War was declared after Germany attacked Poland Sept 1939, the beginning of World War II.

Appel Karel 1921– . Dutch painter and sculptor, founder of "Cobra" 1948, a group of European artists that developed an expressive and dynamic form of abstract painting, with thick paintwork and lurid colors.

appendicitis inflammation of the appendix, a small, blind extension of the bowel in the lower right abdomen. In an acute attack, the pus-filled appendix may burst, causing a potentially lethal spread of infection (see ◊peritonitis). Treatment is by removal (appendectomy).

appendix area of the mammalian intestines, associated with the digestion of cellulose. In herbivores it may be large, containing millions of bacteria secreting enzymes to digest grass. Cellulose is difficult to digest because no vertebrate can produce the correct digestive enzyme. Those herbivores that rely on cellulose for their energy have all evolved specialist mechanisms to make use of the correct type of bacteria.

Appert Nicolas 1750–1841. French pioneer of food preservation by ◊canning. He devised a system of sealing food in glass bottles and subjecting it to heat.

His book *L'art de conserver les substances animales et végétales* appeared in 1810. Shortly after, others applied the same principles to iron or sheet steel containers plated with tin.

apple fruit of *Malus pumila*, a tree of the family Rosaceae. There are several hundred varieties of cultivated apples, grown all over the world, which may be divided into eating, cooking, and cider apples. All are derived from the wild crab apple.

Apple trees grow best in temperate countries with a cool climate and plenty of rain during the winter. The apple has been an important food plant in Eurasia for thousands of years.

Appleseed Johnny. Nickname of US folk legend John ◊Chapman.

Appleton a city in E central Wisconsin, NW of Oshkosh, on the Fox river; seat of Outagamie country. It is a manufacturing center for paper products; population (1990) 65,695. Founded 1847, it claims to have the world's first hydroelectric plant, built 1882.

Appleton Edward Victor 1892–1965. British physicist who worked at Cambridge under Ernest ◊Rutherford from 1920. He proved the existence of the Kennelly–Heaviside layer (now called the E layer) in the atmosphere, and the Appleton layer beyond it, and was involved in the initial work on the atomic bomb. Nobel Prize 1947.

Appleton layer band containing ionized gases in the Earth's upper atmosphere, above the ◊E layer (formerly the Kennelly–Heaviside layer). It can act as a reflector of radio signals, although its ionic composition varies with the sunspot cycle. It is named after the English physicist Edward Appleton.

application a curved line that connects a series of points (or "nodes") in the smoothest possible way. The shape of the curve is governed by a series of complex mathematical formulae. They are used in ◊computer graphics and ◊CAD.

appliqué a type of embroidery used to create pictures or patterns by "applying" pieces of material onto a background fabric. The pieces are cut into the appropriate shapes and sewn on, providing decoration for wall hangings, furnishing textiles, and clothes.

Appomattox village in Virginia, scene of the surrender April 9 1865 of the Confederate army under Robert E Lee to the Union army under Ulysses S Grant, which ended the American Civil War.

The courthouse where the surrender was signed is now a museum, 3 mi/5 km from the modern village of Appomattox.

apricot fruit of *Prunus armeniaca*, a tree of the rose family Rosaceae, closely related to the almond, peach, plum, and cherry. It has yellow-fleshed fruit. Although native to the Far East, it has long been cultivated in Armenia, from where it was introduced into Europe and the US.

April Fools' Day the first day of April, when it is customary in W Europe and the US to expose people to ridicule by a practical joke, causing them to believe some falsehood or to go on a fruitless errand.

a priori (Latin "from what comes before") in logic, an argument that is known to be true, or false, without reference to experience; the converse of ◊a posteriori.

Apuleius Lucius lived c. AD 160. Roman lawyer, philosopher, and author of *Metamorphoses*, or *The Golden Ass*.

Apulia English form of ◊Puglia, region of Italy.

Aqaba, Gulf of gulf extending for 100 mi/160 km between the Negev and the Red Sea; its coastline is uninhabited except at its head, where the frontiers of Israel, Egypt, Jordan, and Saudi Arabia converge. Here are the two ports Eilat (Israeli "Elath") and Aqaba, Jordan's only port.

aquaculture another name for ***fish farming***.

Aquae Sulis Roman name of the city of ◊Bath in W England.

aqualung or ***scuba*** self-contained underwater breathing apparatus worn by divers, developed in the early 1940s by the French diver Jacques Cousteau. Compressed-air cylinders strapped to the diver's back are regulated by a valve system and by a mouth tube provide air to the diver at the same pressure as that of the surrounding water (which increases with the depth).

The vital component of an aqualung is the demand-regulator, a two-stage valve in the diver's mouthpiece. When the diver breathes in, air first passes from the compressed-air cylinders through a valve to the inner chamber of the mouthpiece. There, water that has entered the outer chamber pressurizes the air to the surrounding pressure before the diver takes in the air.

aquamarine a blue variety of the mineral ◊beryl.

aquaplaning phenomenon in which the tires of a road vehicle cease to make direct contact with the road surface, due to the presence of a thin film of water. As a result, the vehicle can go out of control (particularly if the steered wheels are involved).

Aquaplaning can be prevented by fitting tires with a good tread pattern at the correct pressure and by avoiding excessive speed when the roads are wet.

aquarium tank or similar container used for the study and display of living aquatic plants and animals. The same name is used for institutions that exhibit aquatic life. These have been common since Roman times, but the first modern public aquarium was opened in Regent's Park, London, in 1853. A recent development is the oceanarium or seaquarium, a large display of marine life forms.

Aquarius zodiac constellation a little south of the celestial equator near Pegasus. Aquarius is represented as a man pouring water from a jar. The Sun passes through Aquarius from late Feb to early March. In astrology, the dates for Aquarius are between about Jan 20 and Feb 18 (see ◊precession).

aquatic living in water. All life originated in the early oceans, because the aquatic environment has several advantages for organisms. Dehydration is almost impossible, temperatures usually remain stable, and the heaviness of water provides physical support.

aquatint printmaking technique, usually combined with ◊etching to produce areas of subtle tone as well as more precisely etched lines. Aquatint became common in the late 18th century.

The etching plate is dusted with a fine layer of resin that is fixed to the plate by heating. The plate is then immersed in acid, which bites through the resin, causing tiny pits on the surface of the plate. When printed, this results in a fine, grainy tone. Areas of tone can be controlled by varnishing the plate with acid-resisting material. Denser tones are acquired by longer exposure to the acid.

Gainsborough experimented with aquatint but the first artist to become proficient in the technique was J B Le Prince (1733–1781). Others attracted to it include Goya, Degas, Pissarro, Picasso, and Rouault.

Aquaviva Claudius (Claudio) 1543–1615. Fifth general of the Roman Catholic monastic order of Jesuits. Born in Naples, of noble family, he entered the order in 1567 and became its head in 1581. Under his rule they greatly increased in numbers, and the revolt of the Spanish Jesuits was put down. He published a treatise on education.

aqueduct any artificial channel or conduit for water, often an elevated structure of stone, wood, or iron built for conducting water across a valley.

The Greeks built a tunnel 4,200 ft/1,280 m long near Athens, 2,500 years ago. Many Roman aqueducts are still standing, for example the one at Nîmes in S France, built about AD 18 (which is 160 ft/48 m high). The largest Roman aqueduct is that at Carthage in Tunisia, which is 87 mi/141 km long and was built during the reign of Publius Aelius Hadrianus between AD 117 and 138. A recent aqueduct is the California State Water Project taking water from Lake Oroville in the north, through two power plants and across the Tehachapi mountains, more than 110 mi/177 km to S California.

aqueous humor watery fluid found in the space between the cornea and lens of the vertebrate eye. Similar to blood serum in composition, it is renewed every four hours.

aqueous solution a solution in which the solvent is water.

aquifer any rock formation containing water that can be extracted by a well. The rock of an aquifer must be porous and permeable (full of interconnected holes) so that it can absorb water.

An aquifer may be underlain, overlain, or sandwiched between impermeable layers, called aquicludes, which impede water movement. Sandstones and porous limestones make the best aquifers. They are actively sought in arid areas as sources of drinking and irrigation water.

Aquila constellation on the celestial equator (see ◊celestial sphere), near Capricornus. Its brightest star is first-magnitude ◊Altair, flanked by the stars Beta and Gamma Aquilae. It is represented by an eagle.

Aquinas St Thomas c. 1226–1274. Neapolitan philosopher and theologian, the greatest figure of the

Aquino *President Corazón Aquino campaigning in Angeles City, Philippines, Jan 1987.*

school of ◊scholasticism. He was a Dominican monk, known as the "Angelic Doctor." In 1879 his works were recognized as the basis of Catholic theology. His *Summa contra Gentiles/Against the Errors of the Infidels* 1259–64 argues that reason and faith are compatible. He assimilated the philosophy of Aristotle into Christian doctrine.

Aquino (Maria) Corazón (born Cojuangco) 1933– President of the Philippines from 1986, when she was instrumental in the nonviolent overthrow of President Ferdinand Marcos. She has sought to rule in a conciliatory manner, but has encountered opposition from left (communist guerrillas) and right (army coup attempts), and her land reforms have been seen as inadequate.

The daughter of a sugar baron, she studied in the US and in 1956 married the politician Benigno Aquino (1933–1983). The chief political opponent of the right-wing president Marcos, he was assassinated by a military guard at Manila airport on his return from exile. Corazón Aquino was drafted by the opposition to contest the Feb 1986 presidential election and claimed victory over Marcos, accusing the government of ballot rigging. She led a nonviolent "people's power" campaign, which overthrew Marcos Feb 25. A devout Roman Catholic, Aquino enjoyed strong church backing in her 1986 campaign.

The US provided support as well and was instrumental in turning back a 1989 coup attempt.

Aquitaine region of SW France; capital Bordeaux; area 15,942 sq mi/41,300 sq km; population (1986) 2,718,000. It comprises the *départements* of Dordogne, Gironde, Landes, Lot-et-Garonne, and Pyrénées-Atlantiques. Red wines (Margaux, St Julien) are produced in the Medoc district, bordering the Gironde. Aquitaine was an English possession 1152–1452.

history Early human remains have been found in the Dordogne region. Aquitaine coincides roughly with the Roman province of Aquitania and the ancient French province of Aquitaine. Eleanor of Aquitaine married the future Henry II of England 1152 and brought it to him as her dowry; it remained in English hands until 1452.

AR abbreviation for ◊Arkansas.

Arab any of a Semitic (see ◊Semite) people native to the Arabian peninsula, but now settled throughout North Africa and the nations of the Middle East.

Arab Emirates see ◊United Arab Emirates.

arabesque in ballet, a pose in which the dancer stands on one leg, straight or bent, with the other leg raised behind, fully extended. The arms are held in a harmonious position to give the longest possible line from fingertips to toes.

Arabia the peninsula between the Persian Gulf and the Red Sea, in SW Asia; area 1,000,000 sq mi/ 2,590,000 sq km. The peninsula contains the world's richest oil and gas reserves. It comprises the states of Bahrain, Kuwait, Oman, Qatar, Saudi Arabia, the United Arab Emirates, and Yemen.

physical A sandy coastal plain of varying width borders the Red Sea, behind which a mountain chain rises to about 2,000-6,600–8,200 ft/- 2,500 m. Behind this range is the plateau of the Nejd, averaging 3,300 ft/1,000 m. The interior comprises a vast desert area: part of the Hamad (Syrian) desert in the far N; Nafud in northern Saudi Arabia, and Rub'al Khali in S Saudi Arabia.

history The Arabian civilization was revived by Mohammed during the 7th century, but in the new empire created by militant Islam, Arabia became a subordinate state, and its cities were eclipsed by Damascus, Baghdad, and Cairo. Colonialism only touched the fringe of Arabia in the 19th century, and until the 20th century the interior was unknown to Europeans. Nationalism began actively to emerge at the period of World War I (1914–18), and the oil discoveries from 1953 gave the peninsula significant economic power.

Arabian Gulf another name for the ◊Persian Gulf.

Arabian Nights tales in oral circulation among Arab storytellers from the 10th century, probably having their roots in India. They are also known as *The Thousand and One Nights* and include "Ali Baba," "Aladdin," "Sinbad the Sailor," and "The Old Man of the Sea."

They were supposed to have been told to the sultan by his bride Scheherazade to avoid the fate of her predecessors, who were all executed following the wedding night to prevent their infidelity. She began a new tale each evening, which she would only agree to finish on the following night. Eventually the "sentence" was rescinded.

The first European translation was by the French writer Antoine Galland (1646–1715) 1704, although the stories were known earlier. The first English translations were by E W Lane 1838–40 and Richard Burton 1885–88.

Arabian Sea the NW branch of the ◊Indian Ocean.

Arabic language a Semitic language of the Hamito-Semitic family of W Asia and North Africa, originating among the Arabs of the Arabian peninsula. Arabic script is written from right to left.

The language has spread by way of conquest and trade as far west as Morocco and as far east as Malaysia, Indonesia, and the Philippines, and is also spoken in Arab-based communities scattered across the western hemisphere. Forms of colloquial Arabic vary in the countries where it is the dominant language: Algeria, Bahrain, Egypt, Iraq, Jordan, Kuwait, Lebanon, Libya, Mali, Mauretania, Morocco, Oman, Saudi Arabia, Sudan, Syria, Tunisia, the United Arab Emirates, and Yemen. Arabic is also a language of religious and cultural significance in such other countries as Bangladesh, India, Iran, Israel, Pakistan, and Somalia. Arabic-speaking communities are growing in the US and the West Indies.

A feature of the language is its consonantal roots. For example, *s-l-m* is the root for *salaam*, a greeting that implies peace; *Islam*, the creed of submission to God and calm acceptance of his will; and *Muslim*, one who submits to that will (a believer in Islam). The *Koran*, the sacred book of Islam, is "for reading" by a *qari* ("reader") who is engaged in *qaraat* ("reading"). The 7th-century style of the Koran is the basis of Classical Arabic.

Arabic numerals the symbols 0, 1, 2, 3, 4, 5, 6, 7, 8, 9, early forms of which were in use among the Arabs before being adopted by the peoples of Europe during the Middle Ages in place of Roman numerals. They appear to have originated in India and probably reached Europe by way of Spain.

Arab-Israeli Wars a series of wars between Israel and various Arab states in the Middle East since the founding of the state of Israel 1948.

background Arab opposition to an Israeli state began after the Balfour Declaration 1917, which supported the idea of a Jewish national homeland. In the 1920s there were anti-Zionist riots in Palestine, then governed by the UK under a League of Nations mandate. In 1936 an Arab revolt led to the setting up of a British royal commission, which recommended partition (approved by the United Nations 1947, but rejected by the Arabs).

Arab-Israeli Wars *Having crossed the Suez Canal, Israeli troops entered Egypt on Oct 22, 1973. Part of the occupied area was within 45 mi/72 km of Cairo.*

Tension in the Middle East remained high, and the conflict was sharpened and given East–West overtones by Soviet adoption of the Arab cause and US support for Israel. Several wars only increased the confusion over who had a claim to what territory. Particularly in view of the area's strategic sensitivity as an oil producer, pressure grew for a settlement, and in 1978 the ◊Camp David Agreements brought peace between Egypt and Israel, but this was denounced by other Arab countries. Israel withdrew from Sinai 1979–82, but no final agreement on Jerusalem and the establishment of a Palestinian state on the West Bank was reached. The continuing Israeli occupation of the Gaza Strip and the West Bank in the face of a determined uprising (◊intifada) by the residents of these areas hardened attitudes on both sides.

First Arab-Israeli War Oct 14, 1948–Jan 13/ March 24, 1949. As soon as the independent state of Israel had been proclaimed by the Jews in Palestine, it was invaded by combined Arab forces. The Israelis defeated them and went on to annex territory until they controlled 75% of what had been Palestine under British mandate.

Second Arab-Israeli War Oct 29–Nov 4, 1956. After Egypt had taken control of the Suez Canal and blockaded the Straits of Tiran, Israel, with British and French support, invaded and captured Sinai and the Gaza Strip, from which it withdrew under heavy US pressure after the entry of a UN force.

Third Arab-Israeli War June 5–10, 1967, the Six-Day War. It resulted in the Israeli capture of the Golan Heights from Syria; the E half of Jerusalem and the West Bank from Jordan; and, in the south, the Gaza Strip and Sinai Peninsula as far as the Suez Canal.

Fourth Arab-Israeli War Oct 2–22/24 , 1973, the "October War" or Yom Kippur War, so called because of a surprise attack on the Israeli forces on the Day of ◊Atonement. It started with the recrossing of the Suez Canal by Egyptian forces who made initial gains, though there was some later loss of ground by the Syrians in the north.

Fifth Arab-Israeli War From 1978 the presence of Palestinian guerrillas in Lebanon led to Arab raids on Israel and Israeli retaliatory incursions, but on June 6, 1982 Israel launched a full-scale invasion. By June 14 Beirut was encircled, and ◊Palestine Liberation Organization (PLO) and Syrian forces were evacuated (mainly to Syria) Aug 21–31; but in Feb 1985 there was a unilateral Israeli withdrawal from the country without any gain for losses incurred. Israel maintains a "security zone" in S Lebanon and supports the

Arafat *The leader of the Palestine Liberation Organization from 1969, Yasser Arafat.*

South Lebanese Army militia as a buffer against Palestinian guerrilla incursions.

Arabistan former name of the Iranian province of Khuzestan, revived in the 1980s by the 2 million Sunni Arab inhabitants who demand autonomy. Unrest and sabotage 1979–80 led to a pledge of a degree of autonomy by Ayatollah Khomeini.

Arab League organization of Arab states established in Cairo 1945 to promote Arab unity, especially in opposition to Israel. The original members were Egypt, Syria, Iraq, Lebanon, Transjordan (Jordan 1949), Saudi Arabia, and Yemen. In 1979 Egypt was suspended and the league's headquarters transferred to Tunis in protest against the Egypt-Israeli peace, but Egypt was readmitted as a full member May 1989, and in March 1990 its headquarters returned to Cairo.

Arachne (Greek "spider") in Greek mythology, a Lydian woman who was so skillful a weaver that she challenged the goddess Athena to a contest. Athena tore Arachne's beautiful tapestries to pieces and Arachne hanged herself. She was transformed into a spider, and her weaving became a cobweb.

arachnid or ***arachnoid*** a member of a class of arthropods, including spiders, scorpions, and mites. They differ from insects in possessing only two main body regions, the cephalophorax and the abdomen.

Arad Romanian town on the river Mures, 100 mi/160 km NE of Belgrade; population (1985) 185,900. It is a major trading center with many industries.

Arafat Yasser 1929– . Palestinian nationalist politician, cofounder of al-◊Fatah 1956 and president of the ◊Palestine Liberation Organization (PLO) from 1969. In the 1970s his activities in pursuit of an independent homeland for Palestinians made him a prominent figure in world politics, but in the 1980s the growth of factions within the PLO effectively reduced his power. He was forced to evacuate Lebanon 1983, but remained leader of most of the PLO and in 1990 persuaded it to recognize formally the state of Israel.

Arafura Sea the area of the Pacific Ocean between N Australia and Indonesia, bounded by the Timor Sea in the W and the Coral Sea in the E. It is 800 mi/1,290 km long and 350 mi/560 km wide.

Arago Dominique 1786–1853. French physicist and astronomer who made major contributions to the early study of electromagnetism. In 1820 he found out that iron enclosed in a wire coil could be magnetized by the passage of an electric current. Later, in 1824, he was the first to observe the ability of a floating copper disk to deflect a magnetic needle, the phenomenon of magnetic rotation.

Aragón autonomous region of NE Spain including the provinces of Huesca, Teruel, and Zaragoza; area 18,412 sq mi/47,700 sq km; population (1986) 1,215,000. Its capital is Zaragoza, and products include almonds, figs, grapes, and olives. Aragón was an independent kingdom 1035–1479.

history A Roman province until taken in the 5th century by the Visigoths, who lost it to the Moors in the 8th century, it became a kingdom 1035. It was united with Castile 1479 under Ferdinand and Isabella.

Aragon Louis 1897–1982. French poet and novelist. Beginning as a Dadaist, he became one of the leaders of Surrealism, published volumes of verse, and in 1930 joined the Communist party. Taken prisoner in World War II, he escaped to join the Resistance, experiences reflected in the poetry of *Le Crève-coeur* 1942 and *Les Yeux d'Elsa* 1944.

Arakan state of Myanmar (formerly Burma) on the Bay of Bengal coast, some 400 mi/645 km long and strewn with islands; population (1983) 2,046,000. The chief town is Sittwe. It is bounded along its eastern side by the Arakan Yoma, a mountain range rising to 10,000 ft/3,000 m. The ancient kingdom of Arakan was conquered by Burma 1785.

Aral Sea inland sea in the USSR; the world's fourth-largest lake; divided between Kazakhstan and Uzbekistan; former area 24,000 sq mi/62,000 sq km, but decreasing. Water from its tributaries, the Amu Darya and Syr Darya, has been diverted for irrigation and city use, and the sea is disappearing, with long-term consequences for the climate.

Between 1960 and 1990 the water level dropped 40 ft/13 m, reducing the lake to two-thirds of its original area and increasing the area of the surrounding Aralkum salt desert.

Aramaic language a Semitic language of the Hamito-Semitic family of W Asia, the everyday language of Palestine 2,000 years ago, during the Roman occupation and the time of Jesus.

In the 13th century BC Aramaean nomads set up states in Mesopotamia, and during the next 200 years spread into N Syria, where Damascus, Aleppo, and Carchemish were among their chief centers. Aramaic spread throughout Syria and Mesopotamia, becoming one of the official languages of the Persian empire under the Achemenids and serving as a ◊lingua franca of the day. Aramaic dialects survive among small Christian communities in various parts of W Asia, although Arabic spread widely with the acceptance of Islam.

Aran Islands three rocky islands (Inishmore, Inishmaan, Inisheer) in the mouth of Galway Bay, Republic of Ireland; population approximately 4,600. The capital is Kilronan. J M ◊Synge used the language of the islands in his plays.

Aranjuez Spanish town on the river Tagus, 25 mi/40 km SE of Madrid; population (1981) 36,000. The palace was a royal residence for centuries.

Arany János 1817–1882. Hungarian writer. His comic epic *The Lost Constitution* 1846 was followed in 1847 by *Toldi*, a product of the popular nationalist school. In 1864 his epic masterpiece *The Death of King Buda* appeared. During his last years Arany produced the rest of the *Toldi* trilogy, and his most personal lyrics.

Ararat double-peaked mountain on the Turkish-Iranian border; the higher, Great Ararat, 16,900 ft/5,156 m, was the reputed resting place of Noah's Ark after the Flood.

Araucanian Indian a member of a group of South American Indian peoples native to central Chile and the Argentine pampas. They were agriculturalists and hunters, and also renowned warriors, defeating the Incas and resisting the Spanish for 200 years.

araucaria coniferous tree of genus *Araucaria*, allied to the firs, with flat, scalelike needles. Once widespread, it is now native only to the southern hemisphere. Some grow to gigantic size. Araucarias include the monkey-puzzle tree *A. araucana*, the Australian bunya bunya pine *A. bidwillii*, and the Norfolk Island pine *A. heterophylla*.

Arawak member of an indigenous American people of the Caribbean and NE Amazon Basin. They lived mainly by shifting cultivation in tropical for-

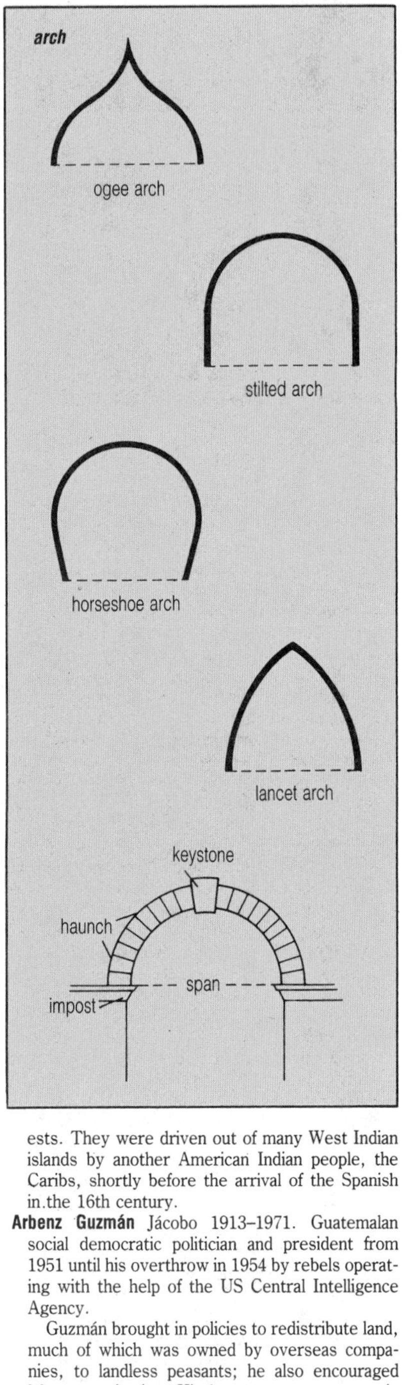
arch
ogee arch
stilted arch
horseshoe arch
lancet arch
keystone
haunch
span
impost

ests. They were driven out of many West Indian islands by another American Indian people, the Caribs, shortly before the arrival of the Spanish in the 16th century.

Arbenz Guzmán Jácobo 1913–1971. Guatemalan social democratic politician and president from 1951 until his overthrow in 1954 by rebels operating with the help of the US Central Intelligence Agency.

Guzmán brought in policies to redistribute land, much of which was owned by overseas companies, to landless peasants; he also encouraged labor organization. His last years were spent in exile in Mexico, Uruguay, and Cuba.

Arbil Kurdish town in a province of the same name in N Iraq. Occupied since Assyrian times, it was the site of a battle in 331 BC at which Alexander the Great defeated the Persians under Darius III. In 1974 Arbil became the capital of a Kurdish autonomous region set up by the Iraqi government. Population (1985) 334,000.

arbitrageur in finance, a person who buys securities (such as currency or commodities) in one country or market for immediate resale in another market, to take advantage of different prices.

Arbitrage became widespread during the 1970s and 1980s with the increasing deregulation of financial markets. The effect of arbitrage is to lessen or eliminate the price differentials among the markets. The term took on additional meaning with the increase in corporate buy-outs in the deregulated atmosphere of the late 1980s. Arbitrageurs speculated on target companies, buying stock and reselling it at the higher buy-out price.

arbitration submission of a dispute to a third, unbiased party for settlement. It may be personal litigation, trade-union issues, or international disputes (as the case of the warship ◊*Alabama*).

The first permanent international court was established at The Hague in the Netherlands 1900, and the League of Nations set up an additional Permanent Court of International Justice 1921 to deal with frontier disputes and the like. The latter was replaced 1945 with the International Court of Justice under the United Nations. Another arbiter is the European Court of Justice, which rules on disputes arising out of the Rome treaties regulating the European Community.

arboretum a collection of trees. An arboretum may have many species or just different varieties of one species—for example, different types of pine tree.

arborvitae any of several coniferous trees or shrubs of the genus *Thuja* of the cypress family, having flattened branchlets covered in overlapping aromatic green scales. In North America, the northern white cedar *Thuja occidentalis* and the western red cedar *T. plicata* are representatives. The Chinese or Oriental species *T. orientalis*, reaching 60 ft/18 m in height, is grown widely as an ornamental.

Arbuckle Fatty (Roscoe Conkling) 1887–1933. Heavyweight US silent-film comedian, also a writer and director. His successful career in such films as *The Butcher Boy* 1917 and *The Hayseed* 1919 ended in 1921 after a sex-party scandal that ended in the death of a starlet. Although acquitted, he was spurned by the public and his films were banned, but he continued writing scripts.

arbutus any evergreen shrub of the genus *Arbutus* of the heath family Ericaceae. The strawberry tree *A. unedo* is grown for its ornamental, strawberrylike fruit.

arc in geometry, a section of a curved line. The arcs of a circle are classified thus: a semicircle, which is exactly half of the circle; minor arcs, which are less than the semicircle; and major arcs, which are greater than the semicircle.

A circle's arcs are measured in degrees. A semicircle is 180°, a minor arc is equal to the measure of its central angle (the angle formed by joining its two ends and the center of the circle), and a major arc is 360° minus the degree measure of its corresponding minor arc.

Arcadia (Greek *Arkadhia*) central plateau of S Greece; area 1,706 sq mi/4,419 sq km; population (1981) 108,000. Tripolis is the capital town.

Arc de Triomphe arch at the head of the Champs Elysées in the Place de l'Etoile, Paris, France, begun by Napoleon 1806 and completed 1836. It was intended to commemorate Napoleon's victories of 1805–06 and commissioned from Jean Chalgrin (1739–1811). Beneath it rests France's "Unknown Soldier."

arch *The Arch of Titus on Via Sacra in the Forum, Rome.*

archeology: chronology

14th–16th centuries	The Renaissance revived interest in Classical Greek and Roman art and architecture, including ruins and buried art and artifacts.
1748	The buried Roman city of Pompeii was discovered under lava from Vesuvius.
1784	Thomas Jefferson dug an Indian burial mound on the Rivanna River in Virginia and wrote a report on his finds.
1790	John Frere identified Old Stone Age (Paleolithic) tools together with large extinct animals.
1822	Champollion deciphered Egyptian hieroglyphics.
1836	C J Thomsen devised the Stone, Bronze, and Iron Age classification.
1840s	A H Layard excavated the Assyrian capital of Nineveh.
1868	Great Zimbabwe ruins in E Africa first seen by Europeans.
1871	Heinrich Schliemann began excavations at Troy.
1879	Stone Age paintings were first discovered at Altamira, Spain.
1880s	A H Pitt-Rivers developed the concept of stratigraphy (identification of successive layers of soil within a site with successive archeological stages; the most recent at the top).
1891	W M F Petrie began excavating Akhetaton in Egypt.
1899–1935	A J Evans excavated Minoan Knossos in Crete.
1900–44	Max Uhle began the systematic study of the civilizations of Peru.
1911	The Inca city of Machu Picchu discovered by Hiram Bingham in the Andes.
1911–12	Piltdown skull "discovered"; proved a fake 1949.
1914–18	Osbert Crawford developed the technique of aerial survey of sites.
1917–27	J E Thompson discovered the great Mayan sites in Yucatán, Mexico.
1922	Tutankhamen's tomb in Egypt opened by Howard Carter.
1926	A kill site in Folsom, New Mexico, was found with human-made spearpoints in association with ancient bison.
1935	Dendrochronology (dating events in the distant past by counting tree rings) developed by A E Douglas; useful where preserved timbers are present.
1939	Anglo-Saxon ship-burial treasure found at Sutton Hoo, England.
1947	The first of the Dead Sea Scrolls discovered.
1948	Proconsul, a fossil, prehistoric ape, discovered by Mary Leakey in Kenya; several early hominid fossils found by Louis Leakey in Olduvai Gorge 1950s–1970s.
1953	Michael Ventris deciphered Minoan Linear B.
1960s	Radiocarbon and thermoluminescence measurement developed as aids for dating remains.
1961	Swedish warship *Wasa* raised at Stockholm.
1963	W B Emery pioneered rescue archeology at Abu Simbel before the site was flooded by the Aswan Dam.
1974	Tomb of Shi Huangdi discovered in China.
1978	Tomb of Philip II of Macedon (Alexander the Great's father) discovered in Greece.
1979	The Aztec capital Tenochtitlán excavated beneath a zone of Mexico City.
1982	The English king Henry VIII's warship *Mary Rose* of 1545 was raised and studied with new techniques in underwater archeology.
1985	The tomb of Maya, Tutankhamen's treasurer, discovered at Saqqara, Egypt.
1988	Turin Shroud established as of medieval date by radiocarbon dating.

Arc de Triomphe, Prix de French horse race run over 2,400 m/1.5 mi at Longchamp, near Paris. It is the leading "open age" race in Europe, and one of the richest. It was first run 1920.

arch a curved structure of masonry that supports the weight of material over an open space, as in a bridge or doorway. The first arches consisted of several wedge-shaped stones supported by their mutual pressure. The Romans are credited with engineering the earliest round keystone arches, used for aqueducts. Other arches include the pointed Gothic arch and the corbeled arch of the Maya. The term is also applied to any curved structure that is an arch in form only.

Archaean or ***Archaeozoic*** earliest period of geologic time; the first part of the Precambrian era, from the formation of Earth up to 2,500 million years ago. Traces of life have recently been found in Archaean rocks.

archaebacteria three groups of bacteria whose DNA differs significantly from that of other bacteria (called the "eubacteria"). All are strict anaerobes, that is, they are killed by oxygen. This is thought to be a primitive condition and to indicate that the archaebacteria are related to the earliest life forms, which appeared about 3.5 billion years ago, when there was little oxygen in the Earth's atmosphere.

archeology the study of prehistory and ancient history, based on the examination of physical remains.

history Interest in the physical remains of the past began in the Renaissance among dealers in and collectors of ancient art. It was further stimulated by discoveries made in Africa, the Americas, and Asia by Europeans during the period of imperialist colonization in the 16th–19th centuries, such as the antiquities discovered during Napoleon's Egyptian campaign in the 1790s.

Toward the end of the 19th century archeology became an academic study, making increasing use of scientific techniques and systematic methodologies.

methods Principal activities include preliminary field (or site) surveys, excavation (where necessary), and the classification, dating, and interpretation of finds. Related disciplines that have been useful in archeological reconstruction include stratigraphy (the study of geologic strata), dendrochronology (the establishment of chronological sequences through the study of tree rings), paleobotany (the study of ancient pollens, seeds, and grains), epigraphy (the study of inscriptions), and numismatics (the study of coins). Since 1958 radiocarbon dating has been used and refined to establish the age of archeological strata and associated materials.

archaeopteryx fossil from the limestone deposits of Bavaria about 160 million years old, and popularly known as "the first bird," although some earlier bird ancestors are now known. *Archaeopteryx* was about the size of a crow and had feathers and wings, but in many respects its skeleton is reptilian (long, bony tail; teeth) and very like some small meat-eating dinosaurs of the time.

Archangel (Russian *Arkhangelsk*) port in northern USSR; population (1987) 416,000. It was made an open port by Boris Godunov and was of prime importance until Peter the Great built St Petersburg. It was used 1918–20 by the Allied interventionist armies in collaboration with the White Army in their effort to overthrow the newly established Soviet state. In World War II it was the receiving station for Anglo-American supplies. An open city in a closed area, it can be visited by foreigners only by air and is a center for ICBMs (intercontinental ballistic missiles). Although the port is blocked by ice during half the year, it

archaeopteryx

wing structure of a flying reptile
wing structure of a bird

is the chief timber-exporting port of the USSR. Plesetsk, to the S, is a launch site for crewed space flight.

archbishop in the Christian church, a bishop of superior rank, who has authority over other bishops in his jurisdiction and often over an ecclesiastical province. The office exists in the Roman Catholic, Eastern Orthodox, and Anglican churches.

archdeacon originally an ordained dignitary of the Christian church charged with the supervision of the deacons attached to a cathedral. Today in the Roman Catholic church the office is purely titular; in the Church of England an archdeacon still has many business duties, such as the periodic inspection of churches. It is not found in other Protestant churches.

archegonium the female sex organ found in bryophytes (mosses and liverworts), pteridophytes (ferns, club mosses, and horsetails), and some gymnosperms. It is a multicellular, flask-shaped structure consisting of two parts: the swollen base or venter containing the egg cell, and the long, narrow neck. When the egg cell is mature, the cells of the neck dissolve, allowing the passage of the male gametes, or ◊antherozoids.

Archer Jeffrey 1940– . English writer and politician. A Conservative member of Parliament 1969–74, he lost a fortune in a disastrous investment, but recouped it as a best-selling novelist and dramatist. His books include *Not a Penny More, Not a Penny Less* 1975, and *First Among Equals* 1984. In 1985 he became deputy chair of the Conservative Party but resigned Nov 1986 after a scandal involving an alleged payment to a prostitute.

archerfish any of a family Toxotidae, especially the genus *Toxotes*, of surface-living fishes native to SE Asia and Australia. It grows to about 10 in/25 cm and is able to shoot down insects up to 5 ft/1.5 m above the water by spitting a jet of water from its mouth.

archery the use of the bow and arrow, originally in hunting and war, now a competitive sport.

Stone arrowheads have been found in Mesolithic archeological deposits, c. 15,000 BC, and bowmen are depicted in the ◊ancient art of the Americas, Europe, and the Near East, as well as later in the art of the early ◊civilizations. Until the introduction of gunpowder in the 14th century, bands of archers were to be found in every European army. By the mid-17th century archery was no longer significant in warfare and interest waned until the 1780s.

Organizations include the world governing body Fédération Internationale de Tir à l'Arc 1931; in the US, the National Archery Association 1879, and, for hunting with the bow, the National Field Archery Association 1940. In competitions, results are based on double FITA rounds, that is 72 arrows at each of four targets at 90, 70, 50, and 30 meters (70, 60, 50, and 30 for women). The best possible score is 2,880.

Archimedes c. 287–212 BC. Greek mathematician who made important discoveries in geometry, hydrostatics, and mechanics. He formulated a law of fluid displacement (Archimedes' principle), and is credited with the invention of the Archimedes screw, a cylindrical device for raising water.

He was born at Syracuse in Sicily. It is alleged that Archimedes' principle was discovered when he stepped into the public bath and saw the water overflow. He was so delighted that he rushed home naked, crying "Eureka! Eureka!" ("I have found it! I have found it!") He used his discovery to prove that the goldsmith of the king of Syracuse had adulterated a gold crown with silver. The Archimedes screw is still used to raise water in the Nile delta. Archimedes designed engines of war for the defense of Syracuse, and was killed when the Romans besieged the town.

Archimedes' principle in physics, law stating that an object totally or partly submerged in a fluid displaces a volume of fluid that weighs the same as the apparent loss in weight of the object (which equals the upthrust on it).

If the weight of the object is less than the force exerted by the fluid, it will float partly or completely above the surface; if its weight is equal to the force, the object will come to equilibrium below the surface.

Archimedes screw one of the earliest kinds of pump, thought to have been invented by Archimedes. It consists of a spiral screw revolving inside a close-fitting cylinder. It is used, for example, to raise water for irrigation.

archipelago a group of islands, or an area of sea containing a group of islands. The islands of an archipelago are usually volcanic in origin, and they sometimes represent the tops of peaks in areas around continental margins flooded by the sea.

Archimedes screw

Volcanic islands are formed either when a hot spot within the Earth's mantle produces a chain of volcanoes on the surface, such as the Hawaiian Archipelago, or at a destructive plate margin (see ◊plate tectonics) where the subduction of one plate beneath another produces an arc-shaped island group, such as the Aleutian Archipelago. Novaya Zemlya in the Arctic Ocean, the northern extension of the Ural Mountains, resulted from continental flooding.

Archipenko Alexander 1887–1964. Russian-born abstract sculptor who lived in France from 1908 and in the US from 1923. He pioneered Cubist works composed of angular forms and spaces and later experimented with clear plastic and sculptures incorporating lights.

architecture the art of designing structures. The term covers design of the visual appearance of structures; their internal arrangements of space; selection of external and internal building materials; design or selection of natural and artificial lighting systems, as well as mechanical, electrical, and plumbing systems; and design or selection of decorations and furnishings. Architectural style may emerge from evolution of techniques and styles particular to a culture in a given time period with or without identifiable individuals as architects or may be attributed to specific individuals or groups of architects working together on a project.

early architecture Little remains of the earliest forms of architecture, but archeologists have examined remains of prehistoric sites and documented ◊Stone Age villages of wooden post buildings with above-ground construction of organic materials such as mud or wattle and daub from the Upper Paleolithic, Mesolithic, and Neolithic periods in Asia, the Near East, Europe, and the Americas. More extensive remains of stone-built structures have given clues to later Neolithic farming communities as well as habitations, storehouses, and religious and civic structures of early civilizations. The best documented are those of ancient Egypt, where exhaustive work in the 19th and 20th centuries revealed much about ordinary buildings, the monumental structures such as the pyramid tombs near modern Cairo, and the temple and tomb complexes concentrated at Luxor and Thebes.

Classical This architecture evolved its basic forms in Greece between the 16th and 2nd centuries BC. Its hallmark characteristic is its post-and-lintel construction of temples and public structures, classified into the Doric, Ionic, and Corinthian orders, defined by simple, scrolled, and acanthus-leaf capitals for support columns, respectively. The Romans copied and expanded on Greek Classical forms, notably introducing bricks and concrete and inventing the vault, arch, and dome for public buildings and aqueducts.

Byzantine This architecture developed primarily in the E Roman Empire from the 4th century, with its center at Byzantium (later named Constantinople, currently known as Istanbul). Its most notable features were construction of churches, some very large, based on the Greek cross plan (Hagia Sophia, Istanbul; St Mark's, Venice), with formalized painted and mosaic decoration.

Islamic This architecture developed from the 8th century, when the Islamic religion spread from its center in the Middle East W to Spain and E to China and parts of the Philippine Islands. Notable features are development of the tower with dome and the pointed arch. Islamic architecture, particularly through Spanish examples such as the Great Mosque at Córdoba and the Alhambra in Granada, profoundly influenced Christian church architecture—for example, by adoption of the pointed arch into the Gothic arch.

Romanesque This architecture in W European Christianity developed from the 8th to the 12th centuries. It is marked by churches with massive walls for structural integrity, rounded arches,

architecture

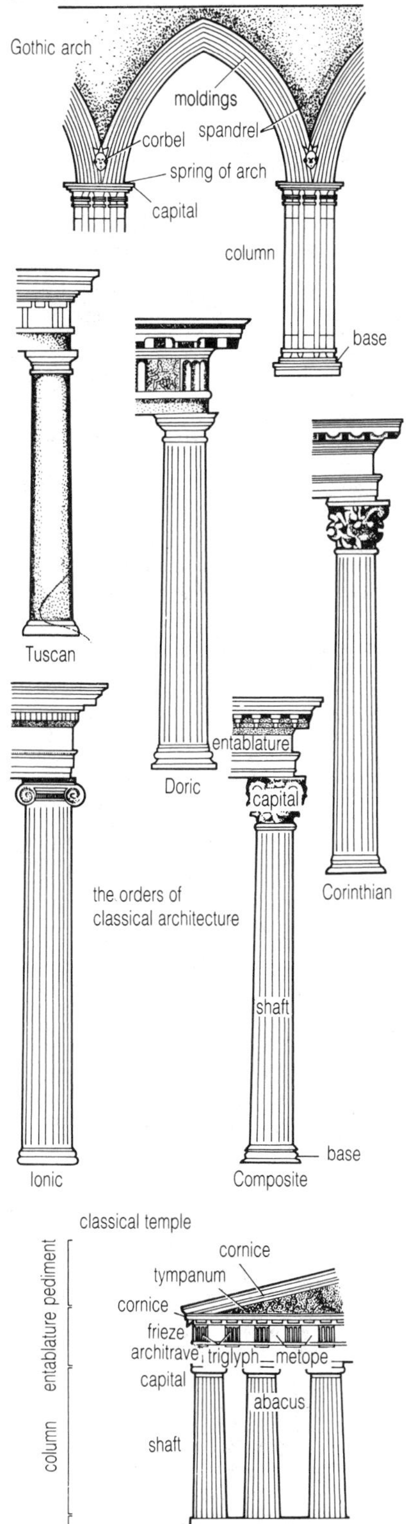
Gothic arch
moldings
corbel
spandrel
spring of arch
capital
column
base
Tuscan
Doric
entablature
capital
Corinthian
Ionic
Composite
base
shaft
the orders of classical architecture
classical temple
cornice
tympanum
cornice
frieze
architrave
triglyph
metope
capital
abacus
shaft
pediment
entablature
column

small windows, and resulting dark volumes of interior space. In England this style is generally referred to as Norman architecture (Durham Cathedral). The style enjoyed a renewal of interest in Europe and the US in the late 19th and early 20th centuries.

Gothic This architecture emerged out of Romanesque, since the pointed arch and flying buttress made it possible to change from thick supporting walls to lighter curtain walls with extensive expansion of window areas (and stained-glass artwork) and resulting increases in interior light. Gothic architecture was developed particularly in France from the 12th to 16th centuries. The style is divided into Early Gothic (Sens Cathedral), High Gothic (Chartres Cathedral), and Late or Flamboyant Gothic. In England the corresponding divisions are Early English (Salisbury Cathedral), Decorated (Wells Cathedral), and Perpendicular (Kings College Chapel, Cambridge). Gothic was also developed extensively in Germany and neighboring countries and in Italy.

Renaissance This architecture of 15th-and 16th-century Europe saw the rebirth of Classical form and motifs in the Italian Neo-Classical movement. A major source of inspiration was the work of the 1st-century BC Roman engineer Vitruvius for Palladio, Alberti, Brunelleschi, Bramante, and Michelangelo, the major Renaissance architects. The Palladian style was extensively used later in England by Inigo Jones and the Classical idiom by Christopher Wren. Classical or Neo-Classical style and its elements have been popular in the US from the 18th century, as evidenced in much of the civic and commercial architecture since the time of the early republic (the US Capitol and Supreme Court buildings in Washington; many state capitols).

Baroque European architecture of the 17th and 18th centuries elaborated on Classical models with exuberant and extravagant decoration. In large-scale public buildings, the style is best seen in the innovative work of Giovanni Bernini and Francesco Borromini in Italy and later by John Vanbrugh, Nicholas Hawksmoor, and Christopher Wren in England. There were numerous practitioners in France and the German-speaking countries; Vienna is especially Baroque.

Rococo This architecture extends the Baroque style with an even greater extravagance of design motifs, using a new lightness of detail and naturalistic elements, such as shells, flowers, and trees.

Neo-Classical European architecture of the 18th and 19th centuries again focused on the more severe Classical idiom (inspired by archeological finds), producing, for example, the large-scale rebuilding of London by Robert Adam and John Nash and later of Paris by Georges Haussman.

Neo-Gothic The late 19th century saw a fussy Gothic revival in Europe and the US, particularly evident in churches (Ralph Adams Cram's work in the US—for example, St John the Divine, New York) and public buildings (Charles Barry's work in the Houses of Parliament, London).

Art Nouveau This architecture arising at the end of the 19th century countered Neo-Gothic, using sinuous, flowing shapes for buildings, room plans, and interior design. The style is characterized by the work of Charles Rennie Mackintosh in Scotland (Glasgow Art School) and Antonio Gaudí in Spain (Church of the Holy Family, Barcelona), and design elements were used especially in France but also in England and the US.

Modernist This architecture is also known as Functionalism or the International Style. It began in the 1900s with the Vienna school and the German Bauhaus but was also seen in the US, Scandinavia, and France. It used spare line and form, an emphasis on rationalism, and the elimination of ornament. It makes great use of technological advances in materials such as glass, steel, and concrete and of construction techniques that allow flexibility of design. Notable practitioners include Frank Lloyd Wright, Mies van der Rohe, and Le Corbusier. Modern architecture also furthered the notion of the planning of extensive multibuilding projects and of whole towns or communities.

Postmodernist This architecture emerged in the US, Japan, and Europe in the 1980s, with one trend toward high-tech forms and another using simplified or geometric elements from earlier styles to decorate plain, functional forms.

archive a collection of historically valuable records, ranging from papers and documents to photographs, films, videotapes, and sound recordings.

The National Archives Hall in Washington, DC contains the original Declaration of Independence, the ◊Constitution, and the ◊Bill of Rights. The National Archives and Records Service is responsible for preserving federal records and for administration of the presidential libraries, usually established in the incumbent's birthplace.

archon (Greek "ruler") in ancient Greece, title of the chief magistrate in many cities.

In Athens, there were originally three: the king archon, the eponymous archon, and the polemarch. Their numbers were later increased to nine, with the extra six keeping a record of judgments. The king archon was the elected king and religious

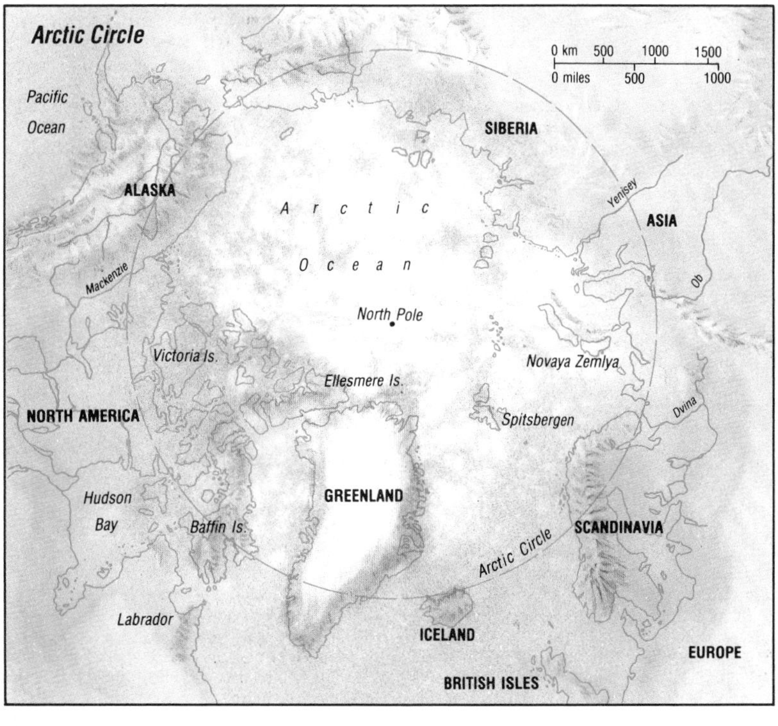
Arctic Circle
0 km 500 1000 1500
0 miles 500 1000
Pacific Ocean
SIBERIA
ALASKA
Yenisey
ASIA
Arctic Ocean
Mackenzie
Ob
North Pole
Victoria Is.
Novaya Zemlya
Ellesmere Is.
NORTH AMERICA
Spitsbergen
Dvina
GREENLAND
Hudson Bay
Baffin Is.
SCANDINAVIA
Arctic Circle
Labrador
ICELAND
EUROPE
BRITISH ISLES

Arctic exploration

60,000–35,000 BC	Ancestors of the Eskimo and American Indians began migration from Siberia to North America by the "lost" landbridge of Beringia.
320 BC	Pytheas, Greek sailor contemporary with Alexander the Great, possibly reached Iceland.
9th–10th centuries AD	Vikings colonized Iceland and Greenland, which then had a much warmer climate.
c. 1000	Leif Ericsson reached Baffin Island (NE of Canada) and Labrador.
1497	Giovanni Caboto first sought the Northwest Passage as a trade route around North America for Henry VII of England.
1553	Richard Chancellor tried to find the Northeast Passage around Siberia and first established direct English trade with Russia.
1576	Martin Frobisher reached Frobisher Bay, but found only "fools' gold" (iron pyrites) for Elizabeth I of England.
1594–97	Willem Barents made three expeditions in search of the Northeast Passage.
1607	Henry Hudson failed to cross the Arctic Ocean, but his reports of whales started the northern whaling industry.
1670	Hudson's Bay Company started the fur trade in Canada.
1728	Vitus Bering passed Bering Strait.
1829–33	John Ross discovered the North Magnetic Pole.
1845	Mysterious disappearance of John Franklin's expedition to the Northwest Passage stimulated further exploration.
1878–79	Nils Nordensköld was the first European to discover the Northeast Passage.
1893–96	Fridtjof Nansen's ship *Fram* drifted across the Arctic, locked in the ice, proving that no Arctic continent existed.
1903–06	Roald Amundsen sailed through the Northwest Passage.
1909	Robert Peary, Matt Henson, and four Eskimo reached the North Pole on Apr 2.
1926	Richard Byrd and Floyd Bennett flew to the Pole on May 9.
1926	Umberto Nobile and Amundsen crossed the Pole (Spitzbergen–Alaska) in the airship Norge on May 12.
1954	First regular commercial flights over the shortcut polar route by Scandinavian Airlines.
1958	The US submarine *Nautilus* crossed the Pole beneath the ice.
1960	From this date a Soviet nuclear-powered icebreaker has kept open a 2,500 mi/4,000 km Asia-Europe passage along the north coast of Siberia 150 days a year.
1969	First surface crossing, by dog sled, of the Arctic Ocean (Alaska–Spitzbergen) by Wally Herbert, British Transarctic Expedition, Feb–May.
1977	The Soviet icebreaker *Arktika* made the first surface voyage to the Pole.
1982	First circumnavigation of Earth (Sept 2, 1979–Aug 29, 1982) via the Poles by Ranulph Fiennes and Charles Burton.
1988	Canadian and Soviet skiers attempted the first overland crossing from the USSR to Canada via the Pole.

representative of the State; the eponymous archon was the head of state and supreme judge; the polemarch was in charge of state security and commanded the army.

arc lamp or ***arc light*** electric light that uses the illumination of an electric arc maintained between two electrodes. The British scientist Humphry Davy developed an arc lamp 1808, and its major use in recent years has been in movie projectors. The lamp consists of two carbon electrodes, between which a very high voltage is maintained. Electric current arcs (jumps) between the two, creating a brilliant light.

The lamp incorporates a mechanism for automatically advancing the electrodes as they gradually burn away. Modern arc lamps (for example, searchlights) have the electrodes enclosed in an inert gas such as xenon.

Arctic, the region N of the Arctic Circle. There is no Arctic continent, merely pack ice (which breaks into ice floes in summer) surrounding the pole and floating on the Arctic Ocean. Pack ice is carried by the S-flowing current into the Atlantic Ocean as ◊icebergs. In winter the Sun disappears below the horizon for a time (and in summer, which only lasts up to two months, remains above it), but the cold is less severe than in parts of E Siberia or Antarctica. Land areas in the Arctic have mainly stunted tundra vegetation, with an outburst of summer flowers. Animals include reindeer, caribou, musk ox, fox, hare, lemming, wolf, polar bear, seal, and walrus. There are few birds, except in summer, when insects, especially mosquitoes, are plentiful. The aboriginal people are the ◊Eskimo of the Siberian/Alaskan/Canadian Arctic and Greenland. The most valuable resource is oil. The International Arctic Sciences Committee was established 1987 by the countries with Arctic coastlines to study ozone depletion and climatic change.

Arctic Circle line encircling the North Pole at latitude 66° 32′ N. Above the Arctic Circle, the Sun remains below the horizon for a period of time during the winter and remains above it during the summer; the length of time for these occurrences increases poleward.

Arctic Ocean ocean surrounding the North Pole; area 5,400,000 sq mi/14,000,000 sq km. Because of the Siberian and North American rivers flowing into it, it has comparatively low salinity and freezes readily.

It comprises:

Beaufort Sea off Canada/Alaska coast, named after British admiral Francis ◊Beaufort; oil drilling allowed only in winter because the sea is the breeding and migration route of the bowhead whales, staple diet of the local Inuit;

Greenland Sea between Greenland and Svalbard;

Norwegian Sea between Greenland and Norway;

And west to east along the N coast of the USSR:

Barents Sea named after Willem ◊Barents, which has oil and gas reserves and is strategically significant as the meeting point of the NATO and Warsaw Pact forces. The ◊White Sea is its southernmost gulf;

Kara Sea renowned for bad weather and known as the "great ice cellar";

Laptev Sea between Taimyr Peninsula and New Siberian Island;

East Siberian Sea and ***Chukchi Sea*** between the USSR and the USA; the seminomadic Chukchi people of NE Siberia finally accepted Soviet rule in the 1930s.

The Arctic Ocean has the world's greatest concentration of nuclear submarines (40 of the 78 Soviet strategic nuclear submarines are here, plus their US counterparts), but at the same time there is much scientific cooperation on exploration, especially since the USSR needs Western aid to develop oil and gas in its areas.

Arcturus or ***Alpha Boötis*** brightest star in the constellation Boötes and the fourth brightest star in the sky. Arcturus is a red giant, 36 light-years away from Earth.

Ardebil town in NW Iran, near the Soviet frontier; population (1983) 222,000. Ardebil exports dried fruits, carpets, and rugs.

Ardèche river in SE France, a tributary of the Rhône. Near Vallon it flows under the Pont d'Arc, a natural bridge. It gives its name to a *département.*

Arden Elizabeth. Adopted name of Florence Nightingale Graham. 1884–1966. Canadian-born US beauty expert and mass merchandiser. Born in Woodbridge, Ontario, she moved to New York 1908. Possessing an extraordinary business sense, she opened a beauty salon 1910 and expanded the firm in 1914 under the corporate name of "Elizabeth Arden," a name she soon adopted herself. She developed and merchandised a line of cosmetic products and also utilized new techniques of mass advertising to introduce her products to the public. She later opened a chain of beauty salons and spas throughout the US.

Ardennes wooded plateau in NE France, SE Belgium, and N Luxembourg, cut through by the river Meuse; also a *département* of ◊Champagne-Ardenne. There was heavy fighting here in World Wars I and II (see ◊Bulge, Battle of the).

are metric unit of area, equal to 100 square meters (119.6 sq yd); 100 ares make one ◊hectare.

Areca genus of palms native to Asia and Australia. The ◊betel nut comes from the species *A. catechu.*

Arecibo site in Puerto Rico of the world's largest single-dish ◊radio telescope, 1,000 ft/305 m in diameter. It is built in a natural hollow, and uses the rotation of the Earth to scan the sky. It has been used both for radar work on the planets and for conventional radio astronomy, and is operated by Cornell University.

Arendt Hannah 1906–1975. German-born US scholar and political scientist. With the rise of the Nazis, she moved to Paris and immigrated to the US 1940. Arendt published a number of important political works, including *The Origins of Modern Totalitarianism* 1951, *The Human Condition* 1958, *On Revolution* 1963, *Eichmann in Jerusalem* 1963, and *On Violence* 1972.

Arendt received her PhD from Heidelberg University 1928. During World War II she was research director for the Conference on Jewish Relations.

Arequipa city in Peru at the base of the volcano El Misti; population (1988) 592,000. Founded by Pizarro 1540, it is the cultural focus of S Peru and a busy commercial (soap, textiles) center.

Ares in Greek mythology, the god of war (Roman ◊Mars). The son of Zeus and Hera, he was worshiped chiefly in Thrace.

arête a sharp narrow ridge separating two ◊glacier valleys (a French term; in the US often called a *combe-ridge*; in German a *grat*). The typical U-shaped cross sections of glacier valleys give arêtes very steep sides. Arêtes are common in glaciated mountain regions such as the Rockies, the Himalayas, and the Alps.

Arethusa in Greek mythology, a nymph of the fountain and spring of Arethusa in the island of Ortygia near Syracuse, on the south coast of Sicily.

Aretino Pietro 1492–1556. Italian writer, born in Arezzo. He earned his living, both in Rome and Venice, by publishing satirical pamphlets while under the protection of a highly placed family. His *Letters* 1537–57 are a unique record of the cultural and political events of his time, and illustrate his vivacious, exuberant character. He also wrote poems and comedies.

Aretino began as a protégé of Pope Leo X, but left Rome after the publication of his lewd verses. He settled in Venice, and quickly became known as the "Scourge of Princes" with his vicious satires on powerful contemporaries; he was also well paid for not taking up his pen.

Arezzo town in the Tuscan region of Italy; 50 mi/80 km SE of Florence; population (1981) 92,100. The writers Petrarch and Aretino were born

Argentina
Republic of
(República Argentina)

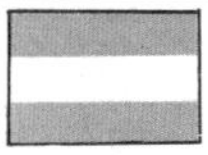

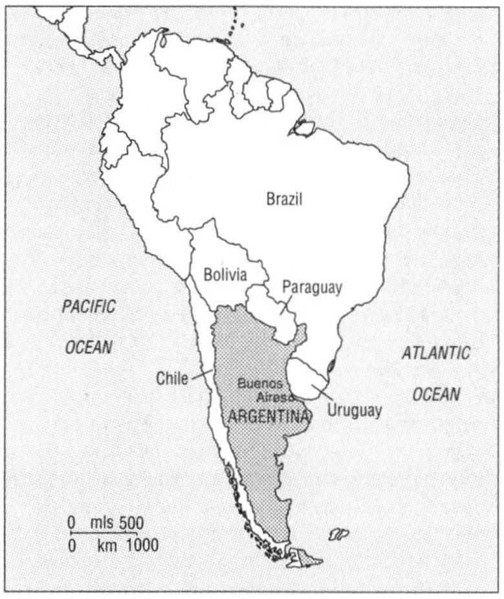
Brazil
Bolivia
Paraguay
PACIFIC
OCEAN
ATLANTIC
OCEAN
Chile
Buenos
Aires
ARGENTINA
Uruguay
0 mls 500
0 km 1000

area 1,073,116 sq mi/2,780,092 sq km
capital Buenos Aires (to move to Viedma)
cities Rosario, Córdoba, Tucumán, Mendoza, Santa Fé; ports are La Plata and Bahía Blanca
physical mountains in W, forest and savanna in N, pampas (treeless plains) in E central area, Patagonian plateau in S; rivers Colorado, Salado, Paraná, Uruguay, Rio de la Plata estuary
territories Tierra del Fuego; disputed claims to S Atlantic islands and part of Antarctica
features Andes mountains, with Aconcagua the highest peak in the W hemisphere; Iguazu Falls
head of state and government Carlos Menem from 1989
political system emergent democratic federal republic
political parties Radical Union Party (UCR), moderate centrist; Justice Party, right-wing Peronist
exports livestock products, cereals, wool, tannin, peanuts, linseed oil, minerals (coal, copper, molybdenum, gold, silver, lead, zinc, barium, uranium); the country has huge resources of oil, natural gas, hydroelectric power
currency austral
population (1989 est) 32,425,000 (mainly of Spanish or Italian origin, only about 30,000 American Indians surviving); growth rate 1.5% p.a.
life expectancy men 66, women 73
language Spanish (official), English, Italian, German, French
religion Roman Catholic (state-supported)
literacy men 96%, women 95% (1985 est)
GDP $70.1 bn (1990); $2,162 per head
chronology
1816 Independence achieved from Spain, followed by civil wars.
1946 Juan Perón elected president, supported by his wife "Evita."
1952 "Evita" Perón died.
1955 Perón overthrown and civilian administration restored.
1966 Coup brought back military rule.
1973 The Perónist party won the presidential and congressional elections. Perón returned from exile in Spain as president, with his third wife, "Isabelita," as vice-president.
1974 Perón died, succeeded by "Isabelita."
1976 Coup resulted in rule by a military junta led by Lt Gen Jorge Videla. Congress dissolved, and hundreds of people, including "Isabelita" Perón, detained.
1976–78 Ferocious campaign against left-wing elements. The start of the "dirty war."
1978 Videla retired. Succeeded by Gen Roberto Viola, who promised a return to democracy.
1981 Viola died suddenly. Replaced by Gen Leopoldo Galtieri.
1982 With a deteriorating economy, Galtieri sought popular support by ordering an invasion of the British-held Falkland Islands. After losing the short war, Galtieri was removed and replaced by Gen Reynaldo Bignone.
1983 Amnesty law passed and 1853 democratic constitution revived. General elections won by Dr Raúl Alfonsín and his party. Armed forces under scrutiny.
1984 Commission on the Disappearance of Persons (CONADEP) reported on over 8,000 people who had disappeared during the "dirty war" of 1976–83.
1985 A deteriorating economy forced Alfonsín to seek help from the IMF and introduce a harsh austerity program.
1986 Unsuccessful attempt on Alfonsín's life.
1988 Unsuccessful army coup attempt.
1989 Carlos Menem, of the Justice Party, elected president. Alfonsín handed over power before required date of Dec 1989. Thirty-day state of emergency declared, after rioting following price measures and dramatic inflation (120% in June, with an annual rate of approximately 12,000%).
1990 Full diplomatic relations with the UK restored. Menem elected Justice Party leader. Revolt by army officers thwarted. Inflation over the year to Nov 1990 now at 1,838%.

here. It is a mining town and also trades in textiles, olive oil, and antiques.

argali wild sheep *Ovis ammon* of Central Asia. The male can grow to 4 ft/1.2 m at the shoulder, and has massive spiral horns.

Argand diagram in mathematics, a method for representing complex numbers by Cartesian coordinates (x, y). Along the x (horizontal) axis are plotted the real numbers, and along the y (vertical) axis the nonreal, or ◊imaginary, numbers.

Argenteuil NW suburb of Paris, France, on the Seine river; population (1982) 96,045.

Argentina country in South America, bounded W and S by Chile, NW by Bolivia, and E by Paraguay, Brazil, Uruguay, and the Atlantic Ocean.

government The return of civilian rule in 1983 brought a return of the 1853 constitution, with some changes in the electoral system. The constitution created a federal system with a president elected by popular vote through an electoral college, serving a six-year term. The president is head of both state and government and chooses the cabinet.

Argentina is a federal union of 22 provinces, one national territory, and the Federal District. The two-chamber Congress consists of a 46-member senate chosen by provincial legislatures for a nine-year term, and a directly elected chamber of 254 deputies serving a four-year term. Each province has its own elected governor and legislature that deal with matters not assigned to the federal government. The two most significant parties are the Radical Union Party (UCR), and the Justice Party.

history Originally inhabited by South American Indian peoples, Argentina was first visited by Europeans in the early 16th century. Buenos Aires was founded first in 1536 and again in 1580 after being abandoned because of Indian attacks. Argentina was made a Spanish viceroyalty in 1776, and in 1810 the population rose against Spanish rule. Full independence was achieved in 1816. After a period of civil wars a stable government was established 1853 and the country developed as a democracy with active political parties.

Since 1930 it has been subject to alternate civilian and military rule. The UCR held power from 1916 until the first military coup in 1930. Civilian government returned in 1932, and a second military coup in 1943 paved the way for the rise of Lt-Gen Juan Domingo ◊Perón. Strengthened by the popularity of his wife, Eva Duarte ◊Perón (the legendary "Evita"), Perón created the Peronista party, based on extreme nationalism and social improvement. Evita Perón died in 1952, and in 1955 her husband was overthrown and civilian rule restored. Perón continued to direct the Peronista movement from exile in Spain.

A coup in 1966 restored military rule, and in 1973 the success of the Peronist party, Frente Justicialista de Liberación, brought Héctor Campora to the presidency. After three months he resigned to make way for Perón, with his third wife, Maria Estela Martinez de Perón ("Isabelita"), as vice-president. Perón died in 1974 and was succeeded by his widow. Two years later, because of concern about the economy, a military coup ousted her and installed a three-man junta, led by Lt-Gen Jorge Videla. The constitution was amended, political and labor union activity banned, and several hundred people arrested.

The years 1976–83 witnessed a ferocious campaign by the junta against left-wing elements, the "dirty war," during which it is believed that between 6,000 and 15,000 people "disappeared." Political activity was banned 1976–80. Although confirmed in office until 1981, Videla retired in 1978, to be succeeded by Gen Roberto Viola, who promised a return to democracy. In 1981 Viola died and was replaced by General Leopoldo ◊Galtieri.

In 1982 Galtieri, seeking popular support and wishing to distract attention from the deteriorating economy, ordered the invasion of the *Islas Malvinas*, the ◊Falkland Islands, over which Britain's claim to sovereignty had long been disputed. After a short war, during which 750 Argentinians were killed, the islands were reoccupied by Britain. US support for Britain pushed Argentina closer to Cuba, Nicaragua, and the ◊nonaligned states.

With the failure of the Falklands invasion, Galtieri was replaced in a bloodless coup by General Reynaldo Bignone. A military inquiry reported in 1983 that Galtieri's junta was to blame for the defeat. Several officers were tried, and some, including Galtieri, given prison sentences. It was announced that the 1853 constitution would be revived, and an amnesty was granted to all those convicted of political crimes during the past ten years. The ban on political and trade-union activity was lifted and general elections were held in Oct 1983. The main parties were the UCR, led by Raúl ◊Alfonsín, and the Peronist Justice Party, led by Italo Luder. Having won the election, Alfonsín announced radical reforms in the armed forces (leading to the retirement of more than half the senior officers) and the trial of the first three military juntas that had ruled Argentina since 1976.

He set up the National Commission on the Disappearance of Persons (CONADEP) to investigate the "dirty war." A report by CONADEP in 1984 listed over 8,000 people who had disappeared and 1,300 army officers who had been involved in the campaign of repression.

Alfonsín's government was soon faced with huge economic problems, resulting in recourse to help from the ◊IMF and an austerity program, described by the president as an "economy of war." The May 1989 presidential election was won by the Justice candidate, Carlos ◊Menem. Alfonsín handed over power in July 1989, five months before his term of office formally ended, to allow Menem to come to grips with the high inflation that threatened to bring about increasing social unrest. The new government soon established a rapport with the UK authorities and full diplomatic relations were restored Feb 1990 (the issue of sovereignty over the Falklands was skirted). In Aug 1990 President Menem was elected leader of the Peronist Justicia Party and in Dec a rebellion by junior army officers was put down.

argon (Greek *argos* "idle") colorless, odorless, nonmetallic, gaseous element, symbol Ar, atomic number 18, atomic weight 39.948. It is grouped with the ◊inert gases, since it was long believed not to react with other substances, but observations now indicate that it can be made to combine with boron fluoride to form compounds. It constitutes almost 1% of the Earth's atmosphere and was discovered in 1894 by the British chemists John Rayleigh (1842–1919) and William Ramsay after all oxygen and nitrogen had been removed chemically from a sample of air. It is used in electric light bulbs and radio tubes.

argonaut or ***paper nautilus*** pelagic octopus, genus *Argonauta*. The 8 in/20 cm female of the common paper nautilus, *A. argo*, secretes a spiralled papery shell for her eggs from the web of the first pair of arms. The male is a 0.4 in/1 cm shell-less dwarf.

Argonauts in Greek legend, the band of heroes who accompanied ◊Jason when he set sail in the *Argo* to find the ◊Golden Fleece.

Argonne wooded plateau in NE France, separating Lorraine and Champagne. It was the scene of much fighting in both world wars.

Argos city in ancient Greece, at the head of the Gulf of Nauplia, which was once a cult center of the goddess Hera. In the Homeric age the name "Argives" was sometimes used instead of "Greeks."

argument in mathematics, a specific value of the independent variable of a ◊function. It is also another name for ◊amplitude.

Argus in Greek mythology, a giant with a hundred eyes. When he was killed by Hermes, Hera transplanted his eyes into the tail of her favorite bird, the peacock.

Argyll Archibald Campbell, 5th Earl of 1530–1573. Adherent of the Scottish presbyterian John ◊Knox. A supporter of Mary Queen of Scots from 1561, he commanded her forces after her escape from Lochleven Castle in 1568. He revised his position and became Lord High Chancellor of Scotland in 1572.

Århus alternate form of ◊Aarhus, Denmark.

aria (Italian "air") solo vocal piece in an opera or oratorio, often in three sections, the third repeating the first after a contrasting central section.

Ariadne in Greek mythology, the daughter of Minos, king of Crete. When Theseus came from Athens as one of the sacrificial victims offered to the Minotaur, she fell in love with him and gave him a ball of thread, which enabled him to find his way out of the labyrinth.

Ariane series of launch vehicles built by the European Space Agency to place satellites into Earth orbit (first flight 1979). The launch site is at Kourou in French Guiana. Ariane is a three-stage rocket using liquid fuels, but small solid-fuel boosters can be attached to its first stage to increase carrying power.

Since 1984 it has been operated commercially by Arianespace, a private company financed by European banks and aerospace industries. Future versions of Ariane may carry astronauts.

Arianism a system of Christian theology that gave God the Father primacy over Christ. It was founded about 310 by ◊Arius, and condemned as heretical at the Council of Nicaea 325.

Some 17th- and 18th-century theologians held Arian views akin to those of ◊Unitarianism (that God is a single being, and that there is no such thing as the Trinity). In the 1970s the question of the heresy arose again for the Vatican in the writings of such theologians as Edouard Schillebeeckx of the Netherlands.

Arias Sanchez Oscar 1940– . Costa Rican politician, president 1986–90, secretary-general of the left-wing National Liberation Party (PLN). He advocated a neutralist policy and in 1987 was the leading promoter of the Central American Peace Plan (see ◊Nicaragua). He was awarded the Nobel Peace Prize in 1990.

Arica port in Chile; population (1987) 170,000. Much of Bolivia's trade passes through it, and there is contention over the use of Arica by Bolivia to allow access to the Pacific Ocean. Arica is Chile's northernmost city.

arid zone infertile area with a small, infrequent rainfall that rapidly evaporates because of high temperatures. There are arid zones in Morocco, Pakistan, Australia, and elsewhere.

Scarcity of water is a problem for the inhabitants of arid zones, and constant research goes into discovering cheap methods of distilling sea water and artificially recharging natural groundwater reservoirs. Another problem is the eradication of salt in irrigation supplies from underground sources or where a surface deposit forms in poorly drained areas.

Ariège river in southern France, a tributary of the Garonne. It gives its name to a *département*.

Aries zodiac constellation in the northern hemisphere between Pisces and Taurus, near Auriga, represented as the legendary ram whose golden fleece was sought by Jason and the Argonauts. Its most distinctive feature is a curve of three stars of decreasing brightness. The brightest of these is Hamal or Alpha Arietis, 85 light-years from Earth. The Sun passes through Aries from late April to mid-May. In astrology, the dates for Aries are between about March 21 and April 19 (see ◊precession).

The spring ◊equinox once lay in Aries, but has now moved into Pisces through the effect of the Earth's precession (wobble).

aril an accessory seed cover other than a ◊fruit; it may be fleshy and sometimes brightly colored, woody, or hairy. In flowering plants, ◊angiosperms, it is often derived from the stalk that originally attached the ovule to the ovary wall. Examples of arils include the bright-red, fleshy layer surrounding the yew seed (yews are ◊gymnosperms so they lack true fruits), and the network of hard filaments that partially covers the nutmeg seed; and yields the spice known as mace.

Another aril, the horny outgrowth found toward one end of the seed of the castor-oil plant *Ricinus communis*, is called a caruncle. It is formed from the integuments (protective layers enclosing the ovule) and develops after fertilization.

Ariosto Ludovico 1474–1533. Italian poet, born in Reggio. He wrote Latin poems and comedies on Classical lines, including the poem ◊*Orlando Furioso* 1516, 1532, an epic treatment of the *Roland* story, and considered to be the perfect poetic expression of the Italian Renaissance.

Ariosto joined the household of Cardinal Ippolito d'Este 1503, and was frequently engaged in ambassadorial missions and diplomacy for the Duke of Ferrara. In 1521 he became governor of a province in the Apennines, and after three years retired to Ferrara, where he died.

Aristarchus of Samos c. 280–264 BC. Greek astronomer. The first to argue that the Earth moves around the Sun, he was ridiculed for his beliefs.

His only surviving work is *Magnitudes and Distances of the Sun and Moon* but Archimedes quotes from another tract that no longer exists. Aristarchus produced methods for calculations that were geometrically correct but rendered useless by inaccuracies in the means of observation.

Aristides c. 530–468 BC. Athenian politician. He was one of the ten Athenian generals at the battle of ◊Marathon 490 BC and was elected chief archon, or magistrate. Later he came into conflict with the democratic leader Themistocles, and was exiled about 483 BC. He returned to fight against the Persians at Salamis 480 BC and in the following year, commanded the Athenians at Plataea.

He was sent into political exile 482 BC because the citizens tired of hearing him praised as "Aristides the Just," probably derived from his just assessment of the contribution to be paid by the Greek states who entered the Delian league against the Persians.

Aristippus c. 435–356 BC. Greek philosopher, founder of the ◊Cyrenaic or ◊hedonist school. A pupil of Socrates, he developed the doctrine that pleasure is the highest good in life. He lived at the court of ◊Dionysius of Syracuse and then with Laïs, a courtesan, in Corinth.

Aristophanes c. 448–380 BC. Greek comedic dramatist. Of his 11 extant plays (of a total of over 40), the early comedies are remarkable for the violent satire with which he ridiculed the democratic war leaders. He also satirized contemporary issues such as the new learning of Socrates in *The Clouds* 423 BC and the power of women in ◊*Lysistrata* 411 BC. The chorus plays a prominent role, frequently giving the play its title, as in *The Wasps* 422 BC, *The Birds* 414 BC, and *The Frogs* 405 BC.

Aristotle 384–322 BC. Greek philosopher who advocated reason and moderation. Aristotle maintained that sense experience is our only source of knowledge, and that by reasoning we can discover the essences of things, that is, their distinguishing qualities. In his works on ethics and politics, Aristotle suggested that human happiness consists in living in conformity with nature. He derived his political theory from the recognition that mutual aid is natural to humankind, and refused to set up any one constitution as universally ideal. Of Aristotle's works some 22 treatises survive through notes taken by his students, dealing with logic, metaphysics, physics, astronomy, meteorology, biology, psychology, ethics, politics, and literary criticism.

Born in Stagira in Thrace, Aristotle studied in Athens, became tutor to ◊Alexander the Great, and in 335 BC opened a school in the Lyceum (grove sacred to Apollo) in Athens. It became known as the "peripatetic school" because he walked up and down as he talked, and his works are a collection of his lecture notes. When Alexander died, Aristotle was forced to flee to Chalcis, where he died.

His works were lost to Europe after the decline of Rome, but they were reintroduced in the Middle Ages by Arab and Jewish scholars and became the basis of medieval ◊scholasticism.

arithmetic branch of mathematics involving the study of numbers. The fundamental operations of arithmetic are addition, subtraction, multiplication, division, and, dependent on these four, raising to ◊powers and extraction of roots. Percentages, fractions, and ratios are developed from these operations. Fractions arise in the process of measurement.

Forms of simple arithmetic existed in prehistoric times. In China, Egypt, Babylon, and early civilizations generally, arithmetic was used for commercial purposes, records of taxation, and astronomy. During the Dark Ages in Europe, knowledge of arithmetic was preserved in India and later among the Arabs. European mathematics revived with the development of trade and overseas exploration. Hindu-Arabic numerals replaced Roman numerals, allowing calculations to be made on paper, instead of by the ◊abacus.

The essential feature of this number system was the introduction of zero, which allows us to have a place-value system. The decimal numeral system employs ten numerals (0,1,2,3,4,5,6,7,8,9) and is said to operate in "base ten." In a base-ten number, each position has a value ten times that of the position to its immediate right; for example, in the number 23 the numeral 3 represents three units (ones), and the number 2 represents two tens. The Babylonians, however, used a complex base-sixty system, residues of which are found today in the number of minutes in each hour and in angular measurement (6×60 degrees). The Mayas used a base-twenty system.

There have been many inventions and developments to make the manipulation of the arithmetic processes easier, such as the invention of ◊logarithms by ◊Napier in 1614 and of the slide rule in the period 1620–30. Since then there have been many forms of ready reckoners invented, such as mechanical and electronic calculators and computers.

Modern computers fundamentally operate in base two, using only two numerals (0,1), known as a binary system. In binary, each position has a value twice as great as the position to its immediate right, so that for example binary 111 (111_2) is equal to 7 in the decimal system, and 1111 (1111_2) is equal to 15. Because the main operations of subtraction, multiplication, and division can be reduced mathematically to addition, digital computers carry out calculations by adding, usually in binary numbers in which the numerals 0 and 1 can be represented by off and on pulses of electric current.

Modular arithmetic, sometimes known as residue arithmetic, can take only a specific number of digits, whatever the value. For example, in modulo 4 (mod 4) the only values any number can take are 0,1,2, or 3. In this system, 7 is written as 3 mod 4, and 35 is also 3 mod 4. Notice 3 is the residue, or remainder, when both 7 and 35 are divided by 4. This form of arithmetic is often illustrated on a circle. It deals with events recurring in regular cycles, and is used in describing the functioning of gasoline engines, electrical generators, and so on. For example, in mod 12, the answer to a question as to what time it will be in five hours if it is now ten o'clock can be expressed $10 + 5 = 3$.

arithmetic sequence or ***arithmetic progression*** or ***arithmetic series*** sequence of numbers or terms that have a common difference between any one term and the next in the sequence. For example, 2, 7, 12, 17, 22, 27, ... is an arithmetic sequence with a common difference of 5. The general formula for the nth term is $a + (n - 1)d$, where a is the first term and d is the common difference. An arithmetic series is the sum of the terms in an arithmetic sequence. The sum S of n terms is given by $S = (n/a)[2a + (n - 1)d]$.

Arius c. 256–336. Egyptian priest whose ideas gave rise to ◊Arianism, a Christian belief which denied the complete divinity of Jesus.

He was born in Libya, and became a priest in Alexandria 311. In 318 he was excommunicated and fled to Palestine, but his theology spread to such an extent that the emperor Constantine called a council at Nicaea 325 to resolve the question. Arius and his adherents were condemned and banished.

Arizona state in SW US; nickname Grand Canyon State
area 113,523 sq mi/294,100 sq km
capital Phoenix
cities Tucson, Scottsdale, Tempe, Mesa, Glendale, Flagstaff
physical Colorado Plateau in the N and E, desert basins and mountains in the S and W, Colorado River, Grand Canyon
features Grand Canyon National Park (the multicolored-rock gorge through which the Colorado River flows, 4–18 mi/6–29 km wide, up to 1.1 mi/1.7 km deep and 217 mi/350 km long); Organ Pipe Cactus National Monument Park; deserts: Painted (including the Petrified Forest of fossil trees), Gila, Sonoran; dams: Roosevelt, Hoover; old London Bridge (transported 1971 to the tourist resort of Lake Havasu City)
products cotton under irrigation, livestock, copper, molybdenum, silver, electronics, aircraft
population (1990) 3,665,228; including 4.5% American Indians (Navaho, Hopi, Apache), who by treaty own a fourth of the state
famous people Cochise, Wyatt Earp, Geronimo, Barry Goldwater, Zane Grey, Percival Lowell, Frank Lloyd Wright
history part of New Spain 1715; part of Mexico 1824; passed to US after Mexican War 1848; territory 1863; statehood 1912.

Arizona is believed to derive its name from the Spanish *arida-zona* ("dry belt"). The first Spaniard to visit Arizona was the Franciscan Marcos de Niza 1539. After 1863 it developed rapidly as a result of the gold rush in neighboring California. Irrigation has been carried out on a colossal scale since the 1920s. The Roosevelt dam on Salt River, and Hoover Dam on the Colorado River between Arizona and Nevada, provide the state with both hydroelectric power and irrigation water. At the end of the 19th century, rich copper deposits were found in Arizona and subsequently deposits of many other minerals. Aided by the use of air conditioning, the post-World War II era has seen heavy influx by retirees and a great increase in tourism. The manufacture of electronic equipment has added considerably to the growth of the state economy.

Arizona

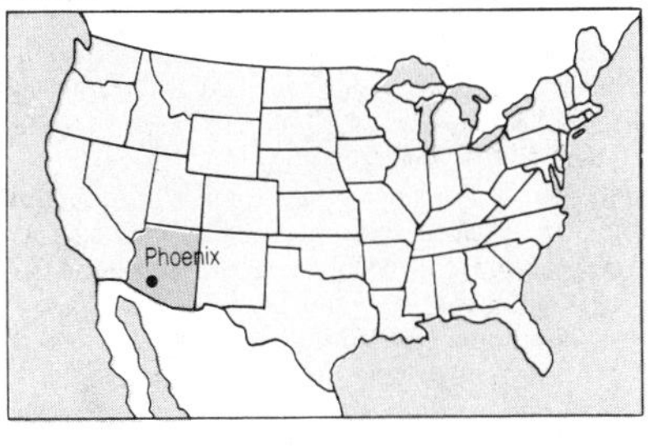
Phoenix

Arkansas

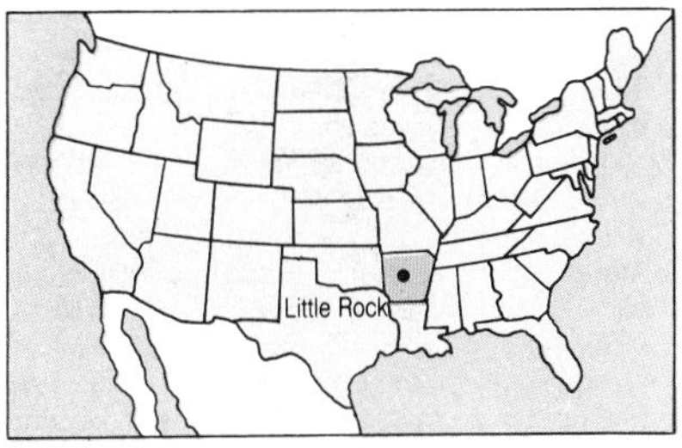
Little Rock

Arjan Indian religious leader, fifth guru (teacher) of Sikhism from 1581. He built the Golden Temple in ◊Amritsar and compiled the *Adi Granth*, the first volume of Sikh scriptures. He died in Muslim custody.

Arjuna Indian prince, one of the two main characters in the Hindu epic *Mahābhārata*.

Arkansas state in S central US; nickname Wonder State/Land of Opportunity
area 53,191 sq mi/137,800 sq km
capital Little Rock
cities Fort Smith, Pine Bluff, Fayetteville
physical Ozark mountains and plateau in the W, lowlands in the E; Arkansas River; many lakes
features Hot Springs National Park
products cotton, soybeans, rice, oil, natural gas, bauxite, timber, processed foods
population (1990) 2,350,725
famous people Johnny Cash, J William Fulbright, Douglas MacArthur, Winthrop Rockefeller
history explored by de Soto 1541; European settlers 1648, who traded with local Indians; part of Louisiana Purchase 1803; statehood 1836.

The first European settlement was Arkansas Post, founded by some of the companions of the French explorer La Salle. After seceding from the Union 1861 (see ◊Confederacy), it was readmitted 1868. In 1957 President Eisenhower sent US troops to enforce a court order to desegregate Central High School in Little Rock after Governor Orval Faubus had called up the National Guard to block integration.

Ark of the Covenant in the Old Testament, the chest that contained the Tablets of the Law as given to Moses. It is now the cupboard in a synagogue in which the ◊Torah scrolls are kept.

Arkwright Richard 1732–1792. English inventor and manufacturing pioneer who developed a machine for spinning cotton (he called it a "spinning frame") 1768. He set up a water-powered spinning factory 1771 and installed steam power in another factory 1790.

Arles town in Bouches-du-Rhône *département*, SE France, on the left bank of the Rhône; population (1982) 50,772. It is an important fruit- and vine-growing district. Roman relics include an amphitheater for 25,000 spectators. The cathedral of St Trophime is a notable Romanesque structure. The painters Van Gogh and Gauguin lived here 1888.

Arlington county in Virginia, and suburb of Washington, DC; population (1990) 170,936. It is the site of the National Cemetery for the dead of the US wars. The grounds were first used as a military cemetery in 1864 during the American Civil War. By 1975, 165,142 military, naval, and civilian persons had been buried there and included the Unknown Soldier of both World Wars, President John F Kennedy, and his brother Robert Kennedy.

Arlington city in N Texas, located between Dallas and Fort Worth. Industries include machinery, paper products, steel, automobile assembly, rubber, and chemicals; population (1990) 261,721.

Armada fleet sent by Philip II of Spain against England 1588. See ◊Spanish Armada.

armadillo mammal of the order Dasypodidae, with an armor of bony plates on its back. Some 20 species live between Texas and Patagonia and range in size from the fairy armadillo at 5 in/13 cm to the giant armadillo, 1.5 m/4.5 ft long. Armadillos feed on insects, snakes, fruit, and carrion. Some can roll into an armored ball if attacked; others rely on burrowing for protection.

The order Edentata ("without teeth") also includes sloths and anteaters. However, only the latter are toothless. Some species of armadillos can have up to 90 peglike teeth.

Armageddon in the New Testament (Revelation 16), the site of the final battle between the nations that will end the world; it has been identified with ◊Megiddo in Israel.

Armagh county town of Armagh, Northern Ireland; population (1981) 13,000. It became the religious center of Ireland in the 5th century when St Patrick was made archbishop. For 700 years it was the seat of the kings of Ulster. The Protestant archbishop of Armagh is nominally "Primate of All Ireland."

Armagnac a deep-colored brandy named after the district of Armagnac in Gascony, SW France, where it is produced.

armature in a motor or generator, the wire-wound coil that carries the current and rotates in a magnetic field. (In alternating-current machines, the armature is sometimes stationary.) "Armature" also means the pole piece of a permanent magnet or electromagnet. The moving, iron part of a solenoid, especially if it acts as a switch, may also be referred to as an armature.

Armenia constituent republic of the Soviet Union 1936–91
area 11,506 sq mi/29,800 sq km
capital Yerevan
towns Leninakan
physical mainly mountainous (including Mt Ararat), wooded
products copper, molybdenum, cereals, cotton, silk

armadillo

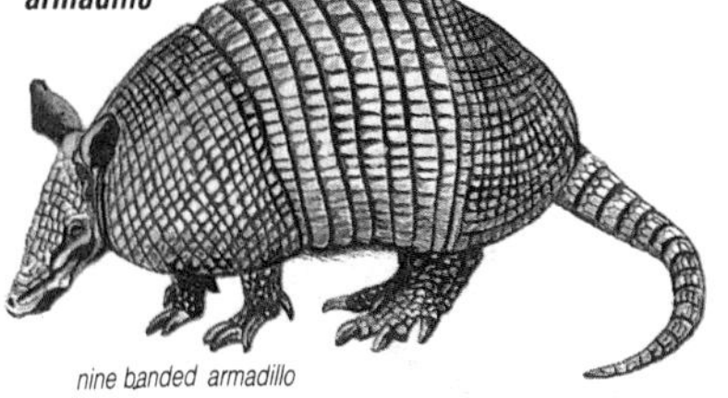

nine banded armadillo

Armenia

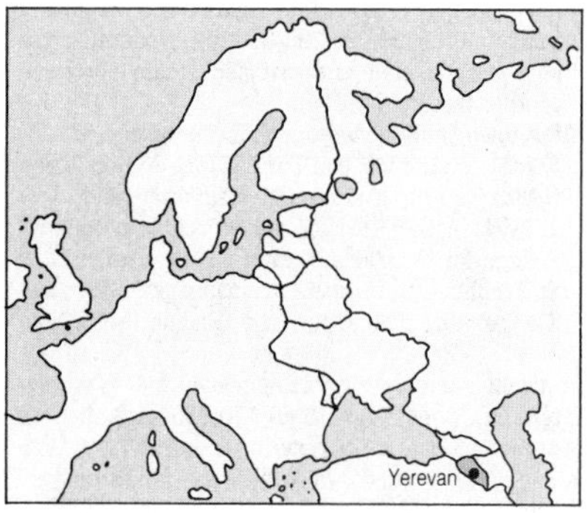
Yerevan

population (1987) 3,412,000; 90% Armenian, 5% Azerbaijani, 2% Russian, 2% Kurd.
language Armenian
religion traditionally Armenian Christian
history an ancient kingdom formerly occupying what is now the Van region of Turkey, part of NW Iran, and what is now the Armenian republic, it became an independent republic 1918, was occupied by the Red Army 1920, and became a constituent republic of the USSR 1936. An earthquake 1988 caused extensive loss of life and property. In 1988, demands for reunion with Nagorno-Karabakh led to riots, strikes and, eventually during 1989–90, to a civil war that had to be queled through the intervention of Soviet troops. The Armenian National Movement, formed Nov 1989, was at the forefront of this nationalist campaign that led to independence 1991.

Armenian church the form of Christianity adopted in Armenia in the 3rd century. The Catholicos, or exarch, is the supreme head, and Echmiadzin (near Yerevan) is his traditional seat.

About 295 Gregory the Illuminator (c. 257–332) was made exarch of the Armenian church, which has developed along national lines. The Seven Sacraments (or Mysteries) are administered, and baptism is immediately followed by confirmation. Believers number about 2 million.

Armenian language one of the main divisions of the Indo-European language family. Old Armenian, the classic literary language, is still used in the liturgy of the Armenian church. Contemporary Armenian, with modified grammar and enriched with words from other languages, is used by a group of 20th-century writers.

Armenian was not written down until the 5th century AD, when an alphabet of 36 (now 38) letters was evolved. Literature flourished in the 4th–14th centuries, revived in the 18th, and continued throughout the 20th.

Armenian massacres series of massacres of Armenians by Turkish soldiers between 1895 and 1915. Reforms promised to Armenian Christians by Turkish rulers never materialized; unrest broke out and there were massacres by Turkish troops 1895. Again in 1909 and 1915, the Turks massacred altogether more than a million Armenians and deported others into the N Syrian desert, where they died of starvation; those who could fled to Russia or Persia. Only some 100,000 were left.

They were declared part of the Transcaucasian Soviet Federated Republic within the USSR and then the Armenian Soviet Socialist Republic 1936.

Armentières town in N France on the Lys river; population about 26,000. The song "Mademoiselle from Armentières" originated during World War I, when the town was held by the British. The town was flattened by German bombardment in 1918 and rebuilt.

Arminius 17 BC–AD 21. German chieftain. An ex-soldier of the Roman army, he annihilated a Roman force led by Varus in the Teutoburger Forest area AD 9, and saved Germany from becoming a Roman province. He thus ensured that the empire's frontier did not extend beyond the Rhine.

Arminius Jacobus. Latinized name of Jakob Harmensen 1560–1609. Dutch Protestant priest who founded Arminianism, a school of Christian theology opposed to Calvin's doctrine of predestination. His views were developed by Simon Episcopius (1583–1643). Arminianism is the basis of Wesleyan ◊Methodism.

armistice a cessation of warfare while awaiting a peace settlement. "The Armistice" refers specifically to the end of World War I between Germany and the Allies on Nov 11, 1918. On June 22, 1940 French representatives signed an armistice with Germany in the same railroad carriage at Compiegne that was used in 1918. No armistice was signed with either Germany or Japan in 1945; both nations surrendered and there was no provision for the suspension of fighting. The Korean armistice signed at Panmunjon on July 27, 1953 terminated the Korean war 1950–1953.

Armistice Day anniversary of the armistice signed Nov 11, 1918, ending World War I. In the US this holiday is now called Veterans' Day.

armor body protection worn in battle. Body armor is depicted in Greek and Roman art. Chain mail was developed in the Middle Ages but the craft of the armorer in Europe reached its height in design in the 15th century, when knights, and to some extent, their horses, were encased in plate armor that still allowed freedom of movement. Medieval Japanese armor was articulated, made of iron, gilded metal, leather, and silk. Contemporary bulletproof vests and riot gear are forms of armor. The term is used in a modern context to refer to a mechanized armored vehicle, such as a tank.

Since World War II armor for tanks and ships has been developed beyond an increasing thickness of steel plate, becoming an increasingly light, layered composite, including materials such as ceramics. More controversial is "reactive" armor, consisting of "shoeboxes" made of armor containing small, quick-acting explosive charges, which are attached at the most vulnerable points of a tank, in order to break up the force of entry of an enemy warhead. This type is used by Israel and the USSR, but the incorporation of explosive material in a tank has potential drawbacks.

The invention of gunpowder led, by degrees, to the virtual abandonment of armor until World War I, when the helmet reappeared as a defense against shrapnel. Suits of armor in the Tower of London were studied by US designers of astronaut wear. Modern armor, used by the army, police, security guards, and people at risk from assassination, uses nylon and fiberglass and is often worn beneath their clothing.

Armory Show exhibition of Modern European art held in Feb 1913 in New York City.

It marked the arrival of abstract art in the US, and influenced US artists. A rioting crowd threatened to destroy Marcel Duchamp's *Nude Descending a Staircase* (now in the Museum of Art, Philadelphia).

Armstrong Edwin Howard 1890–1954. US radio engineer who developed a system known as superheterodyne tuning for reception over a very wide spectrum of radio frequencies and frequency ◊modulation for static-free reception.

Armstrong Louis ("Satchmo") 1901–1971. US jazz cornet and trumpet player and singer, born in New Orleans. His Chicago recordings in the 1920s with the Hot Five and Hot Seven brought him recognition for his warm and pure trumpet tone, his skill at improvisation, and his quirky, gravelly voice. From the 1930s he became equally widely known as a singer, comedian, and film actor.

In 1923 Armstrong joined the Creole Jazz Band led by the cornet player Joe "King" Oliver (1885–1938) in Chicago, but soon broke away and fronted various bands of his own. In 1947 he formed the Louis Armstrong All-Stars. He firmly established the pre-eminence of the virtuoso jazz soloist. He is credited with the invention of scat singing (vocalizing meaningless syllables chosen for their sound).

Armstrong Neil Alden 1930– . US astronaut. In 1969, he was the first person to set foot on the Moon; he said, "That's one small step for a man, one giant leap for mankind." The Moon landing was part of the ◊Apollo project.

Born in Ohio, he gained his pilot's license at 16 and served as a naval pilot in Korea 1949–52 before joining NASA as a test pilot. He was selected to be an astronaut 1962 and landed on the Moon July 20, 1969.

army an organized military force for fighting on the ground. A national army is used to further a political policy by force either within the state or on the territory of another state. Most countries have a national army, maintained by taxation, and raised either by conscription (compulsory military service) or voluntarily (paid professionals). Private

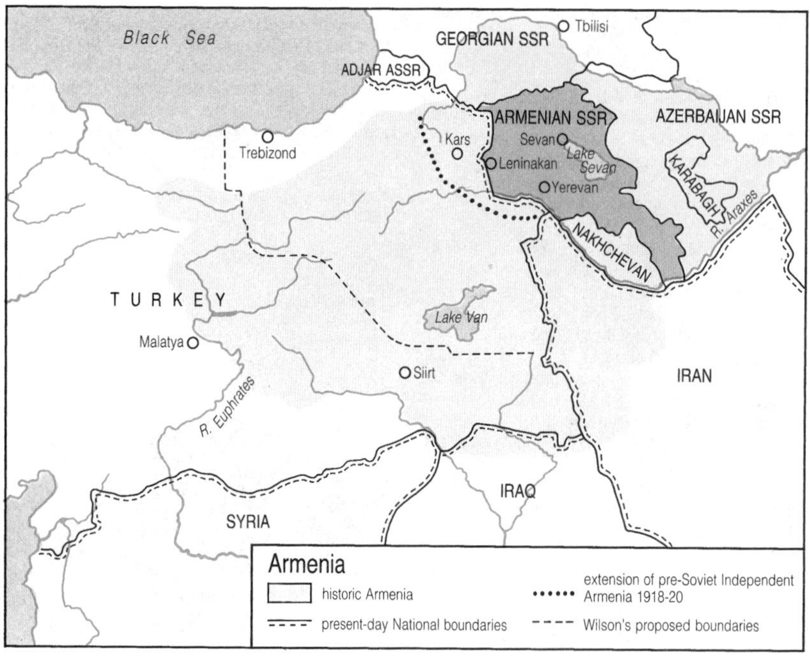
Black Sea
GEORGIAN SSR
Tbilisi
ADJAR ASSR
ARMENIAN SSR
AZERBAIJAN SSR
Kars
Sevan
Lake Sevan
Leninakan
Yerevan
Trebizond
KARABAGH
R. Araxes
NAKHICHEVAN
TURKEY
Malatya
Lake Van
Siirt
IRAN
R. Euphrates
IRAQ
SYRIA
Armenia
historic Armenia
extension of pre-Soviet Independent Armenia 1918-20
present-day National boundaries
Wilson's proposed boundaries

DAGUERRE
Chicago

Armstrong *Jazzman Louis "Satchmo" Armstrong played trumpet and sang scat throughout his long career. In this 1920s picture he is kneeling at the front playing a slide trumpet.*

armies may be employed by individuals and groups.

ancient armies (to 1066) Armies were common to all ancient civilizations. The Spartans trained from childhood for compulsory military service from age 21 to 26 in a full-time regular force as a heavily armed infantryman, or hoplite. Roman armies subjected all citizens to military service in legions of 6,000 men divided into cohorts of 600 men. Cohorts were similarly divided into six centuries of 100 men. The concept of duty to military service continued following the collapse of the Roman Empire. For example, the Anglo-Saxon Fyrd obliged all able-bodied men to serve in defense of Britain against Danish and then Norman invasion.

armies of knights and of mercenaries (1066–1648) Medieval monarchs relied upon mounted men-at-arms, or chevaliers, who in turn called upon serfs on the land. Feudal armies were thus inherently limited in size and could only fight for limited periods. Free yeomen armed with longbows were required by law to practice at the butts and provided an early form of indirect fire as artillery. In Europe paid troops, or soldi, and mounted troops, or serviertes (sergeants), made themselves available as freelances. By the end of the 15th century, battles or battalions or pikemen provided defense against the mounted knight. The hard gun, or arquebus, heralded the coming of infantrymen as known today. Those who wished to avoid military service could do so by paying scutage. For the majority the conpane, or company, was their home; they were placed under royal command by ordonnances and led by crown office holders, or officiers. Increased costs led to the formation of the first mercenary armies. For example, the Great Company of 10,000 men acted as an international racketeer, employing contractors, or condottieri, to serve the highest bidder. By the 16th century the long musket, pikemen, and the use of fortifications combined against the knight. Sappers became increasingly important in the creation and breaking of obstacles such as at Metz, the forerunner to the Maginot Line.

professional armies (1648–1792) The emergence of the European nation-state saw the growth of more professional standing armies which trained in drills, used formations to maximize firepower, and introduced service discipline. The invention of the ring bayonet and the flintlock saw the demise of pikemen and the increased capability to fire from three ranks (today still the standard drill formation in the British Army). Artillery was now mobile and fully integrated into the army structure. The defects of raw levies, noble amateurs, and mercenaries led Oliver Cromwell to create the New Model Army for the larger campaigns of the English Civil War. After the Restoration, Charles II establish a small standing army, which was expanded under James II and William III. In France, a model regiment was set up under de Martinet which set standards of uniformity for all to follow. State taxation provided for a formal system of army administration (uniforms, pay, ammunition). Nevertheless, recruits remained mainly society's misfits and delinquents. Collectively termed other ranks, they were divided from commissioned officers by a rigid hierarchical structure. The sheer cost of such armies forced wars to be fought by maneuver rather than by pitched battle, aiming to starve one's opponent into defeat while protecting one's own logistic chain.

armies of the revolution (1792–1819) Napoleon's organization of his army into autonomous corps of two to three divisions, in turn comprising two brigades of two regiments of two battalions, was a major step forward in allowing a rapid and flexible deployment of forces. Small-scale skirmishing by light infantry, coupled with the increasing devastation created by artillery or densely packed formations, saw the beginnings of the dispersed battlefield. Victory in war was now synonymous with the complete destruction of the enemy in battle. Reservists were conscripted to allow the mass army to fight wars through to the bitter end. (Only Britain, by virtue of the English Channel and the Royal Navy, was able to avoid the need to provide such large land forces.) Officers were now required to be professionally trained; the Royal Military College was set up in Britain 1802, the St Cyr in France 1808, the Kriegsakademie in Berlin 1810, and the Russian Imperial Military Academy 1832. Semaphore telegraph and observation balloons were first steps to increasing the commander's ability to observe enemy movements. The British army, under Wellington, was very strong, but afterwards decreased in numbers and efficiency.

national armies (1815–45) The defeat of Revolutionary France saw a return to the traditions of the 18th century and a reduction in conscription. Meanwhile the railroad revolutionized the deployment of forces, permitting quick mobilization, continuous resupply to the front, and rapid evacuation of casualties to the rear. By 1870, the limitation of supply inherent to the Napoleonic army had been overcome and once again armies of over 1 million could be deployed. By 1914, European national armies numbered as many as 3 million and were based on conscription. General staff were now required to manage these. Breech-loading rifles and machine guns ensured a higher casualty rate.

19th-century armies The 19th century saw the great development of rapidly produced missile

Armstrong *Seen here with fellow* Apollo 11 *crew members Michael Collins (left) and Edwin "Buzz" Aldrin (center) is Neil Armstrong (right), the first person to set foot on the Moon, July 20, 1969.*

weapons and the use of railroads to move troops and materials.

technological armies (1918–45) The advent of the internal-combustion engine allowed new advances in mobility to overcome the supremacy of the defensive over the offensive. The tank and the radio were important to the evolution of armored warfare (blitzkrieg). World War I employed enormous armies in trench warfare; the British army expanded from 750,000 to 5.5 million troops. Armies were able to reorganize into highly mobile formations, such as the German Panzer (tank) Divisions, which utilized speed, firepower, and surprise to overwhelm static defenses and thereby dislocate the army's rear. The armies of World War II were very mobile, especially the Allied forces in the Pacific, which were closely coordinated with the navy and air force. The fueling and maintenance of such huge fleets of vehicles again increased the need for extensive supply lines. The complexity of the mechanized army demanded a wide range of skills not easily found through conscription.

armies of the nuclear age (1945–) The advent of tactical nuclear weapons severely compounded the problems of mass concentration and thus protected mobility assumed greater importance to allow rapid concentration and dispersal of forces in what could be a high chemical threat zone. From the 1960s there were sophisticated developments in tanks and antitank weapons, mortar-locating radar, and heat-seeking missiles. All armies of NATO and the Warsaw Pact are professional, except those of Canada and the UK. In the event of a nuclear war, all armies would be of little value.

Arnauld French family associated with ◊Jansenism, a Christian church movement that began in the 17th century. Antoine Arnauld (1560–1619) was a Parisian advocate, strongly critical of the Jesuits; along with the philosopher Pascal and others, he produced not only Jansenist pamphlets, but works on logic, grammar, and geometry. Many of his 20 children were associated with the abbey of Port Royal, a convent of Cistercian nuns near Versailles which became the center of Jansenism. His youngest child, Antoine (1612–1694), the "great Arnauld," was religious director there.

Arne Thomas Augustus 1710–1778. English composer, whose musical drama *Alfred* 1740 includes the song "Rule Britannia!"

Arnhem, Battle of in World War II, airborne operation by the Allies, 17–Sept 26, 1944, to secure a bridgehead over the Rhine, thereby opening the way for a thrust toward the Ruhr and a possible early end to the war. It was only partly successful. Arnhem is a city in the Netherlands, on the Rhine SE of Utrecht; population (1988) 297,000. It produces salt, chemicals, and pharmaceuticals.

Arnim Ludwig Achim von 1781–1831. German Romantic poet and novelist. Born in Berlin, he wrote short stories, a romance (*Gräfin Dolores/ Countess Dolores* 1810), and plays, but left the historical novel *Die Kronenwächter* 1817 unfinished. With Clemens Brentano he collected the German folk songs in *Des Knaben Wunderhorn/ The Boy's Magic Horn* 1805–08.

Arno Italian river 150 mi/240 km long, rising in the Apennines, and flowing westward to the Mediterranean Sea. Florence and Pisa stand on its banks. A flood in 1966 damaged virtually every Renaissance landmark in Florence.

Arnold Benedict 1741–1801. US soldier and military strategist, who, during the American Revolution won the turning point battle at Saratoga 1777 for the Americans. He is chiefly remembered as a traitor to the American side. A merchant in New Haven, Connecticut, he joined the colonial forces but in 1780 plotted to betray the strategic post at West Point to the British.

Arnold was bitter at having been passed over for promotion, and he contacted Henry Clinton to propose defection. Major André was sent by the British to discuss terms with him, but was caught and hanged as a spy. Arnold escaped to the British, who gave him an army command.

Since the plot failed, he was paid only a fraction of the money promised him.

aromatic compound

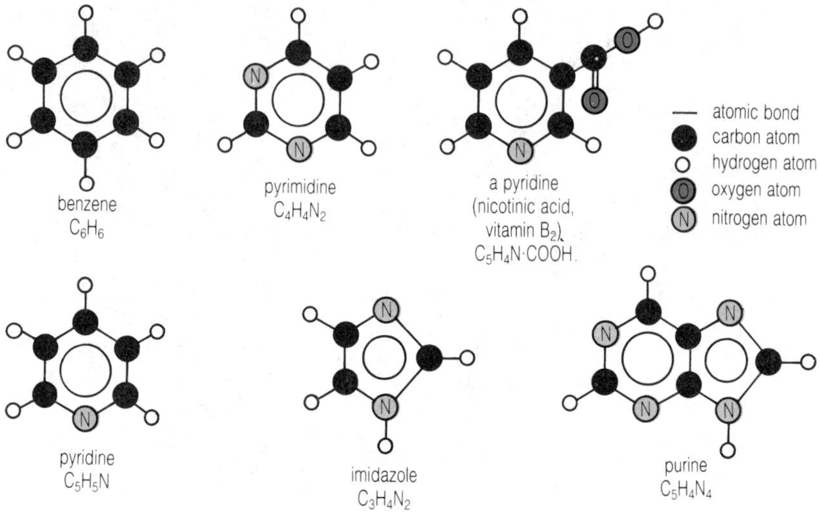
benzene
C_6H_6
pyrimidine
$C_4H_4N_2$
a pyridine
(nicotinic acid,
vitamin B_2)
$C_5H_4N{\cdot}COOH$
atomic bond
carbon atom
hydrogen atom
oxygen atom
nitrogen atom
pyridine
C_5H_5N
imidazole
$C_3H_4N_2$
purine
$C_5H_4N_4$

Arnold Malcolm (Henry) 1921– . English composer. His work is tonal and includes a large amount of orchestral, chamber, ballet, and vocal music. His operas include *The Dancing Master* 1951, and he has written music for more than 80 films, including *The Bridge on the River Kwai* 1957, for which he won an Academy Award.

Arnold Matthew 1822–1888. English poet and critic, son of Thomas Arnold. His poems, characterized by their elegiac mood and pastoral themes, include *The Forsaken Merman* 1849, *Thyrsis* 1867 (commemorating his friend Arthur Hugh Clough), *Dover Beach* 1867, and *The Scholar Gypsy* 1853. Arnold's critical works include *Essays in Criticism* 1865 and 1888, and *Culture and Anarchy* 1869, which attacks 19th-century philistinism.

aromatherapy the use of aromatic essential oils to relieve tension or to induce a feeling of wellbeing, usually in combination with massage. It is also used to relieve minor skin complaints. Common in the Middle East for centuries, the practice was reintroduced to the West in France during the 1960s.

aromatic compound any organic chemical that incorporates a closed chain or ring in its structure, most typically derived from ◊benzene (see also ◊cyclic compounds). Aromatic compounds undergo chemical substitution reactions.

Arp Hans or Jean 1887–1966. French abstract painter and sculptor. He was one of the founders of the ◊Dada movement about 1917, and later was associated with the Surrealists. His innovative wood sculptures use organic shapes in bright colors.

In his early experimental works, such as collages, he collaborated with his wife Sophie Taeuber-Arp (1889–1943).

Arran large mountainous island in the Firth of Clyde, Scotland, in Strathclyde; area 165 sq mi/ 427 sq km; population (1981) 4,726. It is popular as a vacation resort. The chief town is Brodick.

Arras French town on the Scarpe river NE of Paris; population (1982) 80,500 (conurbation). It is the capital of Pas-de-Calais *département*, and was formerly known for tapestry. It was the birthplace of the French revolutionary leader Robespierre.

Arras, Battle of battle of World War I, April–May 1917. It was an effective but costly British attack on German forces in support of a French offensive, which was only partially successful, on the ◊Siegfried Line. British casualties totalled 84,000 as compared to 75,000 German casualties. In World War II the town of Arras was captured 1940 by the Germans in their advance on Dunkirk.

Arras, Congress and Treaty of a meeting in N France 1435 between representatives of Henry VI of England, Charles VII of France, and Philip the Good of Burgundy to settle the Hundred Years' War. The outcome was a diplomatic victory for France. Although England refused to compromise on Henry VI's claim to the French crown, France signed a peace treaty with Burgundy, England's former ally.

Arrau Claudio 1903– . Chilean pianist. A concert performer from the age of five, he specializes in 19th-century music and is known for his thoughtful interpretation.

arrest deprivation of personal liberty by legal authority to stop commission of a crime or to charge someone with violation of a criminal or civil law.

Federal laws, state laws, and local ordinances define circumstances under which individuals may be detained by law officers acting independently, court-issued warrants, or other individuals (citizen's arrest).

Arrhenius Svante August 1859–1927. Swedish scientist, the founder of physical chemistry. Born near Uppsala, he became a professor at Stockholm in 1895, and made a special study of electrolysis (the effects of an electric current passing through a liquid). He wrote *Worlds in the Making* and *Destinies of the Stars*, and in 1903 received the Nobel Prize for Chemistry. In 1905 he is reputed to have predicted global warming as a result of carbon dioxide emission from burning fossil fuels.

arrhythmia disturbance of the natural rhythm of the heart. There are various kinds of arrhythmia, some innocent, some indicative of heart disease.

arrowroot starchy substance derived from the roots and tubers of various tropical plants with thick, clumpy roots. The true arrowroot *Maranta arundinacea* was used by the Indians of South America as an antidote against the effects of poisoned arrows.

The West Indian island of St Vincent is the main source of supply today. The edible starch is easily digested and is good for invalids.

arrowwood any of various North American trees and shrubs, especially of the genus *Viburnum*, named for their long, straight branches, which were used by American Indians to make arrows.

arsenic brittle, greyish-white, semimetallic element (◊metalloid), symbol As, atomic number 33, atomic weight 74.92. It occurs in many ores and occasionally in its elemental state, and is widely distributed, being present in minute quantities in the soil, the sea, and the human body. In larger quantities, it is poisonous. The chief source of arsenic compounds is as a byproduct from metallurgical processes. It is used in making semiconductors, alloys, and solders. The name derives from Latin *arsenicum*.

As it is a cumulative poison, its presence in food and drugs is very dangerous. The symptoms of arsenic poisoning are vomiting, diarrhea, tingling and possibly numbness in the limbs, and collapse.

arson the malicious and willful setting fire to property.

Often arson is a crime committed to claim insurance benefits fraudulently.

art in the broadest sense, all the processes and products of human skill, imagination, and invention; the opposite of nature. In contemporary usage, definitions of art usually reflect esthetic criteria, and the term may encompass literature, music, drama, painting, and sculpture. Popularly, the term is most commonly used to refer to the visual arts. In Western culture, esthetic criteria introduced by the ancient Greeks still influence our perceptions and judgments of art.

Two currents of thought run through our ideas about art. In one, derived from Aristotle, art is concerned with *mimesis* ("imitation"), the representation of appearances, and gives pleasure through the accuracy and skill with which it depicts the real world.

The other view, derived from Plato, holds that the artist is inspired by the Muses (or by God, or by the inner impulses, or by the collective unconscious) to express that which is beyond appearances—inner feelings, eternal truths, or the essence of the age. In the Middle Ages the term "art" was used, chiefly in the plural, to signify a branch of learning which was regarded as an instrument of knowledge. The seven liberal arts consisted of the *trivium*, that is grammar, logic, and rhetoric; and the *quadrivium*, that is arithmetic, music, geometry, and astronomy. In the visual arts of Western civilizations, painting and sculpture have been the dominant forms for many centuries. This has not always been the case in other cultures. Islamic art, for example, is one of ornament, for under the Muslim religion artists were forbidden to usurp the divine right of creation by portraying living creatures. In some cultures masks, tattoos, pottery, and metalwork have been the main forms of visual art. Recent technology has made new art forms possible, such as photography and cinema, and today electronic media have led to entirely new ways of creating and presenting visual images. See also ◊ancient art, ◊medieval art, and the arts of individual countries, such as ◊French art, and individual movements, such as ◊Romanticism, ◊Cubism, and ◊Impressionism.

Artaud Antonin 1896–1948. French theater director. Although his play, *Les Cenci/The Cenci* 1935, was a failure, his concept of the Theatre of Cruelty, intended to release feelings usually repressed in the unconscious, has been an important influence on modern dramatists such as Albert Camus and Jean Genet and on directors and producers. Declared insane 1936, Artaud was confined in an asylum.

Art Deco popular and pervasive style in art and architecture named after a 1925 French exhibition of modern art and industrial design (*Paris Exposition Internationale des Arts Decoratifs et Industriels Modernes*), noted for streamlined shapes and geometric forms. It was popular particularly in France and the US, where it was used extensively in the 1920s and 1930s, in urban architecture such as the Chrysler Building, New York City; in interior design such as in Radio City Music Hall, New York City; and in notable designs for streamlined trains, automobiles, and airplanes. It also influenced industrial design in products such as chinaware, radios, textiles, home furnishings, jewelry, and printed matter. Its use in film sets and costumes helped promote a fascination with Modernism that culminated in the 1939–40 World's Fair in New York City. From the 1970s, a revival of interest in the designs and designers, notably Raymond Loewy, named the style, which in its time was called *moderne*.

artesian well

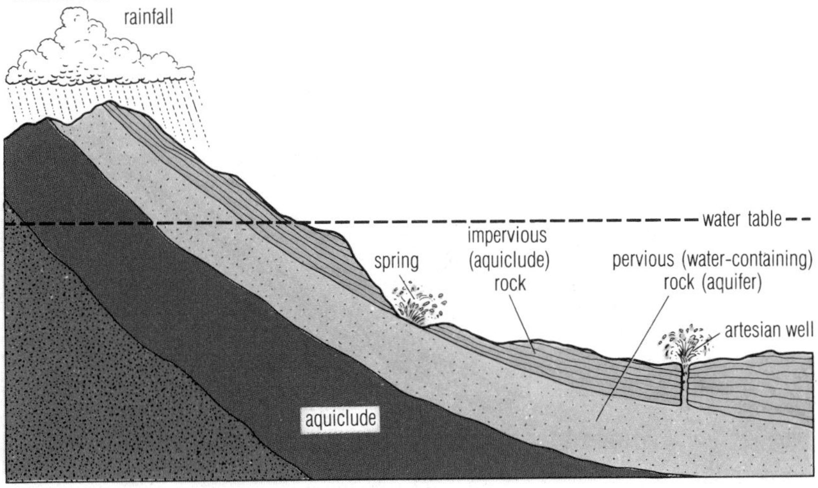
rainfall
water table
impervious (aquiclude) rock
spring
pervious (water-containing) rock (aquifer)
artesian well
aquiclude

Artemis in Greek mythology, the goddess (Roman Diana) of chastity, the Moon, and the hunt. She is the twin sister of ◊Apollo. Her cult center was at Ephesus.

arteriography method of examining the interior of an artery by injecting into it a radio-opaque solution, which is visible on an X-ray photograph. It is used for the arteries of the heart (coronary arteriogram), for example.

arteriosclerosis hardening of the arteries, with thickening and loss of elasticity. It is associated with smoking, aging, and a diet high in saturated fats. The term is used loosely as a synonym for ◊atherosclerosis.

artery vessel that conveys blood from the heart of a vertebrate to the body tissues. The largest of the arteries is the aorta, which in mammals leads from the left ventricle of the heart, up over the heart, and down through the diaphragm into the belly. Arteries are flexible, elastic tubes, consisting of three layers, the middle of which is muscular; its rhythmic contraction aids the pumping of blood around the body.

Not all arteries carry oxygen-rich blood; the pulmonary arteries convey deoxygenated (oxygen-poor) blood from heart to lungs. The cutting of an artery of any size is a dangerous injury. In middle and old age, the arteries normally lose their elasticity; the walls degenerate and can become impregnated with fatty deposits, resulting in ◊atherosclerosis, a condition which can lead to heart disease.

artesian well a well in which water rises from its ◊aquifer under natural pressure. Such a well may be drilled into an aquifer that is confined by impermeable beds both above and below. If the water table (the top of the region of water saturation) in that aquifer is above the level of the well head, hydrostatic pressure will force the water to the surface.

The name comes from Artois, a historical region of N France, on the Strait of Dover, where the phenomenon was first observed.

arthritis inflammation of the joints, with pain, swelling, and restricted motion. Many conditions may cause arthritis, including gout and trauma to the joint.

More common in women, rheumatoid arthritis usually begins in middle age in the small joints of the hands and feet, causing a greater or lesser degree of deformity and painfully restricted movement. It is alleviated by drugs, and surgery may be performed to correct deformity.

arthropod member of the phylum Arthropoda; an invertebrate animal with jointed legs and a segmented body with a horny or chitinous casing (exoskeleton), which is shed periodically and replaced as the animal grows. Included are arachnids such as spiders and mites, as well as crustaceans, millipedes, centipedes, and insects.

Arthur 6th century AD. Legendary English king and hero in stories of ◊Camelot and the quest for the ◊Holy Grail. Arthur is said to have been born in Tintagel, Cornwall, and buried in Glastonbury. He may have been a Romano-British leader against pagan Saxon invaders.

The legends of Arthur and the knights of the Round Table were developed in the 12th century by Geoffrey of Monmouth and the Norman writer Wace. Later writers on the theme include the anonymous author of *Sir Gawayne and the Greene Knight* 1346, Thomas Malory, Tennyson, T H White, and Mark Twain.

Arthur Chester Alan 1830–1886. The 21st president of the US. He was born in Vermont, the son of a Baptist minister, and became a lawyer and Republican political appointee in New York. In 1880, Arthur was chosen as ◊Garfield's vice-president, and was his successor when Garfield was assassinated the following year. Arthur held office until 1885.

artichoke two plants of the composite or sunflower family Compositae. The common or globe artichoke *Cynara scolymus* is native to the Mediterranean and is a form of thistle. It is tall, with purplish blue flowers; the bracts of the unopened flower are eaten.

The Jerusalem artichoke is a sunflower *Helianthus tuberosus*, a native to North America; it has edible tubers, and its common name is a corruption of the Italian for sunflower, *girasole*.

article a grammatical ◊part of speech. There are two articles in English: the definite article *the*, which serves to specify or identify a noun (as in "This is *the* book I need"), and the indefinite article *a* or (before vowels) *an*, which indicates a

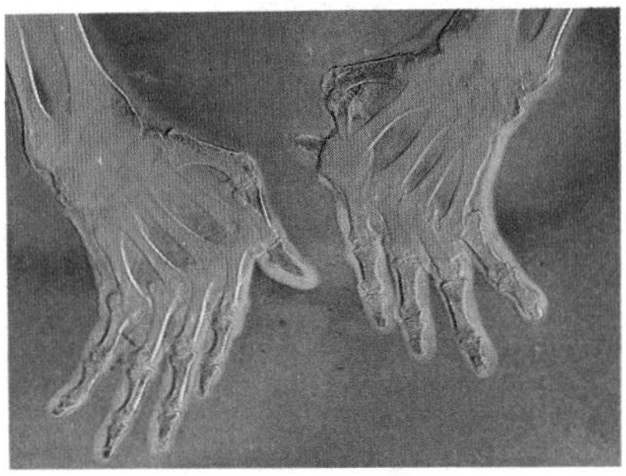

***arthritis** X ray of the hands of a person suffering from extreme rheumatoid arthritis.*

Arthur *The 21st president of the United States of America, Chester A. Arthur, a Republican. 1881–1885.*

single unidentified noun ("They gave me *a* piece of paper and *an* envelope").

artificial insemination (AI) mating achieved by mechanically injecting previously collected semen into the uterus without genital contact. It is commonly used with cattle because it allows farmers to select the type and quality of bull required for a herd; it controls the timing and organization of a breeding program. The practice of artificially inseminating pigs, dogs, horses, and humans has become widespread in recent years.

artificial intelligence (AI) branch of cognitive science concerned with creating computer programs that can perform actions comparable with those of an intelligent human. Current AI research covers areas such as planning (for robot behavior), language understanding, pattern recognition, and knowledge representation.

Early AI programs, developed in the 1960s, attempted simulations of human intelligence or were aimed at general problem-solving techniques. It is now thought that intelligent behavior depends as much on the knowledge a system possesses as on its reasoning power. Present emphasis is on ◊knowledge-based systems, such as ◊expert systems. Britain's largest AI laboratory is at the Turing Institute, University of Strathclyde, Glasgow. In May 1990 the first International Robot Olympics was held there, including table-tennis matches between robots of the UK and the US.

artificial limb device to replace a limb that has been removed by surgery or one that is malformed because of genetic defects. It is one form of ◊prosthesis.

artificial respiration the maintenance of breathing when the natural process is suspended. If breathing is permanently suspended, as in paralysis, an iron lung is used; in cases of electric shock or apparent drowning, for example, the first choice is the expired-air method, the kiss of life by mouth-to-mouth breathing until natural breathing is resumed.

artificial selection in biology, selective breeding of individuals that exhibit particular characteristics that a plant or animal breeder wishes to develop. The development of particular breeds of cattle for improved meat production (such as the Aberdeen Angus) or milk production (such as Holsteins) are examples.

artillery collective term for military ◊firearms too heavy to be carried.

Artillery can be mounted on ships or airplanes and includes cannons and missile launchers.

14th century Cannons came into general use, and were most effective in siege warfare. The term had previously been applied to catapults used for hurling heavy objects.

16th century The howitzer, halfway between a gun and a mortar (muzzle-loading cannon), was first used in sieges.

early 19th century In the Napoleonic period, field artillery became smaller and more mobile.

1914–18 In World War I, howitzers were used to demolish trench systems. Giant cannons were used in the entrenched conditions of the Western Front and at sea against the lumbering, heavily armored battleships, but their accuracy against small or moving targets was poor.

1939–41 In World War II, airplanes and air-mounted artillery were important to both the European and Pacific fronts.

1970s Introduction of electronically operated target devices and remote-control firing.

1980s Howitzers became self-mobile and computer-controlled. Shells may be made to home in automatically on an unseen target, such as a tank.

Art Nouveau art style, named for a shop in Paris that opened in 1895, which makes marked use of sinuous form, stylized flowers and foliage, and flame shapes. In England, it appears in the illustrations of Aubrey Beardsley; in Spain, in the architecture of Antonio Gaudí; in France, in the art glass of René Lalique; in the US, in the lamps and metal work of Louis Comfort Tiffany; and in Scotland, in the interior and exterior designs of Charles Rennie Mackintosh. Art Nouveau was also known as Jugendstil in Germany and Stile Liberty in Italy.

Artois former province of N France, bounded by Flanders and Picardie and almost corresponding with the modern *département* of Pas-de-Calais. Its capital was Arras. Its Latin name *Artesium* lent its name to the artesian well first sunk at Lillers 1126.

Arts and Crafts movement an English social movement, largely antimachine in spirit, based in design and architecture and founded by William Morris in the late 19th century. It was supported by the architect A W Pugin and by John ◊Ruskin and stressed the importance of hand crafting (see also ◊Art Nouveau).

Aruba island in the Caribbean, the westernmost of the Lesser Antilles; an overseas part of the Netherlands

area 75 sq mi/193 sq km

population (1985) 61,000

history Aruba obtained separate status from the other Netherlands Antilles 1986 and has full internal autonomy.

arum any plant of the family Araceae, especially the Old World genus *Arum*. The arum called trumpet lily *Zantedeschia aethiopica*, an ornamental plant, is a native of South Africa.

Jack-in-the-pulpit and skunk cabbage are North American arums belonging to related genera.

Arunachal Pradesh state of India, in the Himalayas on the borders of Tibet and Myanmar

area 32,270 sq mi/83,600 sq km

capital Itanagar

products rubber, coffee, spices, fruit, timber

population (1981) 628,000

language 50 different dialects

history formerly nominally part of Assam, known as the renamed Arunachal Pradesh ("Hills of the Rising Sun"). It became a state 1986.

Arval Brethren (Latin *Fratres Arvales*, brothers of the field) body of priests in ancient Rome who offered annual sacrifices to the *lares* or divinities of the fields to ensure a good harvest. They formed a college of 12 priests, and their chief festival fell in May.

Arvand River Iranian name for the ◊Shatt al-Arab waterway.

Aryan the Indo-European family of languages; also the hypothetical parent language of an ancient people who are believed to have lived between Central Asia and E Europe and to have reached Persia and India in one direction and Europe in another, sometime in the 2nd century BC, diversifying into the various Indo-European language speakers of later times. In ◊Nazi Germany Hitler and other theorists erroneously propagated the idea of the Aryans as a white-skinned, blue-eyed, fair-haired master race.

artificial respiration

This technique – mouth-to-mouth resuscitation – delivers a continuous supply of oxygen to the lungs of an unconscious person who is not breathing.

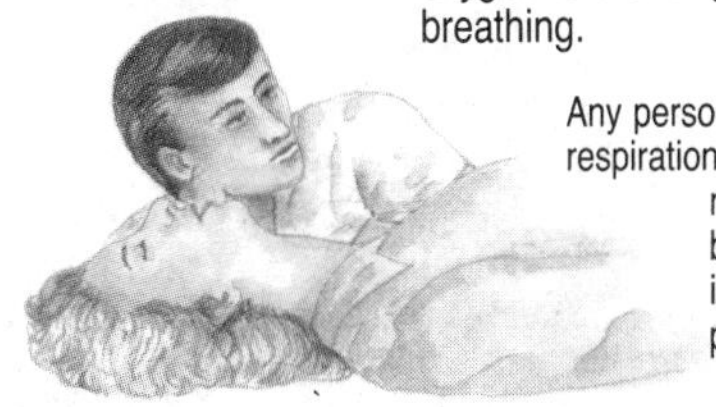

Any person who fails to breathe spontaneously requires artificial respiration immediately. If the vital air supply is interrupted for more than four minutes, brain, heart and other tissues begin to suffer irreversible damage. Warning signs include absence of chest movements and blue-gray pallor.

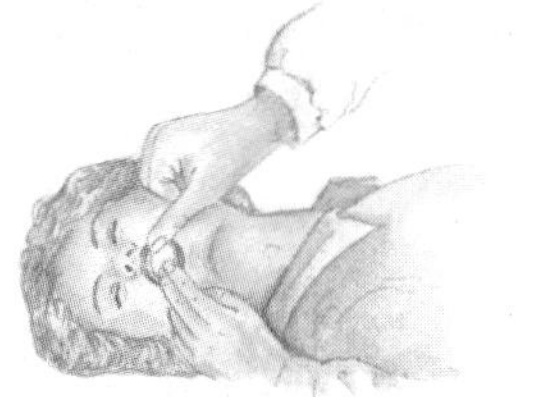

Often the mouth and throat are blocked by blood, stomach contents, or dentures. The victim should be turned onto one side, which may clear the airway. Any obstruction can be removed with the fingers wrapped in a clean cloth. If the person is still not breathing artificial resuscitation should be started at once.

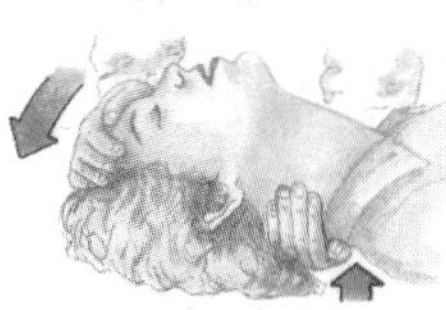

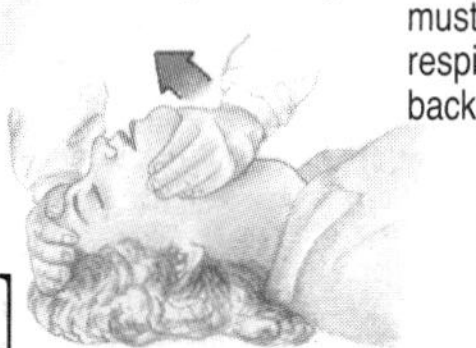

When an unconscious person is placed in the supine position the tongue may drop into the back of the throat, filling the airway and preventing air from reaching the lungs. An open airway must be established before artificial respiration is given. The head is tilted backwards until neck and chest are in a line. Then the jaw is extended to lift the tongue. The position is maintained by keeping one hand on the forehead and the other under the chin.

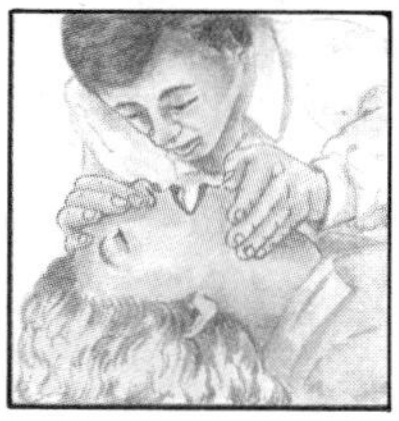

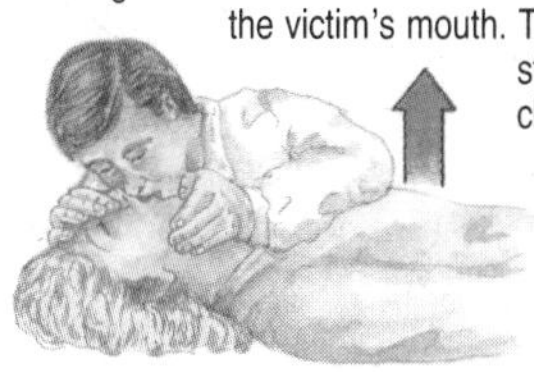

An airtight seal is created by pinching the nostrils between the fingers of the hand on the forehead and placing the lips around the victim's mouth. The lungs are expanded with a steady, gentle breath, and the chest rises visibly. Exhalation occurs naturally, as the victim's mouth is uncovered. For adults, the procedure is repeated 12 times per minute.

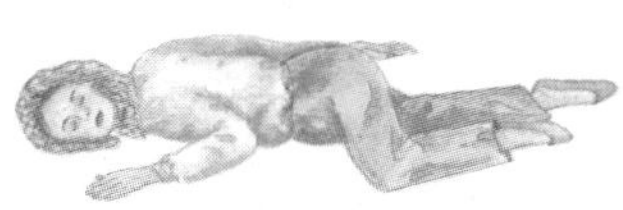

As soon as spontaneous breathing begins the victim should be placed in the recovery position. This keeps the airway clear.

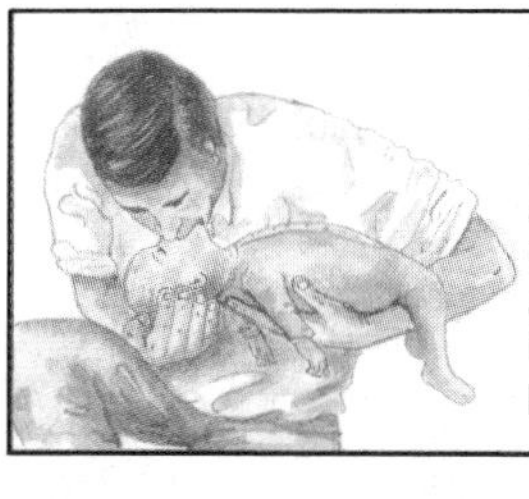

The lips are placed around the nose and mouth of an infant to obtain an airtight seal. No more than little puffs are required to fill the lungs, at a rate of 20 per minute.

Aryana ancient name of Afghanistan.

Aryan language any of the languages of the Aryan peoples of India; a 19th-century name for the ◊Indo-European languages.

Arya Samaj Hindu religious sect founded by Dayanand Saraswati (1825–1888) about 1875. He renounced idol-worship and urged a return to the purer principles of the Vedas (Hindu scriptures). For its time the movement was quite revolutionary in its social teachings, which included forbidding ◊caste practices, prohibiting child-marriage, and allowing widows to remarry.

ASA abbreviation for Association of South East Asia (1961–67), replaced by ASEAN, ◊Association of Southeast Asian Nations.

ASA in photography, a numbering system for rating the speed of films, devised by the American Standards Association. It has now been superseded by ◊ISO, the International Standards Organization.

a.s.a.p. abbreviation for as soon as possible.

ASAT acronym for antisatellite weapon.

asbestos any of several related minerals of fibrous structure that offer great heat resistance because of their nonflammability and poor conductivity. Commercial asbestos is generally made from chrysolite, a ◊serpentine mineral, tremolite (a white ◊amphibole) and riebeckite (a blue amphibole, also known as crocidolite when in its fibrous form). Asbestos usage is now strictly controlled because exposure to its dust can cause cancer.

Asbestos has been used for brake linings, suits for fire fighters and astronauts, insulation of electric wires in furnaces, and fireproof materials for the building industry. Exposure to asbestos is a recognized cause of industrial cancer (mesothelioma), especially in the "blue" form (from South Africa), rather than the more common "white." Asbestosis is a chronic lung inflammation caused by asbestos dust.

ascariasis infection by the roundworm *Ascaris lumbricoides*, an intestinal parasite in humans and other mammals.

Ascension British island of volcanic origin in the S Atlantic, a dependency of ◊St Helena since 1922; population (1982) 1,625. The chief settlement is Georgetown. A Portuguese navigator landed there on Ascension Day 1501, but it remained uninhabited until occupied by Britain in 1815. There are sea turtles and sooty terns. It is known for its role as a staging post to the Falkland Islands.

Ascension Day or ***Holy Thursday*** in the Christian calendar, the feast day commemorating Jesus' ascension into heaven. It is the fortieth day after Easter.

asceticism the renunciation of physical pleasure, for example, in eating, drinking, sexuality, and human company. Often for religious reasons, discomfort or pain may be sought.

ASCII (acronym for American Standard Code for Information Interchange) in computing, a coding system in which numbers (between 0 and 127) are assigned to letters, digits, and punctuation symbols. For example, 45 represents a hyphen and 65 a capital A. The first 32 codes are used for control functions, such as carriage return and backspace. Strictly speaking, ASCII is a seven-bit code, but an eighth bit is often used to provide ◊parity or to allow for extra characters. The system is widely used for the storage of text and for the transmission of data between computers. Although computers work in binary code, ASCII numbers are usually quoted as decimal or ◊hexadecimal numbers.

ascorbic acid or ***vitamin C*** relatively simple organic acid found in fresh fruits such as citrus and vegetables such as potatoes. It is soluble in water and destroyed by prolonged boiling, so soaking or overcooking of vegetables reduces their vitamin C content. Lack of ascorbic acid results in scurvy. In the human body, ascorbic acid is necessary for the correct synthesis of collagen. Lack of it causes skin sores or ulcers, tooth and gum problems, and burst capillaries (scurvy symptoms) since an abnormal type of collagen replaces the normal type in these tissues.

Ascot village in Berkshire, England 6 mi/9.5 km SW of Windsor. Queen Anne established the racecourse on Ascot Heath 1711, and the Royal Ascot meeting is a social, as well as a sporting event. Horse races include the Gold Cup, Ascot Stakes, Coventry Stakes, and King George VI and Queen Elizabeth Stakes.

ASEAN acronym for ◊Association of South East Asian Nations.

asepsis the practice of ensuring that bacteria are excluded from open sites during surgery, wound dressing, blood sampling, and other medical procedures. Aseptic technique is a first line of defense against infection.

asexual reproduction biological term for reproductive processes that are not sexual; they do not involve the manufacture and fusion of ◊gametes, nor the necessity of two parents.

These processes carry a clear advantage in that there is no need to search for a mate nor to develop complex pollinating mechanisms; it can therefore lead to rapid population growth. In evolutionary terms, the disadvantage of asexual reproduction arises from the fact that only identical individuals, or clones, are produced—there is no genetic variation. Populations that can only reproduce asexually are therefore in danger of being unable to adapt to a changing environment or to evolve defenses against a new disease. Many asexually reproducing organisms are therefore capable of reproducing sexually as well.

Asexual processes include ◊binary fission, in which the parent organism splits into two or more "daughter" organisms, and ◊budding, in which a new organism is formed initially as an outgrowth of the parent organism. The asexual production of spores, as in ferns and mosses, is also common, and many plants reproduce asexually by means of runners, rhizomes, bulbs, and corms.

ash

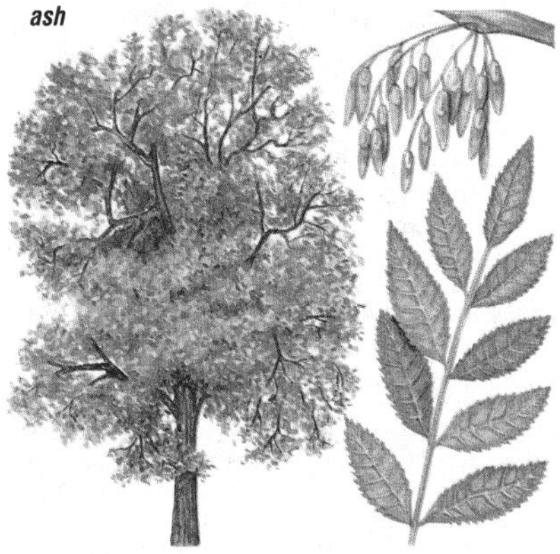

See also ◊vegetative reproduction and ◊parthenogenesis.

Asgard in Scandinavian mythology, the place where the gods lived. It was reached by a bridge called Bifrost, the rainbow.

ash any tree of the genus *Fraxinus*, belonging to the olive family Oleaceae. White ash *F. americana* of the E half of the US is an important timber tree. The leaves of ashes are primately compound, fruits are winged.

Ashanti member of a W African people (Asante culture) living in S central Ghana; the region was formerly a powerful kingdom, active in the slave trade, supplying the British and Dutch. The dialect of Twi spoken there belongs to the Niger-Congo family of languages.

Ashanti or ***Asante*** region of Ghana, W Africa; area 9,700 sq mi/25,100 sq km; population (1984) 2,089,683. Kumasi is the capital. The main crop is cocoa, and the region is noted for its metalwork and textiles. For more than 200 years an independent kingdom, it was lost during the 19th century to the British who sent four expeditions against them and formally annexed their country 1901. Otomfuo Sir Osei Agyeman, nephew of the deposed king, Prempeh I, was made head of the re-established Ashanti confederation 1935 as Prempeh II, and the Golden Stool (actually a chair), symbol of the Ashanti peoples since the 17th century, was returned to Kumasi in 1935 (the rest of the Ashanti treasure is in the British Museum). The Asantahene (King of the Ashanti) still holds ceremonies in which this stool is ceremonially paraded.

Ashanti *The bearer of the king's stool in a procession. An Ashanti king is "enstooled," not crowned.*

Ashbery John 1927– . US poet and art critic. His collections of poetry—including *Self-Portrait in a Convex Mirror* 1975, which won a Pulitzer prize—are distinguished by their strong visual element and narrative power. Other volumes include *Some Trees* 1956, *As We Know* 1979, and *Shadow Train* 1981.

Ashcan school group of US painters active about 1908–14, also known as the Eight. Members included Robert Henri (1865–1929), George Luks (1867–1933), William Glackens (1870–1938), Everett Shinn (1876–1953), and John Sloan (1871–1951). Their style is realist; their subjects centered on city life, the poor, and the outcast. They organized the ◊Armory Show of 1913, which introduced modern European art to the US.

Ashcroft Peggy 1907–. English actress. Her many leading roles include Desdemona in *Othello* (with Paul Robeson), Juliet in *Romeo and Juliet* 1935 (with Laurence Olivier and John Gielgud), and appearances in the British TV play *Caught on a Train* 1980 (BAFTA award), the series *The Jewel in the Crown* 1984, and the film *A Passage to India* 1985.

Ashdod deep water port of Israel, on the Mediterranean 20 mi/32 km S of Tel Aviv, which it superseded in 1965; population (1982) 66,000. It stands on the site of the ancient Philistine stronghold of Askalon.

Ashe Arthur Robert, Jr 1943– . US tennis player and coach. He was the first black to win the US national men's singles title at Forest Hills and the first US Open 1968. Known for his exceptionally strong serve, Ashe turned professional 1969. He won the Australian men's title 1970 and Wimbledon 1975. Cardiac problems ended his playing career 1979, but he continued his involvement with the sport, serving as captain of the US Davis Cup team.

Ashton *The British choreographer, cofounder of the Royal Ballet, Frederick Ashton.*

Born in Richmond, Virginia, Ashe entered the University of California at Los Angeles (UCLA) on a tennis scholarship 1962 and took the National Collegiate Athletic Association (NCAA) men's singles and doubles titles 1966.

Asheville textile town in the Blue Ridge Mountains of North Carolina; population (1990) 61,607.

Asia: history

c. 3000 BC	First dynasties of Sumer in Mesopotamia.
2800–2205	Sage kings in China, earliest Chinese dynasty; civilization spreads to all of China.
2500–1500	Indus Valley civilization.
1950–1282	First Babylonian Empire.
625	Chaldeans established second Babylonian Empire.
563	Birth of Buddha.
551	Birth of Confucius.
538	Cyrus the Great defeated last Babylonian ruler and founded Persian Empire.
334–326	Alexander the Great conquered the Persian Empire.
246	Great Wall of China begun.
AD 166	Tatar invasion of China.
93	Mesopotamia became part of Roman Empire.
320–550	Gupta dynasty in India.
570	Birth of Mohammed.
1192	First Muslim kingdom of India established.
1280	Kublai Khan became emperor of China; Marco Polo visits.
1395	Tamerlane defeated the Golden Horde.
1398	Tamerlane captured Delhi.
1526	Baber established Mogul empire in N India (which lasted until 1857).
1600s	China opened to trade with several European nations despite opposition from the Qing emperors; British East India Company chartered.
1757	Clive defeated the Nawal of Bengal at Plassey.
1839–42	Opium War between Britain and China ended with ceding of Hong Kong to Britain and opening of treaty ports in China.
1854	US Commodore Perry forced Japanese shogun to grant commercial treaty.
1857–58	Sepoy Rebellion in India.
1904–05	Russo-Japanese War.
1931	Japan invaded China.
1941	Japan attacked US fleet at Pearl Harbor.
1947	India and Pakistan gained independence.
1949	Chiang Kai-shek forced by Chinese communists to flee to Formosa, where he set up Republic of China, a US-backed right-wing government.
1950	Korean war.
1954	End of French colonialism in Indochina: Vietnam was divided into the communist north and the noncommunist south.
1955	US sent to advise South Vietnam against Vietcong communist insurgents, backed by North Vietnam and China.
1965	US troops sent to support South Vietnamese in large numbers.
1971	East Pakistan declared independence as Bangladesh.
1975	Fall of South Vietnam to North Vietnam. Khmer Rouge seized power in Cambodia.
1976	Death of Mao Zedong.
1980	Trial of Gang of Four (including Mao's widow Jian Qing).
1980s	Japan became world's richest nation.
1986	Agreement between British and Chinese governments on future 1997 administration of Hong Kong.
1989	Pro-democracy demonstrations in China bloodily repressed by government troops.
1990–91	Iraq occupies Kuwait and is ousted by UN force led by the US and Arab nations.

Showplaces include the 19th-century Biltmore mansion, home of millionaire George W Vanderbilt, and the home of the writer Thomas Wolfe.

Ashkenazi (plural Ashkenazim) a Jew of German or E European descent, as opposed to a Sephardi, of Spanish, Portuguese, or N African descent.

Ashkenazim developed European customs and the ◊Yiddish language during the centuries they remained outside the influence of the Middle East. They were the ◊Zionists who resettled Palestine and who now run the government of Israel, resettling Jews from anywhere in the world.

Ashkenazy Vladimir 1937– . Soviet-born pianist and conductor. His keyboard technique differs slightly from standard Western technique. In 1962 he was joint winner of the Tchaikovsky Competition with John Ogdon. He excels in Rachmaninov, Prokofiev, and Liszt.

After studying in Moscow, he toured the US in 1958. He settled in England in 1963 and moved to Iceland in 1968. He was musical director of the Royal Philharmonic, London, from 1987.

Ashkhabad capital of Republic of Turkmen, USSR; population (1987) 382,000. "Bukhara" carpets are made here.

It was established 1881 as a military fort on the Persian frontier, occupying an oasis on the edge of the Kara-Kum desert. It is the hottest place in the USSR.

Ashland city in NE Kentucky on the Ohio river, E of Louisville. Industries include chemicals, coal, oil, limestone, coke, petroleum products, steel, clothing, and leather goods; population (1990) 23,622.

Ashley Laura (born Mountney) 1925–1985. Welsh designer who established and gave her name to a Neo-Victorian country style in clothes and furnishings beginning in 1953. She founded an international chain of shops.

Ashmore and Cartier Islands group of uninhabited Australian islands comprising Middle, East, and West Islands (the Ashmores), and Cartier Island, in the Indian Ocean, about 120 mi/190 km off the NW coast of Australia; area 5 sq km/2 sq mi. They were transferred to the authority of Australia by Britain 1931. Formerly administered as part of the Northern Territory, they became a separate territory 1978. They are uninhabited, and West Ashmore has an automated weather station. Ashmore reef was declared a national nature preserve 1983.

ashram an Indian community whose members lead a simple life of discipline and self-denial and devote themselves to social service. Noted ashrams are those founded by Mahatma Gandhi at Wardha and the poet Rabindranath Tagore at Santiniketan.

Ashton Frederick 1904–1988. British dancer and choreographer. He studied with Léonid Massine and Marie Rambert before joining the Vic-Wells Ballet 1935 as chief choreographer, creating several roles for Margot Fonteyn. He was director of the Royal Ballet, London, 1963–70.

Ashwander v Tennessee Valley Authority (TVA) a US Supreme Court decision 1936 dealing with the government's authority to utilize navigable waterways as public property. The debate arose over the contracted sale of excess electricity produced by the TVA's Wilson Dam. Power companies unaccustomed to government competition in the industry filed suit to have the TVA contracts canceled. The Court ruled that since the government had acquired the electricity legally, through the exercise of its right to dam waterways, it had full right to dispose of its property.

Ash Wednesday first day of Lent, the period in the Christian calendar leading up to Easter; in the Roman Catholic church the foreheads of the congregation are marked with a cross in ash, as a sign of penitence.

Asia largest of the continents, forming the eastern part of Eurasia to the E of the Ural mountains, one third of the total land surface of the world

area 17,000,000 sq mi/44,000,000 sq km

largest cities (over 5 million) Tokyo, Shanghai, Osaka, Beijing, Seoul, Calcutta, Bombay, Jakarta, Bangkok, Tehran, Hong Kong

physical five main divisions: (1) central triangular mountain mass, including the Himalayas; to the N the great Tibetan plateau, bounded by the Kunlun mountains, to the N of which lie further ranges, as well as the Gobi Desert; (2) the SW plateaus and ranges, forming Afghanistan, Baluchistan, Iran; (3) the northern lowlands, from the central mountains to the Arctic Ocean, much of which is frozen for several months each year; (4) the eastern margin and islands, where much of the population is concentrated; (5) the southern plateau and river plains, including Arabia, the Deccan, and the alluvial plains of the Euphrates, Tigris, Indus, Ganges, and Irrawaddy. The climate shows great extremes and contrasts, the heart of the continent becoming bitterly cold in winter and very hot in summer. This, with the resulting pressure and wind systems, accounts for the Asiatic monsoons, bringing heavy rain to all SE Asia, China, and Japan, between May and Oct

Asia

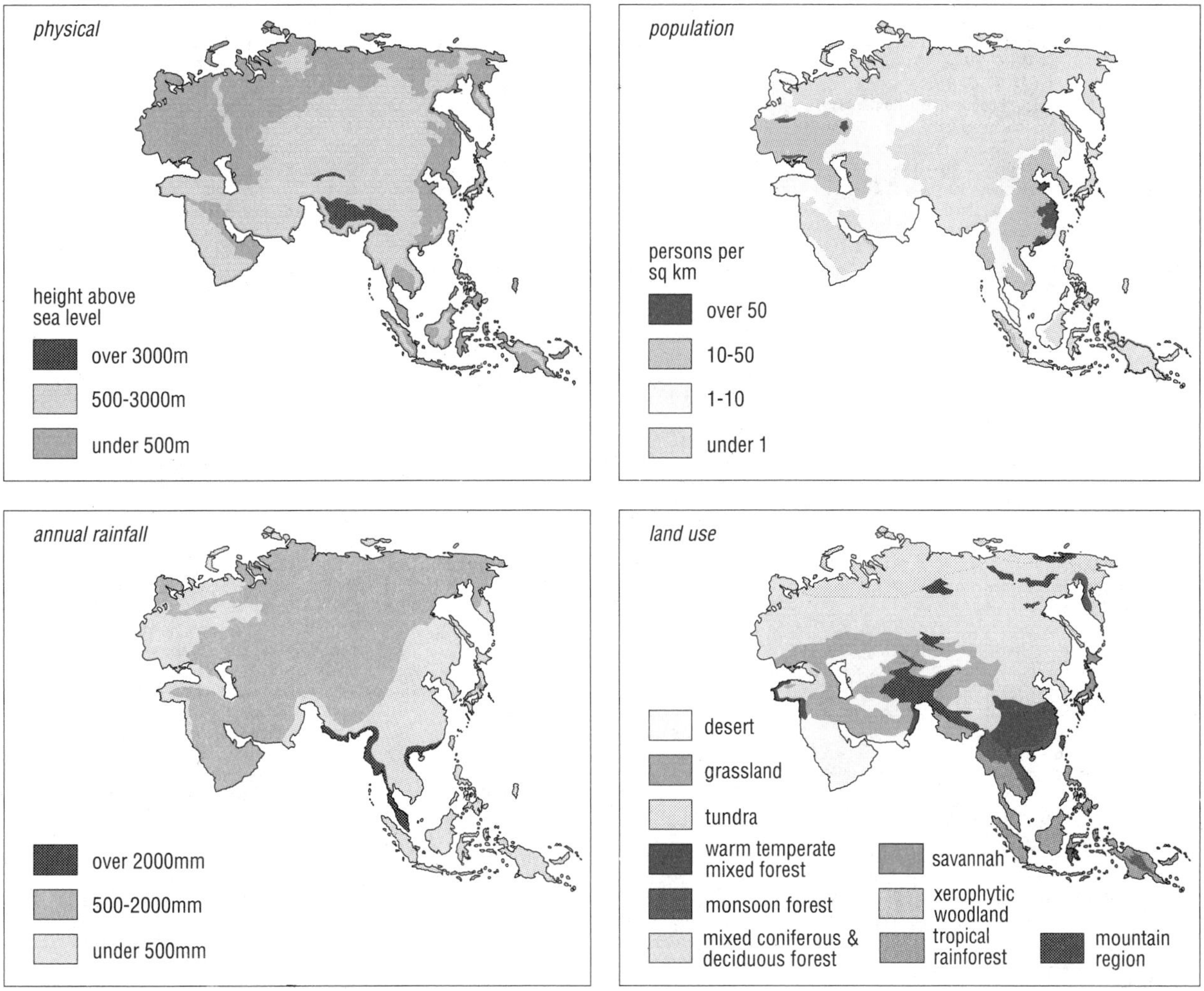
physical
height above sea level
over 3000m
500-3000m
under 500m
population
persons per sq km
over 50
10-50
1-10
under 1
annual rainfall
over 2000mm
500-2000mm
under 500mm
land use
desert
grassland
tundra
warm temperate mixed forest
monsoon forest
mixed coniferous & deciduous forest
savannah
xerophytic woodland
tropical rainforest
mountain region

features rivers (over 2,000 miles): Ob-Irtysh, Chang Jiang, Huang He, Amur, Lena, Mekong, Yenisei, Euphrates; lakes (over 7,000 sq mi/ 18,000 sq km): Caspian and Aral seas, Baikal, Balkhash
population (1984) 3,000 million, the most densely populated of the continents; annual growth rate 1.7% (projected to increase to increase to 3,600 million by AD 2000
language predominantly tonal languages (Chinese, Japanese) in the E, Indo-Iranian languages in central India and Pakistan (Hindi/Urdu), Semitic (Arabic) in the SW
religion Hinduism, Islam, Buddhism, Christianity, Confucianism, Shintoism

Asia Minor historical name for Anatolia, the Asian part of Turkey.

Asian native to or an inhabitant of the continent of Asia, which is the contiguous land mass east of the Ural Mountains, the traditional boundary between Europe and Asia. The region is culturally heterogenous with numerous distinctive ethnic and sociolinguistic groups, totaling over half the Earth's human population (including China, India, and Japan). Asians are of three main racial stocks: Mongoloid in the east; Caucasoid in the west; and Negroid in the Philippines and off-shore islands of the Indian Ocean. The Indians of the Americas were Asian migrants to the New World during the last Ice Age.

Asian Development Bank (ADB) a bank founded 1966 to stimulate growth in Asia and the Far East by administering direct loans and technical assistance. Members include 30 countries within the region and 14 countries of W Europe and North America. The headquarters are in Manila, Philippines.

Japan played a leading role in setting up the ADB, which was established under the aegis of the United Nations Economic and Social Council for Asia and the Pacific (ESCAP).

Asia-Pacific Economic Cooperation Conference (APEC) trade group comprising 12 Pacific Asian countries, formed Nov 1898 to promote multilateral trade and economic cooperation between member states. Its members are the US, Canada, Japan, Australia, New Zealand, South Korea, Brunei, Indonesia, Malaysia, the Philippines, Singapore, and Thailand.

Asia, Soviet Central see ◊Soviet Central Asia.

Asimov Isaac 1920– . Russian-born US author and editor of science fiction and nonfiction.

He has published more than 400 books including his science fiction *I, Robot* 1950 and the *Foundation* trilogy 1951–53, continued in *Foundation's Edge* 1983.

Asimov immigrated to the US as a child. He graduated from Columbia University with a PhD 1948. Trained as a biochemist, Asimov wrote numerous nonfiction works on scientific subjects. These include *Building Blocks of the Universe* 1957; *Until the Sun Dies* 1977, about black holes; and *The Exploding Suns: The Secrets of the Supernovas* 1985. His science-fiction works include short stories, and he has written two autobiographical volumes 1981, 1982.

Asmara or ***Asmera*** capital of Eritrea, Ethiopia; 40 mi/64 km SW of Massawa on the Red Sea; population (1984) 275,385. Products include beer, clothes, and textiles. In 1974, unrest here precipitated the end of the Ethiopian Empire. It has a naval school.

Asnières NW suburb of Paris, France, on the left bank of the Seine; population (1982) 71,220. It is a boating center and pleasure resort.

Asoka lived c. 273–238 BC. Indian emperor, who was a Buddhist convert. He had edicts enjoining the adoption of his new faith carved on pillars and rock faces throughout his dominions, and many survive, among the oldest deciphered texts in India. In Patna there are the remains of a hall built by him.

asp any of several venomous snakes, including *Vipera aspis* of S Europe, allied to the adder, and the Egyptian cobra *Naja haje*, reputed to have been used by the Egyptian queen Cleopatra for her suicide.

asparagus any plant of the genus *Asparagus*, of the lily family Liliaceae, with small scalelike leaves and many needlelike branches. *A. officinalis* is cultivated, and the young shoots are eaten as a vegetable.

Aspasia c. 440 BC. Greek courtesan, the mistress of the Athenian politician ◊Pericles. As a "foreigner" from Miletus, she could not be recognized as his wife, but their son was later legitimized. The philosopher Socrates visited her salon, a meeting place for the celebrities of Athens. Her free thinking led to a charge of impiety, from which Pericles had to defend her.

aspen any of several species of ◊poplar tree, genus *Populus*. The quaking aspen *P. tremula* has flattened leafstalks that cause the leaves to flutter with every breeze.

asphalt type of semisolid brown or black ◊bitumen, used in the construction industry.

Considerable natural deposits of asphalt occur around the Dead Sea and in the Philippines, Cuba, Venezuela, and Trinidad. Bituminous limestone occurs at Neufchâtel, France. Asphalt is mixed with rock chips to form paving material, and the purer varieties are used for insulating material and for waterproofing masonry. Asphalt can be produced artificially by the distillation of ◊petroleum.

asphodel either of two related Old World genera (*Asphodeline* and *Asphodelus*) of plants of the lily family Liliaceae. *Asphodelus albus*, the white asphodel or king's spear, is found in Italy and Greece, sometimes covering large areas, and providing grazing for sheep. *Asphodeline lutea* is the yellow asphodel.

The beautiful plants of *A. lutea* were connected by the Greeks with the dead, and were supposed to grow in the Elysian fields.

asphyxia suffocation; a lack of oxygen that produces a buildup of carbon dioxide waste in the tissues.

Asphyxia may arise from any one of a number of causes, including inhalation of smoke or poisonous gases, obstruction of the windpipe (by water, food, vomit, or foreign object), strangulation, or smothering. If it is not quickly relieved, brain damage or death ensues.

aspidistra Asiatic plant of the genus *Aspidistra* of the lily family Liliaceae. The Chinese *A. elatior* has broad, lanceolate leaves and, like all members of the genus, grows well in warm indoor conditions.

aspirin acetylsalicylic acid, a popular analgesic developed in the early 20th century for headaches and arthritis. It inhibits ◊prostaglandins. It is derived from the white willow tree *Salix alba*.

In the long term, even moderate use may cause stomach bleeding, kidney damage, and hearing defects, and aspirin is no longer considered suitable for children under 12, because of a suspected link with a rare disease, Reye's syndrome (consequently, ◊acetaminophen is often substituted). However, recent medical research suggests that an aspirin a day may be of value in preventing heart attack (myocardial infarction) and thrombosis.

Asplund (Erik) Gunnar 1885–1940. Swedish architect. His early work, for example at the Stockholm South Cemetery (1914), was in the Neo-Classical tradition. Later buildings, such as the Stockholm City Library (1924–27) and Gothenburg City Hall (1934–37), developed a refined Modern-Classical style, culminating in the Stockholm South Cemetery Crematorium (1935–40).

Asquith Herbert Henry, 1st Earl of Oxford and Asquith 1852–1928. British Liberal politician, prime minister 1908–16. As chancellor of the Exchequer he introduced old-age pensions 1908. He limited the powers of the House of Lords and attempted to give Ireland Home Rule.

During World War I, his attitude of "wait and see" was not adapted to all-out war, and in Dec 1916 he was replaced by Lloyd George. In 1918 the Liberal election defeat led to the eclipse of the party.

ass any of several horselike, odd-toed, hoofed mammals of the family Equidae, genus Equus. Species include the African wild ass *Equus asinus*, and the Asian wild ass *Equus hemionus*. They differ from horses in their smaller size, larger ears, tufted tail, and characteristic bray. Donkeys and burros are domesticated asses.

Assad Hafez al 1930– . Syrian Ba'athist politician, president from 1971. He became prime minister after the bloodless military coup 1970, and the following year was the first president to be elected by popular vote. Having suppressed dissent, he was re-elected 1978 and 1985. He is a Shia (Alawite) Muslim.

He has ruthlessly suppressed domestic opposition, and he was Iran's only major Arab ally in its war against Iraq. He has steadfastly pursued military parity with Israel, and he had made himself a key player in any settlement of the Lebanese civil war or Middle East conflict generally.

Assam state of NE India
area 30,262 sq mi/78,400 sq km
capital Dispur
towns Shilling
products half India's tea is grown and half its oil produced here; rice, jute, sugar, cotton, coal
population (1981) 19,903,000, including 12 million Assamese (Hindus), 5 million Bengalis (chiefly Muslim immigrants from Bangladesh), Nepalis, and 2,000,000 native people (Christian and traditional religions)
language Assamese
history a thriving region from 1000 BC; Assam, migrants came from China and Myanmar (Burma). After Burmese invasion 1826, Britain took control; and made it a separate province 1874; included in the Dominion of India, except for most of the Muslim district of Silhet, which went to Pakistan 1947. Ethnic unrest started in the 1960's when Assamese was declared the official language. After protests, the Gara, Khasi, and Jainitia tribal hill districts became the state of ◊Meghalaya 1971; the Mizo hill district became the Union Territory of Mizoram 1972. There were massacres of Muslim Bengalis by Hindus 1983. In 1987 members of Bodo ethnic group began fighting for a separate homeland.

assassination the killing or murder, especially of a political, royal, or public person. The term derives from a sect of Muslim fanatics in the 11th and 12th centuries known as *hashshashin* ("takers of hashish"). They were reputed either to smoke cannabis before they went out to kill or to receive hashish as payment.

assault ship naval vessel designed to land and support troops and vehicles under hostile conditions.

assay in chemistry, the determination of the quantity of a given substance present in a sample. Usually it refers to determining the purity of precious metals.

The assay may be carried out by "wet" methods, when the sample is wholly or partially dissolved in some reagent (often an acid), or by "dry" or "fire" methods, in which the compounds present in the sample are combined with other substances.

assembly line method of mass production in which a product is built up step by step by successive workers adding one part at a time.

US inventor Eli Whitney pioneered the concept of industrial assembly in the 1790s, when he employed unskilled labor to assemble muskets from sets of identical precision-made parts. In 1901 Ransome Olds in the US began mass-producing motor automobiles on an assembly-line principle, a method further refined by the introduction of the moving conveyor belt by Henry ◊Ford 1913 and the time-and-motion studies of F W ◊Taylor. On the assembly line human workers now stand side by side with ◊robots.

asset a business accounting term that covers the

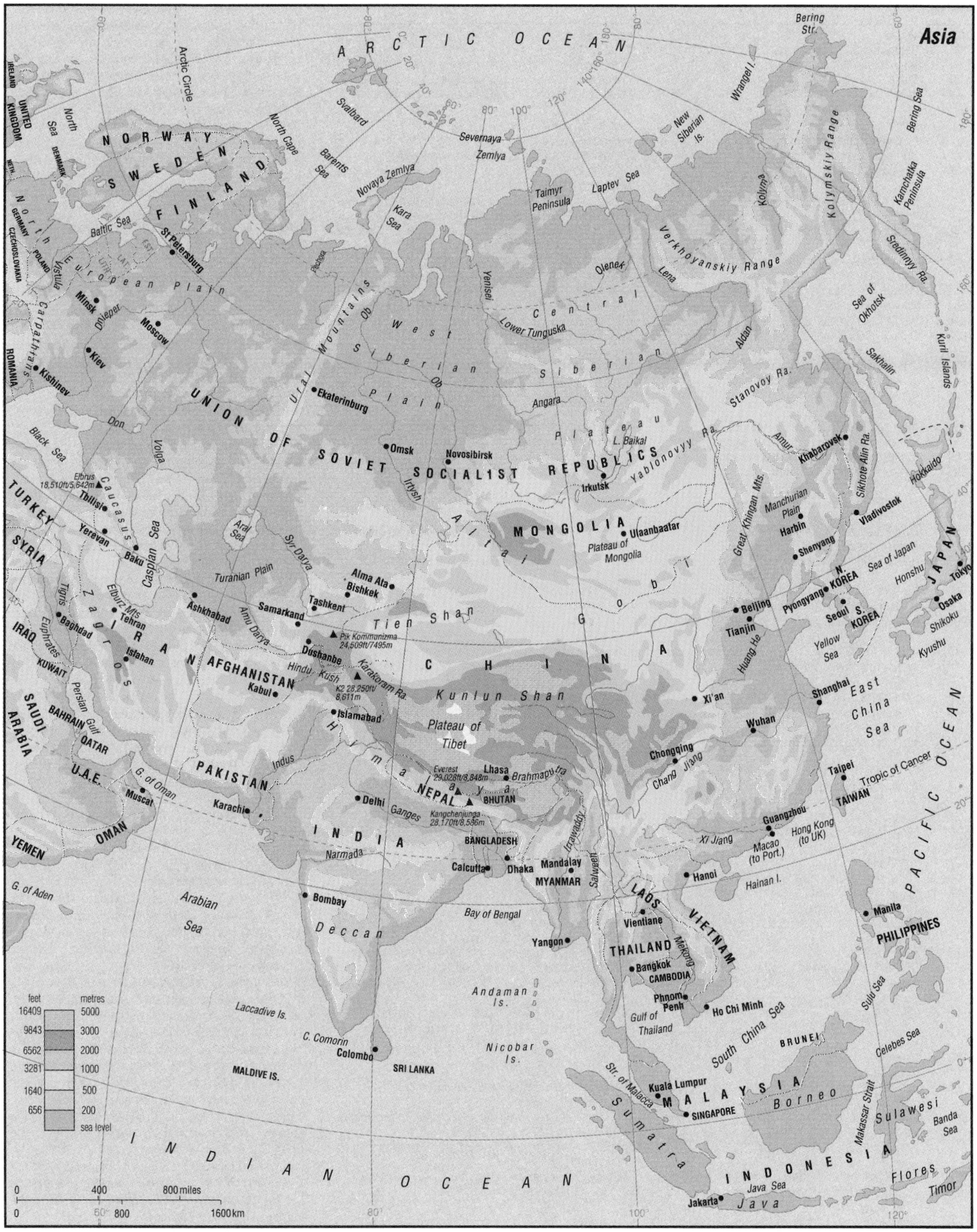
Asia
ARCTIC OCEAN
Bering Str.
Wrangel I.
Bering Sea
Kolymskiy Range
Kamchatka Peninsula
Sredinnyy Ra.
Sea of Okhotsk
Sakhalin
Kuril Islands
New Siberian Is.
Kolyma
Laptev Sea
Taimyr Peninsula
Severnaya Zemlya
Novaya Zemlya
Kara Sea
Barents Sea
Svalbard
North Cape
Arctic Circle
IRELAND
UNITED KINGDOM
North Sea
DENMARK
NETH.
GERMANY
CZECHOSLOVAKIA
POLAND
NORWAY
SWEDEN
FINLAND
Baltic Sea
St Petersburg
North European Plain
Vistula
Minsk
Moscow
Dnieper
Kiev
Carpathians
ROMANIA
Kishinev
Verkhoyanskiy Range
Olenek
Lena
Central Siberian Plateau
Lower Tunguska
Aldan
Yenisei
West Siberian Plain
Ob
Ural Mountains
Ekaterinburg
Stanovoy Ra.
Angara
L. Baikal
Yablonovyy Ra.
Amur
Khabarovsk
Sikhote Alin Ra.
Hokkaido
UNION OF SOVIET SOCIALIST REPUBLICS
Don
Volga
Black Sea
Omsk
Novosibirsk
Irkutsk
Irtysh
Elbrus 18,510ft/5,642m
Caucasus
Tbilisi
Yerevan
Baku
Caspian Sea
Aral Sea
Syr Darya
Turanian Plain
Altai
MONGOLIA
Ulaanbaatar
Plateau of Mongolia
Gobi
Great Khingan Mts.
Manchurian Plain
Harbin
Vladivostok
Shenyang
N. KOREA
Pyongyang
Seoul
S. KOREA
Sea of Japan
Honshu
JAPAN
Tokyo
Osaka
Shikoku
Kyushu
TURKEY
SYRIA
IRAQ
Tigris
Euphrates
Baghdad
Elburz Mts
Tehran
Zagros
IRAN
Isfahan
KUWAIT
SAUDI ARABIA
BAHRAIN
QATAR
U.A.E.
Persian Gulf
G. of Oman
Muscat
OMAN
YEMEN
G. of Aden
Ashkhabad
Samarkand
Amu Darya
Tashkent
Alma Ata
Bishkek
Tien Shan
Pik Kommunizma 24,590ft/7495m
Dushanbe
AFGHANISTAN
Hindu Kush
Kabul
K2 28,250ft/ 8,611m
Karakoram Ra.
Islamabad
Himalaya
PAKISTAN
Indus
Karachi
CHINA
Kunlun Shan
Plateau of Tibet
Beijing
Tianjin
Huang He
Yellow Sea
Xi'an
Wuhan
Shanghai
East China Sea
Chongqing
Chang Jiang
Taipei
TAIWAN
Tropic of Cancer
Everest 29,028ft/8,848m
Lhasa
Brahmaputra
NEPAL
BHUTAN
Kangchenjunga 28,170ft/8,586m
Delhi
Ganges
INDIA
Narmada
BANGLADESH
Calcutta
Dhaka
Mandalay
MYANMAR
Irrawaddy
Salween
Guangzhou
Hong Kong (to UK)
Macao (to Port.)
Xi Jiang
Hanoi
Hainan I.
LAOS
Vientiane
VIETNAM
THAILAND
Mekong
Bangkok
CAMBODIA
Phnom Penh
Ho Chi Minh
Gulf of Thailand
Yangon
Bay of Bengal
Andaman Is.
Nicobar Is.
Bombay
Arabian Sea
Deccan
Laccadive Is.
C. Comorin
Colombo
SRI LANKA
MALDIVE IS.
PACIFIC OCEAN
Manila
PHILIPPINES
Sulu Sea
Celebes Sea
South China Sea
BRUNEI
Kuala Lumpur
MALAYSIA
SINGAPORE
Str. of Malacca
Sumatra
Borneo
Makassar Strait
Sulawesi
Banda Sea
INDONESIA
Flores
Timor
Java Sea
Java
Jakarta
INDIAN OCEAN
feet
metres
16409
5000
9843
3000
6562
2000
3281
1000
1640
500
656
200
sea level
0
400
800 miles
0
800
1600 km

assassinations

BC	*victim*	*details of assassination*
681	Sennacherib of Assyria	Killed by his two sons.
514	Hipparchus, tyrant of Athens	Killed by Harmodius and Aristogeiton, two Athenians.
336	Philip II of Macedon	Killed by Pausanias, a Spartan regent and general.
44	Julius Caesar, Roman dictator	Stabbed by Brutus, Cassius, and others in Senate.
AD	*victim*	*details of assassination*
14	Caligula, Roman emperor	Killed by Cassius Chaerea, an officer of his guard.
96	Domitian, Roman dictator	Stabbed in bedroom by Stephanus, a freed slave.
1170	Thomas à Becket	Killed by four knights (Fitzorse, Tracy, Morville, and Brito) in Canterbury cathedral.
1437	James I of Scotland	Killed in court residence, a Dominican monastery, by assassins led by Sir Robert Graham.
1488	James III of Scotland	Killed following defeat of royal army at Sauchieburn by an unknown person.
1567	Lord Darnley, husband of Mary Queen of Scots	Blown up near Edinburgh while suffering from smallpox; suspected assassin: the Earl of Bothwell.
1584	William the Silent, Prince of Orange	Shot at Delft by Balthasar Gérard.
1589	Henry III of France	Stabbed by Jacques Clément, a fanatical Dominican.
1610	Henry IV of France	Killed by Ravaillac, a Catholic fanatic
1628	Duke of Buckingham	Stabbed at Portsmouth, en route for La Rochelle, by John Felton, a discontented subaltern.
1634	Prince Wallenstein, German general	Killed in private train by Devereux.
1793	Jean Paul Marat, French revolutionary	Stabbed in bath by Charlotte Corday.
1801	Paul I of Russia	Strangled by army officers who had conspired to force his abdication.
1812	Spencer Perceval, British prime minister	Shot while entering lobby of the House of Commons by John Bellingham, a bankrupt Liverpool broker.
1865	Abraham Lincoln, US president	Shot by actor J Wilkes Booth in a theater.
1881	James A Garfield, US president	Shot at station by Charles Guiteau, a disappointed office-seeker.
1881	Alexander II of Russia	Died from injuries after bomb was thrown near his palace by Nihilists.
1882	Lord F Cavendish, chief secretary for Ireland	Killed by "Irish Invincibles" in Phoenix Park, Dublin.
1894	Marie François Carnot, French president	Killed by Italian anarchist in Lyon.
1897	Antonio Cánovas del Castillo, Spanish premier	Shot by Italian anarchist Angiolillo at the bath of Santa Agueda, Vitoria.
1900	Umberto I of Italy	Killed by anarchist G Bresci in Monza.
1901	William McKinley, US president	Shot by anarchist Leon Czolgosz in Buffalo.
1903	Alexander Obrenovich, King of Serbia, and his wife Draga	Killed by military conspirators.
1913	George I of Greece	Killed by a Greek, Schinas, in Salonika.
1914	Archduke Francis Ferdinand	Shot in car by Gavrilo Princip in Sarajevo (sparked World War I); an alleged Serbian plot.
1914	Jean Jaurès, French Socialist	Shot by nationalist in café.
1916	Rasputin, Russian monk	Shot and dumped in river Neva by a group of nobles led by Prince Feliks Yusupov.
1922	Michael Collins, Irish Sinn Fein leader	Killed in an ambush between Bandon and Macroom in Irish Republic.
1934	Dr Engelbert Dollfuss, Austrian chancellor	Shot by Nazis in the Chancellery.
1934	Alexander I of Yugoslavia	Killed; Italian fascists or Croatian separatists suspected.
1935	Huey Long, corrupt American politician	Murdered by Dr Carl Austin Weiss.
1940	Leon Trotsky, exiled Russian communist leader	Killed with an ice-axe in Mexico by Ramon de Rio.
1942	Reinhard Heydrich, second-in-command of the Nazi secret police	Killed by Czech resistance fighters.
1948	Mahatma Gandhi, Indian nationalist leader	Shot by a Hindu fanatic, Nathuran Godse.
1948	Count Folke Bernadotte, Swedish diplomat	Killed by Jewish extremists in ambush in Jerusalem.
1951	Abdullah I of Jordan	Killed by member of Jehad faction.
1951	Liaquat Ali Khan, prime minister of Pakistan	Killed in Rawalpindi by fanatics advocating war with India.
1958	Faisal II of Iraq	Killed with his entire household during a military coup.
1959	S W R D Bandaranaike, Ceylonese premier	Killed by Buddhist monk Talduwe Somarama.
1959	Rafael Trujillo Molina, Dominican Republic dictator	Machine-gunned in car by assassins including General J T Díaz.
1963	John F Kennedy, US president	Shot in car by rifle fire in Dallas, Texas; alleged assassin, Lee Oswald, himself shot two days later while under heavy police escort.
1963	Malcolm X (Little), US leading spokesman for the Black Muslims	Shot at political rally.
1966	Hendrik Frensch Verwoerd, South African premier	Stabbed by parliamentary messenger (later ruled mentally disordered).
1968	Rev Martin Luther King, Jr, US black civil-rights leader	Shot on hotel balcony by James Earl Ray in Memphis, Tennessee.
1968	Robert F Kennedy, US senator	Shot by Arab immigrant Sirhan Sirhan in the Hotel Ambassador, Los Angeles.
1975	King Faisal of Saudi Arabia	Killed by his nephew.
1976	Christopher Ewart Biggs, British ambassador to Republic of Ireland	Car blown up by IRA landmine.
1978	Aldo Moro, president of Italy's Christian Democrats and five times prime minister	Kidnapped by Red Brigade guerrillas and later found dead.
1979	Airey Neave, British Conservative MP and Northern Ireland spokesperson	Killed by IRA bomb while driving out of House of Commons parking garage.
1979	Lord Mountbatten, uncle of Duke of Edinburgh	Killed by IRA bomb in sailing boat off coast of Ireland.
1979	Park Chung Hee, president of South Korea	Shot in restaurant by chief of Korean Central Intelligence Agency.
1980	John Lennon, singer and songwriter	Shot outside his apartment house in New York.
1981	Anwar al-Sadat, president of Egypt	Shot by rebel soldiers while reviewing military parade.
1984	Indira Gandhi, Indian prime minister	Killed by members of her Sikh bodyguard.
1986	Olof Palme, Swedish prime minister	Shot leaving cinema in Stockholm.
1991	Rajiv Gandhi	Shot during election campaign.

land or property of a company or individual, payments due from bills, investments, and anything else owned that can be turned into cash. On a company's balance sheet, total assets must be equal to liabilities (money and services owed).

Assisi town in Umbria, Italy, 12 mi/19 km SE of Perugia; population (1981) 25,000. St Francis was born here and is buried in the Franciscan monastery, completed 1253. The churches of St Francis are adorned with frescoes by Giotto, Cimabue, and others.

Assiut alternative transliteration of ◊Asyut, town in Egypt.

assize in medieval Europe, the passing of laws, either by the king with the consent of nobles, as in the Constitutions of ◊Clarendon 1164 by Henry II, or as a complete system, such as the Assizes of Jerusalem, a compilation of the law of the feudal kingdom of Jerusalem in the 13th century.

Associated State of the UK status of certain ◊Commonwealth countries having full power of internal government, but for which Britain retains responsibility for external relations and defense.

Association of Southeast Asian Nations (ASEAN) regional alliance formed in Bangkok 1967; it took over the nonmilitary role of the Southeast Asia Treaty Organization 1975. Its members are Indonesia, Malaysia, the Philippines, Singapore, Thailand, and (from 1984) Brunei; its headquarters are in Jakarta, Indonesia.

associative law in mathematics, the law that states that the result of performing certain consecutive operations is independent of the order in which they are performed. Thus addition is associative because, for example $3 + (4 + 5)$ gives the same sum as $(3 + 4) + 5$. Multiplication is also associative: for example, $2 \times (3 \times 4)$ gives the same product as $(2 \times 3) \times 4$. Subtraction and division are not associative. For example, $12 \div (4 \div 2) = 6$, but $(12 \div 4) \div 2 = 1.5$.

assortative mating in ◊population genetics, selective mating in a population between individuals that are genetically related or have similar characteristics. If sufficiently consistent, assortative mating can theoretically result in the evolution of new species without geographical isolation (see ◊speciation).

ASSR abbreviation for Autonomous Soviet Socialist Republic.

Assuan alternative transliteration of ◊Aswan.

Assy plateau in Haute-Savoie, E France, 3,280 ft/1,000 m above sea level.

The area has numerous sanatoriums. The church of Nôtre Dame de Toute Grâce, begun 1937 and consecrated 1950, is adorned with works by Braque, Chagall, Matisse, Derain, Rouault, and other artists.

Assyria empire in the Middle East c. 2500–612 BC, in N Mesopotamia (now Iraq); early capital Ashur, later Niniveh. It was initially subject to Sumer and intermittently to Babylon. The Assyrians adopted in the main the Sumerian religion and structure of society. At its greatest extent the empire included Egypt and stretched from the E Mediterranean coast to the head of the Persian Gulf.

The land of Assyria originally consisted of a narrow strip of alluvial soil on each side of the river Tigris. The area was settled about 3500 BC and was dominated by Sumer until about 2350 BC. For nearly 200 years Assyria was subject first to the Babylonian dynasty of Akkad and then to the Gutians, barbarians from the north.

The first Assyrian kings are mentioned during the wars following the decline of the 3rd dynasty of Ur (in Sumer), but Assyria continued under Babylonian and subsequently Egyptian suzerainty until about 1450 BC. Under King Ashur-uballit (reigned about 1380–1340 BC) Assyria became a military power. His work was continued by Adad-nirari I, Shalmaneser I, and Tukulti-enurta I, who conquered Babylonia and assumed the title of king of Sumer and Akkad.

During the reign of Nebuchadnezzar I

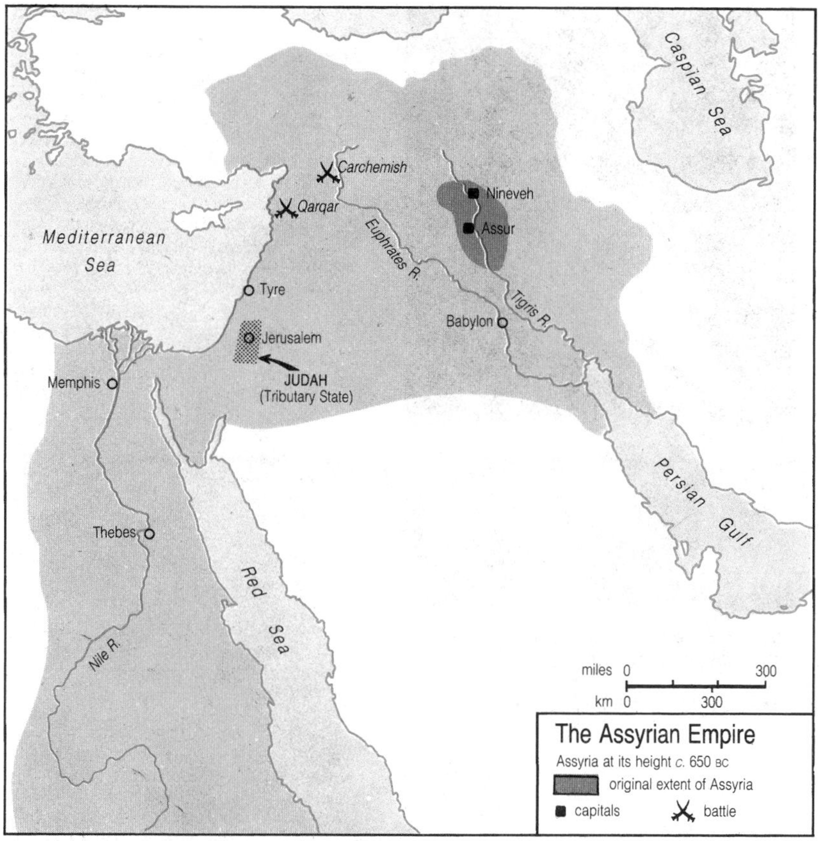
Caspian Sea
Carchemish
Nineveh
Qarqar
Assur
Mediterranean Sea
Euphrates R.
Tigris R.
Tyre
Babylon
Jerusalem
Memphis
JUDAH
(Tributary State)
Persian Gulf
Thebes
Red Sea
Nile R.
miles 0 300
km 0 300
The Assyrian Empire
Assyria at its height c. 650 BC
original extent of Assyria
capitals
battle

(1150–1110 BC), Assyria was again subject to Babylonia, but was liberated by Tiglath-pileser I. In the Aramaean invasions, most of the ground gained was lost. From the accession of Adad-nirari II 911 BC Assyria pursued a course of expansion and conquest, culminating in the mastery over Elam, Mesopotamia, Syria, Palestine, the Arabian marches, and Egypt. Of this period the Old Testament records, and many "documents," such as the Black Obelisk celebrating the conquest of Shalmaneser III in the 9th century BC, survive.

The reign of Ashur-nazir-pal II (885–860 BC) was spent in unceasing warfare; he is said to have introduced "frightfulness," evidenced by many bas-reliefs. Shalmaneser III warred against the Syrian states. At the battle of Qarqar 854 BC the Assyrian advance received a setback, and there followed a period of decline. The final period of Assyrian ascendancy began with the accession of Tiglath-pileser III (746–728 BC) and continued during the reigns of Sargon II, Sennacherib, Esarhaddon, and Ashurbanipal, culminating in the conquest of Egypt by Esarhaddon 671 BC. From this time the empire seems to have fallen into decay. Nabopolassar of Babylonia and Cyaxares of Media (see ◊Mede) united against it; Nineveh was destroyed 612 BC; and Assyria became a Median province and subsequently a principality of the Persian Empire.

Much of Assyrian religion, law, social structure, and artistic achievement was derived from neighboring sources. The Assyrians adopted the cuneiform script (invented by the Sumerians in 3500 BC) and took over the Sumerian pantheon, although the Assyrian god, Ashur (Assur), assumed the chief place in the cult. The library of Ashurbanipal excavated at Nineveh is evidence of the thoroughness with which Babylonian culture had been assimilated.

Astaire Fred. Adopted name of Frederick Austerlitz 1899–1987. US dancer, actor, singer, and choreographer who starred in numerous films, including *Top Hat* 1935, *Easter Parade* 1948, and *Funny Face* 1957, many of which contained inventive sequences he designed and choreographed himself. He made ten classic films with the most popular of his dancing partners, Ginger Rogers. He later played straight dramatic roles, in films such as *On the Beach* 1959.

Born in Omaha, Nebraska, he danced in partnership with his sister Adele (1898–1981) from 1904 until her marriage in 1932. He entered films in 1933. Among his many other films are *Roberta* 1935 and *Follow the Fleet* 1936. Astaire was a virtuoso dancer and a perfectionist known for his elegant style.

Astaire *Dancer Fred Astaire made ten classic films with Ginger Rogers, as pictured here.*

Astarte alternate name for the Babylonian and Assyrian goddess ◊Ishtar.

astatine (Greek *astatos* "unstable") nonmetallic, radioactive element, symbol At, atomic number 85, atomic weight 210. It is a member of the ◊halogen group, and is very rare in nature. Astatine is highly unstable, with many isotopes; the longest lived has a half-life of about eight hours.

aster any plant of the large genus *Aster*, family Compositae, belonging to the same subfamily as the daisy. All asters have starlike flowers with yellow centers and outer rays (not petals) varying from blue and purple to white.

The China aster *Callistephus chinensis* belongs to a closely allied genus; it was introduced to Europe and the US from China in the early 18th century.

The white wood aster *A. divaricatus* grows in open woods throughout most of the US.

asterisk starlike punctuation mark (*) used to link the asterisked word with a note at the bottom of a page, and to mark that certain letters are missing from a word (especially a taboo word such as "f**k").

asteroid or minor planet any of many thousands of small bodies, composed of rock and iron, that orbit the Sun. They range in diameter from under 0.6 mi/1 km to 620 mi/1,000 km. Most asteroids lie in a belt between the orbits of Mars and Jupiter. They are thought to be fragments left over from the formation of the ◊Solar System. About 100,000 may exist, but their total mass is only a few hundredths the mass of the Moon.

They include Ceres (the largest asteroid, 620 mi/1,000 km in diameter), Vesta (which has a light-colored surface, and is the brightest as seen from Earth), ◊Eros, and ◊Icarus. Some asteroids are on orbits that bring them close to the Earth and some, such as the ◊Apollo asteroids, even cross the Earth's orbit. One group, the Trojans, moves along the same orbit as Jupiter, 60° ahead and behind the planet. One unusual asteroid, Chiron, orbits beyond Saturn.

In 1990 asteroids 4147, 4148, 4149, and 4150 (5–10 miles in diameter and too faint to be seen by the naked eye) were renamed for the members of the pop music group the ◊Beatles—John, Paul, George, and Ringo respectively—at the request of their two discoverers, astronomers at the Lowell Observatory, Flagstaff, Arizona.

asthenosphere a division of the Earth's structure lying beneath the ◊lithosphere, at a depth of approximately 45 mi/70 km to 160 mi/260 km. It is thought to be the soft, partially molten layer of the ◊mantle on which the rigid plates of the Earth's surface move to produce the motions of ◊plate tectonics.

asthma difficulty in breathing due to spasm of the bronchi (air passages) in the lungs. Attacks may be provoked by allergy, infection, stress, or emotional upset. It may also be increasing as a result of air pollution and occupational hazards. Treatment is with ◊bronchodilators to relax the bronchial muscles and thereby ease the breathing, and in severe cases by inhaled ◊steroids to reduce inflammation of the bronchi.

Although the symptoms are similar to those of bronchial asthma, cardiac asthma is an unrelated condition and is a symptom of heart deterioration.

Asti town in Piedmont, SE of Turin, Italy; population (1983) 76,439. Asti province is famed for its sparkling wine. Other products include chemicals, textiles, and glass.

astigmatism aberration occurring in lenses, including the eye and mirrors. It results when the curvature differs in two perpendicular planes, so that rays in one may be in focus while rays in the other are not. With astigmatic eyesight, the vertical and horizontal cannot be in focus at the same time; correction is by use of a cylindrical lens that reduces the overall focal length of one plane so that both planes are seen in sharp focus.

Aston Francis William 1877–1945. English physicist who developed the mass spectrometer, which separates ◊isotopes by projecting their ions (charged atoms) through a magnetic field. He received the Nobel Prize for Chemistry 1922.

Astor John Jacob 1763–1848. German-born US merchant who made his fortune trading in furs and New York City real estate. He came to the US 1784 and worked in small shops before entering the fur trade. When he retired 1834, he was the wealthiest man in the US. His estate endowed the Astor library, now a part of The New York Public Library.

Astor made a farsighted agreement with Canadian merchants to import furs to the US from Montreal. He took advantage of the Louisiana Purchase 1803 and extended his trade to the West, creating the Pacific Fur Company 1811 (founding Astoria, now in Oregon, his trading post at the mouth of the Columbia river), a subsidiary of his monopolistic American Fur Company, founded 1808. He sold some of his furs in China through an agreement with the British East India Company. His profits were systematically invested in New York City real estate. When he died he owned most of the southern half of Manhattan, which his sons inherited and administered.

Astor Mary. Adopted name of Lucille Langhanke 1906–1987. US film actress, whose many films included *Don Juan* 1926 and *The Maltese Falcon* 1941. Her memoirs *My Story* 1959 were remarkable for their frankness.

Astrakhan city in the USSR, on the delta of the Volga, capital of Astrakhan region; population (1987) 509,000. In ancient times a Tatar capital, it became Russian 1556. It is the chief port for the Caspian fisheries.

astrolabe ancient navigational instrument, forerunner of the sextant. Astrolabes usually consisted of a flat disk with a sighting rod that could be pivoted to point at the Sun or bright stars. From the altitude of the Sun or star above the horizon, the local time could be estimated.

astrology (Greek *astron* "star"; *legein* "speak") study of the relative position of the planets and stars in the belief that they influence events on Earth. The astrologer casts a ◊horoscope based on the time and place of the subject's birth. Astrology has no proven scientific basis, but has been widespread since ancient times. Western astrology is based on the 12 signs of the zodiac; Chinese astrology is based on a 60-year cycle and lunar calendar.

history A strongly held belief in ancient Babylon, astrology spread to the Mediterranean world, and was widely used by the Greeks and Romans. In Europe during the Middle Ages it had a powerful influence, since kings and other public figures had their own astrologers; astrological beliefs are reflected in Elizabethan and Jacobean literature.

In the US, horoscopes are syndicated in most newspapers and almost everyone, whether professing belief or not, knows his or her astrological sign.

astrometry the measurement of the precise positions of stars, planets, and other bodies in space. Such information is needed for practical purposes including accurate timekeeping, surveying and navigation, and calculating orbits and measuring distances in space. Astrometry is not concerned with the surface features or the physical nature of the body under study.

Before telescopes, astronomical observations were simple astrometry. Precise astrometry has shown that stars are not fixed in position, but have a proper motion caused as they and the Sun orbit the Milky Way galaxy. The nearest stars also show ◊parallax (apparent change in position), from which their distances can be calculated. Above the distorting effects of the atmosphere, satellites can make even more precise measurements than ground telescopes, so refining the distance scale of space.

astronaut *Bruce McCandless floats free above the Earth in his manned maneuvering unit Feb 7, 1984.*

astronaut Western term for a person making flights into space; the Soviet term is cosmonaut.

astronautics the science of space travel. See ◊rocket; ◊satellite; ◊space probe.

astronomical unit unit (abbreviation AU) equal to the mean distance of the Earth from the Sun: 92,955,800 mi/149,597,870 km. It is used to describe planetary distances. Light travels this distance in approximately 8.3 minutes.

astronomy the science of the celestial bodies: the Sun, the Moon, and the planets; the stars and galaxies; and all other objects in the universe. It is concerned with their positions, motions, distances, and physical conditions; and with their origins and evolution. Astronomy thus divides into fields such as astrophysics, celestial mechanics, and cosmology. See also ◊gamma-ray astronomy and ◊ultraviolet astronomy.

Astronomy is perhaps the oldest recorded science; there are observational records from ancient Babylonia, China, Egypt, and Mexico. The first true astronomers, however, were the Greeks, who deduced the Earth to be a spheroid and attempted to measure its size. Ancient Greek astronomers included ◊Thales and ◊Pythagoras. ◊Eratosthenes of Cyrene measured the size of the Earth with considerable accuracy. Star catalogs were drawn up, the most celebrated being that of Hipparchus. The *Almagest*, by ◊Ptolemy of Alexandria, summarized Greek astronomy, and survived in its Arab translation. However, the Greeks still regarded the Earth as the center of the universe, although this was doubted by some philosophers, notably ◊Aristarchus of Samos, who maintained that the Earth moves around the Sun.

Ptolemy, the last famous astronomer of the Greek school, died about AD 180, and little progress was made for some centuries. The Arabs revived the science, carrying out theoretical researches from the 8th and 9th centuries and producing good star catalogs. Unfortunately a general belief in the pseudoscience of astrology continued until the end of the Middle Ages (and has been revived from time to time).

The dawn of a new era came 1543, when a Polish canon, ◊Copernicus, published a work entitled *De Revolutionibus Orbium Coelestium/About the Revolutions of the Heavenly Spheres*, in which he demonstrated that the Sun, not the Earth, is the center of our planetary system. (Copernicus was wrong in many respects—for instance, he still believed that all celestial orbits must be perfectly circular.) ◊Brahe, a Dane, increased the accuracy of observations by means of improved instruments allied to his own personal skill, and his observations were used by the German mathematician ◊Kepler to prove the validity of the Copernican system. Considerable opposition existed, however, for removing the Earth from its central position in the universe; the Catholic Church was openly hostile to the idea and, ironically, Brahe never accepted the idea that the Earth could move around the Sun. Yet before the end of the 17th century, the theoretical work of Isaac ◊Newton had established celestial mechanics.

The refractor telescope was invented about 1608, by ◊Lippershey in Holland, and was first applied to astronomy by the Italian scientist Galileo in the winter of 1609–10. Immediately, Galileo made a series of spectacular discoveries. He found the four largest satellites of Jupiter, which gave strong support to the Copernican theory; he saw the craters of the Moon, the phases of Venus, and the myriad faint stars of our Galaxy, the Milky Way. Galileo's most powerful telescope magnified only 30 times, but before long, larger telescopes were built and official observatories were established.

Galileo's telescope was a refractor; that is to say, it collected its light by means of a glass lens or object glass. Difficulties with this design led Newton, in 1671, to construct a reflector, in which the light is collected by means of a curved mirror.

Theoretical researches continued and astronomy made rapid progress in many directions. New planets were discovered—Uranus 1781 by ◊Herschel, and Neptune 1846, following calculations by ◊Adams and ◊Leverrier. Also significant was the first measurement of the distance of a star, when in 1838 the German astronomer ◊Bessel measured the ◊parallax of the star 61 Cygni and calculated that it lies at a distance of about 6 light-years (about half the correct value). Astronomical spectroscopy was developed, first by Fraunhofer in Germany and then by people such as ◊Secchi and Huggins, while ◊Kirchhoff successfully interpreted the spectra of the Sun and stars. By the 1860s good photographs of the Moon had been obtained and by the end of the century photographic methods had started to play a leading role in research.

William Herschel, probably the greatest observer in the history of astronomy, investigated the shape of the our ◊Galaxy during the latter part of the 18th century and concluded that its stars are arranged roughly in the form of a double-convex lens. asically Herschel was correct, although he placed our Sun near the center of the system; in fact, it is well out toward the edge and lies 25,000 light-years from the galactic nucleus. Herschel also studied the luminous "clouds," or nebulae, and made the tentative suggestion that those nebulae capable of resolution into stars might be separate galaxies, far outside our own Galaxy. It was not until 1923 that Hubble, using the 100-in/2.5-m reflector at the Mount Wilson Observatory, was able to verify this suggestion. It is now known that the "starry nebulae" are galaxies in their own right and that they lie at immense distances. The most distant galaxy visible to the naked eye, the Great Spiral in ◊Andromeda, is 2.2 million light-years away; the most remote galaxy so far measured lies over 10 billion light-years away. It was also found that galaxies tended to form groups and that the groups were apparently receding from each other at speeds proportional to their distances.

This concept of an expanding and evolving universe at first rested largely on ◊Hubble's law, relating the distance of objects to the amount their spectra shift toward red—the ◊red shift. Subsequent evidence derived from objects studied in other parts of the ◊electromagnetic spec-

astronomy: chronology

2300 BC	Chinese astronomers made their earliest observational records.
2000	Babylonian priests made their first observational records.
1900	Stonehenge was constructed: first phase.
365	The Chinese observed the satellites of Jupiter with the naked eye.
3rd century	Aristarchus argued that the Sun is the center of the Solar System.
2nd century AD	Ptolemy's complicated Earth-centered system was promulgated, which dominated astronomy until the Middle Ages.
1543	Copernicus revived the ideas of Aristarchus in De Revolutionibus.
1608	Lippershey invented the telescope, which was first used by Galileo 1609.
1609	Kepler's first two laws of planetary motion were published (the third appeared 1619).
1632	Leiden established the world's first official observatory.
1633	Galileo's theories were condemned by the Inquisition.
1675	The Royal Greenwich Observatory was founded in England.
1687	Newton's *Principia* was published, including his "law of universal gravitation."
1718	Halley predicted the return of the comet named after him, observed 1758: it was last seen 1986.
1781	Herschel discovered Uranus and recognized stellar systems beyond our Galaxy.
1796	Laplace elaborated his theory of the origin of the Solar System.
1801	Piazzi discovered the first asteroid, Ceres.
1814	Fraunhofer first studied absorption lines in the solar spectrum.
1846	Neptune was identified by Galle, following predictions by Adams and Leverrier.
1859	Kirchhoff explained dark lines in the Sun's spectrum.
1887	The earliest photographic star charts were produced.
1889	E E Barnard took the first photographs of the Milky Way.
1890	The first photograph of the spectrum was taken.
1908	Fragment of comet fell at Tunguska, Siberia.
1920	Eddington began the study of interstellar matter.
1923	Hubble proved that the galaxies are systems independent of the Milky Way and by 1930 had confirmed the concept of an expanding universe.
1930	The planet Pluto was discovered by Clyde Tombaugh at the Lowell Observatory, Arizona.
1931	Jansky founded radioastronomy.
1945	Radar contact with the Moon was established by Z Bay of Hungary and the US Army Signal Corps Laboratory.
1948	The 200-in/5-m Hale reflector telescope was installed at Mount Palomar, California.
1955	The Jodrell Bank telescope "dish" in England was completed.
1957	The first Sputnik satellite (USSR) opened the age of space observation.
1962	The first X-ray source was discovered in Scorpius.
1963	The first quasar was discovered.
1967	The first pulsar was discovered by Jocelyn Bell and Antony Hewish.
1969	The first manned Moon landing was made by US astronauts.
1976	A 236-in/6-m reflector telescope was installed at Mount Semirodniki (USSR).
1977	Uranus was discovered to have rings.
1977	The spacecraft *Voyager 1* and *2* were launched, passing Jupiter and Saturn 1979–81.
1978	The spacecraft *Pioneer Venus 1* and *2* reached Venus; a satellite of Pluto, Charon, was discovered by James Christy of the US Naval Observatory.
1979	The UK Infrared Telescope (UKIRT) was established on Hawaii.
1985	Halley's comet returned.
1986	*Voyager 2* flew by Uranus and discovered ten new moons.
1987	Bright supernova visible to the naked eye for the first time since 1604.
1989	*Voyager 2* flew by Neptune and discovered eight moons and three rings.
1990	Hubble Space Telescope was launched into orbit by the US Space Shuttle.

trum, at radio and X-ray wavelengths, has provided confirmation. ◊Radio astronomy established its place in probing the structure of the universe by demonstrating in 1954 that an optically visible distant galaxy was identical with a powerful radio source known as Cygnus A. Later analysis of the comparative number, strength, and distance of radio sources suggested that in the distant past these, including the ◊quasars discovered 1963, had been much more powerful and numerous than today. This fact suggested that the universe has been evolving from an origin and is not of infinite age as expected under a ◊steady-state theory. The discovery 1965 of microwave background radiation suggested that a residue survived the tremendous thermal power of the giant explosion, or Big Bang, that brought the universe into existence.

In 1986 *Voyager 2* discovered six new moons around Uranus. In 1987 Supernova SN1987A flared up in the Large ◊Magellanic Cloud, the first supernova to reach naked-eye visibility since 1604. Also in 1987, the 165-in/4.2-m William Herschel Telescope on La Palma, Canary Islands, and the James Clerk Maxwell Telescope on Mauna Kea, Hawaii, began operation. In 1988 the most distant individual star was recorded; the supernova in one of the galaxies in the AC118 cluster of galaxies is about 5 billion light-years away. In Aug 1989, *Voyager 2* passed by Neptune. See also ◊black hole, ◊cosmology, and ◊infrared radiation.

Although the practical limit in size and efficiency of optical telescopes has apparently been reached, the siting of these and other types of telescope at new observatories in the previously neglected southern hemisphere has opened fresh areas of the sky to search. Australia has been in the forefront of these developments. The most remarkable recent extension of the powers of astronomy to explore the universe is in the use of rockets, satellites, space stations, and space probes. Even the range and accuracy of the conventional telescope may be greatly improved free from the Earth's atmosphere. The US launched a large optical telescope, called the Hubble Space Telescope, permanently in space in April 1990. It is the most powerful optical telescope yet constructed, with a 94.5-in/2.4-m mirror. It detects celestial phenomena seven times more distant (up to 14 billion light-years) than any land telescope.

astrophotography the use of photography in astronomical research. The first successful photograph of a celestial object was the daguerreotype plate of the Moon taken by J W Draper of the US in March 1840. Modern-day astrophotography uses techniques such as ◊charge-coupled devices (CCDs).

Before the development of photography, observations were gathered in the form of sketches made at the telescope. Several successful daguerreotypes were obtained prior to the introduction of wet-plate collodion about 1850. The availability of this more convenient method allowed photography to be used on a more systematic basis, including the monitoring of sunspot activity. Dry plates were introduced in the 1870s, and in 1880 Henry Draper obtained a photograph of the ◊Orion nebula. The first successful image of a comet was obtained 1882 by the Scottish astronomer David Gill, his plate displaying excellent star images. Following this, Gill and J C Kapteyn compiled the first photographic atlas of the southern sky cataloging almost half a million stars.

Modern-day electronic innovations, notably charge-coupled devices, provide a more efficient light-gathering capability than photographic paper as well as enabling information to be transferred to a computer for analysis. However, CCD images are expensive and very small in size compared to photographic plates. Photographic plates are better suited to wide-field images, whereas CCDs are used for individual objects, which may be very faint, within a narrow field of sky.

astrophysics the study of the physical nature of stars, galaxies, and the universe. It began with the development of spectroscopy in the 19th century, which allowed astronomers to analyze the composition of stars from their light. Astrophysicists view the universe as a vast natural laboratory in which they can study matter under conditions of temperature, pressure, and density that are unattainable on Earth.

Asturias autonomous region of N Spain; area 4,092 sq mi/10,600 sq km; population (1986) 1,114,000. Half of Spain's coal is produced from the mines of Asturias. Agricultural produce includes corn, fruit, and livestock. Oviedo and Gijon are the main industrial towns.

It was once a separate kingdom, and the eldest son of a king of Spain is still called prince of Asturias.

Asturias Miguel Ángel 1899–1974. Guatemalan author and diplomat. He published poetry, Guatemalan legends, and novels, such as *El Señor Presidente/The President* 1946, *Men of Corn* 1949, and *Strong Wind* 1950, attacking Latin-American dictatorships and "Yankee imperialism." Nobel Prize 1967.

Astyanax in Greek mythology, the son of ◊Hector and ◊Andromache. After the death of all the sons of ◊Priam in battle, the child Astyanax was thrown from the walls of Troy by the victorious Greeks.

Asunción capital and port of Paraguay, on the Paraguay river; population (1984) 729,000. It produces textiles, footwear, and food products. Founded 1537, it was the first Spanish settlement in the La Plata region.

Aswan winter resort town in Upper Egypt; population (1985) 183,000. It is near the High Dam, built 1960–70, which keeps the level of the Nile constant throughout the year without flooding. It produces steel and textiles.

asymptote in ◊coordinate geometry, a straight line toward which a curve approaches more and more closely but never reaches. If a point on a curve approaches a straight line such that its distance from the straight line is d, then the line is an asymptote to the curve if limit d tends to zero as the point moves toward infinity. Among ◊conic sections (curves obtained by the intersection of a plane and a double cone), a ◊hyperbola has two asymptotes, which in the case of a rectangular hyperbola are at right angles to each other.

Asyut commercial center in Upper Egypt, near the Nile, 200 mi/322 km S of Cairo; population (1985) 274,400. An ancient Graeco-Egyptian city, it has many tombs of 11th-and 12th-dynasty nobles.

Atacama desert in N Chile; area about 31,000 sq mi/80,000 sq km. Inland are mountains, and the coastal area is rainless and barren. There are silver and copper mines and extensive nitrate deposits.

Atatürk *The maker of modern Turkey, Kemal Atatürk was a dictator who introduced many social and administrative reforms that affected Turkish religion, justice, education, language, and the status of women.*

Atahualpa c. 1502–1533. Last emperor of the Incas of Peru. He was taken prisoner 1532 when the Spaniards arrived, and agreed to pay a huge ransom, but was accused of plotting against the conquistador Pizarro and sentenced to be burned. On his consenting to Christian baptism, the sentence was commuted to strangulation.

Atalanta in Greek mythology, a woman hunter who challenged all her suitors to a foot race; if they lost they were killed. Aphrodite gave Milanion three golden apples to drop so that when Atalanta stopped to pick them up, she lost the race.

Atatürk ("Father of the Turks"). Kemal. 1881–1938. Name assumed 1934 by Mustafa Kemal Pasha. Turkish politician and general, first president of Turkey from 1923. After World War I he established a provisional rebel government and in 1921–22 the Turkish armies under his leadership expelled the Greeks who were occupying Turkey. He was the founder of the modern republic, which he ruled as virtual dictator, with a policy of consistent and radical westernization.

Kemal, born in Thessaloniki, was banished 1904 for joining a revolutionary society. Later he was pardoned and promoted in the army, and was largely responsible for the successful defense of the Dardanelles against the British 1915. In 1918, after Turkey had been defeated, he was sent into Anatolia to implement the demobilization of the Turkish forces in accordance with the armistice terms, but instead he established a provisional government opposed to that of Constantinople (under Allied control), and in 1921 led the Turkish armies against the Greeks, who had occupied a large part of Anatolia. He checked them at the Battle of the Sakaria, 23 Aug–Sept 13, 1921, for which he was granted the title of Ghazi (the Victorious), and within a year had expelled the Greeks from Turkish soil. War with the British was averted by his diplomacy, and Turkey in Europe passed under Kemal's control. On Oct 29, 1923, Turkey was proclaimed a republic with Kemal as first president.

atavism (Latin *atavus* "ancestor") in ◊genetics, the reappearance of a characteristic not apparent in the immediately preceding generations; in psychology, the manifestation of primitive forms of behavior.

ataxia loss of muscular coordination due to neurological damage or disease.

Atget Eugène 1857–1927. French photographer. He took up photography at the age of 40, and for 30 years documented urban Paris, leaving some 10,000 photos.

Athabasca lake and river in Alberta and Saskatchewan, Canada, with huge tar-sand deposits (source of the hydrocarbon mixture "heavy oil") to the SW of the lake.

Athanasian creed one of the three ancient ◊creeds of the Christian church. Mainly a definition of the Trinity and Incarnation, it was written many years after the death of Athanasius, but was attributed to him as the chief upholder of Trinitarian doctrine.

Athanasius, St 298–373. Bishop of Alexandria, supporter of the doctrines of the Trinity and Incarnation. He was a disciple of St Anthony the hermit, and an opponent of ◊Arianism in the great Arian controversy. Following the official condemnation of Arianism at the Council of Nicaea 325, Athanasius was appointed bishop of Alexandria 328. The Athanasian creed was not actually written by him, although it reflects his views.

atheism nonbelief in, or the positive denial of, the existence of a god or gods.

Dogmatic atheism asserts that there is no God. Skeptical atheism maintains that the finite human mind is so constituted as to be incapable of discovering that there is or is not a God. Critical atheism holds that the evidence for theism is inadequate. This is akin to philosophical atheism, which fails to find evidence of a God manifest in the universe. Speculative atheism comprises the beliefs of those who, like the German philosopher Kant, find it impossible to demonstrate the existence of God. A related concept is ◊agnosticism.

Buddhism has been called an atheistic religion since it does not postulate any supreme being. The Jains are similarly atheistic, and so are those who adopt the Sankhya system of philosophy in Hinduism.

Following the revolution of 1917 the USSR and later Communist states, such as Albania, adopted an atheist position.

Athelney, Isle of area of firm ground in marshland near Taunton in Somerset, England, in 878 the headquarters of King ◊Alfred the Great when he was in hiding from the Danes.

Athelstan c. 895–939. King of the Mercians and West Saxons. Son of Edward the Elder and grandson of Alfred the Great, he was crowned king 925 at Kingston-upon-Thames. He subdued parts of Cornwall and Wales, and in 937 defeated the Welsh, Scots, and Danes at Brunanburh.

Athena in Greek mythology, the goddess (Roman Minerva) of war, wisdom, and the arts and crafts, who was supposed to have sprung fully grown from the head of Zeus. Her chief cult center was Athens, where the ◊Parthenon was dedicated to her.

Athens city in NE Georgia, on the Oconee river, NE of Atlanta; seat of Clarke county. The University of Georgia was established here 1801. Industries include cotton and electrical products; population (1990) 45,734.

Athens (Greek *Athinai*) capital city of Greece and of ancient Attica; population (1981) 885,000, metropolitan area 3,027,000. Situated 5 mi/8 km NE of its port of Piraeus on the Gulf of Aegina, it is built around the rocky hills of the Acropolis 555 ft/169 m and the Areopagus 368 ft/112 m, and is overlooked from the NE by the hill of Lycabettus 909 ft/277 m. It lies in the S of the central plain of Attica, watered by the mountain streams of Cephissus and Ilissus.

features The Acropolis dominates the city. Remains of ancient Greece include the Parthenon, the Erechtheum, and the temple of Athena Nike. Near the site of the ancient Agora (marketplace) stands the Theseum, and S of the Acropolis is the theater of Dionysus. To the SE stand the gate of Hadrian and the columns of the temple of Olympian Zeus. Nearby is the marble stadium built about 330 BC and restored 1896.

history The site was first inhabited about 3000 BC, and Athens became the capital of a united Attica before 700 BC. Captured and sacked by the Persians 480 BC, subsequently under Pericles it was the first city of Greece in power and culture. After the death of Alexander the Great the city fell into comparative decline, but it flourished as an intellectual center until AD 529, when the philosophical schools were closed by Justinian. In 1458 it was captured by the Turks who held it until 1833; it was chosen as the capital of Greece 1834. Among present day buildings are the royal palace and several museums.

atheroma furring-up of the interior of an artery by deposits, mainly of cholesterol, within its walls.

Associated with atherosclerosis, atheroma has the effect of narrowing the lumen (channel) of the artery, thus restricting blood flow. This predisposes to a number of conditions, including thrombosis, angina, and stroke.

atherosclerosis thickening and hardening of the walls of the arteries, associated with atheroma.

athletics collectively, all the sports, exercises, and contests that utilize and promote such physical skills as speed, agility, and stamina.

Among the Greeks, vase paintings show that competitive athletics were established by at least 1600 BC (see ◊Olympic Games). However, the concept of the unpaid amateur is a recent innovation, ancient athletes having been well paid and sponsored. ◊Aristotle paid the expenses of a boxer contestant at Olympia, and chariot races were sponsored by the Greek city states. Athletics recently became dominated by the drive for new world records. This has led to the use of computer selection for the best potential competitors and the analysis of motion for the greatest speed, distance, and so forth; also the specialization of equipment for maximum performance (for example, fiberglass vaulting poles, foam landing pads, aerodynamically designed javelins, composition running tracks); and the unlawful use of drugs such as ◊anabolic steroids and growth hormones, pain killers, and energizers.

Athos a mountainous peninsula on the Macedonian coast of Greece. Its peak is 6,672 ft/2,033 m high. The promontory is occupied by a community of 20 Basilian monasteries inhabited by some 3,000 monks and lay brothers.

Atlanta capital and largest city of Georgia; population (1990) 394,017, metropolitan area 2,010,000. It was founded 1837 and was partly destroyed by General ◊Sherman 1864. There are Ford and Lockheed assembly plants, and it is the headquarters of Coca-Cola. Atlanta is also the financial, trade, and convention center for the SE US and has one of the busiest and most automated US airports. Educational institutions include Atlanta University, Emory University, the Georgia Institute of Technology, and Georgia State University. The city grew considerably in importance after 1900. In 1990 it was chosen as the host city for the 1996 summer Olympic Games.

Atlantic, Battle of the the German campaign during World War I to prevent merchant shipping from delivering food supplies from the US to the Allies, especially the UK. By 1917, some 875,000 tons of shipping had been lost. The odds were only turned by the belated use of naval convoys and depth charges to deter submarine attack.

Notable action included the British defeat at Coronel off Chile on Nov 1, 1914, the subsequent British success at the Falkland Islands on Dec 8, 1914, and the battle at Jutland on May 31, 1916, which effectively neutralized the German surface fleet for the rest of the war.

Atlantic, Battle of the continuous battle fought in the Atlantic Ocean throughout World War II (1939–45) by the sea and air forces of the Allies and Germany. The number of U-boats destroyed by the Allies during the war was nearly 800. At least 2,200 convoys of 75,000 merchant ships crossed the Atlantic, protected by US naval forces. Before the US entry into the war 1941, destroyers were supplied to the British by the US under the Lend-Lease Act 1941.

The battle opened on the first night of the war, when on Sept 4, 1939 the ocean liner *Athenia*, sailing from Glasgow to New York, was torpedoed by a German submarine off the Irish coast. Germany tried U-boats, surface-raiders, indiscriminate mine-laying, and aircraft, but every method was successfully countered. The U-boats were the greatest menace, especially after the destruction of the German battleship *Bismarck* by British forces on May 27, 1941.

Atlantic Charter declaration issued during World War II by the British prime minister Churchill and the US president Roosevelt after meetings Aug 1941. It stressed their countries' good intentions and war aims and was largely a propaganda exercise to demonstrate public solidarity between the Allies.

The Atlantic Charter stated that Britain and the US sought no territorial gains; desired no territorial changes not acceptable to the peoples concerned; respected the rights of all peoples to choose their own form of government; wished to see self-government restored to the occupied countries; would promote access by all states to trade and raw materials; desired international collaboration for the raising of economic standards; hoped to see a peace affording security to all nations, enabling them to cross the seas without hindrance; and proposed the disarmament of the aggressor states as a preliminary step to general disarmament. This charter was incorporated by reference into the Declaration of the United Nations 1941.

Atlantic City seaside resort in New Jersey; population (1990) 37,986. It is noted for its "boardwalk" and for being the basis of the Monopoly board game; the Miss America contest has been held here since 1921. It is also a convention center. Formerly a family resort, Atlantic City has become a center for casino gambling, which was legalized in 1978.

Atlantic Ocean ocean lying between Europe and Africa to the E and the Americas to the W, probably named after the legendary island ◊Atlantis; area of basin 31,500,000 sq mi/ 81,500,000 sq km; including Arctic Ocean, and Antarctic seas, 41,000,000 sq mi/ 106,200,000 sq km. The average depth is 2 mi/3 km; greatest depth the Milwaukee Depth in the Puerto Rico Trench 28,374 ft/8,648 m. The Mid-Atlantic Ridge, of which the Azores, Ascension, St Helena, and Tristan da Cunha form part, divides it from N to S. Lava welling up from this central area annually increases the distance between South America and Africa. The N Atlantic is the saltiest of the main oceans, and it has the largest tidal range. In the 1960s–80s average wave heights increased by 25%, the largest from 39 ft/ 12 m to 59 ft/18 m.

Atlantis legendary island continent, said to have sunk c. 9600 BC, following underwater convulsions. Although the Atlantic Ocean is probably named after it, the structure of the sea bottom rules out its ever having existed there.

One story told by the Greek philosopher Plato (derived from an account by Egyptian priests) may refer to the volcanic eruption that devastated Santorini in the ◊Cyclades, north of Crete, c. 1500 BC. The ensuing earthquakes and tidal waves brought about the collapse of the empire of Minoan Crete.

Atlas in Greek mythology, one of the ◊Titans who revolted against the gods; as a punishment, Atlas was compelled to support the heavens on his head and shoulders. Growing weary, he asked ◊Perseus to turn him into stone, and he was transformed into Mount Atlas.

atlas a book of maps. The atlas was introduced in the 16th century by ◊Mercator, who began work on it in 1585; it was completed by his son in 1594. Early atlases had a frontispiece showing Atlas supporting the globe.

Atlas Mountains mountain system of NW Africa, stretching 1,500 mi/2,400 km from the Atlantic coast of Morocco to the Gulf of Gabes, Tunisia, and lying between the Mediterranean on the N and the Sahara on the S. The highest peak is Mount Toubkal 13,670 ft/4,167 m.

Geologically the Atlas Mountains compare with the ◊Alps in age, but their structure is much less complex. They are recognized as the continuation of the great Tertiary fold mountain systems of Europe.

The Earth's atmosphere

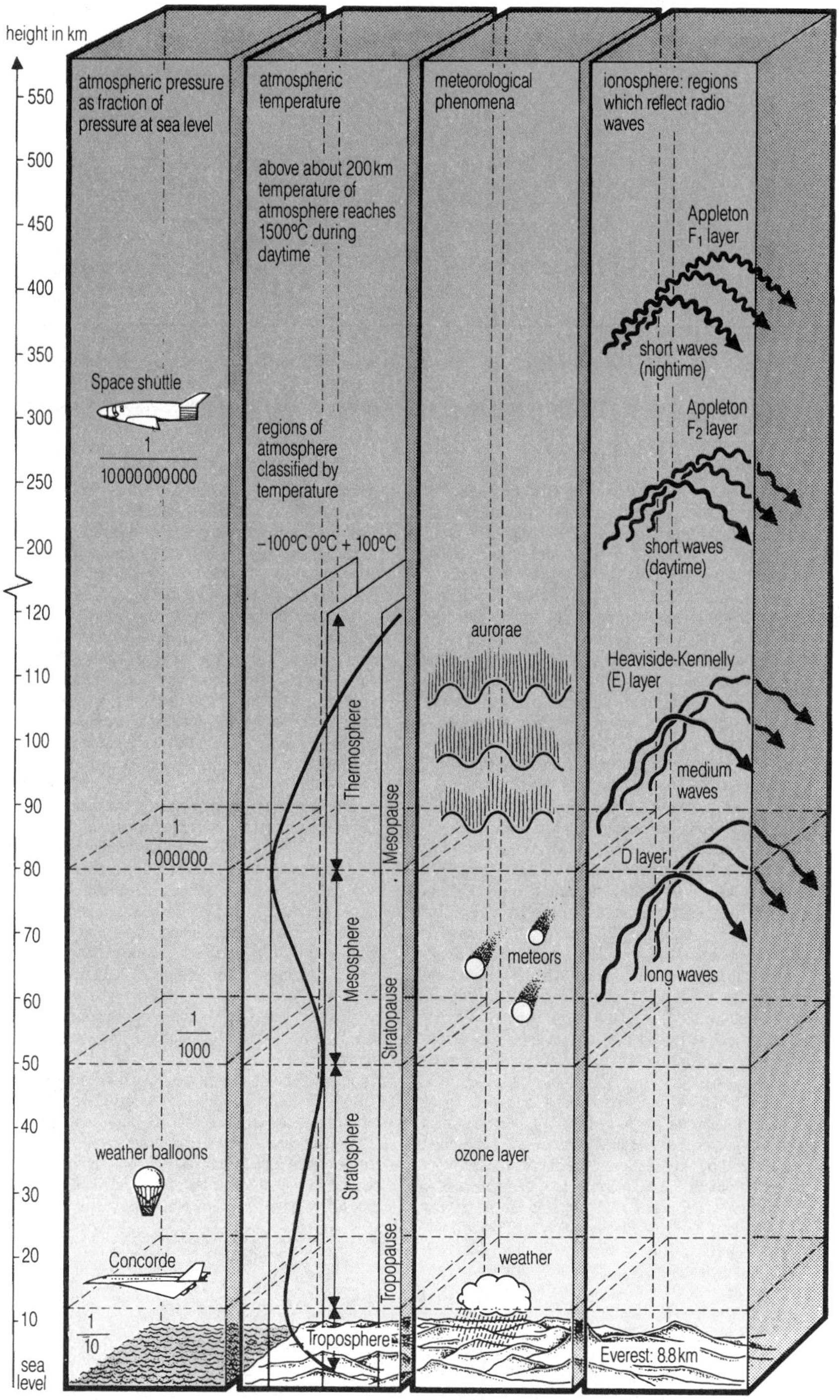
height in km
550
500
450
400
350
300
250
200
120
110
100
90
80
70
60
50
40
30
20
10
sea level
atmospheric pressure as fraction of pressure at sea level
Space shuttle
1/10000000000
1/1000000
1/1000
1/10
weather balloons
Concorde
atmospheric temperature
above about 200km temperature of atmosphere reaches 1500°C during daytime
regions of atmosphere classified by temperature
-100°C 0°C + 100°C
Thermosphere
Mesopause
Mesosphere
Stratopause
Stratosphere
Tropopause
Troposphere
meteorological phenomena
aurorae
meteors
ozone layer
weather
ionosphere: regions which reflect radio waves
Appleton F1 layer
short waves (nightime)
Appleton F2 layer
short waves (daytime)
Heaviside-Kennelly (E) layer
medium waves
D layer
long waves
Everest: 8.8km

Atlas rocket US rocket, originally designed and built as an intercontinental missile but subsequently adapted for space use. Atlas rockets launched astronauts in the Mercury series into orbit, as well as numerous other satellites and space probes.

atman in Hinduism, the individual soul or the eternal essential self.

atmosphere the mixture of gases that surrounds the Earth, prevented from escaping by the pull of the Earth's gravity. Atmospheric pressure decreases with height in the atmosphere. In its lowest layer, the atmosphere consists of nitrogen (78%) and oxygen (21%), both in molecular form (two atoms bound together). The other 1% is largely argon, with very small quantities of other gases, including water vapor and carbon dioxide. The atmosphere plays a major part in the various cycles of nature (the ◊water cycle, ◊carbon cycle, and ◊nitrogen cycle). It is the principal industrial source of nitrogen, oxygen, and argon, which are obtained by fractional distillation of liquid air.

The lowest level of the atmosphere, the ◊troposphere, is heated by the Earth, which is warmed by infrared and visible radiation from the Sun. Warm air cools as it rises in the troposphere, causing rain and most other weather phenomena.

composition of the atmosphere

Gas	Symbol	Volume (%)	Role
nitrogen	N_2	78.08	cycled through human activities and through the action of microorganisms on animal and plant waste
oxygen	O_2	20.94	cycled mainly through the respiration of animals and plants and through the action of photosynthesis
carbon dioxide	CO_2	0.03	cycled through respiration and photosynthesis in exchange reactions with oxygen. It is a also a product of burning fossil fuels
argon	Ar	0.093	chemically inert and with only a few industrial uses
neon	Ne	0.0018	as argon
helium	He	0.0005	as argon
krypton	Kr	trace	as argon
xenon	Xe	trace	as argon
ozone	O_3	0.00006	a product of oxygen molecules split into single atoms by the sun's radiation and unaltered oxygen molecules
hydrogen	H_2	0.00005	unimportant

Infrared and visible radiations form only a part of the Sun's output of electromagnetic radiation. Almost all the shorter-wavelength ultraviolet radiation is filtered out by the upper layers of the atmosphere. The filtering process is an active one: at heights above about 31 mi/50 km ultraviolet photons collide with atoms, knocking out electrons to create a ◊plasma of electrons and positively charged ions. The resulting ionosphere acts as a reflector of radio waves, enabling radio transmissions to "hop" between widely separated points on the Earth's surface. Waves of different wavelengths are reflected best at different heights. The collisions between ultraviolet photons and atoms lead to a heating of the upper atmosphere, although the temperature drops from top to bottom within the zone called the thermosphere as high-energy photons are progressively absorbed in collisions. Between the thermosphere and the tropopause (at which the warming effect of the Earth starts to be felt) there is a "warm bulge" in the graph of temperature against height, at a level called the stratopause. This is due to longer-wavelength ultraviolet photons that have survived their journey through the upper layers; now they encounter molecules and split them apart into atoms. These atoms eventually bond together again, but often in different combinations. In particular, many ◊ozone molecules (oxygen-atom triplets) are formed. Ozone is a better absorber of ultraviolet than ordinary (two-atom) oxygen, and it is the ozone layer that prevents lethal amounts of ultraviolet from reaching the Earth's surface. Far above the atmosphere, as so far described, lie the Van Allen radiation belts. These are regions in which high-energy charged particles traveling outward from the Sun (as the so-called solar wind) have been captured by the Earth's magnetic field. The outer belt (at about 1,000 mi/1,600 km) contains mainly protons, the inner belt (at about 1,250 mi/2,000 km) contains mainly electrons. Sometimes electrons spiral down toward the Earth, noticeably at polar latitudes, where the magnetic field is strongest. When such particles collide with atoms and ions in the thermosphere, light is emitted. This is the origin of the glow visible in the sky as the aurora borealis (northern lights) and the aurora australis (southern lights). A fainter, more widespread, airglow is caused by a similar mechanism.

atmosphere or ***standard atmosphere*** in physics, a unit (abbreviation atm) of pressure equal to 760 torr, 1013.25 millibars, or 1.01325×10^5 newtons per square meter. The actual pressure exerted by the atmosphere fluctuates around this value, which is assumed to be standard at sea level and 32°F/0°C, and is used when dealing with very high pressures.

atmospheric pollution see ◊pollution.

atoll a continuous or broken circle of ◊coral reef and low coral islands surrounding a lagoon.

atom the smallest unit of matter that can take part in a chemical reaction, and which cannot be broken down chemically into anything simpler. An atom is made up of protons and neutrons in a central nucleus surrounded by electrons. The atoms of the various elements differ in atomic number, relative atomic mass, and chemical and physical behavior. There are 109 different types of atom, corresponding with the 109 known elements as listed in the ◊periodic table of the elements.

atom, electronic structure the arrangement of electrons around the nucleus of an atom, in distinct energy levels, also called orbitals or shells (see ◊orbital, atomic). These shells can be regarded as a series of concentric spheres, each of which can contain a certain maximum number of electrons; the noble gases have an arrangement in which every shell contains this number (see ◊noble gas structure). The energy levels are usually numbered beginning with the shell nearest to the nucleus. The outermost shell is known as the ◊valency shell as it contains the valence electrons.

The atomic number of an element indicates the number of electrons in a neutral atom. From this it is possible to deduce its electronic structure. For example, sodium has atomic number 11 ($Z = 11$) and its electronic arrangement (configuration) is two electrons in the first energy level, eight electrons in the second energy level and one electron in the third energy level—generally written as 2.8.1. Similarly for sulfur ($Z = 16$), the electron arrangement will be 2.8.6. The electronic structure dictates whether two elements will combine by ionic or covalent bonding (see ◊bond) or not at all.

atomic bomb bomb deriving its explosive force from nuclear fission (see ◊nuclear energy) as a result of a neutron chain reaction, developed in the 1940s in the US into a usable weapon.

Research began in the UK 1940 and was transferred to the US after its entry into World War II the following year. Known as the Manhattan Project, the work was carried out under the direction of the US physicist Robert Oppenheimer at Los Alamos, New Mexico. After one test explosion, two atomic bombs were dropped on the Japanese cities of Hiroshima (Aug 6, 1945) and Nagasaki (Aug 9, 1945), each nominally equal to 200,000 tons of TNT. The USSR first detonated an atomic bomb in 1949 and the UK in 1952.

atomic clock timekeeping device regulated by various periodic processes occurring in atoms and molecules, such as atomic vibration or the frequency of absorbed or emitted radiation.

The first atomic clock was the ammonia clock, invented at the US National Bureau of Standards 1948. It was regulated by measuring the speed at which the nitrogen atom in an ammonia molecule vibrated back and forth. The rate of molecular vibration is not affected by temperature, pressure, or other external influences, and can be used to regulate an electronic clock.

A more accurate atomic clock is the cesium clock. Because of its internal structure, a cesium atom produces or absorbs radiation of a very precise frequency (9,192,631,770 Hz) that varies by less than one part in 10 billion. This frequency has been used to define the second, and is the basis of atomic clocks used in international timekeeping.

Hydrogen maser clocks, based on the radiation from hydrogen atoms, are the most accurate. The hydrogen maser clock at the US Naval Research Laboratory, Washington, DC, is estimated to lose one second in 1,700,000 years. Cooled hydrogen maser clocks could theoretically be accurate to within one second in 300 million years.

atomic energy former name for ◊nuclear energy.

atomic force microscope (AFM) a microscope developed in the late 1980s that produces a magnified image using a diamond probe, with a tip so fine that it may consist of a single atom, dragged over the surface of a specimen to "feel" the contours of the surface. In effect, the tip acts like the stylus of a phonograph or record player, reading the surface. The tiny up-and-down movements of the probe are converted to an image of the surface by computer, and displayed on a screen. The AFM is useful for examination of biological specimens since, unlike the ◊scanning tunneling microscope, the specimen does not have to be electrically conducting.

atomicity the number of atoms of an ◊element that combine together to form a molecule. A molecule of oxygen (O_2) has atomicity 2; sulfur (S_8) has atomicity 8.

atomic mass unit or ***dalton unit*** (symbol amu or u) of mass that is used to measure the relative mass of atoms and molecules. It is equal to one-twelfth of the mass of a carbon-12 atom, which is equivalent to the mass of a proton or 1.66×10^{-27} kg. The ◊atomic weight of an atom has no units;

atomic bomb *Giant waterspout at Bikini Island in the W Pacific after the explosion of a US atomic bomb in an underwater test. The dark streak in the central column, at left, was the approximate position of the battleship sunk by the blast.*

thus oxygen-16 has an atomic mass of 16 daltons, but a atomic weight of 16.

atomic number or ***proton number*** the number (symbol *Z*) of protons (and electrons) in the nucleus of an atom. It is equal to the positive charge on the nucleus. The 105 elements are numbered 1 (hydrogen) to 109 (unnilennium) in the periodic table of elements. See also ◊nuclear notation and ◊element.

atomic physics former name for ◊nuclear physics.

atomic radiation energy given out by disintegrating atoms during ◊radioactive decay, whether natural or synthesized. The energy may be in the form of fast-moving particles, known as ◊alpha particles and ◊beta particles, or in the form of high-energy electromagnetic waves known as ◊gamma radiation. Overlong exposure to atomic radiation can lead to ◊radiation sickness. Radiation biology studies the effect of radiation on living organisms.

atomic structure the internal structure of an ◊atom. The core of the atom is the ***nucleus***, a particle only one ten-thousandth the diameter of the atom itself. The simplest nucleus, that of hydrogen, comprises a single positively charged particle, the ***proton***. Nuclei of other elements contain more protons and additional particles of about the same mass as the proton but with no electrical charge, ***neutrons***. Each element has its own characteristic nucleus with a unique number of protons, the atomic number. The number of neutrons may vary. Where atoms of a single element have different numbers of neutrons, they are called ◊isotopes. Although some isotopes tend to be unstable and exhibit ◊radioactivity, they all have identical chemical properties.

The nucleus is surrounded by a number of ***electrons***, each of which has a negative charge equal to the positive charge on a proton, but which weighs only 1/1839 times as much. For a neutral atom, the nucleus is surrounded by the same number of electrons as it contains protons. The chemical properties of an element are determined by the ease with which its atoms can gain or lose electrons. This is dependent on both the number of electrons associated with the nucleus and the force exerted on them by its positive charge. High-energy physics research has discovered the existence of other subatomic particles. These include ***antiparticles*** (such as the antiproton and antineutron), which are opposite in some properties but identical in others to known charged and neutral particles; ***hyperons***, with masses greater than protons; and ***mesons***, with masses intermediate between electrons and protons. More than 300 kinds of particle are now known. Experiments by ◊CERN and at the Fermi laboratory (Fermilab) in the USA have suggested that these particles are themselves made up of subparticles, known as ***quarks***, which may be the fundamental building blocks of matter. However, some subatomic particles have been shown to change from one form to another and to behave in a way that is not always predictable (as shown by Werner Heisenberg's ◊uncertainty principle). Atoms are held together by the electrical forces of attraction between each negative electron and the positive protons within the nucleus. The latter repel one another with relatively enormous forces; a nucleus holds together only because other forces, not of a simple electrical character, attract the protons and neutrons to one another. These additional forces act only so long as the protons and neutrons are virtually in contact with one another. If, therefore, a fragment of a complex nucleus, containing some protons, becomes only slightly loosened from the main group of neutrons and protons, the strong natural repulsion between the protons will cause this fragment to fly apart from the rest of the nucleus at high speed. It is by such fragmentation of atomic nuclei (◊nuclear fission) that nuclear energy is released.

atomic time the time as given by ◊atomic clocks, which are regulated by natural resonance frequencies of particular atoms, and display a continuous count of seconds.

In 1967 a new definition of the second was adopted in the SI system of units: the duration of 9,192,631,770 periods of the radiation corresponding to the transition between two hyperfine levels of the ground state of the cesium-133 atom. The International Atomic Time Scale is based on clock data from a number of countries; it is a continuous scale in days, hours, minutes, and seconds from the origin on Jan 1, 1958, when the Atomic Time Scale was made 0 h 0 min 0 sec when Greenwich Mean Time was at 0 h 0 min 0 sec.

atomic weight or ***atomic mass*** the mass of an atom. It depends on the number of protons and neutrons in the atom, the electrons having negligible mass. It is calculated relative to one-twelfth the mass of an atom of carbon-12. If more than one ◊isotope of the element is present, the atomic weight is calculated by taking an average that takes account of the relative proportions of each isotope, resulting in values that are not whole numbers.

atomizer device that produces a spray of fine droplets of liquid. A vertical tube connected with a horizontal tube dips into a bottle of liquid, and at one end of the horizontal tube is a nozzle, at the other a rubber bulb. When the bulb is squeezed, air rushes over the top of the vertical tube and out through the nozzle. Following ◊Bernoulli's effect, the pressure at the top of the vertical tube is reduced, allowing the liquid to rise. The air stream picks up the liquid, breaks it up into tiny drops and carries it out of the nozzle as a spray.

Aton in ancient Egypt, the sun's disk as an emblem of the single deity whose worship was promoted by ◊Ikhnaton in an attempt to replace the many gods traditionally worshiped.

atonality music in which there is an apparent absence of ◊key; often associated with an expressionist style.

Atonality is used by film and television composers for situations of mystery or horror; it exploits dissonance for its power to disturb. For ◊Schoenberg, pioneer of atonal music from 1909, the intention was to liberate tonal expression and not primarily to disturb, and he rejected the term as misleading.

atonement in Christian theology, the doctrine that Jesus suffered on the cross to bring about reconciliation and forgiveness between God and humanity.

Atonement, Day of Jewish holy day (Yom Kippur) held on the tenth day of Tishri (Sept–Oct), the first month of the Jewish year. It is a day of fasting, penitence, and cleansing from sin, ending the Ten Days of Penitence that follow ◊*Rosh Hashanah*, the Jewish New Year.

ATP (adenosine triphosphate) nucleotide molecule found in all cells. It can yield large amounts of energy, and is used to drive the thousands of biological processes needed to sustain life, growth, movement, and reproduction. Green plants use light energy to manufacture ATP as part of the process of ◊photosynthesis. In animals, ATP is formed by the breakdown of glucose molecules, usually obtained from the carbohydrate component of a diet, in a series of reactions termed ◊respiration. It is the driving force behind muscle contraction and the synthesis of complex molecules needed by individual cells.

Atreus the father of ◊Agamemnon and ◊Menelaus (the Atridae) in Greek mythology, son of ◊Pelops, and brother of ◊Thyestes, with whom he contested the throne of ◊Mycenae. As part of the feud, Atreus served the flesh of Thyestes' children to their father at a banquet held to confirm the reconciliation of the two brothers.

atrium in architecture, an inner, open courtyard. It was originally the central court or main room of an ancient Roman house, open to the sky, often with a shallow pool to catch water.

atrium one of the upper chambers of the heart, receiving blood under low pressure as it returns from the body. Atrium walls are thin and stretch easily to allow blood into the heart. On contraction, the atria force blood into the thick-walled ventricles, which then give a second, more powerful beat.

atrophy in medicine, a diminution in size and function, or output, of a body tissue or organ. It is usually due to nutritional impairment, disease, or disuse (muscle).

atropine ◊alkaloid derived from belladonna, a plant with toxic properties. It acts as an ◊anticholinergic and, as atropine sulfate, is administered as a mild antispasmodic drug.

Atropine is named after Atropos, one of the three Greek Fates, who cut people's lives short.

attainder, bill of a legislative device that allowed the English Parliament to declare guilt and impose a punishment on an individual without bringing the matter before the courts. Such bills were used intermittently from the Wars of the Roses until 1798. Some acts of attainder were also passed by US colonial legislators during the American Revolution to deal with "loyalists" who continued to support the English crown.

Bills of attainder were expressly forbidden by the US Constitution. The use of the device has generally been deplored as it did not require the accusers to prove their case.

attar of roses perfume derived from the essential oil of roses (especially damask roses), obtained by crushing and distilling the petals of the flowers.

attempt a partial or unsuccessful commission of a crime. An attempt must be more than preparation for a crime; it must involve actual efforts to commit a crime.

Attenborough David 1926– . English traveler and zoologist, brother of the actor and director Richard Attenborough. He was director of programs for BBC Television 1969–72, and writer and presenter of the television series *Life on Earth* 1979, *The Living Planet* 1983, and *The Trials of Life* 1990.

Attenborough Richard 1923– . English film actor, director and producer. He began his acting career in war films and comedies. His later films include *Séance on a Wet Afternoon* 1964 and *10 Rillington Place* 1970 (as actor), and *Oh! What a Lovely War* 1968, *Gandhi* (which won six Academy Awards) 1982, and *Cry Freedom* 1987 (as director).

Attica (Greek *Attiki*) region of Greece comprising Athens and the district around it; area 1,305 sq mi/3,381 sq km. It is noted for its language, art, and philosophical thought in Classical times. It is a prefecture of modern Greece with Athens as its capital.

Attila c. 406–453. King of the Huns from 434, called the "Scourge of God." He embarked on a career of vast conquests, ranging from the Rhine to Persia. In 451 he invaded Gaul, but was defeated on the ◊Catalaunian Fields by the Roman and Visigoth armies under Aëtius (died 454) and Theodoric I. In 452 Attila led his Huns into Italy and only the personal intervention of Pope Leo I prevented the sacking of Rome.

Attila returned to Pannonia, west of the Danube, where he died on the night of his marriage with Ildico, poison being suspected as the cause. He was said to have been buried with a vast treasure.

Attila Line line dividing Greek and Turkish Cyprus, so called because of a fanciful identification of the Turks with the Huns.

Attis in Classical mythology, a Phrygian god whose death and resurrection symbolized the end of winter and the arrival of spring. Beloved by the goddess ◊Cybele, who drove him mad as a punishment for his infidelity, he castrated himself and bled to death.

Attleboro city in SE Massachusetts, NW of New Bedford. Manufactures include jewelry, tools, silver products, electronics, and paper goods; population (1990) 38,383.

Attlee Clement (Richard), 1st Earl 1883–1967. Brit-

Attenborough *British filmmaker Richard Attenborough (left) and actor Ralph Richardson working on the script of* Oh! What a Lovely War *in 1968. The film won 16 international awards.*

ish Labour politician. In the coalition government during World War II he was Lord Privy Seal 1940–42, dominions secretary 1942–43, and Lord President of the Council 1943–45, as well as deputy prime minister from 1942. As prime minister 1945–51 he introduced a sweeping program of nationalization and a whole new system of social services.

attorney a person who represents another in legal matters. In the US, attorney is the formal title for a lawyer.

See also ◊power of attorney.

attorney general principal law officer.

In the US, the principal officer of the federal government or of a state. The US Attorney General is a member of the cabinet, appointed by the president; state attorneys general are elected to office. Attorneys general act as chief officers for criminal and civil law and as chief legal representatives of their governments in government operations.

Atwood Margaret (Eleanor) 1939– . Canadian novelist, short-story writer, and poet. Her novels, which often treat feminist themes with wit and irony, include *The Edible Woman* 1969, *Life Before Man* 1979, *Bodily Harm* 1981, *The Handmaid's Tale* 1986, and *Cat's Eye* 1989.

Collections of poetry include *Power Politics* 1971, *You are Happy* 1974, and *Interlunar* 1984.

Aube river of NE France, a tributary of the Seine, length 155 mi/248 km; it gives its name to a *département*.

Auber Daniel François Esprit 1782–1871. French operatic composer who studied under the Italian composer and teacher Cherubini. He wrote about 50 operas, including *La Muette de Portici/The Mute Girl of Portici* 1828 and the comic opera *Fra Diavolo* 1830.

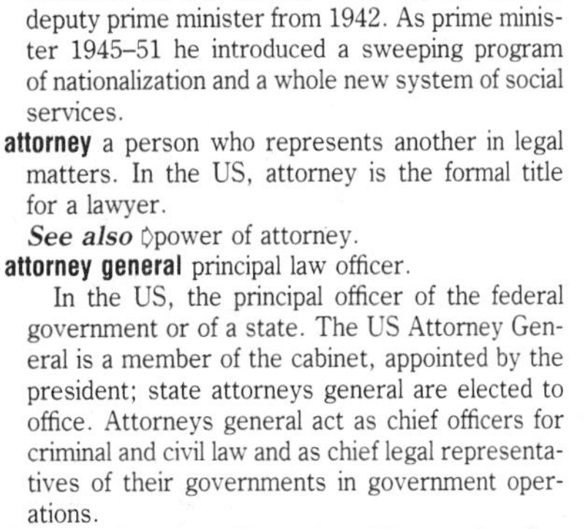

Atwood *Canadian novelist and poet Margaret Atwood.*

aubrieta any spring-flowering dwarf perennial plant of the genus *Aubrieta* of the cress family Cruciferae. All are trailing plants with showy, purple flowers. Native to the Middle East, they are cultivated widely in rock gardens.

Auburn city in SW Maine on the Androscoggin river, W of Lewiston; seat of Androscoggin county. Industries include shoes, textiles, poultry, livestock, and bricks; population (1990) 24,309.

Aubusson town in the *département* of Creuse, France; population (1982) 6,500. Its carpet and tapestry industry dates from the 15th century.

Auchinleck Sir Claude John Eyre 1884–1981. British commander in World War II. He won the First Battle of El ◊Alamein 1942 in N Egypt. In 1943 he became commander in chief in India and founded the modern Indian and Pakistani armies. In 1946 he was promoted to field marshal; he retired in 1947.

Auckland largest city in New Zealand, situated in N North Island; population (1987) 889,000. It fills the isthmus that separates its two harbors (Waitemata and Manukau), and its suburbs spread N across the Harbor Bridge. It is the country's chief port and leading industrial center, having iron and steel plants, engineering, car assembly, textiles, food-processing, sugar-refining, and brewing.

There was a small whaling settlement on the site 1830s, and Auckland was officially founded as New Zealand's capital 1840, remaining so until 1865. The university was founded 1882.

Auckland Islands six uninhabited volcanic islands 300 mi/480 km S of South Island, New Zealand; area 23 sq mi/60 sq km.

auction the sale of goods or property in public to the highest bidder. There are usually conditions of sale by which all bidders are bound.

A bid may be withdrawn at any time before the auctioneer brings down the hammer, and the seller is likewise entitled to withdraw any lot before the hammer falls. It is illegal for the seller or anyone on their behalf to make a bid for their own goods unless their right to do so has been reserved and notified before the sale. "Rings" of dealers agreeing to keep prices down are illegal. A reserve price is kept secret, but an upset price (the minimum price fixed for the property offered) is made public before the sale. An auction where property is first offered at a high price and gradually reduced until a bid is received is known as a "Dutch auction."

auction bridge card game played by two pairs of players using all 52 cards in a standard deck. The chief characteristic is the selection of trumps by a preliminary bid or auction. It has been succeeded in popularity by ◊contract bridge.

Aude river in SE France, 130 mi/210 km long, that gives its name to a *département*. Carcassonne is the main town through which it passes.

Auden W(ystan) H(ugh) 1907–1973. English-born US poet. He wrote some of his most original poetry, such as *Look, Stranger!* 1936, in the 1930s when he led the influential left-wing literary group that included Louis MacNeice, Stephen Spender, and Cecil Day Lewis. He moved to the US 1939, became a US citizen 1946, and adopted a more conservative and Christian viewpoint, for example in *The Age of Anxiety* 1947.

Born in York, Auden was associate professor of English literature at the University of Michigan from 1939, and professor of poetry at Oxford 1956–61. He also wrote verse dramas with Christopher ◊Isherwood, such as *The Dog Beneath the Skin* and *The Ascent of F6* 1951, and opera librettos, notably for Stravinsky's *The Rake's Progress* 1951.

Audenarde French form of ◊Oudenaarde, a town in Belgium.

audiometer electrical instrument used to test hearing.

audit the official inspection of a company's accounts by a qualified accountant as required each year by law to ensure that the company balance sheet reflects the true state of its affairs. Also, any such official inspection of fiduciary affairs, as by the US Internal Revenue Service, of either personal or business accounts.

auditory canal tube leading from the outer ◊ear opening to the eardrum. It is found only in animals whose eardrums are located inside the skull, principally mammals and birds.

Audubon John James 1785–1851. US naturalist and artist. In 1827, after extensive travels and observations of birds, he published the first part of his *Birds of North America*, with a remarkable series of color plates. Later he produced a similar work on North American quadrupeds.

He was born in Santo Domingo (now Haiti) and educated in Paris. The National Audubon Society (founded 1886) has branches throughout the US and Canada for the study and protection of birds.

Auerbach Frank Helmuth 1931– . British artist whose portraits and landscapes blend figurative and abstract work.

Augean stables in Greek mythology, the stables of Augeas, king of Elis in Greece. One of the labors of ◊Heracles was to clean out the stables, which contained 3,000 cattle and had never been cleaned before. He was given only one day to do the labor and so diverted the river Alpheus through their yard.

Augier Émile 1820–1889. French dramatist. In collaboration with Jules Sandeau he wrote *Le Gendre de M Poirier* 1854, a realistic delineation of bourgeois society.

Augrabies Falls waterfalls in the Orange River, NW Cape Province, South Africa. Height 480 ft/148 m.

Augsburg industrial city in Bavaria, West Germany, at the confluence of the Wertach and Lech rivers, 32 mi/52 km NW of Munich; population (1988) 246,000. It is named after the Roman emperor Augustus who founded it 15 BC.

Augsburg, Confession of statement of the Protestant faith as held by the German Reformers, composed by Philip ◊Melanchthon. Presented to the holy Roman emperor Charles V, at the conference known as the Diet of Augsburg 1530, it is the creed of the modern Lutheran church.

Augsburg, Peace of religious settlement following the Diet of Augsburg 1555, which established the right of princes in the Holy Roman Empire (rather than the emperor himself, Ferdinand I) to impose a religion on their subjects—later summarized by the maxim ◊*cuius regio, eius religio* ("those who live in a country shall adopt the religion of its leader"). It initially applied only to Lutherans and Catholics.

augur a member of a college of Roman priests who interpreted the will of the gods from signs or "auspices" such as the flight of birds, the condition of entrails of sacrificed animals, and the direction of thunder and lightning. Their advice was sought before battle and on other important occasions. Consuls and other high officials had the right to consult the auspices themselves, and a campaign was said to be conducted "under the auspices" of the general who had consulted the gods.

Augusta capital of Maine, located in SW part of the state, on the Kennebec river, NE of Lewiston and Auburn. Industries include cotton, timber, and textiles; population (1990) 21,325.

Augusta city in E central Georgia, on the Savannah river on the South Carolina border; seat of Richmond county. It is a manufacturing city and terminal for river barges. Industries include textiles and other cotton products and building materials; population (1990) 44,639. Established 1736 as Fort Augusta, an Indian trading post, it was the site of several battles during the American Revolution and served as Georgia's capital 1786–95.

Augustan age the golden age of the Roman emperor ◊Augustus, during which art and literature flourished. The name is also given to later periods which used Classical ideals, such as that of Queen Anne in England.

Augustin Eugène 1791–1861. French dramatist, the originator and exponent of "well-made" plays, which achieved success but were subsequently forgotten. He wrote *Une Nuit de la Garde Nationale* 1815.

Augustine of Hippo, St 354–430. One of the early Christian leaders and writers known as the Fathers of the Church. He was converted to Christianity by Ambrose in Milan and became bishop of Hippo (modern Annaba, Algeria) 396. Among Augustine's many writings are his *Confessions*, a spiritual autobiography, and *De Civitate Dei/The City of God*, vindicating the Christian church and divine providence in 22 books.

Augustine, St First archbishop of Canterbury, England. He was sent from Rome to convert England to Christianity by Pope Gregory I. He landed at Ebbsfleet in Kent 597, and soon after baptized Ethelbert, King of Kent, along with many of his subjects. He was consecrated bishop of the English at Arles in the same year, and appointed archbishop 601, establishing his see at Canterbury. Feast day May 26.

Augustinian member of a religious community that follows the Rule of St ◊Augustine of Hippo. It includes the Canons of St Augustine, Augustinian Friars and Hermits, Premonstratensians, Gilbertines, and Trinitarians.

Augustus 63 BC–AD 14. Title of Octavian (Gaius Julius Caesar Octavianus), first of the Roman emperors. He joined forces with Mark Antony and Lepidus in the Second Triumvirate. Following Mark Antony's liaison with the Egyptian Queen Cleopatra, Augustus defeated her troops at Actium 31 BC. As emperor (from 27 BC) he reformed the government of the empire, the army, and Rome's public services, and was a patron of the arts. The period of his rule is known as the ◊Augustan Age.

He was the son of a senator who married a niece of Julius Caesar, and he became his great-uncle's adopted son and principal heir. Following Caesar's murder, Octavian formed with Mark Antony and Lepidus the Triumvirate that divided the Roman world between them and proceeded to eliminate the opposition. Antony's victory 42 BC over Brutus and Cassius had brought the republic to an end. Antony then became enamored of Cleopatra and spent most of his time at Alexandria, while Octavian consolidated his hold on the

Augustus *Great-nephew of Julius Caesar, the "venerable" Augustus was the first Roman emperor. He was a ruler of great administrative ability and initative, and his reign marks the golden age of Roman literature.*

western part of the Roman dominion. War was declared against Cleopatra, and the naval victory at Actium left Octavian in unchallenged supremacy, since Lepidus had been forced to retire. After his return to Rome 29 BC, Octavian was created *princeps senatus*, and in 27 BC he was given the title of Augustus ("venerable"). He then resigned his extraordinary powers and received from the Senate, in return, the proconsular command, which gave him control of the army, and the tribunician power, whereby he could initiate or veto legislation. In his program of reforms Augustus received the support of three loyal and capable helpers, Agrippa, Maecenas, and his wife, Livia, while Virgil and Horace acted as the poets laureate of the new regime. A firm frontier for the empire was established: to the N, the friendly Batavians held the Rhine delta, and then the line followed the course of the Rhine and Danube; to the E, the Parthians were friendly, and the Euphrates gave the next line; to the S, the African colonies were protected by the desert; to the W were Spain and Gaul. The provinces were governed either by imperial legates responsible to the *princeps* or by proconsuls appointed by the Senate. The army was made a profession, with fixed pay and length of service, and a permanent fleet was established. Finally, Rome itself received an adequate water supply, a fire brigade, a police force, and a large number of public buildings. The years after 12 BC were marked by private and public calamities: the marriage of Augustus' daughter Julia to his stepson Tiberius proved disastrous; a serious revolt occurred in Pannonia AD 6; and in Germany three legions under Varus were annihilated in the Teutoburg Forest AD 9. Augustus died a broken man, but his work remained secure.

auk any member of the family Alcidae, consisting of marine diving birds including razorbills, puffins, murres, and guillemots. Confined to the northern hemisphere, they feed on fish and use their wings to "fly" underwater in pursuit.

The largest was the great auk *Pinguinis impennis*, 2.5 ft/75 cm and flightless, the last recorded individual being killed in 1844.

The smallest is the least auklet, *Aethia pusilla*, 6 in/15 cm long. It is found along Pacific coasts from Siberia to Alaska.

Aulis anchorage on the eastern coast of Greece, opposite ◊Euboea in Greek mythology, the point of departure for the Greek expedition against ◊Troy.

Aung San 1916–1947. Burmese politician. He was a founder and leader of the Anti-Fascist People's Freedom League, which led Burma's fight for independence from Great Britain. During World War II he collaborated first with Japan and then with the UK. In 1947 he became head of Burma's provisional government but was assassinated the same year by political opponents; Burma (now Myanmar) became independent in 1948.

Aurangzeb or Aurungzebe 1618–1707. Mogul emperor of N India from 1658. Third son of Shah Jehan, he made himself master of the court by a palace revolution. His reign was the most brilliant period of the Mogul dynasty, but his despotic tendencies and Muslim fanaticism aroused much opposition. His latter years were spent in war with the princes of Rajputana and Mahrattas

Aurelian (Lucius Domitius Aurelianus) c. 214–AD 275. Roman emperor from 270. A successful soldier, he was chosen emperor by his troops on the death of Claudius II. He defeated the Goths and Vandals, defeated and captured ◊Zenobia of Palmyra, and was planning a campaign against Parthia when he was murdered. The Aurelian Wall, a fortification surrounding Rome, was built by Aurelian 271. It was made of concrete, and substantial ruins exist. The Aurelian Way ran from Rome through Pisa and Genoa to Antipolis (Antibes) in Gaul.

Aurelius Antoninus Marcus Roman emperor; see ◊Marcus Aurelius Antoninus.

Auric Georges 1899–1983. French composer. He was one of the musical group called ◊*Les Six*. Auric composed a comic opera, several ballets, and incidental music to films of Jean Cocteau.

auricula species of primrose *Primula auricula*, a plant whose leaves are said to resemble bear's ears. It is native to the Alps, but often cultivated in gardens.

Auriga constellation of the northern hemisphere, represented as a man driving a chariot. Its brightest star is first-magnitude Capella about 45 light-years from Earth; Epsilon Aurigae is an ◊eclipsing binary star, with a period of 27 years, the longest of its kind (last eclipse 1983).

The charioteer is usually identified as Erichthonius, legendary king of Athens, who invented the four-horse chariot.

Aurignacian in archeology, an Old Stone Age culture that came between the Mousterian and the Solutrian in the Upper Paleolithic. The name is derived from a cave at Aurignac in the Pyrenees of France. The earliest cave paintings are attributed to the Aurignacian peoples of W Europe about 16,000 BC.

Auriol Vincent 1884–1966. French Socialist politician. He was president of the two Constituent Assemblies of 1946 and first president of the Fourth Republic 1947–54.

aurochs (plural aurochs) extinct species of long-horned wild cattle *Bos primigenius* that formerly roamed Europe, SW Asia, and North Africa. It survived in Poland until 1627. Black to reddish or gray, it was up to 6 ft/1.8 m at the shoulder. It is depicted in many cave paintings, and is considered the ancestor of domestic cattle.

aurora colored light in the night sky, called aurora borealis, "northern lights," in the northern hemisphere and aurora australis in the southern hemisphere. An aurora is usually in the form of a luminous arch with its apex toward the magnetic pole followed by arcs, bands, rays, curtains, and coronas, usually green, but often showing shades of blue and red, and sometimes yellow or white. Auroras are caused at a height of 60 mi/100 km by a fast stream of charged particles, originating in the Sun. These enter the upper atmosphere and, by bombarding the gases in the atmosphere, cause them to emit visible light.

The ◊magnetic field of the Earth divides the concentration into its north and south zones. The

***aurora** The aurora borealis showing multiple bands, near Fairbanks, Alaska.*

French philosopher Gassendi coined the term "northern dawn" 1621.

Aurora Roman goddess of the dawn. The Greek equivalent is Eos.

Aurora city in NE Illinois, on the Fox river, W of Chicago. Manufactures include transportation equipment, glass, and chemicals. It was a pioneer in the use of electric street lights; population (1990) 99,581.

Auschwitz (Polish *Oswiecim*) town near Kraków in Poland, the site of a notorious ◊concentration camp used by the Nazis in World War II to exterminate Jews and other political and social minorities, as part of the "final solution." Each of the four gas chambers could hold 6,000 people.

auscultation evaluation of internal organs by listening, usually with the aid of a stethoscope.

Ausgleich the compromise between Austria and Hungary Feb 8, 1867 that established the Austro-Hungarian Dual Monarchy under Hapsburg rule. It endured until the collapse of Austria-Hungary 1918.

Austen Jane 1775–1817. English novelist whose books are set within the confines of middle-class provincial society, and show her skill at drawing characters and situations with delicate irony.

She was born at Steventon, Hampshire, where her father was rector, and began writing early; the burlesque *Love and Friendship* (sic), published 1922, was written 1790. In 1801 the family moved to Bath and after the death of her father in 1805, to Southampton, finally settling in Chawton, Hampshire, with her brother Edward. Between 1795 and 1798 she worked on three novels. The first to be published (like its successors, anonymously) was *Sense and Sensibility* (drafted in letter form 1797–98). *Pride and Prejudice* (written 1796–97) followed but *Northanger Abbey*, a skit on the contemporary Gothic novel (written 1798, sold to a London publisher 1803, and bought back 1816), did not appear until 1818. The fragmentary *Watsons* and *Lady Susan* written about 1803–05 remained unfinished. The success of her published works, however, stimulated Jane Austen to write in rapid succession *Mansfield Park*, *Emma*, *Persuasion*, and the final fragment *Sanditon* written 1817. She died in Winchester, and is buried in the cathedral.

***Austen** One of the most popular of the classic English novelists, Jane Austen, based on a drawing by her sister Cassandra. Her work appeared anonymously in her lifetime, and she received very little recognition or payment for it, but she has since become one of the most popular English novelists.*

Auster Paul 1947– . US novelist. His experimental use of detective-story techniques to explore modern urban identity is exemplified in his *New York Trilogy*: *City of Glass* 1985, *Ghosts* 1986, and *The Locked Room* 1986.

Austerlitz, Battle of battle on Dec 2, 1805 in which the French forces of Emperor Napoleon defeated those of Alexander I of Russia and Francis II of Austria at a small town in Czechoslovakia (formerly in Austria), 12 mi/19 km E of Brno.

Austin capital of Texas, on the Colorado River; population (1990) 465,622. It is a center for electronic and scientific research. It is the home of the University of Texas and the Lyndon B Johnson Library and Museum. The state capitol, 308 ft/94 m high, is the largest of any state. Austin was founded 1838 and developed as a stop on the Chisholm cattle-drive trail in the 1860s.

Austin Herbert, 1st Baron Austin 1866–1941. English industrialist who began manufacturing automobiles 1905 in Northfield, Birmingham, notably the Austin Seven 1921.

Austin Stephen Fuller 1793–1836. American pioneer and political leader. Born in Austinville, Virginia, he grew up in Missouri and followed his father to Texas 1821. Accepting Mexican citizenship, Austin was granted political privileges and encouraged the settlement of Americans in Texas. However, in 1833 he was imprisoned for his support for Texas autonomy. When he was released 1835, the Texas Revolution was already underway, and Austin was dispatched to the US to gain support for the cause. After the war he was appointed secretary of state of the Republic of Texas. The state capital of Austin was named in his honor.

Australasia loosely applied geographical term, usually meaning Australia, New Zealand, and neighboring islands.

Australia country occupying all of the Earth's smallest continent, situated S of Indonesia, between the Pacific and Indian oceans.

government Australia is an independent sovereign nation within the ◊Commonwealth, retaining the British monarch as head of state and represented by a governor general. The constitution came into effect Jan 1, 1901. As in the British system, the executive, comprising the prime minister and cabinet, is drawn from the federal parliament and is answerable to it. The parliament consists of two chambers: an elected senate of 76 (12 for each of the six states, two for the Australian Capital Territory, and two for the Northern Territory); and a house of representatives of 148, elected by universal adult suffrage. Senators serve for six years, and members of the house for three years. Voting is compulsory; the senate is elected by proportional representation, but the house of representatives is elected as single-member constituencies with preferential voting.

Each state has its own constitution, governor (the monarch's representative), executive (drawn from the parliament), and legislative and judicial system. Each territory has its own legislative assembly. The main political parties are the Liberal Party, the National Party (normally in coalition), the Australian Labor Party, and the Australian Democrats. In 1986 the last relics of UK legislative control over Australia were removed.

history Australia's native inhabitants, the Aborigines, arrived in Australia at least 40,000 years ago, according to present evidence. The first recorded sightings of Australia by Europeans were in 1606, when the Dutch ship *Duyfken* sighted the W shore of Cape York and the Spanish ship of Luis Vaez de Torres sailed N of Cape York and through Torres Strait. Later voyagers include Dirk Hartog 1616, who left an inscribed pewter plate (Australia's most famous early European relic, now in Amsterdam) in W Australia, Abel ◊Tasman, and William ◊Dampier. A second wave of immigration began 1770, when Captain James ◊Cook claimed New South Wales as a British colony.

Exploration of the interior began with the crossing of the barrier of the ◊Blue Mountains 1813. Explorers include Hamilton Hume (1797–1873) and William Hovell (1786–1875) who in 1824 reached Port Phillip Bay and were the first Europeans to see the Murray River; Charles ◊Sturt; Thomas Mitchell (1792–1855), surveyor general for New South Wales 1828–55, who opened up the fertile western area of Victoria; Edward ◊Eyre, Ludwig ◊Leichhardt, Robert ◊Burke and William Wills (1834–61), and John ◊Stuart. In the 1870s the last gaps were filled in by the crossings of W Australia by John ◊Forrest, Ernest Giles (1835–1897) 1875–76, and Peter Warburton (1813–1889) 1873.

The gold rushes, 1851–61 and sporadically until the early 1890s, contributed to the exploration as well as to the economic and constitutional growth of Australia, as did the pioneer work of the ◊overlanders. The creation of other separate colonies followed the first settlement in New South Wales at Sydney 1788: Tasmania 1825, Western Australia 1829, South Australia 1836, Victoria 1851, and Queensland 1859. The system of transportation of convicts from Britain was never introduced in South Australia and Victoria, and ended in New South Wales 1840, Queensland 1849, Tasmania 1852, and Western Australia 1868. The convicts' contribution to the economic foundation of the country was considerable, and many would not have been convicted under a less harsh and capricious penal system than the one operating in Britain at that time.

Australian Prime Ministers

Date of taking office	*Name*	*Party*
1901	Sir Edmund Barton	Liberal
1903	Alfred Deakin	Liberal
1904	John Watson	Labor
1904	Sir G Reid	Free Trade
1905	Alfred Deakin	Liberal
1908	Andrew Fisher	Labor
1909	Alfred Deakin	Liberal
1910	Andrew Fisher	Labor
1913	Sir J Cook	Free Trade
1914	Andrew Fisher	Labor
1915	W M Hughes	Labor
1917	W M Hughes	National
1923	S M Bruce	National
1929	J H Scullin	Labor
1932	J A Lyons	United Australia Party
1939	Sir Earle Page	Country Party
1939	R G Menzies	United Australia Party
1941	A W Fadden	Country Party
1941	John Curtin	Labor
1945	F M Forde	Labor
1945	J B Chifley	Labor
1949	R G Menzies	Liberal
1966	Harold Holt	Liberal
1967	John McEwen	Liberal
1968	J G Gorton	Liberal
1971	William McMahon	Liberal
1972	Gough Whitlam	Labor
1975	Malcolm Fraser	Liberal
1983	Robert Hawke	Labor

In the 1890s there was a halt in the rapid expansion that Australia had enjoyed, and the resulting depression produced the Labor Party and an increase in labor union activity, which has proved such a feature of Australian politics ever since.

Australia
Commonwealth of

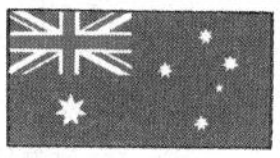

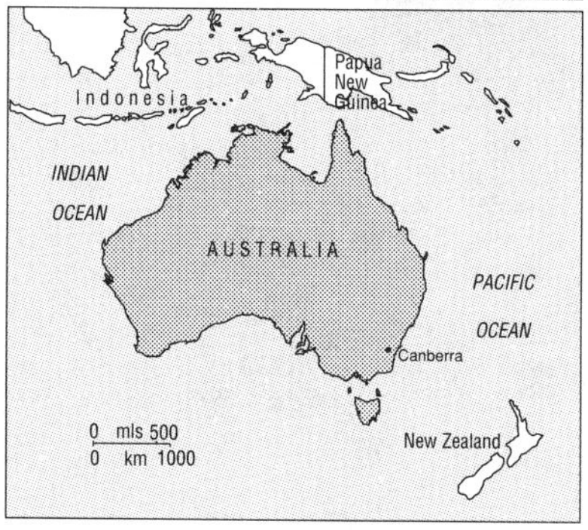
Indonesia
Papua
New
Guinea
INDIAN
OCEAN
AUSTRALIA
PACIFIC
OCEAN
Canberra
0 mls 500
0 km 1000
New Zealand

area 2,966,136 sq mi/7,682,300 sq km
capital Canberra
cities Adelaide, Alice Springs, Brisbane, Darwin, Melbourne, Perth, Sydney, Hobart, Geelong, Newcastle, Townsville, Wollongong
physical the world's smallest, flattest, and driest continent (40% lies in the tropics, one-third is desert, and one-third is marginal grazing); Great Sandy Desert; Great Victoria Desert; Simpson Desert; the Great Barrier Reef (largest coral reef in the world, stretching 1,250 mi/2000 km off E coast of Queensland); Great Dividing Range and Australian Alps in the E; rivers N–S, but Darling River and Murray system E–S; Lake Eyre basin and Nullarbor Plain in the S
territories Norfolk Island, Christmas Island, Cocos (Keeling) Islands, Ashmore and Cartier Islands, Coral Sea Islands, Heard Island and McDonald Islands, Australian Antarctic Territory
features Ayers Rock; Arnhem Land; Gulf of Carpentaria; Great Australian Bight; unique animal species include the kangaroo, koala, platypus, wombat, Tasmanian devil, and spiny anteater; of 800 species of bird, the budgerigar, cassowary, emu, kookaburra, lyre bird, and black swan are also unique as a result of Australia's long isolation from other continents
head of state Elizabeth II from 1952 represented by governor-general
head of government Bob Hawke from 1983
political system federal constitutional monarchy
political parties Australian Labor Party (ALP), moderate left-of-center; Liberal Party of Australia, moderate, liberal, free-enterprise; National Party of Australia, centrist nonmetropolitan
exports world's largest exporter of sheep, wool, diamonds, alumina, coal, lead and refined zinc ores, and mineral sands; other exports include cereals, beef, veal, mutton, lamb, sugar, nickel (world's second-largest producer), iron ore; principal trade partners are Japan, the US, and EC member states
currency Australian dollar
population (1990 est) 16,650,000; growth rate 1.5% p.a.
life expectancy men 75, women 80
language English, Aboriginal
religion Anglican 26%, other Protestant 17%, Roman Catholic 26%
literacy 98.5.% (1988)
GDP $220.96 bn (1988); $14,458 per head
chronology
1901 Creation of Commonwealth of Australia.
1911 Site acquired for capital at Canberra.
1927 Seat of government moved to Canberra.
1942 Statute of Westminster Adoption Act gave Australia autonomy from UK in internal and external affairs.
1944 Liberal Party founded by Robert Menzies.
1951 Australia joined New Zealand and the US as a signatory to the ANZUS Pacific security treaty.
1966 Menzies resigned after being Liberal prime minister for 17 years, and was succeeded by Harold Holt.
1967 A referendum was passed giving Aborigines full citizenship rights.
1968 John Gorton became prime minister after Holt's death.
1971 Gorton succeeded by William McMahon, heading a Liberal–National Party coalition.
1972 Gough Whitlam became prime minister, leading a labor government.
1975 Senate blocked the government's financial legislation; Whitlam declined to resign but was dismissed by the governor-general, who invited Malcolm Fraser to form a Liberal–National Party caretaker government. The action of the governor-general, John Kerr, was widely criticized.
1977 Kerr resigned.
1978 Northern Territory attained self-government.
1983 Australian Labor Party, returned to power under Bob Hawke, convened meeting of employers and unions to seek consensus on economic policy to deal with growing unemployment.
1986 Australia Act passed by UK government, eliminating last vestiges of British legal authority in Australia.
1988 Labor foreign minister Bill Hayden appointed governor general designate. Free trade agreement with New Zealand signed.
1989 Andrew Peacock returned as Liberal Party leader. National Party leader, Ian Sinclair, replaced by Charles Blunt.
1990 Hawke won record fourth election victory, defeating Liberal Party by small majority.
1991 Hawke lost challenge for Labor Party leadership from Paul Keating.

State powers waned following the creation of the Commonwealth 1901. Australia played an important role in both World Wars, and after World War II it embarked on a fresh period of expansion, with new mineral finds playing a large part in economic growth.

Since 1945 Australia has strengthened its ties with India and other SE Asian countries; since Britain's entry into the EC 1973, and under the Labor government, which came to power 1972, there was a growth of nationalism. After heading a Liberal-National Party government for 17 years, Robert Menzies resigned 1966 and was succeeded by Harold Holt, who died in a swimming accident 1967. In 1968 John Gorton became prime minister but lost a vote of confidence in the House and was succeeded by a Liberal-National Party coalition under William McMahon 1971. At the end of 1972, the Australian Labor Party took office, led by Gough Whitlam.

The 1974 general election gave the Labor Party a fresh mandate to govern despite having a reduced majority in the house of representatives. In 1975 the senate blocked the government's financial legislation and, with Whitlam unwilling to resign,, the governor general took the unprecedented step of dismissing him and his cabinet and inviting Malcolm ◊Fraser to form a Liberal-National Party coalition caretaker administration. The wisdom of this action was widely questioned, and eventually, in 1977, governor general John Kerr resigned. In the 1977 general election the coalition was returned with a reduced majority that was further reduced 1980.

In the 1983 general election the coalition was eventually defeated and the Australian Labor Party under Bob ◊Hawke again took office. Hawke called together employers and unions to agree to a wage and price policy and to deal with unemployment. In 1984 he called a general election 15 months early and was returned with a reduced majority. Hawke has placed even greater emphasis than his predecessors on links with SE Asia and has imposed trading sanctions against South Africa as a means of influencing the dismantling of apartheid. In the 1987 general election, Labor marginally increased its majority in the House but did not have an overall majority in the Senate, where the balance was held by the Australian Democrats. The 1990 election was won by Labor, led by Bob Hawke, with a reduced majority in the house of representatives. In Dec 1991, Hawke lost his party leadership to Paul Keating, who assumed the prime ministership.

Australia Day public holiday in Australia, the anniversary of Captain Phillip's arrival on Jan 26, 1788 to found Port Jackson (now Sydney), the first colony.

Australian Aborigine any of the 500 groups of indigenous inhabitants of the continent of Australia, who migrated to this region from S Asia about 40,000 years ago. They are dark-skinned Caucasoids, with fair hair in childhood and heavy dark beards and body hair in adult males. They were hunters and gatherers, living throughout the continent in small kin-based groups before European settlement. Several hundred different languages developed, the most important being Aranda (Arunta), spoken in central Australia, and Murngin, spoken in Arnhem Land. In recent years a movement for the recognition of Aborigine rights has begun, with campaigns against racial discrimination in housing, education, wages, and medical facilities.

Aborigines make up 1% of Australia's population of 16 million. They live in reserves as well as among the general population. They have an infant mortality 4 times the national average and an adult life expectancy 20 years below the average 76 years of other Australians.

Australian Antarctic Territory the islands and territories S of 60° S, between 160° E and 45° E longitude, excluding Adélie Land; area 2,332,984 sq mi/6,044,000 sq km of land and 29,259 sq mi/75,800 sq km of ice shelf. The population on the Antarctic continent is limited to research personnel.

There are scientific bases at Mawson (1954) in MacRobertson Land, named after the explorer; at Davis (1957) on the coast of Princess Elizabeth Land, named in honor of Mawson's second-in-command; at Casey (1969) in Wilkes Land, named after Lord Casey; and at Macquarie Island (1948). It came into being 1933, when established by a British Order in Council.

Australian art art in Australia dates back to early Aboriginal works some 15,000 years ago. These are closely linked with religion and mythology and include rock and bark paintings. True Aboriginal art is now rare. European-style art developed in the 17th century, with landscape painting predominating.

precolonial art Pictures and decorated objects were produced in nearly all settled areas. Subjects included humans, animals, and geometric ornament. The "X-ray style," showing the inner organs in an animal portrait, is unique to Australian Aboriginal art.

17th–18th centuries The first European paintings were topographical scenes of and around Sydney.

late 19th–early 20th century The landscape painters of the Heidelberg School, notably Tom Roberts and later Arthur Streeton (1867–1943), became known outside Australia.

20th century The figurative painters William Dobell, Russell Drysdale, Sidney Nolan, and Albert Namatjira are among Australia's modern artists.

Australian Capital Territory territory ceded to Aus-

Australia

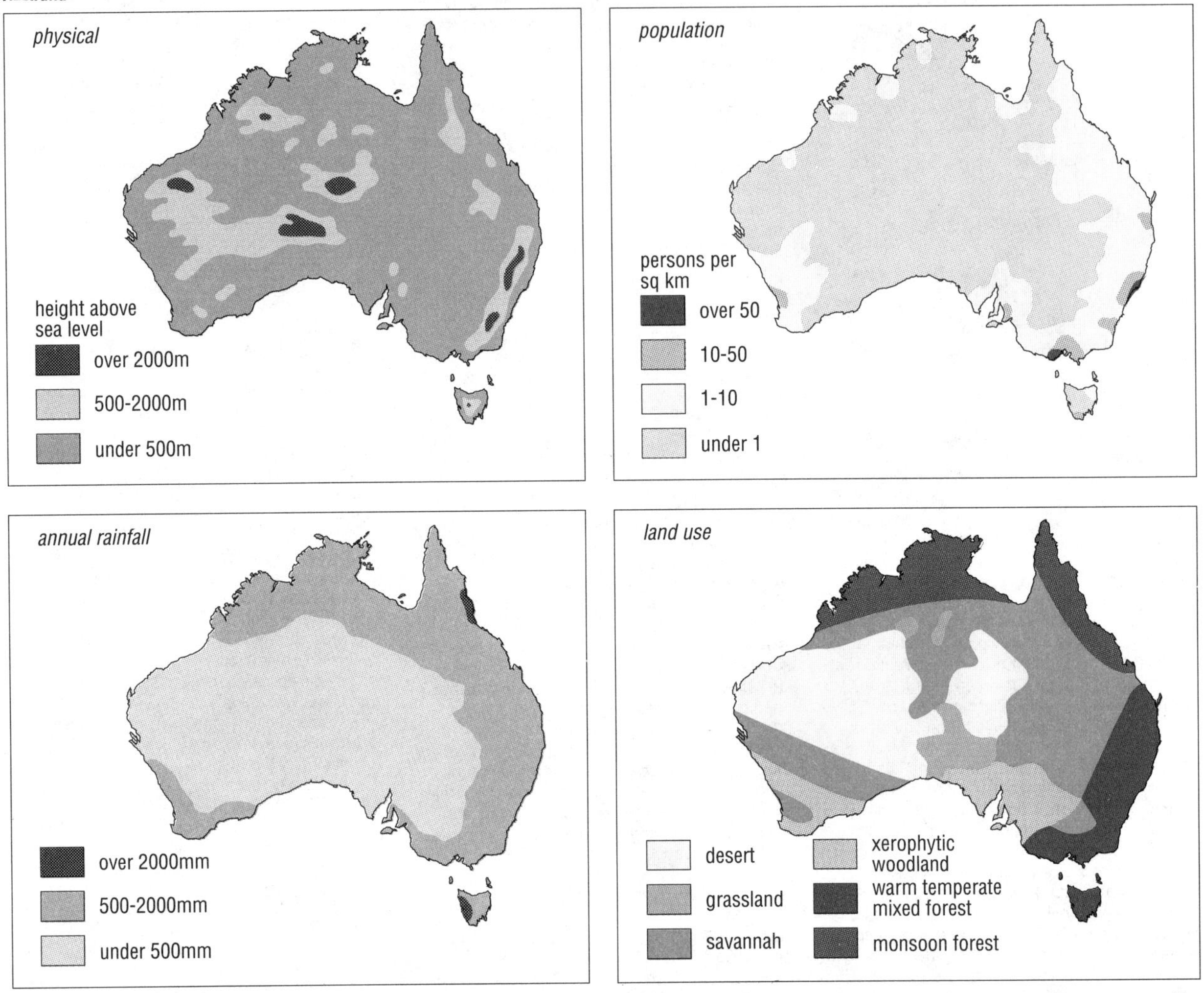
physical
height above
sea level
over 2000m
500-2000m
under 500m
population
persons per
sq km
over 50
10-50
1-10
under 1
annual rainfall
over 2000mm
500-2000mm
under 500mm
land use
desert
grassland
savannah
xerophytic
woodland
warm temperate
mixed forest
monsoon forest

tralia by New South Wales 1911 to provide the site of ◊Canberra, with its port at Jervis Bay, ceded 1915; area 926 sq mi/2,400 sq km; population (1987) 261,000.

Australian literature Australian literature begins with the letters, journals, and memoirs of early settlers and explorers. The first poet of note was Charles Harpur (1813–68); idioms and rhythms typical of the country were developed by, among others, Henry Kendall (1841–82) and Andrew Barton (Banjo) Paterson (1864–1941). More recent poets include Christopher Brennan and Judith Wright, Kenneth Sleesor (1901–71), R D (Robert David) Fitzgerald (1902–), A D (Alec Derwent) Hope (1907–), and James McAuley (1917–76). Among early Australian novelists are Marcus Clarke, Rolfe Boldrewood, and Henry Handel Richardson (1870–1946). Striking a harsh vein in contemporary themes are the dramatist Ray Lawler and novelist Patrick ◊White; the latter received the Nobel Prize for Literature in 1973. Thomas Keneally is a recent Booker prize winner.

Austral Islands alternate name for ◊Tubuai Islands, part of ◊French Polynesia.

Austria landlocked country in central Europe, bounded E by Hungary, SE by Yugoslavia, SW by Italy, W by Switzerland, NW by Germany, and NE by Czechoslovakia.

government Austria is a federal republic consisting of nine provinces (*Länder*), each with its own provincial assembly (*Landtag*), provincial governor, and councillors. The 1920 constitution was amended 1929, suspended during ◊Hitler's regime, and reinstated 1945. The two-chamber federal assembly consists of a national council (*Nationalrat*) and a federal council (*Bundesrat*). The *Nationalrat* has 183 members, elected by universal suffrage through proportional representation, for a four-year term.

The *Bundesrat* has 63 members elected by the provincial assemblies for varying terms. Each province provides a chair for the *Bundesrat* for a six-month term. The federal president, elected by popular vote for a six-year term, is formal head of state and chooses the federal chancellor on the basis of support in the *Nationalrat*. The federal chancellor is head of government and chooses the cabinet. Most significant of several political parties are the Socialist Party of Austria (SPO), the Austrian People's Party (OVP), and the Freedom Party of Austria (FPO).

history Austria was inhabited in prehistoric times by Celtic tribes; the country south of the Danube was conquered by the Romans 14 BC and became part of the Roman Empire. Following the fall of the empire in the 5th century AD, the region was occupied by Vandals, Goths, Huns, Lombards, and Avars. Having conquered the Avars 791, ◊Charlemagne established the East Mark, nucleus of the Austrian empire. In 973 Otto II granted the Mark to the House of Babenburg, which ruled until 1246. Rudolf of Hapsburg, who became king of the Romans and Holy Roman Emperor 1273, seized Austria and invested his son as duke 1282. Until the empire ceased to exist 1806, most of the dukes (from 1453, archdukes) of Austria were elected Holy Roman Emperor.

Austria, which in 1526 acquired control of ◊Bohemia, was throughout the 16th century a bulwark of resistance against the Turks, who besieged Vienna in 1529 without success. The ◊Thirty Years' War (1618–48) did not touch Austria, but it weakened its rulers. A second Turkish siege of Vienna 1683 failed, and by 1697 Hungary was liberated from the ◊Ottoman empire and incorporated in the Austrian dominion. As a result of their struggle with Louis XIV, the Hapsburgs secured the Spanish Netherlands and Milan 1713. When Charles VI, last male Hapsburg in the direct line, died 1740, his daughter Maria Theresa became archduchess of Austria and queen of Hungary, but the elector of Bavaria was elected emperor as Charles VII. Frederick II of Prussia seized Silesia, and the War of the ◊Austrian Succession (1740–48) followed. Charles VII died 1745, and Maria Theresa secured the election of her husband as Francis I, but she did not recover Silesia from Frederick.

The archduke Francis who succeeded 1792 was also elected emperor as Francis II; sometimes opposing, sometimes allied with Napoleon, in 1804 he proclaimed himself emperor of Austria as Francis I, and in 1806 the name Holy Roman Empire fell out of use. Under the Treaty of Vienna 1815, Francis failed to recover the Austrian Netherlands (annexed by France 1797) but received Lombardy and Venetia.

During the ◊revolutions of 1848 the grievances of mixed nationalities within the Austrian empire flared into a rebellion; revolutionaries in Vienna called for the resignation of ◊Metternich, who fled to the UK. By 1851 Austria had crushed all the revolts. As a result of the ◊Seven Weeks' War 1866 with Prussia, Austria lost Venetia to Italy. In the following year Emperor ◊Franz Joseph

Australia: history

30,000–10,000 BC	Aboriginal immigration from S India, Sri Lanka, and SE Asia.
AD 1606	First European sightings of Australia include Dutch ship *Duyfken* off Cape York.
1770	Captain Cook claimed New South Wales for Britain.
1788	Sydney founded.
19th century	The great age of exploration: coastal surveys (Bass, Flinders), interior (Sturt, Eyre, Leichhardt, Burke and Wills, McDouall Stuart, Forrest). Also the era of the bushrangers, overlanders, and squatters, and individuals such as William Buckley and Ned Kelly.
1804	Castle Hill Rising by Irish convicts in New South Wales.
1813	Barrier of the Blue mountains crossed.
1825	Tasmania seceded from New South Wales.
1829	Western Australia formed.
1836	South Australia formed.
1840–68	Convict transportation ended.
1851–61	Gold rushes (Ballarat, Bendigo).
1851	Victoria seceded from New South Wales.
1855	Victoria achieved government.
1856	New South Wales, South Australia, Tasmania achieved government.
1859	Queensland formed from New South Wales and achieved government.
1860	(National) Country Party founded.
1860s	Australian football developed.
1890	Western Australia achieved government.
1891	Depression gave rise to the Australian Labor Party.
1899–1900	South African War—forces offered by the individual colonies.
1901	Creation of the Commonwealth of Australia.
1911	Site for capital at Canberra acquired.
1914–18	World War I—Anzac troops in Europe including Gallipoli.
1939–45	World War II—Anzac troops in Greece, Crete, and North Africa (El Alamein) and the Pacific (Battle of the Coral Sea).
1941	Curtin's appeal to USA for help in World War II marks the end of the special relationship with Britain.
1944	Liberal Party founded by Menzies.
1948–75	Two million new immigrants, the majority from continental Europe.
1950–53	Korean war—Australian troops formed part of the United Nations forces.
1964–72	Vietnam war—Commonwealth troops in alliance with US forces.
1966–74	Mineral boom typified by the Poseidon nickel mine.
1967	Australia becomes a member of ASEAN.
1973	Britain entered the Common Market, and in the 1970s Japan became Australia's chief trading partner.
1974	Whitlam abolished "white Australia" policy.
1975	Constitutional crisis; Prime Minister Whitlam dismissed by the governor general.
1975	United Nations trust territory of Papua New Guinea became independent.
1978	Northern Territory achieved self-government.
1979	Opening of uranium mines in Northern Territory.
1983	Hawke convened first national economic summit.
1988	Nation celebrated Bicentennial

Australia, Commonwealth of

State	*Capital*	*Area sq km*
New South Wales	Sydney	801,600
Queensland	Brisbane	1,727,200
South Australia	Adelaide	984,000
Tasmania	Hobart	67,800
Victoria	Melbourne	227,600
Western Australia	Perth	2,525,500
Territories		
Northern Territory	Darwin	1,346,200
Capital Territory	Canberra	2,400
		7,682,300
Dependencies		
Ashmore and Cartier Islands		5
Australian Antarctic Territory		6,044,000
Christmas Island		140
Cocos (Keeling) Islands		14
Coral Sea Islands		1,000,000
Heard Island and McDonald Islands		410
Norfolk Island		40

established the dual monarchy of Austria–Hungary. The treaty of Berlin 1878 gave Austria the administration of Bosnia and Herzegovina in the Balkans, though they remained nominally Turkish until Austria annexed them 1908.

In 1914 World War I was precipitated by an Austrian attack on Serbia, following the assassination of Archduke Franz Ferdinand (Franz Joseph's nephew) and his wife by Serbian nationalists. Austria–Hungary was defeated 1918, the last Hapsburg emperor overthrown, and Austria became a republic, comprising only Vienna and its immediately surrounding provinces. The Treaty of St Germain in 1919, signed by Austria and the Allies, established Austria's present boundaries. In 1938 Austria was invaded by Hitler's troops and incorporated into the German Reich (the *Anschluss*).

With the conclusion of World War II, Austria returned to its 1920 constitution, with a provisional government led by Dr Karl Renner. The Allies divided both the country and Vienna into four zones, occupied by the USSR, the US, Britain, and France. The first post-war elections resulted in an SPO–OVP coalition government. The country was occupied until independence was formally recognized 1955.

The first postwar noncoalition government was formed 1966 when the OVP came to power with Josef Klaus as chancellor. In 1970 the SPO formed a minority government under Dr Bruno Kreisky and increased its majority in the 1971 and 1975 general elections. In 1978 the government was nearly defeated over proposals to install the first nuclear power plant. The plan was abandoned, but nuclear energy remained a controversial issue.

In 1983 the SPO lost its majority. Kreisky resigned, refusing to join a coalition. The SPO decline was partly attributed to the emergence of two environmentalist groups, the United Green Party (VGO) and the Austrian Alternative List (ALO). Dr Fred Sinowatz, the new SPO chairman, formed an SPO–FPO coalition government.

In 1985 a controversy arose with the announcement that Dr Kurt Waldheim, former UN secretary general, was to be a presidential candidate. Despite allegations of his having been a Nazi officer in Yugoslavia, Waldheim eventually became president 1986, leading to diplomatic isolation by many countries. Later that year Sinowatz resigned as chancellor for what he described as personal reasons and was succeeded by Franz Vranitzky. The SPO–FPO coalition broke up when an extreme right-winger, Jorg Haider, became FPO leader. In the Nov elections the SPO's *Nationalrat* seats fell from 90 to 80, the OVP's from 81 to 77, while the FPO's increased from 12 to 18. For the first time the VGO was represented, winning eight seats. Vranitzky offered his resignation but was persuaded by the president to try to form a "grand coalition" of the SPO and the OVP. Agreement was reached, and Vranitzky remained as chancellor with the OVP leader, Dr Alois Mock, as vice-chancellor. Sinowatz denounced the coalition as a betrayal of Socialist principles and resigned as chairman of the SPO.

In March 1989 Austria announced that it intended to seek membership of the European Community. In the Oct 1990 general election the Socialists won a clear lead over other parties and Vranitzky began another term as prime minister.

In August 1991 the European Community endorsed Austria's earlier application for membership.

Australian Capital Territory

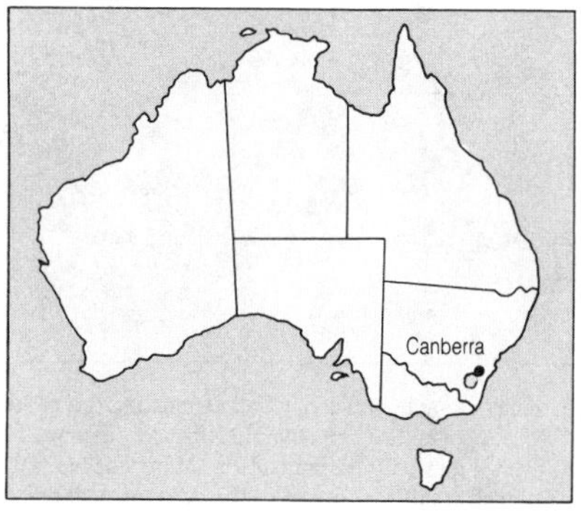
Canberra

Austria: provinces

Province	*Capital*	*Area (sq km)*
Burgenland	Eisenstadt	4,000
Carinthia	Klagenfurt	9,500
Lower Austria	St Pölten	19,200
Salzburg	Salzburg	7,200
Styria	Graz	16,400
Tirol	Innsbruck	12,600
Upper Austria	Linz	12,000
Vienna	Vienna	420
Vorarlberg	Bregenz	2,600

Austrian Succession, War of the 1740–48 war between Austria (supported by England and Holland) and Prussia (supported by France and Spain) ***1740*** The Holy Roman emperor Charles VI died and the succession of his daughter Maria Theresa was disputed by a number of European powers. Frederick the Great of Prussia seized Silesia from Austria.

1743 At Dettingen an army of British, Austrians, and Hanoverians under the command of George II was victorious over the French.

1745 An Austro-English army was defeated at ◊Fontenoy but British naval superiority was confirmed, and so there were gains in the Americas and India. 1748 The war was ended by the Treaty of Aix-la-Chapelle.

Austro-Hungarian empire the Dual Monarchy established with the ◊Ausgleich by the Hapsburg Franz Joseph 1867 between his empire of Austria and his kingdom of Hungary (including territory that

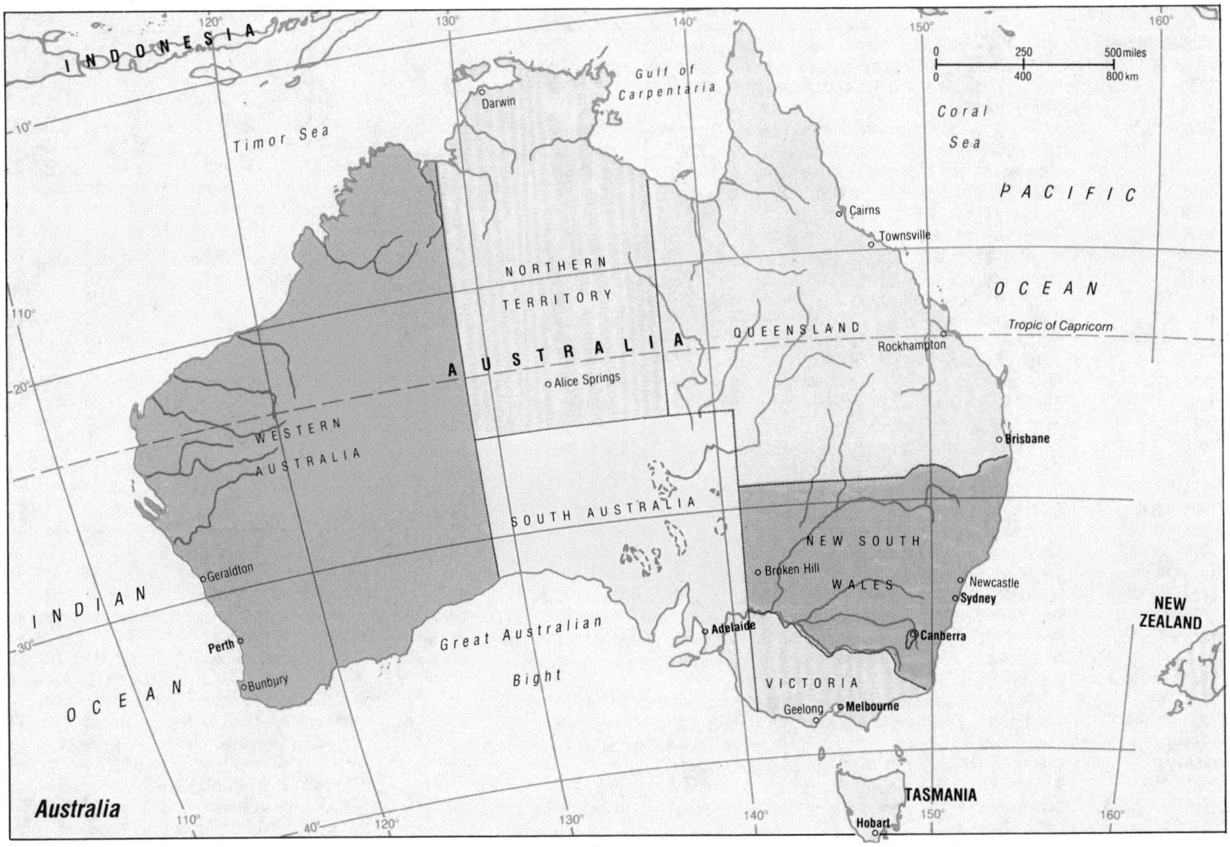
INDONESIA
Timor Sea
Gulf of Carpentaria
Darwin
Coral Sea
PACIFIC
OCEAN
Cairns
Townsville
NORTHERN TERRITORY
QUEENSLAND
Tropic of Capricorn
Rockhampton
AUSTRALIA
Alice Springs
WESTERN AUSTRALIA
Brisbane
SOUTH AUSTRALIA
NEW SOUTH WALES
Broken Hill
Newcastle
Sydney
Geraldton
INDIAN
OCEAN
Perth
Bunbury
Great Australian Bight
Adelaide
Canberra
VICTORIA
Geelong
Melbourne
NEW ZEALAND
TASMANIA
Hobart
0 250 500 miles
0 400 800 km
110° 120° 130° 140° 150° 160°
10° 20° 30° 40°
Australia

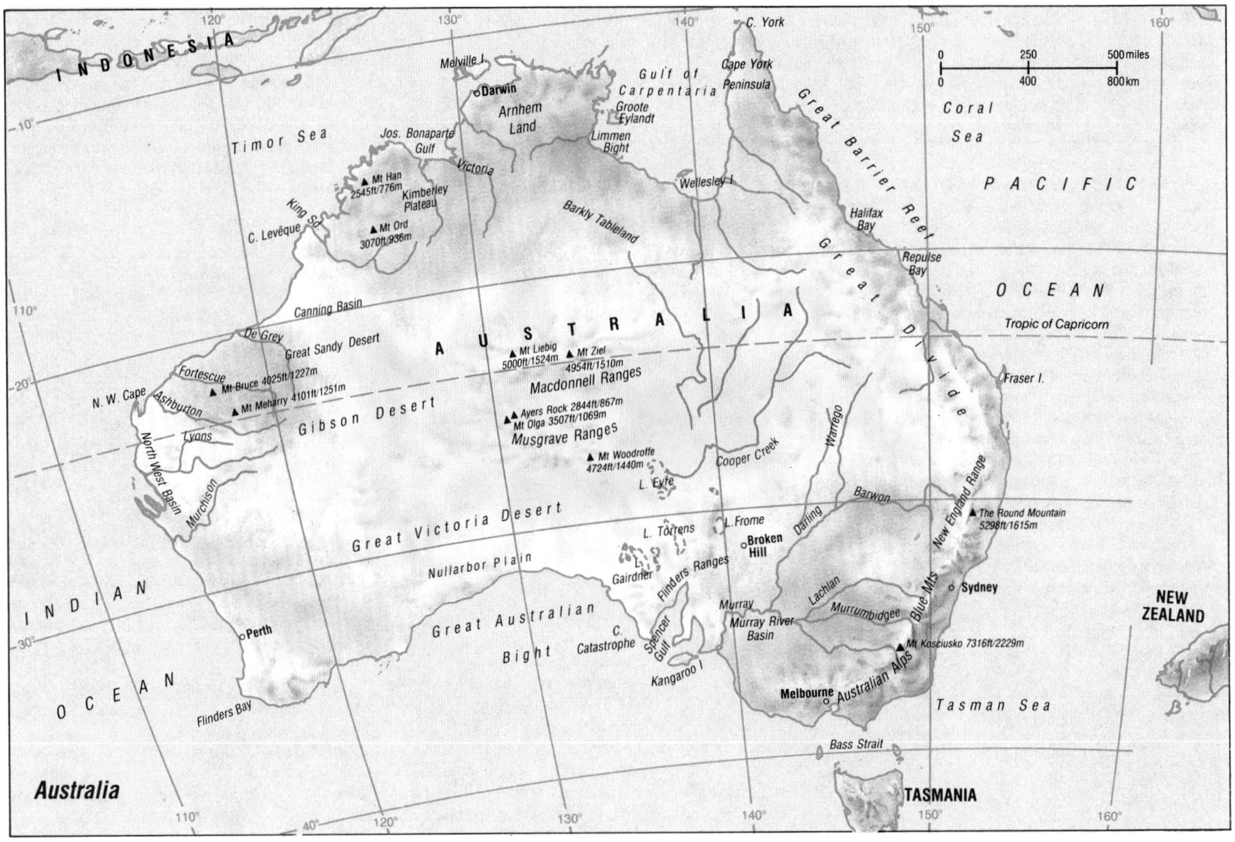
INDONESIA
C. York
Cape York Peninsula
Melville I.
Darwin
Arnhem Land
Gulf of Carpentaria
Groote Eylandt
Limmen Bight
Timor Sea
Jos. Bonaparte Gulf
Victoria
Mt Han 2545ft/776m
Kimberley Plateau
Mt Ord 3070ft/936m
King Sd.
C. Levêque
Barkly Tableland
Wellesley I.
Great Barrier Reef
Halifax Bay
Repulse Bay
Coral Sea
PACIFIC
OCEAN
Tropic of Capricorn
Canning Basin
De Grey
Great Sandy Desert
Fortescue
Mt Bruce 4025ft/1227m
Mt Meharry 4101ft/1251m
N. W. Cape
Ashburton
Lyons
Gibson Desert
AUSTRALIA
Mt Liebig 5000ft/1524m
Mt Ziel 4954ft/1510m
Macdonnell Ranges
Ayers Rock 2844ft/867m
Mt Olga 3507ft/1069m
Musgrave Ranges
Mt Woodroffe 4724ft/1440m
L. Eyre
Cooper Creek
Warrego
Great Dividing Range
Fraser I.
North West Basin
Murchison
Great Victoria Desert
L. Torrens
L. Frome
Broken Hill
Darling
Barwon
New England Range
The Round Mountain 5298ft/1615m
Nullarbor Plain
Gairdner
Flinders Ranges
Blue Mts
Sydney
INDIAN
OCEAN
Perth
Great Australian Bight
C. Catastrophe
Spencer Gulf
Murray
Murray River Basin
Lachlan
Murrumbidgee
Mt Kosciusko 7316ft/2229m
Australian Alps
Kangaroo I.
Melbourne
Tasman Sea
Flinders Bay
NEW ZEALAND
Bass Strait
TASMANIA
0 250 500 miles
0 400 800 km
110° 120° 130° 140° 150° 160°
10° 20° 30° 40°
Australia

became Czechoslovakia as well as parts of Poland, the Ukraine, Romania, Yugoslavia and Italy.) In 1910 it had an area of 100,838 sq mi/ 261,239 sq km with a population of 51 million. It collapsed autumn 1918 with the end of World War I. Only two king-emperors ruled: Franz Joseph 1867–1916 and Charles 1916–18.

autarchy a national economic policy that aims at achieving self-sufficiency and eliminating the need for imports (by imposing tariffs, for example). Such a goal may be difficult, if not impossible, for a small country. Countries that take protectionist

Austria
Republic of
(Republik Österreich)

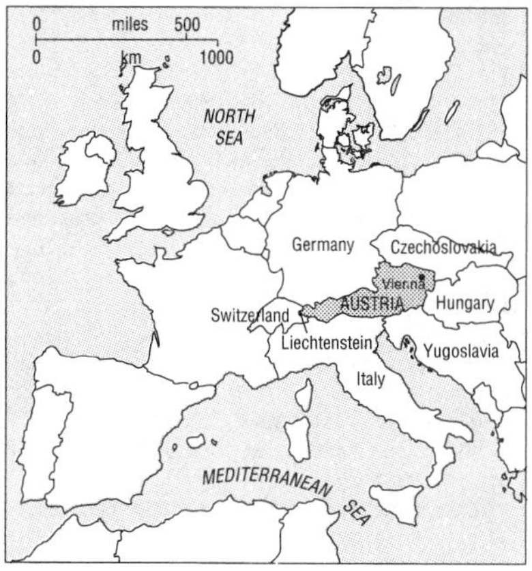
0 miles 500
0 km 1000
NORTH SEA
Germany
Czechoslovakia
Vienna
AUSTRIA
Hungary
Switzerland
Liechtenstein
Yugoslavia
Italy
MEDITERRANEAN SEA

area 32,374 sq mi/83,8500 sq km
capital Vienna
cities Graz, Linz, Salzburg, Innsbruck
physical land-locked mountainous state, with Alps in W and S and low relief in E where most of the population is concentrated
features Austrian Alps (including Grossglockner and Brenner and Semmering passes); Lechtaler and Allgauer Alps N of river Inn; Carnic Alps on Italian border; river Danube
head of state Kurt Waldheim from 1986
head of government Franz Vranitzky from 1986
political system democratic federal republic
political parties Socialist Party of Austria (SPÖ), democratic Socialist; Austrian People's Party (ÖVP), progressive centrist; Freedom Party of Austria (FPÖ), moderate left-of-center; United Green Party of Austria (VGÖ), conservative ecological; Green Alternative Party (ALV), radical ecological
exports lumber, textiles, clothing, iron and steel, paper, machinery and transport equipment, foodstuffs
currency schiling
population (1990 est) 7,595,000; growth rate 0.1% p.a.
life expectancy men 70, women 77
language German
religion Roman Catholic 85%, Protestant 6%
literacy 98% (1983)
GDP $183.3 bn (1987); $11,337 per head
chronology
1867 Emperor Franz Josef established dual monarchy of Austria and Hungary.
1914 Archduke Franz Ferdinand assassinated by Serbian nationalists; Austria–Hungary invaded Serbia, precipitating start of World War I
1918 Hapsburg empire ended, republic proclaimed.
1938 Austria incorporated into German Third Reich by Hitler (the *Anschluss*).
1945 Under Allied occupation, 1920 constitution reinstated and coalition government formed by the SPÖ and the ÖVP.
1955 Allied occupation ended, and the independence of Austria formally recognized.
1966 ÖVP in power with Josef Klaus as chancellor.
1970 SPÖ formed a minority government, with Dr Bruno Kreisky as chancellor.
1983 Kreisky resigned, was replaced by Dr Fred Sinowatz, leading a coalition.
1986 Dr Kurt Waldheim elected president. Sinowatz resigned, succeeded by Franz Vranitzky. No party won an overall majority; Vranitzky formed a coalition of the SPÖ and the ÖVP, with ÖVP leader, Dr Alois Mock, as vice chancellor. Sinowatz denounced the coalition as a betrayal of Socialist principles and resigned his SPÖ chair.
1989 Austria sought European Community membership.
1990 Vranitzky reelected.
1991 Bid for EC membership endorsed by Community.

measures and try to prevent free trade are sometimes described as autarchical.

authoritarianism rule of a country by a dominant elite who repress opponents and the press to maintain their own wealth and power. They are frequently indifferent to activities not affecting their security, and rival power centers, such as labor unions and political parties, are often allowed to exist, although under tight control. An extreme form is ◊totalitarianism.

autism, infantile rare syndrome, generally present from birth, characterized by a withdrawn state and a failure to develop normally in language or social behavior, although the autistic child may show signs of high intelligence in other areas, such as music. Many have impaired intellect, however, and the causes may range from brain damage to heredity.

autobiography a person's own biography, or written account of his or her life, distinguished from the journal or diary by being a connected narrative, and from memoirs by dealing less with contemporary events and personalities. *The Boke of Margery Kempe* c. 1432–36 is the oldest extant autobiography in English.

A form of autobiography is the confession, which is concerned with the inner spiritual life, for example, the *Confessions* of St Augustine.

autochrome in photography, a single-plate additive color process devised by the ◊Lumière brothers 1903. It was the first commercially available process, in use 1907–35.

autoclave pressurized vessel that uses superheated steam to sterilize materials and equipment such as surgical instruments. It is similar in principle to a pressure cooker.

auto-da-fé (Portuguese "act of faith") religious ceremony, including a procession, solemn mass, and sermon, which accompanied the sentencing of heretics by the Spanish ◊Inquisition before they were handed over to the secular authorities for punishment, usually burning.

autogiro or ***autogyro*** heavier-than-air craft that supports itself in the air with a rotary wing, or rotor. The Spanish aviator Juan de la ◊Cierva designed the first successful autogiro 1923. The autogiro's rotor provides only lift and not propulsion; it has been superseded by the helicopter, in which the rotor provides both. The autogiro is propelled by an orthodox propeller.

The three- or four-bladed rotor on an autogiro spins in a horizontal plane on top of the craft, and is not driven by the engine. The blades have an airfoil cross-section, as a plane's wings do. When the autogiro moves forward, the rotor starts to rotate by itself, a state known as autorotation. When traveling fast enough, the rotor develops enough lift from its airfoil blades to support the craft.

autoimmunity in medicine, condition where the body's immune responses are mobilized not against "foreign" matter, such as invading germs, but against the body itself. Diseases considered to be of autoimmune origin include ◊myasthenia gravis, pernicious ◊anemia, rheumatoid ◊arthritis, and ◊lupus erythematosus.

In autoimmune diseases T-lymphocytes reproduce to excess to home in on a target (properly a foreign disease-causing molecule); however, molecules of the body's own tissue that resemble the target may also be attacked, for example insulin-producing cells, resulting in insulin-dependent diabetes; if certain joint membrane cells are attached, then rheumatoid arthritis may result; and if myelin, the basic protein of the nervous system, then multiple sclerosis. In 1990 in Israel a T-cell vaccine was produced that arrests the excessive reproduction of T-lymphocytes attacking healthy target tissues.

Autolycus in Greek mythology, an accomplished thief and trickster, son of the god ◊Hermes, who gave him the power of invisibility.

autolysis in biology, the destruction of a ◊cell after its death by the action of its own ◊enzymes, which break down its structural molecules.

automatic pilot control device that keeps an airplane flying automatically on a given course at a given height and speed. Devised by US businessman Lawrence Sperry 1912, the automatic pilot contains a set of ◊gyroscopes that provide references for the plane's course. Sensors detect when the plane deviates from this course and send signals to the control surfaces—the ailerons, elevators, and rudder—to take the appropriate action. Autopilot is also used in missiles.

automation the widespread use of self-regulating machines in industry. Automation involves the addition of control devices, using electronic sensing and computing techniques, which often follow the pattern of human nervous and brain functions, to already mechanized physical processes of production and distribution; for example, steel processing, mining, chemical production, and road, rail, and air control.

The term was coined by US business consultant John Diebold. Automation builds on the process of ◊mechanization to improve manufacturing efficiency.

automatism the performance of actions without awareness or conscious intent. It is seen in sleepwalking and in some (relatively rare) psychotic states.

automaton mechanical figure imitating human or animal performance. Automatons are usually designed for esthetic appeal as opposed to purely functional robots. The earliest recorded automaton is an Egyptian wooden pigeon of 400 BC.

automobile or ***car*** a small, driver-guided, passenger-carrying motor vehicle; originally the automated version of the horse-drawn carriage, meant to convey people and their goods over streets and roads. Most are four-wheeled and have water-cooled, piston-type internal-combustion engines fueled by gasoline or diesel. Variations have existed for decades that use ingenious and often nonpolluting power plants, but the automobile industry long ago settled on this general formula for the consumer market. Experimental and sports models are streamlined, energy-efficient, and hand-built.

Although it is recorded that in 1479 Gilles de Dom was paid 25 livres by the treasurer of Antwerp in the Low Countries for supplying a self-propelled vehicle, the ancestor of the automobile is generally agreed to be the cumbersome steam carriage made by Nicolas-Joseph Cugnot (1725–1804) in 1769, still preserved in Paris. In 1808, England's Richard Trevithick built a working steam carriage. Steam was an attractive form of power to the English pioneers, and in the 19th century, practical steam coaches were used for public transport until stifled out of existence by the 4 mph/6.4 kph limit, punitive road tolls, and legislation that required someone to walk in front with a red flag by day and a red lantern by night.

In 1885 ◊Benz built and ran the first gasoline-powered automobile. Panhard 1890 (front radiator, engine under hood, sliding-pinion gearbox, wooden ladder-chassis) and Mercédès 1901 (honeycomb radiator, in-line four-cylinder engine, gate-change gearbox, pressed-steel chassis) set the pattern for the modern car. Emerging with Haynes and Duryea in the early 1890s, US demand was so fervent that 300 makers existed by 1895, but only 109 were left by 1900.

In England in 1896 Frederick Lanchester produced an advanced and reliable vehicle, later much copied. The period 1905–06 inaugurated a world automobile boom continuing to the present day.

Among the legendary automobiles of this century are: De Dion Bouton, with the first practical high-speed engines; Mors, notable first for racing and later as a silent touring car; the incomparable Silver Ghost Rolls-Royce; the enduring Model T ◊Ford; and the many types of Bugatti and Delage, from record breakers to luxury touring cars.

After World War I popular motoring began with the era of inexpensive, light (baby) automobiles made by Citroën, Peugeot, and Renault (France); Austin 7, Morris, Clyno, and Swift (England); Fiat (Italy); Volkswagon (Germany); and the slightly bigger Ford, Chevrolet, and Dodge (US). During the interwar years a great deal of auto racing took place, and the experience gained benefited the everyday motorist in improved efficiency, reliability, and safety. There was a divergence between the lighter, economical European car, with good handling on small winding roads, and the heavier US car, cheap, rugged, and well adapted to long distances on straight roads at high speeds.

After World War II small European automobiles tended to fall into three categories: front engine and rear drive, the classic arrangement; front engine and front-wheel drive; rear engine and rear-wheel drive; in about equal numbers, although US automobiles got longer, lower, more powerful (V8 engines) and "styled" with fins. Big automobiles with soft suspensions and low gasoline mileage became the average family's Dreamcar until the OPEC oil crisis of 1973. Air conditioning was a 1950s new "option." From the 1950s a creative resurgence produced in practical form automatic transmission, rubber suspension, transverse engine mounting, self-leveling ride, disk brakes, and safer wet-weather tires. The drive against pollution from the 1960s and the fuel crisis from the 1970s led to experiments for more ecologically responsible powerplants, with steam cars (cumbersome), diesel engines (slow and heavy, although economical), and, a more promising development, a hybrid car using both electricity and gasoline. Nevertheless, the auto industry produced for sale the stratified-charge gasoline engine, using fuel injection to achieve 20% improvement in gasoline consumption; weight reduction in the body by the use of aluminum, fiberglass, and plastics; and "slippery" body designs with low air resistance, or drag. Microprocessors were also developed to measure temperature, engine speed, pressure, and oxygen/ CO_2 content of exhaust gases, and to readjust engine function accordingly. Japanese and European models led the way for US automakers to follow (see also ◊gasoline engine).

automobile chronology

1769 Nicholas-Joseph Cugnot in France built a steam tractor.

1801 Richard Trevithick in England built a steam coach.

1860 Jean Etienne Lenoir built a gas-fueled internal combustion engine.

1865 The British government passed the "Red Flag" Act, requiring a man to precede a "horseless carriage" with a red flag.

1876 Nikolaus August Otto improved the gas engine, making it a practical power source.

1885 Gottlieb Daimler developed a successful lightweight gasoline engine and fitted it to a bicycle to create the prototype of the present-day motorcycle; Karl Benz fitted his lightweight gasoline engine to a three-wheeled carriage to pioneer the motorcar.

1886 Gottlieb Daimler fitted his engine to a four-wheeled carriage to produce a four-wheeled automobile.

1891 René Panhard and Emile Levassor established the present design of automobiles by putting the engine in front.

1896 Frederick Lanchester introduced epicyclic gearing, which foreshadowed automatic transmission.

1899 C. Jenatzy broke 65 mph/100 kph barrier in an electric car *La Jamais Contente* at Achères, France, reaching 65.60 mph/105.85 kph.

1901 The first Mercedes took to the roads. It was the direct ancestor of the present car; Ransome Olds in the US introduced mass production on an assembly line.

1904 L E Rigolly broke the 100 mph barrier, reaching 103.55 mph/166.61 kph in a Gobron-Brillé at Nice, France.

1906 Rolls-Royce introduced the legendary Silver Ghost, which established the company's reputation for superlatively engineered cars.

1908 Henry Ford perfected and accelerated assembly-line production to manufacture his celebrated Model T, nicknamed the Tin Lizzie because it used lightweight sheet steel for the body.

1911 Cadillac introduced the electric starter and dynamo lighting.

1913 Ford introduced the moving conveyor belt to the assembly line, accelerating production of the Model T.

1920 Duesenberg began fitting four-wheel hydraulic brakes.

1922 The Lancia Lambda featured unitary (all-in-one) construction and independent front suspension.

1927 H O D Segrave in England broke the 200 mph barrier in a Sunbeam, reaching 203.79 mph/327.89 kph.

1928 Cadillac introduced the synchromesh gearbox, greatly facilitating gear changing.

1934 Citroën pioneered front-wheel drive in the 7CV model.

1936 Fiat introduced the baby car, the Topolino, 500 cc.

1938 Germany produced its people's car, the Volkswagen "beetle."

1948 Jaguar launched the XK120 sports car; Michelin introduced the radial-ply tire; Goodrich produced the tubeless tire.

1950 Dunlop announced the disk brake.

1951 Buick and Chrysler introduced power steering.

1952 Rover's gas-turbine car set a land-speed record of 152 mph/244 kph.

1954 Bosch introduced fuel injection for automobiles.

1955 Citroën produced the advanced DS-19 "shark-front" car with hydropneumatic suspension.

1957 Felix Wankel built his first rotary gasoline engine.

1965 US automakers were forced to add safety features after the publication of Ralph Nader's *Unsafe at Any Speed.*

1966 California introduced legislation regarding air pollution by automobiles.

1970 American Gary Gabelich drove a rocket-powered car, *Blue Flame*, to a new record speed of 622.287 mph/1,001.473 kph.

1972 Dunlop introduced safety tires, which seal themselves after a puncture.

1973 OPEC oil embargo caused US automakers to design fuel-efficient, smaller automobiles to compete with the economy automobiles of Japan and Europe.

1974 US safety regulations caused Japanese and European makers to produce models that meet import standards.

1979 American Sam Barrett exceeded the speed of sound in the rocket-engined *Budweiser Rocket*, reaching 739.666 mph/1,190.377 kph, a speed not officially recognized as a record because of timing difficulties.

1980 The first mass-produced car with four-wheel drive, the Audi Quattro, was introduced; Japanese car production overtook that of the US.

1981 BMW introduced the on-board computer, which monitored engine performance and indicated to the driver when a service was required.

1983 British driver Richard Noble set an official speed record in the jet-engined *Thrust 2* of 633.468 mph/1,019.4 kph; Austin Rover introduced the Maestro, the first car with a "talking dashboard" that alerted the driver to problems.

1987 The solar-powered *Sunraycer* traveled 1,864 mi/3,000 km from Darwin to Adelaide, Australia, in six days.

automobile racing competitive racing of motor vehicles. It has forms as diverse as hill-climbing, stock-car racing, rallying, sports-car racing, and Formula One Grand Prix racing. The first organized race was from Paris to Rouen 1894.

Road races such as the *Targa Florio* and *Mille Miglia* were tests of a driver's skill and a machine's durability in the 1920s and 1930s. The 24-hour endurance race at ◊Le Mans is now the foremost race for sports automobiles and prototypes.

In Grand Prix racing (instituted 1906) a world championship for drivers has been in existence since 1950, and for builders since 1958. The first six drivers and automobiles in each race are awarded points from nine to one, and the accumulative total at the end of a season (normally 16 races) decides the winners.

Major events include Le Mans Grand Prix d'Endurance, first held in 1923, and the Indianapolis 500, first held 1911.

autonomic nervous system in mammals, the part of the nervous system that controls the involuntary activities of the smooth muscles (of the digestive tract, blood vessels), the heart, and the glands. The sympathetic system responds to stress, when it speeds the heart rate, increases blood pressure and generally prepares the body for action. The parasympathetic system is more important when the body is at rest, since it slows the heart rate, decreases blood pressure, and stimulates the digestive system.

At all times, both types of autonomic nerves carry signals that bring about adjustments in visceral organs. The actual rate of heart beat is the net outcome of opposing signals. Today, it is known that the word "autonomic" is not correct—the reflexes managed by this system are actually integrated by commands from the brain and spinal cord (the central nervous system).

autonomy in politics, term used to describe political self-government.

autopsy or ***post-mortem*** examination of the internal organs and tissues of a dead body, performed to try to establish the cause of death.

autoradiography technique for following the movement of molecules within an organism, especially a plant, by labelling with a radioactive isotope that can be traced on photographs. It is used to study ◊photosynthesis, where the pathway of radioactive carbon dioxide can be traced as it moves through the various chemical stages.

autosome any ◊chromosome in the cell other than a sex chromosome. Autosomes are of the same number and kind in both males and females of a given species.

autosuggestion conscious or unconscious acceptance of an idea as true, without demanding rational proof, but with potential subsequent effect for good or ill. Pioneered by the French psychotherapist Emile Coué (1857–1926) in healing, it is used in modern psychotherapy to conquer nervous habits, and dependence on tobacco, alcohol, and so on.

autotroph any living organism that synthesizes organic substances from inorganic molecules by using light or chemical energy. Autotrophs are the primary producers in all food chains since the materials they synthesize and store are the energy sources of all other organisms. All green plants and many planktonic organisms are autotrophs, using sunlight to convert carbon dioxide and water into sugars by ◊photosynthesis.

The total ◊biomass of autotrophs is far greater than that of animals, reflecting the dependence of animals on plants, and the ultimate dependence of all life on energy from the sun—green plants convert light energy into a form of chemical energy (food) that animals can exploit. Some bacteria use the chemical energy of sulfur compounds to synthesize organic substances. See also ◊heterotroph.

autumnal equinox see ◊equinox.

autumn crocus any member of the genus *Colchicum*, family Liliaceae. One species, the mauve meadow saffron *C. autumnale*, yields colchicine, which is used in treating gout and in plant breeding (it causes plants to double the numbers of their chromosomes, forming ◊polyploids).

Auvergne ancient province of central France now comprising the *départements* Allier, Cantal, Haute-Loire, and Puy-de-Dôme

area 10,036 sq mi/26,000 sq km

population (1986) 1,334,000

capital Clermont-Ferrand

physical it lies at the Central Plateau and is mountainous, composed chiefly of volcanic rocks in several masses

products cattle, wheat, wine, and cheese

history named after the ancient Gallic Avenni tribe whose leader, Vercingetorix, led a revolt aginst the Romans in 52 BC. In the 14th century the Auvergne was divided into a duchy, dauphiny, and countship. The duchy and dauphiny were united by the dukes of Bourbon before being confiscated by Francis I in 1527. The countship united with France in 1615.

Auxerre capital of Yonne *département* France, 106 mi/170 km SE of Paris, on the river Yonne; population about 40,000. The Gothic cathedral, founded 1215, has exceptional sculptures and stained glass.

auxin a plant ◊hormone that promotes stem and root growth in plants. Auxins influence many aspects of plant growth and development, including cell enlargement, inhibition of development of axillary buds, ◊tropisms, and the initiation of roots. Synthetic auxins are used in rooting powders for cuttings, and in some weedkillers, where high auxin concentrations cause such rapid growth that the plants die. They are also used to prevent premature fruitdrop in orchards. The most common naturally occuring auxin is known as indoleacetic acid, or IAA. It is synthesized in the shoot apex and transported to other parts of the plant.

Ava former capital of Burma (now Myanmar), on the river Irrawaddy, founded by Thadomin Payä 1364. Thirty kings reigned there until 1782, when a new capital, Amarapura, was founded by Bodaw Payä. In 1823 the site of the capital was transferred back to Ava by King Baggidaw.

avalanche (from French *avaler* "to swallow") a fall of a mass of snow and ice down a steep slope. Avalanches occur because of the unstable nature of snow masses in mountain areas.

Changes of temperature, sudden sound, or earth-borne vibrations can cause a snowfield to start moving, particularly on slopes of more than 35°. The snow compacts into ice as it moves, and rocks may be carried along, adding to the damage caused.

Avalokiteśvara in Mahāyāna Buddhism, one of the most important ◊bodhisattvas, seen as embodying compassion. Known as Guanyin in China, Kwannon in Japan, he is one of the attendants of Amida Buddha.

Avalon in Celtic legend, the island of the blessed, or paradise; and in the Arthurian legend the land of heroes, ruled over by Morgan le Fay, to which the dead king Arthur was conveyed after his final battle with Mordred. It has been associated with Glastonbury in SW England.

avant-garde (French "advanced guard") in the arts, those artists or works that are in the forefront of new developments in their media. The term was introduced (as was "reactionary") after the French Revolution, when it was used to describe any socialist political movement.

Avar member of a Central Asian nomadic people who in the 6th century invaded the area of Russia N of the Black Sea previously held by the Huns. They extended their dominion over the Bulgarians and Slavs in the 7th century and were finally defeated by Charlemagne 796.

Avatar in Hindu mythology, the descent of a deity to Earth in a visible form, for example the ten Avatars of ◊Vishnu.

Avebury Europe's largest stone circle (diameter 1,352 ft/412 m), Wiltshire, England. It was probably constructed in the Neolithic period 3,500 years ago, and is linked with nearby Silbury Hill. The village of Avebury was built within the circle, and many of the stones were used for building material.

Avedon Richard 1923– . US photographer. A fashion photographer with *Harper's Bazaar* magazine in New York in the mid-1940s, he later became one of the highest-paid commercial photographers.

Born in New York City, Avedon was already pursuing an interest in photography by the age of 10. After studying photography in the US merchant marine and at the New School for Social Research, he turned professional. His primary subject, aside from fashion, was portraits. Many of his dramatic portraits were assembled in such books as *Observations* 1959 (text by Truman Capote) and *Nothing Personal* 1974 (text by James Baldwin).

Ave Maria (Latin "Hail, Mary") Christian prayer to the Virgin Mary, which takes its name from the archangel Gabriel's salutation to the Virgin Mary when announcing that she would be the mother of the Messiah (Luke 11:28).

avens any of several low-growing plants of the genus *Geum* of the rose family Rosaceae. Species are distributed throughout Eurasia and N Africa. Mountain avens *Dryas octopetala* belongs to a different genus and grows in mountain and arctic areas of Eurasia and North America. A creeping perennial, it has white flowers with yellow stamens.

average number or value that represents the typical member of a group or set of numbers. The simplest averages include the arithmetic and geometric means (see ◊mean); the ◊median and the ◊root-mean-square are more complex.

Avernus circular lake, near Naples, Italy. Because it formerly gave off fumes that killed birds, it was thought by the Romans to be the entrance to the lower world.

Averroës (Arabic *Ibn Rushd*) 1126–1198. Arabian philosopher who argued for the eternity of matter and against the immortality of the individual soul. His philosophical writings, including commentaries on Aristotle and on Plato's *Republic*, became known to the West through Latin translations. He influenced Christian and Jewish writers into the Renaissance, and reconciled Islamic and Greek thought in that philosophic truth comes through reason. St Thomas Aquinas opposed this position.

Avery Milton 1893–1965. US painter, whose early work was inspired by Henri ◊Matisse. He typically chose landscapes, beaches, friends, and relatives as his subjects, which he portrayed in thin, flat, richly colored strokes. His later work, although it remained figurative, shows the influence of Mark ◊Rothko and other experimental US artists.

Born in Altmar, New York, Avery received little formal training.

Avery Tex (Frederick Bean) 1907–1980. US cartoon-film director who used violent, sometimes surreal humor. At Warner Brothers he helped develop the characters Bugs Bunny and Daffy Duck, before moving to MGM in 1942 where he created, among others, Droopy and Screwball Squirrel.

Avianus Roman fable writer, placed between the 1st and 6th centuries AD. He wrote 42 fables dedicated to Theodosius.

aviation See ◊flight for the history of aviation and airplanes.

Avicenna (Arabic *Ibn Sina*) 979–1037. Arabian philosopher and physician. He was the most renowned philosopher of medieval Islam. His *Canon Medicinae* was a standard work for many centuries. His philosophical writings were influenced by al-Farabi, Aristotle, and the Neoplatonists, and in turn influenced the scholastics of the 13th century.

Avignon city in Provence, France, capital of Vaucluse *département*, on the river Rhône NW of Marseilles; population (1982) 174,000. It was an important Gallic and Roman city, and has 14th-century walls, a 12th-century bridge (only half still standing), a 13th-century cathedral, and a palace built 1334–42 during the residence here of the popes. Avignon was papal property 1348–1791.

Ávila town in Spain, 56 mi/90 km NW of Madrid; population (1986) 45,000. It is capital of the province of the same name. It has the remains of a Moorish castle, a Gothic cathedral, and the convent and church of St Teresa, who was born here. The town walls are among the best preserved medieval fortifications of those in Europe.

avocado tree *Persea americana* of the laurel family, native to Central America. Its dark-green, thick-skinned, pear-shaped fruit has buttery-textured flesh and is used in salads.

avocet wading bird, genus *Recurvirostra*, family Recurvirostridae, with characteristic long, narrow, upturned bill used in sifting water as it feeds in the shallows. It is about 18 in/45 cm long, and has long legs, partly webbed feet, and black and white plumage. There are four species. Stilts belong to the same family.

Avogadro Amedeo Conte di Quaregna 1776–1856. Italian physicist. His work on gases still has relevance for today's atomic studies.

Avogadro's hypothesis in chemistry, the law stating that equal volumes of all gases, when at the same temperature and pressure, have the same numbers of molecules. This law was first propounded by Count Amadeo Avogadro (1776–1856).

Avogadro's number or ***Avogadro's constant*** the number of carbon atoms in 12 g of the carbon-12 isotope (6.022137×10^{23}). The atomic weight of any element, expressed in grams, contains this number of atoms. It is named after Amadeo Avogadro.

avoirdupois system of weights based on the pound (0.45 kg), which consists of 16 ounces, each of 16 drams, with each dram equal to 27.34 grains (1.772 g).

Avon any of several rivers in England and Scotland. The Avon in Warwickshire is associated with Shakespeare.

The Upper or Warwickshire Avon, 96 mi/154 km, rises in the Northampton uplands near Naseby and joins the Severn at Tewkesbury. The Lower, or Bristol, Avon, 75 mi/121 km, rises in the Cotswolds and flows into the Bristol Channel at Avonmouth. The East, or Salisbury, Avon, 65 mi/104 km, rises S of the Marlborough Downs and flows into the English Channel at Christchurch.

AWACS acronym for Airborne Warning And Control System.

Awash river that rises to the S of Addis Ababa in Ethiopia and flows NE to Lake Abba on the frontier with Djibouti. Although deep inside present-day Ethiopia, the Awash River is considered by Somalis to mark the eastern limit of Ethiopian sovereignty prior to the colonial division of Somaliland in the 19th century.

Axelrod Julius 1912– . US neuropharmacologist who shared the 1970 Nobel Prize for Medicine with the biophysicists Bernard Katz and Ulf von Euler for his work on neurotransmitters (the chemical messengers of the brain).

Axelrod wanted to know why the messengers, once transmitted, ever stopped operating. Through his studies he found a number of specific ◊enzymes that rapidly degraded the neurotransmitters.

axil the upper angle between a leaf (or bract) and the stem from which it grows. Organs developing in the axil, such as flowers, shoots, and buds, are termed axillary, or lateral.

axiom in mathematics, a statement that is assumed to be true and upon which theorems are proved by using logical deduction. ◊Euclid used a series of axioms that he considered could not be demonstrated in terms of simpler concepts to prove his geometrical theorems.

Axis the alliance of Nazi Germany and Fascist Italy before and during World War II. The Rome–Berlin Axis was formed 1936, when Italy was being threatened with sanctions because of its invasion of Ethiopia (Abyssinia). It became a full military and political alliance May 1939. A 10-year alliance between Germany, Italy, and Japan (Rome–Berlin–Tokyo Axis) was signed Sept 1940 and was subsequently joined by Hungary, Bulgaria, Romania, and the puppet states of Slovakia and Croatia. The Axis collapsed with the fall of Mussolini and the surrender of Italy 1943, followed by Germany and Japan 1945.

axis in mathematics, a line from which measurements may be taken, as in a coordinate axis; or a line about which an object may be symmetrical, as in an axis of symmetry; or a line about which an object or plane figure may revolve.

axolotl aquatic larval form ("tadpole") of any of several species of salamander, belonging to the family Ambystomatidae. Axolotls are remarkable because they can breed without changing to the adult form, although individuals do occasionally develop into land-dwelling adults.

Axolotls may be up to 12 in/30 cm long. Species include the Mexican salamander *Ambystomum mexicanum* which lives in mountain lakes near Mexico City, and the tiger salamander *A. tigrinum*, found in North America, from Canada to Mexico. "Axolotl" is an Aztec word; it means "water monster." See also ◊neoteny.

axon the long threadlike extension of a ◊nerve cell that conducts electrochemical impulses away from the cell body toward other nerve cells, or toward an effector organ such as a muscle. Axons terminate in ◊synapses with other nerve cells, muscles, or glands.

Axum alternative transliteration of ◊Aksum, an ancient kingdom in Ethiopia.

Ayacucho capital of a province of the same name in the Andean mountains of central Peru; population (1988) 94,200. The last great battle in the war of independence against Spain was fought near here in Dec 1824.

ayatollah (Arabic "sign of God") honorific title awarded to Shiite Muslims in Iran by popular consent, as, for example, to Ayatollah Ruhollah ◊Khomeini.

Ayckbourn Alan 1939– . English playwright. His prolific output, characterized by comic dialogue, includes *Absurd Person Singular* 1973, the trilogy *The Norman Conquests* 1974, *A Woman in Mind* 1986, *A Small Family Business* 1987, *Man of the Moment* 1988, and scripts for television.

aye-aye

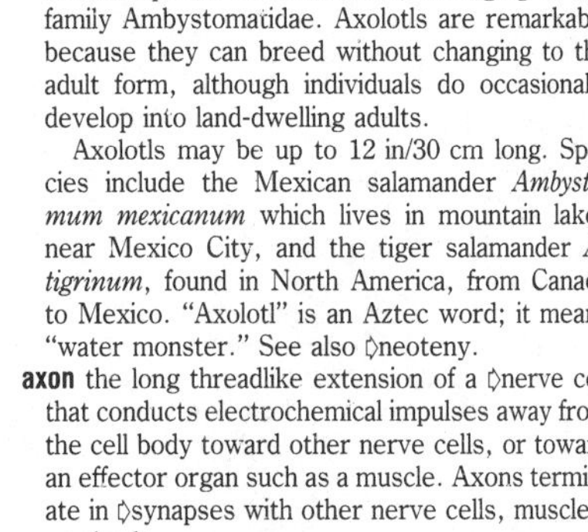

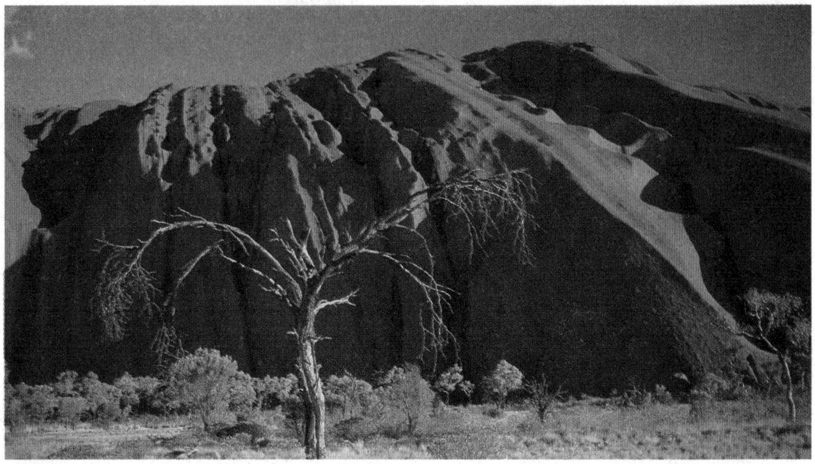

Ayers Rock This monolith in Northern Territory, Australia, is the largest outcrop on Earth. It is known by the Aborigines al Uluru and is a sacred place for them.

aye-aye nocturnal tree-climbing prosimian *Daubentonia madagascariensis* of Madagascar, related to the lemurs. It is just over 3 ft/1 m long, including a tail 20 in/50 cm long.

It has an exceptionally long middle finger with which it probes for insects and their larvae under the bark of trees, and gnawing, rodentlike front teeth, with which it tears off the bark to get at its prey. The aye-aye has become rare through loss of its forest habitat, and is now classified as an endangered species.

Ayer A(lfred) J(ules) 1910–1989. English philosopher. He wrote *Language, Truth and Logic* 1936, an exposition of the theory of "logical positivism," presenting a criterion by which meaningful statements (essentially truths of logic, as well as statements derived from experience) could be distinguished from meaningless metaphysical utterances (for example, claims that there is a God or that the world external to our own minds is illusory).

Ayers Rock vast ovate mass of pinkish rock in Northern Territory, Australia; 1,110 ft/335 m high and 6 mi/9 km around.

It is named after Henry Ayers, a premier of South Australia. For the Aboriginals, whose paintings decorate its caves, it has magical significance.

Ayesha 611–678. Third and favorite wife of the prophet Mohammed, who married her when she was nine. Her father, Abu Bakr, became ◊caliph on Mohammed's death 632, and she bitterly opposed the later succession to the caliphate of Ali, who had once accused her of infidelity.

Aymara member of an ◊American Indian people of Bolivia and Peru, builders of a great culture, who were conquered first by the Incas and then by the Spaniards. Today 1.4 million Aymara farm and herd llamas and alpacas in the highlands; their language survives and their Roman Catholicism incorporates elements of their old beliefs.

Ayr town in Strathclyde, Scotland, at the mouth of the river Ayr; population (1981) 49,500. Auld Brig was built in the 5th century, the New Brig 1788 (rebuilt 1879). Ayr has associations with Robert Burns.

Ayurveda ancient Hindu system of medicine. The main principles are derived from the Vedas of the 1st century AD, and it is still practiced in India, using herbs, purgatives, and liniments, in Ayurvedic hospitals and dispensaries.

AZ abbreviation for ◊Arizona.

azalea any of various deciduous flowering shrubs, genus *Rhododendron*, of the heath family Ericaceae. Azaleas are closely related to the evergreen ◊rhododendrons of the same genus. There are several species of azaleas native to Asia and North America, and from these many cultivated varieties have been derived.

Azaleas, particularly the Japanese varieties, make fine ornamental shrubs. Several species are highly poisonous.

Azaña Manuel 1880–1940. Spanish politician and first prime minister 1931–33 of the second Spanish republic. He was last president of the republic during the Civil War 1936–39, before the establishment of a dictatorship under Franco.

Azerbaijan constituent republic (Azerbaydzhan Soviet Socialist Republic) of the USSR 1936–91
area 33,436 sq mi/86,600 sq km
capital Baku
towns Kirovabad
physical Caspian Sea; the country ranges from semidesert to the Caucasus mountains
products oil, iron, copper, fruit, vines, cotton, silk, carpets
population (1987) 6,811,000; 78% Azerbaijani, 8% Russian, 8% Armenian
language Turkic
religion traditionally Shi'ite Muslim
recent history a member of the Transcaucasian Federation 1917, it became an independent republic 1918, but was occupied by the Red Army 1920. From early 1990, riots led to many deaths. In late 1991 independence was achieved as the USSR collapsed.

Azerbaijan, Iranian two provinces of NW Iran, Eastern Azerbaijan (capital Tabriz), population (1986) 4,114,000, and Western Azerbaijan (capital Orúmiyeh), population 1,972,000. Azeris in Iran as in the USSR, are Muslim (Shi'ite) ethnic Turks, descendants of followers of the Khans from the Mongol Empire.

There are about 5 million in Azerbaijan, and 3 million distributed in the rest of the country, where they form a strong middle class. In 1946, with Soviet backing, they briefly established their

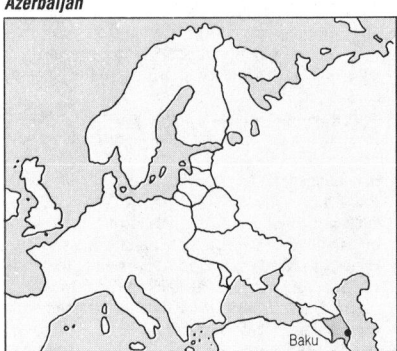

Azerbaijan

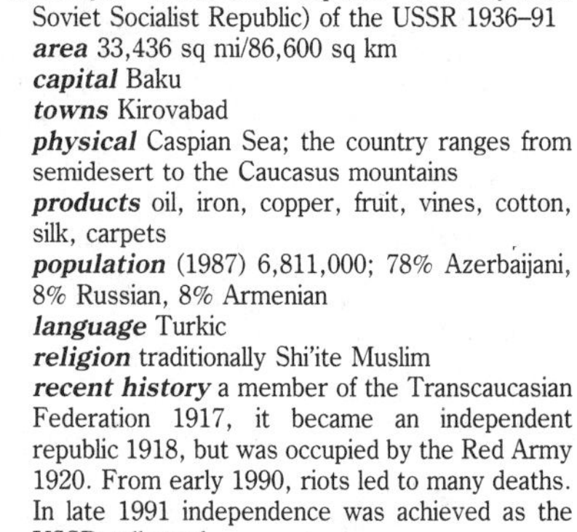
Baku

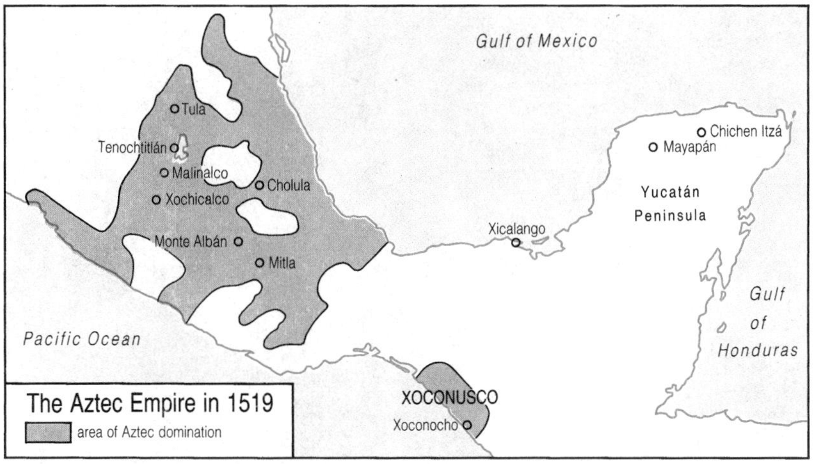
Gulf of Mexico
Tula
Tenochtitlán
Malinalco
Cholula
Xochicalco
Monte Albán
Mitla
Xicalango
Chichen Itzá
Mayapán
Yucatán Peninsula
Gulf of Honduras
Pacific Ocean
XOCONUSCO
Xoconocho
area of Aztec domination

The Aztec Empire in 1519

own republic. Denied autonomy under the Shah, they rose 1979–80 against the supremacy of Ayatollah Khomeini and were forcibly repressed, although a degree of autonomy was promised. Since 1988 there has been a growth in Azer nationalism, spearheaded by the local Azerbaijani Popular Front and fanned by the dispute with neighboring Christian ◊Armenia over ◊Nagorno-Karabakh and ◊Nakhichevan. This dispute, which reawakened centuries-old enmities, flared into a war from Dec 1989 which prompted Azer calls for secession from the USSR and led in Jan 1990 to the despatch of Soviet troops to Baku in an attempt to restore order.

Azhar, El Muslim university and mosque in Cairo, Egypt. Founded 970 by Jawhar, commander in chief of the army of the Fatimid caliph, it is claimed to be the oldest university in the world. It became the center of Islamic learning, with several subsidiary foundations, and is now primarily a school of Koranic teaching.

Azilian an archeological period following the close of the Old Stone (Paleolithic) Age and regarded as one of the cultures of the Mesolithic Age. It was first recognized by Piette at Mas d'Azil, a village in Ariège, France.

azimuth in astronomy, the angular distance eastward along the horizon, measured from due north, between the astronomical ◊meridian (the vertical circle passing through the center of the sky and the north and south points on the horizon) and the vertical circle containing the celestial body whose position is to be measured.

Azores group of nine islands in the N Atlantic, belonging to Portugal; area 867 sq mi/ 2,247 sq km; population (1987) 254,000. They are outlying peaks of the Mid-Atlantic Ridge and are volcanic in origin. The capital is Ponta Delgada on the main island, San Miguel.

Portuguese from 1430, Azores were granted partial autonomy 1976, but remain a Portuguese overseas territory. It has a separatist movement. The Azores command the Western shipping lanes.

Azorín Adopted name of José Martínez Ruiz. 1873–1967. Spanish writer. His works include volumes of critical essays and short stories, plays and novels, such as the autobiographical *La voluntad/The Choice* 1902 and *Antonio Azorín* 1903. He adopted the name of the hero of the latter as his pen name.

Azov (Russian *Azovskoye More*) inland sea of the USSR forming a gulf in the NE of the Black Sea; area 14,500 sq mi/37,555 sq km. Principal ports include Rostov-on-Don, Kerch, and Taganrog. Azov is a good source of freshwater fish.

AZT or ***retrovir***, or ***zidovudine*** trademark for azidothymidine, an antiviral drug used in the treatment of ◊AIDS.

Developed in the mid-1980s and approved for use by 1987, it is not a cure for AIDS but is effective in suppressing the causative virus (HIV) for as long as it is being administered. Taken every four hours, night and day, it reduces the risk of opportunistic infection and relieves many neurological complications. However, frequent blood monitoring is required to control anemia, a potentially life-threatening side-effect of AZT. Blood transfusions are often necessary, and the drug must be withdrawn if liver damage occurs or bone-marrow function is severely affected.

Aztec member of an ancient Mexican civilization that migrated south into the valley of Mexico in the 12th century, and in 1325 began reclaiming lake marshland to build their capital, Tenochtitlán, on the site of present-day Mexico City. Under Montezuma I (reigned from 1440), the Aztecs created a tribute empire in central Mexico. After the conquistador Cortès landed 1519, Montezuma II (reigned from 1502) was killed and Tenochitlán subsequently destroyed. Nahuatal is the Aztec language and it belongs to the Uto-Aztecan family of languages.

The Aztecs are known for their architecture, jewelry (gold, jade, and turquoise), sculpture, and textiles. Their form of writing combined hieroglyphs and pictographs, and they used a complex calendar that combined a sacred period of 260 days with the solar year of 365 days. Propitiatory rites were performed at the intersection of the two, called the "dangerous" period, every 52 years, when temples were rebuilt (useful as a date mark for archeologists). Their main god in a pantheon of gods was Huitzilopochtli (Hummingbird Wizard), but they also worshiped the feathered serpent ◊Quetzalcoatl, inherited from earlier Mexican civilizations. Religious ritual included human sacrifice on a large scale, the priests tearing the heart from the living victim or flaying people alive. War captives were obtained for this purpose, but their own people were also used. The Aztec state was a theocracy with farmers, artisans, and merchants taxed to support the priestly aristocracy. Tribute was collected from a federation of conquered nearby states.

B

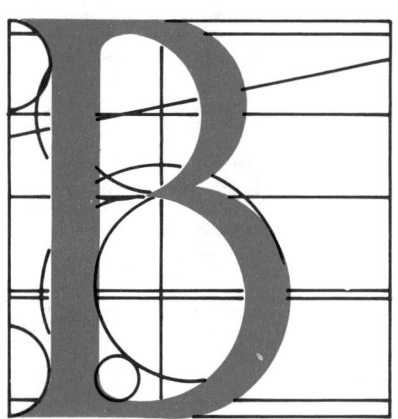

BA in education, abbreviation for Bachelor of Arts degree.

Baabda capital of the province of Jebel Lubnan in central Lebanon and site of the country's presidential palace. Situated to the SE of Beirut, it is the headquarters of the Christian military leader, General Michel Aoun.

Baade Walter 1893–1960. German-born US astronomer who made observations that doubled the distance, scale, and age of the universe. Baade worked at Mount Wilson Observatory and discovered that stars are in two distinct populations according to their age, known as Population I (the younger) and Population II (the older). Later, he found that ◊Cepheid variable stars of Population I are brighter than had been supposed, and that distances calculated from them were wrong. Baade's figures showed that the universe was twice as large as previously thought and twice as old.

Baader Andreas 1943–1977. West German extreme left-wing guerrilla. A former student activist, he formed, with Ulrike ◊Meinhof, the Rote Armee Fraktion/Red Army Faction, an urban guerrilla organization that carried out a succession of terrorist acts in West Germany during the 1970s. Sentenced to life imprisonment in Apr 1977, he took his own life in Oct, following the failure of the Faction's hostage-swap attempt at Mogadishu airport.

Baader-Meinhof gang popular name for the West German guerrilla group the *Rote Armee Fraktion* ("Red Army Faction"), active from 1968 against what it perceived as US imperialism. Its two leaders were Andreas Baader and Ulrike Meinhof who died in prison under mysterious circumstances.

Baal (Semitic "lord" or "owner") a divine title given to their chief male gods by the Phoenicians, or Canaanites. Their worship as fertility gods, often orgiastic and of a phallic character, was strongly denounced by the Hebrew prophets.

Baalbek city of ancient Syria, now in Lebanon, 36 mi/60 km NE of Beirut, 3,000 ft/1,150 m above sea level. It was originally a center of Baal worship. The Greeks identified Baal with Helios, the sun, and renamed Baalbek Heliopolis. Its ruins, including Roman temples, survive; the Temple of Bacchus, built in the 2nd century AD, is still almost intact.

Ba'ath Party Socialist party aiming at the extended union of all Arab countries, active in Iraq and Syria.

Bab, The Name assumed by Mirza Ali Mohammad 1819–1850. Persian religious leader, born in Shiraz, founder of ◊Babism, an offshoot of Islam. In 1844 he proclaimed that he was a gateway to the Hidden Imam, a new messenger of Allah who was to come. He gained a large following whose activities caused the Persian authorities to fear a rebellion, and who were therefore persecuted. The Bab was executed for heresy.

Babangida Ibrahim 1941– . Nigerian politician and soldier, president from 1985. He became head of the Nigerian army in 1983 and in 1985 led a coup against President Buhari, assuming the presidency himself.

Babangida was born in Minna, Niger state; he trained at military schools in Nigeria and the UK. He became an instructor in the Nigerian Defense Academy and by 1983 had reached the rank of major general. In 1983, after taking part in the overthrow of President Shehu Shagari, he was made army commander-in-chief.

Babbage Charles 1792–1871. English mathematician, who devised the precursor of the computer. He designed an ◊analytical engine, a general-purpose mechanical computing device for performing different calculations according to a program input on punched cards (an idea borrowed from the Jacquard loom). This device was never built, but it embodied many of the principles on which present digital computers are based.

As a young man Babbage assisted John Nerschel with his astronomical calculations. He became involved with calculating machines when he worked on his ◊difference engine for the British Admiralty, though this was never completed.

Babbit metal soft, white metal, an ◊alloy of tin, lead, copper, and antimony, used to reduce friction in

Babangida *Nigeria's president since 1985, Ibrahim Babangida. The country's fifth military leader since independence, he has promised a gradual return to civilian democracy.*

Babbage *This prototype of a complex general-purpose calculating device was created by English mathematician Charles Babbage in the 19th century.*

bearings, developed by the US inventor Isaac Babbit 1839.

Babbitt Milton 1916– . US composer. After studying with Roger ◊Sessions he developed a personal style of ◊serialism influenced by jazz. He is a leading composer of electronic music.

Babbitt a satirical novel 1922 by Sinclair Lewis about a Midwestern businessman obsessed with commerce, clubs, and material values. "Babbittry" came to mean a type of Middle American cultureless innocence.

babbler bird of the thrush family Muscicapidae with a loud babbling cry. Babblers, subfamily Timaliinae, are found in the Old World, and there are some 250 species in the group.

Babel Hebrew name for the city of ◊Babylon, chiefly associated with the Tower of Babel which, in the Genesis story in the Old Testament, was erected in the plain of Shinar by the descendants of Noah. It was a ziggurat or staged temple, seven stories high (300 ft/100 m) with a shrine of Marduk on the summit. It was built by Nabopolassar, father of Nebuchadnezzar, and was destroyed when Sennacherib sacked the city 689 BC.

Babel Isaak Emmanuilovich 1894–1939/40. Russian writer. Born in Odessa, he was an ardent supporter of the Revolution and fought with Budyenny's cavalry in the Polish campaign of 1921–22, an experience which inspired *Konarmiya/Red Cavalry* 1926. His other works include *Odesskie rasskazy/Stories from Odessa* 1924, which portrays the life of the Odessa Jews.

Bab-el-Mandeb strait that joins the Red Sea and the Gulf of Aden, and separates Arabia and Africa. The name, meaning "gate of tears," refers to its currents.

Babeuf François-Noël 1760–1797. French revolutionary journalist, a pioneer of practical socialism. In 1794 he founded a newspaper in Paris, later known as the *Tribune of the People*, in which he demanded the equality of all people. He was guillotined for conspiring against the ruling Directory during the French Revolution.

Babi faith alternate name for ◊Baha'i faith.

Babington Anthony 1561–1586. English traitor who hatched a plot to assassinate Elizabeth I and replace her with ◊Mary Queen of Scots; its discovery led to Mary's execution and his own.

babirusa wild pig *Babirousa babyrussa*, becoming increasingly rare, found in the moist forests and by the water of Sulawesi, Buru, and nearby Indonesian islands. The male has large upper

baboon

Hamadryas
baboon

tusks which grow upward through the skin of the snout and curve back toward the forehead. The babirusa is up to 2.5 ft/80 cm at the shoulder. It is nocturnal, and swims well.

Babism religious movement founded 1840's by Mirza Ali Mohammad ("the Bab"). An offshoot of Islam, its main difference lies in the belief that Mohammed was not the last of the prophets. The movement split into two groups after the death of the Bab; Baha'ullah, the leader of one of these groups, founded the ◊Baha'i faith.

Babi Yar site of a massacre of more than 100,000 people (80,000 Jews, the others were Poles, Russians, and Ukrainians) by the Germans in 1941, in Kiev, USSR. The site was ignored until the early 1960s when the poet ◊Yevtushenko immortalized it in a poem of the same name.

baboon type of large monkey, genus *Papio*, with a long doglike muzzle and large canine teeth, spending much of its time on the ground in open country. Males, with head and body up to 3.5 ft/1.1 m long, are larger than females and dominant males rule the "troops" in which baboons live. They inhabit Africa and SW Arabia.

Types include the olive baboon *Papio anubis* from W Africa to Kenya, the chacma *Papio ursinus* from S Africa, and the sacred baboon *Papio hamadryas* from NE Africa and SW Arabia. The male sacred baboon has a "cape" of long hair.

Babrius lived c. 3rd century AD. Roman writer of fables, written in Greek. He probably lived in Syria, where his stories first gained popularity. In 1842 a manuscript of his fables was discovered in a convent on Mount Athos, Greece. There were 123 fables, arranged alphabetically, but stopping at the letter O.

Babur (Arabic "lion") title given to ◊Zahir ud-din Mohammed, founder of the Mogul Empire in N India.

Babylon capital of ancient Babylonia, on the bank of the lower Euphrates River. The site is now in Iraq, 55 mi/88 km S of Baghdad and 5 mi/8 km N of Hilla, which is built chiefly of bricks from the ruins of Babylon. In 1986–89 president Saddam Hussein constructed a replica of the Southern Palace and citadel of Nebuchadnezzar II, on the plans of the German archeologist Robert Koldeway. The hanging gardens of Babylon, one of the ◊seven wonders of the world, were probably

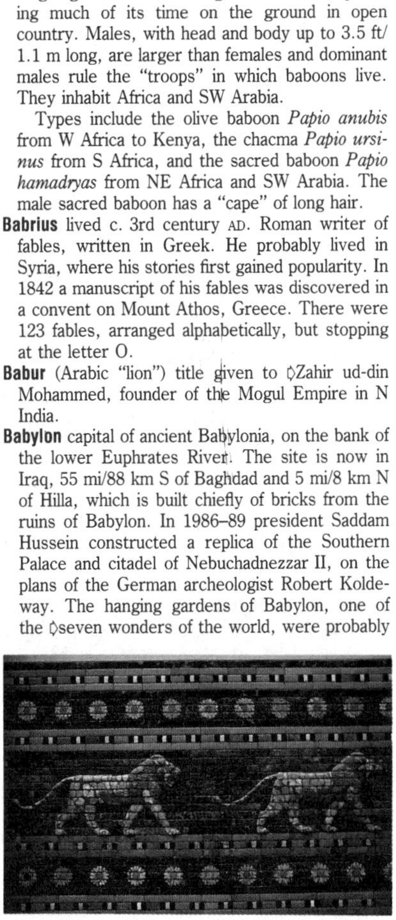

***Babylon** A pair of the 120 lions of the processional way leading from the city wall to the Ishtar Gate, Babylon. These are made of glazed brickwork molded in low relief.*

***Bacall** Lauren Bacall made her début opposite Humphrey Bogart in the film* To Have and Have Not *1944.*

erected on a vaulted stone base, the only stone construction in the mud-brick city. They formed a series of terraces, irrigated by a hydraulic system.

Babylonian captivity the exile of Jewish deportees to Babylon after Nebuchadnezzar II's capture of Jerusalem in 586 BC; according to tradition, the captivity lasted 70 years, but Cyrus of Persia, who conquered Babylon, actually allowed them to go home in 536 BC. By analogy, the name has also been applied to the papal exile to Avignon, France, 1309–77.

Bacall Lauren. Adopted name of Betty Joan Perske 1924– . Striking US actress who became an overnight star when cast by Howard Hawks opposite Humphrey Bogart in *To Have and Have Not* 1944. She and Bogart married in 1945 and starred together in *The Big Sleep* 1946 and several other films. She also appeared in *The Cobweb* 1955 and *Harper* 1966.

Bacău industrial city in Romania, 155 mi/250 km NNE of Bucharest, on the Bistrita; population (1985) 175,300. It is the capital of Bacău county, a leading oil-producing region.

baccarat casino card game with two forms: chemin de fer and baccarat banque. In the former, each player takes it in turn to hold the bank. In the banque variety, all players compete against one banker. Cards are dealt from a wooden holder known as a "shoe."

Bacchus in Greek and Roman mythology, the god of fertility (see ◊Dionysus) and of wine; his rites (the Bacchanalia) were orgiastic.

Bach Carl Philip Emmanuel 1714–1788. German composer, third son of J S Bach. He introduced a new "homophonic" style, light and easy to follow, which influenced Mozart, Haydn, and Beethoven.

In the service of Frederick the Great 1740–67, he left to become master of church music at Hamburg in 1768. He wrote over 200 pieces for keyboard instruments, and published a guide to playing the piano. Through his music and concert performances he helped to establish a leading solo role for the piano in Western music.

Bach Johann Christian 1735–1782. German composer, the 11th son of J S Bach, who became celebrated in Italy as a composer of operas. In 1762 he was invited to London, where he became music master to the royal family. He remained in England until his death, enjoying great popularity as both composer and performer.

Bach Johann Sebastian 1685–1750. German composer. His appointments included positions at the courts of Weimar and Anhalt-Köthen, and from 1723 until his death, he was musical director at St Thomas's choir school in Leipzig. Bach was a master of ◊counterpoint, and his music epitomizes the Baroque polyphonic style. His orchestral music includes the six *Brandenburg Concertos*, other concertos for clavier and violin, and four orchestral suites. Bach's keyboard music, for clavier and organ, his fugues, and his choral music are of equal importance. He also wrote chamber music and songs.

Born at Eisenach, Bach came from a distinguished musical family. At 15 he became a chorister at Lüneburg, and at 19 he was organist at Arnstadt. He married twice and had over 20 children (although several died in infancy). His second wife, Anna Magdalena Wülkens, was a soprano; she also acted as his amanuensis when his sight failed in later years.

Bach's sacred music includes 200 church cantatas, the Easter and Christmas oratorios, the two great Passions, of St Matthew and St John, and the Mass in B minor. His keyboard music includes a collection of 48 preludes and fugues known as the *Well-Tempered Clavier*, the *Goldberg Variations*, and the *Italian Concerto*. Of his organ music the finest examples are the chorale preludes. Two works written in his later years illustrate the principles and potential of his polyphonic art—the *Musical Offering* and *The Art of Fugue*.

Bach Wilhelm Friedemann 1710–1784. German composer, who was also an organist, improviser, and master of ◊counterpoint. He was the eldest son of J S Bach.

Bachelard Gaston 1884–1962. French philosopher and scientist who argued for a creative interplay between reason and experience. He attacked both Cartesian and positivist positions, insisting that science was derived neither from first principles nor directly from experience.

bacillus member of a group of rodlike ◊bacteria that occur everywhere in the soil and air. Some are responsible for diseases such as anthrax or for causing food spoilage.

bacillus of Calmette and Guérin the tuberculosis vaccine ◊BCG.

backcross a breeding technique used to determine the genetic makeup of an individual organism.

backgammon a board game for two players, often used in gambling. It was known in Mesopotamia, ancient Greece and Rome, and in medieval Europe.

The board is marked out in 24 triangular points of alternating colors, 12 to each side. Throwing two dice, the players move their 15 pieces around the board to the six points that form their own

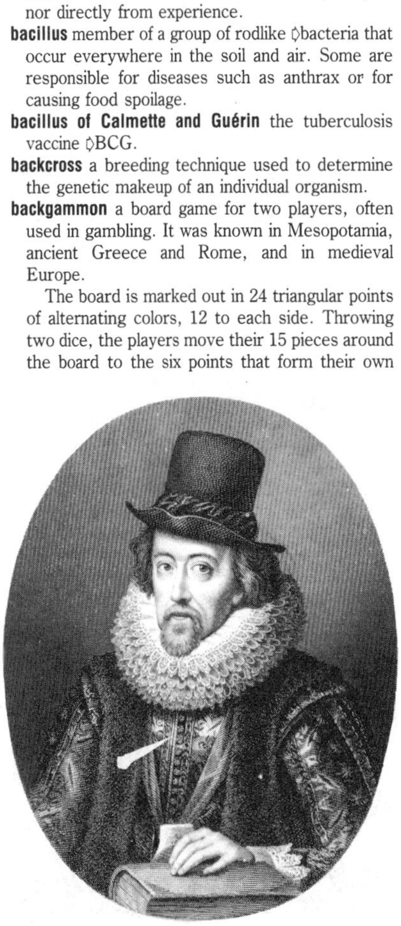

***Bacon** Sir Francis Bacon was a long-serving adviser to Elizabeth I and James I, and a writer on scientific thought and method.*

"inner table"; the first player to move all his or her pieces off the board is the winner.

back to the land a movement in late Victorian England that emphasized traditional values and rural living as a reaction against industrialism and urban society.

For some, this meant moving from city to country and becoming self-supporting; for example, by growing their own food. For others, their participation was limited to encouraging a rebirth of rural crafts and traditions, such as lacemaking, quilting, and folk music.

In the 1960s–80s many Americans took up this movement, some forming ◊communes.

Bacon Francis 1561–1626. English politician, philosopher, and essayist. He became Lord Chancellor 1618, and the same year confessed to bribe-taking, was fined £40,000 (which was paid by the king), and spent four days in the Tower of London. His works include *Essays* 1597, characterized by pith and brevity; *The Advancement of Learning* 1605, a seminal work discussing scientific method; the *Novum Organum* 1620, in which he redefined the task of natural science, seeing it as a means of empirical discovery and a method of increasing human power over nature; and *The New Atlantis* 1626, describing a utopian state in which scientific knowledge is systematically sought and exploited.

His writing helped to inspire the founding of the ◊Royal Society.

Bacon Francis 1909– . British painter, born in Dublin. He came to London in 1925 and taught himself to paint. He practiced abstract art, then developed a distorted Expressionist style with tortured figures presented in loosely defined space. From 1945 he focused on studies of figures, as in his series of screaming popes based on the portrait of Innocent X by Velázquez.

Bacon began to paint about 1930 and held his first show in London in 1949. He destroyed much of his early work. *Three Studies for Figures at the Base of a Crucifixion* 1944 (Tate Gallery, London) is an early example of his mature style.

Bacon Nathaniel 1647–1676. American colonial leader. Born in Suffolk, England, Bacon immigrated to Virginia 1673. As a wealthy planter, he became an opponent of Gov William Berkeley, demanding that frontier settlements be protected against Indian attacks. In 1675 he led a force of colonists on raids against local Indian tribes. Although denounced as a rebel by Berkeley, Bacon gained wide public support. He was eventually proclaimed "General of Virginia" and forced Berkeley to flee from the capital at Jamestown. Bacon's sudden death 1676 ended the rebellion and enabled Berkeley to regain power.

Bacon Roger 1214–1292. English philosopher and scientist, a teacher at Oxford University. In 1266, at the invitation of his friend Pope Clement IV, he began his *Opus Majus/Great Work*, a compendium of all branches of knowledge. In 1268 he sent this with his *Opus Minus/Lesser Work* and other writings to the pope. In 1277 Bacon was condemned and imprisoned by the church for "certain novelties" (heresy) and not released until 1292. He was interested in alchemy, the biological and physical sciences and magic. Many discoveries have been credited to him, including the magnifying lens. He foresaw the extensive use of gunpowder and mechanical automobiles, boats, and planes.

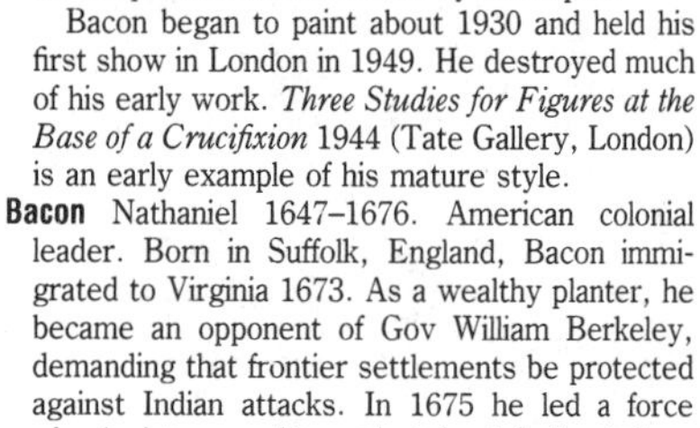

bacteria *False-color electron microscope view of a bacteria about to divide (x 10,000). The cell wall (in red) appears pinched at the point of division.*

bacteria (singular ***bacterium***) microscopic unicellular organisms with prokaryotic cells (see ◊prokaryote). They usually reproduce by ◊binary fission, and since this may occur approximately every 20 minutes, a single bacterium is potentially capable of producing 16 million copies of itself in a day.

Bacteria have a large loop of ◊DNA sometimes called a bacterial chromosome. In addition there are often small, circular pieces of DNA known as ◊plasmids that carry spare genetic information. These plasmids can readily move from one bacterium to another, even though the bacteria are of different species. In a sense they are parasites within the bacterial cell, but they survive by coding their characteristics which promote the survival of their hosts. For example, some plasmids confer antibiotic resistance on the bacteria they inhabit. The rapid and problematic spread of antibiotic resistance among bacteria is due to plasmids, but they are also useful to man in ◊genetic engineering. Although generally considered harmful, certain types of bacteria are vital in many food and industrial processes, while others play an essential role in the ◊nitrogen cycle. In 1990, a British team of food scientists announced a new rapid (five-minute) test for contamination of food by listeria or salmonella bacteria. Fluorescent dyes, added to a liquidized sample of food, reveal the presence of bacteria under laser light.

bacteriology the study of ◊bacteria.

bacteriophage a virus that attacks ◊bacteria. Such viruses are now of use in genetic engineering.

Bactria former region of central Asia (now Afghanistan, Pakistan and Soviet Central Asia) which was partly conquered by ◊Alexander the Great. During the 3rd–6th centuries BC it was a center of East–West trade and cultural exchange.

Bactrian one of the two species of ◊camel, found in Asia.

Badajoz city in Extremadura, Spain, on the Portuguese frontier; population (1986) 126,000. It has a 13th-century cathedral and ruins of a Moorish castle. Badajoz has often been besieged and was stormed by the Duke of Wellington 1812 with the loss of 59,000 British troops.

Baden former state of SW Germany, which had Karlsruhe as its capital. Baden was captured from the Romans in 282 by the Alemanni; later it became a margravate and in 1806, a grand duchy. A state of the German empire 1871–1918, then a republic, and under Hitler a *Gau* (province), it was divided between the *Länder* of Württemberg-Baden and Baden in 1945 and in 1952 made part of ◊Baden-Württemberg.

Baden town in Aargau canton, Switzerland, near Zurich; at an altitude of 1,273 ft/388 m; population (1981) 23,140. Its hot sulfur springs and mineral waters have been visited since Roman times.

Baden-Baden Black Forest spa in Baden-Württemberg, Germany; population (1984) 49,000. Fashionable in the 19th century, it is now a conference center.

Baden-Powell Robert Stephenson Smyth, 1st Baron Baden-Powell 1857–1941. British general, founder of the Scout Association. He fought in defense of Mafeking (now Mafikeng) during the Boer War. After 1907 he devoted his time to developing the Scout movement, which rapidly spread throughout the world. He was created a peer in 1929.

Baden-Württemberg administrative region (German *Land*) of Germany

area 13,819 sq mi/35,800 sq km

capital Stuttgart

towns Mannheim, Karlsruhe, Freiburg, Heidelberg, Heilbronn, Pforzheim, Ulm

physical Black Forest; Rhine boundary S and W; source of the Danube; see also ◊Swabia

products wine, jewelry, watches, clocks, musical instruments, textiles, chemicals, iron, steel, electrical equipment, surgical instruments

badger

American badger

population (1988) 9,390,000

history formed 1952 (following a plebiscite) by the merger of the *Länder* Baden, Württemberg-Baden, and Württemberg-Hohenzollern

badger large mammal of the weasel family with molar teeth of a crushing type adapted to a partly vegetable diet, and short strong legs with long claws suitable for digging. The Eurasian common badger *Meles meles* is about 3 ft/1 m long, with long coarse greyish hair on the back, and a white face with a broad black stripe along each side. Mainly a woodland animal, it is harmless and nocturnal, and spends the day in a system of burrows called a "sett." It feeds on roots, a variety of fruits and nuts, insects, worms, mice, and young rabbits.

The American badger *Taxidea taxus* is a little smaller and lives in open country in North America. Various species of hog badger, ferret badger, and stink badger occur in S and E Asia, the last having the anal scent glands characteristic of the weasel family well developed.

Bad Godesburg SE suburb of ◊Bonn, Germany, formerly a spa, and the meeting place of Chamberlain and Hitler before the Munich Agreement 1938.

badlands a barren landscape cut by erosion into a maze of ravines, pinnacles, gullies and sharp-edged ridges. South Dakota and Nebraska are examples.

badminton racket game played on a court with a feathered shuttlecock instead of a ball. Similar to lawn ◊tennis but played on a smaller court, the object is the same: to create a situation whereby the opposition is unable to return the shuttlecock.

Played by two or four players, the court measures 20 ft/6.1 m by 44 ft/13.4 m. A net, 2.5 ft/0.8 m deep, is stretched across the middle of the court and at a height of 5 ft/1.52 m above the ground to the top of the net. The shuttlecock must be volleyed. Only the server can win points. The sport is named after Badminton House, the seat of the duke of Beaufort, where the game was played in the 19th century. The major tournaments are held on indoor courts; they include the Thomas Cup, an international team championship for men, first held in 1949, and the Uber Cup, a women's international team competition, first held in 1957.

Badoglio Pietro 1871–1956. Italian soldier and Fascist politician. A veteran of campaigns against the peoples of Tripoli and Cyrenaica, in 1935 he became commander in chief in Ethiopia, adopting ruthless measures to break patriot resistance. He was created viceroy of Ethiopia and duke of Addis Ababa in 1936. He resigned during the disastrous campaign into Greece 1940 and succeeded Mussolini as prime minister of Italy from July 1943 to June 1944, negotiating the armistice with the Allies.

Baedeker Karl 1801–1859. German publisher of foreign travel guides; the first was Coblenz 1829. These are now published from Hamburg (before World War II from Leipzig).

Baekeland Leo Hendrik 1863–1944. Belgian-born US chemist. He invented ◊Bakelite, the first commercial plastic, made from ◊formaldehyde and ◊phenol. He later made a photographic paper, Velox, which could be developed in artificial light.

badminton

A volleying game played on an indoor court with rackets and a shuttlecock. It is played as singles or pairs and the object is to play the shuttle over the raised net and to score points by grounding the shuttle in the opponent's half of the court or by forcing an error. Only the server can score points. A game is won when one side reaches 15 points (11 in women's singles).

Shuttles
Shuttles come in two forms. They can be either synthetic or made with 16 goose feathers. The feathered cock is the one used in major tournament play while the plastic cock is used at junior level and for practice.

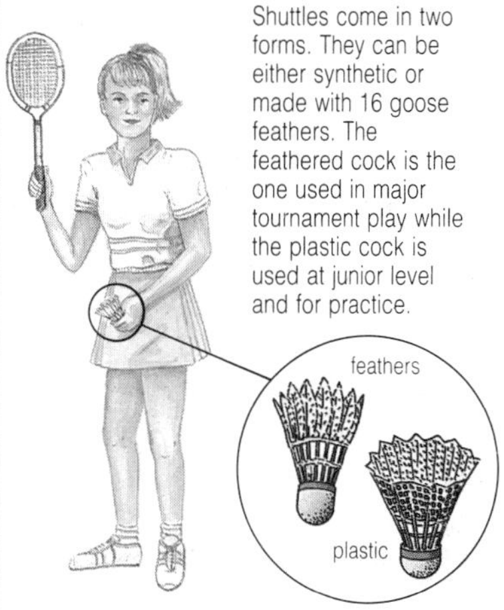
feathers
plastic

Service
The shuttle is dropped from the hand onto the racket and the service must be underhand and hit over the net. Overhand serving, like that in lawn tennis, is not permitted in badminton.

grips

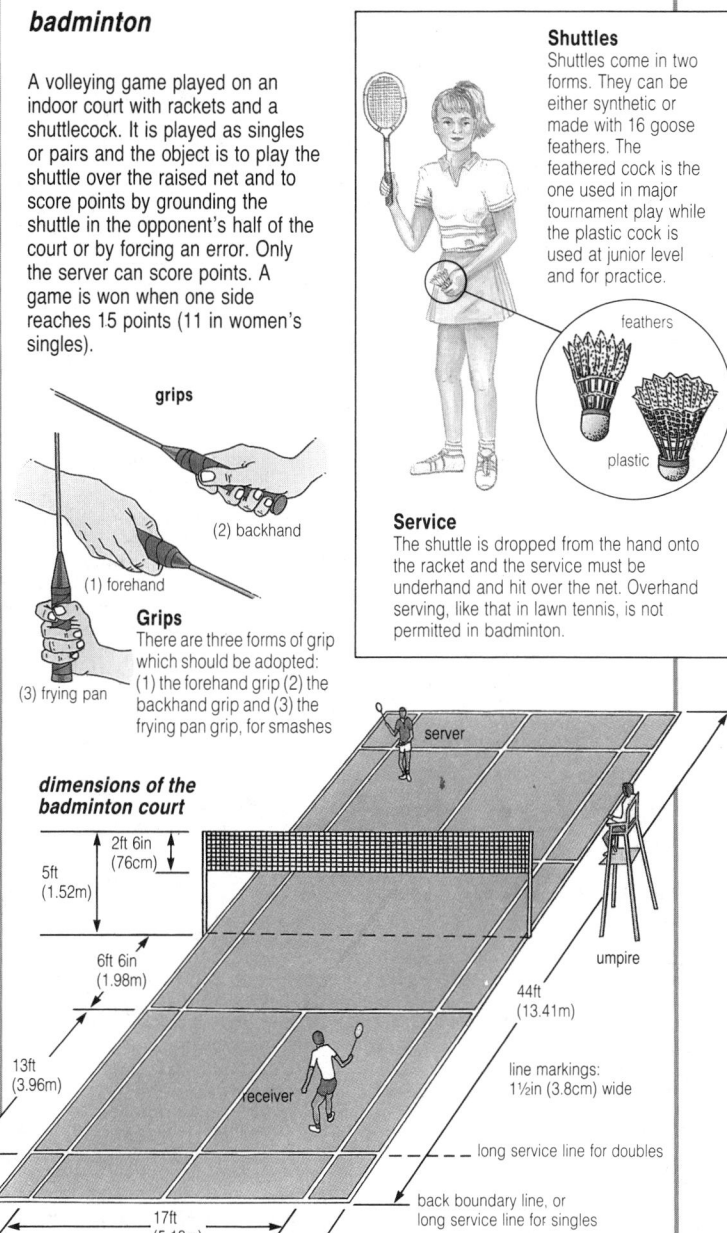

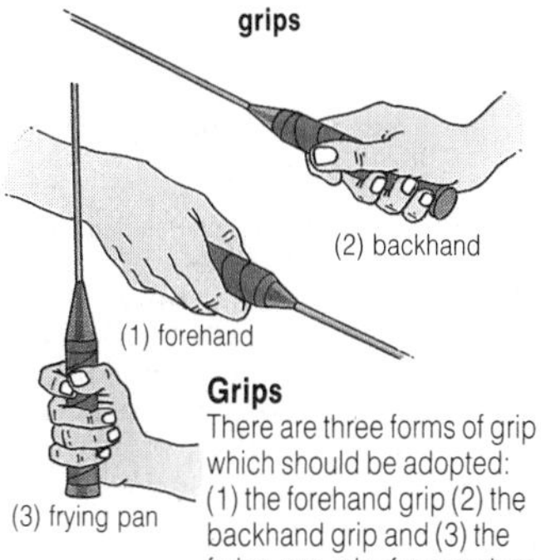
(2) backhand
(1) forehand
(3) frying pan

Grips
There are three forms of grip which should be adopted: (1) the forehand grip (2) the backhand grip and (3) the frying pan grip, for smashes

dimensions of the badminton court

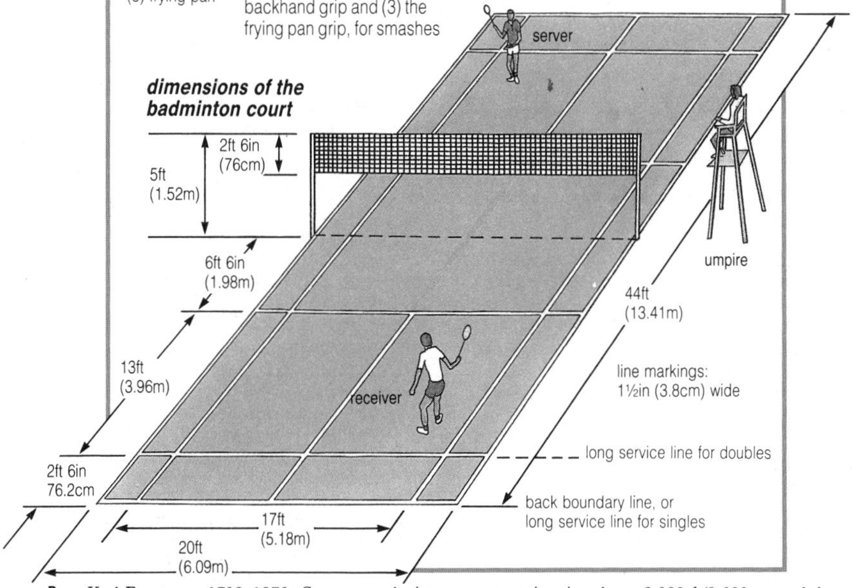
server
2ft 6in
(76cm)
5ft
(1.52m)
6ft 6in
(1.98m)
umpire
44ft
(13.41m)
13ft
(3.96m)
line markings:
1½in (3.8cm) wide
receiver
long service line for doubles
2ft 6in
76.2cm
back boundary line, or
long service line for singles
17ft
(5.18m)
20ft
(6.09m)

Baer Karl Ernst von 1792–1876. German zoologist who was the founder of comparative ◊embryology.

He was born in Estonia and held scientific posts in Königsberg, Germany, and St Petersburg, Russia.

Baez Joan 1941– . US folk singer who achieved fame in the early 1960s with her versions of traditional English and American folk songs such as "Silver Dagger" and "We Shall Overcome," the latter becoming the anthem of anti-Vietnam War protestors. She was a major influence in the popularization of folk music and has also remained active as a pacifist and antiwar campaigner.

Baffin William 1584–1622. English explorer and navigator. In 1616, he and Robert Bylot explored Baffin Bay, NE Canada, and reached latitude 77° 45′ N, which for 236 years remained the "furthest north."

Baffin Island island in the Northwest Territories, Canada

area 195,875 sq mi/507,450 sq km

features largest island in the Canadian Arctic; mountains rise above 6,000 ft/2,000 m, and there are several large lakes. The northernmost part of the strait separating Baffin Island from Greenland forms Baffin Bay, the southern end is Davis Strait.

It is named after William Baffin, who carried out research here 1614 during his search for the ◊Northwest Passage.

bagatelle (French "trifle") in music, a short character piece, often for piano.

bagatelle a game resembling billiards but played on a board with numbered cups instead of pockets. The aim is to get the nine balls into the cups.

In ordinary bagatelle each player delivers all the balls in turn; in French bagatelle two or four players take part alternately.

Baggara a Bedouin people of the Nile Basin, principally in Kordofan, Sudan, W of the White Nile. They are Muslims, traditionally occupied in cattle breeding and big-game hunting.

Baghdad historic city and capital of Iraq, on the Tigris river; population (1985) 4,649,000. Industries include oil refining, distilling, tanning, tobacco processing, and the manufacture of textiles and cement. Founded 762, it became Iraq's capital 1921.

To the SE, on the river Tigris, are the ruins of Ctesiphon, capital of Parthia about 250 BC–AD 226 and of the ◊Sassanian Empire about 226–641; the remains of the Great Palace include the world's largest single-span brick arch 85 ft/26 m wide and 95 ft/29 m high.

A transportation hub from the earliest times, it was developed by the 8th-century caliph Harun al-Rashid, although little of the *Arabian Nights* city remains. It was overrun 1258 by the Mongols, who destroyed the irrigation system. In 1639 it was taken by the Turks. During World War I, Baghdad was captured by General Maude 1917. During the Persian Gulf war 1991, the UN coalition forces bombed it in repeated air raids and destroyed much of the city.

Baghdad Pact military treaty of 1955 concluded by the UK, Iran, Iraq, Pakistan, and Turkey, with the US cooperating; it was replaced by the ◊Central Treaty Organization (CENTO) when Iraq withdrew in 1958.

bagpipe ancient wind instrument used outdoors and incorporating a number of reed pipes powered from a single inflated bag. Known in Roman times, it is found in various forms throughout Europe, including Ireland and Greece. The most famous, that of the Highlands, is the Scottish national instrument.

The bag has the advantage of being more powerful than the unaided lungs and of being able to sustain notes indefinitely. The melody pipe, bent downward, is called a chanter and the accompanying harmony pipes supported on the shoulder are drones, which emit invariable notes to supply a ground bass.

Bagritsky Eduard. Adopted name of Eduard Dzyubin 1895–1934. Soviet poet. One of the Constructivist group, he published the heroic poem *Lay About Opanas* 1926, and collections of verse called *The Victors* 1932 and *The Last Night* 1932.

Baguio summer resort on Luzon island in the Philippines, 125 mi/200 km N of Manila, 4,500 ft/1,370 m above sea level; population (1980) 119,000. It is the official summer residence of the Philippine president.

Bahadur Shah II 1775–1862. Last of the Mogul emperors of India. He reigned, though in name only, as king of Delhi 1837–57, when he was hailed by the mutineers of the ◊Sepoy Rebellion as an independent emperor at Delhi. After the rebellion he was exiled to Burma with his family.

Baha'i religion founded in the 19th century from a Muslim splinter group, ◊Babism, by the Persian ◊Baha'ullah. His message in essence was that all great religious leaders are manifestations of the unknowable God and all scriptures are sacred. There is no priesthood: all Baha'is are expected to teach, and to work toward world unification. There are about 4.5 million Baha'is worldwide.

Great stress is laid on equality regardless of religion, race, or gender. Drugs and alcohol are forbidden, as is celibacy. Marriage is strongly encouraged; there is no arranged marriage, but parental approval must be given. Baha'is are expected to pray daily, but there is no set prayer. From March 2 to 20, adults under 70 fast from sunrise to sunset. Administration is carried out by an elected body, the Universal House of Justice.

Bahamas country comprising a group of about 700 islands and about 2,400 uninhabited islets and cays in the Caribbean, 50 mi/80 km from the SE coast of Florida. They extend for about 760 mi/1,223 km from NW to SE, but only 22 of the islands are inhabited.

government The Bahamas are an independent sovereign nation within the ◊Commonwealth, with the British monarch as head of state and represented by an appointed, resident governor general. The constitution, effective since independence in 1973, provides for a two-chamber parliament with a senate and house of assembly.

Bahamas
Commonwealth of the

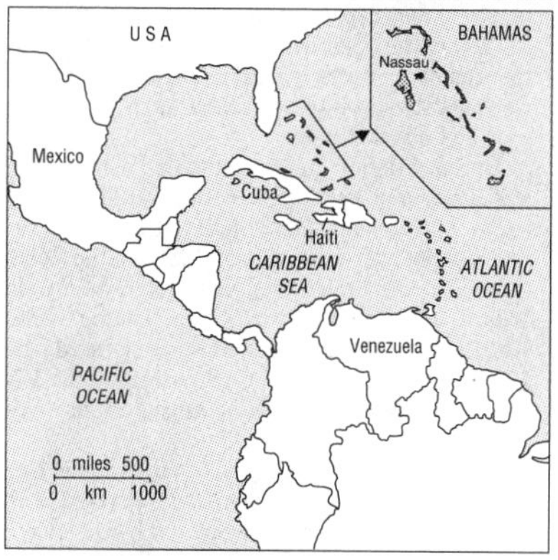
USA
BAHAMAS
Nassau
Mexico
Cuba
Haiti
CARIBBEAN SEA
ATLANTIC OCEAN
Venezuela
PACIFIC OCEAN
0 miles 500
0 km 1000

area 5,352 sq mi/13,864 sq km
capital Nassau on New Providence
cities Alice Town, Andros Town, Hope Town, Spanish Wells, Freeport, Moss Town, George Town
physical comprises 700 tropical coral islands and about 1,000 cays
features desert islands: only 30 are inhabited; Blue Holes of Andros, the world's longest and deepest submarine caves; the Exumas are a thin spine of 365 islands
principal islands Andros, Grand Bahama, Great Abaco, Eleuthera, New Providence, Berry Islands, Biminis, Great Inagua, Acklins, Exumas, Mayaguana, Crooked Island, Long Island, Cat Island, Rum Cay, San Salvador Island
head of state Elizabeth II from 1973 represented by governor-general
head of government Lynden Oscar Pindling from 1967
political system constitutional monarchy
political parties Progressive Liberal Party (PLP), centrist; Free National Movement (FNM), center-left
exports cement, pharmaceuticals, petroleum products, crawfish, salt, aragonite, rum, pulpwood; over half the islands' employment comes from tourism
currency Bahamian dollar
population (1990 est) 251,000; growth rate 1.8% p.a.
language English and some Creole
religion 29% Baptist, 23% Anglican, 22% Roman Catholic
literacy 95% (1986)
GDP $2.7 bn (1987); $11,261 per head
chronology
1964 Independence achieved from Britain.
1967 First national assembly elections.
1972 Constitutional conference to discuss full independence.
1973 Full independence achieved.
1983 Allegations of drug trafficking by government ministers.
1984 Deputy prime minister and two cabinet ministers resigned. Pindling denied any personal involvement and was endorsed as party leader.
1987 Pindling reelected despite claims of frauds.

The governor general appoints a prime minister and cabinet drawn from and responsible to the legislature. The governor general appoints 16 senate members, nine on the advice of the prime minister, four on the advice of the leader of the opposition, and three after consultation with the prime minister. The house of assembly has 49 members, elected by universal suffrage. Parliament has a maximum life of five years and may be dissolved within that period. The major political parties are the Progressive Liberal Party (PLP), and the Free National Movement (FNM).
history The Bahamas were reached by Christopher Columbus 1492, who first landed at San Salvador. The islands were a pirate area in the early 18th century and became a crown colony 1717 (although they were disputed by the Carolina colony until 1787). The Bahamas achieved internal self-government in 1964, and the first elections for the national assembly on a full voting register were held in 1967. The PLP, drawing its support mainly from voters of African origin, won the same number of seats as the European-dominated United Bahamian Party (UBP). Lynden ◊Pindling became prime minister with support from outside his party. In the 1968 elections the PLP scored a resounding victory, repeated in 1972, enabling Pindling to lead his country to full independence within the Commonwealth in 1973 and increase his majority in 1977.

The main contestants in the 1982 elections were the FNM (consisting of a number of factions that had split and reunited) and the PLP. Despite allegations of government complicity in drug trafficking, the PLP was again successful, and Pindling was unanimously endorsed as leader at a Party convention in 1984. The 1987 general election was won by the PLP, led by Pindling, but with a reduced majority.

Baha'ullah title of Mirza Hosein Ali 1817–1892. Persian founder of the ◊Baha'i religion. Baha'ullah, "God's Glory," proclaimed himself as the prophet the ◊Bab had foretold.

Bahawalpur city in the Punjab, Pakistan; population (1981) 178,000. Once the capital of a former state of Bahawalpur, it is now an industrial town producing textiles and soap. It has a university, established 1975.

Bahia state of E Brazil
area 216,556 sq mi/561,026 sq km
capital Salvador
industry oil, chemicals, agriculture
population (1986) 10,949,000.

Bahía Blanca port in S Argentina, on the river Naposta, 3 mi/5 km from its mouth; population (1980) 233,126. It is a major distribution center for wool and food processing. The naval base of Puerto Belgrano is here.

Bahrain country comprising a group of islands in the Persian Gulf, between Saudi Arabia and Iran.
government The 1973 constitution provided for an elected national assembly of 30 members, but was dissolved in 1975 after the prime minister refused to work with it. The Emir now governs Bahrain by decree, through a cabinet chosen by him. There are no recognizable political parties.
history Traditionally an Arab monarchy, Bahrain was under Portuguese rule during the 16th century and from 1602 was dominated by Persia (now Iran). In 1783 it became a sheikdom under the control of the Khalifa dynasty. British assistance was sought to preserve the country's independence against claims of sovereignty made by Persia and the Ottoman Empire. It became a British protectorate in 1861, with government shared between the ruling sheik and a British adviser. In 1928 Iran (Persia) claimed sovereignty but in 1970 accepted a UN report showing that the inhabitants of Bahrain preferred independence.

In 1968 Britain announced the withdrawal of its forces, and Bahrain joined two other territories under British protection, Qatar and the Trucial States (now the ◊United Arab Emirates), to form a Federation of Arab Emirates. In 1971 Qatar and the Trucial States left the Federation, and Bahrain became an independent state.

In 1973 a new constitution provided for an elected national assembly, but two years later the prime minister, Sheik Khalifa, complained of obstruction by the assembly, which was then dissolved. Since then the Emir and his family have ruled with virtually absolute power.

Since the Iranian revolution of 1979, relations between the two countries have been uncertain, with fears of Iranian attempts to disturb Bahrain's stability. Bahrain has now become a focal point in the Gulf, being the site of the new Gulf University and an international airport, the center of Gulf aviation. A causeway linking Bahrain with mainland Saudi Arabia was constructed in 1986 (at 15.5 mi/25 km it is the longest in the world). During the 1991 Gulf War, Bahrain opposed Iraq's invasion of Kuwait.

Bahrain
State of
(Dawlat al Bahrayn)

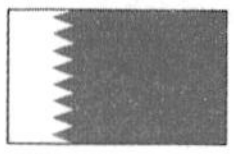

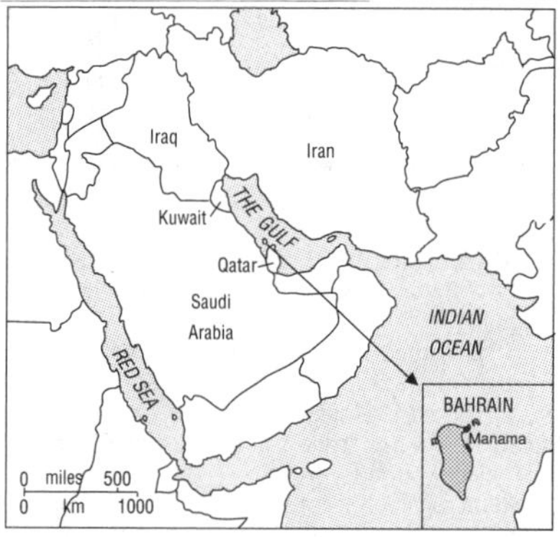
Iraq
Iran
Kuwait
THE GULF
Qatar
Saudi Arabia
INDIAN OCEAN
RED SEA
BAHRAIN
Manama
0 miles 500
0 km 1000

area 266 sq mi/688 sq km
capital Manama on the largest island (also called Bahrain)
cities Muharraq, Jidd Hafs, Isa Town; oil port Mina Sulman
physical 35 islands, composed largely of sand-covered limestone; generally poor and infertile soil; flat and hot
features causeway linking Bahrain to mainland Saudi Arabia; Sitra island is a communications center for the lower Persian Gulf and has a satellite-tracking station
head of state and government Sheikh Isa bin Sulman al-Khalifa (1933–) from 1961
political system absolute emirate
political parties none
exports oil, natural gas, aluminum, fish
currency Bahrain dinar
population (1990 est) 512,000 (two-thirds are nationals); growth rate 4.4% p.a.
life expectancy men 67, women 71
language Arabic (official), Farsi, English, Urdu
religion 85% Muslim (Shiite 60%, Sunni 40%)
literacy men 79%/women 64% (1985 est)
GDP $3.5 bn (1987); $7,772 per head
chronology
1861 Became British protectorate.
1968 Britain announced its intention to withdraw its forces. Bahrain formed, with Qatar and the Trucial States, the Federation of Arab Emirates.
1971 Qatar and the Trucial States withdrew from the federation and Bahrain became an independent state.
1973 New constitution adopted, with an elected national assembly.
1975 Prime minister resigned and national assembly dissolved. Emir and his family assumed virtually absolute power.
1986 A causeway (25 km/15 mi long) linking Bahrain with Saudi Arabia was opened.
1991 Nation joins UN coalition that ousts Iraq from its occupation of Kuwait.

Baikal (Russian *Baykal Ozero*) largest freshwater lake in Asia, (area 12,150 sq mi/31,500 sq km) and deepest in the world (up to 5,710 ft/1,740 m), in S Siberia, USSR. Fed by more than 300 rivers, it is drained only by the Lower Angara. It has sturgeon fisheries and rich fauna.

Baikonur the main Soviet launch site for spacecraft, located at Tyuratam, near the Aral Sea. From there were launched the first satellites and all Soviet space probes and crewed Soyuz missions. It covers an area of 4,675 sq mi/12,200 sq km, much larger than its US equivalent, the ◊Kennedy Space Center in Florida.

bail a security, bonds, or money deposited with the court to obtain the temporary release of an arrested person, on the assurance that the person will obey the court, as by attending a legal proceeding at a stated time and place. If the person does not attend, the bail may be forfeited.

While the US Constitution nominally guarantees individuals right to reasonable bail, in effect availability of bail and amounts of security necessary to secure bail are set by judges, based on judges' evaluations of the likelihood that a defendant will appear, or likelihood of further criminal acts or danger to the public, on the severity of the charge, and on the economic standing of the accused.

bailif an officer of the court whose job, usually in the county courts, is to serve notices and enforce the court's orders involving seizure of the goods of a debtor.

The term orignated in Normandy as the name for a steward of an estate. It retained this meaning in England throughout the Middle Ages, and could also denote a sheriff's assistant. In France, the royal *bailli* or *bayle* was appointed to adminster a large area of territory, the *baillage*, and was a leading local official.

Bailly Jean Sylvain 1736–1793. French astronomer who wrote about the satellites of Jupiter and the history of astronomy. Early in the French Revolution he was president of the National Assembly and mayor of Paris but resigned in 1791; he was guillotined during the Reign of Terror.

Baily's beads bright spots of sunlight seen around the edge of the Moon for a few seconds immediately before and after a total ◊eclipse of the Sun, caused by sunlight shining between mountains at the Moon's edge. Sometimes one bead is much brighter than the others, producing the so-called diamond ring effect. The effect was described 1836 by the English astronomer Francis Baily (1774–1844), a wealthy stockbroker who retired in 1825 to devote himself to astronomy.

Bainbridge Beryl 1933– . English novelist, originally an actress, whose works have the drama and economy of a stage play. They include *The Dressmaker* 1973, *The Bottle Factory Outing* 1974, and the collected short stories in *Mum and Mr Armitage* 1985.

Bainbridge Kenneth Tompkins 1904– . US physicist who was director of the first atomic bomb test at Alamogordo, New Mexico, in 1945.

Bainbridge worked at the Cavendish Laboratory, Cambridge, England, in the 1930s. He also carried out research in radar. From 1961 he was George Vasmer Everett Professor of Physics at Harvard University.

Baird John Logie 1888–1946. Scottish electrical engineer who pioneered television. In 1925 he gave the first public demonstration of television and in 1926 pioneered fiber optics, radar (in advance of Robert ◊Watson-Watt), and "noctovision," a system for seeing at night by using infrared rays.

He also developed video recording on both wax records and magnetic steel disks (1926–27), color TV (1925–28), 3-D color TV (1925–46), and transatlantic TV (1928). In 1944 he developed facsimile television and demonstrated the world's first all-electronic color and 3-D color receiver (500 lines).

Baja California the mountainous peninsula that forms the twin NW states of Lower (Spanish *baja*) California, Mexico; area 55,351 sq mi/143,396 sq km; population (1980) 1,440,600. The N state, Baja California Norte, includes the cities of Mexicali (its capital) and Tijuana; this area bordering the US now contains many factories. The S state, Baja California Sur, attracts many US tourists for fishing, whale-watching (gray whales winter here), swimming, and sunbathing; La Paz is the state capital; Cabo San Lucas is a fashionable resort.

Bakelite the first synthetic ◊plastic, created by Leo ◊Baekeland in 1909. Bakelite is hard, tough, and heatproof, and is used as an electrical insulator. It is made by the reaction of phenol with formaldehyde, producing a powdery resin that sets solid when heated. Objects are made by subjecting the resin to compression molding (simultaneous heat and pressure in a mold).

It is one of the thermosetting plastics, which do not remelt when heated, and is often used for electrical fittings.

Baker James (Addison), III 1930– . US Republican politician. Under President Reagan, he was White House Chief of Staff 1981–85 and Treasury secretary 1985–88. After managing Bush's successful presidential campaign 1988, Baker was appointed secretary of state 1989.

Baker, a lawyer from Houston, Texas, entered politics 1970 as one of the managers of his friend George Bush's unsuccessful campaign for the Senate. He served as undersecretary of commerce 1975–76 in the Ford administration and was deputy manager of the 1976 and 1980 Ford and Bush presidential campaigns. Baker joined the Reagan administration 1981. He has been criticized for the unscrupulousness of the 1988 Bush campaign. The most respected member of the Bush team, he has been described as an effective "prime minister."

Baker Samuel White 1821–1893. English explorer, in 1864 the first European to sight Lake Albert Nyanza (now Lake Mobutu Sese Seko) in central Africa, and discover that the river Nile flowed through it.

Bakersfield city in S California, NE of Santa Barbara, on the Kern river; the seat of Kern county. It is known for its oil wells and oil products; population (1990) 174,820. Oil was discovered 1899.

Baker v Carr a US Supreme Court decision 1962 dealing with the responsibility of federal courts to hear suits against unconstitutional electoral apportionment. The petitioner filed suit against the Tennessee legislature, which, by neglecting to reapportion the state seats according to demographic changes, had allowed a disparity to develop between the voting powers of urban and rural residents. The Court did not decide whether this constituted an infraction of the 14th Amendment right to equal protection. Instead, it empowered federal courts to rule in state apportionment suits.

Bakhtaran formerly (until 1980) Kermanshah capital of Bakhtaran province, NW Iran; population (1986) 561,000. The province (area 9,148 sq mi/23,700 sq km; population 1,463,000) is on the Iraqi border and is mainly inhabited by Kurds. Industries include oil refining, carpets, and textiles.

baking ◊cooking in an oven by dry heat. It is the method used for most breads, cakes, cookies, and pastries, but also meats, poultry, fish, vegetables, and fruits.

Bakst Leon. Assumed name of Leon Rosenberg 1886–1924. Russian painter and theatrical designer. He used intense colors and fantastic images from Oriental and folk art, with an Art Nouveau tendency to graceful surface pattern. His designs for Diaghilev's touring Ballets Russes made a deep impression in Paris 1909–14.

Baku capital city of the Azerbaijan Republic, USSR, and industrial port (oil refining) on the Caspian Sea; population (1987) 1,741,000. Baku is a center of the Soviet oil industry and is linked by pipelines with Batumi on the Black Sea. In Jan 1990 ther were violent clashes between the Azeri majority and the Armenian minority, and Soviet troops were sent to the region. Over 13,000 Armenians subsequently fled from the city.

Bakunin Mikhail 1814–1876. Russian anarchist, active in Europe. In 1848 he was expelled from France as a revolutionary agitator. In Switzerland in the 1860s he became recognized as the leader of the anarchist movement. In 1869 he joined the First International (a coordinating Socialist body) but, after stormy conflicts with Karl Marx, was expelled 1872.

Born of a noble family, Bakunin served in the Imperial Guard but, disgusted with tsarist methods in Poland, resigned his commission and traveled abroad. For his share in a brief revolt at Dresden 1849 he was sentenced to death. The sentence was commuted to imprisonment, and he was handed over to the tsar's government and sent to Siberia 1855. In 1861 he managed to escape to Switzerland. He had a large following, mainly in the Latin American countries. He wrote books and pamphlets, including *God and the State*.

Balaclava, Battle of in the Crimean War, an engagement on Oct 25, 1854 near a town in Ukraine, 6 mi/10 km SE of Sevastopol. It was the scene of the ill-timed Charge of the Light Brigade of British cavalry against the Russian entrenched artillery. Of the 673 soldiers who took part, there were 272 casualties. Balaclava helmets were knitted hoods worn here by soldiers in the bitter weather.

Balakirev Mily Alexeyevich 1837–1910. Russian composer. He wrote orchestral and piano music, songs, and a symphonic poem *Tamara*, all imbued with the Russian national character and spirit. He was leader of the group known as The Five and taught its members, Mussorgsky, Cui, Rimsky-Korsakov, and Borodin.

balalaika Russian musical instrument, resembling a guitar. It has a triangular sound box, frets, and two, three, or four strings played by strumming with the fingers.

balance apparatus for weighing or measuring mass. The various types include the beam balance consisting of a centrally pivoted lever with pans hanging from each end, and the spring balance, in which the object to be weighed stretches (or compresses) a vertical coil spring fitted with a pointer that indicates the weight on a scale. Kitchen and bathroom scales are balances.

balance of nature in ecology, the idea that there is an inherent equilibrium in most ◊ecosystems, with plants and animals interacting so as to produce a stable, continuing system of life on earth. Organisms in the ecosystem are adapted to each other—for example, waste products produced by one species are used by another and resources used by some are replenished by others; the oxygen needed by animals is produced by plants while the waste product of animal respiration, carbon dioxide, is used by plants as a raw material in photosynthesis. The nitrogen cycle, the water cycle, and the control of animal populations by natural predators are other examples. The activities of human beings can, and frequently do, disrupt the balance of nature.

balance of payments in economics, a tabular account of a country's debit and credit transactions with other countries. Items are divided into the current account, which includes both visible trade (imports and exports) and invisible trade (such as transport, tourism, interest, and dividends), and the capital account, which includes investment in and out of the country, international grants, and loans. Deficits or surpluses on these accounts are brought into balance by buying and selling reserves of foreign currencies.

A balance of payments crisis arises when a country's current account deteriorates because the cost of imports exceeds income from exports. In developing countries persistent trade deficits often result in heavy government borrowing overseas, which in turn leads to a ◊debt crisis.

balance of power in politics, the theory that the best way of ensuring international order is to have power so distributed among states that no single state is able to achieve a dominant position. The term, which may also refer more simply to the actual distribution of power, is one of the most enduring concepts in international relations. Since the development of nuclear weapons, it has been asserted that the balance of power has been replaced by a balance of terror.

balance of trade the balance of trade transactions of a country recorded in its current account; it forms one component of the country's ◊balance of payments.

balance sheet a statement of the financial position of a company or individual on a specific date, showing both ◊assets and ◊liabilities.

Balanchine George 1904–1983. Russian-born US choreographer. After leaving the USSR in 1924, he worked with ◊Diaghilev in France. Moving to the US in 1933, he became a major influence on modern dance, starting the New York City Ballet in 1948. He was the most influential 20th-century choreographer of ballet in the US. He developed an "American classic" dance style and made the New York City Ballet one of the world's great companies. He also pioneered choreography in Hollywood films.

His many works include *Appollon Musagéte* 1928 and *The Prodigal Son* 1929 for Diaghilev; several works for music by ◊Stravinsky, such as *Agon* 1957 and *Duo Concertante* 1972; and Broadway musicals such as *On Your Toes* 1936 and *The Boys from Syracuse* 1938.

Balaton lake in W Hungary; area 230 sq mi/600 sq km.

Balboa Vasco Núñez de 1475–1519. Spanish ◊conquistador. He founded a settlement at Darien (now Panama) 1511 and crossed the Isthmus in search of gold, reaching the Pacific Ocean (which he called the South Sea) on Sept 25, 1513, after a 25-day expedition. He was made admiral of the Pacific and governor of Panama but was removed by Spanish court intrigue, imprisoned and executed.

Balcon Michael 1896–1977. British film producer, responsible for the "Ealing Comedies" of the 1940s and early 1950s, such as *Kind Hearts and Coronets* 1949 and *The Lavender Hill Mob* 1951.

Balder in Norse mythology, the son of ◊Odin and ◊Freya and husband of Nanna, and the best, wisest, and most loved of all the gods. He was killed, at ◊Loki's instigation, by a twig of mistletoe shot by the blind god Hodur.

baldness loss of hair from the upper scalp, common in older men. Its onset and extent are influenced by genetic make-up and the level of male sex ◊hormones. There is no cure, and expedients such as hair implants may have no lasting effect. Hair loss in both sexes may also occur as a result of ill health or following radiation treatment, such as for cancer. Alopecia, a condition in which the hair falls out, is different from the "male pattern baldness" described above.

Baldung Grien Hans 1484/85–1545. German Renaissance painter, engraver, and designer, based in Strasbourg. He painted the theme *Death and the Maiden* in several versions.

Baldwin I 1058–1118. King of Jerusalem. A French nobleman, who joined his brother ◊Godfrey de Bouillon on the First Crusade in 1096. Baldwin established the kingdom of Jerusalem in 1100. It was destroyed by Islamic conquest in 1187.

Baldwin James 1924–1987. US writer, born in New York City, who portrayed the condition of black Americans in contemporary society. His works include the novels *Go Tell It on the Mountain* 1953, *Another Country* 1962, and *Just Above My Head* 1979; the play *The Amen Corner* 1955; and the autobiographical essays *Notes of a Native Son* 1955 and *The Fire Next Time* 1963. He was active in the civil rights movement.

***Baldwin** Brought up in Harlem, New York City, with a background of domestic strife and religious fanaticism, author James Baldwin began preaching at the Fireside Pentecostal Church at age 14.*

Baldwin Stanley, 1st Earl Baldwin of Bewdley 1867–1947. British Conservative politician, prime minister 1923–24, 1924–29, and 1935–37; he weathered the general strike 1926, secured complete adult suffrage 1928, and handled the ◊abdication crisis of Edward VIII 1936, but failed to prepare Britain for World War II.

Bâle French form of Basle or ◊Basel, town in Switzerland.

Balearic Islands (Spanish *Baleares*) Mediterranean group of islands forming an autonomous region of Spain; including ◊Majorca, ◊Minorca, ◊Ibiza, Cabrera, and Formentera
area 1,930 sq mi/5,000 sq km
capital Palma de Mallorca
products figs, olives, oranges, wine, brandy, coal, iron, slate; tourism is crucial
population (1986) 755,000
history a Roman colony from 123 BC, the Balearic Islands were an independent Moorish kingdom 1009–1232; they were conquered by Aragón 1343.

Balewa alternative title of Nigerian politician ◊Tafawa Balewa.

Balfour Arthur James, 1st Earl of 1848–1930. British Conservative politician, prime minister 1902–05 and foreign secretary 1916–19, when he issued the Balfour Declaration 1917 and was involved in peace negotiations after World War I, signing the Treaty of Versailles.

Balfour Declaration letter, dated Nov 2, 1917, from the British foreign secretary A J Balfour to Lord Rothschild (chair, British Zionist Federation) stating: "HM government view with favor the establishment in Palestine of a national home for the Jewish people." It led to the foundation of Israel 1948.

Balearic Islands

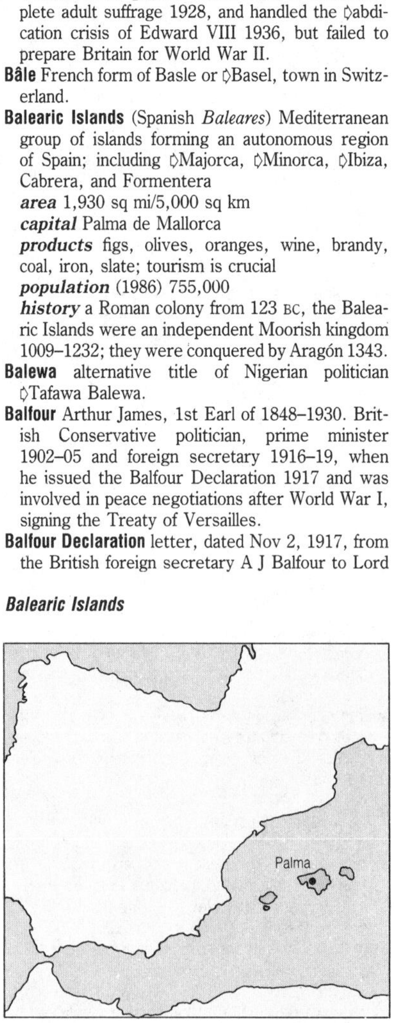
Palma

Bali island of Indonesia, E of Java, one of the Sunda Islands
area 2,240 sq mi/5,800 sq kmFrench
capital Denpasar
physical volcanic mountains
features Balinese dancing, music, drama
products gold and silver work, woodcarving, weaving, çopra, salt, coffee
population (1980) 2,470,000
history Bali's Hindu culture goes back to the 7th century; the Dutch gained control of the island by 1908.

Balikesir city in NW Turkey, capital of Aydin province; population (1985) 152,000. There are silver mines nearby.

Balikpapan port in Indonesia, on the E coast of S Kalimantan, Borneo; population (1980) 280,900. It is an oil-refining center.

Baliol John de c. 1250–1314. King of Scotland 1292–96. As an heir to the Scottish throne on the death of Margaret, the Maid of Norway, his cause was supported by the English king, Edward I, against 12 other claimants. Having paid homage to Edward, Baliol was proclaimed king but soon rebelled and gave up the kingdom when English forces attacked Scotland.

Bali Strait a narrow strait between the two islands of Bali and Java, Indonesia. It was the scene on 19–Feb 20, 1942 of a naval action between Japanese and Dutch forces that served to delay slightly the Japanese invasion of Java.

Balkans (Turkish "mountains") peninsula of SE Europe, stretching into the Mediterranean Sea between the Adriatic and Aegean seas, comprising Albania, Bulgaria, Greece, Romania, Turkey-in-Europe, and Yugoslavia. It is joined to the rest of Europe by an isthmus 750 mi/1,200 km wide between Rijeka on the W and the mouth of the Danube on the Black Sea to the E.

The Balkans is a byword for political dissension historically, a tendency fostered by the great ethnic diversity resulting from successive waves of invasion. The Balkans' economy developed comparatively slowly until after World War II, largely because of the predominantly mountainous terrain, apart from the plains of the Save-Danube basin in the N. Political differences have remained strong—for example, the confrontation of Greece and Turkey over Cyprus, and the differing types of Communism prevailing in the rest—but in the later years of the 20th century a tendency to regional union emerged. To "Balkanize" is to divide into small warring states.

Balkan Wars two wars 1912–13 and 1913 (preceding World War I) which resulted in the expulsion by the Balkan states of Ottoman Turkey from Europe, except for a small area around Istanbul.
The First Balkan War, 1912, of Bulgaria, ◊Serbia, Greece, and Montenegro against Turkey, forced the Turks to ask for an armistice, but the London-held peace negotiations broke down when the Turks, while agreeing to surrender all Turkey-in-Europe W of the city of Edirne (formerly Adrianople), refused to give up the city itself. In Feb 1913 hostilities were resumed. Edirne fell on March 26 and on May 30, by the Treaty of London, Turkey retained in Europe only a small piece of E Thrace and the Gallipoli peninsula.
The Second Balkan War, June–July 1913, took place when the victors fought over acquisitions in Macedonia, from most of which Bulgaria was excluded. Bulgaria attacked Greece and Serbia, which were joined by Romania. Bulgaria was defeated, and Turkey retained Thrace.

Balkhash salt lake in Kazakhstan, USSR; area 6,678 sq mi/17,300 sq km. It is 375 mi/600 km long, receives several rivers, but has no outlet. Very shallow, it is frozen throughout the winter.

Ballesteros *Golfer Seve Ballesteros at the British Open, 1988.*

Balkhash town on the N shore of Lake Balkhash in Kazhakstan, USSR; population (1985) 112,000. It was founded 1928. Chief industries include copper mining and salt extraction.

Ball John English priest, one of the leaders of the ◊Peasants" Revolt 1381, known as "the mad priest of Kent." A follower of John Wycliffe and a believer in social equality, he was imprisoned for disagreeing with the archbishop of Canterbury. During the revolt he was released from prison, and when in Blackheath, London, preached from the text "When Adam delved and Eve span, who was then the gentleman?" When the revolt collapsed he escaped but was captured near Coventry and executed.

Ball Lucille 1911–1989. US comedy actress, famed as TV's Lucy. She began her film career as a bit player 1933, and appeared in dozens of movies over the next few years, including *Room Service* 1938 (with the Marx Brothers) and *Fancy Pants* 1950 with Bob Hope. From 1951 to 1957 she starred with her husband, Cuban bandleader Desi Arnaz, in *I Love Lucy*,the first US television show filmed before an audience. It was followed by *The Lucy Show* 1962–68 and *Here's Lucy* 1968–74.

Her TV success limited her film output after 1950; her later films include *Mame* 1974. The television series are still shown in many countries.

ballad (Latin *ballare* "to dance") type of popular poem that tells a story. Of simple metrical form and dealing with some strongly emotional event, the ballad is halfway between the lyric and the epic. Most English ballads date from the 15th century. Poets of the Romantic movement both in England and in Germany were greatly influenced by the ballad revival, as seen in, for example, the *Lyrical Ballads* 1798 of Wordsworth and Coleridge. Other later forms are the "broadsheets" with a satirical or political motive, and the testamentary "hanging" ballads of the condemned criminal.

Historically, the ballad was primarily intended for singing at the communal ring-dance, the refrains representing the chorus. Opinion is divided as to whether the authorship of the ballads may be attributed to individual poets or to the community. Later ballads tend to center on a popular folk hero, such as Robin Hood or Jesse James.

ballet *Portrait of the 18th-century ballet dancer Marie-Anne de Cupis de Camargo, by Nicholas Lancret.*

In 19th-century music the refined drawing-room ballad had a vogue, but a more robust tradition survived in the music hall; folk song played its part in the development of pop music, and in this genre slow songs are often called "ballads" regardless of content.

ballade in music, an instrumental piece based on a story; a form used in piano works by ◊Chopin and ◊Liszt. In literature, a poetic form developed in France in the later Middle Ages from the ballad, generally consisting of one or more groups of three stanzas of seven or eight lines each, followed by a shorter stanza or envoy, the last line being repeated as a chorus.

Ballance John 1839–1893. New Zealand politician, born in Northern Ireland; prime minister 1891–93. He emigrated to New Zealand, founded and edited the *Wanganui Herald*, and held many cabinet posts.

ball and socket joint a joint allowing considerable movement in three dimensions, for instance the joint between the pelvis and the femur. To facilitate movement, such joints are lubricated by cartilage and synovial fluid. The bones are kept in place by ligaments and moved by muscles.

Ballarat town in Victoria, Australia; population (1986) 75,200. It was founded in the 1851 gold rush, and the mining village and workings have been restored for tourists. The Eureka Stockade miners' revolt took place here 1854.

Ballard J(ames) G(raham) 1930– . British novelist whose works include science fiction on the theme of disaster, such as *The Drowned World* 1962 and *High-Rise* 1975, and the partly autobiographical *Empire of the Sun* 1984, dealing with his internment in China during World War II.

Ballesteros Seve(riano) 1957– . Spanish golfer who came to prominence 1976 and has won several leading tournaments in the US, including the Masters Tournament. He has also won the British Open three times: in 1979, 1984, and 1988.

CAREER HIGHLIGHTS

British Open: 1979, 1984, 1988
US Masters: 1980, 1983
World Match-play: 1981–82, 1984–85

ballet (Italian *balletto* "a little dance") a theatrical representation in dance form in which music also plays a major part in telling a story or conveying a mood. Some such form of entertainment existed in ancient Greece, but Western ballet as we know it today first appeared in Italy. From there it was brought by Catherine de ◊Médici to France in the form of a spectacle combining singing, dancing, and declamation. In the 20th century Russian ballet has had a vital influence on the Classical tradition in the West, and modern ballet has developed in the US through the work of George ◊Balanchine and Martha ◊Graham, and in the UK through the influence of Marie ◊Rambert.

history The first important dramatic ballet, the *Ballet comique de la reine*, was produced 1581 by the Italian Balthasar de Beaujoyeux at the French court and was performed by male courtiers, with ladies of the court forming the *corps de ballet*. In 1661 Louis XIV founded *L'Académie royale de danse*, to which all subsequent ballet activities throughout the world can be traced. Long, flowing court dress was worn by the dancers until the 1720s when Marie-Anne Camargo, the first great ballerina, shortened her skirt to reveal her feet, thus allowing greater movement *à terre* and the development of dancing *en l'air*. It was not until the early 19th century that a Paris costumier, Maillot, invented tights, thus allowing complete muscular freedom. The first of the great ballet masters was J-G ◊Noverre, and great contemporary dancers were Vestris, Heinel, Dauberval, and Gardel. Carlo Blasis is regarded as the founder of Classical ballet, since he defined the standard conventional steps and accompanying gestures.

Romantic ballet The great Romantic era of ◊Taglioni, Elssler, Grisi, Grahn, and Cerrito began about 1830 but survives today only in the ballets *Giselle* 1841 and *La Sylphide* 1832. Characteristics of this era were the new calf-length Classical white dress and the introduction of dancing on the toes, *sur les pointes*. The technique of the female dancer was developed, but the role of the male dancer was reduced to that of her partner.

Russian ballet was introduced to the West by ◊Diaghilev, who set out for Paris 1909, at about the same time that Isadora ◊Duncan, a rigid opponent of Classical ballet, was touring Europe. Associated with Diaghilev were Fokine, Nijinsky, Pavlova, Massine, Balanchine, and Lifar. Ballets presented by his company, before its break-up after his death 1929, included *Les Sylphides*, *Schéhérazade*, *Petrouchka*, and *Blue Train*. Diaghilev and Fokine pioneered a new and exciting combination of the perfect technique of imperial Russian dancers and the appealing naturalism favored by Isadora Duncan. In the USSR ballet continues to flourish, the two chief companies being the Kirov and the Bolshoi. Best-known ballerinas are Ulanova and Plisetskaya.

Male dancers including Rudolf Nureyev, Mikhail Baryshnikov, and Alexander Godunov are now dancing in the West, as are the husband-and-wife team Vyacheslav Gordeyev and Nadezhda Pavlova.

American ballet was firmly established by the founding of Balanchine's School of American Ballet 1934, and by de Basil's Ballets Russes de Monte Carlo and Massine's Ballet Russe de Monte Carlo, which also carried on the Diaghilev tradition. Since 1948 the New York City Ballet with dancers such as Maria Tallchief, Edward Villella, and Nora Kaye, and choreographers Jerome Robbins and Peter Martins, under the guiding influence of Balanchine, has developed a genuine American classic style.

British ballet Marie Rambert initiated in 1926 the company that developed into the Ballet Rambert, but the national company, the Royal Ballet (so named 1956), grew from foundations laid by Ninette de Valois and Frederick Ashton 1928. British dancers include Margot Fonteyn, Beryl Grey, Alicia Markova, Anton Dolin, Antoinette Sibley, and Anthony Dowell; choreographers include Kenneth MacMillan.

ballet blanc (French "white ballet") a ballet, such as *Giselle*, in which the female dancers wear calf-length white dresses. The costume was introduced by Marie ◊Taglioni in *La Sylphide* 1832.

ballet d'action a ballet with a plot, developed by ◊Noverre in the 18th century.

ballistics study of the motion and impact of projectiles such as bullets, bombs, and missiles. For

the ballet repertory

date	*ballet*	*composer*	*choreographer*	*place*
1670	*Le Bourgeois Gentilhomme*	Lully	Beauchamp	Chambord
1735	*Les Indes Galantes*	Rameau	Blondy	Paris
1761	*Don Juan*	Gluck	Angiolini	Vienna
1778	*Les Petits Riens*	Mozart	Noverre	Paris
1801	*The Creatures of Prometheus*	Beethoven	Viganò	Vienna
1828	*La Fille Mal Gardée*	Hérold	Aumer	Paris
1832	*La Sylphide*	Schneitzhoeffer	F. Taglioni	Paris
1841	*Giselle*	Adam	Coralli/Perrot	Paris
1842	*Napoli*	Gade/Paulli Helsted/Lumbye	Bournonville	Copenhagen
1844	*La Esmeralda*	Pugni	Perrot	London
1869	*Don Quixote*	Minkus	M. Petipa	Moscow
1870	*Coppélia*	Delibes	Saint-Léon	Paris
1876	*Sylvia*	Delibes	Mérante	Paris
1877	*La Bayadère*	Minkus	M. Petipa	St Petersburg
1877	*Swan Lake*	Tchaikovsky	Reisinger	Moscow
1882	*Namouna*	Lalo	L. Petipa	Paris
1890	*The Sleeping Beauty*	Tchaikovsky	M. Petipa	St Petersburg
1892	*Nutcracker*	Tchaikovsky	M. Petipa/Ivanov	St Petersburg
1898	*Raymonda*	Glazunov	M. Petipa	St Petersburg
1905	*The Dying Swan*	Saint-Saëns	Fokine	St Petersburg
1907	*Les Sylphides*	Chopin	Fokine	St Petersburg
1910	*Carnival*	Schumann	Fokine	St Petersburg
1910	*The Firebird*	Stravinsky	Fokine	Paris
1911	*Petrushka*	Stravinsky	Fokine	Paris
1911	*Le Spectre de la Rose*	Weber	Fokine	Monte Carlo
1912	*L'Après-midi d'un Faune*	Debussy	Nijinsky	Paris
1912	*Daphnis and Chloë*	Ravel	Fokine	Paris
1913	*Jeux*	Debussy	Nijinsky	Paris
1913	*The Rite of Spring*	Stravinsky	Nijinsky	Paris
1915	*El Amor Brujo*	Falla	Imperio	Madrid
1917	*Parade*	Satie	Massine	Paris
1919	*La Boutique Fantasque*	Rossini/Respighi	Massine	London
1919	*The Three-Cornered Hat*	Falla	Massini	London
1923	*The Creation of the World*	Milhaud	Börlin	Paris
1923	*Les Noces*	Stravinsky	Nijinska	Paris
1924	*Les Biches*	Poulenc	Nijinska	Monte Carlo
1927	*The Red Poppy*	Glière	Lashchilin/Tikhomirov	Moscow
1928	*Apollon Musagète*	Stravinsky	Balanchine	Paris
1928	*Le Baiser de la fée*	Tchaikovsky	Nijinska	Paris
1928	*Bolero*	Ravel	Nijinska	Paris
1929	*The Prodigal Son*	Prokofiev	Balanchine	Paris
1929	*La Valse*	Ravel	Nijinska	Monte Carlo
1931	*Bacchus and Ariadne*	Roussel	Lifar	Paris
1931	*Façade*	Walton	Ashton	London
1931	*Job*	Vaughan Williams	de Valois	London
1937	*Checkmate*	Bliss	de Valois	Paris
1937	*Les Patineurs*	Meyerbeer/Lambert	Ashton	London
1938	*Billy the Kid*	Copland	Loring	Chicago
1938	*Gaîté Parisienne*	Offenbach/Rosenthal	Massine	Monte Carlo
1938	*Romeo and Juliet*	Prokofiev	Psota	Brno, Moravia
1942	*Gayaneh*	Khachaturian	Anisimova	Molotov-Perm
1942	*The Miraculous Mandarin*	Bartók	Milloss	Milan
1942	*Rodeo*	Copland	de Mille	New York
1944	*Appalachian Spring*	Copland	Graham	Washington
1944	*Fancy Free*	Bernstein	Robbins	New York
1945	*Cinderella*	Prokofiev	Zakharov	Moscow
1949	*Carmen*	Bizet	Petit	London
1951	*Pineapple Poll*	Sullivan/Mackerras	Cranko	London
1956	*Spartacus*	Khachaturian	Jacobson	Leningrad
1957	*Agon*	Stravinsky	Balanchine	New York
1959	*Episodes*	Webern	Balanchine	New York
1962	*A Midsummer Night's Dream*	Mendelssohn	Balanchine	New York
1962	*Pierrot Lunaire*	Schoenberg	Tetley	New York
1964	*The Dream*	Mendelssohn/Lanchbery	Ashton	London
1965	*The Song of the Earth*	Mahler	MacMillan	Stuttgart
1967	*Anastasia*	Martinu	MacMillan	New York
1968	*Enigma Variations*	Elgar	Ashton	London
1969	*The Taming of the Shrew*	Stolze/Scarlatti	Cranko	Stuttgart
1972	*Duo Concertante*	Stravinsky	Balanchine	New York
1974	*Elite Syncopations*	Joplin, etc.	MacMillan	London
1976	*A Month in the Country*	Chopin/Lanchbery	Ashton	London
1978	*Mayerling*	Liszt/Lanchbery	MacMillan	London
1978	*Symphony of Psalms*	Stravinsky	Kylian	Scheveningen, The Netherlands
1980	*Gloria*	Poulenc	MacMillan	London
1980	*Rhapsody*	Rachmaninov	Ashton	London

projectiles from a gun, relevant exterior factors include temperature, barometric pressure, and wind strength; and for nuclear missiles these extend to such factors as the speed at which the Earth turns.

balloon lighter-than-air craft that consists of a gasbag filled with gas lighter than the surrounding air and an attached basket, or gondola, for carrying passengers and/or instruments. The first successful human ascent was in Paris, in 1783, in a hot-air balloon designed by the ◊Montgolfier brothers; this was the first-ever aerial voyage. In 1785, a hydrogen-filled balloon designed by J A C Charles traveled across the English Channel. Coal gas was substituted as a cheap alternative to hydrogen in 1821, and this allowed for voyages by later 19th-century and early 20th-century explorers, scientists, and fairground performers. By the 1920s and 1930s balloons were used for high-altitude scientific research, especially before the development of high-altitude aircraft and Earth-orbiting satellites; for other kinds of research and exploration they were found to be generally unreliable, since they cannot be guided but go where the wind blows. They have become popular for sport and continue in use as instrument-only observers for meteorology, and for monitoring infrared, ultraviolet, and gamma rays.

ballroom dancing collective term for social dances such as the ◊foxtrot, quickstep, ◊tango, and ◊waltz.

ball valve valve that works by the action of external pressure raising a ball and thereby opening a hole. An example is the valve used in toilet water tanks to cut off the water supply when it reaches the correct level. It consists of a flat rubber washer at one end of a pivoting arm and a hollow ball at the other. The ball floats on the water surface, rising as the tank fills, and at the correct level the rubber washer is pushed against the water-inlet pipe, cutting off the flow.

Balmer Johann 1825–1898. Swiss physicist and mathematician who developed a formula that gave the wavelengths of the hydrogen atom spectrum. This simple formula played a central role in the development of spectral theory.

balm, lemon garden herb, see ◊lemon balm.

balsam any of various garden plants of the genus *Impatiens* of the balsam family. They are usually annuals with spurred red or white flowers and pods that burst and scatter their seeds when ripe. In medicine and perfumery, balsam refers to various oily or gummy aromatic plant resins, such as balsam of Peru from the Central American tree *Myroxylon pereirae*.

Baltic Sea large shallow arm of the North Sea, extending NE from the narrow Skagerrak and Kattegat, between Sweden and Denmark, to the Gulf of Bothnia between Sweden and Finland. Its coastline is 5,000 mi/8,000 km long, and its area, including the gulfs of Riga, Finland, and Bothnia, is 163,000 sq mi/422,300 sq km. Its shoreline is

Baltic Sea

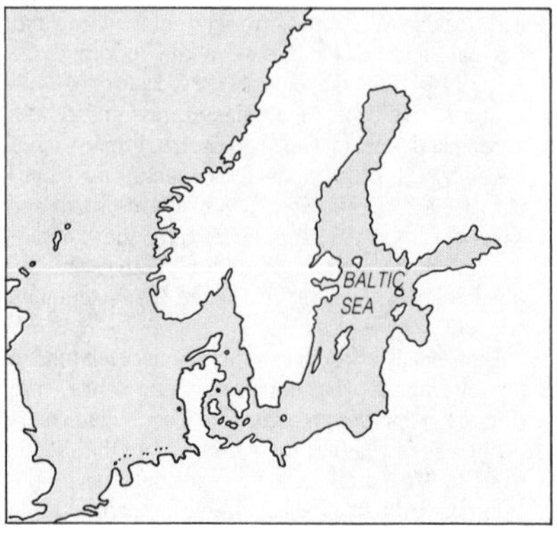
BALTIC
SEA

shared by Denmark, Germany, Poland, the USSR, Finland, and Sweden.

Many large rivers flow into it, including the Oder, Vistula, Niemen, W Dvina, Narva, and Neva. Tides are hardly perceptible, salt content is low; weather is often stormy and navigation dangerous. Most ports are closed by ice from Dec until May. The Kiel canal links the Baltic and North seas; the Göta canal connects the two seas by way of the S Swedish lakes. Since 1975 the Baltic Sea has been linked by the Leningrad–Belomorsk seaway with the White Sea.

Baltic States collective name for the states of ◊Estonia, ◊Latvia, and ◊Lithuania, former constituent republics of the USSR (from 1940). They regained independence Sept 1991.

Baltimore industrial port and largest city in Maryland, on the W shore of Chesapeake Bay, NE of Washington, DC; population (1990) 736,014. Industries include shipbuilding, oil refining, food processing, and the manufacture of steel, chemicals, and aerospace equipment. It is the seat of Johns Hopkins University. The inner harbor area has the National Aquarium, a 30-story World Trade Center, and the first commissioned warship of the US Navy, dating from 1797.

It was named after the founder of Maryland, Lord Baltimore (1606–1675). The city of Baltimore dates from 1729 and was incorporated 1797. At Fort McHenry, Francis Scott Key wrote *The Star Spangled Banner*. The writer Edgar Allan Poe and the baseball player Babe Ruth lived here.

Baltistan a region in the Karakoram range of NE Kashmir held by Pakistan since 1949. It is the home of Balti Muslims of Tibetan origin. The chief town is Skardu, but Ghyari is of greater significance to Muslims as the site of a mosque built by Sayyid Ali Hamadani, a Persian who brought the Shia Muslim religion to Baltistan in the 14th century.

Baluch or ***Baluchi*** native to or an inhabitant of Baluchistan, a region in SW Pakistan and SE Iran on the Arabian Sea. Their common religion is Islam, and they speak Baluchi, a member of the Iranian branch of the Indo-European language family.

Much of Baluchistan is rugged and mountainous, and in the drier areas the Baluchis make use of tents, moving when it becomes too arid. Although they practice nomadic pastoralism, many are settled agriculturalists.

Baluchistan mountainous desert area, comprising a province of Pakistan, part of the Iranian province of Sistán and Balúchestan, and a small area of Afghanistan. The Pakistani province has an area of 134,019 sq mi/347,200 sq km and a population (1985) of 4,908,000; its capital is Quetta. Sistán and Balúchestan has an area of 70,098 sq mi/181,600 sq km and a population (1986) of 1,197,000; its capital is Zahedan. The port of Gwadar in Pakistan is strategically important, on the Indian Ocean and the Strait of Hormuz.

history Originally a loose tribal confederation, Baluchistan was later divided into four principalities that were sometimes under Persian, sometimes under Afghan suzerainty. In the 19th century British troops tried to subdue the inhabitants until a treaty in 1876 gave them autonomy in exchange for British army outposts along the Afghan border and strategic roads. On the partition of India 1947 the khan of Khalat declared Baluchistan independent; the insurrection was crushed by the new Pakistani army after eight months. Three rebellions followed, the last being from 1973 to 1977, when 3,300 Pakistani soldiers and some 6,000 Baloch were killed.

Balzac *French novelist Honoré de Balzac planned to depict every aspect of French life in* La Comédie humaine, *but only managed to complete about 80 of the planned 143 volumes.*

Balzac Honoré de 1799–1850. French novelist. His first success was *Les Chouans/The Chouans* and *La Physiologie du mariage/The Physiology of Marriage* 1829, inspired by Scott. This was the beginning of the long series of novels *La Comédie humaine/The* ◊Human Comedy. He also wrote the Rabelaisian *Contes drolatiques/Ribald Tales* 1833.

Born in Tours, Balzac studied law and worked as a notary's clerk in Paris before turning to literature. His first attempts included tragedies such as *Cromwell* and novels published pseudonymously with no great success. A venture in printing and publishing 1825–28 involved him in a lifelong web of debt. His patroness, Madame de Berny, figures in *Le Lys dans la vallée/The Lily in the Valley* 1836. Balzac intended his major work *La Comédie humaine/The Human Comedy* to comprise 143 volumes, depicting every aspect of society in 19th-century France, but he only managed to complete 80. The series includes *Eugénie Grandet* 1833, *Le Père Goriot* 1834, and *Cousine Bette* 1846. Balzac corresponded constantly with the Polish countess Evelina Hanska after meeting her in 1833, but they married only four months before his death in Paris. He was buried in Père Lachaise cemetery.

Bamako capital and port of Mali on the river Niger; population (1976) 404,022. It produces pharmaceuticals, chemicals, textiles, tobacco, and metal products.

Bamberg town in Bavaria, Germany, on the river Regnitz; population (1985) 70,400. The economy is based on engineering and the production of textiles, carpets, and electrical goods. It has an early 13th-century Romanesque cathedral.

bamboo any of numerous plants of the subgroup Bambuseae within the grass family Gramineae, mainly found in tropical and subtropical countries. Some species grow as tall as 120 ft/36 m. The stems are hollow and jointed and can be used in furniture, house, and boat construction. The young shoots are edible; paper is made from the stem.

Banaba (formerly Ocean Island) island in the Republic of ◊Kiribati.

banana any treelike tropical plant of the genus *Musa* of the family Musaceae, which grow up to 25 ft/8 m high. The edible banana is the fruit of a sterile hybrid form.

The curved yellow fruits of the commercial banana, arranged in rows of "hands," form cylindrical masses of a hundred or more, and are exported green and ripened aboard refrigerated ships. The plant is destroyed after cropping. The plantain, a larger, coarser hybrid variety that is used green as a cooked vegetable, is a dietary staple in many countries. In the wild, bananas depend on bats for pollination.

Banaras alternative transliteration of ◊Varanasi, holy Hindu city in Uttar Pradesh, India.

Banda *Hastings Banda, first president of Malawi.*

Banca alternate form of the Indonesian island ◊Banka.

Bancroft George 1800–1891. US diplomat and historian. A Democrat, he was secretary of the navy 1845 when he established the US Naval Academy at Annapolis, Maryland, and as acting secretary of war (May 1846) was instrumental in bringing about the occupation of California and the ◊Mexican war. He wrote a *History of the United States* 1834–76.

band music group, usually falling into a special category: for example, military, comprising woodwind, brass, and percussion; brass, solely of brass and percussion; marching, a variant of brass; dance, often like a small orchestra; jazz and rock and pop, generally electric guitar, bass, and drums variously augmented; and steel, from the West Indies, in which percussion instruments made from oildrums sound like marimbas.

Banda Hastings Kamuzu 1902– . Malawi politican, president from 1966. He led his country's independence movement and was prime minister of Nyasaland (the former name of Malawi) from 1963. He became Malawi's first president in 1966 and in 1971 was named president for life; his rule has been authoritarian.

Bandar Abbas port and winter resort in Iran on the Ormuz strait, Persian Gulf; population (1983) 175,000. Formerly called Gombroon, it was renamed and made prosperous by Shah Abbas I (1571–1629). It is a naval base.

Bandaranaike Sirimavo (born Ratwatte) 1916– . Sri Lankan politician, who succeeded her husband Solomon Bandaranaike to become the world's first female prime minister 1960–65 and 1970–77, but was expelled from parliament 1980 for abuse of her powers while in office. She was largely responsible for the new constitution 1972.

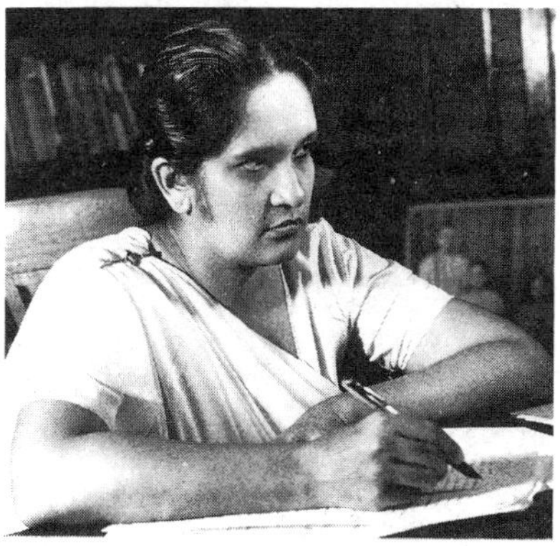

Bandaranaike *In 1960 Sirimavo Bandaranaike of Sri Lanka became the world's first woman prime minister.*

bandicoot

Bandaranaike Solomon West Ridgeway Dias 1899–1959. Sri Lankan nationalist politician. In 1951 he founded the Sri Lanka Freedom party and in 1956 became prime minister, pledged to a Socialist program and a neutral foreign policy. He failed to satisfy extremists and was assassinated by a Buddhist monk.

Bandar Seri Begawan formerly Brunei Town capital of Brunei; population (1983) 57,558.

Bandar Shah port in Iran on the Caspian Sea, and northern terminus of the Trans-Iranian railroad.

bandicoot small marsupial mammal inhabiting Australia and New Guinea. There are about 11 species, family Peramelidae, rat- or rabbit-sized and living in burrows. They have long snouts, eat insects, and are nocturnal. A related group, the rabbit bandicoots or bilbys, is reduced to a single species that is now endangered and protected by law.

Band, The North American rock group 1961–76. They acquired their name when working as Bob Dylan's backing band, and made their solo debut 1968 with *Music from Big Pink*. Their unostentatious ensemble playing and strong original material set a new trend.

Formed in Canada as a backing group for the US rock-and-roll singer Ronnie Hawkins (1935–) and initially known as the Hawks, they took up with Dylan in 1965, touring and recording with him intermittently over the next ten years. *The Band* 1969, *Stage Fright* 1970, and *Northern Lights—Southern Cross* 1975 were all outstanding albums. In their appearance and mysterious lyrics they often evoked a bygone age, as in the song "The Night They Drove Old Dixie Down." Their farewell concert was filmed by Martin Scorsese as *The Last Waltz* 1978.

Bandung commercial city and capital of Jawa Barat province on the island of Java, Indonesia; population (1980) 1,463,000. Bandung is the third-largest city in Indonesia and was the administrative center when the country was the Netherlands East Indies.

Bandung Conference the first conference 1955 of the Afro-Asian nations, proclaiming anticolonialism and neutrality between East and West.

bandy-bandy venomous Australian snake *Vermicella annulata* of the cobra family, which grows to about 2.5 ft/75 cm. It is banded in black and white. It is not aggressive toward humans.

Banff resort city in Alberta, Canada, 62 mi/100 km NW of Calgary; population (1984) 4,246. It is a center for Banff National Park (Canada's first, founded 1885) in the Rocky Mountains.

Bangalore capital of Karnataka state, S India; population (1981) 2,914,000. Industries include electronics, aircraft and machine tools construction, and coffee.

Bangkok capital and port of Thailand, on the river Chao Phraya; population (1987) 5,609,000. Products include paper, ceramics, cement, textiles, and aircraft. It is the headquarters of the South-East Asia Treaty Organization (SEATO).

Bangkok was established as the capital by Phra Chao Tak 1769, after the Burmese had burned down the former capital, Avuthia, about 40 mi/65 km to the N. Features include the temple of the Emerald Buddha and the vast palace complex.

Bangkok *The Royal Palace, Bangkok, contains within its walls some fine temples, including the Chapel Royal of the Emerald Buddha.*

Bangladesh country in S Asia, bounded N, W, and E by India, SE by Myanmar, and S by the Bay of Bengal.

government The 1972 constitution, providing parliamentary democracy, was suspended 1982 after a military coup by Lt-Gen Ershad, who governed first as chief martial law administrator and then, from 1983, as president with an appointed council of ministers. A move back to civilian rule began 1983–85 with local elections, and in 1986 the constitution was revived, with martial law lifted Nov.

At the head of the present system is an executive president, popularly elected for a five-year term by universal suffrage, who serves as head of state and head of the armed forces, appointing cabinet ministers and judicial officers; the head of government is the prime minister. There is also a single-chamber legislative parliament *Jatiya Sangsad*, composed of 300 members directly elected for five-year terms from single-member constituencies and 30 women elected by the legislature itself.

history For history before 1947 see ◊India; for history 1947–1971 see ◊Pakistan. Present-day Bangladesh formerly comprised E Bengal province and Sylhet district of Assam in British India. Predominantly Muslim, it was formed into the eastern province of Pakistan when India was partitioned 1947. Substantially different in culture, language, and geography from the western provinces of Pakistan 1,000 miles away and with a larger population, it resented the political and military dominance exerted by W Pakistan during the 1950s and 1960s. A movement for political autonomy grew after 1954, under the Awami League headed by Sheik Mujibur Rahman. This gained strength as a result of W Pakistan's indifference 1970, when flooding killed 500,000 in E Pakistan.

In Pakistan's first general elections 1970 the Awami League gained an overwhelming victory in E Pakistan and an overall majority in the all-Pakistan National Assembly. Talks on redrawing the constitution broke down, leading to E Pakistan's secession and the establishment of a Bangladesh ("Bengal Nation") government in exile in Calcutta (India) 1971. Civil war resulted in the flight of 10 million E Pakistani refugees to India, administrative breakdown, famine, and cholera. The W Pakistani forces in E Pakistan surrendered 1971 after India intervened on the secessionists' side. A republic of Bangladesh was proclaimed and rapidly gained international recognition 1972.

Sheik Mujibur Rahman became prime minister 1972 under a secular, parliamentary constitution. He introduced a Socialist economic program of nationalization but became intolerant of opposition, establishing a one-party presidential system Jan 1975. In Aug 1975 Sheik Mujibur Rahman, his wife, and close relatives were assassinated in a military coup. The Awami League held power for three months under Khandakar Mushtaq Ahmed before a further military coup Nov 1975 established as president and chief martial law administrator the nonpolitical chief justice Abu Sadat Mohammed Sayem.

In 1976, Maj-Gen Zia ur-Rahman (1936–1981) became chief martial law administrator. Becoming president 1977, he adopted an Islamic constitution, approved by a national referendum in May. In June he won a 4:1 majority in a direct presidential election. Zia's newly formed Bangladeshi Nationalist Party won a parliamentary majority. A civilian government was installed, and martial law and the state of emergency were lifted 1979. The administration was undermined, however, by charges of corruption and by a guerrilla movement in Chittagong 1980. On May 30, 1981 Zia was assassinated in an attempted coup, and interim power was assumed by Vice President Justice Abdus Sattar.

With disorder increasing, the civilian administration was overthrown March 1982 by a coup led by Lt-Gen Mohammad Hussain Ershad (1930–). Martial law was reimposed, and political activity banned. The economy improved and in 1983 a broad opposition coalition, the Movement for the Restoration of Democracy, was formed. Lt-Gen Ershad promised presidential and parliamentary elections 1984, but both were canceled after an opposition threat of a boycott and campaign of civil disobedience if martial law was not first lifted.

In Jan 1986 the ban on political activity was removed, and parliamentary elections were held in May. The Awami League agreed to participate in these elections, but the Bangladesh National Party and many other opposition parties boycotted them. With a campaign marked by violence, widespread abstentions, and claims of ballot-rigging Lt-Gen Ershad and his Jatiya Front party gained the two-thirds majority required to pass a law granting retrospective immunity. In Oct 1986 Ershad was re-elected president in a direct election, and in Nov 1986 martial law was lifted.

During 1987 the opposition Awami League, led by Sheika Hasina Wazed (the daughter of Sheik Mujibur Rahman), and the Bangladesh National Party, led by Begum Khalida Zia (the widow of Maj-Gen Zia ur-Rahman), stepped up their campaign against the Ershad government, demanding the president's resignation and free elections. In the wake of a wave of violent strikes and demonstrations, Ershad proclaimed a state of emergency in Nov 1987. A month later, parliament was dissolved and fresh elections called in March 1988. As a result of both ballot rigging and an opposition boycott, the ruling *Jatiya Dal* gained a sweeping victory. The state of emergency was lifted April 1988, and a bill was passed by parliament June 1988 making Islam the state religion.

In Sept 1988 Bangladesh received the heaviest monsoon rains in 70 years; in the resulting floods several thousand people died and 30 million became homeless. An April 1991 cyclone killed about 140,000 and left 4–10 million homeless.

In June 1989, constitutional amendments were also passed restricting the president to two elected five-year terms and creating the post of elected vice-president.

Bangladesh

People's Republic of
(Gana Prajatantri Bangladesh)
(formerly East Pakistan)

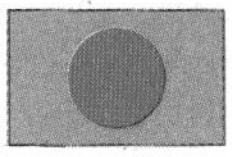

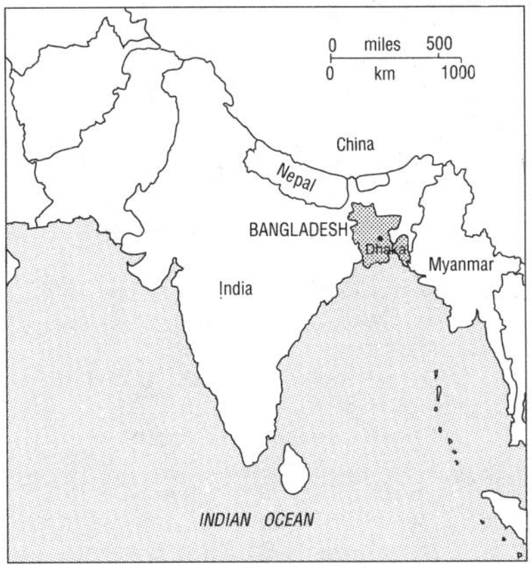
0 miles 500
0 km 1000
China
Nepal
BANGLADESH
Dhaka
Myanmar
India
INDIAN OCEAN

area 55,585 sq mi/144,000 sq km
capital Dhaka (formerly Dacca)
cities ports Chittagong, Khulna
physical flat delta of rivers Ganges (Padma)and Brahmaputra (Jamuna), the largest estuarine delta in the world; annual rainfall of 100 in/2,540 mm; some 75% of the land is less than 10 ft/3 m above sea level and vulnerable to flooding and cyclones; hilly in extreme SE and NE
features tribal cultures with a population of just over 1 million occupy the tropical Chittagong Hill Tracts, Mymensingh and Sylhet districts
head of state Shahabuddin Ahmad (interim president) from Dec 1990
head of government Khaleda Zia from 1991
political system restricted democratic republic
political parties Jatiya Dal (National Party), Islamic nationalist; Awami League, secular, moderate Socialist; Bangladesh National Party (BNP), Islamic right-of-center
exports jute, tea, garments, fish products
currency taka
population (1990 est) 117,980,000; growth rate 2.7% p.a.
life expectancy men 50, women 52
language Bangla (Bengali)
religion Sunni Muslim 85%, Hindu 14%
literacy men 43%/women 22% (1985 est)
GDP $17.6 bn (1987); $172 per head
chronology
1947 Formed into eastern province of Pakistan on partition of British India.
1970 Half a million killed in flood.
1971 Bangladesh emerged as independent nation, under leadership of Sheik Mujibur Rahman, after civil war.
1975 Mujibur Rahman assassinated. Martial law imposed.
1976–77 Maj Gen Zia ur-Rahman assumed power.
1978–79 Elections held and civilian rule restored.
1981 Assassination of Maj Gen Zia.
1982 Lt Gen Ershad assumed power in army coup. Martial law imposed.
1986 Elections held but disputed. Martial law ended.
1987 State of emergency declared in response to opposition demonstrations.
1988 Assembly elections boycotted by main opposition parties. State of emergency lifted. Islam made state religion. Monsoon floods and cyclone left 35 million homeless and thousands dead.
1989 Power devolved to Chittagong Hill Tracts to end 14-year conflict between local people and army-protected settlers.
1990 Following mass antigovernment protests, President Hussain Mohammad Ershad resigned; replaced by Shahabuddin Ahmad pending elections.
1991 Parliamentary elections held; coalition government formed with BNP dominant. Worst cyclone in country's history left 10 million homeless. Former president Ershad jailed for 10 years.

On Dec 4, 1990, following a protracted opposition-led campaign for the government's removal, Hussain Mohammad Ershad resigned as president and the former prime minister, Kazi Zafar Ahmad, went into hiding. The state of emergency was lifted, parliament dissolved, and Ershad was replaced by Shahabuddin Ahmad, the country's chief justice. Immediately, the new president set about removing Ershad-installed personnel from key positions in the military and bureaucracy.

In foreign affairs, Bangladesh has remained a member of the ◊Commonwealth since 1972. It has been heavily dependent on foreign economic aid but has pursued a broader policy of the ◊nonaligned movement.

Bangui capital and port of the Central African Republic, on the River Ubangi; population (1988) 597,000. Industries include beer, cigarettes, office machinery, and timber and metal products.

Banjermasin river port in Indonesia, on Borneo; population (1980) 381,300. It is the capital of Kalimantan Selatan province. It exports rubber, timber, and precious stones. The university was founded 1960.

banjo resonant stringed musical instrument, with a long fretted neck and circular drum-type sound box covered on the topside only by stretched skin (now usually plastic). It is played with a plectrum.

The banjo originated in the American South among black slaves (based on a similar instrument of African origin).

Banjul capital and chief port of Gambia, on an island at the mouth of the river Gambia; population (1983) 44,536. It was known as Bathurst until 1973. It was established as a settlement for freed slaves in 1816.

bank a financial institution that uses funds deposited with it to lend money to companies or individuals, and which also provides financial services to its customers.

A central bank (in the US, the ◊Federal Reserve) issues currency for the government, to provide cash for circulation and exchange. A savings bank serves personal accounts and is licensed by the state in which it and its branches may operate. A commercial bank may have branches throughout the nation, since it services businesses, and sometimes becomes an international institution. There are also various forms of both public and private savings and loan companies that are called banks.

Banka or ***Bang Ka*** island in Indonesia off the E coast of Sumatra
area 4,600 sq mi/12,000 sq km
capital Pangkalpinang
cities Mintok (port)
products tin (one of the world's largest producers)
population (1970) 300,000.

Bank for International Settlements (BIS) a bank established 1930 to handle German reparations settlements from World War I. The BIS (based in Basel, Switzerland) is today an important center for economic and monetary research and assists cooperation of the various national central banks. It also has important trustee duties.

The BIS role as liaison among central banks is its primary function today and the reason it has survived several attempts to terminate it. Its place in the international financial world was greatly restricted by the ◊Bretton Woods Conference 1944 and superseded by the International Monetary Fund.

Bankhead Tallulah 1903–1968. US actress, renowned for her wit and flamboyant lifestyle. Her stage appearances include *Dark Victory* 1934, *The Little Foxes* 1939, and *The Skin of Our Teeth* 1942. Her films include Hitchcock's *Lifeboat* 1943.

Bank of England UK central bank founded by Act of Parliament in 1694. It was entrusted with note issue in 1844 and nationalized in 1946. It is banker to the UK government and assists in implementing financial and monetary policies through intervention in financial and foreign exchange markets.

bankruptcy the process by which the property of a person (in legal terms, an individual or corporation) unable to pay debts is taken away under a court order and divided fairly among the person's creditors, after preferential payments such as taxes and wages. Proceedings may be instituted either by the debtor (voluntary bankruptcy) or by any creditor for a substantial sum (involuntary bankruptcy). Until "discharged," a bankrupt is severely restricted in financial activities.

Federal law distinguishes between complete bankruptcy and protection of the assets of a legal person for purposes of financial reorganization (commonly referred to as Chapter 11 bankruptcy).

Banks Joseph 1744–1820. British naturalist and explorer. He accompanied Capt James ◊Cook on his voyage round the world 1768–71 and brought back 3,600 plants, 1,400 of them never before classified. The *Banksia* genus of shrubs is named after him.

A founder and unofficial first director of the Botanical Gardens, Kew, Banks was president of the Royal Society from 1778 to 1819.

Banks Nathaniel Prentiss 1816–1894. US politician and Civil War general. Born in Waltham, Massachusetts, Banks was elected to the state legislature and US House of Representatives, serving as Speaker of the House 1854–57. He resigned to serve as Massachusetts governor 1857–60. At the outbreak of the Civil War, he was appointed major general in command of the Department of Annapolis. Defeated by Stonewall Jackson in the Shenandoah Valley, he was sent to New Orleans 1863 and took command of the Department of the Gulf. He led the ill-fated 1864 Red River expedition. After the war, he served in Congress until 1891.

Banksia genus of shrubs and trees, family Proteaceae, native to Australia. They have spiny evergreen leaves and include the honeysuckle tree.

Bannister Roger Gilbert 1929–. English track and field athlete, the first person to run a mile in under four minutes. He achieved this feat at Oxford, England, on May 6, 1954 in a time of 3 min 59.4 sec.

Bannockburn a town and battlefield to the S of Stirling, central Scotland.

Bannockburn, Battle of battle on June 24, 1314 in which ◊Robert I of Scotland (known as Robert the Bruce) defeated the English under ◊Edward II, who had come to relieve the besieged Stirling Castle.

bantam small variety of domestic chicken. This can either be a small version of one of the large breeds, or a separate type. Some are prolific layers, and bantam cocks have a reputation as spirited fighters.

banteng wild species of cattle *Bos banteng*, now scarce, but formerly ranging from Myanmar (Burma) through SE Asia to Malaysia and Java, inhabiting hilly forests. Its color varies from pale brown to blue-black, usually with white stockings and rump patch, and it is up to 5 ft/1.5 m at the shoulder.

Banting Frederick Grant 1891–1941. Canadian physician who discovered a technique for isolating the hormone insulin in 1921 when, experimentally, he and his colleague Charles ◊Best tied off the ducts of the ◊pancreas to determine the function of the cells known as the islets of Langerhans. This allowed for the treatment of diabetes. Banting and John J R Macleod, his mentor, shared the 1923 Nobel Prize for Medicine, and Banting divided his prize with Best.

Bantu languages group of related languages spoken widely over the greater part of Africa south of the Sahara, including Swahili, Xhosa, and Zulu. Meaning "people" in Zulu, the word Bantu itself illustrates a characteristic use of prefixes: *mu-ntu* "man," *ba-ntu* "people."

The Bantu-speaking peoples probably originated in N Central Africa. Until 1978, the black people of the Republic of South Africa were officially designated Bantu(s).

Bantustan (or homeland) name until 1978 for the ◊Black National States in the Republic of South Africa.

banyan tropical Asian fig tree *Ficus benghalensis* of the family Moraceae. It produces aerial roots that grow down from its spreading branches, forming supporting pillars that have the appearance of separate trunks.

baobab tree *Adansonia digitata*, family Bombacaceae. It has rootlike branches, hence its nickname "upside-down tree," and edible fruit known as monkey bread.

It may live for 1,000 years and is found in Africa and Australia, a relic of the time when both were part of ◊Gondwanaland.

baptism (Greek "to dip") immersion in or sprinkling with water as a religious rite of initiation. It was practiced long before the beginning of Christianity. In the Christian baptism ceremony, sponsors or godparents make vows on behalf of the child, which are renewed by the child at confirmation. It is one of the seven sacraments. The amrit ceremony in Sikhism is sometimes referred to as baptism.

Baptism was universal in the Christian church from the first days, being administered to adults by immersion. The baptism of infants was not practiced until the 2nd century, but became general in the 6th. Baptism by sprinkling (christening) when the child is named is now general among Western Christians, with the exception of some sects (notably the ◊Baptists) where complete immersion of adults is the rule. The Eastern Orthodox Church also practises immersion.

Baptist member of any of several Protestant and evangelical Christian sects that practice baptism by immersion only upon profession of faith. Baptists seek their authority in the Bible. Baptism originated among English Dissenters who took refuge in the Netherlands in the early 17th century, and spread by emigration and, later, missionary activity. Of the world total of approximately 31 million, some 26.5 million are in the US and 265,000 in the UK.

The first Baptist church in America was organized in Rhode Island 1639. Baptism grew rapidly during the Great Awakening religious revival of the 18th century. After the American Revolution, Baptism spread into the South and among blacks, both slave and free. The Southern Baptist Convention remains the largest Protestant denomination in the US. Other Baptists are scattered among the numerous divisions that developed during the last two centuries. In the 19th century Baptism also spread in Europe and to British colonies. Baptists have been among the most active denominations in missionary work.

bar unit of pressure equal to 10^5 pascals or 10^6 dynes/cm^2, approximately 750 mmHg or 0.987 atm. Its diminutive, the millibar (one-thousandth of a bar), is commonly used by meteorologists.

Bara Theda. Adopted name of Theodosia Goodman 1890–1955. US film actress. She was born in Cincinnati, Ohio, and later became "the vamp," the first movie sex symbol and a national celebrity. Appearing first in a silent film entitled *A Fool There Was* 1915, she went on to play a series of sultry roles in the films *Salome*, *Cleopatra*, and

Barbados

USA
ATLANTIC OCEAN
BARBADOS
Bridgetown
Mexico
Cuba
CARIBBEAN SEA
St Vincent
Grenada
Venezuela
PACIFIC OCEAN
0 miles 500
0 km 1000

area 166 sq mi/430 sq km
capital Bridgetown
cities Speightstown, Holetown, Oistins
physical most easterly island of the West Indies; surrounded by coral reefs; subject to hurricanes June–Nov
features highest point Mount Hillaby 1,115 ft/340 m
head of state Elizabeth II from 1966 represented by governor-general Hugh Springer from 1984
head of government prime minister Erskine Lloyd Sandiford from 1987
political system constitutional monarchy
political parties Barbados Labor Party (BLP), moderate left-of-center; Democratic Labor Party (DLP), moderate left-of-center; National Democratic Party (NDP), center
exports sugar, rum, electronic parts, clothing, cement
currency Barbados dollar
population (1990 est) 260,000; growth rate 0.5% p.a.
life expectancy men 70, women 75
language English and Bajan (Barbadian English dialect)
religion 70% Anglican, 9% Methodist, 4% Roman Catholic
literacy 99% (1984)
GDP $1.4 bn (1987); $5,449 per head
chronology
1627 Became British colony; developed as a sugar plantation economy, initially on basis of slavery (slaves freed 1834).
1951 Universal adult suffrage introduced. BLP won general election.
1954 Ministerial government established.
1961 Independence achieved from Britain. DLP, led by Errol Barrow, in power.
1966 Barbados achieved full independence within Commonwealth. Barrow became the new nation's first prime minister.
1972 Diplomatic relations with Cuba established.
1976 BLP, led by Tom Adams, returned to power.
1983 Barbados supported US invasion of Grenada.
1985 Adams died suddenly; Bernard St John became prime minister.
1986 DLP, led by Barrow, returned to power.
1987 Barrow died, succeeded by Erskine Lloyd Sandiford.
1989 New NDP opposition formed.
1991 DLP, under Erskine Sandifield, won general election.

The Vampire, the movie from which the term "vamp" originated. As the most popular star of the Fox studios, Bara made more than 40 films during her relatively brief film career that extended from 1915 to 1920.

After unsuccessfully attempting a career on the Broadway stage, she retired from show business and lived the rest of her life in relative obscurity.

Barabbas in the New Testament, a condemned robber released by Pilate at Passover instead of Jesus to appease a mob.

barb general name for fish of the genus *Barbus* and some related genera of the family Cyprinidae. As well as the ◊barbel, barbs include many small tropical Old World species, some of which are familiar aquarium species. They are active egglaying species, usually of "typical" fish shape and with barbels at the corner of the mouth.

Barbados An island country in the Caribbean, one of the Lesser Antilles, it is about 300 mi/483 km N of Venezuela.

government The bicameral legislature dates from 1627, when the British settled. The constitution dates from 1966 and provides for a system of parliamentary government on the British model, with a prime minister and cabinet drawn from and responsible to the legislature, which consists of a senate and a house of assembly. The senate has 21 members appointed by the governor general, 12 on the advice of the prime minister, two on the advice of the leader of the opposition, and the rest on the basis of wider consultations. The house of assembly has 27 members elected by universal suffrage. The legislature has a maximum life of five years and may be dissolved within this period. The governor general appoints both the prime minister (on the basis of support in the house of assembly) and the leader of the opposition. The two main political parties are the Barbados Labor Party (BLP) and the Democratic Labor Party (DLP).

history Originally inhabited by Arawak Indians, who were wiped out soon after the arrival of the first Europeans, Barbados became a British colony in 1627 and remained so until independence in 1966. Universal adult suffrage was introduced in 1951, and the BLP won the first general election. Ministerial government was established in 1954, and the BLP leader Grantley Adams became the first prime minister. In 1955 a group broke away from the BLP and formed the DLP. Six years later full internal self-government was achieved, and in the 1961 general election the DLP was victorious under its leader, Errol Barrow.

When Barbados attained full independence in 1966, Barrow became its first prime minister. The DLP was re-elected in 1971, but in the 1976 general election the BLP—led now by Grantley Adams's son, Tom—ended Barrow's 15-year rule. Both parties were committed to maintaining free enterprise and alignment with the US, although the DLP government established diplomatic relations with Cuba in 1972 and the BLP administration supported the US invasion of ◊Grenada in 1983.

In 1981 the BLP was re-elected. After Adams's sudden death in 1985 he was succeeded by his deputy Bernard St John, a former BLP leader. In the 1986 general election the DLP, led by Barrow, was returned to power with 24 of the 27 seats in the house of assembly. Errol Barrow died in 1987 and was succeeded by Erskine Lloyd Sandiford. In March 1989, foreign minister James Tudor resigned in the face of charges that diplomatic staff had been involved in drug smuggling.

Barbarossa nickname "red beard" given to the Holy Roman emperor ◊Frederick I, and also to two brothers, Horuk and Khair-ed-Din, who were Barbary pirates. Horuk was killed by the Spaniards 1518; Khair-ed-Din took Tunis 1534 and died in Constantinople 1546.

Barbarossa, operation German code name for the

plans to invade the USSR during World War II in 1941.

Barbary ape tailless yellowish-brown macaque monkey *Macaca sylvanus*, found in the mountains and wilds of Algeria and Morocco. It was introduced to Gibraltar, where legend has it that the British will leave if the colony dies out.

Barbary Coast the North African coast of the Mediterranean Sea (which was named after the ◊Berbers) from which pirates operated against US and European shipping (taking hostages for ransom) in the 16th–19th centuries.

President ◊Jefferson took action against them, sending in the US Navy with the Marines who landed on "the shores of Tripoli."

barbastelle insect-eating bat *Barbastella barbastellus* with "frosted" black fur and a wingspan of about 10 in/25 cm, occasionally found in the UK but more common in Europe.

barbed wire cheap fencing material made of strands of galvanized wire (see ◊galvanizing), twisted together with sharp barbs at close intervals. In 1873 an American, Joseph Glidden, devised a machine to mass-produce barbed wire. Its use on the open grasslands of 19th-century America led to range warfare between farmers and cattle ranchers, used to driving their herds cross-country.

Barber Samuel 1910–1981. US composer with an increasingly dissonant style, whose works include *Adagio for Strings* 1936 and the opera *Vanessa* 1958, which won him one of his two Pulitzer prizes. Another Barber opera, *Antony and Cleopatra* 1966, was commissioned for the opening of the new Metropolitan Opera House at Lincoln Center, New York City. Barber's music represents the romantic and lyric trends in music. His later works include *The Lovers* and *Fadograph of a Yestern Scene*, both 1971.

barberry any spiny shrub of the genus *Berberia* of the barberry family, having sour red berries and yellow flowers. These shrubs are often used as hedges. The barberry family (Berberidaceae) also includes plants such as the May apple *Podophyllum peltatum* of the E North American woodlands.

barbershop in music, a style of unaccompanied close-harmony singing of sentimental ballads, revived in the US during the 19th century. Traditionally sung by four male voices, since the 1970s it has developed as a style of ◊a cappella choral singing for both male and female voices.

Barbershop originated in 17th-century European barber's shops, which offered dental and medical services. Waiting customers were provided with a cittern or guitar by managements aware of the benefits of music to those undergoing pain.

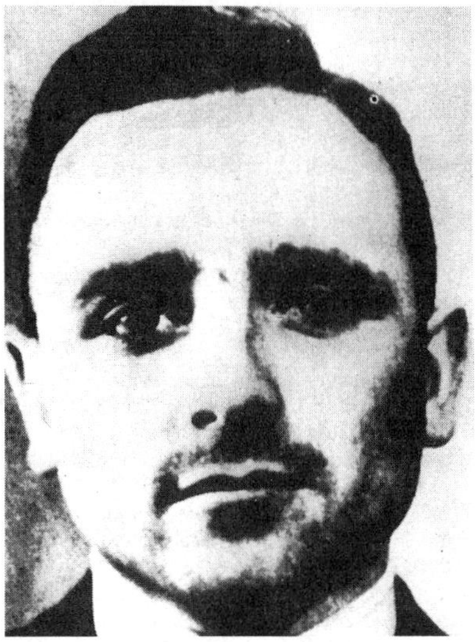

***Barbie** Nazi SS commander of Lyon, France, during World War II, Klaus Barbie was tracked to Bolivia, arrested in 1983, and tried in France. He was convicted of crimes against humanity in 1987.*

barbet small, tropical bird, often brightly colored. There are some 78 species of barbet in the family Capitonidae, about half living in Africa. Barbets eat insects and fruits and, being distant relations of woodpeckers, drill nest holes with their beaks. The name comes from the "little beard" of bristles at the base of the beak.

Barbie Klaus 1913–1991. German Nazi, a member of the ◊SS from 1936. During World War II he was involved in the deportation of Jews from the occupied Netherlands 1940–42 and in tracking down Jews and Resistance workers in France 1942–45. Having escaped capture in 1945, Barbie was employed by the US intelligence services in Germany before moving to Bolivia in 1951 where he made a living as a businessman accompanied by his family. Expelled from there in 1983, he was arrested and convicted of crimes against humanity in France 1987. He died in prison.

His work as SS commander, based in Lyon, included the rounding-up of Jewish children from an orphanage at Izieu and the torture of the Resistance leader Jean Moulin. During this time, his ruthlessness earned him the epithet "Butcher of Lyon."

Barbirolli John 1899–1970. English conductor. He made his name as a cellist, and in 1937 succeeded Toscanini as conductor of the New York Philharmonic Orchestra. He returned to England in 1943, where he remained conductor of the Hallé Orchestra, Manchester, until his death.

barbiturate hypnosedative drug, commonly called "sleeping pills," consisting of any salt or ester of barbituric acid $C_4H_4O_3N_2$. They work by depressing brain activity. Highly addictive, most barbiturates are no longer prescribed and are listed as controlled substances.

Tolerance develops quickly in the user so that increasingly large doses are required to induce sleep. A barbiturate's action persists for hours or days, causing confused, aggressive behavior or disorientation. Overdosage causes death by inhibiting the breathing center in the brain. Short-acting barbiturates are sometimes used as ◊anesthetics to induce general anesthesia.

Barbizon school French school of landscape painters of the mid-19th century, based at Barbizon in the forest of Fontainebleau. Members included Jean-François Millet, Diaz de la Peña (1807–1876), and Théodore Rousseau (1812–1867). They aimed to paint fresh, realistic scenes, sketching and painting their subjects in the open air.

Barbor Philip Pendleton 1783–1841. US jurist and political leader. Born in Barborsville, Virginia, Barbor studied law and briefly practiced in Kentucky before returning to Virginia and beginning a political career. He was elected to the state legislature and the US House of Representatives, serving as Speaker of the House 1821–23. As a strong supporter of states' rights, he was appointed federal district judge by President Jackson 1830. He served on the US Supreme Court 1836–41, consistently ruling in favor of the prerogative of the states over federal authority.

Barbuda one of the islands that form the state of ◊Antigua and Barbuda.

Barcelona capital, industrial city (textiles, engineering, chemicals), and port of Catalonia, NE Spain; population (1986) 1,694,000. As the chief center of anarchism and Catalonian nationalism, it was prominent in the overthrow of the monarchy 1931 and was the last city of the republic to surrender to Franco 1939. In 1992 the city hosted the Summer Olympics.

history Barcelona was founded in the 3rd century BC and its importance grew until, in the 14th century, it had become one of the leading trading cities of the Mediterranean.

features The Ramblas, tree-lined promenades leading from the Plaza de Cataluña, the largest square in Spain; ◊Gaudí's unfinished church of the Holy Family 1883; the Pueblo Español 1929, with specimens of Spanish architecture; a replica of Columbus's flagship the *Santa Maria*, in the Maritime Museum; a large collection of art by Picasso.

bar code

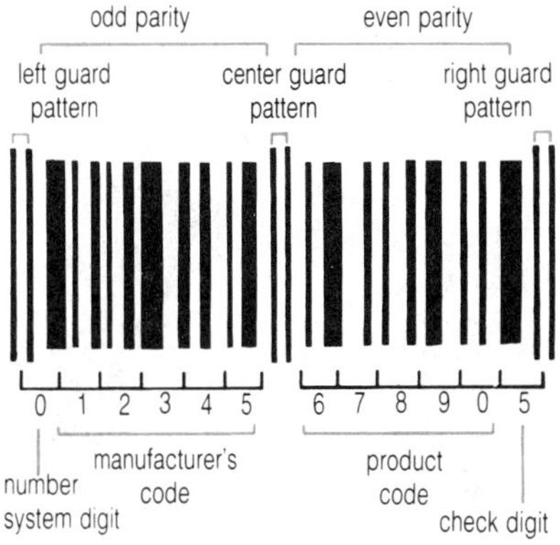
odd parity
even parity
left guard pattern
center guard pattern
right guard pattern
0 1 2 3 4 5
6 7 8 9 0 5
number system digit
manufacturer's code
product code
check digit

bar chart in statistics, a way of displaying data. The heights or lengths of the bars are proportional to the quantities they represent.

bar code pattern of bars and spaces that can be read by a computer. They are widely used in retailing, industrial distribution, and public libraries. The code is read by a ◊scanning device; the computer determines the code from the widths of the bars and spaces.

The technique was patented in 1949 but only became popular in 1973, when the food industry in North America adopted the Universal Product Code system.

Bardeen John 1908–1991. US physicist who won a Nobel Prize 1956, with Walter Brattain and William Shockley, for the development of the transistor in 1948. In 1972 he became the first double winner of a Nobel Prize in the same subject (with Leon Cooper and John Schrieffer) for his work on superconductivity.

Bardot Brigitte 1934– . French film actress, called BB, whose sensual appeal did much to popularize French films internationally. She was a protégée of Roger Vadim and her films include *Et Dieu créa la Femme/And God Created Woman* 1950, *Viva Maria* 1965, and *Shalako* 1968.

Bardo Thodol also known as the ***Book of the Dead*** a Tibetan Buddhist text giving instructions to the newly dead about the Bardo, or state between death and rebirth.

Bareilly industrial city in Uttar Pradesh, India; population (1981) 438,000. It was a Mogul capital 1657 and at the center of the Indian Mutiny 1857.

Barenboim Daniel 1942– . Israeli pianist and conductor, born in Argentina. Pianist/conductor with the English Chamber Orchestra from 1964, he became conductor of the New York Philharmonic Orchestra 1970 and musical director of the Orchestre de Paris 1975. Appointed artistic director of the Opéra Bastille, Paris, July 1987, he was fired from his post a few months before the Opéra's opening in July 1989. He is a celebrated interpreter of Mozart and Beethoven.

Barents Willem c. 1550–1597. Dutch explorer and navigator. He made three expeditions to seek the ◊Northeast Passage; he died on the last voyage. The Barents Sea, part of the Arctic Ocean N of Norway, is named after him.

Barents Sea section of the E ◊Arctic Ocean. It has oil and gas reserves.

Bari capital of Puglia region, S Italy, and industrial port on the Adriatic; population (1988) 359,000. It is the site of Italy's first nuclear power station; the part of the town known as Tecnopolis is the Italian equivalent of ◊Silicon Valley.

Barikot a garrison town in Konar province, E Afghanistan, near the Pakistan frontier. Besieged by Mujaheddin rebels in 1985, the relief of Barikot by Soviet and Afghan troops was one of the larg-

barley

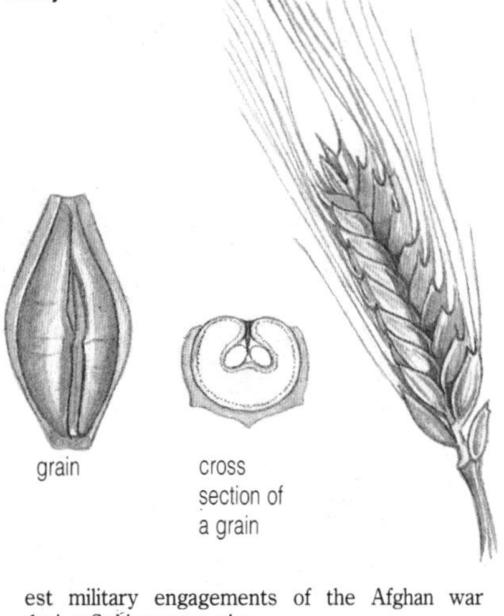
grain
cross section of a grain

est military engagements of the Afghan war during Soviet occupation.

Barisal river port and capital city of Barisal region, S Bangladesh; population (1981) 142,000. It trades in jute, rice, fish, and oilseed.

barium soft, silver-white, metallic element, symbol Ba, atomic number 56, atomic weight 137.33. It is one of the alkaline-earth metals, found in nature as barium carbonate and barium sulfate. As the sulfate it is used in medicine; taken in solution (a "barium meal"), its progress is followed by using X-rays to reveal abnormalities of the alimentary canal. Barium is also used in alloys, pigments, and safety matches and, with strontium, forms the emissive surface in cathode-ray tubes. The name comes from the Greek *barytes*, for "heavy," since it was first discovered in heavy spar.

bark the protective outer layer on the stems and roots of woody plants, composed mainly of dead cells. To allow for expansion of the stem, the bark is continually added to from within, and the outer surface often becomes fissured or is shed as scales. The bark from the cork oak *Quercus suber* is economically important and harvested commercially. The spice ◊cinnamon and the drugs cascara (used as a laxative and stimulant) and ◊quinine all come from bark.

Bark technically includes all the tissues external to the vascular ◊cambium (the ◊phloem, cortex, and periderm), and its thickness may vary from 0.1 in/2.5 mm to 12 in/30 cm or more, as in the giant redwood *Sequoia* where it forms a thick, spongy layer.

bark painting technique of painting on the inner side of strips of tree bark, practiced by Australian Aborigines. In red, yellow, white, brown, and black pigments, the works were often painted with the fingers as the artist lay inside a low bark-roofed shelter.

Barlach Ernst 1870–1938. German Expressionist sculptor, painter, and poet. His simple, evocative figures carved in wood (for example, those in St Catherine's, Lübeck, 1930–32) often express melancholy.

Barletta industrial port on the Adriatic, Italy; population (1981) 83,800. It produces chemicals and soap; as an agriculture center it trades in wine and fruit. There is a Romanesque cathedral and a castle.

barley cereal belonging to the grass family (Gramineae). Cultivated barley *Hordeum vulgare* comprises three main varieties—six-rowed, four-rowed, and two-rowed. Barley was one of the earliest cereals to be cultivated, about 10,000 years ago in the Near East and Egypt, and no other cereal can thrive in so wide a range of climatic conditions; polar barley is sown and reaped well within the Arctic Circle in Europe. Barley is no longer much used in bread-making, but it is used as a cereal grain, in soups and stews and as a starch. Its high-protein form finds a wide use for animal feed; and its low-protein form is used in brewing and distilling alcoholic beverages.

Barlow Joel 1754–1812. US poet and diplomat. Born in Redding, Connecticut, Barlow was educated at Yale. As a member of the literary circle known as the "Connecticut Wits," he published an epic entitled *The Vision of Columbus* 1787. Living as an expatriate in Paris and London, Barlow was deeply affected by the philosophical ideals of the Enlightenment and was granted citizenship in revolutionary France.

In 1795–97 he served as US consul in Algiers, gaining the release of American hostages taken by the Barbary pirates. In 1811 he was sent to France on a diplomatic mission and died while accompanying Napoleon in his retreat from Russia.

bar mitzvah (Hebrew "son of the commandment") in Judaism, initiation of a boy, which takes place at the age of 13, into the adult Jewish community; less common is the bat or bas mitzvah for girls aged 12. The child reads a passage from the Torah in the synagogue on the Sabbath, and is subsequently regarded as a full member of the congregation.

barn a farm building traditionally used for the storage and processing of cereal crops and hay. On older farmsteads, the barn is usually the largest building. It is often characterized by ventilation openings rather than windows and has at least one set of big double doors for access. Before mechanization, wheat was threshed by hand on a specially prepared floor inside these doors.

Tithe barns were used in feudal England to store the produce paid as a tax to the parish priest by the local occupants of the land. In the Middle Ages, monasteries often controlled the collection of tithes over a wide area and, as a result, constructed some enormous tithe barns.

Barnabas, St in the New Testament, a "fellow laborer" with St Paul; he went with St Mark on a missionary journey to Cyprus, his birthplace. Feast day June 11.

barnacle marine crustacean of the subclass Cirripedia. The larval form is free-swimming, but when mature, it fixes itself by the head to rock or floating wood. The animal then remains attached, enclosed in a shell through which the cirri (modified legs) protrude to sweep food into the mouth. Barnacles include the stalked goose barnacle *Lepas anatifera* found on ships' bottoms and the acorn barnacles, such as *Balanus balanoides*, common on rocks.

Barnard Christiaan (Neethling) 1922– . South African surgeon who performed the first human heart transplant in 1967 in Cape Town. The patient, 54-year-old Louis Washkansky, lived for 18 days.

Barnard's star second-closest star to the Sun, six light-years away in the constellation Ophiuchus. It is a faint red dwarf of 9th magnitude, visible only through a telescope. It is named after the US astronomer Edward E Barnard (1857–1923), who discovered in 1916 that it has the fastest proper motion of any star, crossing 1 degree of sky every 350 years. Some observations suggest that Barnard's star may be accompanied by planets.

Barnaul industrial city in S Siberia, USSR; population (1987) 596,000.

Barnet, Battle of in the English Wars of the ◊Roses, the defeat of Lancaster by York on April 14, 1471 in Barnet (now in NW London).

Barnsley town in S Yorkshire, England; population (1981) 128,200. It is an industrial town (iron and steel, glass, paper, carpet, clothing) on one of Britain's richest coalfields.

Barnum Phineas T(aylor) 1810–1891. US showman. In 1871, after an adventurous career, he established the "Greatest Show on Earth" which included the midget "Tom Thumb" comprising a circus, a menagerie, and an exhibition of "freaks,' conveyed in 100 rail automobiles. In 1881, it merged with its chief competitor and has con-

barometer

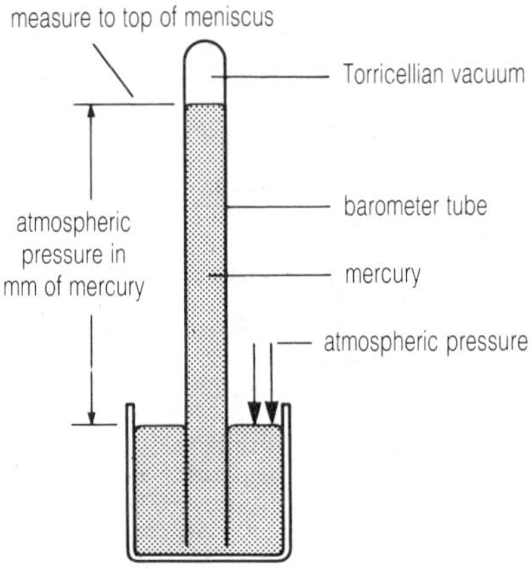
measure to top of meniscus
Torricellian vacuum
barometer tube
atmospheric pressure in mm of mercury
mercury
atmospheric pressure

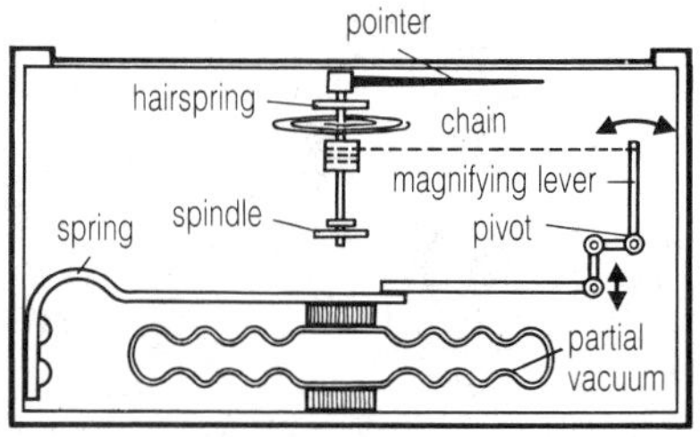
pointer
hairspring
chain
magnifying lever
spring
spindle
pivot
partial vacuum

tinued to this day as the Ringling Brothers and Barnum and Bailey Circus.

In 1850, in an attempt to change his image to that of an art promoter, Barnum managed the hugely successful US concert tour of Swedish soprano Jenny Lind, whom he dubbed "The Swedish Nightingale.'

Barocci Federico c. 1535–1612. Italian artist, born and based in Urbino. He painted religious themes in a highly colored, sensitive style that falls between Renaissance and Baroque. The *Madonna del Graffo* (National Gallery, London) shows the influence of Raphael (also from Urbino) and Correggio on his art.

Baroda former name of ◊Vadodara, in Gujarat, India.

barograph device for recording variations in atmospheric pressure. A pen, governed by the movements of an aneroid ◊barometer, makes a continuous line on a paper strip on a cylinder that rotates over a day or week to create a barogram, or permanent record of variations in atmospheric pressure.

Baroja Pio 1872–1956. Spanish novelist of Basque extraction whose works include a trilogy dealing with the Madrid underworld, *La lucha por la vida/The Struggle for Life* 1904–05, and the multivolume *Memorias de un hombre de acción/Memoirs of a Man of Action* 1913–28.

barometer instrument that measures atmospheric pressure as an indication of weather. Most often used are the mercury barometer and the aneroid barometer.

In a mercury barometer a column of mercury in a glass tube roughly 2.5 ft/0.75 m high (closed at one end, curved upward at the other) is balanced by the pressure of the atmosphere on the open end; any change in the height of the column reflects a change in pressure. An aneroid barometer achieves a similar result by changes in the distance between the faces of a shallow cylindrical metal box which is partly exhausted of air.

baron rank in the ◊peerage of the UK, above a baronet and below a viscount.

Life peers are always of this rank.

baronet hereditary title in the UK below the rank of baron, but above that of knight; the first creations were in 1611 by James I. A baronet does not have a seat in the House of Lords, but is entitled to the style *Sir* before his name.

Barons' Wars civil wars in England:

1215–17 between King ◊John and his barons, over his failure to honor ◊Magna Carta

1264–67 between ◊Henry III (and the future ◊Edward I) and his barons (led by Simon de ◊Montfort)

1264 May 14 Battle of Lewes at which Henry III was defeated and captured

1265 Aug 4 Simon de Montfort was defeated by Edward I at Evesham and killed.

Baroque style of art and architecture characterized by extravagance in ornament, asymmetry of design, and great expressiveness. It dominated European art for most of the 17th century, with artists such as the painter Rubens and the sculptor Bernini. In architecture, it often involved large-scale designs, such as Bernini's piazza in Rome and the palace of Versailles in France. In music, the Baroque period lasted from about 1600 to 1750, and its major composers included Monteverdi, Vivaldi, J S Bach, and Handel.

In painting, Caravaggio, with his bold use of light and forceful compositions, was an early exponent, but the Carracci family was more typical of the early Baroque style, producing grandiose visions in ceiling paintings that deployed illusionistic displays of florid architectural decoration. In sculpture, the greatest master was Bernini, whose *Ecstasy of St Theresa* 1645–52 (Sta Maria della Vittoria, Rome) is a fine example of overt emotionalism. Most masterpieces of the new style emerged in churches and palaces in Rome, but the Baroque influence soon spread through Europe. The Swiss art historian Burckhardt was the first to use the term "baroque." Baroque decorations were applied to building exteriors and interiors including furnishings.

Barossa Valley wine-growing area in the Lofty mountain ranges, South Australia.

Barotseland former kingdom in Western Province of ◊Zambia.

Barquisimeto capital of Lara state, NW Venezuela; population (1981) 523,000.

Barra southernmost of the larger Outer Hebrides, Scotland; area 35 sq mi/90 sq km; population (1981) 1,340. It is separated from South Uist by the Sound of Barra. The main town is Castlebay.

barracuda large predatory fish *Sphyraena barracuda* found in the warmer seas of the world. It can grow over 6 ft/2 m long, and has a superficial resemblance to a pike. Young fish shoal but the older ones are solitary. The barracuda has very sharp shearing teeth, and may attack people.

Barragán Luis 1902–1988. Mexican architect who used rough wooden beams, cobbles, lava, and adobe in his simple designs for houses, walled gardens, and fountains.

Barrancabermeja a port and oil-refining center on the Magdalena River in the department of Santander, NE Colombia. It is a major outlet for oil from the De Mares fields, which are linked by pipeline to Cartagena on the Caribbean coast.

Barranquilla seaport in N Colombia, on the river Magdalena; population (1985) 1,120,900. Products include chemicals, tobacco, textiles, furniture, and footwear.

It is Colombia's chief port on the Caribbean and is the site of Latin America's first air terminal 1919.

Barras Paul François Jean Nicolas, Count 1755–1829. French revolutionary. He was elected to the National Convention 1792 and helped to overthrow Robespierre 1794. In 1795 he became a member of the ruling Directory (see ◊French Revolution). In 1796 he brought about the marriage of his former mistress, Josephine de Beauharnais, with Napoleon and assumed dictatorial powers. After Napoleon's coup d'etat Nov 19, 1799, Barras fell into disgrace.

Barrault Jean Louis 1910– . French actor and director. His films include *La Symphonie fantastique* 1942, *Les Enfants du paradis* 1944, and *La Ronde* 1950.

Barrett Browning *Lyric poet Elizabeth Barrett married poet Robert Browning in 1846, escaping the reclusive life imposed on her by her tyrannical father.*

He was producer and director to the ◊Comédie Française 1940–46 and director of the Théâtre de France (formerly Odéon) from 1959 until his dismissal 1968, because of statements made during the occupation of the theater by student rebels.

barre the wooden bar running along the walls of a ballet studio at waist height, designed to help dancers keep their balance while going through the initial daily exercises.

Barre Raymond 1924– . French politician, member of the center-right Union pour la Démocratie Française; prime minister 1976–81, when he also held the Finance Ministry portfolio and gained a reputation as a tough and determined budget cutter.

barrel a unit of liquid capacity, the value of which depends on the liquid being measured. It is used for petroleum, a barrel of which contains 42 gallons/159 liters; a barrel of alcohol contains 49.9 gallons/189 liters.

barrel a cylindrical container, tapering at each end, made of thick strips of wood bound together by metal hoops. They are used for the bulk storage of fine wines and spirits.

Barrels were made by coopers, whose main skill was the shaping and bending of the wooden strips (staves) so that they fitted together without gaps when secured by the hoops. They were widely used for storing liquids and dry goods until the development of plastic containers.

barrel organ portable pipe organ, played by turning a handle. This works a pump and drives a replaceable cylinder upon which music is recorded as a pattern of ridges controlling the passage of air to the pipes.

Barren Lands/Grounds the ◊tundra region of Canada, W of Hudson Bay.

Barrett Browning Elizabeth 1806–1861. English poet. In 1844 she published *Poems* (including "The Cry of the Children"), which led to her friendship with and secret marriage to Robert Browning in 1846. The *Sonnets from the Portuguese* 1847 were written during their courtship. Later works include *Casa Guidi Windows* 1851 and the poetic novel *Aurora Leigh* 1857.

Barrett Browning was born near Durham. As a child she fell from her pony and injured her spine and was subsequently treated by her father as a confirmed invalid. Freed from her father's oppressive influence, her health improved. She wrote strong verse about social injustice and oppression in Victorian England.

Barrie J(ames) M(atthew) 1860–1937. Scottish playwright and novelist, author of *The Admirable Crichton* 1902 and the children's fantasy *Peter Pan* 1904.

barrier island a long island of sand, lying offshore and parallel to the coast. Some of these islands are over 60 mi/100 km in length. Often several islands lie in a continuous row offshore. Coney Island and Jones Beach near New York City are well-known examples, as is Padre Island, Texas. Barrier islands also fringe the North Sea coast of the Netherlands.

Most barrier islands are derived from marine sands piled up by shallow longshore currents that sweep sand parallel to the seashore. Others are derived from former spits, connected to land and built up by drifted sand, that were later severed from the mainland.

barrier reef a ◊coral reef that lies offshore, separated from the mainland by a shallow lagoon.

Barron v Baltimore a US Supreme Court decision 1833 dealing with the responsibilities of state courts under the Fifth Amendment. The plaintiff, a wharf owner who lost money through the municipally engineered reorganization of Baltimore's harbor, sued the city for damages. Although the Fifth Amendment protects citizens from expropriation without proper compensation, the Maryland courts found against Barron. He appealed to the US Supreme Court, which upheld the Maryland decision, ruling that the intent of the Bill of Rights is protection from the federal government, not from state governments.

barrow burial mound, usually composed of earth but sometimes of stones, examples of which are found in many parts of the world. The two main types are long, dating from the New Stone Age, or Neolithic, and round, from the later Mesolithic peoples of the early Bronze Age.

Barrow northernmost town in the US, at Point Barrow, Alaska; the world's largest Eskimo settlement. Population (1990) 3,469. There is oil at nearby Prudhoe Bay, and the US Naval Research Laboratory is in the vicinity. Barrow developed as a whaling center about 1900.

Barrow Clyde 1900–1934. US criminal; see ◊Bonnie and Clyde.

Barrow Isaac 1630–1677. British mathematician, theologian, and classicist. His *Lectiones geometricae* 1670 contains the essence of the theory of ◊calculus, which was later expanded by Isaac ◊Newton and Gottfried ◊Leibniz.

Barry Charles 1795–1860. English architect of the Neo-Gothic Houses of Parliament at Westminster, London, 1840–60, in collaboration with ◊Pugin.

Barry Comtesse du see ◊Du Barry, mistress of Louis XV of France.

Barrymore US family of actors, the children of British-born Maurice Barrymore and Georgie Drew, both stage personalities.

Lionel Barrymore (1878–1954) first appeared on the stage with his grandmother, Mrs John Drew, in 1893. He played numerous film roles from 1909, including *A Free Soul* 1931 and *Grand Hotel* 1932, but was perhaps best known for his annual radio portrayal of Scrooge in Dickens's *A Christmas Carol.*

Ethel Barrymore (1879–1959) played with the British actor Henry Irving in London in 1898 and in 1928 opened the Ethel Barrymore Theatre in New York; she also appeared in many films from 1914, including *None but the Lonely Heart* 1944.

John Barrymore (1882–1942), a flamboyant actor who often appeared on stage and screen with his brother and sister. In his early years he was a Shakespearean actor. From 1923 he acted almost entirely in films, including *Dinner at Eight* 1933, and became a screen idol, nicknamed "the Profile."

barter the exchange of goods or services without the use of money.

Barth Heinrich 1821–1865. German geographer and explorer who in explorations of N Africa between

Barrymore *US actor John Barrymore was the youngest of the three talented Barrymores, whose parents were also actors.*

1844 and 1855 established the exact course of the river Niger.

He studied the coast of N Africa from Tunis to Egypt 1844–45, traveled in the Middle East 1845–47, crossed the Sahara from Tripoli 1850, and then spent five years exploring the country between Lake Chad and Cameroon which he described in the five-volume *Travels and Discoveries in Central Africa* 1857–58.

Barth John 1930– . US novelist and short-story writer who was influential in the "academic" experimental movement of the 1960s. His works are usually interwoven fictions based on language games, since he is concerned with the relationship of language and reality. They include the novels *The Sot-Weed Factor* 1960, *Giles Goat-Boy* 1966, *Letters* 1979, *Sabbatical: A Romance* 1982, and *The Tidewater Tales* 1987. He also wrote the novella *Chimera* 1972 and *Lost in the Funhouse* 1968, a collection of short stories.

Barth Karl 1886–1968. Swiss Protestant theologian. Socialist in his political views, he attacked the Nazis. His *Church Dogmatics* 1932–62 makes the resurrection of Jesus the focal point of Christianity.

He is generally considered the greatest Christian theologian of the 20th century. His *Theology of Crisis* rejected liberal theology and stressed scripture and the infinite gulf that separates God from humanity, which can be overcome only by the grace of God.

Barthes Roland 1915–1980. French critic and theorist of ◊semiology, the science of signs and symbols. One of the French "new critics," he attacked traditional literary criticism in his early works, including *Sur Racine/On Racine* 1963, and set out his own theories in *Eléments de sémiologie* 1964. He also wrote an autobiographical novel, *Roland Barthes sur Roland Barthes* 1975.

Bartholdi Frédéric Auguste 1834–1904. French sculptor. He designed the Statue of Liberty that now stands on Liberty (formerly Bedloe's) Island in New York Harbor, 1884.

Bartholomew, Massacre of St see ◊St Bartholomew, Massacre of.

Bartholomew, St in the New Testament, one of the apostles. Legends relate that after the Crucifixion he took Christianity to India, or that he was a missionary in Anatolia and Armenia, where he suffered martyrdom by being flayed alive. Feast day 24 Aug.

Bartók Béla 1881–1945. Hungarian composer. Regarded as a child prodigy, he studied music at

Barthes *French critic and exponent of semiology, Roland Barthes.*

the Budapest Conservatory, later working with ◊Kodály in recording and transcribing local folk music for a government project. This led him to develop a personal musical language combining folk elements with mathematical concepts of tone and rhythmic proportion. His large output includes six string quartets, a ballet *The Miraculous Mandarin* 1919, which was banned because of its subject matter, concertos, an opera, and graded teaching pieces for piano. He died in the US having fled from Hungary in 1940.

Bartolommeo Fra, also called Baccio della Porta c. 1472–c. 1517. Italian religious painter of the High Renaissance, active in Florence. His painting of *The Last Judgment* 1499 (Museo di San Marco, Florence) influenced Raphael.

Barton Clara 1821–1912. US health worker. Born in Oxford, Massachusetts, Barton was trained as a teacher, and at the outbreak of the US Civil War she became involved in projects for the welfare of Union soldiers. As a volunteer nurse, she tended the casualties in the 1861 Baltimore riot and at the battles of Antietam and Fredericksburg. In 1864 Gen Benjamin Butler named her superintendent of nurses for his forces. In 1870 Barton traveled to Europe to bring medical supplies to troops in the Franco-Prussian War. She founded

Bartók *Hungarian composer Béla Bartók.*

the American Red Cross 1881 and served as its president until 1904.

Barton Edmund 1849–1920. Australian politician. He was leader of the federation movement from 1896 and first prime minister of Australia 1901–03.

Baruch Bernard (Mannes) 1870–1965. US financier. He was a friend of British prime minister Churchill and a self-appointed, unpaid adviser to US presidents Wilson, F D Roosevelt, and Truman. He strongly advocated international control of nuclear energy.

baryon a hadron; any of a group of ◊elementary particles, including protons, neutrons, and hyperons. They are composed of three quarks.

Baryshnikov Mikhail 1948– . Soviet dancer, now in the US. He joined the Kirov Ballet in 1967 and soon gained fame worldwide as a soloist. After defecting "on artistic, not political grounds" while in Canada in 1974, he danced with various companies, becoming director of the American Ballet Theatre in 1980.

He has created many roles, notably in Twyla Tharp's *Push Comes to Shove* 1976 (music by Haydn/Lamb) and in Jerome Robbins's *Opus 19* 1979 (Prokofiev). He made his film debut in *The Turning Point* 1978 and has since acted in other films, including *White Nights* 1985. He made his legitimate theater debut in *Metamorphosis* 1989.

baryte barium sulfate, $BaSO_4$, the most common mineral of barium. It is white or light-colored, and has a comparatively high density (specific gravity 4.6); the latter property makes it useful in the production of high-density drilling muds. Baryte occurs mainly in ore veins, where it is often found with calcite and with lead and zinc minerals. It crystallizes in the orthorhombic system and can form tabular crystals or radiating fibrous masses.

baryton a complex bowed-stringed instrument producing an intense singing tone. It is based on an 18th-century viol and modified by the addition of up to 40 sympathetic (freely vibrating) strings.

The baryton was a favorite instrument of Prince Nicholas Esterházy, patron of the Austrian composer Franz Joseph Haydn who, to please him, wrote almost 200 trios for violin, baryton, and cello.

Barzun Jacques Martin 1907– . French-born US historian and educator. Barzun immigrated to the US with his parents 1919. His specialty was 19th-century European intellectual life. Among his many historical works, he published *Romanticism and the Modern Ego* 1943. His book *The Modern Researcher* 1970 is recognized as a classic study of historical method.

He was educated at Columbia University, earning a PhD in history 1932, and soon afterward joined the faculty there and became a member of the administration.

basal metabolic rate (BMR) the amount of energy needed by an animal just to stay alive. It is measured when the animal is awake but resting, and includes the energy required to keep the heart beating, sustain breathing, repair tissues, and keep the brain and nerves functioning. Measuring the animal's consumption of oxygen gives an accurate value for BMR, because oxygen is needed to release energy from food.

A cruder measure of BMR estimates the amount of heat given off, some heat being released when food is used up. BMR varies from one species to another, and from males to females. In humans, it is highest in children and declines with age. Disease, including mental illness, can make it rise or fall. Hormones from the ◊thyroid gland control the BMR.

basalt the commonest volcanic ◊igneous rock, and the principal rock type on the ocean floor; it is basic, that is, it contains relatively little silica: under 50%. It is usually dark gray, but can also be green, brown, or black.

The groundmass may be glassy or finely crystalline, sometimes with large ◊crystals embedded. Basaltic lava tends to be runny and flows for great distances before solidifying. Successive eruptions

basalt *The Giant's Causeway in Antrim, Ireland, consisting of several thousand hexagonal pillars of basalt set together in a honeycomb pattern.*

of basalt have formed the great plateaus of Colorado and the Indian Deccan. In some places, such as Fingal's Cave in the Inner Hebrides of Scotland and the Giant's Causeway in Antrim, Northern Ireland, shrinkage during the solidification of the molten lava caused the formation of hexagonal columns.

bascule bridge type of drawbridge in which one or two counterweighted deck members pivot upward to allow shipping to pass underneath. One example is the double bascule Tower Bridge in London.

base

binary (base 2)	*octal (base 8)*	*decimal (base 10)*	*hexadecimal (base 16)*
0	0	0	0
1	1	1	1
10	2	2	2
11	3	3	3
100	4	4	4
101	5	5	5
110	6	6	6
111	7	7	7
1000	10	8	8
1001	11	9	9
1010	12	10	A
1011	13	11	B
1100	14	12	C
1101	15	13	D
1110	16	14	E
1111	17	15	F
10000	20	16	10
11111111	377	255	FF
11111010001	3721	2001	7D1

base in mathematics, the number of different single-digit symbols used in a particular number system. Thus our usual (decimal) counting system of numbers has the base ten (using the symbols 0, 1, 2, 3, 4, 5, 6, 7, 8, 9). In the ◊binary number system, which has only the numbers 1 and 0, the base is two. A base is also a number that, when raised to a particular power (that is, when multiplied by itself a particular number of times as in $10^2 = 10 \times 10 = 100$), has a ◊logarithm equal to the power. For example, the logarithm of 100 to the base ten is 2.

base in chemistry, a substance that accepts protons, such as the hydroxide ion (OH^-) and ammonia (NH_3). Bases react with acids to give a salt. Those that dissolve in water are called ◊alkalis.

Inorganic bases are usually oxides or hydroxides of metals, which react with dilute acids to form a salt and water. Many carbonates also react with dilute acids, additionally giving off carbon dioxide. Many organic compounds that contain nitrogen are bases.

baseball a bat-and-ball game between two teams, played on a field called a diamond, because of the arrangement of the bases. Bats, balls, and gloves constitute the basic equipment. The game is divided into nine innings. During the "top" half of each inning the home team plays defense and the visiting team, offense. In the "bottom" half, the roles are reversed. There are nine defensive positions: the pitcher, who stands on a mound 60.5 ft/18.4 m from home plate; the catcher, who crouches behind home plate; the first, second, and third basemen, who stand at or near their respective bases (90 ft/27.4 m apart), which together with home plate form the diamond-shaped infield: the shortstop, who covers the infield between second and third bases; and the right, center, and left fielders, whose domain is the outfield, the dimensions of which vary from stadium to stadium.

Essentially, an offensive player attempts to get on base and advance around the bases, to score a run by crossing home plate. Batters appear in an assigned order. Assuming a batting stance in front of the catcher, the batter faces the pitcher, who throws the baseball across home plate to the catcher. Standing behind the catcher is an umpire (major-league games have four umpires, one at each base), who calls out a "ball" or "strike" ruling

baseball

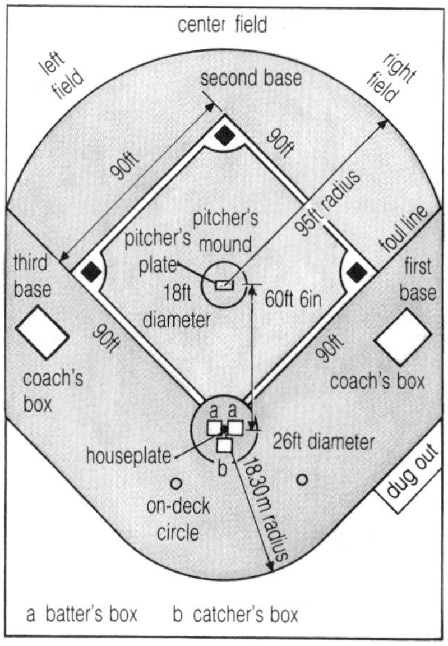
center field
left field
right field
second base
90ft
90ft
95ft radius
pitcher's mound
pitcher's plate
18ft diameter
60ft 6in
foul line
third base
first base
90ft
90ft
coach's box
coach's box
a a
b
26ft diameter
houseplate
1830m radius
on-deck circle
dug out
a batter's box
b catcher's box

for each unhit pitch. A pitch that fails to cross the plate within the batter's "strike zone" is called a ball. However, if such a pitch is swung at and missed, a strike is ruled against the batter. Any unhit pitch that is within the strike zone, whether or not the batter swings, is called a strike. Hit balls that fall outside playing-field bounds are called "foul balls" and are counted as strikes, unless it would be a third strike, when the batter is allowed to continue at bat. A three-strike count is an "out." If the count reaches four balls before the third strike is called the batter earns a "walk" and proceeds to first base; if the batter is hit by a pitched ball, first base is awarded.

When a ball is hit into fair territory, numerous outcomes are possible: among them, the ball could be a "fly ball" caught by a fielder for an out; a "grounder" scooped up and thrown to first base before the batter (now the runner) gets there, also for an out; a "hit," in which the runner reaches a base (first base for a single; second for a double; third for a triple, and home for an inside-the-park home run) before the ball; or a "home run," a hit that usually goes beyond the outfield wall, so the batter (and any baserunners) completes the circuit of base paths that leads back to home plate. The object is to advance runners around the bases, and a "run" is scored each time a runner safely crosses home plate.

During each inning, a team's offensive play continues until three outs occur. After nine innings, the team with the most runs wins. If the game is tied after nine innings, extra innings are played until the tie is broken.

history The legend of Abner ◊Doubleday's invention of baseball in Cooperstown, New York, 1839, was born 1907 when a major-league baseball committee tried to determine the origins of the game. The story was presented as fact, although there was no real evidence to support it, and Doubleday's journals contain no mention of any pastime similar to baseball.

Sports historians vary in their hypotheses, but most agree that baseball was no one person's invention; rather it evolved from numerous ball-and-stick games. Colonial Americans enjoyed several varieties of such English games as rounders and town ball. By the mid-19th century many regional variations of baseball had been developed. The "New York game" became especially popular after 1845, when player A J Cartwright devised such surviving innovations as the nine-man team, the diamond-shaped infield, and the three-outs-per-inning format. Cartwright was a founding member of the New York Knickerbocker Club, which for 13 years exerted its authority over baseball in the greater New York area. When 25 ball clubs formed the National Association of Base Ball Players 1858, the Knickerbockers lost their arbitership, and the game of baseball entered a new era of standardization and organized competition.

In 1871 the National Association of Professional Base Ball Players was born, becoming baseball's first major league. The more stable National League usurped the Association 1876, and for nearly 40 years watched the rise and fall of several rival leagues. By 1916 the "majors" belonged to just two leagues: the National League (NL) and the American League (AL), and so it remains to this day. In 1916 each league was comprised of 8 teams. Today the NL's 12 teams and the AL's 14 teams are divided into east and west divisions. At the end of the regular playing season (Apr–Oct), the division-leading teams compete for their league's championship in a best-of-seven "pennant" series. The two pennant winners meet for the best-of-seven World Series.

The exclusivity of US teams in major-league baseball ended 1969 when Canada's Montreal Expos joined the NL. (Another Canadian team, the Toronto Blue Jays, joined the AL 1977.) In 1973 the AL adopted the "designated hitter" rule, which allows a tenth player to assume the batting role of the pitcher without affecting the pitcher's eligibility to continue defensive play.

Professional baseball also includes the "minors," the majors' training leagues, which is an extensive network across the US. The sport is very popular in Latin America, the Caribbean, and Japan, all of which have baseball leagues similar to those of the US.

Baseball is the quintessential US hometown sport, with American children playing on fields and sandlots from age 3 on. It has been formalized into school leagues and Little League competitions, but most children love to play it for the fun of the game.

Recent World Series Champions

1980 Philadelphia Phillies (NL)
1981 Los Angeles Dodgers (NL)
1982 St Louis Cardinals (NL)
1983 Baltimore Orioles (AL)
1984 Detroit Tigers (AL)
1985 Kansas City Royals (AL)
1986 New York Mets (NL)
1987 Minnesota Twins (AL)
1988 Los Angeles Dodgers (NL)
1989 Oakland Athletics (AL)
1990 Cincinnati Reds (NL)
1991 Minnesota Twins (AL)

Basel or ***Basle*** (French *Bâle*) financial, commercial, and industrial city in Switzerland; population (1987) 363,000. Basel was a strong military station under the Romans. In 1501 it joined the Swiss confederation and later developed as a center for the Reformation.

It has the chemical firms Hoffman–La Roche, Sandoz, and Ciba–Geigy (dyes, vitamins, agrochemicals, dietary products, genetic products). There are trade fairs, and it is the headquarters of the Bank for International Settlements. There is an 11th-century cathedral (rebuilt after an earthquake 1356), a 16th-century town hall, and a university dating from the 15th century.

basenji breed of dog originating in Central Africa, where it is used as a hunter. About 1.3 ft/41 cm tall, it has a wrinkled forehead, curled tail, and short glossy coat. It is remarkable because it has no true bark.

base pair in biochemistry, the linkage of two base (purine or pyrimidine) molecules in ◊DNA. They are found in nucleotides, and form the basis of the genetic code.

One base lies on one strand of the DNA double helix, and one on the other, so that the base pairs link the two strands like the rungs of a ladder. In DNA, there are four bases: adenine and guanine (purines) and cytosine and thymine (pyrimidines). Adenine always pairs with thymine, and cytosine with guanine.

Bashkir autonomous republic of the USSR, with the Ural Mountains on the E
area 143,600 sq km/55, 430 sq mi
capital Ufa
products minerals, oil
population (1982) 3,876,000
history annexed by Russia 1557; became the first Soviet autonomous republic 1919.

Bashkirtseff Marie 1860–1884. Russian diarist and painter whose journals, written in French, were cited by Simone de Beauvoir as the archetypal example of "self-centered female narcissism," but which also revealed the discovery by the female of her independent existence. She died of tuberculosis at 24.

Bashō Adopted name of Matsuo Munefusa 1644–1694. Japanese poet who was a master of the haiku, a 17-syllable poetic form with lines of 5, 7, and 5 syllables, which he infused with subtle allusiveness and made the accepted form of poetic expression in Japan. His most famous work is *Oku-no-hosomichi/The Narrow Road to the Deep North* 1694, an account of a visit to northern Japan, which consists of haikus interspersed with prose passages.

BASIC (acronym for Beginner's All-Purpose Symbolic Instruction Code) a computer-programming language, developed in 1964, originally designed to take advantage of ◊time-sharing computers (which can be used by many people at the same time). Most versions use an ◊interpreter program, which allows programs to be entered and run with no intermediate translation, although recent versions have been implemented as a ◊compiler. The language is relatively easy to learn and popular among microcomputer users.

basic-oxygen process

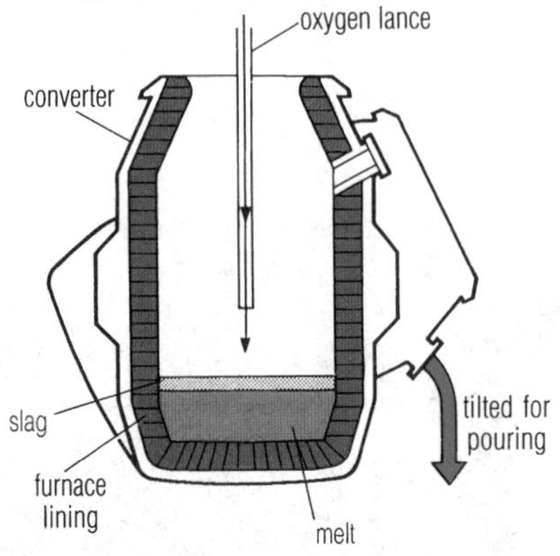
oxygen lance
converter
slag
furnace lining
melt
tilted for pouring

Basic English a simplified form of English devised and promoted by C K ◊Ogden in the 1920s and 1930s as an international auxiliary language; as a route into Standard English for foreign learners; and as a reminder to the English-speaking world of the virtues of plain language. Its name derives from the initial letters of *B*ritish, *A*merican, *s*cientific, *i*nternational, and *c*ommercial.

Basic has a vocabulary of 850 words (plus names, technical terms, and so on), only 18 of which are verbs or "operators."

basic-oxygen process the most widely used method of steelmaking, involving the blasting of oxygen at supersonic speed into molten pig iron.

Pig iron from a blast furnace, together with steel scrap, is poured into a converter, and a jet of oxygen is then projected into the mixture. The excess carbon in the mix and other impurities quickly burn out or form a slag, and the converter is emptied by tilting. It takes only about 45 minutes to refine 400 tons/350 tonnes of steel. The basic-oxygen process was developed in 1948 at a steelworks near the Austrian towns of Linz and Donawitz. It is a version of the ◊Bessemer process.

basidiocarp

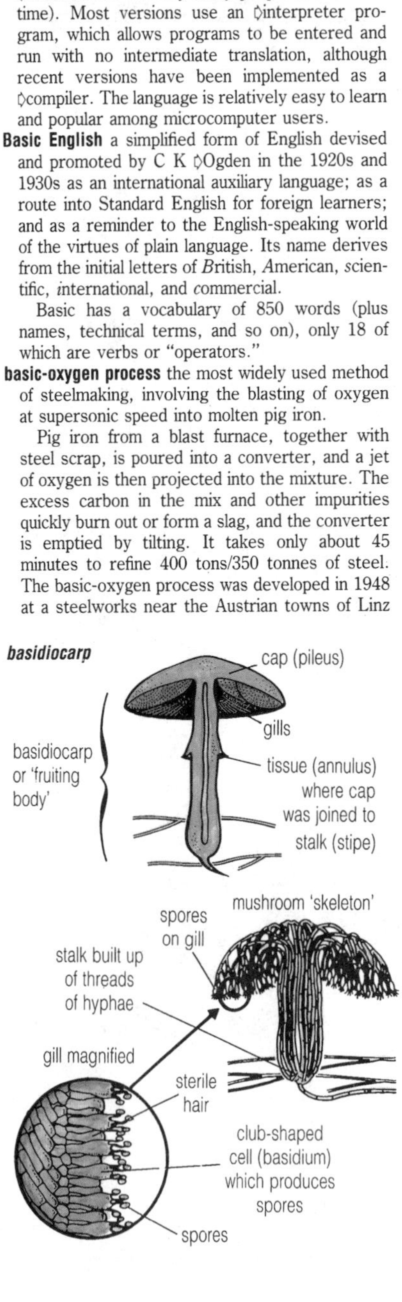
cap (pileus)
gills
basidiocarp or 'fruiting body'
tissue (annulus) where cap was joined to stalk (stipe)
mushroom 'skeleton'
spores on gill
stalk built up of threads of hyphae
gill magnified
sterile hair
club-shaped cell (basidium) which produces spores
spores

basil

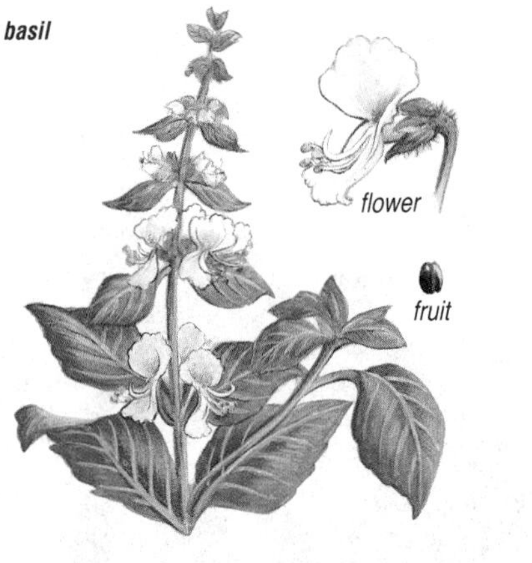
flower
fruit

basidiocarp the spore-bearing body, or "fruiting body," of all basidiomycete ◊fungi (commonly called club fungi), except the rusts and smuts. A well-known example is the edible mushroom *Agaricus brunnescens*. Other types include globular basidiocarps (puffballs) or flat ones that project from tree trunks (brackets). They are made up of a mass of tightly packed, intermeshed ◊hyphae.

The tips of these hyphae develop into the reproductive cells, or basidia, that form a fertile layer known as the hymenium or the gills of the basidiocarp. Four spores are budded off from the surface of each basidium.

Basie Count (William) 1904–1984. US jazz band leader, pianist, and organist who developed the big-band sound and a simplified, swinging style of music. He led impressive groups of musicians in a career spanning more than 50 years.

His solo piano technique was influenced by the style of Fats Waller. Some consider his the definitive dance band. Basie's compositions include "One O'Clock Jump" and "Jumpin at the Woodside."

basil plant *Ocimum basilicum* of the mint family Labiatae. A native of the tropics, it is cultivated in Europe as a culinary herb.

Basil, St c. 330–379. Cappadocian monk, known as "the Great," founder of the Basilian monks. Elected bishop of Caesarea 370, Basil opposed the heresy of ◊Arianism. He wrote many theological works and composed the "Liturgy of St Basil," in use in the Eastern Orthodox Church. Feast day Jan 2.

Basil II c. 958–1025. Byzantine emperor from 976. His achievement as emperor was to contain, and later decisively defeat, the Bulgarians, earning for himself the title "Bulgar-Slayer" after a victory in 1014. After the battle he blinded almost all 15,000 of the defeated, leaving only a few men with one eye to lead their fellows home. The Byzantine empire had reached its largest extent at the time of his death.

Basildon industrial new town in Essex, England; population (1981) 152,500. It was designated as a new town in 1949 from several townships. Industries include chemicals, clothing, printing, and engineering.

basilica type of Roman public building; a large roofed hall flanked by columns, generally with an aisle on each side, used for judicial or other public business. The earliest known basilica, at Pompeii, dates from the 2nd century BC. This architectural form was adopted by the early Christians for their churches.

Basilicata mountainous region of S Italy, comprising the provinces of Potenza and Matera; area 3,860 sq mi/10,000 sq km; population (1988) 622,000. Its capital is Potenza. It was the Roman province of Lucania.

basilisk South American lizard, genus *Basiliscus*. It is able to run on its hind legs when traveling

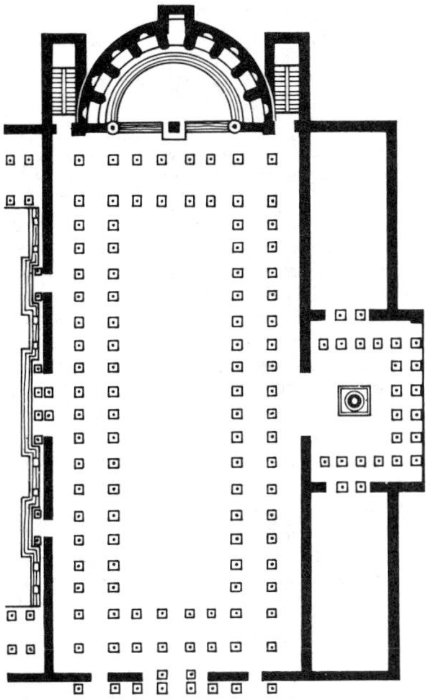

basilica *Plan of the Basilica Ulpia in Rome.*

fast (about 7 mph/11 kph) and may dash a short distance across the surface of water. The male has a well-developed crest on the head, body, and tail.

Baskerville John 1706–1775. English printer and typographer who experimented in casting types from 1750 onward. The Baskerville typeface is named after him.

basketball ball game between two teams of five players, played on both indoor and outdoor rectangular courts. Players move the ball by passing it or by dribbling it (bouncing it on the floor) while running. Basketball is played worldwide by both men and women and, with soccer, is one of the two most popular sports.

In the US the standard court is 94 ft/28.7 m long and 54 ft/16.5 m wide, with a backboard at the center of each end of the court. A circular metal hoop, whose rim is 10 ft/3 m from the floor, is attached to each backboard. The object of the game is to score the most points by throwing the inflated ball through the hoop, also called a basket, with two points scored for each field goal, or basket, shot from the field. Under certain rules, three points are awarded for field goals made beyond a specified distance from the basket. One point is scored for each foul shot (awarded after certain types of rules infractions by the opposing team). Foul shots, also called free throws, are taken from a line 15 ft/4.6 m from the backboard. The court has lines from the foul line to the court's base line. The lane between the lines cannot be entered by players until the foul shot has been released by the shooter. During regular play, offensive players may remain in the lane for only three conseutive seconds. The court dimensions and markings vary slightly among US amateur, US professional, and international rules. If a regulation game ends in a tie, overtime periods are played until one team wins.

Time limits for games vary: 8-min quarters in high school; 20-min halves in college; 12-min quarters in professional contests. Under some rules the team with possession of the ball must shoot within a certain time period: 24 sec in professional games; 30 sec in international amateur; 45 sec in college. A player must leave the game after accumulating five (high school, college, and international amateur) or six (professional) fouls.

history basketball was invented by James Naismith, a Canadian who was a physical education instructor at what is now Springfield College (Massachusetts). The first game was played 1891, and the first formal rules were set out 1892. It rapidly became popular, especially in the E US, and the first college and professional games were played before 1900. Today, the premier professional league is the National Basketball Association (NBA), formed 1949. Perhaps the most famous professional team is the Harlem Globetrotters, an independent team composed of black players, founded 1927. Its tours of the world have greatly increased basketball's popularity. Basketball has been played in the summer Olympic Games since 1936.

Recent NBA Champions

1980	Los Angeles Lakers
1981	Boston Celtics
1982	Los Angeles Lakers
1983	Philadelphia 76ers
1984	Boston Celtics
1985	Los Angeles Lakers
1986	Boston Celtics
1987	Los Angeles Lakers
1988	Los Angeles Lakers
1989	Detroit Pistons
1990	Detroit Pistons
1991	Chicago Bulls

basketry an ancient craft (Mesolithic–Neolithic) used to make a wide range of objects, from sandals and baskets to furniture, by interweaving or braiding rushes, cane, or other equally strong, natural fibers. Wickerwork is a more rigid type of basketry worked onto a sturdy frame, usually made from strips of willow.

Basle alternate form of ◊Basel, city in Switzerland.

Basov Nikolai Gennadievich 1912– . Soviet physicist who in 1953, with his compatriot Aleksandr Prokhorov, developed the microwave amplifier called a ◊maser. They were awarded the Nobel Prize for Physics 1964, which they shared with Charles Townes of the US.

Basque a member of a people who occupy the autonomous Basque region (created 1980) of NE Spain and the adjoining French *département* of Pyr-

basketball

An indoor sport played on a court by five members per side. The object is, via a series of dribbling and passing moves with the hands, to get the ball into the opposing half of the court and score goals by tossing the ball into the opposing basket.

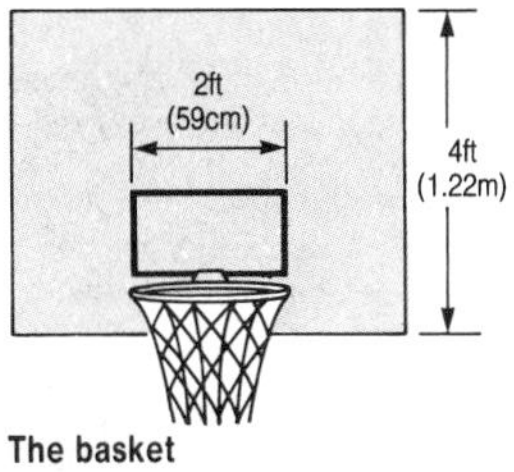
2ft
(59cm)
4ft
(1.22m)

The basket

The basket is a piece of netting which hangs from a metal rim and is open at both ends to allow the ball to pass through. The rim is attached to a backboard and points can be scored by bouncing the ball off the backboard and into the basket.

Play

Play is started with a jumpball. Two players, one from each team, face each other and the referee tosses the ball into the air between the two players who attempt to tap the ball to a teammate. The ball can only be played after it has reached its greatest height. A player in the jumpball can only play the ball twice after which it must be played to a player not involved.

dimensions of the international court

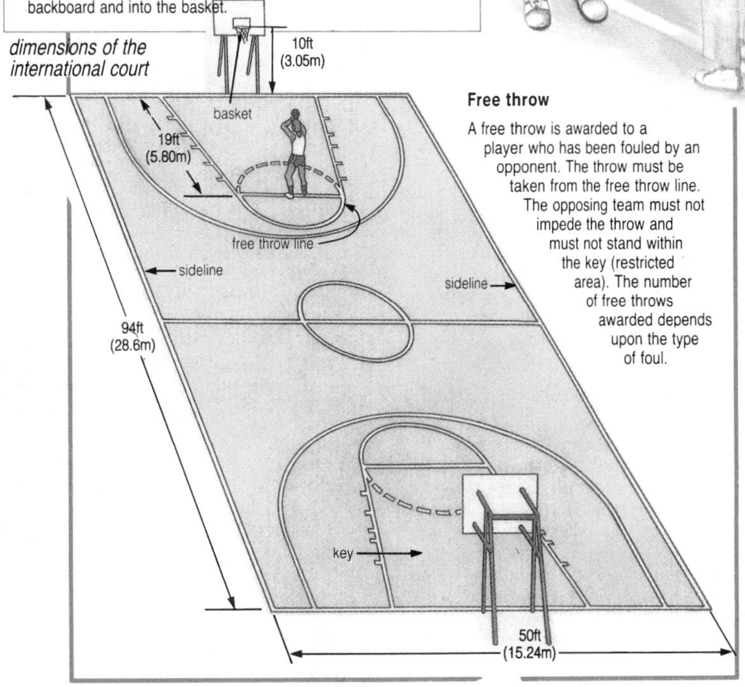
10ft
(3.05m)
basket
19ft
(5.80m)
free throw line
sideline
sideline
94ft
(28.6m)
key
50ft
(15.24m)

Free throw

A free throw is awarded to a player who has been fouled by an opponent. The throw must be taken from the free throw line. The opposing team must not impede the throw and must not stand within the key (restricted area). The number of free throws awarded depends upon the type of foul.

énées-Atlantiques. The Basques are a pre-Indo-European people who largely maintained their independence until the 19th century and speak their own Euskara tongue. During the Spanish Civil War 1936–39 they were on the Republican side and were defeated by Franco. The Basque separatist movement ETA (*Euskadi ta Azkatasuna*, "Basque Nation and Liberty") and the French organization *Enbata* ("Ocean Wind") have engaged in guerrilla activity from 1968 in an unsuccessful attempt to secure a united Basque state.

Basque Country (French *Pays Basque*) homeland of the Basque people in the W Pyrenees. The Basque Country includes the Basque Provinces of N Spain and the French arrondissements of Bayonne and Maulaon.

Basque language language of W Europe known to its speakers, the Basques, as Euskara, and apparently unrelated to any other language. It is spoken by some half million people in N Spain and SW France, around the Bay of Biscay ("the Basque bay"), as well as by emigrants in both Europe and the Americas.

Although officially discouraged in the past, Basque is now accepted as a regional language in both France and Spain and is of central importance to the Basque nationalist movement.

Basque Provinces (Spanish *Vascongadas*, Basque *Euskadi*) autonomous region of NW Spain, comprising the provinces of Vizcaya, Álava, and Guipúzcoa; area 2,818 sq mi/7,300 sq km; population (1986) 2,133,000.

Basra (Arabic *al-Basrah*) principal port in Iraq, in the Shatt-al-Arab delta, 60 mi/97 km from the Persian Gulf; population (1985) 617,000. Exports include wool, oil, cereal, and dates.

bass long-bodied scaly sea fish *Morone labrax* found in the N Atlantic and Mediterranean. They grow to 3 ft/1 m, and are often seen in shoals.

Other fish of the same family (Serranidae) are also called bass, as are North American freshwater fishes of the family Centrarchidae, such as black bass and small-mouthed bass.

bass (1) lowest range of male voice; (2) lower regions of musical pitch; (3) a double bass (see ◊violin family).

Bass George 1763–c. 1808. English naval surgeon who with Matthew ◊Flinders explored the coast of New South Wales and the strait that bears his name between Tasmania and Australia 1795–98.

Bassein port in Myanmar (Burma), in the Irrawaddy delta, 78 mi/125 km from the sea; population (1983) 355,588. Bassein was founded in the 13th century.

Basse-Normandie or ***Lower Normandy*** coastal region of NW France lying between Haute-Normandie and Brittany (Bretagne). It includes the *départements* of Calvados, Manche, and Orne; area 6,794 sq mi/17,600 sq km; population (1986) 1,373,000. Its capital is Caen. Apart from stock farming, dairy farming and the production of textiles, the area produces Calvados (apple brandy).

The invasion of Europe by Allied forces began in June 1944 when troops landed on the beaches of Calvados.

basset type of dog with a long low body, wrinkled forehead, and long pendulous ears, originally bred in France for hunting hares.

Basseterre capital and port of St Kitts–Nevis, in the Leeward Islands; population (1980) 14,000. Industries include data processing, rum, clothes, and electrical components.

Basse-Terre port on the Leeward Island Basse-Terre; population (1982) 13,600. It is the capital of the French overseas *département* of Guadeloupe.

Basse-Terre main island of the French West Indian island group of Guadeloupe; area 327 sq mi/848 sq km; population (1982) 141,300. It has an active volcano, Grande Soufrière, rising to 4,870 ft/1,484 m.

basset horn a musical ◊woodwind instrument resembling a clarinet, pitched in F and ending in a brass bell. Its range lies between the clarinet and the bass clarinet.

bassoon a double-reed ◊woodwind instrument, the bass of the oboe family. It doubles back on itself in a tube about 7.5 ft/2.5 m long. Its tone is rich and deep.

It is descended from the bass pommer, which was approximately 6 ft/2 m in length and perfectly straight.

Bass Strait channel between Australia and Tasmania, named after the British explorer George Bass (1763–1808); oil was discovered there in the 1960s.

bastard feudalism a late medieval development of ◊feudalism in which grants of land were replaced by money as rewards for service.

Conditions of service were specified in a contract, or indenture, between lord and retainer. The system allowed large numbers of men to be raised quickly for wars or private feuds.

Bastia port and commercial center in NE Corsica, France; population (1983) 50,500.

Bastille the castle of St Antoine, built about 1370 as part of the fortifications of Paris. It was made a state prison by Cardinal ◊Richelieu and was stormed by the mob that set the French Revolution in motion July 14, 1789. Only seven prisoners were found in the castle; the governor and most of the garrison were killed, and the Bastille was razed.

Bastos Augusto Roa 1917– . Paraguayan writer of short stories and novels, including *Son of Man* 1960 about the Chaco War between Bolivia and Paraguay, in which he fought.

Basutoland former name for ◊Lesotho.

bat flying mammal in which the forelimbs are developed as wings capable of rapid and sustained flight. There are two main groups of bats: megabats, or flying foxes, which eat fruit, and microbats, which mainly eat insects. Although by no means blind, many microbats rely largely on echolocation for navigation and finding prey, sending out pulses of high-pitched sound and listening for the echo. Bats are nocturnal, and those native to temperate countries hibernate in winter. There are about 1,000 species of bats forming the order Chiroptera, making this the second-largest mammalian order; bats make up nearly one fourth of the world's mammals. Although bats are widely distributed, bat populations have declined alarmingly and many species are now endangered.

megabats The Megachiroptera live in the tropical regions of the Old World, Australia, and the Pacific, and feed on fruit, nectar and pollen. The hind feet have five toes with sharp hooked claws which suspend the animal head downward when resting. Relatively large, up to 900 gm/2 lb and 5 ft/1.5 m wingspan, they have large eyes and a long face earning them the name "flying fox." Many rainforest trees depend on bats for pollination and seed dispersal, and some 300 bat-dependent plant species yield more than 450 economically valuable products. Some bats are keystone species on whose survival whole ecosystems may depend.

microbats Most bats are Microchiroptera, mainly small and insect-eating, though some species eat blood (◊vampire bats), frogs, or fish. They roost in caves, crevices, and hollow trees. A single bat may eat 3,000 insects in one night.

A bat's wings consist of a thin hairless skin stretched between the four fingers of the hand, and from the last finger down to the hindlimb. The thumb is free and has a sharp claw to help in climbing. Some bats live to be over 30 years old. An adult female bat usually rears only one pup a year. The bumblebee bat, inhabiting SE Asian rainforests, is the smallest mammal in the world. In China bats are associated with good luck.

Bataan peninsula in Luzon, the Philippines, which was defended against the Japanese in World War II by US and Filipino troops under General MacArthur 1 Jan–9 Apr 1942. MacArthur was evacuated, but some 67,000 Allied prisoners died on the Bataan Death March to camps in the interior.

Batak member of the several distinct but related peoples of N Sumatra in Indonesia. Numbering approximately 2.5 million, the Batak speak languages belonging to the Austronesian family.

The most numerous and most centrally located are the Toba Batak who live S and W of Lake Toba. Although the Batak possess distinctive traditional beliefs, they were influenced by Hinduism between the 2nd and 15th centuries. The syllabic script of the Batak, which was inscribed on bamboo, horn, bone, and tree bark, is based on Indian scripts. Although the island of Sumatra has many Muslim peoples, most Batak did not adopt Islam. Since 1861 German and other missionaries have been active in N Sumatra and today over 80% of the Batak profess Christianity. Many Batak are rice farmers and produce handicrafts such as dyed textiles.

Batavia former name until 1949 for ◊Jakarta, capital of Indonesia on Java.

Batavian Republic name given to the ◊Netherlands by the French 1795; it lasted until the establishment of the kingdom of the Netherlands 1814 at the end of the Napoleonic Wars.

Bates Alan 1934– . English actor, a versatile male lead in over 60 plays and films. His films include *Zorba the Greek* 1965, *Far from the Madding Crowd* 1967, *Women in Love* 1970, *The Go-Between* 1971, *The Shout* 1978, and *Duet for One* 1986.

Bates H(enry) W(alter) 1825–1892. English naturalist and explorer, who spent 11 years collecting animals and plants in South America and identified 8,000 new species of insects. He made a special study of ◊camouflage in animals, and his observation of insect imitation of species unpleasant to predators is known as "Batesian mimicry."

Bates H(erbert) E(rnest) 1906–1974. English author. Of his many novels and short stories, *The Jacaranda Tree* 1949 and *The Darling Buds of May* 1958 demonstrate the fineness of his natural observation and compassionate portrayal of character. *Fair Stood the Wind for France* 1944 was based on his experience as a Squadron Leader in World War II.

Bath historic city in Avon, England; population (1981) 75,000

features hot springs; the ruins of the baths for which it is named, as well as a great temple, are the finest Roman remains in Britain. Excavations in 1979 revealed thousands of coins and "curses," offered at a place which was thought to be the link between the upper and lower worlds. The Gothic Bath Abbey has an unusually decorated W front and fan vaulting. There is much 18th-century architecture, notably the Royal Crescent by John France Wood. The Assembly Rooms 1771 were destroyed in an air raid in 1942 but reconstructed in 1963. The University of Technology was established 1966. The Bath Festival Orchestra is based here.

history the Roman city of Aquae Sulis ("waters of Sul" – the British goddess of wisdom) was built in the first 20 years after the Roman invasion. In medieval times the hot springs were crown property, administered by the church, but the city was transformed in the 18th century to a fashionable spa, presided over by "Beau" ◊Nash. At his home here the astronomer Herschel discovered Uranus 1781. Visitors included the novelists Smollett, Fielding, and Jane Austen.

batholith a large, irregular, deep-seated mass of igneous rock, usually granite, with an exposed surface of more than 40 sq mi/100 sq km. The mass forms by intrusion or upswelling of magma through the surrounding rock. Batholiths form the core of all major mountain ranges.

According to plate tectonic theory, magma rises in subduction zones along continental margins where one plate sinks beneath another. The solidified magma becomes the central axis of a

battery

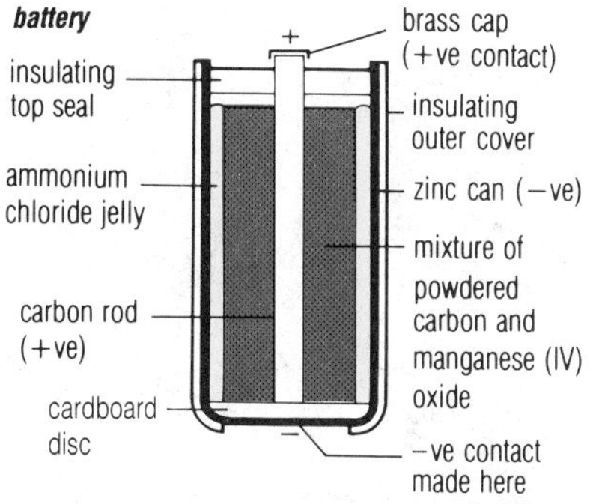
insulating top seal
ammonium chloride jelly
carbon rod (+ve)
cardboard disc
brass cap (+ve contact)
insulating outer cover
zinc can (−ve)
mixture of powdered carbon and manganese (IV) oxide
−ve contact made here
+
−

rising mountain range, resulting in the deformation (folding and overthrusting) of rocks on either side. Gravity measurements indicate that the downward extent or thickness of many batholiths is some 6–9 mi/10–15 km.

Bath, Order of the British order of knighthood, believed to have been founded in the reign of Henry IV (1399–1413). Formally instituted 1815, it included civilians from 1847 and women from 1970.

Báthory Stephen 1533–1586. King of Poland, elected by a diet convened in 1575 and crowned in 1576. Báthory succeeded in driving the Russian troops of Ivan the Terrible out of his country. His military successes brought potential conflicts with Sweden, but he died before these developed.

bathyal zone the upper part of the ocean, which lies on the Continental shelf at a depth of between 200 and 2,000 meters.

bathyscaph or ***bathyscaphe*** or ***bathyscape*** deep-sea diving apparatus used for exploration at great depths in the ocean. In 1960, Jacques Piccard and Don Walsh took the bathyscaph *Trieste* to a depth of 35,820 ft/10,917 m in the Challenger deep in the ◊Mariana Trench off the island of Guam in the Pacific Ocean.

bathysphere watertight steel sphere used for observation in deep-sea diving. It is lowered into the ocean by cable to a maximum depth of 3,000 ft/900 m.

batik Javanese technique of hand-applied color design for fabric; areas to be left undyed in a color are covered with wax. Practiced throughout Indonesia, the craft was introduced to the West by the Dutch.

Batista Fulgencio 1901–1973. Cuban dictator 1933–44 and 1952–59, whose authoritarian methods enabled him to jail his opponents and amass a large personal fortune. He was overthrown by rebel forces led by Fidel ◊Castro 1959.

Baton Rouge deepwater port on the Mississippi River; the capital of Louisiana; population (1990) 219,531. Industries include oil refining, petrochemicals, and iron. The port has become one of the nation's largest. Baton Rouge is the home of Louisiana State and Southern universities. It was settled in 1719 and was, successively, under French, British, Spanish, French, and Spanish rule before the residents rebelled against Spain 1819 and joined it to the US.

Battenberg title (conferred 1851) of German noble family; ~~its~~ members included ◊Louis, Prince of Battenberg, and Louis Alexander, Prince of Battenberg, who anglicized his name to Mountbatten 1917.

battery any energy storage device allowing release of electricity on demand. A battery is made up of one or more cells, each containing two conducting ◊electrodes (one positive, one negative) immersed in an ◊electrolyte, in a container. When an outside connection (such as through a light bulb) is made between the electrodes, a current flows through the circuit, and chemical reactions releasing energy take place within the cells.

Primary cell batteries are disposable; secondary cell batteries are rechargeable. The common dry cell is a primary cell battery based on the ◊Leclanche cell, and consists of a central carbon electrode immersed in a paste of manganese dioxide and ammonium chloride as the electrolyte. The zinc casing forms the other electrode. The lead-acid car battery is a group of rechargeable secondary cells. The car's alternator (◊generator) continually recharges the battery. It consists of sets of lead (positive) and lead peroxide (negative) plates in an electrolyte of sulfuric acid.

Baudelaire Perhaps the first great poet of the modern city, celebrating its contrasts of rich and poor, beauty and ugliness, Baudelaire spent almost all his adult life in Paris.

The introduction of rechargeable nickel-cadmium batteries has revolutionized portable electronic newsgathering (sound recording, video) and information processing (computing). These batteries offer a stable, short-term source of power free of noise and other hazards associated with mains electricity.

Battle Creek city in S Michigan, directly E of Kalamazoo. It became known as the cereal capital of the world after J H Kellogg, W K Kellogg, and C W Post established dry cereal and grain factories here; population (1990) 53,540. Battle Creek was also a station on the ◊Underground Railroad.

battleship a class of large warships with the biggest guns and heavist armor. In 1990, four US battleships were in active service.

Batumi port and capital in the Republic of Adzhar, USSR; population (1984) 111,000. Main industries include oil refining, food canning, and engineering.

baud in engineering, a unit of telegraph signaling speed equal to one pulse per second; also the number of bits per second that can be transmitted in a computer system.

Baudelaire Charles Pierre 1821–1867. French poet, whose work combined rhythmical and musical perfection with a morbid romanticism and eroticism, finding beauty in decadence and evil. His first book of verse was *Les Fleurs du mal*/◊*Flowers of Evil* 1857.

Baudouin 1930– . King of the Belgians from 1951. In 1950 his father, ◊Leopold III, abdicated and Baudouin was known until his succession in July 1951 as *Le Prince Royal*. In 1960 he married Fabiola de Mora y Aragón (1928–), member of a Spanish noble family.

Bauhaus a German school of Modern architecture and design founded 1919 by the architect Walter ◊Gropius at Weimar in Germany, in an attempt to fuse all arts, design, architecture and crafts into a functional, unified whole. Moved to Dessau under political pressure 1925, it was closed by the Nazis 1933 because of "decadence." Associated with the Bauhaus were the artists Klee and Kandinsky and the architect Mies van der Rohe. Gropius and Marcel Breuer worked together in the USA 1937–40. The international style of Modern architecture spread worldwide from there and in 1972 the Bauhaus Archive was installed in new premises in W Berlin.

bay

Bāul member of a Bengali mystical sect that emphasizes freedom from compulsion, from doctrine, and from social caste; they avoid all outward forms of religious worship. Not ascetic, they aim for harmony between physical and spiritual needs.

An oral tradition is passed down by gurus (teachers). The Bāuls make great use of music and poetry.

Baum L(yman) Frank 1856–1919. US writer, author of the children's fantasy *The Wonderful Wizard of Oz* 1900 and its 13 sequels. The series was continued by another author after his death. The film *The Wizard of Oz* 1939 was one of the most popular of all time.

Bausch Pina 1940– . German dance choreographer and director of the unique Wuppertal Tanztheater. Her works incorporate dialogue, elements of psychoanalysis, comedy, and drama. She never accepts requests to restage her creations.

bauxite the principal ore of ◊aluminum, consisting of a mixture of hydrated aluminum oxides and hydroxides, generally contaminated with compounds of iron, which give it a red color. Chief producers of bauxite are Australia, Guinea, Jamaica, the USSR, Suriname, and Brazil.

Bavaria (German Bayern) administrative region (German *Land*) of Germany
area 27,252 sq mi/70,600 sq km
capital Munich
towns Nuremberg, Augsburg, Würzburg, Regensburg
features largest of the German *Länder*; forms the Danube basin; festivals at Bayreuth and Oberammergau
products beer, electronics, electrical engineering, optics, automobiles, aerospace, chemicals, plastics, oil-refining, textiles, glass, toys
population (1988) 11,083,000
famous people Lucas Cranach, Hitler, Franz Josef Strauss, Richard Strauss
religion 70% Roman Catholic, 26% Protestant
history the last king, Ludwig III, abdicated 1918, and Bavaria declared itself a republic.

The original Bavarians were Teutonic invaders from Bohemia who occupied the country at the end of the 5th century. They were later ruled by dukes who recognized the supremacy of the emperor. The house of Wittelsbach ruled parts or all of Bavaria 1181–1918; Napoleon made the ruler a king 1806. In 1871 Bavaria became a state of the German Empire.

bay various species of ◊laurel, genus *Laurus*. The aromatic evergreen leaves are used for flavoring in cooking. There is also a golden-leaved variety.

Bay City industrial city in Michigan; population

(1990) 38,936. Industries include shipbuilding and engineering.

Bayern German name for ◊Bavaria, region of Germany.

Bayes Thomas 1702–1761. English mathematician, whose investigations into probability led to what is now known as Bayes' theorem.

Bayesian statistics a form of statistics that uses the knowledge of prior probability together with the probability of actual data to determine posterior probabilities, using Bayes' theorem.

Bayes' theorem in statistics, a theorem relating the ◊probability of particular events taking place to the probability that events conditional upon them have occurred.

For example, the probability of picking an ace at random out of a pack of cards is $4/52$. If two cards are picked out, the probability of the second card being an ace is conditional on the first card: if the first card was an ace the probability will be $3/51$; if not it will be $4/51$. Bayes' theorem gives the probability that given that the second card is an ace, the first card is also.

Bayeux town in N France; population (1982) 15,200. Its museum houses the Bayeux Tapestry. There is a 13th-century Gothic cathedral. Bayeux was the first town in W Europe to be liberated by the Allies in World War II, June 8, 1944.

Bayeux Tapestry a linen hanging 231 ft/70 m long and 20 in/50 cm wide, made about 1067–70, which gives a vivid pictorial record of the invasion of England by ◊William I (the Conqueror) 1066. It is an embroidery rather than a true tapestry, sewn with woolen threads in blue, green, red, and yellow, containing 72 separate scenes with descriptive wording in Latin. It is exhibited at the museum of Bayeaux in Normandy, France.

Bayle Pierre 1647–1706. French critic and philosopher. He was suspended from the chair of philosophy at Rotterdam under suspicion of religious skepticism in 1693. Three years later his *Dictionnaire historique et critique* appeared, which influenced among others the French Encyclopedists.

Bayliss William Maddock 1860–1924. English physiologist, who discovered the digestive hormone secretin with E H ◊Starling in 1902. During World War I, Bayliss introduced the use of saline (salt water) injections to help the injured recover from ◊shock.

Bay of Pigs inlet on the S coast of Cuba about 90 mi/145 km SW of Havana, the site of an unsuccessful invasion attempt by 1,500 US-sponsored Cuban exiles Apr 17–20, 1961; 1,173 were taken prisoner.

The creation of this anti-revolutionary force by the CIA had been authorized by the Eisenhower administration, and the project was executed under that of J F Kennedy. In 1962 most of the Cuban prisoners were ransomed for $53 million in food and medicine.

bayonet a short sword attached to the muzzle of a firearm. The bayonet was placed inside the barrel of the muzzle-loading muskets of the late 17th century. The *sock* or ring bayonet, invented 1700, allowed a weapon to be fired without interruption, leading to the demise of the pike.

Since the 1700s, bayonets have evolved into a variety of types. During World War I, the French used a long needle bayonet, while the Germans attached a bayonet, known as the butcher's knife, to their Mauser 98s. As armies have become more mechanized, bayonets have tended to decrease in length.

Although many military leaders have advocated the use of the bayonet, in practice it has been rarely used. For example, at Inkerman during the Crimean War 1854, only 6% of casualties were attributed to the bayonet. However, the morale effects associated with the fixing of bayonets has generally been considered to outweigh their disadvantages, which include restriction of movement and lack of real utility.

Bayonne river port in SW France; population (1983) 127,000. It trades in timber, steel, fertilizer, and brandy. It is a center of ◊Basque life. The bayonet was invented here.

bayou (corruption of French *boyau* "gut") in the Gulf States, an ◊oxbow lake or marshy offshoot of a river.

Bayous may be formed, as in the lower Mississippi, by a river flowing in wide curves or meanders in flat country, and then cutting a straight course across them in times of flood, leaving loops of isolated water behind.

Bay Psalm Book Puritan rendering of the psalms into meter, printed in 1639; it is considered the first work of American literature.

Written by Richard Mather, John Eliot, and 28 other ministers of the Massachusetts Bay Colony, it was published by Stephen Day in Cambridge, with an edition of 1,700 copies.

Bayreuth town in Bavaria, West Germany; population (1983) 71,000. It was the home of composer Richard ◊Wagner. The Wagner theater was established 1876, and opera festivals are held there every summer.

Bazaine Achille François 1811–1888. Marshal of France. From being a private soldier in 1831 he rose to command the French troops in Mexico 1862–67 and was made a marshal in 1864. In the Franco-Prussian War Bazaine allowed himself to be taken in the fortress of Metz, surrendering on Oct 27, 1870 with nearly 180,000 men. For this he was court-martialed in 1873 and imprisoned but in 1874 escaped to Spain.

BBC abbreviation for ◊British Broadcasting Corporation.

BC in the Christian calendar, abbreviation for before Christ; used with dates.

BCE abbreviation for before the Common (or Christian) Era; used with dates (instead of BC) by archeologists in the Near East who are not Christian.

B cell or ***B ◊lymphocyte*** immune cell in the blood that produces ◊antibodies. Each B cell produces just one type of antibody, specific to a single ◊antigen. Lymphocytes are related to ◊T cells.

BCG abbreviation for bacillus of ◊Calmette and Guérin, used as a vaccine to confer active immunity to ◊tuberculosis (TB).

BCG was developed in France after World War I from live bovine TB bacilli. These bacteria were bred in the laboratory over many generations until they became attenuated (weakened). Each inoculation contains just enough live, attenuated bacilli to provoke an immune response: the formation of specific ◊antibodies. The recipient then has lifelong protection against TB.

beach strip of land bordering the sea, normally consisting of boulders and pebbles on exposed coasts or sand on sheltered coasts. It is usually defined by the high-and low-water marks.

The material of the beach consists of a rocky debris eroded from exposed rocks and headlands. The material is transported to the beach, and along the beach, by waves that hit the coastline at an angle, resulting in a net movement of the material in one particular direction. This movement is known as longshore drift. Attempts are often made to halt longshore drift by erecting barriers, or jetties, at right angles to the movement. Pebbles are worn into round shapes by being battered against one another by wave action and the result is called shingle. The finer material, the sand, may be subsequently moved about by the wind and form sand dunes. Apart from the natural process of longshore drift, a beach may be threatened by the commercial use of sand and aggregate, by the mineral industry—since particles of metal ore are often concentrated into workable deposits by the wave action—and by pollution.

Beach Boys, The US pop group formed 1961. They began as exponents of vocal-harmony surf music with Chuck Berry guitar riffs (their hits include "Surfin' USA" 1963, and "Help Me, Rhonda" 1965) but the compositions, arrangements, and production by Brian Wilson (1942–) became

bear

highly complex under the influence of psychedelic rock, peaking with "Good Vibrations" 1966. Wilson spent most of the next 20 years in retirement but returned with a solo album 1988.

Beadle George Wells 1903–1989. US biologist. Born in Wahoo, Nebraska, he was professor of biology at the California Institute of Technology 1946–61. In 1958 he shared a Nobel Prize with Edward L Tatum for his work in biochemical genetics, forming the "one-gene-one-enzyme" hypothesis (a single gene codes for a single kind of enzyme).

beagle shorthaired hound with pendant ears, sickle tail, and belllike voice for hunting hares on foot ("beagling").

Beagle Channel channel to the S of Tierra del Fuego, South America, named after the ship of Charles ◊Darwin's voyage. Three islands at its E end, with krill and oil reserves within their 200 mi/322 km territorial waters, and the dependent sector of the Antarctic with its resources, were disputed between Argentina and Chile and awarded to Chile 1985.

beak the horn-covered projecting jaws of a bird, or other horny jaws such as those of the tortoise or octopus. The beaks of birds are adapted by shape and size to specific diets.

Beaker people people thought to be of Iberian origin who spread out over Europe in the 2nd millennium BC, and who began Stonehenge in England. They were skilled in metal-working, and their remains include earthenware beakers that distinguish them from other cultures of that time, hence the name.

beam balance instrument for measuring mass (or weight). A simple form consists of a beam pivoted at its midpoint with a pan hanging at each end. The mass to be measured, in one pan, is compared with a variety of standard masses placed in the other. When the beam is balanced, the masses' turning effects or moments under gravity, and hence the masses themselves, are equal.

bean any seed of numerous leguminous plants. Beans are rich in nitrogenous or protein matter and are grown both for human consumption and as food for cattle and horses. Varieties of bean are grown throughout Europe, the US, South America, China, Japan, and SE Asia.

The broad bean *Vicia faba* has been cultivated in Europe since prehistoric times. The French bean, kidney bean, or haricot *Phaseolus vulgaris* is probably of South American origin; the runner bean *Phaseolus coccineus* is closely allied to it, but differs in its climbing habit. Among beans of warmer countries are the lima or butter bean *Phaseolus lunatus* of South America; the soy bean *Glycine max*, extensively used in China and Japan; and the winged bean *Psophocarpus tetragonolobus* of SE Asia. The tuberous root of the winged bean has potential as a main crop in tropical areas where protein deficiency is common. The Asian mung bean *Phaseolus mungo* yields the bean sprouts used in Chinese cooking. Canned baked beans are usually a variety of *Phaseolus vulgaris*, which grows well in the US.

bear large mammal with a heavily built body, short powerful limbs, and very short tail. Bears breed once a year, producing one to four cubs. In northern regions they hibernate, and the young are born in the winter den. They are found mainly in North America and N Asia. The skin of the polar bear is black to conserve 80–90% of the solar energy trapped and channelled down the hollow hairs of its fur.

Bears walk on the soles of the feet and have long, nonretractable claws. There are seven species of bear, including the brown bear *Ursus arctos*, formerly ranging across most of Europe, N Asia, and North America, but now reduced in number. It varies in size from under 7 ft/2 m long in parts of the Old World to 9 ft/2.8 m long and 1,700 lb/780 kg in Alaska. The grizzly bear is a North American variety of this species and another subspecies, the Kodiak bear of Alaska, is the largest living land carnivore. The white polar bear *Thalarctos maritimus* is up to 8 ft/2.5 m long, has furry undersides to the feet, and feeds mainly on seals. It is found in the North polar region. The North American black bear *Euarctos americanus* and the Asian black bear *Selenarctos thibetanus* are smaller, only about 5 ft/1.6 m long. The latter has a white V-mark on its chest. The spectacled bear *Tremarctos ornatus* of the Andes is similarly sized, as is the sloth bear *Melursus ursinus* of India and Sri Lanka, which has a shaggy coat and uses its claws and protrusible lips to obtain termites, one of its preferred foods. The smallest bear is the Malaysian sun bear *Helarctos malayanus*, rarely more than 4 ft/1.2 m long, a good climber, whose favorite food is honey. The bear family, Ursidae, is related to carnivores such as dogs and weasels, and all are capable of killing prey. The panda is probably related to both bears and raccoons.

bear in business, a speculator who sells stocks or shares on the stock exchange expecting a fall in the price in order to buy them back at a profit, the opposite of a ◊bull. In a bear market, prices fall, and bears prosper.

bearberry any of several species of evergreen trailing shrub, genus *Arctostaphylos*, of the heath family, found on uplands and rocky places. Most bearberries are North American but *A. uva-ursi* is also found in Asia and Europe in northern mountainous regions. It bears small pink flowers in spring, followed by red berries that are edible but dry.

Beard Charles Austin 1874–1948. US historian. Born near Knightstown, Indiana, Beard earned a

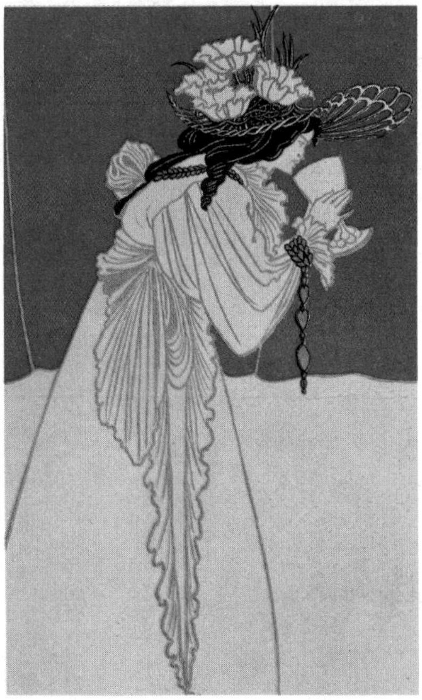

Beardsley *Isolde by Aubrey Beardsley (private collection).*

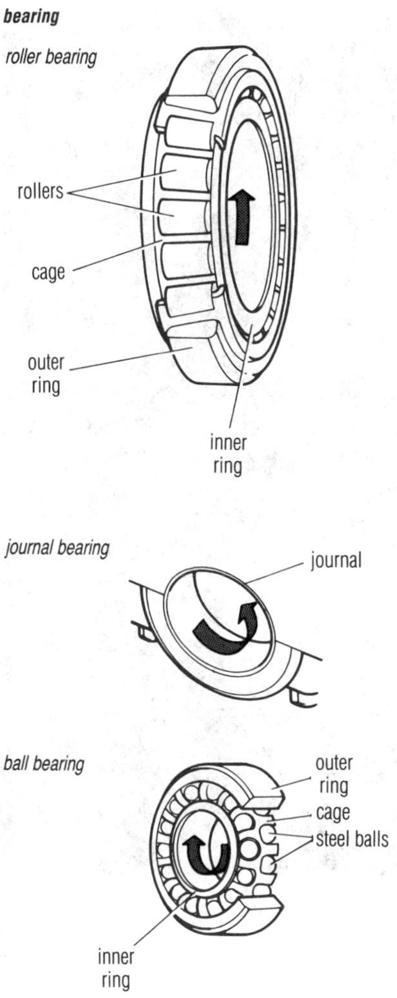
bearing
roller bearing
rollers
cage
outer ring
inner ring
journal bearing
journal
ball bearing
outer ring
cage
steel balls
inner ring

PhD from Columbia University 1904. A leading exponent of critical economic history, he published *An Economic Interpretation of the Constitution of the United States* 1913 and *The Economic Origins of Jeffersonian Democracy* 1915. He was a leader of the Progressive Movement and resigned from the Columbia faculty 1917 over issues of academic freedom. He helped found the New School for Social Research 1918. With his wife, Mary, he wrote *A Basic History of the United States* 1944, long a standard textbook.

Beardsley Aubrey (Vincent) 1872–1898. British illustrator. His meticulously executed black-and-white work displays the sinuous line and decorative mannerisms of Art Nouveau and was often charged with being grotesque and decadent.

Bear, Big and Little common names (and translations of the Latin) for the constellations ◊Ursa Major and ◊Ursa Minor respectively.

bearing device used in a machine to allow free movement between two parts, typically the rotation of a shaft in a housing. Ball bearings consist of two rings, one fixed to a housing, one to the rotating shaft. Between them is a set, or race, of steel balls. They are widely used to support shafts, as in the spindle in the hub of a bicycle wheel.

The sleeve, or journal, bearing is the simplest bearing. It is a hollow cylinder, split into two halves. It is used for the big-end and main bearings on a car ◊crankshaft.

In some machinery the balls of ball bearings are replaced by cylindrical rollers or thinner, needle bearings.

In precision equipment such as watches and aircraft instruments, bearings may be made from material such as ruby and are known as jewel bearings.

For some applications bearings made from nylon and other plastics are used. They need no lubrication because their surfaces are naturally waxy.

bearing angle that a fixed, distant point makes with true or magnetic north at the point of observation, or the angle of the path of a moving object with respect to the north lines. Bearings are measured in degrees and given as three-digit numbers increasing clockwise. For instance, NW would be denoted as 045M or 045T, depending whether the reference line were magnetic (M) or true (T) north.

Beas river in Himachal Pradesh, India, an upper tributary of the Sutlej, which in turn joins the Indus. It is one of the five rivers that give the Punjab its name. The ancient Hyphasis, it marked the limit of the invasion of India by Alexander the Great.

Beat Generation or ***Beat Movement*** the beatniks of the 1950s and 1960s, usually in their teens and early twenties, who rejected conventional lifestyles and opted for life on the road, drug experimentation, and antimaterialist values; and the associated literary movement whose members included William S Burroughs, Lawrence Ferlinghetti, Allen ◊Ginsberg, and Jack ◊Kerouac (who is credited with coining the term).

Beat literature has a free, unstructured style; the most important example is Ginsberg's poem *Howl* 1956. Jazz music, Zen, and hallucinogenic visions had a major influence on the attitudes and vocabulary of the Beats, who indicted the "madness" of modern society.

beatification in the Catholic church, the first step toward ◊canonization. Persons who have been beatified can be prayed to, and the title "Blessed" can be put before their names.

Beatitudes in the New Testament, the sayings of Jesus reported in Matthew 6: 1–12 and Luke 6: 20–38, depicting the spiritual qualities that characterize members of the Kingdom of God.

Beatles, The English pop group 1960–70. The members, all born in Liverpool, were John Lennon (1940–80, rhythm guitar, vocals), Paul McCartney (1942– , bass, vocals), George Harrison (1943– , lead guitar, vocals), and Ringo Starr (formerly Richard Starkey, 1940– , drums). Using songs written largely by Lennon and McCartney, the Beatles dominated rock music and pop culture in the 1960s.

In addition to experimenting with a wide range of musical styles, they greatly influenced subsequent bands, made films and toured extensively. Their hit songs include "She Loves You" 1963, "Can't Buy Me Love" 1964, and "Yesterday" 1965. Their films include *A Hard Day's Night* 1964, *Help* 1965, and the animated feature *Yellow Submarine* 1968, for which they provided the soundtrack. The Beatles continued to have an impact on the dress, hair, lifestyle, and thought of young people even after they pursued separate careers.

beat music style of pop music that evolved in the UK in the early 1960s, known in its purest form as ◊Mersey beat, and as British Invasion in the US. The beat groups characteristically had a simple, guitar-dominated line-up, vocal harmonies, and catchy tunes. They included the Beatles (1960–70), the Hollies (1962–), and the Zombies (1962–67).

Beaton Cecil 1904–1980. English portrait and fashion photographer, designer, illustrator, diarist, and conversationalist. He produced portrait studies and also designed scenery and costumes for ballets, and Art Deco sets for plays and films.

Beatrix 1936– . Queen of the Netherlands. The eldest daughter of Queen ◊Juliana, she succeeded to the throne on her mother's abdication 1980. In 1966, she married W German diplomat Claus von Amsberg (1926–).

Beatles, The *(Left to right) John Lennon, Ringo Starr, George Harrison, and Paul McCartney in 1963, at the start of their career.*

beats regular variations in the loudness of the sound when two notes of nearly equal pitch or ◊frequency are heard together. The beats result from the ◊interference between the sound of waves of the notes. The frequency of the beats equals the difference in frequency of the notes.

Musicians use the effect when tuning their instruments. A similar effect can occur in electrical circuits when two alternating currents are present, producing regular variations in the overall current.

Beaton *British photographer and designer Cecil Beaton in 1951.*

Beatty David, 1st Earl 1871–1936. British admiral in World War I. He commanded the cruiser squadron 1912–16 and bore the brunt of the Battle of Jutland.

Beatty Warren. Adopted name of Warren Beaty 1937– . US film actor and director, popular for such films as *Splendor in the Grass* 1961, *Bonnie and Clyde* 1967 and *Heaven Can Wait* 1978. His more recent productions include *Reds* 1981 (Academy Award for Best Producer) and *Dick Tracy* 1990.

Beaufort Francis 1774–1857. British admiral, hydrographer to the Royal Navy from 1829; the Beaufort scale and the Beaufort Sea in the Arctic Ocean are named after him.

Beaufort Henry 1375–1447. English priest, bishop of Lincoln from 1398, of Winchester from 1405. As chancellor of England, he supported his half-brother Henry IV, and made enormous personal loans to Henry V to finance war against France. As a guardian of Henry VI from 1421, he was in effective control of the country until 1426. In the same year he was created a cardinal. In 1431 he crowned Henry VI as king of France in Paris.

Beaufort scale system of recording wind velocity, devised in 1806 by Francis Beaufort. It is a numerical scale ranging from 0 to 17, calm being indicated by 0 and a hurricane by 12; 13–17 indicate degrees of hurricane force.

In 1874, the scale received international recognition; it was modified in 1926. Measurements are made at 33 ft/10 m above ground level.

Beaufort Sea section of the Arctic Ocean off Alaska and Canada, named after Francis Beaufort. Oil drilling is allowed only in the winter months because the sea is the breeding and migration route of bowhead whales, the staple diet of local Eskimo.

Beauharnais Alexandre, Vicomte de 1760–1794. French liberal aristocrat and general who served in the American Revolution and became a member of the National Convention in the early days of the French Revolution. He was the first husband of Josephine (consort of Napoleon I). Their daughter Hortense (1783–1837) married Louis, a younger brother of Napoleon, and their son became ◊Napoleon III. Beauharnais was guillotined during the Terror for his alleged lack of zeal for the revolutionary cause and his lack of success as Commander of the Republican Army of the North.

Beaujolais light, fruity red wine produced in the area S of Burgundy in E France. Beaujolais is best drunk while young; the broaching date is the third Thursday in Nov, when the new vintage is rushed to the US, the UK, Japan and other countries, so that the Beaujolais *nouveau* (new Beaujolais) may be marketed.

Beaumarchais Pierre Augustin Caron de 1732–1799. French dramatist. His great comedies *Le Barbier de Seville/The Barber of Seville* 1775 and *Le Mariage de Figaro/The Marriage of Figaro* (1778, but prohibited until 1784) form the basis of operas by ◊Rossini and ◊Mozart.

Louis XVI entrusted Beaumarchais with secret missions, notably for the profitable shipment of arms to the American colonies during the War of Independence. Accused of treason in 1792, he fled to Holland and England, but in 1799 he returned to Paris.

Beaumont city and port in SE Texas, NE of Houston, on the Neches river; seat of Jefferson county. It is an oil-processing center for the surrounding oil fields and a shipping point via the Sabine–Neches canal to the Gulf of Mexico. Shipbuilding and paper production are also industries; population (1990) 114,323. In 1901, when a successful oil

Beaufort scale

Number and Description	*Features*	*Air speed mi per hr*	*m per sec*
0 calm	smoke rises vertically; water smooth	less than 1	less than 0.3
1 light air	smoke shows wind direction; water ruffled	1–3	0.3–1.5
2 slight breeze	leaves rustle; wind felt on face	4–7	1.6–3.3
3 gentle breeze	loose paper blows around	8–12	3.4–5.4
4 moderate breeze	branches sway	13–18	5.5–7.9
5 fresh breeze	small trees sway, leaves blown off	19–24	8.0–10.7
6 strong breeze	whistling in telephone wires; sea spray from waves	25–31	10.8–13.8
7 moderate gale	large trees sway	32–38	13.9–17.1
8 fresh gale	twigs break from trees	39–46	17.2–20.7
9 strong gale	branches break from trees	47–54	20.8–24.4
10 whole gale	trees uprooted, weak buildings collapse	55–63	24.5–28.4
11 storm	widespread damage	64–72	28.5–32.6
12 hurricane	widespread structural damage	above 73	above 32.7

Beaumarchais *French comic dramatist Pierre Augustin Caron de Beaumarchais. He was forced to flee France during the Revolution.*

well was drilled at Spindletop Field, the modern oil industry began in the West.

Beaumont Francis 1584–1616. English dramatist and poet. From about 1608 he collaborated with John ◊Fletcher. Their joint plays include *Philaster* 1610, *The Maid's Tragedy* about 1611, and *A King and No King* about 1611. *The Woman Hater* about 1606 and *The Knight of the Burning Pestle* about 1607 are ascribed to Beaumont alone.

Beaumont William 1785–1853. US surgeon who conducted pioneering experiments on the digestive system. In 1882 he saved the life of a Canadian trapper wounded in the side by a gun blast; the wound only partially healed and, through an opening in the stomach wall, Beaumont was able to observe the workings of the stomach. His *Experiments and Observations on the Gastric Juice and the Physiology of Digestion* was published in 1833.

Beaune town SW of Dijon, France; population (1982) 21,100. It is the center of the Burgundian wine trade, and has a wine museum. Other products include agricultural equipment and mustard.

Beauregard Pierre Gustave Toutant (1818–1893) US military leader and Confederate general. His military successes were clouded by his conflicts with Confederate President Jefferson Davis.

Beauregard was born in Louisiana and graduated from West Point in 1838. He distinguished himself during the Mexican War and then returned to Louisiana. In 1861 he was appointed superintendent of West Point, but resigned after four days to join the South.

At the outset of the Civil War, Beauregard achieved fame immediately for his attack on Fort Sumter. He played a leading role in the Confederate victory at the 1st Battle of Bull Run and prevented disaster at Shiloh (1862) through an orderly withdrawal. His disagreements with Davis, however, resulted in frequent changes in his commands. In 1865 he helped to delay the Union advance on Petersburg, Virginia. He spent his postwar years in New Orleans, where he was prominent in business and politics.

Beauvais town 47 mi/76 km NW of Paris, France; population (1982) 54,150. It is a market town trading in fruit, dairy produce, and agricultural machinery. It has a Gothic cathedral, the tallest in France: (223 ft/68 m), and is reknowned for tapestries (◊Gobelin), now made in Paris.

Beauvoir Simone de 1908–1986. French Socialist, feminist, and writer, who taught philosophy at the Sorbonne university in Paris 1931–43. Her book *Le Deuxième sexe/The Second Sex* 1949 became a seminal work for many feminists.

Her novel of postwar Paris, *Les Mandarins/ The Mandarins* 1954, has characters resembling the writers Albert Camus, Arthur Koestler, and Jean-Paul ◊Sartre. She also published autobiographical volumes.

beaver aquatic rodent *Castor fiber* with webbed hind feet, broad flat scaly tail, and thick waterproof fur. It has very large incisor teeth and fells trees to feed on the bark and to use the logs to construct the "lodge," in which the young are reared, food is stored, and where much of the winter is spent.

Beavers can construct dams on streams, and thus modify the environment considerably. They once ranged across Europe, N Asia, and North America, but in Europe now only survive where they are protected, and are reduced elsewhere, partly through trapping for the fur.

Beaverbrook (William) Max(well) Aitken, 1st Baron 1879–1964. British newspaper proprietor and politician, born in Canada. He bought a majority interest in the *Daily Express* 1919, founded the *Sunday Express* 1921, and bought the London *Evening Standard* 1929. He served in Lloyd George's World War I cabinet and Churchill's World War II cabinet.

Bebel August 1840–1913. German Socialist and founding member of the Verband deutsche Arbeitervereine (League of German Workers' Clubs), together with Wilhelm Liebknecht 1869. Also known as the Eisenach Party, he became its leading speaker in the Reichstag; it was based in Saxony and SW Germany before being incorporated into the SPD (Sozialdemokratische Partei Deutschlands/German Social Democratic Party) 1875.

bebop or *bop* a rhythmically complex, virtuosic, highly improvisational, "hot" jazz style that was developed in the US 1945–55 by Charlie Parker, Dizzy Gillespie, Thelonius Monk, and other disaffected black musicians who were engaged in "protest" performances.

Beccaria Cesare, Marese di Beccaria 1738–1794. Italian philanthropist, born in Milan. He opposed capital punishment and torture; advocated education as a crime preventative; influenced ◊Bentham; and coined the phrase "the greatest happiness of the greatest number," the tenet of ◊utilitarianism.

Bechet Sidney (Joseph) 1897–1959. US jazz musician, born in New Orleans. He played clarinet and was the first to forge an individual style on soprano saxophone. Bechet was based in Paris in the late 1920s and the 1950s, where he was recognized by Classical musicians as a serious artist.

Bechuanaland former name until 1966 of ◊Botswana.

Becker Boris 1967– . German tennis player. In 1985 he became the youngest winner of a singles title at Wimbledon at the age of 17. He has won the title three times and helped West Germany to win the Davis Cup 1988 and 1989. He also won the US Open 1989.

Beauvoir *Simone de Beauvoir, the distinguished French literary figure and philosopher of the feminist movement.*

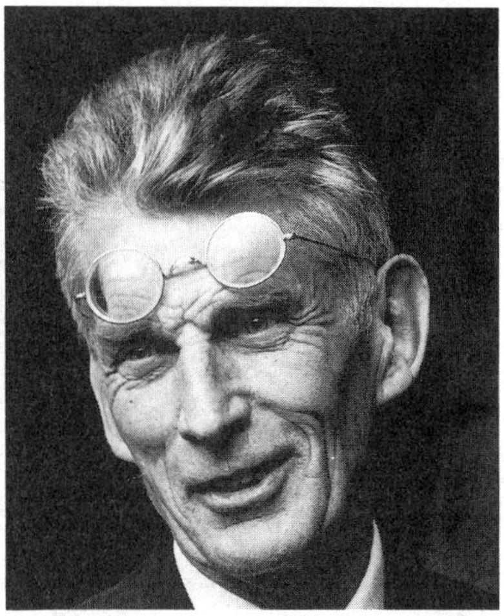

Beckett *Irish novelist and dramatist Samuel Beckett, winner of the Nobel Prize for Literature in 1969.*

Becket St Thomas à 1118–1170. English priest and politician. He was chancellor to ◊Henry II 1155–62, when he was appointed archbishop of Canterbury. The interests of the church soon conflicted with those of the crown and Becket was assassinated; he was canonized 1172.

He resisted Henry's attempts to regulate relations between church and state, and was murdered by four knights before the altar of Canterbury cathedral.

Beckett Samuel 1906–1989. Irish novelist and dramatist, who wrote in French and English. His *En attendant Godot/Waiting for Godot* 1952 is possibly the most universally known example of Theater of the ◊Absurd (in which life is taken to be meaningless). This genre is taken to further extremes in *Fin de Partie/Endgame* 1957 and *Happy Days* 1961. Nobel Prize for Literature 1969.

Beckmann Max 1884–1950. German Expressionist painter who fled the Nazi regime in 1933 for the US. After World War I his art was devoted to themes of cruelty in human society, portraying sadists and their victims with a harsh style of realism.

Beckmann was born in Leipzig. He fought in World War I and was discharged following a breakdown, reflected in the agony of his work; pictures include *Carnival* and *The Titanic*. He later painted enormous triptychs, full of symbolic detail. He died in New York.

becquerel SI unit (abbreviation Bq) of ◊radioactivity, equal to one radioactive disintegration (change in the nucleus of an atom when a particle or ray is given off) per second.

The becquerel is much smaller than the previous standard unit, the ◊curie, and so can be used for measuring smaller quantities of radioactivity. It is named after Antoine Becquerel.

Becquerel Antoine Henri 1852–1908. French physicist who discovered penetrating radiation coming from uranium salts, the first indication of ◊radioactivity, and shared a Nobel Prize with Marie and Pierre ◊Curie in 1903.

bed in geology, a single ◊sedimentary rock unit with a distinct set of physical characteristics or contained fossils, readily distinguishable from those of beds above and below. Well-defined partings called bedding planes separate successive beds or strata.

The depth of a bed can vary from a fraction of a centimeter to several meters or feet, and can extend over any area. The term is also used to indicate the floor beneath a body of water (lake bed) and a layer formed by a fall of particles (lava bed).

bedbug flattened wingless red-brown insect *Cimex*

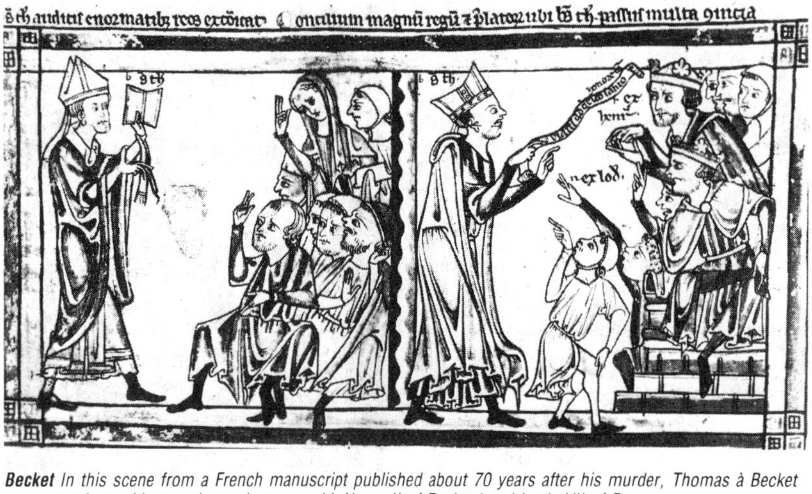

Becket *In this scene from a French manuscript published about 70 years after his murder, Thomas à Becket excommunicates his enemies and argues with Henry II of England and Louis VII of France.*

lectularius with piercing mouthparts. It hides by day in crevices or bedclothes and emerges at night to suck human blood.

Bede c. 673–735. English theologian and historian, known as the Venerable Bede, active in Durham and Northumbria. He wrote many scientific, theological, and historical works. His *Historia Ecclesiastica Gentis Anglorum/Ecclesiastical History of the English People* 731 is a seminal source for early English history.

Bedford administrative headquarters of Bedfordshire, England; population (1983) 89,200. Industries include agricultural machinery and airships. John Bunyan wrote *The Pilgrim's Progress* (1678) while imprisoned here.

Bedlam abbreviation of Bethlehem, the earliest mental hospital in Europe. The hospital was opened in the 14th century in London and is now sited in Surrey. It is now used as a slang word meaning chaos.

Bedlington breed of ◊terrier with short body, long legs, and curly hair, usually gray, named after a district of Northumberland, England.

Bedouin an Arab of any of the nomadic tribes occupying the desert regions of Arabia, Syria, and North Africa, now becoming increasingly settled. Their traditional livelihood was the rearing and trading of horses and camels.

bee four-winged insect of the super-family Apoidea in the order Hymenoptera, usually with a sting. There are over 12,000 species, of which less than 1 in 20 are social in habit.

Most familiar is the bumblebee, genus *Bombus*, which is larger and stronger than the hive bee and so is adapted to fertilize plants in which the pollen and nectar lie deep, as in red clover; they can work in colder weather than the hive bee. The hive or honey bee *Apis mellifera* establishes perennial colonies of about 80,000, the majority being infertile females (workers), with a few larger fertile males (drones), and a single very large fertile female (the queen).

Solitary bees include species useful in pollinating orchards in spring, and may make their nests in tunnels under the ground or in hollow plant stems; "cuckoo" bees lay their eggs in the nests of bumblebees, which they closely resemble.

Social bees, apart from the bumblebee and the hive bee, include the stingless South American vulture bee *Trigona hypogea*, discovered in 1982, which is solely carnivorous.

Bees transmit information to each other about food sources by a "dance," each movement giving rise to sound impulses which are picked up by tiny hairs on the back of the bee's head, the orientation of the dance also having significance. They use the sun in navigation (see also under ◊migration). Besides their use in crop pollination and production of honey and wax, bees (by a measure of contaminants brought back to their hives) can provide an inexpensive and effective monitor of industrial and other pollution of the atmosphere and soil.

Most bees are pacific unless disturbed, but some South American species are aggressive. Bee stings may be fatal to people who are allergic to them, but this is comparatively rare. A vaccine treatment against bee stings, which uses concentrated venom, has been developed; see ◊melitin.

bee

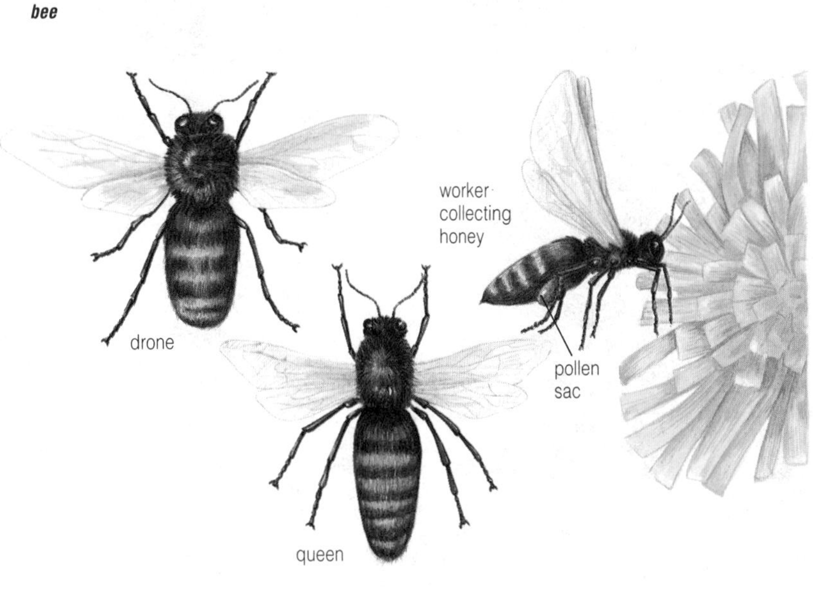
drone
worker collecting honey
pollen sac
queen

bee *The head of a honey worker bee.*

Beebe Charles 1877–1962. US naturalist, explorer, and writer. His interest in deep-sea exploration led to a collaboration with the engineer Otis Barton and the development of a spherical diving vessel, the bathysphere. On August 24, 1934 the two men made a record-breaking dive to 3028 ft/ 923 m. Beebe's expeditions are described in a series of memoirs.

beech genus of trees *Fagus*, of the family Fagaceae. Of the ten species in this genus only one is native to North America; others grow in Europe. The American beech *F. grandifolia* grows to 100 ft/ 30 m, with blue-gray bark; a broad, rounded crown; and leaves that are lanceolate, serrate, triangular and edible.

Beecham Thomas 1879–1961. British conductor and impresario. He established the Royal Philharmonic Orchestra in 1946 and fostered the works of composers such as Delius, Sibelius, and Richard Strauss.

Beecher Henry Ward 1813–1887. US Congregational minister and militant opponent of slavery, son of the pulpit orator Lyman ◊Beecher and brother of the writer Harriet Beecher ◊Stowe.

He traveled to Britain and did much to turn sentiment against the South.

Beecher Lyman 1775–1863. Congregational and Presbyterian minister, one of the most influential pulpit orators of his time. As a pastor in Connecticut and Boston, he preached against Unitarianism and Roman Catholicism and contributed to the development of the New Haven theology of evangelical Calvinism. He was the father of Harriet Beecher ◊Stowe and Henry Ward Beecher.

bee-eater bird *Merops apiaster* found in Africa, S Europe, and Asia. It feeds on a variety of insects, including bees, which it catches in its long narrow bill. Chestnut, yellow, and blue-green, it is gregarious, and generally nests in river banks and sandpits.

beech

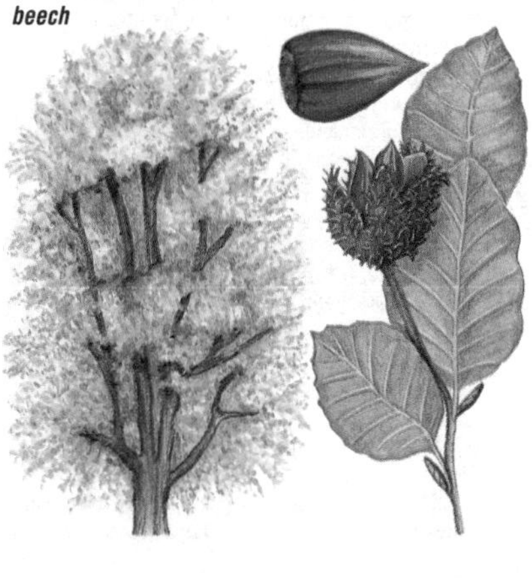

Beelzebub (Hebrew "lord of the flies") in the New Testament, the leader of the devils, sometimes identified with Satan and sometimes with his chief assistant (see ◊devil). In the Old Testament Beelzebub was a fertility god worshiped by the Philistines and other Semitic groups (Baal).

beer alcoholic drink made from water and malt (fermented barley or other grain), flavored with hops. Beer contains between 1% and 6% alcohol. One of the oldest alcoholic drinks, it was brewed in ancient China, Egypt, and Babylon.

The distinction between beer (containing hops) and ale (without hops) was made in medieval times. Beer is now a generic term including pilsner and lager. Stout is top fermented but is sweet and strongly flavored with roasted grain; lager (German "store") is a light beer, bottom fermented and matured over a longer period. Modern ales are made with hops like beer, but fermented more rapidly at relatively high temperatures. In the US, light beers and lite beers are made with more water, fewer calories, and less alcohol.

Beerbohm Max 1872–1956. British caricaturist and author, the half brother of the actor and manager Herbert Beerbohm Tree (1853–1917). A perfectionist in style, he contributed to *The Yellow Book* in 1894; wrote the novel of Oxford undergraduate life, *Zuleika Dobson* 1911; and published volumes of caricature, including *Rossetti and His Circle* 1922. He succeeded G B Shaw as critic to the *Saturday Review* 1898.

Beersheba industrial town in Israel; population (1987) 115,000. It is the chief center of the Negev desert and has been a settlement from the Stone Age.

beet plant of the genus *Beta* of the goosefoot family Chenapodiaceae. The common beet *B. vulgaris* is used in one variety to produce sugar, and another, the mangelwurzel, is grown as cattle fodder. The beetroot or red beet *B. rubra* is a salad plant.

Beethoven Ludwig van 1770–1827. German composer and pianist, whose mastery of musical expression in every genre made him the dominant influence on 19th-century music. Beethoven's repertoire includes concert overtures; the opera *Fidelio*; seven complete piano concertos and two for violin (one unfinished); 32 piano sonatas, including the *Moonlight* and *Appassionata*; 17 string quartets; the *Mass in D* (*Missa solemnis*); and nine complete symphonies, as well many youthful works. He usually played his own piano pieces and conducted his orchestral works until he was hampered by deafness 1801; nevertheless he continued to compose.

Born in Bonn, the son and grandson of musicians, Beethoven became deputy organist at the court of the Elector of Cologne at Bonn before he was 12; later he studied under ◊Haydn and possibly ◊Mozart, whose influence dominated his early work. Beginning in 1809 he received a small allowance from aristocratic patrons.

beetle common name of insects in the order Coleoptera (Greek "sheath-winged") with leathery forewings folding down in a protective sheath over the membranous hindwings, which are those used for flight. They pass through a complete metamorphosis. They include some of the largest and smallest of all insects; the largest is the Hercules beetle *Dynastes hercules* of the South American rainforests, 6 in/15 cm long, the smallest only 0.02 in/0.05 cm. Comprising more than 50% of the animal kingdom, beetles number some 370,000 named species, with many not yet described.

Beetles are found in virtually every land and freshwater habitat, and feed on virtually anything edible. Examples include: click beetle or skipjack species of the family Elateridae, so called because if they fall on their backs they right themselves with a jump and a loud click; the larvae, known as wireworms, feed on the roots of crops. In some tropical species of Elateridae the beetles

Begin *Israeli politician Menachem Begin.*

have luminous organs between the head and abdomen and are known as fireflies. The potato pest Colorado beetle *Leptinotarsa decemlineata* is striped in black and yellow. The blister beetle *Lytta vesicatoria*, a shiny green species from S Europe, was once sold pulverized as an aphrodisiac and contains the toxin cantharidin. The furniture beetle *Anobium punctatum* and its relatives are serious pests of timber buildings and furniture through their "woodworm" larvae.

begging soliciting, usually for money and food. It is prohibited in many Western countries and stringent measures are taken against begging in the USSR. In the Middle East and Asia, almsgiving is often considered a religious obligation.

Begin Menachem 1913– . Israeli politician, born in Poland. He was a leader of the extremist Irgun Zvai Leumi organization in Palestine from 1942; was prime minister of Israel 1977–83, as head of the right-wing Likud party; and in 1978 shared a Nobel Peace Prize with President Sadat of Egypt for work on the ◊Camp David Agreements for a Middle East peace settlement.

begonia any plant of the genus *Begonia* of the tropical and subtropical plant family Begoniaceae. Begonias have fleshy and succulent leaves, and some have large, brilliant flowers. There are numerous species native to the tropics, in particular South America and India.

Behan Brendan 1923–1964. Irish dramatist. His early experience of prison and knowledge of the workings of the ◊IRA (recounted in his autobiography *Borstal Boy* 1958) provided him with two recurrent themes in his plays. *The Quare Fellow* 1954 was followed by the tragicomedy *The Hostage* 1958, first written in Gaelic.

behaviorism school of psychology originating in the US, of which the leading exponent was John Broadus ◊Watson. Behaviorists maintain that all human activity can ultimately be explained in terms of conditioned reactions or reflexes and habits formed in consequence. Leading behaviorists include ◊Pavlov and B F ◊Skinner.

behavior therapy in psychology, the application of behavioral principles, derived from learning theories, to the treatment of clinical conditions such as ◊phobias, ◊obsessions, and sexual and interpersonal problems. For example, in treating a phobia the person is taken into the feared situation in gradual steps. Over time, the fear typically reduces, and the problem becomes less acute.

behemoth (Hebrew "beasts") in the Old Testament (Job 40), an animal cited by God as evidence of his power; usually thought to refer to the hippopotamus. It is used proverbially to mean any giant and powerful creature.

Behn Aphra 1640–1689. English novelist and playwright, the first woman in England to earn her living as a writer. Her writings were criticized for their explicitness; they frequently present events from a woman's point of view. Her novel *Oronooko* 1688 is an attack on slavery.

Between 1670 and 1687 fifteen of her plays were produced, including *The Rover*, which attacked forced and mercenary marriages. She had the patronage of James I and was employed as a government spy in Holland in 1666.

Behrens Peter 1868–1940. German architect. He pioneered the adaptation of architecture to industry, and designed the AEG turbine factory in Berlin 1909, a landmark in industrial design. He influenced ◊Le Corbusier and ◊Gropius.

Behring Emil von 1854–1917. German physician who discovered that the body produces antitoxins, substances able to counteract poisons released by bacteria. Using this knowledge, he developed new treatments for diseases such as ◊diphtheria.

Educated in Berlin, Behring was Robert ◊Koch's assistant before becoming professor of hygiene at Halle and Marburg. He won the 1901 Nobel Prize for Medicine.

Beiderbecke Bix (Leon Bismarck) 1903–1931. US jazz cornetist, composer, and pianist. A romantic soloist with the King Oliver, Louis Armstrong, and Paul Whiteman orchestras, Beiderbecke was the first acknowledged white jazz innovator. He was inspired by the Classical composers Debussy, Ravel, and Stravinsky.

His reputation grew after his early death with the publication of Dorothy Baker's novel *Young Man with a Horn* 1938.

Beijing or ***Peking*** capital of the People's Republic of China; part of its NE border is formed by the Great Wall of China; population (1986) 5,860,000. The municipality of Beijing has an area of 6,871 sq mi/17,800 sq km and a population (1986) of 9,750,000. Industries include textiles, petrochemicals, steel, and engineering.

Features include Tianamen Gate (Gate of Heavenly Peace) and Tianamen Square, where, in 1989, Chinese troops massacred over 1,000 students and civilians demonstrating for greater freedom and democracy; the Forbidden City, built between 1406 and 1420 as Gu Gong (Imperial Palace) of the Ming Emperors, where there were 9,000 ladies in waiting and 10,000 eunuchs in service (it is now the seat of the government); the Great Hall of the People 1959 (used for official banquets); museums of Chinese history and of the Chinese revolution; Chairman Mao Memorial Hall 1977 (shared from 1983 with Zhou Enlai, Zhu De, and Liu Shaoqi); the Summer Palace built by the dowager empress Zi Xi (damaged by the European powers 1900, but restored 1903); Temple of Heaven (Tiantan); and Ming tombs 30 mi/50 km to the NW.

history Beijing, founded 2,000 years ago, was the 13th-century capital of the Mongol emperor Kublai Khan. Later replaced by Nanking, it was again capital from 1421, except from 1928 to 1949, when it was renamed Peiping.

Beijing was held by Japan 1937–45.

Beira port at the mouth of the river Pungwe, Mozambique; population (1986) 270,000. It is a major port, and exports minerals, cotton, and food products. A railroad through the Beira Corridor links the port with Zimbabwe.

Beirut or ***Beyrouth*** capital and port of Lebanon, devastated by civil war in the 1970s and 1980s and occupied by armies of neighboring countries; population (1980) 702,000. The city is divided into a Christian eastern and a Muslim western sector by the Green Line.

history Beirut dates back to at least 1400 BC. Until the civil war 1975–76, Beirut was an international financial and educational center, with four universities (Lebanese, Arab, French, and US); it was also a center of espionage. It was besieged and virtually destroyed by the Israeli army July–Sept 1982 to ensure the withdrawal of the forces of the Palestinian Liberation Organization. After the ceasefire, 500 Palestinians were massacred in the Sabra–Chatila camps Sept 16–18, 1982, by dissident ◊Phalangist and ◊Maronite troops, with alleged Israeli complicity. Civil disturbances continued, characterized by sporadic street fighting and hostage taking. In 1987 Syrian troops were sent in but fighting and disruption continued.

Bejaia formerly ***Bougie*** port in Algeria, 120 mi/193 km E of Algiers; population (1982) 145,000. It is linked by pipeline with oil wells at Hassi Messaoud. It exports wood and hides.

Bekka, the or ***El Beqa'a*** a governorate of E Lebanon separated from Syria by the Anti-Lebanon mountains. The Bekka Valley has been of strategic importance in the Syrian struggle for control of N Lebanon. In the early 1980s the valley was penetrated by Shia Muslims who established an extremist Hezbollah stronghold with the support of Iranian Revolutionary Guards. Zahlé and the ancient city of Baalbek are the chief towns.

Belasco David 1859–1931. US playwright and producer. His works include *Madame Butterfly* 1900 and *The Girl of the Golden West* 1905, both of which ◊Puccini used as libretti for operas. Many of his plays were written in collaboration with others, including J A Herne. As a producer, Belasco was known more for his technical innovations than for the quality of the plays he chose. His name was a big draw for theater audiences, and he made stars out of many unknown performers.

Belaúnde Terry Fernando 1913– . President of Peru from 1963 to 1968 and from 1980 to 1985. He championed land reform and the construction of roads to open up the Amazon valley. He fled to the US in 1968 after being deposed by a military junta. After his return, his second term in office was marked by rampant inflation, enormous foreign debts, terrorism, mass killings, and human-rights violations by the armed forces.

Belau, Republic of formerly Palau self-governing island group in Micronesia; area 193 sq mi/500 sq km; population (1988) 14,000. It is part of the US Trust Territory, and became internally self-governing 1980.

There are 26 larger islands (8 inhabited) and about 300 islets. Three referendums have shown that Belau wishes to remain "nonnuclear," although the US is exerting strong pressure to secure nuclear facilities for itself.

Spain held the islands from about 1600, and sold them to Germany 1899. Japan seized them in World War I, administered them by League of Nations mandate, and used them as a naval base during World War II. They were captured by the US 1944, and became part of its Trust Territory 1947.

bel canto (Italian "beautiful song") in music, an 18th-century Italian style of singing with emphasis on perfect technique and beautiful tone. The style reached its peak in the operas of Rossini, Donizetti, and Bellini.

Belém port and naval base in N Brazil; population (1980) 758,000. The chief trade center of the Amazon Basin, it is also known as Pará, the name of the state of which it is capital. It was founded about 1615 as Santa Maria de Belém do Grãs Pará.

belemnite extinct relative of the squid, with rows of little hooks rather than suckers on the arms. The parts of belemnites most frequently found as fossils are the bullet-shaped shells that were within the body. Like squid, these animals had an ink sac which could be used to produce a smokescreen when attacked.

Belfast industrial port (shipbuilding, engineering, electronics, textiles, tobacco) and capital of Northern Ireland since 1920; population (1985) 300,000. From 1968 it has been heavily damaged by guerrilla activities.

history Belfast grew up around a castle built in 1177 by John de Courcy. With the settlement of English and Scots, Belfast became a center of Irish Protestantism in the 17th century. An influx of Huguenots after 1685 extended the linen industry, and the 1800 Act of Union with England resulted in the promotion of Belfast as an industrial center. It was created a city in 1888, with a lord mayor from 1892. The former parliament buildings are to the S at Stormont.

Belfort town in NE France; population (1983) 54,500. It is in the strategic Belfort Gap between the Vosges and Jura mountains and is the capital of the *département* of Territoire de Belfort. Industries include chemicals, engineering, plastics, and textiles.

Belgae a people who lived in Gaul in Roman times, N of the Seine and Marne rivers. They were defeated by Caesar in 57 BC. Many of the Belgae settled in SE England during the 2nd century BC.

Belgaum city in Karnataka, S India; population (1981) 300,000. The main industry is cotton manufacture. It is also known for its Jain temples.

Belgian Congo former name 1908–60 of ◊Zaïre.

Belgian literature writers in French have included Georges Eekhoud (1854–1927), who wrote of Flemish peasant life; Emile Verhaeren (1855–1916); and Maurice Maeterlinck. For writers in Flemish, see ◊Flemish literature.

Belgium country in N Europe, bounded N by the Netherlands, NW by the North Sea, S and W by France, E by Luxembourg and Germany

government A parliamentary democracy under a constitutional monarch, with nine provinces, Belgium's constitution dates from 1831 and was most recently revised 1971. The prime minister and cabinet are drawn from and answerable to the legislature, which exercises considerable control over the executive. The legislature consists of a senate and a chamber of representatives. The senate has 182 members: 106 nationally elected, 50 representing the provinces, 25 coopted and, by right, the heir to the throne. Senators are elected for four years. The chamber of representatives has 212 members elected by universal suffrage, through a system of proportional representation, for a four-year term. On the basis of parliamentary support, the monarch appoints the prime minister, who chooses the cabinet.

The multiplicity of political parties reflects the linguistic and social divisions. The main parties are the Dutch-speaking Social Christian Party (CVP), the French-speaking Social Christian Party (PSC), the Dutch-speaking Socialist Party (SP), the French-speaking Socialist Party (PS), the Dutch-speaking Liberal Party (PVV), the French-speaking Liberal Party (PRL), and the Flemish People's Party (VU).

history The first recorded inhabitants were the Belgae, an ancient Celtic people. Conquered by the Romans, the area was known from 15 BC as the Roman province of Belgica; from the 3rd century AD onward it was overrun by the Franks. Under ◊Charlemagne, Belgium became the center of the Carolingian dynasty, and the peace and order during this period fostered the growth of such towns as Ghent, Bruges, and Brussels. Following the division of Charlemagne's empire in 843 the area became part of Lotharingia. By the 11th century seven feudal states had emerged: the counties of Flanders, Hainault, and Namur, the duchies of Brabant, Limburg, and Luxembourg, and the bishopric of Liège, all nominally

Belgium
Kingdom of
(French *Royaume de Belgique*, Flemish *Koninkrijk België*)

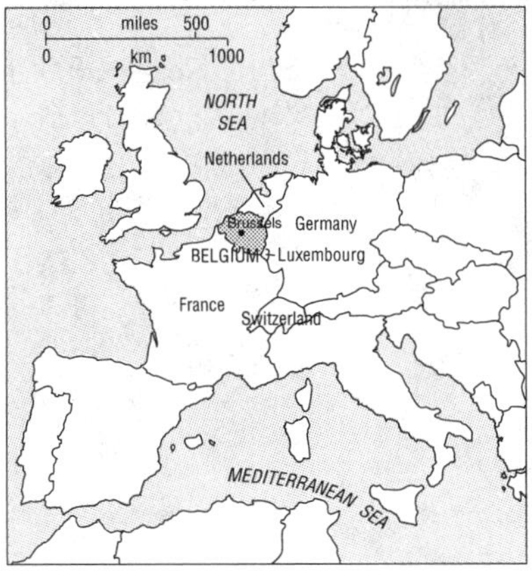
0 miles 500
0 km 1000
NORTH SEA
Netherlands
Brussels
Germany
BELGIUM
Luxembourg
France
Switzerland
MEDITERRANEAN SEA

area 11,784 sq mi/30,510 sq km
capital Brussels
cities Ghent, Liège, Charleroi, Bruges, Mons, Namur, Leuven; ports are Antwerp, Ostend, Zeebrugge
physical fertile coastal plain in NW, central rolling hills rise eastward, hills and forest in SE
features Ardennes Forest; rivers Scheldt and Meuse
head of state King Baudouin from 1951
head of government Wilfried Martens from 1981
political system liberal democracy
political parties Flemish Social Christian Party (CVP), center-left; French Social Christian Party (PSC), center-left; Flemish Socialist Party (SP), left-of-center; French Socialist Party (PS), left-of-center; Flemish Liberal Party (PVV), moderate centrist; French Liberal Reform Party (PRL), moderate centrist; Flemish People's Party (VU), federalist; Flemish Green Party (Agalev); French Green Party (Ecolo)
exports iron, steel, textiles, manufactured goods, petrochemicals, plastics, vehicles, diamonds
currency Belgian franc
population (1990 est) 9,895,000 (comprising Flemings and Walloons); growth rate 0.1% p.a.
life expectancy men 72, women 78
language in the N (Flanders) Flemish (a Dutch dialect, known as *Vlaams*) 55%; in the S (Wallonia) Walloon (a French dialect) 32%; bilingual 11%; German (E border) 0.6%; all are official
religion Roman Catholic 75%
literacy 98% (1984)
GDP $111 bn (1986); $9,230 per head
chronology
1830 Belgium became an independent kingdom.
1914 Invaded by Germany.
1940 Again invaded by Germany.
1948 Belgium became founding member of Benelux Customs Union.
1949 Belgium became founding member of Council of Europe and NATO.
1951 Leopold III abdicated in favor of his son Baudouin.
1952 Belgium became founding member of European Coal and Steel Community (ECSC).
1957 Belgium became founding member of the European Economic Community (EEC).
1971 Steps toward regional autonomy taken.
1972 German-speaking members of the cabinet included for the first time.
1973 Linguistic parity achieved in government appointments.
1974 Separate regional councils and ministerial committees established.
1978 Wilfried Martens succeeded Leo Tindemans as prime minister.
1980 Open violence over language divisions. Regional assemblies for Flanders and Wallonia and a three-member executive for Brussels created.
1981 Short-lived coalition led by Mark Eyskens was followed by the return of Martens.
1987 Martens head of caretaker government after break-up of coalition.
1988 Following a general election, Martens formed a new CVP–PS–SP–PSC–VU coalition.

Belgium
North Sea
NETHERLANDS
Turnhout
Antwerp
Ostend (Oostende)
Bruges (Brugge)
Ghent (Gand)
Hasselt
GERMANY
Courtrai (Kortrijk)
Brussels (Bruxelles)
Louvain (Leuven)
Scheldt (Schelde)
Tournai
B E L G I U M
Meuse
Liège (Luik)
Mons
Namur (Namen)
Malmédy
Sambre
Charleroi
Philippeville
FRANCE
Bastogne
N
Bouillon
LUXEMBOURG
Arlon
0 km 20
0 miles 20

subject to the French kings or the German emperor, but in practice independent. From the 12th century the economy flourished; Bruges, Ghent, and Ypres became centers of the textile industry, while the artisans of Dinant and Liège exploited the copper and tin of the Meuse valley. During the 15th century the states came one by one under the rule of the dukes of Burgundy, and in 1477, by the marriage of Mary (heir of Charles the Bold, duke of Burgundy) to Maximilian (archduke of Austria) passed into the ◊Hapsburg dominions.

Other dynastic marriages brought all the Low Countries under Spain, and in the 16th century the religious and secular tyranny of Philip II led to revolt in the Netherlands. The independence of the Netherlands as the Dutch Republic was recognized 1648; the south, reconquered by Spain, remained Spanish until the Treaty of ◊Utrecht 1713 transferred it to Austria. In 1719 the Austrian Netherlands was annexed by revolutionary France. The ◊Congress of Vienna 1815 reunited North and South Netherlands as one kingdom under William, King of Orange-Nassau; but historical differences, and the fact that the language of the wealthy and powerful in the south was (as it remains) French, made the union uneasy. An uprising 1830 of the largely French-speaking people in the south, and continuing disturbances, led in 1839 to the Great Powers' recognition of the South Netherlands as the independent and permanently neutral kingdom of Belgium, with Leopold of Saxe-Coburg (widower of Charlotte, daughter of George IV of England) as king, and a parliamentary constitution.

Although Prussia had been a party to the treaty 1839 recognizing Belgium's permanent neutrality, Germany invaded Belgium 1914 and occupied a large part of it until 1918. Again in 1940 Belgium was overrun by Germany, to whom Leopold III surrendered. His government escaped to London, and Belgium had a strong resistance movement. After Belgium's liberation by the Allies 1944–45 the king's surrender caused acute controversy, ended only by his abdication 1951 in favor of his son Baudouin.

Since 1945 Belgium has been a major force for international cooperation in Europe, being a founding member of the ◊Benelux Economic Union, the Council of Europe, and the European Community.

Belgium's main problems stem from the division between French- and Flemish-speaking members of the population, aggravated by the polarization between the predominantly conservative Flanders in the north, and the mainly Socialist French-speaking Wallonia in the south. About 55% of the population speak Flemish, 44% French, and the remainder German.

From 1971–73, attempts to close the linguistic and social divisions included the transfer of greater power to the regions, the inclusion of German-speaking members in the cabinet, and linguistic parity in the government. In 1974 separate regional councils and ministerial committees were established.

In 1977 a coalition government, headed by Leo Tindemans (CVP) proposed the creation of a federal Belgium, based on Flanders, Wallonia, and Brussels, but the proposals were not adopted, and in 1978 Tindemans resigned. He was succeeded by Wilfried ◊Martens, heading another coalition.

In 1980 the language conflict developed into open violence, and it was eventually agreed that Flanders and Wallonia should be administered by separate regional assemblies, with powers to spend up to 10% of the national budget on cultural facilities, health, roads, and urban projects. Brussels was to be governed by a three-member executive. Such was the political instability that by 1980 Martens had formed no less than four coalition governments. In 1981 a new coalition, led by Mark Eyskens (CVP), lasted less than a year, and Martens again returned to power.

In 1981–82 economic difficulties resulted in a series of public sector strikes, and in 1983 linguistic divisions again threatened the government. Between 1983 and 1985 there was much debate about the siting of US cruise missiles in Belgium before a majority vote in parliament allowed their installation. The 1985 elections led to Martens forming another coalition. The 1987 general election produced no decisive result and Martens formed a new five-party coalition government that broke up March 1987, when the king asked Martens to form a new caretaker government pending a general election and the adoption of a new constitution, devolving more power to the regions. In 1988, Martens formed a new coalition government, following a general election.

Belgrade (Serbo-Croat *Beograd*) capital of Yugoslavia and Serbia, and Danube river port linked with the port of Bar on the Adriatic; population (1981) 1,470,000. Industries include light engine-

Belize
(formerly British Honduras)

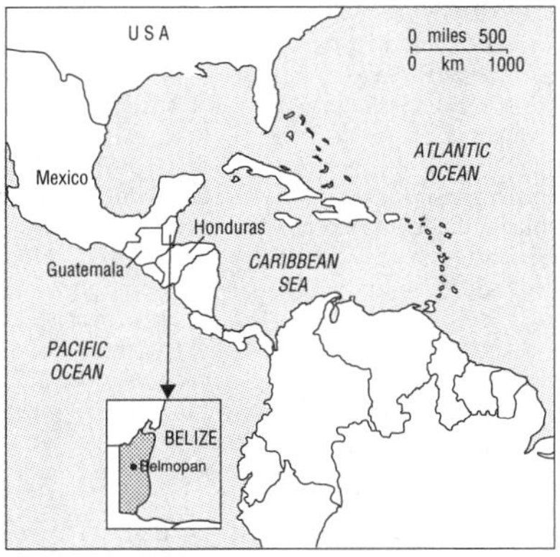
USA
0 miles 500
0 km 1000
ATLANTIC OCEAN
Mexico
Honduras
Guatemala
CARIBBEAN SEA
PACIFIC OCEAN
BELIZE
Belmopan

area 8,864 sq mi/22,963 sq km
capital Belmopan
cities ports Belize City, Dangriga and Punta Gorda; Orange Walk, Corozal
physical tropical swampy coastal plain, Maya Mountains in S, over 90% under forest
features world's second-longest barrier reef; Maya ruins
head of state Elizabeth II from 1981 represented by governor general
head of government George Price from 1989
political system constitutional monarchy
political parties People's United Party (PUP), left-of-center; United Democratic Party (UDP), moderate conservative
exports sugar, citrus, rice, fish products, bananas
currency Belize dollar
population (1990 est) 180,400 (including Mayan minority in the interior); growth rate 2.5% p.a.
life expectancy (1988) 60 years
language English (official), Spanish (widely spoken), native Creole dialects
religion Roman Catholic 60%, Protestant 35%
literacy 93% (1988)
GDP $247 million (1988); $1,220 per head
chronology
1862 Belize became a British colony.
1954 Constitution adopted, providing for limited internal self-government. General election won by George Price.
1964 Self-government achieved from Britain (universal adult suffrage introduced).
1965 Two-chamber national assembly introduced, with Price as prime minister.
1970 Capital moved from Belize City to Belmopan.
1974 British Honduras became Belize.
1975 British troops sent to defend the disputed frontier with Guatemala.
1977 Negotiations undertaken with Guatemala but no agreement reached.
1980 United Nations called for full independence.
1981 Full independence achieved. Price became prime minister.
1984 Price defeated in general election. Manuel Esquivel formed the government. Britain reaffirmed its undertaking to defend the frontier.
1988 Negotiations with Guatemala resumed.
1989 Price and the PUP won the general election.

ering, food processing, textiles, pharmaceuticals, and electrical goods.

Belgrano Manuel 1770–1820. Argentinian revolutionary. He was a member of the military group that led the 1810 revolt against Spain. Later, he commanded the revolutionary army until he was replaced by José de ◊San Martín in 1814.

Belisarius c. 505–565. Roman general under Emperor ◊Justinian I.

Belitung alternate name for the Indonesian island of ◊Billiton.

Belize country in Central America, bounded N by Mexico, W and S by Guatemala, and E by the Caribbean Sea.

government The 1981 constitution provides for a parliamentary government on the British model, with a prime minister and cabinet drawn from the legislature and accountable to it. The national assembly consists of a senate and a house of representatives. The senate has eight members appointed by the governor general for a five-year term, five on the advice of the prime minister, two on the advice of the leader of the opposition, and one after wider consultations. The house of representatives has 28 members elected by universal suffrage. The governor general appoints both the prime minister and the leader of the opposition.

history Once part of the ◊Maya civilization, and colonized in the 17th century, British Honduras (as it was called until 1973) became a recognized British colony in 1862. A 1954 constitution provided for internal self-government, with Britain responsible for defense, external affairs, and internal security.

The first general election under the the new constitution, and all subsequent elections until 1984, were won by the People's United Party (PUP), led by George Price. In 1964 full internal self-government was granted, and Price became prime minister. In 1970 the capital was moved from Belize City to the new town of Belmopan. In 1975 British troops were sent to defend the long-disputed frontier with Guatemala. Negotiations begun in 1977 were inconclusive.

In 1980 the UN called for full independence for Belize. A constitutional conference in 1981 broke up over Guatemala's demand for territory rather than just access to the Caribbean. In 1981, full independence was achieved with George Price as the first prime minister. Britain agreed to protect the frontier and to assist in the training of Belizean forces. In 1984 the PUP's uninterrupted 30-year rule ended when the United Democratic Party (UDP) leader, Manuel Esquivel, became prime minister. Britain reaffirmed its undertaking to protect Belize's disputed frontier. Still led by George Price, the PUP unexpectedly won the Sept 1989 general election by a margin of 15 to 13 seats in the house of representatives.

Belize City chief port of Belize, and capital until 1970; population (1980) 40,000. After the city was destroyed by a hurricane 1961 it was decided to move the capital inland, to Belmopan.

Bell Alexander Graham 1847–1922. Scottish-born US scientist and inventor of the telephone. He patented his invention in 1876, later experimented with a type of phonograph, and in aeronautics invented the tricycle undercarriage.

Born in Edinburgh, Bell was educated at the universities of Edinburgh and London and studied under his father, who developed a method for teaching the deaf to speak. In 1870 the family moved to Canada and Bell came to the US, where he opened a school 1872 for teachers of the deaf in Boston. In 1873 he began teaching vocal physiology at Boston University. He became a US citizen 1882. Bell also worked on converting seawater to drinking water and on air conditioning and sheep breeding.

belladonna or ***deadly nightshade*** poisonous plant *Atropa belladonna*, found in Europe and Asia. The dried powdered leaves contain ◊alkaloids. Belladonna extract acts medicinally as an ◊anticholinergic, and is highly toxic in large doses.

Bell *Alexander Graham Bell patented the telephone in 1876 and formed the Bell Telephone Co by 1877.*

Belladonna is of the nightshade family, *Solanaceae*. It grows to 5 ft/1.5 m, with dull green leaves to 8 in/20 cm and solitary greenish flowers that produce deadly black berries. The alkaloids contained are hyoscyamine, atropine, hyoscine, and belladonnine.

Bellamy Edward 1850–1898. US author and social critic. In 1888, deeply concerned with the social problems of the day, he published *Looking Backward: 2000–1887*, a utopian novel. A huge bestseller, it inspired wide public support for Bellamy's political program of state socialism. Bellamy later founded the *New Nation* newspaper and published a second utopian novel, *Equality* 1897.

Born in Chicopee Falls, Massachusetts, Bellamy wrote for the New York *Post* and the Springfield *Union*. In 1880 he founded the Springfield *Daily News* but soon afterward abandoned journalism to become a full-time author.

Bellarmine Roberto Francesco Romolo 1542–1621. Italian Roman Catholic theologian and cardinal. He taught at the Jesuit College in Rome, and became archbishop of Capua in 1602. His *Disputationes de controversersiis fidei christianae* 1581–93 was a major defense of Catholicism in the 16th century. He was canonized in 1930.

Bellay Joaquim du c. 1522–1560. French poet and prose writer, who published the great manifesto of the new school of French poetry, the Pléiade: *Défense et illustration de la langue française* 1549.

Bellerophon in Greek mythology, a victim of slander who was sent against the monstrous ◊Chimera, which he killed with the help of his winged horse ◊Pegasus. After further trials, he ended his life as a beggar. His story was dramatized by ◊Euripides.

Belleville city in SW Illinois, SE of East St Louis; seat of St Clair county. Industries include coal, beer, furnaces and boilers, and clothing; population (1990) 42,785.

bellflower general name for many plants of the family Campanulaceae, especially those of the genus *Campanula*. The white, pink, or blue flowers are bell-shaped and showy. The varied-leaf bluebell (*C. rotundifolia*) grows in N North America and Europe.

The clustered bellflower *C. glomerata* is characteristic of chalk grassland, and found in Europe and N Asia. Erect and downy, it has tight clusters of violet bell-shaped flowers in late summer.

Bellingham city and port in NW Washington just S of the Canadian border, on Bellingham Bay in the Strait of Georgia. A port of entry for the logging and paper industry; shipbuilding and food processing are also carried on; population (1990) 52,179.

Bellini *Venetian artist Giovanni Bellini painted* The Doge Leonardo Loredan *c. 1501 (National Gallery, London).*

Bellingshausen Fabian Gottlieb von 1779–1852. Russian Antarctic explorer, the first to sight and circumnavigate the Antarctic continent 1819–21, although he did not realize what it was.

Bellingshausen Sea the section of the S Pacific off the Antarctic coast. It is named after the Russian explorer Fabian Gottlieb von Bellingshausen.

Bellini family of Italian Renaissance painters, founders of the Venetian school.

Jacopo (c. 1400–1470) was father to Gentile and Giovanni. Little of his work has survived, but two of his sketchbooks (exhibited in the British Museum and the Louvre) contain his ideas and designs.

Gentile (c. 1429–1507) assisted in the decoration of the Doge's Palace 1474 and worked in the court of Mohammed II at Constantinople (a portrait of the sultan is in the National Gallery, London). His also painted processional groups (Accademia, Venice).

Giovanni (c. 1430–1516), Gentile's younger brother, studied under his father, and painted portraits and various religious subjects. Giovanni Bellini's early works show the influence of his brother-in-law, Mantegna. His style developed from the static manner of mid-15th century Venetian work toward a High Renaissance harmony and grandeur, as in the altarpiece 1505 in Sta Zaccaria, Venice. He introduced softness in tone, harmony in composition, and a use of luminous color that influenced the next generation of painters (including his pupils Giorgione and Titian). He worked in oil rather than tempera, a technique adopted from Antonello da Messina.

Bellini Vincenzo 1801–1835. Italian composer, born in Catania, Sicily. His operas include *La Sonnambula* 1831, *Norma* 1831, and *I Puritani* 1835.

Bellinzona town in Switzerland, on the river Ticino; 10 mi/16 km from Lake Maggiore; population (1980) 17,000. It is the capital of Ticino canton and a traffic center for the St Gotthard Pass. It is a tourist center.

Belloc (Joseph) Hilaire Pierre 1870–1953. British author, remembered primarily for his nonsense verse for children *The Bad Child's Book of Beasts* 1896 and *Cautionary Tales* 1907. With G K ◊Chesterton, he advocated a return to the late medieval ◊guild system of commercial association in place of capitalism or socialism.

Bellona Roman goddess of war, wife or sister of ◊Mars, with a temple in the Campus Martius, near the altar of Mars.

Bellow Saul 1915– . Canadian-born US novelist, whose finely styled works and skilled characterizations of life, especially contemporary Jewish-American life, won him the Nobel Prize for Literature 1976. His works usually portray an individual's frustrating relationship with the ongoing events of an indifferent society.

Bellow moved 1924 to the US with his family and graduated from Northwestern University 1937. He taught at various colleges, including Princeton, Bard, and the University of Chicago. His works include *The Adventures of Augie March* 1953, *Herzog* 1964, *Humboldt's Gift* 1975, *The Dean's December* 1982, *Him With His Foot in His Mouth* 1984, and *More Die of Heartbreak* 1987. He won the National Book award 1954, 1964 and a Pulitzer prize 1976.

Bellows George Wesley 1882–1925. US painter. Born in Columbus, Ohio, he painted in the realism of the Ashcan school. Taught by Robert ◊Henri, he became the youngest academician of his time. Known for his vigorous style, his paintings portray the drama of street life and sport. His most famous works, such as *Stag at Sharkey's* 1909, show the violence and excitement of illegal boxing matches. He was involved in the progressive artists movement and the creation of the Armory Show 1913.

bells nautical term applied to half-hours of watch. A day is divided into seven watches, five of four hours each and two, called dogwatches, of two hours. Each half-hour of each watch is indicated by the striking of a bell, eight bells signaling the end of the watch.

Bell's theorem hypothesis of Swiss physicist John S Bell, that an unknown force, of which space, time, and motion are all aspects, continues to link separate parts of the universe that were once united, and that this force travels faster than the speed of light.

Belmondo Jean Paul 1933– . French film actor who became a star in Jean-Luc Godard's *A bout de souffle/Breathless* 1960. He is best known for his racy personality in French vehicles, many of which he has produced. He is also known for *That Man from Rio* 1964, *Borsalino* 1970, and *Stavisky* 1974.

Belmont August 1816–1890. German-born US financier. Belmont was employed by the Rothschild banking house and traveled widely throughout Europe. In 1837 he came to New York and established a private bank, becoming the Rothschilds' exclusive representative in the US. Belmont became a naturalized American citizen 1844, was a friend to the Astors and a leading member of New York City society's "400," and was instrumental in financing the costs of the Mexican War.

An active Democrat, he supported the presidential candidacy of Stephen Douglas 1860 but remained a strong unionist after Lincoln's election. He served as the Democratic National Chairman 1872.

Bellow *US novelist Saul Bellow.*

Belmopan capital of Belize from 1970; population (1980) 3,000. It replaced Belize City as administrative center of the country.

Belo Horizonte industrial city (steel, engineering, textiles) in SE Brazil, capital of the fast-developing state of Minas Gerais; population (1985) 3,060,000. Built in the 1890s, it was Brazil's first planned modern city.

Beloit city in SE Wisconsin, on the Rock river, SE of Madison. Industries include electrical machinery, shoes, generators, and diesel engines; population (1990) 35,573.

Belorussia alternate spelling for ◊Byelorussia.

Belsen site of a Nazi ◊concentration camp in Lower Saxony, West Germany.

Belshazzar in the Old Testament, the last king of Babylon, son of Nebuchadnezzar. During a feast (known as Belshazzar's Feast) he saw a message, interpreted by ◊Daniel as prophesying the fall of Babylon and death of Belshazzar.

All of this is said to have happened the same night that the city was invaded by the Medes and Persians (539 BC).

Bemba member of a people native to NE Zambia and neighboring areas of Zaïre and Zimbabwe, although many reside in urban areas such as Lusaka and Copperbelt. The Bemba language belongs to the Bantu branch of the Niger-Congo family.

Ben Ali Zine el Abidine 1936– . Tunisian politician, president from 1987. After training in France and the US, he returned to Tunisia and became director-general of national security. He was made minister of the interior and then prime minister under the aging president for life, Habib ◊Bourguiba, whom he deposed in 1987 by a bloodless coup with the aid of ministerial colleagues. He assumed the presidency, promising greater democracy through constitutional reform.

Benares alternative transliteration of ◊Varanasi, holy city in India.

Ben Barka Mehdi 1920–1965. Moroccan politician. He became president of the National Consultative Assembly in 1956 on the country's independence from France. He was assassinated by Moroccan agents with the aid of French secret-service men as a result of his alleged involvement in an attempt on King Hassan's life and for supporting Algeria in Algerian-Moroccan border disputes.

Ben Bella Ahmed 1916– . Algerian leader of the National Liberation Front (FLN) from 1952; prime minister of independent Algeria 1962–65, when he was overthrown by ◊Boumédienne and detained until 1980. He founded a new party, Mouvement pour la Démocratie en Algérie, in 1985. In 1990 he returned to Algeria.

Benchley Robert 1889–1945. US humorist, actor, and drama critic whose books include *Of All Things* 1921 and *Benchley Beside Himself* 1943. His film skit *How to Sleep* illustrates his ability to extract humor from everyday life.

Born in Massachusetts, he was associated with the writer Dorothy Parker, *The New Yorker* magazine, and the circle of wits at the Algonquin Round Table in New York. He was a master of gentle satire, left New York City for Hollywood, and wrote and appeared in several 1930s and 1940s films.

Benda Julien 1867–1956. French writer and philosopher. He was an outspoken opponent of the philosophy of ◊Bergson, and in 1927 published a manifesto on the necessity of devotion to the absolute truth, which he felt his contemporaries had betrayed, *La Trahison des clercs/The Treason of the Intellectuals*.

Bendigo city in Victoria, Australia, about 75 mi/120 km NNW of Melbourne; population (1986) 62,400. Founded 1851 at the start of a gold rush, the town takes its name from the pugilist William Thompson (1811–1889), known as "Bendigo."

Ben Bella *Algerian leader Ahmed Ben Bella worked for independence and was imprisoned in France before becoming prime minister of independent Algeria in 1962.*

bends popular name for a paralytic affliction of deep-sea divers, arising from too rapid a release of nitrogen from solution in their blood under pressure. Immediate treatment is compression and slow decompression in a special chamber.

Benedict, St c. 480–c. 547. Founder of Christian monasticism in the West and of the ◊Benedictine order. He founded the monastery of Monte Cassino, Italy. Here he wrote out his rule for monastic life, and was visited shortly before his death by the Ostrogothic king Totila, whom he converted to the Christian faith. Feast day July 11.

Benedict XV 1854–1922. Pope from 1914. During World War I he endeavored to bring about a peace settlement, and it was during his papacy that British, French, and Dutch official relations were renewed with the Vatican.

Benedictine order religious order of monks and nuns in the Roman Catholic church, founded by St ◊Benedict at Subiaco, Italy, in the 6th century. It had a stong influence on medieval learning and reached the height of its prosperity early in the 14th century.

Benedict, St *The founder of Western monasticism was the Italian St Benedict. The Benedictine order was established in the 6th century.*

There are Benedictine monasteries in the US in Latrobe, Pennsylvania, and St Meinrad, Indiana. In 1985 there were 9,453 monks and 7,911 nuns living in convents.

benefice in the early Middle Ages, a donation of land or money to the Christian church as an act of devotion, but from the 12th century, the income enjoyed by clergy.

Under the ◊Carolingian dynasty, "benefice" was used to mean a gift of land from a lord to a ◊vassal, in which sense it is often indistinguishable from a ◊fief.

Benelux customs union of Belgium, the Netherlands, and Luxembourg (agreed 1944, fully effective 1960); precursor of the European Community.

Beneš Eduard 1884–1948. Czechoslovak politician. He worked with Thomas ◊Masaryk toward Czechoslavak nationalism from 1918 and was foreign minister and representative at the League of Nations. He was president of the republic from 1935 until forced to resign by the Germans; he headed a government in exile in London during World War II. He returned home as president 1945 but resigned again after the Communist coup 1948.

Benét Stephen Vincent 1898–1943. US poet, novelist, and short-story writer noted for his Pulitzer prize-winning 1929 narrative poem of the Civil War *John Brown's Body* 1928. One of his short stories, "The Devil and Daniel Webster," became a classic and was made into a play, an opera, and a film (*All That Money Can Buy*). He published more than 17 volumes of verse and prose.

Benevento historic town in Campania, S Italy; population (1981) 62,500. It is known for the production of Strega liqueur.

Bengal former province of British India, divided 1947 into ◊West Bengal, a state of India, and East Bengal, from 1972 ◊Bangladesh. The famine in 1943, caused by a slump in demand for jute and a bad harvest, resulted in over 3 million deaths.

Bengali language member of the Indo-Iranian branch of the Indo-European language family, the official language of Bangladesh and of the state of Bengal in E India.

Benghazi or ***Banghazi*** historic city and industrial port in N Libya on the Gulf of Sirte; population (1982) 650,000. It was controlled by Turkey between the 16th century and 1911, and by Italy 1911–1942; a major naval supply base during World War II.

Colonized by the Greeks in the 7th century BC (*Euhesperides*), Benghazi was taken by Rome in the 1st century BC (*Berenice*) and by the Vandals in the 5th century AD. It became Arab in the 7th century. With Tripoli, it was cocapital of Libya 1951–72.

Benguela port in Angola, SW Africa; population (1970) 41,000. It was founded 1617. Its railroad runs inland to the copper mines of Zaïre and Zambia.

Benguela current the cold ocean current in the S Atlantic Ocean, moving northward along the west coast of Southern Africa and merging with the south equatorial current at a latitude of 15° S. Its rich plankton supports large, commercially exploited fish populations.

Ben-Gurion David. Adopted name of David Gruen 1886–1973. Israeli statesman and Socialist politician, one of the founders of the state of Israel, the country's first prime minister 1948–53, and again 1955–63.

He was born in Poland, and went to Palestine in 1906 to farm. He was a leader of the Zionist movement, and as defense minister he presided over the development of Israel's armed forces into one of the strongest armies in the Middle East.

Benin country in W Africa, bounded E by Nigeria, N by Burkina Faso and Niger, W by Togo, and S by the Gulf of Guinea.

government The constitution is based on the Fundamental Law (*Loi Fondamentale*) of 1977, which established a national revolutionary assembly with 196 members (representing socioprofessional classes rather than geographical constituencies) elected for a five-year term by universal suffrage. The assembly elects the president (head of state) also to serve a five-year term. From 1975 to 1989 Benin was a one-party state, committed to "scientific socialism." The party is the Party of the People's Revolution of Benin (PRPB) and is chaired by the president.

history In the 12th–13th centuries the country was settled by the Aja, whose kingdom reached its peak in the 16th century. In the 17th–19th centuries the succeeding Dahomey kingdom (which gave the country its name until 1975) captured and sold its neighbors as slaves to Europeans.

Under French influence from the 1850s, Dahomey formed part of French West Africa from 1899, and in 1958 became a self-governing dominion within the French Community. In 1960 it became fully independent.

Dahomey went through a period of political instability 1960–72, with swings from civilian to military rule and disputes between regions. In 1972 the deputy chief of the army, Mathieu Kerekou, established a military regime pledged to give fair representation to each region. His initial instrument of government was the National Council of the Revolution (CNR). In 1974 Kerekou announced that as the People's Republic of Benin the country would follow "scientific socialism," based on Marxist-Leninist principles.

In 1977 CNR was dissolved, and a civilian government formed. A fundamental law established a national revolutionary assembly that in 1980 elected Kerekou as president and head of state. He was reelected in 1984 and, after initial economic and social difficulties, his government grew more stable; relations with France (Benin's biggest trading partner) improved considerably. In 1983 President Mitterrand became the first French head of state to visit Benin.

In Aug 1989 President Kerekou was reelected for another five-year term. It was announced Dec 1989 that Marxism-Leninism was no longer the official ideology of Benin and that further constitutional reforms—allowing for more private enterprise—would be agreed upon. A preliminary referendum in Dec 1990 showed overwhelming support for a multiparty political system.

Benin
People's Republic of
(République Populaire du Bénin)

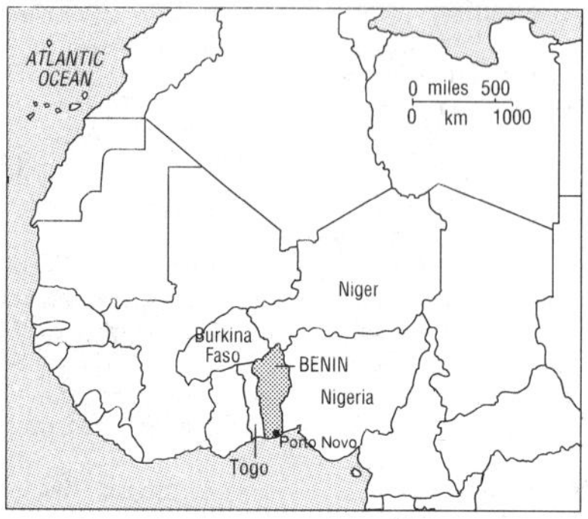
ATLANTIC
OCEAN
0 miles 500
0 km 1000
Niger
Burkina
Faso
BENIN
Nigeria
Porto Novo
Togo

area 43,472 sq mi/112,622 sq km
capital Porto Novo (official), Cotonou (de facto)
cities Abomey, Natitingou, Parakou; chief port Cotonou
physical flat to undulating terrain; hot and humid in S; semiarid in N
features coastal lagoons with fishing villages on stilts; Niger River in NE
head of state and government Nicephore Soglo from 1991
political system Socialist pluralist republic
political parties Party of the People's Revolution of Benin (PRPB); other parties from 1990
exports cocoa, peanuts, cotton, palm oil, petroleum, cement, sea products
currency CFA franc
population (1990 est) 4,840,000; growth rate 3% p.a.
life expectancy men 42, women 46
language French (official); Fon 47% and Yoruba 9% in S; six major tribal languages in N
religion animist 65%, Christian 17%, Muslim 13%
literacy men 37%/women 16% (1985 est)
GDP $1.6 bn (1987); $365 per head
chronology
1851 Under French control.
1958 Became self-governing dominion within the French Community.
1960 Independence achieved from France.
1960–72 Acute political instability, with switches from civilian to military rule.
1972 Military regime established by Gen Mathieu Kerekou.
1974 Kerekou announced that the country would follow a path of "scientific socialism."
1975 Name of country changed from Dahomey to Benin.
1977 Return to civilian rule under a new constitution.
1980 Kerekou formally elected president by the national revolutionary assembly.
1989 Marxism-Leninism dropped as official ideology. Strikes and protests against Kerekou's rule mounted; he banned demonstrations and deployed the army against protesters.
1990 Referendum support for multiparty politics.
1991 Multiparty elections held. Kerekou defeated in presidential elections by Nicephore Soglo.

Benin former African kingdom 1200–1897, now part of Nigeria. It reached the height of its power in the 14th–17th centuries when it ruled the area between the Niger Delta and Lagos. Benin traded in spices, ivory, palm oil, and slaves until its decline and eventual incorporation into Nigeria. The Oba (ruler) of Benin continues to rule his people as a divine monarch. The present Oba is considered an enlightened leader and one who is helping his people to become part of modern Nigeria.

Artworks honoring the Oba of Benin were looted by a British military expedition 1897. They included cast bronzes and carved ivories and have since found their way into museums and into the hands of collectors worldwide. See ◊African art.

Benioff zone a seismically active zone dipping beneath a continent or continental margin behind a deep-sea trench. The zone is named after Hugo Benioff, a US seismologist who first described this feature. The zone is equivalent to what is called a subduction zone in plate tectonic theory, where one plate descends beneath another.

Benjamin Arthur 1893–1960. Australian pianist and composer who taught composition at the Royal College of Music in London from 1925, where ◊Britten was one of his pupils. His works include *Jamaican Rumba*, inspired by a visit to the West Indies in 1937.

Benjamin Judah Philip 1811–1884. US Confederate official. Born in St Thomas, Virgin Islands, Benjamin was raised in South Carolina and was educated at Yale. After entering the legal profession in New Orleans, he served in the state legislature and was elected to the US Senate 1852. As a strong proponent of Southern secession, he resigned from the Senate 1861. Benjamin became one of the leaders of the Confederacy, serving as attorney general, secretary of war, and secretary of state. At the end of the war, he escaped to England, where he spent the rest of his life practicing law.

Bennett (Enoch) Arnold 1867–1931. English novelist. He became a London journalist 1893 and editor of *Woman* 1896. His books include *Anna of the Five Towns* 1904, *The Old Wives' Tale* 1908, and the trilogy *Clayhanger*, *Hilda Lessways*, and *These Twain* 1910–16.

Bennett Richard Rodney 1936– . English composer of jazz, film music, symphonies, and operas. His film scores for *Far from the Madding Crowd* 1967, *Nicholas and Alexandra* 1971, and *Murder on the Orient Express* 1974 all received Oscar nominations. His operas include *The Mines of Sulfur* 1963 and *Victory* 1970.

Ben Nevis highest mountain in the British Isles (4,406 ft/1,342 m), in the Grampians, Scotland.

Benny Jack. Adopted name of Benjamin Kubelsky 1894–1974. US comedian. Over the years, Benny appeared on the stage, in films, and on radio and television. His radio program, which began 1932, made him a national institution. Featuring his wife, Mary Livingston; singer Dennis Day; announcer Don Wilson; and valet Eddie "Rochester" Anderson, it was produced for television in the 1950s.

Born in Chicago, he began a musical career in local theater orchestras (playing the violin) and joined a vaudeville troupe. During the 1920s, he turned to comedy, taking the stage name "Jack Benny" and developing his familiar miserly, yet harmless character. His film appearances, mostly in the 1930s and 1940s, included a starring role in *To Be or Not To Be* 1942. He also played in *Charley's Aunt* 1941, *It's In the Bag* 1945, and *A Guide for the Married Man* 1967.

Benoni city in the Transvaal, South Africa, 17 mi/27 km E of Johannesburg; population (1980) 207,000. It was founded 1903 as a gold-mining center.

bent or ***bent grass*** any grasses of the genus *Agrostis*. Creeping bent grass *A. stolonifera*, also known as fiorin, is common in N North America and Eurasia, including lowland Britain. It spreads by ◊stolons and bears large attractive panicles of yellow or purple flowers on thin stalks. It is often used on lawns and golf courses.

Bentham Jeremy 1748–1832. English philosopher, legal and social reformer, and founder of ◊utilitarianism. The essence of his moral philosophy is found in the pronouncement of his *Principles of Morals and Legislation* (written 1780, published 1789): that the object of all legislation should be "the greatest happiness for the greatest number."

Bentham declared that the "utility" of any law is to be measured by the extent to which it promotes the pleasure, good, and happiness of the people concerned. In 1776, he published *Fragments on Government*. He made suggestions for the reform of the poor law 1798, which formed the basis of the reforms enacted in 1834, and in his *Catechism of Parliamentary Reform* 1817 he proposed annual elections, the secret ballot, and universal male suffrage. He was also a pioneer of prison reform. In economics he was an apostle of *laissez-faire*, and in his *Defence of Usury* 1787 and *Manual of Political Economy* 1798 he contended that his principle of "utility" was best served by allowing every man (sic) to pursue his own interests unhindered by restrictive legislation. He was made a citizen of the French Republic in 1792.

Bentiu an oil-rich region to the W of the White Nile, in the Upper Nile province of S Sudan.

Bentley Richard 1662–1742. British Classical scholar, whose textual criticism includes *Dissertation upon the Epistles of Phalaris* 1699. He was Master of Trinity College, Cambridge University, from 1700.

Benton Thomas Hart 1782–1858. US political leader. Moving to St Louis 1815, he opened a law practice and published the *Missouri Enquirer* 1818–20. Elected to the US Senate 1820, Benton served in that body for the next 30 years, distinguishing himself as an outspoken opponent of the Bank of the United States and the extension of slavery and as a strong supporter of westward expansion.

benzene

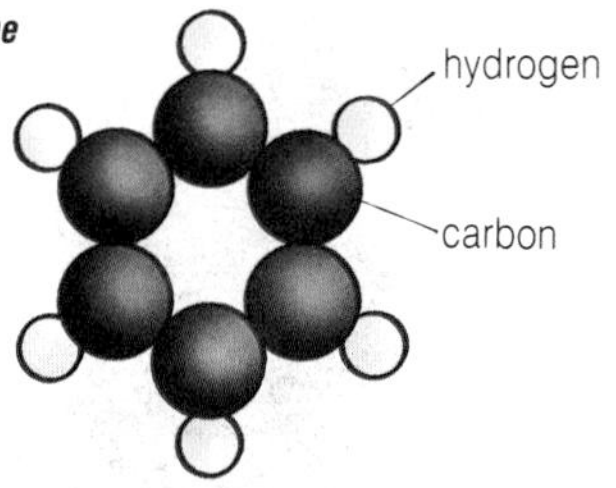
hydrogen
carbon

Born in Hillsboro (now Hillsborough), North Carolina, Benton moved to Tennessee and was admitted to the bar 1806. During the War of 1812, he served as Gen Andrew Jackson's aide-de-camp, eventually rising to the rank of colonel.

Benton Harbor city in SW Michigan, NE of Chicago, Illinois, which is across Lake Michigan. Industries include iron and other metal products and food processing; population (1990) 12,818. The religious sect, House of David, was established here 1903.

bentonite type of clay, consisting mainly of montmorillonite and resembling ◊fuller's earth, which swells when wet. It is used in papermaking, molding sands, drilling muds for oil wells, and as a decolorant in food processing.

bentwood originally a country style of wooden furniture, mainly chairs, made by steam-heating and then bending rods of wood to form the back, legs, and seat frame. Twentieth-century designers such as Marcel ◊Breuer and Alvar ◊Aalto developed a different form by bending sheets of plywood.

Benue river in Nigeria, largest affluent of the Niger; it is navigable for most of its length of 870 mi/1,400 km.

Benz Karl 1844–1929. German automobile engineer, who produced the world's first gasoline-driven motor vehicle. He built his first model engine in 1878 and the gasoline-driven car in 1885.

Benzedrine a trade name for ◊amphetamine, a stimulant drug.

benzene C_6H_6 a clear liquid hydrocarbon of characteristic odor, occurring in coal tar. It is used as a solvent and in the synthesis of many chemicals.

The benzene molecule consists of a ring of six carbon atoms, all of which are in a single plane, and it is one of the simplest ◊cyclic compounds. Benzene is the simplest of a class of compounds collectively known as aromatic compounds. Some are considered carcinogenic (cancer-inducing).

benzodiazepine any of a group of mood-altering drugs (tranquilizers), for example Librium and Valium. They are addictive and interfere with the process by which information is transmitted between brain cells, and various ill effects arise from continued use. They were originally developed as a muscle relaxant, and then excessively prescribed in the West as anxiety-relaxing drugs.

benzoic acid C_6H_5COOH a white crystalline solid, sparingly soluble in water, that is used as a preservative for certain foods and as an antiseptic. It is obtained chemically by the direct oxidation of benzaldehyde and occurs in certain natural resins, some essential oils, and as hippuric acid.

benzoin resin obtained by making incisions in the bark of *Styrax benzoin*, a tree native to the East Indies. Benzoin is used in the preparation of cosmetics, perfumes, and incense.

The name is also used for several bushes of the genus *Lindera* of the laurel family, growing in E North America, especially the common spicebush *L. benzoin*.

Ben Zvi Izhak 1884–1963. Israeli politician, president 1952–63. He was born in Atpoltava, Russia, and became active in the Zionist movement in Ukraine. In 1907 he went to Palestine but was deported in 1915 with ◊Ben-Gurion. They served in the Jewish Legion under Gen Allenby, who commanded the British forces in the Middle East.

Beograd the Serbo-Croatian form of ◊Belgrade, capital of Yugoslavia.

Beowulf Anglo-Saxon poem (composed c. 700), the only complete surviving example of Germanic folk-epic. It exists in a single manuscript copied about 1000 in the Cottonian collection of the British Museum.

Béranger Pierre Jean de 1780–1857. French poet, who wrote light satirical lyrics dealing with love, wine, popular philosophy, and politics.

Berber member of a non-Semitic Caucasoid people of North Africa, who since prehistoric times inhabited Barbary, the Mediterranean coastlands from Egypt to the Atlantic. Their language, present-day Berber (a member of the Afro-Asiatic language family), is spoken by about one-third of Algerians and nearly two-thirds of Moroccans, 10 million people. Berbers are mainly agricultural, but some are still nomadic.

Berbera seaport in Somalia, with the only sheltered harbor on the S side of the Gulf of Aden; population (1982) 55,000. It is in a strategic position on the oil route and has a new deep-sea port completed 1969. It was under British control 1884–1960.

Berchtesgaden village in SE Bavaria, Germany, site of Hitler's country residence, the Berghof, which was captured by US troops May 4, 1945, and destroyed.

Berchtold Count Leopold von 1863–1942. Prime minister and foreign minister of Austria-Hungary 1912–15 and a crucial figure in the events that led to World War I, because his indecisive stance caused tension with Serbia.

Berdichev town in Ukraine, USSR, 30 mi/48 km S of Zhitomir; population (1980) 60,000. Industries include engineering and food processing.

Berdyaev Nikolai Alexandrovich 1874–1948. Russian philosopher who often challenged official Soviet viewpoints after the Revolution of 1917. Although appointed professor of philosophy in 1919 at Moscow University, he was exiled 1922 for defending Orthodox Christian religion. His books include *The Meaning of History* 1923 and *The Destiny of Man* 1935.

Berdyansk city and port on the Berdyansk Gulf of the Sea of Azov, in SE Ukraine, USSR; population (1985) 130,000.

Berengaria of Navarre 1165–1230. The only English queen never to set foot in England. Daughter of King Sancho VI of Navarre, she married Richard I of England in Cyprus 1191, and accompanied him on his crusade to the Holy Land.

Berenson Bernard 1865–1959. US art expert, born in Lithuania, once revered as a leading scholar of the Italian Renaissance. He amassed a great fortune, and many of his attributions of previously anonymous Italian paintings were later disproved.

Berezniki city in the USSR, on the Kama river N of Perm; population (1987) 200,000. It was formed 1932 by the amalgamation of several older towns. Industry includes chemicals and paper.

Berg Alban 1885–1935. Austrian composer. He studied under ◊Schoenberg and was associated with him as one of the leaders of the serial, or 12-tone, school of composition. His output includes orchestral, chamber, and vocal music as well as two operas, *Wozzeck* 1925, a grim story of working-class life, and the unfinished *Lulu* 1929–35.

His music is emotionally expressive, and sometimes anguished, but can also be lyrical, as in the *Violin Concerto* 1935.

Berg Paul 1926– . US molecular biologist. In 1972, using gene-splicing techniques developed by others, Berg spliced and combined into a single hybrid ◊DNA from an animal tumor virus (SV40) and DNA from a bacterial virus. Berg's work aroused fears in other workers and excited con-

Berg *Austrian composer Alban Berg.*

tinuing controversy. For his work on recombinant DNA, Berg shared the 1980 Nobel Prize for Chemistry with Walter ◊Gilbert and Frederick ◊Sanger.

Bergama modern form of ◊Pergamum, ancient city in W Turkey.

Bergamo city in Lombardy, Italy; 30 mi/48 km NE of Milan; population (1988) 119,000. Industries include silk and metal. The Academia Carrara holds a collection of paintings.

bergamot small, evergreen tree *Citrus bergamia* of the rue family Rutaceae. From the rind of its fruit a fragrant orange-scented essence used as a perfume is obtained. The sole source of supply is S Calabria, Italy, but the name comes from the town of Bergamo, in Lombardy.

Bergen industrial port (shipbuilding, engineering, fishing) in SW Norway; population (1988) 210,000. Founded 1070, Bergen was a member of the Hanseatic League.

Bergisch Gladbach industrial city in North Rhine–Westphalia, Germany; population (1988) 102,000.

Bergius Friedrich Karl Rudolph 1884–1949. German research chemist who invented processes for converting coal into oil and wood into sugar. Nobel Prize 1931.

Bergman Ingmar 1918– . Swedish film producer and director. His work deals with complex moral psychological, and metaphysical problems and is often heavily tinged with pessimism. His films include *Wild Strawberries* 1957, *Persona* 1966, and *Fanny and Alexander* 1982.

Bergman Ingrid 1917–1982. Swedish actress, whose early films include *Intermezzo* 1939, *Casablanca*, *For Whom the Bell Tolls* both 1943, and *Gaslight* 1944, for which she won an Academy

Bergius *German chemist and Nobel Prizewinner in 1931, Friedrich Bergius.*

Bergman *The Swedish actress Ingrid Bergman, photographed in 1971.*

Award. By leaving her husband to have a child with director Roberto Rossellini, she broke an unofficial moral code of Hollywood "star" behavior and was ostracized for some years. During her "exile," she made films in Europe such as *Stromboli* 1949 (directed by Rossellini). Later films include *Anastasia* 1956, for which she won an Academy Award.

Her last film, *Autumn Sonata* 1978, was made by Ingmar Bergman. She also did stage plays and received an Emmy for the television film *A Woman Called Golda* 1982, portraying the Israeli prime minister.

Bergson Henri 1859–1941. French philosopher who believed that time, change, and development were the essence of reality. He thought that time was not a succession of distinct and separate instants but a continuous process in which one period merged imperceptibly into the next. Nobel Prize for Literature 1928.

Beria Lavrenti 1899–1953. Soviet politician who became head of the Stalinist police force in 1938 that imprisoned, liquidated and transported millions of Soviet citizens. On Stalin's death in 1953, he attempted to seize power but was foiled and shot after a secret trial. Apologists for Stalin blame Beria for the excesses above.

beriberi endemic polyneuritis, an inflammation of the nerve endings, mostly occurring in the tropics and resulting from a deficiency of vitamin B_1 (thiamine).

Bering Vitus 1681–1741. Danish explorer, the first European to sight Alaska. He died on Bering Island in the Bering Sea, both named after him, as is the Bering Strait, which separates Asia (USSR) from North America (Alaska).

Beringia or ***Bering Land Bridge*** former land bridge 1,000 mi/1,600 km wide between Asia and North America; it existed during the ice ages that occurred before 35,000 BC and during the period 24,000–9000 BC. It is now covered by Bering Strait and Chukchi Sea.

Bering Sea section of the N Pacific between Alaska and Siberia, from the Aleutian Islands N to Bering Strait.

Bering Strait strait between Alaska and Siberia, linking the N Pacific and Arctic oceans.

Berio Luciano 1925– . Italian composer. His style has been described as graceful ◊serialism, and he has frequently experimented with electronic music and taped sound. His works include nine *Sequenzas/Sequences* 1957–75 for various solo instruments or voice, *Sinfonia* 1969 for voices and orchestra, *Points on the curve to find*... 1974, and a number of dramatic works, including the opera *Un re in ascolto/A King Listens* 1984, loosely based on Shakespeare's *The Tempest*.

Berkeley city on San Francisco Bay in California; population (1990) 102,724. It is the site of an acclaimed branch of the University of California, noted for its nuclear research at the Lawrence Berkeley Laboratory. Berkeley was settled 1853.

Berkeley Busby. Adopted name of William Berkeley Enos 1895–1976. US choreographer and film director. He was famous for his ingenious and extravagant sets, choreography, and costumes. After he choreographed more than 20 Broadway musicals, producer Samuel Goldwyn hired him for the musical film *Whoopee* 1930. His musical extravaganzas include the films *Gold Diggers of 1933* and *Footlight Parade* 1933, where dozens of dancers are filmed from above and all sides, creating patterns with movement and costume, giving the appearance of a kaleidoscope.

Berkeley George 1685–1753. Irish philosopher and cleric who believed that nothing exists apart from perception, and that the all-seeing mind of God makes possible the continued apparent existence of things. For Berkeley, everyday objects are collections of ideas or sensations, hence the dictum *esse est percipi* ("to exist is to be perceived"). He became bishop of Cloyne 1734.

Berkeley Sir William 1606–1677. British colonial administrator. Born in Bruton, England, and educated at Oxford, Berkeley was knighted by Charles I 1639 and appointed governor of Virginia 1641. Although at first an able administrator, he was drawn into English political struggles. Taking the side of the Royalists in the English Civil War, he was removed from office by Cromwell 1652. With the Restoration 1660, Berkeley was reappointed by Charles II, but he faced the growing opposition that culminated in Bacon's Rebellion 1676. In 1677, Berkeley was removed from office for his brutal repression of that uprising.

berkelium synthesized, radioactive, metallic element of the ◊actinide series, symbol Bk, atomic number 97, atomic weight 247. It was first produced in 1949 by Glenn ◊Seaborg and his team, at the University of California at Berkeley, for which it is named.

Berlin industrial city (machine tools, electrical goods, paper, printing) and capital of the Federal Republic of Germany; population (1990) 3,102,500. The Berlin Wall divided the city from 1961 to 1989, but in Oct 1990 Berlin became the capital of a unified Germany once more with East and West Berlin reunited as the 16th *Land* (state) of the Federal Republic.

Unter den Linden, the tree-lined avenue once the whole city's focal point, has been restored in what was formerly East Berlin. The fashionable Kurfürstendamm and the residential Hansa quarter form part of what was once West Berlin. Prominent buildings include the Reichstag (former parliament building); Schloss Bellevue (Berlin residence of the president); Schloss Charlottenburg (housing several museums); Congress Hall; restored 18th-century State Opera; Dahlem picture gallery. The environs of Berlin include the Grünewald forest and Wannsee lake.

First mentioned about 1230, the city grew out

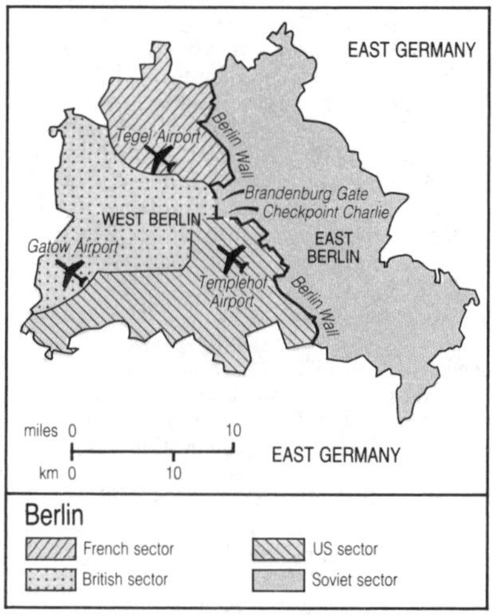
EAST GERMANY
Tegel Airport
Berlin Wall
Brandenburg Gate
Checkpoint Charlie
WEST BERLIN
EAST BERLIN
Gatow Airport
Templehof Airport
Berlin Wall
miles 0 10
km 0 10
EAST GERMANY
Berlin
French sector
US sector
British sector
Soviet sector

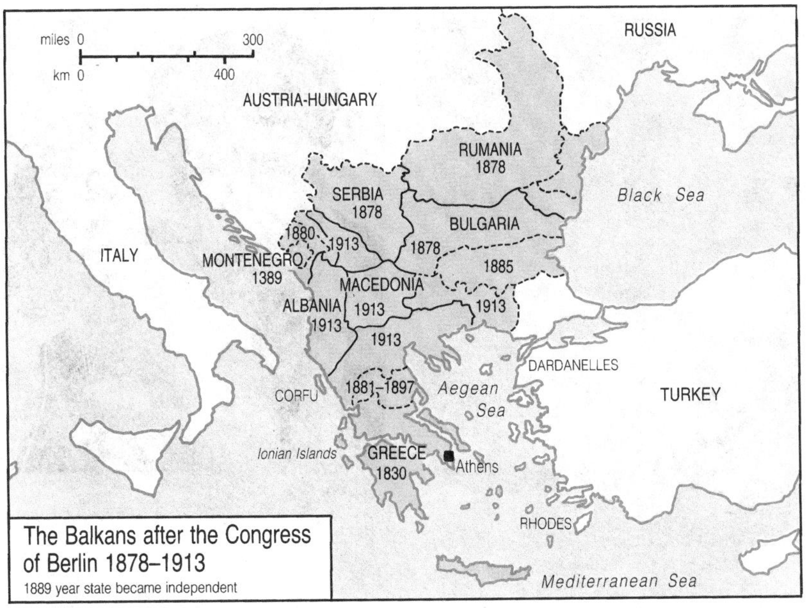
miles 0
300
km 0
400
RUSSIA
AUSTRIA-HUNGARY
RUMANIA
1878
SERBIA
1878
Black Sea
BULGARIA
1880
1913
1878
ITALY
MONTENEGRO
1389
1885
MACEDONIA
ALBANIA
1913
1913
1913
1913
DARDANELLES
CORFU
1881–1897
Aegean
Sea
TURKEY
Ionian Islands
GREECE
1830
Athens
RHODES
Mediterranean Sea
The Balkans after the Congress of Berlin 1878–1913
1889 year state became independent

of a fishing village, joined the Hanseatic League in the 15th century, became the permanent seat of the Hohenzollerns, and was capital of the Brandenburg electorate 1486–1701, of the kingdom of Prussia 1701–1871, and of united Germany 1871–1945. From the middle of the 18th century it developed into a commercial and cultural center. In World War II air raids and conquest by the Soviet army 23 April–May 2, 1945, destroyed much of the city. After the war, Berlin was divided into four sectors—British, US, French, and Soviet—and until 1948 was under quadripartite government by the Allies; in that year the USSR withdrew from the combined board, blockaded the city for 327 days (supplies were brought in by air by the Allies), and created a separate municipal government in its sector. The other three sectors (West Berlin) were made a *Land* of the Federal Republic May 1949, and in Oct 1949 East Berlin was proclaimed capital of East Germany.

Berlin Irving. Adopted name of Israel Baline. 1888–1989. Russian-born American composer, whose song hits include "Alexander's Ragtime Band," "Always," "God Bless America," and "White Christmas." He wrote the musicals *Annie Get Your Gun* 1946 and *Call Me Madam* 1950.

He also wrote the scores for films such as *Top Hat* 1935, *Holiday Inn* 1942, and *Easter Parade* 1946. The son of a poor Jewish cantor, Berlin learned music by ear. He was instrumental in the development of the popular song, taking it from jazz and ragtime to swing and romantic ballads. Many of his songs are "standards," the most popular and enduring of all time.

Berlin Isaiah 1909– . Latvian-born British philosopher, professor of social and political theory at Oxford 1957–67. He wrote about Tolstoy's theory of irresistible historical forces and about Marxism; his books include *Historical Inevitability* 1954 and *Four Essays on Liberty* 1969.

Berlin blockade in June 1948, the closing of entry to Berlin from the west by Soviet forces. It was an attempt to prevent the other Allies (USA, France, and Britain) unifying the western part of Germany. The British and US forces responded by sending supplies to the city by air for over a year (the Berlin airlift). In May 1949 the blockade was lifted; the airlift continued until Sept. The blockade marked the formal division of the city into Eastern and Western sectors.

Berlin, Conference of a conference 1884–85 of the major European powers (France, Germany, the UK, Belgium and Portugal) called by Chancellor Otto von Bismarck to decide on the colonial partition of Africa.

Also discussed were a neutral Congo Basin with free trade, and an independent Congo Free State; the slave trade was forbidden.

Berlin, Congress of congress of the European powers (Russia, Turkey, Austria-Hungary, Britain, France, Italy, and Germany) held at Berlin in 1878 to determine the boundaries of the Balkan states after the Russo-Turkish war.

Berlinguer Enrico 1922–1984. Italian Communist who freed the party from Soviet influence. By 1976 he was near to the premiership, but the murder of Aldo Moro, the prime minister, by Red Brigade guerrillas, prompted a move of support to the Socialists.

Berlin Wall the dividing barrier between East and West Berlin 1961–89, erected by East Germany to keep its citizens in. Escapers from East to West were shot on sight.

Beginning Aug 13, 1961, the East German security forces sealed off all but 12 of the 80 crossing points to West Berlin with a barbed wire barrier. It was reinforced with concrete by the Soviets to prevent the escape of unwilling inhabitants of East Berlin to the rival political and economic system of West Berlin. The interconnecting link between East and West Berlin was Checkpoint Charlie, where both sides exchanged captured spies. On Nov 9, 1989 the East German government opened its borders to try to halt the mass exodus of its citizens to the West via other Eastern bloc countries, and the wall was gradually dismantled.

Berlioz (Louis) Hector 1803–1869. French romantic composer and the founder of modern orchestration. Much of his music was inspired by drama and literature and has a theatrical quality. He wrote symphonic works, such as *Symphonie fantastique* and *Roméo et Juliette*; dramatic cantatas including *La Damnation de Faust* and *L'Enfance du Christ*; sacred music; and three operas, *Béatrice et Bénédict*, *Benvenuto Cellini*, and *Les Troyens*.

Berlioz studied music at the Paris Conservatoire. He won the Prix de Rome 1830, and spent two years in Italy. In 1833 he married Harriet Smithson, an Irish actress playing Shakespearean parts in Paris, but they separated in 1842. After some years of poverty and public neglect, he went to Germany in 1842 and conducted his own works. He subsequently visited Russia and England. In 1854 he married Marie Recio, a singer.

Bermuda British colony in the NW Atlantic

bermuda

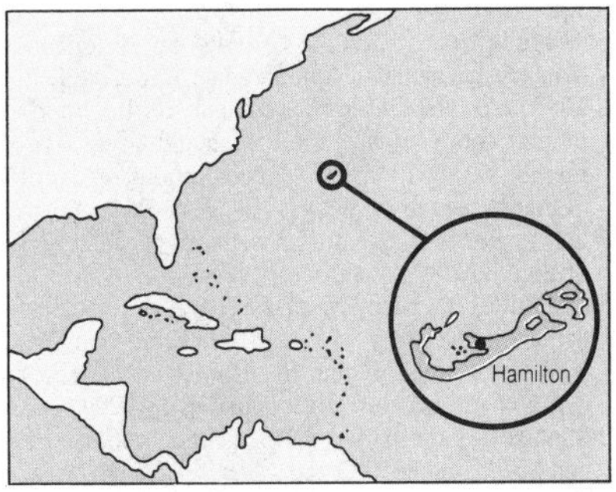
Hamilton

area 21 sq mi/54 sq km
capital and chief port Hamilton
features consists of about 150 small islands, of which 20 are inhabited, linked by bridges and causeways; Britain's oldest colony.
products Easter lilies, pharmaceuticals; tourism and banking are important
population (1988) 58,100 (66% black; 34% white)
language English
religion Christian
government under the constitution of 1968, Bermuda is a fully self-governing British colony, with a governor, senate, and elected House of Assembly (premier from 1982 John Swan, United Bermuda Party)
history the islands were named after Juan de Bermudez, who visited them in 1515, and were settled by British colonists in 1609. Indian and African slaves were transported from 1616, and soon outnumbered the white settlers. Racial violence in 1977 led to intervention, at the request of the government, by British troops.

Bermuda Triangle the sea area bounded by Bermuda, Florida, and Puerto Rico, which gained the nickname "Deadly Bermuda Triangle" in 1964 when it was suggested that unexplained disappearances of ships and aircraft were exceptionally frequent there; analysis of the data did not eventually confirm the idea.

Bern (French *Berne*) capital of Switzerland and of Bern canton, in W Switzerland on the Aare River; population (1987) 300,000. It joined the Swiss confederation 1353 and became the capital 1848. Industries include textiles, chocolate, pharmaceuticals, light metal, and electrical goods.

It was founded 1191 and made a free imperial city by Frederick II 1218. Its name is derived from the bear in its coat of arms, and there has been a bear pit in the city since the 16th century. The minster was begun 1421, the town hall 1406, and the university 1834. It is the seat of the Universal Postal Union.

Bernadette, St 1844–1879. French saint, born in Lourdes in the French Pyrenees. In Feb 1858 she had a vision of the Virgin Mary in a grotto, and it became a center of pilgrimage. Many sick people who were dipped in the water of a spring

Berlin Wall *The day after the breaching of the Berlin Wall on Nov 9, 1989, unarmed soldiers of the German Democratic Republic took up positions at the Brandenburg Gate.*

there were said to have been cured. Feast day Apr 16.

Bernadotte Count Folke 1895–1948. Swedish diplomat and president of the Swedish Red Cross. In 1945 he conveyed the Nazi commander Himmler's offer of capitulation to the British and US governments, and in 1948 was United Nations mediator in Palestine, where he was assassinated by Stern Gang guerrillas. He was a nephew of Gustaf VI of Sweden.

Bernadotte Jean-Baptiste Jules 1764–1844. Marshal in Napoleon's army who in 1818 became ◊Charles XIV of Sweden. Hence, Bernadotte is the family name of the present royal house of Sweden.

Bernanos Georges 1888–1948. French author. He achieved fame in 1926 with *Sous le soleil de Satan/The Star of Satan*. His strongly Catholic viewpoint is also expressed in his *Journal d'un curé de campagne/The Diary of a Country Priest* 1936.

Bernard Claude 1813–1878. French physiologist and founder of experimental medicine. Bernard first demonstrated that digestion is not restricted to the stomach, but takes place throughout the small intestine. He discovered the digestive input of the pancreas, several functions of the liver, and the vasomotor nerves which dilate and contract the blood vessels and thus regulate body temperature. This led him to the concept of the *milieu intérieur* ("internal environment") whose stability is essential to good health. Bernard was a member of the Académie Française and served in the French Senate.

Bernard of Clairvaux, St 1090–1153. Christian founder in 1115 of Clairvaux monastery in Champagne, France. He reinvigorated the ◊Cistercian order, preached in support of the Second Crusade in 1146, and had the scholastic philosopher Abelard condemned for heresy. He is often depicted with a beehive. Feast day Aug 20.

Bernard of Menthon, St or ***Bernard of Montjoux*** 923–1008. Christian priest, founder of the hospices for travelers on the Alpine passes that bear his name. The large, heavily built St Bernard dogs, formerly employed to find travelers lost in the snow, were also named after him. He is the patron saint of mountaineers. Feast day May 28.

Bernese Oberland or ***Bernese Alps*** the mountainous area in the S of Berne canton. It includes the Jungfrau, Eiger, and Finsteraarhorn peaks. Interlaken is the chief town.

Bernhard Prince of the Netherlands 1911– . Formerly Prince Bernhard of Lippe-Biesterfeld, he married Princess ◊Juliana in 1937. When Germany invaded the Netherlands in 1940, he escaped to England and became liaison officer for the Dutch and British forces, playing a part in the organization of the Dutch Resistance.

Bernhardt Sarah. Adopted name of Rosine Bernard 1845–1923. French actress who dominated the stage of her day, frequently performing at the Comédie-Française in Paris. She exceled in tragic roles, including Cordelia in Shakespeare's *King Lear*, the title role in Racine's *Phèdre*, and the male roles of Hamlet and of Napoleon's son in Edmond ◊Rostand's *L'Aiglon*.

Bernini Giovanni Lorenzo 1598–1680. Italian sculptor, architect, and painter, a leading figure in the development of the Baroque style. His work in Rome includes the colonnaded piazza in front of St Peter's Basilica (1656), fountains (as in the Piazza Navona), and papal monuments. His sculpture includes *The Ecstasy of St Theresa* 1645–52 (Sta Maria della Vittoria, Rome) and numerous portrait busts.

Bernini's sculptural style is full of movement and drama, as captured in billowing drapery and facial expressions. His subjects are religious and mythological. A fine example is the marble *Apollo and Daphne* for the Cardinal Borghese, 1622–25 (Borghese Palace, Rome), with the figures shown in full flight. Inside St Peter's, he created several marble monuments and the elaborate canopy over the high altar. He also produced many fine portrait busts, such as one of Louis XIV of France.

Bernhardt *French tragic actress Sarah Bernhardt, called by Oscar Wilde "the divine Sarah," in her role as Marguérite in* La Dame aux Camélias *1881.*

Bernoulli Swiss family that produced many capable mathematicians and scientists in the 17th, 18th, and 19th centuries, in particular the brothers Jakob (1654–1705) and Johann (1667–1748).

Jakob and Johann were pioneers of ◊Leibniz's calculus. Jakob used calculus to study the forms of many curves arising in practical situations, and studied mathematical probability (*Ars conjectandi* 1713); Bernoulli numbers are named after him. Johann developed exponential calculus and contributed to many areas of applied mathematics, including the problem of a particle moving in a gravitational field. His son, Daniel (1700–1782) worked on calculus and probability, and in physics proposed Bernoulli's principle, which states that the pressure of a moving fluid decreases the faster it flows (which explains the origin of lift on the airfoil of an aircraft's wing). This and other work on hydrodynamics was published in *Hydrodynamica* 1738.

Bernoulli's principle statement that the speed of a fluid varies inversely with the pressure, an increase in speed producing a decrease in pressure (such as a drop in hydraulic pressure as the fluid speeds up flowing through a constriction in a pipe) and vice versa. The principle also explains the pressure differences on each surface of an airfoil, which gives lift to the wing of an aircraft. The principle was named after the Swiss physicist Daniel Bernoulli.

Bernstein Edouard 1850–1932. German Socialist thinker, journalist and politician. He was elected to the Reichstag 1902. He was a proponent of reformist rather than revolutionary socialism, whereby a Socialist society could be achieved within an existing parliamentary structure merely by workers" parties obtaining a majority.

Bernstein Leonard 1918–1990. US composer, conductor, and pianist. His works, which established a vogue for realistic, contemporary themes, include symphonies such as *The Age of Anxiety* 1949; ballets such as *Fancy Free* 1944; scores for musicals including *Wonderful Town* 1953 and *West Side Story* 1957; and *Mass* 1971 in memory of President J F Kennedy.

Born in Lawrence, Massachussetts, he was educated at Harvard University and the Curtis Institute of Music. From 1958 to 1970 he was musical director of the New York Philharmonic. Among his other works are *Jeremiah* 1944, *Facsimile* 1946, *Candide* 1956, and the *Chichester Psalms* 1965.

Berri Nabih 1939– . Lebanese politician and soldier, leader of Amal ("Hope"), the Syrian-backed Shiite nationalist movement. He was minister of justice in the government of President ◊Gemayel from 1984. In 1988 Amal was disbanded after defeat by the Iranian-backed Hezbollah ("Children of God") during the Lebanese civil wars, and Berri joined the cabinet of Salim al-Hoss in 1989.

Berry *US singer, songwriter, and guitarist Chuck Berry was one of the first musicians to popularize rock and roll.*

Berrigan Daniel 1921– and Philip 1924– . US Roman Catholic priests. The brothers, opponents of the Vietnam war, broke into the draft-records offices at Catonsville, Maryland, to burn the files with napalm. They were sentenced in 1968 to three and six years' imprisonment respectively, but went underground. Subsequently Philip Berrigan was tried with others in 1972 for allegedly conspiring to kidnap President Nixon's adviser Henry Kissinger and blow up government offices in Washington, DC; he was then sentenced to two years' imprisonment.

berry a fleshy, many-seeded ◊fruit that does not split open to release the seeds. The outer layer of tissue, the exocarp, forms an outer skin that is often brightly colored to attract birds to eat the fruit and thus disperse the seeds. Examples of berries are the tomato and the grape.

A pepo is a type of berry that has developed a hard exterior, such as the cucumber fruit. Another type is the hesperidium, which has a thick, leathery outer layer, such as that found in citrus fruits, and fluid-containing vesicles within, which form the segments.

Berry Chuck (Charles Edward) 1926– . US musician. He made his first recording, of the song "Maybellene," at Chess Records in Chicago 1955. Widely promoted by New York disk jockey Alan Freed, it became an early rock-and-roll classic. Recognized as one of the fathers of rock and roll, Berry enjoyed a revival of popularity in the 1970s and 1980s.

Born in St Louis, Missouri, Berry began his musical career as a blues guitarist in local clubs. Berry's other early tunes, among them "Roll over Beethoven," "Rock 'n' Roll Music," "Sweet Little Sixteen," and "Johnny B. Goode," featured his trademark guitar solos.

Berryman John 1914–1972. US poet, whose somber, complex, and personal works have much in common with that of the "confessional" poets, but his use of humor sets it apart. His poetry collections include *Homage to Mistress Bradstreet* 1956, *77 Dream Songs* 1964 (Pulitzer prize 1965), *His Toy, His Dream, His Rest* 1968, and *Delusions, etc.* 1972. He also wrote short stories and a biography of Stephen Crane 1950. Berryman, an alcoholic, committed suicide.

Berthelot Pierre Eugène Marcellin 1827–1907. French chemist and politician who carried out research into dyes and explosives, proving that hydrocarbons and other organic compounds can be synthesized from inorganic materials.

Bertholet Claude Louis 1748–1822. French chemist, who carried out research on dyes and bleaches (introducing the use of ◊chlorine as a bleach) and determined the composition of ◊ammonia. Modern chemical nomenclature is based on a system worked out by Bertholet and Antoine ◊Lavoisier.

Bertolucci Bernardo 1940– . Italian film director whose work combines political and historical perspectives with an elegant and lyrical visual appeal. His films include *The Spider's Stratagem* 1970, *Last Tango in Paris* 1972, *The Last Emperor* 1987, for which he received an Academy Award, and *The Sheltering Sky* 1990.

He is regarded as one of the most talented of the younger generation of Italian film directors. Among his other films are *The Conformist* 1970 and *1900* 1976.

Bertrand de Born c. 1140–c. 1215. Provençal ◊troubador. He was viscount of Hautefort in Périgord, accompanied Richard the Lion-Hearted to Palestine, and died a monk.

beryl a mineral, beryllium aluminum silicate, $Be_3Al_2Si_6O_{18}$, which forms crystals chiefly in granite. It is the chief ore of beryllium. Two of its gem forms are aquamarine (light-blue crystals) and emerald (dark-green crystals).

Well-formed crystals of up to 200 tons have been found.

beryllium hard, lightweight, silver-white, metallic element, symbol Be, atomic number 4, atomic weight 9.012. It is one of the ◊alkaline-earth metals, with chemical properties similar to those of magnesium; in nature it is found only in combination with other elements. It is used to make sturdy, light alloys and to control the speed of neutrons in nuclear reactors. It was discovered in 1798 by French chemist Louis-Nicolas Vauquelin (1763–1829). The name comes from Latin *beryllus*.

Berzelius Jöns Jakob 1779–1848. Swedish chemist who accurately determined more than 2,000 relative atomic and molecular masses. He devised (1813–14) the system of chemical symbols and formulae now in use and proposed oxygen as a reference standard for atomic masses. His discoveries include the elements selenium (1817), cerium, and thorium (1828); he was the first to prepare silicon in its amorphous form and to isolate zirconium. The words isomerism, allotropy, and protein were coined by him.

Berzelius *Swedish chemist John Jacob Berzelius devised the system of chemical symbols now in use and determined atomic and molecular weights in the 19th century.*

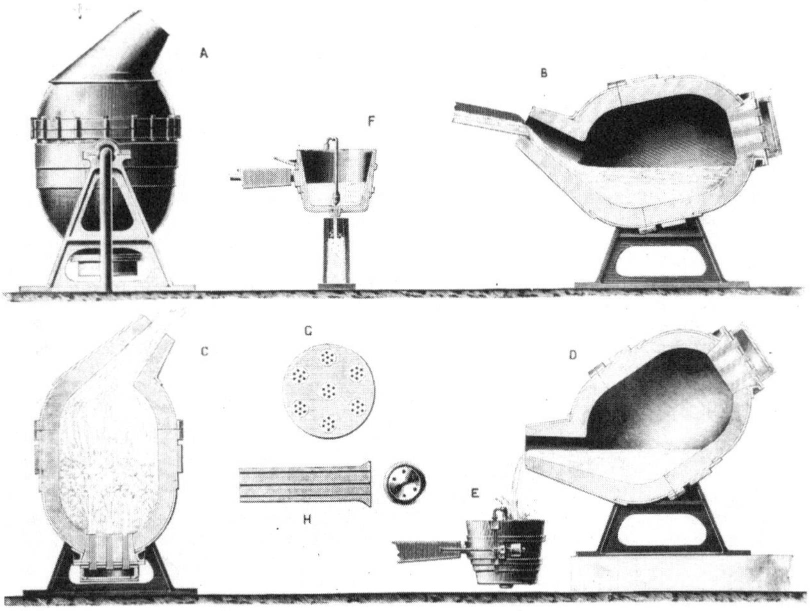
A
B
C
C
D
E
F
G
H

Bessemer *The British metallurgist Henry Bessemer patented an economical process by which pig iron blasted by a current of air is turned directly into steel. This is a diagram of the first moveable form of his converter and ladle, taken from his autobiography.*

Bes in Egyptian mythology, the god of music and dance, usually shown as a grotesque dwarf.

Besançon town on the river Doubs, France; population (1983) 120,000. It is the capital of Franche-Comté. The first factory to produce artificial fibers was established here 1890. Industries include textiles and clock-making. It has fortifications by ◊Vauban, Roman remains, and a Gothic cathedral. The writer Victor Hugo and the Lumière brothers, inventors of cinematography, were born here.

Besant Annie 1847–1933. British Socialist and feminist activist. Separated from her clerical husband in 1873 because of her freethinking views, she was associated with the radical atheist Charles Bradlaugh and the Socialist ◊Fabian Society. She and Bradlaugh published a treatise advocating birth control and were prosecuted; as a result she lost custody of her daughter. In 1889 she became a disciple of Madame ◊Blavatsky. She thereafter preached theosophy and went to India. As a supporter of Indian independence, she founded the Central Hindu College 1898 and the Indian Home Rule League 1916, and became president of the Indian National Congress in 1917.

Bessarabia territory in SE Europe, annexed by Russia 1812, that broke away at the Russian Revolution to join Romania. The cession was confirmed by the Allies, but not by Russia, in a Paris treaty of 1920; Russia reoccupied it 1940 and divided it between the Moldavian and Ukrainian republics. Romania recognized the position in the 1947 peace treaty.

Bessel Friedrich Wilhelm 1784–1846. German astronomer and mathematician, the first person to find the approximate distance to a star by direct methods when he measured the ◊parallax (annual displacement) of the star 61 Cygni in 1838. In mathematics, he introduced the series of functions now known as Bessel functions.

Bessemer Henry 1813–1898. British civil engineer who invented a method of converting molten pig iron into steel (the Bessemer process).

Bessemer process the first cheap method of making ◊steel, invented by Henry Bessemer in England 1856. It has since been superseded by more efficient steelmaking processes, such as the ◊basic-oxygen process. In the Bessemer process compressed air is blown into the bottom of a converter, a furnace shaped like a cement mixer, containing molten pig iron. The excess carbon in the iron burns out, other impurities form a slag, and the furnace is emptied by tilting.

Bessmertnykh Aleksandr 1934– . Soviet politician and foreign minister. Born in southern Siberia, the son of a civil servant, after graduating at Mgimo, (the Moscow international relations institute), he began his diplomatic career. He worked mostly in the US, at the United Nations headquarters in New York and the Soviet embassy in Washington. He succeeded Edvard Shevardnadze as foreign minister in 1991.

Best Charles Herbert 1899–1978. Canadian physiologist, one of the team of Canadian scientists including Frederick ◊Banting whose research resulted in 1922 in the discovery of insulin as a treatment for diabetes.

A Banting–Best Department of Medical Research was founded in Toronto, and Best was its director 1941–67.

bestiary in medieval times, a book with stories and illustrations which depicted real and mythical animals or plants to illustrate a (usually Christian) moral. The stories were initially derived from the Greek *Physiologus*, a collection of 48 such stories, written in Alexandria around the 2nd century AD.

Translations of the *Physiologus* into vernacular languages (French, Italian, and English) date from the 13th century; illustrated versions are known from the 9th century. Much of later and contemporary folklore about animals derives from the bestiary, such as the myth of the phoenix burning itself to be born again.

bestseller a book that achieves large sales. Listings are based upon sales figures from bookstores and other retail stores.

The Bible has sold more copies than any other book over time, but popular and commercial examples include Charles Monroe Seldon's *In His Steps* 1897, Margaret Mitchell's *Gone With the Wind* 1936, and Dale Carnegie's *How to Win Friends and Influence People* 1937. Current bestseller lists appear in newspapers, magazines, and book trade publications.

beta-blocker any of a class of drugs that block impulses that stimulate certain nerve endings (beta receptors) serving the heart muscles. This reduces the heart rate and the force of contraction, which in turn reduces the amount of oxygen (and therefore the blood supply) required by the heart. Beta-blockers are banned from use in competitive sports. They may be useful in the treatment of angina, arrhythmia, and raised blood pressure, and following myocardial infarctions. They must be withdrawn from use gradually.

beta decay the spontaneous alteration of the nucleus of a radioactive atom, which transmutes the atom from one atomic number to another through the emission of either an electron (beta-minus decay) or a positron (beta-plus decay). In the more commonly occurring of the two, beta-minus decay, the atomic number increases by one (through the decay of a neutron, which converts to a proton emitting an electron and an antineutrino); in the less commonly occurring beta-plus decay, the atomic number decreases by one (the proton converts to a neutron, emitting a positron and a neutrino). The symbol used for the electron in beta-minus decay is β^-; the symbol for the positron in beta-plus decay is β^+.

beta particle an electron or positron emitted with great velocity from a radioactive atom that is undergoing spontaneous disintegration. Beta particles do not exist in the nucleus but are created upon disintegration.

The process of disintegration is known as ◊beta decay (both beta-minus and beta-plus), and it transmutes one element into another.

Betelgeuse or ***Alpha Orionis*** red supergiant star in the constellation of Orion and the tenth brightest star in the sky, although its brightness varies. It is over 300 times the diameter of the Sun, about the same size as the orbit of Mars, and lies 650 light-years from Earth.

betel nut fruit of the areca palm (*Areca catechu*), used together with lime and betel pepper as a masticatory stimulant by peoples of the East. Chewing it results in blackened teeth and a mouth stained deep red.

Bethe Hans Albrecht 1906– . German-born US physicist who worked on the first atomic bomb. He was awarded a Nobel Prize 1967 for his discoveries concerning energy production in stars.

Bethe left Germany for England in 1933, and worked at Manchester and Bristol universities. In 1935 he moved to the US where he became professor of theoretical physics at Cornell University; his research was interrupted by the war and by his appointment as head of the theoretical division of the Los Alamos atomic bomb project. He has since become a leading peace campaigner, and opposed the US government's Strategic Defense Initiative (Star Wars) program.

Bethlehem city in E Pennsylvania; population (1990) 71,428. Its former steel industry has been replaced by high technology. Lehigh University is here. Bethlehem was founded 1741 by German immigrants.

Bethlehem (Hebrew *Beit-Lahm*) town on the W bank of the river Jordan, S of Jerusalem. Occupied by Israel in 1967; population (1980) 14,000. In the Bible it is mentioned as the birthplace of King David and Jesus.

Bethmann Hollweg Theobald von 1856–1921. German politician, imperial chancellor 1909–17, largely responsible for engineering popular support for World War I in Germany, but his power was overthrown by a military dictatorship under ◊Ludendorff and ◊Hindenburg.

Béthune city in N France, W of Lille; population (1982) 258,400. Industries include textiles, machinery, and tires.

Bettelheim Bruno 1903–1990. Austrian-born US psychologist. He fled Europe in 1939 and came to the US, where he joined the faculty of the University of Chicago. He later became involved in the treatment of severely disturbed children. Among his most influential books are *Love Is Not Enough* 1950, *Truants from Life* 1954, and *Children of the Dream* 1962.

He received his PhD from the University of Vienna 1938. With the Nazi occupation of Austria, he was arrested and sent to the concentration camps at Dachau and Buchenwald, where he began a long-term study of the psychological effects of totalitarianism.

Betti Ugo 1892–1953. Italian poet and dramatist. His plays include *Delitto all'isola delle capre/Crime on Goat Island* 1948 and *La Regina e gli insorte/The Queen and the Rebels* 1949.

betting wagering money on the outcome of a game, race, or other event, not necessarily a sporting event.

Bevan Aneurin 1897–1960. British Labor politician. Son of a Welsh miner, and himself a miner at 13, he became member of Parliament for Ebbw Vale 1929–60. As minister of health 1945–51, he inaugurated the National Health Service (NHS); he was minister of labor Jan–April 1951, when he resigned (with Harold Wilson) on the introduction of NHS charges and led a Bevanite faction against the government. He was a good speaker.

beverage any liquid for drinking other than pure water. Beverages are made with plant products to impart pleasant flavors, nutrients, and stimulants to people's fluid intake. Examples include juices, tea, coffee, cocoa, soft drinks, and alcoholic beverages.

The juices of grapes and other fruits are fermented to produce wines, while fermented cereals form the basis of beers and liquors.

See also ◊alcoholic beverage.

Beverly Hills residential city and a part of greater Los Angeles, California, known as the home of Hollywood film stars. Rodeo Drive is a popular shopping area for prestige goods. Population (1990) 31,971.

Beza Théodore (properly De Bèsze) 1519–1605. French church reformer. He settled in Geneva, Switzerland, where he worked with the Protestant leader John Calvin and succeeded him as head of the reformed church there 1564. He wrote in defense of the burning of ◊Servetus (1554) and translated the New Testament into Latin.

Bezier curve curved line that connects a series of points (or "nodes") in the smoothest possible way. The shape of the curve is governed by a series of complex mathematical formulae. They are used in ◊computer graphics and ◊CAD.

Béziers city in Languedoc-Roussillon, S France; population (1983) 84,000. It is a center of the wine trade. It was once a Roman station and was the site of a massacre 1209 in the Albigensian Crusade.

Bhagalpur town in N India, on the river Ganges; population (1981) 225,000. It manufactures silk and textiles. Several Jain temples are here.

Bhagavad-Gītā (Hindu "the Song of the Blessed") religious and philosophical Sanskrit poem, dating from around 300 BC, forming an episode in the sixth book of the *Mahābhārata*, one of the two great Hindu epics. It is the supreme religious work of Hinduism.

bhakti (Sanskrit "devotion") in Hinduism, a tradition of worship that emphasizes love and devotion rather than ritual, sacrifice, or study.

Bhamo town in Myanmar (Burma), near the Chinese frontier, on the Irrawaddy river. It is the inland limit of steam navigation and is mainly a trading center.

bhang another name for ◊cannabis.

Bharat Hindi name for ◊India.

Bharat Natyam type of Indian Classical dancing.

Bhatgaon Bhadgaon or Bhaktapur town in Nepal, 7 mi/11 km SE of Katmandu; population (1981) 48,500. A religious center from the 9th century, it has a palace.

Bhavnagar port in Gujarat, NW India, in the Kathiawar peninsula; population (1981) 308,000. It is a center for textile industry. It was capital of the former Rajput princely state of Bhavnagar.

bhikku a Buddhist monk who is totally dependent on alms and the monastic community (*sangha*) for support.

Bhindranwale Sant Jarnail Singh 1947–1984. Indian Sikh fundamentalist leader who campaigned for the creation of a separate state of Khalistan during the early 1980s, precipitating a bloody Hindu-Sikh conflict in the Punjab. Having taken refuge in the Golden Temple complex in Amritsar and built up an arms cache for guerrilla activities, Bhindranwale, along with around 500 followers, died at the hands of Indian security forces who stormed the temple in "Operation Blue Star" June 1984.

Bhopal industrial city (textiles, chemicals, electrical

Bhutan
Kingdom of
(*Druk-yul*)

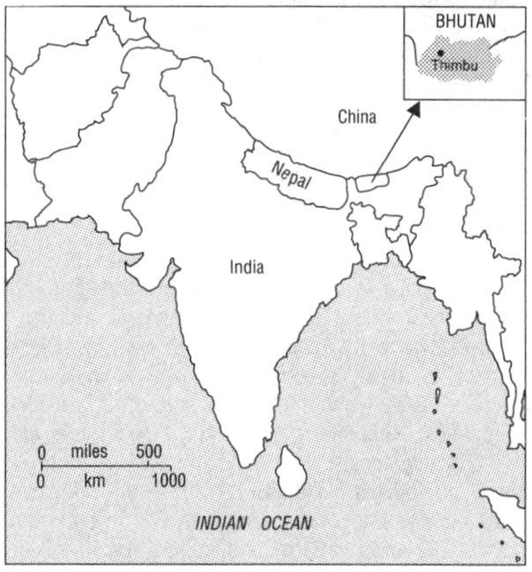
BHUTAN
Thimbu
China
Nepal
India
0 miles 500
0 km 1000
INDIAN OCEAN

area 17,954 sq mi/46,500 sq km
capital Thimbu (Thimphu)
cities Paro, Punakha, Mongar
physical occupies S slopes of the Himalayas; cut by valleys formed by tributaries of the Brahmaputra; thick forests in S
features Gangkar Punsum (24,700 ft/7,529 m) is one of the world's highest unclimbed peaks
head of state and government Jigme Singye Wangchuk from 1972
political system absolute monarchy
political parties none officially; illegal Bhutan People's Party (BPP)
exports timber, talc, fruit and vegetables, cement, distilled spirits, calcium carbide
currency ngultrum
population (1990 est) 1,566,000; growth rate 2% p.a. (75% Ngalops and Sharchops, 25% Nepálese)
life expectancy men 44, women 43
language offical Dzongkha (a Tibetan dialect), Sharchop, Bumthap, Nepali, and English
religion 75% Lamaistic Buddhist (state religion), 25% Hindu
literacy 5%
GDP $250 million (1987); $170 per head
chronology
1865 Trade treaty with Britain signed.
1907 First hereditary monarch installed.
1910 Anglo-Bhutanese Treaty signed.
1945 Indo-Bhutan Treaty of Friendship signed.
1952 King Jigme Dorji Wangchuk installed.
1953 National assembly established.
1959 4,000 Tibetan refugees given asylum.
1968 King established first cabinet.
1972 King died and was succeeded by his son Jigme Singye Wangchuk.
1979 Tibetan refugees told to take Bhutanese citizenship or leave; most stayed.
1983 Bhutan became a founding member of the South Asian Regional Cooperation organization (SARC).
1988 King imposes "code of conduct" suppressing Nepalese customs.
1989 People's Forum of Human Rights founded.
1990 Prodemocracy demonstrations took place.

goods, jewelry); capital of Madhya Pradesh, central India; population (1981) 672,000. Nearby Bhimbetka Caves, discovered 1973, have the world's largest collection of prehistoric paintings, which are about 10,000 years old. In 1984 some 2,000 people died from an escape of poisonous gas from a factory owned by the US company Union Carbide; the long-term effects are yet to be discovered.

The city was capital of the former princely state of Bhopal, founded 1723, which became allied to Britain in 1817. It was merged with Madhya Pradesh in 1956.

Bhubaneswar city in NE India; population (1981) 219,200. It is the capital of Orissa. Utkal University was founded 1843. A place of pilgrimage and center of Siva worship, it has temples of the 6th–12th centuries.

Bhumibol Adulyadej 1927– . King of Thailand from 1946. Born in the US and educated in Bangkok and Switzerland, he succeeded to the throne on the assassination of his brother. In 1973 he was active, with popular support, in overthrowing the military government of Marshal Thanom Kittikachorn and thus ended a sequence of army-dominated regimes in power from 1932.

Bhutan mountainous, landlocked country in eastern Himalayas (SE Asia), bounded N and E by Tibet (China) and to the S and W by India.

government Bhutan is a hereditary monarchy and although since 1953 there has been an elected national assembly (*Tshogdu*) and since 1965 a partially elected royal advisory council with whom the monarch shares power, in the absence of a written constitution or political parties it is in effect an absolute monarchy. There are, however, certain written rules governing the methods of electing members of the royal advisory council and Tshogdu. A gradual trend toward greater democracy is occurring.

history Bhutan was ruled by Tibet from the 16th century and by China from 1720. In 1774 the British East India Company concluded a treaty with the ruler of Bhutan, and British influence grew during the 19th century. A short border war in 1863 ended with a treaty in 1865, under which an annual subsidy was paid by Britain to Bhutan. In 1907 the first hereditary monarch was installed, and under the Anglo-Bhutanese Treaty signed three years later Bhutan was granted internal autonomy while foreign relations were placed under the control of the British government in India.

When India became independent in 1945, an Indo-Bhutan treaty of friendship was signed, under which Bhutan agreed to seek Indian advice on foreign relations but not necessarily to accept it. There is no formal defense treaty, but India would regard an attack on Bhutan as an act of aggression against itself. In 1952 King Jigme Dorji Wangchuk came to power, and in 1953 a national assembly was established.

In 1959, after the Chinese annexation of Tibet, Bhutan gave asylum to some 4,000 Tibetan refugees who in 1979 were given the choice of taking Bhutanese citizenship or returning to Tibet. Most became citizens, and the rest went to India. In 1968, as part of a move toward greater democracy, the king appointed his first cabinet. He died in 1972 and was succeeded by his Western-educated son Jigme Singye Wangchuk.

In 1983 Bhutan became a founding member of the South Asia Regional Co-operation organization (SARC), and in 1985 the first meeting of SARC foreign ministers was held in Bhutan.

Agitation in the non-Drukpa southern plains against the autocratic rule of the Buddhist Drukpa ethnic minority, headed by King Jigme Singye Wangchuk, has since 1988 imposed its own language, religious practices, and national dress on the divided (although principally Hindu-Nepali) majority community and suppressd the Nepalese language and customs.

Bhutto Benazir 1953– . Pakistani politician, leader

Bhutto *The first woman leader of a Moslem state was Benazir Bhutto, prime minister of Pakistan 1988–1990.*

of the PakistanPeople's Party (PPP) from 1984 (in exile until 1986), and prime minister of Pakistan 1988–90. She was the first female leader of a Muslim state.

Benazir Bhutto was educated at Harvard and Oxford universities. She returned to Pakistan 1977 but was placed under house arrest after Gen ◊Zia ul Haq seized power from her father, Prime Minister Zulfiqar Ali Bhutto. On her release she moved to the UK and became, with her mother Nusrat (1934–), the joint leader in exile of the opposition PPP. When martial law had been lifted, she returned to Pakistan Apr 1986 to launch a campaign for open elections. In her first year in office she struck an uneasy balance with the military establishment and improved Pakistan's relations with India. She led her country back into the Commonwealth 1989.

In Aug 1990, she was removed from office by presidential decree, and a caretaker government installed. Charges of corruption and abuse of power were leveled, and her party was defeated in the subsequent general election.

Bhutto Zulfikar Ali 1928–1979. Pakistani politician, president 1971–73; prime minister from 1973 until the 1977 military coup led by Gen ◊Zia ul Haq. In 1978 he was sentenced to death for conspiring to murder a political opponent and was hanged the following year.

Biafra, Bight of name until 1975 of the Bight of ◊Bonny, W Africa.

Biafra, Republic of African state proclaimed in 1967 when fears that Nigerian central government was increasingly in the hands of the rival Hausa tribe led the predominantly Ibo Eastern Region of Nigeria to secede under Lt Col Odumegwu Ojukwu. On the proclamation of Biafra, civil war ensued with the rest of the federation. In a bitterly fought campaign federal forces confined the Biafrans to a shrinking area of the interior by 1968, and by 1970 Biafra ceased to exist.

Białystok city in E Poland; population (1985) 245,000. It is the capital city of Białystok region. Industries include textiles, chemicals, and tools. Founded 1310, the city belonged to Prussia 1795–1807 and to Russia 1807–1919.

Biarritz town on the Bay of Biscay, France, near the Spanish border; population (1982) 28,000. A seaside resort and spa town, it was popularized by Queen Victoria and Edward VII.

biathlon an athletic competition that combines cross-country skiing with rifle marksmanship. Basic equipment consists of cross-country skis, poles, and boots and bolt-action (nonautomatic) rifles. The course (defined in metric terms) is usually 12.5 mi/20 km long and follows terrain that is uphill, downhill, and level (with approximately equal distances of each). Between the 5th km/3rd mi and the 18th km/11th mi there are 4 stations, at which the biathlete must fire 5 shots at targets that vary from 110 yd/100 m to 275 yd/250 m away. Firing positions alternate between prone and standing.

In standard team competition, a team's score is the total corrected time (penalties are imposed for missed targets) of the team's 3 leading entrants. The typical biathlon relay is a 4-person,

the Bible

The Books of the Old Testament		
Name of book	*Chapters*	*Date written*
The Pentateuch or the Five Books of Moses		
Genesis	50	mid 8th-century BC
Exodus	40	950–586 BC
Leviticus	27	mid 7th-century BC
Numbers	36	850–650 BC
Deuteronomy	34	mid-7th century BC
Joshua	24	c. 550 BC
Judges	21	c. 550 BC
Ruth	4	end 3rd century BC
1 Samuel	31	c. 900 BC
2 Samuel	24	c. 900 BC
1 Kings	22	550–600 BC
2 Kings	25	550–600 BC
1 Chronicles	29	c. 300 BC
2 Chronicles	36	c. 300 BC
Ezra	10	c. 450 BC
Nehemiah	13	c. 450 BC
Esther	10	c. 200 BC
Job	42	600–400 BC
Psalms	150	6th–2nd century BC
Proverbs	31	350–150 BC
Ecclesiastes	12	c. 200 BC
Song of Solomon	8	3rd century BC
Isaiah	66	end 3rd century BC
Jeremiah	52	604 BC
Lamentations	5	586–536 BC
Ezekiel	48	6th century BC
Daniel	12	c. 166 BC
Hosea	14	c. 732 BC
Joel	3	c. 500 BC
Amos	9	775–750 BC
Obadiah	1	6th–3rd century BC
Jonah	4	600–200 BC
Micah	7	end 3rd century BC
Nahum	3	c. 626 BC
Habakkuk	3	c. 600 BC
Zephaniah	3	3rd century BC
Haggai	2	c. 520 BC
Zechariah	14	c. 520 BC
Malachi	4	c. 430 BC
The Books of the New Testament		
Name of books	*Chapters*	*Date written*
The Gospels		
Matthew	28	before AD 70
Mark	16	before AD 70
Luke	24	AD 70–80
John	21	AD 90–100
The Acts	28	AD 70–80
Romans	16	AD 120
1 Corinthians	16	AD 57
2 Corinthians	13	AD 57
Galatians	6	AD 53
Ephesians	6	AD 140
Philippians	4	AD 63
Colossians	4	AD 140
1 Thessalonians	5	AD 50–54
2 Thessalonians	3	AD 50–54
1 Timothy	6	before AD 64
2 Timothy	4	before AD 64
Titus	3	before AD 64
Philemon	1	AD 60–62
Hebrews	13	AD 80–90
James	5	before AD 52
1 Peter	5	before AD 64
2 Peter	3	before AD 64
1 John	5	AD 90–100
2 John	1	AD 90–100
3 John	1	AD 90–100
Jude	1	AD 75–80
Revelation	22	AD 81–96

Two plates from the Bible Pauperum c. 1470. The left-hand page shows Joseph in the pit, the burial of Jesus, and Jonah. The right-hand plate shows David slaying Goliath, the resurrection of Christ, and Samson and the lion.

7.5-km/4.7-mi event, in which a 200-m/220-yd penalty loop must be skied for each missed target.

The biathlon can be traced to Sweden, where it began as informal competition among hunters. By 1908 the sport had become organized enough to inspire international military ski races in Europe. The first modern biathlon event in the US was at Camp Hale, Colorado, 1956. In 1960, at the Winter Games in Squaw Valley, California, the sport became an Olympic event. Relay competition was added 1968.

Biber Heinrich von 1644–1704. Bohemian composer, kapellmeister at the archbishop of Salzburg's court. A virtuoso violinist, he composed a wide variety of musical pieces including the *Nightwatchman Serenade*.

Bible (Greek *ta biblia* "the books") the sacred book of the Jewish and Christian religions. The Hebrew Bible, recognized by both Jews and Christians, is called the ◊Old Testament by Christians. The ◊New Testament comprises books recognized by the Christian church from the 4th century as canonical. The Roman Catholic Bible also includes the ◊Apocrypha. The first English translation of the entire Bible was by a priest, Miles Coverdale, 1535; the King James Version or King James Bible 1611 was long influential for the clarity and beauty of its language. A revision of the King James Version carried out 1959 by the British and Foreign Bible Society produced the widely used Revised Standard Version. A conference of British churches 1946 recommended a completely new translation into English from the original Hebrew and Greek texts; work on this was carried out over the following two decades, resulting in the publication of the New English Bible (New Testament 1961, Old Testament and Apocrypha 1970). Another major new translation is the Jerusalem Bible, completed by Catholic scholars in 1966.

Missionary activity led to the translation of the Bible into the languages of people they were trying to convert, and by 1975 parts of the Bible had been translated into over 1,500 different languages, with 261 complete translations.

Bible society society founded for the promotion of translation and distribution of the Scriptures. The four largest branches are the British and Foreign Bible Society, founded in 1804, the American Bible Society, the National Bible Society of Scotland, and the Netherlands Bible Society.

Biblical criticism study of the content and origin of the Bible. Lower or textual criticism is directed toward the recovery of the original text; higher or documentary criticism is concerned with questions of authorship, date, and literary sources; historical criticism seeks to ascertain the actual historical content of the Bible, aided by archeological discoveries and the ancient history of neighboring peoples.

bicarbonate of soda or ***baking soda*** $NaHCO_3$ (technical name sodium hydrogencarbonate) white crystalline solid that neutralizes acids and is used in medicine to treat acid indigestion. It is also used in baking powders and effervescent drinks.

Bichat Marie François Xavier 1771–1802. French physician and founder of ◊histology, the study of tissues. He studied the organs of the body, their structure, and the ways in which they are affected by disease. This led to his discovery and naming of "tissue," a basic biological and medical concept; he identified 21 types. He argued that disease does not affect the whole organ but only certain of its constituent tissues.

bichir African fish, genus *Polypterus*, found in tropical swamps and rivers. Cylindrical in shape, some species grow to 2.3 ft/70 cm or more. They show many "primitive" features, such as breathing air by using the swimbladder, having a spiral valve in the intestine, having heavy bony scales, and having a larva with external gills. These, and the fleshy fins, lead some scientists to think they are related to lungfish and coelacanths.

bicycle pedal-driven two-wheeled vehicle used in ◊cycling. It consists of a metal frame mounted on two large wire-spoked wheels, with handlebars in front and a seat between the front and back wheels. The bicycle is an energy-efficient, nonpolluting form of transport and is used throughout the world. China, India, Denmark, and the Netherlands are countries with a high use of bicycles.

Bidault Georges 1899–1983. French politician. He was a leader of the French resistance during World War II and foreign minister and president in De Gaulle's provisional government. He left the Gaullists over Algerian independence and in 1962 became head of the ◊Organisation de l'Armée Secrète (OAS), he was charged with treason in 1963 and left the country, but was allowed to return in 1968.

Biddle Nicholas 1786–1844. US financier and public figure. Born in Philadelphia, Biddle was admitted to the Pennsylvania bar 1809 and elected to the state legislature 1814. As an acknowledged expert in international commerce, he was appointed a director of the Bank of the United States by President Monroe 1819. He became president of the bank 1822, but as an extreme fiscal conservative, Biddle became the focus of Andrew ◊Jackson's antibank campaigns in 1828 and 1832. After the withdrawal of the bank's federal charter 1836, he remained its president under a state charter.

Biedermeier Germanic style of art and furniture design 1816–48, derogatorily named after Gottlieb Biedermeier, a humorous pseudonym used by several German poets, embodying bourgeois taste. Inexpensive and comfortable, it offered a simple version of 18th-century Empire, Directoire, and English styles.

Biel (French *Bienne*) town in NW Switzerland; population (1987) 83,000. Its main industries include engineering, scientific instruments, and watchmaking.

Bielefeld city in North Rhine–Westphalia, Germany, 34 mi/55 km E of Münster; population (1988) 299,000. Industries include textiles, drinks, chemicals, machinery, and motorcycles.

Bielostok Russian form of ◊Białystok, city in Poland.

Bienne French form of ◊Biel, town in Switzerland.

biennial plant a plant that completes its life cycle in two years. During the first year it grows vegetatively and the surplus food produced is stored in its ◊perennating organ, usually the root. In the following year these food reserves are used for the production of leaves, flowers and seeds, after which the plant dies. Many root vegetables are biennials, including the carrot *Daucus carota* and parsnip *Pastinaca sativa*. Some garden plants that are grown as biennials are actually perennials, for example, the wallflower *Cheiranthus cheiri*.

Bienville Jean Baptiste Le Moyne, Sieur de 1680–1768. French colonial administrator. Born in Ville-Marie (now Montreal), Quebec, Bienville saw service in the French navy and in 1698 accompanied ◊Iberville on a mission to establish a French colony at the mouth of the Mississippi river. Serving his first term as governor of Louisiana 1706–13, he founded the settlement at Mobile. In his second term 1717–23, he established the colonial capital at New Orleans. During Bienville's third and final term 1733–43, he was drawn into a costly and ultimately unsuccessful war with the Indians of the lower Mississippi Valley.

Bierce Ambrose (Gwinett) 1842–c. 1914. US author. He established his reputation as a master of supernatural and psychological horror with *Tales of Soldiers and Civilians* 1891 and *Can Such Things Be?* 1893. He also wrote *The Devil's Dictionary* 1911 (first published as *The Cynic's Word Book 1906), a collection of ironic definitions*. He disappeared in Mexico 1913.

He was writer-editor of the *San Francisco Newletter*, publisher of short stories by Mark Twain and Bret Harte, and the satirical columnist known as "The Prattler" 1887–1906.

Bierstadt Albert 1830–1902. German-born US landscape painter. His spectacular panoramas of the American wilderness fell out of favor after his death until interest in the Hudson River School rekindled late in the century. A classic work is *Thunderstorm in the Rocky Mountains* 1859 (Museum of Fine Arts, Boston).

His *Discovery of the Hudson* hangs in the Capitol in Washington, DC.

bigamy in law, the offense of marrying a person while already lawfully married to another in a monogamous legal jurisdiction. In some countries marriage to more than one wife or husband is lawful; see also ◊polygamy.

big band jazz sound ◊swing music created in the late 1930s and 1940s by bands of 15 or more players, such as those of Duke ◊Ellington and Benny ◊Goodman.

Big Bang in astronomy, the hypothetical "explosive" event that marked the origin of the universe as we know it. At the time of the Big Bang, the entire universe was squeezed into a hot, superdense state, which was, according to some calculations, 300 million times smaller than the universe is today. The Big Bang explosion threw this compacted material outward, producing the expanding universe (see ◊red shift). The cause of the Big Bang is unknown; observations of the current rate of expansion of the universe suggest that it took place almost 20 billion years ago. See also ◊cosmology.

Big Bertha any of three large German howitzer guns that were mounted on freight cars during World War I.

Big Dipper American name for the seven brightest and most prominent stars in the constellation ◊Ursa Major, which in outline resemble a large dipper.

bight a coastal indentation, such as the Bight of ◊Bonny in W Africa and the Great Australian Bight.

Bihar or Behar state of NE India

area 67,125 sq mi/173,900 sq km

capital Patna

features river Ganges in the N, Rajmahal Hills in the S

products copper, iron, coal, rice, jute, sugar cane, grain, oilseed

population (1981) 69,823,000

language Hindi, Bihari

famous people Chandragupta, Asoka

history the ancient kingdom of Magadha roughly corresponded to central and S Bihar.

Bijapur ancient city in Karnataka, India. It was founded around AD 1489 Yusuf Adil Shah (died 1511), the son of Murad II, as the capital of the Muslim kingdom of Biafra. The city and kingdom was annexed by the Mogul emperor Aurangzeb in 1686.

Bikaner city in Rajasthan, N India; population (1981) 280,000. Once capital of the Rajput state of Bikaner, it is now a center for carpet-weaving.

Bikini atoll in the ◊Marshall Islands, N Pacific, where atomic and hydrogen bomb tests (some underwater) were carried out by the US between 1946 and 1958. Some of the islanders, who had been relocated by the US before 1946, returned in the late 1960s, but they were again removed in the late 1970s because of continuing harmful levels of radiation.

Biko Steve (Stephen) 1946–1977. South African civil rights leader. An active opponent of ◊apartheid, he was arrested in Sept 1977; he died in detention six days later. Since his death in the custody of South African police he has been a symbol of the antiapartheid movement.

bilateralism in economics, a trade agreement between two countries or groups of countries in which they give each other preferential treatment. Usually the terms agreed result in balanced trade and are favored by countries with limited foreign exchange reserves. Bilateralism is incompatible with free trade.

Bilbao industrial port (iron and steel, chemicals, cement, food) in N Spain, capital of Biscay province; population (1986) 378,000.

bilberry several species of shrubs of the genus *Vaccinium* of the heath family Ericaceae, closely related to North American blueberries.

bilby a rabbit-eared bandicoot *Macrotis lagotis*, a lightly built marsupial with big ears and long nose. This burrowing animal is mainly carnivorous, and its pouch opens backwards.

Bildungsroman (German "education novel") novel that deals with the psychological and emotional development of its protagonist, tracing his or her life from inexperienced youth to maturity. The first example of the type is generally considered to be ◊Wieland's *Agathon* 1765–66, but it was ◊Goethe's *Wilhelm Meisters Lehrjahr/Wilhelm Meister's Apprenticeship* 1795–96 that established the genre. Although taken up by writers in other languages, it remained chiefly a German form; later examples includ ◊Mann's *Der Zauberberg/The Magic Mountain* 1924.

bile brownish fluid produced by the liver. In most vertebrates, it is stored in the gall bladder and emptied into the small intestine as food passes through. Bile consists of bile salts, bile pigments, cholestrol, and lecithin. Bile salts assist in the breakdown and absorption of fats; bile pigments are the breakdown products of old red blood cells that are passed into the gut to be eliminated with the feces.

bilharzia or ***schistosomiasis*** disease that causes anemia, inflammation, formation of scar tissue, dysentery, enlargement of the spleen and liver, and cirrhosis of the liver. It is contracted by bathing in water contaminated with human sewage. Some 300 million people are thought to suffer from this disease in the tropics.

Freshwater snails that live in this water act as host to the first larval stage of flukes of the genus *Schistosoma*; when these larvae leave the snail in their second stage of development, they are able to pass through human skin, become sexually mature, and produce quantities of eggs, which pass to the intestine or bladder. The human host eventually dies of the infestation, but before then numerous eggs have passed from the body in urine or feces to continue the cycle. Treatment is by means of drugs, usually containing antimony, to kill the parasites.

billiards indoor game played, normally, by two players, with tapered poles (called cues) and composition balls (one red, two white) on a rectangular table covered with a green, feltlike cloth (baize) without pockets. Scoring strokes are made by sinking the red ball, sinking the opponent's ball, or sinking another ball off one of these two. The cannon (when the cue ball hits the two other balls on the table) is another scoring stroke.

Billings city in S central Montana on the N shore of the Yellowstone river; seat of Yellowstone county. It is a center for transporting livestock and animal products and for vegetable and grain processing; population (1990) 81,151. Nearby, to the SE, is Big Horn Indian reservation where the Battle of Little Big Horn took place 1876.

billion the cardinal number represented by a 1 followed by nine zeros (1,000,000,000), equivalent to a thousand million.

Billiton Indonesian island in the Java Sea, between Borneo and Sumatra, one of the Sunda Islands; area 1,860 sq mi/4,830 sq km. The chief port is Tanjungpandan. Tin mining is the chief industry.

bill of exchange or ***bank draft*** a written order in which a *drawer* orders a *drawee* to pay a specified sum to a *payee*. For example, a check is a bill of exchange drawn on a bank or banker. Once signed and endorsed, it becomes negotiable and can be discounted (sold for cash before the maturity date under face value) at current short-term interest rates.

In the US, major corporations make use of short-term "paper" to meet general financial obligations as well as foreign trade transactions.

Bill of Rights in the US, the first ten amendments to the US ◊Constitution:

1. guarantees freedom of worship, of speech, of the press, of assembly, and to petition the government;

2. grants the right to keep and bear arms;

3. prohibits billeting of soldiers in private homes in peacetime;

4. forbids unreasonable search and seizure;

5. guarantees none be "deprived of life, liberty or property without due process of law" or be compelled in any criminal case to be a witness against oneself;

6. grants the right to speedy trial, to call witnesses, and to have defense counsel;

7. grants the right to a trial by jury of one's peers;

8. prevents the infliction of excessive bail or fines, or "cruel and unusual punishment";

9, 10. provide a safeguard to the states and the people for all rights not specifically delegated to the central government.

Not originally part of the draft of the Constitution, the need for a Bill of Rights emerged during the period of ratification. Twelve amendments were proposed by Congress in 1789; the ten now called the Bill of Rights were ratified 1791.

***Billy the Kid** An outlaw of the Old West, Billy the Kid was only 21 when shot and killed by Sheriff Pat Garrett.*

Billy the Kid 1859–1881. Nickname of William H Bonney, US outlaw, born in Brooklyn, New York. His family moved west, to Kansas and then New Mexico, where he led a gang in the 1878 Lincoln County cattle war. He was sentenced to death for murdering a sheriff, but escaped (killing two guards) and was finally shot by Sheriff Pat Garrett while trying to avoid recapture. He allegedly had killed a man at age 12 and was reputed to have killed 21 men by age 22, when he died.

Biloxi port in Mississippi; population (1990) 46,319. Chief occupations include tourism and seafood canning. It is a major fishing port. Named after a local Indian people, Biloxi was founded 1719 by the French. The city suffered heavy damage from Hurricane Camille 1969, but rebuilding was rapid.

bimetallic strip strip made from two metals each having a different coefficient of ◊thermal expansion; it therefore bends when subjected to a change in temperature. Such strips are used widely for temperature measurement and control.

bimetallism monetary system in which two metals, traditionally gold and silver, both circulate at a ratio fixed by the state, are coined by the ◊mint on equal terms, and are legal tender to any amount. The system was in use in the 19th century.

Advocates of bimetallism have argued that the "compensatory action of the double standard" makes for a currency more stable than one based only on gold, since the changes in the value of the two metals taken together may be expected to be less than the changes in one of them. One of the many arguments against the system is that the ratio of the prices of the metals is frozen regardless of the supply and demand.

bimodal in statistics, a frequency distribution of data that has two distinct peaks.

binary fission in biology, a form of ◊asexual reproduction, whereby a single-celled organism divides into two smaller "daughter" cells. It can also occur in a few simple multicellular organisms, such as sea anemones, producing two smaller sea anemones of equal size.

binary number system or ***binary number code*** system of numbers to ◊base two, using combinations of the digits 1 and 0. Binary numbers play a key role in digital computers, in which they form the basis of the internal coding of information, the values of ◊bits (short for "binary digits") being represented as on/off (1 and 0) states of switches and high/low voltages in circuits.

The value of any position in a binary number increases by powers of 2 (doubles) with each move from right to left (1, 2, 4, 8, 16, and so on). For example, 1011 in the binary number system means $(1 \times 8) + (0 \times 4) + (1 \times 2) + (1 \times 1)$, which adds up to 11 in the decimal system.

binary star pair of stars moving in orbit around their common center of mass. Observations show that most stars are binary, or even multiple—for example, the nearest star system to the Sun, ◊Alpha Centauri.

A spectroscopic binary is a binary in which the two stars are so close together that they cannot be seen separately, but their separate light spectra can be distinguished by a spectroscope. Another type is the ◊eclipsing binary.

binary weapon in chemical warfare, weapon consisting of two substances that in isolation are harmless but when mixed together form a poisonous nerve gas. They are loaded into the delivery system separately and combine after launch.

binding energy in physics, the amount of energy needed to break the nucleus of an atom into the neutrons and protons of which it is made.

Bingham George Caleb 1811–1879. US painter. Born near Charlottesville, Virginia, he grew up in Missouri and studied at the Pennsylvania Academy of the Fine Arts 1837. After painting in New York and Washington, he returned to Missouri. The influence of the Hudson River School is evident in such frontier landscapes as *Fur Traders Descending the Missouri* 1845.

Bingham Hiram 1875–1919. US explorer and politician, who from 1907 visited Latin America, discovering ◊Machu Picchu, Vitcos, and other Inca settlements in Peru. He later entered politics, becoming a senator.

Binghampton city in S central New York where the Chenango river meets the Susquehanna river. Its industries include electronic, computer, and camera equipment and textiles. Johnson City and Endicott, directly to the W on the Susquehanna river, form the Triple Cities with Binghampton; population (1990) 53,008.

binoculars optical instrument for viewing an object in magnification with both eyes; for example, field glasses and opera glasses. Binoculars consist of two telescopes containing lenses and prisms, which produce a stereoscopic effect as well as magnifying the image. Use of prisms has the effect of "folding" the light path, allowing for a compact design.

The first binocular telescope was constructed by the Dutch inventor Hans Lippershey (c. 1570–c. 1619), in 1608. Later development was largely due to the German Ernst Abbé (1840–1905) of Jena, who at the end of the 19th century designed prism binoculars that foreshadowed the instruments of today, in which not only magnification but also stereoscopic effect is obtained.

binoculars

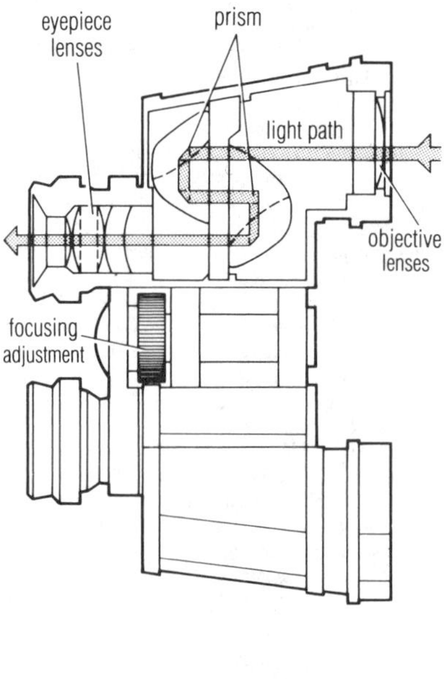
eyepiece
lenses
prism
light path
objective
lenses
focusing
adjustment

binomial in algebra, an expression consisting of two terms, such as $a + b$ or $a - b$. The binomial theorem, discovered by Isaac ◊Newton and first published in 1676, is a formula whereby any power of a binomial quantity may be found without performing the progressive multiplications.

binomial system of nomenclature in biology, the system in which all organisms are identified by a two-part Latinized name. Devised by the biologist ◊Linnaeus, it is also known as the Linnean system. The first name is capitalized and identifies the ◊genus; the second identifies the ◊species within that genus.

binturong shaggy-coated mammal *Arctitis binturong*, the largest member of the mongoose family, nearly 3 ft/1 m long excluding a long muscular tail with a prehensile tip. Mainly nocturnal and tree-dwelling, the binturong is found in the forests of SE Asia, feeding on fruit, eggs, and small animals.

Bío-Bío longest river in Chile; length 230 mi/370 km from its source in the Andes to its mouth on the Pacific. The name is an Araucanian term meaning "much water."

biochemistry science concerned with the chemistry of living organisms: the structure and reactions of proteins such as enzymes, nucleic acids, carbohydrates, and lipids.

The study of biochemistry has increased our knowledge of how animals and plants react with their environment, for example, in creating and storing energy by photosynthesis, taking in food and releasing waste products, and passing on their characteristics through their genes. It plays a part in many areas of research, including medicine and agriculture.

biodegradable capable of being broken down by living organisms, principally bacteria and fungi. Biodegradable substances, such as food and sewage, can therefore be rendered harmless by natural processes. The process of decay leads to compaction and liquefaction, and to the release of nutrients that are then recycled by the ecosystem. Nonbiodegradable substances, such as glass, heavy metals, and most types of plastic, present major problems of disposal.

bioeconomics theory put forward in 1979 by Chicago economist Gary Becker that the concepts of sociobiology apply also in economics. The competitiveness and self-interest built into human genes are said to make capitalism an effective economic system, whereas the selflessness and collectivism proclaimed as the Socialist ideal are held to be contrary to human genetic make-up and to produce an ineffective system.

bioengineering the application of engineering to biology and medicine. Common applications include the design and use of artificial limbs, joints, and organs, including hip joints and heart valves.

biofeedback modification or control of a biological system by its results or effects. For example, a change in the position or ◊trophic level of one species affects all levels above it.

Many biological systems are controlled by negative feedback. When enough of the hormone thyroxine has been released into the blood, the hormone adjusts its own level by "switching off" the gland that produces it. In ecology, as the numbers in a species rise, the food supply available to each individual is reduced. This acts to reduce the population to a sustainable level.

biogenesis biological term coined 1870 by T H Huxley to express the hypothesis that living matter always arises out of other similar forms of living matter. It superseded the opposite idea of ◊spontaneous generation or abiogenesis (that is, that living things may arise out of nonliving matter).

biogeography the study of how and why plants and animals are distributed around the world, in the past as well as in the present; more specifically, a theory describing the geographical distribution of ◊species developed by Robert MacArthur and E O ◊Wilson. The theory argues that for many species, ecological specializations mean that suitable habitats are patchy in their occurrence. Thus for a dragonfly, ponds in which to breed are separated by large tracts of land, and for edelweiss adapted to alpine peaks the deep valleys between cannot be colonized.

biography an account of a person's life. When it is written by that person, it is an ◊autobiography. Biography can be simply a factual narrative, but it was also established as a literary form in the 18th and 19th centuries. Among ancient biographers are Xenophon, Plutarch, Tacitus, Suetonius, and the authors of the Gospels of the New Testament. In the English language Lytton Strachey's *Eminent Victorians* opened the new era of frankness; 20th-century biographers include Richard Ellmann (James Joyce and Oscar Wilde), Michael Holroyd (1935–) (Lytton Strachey and George Bernard Shaw) and Elizabeth Longford (Queen Victoria and Wellington).

Medieval biography was mostly devoted to religious edification and produced chronicles of saints and martyrs; among the biographies of laymen are Einhard's *Charlemagne* and Asser's *Alfred*. In England true biography begins with the early Tudor period and such works as *Sir Thomas More* 1626, written by his son-in-law William Roper (1498–1578). By the 18th century it became a literary form in its own right through Johnson's *Lives of the Most Eminent English Poets* 1779–81 and Boswell's biography of Johnson 1791. Nineteenth-century biographers include Southey, Elizabeth Gaskell, G H Lewes, J Morley, and Thomas Carlyle. The general tendency was to provide irrelevant detail and suppress the more personal facts.

The earliest biographical dictionary in the accepted sense was that of Pierre Bayle 1696, followed during the 19th century by the development of national biographies in Europe, and the foundation of the *English Dictionary of National Biography* in 1882 and the *Dictionary of American Biography* in 1928.

In the US, notable biographers include William Manchester (John F Kennedy and Douglas MacArthur), Leon Edel (Henry James), and Joseph Lash (Franklin and Eleanor Roosevelt and Helen Keller).

Bioko island in the Bight of Bonny, W Africa, part of Equatorial Guinea; area 786 sq mi/2,017 sq km; produces coffee, cacao, and copra; population (1983) 57,190. Formerly a Spanish possession, as Fernando Po, it was known 1973–79 as Macías Nguema Bijogo.

biological clock a regular internal rhythm of activity, produced by unknown mechanisms, and not dependent on external time signals. Such clocks are known to exist in almost all animals, and also in many plants, fungi, and unicellular organisms. In higher organisms, there appears to be a series of clocks of graded importance. For example, although body temperature and activity cycles in human beings are normally "set" to 24 hours, the two cycles may vary independently, showing that two clock mechanisms are involved. Exposing humans to bright light can change the biological clock and help, for example, people suffering from ◊seasonal affective disorder.

biological control the control of pests such as insects and fungi through biological means, rather than the use of chemicals. This can include breeding resistant crop strains; inducing sterility in the pest; infecting the pest species with disease organisms; or introducing the pest's natural predator. Biological control tends to be naturally self-regulating, but as ecosystems are so complex, it is difficult to predict all the consequences of introducing a biological controlling agent.

biological oxygen demand (BOD) the amount of dissolved oxygen taken up by microorganisms in a sample of water. Since these microorganisms live by decomposing organic matter, and the amount of oxygen used is proportional to their number and metabolic rate, BOD can be used as a measure of the extent to which the water is polluted with organic compounds.

biological warfare use of living organisms, or of infectious material derived from them, to bring about death or disease in humans, animals, or plants. It was condemned by the Geneva Convention 1925, to which the United Nations has urged all states to adhere. Nevertheless research in this area continues; the Biological Weapons Convention permits research for defense purposes but does not define how this differs from offensive weapons development. In 1990 the US Department of Defense allocated $60 million to research, develop and test defense systems. Advances in genetic engineering make the development of new varieties of potentially offensive biological weapons more likely. At least ten countries have this capability. See also ◊chemical warfare.

biology the science of life. Strictly speaking, biology includes all the life sciences—for example, anatomy and physiology, cytology, zoology and botany, ecology, genetics, biochemistry and biophysics, animal behavior, embryology, and plant breeding. During the 1990s an important focus of biological research will be the international Human Genome Project, which will attempt to map the entire genetic code contained in the 23 pairs of human chromosomes.

bioluminescence the production of light by living organisms. It is a feature of many fishes, crustaceans, and other marine animals, especially deep-sea organisms. On land, bioluminescence is seen in some nocturnal insects such as glowworms and fireflies, and in certain bacteria and fungi. Light is usually produced by the oxidation of luciferin, a reaction catalyzed by the ◊enzyme luciferase. This reaction is unique, being the only known biological oxidation that does not produce heat. Animal luminescence is involved in communication, camouflage, or the luring of prey, but its function in other organisms is unclear.

biomass the total mass of living organisms present in a given area. It may be specified for a particular species (such as earthworm biomass) or for a general category (such as herbivore biomass). Estimates also exist for the entire global plant biomass. Measurements of biomass can be used to study interactions between organisms, the stability of those interactions, and variations in population numbers.

biome a broad natural assemblage of plants and animals shaped by common patterns of vegetation and climate. Examples include the tundra biome and the desert biome.

biometry literally, the measurement of living things, but generally used to mean the application of mathematics to biology. The term is now largely obsolete, since mathematical or statistical work is an integral part of most biological disciplines.

bionics (from "biological electronics") design and development of electronic or mechanical artificial systems that imitate those of living things. The bionic arm, for example, is an artificial limb that uses electronics to amplify minute electrical signals generated in body muscles to work electric motors, which operate the joints of fingers and wrist.

The first person to receive two bionic ears was Peter Stewart, an Australian journalist, in 1989. His left ear was fitted with an array of 22 electrodes, replacing the hairs that naturally convert sounds into electrical impulses. Five years previously he had been fitted with a similar device in his right ear. See ◊prosthesis.

biophysics the application of physical laws to the properties of living organisms. Examples include using the principles of ◊mechanics to calculate the strength of bones and muscles, and ◊thermodynamics to study plant and animal energetics.

biopsy removal of a living tissue sample from the body for diagnostic examination.

biorhythms rhythmic changes, mediated by ◊hormones, in the physical state and activity patterns of certain plants and animals that have seasonal activities. Examples include winter hibernation, spring flowering or breeding, and periodic migration. The hormonal changes themselves are often a response to changes in day length (◊photoperiodism); they signal the time of year to the animal or plant. Other biorhythms are innate and continue even if external stimuli such as day length are removed. These include a 24-hour or ◊circadian rhythm, a 28-day or circalunar rhythm (corresponding to the phases of the moon), and even a year-long rhythm in some organisms.

Such innate biorhythms are linked to an internal or ◊biological clock, whose mechanism is still poorly understood. Often both types of rhythm operate; thus many birds have a circalunar rhythm that prepares them for the breeding season, and a photoperiodic response. There is also a non-scientific and unproven theory that human activity is governed by three biorhythms: the intellectual (33 days), the emotional (28 days), and the physical (23 days). Certain days in each cycle are regarded as "critical," even more so if one such day coincides with that of another cycle.

biosensor a device based on microelectronic circuits that can directly measure medically significant variables for the purpose of diagnosis or monitoring treatment. One such device measures the blood sugar level of diabetics using a single drop of blood, and shows the result on a liquid crystal display within a few minutes.

biosphere the narrow zone that harbors life on our planet. It is limited to the waters of the Earth, a fraction of its crust, and the lower regions of the atmosphere.

biosynthesis the synthesis of organic chemicals from simple inorganic ones by living cells—for example, the conversion of carbon dioxide and water to glucose by plants during ◊photosynthesis. Other biosynthetic reactions produce cell constituents including proteins and fats.

biotechnology the industrial use of living organisms to manufacture food, drugs, or other products. The brewing and baking industries have long relied on the yeast microorganism for ◊fermentation purposes, while the dairy industry employs a range of bacteria and fungi to convert milk into cheeses and yogurts. Recent advances include ◊genetic engineering, in which single-celled organisms with modified ◊DNA are used to produce insulin and other drugs. ◊Enzymes, whether extracted from cells or produced artificially, are central to most biotechnological applications.

biotic factor organic variable affecting an ecosystem, for example the changing population of elephants and its effect on the African savanna.

biotin a vitamin of the B complex, also called vitamin H. It is found in many different kinds of food; egg yolk, liver, and legumes contain large amounts.

biotite dark mica, $K(Mg,Fe)_3Al\ Si_3O_{10}(OH,F)_2$, a common silicate mineral It is colorless to silvery white with shiny surfaces, and like all micas, it splits into very thin flakes along its one perfect cleavage. Biotite is a mineral of igneous rocks such as granites, and metamorphic rocks such as schists and gneisses.

birch any tree of the genus *Betula*, including about 40 species found in cool temperate parts of the northern hemisphere. Birches grow rapidly, and their hard, beautiful wood is used for veneers and cabinet work.

Paper birch *B. papyrifera* is native to the N half of North America.

Birch John M 1918–1945. American Baptist missionary, commissioned by the US Air Force to carry

biology: chronology

c 500 BC	First studies of the structure and behavior of animals, by the Greek Alcmaeon of Creton.
c 450	Hippocrates of Cos undertook the first detailed studies of human anatomy.
c 350	Aristotle laid down the basic philosophy of the biological sciences and outlined a theory of evolution.
c 300	Theophrastus carried out the first detailed studies of plants.
c AD 175	Galen established the basic principles of anatomy and physiology.
c 1500	Leonardo da Vinci studied human anatomy to improve his drawing ability and produced detailed anatomical drawings.
1628	William Harvey described the circulation of the blood and the function of the heart as a pump.
1665	Robert Hooke used a microscope to describe the cellular structure of plants.
1672	Marcelle Malphigi undertook the first studies in embryology by describing the development of a chicken egg.
1677	Anthony van Leeuwenhoek greatly improved the microscope and used it to describe spermatozoa as well as many microorganisms.
1682	Nehemiah Grew published the first textbook in botany.
1736	Carolus (Carl) Linnaeus published his systematic classification of plants, so establishing taxonomy.
1768–79	James Cook's voyages of discovery in the Pacific revealed an undreamed-of diversity of living species, prompting the development of theories to explain their origin.
1796	Edward Jenner established the practice of vaccination against smallpox, laying the foundations for theories of antibodies and immune reactions.
1809	Jean-Baptiste Lamarck advocated a theory of evolution through inheritance of acquired characters.
1839	Theodor Schwann proposed that all living matter is made up of cells.
1857	Louis Pasteur established that microorganisms are responsible for fermentation, creating the discipline of microbiology.
1859	Charles Darwin published *On the Origin of Species*, expounding his theory of the evolution of species by natural selection.
1866	Gregor Mendel pioneered the study of inheritance with his experiments on peas, but achieved little recognition.
1883	August Weismann proposed his theory of the continuity of the germ plasm.
1900	Mendel's work was rediscovered and the science of genetics founded.
1935	Konrad Lorenz published the first of many major studies of animal behavior, which founded the discipline of ethology.
1953	James Watson and Francis Crick described the molecular structure of the genetic material, DNA.
1964	William Hamilton recognized the importance of inclusive fitness, so paving the way for the development of sociobiology.
1975	Discovery of endogenous opiates (the brain's own painkillers) opened up a new phase in the study of brain chemistry.
1976	Har Gobind Khorana and his colleagues constructed the first artificial gene to function naturally when inserted into a bacterial cell, a major step in genetic engineering.
1982	Establishment of gene databases at Heidelberg, Germany, for the European Molecular Biology Laboratory, and at Los Alamos, US, for the US National Laboratories.
1985	Isolation of the first human cancer gene, retinoblastoma, by researchers at the Massachusetts Eye and Ear Infirmary and the Whitehead Institute, Massachusetts.
1988	Human Genome Organization (HUGO) established in Washington, DC, with the aim of mapping the complete sequence of DNA.

out intelligence work behind the Chinese lines where he was killed by the communists; the US extreme right-wing John Birch Society 1958 is named after him.

bird backboned animal of the class Aves, the biggest group of land vertebrates, characterized by warm blood, feathers, wings, breathing through lungs, and egg-laying by the female.

Birds are bipedal, with the front limb modified to form a wing and retaining only three digits. The heart has four chambers, and the body is maintained at a high temperature (about 106°F/41°C). Most birds fly, but some groups (such as ostriches) are flightless, and others include flightless members. Many communicate by sounds, or by visual displays, in connection with which many species are brightly colored, usually the males. Birds have highly developed patterns of instinctive behavior. Hearing and eyesight are well developed, but the sense of smell is usually poor. Typically the eggs are brooded in a nest and, on hatching, the young receive a period of parental care. There are nearly 8,500 species of birds.

Bird Isabella 1832–1904. British traveler and writer who wrote extensively of her journeys in the US, Persia, Tibet, Kurdistan, China, Japan, and Korea.

Her published works include *The Englishwoman in America* 1856, *A Lady's Life in the Rocky Mountains* 1874, *Unbeaten Tracks in Japan* 1880, *Among the Tibetans* 1894, and *Pictures from China* 1900. Her last great journey was made in 1901 when she traveled over 1,000 mi/1,600 km in Morocco.

bird of paradise one of 40 species of crowlike birds, family Paradiseidae, native to New Guinea and neighboring islands. Females are drably colored, but the males have bright and elaborate plumage used in courtship display. Hunted almost to extinction for their plumage, they are now subject to conservation.

Birdseye Clarence 1886–1956. US inventor who pioneered food refrigeration processes. While working as a fur trader in Labrador 1912–16 he was struck by the ease with which food could be preserved in an Arctic climate. Back in the USA he found that the same effect could be obtained by rapidly freezing prepared food between two refrigerated metal plates. To market his products he founded the General Sea Foods Co. 1924, which he sold to General Foods 1929.

Birkenhead seaport in Merseyside, England, on the Mersey estuary opposite Liverpool; population (1981) 123,884. Chief industries include shipbuilding and engineering. The rail Mersey Tunnel 1886 and road Queensway Tunnel 1934 link Birkenhead with Liverpool.

Birmingham industrial city in the West Midlands, second-largest city of the UK; population (1989) 998,200, metropolitan area 2,632,000. Industries include motor vehicles, machine tools, aerospace control systems, plastics, chemicals, and food.

It is the site of the National Exhibition Center and Sports Arena. Aston University is linked to a ◊science park; a school of music and symphony orchestra; the art gallery has a Pre-Raphaelite collection; the repertory theater was founded 1913 by Sir Barry Jackson (1897–1961).

Lawn tennis was invented here. Sutton Park, in the residential suburb of Sutton Coldfield, has been a public country recreational area since the 16th century. As mayor, Joseph ◊Chamberlain carried out reforms in the 1870s.

Birmingham commercial and industrial city (iron, steel, chemicals, building materials, computers, cotton textiles) and largest city in Alabama; population (1990) 265,968. Although the 55 ft/17 m statue of Vulcan (Roman god of the forge) still dominates the city from a nearby summit, US Steel shut down its works in what used to be the steelmaking center of the South. Settled 1813, Birmingham became notorious in the early 1960s for its enforcement of segregation, and the 1963 bombing of a church in which four black girls were killed aroused international attention. In 1979 the city, with a black majority population, elected a black mayor.

Birobijan town in Kharabovsk Territory, E USSR, near the Chinese border; population (1981) 72,000. Industries include lumber mills and clothing. It was capital of the Jewish Autonomous Region 1928–51 (sometimes also called Birobijan).

birth the act of producing live young from within the body of female animals. Both viviparous and ovoviviparous animals give birth to young. In viviparous animals, embryos obtain nourishment from the mother via a ◊placenta or other means. In ovoviviparous animals, fertilized eggs develop and hatch in the oviduct of the mother and gain little or no nourishment from maternal tissues. See also ◊pregnancy.

birth control another name for ◊family planning.

Birth of a Nation, The epic silent film about ◊Reconstruction, the period after the Civil War during which the US South was assimilated into the Union. Directed 1915 by D W ◊Griffith, it was considered by many to be the first cinematic masterpiece.

birth rate is measured as births per year per thousand of the population.

Biscay, Bay of bay of the Atlantic Ocean between N Spain and W France, known for rough seas and exceptionally high tides.

bishop (Greek "overseer") priest next in rank to an archbishop in the Roman Catholic, Eastern Orthodox, Anglican or episcopal churches. A bishop has charge of a district called a diocese.

Originally bishops were chosen by the congregation, but in the Roman Catholic church they are appointed by the pope, although in some countries, such as Spain, the political authority nominates appointees. In the Eastern Orthodox church bishops are always monks. In the Church of England the prime minister selects bishops on the advice of the archbishop of Canterbury; when a diocese is very large, assistant (suffragan) bishops are appointed. Bishops are responsible for meeting to settle matters of belief or discipline; they ordain priests and administer confirmation (as well as baptism in the Orthodox church). In the Methodist and Lutheran churches the bishop's role is mostly that of a supervisory official. In 1989 Barbara Harris of the US Episcopalian church was elected the first woman bishop in the Anglican Communion.

Bishops with more limited authority have the highest rank in certain Lutheran denominations and in the Methodist church.

Bishop Isabella Married name of the travel writer Isabella ◊Bird.

Biskra oasis town in Algeria on the edge of the Sahara; population (1968) 60,000.

Bismarck capital of North Dakota, on the Missouri river in Burleigh county, in the S part of the state. It is a shipping point for the region's agricultural and livestock products from surrounding farms and for oil products from nearby oil wells; population (1990) 49,256. Serving as the capital of

bird

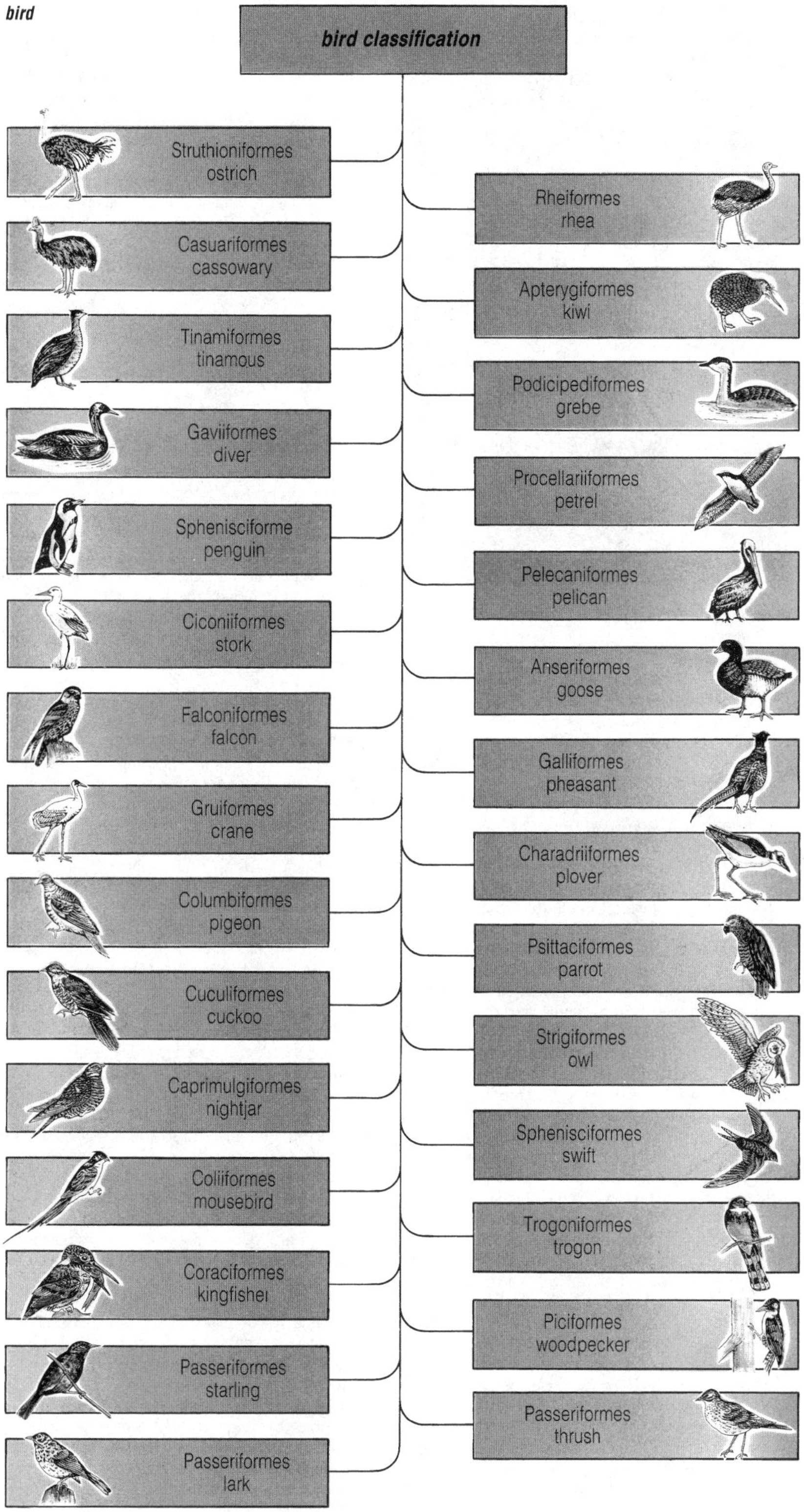
bird classification
Struthioniformes
ostrich
Casuariformes
cassowary
Tinamiformes
tinamous
Gaviiformes
diver
Sphenisciforme
penguin
Ciconiiformes
stork
Falconiformes
falcon
Gruiformes
crane
Columbiformes
pigeon
Cuculiformes
cuckoo
Caprimulgiformes
nightjar
Coliiformes
mousebird
Coraciformes
kingfishei
Passeriformes
starling
Passeriformes
lark
Rheiformes
rhea
Apterygiformes
kiwi
Podicipediformes
grebe
Procellariiformes
petrel
Pelecaniformes
pelican
Anseriformes
goose
Galliformes
pheasant
Charadriiformes
plover
Psittaciformes
parrot
Strigiformes
owl
Sphenisciformes
swift
Trogoniformes
trogon
Piciformes
woodpecker
Passeriformes
thrush

the Dakota Territory from 1883, it remained the capital when North Dakota became a state 1889. Named for German chancellor Otto von Bismarck, it was the terminus of the heavily German-funded Northern Pacific Railroad.

Bismarck Otto Eduard Leopold, Prince von 1815–1898. German politician, prime minister of Prussia 1862–90 and chancellor of the German Empire 1871–90. He pursued an aggressively expansionist policy, waging wars against Denmark 1863–64, Austria 1866, and France 1870–71, which brought about the unification of Germany.

Bismarck was ambitious to establish Prussia's leadership within Germany and eliminate the influence of Austria. He secured Austria's support for his successful war against Denmark then, in 1866, went to war against Austria and its allies (the ◊Seven Weeks' War), his victory forcing Austria out of the German Bund and unifying the N German states into the North German Confederation under his own chancellorship 1867. He then defeated France, under Napoleon III, in the Franco-Prussian War 1870–71, proclaimed the German Empire 1871, and annexed Alsace-Lorraine. He tried to secure his work by the ◊Triple Alliance 1881 with Austria and Italy but ran into difficulties at home with the Roman Catholic church and the Socialist movement and was forced to resign by Wilhelm II March 18, 1890.

***Bismarck** Prince Otto von Bismarck unified Germany and became first chancellor of the German Empire. 1871–1890.*

Bismarck Archipelago group of over 200 islands in SW Pacific Ocean, part of ◊Papua New Guinea; area 19,200 sq mi/49,660 sq km. Largest island New Britain.

bismuth hard, brittle, pinkish-white, metallic element, symbol Bi, atomic number 83, atomic weight 208.98. It is the last of the stable elements; all from atomic number 84 up are radioactive. Bismuth occurs in ores and occasionally as a free metal. It is a poor conductor of heat and electricity; it is used in alloys of low melting point and in medical compounds to soothe gastric ulcers.

The name comes from the Latin *besemutum*, from the earlier German *Wismut*.

bison large, hoofed mammal of the bovine family. There are two species, both brown. The European bison or wisent, *Bison bonasus*, of which only a few protected herds survive, is about 7 ft/2 m high and weighs a ton. The North American bison (often known as "buffalo") *Bison bison* is slightly smaller, with a heavier mane and more sloping hindquarters. Formerly roaming the prairies in vast numbers, it was almost exterminated (by white hunters for their hides) in the 19th century, but it survives in protected areas.

Crossed with domestic cattle, the latter has produced a hardy hybrid, the "beefalo," producing a lean carcass on an economical grass diet.

Bismarck Archipelago

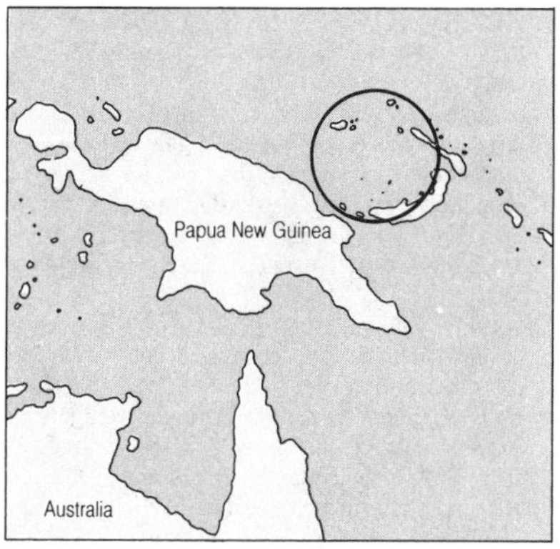
Papua New Guinea
Australia

Bissau capital and chief port of Guinea-Bissau, on an island at the mouth of the Geba river; population (1988) 125,000. Originally a fortified slave-trading center, Bissau became a free port 1869.

bit in computing, the smallest unit of information; a binary digit or place in a binary number. A ◊byte contains 8 bits.

bit in building and construction, the cutting, drilling, or boring part of any tool, as in a carpenter's brace and bit, drill press, or electric drill. It also refers to the blade of a plane.

Bithynia district of NW Asia which became a Roman province 74 BC.

Bitolj or ***Bitola*** town in Yugoslavia, 20 mi/32 km N of the Greek border; population (1981) 137,800.
history Held by the Turks (under whom it was known as Monastir) from 1382, it was taken by the Serbs in 1912 during the First ◊Balkan War. Retaken by Bulgaria in 1915, it was again taken by the Allies Nov 1916.

bittern any of several small herons, in particular the common bittern *Botaurus stellaris* of Europe and Asia. It is shy, stoutly built, has a streaked camouflage pattern and a loud, booming call. An inhabitant of marshy country, it is now quite rare in Britain.

bitumen an impure mixture of hydrocarbons, including such deposits as petroleum, asphalt, and natural gas, although sometimes the term is restricted to a soft kind of pitch resembling asphalt.

Solid bitumen may have arisen as a residue from the evaporation of petroleum. If evaporation took place from a pool or lake of petroleum, the residue might form a pitch or asphalt lake, such as Pitch Lake in Trinidad. Bitumen was used in ancient times as a mortar, and by the Egyptians for embalming.

bivalent in biology, a name given to the pair of homologous chromosomes during reduction division (◊meiosis). In chemistry, the term is sometimes used to describe an element or group with a ◊valency of two, although the term "divalent" is more common.

bivalve marine or freshwater mollusk whose body is enclosed between two shells hinged together by a ligament on the dorsal side of the body.

The shell is closed by strong "adductor" muscles. Ventrally, a retractile "foot" can be put out to assist movement in mud or sand. Two large platelike gills are used for breathing and also, with the ◊cilia present on them, make a mechanism for collecting the small particles of food on which bivalves depend. The bivalves form one of the five classes of mollusks, the Lamellibranchiata, otherwise known as Bivalvia or Pelycypoda, containing about 8,000 species.

Bizerta or ***Bizerte*** port in Tunisia, N Africa; population (1984) 94,500. Chief industries include fishing, oil refining, and metal works.

Bizet Georges (Alexandre César Léopold) 1838–1875. French composer of operas, among them *Les Pêcheurs de perles/The Pearl Fishers* 1863, and *La jolie Fille de Perth/The Fair Maid of Perth* 1866. He also wrote the concert overture *Patrie* and incidental music to Daudet's *L'Arlésienne*. His operatic masterpiece *Carmen* was produced a few months before his death in 1875.

Bizonia name given to the unified US and British occupied zones of Germany after 1 Jan 1947. This unification was brought about largely by increasing East–West tensions and the need for integrated economic planning. Bizonia became Tri-zone in April 1948 with the inclusion of the French zone.

Björneborg Swedish name of the town of ◊Pori, Finland.

Björnson Björnstjerne 1832–1910. Norwegian novelist, playwright, poet, and journalist. His plays include *The Newly Married Couple* 1865 and *Beyond Human Power* 1883, dealing with politics and sexual morality. Among his novels is *In God's Way* 1889. Nobel Prize for Literature 1903.

black English term first used in 1625 to describe West Africans, now used to refer to Africans south of the Sahara and to people of African descent living outside Africa. In the UK and some other countries (but not in North America) the term is sometimes also used for people originally from the Indian subcontinent, for Australian Aborigines, and peoples of Melanesia.

***Bizet** French composer Georges Bizet's best-known work is the opera* Carmen *1875.*

The term "black," at one time considered offensive by many people, was first adopted by militants in the US in the mid-1960s to emphasize ethnic pride; they rejected the terms "colored" and "Negro" as euphemistic. "Black" has since become the preferred term in the US and largely in the UK. Currently, some US blacks prefer the term "African-American" or "African American."
history Black Africans were first brought to the West Indies in large numbers as slaves by the Spanish in the early 16th century and to the North American mainland in the early 17th century. They were brought to South America by both the Spanish and Portugese from the 16th century. African blacks were also taken to Europe to work as slaves and servants. Some of the indigenous coastal societies in W Africa were heavily involved in the slave trade and became wealthy on its proceeds. Sometimes, black sailors settled in European ports on the Atlantic seaboard, such as Liverpool and Bristol, England. Although blacks fought beside whites in the American Revolution, the US Constitution, ratified 1788, did not redress the slave trade, and slaves were given no ◊civil rights. Slavery was gradually abolished in the northern US states during the early 19th century, but as the South's economy had been based upon slavery, it was one of the issues concerning states' rights that led to the secession of the South, which provoked the American Civil War 1861–65. During the Civil War about 200,000 blacks fought in the Union (Northern) army, but in segregated units led by white officers.

The Emancipation Proclamation 1863 of President Abraham Lincoln officially freed the slaves (about 4 million), but it could not be enforced until the Union victory 1865 and the period after the war known as ◊Reconstruction. Freed slaves were often resented by poor whites as economic competitors, and vigilante groups in the South, such as the ◊Ku Klux Klan were formed to intimidate them. In addition, although freed slaves had full US citizenship under the 14th Amendment to the Constitution, and were thus entitled to vote, they were often disenfranchised in practice by state and local literacy tests and poll taxes.

A "separate but equal" policy was established when the US Supreme Court ruled 1896 (*Plessy* v. *Ferguson*) that segregation was legal if equal facilities were provided for blacks and whites. The ruling was overturned 1954 (*Brown* v. *Board of Education*) with the Supreme Court decision outlawing segregation in state schools. This led to a historic confrontation in Little Rock, Arkansas, 1957 when Governor Orval Faubus attempted to prevent black students from entering Central High School, and President Eisenhower sent federal troops to enforce their right to attend.

Another landmark in the blacks' struggle for civil rights was the ◊Montgomery bus boycott in Alabama 1955, which first brought Martin Luther ◊King Jr to national attention. In the early 1960s the civil-rights movement had gained impetus, largely under the leadership of King, who in 1957 had founded the ◊Southern Christian Leadership Conference (SCLC), a coalition group advocating nonviolence. Moderate groups such as the National Association for the Advancement of Colored People (NAACP) had been active since early in the century; for the first time they were joined in large numbers by whites, in particular students, as in the historic march converging on Washington, DC 1963 from all over the US. At about this time, impatient with the lack of results gained through moderation, the militant ◊Black Power movements began to emerge, such as the Black Panther Party founded 1966, and black separatist groups such as the ◊Black Muslims gained support.

Increasing pressure led to the passage of federal legislation, the Civil Rights acts of 1964 and 1968, and the Voting Rights Act of 1965, under President Johnson; they guaranteed equal rights under the law and prohibited discrimination in public facilities, schools, employment, and voting. However, in the 1980s, despite some advances, legislation, and affirmative action (positive discrimination), blacks, who comprise some 12% of the US population, continued to suffer discrimination and inequality of opportunities in practice in such areas as education, employment, and housing. Despite these obstacles, many blacks have made positive contributions in the arts, the sciences, and politics.

Black Davidson 1884–1934. Canadian anatomist. In 1927, when professor of anatomy at the Union Medical College, Peking, he unearthed the remains of ◊Peking man, an example of one of our human ancestors.

Black Hugo LaFayette 1886–1971. US jurist. Born in Harlan, Alabama, Black was admitted to the bar 1906. After serving as judge and prosecuting attorney in Birmingham, he was elected to the US Senate 1926. Despite his earlier association with the Ku Klux Klan, Black distinguished himself as a progressive populist. He was appointed to the US Supreme Court by F D Roosevelt 1937 and resigned from the Court shortly before his death.

Among his decisions concerning personal and civil rights were those rendered in *Board of Education* v *Barnette* 1943, *Korematsu* v *US* 1944, and *Gideon* v *Wainwright* 1963.

Black James 1924– . British physiologist, director of therapeutic research at Wellcome Laboratories (near London) from 1978. He was active in the development of ◊beta-blockers (which reduce the rate of heartbeat) and antiulcer drugs. Nobel Prize for Medicine 1988.

Black Joseph 1728–1799. Scottish physicist and chemist who in 1754 discovered carbon dioxide (which he called "fixed air"). By his investigations in 1761 of latent heat and specific heat, he laid the foundation for the work of his pupil, James Watt.

Born in Bordeaux, France, Black qualified as a doctor in Edinburgh. In chemistry, he prepared the way for the scientists Henry Cavendish, Joseph Priestley, and Antoine Lavoisier.

Black and Tans nickname of a special force of military police employed by the British in 1920–21 to combat the Sinn Feiners (Irish nationalists) in Ireland; the name derives from the colors of the uniforms, khaki with black hats and belts.

Black Beauty the story of a horse's life, by Anna ◊Sewell, published in 1877. The book, which describes the experiences of the horse, Black Beauty, under many different owners, revived the genre of "animal autobiography" popular in the late 18th and early 19th centuries.

blackberry prickly shrub *Rubus fruticosus*, of the rose family, closely allied to raspberries and dewberries, that is native to northern parts of Europe. It produces pink or white blossoms and edible, black, compound fruits.

The North American blackberry *R. allegheniensis* has white blossoms and grows wild in Canada and E US.

blackbird bird *Turdus merula* of the thrush family. The male is black with yellow bill and eyelids, the female dark brown with a dark beak. About 10 in/25 cm long, it lays three to five blue-green eggs with brown spots. Its song is rich and flutelike.

Found across Europe and Asia, the blackbird adapts well to human presence and gardens, and is one of the most common British bird. North American "blackbirds" belong to a different family of birds, the Icteridae.

black body in physics, a hypothetical object that completely absorbs all thermal (heat) radiation striking it. It is also a perfect emitter of thermal radiation.

Although a black body is hypothetical, a practical approximation can be made by using a small hole in the wall of a constant-temperature enclosure. The radiation emitted by a black body is of all wavelengths, but with maximum radiation at a particular wavelength that depends on the body's temperature. As the temperature increases, the wavelength of maximum intensity becomes shorter (see ◊Wien's law). The total energy emitted at all wavelengths is proportional to the fourth power of the temperature (see ◊Stefan's law). Attempts to explain these facts failed until the development of ◊quantum theory in 1900.

black box popular name for the unit containing an airplane's flight and voice recorders. These monitor the plane's behavior and the crew's conversation, thus providing valuable clues to the cause of a disaster. The box is nearly indestructible and usually painted orange for easy recovery. The name also refers to any compact electronic device that can be quickly connected or disconnected as a unit.

The maritime equivalent is the voyage recorder, installed in ships from 1989. It has 350 sensors to record the performance of engines, pumps, navigation lights, alarms, radar, and hull stress.

Black Boy autobiography of the US left-wing writer Richard Wright, published 1945, that summarizes the experience of growing up black in the US.

blackbuck antelope *Antilope cervicapra* found in central and NW India. It is related to the gazelle, from which it differs in having spirally-twisted horns. The male is black above and white beneath, whereas the female and young are fawn-colored above. It is about 2.5 ft/76 cm in height.

Blackburn industrial town (engineering) in Lancashire, England, 20 mi/32 km NW of Manchester; population (1981) 88,000. It was primarily a cotton-weaving town until World War II.

blackcock large grouse *Lyrurus tetrix* found on moors and in open woods in N Europe and Asia. The male is mainly black with a lyre-shaped tail, and grows up to 1.7 ft/54 cm in height. The female is speckled brown and only 40 cm/1.3 ft high.

Black Country central area of England, around and to the N of Birmingham. Heavily industrialized, it gained its name in the 19th century from its belching chimneys, but antipollution laws have changed its aspect.

blackcurrant a variety of ◊currant.

Black Death great epidemic of bubonic ◊plague that ravaged Europe in the 14th century, killing between one third and one half of the population. The cause of the plague was the bacterium *Pasteurella pestis*, transmitted by fleas borne by migrating Asian black rats. The name Black Death was first used in England in the early 19th century.

black earth exceedingly fertile soil, a kind of ◊loess, that covers a belt of land in NE North America, Europe, and Asia.

In Europe and Asia it extends from Bohemia through Hungary, Romania, S Russia, and Siberia, as far as Manchuria, having been deposited when the great inland ice sheets melted at the close of the last ◊ice age. In North America, it extends from the Great Lakes E through New York State, having been deposited when the last glaciers melted from the terminal moraine.

black economy See ◊underground economy.

Blackett Patrick Maynard Stuart, Baron Blackett 1897–1974. British physicist. He was awarded a Nobel Prize in 1948 for work in cosmic radiation and his perfection of the Wilson cloud chamber.

blackfly human-and plant-sucking insect, a type of ◊aphid. It is especially hungry for human blood in the NE of the US and attacks in May–July, during Blackfly Season.

Blackfoot member of a ◊Plains American Indian people consisting of some 10,000 in three subtribes: the Blackfoot proper, the Blood, and the Piegan, who live in Montana, Saskatchewan, and Alberta. They were skilled horse-riding buffalo hunters until their territories were settled by Europeans. Their name derives from their black moccasins, and their language belongs to the Algonquian family.

Black Forest (German Schwarzwald) mountainous region of coniferous forest in Baden-Württemberg, W Germany. Bounded W and S by the Rhine, which separates it from the Vosges, it has an area of 1,800 sq mi/4,660 sq km and rises to 4,905 ft/1,493 m in the Feldberg. Parts of the forest have recently been affected by ◊acid rain.

Black Friday the day, Sept 24, 1869, on which the stock manipulators, Jay Gould (1836–1892) and James Fisk (1834–1872), attempted to corner the gold market by trying to prevent the US government from selling gold. President Grant refused to agree, but they spread the rumor that the president was opposed to the sales. George S Boutweel (1818–1905) with Grant's approval ordered the sale of $4 million in gold. The gold price plunged and many speculators were ruined. The two men made about $11 million.

Black Hawk or ***Black Sparrow Hawk*** (Sauk name Makataimeshekiakiak). 1767–1838. Sauk Indian leader. He was born on the Rock River near present-day Rock Island, Illinois, and became a leading opponent of the cession of Indian lands to the US government. During the War of 1812, Black Hawk sided with the British and served under the Shawnee leader Tecumseh. After the war, he accompanied his people in their removal to Iowa. In 1832 he led a large contingent back to Illinois to resettle the Sauk homeland. Defeated by Illinois militia in the bloody "Black Hawk War," he was captured by the Illinois forces and permanently exiled to Iowa.

Black Hills mountains in the Dakotas and Wyoming. It occupies about 6,000 sq mi/15,500 sq km and rises to 7,242 ft/2,207 m at Harney Peak, South Dakota. The Black Hills include a national forest and Mt Rushmore, which has the visages of four presidents (Washington, Jefferson, Lincoln, T Roosevelt) carved on a cliff face. Gold, discovered in 1874, is still mined here.

black hole tiny object in space whose gravity is so great that nothing can escape from it, not even light. Thought to form when massive stars shrink at the ends of their lives, a black hole sucks in more matter, including other stars, from the space around it. Matter that falls into a black hole is squeezed to infinite density at the center of the hole. Black holes can be detected only because gas falling toward them becomes so hot that it emits X-rays.

Satellites above the Earth's atmosphere have detected X-rays from a number of objects in our Galaxy that might be black holes. Massive black holes containing the compressed mass of millions of stars are thought to lie at the centers of ◊quasars. Microscopic black holes may have been formed in the chaotic conditions of the ◊Big Bang. The English physicist Stephen ◊Hawking has shown that such tiny black holes could "evaporate" and explode in a flash of energy.

Black Hole of Calcutta incident in Anglo-Indian history: according to tradition, the nawab (ruler) of Bengal confined 146 British prisoners on the night of June 20, 1756 in one small room, of whom only 23 allegedly survived. Later research reduced the death count to 43, assigning negligence rather than intention.

blackmail criminal offense of extorting money with menacing of violence or threats of detrimental action, such as exposure of some misconduct on the part of the victim.

black market illegal trade in rationed or otherwise scarce goods (for example, food, gasoline and clothing, during World War II and after).

Black Monday a worldwide stockmarket crash that began Oct 19, 1987, prompted by the announcement of worse-than-expected US trade figures and the response by US Secretary of the Treasury James Baker, who indicated that the sliding dollar needed to decline further. This caused a world panic as fears of the likely impact of a US recession were voiced by the major industrialized countries. Between Oct 19 and 23, the New York Stock Exchange fell by 33%, the London Stock Exchange Financial Times 100 Index by 25%, the European index by 17%, and Tokyo by 12%. The total paper loss on the London Stock Exchange and other City of London institutions was ££94 billion. The expected world recession did not occur; by the end of 1988 it was clear that the main effect had been a steadying in stock market activity and only a slight slowdown in world economic growth.

Blackmore R(ichard) D(oddridge) 1825–1900. English novelist, author of *Lorna Doone* 1869, a romance set on Exmoor, SW England, in the late 17th century.

Black Mountain poets group of experimental US poets of the 1950s who were linked with Black Mountain College, a liberal arts college in North Carolina. They rejected the formalistic constraints of rhyme and meter. Leading members included Charles Olson (1910–70) and Robert Creeley (1926–).

Black Muslim member of a religious group founded 1929 in the US and led, from 1934, by Elijah Mohammed (then Elijah Poole) (1897–1975) after he had a vision of ◊Allah. Its growth from 1946 as a black separatist organization was due to Malcolm X (1926–65), son of a Baptist minister who, in 1964, broke away and founded his own Organization for African-American Unity, preaching "active self-defense."

black nationalism a movement toward black separatism in the US during the 1960s see ◊Black Power.

Black National State area in the Republic of South Africa set aside for development toward self-government by black Africans in accordance with ◊apartheid. Before 1980 these areas were known as black homelands or bantustans. They make up less than 14% of the country, tend to be in arid areas (although some have mineral wealth), and may be in scattered blocks. Those that have so far achieved nominal independence are Transkei 1976, Bophuthatswana 1977, Venda 1979, and Ciskei 1981. They are not recognized outside South Africa because of their racial basis. Eleven million blacks live permanently in the country's white-designated areas.

blackout temporary loss of consciousness, or of electrical power; in wartime, the policy of keeping

Black Sea

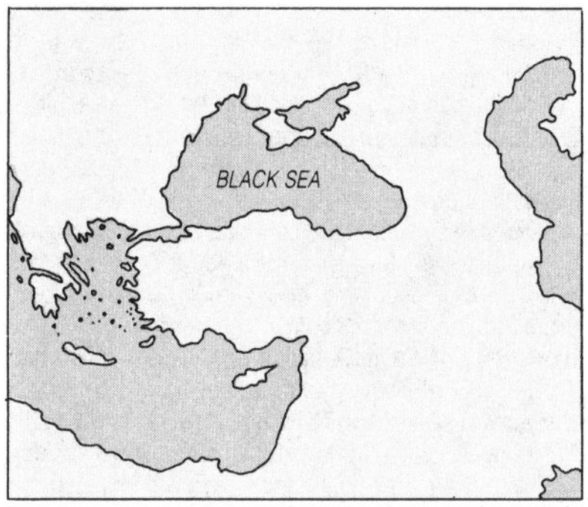
BLACK SEA

cities in darkness to conceal them from enemy aircraft at night.

Blackpool seaside resort in Lancashire, England, 28 mi/45 km N of Liverpool; population (1981) 148,000. The largest vacation resort in N England, the amusement facilities include 7 mi/11 km of promenades, known for their "illuminations" of colored lights, fun fairs, and a tower 500 ft/152 m high. Political party conferences are often held here.

Black Power movement toward black separatism in the US during the 1960s, embodied in the Black Panther Party founded 1966 by Huey Newton and Bobby Seale. Its declared aim was the establishment of a separate black state in the US established by a black plebiscite under the aegis of the United Nations. Following a National Black Political Convention in 1972, a National Black Assembly was established to exercise pressure on the Democratic and Republican parties.

The Black Power concept arose when existing ◊civil rights organizations such as the National Association for Advancement of Colored People and the Southern Christian Leadership Conference were perceived to be ineffective in producing major change in the status of black people. Stokely Carmichael then advocated the exploitation of political and economic power and abandonment of nonviolence, with a move toward the type of separatism first developed by the ◊Black Muslims. Leaders such as Martin Luther King rejected this approach, but the Black Panther Party (so named because the panther, though not generally aggressive, will fight to the death under attack) adopted it fully and, for a time, achieved nationwide influence.

Black Prince nickname of ◊Edward, Prince of Wales, eldest son of Edward III of England.

Black Sea (Russian *Chernoye More*) inland sea in SE Europe, linked with the seas of Azov and Marmara, and via the Dardanelles with the Mediterranean. Uranium deposits beneath it are among the world's largest.

Black September guerrilla splinter group of the ◊Palestine Liberation Organization formed in 1970. Operating from bases in Syria and Lebanon, it was responsible for the kidnappings at the Munich Olympics 1972 that led to the deaths of 11 Israelis, and for more recent hijack and bomb attempts. The group is named after the month in which Palestinian guerrillas were expelled from Jordan by King Hussein.

Blackshirts term widely used to describe fascist paramilitary organizations. Originating with Mussolini's fascist Squadristi in the 1920s, it was also applied to the Nazi SS (*Schutzstaffel*) and to the followers of Oswald Mosley's British Union of Fascists.

blacksnake several species of snake. The blacksnake *Pseudechis porphyriacus* is a venomous snake of the cobra family found in damp forests and swamps in E Australia. The blacksnake *Coluber constrictor* from the E USA, is a relative of the grass snake, growing up to 4 ft/1.2 m long, and without venom.

Black Stone in Islam, sacred stone built into the east corner of the ◊Kaaba which is a focal point of the *hajj*, or pilgrimage, to Mecca. There are a number of stories concerning its origin, one of which states that it was sent to Earth at the time of the first man, Adam; Mohammed declared that it was given to Abraham by Gabriel. It has been suggested that it is of meteoric origin.

Blackstone William 1723–1780. English jurist, who published his *Commentaries on the Laws of England* 1765–70. This series of lectures has been very influential in legal education, since they present the first comprehensive account of ◊English law, hence Blackstone is synonymous with the law.

Black Stump, the in Australia, an imaginary boundary between civilization and the outback, as in the phrase *this side of the black stump*.

blackthorn densely branched spiny European bush *Prunus spinosa*, family Rosaceae. It produces white blossom on black and leafless branches in early spring. Its sour, plumlike, blue-black fruit, the sloe, is used to flavor gin.

Black Thursday day of the Wall Street stock market crash Oct 29, 1929, which precipitated the ◊Depression in the US and throughout the world.

Blackwell Elizabeth 1821–1910. US physician, born in England, the first woman to qualify in medicine in the US (1849) and the first woman to be recognized as a qualified physician in the UK (1869).

Blackwell was taken to the US as a child. She studied at Geneva Medical School of western New York and then opened a private clinic in New York City. After her return to Britain 1869, she became professor of gynecology at the London School of Medicine for Women 1875–1907. Her example inspired many other aspiring female doctors.

black widow North American spider *Latrodectus mactans*. The male is small and harmless, but the female is 0.5 in/1.3 cm long with a red patch below the abdomen and a powerful venomous bite. The bite causes pain and fever in human victims, but they usually recover.

bladder hollow elastic-walled organ in the ◊urinary systems of some fishes, most amphibians, some reptiles, and all mammals. Urine enters the bladder through two ureters, one leading from each kidney, and leaves it through the urethra.

bladderwort any of a large genus *Utricularia* of carnivorous aquatic plants of the family Lentibulariaceae. They have leaves with bladders that entrap small aquatic animals.

Blagonravov Anatoly Arkadievich 1894–1975. Russian engineer, a specialist in rocketry and instrumentation. He directed the Earth satellite program leading to the launching of *Sputnik 1* and *2*.

Blaine James Gillespie 1830–1893. US politician and diplomat. Born in West Brownsville, Pennsylvania, Blaine moved to Maine 1854. After serving in the state legislature 1858–62, he was elected to the US House of Representatives and became Speaker of the House 1868. He unsuccessfully sought the Republican presidential nomination 1876 and 1880 and served briefly as James Garfield's secretary of state. Gaining the Republican presidential nomination 1884, he was defeated by Democrat Grover Cleveland. During the Benjamin Harrison administration 1889–93, Blaine again served as secretary of state.

Blake William 1757–1827. English painter, engraver, poet, and mystic, a leading figure in the Romantic period. His visionary, symbolic poems include *Songs of Innocence* 1789 and *Songs of Experience* 1794. He engraved the text and illustrations for his works and hand-colored them, mostly in watercolor. He also illustrated works by John Milton and William Shakespeare.

Blake was born in Soho, London, and apprenticed to an engraver 1771–78. He illustrated the Bible, works by Dante and Shakespeare, and his own poems. His figures are heavily muscled, with elongated proportions. In his later years he attracted a group of followers, including Samuel Palmer, who called themselves the Ancients.

***Blake** English poet and artist William Blake was a mystic and visionary. He also illustrated works, as in this engraving, "Satan arouses the rebel angels after the fall" from Book One of Milton's* Paradise Lost.

Henry Fuseli was another admirer. Blake's poem *Jerusalem* 1820 was set to music by Charles Parry (1848–1918).

Blakey Art. Muslim name Abdullah Ibn Buhaina 1919–1990. US jazz drummer, known for his dynamic style in 1940s ◊swing bands. He formed and led the Jazz Messengers from 1955, and widely expanded percussion possibilities, including the assimilation of African rhythms.

Blamey Thomas Albert 1884–1951. The first Australian field marshal. Born in New South Wales, he served at Gallipoli, Turkey, and on the Western Front in World War I. In World War II he was Commander in Chief of the Allied Land Forces in the SW Pacific 1942–45.

Blanc Louis 1811–1882. French Socialist and journalist. In 1839 he founded the *Revue du progrès*, in which he published his *Organisation du travail*, advocating the establishment of cooperative workshops and other Socialist schemes. He was a member of the provisional government of 1848 (see ◊revolutions of 1848) and from its fall lived in the UK until 1871.

Blanchard Jean Pierre 1753–1809. French balloonist who made the first hot air balloon flight across the English Channel with John Jeffries in 1785. He made the first balloon flight in the US in 1793.

Blanche of Castile 1188–1252. Queen of France, wife of ◊Louis VIII of France, and regent for her son Louis IX (St Louis of France) from the death of her husband in 1226 until Louis IX's majority in 1234, and again from 1247 while he was on a Crusade.

She quelled a series of revolts by the barons and in 1229 negotiated the Treaty of Paris, by which Toulouse came under control of the monarchy.

blank verse in literature, the unrhymed iambic pentameter or ten-syllable line of five stresses. First used by the Italian Gian Giorgio Trissino in his tragedy *Sofonisba* 1514–15, it was introduced to England about 1540 by the Earl of Surrey, and developed by Christopher Marlowe. More recent exponents of blank verse in English include Thomas Hardy, T S Eliot, and Robert Frost.

After its introduction from Italy, blank verse was used with increasing freedom by Shakespeare, John Fletcher, John Webster, and Thomas Middleton. It was remodeled by Milton, who was imitated in the 18th century by James Thomson, Edward Young, and William Cowper; and revived in the early 19th century by Wordsworth, Shelley, and Keats, and later by Tennyson, Robert Browning, and Algernon Charles Swinburne.

Blanqui Louis Auguste 1805–1881. French revolutionary politician. He formulated the theory of the "dictatorship of the proletariat," used by Karl Marx, and spent a total of 33 years in prison for insurrection. Although in prison, he was elected president of the Commune of Paris 1871. His followers, the Blanquists, joined with the Marxists in 1881.

Blantyre-Limbe chief industrial and commercial center of Malawi, in the Shire highlands; population (1985) 355,000. It produces tea, coffee, rubber, tobacco, and textiles.

It was formed by the union of the towns of Blantire (named after the explorer Livingstone's birthplace) and Limbe in 1959.

Blarney small town in County Cork, Republic of Ireland, possessing, inset in the wall of the 15th-century castle, the Blarney Stone, reputed to give persuasive speech to those kissing it.

Blasis Carlo 1797–1878. Italian ballet teacher of French extraction. He was successful as a dancer in Paris and in Milan, where he established a dancing school in 1837. His celebrated treatise on the art of dancing, *Traité élémentaire, théoretique et pratique de l'art de la danse* 1820, forms the basis of Classical dance training.

blasphemy (Greek "evil-speaking") written or spoken insult directed against religious belief or sacred things with deliberate intent to outrage believers.

There are numerous laws in the US against blasphemy, but they are rarely, if ever, enforced.

blast furnace smelting furnace in which temperature is raised by the injection of an air blast. It is employed in the extraction of metals from their ores, chiefly pig iron from iron ore.

The principle has been known for thousands of years, but the present blast furnace is a heavy engineering development combining a number of special techniques.

blastocyst in mammals, a stage in the development of the ◊embryo that is roughly equivalent to the ◊blastula of other animal groups.

blastomere in biology, a cell formed in the first stages of embryonic development (the morula) before the development of a ◊blastula or blastocyst.

blastula early stage in the development of a fertilized egg, when the egg changes from a solid mass of cells (the morula) to a hollow ball of cells (the blastula), containing a fluid-filled cavity (the blastocoel). See also ◊embryology.

Blaue Reiter, der (German "the Blue Rider") a group of German Expressionist painters based in Munich, some of whom had left *die* ◊*Brücke*. They were interested in the value of colors, in folk art, and in the necessity of painting "the inner, spiritual side of nature," but styles were highly varied. Wassily Kandinsky and Franz Marc published a book of their views in 1912, and there were two exhibitions (1911, 1912).

Blavatsky Helena Petrovna (born Hahn) 1831–1891. Russian spiritualist and mystic, cofounder of the Theosophical Society (see ◊Theosophy) 1875, which has its headquarters near Madras, India. In Tibet she underwent spiritual training and later became a Buddhist. Her books include *Isis Unveiled* 1877 and *The Secret Doctrine* 1888. She was declared a fraud by the London Society for Psychical Research 1885.

bleaching decolorization of colored materials. The two main types of bleaching agent are the oxidizing bleaches that add oxygen and remove hydrogen, and include the ultraviolet rays in sunshine, hydrogen peroxide, and chlorine in household bleaches, and the reducing bleaches, which add hydrogen or remove oxygen, for example sulfur dioxide.

Bleaching processes have been known from antiquity, mainly those acting through sunlight. Both natural and synthetic pigments usually possess highly complex molecules, the color property often being due only to a part of the molecule. Bleaches usually attack only that small part, yielding another substance similar in chemical structure but colorless.

***Blavatsky** Theosophist Madame Blavatsky convinced a large following of her intuitive insight into the nature of the divine during the 19th century.*

bleeding loss of blood from the circulation; see ◊hemorrhage.

blenny any fish of the family Blenniidae, mostly small fishes found near rocky shores, with elongated slimy bodies tapering from head to tail, no scales, and long pelvic fins set far forward.

Blériot Louis 1872–1936. French aviator who, in a 24-horsepower monoplane of his own construction, made the first flight across the English Channel on July 25, 1909.

blesbok African antelope *Damaliscus albifrons*, about 3 ft/1 m high, with curved horns, brownish body, and a white blaze on the face. It was seriously depleted in the wild at the end of the 19th century. A few protected herds survive in South Africa. It is farmed for meat.

***Bligh** Captain Bligh inspired the mutiny on the* Bounty.

Bligh William 1754–1817. British admiral. Bligh accompanied Captain James ◊Cook on his second voyage around the world 1772–74, and in 1787 commanded HMS *Bounty* on an expedition to the Pacific. On the return voyage the crew mutinied 1789, and Bligh was cast adrift in a boat with 18 men. He was appointed governor of New South Wales in 1805, where his discipline again provoked a mutiny 1808 (the Rum Rebellion). He returned to Britain, and was made an admiral in 1811.

Bligh went to Tahiti with the *Bounty* to collect breadfruit-tree specimens shortly before the mutiny, and gained the nickname "Breadfruit Bligh." In protest against harsh treatment, he and those of the crew who supported him were put in a small craft with no map and few provisions. They survived, after many weeks reaching Timor, near Java, having drifted 3,618 mi/5,822 km. Many of the crew members settled in the ◊Pitcairn Islands.

blight number of plant diseases caused mainly by parasitic species of ◊fungus, which produce a whitish appearance on leaf and stem surfaces—

L'AÉRO-CLUB
DE FRANCE
PARIS
Certifie
que M Louis
Blériot
a été nommé
PILOTE-AVIATEUR
le 7 Janvier 1909
LE PRÉSIDENT

***Blériot** The pilot's license of French aviator Louis Blériot. He made the first flight across the English Channel from Baraques to Dover.*

for instance potato blight *Phytophthora infestans*. General damage caused by aphids or pollution is sometimes known as blight.

blimp an airship: any self-propelled, lighter-than-air craft that can be steered. A blimp with a soft frame is also called a dirigible; a ◊zeppelin is rigid-framed.

blindness complete absence or impairment of sight. It may be caused by heredity, accident, disease, or deterioration with age.

Education of the blind was begun by Valentin Haüy, who published a book with raised lettering 1784, and founded a school. Aids to the blind include the use of the ◊Braille and ◊Moon alphabets in reading and writing, and of electronic devices now under development that convert print to recognizable mechanical speech; guide dogs; and sonic flashlights.

blind spot area where the optic nerve and blood vessels pass through the retina of the ◊eye. No visual image can be formed as there are no light-sensitive cells in this part of the retina.

Blitz, the (German "lightning") in Britain during World War II, the attempted saturation bombing of London by the German air force between Sep 1940 and May 1941.

Blitzkrieg (German "lightning war") a swift military campaign, as used by Germany at the beginning of World War II 1939–41. The abbreviated Blitz was applied to the German air raids on London 1940–41.

Blitzstein Marc 1905–1964. US composer. Born in Philadelphia, he was a child prodigy as a pianist at the age of six. He served with the US Army 8th Air Force 1942–45, for which he wrote *The Airborne* 1946, a choral symphony. His operas include *The Cradle Will Rock* 1937.

Blixen Karen, born Karen Dinesen 1885–1962. Danish writer. Her autobiography *Out of Africa* 1937 is based on her experience of running a coffee plantation in Kenya. She wrote fiction, mainly in English, under the pen name Isak Dinesen.

BL Lacertae object starlike object that forms the center of a distant galaxy, with a prodigious energy output. BL Lac objects, as they are called, seem to be intermediate between ◊quasars and ◊Seyfert galaxies. They are so named because the first to be discovered lies in the small constellation Lacerta.

bloc (French) a group, generally used to describe politically allied countries, as in "the Soviet bloc."

Bloch Ernest 1880–1959. US composer, born in Geneva, Switzerland. He went to the US in 1916 and became founder-director of the Cleveland Institute of Music 1920–25. Among his works are the lyrical drama *Macbeth* 1910, *Schelomo* for cello and orchestra 1916, five string quartets, and *Suite Hébraique*, for viola and orchestra 1953. He often used themes based on Jewish liturgical music and folk song.

Bloch Felix 1905–1983. Swiss-US physicist. He received a Nobel Prize jointly with E M Purcell in 1952 for his work on nuclear magnetic resonance (NMR) spectroscopy.

He was born in Zürich, and was professor of physics at Stanford University 1934–71.

Bloch Konrad 1912– . US chemist whose research concerned cholesterol. Making use of the ◊radioisotope carbon-14 (the radioactive form of carbon), Bloch was able to follow the complex steps by which the body chemically transforms acetic acid into cholesterol. For his ability in this field Bloch shared the 1964 Nobel Prize for Medicine with Feodor Lynen (1911–).

Block Herbert Lawrence. Real name of US cartoonist ◊Herblock.

blockade the closing off of a locale by military forces by land, sea, or air to prevent any movement to or fro, in order to compel a surrender without attack. For example, during World War I Germany attempted to blockade Britain with intensive submarine warfare, and Britain attempted to blockade Germany. In 1948 the Soviets blockaded the land routes into West Berlin but the Americans and British organized an airlift of essential supplies. The blockade was lifted in May 1949. In 1990 a United Nations Resolution stated the determination of the member countries to effect a blockade in an attempt to force Iraq (under the leadership of President Saddam Hussein) to withdraw its military forces from Kuwait.

No nation has the right to declare a blockade unless it has the power to enforce it, according to international law. The Declaration of London 1909 laid down that a blockade must not be extended beyond the coasts and ports belonging to or occupied by an enemy.

block and tackle type of ◊pulley.

Bloemfontein capital of the Orange Free State and judicial capital of the Republic of South Africa; population (1985) 204,000. Founded 1846, the city produces canned fruit, glassware, furniture, and plastics.

Blois town on the river Loire in central France; population (1983) 49,500. It has a château partly dating from the 13th century.

Blok Alexander Alexandrovich 1880–1921. Russian poet who, as a follower of the French Symbolist movement, used words for their symbolic rather than actual meaning. He backed the 1917 Revolution, as in his most famous poems *The Twelve* 1918, and *The Scythians* 1918, the latter appealing to the West to join in the revolution.

Blomberg Werner von 1878–1946. German soldier and Nazi politician, minister of defense 1933–35, minister of war, and head of the *Wehrmacht* (army) 1935–38 under Hitler's chancellorship. He was discredited by his marriage to a prostitute and dismissed in Jan 1938, enabling Hitler to exercise more direct control over the armed forces. In spite of his removal from office, Blomberg was put on trial for war crimes in 1946 at Nuremberg.

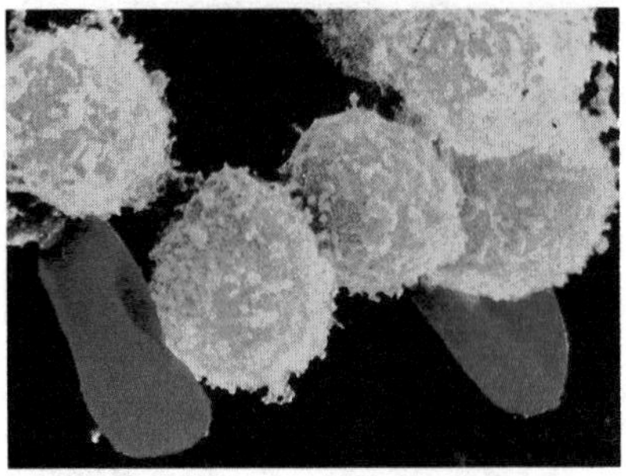

blood False-color electron microscope view of human blood showing a number of lymphocytes and two red blood cells (x 880).

blood liquid circulating in the arteries, veins, and capillaries of vertebrate animals. In humans it makes up 5% of the body weight, occupying a volume of 12 pt/5.5 l in the average adult. It consists of a colorless, transparent liquid called plasma, containing microscopic cells of three main varieties. Red cell (erythrocytes) form nearly half the volume of the blood, with 2.4 billion cells per pint (5 billion cells per liter). They carry oxygen and carbon dioxide. Their red color is caused by ◊hemoglobin. White cells (◊leukocytes) are of several kinds. Some phagocytes ingest invading bacteria and so protect the body from disease; these also help to repair injured tissues. Others (◊lymphocytes) produce antibodies, which help provide immunity. Blood platelets (thrombocytes), which are bits of cytoplasm pinched off of larger cells, assist in the clotting of blood.

Blood cells constantly wear out and die, and are replaced from the bone marrow. Dissolved in the plasma are plasma proteins (such as gamma globulins, ◊albumins, and fibrinogen), salts, proteins, sugars, fats, hormones, vitamins, and dissolved gases, which are transported around the body. The term "blood" also refers to the corresponding fluid in those invertebrates that possess a closed ◊circulatory system.

Blood and Iron (German: *Blut und Eisen*) description of the methods used by German chancellor, ◊Bismarck to unify Germany 1862–1871. The phrase came from Bismarck's speech in which he declared that "the great questions of the day will be decided, not by speeches and majority votes ... but by iron and blood.'

blood–brain barrier theoretical term for the defense mechanism that prevents many substances circulating in the bloodstream (including some germs) from invading the brain.

The blood–brain barrier is not a single entity, but a defensive complex comprising various physical features and chemical reactions to do with the permeability of cells. It ensures that "foreign" proteins, carried in the blood vessels supplying the brain, do not breach the vessel walls and enter the brain tissue. Many drugs are unable to cross the blood–brain barrier.

blood group the classification of human blood types according to antigenic activity. Red blood cells of one individual may carry molecules on their surface that act as ◊antigens in another individual whose red blood cells lack these molecules. The two main antigens are designated A and B. These give rise to four blood groups: having A only (A), having B only (B), having both (AB), and having neither (O). Each of these groups may or may not contain the ◊rhesus factor. Correct typing of blood groups is vital in transfusion, since incompatible types of donor and recipient blood will result in blood clotting, with possible death of the recipient.

These ABO blood groups were first described by Karl ◊Landsteiner in 1902. Subsequent research revealed at least 14 main types of blood groupings, 11 of which are involved with induced ◊antibody production. Blood typing is also of importance in forensic medicine, cases of disputed paternity, and in anthropological studies.

bloodhound ancient breed of dog. Black and tan in color, it has long, pendulous ears and distinctive wrinkled head and face. It grows to a height of about 26 in/65 cm at the shoulder. The breed originated as a hunting dog in Belgium in the Middle Ages, and its excellent powers of scent have been employed in tracking and criminal detection from very early times.

blood poisoning infection caused by bacteria or bacterial toxins present in the blood (septicemia); treatment is by antibiotics.

blood pressure the pressure, or tension, of the blood against the inner walls of blood vessels, especially the arteries, due to the muscular pumping activity of the heart. Abnormally high blood pressure (see ◊hypertension) may be associated with various conditions or arise with no obvious cause; abnormally low blood pressure occurs in ◊shock.

In mammals, the left ventricle of the ◊heart pumps blood into the arterial system. This pumping is assisted by waves of muscular contraction by the arteries themselves, but resisted by the elasticity of the inner and outer walls of the same arteries. Pressure is greatest when the heart ventricle contracts (systolic pressure) and least when the ventricle is filling up with blood and pressure is solely maintained by the elasticity of the arteries (diastolic pressure). Blood pressure is measured in millimeters of mercury (the height of a column on the measuring instrument, a sphygmomanometer). Normal human blood pressure is around 120/80 mm Hg; the first number represents the systolic pressure and the second the diastolic. Large deviations from this figure usually indicate ill health.

blood test laboratory evaluation of a blood sample. There are numerous blood tests, from simple typing to establish the ◊blood group to sophisticated biochemical assays of substances, such as hormones, present in the blood only in minute quantities.

The majority of tests fall into one of three categories: hematology (testing the state of the blood itself), microbiology (identifying infection), and blood chemistry (reflecting chemical events elsewhere in the body). Before operations, a common test is hemoglobin estimation to determine how well a patient might tolerate blood loss during surgery.

blood vessel specialized tube that carries blood around the body of multicellular animals. Blood vessels are highly evolved in vertebrates where the three main types, the arteries, veins, and capillaries, are all adapted for their particular role within the body.

bloom whitish powdery or waxlike coating over the surface of certain fruits that easily rubs off when handled. It often contains ◊yeasts that live on the sugars in the fruit. The term bloom is also used to describe a rapid increase in number of certain species of algae found in lakes, ponds, and oceans.

Bloom Claire 1931– . British actress. Born in London, she first made her reputation on the stage in Shakespearean roles. Her films include *Richard III* 1956 and *The Brothers Karamazov* 1958, and television appearances include *Brideshead Revisited* 1980.

Bloomer Amelia Jenks 1818–1894. US campaigner for women's rights. In 1849, when unwieldy crinolines were the fashion, she introduced a knee-length skirt combined with loose trousers gathered at the ankles, which became known as bloomers (also called "rational dress"). She published the magazine *The Lily* 1849–54, which campaigned for women's rights and dress reform, and lectured with Susan B ◊Anthony in New York.

Bloomington city in S central Indiana SW of Indianapolis; seat of Monroe county. It is an exporter of limestone from nearby quarries. It is also a center for the manufacture of electrical products and elevators. Indiana University 1820 is located here; population (1990) 42,156.

Bloomsbury Group group of writers and artists based in ◊Bloomsbury, London. The group included the artists Duncan Grant and Vanessa Bell, and the writers Lytton ◊Strachey and Leonard and Virginia ◊Woolf.

blowfly fly, genus *Calliphora*, also known as bluebottle, or of the related genus *Lucilia*, when it is greenbottle. It lays its eggs in dead flesh, on which the maggots feed.

Bloy Léon-Marie 1846–1917. French author. He achieved a considerable reputation with his literary lampoons in the 1880s.

blubber thick layer of ◊fat under the skin of marine mammals, which provides an energy store and an effective insulating layer, preventing the loss of body heat to the surrounding water. Blubber has been used (when boiled down) in engineering, food processing, cosmetics and printing, but all of these products can now be produced synthetically, thus saving the lives of animals.

Blücher Gebhard Leberecht von 1742–1819. Prussian general and field marshal, popular as "Marshal Forward." He took an active part in the patriotic movement, and in the War of German Liberation defeated the French as commander in chief at Leipzig 1813, crossed the Rhine to Paris 1814, and was made prince of Wahlstadt (Silesia).

In 1815 he was defeated by Napoleon at Ligny but came to the aid of British commander Wellington at ◊Waterloo.

Bluebeard folktale character, popularized by the writer Charles Perrault in France about 1697, and historically identified with Gilles de ◊Rais. He murdered six wives for disobeying his command not to enter a locked room, but was himself killed before he could murder the seventh.

blueberry any of various acid-soil shrubs of the genus *Vaccinium* of the heath family. The genus also includes huckleberries, bilberries, deerberries, and cranberries, many of which resemble each other and are difficult to distinguish from blueberries. All have small, elliptical short-stalked leaves, slender green or reddish twigs, and whitish belllike blossoms. Only true blueberries, however, have tiny granular speckles on their twigs. Blueberries have black or blue edible fruits, often covered with a white powder.

bluebird three species of a North American bird, genus *Sialia*, belonging to the thrush subfamily, Turdinae. The eastern bluebird *Sialia sialis* was regarded as the herald of spring, but with DDT, deforestation, and the removal of orchards it has almost become extinct. About 7 in/18 cm long, it has a reddish breast, the upper plumage being sky-blue, and a distinctive song.

bluebuck any several species of antelope, including the blue ◊duiker *Cephalophus monticola* of South Africa, about 13 in/33 cm high. The male of the Indian ◊nilgai antelope is also known as the bluebuck.

The bluebuck or blaubok, *Hippotragus leucophaeus*, was a large blue-gray South African antelope. Once abundant, it was hunted to extinction, the last being shot in 1800.

blue chip in business and finance, a stock that is considered strong and reliable in terms of the dividend yield and capital value. Blue chip companies are favored by stock market investors more interested in security than risk taking.

Bluefields one of three major port facilities on the E coast of Nicaraguà, situated on an inlet of the Caribbean Sea.

bluegrass dense, spreading grass of the genus *Poa*, which is blue-tinted and grows in clumps. Various species are known from the northern hemisphere. Kentucky bluegrass *P. pratensis*, introduced from Europe, provides pasture for horses.

blue-green algae single-celled, primitive organisms that resemble bacteria in their internal cell organization, sometimes joined together in colonies or filaments. Blue-green algae are among the oldest known living organisms; remains have been found in rocks up to 3.5 billion years old. They are widely distributed in aquatic habitats, on the damp surfaces of rocks and trees, and in the soil.

Blue-green algae and bacteria are ◊prokaryotic organisms. Some can fix nitrogen and thus are necessary to the nitrogen cycle, while others follow a symbiotic existence—for example, living in association with fungi to form lichens.

blue gum Australian tree *Eucalyptus globulus* of the myrtle family, with bluish bark, a chief source of eucalyptus oil. It is cultivated extensively in California.

Blue Mountains part of the ◊Great Divide, New South Wales, Australia, ranging 2,000–3,600 ft/600–1,100 m and blocking Sydney from the interior until the crossing 1813 by surveyor William Lawson, Gregory Blaxland, and William Wentworth.

Blue Nile (Arabic *Bahr el Azraq*) river rising in the mountains of Ethiopia. Flowing W then N for 1,250 mi/2,000 km, it eventually meets the White Nile at Khartoum. The river is dammed at Roseires where a hydroelectric scheme produces 70% of Sudan's electricity.

blueprint photographic process used for copying engineering drawings and architectural plans, so called because it produces a white copy of the original against a blue background.

The plan to be copied is made on transparent tracing paper, which is placed in contact with paper sensitized with a mixture of iron ammonium citrate and potassium hexacyanoferrate. The paper is exposed to ◊ultraviolet radiation and then washed in water. Where the light reaches the paper, it turns blue (Prussian blue). The paper underneath the lines of the drawing is unaffected, so remains white.

Blue Ridge Mountains range extending from West Virginia to Georgia, and including Mount Mitchell 6,712 ft/2,045 m; part of the ◊Appalachians.

blues African-American or black music that originated in the rural South in the late 19th century, characterized by a 12-bar construction and often melancholy lyrics. Blues guitar and vocal styles have played a vital part in the development of jazz and pop music in general.

1920s–1930s The rural or delta blues was usually performed solo with guitar or harmonica, by artists such as Robert Johnson (1911–1938) and Bukka White (1906–1977), but the earliest recorded style, classic blues, by musicians such as W C Handy (1873–1958) and Bessie Smith (1894–1937), was sung with a small band.

1940s–1950s Urban blues, using electric amplification, emerged in the northern cities, chiefly Chicago. As exemplified by Howlin' Wolf (adopted name of Chester Burnett, 1910–1976), Muddy Waters (adopted name of McKinley Morganfield, 1915–1983), and John Lee Hooker (1917–), urban blues became rhythm and blues.

1960s The jazz-influenced guitar style of B B King (1925–) inspired many musicians of the British blues boom, including Eric Clapton (1945–).

1980s The "blues *noir*" of Robert Cray (1953–) found a wide audience.

blue shift in astronomy, a manifestation of the ◊Doppler effect in which an object appears bluer when it is moving toward the observer or when the observer is moving toward it (blue light is of a higher frequency than other colors in the spectrum). The blue shift is the opposite of the ◊red shift.

Blum Léon 1872–1950. French politician. He was converted to socialism by the ◊Dreyfus affair 1899 and in 1936 became the first Socialist prime minister of France. He was again premier for a few weeks 1938. Imprisoned under the ◊ Vichy government 1942 as a danger to French security, he was released by the Allies 1945. He again became premier for a few weeks 1946.

Blunt Anthony 1907–1983. British art historian and double agent. As a Cambridge lecturer, he recruited for the Soviet secret service and, as a member of the British Secret Service 1940–45, passed information to the USSR. In 1951 he assisted the defection to the USSR of the British agents Guy ◊Burgess and Donald Maclean (1913–83). He was author of many respected works on French and Italian art. Unmasked in 1964, he was given immunity after his confession.

boa any of various nonvenomous snakes of the family Boidae, found mainly in tropical and subtropical parts of the New World. Boas feed mainly on small mammals and birds. They catch these in their teeth or kill them by constriction (crushing the creature within their coils until it suffocates). The boa constrictor *Constrictor constrictor*, can grow up to 18.5 ft/5.5 m long, but rarely reaches more than 12 ft/4 m. Other boas include the anaconda and the emerald tree boa *Boa canina*, about 6 ft/2 m long and bright green.

Some small burrowing boas live in N Africa and W Asia, while other species live on Madagascar and some Pacific islands, but the majority of boas live in South and Central America. The name boa is sometimes used loosely to include the pythons of the Old World, which also belong to the Boidae family, and which share with boas vestiges of hind limbs and constricting habits.

Boadicea alternate spelling of British queen ◊Boudicca.

boar wild member of the pig family, such as the Eurasian wild boar *Sus scrofa*, from which domestic pig breeds derive. The wild boar is sturdily built, being 4.5 ft/1.5 m long and 3 ft/1 m high, and possesses formidable tusks. Of gregarious nature and mainly woodland-dwelling, it feeds on roots, nuts, insects, and some carrion.

The dark coat of the adult boar is made up of coarse bristles with varying amounts of underfur, but the young are striped. The male domestic pig is also known as a boar, the female as a sow.

Boas Franz 1858–1942. German-born US anthropologist. Joining the faculty of Clark University 1888, Boas became one of America's first academic anthropologists; he stressed the need to study "four fields"—ethnology, linguistics, physical anthropology, and archeology—before generalizations might be made about any one culture or comparisons about any number of cultures. In 1896 he was appointed professor at Columbia University, where he trained the first generation of US anthropologists, such as Alfred Kroeber and Margaret Mead. From 1901 to 1905 he also served as curator of the American Museum of Natural History in New York City. Boas spent much of his later career battling unscientific theories of racial inequality.

He began his career in geography but switched to ethnology when he joined a German scientific expedition to the Arctic 1883. In 1886 he traveled to the Pacific Northwest to study the culture of the Kwakiutl Indian people, including their language.

boat people those Vietnamese who left their country following the takeover of South Vietnam 1975 by North Vietnam. One hundred sixty thousand Vietnamese fled to Hong Kong, many being attacked at sea by Thai pirates, and in 1989 50,000 remained there in cramped, squalid refugee camps. The UK government began forced repatriation in 1990. The term "boat people" has also been used for Haitian refugees who reach Florida by boat.

Only 10% of those who have arrived in Hong Kong since the policy of "screening" (questioning about reasons for leaving Vietnam) began in 1988 have been given refugee status; the others are classified as "economic migrants." In 1990 the total number of boat people in SE Asia was about 90,000, an increase of 30,000 from 1988.

bobcat cat *Felis rufa* living in a variety of habitats from S Canada through to S Mexico. It is similar to the lynx, but only 2.5 ft/75 cm long, with reddish fur and less well-developed ear-tufts.

bobolink North American songbird *Dolichonyx oryzivorus*. The distinctive call of the male has given rise to its name. Breeding males are mostly black, with a white rump. Breeding females are buff-colored with dark streaks. These birds are about 7 in/18 cm long, and build their nests on the ground in hayfields and weedy meadows.

Bobruisk town in Byelorussia, USSR, on the Beresina River; population (1987) 232,000. Industries include timber, machinery, tires, and chemicals.

bobsledding the sport of racing steel-bodied, steerable toboggans, crewed by two or four people, down mountain ice-chutes at speeds of up to 80 mph/130 kph. It was introduced as an Olympic event in 1924, and world championships have been held every year since 1931. Included among the major bobsledding events are the Olympic Championships (the four-crew event was introduced at the 1924 Winter Olympics and the two-crew in 1932); also the World Championships, the four-crew championship introduced in 1924 and the two-crew in 1931; in Olympic years winners automatically become world champions.

Boca Raton city in SE Florida on the Atlantic Ocean, N of Miami. Although it is mainly a resort and residential area, there is some light industry; population (1990) 61,492.

Boccaccio Giovanni 1313–1375. Italian poet, chiefly known for the collection of tales called the ◊*Decameron* 1348–53.

Son of a Florentine merchant, he lived in Naples 1328–41, where he fell in love with the unfaithful "Fiametta" who inspired his early poetry. Before returning to Florence in 1341 he had written *Filostrato* and *Teseide* (used by Chaucer in his *Troilus and Criseyde* and *Knight's Tale*). He was much influenced by ◊Petrarch, whom he met in 1350.

Boccherini (Ridolfo) Luigi 1743–1805. Italian composer and cellist. He studied in Rome, made his mark in Paris in 1768, and was court composer in Prussia and Spain. Boccherini composed some 350 instrumental works, an opera, and oratorios.

Boccioni Umberto 1882–1916. Italian painter and sculptor. One of the founders of the ◊Futurist movement, he was a pioneer of abstract art.

Bochum town in the Ruhr district, Germany; population (1988) 381,000. Industry includes metallurgy, vehicles, and chemicals.

Böcklin Arnold 1827–1901. Swiss Romantic painter. His mainly imaginary landscapes have a dreamlike atmosphere: for example, *Island of the Dead* 1880 (Metropolitan Museum of Art, New York).

He was strongly attracted to Italy and lived for years in Rome. Many of his paintings are peopled with mythical beings, such as nymphs and naiads.

Bode Johann Elert 1747–1826. German astronomer, director of the Berlin observatory. He published the first atlas of all stars visible to the naked eye, *Uranographia* 1801, and devised Bode's Law.

Bode's law is a numerical sequence that gives the approximate distances, in astronomical units (distance between Earth and Sun = one astronomical unit), of the planets from the Sun by adding 4 to each term of the series 0, 3, 6, 12, 24, ... and then dividing by 10. Bode's law predicted the existence of a planet between ◊Mars and ◊Jupiter, which led to the discovery of the asteroids. The "law" breaks down for ◊Neptune and ◊Pluto. The relationship was first noted by the German mathematician Johann Titius (1729–1796) in 1772 (it is also known as the Titius–Bode law).

Bodensee German name for Lake ◊Constance, N of the Alps.

Bodhidharma 6th century AD. Indian Buddhist. He entered China from S India about 520, and was the founder of Zen, the school of Mahāyāna Buddhism in which intuitive meditation, prompted by contemplation, leads to enlightenment.

bodhisattva in Mahāyāna Buddhism, someone who seeks ◊enlightenment in order to help other living beings. A bodhisattva is free to enter ◊nirvana but voluntarily chooses to be reborn until all other beings have attained that state.

Bodin Jean 1530–1596. French political philosopher whose six-volume *De la République* 1576 is considered the first work on political economy.

Bodoni Giambattista 1740–1813. Italian printer who managed the printing press of the Duke of Parma and produced high-quality editions of the classics. He designed several typefaces, including one bearing his name, which is in use today.

Boehme Jakob 1575–1624. German mystic. He claimed divine revelation of the unity of everything and nothing, and found in God's eternal nature a principle to reconcile good and evil. He was the author of the treatise *Aurora* 1612. He had many followers in Germany, Holland, and England.

Boeing William Edward 1881–1956. US industrialist, founder of the Boeing Airplane Company 1917. Its military aircraft include the Flying Fortress bombers used in World War II and the Chinook helicopter; its commercial craft include the ◊jetfoil, and the Boeing 707 and 747 jets.

Boeotia ancient district of central Greece, of which ◊Thebes was the chief city; the Boeotian League (formed by 10 city states in the 6th century BC) superseded ◊Sparta in the leadership of Greece in the 4th century BC.

Boer a Dutch settler or descendant of Dutch and Huguenot settlers in South Africa; see also ◊Afrikaner.

Boer War the second of the ◊South African Wars 1889–1902; war between the Dutch settlers in South Africa and the British.

Boethius Anicius Manilus Severinus AD 480–524. Roman philosopher. While imprisoned on suspicion of treason by the emperor ◊Theodoric, he wrote treatises on music and mathematics and *De Consolatione Philosophiae/The Consolation of Philosophy*, a dialogue in prose. It was translated into European languages during the Middle Ages; English translations by Alfred the Great, Geoffrey Chaucer, and Queen Elizabeth I.

bog an area of soft, wet, spongy ground consisting of decaying vegetable matter or ◊peat. Bogs occur on the uplands of cold or temperate areas where drainage is poor.

The typical bog plant is sphagnum moss; rushes, cranberry, cotton grass, and sundew also grow under these conditions. Unlike marshes, bogs usually have little open water, and the water is acidic and low in oxygen.

***Bogart** Hollywood star Humphrey Bogart was admired for his tough-guy roles and his fine acting abilities.*

Bogarde Dirk. Adopted name of Derek van den Bogaerde 1921– . English film actor who appeared in comedies and adventure films such as *Doctor in the House* 1954 and *Campbell's Kingdom* 1957, before acquiring international recognition for complex roles in films such as *The Servant* 1963 and *Accident* 1967, made with director Joseph Losey, and Luchino Visconti's *Death in Venice* 1971.

He has also written autobiographical books and novels, for example, *A Postillion Struck by Lightning* 1977, *Snakes and Ladders* 1978, *Orderly Man* 1983, and *Backcloth* 1986.

Bogart Humphrey 1899–1957. US film actor who achieved fame with his portrayal of a gangster in *The Petrified Forest* 1936. He became an international cult figure as the romantic, tough "loner" in such films as *The Maltese Falcon* 1941 and *Casablanca* 1943, a status resurrected in the 1960s and still celebrated today. He won an Academy Award for his role in *The African Queen* 1952.

He costarred in *To Have and Have Not* 1944 and *The Big Sleep* 1946 with Lauren Bacall, who became his fourth wife.

bog asphodel any swamp-growing herbaceous plant of the genus *Narthecium* of the lily family. There are three species in North America, of which the grasslike yellow asphodel (*Narthecium americanum*) of the E coastal plain is the best known.

Boğazköy village in Turkey 90 mi/145 km E of Ankara. It is on the site of Hattusas, the ancient ◊Hittite capital established about 1640 BC. Thousands of tablets discovered by excavations here over a number of years by the German Oriental Society revealed, when their cuneiform writing was deciphered by Bedrich Hrozny (1879–1952), a great deal about the customs, religion, and history of the Hittite people.

bogbean or ***buckbean*** aquatic or bog plant *Menyanthes trifoliata* of the gentian family, with a creeping rhizome and leaves and pink flower spikes held above water. It is found over much of the northern hemisphere.

Bogdanovich Peter 1939– . US film director, screenwriter, and producer, formerly a critic. *The Last Picture Show* 1971 was followed by two films that attempted to capture the style of old Hollywood, *What's Up Doc?* 1972 and *Paper Moon* 1973. Both made money but neither was a critical success. In 1990 he made *Texasville*, a sequel to *The Last Picture Show*.

Bogomils Christian heretics who originated in 10th-century Bulgaria and spread throughout the Byzantine empire. Their name derives from Bogomilus, or Theophilus, who taught in Bulgaria 927–950. Despite persecution, they were expunged by the Ottomans only after the fall of Constantinople 1453.

Bogotá capital of Colombia, South America; 8,660 ft/2,640 m above sea level on the edge of the plateau of the E Cordillera; population (1985) 4,185,000. It was founded 1538.

Bohemia area of W Czechoslovakia, a kingdom of central Europe from the 9th century. It was under Hapsburg rule 1526–1918, when it was included in Czechoslovakia. The name Bohemia derives from the Celtic Boii, its earliest known inhabitants.

It became part of the Holy Roman Empire as the result of Charlemagne's establishment of a protectorate over the Celtic, Germanic, and Slav tribes settled in this area. Christianity was introduced 9th century, the See of Prague being established 975, and feudalism was introduced by King Ottaker I of Bohemia (1197–1230). From the 12th century onward, mining attracted large numbers of German settlers, leading to a strong Germanic influence in culture and society. In 1310, John of Luxemburg (died 1346) founded a German-Czech royal dynasty that lasted until 1437. His son, Charles IV, became Holy Roman Emperor 1355, and during his reign the See of Prague was elevated to an archbishopric and a university was founded there. During the 15th century, divisions within the nobility and religious conflicts culminating in the Hussite Wars (1420–36) led to decline.

Böhm Karl 1894–1981. Austrian conductor, known for his interpretation of Beethoven, and of the Mozart and Strauss operas.

Bohr Aage 1922– . Danish physicist, the son of Niels Bohr, who produced a new model of the atomic nucleus in 1952, known as the collective model. For this work, he shared the 1975 Nobel Prize for Physics.

Bohr Niels Henrik David 1885–1962. Danish physicist. He founded the Institute of Theoretical Physics in Copenhagen, of which he became director in 1920. He won a Nobel Prize 1922. In 1952, he helped to set up ◊CERN, the European nuclear research organization, in Geneva. He fled from the Nazis in World War II and took part in work on the atomic bomb in the US. His son, Aage Bohr was also a physicist.

Boiardo Matteo Maria, Count 1434–1494. Italian poet, famed for his *Orlando innamorato/Roland in Love* 1486.

boil small abscess originating around a hair follicle or in a sweat gland, most likely to form if resistance is low or diet inadequate.

Boileau Nicolas 1636–1711. French poet and critic. After a series of contemporary satires, his *Epîtres/Epistles* 1669–77 led to his joint appointment with Racine as royal historiographer in 1677. Later works include *L'Art poétique/The Art of Poetry* 1674 and the mock-heroic *Le Lutrin/The Lectern* 1674–83.

boiler any vessel that converts water into steam. Boilers are used in conventional power stations to generate steam to feed steam ◊turbines, which drive the electricity generators. They are also used in steamships, which are propelled by steam turbines, and in steam locomotives. Every boiler has a furnace in which fuel (coal, oil, or gas) is burned to produce hot gases, and a system of tubes in which heat is transferred from the gases to the water.

The common kind of boiler used in ships and power stations is the water-tube type, in which the water circulates in tubes surrounded by the hot furnace gases. The water-tube boilers at power stations produce steam at a pressure of up to 300 atmospheres and at a temperature of up to 1,100°F/600°C to feed to the steam turbines. It is more efficient than the fire-tube type that is used in steam locomotives. In this boiler the hot furnace gases are drawn through tubes surrounded by water.

boiling point for any given liquid, the temperature at which the application of heat raises the temperature of the liquid no further, but converts it to vapor.

The boiling point of water under normal pressure is 212°F/100°C. The lower the pressure, the lower the boiling point and vice versa.

Bokassa *Marshal Jean Bokassa changed his country's name to the Central African Empire, and crowned himself emperor in 1977.*

Boise capital of Idaho, located in the W part of the state, on the Boise river in the W foothills of the Rocky mountains. It serves as a center for the farm and livestock products of the region and has meatpacking and food-processing industries. Steel and lumber products are also manufactured; population (1990) 125,738. It was founded during the Idaho gold rush of 1862 and served as territorial capital 1864–90, when Idaho became a state.

Bois-le-Duc French form of ◊'sHertogenbosch, a town in North Brabant, the Netherlands.

Bokassa Jean-Bédel 1921– . President and later self-proclaimed emperor of the Central African Republic 1966–79. Commander in chief from 1963, in Dec 1965 he led the military coup that gave him the presidency. On 4 Dec 1976 he proclaimed the Central African Empire and one year later crowned himself as emperor for life. His regime was characterized by arbitrary state violence and cruelty. Overthrown in 1979, Bokassa was in exile until 1986. Upon his return he was sentenced to death, but this was commuted to life imprisonment 1988.

Bokhara another form of ◊Bukhara, city in Asian USSR.

Bol Ferdinand 1610–1680. Dutch painter, a pupil and for many years an imitator of ◊Rembrandt. After the 1660s he developed a more independent style and prospered as a portraitist.

bolero a Spanish dance in triple time for a solo dancer or a couple, usually with castanet accompaniment. It was used as the title of a one-act ballet score by Ravel, choreographed by Nijinsky for Ida Rubinstein in 1928.

boletus genus of fleshy fungi belonging to the class Basidiomycetes, with thick stems and caps of various colors. The European *Boletus edulis* is edible, but some species are poisonous.

Boleyn Anne 1507–1536. Queen of England, the woman for whom Henry VIII broke with the pope and founded the Church of England (see ◊Reformation). Second wife of Henry, she was married to him in 1533 and gave birth to the future Queen Elizabeth I in the same year. Accused of adultery and incest with her half-brother (a charge invented by Thomas ◊Cromwell), she was beheaded.

Bolívar *A portrait of Simón Bolívar, the Liberator, by an unknown artist.*

Bolingbroke title of Henry of Bolingbroke, ◊Henry IV of England.

Bolívar Simón 1783–1830. South American revolutionary leader, known as "the Liberator," who freed much of South America from Spanish rule.

Born in Venezuela, he joined that country's revolution against Spain in 1810, and in the following year he declared Venezuela independent. His army was soon defeated by the Spanish, however, and he was forced to flee. Many battles and defeats followed, and it was not until 1819 that Bolívar won his first major victory, defeating the Spanish in Colombia and winning independence for that country. He went on to liberate Venezuela 1821 and Ecuador 1822. These three countries were united into the republic of Gran Colombia with Bolívar as its president. In 1824 Bolívar helped bring about the defeat of Spanish forces in Peru, and the area known as Upper Peru was renamed "Bolivia" in Bolívar's honor. Within the next few years, Venezuela and Ecuador seceded from the union, and in 1830 Bolívar resigned as president. He died the same year, despised by many for his dictatorial ways but since revered as South America's greatest liberator.

Bolivia landlocked country in central Andes mountains in South America, bordered N and E by Brazil, SE by Paraguay, S by Argentina, and W by Chile and Peru.

government Achieving independence in 1825 after nearly 300 years of Spanish rule, Bolivia

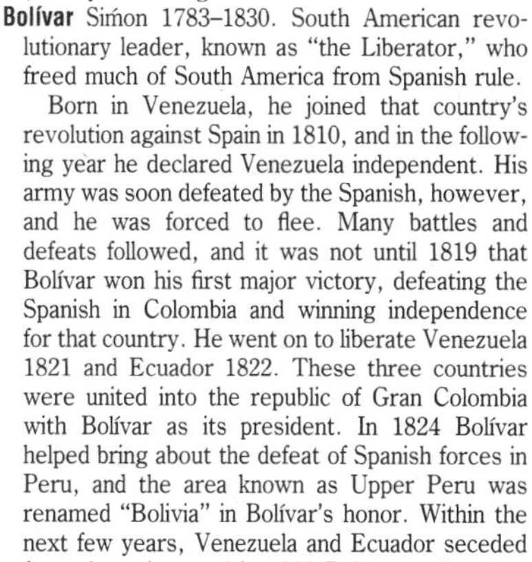

Boleyn *Portrait of Anne Boleyn by an unknown artist (1530s) National Portrait Gallery, London.*

Bolivia
Republic of
(República de Bolivia)

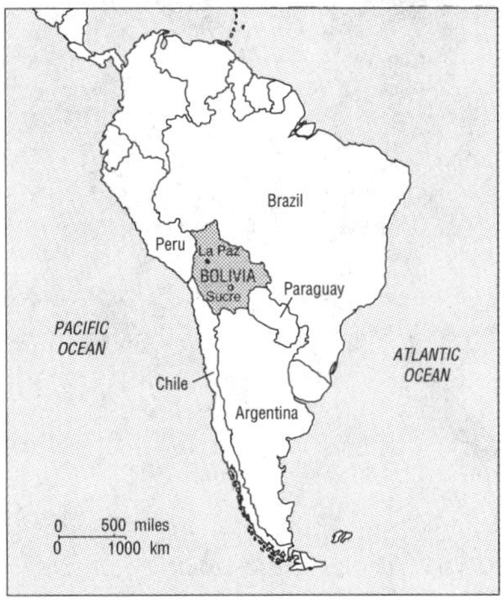
Brazil
Peru
La Paz
BOLIVIA
Sucre
Paraguay
PACIFIC OCEAN
ATLANTIC OCEAN
Chile
Argentina
0 500 miles
0 1000 km

area 424,052 sq mi/1,098,581 sq km
capital La Paz (seat of government), Sucre (legal capital and seat of judiciary)
cities Santa Cruz, Cochabamba, Oruro, Potosí
physical high plateau (altiplano) between mountain ridges (cordilleras); forest and lowlands (llano) in the E
features Andes, lakes Titicaca (the world's highest navigable lake, 12,500 ft/3,800 m) and Poopó; La Paz is world's highest capital city (11,800 ft/3,600 m)
head of state and government Jaime Paz Zamora from 1989
political system emergent democratic republic
political parties National Revolutionary Movement (MNR), center-right; Nationalist Democratic Action Party (ADN), extreme right-wing; Movement of the Revolutionary Left (MIR), left-of-center
exports tin, antimony (second-largest world producer), other nonferrous metals, oil, gas (piped to Argentina), agricultural products, coffee, sugar, cotton
currency boliviano
population (1990 est) 6,730,000; (Quechua 25%, Aymara 17%, Mestizo 30%, European 14%); growth rate 2.7% p.a.
life expectancy men 51, women 54
language Spanish, Aymara, Quechua (all official)
religion Roman Catholic 95% (state-recognized)
literacy men 84%/women 65% (1985 est)
GDP $4.2 bn (1987); $617 per head
chronology
1825 Liberated from Spanish rule by Simón Bolívar; independence achieved (formerly known as Upper Peru).
1952 Dr Víctor Paz Estenssoro elected president.
1956 Dr Hernan Siles Zuazo became president.
1960 Estenssoro returned to power.
1964 Army coup led by vice-president.
1966 Gen René Barrientos became president.
1967 Uprising, led by "Che" Guevara, put down with US help.
1969 Barrientos killed in plane crash, replaced by Vice President Siles Salinas. Army coup deposed him.
1970 Army coup put Gen Juan Torres Gonzalez in power.
1971 Torres replaced by Col Hugo Banzer Suarez.
1973 Banzer promised a return to democratic government.
1974 Attempted coup prompted Banzer to postpone elections and ban political and labor union activity.
1978 Elections declared invalid after allegations of fraud.
1980 More inconclusive elections followed by another coup, led by Gen Garcia. Allegations of corruption and drug trafficking led to cancellation of US and EC aid.
1981 Garcia forced to resign. Replaced by Gen Celso Torrelio Villa.
1982 Torrelio resigned. Replaced by military junta led by Gen Vildoso. Because of worsening economy, Vildoso asked congress to install a civilian administration. Dr Siles Zuazo chosen as president.
1983 Economic aid from USA and Europe resumed.
1984 New coalition government formed by Siles. Abduction of president by right-wing officers. The president undertook a five-day hunger strike as an example to the nation.
1985 President Siles resigned. Election result inconclusive. Dr Paz Estenssoro, at the age of 77, chosen by congress.
1989 Jaime Paz Zamora (MIR) elected president in power-sharing arrangement with Hugo Banzer Suarez; pledged to maintain fiscal and monetary discipline and preserve free-market policies.

adopted its first constitution in 1826, and since then a number of variations have been produced. The present one provides for a congress consisting of a 27-member senate and a 130-member chamber of deputies, both elected for four years by universal suffrage. The president, directly elected for a four-year term, is head of both state and government and chooses the cabinet. For administrative purposes, the country is divided into nine departments, each governed by a prefect appointed by the president. Most significant among the many political parties are the National Revolutionary Movement (MNR), and the Nationalist Democratic Action Party (ADN).

history Once part of the ◊Inca civilization, Bolivia was conquered by Spain in 1538 and remained under Spanish rule until liberated by Simón Bolívar in 1825 (after whom the country took its name). Bolivia formed a Peruvian-Bolivian Confederation 1836–39 under Bolivian President Andrés Santa Cruz, a former president of Peru. Chile declared war on the confederation, Santa Cruz was defeated, and the confederation dissolved. Bolivia was again at war with Chile 1879–84, when it lost its coastal territory and land containing valuable mineral deposits, and with Paraguay (the Chaco War) 1932–35, again losing valuable territory.

In the 1951 election, Dr Victor Paz Estenssoro, the MNR candidate exiled in Argentina since 1946, failed to win an absolute majority, and an army junta took over. A popular uprising, supported by MNR and a section of the army, demanded the return of Paz, who became president and began a program of social reform. He lost the 1956 election but returned to power in 1960. In 1964 a coup, led by Vice-President General René Barrientos, overthrew Paz and installed a military junta. Two years later Barrientos won the presidency. He was opposed by left-wing groups and in 1967 a guerrilla uprising led by Dr Ernesto "Che" ◊Guevara was only put down with US help.

In 1969 President Barrientos died in an airplane crash and was replaced by the vice-president. He was later replaced by General Alfredo Ovando, who was ousted by General Juan Torres, who in turn was ousted by Col Hugo Banzer in 1971. Banzer announced a return to constitutional government, but another attempted coup in 1974 prompted him to postpone elections, ban all labor union and political activity, and proclaim that military government would last until at least 1980. Banzer agreed to elections in 1978, but there were allegations of fraud, and, in that year, two more military coups.

In the 1979 elections Dr Siles and Dr Paz received virtually equal votes, and an interim administration was installed. An election in 1980 proved equally inconclusive and was followed by the 189th military coup in Bolivia's 154 years of independence. General Luis García became president but resigned the following year after allegations of drug trafficking. He was replaced by General Celso Torrelio, who promised to fight corruption and return the country to democracy within three years. In 1982 a mainly civilian cabinet was appointed, but rumors of an impending coup resulted in Torrelio's resignation. A military junta led by the hardline General Guido Vildoso was installed.

With the economy deteriorating, the junta asked congress to elect a president, and Dr Siles Zuazo was chosen to head a coalition cabinet. Economic aid from Europe and the US, cut off in 1980, was resumed, but the economy continued to deteriorate. The government's austerity measures proved unpopular, and in June the president was temporarily abducted by a group of right-wing army officers. In an attempt to secure national unity, President Siles embarked on a five-day hunger strike.

Siles resigned in 1985 and an election was held. No candidate won an absolute majority and Dr Victor Paz Estenssoro, aged 77, was chosen by congress. Austerity measures imposed by Estenssoro's administration reduced inflation from 24,000% in 1985 to 3% in the first half of 1989.

In the 1989 congressional elections the MNR won marginally more votes in the chamber of deputies than the ADN, but did not obtain a clear majority. After an indecisive presidential contest Jaime Paz Zamora, of the Movement of the Revolutionary Left (MIR), was elected president by the congress after he negotiated a power-sharing arrangement with former military dictator, Hugo Banzer Suarez.

Bolkiah Hassanal 1946– . Sultan of Brunei from 1967, following the abdication of his father, Omar Ali Saifuddin (1916–1986). On independence, in 1984, Bolkiah also assumed the posts of prime minister and defense minister.

As head of an oil- and gas-rich micro-state, the sultan is reputedly the world's richest individual, with an estimated total wealth of $22 billion, which includes the Dorchester and Beverly Hills hotels in London and Los Angeles, and, at a cost of $40 million, the world's largest palace. He was educated at a British military academy.

Böll Heinrich 1917–1985. West German novelist. A radical Catholic and anti-Nazi, he attacked Germany's political past and the materialism of its contemporary society. His many publications include poems, short stories, and novels which satirize German society, for example *Billard um Halbzehn/Billiards at Half-Past Nine* 1959 and *Gruppenbild mit Dame/Group Portrait with Lady* 1971. Nobel Prize for Literature 1972.

Bollandist member of a group of Belgian Jesuits who edit and publish the *Acta Sanctorum*, the standard collection of saints' lives and other scholarly publications. They are named after John Bolland (1596–1665), who published the first two volumes in 1643.

boll-weevil small American beetle *Anthonomus grandis* of the weevil group. The female lays her eggs in the unripe pods or "bolls" of the cotton plant, and on these the larvae feed, causing great destruction.

Bologna industrial city and capital of Emilia-Romagna, Italy, 50 mi/80 km N of Florence; population (1988) 427,000. It was the site of an Etruscan town, later of a Roman colony, and became

PERSHING II
CRUISE MISSILES
NEIN!

Böll West German writer Heinrich Böll speaking at a peace rally in Bonn in 1983.

a republic in the 12th century. It came under papal rule 1506 and was united with Italy 1860.

The city has a cathedral and medieval towers, and the university, which dates from the 11th century, laid the foundations of the study of anatomy and was attended by the poets Dante, Petrarch, and Tasso and the astronomer Copernicus.

bolometer sensitive ◊thermometer that measures the energy of radiation by registering the change in electrical resistance of a fine wire when it is exposed to heat or light. The US astronomer Samuel Langley devised it in 1880 for measuring radiation from stars.

Bolshevik (from Russian *bolshinstvo*, "a majority") member of the majority of the Russian Social Democratic Party who split from the ◊Mensheviks 1903. The Bolsheviks, under ◊Lenin, advocated the destruction of capitalist political and economic institutions, and the setting-up of a Socialist state with power in the hands of the workers. The Bolsheviks set the ◊Russian Revolution 1917 in motion.

They maintained power after the Civil War 1918–1921.

bolson a basin without outlet, found in desert regions. Bolsons often contain temporary lakes, called playa lakes, and become filled with alluvial deposits from inflowing intermittent streams.

Bolt Robert (Oxton) 1924– . British dramatist, known for his historical plays, such as *A Man for All Seasons* 1960 (filmed 1967), about Thomas More, and for his screenplays, including *Lawrence of Arabia* 1962 and *Dr Zhivago* 1965.

Bolton city in Greater Manchester, England, 11 mi/18 km NW of Manchester; population (1985) 261,000. Industries include chemicals and textiles.

Boltzmann Ludwig 1844–1906. Austrian physicist who studied the kinetic theory of gases, which explains the properties of gases by reference to the motion of their constituent atoms and molecules.

He derived a formula, the Boltzmann distribution, which gives the number of atoms or molecules with a given energy at a specific temperature. The constant in the formula is called the Boltzmann constant.

Boltzmann constant in physics, the constant (abbreviation k) that relates the kinetic energy (energy of motion) of a gas atom or molecule to temperature. Its value is 1.380662×10^{-23} joules per Kelvin. It is equal to the gas constant R, divided by ◊Avogadro's number.

Bolzano (German *Bozen*) town in Italy, in Trentino–Alto Adige region on the Isarco in the Alps; population (1988) 101,000. Bolzano belonged to Austria until 1919. The people are mostly German-speaking.

Boma port in Zaïre, on the estuary of the river Zaïre 55 mi/88 km from the Atlantic; population (1976) 93,965. The oldest European settlement in Zaïre, it was a center of the slave trade, and capital of the Belgian Congo until 1927.

bomb a container filled with explosive or chemical material and generally used in warfare. There are also ◊incendiary bombs and nuclear bombs and missiles (see ◊nuclear warfare). Any object designed to cause damage by explosion can be called a bomb (car bombs, letter bombs). Initially dropped from airplanes (from World War I), bombs were in World War II also launched by rocket (◊V1, V2). The 1960s saw the development of missiles that could be launched from aircraft, land sites, or submarines. In the 1970s laser guidance systems were developed to hit small targets with accuracy.

Bombay industrial port (textiles, engineering, pharmaceuticals, diamonds), commercial center, and capital of Maharashtra, W India; population (1981) 8,227,000. It is the center of the Hindi film industry.

features World Trade Centre 1975, National Centre for the Performing Arts 1969.

history Bombay was founded 13th century, came under Mogul rule, was occupied by Portugal 1530, and passed to Britain 1662 as part of Catherine of Bragança's dowry. It was headquarters of the East India Company 1685–1708. The city expanded rapidly with the development of the cotton trade and the railroad in the 1860s.

bombay duck small fish *Harpodon nehereus*, also called the bummalow, found in the Indian Ocean. It has a thin body, up to 16 in/40 cm long, and sharp, pointed teeth. It feeds on shellfish and other small fish. It is valuable as a food fish, and is eaten, salted and dried, with dishes such as curry.

bona fide (Latin "in good faith") legal phrase used to signify that a contract is undertaken without intentional misrepresentation.

Bonampak site of Classic ◊Mayan city, on the river Usumacinta near the Mexico and Guatemala border, with extensive remains of wall paintings depicting battles, torture, and sacrifices. Rediscovered 1948, the paintings shed new light on Mayan society, which to that date had been considered peaceful.

Bonaparte Corsican family of Italian origin that gave rise to the Napoleonic dynasty: see ◊Napoleon I, ◊Napoleon II, and ◊Napoleon III. Others were the brothers and sister of Napoleon I:

Joseph 1768–1844, whom Napoleon made king of Naples 1806 and Spain 1808.

Lucien 1775–1840, whose handling of the Council of Five Hundred on Nov 10, 1799 ensured Napoleon's future.

Louis 1778–1846, made king of Holland 1806–10, who was the father of Napoleon III.

Caroline 1782–1839, who married Joachim ◊Murat in 1800.

Jerome 1784–1860, made king of Westphalia in 1807.

Bonaventura, St (John of Fidanza) 1221–1274. Italian Roman Catholic theologian. He entered the Franciscan order in 1243, became professor of theology in Paris, and in 1256 general of his order. In 1273 he was created cardinal and bishop of Albano. Feast day July 15.

bond in chemistry, the result of the forces of attraction that hold together atoms of an element or elements to form a molecule. The principle types of bonding are ◊ionic, ◊covalent, ◊metallic, and ◊intermolecular (such as hydrogen bonding).

bond in commerce, a security issued against a loan by a government, local authority, company, bank, or other institution on fixed interest. Usually a long-term security, a bond may be irredeemable,

bone

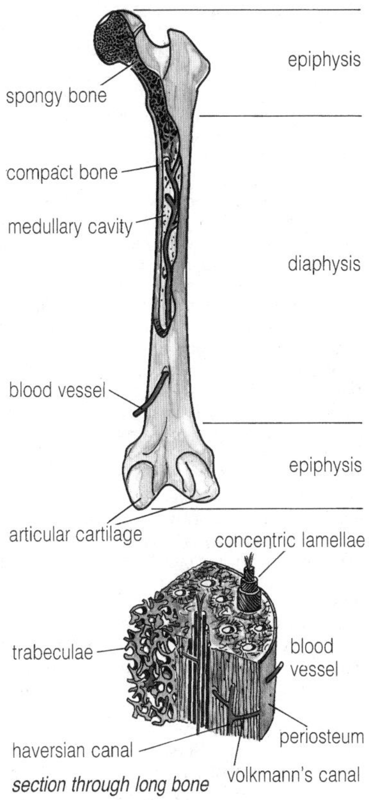
spongy bone
epiphysis
compact bone
medullary cavity
diaphysis
blood vessel
epiphysis
articular cartilage
concentric lamellae
trabeculae
blood vessel
haversian canal
periosteum
volkmann's canal

section through long bone

secured or unsecured, but may be held to maturity or traded on the bond market. Property bonds are nonfixed securities with the yield fixed to property investment. See also ◊Eurobond.

Bondi Hermann 1919– . British cosmologist, born in Austria. In 1948 he joined with Fred ◊Hoyle and Thomas Gold (1920–) in developing the steady-state theory of cosmology, which suggested that matter is continuously created in the universe.

bondservant another term for a slave or serf used in the Caribbean in the 18th and 19th centuries; a person who was offered a few acres of land in return for some years of compulsory service. The system was a means of obtaining labor from Europe.

bone the hard connective tissue comprising the ◊skeleton of most vertebrate animals. It consists of a network of collagen fibers impregnated with inorganic salts, especially calcium phosphate. Enclosed within this solid matrix are bone cells, blood vessels, and nerves. In strength, the toughest bone is comparable with reinforced concrete. There are two types of bone: those that develop by replacing ◊cartilage and those that form directly from connective tissue. The latter are usually platelike in shape, and form in the skin of the developing embryo. Humans have about 206 distinct bones in the skeleton. The interior of long bones consists of a spongy matrix filled with a soft marrow that produces blood cells.

Bône (or Bohn) former name of ◊Annaba, Algerian port.

bone china (softpaste) semiporcelain made of 5% bone ash added to 95% kaolin; first made in the West as an attempt at imitating Chinese porcelain, whose formula was kept secret by the Chinese.

bone marrow in vertebrates, soft tissue in the center of some large bones that manufactures red and white blood cells.

bongo Central African antelope *Boocercus eurycerus*, living in dense humid forests. Up to 4.5 ft/1.4 m at the shoulder, it has spiral-shaped horns which may be 2.6 ft/80 cm or more in length. The body is rich chestnut, with narrow white stripes running vertically down the sides, and a black belly.

Bonheur Rosa (Marie Rosalie) 1822–1899. French animal painter. Her realistic animal portraits include *Horse Fair* 1853 (Metropolitan Museum of Art, New York).

She exhibited at the Paris Salon every year from 1841, and received international awards. In 1894 she became the first woman Officer of the Légion d'Honneur.

Bonhoeffer Dietrich 1906–1945. German Lutheran theologian and opponent of Nazism. Involved in an anti-Hitler plot, he was executed by the Nazis in Flossenburg concentration camp. His *Letters and Papers from Prison* 1953 became the textbook of modern radical theology, advocating the idea of a "religionless" Christianity.

Boniface name of nine popes, including:

Boniface VIII Benedict Caetani c. 1228–1303. Pope from 1294. He clashed unsuccessfully with Philip IV of France over his taxation of the clergy, and also with Henry III of England.

Boniface exempted the clergy from taxation by the secular government in a bull (edict) in 1296, but was forced to give way when the clergy were excluded from certain lay privileges. His bull of 1302 *Unam sanctam*, asserting the complete temporal and spiritual power of the papacy, was equally ineffective.

Boniface, St 680–754. English Benedictine monk, known as the "Apostle of Germany"; originally named Wynfrith. After a missionary journey to Frisia in 716, he was given the task of bringing Christianity to Germany by Pope Gregory II in 718, and was appointed archbishop of Mainz in 746. He returned to Frisia in 754 and was martyred near Dockum. Feast day June 5.

Bonin and Volcano islands Japanese islands in the Pacific, N of the Marianas and 800 mi/1,300 km E of the Ryukyu islands. They were under US control 1945–68. The Bonin Islands (Japanese *Ogasawara Gunto*) number 27 (in 3 groups), the largest being Chichijima: area 40 sq mi/ 104 sq km, population (1970) 300. The Volcano Islands (Japanese *Kazan Retto*) number 3, including ◊Iwo Jima, scene of some of the fiercest fighting of World War II; total area 11 sq mi/ 28 sq km.

bonito various medium-sized tuna, predatory fish of the genus *Sarda*, in the mackerel family. The ocean bonito *Katsuwonus pelamis* grows to 3 ft/ 1 m and is common in tropical seas. The Atlantic bonito *Sarda sarda* is found in the Mediterranean and tropical Atlantic and grows to the same length but has a narrower body.

Bonn industrial city (chemicals, textiles, plastics, aluminum), and seat of government of the Federal Republic of Germany, 15 mi/18 km SSE of Cologne, on the left bank of the Rhine; population (1988) 292,000.

Once a Roman outpost, Bonn was captured by the French 1794, annexed 1801, and was allotted to Prussia 1815. Beethoven was born here. It was capital of West Germany 1949–90.

Bonnard Pierre 1867–1947. French Post-Impressionist painter. With other members of les ◊Nabis, he explored the decorative arts (posters, stained glass, furniture). He painted domestic interiors and nudes.

Bonner Yelena 1923– . Soviet human-rights campaigner. Disillusioned by the Soviet invasion of Czechoslovakia 1968, she resigned from the Communist party after marrying her second husband, Andrei ◊Sakharov, in 1971, and became active in the dissident movement.

Bonneville Salt Flats bed of a prehistoric sea in Utah, of which the Great Salt Lake is the surviving remnant. The flats, near the Nevada border, have been used to set many land speed records.

Bonney William H see ◊Billy the Kid.

Bonnie and Clyde Bonnie Parker (1911–1934) and Clyde Barrow (1900–1934). Infamous US criminals who carried out a series of small-scale robberies in Texas, Oklahoma, New Mexico, and Missouri between Aug 1932 and May 1934. They were eventually betrayed and then killed in a police ambush.

Much of their fame emanated from encounters with the police and their coverage by the press. Their story was filmed as *Bonnie and Clyde* 1967 by the US director Arthur Penn.

Bonny, Bight of name since 1975 of the former Bight of Biafra, an area of sea off the coasts of Nigeria and Cameroon.

bonsai (Japanese "bowl cultivation") the art of producing miniature trees by selective pruning. It originated in China many centuries ago and later spread to Japan. Some specimens in China are about 1,000 years old and some in the imperial Japanese collection are more than 300 years old.

Bonus Army or ***Bonus Expeditionary Force*** in US history, a march on Washington, DC by unemployed ex-servicemen during the great ◊Depression to lobby Congress for immediate cash payment of a promised war veterans's bonus.

During the spring of 1932, some 15,000 veterans camped by the Potomac River or squatted in disused government buildings. They were eventually dispersed by troops.

boobook owl *Ninox novaeseelandiae* found in Australia, so named because of its call.

booby tropical seabird of the genus *Sula*, in the same family, Sulidae, as the northern ◊gannet. There are six species, including the circumtropical brown booby *Sula leucogaster*. They inhabit coastal waters, and dive to catch fish. Their name was given to them by sailors who saw their tameness as stupidity.

One species, Abbott's booby, breeds only on Christmas Island, in the western Indian Ocean. Unlike most boobies and gannets it nests high up in trees. Large parts of its breeding ground have been destroyed by phosphate mining, but conservation measures now protect the site.

boogie-woogie a form of jazz played on the piano, using a repeated motif for the left hand. It was common in the US from around 1900 to the 1950s. Boogie-woogie players included Pinetop Smith (1904–1929), Meade "Lux" Lewis (1905–1964), and Jimmy Yancey (1898–1951).

book a portable written record. Substances used to make early books included leaves, bark, linen, silk, clay, leather, and papyrus. In about AD 100–150, the codex or paged book, as opposed to the roll or scroll, began to be adopted. Vellum (parchment of calfskin, lambskin, or kidskin) was generally used for book pages by the beginning of the 4th century, and its use lasted until the 15th. It was superseded by paper, which came to Europe from China (where it was made as early as AD 105, a mixture of bark and hemp fibers). Books only became widely available after the invention of the ◊printing press in the 15th century. Printed text is also reproduced and stored in ◊microform.

booby

Abbott's booby

bookbinding the securing of the pages of a book between protective covers by sewing and/or gluing. Cloth binding was first introduced in 1822, but since World War II synthetic bindings have been increasingly employed, and most hardcover books are bound by machine.

Bookbinding did not emerge as a distinct craft until ◊printing was introduced to Europe in the 15th century. Until that time scrolls, not books, were usual. Gold tooling, the principal ornament of leather bookbinding, was probably introduced to Europe from the East by the Venetian Aldus Manutius (1450–1515).

bookkeeping process of recording commercial transactions in a systematic and established procedure. These records provide the basis for the preparation of accounts.

booklouse any of numerous species of tiny wingless insects of the order Psocoptera, especially *Atropus pulsatoria* that lives in books and papers, feeding on starches and molds.

Most of the other species live in bark, leaves, and lichens. They thrive in dark, damp conditions.

Book of the Dead ancient Egyptian book, known as the *Book of Coming Forth by Day*, buried with the dead as a guide to reaching the kingdom of Osiris, the god of the underworld.

Books of Hours see ◊Hours, Books of.

Boole George 1814–1864. English mathematician whose work *The Mathematical Analysis of Logic* 1847 established the basis of modern mathematical logic, and whose Boolean algebra can be used in designing computers.

boom a sudden increase in importance, activity, or profits, as in the boom and bust cycle of business.

boomerang hand-thrown, flat wooden hunting missile shaped in a curved angle, developed by the Australian Aborigines. It is used to kill game and as a weapon; some are specifically made to return to the thrower if the target is missed.

boomslang rear-fanged venomous African snake *Dispholidus typus*, often green but sometimes brown or blackish. It lives in trees, and feeds on tree-dwelling lizards such as chameleons. Its venom can be fatal to humans; however, boomslangs rarely attack people.

Boone Daniel 1734–1820. American pioneer, who explored the Wilderness Road (East Virginia/Kentucky) in 1775 and paved the way for the first westward migration of settlers.

Boone was born in Pennsylvania and spent most of his youth in North Carolina. During the American Revolution, he led militias against Indians allied with the British. He was captured by a Shawnee war party and so impressed the chief that he was adopted by the tribe. He left the Indians and continued to explore westward.

Boorman John 1933– . English film director who, after working in television, subsequently directed successful films both in Hollywood (*Deliverance* 1972, *Point Blank* 1967) and in Britain (*Excalibur* 1981, *Hope and Glory* 1987).

booster the first-stage rockets of a space-launching vehicle, or additional rockets strapped to the main rocket to assist takeoff.

The US Delta rocket, for example, has a cluster of nine strap-on boosters that fire on lift-off. Europe's Ariane 3 rocket uses twin strap-on boosters, as does the US space shuttle.

Boötes constellation of the northern hemisphere represented by a herdsman driving a bear (Ursa Major) around the pole. Its brightest star is ◊Arcturus (or Alpha Boötis) about 36 light-years from Earth.

Booth Edwin Thomas 1833–1893. US actor. Born near Bel Air, Maryland, elder brother of John Wilkes ◊Booth, and member of a distinguished theatrical family, he was one of America's most acclaimed Shakespearean actors. As lead performer, theater manager, and producer, he successfully brought to the New York stage numerous Shakespearean tragedies, becoming famous for his portrayal of Hamlet.

After the public disgrace of his brother's

assassination of Lincoln, Booth suffered a series of financial reverses and spent his later years in performance tours of Europe, the British Isles, and the US.

Booth John Wilkes 1839–1865. US actor and fanatical Confederate sympathizer who assassinated President Abraham ◊Lincoln April 14, 1865; he escaped with a broken leg and was later shot in a barn in Virginia when he refused to surrender.

He had earlier conceived a plan to kidnap Lincoln and decided to kill him in vengeance when the plan failed.

Booth William 1829–1912. British founder of the Salvation Army in 1878, and its first "general."

Boothe Claire see ◊Luce, Claire Boothe.

bootlegging the illegal manufacture, distribution, or sale of a product. The term originated in the US, when the sale of alcohol to American Indians was illegal and bottles were hidden for sale in the legs of the jackboots of unscrupulous traders. The term was later used for all illegal liquor sales during the period of ◊Prohibition in the US 1920–33, and is often applied to unauthorized commercial tape recordings and the copying of computer software.

bop short for ◊bebop, a style of jazz.

Bophuthatswana Republic of; self-governing black "homeland" within South Africa

area 15,571 sq mi/40,330 sq km

capital Mmbatho or Sun City, a casino resort frequented by many white South Africans

features divided into six "blocks"

exports platinum, chromium, vanadium, asbestos, manganese

population (1985) 1,627,000

language Setswana, English

religion Christian

government executive president elected by the Assembly: Chief Lucas Mangope

recent history first "independent" Black National State from 1977, but not recognized by any country other than South Africa.

Bora-Bora one of the 14 Society Islands of French Polynesia. Situated 140 mi/225 km NW of Tahiti. Area 15 sq mi/39 sq km. Exports include mother-of-pearl, fruit and tobacco.

Borah William Edgar 1865–1940. US Republican politician. Born in Illinois, he was a senator for Idaho from 1906. An arch-isolationist, he was one of those chiefly responsible for the US's repudiation of the League of Nations following World War I.

He also resisted US participation in the World Court (see ◊International Court of Justice; and the ◊United Nations).

Borås town in SW Sweden; population (1982) 211,197. Chief industries include textiles and engineering.

borax hydrous sodium borate, $Na_2B_4O_7.10H_2O$, found as soft, whitish crystals or encrustations on the shores of hot springs and in the dry beds of salt lakes in arid regions, where it occurs with other borates, halite, and ◊gypsum. It is used in bleaches and washing powders.

A large industrial source is Borax Lake, California. Borax is also used in glazing pottery, in soldering, as a mild antiseptic, and as a metallurgical flux.

Borchert Wolfgang 1921–1947. German playwright and prose writer. Borchert was sent home wounded during World War II while serving on the Russian front, where he had been sent for making anti-Nazi comments. *Draussen vor der Tür/The Outsider* 1947 is a surreal play about the chaotic conditions that a German soldier finds when he returns to Germany after walking home from the Russian front.

Bordeaux port on the Garonne, capital of Aquitaine, SW France, a center for the wine trade, oil refining, and aeronautics and space industries; population (1982) 640,000. Bordeaux was under the English crown for three centuries until 1453. In 1870, 1914, and 1940 the French government was moved here because of German invasion.

Bordet Jules 1870–1961. Belgian bacteriologist and immunologist who researched the role of blood serum in the human immune response. He was the first to isolate, in 1906, the whooping cough bacillus.

bore a surge of tidal water up an estuary or a river, caused by the funneling of the rising tide by a narrowing river mouth. A very high tide, possibly fanned by wind, may build up when it is held back by a river current in the river mouth. The result is a broken wave, a few feet or a meter high, that rushes upstream.

Famous bores are found in the rivers Severn (England), Seine (France), Hooghly (India), and Chiang Jiang (China), where bores of over 13 ft/4 m have been reported.

Borelli Giovanni Alfonso 1608–1679. Italian scientist who explored the links between physics and medicine, and showed how mechanical principles could be applied to animal ◊physiology. This approach, known as iatrophysics, has proved basic to understanding how the mammalian body works.

Borg Bjorn 1956– . Swedish tennis player who won the men's singles title at Wimbledon five times 1976–80, a record since the abolition of the challenge system 1922. In 1990 Borg announced tentative plans to return to professional tennis.

CAREER HIGHLIGHTS

Wimbledon singles: 1976–80
French Open singles: 1974–75, 1978–81
Davis Cup 1975 (member of winning Sweden team)
Grand Prix Masters 1980–81
WCT Champion 1976
ITF World Champion 1978–80

Borges Jorge Luis 1899–1986. Argentinian poet and short-story writer. In 1961 he became director of the National Library, Buenos Aires, and was professor of English literature at the university there. He is known for his fantastic and paradoxical work *Ficciones/Fictions* 1944.

Borgia Cesare 1476–1507. Italian general, illegitimate son of Pope ◊Alexander VI. Made a cardinal at 17 by his father, he resigned to become captain-general of the papacy, campaigning successfully against the city republics of Italy. Ruthless and treacherous in war, he was an able ruler (the model for Machiavelli's *The Prince*), but his power crumbled on the death of his father. He was a patron of artists, including Leonardo da Vinci.

Borgia Lucrezia 1480–1519. Duchess of Ferrara from 1501. She was the illegitimate daughter of Pope ◊Alexander VI and sister of Cesare Borgia. She was married at 12 and again at 13 to further her father's ambitions, both marriages being annulled by him. At 18 she was married once more, but her husband was murdered in 1500 on the order of her brother, with whom (as well as with her father) she was said to have committed incest. Her final marriage was to the duke of Este, the son and heir of the duke of Ferrara. She made the court a center of culture and was a patron of authors and artists such as Ariosto and Titian.

Borglum Gutzon 1871–1941. US sculptor. He created a six-ton marble head of Lincoln in Washington, DC, and the series of giant heads of presidents Washington, Jefferson, Lincoln, and Theodore Roosevelt carved on Mount Rushmore, in South Dakota (begun 1930).

boric acid or ***boracic acid*** H_3BO_3, an acid formed by the combination of hydrogen and oxygen with nonmetallic boron. It is a weak antiseptic and is used in the manufacture of glass and enamels. It is also an efficient insecticide against cockroaches.

Boris III 1894–1943. Tsar of Bulgaria from 1918, when he succeeded his father, Ferdinand I. From 1934 he was virtual dictator until his sudden and mysterious death following a visit to Hitler. His son Simeon II was tsar until deposed in 1946.

Boris Godunov 1552–1605. See Boris ◊Godunov, tsar of Russia from 1598.

Borlaug Norman Ernest 1914– . US microbiologist and agronomist. He developed high-yielding

Borges *The Argentinian author and former university professor Jorge Luis Borges is seen here after receiving an honorary degree at the University of Oxford in 1970.*

varieties of wheat and other grain crops to be grown in Third World countries, and was the first to use the term "Green Revolution." Nobel Prize for Peace 1970.

Bormann Martin 1900–1945. German Nazi leader. He took part in the abortive Munich ◊putsch (uprising) of 1923 and rose to high positions in the Nazi (National Socialist) Party, becoming party chancellor in May 1941. He was believed to have escaped the fall of Berlin in May 1945 and was tried in his absence and sentenced to death at the ◊Nuremberg trials 1945–46, but a skeleton uncovered by a mechanical excavator in Berlin in 1972 was officially recognized as his by forensic experts in 1973.

Born Max 1882–1970. German physicist, who received a Nobel Prize in 1954 for fundamental work on the ◊quantum theory. He left Germany for the UK during the Nazi era.

Borneo third-largest island in the world, one of the Sunda Islands in the W Pacific; area

Born *German physicist Max Born seated surrounded by his colleagues at Göttingen in 1922; left to right: William Osler, Niels Bohr, James Franck, and Oscar Klein.*

290,000 sq mi/754,000 sq km. It comprises the Malaysian territories of ◊Sabah and ◊Sarawak; ◊Brunei; and, occupying by far the largest part, the Indonesian territory of ◊Kalimantan. It is mountainous and densely forested. In coastal areas the people of Borneo are mainly of Malaysian origin, with a few Chinese, and the interior is inhabited by the indigenous Dayaks. It was formerly under both Dutch and British colonial influence until Sarawak was formed in 1841.

Bornholm Danish island in the Baltic Sea, 22 mi/35 km SE of the nearest point of the Swedish coast. It constitutes a county of the same name.
area 227 sq mi/587 sq km
capital Rönne
population (1985) 47,164

Bornu kingdom of the 9th–19th centuries to the west and south of Lake Chad, W central Africa. Converted to Islam in the 11th century, it reached its greatest strength in the 15th–18th centuries. From 1901 it was absorbed in the British, French, and German colonies in this area, which became the states of Niger, Cameroon, and Nigeria. The largest section of ancient Bornu is now the state of Bornu in Nigeria.

Borobudur site of Buddhist shrine near ◊Yogyakarta, Indonesia.

Borodin Alexander Porfir'yevich 1833–1887. Russian composer. Born in St Petersburg, the illegitimate son of a Russian prince, he became by profession an expert in medical chemistry, but in his spare time devoted himself to music. His principal work is the opera *Prince Igor*; left unfinished, it was completed by Rimsky-Korsakov and Glazunov and includes the Polovtsian Dances.

Borodino village 70 mi/110 km NW of Moscow. French troops under Napoleon defeated the Russians under Kutusov here Sept 7, 1812.

boron nonmetallic element, symbol B, atomic number 5, atomic weight 10.811. In nature it occurs only in compounds, as with sodium and oxygen in borax. It exists in two allotropic forms: a brown amorphous powder and very hard, brilliant crystals. Its compounds are used in the preparation of boric acid, water softeners, soaps, enamels, glass, and pottery glazes. In alloys it is used to harden steel. Because it absorbs slow neutrons, it is used to make boron carbide control rods for nuclear reactors. It is a necessary trace element in human nutrition.

It was named by Humphry Davy, who isolated it 1808, from *bor*ax + -on, as in carb*on*.

Borromeo, St Carlo 1538–1584. Italian Roman Catholic saint and cardinal. He was instrumental in bringing the Council of Trent (1562–3) to a successful conclusion, and in drawing up the catechism that contained its findings. Feast day Nov 4.

Born at Arona of a noble Italian family, Borromeo was created a cardinal and archbishop of Milan by his uncle Pope Pius IV in 1560. He lived the life of an ascetic, and in 1578 founded the community later called the Oblate Fathers of St Charles. He was canonized 1610.

Borromini Francesco 1599–1667. Italian architect. He was the main rival of Bernini and brought the Baroque style to its peak in Rome, where his major work was executed. He had a highly individual style that set his work off from the rest of the Baroque masters, and his genius may be seen in the cathedrals of St Carlo 1641, St Ivo 1660, and the oratorio of St Filippo Neri 1650.

borzoi (Russian "swift") large breed of dog originating in Russia, 2.5 ft/75 cm or more at the shoulder. It is of the greyhound type, white with darker markings, with a thick, silky coat.

Bosch Hieronymus (Jerome) 1460–1516. Early Netherlandish painter. His fantastic visions of weird and hellish creatures, as shown in *The Garden of Earthly Delights* about 1505–10 (Prado, Madrid), show astonishing imagination and a complex imagery. His religious subjects focused not on the holy figures but on the mass of ordinary witnesses, placing the religious event in a contemporary Netherlandish context and creating cruel caricatures of human sinfulness.

Bosch is named after his birthplace, 'sHertogenbosch, in Brabant (now in Belgium). His work foreshadowed Surrealism and was probably inspired by a local religious brotherhood. However, he was an orthodox Catholic and a prosperous painter, not a heretic, as was once believed. After his death, his work was collected by Philip II of Spain.

Bosch Juan 1909– . President of the Dominican Republic 1963. His left-wing Partido Revolucionario Dominicano won a landslide victory in the 1962 elections. In office, he attempted agrarian reform and labor legislation. Opposed by the US, he was overthrown by the army. His achievement was to establish a democratic political party after three decades of dictatorship.

Boscovich Ruggiero 1711–1787. Italian scientist. An early supporter of Newton, he developed a theory of the atom as a single point with surrounding fields of repulsive and attractive forces that was popular in the 19th century.

Bose Jagadis Chunder 1858–1937. Indian physicist and plant physiologist. Born near Dakha, he was professor of physical science at Calcutta 1885–1915, and studied the growth and minute movements of plants, and their reaction to electrical stimuli. He founded the Bose Research Institute, Calcutta.

Bose Satyendra Nath 1894–1974. Indian physicist who formulated the Bose–Einstein law of quantum mechanics with ◊Einstein. He was professor of physics at the University of Calcutta 1945–58.

Bosnia and Herzegovina (Serbo-Croat *Bosna-Hercegovina*) constituent republic of Yugoslavia
area 19,725 sq mi/51,100 sq km
capital Sarajevo
features barren, mountainous country
population (1986) 4,360,000; including 30% Serbs, 17% Croats
language Serbian variant of Serbo-Croat
religion Sunni Muslim, Serbian Orthodox, Roman Catholic
history once the Roman province of ◊Illyria, the region enjoyed brief periods of independence in medieval times, then was ruled by the Ottoman Empire 1463–1878 and Austria 1878–1918, when it was incorporated in the future Yugoslavia. In 1943 Marshall Tito set up a provisional government at liberated Jajce and declared the Yugoslav Federal Republic in 1945, after the expulsion of remaining German forces. Islamic nationalist unrest broke out in the 1980s, and Muslim-Serb violence worsened 1989–1990. During Yugoslavia's civil warfare 1991, the republic suffered heavy damage and loss of life.

Bosnian Crisis period of international tension 1908 when Austria attempted to capitalize on Turkish weakness after the ◊Young Turk revolt by annexing the provinces of Bosnia and Herzegovina. Austria obtained Russian approval in exchange for conceding Russian access to the Bosporus Straits.

The speed of Austrian action took Russia by surprise, and domestic opposition led to the resignation of Russian foreign minister Izvolsky. Russia also failed to obtain necessary French and British agreements on the straits.

Bosporus (Turkish *Karadeniz Boğazi*) literally "oxford." Strait 17 mi/27 km long joining the Black Sea with the Sea of Marmara and forming part of the water division between Europe and Asia. Istanbul stands on its W side. The Bosporus Bridge 1973 links Istanbul and Turkey-in-Asia (5,320 ft/1,621 m). In 1988 a second bridge across the straits was opened, linking Asia and Europe. The name may be derived from the Greek legend of ◊Io.

Boston industrial and commercial center, capital of Massachusetts; population (1990) 574,283, metropolitan area 4,171,643. It is a publishing center and industrial port on Massachusetts Bay, but the economy is dominated by financial and health services and government. Boston and Northeastern universities are here; Harvard University and the Massachusetts Institute of Technology are in neighboring Cambridge, across the Charles River.
features Faneuil Hall, Old North Church, Paul Revere house, USS *Constitution* ("Old Ironsides")
history founded by Puritans 1630, Boston was a center of opposition to British trade restrictions, culminating in the Boston Tea Party 1773. After the first shots of the American Revolution in 1775 at nearby Lexington and Concord, the Battle of Bunker Hill was fought outside the city. The British withdrew from the city 1776. In the 19th century, Boston became the metropolis of New England. Urban redevelopment and the growth of service industries have compensated for the city's industrial decline.

Boston Tea Party protest in 1773 against the British tea tax by colonists in Massachusetts before the ◊American Revolution.

When a valuable consignment of tea (belonging to the East India Company), and intended for sale in the American colonies, arrived in Boston Harbor aboard three ships from England, it was thrown overboard by a group of Bostonians disguised as Indians, during the night of Dec 16, 1773 from the three ships that had brought it from England. The British government, angered by this and other colonial protests against British policy, took retaliatory measures 1774, including the closing of the port of Boston.

Boswell James 1740–1795. Scottish biographer and diarist. He was a member of Samuel ◊Johnson's London Literary Club and in 1773 the two men traveled to Scotland together, as recorded in Boswell's *Journal of the Tour to the Hebrides* 1785. His classic English biography, *Life of Samuel Johnson*, was published 1791. His long-lost personal papers were acquired for publication by Yale University 1949, and the *Journals* are of exceptional interest.

Born in Edinburgh, Boswell studied law but centered his ambitions on literature and politics. He first met Johnson in 1763, before setting out on a European tour during which he met the French thinkers Rousseau and Voltaire, and the Corsican nationalist general Paoli (1726–1807), whom he commemorated in his popular *Account of Corsica* 1768. In 1766 he became a lawyer, and in 1772 renewed his acquaintance with Johnson in London.

Boswell *Diarist James Boswell immortalized Dr Johnson, a leading figure of the 18th century. They met in 1763, traveled throughout Europe, and visited with many of the notables of their day. The sketch is by George Dance 1793.*

Bosworth, Battle of last battle of the Wars of the ◊Roses, fought on Aug 22, 1485. Richard III, the Yorkist king, was defeated and slain by Henry of Richmond, who became Henry VII. The battlefield is near the village of Market Bosworth, 12 mi/19 km W of Leicester, England.

botanical garden a place where a wide range of plants is grown, providing the opportunity to see a botanical diversity not likely to be encountered naturally. Among the earliest forms was the physic garden, devoted to the study and growth of medicinal plants; an example is the Chelsea Physic Garden in London, established in 1673 and still in existence. Following increased botanical exploration, botanical gardens were used to test the commercial potential of new plants being sent back from all parts of the world.

Today a botanical garden serves many purposes: education, science, and conservation. Many are associated with universities and also maintain large collections of preserved specimens (see ◊herbarium), libraries, research laboratories, and gene banks.

In the US, there are both publicly and privately funded botanical gardens. Some botanical gardens and arboretums are devoted to local or New World plants while others preserve, protect, and propagate specialties, such as ornamentals. Most botanical gardens are open year round, with greenhouses and conservatories as well as extensive landscaped grounds and an exhibit hall that sells plants and offers an advisory service. The New York Botanical Society runs the botanical garden at the Bronx Zoo in this way. Winterthur, the former du Pont estate, and Mount Vernon, the former home of George Washington, are now run as private historical sites and botanical gardens.

botany the study of plants. It is subdivided into a number of specialized studies, such as the identification and classification of plants (taxonomy), their external formation (plant morphology), their internal arrangement (plant anatomy), their microscopic examination (plant histology), their functioning and life history (plant physiology), and their distribution over the Earth's surface in relation to their surroundings (plant ecology). Paleobotany concerns the study of fossil plants, while economic botany deals with the utility of plants. Horticulture, agriculture, and forestry are specialized branches of botany.

history The most ancient botanical record is carved on the walls of the temple at Karnak, Egypt, about 1500 BC. The Greeks in the 5th and 4th centuries BC used many plants for medicinal purposes, the first Greek *Herbal* being drawn up about 350 BC by Diocles of Carystus. Botanical information was collected into the works of Theophrastus of Eresus (380–287 BC), a pupil of Aristotle, who founded technical plant nomenclature. Cesalpino in the 16th century sketched out a system of classification based on flowers, fruits, and seeds, while Jung (1587–1658) used flowers only as his criterion. John Ray (1627–1705) arranged plants systematically, based on his findings on fruit, leaf, and flower, and described about 18,600 plants.

The Swedish botanist Carl von Linné, or ◊Linnaeus, who founded systematics in the 18th century, included in his classification all known plants and animals, giving each a ◊binomial descriptive label. His work greatly aided the future study of plants, as botanists found that all plants could be fitted into a systematic classification based on Linnaeus' work. Linnaeus was also the first to recognize the sexual nature of flowers. This was followed up later by Charles ◊Darwin and others.

Later work revealed the detailed cellular structure of plant tissues and the exact nature of ◊photosynthesis. Julius von Sachs (1832–1897) defined the function of ◊chlorophyll and the significance of plant ◊stomata. In the second half of the 20th century, much has been learned about cell function, repair, and growth by the hybridization of plant cells (the combination of the nucleus of one cell with the cytoplasm of another).

Botany Bay inlet on the E coast of Australia, 5 mi/8 km S of Sydney, New South Wales. Chosen in 1787 as the site for a penal colony, it proved unsuitable. Sydney now stands on the site of the former settlement. The name Botany Bay continued to be popularly used for any convict settlement in Australia.

Botero Fernando 1932– . Colombian painter. He studied in Spain and gained an international reputation for his paintings of fat, vulgar figures, often of women, parodies of conventional sensuality.

botfly any fly of the family Oestridae. The larvae are parasites that feed on the skin (warblefly of cattle) or in the nasal cavity (nostril-flies of sheep and deer). The horse botfly belongs to another family, the Gasterophilidae. It has a parasitic larva that feeds in the horse's stomach.

Botha Louis 1862–1919. South African soldier and politician, a commander in the Boer War. In 1907 Botha became premier of the Transvaal and in 1910 of the first Union South African government. On the outbreak of World War I in 1914 he rallied South Africa to the Commonwealth, suppressed a Boer revolt, and conquered German South West Africa.

Botha P(ieter) W(illem) 1916– . South African politician. Prime minister from 1978, he initiated a modification of ◊apartheid, which later slowed in the face of Afrikaner (Boer) opposition. In 1984 he became the first executive state president. In 1989 he unwillingly resigned both party leadership and presidency after suffering a stroke, and was succeeded by F W de Klerk.

Bothe Walther 1891–1957. German physicist who showed in 1929 that the cosmic rays bombarding the Earth are composed not of photons but of more massive particles. Nobel Prize for Physics 1954.

Bothwell James Hepburn, 4th Earl of c. 1536–1578. Scottish nobleman, third husband of ◊Mary Queen of Scots, 1567–70, alleged to have arranged the explosion that killed Darnley, her previous husband, in 1567.

Tried and acquitted a few weeks after the assassination, he abducted Mary and married her on May 15th. A revolt ensued, and Bothwell fled. In 1570 Mary obtained a divorce, and Bothwell was confined in a castle in mainland Europe, where he died insane.

bo tree or ***peepul*** Indian ◊fig tree *Ficus religiosa*, said to be the tree under which Buddha became enlightened.

Botswana landlocked country in central southern Africa, bounded S and E by South Africa, W and N by Namibia, and NE by Zimbabwe.

government The 1966 constitution blends the British system of parliamentary accountability with representation for each of Botswana's major ethnic groups. It provides for a national assembly of 40 members – 34 elected by universal suffrage, four by the assembly itself, plus the speaker and the attorney general—and has a life of five years. The president is elected by the assembly for its duration and is an ex-officio member of that body and answerable to it. There is also a 15-member house of chiefs, consisting of the chiefs of Botswana's eight principal ethnic groups, plus four members elected by the chiefs themselves and three elected by the house in general. The president may delay a bill for up to six months and then either sign it or dissolve the assembly and call a general election. The house of chiefs is consulted by the president and the assembly in matters affecting it. The president appoints a cabinet that is answerable to the assembly. Most significant of the seven political groupings are the Botswana Democratic Party (BDP), and the Botswana National Front (BNF).

history The first inhabitants were the ◊Bushmen, the hunter-gatherer groups living chiefly in the Kalahari Desert; from the 17th century the Tswana people became the principal inhabitants of the area, followed by the arrival of Bantu peoples in the early 19th century. Fearing an invasion by Boer farmers, the local rulers appealed to Britain and in 1885 Bechuanaland (as it was originally called) became a British protectorate.

On passing the Union of South Africa Act in 1910, making South Africa independent, the British Parliament provided for the possibility of Bechuanaland becoming part of South Africa, but stipulated that this would not happen without popular consent. Successive South African governments requested the transfer, but Botswana preferred full independence.

The 1960 constitution provided for a legislative council, although remaining under British High Commission control. In 1963 High Commission rule ended, and in the legislative assembly elections the newly formed Bechuanaland Democratic Party (BDP) won a majority. Its leader, Seretse ◊Khama, had been deposed as chief of the Bangangwato Tribe in 1950 and had since lived in exile, after marrying an English woman two years before.

In 1966 the country, renamed Botswana, became an independent state within the ◊Commonwealth with Sir Seretse Khama, as he had now become, as president. He continued to be re-elected until his death in 1980 when he was succeeded by the vice president, Dr Quett Masire, who was re-elected in 1984. In the Oct 1989 elections the BDP won 31 of the 34 national assembly seats and Quett Masire was again re-elected.

Since independence Botswana has earned a reputation for stability. It is a member of the ◊nonaligned movement. South Africa has accused it of providing bases for the African National Congress (ANC) and Botswana was the target of several cross-border raids by South African forces. The presence of ANC bases has always been denied by both Botswana and the ANC itself. South Africa has persistently pressed Botswana to sign a nonaggression pact, similar to the Nkomati Accord between South Africa and Mozambique.

Botticelli Sandro 1445–1510. Florentine painter of religious and mythological subjects. He was patronized by the ruling ◊Medici family, for whom he painted *Primavera* 1478 and *The Birth of Venus* about 1482–84 (both in the Uffizi, Florence). From the 1490s he was influenced by the religious fanatic ◊Savonarola and developed a harshly expressive and emotional style.

His real name was Filipepi, but his elder brother's nickname Botticelli "little barrel" was passed on to him. His work for the Medicis was designed to cater to the educated Classical tastes of the day. As well as his sentimental, beautiful young Madonnas, he produced a series of inventive compositions, including *tondi*, circular paintings. He broke with the Medicis after their execution of Savonarola.

bottlebrush tree or shrub common in Australia, belonging to the genera *Melaleuca* and *Callistemon* of the myrtle family, with characteristic cylindrical, composite flower heads, often brightly colored.

Bottrop city in North Rhine–Westphalia, Germany; population (1988) 112,000.

botulism rare, often fatal type of ◊food poisoning. Symptoms include muscular paralysis and disturbed breathing and vision. It is caused by a toxin produced by the bacterium *Clostridium botulinum*, sometimes found in improperly canned food.

Thorough cooking destroys the toxin, which otherwise suppresses the cardiac and respiratory centers of the brain.

Boucher François 1703–1770. French Rococo painter, court painter from 1765. He was much patronized for his light-hearted, decorative scenes: for example *Diana Bathing* 1742 (Louvre, Paris).

He also painted portraits and decorative chinoiserie for Parisian palaces. He became director of the Gobelin tapestry works, Paris, in 1755.

Botswana
Republic of

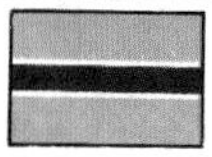

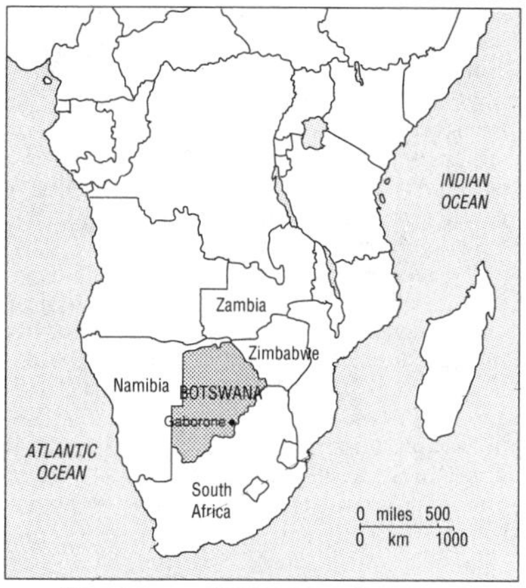
Zambia
Zimbabwe
Namibia
BOTSWANA
Gaborone
ATLANTIC OCEAN
INDIAN OCEAN
South Africa
0 miles 500
0 km 1000

area 225,000 sq mi/582,000 sq km
capital Gaborone
cities Mahalpye, Serowe, Tutume, Francistown
physical desert in SW, plains in E, fertile lands and swamp in N
features the Kalahari Desert in SW; Okavango Swamp in N, remarkable for its wildlife; Makgadikgadi salt pans in E; diamonds mined at Orapa and Jwaneng in partnership with De Beers of South Africa
head of state and government Quett Ketamile Joni Masire from 1980
political system democratic republic
political parties Botswana Democratic Party (BDP), moderate centrist; Botswana National Front (BNF), moderate left-of-center
exports diamonds (third-largest producer in world), copper, nickel, meat products, textiles
currency pula
population (1990 est) 1,218,000 (80% Bamangwato, 20% Bangwaketse); growth rate 3.5% p.a.
life expectancy (1988) 59 years
language English (official); Setswana (national)
religion Christian 50%, animist 50%
literacy (1988) 84%
GDP $2.0 bn (1988); $1,611 per head
chronology
1885 Became a British protectorate.
1960 New constitution created a legislative council.
1963 End of rule by high commission.
1965 Capital transferred from Mafeking to Gaborone. Internal self-government granted. Seretse Khama elected head of government.
1966 Independence achieved from Britain. New constitution came into effect; name changed from Bechuanaland to Botswana; Seretse Khama elected president.
1980 Seretse Khama died; succeeded by Vice President Quett Masire.
1984 Masire reelected.
1985 South African raid on Gaborone.
1987 Joint permanent commission with Mozambique established, to improve relations.
1989 The BDP and Masire reelected.

Botticelli The Mystic Nativity *(1500) National Gallery, London.*

Boucher de Crèvecoeur de Perthes Jacques 1788–1868. French geologist, whose discovery of Paleolithic hand-axes in 1837 challenged the accepted view of human history dating only from 4004 BC, as proclaimed by the calculations of Bishop James Usher.

Boudicca died AD 60. Queen of the Iceni (native Britons), often referred to by the Latin form Boadicea. Her husband, King Prasutagus, had been a tributary of the Romans, but on his death AD 60 the territory of the Iceni was violently annexed. Boudicca was scourged and her daughters raped. Boudicca raised the whole of SE England in revolt, and before the main Roman armies could return from campaigning in Wales she burned London, St Albans, and Colchester. Later the Romans under governor Suetonius Paulinus defeated the British somewhere between London and Chester; they were virtually annihilated and Boudicca poisoned herself.

Boudin Eugène 1824–1898. French artist, a forerunner of the Impressionists, known for his fresh seaside scenes painted in the open air.

Bougainville island province of Papua New Guinea; largest of the Solomon Islands archipelago
area 4,100 sq mi/10,620 sq km
capital Kieta
products copper, gold and silver
population (1989) 128,000
history named after the French navigator ◊Bougainville who arrived in 1768. In 1976 Bougainville became a province (with substantial autonomy) of Papua New Guinea. A state of emergency declared 1989 after secessionist violence.

Bougainville Louis Antoine de 1729–1811. French navigator. After service with the French in Canada during the Seven Years' War, he made the first French circumnavigation of the world in 1766–69 and the first systematic observations of longitude.

Several Pacific islands are named after him, as is the climbing plant bougainvillea.

bougainvillea genus of South American tropical vines of the four o'clock family Nyctaginaceae, now cultivated in warm countries throughout the world for the red and purple bracts that cover the flowers. They are named after the French navigator Louis Bougainville.

Bougie name until 1962 of ◊Bejaia, port in Algeria.

Bouguer anomaly in geophysics, an increase in the Earth's gravity observed near a mountain or dense rock mass. This is due to the gravitational force exerted by the rock mass. It is named after its discoverer, the French mathematician Pierre Bouguer (1698–1758), who first observed it in 1735.

Bouguereau Adolphe William 1825–1905. French academic painter of historical and mythological subjects. He was respected in his day but his style is now thought to be insipid.

Bou Kraa the principal phosphate-mining center of Western Sahara, linked by conveyor belt to the Atlantic coast near La'youn.

Boulanger George Ernest Jean Marie 1837–1891. French general. He became minister of war 1886, and his anti-German speeches nearly provoked war with Germany 1887. In 1889 he was suspected of aspiring to dictatorship by a coup d'état. Accused of treason, he fled into exile and committed suicide on the grave of his mistress.

Boulanger Nadia (Juliette) 1887–1979. French music teacher and conductor. A pupil of Fauré, and admirer of Stravinsky, she included among her composition pupils at the American Conservatory in Fontainebleau (from 1921) Aaron Copland, Roy Harris, Walter Piston, and Philip Glass.

She was the first woman to conduct the Royal Philharmonic, London 1937, and the Boston Symphony, the New York Philharmonic, and the Philadelphia Orchestra 1938.

Boulder city in N central Colorado, NW of Denver, in the E foothills of the Rocky mountains. A center of scientific research, especially that of space, it is the site of the University of Colorado 1876. Other industries include agriculture, mining, and tourism; population (1990) 83,312.

boules (French "balls") a French lawn bowling game (also called *boccie* and *pétanque*) between two players or teams; it is similar to bowls.

Boules is derived from the ancient French game *jeu provençal*. The object is to deliver a boule (or boules) from a standing position to land as near the jack (target) as possible. The boule is approximately 3 in/8 cm in diameter and weighs 22–28 oz/620–800 g. The standard length of the court, normally with a sand base, is 90 ft/27.5 m.

Boulez Pierre 1925– . French composer and conductor. He studied with ◊Messiaen and promoted contemporary music with a series of innovative *Domaine Musical* concerts and recordings in the 1950s, as conductor of the BBC Symphony and New York Philharmonic orchestras during the 1970s, and as founder-director of IRCAM, a music research studio in Paris opened in 1976.

His music, strictly serial and expressionistic in style, includes the cantatas *Le Visage nuptial* 1946–52 and *Le Marteau sans maître* 1955, both to texts by René Char; *Pli selon pli* 1962 for soprano and orchestra; and *Répons* 1981 for soloists, orchestra, tapes and computer-generated sounds.

boulle or ***buhl*** a type of ◊marquetry, in brass and tortoise shell. Originally Italian, it has acquired the name of one of its most skillful exponent, the French artisan André-Charles Boulle (1642–1732).

Boulogne-sur-Mer town on the English Channel, Pas-de-Calais *département*, France; population (1983) 99,000. Industries include oil refining, food processing, and fishing. It is also a ferry port (connecting with Dover and Folkestone) and seaside resort. Boulogne was a medieval countship, but became part of France 1477.

Boult Adrian (Cedric) 1889–1983. British conductor of the BBC Symphony Orchestra 1930–50 and the London Philharmonic 1950–57. He promoted the work of Holst and Vaughan Williams, and was a celebrated interpreter of Elgar.

Boumédienne Houari. Adopted name of Mohammed Boukharouba 1925–1978. Algerian politician who brought the nationalist leader Ben Bella to power by a revolt 1962, and superseded him as president in 1965 by a further coup.

Boundary Peak highest mountain in Nevada, rising to 13,143 ft/4,006 m on the Nevada-California frontier.

***Bounty*, Mutiny on the** naval mutiny in the Pacific 1789 against British captain William ◊Bligh.

Bourbon name 1649–1815 of the French island of ◊Réunion, in the Indian Ocean.

Bourbon, duchy of originally a seigneury (feudal domain) created in the 10th century in the county of Bourges, central France, held by the Bourbon family. It became a duchy 1327.

The lands passed to the Capetian dynasty (see ◊Capet) as a result of the marriage of the Bourbon heiress Beatrix to Robert of Clermont, son of Louis IX. Their son Pierre became the first duke of Bourbon 1327. The direct line ended with the death of Charles, Duke of Bourbon, in 1527.

Bourbon French royal house (succeeding that of ◊Valois) beginning with Henry IV, and ending with Louis XVI, with a brief revival under Louis VIII, Charles X, and Louis Philippe. The Bourbons also ruled Spain almost uninterruptedly from Philip V to Alfonso XIII and were restored in 1975 (◊Juan Carlos); at one point they also ruled Naples and several Italian duchies. The Grand Duke of Luxembourg is also a Bourbon by male descent.

Bourdon Eugène 1808–1884. French engineer and instrument maker who invented the pressure gauge that bears his name.

Bourdon gauge instrument for measuring pressure, invented by Eugène Bourdon 1849. The gauge contains a C-shaped tube, closed at one end and oval in cross section, which straightens and changes circumference slightly when a gas or liquid under pressure flows into it. Levers and gears make the movement at the end of the tube work a pointer, which indicates pressure on a circular scale.

bourgeois (French) a member of the middle class, implying that a person is unimaginative, conservative, and materialistic.

Bourgeois Léon Victor Auguste 1851–1925. French politician. Entering politics as a Radical, he was prime minister in 1895, and later served in many cabinets. He was one of the pioneer advocates of the League of Nations. He was awarded the Nobel Peace Prize 1920.

bourgeoisie (French) the middle classes. The French word originally meant "the freemen of a borough." It came to mean the whole class above the workers and peasants, and below the nobility. Bourgeoisie (and *bourgeois*) has also acquired a contemptuous sense, implying commonplace, philistine respectability. By Socialists it is applied to the whole propertied class, as distinct from the proletariat.

Bourges city in central France, 125 mi/200 km S of Paris; population (1982) 92,000. Industries include aircraft, engineering, and tires. It has a 13th-century Gothic cathedral and notable art collections.

Bourgogne region of France, that includes the *départements* of Côte-d'Or, Nièvre, Saône-et-Loire, and Yonne; area 12,198 sq mi/31,600 sq km; population (1986) 1,607,000. Its capital is Dijon. It is renowned for its wines, such as Chablis and Nuits-Saint-Georges, and for its cattle (the Charolais herdbook is maintained at Nevers). A former independent kingdom and duchy (English name ◊Burgundy), it was incorporated into France 1477.

Bourguiba Habib ben Ali 1903– . Tunisian politician, first president of Tunisia 1957–87. Educated at the University of Paris, he became a journalist and was frequently imprisoned by the French for his nationalist aims as leader of the Néo-Destour party. He became prime minister 1956, president (for life from 1974) and prime minister of the Tunisian republic 1957; he was overthrown in a coup 1987.

Bourke-White Margaret 1906–1971. US photographer. Serving as an editor of *Fortune* magazine 1929–33, she traveled extensively in the Soviet Union, publishing several collections of photographs. Later, with husband Erskine Caldwell, she published photo collections of American and European subjects. Named to the staff of *Life* magazine 1936, she covered combat in World War II and documented India's postwar struggle for independence.

Born in New York and educated at Cornell University, Bourke-White began her career as a freelance industrial and architectural photographer.

Bournemouth seaside resort in Dorset, England; population (1981) 145,000.

Bournonville August 1805–1879. Danish dancer and choreographer. He worked with the Royal Danish Ballet for most of his life, giving Danish ballet a worldwide importance. His ballets, many of which have been revived in the last 50 years, include *La Sylphide* 1836 (music by Lövenskjöld) and *Napoli* 1842.

Bouts Dierick c. 1420–1475. Early Netherlandish painter. Born in Haarlem, he settled in Louvain, painting portraits and religious scenes influenced by Rogier van der Weyden. *The Last Supper* 1464–68 (St Pierre, Louvain) is one of his finest works.

Bouvet Island uninhabited island in the S Atlantic Ocean, a dependency of Norway since 1930; area 19 sq mi/48 sq km. Discovered by the French captain Jacques Bouvet in 1738, it was made the subject of a claim by Britain in 1825, but this was waived in Norway's favor in 1928.

Bouvines, Battle of a victory for Philip II (Philip Augustus) of France in 1214, near the village of Bouvines in Flanders, over the Holy Roman emperor Otto IV and his allies. The battle, one of the most decisive in medieval Europe, ensured the succession of Frederick II as emperor and confirmed Philip as ruler of the whole of N France and Flanders; it led to the renunciation of all English claims to the region.

Bovet Daniel 1907– . Swiss physiologist. He pioneered research into antihistamine drugs used in the treatment of nettle rash and hay fever, and was awarded a Nobel Prize for Medicine 1957 for his production of a synthetic form of curare, used as a muscle relaxant in anesthesia.

bovine spongiform encephalopathy (BSE) disease of cattle, allied to ◊scrapie, that renders the brain spongy and may drive an animal mad. It has been identified only in the UK, where more than 13,400 cases had been confirmed between the first diagnosis Nov 1986 and Feb 1990.

Bow Clara 1905–1965. US film actress known as a Jazz Baby and the "It Girl" after her portrayal of a glamorous flapper in the silent film *It* 1927. She made a smooth transition to sound with *The Wild Party* 1929.

Earlier films included *Down to the Sea in Ships* 1925 and *The Plastic Age, Kid Boots, Mantrap*, and *Dancing Mothers*, all 1926. Later films include *Rough House Rosie* 1927, *Red Hair* 1928, *Three Weekends* 1928, and *The Saturday Night Kid* 1929. She made her last film *Hoopla* 1933 and retired to her husband's ranch in Nevada.

Bowditch Nathaniel 1773–1838. US astronomer. Having discovered many inaccuracies in the standard navigation guide of the day, he published his own guide, *The New American Practical Navigator* 1802. Later, as a maritime insurance actuary, Bowditch continued his private study and published works on astronomical observations—among them, *Celestial Mechanics* 1829–39, a translation of the first four volumes of Laplace's *Mécanique céleste*. In 1829 he became president of the American Academy of Arts and Sciences.

Born in Salem, Massachusetts, Bowditch had little formal education but read widely as a merchant seaman during the years 1795–1803.

Bowie British pop singer and songwriter David Bowie has also acted in films, notably The Man Who Fell to Earth *1976.*

Bowdler Thomas 1754–1825. British editor whose prudishly expurgated versions of Shakespeare and other authors gave rise to the verb *bowdlerize*.

Bowdoin James 1726–1790. American public official. Born in Boston, Bowdoin was educated at Harvard and began his public career with election to the Massachusetts General Court 1753. Chosen as a member of the Governor's Council 1757, he became a strong supporter of the cause of American independence, serving on the Massachusetts Executive Council 1775–76. Bowdoin later served as president of the state constitutional convention 1779–80 and as governor 1785–87. He was also the first president of the American Academy of Arts and Sciences. Bowdoin College in Brunswick, Maine, is named in his honor.

bower-bird New Guinean and N Australian bird of the family Ptilonorhynchidae, related to the ◊birds of paradise. The males are dull-colored, and build elaborate bowers of sticks and grass, decorated with shells, feathers, or flowers, and even painted with the juice of berries, to attract the females. There are 17 species.

bowfin North American fish *Amia calva* with a swim bladder highly developed as an air sac, enabling it to breathe air. It is the only surviving member of a primitive group of bony fishes.

bowhead Arctic whale *Balena mysticetus* with strongly curving upper jawbones supporting the plates of baleen with which it sifts planktonic crustaceans from the water. Averaging 50 ft/15 m long and 90 tons in weight, these slow-moving, placid whales were once extremely common, but by the 17th century were already becoming scarce through hunting. Only an estimated 3,000 remain, and continued hunting by the Eskimo may result in extinction.

Bowie David. Adopted name of David Jones 1947– . British pop singer, songwriter, and actor, born in Brixton, London. He became a glam-rock star in the early 1970s with the release of *The Rise and Fall of Ziggy Stardust and the Spiders from Mars* album in 1972, and collaborated in the mid-1970s with the electronic virtuoso Brian Eno (1948–) and Iggy Pop. He has also acted in plays and films, including Nicolas Roeg's *The Man Who Fell to Earth* 1976.

Bowie James "Jim" 1796–1836. US frontiersman and folk hero. A colonel in the Texan forces during the Mexican War, he is said to have invented the single-edge, guarded hunting and throwing knife known as a Bowie knife. He was killed in the battle of the ◊Alamo.

Bowles Paul 1910– . US novelist and composer. Born in New York City, he studied with Aaron Copland and Virgil Thomson, writing scores for ballets, films, and an opera, *The Wind Remains* 1943, as well as incidental music for plays. He settled in Morocco, the setting of his novels *The Sheltering Sky* 1949 and *Let It Come Down* 1952. His autobiography, *Without Stopping*, was published in 1972.

bowling indoor sport played in a bowling alley in which a ball is rolled into a target of standing pins. There are many forms of the sport, but the term "bowling" usually refers to the most popular variety, tenpin. The ball used in tenpin bowling is sometimes plastic but more commonly hard rubber. An official ball (one allowed in league play) must weigh 10–16 lb/4.5–7.3 kg and may not exceed 8.6 in/21.8 cm in diameter. Finger holes are drilled into each ball. Methods of gripping differ from bowler to bowler but most common is the underhand three-finger grip (thumb, middle finger, and ring finger).

Each of the bottle-shaped maple pins is 15 in/38 cm high, at least 5.25 in/13.34 cm in circumference at the neck, and at most 15 in/38 cm in circumference at the widest part. Pins are arranged in a triangular pattern at the end of a wooden lane 60 ft/18.3 m long from the headpin to the foul line. A bowler makes an approach toward the foul line, which may not be crossed, bringing the ball into a backswing and then swinging it forward for release. The ball travels down the lane, the object being to "bowl over" as many pins as possible.

A game of tenpins is divided into ten frames. In each frame, the bowler has two attempts to knock down all ten pins. Each toppled pin is scored as one point. If all ten pins go down on a first roll, it is called a "strike" and counts ten points plus the number of pins knocked down by the bowler's next two rolls. When all ten pins are toppled by two rolls, it is a "spare" and counts ten points plus the number of pins knocked down by the bowler's first roll of the next frame. A perfect game is 12 consecutive strikes, for a score of 300.

Whereas tenpin is called big-pin bowling, several other forms of the game are classified as small-pin bowling, the most popular being duckpin and candlepin. Both use a much smaller ball than tenpin. The stubby duckpins are 9.4 in/23.9 cm high; the narrow, tapered candlepins are 15.75 in/40.00 cm high and can stand upright on either end.

history Bowling in its most rudimentary form can be traced to ancient Egypt. Bowling-type equipment was found in the tomb of an Egyptian boy who died about 5200 BC. Other ancient cultures enjoyed their own variations of the sport, but what is considered the precursor of modern bowling generally is dated to medieval Europe, where *kegels* (the pins) were knocked down by thrown or rolled rocks.

Ninepins, a Dutch version of bowling, was introduced to the Americas in the 17th century. By the 1800s it not only had become very popular in New England but it had evolved into a major gambling activity. When Connecticut put a ban on "bowling at nine pins" in 1841, enterprising bowlers overstepped the law by adding a pin to the game–hence, tenpin bowling.

In 1895 the American Bowling Congress was organized, and under its authority the rules and equipment specifications of bowling in the US became standardized. In 1916 the Women's International Bowling Congress was founded; today it is the largest women's sports organization in the world. Professional bowling is a lucrative occupation for top contenders. The Professional Bowlers Association and the Ladies Pro Bowlers Tour sponsor high-stake tournaments throughout the US and in several other countries as well (Canada, Japan, and Latin America have shown particular interest in the game). Bowling "alleys" are businesses run to attract recreational bowlers; often leagues are formed and competitions or league events are held at them.

bowls a lawn bowling game played on a bowling green and indoors.

Bowman's capsule in the vertebrate kidney, a microscopic filtering device used in the initial stages of waste-removal and urine formation.

There are approximately a million of these capsules in a human kidney, each made up of a tight knot of capillaries and each leading into a kidney tubule or nephron. Blood at high pressure passes into the capillaries where water, dissolved nutrients, and urea move through the capillary wall into the tubule.

box small evergreen trees and shrubs, genus *Buxus*, of the family Buxaceae, with small, leathery leaves. Some species are used as hedge plants and for shaping into garden ornaments.

boxer breed of dog, about 2 ft/60 cm tall, with a smooth coat and a set-back nose. The tail is usually docked. Boxers are usually brown but may be brindled or white.

Boxer member of the *I ho ch'üan* ("Righteous Harmonious Fists"), an antiforeign society of Chinese nationalists who, in 1900 at the instigation of the empress dowager, besieged the European and US legations in Beijing and murdered missionaries and thousands of Chinese Christian converts (the Boxer Rebellion or Uprising). An international punitive force was dispatched, Beijing was captured Aug 14, 1900, and China agreed to pay a large indemnity.

boxfish any fish of the family Ostraciodontidae, with scales that are hexagonal bony plates fused to form a box covering the body, only the mouth and fins being free of the armor.

Boxfishes, also known as trunkfishes, swim slowly. The cowfish, genus *Lactophrys*, with two "horns" above the eyes, is a member of this group.

boxing fighting with gloved fists in a square area bordered by ropes, called a "ring," in timed rounds, almost entirely a male sport. Boxing dates from the 18th century, when fights were fought with bare knuckles and untimed rounds, which ended with a knockdown. Fighting with gloves became the accepted form in the latter part of the 19th century after the formulation of the Queensberry Rules 1867. The last bare-knuckle championship fight was between John L Sullivan and Jake Kilrain 1899.

Jack Broughton (1704–1889) was one of the early champions and in 1743 drew up the first set of boxing rules. Today all boxing follows the original Queensberry Rules, but with modifications. Contests take place in a square, roped ring 14–20 ft/4.3–6.1 m square. All rounds last 3 min. Amateur bouts last three rounds and professional championship bouts for as many as 12 or 15 rounds. Boxers are classified according to weight and may not fight in a division lighter than their own. The weight divisions in professional boxing range from straw-weight (also known as paperweight and mini-flyweight), under 108 lb/49 kg, to heavyweight, over 195 lb/88 kg. Boxing has school, amateur, semiprofessional, and professional matches.

boxing: recent winners

World Champions (WBC = World Boxing Council; WBA = World Boxing Association; IBF = International Boxing Federation; WBO = World Boxing Organization)

heavyweight

1986 Tim Witherspoon *US* (WBA)
1986 Trevor Berbick *Canada* (WBC)
1986 Mike Tyson *US* (WBC)
1986 James Smith *US* (WBA)
1987 Mike Tyson *US* (WBA)
1987 Tony Tucker *US* (IBF)
1987 Mike Tyson *US* (undisputed)
1989 Francesco Damiani *(Italy)* (WBO)
1990 James Douglas *(US)* (undisputed)
1990 Evander Holyfield *(US)* (undisputed)

Great heavyweight champions include:

John L Sullivan (bare-knuckle champion) 1882–92
Jim Corbett (first Marquess of Queensberry champion) 1892–97
Jack Dempsey 1919–26
Joe Louis 1937–49
Rocky Marciano 1952–56
Muhammad Ali 1964–67, 1974–78, 1978–79
Larry Holmes 1978–85
Mike Tyson 1986–1990

boyar a landowner in the Russian aristocracy. During the 16th century boyars formed a powerful interest group threatening the tsar's power, until their influence was decisively broken in 1565 when Ivan the Terrible confiscated much of their land.

Boycott Charles Cunningham 1832–1897. English land agent in County Mayo, Ireland, who strongly opposed the demands for agrarian reform by the Irish Land League 1879–81, with the result that the peasants refused to work for him; hence the word *boycott*.

Boyd-Orr John 1880–1971. British nutritionist and health campaigner. He was awarded the Nobel Prize for Peace in 1949 in recognition of his work toward alleviating world hunger.

Boyer Charles 1899–1978. French film actor, who made his name in Hollywood in the 1930s as a screen "lover" in such films as *The Garden of Allah* 1936 and *Mayerling* 1937. He played a definitive Napoleon in *Conquest* 1937 with Garbo and continued as a leading man into the 1950s.

Boyle Charles, 4th Earl of Orrery 1676–1731. Irish soldier and diplomat. The orrery, a mechanical model of the Solar System in which the planets move at the correct relative velocities, is named after him.

Boyle Robert 1627–1691. Irish physicist and chemist, who published the seminal *The Skeptical Chymist* 1661. He formulated Boyle's law in 1662.

Boyle's law in physics, law stating that the volume of a given mass of gas at a constant temperature is inversely proportional to its pressure. It was discovered in 1662 by Robert Boyle.

Boyne a river in the Irish Republic. Rising in the Bog of Allen in County Kildare, it flows 69 mi/110 km NE to the Irish Sea near Drogheda. The Battle of the Boyne was fought at Oldbridge near the mouth of the river in 1690.

Boyne, Battle of the battle fought July 1, 1690 in E Ireland, in which James II was defeated by William III and fled to France. It was the decisive battle of the War of English Succession, confirming a Protestant monarch. It took its name from the river Boyne in the Republic of Ireland 70 mi/113 km long, flowing past Drogheda into the Irish Sea.

Boyoma Falls series of seven cataracts in under 60 mi/100 km in the Lualaba (upper Zaïre river) above Kisangani, central Africa. They have a total drop of over 200 ft/60 m.

Boy Scout a member of the ◊Scout organization.

Bozen German form of ◊Bolzano, town in Italy.

Bo Zhu Yi 772–846. Chinese poet (formerly known as Po Chü-i). President from 841 of the imperial war department, he criticized government policy. He is said to have checked his work with an old peasant woman for clarity of expression.

Brabançonne, La national anthem of Belgium, written and composed during the revolution of 1830.

Brabant (Flemish *Braband*) former duchy of W Europe, comprising the Dutch province of ◊North Brabant and the Belgian provinces of Brabant and Antwerp. They were divided when Belgium became independent 1830. The present-day

Boyle *The law of the compressibility of gases, known as Boyle's law, was published in 1662. Robert Boyle was the 14th child of the Earl of Cork.*

Belgian province of Brabant has an area of 1,312 sq mi/3,400 sq km and a population (1987) of 2,222,000.

During the Middle Ages it was an independent duchy, and after passing to Burgundy, and thence to the Spanish crown, was divided during the Dutch War of Independence. The southern portion was Spanish until 1713, then Austrian until 1815, when the whole area was included in the Netherlands. In 1830 the French-speaking part of the population in the S Netherlands rebelled, and when Belgium was recognized 1839, S Brabant was included in it.

brachiopod any member of the phylum Brachiopoda, marine invertebrateswith two shells, resembling but totally unrelated to bivalves. There are about 300 living species; they were much more numerous in past geologic ages. They are suspension feeders, ingesting minute food particles from water. A single internal organ, the iophophore, handles feeding, aspiration, and excretion.

bracken large fern, especially *Pteridium aquilinum*, abundant in the northern hemisphere. A perennial rootstock throws up coarse fronds.

bracket fungus any ◊fungus of the class Basidiomycetes, with fruiting bodies that grow like shelves from trees.

bract a leaflike structure, in whose ◊axil a flower or inflorescence develops. Bracts are generally green and smaller than the true leaves. However, in some plants they may be brightly colored and conspicuous, taking over the role of attracting pollinating insects to the flowers, whose own petals are small; examples include poinsettia *Euphorbia pulcherrima* and bougainvillea.

A whorl of bracts surrounding an ◊inflorescence is termed an involucre. A bracteole is a leaflike organ that arises on an individual flower stalk, between the true bract and the ◊calyx.

Bradbury Ray 1920– . US science-fiction writer, responsible for making the genre "respectable" to a wider readership. His work shows nostalgia for small-town Midwestern life, and includes *The Martian Chronicles* 1950, *Fahrenheit 451* 1953, *R is for Rocket* 1962, and *Something Wicked This Way Comes* 1962.

Some of his short stories are collected in *The Stories of Ray Bradbury* 1980. He also has written several volumes of poetry, television and motion-picture screenplays, radio dramas, and children's stories.

Bradenton city in W Florida on the S shores of Tampa Bay, SW of Tampa; seat of Manatee county. It is a resort center during the winter months. Some travertine, a sparkling sheet of calcium carbonate formed on cave walls and floors, is quarried here; population (1990) 43,779.

Bradford industrial city (engineering, machine tools, electronics, printing) in West Yorkshire, England, 9 mi/14 km W of Leeds; population (1981) 281,000.

Bradford William 1590–1657. First governor of Plymouth Colony. In 1620 he sailed for American aboard the *Mayflower*. Bradford was among the signers of the Mayflower Compact, the first written constitution in the New World. In the spring of 1621 he was chosen as governor of Plymouth and served in that office almost continuously for the next 35 years. His memoirs, *History of Plimoth Plantation*, are an important source for the colony's early history.

Born in Yorkshire, England, Bradford joined the Puritan Separatists (later known as the ◊Pilgrims) at an early age and lived with them in exile in Leiden, Holland, 1609–20.

Bradley Francis Herbert 1846–1924. British philosopher. In *Ethical Studies* 1876 and *Principles of Logic* 1883 he attacked the utilitarianism of J S Mill, and in *Appearance and Reality* 1893 and *Truth and Reality* 1914 he outlined his Neo-Hegelian doctrine of the universe as a single ultimate reality.

Bradley James 1693–1762. English astronomer who in 1728 discovered the ◊aberration of starlight. From the amount of aberration in star positions, he was able to calculate the speed of light. In 1748, he announced the discovery of ◊nutation (variation in the Earth's axial tilt).

Bradley Omar Nelson 1893–1981. US general in World War II. In 1943 he commanded the 2nd US Corps in their victories in Tunisia and Sicily, leading to the surrender of 250,000 Axis troops, and in 1944 led the US troops in the invasion of France. His command, as the 12th Army Group, grew to 1.3 million troops, the largest US force ever assembled.

Born in Clark, Missouri, Bradley graduated from West Point 1915 and served in World War I. After World War II, he headed the Veterans Administration 1945–47, was chief of staff of the US Army 1948–49, and was the first chairman of the joint chiefs of staff 1949–53. He was appointed general of the army 1950 and retired from the army 1953. He wrote his memoirs in *A Soldier's Story*.

Brady Mathew B c. 1823–1896. US photographer. Famed for his skill in photographic portraiture, he published *The Gallery of Illustrious Americans* 1850. With the outbreak of the Civil War, Brady and his staff became the foremost photographers of battle scenes and military life. Although his war photos were widely reproduced, Brady himself later suffered a series of financial reverses and died in poverty.

Born in Warren County, New York, Brady served as an apprentice to a portrait painter. Learning the rudiments of photography from Samuel ◊Morse, Brady established his own ◊daguerreotype studio in New York 1844.

Braga city in N Portugal 30 mi/48 km NNE of Oporto; population (1981) 63,800. Industries include textiles, electrical goods, and vehicle manufacture. It has a 12th-century cathedral, and the archbishop is primate of the Iberian peninsula. As Bracara Augusta it was capital of the Roman province Lusitania.

Bragança name of the royal house of Portugal whose members reigned 1640– 1853; another branch were emperors of Brazil 1822–89.

Braganua capital of a province of the same name in NE Portugal, 110 mi/176 km NE of Oporto. Population (1981) 13,900. It was the original family seat of the House of Braganua which ruled Portugal 1640–1910.

Bragg William Henry 1862–1942. British physicist. In 1915 he shared with his son (William) Lawrence Bragg (1890–1971) the Nobel Prize for Physics for their research work on X-rays and crystals.

Brahe Tycho 1546–1601. Danish astronomer who made accurate observations of the planets from which the German astronomer and mathematician Johann ◊Kepler proved that planets orbit the Sun in ellipses. His discovery and report of the 1572 supernova brought him recognition and his observations of the comet of 1577 proved that it moved on an orbit among the planets, thus disproving the Greek view that comets were in the Earth's atmosphere.

Brahe was a colorful figure who had to wear a metal nose after his own was cut off in a duel, and who took an interest in alchemy. In 1576 Frederick II of Denmark gave him the island of Hven, where he set up an observatory. Brahe was the greatest observer in the days before telescopes, making the most accurate measurements of the positions of stars and planets. He moved to Prague as imperial mathematician in 1599, where he was joined by Kepler, who inherited his observations when he died.

Brahma in Hinduism, the creator of the cosmos, who forms with Vishnu and Siva the Trimurti, or three aspects of the absolute spirit.

In the Hindu creation myth, Brahma, the demiurge, is born from the unfolding lotus flower that grows out of Vishnu's navel; after Brahma creates the world, Vishnu wakes and governs it for the duration of the cosmic cycle *kalpa*, the "day of Brahma," which lasts for 4,200 million earthly years. Unlike Brahman, which is an impersonal principle and of neuter gender, Brahma is a personified god and of masculine gender.

***Brahms** The composer in his study.*

Brahman in Hinduism, the supreme being, an abstract, impersonal world-soul into whom the *atman*, or individual soul, will eventually be absorbed when its cycle of rebirth is ended.

Brahmanism the earliest stage in the development of ◊Hinduism. Its sacred scriptures are the ◊Vedas, with their accompanying literature of comment and explanation known as Brahmanas, Aranyakas, and Upanishads.

Brahmaputra river in Asia 1,800 mi/2,900 km long, a tributary of the Ganges.

It rises in the Himalayan glaciers as Zangbo and runs E through Tibet, to the mountain mass of Namcha Barwa. Turning S, as the Dihang, it enters India and flows into the Assam valley near Sadiya, where it is now known as the Brahmaputra. It flows generally W until, shortly after reaching Bangladesh, it turns S and divides into the Brahmaputra proper, without much water, and the main stream, the Jamuna, which joins the Padma arm of the Ganges. The river is navigable for 800 mi/1,285 km from the sea.

Brahma Samaj Indian monotheistic religious movement, founded in 1830 in Calcutta by Ram Mohun Roy, who attempted to recover the simple worship of the Vedas and purify Hinduism. The movement had split into a number of sects by the end of the 19th century and is now almost defunct.

Brahms Johannes 1833–1897. German composer, pianist, and conductor. Considered one of the greatest composers of symphonic music and of songs, his works include four symphonies; ◊lieder (songs); concertos for piano and for violin; chamber music; sonatas; and the choral *A German Requiem* 1868. He performed and conducted his own works.

In 1853 the violinist Joachim introduced him to Liszt and Schumann. From 1868 Brahms made his home in Vienna. Although his music has romantic qualities, it is essentially a sophistication of the Classical tradition from the point to which Beethoven had brought it.

Brăila port in Romania on the river Danube; 106 mi/170 km from its mouth; population (1983) 226,000. It is a naval base. Industries include the manufacture of artificial fibers, iron and steel, machinery, and paper. It was controlled by the Ottoman Empire 1544–1828.

Braille system of writing for the blind. Letters are represented by a combination of raised dots on paper or other materials, which are then read by touch. It was invented in 1829 by Louis Braille (1809–52), who became blind at the age of three.

brain in higher animals, a mass of interconnected ◊nerve cells, forming the anterior part of the ◊central nervous system, whose activities it coordinates and controls. In ◊vertebrates, the brain is

brain

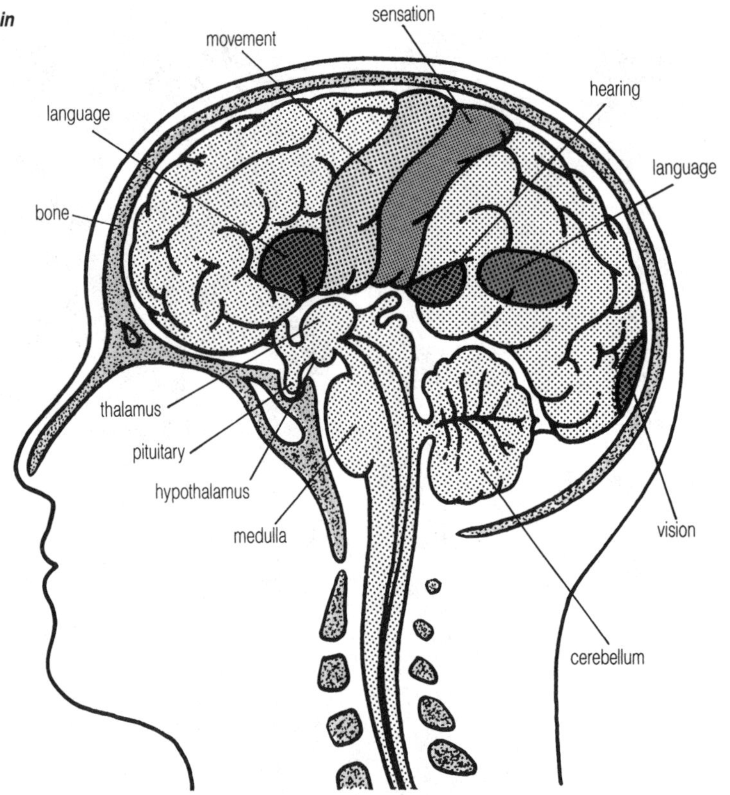
sensation
movement
hearing
language
language
bone
thalamus
pituitary
hypothalamus
medulla
vision
cerebellum

brain *Cross-section of a human brain, showing the surface of the left half of the cerebrum and sections through the midbrain, pons, medulla oblongata, and cerebellum.*

contained by the skull. An enlarged portion of the upper spinal cord, the medulla oblongata, contains centers for the control of respiration, heartbeat rate and strength, and blood pressure. Overlying this is the cerebellum, which is concerned with coordinating complex muscular processes such as maintaining posture and moving limbs. The cerebral hemispheres (cerebrum) are paired outgrowths of the front end of the forebrain, in early vertebrates mainly concerned with the senses, but in higher vertebrates greatly developed and involved in the integration of all sensory input and motor output, and in intelligent behavior.

In vertebrates, many of the nerve fibers from the two sides of the body cross over as they enter the brain, so that the left cerebral hemisphere is associated with the right side of the body and vice versa. In humans, a certain asymmetry develops in the two halves of the cerebrum. In right-handed people, the left hemisphere seems to play a greater role in controlling verbal and some mathematical skills, whereas the right hemisphere is more involved in spatial perception. In general, however, skills and abilities are not closely localized. In the brain, nerve impulses are passed across ◊synapses by neurotransmitters, in the same way as in other parts of the nervous system.

In mammals the cerebrum is the largest part of the brain, carrying the cerebral cortex. This consists of a thick surface layer of cell bodies (gray matter), below which fiber tracts (white matter) connect various parts of the cortex to each other and to other points in the central nervous system. As cerebral complexity grows, the surface of the brain becomes convoluted into deep folds. In higher mammals, there are large unassigned areas of the brain that seem to be connected with intelligence, personality, and higher mental faculties. Language is controlled in two special regions usually in the left side of the brain: Broca's area governs the ability to talk, and Wernicke's area is responsible for the comprehension of spoken and written words. In 1990, scientists at Johns Hopkins University, Baltimore, succeeded in culturing human brain cells.

brain damage impairment that can be caused by trauma (for example, accidents) or disease (such as encephalitis), or which may be present at birth. Depending on the area of the brain that is affected, language, movement, sensation, judgment, or other abilities may be impaired.

Braine John 1922–1986. English novelist. His novel *Room at the Top* 1957 created the character of Joe Lampton, one of the first of the northern working-class antiheroes.

brainstem central core of the brain, where the top of the spinal cord merges with the undersurface of the brain.

The oldest part of the brain in evolutionary terms, the brainstem is the body's life-support center, containing regulatory mechanisms for vital functions such as breathing, heart rate, and blood pressure. It is also involved in controlling the level of consciousness by acting as a relay station for nerve connections to and from the higher centers of the brain.

In many countries, death of the brainstem is now formally recognized as death of the person as a whole. Such cases are the principal donors of organs for transplant. So-called "beating-heart donors" can be maintained for a limited period by life-support equipment.

Brain Trust nickname applied to an informal group of experts who advised US president F D Roosevelt on his New Deal policy.

brake device used to slow down or stop the movement of a moving body or vehicle. The mechanically applied caliper brake used on bicycles uses a scissor action to press hard rubber blocks against the wheel rim. The main braking system of a car works hydraulically: when the driver depresses the brake pedal, liquid pressure forces pistons to apply brakes on each wheel.

Two types of car brakes are used. Disc brakes are used on the front wheels of some automobiles and on all wheels of sports and performance automobiles, since they are the more efficient and less prone to fading (losing their braking power) when they get hot. Braking pressure forces brake pads against both sides of a steel disk that rotates with the wheel. Drum brakes are fitted on the rear wheels of some automobiles and on all wheels of some passenger automobiles. Braking pressure forces brake shoes to expand outward into contact with a drum rotating with the wheels. The brake pads and shoes have a tough ◊friction lining that grips well and withstands wear.

Many trucks and trains have air brakes, which work by compressed air. On landing, jet planes reverse the thrust of their engines to reduce their speed quickly. Space vehicles use retrorockets for braking in space, and use the air resistance, or drag of the atmosphere, to slow down when they return to Earth.

Bramante Donato c. 1444–1514. Italian Renaissance architect and artist. Inspired by Classical designs, he was employed by Pope Julius II in rebuilding part of the Vatican and St Peter's in Rome.

bramble any prickly bush of a genus *Rubus* belonging to the rose family Rosaceae. Examples are ◊blackberry, raspberry, and dewberry.

Branagh Kenneth 1960– . British actor and director. He launched his Renaissance Theatre Company in 1987, was a notable Hamlet and Touchstone in 1988, and in 1989 directed and starred in a film of Shakespeare's *Henry V*.

Brancusi Constantin 1876–1957. Romanian sculptor, active in Paris from 1904, a pioneer of abstract forms and conceptual art. He was one of the first sculptors in the 20th century to carve directly from his material, working with marble, granite, wood, and other materials. He developed increasingly simplified natural or organic forms, such as the sculpted head that gradually came to resemble an egg (*Sleeping Muse* 1910, Musée National d'Art Moderne, Paris). By the 1930s he had achieved monumental simplicity with structures of simple repeated forms (*Endless Column* and other works in Tirgu Jiu public park, Romania). Brancusi was revered by his contemporaries and remains a seminal figure in 20th-century sculpture.

In 1904 he walked from Romania to Paris, where he worked briefly in Rodin's studio. He began to explore direct carving in marble (producing many versions of Rodin's *The Kiss*).

Brand Dollar (Adolf Johannes) 1934– . Former name of the South African jazz musician Abdullah ◊Ibrahim.

Brandeis Louis Dembitz 1856–1941. US jurist. Born in Louisville, Kentucky, Brandeis was educated at Harvard and was admitted to the bar 1877. As a crusader for progressive causes, Brandeis helped draft social welfare and labor legislation. In 1916, with his appointment to the US Supreme Court by President Wilson, he became the first Jewish justice and maintained his support of individual rights in his opposition to the 1917 Espionage Act and in his dissenting opinion in the first wiretap case, *Olmstead* v *US* 1928. Brandeis University in Waltham, Massachusetts, is named in his honor.

Brandenburg administrative *Land* (state) of the Federal Republic of Germany
area 10,000 sq mi/25,000 sq km
capital Potsdam
towns Cottbus, Brandenburg, Frankfurt-on-Oder
products iron and steel, paper, pulp, metal products, semiconductors
population (1990) 2,700,000
history the Hohenzollern rulers who took control of Brandenburg in 1415 later acquired the powerful duchy of Prussia and became emperors of Germany. At the end of World War II, Brandenburg lost over 5,000 sq mi/12,950 sq km of territory when Poland advanced its frontier to the line of the Oder and Neisse rivers. The remainder, which became a region of East Germany, was divided 1952 into the districts of Frankfurt-on-

brake

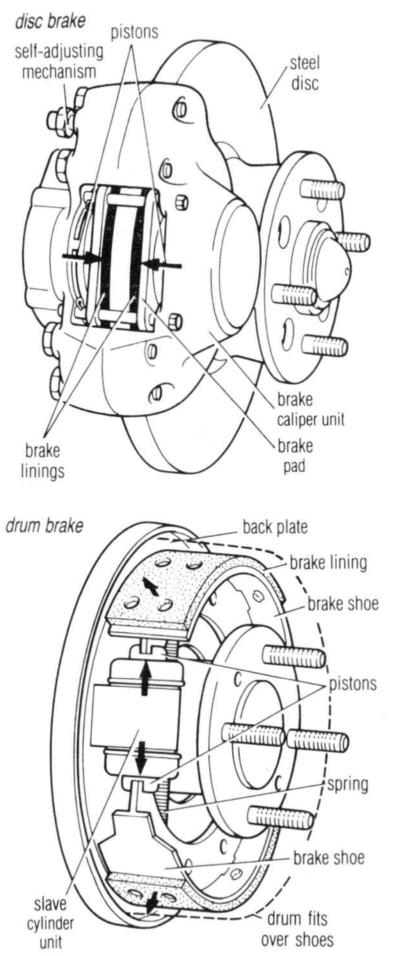
disc brake
pistons
self-adjusting mechanism
steel disc
brake caliper unit
brake pad
brake linings
drum brake
back plate
brake lining
brake shoe
pistons
spring
brake shoe
slave cylinder unit
drum fits over shoes

Oder, Potsdam, and Cottbus. When Germany was reunited 1990, Brandenburg reappeared as a state of the Federal Republic.

Brandenburg town in the Federal Republic of Germany, on the river Havel; 36 mi/60 km W of Berlin; population (1981) 94,700. Industries include textiles, automobiles, and aircraft. It has a 12th-century cathedral.

Brando Marlon 1924– . Actor Marlon Brando, whose casual style, mumbling speech, and use of ◊Method acting earned him a place as a distinctive actor. He won best-actor Academy Awards for *On the Waterfront* 1954 and *The Godfather* 1972. He made his Broadway debut in *I Remember Mama* 1944, appeared in *Candida* 1946, and achieved fame in *A Streetcar Named Desire* 1947.

His films include *The Men* 1950, *A Streetcar Named Desire* 1951, *Julius Caesar* 1953, *The Wild One* 1954, *Mutiny on the Bounty* 1962, *Last Tango in Paris* 1973, *Apocalypse Now* 1979, and *The Freshman* 1990.

Brandt Bill 1905–1983. British photographer who produced a large body of richly printed and romantic black-and-white studies of people, London life, and social behavior.

Brandt Willy. Adopted name of Karl Herbert Frahm 1913– . German Socialist politician, federal chancellor (premier) of West Germany 1969–74. He played a key role in the remolding of the Social Democratic Party (SPD) as a moderate Socialist force (leader 1964–87). As mayor of West Berlin 1957–66, Brandt became internationally known during the Berlin Wall crisis 1961. He received the Nobel Peace Prize 1971.

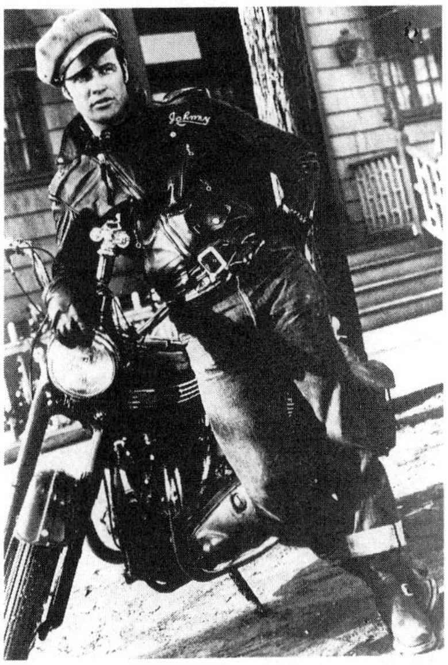

Brando *Marlon Brando as the rebellious biker Johnny in* The Wild One *1954.*

Brandt, born in Lübeck, changed his name when he fled to Norway 1933 and became active in the anti-Nazi resistance. He returned 1945 and entered the Bundestag (federal parliament) 1949. In the "grand coalition" 1966–69 he served as foreign minister and introduced Ostpolitik, a policy of reconciliation between East and West Europe, which was continued when he became federal chancellor 1969, and culminated in the 1972 signing of the Basic Treaty with East Germany.

He resigned from the chancellorship 1974 following the discovery that an aide had been an East German spy. Brandt continued to wield considerable influence in the SPD, in particular over the party's new radical left wing. He chaired the ◊Brandt Commission on Third World problems 1977–83 and was a member of the European Parliament 1979–83.

Brandt Commission officially the Independent Commission on International Development Issues, established in 1977 and chaired by the former West German chancellor Willy ◊Brandt. Consisting of 18 eminent persons acting independently of governments, the commission examined the problems of developing countries and sought to identify corrective measures that would command international support. It was disbanded in 1983.

Its main report, published in 1980 under the title *North-South: A Program for Survival*, made detailed recommendations for accelerating the development of poorer countries (involving the transfer of resources to the latter from the rich countries).

brandy (Dutch brandewijn "burned wine") alcoholic liquor distilled from fermented grape juice (wine). Best-known examples are produced in France, notably Armagnac and Cognac. Brandy can also be prepared from other fruits, for example, apples (Calvados) and cherries (Kirschwasser). Brandies contain up to 55% alcohol.

Braque Georges 1882–1963. French painter who, with Picasso, founded the Cubist movement around 1907–10. They worked together at L'Estaque in the south of France and in Paris. Braque began to experiment in collages and invented a technique of gluing paper, wood, and other materials to canvas. His later work became more decorative.

Brasília capital of Brazil from 1960, 3,000 ft/1,000 m above sea level; population (1980) 411,500. It was designed by Lucio Costa (1902–1963), with Oscar Niemeyer as chief archi-

brass

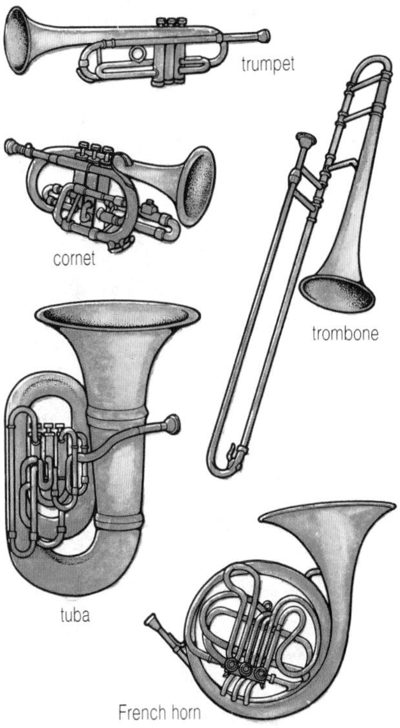
trumpet
cornet
trombone
tuba
French horn

tect, as a completely new city to bring life to the interior.

Braşov (Hungarian *Brassó*, German *Krondstadt*) industrial city (machine tools, industrial equipment, chemicals, cement, woolens) in central Romania at the foot of the Transylvanian Alps; population (1985) 347,000. It belonged to Hungary until 1920.

brass metal ◊alloy of copper and zinc, with not more than 5% or 6% of other metals. The zinc content ranges from 20% to 45%, and the color of brass varies accordingly from coppery to whitish yellow. Brasses are characterized by the ease with which they may be shaped and machined; they are strong and ductile, resist many forms of corrosion, and are used for electrical fittings, ammunition cases, screws, household fittings, and ornaments.

Brasses are usually classed into those that can be worked cold (up to 25% zinc) and those that are better worked hot (about 40% zinc).

brass in music, instruments made of brass or other metal, which are directly blown through a "cup" or "funnel" mouthpiece.

In the symphony orchestra they comprise: the French horn, a descendant of the natural hunting horn, valved, and curved into a circular loop, with a wide bell; the trumpet, a cylindrical tube curved into an oblong, with a narrow bell and three valves (the state fanfare trumpet has no valves); the trombone, an instrument with a "slide" to vary the effective length of the tube (the sackbut, common from the 14th century, was its forerunner); the tuba, normally the lowest-toned instrument of the orchestra; valved and with a very wide bore to give sonority, it has a bell that points upward.

In the brass band (in descending order of pitch) they comprise: the cornet, three-valved instrument, looking like a shorter, broader trumpet, and with a wider bore; the flugelhorn, valved instrument, rather similar in range to the cornet; the tenor horn; B-flat baritone; euphonium; trombone; and bombardon (bass tuba). A brass band normally also includes bass and side drums, triangle, and cymbals.

Brassäi Adopted name of Gyula Halesz 1899–1986. French photographer of Hungarian origin. From the early 1930s on he documented, mainly by flash, the nightlife of Paris, before turning to more abstract work.

Brassica genus of plants of the family Cruciferae. The most familiar species is the common cabbage *Brassica oleracea*, with its varieties broccoli, cauliflower, kale, and brussels sprouts.

In 1990 US experiments in cross-pollinating the wild cabbage *B. campestris* with related varieties of cultivated cabbage, turnip, and rutabaga produced a new plant having a life cycle of only five weeks. It is now being used in US schools to enable pupils to carry out plant-breeding experiments that can produce ten generations in one year.

Bratislava (German *Pressburg*) industrial port (engineering, chemicals, oil refining) in Czechoslovakia, on the river Danube; population (1986) 417,000. It was the capital of Hungary 1526–1784 and is now capital of the Slovak Socialist Republic and second-largest city in Czechoslovakia.

Brattain Walter Houser 1902–1987. US physicist. In 1956 he was awarded a Nobel Prize jointly with William Shockley and John Bardeen for their work on the development of the transistor, which replaced the comparatively costly and clumsy vacuum tube in electronics.

He was born in Amoy, China, the son of a teacher. From 1929 to 1967 he was on the staff of Bell Telephone Laboratories.

Brauchitsch Walther von 1881–1948. German field marshal. A staff officer in World War I, he became in 1938 commander in chief of the army and a member of Hitler's secret cabinet council. He was dismissed after his failure to invade Moscow 1941. Captured in 1945, he died before being tried in the ◊Nuremburg trials.

Braun Eva 1910–1945. German mistress of Adolf Hitler. Secretary to Hitler's photographer and personal friend, Heinrich Hoffmann, she became Hitler's mistress in the 1930s and married him in the air-raid shelter of the Chancellery in Berlin on April 29, 1945. The next day they committed suicide together.

Braunschweig German form of ◊Brunswick.

Brautigan Richard 1935–1984. US novelist, author of playful fictions set in California, such as *Trout Fishing in America* 1967, and Gothic works like *The Hawkline Monster* 1974.

Brazil Largest country in South America, (almost half the continent) bounded SW by Uruguay, Argentina, Paraguay and Bolivia; W by Peru and Colombia; N by Venezuela, Guyana, Suriname, and French Guiana; and E by the Atlantic Ocean.

government Brazil is a federal republic of 23 states, three territories, and a federal district (Brasília). A two-chamber national congress consisting of a senate of 69 members (on the basis of one senator per state) elected for an eight-year term, and a chamber of deputies, whose numbers vary, elected for a four-year term. The number of deputies is determined by the population of each state, and each territory is represented by one deputy. Elections to both chambers are by universal suffrage. The cabinet is chosen by the president, who is elected by universal adult suffrage for a five-year term and is not eligible for re-election. The states and the federal district each have an elected governor.

history Inhabited by various South American Indians, Brazil was colonized by the Portuguese from AD 1500. In 1808, after ◊Napoleon invaded Portugal, King John VI moved his capital from Lisbon to Rio de Janeiro. In 1821 he returned to Lisbon, leaving his son, Crown Prince Pedro, as regent. In 1822 Pedro declared Brazil an independent kingdom, and took the title Emperor Pedro I. His son, Pedro II, persuaded large numbers of Portuguese to emigrate, and the center of Brazil developed quickly, largely on the basis of slavery. In 1888 slavery was abolished and in 1889 a republic was founded, followed by the adoption of a constitution for a federated nation in 1891.

After social unrest in the 1920s, the world economic crisis of 1930 produced a revolt that brought Dr Getúlio Vargas to the presidency. He held office, as a benevolent dictator, until the army forced him to resign in 1945 and General Eurico Dutra became president. In 1951 Vargas returned to power but committed suicide in 1954 and was succeeded by Dr Juscelino Kubitschek.

In 1961 Dr Jânio Quadros became president but resigned after seven months, to be succeeded by Vice President Joâo Goulart. Suspecting him of left-wing leanings, the army forced a restriction of presidential powers and created the office of prime minister. A referendum in 1963 brought back the presidential system, with Goulart choosing his own cabinet.

In a bloodless coup in 1964, General Castelo Branco assumed dictatorial powers and banned all political groupings except for two artificially created parties, the pro-government National Renewal Alliance (ARENA) and the opposition Brazilian Democratic Movement Party (PMBD). In 1967 Branco named Marshal da Costa e Silva as his successor, and a new constitution was adopted. In 1969 da Costa e Silva resigned because of ill health, and a military junta took over. In 1974 General Ernesto Geisel became president until succeeded by General Baptista de Figueiredo in 1978. In 1979 the ban on opposition parties was lifted.

President Figueiredo held office until 1985, his last few years as president witnessing economic decline, strikes, and calls for the return of democracy. In 1985 Tancredo Neves became the first civilian president in 21 years, but died within months of taking office. He was succeeded by Vice President José ◊Sarney, who continued to work with Neves's cabinet and policies. The constitution was again amended to allow direct presidential elections. In March 1989 the moderate members of PMDB and the Liberal Party Front (PFL), pulled out of their coalition with PMDB, forcing President Sarney to reconstruct the government.

In the Dec 1989 presidential election Fernando Collor of the National Reconstruction Party (PRN) narrowly defeated Luis Inacio da Silva of the Workers' Party. He advocated free-market economic policies and a crackdown on government corruption. Collor de Mello created his own political party, the National Reconstruction Party. In the Oct 1990 general elections, despite wins for

Brazil
Federative Republic of
(República Federativa do Brasil)

Guyana
Venezuela
Surinam
Fr. Guiana
Colombia
BRAZIL
Peru
Brasília
Bolivia
Rio de Janeiro
São Paulo
PACIFIC OCEAN
Paraguay
ATLANTIC OCEAN
Uruguay
0 500 miles
0 1000 km

area 3,285,618 sq mi/8,511,965 sq km
capital Brasília
cities São Paulo, Belo Horizonte, Curitiba, Manaus, Fortaleza; ports are Rio de Janeiro, Belém, Recife, Pôrto Alegre, Salvador
physical the densely forested Amazon basin covers the northern half of the country with a network of rivers; the south is fertile; enormous energy resources, both hydroelectric (Itaipú dam on the Paraná, and Tucurui on the Tocantins) and nuclear (uranium ores)
features Mount Roraima, Xingu National Park; Amazon delta; Rio harbor
head of state and government Fernando Affonso Collor de Mello from 1989
political system emergent democratic federal republic
political parties Social Democratic Party (PDS), moderate left-of-center; Brazilian Democratic Movement Party (PMDB), center-left; Liberal Front Party (PFL), moderate left-of-center; Workers' Party, left-of-center; National Reconstruction Party (PRN), center-right
exports coffee, sugar, soybeans, cotton, textiles, timber, motor vehicles, iron, chrome, manganese, tungsten and other ores, as well as quartz crystals, industrial diamonds, gemstones; the world's sixth-largest arms exporter
currency cruzado
population (1990 est) 153,770,000 (including 200,000 Indians, survivors of 5 million, especially in Rondonia and Mato Grosso, mostly living on reservations); growth rate 2.2% p.a.
life expectancy men 61, women 66
language Portuguese (official); 120 Indian languages
religion Roman Catholic 89%; Indian faiths
literacy men 79%/women 76% (1985 est)
GDP $352 bn (1988); $2,434 per head
chronology
1822 Independence achieved from Portugal; ruled by Dom Pedro, son of the refugee King John VI of Portugal.
1889 Monarchy abolished, and republic established.
1891 Constitution for a federal state adopted.
1930 Dr Getulio Vargas became president.
1945 Vargas deposed by the military.
1946 New constitution adopted.
1951 Vargas returned to office.
1954 Vargas committed suicide.
1956 Juscelino Kubitschek became president.
1960 Capital moved to Brasília.
1961 João Goulart became president.
1964 Bloodless coup made Gen Castelo Branco president; he assumed dictatorial powers, abolishing free political parties.
1967 New constitution adopted. Branco succeeded by Marshal da Costa e Silva.
1969 Da Costa e Silva resigned, and a military junta took over.
1974 Gen Ernesto Geisel became president.
1978 Gen Baptista de Figueiredo became president.
1979 Political parties legalized again.
1984 Mass calls for a return to fully democratic government.
1985 Tancredo Neves became first civilian president in 21 years. Neves died and was succeeded by the vice-president, José Sarney.
1988 New constitution approved, transferring power from the president to the congress. Measures announced to halt large-scale burning of Amazonian rainforest for cattle grazing.
1989 Forest Protection Service and Ministry for Land Reform abolished; Fernando Collor (PRN) elected president Dec, pledging free-market economic policies.
1990 Government won the general election offset by mass abstentions.

the PRN, widespread abstentions showed disillusionment with President Collor's policies.

Brazil nut seed, rich in oil and highly nutritious, of the gigantic South American tree *Bertholletia excelsa*. The seeds are enclosed in a hard outer casing, each fruit containing 10–20 seeds arranged like the segments of an orange. The timber of the tree is also valuable.

brazing method of joining two metals by melting an ◊alloy into the joint. It is similar to soldering but takes place at a much higher temperature. Copper and silver alloys are widely used for brazing, at temperatures up to about 1,650°F/900°C.

Brazzaville capital of the Congo, industrial port (foundries, railroad repairs, shipbuilding, shoes, soap, furniture, bricks) on the river Zaïre, opposite Kinshasa; population (1984) 595,000.

There is a cathedral 1892 and the Pasteur Institute 1908. It stands on Pool Malebo (Stanley Pool).

Brazzaville was founded by the Italian Count Pierre Savorgnan de Brazza (1852–1905), employed in African expeditions by the French government. It was the African headquarters of the Free (later Fighting) French during World War II.

bread food baked from a kneaded dough or batter made with ground cereals, usually wheat, and water; many other ingredients may be added. The dough may be unleavened or raised (usually with yeast).

Bread has been a staple of human diet in many civilizations as long as agriculture has been practiced, and some hunter-gatherer peoples made it from crushed acorns or beech nuts. Potato, banana and cassava bread are among some local varieties, but most breads are made from fermented cereals which form glutens when mixed with water. The earliest bread was unleavened and was made from a mixture of flour and water and dried in the sun on flat stones. Leavened bread was first made in the ancient Near East and Egypt in brick ovens similar to ceramic kilns. The yeast creates gas, making the dough rise. Traditionally, bread has been made from whole grains: wheat, barley, rye and oats, ground into a meal. Modern manufacturing processes have changed this to optimize the profit and shorten the manufacturing time. Fermentation is speeded up using ascorbic acid and potassium bromide with fast-acting flour improvers. White bread was developed by the end of the 19th century by roller-milling, which removed the wheat germ to satisfy fashionable consumer demand. In modern bread, some of the nutrients removed in processing are replaced with synthetics, such as vitamins.

breadfruit fruit of the tropical trees *Artocarpus communis* and *A. altilis* of the mulberry family Moraceae. It is highly nutritious and when baked is said to taste like bread. It is native to many South Pacific islands.

Breakspear Nicholas. Original name of ◊Adrian IV, the only English pope.

bream deep-bodied, flattened fish *Abramis brama* of the carp family, growing to about 1.6 ft/50 cm, typically found in lowland rivers across Europe.

The sea-breams are also deep-bodied flattened fish, but belong to the family Sparidae, and are unrelated to the true breams. The red sea-bream *Pagellus bogaraveo* up to 1.5 ft/45 cm, is heavily exploited as a food fish in the Mediterranean.

Bream Julian (Alexander) 1933– . British virtuoso of the guitar and lute. He has revived much Elizabethan lute music and encouraged composition by contemporaries for both instruments. Britten and Henze have written for him.

breast one of a pair of organs on the upper front of the human female, also known as a ◊mammary gland. Each of the two breasts contains milk-producing cells, and a network of tubes or ducts that lead to an opening in the nipple.

Milk-producing cells in the breast do not become active until a woman has given birth to a baby. Breast milk is made from substances

breast

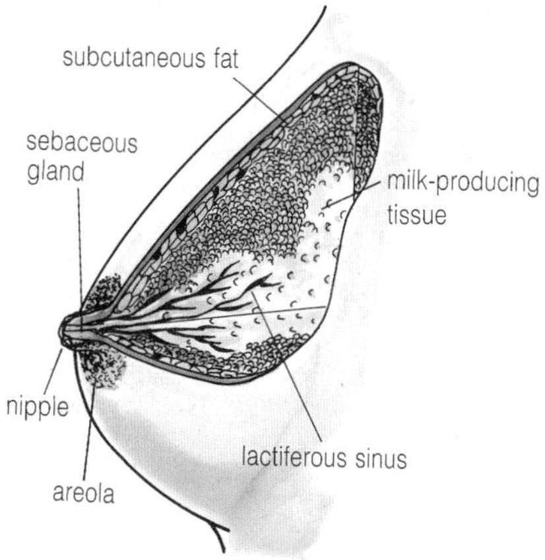
subcutaneous fat
sebaceous gland
milk-producing tissue
nipple
lactiferous sinus
areola

extracted from the mother's blood as it passes through the breasts. It contains all the nourishment a baby needs, including antibodies to help fight infection.

Breasted James Henry 1865–1935. US Orientalist. Born in Rockford, Illinois, Breasted was first trained as a pharmacist but later pursued studies in Egyptology at Yale University and the University of Berlin. He joined the faculty of the University of Chicago 1896, published *A History of Egypt* 1905, and directed the Chicago expedition to Egypt and Sudan 1905–07. Well known as the author of textbooks and popular works on the history of the ancient Near East, Breasted was the founder of the University of Chicago Oriental Institute, funded by John D Rockefeller, as a center of American archeological research.

Breathalyzer instrument for on-the-spot checking by the police of the amount of alcohol consumed by a suspect driver, who breathes into a plastic bag connected to a tube containing a chemical (such as a diluted solution of potassium dichromate in 50% sulfuric acid) that changes color. Another method is to use a gas chromatograph, again from a breath sample.

breathing in terrestrial animals, the muscular movements whereby air is taken into the lungs and then expelled, a form of ◊gas exchange. Breathing is sometimes referred to as external respiration, for true respiration is a cellular (internal) process.

Lungs are specialized for gas exchange but are not themselves muscular, consisting of spongy material. In order for oxygen to be passed to the blood and carbon dioxide removed, air is forced in and out of the chest region by the ribs and accompanying intercostal muscles, the rate of breathing being controlled by the brain. High levels of activity lead to a greater demand for oxygen and a subsequent higher rate of breathing.

breccia a coarse clastic ◊sedimentary rock, made up of broken fragments (clasts) of pre-existing rocks. It is similar to ◊conglomerate but the fragments in breccia are large and jagged.

Brecht Bertolt 1898–1956. German dramatist and poet, who aimed to destroy the "suspension of disbelief" usual in the theater and to express Marxist ideas. He adapted John Gay's *Beggar's Opera* as *Die Dreigroschenoper/The Threepenny Opera* 1928, set to music by Kurt Weill. Later plays include *Mutter Courage/Mother Courage* 1941, set during the Thirty Years' War, and *Der kaukasische Kreidekreis/The Caucasian Chalk Circle* 1949.

As an anti-Nazi, he left Germany in 1933 for Scandinavia and the US. He became an Austrian citizen after World War II; in 1949 he established the Berliner Ensemble theater group in East Germany.

Breda town in North Brabant, the Netherlands; population (1988) 156,000. It was here that

Brecht *German dramatist and poet Bertolt Brecht.*

Charles II of England made the declaration that paved the way for his restoration 1660.

Breda, Treaty of 1667 treaty that ended the Second Anglo-Dutch War (1664–67). By the terms of the treaty, England gained New Amsterdam, which was renamed New York.

breed a recognizable group of domestic animals, within a species, with distinctive characteristics that have been produced by ◊artificial selection.

breeder reactor in nuclear physics, a reactor in which more fissionable material is produced (breeding) than is consumed in running it. Breeder reactors are typically operated by and for the military to produce plutonium-239, the fissile material used in the nuclear weapons industry. Although uranium-235 is fissile, it comprises less than 1% of uranium ore, an amount too small to supply the weapons industry. Therefore, non-fissile uranium-238, which is plentiful, comprising 99% of uranium ore, is used instead, in breeder reactors, to manufacture fissile plutonium-239.

This is done by wrapping a blanket of U-238 around the core of a nuclear reactor. The fission process of the reactor-core material (usually U-235) produces excess neutrons that are captured by the U-238, which transmutes by beta decay into the highly unstable isotope U-239, which in turn through beta decay transmutes into the highly unstable isotope neptunium-239, which in turn undergoes beta decay to transmute into fissile Pu-239.

breeding in biology, the crossing and selection of animals and plants to change the characteristics of an existing ◊breed or ◊cultivar (variety), or to produce a new one.

Bremen industrial port (iron, steel, oil refining, chemicals, aircraft, shipbuilding, cars) in Germany, on the Weser 43 mi/69 km from the open sea; population (1988) 522,000.

Bremen was a member of the ◊Hanseatic League, and a free imperial city from 1646. It became a member of the North German Confederation 1867 and of the German Empire 1871.

Bremen administrative region (German *Land*) of Germany, consisting of the cities of Bremen and Bremerhaven; area 154 sq mi/400 sq km; population (1988) 652,000.

Bremerhaven formerly (until 1947) Wesermünde port at the mouth of the Weser, Germany; population (1988) 132,000. Industries include fishing and shipbuilding. It serves as an outport for Bremen.

Bremerton city in W Washington, SW of Seattle and NW of Tacoma, on an inlet of Puget Sound. It serves as a port for the area's fish, dairy, and lumber products. Tourism is also important to the economy; population (1990) 38,142.

Brendel Alfred 1931– . Austrian pianist, known for his fastidious and searching interpretations of Beethoven, Schubert, and Liszt. The author of *Musical Thoughts and Afterthoughts* 1976 and *Music Sounded Out* 1990.

Brennan Christopher (John) 1870–1932. Australian Symbolist poet, influenced by Baudelaire and Mallarmé. Although one of Australia's greatest poets, he is virtually unknown outside his native country. His complex, idiosyncratic verse includes *Poems* 1914 and *A Chant of Doom and Other Verses* 1918.

Brennan Walter 1894–1974. US actor, often seen in Westerns as the hero's sidekick. His work includes *The Westerner* 1940, *Bad Day at Black Rock* 1955, and *Rio Bravo* 1959.

Brennan William Joseph, Jr 1906– US jurist and associate justice of the US Supreme Court 1956–90. Considered a moderate liberal, his vote was usually cast with the majority during the years of the Court under Chief Justice Earl ◊Warren, but he became a key liberal influence when the court majority, under chief justices ◊Burger and ◊Rehnquist, shifted to the conservative side in the 1980s. He is especially noted for writing the majority opinions in *Baker* v *Carr* 1962, in which state voting reapportionment ensured "one person, one vote," and in *US* v *Eichman* 1990, which ruled that the law banning desecration of the flag was a violation of the right to free speech as provided for in the First Amendment.

Born in Newark, New Jersey, Brennan graduated from the University of Pennsylvania and Harvard Law School. A New Jersey superior court 1949–52 and supreme court 1952–56 judge, he was appointed to the US Supreme Court by President Eisenhower. Brennan wrote many important Supreme Court majority decisions that assured the freedoms set forth in the First Amendment and established the rights of minority groups. He retired from the Court 1990, citing health reasons.

Brenner Sidney 1927– . South African scientist, one of the pioneers of genetic engineering. Brenner discovered messenger ◊RNA (a link between ◊DNA and the ◊ribosomes in which proteins are synthesized) 1960. Brenner first studied medicine, but then moved into molecular biology at Oxford University. He worked for many years with Francis Crick, doing much research on nematode worms.

Brenner Pass lowest of the Alpine passes, 4,495 ft/1,370 m; it leads from Trentino–Alto Adige, Italy, to the Austrian Tirol, and is 12 mi/19 km long.

Brentano Franz 1838–1916. German-Austrian philosopher and psychologist whose *Psychology from the Empirical Standpoint* 1874 developed the concept of "intentionality," the directing of the mind to an object; for example, in perception.

Brentano Klemens 1778–1842. German writer, leader of the Young ◊Romantics. He published a seminal collection of folktales and songs with Ludwig von ◊Arnim (*Des Knaben Wunderhorn*) 1805–08, and popularized the legend of the Lorelei (a rock in the river ◊Rhine). He also wrote mystic religious verse, as in *Romanzen vom Rosenkranz* 1852.

Brescia (ancient *Brixia*) historic and industrial city (textiles, engineering, firearms, metal products) in N Italy, 52 mi/84 km E of Milan; population (1988) 199,000. It has medieval walls and two cathedrals (12th and 17th centuries).

Breslau German name of ◊Wrocław, town in Poland.

Brest naval base and industrial port (electronics, engineering, chemicals) on Rade de Brest (Brest Roads), a great bay at the western extremity of Bretagne, France; population (1983) 201,000. Occupied as a U-boat base by the Germans 1940–44, the town was destroyed by Allied bombing and rebuilt.

Brest town in Byelorussia, USSR, on the river Bug and the Polish frontier; population (1987) 238,000. It was in Poland (*Brześć nad Bugiem*) until 1795 and again 1921–39. The Treaty of ◊Brest-Litovsk (an older Russian name of the town) was signed here.

Brest-Litovsk, Treaties of treaty signed by Russia with Germany, Austria-Hungary, and their allies toward the end of World War I. Under the second, Russia agreed to recognize the independence of Georgia, Ukraine, Poland and the Baltic states, and to pay heavy compensation. Under the Nov 1918 Armistice that ended World War I, they were annulled, since Russia was one of the winning allies.

Bretagne region of NW France, see ◊Brittany.

Brétigny, Treaty of treaty made between Edward III of England and John II of France in 1360 at the end of the first phase of the Hundred Years' War, under which Edward received Aquitaine and its dependencies in exchange for renunciation of his claim to the French throne.

Breton André 1896–1966. French author, among the leaders of the ◊Dadaart movement. *Les Champs magnétiques/Magnetic Fields* 1921, an experiment in automatic writing, was one of the products of the movement. He was also a founder of ◊Surrealism, publishing *Le Manifeste de surréalisme/Surrealist Manifesto* 1924. Other works include *Najda* 1928, the story of his love affair with a medium.

Breton language member of the Celtic branch of the Indo-European language family; the language of Brittany in France, related to Welsh and Cornish, and descended from the speech of Celts who left Britain as a consequence of the Anglo-Saxon invasions of the 5th and 6th centuries. Officially neglected for centuries, Breton is now a recognized language of France.

Bretton Woods township in New Hampshire where the United Nations Monetary and Financial Conference was held in 1944 to discuss postwar international payments problems. The agreements reached on financial assistance and measures to stabilize exchange rates led to the creation of the International Bank for Reconstruction and Development in 1945 and the International Monetary Fund (IMF).

There were 44 nations represented at the conference, which considered proposals by the US, UK, and Canadian governments. The IMF became a specialized agency of the UN 1947. The "Bretton Woods" system was based on a policy of fixed exchange rates, the elimination of exchange restrictions, currency convertibility, and a multilateral system of international payments.

Breuer Josef 1842–1925. Viennese physician, one of the pioneers of psychoanalysis. He applied it successfully to cases of hysteria, and collaborated with Freud in *Studien über Hysterie/Studies in Hysteria* 1895.

Breuer Marcel 1902–1981. Hungarian-born architect and designer who studied and taught at the ◊Bauhaus school in Germany. His tubular steel chair 1925 was the first of its kind. He moved to England, then to the US, where he was in partnership with Walter Gropius 1937–40. His buildings show an affinity with natural materials; they include the Bijenkorf, in Rotterdam (with Elzas) 1953.

Breuil Henri 1877–1961. French prehistorian, professor of historic ethnography and director of research at the Institute of Human Paleontology, Paris, from 1910. He established the genuine antiquity of Paleolithic cave art and stressed the anthropological approach to human prehistory.

breviary (Latin, "a summary or abridgement") in the Roman Catholic church, the book of instructions for reciting the daily services. It is usually in four volumes, one for each season.

brewing the making of ◊beer, ale, or other alcoholic beverage from ◊malt and ◊barley by steeping (mashing), boiling, and fermenting. The term is also used to describe the industry that makes all alcoholic drinks.

Mashing the barley releases the sugar maltose. Yeast is then added, which contains the enzymes needed to convert the maltose into ethanol (alcohol) and carbon dioxide. Hops are added to give a bitter taste.

brewster unit (abbreviation B) for measuring the reaction of optical materials to stress, defined in terms of the slowing down of light passing through the material when it is stretched or compressed.

***Brezhnev** Soviet leader Leonid Brezhnev. Appointed General Secretary of the Communist Party in 1964 and President in 1977, he held both offices until his death.*

Brezhnev Leonid Ilyich 1906–1982. Soviet leader. A protégé of Stalin and Khrushchev, he came to power (after he and ◊Kosygin forced Khrushchev to resign) as general secretary of the Soviet Communist Party (CPSU) 1964–82 and was president 1977–82. Domestically he was conservative; abroad the USSR was established as a military and political superpower during the Brezhnev era, extending its influence in Africa and Asia.

Brezhnev, born in the Ukraine, joined the CPSU in the 1920s. In 1938 he was made head of propaganda by the new Ukrainian party chief Khrushchev and ascended in the local party hierarchy. After World War II he caught the attention of the CPSU leader Stalin, who inducted Brezhnev into the secretariat and Politburo 1952. Brezhnev was removed from these posts after Stalin's death 1953, but returned 1956 with Khrushchev's patronage. In 1960, as criticism of Khrushchev mounted, Brezhnev was moved to the ceremonial post of state president and began to criticize Khrushchev's policies.

Brezhnev stepped down as president 1963 and returned to the Politburo and secretariat. He was elected CPSU general secretary 1964, when Khrushchev was ousted, and gradually came to dominate the conservative and consensual coalition. In 1977 he regained the additional title of state president under the new constitution. He suffered an illness (thought to have been a stroke or heart attack) March–April 1976 that was believed to have affected his thought and speech so severely that he was not able to make decisions. These were made by his entourage, for example committing the troops to Afghanistan to prop up the government. Within the USSR, economic difficulties mounted; the Brezhnev era was a period of caution and stagnation, although outwardly imperialist.

Brezhnev Doctrine Soviet doctrine 1968 designed to justify the invasion of Czechoslovakia. It laid down for the USSR as a duty the direct maintenance of "correct" socialism in countries within the Soviet sphere of influence. In 1979 it was extended, by the invasion of Afghanistan, to the direct establishment of "correct" socialism in countries not already within its sphere. The doctrine was renounced by Mikhail ◊Gorbachev in 1989. Soviet troops were withdrawn from Afghanistan and the satellite states of E Europe were allowed to decide their own forms of government, with non-communist and "reform communist" governments being established from Sept 1989.

Brian Havergal 1876–1972. English composer of 32 symphonies in visionary romantic style, including the *Gothic* 1919–27 for large choral and orchestral forces.

Brian known as Brian Boru ("Brian of the Tribute") 926–1014. High king of Ireland from 976, who took Munster, Leinster, and Connacht to become ruler of all Ireland. He defeated the Norse at Clontarf, thus ending Norse control of Dublin, although he was himself killed. He was the last high king with jurisdiction over most of Scotland. His exploits were celebrated in several chronicles.

Briand Aristide 1862–1932. French radical Socialist politician. He was prime minister 1909–11, 1913, 1915–17, 1921–22, 1925–26 and 1929, and foreign minister 1925–32. In 1925 he concluded the ◊Locarno Pact (settling Germany's western frontier) and in 1928 the ◊Kellogg-Briand Pact renouncing war; in 1930 he outlined a scheme for a United States of Europe.

brick common building material, rectangular in shape, made of clay that has been fired in a kiln. Bricks are made by kneading a mixture of crushed clay and other materials into a stiff mud and extruding it into a ribbon. The ribbon is cut into individual bricks, which are fired at a temperature of up to about 1,800°F/1,000°C. Bricks may alternatively be pressed into shape in molds.

Refractory bricks used to line furnaces are made from heat-resistant materials such as silica and dolomite. They must withstand operating temperatures of 2,700°F/1,500°C or more. Sun-dried bricks of mud reinforced with straw were first used in Mesopotamia some 8,000 years ago. Similar mud bricks, called adobe, are still used today in Mexico and other areas where the climate is warm and dry.

bridewealth or ***brideprice*** goods or property presented by a man's family to his prospective wife's as part of the marriage agreement. It was the usual practice among many societies in Africa, Asia, and the Pacific, and among many American Indian groups. In most European and S Asian countries the alternative custom was called ◊dowry.

Bridewealth is regarded as compensation to the woman's family for giving her away in marriage, and it usually means that the children she bears will belong to her husband's family group rather than her own. It may require a large amount of valuables such as livestock, shell items, or cash.

bridge structure that provides a continuous path for pedestrians or vehicles over water, valleys, ravines, or other roads. Three basic designs and composites of these are based on the way they bear the weight of the bridge and its load. Beam, or girder, bridges are supported at each end by the ground with the weight thrusting downward. (Cantilever bridges are a complex form of girder.) Arch bridges thrust outward but downward at their ends; they are in compression. Suspension bridges use cables under tension to pull inward against anchorages on either side of the span, so that the roadway hangs from the main cables by the network of vertical cables. Some bridges are too low to allow traffic to pass beneath easily, so they are designed with movable parts, such as swing, vertical-lift and draw bridges.

In prehistory, people used logs or wove vines into ropes that were thrown across the obstacle. By 4,000 BC arched structures of stone and/or brick were used in the Near East, and the Romans are renowned for their long arched spans, many of which are still standing. Wooden bridges proved vulnerable to fire and rot and many were replaced with cast and wrought iron, but these too were disadvantaged by low tensile strength. The ◊Bessemer process produced steel that revolutionized bridgebuilding, since it became possible to design and construct long-lived framed structures that support great weight over long spans.

Today the longest spans are suspension bridges, with the measurement referring only to that part of the bridge actually suspended by cables.

bridge

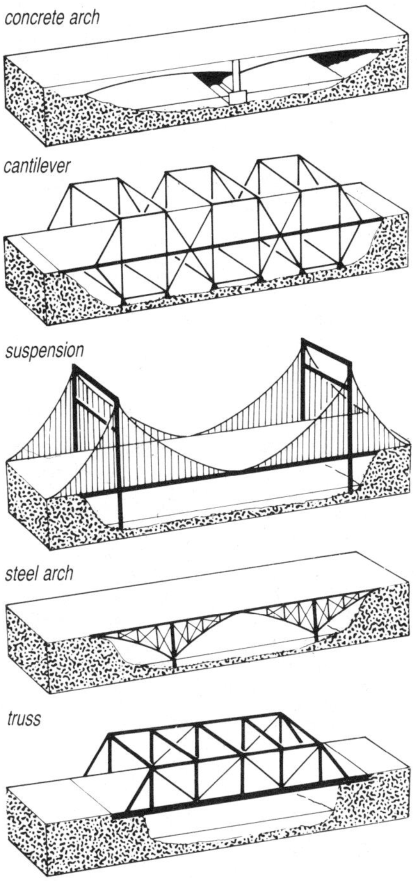
concrete arch
cantilever
suspension
steel arch
truss

bridge card game derived from whist. First played among members of the Indian Civil Service about 1900, bridge was brought to England in 1903 and played at the Portland Club in 1908. It is played in two forms: ◊auction bridge and ◊contract bridge.

Bridgeport city in Connecticut, on Long Island Sound; population (1990) 141,686. Industries include metal goods, electrical appliances, and aircraft, but many factories closed in the 1970s. The University of Bridgeport was established 1927. The P T Barnum Museum and Tom Thumb statue are here. Bridgeport was settled 1639.

Bridges Harry 1901–1990. US labor leader. Born in Melbourne, Australia, he ran away to sea and settled in San Francisco. In 1931 he formed a labor union of dockworkers, and in 1934, after police opened fire on a picket line, killing two strikers, he organized a successful general strike. He remained head of the International Longshoremen's and Warehousemen's Union for many years, despite Federal Bureau of Investigation objections (later proved false) that he had concealed membership in the Communist Party on his immigration papers.

Bridges Robert (Seymour) 1844–1930. British poet, poet laureate from 1913, author of *The Testament of Beauty* 1929, a long philosophical poem. In 1918 he edited and published posthumously the poems of Gerard Manley ◊Hopkins.

Bridgeton city in SW New Jersey at the head of the Cohansey river; seat of Cumberland county. Industries include food processing, glassmaking, clothing, and dairy products; population (1990) 18,942.

Bridgetown port and capital of Barbados, founded 1628; population (1987) 8,000. Sugar is exported through the nearby deep-water port.

Bridget, St 453–523. A patron saint of Ireland, also known as St Brigit or St Bride. She founded a church and monastery at Kildare, and is said to have been the daughter of a prince of Ulster. Feast day Feb 1.

Bridgman Percy Williams 1882–1961. US physicist. His research into machinery producing high pressure led in 1955 to the creation of synthetic diamonds by General Electric.

Born in Cambridge, Massachusetts, he was educated at Harvard, where he was Hollis Professor of Mathematics and Natural Philosophy 1926–50 and Higgins university professor 1950–54.

Brieux Eugène 1858–1932. French dramatist, an exponent of the naturalistic problem play attacking social evils. His most powerful plays are *Les trois filles de M Dupont* 1897; *Les Avariés/Damaged Goods* 1901, long banned for its outspoken treatment of syphilis; and *Maternité*.

Bright Richard 1789–1858. British physician who described many conditions and linked edema to kidney disease. Bright's disease, an inflammation of the kidneys, is named after him; see ◊nephritis.

Brighton resort on the E Sussex coast, England; population (1981) 146,000. It has Regency architecture and The Royal Pavilion 1782 in Oriental style. There are two piers and an aquarium. The University of Sussex was founded 1963.

history Originally a fishing village called Brighthelmstone, it became known as Brighton at the beginning of the 19th century, when it was already a fashionable health resort patronized by the Prince Regent, afterwards George IV. In 1990 the Royal Pavilion reopened after nine years of restoration.

brill flatfish *Scophthalmus levis*, living in shallow water over sandy bottoms in the NE Atlantic and Mediterranean.

Brillat-Savarin Jean Anthelme 1755–1826. French gastronome, author of *La Physiologie du Goût/ The Physiology of Taste* 1825, a compilation of observations on food and drink regarded as the first great classic of gastronomic literature. Most of his professional life was spent as a politician.

Brindisi (ancient *Brundisium*) port and naval base on the Adriatic, in Puglia, on the heel of Italy; population (1981) 90,000. Industries include food processing and petrochemicals. It is one of the oldest Mediterranean ports, at the end of the Appian Way from Rome. The poet Virgil died here 19 BC.

brine common name for salt water, a solution of sodium chloride (NaCl) in water. Brines are used extensively in the food manufacturing industry for canning vegetables, pickling vegetables (sauerkraut manufacture), and curing meat. Industrially, brine is the source from which chlorine, caustic soda (sodium hydroxide), and sodium carbonate are made.

Brinell Johann Auguste 1849–1925. Swedish engineer who devised the Brinell hardness test, for measuring the hardness of substances, in 1900.

Brinell hardness test test for the hardness of a substance according to the area of indentation made by a 0.4-in/10-mm hardened steel or sintered tungsten carbide ball under standard loading conditions in a test machine. The resulting Brinell number is equal to the load (kg) divided by the surface area (mm^2) and is named after its inventor Johann Brinell.

Brisbane industrial port (brewing, engineering, tanning, tobacco, shoes; oil pipeline from Moonie), capital of Queensland, E Australia, near the mouth of Brisbane river, dredged to carry ocean-going ships; population (1986) 1,171,300

brisling the processed form of sprat *Sprattus sprattus* a small herring, fished in Norwegian fjords, then seasoned and canned.

Brissot Jacques Pierre 1754–1793. French revolutionary leader, born in Chartres. He became a member of the legislative assembly and the National Convention, but his party of moderate republicans, the ◊Girondins, or Brissotins, fell foul of Robespierre, and Brissot was guillotined.

bristlecone pine see ◊pine.

bristletail primitive wingless insect of the order Thysanura. Up to 0.8 in/2 cm long, bristletails have a body tapering from front to back, two long antennae and three "tails" at the rear end.

They include the silverfish *Lepisma saccharina* and the firebrat *Thermobia domestica*. Two-tailed bristletails constitute another insect order, the Diplura. They live under stones and fallen branches, feeding on decaying material.

Bristol industrial port (aircraft engines, engineering, microelectronics, tobacco, chemicals, paper, printing), administrative headquarters of Avon, SW England; population (1986) 391,000. The old docks have been redeveloped for housing, industry, yachting facilities, and the National Lifeboat Museum. Further developments include a new city center, with Brunel's Temple Meads railroad station at its focus, and a weir across the Avon nearby to improve the waterside environment.

features 12th-century cathedral; 14th-century St Mary Redcliffe; 16th-century Acton Court, built by Sir Nicholas Poynz, a courtier of Henry VIII; the Georgian residential area of Clifton; the Clifton Suspension Bridge designed by Brunel and his *SS Great Britain*, which is being restored in dry dock.

history John Cabot sailed from here 1497 to Newfoundland, and there was a great trade with the American colonies and the West Indies in the 17th–18th centuries, including slaves. The poet Chatterton was born here.

Bristol city located in Virginia and Tennessee (the states' border runs through the center of the city), NE of Knoxville. This dual city is divided politically, but one unit economically. Manufactures include lumber, steel, office machines, pharmaceuticals, missile parts, and textiles; population (1990) 23,421 (Tennessee), 18,426 (Virginia).

Bristol city in central Connecticut, SW of Hartford. Known as the clock-making capital of the US, its manufactures also include tools and machinery parts; population (1990) 60,640.

Britain or Great Britain island off the NW coast of Europe, one of the British Isles. It consists of ◊England, ◊Scotland, and ◊Wales, and is part of the ◊United Kingdom. The name is derived from the Roman name Britannia, which in turn is derived from ancient Celtic name of the inhabitants, *Bryttas*.

Britain, ancient the period in the British Isles, excluding Ireland, from prehistory to the Roman occupation. After the last glacial retreat of the Ice Age about 15,000 BC, Britain was inhabited by hunters who became neolithic farming villagers. They built stone circles and buried their chiefs in ◊barrow mounds. Around 400 BC Britain was conquered by the ◊Celts and 54 BC by the Romans under Julius Caesar; ◊Boudicca led an uprising against their occupation.

Britain, Battle of World War II air battle between German and UK air forces over Britain lasting from July 10 to Oct 12, 1940.

At the outset the Germans had the advantage because they had seized airfields in the Netherlands, Belgium, and France, which were basically safe from attack and from which SE England was within easy range. On Aug 1, 1940 the Luftwaffe had about 4,500 aircraft of all kinds, compared to about 3,000 for the RAF. The Battle of Britain had been intended as a preliminary to the German invasion plan *Seelöwe* (Sea Lion), which Hitler indefinitely postponed Sept 17 and abandoned Oct 10, choosing instead to invade the USSR.

Britannicus Tiberius Claudius c. AD 41–55. Roman prince, son of the Emperor Claudius and Messalina; so-called from his father's expedition to Britain. He was poisoned by Nero.

British Antarctic Territory colony created in 1962 and comprising all British territories S of latitude 60° S: the South Orkney Islands, the South Shetland Islands, the Antarctic Peninsula and all adjacent lands, and Coats Land, extending to the South Pole; total land area 170,874 sq mi/ 660,000 sq km. Population (exclusively scientific personnel): about 300.

British Columbia

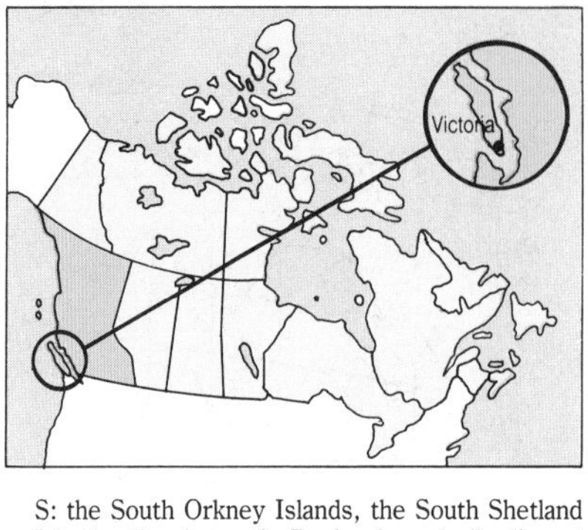

British Broadcasting Corporation (BBC) in the UK, the state-owned broadcasting network. It operates television and national and local radio stations, and is financed solely by the sale of television viewing licenses. It is not allowed to carry advertisements, but overseas radio broadcasts (World Service) have a government subsidy.

The BBC was converted from a private company (established 1922) to a public body 1927.

British Columbia province of Canada on the Pacific

area 365,851 sq mi/947,800 sq km

capital Victoria

towns Vancouver, Prince George, Kamloops, Kelowna

physical Rocky Mountains and Coast Range; deeply indented coast; rivers include the Fraser and Columbia; over 80 lakes; more than half the land is forested

products fruit and vegetables; timber and wood products; fish; coal, copper, iron, lead; oil and natural gas; hydroelectricity

population (1986) 2,889,000

history Captain Cook explored the coast in 1778; a British colony was founded on Vancouver Island in 1849, and the gold rush of 1858 extended settlement to the mainland; it became a province in 1871. In 1885 the Canadian Pacific Railroad linking British Columbia to the E coast was completed.

British Commonwealth of Nations former official name of the ◊Commonwealth.

British East India Company a commercial company 1600–1858 chartered by Queen Elizabeth I and given a monopoly of trade between England and the Far East. In the 18th century it became, in effect, the ruler of a large part of India, and a form of dual control by the company and a committee responsible to Parliament in London was introduced by Pitt's India Act 1784. The end of the monopoly of China trade came 1834, and after the ◊Sepoy Rebellion 1857 the crown took complete control of the government of British India; the India Act 1858 abolished the company.

British Empire the various territories all over the world conquered or colonized by Britain from about 1600, most now independent or ruled by other powers; the British Empire was at its largest at the end of World War I, with over 25% of the world's population and area. The ◊Commonwealth is composed of former and remaining territories of the British Empire.

The first successful British colony was Jamestown, Virginia, founded 1607. British settlement spread up and down the east coast of North America and by 1664, when the British secured New Amsterdam (New York) from the Dutch, continuous colonies existed from the present South Carolina to what is now New Hampshire. The attempt of George III and his minister Lord North to coerce the colonists into paying special taxes to Britain roused them to resistance, which came to a head in the ◊American Revolution 1775–81 and led to the creation of the United States of America from the 13 English colonies then lost.

Colonies and trading posts were set up in many parts of the world by the British, who also captured them from other European empire builders. Settlements were made in Gambia and on the Gold Coast of Africa 1618; in Bermuda 1609 and other islands of the West Indies; Jamaica was taken from Spain 1655; in Canada, Acadia (Nova Scotia) was secured from France by the Treaty of Utrecht 1713, which recognized Newfoundland and Hudson Bay (as well as Gibraltar in Europe) as British. New France (Québec), Cape Breton Island, and Prince Edward Island became British as a result of the Seven Years' War 1756–63.

In the Far East, the ◊East India Company, chartered 1600, set up trading posts. The company steadily increased its possessions up to the eve of the Indian Mutiny (or Sepoy Rebellion) 1857. Although this revolt was put down, it resulted in the taking over of the government of British India by the crown 1858; Queen Victoria was proclaimed empress of India Jan 1, 1877. Ceylon (now Sri Lanka) had also been annexed to the East India Company 1796, and Burma (now Myanmar), after a series of Anglo-Burmese Wars from 1824, became a province of British India 1886. Burma and Ceylon became independent 1948 and the republic of Sri Lanka dates from 1972. British India, as the two dominions of India and Pakistan, was given independence in 1947. In 1950 India became a republic but remained a member of the Commonwealth.

Constitutional development in Canada started with an act of 1791 which set up Lower Canada (Québec), mainly French-speaking, and Upper Canada (Ontario), mainly English-speaking. Discontent led to rebellion in both Canadas 1837. After the suppression of these uprisings, Lord Durham was sent out to advise on the affairs of British North America. In accordance with his recommendations, the two Canadas were united 1840 and given a representative legislative council. With the British North America Act 1867, the self-governing dominion of Canada came into existence.

In New Zealand and Australia, colonization began with the desire to find a place for penal settlement after the loss of the original American colonies. The first shipload of British convicts landed in Australia 1788 on the site of the future city of Sydney. New South Wales was opened to free settlers 1819, and in 1853 transportation of convicts was abolished. An act of Parliament created the federal commonwealth of Australia, an independent dominion, 1901. New Zealand was created a dominion 1907.

The Cape of Good Hope in South Africa was occupied by two English captains 1620, but neither the home government nor the East India Company was interested. The Dutch occupied it from 1650 until 1795 when, French revolutionary armies having occupied the Dutch Republic, the British seized it to keep it from the French. Under the Treaty of Paris 1814 Britain bought it from the Netherlands. It was proclaimed a British colony 1843.

The need to find new farmland and establish independence from British rule led a body of Boers (Dutch "farmers") from the Cape to make the Great Trek northeast 1836, to found Transvaal and Orange Free State. Conflict between the British government and the Boers culminated in the Boer War 1899–1902, which brought Transvaal and Orange Free State under British sovereignty. Given self-government 1907, they were formed, with Cape Colony and Natal, into the Union of South Africa 1910. The British South Africa Company, chartered 1889, extended British influence over Southern Rhodesia and Northern Rhodesia; with Nyasaland, the Rhodesias were formed into a federation 1953–63 with

British Empire

current name	colonial names and history	colonized	independent
India	British E India Co. 18th cent.–1858	18th cent.	1947
Pakistan	British E India Co. 18th cent.–1858	18th cent.	1947
Sri Lanka	Portuguese, Dutch 1602–1796; Ceylon 1802–1972	16th cent.	1948
Ghana	Gold Coast	1618	1957
Nigeria		1861	1960
Cyprus	Turkish to 1878, then British rule	1878	1960
Sierra Leone	British protectorate	1788	1961
Tanzania	German E Africa to 1921; British mandate from League of Nations/UN as Tanganyika	19th cent.	1961
Jamaica	Spanish to 1655	16th cent.	1962
Trinidad & Tobago	Spanish 1532–1797; British 1797–1962	1532	1962
Uganda	British protectorate	1894	1962
Kenya	British colony from 1920	1895	1963
Malaysia	British interests from 1786; Federation of Malaya 1957–63	1874	1963
Malawi	British protectorate of Nyasaland 1907–53; Federation of Rhodesia & Nyasaland 1953–64	1891	1964
Malta	French 1798–1814	1798	1964
Zambia	N Rhodesia—British protectorate; Federation of Rhodesia & Nyasaland 1953–64	1924	1964
The Gambia		1888	1965
Singapore	Federation of Malaya 1963–65	1858	1965
Guyana	Dutch to 1796; British Guiana 1796–1966	1620	1966
Botswana	Bechuanaland—British protectorate	1885	1966
Lesotho	Basutoland	1868	1966
Bangladesh	British E India Co. 18th cent.–1858; British India 1858–1947; E Pakistan 1947–71	18th cent.	1971
Zimbabwe	S Rhodesia from 1923; UDI under Ian Smith 1965–79	1895	1980

representative government. Uganda was made a British protectorate 1894. Kenya became a colony 1920.

In W Africa, Sierra Leone colony was founded 1788 with the cession of a strip of land to provide a home for liberated slaves; a protectorate was established over the hinterland 1896. British influence in Nigeria began through the activities of the National Africa Company (the Royal Niger Company from 1886) which bought Lagos from an African chief 1861; in 1900 the two protectorates of N and S Nigeria were proclaimed. In 1921–22, under League of Nations mandate, some German colonies were ceded to Britain: Tanganyika was transferred to British administration, SW Africa to South Africa; and Cameroons and Togoland were divided between Britain and France.

The establishment of the greater part of Ireland as the Irish Free State, with dominion status, occurred 1922. A new constitution 1937 dropped the name and declared Ireland (Eire) to be a "sovereign independent state"; in 1949 Ireland became a republic outside the Commonwealth, though remaining in a special relationship with Britain.

British Expeditionary Force (BEF) a British army serving in France in World War I 1914–18. Also the 1939–40 army in Europe in World War II, which was evacuated from Dunkirk, France.

British Honduras former name of ◊Belize.

British Indian Ocean Territory British colony in the Indian Ocean directly administered by the Foreign and Commonwealth Office. It consists of the Chagos Archipelago some 1,200 mi/1,900 km NE of Mauritius

area 23 sq mi/60 sq km

features lagoons; US naval and air base on Diego Garcia

products copra, salt fish, tortoiseshell

population (1982) 3,000

history purchased in 1965 for $3 million by Britain from Mauritius to provide a joint US/UK base.

The island of Aldabra, Farquhar, and Desroches, some 300 mi/485 km N of Madagascar, originally formed part of the British Indian Ocean Territory but were returned to the administration of the Seychelles in 1976.

British Isles group of islands off the NW coast of Europe, consisting of Great Britain (England, Wales, and Scotland), Ireland, the Channel Islands, the Orkney and Shetland islands, the Isle of Man, and many other islands that are included in various counties, such as the Isle of Wight, Scilly Isles, Lundy Island, and the Inner and Outer Hebrides. The islands are divided from Europe by the North Sea, Strait of Dover, and the English Channel, and face the Atlantic to the W.

British Museum largest museum of the UK. Founded in 1753, it opened in London in 1759. Rapid additions led to the construction of the present buildings by 1852. In 1881 the Natural History Museum was transferred to South Kensington.

British Somaliland a British protectorate over 67,980 sq mi/176,000 sq km of territory on the Somali coast of Africa from 1884 until the independence of Somalia in 1960. British authorities were harassed by a self-proclaimed messiah known as the "Mad Mullah" from 1901 until 1910.

British thermal unit imperial unit (abbreviation Btu) of heat, now replaced in the SI system by the ◊joule (one British thermal unit is approximately 1,055 joules). Burning one cubic foot of natural gas releases about 1,000 Btu of heat.

One British thermal unit is defined as the amount of heat required to raise the temperature of 1 lb/0.45 kg of water by 1°F. The exact value depends on the original temperature of the water.

British Virgin Islands part of the ◊Virgin Islands group in the West Indies.

Brittany (French *Bretagne*) region of NW France in the Breton peninsula between the Bay of Biscay and the English Channel; area 10,499 sq mi/27,200 sq km; population (1987) 2,767,000. Its capital is Rennes and includes the *départements* of Côte-du-Nord, Finistère, Ille-et-Vilaine, and Morbihan. It is a farming region.

Bretagne was established by the Celts in the 5th century and was the Gallo-Roman province of Armorica after being conquered by Julius Caesar 56 BC. It was devastated by Norsemen after the Roman withdrawal. During the Anglo-Saxon invasion of Britain so many Celts migrated across the Channel that it was called Brittany. It became a strong, expansionist state that maintained its cultural and political independence, despite pressure from the Carolingians, Normans, and Capetians. In 1171, the duchy of Brittany was inherited by Geoffrey, son of Henry II of England, and remained in the Angevin dynasty's possession until 1203, when Geoffrey's son Arthur was murdered by King ◊John, and the title passed to the

Britten *English composer Benjamin Britten.*

Capetian Peter of Dreux. Under the Angevins, feudalism was introduced, and French influence increased under the Capetians. By 1547 it had been formally annexed by France, and the ◊Breton language was banned in education. A separatist movement developed after World War II, and there has been guerrilla activity.

Britten (Edward) Benjamin, 1913–1976. English composer. He often wrote for the individual voice; for example, the role in the opera *Peter Grimes* 1945, based on verses by Crabbe, was created for Peter ◊Pears. Among his many works are the *Young Person's Guide to the Orchestra* 1946; the chamber opera *The Rape of Lucretia* 1946; *Billy Budd* 1951; *A Midsummer Night's Dream* 1960; and *Death in Venice* 1973.

He studied at the Royal College of Music. From 1939 to 1942 he worked in the US, then returned to England and devoted himself to composing at his home in Aldeburgh, Suffolk, where he established an annual music festival. His oratorio *War Requiem* 1962 was written for the rededication of Coventry Cathedral.

brittle-star any member of the echinoderm class Ophiuroidea. A brittle star resembles a starfish, and has a small, central, rounded body and long, flexible, spiny arms used for walking. The small brittle-star *Amphipholis squamata* is greyish, about 2 in/4.5 cm across, and found on sea bottoms worldwide. It broods its young, and its arms can be luminous.

About 2,000 species of brittle-stars and basket-stars, whose arms are tangled and rootlike, are included in this group.

Brno industrial city in central Czechoslovakia (chemicals, arms, textiles, machinery); population (1984) 380,800. Now the third-largest city in Czechoslovakia, Brno was formerly capital of the Austrian crown land of Moravia.

broadbill primitive perching bird of the family Eurylaimidae, found in Africa and S Asia. Broadbills are forest birds and are often found near water. They are gregarious and noisy, have brilliant coloration and wide bills, and feed largely on insects.

broadcasting the transmission of sound and vision programs by ◊radio and ◊television.

In the US, broadcasting licenses are issued to public organizations and competing commercial companies by the Federal Communications Commission.

Television broadcasting entered a new era with the introduction of high-powered communications satellites in the 1980s. The signals broadcast by these satellites are sufficiently strong to be picked up by a small dish aerial located, for example, on the roof of a house. Direct broadcast by satellite thus became a feasible alternative to land-based television services. See also ◊cable television.

broad-leaved tree another name for a tree belonging to the ◊angiosperms, such as ash, beech, oak, maple, or birch. Their leaves are generally broad and flat, in contrast to the needlelike leaves of most ◊conifers. See also ◊deciduous tree.

Broadway major avenue in New York running from the tip of Manhattan NW and crossing Times Square at 42nd Street, at the heart of the theater district, where Broadway is known as "the Great White Way." New York theaters situated outside this area are described as off-Broadway; those even smaller and farther away are off-off-Broadway.

broccoli a variety of ◊cabbage.

Broch Hermann 1886–1951. Austrian novelist, who used experimental techniques in *Die Schlafwandler/The Sleepwalkers* 1932, *Der Tod des Vergil/The Death of Virgil* 1945, and *Die Schuldlosen/The Guiltless*, a novel in 11 stories. He moved to the US 1938 after being persecuted by the Nazis.

Brocken highest peak of the Harz Mountains (3,746 ft/1,142 m) in East Germany. On May 1 (Walpurgis night), witches are said to gather here.

brocket name for a male European red deer in its second year, when it has short, straight, pointed antlers. Brocket deer, genus *Mazama* include a number of species of small, shy, solitary deer found in Central and South America. They are up to 4 ft/1.3 m in body length and 2 ft/65 cm at the shoulder, and have similar small, straight antlers even when adult.

Brockton city in SW Massachusetts, S of Boston. Industries include footwear, tools, and electronic equipment; population (1990) 92,788.

broderie anglaise (French "English embroidery") a type of embroidered fabric, usually white cotton, in which holes are cut in patterns and oversewn, often to decorate lingerie, shirts, and skirts.

Brodsky Joseph 1940– . Russian poet, who emigrated to the US in 1972. His work, often dealing with themes of exile, is admired for its wit and economy of language, particularly in its use of understatement. Many of his poems, written in Russian, have been translated into English (*A Part of Speech* 1980). More recently he has also written in English. Nobel Prize 1987.

Broglie, de Louis, 7th Duc de Broglie 1892–1987. French theoretical physicist. He established that all subatomic particles can be described either by particle equations or by wave equations, thus laying the foundations of wave mechanics. He was awarded the 1929 Nobel Prize for Physics.

Broglie, de Maurice, 6th Duc de Broglie 1875–1960. French physicist. He worked on X-rays and gamma rays, and helped to establish the Einsteinian description of light in terms of photons. He was the brother of Louis de Broglie.

Broken Hill mining town in New South Wales, Australia; population (1981) 27,000. It is the base of the Royal Flying Doctor Service.

Broken Hill former name (until 1967) of ◊Kabwe, town in Zambia.

brolga or ***native companion***, Australian crane *Grus rubicunda*, about 5 ft/1.5 m tall, mainly gray with a red patch on the head.

Bromberg German name of ◊Bydgoszcz, port in Poland.

brome grass any annual grasses of the genus *Bromus* of the temperate zone; some are used for forage, but many are weeds.

bromeliad any tropical or subtropical plant of the pineapple family Bromeliaceae, usually with stiff leathery leaves and bright flower spikes.

Many tropical species are epiphytes on rainforest trees. The pineapple plant *Ananas comosus* is widely cultivated for its fleshy collective fruit, resembling a pine cone, developed from a flower spike. Spanish moss *Tillandsia usneoides*, another bromeliad, grows in long strands from the branches of trees in the SE US and tropical America.

Bromfield Louis 1896–1956. US novelist. Among his books are *The Strange Case of Miss Annie Spragg* 1928, *The Rains Came* 1937, and *Mrs Parkington* 1943, dealing with the golden age of New York society.

Broglie, de *1929 Nobel Prizewinner for physics, Louis de Broglie was a prominent member of the French Academy of Sciences.*

bromine (Greek *bromos* "stench") dark reddish-brown, nonmetallic element, a volatile liquid at room temperature, symbol Br, atomic number 35, atomic weight 79.904. It is a member of the ◊halogen group, has an unpleasant odor, and is very irritating to mucous membranes. Its salts are known as bromides.

Bromine was formerly extracted from salt beds, but is now mostly obtained from sea water, where it occurs in small quantities. Its compounds are used in photography and in the chemical and pharmaceutical industries.

bromocriptine drug that mimics the actions of the naturally occurring biochemical substance dopamine, a neurotransmitter. Bromocriptine acts on the pituitary gland to inhibit the release of prolactin, the hormone that regulates lactation, and thus reduces or suppresses milk production. It is also used in the treatment of ◊Parkinson's disease.

Bromocriptine may also be given to control excessive prolactin secretion and to treat prolactinoma (a hormone-producting tumor). Recent research has established its effectiveness in reversing some cases of infertility.

bronchiole small-bore air tube found in the vertebrate lung responsible for delivering air to the main respiratory surfaces. Bronchioles lead off from the larger bronchus and branch extensively before terminating in the many thousand alveoli that form the bulk of lung tissue.

bronchitis inflammation of the bronchi (air passages) of the lungs, usually caused initially by a viral infection, such as a cold or flu. It is aggravated by environmental pollutants, especially smoking, and results in a persistent cough, irritated mucus-secreting glands, and large amounts of sputum.

bronchodilator drug that relieves obstruction of the airways by causing the bronchi and bronchioles to relax and widen. It is most useful in the treatment of ◊asthma.

bronchus one of a pair of large tubes (bronchii) splitting off from the windpipe and passing into the vertebrate lung. Apart from their size, bronchii differ from the bronchioles in possessing cartilaginous rings, which give rigidity and prevent collapse during breathing movements.

Numerous glands secrete a slimy mucus, which traps dust and other particles; the mucus is constantly being propelled upward to the mouth by thousands of tiny hairs or cilia. The bronchus is adversely effected by several respiratory diseases and by smoking, which damages the cilia and therefore the lung cleaning mechanism.

Bronson Charles. Adopted name of Charles Bunchinsky 1922– . US film actor. His films are mainly violent thrillers such as *Death Wish* 1974. He was one of *The Magnificent Seven* 1960.

rontë family of English writers, including the three sisters Charlotte (1816–55), Emily Jane (1818–48) and Anne (1820–49), and their brother Patrick Branwell (1817–48). Their most enduring works are Charlotte Brontë's *Jane Eyre* 1847 and Emily Brontë's *Wuthering Heights* 1847. Later works include Anne's *The Tenant of Wildfell Hall* 1848 and Charlotte's *Shirley* 1849 and *Villette* 1853.

The Brontës were brought up by an aunt at Haworth rectory (now a museum) in Yorkshire. In 1846 the sisters published a volume of poems under the pen names Currer (Charlotte), Ellis (Emily) and Acton (Anne) Bell. In 1847 (using the same names), they published the novels *Jane Eyre*, *Wuthering Heights*, and *Agnes Grey*, Anne's much weaker work. During 1848–49 Branwell, Emily, and Anne all died of tuberculosis, aided in Branwell's case by alcohol and opium addiction; he is remembered for his portrait of the sisters. Charlotte married her father's curate, A B Nicholls, in 1854, and died during pregnancy.

brontosaurus former name of a type of large, plant-eating dinosaur, now known as ◊apatosaurus.

Bronx, the borough of New York City, NE of the Harlem River; area 109 sq km/ 42 sq mi; population (1990) 1,169,000. Largely residential, it is named after an early Dutch settler, James Bronck. The New York Zoological Society and Gardens are here, popularly called the Bronx Zoo and the Bronx Botanical Gardens.

bronze ◊alloy of copper and tin, yellow or brown in color. It is harder than pure copper, more suitable for ◊casting, and also resists ◊corrosion. Bronze may contain as much as 25% tin, together with small amounts of other metals, mainly lead.

Bronze is one of the first metallic alloys known and used widely by early peoples during the period of history known as the ◊Bronze Age.

Bell metal, the bronze used for casting bells, contains 15% or more tin. Phosphor bronze is hardened by the addition of a small percentage of phosphorus. Silicon bronze (for telegraph wires) and aluminum bronze are similar alloys of copper with silicon or aluminum and small amounts of iron, nickel, or manganese, but usually no tin.

Bronze Age stage of prehistory and early history when bronze became the first metal worked extensively and used for tools and weapons. It developed out of the Stone Age, preceded the Iron Age and may be dated 5000–1200 BC in the Middle East and about 2000–500 BC in Europe. Recent discoveries in Thailand suggest that the Far East, rather than the Middle East, was the cradle of the Bronze Age.

Mining and metalworking were the first specialized industries, and the invention of the wheel during this time revolutionized transport. Agricultural productivity (which began during the New Stone Age, or Neolithic, about 10,000 BC), and

Brontë *Emily, Anne, and Charlotte Brontë painted by their brother, Patrick Branwell, c. 1835.*

Brooks *Actress Louise Brooks started a rage for this hairstyle, which she used in her role of Lulu in* Pandora's Box *1928.*

hence the size of the population that could be supported, was transformed by the ox-drawn plow.

Bronzino Agnolo 1503–1572. Italian painter active in Florence, court painter to Cosimo I, Duke of Tuscany. He painted in an elegant, Mannerist style and is best known for portraits and the allegory *Venus, Cupid, Folly and Time* about 1545 (National Gallery, London).

Brooke Rupert Chawner 1887–1915. English poet, symbol of the World War I "lost generation." The five war sonnets (including "Grantchester" and "The Great Lover") and other poems, were published posthumously.

Brook Farm farm in W Roxbury, near Boston, Massachusetts, which was the scene of an idealistic experiment in communal living in 1841–47, led by George Ripley (1802–1880), a former Unitarian minister. Financial difficulties and a fire led to the community's dissolution.

Brooklyn borough of New York City, occupying the SW end of Long Island. It is linked to Manhattan Island by the Brooklyn-Battery Tunnel, the Brooklyn Bridge 1883, the Williamsburg and the Manhattan bridges, and to Staten Island by the Verrazano-Narrows Bridge 1964. Of the more than 60 parks, Prospect is the largest. There is also a museum, botanical garden, and the beach and amusement area at Coney Island.

Brooks Louise 1906–1985. US actress, known for her roles in silent films such as *Die Büchse der Pandora/Pandora's Box* 1928 and *Das Tagebuch einer Verlorenen/Diary of a Lost Girl* 1929, both directed by G W ◊Pabst. She retired from the screen 1938.

Brooks Mel. Adopted name of Melvin Kaminsky 1926– . US film director and comedian, known for madcap and slapstick verbal humor. He became well known with his record album *The 2,000-Year-Old Man* 1960. His films include *The Producers* 1968, *Blazing Saddles* 1974, *Young Frankenstein* 1975, *History of the World Part I* 1981, and *To Be or Not To Be* 1983.

Brooks Van Wyck 1886–1963. US literary critic and biographer. His five-volume *Makers and Finders: A History of the Writer in America, 1800-1915* 1936–52 was an influential series of critical works on US literature. The first volume *The Flowering of New England* 1936 won a Pulitzer prize.

An earlier work, *America's Coming-of-Age* 1915, concerned the Puritan heritage and its effects on American literature. His other works include studies of Mark Twain, Henry James, and Ralph Waldo Emerson.

broom any shrub of the legume family Leguminosae, especially species of the *Cytisus* and *Spartium*, often cultivated for their bright yellow flowers.

Brothers Karamazov, The a novel by Dostoievsky, published 1879–80. It describes the reactions and emotions of four brothers after their father's murder. One of them is falsely convicted of the crime, although his illegitimate brother is guilty.

Brouwer Adriaen 1605–1638. Flemish painter who studied with Frans Hals. He exceled in scenes of peasant revelry.

Brown "Capability" (Lancelot) 1715–1783. English landscape gardener. He acquired his nickname because of his continual enthusiam for the "capabilities" of natural landscapes.

Brown Charles Brockden 1771–1810. US novelist and magazine editor. He introduced the American Indian into fiction and is called the "father of the American novel" for his *Wieland* 1798, *Ormond* 1799, *Edgar Huntly* 1799, and *Arthur Mervyn* 1800. His works also pioneered the Gothic and fantastic traditions in US fiction.

Brown Ford Madox 1821–1893. British painter associated with the ◊Pre-Raphaelite Brotherhood. His pictures include *The Last of England* 1855 (Birmingham Art Gallery) and *Work* 1852–65 (City Art Gallery, Manchester), packed with realistic detail and symbolic incident.

Brown (James) Gordon 1951– . British Labor politician. He entered Parliament in 1983, rising quickly to the opposition front bench, with a reputation as an outstanding debater.

Brown John 1825–1883. Scottish servant and confidant of Queen Victoria from 1858.

Brown John 1800–1859. US slavery abolitionist. With 18 men, he seized, on the night of Oct 16, 1859, the government arsenal at Harper's Ferry in W Virginia, apparently intending to distribute weapons to runaway slaves who would then defend the mountain stronghold, which Brown hoped would become a republic of former slaves. On Oct 18 the arsenal was stormed by US Marines under Col Robert E ◊Lee. Brown was tried and hanged on Dec 2, becoming a martyr and the hero of the popular song "John Brown's Body" c. 1860.

Born in Connecticut, he settled as a farmer in Kansas in 1855. In 1856 he was responsible for the "Pottawatomie massacre" when five pro-slavery farmers were killed. In 1858 he formed the plan for a refuge for runaway slaves in the mountains of Virginia.

Brown Robert 1773–1858. Scottish botanist, a pioneer of plant classification and the first to describe and name the cell nucleus.

On an expedition to Australia in 1801 he collected 4,000 species of plant and later classified them using the "natural" system of Bernard de Jussieu (1699–1777) rather than relying upon the system of Carolus ◊Linnaeus. The agitated movement of small particles suspended in water, now explained by kinetic theory, was described by Brown in 1827 and later became known as Brownian motion.

Browne Robert 1550–1633. English Puritan leader, founder of the Brownists. He founded a community in Norwich, East Anglia, and in the Netherlands, which developed into present-day ◊Congregationalism.

Brownian movement the continuous random motion of particles in a fluid medium (gas or liquid) as they are subjected to impact from the molecules of the medium. The phenomenon was explained by Albert Einstein in 1905 but was observed as long ago as 1827 by the Scottish botanist Robert Brown (1773–1858).

Browning Robert 1812–1889. English poet, married to Elizabeth ◊Barrett Browning. His work is characterized by the use of dramatic monologue and an interest in obscure literary and historical figures. It includes the play *Pippa Passes* 1841 and the poems "The Pied Piper of Hamelin" 1842, "My Last Duchess" 1842, "Home Thoughts from Abroad" 1845, and "Rabbi Ben Ezra" 1864.

Browning, born in Camberwell, London, wrote his first poem "Pauline" 1833 under the influence of Shelley; it was followed by "Paracelsus" 1835 and "Sordello" 1840. From 1837 he achieved moderate success with his play *Strafford* and several other works. In the pamphlet series of *Bells and Pomegranates* 1841–46, which contained *Pippa Passes*, *Dramatic Lyrics* 1842 and *Dramatic Romances* 1845, he included the dramas *King Victor and King Charles*, *Return of the Druses*, and *Colombe's Birthday*.

Browning *Admired for his innovative works incorporating psychological analysis and obscure historical characters, Robert Browning was one of the most popular Victorian poets.*

In 1846 he met Elizabeth Barrett; they married the same year and went to Italy. There he wrote *Christmas Eve and Easter Day* 1850 and *Men and Women* 1855, the latter containing some of his finest love poems and dramatic monologues, which were followed by *Dramatis Personae* 1864 and *The Ring and the Book* 1868–69, based on an Italian murder story. After his wife's death in 1861 Browning settled in England and enjoyed an established reputation, although his later works, such as *Red-Cotton Night-Cap Country* 1873, *Dramatic Idylls* 1879–80, and *Asolando* 1889, prompted opposition by their rugged obscurity of style.

Browns Ferry site of a nuclear power station on the Alabama River, central Alabama. A nuclear accident in 1975 resulted in the closure of the plant for 18 months. This incident marked the beginning of widespread disenchantment with nuclear power in the US.

Brownshirts the SA (*Sturmabteilung*), or Storm Troops, the private army of the German Nazi party who derived their name from the color of their uniform.

Brownsville city in S Texas on the Rio Grande just before it flows into the Gulf of Mexico, S of Corpus Christi and N of Matamoros, Mexico; seat of Cameron county. It is a port of entry to the US. Industries include chemicals and food products. Tourism is also important; population (1990) 98,962. Originally Fort Taylor 1846, it was an important Confederate port during the Civil War.

Brown v Board of Education (of Topeka Kansas) a US Supreme Court decision 1954 that consolidated several suits challenging segregation laws in four states and the District of Columbia. The petitioner, Brown, was the father of a schoolgirl who lived near a school but was forced to travel across town to attend class in an all-black school. In a landmark decision the Court did away with the long-standing "separate but equal" doctrine of ◊*Plessy* v *Ferguson*, ruling that segregated educational facilities are intrinsically unequal and are therefore in violation of the 14th Amendment. Lower courts were directed to desegregate schools with all deliberate speed.

Brubeck Dave (David Warren) 1920– . US jazz pianist, a student of the French composer Milhaud and Arnold Schoenberg, inventor of the 12-tone

Bruckner *Austrian composer Anton Bruckner. He was often persuaded to abridge and modify the orchestration of his lengthy works, so there are problems in establishing authentic versions.*

composition system. The Dave Brubeck Quartet (formed 1951) combined improvisation with Classical discipline. Included in his large body of compositions is the internationally popular "Take Five."

Bruce one of the chief Scottish noble houses. Robert I (Robert the Bruce) and his son, David II, were both kings of Scotland descended from Robert de Bruis (died 1094), a Norman knight who came to England with William the Conqueror 1066.

Bruce James 1730–1794. Scottish explorer, the first European to reach the source of the Blue Nile 1770 and to follow the river downstream to Cairo 1773.

He was British consul at Algiers 1763–65.

Bruce Robert. King of Scotland; see ◊Robert I.

Bruce Stanley Melbourne, 1st Viscount Bruce of Melbourne 1883–1967. Australian National Party politician, prime minister 1923–29. He was elected to parliament in 1918. As prime minister he introduced a number of social welfare measures.

brucellosis disease of cattle, goats, and pigs, also known when transmitted to humans as undulant fever since it remains in the body and recurs. It was named after Australian doctor David Bruce (1855–1931), and is caused by bacteria (genus *Brucella*) present in the milk of infected cattle.

It has largely been eradicated in the West through vaccination of the animals and pasteurization of milk.

Bruch Max 1838–1920. German composer, professor at the Berlin Academy 1891. He wrote three operas including *Hermoine* 1872. Among the most celebrated of his works are the *Kol Nidrei* 1880 for cello and orchestra, the *Scottish Fantasy* for violin and orchestra, violin concertos, and many choral pieces.

Brücke, die (German "the bridge") German Expressionist art movement 1905–13, formed in Dresden. Ernst Ludwig Kirchner was one of its founders, and Emil Nolde, a member 1906–07. Influenced by African art, they strove for spiritual significance, using raw colors to express different emotions. In 1911 the ◊Blaue Reiter took over as the leading group in German art.

Bruckner (Joseph) Anton 1824–1896. Austrian Romantic composer. He was cathedral organist at Linz 1856–68, and from 1868 he was professor at the Vienna Conservatoire. His works include many choral pieces and twelve symphonies, the last two unfinished. His compositions were influenced by Richard ◊Wagner and Beethoven.

Bruderhof (German "Society of Brothers") Christian Protestant sect with beliefs similar to the ◊Mennonites. In the US they are known as Hutterites. They originated as an Anabaptist sect in Moravia in 1529. Jacob Hutter, a Swiss minister, was their leader until martyred 1536. They survived relentless persecution in the 16th and 17th centuries. Many emigrated to South Dakota in the 19th century and later to Canada. They live in groups of families (single persons are assigned to a family), marry only within the sect (divorce is not allowed), and retain a "modest" dress for women (cap or head scarf and long skirts).

Brueghel family of Flemish painters. Pieter Brueghel (c. 1525–1569) was one of the greatest artists of his time. He painted satirical and humorous pictures of peasant life, many of which include symbolic details illustrating folly and inhumanity, and a series of Months, (five survive), including *Hunters in the Snow* (Kunsthistorisches Museum, Vienna).

The elder Pieter was nicknamed "Peasant" Brueghel. Two of his sons were painters. Pieter Brueghel the Younger (1564–1638), called "Hell" Brueghel, specialized in religious subjects, and another son, Jan Brueghel (1568–1625), called "Velvet" Brueghel, painted flowers, land- and seascapes.

Bruges (Flemish *Brugge*) historic city in NW Belgium; capital of W Flanders province, 10 mi/16 km from the North Sea, with which it is connected by canal; population (1985) 117,700. Bruges was the capital of medieval ◊Flanders and was the chief European wool manufacturing town as well as its chief market.

features Among many fine buildings are the 14th-century cathedral, the church of Nôtre Dame with a Michelangelo statue of the Virgin and Child, the Gothic town hall and market hall; there are remarkable art collections. It was named for its many bridges. The College of Europe is the oldest center of European studies. The contemporary port handles coal, iron ore, oil, and fish. Local manufactures include lace, textiles, paint, steel, beer, furniture, and motors.

Brugge Flemish form of ◊Bruges, town in Belgium.

Brulé Étienne c. 1592–1632. French adventurer and explorer. He traveled with ◊Champlain to the New World in 1608 and settled in Québec, where he lived with the Algonquin Indians. He explored the Great Lakes and traveled as far south as Chesapeake Bay. Returning north, he was killed and eaten by Huron Indians.

Brummell Beau (George Bryan) 1778–1840. British dandy and leader of fashion. He introduced long trousers as conventional day and evening wear for men. A friend of the Prince of Wales, the future George IV, he later quarrelled with him, and was driven by gambling losses to exile in France in 1816 and died in an asylum.

Brundtland Gro Harlem 1939– . Norwegian Labor politician. Environment minister 1974–76, she briefly took over as prime minister 1981, and was elected prime minister in 1986 and again in 1990.

She chaired the World Commission on Environment and Development which produced the *Brundtland Report* 1987.

Brunei country on the N coast of the island of Borneo, bounded to landward side by Sarawak and to the N by the South China Sea.

government The 1959 constitution gives supreme authority to the sultan, advised by various councils. Since the constitution was suspended after a revolution in 1962, the sultan rules by decree. One political party is allowed, the Brunei National United Party (BNUP), a multiethnic splinter group formed by former members of the Brunei National Democratic Party (BNDP). While loyal to the sultan, it favors the establishment of an elected prime ministerial system. Other parties have been banned or have closed down.

history An independent Islamic sultanate from the 15th century, Brunei was a powerful state by the early 16th century, with dominion over all of Borneo, its neighboring islands, and parts of the Philippines. With the growing presence of the Portuguese and Dutch in the region its influence declined in the late 16th century.

In 1888 Brunei became a British protectorate, and under an agreement of 1906 accepted the appointment of a British Resident as adviser to the sultan. The discovery of large oil fields in the 1920s brought economic prosperity to Brunei. The country was occupied by the Japanese in 1941 and liberated by the Australians in 1945, when it was returned to Britain. In 1950 Sir Muda Omar Ali Saiffuddin Saadul Khairi Waddien (1916–86), popularly known as Sir Omar, became sultan.

In 1959, a new constitution gave Brunei internal self-government but made Britain responsible for defense and external affairs; a proposal in 1962 that Brunei should join the Federation of Malaysia was opposed by a revolution that was put down with British help. As a result the sultan decided to rule by decree. In 1967, he abdicated in favor of his son, Hassanal Bolkiah, but continued to be his chief adviser. In 1971 Brunei gained full internal self-government. In 1984 full independence was achieved, the sultan becoming prime minister, and minister of finance and home affairs, presiding over a cabinet of six, three of whom were close relatives. Britain agreed to maintain a small force to protect the oil and gas fields that make Brunei the wealthiest nation, per head, in Asia.

In 1985, the sultan cautiously allowed the formation of the loyal and reliable Brunei National Democratic Party (BNDP), an organization dominated by businessmen. A year later, ethnic Chinese and government employees (who were debarred from joining the BNDP) formed, with breakaway members of the other party, the Brunei National United Party (BNUP), the country's only political party after the dissolution of the BNDP 1988. Since the death of the sultan's father, Sir Omar, in 1986 the pace of political reform has quickened, with key cabinet portfolios being assigned to nonmembers of the royal family. A more nationalist socioeconomic policy has also begun, with preferential treatment given to native Malays in the commercial sphere rather than the traditional Chinese, and an Islamic state is being constructed.

During the Iranian arms scandal in 1987, it was revealed that the sultan of Brunei donated $10 million to the Nicaraguan *contras*.

Brunei Town former name (until 1970) of ◊Bandar Seri Begawan, Brunei.

Brunel Isambard Kingdom 1806–1859. British engineer and inventor. In 1833 he became engineer to the Great Western Railway, which adopted the 7 ft/2.1 m gauge on his advice. He built the Clifton Suspension Bridge over the Avon river at Bristol and the Saltash Bridge over the Tamar river near Plymouth. His shipbuilding designs include the *Great Western* 1838, the first steamship to cross the Atlantic regularly; the *Great Britain* 1845, the first large iron ship to have a screw propeller; and the *Great Eastern* 1858, which laid the first transatlantic telegraph cable.

Brunelleschi Filippo 1377–1446. Italian Renaissance architect. One of the earliest Renaissance architects, he pioneered the scientific use of perspective. He was responsible for the construction of the dome of Florence Cathedral (completed 1438), a feat deemed impossible by many of his contemporaries.

Bruning Heinrich 1885–1970. German politician. Elected to the Reichstag (parliament) 1924, he led the Catholic Centre Party from 1929 and was federal chancellor (premier) 1930–32 when political and economic crisis forced his resignation.

Brünn German form of ◊Brno, a town in Czechoslovakia.

Brunei

The Islamic Sultanate of
(Negara Brunei Darussalam)

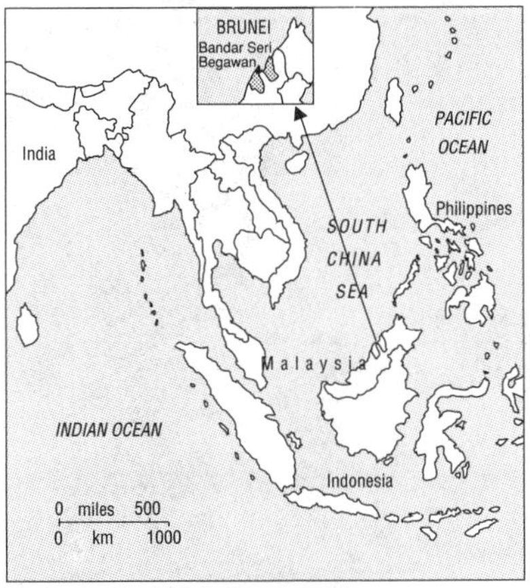
BRUNEI
Bandar Seri Begawan
India
PACIFIC OCEAN
Philippines
SOUTH CHINA SEA
Malaysia
INDIAN OCEAN
Indonesia
0 miles 500
0 km 1000

area 2,225 sq mi/5,765 sq km
capital and chief port Bandar Seri Begawan
cities Tutong, Seria, Kuala Belait
physical flat coastal plain with hilly lowland in W and mountains in E; 75% of the area is forested; the Limbang valley splits Brunei in two, and its cession to Sarawak 1890 is disputed by Brunei
features Temburong, Tutong, and Belait rivers; Mount Pagon (6,070 ft/1,850 m)
head of state and of government HM Muda Hassanal Bolkiah Mu'izzaddin Waddaulah, Sultan of Brunei, from 1968
political system absolute monarchy
political parties Brunei National United Party (BNUP), Brunei National Democratic Party (banned 1988)
exports liquefied natural gas (world's largest producer) and oil, both expected to be exhausted by the year 2000
currency Brunei dollar
population (1990 est) 372,000 (65% Malay, 20% Chinese—few Chinese granted citizenship); growth rate 12% p.a.
life expectancy 74 years
language Malay (official), Chinese (Hokkien), English
religion 60% Muslim (official)
literacy 95%
GDP $3.4 bn (1985); $20,000 per head
chronology
1888 Brunei became a British protectorate.
1941–45 Occupied by Japan.
1959 Written constitution made Britain responsible for defense and external affairs.
1962 Sultan began rule by decree.
1963 Proposal to join Malaysia abandoned.
1967 Sultan abdicated in favor of his son, Hassanal Bolkiah.
1971 Brunei given internal self-government.
1975 UN resolution called for independence for Brunei.
1984 Independence achieved from Britain, with Britain maintaining a small force to protect the oil and gas fields.
1985 A "loyal and reliable" political party, the Brunei National Democratic Party (BNDP), legalized.
1986 Death of former sultan, Sir Omar. Formation of multiethnic Brunei National United Party (BNUP).
1988 BNDP banned.

Brunel *Isambard Kingdom Brunel designed and built the* Great Western *1836, the first steamship to cross the Atlantic on a regular schedule, and the* Great Eastern *1858, which laid the transatlantic cable.*

Bruno Giordano 1548–1600. Italian philosopher. He entered the Dominican order of monks 1563, but his skeptical attitude to Catholic doctrines forced him to flee Italy 1577. After visiting Geneva and Paris, he lived in England 1583–85, where he wrote some of his finest works. After returning to Europe, he was arrested by the ◊Inquisition 1593 in Venice and burned at the stake for his adoption of Copernican astronomy and his heretical religious views.

Bruno, St 1030–1101. German founder of the monastic Catholic ◊Carthusian order. He was born in Cologne, became a priest, and controlled the cathedral school of Rheims 1057–76. Withdrawing to the mountains near Grenoble after an ecclesiastical controversy, he founded the monastery at Chartreuse in 1084. Feast day Oct 6.

Brunswick (German *Braunschweig*) former independent duchy, a republic from 1918, which is now part of ◊Lower Saxony, Germany.

Brunswick (German *Braunschweig*) industrial city (chemical engineering, precision engineering, food processing) in Lower Saxony, Germany; population (1988) 248,000. It was one of the chief cities of N Germany in the Middle Ages and a member of the ◊Hanseatic League. It was capital of the duchy of Brunswick from 1671.

Brusa alternate form of ◊Bursa, a town in Turkey.

Brussels (Flemish *Brussel*; French *Bruxelles*) capital of Belgium, industrial city (lace, textiles, machinery, chemicals); population (1987) 974,000 (80% French-speaking, the suburbs Flemish-speaking). It is the headquarters of the European Economic Community and since 1967 of the international secretariat of ◊NATO. First settled in the 6th century, and a city from 1312, Brussels became the capital of the Spanish Netherlands 1530 and of Belgium 1830.
features It has fine buildings including the 13th-century church of Sainte Gudule; the Hôtel de Ville, Maison du Roi, and others in the Grand Place; the royal palace. The Musées Royaux des Beaux-Arts de Belgique hold a large art collection. The bronze fountain statue of a tiny naked boy urinating, the Manneken Pis (1388) is to be found here.

Brussels sprout one of the small edible buds along the stem of a variety (*Brassica oleracea* var. *gemmifera*) of ◊cabbage.

Brussels, Treaty of pact of economic, political, cultural, and military alliance established March 17, 1948, for 50 years, by the UK, France, and the Benelux countries, joined by West Germany and Italy 1955. It was the forerunner of the North Atlantic Treaty Organization and the European Community.

Brussilov Aleksei Alekseevich 1853–1926. Russian general, military leader in World War I who achieved major successes against the Austro-Hungarian forces in 1916. Later he was commander of the Red Army 1920, which drove the Poles to within a few miles of Warsaw before being repulsed by them.

Brutus Marcus Junius c. 78–42 BC. Roman soldier, a supporter of ◊Pompey (against Caesar) in the civil war. Pardoned by ◊Caesar and raised to high office by him, he nevertheless plotted Caesar's assassination to restore the purity of the Republic. Brutus committed suicide when he was defeated (with ◊Cassius) by ◊Mark Antony, Caesar's lieutenant, at Philippi 42 BC.

Bryan city in E Texas, NW of Houston; seat of Brazos county. Its industries include the manufacture of cotton gins; population (1990) 55,002.

Bryan William Jennings 1860–1925. US politician who campaigned unsuccessfully for the presidency three times: as the Populist and Democratic nominee 1896, as an anti-imperialist Democrat 1900, and as a Democratic tariff reformer 1908. He served as President Wilson's secretary of state 1913–15. In the early 1920s he was a leading fundamentalist and opponent of Clarence Darrow in the ◊Scopes monkey trial. He died shortly after from the strain.

Bryansk city in W central USSR, SW of Moscow on the Desna; population (1987) 445,000. Industries include lumber mills, textiles, and steel.

Bryant William Cullen 1794–1878. US poet and literary figure. His most famous poem, "Thanatopsis," was published 1817. He was coowner and coeditor of the *New York Evening Post* 1829–78

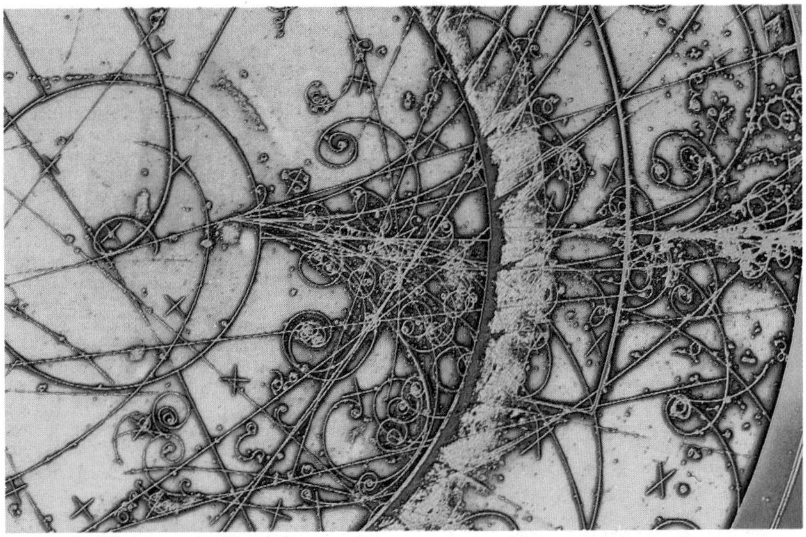

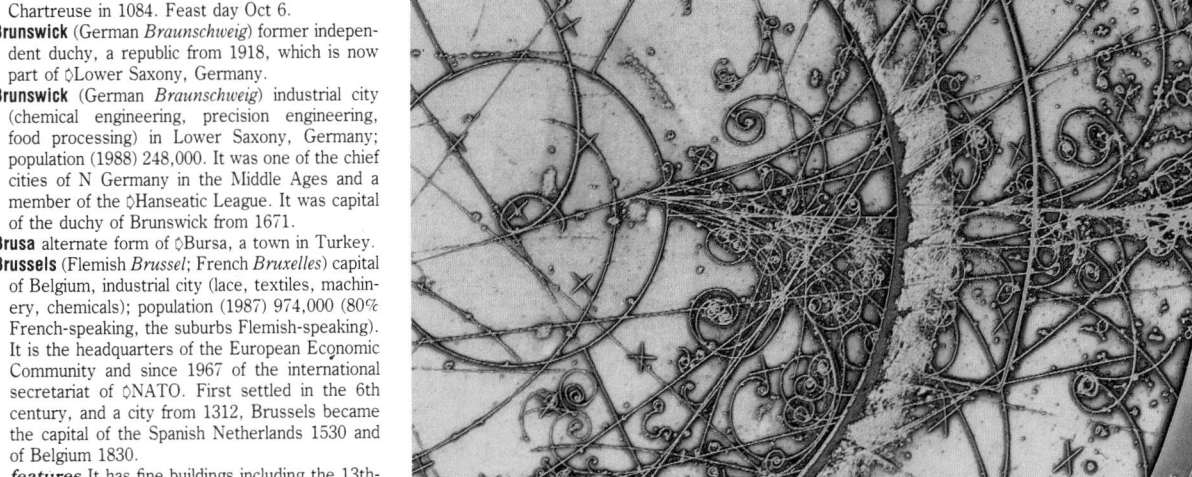

bubble chamber *Artificially colored bubble chamber at CERN, the European particle-physics laboratory, near Geneva, Switzerland.*

and was involved in Democratic party politics. However, his resolute opposition to slavery eventually caused him to become a supporter of the Republican party from its inception 1856.

Born in Cummington, Massachusetts, Bryant briefly attended Williams College and was trained as a lawyer but throughout his life maintained a deep personal interest in poetry.

Brynner Yul. Adopted name of Youl Bryner 1915–1985. US actor who made baldness his trademark. He played the king in *The King and I* both on stage 1951 and on film 1956; he is also memorable as the leader of *The Magnificent Seven* 1960.

bryophyte member of the Bryophyta, a division of the plant kingdom containing three classes, the Hepaticae (◊liverwort), Musci (◊moss), and Anthocerotae (◊hornwort). Bryophytes are generally small, low-growing, terrestrial plants with no vascular (water-conducting) system as in higher plants. Their life cycle shows a marked ◊alternation of generations. Bryophytes chiefly occur in damp habitats and require water for the dispersal of the male gametes (◊antherozoids).

In bryophytes, the ◊sporophyte, consisting only of a spore-bearing capsule on a slender stalk, is wholly or partially dependent on the ◊gametophyte for water and nutrients. In some liverworts the plant body is a simple ◊thallus, but in the majority of bryophytes it is differentiated into stem, leaves, and ◊rhizoids.

Bryusov Valery 1873–1924. Russian Symbolist poet, novelist and critic, author of *The Fiery Angel* 1908.

Brześć nad Bugiem Polish form of ◊Brest, a town in the USSR.

Brzezinski Zbigniew 1928– . US Democratic politician, born in Poland; he taught at Harvard University, and became a US citizen 1949. He was national security adviser to President Carter 1977–81 and chief architect of Carter's human-rights policy.

BSc abbreviation for Bachelor of Science degree.

Btu symbol for ◊British thermal unit.

bubble chamber in physics, a device for observing the nature and movement of atomic particles, and their interaction with radiations. It is a vessel filled with a superheated liquid through which ionizing particles move and collide. The paths of these particles are shown by strings of bubbles, which can be photographed and studied. By using a pressurized liquid medium instead of a gas, it overcomes drawbacks inherent in the earlier ◊cloud chamber. It was invented by Donald ◊Glaser in 1952.

bubble memory in computing, a memory device based on the creation of small "bubbles" on a magnetic surface. Bubble memories typically store up to 4 megabits (4 million ◊bits) of information. They are not sensitive to shock and vibration, unlike other memory devices such as disk drives, yet, like magnetic disks, they do not lose their information when the computer is switched off.

Buber Martin 1878–1965. Austrian-born Israeli philosopher, a Zionist and advocate of the reappraisal of ancient Jewish thought in contemporary terms. His book *I and Thou* 1923 posited a direct dialogue between the individual and God; it had great impact on Christian and Jewish theology. When forced by the Nazis to abandon a professorship in comparative religion at Frankfurt, he went to Jerusalem and taught social philosophy at the Hebrew University 1937–51.

Bubiyan an island off Kuwait, occupied by Iraq 1990 after an ultimatum to Kuwait to give it up was refused. Kuwait regained possession after the Gulf War 1991.

bubonic plague epidemic disease of the Middle Ages; see ◊plague and ◊Black Death.

Bucaramanga industrial (coffee, tobacco, cacao, cotton) and commercial city in N central Colombia; population (1985) 493,929. It was founded by the Spanish in 1622.

***Buchanan** The 15th president of the United States of America, James Buchanan, a Democrat. 1857–1861.*

buccaneer member of various groups of seafarers who plundered Spanish ships and colonies on the Spanish American coast in the 17th century. Unlike true pirates, they were acting on (sometimes spurious) commission.

Bucer Martin 1491–1551. German Protestant reformer, regius professor of divinity at Cambridge University from 1549, who tried to reconcile the views of his fellow Protestants Luther and Zwingli with the significance of the eucharist.

Buchanan James 1791–1868. 15th president of the US 1857–61. Born near Mercersburg, Pennsylvania, Buchanan was trained as a lawyer and was admitted to the bar 1812. He served as a member of the state legislature 1814–16 and the US House of Representatives 1821–31. He was US minister to Russia 1832–34 before being elected to the Senate 1834. An accommodationist on the issue of slavery, he left his Senate seat to serve as US secretary of state during the Mexican War. Nominated by the Democrats and elected president 1856, Buchanan could do little to avert the secession of the South over the issue of slavery.

Bucharest (Romanian *București*) capital and largest city of Romania; population (1985) 1,976,000, the conurbation of Bucharest district having an area of 587 sq mi/1,520 sq km and a population of 2,273,000. Originally a citadel built by Vlad the Impaler (see ◊Dracula) to stop the advance of the Ottoman invasion in the 14th century. It became the capital of the princes of Wallachia 1698 and of Romania 1861. Savage fighting took place in the city during Romania's 1989 revolution.

Buchenwald site of a Nazi ◊concentration camp 1937–45 at a village NE of Weimar, E Germany.

Buchner Eduard 1860–1917. German chemist who researched the process of fermentation. In 1897 he observed that fermentation could be produced mechanically, by cell-free extracts. Buchner argued that it was not the whole yeast cell that produced fermentation, but only the presence of the enzyme he named zymase. Nobel Prize 1907.

Buck Pearl S 1892–1973. US novelist. Daughter of missionaries to China, she spent much of her life there and wrote novels about Chinese life, such as *East Wind–West Wind* 1930 and *The Good Earth* 1931, for which she received a Pulitzer prize 1932. She received the Nobel Prize for Literature in 1938. She wanted to make the East understandable to the West.

Buckingham George Villiers, 1st Duke of 1592–1628. English courtier, adviser to James I and later Charles I. After Charles's accession, Buckingham attempted to form a Protestant coalition in Europe, which led to war with France, but he failed to relieve the Protestants (Huguenots) besieged in La Rochelle 1627. This added to his unpopularity with Parliament, and he was assassinated.

Buckingham Palace London home of the British sovereign, built 1703 for the duke of Buckingham, but bought by George III in 1762 and recon-

***Budapest** The Parliament building on the eastern side of the river Danube.*

structed by John ◊Nash 1821–36; a new front was added in 1913.

Buckley William F(rank) 1925– . US conservative political writer, novelist, and founder-editor of the *National Review* 1955. In such books as *Up from Liberalism* 1959, and in a weekly television debate "Firing Line," he represented the "intellectual" right-wing, antiliberal stance in US political thought.

buckwheat any of several herbaceous plants of the genus *Fagopyrum*, family Polygonaceae, especially *F. esculentum*, which grows to about 3 ft/1 m and can grow on poor soil in a short summer. The highly nutritious black, triangular seeds (groats) are consumed by both animals and humans. They can be eaten either cooked whole or as a roasted cracked meal (kasha) or ground into flour, often made into pancakes.

bud an undeveloped shoot usually enclosed by protective scales; inside is a very short stem and numerous undeveloped leaves, or flower parts, or both. Terminal buds are found at the tips of shoots, while axillary buds develop in the ◊axils of the leaves, often remaining dormant unless the terminal bud is removed or damaged. Adventitious buds may be produced anywhere on the plant, their formation sometimes stimulated by an injury, such as that caused by pruning.

Budaeus Latin form of the name of Guillaume Budé 1467–1540. French scholar. He persuaded Francis I to found the Collège de France, and also the library that formed the nucleus of the French national library, the Bibliothèque Nationale.

Budapest capital of Hungary, industrial city (chemicals, textiles) on the river Danube; population (1985) 2,089,000. Buda, on the right bank of the Danube, became the Hungarian capital 1867 and was joined with Pest, on the left bank, 1872.

Budapest saw fighting between German and Soviet troops in World War II 1944–45 and between the Hungarians and Soviet troops in the uprising of 1956.

Buddenbrooks a novel by the German writer Thomas Mann, published 1901. Set in N Germany during the 19th century, it describes the decline of a family.

Buddha "enlightened one," title of Prince Gautama Siddhārtha c. 563–483 BC. Religious leader, founder of Buddhism, born at Lumbini in Nepal. At the age of 29, he left his wife and son and a life of luxury, to escape from the material burdens of existence. After six years of austerity he realized that asceticism, like overindulgence, was futile, and chose the middle way of meditation. He became enlightened under a bo tree near Buddh Gaya in Bihar, India. He began teaching at Varanasi, and founded the Sangha, or order of monks. He spent the rest of his life traveling around N India, and died at Kusinagara in Uttar Pradesh.

Buddha's teaching consisted of the Four Noble Truths: the fact of frustration or suffering; that suffering has a cause; that it can be ended; and that it can be ended by following the Noble Eightfold Path—right views, right intention, right speech, right action, right livelihood, right effort, right mindfulness, and right concentration—eventually arriving at nirvana, the extinction of all craving for things of the senses and release from the cycle of rebirth.

Buddh Gaya village in Bihar, India, where Gautama became ◊Buddha while sitting beneath a bo (*bodhi*, wisdom) tree; a descendant of the original bo tree (*Ficus religiosa*, peepul tree) is preserved.

Buddhism one of the great world religions, which originated in India about 500 BC. It derives from the teaching of Buddha, who is regarded as one of a series of such enlightened beings; there are no gods. The chief doctrine is that of karma, good or evil deeds meeting an appropriate reward or punishment either in this life or (through reincarnation) a long succession of lives. The main divisions in Buddhism are Theravāda (or Hīnayāna) in SE Asia and Mahāyāna in N Asia; Lamaism in Tibet and Zen in Japan are among the many Mahāyāna sects. Its symbol is the lotus. There are over 247.5 million Buddhists worldwide.

***Buddha** 13th century Thai bronze Buddha.*

scriptures The only complete canon of the Buddhist scriptures is that of the Sinhalese (Sri Lanka) Buddhists, in Pāli, but other schools have essentially the same canon in Sanskrit. The scriptures, known as *pitakas* (baskets), date from the 2nd to 6th centuries AD. There are three divisions: vinaya (discipline), listing offenses and rules of life; the sūtras (discourse), or dharma (doctrine), the exposition of Buddhism by Buddha and his disciples; and abhidharma (further doctrine), later discussions on doctrine.

beliefs The self is not regarded as permanent, and the aim of following the Noble Eightfold Path is to break the chain of karma and achieve dissociation from the body by attaining nirvana ("blowing out")—the eradication of all desires, either in annihilation or by absorption of the self in the infinite. Supreme reverence is accorded to the historical Buddha (Śākyamuni, or, when referred to by his clan name, Gautama), who is seen as one in a long and ongoing line of Buddhas, the next one (Maitreya) being due *c.* AD 3000.

divisions Theravāda Buddhism, the School of the Elders, also known as Hīnayāna or Lesser Vehicle, prevails in SE Asia (Sri Lanka, Thailand, and Burma), and emphasizes the mendicant, meditative life as the way to break the cycle of samsāra, or death and rebirth. Its scriptures are written in Pāli, an Indo-Aryan language with its roots in N India. In India itself Buddhism was replaced by Hinduism, but still has 5 million devotees and is growing. Mahāyāna, or Greater Vehicle, which arose at the beginning of the Christian era, exhorts the individual not merely to attain personal nirvana, but to become a trainee Buddha, or bodhisattva, and so save others; this meant the faithful could be brought to enlightenment by a bodhisattva without following the austerities of Theravāda, and the cults of various Buddhas and bodhisattvas arose. Mahāyāna Buddhism prevails in N Asia (China, Korea, Japan, and Tibet). ◊Zen originated about AD 520 in China, and from the 12th century was adopted in Japan; Japan also has the lay organization Sōka Gakkai (Value Creation Society), founded 1937, which equates absolute faith with immediate material benefit; by the 1980s it was followed by more than 7 million households.

budding a type of ◊asexual reproduction in which an outgrowth develops from a cell to form a new individual. Most yeasts reproduce in this way.

In a suitable environment, yeasts grow rapidly, forming long chains of cells as the buds themselves produce further buds before being separated from the parent. Simple invertebrates, such as ◊hydra, can also reproduce by budding.

In horticulture, the term is used for a technique of plant propagation whereby a bud (or scion) and a sliver of bark from one plant are transferred to an incision made in the bark of another plant (the stock). This method of ◊grafting is often used for roses.

buddleia tropical genus of shrubs and trees, family Buddleiaceae, to which the the butterfly bush *Buddleia davidii* belongs. Its purple or white flower heads are attractive to insects and it is widely cultivated.

Budge Donald 1915– . US tennis player. He was the first to perform the Grand Slam when he won the Wimbledon, French, US, and Australian championships all in 1938.

He won 14 Grand Slam events, including Wimbledon singles twice. He turned professional 1938.

CAREER HIGHLIGHTS

Wimbledon
singles: 1937–38
doubles: 1937–38
mixed: 1937–38
US Open
singles: 1937–38
doubles: 1936, 1938
mixed: 1937–38
French Open
singles: 1938
Australian Open
singles: 1938

budgerigar small Australian parakeet *Melopsittacus undulatus* that feeds mainly on grass seeds. Normally it is bright green, but yellow, white, blue, and mauve varieties have been bred for the pet market.

budget an estimate of income and expenditure for some future period, used in financial planning. National budgets set out estimates of government income and expenditure and generally include projected changes in taxation and growth. Interim budgets are not uncommon, in particular, when dramatic changes in economic conditions occur. Governments will sometimes construct a budget deficit or surplus as part of macroeconomic policy.

budget deficit the amount of shortfall that occurs when expenditures exceed revenues. While individuals and private enterprises can have budget deficits, the most economically significant deficit is the federal budget deficit. The deficit must be covered through the sale of government securities on the financial market or through the printing of money. Since printing money would be unacceptably inflationary, the government sells bonds and other financial instruments, promising to repay the face value plus interest in a specified time. The accumulation of obligations constitutes the ◊national debt.

In the US during the Reagan administrations, tax cuts and increased defense spending combined to create massive budget deficits. Because there is a limited amount of investment capital available, the debt has been sold increasingly to foreigners. Debt service now consumes 15% of the federal budget, and federal borrowing has distorted financial markets, squeezing out private borrowers. Interest on the debt is the fourth-largest component of the budget. Public debt is the total net government debt, including net federal and net state and local government debt.

Budějovice see ◊České Budějovice, town in Czechoslovakia.

Budweis German form of České Budějovice, a town in Czechoslovakia.

Buenos Aires capital and industrial city of Argentina, on the S bank of the river Plate; population (1980) 2,922,829, metrolpolitan area 9,969,826. It was founded 1536, and became the capital 1853.

features Palace of Congress; on the Plaza de Mayo, the cathedral and presidential palace (known as the Pink House); university 1821.

buffalo two species of wild cattle. The Asiatic water buffalo *Bubalis bubalis* is found domesticated throughout S Asia and wild in parts of India and Nepal. It likes moist conditions. Usually gray or black, up to 6 ft/1.8 m high, both sexes carry large horns. The African buffalo *Syncerus caffer* is found in Africa, south of the Sahara, where there is grass, water, and cover in which to retreat. There are a number of subspecies, the biggest up to 5 ft/1.6 m high, and black, with massive horns set close together over the head. The name is also commonly applied to the American bison.

Buffalo industrial port in W New York, at the NE end of Lake Erie; population (1990) 328,123. It is linked with New York City by the New York State Barge Canal. Grain from Buffalo's elevators is shipped overseas via the St Lawrence Seaway. An industrial city, Buffalo was hard hit by the closing of steel mills and auto factories in the late 1970s and early 1980s. The State University of New York at Buffalo and Canisius College are here. Settled in 1780, Buffalo was burned by the British during the War of 1812 but was soon rebuilt and flourished with the completion of the Erie Canal 1825.

***Buenos Aires** The Congress National and Plaza in Buenos Aires, Argentina.*

buffer in computing, part of the memory used to hold data while it is waiting to be used. For example, a program might store data in a printer buffer until the printer is ready to print it.

buffer a mixture of chemical compounds chosen to maintain a steady ◊pH. The commonest buffers consist of a mixture of a weak organic acid and one of its salts or a mixture of acid salts of phosphoric acid. The addition of either an acid or a base causes a shift in the chemical equilibrium, thus keeping the pH constant.

Buffet Bernard 1928– . French figurative painter who created distinctive, thin, spiky forms with bold, dark outlines. He was a precocious talent in the late 1940s.

Buffon George Louise Leclerc, Comte de 1707–1778. French naturalist and author of the 18th century's most significant work of natural history, the 44-volume *Histoire naturelle* (1749–1804), 36 volumes of which he completed before his death. In *The Epochs of Nature*, one of the volumes, he questioned biblical chronology for the first time, and raised the Earth's age from the traditional figure of 6,000 years to the seemingly colossal estimate of 75,000 years.

Bug two rivers in E Europe: the West Bug rises in SW Ukraine and flows to the Vistula, and the South Bug rises in W Ukraine and flows to the Black Sea.

bug in computing, an error in a program. It can be an error in the logical structure of a program or a syntactic error, such as a spelling mistake. Some bugs cause a program to fail immediately; others remain dormant, causing problems only when a particular combination of events occurs. See also ◊debugging.

bug in entomology, insects belonging to the order Hemiptera. All these have two pairs of wings with forewings partly thickened. They also have piercing mouthparts adapted for sucking the juices of plants or animals, the "beak" being tucked under the body when not in use.

They include: the bedbug, which sucks human blood; the shieldbug, or stinkbug, which has a strong odor and feeds on plants; the water boatman and other water bugs.

Buganda two provinces (North and South Buganda) of Uganda, home of the Baganda people and formerly a kingdom from the 17th century. The *kabaka* or king, Edward Mutesa II (1924–1969), was the first president of independent Uganda 1962–66, and his son Ronald Mutebi (1955–) is *sabataka* (head of the Baganda clans).

bugle in music, a valveless brass instrument with a shorter tube and less expanded bell than the trumpet. Constructed of copper plated with brass, it has long been used as a military instrument for giving a range of signals based on the tones of a harmonic series.

bugle any of a genus *Ajuga* of low-growing plants of the mint family Labiatae, with spikes of white, pink, or blue flowers. They are often grown as ground covers.

bugloss plants of several genera of the borage family Boraginaceae, distinguished by their rough, bristly leaves and small blue flowers.

buhl alternate spelling for ◊boulle, a type of marquetry.

Bujumbura capital of Burundi; population (1986) 272,600. Formerly called *Usumbura* (until 1962), it was founded in 1899 by German colonists. The university was established 1960.

Bukavu port in E Zaïre, on Lake Kivu; population (1982) 209,050. Mining is the chief industry. Called Costermansville until 1966, it is the capital of Itivu region.

Bukhara city in Uzbekistan, USSR; population (1987) 220,000. It is the capital of Bukhara region, which has given its name to carpets (made in

Ashkhabad). It is an Islamic center, with a Muslim theological training center. An ancient city in central Asia, it was formerly the capital of the independent emirate of Bukhara, annexed to Russia 1868.

Bukharest alternate form of ◊Bucharest, capital of Romania.

Bukharin Nikolai Ivanovich 1888–1938. Soviet politician and theorist. A moderate, he was the chief Bolshevik thinker after Lenin. Executed on Stalin's orders for treason in 1938, he was posthumously rehabilitated in 1988.

He wrote the major defense of war communism in his *Economics of the Transition Period* 1920. He drafted the Soviet constitution of 1936 but in 1938 was imprisoned and tried for treason in one of Stalin's "show trials." He pleaded guilty to treason, but defended his moderate policies and denied criminal charges. Nevertheless, he was executed, as were all other former members of Lenin's Politburo except Trotsky, who was murdered, and Stalin himself.

Bukovina region in SE Europe, divided between the USSR and Romania. It covers 4,050 sq mi/10,500 sq km.

history Part of Moldavia during the Turkish regime, it was ceded by the Ottoman Empire to Austria 1777, becoming a duchy of the Dual Monarchy 1867–1918; then it was included in Romania. N Bukovina was ceded to the USSR 1940 and included in Ukraine as the region of Chernovtsy; the cession was confirmed by the peace treaty 1947, but the question of its return has been raised by Romania. The part of Bukovina remaining in Romania became the district of Suceava.

Bulawayo industrial city and railroad junction in Zimbabwe; population (1982) 415,000. It lies at an altitude of 4,450 ft/1,355 m on the river Matsheumlope, a tributary of the Zambezi, and was founded on the site of the kraal (enclosed village), burned down 1893, of the Matabele chief, Lobenguela. It produces agricultural and electrical equipment. The former capital of Matabeleland, Bulawayo developed with the exploitation of goldmines in the neighborhood.

bulb underground bud with fleshy leaves containing a reserve food supply and with roots growing from its base. Bulbs function in vegetative reproduction and are characteristic of many monocotyledenous plants such as the daffodil, snowdrop, and onion. Bulbs are grown on a commercial scale in temperate countries, such as England and the Netherlands.

bulbil a small bulb that develops above ground from a bud. Bulbils may be formed on the stem from axillary buds, as in members of the saxifrage family, or in the place of flowers, as seen in many species of onion *Allium*. They drop off the parent plant and develop into new individuals, providing a means of ◊vegetative reproduction and dispersal.

bulbul small fruit-eating passerine bird of the family Pycnonotidae. There are about 120 species, mainly in the forests of the Old World tropics.

Bulfinch Charles 1763–1844. US architect. Born in Boston, Bulfinch was educated at Harvard and traveled widely in Europe. In 1787 his design for the Massachusetts State House was accepted, and he went on to become one of New England's leading architects, planning such important structures as the Hollis Street Church, Harvard's University Hall, the Massachusetts General Hospital, and the Connecticut State House. Deeply involved in the municipal affairs of Boston, Bulfinch served on its board of selectmen 1791–1817. In 1817 he was appointed architect of the US Capitol by President Monroe.

Bulgakov Mikhail Afanasyevich 1891–1940. Russian novelist and playwright. His novel *The White Guard* 1924, dramatized as *The Days of the Turbins* 1926, deals with the Revolution and the civil war.

His satiric approach made him unpopular with the Stalin regime, and he was unpublished from the 1930s. *The Master and Margarita*, a fantasy about the devil in Moscow, was not published until 1967.

Bulganin Nikolai 1895–1975. Soviet statesman. His career began in 1918 when he joined the Cheka, the Soviet secret police. He helped to organize Moscow's defense in World War II, became a marshal of the USSR 1947, and was minister of defense 1947–49 and 1953–55. On the fall of Malenkov he became prime minister (chair of Council of Ministers) 1955–58 and in the attempt to oust Khrushchev in 1957 was himself dismissed.

Bulgaria country in SE Europe, bounded N by Romania, W by Yugoslávia, S by Greece, SE by Turkey, and E by the Black Sea.

government Under the 1971 constitution the supreme legislative and executive body in Bulgaria is the 400-member national assembly, elected every five years by universal adult suffrage. It meets at least three times a year but elects a permanent 28-member state council, headed by a president who acts as head of state, to take over its functions in its absence. The national assembly also elects a council of ministers, headed by a prime minister, that forms the executive government. The controlling force has traditionally been the Bulgarian Communist Party (BCP), now renamed 1989/90 the Bulgarian Socialist Party.

history In the ancient world Bulgaria comprised ◊Thrace and Moesia and was the Roman province of Moesia Inferior. It was occupied in the 6th century by the Slavs (from whom the language derives), followed by Bulgars from Asia in the 7th century. In 865 Khan Boris adopted Easern Orthodox Christianity, and under his son Simeon (893–927), who assumed the title Tsar, Bulgaria became a leading power. It was ruled by ◊Byzantium from the 11th century, and although a second Bulgarian empire was founded after the 14th century, Bulgaria formed part of the ◊Ottoman empire for almost 500 years, becoming an independent kingdom in 1908.

Bulgaria allied itself with Germany during World War I. From 1919 a government of the leftist Agrarian Party introduced land reforms, but was overthrown in 1923 by a facist coup. A monarchical-facist dictatorship was established 1934 under King ◊Boris III. During World War II Bulgaria again allied itself with Germany, being occupied in 1944 by the USSR. In 1946 the monarchy was abolished, and a republic was proclaimed under a communist-leaning alliance, the Fatherland Front, led by Georgi ◊Dimitrov (1882–1949). Bulgaria reverted largely to its 1919 frontiers.

The new republic adopted a Soviet-style constitution in 1947, with nationalized industries and cooperative farming introduced. Vulko Chervenkov, Dimitrov's brother-in-law, became the dominant political figure 1950–54, introducing a Stalinist regime. He was succeeded by the more moderate Todor ◊Zhivkov, under whom Bulgaria became one of the Soviet Union's most loyal satellites.

During the 1980s the country faced mounting economic problems, chiefly caused by the rising cost of energy imports. During 1985–89, under the promptings of the Soviet leader ◊Gorbachev, a haphazard series of administrative and economic

Bulgaria
People's Republic of
(Narodna Republika Bulgaria)

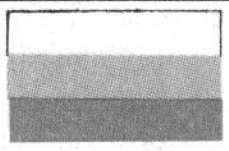

0 miles 500
0 km 1000
Romania
Yugoslavia
Italy
BULGARIA
Sofia
Turkey
Greece
MEDITERRANEAN SEA

area 42,812 sq mi/110,912 sq km
capital Sofia
cities Plovdiv, Ruse; Black Sea ports Burgas and Varna
physical lowland plains in N and SE separated by mountains which cover three-quarters of the country
features key position on land route from Europe to Asia; Black Sea coast; Balkan and Rhodope mountains; Danube River in N
head of state Zhelyo Zhelev from 1990
head of government Dimitur Popov from 1990
political system Socialist pluralist republic
political parties Bulgarian Socialist Party (BSP), the former communist party; Bulgarian Agrarian People's Union (BZNS); Union of Democratic Forces (UDF)
exports textiles, leather, chemicals, nonferrous metals, timber, machinery, tobacco, cigarettes (world's largest exporter)
currency lev
population (1990 est) 8,978,000 (including 900,000–1,500,000 ethnic Turks, concentrated in S and NE); growth rate 0.1% p.a.
life expectancy men 69, women 74
language Bulgarian, Turkish
religion Eastern Orthodox Christian 90%, Sunni Muslim 10%
literacy 98%
GDP $25.4 bn (1987); $2,836 per head
chronology
1908 Bulgaria became a kingdom independent of Turkish rule.
1944 Soviet invasion of German-occupied Bulgaria.
1946 Monarchy abolished and communist-dominated people's republic proclaimed.
1947 Soviet-style constitution adopted.
1949 Death of Georgi Dimitrov, the communist government leader.
1954 Election of Todor Zhivkov as Communist Party general secretary; made nation a loyal satellite of USSR.
1971 Constitution modified; Zhivkov elected president.
1985–88 Large administrative and personnel changes made haphazardly under Soviet stimulus.
1987 New electoral law introduced multicandidate elections.
1989 Large-scale land reform announced, with break-up of large collective farms and opportunity for leasing farmland. The banning of the Turkish language led to conflicts between Bulgarians and Turks, and 310,000 ethnic Turks fled in opposition to the "Bulgarianization" campaign of forced assimilation. Zhivkov ousted by Petar Mladenov Nov and expelled from BCP. Sweeping pluralist reforms instituted, and opposition parties allowed to form; Bulgarianization abandoned; official corruption investigated.
1990 Alexander Lilov elected new BCP leader and Andrey Loukanov prime minister Feb, the latter replaced Dec by Popov heading a coalition government.
1991 Food shortages and price rises accompanied the move to a market economy.

reforms was instituted. This proved insufficient, however, to placade reformists both inside and outside the BCP. In Nov 1989, influenced by the democratization movements sweeping other East European countries and backed by the Army and the USSR, the foreign secretary, Petar ◊Mladenov, ousted Zhivkov and other members of the "old guard" in a skillful committee coup. Mladenov became leader of the BCP and president of the state council, and quickly promoted genuine political pluralism. In Dec 1989 legislation was passed to end the BCP's "leading role" in the state and allow the formation of free opposition parties and labor unions; political prisoners were freed; the secret police wing responsible for dissident surveillance was abolished; and free elections were promised for 1990. In Feb 1990 Alexander Lilov, a reformer, was elected party chief, and Andrey Loukanov became prime minister. A special commission was established to investigate allegations of nepotism and high-level embezzlement of state funds under Zhivkov. Zhivkov was placed under house arrest, and later imprisoned, pending trial on charges of corruption and abuse of power.

Bulgaria's relations with neighboring Turkey deteriorated during 1989, following the flight of 310,000 ethnic Turks from Bulgaria to Turkey after the Bulgarian government's violent suppression of their protests at the program of "Bulgarianization" (forcing them to adopt Slavic names and resettle elsewhere). The new Mladenov government announced Dec 1989 that the forced assimilation program would be abandoned; this provoked demonstrations by anti-Turk nationalists (abetted by BCP conservatives) but encouraged more than 100,000 refugees to return from Turkey.

In Feb 1990 a government decree relegalized private farming and in April 1990 a phased lifting of price controls commenced, as part of a drive toward a market economy.

Petar Mladenov resigned as president July 1990 and in Aug the opposition leader Zhelyu Zelev was elected in his place. In Nov 1990, following mass demonstrations in Sofia, a general strike, and a boycott of parliament by opposition deputies, the reform-communist government of Andrei Lukanov resigned. He was replaced in Dec 1990 by a nonparty politician, Dimitar Popov, who headed a caretaker government pending fresh elections and the drafting of a new constitution 1991.

Bulge, Battle of the or ***Ardennes offensive*** in World War II, Hitler's plan, code-named "Watch on the Rhine," for a breakthrough by his field marshal ◊Rundstedt aimed at the US line in Ardennes Dec 16, 1944–Jan 28, 1945. There were 77,000 Allied casualties and 130,000 German, including Hitler's last powerful reserve, his Panzer elite.

bulimia (Greek "ox hunger") condition of continuous, uncontrolled hunger. Considered a counteraction to stress or depression, this eating disorder is found chiefly in young women. When compensated for by forced vomiting or overdoses of laxatives, the condition is called bulimia nervosa. It is sometimes associated with ◊anorexia.

bull a speculator who buys stocks or shares on the stock exchange expecting a rise in the price in order to sell them later at a profit, the opposite of a ◊bear. In a bull market, prices rise and bulls profit.

bull papal document or edict issued by the pope; so called from the circular seals (medieval Latin *bulla*) attached to them. Some of the most celebrated bulls include Leo X's condemnation of Luther in 1520 and Pius IX's proclamation of papal infallibility in 1870.

Bull John. Typical Englishman, as represented in cartoons and caricatures: a stocky figure, regarded as stubborn and honest.

Bull Olaf 1883–1933. Norwegian lyric poet, son of humorist and fiction writer Jacob Breda Bull (1853–1930). He often celebrated his birthplace Christiania (now Oslo) in his poetry.

bulldog British dog of ancient but uncertain origin. The head is broad and square, with deeply wrinkled cheeks, small folded ears, and the nose laid back between the eyes. The bulldog grows to about 18 in/45 cm at the shoulder.

It was bred for bull-baiting, the peculiar set of the lower jaw making it difficult for the dog to release its grip.

bulldozer earth-moving machine widely used in construction work for clearing rocks and tree stumps and leveling a site. The bulldozer is a kind of ◊tractor with a powerful engine and a curved, shovellike blade at the front, which can be lifted and forced down by hydraulic rams. It usually has ◊caterpillar tracks so that it can move easily over rough ground.

bullfighting the national "sport" of Spain, (where there are more than 400 bullrings), which is also popular in Mexico, Portugal, and much of Latin America. It involves the ritualized taunting of a bull in a circular ring, by men, and men on horseback, until its eventual death at the hands of the matador. Originally popular in ancient Greece and Rome, it was introduced into Spain by the Moors in the 11th century.

Picadores on horseback first taunt the bull and wound it with lances before the banderillos pierce the bull's neck with darts. The final act, the kill, is performed by the matador, who is armed with a red cape and sword. He teases the bull further with the cape and then kills it by plunging the sword between its shoulder blades. In some parts of France and in Portugal it is illegal to kill the bulls; where the bulls are killed the meat is donated to charities. Opponents of the sport are appalled by the cruelty involved and efforts have been made to outlaw it.

bullfinch Eurasian finch *Pyrrhula pyrrhula*, with a thick head and neck, and short heavy bill. It is small and blue-gray or black, the males being reddish and the females brown on the breast. Bullfinches are 6 in/15 cm long, and usually seen in pairs. They feed on tree buds as well as seeds and berries, and are usually seen in woodland. They also live in the Aleutians and on the Alaska mainland.

bullhead any of a North American family, Ictaluridae, of small freshwater catfish, for example, the black bullhead *Ictalurus melas*. Also, another name for the sculpin or other members of the family Cottidae.

bullroarer musical instrument consisting of a piece of wood fastened by one of its pointed ends to a cord. It is twirled around the head to make a whirring noise, and is used by Australian Aborigines during religious rites.

Bull Run, Battles of in the American Civil War, two victories for the Confederate army under General Robert E ◊Lee at Manassas Junction, NE Virginia: First Battle of Bull Run July 21, 1861. 34,000 Confederate troops routed 30,000 Union troops and challenged the North's complacent expectation of quick victory. Second Battle of Bull Run Aug 29–30, 1862. Lee led 54,000 soldiers in a victory over Union forces, routing 63,000 Northern troops and opening an invasion route to the North.

bull terrier heavily built, smooth-coated breed of dog, usually white, originating as a cross between terrier and bulldog. It grows to about 16 in/40 cm tall, and was formerly used in bull-baiting. Pit-bull terriers are used in illegal dog fights.

Bülow Bernhard, Prince von 1849–1929. German diplomat and politician. He was chancellor of the German Empire 1900–09 under Kaiser Wilhelm II and, holding that self-interest was the only rule for any state, adopted attitudes to France and Russia that unintentionally reinforced the trend toward opposing European power groups: the ◊Triple Entente (Britain, France, Russia) and ◊Triple Alliance (Germany, Austria-Hungary, Italy).

He resigned after losing the confidence of Emperor William II and the Reichstag.

Bülow Hans (Guido) Frieherr von 1830–1894. German conductor and pianist. He studied with Richard ◊Wagner and Franz ◊Liszt, and in 1857 married Cosima, daughter of Liszt. From 1864 he served Ludwig II of Bavaria, conducting first performances of Wagner's *Tristan und Isolde* and *Die Meistersinger*. His wife left him and married Wagner in 1870.

bulrush any of a number of marsh plants (especially of the genus *Scirpus*) belonging to the ◊sedge family, having long, slender, solid stems tipped with brown spikelets of tiny flowers. Bulrushes are used in basket-making and thatching.

Bulwer-Lytton Edward George Earle Lytton, Ist Baron Lytton 1803–1873. See ◊Lytton.

bumblebee any large ◊bee, 1–2 in/2–5 cm, usually dark-colored but banded with yellow, orange or white, belonging to the genus *Bombus*. Most species live in small colonies, usually underground, often in an old mousehole. The queen lays her eggs in a hollow nest of moss or grass at the beginning of the season. The larvae are fed on pollen and honey, and develop into workers. All the bees die at the end of the season except fertilized females, which hibernate and produce fresh colonies in the spring. Bumblebees are found naturally all over the world, with the exception of Australia, where they have been introduced to facilitate the pollination of some cultivated varieties of clover.

Bunche Ralph 1904–1971. US diplomat. Grandson of a slave, he was principal director of the UN Department of Trusteeship 1947–54, and UN undersecretary acting as mediator in Palestine 1948–49 and as special representative in the Congo 1960. He taught at Harvard and Howard universities and was involved in the planning of the ◊United Nations. In 1950 he was awarded the Nobel Prize for Peace, the first ever awarded to a black man.

Bunin Ivan Alexeyevich 1870–1953. Russian writer, author of *Derevnya/The Village* 1910, which tells of the passing of peasant life; and *Gospodin iz San Frantsisko/The Gentleman from San Francisco* 1916 (about the death of a millionaire on Capri), for which he received a Nobel Prize in 1933. He was also a poet and translated Byron into Russian.

Bunker Hill, Battle of the first significant engagement in the ◊American Revolution, June 17, 1775, near a small hill in Charlestown (now part of Boston), Massachusetts; the battle actually took place on Breed's Hill. Although the colonists were defeated, they were able to retreat to Boston and suffered far fewer casualites than the British. The failure to defeat the rebels soundly resulted in the replacement of General Thomas ◊Gage as British commander.

Bunsen Robert Wilhelm von 1811–1899. German chemist, credited with the invention of the Bunsen burner. His name is also given to the carbon–zinc electric cell, which he invented in 1841 for use in arc lamps. In 1859 he discovered two new elements, cesium and rubidium.

Bunshaft Gordon 1909–1990. US architect whose Modernist buildings include the first to be completely enclosed in curtain walling (walls that hang from a rigid steel frame), the Lever Building 1952 in New York City. He also designed the Heinz Company's UK headquarters 1965 at Hayes Park, London.

bunting any of a number of sturdy, finchlike, passerine birds with short, thick bills, of the family Emberizidae, especially the genera *Passerim* and *Emberiza*. Most of these brightly colored birds are native to the New World.

Buntline Ned. Adopted name of US author Edward Z C ◊Judson.

Buñuel Luis 1900–1983. Spanish ◊Surrealist film director. He collaborated with Salvador Dalí in *Un Chien andalou* 1928, and established his solo career with *Los Olvidados/The Young and the*

***Bunyan** Portrait of John Bunyan by Thomas Sadler (1684–85) National Portrait Gallery, London.*

Damned 1950. His works are often anticlerical, with black humor and erotic imagery.

Later films include *Le Charme discret de la bourgeoisie/The Discreet Charm of the Bourgeoisie* 1972 (Academy Award winner) and *Cet Obscur Objet du désir/That Obscure Object of Desire* 1977.

Bunyan John 1628–1688. English author. A Baptist, he was imprisoned in Bedford 1660–72 for unlicensed preaching. During a second jail sentence in 1675 he started to write *Pilgrim's Progress*, the first part of which was published in 1678. Other works include *Grace Abounding* 1666, *The Life and Death of Mr Badman* 1680, and *The Holy War* 1682.

buoy floating object used to mark channels for shipping or warn of hazards to navigation. Buoys come in different shapes, such as a pole (spar buoy), cylinder (car buoy), and cone (nun buoy). Light buoys carry a small tower surmounted by a flashing lantern, and bell buoys house a bell, which rings as the buoy moves up and down with the waves. Mooring buoys are heavy and have a ring on top to which a ship can be tied.

buoyancy the lifting effect of a fluid on a body wholly or partly immersed in it. This was studied by ◊Archimedes in the 3rd century BC.

bur in botany, a type of "false fruit" or ◊pseudocarp, surrounded by numerous hooks. An example is that of burdock *Arctium*, where the hooks are formed from bracts surrounding the flowerhead. The term is also used to include any type of fruit or seed with hooks, such as that of sandbur *Cenchrus*, a grass, and white avens *Geum canadese*. Burs catch in the feathers or fur of passing animals and thus may be dispersed over considerable distances.

Burbage Richard c. 1567–1619. English actor, thought to have been ◊Shakespeare's original Hamlet, Othello, and Lear. He also appeared in first productions of works by Ben Jonson, Thomas Kyd, and John Webster. His father James Burbage (c. 1530–1597) built the first English playhouse, known as "the Theatre"; his brother Cuthbert Burbage (c. 1566–1636) built the original ◊Globe Theatre 1599 in London.

burbot long, rounded fish *Lota lota* of the cod family, the only one living entirely in fresh water. Up to 3 ft/1 m long, it lives on the bottom of clear lakes and rivers, often in holes or under rocks, throughout Europe, Asia, and North America.

Burckhardt Jacob 1818–1897. Swiss art historian, professor of history at Basel University 1858–93. His *The Civilization of the Renaissance in Italy* 1860, intended as part of a study of world cultural history, influenced thought on the significance of this period.

Burckhardt Johann Ludwig 1784–1817. Swiss traveler whose knowledge of Arabic enabled him to travel throughout the Middle East, visiting Mecca disguised as a Muslim pilgrim in 1814. In 1817 he discovered the ruins of Petra.

burden of proof in court proceedings, the duty of a party to produce sufficient evidence to prove that his case is true.

In English and US law a higher standard of proof is required in criminal cases (beyond all reasonable doubt), than in civil cases (on the balance of probabilities).

In the US, the burden of proof is on the court, since the accused is presumed innocent; in many other countries, the accused is presumed guilty until cleared, thus putting the burden or proof on the defense.

burdock any of the bushy herbs belonging to the genus *Arctium* of the family Compositae, characterized by hairy leaves and ripe fruit enclosed in ◊burs with strong hooks.

bureaucracy an organization whose structure and operations are governed to a high degree by written rules and a hierarchy of offices; in its broadest sense, all forms of administration, and in its narrowest, rule by officials.

The early civilizations of Mesopotamia, Egypt, China, and India were organized hierarchically, thus forming the bureaucratic tradition of government. The German sociologist Max Weber saw the growth of bureaucracy in industrial societies as an inevitable reflection of the underlying shift from traditional authority to a rational and legal system of organization and control. In Weber's view, bureaucracy established a relation between legally enstated authorities and their subordinate officials. This relationship is characterized by defined rights and duties prescribed in written regulations.

Contemporary writers have highlighted the problems of bureaucracy, such as its inflexibility and rigid adherence to rules, so that today the term is often used as a criticism rather than its original neutral sense.

Burgas Black Sea port and resort in Bulgaria; population (1987) 198,000.

Burgenland federal state of SE Austria, extending from the Danube S along the W border of the Hungarian plain; area 1,544 sq mi/4,000 sq km; population (1987) 267,000. It is a largely agricultural region adjoining the Neusiedler See, and produces timber, fruit, sugar, wine, lignite, antimony, and limestone. Its capital is Eisenstadt.

Bürger Gottfried 1747–1794. German Romantic poet, remembered for his ballad "Lenore" 1773.

Burger Warren Earl 1907– . US jurist and chief justice of the United States (1969–86). In 1969 Burger was named to the US Supreme Court, succeeding Chief Justice Earl Warren. His term was marked by a conservative turn in civil rights matters. His majority decision in the Watergate tapes case *US* v *Nixon* 1974 was instrumental in bringing about Nixon's resignation. Burger retired from the Court 1986 and was succeeded by William Rehnquist.

Born in St Paul, Minnesota, Burger was educated at the University of Minnesota and was admitted to the bar 1931. President Eisenhower appointed him judge of the US Court of Appeals 1956.

Burgess Anthony. Adopted name of Anthony John Burgess Wilson 1917– British novelist, critic, and composer. His prolific work includes *A Clockwork Orange* 1962, set in a future London terrorized by teenage gangs, and the panoramic *Earthly Powers* 1980. His vision has been described as bleak and pessimistic, but his work is also comic and satiric, as in his novels featuring the poet Enderby.

Burgess Guy (Francis de Moncy) 1910–1963. British spy, a diplomat recruited by the USSR as agent; linked with Kim ◊Philby, Donald Maclean (1913–1983), and Anthony ◊Blunt.

Burgess Shale Site the site of unique fossil-bearing rock formations, 530 million years old, in Yoho National Park, British Colombia The shales in this corner of the Rocky Mountains contain more than 120 species of marine invertebrate fossils. Although discovered in 1909 by Charles Walcott, the Burgess Shales have only recently been used as evidence in the debate concerning the evolution of life. In 1990 Stephen Jay Gould drew attention to a body of scientific opinion interpreting the fossil finds as evidence of parallel early evolutionary trends extinguished by chance rather than natural selection.

burgh (burh or borough) a term originating in Germanic lands 9th–10th centuries referring to a fortified settlement, usually surrounding a monastery or castle. Later, it was used to mean new towns, or towns that enjoyed particular privileges relating to government and taxation and whose citizens were called burghers.

Burgh Hubert de died 1243. English ◊justiciar and regent of England. He began his career in the administration of Richard I, and was promoted to the justiciarship by King John; he remained in that position under Henry III from 1216 until his dismissal. He was a supporter of King John against the barons, and ended French intervention in England by his defeat of the French fleet in the Strait of Dover in 1217. He reorganized royal administration and the Common Law.

burgher a term used from the 11th century to describe citizens of ◊burghs who were freemen of a burgh, and had the right to participate in its government. They usually had to possess a house within the burgh.

Burghley William Cecil, Baron Burghley 1520–1598. English politician, chief adviser to Elizabeth I as secretary of state from 1558 and Lord High Treasurer from 1572. He was largely responsible for the religious settlement of 1559, and took a leading role in the events preceding the execution of Mary Queen of Scots in 1587.

burglary in law, the offense of breaking into a building as a trespasser with the intent to commit theft or other serious crime.

Burgos city in Castilla-León, Spain, 135 mi/217 km N of Madrid; population (1986) 164,000. It produces textiles, motor parts, and chemicals. It was capital of the old kingdom of Castile, and the national hero El Cid is buried in the Gothic cathedral, built 1221–1567.

Burgoyne John 1722–1792. British general and dramatist. He served in the American War of Independence and surrendered 1777 to the colonists at Saratoga, New York State, in one of the pivotal battles of the war. He wrote comedies, among them *The Maid of the Oaks* 1775 and *The Heiress* 1786. He figures in George Bernard Shaw's play *The Devil's Disciple*.

Burgundy ancient kingdom and duchy in the valleys of the rivers Saône and Rhône, France. The Burgundi were a Teutonic tribe that overran the country about 400. From the 9th century to the death of Duke ◊Charles the Bold in 1477, it was the nucleus of a powerful principality. On Charles's death the duchy was incorporated into France. The capital of Burgundy was Dijon. Today the region to which it corresponds is ◊Bourgogne.

Burke Edmund 1729–1797. British Whig politician and political theorist, born in Dublin, Ireland. In Parliament from 1765, he opposed the government's attempts to coerce the American colonists, for example in *Thoughts on the Present Discontents* 1770, and supported the emancipation of Ireland, but denounced the French Revolution, for example in *Reflections on the Revolution in France* 1790.

Burke Martha Jane c. 1852–1903. Real name of US heroine ◊Calamity Jane.

Burke's Peerage popular name of the *Genealogical and Heraldic History of the Peerage, Baronetage, and Knightage of the United Kingdom*, first issued by John Burke in 1826. The most recent edition was in 1970.

Burkina Faso (formerly Upper Volta) landlocked country in W Africa, bounded E by Niger, NW and W by Mali, S by Ivory Coast, Ghana, Togo, and Benin.

government A military coup in 1980 suspended the 1977 constitution and after two further coups in 1982 and 1983, power was taken by a national revolutionary council, comprising the only political factions: the Patriotic League for Development

Burkina Faso

The People's Democratic Republic of (former name Upper Volta)

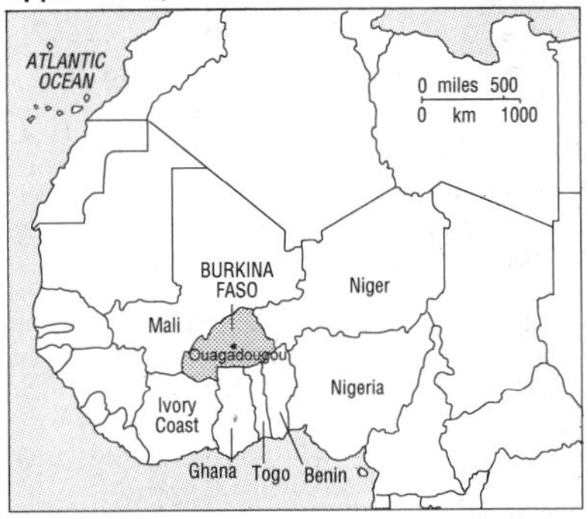
ATLANTIC
OCEAN
0 miles 500
0 km 1000
BURKINA
FASO
Niger
Mali
Ouagadougou
Nigeria
Ivory
Coast
Ghana
Togo
Benin

area 105,811 sq mi/274,122 sq km
capital Ouagadougou
cities Bobo-Dioulasso, Koudougou
physical landlocked plateau with hills in W and SE; headwaters of the river Volta; semiarid in N, forest and farm land in S
features linked by rail to Abidjan on Ivory Coast, its only outlet to the sea
head of state and government Blaise Compaore from 1987
political system one-party military republic
political parties Organization for Popular Democracy–Workers' Movement (ODP–MT), nationalist left-wing
exports cotton, groundnuts, livestock, hides, skins, sesame, cereals
currency CFA franc
population (1990 est) 8,941,000; growth rate 2.4% p.a.
life expectancy men 44, women 47
language French (official); about 50 native Sudanic languages spoken by 90% of population
religion animist 53%, Sunni Muslim 36%, Roman Catholic 11%
literacy men 21%/women 6% (1985 est)
GDP $1.6 bn (1987); $188 per head
chronology
1958 Became a self-governing republic within the French Community.
1960 Independence achieved from France, with Maurice Yameogo as the first president.
1966 Military coup led by Col Lamizana. Constitution suspended, political activities banned, and a supreme council of the armed forces established.
1969 Ban on political activities lifted.
1970 Referendum approved a new constitution leading to a return to civilian rule.
1974 After experimenting with a mixture of military and civilian rule, Lamizana reassumed full power.
1977 Ban on political activities removed. Referendum approved a new constitution based on civilian rule.
1978 Lamizana elected president.
1980 Lamizana overthrown in bloodless coup led by Col Zerbo.
1982 Zerbo ousted in a coup by junior officers. Major Ouédraogo became president, and Thomas Sankara, prime minister.
1983 Sankara seized complete power.
1984 Upper Volta renamed Burkina Faso, "land of upright man."
1987 Sankara killed in coup led by Blaise Compaore.
1989 New government party ODP–MT formed by merger of other progovernment parties. Coup against Compoare foiled.
1991 New constitution approved.

(LIPAD), the Union of the Communist Struggle (ULC), and the Communist Officers' Regrouping (ROC).

history The area known from 1984 as Burkina Faso was invaded in the 11th to 13th century by the Mossi people, whose powerful warrior kingdoms lasted for over 500 years. In the 1890s it became a province of French West Africa, known as Upper Volta.

In 1958 it became a self-governing republic and in 1960 achieved full independence with Maurice Yameogo as president. A military coup in 1966 removed Yameogo and installed Colonel Sangoulé Lamizana as president and prime minister. He suspended the constitution, dissolved the national assembly, banned political activity, and set up a supreme council of the armed forces as the instrument of government.

In 1969 the ban on political activity was lifted, and in 1970 a referendum approved a new constitution, based on civilian rule, that was to come into effect after four years of combined military and civilian government. After disagreements between military and civilian members of the government, General Lamizana announced in 1974 a return to army rule and dissolved the national assembly.

In 1977 political activity was allowed again, and a referendum approved a constitution that would create a civilian goverment. In the 1978 elections the Volta Democratic Union (UDV) won a majority in the national assembly, and Lamizana became president. But a deteriorating economy led to strikes, and a bloodless coup led by Col Zerbo overthrew Lamizana in 1980. Zerbo formed a government of national recovery, suspended the constitution, and dissolved the national assembly.

In 1982 Zerbo was ousted, and Major Jean-Baptiste Ouédraogo emerged as leader of a military regime, with Capt Thomas Sankara as prime minister. In 1983 Sankara seized power in another coup, becoming president and ruling through a council of ministers. Opposition members were arrested, the national assembly was dissolved, and a National Revolutionary Council (CNR) set up. In 1984 Sankara announced that the country would be known as Burkina Faso ("land of upright men"), symbolizing a break with its colonial past; his government strengthened ties with Ghana and established links with Benin and Libya. Sankara was killed in Oct 1987 in a military coup led by a former close colleague, Capt Blaise Compaore (1951–). In April 1989 a restructuring of the ruling political groupings took place, and Sept 1989 a plot to oust Compaore was discovered and foiled.

burlesque in the 17th and 18th centuries, a form of satirical comedy parodying a particular play or dramatic genre. For example, ◊Gay's *The Beggar's Opera* 1728 is a burlesque of 18th-century opera, and ◊Sheridan's *The Critic* 1777 satirizes the sentimentality in contemporary drama. In the US from the mid-19th century, burlesque referred to a sex and comedy show invented by Michael Bennett Leavitt in 1866 with acts including acrobats, singers, and comedians. During the 1920s striptease was introduced in order to counteract the growing popularity of the movies; Gypsy Rose Lee was the most famous stripper. Burlesque was frequently banned in the US.

Burlington city in N central North Carolina, NW of Durham. Industries include textiles, chemicals, furniture, and agricultural products; population (1990) 39,498.

Burlington city in NW Vermont, on the E shore of Lake Champlain; seat of Chittenden county. It is a port of entry and the largest city in Vermont. Industries include computer parts, steel, marble, lumber, dairy products, and tourism. It is the site of the University of Vermont 1791; population (1990) 39,127. It was a naval base during the War of 1812.

Burma former name (to 1989) of ◊Myanmar.

Burma War war 1942–45 during which Burma (now ◊Myanmar) was occupied by Japan.

Burmese native to or inhabitant of Myanmar (formerly Burma), a state with over 20 ethnic groups, all of whom have the right to Burmese nationality. The largest group are the Burmans, speakers of a Sino-Tibetan language, who migrated from the hills E of Tibet, settling in the area around Mandalay by the 11th century AD.

From the Mons, speakers of a Mon-Khmer language, the Burmans acquired Hīnyāna Buddhism and a written script based on Indian syllables. The Burmans are mainly settled in the valleys where they cultivate rice in irrigated fields. The highland people often use shifting cultivation methods and, although there are many minorities, the major groupings are Karen, Kachin, Chin, Naga, Palaung, and Wa.

burn destruction of body tissue by extremes of temperature, corrosive chemicals, electricity, or radiation. First-degree burns may cause reddening; second-degree burns cause blistering and irritation but usually heal spontaneously; third-degree burns are disfiguring and may be life-threatening.

Burns cause plasma, the fluid component of the blood, to leak from the blood vessels, and it is this loss of circulating fluid that engenders ◊shock. Emergency treatment is needed for third-degree burns in order to replace the fluid volume, prevent infection (a dire threat to the severely burned), and reduce the pain. Plastic, or reconstructive, surgery, including skin grafting, may be required to compensate for damaged tissue and minimize disfigurement.

Burnaby Frederick 1842–1885. English soldier, traveler, and founder of the weekly critical journal *Vanity Fair*. He traveled to Spain, Sudan, and Russian Asia during his leave from the Horse Guards. His books include *A Ride to Khiva* 1876 and *On Horseback through Asia Minor* 1877. Burnaby joined the British Nile expedition to relieve General Gordon, under siege in Khartoum, Sudan, and was killed in action at the battle of Abu Klea.

Burne-Jones Edward Coley 1833–1898. British painter. In 1856 he was apprenticed to the Pre-Raphaelite painter ◊Rossetti, who remained a dominant influence. His paintings, inspired by legend and myth, were characterized by elongated forms as in *King Cophetua and the Beggar Maid* 1880–84 (Tate Gallery, London). He later moved toward Symbolism. He also designed tapestries and stained glass in association with William ◊Morris.

Burnell (Susan) Jocelyn (Bell) 1943– . British astronomer. In 1967 she discovered the first ◊pulsar (rapidly flashing star) with Antony ◊Hewish and colleagues at Cambridge University, England.

Burnes Alexander 1805–1841. Scottish soldier, linguist, diplomat, and traveler in Central Asia. Following journeys to Rajputana and Lajhore he led an expedition across the Hindu Kush to Bokhara described in his *Travels into Bokhara* 1834. In 1836–37 he led a diplomatic mission to the Afghan leader Dost Mohammed, described in his book *Kabul* 1842. He was killed in Kabul during a rising that sparked off the first Afghan War.

burnet herb *Sanguisorba minor* of the rose family, also known as salad burnet. It smells of cucumber and can be used in salads. The term is also used for other members of the genus *Sanguisorba*.

Burnett Frances (Eliza) Hodgson 1849–1924. English writer, living in the US from 1865, whose novels for children include the rags-to-riches tale *Little Lord Fauntleroy* 1886 and the sentimental *The Secret Garden* 1909.

Burney Frances (Fanny) 1752–1840. English novelist and diarist, daughter of the musician Dr Charles Burney (1726–1814). She achieved success with *Evelina*, published anonymously 1778, became a member of Dr ◊Johnson's circle, received a post at court from Queen Charlotte, and in 1793 married the émigré General d'Arblay. She published three further novels, *Cecilia* 1782, *Camilla* 1796, and *The Wanderer* 1814; her diaries and letters appeared in 1842.

Burnham Forbes 1923–1985. Guyanese Marxist-Leninist politician. He was prime minister 1964–80, leading the country to independence 1966 and declaring it the world's first cooperative republic 1970. He was executive president 1980–85. Resistance to the US landing in Grenada 1983 was said to be due to his forewarning the Grenadans of the attack.

Burnley town in Lancashire, England, 12 mi/19 km NE of Blackburn; population (1983) 92,000. Formerly a cotton-manufacturing town.

Burns Robert 1759–1796. Scottish poet who used the Scots dialect at a time when it was not considered suitably "elevated" for literature. Burns' first volume, *Poems, Chiefly in the Scottish Dialect*, appeared in 1786. In addition to his poetry Burns wrote or adapted many songs, including "Auld Lang Syne."

Burns' fame rests equally on his poems (such as "Holy Willie's Prayer," "Tam o'Shanter," "The Jolly Beggars," and "To a Mouse") and his songs—sometimes wholly original, sometimes adaptations—of which he contributed some 300 to Johnson's *Scots Musical Museum* 1787–1803 and Thomson's *Scottish Airs with Poetry* 1793–1811.

Burnside Ambrose Everett 1824–1881. US military leader and politician. Born in Liberty, Indiana, Burnside attended West Point and was appointed brigadier general in the Union army soon after the outbreak of the Civil War. Named as ◊McClellan's successor as commander of the Army of the Potomac, Burnside served briefly in that position before being transferred to the West. Later blamed for the Union defeat at Petersburg 1864, Burnside retired from active service.

Entering politics after the war, he was elected governor of Rhode Island 1866–69 and US Senator 1874–81. His distinctive side whiskers and mustache framing a clean-shaven chin became popularly known as "burnsides," of which "sideburns" is a modification.

Burr Aaron 1756–1836. US politician. He was on George Washington's staff during the ◊American Revolution but was critical of the general and was distrusted in turn. He tied with Thomas Jefferson in the presidential election of 1800, but Alexander ◊Hamilton, Burr's longtime adversary, influenced the House of Representatives to vote Jefferson in, Burr becoming vice-president. Burr briefly faced murder charges after killing Hamilton in a duel in 1804. He had to leave the US for some years following the "Burr conspiracy," which implicated him variously in a scheme to conquer Mexico, or part of Florida, or to rule over a seceded Louisiana.

He was tried and acquitted on treason charges and while in Europe sought British and French aid in overthrowing Jefferson. He died in poverty at the age of 80.

Burr Raymond 1917– . Canadian-born character actor who played Perry Mason in the television series of the same name and in several films. He played the murderer in Alfred Hitchcock's *Rear Window* 1954, and his other films include *The Blue Gardinia*, *The Adventures of Don Juan* 1948, and *Godzilla* (English-language version) 1956.

Burroughs Edgar Rice 1875–1950. US novelist, born in Chicago. He wrote *Tarzan of the Apes* 1914, the story of an aristocratic child lost in the jungle and reared by apes and followed it with over 20 more books about the Tarzan character. He also wrote about life on Mars.

Burroughs William S 1914– . US novelist, born in St Louis, Missouri. He "dropped out" and, as part of the ◊beat generation, wrote *Junkie* 1953, *The Naked Lunch* 1959, *The Soft Machine* 1961, and *Dead Fingers Talk* 1963. His later novels include *Queer* and *Mind Wars*, both 1985.

Burundi
Republic of
(Republika y'Uburundi)

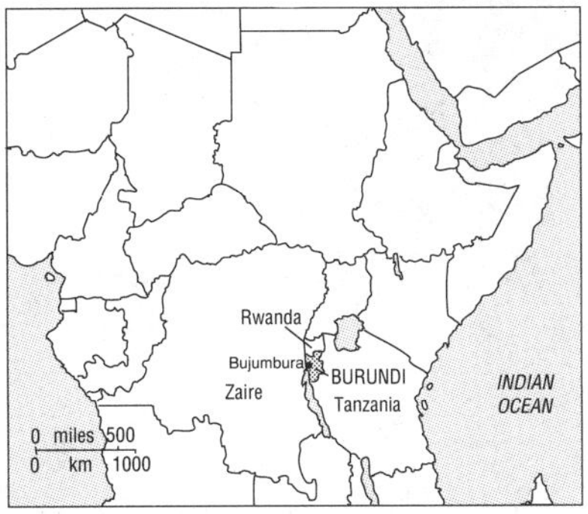
Rwanda
Bujumbura
BURUNDI
Zaire
Tanzania
INDIAN OCEAN
0 miles 500
0 km 1000

area 10,744 sq mi/27,834 sq km
capital Bujumbura
cities Gitega, Bururi, Ngozi, Muyinga
physical landlocked grassy highland straddling watershed of Nile and Congo
features Lake Tanganyika, Great Rift Valley
head of state and government Pierre Buyoya from 1987
political system one-party military republic
political parties Union for National Progress (UPRONA), nationalist Socialist
exports coffee, cotton, tea, nickel, hides, livestock, cigarettes, beer, soft drinks; there are 500 million tons of peat reserves in the basin of the Akanyaru River
currency Burundi franc
population (1990 est) 5,647,000 (of whom 15% are the Nilotic Tutsi, still holding most of the land and political power, 1% are Pygmy Twa, and the remainder Bantu Hutu); growth rate 2.8% p.a.
life expectancy men 45, women 48
language Kirundi (a Bantu language) and French (official); Kiswahili
religion Roman Catholic 62%, Protestant 5%, Muslim 1%, animist 32%
literacy men 43%/women 26% (1985)
GDP $1.1 bn (1987); $230 per head
chronology
1962 Separated from Ruanda-Urundi, as Burundi, and given independence as a monarchy under King Mwambutsa IV.
1966 King deposed by his son Charles, who became Ntare V; he was in turn deposed by his prime minister, Capt Michel Micombero, who declared Burundi a republic.
1972 Ntare V killed, allegedly by the Hutu ethnic group. Massacres of 150,000 Hutus by the rival Tutsi ethnic group, of which Micombero was a member.
1973 Micombero made president and prime minister.
1974 UPRONA declared the only legal political party, with the president as its secretary general.
1976 Army coup deposed Micombero. Col Jean-Baptiste Bagaza appointed president bv the Supreme Revolutionary Council.
1981 New constitution adopted, providing for a national assembly.
1984 Bagaza elected president as sole candidate.
1987 Bagaza deposed in coup Sept. Major Pierre Buyoya headed new Military Council for National Redemption.
1988 Some 24,000 majority Hutus killed by Tutsis. First Hutu prime minister appointed.

Burroughs William Steward 1857–1898. US industrialist who invented the first hand-operated adding machine to give printed results.

Bursa city in NW Turkey, with a port at Mudania; population (1985) 614,000. It was the capital of the Ottoman Empire 1326–1423.

Burton Richard Francis 1821–1890. British explorer and translator (he knew 35 oriental languages). He traveled mainly in the Middle East and NE Africa, often disguised as a Muslim; made two attempts to find the source of the Nile, 1855 and 1857–58 (on the second, with ◊Speke, he reached Lake Tanganyika); and wrote many travel books. He translated oriental erotica and the *Arabian Nights* 1885–88.

After military service in India, Burton explored the Arabian peninsula and Somaliland. In 1853 he visited Mecca and Medina disguised as an Afghan pilgrim; he was then commissioned by the Foreign Office to explore the sources of the Nile. Later travels took him to North and South America. His translations include the *Kama Sutra of Vatsyayana* 1883 and *The Perfumed Garden* 1886. His wife, who had accompanied him on some journeys, burned his unpublished manuscripts and diaries after his death.

Burton Richard. Adopted name of Richard Jenkins 1925–1984. Welsh-born actor. He was remarkable for the dramatic quality of his voice, and for his marital and acting partnership with Elizabeth Taylor, with whom he appeared in several films including *Cleopatra* 1962 and *Who's Afraid of Virginia Woolf?* 1966. Among his later films are *Equus* 1977 and *1984* 1984.

He also won acclaim for his stage performances in both Shakespearian and contemporary dramas throughout his film career.

Burton Robert 1577–1640. English philosopher who wrote an analysis of depression, *Anatomy of Melancholy* 1621, a compendium of information on the medical and religious opinions of the time, much used by later authors.

Burton upon Trent town in Staffordshire, England, NE of Birmingham; population (1983) 57,725. Industries include brewing, tires, and engineering.

Burundi country in east central Africa, bounded N by Rwanda, W by Zaïre, S by Lake Tanganyika, and SE and E by Tanzania.

government Under its 1981 constitution, Burundi's only political party is the Union for National Progress (UPRONA). The president is elected by universal suffrage for a five-year term, and a 65-member national assembly has the same period of tenure, 52 of its members being elected by suffrage and 13 appointed by the president. Ultimate power lies with UPRONA.

history Originally inhabited by the pygmy Twa, Burundi was taken over by Bantu Hutus in the 13th century, and overrun in the 15th century by the Tutsi. In 1890, ruled by a Tutsi king and known as Urundi, it became part of German East Africa and during World War I was occupied by Belgium. Later, as part of Ruanda-Urundi, it was administered by Belgium as a League of Nations (and then United Nations) trust territory.

The 1961 elections, supervised by the UN, were won by UPRONA, a party formed by Louis, one of the sons of the reigning king, Mwambutsa IV. Louis was assassinated after only two weeks as prime minister and was succeeded by his brother-in-law, André Muhirwa. In 1962 Urundi separated from Ruanda and, as Burundi, was given internal self-government and then full independence.

In 1966 King Mwambutsa IV, after a 50-year reign, was deposed by another son, Charles, with army help, and the constitution was suspended. Later that year Charles, now Ntare V, was deposed by his prime minister, Capt Michel Micombero, who declared Burundi a republic. Micombero was a Tutsi, whose main rivals were the numerically superior Hutu. In 1972 the deposed

Ntare V was killed, allegedly by the Hutu, giving the Tutsi an excuse to massacre large numbers of Hutu.

In 1973 amendments to the constitution made Micombero president and prime minister and in the following year UPRONA was declared the only political party. In 1976 Micombero was deposed in an army coup led by Col Jean-Baptiste Bagaza, who became president, with a prime minister and a new council of ministers. In 1977 the prime minister announced a return to civilian rule and a five-year plan to eliminate corruption and secure social justice, including promoting some Hutu to government positions.

In 1978 the post of prime minister was abolished and in 1981 a new constitution, providing for a national assembly, was adopted after a referendum. Bagaza was re-elected 1984 (he was the only presidential candidate) but was deposed in a military coup Sept 1987, his government being replaced by a "Military Council for National Redemption" headed by Major Pierre Buyoya, believed to be a Tutsi. In Aug 1988 the minority-Tutsi-controlled Burundian army massacred thousands of Hutus in the NE section of the country. Despite the pledges of Major Buyoya to end tribal violence, this massacre was seen by many as a continuation of the strife that began following an abortive Hutu rebellion 1972.

Bury town in Greater Manchester, England, on the river Irwell, 10 mi/16 km N of central Manchester; population (1986) 173,650. Industries include cotton, chemicals, and engineering.

Buryat republic of the USSR, in Soviet central Asia
area 135,600 sq mi/351,300 sq km
capital Ulan-Udé
physical bounded on the S by Mongolia, on the W by Lake Baikal; mountainous and forested
products coal, timber, building materials, fish, sheep, cattle
population (1986) 1,014,000
history settled by Russians 17th century; annexed from China by treaties 1689 and 1727.

bus or ***omnibus*** (Latin "for all") vehicle that carries fare-paying passengers on a fixed route, with frequent stops where passengers can get on and off.

An omnibus appeared briefly on the streets of Paris in the 1660s, when the mathematician Blaise Pascal introduced the first horse-drawn vehicles for public use. But a successful service, again in Paris, was not established until 1827. Two years later George Shillibeer introduced a horse-drawn bus in London.

Gasoline-engine buses came into general use by the 1910s and provide intracity and nationwide service through both public and private companies.

Bush George Herbert Walker 1924– . Forty-first president of the US 1989– . A Republican, he was director of the Central Intelligence Agency (CIA) 1976–81 and US vice-president 1981–89. In 1989, as president, he visited East European countries undergoing reform, held a summit meeting at Malta with Soviet president Gorbachev, and sent US troops to Panama to oust that country's drug-trafficking president, Manuel Noriega. Bush led the UN coalition and sent US forces to Saudi Arabia to prepare for a military strike after Iraq annexed Kuwait 1990. In Jan 1991, he led the coalition war against Iraq that forced Saddam Hussein to remove his troops from Kuwait. He was instrumental in convincing Israel and several of its traditional Arab enemies to convene for a historic fact-to-face meeting in Spain in Nov 1991. Domestic economic problems in 1990–91 dimmed the luster of his foreign policy triumphs.

Born in Milton, Massachusetts, Bush grew up in Connecticut, where his father, Prescott Bush, was a US senator. He graduated from Yale University 1948 and moved to Texas to build up an oil-drilling company. A congressman 1967–70, he was appointed US ambassador to the United Nations 1971–73 and Republican national chairman 1973–74 by President Nixon. During the Ford administration, Bush was a special envoy to China 1974–75. As vice-president during Ronald Reagan's administration he traveled widely and was responsible for overseeing government reform and programs to combat drug smuggling.

Bush *The 41st president of the United States of America, George Bush, a Republican. 1989–*

bushbuck antelope *Tragelaphus scriptus* found over most of Africa S of the Sahara. Up to 3 ft/1 m high, the males have keeled horns twisted into spirals, and are brown to blackish. The females are generally hornless, lighter, and redder. All have white markings, including stripes or vertical rows of dots down the sides. Rarely far from water, bushbuck live in woods and thick brush.

bushel dry measure used for grain and fruit, equal to eight gallons (2,219.36 cu in/36.37 l) in the UK; some US states have different standards according to the goods measured. One bushel equals four pecks.

bushido chivalric code of honor of the Japanese military caste, the ◊samurai. Bushido means "the way of the warrior"; the code stresses simple living, self-discipline, and bravery.

Bushman former term for the Kung, an aboriginal people of southern Africa, still living to some extent nomadically, in the Kalahari Desert. Formerly numerous, only some 26,000 of these characteristically small-statured and brown-skinned people remain. They are traditionally hunters and gatherers and speak a Khoisan language related to that of the Hottentots. Their early art survives in cave paintings.

bushmaster large snake *Lachesis muta*. It is a type of pit viper, and is related to the rattlesnakes. Up to 12 ft/4 m long, it is found in wooded areas of South and Central America, and is the largest venomous snake in the New World. It has a powerful venomous bite. When alarmed, it produces a noise by vibrating its tail among dry leaves.

bushranger Australian armed robber of the 19th century. The first bushrangers were escaped convicts. The last gang was led by Ned ◊Kelly and his brother Dan in 1878–80. They form the subject of many Australian ballads.

business cycle period of time that includes a peak and trough of economic activity, as measured by a country's national income. In Keynesian economics, one of the main roles of the government is to smooth out the peaks and troughs of the business cycle by intervening in the economy, thus minimizing "overheating" and "stagnation."

business school institution for training in management and marketing, such as Harvard in the US, London Business School (LBS) in the UK, and Insead in France. The emphasis has shifted recently to add study of such issues as environmental policy, corporate responsibility, business ethics, and internationalism. The master's in business administration has become a highly prized degree in many professions.

Busoni Ferruccio (Dante Benvenuto) 1866–1924. Italian pianist, composer, and music critic. Much of his music was for the piano, but he also composed several operas including *Doktor Faust*, completed by a pupil after his death.

bust in finance, a failure or bankruptcy, as in the boom and bust cycle of business.

Bustamante (William) Alexander (born Clarke) 1884–1977. Jamaican Socialist politician. As leader of the Labor Party, he was the first prime minister of independent Jamaica 1962–67.

bustard bird of the family Otididae, related to cranes but with a rounder body, a thicker neck, and a relatively short beak. Bustards are found on the ground on open plains and fields.

The great bustard *Otis tarda* is one of the heaviest flying birds at 40 lb/18 kg, and the larger males may have a length of 3 ft/1 m and wingspan of 7.5 ft/2.3 m. It is found in Europe and N Asia.

butane C_4H_{10} one of two gaseous alkanes (◊paraffin hydrocarbon) having the same formula but differing in structure. Normal butane is derived from natural gas; isobutane is a by-product of petroleum manufacture. Liquefied under pressure, it is used as a fuel for industrial and domestic purposes (for example in portable cookers).

Bute island and resort in the Firth of Clyde, Scotland; area 46 sq mi/120 sq km. The chief town is Rothesay. It is separated from the mainland in the north by a winding channel, the Kyles of Bute. With Arran and the adjacent islands it comprised the former county of Bute, merged 1975 in the region of Strathclyde.

Bute John Stuart, 3rd Earl of 1713–1792. British Tory politician, prime minister 1762–63. On the accession of George III in 1760, he became the chief instrument in the king's policy for breaking the power of the Whigs and establishing the personal rule of the monarch through Parliament.

Buthelezi Chief Gatsha 1928– . Zulu leader and politician, chief minister of KwaZulu, a black "homeland" in the Republic of South Africa from 1970. He is founder and president of ◊Inkatha 1975, a paramilitary organization for attaining a nonracial democratic political system.

Butler Samuel 1835–1902. English author who made his name 1872 with a satiric attack on contemporary utopianism, *Erewhon* (*nowhere* reversed), but is now remembered for his autobiographical *The Way of All Flesh* written 1872–85 and published 1903.

Butor Michel 1926– . French writer, a practitioner of the "antinovel" (in which the conventions of the novel are abandoned). His works include *Passage de Milan/Passage from Milan* 1954, *Dégrès/Degrees* 1960, and *L'Emploi du temps/Passing Time* 1963. *Mobile* 1962 is a volume of essays.

butte a steep-sided flat-topped hill, formed in horizontally layered sedimentary rocks, largely in arid areas. A large butte with a pronounced tablelike profile is a ◊mesa.

Buttes and mesas are characteristic of semiarid areas where remnants of resistant rock layers protect softer rock underneath, as in the plateau regions of Colorado, Utah, and Arizona.

Butte mining city in Montana, in the Rocky Mountains; population (1990) 33,941. Butte was founded in 1864 during a rush for gold, soon exhausted; copper was found some 20 years later on what was called "the richest hill on earth." The last mine closed 1983. Butte is the seat of the Montana College of Mineral Science and Technology.

butter solid, edible yellowish fat derived from whole milk. Making butter by hand, which is done by skimming off the cream and churning it, was traditionally a convenient means of preserving milk.

The transfer of butter-making from a farm-based to a factory-based process began in the last fourth of the 19th century, with the introduction of centrifugal separators for the instant separation of cream from milk. It could then be conveyed into large steam-powered churns. Today, most butter is made on a continuous system devised in Germany during World War II. Inside a single machine, the cream is churned, the buttermilk drawn off, and the butter washed, salted, and worked, to achieve an even consistency. A continuous stream of finished butter is extruded from the machine ready for wrapping. Salted butter has a longer shelf-life than sweet butter, salt being added as a preservative.

buttercup any species of the genus *Ranunculus* of the buttercup family with divided leaves and yellow flowers, including the swamp buttercup (*R. septentrionaiis*) of the US.

butterfly insect belonging, like moths, to the order Lepidoptera, in which the wings are covered with tiny scales, often brightly colored. There are some 15,000 species of butterfly, many of which are under threat throughout the world because of the destruction of habitat.

Butterflies have a tubular proboscis through which they suck up nectar, or, in some species, carrion, dung, or urine. ◊Metamorphosis is complete; the pupa, or chrysalis, is usually without the protection of a cocoon. Adult life span may be only a few weeks, but some species hibernate and lay eggs in the spring.

The largest family, Nymphalidae, has some 6,000 species; it includes the peacock, tortoiseshells, and fritillaries. The family Pieridae includes the cabbage white, one of the few butterflies injurious to crops. The Lycaenidae are chiefly small, often with metallic coloration, for example the blues, coppers, and hairstreaks. The large blue *Lycaena arion* (extinct in Britain from 1979, but re-established 1984) has a complex life history: it lays its eggs on wild thyme, and the caterpillars are then taken by Myrmica ants to their nests. The ants milk their honey glands, while the caterpillars feed on the ant larvae. In the spring, the caterpillars finally pupate and emerge as butterflies. The mainly tropical Papilionidae, or swallowtails, are large and very beautiful, especially the South American species. The world's largest butterfly is Queen Alexandra's birdwing *Ornithoptera alexandrae* of Papua New Guinea, with a body 3 in/7.5 cm long and a wingspan of 10 in/25 cm. The most spectacular migrant is the orange and black monarch butterfly *Danaus plexippus*, which may fly from N Canada to Mexico in the autumn.

Butterflies usually differ from moths in having

butterfly

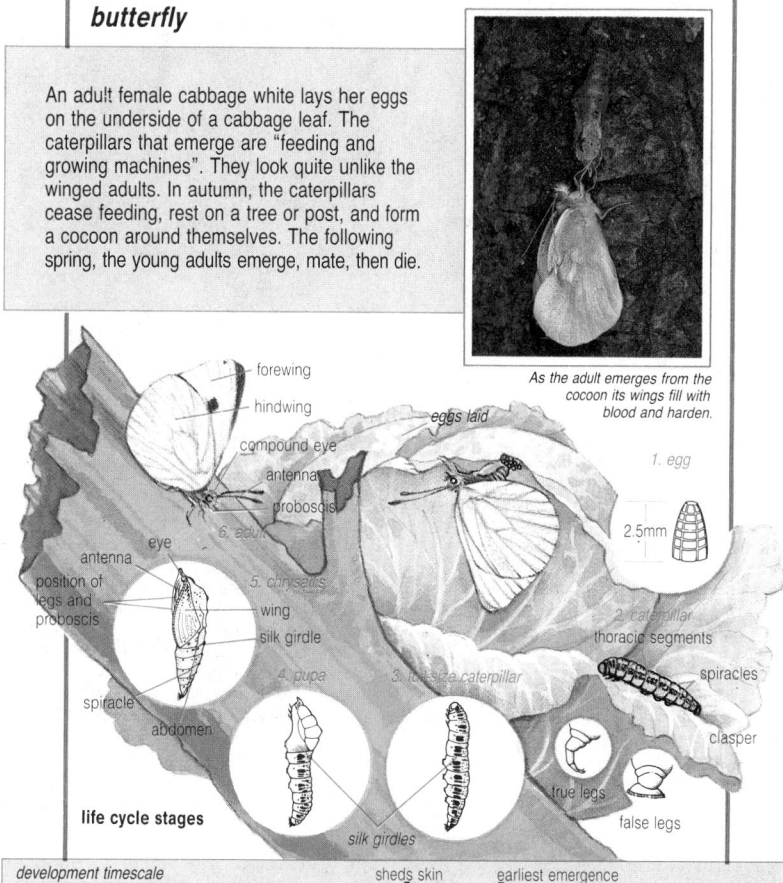

An adult female cabbage white lays her eggs on the underside of a cabbage leaf. The caterpillars that emerge are "feeding and growing machines". They look quite unlike the winged adults. In autumn, the caterpillars cease feeding, rest on a tree or post, and form a cocoon around themselves. The following spring, the young adults emerge, mate, then die.

As the adult emerges from the cocoon its wings fill with blood and harden.

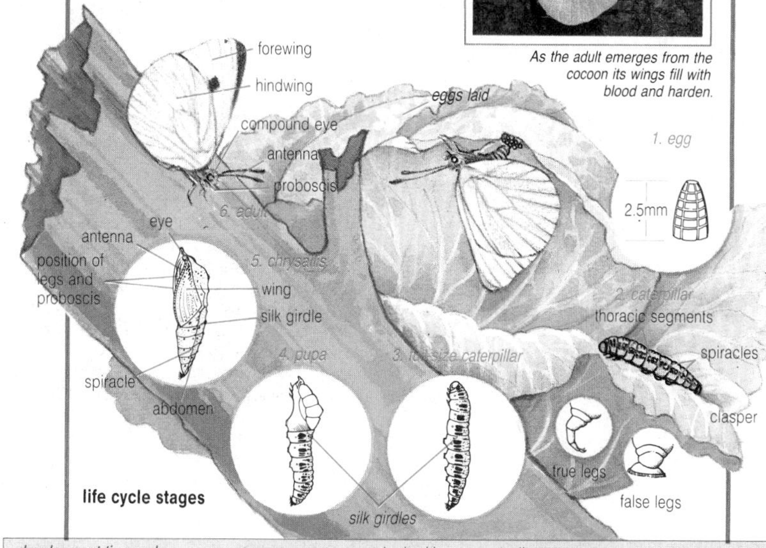
forewing
hindwing
compound eye
antenna
proboscis
6. adult
eggs laid
1. egg
2.5mm
eye
antenna
position of legs and proboscis
5. chrysalis
wing
silk girdle
2. caterpillar
thoracic segments
spiracles
4. pupa
3. full-size caterpillar
spiracle
abdomen
clasper
true legs
false legs
silk girdles

life cycle stages

development timescale						sheds skin		earliest emergence		
stage	1	2				3 & 4		5	can remain pupating for up to 6 months ►	6
weeks	1	2	3	4	5	6	7	8		34

Caterpillars have biting mouthparts and simple eyes. They bite off pieces of leaves with their jaws. Adult butterflies have sucking mouthparts, with which they feed on nectar, and large, compound eyes.

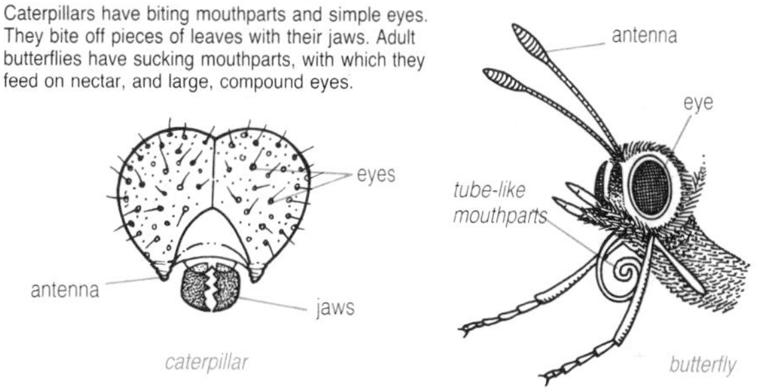
eyes
antenna
jaws
caterpillar
antenna
eye
tube-like mouthparts
butterfly

Byelorussia

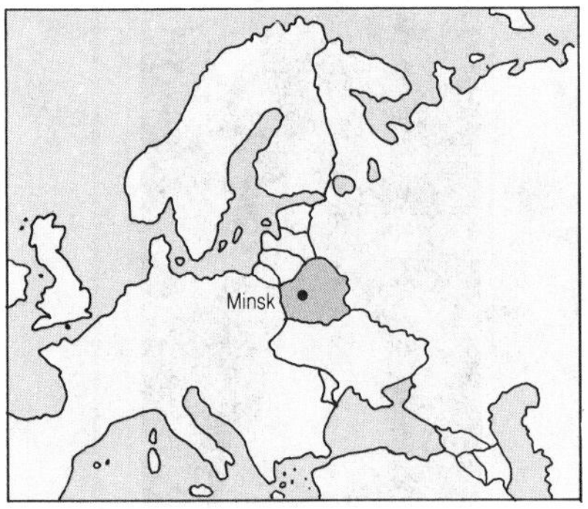
Minsk

the antennae club-shaped rather than plumed or feathery, no "lock" between the fore and hindwing, and resting with the wings in the vertical position rather than flat or sloping.

butterfly fish several fishes, not all related. The freshwater butterfly fish *Pantodon buchholzi* of W Africa can leap from the water and glide for a short distance on its large winglike pectoral fins. Up to 4 in/10 cm long, it lives in stagnant water. The tropical marine butterfly fishes, family Chaetodontidae, are brightly colored with laterally flattened bodies, often with long snouts which they poke into crevices in rocks and coral when feeding.

butterwort insectivorous plant, genus *Pinguicula*, of the bladderwort family, with purplish flowers and a rosette of flat leaves covered with a sticky secretion that traps insects.

Buxtehude Diderik 1637–1707. Danish composer and organist at Lübeck, Germany, who influenced ◊Bach and ◊Handel. He is remembered for his organ works and cantatas, written for his evening concerts or *Abendmusiken*.

buyer's market a market having an excess of goods and services on offer and where prices are likely to be declining. The buyer benefits from the wide choice and competition available.

buzzard any of a number of species of medium-sized hawks with broad wings, often seen soaring.

The common buzzard *Buteo buteo* of Europe and Asia is about 1.8 ft/55 cm long with a wingspan of over 4 ft/1.2 m. It preys on a variety of small animals up to the size of a rabbit. The rough-legged buzzard *Buzzard lagopus* lives in the northern tundra and eats lemmings. The honey buzzard *Pernis apivora* feeds largely, as its name suggests, on honey and insect larvae. It summers in Europe and W Asia and winters in Africa.

Byblos ancient Phoenician city (modern Jebeil), 20 mi/32 km N of Beirut, Lebanon. Known to the Assyrians and Babylonians as Gubla, it had a thriving export of cedar and pinewood to Egypt as early as 1500 BC. In Roman times it boasted an amphitheater, baths, and a temple dedicated to an unknown male god, and was known for its celebration of the resurrection of Adonis, worshiped as a god of vegetation.

Bydgoszcz industrial river port in N Poland, 65 mi/105 km NE of Poznan on the Warta; population (1985) 361,000. As Bromberg it was under Prussian control 1772–1919.

Byelorussia or ***Belorussia*** (Russian *Belaruskaya* or "White Russia") constituent republic of western USSR 1919–91

area 80,154 sq mi/207,600 sq km

capital Minsk

features more than 25% forested; rivers W Dvina, Dnieper and its tributaries, including the Pripet and Beresina; the Pripet Marshes in the E; mild and damp climate

products peat, agricultural machinery, fertilizers, glass, textiles, leather, salt, electrical goods, meat, dairy produce

population (1987) 10,078,000; 79% Byelorussian, 12% Russian, 4% Polish, 2% Ukrainian, 1% Jewish

Guglielmo Bird
Inglese Compositore

Byrd *Early music composer William Byrd is often considered the best of the British composers of his time.*

history In a series of mass executions ordered by Stalin 1937–41, more than 100,000 people were shot. The republic suffered severely under German invasion and occupation during World War II. A Byelorussian Popular Front was established Feb 1989 and in 1991 the republic declared its independence.

Byng Julian, 1st Viscount of Vimy 1862–1935. British general in World War I, commanding troops in Turkey and France, where, after a victory at Vimy Ridge, he took command of the Third Army.

Byrd Richard Evelyn 1888–1957. US aviator and explorer. The first to fly over the North Pole (1926), he also flew over the South Pole (1929), and led five overland expeditions in Antarctica.

At the request of President Franklin Roosevelt, he took command of the US Antarctic Service. Byrd maintained that new techniques could be used as supplements to traditional methods, rather than as replacements for them. In holding this view, he disagreed with Norwegian explorer Roald ◊Amundsen.

Byrd William 1543–1623. British composer. His church choral music (set to Latin words, as he was a firm Catholic) represents his most important work. He also composed secular vocal and instrumental music.

Byrds, the US pioneering folk-rock group 1964–73. Remembered for their 12-string guitar sound and the hits "Mr Tamborine Man" (a 1965 version of Bob Dylan's song) and "Eight Miles High" 1966, they moved toward country rock in the late 1960s.

Byron Augusta Ada 1815–1851. British mathematician, daughter of Lord ◊Byron. She was the world's first computer programmer, working with ◊Babbage's mechanical invention. In 1983 a new, high-level computer language, ADA, was named after her.

Byron George Gordon, 6th Baron Byron 1788–1824. English poet who became the symbol of Romanticism and political liberalism throughout Europe in the 19th century. His reputation was established with the first two cantos of *Childe Harold* 1812. Later works include *The Prisoner of Chillon* 1816, *Beppo* 1818, *Mazeppa* 1819, and, most notably, *Don Juan* 1819–24. He left England in 1816, spending most of his later life in Italy.

Byrd *US explorer Richard Byrd who was the first man to fly to both the North (1926) and South (1929) Poles.*

Born in London and educated at Harrow and Cambridge, Byron published his first volume *Hours of Idleness* 1807 and attacked its harsh critics in *English Bards and Scotch Reviewers* 1809. Overnight fame came with the first two cantos of *Childe Harold*, romantically describing his tours in Portugal, Spain, and the Balkans (third canto 1816, fourth 1818). In 1815 he married the mathematician Anne Milbanke (1792–1860), by whom he had a daughter, Augusta Ada Byron, separating from her a year later amid much scandal. He then went to Europe, where he became friendly with Percy and Mary ◊Shelley. He engaged in Italian revolutionary politics and sailed for Greece in 1823 to further the Greek struggle for independence, but died of fever at Missolonghi. He is remembered for his lyrics, his colloquially easy *Letters*, and as the "patron saint" of romantic liberalism. One of the first biographies of Byron was written by his friend Thomas ◊Moore.

byte in computing, a basic unit of storage of information. A byte contains 8 ◊bits and can hold either a single character (letter, digit, or punctuation symbol) or a number between 0 and 255. Not all computers use bytes, although the unit is widely used in microcomputers.

Byte now also refers to a single memory location; large computer memory size is measured in thousands of bytes (kilobytes or KB) or millions of bytes (megabytes or MB).

Byzantine Empire the Eastern Roman Empire 395–1453, with its capital at Constantinople (formerly Byzantium).

330 Emperor Constantine converted to Christianity and moved his capital to Constantinople.

395 The Roman Empire was divided into eastern and western halves.

476 The Western Empire was overrun by barbarian invaders.

527–565 Emperor Justinian I temporarily recovered Italy, N Africa, and parts of Spain.

7th–8th centuries Syria, Egypt, and N Africa were lost to the Muslims, who twice besieged Constantinople (673–77, 718), but the Christian Byzantines maintained their hold on Anatolia.

8th–9th centuries The ◊Iconoclastic controversy brought the emperors into conflict with the papacy, and in 867 the Greek Orthodox church broke with the Roman.

867–1056 Under the Macedonian dynasty the Byzantine Empire reached the height of its prosperity; the Bulgars proved a formidable danger, but after a long struggle were finally crushed in 1018 by ◊Basil II ("the Bulgar-Slayer"). After Basil's death the Byzantine Empire declined because of internal factions.

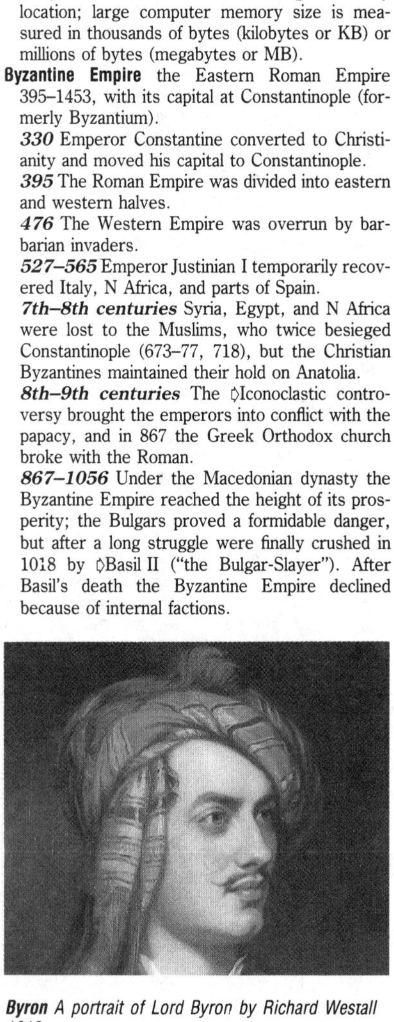

Byron *A portrait of Lord Byron by Richard Westall 1813.*

1071–73 The Seljuk Turks conquered most of Anatolia.

1204 The Fourth Crusade sacked Constantinople and set Baldwin of Flanders (1171–1205) on the throne of the new Latin (W European) Empire.

1261 The Greeks recaptured the Latin (W European) Empire and restored the Byzantine Empire, but it maintained a precarious existence.

1453 The Turks captured Constantinople and founded the ◊Ottoman Empire.

Byzantine literature written mainly in the Greek *koinē*, a form of Greek accepted as the literary language of the 1st century AD and increasingly separate from the spoken tongue of the people, it is chiefly concerned with theology, history, and commentaries on the Greek classics. Its chief authors are the theologians St Basil, Gregory of Nyssa, Gregory of Nazianzus, Chrysostom (4th century AD) and John of Damascus (8th century); the historians Zosimus (about 500), Procopius (6th century), Bryennius and his wife ◊Anna Comnena (about 1100), and Georgius Acropolita (1220–82); and the encyclopedist Suidas (about 975). Drama was nonexistent, and poetry, save for the hymns of the 6th–8th centuries, scanty and stilted, but there were many popular works about the lives of the saints.

Byzantine style a style in the visual arts and architecture that originated in the 4th–5th centuries in Byzantium (the capital of the Eastern Roman Empire), and spread to Italy, throughout the Balkans, and to Russia, where it survived for many centuries. It is characterized by heavy stylization, strong linear emphasis, the use of rigid artistic stereotypes and rich colors such as gold. Byzantine artists excelled in mosaic work and manuscript painting. In architecture, the dome supported on pendentives was in widespread use.

Classical examples of Byzantine architecture are the churches of Sta Sophia, Constantinople, and St Mark's, Venice. Medieval painting styles were influenced by Byzantine art; a more naturalistic style emerged from the 13th century onward in the West. See also ◊medieval art.

Byzantium ancient Greek city on the Bosphorus (modern Istanbul), founded as a colony of the Greek city of Megara, near Corinth, about 660 BC. In AD 330 the capital of the Roman Empire was transferred there by Constantine the Great, who renamed it ◊Constantinople.

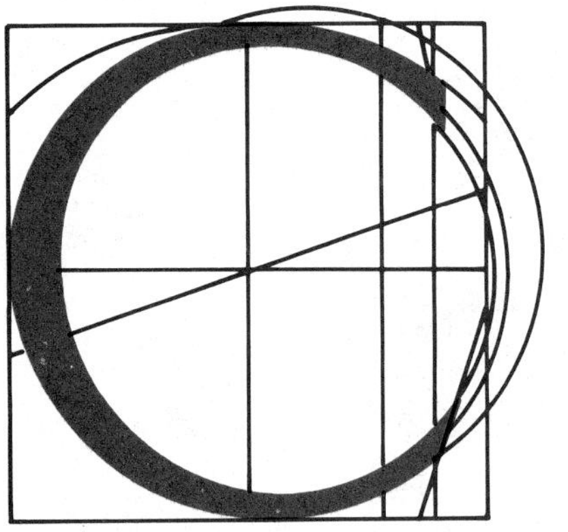

C general-purpose computer-programming language popular on minicomputers and microcomputers. Developed in the early 1970s from an earlier language called BCPL, C is closely associated with the operating system ◊Unix. It is useful for writing fast and efficient systems programs, such as operating systems (which control the operations of the computer).

c. abbreviation for circa (Latin "about"); used with dates that are uncertain.

C abbreviation for centum (Latin "hundred"); century; centigrade; ◊Celsius.

C °C abbreviation for ◊Celsius (temperature scale), formerly called centigrade.

CA abbreviation for ◊California.

Cabal, the (from *kabbala*) group of politicians, the English king Charles II's counselors 1667–73, whose initials made up the word by coincidence—Clifford (Thomas Clifford 1630–1673), Ashley (Anthony Ashley Cooper, 1st Earl of ◊Shaftesbury), ◊Buckingham (George Villiers, 2nd Duke of Buckingham), Arlington (Henry Bennett, 1st Earl of Arlington 1618–1685), and ◊Lauderdale (John Maitland, Duke of Lauderdale).

cabbage plant *Brassica oleracea* of the cress family Cruciferae, allied to the turnip and wild mustard, or charlock. It is a major table vegetable, cultivated as early as 2,000 BC, and the numerous commercial varieties include kale, Brussels sprouts, common cabbage, savoy, cauliflower, sprouting broccoli, and kohlrabi.

cabbala alternate spelling of ◊kabbala.

Cabinda or ***Kabinda*** African coastal enclave, a province of ◊Angola; area 3,000 sq mi/7,770 sq km; population (1980) 81,300. The capital is Cabinda. There are oil reserves. Cabinda, which was attached to Angola in 1886, has made claims to independence.

cabinet in government, a group of advisers to a country's executive. Cabinet members generally advise on, decide, or administer aspects of the government's policy.

The US cabinet consists of the secretaries (heads) of the executive departments, appointed by the president and confirmed by the Senate. The secretaries are not members of Congress; they are advisers to the president.

the US cabinet
Department of State
Department of the Treasury
Department of the Interior
Department of Agriculture
Department of Justice
Department of Commerce
Department of Labor
Department of Defense
Department of Housing and Urban Development
Department of Transportation
Department of Energy
Department of Education
Department of Health and Human Services
Department of Veteran Affairs

cable car method of transporting passengers up steep slopes by cable. In the cable railroad, passenger automobiles are hauled along rails by a cable wound by a powerful winch. A pair of automobiles usually operates together on the funicular principle, one going up as the other goes down. The other main type is the aerial cable car, where the passenger car is suspended from a trolley that runs along an aerial cableway.

A unique form of cable-car system has operated in San Francisco since 1873. The streetcars travel along rails and are hauled by moving cables under the ground.

cable length unit of length, used on ships, originally the length of a ship's anchor cable or 120 fathoms (720 ft/219 m), but in British usage taken as one-tenth of a ◊nautical mile (608 ft/185 m).

cable television distribution of broadcast signals through cable relay systems. Narrowband systems were originally used to deliver services to areas with poor regular reception; systems with wider bands using coaxial and fiber-optic cable are increasingly used for distribution and development of home-based interactive services.

Cabot Sebastian 1474–1557. Italian navigator and cartographer, the second son of Giovanni ◊Caboto. He explored the Brazilian coast and the River Plate for Charles V 1526–30.

He was also employed by Henry VIII, Edward VI, and Ferdinand of Spain. He planned a voyage to China by way of the North-East Passage, the sea route along the N Eurasian coast, encouraged the formation of the Company of Merchant Adventurers of London 1551, and in 1553 and 1556 directed the Company's expeditions to Russia, where he opened British trade.

Caboto Giovanni or John Cabot 1450–1498. Italian navigator. Commissioned, with his three sons, by Henry VII of England to discover unknown lands, he arrived at Cape Breton Island on June 24, 1497, thus becoming the first European to reach the North American mainland (he thought he was in NE Asia). In 1498 he sailed again, touching Greenland, and probably died on the voyage.

Cabral Pedro Alvarez 1460–1526. Portuguese explorer. He set sail from Lisbon for the East Indies March 1500, and accidentally reached Brazil by taking a course too far west. He claimed the country for Portugal Apr 25, as Spain had not followed up Vicente Pinzón's (c. 1460–1523) landing there earlier in the year. Continuing around Africa, he lost seven of his fleet of 13 ships (the explorer Bartolomeu ◊Diaz being one of those drowned), and landed in Mozambique. Proceeding to India, he negotiated the first Indo-Portuguese treaties for trade, and returned to Lisbon July 1501.

cactus

Cabrini Frances or Francesca 1850–1917. (also called "Mother Cabrini") First Roman Catholic US citizen to become a saint. Born in Lombardy, Italy, she founded the Missionary Sisters of the Sacred Heart, and established many schools and hospitals in the care of her nuns. She was canonized 1946. Her feast day is Dec 22.

cacao tropical South American evergreen tree *Theobroma cacao* of the Sterculia family, now also cultivated in West Africa and Sri Lanka. Its seeds are cocoa beans, from which ◊cocoa and chocolate are prepared.

The trees mature at five to eight years and produce two crops per year. The fruit is 6.5 in/17 cm–9.5 in/25 cm long, hard and ridged, with the beans inside. The seeds are called cocoa nibs; when left to ferment, then roasted and separated from the husks, they contain about 50% fat, part of which is removed to make chocolate and cocoa. The Aztecs revered cacao and made a drink for the nobility only from cocoa beans and chilis, which they called chocolatl. In the 16th century the Spanish brought cacao to Europe. It was used to make a drink, which came to rival coffee and tea in popularity.

cacao beans see ◊cocoa and chocolate.

cachalot alternate name for the sperm whale; see ◊whale.

Cacoyannis Michael 1922– . Greek film director and writer whose films include *Zorba the Greek* 1965. Born in Cyprus, he studied law in England before returning to Greece to become a leading film director.

cactus (plural cacti) plant of the family Cactaceae, although the term is commonly applied to many different succulent and prickly plants. True cacti have a woody axis (central core) overlaid with an enlarged fleshy stem, which assumes various forms and is usually covered with spines (actually reduced leaves). They all have special adaptations to growing in dry areas.

Cactus flowers are often large and brightly colored; the fruit is fleshy and often edible, as in the case of the prickly pear. The Cactaceae are a New World family and include the treelike saguaro and the night-blooming cereus with blossoms 12 in/30 cm across.

CAD (acronym from computer-aided design) the use of computers for creating and editing design drawings. CAD also allows such things as automatic testing of designs and multiple or animated three-dimensional views of designs. CAD systems are widely used in architecture, electronics, and engineering, for example in the motor-vehicle industry, where automobiles designed with the assistance of computers are now commonplace. A related development is ◊CAM (computer-assisted manufacture).

caddis fly insect of the order Trichoptera. Adults are generally dull brown, mothlike, with wings covered in tiny hairs. Mouthparts are poorly developed, and many do not feed as adults. They are usually found near water.

The larvae are aquatic, and many live in cases, open at both ends, which they make out of sand or plant remains. Some species make silk nets among aquatic vegetation to help trap food.

cadenza in music, an unaccompanied bravura passage (requiring elaborate, virtuoso execution) in the style of an improvisation for the soloist during a concerto.

Cádiz Spanish city and naval base, capital and seaport of the province of Cádiz, standing on Cádiz Bay, an inlet of the Atlantic, 64 mi/103 km S of Seville; population (1986) 154,000. After the discovery of the Americas 1492, Cádiz became one of Europe's most vital trade ports. The English seaman Francis Drake burned a Spanish fleet here 1587 to prevent the sailing of the ◊Armada.

Probably founded by the Phoenicians about 1100 BC, it was a center for the tin trade with Cornwall, England. It was recaptured from the ◊Moors by the king of Castile 1262. Development was restricted by its peninsular location until a bridge to the opposite shore of Cádiz Bay was completed 1969.

cadmium soft, silver-white, ductile and malleable, metallic element, symbol Cd, atomic number 48, atomic weight 112.40. Cadmium occurs in nature as a sulfide or carbonate in zinc ores. It is a toxic metal that, because of industrial dumping, has become an environmental pollutant. Its uses include batteries, electroplating, and as a constituent of alloys used for bearings with low coefficients of friction; it is also a constituent of an alloy with a very low melting point.

Cadmium is also used in control rods for nuclear reactors, caused by its high absorption of neutrons. It was named in 1817 by German chemist Friedrich Strohmeyer (1776–1835) for Cadmus, in Greek mythology, ruler of Thebes near where ores containing it were found.

Cadmus in Greek mythology, a Phoenician from ◊Tyre, brother of ◊Europa. He founded the city of Thebes in Greece. Obeying the oracle of Athena, Cadmus slew the sacred dragon that guarded the spring of Ares. He sowed the teeth of the dragon from which sprang a multitude of fierce warriors who fought among themselves; the survivors were considered to be the ancestors of the Theban aristocracy.

Cadmus married Harmonia and was credited with the introduction of the (Phoenician) alphabet into Greece.

caecilian tropical amphibian of rather wormlike appearance. There are about 170 species known, forming the amphibian order Apoda (also known as Caecilia or Gymnophiona). Caecilians have a grooved skin that gives a "segmented' appearance, have no trace of limbs, and mostly live below ground. Some species bear live young, others lay eggs.

Caen capital of Calvados *département*, France, on the river Orne; population (1982) 183,526. It is a business center, with ironworks, electric and electronic industries. Caen building stone has a fine reputation. The town is linked by canal with the nearby English Channel to the NE. The church of St Étienne was founded by William the Conqueror, and the university by Henry VI of England in 1432. Caen was captured by the British in World War II on July 9, 1944 after five weeks' fighting, during which the town was badly damaged.

Caernarvon or ***Caernarfon*** administrative headquarters of Gwynedd, N Wales, situated on the SW shore of the Menai Strait; population (1981) 10,000. Formerly a Roman station, it is now a market port city. The first Prince of Wales (later ◊Edward II) was born in Caernarvon Castle; Edward VIII was invested here 1911 and Prince Charles 1969.

Caesar powerful family of ancient Rome, which included Gaius Julius ◊Caesar, whose grandnephew and adopted son ◊Augustus assumed the name of Caesar and passed it on to his adopted son ◊Tiberius. Henceforth, it was used by the successive emperors, becoming a title of the Roman rulers. The titles "tsar" (czar) in Russia and "kaiser" in Germany were both derived from the name Caesar.

***Caesar** Roman general and consul of the Roman republic, Julius Caesar wrote masterful commentaries of his campaigns.*

Caesar Gaius Julius c. 102–44 BC. Roman statesman and general. He formed with Pompey and Crassus the First Triumvirate in 60 BC. He conquered Gaul 58–50 and invaded Britain 55 and 54. He fought against Pompey 49–48 defeating him at Pharsalus. After a period in Egypt Caesar returned to Rome as dictator from 46. He was assassinated by conspirators on the ◊Ides of March, 44 BC.

A patrician, Caesar allied himself with the popular party, and when elected Aedile 65 nearly ruined himself with lavish amusements for the Roman populace. Although a free thinker, he was elected chief pontiff 63 and appointed governor of Spain 61. Returning to Rome 60, he formed with Pompey and Crassus the First Triumvirate. As governor of Gaul, he was engaged in its subjugation 58–50, defeating the Germans under Ariovistus and selling thousands of the Belgic tribes into slavery. In 55 he crossed into Britain, returning for a further campaigning visit 54. A revolt by the Gauls under Vercingetorix 52 was crushed 51. His own commentaries on the campaigns show a mastery worthy of fiction, as does his account of the ensuing Civil War. His governorship of Spain was to end 49, and, Crassus being dead, Pompey became his rival. Declaring "the die is cast," Caesar crossed the Rubicon (the small river separating Gaul from Italy) to meet the army raised against him by Pompey. In the ensuing civil war, he followed Pompey to Epirus 48, defeated him at Pharsalus, and chased him to Egypt, where he was murdered. Caesar stayed some months in Egypt, where Cleopatra, queen of Egypt, gave birth to his son, Caesarion. He executed a lightning campaign 47 against King Pharnaces II (ruled 63–47 BC) in Asia Minor, which he summarized: *Veni vidi vici* "I came, I saw, I conquered." With his final victory over the sons of Pompey at Munda in Spain 45, he established his position, having been awarded a ten-year dictatorship 46. On March 15, 44 he was stabbed to death at the foot of Pompey's statue (see ◊Brutus, ◊Cassius) in the Senate house.

Caesarea ancient city in Palestine (now ◊Qisarya). It was built by Herod the Great 22–12 BC, who also constructed a port (*portus Augusti*). It was the administrative capital of the province of Judea.

Caesarea Mazaca ancient name for the Turkish city of ◊Kayseri.

Caesarean section surgical operation to deliver a baby by cutting through the mother's abdominal and intrauterine walls. It may be recommended for almost any obstetric complication implying a threat to mother or baby. In the US in 1987, 24% of all births were by Caesarean section.

Caesarean section was named after the Roman emperor Julius Caesar, who was born this way. In medieval times, it was performed mostly in attempts to save the life of a child whose mother had died in labor. The Christian church forbade cutting open the mother before she was dead.

Caetano Marcello 1906–1980. Portuguese right-wing politician. Professor of administrative law at Lisbon from 1940, he succeeded the dictator Salazar as prime minister from 1968 until his exile after the military coup of 1974. He was granted political asylum in Brazil.

caffeine one of a group of organic substances called ◊alkaloids. Caffeine is found in tea, coffee, chocolate, maté, and kola nuts; it stimulates the heart and central nervous system. When isolated, it is a bitter crystalline substance, $C_8H_{10}N_4O_2$. Too much caffeine can be detrimental to health (more than six average cups of tea or coffee a day).

Cage John 1912– . US composer. A pupil of ◊Schoenberg, he reassessed musical esthetics and defined the role of music as "purposeless play." He maintained that sounds should be available for musical purposes; for example, he used 24 radios, turned on to random stations, in *Imaginary Landscape No 4* 1951. He also worked to reduce the control of the composer over the music, introducing randomness and inexactitude and allowing sounds to "be themselves."

In one of his most famous pieces, titled *4 Minutes and 33 Seconds* 1952, the pianist sits at the piano reading a score for that length of time but does not play. Cage's unconventional ideas have had a profound impact on 20th-century music. See also ◊aleatory music.

Cagliari capital and port of Sardinia, Italy, on the Gulf of Cagliari; population (1988) 222,000.

Cagnes-sur-Mer capital of the *département* of Alpes-Maritimes; SW of Nice, France; population (1986) 35,214. The château (13th–17th centuries) contains mementoes of the artist Renoir, who lived here 1900–19.

Cagney James 1899–1986. US actor who moved to films from Broadway. Usually associated with gangster roles in films such as *The Public Enemy* 1931, he was an actor of great versatility, playing Bottom in *A Midsummer Night's Dream* 1935 and singing and dancing in *Yankee Doodle Dandy* 1942. He starred in *Mr Roberts* 1955, and *One Two Three* was his last film before retirement; but in 1981 he came back for *Ragtime*.

Cahora Bassa the largest hydroelectric project in Africa, created as a result of the damming of the Zambezi River to form a reservoir 144 mi/230 km long in W Mozambique.

Cain in the Old Testament, the first-born son of Adam and Eve. Motivated by jealousy, he murdered his brother Abel as the latter's sacrifice was more acceptable to God than his own.

Cain James M(allahan) 1892–1977. US novelist. He was the author of *The Postman Always Rings Twice* 1934, *Mildred Pierce* 1941, and *Double Indemnity* 1943, which all became classic motion pictures. These novels epitomized the "hard-boiled" fiction of the 1930s and 1940s.

Caine Michael. Adopted name of Maurice Micklewhite 1933– . English actor, whose long career has seen him mature from cheeky, Cockney roles to an artist of great range and versatility. His cinematic history includes the films *Alfie* 1966, *California Suite* 1978, *Educating Rita* 1983, and *Hannah and her Sisters* 1986.

cairn Scottish breed of ◊terrier. Shaggy, shortlegged, and compact, it can be sandy, greyish brindle, or red. It was formerly used for flushing out foxes and badgers.

Cairngorms mountain group in Scotland, N part of the ◊Grampians, the highest peak being Ben Macdhui 4,296 ft/1,309 m.

Cairo (Arabic *El Qahira*) capital of Egypt, on the E bank of the Nile 8 mi/13 km above the apex of

Caine *English film actor Michael Caine is known for his dry Cockney wit.*

the Delta and 100 mi/160 km from the Mediterranean; the largest city in Africa and in the Middle East; population (1985) 6,205,000, Greater Cairo (1987) 13,300,000. El Fustat (Old Cairo) was founded by Arabs about AD 64, Cairo itself about 1000 by the ◊Fatimid ruler Gowhar. The Great Pyramids and Sphinx are at nearby Gîza.

It is the site of the mosque that houses the El Azhar university 972. The city is 20 mi/32 km N of the site of the ancient Egyptian center of ◊Memphis.

The Mosque of Amr dates from 643; the Citadel, built by Sultan Saladin in the 12th century, contains the impressive 19th-century Mohammed Ali mosque.

The government and business quarters reflect Cairo's position as a leading administrative and commercial center, and the semiofficial newspaper *al Ahram* is an influential voice in the Arab world. At Helwan, 15 mi/24 km to the S, an industrial center is developing, with iron and steel works powered by electricity from the Aswan High Dam. There are two secular universities: Cairo University (1908) and Ein Shams (1950).

caisson hollow cylindrical or boxlike structure, usually of reinforced ◊concrete, that is sunk into a riverbed to form the foundations of a bridge.

An open caisson is open at the top and at the bottom, where there is a wedge-shaped cutting edge. Material is excavated from inside, allowing the caisson to sink. A pneumatic caisson has a pressurized chamber at the bottom, in which workers carry out the excavation. The air pressure prevents the surrounding water entering; the workers enter and leave the chamber through an air lock, allowing for a suitable decompression period to prevent ◊decompression sickness (the so-called bends).

CAL (acronym from computer-assisted learning) the use of computers in education and training: the computer displays instructional material to a student and asks questions about the information given; the student's answers determine the sequence of the lessons.

cal symbol for ◊calorie.

Calabar port and capital of Cross River State, SE Nigeria, on the Cross River, 40 mi/64 km from the Atlantic; population (1983) 126,000. Rubber, timber, and vegetable oils are exported. It was a center of the slave trade in the 18th and 19th centuries.

calabash tropical South American evergreen tree *Crescentia cujete*, family Bignoniaceae, with gourds 20 in/50 cm across, which are used as water containers. The Old World tropical vine bottle gourd *Lagenaria siceraria* of the gourd family Cucurbitaceae is sometimes called calabash, and it produces equally large true gourds.

Calabria mountainous earthquake region occupying the "toe" of Italy, comprising the provinces of Catanzaro, Cosenza, and Reggio; capital Catanzaro; area 5,829 sq mi/15,100 sq km; population (1988) 2,146,000. Reggio is the industrial center.

Calamity Jane *Known as a sharpshooter in the mining towns of South Dakota was Martha Jane Burke, then called Calamity Jane.*

Calais port in N France; population (1982) 101,000. Taken by England's Edward III in 1347, it was saved from destruction by the personal surrender of the Burghers of Calais commemorated in Rodin's sculpture; the French retook it 1558. Following German occupation May 1940–Oct 1944, it surrendered to the Canadians.

Calais, Pas de French name for the Strait of ◊Dover.

calamine $Zn_4Si_2O_7(OH)_2.H_2O$ native zinc silicate, an ore of zinc. The term also refers to a pink powder of zinc oxide mixed with 0.5% ferric oxide, used in lotions and ointments as a topical astringent.

Calamity Jane nickname of Martha Jane Burke c. 1852–1903. US heroine of Deadwood, South Dakota. She worked as a teamster, transporting supplies to the mining camps, adopted male dress and, as an excellent shot, promised "calamity" to any aggressor. Many fictional accounts of the "wild west" featured her exploits.

She was also known as Martha Jane Canary. During a smallpox epidemic 1878, she assisted in caring for the victims who had been abandoned by local citizens.

calceolaria plant of the *Calceolaria* figwort genus, family Scrophulariaceae, with brilliantly colored slipper-shaped flowers. Native to South America, they were introduced to Europe and the US in the 1830s.

Calchas in Greek mythology, a visionary and interpreter of omens for the Greek expedition against ◊Troy, responsible for recommending the sacrifice of ◊Iphigenia by her father ◊Agamemnon, as an atonement for an offense against the goddess ◊Artemis.

calcination the ◊oxidation of metals by burning in air.

calcite a common, colorless, white, or light-colored rock-forming mineral, calcium carbonate, $CaCO_3$. It is the main constituent of ◊limestone and marble, and forms many types of invertebrate shell.

Calcite often forms ◊stalactites and ◊stalagmites in caves and is also found deposited in veins through many rocks because of the ease with which it is dissolved and transported by groundwater; ◊oolite is its spheroidal form. It rates 3 on the ◊Mohs' scale of hardness. Large crystals up to 3 ft/1 m have been found in Oklahoma and Missouri. ◊Iceland spar is a transparent form of calcite used in the optical industry; as limestone it is used in the building industry.

calcium (Latin *calcis* "lime") soft, silver-white, metallic element, symbol Ca, atomic number 20, atomic weight 40.08. It is one of the ◊alkaline-earth metals. One of the most widely distributed elements, it is the fifth most abundant element (the third most abundant metal) in the Earth's crust. It is found mainly as its carbonate $CaCO_3$, which occurs in a fairly pure condition as chalk and limestone (see ◊calcite). Calcium is an essential component of bones, teeth, shells, milk, and leaves, and it forms 1.5% of the human body by mass.

Calcium is very important to ongoing health, and the best source for human utilization is found in plant foods, such as sesame seeds and broccoli. Calcium was named in 1808 by Humphry Davy.

calculator pocket-sized electronic computing device for performing numerical calculations. It can add, subtract, multiply, and divide; many calculators also compute squares and roots, and have advanced trigonometric and statistical functions. Input is by a small keyboard and results are shown on a one-line computer screen, typically a ◊liquid crystal display (LCD) or a light-emitting diode (LED). The first electronic calculator was manufactured by the Bell Punch Company in the US in 1963.

calculus (Latin "pebble") branch of mathematics that permits the manipulation of continuously varying quantities, used in practical problems involving such matters as changing speeds, problems of flight, varying stresses in the framework of a bridge, and alternating current theory. Integral calculus deals with the method of summation or adding together the effects of continuously varying quantities. Differential calculus deals in a similar way with rates of change. Many of its applications arose from the study of the gradients of the tangents to curves.

There are several other branches of calculus, including calculus of errors and calculus of variation. Differential and integral calculus, each of which deals with small quantities which during manipulation are made smaller and smaller, compose the infinitesimal calculus. Differential equations relate to the derivatives of a set of variables and may include the variables. Many give the mathematical models for physical phenomena such as ◊simple harmonic motion. Differential equations are solved generally through integrative means, depending on their degrees. If no known mathematical processes are available, integration can be performed graphically or by computers.

history Calculus originated with Archimedes in the 3rd century BC as a method for finding the areas of curved shapes and for drawing tangents to curves. These ideas were not developed until the 17th century, when the French philosopher Descartes introduced ◊coordinate geometry, showing how geometrical curves can be described and manipulated by means of algebraic expressions. Then the French mathematician Fermat used these algebraic forms in the early stages of the development of differentiation. Later the German philosopher Leibniz and the English scientist Newton advanced the study.

Calcutta largest city of India, on the river Hooghly, the westernmost mouth of the river Ganges, some 80 mi/130 km N of the Bay of Bengal. It is the capital of West Bengal; population (1981) 9,166,000. It is chiefly a commercial and industrial center (engineering, shipbuilding, jute, and other textiles). Calcutta was the seat of government of British India 1773–1912.

Buildings include a magnificent Jain temple, the palaces of former Indian princes; and the Law Courts and Government House, survivals of the British Raj. Across the river is ◊Howrah, and

caldera *Huge caldera of Las Canadas, S Tenerife, Canary Islands. Lava is flowing from the summit in the foreground.*

between Calcutta and the sea there is a new bulk cargo port, Haldia, which is the focus of oil refineries, petrochemical plants, and fertilizer factories.

There is a fine museum; educational institutions include the University of Calcutta (1857), oldest of several universities; the Visva Bharati at Santiniketan, founded by Rabindranath Tagore; and the Bose Research Institute.

history Calcutta was founded 1686–90 by Job Charnock of the East India Company as a trading post. Captured by Suraj-ud-Dowlah in 1756, during the Anglo-French wars in India, in 1757 it was retaken by Robert Clive.

Caldecott Randolph 1846–1886. British artist and illustrator of books for children, including *John Gilpin* 1848.

The Caldecott medal, given annually by the American Library Association to the artist of the year's best illustrated book, is named for him.

Calder Alexander 1898–1976. US abstract sculptor, the inventor of mobiles, suspended shapes that move in the lightest current of air. In the 1920s he began making wire sculptures and stabiles (static mobiles), colored abstract shapes attached by lines of wire. Huge versions adorn Lincoln Center in New York City and UNESCO in Paris.

Calder was born in Philadelphia. An important early influence on him was the Ringling Brothers and Barnum and Bailey Circus, which inspired such works as his miniature *Circus* of wire marionettes. About 1930, his friendship with Miró and Mondrian influenced him to create abstract works. In 1943 the first retrospective of his work was exhibited at the Museum of Modern Art.

caldera in geology, a very large basin-shaped ◊crater. Calderas are found at the tops of volcanoes, where the original peak has collapsed into an empty chamber beneath. The basin, many times larger than the original volcanic vent, may be flooded, producing a crater lake, or the flat floor may contain a number of small volcanic cones, produced by volcanic activity after the collapse.

Typical calderas are Kilauea, Hawaii; Crater Lake, Oregon; and the summit of Olympus Mons, on Mars. Some calderas are wrongly referred to as craters, such as Ngorongoro, Tanzania.

Calderón de la Barca Pedro 1600–1681. Spanish dramatist and poet. After the death of Lope de Vega in 1635, he was considered to be the leading Spanish dramatist. Most celebrated of the 118 plays is the philosophical *La Vida es sueño/Life is a Dream* 1635.

Born in Madrid, Calderón studied law at Salamanca (1613–19). In 1620 and 1622 he was successful in poetry contests in Madrid; while still writing dramas, he served in the army in Milan and the Netherlands (1625–35). By 1636 his first volume of plays was published and he had been made master of the revels at the court of Philip IV, receiving a knighthood in 1637. In 1640 he assisted in the suppression of the Catalan rebellion. After the death of his mistress he became a Franciscan in 1650, was ordained in 1651, and appointed as a prebendary of Toledo in 1653. As honorary chaplain to the king in 1663, he produced outdoor religious plays for the festival of the Holy Eucharist. His works include the tragedies *El pintor de su deshonra/The Painter of His Own Dishonor* 1645, *El Alcalde de Zalamea/The Mayor of Zalamea* 1640, and *El Médico de su honra/The Surgeon of His Honor* 1635; the historical *El Príncipe constante/The Constant Prince* 1629; and the dashing intrigue *La Dama duende/The Phantom Lady* 1629.

Caldwell Erskine (Preston) 1903–1987. US novelist whose *Tobacco Road* 1932 and *God's Little Acre* 1933 are earthy and vivid presentations of poverty-stricken Southern sharecroppers.

D. PETRVS CALDERON DE LA BARCA.

Calderón de la Barca *Spanish poet and dramatist Don Pedro Calderón de la Barca produced his first play at age 13. He went on to write more than 100 plays.*

Born in White Oak, Georgia, Caldwell traveled with his father, a minister, and worked among poor whites in the South as a cotton picker. His other works include *Trouble in July* 1940 and *Georgia Boy* 1943. He was married to photojournalist Margaret Bourke-White, who collaborated with him on three books, notably *You Have Seen Their Faces* 1937, about the rural South.

Caledonian Canal a waterway in NW Scotland, 61 mi/98 km long, linking the Atlantic and the North Sea. Of its total length only a 23 mi/37 km stretch is artificial, the rest being composed of lochs Lochy, Oich, and Ness. The canal was built by Thomas Telford 1803–23.

calendar the division of the ◊year into months, weeks, and days and the method of ordering the years. From year one, an assumed date of the birth of Jesus, dates are calculated backwards (BC "before Christ," or BCE "before common era") and forwards (AD, Latin, *anno domini* "in the year of the Lord" or CE "common era"). The lunar month (period between one new moon and the next) naturally averages 29.5 days, but the Western calendar uses for convenience a calendar month with a complete number of days, 30 or 31 (Feb has 28). For adjustments, since there are slightly fewer than six extra hours a year left over, they are added to Feb as a 29th day every fourth year (leap year), century years being excepted unless they are divisible by 400. For example 1896 was a leap year; 1900 was not.

The month names in most European languages were probably derived as follows: January from Janus, Roman god; February from *Februar*, Roman festival of purification; March from Mars, Roman god; April from Latin *aperire*, "to open"; May from Maia, Roman goddess; June from Juno, Roman goddess; July from Julius Caesar, Roman general; August from Augustus, Roman emperor; September, October, November, December (originally the seventh–tenth months) from the Latin words meaning seventh, eighth, ninth, and tenth, respectively.

The days of the week are Monday named after the Moon; Tuesday from Tiu or Tyr, Anglo-Saxon and Norse god; Wednesday from Woden or Odin, Norse god; Thursday from Thor, Norse god; Friday from Freya, Norse goddess; Saturday from Saturn, Roman god; and Sunday named after the Sun.

All early calendars except the ancient Egyptian were lunar. The word calendar comes from the Latin *Kalendae* or *calendae*, the first day of each month on which, in ancient Rome, solemn proclamation was made of the appearance of the new moon.

The Western or Gregorian calendar derives from the Julian calendar instituted by Julius Caesar 46 BC. It was adjusted by Pope Gregory XIII 1582, who eliminated the accumulated error caused by a faulty calculation of the length of a year and avoided its recurrence by restricting century leap years to those divisible by 400. Other states only gradually changed from ◊Old Style to New Style; Britain and its colonies adopted the Gregorian calendar 1752, when the error amounted to 11 days, and Sept 3, 1752 became Sept 14 (at the same time the beginning of the year was put back from March 25 to Jan 1). Russia did not adopt it until the October Revolution of 1917, so that the event (then Oct 25) is currently celebrated Nov 7.

The Jewish calendar is a complex combination of lunar and solar cycles, varied by considerations of religious observance. A year may have 12 or 13 months, each of which normally alternates between 29 and 30 days; the New Year (Rosh Hashanah) falls between Sept 5 and Oct 5. The calendar dates from the hypothetical creation of the world (taken as Oct 7, 3761 BC).

The Chinese calendar is lunar, with a cycle of 60 years. Both the traditional and, from 1911, the Western calendar are in use in China.

The Muslim calendar, also lunar, has 12

California

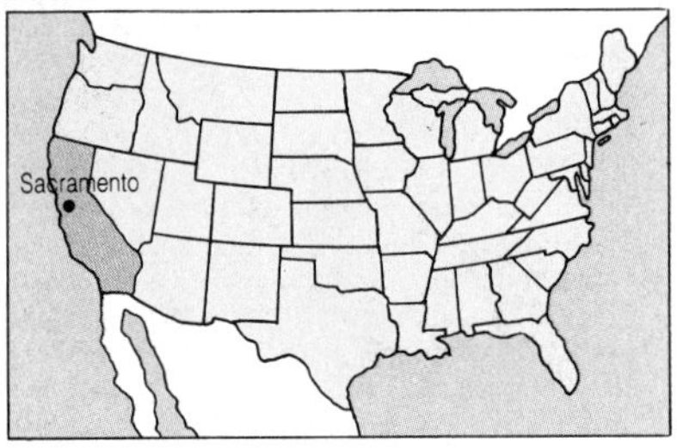
Sacramento

months of alternately 30 and 29 days, and a year of 354 days. This results in the calendar rotating around the seasons in a 30-year cycle, so that when the 9th month of Ramadan (when Muslims fast during the day) occurs in summer, fasting may be very difficult. The era is counted as beginning on the day Mohammed fled from Mecca AD 622.

Calgary city in Alberta, Canada, on the Bow River, in the foothills of the Rockies; at 3,440 ft/1,048 m it is one of the highest Canadian towns; population (1986) 671,000. It is the center of a large agricultural region and is the oil and financial center of Alberta and W Canada. Founded as Fort Calgary by the North West Mounted Police 1875, it was reached by the Canadian Pacific Railway 1885 and developed rapidly after the discovery of oil 1914. The 1988 Winter Olympic Games were held here.

It has oil-linked and agricultural industries, such as fertilizer factories and flour mills, and is also a tourist center; the annual Calgary Exhibition and Stampede is held in July. The University of Calgary became independent of the University of Alberta 1966.

Calhoun John C(aldwell) 1782–1850. US politician; vice-president 1825–29 under John Quincy Adams and 1829–33 under Andrew Jackson. Throughout his vice-presidency, he was a defender of strong states' rights versus an overpowerful federal government and of the institution of slavery. He served in the US Senate 1842–43, 1845–50, where he continued to espouse the right of states to legislate on slavery.

Born near Abbeville, South Carolina, Calhoun was educated at Yale University and studied law in Connecticut. He served in the South Carolina state legislature 1809–11, after which he became a representative to the US Congress. As secretary of war in President Monroe's cabinet, he supported the federal government, but gradually his political philosophy changed as it became evident to him that states' rights had to stay strong to keep slavery in the South, assuming it essential to the cotton industry. As President Tyler's secretary of state 1844–45, he was responsible for effecting the annexation of Texas.

Cali city in SW Colombia, in the Cauca Valley 3,200 ft/975 m above sea level, founded in 1536. Cali has textile, sugar, and engineering industries. Population (1985) 1,398,276.

calibration the preparation of a usable scale on a measuring instrument. A mercury ◊thermometer, for example, can be calibrated with a Celsius scale by noting the heights of the mercury column at two standard temperatures—the freezing point (0°C) and boiling point (100°C) of water—and dividing the distance between them into 100 equal parts and continuing these divisions above and below.

calico a cotton fabric. In the US, a printed cotton; in the UK, a plain woven cotton material. The name derives from Calicut, India, an original source of calico.

California Pacific-coast state of the US; nickname Golden State (originally because of its gold mines, more recently because of its orange groves and sunshine)

area 158,685 sq mi/411,100 sq km

capital Sacramento

cities Los Angeles, San Diego, San Francisco, San José, Fresno

physical Sierra Nevada, including Yosemite and Sequoia national parks, Lake Tahoe, Mount Whitney (14,500 ft/4,418 m, the highest mountain in the lower 48 states); the Coast Range; Death Valley (282 ft/86 m below sea level, the lowest point in the W hemisphere); deserts Colorado, Mohave (Edwards Air Force base is here); Monterey Peninsula; Salton Sea; the San Andreas fault; huge, offshore underwater volcanoes with tops 5 mi/8 km across

features California Institute of Technology (Caltech); Lawrence Berkeley and Lawrence Livermore laboratories of the University of California, which share particle physics and nuclear weapons research with Los Alamos; Stanford University, which has the Hoover Institute and is the powerhouse of ◊Silicon Valley; Paul Getty art museum at Malibu, built in the style of a Roman villa; Hollywood.

products leading agricultural state with fruit (peaches, citrus, grapes in the valley of the San Joaquin and Sacramento rivers), nuts, wheat, vegetables, cotton, and rice, all mostly grown by irrigation, the water being carried by immense concrete-lined canals to the Central and Imperial valleys; beef cattle; timber; fish; oil; natural gas; aerospace technology; electronics (Silicon Valley); food processing; films and television programs; great reserves of energy (geothermal) in the hot water that lies beneath much of the state

population (1990) 29,760,021, the most populous state of the US; 66% non-Hispanic white, 20% Hispanic, 7% black, 7% Asian (including many Vietnamese)

famous people Luther Burbank, Walt Disney, William Randolph Hearst, Jack London, Marilyn Monroe, Richard Nixon, Ronald Reagan, John Steinbeck

history colonized by Spain 1769; ceded to the US after the Mexican War 1848; became a state 1850. The discovery of gold in the Sierra Nevada Jan 1848 was followed by the gold rush 1849-56. The completion of the first transcontinental railroad 1869 fostered economic development. The Los Angeles area flourished with the growth of the film industry after 1910, oil discoveries in the early 1920s, and the development of aircraft plants and shipyards during World War II. Some 100,000 Californians of Japanese ancestry were interned during the war. California became the nation's most populous state in 1962. Northern California benefited from the growth of the electronics industry during the 1970s in what came to be called Silicon Valley.

California current the cold ocean ◊current in the East Pacific Ocean flowing southward down the west coast of North America. It is part of the North Pacific ◊gyre (a vast, circular movement of ocean water).

California, Lower English name for ◊Baja California.

californium synthesized, radioactive, metallic element of the ◊actinide series, symbol Cf, atomic number 98, atomic weight 251. It is produced in very small quantities and used in nuclear reactors as a neutron source. The longest-lived isotope, Cf-251, has a half-life of 800 years.

It is named after the state of California, where it was first synthesized in 1950 by Glenn Seaborg and his team at the University of California at Berkeley.

Caligula Gaius Caesar AD 12–41. Roman emperor, son of Germanicus and successor to Tiberius in AD 37, Caligula was a cruel tyrant and was assassinated by an officer of his guard. Believed to have been mentally unstable, he is remembered for giving a consulship to his horse Incitatus.

calima (Spanish "haze") dust cloud in Europe, coming from the Sahara Desert, which sometimes causes heatwaves and eye irritation.

calipers an instrument used for measuring the thickness or diameter of objects—for example, the internal and external diameter of pipes. Some calipers are made like a drawing compass, having two legs, often curved, pivoting about a screw at one end. The ends of the legs are placed in contact with the object to be measured, and the gap between the ends is then measured against a rule. The slide caliper looks like an adjustible wrench, and carries a scale for direct measuring, usually with a ◊vernier scale for accuracy.

caliph title of civic and religious heads of the world of Islam. The first caliph was ◊Abu Bakr. Nominally elective, the office became hereditary, held by the Ummayyad dynasty 661–750 and then by the ◊Abbasid. During the 10th century the political and military power passed to the leader of the caliph's Turkish bodyguard; about the same time, an independent ◊Fatimid caliphate sprang up in Egypt. After the death of the last Abbasid (1258), the title was claimed by a number of Muslim chieftains in Egypt, Turkey, and India. The most powerful of these were the Turkish sultans of the Ottoman Empire.

The title was adopted by the prophet Mohammed's successors. The last of the Turkish caliphs was deposed by Kemal ◊Atatürk in 1924.

calla alternate name for ◊arum lily.

Callaghan (Leonard) James, Baron Callaghan 1912– . British Labour politician. As chancellor of the Exchequer 1964–67, he introduced corporation and capital-gains taxes, and resigned following devaluation. He was home secretary 1967–70 and prime minister 1976–79 in a period of increasing economic stress. As foreign secretary 1974, Callaghan renegotiated Britain's membership of the European Community. In 1976 he succeeded Harold Wilson as prime minister and in 1977 entered into a pact with the Liberals to maintain his government in office. Strikes in the winter of 1978–79 led to his defeat at the polls May 1979.

Callaghan Morley 1903–1990. Canadian novelist and short-story writer whose realistic novels include *Such Is My Beloved* 1934, *More Joy In Heaven* 1937, and *Close To The Sun Again* 1977.

His other works include *They Shall Inherit The Earth* 1935, *The Loved and the Lost* 1951, *Stories* 1959, and *A Passion in Rome* 1961.

Callao chief commercial and fishing port of Peru, 7 mi/12 km SW of Lima; population (1988) 318,000. Founded 1537, it was destroyed by an earthquake 1746. It is Peru's main naval base, and produces fertilizers.

Callas Maria. Adopted name of Maria Kalogeropoulos 1923–1977. US lyric soprano, born in New York of Greek parents. With a voice of fine range and a gift for dramatic expression, she exceled in operas including *Norma, Madame Butterfly, Aïda, Lucia di Lammermoor,* and *Medea.*

She debuted in Verona, Italy, in 1947 and at New York's Metropolitan Opera in 1956. Although her technique was not considered perfect, she helped to popularize Classical coloratura roles through her expressiveness and charisma.

Callicrates 5th century BC. Athenian architect (with Ictinus) of the ◊Parthenon on the Acropolis.

calligraphy the art of handwriting, regarded in China and Japan as the greatest of the visual arts, and playing a large part in Islamic art because the depiction of the human and animal form is forbidden.

The present letter forms have gradually evolved from originals shaped by the tools used to make them—the flat brush on paper, the chisel on stone, the stylus on wax and clay, and the reed and quill on papyrus and skin.

In Europe during the 4th and 5th centuries, books were written in square capitals ("majuscules") derived from Classical Roman inscriptions (Trajan's Column in Rome is the outstanding example). The rustic capitals of the same period were written more freely, and the uncial capitals, more rounded, were used from the 4th to the 8th centuries. During this period the cursive hand was also developing, and the interplay of this with the formal hands, coupled with the need for speedier writing, led to the small letter forms ("minuscules"). During the 7th century the half-uncial was developed with ascending and descending strokes and was adopted by all countries under Roman rule. The cursive forms developed differently in different countries. In Italy the italic script was evolved and became the model for italic typefaces. Printing and the typewriter undermined the need for calligraphy in the West until the 20th-century revival inspired by Edward Johnston (1872–1944).

Callimachus 310–240 BC. Greek poet and critic known for his epigrams. Born in Cyrene, he taught in Alexandria, Egypt, where he is reputed to have been head of the great library.

Calliope in Greek mythology, the ◊Muse of epic poetry and chief of the Muses.

Callisto in Greek mythology, the ◊nymph beloved by Zeus (Roman Jupiter) who was changed into a she-bear by his jealous wife Hera.

Callisto second-largest moon of Jupiter, 3,000 mi/4,800 km in diameter, orbiting every 16.7 days at a distance of 1.2 million mi/1.9 million km from the planet. Its surface is covered with large craters.

Callot Jacques 1592/93–1635. French engraver and painter. His series of etchings *Great Miseries of War* 1632–33, prompted by his own experience of the Thirty Years' War, are arrestingly composed and full of horrific detail.

callus in botany, a tissue that forms at a damaged plant surface. Composed of large, thin-walled ◊parenchyma cells, it grows over and around the wound, eventually covering the exposed area.

Calmette Albert 1863–1933. French bacteriologist. A student of Pasteur, he developed (with Camille Guérin 1872–1961) the ◊BCG vaccine against tuberculosis in 1921.

calorie unit of heat, now replaced by the ◊joule (one calorie is approximately 4.2 joules). It is the heat required to raise the temperature of one gram of water by 1°C. In dietetics, the calorie or kilocalorie is equal to 1,000 calories.

The kilocalorie measures the energy value of food in terms of its heat output: 1 oz/28 g of protein yields 120 kilocalories, of carbohydrate 110, of fat 270, and of alcohol 200.

calorific value the amount of heat generated by a given mass of fuel when it is completely burned. It is measured in joules per kilogram. Calorific values are measured experimentally with a bomb calorimeter.

calorimeter instrument used in physics to measure heat. A simple calorimeter consists of a heavy copper vessel that is polished (to reduce heat losses by radiation) and covered with insulating material (to reduce losses by convection and conduction).

In a typical experiment, such as to measure the heat capacity of a piece of metal, the calorimeter is filled with water, whose temperature rise is measured using a thermometer when a known mass of the heated metal is immersed in it. Chemists use a bomb calorimeter to measure the heat produced by burning a fuel completely in oxygen.

calotype a paper-based photograph using a wax paper negative, the first example of the ◊negative/positive process invented by the English photographer Fox Talbot around 1834.

Calpe former name of ◊Gibraltar.

Caltanissetta town in Sicily, Italy, 60 mi/96 km SE of Palermo; population (1981) 61,146. It is the center of the island's sulfur industry. It has a baroque cathedral.

Calvados *département* in Basse-Normandie region of France, which has given its name to an apple brandy distilled from cider.

Calvary (Aramaic *Golgotha* "skull") in the New Testament, the site of Jesus's crucifixion at Jerusalem. Two chief locations are suggested: the site where the Church of the Sepulchre now stands, and the hill beyond the Damascus gate.

Calvert George 1579–1632. Founder of Maryland.

***Calvin** John Calvin was the Swiss Protestant reformer who founded Calvinism and the Presbyterian form of church government.*

Born in Yorkshire, England, and educated at Oxford, Calvert became a confidant of King James I, served in parliament and the Privy Council, and was knighted in 1617. Later named secretary of state, Calvert was forced to resign from that office because of his conversion to Roman Catholicism 1625. In the same year, he was named Baron Baltimore by the king. As a supporter of colonization in North America, he was granted land in Newfoundland 1628 but, finding the climate too harsh, obtained a royal charter for Maryland 1632.

Calvin John (also known as Cauvin or Chauvin) 1509–1564. French-born Swiss Protestant church reformer and theologian. He was a leader of the Reformation in Geneva and set up a strict religious community there. His theological system is known as Calvinism, and his church government as ◊Presbyterianism. Calvin wrote (in Latin) *Institutes of the Christian Religion* 1536 and commentaries on the New Testament and much of the Old Testament.

Calvin, born in Noyon, Picardie, studied theology and then law, and about 1533 became prominent in Paris as an evangelical preacher. In 1534 he was obliged to leave Paris and retired to Basel, where he studied Hebrew. In 1536 he accepted an invitation to go to Geneva, Switzerland, and assist in the Reformation, but was expelled 1538 because of public resentment against the numerous and too drastic changes he introduced. He returned to Geneva 1541 and, in the face of strong opposition, established a rigorous theocracy (government by priests). In 1553 he had the Spanish theologian Servetus burned for heresy. He supported the Huguenots in their struggle in France and the English Protestants persecuted by Queen Mary I.

Calvin Melvin 1911– . US chemist who, using radioactive carbon-14 as a tracer, determined the biochemical processes of ◊photosynthesis, in which green plants use ◊chlorophyll to convert carbon dioxide and water into sugar and oxygen. He was awarded a Nobel Prize 1961.

Calvinism Christian doctrine as interpreted by John Calvin and adopted in Scotland, parts of Switzerland, and the Netherlands; by the ◊Puritans in England and New England; and by the subsequent Congregational and Presbyterian churches in the US. Its central doctrine is predestination, under which certain souls (the elect) are predestined by God through the sacrifice of Jesus to salvation, and the rest to damnation. Although Calvinism is rarely accepted today in its strictest interpretation, the 20th century has seen a Neo-Calvinist revival through the work of Karl ◊Barth.

Calypso in Greek mythology, a sea ◊nymph who waylaid the homeward-bound Odysseus for seven years.

calypso in music, a type of West Indian satirical ballad with a syncopated beat.

calyptra in mosses and liverworts, a layer of cells that encloses and protects the young ◊sporophyte (spore capsule), forming a sheathlike hood around the capsule. Also used to describe the root cap, a layer of ◊parenchyma cells covering the end of a root that gives protection to the root tip as it grows through the soil. This is constantly being worn away and replaced by new cells from a special ◊meristem, the calyptrogen.

calyx the collective term for the ◊sepals of a flower, forming the outermost whorl of the ◊perianth. It surrounds the other flower parts and protects them while in bud. In some flowers, for example, the catchflies *Silene* of the pink family, the sepals are fused along their sides, forming a sticky tubular calyx.

cam a part of a machine that converts circular motion to linear motion or vice versa. The edge cam in a car engine is in the form of a rounded projection on a shaft, the camshaft. When the camshaft turns, the cams press against linkages (plungers or followers) that open the valves in the cylinders.

A face cam is a disk with a groove in its face, in which the follower travels. A cylindrical cam carries angled parallel grooves, which impart a to-and-fro motion to the follower when it rotates.

CAM (acronym from computer-aided manufacture) the use of computers to control production processes; in particular, the control of machine tools and ◊robots in factories. In some factories, the whole design and production system has been automated by linking ◊CAD (computer-aided design) to CAM.

Very flexible manufacturing with CAD/CAM can be utilized by computer-based sales and distribution methods to mass-produce semicustomized products.

Camagüey city in Cuba; population (1986) 260,800. It is the capital of Camagüey province in the center of the island. Founded about 1514, it was the capital of the Spanish West Indies during the 19th century. It has a 17th-century cathedral.

Camargo Marie-Anne de Cupis de 1710–1770. French ballet dancer of Spanish descent. Born in Brussels, she became a ballet star in Paris in 1726. She was the first ballerina to wear a shortened skirt, which allowed freedom of movement and increased visibility. She was the first to attain the ◊*entrechat quatre*.

Camargue marshy area of the ◊Rhône delta, south of Arles, France; about 300 sq mi/780 sq km. Bulls and horses are bred there, and the nature preserve, which is known for its bird life, forms the southern part.

cambium a layer of actively dividing cells (lateral ◊meristem), found within stems and roots, that gives rise to ◊secondary growth in perennial plants, causing an increase in girth. There are two main types of cambium: vascular cambium which gives rise to secondary ◊xylem and ◊phloem tissues, and cork cambium (or phellogen) which gives rise to secondary cortex and cork tissues (see ◊bark).

Cambodia formerly Khmer Republic 1970–76, Democratic Kampuchea 1976–77, and People's Republic of Kampuchea 1979–89 country in SE Asia, bordered N and NW by Thailand, N by Laos, E and SE by Vietnam, and SW by the South China Sea.

government Under the 1981 constitution, the sole and supreme legislative body in Cambodia is the national assembly, whose 117 members are elected for five-year terms by universal suffrage. The assembly elects from within its ranks a smaller, permanent council of state, headed by the state president. In addition, it appoints a council of ministers, headed by a prime minister, to carry out day-to-day government. The dominating force in Cambodia is the Communist Party (Kampuchean People's Revolutionary Party) supported

Cambodia

State of
(former official names
Khmer Republic 1970–76,
Democratic Kampuchea 1976–79,
People's Republic of Kampuchea 1979–89)

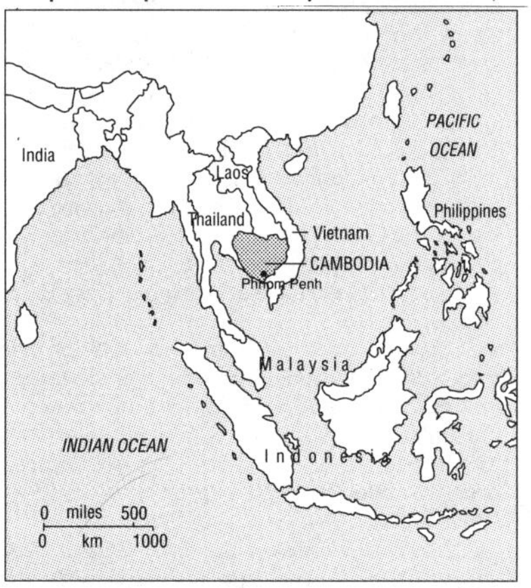
India
PACIFIC
OCEAN
Laos
Thailand
Philippines
Vietnam
CAMBODIA
Phnom Penh
Malaysia
INDIAN OCEAN
Indonesia
0 miles 500
0 km 1000

area 69,880 sq mi/181,035 sq km
capital Phnom Penh
cities Battambang, the seaport Kompong Som
physical mostly flat forested plains with mountains in SW and N; Mekong River runs N–S
features ruins of ancient capital Angkor; Lake Tonle Sap
head of state Heng Samrin from 1979*
head of government Hun Sen from 1985*
*Not internationally recognized. UN seat is held by government in exile formed 1982: Son Sann, premier; Norodom Sihanouk, coalition leader.
political system communism
political parties Kampuchean People's Revolutionary Party (KPRP), Marxist-Leninist; Party of Democratic Kampuchea (Khmer Rouge), exiled ultranationalist communist; Khmer People's National Liberation Front (KPNLF), exiled anticommunist; Sihanoukists, exiled prodemocracy forces allied to Prince Sihanouk
exports rubber, rice, pepper, wood, cattle
currency Cambodian riel
population (1990 est) 6,993,000; growth rate 2.2% p.a.
life expectancy men 42, women 45
language Khmer (official), French
religion Theravada Buddhist 95%
literacy men 78%/women 39% (1980 est)
GDP $592 mn (1987); $83 per head
chronology
1863–1941 French protectorate.
1941–45 Occupied by Japan.
1946 Recaptured by France.
1953 Independence achieved from France.
1970 Prince Sihanouk overthrown by US-backed Lon Nol.
1975 Lon Nol overthrown by Khmer Rouge.
1978–79 Vietnamese invasion and installation of Heng Samrin government.
1982 The three main anti-Vietnamese resistance groups formed an alliance under Prince Sihanouk.
1987 Partial withdrawal of Vietnamese troops.
1988 Vietnamese troop withdrawal continued.
1989 Name of State of Cambodia readopted and Buddhism declared state religion. Vietnamese forces fully withdrawn Sept; civil war intensified; Khmer Rouge captured a provincial capital; Sihanouk declared willingness to consider UN trusteeship pending elections.
1991 Ceasefire agreed and peace talks started but subsequently collapsed before final peace agreement signed in November.

by the mass organization the Kampuchean United Front for National Construction and Defense.

history The area now known as Cambodia was once occupied by the Khmer empire, an ancient civilization that flourished during the 6th–15th centuries. After this, the region was subject to attacks by the neighboring Vietnamese and Thai, and in 1863 became a French protectorate. A nationalist movement began in the 1930s, and in 1940–41 anti-French feeling was fueled when the French agreed to Japanese demands for bases in Cambodia, and allowed Thailand to annex Cambodian territory.

During World War II Cambodia was occupied by Japan. France regained control of the country in 1946, but it achieved semiautonomy within the French Union in 1949 and full independence in 1953. Prince Norodom Sihanouk (1922–), who had been elected king in 1941, abdicated in favor of his parents and became prime minister as leader of the Popular Socialist Community in 1955. In 1960, when his father died, he became head of state.

Sihanouk remained neutral during the ◊Vietnam War and was overthrown by a right-wing revolt led by pro-US Lt-Gen Lon Nol in 1970. Lon Nol first became prime minister (1971–72) and then president (1972–75) of what was termed the new Khmer Republic. His regime was opposed by the exiled Sihanouk and by the communist Khmer Rouge (backed by N Vietnam and China) who merged to form the National United Front of Cambodia. A civil war developed and despite substantial military aid from the US during its early stages, Lon Nol's government fell in 1975. The country was renamed Kampuchea, with Prince Sihanouk as head of state.

The Khmer Rouge proceeded ruthlessly to introduce an extreme communist program, forcing urban groups into rural areas, which led to over 2,500,000 deaths from famine, disease and maltreatment. In 1976 a new constitution removed Prince Sihanouk from power, appointed Khieu Samphan (the former deputy prime minister) president and placed the Communist Party of Kampuchea, led by ◊Pol Pot, in control. The Khmer Rouge developed close links with China and fell out with its former sponsors Vietnam and the Soviet Union.

In a Vietnamese invasion of Kampuchea launched in 1978, Pol Pot was overthrown and a pro-Vietnamese puppet government was set up under Heng Samrin, head of the newly formed Kampuchean National United Front for National Salvation. The defeated regime kept up guerrilla resistance under Pol Pot, causing over 300,000 Kampuchean refugees to flee to Thailand in 1979.

In 1982 the resistance movement broadened with the formation in Kuala Lumpur (Malaysia) of an anti-Vietnamese coalition and Democratic Kampuchea government-in-exile with Prince Sihanouk (then living in North Korea) as president, Khieu Samphan (political leader of the now less extreme Khmer Rouge) as vice-president, and Son Sann (an ex-premier and contemporary leader of the noncommunist Khmer People's National Liberation Front) as prime minister. The coalition received sympathetic support from ◊ASEAN countries and China. However, its 60,000 troops were outnumbered by the 170,000 Vietnamese who supported the Heng Samrin government. With the resistance coalition's base camps being overrun in 1985, a military victory appeared unlikely. From 1982 the US aided the KPNLF and the Sihanoukist National Army (ANS) – allies of the Khmer Rouge – with millions of dollars in "humanitarian" aid and secret "nonlethal" military aid.

Hopes of a political settlement were improved by the retirement of the reviled Pol Pot as Khmer Rouge military leader in 1985 and by the appointment of the reformist Hun Sen as prime minister. A mixed-economy domestic approach was adopted and indigenous Khmers promoted to key government posts; at the same time, prompted by the new Soviet leader Mikhail Gorbachev, the Vietnamese began a phased withdrawal. In spring 1989, following talks with the resistance coalition, the Phnom Penh government agreed to a package of constitutional reforms, including the adoption of Buddhism as the state religion and a change of name to the ideologically neutral State of Cambodia. Despite the breakdown of further talks over possible future power-sharing agreements, withdrawal of the Vietnamese army was completed Sept 1989. However, the United Nations continued to refuse recognition of the Hun Sen government and the civil war intensified, with the Khmer Rouge making advances in the western provinces. The Phnom Penh government was left with an army of 40,000, backed by a 100,000-strong militia, against the resistance coalition's 45,000 guerrillas, half of whom belonged to the Khmer Rouge. In Nov 1990 the five permanent members of the UN Security Council, including the US, USSR, and China, agreed on the final draft of a Cambodian peace settlement, which provided for an immediate ceasefire and the formation of of an interim administration under UN auspices. The Phnom Penh government dismissed it, objecting to the establishment of a UN administration within the country. However, a comprehensive peace agreement was finally signed (by 19 countries) in Oct 1991. The treaty named the United Nations to help adminster the country and to oversee a return to democracy.

Cambrai chief town of Nord *département*, France; on the river Escaut (Scheldt); population (1982) 36,600. Industries include light textiles (cambric is named after the town) and confectionery. The Peace of Cambrai or Ladies' Peace (1529) was concluded on behalf of Francis I of France by his mother Louise of Savoy and on behalf of Charles V by his aunt Margaret of Austria. Cambrai was severely damaged during World War I.

Cambrai, Battles of two battles in World War I at Cambrai in NE France:

First Battle Nov–Dec 1917, the town was almost captured by the British when large numbers of tanks were used for the first time.

Second Battle Aug 26–Oct 5, 1918, the town was taken during the final British offensive.

Cambrian period of geologic time 590–505 million years ago; the first period of the Paleozoic era. All invertebrate animal life appeared, and marine algae were widespread. The earliest fossils with hard shells, such as trilobites, date from this period.

The name comes from Cambria, an old name for Wales, where Cambrian rocks are typically exposed and were first described.

Cambridge city in England, on the river Cam (a river sometimes called by its earlier name, Granta), 50 mi/80 km N of London; population (1989) 101,000. It is the administrative headquarters of Cambridgeshire. The city is centered on Cambridge University (founded 12th century).

history As early as 100 BC, a Roman settlement grew up on a slight rise in the low-lying plain, commanding a ford over the river. Apart from those of Cambridge University, fine buildings include St Benet's church, the oldest building in Cambridge, the round church of the Holy Sepulchre, and the Guildhall 1939.

The Cambridge Science Park was started by Trinity College 1973. Industries include the manufacture of scientific instruments, radio, electronics, paper, flour milling, and fertilizers.

Cambridge city in Massachusetts; population (1990) 95,802. Industries include paper and publishing. Harvard University 1636 (the oldest educational institution in the US, named after John Harvard

1607–38, who bequeathed his library to it along with half his estate), Massachusetts Institute of Technology 1861, and the John F Kennedy School of Government and Memorial Library are here, as well as a park named after him.

Cambridge University English university, one of the earliest in Europe, probably founded in the 12th century, although the earliest of the existing colleges, Peterhouse, was not founded until about 1284.

Famous students of the university include Rupert Brooke, S T Coleridge, Thomas Gray, Christopher Marlowe, John Milton, Samuel Pepys, and William Wordsworth. In 1990, there were 10,000 undergraduate and 3,000 postgraduate students.

Cambridge Colleges

1280–84 Peterhouse	1596 Sidney Sussex
1326 Clare	1800 Downing
1347 Pembroke	1869 Girton
1348 Gonville and Caius	1871 Newnham
1350 Trinity Hall	1882 Selwyn
1352 Corpus Christi	1885 Hughes Hall
1441 King's	1896 St Edmund's House
1448 Queens'	1954 New Hall
1473 St Catherine's	1960 Churchill
1496 Jesus	1964 Darwin
1505 Christ's	1965 Wolfson College
1511 St John's	1966 Lucy Cavendish College
1542 Magdalene	1966 Clare Hall
1546 Trinity	1966 Fitzwilliam
1584 Emmanuel	1978 Robinson College

Cambyses 6th century BC. Emperor of Persia 529–522 BC. Succeeding his father Cyrus, he assassinated his brother Smerdis and conquered Egypt in 525 BC. There he outraged many of the local religious customs and was said to have become insane. He died in Syria on his journey home, probably by suicide.

Camden industrial city of New Jersey, on the Delaware River; population (1990) 87,492. The city is linked with Philadelphia, Pennsylvania, by the Benjamin Franklin suspension bridge (1926). The Walt ◊Whitman House, where the poet lived 1884–92, is now a museum.

Camden Town Group school of British painters 1911–13, based in Camden Town, London, inspired by W R Sickert. The work of Spencer Gore (1878–1914) and Harold Gilman (1876–1919) is typical of the group, rendering everyday town scenes in Post-Impressionist style.

camel large cud-chewing mammal of the even-toed hoofed order Artiodactyla. Unlike typical ruminants, it has a three-chambered stomach. It has two toes which have broad soft soles for walking on sand, and hoofs resembling nails. There are two species, the single-humped Arabian camel (*Camelus dromedarius*), and the twin-humped Bactrian camel (*Camelus bactrianus*) from Asia. They carry a food reserve of fatty tissue in the hump, can go without drinking for long periods, can feed on salty vegetation, and withstand extremes of heat and cold, thus being well adapted to desert conditions.

The Arabian camel has long been domesticated, so that its original range is not known. It is used throughout Arabia and N Africa, and has been taken to other places such as North America and Australia, in the latter country playing a crucial part in the development of the interior. The dromedary is, strictly speaking, a lightly-built, fast, riding variety of the Arabian camel, but often the name is applied to all one-humped camels. Arabian camels can be used as pack animals, for riding, racing, milk production, and for meat.

The Bactrian camel is native to the central Asian deserts, where a small number still live wild, but most are domestic animals. With a head and body length of 10 ft/3 m and shoulder height of about 6 ft/2 m, the Bactrian camel is a large

Cameroon

Republic of

(République du Cameroun)

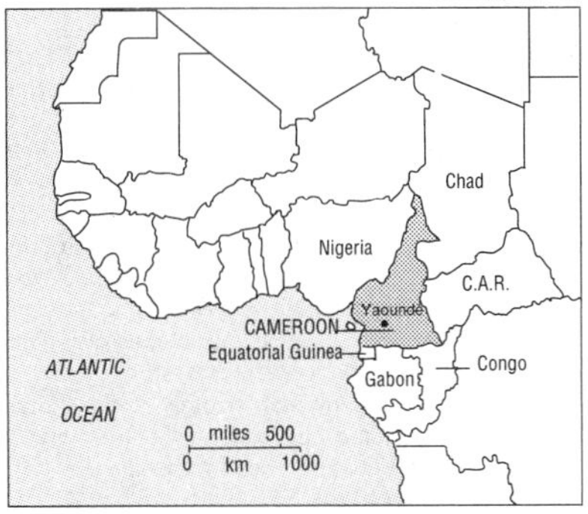
Chad
Nigeria
C.A.R.
CAMEROON
Yaoundé
Equatorial Guinea
Gabon
Congo
ATLANTIC
OCEAN
0 miles 500
0 km 1000

area 183,638 sq mi/475,440 sq km
capital Yaoundé
cities chief port Douala; Nkongsamba, Garova
physical desert in far N in the Lake Chad basin, mountains in W, dry savanna plateau in the intermediate area, and dense tropical rainforest in S
features Mount Cameroon 13,358 ft/4,070 m, an active volcano on the coast, W of the Adamawa Mountains
head of state and of government Paul Biya from 1982
political system one-party authoritarian nationalism; Cameroon is a police state, using torture to oppress dissent
political parties Democratic Assembly of the Cameroon People (RDPC), nationalist left-of-center
exports cocoa, coffee, bananas, cotton, timber, rubber, groundnuts, gold, aluminum, crude oil
currency CFA franc
population (1990 est) 11,109,000; growth rate 2.7% p.a.
life expectancy men 49, women 53
language French and English in pidgin variations (official); there has been some discontent with the emphasis on French—there are 163 indigenous peoples with their own African languages
religion Roman Catholic 35%, animist 25%, Muslim 22%, Protestant 18%
literacy men 68%/women 45% (1985 est)
GDP $12.7 bn (1987); $1,170 per head
chronology
1884 Treaty signed establishing German rule.
1916 Captured by Allied forces in World War I.
1922 Divided between Britain and France.
1946 French and British Cameroons made UN trust territories.
1960 French Cameroon became the independent Republic of Cameroon. Ahmadou Ahidjo elected president.
1961 N part of British Cameroon merged with Nigeria and S part joined the Republic of Cameroon to become the Federal Republic of Cameroon.
1966 One-party regime introduced.
1972 New constitution made Cameroon a unitary state, the United Republic of Cameroon.
1973 New national assembly elected.
1982 Ahidjo resigned and was succeeded by Paul Biya.
1983 Biya began to remove his predecessor's supporters; accused by Ahidjo of trying to create a police state. Ahidjo went into exile in France.
1984 Biya reelected; defeated a plot to overthrow him. Country's name changed to Republic of Cameroon.
1988 Biya reelected.
1991 Widespread public disorder. Biya granted amnesty to political prisoners and promised multiparty elections.

animal, but not so long in the leg as the Arabian. It has a shaggy winter coat.

camellia any oriental evergreen shrub with roselike flowers of the genus *Camellia*, tea family Theaceae. Numerous species, including *C. japonica* and *C. reticulata*, have been introduced into Europe and the US.

Camelot legendary seat of King ◊Arthur.

A possible site is the Iron Age hill fort of South Cadbury Castle in Somerset, England, where excavations from 1967 have revealed remains dating from 3000 BC to AD 1100, including those of a large 6th-century settlement, the time ascribed to Arthur.

Camembert village in Normandy, France, where Camembert cheese originated.

cameo small relief carving of semiprecious stone, shell or glass. A pale-colored surface layer is carved to reveal a darker ground. Fine cameos were produced in ancient Greece and Rome, during the Renaissance, and in the Victorian era. They were used for decorating goblets and vases, and as jewelry.

camera an optical device used in ◊photography.

camera obscura a darkened box with a tiny hole for projecting the inverted image of the scene outside on to a screen inside. For its development as a device for producing photographs, see ◊photography.

Cameron Charles 1746–1812. Scottish architect. He trained under Isaac Ware in the Palladian tradition before being summoned to Russia in 1779. He created the palace complex at Tsarskoe Selo (now Pushkin), planned the town of Sofia, and from 1803, as Chief Architect of the Admiralty, executed many buildings, including the Naval Hospital and barracks at Kronstadt 1805.

Cameron Julia Margaret 1815–1879. British photographer. She made lively, revealing portraits of the Victorian intelligentsia using a large camera, five-minute exposures, and wet plates. Her subjects included Charles Darwin and Alfred Tennyson.

Cameron Simon 1799–1889. US political leader. At the 1860 Republican nominating convention, he threw his support to Lincoln, gaining an appointment as secretary of war. A dismal failure in that position, he was named minister to Russia 1862. After the Civil War he returned to the Senate, serving 1867–77.

Born in Maytown, Pennsylvania, Cameron was trained as a printer, but he eventually became a newspaper editor in Harrisburg and embarked on a political career. Gaining wealth through investments in transportation and industry, he served two partial terms in the US Senate 1845–49, 1857–60.

Cameroon country in W Africa, bounded NW by Nigeria, NE by Chad, E by the Central African Republic, S by Congo, Gabon, and Equatorial Guinea, and W by the Atlantic.

government Cameroon was a federal state until 1972 when a new constitution, revised 1975, made it unitary. The constitution provides for a president and a single-chamber national assembly of 180, each elected for a five-year term. The president has the power to choose the cabinet, to lengthen or shorten the life of the assembly, and may stand for re-election. The only political party is the Democratic Assembly of the Cameroon People (RDPC), formed 1966 by a merger of the governing party of each state of the original federation and the four opposition parties. The state president is also president of the party.

history The area was first visited by Europeans 1472, when the Portuguese began slave trading in the area. In 1884 Cameroon became a German protectorate. After World War I, France governed about 80% of the area under a ◊League of Nations mandate, with Britain administering the

camouflage *A well-camouflaged giant bush cricket or katydid from Aguas Calientes, Peru.*

remainder. In 1946 both became UN trust territories.

In 1957 French Cameroons became a state within the French Community and three years later achieved full independence as the Republic of Cameroon. After a plebiscite 1961, the northern part of British Cameroons merged with Nigeria, and the southern part joined the Republic of Cameroon to form the Federal Republic of Cameroon. The French zone became East Cameroon and the British part West Cameroon.

Ahmadou Ahidjo, who had been the first president of the republic 1960, became president of the federal republic and was re-elected 1965. In 1966 Cameroon was made a one-party state when the two government parties and most of the opposition parties merged into the Cameroon National Union (UNC). Extreme left-wing opposition to the UNC was crushed 1971. In 1972 the federal system was abolished, and a new national assembly was elected 1973.

In 1982 Ahidjo resigned, nominating Paul Biya as his successor. In 1983 Biya began to remove Ahidjo's supporters, and in protest Ahidjo resigned the presidency of UNC. Biya was re-elected 1984, while Ahidjo went into exile in France. Biya strengthened his position by abolishing the post of prime minister and reshuffling his cabinet. He also changed the nation's name from the United Republic of Cameroon to the Republic of Cameroon. Many of Ahidjo's supporters were executed after a failed attempt to overthrow Biya. In 1985 UNC changed its name to RPDC, and Biya tightened his control by more cabinet changes.

In Aug 1986 a volcanic vent under Lake Nyos released a vast quantity of carbon dioxide and hydrogen sulfide, which suffocated large numbers of people and animals.

In April 1988 Biya was re-elected president with 98.75% of the vote.

Camilla a Volscian woman and warrior, enemy of ◊Aeneas and ally of Turnus in ◊Virgil's *Aeneid*.

Camoëns or ***Camões*** Luís Vaz de 1524–1580. Portuguese poet and soldier. He went on various military expeditions, and was shipwrecked in 1558. His poem, *Os Lusiades/The Lusiads*, published 1572, tells the story of the explorer Vasco da Gama and incorporates much Portuguese history; it has become the country's national epic. His posthumously published lyric poetry is also now valued.

Having wounded an equerry of the king in 1552, he was banished to India. He received a small pension, but died in poverty of plague.

Camorra Italian secret society formed about 1820 by criminals in the dungeons of Naples and continued once they were freed. It dominated politics from 1848, was suppressed in 1911, but many members eventually surfaced in the US ◊Mafia. The Camorra still operates in the Naples area.

camouflage colors or structures that allow an animal to blend with its surroundings to avoid detection by other animals. Camouflage can take the form of matching the background color, of countershading (darker on top, lighter below, to counteract natural shadows), or of irregular patterns that break up the outline of the animal's body. More elaborate camouflage involves closely resembling a feature of the natural environment, as with the stick insect; this is closely akin to ◊mimicry.

Camp Walter Chauncey 1859–1925. US football coach who initiated the tradition of selecting an annual All-American football team. Born in New Britain, Connecticut, Camp was educated at Yale University. In 1888, after a brief business career, he returned to Yale as athletic director. As the Yale football coach and member of the Intercollegiate Football Rules Committee, Camp was responsible for instituting some of the most basic rules of the game, including team size, field dimensions, and the four-down system.

Campagna Romana lowland stretch of the Italian peninsula, including and surrounding the city of Rome. Lying between the Tyrrhenian Sea and the Sabine Hills to the NE, and the Alban Hills to the SE, it is drained by the lower course of the river Tiber and a number of small streams, most of which dry up in the summer. Prosperous in Roman times, it later became virtually derelict through over-grazing, lack of water, and the arrival in the area of the malaria-carrying *Anopheles* mosquito. Extensive land reclamation and drainage in the 19th and 20th centuries restored its usefulness.

Campaign for Nuclear Disarmament (CND) nonparty-political British organization advocating the abolition of nuclear weapons worldwide: CND seeks unilateral British initiatives to help start the multilateral process and end the arms race.

The movement was launched by the philosopher Bertrand Russell and Canon John Collins in 1958. It grew out of the demonstration held outside the government's Atomic Weapons Research Establishment at Aldermaston, Berkshire, at Easter 1956. It held annual marches from Aldermaston to London 1959–63, after the initial march in 1958 which was routed from London to Aldermaston. From 1970 CND has also opposed nuclear power.

Campania agricultural region (wheat, citrus, wine, vegetables, tobacco) of S Italy, including the volcano ◊Vesuvius; capital Naples; industrial centers Benevento, Caserta, and Salerno; area 5,250 sq mi/13,600 sq km; population (1988) 5,732,000. There are ancient sites at Pompeii, Herculaneum, and Paestum.

campanile originally a bell tower erected near, or attached to, churches or town halls in Italy. The leaning tower of Pisa is a renowned example; another is the great campanile of Florence, 275 ft/90 m high.

They were used as components of 19th-century American factory architecture in New England.

Campbell Gordon 1886–1953. British admiral in World War I. He commanded Q-ships, which were armed vessels that masqueraded as merchant ships to decoy German U-boats to destruction.

Campbell Malcolm 1885–1948. British racing driver who, at one time, held both land- and water-speed records. His car and boat were both called *Bluebird*.

He set the land-speed record nine times, pushing it up to 301.1 mph/484.8 kph at Bonneville Flats, Utah, in 1935, and three times broke the water-speed record, the best being 141.74 mph/228.2 kph on Coniston Water, England, in 1939.

Campbell Mrs Patrick (born Beatrice Stella Tanner) 1865–1940. British actress whose roles included Paula in Pinero's *The Second Mrs Tanqueray* 1893 and Eliza in *Pygmalion*, written for her by G B Shaw, with whom she had an amusing correspondence.

Campbell-Bannerman Henry 1836–1908. British Liberal politician, prime minister 1905–08. It was during his term of office that the South African colonies achieved self-government, and the Trades Disputes Act 1906 was passed.

Camp David official country home of US presidents, situated in the Appalachian mountains, Maryland; it was originally named Shangri-la by F D Roosevelt, but was renamed Camp David by Eisenhower (after his grandson).

Campin A Woman *National Gallery, London.*

It was briefly known (for security reasons) as Camp Number Four after the Kennedy assassination. It is guarded by Marines, and consists of a series of lodges, Aspen Lodge being the presidential residence. It was the site of talks held by President Carter to bring about an Egypt-Israel peace accord, see ◊Camp David Agreements.

Camp David Agreements two framework agreements signed at Camp David, Maryland, in 1978 by the Israeli prime minister Begin and the Egyptian president Sadat, under the guidance of President Jimmy Carter, covering an Egypt–Israel peace treaty and phased withdrawal of Israel from Sinai, which was completed in 1982, and an overall Middle East settlement including the election by the West Bank and Gaza Strip Palestinians of a "self-governing authority." This issue has stalled repeatedly over issues of who will represent the Palestinians and what form the self-governing body will take.

Campeche port on the Bay of Campeche, Mexico; population (1984) 120,000. It is the capital of Campeche state. Timber and fish are exported, and there is a university, established 1756.

Campeche, Bay of SW area of the Gulf of Mexico, site of a major oil pollution disaster from the field off Yucatán peninsula in 1979.

camphor $C_{10}H_{16}O$ volatile, aromatic ◊ketone substance obtained from the camphor tree *Cinnamomum camphora*. It is distilled from chips of the wood or produced synthetically, and is used in insect repellents and in the manufacture of celluloid.

The camphor tree, a member of the family Lauraceae, is native to South China, Taiwan, and Japan.

Campi family of Italian painters practicing in Cremona, N Italy, in the 16th century, the best-known member being Giulio Campi (c. 1502–1572).

Campin Robert, also known as the Master of Flémalle c. 1378–1444. Netherlandish painter of the early Renaissance, active in Tournai from 1406, one of the first northern masters to use oil. Several altarpieces are attributed to him. Rogier van der Weyden was his pupil.

His outstanding work is *Mérode altarpiece*, about 1425 (Metropolitan Museum of Art, New York), which shows a distinctly naturalistic style,

Camus French novelist and dramatist Albert Camus.

with a new subtlety in modeling and a grasp of pictorial space.

Campinas city of São Paulo, Brazil, situated on the central plateau; population (1980) 566,700. It is a coffee-trading center, which also has metallurgical and food industries.

campion several plants of the genera *Lychnis* and *Silene*, belonging to the pink family (Caryophyllaceae), which include the garden campion *L. coronaria*, introduced from Europe, and the catchflies (genus *Silene*) of E North America.

Campion Edmund 1540–1581. English Jesuit and Roman Catholic martyr.

Born in London, he became a Jesuit in Rome in 1573 and in 1580 was sent to England as a missionary. He was betrayed as a spy in 1581, imprisoned in the Tower of London, and hanged, drawn, and quartered as a traitor.

Campobasso capital of Molise region, Italy, about 120 mi/190 km SE of Rome; population (1981) 48,300. It has a high reputation for its cutlery.

Campo-Formio, Treaty of peace settlement 1797 during the Revolutionary Wars between Napoleon and Austria, by which France gained the region that is now Belgium and Austria was compensated with Venice and part of that area which is now Yugoslavia.

Cam Ranh port in S Vietnam. In the Vietnam war it was a US base; it is now a major staging complex for the Soviet Pacific fleet.

Camus Albert 1913–1960. Algerian-born French writer. A journalist in France, he was active in the Resistance during World War II. His novels, which owe much to ◊existentialism, include *L'Etranger/The Outsider* 1942, *La Peste/The Plague* 1948, and *L'Homme Révolté/The Rebel* 1952. He was awarded the Nobel Prize for Literature 1957.

Canaan ancient region between the Mediterranean and the Dead Sea, called in the Bible the "Promised Land" of the Israelites. Occupied as early as the 3rd millennium BC by the Canaanites, a Semitic-speaking people who were known to the Greeks of the 1st millennium BC as Phoenicians. The capital was Ebla (what is now Tell Mardikh, Syria).

The Canaanite Empire included Syria, Palestine, and part of Mesopotamia. It was conquered by the Israelites during the 13th to 10th centuries BC. Ebla was excavated 1976–77, revealing an archive of inscribed tablets dating from the 3rd millennium BC, which includes place names such as Gaza and Jerusalem (no excavations at the latter had suggested occupation at so early a date).

Canada country occupying northern part of the North American continent, bounded S by the US, N by the Arctic Ocean, NW by Alaska, E by the Atlantic Ocean, and W by the Pacific Ocean.

government The Canada Act of 1982 gave Canada power to amend its constitution and added a charter of rights and freeedoms. This represented Canada's complete independence, though it remains a member of the ◊Commonwealth.

Canada is a federation of ten provinces–Alberta, British Columbia, Manitoba, New Brunswick, Newfoundland, Nova Scotia, Ontario, Prince Edward Island, Québec, and Saskatchewan–and two territories—Northwest Territories and Yukon. Each province has a single-chamber assembly, popularly elected; the premier (the leader of the party with the most seats in the legislature) chooses the cabinet. The two-chamber federal parliament consists of the Senate, whose 104 members are appointed by the government for life or until the age of 75 and who must be resident in the provinces they represent; and the House of Commons, which has 295 members, elected by universal suffrage in single-member constituencies.

The federal prime minister is the leader of the best-supported party in the House of Commons and is accountable, with the cabinet, to it. Parliament has a maximum life of five years. Legislation must be passed by both chambers and then signed by the governor general.

history Inhabited by indigenous Indian and Eskimo groups, Canada was reached by an English expedition led by John Cabot 1497 and a French expedition under Jacques Cartier 1534. Both countries developed colonies from the 17th century, with hostility between them culminating in the French and Indian Wars (1689–1763), in which France was defeated. Antagonism continued, and in 1791 Canada was divided into English-speaking Upper Canada and French-speaking Lower Canada (Ontario and Québec). The two were united as Canada Province 1841–67, when the self-governing Dominion of Canada was founded.

In 1870 the province of Manitoba was added to the confederation, British Columbia joined in 1871, and Prince Edward Island in 1873. The new provinces of Alberta and Saskatchewan were formed out of the Northwest Territories in 1905. An improving economy led to vast areas of fertile prairie land being opened up for settlement; the discovery of gold and other metals, the exploitation of forests for lumber and paper, the development of fisheries and tourism, and investment from other countries gradually transformed Canada's economy into one of the most important manufacturing and trading nations in the world. World War II stimulated further rapid industrialization, and in the postwar period discovery and exploitation of mineral resources took place on a vast scale.

The Progressive Conservatives returned to power 1957, after 22 years of Liberal Party rule.

Canada
Dominion of

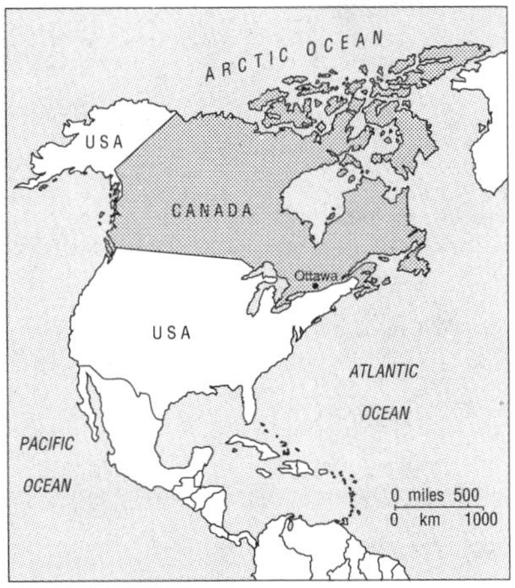
ARCTIC OCEAN
USA
CANADA
Ottawa
USA
ATLANTIC
OCEAN
PACIFIC
OCEAN
0 miles 500
0 km 1000

area 3,849,803 sq mi/9,970,600 sq km
capital Ottawa
cities Toronto, Montréal, Vancouver, Edmonton, Calgary, Winnipeg, Québec, Hamilton, Saskatoon, Halifax
physical mountains in W, with low-lying plains in interior and rolling hills in E. Climate varies from temperate in S to arctic in N
features St Lawrence Seaway, Mackenzie River; Great Lakes; Arctic Archipelago; Rocky Mountains; Great Plains or Prairies; Canadian Shield; Niagara Falls; the world's second-largest country
head of state Elizabeth II from 1952 represented by governor-general
head of government Brian Mulroney from 1984
political system federal constitutional monarchy
political parties Progressive Conservative Party, free-enterprise, right-wing; Liberal Party, nationalist, centrist; New Democratic Party, moderate, left-of-center
political parties Progressive Conservative Party, free-enterprise centrist; Liberal Party, nationalist left-of-center; New Democratic Party, moderate left-of-center
exports wheat, timber, pulp, newsprint, fish (salmon), furs (ranched fox and mink exceed the value of wild furs), oil, natural gas, aluminum, asbestos (world's second-largest producer), coal, copper, iron, zinc and nickel (world's largest producer), uranium (world's largest producer), motor vehicles and parts, industrial and agricultural machinery, fertilizers, chemicals
currency Canadian dollar
population (1990 est) 26,527,000—including 300,000 North American Indians, of whom 75% live on over 2,000 reservations in Ontario and the four western provinces; some 300,000 Métis (people of mixed race) and 19,000 Inuit (or Eskimo, of whom 75% live in the Northwest Territories). Over half Canada's population lives in Ontario and Québec. Growth rate 1.1% p.a.
life expectancy men 72, women 79
language English, French (both official) (about 70% speak English, 20% French, and the rest are bilingual); there are also North American Indian languages and the Eskimo Inuktitut
religion Roman Catholic 46%, Protestant 35%
literacy 99%
GDP $412 bn (1987); $15,910 per head
chronology
1867 Dominion of Canada founded.
1949 Newfoundland joined Canada.
1957 Progressive Conservatives returned to power after 22 years in opposition.
1961 New Democratic Party (NDP) formed.
1963 Liberals elected under Lester Pearson.
1968 Pearson succeeded by Pierre Trudeau.
1979 Joe Clark, leader of the Progressive Conservatives, formed a minority government; defeated on budget proposals.
1980 Liberals under Trudeau returned with a large majority.
1982 Canada Act removed Britain's last legal control over Canadian affairs; "patriation" of Canada's constitution.
1983 Clark replaced as leader of the Progressive Conservatives by Brian Mulroney.
1984 Trudeau retired and was succeeded as Liberal leader and prime minister by John Turner. Progressive Conservatives won the federal election with a large majority, and Mulroney became prime minister.
1988 Conservatives reelected with reduced majority on platform of free trade with the US.
1989 Free trade agreement signed. Turner resigned as Liberal Party leader, and Ed Broadbent as New Democratic Party leader.

Canada: history

c. 35,000 BC	People arrived in North America from Asia by way of Beringia.
c. 2000 BC	Eskimo begin settling Arctic coast from Siberia E to Greenland.
c. AD 1000	Vikings, including Leif Ericsson, landed in NE Canada, and started settlements that did not survive.
1497	John Cabot landed on Cape Breton Island.
1534	Jacques Cartier discovered the Gulf of St Lawrence.
1603	Champlain began his exploration of Canada.
1608	Champlain founded Québec.
1759	Wolfe captured Québec.
1763	France ceded Canada to Britain under the Treaty of Paris.
1775–83	American Revolutionary War caused Loyalist influx to New Brunswick and Ontario.
1791	Canada divided into English-speaking Upper Canada (Ontario) and French-speaking Lower Canada (Québec).
1793	Alexander Mackenzie reached Pacific by land.
1812–14	War of 1812 between Britain and the US. US invasions repelled by both provinces.
1837	Rebellions led by William Lyon Mackenzie in Upper Canada and Louis Joseph Papineau in Lower Canada.
1840	Responsible government granted, and Upper and Lower Canada united.
1866	British Columbia created, entered confederation 1871.
1867	British North America Act created the Dominion of Canada (Ontario, Québec, Nova Scotia, and New Brunswick).
1869	Northwest Territories created and entered confederation; uprising by Louis Riel.
1870	Manitoba created (from Northwest Territories) and joined confederation.
1873	Prince Edward Island entered confederation.
1885	Northwest Rebellion crushed and leader Louis Riel hanged. Canadian Pacific Railway completed.
1905	Alberta and Saskatchewan formed from the Northwest Territories and entered confederation.
1914–18	World War I—Canadian troops at 2nd Battle of Ypres, Vimy Ridge, Passchendaele, the Somme, and Cambrai.
1931	Canada became a self-governing Dominion. Norway renounced her claim to the Sverdrup Islands, confirming Canadian sovereignty in the entire Arctic Archipelago north of the Canadian mainland.
1939–45	World War II—Canadian participation in all theaters.
1949	Newfoundland joined the confederation.
1950–53	Korean War—Canada participated in United Nations force, and subsequently participated in almost all United Nations peacekeeping operations.
1968	Pierre Trudeau becomes prime minister.
1970	FLQ, a separatist guerrilla force in Québec, kills a provincial cabinet minister; War Measures Act invoked.
1972	Adoption of "Third Option" policy to reduce US influence by economic links with Europe and Japan.
1979	Progressive Conservatives elected with Joe Clark as prime minister.
1980	Québec referendum rejected demand for independence. Liberals returned with Trudeau again as PM.
1982	British North America Act amended to patriate the Canadian constitution.
1984	John Turner succeeded Trudeau as leader of the Liberal Party and prime minister. Brian Mulroney and the Conservatives won the general election.
1988	Conservatives re-elected.
1989	Free trade deal signed with the US.
1990	Meech lake accords on constitution fail.
1991	Canada joins anti-Iraq coalition in Gulf War.

In 1963 the Liberals were reinstated in office under Lester Pearson, who was succeeded by Pierre Trudeau 1968. Trudeau maintained Canada's defensive alliance with the US but sought to widen its influence internationally. Faced with the problem of Québec's separatist movement, he set about creating the "Just Society." He won both the 1972 and 1974 elections.

In 1979, with no party having an overall majority in the Commons, the Progressive Conservatives formed a government under Joe Clark. Later that year Trudeau announced his retirement from politics, but when, in Dec 1979, Clark was defeated on his budget proposals, Trudeau reconsidered his decision and won the 1980 general election with a large majority.

Trudeau's third administration was concerned with "patriation," or the extent to which the British Parliament should determine Canada's constitution. The position was resolved with the passing of the Canada Act 1982, the last piece of UK legislation to have force in Canada.

In 1983 Clark was replaced as leader of the Progressive Conservatives by Brian Mulroney, a corporate lawyer who had never run for public office, and in 1984 Trudeau retired to be replaced as Liberal Party leader and prime minister by John Turner, a former minister of finance. Within nine days of taking office, Turner called a general election, and the Progressive Conservatives, under Mulroney, won 211 seats, the largest majority in Canadian history, with the Liberal Party and the New Democratic Party (NDP) winning 40 and 30 seats respectively.

Soon after taking office, Mulroney began an international realignment, placing less emphasis on links established by Trudeau with Asia, Africa, and Latin America and more on cooperation with Europe and a closer relationship with the US. The election of 1988 was fought on the issue of free trade with the US, and the Conservatives won with a reduced majority. Despite the majority of voters opting for the Liberals or NDP, who both opposed free trade, an agreement was signed with the US 1989. Turner and Ed Broadbent, leader of the NDP, both resigned 1989.

The 1990s began inauspiciously with the collapse of the Meech Lake accords, the 1987 compromise among the Canadian provinces aimed at getting Quebec's acceptance of the 1982 constitutional reforms. In 1990–91, Canada joined the coalition opposing Iraq's invasion of Kuwait.

Canadian Prime Ministers

1867	John A Macdonald (*Conservative*)
1873	Alexander Mackenzie (*Liberal*)
1878	John A Macdonald (*Conservative*)
1891	John J Abbott (*Conservative*)
1892	John S D Thompson (*Conservative*)
1894	Mackenzie Bowell (*Conservative*)
1896	Charles Tupper (*Conservative*)
1896	Wilfred Laurier (*Liberal*)
1911	Robert L Bordern (*Conservative*)
1920	Arthur Meighen (*Conservative*)
1921	William Lyon Mackenzie King (*Liberal*)
1926	Arthur Meighen (*Conservative*)
1926	William Lyon Mackenzie King (*Liberal*)
1930	Richard Bedford Bennett (*Conservative*)
1935	William Lyon Mackenzie King (*Liberal*)
1948	Louis Stephen St Laurent (*Liberal*)
1957	John G Diefenbaker (*Conservative*)
1963	Lester Bowles Pearson (*Liberal*)
1968	Pierre Elliot Trudeau (*Liberal*)
1979	Joseph Clark (*Progressive Conservative*)
1980	Pierre Elliot Trudeau (*Liberal*)
1984	John Turner (*Liberal*)
1984	Brian Mulroney (*Progressive Conservative*)

Canada: provinces

Province (Capital)	*Area sq km*
Alberta *(Edmonton)*	661,200
British Columbia *(Victoria)*	947,800
Manitoba *(Winnipeg)*	650,000
New Brunswick *(Fredericton)*	73,400
Newfoundland *(St John's)*	405,700
Nova Scotia *(Halifax)*	55,500
Ontario *(Toronto)*	1,068,600
Prince Edward Island *(Charlottetown)*	5,700
Québec *(Québec)*	1,540,700
Saskatchewan *(Regina)*	652,300
Territory	
Northwest Territories *(Yellowknife)*	3,426,300
Yukon Territory *(Whitehorse)*	483,500

Canadian art painting and sculpture of Canada after colonization. Early painters of Canadian life include Cornelius Krieghoff (1815–1872), who recorded Indian and pioneer life, and Paul Kane (1810–1871), painter of the Plains Indians. In the late 19th century, a Canadian style developed with the landscapes of Tom Thomson (1877–1917) and the "Group of Seven," formed in 1913, that developed an expressive landscape style. Maurice Cullen (1866–1934), an Impressionist, and James Wilson Morrice (1865–1924), a Fauve, introduced new European trends.

Before World War II Emily Carr (1871–1945) was one of the most original talents, developing eloquent studies of nature. Canadian artists have since joined the international arena. The Automatistes, led by the Surrealist Paul-Emile Borduas (1905–1960), rebelled against the Canadian establishment. Jean-Paul Riopelle (1923–) has made a significant contribution to Abstract Expressionism.

Canadian literature Canadian literature in English began early in the 19th century in the Maritime Provinces with the humorous tales of T C Haliburton (1796–1865); Charles Heavysege (1816–1876), a poet of note, was from Kingston, Ontario. The late 19th century brought the lyrical output of Charles G D Roberts (1860–1943), Bliss Carman (1861–1929), Archibald Lampman (1861–1899), and Duncan Campbell Scott (1862–1944).

Realism in fiction developed with Frederick P Grove (1871–1948), Mazo de la Roche (1885–1961), creator of the "Jalna" series, and Hugh MacLennan (1907–). Humor of worldwide appeal emerged in Stephen Leacock (1869–1944); Brian Moore (1921–), author of *The Luck of Ginger Coffey* (1960); and Mordecai ◊Richler. Also widely read outside Canada was Lucy Montgomery (1874–1942), whose *Anne of Green Gables* 1908 became a children's classic. Saul Bellow and Marshall ◊McLuhan were both Canadian-born, as were contemporary novelists Robertson ◊Davies and Margaret ◊Atwood. See also ◊French Canadian literature.

canal artificial waterway or channel, of two types: navigation canals or conveyance canals (for irrigation, power, or drainage). Irrigation canals are the older, dug from ancient times, and provided flood control as well as neolithic farming villages with an expanded area of rich alluvial soil, especially in the Tigris-Euphrates valley and along the Nile, where agricultural surpluses eventually

canals and waterways

name	*country*	*opened*	*length km*	*mi*
Amsterdam	Netherlands	1876	26.6	16.5
Baltic–Volga	USSR	1964	2,430	1,510
Baltic–White Sea	USSR	1933	235	146
Corinth	Greece	1893	6.4	4
Elbe and Trave	Germany	1900	66	41
Erie	USA	1825	580	360
Göta	Sweden	1832	185	115
Grand Canal	China	485 BC–AD 1972	1,050	650
Kiel	Germany	1895	98	61
Manchester	England	1894	57	35.5
Panama	Panama	1914	81	50.5
Princess Juliana	Netherlands	1935	32	20
St Lawrence	Canada	1959	3,770	2,342
Saulte Ste Marie	USA	1855	2.6	1.6
Saulte Ste Marie	Canada	1895	1.8	1.1
Welland	Canada	1929	45	28
Suez	Egypt	1869	166	103

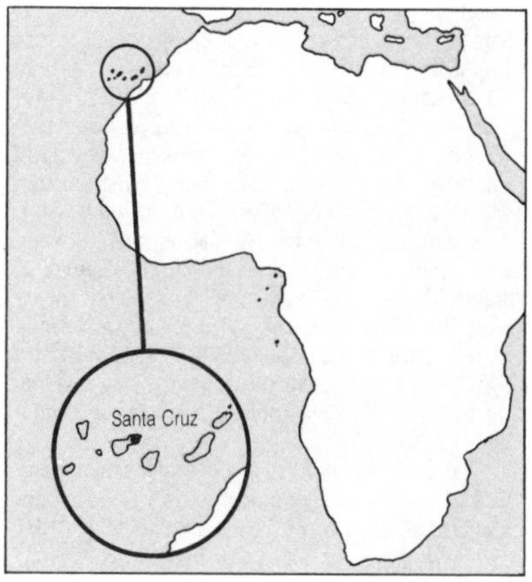
Santa Cruz

allowed for the rise of ◊civilizations. Navigation canals developed after irrigation and drainage canals; often they link two waterways and were at first level and shallow. Soon, those with inclined planes had towpaths along which men and animals towed vessels from one level to the next. ◊Locks were invented to allow passage where great variations in level exist. By the 20th century mechanized tows and self-propelled barges were in use.

The longest navigational canal is the Grand Canal of China, c. 1,000 mi/1,600 m, from Beijing to Hangzhou, which forms an important N-S waterway for millions of tons of freight every year. It was started in the 6th century BC and expanded for 2,000 years. In the US, the Erie Canal 1825 linked the Great Lakes with the Hudson River and opened the NE and midwest commercially. The Suez Canal 1869 and the Panama Canal 1914 eliminated long trips around continents and dramatically shortened shipping routes.

Canaletto Antonio (Giovanni Antoni Canal) 1697–1768. Italian painter celebrated for his paintings of views (*vedute*) of Venice (his native city) and of the river Thames and London 1746–56.

Much of his work is very detailed and precise, with a warm light and a sparkling of tiny highlights on the green waters of canals and rivers. His later style became clumsier and more static.

Canaries current the cold ocean current in the North Atlantic Ocean flowing SW from Spain along the NW coast of Africa. It meets the northern equatorial current at a latitude of 20° N.

canary bird *Serinus canaria* of the finch family, found wild in the Canary Islands and Madeira. It is greenish with a yellow underside. Canaries have been bred as cage-birds in Europe since the 15th century, and many domestic varieties are yellow or orange.

Some canaries are used in mines as detectors of traces of poison gas in the air.

Canary Islands (Spanish *Canarias*) group of volcanic islands 60 mi/100 km off the NW coast of Africa, forming the Spanish provinces of Las Palmas and Santa Cruz de Tenerife; area 2,818 sq mi/ 7,300 sq km; population (1986) 1,615,000.

features The chief centers are Santa Cruz on Tenerife (which also has the highest peak in extracontinental Spain, Pico de Teide 12,186 ft/3,713 m), and Las Palmas on Gran Canaria. The province of Santa Cruz comprises Tenerife, Palma, Gomera, and Hierro; the province of Las Palmas comprises Gran Canaria, Lanzarote, and Fuerteventura. There are also six uninhabited islets. The Northern Hemisphere Observatory (1981) is on the island of Las Palmas, the first in the world to be controlled remotely. Observation conditions are among the best in the world, since there is no moisture, no artificial light pollution, and little natural ◊airglow. The Organization of African Unity (OAU) supports an independent Guanch Republic (so called from the indigenous islanders, a branch of the N African Berbers) and revival of the Guanch language.

Canberra capital of Australia (since 1908), situated in the Australian Capital Territory, enclosed within New South Wales, on a tributary of the Murrumbidgee River; area (Australian Capital Territory including the port at Jervis Bay) 939 sq mi/2,432 sq km; population (1986) 285,800.

It contains the Parliament House, first used by the Commonwealth Parliament in 1927, the Australian National University (1946), the Canberra School of Music (1965), and the National War Memorial.

cancan high-kicking stage dance for women (solo or line of dancers) originating in Paris about 1830. The music usually associated with the cancan is the *galop* from Offenbach's *Orpheus in the Underworld*.

cancer group of diseases characterized by abnormal proliferation of cells. Cancer (malignant) cells are usually degenerate, capable only of reproducing themselves (tumor formation) until they outnumber the surrounding healthy cells. Malignant cells tend to spread from their site of origin by traveling through the bloodstream or lymphatic system.

There are more than 100 types of cancer. Some, like lung or bowel cancer, are common; others are rare. The likely cause remains unexplained. Triggering agents (◊carcinogens) include chemicals such as those found in cigarette smoke, other forms of smoke, asbestos dust, exhaust fumes, and many industrial chemicals. Some viruses can also trigger the cancerous growth of cells (see ◊oncogenes), as can X-rays and radioactivity. Dietary factors are important in some cancers; for example, lack of fiber in the diet may predispose people to bowel cancer and a diet high in animal fats and low in fresh vegetables and fruit increases the risk of breast cancer. Psychological ◊stress may increase the risk of cancer, more so if the person concerned is not able to control the source of the stress. In some families there is

Canaletto The Bacino di San Marco on Ascension Day *(c. 1740) Royal Collection, London.*

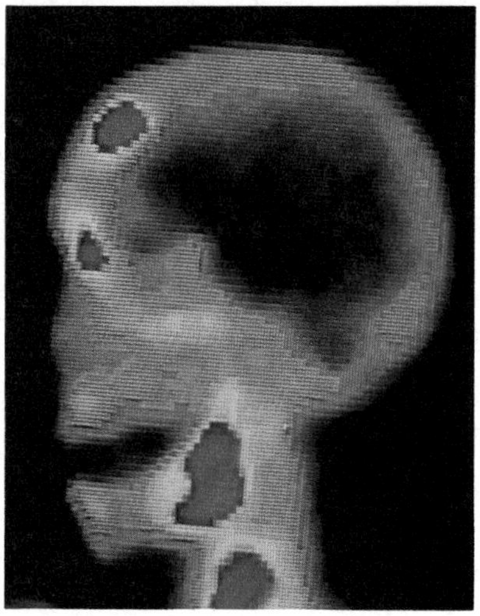

cancer *Skull of a person suffering from bone cancer, showing the areas of cancerous bone in red.*

a genetic tendency toward a particular type of cancer.

Cancer the faintest of the zodiac constellations (its brightest stars are fourth magnitude). It lies in the northern hemisphere, near Ursa Major, and is represented as a crab. Cancer's most distinctive feature is the star cluster Praesepe, popularly known as the Beehive. The Sun passes through the constellation during late July and early Aug. In astrology, the dates for Cancer are between about June 22 and July 22 (see ◊precession).

candela SI unit (abbreviation cd) of luminous intensity, which replaced the old units of candle and standard candle. It measures the brightness of a light itself rather than the amount of light falling on an object, which is called *illuminance* and measured in ◊lux.

One candela is defined as the luminous intensity in a given direction of a source that emits monochromatic radiation of frequency 540 × 10^{-12} Hz and whose radiant energy in that direction is 1/683 watt per steradian.

Candela Felix 1910– . Spanish-born Mexican architect, originator of the hypar (hyperbolic paraboloid) from 1951, in which doubly curved surfaces are built up on a framework of planks sprayed with cement. He was a professor at the National School of Architecture, University of Mexico, from 1953.

Candia Italian name for the Greek island of ◊Crete. Also, formerly the name of Crete's largest city, ◊Iráklion, founded about AD 824.

Candida albicans a yeastlike fungus present in the human digestive tract and in the vagina, which causes no harm in most healthy people. However, it can cause problems if it multiplies excessively, as in vaginal candidiasis or ◊thrush, the main symptom of which is intense itching. The most common form of thrush is oral, which often occurs in those taking steroids or prolonged courses of antibiotics.

Newborn babies may pick up the yeast during birth and suffer an infection of the mouth and throat. There is also some evidence that overgrowth of *Candida* may occur in the intestines, causing diarrhea, bloating and other symptoms, such as headache and fatigue, but this has not yet been proven. Occasionally, *Candida* can infect immunocompromised patients, such as those with AIDS. Treatment for candidiasis is based on antifungal drugs.

Candide a satire by Voltaire, published 1759 , which narrates the misfortunes of the protagonist Candide. The story's conclusion that "all is for the best in the best of all possible worlds," satirizes the philosophies of Leibniz and Jean-Jacques Rousseau.

Candlemas in the Christian church, the Feast of the Purification of the Blessed Virgin Mary and the Presentation of the Infant Christ in the Temple, celebrated on Feb 2; church candles are blessed on this day.

cane reedlike stem of various plants such as the sugar cane and bamboo, and in particular, the group of palms called rattans, consisting of the genus *Calamus* and its allies. Their slender stems are dried and used for making walking sticks, baskets, and furniture.

Canea (Greek *Khania*) principal port of Crete, on the NW coast; population (1981) 47,338. It was founded in 1252 by the Venetians and is surrounded by a wall. Vegetable oils, soap, and leather are exported. Heavy fighting took place here during World War II, after the landing of German parachutists in May 1941. In 1971 it was replaced by Iráklion as administrative capital of Crete.

Canes Venatici constellation of the northern hemisphere near Ursa Major, representing the hunting dogs of ◊Boötes, the herdsman. Its stars are faint and it contains the Whirlpool galaxy (M51), the first spiral galaxy to be recognized.

Canetti The first Bulgarian to win the Nobel Prize for Literature was Elias Canetti in 1981.

Canetti Elias 1905– . Bulgarian-born writer. He was exiled from Austria as a Jew 1938 and settled in England 1939. His books, written in German, include the novel *Die Blendung/Auto da Fé* and an autobiography *The Tongue Set Free* (translated 1988). He was concerned with crowd behavior and the psychology of power. Nobel Prize 1981.

canine or ***canine tooth*** in mammalian carnivores, long, often pointed teeth found at the front of the mouth between the incisors and premolars. They are used for catching prey, for killing, and for tearing flesh. Canines are absent in herbivores such as rabbits and the sheep, and are much reduced in humans.

Canis Major brilliant constellation of the southern hemisphere, representing one of the two dogs following at the heel of Orion. Its main star, Sirius, is the brightest star in the sky.

Canis Minor small constellation along the celestial equator, representing the second of the two dogs of Orion (the other dog is represented by Canis Major). Its brightest star is Procyon.

Cannae village in Puglia, Italy, site of ◊Hannibal's defeat of the Romans 216 BC.

cannabis the dried leaf and female flowers (together called marijuana) and resin (hashish) of certain varieties of ◊hemp *Cannabis sativa*, that are smoked or eaten and have an intoxicating and euphoric effect. Cultivation of cannabis is illegal in the US and UK except under license. Cannabis is a soft drug in that any dependence is psychological rather than physical. It has medicinal use in countering depression and the side effects of cancer therapy (pain and nausea). Cultivation of cannabis is illegal in the UK and US except under license.

Cannes resort in Alpes-Maritimes *département*, S France; population (1982) 73,000, conurbation 296,000. The film industry's most prestigious festival is held here annually. Formerly only a small seaport, in 1834 it attracted the patronage of Lord ◊Brougham and other distinguished visitors and soon became a fashionable vacation resort. A new town (La Bocca) grew up facing the Mediterranean.

cannibalism the practice of eating human flesh, also called anthropophagy. The name is derived from the Caribs, a South American and West Indian people, alleged by the conquering Spaniards to ritually eat their captives.

canning food preservation in hermetically sealed containers by the application of heat. Originated by Nicolas Appert in France 1809 with glass containers, it was developed by Peter Durand in England 1810 with cans made of sheet steel thinly coated with tin to delay corrosion.

Canneries were established in the US before 1820, but the US canning industry began to grow considerably in the 1870s when the manufacture of cans was mechanized and factory methods of processing were used. The quality and taste of early canned food was frequently dubious but by the end of the 19th century, scientific research made greater understanding possible of the food preserving process, and standards improved. Cans for beer and soft drinks are generally made of aluminum. More than half the aluminum cans used in the US are now recycled.

Canning Charles John, 1st Earl 1812–1862. British administrator, first viceroy of India from 1858. As governor general of India from 1856, he suppressed the Indian Mutiny with a fair but firm hand which earned him the nickname "Clemency Canning." He was the son of George Canning.

Canning George 1770–1827. British Tory politician, foreign secretary 1807–10 and 1822–27, and prime minister 1827 in coalition with the Whigs. He was largely responsible, during the Napoleonic Wars, for the seizure of the Danish fleet and British intervention in the Spanish peninsula.

Cannizzaro Stanislao 1826–1910. Italian chemist who revived interest in the work of Avogadro 1811 that had revealed the difference between ◊atoms and ◊molecules, and so established atomic and molecular weights as the basis of chemical calculations.

Cannizzaro also worked in aromatic organic chemistry. In 1853 he discovered reactions (named after him) that make benzyl alcohol and benzoic acid from benzaldehyde.

Cannon Annie Jump 1863–1941. US astronomer who, from 1896, worked at Harvard College Observatory and carried out revolutionary work on the classification of stars by examining their spectra. Her system, still used today, has spectra arranged according to temperature and runs from O through B, A, F, G, K, and M. O-type stars are the hottest, with surface temperatures of 35,000K. She also discovered over 300 ◊variable stars and five ◊novae.

Cano Alonso 1601–1667. Spanish sculptor, painter, and architect, an exponent of the Baroque style in Spain. He was active in Seville, Madrid, and Granada and designed the façade of Granada Cathedral 1667.

From 1637 he was employed by Philip IV to restore the royal collection at the Prado Museum in Madrid. Many of his religious paintings show the influence of the Venetian masters. He also created monumental carved screens, such as the reredos (altar screen) in Lebrija, near Seville, and graceful free-standing polychrome carved figures.

Cano Juan Sebastian del c. 1476–1526. Spanish voyager. It is claimed that he was the first sea captain to sail around the world. He sailed with Magellan in 1519 and, after the latter's death in the Philippines, brought the *Victoria* safely home to Spain.

canoeing sport of propelling a lightweight, shallow boat, pointed at both ends, by paddles or sails. Currently, canoes are often made from aluminum and fiberglass, but the originals were native American craft of wooden construction covered in bark or skin. Canoeing was popularized as a recreational pastime and as a sport in the 19th century. Canoeing and camping/fishing trips are popular at lakes and rivers across the US. Whitewater canoeing is a dangerous but invigorating challenge to the advanced canoer.

Two types of canoe are used: the ***kayak***, and the *Canadian-style* canoe. The kayak, derived from the Eskimo model, has a keel and the canoeist sits. The Canadian style canoe has no keel and the canoeist kneels. In addition to straightforward racing, there are slalom courses, with up to 30 "gates" to be negotiated through rapids and around artificial rock formations. Penalty seconds are added to course time for touching suspended gate poles or missing a gate. One to four canoeists are carried. The sport was introduced into the Olympic Games 1936.

canon type of priest in the Roman Catholic and Anglican churches. Canons, headed by the dean, are attached to a cathedral and constitute the chapter.

canon in theology, the collection of writings that is accepted as authoritative in a given religion, such as the *Tripitaka* in Theravāda Buddhism. In the Christian church, it comprises the books of the ◊Bible.

The canon of the Old Testament was drawn up at the assembly of rabbis held at Jamnia in Palestine between AD 90 and 100; certain excluded books were included in the ◊Apocrypha. The earliest list of New Testament books is known as the Muratorian Canon (c. 160–170). Bishop Athanasius promulgated a list (c. 365) which corresponds with that in modern Bibles.

canon in music, an echo form for two or more parts repeating and following a leading melody at regular time-intervals to achieve a harmonious effect. It is often found in Classical music, for example ◊Vivaldi and J S ◊Bach.

canonical hours in the Catholic church, seven set periods of devotion: matins and lauds, prime, terce, sext, nones, evensong or vespers, compline.

canonization in the Catholic church, the admission of one of its members to the Calendar of ◊Saints. The evidence of the candidate's exceptional piety is contested before the Congregation for the Causes of Saints by the Promotor Fidei, popularly known as the devil's advocate. Papal ratification of a favorable verdict results in ◊beatification, and full sainthood (conferred in St Peter's basilica, the Vatican) follows after further proof.

Under a system laid down mainly in the 17th century, the process of investigation was seldom completed in under 50 years, although in the case of a martyr it took less time. Since 1969 the gathering of the proof of the candidate's virtues has been left to the bishop of the birthplace, and, miracles being difficult to substantiate, stress is placed on extraordinary "favors" or "graces" that can be proved or attested by serious investigation.

canon law the rules and regulations of the Christian church, especially the Greek Orthodox, Roman Catholic, and Anglican churches. Its origin is sought in the declarations of Jesus and the apostles. In 1983 Pope John Paul II issued a new canon law code reducing offenses carrying automatic excommunication, extending the grounds for annulment of marriage, removing the ban on marriage with non-Catholics, and banning labor union and political activity by priests.

The earliest compilations were in the East, and the canon law of the Eastern Orthodox Church is comparatively small. Through the centuries, a great mass of canon law was accumulated in the Western church which, in 1918, was condensed in the *Corpus juris canonici* under Benedict XV. Even so, this is supplemented by many papal decrees.

Canopus second brightest star in the sky (after Sirius), lying in the constellation Carina. It is a yellow-white supergiant about 200 light-years from Earth and thousands of times more luminous than the Sun.

Canova Antonio 1757–1822. Italian Neo-Classical sculptor, based in Rome from 1781. He received commissions from popes, kings, and emperors for his highly finished marble portrait busts and groups. He made several portraits of Napoleon.

Canova was born near Treviso. His reclining marble *Pauline Borghese* 1805–07 (Borghese Gallery, Rome) is a fine example of cool, polished Classicism. He executed the tombs of popes Clement XIII, Pius VII, and Clement XIV. His marble sculptures include *Cupid and Psyche* (Louvre, Paris) and *The Three Graces* (Victoria and Albert Museum, London).

Cánovas del Castillo Antonio 1828–1897. Spanish politician and chief architect of the political system known as the *turno político* through which his own Conservative party, and that of the Liberals under Práxedes Sagasta, alternated in power. Elections were rigged to ensure the appropriate majorities. Cánovas was assassinated in 1897 by anarchists.

Cantabria autonomous region of N Spain; area 2,046 sq mi/5,300 sq km; population (1986) 525,000; capital Santander.

Cantabrian Mountains (Spanish *Cordillera Cantabrica*) mountains running along the N coast of Spain, reaching 8,688 ft/2,648 m in the Picos de Europa massif. The mountains contain coal and iron deposits.

Cantal volcanic mountain range in central France, which gives its name to Cantal *département*. The highest point is the Plomb du Cantal, 6,096 ft/1,858 m.

cantaloupe any of several small varieties of muskmelon, *Cucumis melo*, distinguished by their round, ribbed fruits with orange-colored flesh.

cantata in music, an extended work for voices, from the Italian, meaning "sung," as opposed to ◊sonata ("sounded") for instruments. A cantata can be sacred or secular, sometimes uses solo voices, and usually has orchestral accompaniment. The first printed collection of sacred cantata texts dates from 1670.

Canterbury city in Kent, England, on the river Stour, 62 mi/100 km SE of London; population (1984) 39,000.

The Roman Durovernum, Canterbury was the Saxon capital of Kent. The present name derives from Cantwarabyrig (Old English "fortress of the men of Kent"). In 597 King Ethelbert welcomed ◊Augustine's mission to England here, and the city has since been the metropolis of the Anglican Communion and seat of the archbishop of Canterbury.

Canterbury, archbishop of primate of all England, archbishop of the Church of England (Anglican), and first peer of the realm, ranking next to royalty. He crowns the sovereign, has a seat in the House of Lords, and is a member of the Privy Council. He is appointed by the prime minister.

Canterbury Plains area of rich grassland between the mountains and the sea on the E coast of South Island, New Zealand, source of Canterbury lamb. Area 4,000 sq mi/10,000 sq km.

Canterbury Tales an unfinished collection of stories in prose and verse (c. 1387) by Geoffrey ◊Chaucer, told in Middle English by a group of pilgrims on their way to Thomas á ◊Becket's tomb at Canterbury. The tales and preludes are remarkable for their vivid character portrayal and colloquial language.

cantilever beam or structure that is fixed at one end only, though it may be supported at some point along its length; for example, a diving board. The cantilever principle, widely used in construction engineering, eliminates the need for a second main support at the free end of the beam, allowing for more elegant structures and reducing the amount of materials required. Many large-span bridges have been built on the cantilever principle.

A typical cantilever bridge consists of two beams cantilevered out from either bank, each supported part way along, with their free ends meeting in the middle. The multiple-cantilever Forth Rail Bridge (completed 1890) across the Firth of Forth in Scotland has twin main spans of 1,710 ft/521 m.

canton in France, an administrative district, a subdivision of the *arrondissement*; in Switzerland, one of the 23 subdivisions forming the Confederation.

Canton former name of Kwangchow or ◊Guangzhou in China.

Canton city in NE Ohio, SE of Akron; seat of Stark county. Its products include office equipment, ceramics, and steel; population (1990) 84,161. The home of President William McKinley is here, as is the Football Hall of Fame.

cantor (Latin *cantare* "to sing") in Judaism, the prayer leader and choir master in a synagogue; the cantor is not a rabbi, and the position can be held by any lay person.

Cantor Georg 1845–1918. German mathematician who followed his work on number theory and trigonometry by considering the foundations of mathematics. He defined real numbers and produced a treatment of irrational numbers using a series of transfinite numbers. Cantor's set theory has been used in the development of topology and real function theory.

Canute c. 995–1035. King of England from 1016, Denmark from 1018, and Norway from 1028. Having invaded England 1013 with his father, Sweyn, king of Denmark, he was acclaimed king on his father's death 1014 by his ◊Viking army. Canute defeated ◊Edmund Ironside at Assandun, Essex, 1016, and became king of all England on Edmund's death. He succeeded his brother Harold as king of Denmark 1018, compelled King Malcolm to pay homage by invading Scotland about 1027, and conquered Norway 1028. He was succeeded by his illegitimate son Harold I.

The legend of Canute disenchanting his flattering courtiers by showing that the sea would not retreat at his command was first told by Henry of Huntingdon in 1130.

Canute VI (Cnut VI) 1163–1202. King of Denmark from 1182, son and successor of Waldemar Knudsson. With his brother and successor, Waldemar II, he resisted Frederick I's northward expansion, and established Denmark as the dominant power in the Baltic.

canyon (Spanish *cañon*, "tube") a deep, narrow valley or gorge running through mountains. Canyons are formed by stream down-cutting, usually in areas of low rainfall, where the stream or river receives water from outside the area.

There are many canyons in the western US and in Mexico, for example the Grand Canyon of the Colorado River in Arizona, the canyon in Yellowstone National Park, and the Black Canyon in Colorado.

Cao Chan or Ts'ao Chan 1719–1763. Chinese novelist. His tragic love story *Hung Lou Meng/The Dream of the Red Chamber* published 1792, involves the downfall of a Manchu family and is semiautobiographical.

capacitance, electrical the property of a capacitor that determines how much charge can be stored in it for a given potential difference between its terminals. It is equal to the ratio of the electrical charge stored to the potential difference. It is measured in ◊farads.

capacitor or ***condenser*** device for storing electric charge, used in electronic circuits; it consists of two or more metal plates separated by an insulating layer called a dielectric.

Its capacitance is the ratio of the charge stored on either plate to the potential difference between the plates. The SI unit of capacitance is the farad, but most capacitors have much smaller capacitances, and the microfarad (a millionth of a farad) is the commonly used practical unit.

Cape Breton island forming the northern part of the province of Nova Scotia, Canada; area 3,970 sq mi/10,282 sq km; population (1988) 170,000. Bisected by a waterway, it has road and rail links with the mainland across the Strait of Canso. It has coal resources and steelworks, and there has been substantial development in the strait area, with docks, oil refineries, and newsprint production from local timber. In the N, the surface rises to 1,800 ft/550 m at North Cape, and the coast has many fine harbors. There are cod fisheries. The climate is mild and very moist. The chief towns are Sydney and Glace Bay.

history The first British colony was established in 1629 but was driven out by the French. In 1763 Cape Breton was ceded to Britain and attached to Nova Scotia 1763–84 and from 1820.

Cape Byron the eastern extremity of Australia, in New South Wales, just S of the border with Queensland.

Cape Canaveral promontory on the Atlantic coast of

Florida, 228 mi/367 km N of Miami, used as a rocket launch site by ◊NASA.

First mentioned in 1513, it was known 1963–73 as Cape Kennedy to honor Pres J F Kennedy after his assassination. The ◊Kennedy Space Center is nearby.

Cape Coast port of Ghana, W Africa, 80 mi/130 km W of Accra; population (1982) 73,000. It has been superseded as the main port since 1962 by Tema. The town, first established by the Portuguese in the 16th century, is built on a natural breakwater, adjoining the castle.

Cape Cod hook-shaped peninsula in SE Massachusetts; 60 mi/100 km long and 1–20 mi/1.6–32 km wide. Its beaches and woods make it a popular tourist area. It is separated from the rest of the state by the Cape Cod Canal. The islands of Martha's Vineyard and Nantucket are just south of the cape. Basque and Norse fisherfolk are believed to have visited Cape Cod many years before the English Pilgrims landed at Provincetown 1620. It was named after the cod which were caught in the dangerous shoals of the cape. The ◊Kennedy family home is at the resort of Hyannis Port.

Cape Coloured South African term for people of mixed African and European descent, mainly living in Cape Province.

Cape gooseberry plant *Physalis peruviana* of the potato family. Originating in South America, it is grown in South Africa, from where it takes its name. It is cultivated for its fruit, a yellow berry surrounded by a papery ◊calyx.

Cape Horn southernmost point of South America, in the Chilean part of the archipelago of ◊Tierra del Fuego; notorious for gales and heavy seas. It was named in 1616 by its Dutch discoverer Willem Schouten (1580–1625) after his birthplace (Hoorn).

Čapek Karel (Matelj) 1890–1938. Czech writer whose works often deal with social injustice in an imaginative, satirical way. *R.U.R.* 1921 is a play in which robots (a term he coined) rebel against their controllers; the novel *Valka's Mloky/War With the Newts* 1936 is a science-fiction classic.

Capella brightest star in the constellation Auriga and the sixth brightest star in the sky. It consists of a pair of yellow giant stars 45 light-years from Earth, orbiting each other every 104 days.

Cape of Good Hope South African headland forming a peninsula between Table Bay and False Bay, Cape Town. The first European to sail around it was Bartholomew Diaz in 1488. Formerly named Cape of Storms, it was given its present name by King John II of Portugal.

Cape Province (Afrikaans *Kaapprovinsie*) largest province of the Republic of South Africa, named after the Cape of Good Hope

area 247,638 sq mi/641,379 sq km, excluding Walvis Bay

capital Cape Town

towns Port Elizabeth, East London, Kimberley, Grahamstown, Stellenbosch

physical Orange River, Drakensberg, Table mountain (highest point Maclear's Beacon, 3567 ft/1087 m); Great Karoo Plateau, Walvis Bay

products fruit, vegetables, wine; meat, ostrich feathers; diamonds, copper, asbestos, manganese

population (1985) 5,041,000; officially including 44% Colored; 31% Black; 25% White; 0.6% Asian

history the Dutch occupied the Cape in 1652, but it was taken by the British in 1795 after the French Revolutionary armies had occupied the Netherlands and was sold to Britain for £6 million in 1814. The Cape achieved self-government in 1872. t was an original province of the Union in 1910.

The Orange River was proclaimed the northern boundary in 1825. Griqualand West (1880) and the southern part of Bechuanaland (1895) were later incorporated; Walvis Bay, although formerly administered with Namibia, is legally an integral part of Cape Province.

caper trailing shrub *Capparis spinosa*, native to the Mediterranean and belonging to the family Capparidaceae. Its flower buds are preserved in vinegar as a condiment.

capercaillie large bird *Tetrao uroqallus* of the grouse type found in coniferous woodland in Europe and N Asia. At nearly 3 ft/1 m long, the male is the biggest gamebird in Europe, with a largely black plumage and rounded tail which is fanned out in courtship. The female is speckled brown and about 2 ft/60 cm long.

Hunted to extinction in Britain in the 18th century, the capercaillie was reintroduced from Sweden in the 1830s and has re-established itself in Scotland.

Capet Hugh 938–996. King of France from 987, when he claimed the throne on the death of Louis V. He founded the Capetian dynasty, of which various branches continued to reign until the French Revolution, for example, ◊Valois and ◊Bourbon.

Cape Town (Afrikaans *Kaapstad*) port and oldest town in South Africa, situated in the SW on Table Bay; population (1985) 776,617. Industries include horticulture and trade in wool, wine, fruit, grain, and oil. It is the legislative capital of the Republic of South Africa and capital of Cape Province; it was founded in 1652.

It includes the Houses of Parliament, City Hall, Cape Town Castle (1666), and Groote Schuur, ("great barn"), the estate of Cecil Rhodes (he designated the house as the home of the premier, and a university and the National Botanical Gardens occupy part of the grounds). The naval base of Simonstown is to the SE; in 1975 Britain's use of its facilities was ended by the Labour government in disapproval of South Africa's racial policies.

Cape Verde
Republic of
(República de Cabo Verde)

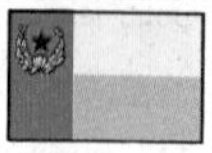

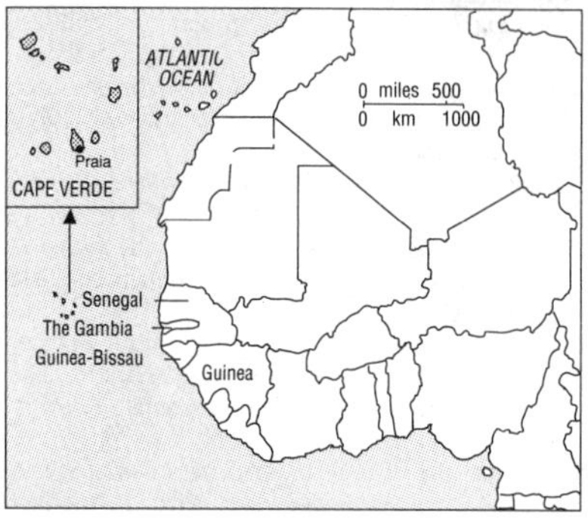
ATLANTIC OCEAN
0 miles 500
0 km 1000
Praia
CAPE VERDE
Senegal
The Gambia
Guinea-Bissau
Guinea

area 1,557 sq mi/4,033 sq km
capital Praia
cities Mindelo, Sal-Rei, Porto Novo
physical archipelago of ten volcanic islands 350 mi/565 km W of Senegal; the windward (Barlavento) group includes Santo Antão, São Vicente, Santa Luzia, São Nicolau, Sal, and Boa Vista; the leeward (Sotovento) group comprises Maio, São Tiago, Fogo, and Brava; all but Santa Luzia are inhabited
features strategic importance guaranteed by its domination of western shipping lanes; Sal, Boa Vista, and Maio lack water supplies but have fine beaches
head of state Mascarenhas Monteiro from 1991
head of government Carlos Viega from 1991
political system Socialist pluralist state
political parties African Party for the Independence of Cape Verde (PAICV), African nationalist; Movement for Democracy (MPD)
exports bananas, salt, fish
currency Cape Verde escudo
population (1990 est) 375,000 (including 100,000 Angolan refugees); growth rate 1.9% p.a.
life expectancy men 57, women 61
language Creole dialect of Portuguese
religion Roman Catholic 80%
literacy men 61%/women 39% (1985)
GDP $158 million (1987); $454 per head
chronology
15th century First settled by Portuguese.
1951–74 Ruled as an overseas territory by Portugal.
1974 Moved toward independence through a transitional Portuguese–Cape Verde government.
1975 Independence achieved from Portugal. National people's assembly elected. Aristides Pereira became the first president.
1980 Constitution adopted providing for eventual union with Guinea-Bissau.
1981 Union with Guinea-Bissau abandoned and the constitution amended; became one-party state.
1991 First multiparty elections held. New party, Movement for Democracy (MPD) won majority in assembly. Pereira replaced by Mascarenhas Monteiro.

Cape Verde group of islands in the Atlantic, W of Senegal (W Africa).

government The 1980 constitution provides for a national people's assembly of 83, elected by universal suffrage for a five-year term, and a president, elected for a similar term by the assembly. The constitution had also provided for union with Guinea-Bissau but this was deleted in 1981 and an amendment inserted replacing the African Party for the Independence of Portuguese Guinea and Cape Verde (PAIGC) with the African Party for the Independence of Cape Verde (PAICV) as the only political party. As well as combining the roles of head of state and head of government, the president is secretary general of PAICV. There is an opposition party, the Independent Democratic Union of Cape Verde (UCID), but it operates from Lisbon.

history The Cape Verde islands were first settled in the 15th century by Portugal, the first black inhabitants being slaves imported from W Africa. Over the next five centuries of Portuguese rule the islands were gradually peopled with Portuguese, African slaves, and people of mixed African-European descent who became the majority. The Cape Verdians kept some African culture but came to speak Portuguese or the Portuguese-derived Creole language, and became Catholics.

A liberation movement developed in the 1950s. The mainland territory to which Cape Verde is linked, Guinea, now Guinea-Bissau, achieved independence in 1974, and a process began for their eventual union. A transitional government was set up, composed of Portuguese and PAIGC members. In 1975 a national people's assembly was elected, and Aristides Pereira, PAIGC secretary general, became president of Cape Verde. The 1980 constitution provided for the union of the two states but in 1981 this aspect was deleted because of insufficient support and the PAIGC became the PAICV. Pereira was re-elected, and relations with Guinea-Bissau improved. Under President Pereira, Cape Verde has adopted a non-aligned policy and achieved considerable respect within the region.

Cape York peninsula, the northernmost point (10° 41′ S) of the Australian mainland, named by Captain James ◊Cook in 1770. The peninsula is about 500 mi/800 km long and 400 mi/640 km wide at its junction with the mainland. Its barrenness deterred early Dutch explorers, although the S is being developed for cattle (Brahmin type). In the N there are large bauxite deposits.

capillarity the spontaneous movement of liquids up or down narrow tubes, or capillaries. The movement is due to unbalanced molecular attraction at the boundary between the liquid and the tube. If liquid molecules near the boundary are more strongly attracted to molecules in the material of the tube than to other nearby liquid molecules, the liquid will rise in the tube. If liquid molecules are less attracted to the material of the tube than to other liquid molecules, the liquid will fall.

capillary the narrowest blood vessel in vertebrates, between 8- and 20-thousandths of a millimeter in diameter, barely wider than a red blood cell. Capillaries are distributed as beds, complex networks connecting arteries and veins. Capillary walls are extremely thin, consisting of a single layer of cells, and so nutrients, dissolved gases, and waste products can easily pass through them. This makes the capillaries the main area of exchange between the fluid (◊lymph) bathing body tissues and the blood.

capillary in physics, a very narrow, thick-walled tube, usually made of glass, such as in a thermometer. Properties of fluids, such as surface tension and viscosity, can be studied using capillary tubes.

capital in architecture, a stone placed on the top of a column, pier, or pilaster, and usually wider on the upper surface than the diameter of the supporting shaft. A capital consists of three parts: the top member, called the abacus, a block that acts as the supporting surface to the superstructure; the middle portion, known as the bell or echinus; and the lower part, called the necking or astragal.

capital in economics, accumulated or inherited wealth held in the form of assets (such as stocks and shares, property, and bank deposits). In stricter terms, capital is defined as the stock of goods used in the production of other goods; it may be fixed capital (such as buildings, plant, and machinery), which is durable, or circulating capital (raw materials and components), which is used up quickly.

capital bond an investment bond that is purchased by a single payment, set up for a fixed period, and offered for sale by a life insurance company. The emphasis is on capital growth of the lump sum invested rather than on income.

capital expenditure spending on fixed assets such as plant and equipment, trade investments, or the purchase of other businesses.

capital-gains tax an income tax levied on the change of value of a person's assets, after they are sold, including securities and real property. It is frequently a politically contentious tax, since if it is set too low, it is seen as a subsidy for the rich who have made large profits on their property. If it is set too high, it can act as a disincentive for investment, and economic activity can slow.

capitalism economic system in which the principal means of production, distribution, and exchange are in private (individual or corporate) hands and competitively operated for profit. A mixed economy combines the private enterprise of capitalism and a degree of state monopoly, as in nationalized industries.

capital punishment punishment by death. Capital punishment, abolished in the UK 1965 for all crimes except treason, is retained in many countries, including the US (37 states), France, and the USSR. Methods of execution include electrocution, lethal gas, hanging, shooting, lethal injection, garrotting, and decapitation.

In the US, the Supreme Court declared capital punishment unconstitutional 1972 (as a cruel and unusual punishment) but decided 1976 that this was not so in all circumstances. It was therefore reintroduced in some states. The first state to abolish capital punishment was Michigan 1847.

capitulum in botany, a flattened or rounded head (inflorescence) of numerous, small, stalkless flowers. The capitulum is surrounded by a circlet of petallike bracts and has the appearance of a large, single flower. It is characteristic of plants belonging to the daisy family Compositae, such as sunflowers *Helianthus*, goldenrods *Solidago*, and dandelions *Taraxacum*. The individual flowers are known as ◊florets.

***Capone** Al Capone (light suit, center) was a notorious Chicago gang leader during Prohibition. Seemingly untouchable, he was arrested for federal tax evasion and imprisoned from 1931 to 1939. This photo was taken when he was under indictment in Chicago Federal Court 1931.*

Capodimonte village, N of Naples, Italy, where porcelain known by the same name was first produced under King Charles III of Naples about 1740. The porcelain is usually white, painted with colorful folk figures, landscapes, or flowers.

Capone Al(phonse) 1898–1947. US gangster, born in Brooklyn, New York, the son of an Italian barber. His nickname was Scarface. During the ◊Prohibition period, Capone built a formidable criminal organization in Chicago. He was brutal in his pursuit of dominance, killing seven members of a rival gang in the St Valentine's Day massacre. He was imprisoned 1931–39 for income-tax evasion, the only charge that could be sustained against him.

Caporetto former name of ◊Kobarid, Yugoslavia.

Capote Truman. Adopted name of Truman Streckfus Persons 1924–1984. US novelist, short-story writer, and playwright. He wrote *Breakfast at Tiffany's* 1958; set a trend with the first "nonfiction novel," *In Cold Blood* 1966, reconstructing a Kansas killing; and mingled recollection and fiction in *Music for Chameleons* 1980.

***Capote** The youthful novelist and journalist Truman Capote.*

His other works range from musicals to screenplays to sketches and essays about travel, celebrities, and other topics. He was a prominent figure in the New York social and literary world in his later years.

Cappadocia ancient region of Asia Minor, in E central Turkey. It was conquered by the Persians in 584 BC but in the 3rd century BC became an independent kingdom. The region was annexed as a province of the Roman Empire in AD 17.

The area includes over 600 Byzantine cave churches cut into volcanic rock, dating mainly from the 10th and 11th centuries.

Capra Frank 1897–1991. Italian-born US film director. His films, satirical social comedies which often have idealistic heroes, include *It Happened One Night* 1934, *Mr Deeds Goes to Town* 1936, and *You Can't Take It With You* 1938, for which he received Academy Awards.

Capri Italian island at the S entrance of the Bay of Naples; 20 mi/32 km S of Naples; area 5 sq mi/13 sq km. It has two towns, Capri and Anacapri, a profusion of flowers, beautiful scenery, and an ideal climate.

capriccio (Italian "caprice") in music, a short instrumental piece, often humorous or whimsical in character.

Capricorn alternative term for Capricornus.

Capricornus zodiac constellation in the southern hemisphere near Sagittarius. It is represented as a fish-tailed goat, and its brightest stars are third magnitude. The Sun passes through it late Jan to mid-Feb. In astrology, the dates for Capricornus are between about Dec 22 and Jan 19 (see ◊precession).

Capricornus contains the ◊globular cluster M30.

Caprivi Strip NE access strip for ◊Namibia to the Zambezi River.

capsicum any pepper plant of the genus *Capsicum* of the nightshade family Solanaceae, native to Central and South America. The differing species produce green to red fruits that vary in size. The small ones are used whole to give the hot flavor of chili, or ground to produce cayenne pepper; the large pointed or squarish pods, known as sweet and bell peppers, are mild-flavored and used as a vegetable.

Caracalla *Marcus Aurelius Antoninus Caracalla, Roman emperor* AD *211–17.*

capsule in botany, a dry, usually many-seeded fruit formed from an ovary composed of two or more fused ◊carpels, which splits open to release the seeds. The same term is used for the spore-containing structure of mosses and liverworts; this is borne at the top of a long stalk or seta.

Capsules burst open (dehisce) in various ways, including lengthwise, by a transverse lid—for example, scarlet pimpernel *Anagallis arvensis*—or by a number of pores, either toward the top of the capsule, as in the poppy *Papaver*, or near the base, as in certain species of bellflower *Campanula*.

Captain Marvel US comic book character created 1940 by C(larence) C(harles) Beale (1910–1989). Captain Marvel is a 15-year-old schoolboy, Billy Batson, who transforms himself by saying "Shazam" into a superhuman hero wearing a red-and-yellow caped athletic suit.

Capua Italian town in Caserta province on the Volturno, in a fertile plain N of Naples; population (1981) 18,000. There was heavy fighting here in 1943 during World War II, which almost destroyed the Romanesque cathedral.

Capuchin a member of the Franciscan order of monks in the Roman Catholic church, instituted by the Italian monk Matteo di Bassi (d. 1552), who wished to return to the literal observance of the rule of St Francis. The Capuchin rule was drawn up in 1529 and the order recognized by the pope in 1619. The name was derived from the French term for the brown habit and pointed hood (*capuche*) that they wore. The order has been involved in missionary activity.

capuchin monkey, genus *Cebus* found in Central and South America, so called because the hairs on the head resemble the cowl of a capuchin monk. Capuchins live in small groups, feed on fruit and insects, and have a tail that is semiprehensile and can give support when climbing through the trees.

capybara largest rodent *Hydrochoerus hydrochaeris*, up to 4 ft/1.3 m long and 110 lb/50 kg in weight. It is found in South America, and belongs to the guinea-pig family. The capybara inhabits marshes and dense vegetation around water. It has thin, yellowish hair, swims well, and can rest underwater with just eyes, ears, and nose above the surface.

car popular name for ◊automobile.

caracal cat *Felis caracal* related to the ◊lynx. It has long black ear-tufts, a short tail, and short reddish-fawn fur. It lives in bush and desert country in Africa, Arabia, and India, hunting birds and small mammals at night. Head and body length is about 2.5 ft/75 cm.

Caracalla Marcus Aurelius Antoninus AD 186–217. Roman emperor. So-called from the celtic cloak (caracalla) that he wore. He succeeded his father Septimus Severus in 211, ruled with cruelty and extravagance, and was assassinated.

caraway

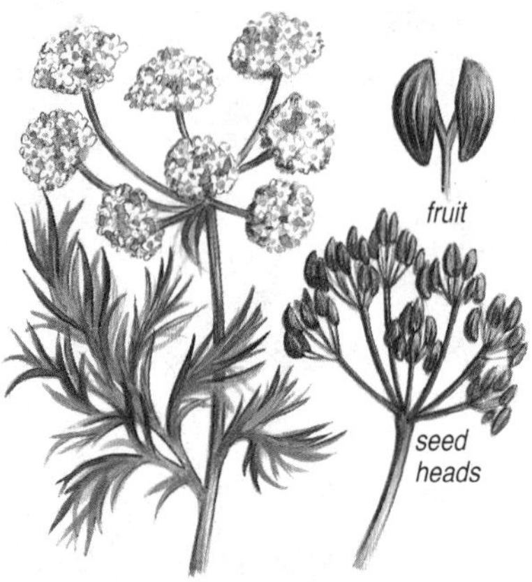
fruit
seed heads

With the support of the army he murdered his brother Geta and thousands of his followers to secure sole possession of the throne. During his reign, Roman citizenship was given to all subjects of the Empire. He built on a grandiose scale, for example the Baths of Caracalla in Rome.

Caracas chief city and capital of Venezuela; situated on the Andean slopes, 8 mi/13 km S of its port La Guaira on the Caribbean coast; population of metropolitan area (1981) 1,817,000. Founded 1567, it is now a major industrial and commercial center, notably for oil companies.

It is the birthplace of Simón ◊Bolívar. It has many fine buildings, including Venezuela University, which forms a city within a city, and has gates guarded by university police. As in most Latin American countries, the university is independent and self-governing, and no state police or soldiers are allowed to enter. The city has suffered several severe earthquakes.

carat unit for measuring the mass of precious stones, derived from the Arabic word *quirrat*, meaning "seed." Originally, 1 carat was the weight of a carob seed; it is now taken as 0.00705 oz/0.2 g, and is part of the troy system of weights. Also, an alternate spelling of ◊karat.

Caravaggio Michelangelo Merisi da 1573–1610. Italian early Baroque painter, active in Rome 1592–1606, then in Naples, and finally in Malta. His life was as dramatic as his art (he had to leave Rome after killing a man). He created a forceful style, using contrasts of light and shade and focusing closely on the subject figures, sometimes using dramatic foreshortening.

He was born in Caravaggio, near Milan. His compositions were unusual, strong designs in the two-dimensional plane with little extraneous material. He painted from models, making portraits of real Roman people as saints and Madonnas, which caused outrage. An example is *The Conversion of St Paul* (Sta Maria del Popolo, Rome).

He had a number of direct imitators (Caravaggisti), and several Dutch and Flemish artists who visited Rome, including Honthorst and Terbrugghen were inspired by him.

caraway herb *Carum carvi* of the carrot family Umbelliferae. It is grown for its spicy, aromatic seeds, which are used in cooking, medicine, and perfumery.

carbide any solid compound of carbon and one other chemical element, usually a metal, silicon, or boron.

Calcium carbide (CaC_2) can be used as the starting material for many basic organic chemical syntheses, by the addition of water and generation of ethyne (acetylene). Some metallic carbides are used in engineering because of their extreme hardness and strength. Tungsten carbide is an essential ingredient of carbide tools and high-speed tools. The "carbide process" was used during World War II to make organic chemicals from coal rather than from oil.

carbohydrate chemical compound composed of carbon, hydrogen, and oxygen, with the basic formula $C_m(H_2O)_n$, and related compounds with the same basic structure but modified ◊functional groups.

The simplest carbohydrates are sugars—monosaccharides, such as glucose and fructose, and disaccharides, such as sucrose—which are soluble compounds, some with a sweet taste. When these basic sugar units are joined together in long chains they form polysaccharides, such as starch and glycogen, which often serve as food stores in living organisms. As such they form a major energy-providing part of the human diet. Even more complex carbohydrates are known, including ◊chitin, which is found in the cell walls of fungi and the hard outer skeletons of insects, and ◊cellulose, which makes up the cell walls of plants. Carbohydrates form the chief foodstuffs of herbivorous animals.

carbolic acid common name for the aromatic compound ◊phenol.

carbon (Latin *carbo* (*carbonaris*) "coal") nonmetallic element, symbol C, atomic number 6, atomic weight 12.011. It is one of the most widely distributed elements, both inorganically and organically, and occurs in combination with other elements in all plants and animals. The atoms of carbon can link with one another in rings or chains, giving rise to innumerable complex compounds. It occurs in nature (1) in the pure state in the crystalline forms of graphite and diamond; (2) as calcium carbonate ($CaCO_3$) in carbonaceous rocks such as chalk and limestone; (3) as carbon dioxide (CO_2) in the atmosphere; and (4) as hydrocarbons in the fossil fuels petroleum, coal, and natural gas. Noncrystalline forms of pure carbon include charcoal and coal. When added to steel, carbon forms a wide range of alloys. In its elemental form, it is widely used as a moderator in nuclear reactors; as colloidal graphite it is a good lubricant, which, when deposited on a surface in a vacuum, obviates photoelectric and secondary emission of electrons. The radioactive isotope C-14 (half-life 5,730 years) is widely used in archeological dating and as a tracer in biological research.

Carbonari a secret revolutionary society in S Italy

carbohydrate

polysaccharide

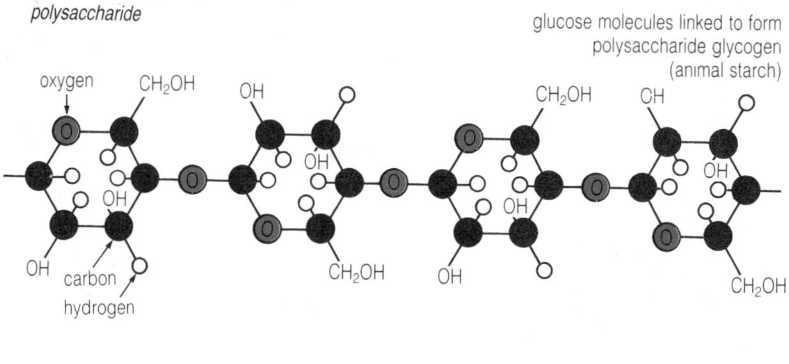
glucose molecules linked to form polysaccharide glycogen (animal starch)
oxygen
CH_2OH
OH
OH
OH
OH
carbon
hydrogen
CH_2OH
OH
CH_2OH
OH
OH
OH
CH_2OH

carbon

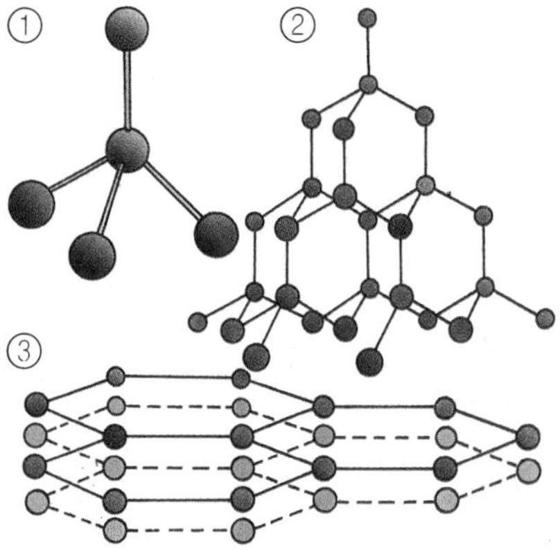
1
2
3

1. the basic unit of the diamond structure
2. *diamond* a giant three dimensional structure
3. *graphite* a two dimensional structure

carbon cycle

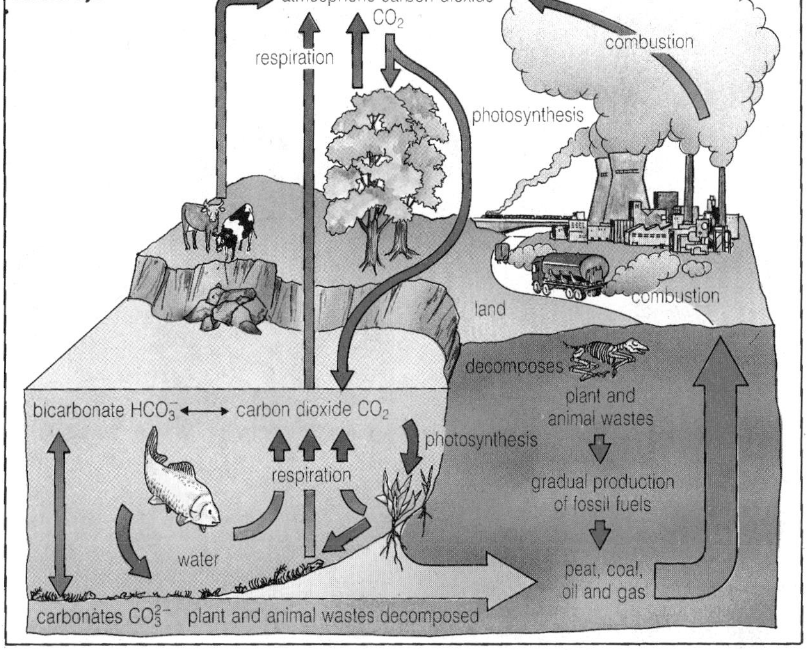
atmospheric carbon dioxide
CO_2
respiration
combustion
photosynthesis
land
combustion
decomposes
plant and
animal wastes
bicarbonate HCO_3^- ←→ carbon dioxide CO_2
photosynthesis
respiration
gradual production
of fossil fuels
water
peat, coal,
oil and gas
carbonates CO_3^{2-} plant and animal wastes decomposed

in the first half of the 19th century that advocated constitutional government. The movement spread to N Italy but support dwindled after the formation of ◊Mazzini's nationalist "Young Italy" movement, although it helped pave the way for the unification of Italy (see ◊Risorgimento).

carbonate CO_3^{2-} ion formed when carbon dioxide dissolves in water, and any salt formed by this ion and another chemical element, usually a metal.

The carbon dioxide (CO_2) dissolved by rain falling through the air, and liberated by decomposing animals and plants in the soil, forms with water carbonic acid (H_2CO_3), which unites with various basic substances to form carbonates. Calcium carbonate ($CaCO_3$) (chalk, limestone, and marble) is one of the most abundant carbonates on Earth, being formed from mollusk shells and the hard outer skeletons of crustaceans.

carbon cycle the sequence by which carbon circulates and is recycled through the natural world. The carbon element from carbon dioxide in the atmosphere is taken up during the process of ◊photosynthesis, and the oxygen component is released back into the atmosphere. Some of this carbon becomes locked up in coal and petroleum and other sediments. Carbon (as carbon dioxide) is released during aerobic respiration of plants and animals. New carbon also enters the atmosphere during volcanic eruptions. Today, the carbon cycle is being altered by the increased consumption of fossil fuels and the burning of large tracts of tropical forests, as a result of which levels of carbon dioxide are building up in the atmosphere and probably contributing to the ◊greenhouse effect.

carbon dating alternate name for ◊radiocarbon dating.

carbon dioxide CO_2 colorless gas formed by the complete oxidation of carbon. It is produced during the process of respiration by living things and by the decay of organic matter. Its increasing density contributes to the ◊greenhouse effect and ◊global warming. Britain has 1% of the world's population, yet it produces 3% of CO_2 emissions; the US has 5% of the world's population and produces 25% of CO_2 emissions.

carbon fiber fine, black, silky filament of pure carbon produced by heat treatment from a special grade of Courtelle acrylic fiber, used for reinforcing plastics. The resulting composite is very stiff and, weight for weight, has four times the strength of high-tensile steel. It is used in aerospace, automobiles, and electrical and sports equipment.

Carboniferous period of geologic time 360–286 million years ago, the fifth period of the Paleozoic era. In the US it is regarded as two periods: the Mississippian (lower) and the Pennsylvanian (upper). Typical of the lower-Carboniferous rocks are shallow-water ◊limestones, while upper-Carboniferous rocks have ◊delta deposits with ◊coal (hence the name). Amphibians were abundant, and reptiles evolved.

carbon monoxide CO colorless, odorless gas formed when carbon is oxidized in a limited supply of air.

It is a poisonous constituent of auto exhaust fumes, forming a stable compound with hemoglobin in the blood, thus preventing the hemoglobin from performing its vital function of transporting oxygen to the body tissues.

carbon tetrachloride CCl chlorinated organic compound that is a very efficient solvent for fats and greases. It is a toxic solvent and its use is restricted.

Carborundum trademark for a very hard, black abrasive, consisting of silicon carbide (SiC), an artificial compound of carbon and silicon. First produced in 1891 by Edward Acheson (1856–1931), it is harder than ◊corundum but not as hard as ◊diamond (9 and 10 respectively, on ◊Mohs' scale).

carbuncle bacterial infection of the skin, similar to a ◊boil but deeper and more widespread. It is treated with drawing salves, lancing, or antibiotics.

carburetion any process involving chemical combination with carbon, especially the mixing or charging of a gas, such as air, with volatile compounds of carbon (gasoline, kerosene, or fuel oil) in order to increase potential heat energy during combustion. Carburation applies to combustion in the cylinders of reciprocating gasoline engines of the types used in aircraft, road vehicles, or marine vessels. The device by which the liquid fuel is atomized and mixed with air is called a carburetor.

Carcassonne city in SW France, capital of Aude *département*, on the river Aude, which divides it into the ancient and modern town; population (1982) 42,450. Its medieval fortifications (restored) are the finest in France.

Carchemish (now Karkamis, Turkey) center of the ◊Hittite New Empire (c. 1400–1200 BC) on the river Euphrates, 50 mi/80 km NE of Aleppo, and taken by Sargon II of Assyria 717 BC. Nebuchadnezzar II of Babylon defeated the Egyptians here 605 BC.

carcinogen any agent that increases the chance of a cell becoming cancerous (see ◊cancer), including various chemical compounds, some viruses, X-rays and other forms of ionizing radiation. The term is often used more narrowly to mean chemical carcinogens only.

carcinoma malignant ◊tumor arising from the skin, the glandular tissues, or the mucous membranes that line the gut and lungs.

Cardano Girolamo 1501–1576. Italian physician, mathematician, philosopher, astrologer, and gambler. He is remembered for his theory of chance, his use of algebra, and many medical publications, notably the first clinical description of typhus fever.

Born at Pavia, he became professor of medicine there in 1543, and wrote two works on physics and natural science, *De Subtilitate rerum* 1551 and *De Varietate rerum* 1557.

Cárdenas Lázaro 1895–1970. Mexican center-left politician and general, president 1934–40. A civil servant in early life, Cárdenas took part in the revolutionary campaigns 1915–29 that followed the fall of President Díaz (1830–1915). As president of the republic, he attempted to achieve the goals of the revolution by building schools, distributing land to the peasants, and developing transport and industry. He was minister of defense 1943–45.

cardiac pertaining to the ◊heart.

Cardiff capital of Wales (from 1955) and administrative headquarters of South and Mid Glamorgan, at the mouth of the Taff, Rhymney, and Ely rivers; population (1983) 279,800. Besides steelworks, there are automotive component, flour milling, paper, cigar, and other industries.

The city dates from Roman times, the later town being built around a Norman castle. The castle was the residence of the earls and marquesses of Bute from the 18th century and was given to the city 1947 by the fifth marquess. Coal was exported until the 1920s. As coal declined, iron and steel exports continued to grow, and an import trade in timber, grain and flour, tobacco, meat, and citrus fruit developed.

Cardin Pierre 1922– . French fashion designer; the first women's designer to show a collection for men, in 1960.

cardinal in the Roman Catholic church, the highest rank next to the pope. Cardinals act as an advisory body to the pope and elect him. Their red hat is the badge of office. The number of cardinals has varied; there were 151 in 1989.

Originally a cardinal was any priest in charge of a major parish, but in 1567 the term was confined

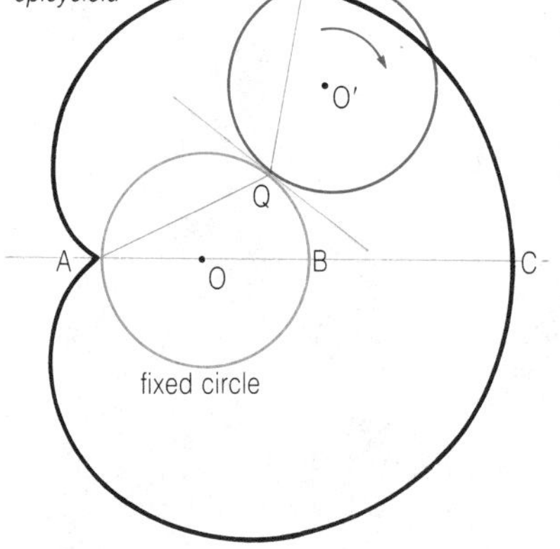
rolling circle
P′
O′
Q
A
O
B
C
fixed circle

cardioid
the cardioid as an epicycloid

to the members of the Sacred College, 120 of whom (below the age of 80) elect the pope and are themselves elected by him (since 1973). They advise on all matters of doctrine, canonizations, convocation of councils, liturgy, and temporal business.

cardinal number in mathematics, one of the series of numbers 0,1,2,3,4,... . Cardinal numbers relate to quantity, whereas ordinal numbers (first, second, third, fourth,...) relate to order.

cardioid heart-shaped curve traced out by a point on the circumference of a circle that rolls around the edge of another circle of the same diameter. The polar equation of the cardioid is of the form $r = a(1 + \cos \theta)$.

Cardozo Benjamin Nathan 1870–1938. US jurist and Supreme Court justice. Cardozo was named to the US Supreme Court by President Hoover 1932. During the F D Roosevelt administration, he upheld the constitutionality of New Deal programs, as in *Ashwander* v *Tennessee Valley Authority* 1936 and the Social Security case *Helvering* v *Davis* 1937.

Born in New York, Cardozo was educated at Columbia University and was admitted to the bar 1891. After a brief career as a corporate counsel, he was elected to the New York Supreme Court 1913. Appointed associate justice of the court of appeals 1917, he became its chief judge 1926.

cards common name for ◊playing cards.

Carducci Giosuè 1835–1907. Italian poet. Born in Tuscany, he was appointed in 1860 professor of Italian literature in Bologna, and won distinction through his lecturing, critical work, and poetry. His revolutionary *Inno a Satana/Hymn to Satan* 1865 was followed by several other volumes of verse, in which his nationalist sympathies are apparent. Nobel Prize 1906.

Carême Antonin 1784–1833. French chef who is regarded as the founder of classic French *haute cuisine*. At various times he was chief cook to the Prince Regent in England and Tsar Alexander I in Russia.

Carey Peter 1943– . Australian novelist. He has combined work in advertising with a writing career since 1962, and his novels include *Bliss* 1981, *Illywhacker* (Australian slang for "con man") 1985, and *Oscar and Lucinda* 1988, which won the Booker prize.

cargo cult Melanesian religious movement, dating from the 19th century. Adherents believe the arrival of cargo is through the agency of a messianic spirit figure, heralding a new paradise free of white dominance. The movement became active during and after World War II with the apparently miraculous dropping of supplies from airplanes.

Carib a member of a group of ◊American Indian people of the N coast of South America and the islands of the S West Indies in the Caribbean. Those who moved north to take the islands from

CATCHING AN ELEPHANT.

caricature *George Rowlandson's* Catching an Elephant *1812, Guildhall Library, London. Rowlandson's caricatures usually focused on the most hideous aspects of the lowest and highest levels of society in Georgian England.*

the Arawak Indians were reputedly fierce cannibals. In 1796, the English in the West Indies deported most of them to Roatan Island, off Honduras.

Caribbean Community and Common Market (CARICOM) organization for economic and foreign policy coordination in the Caribbean region, established by the Treaty of Chaguaramas 1973 to replace the former Caribbean Free Trade Association. Its headquarters are in Georgetown, Guyana. The leading member is Trinidad and Tobago; other members are Antigua, Barbados, Belize, Dominica, Grenada, Guyana, Jamaica, Montserrat, St Christopher–Nevis, Anguilla, St Lucia, and St Vincent. From 1979, a left-wing Grenadan coup led to a progressive regional subgroup including St Lucia and Dominica.

Caribbean Sea W part of the Atlantic Ocean between the S coast of North America and the N coasts of South America. Central America is to the west and the West Indies are the islands within the sea, which is about 1,700 mi/2,740 km long and between 400–900 mi/650–1,500 km wide. It is from here that the ◊Gulf Stream turns toward Europe. A number of continental American nations lie on its shores, and it contains the West Indies archipelago, which consists of independent island nations as well as dependencies of the US, France, the Netherlands, and the UK. The Caribbean Sea is a major maritime trade route for oil, other raw materials, seafood, and tropical agricultural products. It was named for the Carib Indians who inhabited the area when it was discovered by Spanish explorers, beginning with Christopher Columbus in 1492.

caribou the ◊reindeer of North America.

caricature exaggerated portrayal of individuals or types, aiming to ridicule or otherwise expose the subject. Classical and medieval examples survive. Artists of the 18th, 19th, and 20th centuries have often used caricature as a way of satirizing society and politics. Notable exponents include Daumier and Grosz.

Grotesque drawings have been discovered in Pompeii and Herculaneum, and Pliny refers to a grotesque portrait of the poet Hipponax. Humorous drawings were executed by the ◊Carracci family and their Bolognese followers (the Italian "eclectic" school of the 16th century). In 1830, Charles Philipon (1800–1862) founded in Paris *La Caricature*, probably the first periodical to specialize in caricature.

CARICOM abbreviation for ◊Caribbean Community and Common Market.

caries decay and disintegration, usually of the substance of teeth (cavity) or bone.

Carina constellation of the southern hemisphere, representing a ship's keel. Its brightest star is Canopus; it also contains Eta Carinae, a massive and highly luminous star embedded in a gas cloud. It has varied unpredictably in the past; some astronomers think it is likely to explode as a supernova within 10,000 years.

Carinthia (German *Kärnten*) alpine federal province of SE Austria, bordering Italy and Yugoslavia in the S; capital Klagenfurt; area 3,667 sq mi/ 9,500 sq km; population (1987) 542,000. It was an independent duchy from 976 and a possession of the Hapsburg dynasty 1276–1918.

Carissimi Giacomo 1605–1674. Italian composer, a pioneer of the oratorio.

Carl XVI Gustaf 1946– . King of Sweden from 1973. He succeeded his grandfather Gustaf VI, his father having been killed in an airplane crash in 1947. Under the new Swedish constitution, which became effective on his grandfather's death, the monarchy was stripped of all power at his accession.

Carlisle city in NW England; situated on the river Eden at the west end of Hadrian's Wall; population (1981) 71,000. It is the administrative headquarters of Cumbria, and the county town of the former county of Cumberland. It is a leading railroad center; textiles, engineering, and cookie making are the chief industries. There is a Norman cathedral and a castle. The bishopric dates from 1133.

Carlisle city in S Pennsylvania in the Cumberland Valley, SW of Harrisburg; seat of Cumberland county. Manufactures include electronics and steel products. The US Army War College and Dickinson College are here; population (1990) 18,419.

Carlist a supporter of the claims of the Spanish pretender Don Carlos de Bourbon (1788–1855), and his descendants, to the Spanish crown. The Carlist revolt continued, primarily in the Basque provinces, until 1839. In 1977 the Carlist political party was legalized and Carlos Hugo de Bourbon Parma (1930–) renounced his claim as pretender and became reconciled with King Juan Carlos. See also ◊Bourbon.

Carlos four kings of Spain. See ◊Charles.

Carlos I 1863–1908. King of Portugal, of the Braganza-Coburg line, from 1889 until he was assassinated in Lisbon with his elder son Luis. He was succeeded by his younger son Manuel.

Carlos Don 1545–1568. Spanish prince. Son of Philip II, he was recognized as heir to the thrones of Castile and Aragon but became mentally unstable and had to be placed under restraint following a plot to assassinate his father. His story was the subject of plays by Schiller, Alfieri, Otway, and others.

Carlow county in the Republic of Ireland, in the province of Leinster; county town Carlow; area 347 sq mi/900 sq km; population (1986) 41,000. Mostly flat except for mountains in the S, the land is fertile, and well suited to dairy farming.

Carlsbad German name of ◊Karlovy Vary, a spa town in W Bohemia, Czechoslovakia.

Carlson Chester 1906–1968. US scientist who invented ◊xerography. A research worker with Bell Telephone, he lost his job in 1930 during the Depression and set to work on his own to develop an efficient copying machine. By 1938 he had invented the Xerox photocopier.

Carlsson Ingvar (Gösta) 1934– . Swedish Socialist politician, leader of the Social Democratic Party, deputy prime minister 1982–86 and prime minister from 1986. After studying in Sweden and the US, Carlsson became president of the Swedish Social Democratic Youth League in 1961. He was elected to the Riksdag (parliament) in 1964 and became a minister in 1969. With the return to power of the Social Democrats in 1982, Carlsson became deputy to Prime Minister Palme and, on his assassination in 1986, succeeded him.

Carlucci Frank (Charles) 1930– . US politician. A former diplomat and deputy director of the CIA, he was national security adviser 1986–87 and defense secretary 1987–89 under Reagan, supporting Soviet-US arms reduction.

Educated at Princeton and Harvard, Carlucci, after fighting in the Korean War, was a career diplomat during the later 1950s and 1960s. He returned to the US in 1969 to work under presidents Nixon, Ford and Carter, his posts including US ambassador to Portugal and deputy director of the CIA. An apolitical Atlanticist, Carlucci found himself out of step with the hawks in the Reagan administration, and left to work in industry after barely a year as deputy secretary of defense. In Dec 1986, after the ◊Irangate scandal, he replaced John ◊Poindexter as national security adviser.

Carlyle Thomas 1795–1881. Scottish essayist and social historian. His works include *Sartor Resartus* 1833–34, describing his loss of Christian belief, *French Revolution* 1837, *Chartism* 1839, and *Past and Present* 1843. He was a friend of J S ◊Mill and Ralph Waldo ◊Emerson.

Carlyle was born at Ecclefechan in Dumfriesshire. In 1821 he passed through the spiritual crisis described in *Sartor Resartus*. He married Jane Baillie Welsh (1801–66) in 1826 and they moved to her farm at Craigenputtock, where *Sartor Resartus* was written. His reputation was established with the *French Revolution*. The series of lectures he gave 1837–40 included *On Heroes, Hero-Worship and The Heroic in History* (published 1841). He also wrote several pamphlets, including *Chartism*, attacking the doctrine of ◊*laissez-faire*; the notable *Letters and Speeches of Cromwell* 1845; and the miniature life of his friend, John Sterling 1851. Carlyle then began his *History of Frederick the Great* 1858–65, and after the death of his wife in 1866 edited her letters 1883 and prepared his *Reminiscences* 1881, which shed an unfavorable light on his character and his neglect of her, for which he could not forgive himself. His house in Cheyne Row, Chelsea, London, is a museum.

Carmelite order mendicant order of friars in the Roman Catholic church. The order was founded on Mount Carmel in Palestine by Berthold, a crusader from Calabria, about 1155, and spread to Europe in the 13th century. The Carmelites have devoted themselves largely to missionary work and mystical theology. They are known as White Friars because of the white overmantle they wear (over a brown habit).

Traditionally Carmelites originated in the days of Elijah, who according to the Old Testament is supposed to have lived on Mount Carmel. Following the rule which the patriarch of Jerusalem drew up for them about 1210, they lived as hermits in separate huts. About 1240, the Muslim conquests compelled them to move from Palestine and they spread to the west, mostly in France and England, where the order began to live communally. The most momentous reform movement was initiated by St ◊Teresa. In 1562 she founded a convent in Avila and, with the cooperation of St John of the Cross and others, she established a stricter order of barefoot friars and nuns (the Discalced Carmelites).

Carmichael Hoagy (Hoagland Howard) 1899–1981. US composer, pianist, singer, and actor. His best-known songs include "Stardust" 1927, "Rockin' Chair" 1930, "Lazy River" 1931, and "In the Cool, Cool, Cool of the Evening" 1951, for which he won an Academy Award.

While studying law at Indiana University, he began to compose, and he came to perform with such jazz greats as Bix ◊Beiderbecke. Later he worked in Hollywood, where he also appeared in films, including *To Have and Have Not* 1944.

***Carnegie** On his retirement, the industrialist Andrew Carnegie devoted his life to the philanthropic distribution of his vast fortune.*

Carmina Burana medieval lyric miscellany compiled from the work of wandering 13th-century scholars and including secular (love songs and drinking songs) as well as religious verse. A cantata (1937) by Carl ◊Orff is based on the material.

Carnac megalithic site in France where remains of tombs and stone alignments of the period 2000–1500 BC have been found. The largest of the latter has 1,000 stones up to 13 ft/4 m high arranged in 11 rows, with a circle at the western end. Carnac is a village in Brittany; population about 4,000.

Carnap Rudolf 1891–1970. German philosopher, in the US from 1935, an exponent of logical ◊empiricism. He was a member of the Vienna Circle, who adopted Ernst ◊Mach as their guide. His books include *The Logical Syntax of Language* 1934 and *Meaning and Necessity* 1956. He was professor of philosophy at the University of California 1954–62.

Carnarvon alternate spelling of ◊Caernarvon.

carnassial tooth powerful scissorlike pair of molars, found in all mammalian carnivores except seals. Carnassials are formed from an upper premolar and lower molar, and are shaped to produce a sharp cutting surface. Carnivores such as dogs transfer meat to the back of the mouth, where the carnassials slice up the food ready for swallowing.

Carnatic region of SE India, in Madras state. It is situated between the Eastern Ghats and the Coromandel Coast and was formerly a leading trading center.

carnation numerous double-flowered cultivated varieties of a plant *Dianthus caryophyllus* of the pink family. The flowers smell like cloves; they are divided into flake, bizarre, and picotees, according to whether the petals exhibit one or more colors on their white ground, have the color dispersed in strips, or have a colored border to the petals.

carnauba palm *Copernicia cerifera* native to South America. It produces fine timber and a hard wax, used for polishes and lipsticks.

Carné Marcel 1906– . French director of the films *Le Jour se lève/Daybreak* 1939 and *Les Enfants du paradis/Children of Paradise* 1944.

Carnegie Andrew 1835–1919. US industrialist and philanthropist, born in Scotland, who developed the Pittsburgh iron and steel industries, making the US the world's leading producer. He endowed public libraries, education, and various research trusts.

Born in Dunfermline, Scotland, he was taken by his parents to the US in 1848 and at 14 became a telegraph boy in Pittsburgh. He became a railroad employee, rose to be superintendent, introduced sleeping-cars, and invested successfully in oil. In developing the Pittsburgh iron and steel industries, he built up a vast empire, which in 1901 he disposed of to the United States Steel Trust before moving to Skibo castle in Sutherland, Scotland. He used his wealth to endow US libraries and universities, the Carnegie Endowment for International Peace, and other philanthropies. On his death the Carnegie Trusts continued his benevolent activities. Carnegie Hall in New York City, opened in 1891 as The Music Hall, was renamed in 1898 because of his large contribution to its construction.

Carnegie was attacked by some as an exploiter of labor and as an unscrupulous business competitor. However, his innovations transformed the US steel industry, and his philanthropies have had lasting effect.

Carnegie Dale 1888–1955. US author and teacher, best known for the ongoing bestseller on personality improvement *How to Win Friends and Influence People* 1937. His courses in public speaking, which drew huge audiences, first won him fame, and he was asked to publish them as a book. His other books include *Little Known Facts About Well Known People* 1934 and *How to Stop Worrying and Start Living* 1948.

carnelian semiprecious gemstone variety of ◊chalcedony consisting of quartz (silica) with iron impurities, which give it a translucent red color. It is found mainly in Brazil, India, and Japan.

Carniola a former crownland and duchy of Austria, most of which was included in Slovenia, part of the kingdom of the Serbs, Croats, and Slovenes (later Yugoslavia) in 1919. The W districts of Idrija and Postojna, then allocated to Italy, were transferred to Yugoslavia in 1947.

carnivore an animal that eats other animals. Although it is sometimes confined to animals that eat the flesh of ◊vertebrate prey, the term is often used more broadly to include any animal that eats other animals, even microscopic ones. Carrion-eaters may or may not be included.

The mammalian order Carnivora includes civets, raccoons, cats, dogs, and bears.

Carnot Lazare Nicolas Marguerite 1753–1823. French general and politician. A member of the National Convention in the French Revolution, he organized the armies of the republic. He was war minister 1800–01 and minister of the interior 1815 under Napoleon. His work on fortification, *De la défense de places fortes* 1810, became a military textbook. Minister of the interior during the ◊Hundred Days, he was proscribed at the restoration of the monarchy and retired to Germany.

Carnot Nicolas Leonard Sadi 1796–1832. French scientist and military engineer, son of Lazare Carnot, who founded the science of ◊thermodynamics; his pioneering work was *Réflexions sur la puissance motrice du feu/On the Motive Power of Fire*.

Carnot cycle changes in the physical condition of a gas in a reversible heat engine, necessarily in the following order: (1) isothermal expansion (without change of temperature), (2) adiabatic expansion (without change of heat content), (3) isothermal compression, and (4) adiabatic compression.

The principles derived from a study of this cycle are important in the fundamentals of heat and ◊thermodynamics.

carnotite potassium uranium vanadate, $K_2(UO_2)_2(VO_4)_2.3H_2O$, a radioactive ore of vanadium and uranium with traces of radium. A yellow powdery mineral, it is mined chiefly in the Colorado Plateau; Radium Hill, Australia; and Shaba, Zaïre.

carob small Mediterranean tree *Ceratonia siliqua* of the legume family Leguminosae. Its 8 in/20 cm pods are used as animal fodder; they are also the source of a chocolate substitute.

carol song that in medieval times was associated with a round dance; now those that are sung at annual festivals, such as Easter and Christmas.

Christmas carols were common as early as the

Carnot *It is as the founder of thermodynamics that the distinguished military engineer and scientist Sadi Carnot is remembered. He died at the age of 36, victim of a cholera epidemic.*

15th century. The custom of singing carols from house to house, collecting gifts, was called wassailing. Many carols such as "God Rest You Merry, Gentlemen" and "The First Noel," date back at least as far as the 16th century.

Carol two kings of Romania:

Carol I 1839–1914. First king of Romania 1881–1914. A prince of the house of Hohenzollern-Sigmaringen, he was invited to become prince of Romania, then part of the Ottoman Empire, 1866. In 1877, in alliance with Russia, he declared war on Turkey, and the Congress of Berlin 1878 recognized Romanian independence.

He promoted economic development and industrial reforms but failed to address rural problems. This led to a peasant rebellion 1907 which he brutally crushed. At the beginning of World War I, King Carol declared Romania's neutrality but his successor (his nephew King Ferdinand I) declared his support for the Allies.

Carol II 1893–1953. King of Romania 1930–40. Son of King Ferdinand, he married Princess Helen of Greece and they had a son, Michael. In 1925 he renounced the succession and settled in Paris with his mistress, Mme Lupescu. Michael succeeded to the throne 1927, but in 1930 Carol returned to Romania and was proclaimed king. In 1938 he introduced a new constitution under which he practically became an absolute ruler. He was forced to abdicate by the pro-Nazi ◊Iron Guard Sept 1940, went to Mexico, and married his mistress 1947.

Caroline of Anspach 1683–1737. Queen of George II of Great Britain and Ireland. The daughter of the Margrave of Brandenburg-Anspach, she married George, Electoral Prince of Hanover 1705, and followed him to England in 1714 when his father became King George I. She was the patron of many leading writers and politicians such as Alexander Pope, John Gay, and Chesterfield. She supported Sir Robert Walpole and kept him in power and acted as regent during her husband's four absences.

Caroline of Brunswick 1768–1821. Queen of George IV of Great Britain, who unsuccessfully attempted to divorce her on his accession to the throne 1820.

Since they separated in 1796, he forbade her access to their daughter Charlotte and kept her from the coronation 1821; her death a few weeks later led to riots.

Carolines scattered archipelago in Micronesia, Pacific Ocean, consisting of over 500 coral islets; area 463 sq mi/1,200 sq km. The chief islands are Ponape, Kusai, and Truk in the eastern group, and Yap and Belau in the western.

They are well watered and productive. Occupied by Germany 1899, and Japan 1914, and mandated by the League of Nations to Japan 1919, they were fortified, contrary to the terms of the mandate. Under Allied air attack in World War II they remained unconquered. In 1947 they became part of the US Trust Territory of the ◊Pacific Islands.

Carolingian dynasty Frankish dynasty descending from ◊Pepin the Short (died 768) and named after his son Charlemagne; its last ruler was Louis V of France (reigned 966–87), who was followed by Hugh ◊Capet.

carotene a naturally occurring pigment of the ◊carotenoid group. Carotenes produce the orange, yellow, and red colors of carrots, tomatoes, oranges, and crustaceans. They are also involved in ◊photosynthesis as adjuncts to ◊chlorophyll. In vertebrates, carotenes are converted to vitamin A and retinal pigments important in vision.

carotenoids a group of yellow, orange, red, or brown pigments found in many living organisms, particularly in the ◊chloroplasts of plants. There are two main types, the carotenes and the xanthophylls. Both types are long-chain lipids (◊fats).

Some carotenoids act as accessory pigments in ◊photosynthesis, and in certain algae they are the principal light-absorbing pigments functioning more efficiently than ◊chlorophyll in low-intensity light. Carotenes can also occur in organs such as petals, roots, and fruits, giving them their characteristic color, as in the yellow and orange petals of wallflowers *Cheiranthus*. They are also responsible for the autumn colors of leaves, persisting longer than the green chlorophyll, which masks them during the summer.

Carothers Wallace 1896–1937. US chemist, who carried out research into ◊polymerization. By 1930 he had discovered that some polymers were fiber forming, and in 1937 he produced ◊nylon.

carotid artery one of a pair of major blood vessels, one on each side of the neck, supplying blood to the head.

carp fish *Cyprinus carpio* found all over the world. It commonly grows to 1.8 ft/50 cm and 7 lb/3 kg, but may be even larger. It lives in lakes, ponds and slow rivers. The wild form is drab, but cultivated forms (domesticated by the ancient Chinese) may be golden, or may have few large scales (mirror carp) or be scaleless (leather carp). Koi carp are highly prized and can grow up to 3 ft/1 m long with a distinctive pink, red, white or black coloring.

A large proportion of European freshwater fishes belong to the carp family, Cyprinidae, and related fishes are found in Asia, Africa, and North America. Its fast growth, large size, and ability to live in still water with little oxygen have made it a good fish to farm, and it has been cultivated for hundreds of years and spread by human agency. Members of this family have a single nonspiny dorsal fin, pelvic fins well back on the body, and toothless jaws, although teeth in the throat form an efficient grinding apparatus. Minnows, roach, rudd, and many others including goldfish belong to this family. Chinese grass carp *Ctenopharyngodon idella* have been introduced (one sex only) to European rivers for weed control.

Carpaccio Vittorio 1450/60–1525/26. Italian artist who painted scenes of his native Venice. His series *The Legend of St Ursula* 1490–98 (Accademia, Venice) is full of detail of contemporary Venetian life. His other great series is the lives of saints George and Jerome 1502–07 (S Giorgio degli Schiavoni, Venice).

Carpathian Mountains Central European mountain system, forming a semicircle through Czechoslovakia–Poland–the Ukraine–Romania, 900 mi/ 1,450 km long. The central Tatra mountains on the Czechoslovakia–Poland frontier include the highest peak, Gerlachovka, 8,737 ft/2,663 m.

Carpeaux Jean-Baptiste 1827–1875. French sculptor whose lively naturalistic subjects include *La Danse* 1865–69 for the Opéra, Paris.

Another example is the *Neapolitan Fisherboy* 1858 (Louvre, Paris). The Romantic charm of his work belies his admiration of Michelangelo. He studied in Italy 1856–62 and won the Prix de Rome scholarship 1854.

carpel a female reproductive unit in flowering plants (◊angiosperms). It usually comprises an ◊ovary containing one or more ovules, the stalk or style, and a ◊stigma at its top which receives the pollen. A flower may have one or more carpels, and they may be separate or fused together. Collectively the carpels of a flower are known as the ◊gynoecium.

Carpentaria, Gulf of shallow gulf opening out of the Arafura Sea on the N of Australia. It was discovered by Tasman in 1606 and named in 1623 in honor of Pieter Carpentier, governor general of the Dutch East Indies.

Carpenter John 1948– . US director of horror and science fiction films. His career began with *Dark Star* 1974 and *Halloween* 1978, and continued with such films as *The Thing* 1982; *Christine* 1983, adapted from a Stephen King story about a vindictive car; the underrated, gentle *Starman* 1984; and *They Live* 1988. He composes his own film scores, which have often added to the atmosphere of menace that haunt his more scary movies.

carpetbagger in US history, derogatory name for the entrepreneurs and politicians from the North who moved to the Southern states during ◊Reconstruction 1865–76 after the Civil War.

With the votes of newly enfranchised blacks and some local white people (called scalawags), they won posts in newly created Republican state governments, but were resented by many white Southerners as outsiders and opportunists. The term thus came to mean a corrupt outsider who profits from an area's political instability, although some arrivals had good motives. They were so called because they were supposed to own no property except what they carried in their small satchels made of carpeting.

Carpini Johannes de Plano 1182–1252. Franciscan friar and traveler. Sent by Pope Innocent IV on a mission to the Great Khan, he visited Mongolia 1245–47 and wrote a history of the Mongols.

Carracci Italian family of painters in Bologna whose forte was murals and ceilings. The foremost of them, Annibale Carracci (1560–1609), decorated the Farnese Palace, Rome, with a series of mythological paintings united by simulated architectural ornamental surrounds (completed 1604).

Ludovico Carracci (1555–1619), with his cousin Agostino Carracci (1557–1602), founded Bologna's Academy of Art. Agostino collaborated with his brother Annibale on the Farnese Palace decorative scheme, which paved the way for a host of elaborate murals in Rome's palaces and churches, ever-more inventive illusions of pictorial depth and architectural ornament. Annibale also painted early landscapes such as *Flight into Egypt* 1603 (Doria Gallery, Rome).

Carradine John (Richmond Reed) 1906–1988. US film actor who often played sinister roles. He appeared in many major Hollywood films, such as *Stagecoach* 1939 and *The Grapes of Wrath* 1940, but was later seen mostly in "B" horror films, including *House of Frankenstein* 1944.

carragheen species of deep-reddish, branched seaweed *Chondrus crispus*. Named after Carragheen in Ireland, it is found on rocky shores on both sides of the Atlantic. It is exploited commercially in food and medicinal preparations and as cattle feed.

Carrara town in Tuscany, Italy, 37 mi/60 km NW of Livorno; population (1981) 66,000. It is celebrated for its quarries of fine white marble, which were worked by the Romans, abandoned in the 5th century, and came into use again with the revival of sculpture and architecture in the 12th century.

Carrel Alexis 1873–1944. US surgeon born in France, whose experiments paved the way for organ transplant. Working at the Rockefeller

Carroll *Charles Lutwidge Dodgson—Lewis Carroll—who, as well as being a mathematician and author of the* Alice *books, was a pioneer of portrait photography.*

Carson *US frontiersman "Kit" Carson.*

Institute in New York City, he devised a way of joining blood vessels end to end (anastomosing). This was a key move in the development of transplant surgery, as was his work on keeping organs viable outside the body, for which he was awarded the Nobel Prize for Medicine in 1912.

Carreras José 1947– . Spanish tenor, whose roles include Handel's Samson, and whose recordings include *West Side Story* 1984. In 1987, he became seriously ill with leukemia, but resumed his career in 1988.

Carrhae, Battle of battle in which the invading Roman general Crassus was defeated and killed by the Parthians in 53 BC. The ancient town of Carrhae is near Haran, Turkey.

Carrickfergus seaport on Belfast Lough, County Antrim, N Ireland; population (1985) 30,000.

carrier in medicine, anyone who harbors an infectious organism without ill effects but can pass the infection to others. The term is also applied to those who carry a recessive gene for a disease or defect without manifesting the condition.

Carroll Charles 1737–1832. American public official and signer of the Declaration of Independence.

Born in Annapolis, Maryland, Carroll was educated in France and England, returning to administer Carrollton, the family estate in Maryland. Because of his Catholic faith, he was not allowed to enter political life but was a strong supporter of the cause of American independence. In 1776 Carroll accompanied Benjamin Franklin on a diplomatic mission to Canada and in July of that year, as a member of the Continental Congress, was one of the signers of the Declaration of Independence. Carroll became one of Maryland's first two US senators 1789–92.

Carroll Lewis. Adopted name of Charles Lutwidge Dodgson 1832–1898. English mathematician and writer of children's books. He wrote the children's classics *Alice's Adventures in Wonderland* 1865 and its sequel *Through the Looking Glass* 1872. He also published mathematics books under his own name.

Born in Daresbury, Cheshire, Dodgson was a mathematics lecturer at Oxford 1855–1881. *Alice's Adventures in Wonderland* grew out of a story told by Dodgson to amuse three little girls, including the original "Alice," the daughter of Dean Liddell, Dean of Christ Church. During his lifetime Dodgson refused to acknowledge any connection with any books not published under his own name. Among later works was the mock-heroic nonsense poem "The Hunting of the Snark" 1876. He was among the pioneers of portrait photography.

carrot hardy European biennial *Daucus carota* of the family Umbelliferae. Cultivated since the 16th century for its edible root, it has a high sugar content and also contains carotene, which is converted by the human liver to vitamin A.

carrying capacity in ecology, the maximum number of animals of a given species that a particular area can support. When the carrying capacity is exceeded, there is insufficient food (or other resources) for the members of the population. The population may then be reduced by emigration, reproductive failure, or death through starvation.

Carson Christopher "Kit" 1809–68. US frontiersman, guide, and Indian agent, who later fought for the Federal side in the Civil War. Carson City, Nevada, was named after him.

Carson Rachel 1907–1964. US naturalist. An aquatic biologist with the US Fish and Wildlife Service 1936–49, she then became its editor-in-chief until 1952. In 1951 she published *The Sea Around Us* and in 1963 *Silent Spring*, attacking the indiscriminate use of pesticides.

Carson City capital of Nevada; population (1990) 40,443. Settled as a trading post 1851, it was platted and named for Kit Carson in 1858. It flourished as a boom town after the discovery of the nearby Comstock silver-ore lode 1859.

Cartagena city in the province of Murcia, Spain, on the Mediterranean; population (1986) 169,000. It is a seaport and naval base. It was founded as Carthago Nova about 225 BC by the Carthaginian Hasdrubal, son-in-law of Hamilcar Barca. It continued to flourish under the Romans and the Moors and was conquered by the Spanish 1269. It has a 13th-century cathedral and Roman remains.

Cartagena or ***Cartagena de los Indes*** port, industrial center, and capital of the department of Bolívar, NW Colombia; population (1985) 531,000. Plastics and chemicals are produced here.

It was founded 1533 and taken by Francis Drake 1586. A pipeline brings petroleum to the city from the De Manes oil-fields.

cartel (German *Kartell* "a group") an agreement among national or international firms that remain independent but enter into agreement to set mutually acceptable prices for their products. A cartel may restrict supply, or output, or raise prices to prevent entrants to the market and increase member profits. It therefore represents a form of ◊oligopoly. ◊OPEC, for example, is an oil cartel.

National laws concerning cartels differ widely, and international agreement is difficult to achieve. In the US, cartels are generally illegal, since the Sherman Antitrust Act 1890 prohibited cartels, but legislation passed during the Great Depression permitted industries to enact "codes of fair competition." These were declared unconstitutional 1935, and public cartels in coal mining, oil production, and agriculture largely ended after World War II. In Germany, cartels are the most common form of monopolistic organization.

Carter Elliott (Cook) 1908– . US composer. His early music shows the influence of ◊Stravinsky, but after 1950 it became increasingly intricate and densely written in a manner resembling ◊Ives. He invented "metrical modulation" which allows different instruments or groups to stay in touch while playing at different speeds. He has written four string quartets, the *Symphony for Three Orchestras* 1967, and the song cycle *A Mirror on Which to Dwell* 1975.

Carter Jimmy (James Earl) 1924– . the 39th president of the US 1977–81, a Democrat. In 1976 he narrowly wrested the presidency from Gerald Ford. Features of his presidency were the return of the Panama Canal Zone to Panama, the Camp David Agreements for peace in the Middle East, and the Iranian seizure of US embassy hostages. He was defeated by Ronald Reagan 1980.

Born in Plains, Georgia; he served in the navy, studied nuclear physics, and after a spell as a peanut farmer entered politics 1953.

Carter Doctrine assertion in 1980 by President Carter of a vital US interest in the Persian Gulf region (prompted by the Soviet invasion of Afghanistan and instability in Iran): any outside attempt at control would be met by military force if necessary.

Carteret Philip d 1796, English navigator who discovered the Pitcairn Islands in 1767 during a round-the-world expedition 1766–69. He retired in 1794 with the rank of rear admiral.

Cartesian coordinates in ◊coordinate geometry, the components of a system used to represent vectors or to denote the position of a point on a plane (two dimensions) or in space (three dimensions) with reference to a set of two or more axes. The Cartesian coordinate system can be extended to any finite number of dimensions (axes), and is used thus in theoretical mathematics. It is named after Descartes.

For a plane defined by two axes at right angles (a horizontal x-axis and a vertical y-axis), the coordinates of a point are given by its perpendicular distances from the y-axis and x-axis, written in the form (x,y). For example, a point P that lies three units from the y-axis and four units from the x-axis has Cartesian coordinates (3,4). In three-dimensional coordinate geometry, points are located with reference to a third, z-axis. The system is useful in creating technical drawings of machines or buildings, and in computer-aided design (◊CAD).

Carthage ancient Phoenician port in N Africa; it lay 10 mi/16 km N of Tunis, Tunisia. A leading trading center, from the 6th century BC it was in conflict with Greece, and then with Rome, and was destroyed by Roman forces 146 BC at the end of the ◊Punic Wars. About 45 BC, Roman colonists settled in Carthage, and it became the wealthy capital of the province of Africa. After its capture by the Vandals in AD 439 it was little more than a pirate stronghold. From 533 it formed part of the Byzantine Empire until its final destruction by Arabs in 698, during their conquest in the name of Islam.

Carthage is said to have been founded in 814 BC by Phoenician emigrants from Tyre, led by Princess Dido. It developed an extensive commerce throughout the Mediterranean and traded with the Tin Islands, whose location is believed to have been either Cornwall, England, or SW Spain. After the capture of Tyre by the Babylonians in the 6th century BC, it became the natural leader of the Phoenician colonies in N Africa and Spain, and there soon began a prolonged struggle with the Greeks, which centered mainly on Sicily, the east of which was dominated by Greek colonies, while the west was held by Carthaginian trading stations. About 540 BC the Carthaginians defeated a Greek attempt to land in Corsica, and in 480 BC

Carter *The 39th President of the United States of America, Jimmy (James Earl) Carter, a Democrat. 1977–1981.*

a Carthaginian attempt to conquer the whole of Sicily was defeated by the Greeks at Himera.

The population of Carthage before its destruction by the Romans is said to have numbered over 700,000. The constitution was an aristocratic republic with two chief magistrates elected annually and a senate of 300 life members. The religion was Phoenician, including the worship of the Moon goddess Tanit, the great Sun god Baal-Hammon, and the Tyrian Meklarth; human sacrifices were not unknown. The real strength of Carthage lay in its commerce and its powerful navy; its armies were for the most part mercenaries.

Carthusian order Roman Catholic order of monks and, later, nuns, founded by St Bruno in 1084 at Chartreuse, near Grenoble, France. Living chiefly in unbroken silence, they ate one vegetarian meal a day and supported themselves by their own labors; the rule is still one of severe austerity.

Cartier Georges Etienne 1814–1873. French-Canadian politician. He fought against the British in the rebellion 1837, was elected to the Canadian parliament 1848, and was joint prime minister with John A Macdonald 1858–62. He brought Québec into the Canadian federation 1867.

Cartier Jacques 1491–1557. French navigator who was the first European to sail up the St Lawrence river in 1534. He named the site of Montreal.

Cartier-Bresson Henri 1908– . French photographer, considered one of the greatest photographic artists. His documentary work was shot in black and white, using a small format camera. His work is remarkable for its tightly structured composition and his ability to capture the decisive moment.

cartilage flexible bluish-white connective ◊tissue made up of the protein collagen. In cartilaginous fish it forms the skeleton; in other vertebrates it forms the greater part of the the embryonic skeleton, and is replaced by ◊bone in the course of development, except in areas of wear such as bone endings, and the disks between the backbones. It also forms structural tissue in the larynx, nose, and external ear of mammals.

Cartland Barbara 1904– . English romantic novelist. She published her first book, *Jigsaw*, in 1921, and since then has produced a prolific stream of stories of chastely romantic love, usually in idealized or exotic settings, for a mainly female audience (such as *Love Climbs In* 1978 and *Moments of Love* 1981).

cartography the art and practice of drawing ◊maps.

cartomancy practice of telling fortunes by cards, often ◊tarot cards.

cartoon humorous or satirical drawing or ◊caricature; a strip cartoon or ◊comic strip; traditionally, the base design for a large fresco, mosaic, or tapestry, transferred to wall or canvas by tracing or picking out (pouncing). Surviving examples include Leonardo da Vinci's *Virgin and St Anne* (National Gallery, London).

Cartwright Edmund 1743–1823. British inventor. He patented the power loom 1785, built a weaving mill 1787, and patented a wool-combing machine 1789.

Caruso Enrico 1873–1921. Italian operatic tenor. In 1902 he starred, with Nellie Melba, in Puccini's *La Bohème*. He was one of the first opera singers to profit from phonograph recordings

Carver George Washington 1864–1943. US agricultural chemist. Born a slave in Missouri, he was kidnapped and raised by his former owner, Moses Carver. He devoted his life to improving the economy of the US South and the condition of blacks. He advocated the diversification of crops, promoted peanut production, and was a pioneer in the field of plastics.

Carver was honored as one of America's most influential and innovative agronomists.

Carver Raymond 1939–1988. US short-story writer and poet, author of vivid tales of contemporary US life, a collection of which were published in *Cathedral* 1983; *Fires* 1985 includes his essays and poems.

Cary (Arthur) Joyce (Lunel) 1888–1957. British novelist. He used his experiences gained in Nigeria in the Colonial Service (which he entered in 1918) as a backdrop to such novels as *Mister Johnson* 1939. Other books include *The Horse's Mouth* 1944.

caryatid building support or pillar in the shape of a woman, the name deriving from the Karyatides, who were priestesses at the temple of Artemis at Karyai; a male figure is a telamon or atlas.

caryopsis a dry, one-seeded ◊fruit in which the wall of the seed becomes fused to the carpel wall during its development. It is a type of ◊achene, and therefore develops from one ovary and does not split open to release the seed. Caryopses are typical of members of the grass family (Gramineae), including the cereals.

Casablanca (Arabic *Dar el-Beida*) port, commercial and industrial center on the Atlantic coast of Morocco; population (1981) 2,409,000. It trades in fish, phosphates, and manganese. The Great Hassan II Mosque, completed 1989, is the world's largest; it is built on a platform (430,000 sq ft/40,000 sq m) jutting out over the Atlantic, with walls 200 ft/60 m high, topped by a hydraulic sliding roof, and a minaret 574 ft/175 m high.

Casablanca was occupied by the French from 1907 until Morocco became independent 1956.

Casablanca Conference World War II meeting of the US and UK leaders Roosevelt and Churchill, Jan 14–24, 1943, at which the Allied demand for the unconditional surrender of Germany, Italy, and Japan was issued.

Casals Pablo 1876–1973. Catalan cellist, composer, and conductor. As a cellist, he was celebrated for his interpretations of J S Bach's unaccompanied suites. He left Spain in 1939 to live in Prades, in the French Pyrenees, where he founded an annual music festival. He wrote instrumental and choral works, including the Christmas oratorio *The Manger*.

In 1919 Casals founded the Barcelona orchestra, which he conducted until leaving Spain at the outbreak of the Spanish Civil War in 1936. He

caryatid The Erectheon, Porch of the Caryatids at the Parthenon, Athens, Greece.

was an outspoken critic of fascism, and a tireless crusader for peace. In 1956 he moved to Puerto Rico where he launched the Casals Festival 1957 and toured extensively in the US. He married three times; his first wife was the Portuguese cellist Guilhermina Suggia.

Casanova de Seingalt Giovanni Jacopo 1725–1798. Italian adventurer, spy, violinist, librarian, and, according to his *Memoirs*, one of the world's great lovers. From 1774 he was a spy in the Venetian police service. In 1782 a libel got him into trouble, and after more wanderings he was in 1785 appointed librarian to Count Waldstein at his castle of Dûx in Bohemia. Here Casanova wrote his *Memoirs* (published 1826–38, although the complete text did not appear until 1960–61).

Cascade Range volcanic mountains in western US and Canada, extending 700 mi/1,120 km/ from N California through Oregon and Washington to the Fraser River. They include Mount St Helens and Mount Rainier (the highest peak, 14,408 ft/ 4,392 m), which is noteworthy for its glaciers. The mountains are the most active in the US, excluding Alaska and Hawaii.

Cascais fishing port and resort town on the Costa do Sol, 16 mi/25 km W of Lisbon, Portugal.

case grammar theory of language structure that proposes that the underlying structure should contain some sort of functional information about the roles of its components; thus in the sentence "The girl opened the door," the phrase *the girl* would have the role of agent, not merely that of grammatical subject.

casein main protein of milk, from which it can be separated by the action of acid, the enzyme rennin, or bacteria (souring); it is also the main component of cheese. Casein is used commercially in cosmetics, glues, and as a sizing for coating paper.

Casement Roger David 1864–1916. Irish nationalist. While in the British consular service, he exposed the ruthless exploitation of the people of the Belgian Congo and Peru, for which he was knighted in 1911 (degraded 1916). He was hanged for treason by the British for his part in the Irish republican Easter Rising.

Caserta town in S Italy 21 mi/33 km NE of Naples; population (1981) 66,318. It trades in chemicals, olive oil, wine, and grain. The base for Garibaldi's campaigns in the 19th century, it was the Allied headquarters in Italy 1943–45, and the German forces surrendered to Field Marshal Alexander here in 1945.

Cash Johnny 1932– . US country singer, songwriter, and guitarist. His early hits, recorded for Sun Records in Memphis, Tennessee, include the million-selling "I Walk the Line" 1956. Many of his songs have become classics. He is also known as "The Man in Black" because of his penchant for dressing entirely in that color.

cash crop crop grown solely for sale rather than for the farmer's own use, for example, coffee, cotton, or sugar beet. Many Third World countries grow cash crops to meet their debt repayments rather than grow food for their people. The price for these crops depends on financial interests, such as those of the multinational companies and the International Monetary Fund.

cashew tropical American tree *Anacardium occidentale*, family Anacardiaceae. Extensively cultivated in India and Africa, it produces poisonous kidney-shaped nuts that become edible after being roasted.

cashmere a natural fiber originating from the wool of the goats of Kashmir, India. Used for shawls, scarves, sweaters, and coats, it can also be made artificially.

Casper city in E central Wyoming, on the North Platte river, NW of Cheyenne; seat of Natrona county. The largest city in Wyoming, it serves as the marketing center for the region's livestock and petroleum products; population (1990) 46,742.

Caspian Sea world's largest inland sea, divided between Iran and the USSR. Area about 155,000 sq mi/400,000 sq km, with a maximum depth of 3,250 ft/1,000 m. The chief ports are Astrakhan and Baku. It is now approximately 90 ft/28 m below sea level due to drainage in the N, and the damming of the Volga and Ural rivers for hydroelectric power.

An underwater ridge divides it into two halves, of which the shallow N is almost salt-free. There are no tides. The damming has led to shrinkage over the last 50 years, and the growth of industry along its shores has caused pollution and damaged the Russian and Iranian caviar industries.

Cass Lewis 1782–1866. US political leader and diplomat. Born in Exeter, New Hampshire, Cass studied law in Ohio and was admitted to the bar 1802. During the War of 1812, Cass rose to the rank of brigadier general and was appointed governor of the Michigan Territory 1813. President Jackson chose him as his secretary of war 1831, and he served as US minister to France 1836–42. After a partial term in the US Senate, Cass was the unsuccessful Democratic presidential candidate in 1848. He returned to the Senate 1849–57 and later served as secretary of state in the Buchanan administration.

Cassandra in Greek mythology, the daughter of ◊Priam, king of Troy. Her prophecies (for example, of the fall of Troy) were never believed, because she had rejected the love of Apollo. She was murdered with Agamemnon by his wife Clytemnestra.

Cassatt Mary 1845–1926. US Impressionist painter and printmaker. Born to a wealthy Philadelphia family, in 1868 she settled in Paris and exhibited with the Impressionists 1879–81, 1886, the only American to do so. Her popular, colorful pictures of mothers and children show the then-new influence of Japanese prints: for example, *The Bath* 1892.

She also excelled in etching and pastels. Her work, always respected in France, has gained recognition in the US in recent years, the largest collection being on view at the Philadelphia Art Museum.

cassava or ***manioc*** plant *Manihot utilissima*, belonging to the spurge family Euphorbiaceae. Native to South America, it is now widely grown throughout the tropics for its starch-containing roots, from which tapioca and bread are made.

Cassavetes John 1929–1989. US film director and actor who directed experimental, apparently improvised films, including *Shadows* 1960, and *The Killing of a Chinese Bookie* 1980. His acting appearances included *The Dirty Dozen* 1967, and *Rosemary's Baby* 1968.

Cassel alternate spelling of ◊Kassel, an industrial town in western Germany.

cassia bark of a SE Asian plant *Cinnamomum cassia*, of the laurel family Lauraceae. It is aromatic and closely resembles true cinnamon, for which it is a widely used substitute. *Cassia* is also a genus of pod-bearing tropical plants of the family Caesalpiniaceae, many of which have strong purgative properties; *Cassia senna* is the source of the laxative drug senna.

Cassini Giovanni Domenico 1625–1712. Italian-French astronomer who discovered four moons of Saturn and the gap in the rings of Saturn now called the Cassini division.

Born in Italy, he became director of the Paris Observatory in 1671. His son, grandson, and great-grandson in turn became directors of the Paris Observatory.

Cassino town in S Italy, 50 mi/80 km NW of Naples; at the foot of Monte Cassino; population (1981) 31,139. It was the scene of heavy fighting during World War II in 1944, when most of the town was destroyed. It was rebuilt 1 mi/1.5 km to the N. The abbey on the summit of Monte Cassino, founded by St Benedict in 529, was rebuilt in 1956.

Cassiopeia in Greek mythology, the mother of ◊Andromeda.

Cassatt *The Paris Basin, Musée du Petit Palais, Paris, by US artist Mary Cassatt. Cassatt settled in France in her early thirties, where she worked closely with the Impressionists.*

Castiglione *Perhaps the best expression of the Renaissance spirit has come from the Italian author and diplomat Count Baldassare Castiglione, in his celebrated dialogue on courtly life,* Il Cortegiano.

Cassiopeia prominent constellation of the northern hemisphere, representing the mother of Andromeda. It has a distinctive W-shape and contains one of the most powerful radio sources in the sky, Cassiopeia A, the remains of a ◊supernova (star explosion), as well as open and globular clusters.

cassiterite or tinstone chief ore of tin, consisting of reddish-brown to black stannic oxide (SnO_2), usually found in granite rocks. When fresh it has a bright ("adamantine") luster. It was formerly extensively mined in Cornwall, England; today Malaysia is the world's major supplier. Other sources of cassiterite are in Africa, Indonesia, and South America.

Cassius Gaius died 42 BC. Roman soldier, one of the conspirators who killed Julius ◊Caesar in 44. He fought at Carrhae 53, and with the republicans against Caesar at Pharsalus 48, was pardoned and appointed praetor, but became a leader in the conspiracy of 44, and after Caesar's death joined Brutus. He committed suicide after his defeat at ◊Philippi 42 BC.

cassowary large flightless bird, genus *Casuarius*, found in New Guinea and N Australia, usually in forests. Cassowaries are related to emus, but have a bare head with a horny casque, or helmet, on top, and brightly colored skin on the neck. The loose plumage is black and the wings are tiny, but cassowaries can run and leap well, defending themselves by kicking. They stand up to 5 ft/ 1.5 m tall.

Castagno Andrea del c. 1421–1457. Italian Renaissance painter, active in Florence. In his frescoes in Sta Apollonia, Florence, he adapted the pictorial space to the architectural framework and followed ◊Masaccio's lead in perspective.

Castagno's work is sculptural and strongly expressive, anticipating the Florentine late 15th-century style, as in his *David*, about 1450–57 (National Gallery, Washington, DC).

Castalia a spring near ◊Delphi in Greece, sacred to ◊Apollo and the ◊Muses in Classical times.

castanets Spanish percussion instrument made of two hollowed wooden shells, held in the hand to produce a rhythmic accompaniment to dance.

caste (Portuguese *casta* "race") the stratifying of Hindu society, dating from ancient times, into four main groups from which over 3,000 subsequent divisions derive: Brahmans (priests), Kshatriyas, (nobles and warriors), Vaisyas (traders and farmers), and Sudras (servants); plus a fifth group, Harijan (untouchables). No upward or downward mobility exists, as in classed societies.

In Hindu tradition, the four main castes are said to have originated from the head, arms, thighs, and feet respectively of Brahma, the creator: the members of the fifth were probably the aboriginal inhabitants of the country, known variously as the Scheduled Castes, Depressed Classes, Untouchables, or Harijan (name coined by Gandhi, "children of God"). This lowest caste handled animal products, garbage, and human waste, and so was considered polluting by touch, or even by sight, to others. Discrimination against them was made illegal in 1947 when India became independent, but persists.

Castel Gandolfo village in Italy 15 mi/24 km SE of Rome. The castle, built by Pope Urban VIII in the 17th century, is still used by the pope as a summer residence.

Castellón de la Plana port in Spain, facing the Mediterranean to the E; population (1981) 124,500. It is the capital of Castellón province and is the center of an orange-growing district.

Castelo Branco Camilo 1825–1890. Portuguese novelist. His work fluctuates between mysticism and bohemianism, and includes *Amor de perdição/Love of Perdition* 1862, written during his imprisonment for adultery, and *Novelas do Minho* 1875, stories of the rural north.

Born illegitimately and then orphaned, he led a dramatic life. Other works include *Onde está a felicidade?/Where is Happiness?* 1856 and *A brazileira de Prazins/The Brazilian Girl from Prazins* 1882. Made a viscount in 1885, he committed suicide when overtaken by blindness.

cassowary

Castiglione Baldassare, Count Castiglione 1478–1529. Italian author and diplomat, who described the perfect Renaissance gentleman in *Il Cortegiano/The Courtier* 1528.

Born near Mantua, Castiglione served the Duke of Milan, and in 1506 was engaged by the Duke of Albino on a mission to Henry VII of England. While in Spain in 1524 he was made bishop of Avila.

Castile kingdom founded in the 10th century, occupying the central plateau of Spain. Its union with ◊Aragon in 1479, based on the marriage of ◊Ferdinand and Isabella, effected the foundation of the Spanish state, which at the time was occupied and ruled by the ◊Moors. Castile comprised the two great basins separated by the Sierra de Gredos and the Sierra de Guadarrama, known traditionally as Old and New Castile. The area now forms the regions of ◊Castilla-León and ◊Castilla-La Mancha.

The kingdom of Castile grew from a small area in the north. In the 11th century, Old Castile was united with León; in 1085 the kingdom of Toledo was captured from the Moors and became New Castile, with Toledo the capital of the whole. Castile was united with Aragon in 1479, and in 1492, after routing the Moors, Ferdinand and Isabella established the Catholic kingdom of Spain.

Castilian language member of the Romance branch of the Indo-European language family, originating in NW Spain, in the provinces of Old and New Castile. It is the basis of present-day standard Spanish (see ◊Spanish language) and is often seen as the same language, the terms *castellano* and *español* being used interchangeably in both Spain and the Spanish-speaking countries of the Americas.

Castilla Ramón 1797–1867. President of Peru 1841–51 and 1855–62. He dominated Peruvian politics for over two decades, bringing political stability. Income from guano exports was used to reduce the national debt and improve transport

castle (Top) Stokesay Castle in Shropshire, England, built between the 12th and 13th centuries. (Bottom) Bodiam Castle, built by Sir Edward Dalyngrigge in the 14th century.

and educational facilities. He abolished black slavery and the head tax on Indians.

Castilla-La Mancha autonomous region of central Spain; area 30,571 sq mi/79,200 sq km; population (1986) 1,665,000. It includes the provinces of Albacete, Ciudad Real, Cuenca, Guadalajara, and Toledo. Irrigated land produces grain and chickpeas, and merino sheep graze here.

Castilla-León autonomous region of central Spain; area 36,323 sq mi/94,100 sq km; population (1986) 2,600,000. It includes the provinces of Ávila, Burgos, León, Palencia, Salamanca, Segovia, Soria, Valladolid, and Zamora. Irrigated land produces wheat and rye. Cattle, sheep, and fighting bulls are bred in the uplands.

casting the process of producing solid objects by pouring molten material into a shaped mold and allowing it to cool. Casting is used to shape such materials as glass, plastics, as well as metals and alloys.

The casting of metals has been practiced for more than 6,000 years, using first copper, bronze, then iron. The traditional method of casting metal is sand casting. Using a model of the object to be produced, a hollow mold is made in a damp sand and clay mix. Molten metal is then poured into the mold, taking its shape when it cools and solidifies. The sand mold is broken up to release the casting. Permanent metal molds called dies are also used for casting, in particular, small items in mass-production processes where molten metal is injected under pressure into cooled dies. Continuous casting is a method of shaping bars and slabs that involves pouring molten metal into a hollow, water-cooled mold of the desired cross section.

cast iron cheap but invaluable constructional material, most commonly used for car engine blocks. Cast iron is partly refined pig (crude) ◊iron, which is very fluid when molten and highly suitable for shaping by ◊casting, as it contains too many impurities, such as carbon, to be readily shaped in any other way. Solid cast iron is heavy and can absorb great shock but is very brittle.

castle (Latin *castellum* "small fortification") the private fortress of a king or noble during the Middle Ages. At first a building on a mound surrounded by a wooden fence, this was later copied in stone.

castle

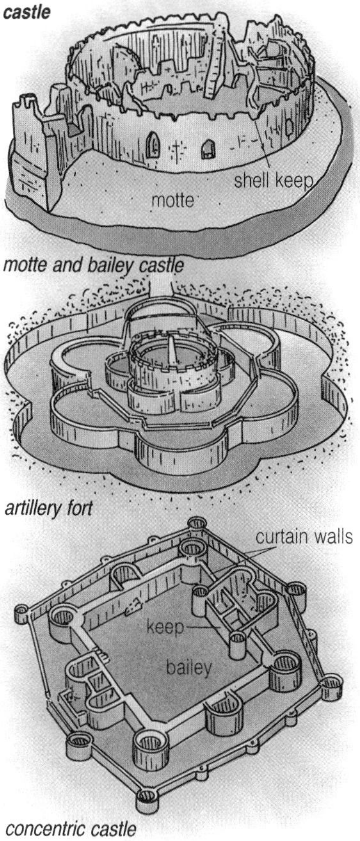
motte
shell keep
motte and bailey castle
artillery fort
curtain walls
keep
bailey
concentric castle

The earliest castles in Britain were built following the ◊Norman Conquest, and the art of castle building reached a peak in Europe during the 13th century. By the 15th century, the need for castles for domestic defense had largely disappeared, and the advent of gunpowder had made them largely useless against attack. See also ◊château.

The main parts of a typical castle are the keep, a large central tower containing storerooms, soldiers' quarters, and a hall for the lord and his family; the inner bailey, or walled courtyard surrounding the keep; the outer bailey, or second courtyard, separated from the inner bailey by a wall; crenelated embattlements through which missiles could be discharged against an attacking enemy; rectangular or round towers projecting from the walls; the portcullis, a heavy grating that could be let down to close the main gate; and the drawbridge crossing the ditch or moat surrounding the castle. Sometimes a tower called a barbican was constructed over a gateway as an additional defensive measure.

Early castles (11th century) consisted of an earthen hill (motte) surrounded by wooden palisades enclosing a courtyard (bailey). The motte supported a wooden keep. Later developments substituted stone for wood and utilized more elaborate defensive architectural detail. After introduction of gunpowder in the 14th century, castles became less defensible. Increases in civil order led to their replacement by unfortified manor houses by the 16th century. Large stone fortifications became popular again in the 18th century, particularly those modeled after the principles of fortification introduced by the French architect Vauban, and were built as late as the first half of the 19th century. In the late 19th century, castle-like buildings were built as residences for the wealthy as part of the Romantic revival in Europe and America.

Castlereagh Robert Stewart, Viscount 1769–1822. British Tory politician. As chief secretary for Ireland 1797–1801, he suppressed the rebellion of 1798 and helped the younger Pitt secure the union of England, Scotland, and Ireland in 1801. As foreign secretary 1812–22 he coordinated European opposition to Napoleon and represented Britain at the Congress of Vienna 1814–15.

Castor or Alpha Geminorum second brightest star in the constellation Gemini and the 23rd brightest star in the sky. Along with ◊Pollux, it forms a prominent pair at the eastern end of Gemini.

Castor is 45 light-years from Earth and is one of the finest ◊binary stars in the sky for small telescopes. The two main components orbit each other over a period of 400–500 years. A third, much fainter, star orbits the main pair over a period probably exceeding 10,000 years. Each of the three visible components is a spectroscopic binary, making Castor a sextuple star system.

Castor and Pollux/Polydeuces in Greek mythology, twin sons of Leda (by ◊Zeus), brothers of ◊Helen and ◊Clytemnestra. Protectors of mariners, they were transformed at death into the constellation Gemini.

castoreum the preputial follicles of the beaver, abbreviated as "castor," and used in perfumery.

castor-oil plant tall, tropical and subtropical shrub *Ricinus communis* of the spurge family Euphorbiaceae. The seeds, in North America called castor beans, yield the purgative castor oil and also ricin, one of the most powerful poisons known, which can be targeted to destroy cancer cells, while leaving normal cells untouched.

castration removal of the testicles. Male domestic animals may be castrated to prevent reproduction, make them larger or more docile, or remove a disease site.

Castration of humans was used in ancient and medieval times and occasionally later to preserve the treble voice of boy singers or, by Muslims, to provide trustworthy harem guards, called eunuchs. If done in childhood, it greatly modifies the secondary sexual characteristics: for instance, the voice may remain high, and growth of hair on the face and body may become weak or cease, caused by the removal of the hormones normally secreted by the testes.

Male domestic animals, especially stallions and bovine bulls, are castrated to prevent undesirable sires from reproducing, to moderate their aggressive and savage disposition and, for bulls, to improve their value as beef cattle (castrated bovines are called steer). Roosters are castrated (capons) to improve their flavor and increase their size. The effects of castration can also be achieved by chemical means, by administration of hormones, in humans and animals. If done in adulthood, the sexual function may be retained (although infertile) as well as masculine features already established.

castrato in music, a high male voice of unusual brilliance and power achieved by castration before puberty. The practice was outlawed in the mid-19th century.

Castries port and capital of St Lucia, on the NW coast of the island in the Caribbean; population (1988) 53,000. It produces textiles, chemicals, tobacco, and wood and rubber products.

The town was rebuilt after destruction by fire 1948.

Castro Cipriano 1858–1924. Venezuelan dictator 1899–1908, known as "the Lion of the Andes." When he refused to pay off foreign debts in 1902, British, German, and Italian ships blockaded the country. He presided over a corrupt government. There were frequent rebellions during his rule, and opponents of his regime were exiled or murdered.

Castro (Ruz) Fidel 1927– . Cuban revolutionary; prime minister 1959–76, following his overthrow of the military dictatorship of Fulgencio Batista; and president from 1976.

Of wealthy parentage, Castro was educated at Jesuit schools and studied law at the University of Havana. He strongly opposed the Batista dic-

Castro *Cuban revolutionary and premier Fidel Castro.*

cat

Manx
Persian
White Longhair
European wild cat
Siamese
Japanese bob tail
Egyptian mau
Sphynx
Balinese
blue point
Turkish angora

tatorship, and in 1953, with his brother Raúl, he took part in an unsuccessful attack on a Cuban army barracks. After spending time in jail and in exile in the US and Mexico, Castro attempted a secret landing in Cuba 1956, in which all but 11 of his supporters were killed. Castro escaped into the Sierra Maestra, where, with the support of the peasants, he built a guerrilla force of more than 5,000. On Jan 1, 1959, Castro's forces overthrew Batista, and Castro became prime minister. He seized the property of wealthy Cubans, Americans, and other foreigners, resulting in the severance of relations by the US, an economic embargo, and US attempts to subvert Cuba's government (see also ◊Bay of Pigs). Castro declared Cuba a MarxistLeninist state. The USSR replaced the US as Cuba's major trading partner and provided Cuba with substantial aid (see also ◊Cuban Missile Crisis). Castro built a strong military force and attempted to export his revolution to other Latin American countries. He also improved education, housing, and health care for the majority of Cubans but lost the support of the middle class, hundreds of thousands of whom fled the country.

casuarina tree or shrub of the genus *Casuarina*, family Casuarinaceae, which includes many species native to Australia and New Guinea but is also found in Africa and Asia. The river she-oak *C. cunninghamiana* has fronded branches resembling cassowary feathers, hence the Latin name.

cat small, domesticated (by the ancient Egyptians), carnivorous mammal *Felis catus* often kept as a pet or for catching small pests such as rodents. Found in many color variants, it may have short, long, or no hair, but the general shape and size is constant. All cats walk on the pads of their toes, and have retractile claws. They have strong limbs, large eyes, and acute hearing. The canine teeth are long and well-developed, as are the shearing teeth in the side of the mouth.

Domestic cats have a common ancestor, the African wild cat *Felis libyca*, found across Africa and Arabia. This is similar to the European wild cat *Felis silvestris*. Domestic cats can interbreed with either of these wild relatives. Various other species of small wild cat live in all continents except Antarctica and Australia. Large cats such as the lion and tiger also belong to the cat family Felidae.

catabolism in biology, the destructive part of ◊metabolism where living tissue is changed into energy and waste products. It is the opposite of anabolism. It occurs continuously in the body, but is accelerated during many disease processes, such as fever, and in starvation.

catacomb underground cemetery, such as the catacombs of the early Christians, including those beneath the basilica of St Sebastian in Rome, where bodies were buried in niches in the walls of the tunnels.

Catalan language member of the Romance branch of the Indo-European language family, an Iberian language closely related to Provençal in France. It is spoken in Catalonia in NE Spain, the Balearic Isles, Andorra, and a corner of SW France.

Since the end of the Franco regime in Spain in 1975, Catalan nationalists have vigorously promoted their regional language as being coequal in Catalonia with Castilian Spanish.

Catalaunian Fields plain near Troyes, France, scene of the defeat of Attila the Hun by the Romans and Goths under the Roman general Aëtius (died 454) in 451.

catalepsy in medicine, an abnormal state in which the patient is apparently or actually unconscious and the muscles become rigid.

There is no response to stimuli, and the rate of heartbeat and breathing is slow. A similar condition can be drug-induced or produced by hypnosis, but catalepsy as ordinarily understood occurs spontaneously in epilepsy, schizophrenia, and other nervous disorders.

Catal Hüyük Neolithic site (6000 BC) in Turkey-in-Asia, SE of Konya. It was a fortified city and had temples with wall paintings, and objects like jewelry, obsidian, and mirrors. Finds at Jericho and Catal Hüyük together indicated much earlier development of urban life in the ancient world than was previously imagined.

Catalonia (Spanish *Cataluña*) autonomous region of NE Spain; area 12,313 sq mi/31,900 sq km; population (1986) 5,977,000. It includes Barcelona (the capital), Gerona, Lérida, and Tarragona.

Industries include wool and cotton textiles; hydroelectric power is produced.

The N is mountainous, and the Ebro basin breaks through the Castellón mountains in the S. The soil is fertile, but the climate in the interior is arid. Catalonia leads Spain in industrial development. Tourist resorts have developed along the Costa Brava.

history The region has a long tradition of independence. It enjoyed autonomy 1932–39 but lost its privileges for supporting the Republican cause in the ◊Spanish Civil War. Autonomy and official use of the Catalan language were restored 1980.

French Catalonia is the adjacent *département* of Pyrénées-Orientales.

catalpa any of a genus *Catalpa* of trees belonging to the trumpet creeper Bignoniaceae family, found in North America, China, and the West Indies. The northern catalpa *C. speciosa* of North America grows to 100 ft/30 m and has heart-shaped, deciduous leaves and tubular white flowers with purple borders.

catalyst substance that alters the speed of or makes possible a chemical or biochemical reaction but that remains unchanged at the end of the reaction. ◊Enzymes are natural biochemical catalysts. In practice most catalysts are used to speed up reactions.

catalytic converter device for reducing toxic emissions from the internal-combustion engine. It converts harmful exhaust products to relatively harmless ones by passing exhaust gases over a mixture of catalysts. Oxidation catalysts convert hydrocarbons into carbon dioxide and water; three-way catalysts convert oxides of nitrogen back into nitrogen. Catalytic converters are standard in the US, where a 90% reduction in pollution from automobiles was achieved without loss of engine performance or fuel economy.

catamaran (Tamil "tied log") twin-hulled sailing vessel, based on the aboriginal craft of South America and the Indies, made of logs lashed together, with an outrigger. A similar vessel with three hulls is known as a trimaran. Car ferries with a wave-piercing catamaran design are also in use in parts of Europe and North America. They have a very pointed main hull and two outriggers and travel at a speed of 35 knots (52.5 mph/ 84.5 kph).

Catania industrial port in Sicily; population (1988) 372,000. It exports local sulfur.

cataract eye disease in which the crystalline lens or its capsule becomes opaque, causing blindness. Fluid accumulates between the fibers of the lens and gives place to deposits of ◊albumin. These coalesce into rounded bodies, the lens fibers break down, and areas of the lens or the lens capsule become filled with opaque products of degeneration.

The condition nearly always affects both eyes, usually one more than the other. In most cases, the treatment is replacement of the lens with an artificial implant.

catarrh inflammation of any mucous membrane, especially of the nose and throat, with increased production of mucus.

catastrophe theory mathematical theory developed by René Thom in 1972, in which he showed that the growth of an organism proceeds by a series of gradual changes that are triggered by, and in turn trigger, large-scale changes or "catastrophic" jumps. It also has applications in engineering—for example, the gradual strain on the structure of a bridge that can eventually result in a sudden collapse—and has been extended to economic and psychological events.

catastrophism theory that the geologic features of the Earth were formed by a series of sudden, violent "catastrophes" beyond the ordinary workings of nature. The theory was largely the work of Georges ◊Cuvier. It was later replaced by the concepts of ◊uniformitarianism and ◊evolution.

Catch-22 black humor novel by Joseph Heller, published 1961, about a US squadron that is ordered to fly an increased number of bombing missions in Italy in World War II; the crazed military justifications involved were described by the novel's phrase "Catch-22," which has come to represent the dilemma of all false authoritarian logic.

A man "would be crazy to fly more missions and sane if he didn't but if he was sane, he had to fly them. If he flew them he was crazy and didn't have to; but if he didn't, he was sane and had to."

catchment area

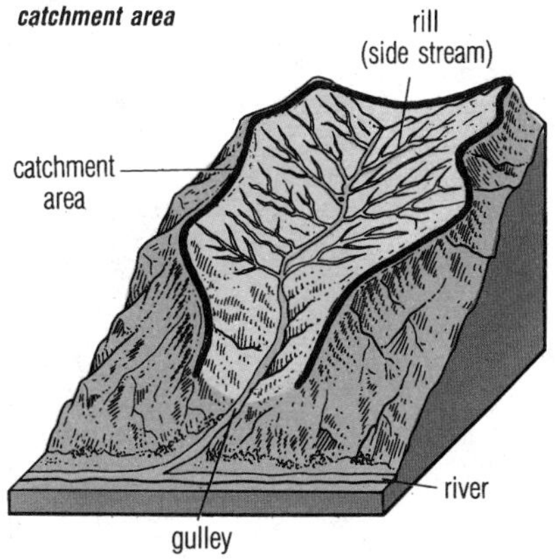
rill
(side stream)
catchment
area
river
gulley

catch crop crop that is inserted between two principal crops in a rotation in order to provide some quick livestock feed or soil improvement at a time when the land would otherwise be lying idle.

In the gap between harvesting a crop of winter-sown wheat and sowing a spring variety of barley, for example, an additional catch crop of turnips or ryegrass can be produced for animal feed in the late winter period when other green fodder is scarce. When the catch crop is plowed under, the succeeding spring crop benefits from the improvement to the soil.

Catcher in the Rye, The 1951 novel of a young man's growing up and his fight to maintain his integrity in a "phony" adult world; written by J D Salinger, it has become an international classic.

catchment area area from which water is collected by a river and its tributaries.

Cateau-Cambresis, Treaty of treaty that ended the dynastic wars between the Valois of France and the Hapsburg Empire, April 2–3, 1559.

catechism teaching by question and answer on the Socratic method, but chiefly as a means of instructing children in the basics of the Christian creed. A person being instructed in this way in preparation for baptism or confirmation is called a catechumen.

A form of catechism was used for the catechumens in the early Christian church. Little books of catechism were written by Luther and Calvin at the Reformation.

catecholamine chemical that functions as a ◊neurotransmitter or a ◊hormone. Dopamine, epinephrine (adrenaline), and norepinephrine (noradrenaline) are catecholamines.

catechu extract of the leaves and shoots of *Acacia catechu*, an East Indian plant. It is rich in tannic acid, which is released slowly, a property that makes it a useful intestinal astringent in diarrhea.

categorical imperative a technical term in ◊Kant's moral philosophy designating the supreme principle of morality for rational beings. The imperative orders us to act only in such a way that we can wish a maxim, or subjective principle, of our action to be a universal law.

category in philosophy, a fundamental concept applied to being that cannot be reduced to anything more elementary. Aristotle listed ten categories: substance, quantity, quality, relation, place, time, position, state, action, passion.

catenary a curve taken up by a flexible cable suspended between two points, under gravity; for example, the curve of overhead suspension cables that hold the conductor wire of an electric railroad or trolley.

caterpillar larval stage of a ◊butterfly or ◊moth. Wormlike in form, the body is segmented, may be hairy, and often has scent glands. The head has strong biting mandibles, silk glands, and a spinneret.

Many caterpillars resemble the plant on which they feed, dry twigs, or rolled leaves. Others are highly colored and rely for their protection on their irritant hairs, disagreeable smell, or on their power to eject a corrosive fluid. Yet others take up a "threat attitude" when attacked.

Caterpillars emerge from eggs that have been laid by the female insect on the food plant and feed greedily, increasing greatly in size and casting their skins several times, until the pupal stage is reached. The abdominal segments bear a varying number of "pro-legs" as well as the six true legs on the thoracic segments.

caterpillar track endless flexible belt of metal plates on which certain vehicles such as tanks and bulldozers run, which takes the place of tired wheels. A track-laying vehicle has a track on each side, and its engine drives small cogwheels that run along the top of the track in contact with the ground. The advantage of such tracks over wheels is that they distribute the vehicle's weight over a wider area and are thus ideal for use on soft and waterlogged as well as rough and rocky ground.

catfish fish belonging to the order Siluriformes, in which barbels (feelers) on the head are well-developed, so giving a resemblance to the whiskers of a cat. Catfishes are found worldwide, mainly but not exclusively in fresh water, and are plentiful in South America.

The East European giant catfish or wels *Silurus glanis* grows to 5 ft/1.5 m long or more. It has been introduced to several places in Britain.

The unrelated marine wolf-fish *Anarhicas lupus*, a deep-sea relative of the blenny, growing 4 ft/1.2 m long, is sometimes called a catfish.

Cathar (medieval Latin "the pure") member of a sect in medieval Europe usually numbered among the Christian heretics. Influenced by ◊Manichaeism, they started about the 10th century in the Balkans where they were called "Bogomils," spread to SW Europe where they were often identified with the ◊Albigenses, and by the middle of the 14th century had been destroyed or driven underground by the Inquisition.

The Cathars believed that this world is under the domination of Satan, and men and women are the terrestrial embodiment of spirits who were inspired by him to revolt and were driven out of heaven. At death, the soul will be reincarnated (whether in human or animal form) unless it has been united through the Cathar faith with Christ.

cathedral (Latin *cathedra*, a seat or throne) Christian church containing the throne of a bishop or archbishop, which is usually situated on the south side of the choir. There are cathedrals in most of the major cities of the world, built in a wide variety of architectural styles.

Cather Willa (Sibert) 1876–1947. US novelist and

catenary

A suspension bridge takes up a catenary curve

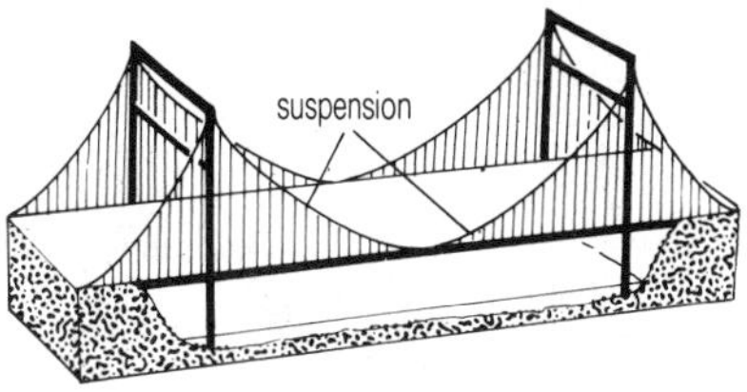
suspension

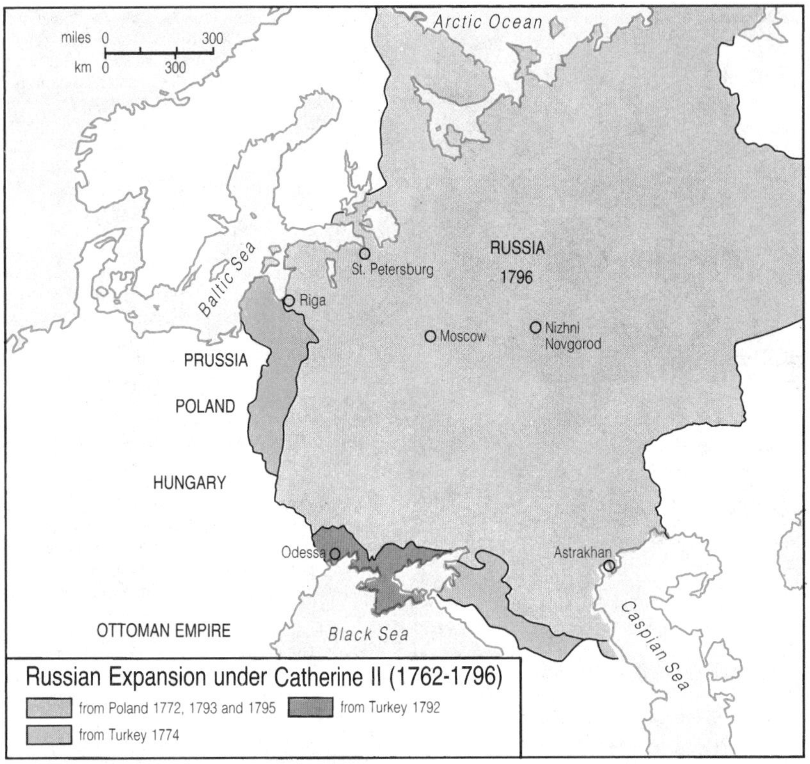
miles 0 300
km 0 300
Arctic Ocean
RUSSIA
1796
St. Petersburg
Baltic Sea
Riga
Moscow
Nizhni Novgorod
PRUSSIA
POLAND
HUNGARY
Odessa
Astrakhan
OTTOMAN EMPIRE
Black Sea
Caspian Sea
Russian Expansion under Catherine II (1762-1796)
from Poland 1772, 1793 and 1795
from Turkey 1792
from Turkey 1774

***Catherine II** An intelligent ruler and patron of the arts, Catherine the Great of Russia is remembered as a benevolent despot who significantly increased Russia's territory, into Turkey, Sweden, and Poland.*

short-story writer. Born in Virginia, she moved to Nebraska as a child. Her novels frequently explore life in the pioneer West, both in her own time and in past eras; for example, *O Pioneers!* 1913 and *My Antonia* 1918, and *A Lost Lady* 1923. *Death Comes for the Archbishop* 1927 is a celebration of the spiritual pioneering of the Catholic church in New Mexico. She also wrote poetry and essays on fiction.

Catherine I 1684–1727. Empress of Russia from 1725. A Lithuanian peasant girl, born Martha Skavronsky, she married a Swedish dragoon and eventually became the mistress of Peter the Great. In 1703 she was rechristened as Katarina Alexeievna, and in 1711 the tsar divorced his wife and married Catherine 1712. She accompanied him on his campaigns, and showed tact and shrewdness. In 1724 she was proclaimed empress, and after Peter's death 1725 she ruled capably with the help of her ministers. She allied Russia with Austria and Spain in an anti-English bloc.

Catherine II the Great 1729–1796. Empress of Russia from 1762, and daughter of the German prince of Anhalt-Zerbst. In 1745, she married the Russian grand duke Peter. Catherine was able to dominate him; six months after he became Tsar Peter III 1762, he was murdered in a coup and Catherine ruled alone. During her reign Russia extended its boundaries to include territory from wars with the Turks 1768–72, 1787–92, and from the partitions of Poland 1772, 1793, and 1795.

Catherine's private life was notorious throughout Europe, but except for Grigory ◊Potemkin she did not let her lovers influence her policy.

She admired and aided the French ◊Encyclopédistes.

Catherine de' Medici 1519–1589. French queen consort of Henry II, whom she married 1533; daughter of Lorenzo de' Medici, duke of Urbino; and mother of Francis II, Charles IX, and Henry III. At first outshone by Henry's mistress Diane de Poitiers (1490–1566), she became regent 1560–63 for Charles IX and remained in power until his death 1574.

During the religious wars of 1562–69, she first supported the Protestant ◊Huguenots against the Roman Catholic Guises to ensure her own position as ruler; she later opposed them, and has been traditionally implicated in the Massacre of ◊St Bartholomew 1572.

Catherine of Alexandria, St Christian martyr. According to legend she disputed with 50 scholars, refusing to give up her faith and marry Emperor Maxentius. Her emblem is a wheel, on which her persecutors tried to kill her (the wheel broke and she was beheaded). Feast day Nov 25.

Catherine of Aragon 1485–1536. First queen of Henry VIII of England, 1509–33, and mother of Mary I; Henry divorced her without papal approval, thus beginning the English ◊Reformation.

Catherine had married Henry's elder brother Prince Arthur 1501 and on his death 1502 was betrothed to Henry, marrying him on his accession 1509. Of their six children, only Mary lived. Wanting a male heir, Henry sought an annulment 1526 when Catherine was too old to bear children. When the pope demanded that the case be referred to him, Henry married Anne Boleyn, afterwards receiving the desired decree of nullity from Cranmer, the archbishop of Canterbury, in 1533. The Reformation in England followed, and Catherine went into retirement until her death.

Catherine of Braganza 1638–1705. Queen of Charles II of England 1662–85. The daughter of John IV of Portugal (1604–1656), she brought the Portuguese possessions of Bombay and Tangier as her dowry and introduced tea drinking and citrus fruits to England. Her childlessness and practice of her Catholic faith were unpopular, but Charles resisted pressure for divorce. She returned to Lisbon 1692, after his death.

Catherine of Genoa, St 1447–1510. Italian mystic, who devoted herself to the sick and to meditation. Her feast day is Sept 15.

Catherine of Siena 1347–1380. Italian mystic, born in Siena, Italy. She persuaded Pope Gregory XI to return to Rome from Avignon 1376. In 1375 she is said to have received on her body the stigmata, the impression of Jesus' wounds. Her *Dialogue* is a classic mystical work. Feast day Apr 29.

Catherine of Valois 1401–1437. Queen of Henry V of England, whom she married 1420; the mother of Henry VI. After the death of Henry V, she secretly married Owen Tudor (c. 1400–1461) about 1425, and their son Edmund Tudor became the father of Henry VII.

Catherwood Frederick 1799–1854. British topographical artist and archaeological illustrator who accompanied John Lloyd ◊Stephens in his exploration of central America 1839–40 and the Yucatan 1841–42. His engravings, published 1844, were the first accurate representation of Mayan civilization in the West.

catheter fine tube inserted into the body to introduce or remove fluids. The original catheter was the urinary one, passed by way of the urethra (the duct that leads urine away from the bladder). In today's practice, catheters can be inserted into blood vessels, either in the limbs or trunk, to provide blood samples and local pressure measurements, and to deliver drugs and/or nutrients directly into the bloodstream.

cathode the negative electrode toward which positive particles (cations) move within a device such

***Catherine de' Medici** During her regency Catherine de' Medici exacerbated the rivalry between the Protestant Huguenots and the Catholic Guises in order to ensure her position as ruler.*

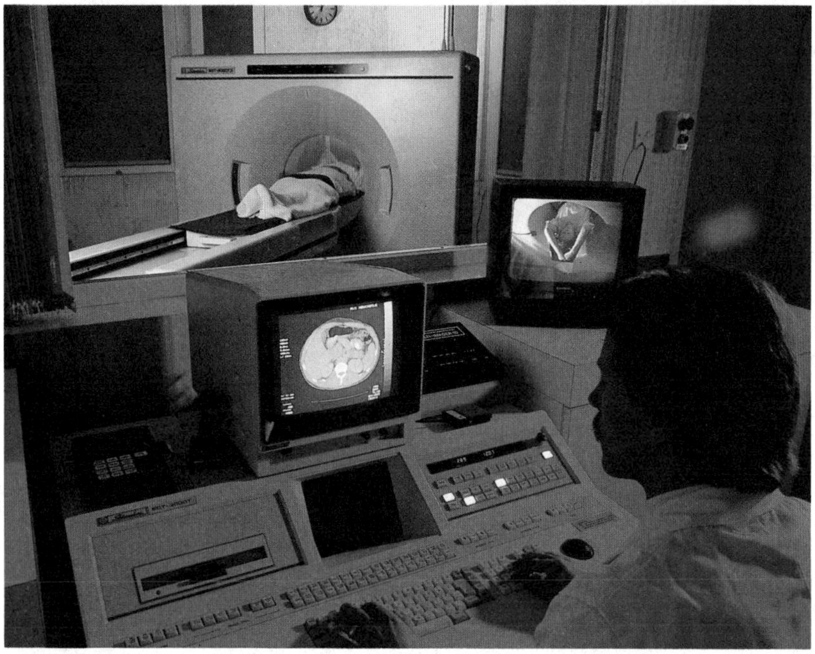

CAT scan *CAT scan in progress, showing the scanner and patient in the background and the radiographer working at the scanner's computer terminal.*

as a cell in a battery, an electrolytic cell, or a diode.

cathode-ray tube a type of vacuum tube in which a beam of electrons is produced and focused onto a fluorescent screen. It is an essential component of television receivers, computer visual display units, and oscilloscopes.

Catholic church the whole body of the Christian church, though usually referring to the Roman Catholic Church.

Catiline (Lucius Sergius Catilina) c. 108–62 BC. Roman politician. Twice failing to be elected to the consulship in 64/63 BC, he planned a military coup, but ◊Cicero exposed his conspiracy. He died at the head of the insurgents.

cation ◊ion carrying a positive charge. During electrolysis, cations in the electrolyte move to the cathode (negative electrode).

catkin in flowering plants (◊angiosperms), a pendulous inflorescence, bearing numerous small, usually unisexual flowers. The tiny flowers are stalkless and the petals and sepals are usually absent or much reduced in size. Many types of trees bear catkins, including willows, poplars, and birches. Most plants with catkins are wind-pollinated, so the male catkins produce large quantities of pollen. Some ◊gymnosperms also have catkinlike structures that produce pollen, for example, the swamp cypress *Taxodium*.

Catlin George 1796–1872. US explorer and artist. Born in Wilkes-Barre, Pennsylvania, Catlin briefly practiced law before embarking on a career as a portrait painter. His deep interest in the Indians of the West then led him to travel widely, recording pictorially the lifeways and customs of the tribes of the Rocky Mountains and Great Plains 1832–40.

His *Letters and Notes on the Manners, Customs, and Conditions of the North American Indians* 1841 is among the most important of his published works. After Catlin's death, his collection of paintings and sketches was donated to the Smithsonian Institution.

Cato Marcus Porcius 234–149 BC. Roman politician. Appointed censor (senior magistrate) in 184, he excluded from the Senate those who did not meet his high standards. He was so impressed by the power of ◊Carthage, on a visit in 157, that he ended every speech by saying "Carthage must be destroyed." His farming manual is the earliest surviving work in Latin prose.

Cato Street Conspiracy in British history, unsuccessful plot hatched in Cato Street, London, to murder the Tory foreign secretary Castlereagh and all his ministers on Feb 20, 1820. The leader, the Radical Arthur Thistlewood (1770–1820), who intended to set up a provisional government, was hanged with four others.

CAT scan or ***CT scan*** (acronym for *c*omputerized *a*xial *t*omography) in medicine, a sophisticated method of X-ray imaging. Quick and noninvasive, CAT scanning is an aid to diagnosis, helping to pinpoint problem areas without the need for exploratory surgery.

The CAT scanner passes a narrow fan of X rays through successive slices of the suspect body part. These slices are picked up by crystal detectors in a scintillator and converted electronically into cross-sectional images displayed on a viewing screen. Gradually, using views taken from various angles, a three-dimensional picture of the organ or tissue can be built up and suspect irregularities analyzed.

CAT scanner or ***CT scanner*** medical device used to obtain detailed X-ray pictures of the inside of a patient's body. The body is examined in slices, and an overall picture is built up from the results by computer. This technique is called ◊tomography.

cat's cradle worldwide ancient children's game still played on the fingers with looped string.

Catskills low mountain range, mainly in SE New York, W of the Hudson River. The highest point is Slide mountain 4,204 ft/1,281 m. Long a vacation and resort center for New York City residents, the Catskills offer hiking, skiing, hunting and fishing, and the picturesque trails and scenes of woods, waterfalls, lakes, and streams that have attracted such painters as Frederic Church and Thomas Cole. It is the setting for *Rip Van Winkle*, one of Washington Irving's most popular tales.

cattle large, ruminant, even-toed, hoofed mammals of the genus *Bos*, family Bovidae, including wild species such as yak, gaur, gayal, banteng, and kouprey, as well as domesticated breeds. Asiatic water buffalos *Bubalus*, African buffalos *Syncerus*, and American bison *Bison* are not considered true cattle. Cattle were first domesticated in the Near East during the Neolithic, about 8,000 BC. They were brought north into Europe and south into Africa by migrating Neolithic farmers.

Fermentation in the four-chambered stomach allows cattle to make good use of the grass that is normally the main part of the diet. There are two main types of domesticated cattle: the European breeds, variants of *Bos taurus* descended from the ◊aurochs, and the various breeds of zebu *Bos indicus*, the humped cattle of India, which are useful in the tropics for their ability to withstand the heat and diseases to which European breeds succumb. Cattle are bred to achieve maximum yields of meat (beef cattle) or milk (dairy cattle). The old established beef breeds are mostly British in origin. The Hereford, for example, is the premier English breed, ideally suited to rich lowland pastures but it will also thrive on poorer land such as that found in the US Midwest and the Argentine pampas. Of the Scottish beef breeds, the Aberdeen Angus, a black and hornless variety, produces high-quality meat through intensive feeding methods. Other breeds include the Devon, a hardy early-maturing type, and the Beef Shorthorn, now less important than formerly, but still valued for an ability to produce good calves when crossed with less promising cattle. In recent years, more interest has been shown in other European breeds, their tendency to have less fat being more suited to modern tastes. Examples include the Charolais and the Limousin from central France, and the Simmental, originally from Switzerland. In the US, four varieties of zebus, called Brahmans, have been introduced. They interbreed with *B. taurus* varieties and produce valuable hybrids that resist heat, ticks, and insects. For dairying purposes, a breed raised in many countries is variously known as the Fresian, Holstein, or Black and White. It can give enormous milk yields, up to 3,450 gal/13,000 l in a single lactation, and it will produce calves ideally suited for intensive beef production. Other dairying types include the Jersey and Guernsey, whose milk has a high butterfat content, and the Ayrshire, a smaller breed capable of being outdoors year-round.

Catullus Gaius Valerius c. 84–54 BC. Roman lyric poet, born in Verona of a well-to-do family. He moved in the literary and political society of Rome and wrote lyrics describing his unhappy love affair with Clodia, probably the wife of the consul Metellus, calling her Lesbia. His longer poems include two wedding songs. Many of his poems are short verses to his friends.

Caucasoid referring to one of the three major varieties (see ◊race) of humans, *Homo sapiens sapiens*, including the indigenous peoples of Europe, the Near East, North Africa, India, and Australia. Caucasoids exhibit the widest range of variation in physical traits, including straight to curly hair; fair to dark skin; blue, hazel, and brown eyes; blond, red, brown, and black hair; medium to heavy beard and body hair; small to high-bridged noses; medium to thin lips. The term was coined by the German anthropologist J F Blumenbach (1752–1840), who erroneously theorized that they originated in the Caucasus region. See also ◊Mongoloid, ◊Negroid.

Caucasus series of mountain ranges between the Caspian and Black Seas, USSR; 750 mi/1,200 km long. The highest is Elbruz, 18,480 ft/5,633 m.

Cauchy Augustin Louis 1789–1857. French mathematician, celebrated for his rigorous methods of analysis. His prolific output included work on complex functions, determinants, and probability, and on the convergence of infinite series. In calculus, he refined the concepts of the limit and the definite integral.

In 1843 he published a defense of academic freedom of thought that was instrumental in the abolition of the oath of allegiance soon after the fall of Louis Philippe in 1848.

caucus a closed meeting of regular political party

members (the "smoke-filled" room); for example, to choose a candidate for office. The term was originally used in the 18th century in Boston, Massachusetts.

cauda tail, or taillike appendage; part of the *cauda equina*, a bundle of nerves at the bottom of the spinal cord in vertebrates.

cauliflower variety of ◊cabbage *Brassica oleracea*, distinguished by its large, flattened head of fleshy, aborted flowers. It is similar to broccoli but less hardy.

causality in philosophy, a consideration of the connection between cause and effect, usually referred to as the "causal relationship." If an event is assumed to have a cause, two important questions arise: what is the relationship between cause and effect, and must it follow that every event is caused? The Scottish philosopher David Hume considered these questions to be, in principle, unanswerable.

caustic soda former name for sodium hydroxide, NaOH.

cauterization in medicine, the use of special instruments to burn or fuse small areas of body tissue to destroy dead cells, prevent the spread of infection, or seal tiny blood vessels to minimize blood loss during surgery.

Cauvery or *Kaveri* river of S India, rising in the W Ghats and flowing 475 mi/765 km SE to meet the Bay of Bengal in a wide delta. A major source of hydroelectric power since 1902 when India's first hydropower plant was built on the river.

Cavaco Silva Anibal 1939– . Portuguese politician, finance minister 1980–81, and prime minister and Social Democratic Party (PSD) leader from 1985. Under his leadership Portugal joined the European Community 1985 and the Western European Union 1988.

Cavaco Silva was born in Loule, studied economics in Britain and the US, and was a university teacher and research director in the Bank of Portugal. In 1978, with the return of constitutional government, he entered politics. His first government fell in 1987, but an election later that year gave him Portugal's first absolute majority since democracy was restored.

Cavafy Constantinos. Adopted name of Konstantínos Pétrou 1863–1933. Greek poet. An Alexandrian, he shed light on Greek history, recreating the Classical period with zest. He published only one book of poetry and remained almost unknown until translations of his works appeared in 1952.

cavalier horseman of noble birth, but mainly used to describe a male supporter of Charles I in the English Civil War, typically with courtly dress and long hair (as distinct from a Roundhead); also a supporter of Charles II after the Restoration.

Cavalier poets poets of Charles I's court, including Thomas Carew, Robert Herrick, Richard Lovelace, and John Suckling. They wrote witty, lighthearted love lyrics.

Cavalli (Pietro) Francesco 1602–1676. Italian composer, organist at St Mark's, Venice, and the first to make opera a popular entertainment with such works as *Xerxes* 1654, later performed in honor of Louis XIV's wedding in Paris. 27 of his operas survive.

cave a roofed-over cavity in the Earth's crust usually produced by the action of underground water or by waves on a seacoast. Caves of the former type commonly occur in areas underlain by limestone, such as Kentucky and many Balkan regions, but not in chalk country where the rocks are soluble in water. A pothole is a vertical hole in rock caused by water descending a crack and is thus open to the sky. Cave animals often show loss of pigmentation or sight, and under isolation, specialized species may develop. The scientific study of caves is called speleology.

During the ◊Ice Age, humans began living in caves leaving many layers of debris that archeologists have unearthed and dated in the Old World and the New. They also left cave art, paintings of extinct animals often with hunters on their trail. See also ◊Altamira and ◊ancient art.

Celebrated caves include the Mammoth Cave in Kentucky, 4 mi/6.4 km long and 125 ft/38 m high; the Caverns of Adelsberg (Postumia) near Trieste, Italy which extend for many miles; Carlsbad Cave, New Mexico, the largest in the US; the Cheddar caves, England; Fingal's Cave, Scotland, renowned for its range of basalt columns; and Peak Cavern, England.

caveat emptor (Latin "let the buyer beware") dictum that professes the buyer is responsible for checking the quality of nonwarrantied goods purchased.

cavefish cave-dwelling fish, which may belong to one of several quite unrelated groups, independently adapted to life in underground waters. They have in common a tendency to blindness and atrophy of the eye, enhanced touch-sensitive organs in the skin, and loss of pigment.

The Kentucky blind-fish *Amblyopsis spelea*, which lives underground in limestone caves, has eyes which are vestigial and beneath the skin, and a colorless body. The Mexican cave characin is a blind, colorless form of *Astyanax fasciatus* found in surface rivers of Mexico.

Cavendish Henry 1731–1810. British physicist. He discovered hydrogen (which he called "inflammable air") 1766, and determined the compositions of water and of nitric acid.

The ◊Cavendish experiment was a device of his to discover the mass and density of the Earth.

Cavendish experiment measurement of the gravitational attraction between lead and gold spheres, which enabled Henry ◊Cavendish to calculate a mean value for the mass and density of Earth, using Newton's Law of Universal Gravitation.

caviar the salted roe (eggs) of sturgeon, salmon and other fishes. Caviar is prepared by beating and straining the egg sacs until the eggs are free from fats, then adding salt. The USSR and Iran are the main exporters of the most prized variety of caviar, derived from Caspian Sea sturgeon. Iceland produces various high-quality, lower-priced caviars.

cavitation the formation of partial vacuums in fluids at high velocities, produced by propellers or other machine parts in hydraulic engines, in accordance with the ◊Bernoulli effect. When these vacuums collapse, pitting, vibration, and noise can occur in the metal parts in contact with the fluids.

Cavite port city of the Philippine Republic; 8 mi/13 km S of Manila; population (1980) 88,000. It is the capital of Cavite province, Luzon. It was in Japanese hands Dec 1941–Feb 1945. After the Philippines achieved independence in 1946, the US Seventh Fleet continued to use the naval base.

cavity in dentistry, decay of tooth enamel by the acids produced by mouth bacteria. Continuing decay undermines the inner tooth and attacks the nerve, causing toothache. Measures can be taken to save teeth by cleaning out the decay (drilling) and filling the tooth with a plastic substance such as silver amalgam or covering the cavity with a inlay or crown.

Cavour Camillo Benso di, Count 1810–1861. Italian nationalist politician. Editor of *Il* ◊*Risorgimento* from 1847. As prime minister of Piedmont 1852–59 and 1860–61, he enlisted the support of Britain and France for the concept of a united Italy achieved in 1861; after expelling the Austrians 1859, he assisted Garibaldi in liberating Southern Italy 1860.

Cavour was born in Turin, served in the army in early life and entered politics in 1847. From 1848 he sat in the Piedmontese parliament and held cabinet posts 1850–52. As prime minister, he sought to secure French and British sympathy for the cause of Italian unity by sending Piedmontese troops to fight in the Crimean War. In 1858 he had a secret meeting with Napoleon III at Plombières, where they planned the war of 1859 against Austria, which resulted in the union of Lombardy with Piedmont. Then the central Italian states joined the kingdom of Italy, although Savoy and Nice were to be ceded to France. With Cavour's approval Garibaldi overthrew the Neapolitan monarchy, but Cavour occupied part of the Papal States which, with Naples and Sicily were annexed to Italy, to prevent Garibaldi from marching on Rome.

cavy a type of short-tailed South American rodent, family Caviidae, of which the guinea-pig *Cavia porcellus* is an example. Wild cavies are greyish or brownish with rather coarse hair. They live in small groups in burrows, and have been kept for food since ancient times.

Cawnpore former spelling of ◊Kanpur, Indian city.

Caxton William c. 1422–1491. First English printer. He learned the art of printing in Cologne, Germany 1471 and set up a press in Belgium, where he produced the first book printed in English, his own version of a French romance, *Recuyell of the Historyes of Troye* 1474. Returning to England in 1476 he established himself in London, where he produced the first book printed in England, *Dictes or Sayengis of the Philosophres* 1477.

Born in Kent, Caxton was apprenticed to a London cloth dealer 1438, and set up his own business in Bruges 1441–70; he became governor of the English merchants there, negotiating on their behalf with the dukes of Burgundy. In 1471 he went to Cologne, where he learned the art of printing, and then set up his own press in Bruges in partnership with Colard Mansion, a calligrapher. The books from Caxton's press in Westminster included editions of the poets Chaucer, Gower, and John Lydgate (c. 1370–1449). He translated many texts from French and Latin and revised some English ones, such as Malory's *Morte d'Arthur*. Altogether he printed about 100 books.

A typeface is named for him.

Cayenne capital and chief port of French Guiana, on Cayenne island at the mouth of the river Cayenne; population (1982) 38,135.

It was founded in 1634, and used as a penal settlement from 1854 to 1946.

cayenne pepper condiment derived from the dried fruits of various species of ◊capsicum (especially *Capsicum frutescens*), a troical American genus of plants of the family Solanaceae. It is wholly distinct in its origin from black or white pepper, which is derived from an East Indian plant (*Piper nigrum*).

Cayley Arthur 1821–1895. British mathematician, who developed matrix algebra, used by ◊Heisenberg in his elucidation of quantum mechanics.

Cayley George 1773–1857. British aviation pioneer, inventor of the first piloted glider in 1853, and the caterpillar tractor.

Cavour *As prime minister of Piedmont, Cavour was largely responsible for achieving the unification of Italy in 1861.*

Cayman Islands

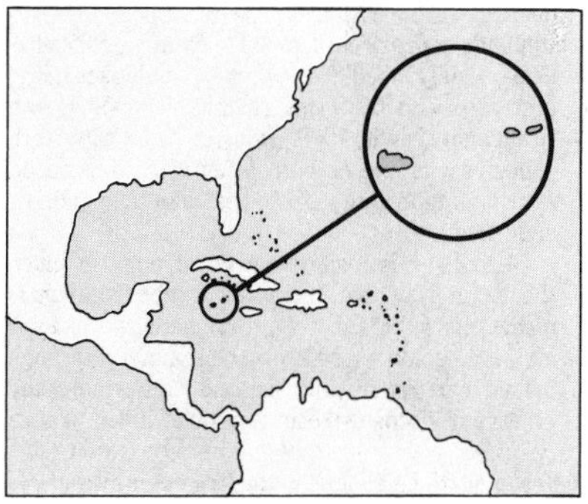

cayman or ***caiman*** large reptile, resembling the ◊crocodile.

Cayman Islands British island group in the West Indies
area 100 sq mi/260 sq km
features comprises three low-lying islands: Grand Cayman, Cayman Brac, and Little Cayman
exports seawhip coral, a source of ◊prostaglandins; shrimps; honey; jewelry
population (1988) 22,000
language English
government governor, executive council, and legislative assembly
history settled by military deserters in the 17th century, the islands became a pirate lair in the 18th century. Administered with Jamaica until 1962, when the Caymans became a separate colony, they are now a tourist resort, international financial center, and tax haven.

CB abbreviation for ◊citizens' band (radio).

cc abbreviation for cubic centimeter and for carbon copy/copies.

CD abbreviation for Corps Diplomatique (French "Diplomatic Corps"); compact disc; certificate of deposit.

CD-ROM in computing, a storage device, consisting of a metal disk with a plastic coating, on which information is etched in the form of microscopic pits. A CD-ROM typically holds about 550 ◊megabytes of data. CD-ROMs cannot have information written on to them by the computer, but must be manufactured from a master.

They are used for distributing large quantities of text, such as dictionaries, encyclopedias, and technical manuals. The technology is similar to that of the audio compact disk.

CE abbreviation for Common Era (see ◊calendar); Church of England (often C of E).

Ceauşescu Nicolae 1918–1989. Romanian politician, leader of the Romanian Communist Party (RCP), in power 1965–89. He pursued a policy line independent of and critical of the USSR. He appointed family members, including his wife Elena Ceauşescu, to senior state and party posts, and governed in an increasingly repressive manner, zealously implementing schemes that impoverished the nation. The Ceauşescus were overthrown in a bloody revolutionary coup Dec 1989 and executed.

Ceauşescu joined the underground RCP in 1933 and was imprisoned for antifascist activities 1936–38 and 1940–44. After World War II he was elected to the Grand National Assembly and was soon given ministerial posts. He was inducted into the party secretariat and Politburo in 1954–55. In 1965 Ceauşescu became leader of the RCP and from 1967 chair of the state council. He was elected president in 1974. As revolutionary changes rocked E Europe 1989, protests in Romania escalated until the Ceauşescu regime was toppled. Following his execution, the full extent of his repressive rule and personal extravagance became public.

***Ceauşescu** Former Romanian communist leader Nicolae Ceauşescu. A neo-Stalinist, he held sway over the country from 1965 until his popular overthrow and execution in Dec 1989.*

Cebu chief city and port of the island of Cebu in the Philippines; population (1980) 490,000; area of the island 1,964 sq mi/5,086 sq km and population (1980) 1,234,000.

The oldest city of the Philippines, founded as San Miguel in 1565, it became the capital of the Spanish Philippines.

Cecil Robert, 1st Earl of Salisbury 1563–1612. Secretary of state to Elizabeth I of England, succeeding his father, Lord Burghley; he was afterwards chief minister to James I, who created him Earl of Salisbury 1605.

Cecilia, St Christian patron saint of music, martyred in Rome in the 2nd or 3rd century, who is said to have sung hymns while undergoing torture. Feast day Nov 22.

cedar any of an Old World genus *Cedrus* of coniferous trees of the pine family Pinaceae. The cedar of Lebanon *Cedrus libani* grows to great heights and age in the mountains of Syria and Asia Minor. Of the historic forests on Mount Lebanon itself, only a few stands of trees remain.

The name cedar is also applied to species of several genera of other coniferous trees in several families—for example, some ◊junipers, ◊cypresses, and ◊redwoods.

Cedar Falls city in NE Iowa on the Cedar river, W of Waterloo. Industries include farm and other heavy equipment, rotary pumps, and tools; population (1990) 34,298.

Cedar Rapids city in E Iowa; population (1990) 108,751. It produces communications equipment, construction machinery, and processed foods. Coe College is here. Cedar Rapids was settled 1837.

cedar

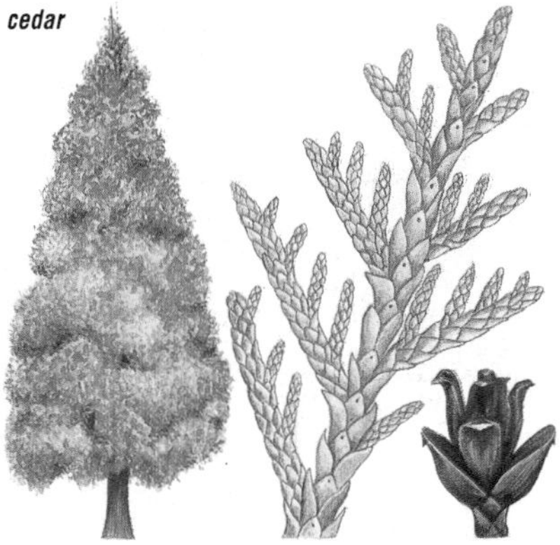

Cela Camilo José 1916– . Spanish novelist. Among his novels, characterized by their violence and brutal realism, are *La familia de Pascual Duarte/The Family of Pascal Duarte* 1942, and *La colmena/The Hive* 1951. He was awarded the Nobel Prize for Literature 1989.

celandine two plants belonging to different families, and resembling each other only in their bright yellow flowers. The greater celandine *Chelidonium majus* belongs to the poppy family (Papaveraceae) and is a common introduced European weed on wooded slopes in the US. The lesser celandine (*Ranunculus ficaria* is a European member of the buttercup family.

Celebes English name for ◊Sulawesi, an island of Indonesia.

celeriac variety of garden celery *Apium graveolens* var. *rapaceum* of the parsley family (Umbelliferae), with an edible, turniplike root and small, bitter stems.

celery Old World plant *Apium graveolens* of the carrot family Umbelliferae. It grows wild in ditches and salt marshes and has a coarse texture and acrid taste. Cultivated varieties of celery are grown under cover to make them less bitter.

celesta a keyboard glockenspiel producing sounds of disembodied purity. It was invented by Auguste Mustel 1886 and first used to effect by Tchaikovsky in *The Nutcracker* ballet music.

celestial mechanics the branch of astronomy that deals with the calculation of the orbits of celestial bodies, their gravitational attractions (such as those that produce Earth's tides), and also the orbits of artificial satellites and space probes. It is based on the laws of motion and gravity laid down by ◊Newton.

Celestial Police group of astronomers in Germany 1800–15 who set out to discover a supposed missing planet thought to be orbiting the Sun between Mars and Jupiter, a region now known to be occupied by types of ◊asteroid. Although they did not discover the first asteroid (found 1801), they discovered the second, Pallas (1802), third, Juno (1804), and fourth, Vesta (1807).

The first asteroid was actually discovered by the Italian Giuseppe Piazzi at the Palermo Observatory, Sicily, Jan 1, 1801.

celestial sphere imaginary sphere surrounding the Earth on which the celestial bodies seem to lie. The positions of bodies such as stars, planets, and galaxies are specified by their coordinates on the celestial sphere. The equivalents of latitude and longitude on the celestial sphere are called ◊declination and ◊right ascension (which is measured in hours from 0 to 24). The celestial poles lie directly above the Earth's poles, and the celestial equator lies over the Earth's equator. The celestial sphere appears to rotate once around the Earth each day, actually a result of the rotation of the Earth on its axis.

celestine or ***celestite*** mineral consisting of strontium sulfate, $SrS0_4$, occurring as white or light blue crystals. It is the principal source of strontium.

Celestine is found in small quantities in Germany, Italy, and the US.

celiac disease deficiency disease, usually in young children, due to disorder of the absorptive surface of the small intestine. It is mainly associated with an intolerance to gluten (a constituent of wheat) and characterized by diarrhea and malnutrition.

celibacy a way of life involving voluntary abstinence from sexual intercourse. In some religions, such as Christianity and Buddhism, celibacy is a requirement for certain religious roles, such as the priesthood or a monastic life. Other religions, including Judaism, strongly discourage celibacy.

Céline Louis Ferdinand. Adopted name of Louis Destouches 1884–1961. French novelist, whose writings (the first of which was *Voyage au bout de la nuit/Journey to the End of the Night* 1932) aroused controversy over their cynicism and misanthropy.

cell in biology, a discrete, membrane-bound portion

celestial sphere

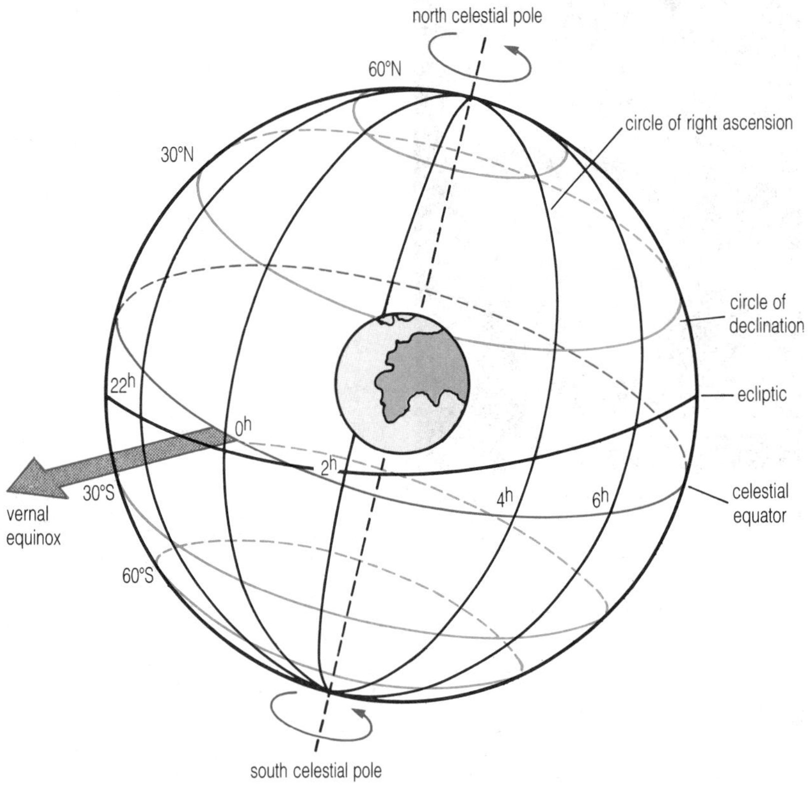
north celestial pole
60°N
circle of right ascension
30°N
circle of declination
ecliptic
22h
0h
2h
4h
6h
celestial equator
30°S
vernal equinox
60°S
south celestial pole

of living matter, the smallest unit capable of an independent existence. All living organisms consist of one or more cells, with the exception of ◊viruses. Bacteria, protozoa and many other microorganisms consist of single cells, whereas a human is made up of billions of cells. Essential features of a cell are the membrane, which encloses it and restricts the flow of substances in and out; the jellylike material within, often known as ◊protoplasm, the ◊ribosomes, which carry out protein synthesis, and the ◊DNA, which forms the hereditary material.

cell division the process by which a cell divides, either ◊meiosis, associated with sexual reproduction, or ◊mitosis, associated with growth, cell replacement or repair. Both forms involve the duplication of DNA and the splitting of the nucleus.

cell, electric in physics, an apparatus in which chemical energy is converted into electrical energy; the popular name is "battery," but this actually refers to a collection of cells in one unit.

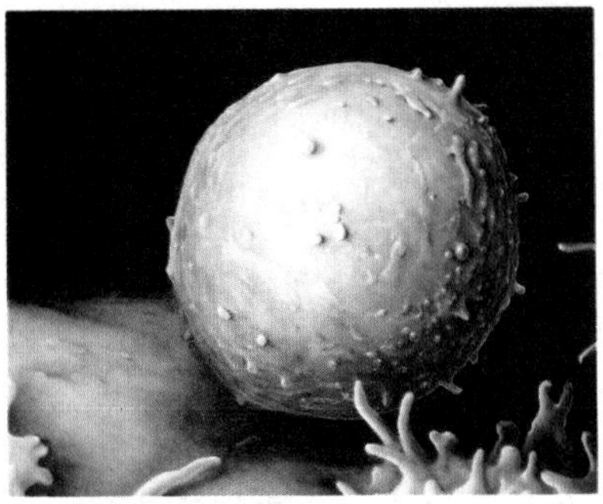

***cell** The drawing of the animal cell is based on an electron microscope view of a lymphocyte, a type of white blood cell, about 0.01 mm across. These cells help defend the body against viruses and some bacteria.*

A primary electric cell cannot be replenished, whereas in a secondary cell or storage battery, the action is reversible and the original condition can be restored by an electric current.

The first cell was made by Volta in 1800. Types of primary cells include the Daniell, Lalande, Leclanché, and so-called "dry" cells; secondary cells include Planté, Faure, and Edison. Newer types include the Mallory (mercury depolarizer), which has a very stable discharge curve and can be made in very small units (for example, for hearing aids), and the Venner battery, which can be made substantially solid for some purposes. See also battery.

Cellini Benvenuto 1500–1571. Italian sculptor and goldsmith working in the Mannerist style; author of an arrogant autobiography (begun 1558). Among his works are a graceful bronze *Perseus* 1545–54 (Loggia dei Lanzi, Florence) and a gold salt cellar made for Francis I of France 1540–43 (Kunsthistorisches Museum, Vienna), topped by nude reclining figures.

Cellini was born in Florence and apprenticed to a goldsmith. In 1519 he went to Rome, later worked for the papal mint, and was once imprisoned on a charge of having embezzled pontifical jewels. He worked for a time in France at the court of Francis I, but finally returned to Florence in 1545.

cell membrane or ***plasma membrane*** thin layer of protein and fat surrounding cells that controls substances passing between the cytoplasm and the intercellular space. Cell membrane is "semipermeable," allowing some substances to pass through and some not.

Generally, small molecules such as water, glucose, and amino acids can penetrate the membrane, while large molecules such as starch cannot. Membranes also play a part in active transport, hormonal response, and cell metabolism.

cello abbreviation for violoncello, a member of the ◊violin family and the lowest member of a string quartet.

cellophane transparent film made from wood ◊cellulose, widely used for wrapping and packaging, first produced by Swiss chemist Jacques Edwin Brandenberger in 1908. Rolls of cellophane with adhesives on one or both faces were introduced as Scotch tape in the US and as cello-tape in other countries.

Cellophane is made from wood pulp, in much the same way that the artificial fiber ◊rayon is made: the pulp is dissolved in chemicals to form a viscose solution, which is then pumped through a long narrow slit into an acid bath where the emergent viscose stream turns into a film of pure cellulose.

cell sap dilute fluid found in the large central vacuole of many plant cells. It is made up of water, amino acids, glucose, and salts. The sap has many functions, including storage of useful materials, and provides mechanical support for nonwoody plants.

cellular phone mobile radio telephone, one of a network connected to the telephone system by a computer-controlled communication system. Service areas are divided into small "cells," about 3 mi/5 km across, each with a separate low-power transmitter.

The cellular system allows the use of the same set of frequencies with the minimum risk of interference. Nevertheless, in crowded city areas, cells can become overloaded. This has led to a move away from analog transmissions to digital methods that allow more calls to be made within a limited frequency range.

cellulite fatty compound alleged by some dietitians to be produced in the body by liver disorder and to cause lumpy deposits on the hips and thighs. Medical opinion generally denies its existence, attributing the lumpy appearance to a type of subcutaneous fat deposit.

cellulitis inflammation of body tissue, especially subcutaneous tissue, accompanied by swelling, redness, and pain.

celluloid transparent or translucent, highly flammable, plastic material (a thermoplastic made from nitrocellulose and camphor) once used for toilet articles, novelties, and photographic film. It has been replaced by the nonflammable substance cellulose acetate.

cellulose a complex ◊carbohydrate composed of long chains of glucose units. It is the principal constituent of the cell wall of higher plants, and a vital ingredient in the diet of many ◊herbivores. Molecules of cellulose are organized into long, unbranched microfibrils that give support to the cell wall. No mammal produces the enzyme (cellulase) necessary for digesting cellulose; mammals such as rabbits and cows are only able to digest grass because the bacteria present in their gut manufacture the appropriate enzyme.

Cellulose is the most abundant substance found in the plant kingdom. It has numerous uses in industry: in rope-making; as a source of textiles (linen, cotton, viscose, and acetate) and plastics (cellophane and celluloid); in the manufacture of nondrip paint; and in foods such as whipped dessert toppings.

Celsius temperature scale in which one division or degree is taken as one hundredth part of the interval between the freezing point (0°C) and the boiling point (100°C) of water at standard atmospheric pressure.

The degree centigrade (°C) was officially renamed Celsius in 1948 to avoid confusion with the angular measure known as the centigrade (one hundredth of a grade). The Celsius scale is named after the Swedish astronomer Anders Celsius (1701–44), who devised it in 1742, but in reverse (freezing point was 100°; boiling point 0°).

Celt (Greek *Keltoi*) a member of a people of alpine Europe and Iberia whose first known territory was in central Europe about 1200 BC, in the basin of the upper Danube, the Alps, and parts of France and S Germany. In the 6th century they

cell

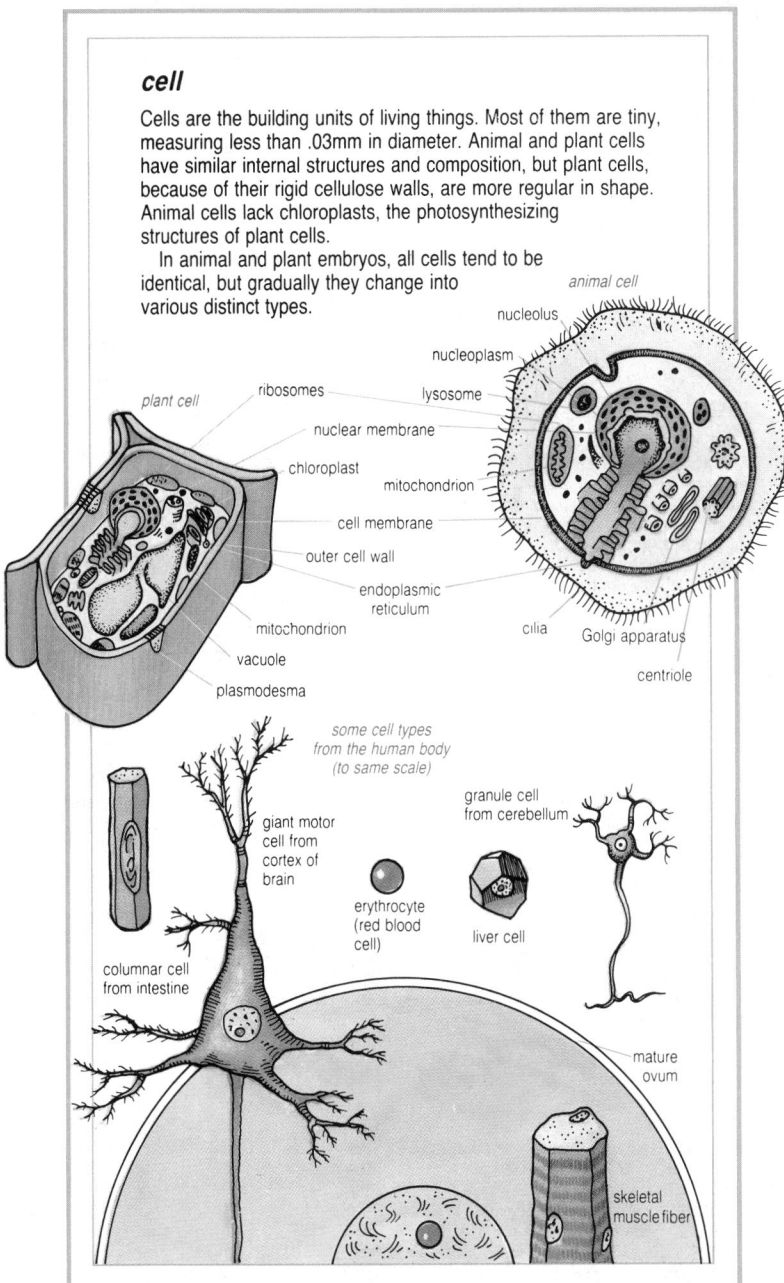

Cells are the building units of living things. Most of them are tiny, measuring less than .03mm in diameter. Animal and plant cells have similar internal structures and composition, but plant cells, because of their rigid cellulose walls, are more regular in shape. Animal cells lack chloroplasts, the photosynthesizing structures of plant cells.

In animal and plant embryos, all cells tend to be identical, but gradually they change into various distinct types.

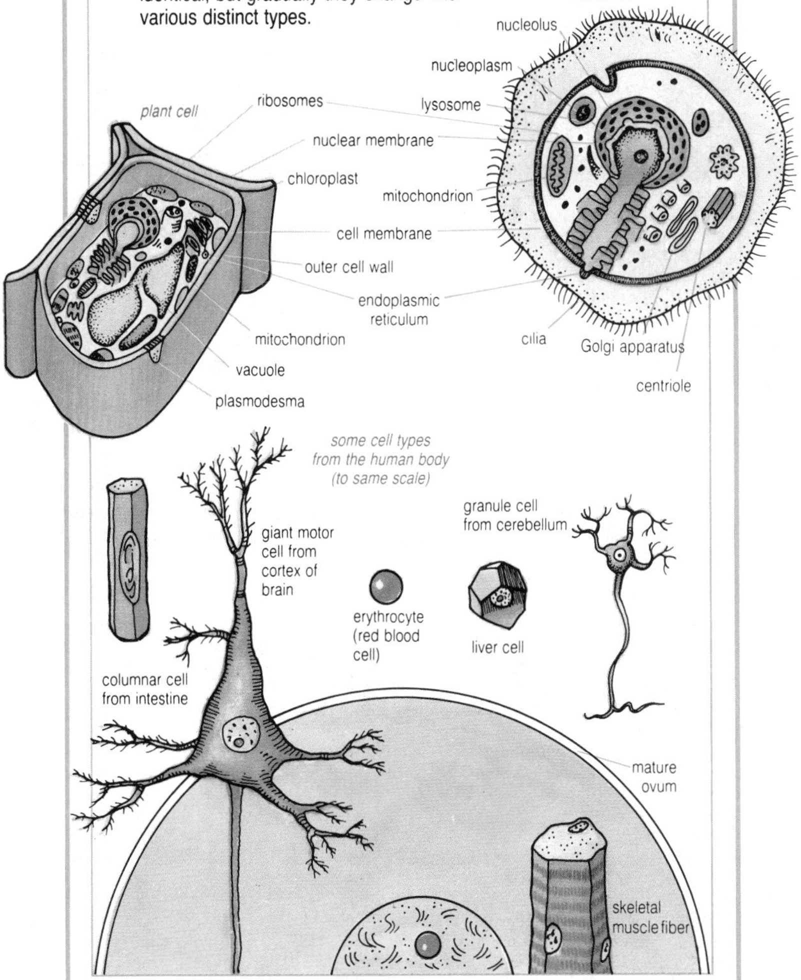
animal cell
nucleolus
nucleoplasm
plant cell
ribosomes
lysosome
nuclear membrane
chloroplast
mitochondrion
cell membrane
outer cell wall
endoplasmic reticulum
mitochondrion
vacuole
plasmodesma
cilia
Golgi apparatus
centriole
some cell types from the human body (to same scale)
giant motor cell from cortex of brain
granule cell from cerebellum
erythrocyte (red blood cell)
liver cell
columnar cell from intestine
mature ovum
skeletal muscle fiber

spread into Spain and Portugal. Over the next 300 years, they also spread into the British Isles (see ◊Britain, ancient), N Italy (sacking Rome 390 BC), Greece, the Balkans, and parts of Asia Minor, although they never established a united empire. In the 1st century BC they were defeated by the Roman Empire and by Germanic tribes and confined largely to Britain, Ireland, and N France.

Between the Bronze and Iron Ages, in the 9th–5th centuries BC, they developed a transitional culture (named the Hallstatt culture after its archeological site SW of Salzburg). They farmed, raised cattle, and were pioneers of ironworking, reaching their peak in the period from the 5th century to the Roman conquest (the La Tène culture). Celtic languages survive in Ireland, Wales, Scotland, the Isle of Man, and Brittany.

Celtic art a style of art that originated in about 500 BC, probably on the Rhine, and spread westward to Gaul and the British Isles and southward to Italy and Turkey. Celtic manuscript illumination and sculpture from Ireland and Anglo-Saxon Britain of the 6th–8th centuries has intricate spiral and geometric ornament, as in *The Book of Kells* (Trinity College, Dublin) and the *Lindisfarne Gospels* (British Museum, London).

Celtic languages branch of the Indo-European family, divided into two groups: the Brythonic or P-Celtic (Welsh, Cornish, Breton, and Gaulish) and the Goidelic or Q-Celtic (Irish, Scottish, and Manx Gaelic). Celtic languages once stretched from the Black Sea to Britain, but have been in decline for centuries, limited to the so-called "Celtic Fringe" of western Europe.

As their names suggest, a major distinction between the two groups is that where Brythonic has *p* (as in Old Welsh *map*, "son") Goidelic has a *q* sound (as in Gaelic *mac*, "son"). Gaulish is the long-extinct language of ancient Gaul; Cornish died out as a natural language in the late 18th century and Manx in 1974. All surviving Celtic languages have experienced official neglect in recent centuries and have suffered from emigration; currently, however, governments are more inclined than in the past to encourage their use.

Celtic Sea name commonly used by workers in the oil industry for the sea area bounded by Wales, Ireland, and SW England, to avoid nationalist significance. It is separated from the Irish Sea by St George's Channel.

cembalo an accompanying keyboard instrument in Classical music.

cement any bonding agent used to unite particles in a single mass or to cause one surface to adhere to another. Portland cement is a powder obtained from burning together a mixture of lime (or chalk) and clay, and when mixed with water and sand or gravel, turns into mortar or concrete. In geology, a chemically precipitated material such as carbonate that occupies the interstices of clastic rocks is called cement.

The term cement covers a variety of materials, such as fluxes and pastes, and also bituminous products obtained from tar. In 1824 Joseph Aspdin, an English bricklayer, created and patented the first Portland cement, so named because its color in the hardened state resembled that of Portland stone, a limestone used in building.

cenotaph (Greek "empty tomb") monument to commemorate a person or persons not actually buried at the site, as in the Whitehall Cenotaph, London, designed by Edwin Lutyens to commemorate the dead of both World Wars.

Cenozoic or Caenozoic era of geologic time that began 65 million years ago and is still in process. It is divided into the Tertiary and Quaternary periods. The Cenozoic marks the emergence of mammals as a dominant group, including humans, and the formation of the mountain chains of the Himalayas and the Alps.

censor in ancient Rome, either of two senior magistrates, high officials elected every five years to hold office for 18 months. Their responsibilities included public morality, a census of the citizens, and a revision of the Senatorial list.

censor in Freudian psychology, the psychic function that prevents unacceptable unconscious impulses from reaching the conscious mind. This function leads to ◊repression of intolerable ideas, memories or impulses.

censorship the suppression by authority of material considered immoral, heretical, subversive, libelous, damaging to state security, or otherwise offensive. It is generally more stringent under totalitarian or strongly religious regimes and in wartime.

Despite First Amendment protection of free speech, attempts at censorship are made by government agencies or groups; the question is often tested in the courts, especially with respect to sexually explicit material. Recently, efforts have been made to suppress certain pieces of music and works of art, on such grounds as racial harassment and social depravity.

censorship, film control of the content and presentation of films. Film censorship dates back almost as far as the cinema. In the US, censorship was not established until 1922 with the founding of the self-regulating Motion Picture Producers and Distributors of America (see ◊Hays Office).

census official count of the population of a country, originally for military call-up and taxation, later for assessment of social trends as other information regarding age, sex, and occupation of each individual was included. They may become unnecessary as computerized databanks are developed.

The first US census was taken in 1790.

centaur in Greek mythology, a creature half man and half horse. Centaurs were supposed to live in Thessaly, and be wild and lawless; the mentor of Heracles, Chiron, was an exception.

The earliest representations of centaurs (c. 1800–1000 BC) were excavated near Famagusta, Cyprus, in 1962, and are two-headed. Some female representations also exist.

Centaurus large bright constellation of the southern

hemisphere, represented as a centaur. It contains the closest star to the Sun, Proxima Centauri. Omega Centauri, the largest and brightest globular cluster of stars in the sky, is 16,000 light-years away. Centaurus A, a peculiar galaxy 15 million light-years away, is a strong source of radio waves and X-rays.

CentCom abbreviation for US ◊Central Command, a military strike force.

center of gravity the point in or near an object from which its total weight appears to originate and can be assumed to act. A symmetrical homogeneous object such as a sphere or cube has its center of gravity at its physical center; a hollow shape (such as a cup) may have its center of gravity in space inside the hollow.

For an object to be in stable equilibrium, a perpendicular line down through its center of gravity must run within the boundaries of its base; if tilted until this line falls outside the base, the object becomes unstable and topples over.

Center Party (German *Zentrumspartei*) German political party established 1871 to protect Catholic interests. Although alienated by Chancellor Bismarck's ◊*Kulturkampf* 1873–78, in the following years the *Zentrum* became an essential component in the government of imperial Germany. The party continued to play a part in the politics of Weimar Germany before being barred by Hitler in the summer of 1933.

centigrade common name for the ◊Celsius temperature scale.

centipede jointed-legged animal of the group Chilopoda, members of which have a distinct head and a single pair of long antennae. Their bodies are composed of segments (which may number nearly 200), each of similar form and bearing a single pair of legs. Most are small, but the tropical *Scolopendra gigantea* may reach 1 ft/30 cm in length. Millipedes, class Diplopoda, have fewer segments (up to 100), but have two pairs of legs on each.

Nocturnal, frequently blind, and all carnivorous, they eat animal food usually when rotten, live in moist, dark places, and protect themselves by a poisonous secretion. They have a pair of poison claws, and strong jaws with poison fangs. The bite of some tropical species is dangerous to humans. Several species live in Britain, *Lithobius forficatus* being the most common.

CENTO abbreviation for ◊Central Treaty Organization.

Central African Republic
(*République Centrafricaine*)

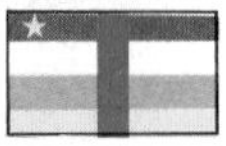

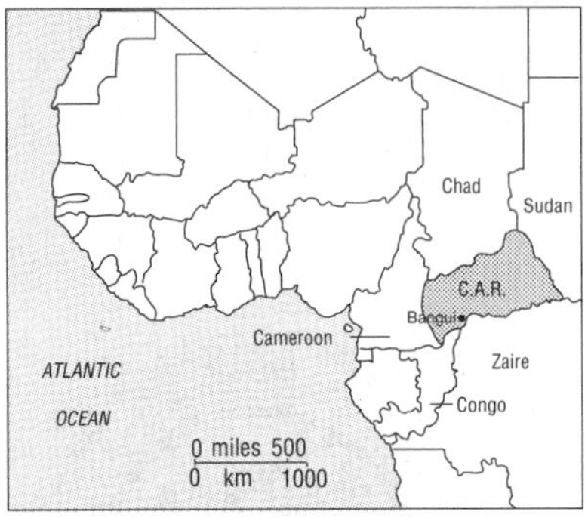
Chad
Sudan
C.A.R.
Bangui
Cameroon
Zaire
Congo
ATLANTIC
OCEAN
0 miles 500
0 km 1000

area 240,260 sq mi/622,436 sq km
capital Bangui
cities Berberati, Bovar, Bossangoa
physical landlocked flat plateau, with rivers flowing N and S, and hills in NE and SW. Dry in N, rainforest in SW
features Kotto and Mbali river falls; the Oubangui River rises 20 ft/6 m at Bangui during the wet season (June–Nov)
head of state and government André Kolingba from 1981
political system one-party military republic
political parties Central African Democratic Assembly (RDC), nationalist
exports diamonds, uranium, coffee, cotton, timber, tobacco
currency CFA franc
population (1990 est) 2,879,000 (more than 80 ethnic groups); growth rate 2.3% p.a.
life expectancy men 41, women 45
language Sangho (national), French (official); also Arabic, Hunsa, and Swahili
religion animist 35%; Roman Catholic 25%; Protestant 25%; Muslim 15%
literacy men 53%/women 29% (1985 est)
GDP $1 bn (1987); $374 per head
chronology
1960 Central African Republic achieved independence from France; David Dacko elected president.
1962 The republic made a one-party state.
1965 Dacko ousted in military coup led by Col Bokassa.
1966 Constitution rescinded and national assembly dissolved.
1972 Bokassa declared himself president for life.
1976 Bokassa made himself emperor of the Central African Empire.
1979 Bokassa deposed by Dacko following violent repressive measures by the self-styled emperor, who went into exile.
1981 Dacko deposed in a bloodless coup, led by General André Kolingba, and an all-military government established.
1983 Clandestine opposition movement formed.
1984 Amnesty for all political party leaders announced. President Mitterrand of France paid a state visit.
1985 New constitution promised, with some civilians in the government.
1986 Bokassa returned from France, expecting to return to power; he was imprisoned and his trial started. Gen Kolingba reelected.
1988 Bokassa found guilty and received death sentence, later commuted to life imprisonment.
1990 Public called for a return to multiparty politics.
1991 Further calls for political reform.

Central African Republic landlocked country in Central Africa, bordered NE and E by Sudan, S by Zaïre and the Congo, W by Cameroon, and NW by Chad.

government After a coup in Sept 1981, the constitution of Feb the same year was suspended, and all executive and legislative powers placed in the hands of a Military Committee for National Recovery (CMRN). Four years later CMRN was dissolved and a new 22-member council of ministers, composed of both military and civilian members, was established. The president is head of both state and government and presides over the council of ministers. All political activity has been banned since the coup, but the main opposition groups, although passive, still exist. They are the Patriotic Front Ubangi Workers" Party (FPO-PT), the Central African Movement for National Liberation (MCLN), and the Movement for the Liberation of the Central African People (MPLC). A new constitution was approved by referendum 1986, providing for a 52-member national assembly elected for a five-year term at the summons of the president. Despite this manifesto, however, the country remains under military rule.

history A French colony from the late 19th century, the territory of Ubangi-Shari became self-governing within French Equatorial Africa in 1958 and two years later achieved full independence. Barthélémy Boganda, who had founded the Movement for the Social Evolution of Black Africa (MESAN), had been a leading figure in the campaign for independence and became the country's first prime minister. A year before full independence he was killed in an airplane crash and was succeeded by his nephew, David Dacko, who became president in 1960 and in 1962 established a one-party state, with MESAN as the only political organization. Dacko was overthrown in a military coup in Dec 1965, and the commander-in-chief of the army, Col Jean-Bédel ◊Bokassa, assumed power.

Bokassa annulled the constitution and made himself president-for-life in 1972 and marshal of the Republic in 1974. An authoritarian regime was established, and in 1976 ex-president Dacko was recalled to be the president's personal adviser. At the end of that year the republic was restyled the Central African Empire (CAE), and in 1977 Bokassa was crowned emperor at a lavish ceremony his country could ill afford. His rule became increasingly dictatorial and idiosyncratic, leading to revolts by students and, in April 1979, by school children who objected to the compulsory wearing of school uniforms made by a company owned by the Bokassa family. Many of the children were imprisoned, and it is estimated that at least 100 were killed, with the emperor allegedly personally involved.

In Sept 1979, while Bokassa was in Libya, Dacko ousted him in a bloodless coup, backed by France. The country became a republic again, with Dacko as president. He initially retained a number of Bokassa's former ministers but, following student unrest, they were dropped, and in Feb 1981 a new constitution was adopted, with an elected national assembly. Dacko was elected president for a six-year term in March, but opposition to him grew and in Sept 1981 he was deposed in another bloodless coup, led by the armed forces' chief of staff, General André Kolingba. The constitution and all political organizations were suspended, and a military government installed. Undercover opposition to the Kolingba regime continued, with some French support, but relations with France were improved by an unofficial visit by President Mitterrand in Oct 1982.

By 1984 there was evidence of a gradual return to constitutional government. The leaders of the banned political parties were granted an amnesty, and at the end of the year the French president paid a state visit. In Jan 1985 proposals for a new constitution were announced and in Sept civilians were included into Kolingba's administration. In 1986 Bokassa returned from exile in France, expecting to be returned to power. Instead, he was tried for his part in the killing of the school children in 1979. Condemned to death, the sentence was commuted to life imprisonment 1988. In Oct 1990 there were widespread demonstrations calling for the restoration of multiparty politics.

Central America the part of the Americas that links Mexico with the Isthmus of Panama, comprising Belize, Costa Rica, El Salvador, Guatemala, Honduras, Nicaragua, and Panama. It is also an isthmus, crossed by mountains that form part of the Cordilleras, rising to a maximum height of 13,845 ft/4,220 m, with numerous active volcanoes. Central America is about 200,000 sq mi/523,000 sq km in area and has a population (1980) estimated at 22,700,000, mostly Indians or mestizos (of mixed white-Indian ancestry) but also whites, blacks, and Asians. Tropical agricultural products and other basic commodities and raw materials are exported.

Much of Central America was included in the ◊Maya civilization. The region was discovered by Christopher Columbus 1502. Spanish settlers married indigenous women, and the area remained out of the mainstream of Spanish Empire history. When the Spanish Empire collapsed in the early 1800s, the Central American Federation was formed, with a constitution based

central nervous system

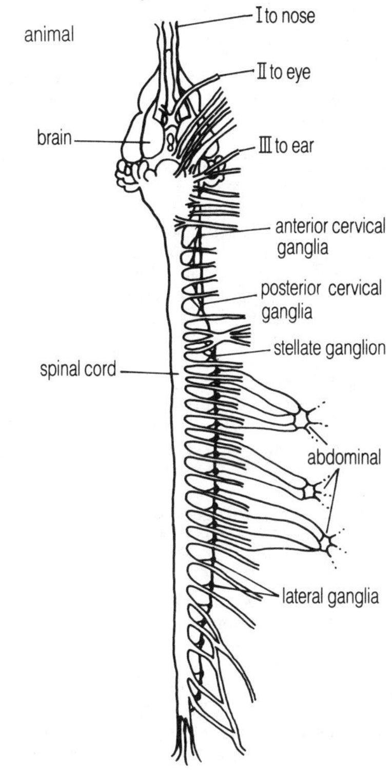
animal
I to nose
II to eye
brain
III to ear
anterior cervical ganglia
posterior cervical ganglia
stellate ganglion
spinal cord
abdominal
lateral ganglia

central processing unit

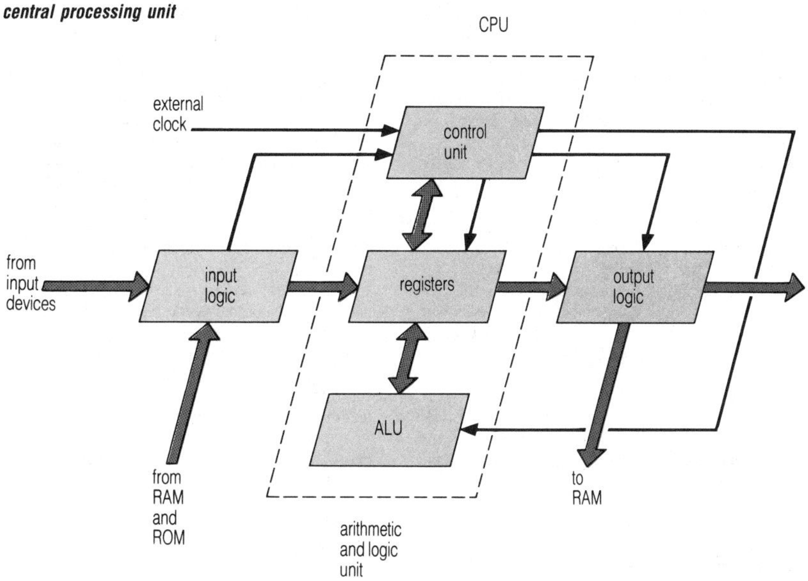
CPU
external clock
control unit
from input devices
input logic
registers
output logic
ALU
from RAM and ROM
arithmetic and logic unit
to RAM

on that of the US. The federation disintegrated 1840, however. Completion of the Panama Canal 1914 enhanced the region's position as a strategic international crossroads. Demand for cash crops (bananas, coffee, cotton), especially from the US, created a strong landowning industrialist class (representing the United Fruit Co) controlling a serflike peasantry by military means. There has been US military intervention in the area since President T Roosevelt's Big Stick policy–for example, in Nicaragua, where the dynasty of General Anastasio Somoza was founded. President ◊Carter reversed support for such regimes, but in the 1980s the ◊Reagan and ◊Bush administrations again favored military and financial aid to selected political groups, including the ◊Contras in Nicaragua and the ruling regime in El Salvador. Continuing US interest was underscored by its invasion of Panama Dec 1989.

Central American Common Market ODECA (*Organización de Estados Centro-americanos*) economic alliance established in 1960 by El Salvador, Guatemala, Honduras (seceded 1970), and Nicaragua; Costa Rica joined in 1962.

Central Command a military strike force consisting of units from the US army, navy, and air force, which operates in the Middle East and North Africa. Its headquarters are at McDill Air Force Base, Florida. It was established 1979, following the Iranian hostage crisis and the Soviet invasion of Afghanistan, and was known as the Rapid Deployment Force until 1983.

Plagued by organizational problems, interservice rivalries, equipment shortages, and lack of access to bases in the Middle East, it was reorganized by President Reagan in 1983 as the US Central Command.

central dogma in genetics and evolution, the fundamental belief that ◊genes can affect the nature of the physical body, but that changes in the body (for example, through use or accident) cannot be translated into changes in the genes.

central heating a system of heating from a central source, typically of a house, larger building or group of buildings, as opposed to heating each room individually. Steam heat and hot-water heat are the most common systems in use. Water is heated in a furnace burning oil, gas or solid fuel, and, as steam or hot water, is then pumped through radiators in each room. The level of temperature can be selected by adjusting a thermostat on the burner or in a room.

Central heating has its origins in the ◊hypocaust heating system introduced by the Romans nearly 2,000 years ago. Central heating systems are usually switched on and off by a time switch. Another kind of central heating system uses hot air, which is pumped through ducts (called risers) to grills in the rooms. Underfloor heating (called radiant heat) is used in some houses, the heat coming from electric elements buried in the floor.

Central Intelligence Agency (CIA) US intelligence-gathering organization established 1947 under President Truman. It belongs to the executive branch of government and acts on the president's orders. Historically, it runs both covert (secret) and overt (open) operations in the name of national security and was intended to centralize espionage and counterespionage intelligence in the ◊Cold War. It has actively intervened overseas, generally to undermine left-wing regimes or to protect US financial interests; for example, in the Congo (now Zaïre) and Nicaragua. William Webster became director 1987. From 1980 all covert activity by the CIA has by law to be reported to Congress, preferably beforehand, and must be authorized by the president.

Developed from the wartime Office of Strategic Services (OSS) and set up by Congress, as part of the National Security Act, on the lines of the British Secret Service. It was involved in, for example, the restoration of the shah of Iran 1953, South Vietnam (during the Vietnam war), Chile (the coup against President Allende), and Cuba (the ◊Bay of Pigs). On the domestic front, it was illegally involved in the ◊Watergate political scandal and in the 1970s lost public confidence when US influence collapsed in Iran, Afghanistan, Nicaragua, Yemen, and elsewhere. Past directors include William Casey, Richard ◊Helms, and George ◊Bush. Domestic intelligence functions are performed by the ◊Federal Bureau of Investigation.

Central Mount Stuart flat-topped mountain 2,770 ft/844 m high, at approximately the central point of Australia.

central nervous system the part of the nervous system with a concentration of ◊nerve cells which coordinates various body functions. In ◊vertebrates, the central nervous system consists of a brain and a dorsal nerve cord (the spinal cord) within the spinal column. In worms, insects, and crustaceans, it consists of a paired ventral nerve cord with concentrations of nerve cells, known as ◊ganglia in each segment, and a small brain in the head.

Some simple invertebrates, such as sponges and jellyfishes, have no central nervous system but a simple network of nerve cells called a nerve net.

Central Powers originally the signatories of the ◊Triple Alliance 1882; Germany, Austria and Hungary. During the World War I, Italy remained neutral before joining the ◊Allies.

central processing unit (CPU) the key controlling component of a computer, the part that executes individual program instructions and controls the operation of other parts. It is also called a central processor or, in modern computers, a ◊microprocessor.

It comprises five main elements: the ◊ALU (arithmetic and logic unit), which contains the basic operations (its "instruction set") and applies them to data; a program counter to keep track of the program being executed; a number of ◊registers for storing intermediate results and data awaiting processing; (normally) an electronic clock, which emits regular pulses that coordinate the CPU's activities; and a control unit for organizing the processing.

Central Provinces and Berar former British province of India, now part of ◊Madhya Pradesh.

Central Treaty Organization (CENTO) military alliance that replaced the ◊Baghdad Pact 1959; it collapsed when the withdrawal of Iran, Pakistan, and Turkey 1979 left the UK as the only member.

Centre region of N central France; area 15,131 sq mi/39,200 sq km; population (1986) 2,324,000. It includes the *départements* of Cher, Eure-et-Loire, Indre, Indre-et-Loire, Loire-et-Cher, and Loiret. Its capital is Orléans.

centrifugal force useful concept in physics, based on an apparent (but not real) force. It may be regarded as a force that acts radially outward from a spinning or orbiting object, thus balancing the ◊centripetal force (which is real). For an object of mass m moving with a velocity v in a circle of radius r, the centrifugal force F equals mv^2/r (outward).

centrifuge apparatus that rotates containers at high speeds, creating centrifugal forces. One use is for separating mixtures of substances of different densities. A common example is the separation of the lighter plasma from the heavier blood corpuscles in certain blood tests.

The mixtures are placed in the containers and the rotation sets up centrifugal forces, causing them to separate according to their densities. The ultracentrifuge is a very high-speed centrifuge, used in biochemistry for separating ◊colloids and organic substances; it may operate at several million revolutions per minute. Large centrifuges are used for physiological research—for example, in astronaut training where bodily response to many times the normal gravitational force is tested.

centriole a structure found in the ◊cells of animals that plays a role in the processes of ◊meiosis and ◊mitosis (cell division).

centripetal force force that acts radially inward on an object moving in a curved path. For example, with a weight whirled in a circle at the end of a length of string, the centripetal force is the tension in the string. For an object of mass m moving with a velocity v in a circle of radius r, the centripetal force F equals mv^2/r (inward). The reaction to this force is the ◊centrifugal force.

centromere part of the ◊chromosome where there are no ◊genes. Under the microscope, it usually appears as a constriction in the strand of the chromosome, and is the point at which the spindle fibers are attached during ◊meiosis and ◊mitosis (cell division).

Cephalonia English form of ◊Kefallinia, largest of the Ionian islands, off the W coast of Greece.

cephalopod type of predatory marine mollusk with the mouth and head surrounded by tentacles. They are the most intelligent, the fastest-moving, and the largest of all animals without backbones, and there are remarkable luminescent forms which swim or drift at great depths. Cephalopods have the most highly developed nervous and sensory systems of all invertebrates, the eye in some paralleling closely that found in vertebrates. Examples include octopus, squid, and cuttlefish. Shells are rudimentary or absent in most cephalopods.

Typically they move by swimming with the mantle (fold of outer skin) aided by the arms, but can squirt water out of the siphon (funnel) to propel themselves backwards by jet propulsion. They grow very rapidly and may be mature in a year. The female common octopus lays 150,000 eggs after copulation, and stays to brood them for as long as six weeks. After they hatch the female dies, and, although reproductive habits of many cephalopods are not known, it is thought that dying after spawning may be typical.

cephalosporin any of a class of broad-spectrum antibiotics derived from a fungus (genus *Cephalosporium*). It is similar to penicillin and is used on penicillin-resistant infections.

The first cephalosporin was extracted from sewage-contaminated water, and other naturally occurring ones have been isolated from molds taken from soil samples. Synthetic cephalosporins can be designed to be effective against a particular ◊pathogen.

Cepheid variable yellow supergiant star that varies regularly in brightness every few days or weeks as a result of pulsations. The time that a Cepheid variable takes to pulsate is directly related to its average brightness; the longer the pulsation period, the brighter the star.

This relationship, the period luminosity law (discovered by ◊Leavitt), allows astronomers to use Cepheid variables as "standard candles" to measure distances in our Galaxy and to nearby galaxies. They are named after their prototype, Delta Cephei, whose light variations were observed 1784 by the English astronomer John Goodricke (1764–1786).

Cepheus constellation of the north polar region, representing King Cepheus of Greek mythology, husband of Cassiopeia and father of Andromeda. It contains the Garnet Star (Mu Cephei), a red supergiant of variable brightness that is one of the reddest stars known, and Delta Cephei, prototype of the ◊Cepheid variables.

Ceram or *Seram* Indonesian island, in the Moluccas; area 6,621 sq mi/17,142 sq km. The principal town is Ambon.

ceramic nonmetallic mineral (clay) used in plastic form to fashion objects that are then fired at high temperatures creating a hard, stonelike product. Ceramics are divided into heavy clay products (bricks, roof tiles, drainpipes, sanitary ware), refractories or high-temperature materials (linings for furnaces used to manufacture steel, fuel elements in nuclear reactors), and ◊pottery, which uses kaolinite, ball clay, china stone, and flint. Super-ceramics, such as silicon carbide, are lighter, stronger, and more heat-resistant than steel for use in motor and aircraft engines and have to be cast to shape since they are too hard to machine.

The earliest ceramics date back to the beginning of the Neolithic in the Near East, Asia, the Americas, Europe, and Africa.

Cerberus in Greek mythology, the three-headed dog guarding the entrance to ◊Hades, the underworld.

cereal grass grown for its edible starch seeds. The term refers primarily to grains–wheat, oats, rye, and barley, but may also refer to corn, millet, and rice. Cereals contain about 75% complex carbohydrates and 10% protein, plus fats and roughage. They store well. In 1984, world production exceeded 2 billion tons. If all the world's cereal crop were consumed as wholegrain products directly by humans, everyone could obtain adequate protein and complex carbohydrate; however, a large proportion of cereal production, especially in affluent nations, is used as animal feed to boost the production of meat, milk, butter, and eggs.

cerebellum part of the brain of ◊vertebrate animals which controls muscular movements, balance, and coordination. It is relatively small in lower animals such as newts and lizards, but large in birds since flight demands precise coordination. The human cerebellum is also well developed, because of the need for balance when walking or running, and for coordinated hand movements.

cerebral pertaining to the brain, especially the part known as the cerebral hemispheres, concerned with higher brain functions.

cerebral hemorrhage or ***apoplectic fit*** in medicine, a stroke in which a blood vessel bursts in the brain, caused by factors such as high blood pressure combined with hardening of the arteries (an ◊aneurysm), or chronic poisoning with lead or alcohol. It may cause death or damage parts of the brain, leading to paralysis or mental impairment. The effects are usually long-term and the condition may recur.

cerebral hemisphere one of the two halves of the ◊cerebrum.

cerebral palsy any abnormality of the brain caused by oxygen deprivation before birth, injury during birth, hemorrhage, meningitis, viral infection, or faulty development. It is characterized by muscle spasm, weakness, lack of coordination, and impaired movement. Intelligence is not always affected.

cerebrovascular accident (CVA) alternate name for ◊stroke.

cerebrum part of the vertebrate ◊brain, formed from the two paired cerebral hemispheres. In birds and mammals it is the largest part of the brain. It is covered with an infolded layer of gray matter, the cerebral cortex, which integrates brain functions. The cerebrum coordinates the senses, and is responsible for learning and other higher mental faculties.

Ceres the largest asteroid, 634 mi/1,020 km in diameter, and the first to be discovered (by Giuseppe Piazzi 1801). Ceres is a rock that orbits the Sun every 4.6 years at an average distance of 260 million mi/420 million km. Its mass is about one-sixtieth (0.017) of that of the Moon.

Ceres in Roman mythology, the goddess of agriculture; see ◊Demeter.

Cerf Bennett Alfred 1898–1971. US editor and publisher. In 1925 he and a partner purchased the rights to the Modern Library series, and on that base Cerf founded Random House 1927. As that company grew to be one of the world's major publishing houses, Cerf gained a reputation as a celebrity in his own right.

Born in New York, Cerf was educated at Columbia University and briefly worked as a reporter for the *New York Herald Tribune*. He published several collections of humor and appeared as a regular panelist on the popular television show "What's My Line?'

cerium gray, malleable and ductile, metallic element, symbol Ce, atomic number 58, atomic weight 140.12. It is the most abundant member of the ◊lanthanide series, and is used in alloys, electronic components, nuclear fuels, and lighter flints. It was discovered in 1804 by Jöns Berzelius and Wilhelm Hisinger (1766–1852).

It was named for the then recently discovered asteroid Ceres.

cermet bonded material containing ceramics and metal, widely used in jet engines and nuclear reactors. Cermets behave much like metals but have the great heat resistance of ceramics. Tungsten carbide, molybdenum boride, and aluminum oxide are among the ceramics used; iron, cobalt, nickel, and chromium are among the metals.

CERN nuclear research organization founded 1954 as a cooperative enterprise among European governments. It has laboratories at Meyrin, near Geneva, Switzerland. It was originally known as the *Conseil Européen pour la Recherche Nucléaire* but subsequently renamed *Organisation Européene pour la Recherche Nucléaire*, although still familiarly known as CERN. It houses the world's largest particle ◊accelerator the ◊Large Electron–Positron Collider (LEP) with which notable advances have been made in ◊particle physics.

In 1965 the original laboratory was doubled in size by extension across the border from Switzerland into France.

Cernăuţi Romanian form of ◊Chernovtsy.

Cervantes Saavedra, Miguel de 1547–1616. Spanish novelist, playwright, and poet, whose masterpiece, ◊*Don Quixote* (in full *El ingenioso hidalgo Don Quixote de la Mancha*) was published 1605. In 1613, his *Novelas Ejemplares/Exemplary Novels* appeared, followed by *Viaje del Parnaso/The Voyage to Parnassus* 1614. A spurious second part of *Don Quixote* prompted Cervantes to bring out his own second part in 1615, often considered superior to the first in construction and characterization.

Born at Alcalá de Henares, he entered the army in Italy, and was wounded in the battle of Lepanto 1571. While on his way back to Spain 1575, he was captured by Barbary pirates and taken to Algiers, where he became a slave until ransomed 1580. Returning to Spain, he wrote several plays, and in 1585 his pastoral romance *Galatea* was printed. He was employed in Seville 1587 provisioning the Armada. While working as a tax collector, he was imprisoned more than once for deficiencies in his accounts. He sank into poverty, and little is known of him until 1605 when he published *Don Quixote*. The novel was an immediate success and was soon translated into English and French.

cervical cancer ◊cancer of the cervix (the neck of the womb).

cervical cap see ◊contraceptive.

cervical smear removal of a small sample of tissue from the cervix (neck of the womb) to screen for changes implying a likelihood of cancer. The procedure is also known as the Pap test after its originator, George Papanicolau.

cervix (Latin "neck") abbreviation for *cervix uteri*: the neck of the womb.

César adopted name of César Baldaccini 1921– French sculptor who uses iron and scrap metal and, in the 1960s, crushed car bodies. His subjects are imaginary insects and animals.

cesium soft, silvery-white, ductile, metallic element, symbol Cs, atomic number 55, atomic weight 132.905. It is one of the ◊alkali metals, the most electropositive of all the elements. In air it ignites spontaneously, and it reacts vigor-

Cézanne Mountains in Provence *(c. 1886) National Gallery, London.*

ously with water. It is used in the manufacture of photoelectric cells.

The rate of vibration of cesium atoms is used as the standard of measuring time. Its radioactive isotope Cs-137 (half-life 30.17 years) is one of the most dangerous waste products of the nuclear industry, because it is a highly radioactive biological analog for potassium, produced as a fission product of nuclear explosions and in the reactors of nuclear power plants.

It was named in 1860 by Robert Bunsen, German chemist, from the blueness of its spectral line, for the Latin *caesius*, "blue-gray."

České Budějovice (German *Budweis*) town in Czechoslovakia, on the river Vltava; population (1984) 92,800. It is a commercial and industrial center for S Bohemia, producing beer, timber, and metal products.

Cetewayo (Cetshwayo) c. 1826–1884. King of Zululand, South Africa 1873–83, whose rule was threatened by British annexation of the Transvaal 1877. Although he defeated the British at Isandhlwana 1879, he was later that year defeated by them at Ulundi. Restored to his throne 1883, he was then expelled by his subjects.

Cetinje town in Montenegro, Yugoslavia, 12 mi/19 km SE of Kotor; population (1981) 20,213. Founded 1484 by Ivan the Black, it was capital of Montenegro until 1918. It has a palace built by Nicholas, the last king of Montenegro.

Cetus (Latin "whale") constellation straddling the celestial equator (see ◊celestial sphere), representing the whale. Its brightest star is Diphda (Beta Ceti), about 69 light-years from Earth. Cetus contains the long-period variable star ◊Mira, and ◊Tau Ceti, one of the nearest stars visible with the naked eye.

Ceuta Spanish seaport and military base in Morocco, Spanish N Africa; 17 mi/27 km S of Gibraltar and overlooking the Mediterranean approaches to the Straits of Gibraltar; area 7 sq mi/18 sq km; population (1986) 71,000. It trades in tobacco and gasoline products.

Cévennes a series of mountain ranges on the S, SE. and E borders of the Central Plateau of France. The highest peak is Mt Mézenc 5,755 ft/1,754 m.

Ceylon former name of ◊Sri Lanka.

Cézanne Paul 1839–1906. French Post-Impressionist painter, a leading figure in the development of modern art. He broke away from the Impressionists' spontaneous vision to develop a style that captured not only light and life, but the structure of natural forms in landscapes, still lifes, portraits, and his series of bathers.

He was born in Aix-en-Provence, where he studied, and was a friend of the novelist Emile Zola. In 1872 Cézanne met Pissarro and lived near him in Pontoise, outside Paris, but soon abandoned Impressionism. His series of paintings of Mont Sainte-Victoire in Provence from the 1880s into the 1900s show an increasing fragmentation of the painting's surface and a movement toward abstraction, with layers of color and square brushstrokes achieving monumental solidity. He was greatly revered by early abstract painters, notably Picasso and Braque.

cf. abbreviation for confer (Latin "compare").

CFC abbreviation for ◊chlorofluorocarbon.

Chablis town in the Yonne *département* of central France; it produces white burgundy wine of the same name.

Chabrier (Alexis) Emmanuel 1841–1894. French composer who wrote *España* 1883, an orchestral rhapsody, and the light opera *Le Roi malgré lui/King Against His Will* 1887. His orchestration inspired Debussy and Ravel.

Chabrol Claude 1930– . French film director. Originally a critic, he was one of the French "New Wave" of directors. His works of murder and suspense, which owe much to Hitchcock, include *Les Biches/The Girlfriends* 1968, *Le Boucher/The Butcher* 1970, and *Cop au Vin* 1984.

chacma a type of ◊baboon.

Chaco province of Argentina; area 38,458 sq mi/99,633 sq km; population (1980) 701,400. Its capital is Resistencia, in the southeast. The chief crop is cotton, and there is forestry.

It includes many lakes, swamps, and forests, producing timber and quebracho (a type of wood used in tanning). Until 1951 it was a territory, part of Gran Chaco, a great zone, mostly level, stretching into Paraguay and Bolivia. The N of Gran Chaco was the scene of the Bolivia-Paraguay border dispute 1932–35, settled by arbitration 1938.

Chaco War war between Bolivia and Paraguay 1932–35 over boundaries in the N Gran Chaco, settled by arbitration 1938.

Chad landlocked country in central N Africa, bounded N by Libya, E by Sudan, S by the Central African Republic, and W by Cameroon, Nigeria, and Niger.

government The 1982 provisional constitution provides for a president who appoints and leads a council of ministers that exercises executive and legislative power. In 1984 a new regrouping, the National Union for Independence and Revolution (UNIR), was undertaken in an attempt to consolidate the president's position, but a number of opposition groups exist.

history Called Kanem when settled by Arabs in the 7th–13th centuries, the area later became known as Bornu and in the 19th century was conquered by Sudan. From 1913 a province of French Equatorial Africa, Chad became an autonomous state within the French Community in 1958, with François Tombalbaye as prime minister.

Full independence was achieved in 1960, and Tombalbaye became president. He soon faced disagreements between the Arabs of the north, who saw Libya as an ally, and the black African Christians of the south, who felt more sympathy for Nigeria. In the north the Chadian National Liberation Front (Frolinat) revolted against the government. In 1975 Tombalbaye was killed in a coup led by former army Chief of Staff Félix Malloum, who became president of a supreme military council and appealed for national unity. Frolinat continued its opposition, however, supported by Libya, which held a strip of land in the north, believed to contain uranium.

By 1978 Frolinat, led by General Goukouni Oueddi, had expanded its territory but was halted with French aid. Malloum tried to reach a settlement by making former Frolinat leader, Hissène Habré, prime minister, but disagreements developed between them.

In 1979 fighting broke out again between government and Frolinat forces, and Malloum fled the country. Talks resulted in the formation of a provisional government (GUNT), with Goukouni holding the presidency with Libyan support. A

Chad
Republic of
(République du Tchad)

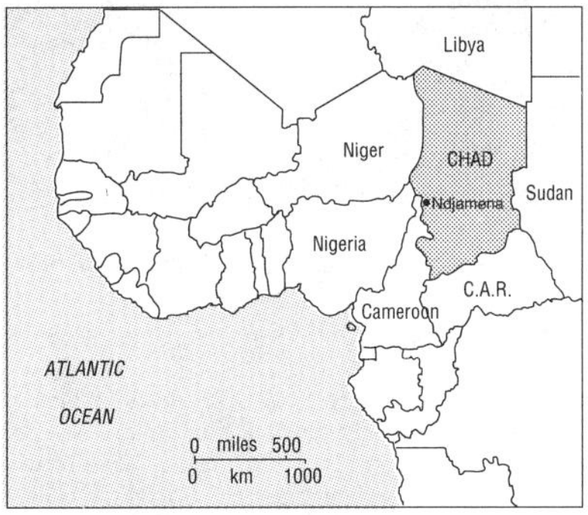
Libya
Niger
CHAD
Sudan
Ndjamena
Nigeria
C.A.R.
Cameroon
ATLANTIC
OCEAN
0 miles 500
0 km 1000

area 495,624 sq mi/1,284,000 sq km
capital N'djamena (formerly Fort Lamy)
cities Sarh, Moundou, Abéché
physical landlocked state with mountains and part of Sahara Desert in N; moist savanna in S; rivers in S flow N to Lake Chad
features nomadic tribes move N–S seasonally in search of water
head of state and government Idriss Deby from 1990
political system emergent democracy
political parties National Union for Independence (UNIR), nationalist
exports cotton, meat, livestock, hides, skins
currency CFA franc (498.25 = £July 1, 1991)
population (1990 est) 5,064,000; growth rate 2.3% p.a.
life expectancy men 42, women 45
language French, Arabic (both official), over 100 African dialects spoken
religion Muslim 44% (N); Christian 33%; animist 23% (S)
literacy men 40%/women 11% (1985 est)
GDP $980 million (1986); $186 per head
chronology
1960 Independence achieved from France, with François Tombalbaye as president.
1963 Violent opposition in the Muslim north, led by the Chadian National Liberation Front (Frolinat), backed by Libya.
1968 Revolt quelled with France's help.
1975 Tombalbaye killed in military coup led by Felix Malloum. Frolinat continued its resistance.
1978 Malloum tried to find a political solution by bringing the former Frolinat leader Hissène Habré into his government but they were unable to work together.
1979 Malloum forced to leave the country; an interim government was set up under Gen Goukouni. Habré continued his opposition with his Army of the North (FAN).
1981 Habré now in control of half the country, forcing Goukouni to flee to Cameroon and then Algeria, where, with Libya's support, he set up a "government in exile."
1983 Habré's regime recognized by the Organization for African Unity (OAU), but in north Goukouni's supporters, with Libya's help, fought on. Eventually a ceasefire was agreed, with a "red line" declared by France at latitude 16° N.
1984 Libya and France agreed to a withdrawal of forces.
1985 Fighting between Libyan-backed and French-backed forces intensified.
1987 Chad, France, and Libya agreed on ceasefire proposed by OAU.
1988 Full diplomatic relations with Libya restored.
1989 Libyan troop movements reported on border; elections retained Habré in power, amended constitution.
1990 President Habré ousted in coup led by Idriss Deby. New constitution adopted.

proposed merger with Libya was rejected, and Libya withdrew most of its forces.

The Organization for African Unity (OAU) set up a peacekeeping force but civil war broke out and by 1981 Hissène Habré's Armed Forces of the North (FAN) controlled half the country. Goukouni fled and set up a "government in exile." In 1983 a majority of OAU members agreed to recognize Habré's regime, but Goukouni, with Libyan support, fought on.

After Libyan bombing, Habré appealed to France for help. Three thousand troops were sent as instructors, with orders to retaliate if attacked. Following a Franco-African summit in 1983, a ceasefire was agreed, with latitude 16° N dividing the opposing forces. Libyan president Col Khaddhafi's proposal of a simultaneous withdrawal of French and Libyan troops was accepted. By Dec all French troops had left, but Libya's withdrawal was doubtful.

Habré dissolved the military arm of Frolinat and formed a new party, the National Union for Independence and Revolution (UNIR), but opposition to his regime grew. In 1987 Goukouni was reported to be under house arrest in Tripoli. Meanwhile Libya intensified its military operations in northern Chad, Habré's government retaliated, and France renewed (if reluctantly) its support. It was announced in March 1989 that France, Chad, and Libya had agreed to observe a ceasefire proposed by the Organization of African Unity (OAU). A meeting in July 1989 between Habré and Khaddhaffi reflected the improvement in relations between Chad and Libya. Habré was endorsed as president Dec 1989 for another seven-year term, under a revised constitution. The new constitution was introduced in July 1990, providing for a new national assembly of 123 elective seats to replace the appointed National Consultative Council. In Dec 1990 the government fell to rebel opposition forces, Hissène Habré was reported killed, and the rebel leader Idriss Deby became president.

Chad, Lake lake on the NE boundary of Nigeria. It once varied in extent between rainy and dry seasons from 20,000 sq mi/50,000 sq km to 7,000 sq mi/20,000 sq km, but a series of droughts 1979–89 reduced its area by 80%. The Lake Chad basin is being jointly developed for oil and natron by Cameroon, Chad, Niger, and Nigeria. The lake was first seen by European explorers 1823.

Chadli Benjedid 1929– . Algerian Socialist politician, president 1979–92. An army colonel, he supported Boumédienne in the overthrow of Ben Bella 1965, and succeeded Boumédienne 1979, pursuing more moderate policies. He prevailed in a power struggle Sept 1989 with Prime Minister Kasdi Merbah, replacing him with Mouloud Hamrouche. Chadli resigned in Jan 1992 as religious fundamentalists neared an election victory.

chador (Hindi "square of cloth") all-enveloping black garment for women worn by some Muslims and Hindus.

The origin of the chador dates to the 6th century BC under Cyrus the Great and the Achemenian empire in Persia. Together with the ◊purdah (Persian "veil") and the idea of female seclusion, it persisted under Alexander the Great and the Byzantine Empire, and was adopted by the Arab conquerors of the Byzantines. Its use was revived in Iran in the 1970s by Ayatollah Khomeini in response to the Koranic request for "modesty" in dress.

Chadwick James 1891–1974. British physicist. In 1932 he discovered the particle in the nucleus of an atom that became known as the neutron because it has no electric charge. He was awarded a Nobel Prize 1935.

chafer type of beetle, family Scarabeidae. The adults eat foliage or flowers, and the underground larvae feed on roots, especially of grasses and cereals, and can be very destructive. Examples include the ◊cockchafer and the rose chafer

CHAGALL

Chagall The Blue Circus *(1950) Tate Gallery, London.*

Cetonia aurata, about 0.8 in/2 cm long and bright green.

chaffinch bird *Fringilla coelebs* of the finch family, common throughout much of Europe and W Asia. About 6 in/15 cm long, the male is olive-brown above, with a bright chestnut breast, a bluish-gray cap, and two white bands on the upper part of the wing; the female is duller.

Chagall Marc 1887–1985. Russian-born French painter and designer; much of his highly colored, fantastic imagery was inspired by the village life of his boyhood. He also designed stained glass, mosaics (for Israel's Knesset in the 1960s), tapestries, and stage sets.

Chagall is an original figure, often seen as a precursor of Surrealism, as in *The Dream* (Metropolitan Museum of Art, New York). He lived mainly in France from 1922. His stained glass can be found in, notably, a chapel in Venice, the south of France, 1950s, and a synagogue near Jerusalem. He also produced illustrated books.

Chagas' disease disease common in Central and South America, caused by a trypanosome parasite transmitted by insects; it results in incurable damage to the heart, intestines, and brain. It is named after Brazilian doctor Carlos Chagas (1879–1934).

Chagos Archipelago island group in the Indian Ocean; area 23 sq mi/60 sq km. Formerly a dependency of ◊Mauritius, it now forms the ◊British Indian Ocean Territory. The chief island is Diego Garcia, now a US/UK strategic base.

Chaillu Paul Belloni du 1835–1903. French-born US explorer. In 1855 he began a four-year journey of exploration in West Africa. His *Explorations and Adventures in Equatorial Africa* 1861 describes his discovery of the gorilla in Gabon.

Chain Ernst Boris 1906–1979. German-born British biochemist who worked on the development of ◊penicillin. Chain fled to Britain from the Nazis 1933. After the discovery of penicillin by Alexander Fleming, Chain worked to isolate and purify it. For this work, he shared the 1945 Nobel Prize for Medicine with Fleming and Howard Florey. Chain also discovered penicillinase, an enzyme that destroys penicillin.

chain reaction in nuclear physics, a fission reaction that is maintained because neutrons released by the splitting of some atomic nuclei themselves go on to split others, releasing even more neutrons. Such a reaction can be controlled (as in a nuclear reactor) by using moderators to absorb excess neutrons. Uncontrolled, a chain reaction produces a nuclear explosion (as in a nuclear weapon).

chain reaction in chemistry, mechanism that produces very fast, ◊exothermic reactions, as in the formation of flames and explosions.

The reaction begins with the formation of a

chalk *Cliffs near Lulworth, Dorset, provide some of the finest coastal scenery in England.*

single reactive molecule. This combines with an inactive molecule to form two reactive molecules. These two produce four (or more) reactive molecules; very quickly, very many reactive molecules are produced, so the reaction rate accelerates dramatically. The reactive molecules contain an unpaired electron and are called ◊free radicals; they last only a short time because they are so reactive.

Chaka alternate spelling of ◊Shaka, Zulu chief.

Chalatenango a department on the N frontier of El Salvador; area 968 sq mi/2507 sq km; population (1981) 235,700; capital Chalatenango. It is largely controlled by FMLN guerrilla insurgents.

Chalcedon, Council of an ecumenical council of the early Christian church, convoked 451 by the Roman emperor Marcian, and held at Chalcedon (now Kadiköy, Turkey). The council, attended by over 500 bishops, resulted in the Definition of Chalcedon, an agreed doctrine for both the eastern and western churches.

The council was assembled to repudiate the ideas of Eutyches (378–454) on Jesus' divine nature subsuming the human; it also rejected the ◊Monophysite doctrine that Jesus had only one nature, and repudiated ◊Nestorianism. It reached a compromise definition of Jesus' nature which it was hoped would satisfy all factions: Jesus was one person in two natures, united "unconfusedly, unchangeably, indivisibly, inseparably."

chalcedony a form of quartz, SiO_2, in which the crystals are so fine-grained that they are impossible to distinguish with a microscope (cryptocrystalline). Agate, onyx, tiger's eye, and carnelian are ◊gem varieties of chalcedony.

chalcopyrite copper iron sulfide, $CuFeS_2$, the most common ore of copper. It is brassy yellow in color and may have an iridescent surface tarnish. It occurs in many different types of mineral vein, in rocks ranging from basalt to limestone.

Chaldaea an ancient region of Babylonia.

Chaliapin Fyodor Ivanovich 1873–1938. Russian bass singer, born in Kazan of peasant parentage. His greatest role was that of Boris Godunov in Mussorgsky's opera of the same name. Chaliapin left the USSR in 1921 to live and sing in the world's capitals.

chalk soft, fine-grained, whitish rock composed of calcium carbonate $CaCO_3$, extensively quarried for use in cement, lime, and mortar, and in the manufacture of cosmetics and toothpaste. Blackboard chalk in fact consists of ◊gypsum (calcium sulfate, $CaSO_4$).

Chalk was once thought to derive from the remains of microscopic animals or foraminifera. In 1953, however, it was seen under the electron microscope to be composed chiefly of coccoliths, unicellular lime-secreting algae, and hence primarily of plant origin. It is formed from deposits of deep-sea sediments called oozes.

Châlons-sur-Marne capital of the *département* of Marne, NE France; population (1982) 54,400. It is a market town and trades mainly in Champagne. Tradition has it that Attila was defeated in his attempt to invade France, at the Battle of Châlons (451), by the Roman general Aëtius and the Visigoth Theodoric.

Chalon-sur-Saône town in the *département* of Saône-et-Loire, France, on the river Saône and the Canal du Centre; population (1982) 58,000. It has mechanical and electrical engineering and chemical industries.

Chamberlain (Arthur) Neville 1869–1940. British Conservative politician, son of Joseph Chamberlain. He was prime minister 1937–40; his policy of appeasement toward the fascist dictators Mussolini and Hitler (with whom he concluded the ◊Munich Agreement 1938) failed to prevent the outbreak of World War II. He resigned 1940 following the defeat of the British forces in Norway.

In 1938 Chamberlain went to Munich, Germany, and negotiated with Hitler on the Czechoslovak question. He was ecstatically received on his return and claimed that the Munich Agreement brought "peace in our time." However, Germany advanced against British allies and within a year Britain was at war.

Chamberlain Joseph 1836–1914. British politician, reformist mayor of and member of Parliament for Birmingham; in 1886, resigned from the cabinet over Gladstone's policy of home rule for Ireland, and led the revolt of the Liberal-Unionists.

Chamberlain (Joseph) Austen 1863–1937. British Conservative politician, elder son of Joseph Chamberlain; as foreign secretary 1924–29 he negotiated the Pact of ◊Locarno, for which he won the Nobel Peace Prize 1925, and signed the ◊Kellogg–Briand pact to outlaw war 1928.

Chamberlain Owen 1920– . US physicist whose graduate studies were interrupted by wartime work on the Manhattan project at Los Alamos. After World War II, working with Italian physicist Emilio Segrè, he discovered the existence of the antiproton. Both men were awarded the Nobel Prize for Physics in 1959.

Chamberlain Wilt (Wilton Norman) 1936– . US basketball player, who set a record by averaging 50.4 points a game during the 1962 season, and was the only man to score 100 points in a game.

He played professionally for the Philadelphia Warriors, Philadelphia 76ers, Los Angeles Lakers, and briefly for the ◊Harlem Globetrotters. Playing against the New York Knickerbockers 1962 he became the only man to score 100 points in a National Basketball Association (NBA) game. He was the only center to lead the league in assists. He led the league in scoring 1960–66, was NBA Most Valuable Player 1960, 1966–68, and retired 1973 after a 13-year career.

CAREER HIGHLIGHTS

Total games: 1,045
Points: 31,419 (average 30.1 per game)
Records: most points in a game: 100 v New York Knickerbockers (1962)
Most points in a season: 4,029 (1962) (average 50.4 per game)
Most seasons as NBA top scorer: 7 (1960–66)

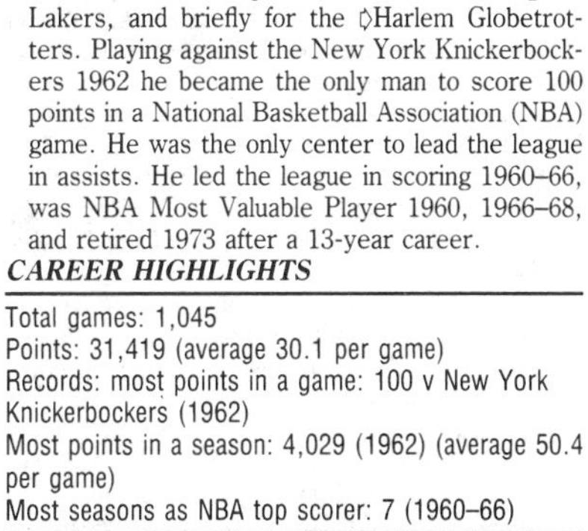

Chamberlain *British prime minister Neville Chamberlain is at front left, holding the Munich Agreement, an appeasement negotiated with Hitler in 1938.*

chameleon

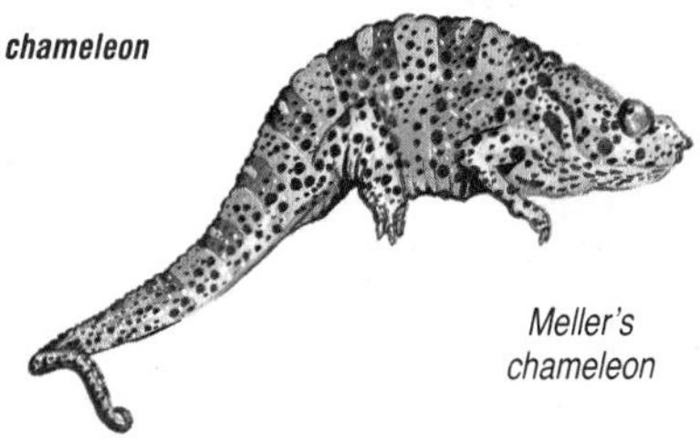

Meller's chameleon

chamber music music suitable for performance in a small room or chamber, rather than in the concert hall, and usually written for instrumental combinations, played with one instrument to a part, as in the string quartet.

It came into use as a reaction to earlier music for voices such as the madrigal, which allowed accompanying instruments little freedom for technical display. At first a purely instrumental style, it developed through Haydn and Beethoven into a private and often experimental medium making unusual demands on players and audiences alike. During the 20th century the limitations of recording and radio have encouraged many composers to scale down their orchestras to chamber proportions, as in Berg's *Chamber Concerto* and Stravinsky's *Agon*.

Chambers William 1726–1796. British architect and popularizer of Chinese influence (for example, the pagoda in Kew Gardens, London) and designer of Somerset House, London.

Chambéry former capital of Savoy, now capital of Savoie *département*, France; population (1982) 96,000. It is the seat of an archbishopric and has some industry; it is also a vacation and health resort. The town gives its name to a French vermouth.

chameleon type of lizard, some 80 or so species of family Chameleontidae. Some species have highly developed color-changing abilities, which are caused by changes in the intensity of light, of temperature, and of emotion, which affect the dispersal of pigment granules in the layers of cells beneath the outer skin.

The tail is long and highly prehensile, assisting the animal when climbing. Most chameleons live in trees and move very slowly. The tongue is very long, protrusile, and covered with a viscous secretion; it can be shot out with great rapidity to 8 in/20 cm for the capture of insects. The eyes are on "turrets," move independently, and can swivel forward to give stereoscopic vision for "shooting." Most live in Africa and Madagascar, but the common chameleon *Chameleo chameleon* is found in Mediterranean countries; two species live in SW Arabia, and one species in India and Sri Lanka.

Chamisso Adelbert von. Adopted name of Louis-Charles-Adélaide Chamisso de Boncourt 1781–1831. German writer of the story "Peter Schlemihl," about the man who sold his shadow. He was born into a French family who left France because of the French Revolution; subsequently he went as a botanist on Otto von Kotzebue's trip around the world 1815–18, recounted in *Reise um de Welt* 1821. His verse includes the cycle of lyrics *Frauenliebe und Frauenleben* 1831, set to music by Schumann.

chamois goatlike mammal *Rupicapra rupicapra* found in mountain ranges of S Europe and Asia Minor. It is brown, with dark patches running through the eyes, and can be up to 2.6 ft/80 cm high. Chamois are very sure footed, and live in herds of up to 30 members.

Both sexes have horns which may be 8 in/20 cm long. These are set close together and go up vertically, forming a hook at the top. Chamois skin is very soft, and excellent for cleaning glass, but the chamois is now comparatively rare and "chamois leather" is often made from the skin of sheep and goats.

Chamonix vacation resort at the foot of Mont Blanc,

in the French Alps; population (1982) 9,255. Site of the first Winter Olympics 1924.

Champagne sparkling white wine made from a blend of grapes, *pinot noir* and *pinot chardonnay*, which originated in the Marne River region around Rheims and Epernay, in Champagne, NE France. After a first fermentation, sugar and yeast are added to the still wine, which, when bottled, undergoes a second fermentation to produce the sparkle. Sugar syrup may be added to make the wine sweet (*sec*) or dry (*brut*).

Champagne has become a symbol of luxurious living and is used worldwide to celebrate special occasions. Demand has given rise to the production of similar wines outside France, in the US, for example, and Spain. Although these wines imitate Champagnes closely, they are referred to as *méthode champenoise*; only wines produced in the Champagne region of France can be termed "Champagne."

Champagne-Ardenne region of NE France; area 9,882 sq mi/25,600 sq km; population (1986) 1,353,000. Its capital is Reims, and it comprises the *départements* of Ardennes, Aube, Marne, and Haute-Marne. It has sheep and dairy farming and vineyards.

It forms the plains E of the Paris basin. Its chief towns are Epernay, Troyes, and Chaumont. The capital of the ancient province of Champagne was Troyes.

Champaign city in E central Illinois, directly W of Urbana. Industries include electronic equipment, academic clothing, and air-conditioning equipment. Together with Urbana, it is the site of the activities of the University of Illinois; population (1990) 63,502.

Champaigne Philippe de 1602–1674. French artist, the leading portrait painter of the court of Louis XIII. Of Flemish origin, he went to Paris 1621 and gained the patronage of Cardinal Richelieu. His style is elegant, cool, and restrained.

champignon fungus *Marasmius oreades*, family Agaricaceae, which is edible and a popular food in parts of Europe. It is known as the fairy-ring champignon because the fruiting bodies (mushrooms) occur in rings around the outer edge of the underground mycelium (threadlike tubes) of the fungus. Several other edible agarics are also called champignons.

Champion v Ames a US Supreme Court decision 1903 that gave judicial sanction to the use of federal police power. Champion, arrested for shipping lottery tickets across state lines, in violation of the Federal Lottery Act 1895, filed suit against the federal government, arguing that the act infringed on the police power of the states. The Court upheld the Lottery Act 5–4, ruling that the federal government had the right to use its regulatory and prohibitive powers in the interest of the public good.

Champlain lake in NE US (extending some 6 mi/10 km into Canada) on the New York-Vermont border; length 125 mi/201 km; area 430 sq mi/692 sq km. Named for explorer Samuel de ◊Champlain, who saw it in 1609, it is linked by canal to the St Lawrence and Hudson rivers. The largest city on its shores is Burlington, Vermont. Lake Champlain was the scene of a US naval victory over the British in 1814.

Champlain Samuel de 1567–1635. French pioneer, soldier, and explorer in Canada. Having served in the army of Henry IV and on an expedition to the West Indies, he began his exploration of Canada 1603. In a third expedition 1608 he founded and named Québec, and was appointed Lieutenant-Governor of French Canada 1612.

Champollion Jean François, le Jeune 1790–1832. French Egyptologist who in 1822 deciphered Egyptian hieroglyphics with the aid of the ◊Rosetta Stone.

chance the theory of ◊probability. As a science, it originated when the Chevalier de Méré consulted ◊Pascal about how to reduce his gambling losses. In correspondence with another mathematician, ◊Fermat, Pascal worked out the foundations of the theory of chance. This underlies the science of statistics.

chancel the part of a Christian church where the choir and clergy sit, formerly kept separate from the nave.

The term originated in the early Middle Ages, when chancels were raised above the level of the nave, from which they were separated by a rood screen, a pierced partition bearing the image of the Crucifixion. The chancel has usually been regarded as the preserve and responsibility of the clergy, while the upkeep and repair of the nave was left to the parishioners.

Chan Chan capital of the pre-Inca ◊Chimu kingdom in Peru.

chancroid an acute localized, sexually transmitted ulcer on or about the genitals caused by the bacterium *Hemophilus ducreyi*. The ulcer forms at the point of inoculation from a sexual partner and leads to painful enlargement and suppuration of lymph nodes in the groin area.

Chandernagore ("city of sandalwood") city, on the river Hooghly, India, in the state of West Bengal; population (1981) 102,000. Formerly a French settlement, it was ceded to India by treaty in 1952.

Chandigarh city of N India, in the foothills of the Himalayas; population (1981) 421,000. It is also a Union Territory; area 44 sq mi/114 sq km; population (1981) 450,000.

Planned by the architect Le Corbusier, it was inaugurated 1953 to replace Lahore (capital of British Punjab), which went to Pakistan under partition 1947. Since 1966, when it became a Union Territory, it has been the capital city of both Haryana and Punjab, until a new capital is built for the former.

Chandler Happy (Albert Benjamin) 1898–1991. US politician and sports administrator. Born in Corydon, Kentucky, Chandler studied law at the University of Kentucky and was admitted to the bar 1924. Entering politics, he served in the state legislature and was elected governor 1934, resigning from that office 1939 to fill a vacancy in the US Senate. In 1945 Chandler was appointed baseball commissioner but resigned 1951 due in large measure to personality conflicts with several team owners. He again served as governor of Kentucky 1955–59.

Chandler Raymond 1888–1959. US crime writer, who created the hard-boiled private eye Philip Marlowe in books that include *The Big Sleep* 1939, *Farewell, My Lovely* 1940, and *The Long Goodbye* 1954.

Many of his books have been made into popular Hollywood films. He also wrote numerous screenplays, notably *Double Indemnity* 1944 and *Strangers on a Train* 1951.

Chandragupta Maurya ruler of N India c. 321–c. 297 BC, founder of the Maurya dynasty. He overthrew the Nanda dynasty 325 and then conquered the Punjab 322 after the death of ◊Alexander the Great, expanding his empire W to Persia. He is credited with having united most of India.

Chandrasekhar Subrahmanyan 1910– . Indian-born US astrophysicist who made pioneering studies of the structure and evolution of stars. The Chandrasekhar limit of 1.4 Suns is the maximum mass of a ◊white dwarf before it turns into a ◊neutron star. Born in Lahore, he studied in Madras, India, and Cambridge, England, before emigrating to the US. He was awarded the 1983 Nobel Prize for Physics.

Chanel Coco (Gabrielle) 1883–1971. French fashion designer, creator of the "little black dress," informal cardigan suit, costume jewelry, and perfumes.

Chaney Lon (Alonso) 1883–1930. US star of silent films, often in grotesque or monstrous roles such as *The Phantom of the Opera* 1925. A master of make-up, he was nicknamed "The Man of a Thousand Faces." He sometimes employed extremely painful devices for added effectiveness, as in the title role in *The Hunchback of Notre Dame* 1923, when he carried over 70 lbs of costume in the form of a heavy hump and harness.

Chanel *French couturier Coco Chanel modernized women's wear by softening the lines and fabrics of both undergarments and day wear in the early 20th century.*

Chaney Lon, Jr (Creighton) 1906–1973. US actor, son of Lon Chaney, who gave an acclaimed performance as Lennie in *Of Mice and Men* 1940. He went on to star in many 1940s' horror films, including the title role in *The Wolfman* 1941. His other work includes *My Favorite Brunette* 1947 and *The Haunted Palace* 1963.

Changchiakow alternative transliteration of ◊Zhangjiakou, trading center in Hesei province, China.

Chang Ch'ien lived 2nd century BC. Chinese explorer who pioneered the Silk Route.

Changchun industrial city and capital of Jilin province, China; population (1986) 1,860,000. Machinery and motor vehicles are manufactured. It is also the center of an agricultural district.

As Hsingking ("new capital") it was the capital of Manchukuo 1932–45 during Japanese occupation.

Chang Jiang longest river (formerly Yangtze Kiang) of China, flowing about 3,900 mi/6,300 km from Tibet to the Yellow Sea. It is a major commercial waterway.

It has 127 mi/204 km of gorges, below which is Gezhou Ba, the first dam to harness the river. The entire length of the river was first navigated 1986.

Changsha river port, on the river Chang Jiang, capital of Hunan province, China; population (1986) 1,160,000. It trades in rice, tea, timber, and nonferrous metals; works antimony, lead, and silver; and produces chemicals, electronics, porcelain, and embroideries.

Mao Zedong was a student here 1912–18.

Channel, English stretch of water between England and France, leading in the west to the Atlantic Ocean, and in the east via the Strait of Dover to the North Sea; also known as La Manche (French "the sleeve") from its shape.

Channel Islands a group of islands in the English Channel, off the NW coast of France; they are a possession of the British crown; they comprise the islands of Jersey, Guernsey, Alderney, Great and Little Sark, with the lesser Herm, Brechou, Jethou, and Lihou.

Channel swimming popular test of endurance since Captain Matthew Webb (1848–1883) first swam across the English Channel from Dover to Calais in 1875. His time was 21 hr 45 min for the 21 mi/34 km journey.

The current record is 7 hr 40 min by Penny Dean of the US 1978. The first to swim nonstop in both directions was the Argentine Antonio Abertondo in 1961. The Channel Swimming Association was formed 1927, and records exist for various feats; double crossing, most cross-

Channel tunnel

The rail link between the UK and France has the potential to reduce the travel time between London and Paris to about three hours, matching the total time of a journey by air. An Anglo-French consortium raised money for work to begin at both ends of the projected route in 1987, with a deadline for completion of 1993.

The machines used to bore the Channel tunnel each weigh almost 500 tons. They have rotating heads with tungsten-carbide "picks," and special trains travel behind them to deliver equipment and remove debris. 700,000 concrete segments will form the tunnel lining, and trackwork, mechanical and electrical equipment and signals will be installed.▶

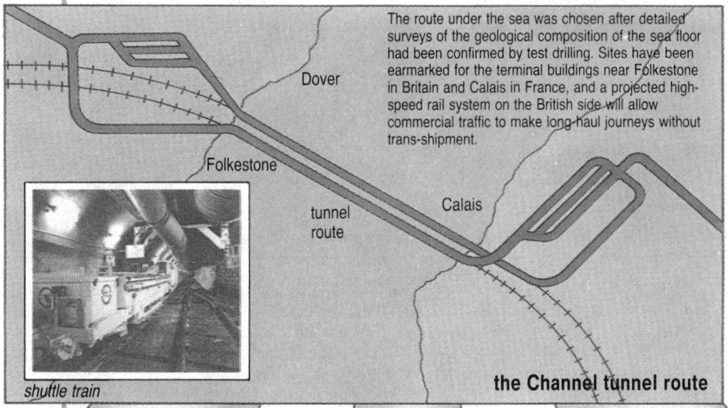
The route under the sea was chosen after detailed surveys of the geological composition of the sea floor had been confirmed by test drilling. Sites have been earmarked for the terminal buildings near Folkestone in Britain and Calais in France, and a projected high-speed rail system on the British side will allow commercial traffic to make long-haul journeys without trans-shipment.
Dover
Folkestone
tunnel route
Calais
shuttle train
the Channel tunnel route

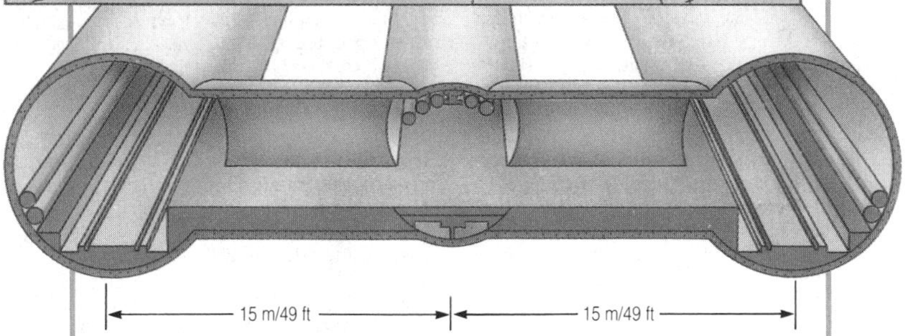
15 m/49 ft
15 m/49 ft

There are two main tunnels, each carrying trains travelling in one direction only. Between them is a service tunnel, supplying fresh air to the system. Special precautions are being taken to prevent rabid animals from using the tunnel to reach Britain, which is rabies-free.

ings, and youngest and oldest to complete a crossing.

Channel tunnel tunnel built beneath the English Channel, linking Britain with mainland Europe. It comprises twin rail tunnels, 31 mi/50 km long and 24 ft/7.3 m in diameter, located 130 ft/40 m beneath the seabed. Specially designed shuttle trains carrying automobiles and trucks will run between terminals at Folkestone, Kent, and Sangatte, W of Calais, France. It was begun 1986 and is scheduled to be operational 1993.

A channel tunnel is not a new idea. In the 1880s British financier and railroad promoter Edward Watkin started boring a tunnel near Dover, abandoning it 1894 because of governmental opposition after driving some 1 mi/1.6 kmle out to sea. In 1973 Britain and France agreed to back a tunnel, but a year later Britain pulled out following a change of government. The estimated costs has continually been revised upward and in 1989 was £6 billion. In 1990 the French and British tunneling teams met underneath the Channel.

Channing William Ellery 1780–1842. US minister and theologian. Born in Newport, Rhode Island, Channing was educated at Harvard and was appointed minister of the Federal Street Congregationalist Church in Boston 1803. In 1819, during a theological conflict between liberals and conservatives, he became a leader of the Unitarian movement in its opposition to the strict Calvinism of the New England Congregationalist churches. He was an instrumental figure in the establishment of the American Unitarian Association. In his later years, Channing devoted his energies to the cause of abolitionism.

chanson a type of song common in France and Italy, often based on a folk tune that originated with the ◊troubadors. Josquin ◊Desprez was a chanson composer.

chanson de geste the epic poetry of the High Middle Ages. It probably developed from oral poetry recited in royal or princely courts, and takes as its subject the exploits of heroes, such as those associated with Charlemagne and the Crusades.

***Chaplin** The greatest of the silent comedy stars, Charlie Chaplin wrote, directed, produced, and starred in his own films. He is seen here with Jackie Coogan in* The Kid *1920.*

Chanson de Roland an early 12th-century epic poem which tells of the real and imaginary deeds of Roland and other knights of Charlemagne, and their last stand against the Basques at Roncesvalles.

It is an example of the *chanson de geste*, a type of epic poem probably originating in the 11th century, and which often took the lives of knights, and their exemplary virtues, as its subject.

chant word used in common speech to denote any vocal melody or song, especially of a slow and solemn character; in music, a type of simple melody used in services of the Christian Church, for singing psalms and canticles, and in some forms of Buddhism. The Ambrosian and ◊Gregorian chants are forms of ◊plainsong melody.

chanterelle edible fungus *Cantharellus cibarius* that is bright yellow and funnel-shaped. It grows in deciduous woodland.

Chantilly town in Oise *département*, France, NE of Paris; population (1982) 10,208. It is the center of French horseracing and was the headquarters of the French military chief Joffre 1914–17. It was formerly renowned for its lace and porcelain.

chantry in medieval Europe, a religious ceremony in which, in return for an endowment of land, the souls of the donor, his family, and his friends would be prayed for. A chantry could be held at an existing altar, or in a specially constructed chantry chapel, in which the donor's body was usually buried.

Chao Phraya chief river (formerly Menam) of Thailand, flowing 750 mi/1,200 km into the Bight of Bangkok, an inlet of the Gulf of Thailand.

chaos theory or ***chaology*** branch of mathematics used to deal with chaotic systems—for example, an engineered structure, such as an oil platform, that is subjected to irregular, unpredictable wave stress.

chaparral thick scrub country of southwest US. Thorny bushes have replaced what was largely evergreen oak trees.

chapel a place of worship used by some Christian denominations; also, a part of a building used for Christian worship. A large church or cathedral may have several chapels.

Chaplin Charlie (Charles Spencer) 1889–1977. English-born US film actor-director. He made his reputation as a tramp with a smudge moustache, bowler hat, and twirling cane in silent comedies from the mid-1910s, including *The Rink* 1916, *The Kid* 1921, and *The Gold Rush* 1925. His work often contrasts buffoonery with pathos, and his later films combine dialogue with mime and music, as in *The Great Dictator* 1940, and *Limelight* 1952. With Douglas Fairbanks, Mary Pickford, and D W Griffith he formed United Artists 1919. Until sound films became common, he was the best known and most popular film star of his day.

Born in south London, he first appeared on the stage at the age of five. His other films include *City Lights* 1931, *Modern Times* 1936, and *Monsieur Verdoux* (in which he spoke for the first time) 1947. *Limelight* 1952 was awarded an Oscar for Chaplin's musical theme. When accused of Communist sympathies during the McCarthy witch hunt (anticommunist ◊HUAC investigations), he left the US in 1952 and moved to Switzerland. He was married four times, his third wife being actress Paulette Goddard, and his fourth, Oona, was the daughter of the dramatist Eugene O'Neill. He received special Oscars 1928 and 1972.

Chapman Frederick Spencer 1907–1971. British explorer, mountaineer, and writer, who explored Greenland, the Himalayas, and Malaysia. He accompanied Gino Watkins on the British Arctic Air Routes Expedition 1930–31, recalled in *Northern Lights* 1932, and in 1935 he joined a climbing expedition to the Himalayas. For two years he participated in a government mission to Tibet described in *Lhasa, the Holy City* 1938, before setting out to climb the 24,000 ft/7,315 m peak, Chomollari.

Chapman George 1559–1634. English poet and dramatist. His translations of Homer (completed 1616) were celebrated; his plays include the comedy *Eastward Ho!* (with Jonson and Marston) 1605 and the tragedy *Bussy d'Amboise* 1607.

Chapman John 1774–1845. US pioneer and folk hero. Better known as "Johnny Appleseed," Chapman was born in Leominster, Massachusetts, and roamed westward from Pennsylvania in the years after 1800. Planting apple seeds in Ohio and Indiana, he was credited with establishing orchards throughout the Midwest. Becoming famous as the subject of local legends and folk tales, Chapman was described as a religious visionary with boundless generosity. However, few specific details about his later life, especially during the War of 1812, can be verified.

chapter the collective assembly of canons (priests) who together administer a cathedral.

char or ***charr*** fish *Salvelinus alpinus* related to the trout, living in the Arctic coastal waters, and also in Europe and North America in some upland lakes. It is one of Britain's rarest fish, and is at risk from growing acidification.

Numerous variants have been described, but they probably all belong to the same species.

characin freshwater fish belonging to the family Characidae. There are over 1,300 species, mostly in South and Central America, but also in Africa. Most are carnivores. In typical characins, unlike the somewhat similar carp family, the mouth is toothed, and there is a small dorsal adipose fin just in front of the tail.

Characins are small fishes, often colorful, and they include ◊tetras and ◊piranhas.

characteristic in mathematics, the integral part (whole number) of a ◊logarithm. For example, in base ten, $10^0 = 1$, $10^1 = 10$, $10^3 = 100$, and so on; the powers to which 10 is raised are the characteristics. To determine the power to which 10 must be raised to obtain a number between 10 and 100, say 20, the logarithm for 2 is found (0.3010), and the characteristic 1 added to make 1.3010. The fractional part (in this case 0.3010) is the ◊mantissa.

charcoal black, porous form of ◊carbon, produced by heating wood or other organic materials in the absence of air (a process called destructive distillation). It is used as a fuel, for smelting metals such as copper and zinc; in the form of activated charcoal, for purifying and filtration of drinking water and other liquids and gases; and by artists for making black line drawings.

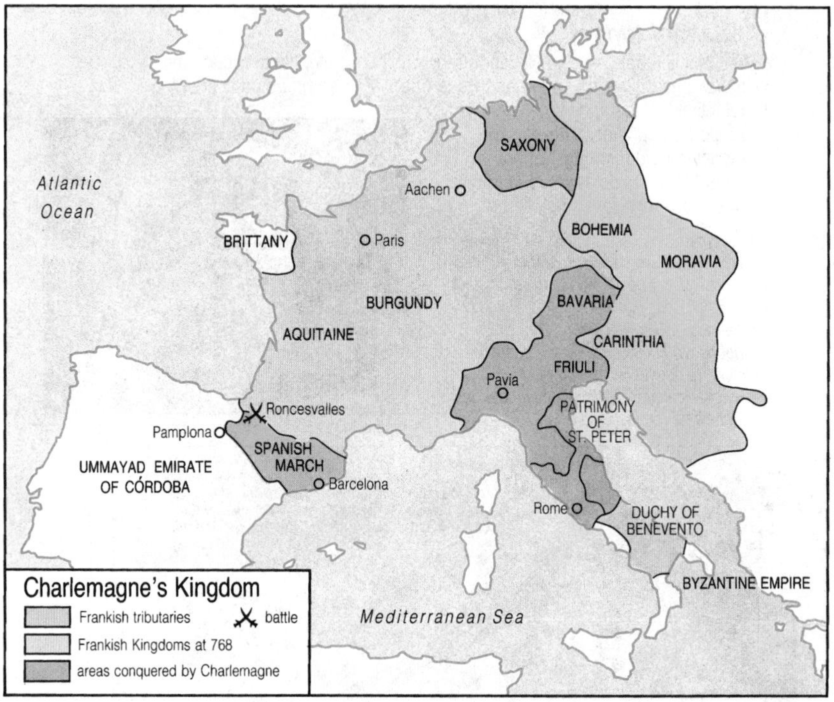
Atlantic Ocean
SAXONY
Aachen
BOHEMIA
MORAVIA
BRITTANY
Paris
BURGUNDY
BAVARIA
AQUITAINE
CARINTHIA
FRIULI
Pavia
Roncesvalles
PATRIMONY OF ST. PETER
Pamplona
SPANISH MARCH
UMMAYAD EMIRATE OF CÓRDOBA
Barcelona
Rome
DUCHY OF BENEVENTO
BYZANTINE EMPIRE
Mediterranean Sea
Charlemagne's Kingdom
Frankish tributaries
battle
Frankish Kingdoms at 768
areas conquered by Charlemagne

Charcoal was traditionally produced by burning dried wood in a kiln, a process lasting several days. The kiln was either a simple hole in the ground, or an earth-covered mound. Today kilns are of brick or iron, both of which allow the waste gases to be collected and used.

Charcoal had many uses in earlier centuries. Because of the high temperature at which it burns (1,100°C), it was used in furnaces and blast furnaces before the development of ◊coke. It was also used in an industrial process for obtaining ◊acetic acid, in producing wood tar and wood pitch, and (when produced from alder or willow trees) as a component of gunpowder.

Charcot Jean-Martin 1825–1893. French neurologist who studied hysteria, sclerosis, locomotor ataxia, and senile diseases. Among his pupils was Sigmund ◊Freud.

Chardin Jean-Baptiste-Siméon 1699–1779. French painter of naturalistic still lifes and quiet domestic scenes that recall the Dutch tradition. His work is a complete contrast to that of his contemporaries, the Rococo painters. He developed his own technique using successive layers of paint to achieve depth of tone and is generally considered one of the finest exponents of the genre.

Chardonnet Hilaire Bernigaud 1839–1924. French chemist who developed artificial silk in 1883, the first artificial fiber.

Charente French river, rising in Haute-Vienne *département* and flowing past Angoulême and Cognac into the Bay of Biscay below Rochefort. Length 225 mi/360 km. Its wide estuary is much silted up. It gives its name to two *départements*, Charente and Charente-Maritime (formerly Charente-Inférieure).

charge see ◊electric charge.

charge-couple device (CCD) device for forming images electronically, using a layer of silicon that releases electrons when struck by incoming light. The electrons are stored in individual picture elements (pixels) and read off into a computer at the end of exposure. CCDs have now almost entirely replaced photographic film for applications such as astrophotography where extreme sensitivity to light is required.

charged particle beam high-energy beam of electrons or protons that does not burn through the surface of its target like a ◊laser, but cuts through it. Such beams are being developed as weapons.

Charge of the Light Brigade disastrous attack by the British Light Brigade of cavalry against the Russian entrenched artillery on Oct 25, 1854 during the Crimean War at ◊Balaclava.

chariot a horse-drawn carriage with two wheels, used in ancient Egypt, Greece, and Rome, for fighting, processions, and races; it is thought to have originated in Asia. Typically, the fighting chariot contained a driver and a warrior, who would fight on foot, with the chariot providing rapid mobility.

Julius Caesar and Tacitus both write of chariots being used by the British against Roman armies in the 1st century AD. The most complete remains of a chariot found in Britain were at Llyn Cerrig Bach in Anglesey, Wales, but many parts of chariots, such as axle-caps and harness mounts, have been found.

charismatic a recent movement within the Christian church that emphasizes the role of the Holy Spirit in the life of the individual believer and in the life of the Church. See ◊Pentecostal movement.

Charlemagne Charles I the Great 742–814. King of the Franks from 768 and Holy Roman emperor from 800. By inheritance (his father was ◊Pepin the Short) and extensive campaigns of conquest, he united most of W Europe by 804, when after 30 years of war the Saxons came under his control. He reformed the legal, judicial, and military systems; established schools; and promoted Christianity, commerce, agriculture, arts, and literature. In his capital, Aachen, scholars gathered from all over Europe.

Pepin had been mayor of the palace in Merovingian Neustria until he was crowned king by Pope Stephen II (died 757) in 754, and his sons Carl (Charlemagne) and Carloman were crowned as joint heirs. When Pepin died 768, Charlemagne inherited the N Frankish kingdom, and when Carloman died 771, he also took possession of his domains. He was engaged in his first Saxon campaign when the Pope's call for help against the Lombards reached him; he crossed the Alps, captured Pavia, and took the title of king of the Lombards. The pacification and christianizing of the Saxon peoples occupied the greater part of Charlemagne's reign. From 792 N Saxony was subdued, and in 804 the whole region came under his rule.

In 777 the emir of Zaragoza asked for Charlemagne's help against the emir of Córdoba. Charlemagne crossed the Pyrenees 778 and reached the Ebro but had to turn back from Zaragoza. The rearguard action of Roncesvalles, in which ◊Roland, warden of the Breton March, and other Frankish nobles were ambushed and killed by Basques, was later glorified in the *Chanson de Roland*. In 801 the district between the Pyrenees and the Llobregat was organized as the Spanish March. The independent duchy of Bavaria was incorporated in the kingdom 788, and the ◊Avar people were subdued 791–96 and accepted Christianity. Charlemagne's last campaign was against a Danish attack on his northern frontier 810.

The supremacy of the Frankish king in Europe found outward expression in the bestowal of the imperial title: in Rome, during Mass on Christmas Day 800, Pope Leo III crowned Charlemagne emperor. He enjoyed diplomatic relations with Byzantium, Baghdad, Mercia, Northumbria, and other regions. Jury courts were introduced, the laws of the Franks revised, and other peoples' laws written down. A new coinage was introduced, weights and measures were reformed, and communications were improved. Charlemagne also took a lively interest in theology, organized the church in his dominions, and furthered missionary enterprises and monastic reform.

The Carolingian Renaissance of learning began when he persuaded the Northumbrian scholar Alcuin to enter his service 781. Charlemagne gathered a kind of academy around him. Although he never learned to read, he collected the old heroic sagas, began a Frankish grammar, and promoted religious instruction in the vernacular. He died Jan 28, 814 in Aachen, where he was buried. Soon a cycle of heroic legends and romances developed around him, including epics by Ariosto, Boiardo, and Tasso.

Charlemagne Prize political award established 1949, given annually to those serving European cooperation. Past winners include Winston ◊Churchill, Konrad ◊Adenauer, Robert ◊Schuman, and Edward ◊Heath.

Charleroi town in Belgium on the river Sambre, Hainault province; population (1985) 212,000. Its coal industry declined in the 1970s.

Charles Jacques Alexandre César 1746–1823. French physicist, who studied gases and made the first ascent in a hydrogen-filled balloon 1783. His work on the expansion of gases led to the formulation of ◊Charles's law.

Charles (Mary) Eugenia 1919– . Dominican politician, prime minister from 1980; cofounder and first leader of the centrist Dominica Freedom Party (DFP).

Charles qualified as a lawyer in England and returned to practice in the Windward and Leeward Islands in the West Indies. Two years after Dominica's independence the DFP won the 1980 general election and she became the Caribbean's first female prime minister.

Charles Ray 1930– . US singer, songwriter, and pianist, whose first hits were "I've Got A Woman" 1955, "What'd I Say" 1959, and "Georgia on My Mind" 1960. He has recorded gospel, blues, rock, soul, country, and rhythm and blues.

Charles two kings of Britain:

Charles I 1600–1649. King of Great Britain and Ireland from 1625, son of James I of England (James VI of Scotland). He accepted the ◊Petition of Right 1628 but then dissolved Parliament and ruled without one 1629–40. His advisers were Strafford and ◊Laud, who persecuted the Puritans and provoked the Scots to revolt. The ◊Short Parliament, summoned 1640, refused funds, and the ◊Long Parliament later that year rebelled. Charles declared war on Parliament 1642 but surrendered 1646 and was beheaded 1649. He was the father of Charles II.

Charles II 1630–1685. King of Great Britain and Ireland from 1660, when Parliament accepted the restoration of the monarchy; son of Charles I. His chief minister Clarendon, who arranged his marriage 1662 with Catherine of Braganza, was replaced 1667 with the ◊Cabal of advisers. His plans to restore Catholicism in Britain led to war with the Netherlands 1672–74 and a break with Parliament, which he dissolved 1681. He was succeeded by James II.

When Charles dissolved Parliament, the Whigs fled in terror. He now ruled without a Parliament, financed by Louis XIV. When the Whigs plotted a revolt, their leaders were executed,

Charles (full name Charles Philip Arthur George) 1948– . Prince of the United Kingdom, heir to the British throne, and Prince of Wales since 1958 (invested 1969). He is the first-born child of Queen Elizabeth II and the Duke of Edinburgh. He studied at Trinity College, Cambridge, 1967–70, before serving in the Royal Air Force and Royal Navy. He is the first royal heir since 1659 to have an English wife, Lady Diana Spencer, daughter of the 8th Earl Spencer. They have two sons and heirs, William (1982–) and Henry (1984–).

Charles ten kings of France, including:

Charles I better known as the emperor ◊Charlemagne.

Charles II the Bald; see ◊Charles II, Holy Roman emperor.

Charles III the Simple 879–929. King of France 893–922, son of Louis the Stammerer. He was crowned at Reims. In 911 he ceded what later became the duchy of Normandy to the Norman chief Rollo.

Charles IV the Fair 1294–1328. King of France from 1322, when he succeeded Philip V as the last of the direct Capetian line.

Charles V the Wise 1337–1380. King of France from 1364. He was regent during the captivity of his father, John II, in England 1356–60, and became king on John's death. He reconquered nearly all France from England 1369–80.

Charles VI the Mad or the Well-Beloved 1368–1422. King of France from 1380, succeeding his father Charles V, he was under the regency of his uncles until 1388. He became mentally unstable 1392, and civil war broke out between the dukes of Orleans and Burgundy. Henry V of England invaded France 1415, conquering Normandy, and in 1420 forcing Charles to sign the Treaty of Troyes, recognizing Henry as his successor.

Charles VII 1403–1461. King of France from 1429.

***Charles** The Prince of Wales pictured with the Princess and their two sons, (right) Prince William and Prince Henry. Prince Charles is known for his interest in protecting the environment.*

Son of Charles VI, he was excluded from the succession by the Treaty of Troyes, but recognized by the South of France. In 1429 Joan of Arc raised the siege of Orléans and had him crowned at Reims. He organized France's first standing army and by 1453 he had expelled the English from all of France except Calais.

Charles VIII 1470–1498. King of France from 1483, when he succeeded his father, Louis XI. In 1494 he unsuccessfully tried to claim the Neapolitan crown, and when he entered Naples 1495 was forced to withdraw by a coalition of Milan, Venice, Spain, and the Holy Roman Empire. He defeated them at Fornovo, but lost Naples. He died while preparing a second expedition.

Charles IX 1550–1574. King of France from 1560. Second son of Henry II and Catherine de' Medici, he succeeded his brother Francis II at the age of ten but remained under the domination of his mother's regency for ten years while France was torn by religious wars. In 1570 he fell under the influence of the ◊Huguenot leader Admiral Coligny (1517–72); alarmed by this, Catherine instigated his order for the Massacre of ◊St Bartholomew, which led to a new religious war.

Charles X 1757–1836. King of France from 1824. Grandson of Louis XV and brother of Louis XVI and Louis XVIII, he was known as the comte d'Artois before his accession. He fled to England at the beginning of the French Revolution, and when he came to the throne on the death of Louis XVIII, he attempted to reverse the achievements of the Revolution. A revolt ensued 1830, and he again fled to England.

Charles seven rulers of the Holy Roman Empire:

Charles I better known as ◊Charlemagne.

Charles II the Bald 823–877. Holy Roman emperor from 875 and (as Charles II) king of France from 843. Younger son of Louis I (the Pious), he warred against his eldest brother, Emperor Lothair I. The Treaty of Verdun 843 made him king of the West Frankish Kingdom (now France and the Spanish Marches).

Charles III the Fat 839–888. Holy Roman emperor 881–87; he became king of the West Franks 885, thus uniting for the last time the whole of Charlemagne's dominions, but was deposed.

Charles IV 1316–1378. Holy Roman emperor from 1355 and king of Bohemia from 1346. Son of John of Luxembourg, king of Bohemia, he was elected king of Germany 1346 and ruled all Germany from 1347. He was the founder of the first German university in Prague 1348.

Charles V 1500–1558. Holy Roman emperor 1519–56. Son of Philip of Burgundy and Joanna of Castile, he inherited vast possessions, which led to rivalry from Francis I of France, whose alliance with the Ottoman Empire brought Vienna under siege 1529 and 1532. Charles was also in conflict with the Protestants in Germany until the Treaty of Passau 1552, which allowed the Lutherans religious liberty.

Charles VI 1685–1740. Holy Roman emperor from 1711, father of ◊Maria Theresa, whose succession to his Austrian dominions he tried to ensure, and himself claimant to the Spanish throne 1700, thus causing the War of the ◊Spanish Succession.

Charles VII 1697–1745. Holy Roman emperor from 1742, opponent of ◊Maria Theresa's claim to the Austrian dominions of Charles VI.

Charles (Karl Franz Josef) 1887–1922. Emperor of Austria and king of Hungary from 1916, the last of the Hapsburg emperors. He succeeded his great-uncle, Franz Josef 1916 but was forced to withdraw to Switzerland 1918, although he refused to abdicate. In 1921 he attempted unsuccessfully to regain the crown of Hungary and was deported to Madeira, where he died.

Charles (Spanish *Carlos*) four kings of Spain:

Charles I 1500–1558. See ◊Charles V, Holy Roman emperor.

Charles II 1661–1700. King of Spain from 1665; second son of Philip IV, he was the last of the

Charles II *The Restoration of the monarchy in 1660 was greeted with joy in England and Charles II showed himself to be an exceptionally affable and energetic king. He had many mistresses, including Nell Gwynn. The portrait by Peter Lely shows the face of the bon viveur.*

Spanish Hapsburg kings. Mentally handicapped from birth, he bequeathed his dominions to Philip of Anjou, grandson of Louis XIV, which led to the War of the ◊Spanish Succession.

Charles V *Holy Roman emperor and king of Spain in the 16th century, Charles V aimed to preserve the medieval idea of the Empire. He had persecuted any separatist political or religious movements in order to achieve this unrealistic end.*

Charles III 1716–1788. King of Spain from 1759. Son of Philip V, he became duke of Parma in 1732 and in 1734 conquered Naples and Sicily. On the death of his half brother Ferdinand VI (1713–1759), he became king of Spain, handing over Naples and Sicily to his son Ferdinand (1751–1825). During his reign, Spain was twice at war with Britain: during the Seven Years' War, when he sided with France and lost Florida; and when he backed the colonists in the American Revolution and regained it. At home he carried out a program of reforms and expelled the Jesuits.

Charles IV 1748–1819. King of Spain from 1788, when he succeeded his father, Charles III, but left the government in the hands of his wife and her lover, the minister Manuel de Godoy (1767–1851). In 1808 Charles was induced to abdicate by Napoleon's machinations in favor of his son Ferdinand VII (1784–1833), who was subsequently deposed by Napoleon's brother Joseph. Charles was awarded a pension by Napoleon and died in Rome.

Charles (Swedish *Carl*) 15 kings of Sweden (the first six were local chieftains):

Charles VII King of Sweden from about 1161. He helped to establish Christianity in Sweden.

Charles VIII King of Sweden from 1448. He was elected regent of Sweden 1438, when Sweden broke away from Denmark and Norway. He stepped down 1441 when Christopher III of Bavaria (1418–48) was elected king, but after his death became king. He was twice expelled by the Danes and twice restored.

Charles IX 1550–1611. King of Sweden from 1604, the youngest son of Gustavus Vasa. In 1568 he and his brother John led the rebellion against Eric XIV (1533–77); John became king as John III and attempted to Catholicize Sweden, and Charles led the opposition. John's son Sigismund, king of Poland and a Catholic, succeeded to the Swedish throne 1592, and Charles led the Protestants. He was made regent 1595 and deposed Sigismund 1599. Charles was elected king of Sweden 1604 and was involved in unsuccessful wars with Russia, Poland, and Denmark. He was the father of Gustavus Adolphus.

Charles X 1622–1660. King of Sweden from 1654, when he succeeded his cousin Christina. He waged war with Poland and Denmark and in 1657 invaded Denmark by leading his army over the frozen sea.

Charles XI 1655–1697. King of Sweden from 1660, when he succeeded his father Charles X. His mother acted as regent until 1672 when Charles took over the government. He was a remarkable general and reformed the administration.

Charles XII 1682–1718. King of Sweden from 1697, when he succeeded his father, Charles XI. From 1700 he was involved in wars with Denmark, Poland, and Russia. He won a succession of victories until, in 1709 while invading Russia, he was defeated at Poltava in the Ukraine, and forced to take refuge in Turkey until 1714. He was killed while besieging Fredrikshall.

Charles XIII 1748–1818. King of Sweden from 1809, when he was elected; he became the first king of Sweden and Norway 1814.

Charles XIV (Jean Baptiste Jules ◊Bernadotte) 1763–1844. King of Sweden and Norway from 1818. A former marshal in the French army, in 1810 he was elected crown prince of Sweden under the name of Charles John (*Carl Johan*). Loyal to his adopted country, he brought Sweden into the alliance against Napoleon 1813, as a reward for which Sweden received Norway. He was the founder of the present dynasty.

Charles XV 1826–1872. King of Sweden and Norway from 1859, when he succeeded his father Oscar I. A popular and liberal monarch, his main achievement was the reform of the constitution.

Charles Albert 1798–1849. King of Sardinia from 1831. He showed liberal sympathies in early life, and after his accession introduced some reforms. On the outbreak of the 1848 revolution he granted a constitution and declared war on Austria. His troops were defeated at Custozza and Novara. In 1849 he abdicated in favor of his son Victor Emmanuel and retired to a monastery, where he died.

Charles Edward Stuart 1720–1788. British prince, known as the Young Pretender or Bonnie Prince Charlie, grandson of James II. In the Jacobite rebellion 1745 Charles won the support of the Scottish Highlanders; his army invaded England but was beaten back by the Duke of ◊Cumberland and routed at ◊Culloden 1746. Charles went into exile.

With a price of £30,000 on his head, Charles Edward fled to France, eventually settling in Italy 1766.

Charles Martel c. 688–741. Frankish ruler (Mayor of the Palace) of the E Frankish kingdom from 717 and the whole kingdom from 731. His victory against the Moors at Moussais-la-Bataille near Tours in 732 earned him his nickname of Martel, "the Hammer," because he halted the Islamic advance by the ◊Moors into Europe. An illegitimate son of Pepin of Heristal (Pepin II, Mayor of the Palace c. 640–714), he was a grandfather of Charlemagne.

Charles River Bridge v Warren Bridge a US Supreme Court decision 1837 dealing with the interpretation of corporate charters and states' power to regulate corporations. The owners of the Charles River toll bridge, in fear of economic competition, sued for an injunction against the building of the Warren Bridge, which the state had authorized. They claimed that their 1785 charter implied the exclusive right to bridge the river; the state was impairing that contract by sanctioning a second bridge. The Court ruled implicit rights to be invalid and declared that ambiguous clauses must be interpreted in favor of the public over the corporation.

Charles's law law stated by Jacques Charles in 1787, and independently by Joseph Gay-Lussac (1778–1850) in 1802, which states that the volume of an ideal mass of gas at constant pressure is directly proportional to the absolute temperature; that is, it increases by 1/273 of its volume at 0°C for each °C rise of temperature. That means that the coefficient of expansion (or expansivity) of all gases is the same. The law is only approximately true and the coefficient of expansion is generally taken as 0.003663 per °C.

Charles the Bold Duke of Burgundy 1433–1477. Son of Philip the Good, he inherited Burgundy and the Low Countries from him 1465. He waged wars attempting to free the duchy from dependence on France and restore it as a kingdom. He was killed in battle.

Charles's ambition was to create a kingdom stretching from the mouth of the Rhine to the mouth of the Rhône. He formed the League of the Public Weal against Louis XI of France, invaded France 1471, and conquered the country as far as Rouen. The Holy Roman emperor, the Swiss, and Lorraine united against him; he captured Nancy, but was defeated at Granson and again at Morat 1476. Nancy was lost, and he was killed while attempting to recapture it. His possessions in the Netherlands passed to the Hapsburgs by the marriage of his daughter Mary to Maximilian I of Austria.

Charleston main port and city of South Carolina; population (1990) 80,414. Industries include textiles, clothing, and paper products. A nuclear-submarine naval base and an air-force base are nearby. The city dates from 1670. Fort Sumter, in the sheltered harbor of Charleston, was bombarded by Confederate batteries April 12–13, 1861, thus beginning the Civil War. There are many historic houses and fine gardens. Charleston is the setting for ◊Gershwin's folk opera *Porgy and Bess*. Spoleto Festival USA, dating from 1977, attracts performing-arts groups. Charleston was hard hit by Hurricane Hugo 1989.

Charleston capital and chief city of West Virginia, on the Kanawha River; population (1990) 57,287. It is the center of a region that produces coal, natural gas, salt, clay, timber, and oil, and it is an important chemical-producing center. Charleston, once the home of Daniel Boone, developed from a fort built 1788.

Charleston a back-kicking dance of the 1920s that originated in Charleston, South Carolina, and became an American craze.

Charlotte largest city in North Carolina, on the border with South Carolina; population (1990) 395,934. Industries include data processing, textiles, chemicals, machinery, and food products. It was the gold-mining center of the country until gold was discovered in California 1849. The Mint Museum of Arts has paintings, sculpture, and ceramics. Charlotte is the birthplace of James K Polk, 11th president of the US. The University of North Carolina-Charlotte is here. Settled around 1750, Charlotte enjoyed rapid growth in the 1970s.

Charlotte Amalie capital and tourist resort of the US Virgin Islands; population (1980) 11,756. Located on the island of St Thomas, Charlotte Amalie is a free port, formerly called St Thomas. Boatbuilding and rum distilling are among the economic activities. The College of the Virgin Islands and the Museum of the Virgin Islands are here. It was founded 1672 by the Danish West India Co.

Charlottesville city in central Virginia, in the Blue Ridge mountain foothills, NW of Richmond, on the Rivanna river; seat of Albemarle county. Site of the University of Virginia, established 1819 by Thomas Jefferson. Jefferson's home, Monticello, is nearby, as is Pres James Monroe's home, Ash Lawn. Tourism is an important industry, and some textiles are manufactured; population (1990) 40,341.

Charlottetown capital of Prince Edward Island, Canada; population (1986) 16,000. The city trades in textiles, fish, timber, vegetables, and dairy produce. It was founded by the French in the 1720s.

charm in physics, property possessed by one type of ◊quark (constituents of protons and neutrons), called the charm quark. The effects of charm are only seen in experiments with particle ◊accelerators. See ◊elementary particles.

Charon in Greek mythology, the boatman who ferried the dead over the river Styx to the underworld.

Charpentier Gustave 1860–1956. French composer who wrote an opera about Paris working-class life, *Louise* 1900.

Charpentier Marc-Antoine 1645–1704. French composer. He wrote sacred music including a number of masses; other works include instrumental theater music and the opera *Médée* 1693.

Charrière Isabelle Van Zuylen de 1740–1805. Dutch aristocrat, who settled in Colombier, Switzerland in 1761. Her works include plays, tracts, and novels, including *Caliste* 1786. She had many early feminist ideas.

Charteris Leslie 1907– . British novelist. Born in Singapore, his varied career in many exotic occupations gave authentic background to some 40 novels about Simon Templar, the "Saint," a gentleman-adventurer on the wrong side of the law, which have been adapted for films, radio, and television. The first was *The Saint Meets the Tiger* 1928. He became a US citizen 1946.

Chartism radical British democratic movement, mainly of the working classes, which flourished around 1838–50. It derived its name from the People's Charter, a six-point program comprising: universal male suffrage, equal electoral districts, secret ballot, annual parliaments, abolition of the property qualification for, and payment of, members of Parliament. Greater prosperity, lack of organization, and rivalry in the leadership led to its demise.

Chartres capital of the *département* of Eure-et-Loir, NW France, 59 mi/96 km SW of Paris, on the river Eure; population (1982) 39,243. The city is an agricultural center for the fertile Plaine de la Beauce. Its cathedral of Notre Dame, completed about 1240, is a masterpiece of Gothic architecture.

Chartreuse trademark for a green or yellow liqueur distilled since 1607 by the Carthusian monks at La Grande Chartreuse monastery, France, and also in Tarragona, Spain.

Chartreuse, La Grande the original home of the Carthusian order of Roman Catholic monks, established by St Bruno around 1084, in a remote valley near Grenoble, France. The present buildings date from the 17th century.

Charybdis in Greek mythology, a whirlpool formed by a monster of the same name on one side of the narrow straits of Messina, Sicily, opposite the monster Scylla.

Chase Salmon Portland 1808–1873. US public official and chief justice of the US. He held a US Senate seat 1849–55 and 1860; helped found the Republican party 1854–56; was elected governor of Ohio 1855; became Lincoln's secretary of the treasury 1861; and was appointed chief justice of the US Supreme Court 1864. Chase tempered the abuses of Reconstruction, as in ◊*Ex parte Milligan* 1866, and presided over the impeachment trial of President A ◊Johnson 1868.

Born in Cornish, New Hampshire, and educated at Dartmouth, Chase studied law and was admitted to the bar 1829. Moving to Cincinnati, Ohio, he became an abolitionist, often taking the cases of runaway slaves.

chasing indentation of a design on metal by small chisels and hammers. This method of decoration was familiar in ancient Egypt, Assyria, and Greece; it is used today on fine silverware.

chasuble the outer garment worn by the priest in the celebration of the Christian Mass. The color of the chasuble depends on which feast is being celebrated.

château *The château of Azay le Rideau, France.*

château term originally applied to a French medieval castle, but now used to describe a country house or important residence in France. The château was first used as a domestic building in the late 15th century; by the reign of Louis XIII (1610–43) fortifications such as moats and keeps were no longer used for defensive purposes, but merely as decorative features. The Loire valley contains some fine examples of châteaux.

Chateaubriand François René, vicomte de 1768–1848. French author. In exile from the French Revolution 1794–99, he wrote *Atala* 1801 (written after his encounters with North American Indians); and the autobiographical *René*, which formed part of *Le Génie du christianisme/The Genius of Christianity* 1802.

He visited the US 1791 and, on his return to France, fought for the royalist side which was defeated at Thionville 1792. He lived in exile in England until 1800. When he returned to France, he held diplomatic appointments under Louis XVIII. He later wrote *Mémoires d'outre tombe/Memoirs from Beyond the Tomb* 1849–50.

Châtelet Emilie de Breteuil, Marquise du 1706–1749. French scientific writer, mistress of ◊Voltaire, and translator into French of Newton's *Principia*.

Her marriage to the Marquis du Châtelet in 1725 gave her the leisure to study physics and mathematics. She met Voltaire in 1733, and settled with him at her husband's estate at Cirey, in the Duchy of Lorraine. Her study of Newton, with whom she collaborated on various scientific works, influenced Voltaire's work. She independently produced the first (and only) French translation of Newton's *Principia Mathematica* (published posthumously in 1759).

Chatham town in Kent, England; population (1983) 146,000. The Royal Dockyard 1588–1984 was from 1985 converted to an industrial area, marina, and museum as a focus of revival for the whole Medway area.

Chatham Islands two Pacific islands (Chatham and Pitt), forming a county of South Island, New Zealand; area 371 sq mi/960 sq km; population (1981) 750. The chief settlement is Waitangi.

Chattanooga city in Tennessee, on the Tennessee River; population (1990) 152,466. It is the focus of the Tennessee Valley Authority area. Developed as a salt-trading center after 1835, it now produces chemicals, textiles, and metal products. The Hunter Museum of Art and a campus of the University of Tennessee are here. Chattanooga was laid out 1838 after Cherokee Indians were removed from the area. Union forces captured it from the Confederacy 1863.

Chatterji Bankim Chandra 1838–1894. Indian novelist. Born in Bengal, where he established his reputation with his first book, *Durges-Nandini*

Chaucer *Posthumous portrait of the English poet Geoffrey Chaucer by an unknown artist, National Portrait Gallery, London.*

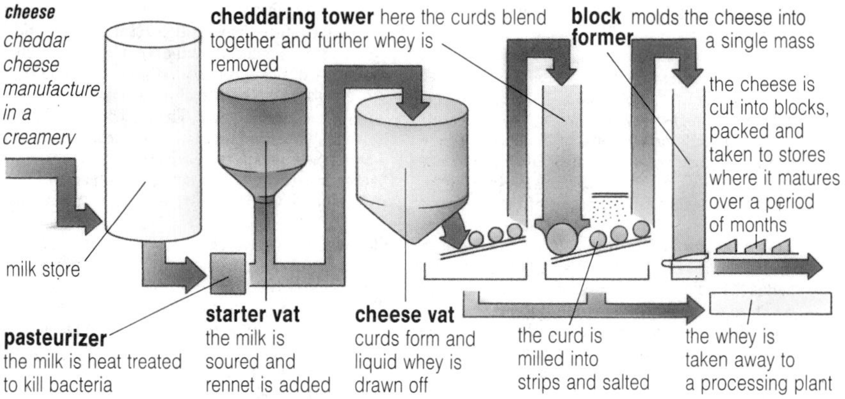
cheese
cheddar cheese manufacture in a creamery
cheddaring tower here the curds blend together and further whey is removed
block former
molds the cheese into a single mass
the cheese is cut into blocks, packed and taken to stores where it matures over a period of months
milk store
pasteurizer
the milk is heat treated to kill bacteria
starter vat
the milk is soured and rennet is added
cheese vat
curds form and liquid whey is drawn off
the curd is milled into strips and salted
the whey is taken away to a processing plant

1864, he became a favorite of the nationalists. His book *Ananda Math* 1882 contains the Indian national song "Bande-Mataram."

Chatterton Thomas 1752–1770. English poet whose medieval-style poems and brief life were to inspire English Romanticism. Born in Bristol, he studied ancient documents he found in the Church of St Mary Redcliffe and composed poems he ascribed to a 15th-century monk, "Thomas Rowley," which were accepted as genuine. He committed suicide in London, after becoming destitute.

Chatwin Bruce 1940–1989. English writer. His works include *The Songlines* 1987, written after living with Aborigines, *Utz* 1988, about a manic porcelain collector in Prague, and *What Am I Doing Here* 1989.

Chaucer Geoffrey c. 1340–1400. English poet, author of *The Canterbury Tales* about 1387, a collection of tales told by pilgrims in Middle English on their way to the Thomas à Becket shrine. He was the most influential English poet of the Middle Ages. Chaucer's other work includes the French-influenced *Romance of the Rose* and an adaptation of Boccaccio's *Troilus and Criseyde*.

Chaucer was born in London. Taken prisoner in the French wars, he had to be ransomed by Edward III 1360. He married Philippa Roet 1366, becoming in later life the brother-in-law of ◊John of Gaunt. He achieved various appointments and was sent on missions to Italy (where he may have met ◊Boccaccio and ◊Petrarch), France, and Flanders. His early work showed formal French influence, as in his adaptation of the French allegorical poem on courtly love, *Romance of the Rose*; more mature works reflected the influence of Italian realism, as in his long narrative poem *Troilus and Criseyde*, adapted from Boccaccio. In *The Canterbury Tales* he showed his own genius for meter and characterization.

chauvinism a warlike, often unthinking, patriotism, as exhibited by Nicholas Chauvin, one of Napoleon I's veterans and his fanatical admirer. In the mid-20th century the expression male chauvinism was coined to mean an assumed superiority of the male sex over the female.

Chávez Carlos 1899–1978. Mexican composer. A student of the piano and of the complex rhythms of his country's folk music, he founded the Mexico Symphony Orchestra. His composed a number of ballets, seven symphonies, and concertos for both violin and piano.

Chavez Cesar Estrada 1927– . US labor organizer. Chavez devoted himself to the cause of unionization and became director of the Community Service Organization 1958. He founded the National Farm Workers Association 1962 and, with the support of the AFL-CIO and other major unions, embarked on a successful campaign to unionize California grape workers. He led boycotts of citrus fruits, lettuce, and grapes in the early 1970s, but disagreement and exploitation of migrant farm laborers continued despite his successes.

Born near Yuma, Arizona, to a family of migrant farm workers, Chavez was deeply influenced by the organizing efforts of Saul Alinsky among agricultural workers in California in the early 1950s.

Chayefsky Paddy (Sidney) 1923–1981. US writer. He established his reputation with the television plays *Marty* 1955 (for which he won an Oscar when he turned it into a film), and *Bachelor Party* 1957. He also won Oscars for *The Hospital* 1971 and *Network* 1976.

Checheno-Ingush autonomous republic in western USSR; area 7,350 sq mi/19,000 sq km; population (1986) 1,230,000. It was conquered in the 1850s, and is a major oil-field. The capital is Grozny. The population includes Chechens (53%) and Ingushes (12%).

check an order written by the drawer to a bank to pay a specific sum on demand from a checking account to a person or an institution.

The check should bear the date on which it is payable, a definite sum of money to be paid, written in words and figures, and be signed by the drawer. It is then payable on presentation at the bank on which it is drawn. In the US checks are widely negotiable for retail purchases and other financial transactions.

checkers board game using a 64-square board of alternating colors. Each of the two players has 12 checkers (disk-shaped pieces) of a single color, and attempts with one move per turn (including "jumps"), either to capture all the opponent's checkers or to block their final movements.

Cheddar village in Somerset, England; population (1983) 3,994. Cheddar cheese was first produced here; it has a limestone gorge and caves with stalactites and stalagmites. In 1962 excavation revealed the site of a Saxon palace.

cheese food made from the curds (solids) of fresh and soured milk from cows, sheep, or goats, separated from the whey (liquid), then salted, put into molds, and pressed into firm blocks. Cheese is ripened with bacteria or surface fungi, and kept for a time to mature before eating.

There are six main types of cheese. Soft cheeses may be ripe or unripe, and include cottage cheese and high-fat soft cheeses such as Bel Paese, Camembert, and Neufchatel. Semi-hard cheeses are ripened by bacteria (Munster) or by bacteria and surface fungi (Port Salut, Gouda, St Paulin); they may also have penicillin molds injected into them (Roquefort, Gorgonzola, Blue Stilton, Wensleydale). Hard cheeses are ripened by bacteria, and include Cheddar, Cheshire, and Cucciocavallo; some have large cavities within them, such as Swiss Emmental and Gruyère. Very hard cheeses, such as Parmesan and Spalen, are made with skimmed milk. Processed cheese is made with dried skim milk powder and additives, and whey cheese is made by heat coagulation of the proteins from whey; examples are Mysost and Primost. In France (from 1980) cheese has the same *appellation controlée* status as wine if made only in a special defined area, for example Cantal and Roquefort, but not Camembert and Brie, which are also made elsewhere.

types of cheese

cheese	*calories*	*protein (%)*	*fat (%)*	*calcium*
soft	300	22.8	23.2	880
semihard	304	24.4	22.9	740
hard	406	26.0	33.5	800
very hard	408	35.1	29.7	1220
processed	311	21.5	25.0	1360

cheesecloth fine muslin or cotton fabric of very loose weave, originally used to press curds during the cheesemaking process.

cheetah large wild cat *Acinonyx jubatus* native to Africa, Arabia, and SW Asia, but now rare in some areas. Yellowish with black spots, it has a slim lithe build. It is up to 3 ft/1 m tall at the shoulder, and up to 5 ft/1.5 m long. It can reach 70 mph/110 kph, but tires after about 440 yds/400 m. Cheetahs live in open country where they hunt small antelopes, hares, and birds.

A cheetah's claws do not retract as fully as in most cats.

Cheever John 1912–1982. US writer, whose stories and novels focus on the ironies of upper-middle-class life in mid-20th-century suburban America. His short stories frequently were published in *The New Yorker*.

Born in Quincy, Massachusetts, Cheever's collections of short stories include *The Way Some People Live* 1943, *The Housebreaker of Shady Hill* 1958, *The Brigadier and the Golf Widow* 1964, and *Stories of John Cheever* 1978 (Pulitzer prize). His first novel was *The Wapshot Chronicle* 1957, for which he won the National Book award. Others include *Bullet Park* 1969, *Falconer* 1977, and *Oh What a Paradise It Seems* 1982.

Chefoo former name of part of ◊Yantai in China.

Cheka secret police operating in the USSR 1918–23. It originated from the tsarist Okhrana and became successively the OGPU (GPU) 1923–34, NKVD 1934–46, and MVD 1946–53, before its present form, the ◊KGB.

The name is formed from the initials *che* and *ka* of the two Russian words meaning "extraordinary commission," formed for "the repression of counter-revolutionary activities and of speculation," and extended to cover such matters as espionage and smuggling.

Chekhov Anton (Pavlovich) 1860–1904. Russian dramatist and writer. He began to write short stories and comic sketches as a medical student. His plays concentrate on the creation of atmosphere and delineation of internal development, rather than external action. His first play *Ivanov* 1887 was a failure, as was *The Seagull* 1896 until revived by Stanislavsky 1898 at the Moscow Art Theatre, for which Chekhov went on to write his major plays: *Uncle Vanya* 1899, *The Three Sisters* 1901 and *The Cherry Orchard* 1904.

Born at Taganrog, he qualified as a doctor 1884, but devoted himself to writing short stories rather than practicing medicine. The collection *Particolored Stories* 1886 consolidated his reputation and gave him leisure to develop his style, as seen in "My Life" 1895, "The Lady with the Dog" 1898 and "In the Ravine" 1900.

Chekiang alternative transliteration of ◊Zhejiang province of SE China.

chela in Hinduism, a follower or pupil of a guru (teacher).

chelate type of chemical compound whose molecules consist of one or more metal atoms or charged ions joined to chains of organic residues by coordinate (or dative covalent) chemical ◊bonds.

The parent organic compound is known as a chelating agent—for example, EDTA (ethylenediaminetetraacetic acid), used in chemical analysis. Chelates are used in analytical chemistry, in agriculture and horticulture as carriers for essential trace metals, in water softening, and in the treatment of thalassemia by removing excess iron, which may build up to toxic levels in the body. Metalloproteins (natural chelates) may influence the performance of enzymes or provide a mechanism for the storage of iron in the spleen and plasma of the human body.

Chelmsford town in Essex, England, 30 mi/48 km NE of London; population (1981) 58,000. It is the administrative headquarters of the county, and a market town with radio, electrical, engineering, and agricultural machinery industries.

Chelsea historic area of the Royal Borough of Kensington and Chelsea, London, immediately N of the Thames, where it is crossed by the Albert and Chelsea bridges.

Chelsea porcelain factory porcelain factory thought to be the first in England. Based in SW London, it dated from the 1740s, when it was known as the Chelsea Porcelain Works. It produced softpaste porcelain in imitation of Chinese high-fired porcelain. Later items are distinguished by the anchor mark on the base. Chelsea porcelain includes plates and other items decorated with botanical, bird, and insect paintings.

Chekhov *Russian writer Anton Chekhov, author of* The Cherry Orchard.

Cheltenham spa at the foot of the Cotswolds, Gloucestershire, England; population (1981) 73,000. There are annual literary and music festivals, a racecourse (the Cheltenham Gold Cup is held annually), and Cheltenham College (founded 1854).

Chelyabinsk industrial town and capital of Chelyabinsk region, W Siberia, USSR; population (1987) 1,119,000. It has iron and engineering works and makes chemicals, motor vehicles, and aircraft.

It lies E of the Ural Mountains, 150 mi/240 km SE of Sverdlovsk. It was founded 1736 as a Russian frontier post.

chemical element alternate name for ◊element.

chemical equation method of indicating the reactants and products of a chemical reaction by using chemical symbols and formulae. A chemical equation gives two basic pieces of information: (1) the reactants (on the left-hand side) and products (right-hand side); and (2) the reacting proportions (stoichiometry), that is how many units of each reactant and product are involved. The equation must balance; that is, the total number of atoms of a particular element on the left-hand side must be the same as the number of atoms of that element on the right-hand side.

$$\underbrace{Na_2CO_3 + 2HCl}_{\text{reactants}} = \underbrace{2NaCl + CO_2 + H_2O}_{\text{products}}$$

This equation states that one molecule of sodium carbonate combines with two molecules of hydrochloric acid to form two molecules of sodium chloride, one of carbon dioxide, and one of water. State symbols and the energy symbol (ΔH) can be used to provide further information. $Na_2CO_{3\,(s)} + 2HCl_{(aq)} = 2NaCl_{(aq)} + CO_{2\,(g)} + H_2O_{(l)} \quad -\Delta H$ Substituting the molecular weights of the substances indicates the proportions of masses involved.

Double arrows indicate that the reaction is reversible—in the formation of ammonia from hydrogen and nitrogen, the direction depends on the temperature and pressure of the reactants.

$$3H_2 + N_2 = 2NH_3$$

chemical warfare use in war of gaseous, liquid, or solid substances intended to have a toxic effect on humans, animals, or plants. Together with biological warfare, it was banned 1925 by the Geneva Convention, although this has not always been observed. In 1989, when the 149-nation Conference on Chemical Weapons unanimously voted to outlaw chemical weapons, the total US stockpile was estimated at 30,000 tons and the Soviet stockpile at 300,000 tons.

In a deal with the US, the USSR offered to eliminate its stocks; the US is destroying its current stocks and replacing them with new "binary" nerve-gas weapons. Some 20 nations currently hold chemical weapons, including Iraq, Iran, Israel, Syria, Libya, South Africa, and China.

There are several types of chemical weapons. Irritant gases may cause permanent injury or death. Examples include chlorine, phosgene (Cl_2CO), and mustard gas ($C_4H_8Cl_2S$), used in World War I (1914–18) and allegedly used by Soviet forces in Afghanistan, by Vietnamese forces in Laos, and by Iraq against Iran during their 1980–88 war. Tear gases, such as CS gas, used in riot control, affect the lungs and eyes, causing temporary blindness. Nerve gases are organophosphorus compounds similar to insecticides, which are taken into the body through the skin and lungs and break down the action of the nervous system. Developed by the Germans for World War II, they were not used.

Incapacitants are drugs designed to put an enemy temporarily out of action by, for example, impairing vision or inducing hallucinations. They have not so far been used. Toxins are poisons to be eaten, drunk, or injected; for example, ricin (derived from the castor-oil plant) and the botulism toxin. Ricin has been used in individual cases, and other toxins have allegedly been used by Soviet forces in Afghanistan and Vietnamese forces in Cambodia. Herbicides are defoliants used to destroy vegetation sheltering troops and the crops of hostile populations. They were used in Vietnam by the US and in Malaysia by the UK. ◊Agent Orange became notorious because it caused cancer and birth abnormalities among Vietnam War veterans and US factory staff. Binary weapons are two chemical components that become toxic in combination, after the shell containing them is fired.

chemiluminescence alternate term for ◊bioluminescence.

chemisorption the attachment, by chemical means, of a single layer of molecules, atoms, or ions of gas to the surface of a solid or, less frequently, a liquid. It is the basis of catalysis (see ◊catalyst) and of great industrial importance.

chemistry the science concerned with the composition of matter and of the changes that take place in it under certain conditions.

All matter can exist in three states: gas, liquid, or solid. It is composed of minute particles termed molecules, which are constantly moving, and may be further divided into ◊atoms. Molecules that contain atoms of one kind only are known as ◊elements; those that contain atoms of different kinds are called ◊compounds.

Examination and possible breakdown of compounds to determine their components is analysis, and the building up of compounds from their components is synthesis. When substances are brought together without changing their molecular structures they are said to be mixtures. Chemical compounds are produced by a chemical action that alters the arrangement of the atoms in the molecule. Heat, light, vibration, catalytic action, radiation, or pressure, as well as moisture (for ionization), may be necessary to produce a chemical change.

Organic chemistry is the branch of chemistry that deals with carbon compounds. Inorganic chemistry deals with the description, properties, reactions, and preparation of all the elements and their compounds, with the exception of carbon compounds. Physical chemistry is concerned with the quantitative explanation of chemical phenomena and reactions, and the measurement of data required for such explanations. This branch studies in particular the movement of molecules and the effects of temperature and pressure, often with regard to gases and liquids.

Symbols are used to denote the elements. The symbol is usually the first letter or letters of the English or Latinized name of the element—for example C for carbon; Ca for calcium; Fe for iron (*ferrum*). These symbols represent one atom of the element; molecules containing more than one atom are denoted by a subscript figure—for example water is H_2O. In some substances a group of atoms acts as a single entity, and these are enclosed in parentheses in the symbol—for example $(NH_4)_2SO_4$ denotes ammonium sulfate. The symbolic representation of a molecule is known as a formula. A figure placed before a formula represents the number of molecules of one substance present in another—for example $2H_2O$ indicates two molecules of water. Chemical reactions are expressed by means of equations. $NaCl + H_2SO_4 \rightarrow NaHSO_4 + HCl$. This equation states the fact that sodium chloride ($NaCl$) on being treated with sulfuric acid (H_2SO_4) is converted into sodium bisulfate (sodium hydrogensulfate, $NaHSO_4$) and hydrogen chloride (HCl).

Elements are divided into metals, which have luster and conduct heat and electricity, and nonmetals, which usually lack these properties. The periodic system, developed by Newlands in 1863 and established by Mendeleyev in 1869, classifies elements according to their atomic weights—that is, the least weight of the element present in a molecular weight of any of its compounds. Those elements that resemble each other in general properties were found to bear a relation to one

chemistry: chronology

AD 1	Gold, silver, copper, lead, iron, tin, and mercury were known.	1869	Mendeleyev expounded his periodic table of the elements.
200	Solution, filtration, and distillation were known.	1895	Radioactivity was discovered; the electron was discovered by Thomson.
1100	Alcohol was first distilled.	1905	Einstein's theory of relativity was announced.
1242	Gunpowder introduced to Europe from the Far East.	1912	Vitamins were discovered by Hopkins.
1604	Galileo invented the thermometer.	1919	Artificial disintegration of atoms by Rutherford.
1620	Scientific method of reasoning expounded by English philosopher Francis Bacon in his *Novum Organum*.	1927	Sidgwick's theory of valency was announced.
1650	Leyden University in the Netherlands set up the first chemistry laboratory.	1929	Penicillin was discovered.
1660	Definition of the element; law concerning effect of pressure on gas was established by English chemist Robert Boyle (Boyle's law).	1933	Heavy hydrogen (deuterium) discovered by US chemist Harold Urey.
1662	The Royal Society was formed in England.	1940	Plutonium was first synthesized by US chemists Glen T Seaborg and Edwin McMillan.
1742	Centigrade scale was invented.	1945	The atomic bomb was exploded.
1756	Black discovered carbon dioxide.	1952	Einsteinium and fermium were synthesized.
1769	Scheele discovered oxygen.	1953	Hydrogen was converted to helium.
1777	Lavoisier explained burning.	1960	The "atomic time clock" established by US chemist Willard Libby to measure the age of objects by measuring their radioactivity.
1792	Volta demonstrated the electrochemical series.	1965	The synthesis of complex organic compounds by US chemist Robert B Woodward.
1803	Dalton expounded his atomic theory.	1979	DNA structure and function mapped by US chemists Paul Berg and Walter Gilbert, and UK chemist Frederick Sanger.
1811	Publication of Italian physicist Amedeo Avogadro's hypothesis on the relation of volumes of gases and numbers of molecules to temperature and pressure.	1981	Quantum mechanics applied to predict course of chemical reactions by US chemist Roald Hoffmann and Kenichi Fukui of Japan.
1818	Berzelius's atomic symbols were elaborated.	1982	Element 109, unnilennium, synthesized; electron transfer understood in chemical reactions by US chemist Henry Taube.
1828	The first organic compounds, alcohol and urea, were synthesized.	1987	Creation of artificial molecules that mimic vital chemical reactions of life processes by US chemists Donald Cram and Charles Pederson, and Jean-Marie Lehn of France.
1834	Faraday expounded the laws of electrolysis.		
1853	Bunsen invented the Bunsen burner.		
1866	Nobel invented dynamite.		
1868	The first plastic substance (celluloid) was made.		

another by weight, and these were placed in groups or families. Certain anomalies in this system were removed by classifying the elements according to their atomic numbers. The latter is equivalent to the positive charge on the nucleus of the atom.

history Ancient peoples were familiar with certain chemical processes—for example, extracting metals from their ores, and making alloys. Medieval alchemists endeavored to turn base metals into gold, and toward the end of the 17th century chemistry evolved from the techniques and insights developed during alchemical experiments. Robert Boyle defined elements as the simplest substances into which matter could be resolved. The alchemical doctrine of the four elements (earth, air, fire, and water) gradually lost its hold, and the theory that all combustible bodies contain a substance called phlogiston (a weightless "fire element" generated during combustion) was discredited in the 18th century by the experimental work of Black, Lavoisier, and Priestley (who discovered the presence of oxygen in air). Cavendish discovered the composition of water, and Dalton put forward the atomic theory, which ascribed a precise relative weight to the "simple atom" characteristic of each element. Much research then took place leading to the development of ◊biochemistry, ◊chemotherapy, and ◊plastics.

Chemnitz industrial city (engineering, textiles, chemicals) in the state of Saxony, Federal Republic of Germany, on the Chemnitz river, 40 mi/65 km SSE of Leipzig; population (1990) 310,000. As a former district capital of East Germany it was named Karl-Marx-Stadt 1953–90.

chemosynthesis method of making ◊protoplasm (contents of a cell) using the energy from chemical reactions, in contrast to the use of light energy employed for the same purpose in ◊photosynthesis. The process is used by certain bacteria, which can synthesize organic compounds from carbon dioxide and water using the energy from special methods of ◊respiration.

Nitrifying bacteria are a group of chemosynthetic organisms which change free nitrogen into a form that can be taken up by plants; nitrobacteria, for example, oxidize nitrites to nitrates. This is a vital part of the ◊nitrogen cycle. As chemosynthetic bacteria can survive without light energy, they can live in dark and inhospitable regions, including the hydrothermal vents of the Pacific ocean. Around these vents, where temperatures reach up to 662°F/350°C, the chemosynthetic bacteria are the basis of a food web supporting fishes and other marine life.

chemotherapy any medical treatment with chemicals. It usually refers to treatment of cancer with cytotoxic and other drugs. The term was coined by the German bacteriologist Paul Ehrlich for the use of synthetic chemicals against infectious diseases.

chemotropism movement by part of a plant in response to a chemical stimulus. The response by the plant is termed "positive" if the growth is toward the stimulus or "negative" if the growth is away from the stimulus.

Fertilization of flowers by pollen is achieved because the ovary releases chemicals that produce a positive chemotrophic response from the developing pollen tube.

Chemulpo former name for ◊Inchon, port and summer resort on the W coast of South Korea.

Chenab a tributary of the river ◊Indus.

Chengchow former name of ◊Zhengzhou, capital of Henan province of China.

Chengde town, formerly Chengteh in Hebei province, China, NE of Beijing; population (1984) 325,800. It is a market town for agricultural and forestry products. It was the summer residence of the Manchu rulers and has an 18th-century palace and temples.

Chengdu or ***Chengtu*** ancient city, capital of Sichuan province, China; population (1986) 2,580,000. It is a busy rail junction and has railroad workshops, and textile, electronics, and engineering industries. It has well-preserved temples.

Chengteh alternative transliteration of ◊Chengde.

Chengtu alternative transliteration of ◊Chengdu.

Chénier André de 1762–1794. French poet, born in Constantinople. His lyrical poetry was later to inspire the Romantic movement, but he was known in his own time for his uncompromising support of the constitutional royalists after the Revolution. In 1793 he went into hiding, but finally he was arrested and, on July 25, 1794, guillotined. While in prison he wrote *Jeune Captive/Captive Girl* and the political *Iambes*, published after his death.

Cher French river that rises in Creuse *département* and flows into the river Loire below Tours, length 220 mi/355 km. It gives its name to a *département*.

Cherbourg French port and naval station at the northern end of the Cotentin peninsula, in Manche *département*; population (1982) 85,500 (conurbation). There is an institute for studies in nuclear warfare, and Cherbourg has large shipbuilding yards. During World War II, Cherbourg was captured June 1944 by the Allies, who thus gained their first large port of entry into France. Cherbourg was severely damaged; restoration of the harbor was completed 1952. There is a nuclear processing plant at nearby Cap la Hague. There are ferry links to England.

Cherenkov Pavel 1904– . Soviet physicist. In 1934 he discovered Cherenkov radiation; this occurs when liquids are exposed to a source of fast gamma radiation. He attributed the luminescence to particles traveling near the speed of light (in vacuo).

Cherenkov discovered that this effect was independent of any medium and depended for its production on the passage of high velocity electrons. The phenomenon has also been claimed as the discovery of the French scientist Lucien Mallet. Cherenkov shared a Nobel Prize 1958 with his colleagues Ilya ◊Frank and Igor Tamm for work resulting in a cosmic-ray counter.

Cherepovets iron and steel city in W USSR, on the Volga-Baltic waterway; population (1985) 299,000.

Chéret Jules 1836–1932. One of the first French ◊poster artists.

Chernenko Konstantin 1911–1985. Soviet politician, leader of the Soviet Communist Party (CPSU) and president 1984–85. He was a protégé of Brezhnev and from 1978 a member of the Politburo.

Chernenko, born in central Siberia, joined the Komsomol (Communist Youth League) 1929 and the CPSU 1931. The future CPSU leader Brezhnev brought him to Moscow to work in the central apparatus 1956 and later sought to establish Chernenko as his successor, but he was passed over in favor of the KGB chief Andropov. When Andropov died Feb 1984 Chernenko was selected as the CPSU's stopgap leader by cautious party colleagues and was also elected president. From July 1984 he gradually retired from public life because of failing health.

Chernigov port city on the river Desna in N Ukraine; population (1987) 291,000. It has an 11th-century cathedral. Lumbering, textiles, chemicals, distilling, and food-canning are among its industries.

Chernobyl town in the Ukraine, USSR. In Apr 1986 a leak, caused by overheating, occurred in a non-pressurized boiling-water nuclear reactor. The resulting clouds of radioactive isotopes were traced as far away as Sweden; over 250 people were killed, and thousands of square miles contaminated.

Chernovtsy city in Ukraine, USSR; population (1987) 254,000. Industries include textiles, clothing, and machinery. Former names: Czernowitz (before 1918), Cernăuţi (1918–1940, when it was part of Romania), Chrenovitsy (1940–44).

Cherokee member of a North ◊American Indian people, formerly living in the S Allegheny Mountains of what is now Alabama, the Carolinas, Georgia, and Tennessee. Their scholarly leader Sequoyah (c. 1770–1843) devised the syllabary used for writing their language. Their language belongs to the Iroquoian family.

In 1829 they were transported to a reservation

in Oklahoma, by forced march, the Trail of Tears, by order of President Andrew Jackson as a punishment for aiding the British during the American Revolution. In 1984, they were permitted to reestablish a tribal center in North Carolina.

cherry any of various trees of the genus *Prunus*, of the rose family, distinguished from plums and apricots by their fruits, which are spherical and smooth and not covered with a bloom.

Most cultivated cherries come from Europe. The common chokecherry *P. virginiana* is a widespread wild cherry tree of the US.

Cherry Orchard, The a play by Anton Chekhov, first produced 1904. Its theme is the demise of the way of life of a landowning family, symbolized by the felling of a cherry orchard after it has been sold to an entrepreneur.

cherub (Hebrew *kerubh*) a type of angel in Christian belief, usually depicted as a young child with wings. Cherubim form the second order of ◊angels.

Cherubini Luigi (Carlo Zanobi Salvadore Maria) 1760–1842. Italian composer. His first opera *Quinto Fabio* 1779 was produced at Alessandria. In 1784 he went to London and became composer to King George III, but from 1788 he lived in Paris, where he produced a number of dramatic works including *Médée* 1797, *Les Deux Journées* 1800, and the ballet *Anacréon* 1803. After 1809 he devoted himself largely to church music.

chervil several plants of the carrot family Umbelliferae. The garden chervil *Anthriscus cerefolium* has leaves with a sweetish odor, resembling parsley. It is used as a garnish and in soups.

Chesapeake Bay largest of the inlets on the Atlantic coast of the US, bordered by Maryland and Virginia. It is about 200 mi/320 km in length and 4–40 mi/6–64 km in width. Among the rivers that flow into the bay are the James, York, Potomac, Rappahannock, Patuxent, and Susquehanna. Deepwater ports on the bay are Newport News, Norfolk, Portsmouth, and Baltimore. The Chesapeake and Delaware Canal links the bay to the Delaware river and the Wilmington-Philadelphia port area. The Chesapeake Bay Bridge Tunnel connects both Virginia shores; farther north the Chesapeake Bay Bridge links the W Maryland shore near Annapolis to Kent Island. Pollution has greatly diminished the once-bountiful shellfish in the bay.

chess board game originating as early as the 2nd century AD. Two players use 16 pieces each, on a board of 64 squares of alternating color, to try and force the opponent into a position where the main piece (the king) is threatened, and cannot move to another position without remaining threatened.

The Fédération Internationale des Echecs (FIDE) was established 1924. Leading players are rated according to the Elo System, and Bobby Fischer (USA) is considered to be one of the greatest Grand Masters of all time with a rating of 2,785.

Chess originated in India, and spread to Russia, China, Japan, and Iran, and from there was introduced to the Mediterranean area by Arab invaders. It reached Britain in the 12th century via Spain and Italy. The first official world championships were recognized in 1886.

chess: recent winners

World champions	
men	
1957	Vassily Smyslov *(USSR)*
1958	Mikhail Botvinnik *(USSR)*
1960	Mikhail Tal *(USSR)*
1961	Mikhail Botvinnik *(USSR)*
1963	Tigran Petrosian *(USSR)*
1969	Boris Spassky *(USSR)*
1972	Bobby Fischer *(USA)*
1975	Anatoly Karpov *(USSR)*
1985	Gary Kasparov *(USSR)*
women	
1950	Lyudmila Rudenko *(USSR)*
1953	Elizaveta Bykova *(USSR)*
1955	Olga Runtsova *(USSR)*
1958	Elizaveta Bykova *(USSR)*
1962	Nona Gaprindashvili *(USSR)*
1978	Maya Chiburdanidze *(USSR)*

chervil

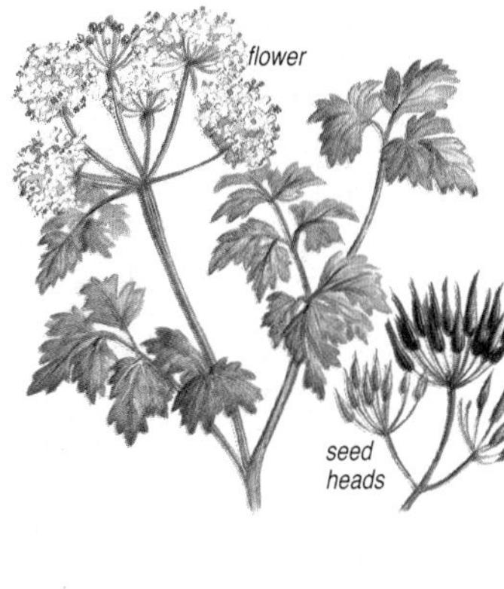
flower
seed heads

Chernobyl *The damaged nuclear reactor at the Chernobyl power plant near Kiev, Ukraine, in 1986. Radioactive materials were dispersed by air and water throughout the world.*

Chester city in Cheshire, England, on the river Dee 16 mi/26 km S of Liverpool; population (1984) 117,000. It is the administrative headquarters of Cheshire. Industries include engineering and the manufacture of car components. Its name derives from the Roman *Castra Devana* ("the camp on the Dee"), and there are many Roman and later remains. It is the only English city to retain its city walls (2 mi/3 km long) intact. The cathedral dates from the 11th century but was restored in 1876. The church of St John the Baptist is a well-known example of early Norman architecture. The "Rows" are covered arcades dating from the Middle Ages.

Chesterfield market town of Derbyshire, England; 25 mi/40 km N of Derby, on the Rother river; population (1981) 78,200. Industries include coal-mining, engineering, and glass. It is the burial place of the engineer George ◊Stephenson. All Saints' Church is renowned for its crooked spire.

Chesterfield Philip Dormer Stanhope, 4th Earl of 1694–1773. English politician and writer, author

chess

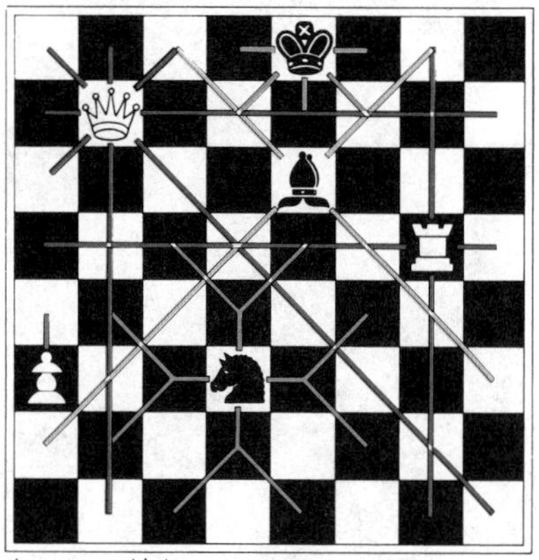

the way each piece can move

arrangement of the chessmen

of *Letters to his Son* 1774—his illegitimate son, Philip Stanhope (1732–68).

A member of the literary circle of Swift, Pope, and Bolingbroke, he incurred the wrath of Dr Samuel ◊Johnson by failing to carry out an offer of patronage.

Chesterton G(ilbert) K(eith) 1874–1936. English novelist, essayist, and satirical poet, author of a series of novels featuring the naive priest-detective Father Brown. Other novels include *The Napoleon of Notting Hill* 1904 and *The Man Who Knew Too Much* 1922.

chestnut tree of the genus *Castanea*, belonging to the beech family Fagaceae. The Spanish or sweet chestnut *C. sativa* produces edible nuts inside husks; its timber is also valuable. Horse chestnuts are quite distinct, belonging to the genus *Aesculus*, family Hippocastanaceae.

Horse chestnuts are also called buckeyes. The American chestnut *C. dentata* was a valued hardwood until it was virtually destroyed by an introduced fungus.

Chetnik member of a Serbian nationalist group that operated underground during the German occupation of Yugoslavia during World War II. Led by Col Draza ◊Mihailovič, the Chetniks initially received aid from the Allies, but this was later transferred to the communist partisans led by Tito.

Chevalier Maurice 1888–1972. French singer and actor. He began as dancing partner to the revue artiste ◊Mistinguett at the ◊Folies-Bergère, and made numerous films including *Innocents of Paris* 1929, which revived his song "Louise," *The Merry Widow* 1934, and *Gigi* 1958.

chestnut

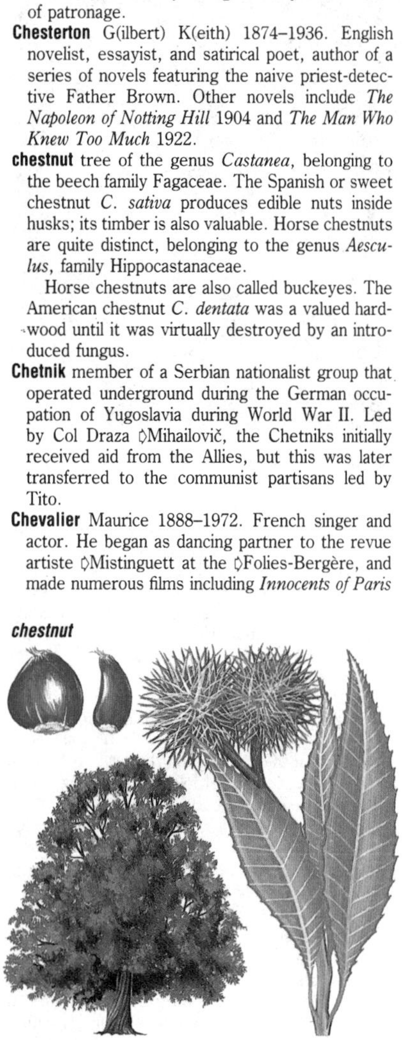

Cheviots range of hills 35 mi/56 km long, mainly in Northumberland, forming the border between England and Scotland for some 30 mi/48 km. The highest point is the Cheviot, 2,676 ft/816 m. For centuries the area was a battleground between the English and the Scots. It gives its name to a breed of sheep.

Chevreul Michel-Eugene 1786–1889. French chemist who studied the composition of fats and identified a number of fatty acids, including "margaric acid," which became the basis of margarine.

Chevreul was Director of the Natural History Museum and Director of Dyeing at the Gobelin tapestry factory.

chewing gum gummy confectionery to be chewed not swallowed. It is composed mainly of chicle (milky juice of the tropical sapodilla tree *Achras zapota* of Central America), usually flavored with mint, sweetened, and pressed flat. The first patent was taken out in the US in 1871. Bubble gum is a variety that allows chewers to blow bubbles.

Cheyenne capital of Wyoming, located in the SE part of the state, just N of the Colorado border in the foothills of the Laramie Mountains. An agricultural and transportation center, its industries include oil refining, fertilizers, electronics, restaurant equipment, and ceramics. Tourism is also important to the economy; population (1990) 50,008.

Chiang Ching alternate spelling of ◊Jiang Qing, Chinese actress, third wife of Mao.

Chiang Ching-kuo 1910–1988. Taiwanese politician, son of Chiang Kai-shek, prime minister 1971–78, president 1978–88.

Chiang Kai-shek Pinyin *Jiang Jie Shi* 1887–1975. Chinese Nationalist ◊Guomindang (Kuomintang) general and politician, president of China 1928–31 and 1943–49, and of Taiwan from 1949, where he set up a US-supported right-wing government on his expulsion from the mainland by the Communist forces. He was a commander in the civil war that lasted from the end of imperial rule 1911 to the Second ◊Sino-Japanese War and beyond, having split with the Communist leader Mao Zedong 1927.

Chiang took part in the revolution of 1911 that overthrew the Qing dynasty of the Manchus, and on the death of the Nationalist Guomindang leader Sun Yat-sen was made commander in chief of the Nationalist armies in S China 1925. Collaboration with the communists, broken 1927, was resumed after the ◊Xian incident 1936, when China needed to pool military strength, and Chiang nominally headed the struggle against the Japanese invaders of World War II, receiving the Japanese surrender 1945. The following year, civil war between the Nationalists and Communists erupted, and in Dec 1949 Chiang and his followers took refuge on the island of Taiwan, maintaining a large army in the hope of reclaiming the mainland. His authoritarian regime enjoyed US support until his death. His son, Chiang Ching-kuo, then became president.

Chiba industrial city (paper, steel, textiles) in Kanton region, E Honshu island, Japan, 25 mi/40 km W of Tokyo; population (1987) 793,000.

Chibcha member of a South American Indian people of Colombia, whose high chiefdom was conquered by the Spanish in 1538. Their practice of covering their chief with gold dust, during rituals, fostered the legend of the "Lost City" of El Dorado (the Golden), which was responsible for many failed expeditions into the interior of the continent.

Chicago financial and industrial (iron, steel, chemicals, electrical goods, machinery, meatpacking and food processing, publishing, fabricated metals, machinery) city in Illinois, on Lake Michigan; third largest US city; population (1990) 2,783,726, metropolitan area (1990) 8,065,063. The famous stockyards are now closed.

The world's first skyscraper was built here 1885 and some of the world's tallest skyscrapers, including the tallest, the Sears Tower, 1,454 ft/443 m, were built here. The Museum of Science and Industry, opened 1893, has "hands-on" exhibits including a coal mine, a World War II U-boat, an Apollo spacecraft and lunar module, and exhibits by industrial firms. The Chicago River cuts the city into three "sides." Chicago is known as the Windy City, so called from the breezes of Lake Michigan, as well as from its citizens' (and, allegedly, politicians') voluble talk; the lake shore ("the Gold Coast") is occupied by luxury apartment buildings. It has a renowned symphony orchestra, an art institute, the University of Chicago (site of the first controlled nuclear reaction), DePaul and Loyola universities, a campus of the University of Illinois, and the Illinois Institute of Technology. Chicago-O'Hare International Airport is the nation's busiest. The Board of Trade, Mercantile Exchange, and Options Exchange are among the world's largest commodity markets.

***Chiang Kai-shek** Chinese nationalist leader Chiang Kai-shek fought a bitter war against the communist troops of Mao Zedong before leaving mainland China to form his own government on Taiwan in 1949.*

The site of Chicago was visited by Jesuit missionaries 1673, and Fort Dearborn, then a frontier fort, was built here 1803. The original layout of Chicago was a rectangular grid, but many outer boulevards have been constructed on less rigid lines. As late as 1831 Chicago was still an insignificant village, but railroads from the E coast reached it by 1852, and by 1871, when it suffered a disastrous fire, it was a city of more than 300,000 inhabitants. Rapid development began again in the 1920s, and during the years of Prohibition 1919–33, the city became notorious for the activities of its gangsters. The opening of the St Lawrence Seaway 1959 brought Atlantic shipping to its docks.

Chicago School of Sociology the first university department of sociology, founded in Chicago 1892, under Albion Small. He was succeeded by Robert E Park, who with W I Thomas, Ernest Burgess, Louis Wirth, and R McKenzie created a center for the social sciences in the 1920s and 1930s, studying urban life, including crime and deviance in Chicago, with its variety of urban communities, lifestyles, and ethnic subcultures.

A neo-Chicagoan school emerged in the 1940s under Erving Goffman and Howard Becker.

Chicano a citizen or resident of the US of Mexican descent. The term was originally used for those who became US citizens after the ◊Mexican War.

Chichen Itzá Toltec city situated among the Mayan city-states of Yucatán, Mexico. It flourished AD 900–1200 and displays Classic and Post-

***Chichen Itzá** The main pyramid of Chichen Itzá, a Mayan/Toltec city in Yucatán, Mexico, is a stepped pyramid with a long stairway leading to a temple at the summit.*

Classic architecture of the Toltec style. The site has temples with sculptures and color reliefs, an observatory, and a sacred well into which sacrifices, including human beings, were cast.

Chichester city and market town in Sussex; 69 mi/111 km SW of London, near Chichester Harbor; population (1981) 24,000. It is the administrative headquarters of West Sussex. It was a Roman township, and the remains of the Roman palace built around AD 80 at nearby Fishbourne are unique outside Italy. There is a cathedral consecrated 1108, later much rebuilt and restored, and the Chichester Festival Theatre (1962).

chicken domestic fowl, domesticated form of the SE Asian jungle fowl *Gallis gallis*; see under ◊poultry.

chickenpox or ***varicella*** common acute disease, caused by a virus of the ◊herpes group and transmitted by airborne droplets. Chickenpox chiefly attacks children under ten. The incubation period is two to three weeks. One attack normally gives immunity for life.

The temperature rises and spots (later inflamed blisters) develop on the torso, then on the face and limbs. The sufferer recovers within a week, but remains infectious until the last scab disappears.

chickpea annual plant *Cicer arietinum*, family Leguminosae, which is grown for food in India, the Middle East, and the Mediterranean region. Its short, hairy pods contain edible pealike seeds.

chickweed any of several low-growing plants of the genera *Stellaria* and *Cerastium* of the pink family Caryophyllaceae, with small, white, starlike flowers.

Chiclayo capital of Lambayeque department, NW Peru; population (1988) 395,000.

chicle milky juice from the sapodilla tree *Achras zapota* of Central America; it forms the basis of chewing gum.

Chico city in N California, NW of Sacramento. Situated in the fertile Sacramento Valley, a farming region, its industries include food processing and lumber products; population (1990) 40,079.

chicory European plant *Cichorium intybus* of the family Compositae. It grows mainly on chalky soils and has large, usually blue, flowers. Its long taproot is used dried and roasted as a coffee substitute. The blanched leaves are used in salads. Endive, escarole, and radicchio are domesticated forms of chicory.

Chiengmai or ***Chiang Mai*** town in N Thailand; population (1982) 104,910. There is a trade in teak and lac (as shellac, a resin used in varnishes and polishes) and many handicraft industries. It is the former capital of the Lan Na Thai kingdom.

chiffchaff bird *Phylloscopus collybita* of the warbler family, found in woodlands and thickets in Europe and N Asia during the summer, migrating south for winter. About 4.3 in/11 cm long, olive above, greyish below, with an eyestripe and usually dark legs, it looks similar to a willow-warbler but has a distinctive song.

Chifley Ben (Joseph Benedict) 1885–1951. Australian Labor prime minister 1945–49. He united the party in fulfilling a welfare and nationalization program 1945–49 (although he failed in an attempt to nationalize the banks 1947) and initiated an immigration program and the Snowy Mountains hydroelectric project.

chigger or ***harvest mite*** scarlet or rusty brown ◊mite of the family Trombiculidae, common in summer and autumn. Their tiny red larvae cause intensely irritating bites.

chihuahua smallest breed of dog, developed in the US from Mexican origins. It may weigh only 2.2 lb/1 kg. The domed head and wide set ears are characteristic, and the skull is large compared to the body. It can be almost any color, and occurs in both smooth (or even hairless) and long-coated varieties.

Chihuahua capital of Chihuahua state, Mexico, 800 mi/1,285 km NW of Mexico City; population (1984) 375,000. Founded in 1707, it is the center of a mining district and has textile mills. The University of Chihuahua is here. The revolutionary leader Pancho Villa had his headquarters here during the early 20th century, and his home is a tourist attraction.

chilblain painful inflammation of the skin of the feet, hands, or ears, due to cold. The parts turn red, swell, itch violently, and are very tender. In bad cases, the skin cracks, blisters, or ulcerates.

Child Lydia Maria 1802–1880. US author and social critic. She is perhaps best remembered for her feminism and popular women's guides *The Frugal Housewife* 1829 and *The Mother's Book* 1831. With her husband, David Child, she worked for the abolitionist cause, advocating educational support for black Americans. The Childs also edited the weekly *National Anti-Slavery Standard* 1840–44.

Born in Medford, Massachusetts, Child received little formal education but read widely and published several historical novels about life in colonial New England.

child abuse the molesting of children by parents and other adults. It can give rise to various criminal charges and has become a growing concern since the early 1980s.

childbirth the expulsion of a baby from its mother's body following ◊pregnancy. In a broader sense, it is the period of time involving labor and delivery of the baby, plus the effort and pain involved.

Child, Convention on the Rights of the United Nations document designed to make the wellbeing of children an international obligation. It was adopted 1989 and covers children from birth up to 18.

It laid down international standards for:
provision of a name, nationality, health care, education, rest, and play;
protection from commercial or sexual exploitation, physical or mental abuse, and engagement in warfare;
participation in decisions affecting a child's own future.

Childe V Gordon 1892–1957. Australian-born British archeologist, director of the London Institute of Archeology 1946–57. He discovered the prehistoric village of Skara Brae in the Orkneys and became the most influential synthesizer of Old World archeology with his publication *The Dawn of European Civilization* 1925. He defined ◊civilization for archeological reconstruction.

child prodigy a young person who has developed a remarkable skill, understanding or talent for one or more subjects or pursuits. Unlike ◊*idiots savants*, child prodigies are usually taught by an adult. ◊Mozart was a child prodigy of musical genius.

Children's Crusade a ◊Crusade by some 10,000 children from France, the Low Countries, and Germany, in 1212, to recapture Jerusalem for Christianity. Motivated by religious piety, many of them were sold into slavery or died of disease.

children's literature works specifically written for children. The earliest known illustrated children's book in English is *Goody Two Shoes* 1765, possibly written by Oliver Goldsmith. Fairy tales were originally part of a vast range of oral literature, credited only to the writer who first recorded them, such as Charles Perrault. During the 19th century several writers, including Hans Christian Andersen, wrote original stories in the fairy tale genre; others, such as the Grimm brothers, collected (and sometimes adapted) existing stories.

Early children's stories were written with a moral purpose; this was particularly true in the 19th century, apart from the unique case of Lewis Carroll's *Alice* books. The late 19th century was the great era of children's literature in the UK, with Lewis Carroll, Beatrix Potter, Charles Kingsley, and J M Barrie. It was also the golden age of illustrated children's books, with such artists as Kate Greenaway and Randolph Caldecott. In the US, Louise May Alcott's *Little Women* 1868 and its sequels found a wide audience. Among the most popular 20th-century children's writers in English have been Kenneth Grahame (*The Wind in the Willows* 1908) and A A Milne (*Winnie the Pooh* 1926) in the UK; and, in the US, Laura Ingalls Wilder (*Little House on the Prairie* 1935), E B White (*Stuart Little* 1945, *Charlotte's Web* 1952), Dr Seuss (*Cat in the Hat* 1957), and Maurice Sendak (*Where the Wild Things Are* 1963). Canadian Lucy Maud Montgomery's series that began with *Anne of Green Gables* 1908 was widely popular. Adventure stories have often appealed to children even when these were written for adults; examples include *Robinson Crusoe* by Daniel Defoe; the satirical *Gulliver's Travels* by Jonathan Swift, and *Tom Sawyer* 1876 and *Huckleberry Finn* 1884 by Mark Twain.

Chile South American country, bounded N by Peru and Bolivia, E by Argentina, and S and W by the Pacific Ocean.

government Since 1973 Chile has been ruled by a military junta. A new constitution announced 1981 took effect 1989. It provides for the election of a president for an eight-year, nonrenewable term and a legislature consisting of a senate with 26 elected and nine appointed members and a

Chile
Republic of
(República de Chile)

Peru
Bolivia
PACIFIC
OCEAN
ATLANTIC
OCEAN
CHILE
Santiago
Argentina
0 500 miles
0 1000 km

area 292,257 sq mi/756,950 sq km
capital Santiago
cities Concepción, Viña del Mar, Temuco; ports Valparaiso, Antofagasta, Arica, Iquique and Punta Arenas
physical Andes mountains along E border, Atacama Desert in N, fertile central valley, grazing land and forest in S
territories Easter Island, Juan Fernandez Islands, half of Tierra del Fuego, claim to part of Antarctica
features Atacama Desert is one of the driest regions in the world
head of state and government Patricio Aylwin from 1990
political system emergent democracy
political parties Christian Democratic Party (PDC), moderate centrist; National Renewal Party (RN), right-wing
exports copper (world's leading producer), iron, molybdenum (world's second-largest producer), nitrate, pulp and paper, steel products, fishmeal, fruit
currency peso
population (1990 est) 13,000,000 (the majority are of European origin or are mestizos, of mixed American Indian and Spanish descent); growth rate 1.6% p.a.
life expectancy men 64, women 73
language Spanish
religion Roman Catholic 89%
literacy 94% (1988)
GDP $18.9 bn (1987); $6,512 per head
chronology
1818 Achieved independence from Spain.
1964 PDC formed government under Eduardo Frei.
1970 Dr Salvador Allende became the first democratically elected Marxist president; he embarked on an extensive program of nationalization and social reform.
1973 Government overthrown by the CIA-backed military, led by Gen Augusto Pinochet. Allende killed. Policy of repression began during which all opposition was put down and political activity banned.
1983 Growing opposition to the regime from all sides, with outbreaks of violence.
1988 Referendum on whether Pinochet should serve a further term resulted in a clear "No" vote.
1989 President Pinochet agreed to constitutional changes to allow pluralist politics; elections in Dec replaced Pinochet with Patricio Aylwin, a Christian Democrat; Pinochet remained as army commander.
1990 Salvador Allende officially restored to favor. Aylwin reached accord on end to military junta government. Pinochet censured by president.

chamber of deputies with 120 elected members, all serving four-year terms. Marxist and "totalitarian" groups and political activity were all banned until 1989. Strikes in the public services are not allowed, and the economy is based on "free market principles."

history The area now known as Chile was originally occupied by the Araucanian Indians and invaded by the ◊Incas in the 15th century. The first European to reach it was ◊Magellan, who in 1520 sailed through the strait now named after him. A Spanish expedition under Pedro de Valdivia founded Santiago 1541, and Chile was subsequently colonized by Spanish settlers who established an agricultural society, although the Indians continued to rebel until the late 19th century. Becoming independent from Spain 1818, Chile went to war with Peru and Bolivia 1879 and gained considerable territory from them.

Most of the 20th century has been characterized by left- versus right-wing struggles. The Christian Democrats under Eduardo Frei held power 1964–70, followed by a left-wing coalition led by Dr Salvador ◊Allende, the first democratically elected Marxist head of state. He promised social justice by constitutional means and began nationalizing industries, including US-owned copper mines.

The ◊CIA saw Allende as a pro-Cuban communist and encouraged opposition to him. In 1973 the army, led by General Augusto ◊Pinochet, overthrew the government. Allende was killed or, as the new regime claimed, committed suicide. Pinochet became president, and his opponents were tortured, imprisoned, or just "disappeared." In 1976 Pinochet proclaimed an "authoritarian democracy" and in 1977 banned all political parties. His policies were "endorsed" by a referendum 1978.

In 1980 a "transition to democracy" by 1989 was announced, but imprisonment and torture continued. By 1983 opposition to Pinochet had increased, with demands for a return to democratic government. He attempted to placate opposition by initiating public works. In 1984 an antigovernment bombing campaign began, aimed mainly at electricity installations, resulting in a 90-day state of emergency, followed by a 90-day state of siege. In 1985, as opposition grew in the Catholic Church and the army as well as among the public, another state of emergency was declared, but the bombings and killings continued.

In Oct 1988 Pinochet's proposal to remain in office for another eight-year term was rejected in a plebiscite. Another plebiscite in Aug 1989 approved constitutional changes leading to a return to pluralist politics and in Dec the moderate PDC candidate, Patricio Aylwin Azocar, was elected president, his term of office beginning March 1990. Pinochet demanded the retention of his post as army commander in chief after his relinquishment of the presidency.

In Jan 1990, the junta approved the disbanding of the secret police of the National Information Center (CNI). The CNI, which replaced the National Information Bureau (DINA) in 1977, is regarded as responsible for 170 assassinations, 1,300 cases of torture, 2,000 illegal detentions, and threats to or illegal surveillance of 4,000 people in its last four years of existence. In Sept 1990 a government commission was set up to investigate some 2,000 political executions 1973–78, 500 political murders 1978–90, and 700 disappearances. In the same month the former discredited politician Salvador Allende was officially recognized by being buried in a marked grave. In the same month President Aylwin censured General Pinochet for trying to return to active politics.

Chilean Revolution in Chile, the presidency of Salvador ◊Allende 1970–73, the Western hemisphere's first democratically elected Marxist-oriented president of an independent state.

chili (North American chili) the pod, or powder made from the pod, of a variety of ◊capsicum, *Capsicum frutescens*, a hot, red pepper.

chiliasm another word for millenarianism; see ◊millennium.

Chilterns range of chalk hills in England, extending for some 45 mi/72 km in a curve from a point north of Reading to the Suffolk border. Coombe Hill, near Wendover, 852 ft/260 m high, is the highest point.

chimaera fish of the group Holocephali. They have thick bodies that taper to a long thin tail, large fins, smooth skin, and a cartilaginous skeleton. They can grow to 4.5 ft/1.5 m. Most chimaeras are deep-water fish, and even *Chimaera monstrosa*, a relatively shallow-living form caught around European coasts, lives at a depth of 1,000–1,600 ft/300–500 m.

Chimbote largest fishing port in Peru; population (1981) 216,000.

chimera in biology, an organism composed of tissues that are genetically different. Chimeras can develop naturally if a ◊mutation occurs in a cell of a developing embryo, but are more commonly produced artificially by implanting cells from one organism into the embryo of another.

chimera or ***chimaera*** in Greek mythology, a fire-breathing animal with a lion's head, a goat's body, and tail in the form of a snake; hence any apparent hybrid of two or more creatures. The chimera was killed by the hero Bellerophon on the winged horse Pegasus.

chimpanzee highly intelligent African ape *Pan troglodytes* that lives mainly in rainforests but sometimes in wooded savannah. They are covered in thin but long black body hair, except for the face, hands, and feet, which may have pink or black skin. Chimpanzees normally walk on all fours, supporting the front of the body on the knuckles of the fingers, but can stand or walk upright for a short distance. They can grow to 4.5 ft/1.4 m tall, and weigh up to 110 lb/50 kg. They are strong, and climb well, but spend time on the ground. They live in loose social groups. The bulk of the diet is fruit, with some leaves, insects, and occasional meat. Chimpanzees can use "tools," fashioning twigs to extract termites from their nests. Chimpanzees are found in an area from W Africa to W Uganda and Tanzania in the east. Studies of chromosomes suggest that chimpanzees are the closest apes to humans, perhaps sharing 99% of the same genes. They can communicate with humans when carefully taught and with the aid of machines or sign language, but are probably precluded from human speech by the position of the voicebox.

Chimu South American civilization that flourished on the coast of Peru from about 1250 to about 1470, when they were conquered by the Incas. They produced fine work in gold, realistic portrait pottery, savage fanged feline images in clay, and possibly a system of writing or recording by painting patterns on beans. They built aqueducts carrying water many miles, and the huge, mazelike city of Chan Chan, 14 sq mi/36 sq km, on the coast near Trujillo.

The Chimu people built enormous adobe brick mounds or *huacas* as the base of temples and palaces. Chan Chan consists of nine complexes, probably built by successive kings to form their eventual tombs. Their agricultural system depended on extensive irrigation; the invading Incas ensured victory by cutting the Chimu aqueducts.

China the largest country in E Asia, bounded N by Mongolia; NW and NE by the USSR; SW by

Chimu *A pottery vessel in the shape of a pan-piper from the ancient Peruvian civilization of Chimu.*

India and Nepal; S by Bhutan, Myanmar (Burma), Laos, and Vietnam; SE by the South China Sea; and E by the East China Sea, North Korea, and the USSR.

government China is divided into 21 provinces, five autonomous regions, and three municipalities (Beijing, Shanghai, and Tianjin), each with an elected local people's government with policy-making power in defined areas.

Ultimate authority resides in the single-chamber National People's Congress (NPC), composed of 2,970 deputies indirectly elected every five years through local people's congresses. Deputies to local people's congresses are directly elected through universal suffrage in constituency contests. The NPC, the "highest organ of state power," meets annually and elects a permanent, 133-member committee to assume its functions between sittings. The committee has an inner body comprising a chairman and 19 vice chairmen. The NPC also elects for a five-year term a State Central Military Commission (SCMC), leading members of the judiciary, the vice-president, and the state president, who must be at least 45 years of age. The president is restricted to two terms in office and performs primarily ceremonial functions. Executive administration is effected by a prime minister and a cabinet (state council) that includes three vice premiers, 31 departmental ministers, eight commission chiefs, an auditor-general, and a secretary general, and is appointed by the NPC.

China's controlling force is the Chinese Communist Party (CCP). It has a parallel hierarchy comprising elected congresses and committees functioning from village level upward and taking orders from above. A national party congress every five years elects a 285-member central committee (175 of whom have full voting powers) that meets twice a year and elects an 18-member Politburo and 5-member secretariat to exercise day-to-day control over the party and to frame state and party policy goals. The Politburo meets weekly and is China's most significant political body.

history for early history see ◊China, history. Imperial rule ended in 1911 with the formation of a republic in 1912. After several years of civil war the nationalist ◊Guomindang, led by ◊Chiang Kai-shek, was firmly installed in power in 1926, with communist aid. In 1927 Chiang Kai-shek began a purge of the communists, who began the "Long March" (1934–36) to Shaanxi, which became their base.

In 1931 Japan began its penetration of Manchuria and in 1937 began the second ◊Sino-Japanese War, during which both communists and nationalists fought Japan. Civil war resumed after the Japanese surrender in 1945, until in 1949, following their elimination of nationalist resistance on the mainland, the communists inaugurated the People's Republic of China, the nationalists having retired to ◊Taiwan.

To begin with, the communist regime concentrated on economic reconstruction. A centralized Soviet-style constitution was adopted in 1954, industries were nationalized, and central planning and moderate land reform introduced. The USSR provided economic aid, while China intervened in the ◊Korean War. Development during this period was based on material incentives and industrialization.

From 1958, under state president and CCP chairman ◊Mao Zedong, China embarked on a major new policy, the ◊Great Leap Forward. This created large self-sufficient agricultural and industrial communes in an effort to achieve classless "true communism." The experiment proved unpopular and impossible to coordinate, and over 20 million people died in the floods and famines of 1959–62. A breach in Sino-Soviet relations brought a withdrawal of Soviet technical advisers in 1960.

The failure of the "Great Leap" reduced Mao's influence 1962–65, and a successful "recovery program" was begun under President Liu Shaoqi. Private farming plots and markets were reintroduced, communes reduced in size, and income differentials and material incentives restored.

Mao struck back against what he saw as a return to capitalism by launching the Great Proletarian Cultural Revolution (1966–69), a "rectification campaign" directed against "rightists" in

China
People's Republic of
(Zhonghua Renmin Gonghe Guo)

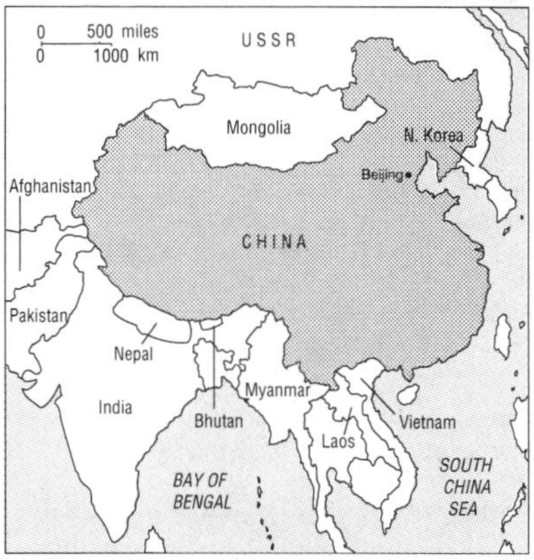
0 500 miles
0 1000 km
USSR
Mongolia
N. Korea
Beijing
Afghanistan
CHINA
Pakistan
Nepal
India
Myanmar
Bhutan
Laos
Vietnam
BAY OF BENGAL
SOUTH CHINA SEA

area 3,599,975 sq mi/9,596,960 sq km
capital Beijing (Peking)
cities Chongqing (Chungking), Shenyang (Mukden), Wuhan, Nanjing (Nanking), Harbin; ports Tianjin (Tientsin), Shanghai, Qingdao (Tsingtao), Lüda (Lü-ta), Guangzhou (Canton)
physical two-thirds of China is mountains or desert (N and W); the low-lying E is irrigated by rivers Huang He (Yellow River), Chang Jiang (Yangtze-Kiang), Xi Jiang (Si Kiang)
features Great Wall of China; Gezhouba Dam; Ming Tombs; Terra-Cotta Warriers (Xi'ain); Gobi Desert; world's most populous country
head of state Yang Shangkun from 1988
head of government Li Peng from 1987
political system communist republic
political parties Chinese Communist Party (CCP), Marxist-Leninist-Maoist
exports tea, livestock and animal products, silk, cotton, oil, minerals (China is the world's largest producer of tungsten and antimony), chemicals, light industrial goods
currency yuan
population (1990 est) 1,130,065,000 (the majority are Han or ethnic Chinese; the 67 million of other ethnic groups, including Tibetan, Uigur, and Zhuang, live in border areas). The number of people of Chinese origin outside China, Taiwan, and Hong Kong is estimated at 15–24 million. Growth rate 1.2% p.a.
life expectancy men 67, women 69
language Chinese, including Mandarin (official), Cantonese and other dialects
religion officially atheist, but traditionally Taoist, Confucianist, and Buddhist; Muslim 13 million; Catholic 3–6 million (divided between the "patriotic" church established 1958 and the "loyal" church subject to Rome); Protestant 3 million
literacy men 82%/women 66% (1985 est)
GDP $293.4 bn (1987); $274 per head

chronology
1949 People's Republic of China proclaimed by Mao Zedong.
1954 Soviet-style constitution adopted.
1956–57 Hundred Flowers Movement encouraged criticism of the government.
1958–60 Great Leap Forward commune experiment to achieve "true communism."
1960 Withdrawal of Soviet technical advisers.
1962 Sino-Indian border war.
1962–65 Economic recovery program under Liu Shaoqi; Maoist "Socialist education movement" rectification campaign.
1966–68 Great Proletarian Cultural Revolution and overthrow of Liu Shaoqi.
1969 Ussuri River border clashes with USSR.
1970–76 Reconstruction under Mao and Zhou Enlai; purge of extreme left.
1971 Entry into United Nations.
1972 US president Nixon visited Beijing.
1975 New state constitution. Unveiling of Zhou's Four Modernizations program.
1976 Deaths of Zhou Enlai and Mao Zedong; appointment of Hua Guofeng as prime minister and Communist party chairman. Deng in hiding. Gang of Four arrested.
1977 Rehabilitation of Deng Xiaoping.
1979 Economic reforms introduced. Diplomatic relations opened with USA. Punitive invasion of Vietnam.
1980 Zhao Ziyang appointed prime minister.
1981 Hu Yaobang succeeded Hua as party chair. Imprisonment of Gang of Four.
1982 New state constitution adopted.
1984 "Enterprise management" reforms for industrial sector.
1986 Student prodemocracy demonstrations.
1987 Hu was replaced as party leader by Zhao, with Li Peng as prime minister. Deng left Politburo but remained influential.
1988 Yang Shangkun became state president. Economic reforms encountered increasing problems; inflation rocketed.
1989 Following the death of Hu Yaobang, prodemocracy student demonstrations in Tiananmen Square, Beijing, were crushed by army, who killed over 2,000 demonstrators. Martial law was declared in Beijing; international sanctions applied; Zhao ousted, replaced as party leader by Jiang Zemin; hardline faction consolidated power; Deng retired from remaining army and party posts but received high-level US delegation.
1991 Having given considerable support to the US line on the Gulf crisis, China was no longer subject to sanctions from the European Community or Japan. Normal relations with USSR resumed. Jiang Qing died, allegedly committing suicide. UK prime minister John Major visited Beijing to sign agreement on new Hong Kong airport—he was the first Western leader to visit China since the Tiananmen Square massacre.

the CCP that sought to re-establish the supremacy of (Maoist) ideology over economics. During the campaign, Mao, supported by People's Liberation Army (PLA) chief ◊Lin Biao and the Shanghai-based ◊Gang of Four (comprising Mao's wife Jiang Qing, radical intellectuals Zhang Chunqiao and Yao Wenyuan, and former millworker Wang Hongwen), encouraged student (Red Guard) demonstrations against party and government leaders.

The chief targets were Liu Shaoqi, ◊Deng Xiaoping (head of the CCP secretariat) and Peng Zhen (mayor of Beijing). All were forced out of office. The campaign grew anarchic during 1967, necessitating PLA intervention and the dispersal of Red Guards into the countryside to "learn from the peasants." Government institutions fell into abeyance during the Cultural Revolution, and new "Three Part Revolutionary Committees," comprising Maoist party officials, labor unionists and PLA commanders, took over administration.

By 1970, Mao sided with pragmatic Prime Minister ◊Zhou Enlai and began restoring order and a more balanced system. A number of "ultra-leftists" were ousted in 1970, and in 1971 Lin Biao died en route to Mongolia after a failed coup. In 1972–73 Deng Xiaoping, finance minister Li Xiannian, and others were rehabilitated, and a policy of détente toward the US began. This reconstruction movement was climaxed by the summoning of the NPC in 1975 for the first time in 11 years to ratify a new constitution and approve an economic plan termed the "Four Modernizations"–agriculture, industry, defense, and science and technology–that aimed at placing China on a par with the West by the year 2000.

The deaths of Zhou Enlai and Mao Zedong in 1976 unleashed a violent succession struggle between the leftist Gang of Four, led by Jiang Qing, and moderate "rightists," grouped around vice-premier Deng Xiaoping. Deng was forced into hiding by the Gang; and Mao's moderate protegé ◊Hua Guofeng became CCP chair and head of government in 1976. Hua arrested the Gang on charges of treason and held power 1976–78 as a stop-gap leader, continuing Zhou Enlai's modernization program.

His authority was progressively challenged, however, by Deng Xiaoping, who returned to office in 1977 after campaigns in Beijing. By 1979, after further popular campaigns, Deng had gained effective charge of the government, controlling a majority in the Politburo. State and judicial bodies began to meet again, Liu Shaoqi was rehabilitated as a party hero, and economic reforms were introduced. These involved the dismantling of the commune system, the introduction of direct farm incentives under a new "responsibility system," and the encouragement of foreign investment in "Special Economic Zones" in coastal enclaves. By June 1981 Deng's supremacy was assured when his protegés ◊Hu Yaobang and ◊Zhao Ziyang became party chair and prime minister and the Gang of Four were sentenced to life imprisonment (Yao Wenyuan received 20 years).

In 1982, Hua Guofeng and a number of senior colleagues were ousted from the Politburo, and the NPC adopted a definitive constitution, restoring the post of state president (abolished since 1975) and establishing a new civil rights code. The new administration was a collective leadership, with Hu Yaobang in control of party affairs, Zhao Ziyang overseeing state administration, and Deng Xiaoping (a party vice-chair and SCMC chair) formulating long-term strategy and supervising the PLA.

The triumvirate pursued a three-pronged policy aimed firstly at streamlining the party and state bureaucracies and promoting to power new, younger, and better-educated technocrats. By 1986 half the CCP's provincial-level officers had been replaced. Secondly, they sought to curb PLA influence by retiring senior commanders and reducing manpower numbers from 4.2 to 3 million. Thirdly, they gave priority to economic modernization by extending market incentives and local autonomy and by introducing a new "open door" policy to encourage foreign trade and investment.

These economic reforms met with substantial success in the agricultural sector (output more than doubled 1978–85) but had adverse side effects, widening regional and social income differentials and fueling a wave of "mass consumerism" that created balance of payments problems. Contact with the West brought demands for full-scale democratization in China. These calls led in 1986 to widespread student demonstrations, and party chief Hu Yaobang was dismissed in 1987 for failing to check the disturbances. Hu's departure imperiled the post-Dengist reform program, as conservative forces, grouped around the veteran Politburo members Chen Yun and Peng Zhen, sought to halt the changes and reestablish central party control, evidenced during 1987 by the launching of a campaign against "bourgeois liberalization" (Western ideas).

Chen Yun, Peng Zhen, and Deng Xiaoping all retired from the Politburo in Oct 1987, and soon after ◊Li Peng (the adopted son of Zhou Enlai) took over as prime minister, Zhao Ziyang having become CCP chairman. With inflation spiraling,

China: provinces

Province	*Former name*	*Capital*	*Area sq km*
Anhui	Anhwei	Hefei	139,900
Fujian	Fukien	Fuzhou	123,100
Gansu	Kansu	Lanzhou	530,000
Guangdong	Kwantung	Guangzhou	231,400
Guizhou	Kweichow	Guiyang	174,000
Hainan		Haikou	34,000
Hebei	Hopei	Shijiazhuang	202,700
Heilongjiang	Heilungkiang	Harbin	463,600
Henan	Honan	Zhengzhou	167,000
Hubei	Hupei	Wuhan	187,500
Hunan		Changsha	210,500
Jiangsu	Kiangsu	Nanjing	102,200
Jiangxi	Kiangsi	Nanchang	164,800
Jilin	Kirin	Changchun	187,000
Liaoning		Shenyang	151,000
Qinghai	Tsinghai	Xining	721,000
Shaanxi	Shensi	Xian	195,800
Shandong	Shantung	Jinan	153,300
Shanxi	Shansi	Taiyuan	157,100
Sichuan	Szechwan	Chengdu	569,000
Yunnan		Kunming	436,200
Zhejiang	Chekiang	Hangzhou	101,800
Autonomous Region			
Guangxi Zhuang	Kwangsi Chuang	Nanning	220,400
Nei Mongol	Inner Mongolia	Hohhot	450,000
Ningxia Hui	Ninghsia-Hui	Yinchuan	170,000
Xinjiang Uygur	Sinkiang Uighur	Urumqi	1,646,800
Xizang	Tibet	Lhasa	1,221,600
Municipality			
Beijing	Peking		17,800
Shanghai			5,800
Tianjin	Tientsin		4,000
		TOTAL	9,139,300

Chinese Dynasties

Dynasty	*Dates*	*Major Events*
Hsia	1994–1523 BC	agriculture, bronze, first writing
Shang or Yin	1523–1027	first major dynasty; first Chinese calendar
Chou	1027–255	developed society using money, iron, written laws; age of Confucius
Qin	255–206	unification after period of Warring States, building of Great Wall begun, roads built
Han	AD 206–220	first centralized and effectively administered empire; introductiion of Buddhism.
San Kuo	220–265	division into three parts, prolonged fighting (Three Kingdoms) and eventual victory of Wei over Chu and Wu; Confucianism superseded by Buddhism and Taoism
Tsin	265–420	beginning of Hun invasions in the north
Sui	581–618	reunification; barbarian invasions stopped; Great Wall refortified
T'ang	618–906	centralized government; empire greatly extended; period of excellence in sculpture, painting and poetry
Wu Tai (Five Dynasties)	907–960	economic depression and loss of territory in northern China, central Asia, and Korea; first use of paper money
Song	960–1279	period of calm and creativity; printing developed (movable type); central government restored; northern and western frontiers neglected and Mongol incursions begun
Yüan	1260–1368	beginning of Mongol rule in China, under Kublai Khan; Marco Polo visited China; dynasty brought to an end by widespread revolts, centered in Mongolia
Ming	1368–1644	Mongols driven out by native Chinese, Mongolia captured by 2nd Ming emperor; period of architectural development; Beijing flourished as new capital
Manchu	1644–1912	China once again under non-Chinese rule, the Qing conquered by nomads from Manchuria; trade with the West flourished, but conservatism eventually led to the dynasty's overthrow by nationalistic revolutionaries led by Sun Yatsen.

China, history

500,000 BC	The oldest human remains found in China were those of "Peking man" (*Sinanthropus pekinensis* now known as *Homo sapiens pekinensis* or *Homo erectus pekinensis*).
25,000 BC	Humans of the Upper Paleolithic modern type (*Homo sapiens sapiens*) inhabited the region.
5000 BC	A simple Neolithic agricultural society was established.
c. 2800–c. 2200 BC	The Sage kings, a period of agricultural development, known only from legend.
c. 2200–c. 1500 BC	The Xia dynasty, a bronze age early civilization, with further agricultural developments, including irrigation, and the first known use of writing in this area.
c. 1500–c. 1066 BC	The Shang dynasty is the first of which we have documentary evidence. Writing became well-developed; bronze vases survive in ceremonial burials. The first Chinese calendar was made.
c. 1066–221 BC	During the Zhou dynasty, the feudal structure of society broke down in a period of political upheaval, though iron, money, and written laws were all in use, and philosophy flourished (see ◊Confucius). The dynasty ended in the "Warring States" period (403–221 BC), with the country divided into small kingdoms.
221–206 BC	The Qin dynasty corresponds to the reign of Shih Huang Ti, who curbed the feudal nobility and introduced orderly bureaucratic government; he had roads and canals built and began the ◊Great Wall of China to keep out invaders from the north.
206 BC–AD 220	The Han dynasty was a long period of peace, during which territory was incorporated, the keeping of historical records was systematized, and an extensive civil service set up. Art and literature flourished, and ◊Buddhism was introduced. The first census was taken in AD 2, registering a population of 57 million. Chinese caravans traded with the Parthians.
220–581	The area was divided under Three Kingdoms: the Wei, Shu, and Wu. Confucianism was superseded by Buddhism and Taoism; glass was introduced from the West. Following prolonged fighting, the Wei became the most powerful kingdom, eventually founding the Jin dynasty (265–304), which expanded to take over from the barbarian invaders who ruled much of China at that time, but from 305 to 580 lost the territory they had gained to the Tatar invaders from the north.
581–618	Reunification came with the Sui dynasty when the government was reinstated, the barbarian invasions stopped, and the Great Wall refortified.
618–907	During the Tang dynasty the system of government became more highly developed and centralized, and the empire covered most of SE and much of central Asia. Sculpture, painting, and poetry flourished again, and trade relations were established with the Islamic world and the Byzantine Empire.
907–960	The period known as the Five Dynasties and Ten Kingdoms held war, economic depression, and loss of territory in N China, central Asia, and Korea, but printing was developed, including the first use of paper money, and porcelain traded to Islamic lands.
960–1279	The Song dynasty was a period of calm and creativity. Central government was restored, and movable type was invented. At the end of the dynasty, the northern and western frontiers were neglected, and Mongol invasions took place. Marco Polo visited the court of the Great Khan in 1275.
1279–1368	The Yuan dynasty saw the beginning of Mongol rule in China, with Kublai Khan on the throne in Beijing 1293; there were widespread revolts. Marco Polo served the Kublai Khan.
1368–1644	The Mongols were expelled by the first of the native Chinese Ming dynasty, who expanded the empire. Chinese ships sailed to the Sunda Islands 1403, Ceylon 1408, and the Red Sea 1430. Mongolia was captured by the second Ming emperor. Architecture developed and Beijing flourished as the new capital. Portuguese explorers reached Macao 1516 and Canton 1517; other Europeans followed. Chinese porcelain arrived in Europe 1580. The Jesuits reached Beijing 1600.
1644–1912	The last of the dynasties was the Manchu or Ching, who were non-Chinese nomads from Manchuria. Initially trade and culture flourished, but during the 19th century it seemed that China would be partitioned among the US and European imperialist nations, since all trade was conducted through treaty ports in their control. The ◊Boxer Rebellion 1900 against Western influence was suppressed by European troops.
1911–12	Revolution broke out, and the infant emperor Henry ◊P'u-i was deposed. For history 1911–present, see ◊Chinese Revolution and ◊China.

economic reform was halted in autumn 1988 and an austerity budget introduced in 1989. This provoked urban unrest and, following Hu Yaobang's death April 1989, a student-led pro-democracy movement was launched in Beijing that rapidly spread to provincial cities. There were mass demonstrations during the Soviet leader Mikhail Gorbachev's visit to China in May. But soon after Gorbachev's departure a brutal crackdown was launched against the demonstrators by Li Peng and President Yang Shangkun, with Deng Xiaoping's support. Martial law was proclaimed and in June 1989 more than 2,000 unarmed protesters were massacred by army troops in the capital's Tiananmen Square. Arrests, executions, martial law, and expulsion of foreign correspondents brought international condemnation and economic sanctions. The US imposed an embargo on sales of military equipment and announced the scaling-back of government contacts. Communist Party general secretary Zhao Ziyang was ousted and replaced by Jiang Zemin (the Shanghai party chief and new protegé of Deng Xiaoping), a move that consolidated the power of the hardline faction of President Yang Shangkun and Premier Li Peng. A crackdown on dissidents was launched, as the pendulum swung sharply away from reform toward conservatism. Deng officially retired from the last of his party and army posts but remained a dominant figure.

In foreign affairs, China's 1960 rift with ◊Khrushchev's Soviet Union over policy differences became irrevocable in 1962 when Russia sided with India during a brief Sino-Indian border war. Relations with the Soviet Union deteriorated further in 1969 after border clashes in the disputed Ussuri River region. China pursued ◊nonaligned strategy, projecting itself as the voice of Third World nations, although it achieved nuclear capability by 1964. During the early 1970s, concern with Soviet expansionism brought rapprochement with the US, bringing about China's entry to the UN in 1971 (at ◊Taiwan's expense), and culminating in the establishment of full Sino-American diplomatic relations in 1979. In recent years there has been a partial rapprochement with the USSR, culminating in Gorbachev's visit in May 1989. However, a new rift became evident in 1990, with the Chinese government denouncing the Soviet leader's "revisionism." In recent years there has been political decentralization and a diminishing of direct party control over government organs. Competition has been introduced into party and state elections, and nonparty bodies—such as the broad-front Chinese People's Political Consultative Conference—have been revived and inducted into the policy-making process. Until the Tiananmen Square massacre in June 1989, relations with the West were warm during the Deng administration, with economic contacts broadening. In Dec 1989 US President Bush sent a surprise mission to China, defending the contacts as an effort to prevent dangerous isolation of the Chinese and as a way to engage them in constructive peace proposals for Cambodia. China's improved relations with the USSR led to the Sino-Soviet border agreement in 1991.

China Sea area of the Pacific Ocean bordered by China, Vietnam, Borneo, the Philippines, and Japan. Various groups of small islands and shoals, including the Paracels, 300 mi/500 km E of Vietnam, have been disputed by China and other powers because they lie in oil-rich areas.

N of Taiwan it is known as the East China Sea and to the S as the South China Sea.

chincherinchee poisonous plant *Ornithogalum thyrsoides* of the lily family Liliaceae. It is native to South Africa, and has spikes of long-lasting, white or yellow, waxlike flowers.

chinchilla South American rodent *Chinchilla laniger* found in high, rather barren areas of the Andes in Bolivia and Chile. About the size of a small rabbit, it has long ears and a long bushy tail, and shelters in rock crevices. These gregarious animals have thick soft silver-gray fur, and were hunted almost to extinction for it. They are now farmed and protected in the wild.

Chindits an Indian division of the British army in World War II that carried out guerrilla operations against the Japanese in Burma (now Myanmar) under the command of Brigadier General Orde Wingate (1903–44). The name derived from the mythical Chinthay–half lion, half eagle– placed at the entrance of Burmese pagodas to scare away evil spirits.

Chinese native to or an inhabitant of China and Taiwan, or a person of Chinese descent. The Chinese comprise more than 25% of the world's population, and the Chinese language (Mandarin) is the largest member of the Sino-Tibetan family.

Chinese traditions are ancient, many going back to at least 3000 BC. They include a range of philosophies and religions, including Confucianism, Taoism, and Buddhism. The veneration of ancestors was an enduring feature of Chinese culture, as were patrilineal-based villages. The extended family was the traditional unit, the five-generation family being the ideal. Recent attempts by the People's Republic of China have included the restriction of traditions and the limit of one child to a married couple.

The majority of Chinese are engaged in agriculture, cultivating irrigated rice fields in the south, and growing millet and wheat in the north. Many other Chinese work in commerce, industry, and government. Descendants of Chinese migrants are found throughout SE Asia, the Pacific, Australia, North and South America, and Europe. Within China many minorities speak non-Chinese languages belonging to the Sino-Tibetan family (such as Tibetan, Miao, and Zhuang). Some peoples speak languages belonging to the Altaic (such as Uigur, Mongol, and Manchu) and Indo-European (such as Russian) families, while in the northeast there are Koreans. The Chinese were governed for long periods by the Mongol (AD 1271–1368) and Manchu (AD 1644–1911) dynasties. See ◊China, History.

Although dialects vary considerably, there is a common written language, a nonphonetic script of characters representing concepts rather than sounds, similar to the way numbers represent quantities but may be pronounced differently in every language.

Chinese architecture the style of building in China. Traditionally of timber construction, few existing buildings predate the Ming dynasty (1368–1644), but records such as the *Ying Tsao Fa Shih/Method of Architecture* (1103) show that Chinese architecture changed little throughout the ages, both for the peasants and for the well-to-do. Curved roofs are a characteristic feature; also typical is the pagoda with a number of curved tiled roofs, one above the other. The Chinese are renowned for their wall-building. The Great Wall of China was built about 228–210 BC as a northern frontier defense, and Beijing's fine city walls, of which only a small section remains, date from the Ming period.

Chinese buildings usually face south, a convention that can be traced back to the "Hall of Brightness," a building from the Zhou dynasty (1050–221 BC), and is still retained in the functionally Western-style Chinese architecture of the present day. Although some sections of Beijing have been destroyed by modernization, the city still contains fine examples of buildings from the Ming dynasty, such as the Altar of Heaven, the ancestral temple of the Ming tombs, and the Five Pagoda Temple. The introduction of Buddhism from India exerted considerable influence on Chinese architecture.

Chinese art the painting and sculpture of China. From the Bronze Age to the Cultural Revolution, Chinese art shows the finest workmanship and a stylistic unity unparalleled in any other culture. From about the 1st century AD Buddhism inspired much sculpture and painting. The Han dynasty (206 BC–AD 220) produced outstanding metalwork, ceramics, and sculpture. The Song dynasty (960–1278) established standards of idyllic landscape and nature painting in a delicate calligraphic style.

Neolithic art Accomplished pottery dates back to about 2500 BC, already showing a distinctive Chinese approach to form.

Bronze Age art Rich burial goods, with bronzes and jade carvings, survive from the second millennium BC, decorated with hieroglyphs and simple stylized animal forms. Astonishing life-size terracotta figures from the Qin period (about 221–206 BC) guard the tomb of Emperor Shi Huangdi in the old capital of Xian. Bronze horses, naturalistic but displaying the soft curving lines of the Chinese style, are a feature of the Han dynasty.

early Buddhist art Once Buddhism was established in China it inspired a monumental art, with huge rock-cut Buddhas and graceful linear relief sculptures at the monasteries of Yungang, about 460–535, and Longmen. Bronze images show the same curving lines and rounded forms. Tang dynasty (618–907) art shows increasing sophistication in idealized images and naturalistic portraits, such as the carved figures of Buddhist monks (Luohan). This period also produced brilliant metalwork and delicate ceramics. It is known that the aims and, broadly speaking, the style of Chinese painting were already well established, but few paintings survive, with the exception of some Tang scrolls and silk paintings.

The Song dynasty The golden age of painting was the Song dynasty (960–1278). The imperial court created its own workshop, fostering a fine calligraphic art, mainly devoted to natural subjects—landscape, mountains, trees, flowers, birds, and horses—though genre scenes of court beauties were also popular. Scrolls, albums, and fans of silk or paper were painted with watercolors and ink, using soft brushes that produced many different textures. Painting was associated with literature, and painters added poems or quotations to their work to intensify the effect. Ma Yuan (c. 1190–1224) and Xia Gui (active c. 1180–1230) are among the painters, and Muqi (1180–c. 1270), was a monk known for exquisite brushwork. The Song dynasty also produced the first true porcelain, achieving a classic simplicity and delicacy in coloring and form.

Ming dynasty (1368–1644) Painters continued the landscape tradition, setting new standards in idealized visions. The painter Dong Qichang wrote a history and theory of Chinese painting. The Song style of porcelain gradually gave way to increasingly elaborate decorative work, and pale shades were superseded by rich colors, as in Ming blue-and-white patterned ware.

Qing dynasty (1644–1911) The so-called Individualist Spirits emerged, painters who developed bolder, personal styles of brushwork. But the strong spirit that supported traditional art began to fade in the 19th and 20th centuries.

Chinese art had a great impact on surrounding countries. The art of Korea was almost wholly inspired by Chinese example for many centuries. Along with Buddhism, Chinese styles of art were established in Japan in the 6th–7th centuries BC and continued to exert a profound influence, although Japanese culture soon developed an independent style.

China *People's power was thwarted when students confronted troops in Tiananmen Square during the summer of 1989. Peaceful demonstrators for increased democracy in China were attacked by the military and more than 2,000 unarmed protesters were killed.*

Chinese art *Part of the Sacred Way to the Ming Tombs, near Beijing, is lined with statues of courtiers, soldiers, politicians, and animals.*

Chinese language language or group of languages of the Sino-Tibetan family, spoken in China, Taiwan, Hong Kong, Singapore, and Chinese communities throughout the world. Varieties of spoken Chinese differ greatly, but all share a written form using thousands of ideographic symbols—characters—which have changed little in 2,000 years. Nowadays, *putonghua* ("common speech"), based on the educated Beijing dialect known as Mandarin Chinese, is promoted throughout China as the national spoken and written language.

Because the writing system has a symbolic form (like numbers and music notes) it can be read and interpreted regardless of the reader's own dialect. The Chinese dialects are tonal, that is, they depend upon the tone of a syllable to indicate its meaning: *ma* with one tone means "mother," with another means "horse." The characters of Chinese script were traditionally written down the page from right to left. Today they are commonly written horizontally and read left to right, using 2,000 simplified characters. A variant of the Roman alphabet has been introduced and is used in schools to help with pronunciation. This, called *Pinyin*, is prescribed for international use by the People's Republic of China for personal and place names (as in *Beijing* rather than *Peking*). Pinyin spellings are generally used in this volume, but they are not accepted by the government of Taiwan.

Chinese literature Poetry Chinese poems, often only four lines long, and written in the ancient literary language understood throughout China, consist of rhymed lines of a fixed number of syllables, ornamented by parallel phrasing and tonal pattern. The oldest poems are contained in the *Book of Songs* (800–600 BC). Some of the most celebrated Chinese poets are the nature poet T'ao Ch'ien (372–427), the master of technique Li Po (701–62), the autobiographical Po Chüi (772–846), and the wide-ranging Su Tung-p'o (1036–1101); and among the moderns using the colloquial language under European influence and experimenting in free verse are Hsu Chih-mo (1895–1931), and Pien Chih-lin (1910–).

Prose histories are not so much literary works as they are collections of edited documents with moral comment, while the essay has long been cultivated under strict rules of form and style. A famous example of the latter genre is *Upon the Original Way* by Han Yü (768–824), recalling the nation to Confucianism. Until the 16th century the short story was confined to the anecdote, startling by its strangeness and written in the literary language (for example, the stories of the poetic Tuan Ch'eng-shih (died 863); but after that time the more novelistic type of short story, written in the colloquial tongue, developed by its side. The Chinese novel evolved from the street storyteller's art and has consequently always used the popular language. The early romances *Three Kingdoms, All Men are Brothers,* and *Golden Lotus* are anonymous, the earliest known author of this genre being Wu Che'ng-en (c. 1505–80); the most realistic of the great novelists is Ts'ao Chan (died 1763). Twentieth-century Chinese novels have largely adopted European form, and have been influenced by Russia, as have the realistic stories of Lu Hsün. In typical Chinese drama, the stage presentation far surpasses the text in importance (the dialogue was not even preserved in early plays), but the present century has seen experiments in the European manner.

Chinese Revolution a series of major political upheavals in China 1911–49 that eventually led to Communist party rule and the establishment of the People's Republic of China. In 1912, a Nationalist revolt overthrew the imperial Manchu (or Ching) dynasty. Led by Sun Yat-sen 1923–25, and by Chiang Kai-shek 1925–49, the Nationalists, or Guomindang, were increasingly challenged by the growing Communist movement. The 6,000 mi/10,000 km Long March to the NW by the Communists 1934–35 to escape from attacks by the Nationalist forces resulted in Mao Zedong's emergence as Communist leader. During World War II 1939–45, the various Chinese political groups pooled military resources against the Japanese invaders. After World War II, the conflict reignited into open civil war 1946–49, until the Nationalists were defeated at Nanking and forced to flee to Taiwan. Communist rule was established in the People's Republic of China under the leadership of Mao.

The Chinese revolution came about with the collapse of the Manchu (or Ching) dynasty, a result of increasing internal disorders, pressure from foreign governments, and the weakness of central government. A Nationalist revolt led to a provisional republican constitution being proclaimed and a government established in Beijing (Peking). Led by Sun Yat Sen and Chiang Kai-shek, the Nationalists were faced with the problems of restoring the authority of central government and meeting the challenges from militaristic factions and the growing Communist movement. After 1930, Chiang launched a series of attacks that encircled the Communists in SE China and led to an attempt by Communist army commander Chu Teh to break out. The resulting Long March to NW China from Oct 1934 to Oct 1935 reduced the Communists' army from over 100,000 to little more than 8,000, mainly as a result of skirmishes with Chiang's forces and the severity of the conditions. During the march, a power struggle developed between Mao Zedong and Chang Kuo T'ao that eventually split the force. Mao's group finally based itself in Yen'an, where it remained throughout the war with the Japanese, forming an uneasy alliance with the Nationalists to expel the invaders. Mao's troops formed the basis of the Red Army that renewed the civil war against the Nationalists 1946 and emerged victorious after defeating them at Nanking 1949. As a result, Communist rule was established in China under Mao's leadership.

chip

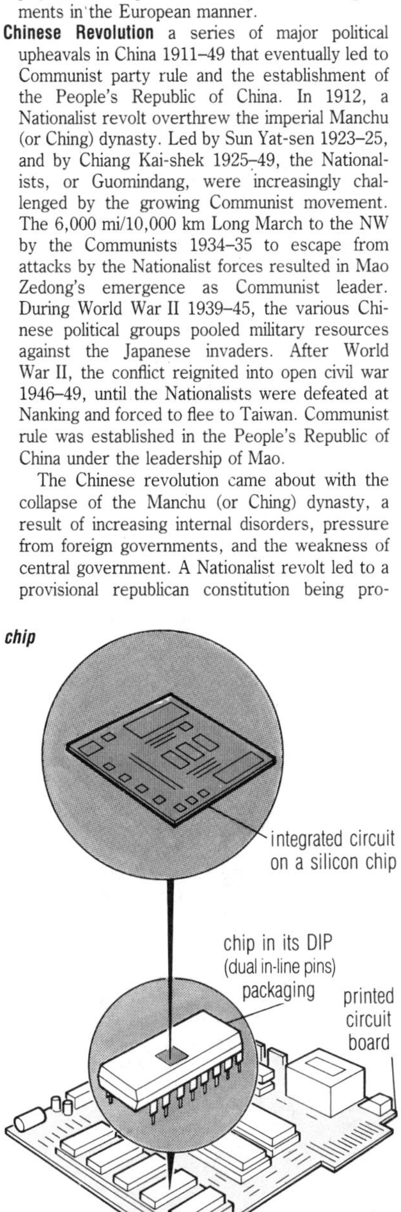
integrated circuit
on a silicon chip
chip in its DIP
(dual in-line pins)
packaging
printed
circuit
board

Chinghai former name of ◊Qinghai, NW province of China.

chinook (American Indian "snow-eater") a warm dry wind that blows downhill on the eastern side of the Rocky Mountains. It often occurs in winter and spring when it produces a rapid thaw, and so is important to the agriculture of the area.

chip complete electronic circuit on a slice of silicon (or other ◊semiconductor) crystal only a few millimeters square. It is also called ◊silicon chip and ◊integrated circuit.

chipmunk several species of small ground squirrel with characteristic stripes along its side. Chipmunks live in North America and E Asia, in a variety of habitats, usually wooded, and take shelter in burrows. They have pouches in their cheeks for carrying food. They climb well but spend most of their time on or near the ground.

The Siberian chipmunk *Eutamias sibiricus*, about 5 in/13 cm long, is found in N Russia, N China, and Japan.

Chippendale Thomas c. 1718–1779. English furniture designer. He set up his workshop in St Martin's Lane, London 1753. His book *The Gentleman and Cabinet Maker's Director* 1754, was a significant contribution to furniture design. He favored Louis XVI, Chinese, Gothic, and Neo-Classical styles, and worked mainly in mahogany.

Chirac Jacques 1932– . French conservative politician, prime minister 1974–76 and 1986–88. He established the neo-Gaullist Rassemblement pour la République (RPR) 1976, and became mayor of Paris 1977.

Chirac held ministerial posts during the Pompidou presidency and gained the nickname "the Bulldozer." In 1974 he became prime minister to President Giscard d'Estaing, but the relationship was uneasy. Chirac contested the 1981 presidential election and emerged as the National Assembly leader for the parties of the right during the Socialist administration of 1981–86. Following the rightist coalition's victory 1986, Chirac was appointed prime minister by President Mitterrand in a "cohabitation" experiment. The term was marked by economic decline, nationality reforms, and student unrest. Student demonstrations in autumn 1986 forced him to abandon plans for educational reform. He ran in the May 1988 presidential elections and was defeated by Mitterrand, who replaced him with the moderate Socialist Michel Rocard.

Chirico Giorgio de 1888–1978. Italian painter born in Greece, whose style presaged Surrealism in its use of enigmatic imagery and dreamlike settings, for example, *Nostalgia of the Infinite* 1911, Museum of Modern Art, New York.

In 1917, with Carlo Carrà (1881–1966), he founded Metaphysical painting, which aimed to convey a sense of mystery and hallucination. This was achieved by distorted perspective, dramatic lighting, and the use of dummies and statues in place of human figures.

Chiron in Greek mythology, the son of Cronos by a sea nymph. A ◊centaur, he was the wise tutor of Jason and Achilles, among others.

Chiron outer asteroid discovered by Charles Kowal 1977, orbiting between Saturn and Uranus. It appears to have a dark surface resembling that of asteroids in the inner Solar System, probably consists of a mixture of ice and dark stony material, and may have a diameter of about 120 mi/200 km.

chiropody the care and treatment of feet.

Originally, it referred to the treatment of hands as well as feet, but is now synonymous with podiatry.

chiropractic maintaining or restoring health by manipulation of the spine and other parts to prevent and relieve conditions claimed to be caused by pressure on the nerve roots as they emerge from the spine. The treatment is not fully recognized by orthodox medicine.

Chisholm Jesse c. 1806–c. 1868. US pioneer. Although little is known of Chisholm's early life, it appears that he gained a reputation as a resourceful guide, trader, and military scout during the early 19th century. Ranging over the S Great Plains, he customarily followed a route from the Mexican border to Kansas, ending at the market town of Abilene. This overland route later became one of the main paths of the yearly Texas cattle drive and became famous among cowboys as the "Chisholm Trail."

Chisholm v Georgia landmark case 1793 in which the US Supreme Court ruled that states are not immune from suits brought by citizens of other states. Alexander Chisholm, a South Carolinian, sued Georgia for payment on Georgia state bonds that were confiscated during the American Revolution. Georgia ignored the case, claiming it was not in federal jurisdiction, but the Supreme Court ruled that Georgia must appear in court to answer the charges. This decision frightened state governments as the number of similar suits grew across the nation. In response to fears about this economic danger to states' survival, the 11th Amendment, passed in 1798, reversed the Chisholm decision.

Chissano Joaquim 1939– . Mozambique nationalist politician, president from 1986; foreign minister 1975–86.

He was secretary to Samora ◊Machel, who led the National Front for the Liberation of Mozam-

Chirac *French politician Jacques Chirac, 1986.*

chive

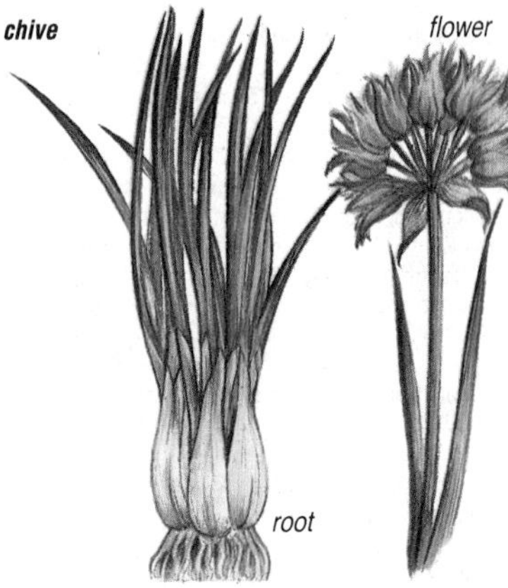
flower
root

bique (Frelimo) during the campaign for independence in the early 1960s. When Mozambique achieved internal self-government in 1974, Chissano was appointed prime minister. After independence he served under Machel as foreign minister and on his death succeeded him as president.

Chita town in E Siberia, USSR, on the Chita River; population (1987) 349,000. It is on the Trans-Siberian railroad, and has chemical and engineering works and coal mines.

chitin complex long-chain compound, or ◊polymer; a nitrogenous derivative of glucose. Chitin is found principally in the ◊exoskeleton of insects and other arthropods. It combines with protein to form a covering that can be hard and tough, as in beetles, or soft and flexible, as in caterpillars and other insect larvae. In crustaceans such as crabs, it is impregnated with calcium carbonate for extra strength.

Chitin also occurs in some ◊protozoans and coelenterates (such as certain jellyfishes), in the jaws of annelid worms, and as the cell-wall polymer of fungi.

Chittagong city and port in Bangladesh, 10 mi/16 km from the mouth of the Karnaphuli River, on the Bay of Bengal; population (1981) 1,388,476. Industries include steel, engineering, chemicals, and textiles.

chivalry the code of gallantry and honor that medieval knights were pledged to observe. The word originally meant the knightly class of the feudal Middle Ages.

chive or ***chives*** bulbous perennial plant *Allium schoenoprasum* of the lily family Liliaceae. It has long, tubular leaves and dense, round flower heads in blue or lilac, and is used as a garnish for salads.

Chkalov name 1938–57 of ◊Orenburg, town in the USSR.

Chladni Ernest Florens Friedrich 1756–1827. German physicist, a pioneer in the field of ◊acoustics.

chlamydia single-celled organism (bacterium) that can only live parasitically in animal cells. Chlamydiae are considered to be descendants of bacteria that have lost certain metabolic processes. In humans, venereally transmitted chlamydiae cause genital and urinary infections as well as ◊trachoma, a leading cause of blindness in the tropics. Psittacosis, another kind of chlamydial infection, is contracted from birds by inhaling particles of dried droppings.

chloracne eruption of the skin, symptomatic of direct contact with chlorinated organic chemicals (hydrocarbons) or an environment contaminated by such chemicals.

chloramphenicol first of the broad-spectrum antibiotics to be used commercially. It was discovered in a Peruvian soil sample containing the bacillus *Streptomyces venezuelae*, which produces the antibiotic substance $C_{11}H_{12}Cl_2N_2O_5$, now synthesized. Because of its toxicity, its use is limited to treatment of life-threatening infections, such as meningitis and typhoid fever.

chlorate any salt from an acid containing both chlorine and oxygen (ClO, ClO_2, ClO_3, and ClO_4). Common chlorates are those of sodium, potassium, and barium. Certain chlorates are used in weedkillers.

chlorella any single-celled, green, freshwater algae of the genus *Chlorella*, 3–10 micrometers in diameter, which can increase their weight by four times in 12 hours. Nutritive content: 50% protein, 20% fat, 20% carbohydrate, 10% phosphate, calcium, and other ◊trace minerals.

chloride negative ion Cl^- formed when hydrogen chloride dissolves in water, and any salt containing this ion, commonly formed by the action of hydrochloric acid (HCl) on various metals or by direct combination of a metal and chlorine. Sodium chloride (NaCl) is common table salt.

chlorine greenish-yellow, gaseous, nonmetallic element with a pungent odor, symbol Cl, atomic number 17, atomic weight 35.453. It is a member of the ◊halogen group and is widely distributed in combination with the ◊alkali metals, as chlorates or chlorides. In nature it is always found in the combined form, as in hydrochloric acid, produced in the mammalian stomach for digestion. It is obtained commercially by the electrolysis of chlorides and is an important bleaching agent and germicide, used for both drinking and swimming-pool water. As an oxidizing agent it finds many applications in organic chemistry. The pure gas is a poison and was used in gas warfare in World War I, where its release seared the membranes of the nose, throat, and lungs, producing pneumonia. Chlorine is responsible for the ◊ozone layer depletion, since as a component of CFCs (chlorofluorocarbons) it is released from the molecule by the action of ultraviolet radiation in the upper atmosphere, making it available to react with and destroy the ozone. It was discovered in 1774 by the German chemist Karl Scheele, but Humphry Davy first proved it to be an element in 1810 and named it for its color, yellow-green, from the Greek *chlōros*.

chlorofluorocarbon (CFC) synthetic chemical, which is odorless, nontoxic, nonflammable, and chemically inert. CFCs are used as propellants in ◊aerosol cans, refrigerants in refrigerators and air conditioners, in the manufacture of foam boxes for takeout food cartons, and as cleaning substances in the electronics industry. They are partly responsible for the destruction of the ◊ozone layer. In June 1990 representatives of 93 nations, including the US and the UK, agreed to phase out production of CFCs and other ozone-depleting chemicals by the end of the 20th century.

When CFCs are released into the atmosphere, they drift up slowly into the stratosphere, where, under the influence of ultraviolet radiation from the Sun, they break down into chlorine atoms, which destroy the ozone layer and allow harmful radiation from the Sun to reach the Earth's surface. CFCs can remain in the atmosphere for more than 100 years. Replacements for CFCs are being developed, and research into safe methods of destroying existing CFCs is being carried out.

chloroform or ***trichloromethane*** CCl_3 clear, colorless, toxic, carcinogenic liquid with a characteristic, pungent, sickly-sweet smell and taste, formerly used as an anesthetic (now superseded by less harmful substances). It is used as a solvent and in the synthesis of organic chemical compounds.

chlorophyll green pigment present in most plants that is responsible for the absorption of light energy during ◊photosynthesis. The pigment absorbs the red and blue-violet parts of sunlight but reflects the green, thus giving plants their most characteristic color.

Chlorophyll is found within chloroplasts, present in large numbers in leaves. Cyanobacteria and other photosynthetic bacteria also have chlorophyll, though of a slightly different type. Chlorophyll is similar in structure to ◊hemoglobin, but with magnesium instead of iron as the reactive part of the molecule.

chloroplast

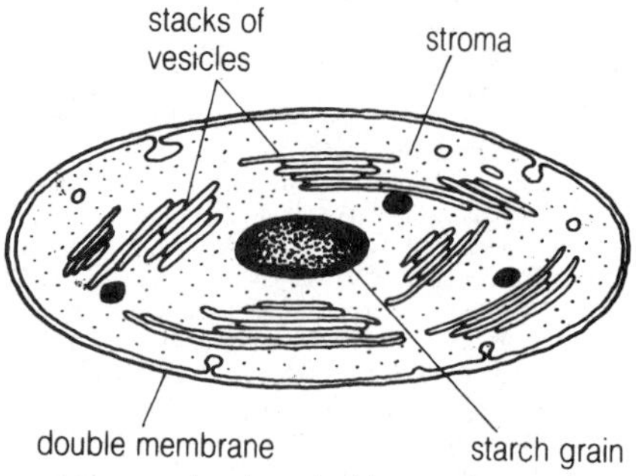
stacks of vesicles
stroma
double membrane
starch grain

chloroplast a structure (◊organelle) within a plant cell containing the green pigment chlorophyll. Chloroplasts occur in most cells of the green plant that are exposed to light, often in large numbers. Typically, they are flattened and disklike, with a double membrane enclosing the stroma, a gellike matrix. Within the stroma are stacks of fluid-containing cavities, or vesicles, where ◊photosynthesis occurs.

It is thought that the chloroplasts were originally free-living cyanobacteria which invaded larger, nonphotosynthetic cells and developed a symbiotic relationship with them. Like ◊mitochondria, they contain a small amount of DNA and divide by fission. Chloroplasts are a type of ◊plastid.

chlorosis an abnormal condition of green plants in which the stems and leaves turn pale green or yellow. The yellowing is due to a reduction in the levels of the green chlorophyll pigments. It may be caused by a deficiency in essential elements (such as magnesium, iron, or manganese), a lack of light, genetic factors, or virus infection.

chocolate a powder, syrup, confectionery, or beverage derived from cacao beans. See ◊cocoa and chocolate.

choir a body of singers, normally divided into two or more parts, and commonly four (soprano, alto, tenor, bass). The words *choir* and *chorus* are frequently interchangeable, although all church groups use the former, while larger groups, which may have several hundred members, invariably use the latter.

Choiseul Étienne François, duc de Choiseul 1719–1785. French politician. Originally a protégé of Mme de Pompadour, the mistress of Louis XV, he became minister for foreign affairs 1758, and held this and other offices until 1770. He banished the Jesuits, and was a supporter of the Enlightenment philosophers Diderot and Voltaire.

cholecystectomy surgical removal of the ◊gall bladder.

cholera any of several intestinal diseases, especially Asiatic cholera, an infection caused by a bacterium *Vibrio cholerae*, transmitted in contaminated water and characterized by violent diarrhea and vomiting. It is prevalent in many tropical areas.

The formerly high death rate during epidemics has been much reduced by treatments to prevent dehydration and loss of body salts. There is an effective vaccine that must be repeated at frequent intervals for people exposed to continuous risk of infection.

cholesterol white, crystalline ◊sterol found throughout the body, especially in fats, blood, nerve tissue, and bile. It is also found in foods such as eggs, meat, and butter. A high level of cholesterol in the blood is thought to contribute to atherosclerosis (hardening of the arteries).

Cholesterol is the starting point for the production of steroid hormones, including the sex hormones; it is an integral part of all cell membranes; it is broken down by the liver into bile salts, which are involved in fat absorption by the digestive system; and it is an essential component of lipoproteins, which transport fats and fatty acids in the blood. Low-density lipoprotein (LDL) cholesterol, when present in excess, can enter the tissues and become deposited on the surface of the arteries, causing atherosclerosis. High-density lipoprotein (HDL) cholesterol acts as a scavenger, transporting fat and cholesterol from the tissues to the liver to be broken down. Blood-cholesterol levels can be altered by eating polyunsaturated fat instead of saturated fat, which helps reduce LDL-cholesterol. HDL-cholesterol (also called "good" cholesterol) can be increased by exercise.

Chomsky Noam 1928– . US professor of linguistics. He proposed a theory of transformational generative grammar, which attracted widespread interest because of the claims it made about the relationship between language and the mind and the universality of an underlying language structure. He is also a leading voice against the imperialist tendencies of the US government.

Chomsky maintained that a fundamental distinction can be made between knowledge and behavior and that the focus of scientific inquiry should be on knowledge. In order to define and describe linguistic knowledge, he posited a set of abstract principles of grammar that seem to be universal and may have a biological basis.

Chongjin capital of North Hamgyong province on the NE coast of North Korea; population (1984) 754,000.

Chongqing or ***Chungking***, also known as ***Pahsien*** city in Sichuan province, China, that stands at the the ◊Chang Jiang and Jialing Jiang rivers; population (1984) 2,733,700. Industries include iron, steel, chemicals, synthetic rubber, and textiles.

For over 4,000 years it has been a major commercial center in one of the most remote and economically deprived regions of China. It was opened to foreign trade in 1891, and it remains a focal point of road, river, and rail transport. When both Beijing and Nanjing were occupied by the Japanese, it was the capital of China 1938–46.

Choonhavan Chatichai 1922– . Thai conservative politician, prime minister of Thailand from 1988. He has promoted a peace settlement in neighboring Cambodia as part of a vision of transforming Indochina into a thriving open-trade zone.

A field marshal's son, Choonhavan fought in World War II and the Korean war, rising to major-general. After a career as a diplomat and entrepreneur, he moved into politics and became leader of the conservative Chat Thai party and, in 1988, prime minister.

Chopin Frédéric (François) 1810–1849. Polish composer and pianist. He made his debut as a pianist at the age of eight. As a performer, Chopin revolutionized the technique of pianoforte-playing, and concentrated on solo piano pieces. His compositions for piano are characterized by their lyrical and poetic quality.

From 1831 he lived in Paris, where he became known in the fashionable salons, although he rarely performed in public. In 1836 Liszt introduced him to Mme Dudevant (George ◊Sand), with whom he had a close relationship 1838–46. During this time she nursed him in Majorca for tuberculosis, while he composed intensively and for a time regained his health. He died Oct 17 1849 and was buried in Père Lachaise cemetery in Paris.

***Chopin** A daguerreotype of the composer Frédéric Chopin.*

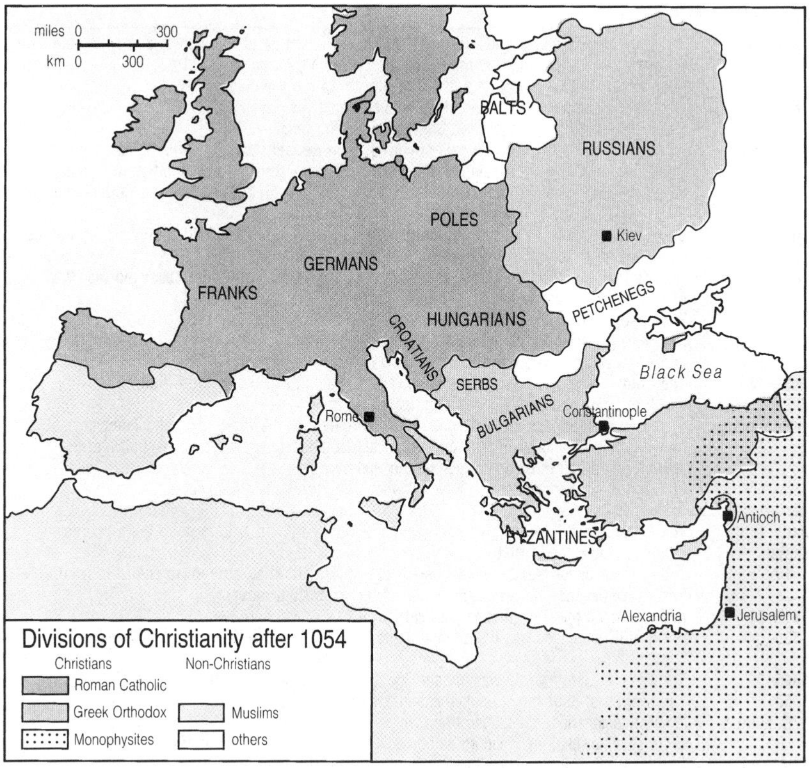
miles 0 300
km 0 300
BALTS
RUSSIANS
POLES
Kiev
GERMANS
FRANKS
HUNGARIANS
PETCHENEGS
CROATIANS
SERBS
Black Sea
BULGARIANS
Constantinople
Rome
BYZANTINES
Antioch
Alexandria
Jerusalem
Divisions of Christianity after 1054
Christians
Non-Christians
Roman Catholic
Greek Orthodox
Muslims
Monophysites
others

Chopin Kate 1851–1904. US novelist and short-story writer. Her novel *The Awakening* 1899, the story of a married New Orleans woman's awakening to her sexuality, is now regarded as a classic of feminist sensibility.

chorale a traditional hymn tune of the German Protestant Church, harmonized in four parts for singing by a congregation.

chord in geometry, a straight line joining any two points on a curve. The chord that passes through the center of a circle (its longest chord) is the diameter. The longest and shortest chords of an ellipse (a regular oval) are called the major and minor axes respectively.

chord in music, a group of three or more notes sounded together. The resulting combination of tones may be either harmonious or dissonant.

chordate animal belonging to the phylum Chordata, which includes vertebrates, sea squirts, amphioxus, and others. All these animals, at some stage of their lives, have a supporting rod of tissue (notochord or backbone) running down their bodies.

chorea disease of the nervous system marked by involuntary movements of the face muscles and limbs, formerly called St Vitus's dance. ◊Huntington's chorea is also characterized by such movements.

choreography the art of creating and arranging ballet and dance for performance; originally, in the 18th century, the art of dance notation.

chorion outermost of the three membranes enclosing the embryo of reptiles, birds, and mammals; the ◊amnion is the innermost membrane.

choroid the black layer found at the rear of the ◊eye beneath the retina. By absorbing light that has already passed through the retina, it stops back-reflection and so aids vision.

chorus a large group of singers; a smaller church group is called a ◊choir.

Chou En-lai alternative transcription of ◊Zhou Enlai.

chough bird *Pyrrhocorax pyrrhocorax* of the crow family, about 15 in/38 cm long, black-feathered, and with red bill and legs. It lives on sea-cliffs and mountains from Europe to E Asia, but is now rare.

The alpine chough *Pyrrhocorax graculus* is similar, but has a yellow bill and is found up to the snowline in mountains from the Pyrenees to Central Asia.

chow chow breed of dog originating in China in ancient times. About 1.5 ft/45 cm tall, it has a broad neck and head, round catlike feet, soft woolly undercoat with a coarse outer coat, and a mane. Its coat should be of one color, and it has an unusual blue-black tongue.

Chrétien de Troyes medieval French poet, born in Champagne about the middle of the 12th century. His epics—which include *Le Chevalier de la charrette*; *Perceval*, written for Philip, Count of Flanders; *Erec*; *Yvain*; and other Arthurian romances—introduced the concept of the ◊Holy Grail.

Christ (Greek *khristos* "anointed one") the ◊Messiah as prophesied in the Old Testament.

Christchurch city on South Island, New Zealand, 7 mi/11 km from the mouth of the Avon River; population (1986) 299,300. Principal city of the Canterbury plains, it is the seat of the University of Canterbury. Industries include fertilizers and chemicals, canning and meat-processing, rail workshops, and shoes.

Christchurch uses as its port a bay in the sheltered Lyttelton Harbor on the N shore of the Banks Peninsula, which forms a denuded volcanic mass. Land has been reclaimed for service facilities, and rail and road tunnels (1867 and 1964 respectively) link Christchurch with Lyttelton.

Christian follower of ◊Christianity, the religion derived from the teachings of Jesus. In the New Testament (Acts 11:26) it is stated that the first to be called Christians were the disciples in Antioch (now Antakya, Turkey).

Christian ten Kings of Denmark and Norway, including:

Christian I 1426–1481. King of Denmark from 1448, and founder of the Oldenburg dynasty. In 1450

Christianity: history

1st century	The Christian church is traditionally said to have originated at Pentecost, and separated from the parent Jewish religion by the declaration of Saints Barnabas and Paul that the distinctive rites of Judaism were not necessary for entry into the Christian church.
3rd century	Christians were persecuted under the Roman emperors Severus, Decius, and Diocletian.
312	Emperor Constantine established Christianity as the religion of the Roman Empire.
4th century	A settled doctrine of Christian belief evolved, with deviating beliefs condemned as heresies. Questions of discipline threatened disruption within the Church; to settle these, Constantine called the Council of Arles 314, followed by the councils of Nicaea 325 and Constantinople 381.
5th century	Councils of Ephesus 431 and Chalcedon 451. Christianity was carried northward by figures such as Saints Columba and Augustine in England.
800	Holy Roman Emperor Charlemagne crowned by the Pope. The Church assisted the growth of the feudal system of which it formed the apex.
1054	The Eastern Orthodox Church split from the Roman Catholic Church.
11th–12th centuries	Secular and ecclesiastical jurisdiction were often in conflict, for example, Emperor Henry IV and Pope Gregory VII, Henry II of England and his archbishop Becket.
1096–1291	The Church supported a series of wars in the Middle East, called the Crusades.
1233	The Inquisition was established to suppress heresy.
14th century	Increasing worldliness (against which the foundation of the Dominican and Franciscan monastic orders was a protest) and ecclesiastical abuses led to dissatisfaction and the appearance of the reformers Wycliffe and Huss.
15th–17th centuries	Thousands of women were accused of witchcraft, tortured, and executed.
early 16th century	The Renaissance brought a re-examination of Christianity in N Europe by the humanists Erasmus, More, and Colet.
1517	The German priest Martin Luther started the Reformation, an attempt to return to a pure form of Christianity, and became leader of the Protestant movement.
1519–64	In Switzerland the Reformation was carried out by Calvin and Zwingli.
1529	Henry VIII renounced papal supremacy and proclaimed himself head of the Church of England.
1545–63	The Counter-Reformation was initiated by the Catholic church at the Council of Trent.
1560	The Church of Scotland was established according to Calvin's Presbyterian system.
17th century	Jesuit missionaries established themselves in China and Japan. Puritans, Quakers, and other sects seeking religious freedom established themselves in North America.
18th century	During the Age of Reason, Christian dogmas were questioned, and intellectuals began to examine society in purely secular terms. In England and America, religious revivals occurred among the working classes in the form of Methodism and the Great Awakening. In England the Church of England suffered the loss of large numbers of Nonconformists.
19th century	The evolutionary theories of Darwin and the historical criticism of the Bible challenged the Book of Genesis. Missionaries converted natives of Africa and Asia, suppressing indigenous faiths and cultures.
1948	The World Council of Churches was founded as part of the ecumenical movement to reunite various Protestant sects and, to some extent, the Protestant churches and the Catholic church.
1950s–80s	Protestant evangelicalism grew rapidly in the US, spread by television.
1969	A liberation theology of freeing the poor from oppression emerged in South America, and attracted papal disapproval.
1972	The United Reformed Church was formed by the union of the Presbyterian Church in England and the Congregational Church. In the US, the 1960s-70s saw the growth of cults, some of them nominally Christian, which were a source of social concern.
1980s	The Roman Catholic Church played a major role in the liberalization of the Polish government; and in the USSR the Orthodox Church and other sects were tolerated and even encouraged under Gorbachev.
1989	Barbara Harris, first female bishop of the Episcopal Church, ordained in the US.

he established the union of Denmark and Norway that lasted until 1814.

Christian III 1503–1559. King of Denmark and Norway from 1535. Under his reign the Reformation was introduced.

Christian IV 1577–1648. King of Denmark and Norway from 1588. He sided with the Protestants in the Thirty Years' War (1618–48), and founded Christiania (now Oslo, capital of Norway). He was succeeded by Frederick II 1648.

Christian VIII 1786–1848. King of Denmark 1839–48. He was unpopular because of his opposition to reform. His attempt to encourage the Danish language and culture in Schleswig and Holstein led to an insurrection there shortly after his death. He was succeeded by Frederick VII.

Christian IX 1818–1906. King of Denmark from 1863. His daughter Alexandra married Edward VII of the UK and another, Dagmar, married Tsar Alexander III of Russia; his second son, George, became king of Greece. In 1864 he lost the duchies of Schleswig and Holstein after a war with Austria and Prussia.

Christian X 1870–1947. King of Denmark and Iceland from 1912, when he succeeded his father Frederick VIII. He married Alexandrine, Duchess of Mecklenburg-Schwerin, and was popular for his democratic attitude. During World War II he was held prisoner by the Germans in Copenhagen. He was succeeded by Frederick IX.

Christiania former name of Norwegian capital of ◊Oslo (1624–1924), after King Christian IV who replanned it after a fire in 1624.

Christianity world religion derived from the teaching of Jesus in the first third of the 1st century, with a present-day membership of about 1 billion. Its main divisions are the ◊Roman Catholic, ◊Eastern Orthodox, and ◊Protestant churches.

beliefs An omnipotent God the Father is the fundamental concept, together with the doctrine of the Trinity, that is, the union of the three persons of the Father, Son, and Holy Spirit in one Godhead (though sects differ on how this is interpreted). Christians believe that Jesus died for the sins of humanity, and his divinity is based on the belief in his resurrection after death and his ascension into Heaven. The main commandments are to love God and to love one's neighbor as oneself, which, if followed successfully, lead to an afterlife in heaven.

Christian Science a sect, the Church of Christ, Scientist, established in the US by Mary Baker Eddy 1879. Christian Scientists believe that since God is good and is a spirit, matter and evil are not ultimately real. Consequently they refuse all medical treatment. It has its own daily newspaper, the *Christian Science Monitor*.

Christian Science is regarded by its adherents as the restatement of primitive Christianity with its full gospel of salvation from all evil, including sickness and disease as well as sin. According to its adherents, Christian Science healing is brought about by the operation of truth in human conscience. There is no ordained priesthood, but there are public practitioners of Christian Science healing who are officially authorized.

The headquarters of the First Church of Christ, Scientist is in Boston, Massachusetts, with branches in most parts of the world. The textbook of Christian Science is Eddy's *Science and Health with Key to the Scriptures* 1875.

Christians of St Thomas sect of Indian Christians on the Malabar Coast, named after the apostle who is supposed to have carried his mission to India. In fact the Christians of St Thomas were established in the 5th century by Nestorians from Persia. They now form part of the Assyrian Church (see under ◊Nestorianism) and have their own patriarch.

Christie Agatha 1890–1976. English detective novelist who created the characters Hercule Poirot and Miss Jane Marple. She wrote more than 70 novels including *The Murder of Roger Ackroyd* 1926 and *Ten Little Indians* 1939, and the play *The Mousetrap* 1952.

Born in Torquay as Agatha Miller, she married Colonel Archibald Christie 1914 and served during World War I as a nurse. Her first crime novel, *The Mysterious Affair at Styles* 1920, introduced Hercule Poirot. She often broke "purist" rules, as in *The Murder of Roger Ackroyd* in which the narrator is the murderer. She caused a nationwide sensation 1926 by disappearing for ten days when her husband fell in love with another woman. After a divorce 1928, she married the archeologist Max Mallowan (1904–78) in 1930.

Christie Julie 1940– . English film actress who became a star in the 1960s following her award-winning performance in *Darling* 1965. She also appeared in *Doctor Zhivago* 1965; *The Go-Between* 1971; *Don't Look Now* 1973; *Memoirs of a Survivor* 1982; and *Power* 1986.

Christina 1626–1689. Queen of Sweden 1632–54. Succeeding her father Gustavus Adolphus at the age of six, she assumed power 1644, but disagreed with the former regent ◊Oxenstjerna. Refusing to marry, she eventually nominated her cousin Charles Gustavus (Charles X) as her successor. As a secret convert to Roman Catholicism, which was then illegal in Sweden, she had to abdicate 1654, and went to live in Rome, twice returning to Sweden unsuccessfully to claim the throne.

Christine de Pisan 1364–1430. French poet and historian. Her works include love lyrics, philosophical poems, a poem in praise of Joan of Arc, a history of Charles V, and various defenses of women, including *La cité des dames/The City of Ladies*.

Born in Venice, she was brought to France as a child when her father entered the service of Charles V. In 1389, after the death of her husband, the Picardian nobleman Etienne Castel, she began writing to support herself and her family.

Christmas Dec 25, a Christian religious holiday, observed throughout the Western world and traditionally marked by feasting and gift-giving. In the Christian church, it is the day on which the birth of Jesus is celebrated, although the actual birth date is unknown. Many of its customs have a non-Christian origin and were adapted from celebrations of the winter solstice.

The choice of a date near the winter solstice owed much to the missionary desire to facilitate conversion of members of older religions, which traditionally held festivals at that time of year.

Christmas Island island in the Indian Ocean, 224 mi/360 km S of Java; area 54 sq mi/140 sq km; population (1986) 2,000. It has phosphate deposits. Found to be uninhabited when reached by Captain W Mynars on Christmas Day 1643, it was annexed by Britain 1888; occupied by Japan 1942–45, and transferred to Australia 1958. After a referendum 1984, it was included in Northern Territory.

Christmas tree any evergreen tree brought indoors and decorated for Christmas. The custom was a medieval German tradition and is now practiced in many Western countries.

Christo adopted name of Christo Javacheff 1935– US sculptor, born in Bulgaria, active in Paris in the 1950s and in New York from 1964. He is known for his wrapped works: structures such as bridges and buildings, and even areas of coastline, are temporarily wrapped in synthetic fabric tied down with rope. The *Running Fence* 1976 across California was another temporary work. In 1991 he simultaneously exhibited a work in both Japan and the US.

Christoff Boris 1918– . Bulgarian bass who made his operatic debut in 1946. His roles included Boris Godunov, Ivan the Terrible, and Mephistopheles.

Christophe Henri 1767–1820. West Indian slave, one of the leaders of the revolt against the French 1791, who was proclaimed king of Haiti 1811. His government distributed plantations to military leaders. He shot himself when his troops deserted him because of his alleged cruelty.

Christopher, St the patron saint of travelers. His feast day on July 25 was dropped from the Roman Catholic liturgical calendar 1969.

Traditionally he was a martyr in Syria in the 3rd century, and legend describes his carrying the child Jesus over the stream; despite his great strength, he found the burden increasingly heavy, and was told that the child was Jesus Christ bearing the sins of all the world.

chromatic scale a musical scale proceeding by semitones. All twelve note steps in the octave are used rather than the seven notes of the diatonic scale.

chromatography technique for separating a mixture, usually in solution, into its constituent components. This is done by passing the mixture (the "mobile phase" through another substance (the "stationary phase"), usually a liquid or solid. The different components of the mixture are absorbed or impeded to different extents, and hence separate. The technique is used for both qualitative and quantitive analyses in biology and chemistry.

chromite iron chromium oxide, Fe,Cr_2O_4, the main ore of chromium. It is one of the spinel group of minerals, and crystallizes in dark colored octahedra of the cubic system. Chromite is usually found in association with ultrabasic and basic rocks; for example in Cyprus it occurs with serpentine, and in South Africa it forms continuous layers in a layered intrusion.

chromium hard, brittle, gray-white, metallic element, symbol Cr, atomic number 24, atomic weight 51.996. It takes a high polish, has a high melting point, and is very resistant to corrosion. It is used in chromium electroplating, to make stainless steel and other alloys, and as a catalyst. Its compounds are used for tanning leather and for ◊alums. In human nutrition it is a vital trace element. In nature, it occurs chiefly as a chrome–iron ore ($FeCr_2O_4$).

The name was given in 1797 by its discoverer French chemist Louis Vauquelin (1763–1829) from Greek *chromos*, "color," for its bright-colored compounds.

chromium ore essentially chromite, Fe,CrO_4, from which chromium is extracted. South Africa and Zimbabwe are major producers.

chromosome a structure in a cell nucleus that carries the ◊genes. Each chromosome consists of one very long strand of DNA, coiled and folded to produce a compact chromosome. The point on a chromosome where a particular gene occurs is known as its locus. Most higher organisms have

chromatography

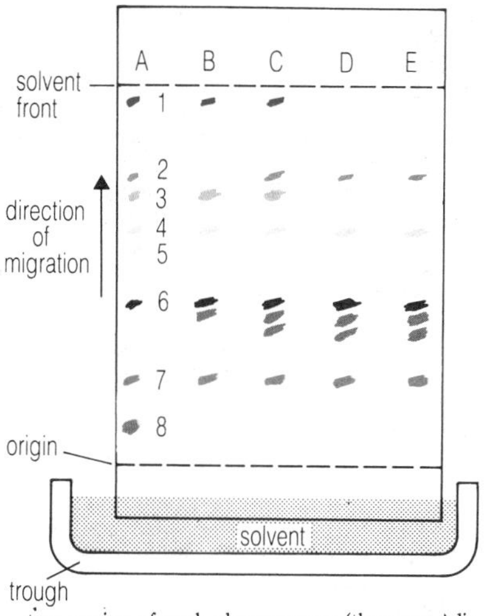

A
B
C
D
E
solvent front
1
2
3
4
5
6
7
8
direction of migration
origin
solvent
trough

two copies of each chromosome (they are ◊diploid) but some have only one (they are ◊haploid). See also ◊mitosis and ◊meiosis.

chromosphere (Greek "color" and "sphere") layer of mostly hydrogen gas about 6,000 mi/10,000 km deep above the visible surface of the Sun (the photosphere). It appears pinkish-red during ◊eclipses of the Sun.

chronic in medicine, description of a condition that is of slow onset and then runs a prolonged course, such as rheumatoid arthritis or chronic bronchitis. In contrast, an acute condition develops quickly and may be of relatively short duration.

Chronicles two books of the Old Testament containing genealogy and history.

chronicles, medieval books modeled on the Old Testament Books of Chronicles. Until the later Middle Ages, they were usually written in Latin by clerics, who borrowed extensively from one another.

Two early examples were written by Gregory of Tours in the 6th century and by ◊Bede. In the later Middle Ages, vernacular chronicles appear, written by laymen, but by then the chronicle tradition was in decline, soon to be supplanted by Renaissance histories.

chronometer instrument for measuring time precisely, originally used at sea. It is designed to remain accurate through all conditions of temperature and pressure. The first accurate marine chronometer, capable of an accuracy of half a minute a year, was made 1761 by John Harrison in England. The term is now applied to scientific time-keeping devices.

chrysanthemum any plant of the genus *Chrysanthemum* of the family Compositae, with about 200 species. There are hundreds of cultivated varieties, whose exact wild ancestry is uncertain. In the Far East the common chrysanthemum has been cultivated for more than 2,000 years and is the national emblem of Japan.

Chrysanthemums may be grown from seed, but are more usually reproduced by cutting or division. They were introduced into the West in 1789.

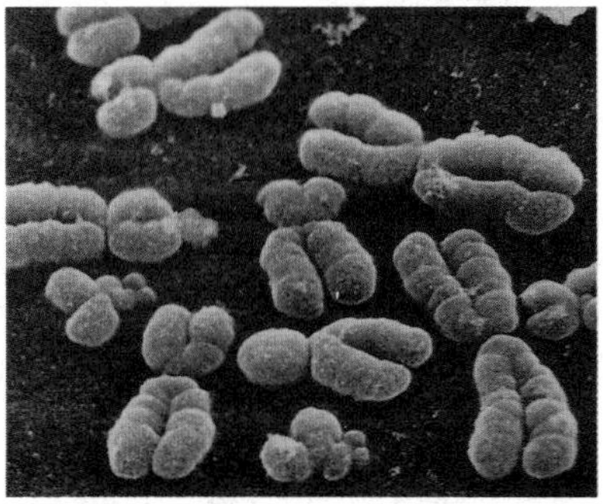

***chromosome** False-color electron microscope view of a group of human chromosomes. Each group consists of two strands joined at their center, and can produce an exact copy of itself.*

Chrysler Walter Percy 1875–1940. US industrialist. Born in Wamego, Kansas, Chrysler worked first as a railroad machinist, rising through the ranks to become manager of the American Locomotive Company in Pittsburgh 1912. Shifting to the auto industry, he was hired by General Motors and was named president of the Buick division 1916. After World War I, he became president of the independent Maxwell Motor Company and founded the Chrysler Corporation 1925. By 1928 he had acquired Dodge and Plymouth, making Chrysler Corporation one of the major forces in the US automotive industry.

chub any of several large minnows of the carp family. Creek chub *Semotelusatromaculatus*, up to 12 in/30 cm, is found widely in North American streams. Also, any of a number of small-mouthed marine fishes of the family Kyphosidae.

Chubu mountainous coastal region of central Honshu island, Japan; population (1986) 20,694,000; area 25,791 sq mi/66,774 sq km. The chief city is Nagoya.

Chufu former name for ◊Qufu, town in Shandong province, China.

Chugoku southwestern region of Honshu island, Japan; population (1986) 7,764,000; area 12,314 sq mi/31,881 sq km. The chief city is Hiroshima.

Chukchi a people of NE Siberia who speak a language belonging to the Paleo-Asiatic family. Numbering approximately 14,000, the reindeer-herding Chukchi were the predominant people of their region and are now citizens of the USSR.

Chukchi Sea part of the Arctic Ocean, situated to the N of Bering Strait between Asia and North America.

Chukovsky Kornei Ivanovitch 1882–1969. Russian critic and poet. The leading authority on the 19th century Russian poet Nekrasov, he was also an expert on the Russian language, as in for example *Zhivoi kak zhizn/A Life as Life* 1963. He was also beloved as "Grandpa" Kornei Chukovsky for his nonsense poems which owe much to the English nursery rhymes and nonsense verse that he admired.

Chun Doo Hwan 1931– . South Korean military ruler who seized power 1979; president 1981–88 as head of the newly formed Democratic Justice Party.

Chun, trained in Korea and the US, served as

church

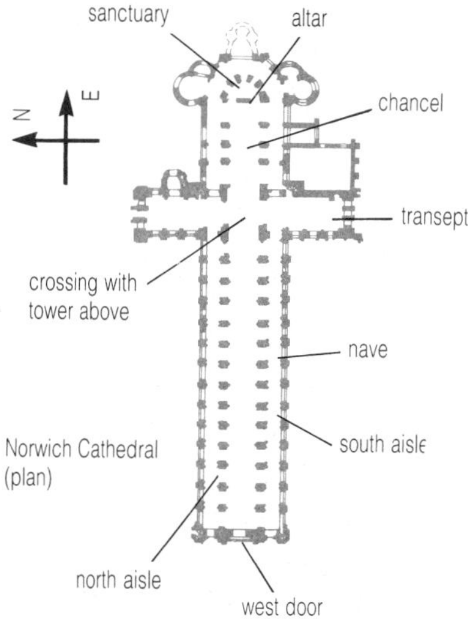

sanctuary
altar
N
E
chancel
transept
crossing with tower above
nave
south aisle
Norwich Cathedral (plan)
north aisle
west door

***Churchill** British Conservative politician Winston Churchill was prime minister during World War II, then again 1951–1955.*

an army commander from 1967 and was in charge of military intelligence 1979 when President Park was assassinated by the chief of the Korean Central Intelligence Agency (KCIA). General Chun took charge of the KCIA and, in a coup, assumed control of the army and the South Korean government. In 1981 Chun was appointed president, and oversaw a period of rapid economic growth, governing in an authoritarian manner. In 1988 he retired to a Buddhist retreat.

Chungking alternative form of ◊Chongqing, city in Sichuan province, China.

church a building designed as a Christian place of worship.

Church Frederic Edwin 1826–1900. US painter, a student of Thomas Cole and follower of the Hudson River school's style of grand landscape. During the 1850s he visited South America and the Arctic.

He is known for his portrayal of light, as in *Heart of the Andes* 1855 and *Niagara Falls* 1857.

Churchill town in the province of Manitoba, Canada, situated on Hudson Bay; population (1986) 1,217. Although the port is ice-free only three months a year, Churchill handles about 500,000 tons of grain annually, as well as fuel oil and bulk cargo. There is a modern airport, and the community is a major center for Arctic research, health programs, and education. The Hudson's Bay Company established a post here and named it for Lord Churchill (later 1st duke of Marlborough). Harbor facilities were completed 1931. A military base was established in World War II, and it continued as a rocket-launching site until the early 1960s.

Churchill Randolph (Henry Spencer) 1849–1895. British Conservative politician, chancellor of the Exchequer and leader of the House of Commons 1886; father of Winston Churchill.

He married Jennie Jerome (1854–1921), daughter of a wealthy New Yorker, 1874.

Churchill Winston (Leonard Spencer) 1874–1965. British Conservative politician. In Parliament from 1900, as a Liberal until 1923, he held a number of ministerial offices, including First Lord of the Admiralty 1911–15 and chancellor of the Exchequer 1924–29. Absent from the cabinet in the 1930s, he returned Sept 1939 to lead a coalition government 1940–45, negotiating with Allied leaders in World War II; he was again prime minister 1951–55. Nobel Prize for Literature 1953.

He was born at Blenheim Palace, the elder son of Lord Randolph Churchill. During the Boer War he was a war correspondent and made a dramatic escape from imprisonment in Pretoria. In 1900 he was elected Conservative member of Parliament for Oldham, but he disagreed with Chamberlain's tariff-reform policy and joined the Liberals.

In 1911 he was appointed First Lord of the Admiralty. In 1915–16 he served in the trenches in France but then resumed his parliamentary duties and was minister of munitions under Lloyd George 1917, when he was concerned with the development of the tank. After the armistice he was secretary for war 1918–21 and then as colonial secretary played a leading part in the establishment of the Irish Free State. During the postwar years he was active in support of the Whites (anti-Bolsheviks) in Russia. From 1929 to 1939 he was out of office as he disagreed with the Conservatives on India, rearmament, and Chamberlain's policy of appeasement.

On the first day of World War II he went back to his old post at the Admiralty. In May 1940 he was called to the premiership as head of an all-party administration and made a much quoted "blood, tears, toil, and sweat" speech to the House of Commons. He had a close relationship with US president Roosevelt and in Aug 1941 concluded the ◊Atlantic Charter with him. In Feb 1945 he met Stalin and Roosevelt at Yalta and agreed on the final plans for victory. On May 8 he announced the unconditional surrender of Germany. On May 23, 1945 the coalition was dissolved, and Churchill formed a caretaker government drawn mainly from the Conservatives. Defeated in the general election in July, he became leader of the opposition until the election Oct 1951, in which he again became prime minister. In Apr 1955 he resigned and retired to paint. After he died his paintings were exhibited in several shows, including a major retrospective in New York City in the 1980s.

Church of England the established form of Christianity in England, a member of the Anglican Communion. It was dissociated from the Roman Catholic Church 1534. There were approximately 1,100,000 regular worshipers 1988.

history

2nd century Christianity arrived in England during the Roman occupation.

597 St Augustine became first archbishop of Canterbury.

1529–34 At the Reformation the chief change was political: the sovereign (Henry VIII) replaced the pope as head of the church and assumed the right to appoint archbishops and bishops.

1536–40 The monasteries were closed down.

1549 First publication of the Book of Common Prayer, the basis of worship throughout the Anglican Church.

1563–1604 The Thirty-Nine Articles, the Church's doctrinal basis, were drawn up, enforced by Parliament, and revised.

17th–18th centuries Colonizers took the Church of England to North America (where three US bishops were consecrated after the American Revolution, and whose successors still lead the Episcopal Church in the US), Australia, New Zealand, and India.

19th century Missionaries were active in Africa. The Oxford Movement eventually developed into Anglo-Catholicism.

20th century There were moves toward reunion with the Methodist and Roman Catholic churches. The ordination of women was accepted by some overseas Anglican churches, for example the US Episcopal Church 1976.

Chuvash autonomous Soviet Socialist Republic of the USSR, it lies W of the Volga, 350 mi/560 km E of Moscow; area 7,100 sq mi/18,300 sq km; population (1986) 1,320,000. The capital is Cheboksary, population (1985) 389,000. The economy is based on lumbering and grain-growing and there are phosphate and limestone deposits and electrical and engineering industries.

CIA abbreviation for ◊Central Intelligence Agency.

Ciano Galeazzo 1903–1944. Italian politician. Son-in-law of Mussolini, the Fascist dictator of Italy, he was foreign minister 1936–43 and member of Fascist Supreme Council. He voted against Mussolini at the meeting of the Grand Council in

***Cicero** Sculpture of Roman orator Cicero. His informal letters, with their references to his wives—both of whom he divorced—and to his daughter, Tulia, who died while still a young woman, show the human side of the public figure.*

July 1943 that overthrew the dictator but was later tried for treason and shot by the Fascists.

cicada insect of the family Cicadidae. Most species are tropical, but a few occur in Europe and North America. Young cicadas live underground, for up to 17 years in some species. The adults live on trees, whose juices they suck. The males produce a loud, almost continuous, chirping by vibrating membranes in resonating cavities in the abdomen.

Cicero 106–43 BC. Roman orator, writer, and politician. His speeches and philosophical and rhetorical works are models of Latin prose, and his letters provide a picture of contemporary Roman life. As consul 63 BC he exposed Catiline's conspiracy in four major orations.

Born in Arpinium, Cicero became an advocate in Rome, spent three years in Greece studying oratory, and after the dictator Sulla's death distinguished himself in Rome on the side of the popular party. When the First Triumvirate was formed 59 BC, Cicero was exiled and devoted himself to literature. He sided with Pompey during the civil war (49–48 BC) but was pardoned by Julius Caesar and returned to Rome. After Caesar's assassination 44 BC he supported Octavian (the future emperor Augustus) and violently attacked Antony in speeches known as the *Philippics*. On the reconciliation of Antony and Octavian he was executed by Antony's agents.

cichlid freshwater fish of the family Cichlidae. Cichlids are somewhat perchlike, but have a single nostril on each side instead of two. They are mostly predatory, and have deep, colorful bodies, flattened from side to side so that some are almost disk shaped. Many are territorial in the breeding season and may show care of the young. There are more than 1,000 species found in South and Central America, Africa, and India.

The discus fish *Symphysodon* produces a skin secretion on which the young feed. Other cichlids, such as those of the genus *Tilapia*, brood their young in the mouth.

Cid, El Rodrigo Díaz de Bivar 1040–1099. Spanish soldier, nicknamed El Cid ("the lord") by the ◊Moors. Born in Castile of a noble family, he fought against the king of Navarre and won his nickname *el Campeador* ("the Champion") by killing the Navarrese champion in single combat. Essentially a mercenary, fighting both with and against the Moors, he died while defending Valencia against them, and in subsequent romances became Spain's national hero.

cider juice pressed from apples as a beverage or for making vinegar. In the US, hard cider refers to fermented apple juice drunk as an alcoholic beverage. Alcoholic cider is produced in large quantities in North and South America, France, England, and Spain.

Cienfuegos port and naval base in Cuba; population (1985) 124,600. It trades in sugar, fruit, and tobacco.

Cierva Juan de la 1895–1936. Spanish engineer. In trying to produce an aircraft that could fly slowly and would not stall, he invented the ◊autogiro.

cigar a compact roll of cured tobacco leaves, contained in a binder leaf, which in turn is surrounded by a wrapper leaf. The cigar was originally a sheath of leaves filled with tobacco, smoked by the Indians of Central America. Cigar smoking was introduced into Spain soon after 1492 and spread all over Europe in the next few centuries. From about 1890 cigar smoking was gradually supplanted in popularity by cigarette smoking.

The first cigar factory was opened in Hamburg, Germany, in 1788, and about that time cigar smoking became popular in Britain and the US. The first cigars were made by hand—as the more expensive cigars still are. From about the 1850s various machine methods have been employed. The best cigars are still hand-rolled in Cuba, hence Havanas.

cigarette (French "little cigar") a thin paper tube stuffed with shredded tobacco for smoking, now often plugged with a filter. The first cigarettes were the *papelitos* smoked in South America about 1750. The habit spread to Spain and then throughout the world; today it is the most general form of tobacco smoking, although it is dangerous to the health of both smokers and nonsmokers who breathe in the smoke.

Since the 1960s warnings from the US Surgeon General have been added to packages, cartons, and advertising, about the dangers of smoking and cancer, lung disease, heart disease, and the effects on the developing fetus.

cilia (singular cilium) small threadlike organs on the surface of some cells, composed of contractile fibers that produce rhythmic waving movements. Some single-celled organisms move by means of cilia. In multicellular animals, they keep lubricated surfaces clear of debris. They also move food in the digestive tracts of some invertebrates.

ciliary muscle ring of muscle surrounding and controlling the lens inside the vertebrate eye, used in ◊accommodation (focusing). Suspensory ligaments, resembling spokes of a wheel, connect the lens to the ciliary muscle and pull the lens into a flatter shape when the muscle relaxes. On contraction, the lens returns to its normal spherical state.

Cilicia ancient region of Asia Minor, now forming part of Turkey, situated between the Taurus Mountains and the Mediterranean.

Successively conquered by the Persians, Alexander the Great, and the Romans under Pompey, Cilicia became an independent Armenian principality in 1080 and a kingdom in 1198. Sometimes referred to as Lesser Armenia, it was absorbed into the Ottoman Empire during the 15th century. Access from the north across the Taurus range is through the Cilician Gates, a strategic pass that has been used for centuries as part of a trade route linking Europe and the Middle East.

Cimabue Giovanni (Cenni de Peppi) c. 1240–1302. Italian painter, active in Florence, traditionally styled the "father of Italian painting." Among the works attributed to him are *Madonna and Child* (Uffizi, Florence), a huge Gothic image of the Virgin that nevertheless has a new softness and solidity that points forward to Giotto.

Cimarosa Domenico 1749–1801. Italian composer of operas that include *Il Matrimonio segreto/The Secret Marriage* 1792.

cimbalom in music, a type of ◊dulcimer.

Cimino Michael 1943– . US film director who established his reputation with *The Deer Hunter* 1978 (which won five Academy Awards). His other films include the financially and critically disastrous *Heaven's Gate* 1981 and *The Year of the Dragon* 1986.

cinchona any shrub or tree of the tropical American genus *Chinchoua* of the madder family Rubiaceae. ◊Quinine is produced from the bark of some species, and these are now cultivated in India, Sri Lanka, the Philippines, and Indonesia.

Cincinnati city and port in Ohio, on the Ohio River; population (1990) 364,040. Chief industries include machinery, clothing, furniture making, wine, chemicals, and meatpacking. Procter and Gamble, a household-products manufacturer, has its headquarters here. Founded in 1788, Cincinnati became a city 1819. It attracted large numbers of European immigrants, particularly Germans, during the 19th century. Xavier University and the University of Cincinnati are here, and it has a major symphony orchestra. William Howard Taft, 27th president of the US, was born in Cincinnati.

Cincinnatus Lucius Quintus 5th century BC. Roman general. Appointed dictator in 458 BC, he defeated the Aequi (an Italian people) in a brief campaign, then resumed life as a yeoman farmer.

Cinderella traditional European fairy tale, of which about 700 versions exist, including one by Charles ◊Perrault. Cinderella is an ill-treated youngest daughter who is enabled by a fairy godmother to attend the royal ball. She captivates Prince Charming but must flee at midnight, losing a tiny glass slipper by which the prince later identifies her.

cinema a 20th-century form of art and entertainment, consisting of "moving pictures" in either black and white or color, projected onto a screen. Cinema borrows from the other arts, such as music, drama, and literature, but is entirely dependent for its origins on technological developments, including the technology of action photography, projection, sound reproduction and film processing and printing (see ◊photography). The audience usually sits in a large hall or theater, in the dark, many designed particularly for film viewing (movie palaces).

film history The first moving pictures were shown in the 1890s. Edison persuaded James J Corbett (1866–1933), the world boxing champion 1892–97, to act a boxing match for a film. Lumière in France, Latham in the US, R W Paul in England, and others were making moving pictures of actual events (for example, *The Derby* 1896, shown in London on the evening of the race), and of simple scenes such as a train coming into a station. In 1902 Georges Méliès of France made the fantasy story film *A Trip to the Moon*, and in 1903 Edwin S Porter directed *The Great Train Robbery* for Edison. This was a story in a contemporary setting and cost about $100 to make. The film was shown all over the world and earned more than $20,000.

film technique For a number of years, films of "indoor" happenings were "shot" out of doors by daylight in New York City and New Jersey before the move (from c. 1910) to Hollywood. The fairly constant sunny climate was the basis of its success as a center of film production. The first film studio was Edison's at Fort Lee, New Jersey, but the Astoria Studios in New York City turned out many popular silents and early "talkies," since it was near Broadway and could therefore make use of the theater stars on its doorstep.

In England, the pioneer company of Cricks and Martin set up a studio at Mitcham (where a romantic domestic drama, *For Baby's Sake*, was made 1908).

D W Griffith, the US director, revolutionized film technique, introducing the close-up, the flashback, the fade-out, and the fade-in. Like other filmmakers, he produced one- and two-reelers before making his first epic, *The Birth of a Nation* 1915, and his second, *Intolerance* 1916, with spectacular scenes in the Babylonian section. Feature-length films had been introduced in 1914.

film personalities At first, players' names were of no importance, although one who appeared nameless in *The Great Train Robbery*, G M Anderson, afterwards became famous as "Bronco Billy" in a series of cowboy films, the first Westerns. The first movie performer to become a name was The Biograph Girl, Florence Lawrence 1910, followed by America's Sweetheart, Mary Pickford; moviegoers found her so attractive that they insisted on knowing who she was 1913–14. World War I virtually stopped film production in Europe, but Hollywood continued to flourish in the 1920s, creating such silent stars as Rudolph Valentino, Douglas Fairbanks Sr, Lillian Gish, Gloria Swanson, Richard Barthelmess, and Greta Garbo (dramatic actors); and Charles Chaplin, Buster Keaton, Harold Lloyd, Ben Blue (comedians).

The introduction of sound from the late 1920s ended the careers of silent stars with unsuitable voices and changed the style of acting to one more natural than mimetic. British stage stars who made the transition to film include Edith Evans, Alec Guinness, Laurence Olivier, and Ralph Richardson. US stars of the golden Hollywood era include Clark Gable, the Marx Brothers, Judy Garland, Greta Garbo, and Joan Crawford. Although many Hollywood stars were "made" by the studios, like Jean Harlow and Shirley Temple, American stage actors such as Humphrey Bogart, Henry Fonda, Spencer Tracy, Katharine Hepburn, and Bette Davis became stars in 1930s Hollywood and continued to act in films for many years.

artistic development Concern for artistry began with Griffith, but also developed in Europe, particularly in the USSR and Germany, where directors exploited film's artistic possibilities during both the silent and the sound eras. Silent films were never completely silent; there was always a musical background, integral to the film, whether played by a solo pianist in a suburban cinema or a 100-piece orchestra in a big city theater. The arrival of sound films (John Barrymore as *Don Juan* 1926 and Al Jolson as *The Jazz Singer* 1927), seen at first as having only novelty value, soon brought about a wider perspective and greater artistic possibilities through the combination of sight and sound. Successful directors of early sound films included Jean Renoir in France, Lang and Murnau in Germany, Mauritz Stiller in Sweden, Hitchcock in Britain, Selznick, Ford, and Capra in the US, and Pudovkin and Eisenstein in the USSR. After World War II Japanese films were first seen in the West (although the industry dates back to the silent days), and India developed a thriving cinema industry.

Apart from story films, the industry produced newsreels of current events and "documentaries" depicting factual life, of which the pioneers were the US filmmaker Robert Flaherty (*Nanook of the North* 1920, *Man of Aran* 1932–34) and the Scot John Grierson (*Drifters* 1929, *Night Mail* 1936); animated cartoon films, which achieved their first success with Patrick Sullivan's *Felix the Cat* 1917, were later surpassed in popularity by Walt Disney's *Mickey Mouse* 1928 and the feature length *Snow White and the Seven Dwarfs* 1938 and others. During the 1930s classic dramas and screwball comedies were made; during the 1940s war films predominated; and during the 1950s *film noir* and Technicolor musicals competed with early television.

the influence of television By the 1960s, increasing competition from television, perceived at the time as a threat to the studio system of film production and distribution, led the film indus-

cinema: chronology

1826–34	Various machines invented to show moving images: the stroboscope, zoetrope, and thaumatrope.
1872	Eadweard Muybridge demonstrated movement of horses' legs by using 24 cameras.
1877	Invention of Praxinoscope; developed as a projector of successive images on screen in 1879 in France.
1878–95	Marey, a French physiologist, developed various types of camera for recording human and animal movements.
1887	Augustin le Prince produced the first series of images on a perforated film; Thomas Edison, having developed the phonograph, took the first steps in developing a motion-picture recording and reproducing device to accompany recorded sound.
1888	William Friese-Green showed the first celluloid film and patented a movie camera.
1889	Edison invented 35 mm film.
1890–94	Edison, using perforated film, developed his Kinetograph camera and Kinetoscope individual viewer; developed commercially in New York, London, and Paris.
1895	The Lumière brothers, Auguste (1862–1954) and Louis (1864–1948), projected, to a paying audience, a film of an oncoming train arriving at a station. Some of the audience fled in terror.
1896	Pathé introduced the Berliner phonograph, using disks in synchronization with film. Lack of amplification, however, made the performances ineffective.
1899	Edison tried to improve amplification by using banks of phonographs.
1900	Attempts to synchronize film and disk were made by Gaumont in France and Goldschmidt in Germany, leading later to the American Vitaphone system.
1902	Georges Méliès (1861–1938) made *Le Voyage dans la Lune/A Trip to the Moon.*
1903	The first "Western" was made in the US: *The Great Train Robbery* by Edwin S Porter.
1906	The earliest color film (Kinemacolor) was patented in Britain by George Albert Smith.
1907–11	The first films shot in the Los Angeles area called Hollywood.
1908–11	In France, Emile Cohl experimented with film animation.
1910	With the influence of US studios and fan magazines, film actors and actresses began to be recognized by name as international stars.
1911	The first Hollywood studio, Horsley's Centaur Film Co, was established followed in 1915 by Carl Laemmle's Universal City and Thomas Ince's studio.
1912	In Britain, Eugene Lauste designed experimental "sound on film" systems.
1914–18	Full newsreel coverage of World War I.
1915	*The Birth of a Nation*, D W Griffith's epic on the American Civil War and the rise of the Ku Klux Klan, was released in the US.
1917	35 mm was officially adopted as the standard format for motion picture film by the Society of Motion Picture Engineers of America.
1918–19	A sound system called Tri-Ergon was developed in Germany, which led to sound being recorded on film photographically. The photography of sound was also developed by Lee De Forrest in his Phonofilm system.
1923	First sound film (as Phonofilm) demonstrated.
1926	*Don Juan*, a silent film with a synchronized music score, was released.
1927	Release of the first major sound film, *The Jazz Singer*, consisting of some songs and a few moments of dialogue, made by Warner Bros, New York. The first Academy Awards (Oscars) were presented.
1928	Walt Disney released his first Mickey Mouse cartoon, *Steamboat Willie*. The first all-talking film, *Lights of New York*, was released.
1930	*The Big Trail*, a Western filmed and shown in 70 mm rather than the standard 35 mm format, was released. 70 mm is still used, but usually only for big-budget epics such as *Lawrence of Arabia.*
1932	Technicolor (three-color) process was used for a Walt Disney cartoon film.
1935	*Becky Sharp*, the first film in three-color Technicolor (a process now abandoned), was released.
1937	Walt Disney released the first feature-length (82 minutes) cartoon, *Snow White and the Seven Dwarfs.*
1939	*Gone With the Wind*, regarded as one of Hollywood's greatest achievements, was released.
1952	Cinerama, a wide-screen presentation using three cameras and three projectors, was introduced in New York.
1953	Commercial 3-D (three-dimensional) cinema and wide-screen CinemaScope were launched in the US. CinemaScope used a single camera and projector to produce a widescreen effect by using an anamorphic lens. The cameras were clumsy and the audiences disliked wearing the obligatory glasses. The new wide-screen cinema was accompanied by the introduction of Stereographic sound, which eventually became standard.
1959	The first film in "Smell-O-Vision," *The Scent of Mystery*, was released. The process did not catch on.
1970	Most major films were released in Dolby Stereo.
1982	3-D made a brief comeback. Some of the films released that used the process, such as *Jaws 3-D* and *Friday the 13th Part 3*, were commercial successes, but the revival was short lived.
1987	US House Judiciary Committee "petitioned" by leading Hollywood filmmakers to protect their work from electronic "colorization," the new process by which black-and-white films were tinted for television transmission.

try to concentrate on special effects (CinemaScope, Cinerama, Todd AO) and wide-screen spectaculars dealing with historical and biblical themes, for example, *Cleopatra* 1963. Also exploited were the horror genre and areas of sexuality and violence considered unsuitable for family television viewing. A distinction was usually made by critics between "art" films and "popular" films; the latter included such genres as the Chinese Western or kung-fu film, which had a vogue in the 1970s, and films controversial for their potential glorification of violence, epitomized by the character Rambo, a loner who takes the law into his own hands, as played by Sylvester Stallone.

Another popular genre was science fiction, such as *Star Wars* 1977, *Close Encounters of the Third Kind* 1977, and *ET* 1982, with expensive special effects. Throughout the 1980s cinema, both as art and as pure entertainment, seemed to be undergoing a revival, partly aided by the growth during the preceding decade of the video industry, which made major films available for viewing on home television screens.

CinemaScope a wide-screen process devised by 20th Century-Fox using anamorphic lenses, in which images are compressed during filming and then extended during projection onto a wide curved screen. The first film to be made in CinemaScope was *The Robe* 1953.

cinema vérité (French "realistic cinema") a style of filmmaking that aims to capture truth on film by observing, recording, and presenting real events and situations as they occur without major directorial, editorial, or technical control.

Cinerama a wide-screen process devised in 1937 by Fred Waller of Paramount's special-effects department. Originally three 35-mm cameras and three projectors were used to record and project a single image. Three aspects of the image were recorded and then projected on a large curved screen with the result that the images blended together to produce an illusion of vastness. The first Cinerama film was *How the West Was Won* 1962. It was eventually abandoned in favor of a single-lens 70-mm process.

cinnabar mercuric sulfide, HgS, the only commercially useful ore of mercury. It is deposited in veins and impregnations near recent volcanic rocks and hot springs. The mineral itself is used as a red pigment, commonly known as ***vermilion***. Cinnabar is found in the US (California), Spain (Almadén), Peru, Italy, and Yugoslavia.

cinnamon dried inner bark of a tree *Cinnamomum zeylanicum* of the laurel family, grown in India and Sri Lanka. The bark is ground to make the spice used in curries and confectionery. Oil of cinnamon is obtained from waste bark and is used as flavoring in food and medicine.

cinquefoil any plant of the genus *Potentilla* of the rose family, usually with five-lobed leaves and brightly colored flowers. It is widespread in northern temperate regions.

Field cinquefoil *P. canadensis* is a low-growing perennial with yellow flowers native to E North America in dry grasslands and barrens.

Cinque Ports group of ports in S England, originally five, Sandwich, Dover, Hythe, Romney, and Hastings, later including Rye, Winchelsea, and others. Probably founded in Roman times, they rose to importance after the Norman conquest and until the end of the 15th century were bound to supply the ships and men necessary against invasion.

circadian rhythm the metabolic rhythm found in most organisms, which generally coincides with the 24-hour day. Its most obvious manifestation is the regular cycle of sleeping and waking, but body temperature and the concentration of ◊hormones that influence mood and behavior also vary over the day. In humans, alteration of habits (such as rapid air travel around the world) may result in the circadian rhythm being out of phase with actual activity patterns, causing malaise until it has had time to adjust.

Circassia former name of an area of the N Caucasus, ceded to Russia by Turkey in 1829 and now part of the Karachai-Cherkess region of the USSR.

Circe in Greek mythology, an enchantress. In the *Odyssey* of Homer she turned the followers of Odysseus into pigs when she held their leader captive.

circle path followed by a point that moves so as to keep a constant distance, the radius, from a fixed point, the center. The longest distance in a straight line from one side of a circle to the other, passing through the center, is called the diameter, and its measure is twice that of the radius. The ratio of the distance all the way around the circle (the circumference) to the diameter is an

◊irrational number called π (pi), roughly equal to 3.14159. A circle of radius r and diameter d has a circumference $C = \pi d$, or $C = 2\pi r$, and an area $A = \pi r^2$.

The area of a circle can be shown by dividing it into very thin sectors and reassembling them to make an approximate rectangle. The proof of $A = \pi r^2$ can be done only by using ◊integral calculus.

circuit in law, the geographic district that constitutes a particular area of jurisdiction.

In the US the Court of Appeals sits in ten judicial areas, or circuits—hence circuit courts—and Washington, DC.

circuit in physics or electrical engineering, an arrangement of electrical components through which a current can flow. There are two basic circuits, series and parallel. In a series circuit, the components are connected end-to-end so that the current flows through all components one after the other. In a parallel circuit, components are connected side-by-side so that part of the current passes through each component. A circuit diagram shows in graphical form how components are connected together, using standard symbols for the components.

circuit breaker switching device designed to protect an electric circuit from excessive current. It has the same action as a ◊fuse, and many houses now have a circuit breaker between the incoming mains supply and the domestic circuits. Circuit breakers usually work by means of ◊solenoids. Those at electricity-generating stations have to be specially designed to prevent dangerous arcing (the release of luminous discharge) when the high-voltage supply is switched off. They may use an air blast or oil immersion to quench the arc.

circulatory system the system of vessels in an animal's body that transports essential substances (blood or other circulatory fluid) to and from the different parts of the body. Except for simple animals such as sponges and coelenterates (jellyfishes, sea anemones, corals), all animals have a circulatory system.

In fishes, blood passes once around the body

circle

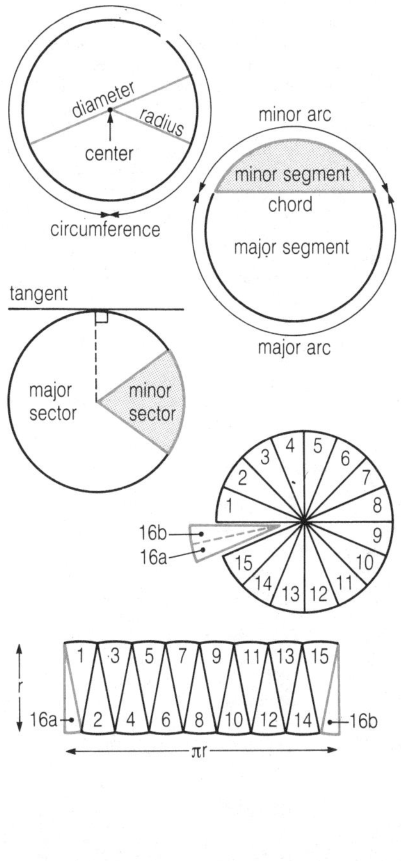
diameter
radius
center
circumference
minor arc
minor segment
chord
major segment
major arc
tangent
major sector
minor sector
16b
16a
r
πr

circulatory system

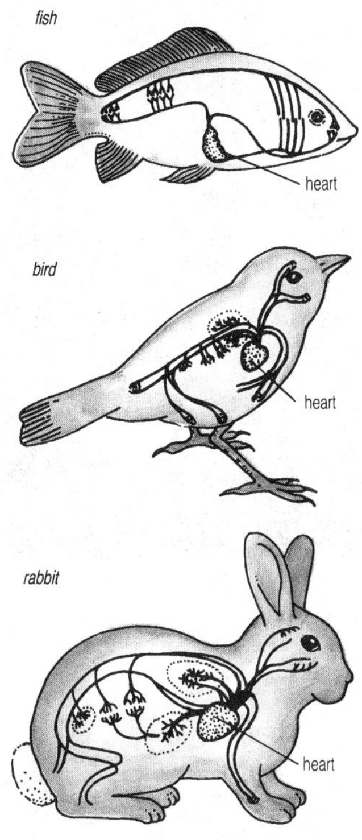
fish
heart
bird
heart
rabbit
heart

before returning to a two-chambered heart (single circulation). In birds and mammals, blood passes to the lungs and back to the heart before circulating around the remainder of the body (double circulation). In all vertebrates, blood flows in one direction. Valves in the heart, large arteries, and veins prevent backflow, and the muscular walls of the arteries assist in pushing the blood around the body. Although most animals have a heart or hearts to pump the blood, normal body movements circulate the fluid in some small invertebrates. In the open system, found in snails and other mollusks, the blood (more correctly called ◊hemolymph) passes from the arteries into a body cavity (hemocoel), and from here is gradually returned to the heart, via the gills, by other blood vessels. Insects and other arthropods have an open system with a heart. In the closed system of earthworms, blood flows directly from the main artery to the main vein, via smaller lateral vessels in each body segment. Vertebrates, too, have a closed system with a network of tiny ◊capillaries carrying the blood from arteries to veins.

circumcision surgical removal of all or part of the foreskin (prepuce) of the penis, usually performed on the newborn; practiced among Jews and Muslims. In Muslim societies in Africa and the Middle East, female circumcision or clitoridectomy (removal of the labia minora and/or clitoris) is practiced on adolescents as well as babies; it is illegal in the West.

Female circumcision has no medical benefit and often causes disease and complications in childbirth; in 1982 an estimated 84 million women had been mutilated in this way. Male circumcision too is usually carried out for cultural reasons, not as a medical necessity. Some evidence indicates that it protects against the development of cancer of the penis later in life and that women with circumcised partners are at less risk from cancer of the cervix, although these theories have not been proved.

Circumcision, Feast of Roman Catholic and Anglican religious festival, celebrated annually on Jan 1 in commemoration of Jesus' circumcision.

circumference in geometry, the curved line that encloses a plane figure, for example a ◊circle or an ellipse. Its length varies according to the nature of the curve, and may be ascertained by the appropriate formula. The circumference of a circle is $2\pi r$, where r is the radius and π is the constant pi, approximately equal to 3.1416.

circumnavigation sailing around the world. The first ship to sail around the world was the *Victoria*, one of the Spanish squadron of five vessels that sailed from Seville in Aug 1519 under the Portuguese navigator Ferdinand Magellan.

Four vessels were lost on the way, but the *Victoria* arrived back in Spain in Sept 1522 under Cano. Magellan himself did not complete the voyage, as he died in the Philippines in 1521. The first English circumnavigator was Drake in 1577–80 in the Golden Hind.

circus (Latin "circle") an entertainment, often held in a large tent ("big top"), involving performing animals, acrobats, and clowns. In 1871 P T ◊Barnum created the "Greatest Show on Earth" in the US. The popularity of animal acts decreased in the 1980s. Originally, in Roman times, a circus was an arena for chariot races and gladiatorial combats.

cirque (Welsh *cwm*; Scottish and English *corrie*) steep-walled hollow in the mountainside of a glaciated area representing the source of a melted glacier. The weight of the ice has ground out the bottom and worn back the sides. It is open at the front, and its sides and back are formed of ◊arêtes. There may be a lake at the bottom.

cirrhosis any degenerative disease in an organ of the body, especially the liver, characterized by excessive development of connective tissue, causing scarring and painful swelling. Cirrhosis of the liver may be caused by an infection such as viral hepatitis, by chronic alcoholism or drug use, blood disorder, or malnutrition. If cirrhosis is diagnosed early, it can be arrested by treating the cause; otherwise it will progress to jaundice, edema, vomiting blood, coma, and death.

Cisalpine Gaul region of the Roman province of Gallia (N Italy) S of the Alps; Transalpine Gaul, the region N of the Alps, comprised Belgium, France, the Netherlands, and Switzerland.

The Cisalpine Republic was the creation of Napoleon in N Italy 1797, known as the Italian Republic 1802–04 and the Kingdom of Italy 1804–15.

Ciskei, Republic of a Bantu homeland in South Africa, which became independent 1981, although this is not recognized by any other country

area 2,974 sq mi/7,700 sq km

capital Bisho

features one of the two homelands of the Xhosa people created by South Africa (the other is Transkei)

products pineapples, timber, metal products, leather, textiles

population (1984) 903,681

language Xhosa

government president, (Brig Oupa Gqozo from 1990) with legislative and executive councils.

Cistercian order Roman Catholic monastic order established at Cîteaux 1098 by St Robert de Champagne, abbot of Molesme, as a stricter form of the Benedictine order. Living mainly by agricultural labor, the Cistercians made many advances in farming methods in the Middle Ages. The ◊Trappists, so called from the original house at La Trappe in Normandy (founded by Dominique de Rancé in 1664), followed a particularly strict version of the rule.

cistron in genetics, the segment of ◊DNA that is required to synthesize a complete polypeptide chain. It is the molecular equivalent of a ◊gene.

CITES abbreviation for Convention on International Trade in Endangered Species, an international agreement signed by 81 countries under the auspices of the ◊IUCN to regulate the trade in ◊endangered species of animals and plants.

cithara ancient musical instrument, resembling a lyre but with a flat back. It was strung with wire

cirque *A perfect cirque overlooking Loch Broom, in the Scottish Highlands.*

and plucked with a plectrum or (after the 16th century) with the fingers. The bandurria and laud, still popular in Spain, are instruments of the same type.

citizens' band (CB) short-range radio communication (around 27 MHz) facility used by members of the public in the US and many European countries to talk to one another or call for emergency assistance.

citizenship status as a member of a nation. In most countries citizenship may be acquired either by birth or by naturalization. The status confers rights such as voting and the protection of the law and also imposes responsibilities such as taxation or military service, in some countries.

Citlaltépetl (Aztec "star mountain") a dormant volcano, the highest mountain in Mexico, height 18,700 ft/5,700 m, N of the city of Orizaba (after which it is sometimes named). It last erupted in 1687.

citric acid $C_6H_8O_7$ organic acid widely distributed in the plant kingdom, found in high concentrations in citrus fruits, with a sharp, sour taste. At one time it was commercially prepared from concentrated lemon juice, but now the main source is the fermentation of sugar with certain molds.

citronella lemon-scented oil used in cosmetics and insect repellents, obtained from the S Asian grass *Cymbopogon nardus*.

citrus tree or shrub of the genus *Citrus* of the rue family Rutaceae. Citruses are found in Asia and other warm parts of the world. They are evergreen and aromatic, and several species—the orange, lemon, lime, citron, and grapefruit—are cultivated for fruit.

city generally, a large and important town.

In the Near East and ancient Europe, and in the ancient civilizations of Mexico and Peru, cities were often states in themselves. In the early Middle Ages, European cities were usually those towns that were episcopal sees (seats of bishops).

In the US, a city is an incorporated municipality whose boundaries and powers of self-government are defined by charter from the state in which it is located.

City of Akron v Akron Center for Reproductive Health a US Supreme Court decision 1983 that reaffirmed the right to privacy in reproduction. The petitioner, an Ohio clinic, challenged a state law that set certain procedural restrictions on second- and third-trimester abortions. The Court found that the Ohio measures, requiring parental consent for minors, a 24-hour waiting period, and "humane disposal" of the fetus, were unconstitutional. The ruling reaffirmed women's constitutional "personal liberty" and the right to abortion.

Ciudad Bolívar city in SE Venezuela, on the river Orinoco, 250 mi/400 km from its mouth; population (1981) 183,000. Gold is mined in the vicinity. The city is linked with Soledad across the river by the Angostura bridge (1967), the first to span the Orinoco. Capital of Bolívar state, it was called Angostura 1824–49.

Ciudad Guayana city in Venezuela, on the S bank of the river Orinoco, population (1981) 314,500. Main industries include iron and steel. The city was formed by the union of Puerto Ordaz and San Felix, and has been opened to ocean-going ships by dredging.

Ciudad Juárez city on the Rio Grande, in Chihuahua, N Mexico, on the US border; population (1986) 596,000. It is a center for cotton.

Ciudad Real city of central Spain; 105 mi/170 km S of Madrid; population (1981) 50,150. It is the capital of Ciudad Real province. It trades in livestock and produces textiles and pharmaceuticals. Its chief feature is its huge Gothic cathedral.

Ciudad Trujillo name 1936–61 of ◊Santo Domingo, capital city and seaport of the Dominican Republic.

civet small to medium-sized carnivorous mammal found in Africa and Asia, belonging to the family Viverridae, which also includes ◊mongooses and ◊genets. Distant relations of cats, they generally have longer jaws and more teeth. All have a scent gland in the inguinal (groin) region.

Extracts from this gland are taken from the African civet *Civettictis civetta* and used in perfumery. This civet is 2.3 ft/70 cm long, darkly spotted, and hunts small animals at night. As well as eating animal matter, many species, for example palm civets such as the SE Asian *Arctogalidia trivirgata*, are fond of fruit.

Civic Forum (Czech Občanske Forum) Czech democratic movement, formed Nov 1989, led by Vaclav ◊Havel. In Dec 1989 it participated in forming a coalition government after the collapse of communist rule in Czechoslovakia. Its Slovak counterpart is ◊Public Against Violence.

civil aviation the operation of passenger and freight transport by air. With increasing traffic, control of air space is a major problem. The Federal Aviation Agency (FAA) is responsible for regulating development of aircraft, air navigation, traffic control, and communications in the US. The Civil Aeronautics Board is the US authority prescribing safety regulations and investigating accidents. The world's largest airline is the Soviet Union's government-owned Aeroflot, which operates 1,300 aircraft over 620,000 mi/1 million km of routes and carries over 110 million passengers a year.

civil defense organized activities by the civilian population of a state to mitigate the effects of enemy attack on them.

During World War II (1939–45) civil-defense efforts were centered on providing adequate warning of air raids to permit the civilian population to reach shelter; then firefighting, food, rescue, communications, and ambulance services were needed. Since then, the threat of nuclear weapons has led to the building of fallout shelters in the US, the USSR, and elsewhere. China has networks of tunnels in the cities that are meant to enable the population to escape nuclear fallout and reach the countryside, but which do not protect against the actual blast.

civil disobedience the deliberate breaking of laws considered unjust, a form of nonviolent direct action; the term was coined by the New England political philosopher Henry David Thoreau in an essay of that name 1849. It was advocated by Mahatma ◊Gandhi to prompt the peaceful withdrawal of the British from India. Civil disobedience has since been employed by, for instance, the US civil-rights movement in the 1960s and the international peace movement in the 1980s.

civil engineering the branch of engineering that is concerned with the construction of roads, bridges, aqueducts, waterworks, tunnels, canals, irrigation works, and harbors.

The term is thought to have been used for the first time by British engineer John Smeaton in about 1750, to distinguish civilian from military engineering projects.

civilization in anthropology, an advanced sociopolitical stage of cultural evolution, whereby a centralized government (over a city, ceremonial center, or larger region called a state) is supported by the taxation of surplus production, and rules the agricultural and, often, mercantile base. Non-food producers become specialists who govern, lead religious ritual, impose and collect taxes, record the past and present, plan and have executed monumental public works (irrigation systems, roads, bridges, buildings, tombs), and elaborate and formalize the style and traditions of the society. These institutions are based on the advantageous use of leisure time to develop writing, mathematics, the sciences, engineering, architecture, philosophy, and the arts.

The earliest civilizations evolved in the Old World from advanced ◊neolithic farming societies in the Near East (Sumer in 3500 BC; Egypt in 3000 BC), the Indus Valley (in 2500 BC), and China (in 2200 BC). In the New World, similar conditions of advanced neolithic farming communities led to the rise of civilizations in Mesoamerica (the Olmec in 1200 BC) and in Peru (the Chavin in 800 BC). Archeological remains of cities and ceremonial centers usually indicate the civilized state, with all the trappings of both style and content mentioned above.

civil law the legal system based on Roman law. It is one of the two main European legal systems, English (common) law being the other. In the US, civil law also means the law relating to matters other than criminal law, such as ◊contract and ◊tort.

civil rights the rights of the individual citizen. In many countries they are specified (as in the Bill of Rights of the US Constitution) and guaranteed by law to ensure equal treatment for all citizens. In the US, the struggle to obtain civil rights for blacks and former slaves and their descendants, both through legislation and in practice, has been a major theme since the Civil War.

Civil Rights Cases five Supreme Court cases 1883 that tested the Civil Rights Act of 1875, which guaranteed protection from racial discrimination by private citizens. Congress considered this protection implicit in the 13th and 14th Amendments, but the Court disagreed. According to an 8–1 ruling, the 13th Amendment only prohibited forced servitude while the 14th Amendment protected citizens only from discrimination by the state, not by private individuals. The Civil Rights Act was struck down, a decision not reversed until 1964 (see ◊*Heart of Atlanta Motel Inc* v *US*).

civil service the body of administrative staff appointed to carry out the policy of a government. In the US, federal employees are restricted in the role they may play in political activity, and they retain their posts (except at senior levels) when there is a change in administration.

civil war war between rival groups within the same country.

Civil War, American also called ***War Between the States*** war 1861–65 between the Southern or Confederate States of America and the Northern or Union states. The former wished to maintain certain "states' rights," in particular the right to determine state law on the institution of slavery, and claimed the right to secede from the Union; the latter fought primarily to maintain the Union, with slave emancipation (1863) a secondary issue.

The war, and in particular its aftermath, when the South was occupied by Northern troops in the period known as ◊Reconstruction, left behind bitterness that lasts to the present day. Industry prospered in the North, while the economy of the South, which had been based on slavery, declined.

chronology

1861 Seven Southern states set up the Confederate States of America (president Jefferson Davis) Feb 8; ◊Fort Sumter, Charleston, captured Apr 12–14; Pierre Beauregard (Confederate) was victorious at the 1st Battle of Bull Run July 21.

1862 Battle of Shiloh Apr 6–7 was indecisive. General Grant (Union) captured New Orleans in May, but the Confederates, under Robert E ◊Lee were again victorious at the 2nd Battle of Bull Run Aug 29–30. Lee's northward advance was then checked by General McClellan at ◊Antietam Sept 17.

1863 The Emancipation Proclamation was issued by President Lincoln Jan 1, freeing the slaves and assuring British and French neutrality; Battle of Gettysburg (Union victory) July 1–4 marked the turning point of the war; Grant overran the Mississippi states, capturing Vicksburg July 4.

1864 In the Battle of Cold Harbor near Richmond, Virginia, June 1–12, Lee delayed Grant in his advance on Richmond. General Sherman (Union) marched through Georgia to the sea, taking Atlanta Sept 1 and Savannah Dec 22, destroying much of the infrastructure as he went.

1865 Lee surrendered to Grant at Appomattox courthouse Apr 9; Lincoln was assassinated Apr 14; last Confederate troops surrendered May 26. There were 359,528 Union and 258,000 Confederate dead. The period of ◊Reconstruction began.

The issue of slavery had brought to a head long-standing social and economic differences between the two oldest sections of the country. A series of political crises was caused by the task of determining whether newly admitted states, such as California, should permit or prohibit slavery in their state constitutions. The political parties in the late 1850s came to represent only sectional interests—Democrats in the South, Republicans in the North. This breakdown of an underlying national political consensus (which had previously sustained national parties) led to the outbreak of hostilities, only a few weeks after the inauguration of the first Republican president, Abraham ◊Lincoln.

Civil War, English in British history, the struggle in the middle years of the 17th century between the king and the Royalists (Cavaliers) on one side, and the Parliamentarians (also called Roundheads) on the other. The Parliamentarians under ◊Cromwell dealt a series of defeats to Charles, executing him 1649, and Cromwell made himself Protector (ruler) until the Restoration of the monarchy 1660.

chronology

1642 On Aug 22 ◊Charles I raised his standard at Nottingham. The Battle of ◊Edgehill on Oct 23 was indecisive.

1644 The Battle of ◊Marston Moor on July 2 was a victory for the Parliamentarians under ◊Cromwell.

1645 The Battle of ◊Naseby on June 14 was a decisive victory for Cromwell.

1646 On May 5, 1646 Charles surrendered to the Scottish army.

1648 A Royalist and Presbyterian uprising from March to Aug was soon crushed by Cromwell and his New Model Army.

1649 Charles was beheaded on Jan 30.

1649–50 Cromwell's invasion of Ireland.

1650 Cromwell defeated the Royalists under the future ◊Charles II at Dunbar, Scotland.

1651 The Battle of Worcester was another victory for Cromwell.

Civil War, Spanish war 1936–39 precipitated by a military revolt led by Gen Franco against the Republican government. Inferior military capability led to the gradual defeat of the Republicans by 1939.

Franco's insurgents (Nationalists, who were supported by Fascist Italy and Nazi Germany) seized power in the south and northwest, but were suppressed in areas such as Madrid and Barcelona by the workers' militia. The loyalists (Republicans) were aided by the USSR and the volunteers of the International Brigade, which included several writers, among them George Orwell.

chronology

1937 Bilbao and the Basque country were bombed into submission by the Nationalists.

1938 Catalonia was cut off from the main Republican territory.

1939 Barcelona fell in Jan and Madrid in April, and Franco established a dictatorship.

Civitavecchia ancient port on the W coast of Italy, in Lazio region; 40 mi/64 km NW of Rome; population (1971) 42,300. Industries include fishing, and the manufacture of cement and calcium carbide.

cladistics a method of biological ◊classification (taxonomy) that uses a formal step-by-step procedure for objectively assessing the extent to which organisms share particular characteristics, and for assigning them to taxonomic groups. These taxonomic groups (◊species, ◊genus, family) are termed clades.

cladode a flattened stem that is leaflike in appearance and function. It is an adaptation to dry conditions because a stem contains fewer ◊stomata than a leaf, and water loss is thus minimized. The true leaves in such plants are usually reduced to spines or small scales. Examples of plants with cladodes are butcher's-broom *Ruscus aculeatus*, asparagus, and certain cacti. Cladodes may bear flowers or fruit on their surface, and this distinguishes them from leaves.

Clair René. Adopted name of René-Lucien Chomette 1898–1981. French filmmaker, originally a poet, novelist, and journalist. His *Sous les toits de Paris/Under the Roofs of Paris* 1930 was one of the first sound films.

clam

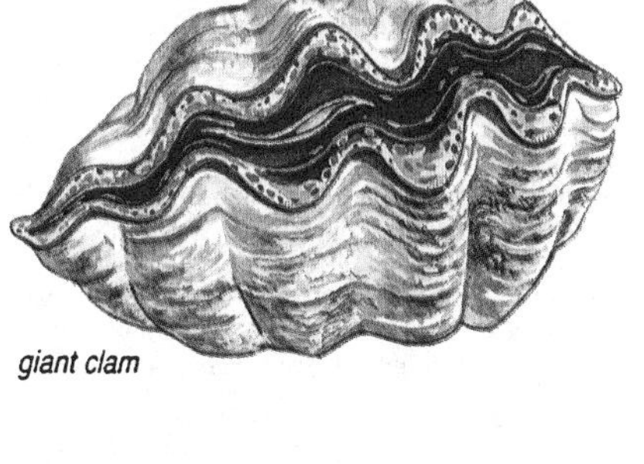

giant clam

clam common name for a ◊bivalve mollusk. The giant clam *Tridacna gigas* of the Indopacific can grow to 3 ft/1 m across in 50 years and weigh, with the shell, 1,000 lb/500 kg.

The term is usually applied to edible species, such as the North American hard clam *Venus mercenaria*, used in clam chowder, and whose shells were formerly used as money by North American Indians.

clan (Gaelic clann "children") social grouping based on ◊kinship. Some traditional societies were organized by clans, which are usually matrilineal or patrilineal, and whose members must marry into another clan in order to avoid in-breeding.

Familiar examples are the Highland clans of Scotland. Theoretically each clan is descended from a single ancestor from whom the name is derived, for example, clan MacGregor ("son of Gregor").

Clapperton Hugh 1788–1827. English explorer who crossed the Sahara from Tripoli with Dixon Denham and discovered Lake Chad 1823. With his servant, Richard Lander, he attempted to reach the Niger, but died at Sokoto. Lander eventually reached the mouth of the river Niger in 1830.

Clapton Eric 1945– . English blues and rock guitarist, singer, and composer, member of the British blues groups the Yardbirds and Cream in the 1960s. One of the pioneers of heavy rock, he later adopted a more laid-back style in his solo career which gave rise to his nickname "Slowhand." His song "Layla" 1973 recorded under the name Derek And The Dominos has become a rock classic.

Clare, St c. 1194–1253. Christian saint. Born in Assisi, Italy, she became at 18 a follower of St Francis, who founded for her the convent of San Damiano. Here she gathered the first members of the Order of Poor Clares. In 1958 she was proclaimed by Pius XII the patron saint of television, since in 1252 she saw from her convent sickbed the Christmas services being held in the Basilica of St Francis in Assisi. Feast day Aug 12.

Clarendon Edward Hyde, 1st Earl of 1609–1674. English politician and historian, chief adviser to Charles II 1651–67. A member of Parliament 1640, he joined the Royalist side 1641. The Clarendon Code (1661–65), a series of acts passed by the government, were directed at Nonconformists (or Dissenters) and were designed to secure the supremacy of the Church of England.

In retirement he wrote the *History of the Rebellion and Civil Wars in England* 1702–04.

claret English term since the 17th century for the dry red wines of Bordeaux, France.

clarinet a musical ◊woodwind instrument with a single reed and a cylindrical tube, broadening at the end, developed in Germany in the 18th century. At the lower end of its range it has a rich "woody" tone, which becomes increasingly brilliant toward the upper register. Its ability both to blend and to contrast with other instruments make it popular for chamber music and as a solo instrument. It is also heard in military and concert bands and as a jazz instrument.

Equally effective both in fast virtuoso passages and as an expressive melodic instrument, the clarinet's potential was quickly exploited, and it found a place in the orchestra by the late 18th century. Music for the instrument is written in one key, for simplicity, but is played in a different key. There are different types of clarinet, varying in range, including the bass clarinet, which has become a regular member of the orchestra.

Clark George Rogers 1752–1818. American military leader and explorer. Born near Charlottesville, Virginia, Clark spent his early adult years surveying and exploring Kentucky and was made commander of the Virginia frontier militia at the outbreak of the Revolutionary War. In 1778–79 he led an attack on the Indian allies of the British to the W of the Ohio river and founded a settlement at the site of Louisville, Kentucky.

Clapton *Eric Clapton (right) with George Harrison (left) at the Live Aid concert, 1985.*

Claudius *One of the most intriguing of the Roman emperors, Claudius wrote historical works and an autobiography, none of which survives. This statue of the deified Claudius is from the Lateran Museum, Rome.*

After the war Clark remained in the Northwest Territory as Indian commissioner, leading an attack on the Wabash 1786. After leaving office, he accepted commissions from the French and Spanish colonial authorities.

Clark Joe (Joseph) Charles 1939– . Canadian Progressive Conservative politician, born in Alberta. He became party leader 1976, and in May 1979 defeated ◊Trudeau at the polls to become the youngest prime minister in Canada's history.

Following the rejection of his government's budget, he was defeated in a second election Feb 1980. He became Secretary of State for External Affairs (foreign minister) in the ◊Mulroney government (1984–).

Clark Kenneth, Lord Clark 1903–1983. British art historian, director of the National Gallery, London, 1934–45. His books include *Leonardo da Vinci* 1939 and *The Nude* 1956.

Clark Mark (Wayne) 1896–1984. US general in World War II. In 1942 he became chief of staff for ground forces, and deputy to General Eisenhower. He led a successful secret mission by submarine to get information in N Africa to prepare for the Allied invasion, and commanded the 5th Army in the invasion of Italy.

Clark, born in New York, fought in France in World War I and between the wars held various military appointments in the US. He was commander in chief of the United Nations forces in the Korean war 1952–53.

Clarke Arthur C(harles) 1917– . English science fiction and nonfiction writer, who originated the plan for the system of communications satellites in 1945. His works include *Childhood's End* 1953 and *2001: A Space Odyssey* 1968 (which was made into a film by Stanley Kubrick), and *2010: Odyssey Two 1982*.

Clarksville city in N Tennessee at the confluence of the Cumberland and Red rivers, NW of Nashville. Manufactures include tobacco products, clothing, air-conditioning and heating equipment, rubber, and cheese; population (1980) 54,777.

class in sociology, the main grouping of social stratification in industrial societies, based primarily on economic, educational, and occupational factors, but also referring to people's style of living or sense of group identity. The basic divisions are upper, middle, and lower.

Within the social sciences, class has been used both as a descriptive category and as the basis of theories about industrial society. Theories of class may see such social divisions either as a source of social stability (see ◊Durkheim) or social conflict (as did ◊Marx).

In the US, little acknowledgment is given to the notion of class. If asked, most Americans' identify themselves as middle class, although social scientists use measurements of education level, income, and occupation to ascribe social strata.

class in biological classification, a group of related ◊orders. For example, all mammals belong to the class Mammalia and all birds to the class Aves. Thus, the class Angiospermae (flowering plants) includes numerous plant orders such as Rosales (currants, acacias, roses, and others). The class Reptilia (reptiles) includes the orders Crocodilia and Chelonia (turtles) among others.

class action in law, a court procedure where one or more claimants represent a larger group of people who are all making the same kind of claim against the same defendant. The court's decision is binding on all the members of the group.

Classical music written in the late 17th and 18th centuries; Western music of any period that does not belong to the folk or popular traditions.

Classical economics school of economic thought that dominated 19th-century thinking. It originated with Adam ◊Smith's *The Wealth of Nations* 1776, which embodied many of the basic concepts and principles of the Classical school. Smith's theories were further developed in the writings of John Stuart Mill and David Ricardo. Central to the theory were economic freedom, competition, and *laissez-faire* government. The idea that economic growth could best be promoted by free trade, unassisted by government, was in conflict with ◊mercantilism.

The belief that agriculture was the chief determinant of economic health was also rejected in favor of manufacturing development, and the importance of labor productivity was stressed. The theories put forward by the Classical economists still influence economists today.

Classicism in literature, music, and art, a style that emphasizes the qualities traditionally considered characteristic of ancient Greek and Roman art, that is, reason, balance, objectivity, restraint, and strict adherence to form. The term Classicism is often used to characterize the culture of 18th-century Europe, as contrasted with 19th-century ◊Romanticism. See ◊Neo-Classicism.

classification in biology, the arrangement of organisms into a hierarchy of groups, on the basis of their similarities in biochemical, anatomical or physiological characters. The basic grouping is a ◊species, several of which may constitute a ◊genus, which in turn are grouped into families, and so on up through orders, classes, phyla (in plants, sometimes called divisions), to kingdoms.

class interval in statistics, the range of each class of data, used when dealing with large amounts of data. To obtain an idea of the distribution, the data are broken down into convenient classes, which must be mutually exclusive and are usually equal. The class interval defines the range of each class; for example, if the class interval is five and the data begin at zero, the classes are 0–4, 5–9, 10–14, and so on.

clathrates compounds formed by small molecules filling in the holes in the structural lattice of another compound—for example, sulfur dioxide molecules in ice crystals. Clathrates are therefore intermediate between mixtures and compounds.

Claude Georges 1870–1960. French industrial chemist, responsible for inventing neon signs. He discovered in 1896 that acetylene, normally explosive, could be safely transported when disolved in acetone. He later demonstrated that neon gas could be used to provide a bright red light in signs. These were displayed publicly for the first time at the Paris Motor Show 1910. As an old man, Claude spent the period 1945–49 in prison as a collaborator.

Claudel Paul 1868–1955. French poet and dramatist. A fervent Catholic, he was influenced by the Symbolists and achieved an effect of mystic allegory in such plays as *L'Annonce faite à Marie/Tidings Brought to Mary* 1912 and *Le Soulier de satin/The Satin Slipper* 1929, set in 16th-century Spain. His verse includes *Cinq grandes odes/Five Great Odes* 1910.

Claude Lorrain (Claude Gellée) 1600–1682. French landscape painter, active in Rome from 1627. His distinctive, luminous, Classical style had great impact on late 17th- and 18th-century taste. His subjects are mostly mythological and historical, with insignificant figures lost in great expanses of poetic scenery, as in *The Enchanted Castle* 1664 (National Gallery, London).

Born in Lorraine, he established himself in Rome, where his many patrons included Pope Urban VIII. His *Liber Veritatis*, which contains some 200 drawings after his finished works, was made to prevent forgeries of his work by contemporaries.

Claudian (Claudius Claudianus) c. 370–404. Last of the great Latin poets of the Roman Empire, probably born in Alexandria, Egypt. He wrote official panegyrics, epigrams, and the epic *The Rape of Proserpine*.

Claudius Tiberius Claudius Nero 10 BC–AD 54. Nephew of ◊Tiberius, made Roman emperor by his troops AD 41, after the murder of his nephew Caligula. Claudius was a scholar, historian, and able administrator. During his reign the Roman Empire was considerably extended, and in 43 he took part in the invasion of Britain.

Lame and suffering from a speech impediment, he was frequently the object of ridicule. He was dominated by his third wife, ◊Messalina, whom he ultimately had executed, and is thought to have been poisoned by his fourth wife, Agrippina the Younger. His life is described by the novelist Robert Graves in his books *I Claudius* 1934 and *Claudius the God* 1934.

Clausewitz Karl von 1780–1831. Prussian officer and writer on war, born near Magdeburg. His book *Vom Kriege/On War* 1833, translated into English 1873, gave a new philosophical foundation to the art of war and put forward a concept of strategy that was influential until World War I.

clausius in engineering, a unit of ◊entropy (the loss of energy as heat in any physical process). It is defined as the ratio of energy to temperature above absolute zero.

Clausius Rudolf Julius Emaneul 1822–1888. German physicist, one of the founders of the science of thermodynamics. In 1850 he enunciated its second law: heat cannot pass from a colder to a hotter body.

claustrophobia a ◊phobia involving fear of enclosed spaces.

claves musical percussion instrument of Latin American origin, consisting of small hardwood batons struck together.

clavichord stringed keyboard instrument, common in Renaissance Europe and in 18th-century Germany. Notes are sounded by a metal blade striking the string. The clavichord was a forerunner of the pianoforte.

clavicle the collar bone of many vertebrates. In humans it is vulnerable to fracture; falls involving a sudden force on the arm may result in excessive stress passing into the chest region by way of the clavicle and other bones.

clavier in music, general term for an early keyboard instrument.

claw hard, hooked pointed outgrowth of the digits of mammals, birds, and most reptiles. Claws are composed of the protein keratin, and grow continuously from a bundle of cells in the lower skin layer. Hooves and nails are modified structures with the same origin as claws.

clay a very fine-grained ◊sedimentary deposit that has undergone a greater or lesser degree of consolidation. When moistened it is plastic, and it hardens on heating, which renders it impermeable. It may be white, gray, red, yellow, blue, or black, depending on its composition. Clay minerals consist largely of hydrous silicates of aluminum and magnesium together with iron, potassium, sodium, and organic substances. The crystals of clay minerals have a layered structure, capable of holding water, and are responsible for its plastic properties. According to international classification, in mechanical analysis of soil, clay has a grain size of less than 0.00008 in/0.002 mm.

Types of clay include adobe, alluvial clay, building clay, brick, cement, kaolinite, ferruginous clay, fireclay, fusible clay, puddle clay, refractory clay, and vitrifiable clay. Clays have a variety of uses, some of which, such as pottery and bricks, date back to prehistoric times.

***Clausewitz** The Prussian army officer Karl von Clausewitz described war as a continuation of politics by other means.*

Clay Cassius Marcellus, Jr see ◊Ali, Muhammad.

Clay Henry 1777–1852. US politician. He stood unsuccessfully three times for the presidency: as a Democratic-Republican 1824, as a National Republican 1832, and as a Whig 1844. He supported the War of 1812 against Britain, and tried to hold the Union together on the slavery issue by the Missouri Compromise of 1820, and again in the compromise of 1850. He was secretary of state 1825–29, and is also remembered for his "American system," which favored the national bank, internal improvements to facilitate commercial and industrial development, and the raising of protective tariffs.

A powerful orator, he was a strong leader of the House of Representatives. He fought a duel over the accusation that he had struck a corrupt deal with John Quincy ◊Adams to ensure the latter would be named president by the House in 1824.

Clay Lucius DuBignon 1897–1978. US Commander-in-Chief of the US occupation forces in Germany 1947–49. He broke the Soviet blockade of Berlin 1948 after 327 days, with an airlift—a term he brought into general use—which involved bringing all supplies into West Berlin by air.

clay mineral one of a group of hydrous silicate minerals that form most of the fine-grained particles in clays. Clay minerals are normally formed by weathering or alteration of other silicates. Virtually all have sheet silicate structures similar to the micas. They exhibit the following useful properties: loss of water on heating, swelling and shrinking in different conditions, cation exchange with other media, and plasticity when wet. Examples are kaolinite, illite, and montmorillonite.

Kaolinite $Al_2Si_2O_5(OH)_4$ is a common white clay mineral derived from alteration of alluminum silicates, especially feldspars. Illite contains the same constituents as kaolinite, plus potassium, and is the main mineral of clay sediments, mudstones, and shales; it is a weathering product of feldspars and other silicates. Montmorillonite contains the constituents of kaolinite plus sodium and magnesium; along with related magnesium- and iron-bearing clay minerals, it is derived from alteration and weathering of basic igneous rocks.

Kaolinite (the mineral name for kaolin or kaolinite) is economically important in the ceramic and paper industries. Illite along with other clay minerals, may also be used in ceramics. Montmorillonite is the chief constituent of fuller's earth, and is also used in drilling muds. Vermiculite (similar to montmorillonite) will expand on heating to produce a material used in insulation.

Clayton Jack 1921– . English film director, originally a producer. His first feature, *Room at the Top* 1958, heralded a new maturity in British cinema. Other works include *The Great Gatsby* 1974 and *The Lonely Passion of Judith Hearne* 1987.

cleanliness unit unit for measuring air pollution: the number of particles greater than 0.5 micrometers in diameter per cubic foot of air. A more usual measure is the weight of contaminants per cubic meter of air.

Clearwater city in W central Florida on the Gulf of Mexico, NW of St Petersburg; seat of Pinellas county. Industries include tourism, citrus fruits, fishing, electronics, and flowers; population (1990) 98,784.

cleavage in mineralogy, the tendency of a mineral to split along defined, parallel planes related to its internal structure. It is a useful distinguishing feature in mineral identification. Cleavage occurs where bonding between atoms is weakest, and cleavages may be perfect, good, or poor, depending on the bond strengths; a given mineral may possess one, two, three, or more orientations along which it will cleave.

Some minerals have no cleavage, for example, quartz will fracture to give curved surfaces similar to those of broken glass. Some other minerals, such as apatite, have very poor cleavage that is sometimes known as a parting. Micas have one perfect cleavage and therefore split easily into very thin flakes. Pyroxenes have two good cleavages and break (less perfectly) into long prisms. Galena has three perfect cleavages parallel to the cube edges, and readily breaks into smaller and smaller cubes. Baryte has one perfect cleavage plus good cleavages in other orientations.

Cleese John 1939–. English actor and comedian who has appeared in both television and films.

He has written for British television including the comic *Monty Python's Flying Circus* and *Fawlty Towers*. His films include *Monty Python and the Holy Grail* 1974, *The Life of Brian* 1979, and *A Fish Called Wanda* 1988.

cleft palate fissure of the roof of the mouth, often accompanied by a harelip, the result of the two halves of the palate failing to join properly during prenatal development.

Cleisthenes late 6th century BC. Ruler of Athens. Inspired by Solon, he is credited with the establishment of democracy in Athens 507 BC.

cleistogamy the production of flowers that never fully open and which are automatically self-fertilized. Cleistogamous flowers are often formed late in the year, after the production of normal flowers, or during a period of cold weather, as seen in several species of violet *Viola*.

Cleland John 1709–1789. English author. He wrote *Fanny Hill, the Memoirs of a Woman of Pleasure* 1748–49 to try to extricate himself from the grip of his London creditors. The book was considered immoral.

clematis genus of temperate woody climbers with showy flowers of the buttercup family Ranunculaceae, often cultivated in gardens.

Rock clematis *C. verticillaris* grows in woods and thickets in most of shady E North America.

Clemenceau Georges 1841–1929. French politician and journalist (prominent in the defense of ◊Dreyfus). He was prime minister 1906–09 and 1917–20. After World War I he presided over the Peace Conference in Paris that drew up the Treaty of ◊Versailles, but failed to secure for France the Rhine as a frontier.

Clemenceau was mayor of Montmartre, Paris, in the war of 1870, and in 1871 was elected a member of the National Assembly at Bordeaux. He was elected a deputy in 1876 after the formation of the Third Republic. An extreme radical, he soon earned the nickname of "the Tiger" on account of his ferocious attacks on politicians whom he disliked. In 1893 he lost his seat and spent the next ten years in journalism. In 1902 he was elected senator for the Var, and was soon one of the most powerful politicians in France. When he became prime minister for the second time in 1917, he made the decisive appointment of Marshal ◊Foch as supreme commander.

Clemens Samuel Langhorne. Real name of the US writer Mark ◊Twain.

Clement VII 1478–1534. Pope 1523–34. He refused to allow the divorce of Henry VIII of England and Catherine of Aragon. Illegitimate son of a brother of Lorenzo di Medici, the ruler of Florence, he commissioned monuments for the Medici chapel in Florence from the Renaissance artist Michelangelo.

Clementi Muzio 1752–1832. Italian pianist and composer. He settled in London in 1782 as a teacher and then as proprietor of a successful piano and music business. He was the founder of the new technique of piano playing, and his series of studies, *Gradus AD Parnassum* 1817, is still in use.

clementine small seedless citrus fruit of the rue family, thought to be a hybrid between a tangerine and an orange, or a variety of tangerine. It has a flowery taste and scent and is in season in winter. It is commonly grown in N Africa and Spain.

Clement of Alexandria c. AD 150–c. 215. Greek theologian who applied Greek philosophical ideas to Christian doctrine, and was the teacher of the theologian Origen.

Clement of Rome, St late 1st century AD. One of the early Christian leaders and writers known as the Fathers of the Church. According to tradition he was the third or fourth bishop of Rome, and a disciple of St Peter. He wrote a letter addressed to the church at Corinth (First Epistle of Clement), and many other writings have been attributed to him.

Clements John 1910–1988. British actor and director whose productions included revivals of Restoration comedies and the plays of George Bernard Shaw.

Cleon Athenian demagogue and military leader in the Peloponnesian War (431–404 BC). After the death of Pericles, to whom he was opposed, he won power as representative of the commercial classes and leader of the party, advocating a vigorous war policy. He was killed fighting the Spartans at Amphipolis.

Cleopatra c. 68–30 BC. Queen of Egypt 51–48 and 47–30 BC. When the Roman general Julius Caesar arrived in Egypt, he restored her to the throne from which she had been ousted. Cleopatra and Caesar became lovers and she went with him to Rome. After Caesar's assassination 44 BC she returned to Alexandria and resumed her position as queen of Egypt. In 41 BC she was joined there by Mark Antony, one of Rome's rulers. In 31 BC Rome declared war on Egypt and scored a decisive victory in the naval Battle of Actium off the W coast of Greece. Cleopatra fled with her 60 ships to Egypt; Antony abandoned the struggle and followed her. Both he and Cleopatra committed suicide.

Cleopatra was Macedonian, and the last ruler of the Macedonian dynasty, which ruled Egypt from 323 until annexation by Rome 31. She succeeded her father Ptolemy XII jointly with her brother Ptolemy XIII, and they ruled together from 51 to 49 BC, when she was expelled by him. Her reinstatement in 48 BC by Caesar caused a war between Caesar and her brother, who was defeated and killed. The younger brother, Ptolemy XIV, was elevated to the throne and married to her, in the tradition of the pharaohs, although she actually lived with Caesar and they had a son, Ptolemy XV, known as Caesarion (he was later killed by Octavian).

After Caesar's death, Cleopatra and Mark Antony had three sons, and in 32 BC he divorced his wife Octavia. She was the sister of Octavian, the ruler of Rome, who then declared war on Egypt. Shakespeare's play *Antony and Cleopatra* recounts that Cleopatra killed herself with an asp (poisonous snake) after Antony's suicide.

Cleopatra's Needle either of two ancient Egyptian granite obelisks erected at Heliopolis in the 15th century BC by Thothmes III, and removed to Alexandria by the Roman emperor Augustus about 14 BC. They have no connection with Cleopatra's reign. One of the pair was taken to England 1878 and erected in London. The other was given by the khedive of Egypt to the US and erected in Central Park, New York, in 1881.

clerihew humorous verse form invented by Edmund Clerihew ◊Bentley, characterized by a first line consisting of a person's name.

The four lines rhyme AABB, but the meter is often distorted for comic effect. An example, from Bentley's *Biography for Beginners* 1905, is: "Sir Christopher Wren/ Said, I am going to dine with some men./ If anybody calls/ Say I am designing St Paul's."

***Cleveland** The 22nd and 24th president of the United States of America, Grover Cleveland, a Democrat. 1885–1889 and 1893–1897.*

Clermont-Ferrand city, capital of Puy-de-Dôme *département*, in the Auvergne region of France; population (1983) 256,000. It is a center for agriculture, and its rubber industry is the largest in France.

Cleveland largest city of Ohio, on Lake Erie at the mouth of the river Cuyahoga; population (1990) 505,616, metropolitan area 2,759,823. Its chief industries are iron and steel and petroleum refining. Iron ore from the Lake Superior region and coal from Ohio and Pennsylvania mines are brought here. Other manufactured goods include machine tools, auto and airplane parts, hardware, trucks, electronic equipment, and appliances. Cleveland has art and natural-history museums, a world-famous symphony orchestra, and Case Western University. It was surveyed 1796 and grew rapidly after a canal linked Lake Erie to the Ohio River 1832. John D Rockefeller established Standard Oil in Cleveland 1870. After surviving a financial crisis in 1978 that resulted from the decline of its industrial base, Cleveland sought vigorously to broaden its economy.

Cleveland (Stephen) Grover 1837–1908. 22nd and 24th president of the US, 1885–89 and 1893–97; the first Democratic president elected after the Civil War and the only president to hold office for two nonconsecutive terms. He attempted to check corruption in the civil service and reduce tariffs. These policies provoked political opposition, and he was defeated by Republican Benjamin Harrison 1888. He was returned to office 1892 and supported the Sherman Silver Purchase Act, which permitted free silver coinage and may have caused the economic panic of 1893. He was a noninterventionist but in 1895 initiated arbitration that settled a boundary dispute between Britain and Venezuela. An unswerving conservative, he refused to involve the government in economic affairs but used federal troops to end the Pullman strike 1894. Within a year of his taking office for the second time, 4 million were unemployed and the US was virtually bankrupt.

Cleveland was born in Caldwell, New Jersey, and trained as a lawyer. He served as mayor of Buffalo, New York, 1881–82 and as governor of New York 1882–84.

click-beetle type of ◊beetle that can regain its feet from lying on its back by jumping into the air and turning over, clicking as it does so.

Cliff Clarice 1899–1972. English pottery designer. Her Bizarre ware, characterized by brightly colored floral and geometric decoration on often geometrically shaped china, became increasingly popular in the 1930s.

Clift Montgomery (Edward) 1920–1966. US film and theater actor. A star of the late 1940s and 1950s in films such as *Red River* 1948, *A Place in the Sun* 1951, and *From Here To Eternity* 1953. He was disfigured in a car accident in 1957 but continued to make films, taking the title role in *Freud* 1962.

climacteric period during the life span when an important physiological change occurs, usually referring to ◊menopause.

climate weather conditions at a particular place over a period of time. Climate encompasses all the meteorological elements and the factors that influence them. The primary factors that determine the variations of climate over the surface of the Earth are: (a) the effect of latitude and the tilt of the Earth's axis to the plane of the orbit about the Sun (66.5°); (b) the large-scale movements of different wind belts over the Earth's surface; (c) the temperature difference between land and sea; (d) contours of the ground; and (e) location of the area in relation to ocean currents. Catastrophic variations to climate may be caused by the impact of another planetary body, or by clouds resulting from volcanic activity.

How much heat the Earth receives from the Sun varies in different latitudes and at different times of the year. In the equatorial region the mean daily temperature of the air near the ground has no large seasonal variation. In the polar regions the temperature in the long winter, when there is no incoming solar radiation, falls far below the summer value. Climate types were first classified by Vladimir Köppen in 1918.

The temperature of the sea, and of the air above it, varies little in the course of day or night, whereas the surface of the land is rapidly cooled by lack of solar radiation. In the same way the annual change of temperature is relatively small over the sea and great over the land. Continental areas are thus colder than the sea in winter and warmer in summer. Winds that blow from the sea are warm in winter and cool in summer, while winds from the central parts of continents are hot in summer and cold in winter.

On average, air temperature drops with increasing land height at a rate of 1.8°F/1°C per 300 ft/90 m. Thus places situated above mean sea level usually have lower temperatures than places at or near sea level. Even in equatorial regions, high mountains are snow-covered during the whole year.

Rainfall is produced by the condensation of water vapor in air. When winds blow against a range of mountains so that the air is forced to ascend, rain results, the amount depending on the height of the ground and the dampness of the air.

The complexity of the distribution of land and sea, and the consequent complexity of the general circulation of the atmosphere, have a direct effect on the distribution of the climate. Centered on the equator is a belt of tropical rainforest, which may be either constantly wet or monsoonal (seasonal with wet and dry seasons in each year). On each side of this is a belt of savannah, with lighter rainfall and less dense vegetation. Usually there is then a transition through ◊steppe (semiarid) to desert (arid), with a further transition through steppe to ◊Mediterranean climate with dry summer, followed by the moist temperate climate of middle latitudes. Next comes a zone of cold climate with moist winter. Where the desert extends into middle latitudes, however, the zones of Mediterranean and moist temperate climates are missing, and the transition is from desert to a cold climate with moist winter. In the extreme east of Asia a cold climate with dry winters extends from about 70° N to 35° N. The polar caps have ◊tundra and glacial climates, with little or no ◊precipitation (rain or snow).

climatology the study of climate, its global variations and causes.

climax community an assemblage of plants and animals that is relatively stable in its environment (for example, beech and maple forest in parts of the US). It is brought about by ecological ◊succession, and represents the final point in a successional series.

climax vegetation the state of equilibrium that is reached after a series of changes have occurred in the vegetation of a particular habitat. It is the final stage in a ◊succession, where the structure and species of a habitat do not develop further, providing conditions remain unaltered.

clinical psychology discipline dealing with the understanding and treatment of health problems, particularly mental disorders. The main problems dealt with include anxiety, phobias, depression, obsessions, sexual and marital problems, drug and alcohol dependence, childhood behavioral problems, psychoses (such as schizophrenia), mental handicap, and brain damage (such as dementia).

Other areas of work include forensic psychology (concerned with criminal behavior) and health psychology. Assessment procedures assess intelligence and cognition (for example, in detecting the effects of brain damage) by using psychometric tests. Behavioral approaches are methods of treatment which apply learning theories to clinical problems. Behavior therapy helps clients change unwanted behaviors (such as phobias, obsessions, sexual problems) and develop new skills (such as improving social interactions). Behavior modification relies on operant conditioning, making selective use of rewards (such as praise) to change behavior. This is helpful for children, the mentally handicapped and for patients in institutions, such as mental hospitals. Cognitive therapy is a new approach to treating emotional problems, such as anxiety and depression, by teaching clients how to deal with negative thoughts and attitudes. Counseling, developed by Rogers, is widely used to help clients solve their own problems. Psychoanalysis, as developed by Freud and Jung, is little used by clinical psychologists today. It emphasizes childhood conflicts as a source of adult problems.

clinometer hand-held surveying instrument for measuring angles of slope.

Clinton De Witt 1769–1828. American political leader and promoter of the Erie Canal. After serving in the state legislature 1797–1802 and the US Senate 1802–03, he was elected mayor of New York City 1803–15. Clinton simultaneously served in the state senate and as lieutenant governor. A strong supporter of the Erie Canal, he was elected governor 1817 and was instrumental in the initiation of that project, completed 1825.

Born in Little Britain, New York, Clinton was educated at Columbia University, studied law, and became the personal assistant of his uncle George Clinton, governor of New York.

Clio in Greek mythology, the inventor of epic poetry and history. One of the nine ◊Muses.

Clive Robert, Baron Clive of Plassey 1725–1774. British soldier and administrator, who established British rule in India by victories over the French 1751 and over the nawab of Bengal 1757. On his return to Britain his wealth led to allegations that he had abused his power. Although aquitted, he committed suicide.

clo unit of thermal insulation of clothing. Standard clothes have an insulation of about 1 clo; the warmest clothing is about 4 clo per 1 in/2.5 cm of thickness. See also ◊tog.

cloaca the common posterior chamber of most vertebrates into which the digestive, urinary, and reproductive tracts all enter; a cloaca is found in most reptiles, birds, and amphibians; many fishes; and, to a reduced degree, marsupial mammals. Placental mammals, however, have a separate digestive opening (the anus) and urinogenital opening instead of one posterior opening to the body, the cloacal aperture, which is controlled by a ring of muscles.

clock any device that measures the passage of time, usually shown by means of pointers moving over a dial or by a digital display. Traditionally a timepiece consists of a train of wheels driven by a spring or weight controlled by a balance wheel or pendulum. The watch is a portable clock.

history In ancient Egypt the time during the day was measured by a shadow clock, a primitive form of ◊sundial, and at night the water clock was used. Up to the late 16th century the only clock available for use at sea was the sand clock, of which the most familiar form is the hourglass. During the Middle Ages various types of sundial were widely used, and portable sundials were in use from the 16th to the 18th century. Watches were invented in the 16th century—the first were made in Nuremberg, Germany, shortly after 1500—but it was not until the 19th century that they became cheap enough to be widely available.

The first known public clock was set up in Milan, Italy, in 1353. The timekeeping of both clocks and watches was revolutionized in the 17th century by the application of pendulums to clocks and of balance springs to watches.

types of clock The marine chronometer is a precision timepiece of special design, used at sea for giving Greenwich mean time (GMT). Electric timepieces were made possible by the discovery early in the 19th century of the magnetic effects of electric currents. One of the earliest and most satisfactory methods of electrical control of a clock was invented by Matthaeus Hipp in 1842. In one kind of electric clock, the place of the pendulum or spring-controlled balance wheel is taken by a small synchronous electric motor, which counts up the alternations (frequency) of the incoming electric supply and, by a suitable train of wheels, records the time by means of hands on a dial. The quartz crystal clock (made possible by the ◊piezoelectric effect of certain crystals) has great precision, with a short term variation in accuracy of about one-thousandth of a second per day. More accurate still is the atomic clock. This utilizes the natural resonance of certain atoms (for example, cesium) as a regulator controlling the frequency of a quartz crystal ◊oscillator. It is accurate to within one millionth of a second per day.

cloisonné ornamental craft technique in which thin metal strips are soldered in a pattern onto a metal surface, and the resulting compartments (cloisons) filled with colored ◊enamels and fired. Cloisonné was first made in the Byzantine Near East and traded to Asia and Europe. It was then made in medieval Europe, but the technique was perfected in Japan and China during the 17th, 18th, and 19th centuries.

cloister in architecture, a covered walk within a convent or monastery, often opening onto an interior courtyard.

Cloisters, The branch of the Metropolitan Museum of Art in Fort Tryon Park, New York City. It consists of a number of medieval buildings, transported to the US from Europe and carefully reassembled; medieval tapestries, sculpture, pictures, and books are among the exhibits. Featured outdoors are period gardens including a medicinal herb garden.

clone line of cells or population of organisms arising by asexual reproduction from a single "parent" individual. Clones therefore have exactly the same genetic make-up. The term has been adopted by computer technology, in which it describes a (nonexistent) device that mimics an actual one to enable certain software programs to run correctly.

closed-circuit television (CCTV) localized television system in which programs are sent over relatively short distances, the camera, receiver, and controls being linked by cable. Closed-circuit TV systems are used in department stores and large offices as a means of internal security, monitoring people's movements.

closed shop any company or firm, public corporation, or other body that requires its employees to be members of the appropriate labor union. Usually demanded by unions, the closed shop may be preferred by employers as simplifying negotiation, but it was condemned by the European Court of Human Rights in 1981.

In the US the closed shop was made illegal by the Taft-Hartley Act 1947, passed by Congress over Truman's veto.

clothes articles made to cover the human body. Clothes can be worn simply for warmth, but they have almost always had the additional purpose of indicating sex and status or of enhancing the appearance.

The earliest clothes were animal skins, replaced by textiles after the discovery of weaving and spinning. Simple woolen clothing predominated in the northern hemisphere but the ancient Mediterranean civilizations made sophisticated use of linens, cotton, and silk. Apart from changing fashions the major developments in the history of clothing are the mass-production of textiles from the early 19th century and the invention of synthetic materials in the 20th century.

clothes moth type of moth whose larvae feed on clothes, upholstery, and carpets. The adults are small golden or silvery moths. The natural habitat of the larvae is in the nests of animals, feeding on remains of hair and feathers, but they have adapted to human households and can cause considerable damage, for example, the common clothes-moth *Tineola bisselliella*.

cloud water vapor condensed into minute water particles that float in masses in the atmosphere. Clouds, like fogs or mists, which occur at lower levels, are formed by the cooling of air charged with water vapor, which generally condenses around tiny dust particles.

Clouds are classified according to the height at which they occur and their shape. Cirrus and cirrostratus clouds occur at 33,000 ft/10,000 m. The former, sometimes called mares'-tails, consist of minute specks of ice and appear as feathery white wisps, while cirrostratus clouds stretch across the sky as a thin white sheet. Three types of cloud are found at 10,000–24,000 ft/3,000–7,500 m: cirrocumulus, altocumulus, and altostratus. Cirrocumulus clouds occur in small or large rounded tufts, sometimes arranged in the familiar pattern called mackerel sky. Altocumulus clouds are similar, but larger, white clouds, also arranged in lines. Altostratus clouds are like heavy cirrostratus clouds and may stretch across the sky as a gray sheet.

The lower clouds, occurring at heights of up to 6,000 ft/1,800 m, may be of two types. Stratocumulus clouds are the dull gray clouds that give rise to a leaden sky which may not yield rain. Nimbus clouds are dark-gray, shapeless rain clouds.

Two types of clouds, cumulus and cumulonimbus, are placed in a special category because they are produced by daily ascending air currents, which take moisture into the cooler regions of the atmosphere. Cumulus clouds have a flat base generally at 4,500 ft/1,400 m where condensation begins, while the upper part is dome-shaped and extends to about 6,000 ft/1,800 m. Cumulonimbus clouds have their base at much the same level, but extend much higher, often up to over 20,000 ft/6,000 m. Short heavy showers and sometimes thunder may accompany them. Stratus clouds, occurring below 3,500 ft/1,000 m, have the appearance of sheets parallel to the horizon and are like high fogs.

cloud chamber apparatus for tracking ionized particles. It consists of a vessel fitted with a piston and filled with air or other gas, supersaturated with water vapor. When the volume of the vessel is suddenly expanded by moving the piston outward, the vapor cools and a cloud of tiny droplets forms on any nuclei, dust, or ions present. As single fast-moving ionizing particles collide with the air or gas molecules, they show as visible tracks.

cloud

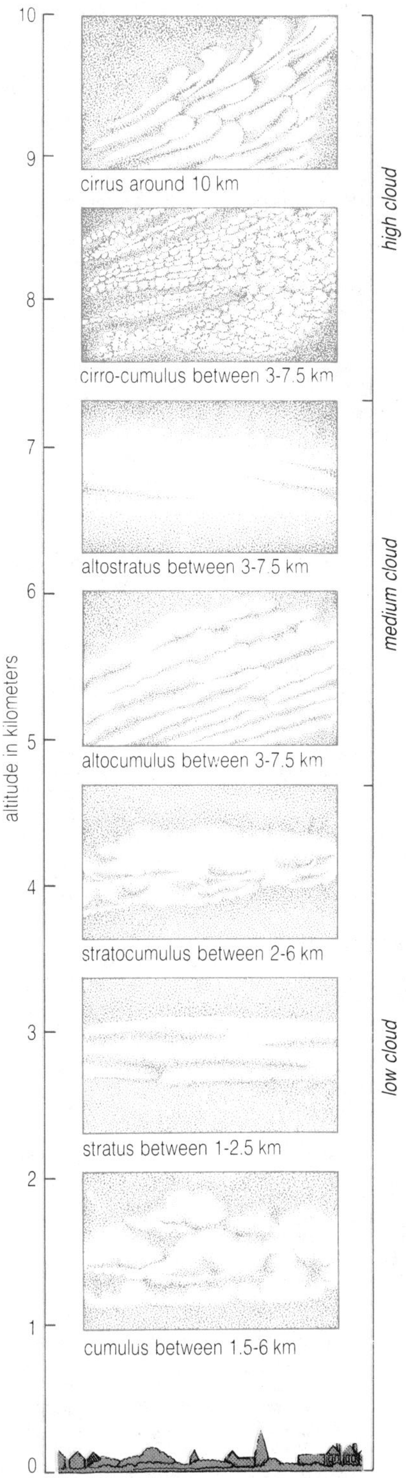
10
9
8
7
6
5
4
3
2
1
0
altitude in kilometers
cirrus around 10 km
cirro-cumulus between 3-7.5 km
altostratus between 3-7.5 km
altocumulus between 3-7.5 km
stratocumulus between 2-6 km
stratus between 1-2.5 km
cumulus between 1.5-6 km
high cloud
medium cloud
low cloud

Much information about interactions between such particles and radiations has been obtained from photographs of these tracks. This system has been improved upon in recent years by the use of liquid hydrogen or helium instead of air or gas (see ◊bubble chamber). The cloud chamber was devised in 1897 by Charles Thomson Rees Wilson (1869–1959) at Cambridge University.

Clouet François c. 1515–1572. French portrait painter who succeeded his father Jean Clouet as court painter. He worked in the Italian style of Mannerism. His half-nude portrait of Diane de Poitiers, *The Lady in Her Bath* 1499–1566 (National Gallery, Washington), is also thought to to be a likeness of Marie Touchet, mistress of Charles IX (1550–74).

Clouet Jean (known as Janet) 1486–1541. French artist, court painter to Francis I. His portraits and drawings, often compared to Holbein's, show an outstanding naturalism.

clove dried, unopened flower bud of the clove tree *Eugenia caryophyllus*. A member of the myrtle family Myrtaceae, the clove tree is a native of the Moluccas. Cloves are used for flavoring in cooking and confectionery. Oil of cloves, which has tonic and carminative qualities, is employed in medicine. The aromatic quality of cloves is shared to a large degree by the leaves, bark, and fruit of the tree.

clover any of an Old World genus *Trifolium* of low-growing leguminous plants, usually with compound leaves of three leaflets and small flowers in dense heads. Sweet clover refers to various species belonging to the related genus *Melilotus*. Red clover *T. pratense* and white clover *T. repens* now grow widely in the US.

The most common honey is made from clover and the most important source of fodder is red clover.

Clovis 465–511. Merovingian king of the Franks from 481. He succeeded his father Childeric as king of the Salian (northern) Franks; defeated the Gallo-Romans (Romanized Gauls) near Soissons 486, ending their rule in France; and defeated the Alemanni, a confederation of Germanic tribes, near Cologne 496. He embraced Christianity and subsequently proved a powerful defender of orthodoxy against the Arian ◊Visigoths, whom he defeated at Poitiers 507. He made Paris his capital.

club a voluntary association of persons formed for leisure, recreational, or political purposes.

club moss or ***lycopod*** any nonseed-bearing plant of the order Lycopodiales belonging to the Pteridophyta family. Club mosses are allied to the ferns and horsetails and, like them, reproduce by spores.

These plants have a wide distribution, but were far more numerous in Paleozoic times, especially the Carboniferous period, when members of this group were large trees. The living species are all of small size.

Lycopodium is the most common genus, with species mostly growing on forest floors.

clubroot a disease affecting cabbages, turnips, and allied plants of the Cruciferae family. It is caused by a ◊slime mold, *Plasmodiophora brassicae*. This attacks the roots of the plant, which send out knotty outgrowths; eventually the whole plant decays.

Cluj (German *Klausenberg*) city in Transylvania, Romania, located on the river Somes; population (1985) 310,000. It is a communications center for Romania and the Hungarian plain. Industries include machine tools, furniture, and knitwear.

There is a 14th-century cathedral, and Romanian (1872) and Hungarian (1945) universities.

Cluny town in Saône-et-Loire *département*, France; on the river Grosne; population (1982) 4,500. Its abbey, now in ruins, was the foundation house 910–1790 of the Cluniac order, originally a reformed branch of the Benedictines. Cluny, once a lace-making center, has a large cattle market.

clusec unit for measuring the power of a vacuum pump.

clutch any device for disconnecting rotating shafts, used especially in an automotive transmission system. In a vehicle with a manual gearbox, the driver depresses the clutch when changing gear, thus disconnecting the engine from the gearbox.

The clutch consists of two main plates, a pressure plate and a driven plate, which is mounted on a shaft leading to the gearbox. When the clutch is engaged, the pressure plate presses the driven

clutch

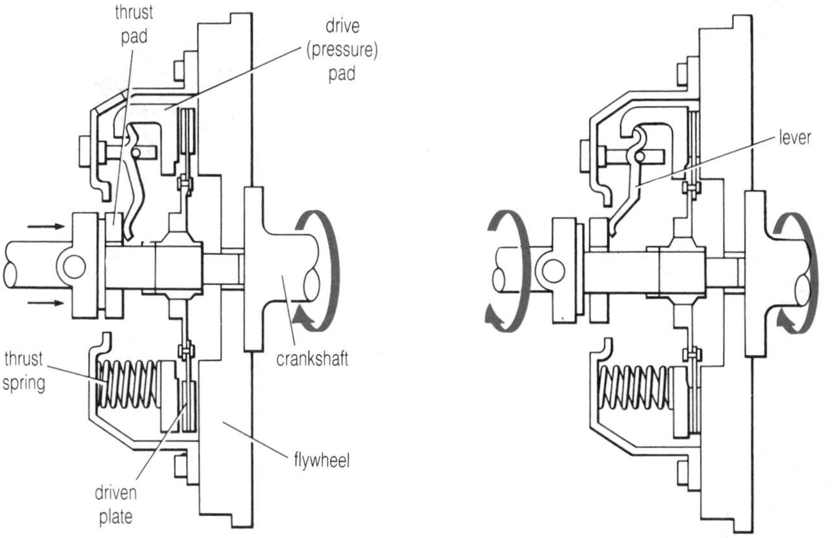
thrust
pad
drive
(pressure)
pad
thrust
spring
crankshaft
flywheel
driven
plate
lever

disengaged (pedal pressed down) *engaged (pedal up)*

plate against the engine ◊flywheel, and drive goes to the gearbox. Depressing the clutch springs the pressure plate away, freeing the driven plate. Vehicles with automatic transmission have no clutch. Drive is transmitted from the flywheel to the automatic gearbox by a liquid coupling or ◊torque converter.

Clutha longest river in South Island, New Zealand, 201 mi/322 km long. It rises in the Southern Alps, has hydroelectric installations, and flows to meet the sea near Kaitangata.

Clyde river in Strathclyde, Scotland; 103 mi/170 km long. The Firth of Clyde and Firth of Forth are linked by the Forth and Clyde canal, 35 mi/56 km long. The shipbuilding yards have declined in recent years.

The nuclear submarine bases of Faslane and Holy Loch are here.

Clytemnestra in Greek mythology, the wife of ◊Agamemnon. With her lover Aegisthus, she murdered her husband and was in turn killed by her son Orestes.

cm abbreviation for centimeter.

Cnossus alternate form of ◊Knossos.

Cnut alternate spelling of ◊Canute.

CO abbreviation for Colorado.

coal black or blackish mineral substance of fossil origin, the result of the transformation of ancient plant matter under progressive compression. It is used as a fuel and in the chemical industry. Coal is classified according to the proportion of carbon and volatiles it contains. The main types are ◊anthracite (shiny, with more than 90% carbon), bituminous coal (shiny and dull patches, more than 80% carbon), and ◊lignite (woody, grading into ◊peat, 70% carbon).

In the second half of the 18th century, coal became the basis of the Industrial Revolution. Coal fields are widely distributed throughout the temperate N hemisphere, the greatest reserves being in Europe, W Siberia, and the US. In the Southern hemisphere, Australia is a major producer.

An increasing use, from 1950–70, of cheap natural gas and oil as fuel and for the production of electricity halted when the energy crisis of the 1970s led to greater exploitation of coal resources.

Coal is becoming a major source of synfuel (synthetic gasoline). In the Fischer–Tropsch process (used in Germany in World War II and today in South Africa), the coal is gasified and then catalysts are used to reconstitute it into diesel and jet fuel. In the degradation process (under development in the US for high-octane motor fuel), a liquid fuel is directly produced by adding hydrogen or removing carbon from the coal.

coal gas gas produced when coal is destructively distilled or heated out of contact with the air. Its main constituents are methane, hydrogen, and carbon monoxide. Coal gas has been superseded by ◊natural gas for domestic purposes.

coalition association of political groups, usually for some limited or short term purpose, such as fighting an election or forming a government when one party has failed to secure a majority in a legislature. In 1990 a coalition of UN military forces was formed to free Kuwait from annexation by Iraq.

coal tar black oily material resulting from the destructive distillation of bituminous coal.

Further distillation of coal tar yields a number of fractions: light oil, middle oil, heavy oil, and anthracene oil; the residue is called pitch. On further fractionation a large number of substances are obtained, about 200 of which have been isolated. They are used as dyes and in medicines.

coastal erosion the sea eroding the land by the constant battering of waves. This produces two effects. The first is a hydraulic effect, in which the force of the wave compresses air pockets in coastal rocks and cliffs, and the air then expands explosively. The second is the effect of abrasion, in which rocks and pebbles are flung against the cliffs, wearing them away.

In areas where there are beaches, the waves cause longshore drift, in which sand and stone fragments are carried parallel to the shore, causing buildups (sandspits) in some areas and beach erosion in others.

coastguard governmental organization whose members patrol a nation's seacoast to prevent smuggling, assist distressed vessels, watch for oil slicks, and so on.

The US Coast Guard 1915 has wide duties, including enforcing law and order on the high seas and navigable waters. During peacetime, it is administered under the Department of Transportation; in time of war, the Department of the Navy.

coati or ***coatimundi*** any of several species of carnivores of the genus *Nasua*, in the same family, Procyonidae, as the raccoons. A coati is a good climber and has long claws, a long tail, a good sense of smell, and a long, flexible piglike snout used for digging. Coatis live in packs in the forests of South and Central America.

The common coati *Nasua nasua* of South America is about 2 ft/60 cm long, with a tail about the same length.

coaxial cable electric cable that consists of a solid or stranded central conductor insulated from and surrounded by a solid or braided conducting tube or sheath. It can transmit the high-frequency signals used in television, telephone, and other telecommunications transmissions.

cobalt hard, lustrous, gray, metallic element, symbol Co, atomic number 27, atomic weight 58.933. It is found in various ores and occasionally as a free metal (see ◊native metal), sometimes in metallic meteorite fragments. It is used in the preparation of magnetic, wear-resistant, and high-strength alloys; its compounds are used in inks, paints, and varnishes.

The isotope Co-60 is radioactive (half-life 5.3 years) and is produced in large amounts for gamma rays to be used in industrial radiography, research, and cancer treatments. It was named in 1730 by Swedish chemist Georg Brandt (1694–1768); the name derives from German *Kobalt*, "goblin," the fact that miners considered its ore worthless because of its arsenic content.

cobalt ore cobalt is extracted from a number of minerals, the main ones being smaltite, $(Co,Ni)As_3$; linneite, Co_3S_4; cobaltite, CoAsS; and glaucodot, (Co,Fe)AsS.

All commercial cobalt is obtained as a byproduct of other metals. Zaïre is the largest producer of cobalt, and it is obtained there as a byproduct of the copper industry. Other producers include Canada and Morocco. Cobalt is also found in the manganese nodules that occur on the ocean floor, and was successfully refined in 1988 from the Pacific Ocean nodules, although this process has yet to prove economic.

Cobb Ty(rus Raymond), nicknamed "the Georgia Peach" 1886–1961. US baseball player, one of the greatest batters and base runners of all time. He played for Detroit and Philadelphia 1905–28, and won the American League batting average championship 12 times. He holds the record for runs scored, 2,254, and batting average, .367. He had 4,191 hits in his career—a record that stood for almost 60 years.

Coblenz alternate spelling of the German city ◊Koblenz.

COBOL (acronym from common business-oriented language) computer-programming language, designed in the late 1950s for business use. COBOL facilitates the writing of programs that deal with large computer files and handle business arithmetic. It has become the major language for commercial data processing.

cobra any of several poisonous snakes, especially the genus *Naja*, of the family Elapidae, found in Africa and S Asia, species of which can grow from 3 ft/1 m to over 14 ft/4.3 m. The neck stretches into a "hood" when the snake is alarmed. Cobra venom contains nerve toxins powerful enough to kill humans.

The Indian cobra *Naja naja* is about 5 ft/1.5 m long, and found over most of S Asia. Some individuals have "spectacle" markings on the hood. The hamadryad *Naja hannah* of S and SE Asia can be 14 ft/4.3 m or more, and eats snakes. The ringhals *Hemachatus hemachatus* of S Africa and the black-necked cobra *Naja nigricollis*, of the African savannah are both about 3 ft/1 m long. Both are able to spray venom toward the eyes of an attacker.

Cobra a group of European abstract painters formed by the Dutch artist Karel Appel 1948. Other leading members were the Dane Asgar Jorn and the Belgian Corneille. They developed an expressive and dynamic form of abstract painting, using thick paint and lurid colors.

Coburg town in Bavaria, Federal Republic of Germany, on the river Itz; 50 mi/80 km SE of Gotha; population (1984) 44,500. Industries include

coastal erosion

The sea erodes the land by the constant battering of waves. The force of the waves creates a hydraulic effect, compressing air to form explosive pockets in the rocks and cliffs. The waves also have an abrasive effect, flinging rocks and pebbles against the cliff faces and wearing them away.

In areas where there are beaches, the waves cause longshore drift, in which sand and stone fragments are carried in a particular direction parallel to the shore.

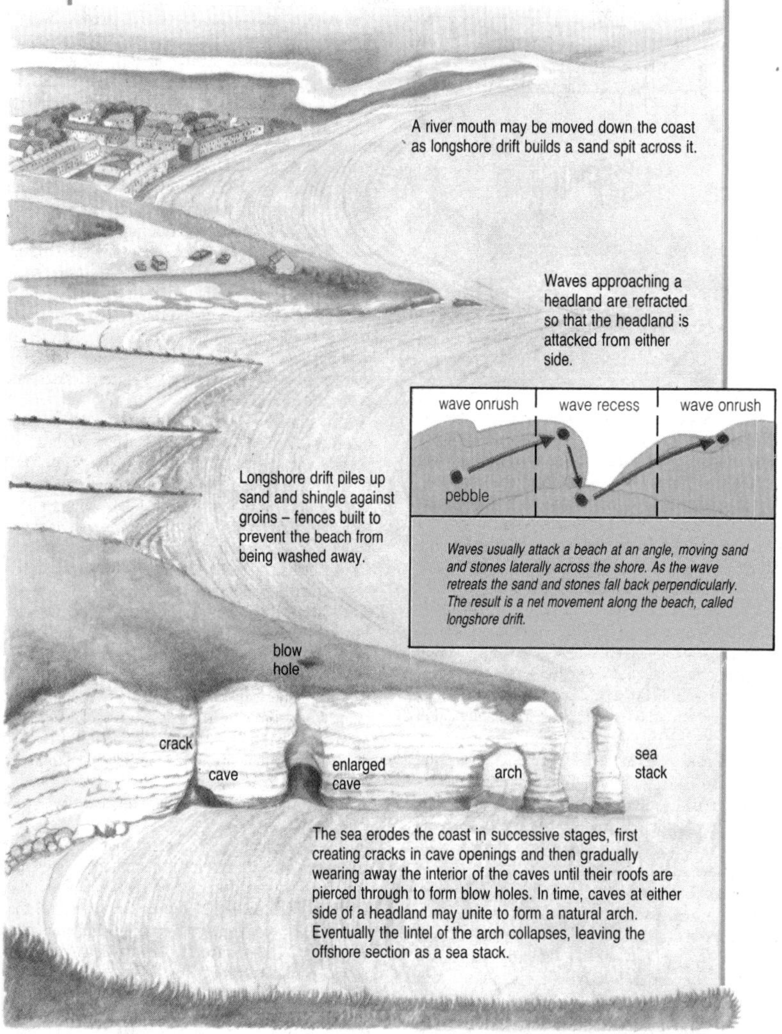
A river mouth may be moved down the coast as longshore drift builds a sand spit across it.
Waves approaching a headland are refracted so that the headland is attacked from either side.
wave onrush
wave recess
wave onrush
pebble
Waves usually attack a beach at an angle, moving sand and stones laterally across the shore. As the wave retreats the sand and stones fall back perpendicularly. The result is a net movement along the beach, called longshore drift.
Longshore drift piles up sand and shingle against groins – fences built to prevent the beach from being washed away.
blow hole
crack
cave
enlarged cave
arch
sea stack
The sea erodes the coast in successive stages, first creating cracks in cave openings and then gradually wearing away the interior of the caves until their roofs are pierced through to form blow holes. In time, caves at either side of a headland may unite to form a natural arch. Eventually the lintel of the arch collapses, leaving the offshore section as a sea stack.

machinery, toys, and porcelain. Formerly the capital of the duchy of Coburg, it was part of Saxe-Coburg-Gotha 1826–1918, and a residence of its dukes.

Coburn James 1928– . US film actor, popular in the 1960s and 1970s. His films include *The Magnificent Seven* 1960, *Our Man Flint* 1966, and *Cross of Iron* 1977.

coca South American shrub *Erythroxylon coca* of the coca family Erythroxylaceae, whose dried leaves are the source of cocaine. It was used as a holy drug by the Andean Indians.

Coca-Cola trade name of a sweetened, carbonated drink, orinally made with coca leaves and flavored with cola nuts, and containing caramel and caffeine. Invented in 1886, Coca-Cola was sold in every state of the US by 1895 and in 155 countries by 1987. As a rule, Fanta, an orange-flavored soda made by Coca-Cola, preceded the cola-flavored soda in the third world. With the increased presence of Americans in third-world nations, US imperialism became known as Coca-Colonialism.

cocaine alkaloid $C_{17}H_{21}NO_4$ extracted from the leaves of the coca tree. It has limited medical application, mainly as a local anesthetic agent that is readily absorbed by mucous membranes (lining tissues) of the nose and throat. It is both toxic and addictive. Its use as a stimulant is illegal. ◊Crack is a derivative of cocaine.

Cocaine was first extracted from the coca plant in Germany in the 19th century. Most of the world's cocaine is produced from coca grown in Peru, Bolivia, Colombia, and Ecuador. Estimated annual production totals 215,000 tons, with most of the processing done in Colombia. Long-term use may cause mental and physical deterioration.

Cochabamba city in central Bolivia, SE of La Paz; population (1985) 317,000. Its altitude is 8,370 ft/2,550 m; it is a center of agricultural trading and oil refining.

Its refinery is linked by pipeline with the Camiri oil-fields. It is the third-largest city in Bolivia.

Cochin former princely state lying W of the Anamalai hills in S India. It was part of Travancore-Cochin from 1949 until merged into Kerala in 1956.

cobra

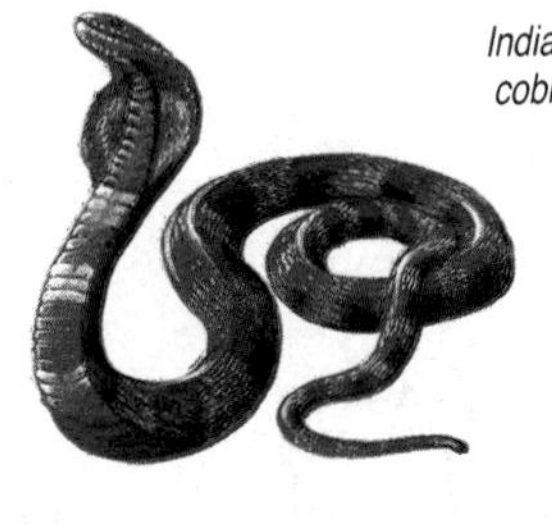

Indian cobra

Cochin seaport in Kerala state, India, on the Malabar coast; population (1983) 686,000. It is a fishing port and naval training base. An industrial center with oil refineries, ropes and clothing are also manufactured here. It exports coir, copra, tea, and spices. Vasco da Gama established a Portuguese factory at Cochin 1502, and St Francis Xavier made it a missionary center 1530. The Dutch held Cochin from 1663 to 1795, when it was taken by the English.

Cochin-China region of SE Asia. With Cambodia it formed part of the ancient Khmer empire. In the 17th–18th centuries it was conquered by Annam. Together with Cambodia it became, 1863–67, the first part of the Indochinese peninsula to be occupied by France. Since 1949 it has been part of Vietnam.

cochineal red dye, obtained from the cactus-eating Mexican ◊scale insect *Dactylopius coccus*, used in coloring food and fabrics.

Cochise c. 1812–1874. Apache leader. Born in Arizona as a member of the Chiricahua band of Apache, Cochise was unjustly arrested by US authorities 1850. Escaping from custody, he took, and later executed, some American hostages, leading to a bitter and long-lasting conflict with the US Government. In his fight to prevent white settlement in his territory, Cochise and his followers joined forces with the Mimbrēno Apache and conducted repeated raids on American posts. In 1862 he successfully held off a large force of California volunteers. Finally apprehended by Gen George Crook 1871, Cochise made peace with the US Government the following year.

cochlea part of the inner ◊ear. It is equipped with approximately 10,000 hair cells, which move in response to sound waves and thus stimulate nerve cells to send messages to the brain. In this way they turn vibrations of the air into electrical signals.

Cockaigne, Land of in medieval English folklore, a mythical country of leisure and idleness, where fine food and drink were plentiful and to be had for the asking.

cockatiel Australian parrot *Nymphicus hollandicus*, about 8 in/20 cm long, with greyish plumage, yellow cheeks, a long tail, and a crest like a cockatoo. They are popular as pets and aviary birds.

cockatoo any of several crested parrots, especially of the genus *Cacatua*. They usually have light-colored plumage with tinges of red, yellow, or orange on the face, and an erectile crest on the head. They are native to Australia, New Guinea, and nearby islands.

There are about 17 species, one of the most familiar being the sulfur-crested cockatoo *C. galerita* of Australia and New Guinea, about 20 in/50 cm long, white with a yellow crest and dark beak.

cockchafer or ***maybug*** European beetle *Melolontha melolontha*, of the scarab family, up to 1.2 in/3 cm long, with clumsy, buzzing flight, seen on early summer evenings. Cockchafers damage trees by feeding on the foliage and flowers.

The larvae live underground for up to four years, feeding on grass and cereal roots.

Cockcroft John Douglas 1897–1967. British physicist. In 1932 he and the Irish physicist Ernest Walton succeeded in splitting the nucleus of an atom for the first time. In 1951 they were jointly awarded a Nobel Prize.

Cockerell Charles 1788–1863. English architect who built mainly in a Neo-Classical style derived from antiquity and from the work of Christopher Wren. His buildings include the Ashmolean Museum and Taylorian Institute in Oxford 1841–45.

cockfighting the pitting of gamecocks with steel spurs fitted to their legs against one another to make sport for onlookers and gamblers. In most countries it is illegal because of its cruelty.

cockle any of over 200 species of bivalve mollusk with ribbed, heart-shaped shells. Some are edible and are sold in W European markets.

The Atlantic strawberry cockle *Americardia media*, about 1 in/2.5 cm across, is a common E North American species.

cock-of-the-rock South American bird *Rupicola peruviana* of the family Cotingidae, which also includes the cotingas and umbrella birds. The male cock-of-the-rock has brilliant orange plumage including the head crest, the female is a duller brown. Males clear an area of ground and use it as a communal display ground, spreading wings, tail, and crest to attract mates.

cockroach any of numerous insects of the family Blattidae, distantly related to mantises and grasshoppers. There are 3,500 species, mainly in the tropics. They have long antennae and biting mouthparts. They can fly, but rarely do so.

The common cockroach, or black-beetle *Blatta orientalis*, is found in human dwellings, is nocturnal, omnivorous, and contaminates food, often spreading hepatitis. The German cockroach *Blattella germanica* and American cockroach *Periplaneta americana* are pests in kitchens, bakeries, and warehouses. In Britain only two innocuous species are native, but several have been introduced with imported food and have become severe pests. They are very difficult to eradicate. Cockroaches have a very high resistance to radiation, making them the only creatures likely to survive a nuclear holocaust.

cocktail effect the effect of two toxic, or potentially toxic, chemicals when taken together rather than separately. Such effects are known to occur with some mixtures of chemicals, with one ingredient making the body more sensitive to another ingredient. This sometimes occurs because both chemicals require the same ◊enzyme to break them down. Chemicals such as pesticides and food additives are only ever tested singly, not in combination with other chemicals that may be consumed at the same time, so no allowance is made for cocktail effects.

cocoa and chocolate (Aztec xocolatl) food products made from the ◊cacao (or cocoa) bean, fruit of a tropical South American tree *Theobroma cacao*, now cultivated mainly in Africa. Chocolate as a drink was introduced to Europe from the New World by the Spanish in the 16th century; eating chocolate was first produced in the late 18th century. Cocoa and chocolate are widely used in confectionery and drinks.

Preparation takes place in the importing country and consists chiefly of roasting, winnowing, and grinding the nib (the edible portion of the bean). If cocoa for drinking is required, a portion of the cocoa butter is removed by hydraulic pressure and the remaining cocoa is reduced by further grinding and sieving to a fine powder. In chocolate all the original cocoa butter remains. Sugar and usually milk are added.

history The cacao tree is indigenous to the forests of the Amazon and Orinoco, and the use of the beans, sacred to the Indians of Mexico, was introduced into Europe after the conquest of Mexico by Cortes. In Mexico cacao was mixed with hot spices, whisked to a froth and drunk cold by the ruling class, during ritual events. A "cocoa-house" was opened in London in 1657; others followed and became fashionable meeting places. In 1828 a press was invented that removed two thirds of the cocoa butter from the beans, leaving a cakelike mass which, when mixed with sugar and spices, made a palatable drink. Joseph Fry combined the cocoa mass with sugar and cocoa butter to obtain a solid chocolate bar, which was turned into milk chocolate by a Swiss, Daniel Pieter, who added condensed milk developed by Henri Nestlé (1814–1890). Cocoa powder was a later development. The Ivory Coast is the world's top cocoa exporter (32% of the world total in 1986).

coconut

cocoa and chocolate

product	*description*
plain chocolate	partly defatted cocoa mass, 30–52%, mixed with a little sugar
coating chocolate	a higher proportion of cocoa butter and a smaller proportion of cocoa solids
milk chocolate	sweetened chocolate with powdered or condensed milk added.
white chocolate	cocoa butter flavored with sugar and vanilla
cooking chocolate	cocoa mass and vegetable fat
cocoa powder	cocoa mass with 18% cocoa butter, sweetened
Dutch cocoa	cocoa treated with weak alkali to improve color, flavor and solubility
drinking chocolate	precooked cocoa powder with added sugar and flavorings

coconut fruit of the coconut palm *Cocos nucifera* of the family Arecaceae, which grows throughout the lowland tropics. The fruit has a large outer husk of fibers, which is split off and used for coconut matting and ropes. Inside this is the nut exported to temperate countries. Its hard shell contains white flesh and coconut milk, both of which are nourishing and palatable.

The white meat can be eaten, or dried prior to the extraction of its oil, which makes up nearly two-thirds of it. The oil is used in the making of soap and margarine and in cooking; the residue is used in cattle feed.

Cocos Islands or *Keeling Islands* group of 27 small coral islands in the Indian Ocean, about 1,720 mi/2,770 km NW of Perth, Australia; area 5.5 sq mi/14 sq km; population (1986) 616. They are owned by Australia.

Discovered by William Keeling 1609, they were uninhabited until 1826, annexed by Britain 1857, and transferred to Australia as the Territory of Cocos (Keeling) Islands 1955. The Australian government purchased them from John Clunies-Ross 1978. In 1984 the islanders voted to become part of Australia.

Cocteau Jean 1889–1963. French poet, dramatist, and film director. A leading figure in European Modernism, he worked with Picasso, Diaghilev, and Stravinsky. He produced many volumes of poetry, ballets such as *Le Boeuf sur le toit/The Nothing Doing Bar* 1920, plays, for example, *Orphée/Orpheus* 1926, and a mature novel of bourgeois French life, *Les Enfants terribles/Children of the Game* 1929, which he made into a film 1950.

cod any fish of the family Gadoidea, especially the Atlantic cod, *Gadus morhua* found in the N Atlantic and Baltic. Brown to gray with spots, white below, it can grow to 5 ft/1.5 m.

The major cod fisheries are in the North Sea, and off the coasts of Iceland and Newfoundland. Much of the catch is salted and dried. Formerly one of the cheapest fish, decline in numbers from overfishing has made it one of the most expensive.

COD abbreviation for cash on delivery.

coda (Italian "tail") in music, a concluding section of a movement added to indicate finality.

codeine opium derivative that provides analgesia in mild to moderate pain. It also suppresses the cough center of the brain. It is an alkaloid $C_{18}H_{21}NO_3$, derived from morphine but less toxic and addictive.

codex (plural codices) book from before the invention of printing: in ancient times wax-coated wooden tablets; later, folded sheets of parchment were attached to the boards, then bound together. The name "codex" was used for all large works, collections of history, philosophy, poetry, and during the Roman Empire designated collections of laws. During the 2nd century AD codices began to replace the earlier rolls. They were widely used by the medieval Christian church to keep records, from about 1200 onward.

Various codices record Mexican Indian civilizations just after the time of the Spanish Conquest about 1520. The *Codex Juris Canonici/Code of Canon Law* is the body of laws governing the Roman Catholic Church since 1918.

cod liver oil oil obtained by subjecting fresh livers of cod and related fish to pressure at a temperature of about 185°F/85°C. It is is highly nutritious, being a valuable source of the vitamins A and D.

codon in genetics, a triplet of bases (see ◊base pair) in a molecule of DNA or RNA that directs the placement of a particular amino acid during the process of protein (polypeptide) synthesis. There are 64 codons in the ◊genetic code.

Cody William Frederick 1846–1917. US scout and performer, known as Buffalo Bill from his contract to supply buffalo carcasses to railroad laborers (over 4,000 in 18 months). From 1883 he toured the US and Europe with a Wild West show which featured the recreation of Indian attacks and, for a time, the cast included Chief ◊Sitting Bull as well as Annie ◊Oakley.

He was a heavy drinker and a trusting investor; he died in poverty after seeing his exploits recounted and exaggerated in novels of the West.

coeducation the education of both boys and girls in one institution.

In most countries coeducation has become favored over single-sex education, although there is some evidence to suggest that girls perform better in a single-sex institution, particularly in math and science. In the US, 90% of schools and colleges are coeducational. In 1954, the USSR returned to its earlier coeducational system,

Cocteau *French playwright, novelist, poet, film director, and artist Jean Cocteau in 1929.*

Cody US showman "Buffalo Bill" Cody. His nickname stemmed from his earlier career supplying buffalo meat to construction gangs.

which was partly abolished in 1944. In Islamic countries, coeducation is discouraged beyond the infant stage on religious principles.

coefficient the number part in front of an algebraic term, signifying multiplication. For example, in the expression $4x^2 + 2xy - x$, the coefficient of x^2 is 4 (because $4x^2$ means $4 \times x^2$), that of xy is 2, and that of x is -1 (because $-1 \times x = -x$).

In general algebraic expressions, coefficients are represented by letters that may stand for numbers; for example, in the equation $ax^2 + bx + c = 0$, a, b, and c are coefficients, which can take any number.

coefficient of relationship the probability that any two individuals share a given gene by virtue of being descended from a common ancestor. In sexual reproduction of diploid species, an individual shares half its genes with each parent, with its offspring, and (on average) with each sibling; but only a quarter (on average) with its grandchildren or its siblings' offspring; an eighth with its great-grandchildren, and so on.

coelacanth lobe-finned fish *Latimeria chalumnae* up to 6 ft/2 m long. It has bone and muscle at the base of the fins, and is distantly related to the freshwater lobefins, which were the ancestors of all land animals with backbones. Coelacanths live in deep water surrounding the Comoros Islands, off the coast of Madagascar. They were believed to be extinct until one was caught in 1938. They are now under threat; a belief that fluid from the spine has a life-extending effect has made them much sought after.

coelom in all but the simplest animals, the fluid-filled body cavity that contains the gut and associated organs.

Coetzee J(ohn) M 1940– . South African author whose novel *In the Heart of the Country* 1975 dealt with the rape of a white woman by a black man. In 1983 he won Britain's prestigious Booker Prize for *The Life and Times of Michael K.*

Other works include *Waiting for the Barbarians* 1982 and *Foe* 1987.

coffee drink made from the roasted and ground beanlike seeds found inside the red berries of any of several species of shrubs of the genus *Coffea*, originally native to Ethiopia and now cultivated throughout the tropics. It contains a stimulant, ◊caffeine.

history Coffee drinking began in Arab regions in the 14th century but did not become common in Europe until 300 years later, when the first coffee houses were opened in Vienna, and soon after in Paris and London. In the American colonies, coffee became the substitute for tea when tea was taxed by the British. After the US became an independent nation, coffee remained the national drink and is so popular that "coffee breaks" are negotiated into labor contracts. Coffee is usually drunk hot, black or with cream and sugar; it is drunk cold as iced coffee, especially in summer.

cultivation naturally about 17 ft/5 m high, the shrub is pruned to about 7 ft/2 m, is fully fruit-bearing in 5 or 6 years, and lasts for 30 years. Coffee grows best on frost-free hillsides with moderate rainfall. The world's largest producers are Brazil, Colombia, and the Ivory Coast; others include Indonesia (Java), Ethiopia, India, Hawaii, and Jamaica.

Cognac town in Charente *département*, France, 25 mi/40 km W of Angoulême; population (1982) 21,000. Situated in a vine-growing district, Cognac has given its name to a brandy. Bottles, corks, barrels, and crates are manufactured here.

cognition in psychology, a general term covering the functions involved in synthesizing with information—for example, perception (seeing, hearing, and so on), attention, memory, and reasoning.

cognitive therapy a treatment for emotional disorders such as ◊depression and ◊anxiety, developed by Professor Aaron T Beck in the US. This approach encourages the client to challenge the distorted and unhelpful thinking that is characteristic of these problems. The treatment includes ◊behavior therapy and has been most helpful for people suffering from depression.

Cohan George M(ichael) 1878–1942. US composer and theatrical personality. He gained celebrity with his 1904 Broadway hit *Little Johnny Jones*, which included his songs "Give My Regards to Broadway" and "Yankee Doodle Boy.' His 1906 song "You're a Grand Old Flag" further associated him with popular patriotism, as did his famous World War I song "Over There" 1917. In 1940 Cohan was honored by Congress. A film version of his life, *Yankee Doodle Dandy*, appeared 1942.

Born in Providence, Rhode Island, to a theatrical family, Cohan spent his youth touring, writing songs, and appearing in musical comedies.

Cohan Robert Paul 1925– . US choreographer and founder of the London Contemporary Dance Theatre 1969–87; now artistic director of the Contemporary Dance Theatre. He was a student of Martha ◊Graham and codirector of her company 1966–69. His ballets include *Waterless Method of Swimming Instruction* 1974 and *Mass for Man* 1985.

coherence in physics, property of two or more waves of a beam of light or other ◊electromagnetic radiation having the same frequency and the same ◊phase, or a constant phase difference.

cohesion in physics, a phenomenon in which interaction between two surfaces of the same material in contact makes them cling together (with two different materials the similar phenomenon is called adhesion). According to kinetic theory, cohesion is caused by attraction between particles at the atomic or molecular level. ◊Surface tension, which causes liquids to form spherical droplets, is caused by cohesion.

coil in medicine, another name for an ◊intrauterine device.

Coimbatore city in Tamil Nadu, S India, on the Noyil River; population (1981) 917,000. It has textile industries and the Indian Air Force Administrative College.

Coimbra city in Portugal, on the Mondego River, 19 mi/32 km from the sea; population (1981) 71,800. It produces fabrics, paper, pottery, and cookies. There is a 12th-century Romanesque cathedral incorporating part of an older mosque, and a university, founded in Lisbon 1290 and transferred to Coimbra 1537. Coimbra was the capital of Portugal 1139–1385.

coin a form of money. The right to make and issue coins is a state monopoly, and the great majority are tokens in that their face value is greater than that of the metal of which they consist. A milled edge, originally used on gold and silver coins to avoid fraudulent "clipping" of the edges of precious-metal coins, is retained in some present-day token coinage.

The invention of coinage is attributed to the Chinese in the 2nd millennium BC, the earliest types being small-scale bronze reproductions of barter objects such as knives and spades. In the Western world, coinage of stamped, guaranteed weight originated with the Lydians of Asia Minor (early 7th century BC) who used electrum, a local natural mixture of gold and silver; the first to issue both gold and silver coins was Croesus of Lydia in the 6th century BC.

coke clean, light fuel produced by the carbonization of certain types of coal. When this coal is strongly heated in airtight ovens (in order to release all volatile constituents), the brittle, silver-gray remains are coke. Coke comprises 90% carbon together with very small quantities of water, hydrogen, and oxygen, and makes a useful industrial and domestic fuel. The process was patented in England 1622, but it was only in 1709 that Abraham Darby devised a commercial method of production.

Coke Edward 1552–1634. Lord Chief Justice of England 1613–17. He was a defender of common law against royal prerogative; against Charles I he drew up the Petition of Right 1628, which defines and protects Parliament's liberties.

cola or ***kola*** any tropical tree of the genus *Cola*, especially *C. acuminata*, family Sterculiaceae. Their nuts are chewed in W Africa for their high caffeine content, and in the West are used to flavor soft drinks.

Colbert Claudette. Adopted name of Claudette Lily Cauchoin 1905– . French-born US film actress who lived in Hollywood from childhood. She was ideally cast in sophisticated, romantic roles, but had a natural instinct for comedy and appeared in several of Hollywood's finest, including *It Happened One Night* 1934, for which she won an Academy Award, and *The Palm Beach Story* 1942.

Colbert Jean-Baptiste 1619–1683. French politician, chief minister to Louis XIV, and controller-general (finance minister) from 1665. He reformed the Treasury, promoted French industry and commerce by protectionist measures, and tried to make France a naval power equal to England or the Netherlands, while favoring a peaceful foreign policy.

Colbert, born in Reims, entered the service of Cardinal Mazarin and succeeded him as chief minister to Louis XIV. In 1661 he set to work to reform the Treasury. The national debt was largely repaid, and the system of tax collection was drastically reformed. Industry was brought under state control, shipbuilding was encouraged by bounties, companies were established to trade with India and America, and colonies were founded in Louisiana, Guiana, and Madagascar. In his later years Colbert was supplanted in Louis's favor by the war minister Louvois (1641–91), who supported a policy of conquests.

Colchester town and river port in England, on the river Colne, Essex; 50 mi/80 km NE of London; population (1981) 82,000. In an agricultural area, it is a market center with clothing manufacture and engineering and printing works. The University of Essex (1961) is at Wivenhoe to the southeast.

Claiming to be the oldest town in England (Latin *Camulodunum*), Colchester dates from the time of ◊Cymbeline (c. AD 10–43). It became a colony of Roman ex-soldiers in AD 50, and one of the most prosperous towns in Roman Britain despite its burning by Boudicca (Boadicea) in 61. Most of the Roman walls remain, as well as ruins of the Norman castle, and St Botolph's priory. Holly Tree Mansion (1718) is a museum of 18th- and 19th-century social life.

cold, common minor disease of the upper respiratory tract, caused by a variety of viruses. Symptoms are headache, chill, nasal discharge, sore throat, and occasionally cough. Research indicates that the virulence of a cold depends on psychological factors and either a reduction or an increase of social or work activity, as a result of stress, in the previous six months.

There is little immediate hope of an effective cure since the viruses transform themselves so rapidly.

coldblooded common name for ◊poikilothermy.

cold fusion in nuclear physics, the fusion of atomic nuclei at room temperature. Were cold fusion to become possible it would provide a limitless, cheap, and pollution-free source of energy, and it has therefore been the subject of research around the world. In 1989, Martin Fleischmann (1927–) and Stanley Pons (1943–) of the University of Utah claimed that they had achieved cold fusion in the laboratory, but their results could not be substantiated.

Fleischmann and Pons reported that they had achieved the fusion of deuterium (heavy hydrogen) nuclei at room temperature by passing an electric current between palladium oxide electrodes suspended in heavy water (water containing deuterium). They claimed that the heat produced in the process could not be explained by any known electrical or chemical effect, and suggested that the palladium had absorbed deuterium atoms from the water, cramming their nuclei together so that they were close enough to fuse. In the following weeks a number of scientists claimed also to have observed the phenomenon, but researchers at the major research laboratories were unable to duplicate Fleischmann and Pons's results. A number of scientists subsequently withdrew their claims and gradually the evidence for cold fusion was undermined. Many now believe that cold fusion is impossible; however, research has continued in some laboratories.

Cold Harbor, Battle of American Civil War engagement near Richmond, Virginia, June 1–12, 1864, in which the Confederate army under Robert E ◊Lee repulsed Union attacks under Ulysses S ◊Grant, inflicting as many as 6,000 casualties in an hour and forcing Grant to adopt a siege of Petersburg. This demonstrated the tenacity of the Confederate forces late in the war and kept Grant's army largely stationary until April 1865.

Colditz town in Germany, near Leipzig, site of a castle used as a high-security prisoner-of-war camp (Oflag IVC) in World War II. Among daring escapes was that of British Captain Patrick Reid and others Oct 1942. It became a museum 1989. In 1990 the castle was being converted to a hotel.

cold war the ideological, political and economic tensions since 1945 between the USSR and Eastern Europe against the US and Western Europe. The cold war was exacerbated by propaganda, covert activity by intelligence agencies, and economic sanctions; it intensified at times of conflict anywhere in the world. Arms reduction agreements between the US and USSR in the late 1980s, and a diminution of Soviet influence in Eastern Europe, symbolized by the opening of the Berlin Wall 1989, led to a reassessment of positions and the "war" officially ended in 1990.

origins Mistrust between the USSR and the West dates from the Russian Revolution 1917 and contributed to the disagreements during and immediately after World War II over the future structure of Eastern Europe. The ◊Atlantic Charter signed 1941 by the US and UK favored self-determination, whereas the USSR insisted on keeping the territory obtained as a result of the Hitler–Stalin pact of August 1939.

After the war the US was eager to have all of Europe open to Western economic interests, while the USSR, afraid of being encircled and attacked by its former allies, saw Eastern Europe as its own sphere of influence and, in the case of Germany, was looking to extract reparations. As the USSR increased its hold on the countries of Eastern Europe, the US pursued a policy of "containment" that involved offering material aid to Western Europe (the ◊Marshall Plan) and to Nazi-victimized countries such as Greece and Turkey. Berlin became the focal point of East-West tension, (since it was zoned for military occupational governments of the US, UK, France and USSR—yet was situated within what was then Soviet-controlled E Germany). This culminated in the Soviet blockade of the US, British and French zones of the city 1948, which was relieved by a sustained airlift of supplies (see ◊Berlin blockade).

The increasing divisions between the capitalist and the communist worlds were reinforced by the creation of military alliances, the ◊North Atlantic Treaty Organization (NATO) 1949 in the West, and the ◊Warsaw Pact 1955 in the East.

cold war: chronology

1947	The term "cold war" was first used by Bernard Baruch in a speech referring to the Truman Doctrine in April.
1950–53	The Korean War.
1956	The USSR intervened in Hungary to put down a revolution.
1962	The Cuban missile crisis.
1964–75	The Vietnam War.
1968	The USSR intervened in Czechoslovakia.
1972	SALT I accord on arms limitation signed by US and USSR, beginning a thaw, or détente, in E–W relations.
1979	The USSR invaded Afghanistan.
1980–81	US support for the Solidarity movement in Poland. US president Reagan called the USSR an "evil empire."
1982–1990	US covert and military intervention in Central America increases to aid anti-Socialist groups.
1983	US president Reagan proposed to militarize space (Star Wars).
1986	Soviet leader Gorbachev made a proposal for nuclear disarmament that was turned down by Reagan.
1988	Soviet and US leaders reach accord on medium-range nuclear missiles.
1989	Poland elects noncommunist government; Hungary declares itself a republic; East Germany opens borders to the West; Czechoslovakia lifts travel restrictions; revolution in Romania topples communist dictatorship; Gorbachev renounces "Brezhnev doctrine" of intervention and withdraws from Afghanistan.
1990	November—the formal end of the cold war.

coldworking method of shaping metal at or near atmospheric temperature.

Cole Thomas 1801–1848. US painter, founder of the Hudson River school of landscape artists.

Cole wrote *An Essay on American Scenery* in 1835. Apart from panoramic views such as *The Oxbow* 1836 (Metropolitan Museum of Art, New York), he painted a dramatic historical series, *The Course of Empire* 1836 (New York Historical Society), influenced by the European artists Claude, Turner, and John Martin.

Coleman Ornette 1930– . US alto saxophonist and jazz composer. In the late 1950s he rejected the established structural principles of jazz for free avant-garde improvisation. He has worked with small and large groups, ethnic musicians of different traditions, and symphony orchestras.

Cole, Old King legendary British king, supposed to be the father of St Helena, who married the Roman emperor Constantius, father of Constantine; he is also supposed to have founded Colchester. The historical Cole was possibly a North British chieftan named Coel, of the 5th century, who successfully defended his land against the Picts and Scots. The nursery rhyme is only recorded from 1709.

coleoptile the protective sheath that surrounds the young shoot tip of a grass during its passage through the soil to the surface. Although of relatively simple structure, most coleoptiles are very sensitive to light, ensuring that seedlings grow upward.

Coleridge Samuel Taylor 1772–1834. English poet, one of the founders of the Romantic movement. A friend of Southey and Wordsworth, he collaborated with the latter on *Lyrical Ballads* 1798. His poems include "The Ancient Mariner," "Christabel," and "Kubla Khan"; critical works include *Biographia Literaria* 1817.

While at Cambridge, Coleridge was driven by debt to enlist in the Dragoons, and then in 1795, as part of an abortive plan to found a Communist colony in the US with Robert Southey, married Sarah Fricker, from whom he afterwards separated. He became addicted to opium and from 1816 lived at Highgate, London, under medical care. As a philosopher, he argued inferentially that even in registering sense-perceptions the mind was performing acts of creative imagination, rather than being a passive arena in which ideas interact mechanistically. As a critic, he used psychological insight to brilliant effect in his *Biographia Literaria* and Shakespearean criticism.

Coleridge-Taylor Samuel 1875–1912. English composer, the son of a West African doctor and an English mother. He wrote the cantata *Hiawatha's Wedding Feast* 1898, a setting in three parts of Longfellow's poem. He was a student and champion of traditional black music.

Colette Sidonie-Gabrielle 1873–1954. French writer. At 20 she married Henri Gauthier-Villars, a journalist known as "Willy" and under whose name and direction her four "Claudine" novels, based on her own early life, were written. Divorced in 1906, she worked as a striptease and mime artist for a while, but continued to write. Works from this later period include *Chéri* 1920, *La Fin de Chéri/The End of Chéri* 1926, and *Gigi* 1944.

Colfax Schuyler 1823–1885. US political leader. Becoming active in Indiana state politics, he was first elected to the US House of Representatives 1854 and served as Speaker of the House 1863–69. A Radical Republican, Colfax was elected vice-president for Grant's first term 1869–73. He was not renominated because of charges of corruption and financial improprieties.

Born in New York, Colfax moved with his family to Indiana 1836 and, although having the benefit of little formal education, worked in a suc-

Coleridge *English poet and critic Samuel Taylor Coleridge, author of "The Ancient Mariner."*

cession of jobs, including county auditor, newspaper reporter, and legal assistant.

colic spasmodic attack of pain in the abdomen, usually in infancy. Colicky pains are caused by air in the intestines, leading to the blockage, and subsequent distension, of a hollow organ; for example, the bowels, gall bladder (biliary colic), or ureter (renal colic). Characteristically the pain is severe during contraction of the muscular wall of the organ, then recedes temporarily as the muscle tires.

colitis inflammation of the colon (large intestine) with diarrhea (often bloody). It may be caused by food poisoning or some types of bacterial dysentery.

collage (French "gluing" or "pasting") a technique of pasting paper and other materials to create a picture. Several artists in the early 20th century used collage: Arp, Braque, Ernst, and Schwitters, among others.

Many artists also experimented with photomontage, creating compositions from pieces of photographs rearranged with often disturbing effects.

collagen a strong, rubbery ◊protein that plays a major structural role in the bodies of ◊vertebrates. Collagen supports the ear flaps and the tip of the nose in humans, as well as being the main constituent of tendons and ligaments. Bones are made up of collagen, with the mineral calcium phosphate providing increased rigidity.

collateral security available in return for a loan. Usually stocks, shares, property, or life insurance policies will be accepted as collateral.

collective bargaining the process whereby management, representing an employer, and a labor union, representing employees, agree to negotiate jointly terms and conditions of employment. Agreements can be company-based or industry-wide.

collective farm (Russian *kolkhoz*) a farm in which a group of farmers pool their land, domestic animals, and agricultural implements, retaining as private property enough only for the members' own requirements. The profits of the farm are divided among its members.

The system was first developed in the USSR in 1917, where it became general after 1930. Stalin's collectivization drive 1929–33 wrecked a flourishing agricultural system and alienated the Soviet peasants from the land: 15 million people were left homeless, 1 million of whom were sent to labor camps and some 12 million deported to Siberia. In subsequent years, millions of those peasants forced into collectives died. Collective farming is practiced in other countries; it was adopted from 1953 in China, and Israel has a large number of collective farms (see ◊kibbutz).

collective security system for achieving international stability by an agreement among all states to unite against any aggressor. Such a commitment was embodied in the post–World War I League of Nations and also in the United Nations, although neither body was able to live up to the ideals of its founders.

collective unconscious in psychology, the term used for the shared pool of memories inherited from ancestors that Carl Jung suggested coexisted with individual ◊unconscious recollections, and which might affect individuals both for ill in precipitating mental disturbance, or for good in prompting achievements (for example, in the arts).

collectivization the policy pursued by Stalin in the USSR after 1928 to reorganize agriculture by taking land into state or collective ownership. Much of this was achieved during the first two ◊Five Year Plans but only with much coercion and loss of life among the peasantry.

College Station city in E central Texas, NW of Houston; adjoining the city of Bryan. Texas A&M University is here; population (1990) 52,456.

collenchyma a plant tissue composed of relatively elongated cells with thickened cell walls, in particular at the corners where adjacent cells meet. It is a supporting and strengthening tissue found in nonwoody plants, mainly in the stems and leaves.

Collins *English rock star Phil Collins*

collie type of sheepdog originally bred in Britain. The rough and smooth collies are about 2 ft/60 cm tall, and have long narrow heads and muzzles. They may be light to dark brown or silver-gray, with black and white markings. The border collie is a working dog, often black and white, about 20 in/50 cm tall, with a dense coat. The bearded collie is about the same size, and is rather like an Old English sheepdog in appearance.

Collier Lesley 1947– . British ballerina, a principal dancer of the Royal Ballet from 1972.

She had major roles in Kenneth MacMillan's *Anastasia* 1971, and *Four Seasons* 1975, Hans van Manen's *Four Schumann Pieces* 1975, Frederick Ashton's *Rhapsody*, and Glen Tetley's *Dance of Albiar* both 1980.

collimator (1) a small telescope attached to a larger optical instrument to fix its line of sight; (2) an optical device for producing a nondivergent beam of light; (3) any device for limiting the size and angle of spread of a beam of radiation or particles.

Collingwood Robin George 1889–1943. English philosopher who believed that any philosophical theory or position could only be properly understood within its own historical context and not from the point of view of the present. His esthetic theory is outlined in *Principles of Art* 1938.

Collins Michael 1890–1922. Irish nationalist. He was a Sinn Féin leader, a founder and director of intelligence of the Irish Republican Army 1919, minister for finance in the provisional government of the Irish Free State 1922 (see ◊Ireland, Republic of), commander of the Free State forces in the civil war and for ten days head of state before being killed.

Collins Phil(lip David Charles) 1951– . English pop singer, drummer, and actor. A member of the group Genesis since 1970, he has also pursued a successful solo career since 1981, with hits (often new versions of old songs) including "In the Air Tonight" 1981 and "Groovy Kind of Love" 1988.

Collins (William) Wilkie 1824–1889. English author of mystery and suspense novels. He wrote *The Woman in White* 1860 (with its fat villain Count Fosco), often called the first English detective novel, and *The Moonstone* 1868 (with Sergeant Cuff, one of the first detectives in English literature).

Collins William 1721–1759. British poet. His *Persian Eclogues* 1742 were followed in 1746 by his series "Odes," including the poem "To Evening."

collision theory theory that explains chemical reactions and the way in which the rate of reaction alters when the conditions alter. For a reaction to occur the reactant particles must collide. Only a certain fraction of the total collisions cause chemical change; these are called fruitful collisions. These fruitful collisions have sufficient energy (activation energy) at the moment of impact to break the existing bonds and form new bonds, resulting in the products of the reaction. Increasing the concentration of the reactants and raising the temperature bring about more collisions and therefore more fruitful collisions, increasing the rate of reaction. When a ◊catalyst undergoes collision with the reactant molecules, less energy is required at the moment of impact for the chemical change to occur, and hence more collisions have sufficient energy for reaction to occur. The reaction rate therefore increases.

Collodi Carlo. Adopted name of Carlo Lorenzini 1826–1890. Italian journalist and writer, who in 1881–83 wrote *The Adventure of Pinocchio*, the children's story of a wooden puppet that became a human boy.

colloid substance composed of extremely small particles whose size is between those in suspension and those in true solution (between 1 and 1,000 microns across). The two components together are the continuous phase; the dispersed phase is distributed in the former. There are various types of colloid: those involving gases include an aerosol (a dispersion of a liquid or solid in a gas, as in fog or smoke) and a foam (a dispersion of a gas in a liquid). Liquids form both the dispersed and continuous phases in an emulsion.

Milk is a natural emulsion (stable colloidal suspension) of liquid fat in a watery liquid; synthetic emulsions such as some paints and cosmetic lotions have chemical emulsifying agents to stabilize the colloid and stop the two phases from separating out. Colloidal solutions (a solid dispersed in a liquid) are called sols. A sol in which both phases contribute to the molecular three-dimensional network of the colloid take on a jellylike form and are known as gels; gelatine, starch "solution" and silica gel are common examples. Colloids were first studied thoroughly by the British chemist Thomas ◊Graham, who defined them as substances that (in solution) will not diffuse through a semipermeable membrane (as opposed to crystalloids, solutions of inorganic salts, which will diffuse through).

Colman Ronald 1891–1958. English actor. His films include *Beau Geste* 1924, *A Tale of Two Cities* 1935, *The Prisoner of Zenda* 1937, *Lost Horizon* 1937, and *A Double Life* 1947, for which he received an Academy Award.

He went to the US in 1920 where he soon found success in romantic Hollywood roles.

Colmar capital of Haut-Rhin *département*, France, between the river Rhine and the Vosges mountains; population (1983) 82,500. It is the center of a wine-growing and market-gardening area. Industries include engineering, food processing, and textiles. The church of St Martin is 13th–14th century, and the former Dominican monastery, now the Unterlinden Museum, contains a Grünewald altarpiece.

Cologne (German *Köln*) industrial and commercial port in North Rhine–Westphalia, Federal Republic of Germany, on the left bank of the Rhine, 22 mi/35 km from Düsseldorf; population (1988) 914,000. To the N is the Ruhr coalfield, on which many of Cologne's industries are based. They include motor vehicles, freight cars, chemicals, and machine tools. Cologne can be reached by ocean-going vessels and has developed into a great transshipment center, and is also the headquarters of Lufthansa, the state airline.

Founded by the Romans 38 BC and made a colony AD 50 under the name Colonia Claudia Arae Agrippinensis (hence the name Cologne), it became a leading Frankish city and during the Middle Ages was ruled by its archbishops. It was a free imperial city from 1288 until the Napoleonic age. In 1815 it passed to Prussia. The great Gothic cathedral was begun in the 13th century, but its towers were not built until the 19th century (completed 1880). Its university (1388–1797) was refounded 1919. Cologne suffered severely from aerial bombardment during World War II; 85% of

Cologne The twin towers of the majestic cathedral dominate the city from every angle. The present building was begun in 1248 but only completed in the 19th century.

the city and its three Rhine bridges were destroyed.

Colombes suburb of Paris, France; population (1983) 83,260. It is the capital of Hauts-de-Seine *département*. Tires, electronic equipment, and chemicals are manufactured.

Colombey-les-Deux-Eglises village (French "Colombey with the two churches") in Haute-Marne, France; population (1981) 700. General ◊de Gaulle lived and was buried here.

Colombia country in South America, bounded N and W by the Caribbean and the Pacific, NW corner by Panama, E and NE by Venezuela, SE by Brazil, and SW by Peru and Ecuador.

government The 1886 constitution provides for a president, a two-chamber congress comprising a senate of 114 members and a house of representatives of 199 members, all elected by universal suffrage for a four-year term. The president appoints the cabinet. Although it does not have a fully federal system, Colombia is divided into 32 regions, enjoying considerable autonomy, with governors appointed by the president and locally elected legislatures. Among many political parties are the Liberal Party and the Conservative Party.

history Until it was conquered by Spain in the 16th century, the area was inhabited by the Chibcha. From 1538 Colombia formed part of a colony known as New Granada, comprising Colombia, Panama, and most of Venezuela. In 1819 the area included Ecuador and became independent as Gran Colombia, a state set up by Simón Bolívar. Colombia became entirely independent in 1886.

In 1948 the left-wing mayor of Bogotá was assassinated, and there followed a decade of near civil war, "La Violencia," during which it is thought that over 250,000 people died. Left-wing guerrilla activity continued. In 1957, in an effort to halt the violence, the Conservative and Liberal Parties formed a National Front, alternating the presidency between them. They were challenged in 1970 by the National Popular Alliance (ANAPO), with a special appeal to the working classes, but the Conservative-Liberal coalition continued, and when in 1978 the Liberals won majorities in both chambers of congress and the presidency, they kept the National Front accord.

In 1982 the Liberals kept their majorities in congress, but Dr Belisario Bentacur won the presidency for the Conservatives. He sought a truce with the left-wing guerrillas by granting them an amnesty and freeing political prisoners. He also embarked on a radical program of public works. His plans suffered a major blow in 1984 when his minister of justice, who had been using harsh measures to curb drug dealing, was assassinated. Betancur reacted by strengthening his antidrug campaign. In the 1986 elections Liberal Virgilio Barco Vargas won the presidency by a record margin. Three months after taking office, he announced the end of the National Front accord, despite a provision in the constitution that the opposition party always has the opportunity to participate in government if it wishes to. The guerrilla activity continued, at first supported, later opposed, by the powerful drug cartels.

President Vargas declared a new campaign against cocaine traffickers following the assassination in Aug of Luis Carlos Galan, the leading candidate for the 1990 presidential elections. Judges, journalists, and more than 100 civilians were victims of a bombing campaign undertaken by the cartels in retaliation for confiscation of property and extradition to the US of leading cartel members. The Colombian security forces scored a major victory in Dec 1989 with the killing in a shoot-out of drug lord José Rodriguez Gacha. President Bush attended an antidrug summit in Colombia Feb 1990. During 1991 several major figures in the Medellín cartel surrendered to the government.

Colombia

Republic of
(República de Colombia)

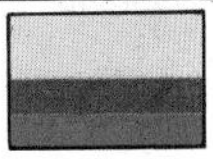

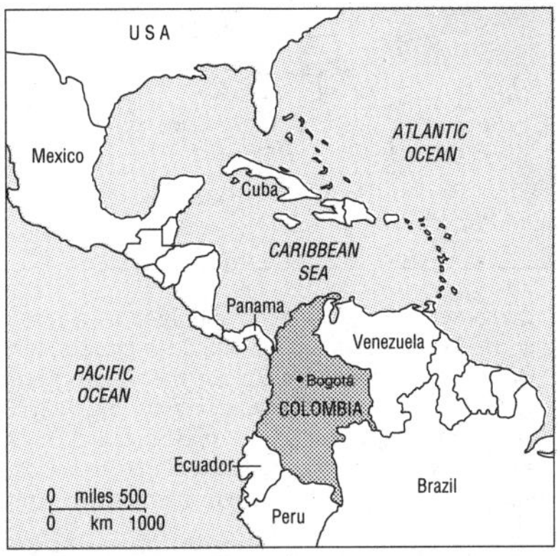
USA
Mexico
ATLANTIC OCEAN
Cuba
CARIBBEAN SEA
Panama
Venezuela
PACIFIC OCEAN
Bogotá
COLOMBIA
Ecuador
Brazil
Peru
0 miles 500
0 km 1000

area 440,715 sq mi/1,141,748 sq km
capital Bogotá
cities Medellín, Cali, Bucaramanga; ports Barranquilla, Cartagena, Buenaventura
physical the Andes mountains run N–S; flat coastland in W and plains (llanos) in E; Magdalena River runs N to Caribbean Sea; includes islands of Providencia, San Andrés, and Mapelo
features Zipaquira salt mine and underground cathedral; Lake Guatavita, source of the legend of "El Dorado"
head of state and government Cesar Gaviria Trujillo from 1990
political system emergent democratic republic
political parties Liberal Party, centrist; April 19 Movement; National Salvation Movement; Conservative Party, right-of-center
exports emeralds (world's largest producer), coffee (second-largest world producer), cocaine (country's largest export), bananas, cotton, meat, sugar, oil, skins, hides, tobacco
currency peso
population (1990 est) 32,598,800 (mestizo 68%, white 20%, Amerindian 1%); growth rate 2.2% p.a.
life expectancy men 61, women 66; Indians 34
language Spanish
religion Roman Catholic 95%
literacy men 89%/women 87% (1987); Indians 40%
GDP $31.9 bn (1987); $1,074 per head
chronology
1886 Full independence achieved from Spain. Conservatives in power.
1930 Liberals in power.
1946 Conservatives in power.
1948 Left-wing mayor of Bogotá assassinated; widespread outcry.
1949 Start of civil war, "La Violencia," during which 280,000 people died.
1957 Hoping to halt the violence, Conservatives and Liberals agreed to form a National Front, sharing the presidency.
1970 National Popular Alliance (ANAPO) formed as a left-wing opposition to the National Front.
1974 National Front accord temporarily ended.
1975 Civil unrest because of disillusionment with the government.
1978 Liberals, under Julio Turbay, revived the accord and began an intensive fight against drug dealers.
1982 Liberals maintained their control of congress but lost the presidency. The Conservative president, Belisario Betancur, attempted to end the violence by granting left-wing guerrillas an amnesty, freeing political prisoners, and embarking on a large public-works program.
1984 Minister of justice assassinated by drug dealers; campaign against them stepped up.
1986 Virgilio Barco Vargas, Liberal, elected president by record margin.
1989 Drug cartel assassinated leading presidential candidate; Vargas declared antidrug war; bombing campaign by drug lords killed hundreds; police killed José Rodríguez Gacha, one of the most wanted cartel leaders.
1990 Cesar Gaviria Trujillo elected president. Liberals maintained control of congress.
1991 Peace talks with rebel leaders. A new constitution was passed prohibiting extradition of Colombians wanted for trial in other countries; shortly afterwards several leading drug traffickers were arrested, including Pablo Escotar Gavicia, head of the Medellín cocaine cartel.

Colombo capital and principal seaport of Sri Lanka, on the W coast near the mouth of the Kelani; population (1981) 588,000, Greater Colombo about 1,000,000. It trades in tea, rubber, and cacao. It has iron and steel works and an oil refinery.

Colombo was mentioned as Kalambu about 1340, but the Portuguese renamed it in honor of the explorer Christopher Columbus. The Dutch seized it 1656 and surrendered it to Britain 1796. Since 1983 the chief government offices have been located at nearby Sri-Jayawardenapura E of the city.

Colombo Matteo Realdo c. 1516–1559. Italian anatomist who discovered pulmonary circulation, the process of blood circulating from the heart to the lungs and back.

This showed that ◊Galen's teachings were wrong, and was of help to ◊Harvey in his work on the heart and circulation. Colombo was a pupil of ◊Vesalius and became his successor at the University of Padua.

Colombo Plan plan for cooperative economic development in S and SE Asia, established 1951. The member countries meet annually to discuss economic and development plans such as irrigation, hydroelectric schemes, and technical training.

The plan has no central fund but technical assistance and financing of development projects are arranged through individual governments or the International Bank for Reconstruction and Development.

colon in anatomy, the part of the large intestine between the cecum and rectum, where water and mineral salts are absorbed from digested food, and the residue formed into feces or fecal pellets.

colon in punctuation, a mark (:) intended to direct the reader's attention forward, usually because what follows explains or develops what has just been written (for example, *The farmer owned a variety of dogs: a spaniel, a pointer, a terrier, a border collie, and three mongrels*).

Colón second-largest city in Panama, at the Caribbean end of the Panama Canal; population (1980) 60,000.

Founded in 1850, and named Aspinwall in 1852, it was renamed Colón in 1890 in honor of the explorer Christopher Columbus.

Colón, Archipiélago de official name of the ◊Galápagos Islands.

colonialism another name for imperialism.

Colonna Vittoria c. 1492–1547. Italian poet. Many of her Petrarchan sonnets idealize her husband, who was killed at the battle of Paria 1525. She was a friend of Michelangelo, who addressed sonnets to her.

colophon originally an inscription on the last page of a book giving the writer or printer's name and the place and year of publication. Today it is a decorative device on the title page or spine of a book, the "trademark" of the individual publisher.

color quality or wavelength of light emitted or reflected from an object. Visible white light consists of electromagnetic radiation of various wavelengths, and if a beam is refracted through a prism, it can be spread out into a spectrum, in which the various colors correspond to different wavelengths. From long to short wavelengths (from about 700 to 400 nanometers) the colors are red, orange, yellow, green, blue, indigo, and violet.

When a surface is illuminated, some parts of the white light are absorbed, depending on the molecular structure of the material and the dyes applied to it. A surface that looks red absorbs light from the blue end of the spectrum, but reflects light from the red, long-wave end. Colors vary in brightness, hue, and saturation (the extent to which they are mixed with white).

Colorado river in North America, rising in the Rocky Mountains and flowing 1,450 mi/2,300 km to the Gulf of California through Colorado, Utah, Arizona (through the Grand Canyon), and NW Mexico. The many dams along its course, including Hoover and Glen Canyon, provide power and irrigation water but have destroyed wildlife and scenery, and very little water now reaches the sea. Its tributaries include the Gunnison, Green, Little Colorado, and Gila rivers. To the W of the river in SE California is the Colorado Desert, an arid area of 2,000 sq mi/5,000 sq km. The Imperial Valley is irrigated by the Colorado River.

Colorado state in W central US; nickname Centennial State

area 104,104 sq mi/269,700 sq km

capital Denver

cities Colorado Springs, Aurora, Lakewood, Fort Collins, Greeley, Pueblo

physical Great Plains in the E; the main ranges of the Rocky Mountains (more than 14,000 ft/4,300 m); high plateaus of the Colorado Basin in the W

features Rocky Mountain National Park; Pike's Peak; prehistoric cliff dwellings of the Mesa Verde National Park; Garden of the Gods (natural sandstone sculptures); Dinosaur and Great Sand Dunes national monuments; mining "ghost" towns; ski resorts, including Aspen, Vail, Steamboat Springs; US Air Force Academy

products cereals, meat and dairy products, oil, coal, molybdenum, uranium, iron, steel, machinery

population (1990) 3,294,394

famous people Jack Dempsey, Douglas Fairbanks

history first visited by Spanish explorers in the 16th century; claimed for Spain 1706; east portion passed to the US 1803 as part of the Louisiana Purchase, the rest in 1845 and 1848 as a result of the Mexican War. It attracted fur traders, and Denver was founded following the discovery of gold 1858. Colorado became a state 1876. Irrigated agriculture, ranching, tourism and outdoor sports, energy development, and the establishment of military bases fueled rapid growth after World War II.

Colorado

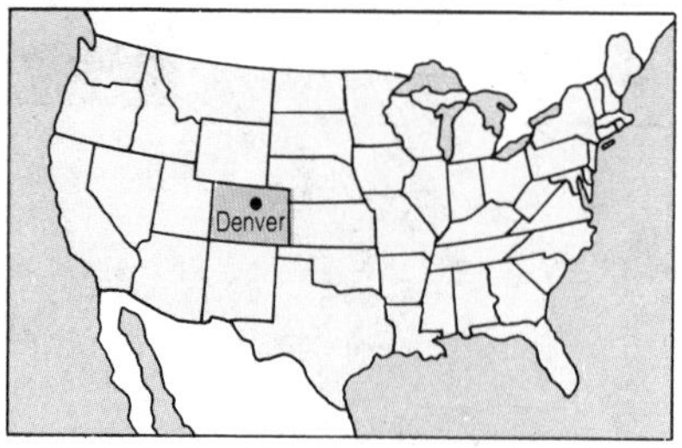
Denver

Colorado Springs city in Colorado, 75 mi/120 km SE of Denver; population (1990) 281,140. At an altitude of about 6,000 ft/1,800 m, and surrounded by magnificent scenery, it was founded as a health resort 1871. A gold strike at nearby Cripple Creek 1892 aided its growth. Colorado Springs is the home of the US Air Force Academy and the operations center of the North American Air Defense Command (NORAD).

color blindness hereditary defect of vision that reduces the ability to discriminate certain colors, especially red and green. The condition is sex-linked, affecting men more than women.

colorings food ◊additives used to alter or improve the color of processed foods. They include artificial colors, such as tartrazine and amaranth, which are made from petrochemicals, and the "natural" colors such as chlorophyll, caramel, and carotene. Some of the natural colors are actually synthetic copies of the naturally occurring substances, and some of these, notably the synthetically produced caramels, may be injurious to health.

colors, military flags or standards carried by military regiments, so-called because of the various combinations of colors employed to distinguish one country or one regiment from another.

Colosseum amphitheater in ancient Rome, begun by the emperor Vespasian to replace the one destroyed by fire during the reign of Nero, and completed by his son Titus AD 80. It was 615 ft/187 m long and 160 ft/49 m high and seated 50,000 people. Early Christians were martyred there by lions and gladiators. It could be flooded for mock sea battles.

Colossians epistle in the New Testament addressed to the church at Colossae; attributed to St Paul.

***Colosseum** The ruins of the Colosseum, where ancient Romans watched gladiators battle lions and each other. Early Christians were also martyred here.*

Colossus of Rhodes bronze statue of Apollo erected at the entrance to the harbor at Rhodes 292–280 BC. Said to have been about 100 ft/30 m high, it was counted as one of the Seven Wonders of the World, but in 224 BC fell as a result of an yearthquake.

Colt Samuel 1814–1862. US gunsmith, who in 1835 invented the revolver, a handgun that bears his name.

Born in Hartford, Connecticut, Colt developed a gun that had an automatic revolving cylinder. When the US Army ordered a large number of guns during the Mexican War, he established his factory first near New Haven, Connecticut, and then at Hartford, where his business grew into an immense arms-manufacturing establishment.

Coltrane John (William) 1926–1967. US jazz saxophonist, who first came to prominence in 1955 with the Miles ◊Davis quintet, later playing with Thelonius Monk 1957. A powerful and individual artist, Coltrane's performances featured much experimentation. His 1960s quartet was highly regarded for its innovations in melody and harmony.

coltsfoot perennial plant *Tussilago farfara*, family Compositae. The solitary yellow flower heads have many narrow rays, and the stems have large, purplish scales. The large leaf, up to 9 in/22 cm across, is shaped like a horse's foot and gives the plant its common name. Coltsfoot grows in Europe, N Asia, and N Africa, often on bare ground and in waste places, and has been introduced to North America.

colugo SE Asian climbing mammal of the genus *Cynocephalus*, order Dermoptera, about 2 ft/60 cm long including tail. It glides between forest trees using a flap of skin that extends from head to forelimb to hindlimb to tail. It may glide 425 ft/130 m or more, losing little height. It feeds largely on buds and leaves, and rests hanging upside down under branches.

There are two species, *C. variegatus* of Indochina and Indonesia, and *C. volans* of the Philippines.

Columba, St 521–597. Irish Christian abbot, missionary to Scotland. He was born in County Donegal of royal descent, and founded monasteries and churches in Ireland. In 563 he sailed with 12 companions to Iona, and built a monastery there that was to play a leading part in the conversion of Britain. Feast day June 9.

From his base on Iona St Columba made missionary journeys to the mainland. Legend has it that he drove a monster from the river Ness, and he crowned Aidan, an Irish king of Argyll.

Columban, St 543–615. Irish Christian abbot. He was born in Leinster, studied at Bangor, and about 585 went to the Vosges, France, with 12 other monks and founded the monastery of Luxeuil. Later, he preached in Switzerland, then went to Italy, where he built the abbey of Bobbio in the Apennines. Feast day 23 Nov.

Columbia city in central Missouri, NE of Jefferson City, seat of Boone county. It is the site of the University of Missouri 1853 and Stephens College 1833; population (1990) 69,101.

Columbia river in W North America, 1,215 mi/1,950 m in length. It rises in British Columbia and flows through Washington to the Pacific below Astoria, after forming much of the boundary between Washington and Oregon. This fast-running river has enormous hydroelectric potential and is harnessed for irrigation and power by the Grand Coulee and other major dams. Although it is famous for salmon fishing, the catch is now much reduced. The mouth of the Columbia was discovered 1792. The explorer David Thompson followed it from its source to its mouth 1811.

Columbia capital of South Carolina, on the Congaree River; population (1990) 98,052. Manufacturing includes textiles, plastics, electrical goods, fertilizers, and hosiery, but the chief products are fuel assemblies for nuclear reactors. The main campus of the University of South Carolina is here. Col-

***Columbus** An engraving of the portrait by Sebastiano del Piombo; the original is in the Uffizi, Florence.*

umbia was laid out as the state capital 1786. It was burned by Union troops 1865, near the close of the Civil War.

Columbia Pictures US film production and distribution company founded 1924. It grew out of a smaller company founded 1920 by Harry and Jack Cohn and Joe Brandt. Under Harry Cohn's guidance, Columbia became a major studio by the 1940s, producing such commercial hits as *Gilda* 1946. After Cohn's death in 1958 the studio remained successful, producing international films such as *Lawrence of Arabia* 1962.

The company now also produces television films through its subsidiary Screen Gems.

columbine any plant of the genus *Aquilegia* of the buttercup family Ranunculaceae. All are perennial herbs with divided leaves and flowers with spurred petals.

The eastern columbine *A. canadensis*, with red flowers, is native to E North America.

columbium (Cb) former name for the chemical element ◊niobium. The name is still used occasionally in metallurgy.

Columbus capital of Ohio, on the rivers Scioto and Olentangy; population (1990) 632,910. It has coal-field and natural gas resources nearby; its industries include the manufacture of automobiles, planes, missiles, and electrical goods.

Columbus city in W central Georgia, SW of Macon, across the Chattahoochee river from Phenix City, Alabama, and just N of US Army infantry base Fort Benning; seat of Muscogee county. It is a distribution center for surrounding farmlands. Industries include processed food, machinery, iron and steel, textiles, cotton, and peanuts; population (1990) 178,681.

Columbus Christopher 1451–1506. Italian explorer whose four voyages to the New World opened the age of European exploration and settlement of the Americas.

Born in Genoa, Italy, Columbus took to the sea while still a teenager, sailing the Mediterranean and the Atlantic as far west as Iceland. In 1485 he went to Spain to ask King Ferdinand and Queen Isabella to support his plan to find a sea route to China by sailing westward. Columbus, like others, thought that India was only 2,500 mi/4,000 km west of Portugal. In 1492 Isabella finally agreed to provide Columbus with ships and supplies. The small fleet, consisting of the *Santa María*, the *Pinta*, and the *Niña*, sailed on Aug 3, 1492 and, after a short stopover in the Canary Islands, reached an island in the Bahamas on Oct 12 that Columbus named San Salvador and that he thought was near China. After exploring the northern coasts of Hispaniola and Cuba, Columbus returned to Spain in March 1493 with some Indians, gold, and trinkets.

During his second voyage (1493–96), Columbus discovered a number of other islands in the Caribbean and established the first European colony in the Americas—Isabella, on the northern coast of Hispaniola. He also explored the southern coast of Cuba, which he thought was the mainland of Asia. During his third voyage (1498), Columbus reached Trinidad and the coast of Venezuela, but he did not know that he had reached the mainland of South America. Upon returning to the colony on Hispaniola, he found the colonists in revolt, for they had discovered little gold or other riches. The new governor, installed by Isabella, sent Columbus back to Spain in chains, but Isabella had him freed, and he soon began his fourth and final voyage (1502–04) to the New World, which he called "the Other World," and which he still thought was near China. Columbus sailed along the coast of Central America and learned that there was another ocean beyond the mountains, but he could not find a passage.

Sailing east into the Caribbean, Columbus was forced to abandon his rotting vessels, and he was marooned on Jamaica for a year. He finally returned to Spain in Nov 1504 and died there two years later, still believing that he had reached Asia. He kept extensive journals, which provide historical data. In 1542 his remains were removed to Hispaniola.

Columbus Day (12 Oct), a public holiday, is named for him.

column in architecture, a structure, round or polygonal in plan, erected vertically as a support for some part of a building. Cretan paintings reveal the existence of wooden columns in Aegean architecture, about 1500 BC. In Classical architecture there are five principal types or ◊orders of column.

The Hittites, Assyrians, and Egyptians also used wooden columns, but the Greeks and Romans used stone, as did later European, Asian, and American builders. Modern architects often design simple but elegant columns, as does the architecture of India, Southeast Asia, China and Japan.

coma in medicine, a state of deep unconsciousness from which the subject cannot be roused and in which the subject does not respond to pain. Possible causes include head injury, liver failure, cerebral hemorrhage, and drug overdose.

coma in optics, one of the geometrical aberrations of a lens, whereby skew rays from a point object make a comet-shaped spot on the image plane instead of meeting at a point.

coma in astronomy, the hazy cloud of gas and dust that surrounds the nucleus of a ◊comet.

Comaneci Nadia 1961– . Romanian gymnast. She won three gold medals at the 1976 Olympics at the age of 14, and was the first gymnast to record a perfect score of 10 in international competition.

CAREER HIGHLIGHTS

Olympic Games:
1976: gold: beam, vault, floor exercise
1980: gold: beam, parallel bars

combine harvester or ***combine*** machine used for harvesting cereals and other crops, so called because it combines the actions of reaping (cutting the crop) and threshing (beating the ears so that the grain separates).

Combines, drawn by horses, were used in the Californian cornfields in the 1850s. Today's mechanical combine harvesters are capable of cutting a swath of up to 30 ft/9 m or more.

combustion burning, defined in chemical terms as rapid combination of a substance with oxygen accompanied by the evolution of heat and usually light. A slow-burning candle flame and the explosion of a mixture of gasoline vapor and air are extreme examples of combustion.

Comecon (Council for Mutual Economic Assistance, or CMEA) economic organization established 1949 and prompted by the ◊Marshall Plan, linking the USSR with Bulgaria, Czechoslovakia, Hungary, Poland, Romania, East Germany (from 1950), Mongolia (from 1962), Cuba (from 1972), and Vietnam (from 1978), with Yugoslavia as an associated member. Albania also belonged 1949–61.

The secretariat is based in Moscow and regular annual meetings are held in the member countries. Trade between member countries is hampered by the lack of a convertible currency, the transferable ruble being merely an accounting device. It was agreed in 1987 that official relations should be established with the European Community, and a free-market approach to trading was adopted 1990.

Comédie Française the French national theater (for both comedy and tragedy) in Paris, founded 1680 by Louis XIV. Its base is the Salle Richelieu on the right bank of the river Seine, and the Théatre de l'Odéon, on the left bank, is a testing ground for avant-garde ideas.

comedy in the simplest terms, a literary work, usually dramatic, with a happy or amusing ending, as opposed to ◊tragedy. The comic tradition has undergone many changes since its Greek and Roman roots; although some comedies are timeless, such as those of Shakespeare and Molière, others are very representative of a particular era, relying upon topical allusion and current fashion.

The comic tradition was established by the Greek dramatists Aristophanes and Menander and the Roman writers Terence and Plautus. In medieval times, the Vices and Devil of the Morality plays developed into the stock comic characters of the Renaissance "Comedy of Humors" with such notable villains as Jonson's Mosca in *Volpone*. The enduring comedies of Shakespeare and Molière were followed during the 17th century in England by the witty "Comedy of Manners" of Restoration writers such as Etherege, Wycherley, and Congreve. Their often coarse but always vital comedy was toned down in the later Restoration dramas of Sheridan and Goldsmith. "Sentimental comedy" dominated most of the 19th century in England and the US, although little of it is remembered or revived today. Its close brought the realistic tradition of Shaw and the elegant social comedy of Wilde.

"Slapstick comedy" went from the stage to silent films from 1900 to 1930. The sophisticated comedy of Coward and Rattigan from the 1920s to the 1940s was performed on stage and in talking films, which also featured "screwball comedy." These were eclipsed during the 1950s and 1960s by a trend toward satire and cynicism, as seen in the works of Samuel Beckett. In the 1970s "black comedy" was dominant in the US and England, but "situation comedy," like Neil Simon's, continued to win audiences of stage, film, and television during the 1970s and 1980s.

comet small, icy body orbiting the Sun, usually on a highly elliptical path. A comet consists of a central nucleus a few miles across, often likened to a dirty snowball because it consists mostly of ice mixed with dust. As the comet approaches the Sun the nucleus heats up, releasing gas and dust which form a tenuous coma, up to 60,000 mi/100,000 km wide, around the nucleus. Gas and dust stream away from the coma to form one or more tails, which may extend for millions of miles.

Comets are believed to have been formed at the birth of the Solar System. Billions of them may reside in a halo (the Oort cloud, named after the Dutch astronomer Jan ◊Oort) beyond Pluto. The gravitational effect of passing stars pushes some toward the Sun, when they eventually become visible from Earth. Most comets swing around the Sun and return to distant space, not to be seen again for thousands or millions of years, although some, called periodic comets, have their orbits altered by the gravitational pull of the planets so that they reappear every 200 years or less. Of the 800 or so comets whose orbits have been calculated, about 160 are periodic. The brightest is ◊Halley's comet. The one with the shortest known period is Encke's comet, which

combine harvester

crop flow through self-propelled combine harvester

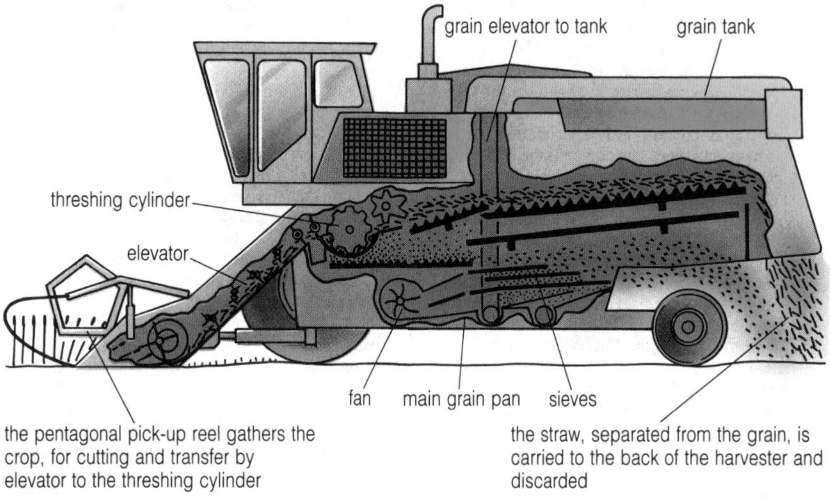
grain elevator to tank
grain tank
threshing cylinder
elevator
fan
main grain pan
sieves
the pentagonal pick-up reel gathers the crop, for cutting and transfer by elevator to the threshing cylinder
the straw, separated from the grain, is carried to the back of the harvester and discarded

orbits the Sun every 3.3 years. A dozen or more comets are discovered every year, some by amateur astronomers.

comfort index estimate of how tolerable conditions are for humans in hot climates. It is calculated as the temperature in degrees Farenheit plus a fourth of the relative ◊humidity, expressed as a percentage. If the sum is less than 95, conditions are tolerable for those unacclimatized to the tropics.

comfrey any plant of the genus *Symphytum* of the borage family Boraginaceae with rough, hairy leaves and small bell-shaped flowers, found in Europe and W Asia.

The European species *S. officinale* was once used as a medicinal plant for treating wounds and various ailments, and is still sometimes used as a poultice.

comic book publication in cartoon-strip form. Most comics are aimed at children, although artistically sophisticated adult comics are produced in Japan and several European countries, notably France; these developed in the 1980s into the graphic novel.

Comic books grew from comic strips in newspapers or, like those of Walt ◊Disney, as spinoffs from animated cartoon films. The first superhero, ◊Superman, created 1938 by Jerome Siegel and Joseph Shuster, soon had his own periodical, and others followed; the Marvel Comics group, formed 1961, was selling 50 million copies a year worldwide by the end of the 1960s and found a cult readership among college students for titles like *Spiderman* and *The Incredible Hulk*. In Japan 1.9 billion comics were sold in 1987 – a third of all publications there.

comic strip or cartoon strip a sequence of several frames of drawings in ◊cartoon style. Strips, which may work independently or form installments of a serial, are usually humorous or satirical in content. Longer stories in comic-strip form are published separately as ◊comic books. Some have been made into animated films.

The first comic strip was "The Yellow Kid" by Richard Felton Outcault, which appeared in the Sunday newspaper *New York World* 1896; it was immediately successful and others soon followed. Some of the most admired early comic strips were the American "Gertie the Dinosaur" and "Happy Hooligan" as well as "Krazy Kat," which began 1910 and ended with the death of its creator, Richard Herriman, in 1944. Current comic strips include "Peanuts" by Charles M Schulz (1922–), which began 1950 and was read daily by 60 million people by the end of the 1960s; the political "Doonesbury" by Garry Trudeau; the British "Andy Capp" by Reginald Smythe (1917–); and the French "Asterix" by Albert Uderzo and René Goscinny, which began in the early 1960s. The most famous and beloved cartoon characters were devised by Walt ◊Disney from the 1930s; and superheroes such as Superman, Batman, and Flash Gordon have staying power.

Cominform Communist Information Bureau 1947–56, established by the Soviet politician Andrei Zhdanov (1896–1948) to exchange information between European communist parties. Yugoslavia was expelled 1948.

Comintern abbreviation of Communist ◊International.

comma a punctuation mark (,) intended to provide breaks or pauses within a sentence; commas may come at the end of a clause, to set off a phrase, or in lists (for example, *apples, pears, plums, and pineapples*).

Many occasional writers, uncertain where sentences properly end, use a comma instead of a period (or full stop), writing *We saw John last night, it was good to see him again*, rather than *We saw John last night. It was good to see him again*. The meaning is entirely clear in both cases. One solution in such situations is to use a ◊semicolon (;), which bridges the gap between the close association of the comma and the sharp separation of the period. For parenthetical commas, see ◊parenthesis.

command language in computing, a set of commands and the rules governing their use, by which users control a program. For example, an ◊operating system may have commands such as SAVE and DELETE, or a payroll program may have commands for adding and amending staff records.

commando member of a specially trained, highly mobile military unit. The term originated in South Africa, where it referred to Boer military reprisal raids against Africans in the nineteenth century and, in the South African Wars, against the British. Commando units have often carried out operations behind enemy lines.

commedia dell'arte popular form of Italian improvised drama in the 16th and 17th centuries, performed by trained troupes of actors and involving stock characters and situations. It exerted considerable influence on writers such as Molière and Goldoni, and on the genres of pantomime, harlequinade, and the ◊Punch and Judy show. It laid the foundation for a tradition of mime, strong in France, that has continued with the contemporary mime of Jean-Louis Barrault and Marcel Marceau.

commensalism a relationship between two ◊species whereby one (the commensal) benefits from the association, whereas the other neither benefits nor suffers. For example, certain species of millipede and silverfish inhabit the nests of army ants and live by scavenging on the refuse of their hosts, but without affecting the ants.

commodity something produced for sale. Commodities may be consumer goods, such as radios, or producer goods, such as copper bars. Commodity markets deal in raw or semiraw materials that are amenable to grading and that can be stored for considerable periods without deterioration.

Commodity markets developed to their present form in the 19th century, when industrial growth facilitated trading in large, standardized quantities of raw materials. Most markets encompass trading in "commodity futures," that is trading for delivery several months ahead. Major commodity markets exist in Chicago, Tokyo, London, and elsewhere. Though specialized markets exist, such as that for silkworm cocoons in Tokyo, most trade relates to cereals, meats, and metals. "Softs" is a term used for most materials other than metals.

Commodus Lucius Aelius Aurelius AD 161–192. Roman emperor from 180, son of Marcus Aurelius Antoninus. He was a tyrant, spending lavishly on gladiatorial combats, confiscating the property of the wealthy, persecuting the Senate, and renaming Rome "Colonia Commodia." There were many attempts against his life, and he was finally strangled at the instigation of his mistress and advisors, who had discovered themselves on the emperor's death list.

Common Agricultural Policy (CAP) system that allows the member countries of the European Community (EC) jointly to organize and control agricultural production within their boundaries. The objectives of the CAP were outlined in the Treaty of Rome: to increase agricultural pro-

major comets

Name	*First recorded sighting*	*Orbital period (years)*	*Interesting facts*
Halley's comet	240 BC	76	parent of Aquarid and Orionid meteor showers
Comet Tempel-Tuttle	AD 1366	33	parent of Leonid meteors
Biela's comet	1772	6.6	broke in half 1846; not seen since 1852
Encke's comet	1786	3.3	parent of Taurid meteors
Comet Swift-Tuttle	1862	120 approx	parent of Perseid meteors; believed lost
Comet Ikeya-Seki	1965	880	so-called "sun-grazing" comet, passed 300,000 mi/500,000 km above surface of Sun on Oct 21 1965
Comet Kohoutek	1973		observed from space by Skylab astronauts; period too long to calculate accurately
Comet West	1975	500,000	nucleus broke into four parts
Comet Bowell	1980		ejected from Solar System after close encounter with Jupiter
Comet IRAS–Araki–Alcock	1983		passed only 2.8 million mi/4.5 million km from Earth on May 11, 1983; period too long to calculate accurately

ductivity, to provide a fair standard of living for farmers and their employees, to stabilize markets, and to assure the availability of supply at a price that was reasonable to the consumer.

common law that part of the English law not embodied in legislation. It consists of rules of law based on common custom and usage and on judicial decisions. English common law became the basis of law in the US and many other English-speaking countries.

Common law developed after the Norman Conquest (1066) as the law common to the whole of England, rather than local law. As the court system became established (under Henry II), and judges' decisions became recorded in law reports, the doctrine of precedent developed. This means that, in deciding a particular case, the court must have regard to the principles of law laid down in earlier reported cases on the same, or similar points, although the law may be extended or varied if the facts of the particular case are sufficiently different. Hence, common law (sometimes called "case law" or "judge-made law") keeps the law in harmony with the needs of the community where no legislation is applicable or where the legislation requires interpretation.

common logarithm another name for a ◊logarithm to the base ten.

Common Market popular name for the ◊European Community (EC).

Common Prayer, Book of the service book of the Church of England, based largely on the Roman breviary.

Commons, House of the lower but more powerful of the two parts of the British and Canadian ◊parliaments. See ◊House of Commons.

commonwealth body politic founded on law for the common "weal" or good. Political philosophers of the 17th century, such as Thomas Hobbes and John Locke, used the term to mean an organized political community. In Britain it was specifically applied to the regime of Oliver ◊Cromwell 1649–1660.

In the US, for example, the state of Massachusetts is officially the Commonwealth of Massachusetts.

Commonwealth conference any consultation between the prime ministers (or defense, finance, foreign, or other ministers) of the sovereign independent members of the British ◊Commonwealth. These are informal discussion meetings, and the implementation of policies is decided by individual governments.

The most notable conference occurred in 1926, which defined the relationship of the self-governing members.

Commonwealth Day a public holiday in parts of the Commonwealth, celebrated on the second Monday in March (the official birthday of Elizabeth II). It was called Empire Day until 1958 and celebrated on May 24 (Queen Victoria's birthday) until 1966.

Commonwealth Games multisport gathering of competitors from British Commonwealth countries. Held every four years, the first meeting (known as the British Empire Games) was at Hamilton, Canada, Aug 1930.

Commonwealth Games: venues

1930	Hamilton, Canada
1934	London, England
1938	Sydney, Australia
1950	Auckland, New Zealand
1954	Vancouver, Canada
1958	Cardiff, Wales
1962	Perth, Australia
1966	Kingston, Jamaica
1970	Edinburgh, Scotland
1974	Christchurch, New Zealand
1978	Edmonton, Canada
1982	Brisbane, Australia
1986	Edinburgh, Scotland
1990	Auckland, New Zealand
1994	Victoria, Canada

Commonwealth, British

country	*capital*	*area sq km*
IN AFRICA		
Botswana	Gaborone	582,000
British Indian Ocean Terr.	Victoria	60
Gambia	Banjul	10,700
Ghana	Accra	238,300
Kenya	Nairobi	582,600
Lesotho	Maseru	30,400
Malawi	Zomba	118,000
Mauritius	Port Louis	2,000
Nigeria	Lagos	924,000
St Helena	Jamestown	100
Seychelles	Victoria	450
Sierra Leone	Freetown	73,000
Swaziland	Mbabane	17,400
Tanzania	Dodoma	945,000
Uganda	Kampala	236,900
Zambia	Lusaka	600
Zimbabwe	Harare	390,300
IN THE AMERICAS		
Anguilla	The Valley	155
Antigua	St John's	400
Bahamas	Nassau	13,900
Barbados	Bridgetown	400
Belize	Belmopan	23,000
Bermuda	Hamilton	54
Brit. Virgin Is.	Road Town	153
Canada	Ottawa	9,958,400
Cayman Islands	Georgetown	300
Dominica	Roseau	700
Falkland Is.	Stanley	12,100
Grenada	St George's	300
Guyana	Georgetown	215,000
Jamaica	Kingston	11,400
Montserrat	Plymouth	100
St Christopher–Nevis	Basseterre	300
St Lucia	Castries	600
St Vincent and the Grenadines	Kingstown	400
Trinidad and Tobago	Port of Spain	5,100
Turks and Caicos Is.	Grand Turk	400
IN THE ANTARCTIC		
Australian Antarctic Terr.		5,403,000
Brit. Antarctic Terr.		390,000
Falklands Is. Dependencies		1,600
(NZ) Ross Dependency		453,000
IN ASIA		
Bangladesh	Dhaka	144,000
Brunei	Bandar Seri Begawan	5,800
Hong Kong	Victoria	1,100
India	Delhi	3,166,800
Malaysia	Kuala Lumpur	329,800
Maldives	Malé	300
Pakistan	Islamabad	803,900
Singapore	Singapore	600
Sri Lanka	Colombo	66,000
IN AUSTRALASIA AND THE PACIFIC		
Australia	Canberra	7,682,300
Norfolk Island		34
Fiji	Suva	18,300
Kiribati	Tawawa	700
*Nauru	Yaren	21
New Zealand	Wellington	268,000
Cook Islands		300
Niue Islands		300
Tokelau Islands		10
Papua New Guinea	Port Moresby	462,800
Pitcairn		5
Solomon Islands	Honiara	27,600
Tonga	Nuku'alofa	700
*Tuvalu	Funafuti	24
Vanuatu	Villa	15,000
Western Samoa	Apia	2,800
IN EUROPE		
*United Kingdom		
England	London	130,400
Wales	Cardiff	21,000
Scotland	Edinburgh	79,000
N. Ireland	Belfast	13,500
Isle of Man	Douglas	600
Channel Islands		200
Cyprus	Nicosia	9,000
Gibraltar	Gibraltar	6
Malta	Valletta	300
total		33,089,900

*special members

Commonwealth of Independent States (CIS) name adopted in Dec 1991 by the former constituent republics of the ◊Union of Soviet Socialist Republics after the Soviet government disintegrated in the wake of the independence of ◊Estonia, ◊Latvia, and ◊Lithuania. Boris ◊Yeltsin became the dominant leader in the CIS.

Commonwealth, the (British) voluntary association of 48 states that have been or still are ruled by Britain (see ◊British Empire). Independent states are full "members of the Commonwealth," while dependent territories, such as colonies and protectorates, rank as "Commonwealth countries." Small self-governing countries, such as Nauru, may have special status. The Commonwealth is founded more on tradition and sentiment than political or economic factors. Queen Elizabeth II is the formal head but not the ruler of member states. The Commonwealth secretariat, headed from Oct 1989 by Nigerian Emeka Anyaoko as secretary general, is based in London.

On May 15, 1917 Jan Smuts, representing South Africa in the imperial war cabinet of World War I, suggested that "British commonwealth of nations" was the right title for the British Empire. The name was recognized in the Statute of Westminster 1931, but after World War II a growing sense of independent nationhood led to the simplification of the title to the Commonwealth.

commune a group of people or families living together, sharing resources and responsibilities.

Communes developed from early 17th-century religious communities such as the Rosicrucians and Muggletonians, to more radical groups such as the ◊Diggers and the ◊Quakers. Many groups moved to America to found communes, such as the Philadelphia Society (1680s) and the Shakers, which by 1800 had ten groups in North America. The Industrial Revolution saw a new wave of utopian communities associated with the ideas of Robert ◊Owen and Charles Fourier. Communes had a revival during the 1960s, when many small groups were founded. In 1970 it was estimated there were 2,000 communes in the US.

The term also refers to a communal division or settlement in a communist country. In China, a policy of Mao Zedong involved the grouping of villages within districts (averaging 30,000 people) and thus, cooperatives were amalgamated into larger units, the communes.

The term can also refer to the 11th-century to 12th-century association of ◊burghers in north and central Italy. The communes of many cities asserted their independence from the overlordship of either the Holy Roman emperor or the pope, only to fall under the domination of oligarchies or despots during the 13th and 14th centuries.

Commune, Paris two periods of government in France; see ◊Paris Commune.

communication in biology, the signaling of infor-

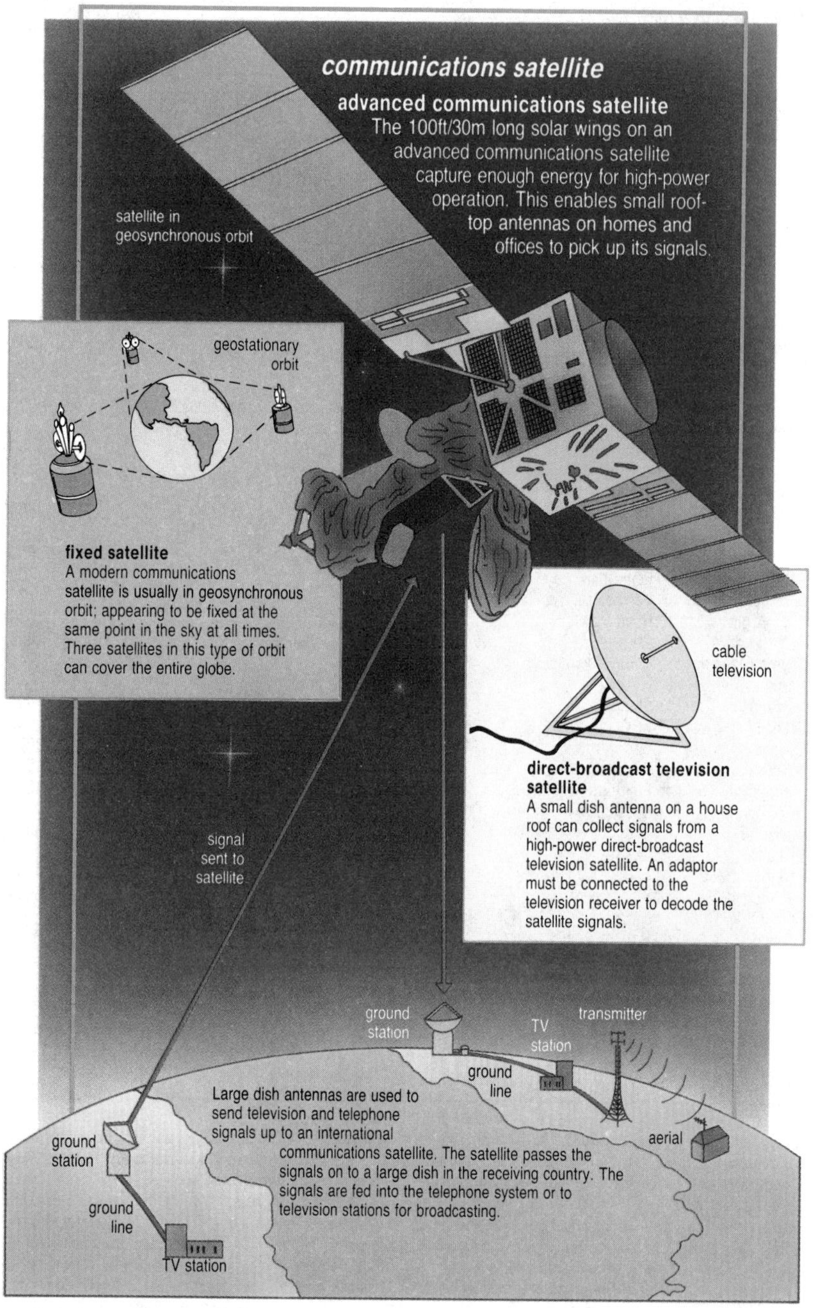
communications satellite
advanced communications satellite
The 100ft/30m long solar wings on an advanced communications satellite capture enough energy for high-power operation. This enables small roof-top antennas on homes and offices to pick up its signals.
satellite in geosynchronous orbit
geostationary orbit
fixed satellite
A modern communications satellite is usually in geosynchronous orbit; appearing to be fixed at the same point in the sky at all times. Three satellites in this type of orbit can cover the entire globe.
cable television
direct-broadcast television satellite
A small dish antenna on a house roof can collect signals from a high-power direct-broadcast television satellite. An adaptor must be connected to the television receiver to decode the satellite signals.
signal sent to satellite
ground station
transmitter
TV station
ground line
Large dish antennas are used to send television and telephone signals up to an international communications satellite. The satellite passes the signals on to a large dish in the receiving country. The signals are fed into the telephone system or to television stations for broadcasting.
aerial
ground station
ground line
TV station

mation by one organism to another, usually with the intention of altering the recipient's behavior. Signals used in communication may be visual (such as the human smile or the display of colorful plumage in birds), auditory (for example, the whines or barks of a dog), olfactory (such as the odors released by the scent glands of a deer), electrical (as in the pulses emitted by electric fish), or tactile (for example, the nuzzling of male and female elephants).

communications satellite relay station in space for sending telephone, television, telex, and other messages around the world. Messages are sent to and from the satellites via ground stations. Most communications satellites are in ◊geosynchronous orbit, appearing to hang fixed over one point on the Earth's surface.

The first satellite to carry TV signals across the Atlantic Ocean was *Telstar* in July 1962. The world is now linked by a system of communications satellites called Intelsat. Other satellites are used by individual countries for internal communications, or for business or military use. A new generation of satellites, called direct broadcast satellites, are powerful enough to transmit direct to small domestic aerials. The power for such satellites is produced by solar panels made up of semiconductor material, usually silicon, which generate electricity when illuminated with sunlight. The total energy requirement of a satellite is small; a typical communications satellite needs about 1.5 kW of power, the same as an electric heater.

Communion, Holy in the Christian church, another name for the ◊Eucharist.

communism (French *commun* "common, general") socialism imposed by revolution, based on the theories of the political philosophers Marx and Engels, emphasizing common ownership of the means of production and a planned economy. The principle held is that each should work according to their capacity and receive according to their needs. Politically, it seeks the overthrow of capitalism through a proletarian revolution. The first communist state was the USSR after the revolution of 1917. Revolutionary Socialist parties and groups united to form communist parties in other countries. After World War II, communism was enforced in those countries that came under Soviet occupation (the Eastern bloc). China became a communist state in 1949 and emerged after 1961 as a rival to the USSR in world communist leadership, and other countries (such as Nicaragua and Chile) attempted to adapt communism to their own needs. The late 1980s saw a movement for more individual freedoms in many communist countries, culminating in the abolition or overthrow of communist rule in some Eastern European countries 1989, and further state repression in China.

Marx and Engels in the *Communist Manifesto* 1848 put forward the theory that human society, having passed through successive stages of slavery, feudalism, and capitalism, must advance to communism. This combines with a belief in economic determinism to form the central communist concept of dialectical materialism. Marx believed that capitalism had become a barrier to progress and needed to be replaced by a dictatorship of the proletariat (working class), which would build a Socialist society.

The Social Democratic parties formed in Europe in the second half of the 19th century professed to be Marxist, but gradually began to aim at reforms of capitalist society rather than at the radical social change envisaged by Marx. The Russian Social Democratic Labor Party, led by Lenin, remained Marxist, and after the Nov 1917 revolution changed its name to Communist Party to emphasize its difference from Social Democratic parties elsewhere. The communal basis of feudalism was still strong in Russia, and Lenin and Stalin were able to impose the communist system.

China's communist revolution was completed 1949 under Mao Zedong. Both China and the USSR took strong measures to maintain or establish their own types of "orthodox" communism in countries on their borders (the USSR in Hungary and Czechoslovakia, and China in North Korea and Vietnam). In more remote areas (the USSR in the Arab world and Cuba, and China in Albania) and (both of them) in the newly emergent African countries, these orthodoxies were installed as the fount of doctrine and the source of technological aid.

In 1956 the Soviet premier Khrushchev denounced Stalinism, and there were uprisings in Hungary and Poland. During the late 1960s and the 1970s it was debated whether the state requires to be maintained as "the dictatorship of the proletariat" once revolution on the economic front has been achieved, or whether it may then become the state of the entire people: Engels, Lenin, Khrushchev, and ◊Liu Shaoqi held the latter view; Stalin and Mao the former.

Many communist parties in capitalist countries, for example, Japan and the Eurocommunism of France, Italy, and the major part of the British Communist Party, have since the 1960s or later rejected Soviet dominance. In the 1980s there was an expansion of political and economic freedom in Eastern Europe: the USSR remained a single-party state, but with a relaxation of strict party orthodoxy and a policy of *perestroika* ("restucturing"), while the other Warsaw Pact countries moved toward an end to communist rule and its replacement by free elections within more democratic political systems. By 1991 the system had essentially collapsed in the USSR, and both the Soviet Union and other E European countries were trying to embrace democracy and a free-world market economy.

In the Third World, Libya has attempted to combine revolutionary socialism with Islam; the extreme communist Khmer Rouge devastated Cambodia (then called Kampuchea) 1975–78; Latin America suffers from the US fear of communism in what it regards as its back yard, with the democratically elected Marxist regime in Chile violently overthrown 1973, and the Socialist government of Nicaragua (until it fell 1990) involved in a prolonged civil war against US-backed guerrillas (Contras).

Communism Peak (Russian *Pik Kommunizma*) highest mountain in the USSR, in the Pamir range in Tadzhikistan; 24,599 ft/7,495 m.

It was known as Mount Garmo until 1933, and Mount Stalin 1933–62.

community in the social sciences, term for the sense of identity, purpose, and companionship that comes from belonging to a particular place, organization, or social group. The concept dominated sociological thinking in the first half of the 20th century, and inspired the academic discipline of community studies.

community in ecology, an assemblage of plants, animals, and other organisms living within a circumscribed area. Communities are usually named by reference to a dominant feature such as characteristic plant species (for example, oak-hickory community), or a prominent physical feature (for example, a freshwater-pond community).

community architecture movement enabling people to work directly with architects in the design and building of their own homes and neighborhoods.

community service provision under which minor offenders are sentenced to work in the service of the community (aiding children, the elderly, or the handicapped), instead of prison.

commutator device in a DC (direct-current) electric motor that reverses the current flowing in the armature coils as the armature rotates. A DC generator, or ◊dynamo, uses a commutator to convert the AC (alternating current) generated in the armature coils into DC. A commutator consists of opposite pairs of conductors insulated from one another, and contact to an external circuit is provided by carbon or metal brushes.

Como city in Lombardy, Italy, on Lake Como at the foot of the Alps; population (1981) 95,500. Motorcycles, glass, silk, and furniture are produced here. The river Adda flows N–S through the lake, and the shores are extremely beautiful. Como has a marble cathedral, built 1396–1732, and is a tourist resort.

Comodoro Rivadavia port in Patagonia, SE Argentina; population (1984) 120,000. Argentina's main oil-fields and natural gas are nearby.

Comorin the southernmost cape of the Indian subcontinent, in Tamil Nadu, where the Indian Ocean, Bay of Bengal, and Arabian Sea meet.

Comoros group of islands in the Indian Ocean between Madagascar and E coast of Africa. Three of them–Njazidja, Nzwani, and Mwali–form the republic of Comoros; the fourth island, Mayotte, is a French dependency.

government Under the 1978 constitution there is a president, elected by universal adult suffrage for a six-year term, with an appointed council of ministers and a single-chamber federal assembly of 42 members elected for five years. Although each of the four main islands has a degree of autonomy, with its own governor and council, the system is a limited form of federalism, since the president appoints the governors and the federal government is responsible for the islands' resources. The Comoros is officially Muslim and since 1979 has been a one-party state although unofficial opposition groups exist.

history Originally inhabited by Asians, Africans, and Indonesians, the Comoros were controlled by Muslim sultans until the French acquired them 1841–1909. The islands became a French colony in 1912 and were attached to Madagascar 1914–47, when they were made a French Overseas Territory. Internal self-government was obtained in 1961, but full independence not achieved until 1975 because of Mayotte's reluctance to sever links with France. Although the Comoros joined the United Nations in 1975, with Ahmed Abdallah as president, Mayotte remained

Comoros
Federal Islamic Republic of
(Jumhurīyat al-Qumur al-Itthādīyah al-Islāmīyah)

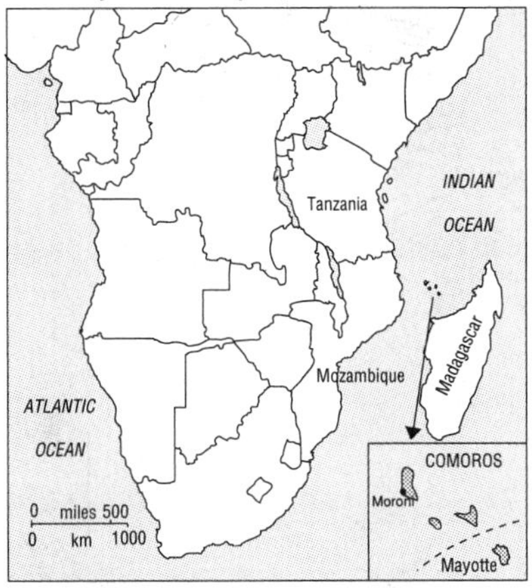
Tanzania
INDIAN
OCEAN
Mozambique
Madagascar
ATLANTIC
OCEAN
COMOROS
Moroni
Mayotte
0 miles 500
0 km 1000

area 719 sq mi/1,862 sq km
capital Moroni
cities Mutsamudu, Domoni, Fomboni
physical comprises the volcanic islands of Njazídja, Nzwani, and Mwali (formerly Grande Comore, Anjouan, Moheli); at N end of Mozambique Channel
features active volcano on Njazídja; poor tropical soil
head of state and government Said Mohammad Djohar (interim administration)
political system authoritarian nationalism
political parties Comoran Union for Progress (Udzima), nationalist Islamic
exports copra, vanilla, cocoa, sisal, coffee, cloves, essential oils
currency CFA franc
population (1990 est) 459,000; growth rate 3.1% p.a.
life expectancy men 48, women 52
language Comorian (Swahili and Arabic dialect), Makua, French, Arabic (official)
religion Muslim (official) 86%, Roman Catholic 14%
literacy 15%
GDP $198 million (1987); $468 per head
chronology
1975 Independence achieved from France, but Mayotte remained part of France. Ahmed Abdallah elected president. The Comoros joined the United Nations.
1976 Abdallah overthrown by Ali Soilih.
1978 Soilih killed by mercenaries working for Abdallah. Islamic republic proclaimed and Abdallah elected president.
1979 The Comoros became a one-party state; powers of the federal government increased.
1985 Constitution amended to make Abdallah head of government as well as head of state.
1989 Abdallah killed by French mercenaries who took control of government; under French and South African pressure mercenaries left Comoros, turning authority over to French administration and interim president Said Mohammad Djohar.
1990 Antigovernment coup foiled.

under French administration. Relations with France deteriorated as Ali Soilih, who had overthrown Abdallah, became more powerful as president under a new constitution. In 1978 he was killed by French mercenaries working for Abdallah. Abdallah's use of mercenaries in his return to power led to the Comoros' expulsion from the Organization of African Unity (OAU).

A federal Islamic republic was proclaimed, a new constitution adopted, and Abdallah reconfirmed as president in an election where he was the only candidate. Diplomatic relations with France were restored. In 1979 the Comoros became a one-party state, and government powers were increased. In the same year a plot to overthrow Abdallah was foiled. In 1984 he was re-elected president, and in the following year the constitution was amended, abolishing the post of prime minister and making Abdallah head of government as well as head of state. Mayotte remains an uneasy member of the federation, with its future uncertain.

In Nov 1989 Abdallah was assassinated during an attack on the presidential palace led by a French mercenary, Col Bob Denard. Denard was subsequently arrested by French army units and returned to France. A provisional military administration was set up, with Said Mohammad Djohar as interim president. In Aug 1990 an attempted antigovernment coup was foiled.

compact disk record disk, about 4.5 in/12 cm across, with up to an hour's playing time on one side. The compact disk is entirely different from a conventional LP (long-playing phonograph record); it is made of aluminum with a transparent plastic coating; the metal disk within is etched by a ◊laser beam with microscopic pits which carry a digital code representing the music. During playback, a laser beam reads the code and produces signals that are changed into near-exact replicas of the original sounds.

CD-ROM, or compact-disk read-only memory, is used to store written text or pictures rather than music. The disks are ideal for large works, such as catalogs and encyclopedias. CD-I, or compact-disk interactive, is a form of CD-ROM used with a computerized reader, which responds intelligently to the user's instructions. These disks are used, for example with audiovisual material, for training. Recordable CDs, called WORMs ("write once, read many times"), are used as computer disks, but are as yet too expensive for home use. Erasable CDs, which can be erased and recorded many times, are also used by the computer industry. These are coated with a compound of cobalt and gadolinium, which alters the polarization of light falling on it. In the reader, the light reflected from the disk is passed through polarizing filters and the changes in polarization are converted into electrical signals.

company see ◊corporation.

compass any instrument for finding direction. The most commonly used is a magnetic compass, consisting of a thin piece of magnetic material with the north-seeking pole indicated, free to rotate on a pivot and mounted on a compass card on which the points of the compass are marked. When the compass is properly adjusted and used, the north-seeking pole will point to the magnetic north, from which true north can be found from tables of magnetic corrections.

Compasses not dependent on the magnet are gyrocompasses, dependent on the ◊gyroscope, and radiocompasses, dependent on the use of radio. These are unaffected by the presence of iron and by magnetic anomalies of the Earth's magnetic field, and are widely used in ships and aircraft.

A compass (or pair of compasses) is also an instrument used for drawing circles or taking measurements, consisting of a pair of pointed legs connected by a central pivot.

compensation point in biology, the point at which there is just enough light for a plant to survive. At this point all the food produced by ◊photosynthesis is used up by ◊respiration. For aquatic plants, the compensation point is the depth of water at which there is just enough light to sustain life (deeper water = less light = less photosynthesis).

competence and performance in linguistics, the potential and actual utterances of a speaker. As

compact disk

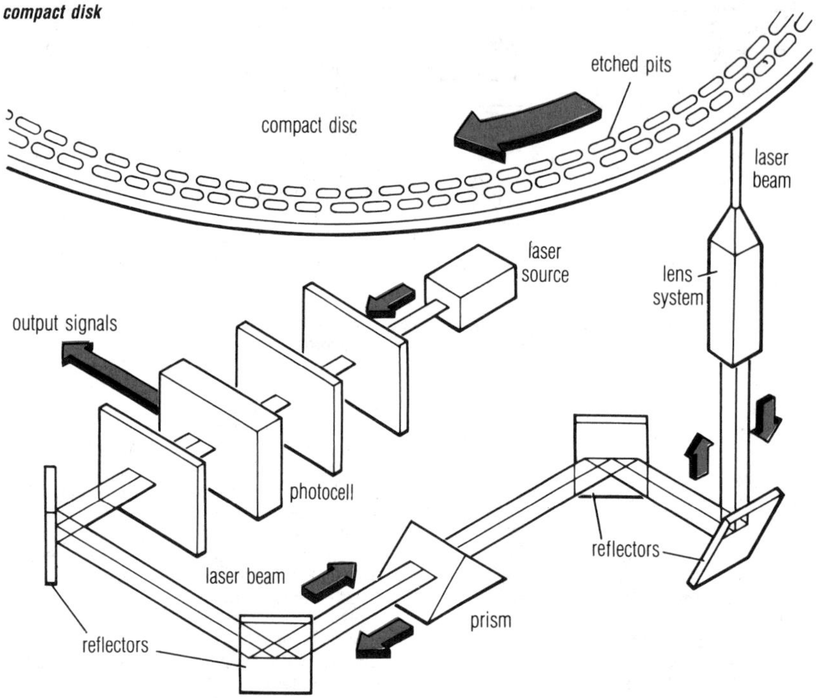
etched pits
compact disc
laser beam
laser source
lens system
output signals
photocell
reflectors
laser beam
prism
reflectors

formulated by the linguist Noam ◊Chomsky, a person's linguistic competence is the set of internalized rules in his or her brain that makes it possible to understand and produce language—rules that stipulate, for example, the order words take to form a sentence. A person's performance consists of the actual phrases and sentences he or she produces on the basis of these inner rules.

competition in commerce, a term used to describe rivalry in the marketplace, usually competition among those who want to sell the same commodities.

compass

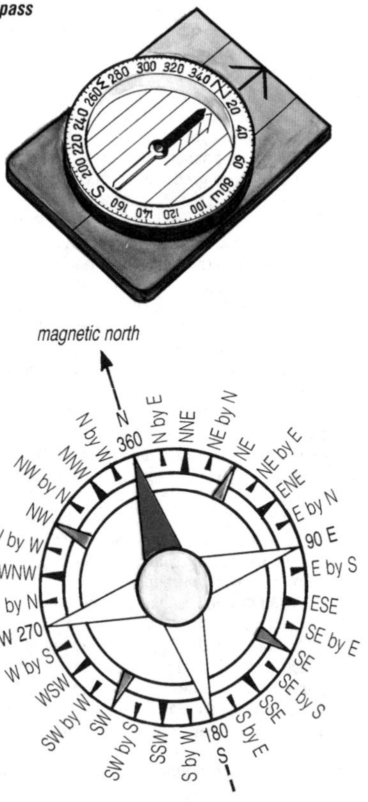
magnetic north
N
N by E
NNE
NE by N
NE
NE by E
ENE
E by N
90 E
E by S
ESE
SE by E
SE
SE by S
SSE
S by E
180
S
S by W
SSW
SW by S
SW
SW by W
WSW
W by S
W 270
W by N
WNW
NW by W
NW
NW by N
NNW
N by W
360

competition in ecology, the interaction between two or more organisms, or groups of organisms (for example, species), that use a common resource which is in short supply. Competition invariably results in a reduction in the numbers of one or both competitors, and in ◊evolution contributes both to the decline of certain species and to the evolution of ◊adaptations.

competition, perfect in economics, a market situation in which there are many potential and actual buyers and sellers, each being too small to be an individual influence on the price; the market is open to all and the products being traded are homogeneous. At the same time, the producers are seeking the maximum profit and consumers the best value for money.

There are many economic, social, and political barriers to perfect competition, not least because the underlying assumptions are unrealistic and in conflict. Nevertheless some elements are applicable in free trade.

Compiègne town in Oise *département*, France, on the river Oise near its confluence with the river Aisne; population (1983) 37,250. It has an enormous chateau, built by Louis XV. The armistices of 1918 and 1940 were signed (the latter by Hitler and Pétain) in a railroad coach in the forest of Compiègne.

compiler computer program that translates other programs into a form in which they can be run by the computer. Most programs are written in high-level languages, designed for the convenience of the programmer. The compiler converts these into ◊machine code, the language the computer understands.

Different compilers are needed for different computer languages (and different dialects of the same language). In contrast to an ◊interpreter, using a compiler adds slightly to the time needed to develop the program, but results in the program running faster.

complement in mathematical set theory, all the members of a universal set that are not members of a particular set. A set and its complement add up to the whole.

complementary angles in geometry, two angles that add up to 90°.

complementary number in number theory, the number obtained by subtracting a number from its base. For example, the complement of 7 in numbers to base ten is 3. Complementary numbers are necessary in computing, as the only mathematical operation of which digital computers (including pocket calculators) are directly capable is addition. Two numbers can be subtracted by adding one number to the complement of the other; two numbers can be divided by using successive subtraction (which, using complements, becomes successive addition); and multiplication can be performed by using successive addition.

The four main operations of arithmetic can thus all be reduced to various types of addition and made with the capability of a digital computer, using the binary number system.

complementation in genetics, the interaction that can occur between two different mutant alleles of a gene in a ◊diploid organism, to make up for each other's deficiencies and allow the organism to function normally.

complex in psychology, a group of ideas and feelings that have become repressed because they are distasteful to the person in whose mind they arose, but which are still active in the depths of the person's unconscious mind, continuing to affect his or her life and actions, even though he or she is no longer fully aware of their existence. Typical examples include the ◊Oedipus complex and the inferiority complex.

complex number in mathematics, a number written in the form $a + ib$, where a and b are ◊real numbers and i is the square root of −1 (that is, $i^2 = -1$); i used to be known as the "imaginary" part of the complex number. Some equations in algebra, such as those of the form $x^2 + 5 = 0$, cannot be solved without recourse to complex numbers, because the real numbers do not include square roots of negative numbers.

The sum of two or more complex numbers is obtained by adding separately their real and imaginary parts, for example, $(a + bi) + (c + di) = (a + c) + (b + d)i$.

Complex numbers can be represented graphically on an Argand diagram, which uses rectangular ◊Cartesian coordinates in which the x-axis represents the real part of the number and the y-axis the imaginary part. Thus the number $z = a + bi$ is plotted as the point (a, b). Complex numbers have applications in various areas of science, such as the theory of alternating currents in electricity.

componential analysis in linguistics, the analysis of the elements of a word's meaning. The word *boy*, for example, might be said to have three basic meaning elements (or semantic properties): "human," "young," and "male"; and so might the word *murder*: "kill," "intentional," and "illegal."

components in mathematics, the vectors produced when a single vector is resolved into two or more parts. The components add up to the original vector.

Compositae the daisy family; dicotyledonous flowering plants characterized by flowers borne in composite heads (see ◊capitulum). It is the largest family of flowering plants, the majority being herbaceous. Birds seem to favor the family for use in nest "decoration," possibly because many species either repel or kill insects (see ◊pyrethrum). Species include the daisy and dandelion; food plants such as the artichoke, lettuce,

complex number

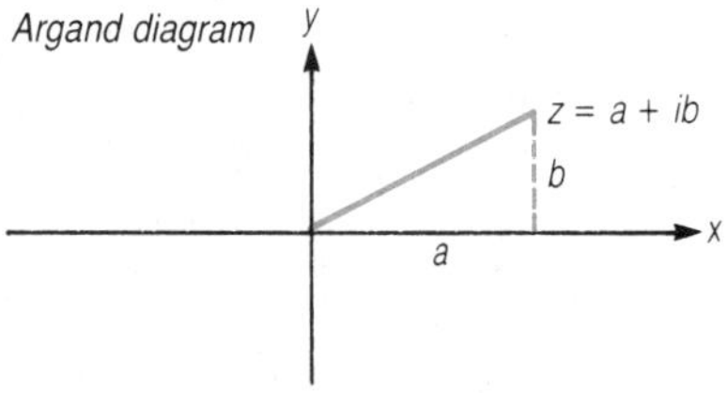
Argand diagram
y
z = a + ib
b
a
x

and safflower; and the garden varieties of chrysanthemum, dahlia, and zinnia.

composite in industry, any purpose-designed engineering material created by combining single materials with complementary properties into a composite form. Most composites have a structure in which one component consists of discrete elements such as fibers (for example, asbestos, glass or carbon steel in continuous or short lengths, or "whiskers," specially grown crystals a few millimeters long, such as silicon carbide) dispersed in a continuous matrix, such as plastics, concrete, or steel.

Composite in Classical architecture, one of the five types of ◊column. See ◊order.

composite function in mathematics, a function made up of two or more other functions carried out in sequence, usually denoted by * or ∘, as in the relation $(f * g)\, x = f\,[g(x)]$.

Usually, composition is not commutative: $(f * g)$ is not necessarily the same as $(g * f)$.

compos mentis (Latin) of sound mind.

compost a mixture of ◊biodegradable vegetation, such as leaves, fruit, and manure, that breaks down as a result of the action of bacteria and fungi. Compost is used as a fertilizer or spread on the soil surface to prevent evaporation and ◊erosion and protect against frost.

As the ◊decomposers feed, they raise the temperature in the center of the compost as high as 150°F/66°C. A compost heap provides food and shelter for a variety of animals.

compound chemical substance made up of two or more ◊elements bonded together, so that they cannot be separated by physical means. Compounds are held together by electrovalent or covalent bonds.

compound interest interest calculated by computing the rate against the original capital plus reinvested interest each time the interest becomes due. When simple interest is calculated, only the interest on the original capital is added.

compressor machine that compresses a gas, usually air, commonly used to power pneumatic tools, such as power drills, paint sprayers, and dentists' drills.

Reciprocating compressors use pistons moving in cylinders to compress the air. Rotary compressors use a varied rotor moving eccentrically inside a casing. The air compressor in jet and ◊gas turbine engines consists of a many-varied rotor rotating at high speed within a fixed casing, where the rotor blades slot between fixed, or stator, blades on the casing.

Compromise of 1850 in US history, legislative proposals designed to resolve the sectional conflict between North and South over the admission of California to the Union in 1850. Slavery was prohibited in California, but a new fugitive slave law was passed to pacify the slave states. The Senate debate on the compromise lasted nine months; acceptance temporarily revitalized the Union.

Compton Arthur Holly 1892–1962. US physicist known for his work on X-rays. Working at Chicago 1923 he found that X-rays scattered by such light elements as carbon increased their wavelengths. Compton concluded from this unexpected result that the X-rays were displaying both wavelike and particlelike properties, since named the Compton effect. He shared the 1927 Nobel Prize with Charles ◊Wilson.

Compton-Burnett Ivy 1892–1969. English novelist. She used dialogue to show reactions of small groups of characters dominated by the tyranny of family relationships. Her novels, set at the turn of the century, include *Pastors and Masters* 1925, *More Women Than Men* 1933, and *Mother and Son* 1955.

computer programmable electronic device that processes data and performs calculations and other symbol-manipulation tasks. There are three types: the ◊digital computer, which manipulates information coded as ◊binary numbers; the ◊analog computer, which works with continuously varying quantities; and the hybrid computer, which has characteristics of both analog and digital computers.

computer

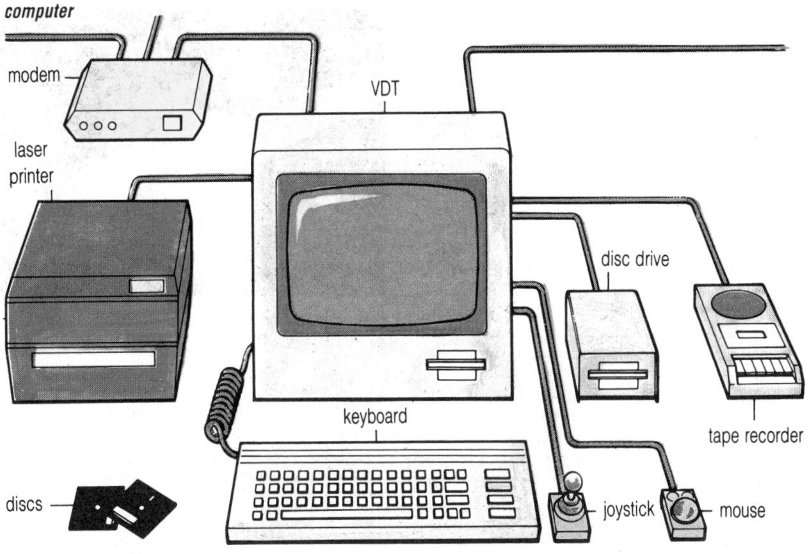
modem
VDT
laser printer
disc drive
tape recorder
keyboard
discs
joystick
mouse

There are four sizes of digital computer, corresponding roughly to their memory capacity and processing speed. Microcomputers are the smallest and most common, used in small businesses, at home, and in schools. They are usually single-user machines. Minicomputers are found in medium-sized businesses and university departments. They may support from perhaps 12 to 30 or so users at once. Mainframes, which can often service several hundreds of users simultaneously, are found in large organizations, such as national companies and government departments. Supercomputers are mostly used for highly complex scientific tasks, such as analyzing the results of nuclear physics experiments and weather forecasting.

history Computers are only one of the many kinds of ◊computing device. The first mechanical computer was conceived by Charles ◊Babbage in 1835, but it never went beyond the design stage. In 1943, more than a century later, Thomas Flowers built Colossus, the first electronic computer. Working with him at the time was Alan Turing, a mathematician who seven years earlier had published a paper on the theory of computing machines that had a major impact on subsequent developments. John von Neumann's computer, EDVAC, built in 1949, was the first to use binary arithmetic and to store its operating instructions internally. This design still forms the basis of today's computers.

basic components At the heart of a computer is the ◊central processing unit (CPU), which performs all the computations. This is supported by memory, which holds the current program and

computing: history

1614	Scottish mathematician John Napier invented logarithms.
1615	William Oughtred (1579–1660) invented the slide rule.
1623	Wilhelm Schickard (1592–1635) invented the mechanical calculating machine.
1645	Blaise Pascal produced a calculator.
1672–74	Leibniz built his first calculator, the Stepped Reckoner.
1801	Joseph-Marie Jacquard developed an automatic loom controlled by punch cards.
1820	First mass-produced calculator, the Arithometer, by Charles Thomas de Colmar (1785–1870).
1822	Charles Babbage's first model for the difference engine.
1830s	Babbage created the first design for the analytical engine.
1890	Herman Hollerith developed the punched card ruler for the US census.
1936	Alan Turing published the mathematical theory of computing.
1938	Konrad Zuse constructed the first binary calculator, using Boolean algebra.
1939	J V Atanasoff of Iowa State University became the first to use electronic means for mechanizing arithmetical operations.
1943	"Colossus" electronic code-breaker developed at Bletchley Park, England; Harvard University Mark I or Automatic Sequence Controlled Calculator (partly financed by IBM): the first program-controlled calculator.
1945	ENIAC (acronym from electronic numerator, integrator, analyzer, and computer) completed at the University of Pennsylvania.
1948	Manchester University (England) Mark I completed: the first stored-program computer.
1951	Ferranti Mark I: the first commercially produced computer; "Whirlwind," the first real-time computer, built for the US air defense system; investigation of transistor.
1952	EDVAC (acronym from electronic discrete variable computer) completed at the Institute for Advanced Study, Princeton (by von Neumann and others).
1953	Magnetic core memory developed.
1958	The first integrated circuit.
1963	The first minicomputer built by Digital Equipment (DEC); the PDP-8; the first electronic calculator (Bell Punch Company).
1964	IBM System/360: the first compatible family of computers.
1965	The first supercomputer: the Control Data CD6600.
1970	The first microprocessor: the Intel 4004.
1974	CLIP–4, the first computer with a parallel architecture.
1975	The first personal computer: Altair 8800.
1981	The Xerox Start system, the first WIMP system (acronym from windows, icons, menus, and pointing devices).
1985	The Inmos T414 Transputer, the first "off the shelf" ◊*RISC* microprocessor for building parallel computers.

data, and "logic arrays," which help move information around the system. A main power supply is needed and, for a mainframe or minicomputer, a cooling system. The computer's "device driver" circuits control the ◊peripheral devices that can be attached. These will normally be keyboards and ◊VDTs for user input and output, disk drive units for mass memory storage, and printers for printed output.

computer game or video game any of various computer-controlled games in which the computer (usually) opposes the human player. Computer games typically employ fast, animated graphics on a ◊VDT, and synthesized sound.

Commercial computer games became possible with the advent of the ◊microprocessor in the mid-1970s and rapidly became popular as amusement arcade games.

computer generations the classification of computers into five broad groups: *first generation* (the earliest computers, developed in the 1940s and 1950s, made from valves and wire circuits); *second generation* (from the early 1960s, based on transistors and printed circuits); *third generation* (from the late 1960s, using integrated circuits and often sold as families of computers, such as the IBM 360 series); *fourth generation* (using ◊microprocessors and large-scale integration, still in current use); and *fifth generation* (based on parallel processors and very large-scale integration, currently under development).

computer graphics the techniques involved in creating images by computer. These are widely used in the film and television industries for producing animated charts and diagrams.

computer literacy the ability to understand and make use of computer technology in an everyday context.

computer numerical control the control of machine tools, most often milling machines, by a computer. The pattern of work for the machine to follow, which often involves performing repeated sequences of actions, is described using a special-purpose programming language.

computer simulation representation of a real-life situation in a computer program. For example, the program might simulate the flow of customers arriving at a bank. The user can alter variables, such as the number of cashiers on duty, and see the effect.

computing device any device built to perform or help perform computations, such as the ◊abacus, ◊slide rule, or ◊computer.

Probably the earliest known example is the abacus. Mechanical devices with sliding scales (similar to the slide rule) date from ancient Greece. In 1642, the French mathematician Blaise Pascal built a mechanical adding machine and, in 1671, the German philosopher Gottfried Leibniz produced a machine to carry out multiplication. The first mechanical computer, the ◊analytical engine, was designed by Charles Babbage in 1835. For the subsequent history of computing see ◊computer.

Comte Auguste 1798–1857. French philosopher, regarded as the founder of sociology, a term he coined 1830. He sought to establish sociology as an intellectual discipline, using a scientific approach ("positivism") as the basis of a new science of social order and social development.

Comte, born in Montpellier, was expelled from the Paris Ecole Polytechnique for leading a student revolt in 1816. From 1816–18 he taught mathematics. In 1818 he became secretary to the Socialist Saint-Simon and was much influenced by him. He began lecturing on the "Positive Philosophy" in 1826, but almost immediately succumbed to a nervous disorder and once tried to commit suicide in the Seine. When he recovered, he resumed his lectures and mathematical teaching.

In his six-volume *Cours de philosophie positive* 1830–42 he argued that human thought and social development evolve through three stages: the theological, the metaphysical, and the positive or scientific. Although he originally sought to proclaim society's evolution to a new golden age of science, industry, and rational morality, his radical ideas were increasingly tempered by the political and social upheavals of his time. His influence, however, continued in Europe and the US until the early 20th century. He divided human knowledge into a hierarchy, with sociology at the top of the academic pyramid. Positivism offered a method of logical analysis and provided an ethical and moral basis for predicting and evaluating social progress.

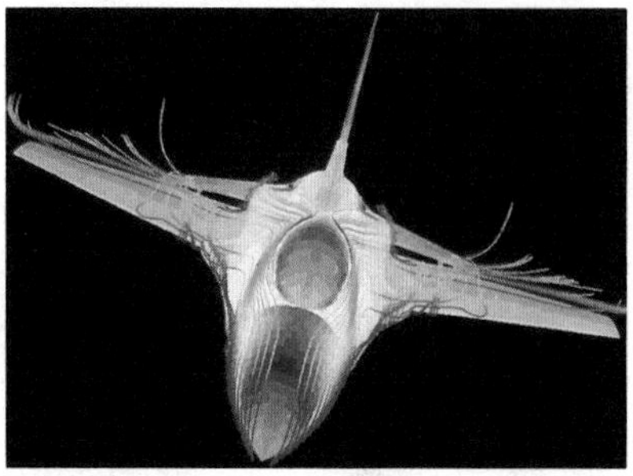

computer graphics *A computer graphics image of air flow over an F-16, as produced on a Cray supercomputer.*

Conakry capital and chief port of the Republic of Guinea; population (1980) 763,000. It is on the island of Tumbo, linked with the mainland by a causeway and by rail with Kankan, 300 mi/480 km NE. Bauxite and iron ore are mined nearby.

concave lens a converging ◊lens—that is, a parallel beam of light gets wider as it passes through such a lens. A concave lens is thinner at its center than at the edges.

Common forms include biconcave (with both surfaces curved inward) and plano-concave (with one flat surface and one concave). The whole lens may be further curved overall (making a convexo-concave or diverging meniscus lens, as in some lenses used for corrective purposes).

concentration camp a prison camp first devised by the British during the Second Boer War in South Africa 1899 for the detention of Afrikaner women and children (with the subsequent deaths of more than 20,000 people). A system of approximately 5,000 concentration camps was developed by the Nazis in Germany and occupied Europe (1933–45) to imprison political and ideological opponents, as well as "unwanted" victims (Jews, gypsies, homosexuals) and other "misfits" after Hitler became chancellor Jan 1933. The camps were established in Germany and occupied Europe, the most infamous being the five secret extermination camps, established 1940, of Auschwitz, Belsen, Dachau, Maidanek, Sobibor, and Treblinka. The total number of people who died at the camps exceeded six million; many died of overwork, disease and/or starvation, some were subjected to medical experimentation before being killed, while millions were sent directly to firing and hanging squads or to gas chambers. The bodies were dumped in mass graves or burned in pyres or in "the ovens."

At Auschwitz-Birkenau, a vast camp complex was created for imprisonment and slave labor as well as the extermination of over four million people. At Maidanek, about 1.5 million people were exterminated, cremated, and their ashes used as fertilizer. Many camp officials and others responsible were tried in Nuremburg after 1945 for war crimes, and executed or imprisoned. Foremost was Adolf ◊Eichmann, the architect of the extermination system, who was found by Nazi-hunters, tried, and executed by the state of Israel in 1961.

concentric circles two or more circles that share the same center.

Concepción city in Chile, near the mouth of the river Bió-Bió; population (1987) 294,000. It is capital of the province of Concepción. It is in a rich agricultural district and is also an industrial center for coal, steel, paper, and textiles.

conceptacle flask-shaped cavities found in the swollen tips of certain brown seaweeds (Phaeophyta), notably rockweed and other large members of the genus *Fucus*. The gametes are formed within them and released into the water via a small pore in the conceptacle, known as an ostiole.

concertina a portable reed organ related to the ◊accordion but smaller in size and rounder in shape, with buttons for keys. It was invented in England in the 19th century.

concert master in music, the leader of an orchestra, usually the principal violinist.

concerto composition, usually in three movements, for solo instrument (or instruments) and orchestra. It developed during the 18th century from the *concerto grosso* form for string orchestra, in which a group of solo instruments is contrasted with a full orchestra.

Corelli and Torelli were early concerto composers, followed by Vivaldi, Handel, and Bach (*Brandenburg concertos*). Mozart wrote about 40 concertos, mostly for piano. Recent concerto composers include Gershwin, Korngold, Schoenberg, Berg, and Bartók, who have developed the form along new lines.

Conchobar in Celtic mythology, king of Ulster whose intended bride, Deirdre, eloped with Noísi. She died of sorrow when Conchobar killed her husband and his brothers.

concilliar movement the 15th-century attempt to urge the supremacy of church councils over the popes, with regard to the ◊Great Schism and the reformation of the church. Councils were held in Pisa 1409, Constance 1414–18, Pavia-Siena 1423–24, Basle 1431–49, and Ferrara-Florence-Rome 1438–47.

After ending the Schism in 1417 with the removal of John XXIII (1410–15), Gregory XII (1406–15), and Benedict XIII (1394–1423), and the election of Martin V (1417–31), the movement fell into disunity over questions of reform, allowing Eugenius IV (1431–47) to use the Ferrara-Florence-Rome council to reunite the church and reasssert papal supremacy.

conclave (Latin "a room locked with a key") A secret meeting, in particular the gathering of cardinals in Rome to elect a new pope. They are locked away in the Vatican Palace until they have reached a decision. The result of each ballot is announced by a smoke signal—black for an undecided vote and white when the choice is made.

Concord capital of New Hampshire, located in the S central part of the state, on the Merrimack river, N of Manchester. Industries include granite, leather goods, electrical equipment, printed products, and wood products; population (1990) 36,006.

Concord town in Massachusetts, 18 mi/29 km NE

concentration camp *Liberation day at Auschwitz, one of the infamous Nazi concentration camps, on May 3, 1945.*

Concorde *The supersonic airliner was the result of Anglo-French cooperation and made its first flight in April 1969. It entered commercial service in 1976 and flies from New York City to London in about 3 hours.*

of Boston; population (1990) 17,076. Site of the first battle of the American Revolution, April 19, 1775. Although electronic equipment, metal products, and leather goods are manufactured, it is mainly a residential suburb of Boston. The Minute Man National Historical Park is here. Concord was settled 1635. The writers Ralph Waldo Emerson, Henry Thoreau, Nathaniel Hawthorne, and Louisa May Alcott lived here.

concordance book containing an alphabetical list of the important words in a major work, with references to the places in which they occur. The first concordance was one prepared to the Latin Vulgate Bible by a Dominican in the 13th century.

Alexander Cruden composed a concordance of the Bible in 1737, of which many editions have appeared. Concordances to Shakespeare, Milton, and other writers also appear in many editions.

concordat agreement regulating relations between the papacy and a secular government, for example, that for France between Pius VII and the emperor Napoleon, which lasted 1801–1905; Mussolini's concordat, which lasted 1929–78 and safeguarded the position of the church in Italy; and one of 1984 in Italy in which Roman Catholicism ceased to be the Italian state religion.

Concorde the only ◊supersonic airliner, which cruises at Mach 2, or twice the speed of sound, about 1,350 mph/2,170 kph. Concorde, the result of Anglo-French cooperation, made its first flight 1969 and entered commercial service seven years later. It is 202 ft/62 m long and has a wing span of nearly 84 ft/26 m.

In 1990 a feasibility study began of providing a replacement for Concorde.

concrete a building material composed of cement, stone, sand, and water. It has been in use since Egyptian and Roman times. During the 20th century, it has been increasingly employed as an economical alternative to materials such as brick and wood.

history

c. 5600 BC Earliest discovered use of concrete at Lepenski Vir, Yugoslavia (hut floors in Stone Age village).

2500 BC Concrete used in Great Pyramid at Giza by Egyptians.

2nd century BC Romans accidentally discovered the use of lime and silican/alumina to produce "pozzolanic" cement.

AD 127 Lightweight concrete (using crushed pumice as aggregate) used for walls of Pantheon, Rome.

medieval times Concrete used for castles (infill in walls) and cathedrals (largely foundation work).

1756 John Smeaton produced the first high-quality cement since Roman times (for rebuilding of Eddystone lighthouse, England).

1824 Joseph Aspdin patented Portland cement in Britain.

1854 William Wilkinson patented reinforced concrete in Britain—first successful use in a building.

1880s First continuous-process rotary cement kiln installed (reducing costs of manufacturing cement).

1926 Eugène Freysinnet began experiments on prestressed concrete in France.

1930s US substituted concrete for limestone during federal building projects of the Great Depression; also used extensively for pavements, roadbeds, bridge approaches, dams, and sports facilities (stadiums, swimming pools, tennis courts, playgrounds).

1940s–1950s Poured concrete used to rebuild war-torn cities of Europe and the Middle East; widespread use of concrete floors for radiant heat in postwar development homes.

1960s Widespread use of concrete in industrialized countries as an economical house and office building material instead of traditional materials.

1980s Move away from concrete as a substitute for brick or stone in house-building due to its comparatively short life span.

concurrent lines two or more lines passing through a single point; for example, the diameters of a circle are all concurrent at the center of the circle.

concussion impaired functioning of an organ, especially the brain, resulting from a violent blow. Temporary unconsciousness is a symptom.

Condé Louis de Bourbon, Prince of Condé 1530–1569. Prominent French ◊Huguenot leader, founder of the house of Condé and uncle of Henry IV of France. He fought in the wars between Henry II and the Holy Roman emperor Charles V, including the defense of Metz.

Condé Louis II 1621–1686. Prince of Condé called the Great Condé. French commander who won brilliant victories during the Thirty Years' War at Rocroi 1643 and Lens 1648, but rebelled 1651 and entered the Spanish service. Pardoned 1660, he commanded Louis XIV's armies against the Spanish and the Dutch.

condensation in physical chemistry, the conversion of a vapor to a liquid as it loses heat. This is frequently achieved by letting the vapor come into contact with a cold surface. It is an essential step in distillation processes.

condensation in organic chemistry, a reaction in which two organic compounds combine to form a larger molecule, accompanied by the removal of a smaller molecule (usually water). This is also known as an addition–elimination reaction. Polyamides (such as nylon) and polyesters are made by condensation polymerization.

condensation number in physics, the ratio of the number of molecules condensing on a surface to the total number of molecules touching that surface.

condenser in optics, a shortfocal-length convex ◊lens or combination of lenses used for concentrating a light source on to a small area, as used in a slide projector or microscope substage lighting unit. A condenser can also be made using a concave mirror. In electricity, another name for ◊capacitor.

Condillac Étienne Bonnot de 1715–1780. French philosopher. He mainly followed ◊Locke, but his *Traité de sensations* 1754 claims that all mental activity stems from the transformation of sensations. He was a collaborator in the French ◊Encyclopédie. Born in Grenoble of noble parentage, he entered the church and was appointed tutor to Louis XV's grandson, the duke of Parma.

conditioning in psychology, two major principles of behavior modification. In classical conditioning, described by Ivan Pavlov, a new stimulus can evoke an automatic response by being repeatedly associated with a stimulus that naturally provokes a response. For example, a bell repeatedly associated with food will eventually trigger salivation, even if presented without food. In operant conditioning, described by Edward Lee Thorndike (1874–1949) and B F Skinner, the frequency of a voluntary response can be increased by following it with a reinforcer or reward.

condom or ***prophylactic*** or ***sheath*** barrier contraceptive, made of rubber or animal skin, which fits over an erect penis and holds in the sperm produced by ejaculation. It is an effective means of

condor

preventing pregnancy if used carefully, preferably with a ◊spermicide. A condom with spermicide is 97% effective; one without spermicide is 85% effective, since they sometimes tear or burst during use. Condoms can also give protection against sexually transmitted diseases and are endorsed for protection from AIDS.

condominium joint rule of a territory by two or more states, for example, Kanton and Enderbury islands in the South Pacific Phoenix group (under the joint control of Britain and the US for 50 years from 1939).

The term has also come into use in North America to describe a type of joint property ownership of, for example, apartment buildings.

condor large bird, a New World vulture *Vultur gryphus*, with wingspan up to 10 ft/3 m, weight up to 28 lb/13 kg, and length up to 3.8 ft/1.2 m. It is black, with some white on the wings and a white frill at the base of the neck. It lives in the Andes and along the South American coast, and feeds on carrion.

The Californian condor *Gymnogyps californianus* is a similar bird, and on the verge of extinction. It lays only one egg at a time and may not breed every year. It is the subject of a special conservation effort.

Condorcet Marie Jean Antoine Nicolas Caritat, Marquis de 1743–1794. French philosopher, mathematician, and politician, associated with the ◊Encyclopédistes. One of the ◊Girondins, he opposed the execution of Louis XVI, and was imprisoned and poisoned himself. His *Esquisse d'un tableau des progrès de l'esprit humain/Historical Survey of the Progress of Human Understanding* 1795 envisaged inevitable future progress, though not the perfectibility of human nature.

conductance the ability of a material to carry an electrical current, usually given the symbol G. For a direct current, it is the reciprocal of resistance: a conductor of resistance R has a conductance of $1/R$. For an alternating current, conductance is the resistance R divided by the impedence Z: $G = R/Z$. Conductance was formerly expressed in reciprocal ohms (or mhos); the SI unit is the Siemens (S).

conductor material that conducts heat or electricity (as opposed to a non-conductor or insulator). A good conductor has a high electrical or heat conductivity, and is generally a substance rich in free electrons such as a metal. A poor conductor (such as the non-metals glass and porcelain) has few free electrons. Carbon is exceptional in being non-metallic and yet (in some of its forms) a relatively good conductor of heat and electricity. Substances such as silicon and germanium, with intermediate conductivities that are improved by heat, light, or voltage, are known as ◊semiconductors.

conductor in music, the leader of the orchestra who rehearses the sections for performance and conceives and controls the overall expression, tempo, and balance of sound.

cone in geometry, a solid or surface generated by rotating an isosceles triangle or framework about its line of symmetry. It can also be formed by the set of all straight lines passing through a fixed point and the points of a circle or ellipse whose plane does not contain the point.

A circular cone of perpendicular height h and base of radius r has a volume $V = \frac{1}{3}\pi r^2 h$. The distance from the edge of the base of a cone to the vertex is called the slant height. In a right circular cone of slant height l, the curved surface area is πrl, and the area of the base is πr^2. Therefore the total surface area $A = \pi rl + \pi r^2 = \pi r(l + r)$.

cone in botany, the reproductive structure of the conifers and cycads; also known as a ◊strobilus. It consists of a central axis surrounded by numerous, overlapping, scalelike sporophylls, modified leaves that bear the reproductive organs. Usually there are separate male and female cones, the former bearing pollen sacs containing pollen grains, and the larger female cones bearing the ovules that contain the ova or egg cells. The pollen is carried from male to female cones by wind (◊anemophily). The seeds develop within the female cone and are released as the scales open in dry atmospheric conditions, which favor seed dispersal.

In some groups (for example, the pines) the cones take two or even three years to reach maturity. The cones of ◊junipers have fleshy cone scales that fuse to form a berrylike structure. One group of ◊angiosperms, the alders, also bear conelike structures; these are the woody remains of the short female catkins, and they contain the alder ◊fruits.

Coney Island seaside resort on a peninsula in Brooklyn, in the SW of Long Island. It has been popular for ocean bathing and its amusement parks since the 1840s and was named for the wild rabbits (the coneys) that inhabited what was originally a small island.

Confederacy in US history, popular name for the Confederate States of America, the government established by 6 (later 11) Southern states Feb 1861 when they seceded from the Union, precipitating the ◊Civil War. Richmond, Virginia, was the capital and Jefferson Davis the president. The Confederacy fell after its army was defeated 1865 and General Robert E Lee surrendered.

The Confederacy suffered from a lack of political leadership as well as a deficit of troops and supplies. Still, Southern forces won many significant victories. Confederate leaders had hoped to enlist support from Britain and France, but the slavery issue and the Confederacy's uncertain prospects prompted the Europeans to maintain neutrality, although they provided supplies for a time. The Union's blockade and the grinding weight of superior resources made the outcome virtually inevitable 1865. The states of the Confederacy were South Carolina, Georgia, Florida, Alabama, Louisiana, Mississippi, Texas, Virginia, Tennessee, Arkansas, and North Carolina.

cone

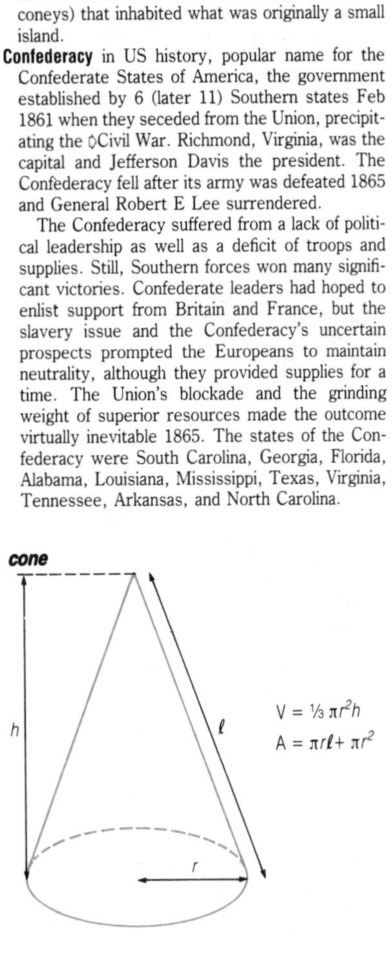
h
ℓ
r
V = ⅓ πr²h
A = πrℓ+ πr²

Confederacy 1861–65

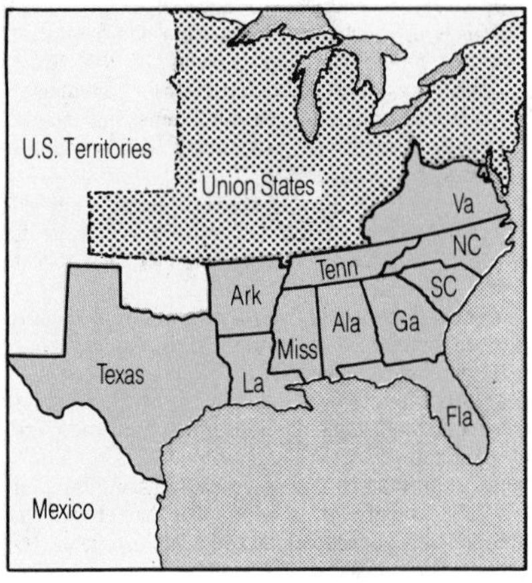
U.S. Territories
Union States
Va
NC
Tenn
SC
Ark
Ala
Ga
Miss
La
Texas
Fla
Mexico

Confederation, Articles of in US history, the initial means by which the 13 former British colonies created a form of national government. Ratified in 1781, the Articles established a unicameral legislature, Congress, with limited powers of raising revenue, regulating currency, and conducting foreign affairs. But because the individual states retained significant autonomy, the confederation was unmanageable. The articles were superseded by the US Constitution in 1788.

conference system a system of international conferences in the 19th century promoted principally by the German chancellor Bismarck to ease the integration of a new powerful German state into the "concert of Europe."

The conferences were intended to settle great power disputes, mainly related to the Balkans, the Middle East, and the designation of colonies in Africa and Asia. Most important of these was the Congress of ◊Berlin 1878. The system fell into disuse with the retirement of Bismarck and the pressures of new European alliance blocks.

confession a religious practice, the confession of sins, practiced in Roman Catholic, Orthodox, and most Oriental Christian churches, and since the early 19th century revived in Anglican and Lutheran churches. The Lateran Council of 1215 made auricular confession (self-accusation by the penitent to a priest, who in Catholic doctrine is divinely invested with authority to give absolution) obligatory once a year.

Both John the Baptist's converts and the early Christian church practiced public confession. The Roman Catholic penitent in recent times has always confessed alone to the priest in a confessional box, but from 1977 such individual confession might be preceded by group discussion, or the confession itself might be made openly by members of the group.

Confindustria in European history, a general confederation of industry established in Italy 1920 with the aim of countering working-class agitation. It contributed large funds to the fascist movement, which, in turn, used its *squadristi* against the workers. After Mussolini's takeover of power in 1922, Confindustria became one of the major groups of the fascist corporative state.

confirmation rite practiced by a number of Christian denominations, including Roman Catholic, Anglican, and Orthodox, in which a previously baptized person is admitted to full membership of the church. In Reform Judaism there is often a confirmation service several years after the bar or bat mitzvah (initiation into the congregation).

Christian confirmation is believed to give the participant the gift of the Holy Spirit. In the Anglican church it consists in the laying on of hands by a bishop, while in the Roman Catholic and Orthodox churches the participant is anointed with oil. Except in the Orthodox churches, where infant confirmation is usual, the rite takes place around early adolescence. Until recently a child preparing for confirmation was required to learn by heart a series of questions and answers known as a ◊catechism.

Confucianism the body of beliefs and practices that are based on the Chinese classics and supported by the authority of the philosopher Confucius (Kong Zi). For about 2,500 years most of the Chinese people have derived from Confucianism their ideas of cosmology, political government, social organization, and individual conduct. Human relationships follow the patriarchal pattern. The origin of things is seen in the union of yin and yang, the passive and active principles.

The writings on which Confucianism is based include the ideas of a group of traditional books edited by Confucius, as well as his own works, such as the *Analects*, and those of some of his pupils. The ◊*I Ching* is included among the Confucianist texts.

doctrine Until 1912 the emperor of China was regarded as the father of his people, appointed by heaven to rule. The Superior Man was the ideal human and filial piety was the chief virtue. Accompanying a high morality was a kind of ancestor worship.

practices Under the emperor, sacrifices were offered to heaven and earth, the heavenly bodies, the imperial ancestors, various nature gods, and Confucius himself. These were abolished at the Revolution in 1912, but ancestor worship (better expressed as reverence and remembrance) remained a regular practice in the home.

Under communism Confucianism continued. The defense minister Lin Biao was associated with the religion, and although the communist leader Mao Zedong undertook an anti-Confucius campaign 1974–76, this was not pursued by the succeeding regime.

Confucius Latinized form of Kong Zi, "Kong the master" 551–479 BC. Chinese sage whose name is given to Confucianism. He devoted his life to relieving suffering among the poor through governmental and administrative reform. His emphasis on tradition and ethics attracted a growing number of pupils during his lifetime. *The Analects of Confucius*, a compilation of his teachings, was published after his death.

Confucius was born in Lu, in what is now the province of Shangdong, and his early years were spent in poverty. Married at 19, he worked as a minor official, then as a teacher. In 517 there was an uprising in Lu, and Confucius spent the next year or two in the adjoining state of Ch'i. As a teacher he was able to place many of his pupils in government posts but a powerful position eluded him. Only in his fifties was he given an office, but he soon resigned because of the lack of power it conveyed. Then for 14 years he wandered from state to state looking for a ruler who could give him a post where he could put his reforms into practice. At the age of 67 he returned to Lu and devoted himself to teaching. At his death five years later he was buried with great pomp, and his grave outside Qufu has remained a center of pilgrimage.

conga Latin American dance, originally from Cuba, in which the participants form a winding line, take three steps forwards or backwards, and then kick.

congenital disease in medicine, a disease that is present at birth. It is not necessarily genetic in origin; for example, congenital herpes may be acquired by the baby as it passes through the mother's birth canal.

conger any of a family, Congridae, of large marine eels, especially the genus *Conger*. Conger eels live in shallow water, hiding in crevices during the day and active by night, feeding on fish and crabs. They are valued for food and angling.

The American conger *C. oceanicus* grows to 4.5 ft/1.4 m in length.

conglomerate a coarse clastic ◊sedimentary rock, composed of rounded fragments (clasts) of pre-existing rocks cemented in a finer matrix, usually sand.

The fragments in conglomerates are pebble- to boulder-sized, and the rock can be regarded as the lithified equivalent of gravel. A ◊bed of conglomerate is often associated with a break in a sequence of rock beds (an unconformity), where it marks the advance of the sea over an old eroded landscape. An oligomict conglomerate contains one type of pebble; a polymict conglomerate has a mixture of pebble types. If the rock fragments are angular, it is called a ◊breccia.

Congo former name 1960–71 of ◊Zaïre.

Congo country in W central Africa, bounded N by Cameroon and the Central African Republic, E and S by Zaïre, W by the Atlantic Ocean, and NW by Gabon.

government The Congo is a one-party state based on the Marxist-Leninist Congolese Labor Party (PTC). The president of the central committee of PTC is automatically elected state president for a five-year term and chairs the council of ministers. The single-chamber legislature is the 153-member people's national assembly, elected by universal suffrage from a list prepared by PTC.

history Occupied from the 15th century by the Bakongo, Bateke, and Sanga, the area was exploited by Portuguese slave traders. From 1889 it came under French administration, becoming part of French Equatorial Africa in 1910.

The Congo became an autonomous republic within the French Community in 1958, and Abbé Fulbert Youlou, a Roman Catholic priest who involved himself in politics and was suspended by the Church, became prime minister and then president when full independence was achieved in 1960. Two years later plans were announced for a one-party state, but in 1963, after industrial unrest, Youlou was forced to resign.

A new constitution was approved, and Alphonse Massamba-Débat, a former finance minister, became president, adopting a policy of "scientific socialism." The National Revolutionary Movement (MNR) was declared the only political party. In 1968 Captain Marien Ngouabi overthrew Massamba-Débat in a military coup, and the national assembly was replaced by a national council of the revolution. Ngouabi proclaimed a Marxist state but kept economic links with France.

In 1970 the nation became the People's Republic of the Congo, with the Congolese Labor Party (PCT) as the only party, and in 1973 a new constitution provided for an assembly chosen from a single party list. In 1977 Ngouabi was assassinated, and Col Joachim Yhombi-Opango took over. He resigned in 1979 after discovering a plot to overthrow him and was succeeded by Denis Sassou-Nguessou, who moved away from Soviet influence and strengthened links with France, the US, and China.

In 1982 President Mitterrand of France paid an official visit to the Congo. In 1984 Sassou-Nguessou was elected for another five-year term. He increased his control by combining the posts of head of state, head of government and president of the central committee of PCT.

In Aug 1990 the ruling PTC announced political reforms, including the abandonment of Marxism-Lenism, the broadening of its membership and an eventual end of the one-party system.

Congregationalism form of church government adopted by those Protestant Christians known as Congregationalists, who let each congregation manage its own affairs, like the people of the Old Testament. The first Congregationalists established themselves in London and were called the Brownists after Robert Browne, who in 1581 defined the congregational principle. They oposed King James I and were supporters of Oliver ◊Cromwell. They became one of the most important forces in the founding of New England.

During the 17th century they joined with Puritans in opposing the Church of England hierarchy. Many fled to Holland to avoid persecution, and in 1620 Congregationalists who left Holland on the *Mayflower* founded Plymouth Colony in Massachusetts. The early Congregational churches in New England were distinguished for their devotion to education—founding Harvard, Yale, and most of the other older private colleges of the region. During the 19th century, Congregationalists lost their semiestablished status in New England, and many congregations turned to ◊Unitarianism, but Congregationalism spread to the Midwest and elsewhere. In 1959, Congregationalists merged with several other groups to form the United Church of Christ.

Congress national legislature of the US, consisting of the House of Representatives (435 members, apportioned to the states of the Union on the basis of population, and elected for two-year terms) and the Senate (100 senators, two for each state, elected for six years, one-third elected every two years). Both representatives and senators are elected by direct popular vote. Congress meets in Washington, DC, in the Capitol Building. An ◊act of Congress is a bill passed by both houses.

The Congress of the United States met for the first time on March 4, 1789. It was preceded by the Congress of the Confederation representing the several states under the Articles of Confederation from 1781 to 1789.

Congress of Racial Equality (CORE) US nonviolent civil-rights organization, founded in Chicago 1942.

Congress Party Indian political party, founded 1885 as the Indian National Congress, which led the movement to end British rule. It has been the governing party for most of the period since independence was attained 1947.

congress system developed from the Congress of Vienna 1814–15, a series of international meetings in Aachen, Germany 1818, Troppali, Austria 1820, and Verona, Italy 1822. British opposition to the use of congresses by ◊Metternich as a weapon against liberal and national movements inside Europe brought them to an end as a system of international arbitration, although congresses continued to meet into the 1830s.

Congreve William 1670–1729. English dramatist and poet. His first success was the comedy *The Old Bachelor* 1693, followed by *The Double Dealer* 1694, *Love for Love* 1695, the tragedy *The Mourning Bride* 1697, and *The Way of the World* 1700. His plays, which satirize the social affectations of the time, are characterized by elegant wit and wordplay.

congruent in geometry, having the same shape and size, as applied to two-dimensional or solid figures. With plane congruent figures, one figure will fit on top of the other exactly, though this may first require rotation and/or reflection (making a mirror image) of one of the figures.

conic section curve obtained when a conical surface is intersected by a plane. If the intersecting plane cuts both extensions of the cone, it yields a ◊hyperbola; if it is parallel to the side of the cone, it produces a ◊parabola. Other intersecting planes produce ◊circles or ◊ellipses.

The Greek philosopher Apollonius (*c.* 262–190 BC) wrote eight books with the title *Conic Sections*, which superseded previous work on the subject by Aristarchus and Euclid.

conidium (plural conidia) an asexual spore formed by some fungi at the tip of a specialized ◊hypha or conidiophore. The conidiophores grow erect, and cells from their ends round off and separate into conidia, often forming long chains. Conidia easily become detached and are dispersed by air movements.

conifer tree or shrub of the class Coniferales, in the gymnosperm or naked-seed-bearing group of plants. They are often pyramidal in form, with leaves that are either scaled or made up of needles; most are evergreen. Conifers include pines, spruces, firs, yews, junipers, monkey puzzles, and larches.

The reproductive organs are the male and female cones, and pollen is distributed by the wind. The seeds develop in the female cones. The processes of maturation, fertilization, and seed ripening may extend over several years.

conjugate in mathematics, a term indicating that two elements are connected in some way; for

Congo
People's Republic of the
(République Populaire du Congo)

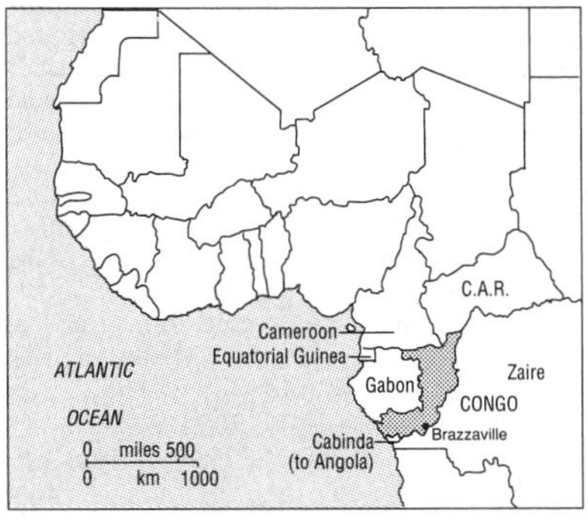
C.A.R.
Cameroon
Equatorial Guinea
ATLANTIC
OCEAN
Gabon
Zaire
CONGO
Brazzaville
Cabinda
(to Angola)
0 miles 500
0 km 1000

area 132,012 sq mi/342,000 sq km
capital Brazzaville
cities chief port Pointe-Noire; N'Kayi, Loubomo
physical narrow coastal plain rises to central plateau then falls into northern basin. Zaïre (Congo) River on the border with Zaïre; half the country is rainforest
features 70% of the population lives in Brazzaville, Pointe-Noire, or in towns along the railroad linking these two places
head of state and government Denis Sassau-Nguesso from 1979
political system one-party Socialist republic
political parties Congolese Labor Party (PCT), Marxist-Leninist
exports timber, petroleum, cocoa, sugar
currency CFA franc
population (1990 est) 2,305,000 (chiefly Bantu); growth rate 2.6% p.a.
life expectancy men 45, women 48
language French (official), many African dialects spoken
religion animist 50%, Christian 48%, Muslim 2%
literacy men 79%/women 55% (1985 est)
GDP $2.1 bn (1983); $500 per head
chronology
1910 Became part of French Equatorial Africa.
1960 Achieved independence from France, with Abbe Youlou as the first president.
1963 Youlou forced to resign. New constitution approved, with Alphonse Massamba-Débat as president.
1964 The Congo became a one-party state.
1968 Military coup, led by Capt Marien Ngouabi, ousted Massamba-Débat.
1970 A Marxist state, the People's Republic of the Congo, was announced, with the PCT as the only legal party.
1977 Ngouabi assassinated. Col Yhombi-Opango became president.
1979 Yhombi-Opango handed over the presidency to PCT, who chose Col Denis Sassou-Ngessou as his successor.
1984 Sassou-Ngessou elected for another five-year term.
1990 PCT abandoned Marxist-Leninism and promised multiparty politics.
1991 1979 constitution suspended pending the introduction of multiparty democracy. Multiparty elections promised.

example, $(a + ib)$ and $(a - ib)$ are conjugate complex numbers.

conjugate angles in geometry, two angles that add up to 360°.

conjugation in biology, the bacterial equivalent of sexual reproduction. A fragment of the ◊DNA from one bacterium is passed along a thin tube, the pilus, into the cell of another bacterium.

conjunction a grammatical ◊part of speech that serves to connect words, phrases, and clauses; for example *and* in "apples and pears" and *but* in "we're going but they aren't."

conjunction in astronomy, the alignment of two celestial bodies so that they have the same position as seen from Earth. Inferior conjunction occurs when an ◊inferior planet (or other object) passes between the Earth and Sun, and has an identical right ascension to the Sun. Superior conjunction occurs when a ◊superior planet (or other object) passes behind, or on the far side of, the Sun, and has the same right ascension as the Sun. Planetary conjunction takes place when a planet is closely aligned with another celestial object, such as the Moon, a star, or another planet, as seen from Earth.

Because the orbital planes of the inferior planets are tilted with respect to the Earth, an inferior planet usually passes either above or below the Sun as seen from Earth. If they line up exactly, a ◊transit will occur.

conjunctiva membrane covering the vertebrate ◊eye. It is continuous with the epidermis of the eyelids, and lies on the surface of the cornea.

conjunctivitis inflammation of the conjunctiva, the delicate membrane that lines the inside of the eyelids and covers the front of the eye. It may be caused by infection, allergy, or other irritant.

Conkling Roscoe 1829–1888. US political leader. Born in Albany, New York, the son of a judge, Conkling was admitted to the bar 1850 and soon named district attorney. Deeply interested in politics, Conkling was one of the founders of the Republican party and served as mayor of Utica 1858. He served in the US House of Representatives 1859–63, 1865–67 and US Senate 1867–81. A Radical Republican, Conkling was an active prosecutor in Andrew ◊Johnson's impeachment trial.

As an opponent of James Garfield, Conkling declined an appointment to the US Supreme Court 1882 and returned to private law practice.

Connecticut state in NE US; nickname Constitution State/Nutmeg State

area 5,018 sq mi/13,000 sq km

capital Hartford

physical highlands in the NW, Connecticut River

features Yale University; Mystic Seaport (reconstruction of 19th-century village, with restored ships)

products dairy, poultry, and market-garden products; tobacco, watches, clocks, silverware, helicopters, jet engines, nuclear submarines, hardware and locks, electrical and electronic equipment, guns and ammunition, optical instruments. Hartford is the center of the nation's insurance industry

population (1990) 3,287,116.

famous people Benedict Arnold, Phineas T Barnum, Jonathan Edwards, Nathan Hale, Katharine Hepburn, Charles Ives, Edward H Land, Eugene O'Neill, Wallace Stevens, Harriet Beecher Stowe, Mark Twain, Eli Whitney

history Dutch navigator Adriaen Block was first European to record the area 1614, and in 1633 Dutch colonists built a trading post near modern Hartford but it soon was settled by Puritan colonists from Massachusetts 1635. It was one of the original 13 colonies and became a state 1788. It prospered in the 19th century from shipbuilding, whaling, and growing industry. In the 20th century it became an important supplier of military equipment. Connecticut is second to Alaska among states in personal income per capita. Many of New York City's most affluent residential suburbs are in SW Connecticut.

Connecticut

Hartford

connectionist machine computing device built from a large number of interconnected simple processors, which are able both to communicate with each other and process information separately. The underlying model is that of the human brain.

These "massively parallel" computers, as they are sometimes known, are still at the development stage.

connective tissue in animals, tissue made up of a noncellular substance, the ◊extracellular matrix, in which some cells are embedded. Skin, bones, tendons, cartilage, and adipose tissue (fat) are the main connective tissues. There are also small amounts of connective tissue in organs such as the brain and liver, where they maintain shape and structure.

Connery Sean 1930– . Scottish film actor, the first, and arguably the best, interpreter of James Bond in several films based on the novels of Ian Fleming. His films include *Dr No* 1962, *From Russia with Love* 1963, *Marnie* 1964, *Goldfinger* 1964, *Diamonds are Forever* 1971, *A Bridge Too Far* 1977, *The Name of the Rose* 1986, and *The Untouchables* 1987,for which he won an Academy Award.

Connors Jimmy 1952– . US tennis player. A popular and entertaining player, he became well known for his "grunting" during play. He won the Wimbledon title 1974, and has since won ten Grand Slam events. He was one of the first players to popularize the two-handed backhand.

Connery *Actor Sean Connery shot to fame as the first James Bond in* Dr No *1962.*

CAREER HIGHLIGHTS

Wimbledon
singles: 1974, 1982
doubles: 1973
US Open
singles: 1974, 1976, 1978, 1982–83
doubles: 1975
Australian Open
singles: 1974

conquistador Spanish word for "conqueror," applied to such explorers and adventurers in the Americas as Cortés (Mexico) and Pizarro (Peru).

Conrad Joseph 1857–1924. British novelist of Polish parentage, born Teodor Jozef Konrad Korzeniowski in the Ukraine. His novels include *Almayer's Folly* 1895, *Lord Jim* 1900, *Heart of Darkness* 1902, *Nostromo* 1904, *The Secret Agent* 1907, and *Under Western Eyes* 1911. His works vividly evoke the mysteries of sea life and exotic foreign settings and explore the psychological isolation of the "outsider."

Conrad several kings of the Germans and Holy Roman emperors, including:

Conrad I King of the Germans from 911, when he succeeded Louis the Child, the last of the German Carolingians. During his reign the realm was harassed by ◊Magyar invaders.

Conrad II King of the Germans from 1024, Holy Roman emperor from 1027. He ceded the Sleswick (Schleswig) borderland, south of the Jutland peninsula, to King Canute, but extended his rule into Lombardy and Burgundy.

Conrad III 1093–1152. Holy Roman emperor from 1138, the first king of the Hohenstaufen dynasty. Throughout his reign there was a fierce struggle between his followers, the ◊Ghibellines, and the ◊Guelphs, the followers of Henry the Proud, duke of Saxony and Bavaria (1108–1139), and later of his son Henry the Lion (1129–1195).

Conrad IV 1228–1254. Elected king of the Germans 1237. Son of the Holy Roman emperor Frederick II, he had to defend his right of succession against Henry Raspe of Thuringia (died 1247) and William of Holland (1227–56).

Conrad V (Conradin) 1252–1268. Son of Conrad IV, recognized as king of the Germans, Sicily, and Jerusalem by German supporters of the ◊Hohenstaufens 1254. He led ◊Ghibelline forces against Charles of Anjou at the battle of Tagliacozzo, N Italy 1266, and was captured and executed.

Conran Terence 1931– . British designer and retailer of furnishings, fashion, and household goods. He was founder of the Habitat and Conran companies, with retail outlets in the UK, the US, and elsewhere.

consanguinity kinship, relationship by descent, whether lineal (for example by direct descent) or collateral (by virtue of a common ancestor). The degree of consanguinity is significant in laws relating to the inheritance of property and also in relation to marriage, which is forbidden in many cultures between parties closely related.

conscientious objector person refusing compulsory service, usually military, on moral, religious, or political grounds.

The term originally denoted parents who objected to compulsory vaccination of their children.

conscription legislation for all able-bodied male citizens (and female in some countries, such as Israel) to serve with the armed forces. It originated in France 1792, and in the 19th and 20th centuries became the established practice in almost all European states. Modern conscription systems often permit alternative national service for conscientious objectors.

In the US conscription (the draft) was introduced during the Civil War—by the Confederates 1862 and by the Union side 1863. In World War I a Selective Service Act was passed 1917, then again 1940 in anticipation of US entry into World War II. It remained in force (except for 15 months 1947–48) until after the US withdrawal from Vietnam 1973, although the system was changed to a lottery based on a registrant's birthday. This was done to rectify the inequities stemming from the deferment system that had allowed college students to delay their service. In 1980 Carter restored registration for a possible military draft for men at 18, but his proposal that it be extended to women was rejected by Congress. The US now has a policy based on all-volunteer armed forces.

consent, age of the age at which consent may legally be given to sexual intercourse by a girl or boy.

In the US it varies according to state statutes.

conservation in the life sciences, action taken to protect and preserve the natural world, usually from pollution, overexploitation, and other harmful features of human activity. Since the 1950s there has been a growing realization that the Earth, together with its atmosphere, animal and plant life, and mineral and agricultural resources, form an interdependent whole, which is in danger of irreversible depletion and eventual destruction unless positive measures are taken to conserve a balance. The late 1980s saw a great increase in concern for the environment, with membership of conservation groups such as ◊Friends of the Earth rising sharply. Globally the most important issues include the depletion of atmospheric ozone by the action of chlorofluorocarbons (CFCs), the greenhouse effect, and the destruction of the tropical rainforests.

conservatism approach to government favoring the maintenance of existing institutions and identified with a number of Western political parties, such as the US Republican, British Conservative, German Christian Democratic, and Australian Liberal parties. It tends to be explicitly nondoctrinaire and pragmatic but generally emphasizes free-enterprise capitalism, minimal government intervention in the economy, rigid law and order, and the importance of national traditions.

Conservative Party although there is a Conservative Party in the US, it is generally a minor element in national elections. The term is most often used in reference to the UK political party, one of the two historic British parties; the name replaced "Tory" in general use from 1830 onward. Traditionally the party of landed interests, it broadened its political base under Disraeli's leadership in the 19th century. The present Conservative Party's free-market capitalism is supported by the world of finance and the management of industry; its economic policies have increased the spending power of the majority, but also the gap between rich and poor; nationalized industries are sold off (see ◊privatization); military spending and close alliance with the US are favored.

Under the leadership of Margaret ◊Thatcher, the Conservative Party returned to power May 1979; she was reelected for a third term in 1987 and resigned 1989.

conspicuous consumption selection and purchase of goods for their social rather than their inherent value. These might include items with an obviously expensive brand-name tag. The term was coined by US economist Thorsten Veblen.

Constable John 1776–1837. English landscape painter. He painted scenes of his native Suffolk including *The Haywain* 1821 (National Gallery, London), and he traveled widely in Britain, depicting castles, cathedrals, landscapes, and coastal scenes. His many sketches are often considered among his best work. The paintings are remarkable for their freshness and influenced French painters such as Delacroix.

Constable inherited the Dutch tradition of somber realism, in particular the style of Jacob ◊Ruisdael, but he aimed to capture the momentary changes of nature as well as to create monumental images of British scenery, such as *The White Horse* 1819 (Frick Collection, New York) and *Flatford Mill* 1825.

Constance (German *Konstanz*) town in Baden-Württemberg, Federal Republic of Germany, on the section of the river Rhine joining Lake Constance and the lake Untersee; population (1983) 69,100. Suburbs stretch across the frontier into Switzerland. Constance has clothing, machinery, and chemical factories and printing works.

Constable Salisbury Cathedral and Archdeacon Fisher's House from the River *(1820) National Gallery, London.*

Constance, Council of council held by the Roman Catholic church 1414–17 in Constance, Germany. It elected Pope Martin V, which ended the Great Schism 1378–1417 when there were rival popes in Rome and Avignon.

Constance, Lake (German *Bodensee*) lake bounded by Germany, Austria, and Switzerland, through which the river Rhine flows; area 200 sq mi/ 530 sq km.

constant in mathematics, a fixed quantity or one that does not change its value in relation to ◊variables. For example, in the algebraic expression $y^2 = 5x - 3$, the numbers 3 and 5 are constants. In physics, certain quantities are regarded as universal constants, such as the speed of light in a vacuum.

Constanța chief Romanian port on the Black Sea, capital of Constanța region, and third-largest city of Romania; population (1985) 323,000. It has refineries, shipbuilding yards, and food factories.

It is the exporting center for the Romanian oilfields, to which it is connected by pipeline. It was founded as a Greek colony in the 7th century BC, and later named after the Roman emperor Constantine I (4th century AD). Ovid, the Roman poet, lived in exile here.

constantan high-resistance alloy of approximately 40% nickel and 60% copper with a very low temperature coefficient. It is used in electrical resistors.

Constant de Rebecque (Henri) Benjamin 1767–1830. French writer and politician. An advocate of the Revolution, he opposed Napoleon and in 1803 went into exile. Returning to Paris after the fall of Napoleon in 1814 he proposed a constitutional monarchy. He published the autobiographical novel *Adolphe* 1816, which reflects his affair with Madame de ◊Staël, and later wrote the monumental study *De la Religion* 1825–31.

Constantine city in Algeria; population (1983) 449,000. It produces carpets and leather goods. It was one of the chief towns of the Roman province of Numidia, but declined and was ruined, then restored 313 by Constantine the Great, whose name it bears. It was subsequently ruled by Arabs, Turks, and Salah Bey 1770–92, who built many of the Muslim buildings. It was captured by the French 1837.

Constantine II 1940– . King of the Hellenes (Greece). In 1964 he succeeded his father Paul I, went into exile 1967, and was formally deposed 1973. He married Princess Anne-Marie of Denmark in 1964.

Constantine the Great AD 274–337. First Christian emperor of Rome and founder of Constantinople. He defeated Maxentius, joint-emperor of Rome 321 and in 313 formally recognized Christianity. As sole emperor of the West of the Empire, he defeated Licinius, emperor of the East, to become ruler of the Roman world 324. He presided over the Church's first council at Nicaea 325. In 330 Constantine moved his capital to Byzantium, renaming it Constantinople.

Born at Naissus (Nish, Yugoslavia), Constantine was the son of Constantius. He was already well known as a soldier when his father died at York in 306 and he was acclaimed by the troops there as joint-emperor in his father's place. A few years later Maxentius, the joint-emperor in Rome (whose sister had married Constantine), challenged his authority and mobilized his armies to invade Gaul. Constantine won a crushing victory outside Rome in 312. During this campaign he was said to have seen a vision of the cross of Jesus superimposed upon the sun, accompanied by the words, "In this sign conquer." By the Edict of Milan 313 he formally recognized Christianity as one of the religions legally permitted within the Roman Empire, and in 314 summoned the bishops of the Western world to the Council of Arles. Sole emperor of the West since 321 by defeating Licinius, the emperor in the East, Constantine became sole Roman emperor 324. He increased the autocratic power of the emperor, issued legislation to tie the farmers and workers to their crafts in a sort of caste system, and enlisted the support of the Christian Church. He summoned, and presided over, the first general council of the Church at Nicaea 325. Constantine moved his capital to Byzantium on the Bosporus 330 and renamed it Constantinople (now Istanbul).

Constantinople former name of Istanbul, Turkey, from 330 to 1453. It was named for the Roman emperor Constantine the Great when he enlarged the Greek city of Byzantium in 328 and declared it the capital of the ◊Byzantine Empire 330. Its elaborate fortifications enabled it to resist a succession of sieges, but it was captured by crusaders 1204, and was the seat of a Latin (Western European) kingdom until recaptured by the Greeks 1261. An attack by the Turks 1422 proved unsuccessful, but it was taken by another Turkish army May 29, 1453 after nearly a year's siege, and became the capital of the Ottoman Empire.

constant prices a series of prices adjusted to reflect real purchasing power. If wages were to rise by 15% from $100 per week (to $115) and the rate of inflation was 10% (requiring $110 to maintain spending power), the real wage would have risen by 5%. Also an index used to create a constant price series, unlike ◊current prices.

constellation one of the 88 areas into which the sky is divided for the purposes of identifying and naming celestial objects. The first constellations were simple, arbitrary patterns of stars in which early civilizations visualized gods, sacred beasts, and mythical heroes.

The constellations in use today are derived from a list of 48 known to the ancient Greeks, who inherited some from the Babylonians. The current list of 88 constellations was adopted by the International Astronomical Union, astronomy's governing body, in 1930.

constitution the fundamental laws of a nation, laying down the system of government and defining the relations of the legislature, executive, and judiciary to each other and to the citizens. Since the French Revolution almost all countries (the UK is one exception) have adopted written constitutions; that of the US (1787) is the oldest.

Constitutional Convention meeting in Philadelphia in 1787 during which the US Constitution was written. Delegates from 12 states (Rhode Island did not attend) had gathered to revise the Articles of Confederation, but eventually decided that the flaws in the Articles were so great that a new form of government was required. The convention, chaired by George Washington, resolved the power struggles between the small and large states and established the tripartite form of government that exists today in the US. The primary authors of the Constitution, whose draft was endorsed in Sept 1787, included James Madison and Alexander Hamilton.

Constructivism revolutionary art movement founded in Moscow 1917 by the Russians Naum ◊Gabo, Antoine Pevsner (1886–1962), and Vladimir Tatlin (1885–1953). Tatlin's abstract sculptures, using wood, metal, and clear plastic, were hung on walls or suspended from ceilings. The brothers Gabo and Pevsner soon left the USSR and joined the European avant-garde.

consul chief magistrate of ancient Rome following the expulsion of the last king in 510 BC. The consuls were two annually elected magistrates, both of equal power; they jointly held full civil power in Rome and the chief military command in the field. After the establishment of the Roman Empire the office became purely honorary.

Today, a consul is a state official, with political and commercial responsibilities, who looks after the nation's citizens in major foreign cities.

consumer durable or durable goods a commodity that is required to satisfy personal requirements and that has a long life, such as furniture and electrical goods, as opposed to food and drink, which are perishables and have to be replaced frequently.

consumer price index a yearly index of the cost of goods and services to the consumer needed for an average standard of living. See also ◊producer price index.

The US Department of Labor reforms its consumer price index (CPI), the most widely used measure of inflation, periodically, establishing a base year at 100. Prices 20% higher than those in the base year would thus be expressed as 120. The index is calculated on the spending habits of salaried employees, wage earners, and retired and unemployed persons in 85 metropolitan areas. The income of almost half the US population is related to the CPI through collective bargaining agreements, alimony, rent, and Social Security payments, all of which are linked to changes in the cost of living. The items making up the "market basket" of typical consumer purchases are also revised periodically, reflecting changes in consumer spending habits.

consumer protection laws and measures designed to ensure fair trading for buyers. Responsibility for checking goods and services for quality, safety, and suitability has in the past few years moved increasingly away from the consumer to the producer.

In earlier days it was assumed that consumers could safeguard themselves by common sense, testing before purchase, and confronting the seller personally if they were dissatisfied. Today the technical complexities of products, the remoteness of outlets from the original producer, and pressures from advertising require protection for the consumer.

In the US both federal and state governments make special provisions for consumer protection. In 1962 President Kennedy set out the four basic rights of the consumer: to safety, to be informed, to choose, and to be heard. There are many private consumer associations, and among the most vociferous of crusaders for greater protection has been Ralph ◊Nader.

Consumers Union a private organization formed to protect consumers' interests, usually in terms of quality and safety.

In the US, Consumers Union publishes *Consumer Reports*, a monthly summary of tests and comparisons conducted by independent researchers. The group is part of a growing movement of consumer advocacy that seeks to inform the public and hold manufacturers responsible for their products. See also Ralph ◊Nader.

consumption the purchase and use of goods and services. In economics, it means a country's total expenditure over a given period (usually a year) on goods and services (including expenditure on raw materials and defense).

consumption (Latin *consumptio* "wasting") former name for the disease ◊tuberculosis.

contact lens a lens, made of soft or hard plastic, that is worn in contact with the cornea and conjunctiva of the eye, beneath the eyelid, to correct defective vision. In special circumstances, contact lenses may be used as protective shells or for cosmetic purposes, such as changing eye color.

The earliest use of contact lenses in the late 19th century was protective, or in the correction of corneal malformation. It was not until the 1930s that simplification of fitting technique by taking eye impressions made general use possible. Recent developments are a type of soft lens that can be worn for lengthy periods without removal, and a disposable soft lens that needs no cleaning but should be discarded after a week of constant wear.

contado in northern and central Italy from the 9th to 13th centuries, the territory under a count's jurisdiction. During the 13th century, this jurisdiction passed to the cities, and it came to refer to the rural area over which a city exerted political and economic control.

Contadora Panamanian island of the Pearl Island group in the Gulf of Panama. It was the first meeting place 1983 of the foreign ministers of Colombia, Mexico, Panama, and Venezuela (now known as the Contadora Group) who came together to discuss the problems of Central America.

Contadora Group an alliance formed between Colombia, Mexico, Panama, and Venezuela Jan 1983 to establish a general peace treaty for Central America.

The process was designed to include the formation of a Central American parliament (similar to the European parliament). Support for Contadora has come from Argentina, Brazil, Peru, and Uruguay, as well as from the Central American states.

containment US policy dating from 1947 designed to prevent the spread of communism beyond the borders of the USSR.

contempt of court behavior that shows contempt for the authority of a court, such as disobeying a court order; behavior that disrupts, prejudices, or interferes with court proceedings; and abuse of judges, inside or outside a court. The court may punish contempt with a fine or imprisonment.

continent any one of the large land masses of Earth, as distinct from ocean. They are Asia, Africa, North America, South America, Europe, Australia, and Antarctica. Continents are constantly moving and evolving (see ◊plate tectonics). A continent does not end at the coastline; its boundary is the edge of the shallow continental shelf (part of the continental ◊crust, made of ◊sial), which may extend several hundred miles or kilometers out to sea.

At the center of each continental mass lies a shield or ◊craton, a deformed mass of old ◊metamorphic rocks dating from Precambrian times. The shield is thick, compact, and solid (the Canadian Shield is an example), having undergone all the mountain-building activity it is ever likely to, and is usually worn flat. Around the shield is a concentric pattern of fold mountains, with older ranges, such as the Rockies, closest to the shield, and younger ranges, such as the coastal ranges of North America, farther away. This general concentric pattern is modified when two continental masses have drifted together and they become welded with a great mountain range along the join, the way Europe and N Asia are joined along the Urals. If a continent is torn apart, the new continental edges have no fold mountains; for instance, South America has fold mountains (the Andes) along its western flank, but none along the east where it tore away from Africa 200 million years ago.

Continental Congress in US history, the federal legislature of the original 13 states, acting as a provisional revolutionary government during the

continent

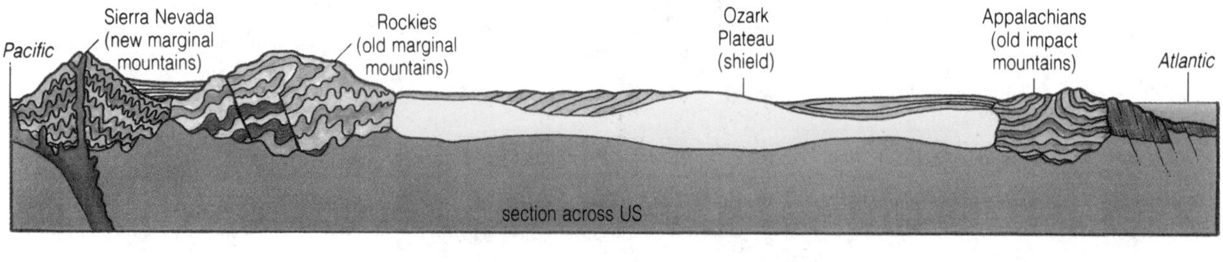
Sierra Nevada
(new marginal
mountains)
Pacific
Rockies
(old marginal
mountains)
Ozark
Plateau
(shield)
Appalachians
(old impact
mountains)
Atlantic
section across US

continental drift

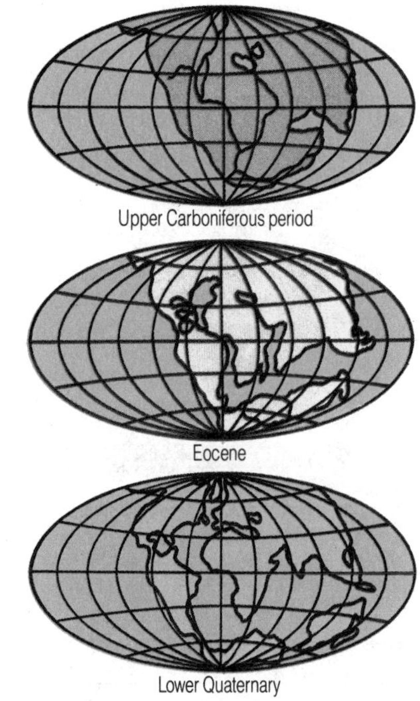
Upper Carboniferous period
Eocene
Lower Quaternary

◊American Revolution. It convened in Philadelphia from 1774 until 1789, when the US Constitution was adopted. The Second Continental Congress, convened May 1775, was responsible for drawing up the ◊Declaration of Independence and, in 1777, the Articles of ◊Confederation. The Congress authorized an army to resist the British and issued paper money to finance the war effort. It also oversaw the deliberations of the Constitutional Convention.

continental drift in geology, theory proposed by the German meteorologist Alfred Wegener in 1915 that, about 200 million years ago, Earth consisted of a single large continent (◊Pangaea) that subsequently broke apart to form the continents known today. Such vast continental movements could not be satisfactorily explained until the study of ◊plate tectonics in the 1960s.

continental rise the portion of the ocean floor rising gently from the abyssal plain toward the steeper continental slope. The continental rise is a depositional feature formed from sediments transported down the slope mainly by turbidity currents. Much of the continental rise actually consists of coalescing submarine alluvial fans bordering the continental slope.

continental slope the sloping, submarine portion of a continent. It extends downward from the continental margin at the edge of the continental shelf. In some places, such as S of the Aleutian Islands of Alaska, continental slopes extend directly to the ocean deeps or abyssal plain. In others, such as the E coast of North America, they grade into the gentler continental rises that in turn grade into the abyssal plains.

Continental System the system of economic preference and protection within Europe created by the French emperor Napoleon in order to exclude British trade. Apart from its function as economic warfare, the system also reinforced the French economy at the expense of other European states. It lasted 1806–13 but failed due to British naval superiority.

continuity in mathematics, property of functions of a real variable that have an absence of "breaks." A function f is said to be continuous at a point a if $\lim f(x) = f(a)$.

continuo abbreviation for *basso continuo*; in music, the bass line on which a keyboard player, often accompanied by a bass stringed instrument, built up a harmonic accompaniment in 17th-century Baroque music.

continuum in mathematics, a ◊set that is infinite and everywhere continuous, such as the set of points on a line.

Contra member of a Central American right-wing guerrilla force attempting to overthrow the democratically elected Nicaraguan Sandinista government 1979–90. The Contras, many of them mercenaries or former members of the deposed Somoza's guard (see ◊Nicaraguan Revolution), operated mainly from bases outside Nicaragua, mostly in Honduras, with covert US funding as revealed by the ◊Irangate hearings 1986–87. In 1989 President Bush announced an agreement with Congress to provide $41 million in "nonlethal" aid to the Contras until Feb 1990. The Sandinista government was defeated in the Feb 1990 elections by the National Opposition Union, a US-backed coalition.

contrabassoon a larger version of the ◊bassoon, sounding an octave lower.

contraceptive any drug, device, or technique that prevents pregnancy. The contraceptive pill (the ◊Pill) contains female hormones that interfere with egg production or the first stage of pregnancy. The "morning-after" pill can be taken after unprotected intercourse. Barrier contraceptives include ◊condoms (sheaths), diaphragms, and cervical caps; they prevent the sperm entering the cervix (neck of the womb). Condoms are available in drugstores; diaphragms must be fitted by a physician and used with a spermicide (cream or jelly); cervical caps, although used in Europe for decades, are only now becoming legal and available in some states of the US. ◊Intrauterine devices, also known as IUDs or coils, are made of plastics and metals and cause a slight inflammation of the lining of the womb; this prevents the fertilized egg from becoming implanted. See also ◊family planning.

Other contraceptive methods include ◊sterilization (women) and ◊vasectomy (men); these are usually nonreversible. "Natural" methods include withdrawal of the penis before ejaculation (coitus interruptus), and avoidance of intercourse at the time of ovulation (◊rhythm method). These methods are unreliable and normally only used on religious grounds. A new development is a sponge impregnated with spermicide that is inserted into the vagina. The use of any contraceptive (birth control) is part of family planning.

The effectiveness of a contraceptive method is often given as a percentage. To say that a method has 95% effectiveness means that, on average, out of 100 healthy couples using that method for a year, 95 will not conceive.

contract agreement between two or more parties that may be enforced by law, according to the intention of the parties.

A contract made in the proper form may be unenforceable if it is made under a mistake, misrepresentation, duress, or undue influence, or if one of the parties does not have the capacity to make it (for example, ◊minors and people who are insane). Illegal contracts are void, including those to commit a crime or civil wrong, those to trade with the enemy, immoral contracts, and contracts in restraint of trade. Contracts by way of gaming and wagering are also void.

In a contract each party mutually obliges himself or herself to the other for exchange of property or performance for a consideration. If the contract is written, the document sets out the conditions of agreement.

contract bridge card game first played 1925. From 1930 it quickly outgrew ◊auction bridge in popularity.

contractile root in botany, a thickened root at the base of a corm, bulb, or other organ that helps position it at an appropriate level in the ground. Contractile roots are found, for example, on the corms of *Crocus*. After they have become anchored in the soil, the upper portion contracts, pulling the plant deeper into the ground.

convergent evolution

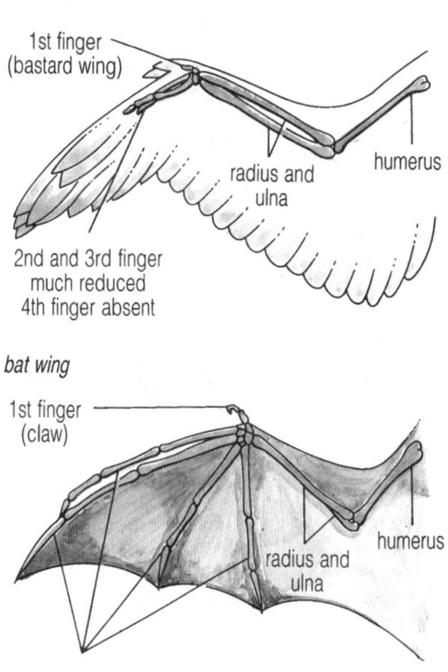
bird wing
1st finger
(bastard wing)
radius and
ulna
humerus
2nd and 3rd finger
much reduced
4th finger absent
bat wing
1st finger
(claw)
radius and
ulna
humerus

contractile vacuole tiny organelle found in many single-celled fresh-water organisms. It slowly fills with water, and then contracts, expelling the water from the cell.

Fresh-water protozoa such as *Amoeba* absorb water by the process of ◊osmosis, and this excess must be eliminated. The rate of vacuole contraction slows as the external salinity is increased, because the osmotic effect weakens; marine protozoa do not have a contractile vacuole.

contrapuntal in music, a work employing ◊counterpoint.

control experiment an essential part of a scientifically valid experiment, designed to show that the factor being tested is actually responsible for the effect observed. In the control experiment all factors, apart from the one under test, are exactly the same as in the test experiments, and all the same measurements are carried out. In drug trials, a placebo (a harmless substance) is given alongside the substance being tested in order to compare effects.

convection heat energy transfer that involves the movement of a fluid (gas or liquid). According to kinetic theory, molecules of fluid in contact with the source of heat expand and tend to rise within the bulk of the fluid. Less energetic, cooler molecules sink to take their place, setting up convection currents. This is the principle of natural convection in many domestic hot-water systems and space heaters.

convent religious house for ◊nuns.

conventionalism the view that ◊a priori truths, logical axioms, or scientific laws have no absolute validity but are disguised conventions representing one of a number of possible alternatives. The French philosopher and mathematician Jules Henri Poincaré introduced this position into philosophy of science.

convergence in mathematics, property of a series of numbers in which the difference between consecutive terms gradually decreases. The sum of a converging series approaches a limit as the number of terms tends to ◊infinity.

convergent evolution the independent evolution of similar structures in species (or other taxonomic groups) that are not closely related, as a result of living in a similar way. Thus, birds and bats have wings, not because they are descended from a common winged ancestor, but because their respective ancestors independently evolved flight.

converse in mathematics, the reversed order of a conditional statement; the converse of the statement "if a, then b" is "if b, then a." The converse does not always hold true; for example, the converse of "if $x = 3$, then $x^2 = 9$" is "if $x^2 = 9$, then $x = 3$," which is not true, as x could also be -3.

convertiplane type of ◊vertical takeoff aircraft with rotors on its wings that spin horizontally for takeoff, but tilt to spin in a vertical plane for forward flight.

At takeoff it looks like a two-rotor helicopter, with both rotors facing skyward. As forward speed is gained, the rotors tilt slowly forward until they are facing directly ahead. There are several different forms of convertiplane. The LTV-Hillier-Ryan XC-142, designed in the US, had wings, carrying the four engines and propellers, that rotated. The German VC-400 had two rotors on each of its wingtips. Neither of these designs went into production. A recent Boeing and Bell design, the Osprey, uses a pair of tilting engines, with propellers 38 ft/11.5 m across, mounted at the end of the wings. It is intended eventually to carry about 50 passengers direct to city centers. The design should also be useful for search and rescue operations and for transport to offshore oil rigs.

convex lens a converging ◊lens – that is, a parallel beam of light passing through it converges and is eventually brought to a focus; it can therefore produce a real image on a screen. Such a lens is wider at its center than at the edges.

Common forms include biconvex (with both surfaces curved outward) and plano-convex (with one flat surface and one convex). The whole lens may be further curved overall, making a concavo-convex or converging meniscus lens, as in some lenses used in corrective eyewear.

conveyancing the administrative process involved in transferring title to land, usually on its sale or purchase.

conveyor a device used for transporting materials. Widely used throughout industry is the conveyor belt, usually a rubber or fabric belt running on rollers. Trough-shaped belts are used, for example in mines, for transporting ores and coal. Chain conveyors are also used in coal mines to remove coal from the cutting machines. Overhead endless chain conveyors are used to carry components and bodies in car assembly works. Other types include bucket conveyors and screw conveyors, powered versions of ◊Archimedes screw.

convolvulus or ***bindweed*** any plants of the genus *Convolvulus* of the morning-glory family Convolvulaceae. They are characterized by their twining stems and by their petals, which are united into a funnel-shaped tube.

The hedge bindweed *C. sepium*, a trailing plant with spear-shaped leaves and large, pinkish-white flowers, is native to N Eurasia and North America.

convoy system grouping of ships to sail together under naval escort in wartime. In World War I (1914–18) navy escort vessels were at first used only to accompany troopships, but the convoy system was adopted for merchant shipping when the unrestricted German submarine campaign began 1917. In World War II (1939–45) it was widely used by the Allies to keep the Atlantic sea lanes open.

convulsion series of violent contractions of the muscles over which the patient has no control. It may be associated with loss of consciousness.

Convulsions may arise from any one of a number of causes, including brain disease (such as ◊epilepsy), injury, high fever, poisoning, and electrocution.

Cook, Mount highest point, 12,353 ft/3,764 m, of the Southern Alps, range of mountains running through New Zealand.

***Cook** Captain James Cook was the English naval explorer who sailed to the south seas, discovering Tahiti, New Zealand, and Australia.*

Cook James 1728–1779. English naval explorer. After surveying the St Lawrence 1759, he made three voyages: 1769–71 to Tahiti, New Zealand, and Australia; 1772–75 to the South Pacific; and 1776–79 to the South and North Pacific, attempting to find the Northwest Passage and charting the Siberian coast. He was killed in Hawaii.

In 1768 Cook was given command of an expedition to the South Pacific to witness Venus eclipsing the sun. He sailed in the *Endeavor* with Joseph ◊Banks and other scientists, reaching Tahiti Apr 1769. He then sailed around New Zealand and made a detailed survey of the E coast of Australia, naming New South Wales and Botany Bay. He returned to England June 12, 1771. Now a commander, Cook set out 1772 with the *Resolution* and *Adventure* to search for the Southern Continent. The location of Easter Island was determined, and the Marquesas and Tonga Islands plotted. He also went to New Caledonia and Norfolk Island. Cook returned July 25, 1775, having sailed 60,000 mi in three years. On June 25, 1776, he began his third and last voyage with the *Resolution* and *Discovery*. On the way to New Zealand, he visited several of the Cook or Hervey Islands and revisited the Hawaiian or Sandwich Islands. The ships sighted the North American coast at latitude 45° N and sailed north hoping to discover the Northwest Passage. He made a continuous survey as far as the Bering Strait, where the way was blocked by ice. Cook then surveyed the opposite coast of the strait (Siberia), and returned to Hawaii early 1779, where he was killed in a scuffle with islanders.

Cook Thomas 1808–1892. Pioneer British travel agent and founder of Thomas Cook & Son. He introduced traveler's cheques (then called "circular notes") in the early 1870s.

Cooke Alistair 1908– . British-born US journalist. He is best known for his writings interpreting US history and culture and for his role as television host of "Omnibus" and "Masterpiece Theatre."

Cooke studied theater at Yale and Harvard universities and returned to the US as a BBC correspondent 1938; he became a US citizen 1941. In 1947 he began his radio broadcast "Letter from America" for the BBC. During the 1970s, he hosted the BBC-produced television series "America" 1972–73 and followed this with the bestselling book *Alistair Cooke's America* 1973, based on the series.

Cooke Sam 1931–1964. US soul singer and songwriter who began his career as a gospel singer and turned to pop music in 1956. His hits include "You Send Me" 1957 and "Wonderful World" 1960 (re-released 1986).

cooking the heat treatment of food to make it more palatable, digestible, and safe. It breaks down connective tissue in meat, making it tender, and softens the cellulose in plant tissue. Some nutrients may be lost in the process, but this does not affect the overall nutritional value of a balanced diet.

cooking

cooking method	*description*
moist heat	
pan broiling	heat through hot dry metal
sautéing	pan broiling with fat
deep frying	food is immersed in hot fat
shallow frying	fat is used to stop sticking
simmering	in pan with water below boiling point
stewing	prolonged simmering
fricasée	sauté and stewing
devilling	grilled or fried after coating food
steaming	cooking by steam
pressure cooking	by steam, above the boiling point, under pressure
dry heat	
baking	cooked in an oven
roasting	cooked in an oven
grilling	direct heat onto food
broiling	direct heat over flame
microwave	
microwaving	microwaves cause oscillation of food molecules, which produces heat
NUTRIENT LOSS DURING COOKING	
cooking method	*nutrients lost*
steaming *and* pressure cooking	40–70% vitamin C, some vitamin B and phosphorus
toasting	10–30% thiamin
baking	some vitamins B and C
microwave	some vitamins B and C
dry heat	20–30% vitamin B

Cookery has been practiced since prehistoric times, becoming fairly sophisticated in the aristocratic societies of ancient civilizations. Professional cooks existed in medieval Europe but cooking as a recognized art originated in 16th-century Italy and was developed in 17th-century France. French pre-eminence in cooking remained unchallenged until the 1940s, when rapidly increasing interest led to the rediscovery and appreciation of traditional cooking styles worldwide.

Cook Islands group of six large and a number of smaller Polynesian islands 1,600 mi/2,600 km NE of Auckland, New Zealand; area 112 sq mi/290 sq km; population (1986) 17,000. Their main products include fruit, copra, and crafts. They became a self-governing overseas territory of New Zealand 1965.

The chief island, Rarotonga, is the site of Avarua, the seat of government. Niue, geographically part of the group, is separately administered. The Cook Islands were visited by Capt Cook 1773, annexed by Britain 1888, and transferred to New Zealand 1901. They have common citizenship with New Zealand.

Cook Strait strait dividing North Island and South Island, New Zealand. A submarine cable carries electricity from South to North Island.

coolabah Australian riverside tree *Eucalyptus microtheca* of the myrtle family Myrtaceae.

Cooley's anemia alternate name for ◊thalassemia.

Coolidge (John) Calvin 1872–1933. the 30th president of the US 1923–29, a Republican. As governor of Massachusetts 1919, he was responsible for crushing a Boston police strike. As Warren ◊Harding's vice-president 1921–23, he succeeded to the presidency upon Harding's death (Aug 2, 1923). He won the 1924 presidential election, and his period of office was marked by great economic prosperity.

Coolidge declined to run for reelection in 1928, supporting his secretary of the interior, Herbert ◊Hoover, who won the presidency.

Cooper Gary 1901–1962. US film actor. He epitomized the lean, true-hearted Yankee, slow of speech but capable of outdoing the "bad guys" in *Lives of a Bengal Lancer* 1935, *Mr Deeds Goes to*

Coolidge *The 30th president of the United States of America, Calvin Coolidge, a Republican. 1923–1929.*

Town (Academy Award for best picture 1936), *Sergeant York* 1940 (Academy Award for best actor 1941), and *High Noon* (Academy Award for best actor 1952).

Cooper James Fenimore 1789–1851. US writer, considered the first great US novelist. He wrote about 50 novels, mostly about the frontier, wilderness life, and the sea. He is best remembered for his ◊Leatherstocking Tales, a series of five novels: *The Pioneers* 1823, *The Last of the Mohicans* 1826, *The Prairie* 1827, *The Pathfinder* 1840, and *The Deerslayer* 1841. All describe the adventures of the frontier hero Natty Bumppo before and after the American Revolution.

Cooper was born in Burlington, New Jersey, son of the wealthy landowner who founded Cooperstown, New York. He grew up in that frontier settlement and after expulsion from Yale sailed as an apprentice seaman in Europe. In 1811 he married the wealthy Susan DeLancey and became a gentleman farmer, achieving success as a writer with his novel *The Spy* 1821. He then moved to New York City, where he became a member of the Knickerbocker Group of writers. Cooper lived and wrote in Europe for seven years before returning to New York 1833 to live in Cooperstown. His many works include *The Pilot* 1823 (the first American novel of the sea) *The Red Rover* 1828, and *Satanstoe* 1845.

Cooper Leon 1930– . British physicist who in 1955 began work on the puzzling phenomena of ◊superconductivity. He proposed that at low temperatures electrons would be bound in pairs (since known as Cooper pairs) and in this state electrical resistance to their flow through solids would disappear. He shared the 1972 Nobel Prize for Physics with ◊Bardeen and Schrieffer.

Cooper Susie. Married name Susan Vera Barker 1902– . English pottery designer. Her style has varied from colorful Art Deco to softer, pastel decoration on more Classical shapes. She started her own company 1929, which later became part of the Wedgwood factory, where she was senior designer from 1966.

cooperative movement the banding together of groups of people for mutual assistance in trade, manufacture, the supply of credit, housing, or other services. The original principles of the cooperative movement were laid down 1844 by the Rochdale Pioneers, under the influence of Robert Owen, and by Charles Fourier in France.

In the US, the period from 1915 to 1930 saw the greatest growth in the number of cooperative associations because they were recognized under statute laws rather than simply under common law. By the 1960s, agricultural cooperatives had declined dramatically because of mergers and more technically advanced marketing procedures. The future for cooperative associations is seen in the areas of consumers' associations, workers' groups, and the housing market.

coordinate in geometry, a number that defines the position of a point relative to a point or axis. ◊Cartesian coordinates define a point by its perpendicular distances from two or more axes drawn through a fixed point at right angles to each other; ◊polar coordinates define a point in a plane by its distance from a fixed point and direction from a fixed line.

coordinate geometry or ***analytical geometry*** a system of geometry in which points, lines, shapes, and surfaces are represented by algebraic expressions. In plane (two-dimensional) coordinate geometry, the plane is usually defined by two axes at right angles to each other, the horizontal x-axis and the vertical y-axis, meeting at O, the origin. A point on the plane can be represented by a pair of ◊Cartesian coordinates, which define its position in terms of its distance along the x-axis and along the y-axis from O. These distances are respectively the x and y coordinates of the point.

Lines are represented as equations; for example, $y = 2x + 1$ gives a straight line, and $y = 3x^2 + 2x$ gives a ◊parabola (a curve). The graphs of varying equations can be drawn by plotting the coordinates of points that satisfy their equations, and joining up the points. One of the advantages of coordinate geometry is that geometrical solutions can be obtained without drawing but by manipulating algebraic expressions. For example, the coordinates of the point of intersection of two straight lines can be determined by finding the unique values of x and y that satisfy both of the equations for the lines, that is, by solving them as a pair of ◊simultaneous equations. The curves studied in simple coordinate geometry are the ◊conic sections (circle, ellipse, parabola, and hyperbola), each of which has a characteristic equation.

coot any of various freshwater birds of the genus *Fulica* in the rail family. Coots are about 1.2 ft/ 38 cm long, and mainly black. They have a white bill, extending up the forehead in a plate, and big feet with lobed toes.

The American coot *F. americana* is found in North and South America and the Caribbean. It feeds on plants, insects, and small fish.

Copán town in W Honduras; population (1983) 19,000. The nearby site of a Mayan city, including a temple and pyramids, was bought by John Stephens of the US in the 1830s for $50.

cope semicircular cape, without sleeves, worn by priests of the Western Christian church in processions and on some other formal occasions, but not when officiating at Mass.

Copenhagen (Danish *København*) capital of Denmark, on the islands of Zealand and Amager; population (1988) 1,344,000 (including suburbs).

To the NE is the royal palace at Amalienborg; the 17th-century Charlottenburg Palace houses the Academy of Arts, and parliament meets in the Christiansborg Palace. The statue of Hans Christian Andersen's "Little Mermaid" (by Edvard Eriksen) is at the harbor entrance. The Tivoli amusement park is on the shore of the Øresund ("The Sound," between Copenhagen and S Sweden).

Copenhagen was a fishing village until 1167, when the bishop of Roskilde built the castle on the site of the present Christiansborg palace. A settlement grew up, and it became the Danish capital 1443. The university was founded 1479. The city was under German occupation Apr 1940–May 1945.

copepod ◊crustacean of the subclass Copepoda, mainly microscopic and found in plankton.

Coper Hans 1920–1981. German potter, originally an engineer. His work resembles Cycladic Greek pots in its monumental quality.

Copernicus Nicolaus 1473–1543. Polish astronomer who believed that the Sun, not Earth, is at the center of the Solar System, thus defying the church doctrine of the time. For 30 years he worked on the hypothesis that the rotation and the orbital motion of Earth were responsible for

Copland *Twentieth-century composer and conductor Aaron Copland.*

the apparent movement of the heavenly bodies. His great work *De Revolutionibus Orbium Coelestium/About the Revolutions of the Heavenly Spheres* was not published until the year of his death.

Born at Torun on the Vistula, then under the Polish king, he studied at Kraków and in Italy, and lectured on astronomy at Rome. On his return to Pomerania 1505 he became physician to his uncle, the bishop of Ermland, and was made canon at Frauenburg, although he did not take holy orders. Living there until his death, he interspersed astronomical work with the duties of various civil offices.

Copland Aaron 1900–1990. US composer and conductor. Copland's early works, such as the piano concerto of 1926, were in the jazz idiom but he gradually developed a gentler symphonic style with a regional flavor drawn from American folk music.

Born in New York, he studied in France with Nadia Boulanger, and in 1940 became instructor in composition at the Berkshire Music Center. After 1945 he was the assistant director. Among his later works are the ballets *Billy the Kid* 1939; *Rodeo* 1942; and *Appalachian Spring* 1944, based on a poem by Hart Crane; and *Inscape for Orchestra* 1967.

Copley John Singleton 1738–1815. American painter. He was the leading portraitist of the colonial period, but from 1775 he lived mainly in London, where he painted lively historical scenes such as *The Death of Major Pierson* 1783 (Tate Gallery, London).

Copley was born in Boston, Massachusetts. Some of his history paintings are unusual in that they portray dramatic events of his time, such as *Brook Watson and the Shark* 1778 (National Gallery, Washington, DC).

copper orange-pink, very malleable and ductile, metallic element, symbol Cu (from Latin *cuprum*), atomic number 29, atomic weight 63.546. It occurs in ores and also as a free metal (see ◊native metal). It is used for its toughness, softness, pliability, high thermal and electrical conductivity, and resistance to corrosion.

It was the first metal used systematically for tools by humans; when mined and worked into utensils it was the basis for the Copper Age in prehistory. When alloyed with tin it forms bronze, which strengthens the copper, allowing it to hold a sharp edge; the systematic production and use of this was the basis for the prehistoric Bronze Age. Brass, another hard copper alloy, includes zinc. The name comes from the Greek for Cyprus (*Kyprios*), which was noted for its copper mines.

copper ore any mineral from which copper is extracted, including native copper, Cu; chalcocite, Cu_2S; chalcopyrite, $CuFeS_2$; bornite, Cu_5FeS_4;

Coppola *Filmmaker Francis Ford Coppola is the genius behind* The Godfather *series.*

azurite, $Cu_3(CO_3)_2(OH)_2$; malachite, $Cu_2CO_3(OH)_2$; and chrysocolla, $CuSiO_3.nH_2O$.

Native copper and the copper sulfides are usually found in veins associated with igneous intrusions. Chrysocolla and the carbonates are products of the weathering of copper-bearing rocks. Copper was one of the first metals to be worked, because it occurred in native form and needed little refining. Today the main producers are the US, the USSR, Zambia, Chile, Peru, Canada, and Zaïre.

coppicing a severe type of pruning where trees are cut down to near ground level at regular intervals, typically every 3–20 years, to promote the growth of numerous shoots from the base.

This form of woodland management was once commonly practiced in Europe, especially on hazel and chestnut, to produce large quantities of thin branches for firewood, fencing, and so on; alder, eucalyptus, maple, poplar, and willow were also coppiced. The resulting thicket was known as a coppice or copse. See also ◊pollarding.

Coppola Francis Ford 1939– . US film director and screenwriter. After an early career working on "B movie" horror films, his first successes were *Finian's Rainbow* 1968 and *Patton* 1969, for which his screenplay won an Academy Award. He directed *The Godfather* 1972, which became one of the biggest money-making films of all time, and its sequel *The Godfather Part II* 1974, which garnered seven Academy Awards. His other films include *The Conversation* 1972, *Apocalypse Now* 1979, *One From the Heart* 1982, *Rumble Fish* 1983, *The Outsiders* 1983, *The Cotton Club* 1984, *Gardens of Stone* 1987, *Tucker: The Man and His Dream* 1988, and *The Godfather Part III* 1990.

copra dried meat from the kernel of the ◊coconut, pressed for coconut oil.

Copt a descendant of those ancient Egyptians who accepted Christianity in the 1st century and refused to adopt Islam after the Arab conquest. They now form a small minority (about 5%) of Egypt's population. The head of the Coptic Church is the Patriarch of Alexandria, currently Shenonda III (1923–), 117th pope of Alexandria. Imprisoned by President Sadat 1981, he is opposed by Muslim fundamentalists.

Before the Arab conquest a majority of Christian Egyptians had adopted Monophysite views (that Christ had "one nature" rather than being both human and divine.) When this was condemned by the Council of Chalcedon 451, they became schismatic and were persecuted by the orthodox party, to which they were opposed on nationalistic as well as religious grounds. They readily accepted Arab rule, but were later subjected to persecution by their new masters. They are mainly town-dwellers, distinguishable in dress and customs from their Muslim compatriots. They rarely marry outside their own sect.

Coptic language member of the Hamito-Semitic language family and a minority language of Egypt. It is descended from the language of the ancient Egyptians and is the ritual language of the Coptic Christian Church. It is written in the Greek alphabet with some additional characters derived from ◊demotic script.

copulation the act of mating in animals with internal ◊fertilization. Male mammals have a ◊penis or other organ, which is used to introduce spermatozoa into the reproductive tract of the female. Most birds transfer sperm by pressing their cloacas (the openings of their reproductive tracts) together.

copyhold a kind of land tenure common from medieval times. The term derives from the copy of the record written by the landowner stating the tenant's rights and dues. The document thus showed legal entitlement to the land.

copyright law applying to literary, musical, and artistic works (including plays, recordings, films, photographs, radio and television broadcasts, and, in the US and Britain, computer programs), which prevents the reproduction of the work, in whole or in part, without the author's consent and terms of payment.

Copyright applies to a work, not an idea. For example, the basic plots of two novels might be identical, but copyright would only be infringed if it was clear that one author had copied from another. A translation is protected in its own right. The copyright holder may assign the copyright to another or license others to reproduce or adapt the work.

In the US (since 1989) copyright lasts for a holder's lifetime plus 50 years, or a flat 75 years for a company copyright. It must be registered with the US Copyright Office of the Library of Congress to bring a court action. Works first federally copyrighted before 1978 must still be renewed in the 28th year to receive the second term of 47 years or it will fall into the public domain at the end of the 28th year. Various conditions apply to works published before 1989 and those between Jan 1, 1978 and March 1 1989. For specific information contact the Copyright Office, Library of Congress, Washington, DC. Copyright is internationally enforceable under the Berne Convention 1886 (ratified by the US March 1, 1989) and the Universal Copyright Convention 1952.

coral marine invertebrate of the class Anthozoa in the phylum Cnidaria, which also includes sea anemones and jellyfish. It has a skeleton of lime (calcium carbonate) extracted from the surrounding water. Corals exist in warm seas, at moderate depths with sufficient light. Some coral is valued for decoration or jewelry, for example Mediterranean red coral *Corallum rubrum*.

Corals live in a symbiotic relationship with microscopic ◊algae (zooxanthellae), which are incorporated into the soft tissue. The algae obtain carbon dioxide from the ◊polyps, and the polyps receive nutrients from the algae. Corals also have a relationship to the fish that rest or take refuge within their branches, and which excrete nutrients that make the corals grow faster. The majority of corals form large colonies; although there are species that live singly. Their accumulated skeletons make up large coral reefs and atolls. The Great Barrier Reef, to the NE of Australia, is about 1,000 mi/1,600 km long.

Coralli Jean 1779–1854. French dancer and choreographer of Italian descent. He made his debut as a dancer in 1802. He choreographed *Le Diable boîteux* 1836 for the Austrian ballerina Fanny Elssler, *Giselle* 1841 and *La Péri* 1843 for the Italian ballerina Grisi; and many other well-known ballets.

coralroot any leafless orchid of the genus *Corallorhiza*, having branched coral-colored roots and small yellowish or purplish flowers. These orchids are either parasitic on the roots of other plants, or saprophytes, living on decaying organic matter.

Coral Sea or *Solomon Sea* part of the Pacific Ocean bounded by NE Australia, New Guinea, the Solo-

coral

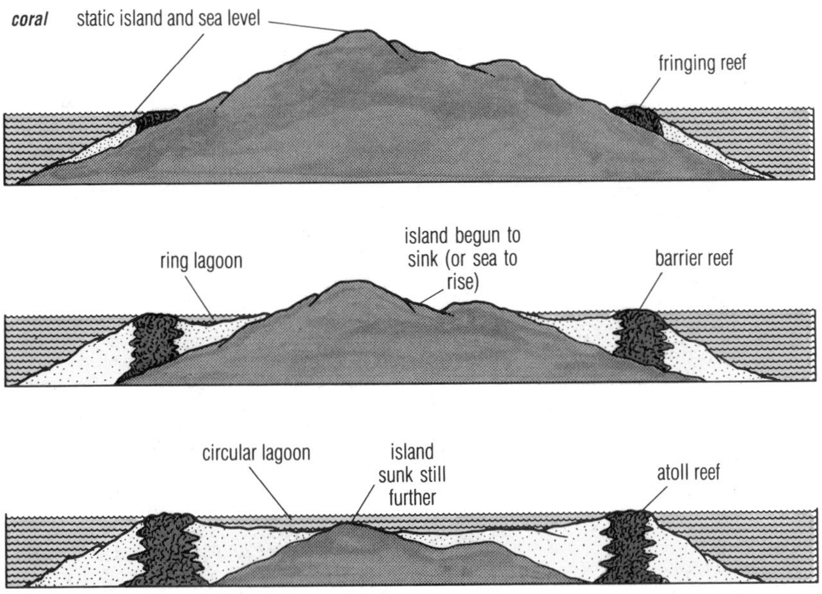
static island and sea level
fringing reef
ring lagoon
island begun to sink (or sea to rise)
barrier reef
circular lagoon
island sunk still further
atoll reef

mon Islands, Vanuatu, and New Caledonia. It contains numerous coral islands and reefs. The Coral Sea Islands are a Territory of Australia; they comprise scattered reefs and islands over an area of about 385,000 sq mi/1,000,000 sq km. They are uninhabited except for a meteorological station on Willis Island. In the World War II Battle of the Coral Sea, May 7–8, 1942, the US fleet prevented the Japanese from landing in SE New Guinea and thus threatening Australia. The Great Barrier Reef lies along the W edge of the sea, just off the E coast of Australia.

cor anglais English horn alto member of the ◊oboe family.

Corbett Gentleman Jim (James John) 1866–1933. US boxer. Corbett was born in San Francisco and after a brief career as a bank clerk became a professional boxer 1886. He eventually gained a national reputation for his elegant manner and his dangerous right hook (a punch that he popularized). Corbett gained the heavyweight title in his 1892 New Orleans fight with reigning champion John L Sullivan; this was the first title bout to be fought with gloves and according to the Marquis of Queensbury rules. Corbett held the title until his defeat 1897 by Robert Fitzsimmons.

Corbière Tristan 1845–1875. French poet. His *Les Amours jaunes/Yellow Loves* 1873 went unrecognized until Verlaine called attention to it in 1884. Many of his poems, such as *La Rhapsodie Foraine/Wandering Rhapsody*, deal with life in his native Brittany.

cord unit for measuring the volume of wood cut for fuel. One cord equals 128 cubic feet (3.456 cubic meters), or a stack 8 feet (2.4 m) long, 4 feet (1.2 m) wide, and 4 feet high.

Corday Charlotte 1768–1793. French Girondin (right-wing republican during the French Revolution). After the overthrow of the Girondins by the more extreme Jacobins May 1793, she stabbed to death the Jacobin leader, Marat, with a bread knife as he sat in his bath in July of the same year. She was guillotined.

cordierite a silicate mineral, $(Mg,Fe)_2Al_4Si_5O_{18}$, blue to purplish in color. It is characteristic of metamorphic rocks formed from clay sediments under conditions of low pressure but moderate temperature; it is the mineral that forms the spots in spotted slate and spotted hornfels.

cordillera a group of mountain ranges and their valleys, all running in a specific direction, formed by the continued convergence of two ◊tectonic plates along a line.

The whole western section of North America, including the Rocky Mountains and the coastal ranges parallel to the contact between the North American and the Pacific plates, is called the Western Cordillera.

Cordilleras, the the mountainous western section of North America, with the Rocky mountains and the coastal ranges parallel to the contact between the North American and the Pacific plates.

Córdoba city in central Argentina, on the Rio Primero; population (1980) 982,000. It is the capital of Córdoba province. Main industries include cement, glass, textiles, and vehicles. Founded in 1573, it has a university founded 1613, a military aviation college, an observatory, and a cathedral.

Córdoba capital of Córdoba province, Spain, on the river Guadalquivir; population (1986) 305,000. Paper, textiles, and copper products are manufactured here. It has many Moorish remains, including the mosque, now a cathedral, founded by 'Abd-ar-Rahman I in 785, which is one of the largest Christian churches in the world. Córdoba was probably founded by the Carthaginians; it was held by the Moors 711–1236.

core the innermost part of the structure of Earth. It is divided into an inner core, the upper boundary of which is 1,060 mi/1,700 km from the center, and an outer core, 1,130 mi/1,820 km thick. Both parts are thought to consist of iron-nickel alloy, with the inner core being solid and the outer core being liquid. The temperature may be 5,400°F/3,000°C.

These hypotheses are based on seismology (the observation of the paths of earthquake waves through the Earth), and calculations of the Earth's density.

Corelli Arcangelo 1653–1713. Italian composer and violinist. He was one of the first virtuoso violinists and his music, marked by graceful melody, includes a set of *concerti grossi* and five sets of chamber sonatas.

Born near Milan, he studied in Bologna and in about 1685 settled in Rome, under the patronage of Cardinal Pietro Ottoboni, where he published his first violin sonatas.

Corfu (Greek *Kérkira*) northernmost, and second largest of the Ionian islands, off the coast of Epirus in the Ionian Sea; area 414 sq mi/1,072 sq km; population (1981) 96,500. Its businesses include tourism, fruit, olive oil, and textiles. Its largest town is the port of Corfu (Kérkira), population (1981) 33,560. Corfu was colonized by the Corinthians about 700 BC. Venice held it 1386–1797, Britain from 1815–64.

Cori Carl 1896– and Gerty 1896–1957. Husband and wife team of US biochemists, both born in Prague, who, together with Bernardo Houssay, received a Nobel Prize 1947 for their discovery of how glycogen—a derivative of ◊glucose – is broken down and resynthesized in the body, for use as a store and source of energy.

coriander a pungent fresh herb, the Eurasian plant *Coriandrum sativum*, a member of the parsley family (Umbelliferae); and, as a spice, the dried ripe fruit. The spice is used commercially as a flavoring in meat products, bakery goods, tobacco, gin, liqueurs, chili, and curry powder. Both are much used in cooking in the Middle East, India, Mexico, and China.

Corinna lived 6th century BC. Greek lyric poet, said to have instructed Pindar. Only fragments of her poetry survive.

Corinth (Greek *Kórinthos*) port in Greece, on the isthmus connecting the Peloponnese with the mainland; population (1981) 22,650. The rocky isthmus is bisected by the 4 mi/6.5 km Corinth

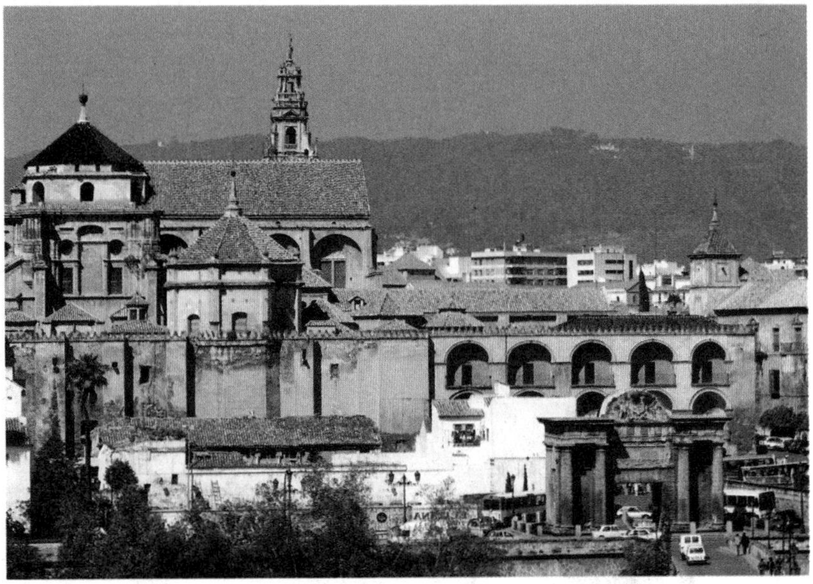

Córdoba *Córdoba's vast horizontal Mezquita was originally a mosque and was transformed into a cathedral in 1236.*

canal, opened 1893. The site of the ancient city-state of Corinth lies 4.5 mi/7 km SW.

Corinth was already a place of some commercial importance in the 9th century BC. At the end of the 6th century BC it joined the Peloponnesian League, and took a prominent part in the ◊Persian and the ◊Peloponnesian wars. In 146 BC it was conquered by the Romans. The emperor Augustus (63 BC–AD 14) made it capital of the Roman province of Achaea. St Paul visited Corinth AD 51 and addressed two epistles to its churches. After many changes of ownership it became part of independent Greece in 1822. Corinth's ancient monuments include the ruined temple of Apollo (6th century BC).

Corinthian in Classical architecture, one of the five types of column; see ◊order.

Corinthians two ◊epistles (Corinthians I, Corinthians II) in the New Testament to the church at Corinth; attributed to ◊Paul.

Coriolis effect a result of the deflective force of the Earth's west to east rotation. Winds, ocean currents, and aircraft are deflected to the right of their direction of travel in the Northern hemisphere and to the left in the Southern hemisphere.

The effect has to be allowed for in launching guided missiles, but despite popular belief it has negligible effect on the clockwise or anticlockwise direction of water running out of a bath. Named after its discoverer, French mathematician Gaspard Coriolis (1792–1843).

Cork city and seaport of county Cork, on the river Lee, at the head of the long inlet of Cork Harbor; population (1986) 174,000. Cork is the second port of the Republic of Ireland. The lower section of the harbor can berth liners, and the town has distilleries, shipyards, and iron foundries. St Finbarr's 7th-century monastery was the original foundation of Cork. It was eventually settled by Danes who were dispossessed by the English 1172.

cork the light, waterproof outer layers of the bark of the stems and roots of almost all trees and shrubs. The cork oak *Quercus suber*, a native of Southern Europe and North Africa, is cultivated in Spain and Portugal; the exceptionally thick outer layers of its bark provide the cork that is used commercially.

corm a short, swollen, underground plant stem, surrounded by protective scale leaves, as seen in *Crocus*. It stores food, provides a means of ◊vegetative reproduction, and acts as a ◊perennating organ.

During the year, the corm gradually withers as the food reserves are used for the production of leafy, flowering shoots formed from axillary buds. Several new corms are formed at the base of these shoots, above the old corm.

Corman Roger 1926– . US film director and producer. He directed a stylish series of Edgar Allan Poe films starring Vincent Price that began with

corm

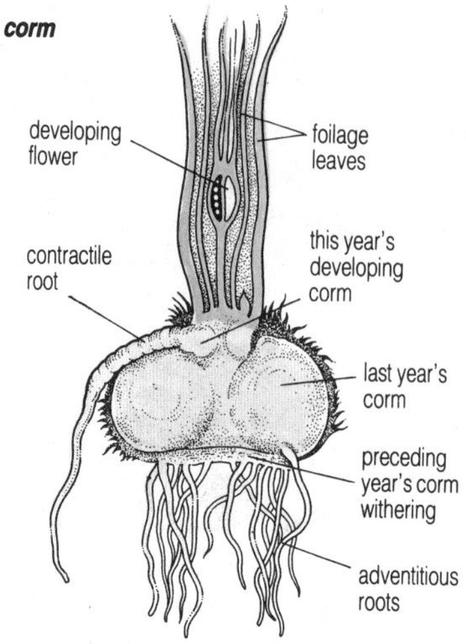
developing flower
foilage leaves
contractile root
this year's developing corm
last year's corm
preceding year's corm withering
adventitious roots

The House of Usher 1960. After 1970 Corman confined himself to production and distribution.

cormorant any of various diving seabirds, mainly of the genus *Phalacrocorax*, about 3 ft/90 cm long, with webbed feet, long neck, hooked beak, and glossy black plumage. There are some 30 species of cormorants worldwide including a flightless form *Nannopterum harrisi* in the Galápagos Islands. Cormorants generally feed on fish and shellfish. Some species breed on inland lakes and rivers.

corn a cultivated New World plant *Zea mays* of the grass family, with the grain borne on cobs enclosed in husks. It is also called corn or Indian corn. It was domesticated by 6,000 BC in Mesoamerica, where it grew wild. It became the staple crop for the ◊neolithic farming villages and ◊civilizations of Mexico and Peru; it was cultivated throughout most of the New World at the point of European contact. It was brought to Europe, Asia, and Africa by the colonizing powers, but its use is mainly for animal feed in those regions. In the US, a corn monoculture dominates the Midwest, where many hybrids have been developed for both human food and animal feed. Today it is grown extensively in all subtropical and warm temperate regions, and its range has been extended to colder zones by hardy varieties developed in the 1960s.

Corn is eaten fresh (on the cob or creamed), canned (niblets), frozen, and in dried forms (cornmeal, popcorn), and is made into hominy, polenta, cornflour, and corn bread. It is pressed for corn oil and fermented into a mash, which, distilled, is corn liquor (whiskey). Most of the methods of storing, processing, and cooking corn can be traced to American Indian recipes. Popcorn has been found in archeological sites in the SW dating from 4,000 BC. Corn stalks are made into paper and hardboard.

Corn Laws in Britain until 1846, laws used to regulate the export or import of cereals in order to maintain an adequate supply for consumers and a secure price for producers.

For centuries the Corn Laws formed an integral part of the mercantile system in England; they were repealed because they became an unwarranted tax on food and a hindrance to British exports. After the Napoleonic wars, with mounting pressure from a growing urban population, the Corn Laws aroused strong opposition because of their tendency to drive up prices. They were modified 1828 and 1842 and, partly as a result of the Irish potato famine, repealed by Robert Peel 1846. A remaining nominal duty was removed 1869.

cornea transparent front section of the vertebrate ◊eye. The cornea is curved and behaves as a fixed lens, so that light entering the eye is partly focused before it reaches the lens.

There are no blood vessels in the cornea and it relies on the fluid in the front chamber of the eye for nourishment. Further protection for the eye is provided by the ◊conjunctiva. In humans, diseased or opaque parts may be replaced by grafts of corneal tissue from a donor.

Corneille Pierre 1606–1684. French dramatist. His many tragedies, such as *Oedipe* 1659, glorify the strength of will governed by reason, and established the French Classical dramatic tradition for the next two centuries. His first play, *Mélite*, was performed 1629, followed by others that gained him a brief period of favor with Cardinal Richelieu. *Le Cid* 1636 was attacked by the Academicians, although it received public acclaim. Later plays were based on Aristotle's unities.

Although Corneille enjoyed public popularity, periodic disfavor with Richelieu marred his career, and it was not until 1639 that Corneille (again in favor) produced plays such as *Horace* 1639, *Polyeucte* 1643, *Le Menteur* 1643, and *Rodogune* 1645, leading to his election to the Académie 1647. His later plays were approved by Louis XIV.

Cornell Katherine 1898–1974. German-born US actress. Her first major success came with an appearance on Broadway in *Nice People* 1921. This debut was followed by a long string of New York stage successes, several of which were directed by her husband, Guthrie McClintic. By 1930 she began to produce her own plays; the most famous of them, *The Barretts of Wimpole Street* 1931, was later taken on tour and produced for television 1956.

Born in Berlin of American parents, Cornell was attracted to the stage at an early age, appearing with the Washington Square Players 1916.

cornet brass band instrument. It is like a shorter, broader trumpet, with a wider bore and mellower tone, and without fixed notes. Notes of different pitch are obtained by over-blowing and by means of three pistons.

cornett a 17th-century woodwind instrument. It has

coriander

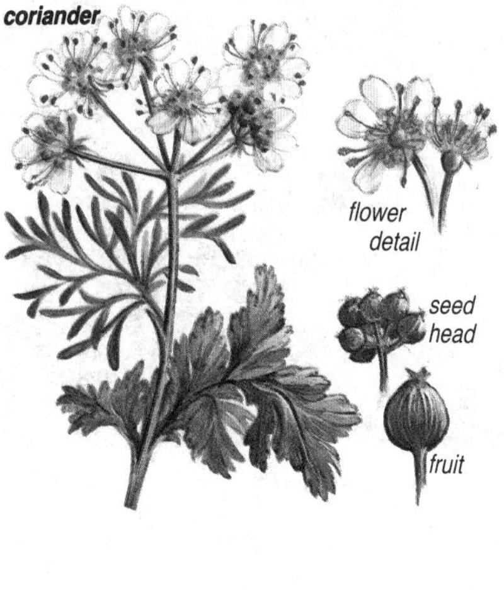
flower detail
seed head
fruit

corn

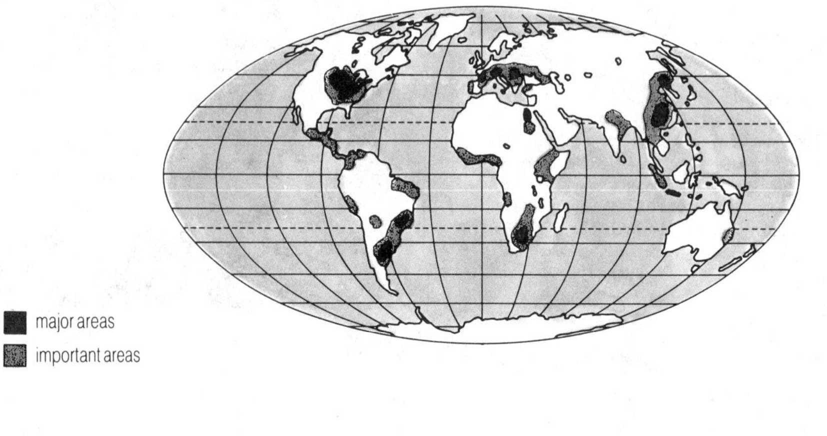
major areas
important areas

a cup mouthpiece and produces a trumpetlike tone.

cornflower plant *Centaurea cyanus* of the family Compositae. It is distinguished from the knapweeds by its deep azure-blue flowers. Formerly a common weed in N European wheat fields, it is now commonly grown in gardens as a herbaceous plant.

Cornforth John 1917– . Australian chemist who settled in England 1941. In 1975 he shared a Nobel Prize with Vladimir Prelog for work using ◊radioisotopes as "markers" to find out how enzymes synthesize chemicals that are mirror images of each other (stereo ◊isomers).

Corniche (French "mountain ledge") *la Grande* (Great) *Corniche*, a road with superb alpine and coastal scenery, built between Nice and Menton, S France, by Napoleon; it rises to 1,700 ft/520 m. *La Moyenne* (Middle) and *la Petite* (Little) *Corniche* are supplementary parallel roads, the latter being nearest the coast.

Cornish language extinct member of the ◊Celtic languages, a branch of the Indo-European language family, spoken in Cornwall, England, until 1777. Written Cornish first appeared in 10th-century documents; some religious plays were written in Cornish in the 15th and 16th centuries, but later literature is scanty, consisting mainly of folk tales and verses.

cornstarch purified, fine, powdery starch made from corn, used as a thickener in cooking and to make corn syrup commercially.

cornucopia (Latin "horn of plenty") in Greek mythology, one of the horns of the goat Amaltheia, which was caused by Zeus to refill itself indefinitely with food and drink. In paintings, the cornucopia is depicted as a horn-shaped container spilling over with fruit and flowers.

Cornwall county in SW England including ◊Scilly Islands (Scillies)

area (excluding Scillies) 1,370 sq mi/3,550 sq km

towns Truro (administrative headquarters), Camborne, Launceston; resorts of Bude, Falmouth, Newquay, Penzance, St Ives

physical Bodmin Moor (including Brown Willy 1,375 ft/419 m), Land's End peninsula, St Michael's Mount, rivers Tamar, Fowey, Fal, Camel

features Poldhu, site of first transatlantic radio signal 1901. The Stannary has six members from each of the four Stannary towns: Losthwithiel, Launceston, Helston, and Truro. The flag of St ◊Piran, a white St George's cross on a black ground, is used by separatists

products electronics, spring flowers, tin (mined since the Bronze Age, some workings renewed in 1960s, although the industry has all but disappeared), kaolin (St Austell), fish

population (1987) 453,000

famous people John Betjeman, Humphry Davy, Daphne Du Maurier, William Golding

history the Stannary or Tinners Parliament, established in the 11th century, ceased to meet 1752 but its powers were never rescinded at Westminster, and it was revived 1974 as a separatist movement.

Cornwallis Charles, 1st Marquess 1738–1805. British general in the ◊American Revolution until 1781, when his defeat at Yorktown led to final surrender and ended the war. He then served twice as governor general of India and once as viceroy of Ireland.

corolla a collective name for the petals of a flower. In some plants the petal margins are partially or completely fused to form a corolla tube, for example in morning glories *Convolvulus*.

Coromandel the E coast of Tamil Nadu, India.

Coromandel Peninsula peninsula on North Island, New Zealand, E of Auckland.

corona faint halo of hot (about 3,600,000°F/2,000,000°C) and tenuous gas around the Sun, which boils from the surface. It is visible at solar ◊eclipses or through a coronagraph, an instrument that blocks light from the Sun's brilliant disk. Gas flows away from the corona to form the ◊solar wind.

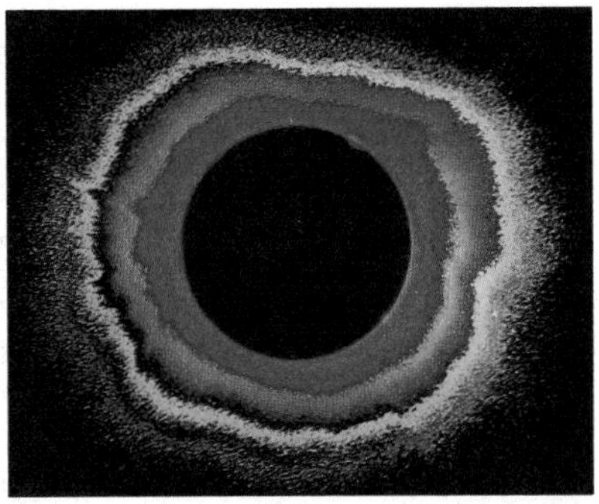

***corona** The corona, the Sun's outer atmosphere, which can be seen only during a total solar eclipse.*

Corona Australis or Southern Crown constellation of the southern hemisphere, located near the constellation Sagittarius.

Corona Borealis or ***Northern Crown*** constellation of the northern hemisphere, between Hercules and Boötes, representing the headband of Ariadne that was cast into the sky by Bacchus. Its brightest star is Alphecca (or Gemma), which is 78 light-years from Earth.

Coronado Francisco de c. 1500–1554. Spanish explorer who sailed to the New World in 1535 in search of gold. In 1540 he set out with several hundred men from the Gulf of California on an exploration of what are today the Southern states. Although he failed to discover any gold, his expedition came across the impressive Grand Canyon of the Colorado and introduced the use of the horse to the indigenous Indians.

coronary artery disease (Latin *corona* "crown," from the arteries' encircling of the heart) condition in which the fatty deposits of ◊atherosclerosis form in the coronary arteries that supply the heart muscle, making them too narrow.

These arteries may already be hardened (arteriosclerosis). If the heart's oxygen requirements are increased, as during exercise, the blood supply through the narrowed arteries may be inadequate, and the pain of ◊angina results. A heart attack occurs if the blood supply to an area of the heart is cut off, for example because a blood clot (thrombus) has blocked one of the coronary arteries. The subsequent lack of oxygen damages the heart muscle (infarct), and if a large area of the heart is affected, the attack may be fatal. Coronary artery disease tends to run in families and is linked to smoking, lack of exercise, and a diet high in saturated (mostly animal) fats, which tends to increase the level of blood ◊cholesterol. It is a common cause of death in many industrialized countries; older men are the most vulnerable group.

coronation ceremony of investing a sovereign with the emblems of royalty, as a symbol of inauguration in office. Since the coronation of Harold 1066, English sovereigns have been crowned in Westminster Abbey, London.

coroner or ***medical examiner*** an official who investigates the deaths of persons who have died suddenly at home, by acts of violence, or under suspicious circumstances, by holding an inquest or ordering a post-mortem examination (autopsy).

Corot Jean-Baptiste-Camille 1796–1875. French painter, creator of a distinctive landscape style with cool colors and soft focus. His early work, including Italian scenes in the 1820s, influenced the Barbizon school of painters. Like them, Corot worked outdoors, but he also continued a conventional academic tradition with more romanticized paintings.

corporal punishment physical punishment of wrongdoers—for example by whipping. It is still used as a punishment for criminals in many countries, especially under Islamic law.

corporation a number of people grouped together in a legally constituted joint enterprise, usually for the conduct of business and for tax advantages. Types of corporations include publicly traded corporations, which sell stock to the public to raise capital, and privately held corporations. Corporations are legal entities filed with state governments and distinct from the individuals who manage their affairs or the owners of their stock. Only about 15% of the businesses in the US are corporations, but they produce 80% of sales.

The legal status of a corporation as a unique entity gives the owners and managers freedom from liability for the corporation's actions. The corporation can be sued and can sue, and it can make contracts. This limitation of liability is essential for growth and development, since large amounts of capital must be raised from many sources. The affairs of the corporation are governed by bylaws and managed by a board of directors. Laws vary from state to state and nation to nation as to how many directors are required and whether they must be stockholders. The board acts on behalf of the stockholders and can be held accountable for failure to abide by the bylaws or for faulty judgment that results in losses.

The development of multinational corporations, enterprises that operate in a number of countries, has been a subject of increasing controversy since they operate only in their own interest, often at odds with government policies in those countries. They also can cause disruptions in domestic economies as they shift facilities and marketing operations in search of the greatest advantage.

corporation tax a tax levied on a company's profits by public authorities. It is a form of income tax, and rates vary according to country, but there is usually a flat rate. It is a large source of revenue for governments.

corps de ballet the dancers in a ballet company who usually dance in groups, in support of the soloists. At the Paris Opéra this is the name given to the whole company.

Corpus Christi feast celebrated in the Roman Catholic and Orthodox churches, and to some extent in the Anglican Church, on the Thursday after Trinity Sunday. It was instituted in the 13th century through the devotion of St Juliana, prioress of Mount Cornillon, near Liège, in honor of the Real Presence of Christ in the Eucharist.

Corpus Christi city in SE Texas, on the Gulf of Mexico at the mouth of the Nueces river, SE of San Antonio; seat of Nueces county. A port of entry to the US, its main industries are oil refining and shipping, commercial fishing, and the processing and shipping of agricultural products; population (1990) 257,453. Corpus Christi began as a small trading post. It was used as a base by General Zachary Taylor during the Mexican–American War 1845–58 and was captured by Union troops 1864 during the Civil War.

corpuscular theory hypothesis about the nature of light championed by Isaac Newton, who postulated that it consists of a stream of particles or corpuscles. The theory was superseded at the beginning of the 19th century by Thomas ◊Young's wave theory. ◊Quantum theory and wave mechanics embody both concepts.

corpus luteum temporary endocrine gland found in the mammalian ◊ovary. It is formed after ovulation from the Graafian follicle, a group of cells associated with bringing the egg to maturity, and secretes the hormone progesterone.

After the release of an egg the follicle enlarges under the action of luteinizing hormone, released from the pituitary. The corpus luteum secretes the hormone progesterone, which maintains the uterus wall ready for pregnancy. If pregnancy does not occur the corpus luteum breaks down.

Correggio Antonio Allegri da c. 1494–1534. Italian painter of the High Renaissance whose style followed the Classical grandeur of Leonardo and

Titian but anticipated the Baroque in its emphasis on movement, softer forms, and contrasts of light and shade.

Based in Parma, he painted splendid illusionistic visions in the cathedral there. His religious paintings, including the night scene *Adoration of the Shepherds* about 1527–30 (Gemäldegalerie, Dresden), and mythological scenes, such as *The Loves of Jupiter* (Wallace Collection, London), were much admired in the 18th century.

Corregidor an island fortress off the Bataan Peninsula at the mouth of Manila Bay, Luzon, the Philippines. On May 6, 1942, Japanese forces captured Corregidor and its 10,000 Americans and Filipino defenders, completing their conquest of the Philippines. US forces recaptured Corregidor Feb 1945.

correlation a relation or form of interdependence between two sets of data. In ◊statistics, such relations are measured by the calculation of ◊coefficients. These generally measure correlation on a scale with 1 indicating perfect positive correlation, 0 no correlation at all, and –1 perfect inverse correlation.

Correlation coefficients for assumed linear relations include the Pearson product moment correlation coefficient (known simply as the correlation coefficient), Kendall's tau correlation coefficient, or Spearman's rho correlation coefficient, which is used in nonparametric statistics (where the data are measured on ordinal rather than interval scales). A high correlation does not always indicate dependence between two variables; it may be that there is a third (unstated) variable upon which both depend.

correspondence in mathematics, the relation between two sets where an operation on the members of one set maps some or all of them onto one or more members of the other. For example, if *A* is the set of members of a family and *B* is the set of months in the year, *A* and *B* are in correspondence if the operation is: "...has a birthday in the month of...."

corresponding societies organizations which began with the London Corresponding Society in 1792. Founded by politicians Thomas Hardy (1752–1832) and John Horne Tooke (1736–1812), the society was one of the first independent organizations for the working classes and advocated annual parliaments and universal male suffrage. It later established branches in Scotland and the provinces. Many of its activities had to be held in secret and government fears about the spread of revolutionary doctrines led to its banning in 1799.

Corrèze river of central France flowing 55 mi/89 km from the Plateau des Millevaches, past Tulle, capital of Corrèze *département* (to which it gives its name), to join the Vézère. It is used for generating electricity at Bar, 6 mi/9.5 km NW of Tulle.

Corrientes city and river port of Argentina, on the Paraná River; population (1980) 180,000. Capital of Corrientes province, it is a stock-raising district. Industries include tanning, lumber milling, and textiles.

corrigendum (Latin) something to be corrected.

corroboree Australian Aboriginal dance. Some corroborees record events in history; others have a religious significance, connected with fertility and rejuvenation; some are theatrical entertainment.

corrosion the eating away and eventual destruction of metals and alloys by chemical attack. The rusting of ordinary iron and steel is the most common form of corrosion. Rusting takes place in moist air: the iron combines with oxygen and water to form a brown-orange deposit of ◊rust, hydrated iron oxide. The rate of corrosion is increased where the atmosphere is polluted with sulfur dioxide. Salty road and air conditions accelerate the rusting of car bodies.

Corrosion is largely an electrochemical process, and acidic and salty conditions favor the establishment of electrolytic cells on the metal, which cause it to be eaten away. Other examples of corrosion include the green deposit that forms on copper and bronze, called verdigris, a basic copper carbonate. The tarnish on silver is a corrosion product, a film of silver sulfide.

Corsica

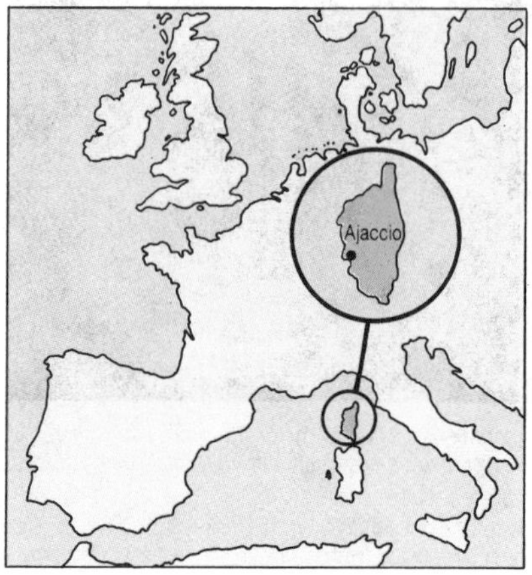
Ajaccio

corsair a pirate based on the North African Barbary Coast. From the 16th century onward the corsairs plundered shipping in the Mediterranean and Atlantic, holding hostages for ransom or selling them as slaves. Although many punitive expeditions were sent against them, they were not suppressed until France occupied Algiers 1830.

Most pirates were Turkish or North African, but there were also many Europeans, such as the Englishman Sir Francis Verney, half brother of Edmund Verney.

Corse French name for Corsica.

Corsica (French *Corse*) island region of France, in the Mediterranean off the W coast of Italy, N of Sardinia; it comprises the *départements* of Haute Corse and Corse du Sud

area 3,358 sq mi/8,700 sq km

capital Ajaccio (port)

features ◊maquis vegetation. Its mountain bandits were eradicated 1931, but the tradition of the vendetta or blood feud lingers; it is the main base of the ◊Foreign Legion

government its special status involves a 61-member regional parliament with the power to scrutinize French National Assembly bills applicable to the island and propose amendments

products wine, olive oil

population (1986) 249,000; including just under 50% native Corsicans. There are about 400,000 *émigrés*, mostly in Mexico and Central America, who return to retire

language French (official); the majority speak Corsican, an Italian dialect

famous people Napoleon.

history The Phocaeans of Ionia founded Alalia about 570 BC, and were succeeded in turn by the Etruscans, the Carthaginians, the Romans, the Vandals, and the Arabs. In the 14th century Corsica fell to the Genoese, and in the second half of the 18th century a Corsican nationalist, Pasquale Paoli (1725–1807), led an independence movement. Genoa sold Corsica to France 1768. In World War II Corsica was occupied by Italy 1942–43. From 1962, French *pieds noir* (refugees from Algeria, mainly vine growers, were settled in Corsica, and their prosperity helped to fan nationalist feeling, which demands an independent Corsica. This fueled a "national liberation front" (FNLC), banned 1983.

Cort Henry 1740–1800. British iron manufacturer. For the manufacture of ◊wrought iron, he invented the puddling process and developed the rolling mill, both of which were significant in the Industrial Revolution.

Cortázar Julio 1914–1984. Argentine writer, born in Brussels, whose novels include *The Winners* 1960, *Hopscotch* 1963, and *Sixty-two: A Model Kit* 1968. His several volumes of short stories include "Blow-up," adapted for a film by the Italian director Antonioni.

Cortés *The conquistador Ferdinand Cortés who destroyed the Aztec empire for the glory of Spain and Christendom.*

Cortés Hernán (Ferdinand) 1485–1547. Spanish conquistador. He conquered the Aztec empire 1519–21, and secured Mexico for Spain.

Cortés went to the West Indies as a young man and in 1518 was given command of an expedition to Mexico. Landing with only 600 men, he was at first received as a god by the Aztec emperor ◊Montezuma II but was expelled from Tenochtitlán (Mexico City) when he was found not to be "divine."

With the aid of Mexican Indian allies he recaptured the city 1521 and took the Aztec empire. His conquests eventually included most of Mexico and N Central America.

cortex in biology, the outer layer of a structure such as the brain, kidney, or adrenal gland. In botany the cortex includes non-specialized cells lying just beneath the surface cells of the root and stem.

corticosteroid any of several steroid hormones secreted by the cortex of the ◊adrenal glands; also synthetic forms with similar properties. Corticosteroids have anti-inflammatory and ◊immunosuppressive effects and may be used to treat a number of conditions including rheumatoid arthritis, severe allergies, asthma, some skin diseases, and some cancers. Side effects can be serious, and therapy must be withdrawn very gradually.

The two main groups of corticosteroids include glucocorticoids (◊cortisone, hydrocortisone, prednisone, and dexamethasone), which affect carbohydrate metabolism, and mineralocorticoids (aldosterone, fludrocortisone), which control the balance of water and salt in the body.

cortisone natural corticosteroid produced by the ◊adrenal gland, now synthesized for its anti-inflammatory qualities and used in the treatment of rheumatoid arthritis.

Cortisone was discovered by Tadeus Reichstein of Basel, Switzerland, and put to practical clinical use for rheumatoid arthritis by Philip Hench (1896–1965) and Edward Kendall (1886–1972) in the US (all three shared a Nobel Prize 1950). A product of the adrenal gland, it was first synthesized from a constituent of ox bile, and is now produced commercially from a Mexican yam and from a byproduct of the sisal plant. It is used for treating allergies and certain cancers, as well as rheumatoid arthritis. The side effects of cortisone steroids include muscle wasting, fat redistribution, diabetes, bone thinning, and high blood pressure.

Cortona town in Tuscany, N Italy, 13 mi/22 km SE of Arezzo; population (1981) 22,000. One of Europe's oldest cities. It is encircled by walls built by the Etruscans and has a medieval castle and an 11th-century cathedral.

Cortona Pietro da. Alternate name for Italian Baroque painter ◊Pietro da Cortona.

corundum aluminum oxide, Al_2O_3, the second hardest naturally occurring mineral (diamond rates 10, corundum 9 on the Mohs' scale); lack of ◊cleavage also increases its durability. Gem quality corundum is ruby (red) or sapphire (any other color including blue). Material of lesser quality is used as an abrasive and for other industrial purposes; synthetic corundum is also used in industry.

Corundum forms in silica-poor igneous and metamorphic rocks. It is a constituent of emery, which is metamorphosed bauxite. Crystals are barrel-shaped prisms of the trigonal system.

Corunna (Spanish *La Coruña*) city in the extreme NW of Spain; population (1986) 242,000. It is the capital of Corunna province. Industry is centered on the fisheries; tobacco, sugar refining, and textiles are also important. The ◊Armada sailed from Corunna 1588, and the town was sacked by Francis Drake 1589.

corvette term, now obsolete, revived from sailing days for small-armed vessels, such as those escorting convoys in World War II.

Cos alternate spelling of ◊Kos, a Greek island.

cosecant in trigonometry, a ◊function of an angle in a right triangle found by dividing the length of the hypotenuse (the longest side) by the length of the side opposite the angle. Thus the cosecant of an angle A, usually shortened to cosec A, is always greater than 1. It is the reciprocal of the sine of the angle, that is, cosec $A = 1/\sin A$.

Cosenza town in Calabria, S Italy; at the junction of the rivers Crati and Busento; population (1988) 106,000. It is the capital of Cosenza province and is an archepiscopal see. ◊Alaric, king of the Visigoths, is buried here.

Cosgrave Liam 1920– . Irish Fine Gael politician, prime minister of the Republic of Ireland 1973–77. As party leader 1965–77, he headed a Fine Gael–Labor coalition government from 1973. Relations between the Irish and UK governments improved under his premiership.

Cosgrave William Thomas 1880–1965. Irish politician. He took part in the ◊Easter Rising 1916 and sat in the Sinn Féin cabinet of 1919–21. Head of the Free State government 1922–33, he founded and led the Fine Gael opposition 1933–44. His eldest son is Liam Cosgrave.

cosine in trigonometry, a function of an angle in a right triangle found by dividing the length of the side adjacent to the angle by the length of the hypotenuse (the longest side). It is usually shortened to cos.

cosmic background radiation the electromagnetic radiation, also known as the 3° radiation, left over from the original formation of the universe in the Big Bang around 15 billion years ago. It corresponds to an overall background temperature of 3K (–454°F/–270°C), or 3°C above absolute zero.

cosmic radiation streams of high-energy particles from outer space, consisting of protons, alpha particles, and light nuclei, which collide with atomic nuclei in the Earth's atmosphere, and produce secondary nuclear particles (chiefly ◊mesons, such as pions and muons) that shower the Earth.

Those of low energy seem to be galactic in origin, and detectors (such as the water-Cherenkov detector near Leeds, England, with an area of 4.5 sq mi/12 sq km) are in use to detect extragalactic sources of high-energy rays (possibly the rotating disks of infalling matter around black holes).

cosmogony (Greek "universe" + "creation") the study of the origin and evolution of cosmic objects, especially the Solar System.

cosmology the study of the structure of the universe. Modern cosmology began in the 1920s with the discovery that the universe is expanding, which suggested that it began in an explosion, the ◊Big Bang. An alternative view, the ◊steady-state theory, claimed that the universe has no origin but is expanding because new matter is being continually created.

cosmonaut *The Soviet pioneers of human space flight, photographed in 1965. Left to right, seated: Yuri Gagarin, Pavel Belyayev, Valentina Tereshkova, Alexei Leonov, and Vladimir Komarov; standing: Pavel Popovich, Gherman Titov, Konstantin Feoktistov, Boris Yegorov, Andrian Nikolayev, and Valeri Bykovsky.*

cosmonaut Soviet term for a person who travels in space; the West's term is astronaut.

Cosmos name used since the early 1960s for nearly all Soviet artificial satellites. Nearly 2,000 Cosmos satellites have been launched.

Cossack member of any of several, formerly horse-raising, Tatar groups of S and SW Russia, the Ukraine, and Poland, who took in escaped serfs and lived in independent communal settlements (military brotherhoods) from the 15th to the 19th centuries. Later they held land in return for military service in the cavalry under Russian and Polish rulers. After 1917, the various Cossack communities were incorporated into the Soviet administrative and collective system.

Cossyra ancient name for ◊Pantelleria, Italian island in the Mediterranean.

Costa Rica country in Central America, bounded N by Nicaragua, S by Panama, E by the Caribbean, and W by the Pacific Ocean.

government The 1949 constitution provides for a president elected for a four-year term by compulsory adult suffrage, two elected vice-presidents, and an appointed cabinet. There is a single-chamber legislature, the 57-member assembly, also serving a four-year term. The principal political parties are the National Liberation Party (PLN), and the Christian Socialist Unity Party (PUSC).

history Originally occupied by Guaymi Indians, the area was visited by Christopher ◊Columbus in 1502 and was colonized by Spanish settlers from the 16th century, becoming independent 1821. Initially part of the ◊Mexican empire, then—with El Salvador, Guatemala, Honduras, and Nicaragua—part of the Central American Federation from 1824, Costa Rica became a republic 1838. Apart from a military dictatorship 1870–82 and a brief civil war 1948 after a disputed presidential election, it has been one of the most democratically governed states in Latin America.

In 1949 a new constitution abolished the army, leaving defense to the Civil Guard. José Figueres, leader of the antigovernment forces in the previous year, became president. He cofounded the PLN, nationalized the banks, and introduced a social security system. He was re-elected 1953.

There followed 16 years of mostly conservative rule, with the reversal of some PLN policies. In 1974 Daniel Oduber won the presidency for the PLN. He returned to Socialist policies, extended the welfare state, and established friendly relations with communist states. Communist and left-wing parties were legalized.

In 1978 Rodrigo Carazo of the conservative Unity Coalition (CU) became president. His presidency was marked by economic collapse and allegations of his involvement in illegal arms trafficking between Cuba and El Salvador.

In 1982 Luis Alberto Monge, a former labor union official and cofounder of PLN, won a convincing victory in the presidential election. To reverse the damage done by the Carazo government, he introduced a 100-day emergency economic program.

The Monge government came under pressure from the US to abandon its neutral stance and condemn the left-wing Sandinista regime in Nicaragua. It was also urged to re-establish its army. Monge resisted the pressure and in 1983 reaffirmed his country's neutrality, but relations with Nicaragua deteriorated after border clashes between Sandinista forces and the Costa Rican Civil Guard. In 1985 Monge agreed to create a US-trained antiguerrilla guard, increasing doubts about Costa Rica's neutrality. In 1986 Oscar Arias Sánchez became president on a neutralist platform, defeating the pro-US candidate, Rafael Angel Calderón. Arias worked tirelessly for peace in the region, hosting regional summit meetings and negotiating framework treaties, winning the Nobel Peace Prize 1987 for his efforts. However, Calderón won the 1990 presidential election.

cost benefit analysis the process whereby a project is assessed for its social and welfare benefits in addition to considering the financial return on investment. For example, this might take into account the environmental impact of an industrial plant or convenience for users of a new railroad.

Costello Elvis. Adopted name of Declan McManus 1954– . English rock singer, songwriter, and guitarist, renowned for his stylistic range and intricate lyrics. His albums with his group the Attractions include *Armed Forces* 1979, *Trust* 1981, *Blood and Chocolate* 1986, and *Spike* 1989.

Coster Laurens Janszoon 1370–1440. Dutch printer. According to some sources, he invented moveable type, but after his death an apprentice ran off to Mainz with the blocks and, taking ◊Guten-

Costa Rica
Republic of
(República de Costa Rica)

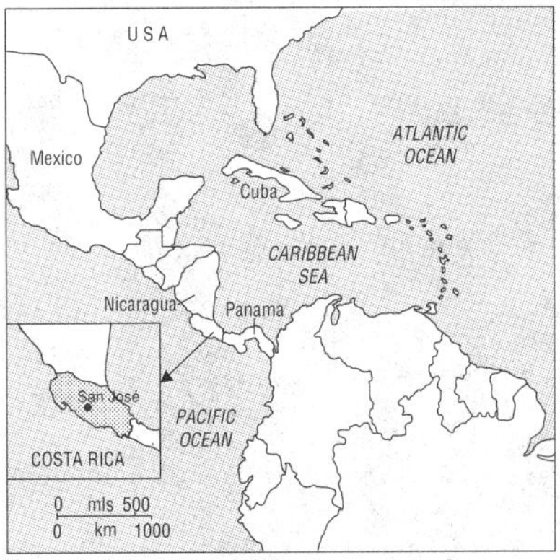
USA
Mexico
ATLANTIC OCEAN
Cuba
CARIBBEAN SEA
Nicaragua
Panama
San José
PACIFIC OCEAN
COSTA RICA
0 mls 500
0 km 1000

area 19,735 sq mi/51,100 sq km
capital San José
cities ports Limón, Puntarenas
physical high central plateau and tropical coasts; Costa Rica was once entirely forested, containing an estimated 5% of the Earth's flora and fauna. By 1983 only 17% of the forest remained; half of the arable land had been cleared for cattle ranching, which led to landlessness and unemployment (except for 2,000 politically powerful families) and soil erosion; the massive environmental destruction also caused incalculable loss to the gene pool
features Poas Volcano; Guayabo pre-Colombian ceremonial site
head of state and government Rafael Calderón from 1990
political system liberal democracy
political parties National Liberation Party (PLN), left-of-center; Christian Socialist Unity Party (PUSC), centrist coalition; ten minor parties
exports coffee, bananas, cocoa, sugar, beef
currency colón
population (1990 est) 3,032,000 (including 1,200 Guaymi Indians); growth rate 2.6% p.a.
life expectancy men 71, women 76
language Spanish (official)
religion Roman Catholic 95%
literacy men 94%/women 93% (1985 est)
GDP $4.3 bn (1986); $1,550 per head
chronology
1821 Independence achieved from Spain.
1949 New constitution adopted. National army abolished. José Figueres, cofounder of the PLN, elected president; he embarked on ambitious Socialist program.
1958–73 Mainly conservative administrations.
1974 PLN regained the presidency and returned to Socialist policies.
1978 Rodrigo Carazo, conservative, elected president. Sharp deterioration in the state of the economy.
1982 Luis Alberto Monge of the PLN elected president. Harsh austerity program introduced to rebuild the economy. Pressure from the US to abandon neutral stance and condemn Sandinista regime in Nicaragua.
1983 Policy of neutrality reaffirmed.
1985 Following border clashes with Sandinista forces, a US-trained antiguerrilla guard formed.
1986 Oscar Arias Sanchez won the presidency on a neutralist platform.
1987 Oscar Arias Sanchez won Nobel Peace Prize for devising a Central American peace plan.
1990 Rafael Calderón (PUSC) elected president.

berg into his confidence, began a printing business with him.

cost of living see ◊consumer price index.

cotangent in trigonometry, a ◊function of an angle in a right triangle found by dividing the length of the side adjacent to the angle by the length of the side opposite it. It is usually written as cotan, or cot and it is the reciprocal of the tangent of the angle, so that cot $A = 1/\tan A$, where A is the angle in question.

crib death death of an apparently healthy baby during sleep, also known as sudden infant death syndrome (SIDS). It is most common in the winter months, and strikes boys more than girls. The cause is not known.

Côte d'Azur the Mediterranean coast from Menton to St Tropez, France, renowned for its beaches; part of ◊Provence–Côte d'Azur.

cotoneaster any plant of the Eurasian genus *Cotoneaster* of trees and shrubs of the rose family Rosaceae, closely allied to the hawthorn and medlar. The fruits, though small and unpalatable, are usually bright red and conspicuous, often persisting through the winter. Some of the shrubs are cultivated for their attractive appearance.

Cotonou chief port and largest city of Benin, on the Bight of Benin; population (1982) 487,000. Palm products and timber are exported.

Although not the official capital, it is the seat of the president, and the main center of commerce and politics.

cotangent

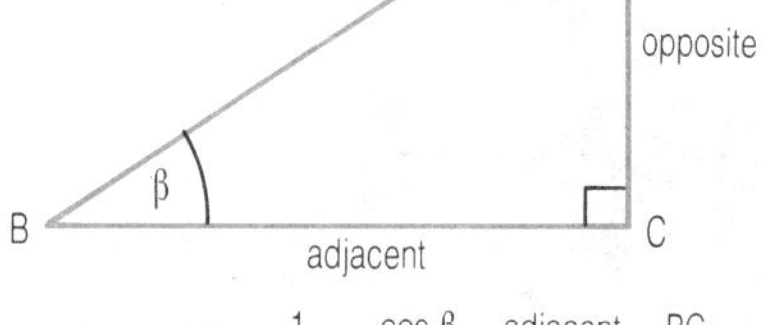
A
opposite
B
β
C
adjacent

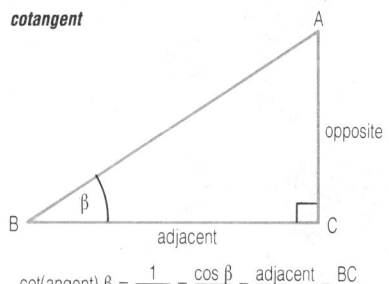

$$\text{cot(angent)}\ \beta = \frac{1}{\tan\beta} = \frac{\cos\beta}{\sin\beta} = \frac{\text{adjacent}}{\text{opposite}} = \frac{BC}{AC}$$

Cotopaxi (Quechua "shining peak") an active volcano, situated to the S of Quito in Ecuador. It is 19,347 ft/5,897 m high and was first climbed 1872.

Cotswolds range of hills in Avon-Gloucestershire, England, 50 mi/80 km long, between Bristol and Chipping Camden. They rise to 1,086 ft/333 m at Cleeve Cloud, but average about 600 ft/200 m.

cottage industry an industry undertaken by employees in their homes and often using their own equipment. Cottage industries frequently utilize a traditional craft such as weaving or pottery, but may also use high technology, such as word processing.

Cottbus industrial city (textiles, carpets, glassware) in the state of Brandenburg, Federal Republic of Germany; population (1990) 128,000. Formerly capital of the East German district of Cottbus 1952–90.

cotton tropical and subtropical herbaceous plant of the genus *Gossypium* of the mallow family Malvaceae. Fibers surround the seeds inside the ripened fruits, or bolls, and these are spun into yarn for cloth.

Cotton disease (byssinosis), caused by cotton dust, affects the lungs of those working in the industry. The seeds are used to produce cooking oil and livestock feed, and the pigment gossypol has potential as a male contraceptive in a modified form. See also ◊cotton gin.

Cotton John 1585–1652. American religious leader. Born in Derby, England, and educated at Cambridge University, Cotton was named vicar in Boston, Lincolnshire, 1612. His extreme Puritan views led to charges of heterodoxy being filed against him in 1633. In the same year, he immigrated to the Massachusetts Bay Colony, where he was named teacher of Boston's First Congregational Church. A leader in the public prosecution of Anne ◊Hutchinson and Roger ◊Williams, Cotton was, throughout his career, a powerful conservative force in the colony and published widely circulated sermons and theological works.

Cotton Joseph 1905– . US actor who was brought into films by Orson Welles. He appeared in many international productions, until the early 1980s, often in leading or important roles, including *Citizen Kane* 1941, *Shadow of a Doubt* 1943, *The Third Man* 1949, and *The Abominable Dr Phibes* 1971.

cotton gin a machine that separates cotton fibers from the seed boll. Production of the gin (then called an engine) by US inventor Eli Whitney 1793 was a milestone in textile history.

The modern gin consists of a roller carrying a set of circular saws. These project through a metal grill in a hopper containing the seed bolls. As the roller rotates, the saws pick up the cotton fibers, leaving the seeds behind.

cotton grass any grasslike plant of the genus *Eriophorum* of the sedge family Cyperaceae. White tufts cover the fruiting heads in midsummer; these break off and are carried long distances on the wind. Cotton grass is found in wet places throughout the Arctic and northern temperate regions, most species being found in acid bogs.

cotton spinning creating thread or fine yarn from the cotton plant by spinning the raw fiber contained within the seed-pods. The fiber is separated from the pods by a machine called a ◊cotton gin. It is then cleaned and the fibers are separated out (carding). Finally the fibers are drawn out to the desired length and twisted together to form strong thread.

cottonwood any of several species of North American poplar (genus *Populus*) with seeds topped by a thick tuft of silky hairs. The eastern cottonwood *P. deltoides*, growing to 100 ft/30 m, is native to the eastern US. The name cottonwood is also given to the downy-leaved Australian tree *Bedfordia salaoina*.

cotyledon a structure in the embryo of a seed plant that may form a "leaf" after germination and is commonly known as a seed leaf. The number of cotyledons present in an embryo is an important character in the classification of flowering plants (◊angiosperms).

Monocotyledons (such as grasses, palms, and lilies) have a single cotyledon, whereas dicotyledons (the majority of plant species) have two. In seeds that also contain ◊endosperm (nutritive tissue), the cotyledons are thin, but where they are the primary food-storing tissue, as in peas and beans, they may be quite large. After germination the cotyledons either remain below ground (hypogeal) or, more commonly, spread out above soil level (epigeal) and become the first green leaves. In gymnosperms there may be up to a dozen cotyledons within each seed.

couch grass European grass *Agropyron repens* of the family Gramineae. It spreads rapidly by underground stems. It is considered a troublesome weed in North America, where it has been introduced.

Coué ˙Emile 1857–1926. French psychological healer, the pioneer of autosuggestion. He coined the slogan "Every day, and in every way, I am becoming better and better." "Couéism" reached the height of its popularity in the 1920s.

cougar another name for the ◊puma, a large North American cat.

coulomb SI unit (abbreviation C) of electrical charge. One coulomb is the quantity of electricity conveyed by a current of one ◊ampere in one second.

Coulomb Charles Auguste de 1736–1806. French scientist, inventor of the torsion balance for measuring the force of electric and magnetic attraction. The coulomb was named after him.

Council for Mutual Economic Assistance (CMEA)

full name for ◊Comecon, organization established 1949 by Eastern bloc countries.

Council of Europe body constituted 1949 at Strasbourg, France (still its headquarters) to secure "a greater measure of unity between the European countries." The widest association of European states, it has a Committee of foreign ministers, a Parliamentary Assembly (with members from national parliaments), and a European Commission investigating violations of human rights.

The first session of the Consultative Assembly opened Aug 1949, the members then being the UK, France, Italy, Belgium, the Netherlands, Sweden, Denmark, Norway, the Republic of Ireland, Luxembourg, Greece, and Turkey; Iceland, West Germany, Austria, Cyprus, Switzerland, Malta, Portugal, Spain, and Liechtenstein joined subsequently.

counseling an approach to treating problems, usually psychological ones, in which clients are encouraged to solve their own problems with support from a counselor or therapist.

counterfeiting fraudulent imitation, usually of legal tender, artwork, or other objects of value. The counterfeiting of money is thwarted by special papers, elaborate watermarks, skilled printing, and sometimes the insertion of a metallic strip. ◊Forgery is also a form of counterfeiting.

counterpoint in music, the art of combining different forms of an original melody with apparent freedom and yet to harmonious effect. ◊Palestrina and J S ◊Bach were masters of counterpoint.

It originated in ◊plainsong, with two independent vocal lines sung simultaneously (Latin *punctus contra punctum* "note against note").

Counter-Reformation a movement initiated by the Catholic church at the Council of Trent 1545–63 to counter the spread of the ◊Reformation. Extending into the 17th century, its dominant forces included the rise of the Jesuits as an educating and missionary group and the deployment of the Spanish ◊Inquisition in other countries.

countervailing power in economics, the belief that too much power held by one group or company can be balanced or neutralized by another, creating a compatible relationship, such as labor unions in the case of strong management in a large company, or an opposition party facing an authoritarian government.

country and western the popular music of the white US South and West; it evolved from the folk music of the English, Irish, and Scottish settlers and has a strong blues influence. Characteristic instruments are slide guitar, mandolin, and fiddle.

Lyrics typically extol family values and traditional sex roles. Country music encompasses a variety of regional styles, and ranges from mournful ballads to fast and intricate dance music.

It is played on radio stations throughout the US, and the 1980s saw its popularity spread even into Eastern urban centers like New York City, which had not been part of the country-and-western tradition.

history

1920s Jimmie Rodgers (1897–1933) wrote a series of "Blue Yodel" songs that made him the first country music recording star.

1930s Nashville, Tennessee, became a center for the country-music industry, with the Grand Ole Opry a showcase for performers. The Carter Family arranged and recorded hundreds of traditional songs. Hollywood invented the singing cowboy.

1940s Hank Williams (1923–1953) emerged as the most significant singer and songwriter; western swing spread from Texas.

1950s The honky-tonk sound; Kentucky bluegrass; ballad singers included Jim Reeves (1923–1964) and Patsy Cline (1932–1963).

1960s Songs of the Bakersfield, California, School, dominated by Buck Owens (1929–) and Merle Haggard (1937–), contrasted with lush Nashville productions of singers such as George Jones (1931–) and Tammy Wynette (1942–).

1970s Dolly Parton (1946–) and Emmylou Harris (1947–); the Austin, Texas, outlaws Willie Nelson (1933–) and Waylon Jennings (1937–); country rock pioneered by Gram Parsons (1946–1973).

1980s Neotraditionalist new country represented by Randy Travis (1963–), Dwight Yoakam (1957–), and Nanci Griffith (1954–).

county administrative unit of a country or state. In the US a county is a subdivision of a state; the power of counties differs widely between states. In the UK it is nowadays synonymous with "shire," although historically the two had different origins. Many of the English counties can be traced back to Saxon times. The Republic of Ireland has 26 geographical and 27 administrative counties.

coup d'état or ***coup*** forcible takeover of the government of a country by elements from within that country, generally carried out by violent or illegal means. It differs from a revolution in typically being carried out by a small group (for example, of army officers or opposition politicians) to install its leader as head of government, rather than being a mass uprising by the people.

Early examples include the coup of 1799, in which Napoleon overthrew the Revolutionary Directory to declare himself first consul of France and the coup of 1851 in which Louis Napoleon (then president) dissolved the French national assembly and a year later declared himself emperor. Coups of more recent times include the overthrow of the Socialist government of Chile in 1973 by a right-wing junta and the military seizure of power in Fiji by Colonel Rabuka in Sept 1987.

Couperin François *le Grand* 1668–1733. French composer. He held various court appointments under Louis XIV and wrote vocal, chamber, and harpsichord music.

couplet in literature, a pair of lines of verse, usually of the same length and rhymed.

The heroic couplet, consisting of two rhymed lines in iambic pentameter, was widely adopted for epic poetry, and was a convention of both serious and mock-heroic 18th-century English poetry, as in the work of Alexander ◊Pope. An example, from Pope's *An Essay on Criticism*, is: "A little learning is a dang'rous thing;/Drink deep, or taste not the Pierian spring."

Courbet Gustave 1819–1877. French artist, a portrait, genre, and landscape painter. Reacting against academic trends, both Classicist and Romantic, he sought to establish a new realism based on contemporary life. His *Burial at Ornans* 1850 (Louvre, Paris), showing ordinary working people gathered around a village grave, shocked the public and the critics with its "vulgarity."

His spirit of realism was to be continued by Manet. In 1871 Courbet was active in the ◊Paris Commune and was later imprisoned for six months for his part in it.

Courrèges André 1923– . French couturier. Originally with Balenciaga, he founded his own firm 1961 and is credited with inventing the mini-skirt in 1964.

Court Margaret (born Smith) 1942– . Australian tennis player. The most prolific winner in the women's game, she won a record 64 Grand Slam titles, including 25 at singles.

Court was the first from her country to win the women's title at Wimbledon (1963) and the second woman after Maureen Connolly to complete the Grand Slam (1970).

CAREER HIGHLIGHTS

Wimbledon
singles: 1963, 1965, 1970
doubles: 1964, 1969
mixed: 1963, 1965–66, 1968, 1975
US Open
singles: 1962, 1965, 1968–70, 1973
doubles: 1963, 1968–70, 1973, 1975
mixed: 1961–65, 1969–70, 1972
French Open
singles: 1962, 1964, 1969–70, 1973
doubles: 1964–66, 1973
mixed: 1963–65, 1969
Australian Open
singles: 1960–66, 1969–71, 1973
doubles: 1961–63, 1965, 1969–71, 1973
mixed: 1963–64

courtly love a medieval code of amorous conduct between noblemen and noblewomen.

Originating in 11th-century Provence, it was popularized by troubadors under the patronage of Eleanor of Aquitaine, and codified by André le Chapelain. Essentially, it was concerned with the (usually) unconsummated love between a young bachelor knight and his lord's lady. The affair between Lancelot and Guinevere is a classic example. This theme was usually treated in an idealized form, but the relationship did reflect the social realities of noble households, in which the lady of the household might be the only noblewoman among several young unmarried knights. It inspired a great deal of medieval and 16th-century art and literature, including the 14th-century *Romance of the Rose* and Chaucer's *Troilus and Criseyde*, and was closely related to concepts of ◊chivalry.

court martial court convened for the trial of persons subject to military discipline who are accused of violations of military laws.

The Uniform Code of Military Justice establishes military law and procedures for courts-martial in the US military.

Courtrai (Flemish *Kortrijk*) town in Belgium on the river Lys, in West Flanders; population (1985) 76,110. It is connected by canal with the coast, and by river and canal with Antwerp and Brussels. It has a large textile industry, including damask, linens, and lace.

Courtrai, Battle of defeat of French knights by the Flemings of Ghent and Bruges on July 11, 1302. It is also called the "Battle of the Spurs" because 800 gilt spurs were hung in Courtrai cathedral to commemorate the victory of billmen over unsupported cavalry.

courtship behavior exhibited by animals as a prelude to mating. The behavior patterns vary considerably from one species to another, but are often ritualized forms of behavior not obviously related to courtship or mating (for example, courtship feeding in birds).

court tennis racket and ball game played in France from about the 12th century, over a central net in an indoor court, but with a sloping roof let into each end and one side of the court, against which the ball may be hit. It is now played in several countries including the US, but there are very few courts. Basic scoring is as for ◊tennis, but with various modifications. It is the game on which tennis was based.

Cousin Victor 1792–1867. French philosopher who helped to introduce German philosophical ideas into France. In 1840 he was minister of public instruction and reorganized the system of elementary education.

Cousteau Jacques-Yves 1910– . French oceanographer, celebrated for his researches in command of the *Calypso* from 1951, his film and television documentaries, and his many books; he pioneered the invention of the aqualung 1943 and techniques in underwater filming.

couvade custom in some societies of a man behaving as if he were about to give birth when his child is being born, which may include feeling or appearing to feel real pain. It has been observed since antiquity in many cultures and may have begun either as a magic ritual or as a way of asserting paternity.

covalence in chemistry, a form of ◊valence in which two atoms unite by sharing electrons in pairs, so that each atom provides half the shared electrons (see also ◊bond).

Covent Garden London square (named after the con-

courtship

gulls courting, indulging in neck arching (left) and sky-pointing (right)

vent garden once on the site) laid out by Inigo ◊Jones in 1631. The buildings that formerly housed London's fruit and vegetable market (moved to Nine Elms, Wandsworth, in 1973) were adapted for shops and restaurants. The Royal Opera House, also housing the Royal Ballet, is here; also the London Transport Museum.

Coventry industrial city in West Midlands, England; population (1981) 313,800. Manufacturing includes automobiles, electronic equipment, machine tools, and agricultural machinery.

history It originated when Leofric, Earl of Mercia and husband of Lady ◊Godiva, founded a priory in 1043. Industry began with bicycle manufacture in 1870. Features include the cathedral, designed by Basil Spence, and incorporating the steeple of the church built 1373–95 and destroyed in an air raid Nov 1940; St Mary's Hall, built 1394–1414 as a guild center; two gates of the old city walls 1356; Belgrade Theatre 1958; Art Gallery and Museum; Museum of British Road Transport; and Lanchester Polytechnic.

Cousteau *Oceanographer Jacques Cousteau has pioneered the exploration of sea life and filmed much of his results, familiarizing us with the beauties of the deep.*

Coward Noël 1899–1973. English playwright, actor, producer, director, and composer, who epitomized the witty and sophisticated man of the theater. From his first success with *The Young Idea* 1923, he wrote and appeared in plays and comedies on both sides of the Atlantic such as *Hay Fever* 1925, *Private Lives* 1930 with Gertrude Lawrence, *Design for Living* 1933, and *Blithe Spirit* 1941.

Coward also wrote for and acted in films, including the patriotic *In Which We Serve* 1942 and the sentimental *Brief Encounter* 1945. After World War II he became a nightclub and cabaret entertainer, performing songs like "Mad Dogs and Englishmen."

cowfish kind of ◊boxfish.

cowrie marine snail of the family Cypreidae, in which the interior spiral form is concealed by a double outer lip. The shells are hard, shiny, and often colored. Most cowries are shallow-water forms, and are found in many parts of the world, particularly the tropical Indopacific. Cowries have been used as ornaments and fertility charms, and also as currency, for example the Pacific money cowrie *Cypraea moneta*.

Four species are found in the SE US and one in California.

cowslip European plant (*Primula veris*) of the same genus as the ◊primrose, in the family Primulaceae, with yellow or purple flowers. The name American cowslip is sometimes given to the marsh marigold (*Caltha palustris*) of the buttercup family, native to NE North America.

Cox Jacob Dolson 1828–1900. Canadian-born US educator and public figure. Born in Montreal, Cox was raised in New York and educated at Oberlin College. Serving briefly as superintendent of schools in Warren, Ohio, he studied law and was elected to the state legislature 1859. During the US Civil War, Cox was appointed brigadier general of volunteers and saw action in West Virginia and at Antietam. He was elected governor of Ohio 1866 and served as secretary of the interior under Grant. After service in the US Congress 1876–79, Cox was president of the University of Cincinnati 1885–89.

coyote wild dog *Canis latrans*, in appearance like a small wolf, living from Alaska to Central America and E to New York. Its head and body are about 3 ft/90 cm long and brown, flecked with gray or black. Coyotes live in open country and can run at 40 mph/65 kph. Their main foods are rabbits and rodents. Although persecuted by humans for over a century, the species is very successful.

coypu another name for ◊nutria.

Coysevox Antoine 1640–1720. French Baroque sculptor. He was employed at the palace of Versailles, contributing a stucco relief of a triumphant Louis XIV to the Salon de la Guerre.

He also produced portrait busts, for example a terracotta of the artist Le Brun 1676 (Wallace Collection, London), and more somber monuments, such as the *Tomb of Cardinal Mazarin* 1689–93 (Louvre, Paris).

Cozens John Robert 1752–1797. British landscape painter, a watercolorist, whose Romantic views of Europe, painted on tours in the 1770s and 1780s, influenced both Thomas Girtin and J M W Turner.

CP/M (acronym for control program/monitor or control program for microcomputers) ◊operating system, produced by Digital Research, which became a standard for microcomputers based on the Intel 8080 and Zilog Z80 8-bit microprocessors. In the 1980s it was superseded by ◊MS-DOS, written for 16-bit microprocessors.

CPR abbreviation for cardiopulmonary ◊resuscitation.

CPU see ◊central processing unit.

crab any decapod (ten-legged) crustacean of the division Brachyura, with a broad, rather round, upper body shell (carapace) and a small ◊abdomen tucked beneath the body. They are related to lobsters and crayfish. Mainly marine, some crabs live in fresh water or on land. They are alert carnivores and scavengers. They have a typical sideways walk, and strong pincers on the first pair of legs, the other four pairs being used for walking. Periodically, the outer shell is cast to allow for growth. The name crab is sometimes used for similar arthropods, such as the horseshoe crab, which is neither a true crab nor a crustacean.

There are many species of true crabs worldwide. The North American blue crab *Callinectes sapidus*, called the soft-shelled crab after molting, is about 6 in/15 cm wide. It is extensively fished along the Atlantic and Gulf coasts. Other true crabs include fiddler crabs (Uca), the males of which have one enlarged claw to wave at and attract females, and spider crabs, with small bodies and very long legs, including the Japanese spider crab *Macrocheira kaemperi* with a leg span of 11 ft/3.4 m. Hermit crabs (division Anomura) have a soft, spirally twisted abdomen and make their homes in empty shells of sea snails for protection. Some tropical hermit crabs are found a considerable distance from the sea. The robber crab *Birgus latro* grows large enough to climb palm trees and feed on coconuts.

crab apple any of 25 species of wild ◊apple trees (genus *Malus*) native to temperate regions of the northern hemisphere. Numerous varieties of cultivated apples have been derived from *M. pumila*, the common native crab apple of SE Europe and central Asia. The fruit of native species is smaller and more bitter than that of cultivated varieties.

Crab nebula cloud of gas 6,000 light-years from Earth, in the constellation Taurus. It is the remains of a star that exploded as a ◊supernova (observed as a brilliant point of light on Earth 1054). At its center is a ◊pulsar that flashes 30 times a second. The name comes from its crablike appearance.

crack chemical (bicarbonate) derivative of ◊cocaine in hard, crystalline lumps; for a drug "high," it is heated in pipes and inhaled (smoked). It was first used in San Francisco in the early 1980s and is highly addictive.

Its use has led to numerous deaths but it is the fastest-growing sector of the illegal drug trade, since it is less expensive than cocaine.

cracking method of distilling ◊petroleum products; see also ◊fractionation.

Cracow alternate form of ◊Kraków, Polish city.

Craig Edward Gordon 1872–1966. British director and stage designer. His innovations and theories on stage design and lighting effects, expounded in *On the Art of the Theatre* 1911, had a profound

crane
whooping crane

influence on stage production in Europe and the US.

Craigavon town in Armagh, Northern Ireland; population (1981) 73,000. It was created from 1965 by the merging of Lurgan and Portadown and named after the first prime minister of Northern Ireland.

Craiova town in S Romania, near the river Jiu; population (1985) 275,000. Industries include electrical engineering, food processing, textiles, fertilizers, and farm machinery.

Cranach Lucas 1472–1553. German painter, etcher, and woodcut artist, a leading light in the German Renaissance. He painted many full-length nudes and precise and polished portraits, such as *Martin Luther* 1521 (Uffizi, Florence).

Born at Kronach in Bavaria, he settled at Wittenberg in 1504 to work for the elector of Saxony. He is associated with the Christian reformer Martin Dürer and Altdorfer and was a close friend of Luther, whose portrait he painted several times. His religious paintings feature splendid landscapes. His second son, Lucas Cranach the Younger (1515–1586), had a similar style and succeeded his father as director of the Cranach workshop.

cranberry any of several trailing evergreen plants of the genus *Vaccinium* in the heath family Ericaceae, allied to bilberries and blueberries. They are common to the NE of the US, grow in marshy places, and bear small, acid, edible, crimson berries extremely high in vitamin C.

crane in engineering, a machine for raising, lowering, or placing in position heavy loads. The three main types are the jib crane, the overhead traveling crane, and the tower crane. Most cranes have the machinery mounted on a revolving turntable. This may be mounted on trucks or be self-propelled, often being fitted with ◊caterpillar tracks.

The main features of a jib crane are a power winch, a rope or cable, and a moveable arm or jib. The cable, which carries a pulley block, hangs from the end of the jib and is wound up and down by the winch. The overhead traveling crane, chiefly used in workshops, consists of a fixed horizontal arm, along which runs a trolley carrying the pulley block. Tower cranes, seen on large building sites, have a long horizontal arm able to revolve on top of a tall tower. The arm carries the trolley.

crane in zoology, a large, wading bird of the family Gruidae, with long legs and neck, and powerful wings. Cranes are marsh- and plains-dwelling birds, feeding on plants as well as insects and small animals. They fly well and are usually migratory. Their courtship includes frenzied, leaping dances. They are found in all parts of the world except South America.

The common crane *Grus grus* is still common in many parts of Europe, and winters in Africa and India. It stands over 3 ft/1 m high. The plumage of the adult bird is gray, varied with black and white, and a red patch of bare skin on the head and neck. All cranes have suffered through hunting and loss of wetlands; the population of the North American whooping crane *Grus americana* fell to 21 wild birds in 1944. Due to careful conservation, numbers have now risen to about 200.

The sandhill crane of North America *Grus canadensis* reaches a height of 3.5 ft/1 m and has greyish plumage, with a red patch on the head. It winters in Mexico and breeds in the far N.

Crane (Harold) Hart 1899–1932. US poet. His long mystical poem *The Bridge* (1930) uses the Brooklyn Bridge as a symbol. In his work he attempted to link humanity's present with its past, in an epic continuum. His poetry is highly original. He drowned after jumping overboard from a steamer bringing him back to the US after a visit to Mexico.

Crane Stephen 1871–1900. US writer who introduced grim realism into the US novel. His book *The Red Badge of Courage* 1895 deals vividly with the US Civil War.

Born in Newark, New Jersey, Crane became a journalist. His first novel, self-published, *Maggie: A Girl of the Streets* 1893, was rejected by many editors because of its unpleasant subject of New York slum life. His free-verse poetry is collected in *The Black Riders* 1895. His critically acclaimed short stories include "The Open Boat," based on a true experience of shipwreck during a journalistic assignment to Cuba 1897.

crane fly or ***daddy-longlegs*** any fly of the family Tipulidae, with long, slender, fragile legs. They look like giant mosquitoes, but the adults are quite harmless. The larvae live in soil or water.

craniotomy operation to remove or turn back a small flap of skull bone to give access to the living brain.

cranium the dome-shaped area of the vertebrate skull, consisting of several fused plates, that protects the brain. Fossil remains of the human cranium have aided the development of theories concerning human evolution.

The cranium has been studied as a possible indicator of intelligence or even of personality. The Victorian argument that a large cranium implies a large brain, which in turn implies a more profound intelligence, has been rejected.

crank handle bent at right angles and connected to the shaft of a machine; it is used to transmit motion or convert reciprocating (back-and-forwards or up-and-down) movement into rotary movement, or vice versa.

The earliest recorded use of a crank is in a water-raising machine by al-Jazari in the 17th century, 200 years before it appeared in Europe.

crankshaft an essential component of piston engines that converts the up-and-down (reciprocating) motion of the pistons into useful rotary motion. The car crankshaft carries a number of cranks. The pistons are connected to the cranks by connecting rods and ◊bearings; when the pistons move up and down, the connecting rods force the offset crank pins to describe a circle, thereby rotating the crankshaft.

Cranmer Thomas 1489–1556. English cleric, archbishop of Canterbury from 1533. A Protestant convert, under Edward VI he helped to shape the doctrines of the Church of England.

Condemned for heresy under the Catholic Mary Tudor, he at first recanted, but when his life was not spared, resumed his position and was burned at the stake, first holding to the fire the hand which had signed his recantation.

craps casino game adapted from the game *hazard* by Bernard de Mandeville in the early 19th century. Played with two dice, a throw of 7 or 11 wins; a throw of 2, 3, or 12 loses.

If none of the above show on the first toss, the "shooter" tries to repeat the number originally thrown before throwing a 7 or 11.

Crassus Marcus Licinius c. 108–53 BC. Roman general who crushed the ◊Spartacus uprising 71 BC. In 60 BC he joined with Caesar and Pompey in the First Triumvirate and obtained command in the East 55 BC. Invading Mesopotamia, he was defeated by the Parthians at the battle of Carrhae, captured, and put to death.

crater a bowl-shaped topographic feature, usually round and with steep sides. Craters are formed by explosive events such as the eruption of a volcano or by the impact of a meteorite. A ◊caldera is a much larger feature.

The Moon has more than 300,000 craters over 6 mi/1 km in diameter, formed by meteorite bombardment; similar craters on Earth have mostly been worn away by erosion. Craters are found on many other bodies in the Solar System.

craton or shield the core of a continent, a vast tract of highly deformed ◊metamorphic rock around which the continent has been built. Intense mountain-building periods shook these shield areas in Precambrian times before stable conditions set in.

Cratons exist in the hearts of all the continents, a typical example being the Canadian Shield.

Crawford Joan. Adopted name of Lucille Le Sueur 1908–1977. US film actress. Beginning her career as a chorus girl 1924, her first film appearance was in 1925. She became a star with her performance as the definitive "flapper' in *Our Dancing Daughters* 1928. In the 1930s she played in many Clark Gable films, and in *Grand Hotel* 1932. In the 1940s and 1950s she appeared as a sultry, mature woman, as in *Mildred Pierce* 1945 (for which she won an Academy Award) and *Password* 1947. *Whatever Happened to Baby Jane?* 1962 was her last "great" film, before cameo appearances and *Trog* 1970.

Crawford Osbert Guy Stanhope 1886–1957. British archeologist who introduced aerial survey as a means of finding and interpreting remains, an idea conceived in World War I.

Crawley town in West Sussex, England, NE of Horsham; population (1981) 73,000. It was chartered by King John 1202 and developed as a "new town" from 1946. Industries include plastics, engineering, and printing.

Craxi Bettino 1934– . Italian Socialist politician, leader of the Italian Socialist Party (PSI) from 1976, prime minister 1983–87.

Craxi, born in Milan, became a member of the Chamber of Deputies 1968 and in 1976 general secretary of the PSI. In 1983 he became Italy's first Socialist prime minister, successfully leading a broad coalition until 1987.

crayfish freshwater decapod (ten-limbed) crustacean belonging to several families structurally similar to, but smaller than, the lobster. Crayfish are brownish-green scavengers and are found in all parts of the world except Africa. They are edible, and some species are farmed.

The spiny lobster *Palinurus vulgaris*, is sometimes called crayfish; it is actually a marine lobster without pincers, and grows up to 20 in/50 cm long.

Crazy Horse 1849–1877. Sioux Indian chief, one of the Indian leaders at the massacre of ◊Little Bighorn. He was killed when captured.

creationism a theory concerned with the origins of matter and life, claiming, as does the Bible in Genesis, that the world and humanity were created by a supernatural Creator, not more than 6,000 years ago. It was developed in response to Darwin's theory of ◊evolution; it is not recognized by most scientists as having a factual basis.

After a trial 1981–82 a US judge ruled unconstitutional an attempt in Arkansas schools to enforce equal treatment to creationism and evolutionary theory.

creation myth legend of the origin of the world. All cultures have ancient stories of the creation of the Earth or its inhabitants. Often this involves the violent death of a primordial being from whose body everything then arises; the giant Ymir in Scandinavian mythology is an example. Marriage between heaven and earth is another common explanation, as in Greek mythology (Uranus and Gaia).

creative accounting the practice of organizing and

crater *An aerial view of Meteor Crater, near Winslow, Arizona, shows the result of an impact with a large meteorite some 25,000 years ago. It is half a mile wide by about 600 feet deep.*

presenting company accounts in a way that, although desirable for the company concerned, relies on a liberal and unorthodox interpretation of general accounting procedures.

The US government has used creative accounting methods to disguise the size of the budget deficit. One method under scrutiny by Congress is the application of surpluses from the Social Security trust fund to current operating budgets, thereby showing less of a deficit. Creative accounting methods are used by administrators and political leaders at all levels to display a desired result.

Crécy, Battle of first major battle of the Hundred Years' War, 1346. Philip VI of France was defeated by Edward III of England at the village of Crécy-en-Ponthieu, now in Somme *département*, France, 11 mi/18 km NE of Abbeville.

credit in economics, means by which goods or services are obtained without immediate payment, usually by agreeing to pay interest. The three main forms are consumer credit (usually extended to individuals by retailers), bank credit (such as overdrafts or personal loans) and trade credit (common in the commercial world both within countries and internationally). Consumer credit is increasingly used to pay for goods. In the US in 1989 it amounted to $711.8 billion, with about 18.5% of disposable income expended on installment buying and credit card payments.

Crawford *Hollywood star Joan Crawford began her career in silents and had the staying power to span the Golden Age of filmmaking.*

credit card plastic-coated (or plastic) card issued by a credit company, retail outlet, or bank, which enables the holder to obtain goods or services on credit (usually to a specified limit), payable on specified terms. This may be called "paying with plastic." The first credit card was introduced 1950 in the US.

Some credit cards also act as bank cards to enable customers to obtain money from various bank branches or from automated teller machines (ATMs). "Intelligent" credit cards are now being introduced that contain coded information about the customer and the amount of credit still available. This can be "read" by a terminal connected with the company's central computer.

credit rating measure of the willingness or ability to pay for goods, loans, or services rendered by an individual, company, or country. A country with a good credit rating will attract loans on favorable terms.

Cree member of a North American Indian people whose language belongs to the Algonquian family. The Cree are distributed over a vast area in Canada from Québec to Alberta. In the US the majority of Cree live in the Rocky Boys reservation in Montana.

creed in general, any system of belief; in the Christian church the verbal confessions of faith expressing the accepted doctrines of the church. The different forms are the ◊Apostles' Creed, the ◊Nicene Creed, and the ◊Athanasian Creed. The only creed recognized by the Orthodox Church is the Nicene.

The oldest is the Apostles' Creed, which, though not the work of the apostles, was probably first formulated in the 2nd century. The full version of the Apostles' Creed, as now used, first appeared about 750.

The use of creeds as a mode of combating heresy was established by the appearance of the Nicene Creed, introduced by the Council of Nicaea in 325 when ◊Arianism was widespread, and giving the orthodox doctrine of the Trinity. The Nicene Creed used today is substantially the same as the version adopted at the church council in Constantinople in 381, with a ◊filioque clause added during the 5th and 8th centuries in the Western church.

The Athanasian Creed is thought to be later in origin than the time of Athanasius (died 373), although it represents his views in a detailed exposition of the doctrines of the Trinity and the incarnation. Some authorities suppose it to have been composed in the 8th or 9th century but others place it as early as the 4th or 5th century.

creep in civil and mechanical engineering, property of a solid, typically a metal, under continuous stress that causes it to deform below its yield point (the point at which any elastic solid normally stretches without any increase in load or stress). Lead, tin, and zinç, for example, exhibit creep at ordinary temperatures, as seen in the movement of the lead sheeting on the roofs of old buildings.

Copper, iron, nickel, and their alloys also show creep at high temperatures.

creeper any small, shortlegged passerine bird of the family Certhidae. They spiral with a mouselike movement up tree trunks, searching for insects and larvae with their thin, down-curved beaks.

The brown creeper *Certhia familiaris* is 5 in/ 12 cm long, brown above, white below, and is found across North America and Eurasia.

cremation disposal of the dead by burning. The custom was universal among ancient Indo-European peoples, for example, the Greeks, Romans, and Teutons. It was discontinued among Christians until the late 19th century because of their belief in the bodily resurrection of the dead. Overcrowded urban cemetries gave rise to its revival in the West. It has remained the usual method of disposal in the East.

Cremona city in Lombardy, Italy, on the river Po, 45 mi/72 km SE of Milan; population (1981) 81,000. It is the capital of Cremona province. Once a violin-making center, it now produces food products and textiles. It has a 12th-century cathedral.

Creole in the West Indies and Spanish America, originally someone of European descent born in the New World; later someone of mixed European and African descent. In Louisiana and other states on the Gulf of Mexico, it applies either to someone of French or Spanish descent or (popularly) to someone of mixed French or Spanish and African descent. Also, a patois or dialect based on French, Dutch, or English, as spoken in the West Indies.

creole language any ◊pidgin language that has ceased to be simply trade jargon in ports and markets and has become the mother tongue of a particular community. Many creoles have developed into distinct languages with literatures of their own; for example, Jamaican Creole, Haitian Creole, Krio in Sierra Leone, and Tok Pisin, now the official language of Papua New Guinea.

The name *creole* derives through French from Spanish and Portuguese, in which it originally referred both to children of European background born in tropical colonies and to house slaves on colonial plantations. The implication is that such groups picked up the pidgin forms of colonists' languages (Portuguese, Spanish, Dutch, French, and English) as they were used in and around the Caribbean, in parts of Africa, and in island communities in the Indian and Pacific Oceans. According to circumstance, in such places as Jamaica, Haiti, Mauritius, and W Africa there may be a "creole continuum" of usage between the strongest forms of a creole and the standard version of the language with which the creole is associated.

Creon in Greek mythology, brother of ◊Jocasta, father of Haemon, and king of Thebes in ◊Sophocles' *Antigone*.

creosote black, oily liquid derived from coal tar,

Crete

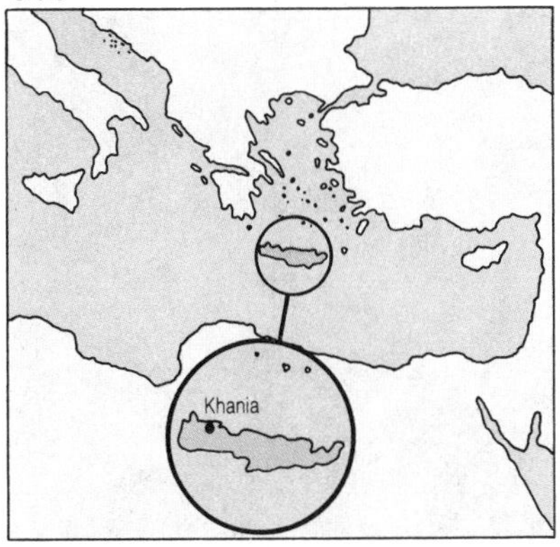
Khania

cricket

A good captain will position fielders according to the strength of the opposition's bowler, the state of the pitch and the stage the match has reached. An attacking field, with fielders close in to the batsmen, is employed when using a fast bowler. A defensive field with the fielders spread out around the boundary, is used when the batting team needs a lot of runs but has few overs remaining. With this type of field, only singles or twos are generally scored. Tactical fielding is more evident in one-day matches when each side plays a limited number of overs.

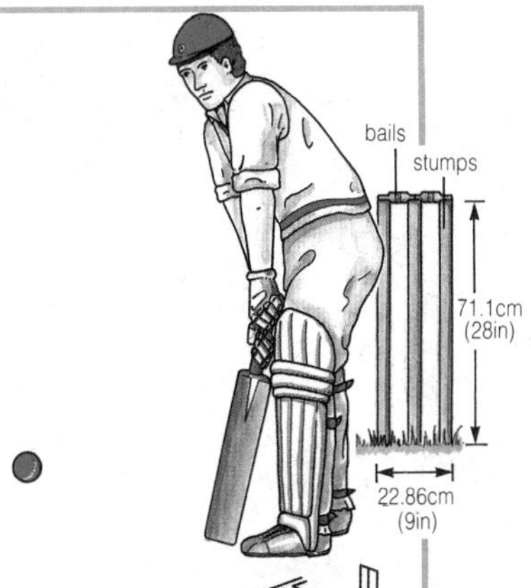
bails
stumps
71.1cm
(28in)
22.86cm
(9in)

the pitch

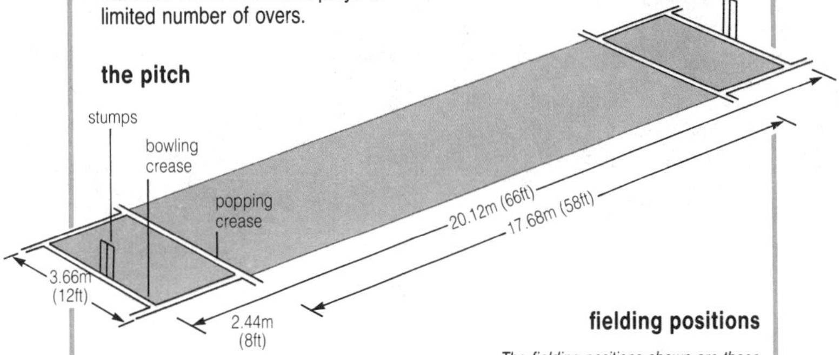
stumps
bowling
crease
popping
crease
20.12m (66ft)
17.68m (58ft)
3.66m
(12ft)
2.44m
(8ft)

fielding positions

The fielding positions shown are those available to the defending captain.

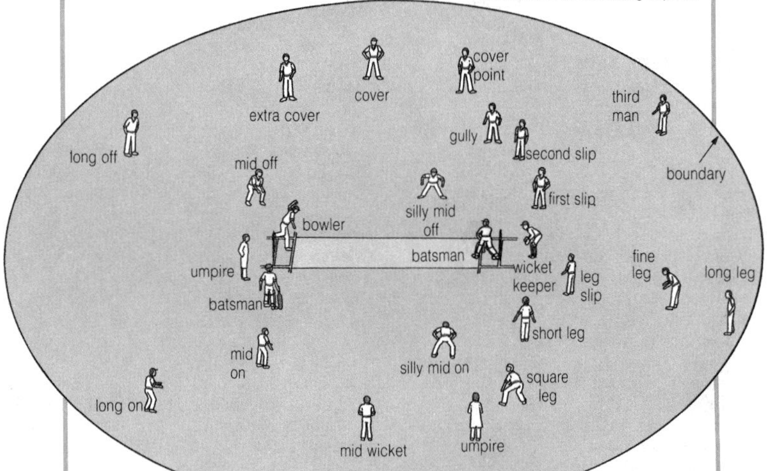
cover
point
cover
extra cover
third
man
gully
second slip
long off
mid off
boundary
silly mid
off
first slip
bowler
batsman
fine
leg
long leg
umpire
wicket
keeper
leg
slip
batsman
short leg
mid
on
silly mid on
square
leg
long on
mid wicket
umpire

used as a wood preservative. Medicinal creosote, which is transparent and oily, is derived from wood tar.

crescent the curved shape of the Moon when it appears less than half-illuminated. It also refers to any object or symbol resembling the crescent Moon. Often associated with Islam, it was first used by the Turks on their standards after the capture of Constantinople 1453 and appears on the flags of many Muslim countries. The Red Crescent is the Muslim equivalent of the Red Cross.

cress any of several plants of the Cruciferae family, characterized by a pungent taste. The common European garden cress *Lepidium sativum* is cultivated worldwide.

Cretaceous (Latin "creta" chalk) period of geologic time 144–65 million years ago. It is the last period of the Mesozoic era, during which angiosperm (seed-bearing) plants evolved, and dinosaurs and other reptiles reached a peak before almost complete extinction at the end of the period. Chalk is a typical rock type of the second half of the period.

Crete (Greek *Kríti*) the largest Greek island, in the E Mediterranean Sea, 62 mi/100 km SE of mainland Greece
area 3,234 sq mi/8,378 sq km
capital Iráklion
towns Khaniá (Canea), Rethymnon, Aghios Nikolaos
products citrus fruit, olives, wine
population (1981) 502,000
language Cretan dialect of Greek
history it has remains of the ◊Minoan civilization 3000–1400 BC, (see ◊Knossos) and was successively under Roman, Byzantine, Venetian, and Turkish rule. The island was annexed by Greece 1913.

In 1941 it was captured by German forces from Allied troops who had retreated from the mainland and was retaken by the Allies 1944.

Creuse river in central France flowing 158 mi/255 km generally north from the Plateau des Millevaches to the Vienne River. It traverses Creuse *département*, to which it gives its name.

Creusot, Le town in Saône-et-Loire *département*, France; population (1982) 32,100. It is a coal mining center and has foundries, locomotive shops, and armaments factories.

cribbage card game, invented in the 17th century by the English poet John Suckling, which is played with a holed board for keeping score. It can be played as singles or in pairs, the number of cards per player depending upon number of players. There is always a "spare hand," which each player takes in turn to "own." Cards are discarded one at a time until the face values of discarded cards total 31. When all players have discarded their cards, the total of each player's hand is calculated according to the cards held, whether they be in pairs, three of a kind, four of a kind and so on.

Crick Francis 1916–. British molecular biologist. From 1949 he and James D ◊Watson researched and finally discovered the molecular structure of DNA. For this work he was awarded a Nobel Prize (with Maurice Wilkins (1916–) and James D Watson).

cricket the national summer sport in England. The game is played between two sides of 11 players each on a field 22 yd/20 m long with a wicket at each end. The object of the game is to score more runs than the opponents. A run is normally scored by the batsman after striking the ball and exchanging ends with his or her partner, or by hitting the ball to the boundary line for an automatic four or six runs.

A batsman stands at each wicket and is bowled a stipulated number of balls (usually six), after which another bowler bowls from the other wicket. A batsman can make an "out" in several ways. Games comprise either one or two innings per team.

The exact origins are unknown. The first rules were drawn up in 1774 and modified following the formation of the Marylebone Cricket Club (MCC) in 1787.

cricket in zoology, an insect belonging to various families, especially the Grillidae, of the order Orthoptera. They are related to grasshoppers. Crickets are somewhat flattened and have long antennae. The males make a chirping noise by rubbing together special areas on the forewings. The females have a long needle-like egglaying organ (ovipositor). There are some 900 species known worldwide.

Crimea northern peninsula on the Black Sea, a region of ◊Ukraine Republic, USSR, from 1954
area 10,425 sq mi/27,000 sq km capital Simferopol
cities Sevastopol, Yalta
features mainly steppe, but the southern coast is a vacation resort
products iron, oil
recent history under Turkish rule 1475–1774, a subsequent brief independence was ended by Russian annexation 1783. It was the republic of

Crimean War *English and French allies fighting together in the Crimean War share a drink. The photograph is by Roger Fenton.*

Crispi *Resolutely anti-French and anticlerical, Francesco Crispi was Italian premier 1887–91 and 1893–96.*

Taurida 1917–20 and the Crimean Autonomous Soviet Republic from 1920 until occupied by Germany July 1942–May 1944. It was then reduced to a region, its Tatar people being deported to Uzbekistan for collaboration. Although they were exonerated 1967 and some were allowed to return, others were forcibly reexiled 1979.

Crime and Punishment a novel by Dostoievsky, published 1866. It analyzes the motives of a murderer and his reactions to the crime he has committed.

Crimean War war 1853–56 between Russia and the allied powers of England, France, Turkey, and Sardinia. The war arose from British and French mistrust of Russia's ambitions in the Balkans. It began with an allied Anglo-French expedition to the Crimea to attack the Russian Black Sea city of Sevastopol. The battles of the River Alma, Balaclava (including the charge of the Light Brigade), and Inkerman 1854 led to a siege which, due to military mismanagement, lasted for a year until Sept 1855. The war was ended by the Treaty of Paris 1856. The scandal surrounding French and British losses through disease led to the organization of proper military nursing services by Florence Nightingale.

1853 Russia invaded the Balkans (from which they were compelled to withdraw by Austrian intervention) and sank the Turkish fleet at Sinope.

1854 Britain and France declared war on Russia, invaded the Crimea and laid siege to Sevastopol (Sept 1854–Sept 1855). Battles of ◊Balaclava Oct 25 (including the charge of the Light Brigade), ◊Inkerman Nov 5, and the Alma.

1855 Sardinia declared war on Russia.

1856 The Treaty of Paris in Feb ended the war.

crime, organized a type of ◊gangsterism.

criminal law the body of law that defines the public wrongs (crimes) that are punishable by the nation, state and local governments, and establishes methods of prosecution and punishment. It is distinct from ◊civil law, which deals with legal relationships between individuals (including organizations), such as contract law.

The laws of each country specify which actions or omissions are criminal. These include serious moral wrongs, such as murder; wrongs that endanger the security of the nation, such as treason; wrongs that disrupt an orderly society, such as evading taxes; and wrongs against the community, such as dropping litter. An action may be considered a crime in one country but not in others, such as homosexuality or drinking alcohol. Some actions, such as assault, are both criminal and civil wrongs; the offender can be both prosecuted and sued for compensation.

Criminal offenses are either ◊felonies or ◊misdemeanors. Felonies are more likely to require a formal charge, called an indictment, by a grand jury. Punishments include imprisonment, fines, suspended terms of imprisonment, probation, and ◊community service.

Crispi Francesco 1819–1907. Italian prime minister 1887–91 and 1893–96. He advocated the ◊Triple Alliance of Italy with Germany and Austria, but was deposed 1896.

Criterion, The English quarterly literary review 1922–39 edited by T S Eliot. His poem *The Waste Land* was published in its first issue. It also published Auden, Pound, Joyce, and D H Lawrence, and introduced the French writers Proust and Valéry to English-language readers.

crith unit of mass used for weighing gases. One crith is the mass of one liter of hydrogen gas (H_2) at standard temperature and pressure.

critical angle in optics, for a ray of light passing from a denser to a less dense medium (such as from glass to air), the smallest angle of incidence at which the emergent ray grazes the surface of the denser medium—at an angle of refraction of 90°.

When the angle of incidence is less than the critical angle, the ray does not pass out into the less dense medium; when the angle of incidence is greater than the critical angle, the ray is not reflected back into the denser medium.

critical mass in nuclear physics, the minimum mass of fissile material that can undergo a continuous ◊chain reaction. Below this mass, too many ◊neutrons escape from the surface for a chain reaction to carry on; above the critical mass, the reaction may accelerate into a nuclear explosion.

critical temperature temperature above which a particular gas cannot be converted into a liquid by pressure alone. It is also the temperature at which a magnetic material loses its magnetism (the Curie temperature or point).

Crivelli Carlo 1435/40–1495/1500. Italian painter in the early Renaissance style, active in Venice. He painted extremely detailed, decorated religious works, sometimes festooned with garlands of fruit. His figure style is strongly Italian, reflecting the influence of Mantegna.

Croatia (Serbo-Croat *Hrvatska*) constituent republic of Yugoslavia

area 21,809 sq mi/56,500 sq km

capital Zagreb

physical Adriatic coastline with large islands; very mountainous, with part of the Karst region and the Julian and Styrian Alps; some marshland

population (1985) 4,660,000; including 75% Croats, 11% Serbs, and 0.5% Hungarians

language the Croatian variant of Serbo-Croat

history part of Pannonia in Roman times; settled by Carpathian Croats 7th century; for 800 years from 1102 an autonomous kingdom under the Hungarian crown; Austrian crownland 1849; Hungarian crownland 1868; included in the kingdom of the Serbs, Croats, and Slovenes (called Yugoslavia from 1931) 1918. It was a Nazi puppet state during World War II, and has been a center for nationalist and separatist demands from the 1970s. Tension between majority Croat and minority Serbian populations increased following the election April–May 1990 of a right-wing Croat nationalist government led by Franje Tudman, which asserted regional autonomy. A multiparty system was adopted, and in Feb 1991 the new government called for secession.

Worsening Serb-Croatia hostilities led to clashes in May 1991. The federal army intervened, but fighting continued through the summer, despite several attempts to bring about a ceasefire. In Sept 1991 President Bush accused the Serb-dominated federal army of adopting an aggressive stance toward Croatia and the EC intervened, arranging peace talks and deploying some 200 ceasefire monitors at strategic points in Yugoslavia. When these measures failed, the United Nations imposed sanctions on Yugoslavia in Nov 1991. A cease fire was reached in Jan 1992.

Croce Benedetto 1866–1952. Italian philosopher, historian, and literary critic; an opponent of fascism. His *Philosophy of the Spirit* 1902–17 was a landmark in idealism. Like Hegel, he held that ideas do not represent reality but *are* reality; but unlike Hegel, he rejected every kind of transcendence.

crochet a technique similar to both knitting and lacemaking, in which one hooked needle is used to produce a looped network of wool or cotton. Dating from the 19th century, crochet can be almost as fine and complex as lace or as simple as knitting. Both garments and trims are produced by crochetting.

Crockett Davy 1786–1836. US folk hero, born in

critical angle

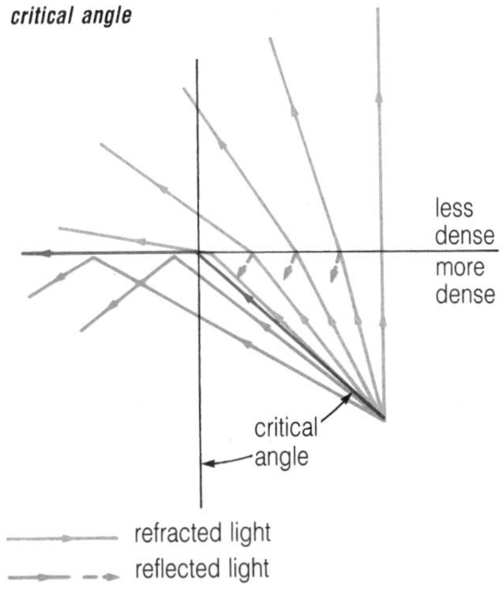
less
dense
more
dense
critical
angle
refracted light
reflected light

Tennessee, he became a Democratic Congressman 1827–31 and 1833–35. A series of books, of which he may have been part-author, made him into a mythical hero of the frontier, but their Whig associations cost him his office.

He clashed with Andrew ◊Jackson, claiming Jackson had betrayed his frontier constituency. In bitterness, he left for Texas and died in the battle of the ◊Alamo during the war for Texan independence. (See ◊Mexican War).

crocodile large aquatic carnivorous reptile of the family Crocodiliae, related to alligators and caimans, but distinguished from them by a more pointed snout, and a notch in the upper jaw into which the fourth tooth in the lower jaw fits. They can grow up to 20 ft/6 m, and have long, powerful tails that propel them when swimming. They can live up to 100 years.

Crocodiles are fierce hunters, larger specimens attacking animals the size of antelopes or, occasionally, people. In some species, the female lays over 100 hard-shelled eggs in holes or nest mounds of vegetation, which she guards until the eggs hatch. When in the sun, crocodiles cool themselves by opening their mouths wide, which also enables scavenging birds to pick their teeth. They can stay underwater for long periods, but must surface to breathe. The nostrils can be closed underwater. They ballast themselves with stones to adjust their buoyancy. They have remained virtually unchanged for 200 million years.

About a dozen species of crocodiles, all of them endangered, are found in tropical parts of Africa, Asia, Australia, and Central America. The largest is the saltwater crocodile *Crocodylus porosus*, which can grow to 20 ft/6 m or more, and is found in E India, Australia, and the W Pacific. The Nile crocodile *C. niloticus* is found in Africa and Madagascar. The American crocodile *C. acutus*, about 15 ft/4.6 m long, is found from S Florida to Ecuador. The gharial, or gavial, *Gavialis gangeticus* is sometimes placed in a family of its own. It is an Indian species which grows to 15 ft/4.5 m or

crocodile

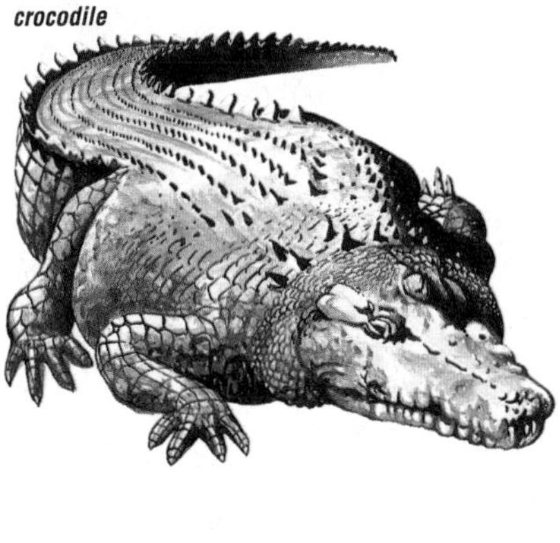

crocus

more, and has a very long narrow snout specialized for capturing and eating fish.

crocus any plant of the genus *Crocus* of the iris family Iridaceae, native to northern parts of the Old World, especially S Europe and Asia Minor. It has single yellow, purple, or white flowers and narrow, pointed leaves.

During the dry season of the year they remain underground in the form of a corm, and produce fresh shoots and flowers in spring or autumn. At the end of the season of growth fresh corms are produced. Several species are cultivated as garden plants, the familiar mauve, white, and orange forms being varieties of *C. vernus*, *C. versicolor*, and *C. aureus*. To the same genus belongs the saffron *C. sativus*. The so-called ◊autumn crocus or meadow saffron *Colchicum autumnale* is not a true crocus but belongs to the lily family.

Croesus last king of Lydia, famed for his wealth. His court included ◊Solon, who warned him that no man could be called happy until his life had ended happily. When Croesus was overthrown by Cyrus the Great 546 BC and condemned to be burned to death, he called out Solon's name. Cyrus, having learned the reason, spared his life.

croft small farm in the Highlands of Scotland, traditionally farming common land cooperatively; the 1886 Crofters Act gave security of tenure to crofters. Today, although grazing land is still shared, arable land is typically enclosed.

Crohn's disease chronic imflammatory bowel disease, also known as regional ileitis or regional enteritis. It tends to flare up for a few days at a time, causing diarrhea, abdominal cramps, loss of appetite, and mild fever. The cause of Crohn's disease is unknown, although stress may be a factor.

Crohn's disease may occur in any part of the digestive system, from the mouth to the anus, but usually affects the small intestine. It is characterized by ulceration, abscess formation, small perforations, and the development of adhesions binding the loops of the small intestine. Affected segments of intestine may constrict, causing obstruction, or may perforate. It is treated by surgical removal of badly affected segments, and by corticosteroids. Mild cases respond to rest, bland diet, and drug treatment. Crohn's disease is often seen in young adults.

Cro-Magnon a prehistoric human, *Homo sapiens sapiens*, believed to be ancestral to Europeans, the first skeletons of which were found 1868 in the Cro-Magnon cave near Les Eyzies, in the Dordogne region of France. They are thought to have superseded the Neanderthals in the Near East, Africa, Europe, and Asia about 40,000 years ago. Although modern in skeletal form, they were more robust in build than some present-day humans. They hunted bison, reindeer, and horses, and are associated with Upper Paleolithic cultures, which produced fine flint and bone tools, jewelry, and naturalistic cave paintings.

Cromwell Oliver 1599–1658. English general and politician, Puritan leader of the Parliamentary side in the ◊Civil War. He raised cavalry forces (later called Ironsides) which aided the victories at Edgehill 1642 and ◊Marston Moor 1644, and organized the New Model Army, which he led (with General Fairfax) to victory at Naseby 1645. As Lord Protector (ruler) from 1653, he established religious toleration and raised Britain's prestige in Europe on the basis of an alliance with France against Spain.

Cromwell was a critic of Charles I and became active in events leading to the Civil War. He signed the king's death warrant in 1648 and in the power struggle that followed sided with the army and the establishment of the Commonwealth. He expelled parliament and established the Protectorate. His foreign policy was dictated by religious and commercial considerations; he found no constitutional basis for his rule and refused the crown 1657.

Cromwell Richard 1626–1712. Son of Oliver ◊Cromwell, he succeeded his father as Lord Protector but resigned May 1659, having been forced to abdicate by the army. He lived in exile after the Restoration until 1680, when he returned.

Cromwell Thomas, Earl of Essex c. 1485–1540. English politician who drafted the legislation making the Church of England independent of Rome. Originally in Lord Chancellor Wolsey's service, he became secretary to Henry VIII 1534 and the real director of government policy; he was executed for treason.

Cromwell had Henry divorced from Catherine of Aragon by a series of acts that proclaimed him head of the church. From 1536 to 1540 Cromwell suppressed the monasteries, ruthlessly crushed all opposition, and favored Protestantism, which denied the divine right of the pope. His mistake in arranging Henry's marriage to Anne of Cleves (to cement an alliance with the German Protestant princes against France and the Holy Roman Empire) led to his being accused of treason and beheaded.

Cronkite Walter 1916– . US broadcast journalist, who enjoyed wide popularity throughout the US as anchorman of the national evening news program for CBS television network, from 1962 to 1981.

Cronus or ***Kronus*** in Greek mythology, ruler of the world and one of the ◊Titans. He was the father of Zeus, who overthrew him.

Crookes William 1832–1919. English scientist, whose many chemical and physical discoveries included the metallic element thallium 1861, the radiometer 1875, and Crookes' high-vacuum tube used in X-ray techniques.

crop in birds, the thin-walled enlargement of the digestive tract between the esophagus and stomach. It is an effective storage organ especially in seed-eating birds; a pigeon's crop can hold about 500 cereal grains. Digestion begins in the crop, by the moisturizing of food. A crop also occurs in insects and annelid worms.

crop any plant product grown or harvested for human use. Over 80 major crops are grown worldwide, providing people with the majority of their food and supplying fibers, rubber, pharmaceuticals, dyes, and other materials.

There are four main groups of crops: food, forage, fibers, and the miscellaneous materials used for many products. Food crops provide the bulk of people's food worldwide. The major types are cereals, roots, pulses (peas, beans), vegetables, fruits, oil crops, tree nuts, sugar, and spices. Cereals make the largest contribution to human nutrition. Forage crops are those such as grass and clover, which are grown to feed livestock; they cover a greater area of the world than food crops. Grasses, which dominate this group, form the world's most abundant crop, consisting mostly of wild species grown in an unimproved state. Fiber crops produce vegetable fibers. Temperate areas produce flax and hemp, but the most valuable fiber crops are cotton, jute, and sisal, which are grown mostly in the tropics. Cotton dominates fiber crop production. Miscellaneous crops include tobacco, rubber, ornamental flowers, and plants that produce perfumes, pharmaceuticals, and dyes. See also ◊catch crop.

crop rotation the system of regularly changing the crops grown on a piece of land. The crops are grown in a particular order to utilize and add to the nutrients in the soil and to prevent the buildup of insect and fungal pests.

In the 18th-century, a four year rotation was widely adopted with autumn-sown cereal, followed by a root crop, then spring cereal, and ending with a leguminous crop. Since then, more elaborate rotations have been devised with two, three, or four successive cereal crops, and with the root crop replaced by a cash crop such as sugar beet or potatoes, or by a legume crop such as peas or beans.

croquet outdoor game played with mallets and balls on a level lawn measuring 90 ft/27 m by 60 ft/18 m. Played in France in the 16th and 17th centuries, it gained popularity in the US and England in the 1850s. Two or more players can play, and the object is to drive the balls though a series of hoops (wickets) in rotation. A player's ball may be advanced or retarded by another ball.

Crosby Bing (Harry Lillis) 1904–1977. US film actor and singer who achieved world success with his distinctive style of 1920s and 1930s crooning in such songs as "Pennies from Heaven" and "White Christmas," later featured in films of the same names. He won an acting Oscar for *Going My Way* 1944, and made a series of "road" film comedies with Dorothy Lamour and Bob Hope, the last being *Road to Hong Kong* 1962.

crossbill species of bird, a ◊finch of the genus *Loxia*, in which the hooked tips of the upper and lower beak cross one another, an adaptation for extracting the seeds from conifer cones. The red crossbill *Loxia curvirostra* is found in parts of Eurasia and North America.

The parrot crossbill *Loxia pytopsittacus* of Europe, and the white-winged crossbill *Loxia leucoptera* of N Asia and North America feed on pine and larch respectively.

cross-eye alternative term for ◊squint.

crossing over in biology, a process that occurs during ◊meiosis. While the chromosomes are lying alongside each other in pairs, each partner may twist around the other and exchange corresponding chromosomal segments. It is a form of genetic ◊recombination, which increases variation and thus provides the raw material of evolution.

crossword a puzzle in which a grid of open and blacked-out squares (often in a designed pattern) must be filled with interlocking words, to be read horizontally and vertically, according to numbered clues. The first crossword was devised by Arthur Wynne of Liverpool, England, in the *New York World* 1913.

croup inflammation (usually viral) of a child's larynx and trachea, with croaking breathing and hoarse coughing.

crow any of 35 species of the genus *Corvus*, family Corvidae, which also includes jays and magpies. Ravens belong to the same genus as crows. Crows are usually about 1.5 ft/45 cm long, black, with a strong bill feathered at the base, and omnivorous with a bias toward animal food. They are considered to be very intelligent.

Crowley John 1942– . US writer of science fiction and fantasy, notably *Little, Big* 1980 and *Aegypt* 1987, which contain esoteric knowledge and theoretical puzzles.

crown an official headdress worn by a king or queen. The modern crown originated with the diadem, an embroidered fillet worn by Eastern rulers, for which a golden band was later substituted. A laurel crown was granted by the Greeks to a victor in the games, and by the Romans to a triumphant general. Crowns came into use among the Byzantine emperors and the European kings after the fall of the Western Empire.

Perhaps the oldest in Europe is the Iron Crown of Lombardy, made in 591. The crown of Charlemagne, preserved in Vienna, consists of eight gold plates.

crown colony any British colony that is under the direct legislative control of the crown and does not possess its own system of representative government. Crown colonies are administered by a crown-appointed governor or by elected or nominated legislative and executive councils with an official majority. Usually the crown retains rights of veto and of direct legislation by orders in council.

crucifixion death by fastening to a cross, a form of capital punishment used by the ancient Romans, Persians, and Carthaginians, and abolished by the Roman emperor Constantine. Specifically, the Crucifixion refers to the execution by the Romans of ◊Jesus in this manner.

Cruelty, Theater of a theory advanced by Antonin ◊Artaud in his book *Le Theâtre et son double* 1938 and adopted by a number of writers and directors. It aims to shock the audience into an awareness of basic, primitive human nature through the release of feelings usually repressed by conventional behavior.

Cruikshank George 1792–1878. British painter and illustrator, remembered for his political cartoons and illustrations for Charles Dickens's *Oliver Twist* and Daniel Defoe's *Robinson Crusoe*.

cruise missile a long-range guided missile that has a terrain-seeking radar system and flies at moderate speed and low altitude. It is descended from the German V-1 of World War II. Initial trials in the 1950s demonstrated the limitations of cruise missiles, which included high fuel consumption and relatively slow speeds (when compared to intercontinental ballistic missiles—ICBMs) as well as inaccuracy and a small warhead. Improvements to guidance systems by the use of terrain-contour matching (TERCOM) ensured pinpoint accuracy on low-level flights after launch from a mobile ground launcher (ground-launched cruise missile—GLCM), from an aircraft (air-launched cruise missile—ALCM), or from a submarine or ship (sea-launched cruise missile—SLCM).

crusade European war against non-Christians and

First Crusade 1095–99

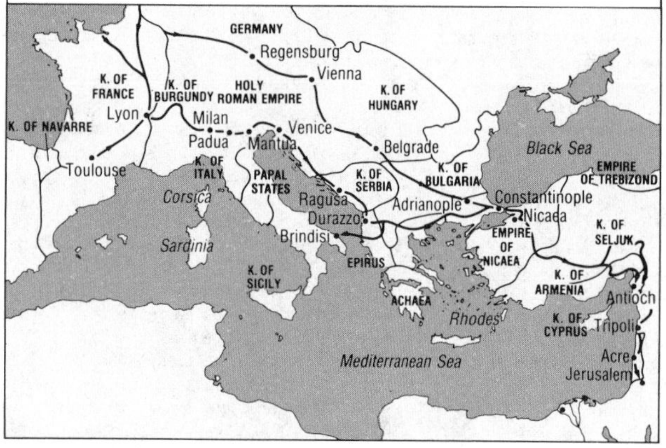
GERMANY
Regensburg
Vienna
K. OF FRANCE
K. OF BURGUNDY
HOLY ROMAN EMPIRE
K. OF HUNGARY
Lyon
K. OF NAVARRE
Milan
Venice
Padua
Mantua
Belgrade
Black Sea
Toulouse
K. OF ITALY
PAPAL STATES
K. OF SERBIA
K. OF BULGARIA
EMPIRE OF TREBIZOND
Corsica
Ragusa
Adrianople
Constantinople
Durazzo
Nicaea
Brindisi
EMPIRE OF NICAEA
K. OF SELJUK
Sardinia
EPIRUS
K. OF SICILY
K. OF ARMENIA
ACHAEA
Antioch
Rhodes
K. OF CYPRUS
Tripoli
Mediterranean Sea
Acre
Jerusalem

Second Crusade 1147–49

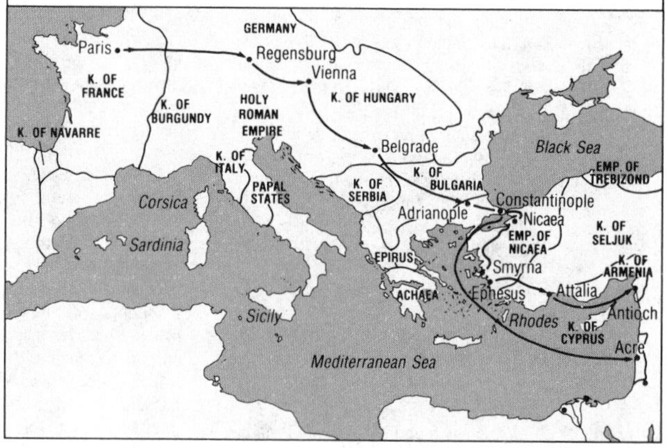
GERMANY
Paris
Regensburg
Vienna
K. OF FRANCE
K. OF BURGUNDY
HOLY ROMAN EMPIRE
K. OF HUNGARY
K. OF NAVARRE
Belgrade
Black Sea
K. OF ITALY
K. OF BULGARIA
EMP. OF TREBIZOND
Corsica
PAPAL STATES
K. OF SERBIA
Constantinople
Adrianople
Nicaea
Sardinia
EMP. OF NICAEA
K. OF SELJUK
EPIRUS
Smyrna
K. OF ARMENIA
ACHAEA
Ephesus
Attalia
Sicily
Rhodes
K. OF CYPRUS
Antioch
Acre
Mediterranean Sea

Third Crusade 1189–92

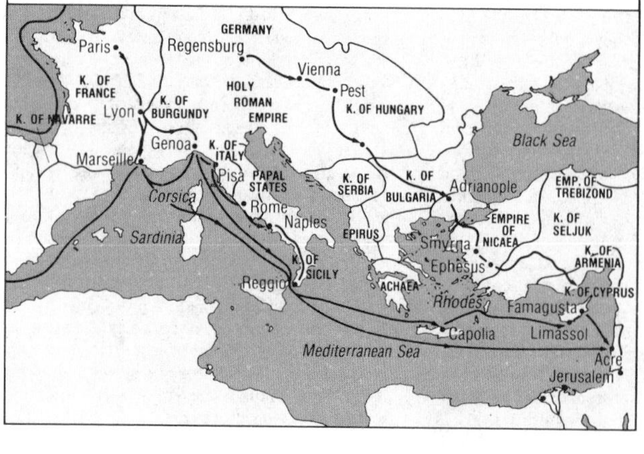
GERMANY
Paris
Regensburg
Vienna
K. OF FRANCE
HOLY ROMAN EMPIRE
Pest
K. OF BURGUNDY
K. OF HUNGARY
K. OF NAVARRE
Lyon
Black Sea
Genoa
K. OF ITALY
Marseille
Pisa
PAPAL STATES
K. OF SERBIA
K. OF BULGARIA
Adrianople
EMP. OF TREBIZOND
Corsica
Rome
Naples
EMPIRE OF NICAEA
K. OF SELJUK
Sardinia
EPIRUS
Smyrna
K. OF ARMENIA
Ephesus
K. OF SICILY
Reggio
ACHAEA
K. OF CYPRUS
Rhodes
Famagusta
Capolia
Limassol
Mediterranean Sea
Acre
Jerusalem

Fourth Crusade, Venice–Constantinople 1202–04

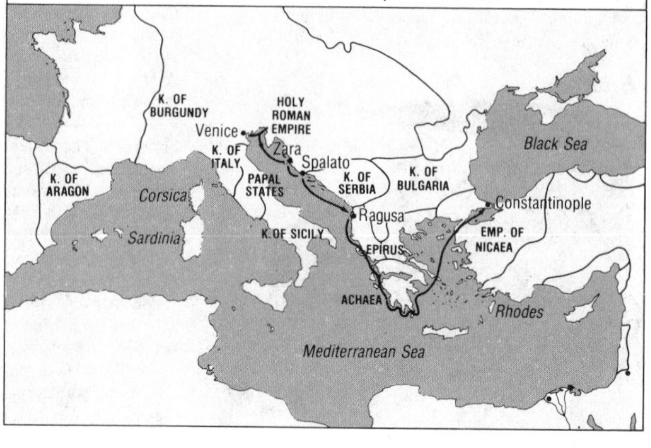
K. OF BURGUNDY
HOLY ROMAN EMPIRE
Venice
Zara
K. OF ITALY
Black Sea
Spalato
K. OF ARAGON
PAPAL STATES
K. OF SERBIA
K. OF BULGARIA
Corsica
Constantinople
Ragusa
Sardinia
K. OF SICILY
EMP. OF NICAEA
EPIRUS
ACHAEA
Rhodes
Mediterranean Sea

crust

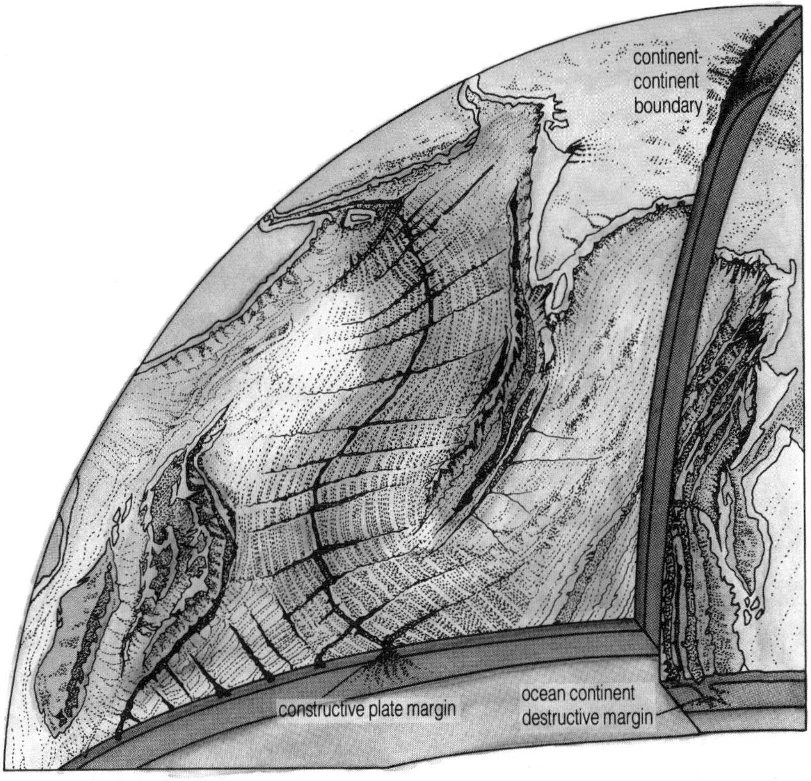
continent-
continent
boundary
constructive plate margin
ocean continent
destructive margin

heretics, sanctioned by the pope; in particular, a series of wars 1096–1291 undertaken by European rulers to recover Palestine from the Muslims. Motivated by religious zeal, the desire for land, and the trading ambitions of the major Italian cities, the Crusades were varied in their aims and effects.

1st Crusade 1095–99 led by Baldwin of Boulogne, Godfrey of Bouillon, and Peter the Hermit. Motivated by occupation of Anatolia and Jerusalem by the Seljuk Turks. The crusade succeeded in recapturing Jerusalem and establishing a series of Latin kingdoms on the Syrian coast.

2nd Crusade 1147–49 led by Louis VII of France and Emperor Conrad III; a complete failure.

3rd Crusade 1189–92 led by Philip II Augustus of France and Richard I of England. Failed to recapture Jerusalem, which had been seized by Saladin 1187.

4th Crusade 1202–04 led by William of Montferrata, and Baldwin of Hainault. Directed against Egypt but diverted by the Venetians to sack and divide Constantinople.

Children's Crusade 1212 thousands of children crossed Europe on their way to the Holy Land but many were sold into slavery at Marseille, or died of disease and hunger.

5th Crusade 1218–21 led by King Andrew of Hungary, Cardinal Pelagius, King John of Jerusalem, and King Hugh of Cyprus. Captured and then lost Damietta, Egypt.

6th Crusade 1228–29 led by the Holy Roman emperor Frederick II. Jerusalem recovered by negotiation with the sultan of Egypt, but the city was finally lost 1244.

7th and 8th Crusades 1249–54, 1270–72 both led by Louis IX of France. Acre, the last Christian fortress in Syria, was lost 1291.

crust the outermost part of the structure of Earth, consisting of two distinct parts, the oceanic crust and the continental crust. The oceanic crust is on average about 6.2 mi/10 km thick and consists mostly of basaltic types of rock. By contrast, the continental crust is primarily granitic in composition and more complex in its structure. Because of the movements of ◊plate tectonics, the oceanic crust is in no place older than about 200 million years. However, parts of the continental crust are over three billion years old.

Beneath a layer of surface sediment, the oceanic crust is made up of a layer of basalt, followed by a layer of gabbro. The composition of the oceanic crust overall shows a high proportion of silicon and magnesium oxides, hence named sima by geologists. The continental crust varies in thickness between about 25–43 mi/40–70 km, being deeper beneath mountain ranges. The surface layer consists of many kinds of sedimentary and igneous rocks. Beneath lies a zone of metamorphic rocks built on a thick layer of granodiorite. Silicon and aluminum oxides dominate the composition and the name sial is given to continental crustal material.

crustacean one of the class of arthropods that includes crabs, lobsters, shrimps, pillbugs, and barnacles. The external skeleton is made of protein and chitin hardened with lime. Each segment bears a pair of appendages that may be modified as sensory feelers (antennae), as mouthparts, or as swimming, walking, or grasping structures.

Crux constellation of the southern hemisphere, popularly known as the Southern Cross, the smallest of the 88 constellations. Its brightest star, Alpha Crucis (or Acrux), is a ◊double star about 360 light-years from Earth. Near Beta Crucis lies a glittering star cluster known as the Jewel Box. The constellation also contains the Coalsack, a dark cloud of dust silhouetted against the bright starry background of the Milky Way.

cryogenics science of very low temperatures (approaching ◊absolute zero), including the production of very low temperatures and the exploitation of special properties associated with them, such as the disappearance of electrical resistance (◊superconductivity).

Low temperatures can be produced by the Joule–Thomson effect (cooling a gas by making it do work as it expands; gases such as oxygen, hydrogen, and helium may be liquefied in this way, and temperatures of 0·3K can be reached. Further cooling requires magnetic methods; a magnetic material, in contact with the substance to be cooled and with liquid helium, is magnetized by a strong magnetic field. The heat generated by the process is carried away by the helium. When the material is then demagnetized, its temperature falls; temperatures of around 10^{-3}K have been achieved in this way. A similar process, called nuclear adiabatic expansion, was used to produce the lowest temperature recorded: 3×10^{-8}K, produced in 1984 by a team of Finnish scientists.

At temperatures near absolute zero, materials can display unusual properties. Some metals, such as mercury and lead, exhibit superconductivity. Liquid helium loses its viscosity and becomes a "superfluid" when cooled to below 2K; in this state it flows up the sides of its container.

Cryogenics has several practical applications. Cryotherapy is a process used in eye surgery, in which a freezing probe is briefly applied to the outside of the eye to repair a break in the retina. Electronic components called ◊Josephson junctions, which could be used in very fast computers, need low temperatures to function. Magnetic levitation (◊maglev) systems must be maintained at low temperatures. Food can be frozen for years, and it has been suggested that space travelers could be frozen for long journeys. Freezing people with terminal illnesses, to be revived when a cure has been developed, has also been suggested.

cryolite rare granular crystalline mineral, sodium aluminum fluoride (Na_3AlF_6), used in the electrolyte reduction of ◊bauxite to aluminum. It is chiefly found in Greenland.

Cryolite also occurs in Colorado at Pike's Peak.

cryonics practice of freezing a body at the moment of clinical death with the aim of enabling eventual resuscitation. The body, drained of blood, is indefinitely preserved in a thermos-type container filled with liquid nitrogen at –321°F/–196°C.

The first human treated was James H Bedford, a lung-cancer patient of 74, in the US in 1967.

cryptogam an obsolete name applied to the lower plants. It included the algae, liverworts, mosses, and ferns (plus the fungi and bacteria in very early schemes of classification). In such classifications seed plants were known as ◊phanerogams.

cryptography science of creating and reading codes; for example, those produced by the Enigma coding machine used by the Germans in World War II (as in ◊Ultra) and those used in commerce by banks encoding electronic fund-transfer messages, business firms sending computer-conveyed memos between headquarters, and in the growing field of electronic mail. No method of encrypting is completely unbreakable, but decoding can be made extremely complex and time consuming.

cryptorchism or ***cryptochidism*** condition marked by undescended testicles; failure of the testes to complete their descent into the scrotum before birth. When only one testicle has descended, the condition is known as monorchism.

About 10% of boys are born with one or both testes undescended. Usually the condition resolves within a few weeks of birth. Otherwise, an operation is needed to bring the testes down and ensure normal sexual development.

crystal substance with an orderly three-dimensional arrangement of its atoms or molecules, thereby creating an external surface of clearly defined smooth faces having characteristic angles between them. Examples are common salt and quartz.

Each geometrical figure or form, many of which may be combined in one crystal, consists of two or more faces—for example, dome, prism, and pyramid.

Crystals fall into seven crystal systems or

crystal

sodium chloride

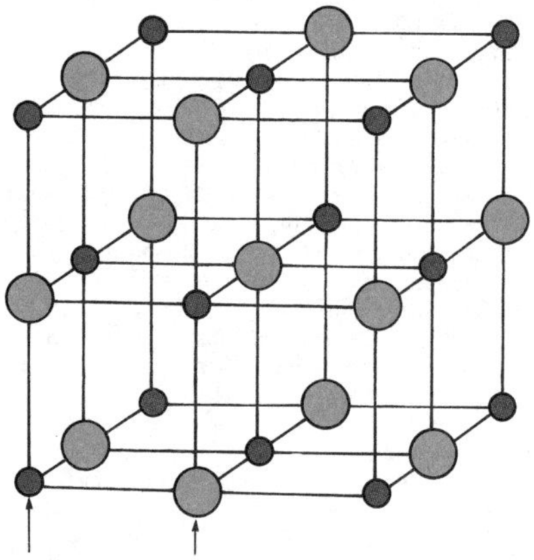
sodium
atom (Na)
chlorine
atom (Cl)

groups, classified on the basis of the relationship of three or four imaginary axes that intersect at the center of any perfect, undistorted crystal form. A mineral can often be identified by the shape of its crystals and the crystal system determined. A single crystal can vary in size from a submicroscopic particle to a mass some 100 ft/30 m in length.

crystallography the scientific study of crystals. In 1912, it was found that the shape and size of the unit cell of a crystal can be discovered by X rays, thus opening up an entirely new way of "seeing" atoms. This means of determining the atomic patterns in a crystal is known as X-ray diffraction. By this method it has been found that many substances have a unit cell that exhibits all the symmetry of the whole crystal. In table salt (sodium chloride, NaCl), for instance, the unit cell is an exact cube. It has been shown that even purified biomolecules, such as proteins and DNA, can form crystals, and such compounds may now be studied by the same method. Another field of application of X-ray analysis lies in the study of metals and alloys. Crystallography is also of use to the geologist studying rocks and soils. Many materials were not even suspected of being crystals until they were examined by X-ray crystallography.

Crystal Palace glass and iron building designed by ◊Paxton, housing the Great Exhibition of 1851 in Hyde Park, London; later rebuilt in modified form at Sydenham Hill 1854 (burned down 1936).

crystal system all known crystalline substances crystallize in one of the seven crystal systems defined by symmetry. The elements of symmetry used for this purpose are: (1) planes of mirror symmetry, across which a miror image is seen, and (2) axes of rotational symmetry, about which, in a 360° rotation of the crystal, equivalent faces are seen twice, three, four, or six times. To be assigned to a particular crystal system, a mineral must possess a certain minimum symmetry, but it may also possess additional symmetry elements. Since crystal symmetry is related to internal structure, a given mineral will always crystallize in the same system, although the crystals may not always grow into precisely the same shape. In cases where two minerals have the same chemical composition (for example graphite and diamond, or quartz and crystobalite), they will generally have different crystal systems because their internal structures are different.

CSCE abbreviation for Conference on Security and Cooperation in Europe, popularly known as the ◊Helsinki Conference.

CT abbreviation for ◊Connecticut.

Ctesiphon ruined royal city of the Parthians, and later capital of the Sassanian Empire, 12 mi/19 km SE of Baghdad, Iraq. A palace of the 4th century still has its throne room standing, spanned by a single vault of unreinforced brickwork some 80 ft/24 m across.

cu abbreviation for cubic (measure).

Cuba island in the Caribbean, the largest of the West Indies, off the south coast of Florida.

government The 1976 constitution created a Socialist state with the National Assembly of People's Power as its supreme organ. It consists of 510 deputies elected by universal suffrage for a five-year term and elects 31 of its members to form the Council of State. It also elects the head of state, who is president of the council, head of government, and first secretary and chairman of the political bureau of the only party, the Cuban Communist Party (PCC). Fidel ◊Castro thus occupies all the key positions within the state and the party.

history The first Europeans to visit Cuba were those of the expedition of Christopher ◊Columbus 1492, who found Arawak Indians there. From 1511 Cuba was a Spanish colony, its economy based on sugar plantations worked by slaves, who were first brought from Africa in 1523 to replace the decimated Indian population. Slavery was not abolished until 1886. Cuba was ceded to the US in 1898, at the end of the ◊Spanish-American War. A republic was proclaimed in 1901, but the US retained its naval base and asserted a right to intervene in internal affairs until 1934.

In 1933 an army sergeant, Fulgencio ◊Batista, seized and held power until he retired in 1944. In 1952 he regained power in a bloodless coup and began another period of rule that many Cubans found oppressive. In 1953 a young lawyer and son of a sugar planter, Dr Fidel Castro, tried to overthrow him but failed. He went into exile to prepare for another coup in 1956 but was again defeated. He fled to the hills with Dr Ernesto "Che" ◊Guevara and ten others to form a guerrilla force.

In 1959 Castro's force of 5,000 men deposed Batista, to great popular acclaim. The 1940 constitution was suspended and replaced by a "Fundamental Law," power being vested in a council of ministers with Castro as prime minister, his brother Raul as his deputy, and Che Guevara, reputedly, as the next in command. In 1960 the US broke off diplomatic relations after all US businesses in Cuba were nationalized without compensation. In 1961 it went further, sponsoring a full-scale (but abortive) invasion, the ◊Bay of Pigs episode. In Dec of that year Castro proclaimed a communist state whose economy would develop along Marxist-Leninist lines.

In 1962 Cuba was expelled from the Organization of American States (OAS) – originally

Cuba
Republic of
(República de Cuba)

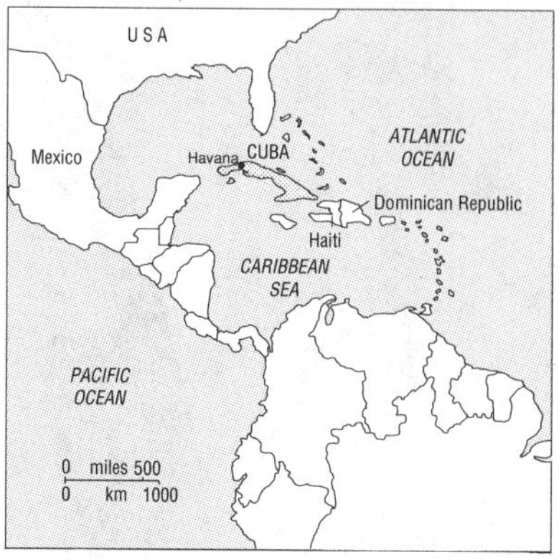
USA
Mexico
Havana
CUBA
ATLANTIC
OCEAN
Dominican Republic
Haiti
CARIBBEAN
SEA
PACIFIC
OCEAN
0 miles 500
0 km 1000

area 42,820 sq mi/110,860 sq km
capital Havana
cities Santiago de Cuba, Camagüey
physical comprises Cuba, the largest and westernmost of the West Indies, and smaller islands including Isle of Youth; low hills; Sierra Maestra mountains in SE
features 2,100 mi/3,380 km of coastline, with deep bays, sandy beaches, coral islands and reefs; more than 1,600 islands surround the Cuban mainland
head of state and government Fidel Castro Ruz from 1959
political system communist republic
political parties Communist Party of Cuba (PCC), Marxist-Leninist
exports sugar, tobacco, coffee, nickel, fish
currency Cuban peso
population (1990 est) 10,582,000 (plus 125,000 refugees—*marielitos*—from the Cuban port of Mariel in US); 37% are white of Spanish descent, 51% mulatto, and 11% are of African origin; growth rate 0.6% p.a.
life expectancy men 72, women 75
language Spanish
religion Roman Catholic 85%; also Episcopalians and Methodists
literacy men 96%/women 95% (1988)
disposable national income $15.8 bn (1983); $1,590 per head

chronology
1901 Cuba achieved independence from Spain; Tomás Estrada Palma became first president of the Republic of Cuba.
1933 Fulgencia Batista seized power.
1944 Batista retired.
1952 Batista seized power again to begin an oppressive regime.
1953 Fidel Castro led an unsuccessful coup against Batista, and again in 1956.
1959 Batista overthrown by Castro. Constitution of 1940 replaced by a "Fundamental Law," making Castro prime minister, his brother Raúl Castro his deputy, and Ché Guevara his number three.
1960 All US businesses in Cuba appropriated without compensation; US broke off diplomatic relations.
1961 US sponsored an unsuccessful invasion at the Bay of Pigs. Castro announced that Cuba had become a Communist state, with a Marxist-Leninist program of economic development.
1962 Cuba expelled from the Organization of American States (OAS). Soviet nuclear missiles removed from Cuba at US insistence.
1965 Cuba's sole political party renamed Cuban Communist Party (PCC). With Soviet help, Cuba began to make considerable economic and social progress.
1972 Cuba became a full member of the Moscow-based Council for Mutual Economic Assistance (CMEA).
1976 New Socialist constitution approved; Castro elected president.
1976–81 Castro became involved in extensive international commitments, sending troops as Soviet surrogates, particularly to Africa.
1982 Cuba joined other Latin American countries in giving moral support to Argentina in its dispute with Britain over the Falklands.
1984 Castro tried to improve US-Cuban relations by discussing the exchange of US prisoners in Cuba with Cuban "undesirables" in the US.
1988 Peace accord with South Africa signed, agreeing to withdrawal of Cuban troops from Angola.
1989 Reduction in Cuba's overseas military activities. Castro reaffirmed Communist orthodoxy.

formed as a regional agency of the UN but increasingly dominated by the US—which initiated a full political and economic blockade. Castro responded by tightening relations with the USSR that, in the same year, supplied missiles with atomic warheads for installation in Cuba. The ◊"Cuban missile crisis" brought the US and USSR to the brink of nuclear war, but conflict was averted when the USSR agreed to dismantle the missiles at the US president's insistence.

In 1965 Guevara left Cuba and was killed in Bolivia during an attempted uprising. Cuba's only political party later changed its name to the Cuban Communist Party (PCC). With Soviet help, Cuba made substantial economic and social progress 1965–72, in 1972 becoming a member of the Council for Mutual Economic Assistance (CMEA), a Moscow-based organization linking communist states.

In 1976 a referendum approved a Socialist constitution, and Fidel Castro and his brother were elected president and vice-president. During the following five years Cuba played a larger role in world affairs, particularly in Africa, to the disquiet of the US. Cuban troops played an important role in Angola, supporting the Luanda government against South African-backed rebels.

Re-elected in 1981, Castro offered to discuss foreign policy with the US but Cuba's support for Argentina, against Britain, cooled relations and drew it closer to other Latin American countries. The 1983 US invasion of Grenada lowered the diplomatic temperature still further, though Cuba has since adopted a more conciliatory position toward the US. Cuban support of leftist rebels seeking to overthrow the government of El Salvador caused continuing strains with the US. Castro also reaffirmed his communist orthodoxy in the light of events in eastern Europe in 1989–90. The advent of ◊Gorbachev and the USSR's abandonment of its policy of supporting Third World revolutions led in 1989 to a curtailment of Cuba's foreign military interventions.

Cubango Portuguese name for the ◊Okavango River in Africa.

Cuban Missile Crisis a crisis in international relations in Oct 1962, when Soviet nuclear missiles had been installed in Cuba and President Kennedy compelled ◊Khrushchev, by an ultimatum, to remove them. The US imposed a naval "quarantine" around the island, and the two superpowers came closer to possible nuclear war than at any other time. Soviet inferiority in nuclear weapons forced a humiliating capitulation to Kennedy's demands. Some historians maintain that Kennedy's lack of resolve during the ◊Bay of Pigs operation gave Khrushchev reason to believe that the US would not resist the introduction of Soviet missiles into Cuba. The drive by the USSR to match the US in nuclear weaponry dates from this event.

In Aug 1979 a lesser Cuban crisis occurred, when President Carter discovered a Soviet combat brigade on the island but failed to enforce its withdrawal.

cube in geometry, a solid figure whose faces are all squares. It has six equal-area faces and 12 equal-length edges. If the length of one edge is l, the volume V of the cube is given by $V = l^3$ and its surface area $A = 6l^2$.

cubic measure measure of volume, indicated either by the prefix cubic followed by a linear measure, as in "cubic foot," or the suffix cubed, as in "meter cubed."

Cubism revolutionary movement in early 20th-century painting, pioneering abstract art. Its founders, Braque and Picasso, were admirers of Cézanne and were inspired by his attempt to create a structure on the surface of the canvas. About 1907–10 the Cubists began to "abstract" images from nature, gradually releasing themselves from the imitation of reality. Cubism announced that a work of art exists in its own right rather than as a representation of the real world. It attracted such artists as Juan Gris, Fernand Léger, and Robert Delaunay.

cubit earliest-known unit of length, which originated between 2800 and 2300 BC. Approximately 20.6 in/50.5 cm long, which is about the length of the human forearm, measured from the tip of the middle finger to the elbow.

cuboid a six-sided three-dimensional prism whose faces are all rectangles. A brick is a cuboid.

Cuchulain in Celtic mythology, a legendary hero, the chief figure in a cycle of Irish legends. He is associated with his uncle Conchobar, king of Ulster; his most famous exploits are described in *Tain Bó Cuailnge/The Cattle-Raid of Cuchulain*.

cuckoo species of bird, any of about 200 members of the family Cuculidae, especially the Eurasian cuckoo *Cuculus canorus*, whose name derives from its characteristic call. Somewhat hawklike, it is about 1.1 ft/33 cm long, bluish-gray and barred beneath (females sometimes reddish), and has a long, typically rounded tail. Cuckoos feed on insects, including hairy caterpillars that are distasteful to most birds. It is a "brood parasite," laying its eggs singly, at intervals of about 48 hours, in the nests of small insectivorous birds. As soon as the young cuckoo hatches, it ejects all other young birds or eggs from the nest and is tended by its "foster-parents" until fledging. American species hatch and rear their own young.

The North American roadrunner *Geococcyx californianus* is a member of the cuckoo family.

cuckoo spit the frothy liquid surrounding and exuded by the larvae of the spittlebug (◊froghopper).

cucumber trailing annual plant *Cucumis sativus* of the gourd family Cucurbitaceae, producing long, green-skinned fruit with crisp, translucent, edible flesh. Small cucumbers, called gherkins, usually the fruit of *C. anguria*, are often pickled.

Cúcuta capital of Norte de Santander department, NE Colombia; population (1985) 379,000. It is situated in a tax-free zone close to the Venezuelan border, and trades in coffee, tobacco, and cattle. It was a focal point of the independence movement and meeting place of the first Constituent Congress 1821.

Cuenca city in S Ecuador; population (1980) 140,000. It is capital of Azuay province. Industries include chemicals, food processing, agricultural machinery, and textiles. It was founded by the Spanish in 1557.

Cuenca city in Spain, at the confluence of the rivers Júcar and Huécar; 84 mi/135 km SE of Madrid; population (1981) 42,000. It is the capital of Cuenca province. It has a 13th-century cathedral.

Cugnot Nicolas-Joseph 1728–1804. French engineer who produced the first high-pressure steam engine. While serving in the French army, he was asked to design a steam-operated gun carriage. After several years, he produced a three-wheeled, high-pressure carriage capable of carrying 400 gal/1800 l of water and four passengers at a speed of 3 mph/5 kph. Although he worked further on the carriage, the political upheavals of the French revolutionary era obstructed progress and his invention was ignored.

Cui Casar Antonovich 1853–1918. Russian composer of operas and chamber music. A professional soldier, he joined ◊Balakirev's Group of Five and promoted a Russian national style.

Cuiaba town in Brazil, on the Cuiaba river; population (1980) 168,000. It is the capital of Mato Grosso state. Gold and diamonds are worked nearby.

Cukor George 1899–1983. US film director. He moved to films from the theater, and was praised for his skilled handling of stars such as Greta ◊Garbo (in *Camille* 1937) and Katharine Hepburn (in *The Philadelphia Story* 1940). His films were usually sophisticated dramas or light comedies.

Culiacán Rosales capital of Sinaloa state, NW Mexico; population (1980) 560,000. It trades in vegetables and textiles.

Culloden, Battle of defeat 1746 of the Jacobite rebel army of the British Prince ◊Charles Edward Stuart by the Duke of ◊Cumberland on a stretch of moorland in Inverness-shire, Scotland. This battle effectively ended the military challenge of the Jacobite rebellion.

cultivar a variety of a plant developed by horticultural or agricultural techniques. The term derives from "cultivated variety."

Cultural Revolution a mass movement begun by Chinese Communist party chairman Mao Zedong 1966, directed against the upper middle class–bureaucrats, artists, and university intellectuals, who were killed, imprisoned, humiliated, or "resettled." Intended to "purify" Chinese communism, it was also an attempt by Mao to renew his political and ideological pre-eminence inside China. The "revolution" was characterized by the violent activities of the semimilitary Red Guards, most of them students. Many established and learned people were humbled and eventually sent to work on the land, and from 1966 to 1970 universities were closed. Although the revolution was brought to an end in 1969, the resulting bureaucratic and economic chaos had many long-term effects.

culture in biology, the growing of living cells and tissues in laboratory conditions.

culture in sociology and anthropology, the way of life of a particular society or group of people, including patterns of thought, beliefs, behavior, customs, traditions, rituals, dress, and language, as well as art, music, and literature. Sociologists and anthropologists use culture as a key concept in describing and analyzing human societies.

Cumae ancient city in Italy, on the coast about 10 mi/16 km W of Naples. In was the seat of the oracle of the Cumaean Sibyl.

Cuman member of a powerful Turki federation of the Middle Ages, which dominated the steppes in the 11th and 12th centuries and built an empire reaching from the Volga to the Danube.

For a generation they held up the Mongol advance on the Volga, but in 1238 a Cuman and Russian army was defeated near Astrakhan, and 200,000 Cumans took refuge in Hungary, where they settled and where their language died out only about 1775. The Mameluke dynasty of Egypt was founded by Cuman ex-slaves. Most of the so-called Tatars of S Russia were of Cuman origin.

Cumberland city in NW Maryland, in the Allegheny mountains, on the Potomac river, directly S of Johnstown, Pennsylvania; seat of Allegheny county. Its industries include the mining and shipping of coal, sheet metal, iron products, and tires; population (1990) 23,706. It was first an Indian village and then a trading post and fort before it was incorporated 1815.

cumin seedlike fruit of the herb *Cuminum cyminum* of the carrot family Umbelliferae, with a bitter flavor. It is used as a spice in cooking.

cummings e e. Literary signature of Edward Estlin Cummings 1894–1962. US poet and novelist. He made his reputation with collections of poetry such as *Tulips and Chimneys* 1923. At first the poems gained notoriety for their idiosyncratic punctuation and typography (using only lowercase letters, for example), but their lyric power has gradually been recognized.

Born in Cambridge, Massachusetts, Cummings graduated from Harvard University and served in the ambulance corps during World War I. He was imprisoned for a brief period for alleged treasonous statements in his correspondence. Out of this experience came his novel, *The Enormous Room* 1922. Other collections of poetry include *XLI*, 1925, *ViVa* 1931, and *1 × 1* 1944. *Him* 1927 was an expressionist drama. Also notable are his paintings, lectures, and the essays *Eimi* 1933, his impressions of the USSR.

cumulative frequency in statistics, the total frequency up to and including a certain point. It is used to draw the cumulative frequency curve, the ogive.

cuneiform ancient writing system formed of combinations of wedge-shaped strokes, usually

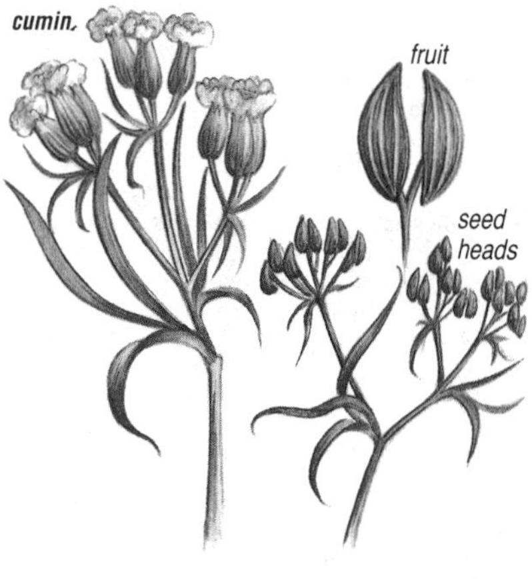
cumin
fruit
seed heads

impressed on clay. It was probably invented by the Sumerians, and was in use in Mesopotamia as early as the middle of the 4th millennium BC.

It was adopted and modified by the Assyrians, Babylonians, Elamites, Hittites, Persians, and many other peoples with different languages.

In the 5th century BC it fell into disuse, but sporadically reappeared in later centuries. The decipherment of cuneiform scripts was pioneered by the German G F Grotefend 1802 and the British orientalist H C Rawlinson 1846.

Cunene or ***Kunene*** river rising near Nova Lisboa in W central Angola. It flows south to the frontier with Namibia, then west to the Atlantic. Length 15 mi/250 km.

Cunha Euclydes da 1866–1909. Brazilian writer. His novel *Os Sertões/Rebellion in the Backlands* 1902 describes the Brazilian *sertão* (backlands), and how a small group of rebels resisted government troops.

Cunningham Merce 1919– . US dancer and choreographer. Influenced by Martha ◊Graham, with whose company he was soloist 1939–45, he formed his own avant-garde dance company and school in New York in 1953. His works include *The Seasons* 1947, *Septet* 1953, *Suite for Five* 1956, *Antic Meet* 1958, *Crises* 1960, *Winterbranch* 1964, *Scramble* 1967, *Signals* 1970, *Sounddance* 1974, *Squaregame* 1976, and *Arcade* 1985. Cunningham worked closely with composers and artists when staging his works.

Cuno Wilhelm 1876–1933. German industrialist and politician who was briefly chancellor of the Weimar Republic 1923.

Cupid in Roman mythology, the god of love, identified with the Greek god ◊Eros.

cuprite Cu_2O ore (copper(I) oxide), found in crystalline form or in earthy masses. It is red to black in color, and is often called ruby copper.

cupronickel a copper alloy (75% copper and 25% nickel), used in hardware products and for coinage.

US coins made with cupronickel include the dime, quarter, half-dollar, and dollar.

Curaçao island in the West Indies, one of the ◊Netherlands Antilles; area 171 sq mi/444 sq km; population (1981) 147,000. The principal industry, dating from 1918, is the refining of Venezuelan petroleum. Curaçao was colonized by Spain 1527, annexed by the Dutch West India Company 1634, and gave its name from 1924 to the group of islands renamed Netherlands Antilles in 1948. Its capital is the port of Willemstad.

Curaçao a sweet liqueur made by flavoring alcohol (obtained from distillation) with sugar and the dried peels of bitter oranges. Originally from the Caribbean island of Curaçao, it is now made elsewhere. The alcohol content varies between 36% and 40%.

curare black, resinous poison extracted from the bark and juices of various South American trees and plants. Originally used on arrowheads by Amazonian hunters to paralyze prey, it blocks nerve stimulation of the muscles. Alkaloid derivatives (called curarines) are used in medicine as muscle relaxants during surgery.

Curie Marie Curie won the Nobel Prize for Chemistry in 1911 for her pioneering work on radioactive elements. She is photographed here in her Paris laboratory.

Curia Romana the judicial and administrative bodies through which the pope carries on the government of the Roman Catholic Church. It includes certain tribunals; the chancellery, which issues papal bulls; various offices including that of the cardinal secretary of state; and the Congregations, or councils of cardinals, each with a particular department of work.

curie former unit (abbreviation Ci) of radioactivity, equal to 37×10^9 ◊becquerels. One gram of radium has a radioactivity of about one curie. It was named after French physicist Pierre Curie.

Curie Marie (born Sklodovska) 1867–1934. Polish-born French scientist, who investigated radioactivity in Paris with her husband Pierre (1859–1906). They discovered radium and polonium.

Born in Warsaw, she studied in Paris from 1891. Impressed by the publication of ◊Becquerel's experiments, Marie Curie decided to investigate the nature of uranium rays. In 1898 she reported the possible existence of some new powerful radioactive element in pitchblende ores. Her husband abandoned his own researches to assist her, and in the same year they announced the existence of polonium and radium. They isolated the pure elements in 1902.

Both scientists refused to take out a patent on their discovery and were jointly awarded the Davy Medal (1903) and the Nobel Prize for Physics (1903; with Becquerel). In 1904 Pierre was appointed to a chair in physics at the Sorbonne, and on his death in a street accident was succeeded by his wife. She wrote a *Treatise on Radioactivity* in 1910, and was awarded the Nobel Prize for Chemistry in 1911. She died a victim of radiation poisoning.

Curie temperature the temperature above which a magnetic material cannot be strongly magnetized. Above the Curie temperature, the energy of the atoms is too great for them to join together to form the small areas of magnetized material, or ◊domains, which combine to produce the strength of the overall magnetization.

Curitiba city in Brazil, on the Curitiba river; population (1980) 844,000. The capital of Paraná state, it dates from 1654. It has a university (1912) and makes paper, furniture, textiles, and chemicals. Coffee, timber, and maté are exported.

curium synthesized, radioactive, metallic element of the ◊actinide series, symbol Cm, atomic number 96, atomic weight 247. It is usually produced by neutron irradiation of plutonium or americium. The longest-lived isotope has a half-life of 1.7×10^7 years.

Curium is used to generate heat and power in satellites or in remote places. It was first synthesized in 1944 at the University of California at Berkeley and was named in 1946 for Pierre and Marie Curie by Glenn Seaborg, its synthesizer, by analogy with the corresponding ◊lanthanide, gadolinium (see ◊periodic table of the elements).

curlew wading bird of the genus Numenius of the sandpiper family, Scolopacidae. The curlew is between 14 in/36 cm and 1.8 ft/55 cm in length, and has mottled brown plumage, long legs, and a long, thin, downcurved bill. Several species live in Northern Europe, Asia, and North America. The name derives from its haunting flutelike call.

One species, the Eskimo curlew, is almost extinct, never having recovered from relentless hunting in the late 19th century.

Curley James Michael 1874–1958. US politician. He served in the US House of Representatives 1912–14 as a Democrat, before being elected mayor of Boston 1914. He served in that post on and off until 1934, when, having established a powerful political organization, he was elected governor. He lost a bid for the US Senate 1936 and did not hold political office again until elected to the House 1942. His fourth and last mayoral term began 1946, during which time he spent six months in federal prison on a mail-fraud conviction. The flamboyant Curley's political career inspired Edwin O'Connor's *The Last Hurrah* 1956.

Born in Boston, Curley became active in the local Democratic party soon after leaving school. He served in the state legislature 1902–03, and on the Boston Board of Aldermen 1904–09, on the Boston City Council 1910–11.

curling game played on ice with stones; sometimes

curlew *eskimo*

described as "bowls on ice." One of the national games of Scotland, it has spread to many countries. It can also be played on artificial (cement or asphalt) ponds.

Curnonsky pseudonym of Maurice Edmond Sailland 1872–1956. French gastronome and cooking writer, who was a pioneer in the cataloging of French regional cuisine.

currant berry of a small seedless variety of cultivated grape *Vitis vinifera*. Currants are grown on a large scale in Greece and California and used dried in cooking and baking. Because of the similarity of the fruit, the name currant is also given to several species of shrubs in the genus *Ribes*, family Grossulariaceae.

The garden red currant *Ribes rubrum* is a native of S Europe and Asia, now also growing in North America. The European black currant *R. nigrum* is widely cultivated. The American black currant *R. americanum* is native to E North America, as is the skunk currant *R. glandulosum*.

currency the type of money in use in a country, for example the US dollar, the UK pound sterling, the German Deutschmark, and the Japanese yen.

current the flow of a body of water or air moving in a definite direction. There are three basic types of oceanic currents: drift currents are broad and slow-moving; stream currents are narrow and swift-moving; and upwelling currents bring cold, nutrient-rich water from the ocean bottom.

Stream currents include the ◊Gulf Stream and the ◊Japan (or Kuroshio) Current. Upwelling currents, such as the Gulf of Guinea Current and the Peru (Humboldt) Current, provide food for plankton, which in turn supports fish and sea birds. At approximate ten-year intervals, the Peru Current that runs from the Antarctic up the west coast of South America, turns warm, with heavy rain and rough seas, and has disastrous results (as in 1982–83) for Peruvian wildlife and for the anchovy industry. The phenomenon is called ◊El Niño (Spanish "the Child") because it occurs toward Christmas.

current account in economics, that part of the balance of payments concerned with current transactions, as opposed to capital movements. It includes trade (visibles) and service transactions, such as investment, insurance, shipping, and tourism (invisibles). The state of the current account is regarded as a barometer of overall economic health.

In some countries, such as Italy, Spain, and Portugal, visibles make a large contribution to the current account and may more than offset trade deficits.

current prices a series of prices that express values pertaining to a given time but that do not take account of the changes in purchasing power, unlike ◊constant prices.

curriculum in education, the range of subjects offered within an institution or course.

The term also refers to the specific series of courses required for graduation and to the series of topics taught within any one course during a semester.

Curtin John 1885–1945. Australian Labor politician, prime minister and minister of defense 1941–45. He was elected leader of the Labor Party 1935. As prime minister, he organized the mobilization of Australia's resources to meet the danger of Japanese invasion during World War II.

Curtis Tony. Adopted name of Bernard Schwartz 1925– . US film actor who starred in the 1950s and 1960s in such films as *The Vikings* 1958 and *The Boston Strangler* 1968, as well as specializing in light comedies such as *Some Like it Hot* 1959, with Jack Lemmon and Marilyn Monroe.

Curtiss Glenn Hammond 1878–1930. US aeronautical inventor, pioneer aviator, and aircraft designer. He belonged to Alexander Graham Bell's Aerial Experiment Assoc 1907–09 and in 1908 made the first public flights in the US, including the 1-mile flight. It was followed by his sensational flight down the Hudson from Albany to New York City in 1910. Curtiss had established the first flying school in 1909, and in 1916 organized the Curtiss Airplane and Motor Corp, based on his invention of ◊ailerons in 1911, which he designed for the first ◊seaplanes (also 1911). He designed and constructed many planes for the Allied nations during World War I, and after the war continued to make improvements in both plane and motor designs.

Curtiz Michael. Adopted name of Mihaly Kertesz 1888–1962. Hungarian-born US film director who worked in Austria, Germany, and France before moving to the US in 1926, where he made several films with Errol Flynn, directed *Mildred Pierce* 1945, which revitalized Joan Crawford's career, and *Casablanca* 1942, for which he won an Academy Award.

His wide range of films includes *Doctor X* 1932; *The Adventures of Robin Hood* 1938; and *White Christmas* 1954.

curve in geometry, the ◊locus of a point moving according to specified conditions. The circle is the locus of all points equidistant from a given point (the center). Other common geometrical curves are the ◊ellipse, ◊parabola, and ◊hyperbola, which are also produced when a cone is cut by a plane at different angles.

Many curves have been invented for the solution of special problems in geometry and mechanics—for example, the cissoid (the inverse of a parabola) and the ◊cycloid.

Curzon George Nathaniel, 1st Marquess Curzon of Kedleston 1859–1925. British Conservative politician, viceroy of India 1899–1905. During World War I, he was a member of the cabinet 1916–19. As foreign secretary 1919–22, he set up a British protectorate over Persia.

Curzon Robert, Lord Zouche 1810–1873. English diplomat and traveler, author of *Monasteries in the Levant* 1849.

Curzon Line Polish-Soviet frontier proposed after the Russo-Polish war 1919–20. It was based on the eastward limit of areas with a predominantly Polish population and acquired its name 1920 after Lord Curzon suggested that the Poles, who had invaded the USSR, should retire to this line pending a peace conference. The frontier established 1945 in general follows the Curzon Line.

Cushing Harvey Williams 1869–1939. US neurologist who pioneered neurosurgery. He developed a range of techniques for the surgical treatment of brain tumors, and also studied the link between the ◊pituitary gland and conditions such as dwarfism.

Cushing Peter 1913– . British actor who specialized in horror roles in films made at Hammer studios 1957–73, including *Dracula* 1958; *The Mummy* 1959; *Frankenstein Must be Destroyed* 1969. Other films include *Doctor Who and the Daleks* 1966, *Star Wars* 1977 and *Top Secret* 1984.

Cushing's syndrome condition in which the body chemistry is upset by excessive production of ◊steroid hormones from the adrenal cortex.

Symptoms include weight gain in the face and trunk, raised blood pressure, excessive growth of facial and body hair (hirsutism), demineralization of bone, and, sometimes, diabeteslike effects. The underlying cause may be an adrenal or pituitary tumor, or prolonged high-dose therapy with ◊corticosteroid drugs.

Custer *George Armstrong Custer is best remembered for his disastrous last stand at the Battle of the Little Big Horn River in 1876.*

cusp a point where two branches of a curve meet and the tangents to each branch coincide.

custard apple any of numerous, primarily tropical trees and shrubs of the family Annonaceae. Several are cultivated for their large, edible, heart-shaped fruits. The pawpaw *A. simina triloba* of the E US, and the pond-apple *Annona glabra* of the West Indies are representatives.

Custer George A(rmstrong) 1839–1876. US Civil War general, the Union's youngest brigadier general as a result of a brilliant war record. Reduced in rank in the regular army at the end of the Civil War, he campaigned against the Sioux from 1874, and was killed with a detachment of his troops by the forces of Sioux chief Sitting Bull in the Battle of the Little Big Horn, Montana: also called Custer's last stand, June 25, 1876.

Some historians accuse Custer of a reckless desire to advance his career.

Customs and Excise government department responsible for taxes levied on imports. Excise duties are levied on goods produced domestically or on licenses to carry on certain trades (such as sale of wines and spirits) or other activities (theatrical entertainments, betting, and so on) within a country.

Cuthbert, St died 687. Christian saint. A shepherd in Northumbria, England, he entered the monastery of Melrose, Scotland after receiving a vision. He traveled widely as a missionary and because of his alleged miracles was known as the "wonder-worker of Britain."

cuticle in zoology, the horny noncellular surface layer of many invertebrates such as insects; in botany, the waxy surface layer on those parts of plants that are exposed to the air, continuous except for ◊stomata and ◊lenticels. All types are secreted by the cells of the ◊epidermis. A cuticle reduces water loss and, in arthropods, acts as an ◊exoskeleton.

Cuttack city and river port in E India, on the Mahanadi River delta; population (1981) 327,500. It was the capital of Orissa state until 1950. The old fort (Kataka) from which the town takes its name is in ruins.

cuttlefish any of a family, Sepiidae, of squidlike cephalopods with an internal calcareous shell (cuttlebone). The common cuttle *Sepia officinalis* of the Atlantic and Mediterranean, is up to 1 ft/30 cm long. It swims actively by means of the fins into which the sides of its oval, flattened body are expanded, and jerks itself backwards by shooting a jet of water from its "siphon."

Cuvier *Georges Cuvier, the founder of paleontology and comparative anatomy, believed that the Earth was periodically flooded, and explained fossils as remnants of lifeforms that had been destroyed in the most recent deluge.*

Cuzco *In Peru, the ancient Inca capital of Cuzco now has Spanish and recent buiding among the remains of older Inca structures.*

cycling *The 1988 Tour de France.*

It is capable of rapid changes of color and pattern. The large head has conspicuous eyes, and the ten arms are provided with suckers. Two arms are very much elongated, and with them the cuttle seizes its prey. It has an "ink sac" from which a dark fluid can be discharged into the water, distracting predators from the cuttle itself. The dark brown pigment, sepia, is obtained from the ink sacs of cuttlefish.

Cuvier Georges, Baron Cuvier 1769–1832. French comparative anatomist. In 1799 he showed that some species have become extinct by reconstructing extinct giant animals that he believed were destroyed in a series of giant deluges. These ideas are expressed in *Recherches sur les ossaments fossiles de quadrupèdes* 1812 and *Discours sur les révolutions de la surface du globe* 1825.

In 1798 Cuvier produced *Tableau élémentaire de l'histoire naturelle des animaux,* in which his scheme of classification is outlined. He was professor of natural history in the Collège de France from 1799 and at the Jardin des Plantes from 1802; at the Restoration in 1815 he was elected chancellor of the University of Paris. Cuvier was the first to relate the structure of ◊fossil animals to that of their living relatives. His great work *Le Règne animal/The Animal Kingdom* 1817 is a systematic survey.

Cuxhaven seaport in Germany on the southern side of the Elbe estuary, at its entrance into the North Sea; population (1983) 57,800. It acts as an outport for Hamburg.

Cuyp Aelbert 1620–1691. Dutch painter of countryside scenes, seascapes, and portraits. His idyllically peaceful landscapes are bathed in golden light: for example, *A Herdsman with Cows by a River* (c. 1650 National Gallery, London). His father, Jacob Gerritsz Cuyp (1594–1652), was also a landscape and portrait painter.

Cuzco city in S Peru, capital of Cuzco department, in the Andes, over 11,000 ft/3,350 m above sea level and 350 mi/560 km SE of Lima; population (1988) 255,000. It was founded in the 11th century as the ancient capital of the ◊Inca empire and was captured by Pizarro 1533.

The university was founded 1598. The city has a Renaissance cathedral and other relics of the early Spanish conquerors. There are many Inca remains and in the 1970s and 1980s the Inca irrigation canals and terracing nearby were being restored to increase cultivation.

CV abbreviation for ◊curriculum vitae.

CVA abbreviation for cerebrovascular accident; see ◊stroke.

cwt symbol for ◊hundredweight, a unit of weight equal to 100 lb (45.36 kg) in the US and 112 lb (50.8 kg) in the UK and Canada.

cyanide CN^- ion derived from hydrogen cyanide (HCN); any salt containing this ion (produced when hydrogen cyanide is neutralized by alkalis), such as potassium cyanide (KCN). The principal cyanides are potassium, sodium, calcium, mercury, gold, and copper. Certain cyanides are poisons.

cyanocobalamin chemical name for ◊vitamin B12, which is normally produced by microorganisms in the alimentary canal. The richest natural sources are raw liver and seaweeds, but it is common in meats. The deficiency disease pernicious anemia is the poor development of red blood cells with possible degeneration of the spinal chord. Sufferers develop extensive bruising and recover slowly from even minor injuries.

cyanosis bluish discoloration of the skin or mucous membranes, usually around the mouth, due to diminished uptake of oxygen. It is most often seen in diseases of the heart, lungs, or blood.

Cybele in Phrygian mythology, an earth goddess, identified by the Greeks with ◊Rhea and honored in Rome.

cybernetics (Greek *kubernan* "to steer") science concerned with how systems organize, regulate, and reproduce themselves, and also how they evolve and learn. In the laboratory, inanimate objects are created that behave like living systems. Applications range from the creation of electronic artificial limbs to the running of the fully automated factory where decision-making machines operate up to managerial level.

Cybernetics was founded and named in 1947 by US mathematician Norbert Wiener. Originally, it was the study of control systems using feedback to produce automatic processes.

cycad plant of the order Cycadales belonging to the gymnosperms. Some have a superficial resemblance to palms, others to ferns. Their large cones contain fleshy seeds. There are ten genera and about 80–100 species, native to tropical and subtropical countries. The stems of many species yield an edible starchy substance resembling sago. Cycads were widespread during the Mesozoic era.

Cyclades (Greek *Kikládhes*) group of about 200 Greek islands in the Aegean Sea, lying between mainland Greece and Turkey; area 996 sq mi/ 2,579 sq km; population (1981) 88,500. They include Andros, Melos, Paros, Naxos, and Siros, on which is the capital Hermoupolis.

cyclamate derivative of cyclohexysulfamic acid, formerly used as an artificial sweetener.

Its use in foods was banned in the US and the UK from 1970, when studies showed that massive doses caused cancer in rats.

cyclamen genus of perennial plants of the primrose family Primulaceae, with heart-shaped leaves and petals that are twisted at the base and bent back. The flowers are usually white or pink, and several species are cultivated.

cycle in physics, a sequence of changes that moves a system away from, and then back to, its original state. An example is a vibration that moves a particle first in one direction and then in the opposite direction, with the particle returning to its original position at the end of the vibration.

cyclic in geometry, describing a polygon of which each vertex (corner) lies on the circumference of a circle. The term is also used in ◊group theory and ◊permutations.

cyclic compound any of a group of organic chemicals that have rings of atoms in their molecules, giving them a closed-chain structure.

cycling riding a ◊bicycle for sport, pleasure, or transport. Cycle racing can take place on oval artificial tracks or on the road or across country (cyclo-cross).

Stage races are run over grueling terrain and can last anything from three to five days up to three and a half weeks, like the ◊Tour de France, Tour of Italy, and Tour of Spain. Criteriums are fast, action-packed races around the closed streets of town or city centers. Each race lasts about an hour. Road races are run over a prescribed circuit, which the riders will lap several times. Such a race will normally cover a distance of approximately 100 mi/160 km. Track racing takes place on either a concrete or wooden banked circuit, either indoors or outdoors. In time trialing each rider races against the clock, with all the competitors starting at different intervals. Among the major events are the Tour de France, first held in 1903; the Tour of Britain (formerly called the Milk Race), first held in 1951; and the World Professional Road Race Championship first held at the Nuburgring, West Germany in 1927.

cycloid in geometry, a curve resembling a series of arches traced out by a point on the circumference

cycloid

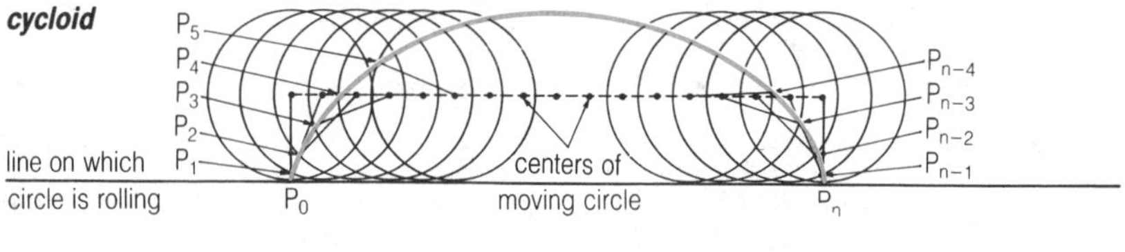
P5
P4
P3
P2
P1
line on which circle is rolling
P0
centers of moving circle
Pn−4
Pn−3
Pn−2
Pn−1
Pn

cylinder

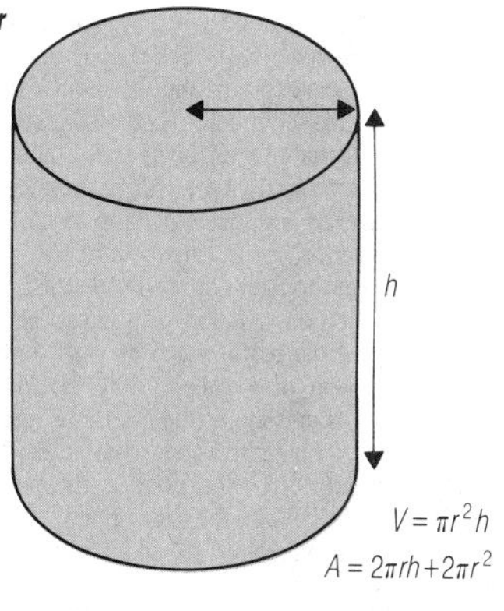
h
$V = \pi r^2 h$
$A = 2\pi rh + 2\pi r^2$

of a circle that rolls along a straight line. Its applications include the study of the motion of wheeled vehicles along roads and tracks.

cyclone an area of low atmospheric pressure. Cyclones are formed by the mixture of cold, dry polar air with warm, moist equatorial air. These masses of air meet in temperate latitudes; the warm air rises over the cold, resulting in rain.

Winds blow in toward the center in an anticlockwise direction in the northern hemisphere, clockwise in the southern hemisphere; the systems are characterized by variable weather. They bring rain or snow, winds up to gale force, low cloud, and sometimes fog. Tropical cyclones are a great danger to shipping. A ◊tornado is a rapidly moving cyclone. In middle and high latitudes low-pressure systems are referred to as depressions or lows, rather than cyclones.

Cyclops in Greek mythology, one of a legendary nation of giants who lived in Sicily, had one eye in the middle of the forehead, and lived as shepherds; Odysseus fought and overcame them in Homer's *Odyssey*.

cyclosporin an ◊immunosuppressive drug derived from a fungus (*Tolypocladium inflatum*). In use by 1978, it revolutionized transplant surgery by reducing the incidence and severity of rejection of donor organs.

It suppresses the T-cells (see ◊lymphocyte) that reject foreign tissue without suppressing other cells that fight infection and cancer.

cyclotron circular type of particle ◊accelerator.

Cygnus large prominent constellation of the northern hemisphere, representing a swan. Its brightest star is first-magnitude ◊Deneb.

cylinder in geometry, a surface generated by a set of lines that are parallel to a fixed line and pass through a plane curve not in the plane of the fixed line. A cylinder is a tubular solid figure with a circular base. In everyday use, the term applies to a right cylinder, the curved surface of which is at right angles to the base.

The volume V of a cylinder is given by $V = \pi r^2 h$, where r is the radius of the base and h is the height of the cylinder. Its total surface area A has the formula $A = 2\pi r(h + r)$, where $2\pi rh$ is the curved surface area, and $2\pi r^2$ is the area of both circular ends.

cymbal ancient musical instrument of percussion, consisting of a shallow circular brass dish held together at the center; either used in pairs clashed together or singly, struck with a beater. Smaller finger cymbals or crotala, used by Debussy and Stockhausen, are more solid and have loose rivets to extend the sound.

Cymbeline play by Shakespeare, first acted about 1610 and printed 1623. It combines various sources to tell the story of Imogen (derived from Ginevra in Boccaccio's *Decameron*), the daughter of the legendary British king Cymbeline, who proves her virtue and constancy after several ordeals.

Cymbeline or ***Cunobelin*** 1st century AD. King of the Catuvelauni AD 5–40, who fought unsuccessfully against the Roman invasion of Britain. His capital was at Colchester.

Cynewulf early 8th century Anglo-Saxon poet. He is thought to have been a Northumbrian monk and is the undoubted author of "Juliana" and part of the "Christ" in the Exeter Book (a collection of poems now in Exeter Cathedral), and of the "Fates of the Apostles" and "Elene" in the Vercelli Book (a collection of Old English manuscripts housed at Vercelli, Italy), in all of which he inserted his name by using runic acrostics.

Cynic a school of Greek philosophy, founded in Athens about 400 BC by Antisthenes, a disciple of Socrates, who advocated a stern and simple morality and a complete disregard of pleasure and comfort.

His followers, led by ◊Diogenes (c. 340 BC), not only showed a contemptuous disregard for pleasure, but despised all human affection as a source of weakness. Their "snarling contempt" for ordinary people earned them the name of Cynic, which in Greek means "doglike."

cypress any coniferous tree or shrub of the genera *Cupressus* and *Chamaecyparis*, family Cupressaceae. There are about 20 species, found mainly in the temperate regions of the northern hemisphere. They have minute, scalelike leaves and small cones made up of woody, wedge-shaped scales and containing an aromatic resin.

All species of cypress native to the US occur in the west. Baldcypresses (genus *Taxodium*) belong to the redwood family and are found only in the S US and Mexico.

Cyprian, St c. 210–258. Christian martyr, one of the earliest Christian writers, and bishop of Carthage about 249. He wrote a treatise on the unity of the church. Feast day Sept 16.

Cyprus island in the Mediterranean, off the southern coast of Turkey and western coast of Syria.

government Under the 1960 constitution, power is shared between Greek and Turkish Cypriots, but in 1963 the Turks ceased participating and in 1964 set up a separate community in northern Cyprus, refusing to acknowledge the Greek government in the south.

The Greek Cypriot government claims to be the government of all Cyprus and is generally accepted as such, except by the Turkish community. There are, therefore, two republics, each with a president, council of ministers, legislature, and judicial system. The "Turkish Republic of Northern Cyprus" has its own representatives overseas.

Greek Cyprus has a president who appoints and heads a council of ministers, elected for five years by universal adult suffrage, and a single-chamber legislature, the 80-member house of representatives, also elected for five years. The four main political parties are the Democratic Front (DIKO), the Progressive Party of the Working People (AKEL) the Democratic Rally (DISY), and the Socialist Party (EDEK).

Cyprus

Greek **Republic of Cyprus** (*Kypriaki Dimokratia*) in the south, and Turkish **Republic of Northern Cyprus** (*Kibris Cumhuriyeti*) in the north

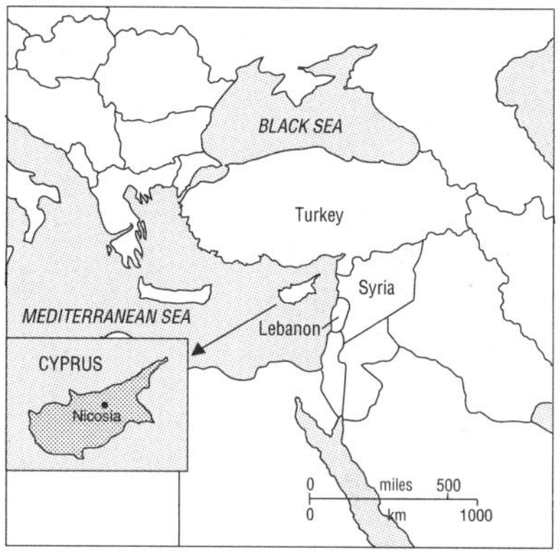
BLACK SEA
Turkey
Syria
MEDITERRANEAN SEA
Lebanon
CYPRUS
Nicosia
0 miles 500
0 km 1000

area 3,571 sq mi/9,251 sq km, 37% in Turkish hands
capital Nicosia (divided between Greeks and Turks) towns ports Paphos, Limassol, and Larnaca (Greek); Morphou, and ports Kyrenia and Famagusta (Turkish)
physical central plain between two E–W mountain ranges
features archeological and historic sites; Mount Olympus 6,406 ft/1,953 m (highest peak); beaches
heads of state and government Georgios Vassilou (Greek) from 1988, Rauf Denktas (Turkish) from 1976
political system democratic divided republic
political parties Democratic Front (DIKO), center-left; Progressive Party of the Working People (AKEL), Socialist; Democratic Rally (DISY), centrist; Socialist Party (EDEK), Socialist; *Turkish zone*: National Unity Party (NUP), Communal Liberation Party (CLP), Republican Turkish Party (RTP), New British Party (NBP)
exports citrus, grapes, raisins, Cyprus sherry, potatoes, clothing, footwear
currency Cyprus pound
population (1990 est) 708,000 (Greek Cypriot 78%, Turkish Cypriot 18%); growth rate 1.2% p.a.
life expectancy men 72, women 76
language Greek and Turkish (official); English
religion Greek Orthodox 78%, Sunni Muslim 18%
literacy 99% (1984)
GDP $3.7 bn (1987); $5,497 per head
chronology
1878 Came under British administration.
1955 Guerrilla campaign began against the British for *enosis* (union with Greece), led by Archbishop Makarios and Gen Grivas.
1956 Makarios and *enosis* leaders deported.
1959 Compromise agreed and Makarios returned to be elected president of an independent Greek-Turkish Cyprus.
1960 Independence achieved from Britain, with Britain retaining its military bases.
1963 Turks set up their own government in northern Cyprus; fighting broke out between the two communities.
1964 UN peacekeeping force installed.
1971 Grivas returned to start a guerrilla war against the Makarios government.
1974 Grivas died. Military coup deposed Makarios, who fled to Britain. Nicos Sampson appointed president. Turkish army sent to northern Cyprus to confirm Turkish Cypriots' control; military regime in southern Cyprus collapsed; Makarios returned. Northern Cyprus declared itself the Turkish Federated State of Cyprus (TFSC), with Rauf Denktas as president.
1977 Makarios died; succeeded by Spyros Kyprianou. 1983 An independent Turkish Republic of Northern Cyprus (TRNC) proclaimed but recognized only by Turkey.
1984 UN peace proposals rejected.
1985 Summit meeting between Kyprianou and Denktas failed to reach agreement.
1988 Georgios Vassilou elected president. Talks with Denktas began, under UN auspices.
1989 Vassilou and Denktas agreed to draft an agreement for the future reunification of the island, but peace talks were abandoned Sept.
1991 Turkish offer of peace talks rejected by Cyprus and Greece.

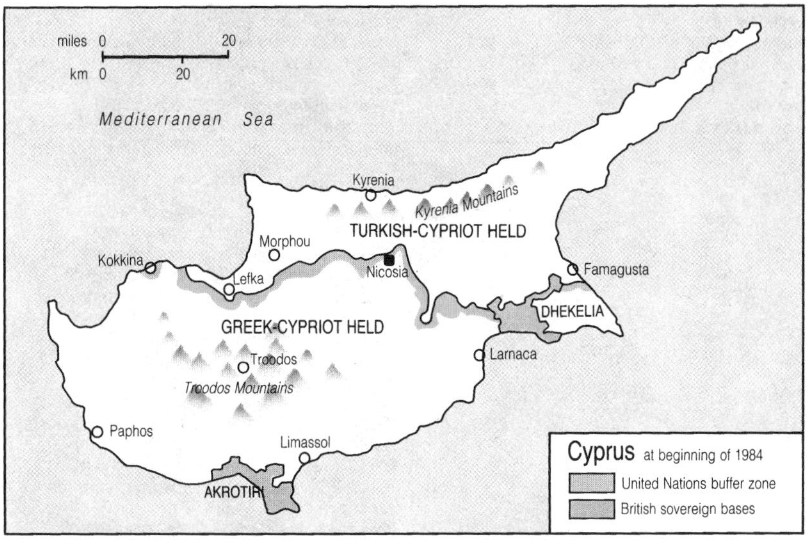
miles 0 20
km 0 20
Mediterranean Sea
Kyrenia
Kyrenia Mountains
TURKISH-CYPRIOT HELD
Morphou
Kokkina
Lefka
Nicosia
Famagusta
DHEKELIA
GREEK-CYPRIOT HELD
Troodos
Troodos Mountains
Larnaca
Paphos
Limassol
AKROTIRI
Cyprus at beginning of 1984
United Nations buffer zone
British sovereign bases

Under the separate constitution adopted by Turkish Cyprus 1985, there is a president, council of ministers, and legislature similar to that in the south. Turkey is the only country to have recognized this government.

history For early history, see ◊Greece, ancient. The strategic position of Cyprus has long made it a coveted territory, and from the 15th century BC it was colonized by a succession of peoples from the mainland. In the 8th century it was within the Assyrian empire, then the Babylonian, Egyptian, and Persian. As part of Ptolemaic Egypt, it was seized by Rome 58 BC. From AD 395 it was ruled by Byzantium, until taken 1191 by England during the Third ◊Crusade. In 1489 it was annexed by Venice, and became part of the Ottoman empire 1571. It came under British administration 1878 and was annexed by Britain 1914, becoming a crown colony in 1925.

In 1955 a guerrilla war against British rule was begun by Greek Cypriots seeking "Enosis," or unification with ◊Greece. The chief organization in this campaign was the National Organization of Cypriot Combatants (EOKA), and its political and military leaders were the head of the Greek Orthodox Church in Cyprus, Archbishop Makarios, and General Grivas.

In 1956 Makarios and other Enosis leaders were deported by the British government. After years of negotiation, Makarios was allowed to return to become president of a new, independent Greek-Turkish Cyprus, retaining British military and naval bases.

In 1963 the Turks withdrew from power-sharing, and fighting began. The following year a United Nations peacekeeping force was set up to keep the two sides apart. After a prolonged period of mutual hostility, relations improved and talks were resumed, with the Turks arguing for a federal state and the Greeks wanting a unitary one.

In 1971 General Grivas returned to the island and began a guerrilla campaign against the Makarios government, which he believed had failed the Greek community. Three years later he died, and his supporters were purged by Makarios, who was himself deposed 1974 by Greek officers of the National Guard and an Enosis extremist, Nicos Sampson, who became president. Makarios fled to Britain.

At the request of the Turkish Cypriot leader Rauf Denktas, Turkey sent troops to the island, taking control of the north and dividing Cyprus along what became known as the ◊Attila Line, cutting off about a third of the total territory. Later in 1975 Sampson resigned, the military regime that had appointed him collapsed, and Makarios returned. The Turkish Cypriots established an independent government for what they called the "Turkish Federated State of Cyprus" (TFSC), with Denktas as president.

In 1977 Makarios died and was succeeded by Spyros Kyprianou, who had been president of the house of representatives. In 1980 UN-sponsored peace talks were resumed. The Turkish Cypriots offered to hand back about 4% of the 35% of the territory they controlled and to resettle 40,000 of the 200,000 refugees who had fled to the north, but stalemate was reached on a constitutional settlement.

The Turks wanted equal status for the two communities, equal representation in government, and firm links with Turkey. The Greeks, on the other hand, favored an alternating presidency, strong central government, and representation in the legislature on a proportional basis.

Between 1982 and 1985 several attempts by the Greek government in Athens and the UN to find a solution failed, and the Turkish Republic of Northern Cyprus (TRNC), with Denktas as president, was formally declared, but recognized only by Turkey.

In 1985 a meeting between Denktas and Kyprianou failed to reach agreement, and the UN secretary general drew up proposals for a two-zone federal Cyprus, with a Greek president and a Turkish vice-president, but this was not found acceptable. Meanwhile, both Kyprianou and Denktas had been reelected.

In 1988 Georgios Vassiliou was elected president of the Greek part of Cyprus, and in Sept talks began between him and Denktas. However, these were abandoned in Sept 1989, reportedly because of Denktas's intransigence. The dispute between the communities remains unresolved, but, because of its strategic importance in the Mediterranean, Cyprus causes concern.

Cyrano de Bergerac Savinien de 1619–1655. French writer. He joined a corps of guards at 19 and performed heroic feats which brought him fame. He is the hero of a classic play by ◊Rostand, in which his excessively long nose is used as a counterpoint to his chivalrous character.

Cyrenaic a school of Greek ◊hedonistic philosophy founded about 400 BC by Aristippus of Cyrene. He regarded pleasure as the only absolutely worthwhile thing in life but taught that self-control and intelligence were necessary to choose the best pleasures.

Cyrenaica area of E Libya, colonized by the Greeks in the 7th century BC; later held by the Egyptians, Romans, Arabs, Turks, and Italians. Present cities in the region are Benghazi, Derna, and Tobruk.

The Greek colonies passed under the rule of the Ptolemies 322 BC, and in 174 BC Cyrenaica became a Roman province. It was conquered by the Arabs in the AD 7th century, by Turkey in the 16th, and by Italy 1912, when it was developed as a colony. It was captured by the British 1942, and under British control until it became a province of the new kingdom of Libya from 1951. In 1963 it was split into a number of smaller divisions under the constitutional reorganization. There are archeological ruins at Cyrene and Apollonia.

Cyril and Methodius, Sts two brothers, both Christian saints: Cyril 826–869 and Methodius 815–885. Born in Thessalonica, they were sent as missionaries to what is today Moravia. They invented a Slavonic alphabet, and translated the Bible and the liturgy from Greek to Slavonic.

The language (known as Old Church Slavonic) remained in use in churches and for literature among Bulgars, Serbs, and Russians up to the 17th century. The cyrillic alphabet is named after Cyril and may also have been invented by him. Feast day Feb 14.

Cyril of Alexandria, St 376–444. Bishop of Alexandria from 412, persecutor of Jews and other non-Christians, and suspected of ordering the murder of Hypatia (c. 370–c. 415), a philosopher whose influence was increasing at the expense of his. He was violently opposed to ◊Nestorianism.

Cyrus the Great died 529 BC. Founder of the Persian Empire. As king of Persia, originally subject to

Czechoslovakia *Czechoslovak protesters demonstrating against the Soviet invasion 1968.*

the ◊Medes, whose empire he overthrew 550 BC. He captured ◊Croesus 546 BC, and conquered all Asia Minor, adding Babylonia (including Syria and Palestine) to his empire 539, allowing exiled Jews to return to Jersualem. He died fighting in Afghanistan.

cystic fibrosis hereditary disease involving defects of various tissues, including the sweat glands, the mucous glands of the bronchi (air passages), and the pancreas. The sufferer experiences repeated chest infections and digestive disorders and generally fails to thrive.

It was once universally fatal at an early age; now, although there is no definitive cure, treatments have raised both the quality and expectancy of life. Management is by diets and drugs, physiotherapy to keep the chest clear, and use of antibiotics to combat infection and minimize damage to the lungs. Some sufferers have benefited from heart-lung transplants. In 1989 the gene for cystic fibrositis was identified by teams of researchers in Michigan and Toronto. This discovery promises more reliable diagnosis of the disease in babies before birth.

cystitis inflammation of the bladder, usually caused by bacterial infection, and resulting in frequent and painful urination. Treatment is by antibiotics and copious fluids with vitamin C.

cytochrome one of a number of iron-containing, red proteins responsible for part of the process of ◊respiration by which food molecules are broken down in ◊aerobic organisms. Cytochromes are also used for the part of the process of ◊photosynthesis by which molecules of water are oxidized to oxygen gas. Cytochromes are part of the electron transport chain, by which energized electrons are passed along to release energy and to make ◊ATP.

cytokine in biology, chemical messengers that carry information from one cell to another, for example the ◊lymphokines.

cytokinin a type of ◊plant hormone that stimulates cell division. Cytokinins affect several different aspects of plant growth and development, but only if ◊auxin is also present. They may delay the process of senescence or aging, break the dormancy of certain seeds and buds, and induce flowering.

cytology the study of ◊cells and their functions. Major advances have been made possible in this field by the development of ◊electron microscopes.

cytoplasm the part of the cell outside the ◊nucleus. Strictly speaking, this includes all the ◊organelles (mitochondria, chloroplasts, and so on), but often cytoplasm refers to the jellylike matter in which the organelles are embedded (correctly termed the cytosol).

In many cells, the cytoplasm is made up of two parts: the ectoplasm (or plasmagel), a dense gelatinous outer layer concerned with cell movement, and the endoplasm (or plasmasol), a more fluid inner part where most of the organelles are found.

cytoskeleton in a living cell, a matrix of protein filaments and tubules that occurs within the cytosol (the liquid part of the cytoplasm). It gives the cell a definite shape, transports vital substances around the cell, and may also be involved in cell movement.

cytotoxic drug any drug used to kill the cells of a malignant tumor, or as an ◊immunosuppressive following organ transplant; it may also damage healthy cells. Side effects include nausea, vomiting, hair loss, and bone-marrow damage.

czar alternate form of tsar, an emperor of Russia.

Czechoslovakia landlocked country in E central Europe, bounded NE by Poland, E by the USSR, S by Hungary and Austria, and W and NW by Germany.

government Since 1968 Czechoslovakia has been a federation of two national republics, Czech and Slovak. The supreme legislative body of the Czech and Slovak Federative Republic is the federal assembly, *Federalni Shromazdeni*, composed of two chambers having equal rights, the directly elected, 200-deputy chamber of the people and the 150-deputy chamber of nations. The first is elected for five-year terms and has a 2:1 Czech majority. The second is divided equally between members chosen by each of the Czech and Slovak National Councils.

The federal assembly elects for a five-year term the president of the Republic, who appoints a prime minister and federal government accountable to the federal assembly. Traditionally, if the president is Czech, the prime minister will be Slovak, and vice versa. The federal government has authority in defense and foreign affairs. In other areas, power is shared with the national councils elected by the national republics.

Formerly, the controlling force was the Czechoslovak Communist Party (CCP). Political pluralism began in 1989, with the emergence of Civic Forum, an intelligensia-led reform coalition embracing liberals, Christian Democrats and social democrats. Other political parties include the Agrarian Party, Czechoslovak Socialist Party and Czechoslovak Freedom Party (former allies of the CCP), and the Green Party.

history Czechoslovakia came into existence as an independent republic 1918 after the break-up of the ◊Austro-Hungarian empire at the end of World War I. It consisted originally of the Bohemian crownlands (◊Bohemia, ◊Moravia, and part of ◊Silesia) and ◊Slovakia, the area of Hungary inhabited by Slavonic peoples; to this was added as a trust, part of Ruthenia when the Allies and Associated Powers recognized the new republic under the treaty of St Germain-en-Laye. Besides the Czech and Slovak peoples, the country included substantial minorities of German origin, long settled in the north, and of Hungarian (or Magyar) origin in the south. But despite the problems of welding into a nation such a mixed group of people, Czechoslovakia made considerable political and economic progress until the troubled 1930s. It was the only East European state to retain a parliamentary democracy throughout the interwar period, with five coalition governments (dominated by the Agrarian and National Socialist parties), with Thomas ◊Masaryk serving as president. It also had a highly developed industrial sector.

The rise to power of ◊Hitler in Germany brought a revival of opposition among the Ger-

Czechoslovakia
Czech and Slovak Federative Republic
(Česká a Slovenská federativní)

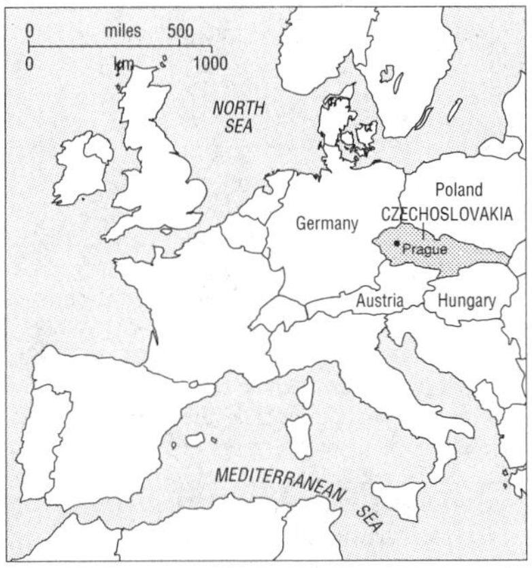
0 miles 500
0 km 1000
NORTH SEA
Poland
Germany
CZECHOSLOVAKIA
Prague
Austria
Hungary
MEDITERRANEAN SEA

area 49,371 sq mi/127,903 sq km
capital Prague
cities Brno, Bratislava, Ostrava
physical Carpathian Mountains; rivers Morava, Labe (Elbe), Vltava (Moldau); hills and plateau; Danube plain in S
features divided by valley of the Morava into the densely populated Czech area with good communications in W, and the sparsely populated, mainly agricultural Slovak area in E; summer and winter resort areas in Western Carpathian, Bohemian, and Sudetes mountain ranges
head of state Václav Havel from 1989
head of government Marián Čalfa from 1989 (resigned from Communist Party 1990 but remained premier)
political system emergent democracy
political parties Communist Party of Czechoslovakia (CCP), Marxist-Leninist; Civic Forum, Czech pluralist reform coalition; Public Against Violence, Slovak equivalent of Civic Forum; Agrarian Party, farmers' party supporting collectivization; Czechoslovak Socialist Party and Czechoslovak Freedom Party (pre-1989 allies of CCP); Green Party
exports machinery, vehicles, timber, ceramics, glass, textiles, lignite, magnesite, mercury
currency koruna
population (1990 est) 15,695,000 (63% Czech, 31% Slovak, with Hungarian, Polish, German, Russian, and other minorities); growth rate 0.4% p.a.
life expectancy men 68, women 75
language Czech and Slovak (official)
religion Roman Catholic 75%, Protestant 15%
literacy 99% (1981)
GDP $148.5 bn (1987); $3,127 per head
chronology
1918 Independence achieved from Austro-Hungarian Empire; Czechs and Slovaks formed Czechoslovakia as independent nation.
1938 Infamous Munich Agreement gave Sudetenland to Nazi Germany, as "appeasement," but six months later Hitler occupied entire nation. Benes headed government in exile until 1945.
1945 Liberation of Czechoslovakia from Nazis by USSR and US.
1948 Communists assumed power in coup, and new constitution framed.
1968 "Prague Spring" experiment with liberalization ended by Soviet invasion and occupation.
1969 Czechoslovakia became a federal state; Husák elected Communist party leader.
1977 Emergence and suppression of Charter 77 human-rights movement.
1985–86 Criticism of Husák rule by new Soviet leadership.
1987 Husák resigned as Communist leader, remaining president; replaced by Miloš Jakeš.
1988 Personnel overhaul of party and state bodies, including replacement of Prime Minister Štrougal by the technocrat Adamec.
1989 Communist regime of Jakeš, Husák, and Adamec overthrown in Nov–Dec bloodless "gentle revolution," following mass prodemocracy protests in Prague and throughout country, directed by newly formed Civic Forum. Communist monopoly of power ended, with new "Grand Coalition" government formed; Václav Havel appointed state president and Alexander Dubček chair of national parliament.
1990 Jan: 22,000 prisoners released. Feb: Havel announced agreement with USSR for complete withdrawal of Soviet troops by May 1991. Dec: devolution of more powers to federal republics.
1991 Bill of rights passed. May: legislation approved for restitution of property nationalized post-1948. June: privatization program announced for large industrial enterprises and small businesses. Last Soviet troops departed.

man-speaking population, and nationalism among the Magyar speakers. In addition, the Slovakian clerical party demanded autonomy for Slovakia. In 1938 the ◊Munich Agreement was made between Britain, France, Germany, and Italy, without consulting Czechoslovakia, resulting in the Sudetenland being taken from Czechoslovakia and given to Germany. Six months later Hitler occupied all Czechoslovakia. A government in exile was established in London under Eduard ◊Beneš until the liberation 1945 by Soviet and US troops. In the same year some two million Sudeten Germans were expelled, and Czech Ruthenia was transferred to Ukraine, USSR. Elections 1946 gave the left a slight majority, and in Feb 1948 the communists seized power, winning an electoral victory in May. Beněs, who had been president since 1945, resigned. The country was divided into 19 and then, in 1960, into ten regions plus Prague and Bratislava.

There was a Stalinist regime during the 1950s, under Presidents Klement Gottwald (1948–53), Antonin Zapotocky (1953–57), and Antonin Novotný (1957–68). Pressure from students and intellectuals brought about policy changes from 1965. Following Novotný's replacement as CCP leader by Alexander ◊Dubček and as president by war hero General Ludvík Svoboda (1895–1979), and the appointment of Oldřich Černik as prime minister, a liberalization program began in 1968. This "Socialist Democratic Revolution," as it was known, promised the return of freedom of assembly, speech, and movement, and the imposition of restrictions on the secret police, all with the goal of creating "socialism with a human face."

Despite assurances that Czechoslovakia would remain within the ◊Warsaw Pact, the USSR viewed these events with suspicion, and in Aug 1968 sent 600,000 troops from Warsaw Pact countries to restore the orthodox line. After the invasion a purge of liberals began in the CCP, with Dr Gustáv ◊Husák (a Slovak Brezhnevite) replacing Dubček as CCP leader 1969 and Lubomír Štrougal (a Czech) becoming prime minister 1970. Svoboda remained as president until 1975 and negotiated the Soviet withdrawal.

In 1968 a new constitution transformed unitary Czechoslovakia into a federal state. In 1973 an amnesty was extended to some of the 40,000 who had fled after the 1968 invasion, signaling a slackening of repression. In 1977, following the signature of a human rights manifesto ("Charter 77") by over 700 intellectuals and former party officials in response to the 1975 ◊Helsinki Conference, a new crackdown commenced. The arrest of dissidents continued during the events of 1981 in ◊Poland.

Czechoslovakia under Dr Husák emerged as a loyal ally of the USSR during the 1970s and early 1980s. However, following Mikhail ◊Gorbachev's accession to the Soviet leadership in 1985, pressure for economic and administrative reform mounted. In Dec Husák, while remaining president, was replaced as CCP leader by Miloš Jakeš (1923–), a Czech-born economist. Working with prime minister Ladislav Adamec, a reformist, he began to introduce a reform program (*prestavba*, "restructuring") on the USSR's ◊perestroika model. However, his approach was cautious and dissident activity, which became increasingly widespread 1988–89, was suppressed. Influenced by events elsewhere in East Europe, a series of initially student-led prodemocracy rallies were held in Prague's Wenceslas Square from Nov 17, 1989. Support for the protest movement rapidly increased following the security forces' brutal suppression of the early rallies; by Nov 20 there were more than 200,000 demonstrators in Prague, and a growing number in Bratislava. An umbrella opposition movement, Civic Forum, was swiftly formed under the leadership of playwright and Charter 77 activist Václav ◊Havel, which attracted the support of prominent members of the small political parties that were members of the ruling CCP-dominated National Front coalition.

With the protest movement continuing to grow, Jakeš resigned as CCP leader Nov 24 and was replaced by Karel Urbanek (1941–), a South Moravian, and the politburo was purged. This was not enough, however, to satisfy the opposition and less than a week later, following a brief general strike, the national assembly voted to amend the constitution to strip the CCP of its "leading role" in the government, and thus of its monopoly on power. Opposition parties, beginning with Civic Forum and its Slovak counterpart, Public Against Violence, were legalized. On Dec 7 Adamec resigned as prime minister and was replaced by Marián Čalfa, who formed a coalition government in which key posts, including the foreign, financial, and labor ministries, were given to former dissidents. Čalfa resigned from the CCP in Jan 1990, but remained premier.

On Dec 27, 1989 the rehabilitated Dubček was sworn in as chair of the federal assembly, and on Dec 29 Havel became president of Czechoslovakia. The new reform government immediately extended an amnesty to 22,000 prisoners, secured agreements from the CCP that it would voluntarily give up its existing majorities in the federal and regional assemblies and state agencies, and promised multiparty elections for June 1990. It also announced plans for reducing the size of the armed forces, called on the USSR to pull out its 75,000 troops stationed in the country by the end of 1990, and applied for membership of the International Monetary Fund and World Bank. Václav Havel was reelected as president, unopposed, for a further two years by the assembly on July 5, 1990.

Fresh initiatives included a new democratic constitution being drafted and a government program being implemented, giving high priority to environmental issues, price liberalization and privatization.

Some devolution of power was introduced 1990 to ameliorate friction between the Czech and Slovak republics. A bill of rights was passed Jan 1991, and moves were made toward price liberalization and privatization of small businesses. In Feb 1991 a bill was passed to return property nationalized after 1948 to its original owners, the first such restitution measure in E Europe. The name "Czech and Slovak Federative Republic" was adopted April 1990. In Nov 1990 the Slovak Republic declared Slovak the official language of the republic.

Czerny Carl 1791–1857. Austrian composer and pianist. He wrote an enormous quantity of religious and concert music, but is chiefly remembered for his books of graded studies and technical exercises used in piano teaching.

Częstochowa town in Poland, on the river Vistula; 120 mi/193 km SW of Warsaw; population (1985) 247,000. It produces iron goods, chemicals, paper, and cement. The basilica of Jasna Góra is a center for Catholic pilgrims (it contains the painting known as the Black Madonna).

D abbreviation for 500 in the Roman numeral system.

DA abbreviation for district attorney.

dab small marine flatfish of the flounder family, especially the genus *Limanda*. Dabs live in the N Atlantic and around the coasts of Britain and Scandinavia. Species include the dab *L. limanda* which grows to about 16 in/40 cm, and the American dab *L. proboscida*, which grows to 12 in/30 cm. Both have both eyes on the right side of their bodies. The left, or blind, side is white, while the rough-scaled right side is light-brown or gray, with dark-brown spots.

Dacca alternate name for ◊Dhaka, capital of Bangladesh.

Dachau site of a Nazi ◊concentration camp during World War II, in Bavaria, Germany.

dachshund (German "badger-dog") small dog of German origin, bred originally for digging out badgers. It has a long body and short legs. Several varieties are bred: standard size (up to 22 lb/10 kg), miniature (11 lb/5 kg or less), long-haired, smooth-haired, and wire-haired.

Dacia ancient region forming much of modern Romania. The various Dacian tribes were united around 60 BC, and for many years posed a threat to the Roman empire; they were finally conquered by the Roman emperor Trajan AD 101–106, and the region became a province of the same name. It was abandoned to the invading Goths in about 275.

dacoit historically a member of an armed gang of robbers, formerly active in India and Myanmar.

Dada artistic and literary movement founded 1915 in Zürich, Switzerland, by the Romanian poet Tristan Tzara (1896–1963) and others in a spirit of rebellion and disillusionment during World War I. Other Dadaist groups were soon formed by the artists ◊Duchamp and ◊Man Ray in New York and ◊Picabia in Barcelona. Dada had a considerable impact on early 20th-century art, questioning established artistic rules and values.

With the German writers Hugo Ball and Richard Huelsenbeck, the Rumanian poet Tristan Tzara founded the Cabaret Voltaire in Zürich 1916, where works by Hans Arp, the pioneer Surrealist Max Ernst, and others were exhibited. In New York in the same period the artist Man Ray met Duchamp and Picabia and began to apply Dadaist ideas to photography. During the 1920s Dada evolved into Surrealism.

Dadra and Nagar Haveli since 1961 a Union Territory of W India; capital Silvassa; area 189 sq mi/490 sq km; population (1981) 104,000. Formerly part of Portuguese Daman. It produces rice, wheat, millet, and timber.

Daedalus in Greek mythology, an Athenian artisan supposed to have constructed for King Minos of Crete the labyrinth in which the ◊Minotaur was imprisoned. He fled from Crete with his son ◊Icarus using wings made by them from feathers fastened with wax.

daffodil any of several Old World species of the genus *Narcissus*, family Amaryllidaceae, distinguished by their trumpet-shaped flowers. The common daffodil of N Europe *N. pseudonarcissus* has large yellow flowers and grows from a large bulb. There are numerous cultivated forms.

Dafydd ap Gwilym c. 1340–c. 1400. Welsh poet. His work is notable for its complex but graceful style, its concern with nature and love rather than with heroic martial deeds, and for its references to Classical and Italian poetry.

Dagestan autonomous republic of western USSR, situated E of the ◊Caucasus, bordering the Caspian Sea. Capital Makhachkala; area 19,421 sq mi/50,300 sq km; population (1982) 1,700,000. It is mountainous, with deep valleys, and its numerous ethnic groups speak a variety of distinct languages. Annexed 1723 from Iran, which strongly resisted Russian conquest, it became an autonomous republic in 1921.

Daguerre Louis Jacques Mande 1789–1851. French pioneer of photography. Together with Niépce, he is credited with the invention of photography (though others were reaching the same point simultaneously). In 1838 he invented the ◊daguerreotype, a single-image process, superseded ten years later by ◊Talbot's negative/positive process.

daguerreotype in photography, a single-image process using mercury vapor and an iodine-sensitized silvered plate; discovered by Daguerre in 1838.

Dahl Johann Christian 1788–1857. Norwegian landscape painter in the Romantic style. He trained in Copenhagen but was active chiefly in Dresden from 1818. He was the first great painter of the Norwegian landscape, in a style that recalls the Dutch artist ◊Ruisdael.

Dahl Roald 1916–1990. British writer, celebrated for short stories with a twist, for example, *Tales of the Unexpected* 1979, and for children's books, including *Charlie and the Chocolate Factory* 1964.

dahlia any perennial plant of the genus *Dahlia*, family Compositae, comprising 20 species and many cultivated forms. Dahlias are stocky plants with showy flowers that come in a wide range of colors. They are native to Mexico and Central America.

daffodil

Daguerre *The discovery of the daguerreotype was the result of Louis Daguerre's observation of some accidentally spilled iodine on his silvered plates.*

Dahomey former name (until 1975) of the People's Republic of ◊Benin.

Daimler Gottlieb 1834–1900. German engineer who pioneered the modern automobile. In 1886 he produced his first motor vehicle and a motorbicycle. He later joined forces with Karl ◊Benz and was one of the pioneers of the high-speed four-stroke gasoline engine.

Dairen former name for the Chinese port of Dalian, part of ◊Lüda.

dairying the business of producing and handling ◊milk and milk products.

In the US and the UK, over 70% of the milk produced is consumed in its liquid form, whereas New Zealand relies on easily transportable milk products such as butter, cheese, and condensed and dried milk. It is now usual for dairy farms to concentrate on the production of milk and for factories to take over the handling, processing, and distribution of milk as well as the manufacture of dairy products.

daisy any of numerous species of perennial plants in the family Compositae, especially the field daisy of Europe *Chrysanthemum leucanthemum* and the English common daisy *Bellis perennis*, with a single white or pink flower rising from a rosette of leaves.

daisy bush genus *Olearia* of Australian and New Zealand shrubs, family Compositae, with flowers like daisies and felted or hollylike leaves.

Dakar capital and chief port (with artificial harbor) of Senegal; population (1984) 1,000,000.

It is an industrial center, and there is a university 1957. Founded 1862, it was formerly the seat of government of ◊French West Africa. In July 1940 an unsuccessful naval action was undertaken by British and Free French forces to seize Dakar as an Allied base.

Daladier Edouard 1884–1970. French Radical politician. As prime minister April 1938–March 1940, he signed the ◊Munich Agreement 1938 (by which the Sudeten districts of Czechoslovakia were ceded to Germany) and declared war on Germany 1939. He resigned 1940 because of his unpopularity for failing to assist Finland against Russia; arrested on the fall of France 1940, he was a prisoner in Germany 1943–45. Following the end

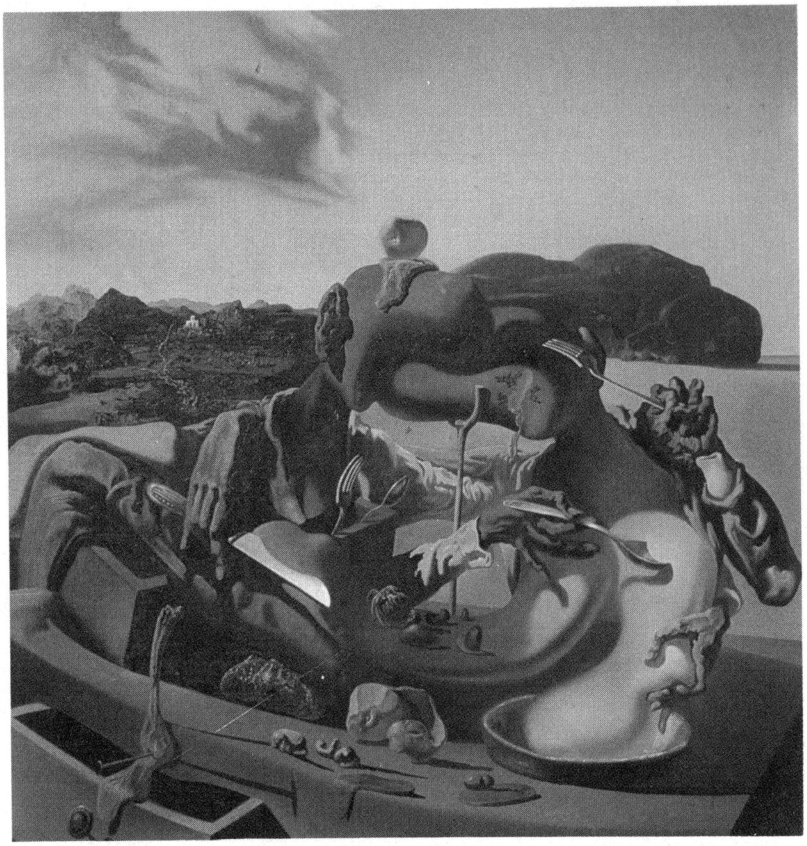

Dali *Dali's* Autumnal Cannibalism *(1936) Tate Gallery, London.*

of World War II he was re-elected to the Chamber of Deputies 1946–58.

Dalai Lama 14th incarnation 1935– . Spiritual and temporal head of the Tibetan state until 1959, when he went into exile in protest against Chinese annexation and oppression. Tibetan Buddhists believe that each Dalai Lama is a reincarnation of his predecessor and also of Avalokiteśvara.

Enthroned 1940, the Dalai Lama temporarily fled 1950–51 when the Chinese overran Tibet, and in March 1959—when a local uprising against Chinese rule was suppressed—made a dramatic escape from Lhasa to India. He then settled at Dharmsala in the Punjab. His people continue to demand his return, and the Chinese offered to lift the ban on his living in Tibet, providing he would refrain from calling for Tibet's independence. His deputy, the Panchen Lama, has cooperated with the Chinese but failed to protect the monks. Nobel Peace Prize 1989 in recognition of his commitment to the nonviolent liberation of his homeland.

Dalcroze Emile Jaques see ◊Jaques-Dalcroze, Emile.

d'Alembert see ◊Alembert, French mathematician.

Dalen Nils 1869–1937. Swedish industrial engineer who invented the light-controlled valve. This allowed lighthouses to operate automatically and won him the 1912 Nobel Prize for Physics.

Daley Richard Joseph 1902–1976. US politician and controversial mayor of Chicago. Born in Chicago, Daley became deeply involved in local Democratic politics and attended law school at DePaul University, gaining admission to the bar 1933. He served in the Illinois legislature 1936–46. He became Cook County clerk 1953 and was elected mayor of Chicago 1955, a post that he held until his death. As mayor, Daley built a formidable political machine and became a force in national Democratic politics, ensuring a Democratic victory 1960 and hosting the turbulent national Democratic convention 1968.

Dalgarno George 1626–1687. Scottish schoolteacher and inventor of the first sign-language alphabet 1680.

Dali Salvador 1904–1989. Spanish painter. In 1928 he collaborated with Buñuel on the film *Un chien andalou*. In 1929 he joined the Surrealists and became notorious for his flamboyant eccentricity. Influenced by the psychoanalytic theories of Freud, he developed a repertoire of dramatic images, including the distorted human body, limp watches, and burning giraffes. These are painted with a meticulous, polished clarity; *The Persistence of Memory* 1931 (Museum of Modern Art, New York) is typical. He also painted religious themes and many portraits of his wife Gala.

Dali, born near Barcelona, initially came under the influence of the Italian Futurists. He is credited as cocreator of *Un chien andalou*, but his role is thought to have been subordinate; he abandoned film after collaborating on the script for Buñuel's *L'Age d'or* 1930. He designed ballet costumes, scenery, jewelry, and furniture. The books *Secret Life of Salvador Dali* 1942 and *Diary of a Genius* 1966 are autobiographical. He was buried beneath a crystal dome in the museum of his work at Figueras on the Costa Brava, Spain.

Dalian one of the two cities comprising the Chinese port of ◊Lüda.

Dallapiccola Luigi 1904–1975. Italian composer. In his early years he was a Neo-Classicist in the manner of Stravinsky, but he soon turned to Serialism, which he adapted to his own style. His works include the operas *Il Prigioniero/The Prisoner* 1949 and *Ulisse/Ulysses* 1968, as well as many vocal and instrumental compositions.

Dallas commercial city in Texas; population (1990) 1,006,877, metropolitan area (with Fort Worth) 3,885,415. Industries include banking, insurance, oil, aviation, aerospace, and electronics. Dallas–Fort Worth Regional Airport (opened 1973) is one of the world's largest. John F ◊Kennedy was assassinated here 1963.

It is a cultural center, with a symphony orchestra, opera, ballet, and theater; there is an annual Texas State Fair. Southern Methodist University is here. Founded as a trading post 1844, it developed as the focus of a cotton area and then as a mineral and oil-producing center, with banking and insurance operations. After World War II, growth increased rapidly.

Dalmatia region of Croatia, Bosnia and Herzegovina, and Montenegro in Yugoslavia. The capital is Split. It lies along the eastern shore of the Adriatic sea and includes a number of islands. The interior is mountainous. Important products are wine, olives, and fish. Notable towns in addition to the capital are Zadar, Sibenik, and Dubrovnik.

history Dalmatia became Austrian 1815 and by the treaty of Rapallo 1920 became part of the kingdom of the Serbs, Croats, and Slovenes (Yugoslavia from 1931), except for the town of Zadar (Zara) and the island of Lastovo (Lagosta), which, with neighboring islets, were given to Italy until transferred to Yugoslavia 1947. Dalmatia was made a region of Croatia 1949.

dalmatian breed of dog, about 2 ft/60 cm tall at the shoulder, white with spots that are black or brown. Dalmatians are born white; the spots appear later on. They were formerly used as coach dogs, walking beside horse-drawn carriages to fend off highwaymen.

dalmatic the outer liturgical vestment of the deacon in the Roman Catholic Church; a mantle worn at Mass and in solemn processions.

Dalton John 1766–1844. British chemist, the first in modern times to propose the existence of atoms, which he considered to be the smallest parts of matter. He also produced the first list of atomic weights in *Absorption of Gases* 1805. He was the first scientist to note and record color blindness (he was himself color blind).

Daly Augustin 1838–1899. US theater manager. He began as a drama critic and playwright before building his own theater in New York 1879 and another, Daly's, in Leicester Square, London 1893.

dam a structure built to hold back water in order to prevent flooding, provide water for irrigation and storage, and to provide hydroelectric power. The biggest dams are of the earth-and rock-fill type, also called embankment dams. Early dams in Britain, built before about 1800, had a core made from puddle clay (clay which has been mixed with water to make it impervious). Such dams are generally built on broad valley sites. Deep, narrow gorges dictate a concrete dam, where the strength of reinforced concrete can withstand the water pressures involved. The first major all-concrete dam in Britain was built at Woodhead in 1876. The first dam where concrete was used to seal the joints in the rocks below was at Tunstall in 1879.

A valuable development in arid regions, as in parts of Brazil, is the underground dam, where water is stored on a solid rock base, with a wall to ground level, so avoiding rapid evaporation. Many concrete dams are triangular in cross section, with their vertical face pointing upstream. Their sheer weight holds them in position, and they are called gravity dams. Other concrete dams are more slightly built in the shape of an arch, with the curve facing upstream: the arch dam derives its strength from the arch shape, just as an arch bridge does.

Major dams include: Rogun (USSR), the world's highest at 1,067 ft/325 m; New Cornelia Tailings (USA), the world's biggest in volume, 7.4 billion cu ft/209 million cu m; Owen Falls (Uganda), the world's largest reservoir capacity, 7.2 trillion cu ft/204.8 billion cu m; and Itaipu (Brazil/Paraguay), the world's most powerful, producing 12,700 megawatts of electricity.

Dam Carl 1895–1976. Danish biochemist who dis-

dam

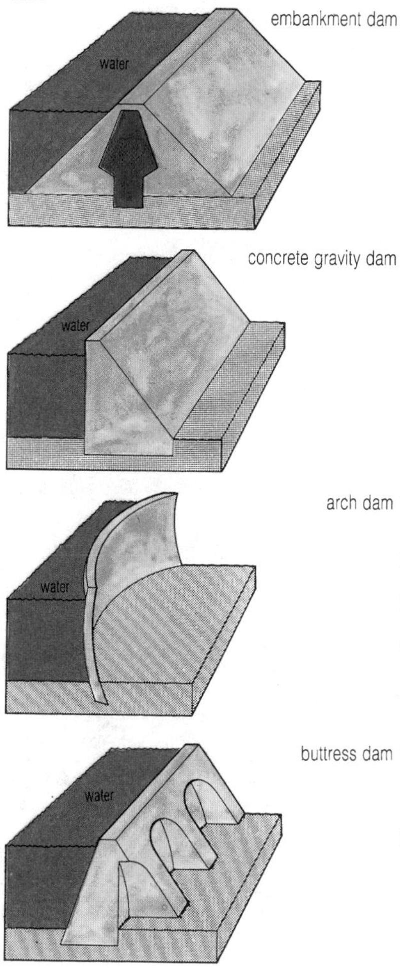
embankment dam
water
concrete gravity dam
water
arch dam
water
buttress dam
water

covered vitamin K. For his success in this field he shared the 1943 Nobel Prize for Medicine with US biochemist Edward Doisy (1893–1986).

In 1928 Dam began a series of experiments to see if chickens could live on a cholesterol-free diet. The birds, it turned out, were able to metabolize their own supply. Yet they continued to die from spontaneous hemorrhages. Dam concluded that their diet lacked an unknown essential ingredient, which he eventually found in abundance in green leaves. As it controlled coagulation, Dam named the new compound vitamin K.

damages in law, compensation for a ◊tort (such as personal injuries caused by negligence) or breach of contract. In the case of breach of contract the complainant can claim all the financial loss he or she has suffered. Damages for personal injuries include compensation for loss of earnings, as well as for the injury itself. The court might reduce the damages if the claimant was partly to blame. In the majority of cases, the parties involved reach an out-of-court settlement (a compromise without going to court).

Daman or *Damão* part of the Union Territory of Daman and ◊Diu, India; area 42 sq mi/110 sq km; capital Panaji; population (1981) 79,000. Daman has an area of 28 sq mi/72 sq km and a population (1981) of 49,000. The town of Daman is a port on the W coast of India, 100 mi/160 km N of Bombay; population (1981) 21,000. Daman was seized by Portugal 1531 and ceded to Portugal by the Shar of Gujarat 1539. It was annexed by India 1961 and was part of the Union Territory of ◊Goa, Daman, and Diu until Goa became a separate state 1987. The economy is based on tourism and fishing.

Damaraland central region of Namibia, home of the nomadic Bantu-speaking ◊Hereros.

Damascus (Arabic *Dimashq*) capital of Syria, on the river Barada, SE of Beirut; population (1981) 1,251,000. It produces silk, wood products, and brass and copper ware. Said to be the oldest continuously inhabited city in the world, Damascus was an ancient city even in Old Testament times; most notable of the old buildings is the Great Mosque, completed as a Christian church in the 5th century.

The Assyrians destroyed it about 733 BC. In 332 BC it fell to one of the generals of Alexander the Great; in 63 BC it came under Roman rule. In AD 635 it was taken by the Arabs, and has since been captured many times, by Egyptians, Mongolians, and Turks. In 1918, during World War I, it was taken from the Turks by the British with Arab aid and in 1920 became the capital of French-mandated Syria.

The "street which is called straight" is associated with St Paul, who was converted while on the road to Damascus. The tomb of ◊Saladin is here. The fortress dates from 1219.

damask textile of woven linen, cotton, wool, or silk, with a reversible figured pattern. It was first made in the city of Damascus, Syria.

Damien, Father 1840–1889. Name adopted by Belgian missionary Joseph de ◊Veuster.

Damietta English name for the Egyptian port of ◊Dumyat.

daminozide (trade name Alar) a chemical used by fruit growers to make apples redder and crisper. It was found to be linked to cancer, and the US Environment Protection Agency (EPA) called for an end to its use.

damnation in Christian and Muslim belief, a state of eternal punishment which will be undergone by those who are not worthy of salvation; sometimes equated with ◊hell.

Damocles lived 4th century BC. In Classical legend, a courtier of the elder Dionysius, ruler of Syracuse, Sicily. Having extolled the happiness of his sovereign, Damocles was invited by him to a feast, during which he saw above his head a sword suspended by a single hair. He recognized this as a symbol of the insecurity of the great.

Damodar Indian river flowing 350 mi/560 km from Chota Nagpur plateau in Bihar, through Bihar and West Bengal states to join the ◊Hooghly river 25 mi/40 km SW of Calcutta. The Damodar Valley is an industrial center with a hydroelectric project, combined with irrigation works.

Damon and Pythias in Greek legend, devoted friends. When Pythias was condemned to death by a tyrant, Damon offered his own life as security to allow Pythias the freedom to go and arrange his affairs. When Pythias returned, they were both pardoned.

damper any device that deadens or lessens vibrations or oscillations; for example, to check vibrations in the strings of a piano. The term is also used for the moveable plate in the flue of a stove or furnace for controlling the draft.

Dampier William 1652–1715. English explorer and hydrographic surveyor who circumnavigated the world three times.

damselfly long, slender, colorful dragonfly of the suborder Zygoptera, with two pairs of similar wings that are generally held vertically over the body when at rest, unlike those of other dragonflies.

damson cultivated variety of ◊plum tree *Prunus domestica* var. *institia*, distinguished by its small, oval, edible fruit, which is dark purple or blue to black in color.

Dana Charles Anderson 1819–1897. US journalist. Born in Hinsdale, New Hampshire, and educated at Harvard, Dana left college before graduating to become manager of Brook Farm, an experimental community in West Roxbury, Massachusetts, 1841–47. After its breakup he embarked on a journalistic career and became city editor of the *New York Tribune* 1847. He covered the European revolutions of 1848 and earned a reputation as one of America's most able foreign correspondents. During the US Civil War he served as assistant secretary of war 1863–65 and in 1868 purchased the *New York Sun*, with which he pioneered the daily tabloid format.

Dana Richard Henry 1815–1882. US author and lawyer who went to sea and worked for his passage around Cape Horn to California and back, then wrote an account of the journey *Two Years before the Mast* 1840. He also published *The Seaman's Friend* 1841, a guide to maritime law.

Danaë in Greek mythology, daughter of Acrisius, king of Argos. He shut her up in a bronze tower because of a prophecy that her son would kill his grandfather. Zeus became enamored of her and descended in a shower of gold, and by him she became the mother of ◊Perseus.

Da Nang port city (formerly Tourane) of S Vietnam, 50 mi/80 km SE of Hué; population (1975) 500,000. Following the reunion of North and South Vietnam, the major part of the population was dispersed 1976 to rural areas. A US base in the Vietnam War, it is now used by the USSR.

Danbury city in SW Connecticut, NW of Bridgeport. Long a center for the manufacturing of hats, Danbury's newer industries include electronics, publishing, chemicals, and furniture; population (1980) 60,470.

Danbury Hatters Case a US Supreme Court case (*Loewe* v *Lawler*) 1908 dealing with the right of the federal government to prohibit certain labor union activities. Dietrich Loewe, owner of the Danbury Hat Co in Connecticut filed suit for damages resulting from a boycott of Danbury Hat products. The boycott was initiated by the United Hatters of North America in support of a strike by the Danbury hatters. The Court ruled unanimously that this sort of secondary boycott was a conspiracy for the restraint of trade, a violation of the Sherman Antitrust act.

dance rhythmic movement of the body, usually performed in time to music. Its primary purpose may be religious, magical, martial, social, or artistic—the last two being characteristic of nontraditional societies. The pre-Christian era had a strong tradition of ritual dance, and ancient Greek dance still exerts an influence on dance movement today. Although Western folk and social dances have a long history, the Eastern dance tradition long predates the Western. The European Classical tradition dates from the 15th century in Italy, the first printed dance text from 16th-century France, and the first dance school in Paris from the 17th century. The 18th century saw the development of European Classical ballet as we know it today, and the 19th century saw the rise of Romantic ballet. In the 20th century many divergent styles and ideas have grown from a willingness to explore a variety of techniques and amalgamate different traditions.

history European dance is relatively young in comparison to that of the rest of the world. The first Indian book on dancing, the *Natya Sastra*, existed a thousand years before its European counterpart. The *bugaku* dances of Japan, with orchestra accompaniment, date from the 7th century and are still performed at court. When the Peking (Beijing) Opera dancers first astonished Western audiences during the 1950s, they were representatives of a tradition stretching back to 740, the year in which Emperor Ming Huang established the Pear Garden Academy. The first comparable European institution, *L'Académie royale de danse*, was founded by Louis XIV 1661.

Social dances have always tended to rise upward through the social scale; for example, the medieval court dances derived from peasant country dances. One form of dance tends to typify a whole period, thus the galliard represents the 16th century, the minuet the 18th, the waltz the 19th, and perhaps the quickstep the 20th.

The nine dances of the modern world cham-

dance chronology

1581	In Paris, the first modern-style unified ballet, the *Ballet Comique de la Reine*, was staged at the court of Catherine de Médici.
1588	Dance and ballet's first basic text, *L'Orchésographie*, by the priest Jehan Tabouret, was printed in Langres, near Dijon.
1651	In London, John Playford published *The English Dancing Master*. The 18th edition (1728) described 900 country dances.
1661	Louis XIV founded L'Académie Royale de Danse in Paris.
1670	The first classic ballet, *Le Bourgeois Gentilhomme*, was produced in Chambord, France.
1681	In Paris, women appeared in ballet for the first time in the opera-ballet *Le Triomphe de L'amour*.
1734	The dancer Marie Sallé streamlined the traditional costume, and Marie Camargo shortened her skirts.
1760	The great dancer and choreographer Jean-Georges Noverre published in Lyons *Lettres sur la Danse et sur les Ballets*, one of the most influential of all ballet books.
1778	Noverre and Mozart collaborated on *Les Petits Riens* in Paris. The cast included the celebrated Auguste Vestris.
late 1700s	The waltz originated in Austria and Germany from a popular folk dance, the *Ländler*.
1820	Carlo Blasis, teacher and choreographer, published his *Traité élémentaire théoretique et pratique de l'arte de la danse* in Milan which, together with his later works of dance theory, codified techniques for future generations of dancers.
1821	The first known picture of a ballerina *sur les pointes*, the French Fanny Bias by F Waldeck, dates from this year.
1832	The first performance of *La Sylphide* at the Paris Opéra opened the Romantic era of ballet and established the central significance of the ballerina. Marie Taglioni, the producer's daughter, who took the title role, wore the new-style diaphanous dress.
1841	Ballet's Romantic masterpiece *Giselle* with Carlotta Grisi in the leading role, was produced in Paris.
1866	*The Black Crook*, the ballet extravaganza from which US vaudeville and musical comedy developed, began its run of 474 performances in New York.
1870	*Coppélia*, 19th-century ballet's comic masterpiece, was presented in Paris.
1877	*Swan Lake* was premiered in Moscow, but failed through poor production and choreography. The Petipa-Ivanov version, in which Pierina Legnani performed 32 *fouettés*, established the work 1895.
1897	Anna Pavlova made her debut in St Petersburg with the Imperial Russian Ballet.
1905	Isadora Duncan appeared in Russia, making an immense impression with her "antiballet" innovations derived from Greek dance.
1906	Vaslav Nijinsky made his debut in St Petersburg.
1909	The first Paris season given by Diaghilev's troupe of Russian dancers, later to become known as the Ballets Russes, marked the beginning of one of the most exciting periods in Western ballet.
1913	The premiere of Stravinsky's *The Rite of Spring* provoked a scandal in Paris.
1914	The foxtrot developed from the two-step in the US.
1926	Martha Graham, one of the most innovative figures in modern dance, gave her first recital in New York. In England, students from the Rambert School of Ballet, opened by Marie Rambert in 1920, gave their first public performance in *A Tragedy of Fashion*, the first ballet to be choreographed by Frederick Ashton.
1928	The first performance of George Balanchine's *Apollon Musagète* in Paris, by the Ballets Russes, marked the birth of Neo-Classicism in ballet.
1931	Ninette de Valois's Vic-Wells Ballet gave its first performance in London. In 1956 the company became the Royal Ballet.
1933	The Hollywood musical achieved artistic independence through Busby Berkeley's kaleidoscopic choreography in *Forty-Second Street* and Dave Gould's airborne finale in *Flying down to Rio*, in which Fred Astaire and Ginger Rogers appeared together for the first time.
1940	The Dance Notation Bureau was established in New York for recording ballets and dances.
1948	The New York City Ballet was founded with George Balanchine as principal choreographer. The film *The Red Shoes* appeared, choreographed by Massine and Robert Helpmann, starring Moira Shearer.
1950	The Festival Ballet, later to become the London Festival Ballet, was created by Alicia Markova and Anton Dolin, who had first danced together with the Ballets Russes de Monte Carlo 1929.
1952	Gene Kelly starred and danced in the film *Singin' in the Rain*.
1953	The US experimental choreographer Merce Cunningham, who often worked with the composer John Cage, formed his own troupe.
1956	The Bolshoi Ballet opened its first season in the West at Covent Garden in London, with Galina Ulanova dancing in *Romeo and Juliet*.
1957	Jerome Robbins choreographed Leonard ◊Bernstein's *West Side Story*, demonstrating his outstanding ability to work in both popular and Classical forms.
1960	The progressive French choreographer Maurice Béjart became director of the Brussels-based *Ballet du XXième Siècle* company.
1961	Rudolf Nureyev defected from the USSR while dancing with the Kirov Ballet in Paris. He was to have a profound influence on male dancing in the West. South African choreographer John Cranko became director of the Stuttgart Ballet, for which he was to produce several major ballets.
1962	Glen Tetley's ballet *Pierrot Lunaire*, in which he was one of the three dancers, was premiered in New York. In the same year he joined the Nederlands Dans Theater.
1965	US choreographer Twyla Tharp produced her first works.
1966	The School of Contemporary Dance was founded in London, from which Robin Howard and the choreographer Robert Cohan created the London Contemporary Dance Theatre, later to become an internationally renowned company. The choreographer Norman Morrice joined the Ballet Rambert and the company began to concentrate on contemporary works.
1968	Arthur Mitchell, the first black dancer to join the New York City Ballet, founded the Dance Theatre of Harlem.
1974	Mikhail Baryshnikov defected from the USSR while dancing with a Bolshoi Ballet group in Toronto.
1977	The release of Robert Stigwood's film *Saturday Night Fever* popularized disco dancing worldwide.
1980	Natalia Makarova, who had defected from the USSR 1979, staged the first full-length revival of Petipa's *La Bayadère* in the West with the American Ballet Theatre in New York.
1981	Wayne Sleep, previously principal dancer with the Royal Ballet, starred as lead dancer in Andrew Lloyd-Webber's musical *Cats*, choreographed by Gillian Lynne.
1983	Peter Martins, principal dancer with the New York City Ballet, became choreographer and codirector with Jerome Robbins on the death of Balanchine. Break dancing became widely popular in Western inner cities.
1984	The avant-garde group Michael Clark and Company made its debut in London.

pionships in ◊ballroom dancing are the standard four (◊waltz, ◊foxtrot, ◊tango, and quickstep), the Latin-American styles (samba, rumba, cha-cha-cha, and paso doble), and the Viennese waltz.

Popular dance crazes have included the Charleston in the 1920s, jitterbug in the 1930s and 1940s, ◊jive in the 1950s, the twist in the 1960s, disco dancing in the 1970s, and break dancing in the 1980s. In general, since the 1960s popular dance in the West has moved away from any prescribed sequence of movements and physical contact between participants, the dancers performing as individuals with no distinction between the male and the female role. Dances requiring skilled athletic performance, such as the hustle and the New Yorker, have been developed.

In Classical dance, the second half of the 20th century has seen a great cross-fertilization from dances of other cultures. Troupes have visited from both the East and the West, including the USSR and Eastern Europe, Indonesia, Japan, South Korea, Nigeria, and Senegal. In the 1970s jazz dance, pioneered in the US by Matt Mattox, became popular. It includes elements of ballet, modern, tap, Indian Classical, Latin American, and African-American dance, and may be summed up as "free-style dance."

Dance Charles 1946–. English film and television actor who achieved fame in *The Jewel in the Crown* 1984. He has also appeared in *Plenty* 1986, *Good Morning Babylon*, *The Golden Child* 1987, and *White Mischief* 1988.

His television appearances include *First Born* 1989. He played Coriolanus in the Royal Shakespeare Company's 1989 production.

dandelion plant *Taraxacum officinale* belonging to the Compositae family. The stalk rises from a rosette of leaves that are deeply indented like a lion's teeth, hence the name (from French *dent de lion*). The flower heads are bright yellow. The fruit is surmounted by the hairs of the calyx which constitute the familiar dandelion "puff."

The milky juice of the dandelion has laxative properties, and the young leaves are sometimes

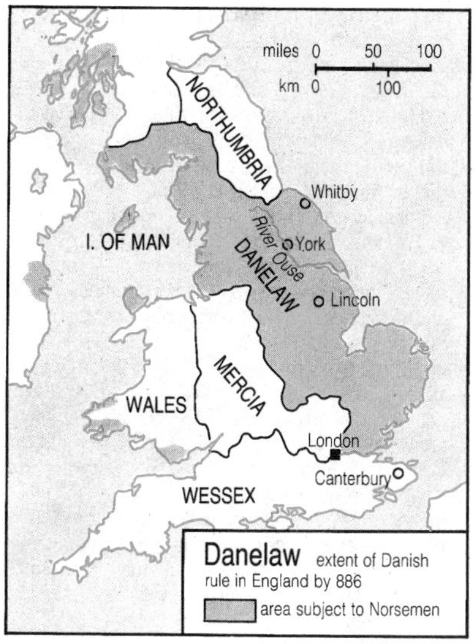
miles 0 50 100
km 0 100
NORTHUMBRIA
Whitby
I. OF MAN
River Ouse
York
DANELAW
Lincoln
MERCIA
WALES
London
Canterbury
WESSEX
Danelaw extent of Danish rule in England by 886
area subject to Norsemen

eaten in salads. In the Russian species *Taraxacum koksaghyz*, the juice forms an industrially usable latex, relied upon especially during World War II.

Dandelions, introduced from Europe, now grow throughout North America.

Dandie Dinmont breed of ◊terrier that originated in the Scottish border country. It is about 10 in/ 25 cm tall, shortlegged and long-bodied, with drooping ears and a long tail. Its hair, about 2 in/ 5 cm long, can be grayish or yellowish. It is named after the character Dandie Dinmont in Walter Scott's novel *Guy Mannering* 1815.

Dandolo Venetian family that produced four doges (rulers), of whom the most outstanding, Enrico (c. 1120–1205), became doge in 1193. He greatly increased the dominions of the Venetian republic and accompanied the crusading army that took Constantinople in 1203.

Dane native to or inhabitant of Denmark; in English history, a ◊Viking.

danegeld in English history, a tax imposed from 991 by Anglo-Saxon kings to pay tribute to the Vikings. After the Norman Conquest the tax continued to be levied until 1162, and the Normans used it to finance military operations.

Danelaw 11th-century name for the area of N and E England settled by the Vikings in the 9th century. It occupied about half of England, from the river Tees to the river Thames. Within its bounds, Danish law, customs, and language prevailed. Its linguistic influence is still apparent.

Daniel 6th century BC. Jewish folk hero and prophet at the court of Nebuchadnezzar; also the name of a book of the Old Testament, probably compiled in the 2nd century BC. It includes stories about Daniel and his companions Shadrach, Meshach, and Abednego, set during the Babylonian captivity of the Jews.

One of the best-known stories is that of Daniel in the den of lions, where he was thrown for refusing to compromise his beliefs, and was preserved by divine intervention. The book also contains a prophetic section dealing with the rise and fall of a number of empires.

Daniel Glyn 1914–1986. British archeologist. Prominent in the development of the subject, he was Disney professor of archeology, Cambridge, 1974–81. His books include *Megaliths in History* 1973 and *A Short History of Archeology* 1981.

Daniell John Frederic 1790–1845. British chemist and meteorologist who invented a primary electrical cell in 1836, the Daniell cell consists of a central zinc cathode dipping into a porous pot containing zinc sulfate solution. The porous pot is, in turn, immersed in a solution of copper sulfate contained in a copper can, which acts as the cell's anode. The use of a porous barrier prevents polarization (the covering of the anode with small bubbles of hydrogen gas) and allows the cell to generate a continuous current of electricity.

Danish language member of the North Germanic group of the Indo-European language family, spoken in Denmark and Greenland and related to Icelandic, Faroese, Norwegian, and Swedish. As one of the languages of the Vikings, who invaded and settled in parts of Britain during the 9th to 11th centuries, Old Danish had a strong influence on English.

Danish literature Danish writers of international fame emerged in the 19th century: Hans Christian Andersen, the philosopher Soren Kierkegaard, and the critic Georg Brandes (1842–1927), all of whom played a major part in the Scandinavian literary awakening, encouraging Ibsen and others. The novelists Henrik Pontoppidan (1857–1943), Karl Gjellerup (1857–1919), and Johannes Jensen (1873–1950) were all Nobel Prizewinners, but have not achieved an enduring reputation outside Scandinavia.

Dankworth John 1927– . British jazz musician, composer, and bandleader, leading figure in the development of British jazz from about 1950. His film scores include *Saturday Night and Sunday Morning* 1960 and *The Servant* 1963.

D'Annunzio Gabriele 1863–1938. Italian poet, novelist, and playwright. Marking a departure from 19th-century Italian literary traditions, his use of language and style of writing earned him much criticism in his own time.

His first volume of poetry, *Primo vere/In Early Spring* 1879, was followed by further collections of verse, short stories, novels, and plays (he wrote the play *La Gioconda* for the actress Eleonora Duse in 1898).

After serving in World War I, he led an expedition of volunteers in 1919 to capture Fiume, which he held until 1921. He became a national hero, and was created Prince of Montenevoso in 1924. Influenced by Nietzsche's writings, he later became an ardent exponent of Fascism.

Dante Alighieri 1265–1321. Italian poet. His masterpiece *La Divina Commedia/The Divine Comedy* 1307–21 is an epic account in three parts of his journey through Hell, Purgatory, and Paradise, during which he is guided part of the way by the poet Virgil; on a metaphorical level the journey is also one of Dante's own spiritual development. Other works include the philosophical prose treatise *Convivio/The Banquet* 1306–08, the first major work of its kind to be written in Italian rather than Latin; *Monarchia/On World Government* 1310–13, expounding his political theories; *De vulgari eloquentia/Concerning the Vulgar Tongue* 1304–06, an original Latin work on Italian, its dialects, and kindred languages; and *Canzoniere/Lyrics*, containing his scattered lyrics.

Dante was born in Florence, where he first met Beatrice (Portinari) in 1274, for whom he conceived a lasting love (described in *La Vita Nuova/New Life* 1283–92) that survived her marriage to another and her death in 1290 at the age of 24.

Daniell cell

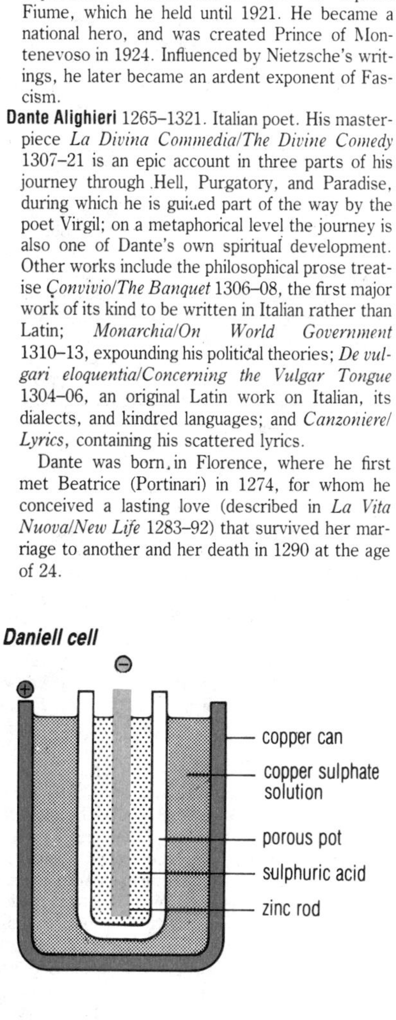
copper can
copper sulphate solution
porous pot
sulphuric acid
zinc rod

Dante Alighieri *Painting of the Italian poet Dante Alighieri by Andrea del Castagno.*

In 1289 Dante fought in the battle of Campaldino, won by Florence against Arezzo, and from 1295 took an active part in Florentine politics. In 1300 he was one of the six Priors of the Republic, favoring the moderate "White" Guelph party rather than the extreme papal "Black" faction; when the Blacks seized power in 1302, he was convicted in his absence of misapplication of public moneys, and sentenced first to a fine and then to death. He escaped Florence and spent the remainder of his life in exile, in central and northern Italy.

Danton Georges Jacques 1759–1794. French revolutionary. Originally a lawyer, during the early years of the Revolution he was one of the most influential people in Paris. He organized the uprising Aug 10, 1792 that overthrew the monarchy, roused the country to expel the Prussian invaders, and in April 1793 formed the revolutionary tribunal and the Committee of Public Safety, of which he was the leader until July of that year. Thereafter he lost power to the ◊Jacobins, and, when he attempted to recover it, was arrested and guillotined.

Danube (German *Donau*) second longest of European rivers, rising on the E slopes of the Black Forest, and flowing 1,776 mi/2,858 km across Europe to enter the Black Sea in Romania by a swampy delta.

The head of river navigation is Ulm, in Baden-Württemberg; Braila, Romania, is the limit for ocean-going ships. Cities on the Danube include Linz, Vienna, Bratislava, Budapest, Belgrade, Ruse, Braila, and Galati. A canal connects the Danube with the river ◊Main, and thus with the Rhine river system. Plans to dam the river for hydroelectric power at Nagymaros in Hungary, with participation by Austria and Czechoslovakia, were abandoned on environmental grounds 1989.

Danville city in S Virginia, just above the North Carolina border, on the Dan river, SE of Roanoke; seat of Averett county. Danville is situated in a tobacco-growing area. Industries include tobacco

Danton *French revolutionary leader Georges Jacques Danton, organizer of the uprising in France 1792, who was overthrown and guillotined by Robespierre and the leaders of the Reign of Terror.*

processing and marketing and the manufacture of tools, textiles, and building materials; population (1990) 53,056. The Confederate government moved from Richmond to Danville during the last days of the Civil War 1865.

Danzig German name for the Polish port of ◊Gdańsk.

Daphne in Greek mythology, a nymph who was changed into a laurel tree to escape from Apollo's amorous pursuit.

darcy unit (abbreviation D) of permeability, used mainly in geology to describe the permeability of rock (for example, to oil, gas, or water).

Dardanelles Turkish strait connecting the Sea of Marmara with the Aegean Sea (ancient name Hellespont, Turkish name *Canakkale Boğazi*; its shores are formed by the ◊Gallipoli peninsula on the NW and the mainland of Turkey-in-Asia on the SE. It is 47 mi/75 km long and 3–4 mi/5–6 km wide.

Dare Virginia 1587–?. First English child born in America. Dare was the daughter of settlers to the Roanoke colony (now in North Carolina) and granddaughter of the colony's governor, John White. Soon after her birth, White returned to England, and because of the sea war with Spain, English communication with Roanoke was cut off for nearly four years. An English ship arriving in 1591 found the colony deserted, with only the enigmatic inscription "Croatan" carved in a tree, as a clue that perhaps the settlers, fearful of hostile Indians, had taken refuge with the friendly Croatan.

Danube River

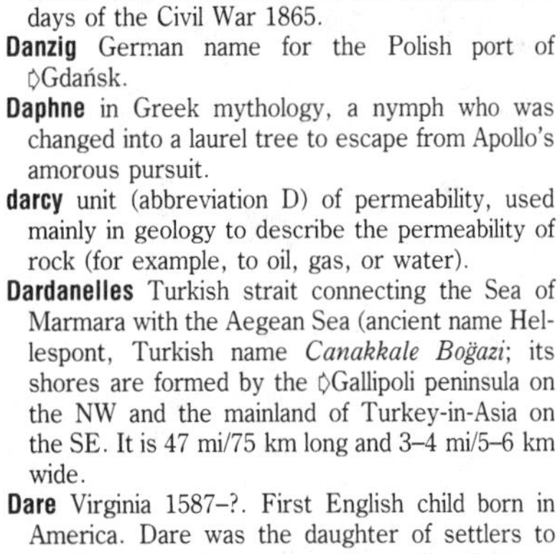
Danube

Dar el-Beida Arabic name for the port of ◊Casablanca, Morocco.

Dar es Salaam (Arabic "haven of peace"); chief seaport in Tanzania, on the Indian Ocean, and capital of Tanzania until its replacement by ◊Dodoma in 1974; population (1985) 1,394,000.

It is the Indian Ocean terminus of the TanZam Railway, and a line also runs to the lake port of Kigoma; a road links it with Ndola in the Zambian copperbelt, and oil is carried to Zambia by pipeline from Dar es Salaam's refineries. University College (1963) became the University of Dar es Salaam in 1970.

Darfur province in the W of the Republic of Sudan; area 75,920 sq mi/196,555 sq km; population (1983) 3,093,699. The capital is El Fasher (population 30,000). The area is a vast rolling plain producing gum arabic, and there is also some stock raising. Darfur was an independent sultanate until conquered by Egypt in 1874.

Darien former name for the Panama isthmus as a whole, and still the name of an eastern province of Panama; area 6,490 sq mi/16,803 sq km; population (1980) 26,500. The Gulf of Darien, part of the Caribbean sea, lies between Panama and Colombia. The Darien Gap is the complex of swamp, jungle, and ravines, which long prevented the linking of the North and South American sections of the Pan-American Highway, stretching about 200 mi/300 km between Canitas, Panama, and Chigorodo, Colombia. At the Colombian end is the Great Atrato Swamp, 35 mi/60 km across and over 1,000 ft/300 m deep. The Darien Expedition was a Scottish attempt to colonize the isthmus 1698–99, which failed disastrously caused by the climate and Spanish hostility. The British Trans-Americas Expedition, led by John Blashford-Snell, made the first motorized crossing in 1972.

Darío Rubén. Adopted name of Félix Rubén García Sarmiento 1867–1916. Nicaraguan poet. His first major work *Azul/Azure* 1888, a collection of prose and verse influenced by French Symbolism, created a sensation. He went on to establish *modernismo*, the Spanish-American modernist literary movement, distinguished by an idiosyncratic and deliberately frivolous style that broke away from the prevailing Spanish provincialism and adapted French poetic models. His vitality and eclecticism influenced every poet writing in Spanish after him, both in the New World and in Spain.

Darius I the Great c. 558–486 BC. King of Persia 521–48 BC. A member of a younger branch of the Achemenid dynasty, he won the throne from the usurper Gaumata (died 522 BC) and reorganized the government. In 512 BC he marched against the Scythians, a people north of the Black Sea, and subjugated Thrace and Macedonia.

An expedition in 492 BC to crush a rebellion in Greece failed, and the army sent into Attica 490 BC was defeated at the battle of Marathon. Darius had an account of his reign inscribed on the mountain at Behistun, Persia.

Darjeeling town and health resort in West Bengal, India; situated 7,000 ft/2,150 m above sea level, on the southern slopes of the Himalayas; population (1981) 57,600. It is connected by rail with Calcutta, 370 mi/595 km to the S. It is the center of a tea-producing district.

Darkhan or ***Darhan*** industrial town in Outer Mongolia, near the border with the USSR; population (1988) 80,000. Industries include the manufacture of cement and bricks, and to the S is Erdenet, where copper and molybdenum are mined.

Darling river in SE Australia, a tributary of the river Murray, which it joins at Wentworth. It is 1,910 mi/3,075 km long, and its waters are conserved in Menindee Lake (60 sq mi/155 sq km) and others nearby. The name comes from Sir Ralph Darling (1775–1858), governor of New South Wales 1825–31. The Darling Range, a ridge in W Australia, has a highest point of about 1,669 ft/582 m.

Darlington industrial town in Durham, England, on the river Skerne, near its junction with the river Tees; population (1981) 85,400. It has coal and ironstone mines, and produces iron and steel goods, and knitting wool. The world's first passenger railroad was opened between Darlington and Stockton on Sept 27, 1825.

Darmstadt town in the *Land* of Hessen, Federal Republic of Germany, 18 mi/29 km S of Frankfurt-am-Main; population (1988) 134,000. Industries include iron founding and the manufacture of chemicals, plastics, and electronics. It is a center of the European space industry. It has a ducal palace and a technical university.

Darnley Henry Stewart or Stuart, Lord 1545–1567. British aristocrat, second husband of Mary Queen of Scots from 1565, and father of James I of England (James VI of Scotland). On the advice of her secretary, David ◊Rizzio, Mary refused Darnley the crown matrimonial; in revenge, Darnley led a band of nobles who murdered Rizzio in Mary's presence. Darnley was assassinated 1567.

He was killed in an explosion (while ill in bed), probably by ◊Bothwell, who became Mary's third husband. Mary's role in the plot remains controversial.

Darrow Clarence (Seward) 1857–1938. US lawyer, born in Ohio, a champion of liberal causes and

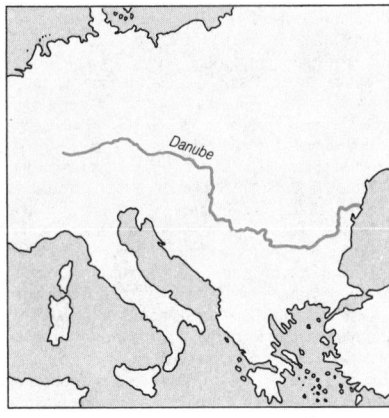

Dardanelles

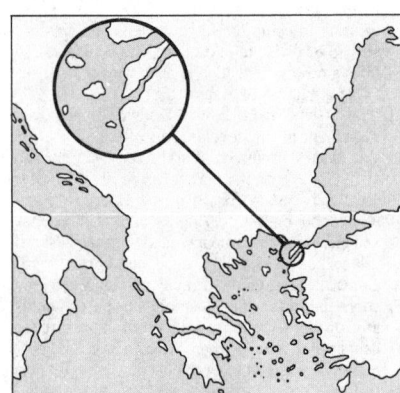

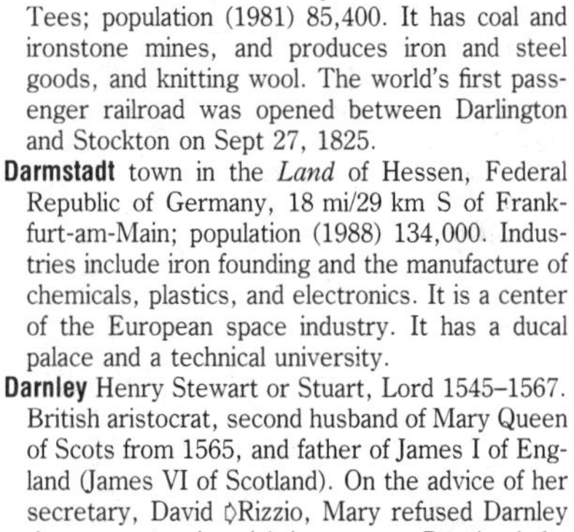

defender of the underdog. He defended many trade-union leaders, including Eugene ◊Debs 1894. He was counsel for the defense in the Nathan Leopold and Richard Loeb murder trial in Chicago 1924, and in the ◊Scopes monkey trial. Darrow matched wits in the trial with prosecution attorney William Jennings ◊Bryan. He was an opponent of capital punishment.

Dart Raymond 1893–1988. Australian-born South African paleontologist and anthropologist who in 1924 discovered the first fossil remains of the Australopithecenes, early hominids, near Taungs in Botswana. He named them *Australopithecus africanus*, and spent many years trying to prove to skeptics that they were early humans, since their cranial and dental characteristics were not apelike in any way. In the 1950s and 1960s, the ◊Leakey family found more fossils of this type and of related types in the Olduvai Gorge of E Africa, establishing that Australopithecines were hominids, walked erect, made tools, and lived as early as 5.5 million years ago. After further discoveries in the 1980s, they are today classified as *Homo sapiens australopithecus*, and Dart's assertions have been validated.

Dartmoor plateau of SW Devon, England, over 400 sq mi/1,000 sq km in extent, of which half is some 1,000 ft/300 m above sea level. Most of Dartmoor is a National Park. The moor is noted for its wild aspect, and rugged blocks of granite, or "tors," crown its higher points. The highest being Yes Tor 2,028 ft/618 m and High Willhays 2,039 ft/621 m. Devon's chief rivers have their sources on Dartmoor. There are numerous prehistoric remains. Near Hemerdon there are tungsten reserves.

Dartmoor Prison, opened in 1809 originally to house French prisoners-of-war during the Napoleonic Wars, is at Princetown in the center of the moor, 7 mi/11 km E of Tavistock. It is still used for category B prisoners.

Dartmouth English seaport at the mouth of the river Dart; 27 mi/43 km E of Plymouth, on the Devon coast; population (1981) 62,298. It is a center for yachting and has an excellent harbor. The Britannia Royal Naval College dates from 1905.

Dartmouth port in Nova Scotia, Canada, on the NE of Halifax harbor; population (1986) 65,300. It is virtually part of the capital city. Industries include oil refining and shipbuilding.

Dartmouth College Case a US Supreme Court case (officially *Trustees of Dartmouth College* v *Woodward*) 1819 dealing with the protection of private corporations from state intervention under contract law. After some dissension among the trustees of the college, the New Hampshire legislature revised Dartmouth's original corporate charter 1769, placing the administration under the control of a state-appointed board. The trustees sued the new secretary of the college, William H Woodward, for recovery of the official seal and documents. The Supreme Court voted 4 to 1 to uphold the original royal charter, ruling that corporations have contractual obligations and therefore are protected from impairment by states.

darts indoor game played on a circular board. Darts (like small arrow shafts) about 5 in/13 cm long are thrown at segmented targets and score points according to their landing place.

The game may have derived from target practice with broken arrow-shafts in days when archery was a compulsory military exercise. The Pilgrim Fathers are believed to have played darts aboard the *Mayflower* 1620.

Darwin capital and port in Northern Territory, Australia, in NW Arnhem Land; population (1986) 69,000. It serves the uranium mining site at Rum Jungle to the S. Destroyed 1974 by a cyclone, the city was rebuilt on the same site.

Darwin is the N terminus of the rail line from Birdum; commercial fruit and vegetable growing is being developed in the area. Founded 1869, under the name of Palmerston, the city was renamed after Charles Darwin 1911.

CHARLES ROBERT DARWIN, LL.D., F.R.S.

IN HIS *DESCENT OF MAN* HE BROUGHT HIS OWN SPECIES DOWN AS LOW AS POSSIBLE—*I.E.*, TO "A HAIRY QUADRUPED FURNISHED WITH A TAIL AND POINTED EARS, AND PROBABLY *ARBOREAL* IN ITS HABITS"—WHICH IS A REASON FOR THE VERY GENERAL INTEREST IN A "FAMILY TREE." HE HAS LATELY BEEN TURNING HIS ATTENTION TO THE "POLITIC WORM."

Darwin *Cartoon of the 19th-century evolutionist Charles Robert Darwin by Linley Sambourne.*

Darwin Charles Robert 1809–1882. English scientist who developed the modern theory of ◊evolution and proposed, with Alfred Russel Wallace, the principle of ◊natural selection. After research in South America and the Galápagos Islands as naturalist on HMS *Beagle* 1831–36, Darwin published *On the Origin of Species by Means of Natural Selection or the Preservation of Favoured Races in the Struggle for Life* 1859. This explained the evolutionary process through the principles of natural and sexual selection. It aroused bitter controversy because it disagreed with the literal interpretation of the Book of Genesis in the Bible.

Darwin Erasmus 1731–1802. British poet, physician, naturalist, and grandfather of Charles Darwin. He anticipated aspects of evolutionary theory, but tended to ◊Lamarck's interpretation.

Darwinism, social in US history, an influential but misleading social theory, based upon the work of Charles Darwin and Herbert Spencer, which claimed to offer a scientific justification for late 19th-century *laissez-faire* capitalism (the principle of unrestricted freedom in commerce).

Popularized by academics and by entrepreneurs such as Andrew ◊Carnegie, social Darwinism was used to legitimize competitive individualism and a market economy unregulated by government; it argued that only the strong and resourceful businesses and individuals would thrive in a free environment.

Dasam Granth a collection of the writings of the tenth Sikh guru (teacher), Gobind Singh, and of poems by a number of other writers. It is written in a script called Gurmukhi, the written form of Punjabi popularized by Guru Angad. It contains a retelling of the Krishna legends, devotional verse, and amusing anecdotes.

Dasht-e-Kavir Desert or ***Dasht-i-Davir Desert*** salt desert SE of Tehran, Iran; US forces landed here in 1980 in an abortive mission to rescue hostages held at the American Embassy in Tehran.

Das Kapital Karl Marx's exposition of his theories on economic production, published in three volumes 1867–95. It focuses on the exploitation of the worker and appeals for a classless society where the production process and its rewards are shared equally.

dasyure any ◊marsupial of the family Dasyuridae, also known as a "native cat," found in Australia and New Guinea. Various species have body lengths from 10 in/25 cm to 2.5 ft/75 cm. Dasyures have long, bushy tails and dark coats with white spots. They are agile, nocturnal carnivores, able to move fast and climb.

data facts, figures, and symbols, especially as stored in computers. The term is often used to mean raw, unprocessed facts, as distinct from information to which a meaning or interpretation has been applied.

database in computing, a structured collection of data. The database makes data available to the various programs that need it, without the need for those programs to be aware of how the data are stored. There are three main types (or "models"): hierarchical, network, and ◊relational, of which relational is the most widely used. A free-text database is one that holds the text of articles or books in a form that permits rapid searching.

A collection of databases is known as a databank. A database-management system (DBMS) program ensures that the integrity of the data is maintained by controlling the degree of access of the application programs using the data. Databases are normally used by large organizations with mainframes or minicomputers.

A telephone directory stored as a database might allow all the people whose names start with the letter B to be selected by one program, and all those living in Chicago by another.

data compression in computing, techniques for reducing the amount of storage needed for a given amount of data. They include word tokenization (in which frequently used words are stored as shorter codes), variable bit lengths (in which common characters are represented by fewer ◊bits than less common ones), and run-length encoding (in which a repeated value is stored once along with a count).

data-flow diagram in computing, a diagram illustrating the route taken by data through the various programs in an application.

data processing (DP) the use of computers for performing clerical tasks such as stock control, payroll, and dealing with orders. DP systems are typically batch systems, running on mainframe computers. DP is sometimes called EDP (electronic data processing).

A large organization usually has a special department to support its DP activities, which might include the writing and maintenance of software (programs), control and operation of the computers, and an analysis of the organization's information requirements.

date palm tree of the genus *Phoenix*. The female tree produces the fruit, dates, in bunches weighing 20–25 lb/9–11 kg.

Dates are an important source of food in the Middle East, being rich in sugar; they are dried for export. The tree also supplies timber, and materials for baskets, rope, and animal feed. The most important species is *P. dactylifera*; native to N Africa, SW Asia, and parts of India, it grows up to 80 ft/25 m high.

dating the science of determining the age of geologic structures, rocks, and fossils, and placing them in the context of geologic time.

Dating can be carried out by identifying fossils of creatures that lived only at certain times (marker fossils), by looking at the physical relationships of rocks to other rocks of a known age, or by measuring how much of a rock's radioactive elements have changed since the rock was formed, using the process of ◊radiometric dating.

dative in the grammar of certain inflected languages (see ◊language) such as Latin, the dative case is the form of a noun, pronoun, or adjective used for the indirect object of a verb. It is also used with some prepositions.

Datura genus of plants, family Solanaceae, such as jimson weed, with handsome trumpet-shaped blooms. Species in this genus have narcotic properties.

Daudet Alphonse 1840–1897. French novelist. He wrote about his native Provence in *Lettres de mon moulin/Letters from My Mill* 1866, and created the character Tartarin, a hero epitomizing southern temperament, in *Tartarin de Tarascon* 1872 and two sequels.

Other works include the play *L'Arlésienne/The Woman from Arles* 1872, for which Bizet composed the music; and *Souvenirs d'un homme de lettres/Recollections of a Literary Man* 1889.

Daudet Léon 1867–1942. French writer and journalist, who founded the militant right-wing royalist periodical *Action française* in 1899 after the Dreyfus case. During World War II he was a collaborator with the Germans. He was the son of Alphonse Daudet.

Daugavpils (Russian *Dvinsk*) town in Latvia, USSR, on the river Daugava (West Dvina); population (1985) 124,000. A fortress of the Livonian Knights 1278, it became the capital of Polish ◊Livonia. Industries include timber, textiles, engineering, and food products.

Daumier Honoré 1808–1879. French artist. His sharply dramatic and satirical cartoons dissected Parisian society. He produced over 4,000 lithographs and, mainly after 1860, powerful satirical oil paintings that were little appreciated in his lifetime.

Daumier drew for *La Caricature*, *Charivari*, and other periodicals. He created several fictitious stereotypes of contemporary figures and was once imprisoned for an attack on Louis Philippe. His paintings show a fluent technique and mainly monochrome palette. He also produced sculptures of his caricatures, such as the bronze statuette of *Ratapoil* about 1850 (Louvre, Paris).

dauphin title of the eldest son of the kings of France, derived from the personal name of a count, whose lands, the Dauphiné (capital Grenoble), traditionally passed to the heir to the throne from 1349 to 1830.

Dauphiné ancient province of France, comprising the modern *départements* of Isère, Drôme, and Hautes-Alpes.

After the collapse of the Roman Empire it belonged to Burgundy, then was under Frankish domination. Afterwards part of Arles, it was sold by its ruler to France in 1349 and thereafter was used as the personal fief of the heir to the throne (the dauphin) until 1560, when it was absorbed into the French kingdom. The capital was Grenoble.

Davao town in the Philippine Republic, at the mouth of the Davao river on the island of Mindanao; population (1980) 611,310. It is the capital of Davao province. It is the center of a fertile district and trades in pearls, copra, rice, and corn.

Davenport city in SE Iowa, S of Dubuque, directly across from Rock Island, Illinois, on the Mississippi river; seat of Scott county. It forms the "Quad Cities" metropolitan area with the Illinois cities of Rock Island, Moline, and East Moline. Industries include aluminum, agriculture, and machinery parts; population (1990) 95,333.

David c. 1060–970 BC. Second king of Israel. According to the Old Testament he played the harp for King Saul to banish Saul's melancholy; he later slew the Philistine giant Goliath with a sling and stone. After Saul's death David was anointed king at Hebron, took Jerusalem, and made it his capital.

David sent Uriah (a soldier in his army) to his death in the front line of battle so that he might marry his widow, Bathsheba. Their son Solomon became the third king.

David probably wrote a few of the psalms (of the Book of Psalms) and was celebrated as a secular poet. In both Jewish and Christian belief, the messiah would be a descendant of David; Christians hold this prophecy to have been fulfilled by Jesus Christ.

David Gerard c. 1450–1523. Netherlandish painter active chiefly in Bruges from about 1484. His style follows that of van der Weyden, but he was also influenced by the taste in Antwerp for Italianate ornament. *The Marriage at Cana* about 1503 (Louvre, Paris) is an example of his work.

David Jacques Louis 1748–1825. French painter in the Neo-Classical style. He was an active supporter of and unofficial painter to the republic during the French Revolution, for which he was imprisoned 1794–95.

He won the Prix de Rome 1774 and studied in Rome 1776–80. On his return to Paris, his strongly Classical themes and polished style soon earned success; a picture from this period is *The Oath of the Horatii* 1784 (Louvre, Paris). During the Revolution he was elected to the Convention and became a member of the Committee of Public Safety and narrowly escaped the guillotine. He was later appointed court painter to the emperor Napoleon, of whom he created images such as the horseback figure of *Napoleon Crossing the Alps* 1800 (Louvre, Paris). In his *Death of Marat* 1793, he turned political murder into a Classical tragedy. Later he devoted himself to the empire in paintings such as the enormous, pompous *Coronation of Napoleon* 1805–07 (Louvre, Paris). After Napoleon's fall, David was banished by the Bourbons and settled in Brussels.

David two kings of Scotland:

David I 1084–1153. King of Scotland from 1124. The youngest son of Malcolm III Canmore and St ◊Margaret, he was brought up in the English court of Henry I, and in 1113 married ◊Matilda, widow of the 1st earl of Northampton. He invaded England 1138 in support of Queen Matilda, but was defeated at Northallerton in the Battle of the Standard, and again 1141.

David II 1324–1371. King of Scotland from 1329, son of ◊Robert I (the Bruce). David was married at the age of four to Joanna, daughter of Edward II of England. In 1346 David invaded England, was captured at the battle of Neville's Cross and imprisoned for 11 years.

David Copperfield a novel by Charles Dickens, published 1849–50. The story follows the orphan David Copperfield from his schooldays and early poverty to eventual fame as an author. Among the characters he encounters are Mr Micawber, Mr Peggotty, and Uriah Heep.

David, St or ***Dewi*** 5th–6th century. Patron saint of Wales, Christian abbot and bishop. According to legend he was the son of a prince of Dyfed and uncle of King Arthur; he was responsible for the adoption of the leek as the national emblem of Wales, but his own emblem is a dove. Feast day Mar 1.

Davies Peter Maxwell 1934– . English composer and conductor. His music combines medieval and

***Davis** During the Civil War, Jefferson Davis was President of the Confederacy 1861–65.*

***Davis** Hollywood legend Bette Davis.*

serial codes of practice with a heightened Expressionism as in his opera *Taverner* 1962–68.

Davies Robertson 1913– . Canadian novelist. He published the first novel of his Deptford trilogy *Fifth Business* 1970, a panoramic work blending philosophy, humor, the occult, and ordinary life. Other works include *A Mixture of Frailties* 1958, *The Rebel Angels* 1981, and *What's Bred in the Bone* 1986.

Da Vinci see ◊Leonardo da Vinci, Italian Renaissance artist.

Davis Angela 1944– . US left-wing activist for black rights, prominent in the student movement of the 1960s. In 1970 she went into hiding after being accused of supplying guns used in the murder of a judge who had been seized as a hostage in an attempt to secure the release of three black convicts. She was captured, tried, and acquitted. At the University of California she studied under Herbert Marcuse, and was assistant professor of philosophy at UCLA 1969–70. In 1980 she was the Communist vice-presidential candidate.

Davis Bette 1908–1989. US actress. She entered films in 1930, establishing a reputation as a forceful dramatic actress with *Of Human Bondage* 1934. Later films included *Dangerous* 1935 and *Jezebel* 1938, both winning her Academy Awards, *All About Eve*, which won the 1950 Academy Award for best picture, and *Whatever Happened to Baby Jane?* 1962. She continued to make films throughout the 1980s such as *How Green Was My Valley* for television, and *The Whales of August* 1987, in which she costarred with Lillian Gish.

Davis Colin 1927– . English conductor. He was musical director at Sadler's Wells 1961–65, chief conductor of the BBC Symphony Orchestra 1967–71, musical director of the Royal Opera 1971–86, and chief conductor of the Bavarian Radio Symphony Orchestra 1983.

Davis Jefferson 1808–1889. US politician, president of the short-lived Confederate States of America 1861–65. He was a leader of the Southern Democrats in the US Senate from 1857, and a defender of "humane" slavery; in 1860 he issued a declaration in favor of secession from the US. During the Civil War he assumed strong political leadership, but often disagreed with military policy. He was imprisoned for two years after the war, one of the few cases of judicial retribution against Confederate leaders.

Born in Kentucky, he graduated from ◊West Point military academy and served in the US army before becoming a cotton planter in Mississippi. He sat in the US Senate 1847–51, was secretary of war 1853–57, and returned to the Senate 1857. His fiery temper and self-righteousness served badly in the effort to achieve broad unity among the Southern states. His call for conscription in the South raised protests that he was a military dictator, violating the very ideals of freedom for which the Confederacy was fighting.

Davis John 1550–1605. English navigator and explorer. He sailed in search of the Northwest Passage through the Canadian Arctic to the Pacific Ocean 1585, and in 1587 sailed to Baffin Bay through the straits named after him. He was the first European to see the Falkland Islands 1592.

Davis Miles (Dewey, Jr) 1926–1991. US jazz trumpeter, composer, and bandleader. He recorded bebop with Charlie Parker 1945, pioneered "cool jazz" in the 1950s and jazz-rock fusion beginning in the late 1960s. His significant albums include *Birth of the Cool* 1949, *Sketches of Spain* 1959, and *Bitches' Brew* 1970.

Davis Sammy, Jr 1925–1990. US entertainer. His starring role in the Broadway show *Mr Wonderful* 1956, his television work, and his roles in films with Frank Sinatra's "rat pack" – among them, *Ocean's Eleven* 1960 and *Robin and the Seven Hoods* 1964 – made him a national celebrity. He published two memoirs, *Yes I Can* 1965 and *Why Me?* 1989.

Born in New York City, Davis appeared on stage at age four and became a member of the Will Mastin Trio 1932. Recognized as one of the best tap dancers in the country, Davis served as an army entertainer during World War II and became a nightclub headliner in the 1950s.

Davis Stuart 1894–1964. US abstract painter. He used hard-edged geometric shapes in primary colors and experimented with collage. Much of his work shows the influence of jazz tempos. In the 1920s he produced paintings of commercial packaging, such as *Lucky Strike* 1921 (Museum of Modern Art, New York), that foreshadow Pop art.

His early abstracts reflect the impact of Cubism, and he was deeply influenced by the ◊Armory Show in New York 1913. He often used numbers or letters as the focus for his compositions.

Davis Cup annual tennis tournament for men's international teams, first held 1900 after Dwight Filley Davis (1879–1945) donated the trophy.

recent winners

1980	Czechoslovakia
1981	US
1982	US
1983	Australia
1984	Sweden
1985	Sweden
1986	Australia
1987	Sweden
1988	West Germany
1989	West Germany
1990	US
1991	France

The Davis Cup was held on a challenge basis up to 1971. Since then it has been organized on an elimination basis, with countries divided into zonal groups, with a promotion and relegation system.

***Davis** US jazz trumpeter, composer, and bandleader Miles Davis was one of the originators of cool jazz.*

***Davy** Pioneer chemist Sir Humphry Davy, who discovered the elements sodium, potassium, calcium, magnesium, strontium, and barium in the early 19th century.*

Davisson Clinton Joseph 1881–1958. US physicist. With Lester Germer (1896–1971), he discovered that electrons can undergo diffraction, so proving Louis de Broglie's theory that electrons, and therefore all matter, can show wavelike structure. G P ◊Thomson carried through the same research independently, and in 1937 the two men shared the Nobel Prize for Physics.

Born in Illinois, Davisson worked under O W ◊Richardson at Princeton before joining Bell Telephone Labs in 1917.

Davitt Michael 1846–1906. Irish nationalist. He joined the Fenians (forerunners of the Irish Republican Army) 1865, and was imprisoned for treason 1870–77. After his release, he and the politician Charles Parnell founded the ◊Land League 1879. Davitt was jailed several times for land-reform agitation. He was a member of Parliament 1895–99, advocating the reconciliation of extreme and constitutional nationalism.

Davos town in an Alpine valley in Grisons canton, Switzerland; 5,115 ft/1,559 m above sea level; population (1980) 10,500. It is recognized as a health resort and as a winter sports center.

Davy Humphry 1778–1829. English chemist. In 1799 he discovered the respiratory effects of laughing gas (nitrous oxide). He discovered, by electrolysis, the metallic elements sodium and potassium in 1807, and calcium, boron, magnesium, strontium, and barium in 1808. In addition, he established that chlorine is an element and proposed that hydrogen is present in all acids. He invented the "safety lamp" for use in mines where methane was present, enabling the miners to work in previously unsafe conditions.

Davy Jones personification of a malevolent spirit of the sea. The phrase "gone to Davy Jones's locker" is used by sailors referring to those drowned at sea.

Dawes Charles Gates 1865–1951. US Republican politician. In 1923 he was appointed by the Allied Reparations Commission president of the committee that produced the Dawes Plan, a $200 million loan that enabled Germany to pay enormous war debts after World War I. It reduced tensions temporarily in Europe but was superseded by the ◊Young Plan (which reduced the total reparations bill) 1929. Dawes was elected US vice-president (under Calvin Coolidge) 1924, received the Nobel

Peace Prize 1925, and was ambassador to Britain 1929–32.

dawn raid in business, sudden and unexpected buying of a significant proportion of a company's shares, usually as a prelude to a takeover bid. The aim is to prevent the target company from having time to organize opposition to the takeover. "Corporate raiders" have gotten bolder and more numerous since the deregulation efforts of the Reagan administration. These acquisitions are ostensibly controlled and monitored by the Securities and Exchange Commission (SEC) and governed under antitrust laws. Recent court decisions have made mergers easier in the US. See also ◊leveraged buyout; ◊poison pill; ◊white knight.

Dawson City town in Canada, capital until 1953 of ◊Yukon Territory, at the junction of the Yukon and Klondike rivers; population (1986) 1,700. It was founded 1896, at the time of the Klondike gold rush, when its population was 25,000.

Dawson Creek town in British Columbia, Canada; population (1981) 11,500. It is the SE terminus of the Alaska Highway.

day the time taken for the Earth to rotate once on its axis. The solar day is the time that the Earth takes to rotate once relative to the Sun. It is divided into 24 hours and is the basis of our civil day. The sidereal day is the time that the Earth takes to rotate once relative to the stars. It is 3 minutes 56 seconds shorter than the solar day because the Sun's position against the background of stars as seen from Earth changes as the Earth orbits it.

Day Clarence Shephard, Jr 1874–1935. US cartoonist and author. His autobiographical memoir *Life with Father* 1935 became a national bestseller, a long-running Broadway play from 1939, and a popular feature film 1947. Day's sequels to that work, *Life with Mother* 1937 and *Father and I* 1940, were published after his death.

Born in New York and educated at Yale, Day joined his father's Wall Street firm soon after graduation. Poor health forced his retirement from business at an early age, and he devoted himself to freelance cartooning and humor writing for a number of New York-based magazines.

Day Doris. Adopted name of Doris von Kappelhoff 1924– . US film actress and singing star of the 1950s and early 1960s, mostly in musicals and, later, coy sex comedies. Her films include *Tea for Two* 1950, *Calamity Jane* 1953, *Love Me or Leave Me* 1955, and Hitchcock's *The Man Who Knew Too Much* 1956. With *Pillow Talk* 1959, *Lover Come Back* 1962, and other 1960s light sex comedies, she played a self-confident but coy woman who manipulated some of the biggest male stars to capitulate.

Dayan Moshe 1915–1981. Israeli general and politician. As minister of defense 1967 and 1969–74, he was largely responsible for the victory over neighboring Arab states in the 1967 Six-Day War, but he was criticized for Israel's alleged unpreparedness in the 1973 October War and resigned along with Prime Minister Golda Meir. Foreign minister from 1977, Dayan resigned in 1979 in protest over the refusal of the Begin government to negotiate with the Palestinians.

dayflower any plant of the genus *Commelina* of the spiderwort family. All have pointed leaves and creeping stems that form roots. The flowers, usually blue, open in the morning and wither by day's end throughout the summer and fall.

Day Lewis Cecil 1904–1972. Irish poet, British poet laureate 1968–1972. With Auden and Spender, he was one of the influential left-wing poets of the 1930s. He also wrote detective novels under the pseudonym Nicholas Blake.

Born at Ballintubber, Ireland, he was educated at Oxford and then taught at Cheltenham College 1930–35. His work, which includes *From Feathers to Iron* 1931, and *Overtures to Death* 1938, is marked by accomplished lyrics and sustained narrative power. Professor of poetry at Oxford

DDT

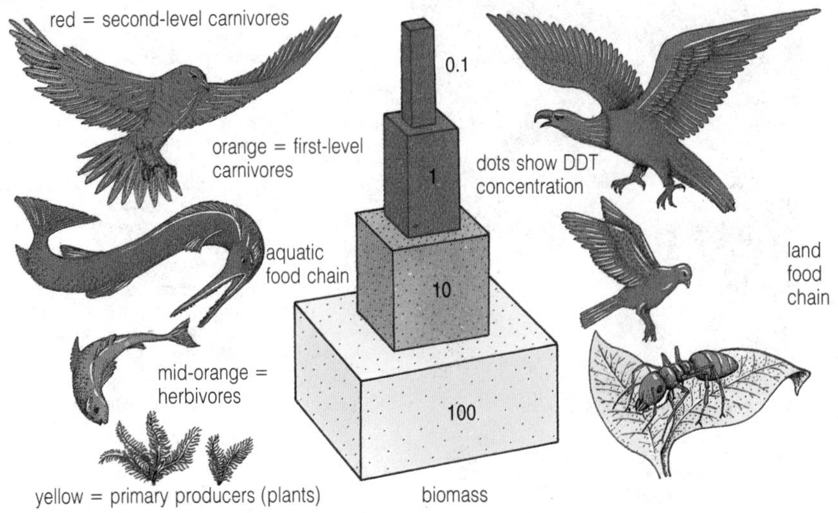
red = second-level carnivores
0.1
orange = first-level carnivores
1
dots show DDT concentration
aquatic food chain
10
land food chain
mid-orange = herbivores
100
yellow = primary producers (plants)
biomass

1951–56, he published critical works and translations from Latin of Virgil's *Georgics* and the *Aeneid*.

daylight saving time legal time for a given zone that is one hour later than the standard time based on universal time coordinated (see ◊time). It is used to provide additional daylight during the summer at the end of the usual working day.

Dayton city in Ohio; population (1990) 182,044. It produces precision machinery, household appliances, and electrical equipment. It has an aeronautical research center and a Roman Catholic university and was the home of aviators Wilbur and Orville Wright.

The Aviation Hall of Fame is in the city, and Wright-Patterson Air Force Base, which has an aviation museum, is nearby. Dayton was settled in 1796.

Dayton town in Tennessee; the scene of the ◊Scopes monkey trial 1925.

Daytona Beach city on the Atlantic coast of Florida; population (1990) 61,921. Economic activities include printing, commercial fishing, and manufacture of electronic equipment and metal products. It is also a resort. The Daytona International Speedway for automobile racing is here.

Dazai Osamu. Adopted name of Shuji Tsushima 1909–1948. Japanese novelist. The title of his novel *The Setting Sun* 1947 became identified in Japan with the dead of World War II.

dBASE family of microcomputer programs for manipulating large quantities of data; also, a related ◊fourth-generation language. The first version, dBASE II, appeared in the early 1980s, since when it has become widely used.

DC in music, the abbreviation for da capo (Italian "from the beginning"); in physics, the abbreviation for direct current (electricity); the District of Columbia.

DD abbreviation for Doctor of Divinity.

D Day June 6, 1944, the day of the Allied invasion of Normandy under the command of General Eisenhower, with the aim of liberating Western Europe from German occupation. The Anglo-American invasion fleet landed on the Normandy beaches on the stretch of coast between the Orne River and St Marcouf. Artificial harbors known as "Mulberries" were constructed and towed across the Channel so that equipment and armaments could be unloaded onto the beaches. After overcoming fierce resistance the Allies broke through the German defenses; Paris was liberated on August 25, and Brussels on September 2.

D Day is also military jargon for any day on which a crucial operation is planned.

DDT abbreviation for dichloro-diphenyl-trichloroethane $(ClC_6H_4)_2CHCHCl_2$ insecticide discovered in 1939 by Swiss chemist Paul Müller. It is useful in the control of insects that spread malaria, but resistant strains develop. DDT is highly toxic and persists in the environment and in living tissue. Its use is now banned in most countries, but it continues to be used on food plants in Latin America.

DE abbreviation for ◊Delaware.

deacon In the Roman Catholic and Anglican churches an ordained minister who ranks immediately below a priest. In the Protestant churches a deacon is in training to become a minister or is a lay assistant.

deadly nightshade another name for ◊belladonna, a poisonous plant.

Dead Sea large lake, partly in Israel and partly in Jordan; area 394 sq mi/1,020 sq km; lying 1,293 ft/394 m below sea level. The chief river entering it is the Jordan; it has no outlet and the water is very salty.

Since both Israel and Jordan are using the waters of the Jordan river, the Dead Sea is now dried up in the center and divided into two halves, but in 1980 Israel announced a plan to link it by canal with the Mediterranean. The Dead Sea Rift is part of the fault between the African and Arab plates.

Dead Sea Scrolls collection of ancient scrolls (rolls of writing) and fragments of scrolls found 1947–56 in caves on the west side of the Jordan 7 mi/12 km S of Jericho and 1 mi/2 km from the north end of the Dead Sea, at ◊Qumran. They include copies of Old Testament books a thousand years older than those previously known to be extant. The documents date mainly from about 150 BC–AD 68, when the monastic community that owned them, the Essenes, was destroyed by the Romans because of its support for a revolt against their rule. Some scrolls were found still intact in their storage jars.

deafness lack or deficiency in the sense of hearing, either inborn or caused by injury or disease of the middle or inner ear.

Of assistance are hearing aids, lip-reading, a cochlear implant in the ear in combination with a special electronic processor, sign language (signs for concepts), and "cued speech" (manual clarification of ambiguous lip movement during speech).

Deakin Alfred 1856–1919. Australian Liberal politician, prime minister 1903–04, 1905–08, and 1909–10. In his second administration, he enacted legislation on defense and pensions.

Deal port and resort on the E coast of Kent, England; population (1981) 26,000. It was one of the ◊Cinque Ports. Julius Caesar is said to have landed here in 55 BC. The castle was built by Henry VIII and houses the town museum.

deamination the removal of the amino group (-NH2) from an unwanted ◊amino acid. This is the nitro-

Deakin *Alfred Deakin was a leading figure in the negotiations to establish the Australian Commonwealth, and in drafting the constitution.*

gen-containing part, and it is converted into ammonia, uric acid, or urea (depending on the type of animal) to be excreted in the urine. In vertebrates, deamination occurs in the ◊liver.

dean in education, in universities and medical schools, the head of administration; in the colleges of Oxford and Cambridge, the member of the teaching staff charged with the maintenance of discipline; in Roman Catholicism, senior cardinal bishop, head of the college of cardinals; in the Anglican Communion, head of the chapter of a cathedral or collegiate church; a rural dean presides over a division of an archdeaconry.

Dean Dizzy (Jay Hanna) 1911–1974. US baseball player. In 1930 he signed with the St Louis Cardinals and made his major-league pitching debut 1932. The offbeat brashness and good-natured arrogance that won him the nickname "Dizzy" are as legendary as his explosive fast-ball pitch. Winning 30 games and leading the Cardinals to a World Series win, he was voted the National League's most valuable player 1934. Following an injury in the 1937 All-Star Game, his pitching suffered. He was traded to the Chicago Cubs, for whom he pitched until his retirement 1941. Dean was elected to the Baseball Hall of Fame 1953.

Born in Lucas, Arkansas, Dean worked as a farmhand until he was old enough to join the army, where his pitching skills were recognized.

Dean James (Byron) 1931–1955. US actor. Killed in an auto accident after only his first film, *East of Eden* 1955, had been shown, he posthumously became a cult hero with *Rebel Without a Cause* and *Giant*, both 1956.

Dean *Legendary actor and cult hero James Dean.*

He has become a symbol of teenage rebellion against American middle-class values.

Deane Silas 1737–1789. American public leader and diplomat. Born in Groton, Connecticut, and educated at Yale, Dean was admitted to the bar 1761. A supporter of American independence, he served in the colonial legislature 1772, on the Connecticut Committee of Correspondence 1773, and in the Continental Congress 1774–76. Dispatched to Paris to obtain aid and support from the French government, Deane recruited Lafayette, Pulaski, and Steuben for the Continental army. Falsely accused of financial improprieties, he was discharged from his post; he was exonerated posthumously by Congress 1842.

Dearborn city in Michigan; on the Rouge River; 10 mi/16 km SW of Detroit; population (1990) 89,286. Settled in 1795, it was the birthplace and home of Henry ◊Ford, who built his first car factory here. Automobile manufacturing is still the main industry. Dearborn also makes aircraft parts, steel, and bricks.

death permanent ending of all the functions that keep an organism alive. Death used to be pronounced when a person's breathing and heartbeat stopped. The advent of mechanical aids has made this point sometimes difficult to determine, and in controversial cases a person is now pronounced dead when the brain ceases to control the vital functions even if breath and heartbeat are maintained.

For removal of vital organs in transplant surgery, the World Health Organization in 1968 set out that the donor should exhibit no brain–body connection, muscular activity, blood pressure, or ability to breathe unaided by machine.

In religious belief death may be seen as the prelude to rebirth (as in Hinduism and Buddhism); under Islam and Christianity, there is the concept of a day of judgment and consignment to heaven or hell; Judaism concentrates not on an afterlife but on survival through descendants who honor tradition.

death cap fungus ◊*Amanita phalloides*, the most poisonous mushroom known. The fruiting body has a scaly white cap and a collarlike structure near the base of the stalk.

Death of a Salesman 1949 Broadway play by Arthur Miller, the story of the defeated sales representative Willy Loman, which captured the limitations and deceptions of the American dream of success.

death penalty another name for ◊capital punishment.

Death Valley depression 140 mi/225 km long and 4–16 mi/6–26 km wide, in SE California. At 280 ft/85 m below sea level, it is the lowest point in the W hemisphere. Bordering mountains rise to 10,000 ft/3,000 m. It is one of the world's hottest and driest places, with temperatures sometimes exceeding 125°F/51°C and an annual rainfall of less than 2 in/5.1 cm. Borax, iron ore, tungsten, gypsum, and salts are extracted.

deathwatch beetle any of the family Anobiidae, of wood-boring beetles, especially *Xestobium rufovillosum*. The larvae live in oaks and willows, and sometimes cause damage by boring in old furniture or structural timbers. To attract the female, the male beetle produces a ticking sound by striking his head on a wooden surface, and this is taken by the superstitious as a warning of approaching death.

Deborah in the Old Testament, a prophet and judge (leader). She helped lead an Israelite army against the Canaanite general Sisera, who was killed trying to flee; her song of triumph at his death is regarded as an excellent example of early Hebrew poetry.

Debray Régis 1941– . French Marxist theorist. He was associated with Che ◊Guevara in the revolutionary movement in Latin America in the 1960s. In 1967 he was sentenced to 30 years' imprisonment in Bolivia but was released after three years. His writings on Latin American politics include *Strategy for Revolution* 1970. He became a specialist adviser to President Mitterrand of France on Latin American affairs.

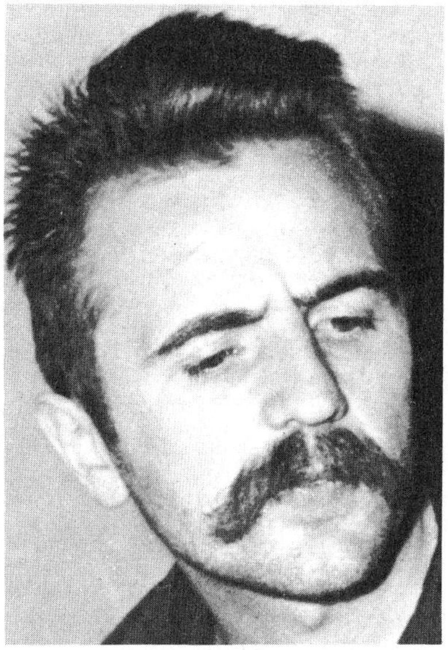

Debray *One of the influential theorists of the revolutionary liberation movements in Latin America, Régis Debray was a friend of Che Guevara and was imprisoned in Bolivia in the 1960s.*

Debrecen third-largest city in Hungary, 120 mi/193 km E of Budapest, in the Great Plain (*Alföld*) region; population (1988) 217,000. It produces tobacco, agricultural machinery, and pharmaceuticals. ◊Kossuth declared Hungary independent of the ◊Hapsburgs here 1849. It is a commercial center and has a university founded 1912.

debridement removal of dead or contaminated tissue from a wound to prevent infection.

de Broglie see ◊Broglie, de.

Debs Eugene Victor 1855–1926. US labor leader and Socialist, who organized the Social Democratic Party 1897. He was the founder and first president of the American Railway Union in 1893, and was imprisoned for six months in 1894 for defying a federal injunction to end the Pullman strike in Chicago. He was Socialist candidate for the presidency in every election from 1900 to 1920, except that of 1916.

Debs was born in Terre Haute, Indiana. He opposed US intervention in World War I and was imprisoned 1918–21 for allegedly advocating resistance to conscription, but was pardoned by President Harding 1921. In 1920 he polled nearly one million votes, the highest Socialist vote ever in US presidential elections, despite having to conduct the campaign from a federal penitentiary in Atlanta, Georgia.

His powerful oratory and his evocation of homespun American ideals were the source of his appeal rather than any doctrinaire adherence to Socialist theory.

debt something that is owed by a person or organization, usually money, goods, or services, usually as a result of borrowing. Debt servicing is the payment of interest on a debt. The national debt of a country is the total money owed by the national government to private individuals, banks, and so on; international debt, the money owed by one country to another, began on a large scale with the investment in foreign countries by newly industrialized countries in the late 19th–early 20th centuries. International debt became a global problem as a result of the oil crisis of the 1970s.

As a result of the ◊Bretton Woods conference in 1944, the World Bank (officially called the ◊International Bank for Reconstruction and Development) was established 1945 as an agency of the United Nations to finance international development by providing loans where private capital was not forthcoming. Loans were made largely at prevailing market rates ("hard loans") and therefore generally to the developed countries, who could afford them.

In 1960 the International Development Association (IDA) was set up as an offshoot of the World Bank to provide interest-free ("soft") loans over a long period to finance the economies of developing countries and assist their long-term development. The cash surpluses of Middle Eastern oil-producing countries were channeled by Western banks to Third World countries. However, a slump in both the world economy and in increases in interest rates have resulted in the debtor countries paying an ever-increasing percentage share of their national output in debt-servicing (paying off the interest on a debt, rather than paying off the debt itself). As a result, many loans had to be rescheduled (renegotiated so that repayments were made over a longer term).

During the early 1980s, Poland and Brazil suspended some payments on their debt, and others threatened to follow suit. With debt-servicing ratios (proportion of export earnings required to pay debt obligations) of more than 50% in some countries, the debt crisis threatened the stability of governments and the international, especially US, banking system. In 1987, one US bank announced that it was writing off $3 billion of international loans. The banks and the borrowing countries both recognized the need for relief, as debtor states could only pay the interest on existing loans by securing new loans. Disagreement over who should bear the cost of debt relief has delayed any real reform. Austerity measures imposed by the International Monetary Fund (IMF) in exchange for loans have provoked riots and an increase in nationalist sentiment, but Brazil began making payments on its debt in 1988, and the US and Mexico have negotiated reduction plans. Poland received substantial loans 1990 from the US and W Europe to assist its transition to a market-based economy.

debt crisis any situation in which an individual, company, or country owes more to others than it can repay or pay interest on; more specifically, the massive indebtedness of many Third World countries that became acute in the 1980s, threatening the stability of the international banking system as many debtor countries became unable to service their debts.

Debussy (Achille-) Claude 1862–1918. French composer. He broke with the dominant tradition of German Romanticism and introduced new qualities of melody and harmony based on the whole-tone scale, evoking oriental music. His work includes *Prélude à l'après-midi d'un faune* 1894 and the opera *Pelléas et Mélisande* 1902.

Among his other works are numerous piano pieces, songs, orchestral pieces such as *La Mer* 1903–05, and the ballet *Jeux* 1910–13. Debussy also wrote with humor about the music of his day, using the fictional character Monsieur Croche "antidilettante" (professional debunker).

Debye Peter 1884–1966. Dutch physicist. A pioneer of X-ray powder crystallography, he also worked on polar molecules, dipole moments, and molecular structure. In 1940, he went to the US where he was professor of chemistry at Cornell University 1940–52. He was awarded the 1936 Nobel Prize for Chemistry.

decagon ten-sided ◊polygon.

Decalogue the ten commandments which, according to the Old Testament, were delivered by God to ◊Moses on Mt Sinai, as stated in the books Exodus 20:1–17 and Deuteronomy 5:6–21. The Decalogue is recognized as the basis of morality by Jews and Christians.

Decameron, The a collection of tales by the Italian writer Boccaccio, brought together 1348–53. Ten young people, fleeing plague-stricken Florence, amuse their fellow travelers by each telling a story on the ten days they spend together. The work had a great influence on English literature, particularly Chaucer's *Canterbury Tales*.

decathlon a two-day athletic competition for men consisting of ten events: 100 meters, long jump, shot put, high jump, 400 meters (day one); 110 meters hurdles, discus, pole vault, javelin, 1,500 meters (day two). Points are awarded for performances and the winner is the athlete with the greatest aggregate score. The decathlon is an Olympic event.

Decatur city in central Illinois, on Lake Decatur, population (1990) 83,885. It has engineering, food processing, and plastics industries. It was founded in 1829 and named after Stephen ◊Decatur.

Decatur Stephen 1779–1820. US naval hero, who distinguished himself in the war with the Barbary pirates at Tripoli 1801–05 when he succeeded in boarding and burning the *Philadelphia*, a US frigate captured by the enemy. During the War of 1812, he commanded three vessels, captured the British frigate *Macedonian*, and was blockaded by the British. Then in Jan 1815, unaware that the war was over, he battled four British ships, taking one but surrendering to the three pursuers. In 1815 he was again sent to the Barbary Coast, where he forced the bey of Algiers to sign the treaty ending US tribute to Algeria.

Born in Sinepuxent, Maryland, Decatur was killed in a duel with Commodore James Barron, whose return to duty he had opposed following the Chesapeake-Leopard Incident in 1807, one of the events leading to the ◊War of 1812. Decatur is known for the phrase "Our country, right or wrong," coined while giving a toast.

Deccan triangular tableland in eastern India, stretching between the Vindhya Hills in the N, and the Western and Eastern Ghats in the S.

decibel unit (abbreviation dB) of measure, used originally to compare sound densities, and subsequently electrical or electronic power outputs; now also used to compare voltages. An increase of 10 dB is equivalent to a 10-fold increase in intensity or power, and a 20-fold increase in voltage. A whisper has an intensity of 20 dB; 140 dB (a jet aircraft taking off nearby) is the threshold of pain.

The difference in decibels between two levels of intensity (or power) L_1 and L_2 is 10 $\log_{10}(L_1/L_2)$; a difference of 1 dB thus corresponds to a change of about 25%. For two voltages V_1 and V_2, the difference in decibels is 20 $\log_{10}(V_1/V_2)$; 1 dB corresponding in this case to a change of about 12%. Commonly such differences are given now not as ratios but as absolute values; for example, 10 dBV corresponds to the voltage level V_1 with V_2 set equal to 1 volt. In acoustics, the absolute reference used in the power ratio is 10^{-16} watt per sq cm.

deciduous describing trees and shrubs that shed their leaves before the onset of winter or a dry season (see ◊abscission). In temperate regions there is little water available during winter, and leaf fall is an adaptation to reduce ◊transpiration.

Most deciduous trees belong to the ◊angiosperms, and the term "deciduous tree" is sometimes used to mean "angiosperm tree," despite the fact that many angiosperms are evergreen, especially in the tropics, and a few ◊gymnosperms (such as larches) are deciduous. The term broad-leaved is now preferred to "deciduous" for this reason.

Examples of deciduous trees are oak and maple.

decimal fractions the system of ◊fractions expressed by the use of the decimal point, that is, fractions in which the denominator is any higher power of 10. Thus $\frac{3}{10}$, $\frac{51}{100}$, $\frac{23}{1,000}$ are decimal fractions and are normally expressed as 0.3, 0.51, 0.023. The use of decimals greatly simplifies addition and multiplication of fractions, though not all fractions can be expressed exactly as decimal fractions. The regular use of the decimal point appears to have been introduced about 1585, but the occasional use of decimal fractions can be traced back as far as the 12th century.

decision table in computing, a method of describing a procedure for a program to follow, based on comparing possible decisions and their consequences. It is often used as an aid in systems design.

The top part of the table contains the conditions for making decisions (for example, if a number is negative rather than positive and is less than 1), the bottom part describes the outcomes when those conditions are met: the program either ends or repeats the operation.

Decius Gaius Messius Quintus Traianus 201–251. Roman emperor from 249. He fought a number of campaigns against the ◊Goths but was finally beaten and killed by them near Abritum. He ruthlessly persecuted the Christians.

Declaration of Independence historic US document stating the theory of government on which the US was founded, based on the right "to life, liberty, and the pursuit of happiness." The statement was issued by the American Continental Congress on July 4, 1776, renouncing all allegiance to the British crown and ending the political connection with Britain.

Following a resolution moved on June 7, by Richard Henry Lee, "that these United Colonies are, and of right ought to be, free and independent States," a committee including Thomas Jefferson and Benjamin Franklin was set up to draft a declaration; most of the work was done by Jefferson. The resolution, coming almost a year after the outbreak of hostilities, was adopted by the representatives of 12 colonies (New York at first abstaining) on July 2, and the Declaration on July 4; the latter date has ever since been celebrated as Independence Day in the US. The representatives of New York announced their adhesion on July 15, and the Declaration was afterwards signed by the members of Congress on Aug 2.

The declaration enumerated the grievances the colonists harbored against the king, which included his use of Indians to attack colonists, taxation without representation, and denial of civil liberties.

Declaration of Rights in Britain, the statement issued by the Convention Parliament Feb 1689, laying down the conditions under which the crown was to be offered to ◊William III and Mary. Its clauses were later incorporated in the ◊Bill of Rights.

declination in astronomy, the coordinate on the ◊celestial sphere (imaginary sphere surrounding the Earth) that corresponds to latitude on the Earth's surface. Declination runs from 0° at the celestial equator to 90° at the north and south celestial poles.

Decline and Fall of the Roman Empire, The History of the a historical work by Edward Gibbon, published in the UK 1776–88. Arranged in three parts, the work spans 13 centuries and covers the history of the empire from Trajan and the Antonines through to the Turkish seizure of Constantinople in 1453.

decolonization the gradual achievement of independence by former colonies of the European imperial powers which began after World War I.

The process of decolonization accelerated after World War II and the movement affected every continent: India and Pakistan gained independence from Britain 1947; Algeria gained independence from France 1962.

decomposer in biology, any organism that breaks down dead matter. Decomposers play a vital role in the ◊ecosystem by freeing important chemical substances, such as nitrogen compounds, locked up in dead organisms or excrement. They feed on some of the released organic matter, but leave the rest to filter back into the soil or pass in gas form into the atmosphere. The principal decomposers are bacteria and fungi, but earthworms and many other invertebrates are often included in this group. The ◊nitrogen cycle relies on the actions of decomposers.

decomposition the process whereby a chemical compound is reduced to its component substances. In biology, it is the destruction of dead organisms either by chemical reduction or by the action of decomposers.

decompression sickness illness brought about by a sudden and substantial change in atmospheric pressure. It is caused by a too rapid release of nitrogen that has been dissolved into the bloodstream under pressure; when the nitrogen bubbles it causes the ◊bends. It causes breathing difficulties, joint and muscle pain, and cramps, and is experienced mostly by deep-sea divers who surface too quickly.

After a one-hour dive at 100 ft/30 m, 40 minutes of decompression are needed, according to US Navy tables.

decontamination factor in radiological protection, a measure of the effectiveness of a decontamination process. It is the ratio of the original contamination to the remaining radiation after decontamination: 1,000 and above is excellent; 10 and below is poor.

decretal in medieval Europe, a papal ruling on a disputed point, sent to a bishop or abbot in reply to a request or appeal. The earliest dates from Siricius in 385. Later decretals were collected to form a decretum.

decretum a collection of papal decrees. The best known is that collected by Gratian (died 1159) in about 1140, comprising some 4,000 items. The decretum was used as an authoritative source of canon law (the rules and regulations of the church).

Dedekind Richard 1831–1916. German mathematician, who made contributions to number theory. In 1872 he introduced the Dedekind cut (which divides a line of infinite length representing all ◊real numbers) to categorize ◊irrational numbers as fractions and thus increase their usefulness.

dedicated computer computer built into another device for the purpose of controlling or supplying information to it. Its use has increased dramatically since the advent of the ◊microprocessor: washing machines, digital watches, cars, and video recorders all have their own processors.

A dedicated system is a general-purpose computer system confined to performing only one function for reasons of efficiency or convenience A word processor is an example.

deduction in philosophy, a form of argument in which the conclusion necessarily follows from the premises. It would be inconsistent ◊logic to accept the premises but deny the conclusion.

Dee river in Grampian region, Scotland; length 87 mi/139 km. From its source in the Cairngorms, it flows E into the North Sea at Aberdeen (by an artificial channel). It is noted for salmon fishing.

deed a legal document that passes an interest in property or binds a person to perform or abstain from some action. Deeds are of two kinds: indenture and deed poll. Indentures bind two or more parties in mutual obligations. A deed poll is made by one party only, such as when a person changes his or her name.

Bargain sale deeds convey title to property by contract but do not guarantee title unless they include a specific covenant to that effect; quitclaim deeds convey a grantor's interest but do not guarantee title; warranty deeds convey interest and guarantee title to the subject property.

deep freezing method of preserving food by rapid freezing and storage at 0°F/–18°C. Commercial freezing is usually done by one of the following methods: blast, the circulation of air at –40°F/–40°C; contact, in which a refrigerant is circulated through hollow shelves; immersion, for example, fruit in a solution of sugar and glycerol; or cryogenic means, for example, by liquid nitrogen spray.

Rapid freezing avoids structural change that would affect the taste or appearance of the food, as in the shrinkage and distortion of cells by formation of enlarged ice crystals in the extracellular spaces. Some "quick-frozen" foods require thawing before use, and cooking must then be prompt.

Accelerated freeze drying (AFD) involves rapid freezing followed by heat drying in a vacuum, for example, shrimps for later rehydration. The product does not have to be stored in frozen condition.

Freezing was developed in the late 19th century and found early commercial application in the transportation of large quantities of meat on long sea voyages.

Deep-Sea Drilling Project a research project initiated by the US in 1968 to sample the rocks of the ocean ◊crust. The operation became international in 1975, when Britain, France, Germany, Japan, and the USSR also became involved.

Over 800 boreholes were drilled in all the oceans using the ship *Glomar Challenger*, and knowledge of the nature and history of the ocean basins was increased dramatically. The technical difficulty of drilling the seabed to a depth of 6,500 ft/2,000 m was overcome by keeping the ship in position with side-thrusting propellers and satellite navigation, and by guiding the drill using a radiolocation system.

deep-sea trench a long and narrow, deep trough (◊ocean trench) in the seafloor, marking the line where one of the plates of the ◊lithosphere is sliding beneath another (see ◊plate tectonics). At this depth (below 3.6 mi/6 km) there is no light and very high pressure; deep-sea trenches are inhabited by crustaceans, coelenterates (for example, sea anemones), polychaetes (a type of worm), mollusks, and echinoderms.

deer any of various ruminant, even-toed, hoofed mammals belonging to the family Cervidae. The male typically has a pair of antlers, shed and regrown each year. Most species of deer are forest-dwellers and are distributed throughout Eurasia and North America, but are absent from Australia and Africa S of the Sahara.

Native to North America are white-tailed deer *Odocoileus viginianus*, mule deer *O. hemionus*, wapiti or elk *Cervus canadensis*, moose *Alces alces*, and caribou or reindeer *Rangifer tarandus*. The last two also occur in Eurasia. Red deer *Cervus elaphus*, roe deer *Capreolus capreolus*, and fallow deer *Dama dama* are typical Eurasian species.

deerhound large, rough-coated dog, formerly used for hunting and killing deer. Slim and long-legged, it grows to 2.5 ft/75 cm or more, usually with a bluish-gray coat.

de Falla Manuel Spanish composer. See ◊Falla, Manuel de.

defamation in law, an attack on a person's reputation by libel or slander.

default in commerce, failure to meet an obligation, usually financial.

Defense, Department of US government department presided over by the secretary of defense, headquartered in the ◊Pentagon. The secretary holds a seat in the president's cabinet; each of the three military services has a civilian secretary, not of cabinet rank, at its head. It was established when the army, navy, and air force were unified by the National Security Act 1947.

defibrillation the use of electrical stimulation to restore a chaotic heartbeat to a rhythmical pattern. In fibrillation, which may occur in most kinds of heart disease, the heart muscle contracts irregularly; the heart is no longer working as an efficient pump. Paddles are applied to the chest wall, and one or more electric shocks are delivered to normalize the beat.

deficit financing in economics, a planned excess of expenditure over income, dictated by government policy, creating a shortfall of public revenue which is met by borrowing. The decision to create a deficit is taken to stimulate an economy by increasing consumer purchasing and at the same time to create more jobs.

Defoe Author of Robinson Crusoe *1719, English novelist Daniel Defoe.*

deflation in economics, a reduction in the level of economic activity, usually caused by an increase in interest rates and reduction in the money supply, increased taxation, or a decline in government expenditure.

Deflation may be chosen as an economic policy to improve the balance of payments, through a reduction in demand and therefore of imports, and reducing inflation to stimulate exports. It can reduce wage increases but may also reduce the level of employment.

Defoe Daniel 1660–1731. English novelist and journalist, who wrote *Robinson Crusoe* 1719, which was greatly influential in the development of the novel. An active pamphleteer and political critic, he was imprisoned 1702–04 following publication of the ironic *The Shortest Way With Dissenters*. Fictional works include *Moll Flanders* 1722 and *A Journal of the Plague Year* 1724. Altogether he produced over 500 books, pamphlets, and journals.

Defoe wrote numerous pamphlets and first achieved fame with the satire *The True-Born Englishman* 1701. His version of the contemporary short story "True Relation of the Apparition of one Mrs Veal" 1706 first revealed a gift for realistic narrative.

de Forest Lee 1873–1961. US inventor, who held more than 300 patents, including the triode tube, precursor to the radio tube and one of the most influential inventions of the century 1906, called by him the audion. It generated, detected, and amplified radio waves. He also developed a movie-sound system and contributed to the phonograph, telephone, television, radar, and diathermy.

deforestation the destruction of forest for timber (see ◊forestry) and clearing for grazing and agriculture, without planting new trees to replace those lost (reforestation). Deforestation causes fertile soil to be blown away or washed into rivers, leading to soil ◊erosion, drought, and flooding.

As a result of deforestation in the Himalayas, disastrous floods occur in lowland areas of India and Bangladesh. In 1989 Thailand banned all logging in an effort to prevent further decline in forests (which then covered only 18% of land surfaces compared to the 70% forest cover of 1945).

Degas (Hilaire Germain) Edgar 1834–1917. French Impressionist painter and sculptor. He devoted himself to lively, informal studies, often using pastels, of ballet, horse racing, and young women

Degas Woman at her Toilet *(c. 1894), Tate Gallery, London.*

working. From the 1890s he turned increasingly to sculpture, modeling figures in wax in a fluent, naturalistic style.

Degas studied under a pupil of Ingres and worked in Italy in the 1850s, painting Classical themes. In 1861 he met Manet, and they developed Impressionism. Degas' characteristic style soon emerged, showing the influence of Japanese prints and of photography in inventive compositions and unusual viewpoints. An example of his sculpture is *The Little Dancer* 1881 (Tate Gallery, London).

de Gaulle Charles André Joseph Marie 1890–1970. French general and statesman; president 1959–69. He organized the ◊Free French troops fighting the Nazis 1940–44, was head of the provisional French government 1944–46, and leader of his own Gaullist party. In 1958 the national assembly asked him to form a government during France's economic recovery and to solve the crisis in Algeria. Having changed the constitution he became president 1959–69. In 1969 he resigned the presidency after the defeat of the government in a referendum on constitutional reform. He retired to the village of Colombey-les-Deux-Eglises in NE France.

de Gaulle *Leader of the Free French during World War II, Charles de Gaulle became premier of France.*

Born in Lille, he graduated from Saint-Cyr 1911 and was severely wounded and captured by the Germans 1916. In June 1940 he refused to accept the new prime minister Pétain's truce with the Germans and became leader of the Free French in England. In 1944 he entered Paris in triumph and was briefly head of the provisional government before resigning over the new constitution of the Fourth Republic 1946. In 1947 he founded the *Rassemblement du Peuple Français*, a nonparty constitutional reform movement, and when national bankruptcy and civil war loomed 1958, de Gaulle was called to form a government.

As premier he promulgated a constitution subordinating the legislature to the presidency and took office as president 1959. Economic recovery and Algerian independence after a bloody war followed. A nationalist, he opposed "Anglo-Saxon" influence in Europe. Re-elected president 1965, he violently quelled student demonstrations May 1968 when they were joined by workers. The Gaullist party, reorganized as *Union des Democrats pour la Cinquième République*, won an overwhelming majority in the elections of the same year.

degaussing neutralization of the magnetic field around a body by encircling it with a conductor through which a current is maintained. Ships were degaussed in World War II to avoid their detonating magnetic mines.

degree in mathematics, a unit (symbol °) of measurement of an angle or arc. A circle is divided into 360°; a degree is subdivided into 60 minutes (symbol ′). Temperature is also measured in degrees, which are divided on a decimal scale. See also ◊Celsius and ◊circle.

A quarter-turn (90°) is a right angle; a half-turn (180°) is the angle on a straight line. A degree of latitude is the length along a meridian such that the difference between its north and south ends is 1°. A degree of longitude is the length between two meridians making an angle of 1° at the center of the Earth.

de Havilland Geoffrey 1882–1965. British aircraft designer who designed and whose company produced the Moth biplane, the Mosquito fighter-bomber of World War II, and the postwar Comet, the world's first jet-powered airliner to enter commercial service.

De Havilland Olivia 1916– . US actress, a star in Hollywood from the age of 19, when she appeared in *A Midsummer Night's Dream* 1935. She later successfully played more challenging dramatic roles in films such as *Gone with the Wind* 1939, *To Each His Own* (Academy Award) and *Dark Mirror* 1946, and *The Snake Pit* 1948. She won her second Academy Award for *The Heiress* 1949, played *Lady In A Cage* and *Hush, Hush, Sweet Charlotte*, both 1964.

Dehra Dun town in Uttar Pradesh, India; population (1981) 220,530. It is the capital of Dehra Dun district. It has a military academy, a forest research institute, and a Sikh temple built in 1699.

dehydration a process to preserve food. Moisture content is reduced to 10–20% in fresh produce, and this provides good protection against molds. Bacteria are not inhibited by drying, so the quality of raw materials is vital.

The process was developed commercially in France about 1795 to preserve sliced vegetables, using a hot-air blast. The earliest large-scale application was to starch products such as pasta, but after 1945 it was extended to milk, potato, soups, instant coffee, and prepared baby and pet foods. A major benefit to food manufacturers is reduction of weight and volume of the food products, lowering distribution cost.

Deianira in Greek mythology, wife of ◊Heracles, who won her in combat, and mother of his sons, considered ancestors of the ◊Dorian Greeks. She killed Heracles by mistake, giving him poison instead of an aphrodisiac, and in her grief committed suicide. Her story is dramatized in ◊Sophocles's *Women of Trachis*.

Deighton Len 1929– . British author of spy fiction, including *The Ipcress File* 1963 and the trilogy *Berlin Game, Mexico Set,* and *London Match* 1983–85, featuring the spy Bernard Samson. Samson was also the main character in *Spy Hook* 1989, which began a second trilogy.

Deimos one of the two moons of Mars. It is irregularly shaped, 9 × 7.5 × 7 mi/15 × 12 × 11 km, orbits at a height of 15,000 mi/24,000 km every 1.26 days, and is not as roughly featured as the other moon, Phobos. Deimos was discovered 1877 by US astronomer Asaph Hall (1829–1907) and is thought to be an asteroid captured by Mars's gravity.

deindustrialization a decline in the share of manufacturing industries in a country's economy. Typically, industrial plants are closed down and not replaced, and service industries increase.

Deirdre in Celtic mythology, beautiful intended bride of ◊Conchobar.

deism belief in a supreme being; but the term usually refers to a movement of religious thought in the 17th and 18th centuries, characterized by the belief in a rational "religion of nature" as opposed to the orthodox beliefs of Christianity. Deists believed that God is the source of natural law but does not intervene directly in the affairs of the world, and that the only religious duty of humanity is to be virtuous.

Deism emerged in England in the writings of Lord Herbert of Cherbury (1583–1648). John Toland (1670–1722) and Matthew Tindal (1657–1733) were among its major exponents. In France, the writer Voltaire was the most prominent advocate of deism. In the US, many of the founding fathers, including Benjamin Franklin and Thomas Jefferson, were essentially deists. See also ◊theism.

Dekker Thomas c. 1572–c. 1632. English dramatist and pamphleteer, who wrote mainly in collaboration with others. His play *The Shoemaker's Holiday* 1600 was followed by collaborations with Thomas Middleton, John Webster, Philip Massinger, and others. His pamphlets include *The Gull's Hornbook* 1609, a lively satire on the fashions of the day.

De Klerk F(rederik) W(illem) 1936– . South Afri-

De Klerk South African state president and National Party leader F W De Klerk. Since coming to power in 1989 he has embarked on a program of reform.

can National Party politician, president from 1989. Trained as a lawyer, he entered the South African parliament in 1972. He served in the cabinets of B J Vorster and P W Botha 1978–89, and in Feb and Aug 1989 successively replaced Botha as National Party leader and state president. Projecting himself as a pragmatic conservative who sought gradual reform of the apartheid system, he won the Sept 1989 elections for his party, but with a reduced majority. In Feb 1990 he ended the ban on the ◊African National Congress opposition movement and released its effective leader, Nelson Mandela. In 1991 measures advocated by him effectively dismantled the apartheid system.

de Kooning Willem 1904– . Dutch-born US painter who immigrated to the US 1926 and worked as a commercial artist. After World War II he became, together with Jackson Pollock, one of the leaders of the Abstract Expressionist movement. His *Women* series, exhibited in 1953, was criticized for its grotesque figurative style.

De Kooning joined the faculty of the Yale Art School and became a member of the National Institute of Arts 1960 and received the Presidential Medal of Freedom 1964. His paintings were commissioned for numerous WPA (Work Projects Administration) projects, and he won praise for his mural in the Hall of Pharmacy at the 1939 New York World's Fair.

Delacroix Eugène 1798–1863. French Romantic painter. His prolific output included religious and historical subjects and portraits of friends, among them the musicians Paganini and Chopin. Against French academic tradition, he evolved a highly colored, fluid style, as in *The Death of Sardanapalus* 1827 (Louvre, Paris).

The *Massacre at Chios* 1824 (Louvre, Paris) shows Greeks enslaved by wild Turkish horsemen, a contemporary atrocity (his use of a contemporary theme recalls Géricault's example). His style was influenced by the English landscape painter Constable. Delacroix also produced illustrations for Shakespeare, Dante, and Byron. His *Journal* is a fascinating record of his times.

de la Mare Walter 1873–1956. English poet, known for his verse for children, such as *Songs of Childhood* 1902, and the novels *The Three Royal Monkeys* 1910 for children and, for adults, *The Memoirs of a Midget* 1921.

Delaroche Paul 1797–1856. French historical artist. His melodramatic, often sentimental, historical paintings achieved great contemporary popularity;

Delacroix A self-portrait by the leader of the French Romantic school.

an example is *Lady Jane Grey* 1833 (National Gallery, London).

Delaunay Robert 1885–1941. French painter, a pioneer in abstract art. With his wife Sonia Delaunay-Terk he invented Orphism, an early variation on Cubism, focusing on the effects of pure color.

In 1912 he painted several series, notably *Circular Forms* (almost purely abstract) and *Windows* (inspired by Parisian cityscapes).

Delaunay-Terk Sonia 1885–1979. French painter and textile designer born in Russia, active in Paris from 1905. With her husband Robert Delaunay, she was a pioneer of abstract art.

De Laurentis Dino 1919– . Italian producer. His early films, including Fellini's *La Strada/The Street* 1954, brought more acclaim than later epics such as *Waterloo* 1970. He then produced a series of Hollywood films: *Death Wish* 1974, *King Kong* (remake) 1976, and *Dune* 1984.

Delaware state in NE US; nickname First State/Diamond State
area 2,046 sq mi/5,300 sq km
capital Dover
cities Wilmington, Newark
physical two main divisions: (1) hilly and wooded; (2) gently undulating to the sea
features one of the most industrialized states; headquarters of the Du Pont chemical firm; Rehoboth Beach; Winterthur Museum
products dairy, poultry, and market-garden produce; chemicals; motor vehicles; textiles
population (1990) 666,168
famous people Du Pont family, J P Marquand
history the first settlers were Dutch 1631 and Swedes 1638, but in 1664 the area was captured by the British and transferred to William Penn. A separate colony from 1704, it fought in the American Revolution as a state 1776, was one of the original 13 states, and was the first state to ratify the US Constitution, Dec 7, 1787. In 1802 the Du Pont gunpowder mill was established near Wilmington. Completion of the Philadelphia-Baltimore railroad line 1838, through Wilmington, fostered development. Delaware was famous as a chemical center by the early 1900s. Two auto-assembly plants and an oil refinery were built after World War II.

Delaware

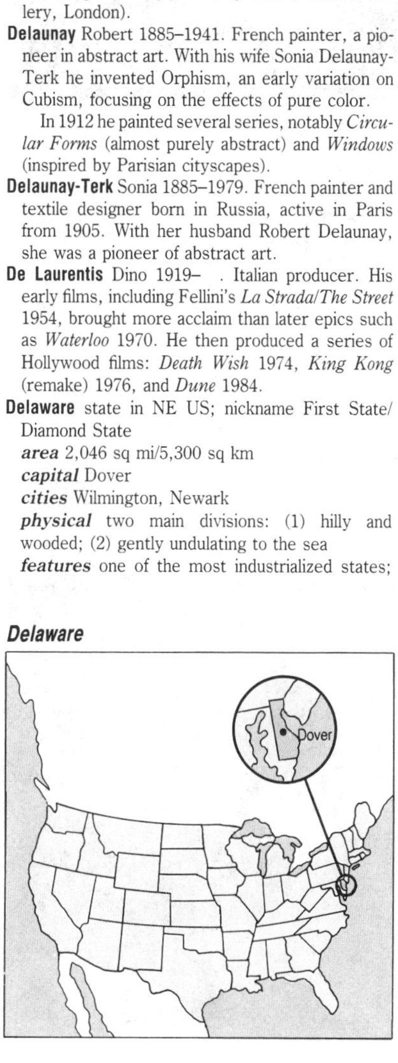
Dover

de la Warr Thomas West, Baron de la Warr 1577–1618. US colonial administrator, known as Delaware. Appointed governor of Virginia 1609, he arrived 1610 just in time to prevent the desertion of the Jamestown colonists, and by 1611 had revitalized the settlement. He fell ill, returned to England, and died during his return voyage to the colony in 1618. Both the river and state are named after him.

Delbruck Max 1906–1981. German-born US biologist who pioneered techniques in molecular biology, studying genetic changes occurring when viruses invade bacteria. Nobel Prize for Medicine 1969.

De Lesseps Ferdinand, Vicomte French engineer; see de ◊Lesseps.

Delft town in the Netherlands in the province of S Holland, 9 mi/14 km NW of Rotterdam; population (1984) 87,000. It produces pottery and porcelain. The Dutch nationalist leader William the Silent was murdered here in 1584. It is the birthplace of the artist Vermeer.

Delhi Union Territory of the Republic of India from 1956; capital New Delhi; area 579 sq mi/1,500 sq km; population (1981) 6,196,000. It produces grains, sugar cane, fruits, and vegetables.

Delibes (Clement Philibert) Léo 1836–1891. French composer. His works include the ballets *Coppélia* 1870, *Sylvia* 1876, and the opera *Lakmé* 1833.

Delilah in the Old Testament, the Philistine mistress of ◊Samson, who cut his hair and thereby stole his power.

deliquescence the phenomenon of a substance absorbing so much moisture from the air that it ultimately dissolves in it to form a solution.

Deliquescent substances make very good drying agents in the bottoms of ◊desiccators. Calcium chloride ($CaCl_2$) is one of the commonest.

delirium in medicine, a state of temporary confusion in which the subject is incoherent, frenzied, and out of touch with reality. It is often accompanied by delusions or hallucinations.

Delirium may occur in feverish illness, some forms of mental illness, and as a result of drug or alcohol intoxication. In chronic alcoholism, attacks of delirium tremens (DTs), marked by hallucinations, sweating, trembling, and anxiety, may persist for several days.

Delius Frederick (Theodore Albert) 1862–1934. English composer. His works include the the opera *A Village Romeo and Juliet* 1901; the choral pieces *Appalachia* 1903, *Sea Drift* 1904, *A Mass of Life* 1905; orchestral works such as *In a Summer Garden* 1908, *A Song of the High Hills* 1911; chamber music; and songs.

His romantic style of writing was influenced by Grieg.

della Robbia Italian family of artists, see ◊Robbia, della.

Delon Alain 1935– . French actor who appeared in the films *Purple Noon* 1960, *Rocco e i suoi Fratelli/Rocco and his Brothers* 1960, *Il Gatto-*

Delphi *The Sanctuary of Athena (Marmaria) at Delphi, Greece.*

pardo/The Leopard 1963, *Texas across the River* 1966, *Scorpio* 1972, and *Swann in Love* 1984.

Delos Greek island, smallest in the ◊Cyclades group, in the SW Aegean sea; area about 2 sq mi/5 sq km. The great temple of Apollo (4th century BC) is still standing.

Delphi city of ancient Greece, situated in a rocky valley N of the gulf of Corinth, on the southern slopes of Mount Parnassus, site of a famous ◊oracle in the temple of Apollo. In the same temple was the *Omphalos*, a conical stone supposed to stand at the center of the Earth. The oracle was interpreted by priests from the inspired utterances of the Pythian priestess until it was closed down by the Roman emperor Theodosius in AD 390.

delphinium any plant of the genus *Delphinium* belonging to the buttercup family Ranunculaceae. There are some 250 species, including the great flowered larkspur *D. grandiflorum*, an Asian form and one of the ancestors of the garden delphinium. Most species have blue, purple, or white flowers in a long spike.

Delray Beach city in SE Florida on the Atlantic Ocean, N of Ft Lauderdale. A tourist resort, it also relies economically on the cultivation of flowers; population (1990) 47,181.

del Sarto Andrea 1486–1531. See ◊Andrea del Sarto, Italian Renaissance painter.

delta a roughly fanlike tract of land at a river's mouth, formed by deposited silt or sediment. Familiar examples of large deltas are those of the Mississippi, Ganges and Brahmaputra, Rhône, Po, Danube, and Nile; the shape of the Nile delta is like the Greek letter Δ, and thus gave rise to the name.

The arcuate delta of the Nile is only one form. Others are birdfoot deltas, like that of the Mississippi, which is a seaward extension of the river's levee system; and tidal deltas, like that of the Mekong in which most of the material is swept to one side by sea currents.

Delta Force US antiguerrilla force, based at Fort Bragg, North Carolina, and modeled on the British Special Air Service.

Delta rocket US rocket used to launch many scientific and communications satellites since 1960, based on the Thor ballistic missile. Several increasingly powerful versions were produced as satellites became larger and heavier. Solid-fuel boosters were attached to the first stage to increase lifting power.

delta wing aircraft wing shaped like the Greek letter Δ. Its design enables an aircraft to pass through the ◊sound barrier with little effect. The supersonic airliner Concorde and the US space shuttle have delta wings.

delta

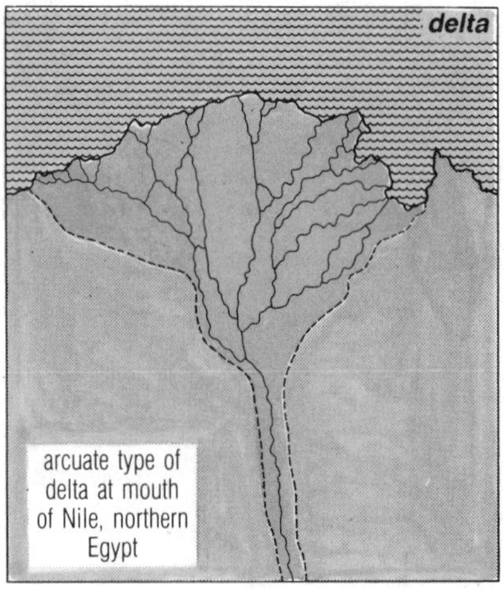

arcuate type of delta at mouth of Nile, northern Egypt

de Maiziere Lothar 1940– . German politician, leader 1989–90 of the conservative Christian Democratic Union in East Germany. He became premier after East Germany's first democratic election in Apr 1990 and negotiated the country's reunion with West Germany.

demand in economics, the quantity of a product or service that customers want to buy at any given price. Also, the desire for a commodity, together with ability to pay for it.

dementia mental deterioration as a result of physical changes in the brain. It may be due to degenerative change, circulatory disease, infection, injury, or chronic poisoning.

Dementia is distinguished from amentia, or severe congenital mental insufficiency.

Demerara river in Guyana, 215 mi/346 km long, which gives its name to the country's chief sugarcane growing area, after which Demerara sugar is named.

demesne in the Middle Ages in Europe, land kept in the lord's possession, not leased out, but, under the system of ◊villeinage, worked by villeins to supply the lord's household.

Demeter in Greek mythology, goddess of agriculture (identified with Roman ◊Ceres), daughter of Cronus and Rhea, and mother of Persephone by Zeus. She is identified with the Egyptian goddess Isis and had a temple dedicated to her at Eleusis where ◊mystery religions were celebrated.

Demetrius Donskoi ("of the Don") 1350–1389. Grand prince of Moscow from 1363. He achieved the first Russian victory over the Tatars on the plain of Kulikovo, next to the river Don (hence his nickname) 1380.

De Mille Agnes George 1905– . US choreographer. After becoming a member of the Ballet Theatre, she choreographed a long string of Broadway hits, including *Oklahoma!* 1943, *Carousel* 1945, *Brigadoon* 1947, *Gentlemen Prefer Blondes* 1949, and *Paint Your Wagon* 1951. She founded the Agnes De Mille Dance Theater 1953.

Born in New York City, the niece of film director Cecil B De Mille, she was trained in Classical ballet and made her stage debut 1928. She later concentrated on choreography, directing the dance movements of the stage adaptation of *Romeo and Juliet* 1936.

De Mille Cecil B(lount) 1881–1959. US film director and producer. He entered films with Jesse Lasky 1913, with whom he later established Paramount Pictures. He specialized in biblical epics, such as *The Sign of the Cross* 1932 and *The Ten Commandments* 1923; remade 1956. He also made the 1952 Academy Award-winning *The Greatest Show on Earth*.

Demirel Suleyman 1924– . Turkish politician. Leader from 1964 of the Justice Party, he was prime minister 1965–71, 1975–77, and 1979–80. He favored links with the West, full membership in the European Community, and foreign investment in Turkish industry.

De Mita Luigi Ciriaco 1928– . Italian conservative politician, leader of the Christian Democratic Party (DC) from 1982, prime minister from 1988. He entered the Chamber of Deputies in 1963 and held a number of ministerial posts in the 1970s before becoming DC secretary-general.

democracy (Greek *demos* "the community," *kratos* "sovereign power") government by the people, usually through elected representatives. In the modern world, democracy has developed from the American and French revolutions.

Representative parliamentary government existed in Iceland from the 10th century and in England from the 13th century, but the British working classes were excluded almost entirely from the ◊vote until 1867, and women were admitted and property qualifications abolished only in 1918.

In direct democracy the whole people meets for the making of laws or the direction of executive officers, for example in Athens in the 5th century

BC (and allegedly in modern Libya). Direct democracy today is represented mainly by the use of the ◊referendum, as in the UK, Switzerland, and certain states of the US.

The Western concept of democracy differs from that in communist countries: the former emphasizes the control of the government by the electorate, with freedom of speech and the press; in the latter, both political and economic power rest in the Communist party.

Democratic Party one of the two main political parties of the US. It tends to be the party of the working person, as opposed to the Republicans, the party of big business, but the divisions between the two are not clear cut. Its stronghold since the Civil War has traditionally been industrial/urban centers and the Southern states, but conservative Southern Democrats were largely supportive of Republican positions and helped elect President Reagan.

Originally called Democratic Republicans, the party was founded by Thomas Jefferson 1792 to defend the rights of the individual states against the centralizing policy of the Federalists. The Democratic Party held power almost continuously 1800–60, and later returned with the presidencies of Cleveland, Wilson, F D Roosevelt, Truman, Kennedy, L B Johnson, and Carter. In the 20th century it has had more liberal social reform policies than the Republicans.

Democritus c. 460–361 BC. Greek philosopher and speculative scientist. His most important contribution is his atomic theory of the universe: all things originate from a vortex of atoms and differ according to the shape and arrangement of their atoms.

His concepts come to us through Aristotle's work in this area. His discussion of the constant motion of atoms to explain the origins of the universe was the most scientific theory proposed in his time.

demodulation in radio, the technique of separating a transmitted audio frequency signal from its modulated radio carrier wave. At the transmitter the audio frequency signal (representing speech or music, for example) may be made to modulate the amplitude (AM broadcasting) or frequency (FM broadcasting) of a continuously transmitted radio-frequency carrier wave. At the receiver, the signal from the aerial is demodulated to extract the required speech or sound component. In early radio systems, this process was called detection.

demography the study of the size, structure, dispersement, and development of human populations to establish reliable statistics on such factors as birth and death rates, marriages and divorces, life expectancy, and migration.

Demography is important in the social sciences as the basis for industry and for government planning in such areas as education, housing, welfare, transport, and taxation.

demonstration public show of support for, or opposition to, a particular political or social issue, typically by a group of people holding a rally, displaying placards, and making speeches. They usually seek some change in official policy by drawing attention to their cause with a media-worthy event.

Demonstrations can be static or take the form of elementary street theater or processions. A specialized type of demonstration is the picket, in which striking or dismissed workers try to dissuade others from using or working in the premises of the employer.

In the US, pickets are closely regulated. Violence and intimidation are beyond the protections of the First Amendment and are illegal. The Supreme Court has also held (1957) that picketing for the purpose of coercing employers as part of a union-organizing campaign is not protected as free speech.

Demosthenes c. 384–322 BC. Athenian orator and politician. From 351 BC he led the party that advocated resistance to the growing power of ◊Philip of Macedon, and in his *Philippics* incited the Athenians to war. This policy resulted in the defeat of Chaeronea 338, and the establishment of Macedonian supremacy. After the death of Alexander he organized a revolt; when it failed, he took poison to avoid capture by the Macedonians

Demosthenes *Athenian orator and politician Demosthenes.*

Demotic Greek the common or vernacular variety of the modern ◊Greek language.

demotic script cursive (joined) writing derived from Egyptian hieratic script, itself a cursive form of ◊hieroglyphic. Demotic documents are known from the 6th century BC to about AD 470. It was written horizontally, from right to left.

Dempsey Jack. Nicknamed "the Manassa Mauler." 1895–1983. US heavyweight boxing champion. He beat Jess Willard 1919 to win the title and held it until losing to Gene Tunney 1926. He engaged in the "Battle of the Long Count" with Tunney 1927.

denaturation irreversible changes occurring in the structure of proteins such as enzymes, usually caused by changes in pH or temperature. An example is the heating of egg albumen resulting in solid egg white.

The enzymes associated with digestion and metabolism become inactive if given abnormal conditions. Heat will damage their complex structure so that the usual interactions between enzyme and substrate can no longer occur.

dendrite part of a ◊nerve cell or neuron. The dendrites are slender filaments projecting from the cell body. They receive incoming messages from many other nerve cells and pass them on to the cell body. If the combined effect of these messages is strong enough, the cell body will send an electrical impulse along the axon (the threadlike extension of a nerve cell). The tip of the axon passes its message to the dendrites of other nerve cells.

Dempsey *A fearless and aggressive boxer, Jack Dempsey (left) was world heavyweight champion from 1919–1926.*

dendrochronology the analysis of the ◊annual rings of trees to date past events. Samples of wood are obtained by means of a narrow metal tube that is driven into a tree to remove a core extending from the bark to the center. Samples taken from timbers at an archeological site can be compared with a master core on file for that region or by taking cores from old, living trees; the year when they were felled can be determined by locating the point where the rings of the two samples correspond and counting back from the present.

Since annual rings are formed by variations in the water-conducting cells produced by the plant during different seasons of the year, they also provide a means of determining past climatic conditions in a given area. In North America, sequences of tree rings extending back over 8,000 years have been obtained for the SW and N Mexico by using cores from the bristle-cone pine *Pinus aristata*, which can live for over 4,000 years in that region. Also, the dryness of the area has preserved wood in SW archeological sites; in wet temperate regions the soil acidity usually absorbs wood, so this dating technique cannot be used.

Dene term used in Canada since the 1970s to describe the Native Americans (Athabaskan Indians) in the Northwest Territories. The official body representing them is called the Dene Nation.

Deneb brightest star in the constellation Cygnus and the 19th brightest star in the sky. It is one of the greatest supergiant stars known, with a true luminosity about 60,000 times that of the Sun. Deneb is about 1,800 light-years from Earth.

Deneuve Catherine 1943– . French actress acclaimed for her blonde beauty and her performance in Roman Polanski's film *Repulsion* 1965. She also appeared in *Les Parapluies de Cherbourg/Umbrellas of Cherbourg* 1964, *Belle de jour* 1967, *The Last Metro* 1980, and *The Hunger* 1983.

dengue tropical viral fever transmitted by mosquitoes and accompanied by joint pains, a rash, and glandular swelling. The incubation time is a week and the fever also lasts about a week. A more virulent form, dengue hemorrhagic fever, thought to be caused by a second infection on top of the first, also causes internal bleeding.

Deng Xiaoping or Teng Hsiao-ping 1904– Chinese political leader. A member of the Chinese Communist Party (CCP) from the 1920s, he took part in the Long March 1934–36. He was in the Politburo from 1955 until ousted in the Cultural Revolution 1966–69. Reinstated in the 1970s, he gradually took power and introduced a radical economic modernization program. He retired from the Politburo in 1987 and from his last official position (as chair of State Military Commission) March 1990, but remained influential behind the scenes.

Deng, born in Sichuan province into a middle-class landlord family, joined the CCP as a student in Paris, where he adopted the name Xiaoping (Little Peace) 1925, and studied in Moscow 1926. After the Long March, he served as a political commissar to the People's Liberation Army during the civil war of 1937–49. He entered the CCP Politburo 1955 and headed the secretariat during the early 1960s, working closely with President Liu Shaoqi. During the Cultural Revolution Deng was dismissed as a "capitalist roader" and sent to work in a tractor factory in Nanchang for "re-education."

Deng was rehabilitated by his patron Zhou Enlai 1973 and served as acting prime minister after Zhou's heart attack 1974. On Zhou's death Jan

Deng Xiaoping China's "paramount ruler" Deng Xiaoping. In effective charge of the country since 1978, he has promoted greater economic but not political liberalization.

1976 he was forced into hiding but returned to office as vice premier July 1977. By Dec 1978, although nominally a CCP vice chair, state vice premier, and Chief of Staff to the PLA, Deng was the controlling force in China. His policy of "socialism with Chinese characteristics," misinterpreted in the West as a drift to capitalism, had success in rural areas. He helped to oust ◊Hua Guofeng in favor of his protégés ◊Hu Yaobang (later in turn ousted) and ◊Zhao Ziyang.

When Deng officially retired from his party and army posts, he claimed to have renounced political involvement. His reputation, both at home and in the West, was tarnished by his sanctioning of the army's massacre of more than 2,000 pro-democracy demonstrators in Tiananmen Square, Beijing, in June 1989.

Den Helder port in North Holland province, the Netherlands, 40 mi/65 km N of Amsterdam, on the entrance to the North Holland Canal from the North Sea; population (1985) 63,538. It is a fishing port and naval base.

denier unit used in measuring the fineness of yarns, equal to the mass in grams of 9,000 meters of yarn. Thus 9,000 meters of 15 denier nylon, used in nylon stockings, weighs 0.5 oz/15 g, and in this case the thickness of thread would be 0.0017 in/0.00425 mm. The term is derived from the French silk industry; the *denier* was an old French silver coin.

In the US and Canada a unit called the drex, equal to the mass of 10,000 meters is used. The tex, equal to the mass of 1,000 meters, is the most common unit in the textile industry.

Denikin Anton Ivanovich 1872–1947. Russian general. He distinguished himself in the ◊Russo-Japanese War 1904–05 and World War I. After the outbreak of the Bolshevik Revolution 1917 he organized a volunteer army of 60,000 Whites (loyalists) but in 1919 was routed and escaped to France. He wrote a history of the Revolution and the Civil War.

De Niro Robert 1943– . US actor. He won Oscars for *The Godfather Part II* 1974 and *Raging Bull* 1979, for which role he deliberately put on weight in the interests of authenticity as the boxer gone to seed, Jake LaMotta. His other films include *Taxi Driver* 1976, *The Deer Hunter* 1978, *The Untouchables* 1987, and *Midnight Run* 1988. He showed his versatility in *King of Comedy* 1982 and other Martin Scorsese vehicles.

Denison city in NE Texas, near the Red river and the Oklahoma border, N of Dallas. A distribution center for grain and dairy products, its industries include textiles, wood products, and food processing; population (1990) 21,505.

Denis, St 3rd century AD. First bishop of Paris and one of the patron saints of France, who was martyred by the Romans. Feast day Oct 9.

denitrification a process occurring naturally in soil, where bacteria break down ◊nitrates to give nitrogen gas, which returns to the atmosphere.

Denktas Rauf R 1924– . Turkish-Cypriot politician. In 1975 the Turkish Federated State of Cyprus (TFSC) was formed in the northern third of the island, with Denktas as its head, and in 1983 he became president of the breakaway Turkish Republic of Northern Cyprus (TRNC).

Denktas held law-officer posts under the British crown before independence in 1960. Relations between the Greek and Turkish communities progressively deteriorated, leading to the formation of the TFSC. In 1983 the TRNC, with Denktas as its president, was formally constituted, but recognized internationally only by Turkey. The accession of the independent politician Georgios Vassilou to the Cyprus presidency offered hopes of reconciliation, but meetings between him and Denktas, under UN auspices, during 1989 failed to produce an agreement.

Denmark peninsula and islands in N Europe, bounded N by the Skagerrak, E by the Kattegat, S by Germany, and W by the North Sea.

government Under the 1849 constitution (last revised 1953) there is a hereditary monarch with no personal political power and a single-chamber parliament, the *Folketing*. The prime minister and cabinet are drawn from and responsible to the *Folketing*, which has 179 members elected by adult franchise – 175 representing metropolitan Denmark, two for the Faroe Islands, and two for Greenland. Voting is by proportional representation; the *Folketing* has a life of four years but may be dissolved within this period if the government is defeated on a vote of confidence. The government, however, need only resign on what it itself defines as a "vital element" of policy. Most significant of the 12 political parties are the Social Democrats, the Conservative People's Party, the Liberals, the Socialist People's Party, the Radical Liberals, the Centre Democrats, the Progress Party, the Christian People's Party, and the Left Socialists.

history The original home of the Danes was Sweden, and they migrated in the 5th and 6th centuries. Ruled by local chieftains, they terrified Europe by their piratical raids during the 8th–10th centuries, until Harald Bluetooth (c. 940–985) unified Denmark and established Christianity. King ◊Canute (ruled 1014–35) founded an empire embracing Denmark, England, and Norway, which fell apart at his death. After a century of confusion Denmark again dominated the Baltic under Valdemar I, Canute VI, and Valdemar II (1157–1241). Domestic conflict then produced anarchy, until Valdemar IV (1340–75) restored order. Denmark, Norway, and Sweden were united under one sovereign 1397. Sweden broke away 1449 and after a long struggle had its independence recognized 1523. Christian I (1448–81) secured the duchies of Schleswig and Holstein, fiefs of the ◊Holy Roman Empire, in 1460, and they were held by his descendants until 1863. Christian II (ruled 1513–23) was deposed in favor of his uncle Frederick, whose son Christian III (ruled 1534–59) made ◊Lutheranism the established religion 1536. Attempts to regain Sweden led to disastrous wars with that country 1563–70, 1643–45, 1657–60; equally disastrous was Christian V's intervention, 1625–29, on the Protestant side of the ◊Thirty Years' War.

Frederick III (ruled 1648–70) made himself absolute monarch 1665 and ruled through a burgher bureaucracy. Serfdom was abolished 1788. Denmark's adherence 1780 to the armed neutrality against Britain resulted in the naval defeat of Copenhagen 1801, and in 1807 the British bombarded Copenhagen and seized the Danish fleet to save it from ◊Napoleon. This incident drove Denmark into the arms of France, and the Allies at the Congress of ◊Vienna took Norway from Denmark and gave it to Sweden 1815. A liberal movement then arose that in 1848–49 compelled Frederick VII (ruled 1848–63) to grant a democratic constitution. The Germans in Schleswig-Holstein revolted with Prussian support 1848–50, and Prussia seized the provinces 1864 after a short war. North Schleswig was recovered after a plebiscite 1920.

Neutral in World War I, Denmark tried to preserve its neutrality 1939 by signing a pact with Hitler, but was occupied by Germany 1940–45. Although traditionally neutral, Denmark joined ◊NATO 1949 and the ◊European Free Trade Association (EFTA) 1960 but resigned 1973 to join the EEC.

◊Iceland was part of the Danish kingdom until 1945 and the other parts of nonmetropolitan Denmark, the Faroe Islands and Greenland, were given special recognition by a constitution that has been adapted to meet changing circumstances. In 1953 provision was made for a daughter to succeed to the throne in the absence of a male heir, and a system of voting by proportional representation was introduced.

Left-wing policies have dominated Danish politics, and proportional representation (often resulting in minority or coalition governments) has encouraged a moderate approach. In the March 1989 general election, the center-right coalition lost seven seats, but Prime Minister Schluter decided to continue with a minority government, holding 70 of the *Folketing* seats.

De Niro Actor Robert De Niro as he appeared in The Untouchables *1987, portraying Al Capone, the Chicago gang leader.*

Dennis et al v US a US Supreme Court decision 1951 dealing with the power of Congress to suppress certain political activities by revoking First Amendment rights. The case was brought by Dennis, a Communist Party official, and others to test the Smith Act 1940, which outlawed advocacy of the violent overthrow of the government. The Court upheld the Smith Act, implicitly returning to the "bad tendency" doctrine by defining any teaching that suggests the overthrow of the government as a clear and present danger to society. This definition gave Congress the right to restrict speech and assembly of anyone affiliated with the Communist Party.

Denpasar capital town of Bali in the Lesser Sunda Islands of Indonesia. Population (1980) 88,100.

density measure of the compactness of a substance; the mass per unit volume, measured in lb per cubic foot/kg per cubic meter. ◊Relative density is the ratio of the density of a substance to that of water at 4°C.

There are also other usages for the term "density": in photography, it is the degree of opacity of the negative; in population studies, it is the quantity or number per unit of area; in electricity, current density is the amount of current passing through a cross-sectional area of a conductor in a

Denmark
Kingdom of
(Kongeriget Danmark)

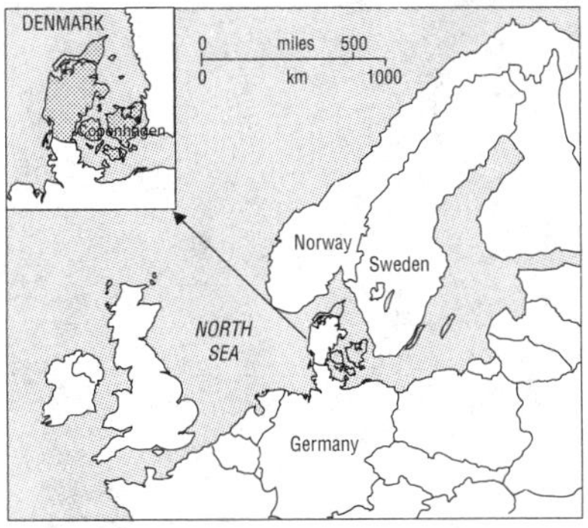
DENMARK
0 miles 500
0 km 1000
Norway
Sweden
NORTH SEA
Germany

area 16,627 sq mi/43,075 sq km
capital Copenhagen
cities Aarhus, Odense, Aalborg, Esbjerg, all ports
physical comprises the Jutland peninsula and about 500 islands (100 inhabited) including the island of Bornholm in the Baltic Sea; the land is flat and cultivated; sand dunes and lagoons on the W coast and long inlets (fjords) on the E; the main island is Sjælland (Zealand), where most of Copenhagen is located (the rest of it is on the island of Amager)
territories the dependencies of Faeroe Islands and Greenland
features Kronborg Castle in Helsingør (Elsinore); Tivoli Gardens (Copenhagen); Legoland Park in Sillund
head of state Queen Margrethe II from 1972
head of government Poul Schlüter from 1982
political system liberal democracy
political parties Social Democrats (SD), left-of-center; Conservative People's Party (KF), moderate center-right; Liberal Party (V), center-left; Socialist People's Party (SF), moderate left-wing; Radical Liberals (RV), radical internationalist left-of-center; Centre Democrats (CD), moderate centrist; Progress Party (FP), radical antibureaucratic; Christian People's Party (KrF), interdenominational, family values
exports bacon, dairy produce, eggs, fish, mink pelts, car and aircraft parts, electrical equipment, textiles, chemicals
currency kroner
population (1990 est) 5,134,000; growth rate 0% p.a.
life expectancy men 72, women 78
language Danish (official); there is a German-speaking minority
religion Lutheran 97%
literacy 99% (1983)
GDP $85.5 bn (1987); $16,673 per head
chronology
1940–45 Occupied by Germany.
1945 Iceland's independence recognized.
1947 Frederik IX succeeded Christian X.
1948 Home rule granted for Faeroe Islands.
1949 Became a founding member of NATO.
1960 Joined European Free Trade Association (EFTA).
1972 Margrethe II became Denmark's first queen in nearly 600 years.
1973 Left EFTA and joined European Community.
1979 Home rule granted for Greenland.
1985 Strong nonnuclear movement in evidence.
1990 General election; another coalition government formed.

given amount of time, usually given in amperes per square inch or amperes per square centimeter.

dental formula a way of showing what an animal's teeth are like. The dental formula consists of eight numbers separated by a line into two rows. The four above the line represent the teeth in one side of the upper jaw, starting at the front. If this reads 2 1 2 3 (as for humans) it means two incisors, one canine, two premolars, and three molars (see ◊tooth). The numbers below the line represent the lower jaw. The total number of teeth can be calculated by adding up all the numbers and multiplying by two.

dentistry care and treatment of the teeth and gums. Orthodontics deals with the straightening of the teeth for esthetic and clinical reasons, and periodontics with care of the supporting tissue (bone and gums).

The bacteria that start the process of dental decay are normal, nonpathogenic members of a large and varied group of microorganisms present in the mouth. They are strains of oral streptococci, and it is only in the presence of sucrose (from refined sugar) in the mouth that they become damaging to the teeth. ◊Fluoride in the water supply has been one attempted solution, and in 1979 a vaccine was developed from a modified form of the bacterium *Streptococcus mutans*.

The earliest dental school was opened in Baltimore, Maryland, 1839.

dentition the type and number of teeth in a species. Different kinds of teeth have different functions, and a grass-eating animal will have well developed molars for grinding its food, whereas a meat-eater will need large canines for catching and killing its prey. The teeth that are less useful may be reduced in size or missing altogether. An animal's dentition is represented diagramatically by a ◊dental formula.

denudation the natural loss of soil and rock debris, blown away by wind or washed away by running water, that lays bare the rock below. Over millions of years, denudation causes a general leveling of the landscape.

Denver city and capital of Colorado, on the South Platte River, near the foothills of the Rocky Mountains; population (1990) 467,610. Denver-Boulder metropolitan area (1990) 1,848,319. It is a processing and distribution center for a large agricultural area and for natural resources (minerals, oil, gas). It was the center of a gold and silver boom in the 1870s and 1880s, and for oil in the 1970s.

Denver was founded 1858 with the discovery of gold, becoming a mining-camp supply center; coal also is mined nearby. There is a university, a mining school, many medical institutions, and a branch of the US mint.

deodar Himalayan ◊cedar tree *Cedrus deodara*, often planted as a rapid-growing ornamental. It has fragrant, durable wood valuable as timber.

deontology ethical theory that the rightness of an action consists in its conformity to duty, regardless of the consequences that may result from it. Deontological ethics is thus opposed to any form of utilitarianism or pragmatism.

deoxyribonucleic acid the full name of ◊DNA.

De Palma Brian 1941– . US film director, especially of thrillers. His technical mastery and enthusiasm for spilling blood are shown in films such as *Sisters* 1973, *Carrie* 1976, and *The Untouchables* 1987.

Depardieu Gerard 1948– . Versatile French actor who has appeared in the films *Deux hommes dans la ville* 1973, *Le camion* 1977, *Mon oncle d'Amérique* 1980, *The Moon in the Gutter* 1983, *Jean de Florette* 1985, and *Cyrano de Bergerac* 1990.

depilatory any instrument or substance used to remove growing hair, usually for cosmetic reasons. Permanent eradication is by electrolysis, the destruction of each individual hair root by an electrolytic needle or an electrocautery, but there is a danger of some regrowth as well as scarring.

deposit account in banking, an account where money is left to attract interest, sometimes for a fixed term. Unlike a current account, the deposit account does not give constant access.

depreciation in economics, decline of a currency's value in relation to other currencies. Depreciation also describes the fall in value of an asset (such as factory machinery) resulting from age, wear and tear, or other circumstances. It is an important factor in assessing company profits and tax liabilities.

depression an emotional state characterized by sadness, unhappy thoughts, apathy, and dejection. Sadness is a normal response to major losses such as bereavement or unemployment. However, clinical depression, which is prolonged or unduly severe, often requires treatment, such as antidepressant medication, ◊cognitive therapy, or, in very rare cases, electroconvulsive therapy (ECT), in which an electrical current is passed through the brain.

depression in economics, a period of exceptionally low output and investment, with high unemployment. Specifically, the term describes two periods of crisis in world economy 1873–96 and 1929–39, also known as panics.

The term is most often used to refer to the world economic crisis precipitated by the Wall Street crash of Oct 29, 1929, when millions of (inflated and margined) dollars were wiped off US stock values by panic selling in a matter of hours. This forced the closing of many US banks whose reserves were involved in stock speculation and led to the recall of US overseas investments. This loss of US credit had serious repercussions on the European economy, especially that of Germany (still recovering from World War I), and led to a steep fall in the levels of international trade as countries attempted to protect their own economies.

Despite unprecedented federal government intervention and employment programs under President Franklin D Roosevelt's New Deal, the US economy began a real recovery only after the rearmament programs of the late 1930s and early 1940s boosted employment and output.

de Quincey Thomas 1785–1859. English author whose works include *Confessions of an English Opium-Eater* 1821 and the essays "On the Knocking at the Gate in Macbeth" 1823 and "On Murder Considered as One of the Fine Arts" 1827. He was a friend of the poets Wordsworth and Coleridge.

Born in Manchester, de Quincey ran away from school there to wander and study in Wales. He then went to London, where he lived in extreme poverty but with the constant companionship of the young orphan Ann, of whom he writes in the *Confessions*. In 1803 he was reconciled to his guardians and was sent to university at Oxford, where his opium habit began. In 1809 he settled with the Wordsworths and Coleridge in the Lake District. He moved to Edinburgh 1828, where he eventually died. De Quincey's work had a powerful influence on ◊Baudelaire and ◊Poe among others.

Derain André 1880–1954. French painter. He experimented with strong, almost primary colors and exhibited with the ◊Fauves but later developed a more somber landscape style. His work includes costumes and scenery for Diaghilev's Ballets Russes.

Derby industrial city in Derbyshire, England; population (1981) 216,000

products rail locomotives, Rolls-Royce automobiles and airplane engines, chemicals, paper, electrical, mining and engineering equipment.

Derby Edward (George Geoffrey Smith) Stanley, 14th Earl of 1799–1869. British politician, prime minister 1852, 1858–59, and 1866–68. Originally a Whig, he became secretary for the colonies

FREE
SOUP COFFEE & DOUGHNUTS
FOR THE UNEMPLOYED
FREE SOUP
PARK

depression *A soup kitchen in Chicago during the Great Depression.*

Descartes *An engraving of French philosopher and mathematician René Descartes from a portrait by Frans Hals.*

1830, and introduced the bill for the abolition of slavery. He joined the Tories 1834, and the split in the Tory Party over Robert Peel's free-trade policy gave Derby the leadership for 20 years.

Derbyshire county in N central England
area 1,015 sq mi/2,630 sq km
towns Matlock (administrative headquarters), Derby, Chesterfield, Ilkeston
features Peak District National Park (including Kinder Scout 2,088 ft/636 m); rivers: Derwent, Dove, Rother, Trent; Chatsworth House, Bakewell (seat of Duke of Devonshire); Haddon Hall
products cereals; dairy and sheep farming

deregulation action to abolish or reduce government controls and supervision over private economic activities, as with the deregulation of the US airline industry 1978. Its purpose is to improve competition. Increased competition had the effect, in some areas, of driving smaller companies out of business. A tremendous increase in mergers, acquisitions, and bankruptcies followed deregulation as the stronger companies consumed the weaker. A wider array of services and lower prices in some industries also have resulted; see also ◊monetarism; ◊privatization.

derivative or ***differential coefficient*** in mathematics, the limit of the gradient of a chord between two points on a curve as the distance between the points tends to zero; for a function with a single variable, $y = f'(x)$, it is denoted by $f'(x)$, $Df(x)$, or dy/dx, and is equal to the gradient of the curve.

dermatitis inflammation of the skin (see ◊eczema), usually related to allergy. Dermatosis refers to any skin disorder and may be caused by contact or systemic problems.

De Roburt Hammer 1923– . President of Nauru 1968–89, out of office 1976–78 and briefly in 1986. During the country's occupation 1942–45, he was deported to Japan. He became head chief of Nauru in 1956 and was elected the country's first president in 1968. In 1989 he was ousted on a no-confidence motion.

derrick simple lifting machine consisting of a pole carrying a block and tackle. Derricks are commonly used on ships that carry freight. In the oil industry the tower used for hoisting the drill pipes is known as a derrick.

derris climbing plant of SE Asia *Derris elliptica* of the legume family Leguminosae. Its roots contain rotenone, a strong insecticide.

Derry county of Northern Ireland
area 799 sq mi/2,070 sq km
cities Derry (county town, formerly Londonderry), Coleraine, Portstewart
features rivers Foyle, Bann, and Roe; borders Lough Neagh
products mainly agricultural, but farming is hindered by the very heavy rainfall; flax, cattle, sheep, food processing, textiles, light engineering
population (1981) 187,000
famous people Joyce Cary.

dervish in Iran and Turkey, a religious mendicant; throughout the rest of Islam a member of an Islamic religious brotherhood, not necessarily mendicant in character. The Arabic equivalent is fakir. There are various orders of dervishes, each with its rule and special ritual. The "whirling dervishes" claim close communion with the deity through ecstatic dancing; the "howling dervishes" gash themselves with knives to demonstrate the miraculous feats possible to those who trust in Allah.

Derwent river in N Yorkshire, NE England; length 70 mi/112 km. Rising in the N Yorkshire moors, it joins the river Ouse SE of Selby.

Desai Morarji 1896– . Indian politician. An early follower of Mahatma Gandhi, he was prime minister 1977–79, as leader of the ◊Janata party, after toppling Indira Gandhi. Party infighting led to his resignation of both the premiership and the party leadership.

desalination the removal of salt, usually from sea water, to produce fresh water for irrigation or drinking. Distillation has usually been the method adopted, but in the 1970s a cheaper process, using certain polymer materials that filter the molecules of salt from the water by reverse osmosis, was developed.

Descartes René 1596–1650. French mathematician and philosopher. He believed that commonly accepted knowledge was doubtful because of the subjective nature of the senses, and attempted to rebuild human knowledge using as his foundation "*cogito ergo sum*" ("I think, therefore I am"). He also believed that the entire material universe could be explained in terms of mathematical physics. He is regarded as the discoverer of analytical geometry and the founder of the science of optics, and also helped to shape contemporary theories of astronomy and animal behavior.

Born near Tours, Descartes served in the army of Prince Maurice of Orange, and in 1619, while traveling through Europe, decided to apply the methods of mathematics to metaphysics and science. He settled in the Netherlands in 1628, where he was more likely to be free from interference by the ecclesiastical authorities. In 1649 he visited the court of Queen Christina of Sweden, and shortly thereafter he died in Stockholm.

His works include *Discourse on Method* 1637, *Meditations on the First Philosophy* 1641, and *Principles of Philosophy* 1644, and numerous books on physiology, optics, and geometry.

Coordinate geometry, as a way of defining and manipulating geometrical shapes by means of algebraic expressions, was determined by Leibniz, and only later called ◊Cartesian coordinates in honor of Descartes.

Descartes identified the "thinking thing" (*res cogitans*) or mind with the human soul or consciousness; the body, though somehow interacting with the soul, was a physical machine, secondary to, and in principle separable from, the soul. He held that everything has a cause; nothing can result from nothing. He believed that, although all matter is in motion, matter does not move of its own accord; the initial impulse comes from God. He also postulated two quite distinct substances—spatial substance, or matter, and thinking substance, or mind. This is called "Cartesian dualism," and it preserved him from serious controversy with the church.

Deschamps Eustache 1346–1406. French poet, born in Champagne. He was the author of more than 1,000 ballades, and the *Miroir de mariage/The Mirror of Marriage*, an attack on women.

desert area without sufficient rainfall and, consequently, vegetation to support human life. Scientifically, this term includes the ice areas of the polar regions. Almost 33% of Earth's land surface is desert, and this proportion is increasing.

The tropical desert belts of latitudes from 5° to 30° are caused by the descent of air that is heated over the warm land and therefore tends to retain its moisture. Other natural desert types are the continental deserts, such as the Gobi, that are too far from the sea to receive any moisture;

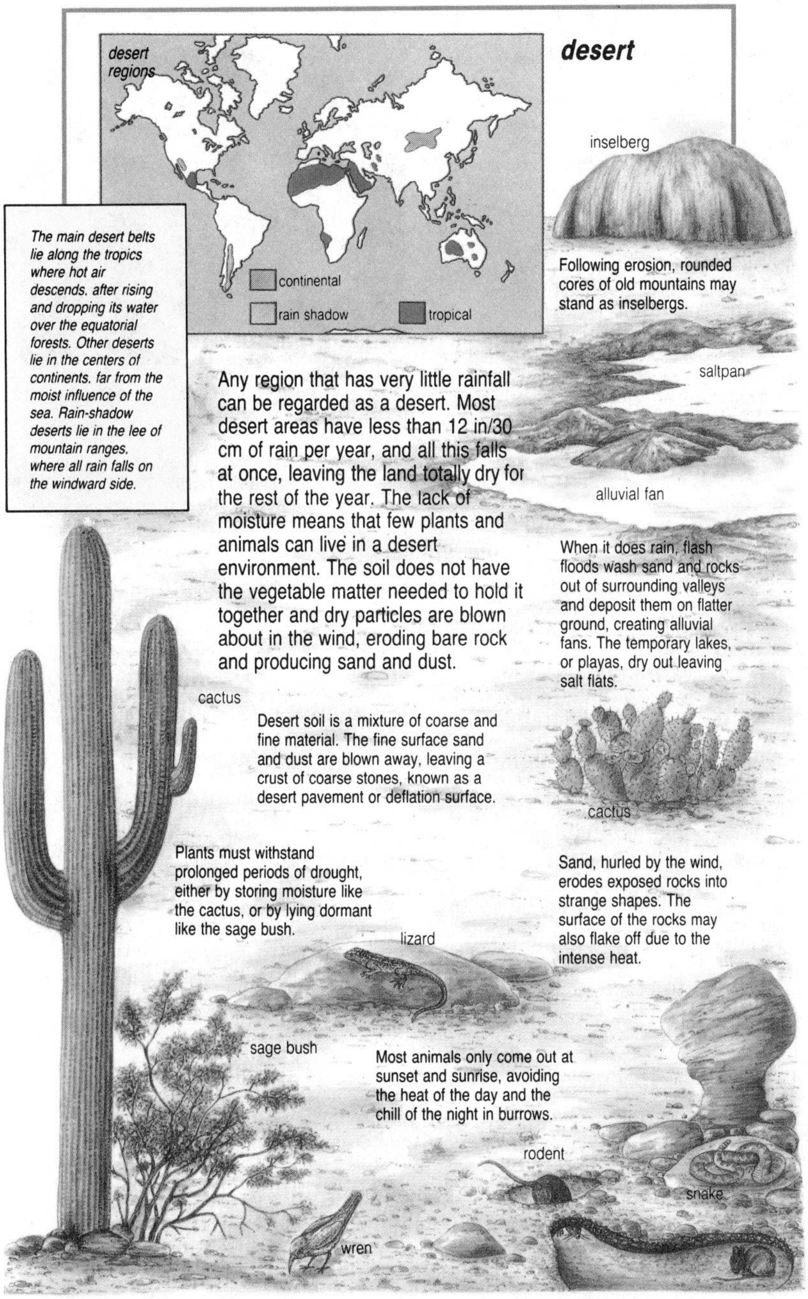
desert
desert regions
continental
rain shadow
tropical
The main desert belts lie along the tropics where hot air descends, after rising and dropping its water over the equatorial forests. Other deserts lie in the centers of continents, far from the moist influence of the sea. Rain-shadow deserts lie in the lee of mountain ranges, where all rain falls on the windward side.
inselberg
Following erosion, rounded cores of old mountains may stand as inselbergs.
saltpan
Any region that has very little rainfall can be regarded as a desert. Most desert areas have less than 12 in/30 cm of rain per year, and all this falls at once, leaving the land totally dry for the rest of the year. The lack of moisture means that few plants and animals can live in a desert environment. The soil does not have the vegetable matter needed to hold it together and dry particles are blown about in the wind, eroding bare rock and producing sand and dust.
alluvial fan
When it does rain, flash floods wash sand and rocks out of surrounding valleys and deposit them on flatter ground, creating alluvial fans. The temporary lakes, or playas, dry out leaving salt flats.
cactus
Desert soil is a mixture of coarse and fine material. The fine surface sand and dust are blown away, leaving a crust of coarse stones, known as a desert pavement or deflation surface.
cactus
Plants must withstand prolonged periods of drought, either by storing moisture like the cactus, or by lying dormant like the sage bush.
lizard
Sand, hurled by the wind, erodes exposed rocks into strange shapes. The surface of the rocks may also flake off due to the intense heat.
sage bush
Most animals only come out at sunset and sunrise, avoiding the heat of the day and the chill of the night in burrows.
rodent
snake
wren

rain-shadow deserts, such as California's Death Valley, that lie in the lee of mountain ranges, where the ascending air drops its rain only on the windward slopes; and coastal deserts, such as the Namib, where cold ocean currents cause local dry air masses to descend. Desert surfaces are usually rocky or gravelly, with only a small proportion being covered with sand. Deserts can be created by changes in climate, or by the human-aided process of desertification.

Desert Rats nickname of the British 8th Army in N Africa during World War II. Their uniforms had a shoulder insignia bearing a jerboa (N African rodent, capable of great leaps).

de Sica Vittorio 1902–1974. Italian director and actor. He won his first Oscar with *Bicycle Thieves* 1948, a film of subtle realism. Later films included *Umberto D* 1952, *Two Women* 1960, and *The Garden of the Finzi-Continis* 1971.

desiccator airtight vessel, traditionally made of glass, in which materials may be stored either to dry them or to prevent them, once dried, from reabsorbing moisture.

The base of the desiccator is a chamber in which is placed a substance with a strong affinity for water (such as calcium chloride or silica gel), which removes water vapor from the desiccator atmosphere and from substances placed in it.

desktop publishing (DTP) the use of microcomputers for small-scale typesetting and page makeup. DTP systems are capable of producing camera-ready pages (pages ready for photographing and printing), made up of text and graphics, with text set in different typefaces and sizes. The page can be previewed on the screen before final printing on a laser printer.

Des Moines capital and largest town in Iowa, on the Des Moines River, a tributary of the Mississippi; population (1990) 193,187. It is a major road, railroad, and air center. Industries include printing, banking, insurance, and food processing.

Drake University is here. The Des Moines Art Center was designed by Eliel Saarinen. Incorporated 1851, Des Moines became the state capital 1857.

Desmoulins Camille 1760–1794. French revolutionary who summoned the mob to arms on July 12, 1789, so precipitating the revolt that culminated in the storming of the Bastille. A prominent ◊Jacobin, he was elected to the National Convention 1792. His *Histoire des Brissotins* was largely responsible for the overthrow of the ◊Girondins, but shortly after he was sent to the guillotine as too moderate.

de Soto Hernando c. 1496–1542. Spanish explorer who sailed with d'Avila (c. 1400–1531) to Darien, Central America, 1519, explored the Yucatán Peninsula 1528, and traveled with Pizarro in Peru 1530–35. In 1538 he was made governor of Cuba and Florida. In his expedition of 1539, he explored Florida, Georgia, and the Mississippi River.

Emperor Charles V appointed de Soto governor of Florida in 1537. His expeditions may have penetrated Missouri and Louisiana. Upon his death on May 21, 1542, his companions buried his body in a river to preserve the local Indians' belief that de Soto had descended from heaven.

Desprez Josquin 1440–1521. Franco-Flemish composer, see ◊Josquin Desprez.

Dessalines Jean Jacques c. 1758–1806. Emperor of Haiti 1804–06. Born in Guinea, he was taken to Haiti as a slave, where in 1802 he succeeded ◊Toussaint L'Ouverture as leader of the black revolt against the French. After defeating the French, he proclaimed Haiti's independence and made himself emperor. He was killed when trying to suppress an uprising provoked by his cruelty.

Dessau town in the state of Saxony-Anhalt, Federal Republic of Germany, on the river Mulde, 70 mi/115 km SW of Berlin; population (1990) 120,000. It is the former capital of Anhalt duchy and state. It manufactures chemicals, machinery, and chocolate and was the site of the Junkers airplane works. The Bauhaus school of art was based in Dessau 1925–33.

Dessau Paul 1894–1979. German composer. His work includes incidental music to Bertolt Brecht's theater pieces, an opera, *Der Verurteilung des Lukullus* 1949, also to a libretto by Brecht, and numerous choral works and songs.

He studied in Berlin, becoming a theater conductor until moving to Paris in 1933, where he studied Schoenberg's serial method with Rena Leibowitz. He collaborated with Brecht from 1942, when they met as political exiles in the US, returning with him to East Berlin 1948.

destroyer small, fast warship designed for antisubmarine work. They played a critical role in the ◊convoy system in World War II. Modern destroyers often carry guided missiles and displace 3,700–5,650 tons.

detective fiction novels or short stories in which a mystery is solved mainly by the action of a professional or amateur detective. Where the mystery to be solved concerns a crime, the work may be called crime fiction. The earliest work of detective fiction as understood today was *Murders in the Rue Morgue* 1841 by Edgar Allan Poe, and his detective Dupin became the model for those who solved crimes by deduction from a series of clues. The most popular deductive sleuth was Sherlock Holmes in the stories by Arthur Conan Doyle.

The "golden age" of the genre was the period from the 1920s to the 1940s, when the leading writers were women—Agatha Christie, Margery Allingham, and Dorothy L Sayers. Types of detective fiction include the police procedural, where the mystery is solved by detailed police work, as in the work of Swedish writers Maj Sjowall and Per Wahloo; the inverted novel, where the identity of the criminal is known from the beginning and only the method or the motive remains to be discovered, as in *Malice Aforethought* by Francis Iles; and the hard-boiled school of private investigators begun by Raymond Chandler and Dashiell Hammett, which became known for its social realism and explicit violence. More recently, the form and traditions of the genre have been used as a framework within which to explore other concerns, as in *Innocent Blood* and *A Taste for Death* by P D James, *The Name of the Rose* by Umberto Eco, and the works of many women writers who explore feminist ideas, as in *Murder in the Collective* by Barbara Wilson.

Like most genres, crime fiction has produced its oddities. *Murder in Pastiche* by Marion Mainwaring is written in the styles of nine famous writers. Agatha Christie, Georgette Heyer, and Ellis Peters have all written detective novels with historical settings. *Murder Off Miami* by Dennis Wheatley was a dossier containing real clues such as photographs, ticket stubs, and hairpins for the reader to use in solving the mystery; the solution was in a closed envelope at the back of the book.

détente (French) a reduction of political tension and the easing of strained relations between nations. For example, the ending of the Cold War 1989–90, although it was first used in the 1970s to describe the easing East-West relations, trade agreements, and cultural exchanges.

detergent surface-active cleansing agent. The common detergents are made from ◊fats (hydrocarbons) and sulfuric acid, and their long-chain molecules have a type of structure similar to that of ◊soap molecules: a salt group at one end attached to a long hydrocarbon "tail." They have the advantage over soap in that they do not produce scum by forming insoluble salts with the calcium and magnesium ions present in hard water.

To remove dirt, which is generally attached to materials by oil or grease, the hydrocarbon "tails" (soluble in oil or grease) penetrate the oil or grease drops, while the "heads" (soluble in water but insoluble in grease) remain in the water and, being salts, become ionized. Consequently the oil drops become negatively charged and tend to repel one another; thus they remain in suspension and are washed away with the dirt.

Detergents were first developed from coal tar in Germany during World War I, and synthetic organic detergents came into increasing use after World War II. Domestic powder detergents for use in hot water have alkyl benzene as their main base, and may also include bleaches and fluorescers as whiteners, perborates to free stain-removing oxygen, and water softeners. Environment-friendly detergents contain no phosphates or bleaches. Liquid detergents for washing dishes are based on ethylene oxide. Cold-water detergents consist of a mixture of various alcohols, plus an ingredient for breaking down the surface tension of the water, so enabling the liquid to penetrate fibers and remove the dirt. When surface-active materials escape the normal processing of sewage, they cause troublesome foam in rivers; phosphates in some detergents can also enrich the vegetation in rivers and lakes, causing ◊eutrophication.

determinism in philosophy, the view that denies human freedom of action. Everything is strictly governed by the principle of cause and effect, and human action is no exception. It is the opposite of free will, and rules out moral choice and responsibility.

In antiquity, the theory of determinism was a feature of ◊Stoicism. In Christian theology, the Calvinist doctrine of predestination is deterministic. Quantum mechanics and the ◊uncertainty principle lend support to free will.

deterrence the underlying conception of the nuclear arms race: the belief that a potential aggressor will be discouraged from launching a "first strike" nuclear attack by the knowledge that the adversary is capable of inflicting "unacceptable damage" in a retaliatory strike. This doctrine is widely known as that of mutual assured destruction (MAD). Three essential characteristics of deterrence are: the "capability to act," "credibility," and the "will to act."

de Tocqueville Alexis 1805–1859. French politician, see ◊Tocqueville, Alexis de.

detonator or ***blasting cap*** or ***percussion cap*** small explosive charge used to trigger off a main charge of high explosive. The relatively unstable compounds mercury fulminate and lead acid are often used in detonators, being set off by a lighted fuse or, more commonly, an electric current.

detritus in biology, the organic debris produced during the ◊decomposition of animals and plants.

Detroit city in Michigan, situated on Detroit River; population (1990) 1,027,974, metropolitan area (1990) 4,665,236. It is an industrial center with the headquarters of Ford, Chrysler, and General Motors, hence its nickname, Motown (from "motor town"). Other manufactured products include metal products, machine tools, chemicals, office machines, and pharmaceuticals. Detroit is a port on the St Lawrence Seaway and the home of Wayne State University and its Medical Center complex. The University of Detroit and the Detroit Institute of Arts are also here.

It was founded 1701 and is the oldest US city of any size W of the original colonies. It was captured from the French by the British in 1760 and passed to the US in 1796. In 1805 it was completely destroyed by fire but was soon rebuilt. The opening of the Erie Canal 1825 aided development. Detroit grew rapidly after the building of the first automobile factories, 1899–1903.

There were significant race riots in 1943 and 1967; a black mayor was elected in 1973.

A recent major development is the waterfront Renaissance Center complex. During the 1960s and 1970s Detroit became associated with the "Motown Sound" of rock and soul music.

Detsko Selo former name of ◊Pushkin, near Leningrad, which was renamed after the Russian poet in 1937.

Deucalion in Greek mythology, son of ◊Prometheus, and an equivalent of ◊Noah in the Old Testament. Warned by his father of a coming flood, he and his wife Pyrrha built an ark. After the waters had subsided, the stones they were instructed by a god to throw over their shoulders became men and women.

deus ex machina (Latin "a god from a machine") a far-fetched or unlikely event that resolves an intractable difficulty. The phrase was originally used in drama to indicate a god descending from heaven to resolve the plot.

deuterium naturally occuring heavy isotope of hydrogen, mass number 2 (one proton and one neutron), discovered by Harold Urey 1932. In nature, about one in every 6,500 hydrogen atoms is deuterium. The symbol D is sometimes used for it. Combined with oxygen, it produces "heavy water" (D_2O), used in the nuclear industry.

deuteron nucleus of an atom of deuterium (heavy hydrogen). It consists of one proton and one neutron, and is used in the bombardment of chemical elements to synthesize other elements.

Deuteronomy book of the Old Testament; 5th book of the ◊Torah. It contains various laws, including the laws for ◊kosher and the ten commandments, and gives an account of the death of Moses.

Deutschmark or Deutsche Mark (DM) the standard currency of Germany.

de Valera Eamon 1882–1975. Irish nationalist politician, prime minister of the Irish Free State/Eire/Republic of Ireland 1932–48, 1951–54, and 1957–59, and president 1959–73. Repeatedly imprisoned, he participated in the Easter Rising 1916 and was leader of the nationalist ◊Sinn Féin party 1917–26, when he formed the republican Fianna Fáil party; he directed negotiations with Britain 1921 but refused to accept the partition of Ireland until 1937.

He was sentenced to death for his part in the Easter Rising, but the sentence was commuted, and he was released under an amnesty 1917. He directed the negotiations of 1921 but refused to accept the ensuing treaty that divided Ireland into the Free State and the North.

de Valera *Eamon de Valera, Irish politician, shortly before his imprisonment 1923.*

Civil war followed. De Valera formed a new party, Fianna Fáil 1926, which secured a majority in 1932. De Valera became prime minister and foreign minister of the Free State. Throughout World War II he maintained a strict neutrality, rejecting an offer by Churchill 1940 to recognize the principle of a united Ireland in return for Eire's entry into the war. He resigned after his defeat at the 1948 elections but was again prime minister in the 1950s and then president of the republic.

de Valois Ninette. Adopted name of Edris Stannus 1898– . Irish dancer, choreographer, and teacher. A pioneer of British national ballet, she worked with Diaghilev in Paris before opening a dance academy in London 1926. Collaborating with Lilian Baylis at the ◊Old Vic, she founded the Vic-Wells Ballet 1931, which later became the Royal Ballet and Royal Ballet School. Among her works are *Job* 1931 and *Checkmate* 1937.

devaluation in economics, lowering of the official value of a currency against other currencies, so that exports become cheaper and imports more expensive. Used when a country is badly in deficit in its balance of trade, it results in the goods the country produces being cheaper abroad, so that the economy is stimulated by increased foreign demand.

The increased cost of imported food, raw materials, and manufactured goods as a consequence of devaluation may, however, stimulate an acceleration in inflation, especially when commodities are rising in price because of increased world demand. ***Revaluation*** is the opposite process.

Devaluations of important currencies upset the balance of the world's money markets and encourage speculation. Significant devaluations include that of the German mark in the 1920s and Britain's devaluation of sterling in the 1960s. To promote greater stability, many countries have allowed the value of their currencies to "float," that is, to fluctuate in value.

developing in photography, the process that produces a visible image on exposed photographic film. Developing involves treating the emulsion with chemical developer, a reducing agent that changes the light-altered salts into dark metallic silver. The developed image is a negative: darkest where the strongest light hit the emulsion, lightest where the least light hit it.

development in the social sciences, the acquisition by a society of industrial techniques and technology; hence the common classification of the "developed" nations of the First and Second Worlds and the poorer, "developing" or "underdeveloped" nations of the Third World. The assumption that development in the sense of industrialization was inherently good has been increasingly questioned since the 1960s.

Human societies have developed in other areas as well—the arts, religion, economics, politics—

but technology has always been available for assessment, since ◊prehistory. Many universities today have academic departments of development studies, which address the theoretical questions involved in proposing practical solutions to the problems of development in the Third World.

development aid see ◊aid, foreign.

developmental psychology the study of development of cognition and behavior from birth to adulthood.

Deventer town in Overijssel province, the Netherlands, on the river Ijssel, 28 mi/45 km S of the Ijssel Meer; population (1984) 64,800. It is an agricultural and transport center and produces carpets, precision equipment and packaging machinery.

deviance abnormal behavior; that is, behavior that deviates from the norms or the laws of a society or group, and so invokes social sanctions, controls, or stigma. Deviance is a relative concept: what is considered deviant in some societies may be normal in others. In a particular society the same act (killing someone, for example) may be either normal or deviant depending on the circumstances (in wartime or for money, for example). Some sociologists, such as Howard Becker, argue that the reaction of others, rather than the act itself, is what determines whether an act is deviant, and that deviance is merely behavior other people so label.

devil in Jewish, Christian, and Muslim theology, the supreme spirit of evil (Beelzebub, Lucifer, Iblis), or an evil spirit generally.

The devil, or Satan, is mentioned only in the more recently written books of the Old Testament, but the later Jewish doctrine is that found in the New Testament.

The concept of the devil passed into the early Christian church from Judaism, and theology until at least the time of St Anselm represented the Atonement as primarily the deliverance, through Christ's death, of mankind from the bondage of the devil. Jesus recognized as a reality the kingdom of evil, of which Satan or Beelzebub was the prince. In the Middle Ages the devil in popular superstition assumed the attributes of the horned fertility gods of paganism, and was regarded as the god of witches. The belief in a personal devil was strong during the Reformation, and the movement's leader Luther regarded himself as the object of a personal Satanic persecution. With the development of liberal Protestantism in the 19th century came a strong tendency to deny the existence of a positive spirit of evil, and to explain the devil as merely a personification. However, the traditional conception was never abandoned by the Roman Catholic Church, and theologians, such as C S Lewis, have maintained the existence of a power of evil.

In Muslim theology, Iblis is one of the *jinn* (beings created by Allah from fire) who refused to prostrate himself before Adam, and who tempted Adam and his wife Hawwa (Eve) to disobey Allah, an act which led to their expulsion from Paradise. He continues to try to lead people astray, but at the Last Judgment he and his hosts will be consigned to hell.

devil ray any of several large fish, rays of the genera *Manta* and *Mobula*, in which two "horns" project forward from the sides of the huge mouth. These flaps of skin guide the plankton on which the fishes feed into the mouth. The largest of these rays can be 23 ft/7 m across, and weigh 2,200 lb/1,000 kg. They live in warm seas.

Devil's Island (French *Île du Diable*) smallest of the Îles du Salut, off French Guiana, 27 mi/43 km NW of Cayenne. The group of islands was collectively and popularly known by the name Devil's Island and formed a penal colony notorious for its terrible conditions.

Alfred ◊Dreyfus was imprisoned here 1895–99. Political prisoners were held on Devil's Island, and dangerous criminals on St Joseph, where they were subdued by solitary confinement in tiny cells or subterranean cages. The largest island, Royale, now has a tracking station for the French rocket site at Kourou.

devil wind minor form of ◊tornado, usually occurring in fine weather; formed from rising thermals of warm air (as is a ◊cyclone). A fire creates a similar updraft.

A fire devil or firestorm may occur in oil-refinery fires, or in the firebombings of cities, for example Dresden, Germany, in World War II.

Devolution, War of war waged unsuccessfully 1667–68 by Louis XIV of France to gain Spanish territory in the Netherlands, of which ownership had allegedly "devolved" on his wife Maria Theresa.

During the course of the war the French marshal Turenne (1611–75) conducted a series of seiges. An alliance of England, Sweden, and the Netherlands threatened intervention, so peace was made at Aix-la-Chapelle.

Devon or *Devonshire* county in SW England

area 2,594 sq mi/6,720 sq km

towns Exeter (administrative headquarters), Plymouth; resorts: Paignton, Torquay, Teignmouth, and Ilfracombe

features rivers: Dart, Exe, Tamar; National Parks: Dartmoor, Exmoor

products mainly agricultural, with sheep and dairy farming; cider and clotted cream; kaolin in the S; Honiton lace; Dartington glass

population (1987) 1,010,000

famous people Francis Drake, John Hawkins, Charles Kingsley, Robert F Scott.

Devonian period of geologic time 408–360 million years ago, the fourth period of the Paleozoic era. Many desert sandstones from North America and Europe date from this time. The first land plants flourished in the Devonian period, corals were abundant in the seas, amphibians evolved from air-breathing fish, and insects developed on land.

The name comes from the county of Devon in SW England, where Devonian rocks were first studied.

Devonshire, 8th Duke of see ◊Hartington, Spencer Compton Cavendish, British politician.

devotio moderna movement of revived religious spirituality which emerged in the Netherlands at the end of the 14th century and spread into the rest of W Europe. Its emphasis was on individual, rather than communal, devotion, including the private reading of religious works.

Its followers were drawn from the laity, including women, and clergy. Lay followers formed themselves into associations known as Brethren of the Common Life. Among its followers was Thomas à Kempis (c. 1380–1471), author of *Imitatio Christi*.

De Vries Hugo 1848–1935. Dutch botanist who conducted important research on osmosis in plant cells and was a pioneer in the study of plant evolution. His work led to the rediscovery of ◊Mendel's laws and the discovery of spontaneously occurring ◊mutations.

devsirme a levy of one in four males aged 10–20 taken by the Ottoman rulers of their Balkan provinces. All were brought to Constantinople and converted to Islam before being trained for the army or the civil service. This practice lasted from the 14th to the mid-17th centuries.

dew precipitation in the form of moisture that collects on the ground. It forms after the temperature of the ground has fallen below the ◊dew point of the air in contact with the ground. As the temperature falls during the night, the air and its water vapor become chilled, and condensation takes place on the cooled surfaces.

When moisture begins to form, the surrounding air is said to have reached its dew point. If the temperature falls below freezing point during the night, the dew will freeze, or if the temperature is low and the dew point is below freezing point, the water vapor condenses directly into ice; in both cases hoar frost is formed.

Dewar James 1842–1923. Scottish chemist and physicist who invented the vacuum flask (Thermos) 1872, during his research into the properties of matter at extremely low temperatures.

de Wet Christiaan Rudolf 1854–1922. Boer general and politician. He served in the South African Wars 1880 and 1899. When World War I began, he headed a pro-German uprising of 12,000 Afrikaners but was defeated, convicted of treason, and imprisoned.

Dewey George 1837–1917. US naval officer. A specialist in naval administration, he was named chief of the Bureau of Equipment 1889 and of the Board of Inspection and Survey 1895. As commodore, Dewey was dispatched to the Pacific 1896. He destroyed the Spanish fleet in Manila harbor at the outbreak of the Spanish-American War 1898. Dewey was promoted to the rank of admiral of the navy (the highest naval rank ever awarded) 1899 and retired from active service 1900.

Born in Montpelier, Vermont, and educated at the US Naval Academy, Dewey saw action on the Mississippi river and in the blockade of Southern ports during the Civil War.

Dewey John 1859–1952. US philosopher who believed that the exigencies of a democratic and industrial society demanded new educational techniques. He expounded his ideas in numerous writings, including *School and Society* 1899, and founded a progressive school in Chicago. A ◊pragmatist thinker, influenced by William James, Dewey maintained that there is only the reality of experience and made "inquiry" the essence of logic.

He was born in Vermont and from 1904 was professor of philosophy at Columbia University, New York.

Dewey Melvil 1851–1931. US librarian. In 1876, he devised the Dewey decimal system of classification for accessioning, storing, and retrieving books, widely used in libraries.

The system uses the numbers 000 to 999 to designate the major fields of knowledge, then breaks these down into more specific subjects by the use of decimals. Dewey founded the American Library Association 1876 and the first school of library science, at Columbia University, 1887.

Dewey Thomas Edmund 1902–1971. US public official. Born in Owosso, Michigan, Dewey received a law degree from Columbia University 1925. He was appointed chief assistant to the US attorney in the Southern District of New York 1931. He gained a reputation as a crime fighter while serving as special investigator of organized crime 1935–37. He was Manhattan district attorney 1937–38 and served as governor of New York 1942–54. Dewey was twice the Republican presidential candidate, losing to F D Roosevelt 1944 and to Truman 1948, the latter race being considered one of the greatest electoral upsets in US history.

dew point the temperature at which the water vapor in the air is saturated. At temperatures below the dew point, water vapor condenses out of the air as droplets, which if small form a suspension as mist or fog, or if larger become deposited on objects on or near the ground as ◊dew.

Dhaka or ***Dacca*** capital of Bangladesh from 1971, in Dhaka region, W of the river Meghna; population (1984) 3,600,000. It trades in jute, oilseed, sugar, and tea and produces textiles, chemicals, glass, and metal products.

history A former French, Dutch, and English trading post, Dhaka became capital of East Pakistan 1947; it was handed over to Indian troops Dec 1971 to become capital of the new country of Bangladesh.

dharma (Sanskrit "justice, order") in Hinduism, the consciousness of forming part of an ordered universe, and hence the moral duty of accepting one's station in life. In Buddhism, dharma is anything that increases generosity and wisdom, and so leads toward enlightenment.

For Hindus, correct performance of dharma has

a favorable effect on their karma; this may enable them to be reborn to a higher caste or on a higher plane of existence, thus coming closer to the final goal of liberation from the cycle of reincarnation.

Dhaulagiri mountain in the ◊Himalayas of W central Nepal, rising to 26,811 ft/8,172 m.

Dhofar mountainous western province of ◊Oman, on the border with South Yemen; population (1982) 40,000. South Yemen supported guerrilla activity here in the 1970s, while Britain and Iran supported the government's military operations. The capital is Salalah, which has a port at Rasut.

dhole wild dog *Cuon alpinus* found in Asia from Siberia to Java. With head and body up to 3 ft/1 m long, variable in color but often reddish above and lighter below, the dhole lives in groups of from 3 to 30 individuals. The species is becoming rare and is protected in some areas.

Dholes can chase prey for long distances; a pack is capable of pulling down deer and cattle as well as smaller prey. They are even known to have attacked tigers and leopards.

diabase an igneous rock formed below the Earth's surface, a form of basalt, containing relatively little silica (basic in composition).

Dolerite is a medium-grained (hypabyssal) basalt and forms in minor intrusions, such as dykes, which cut across the rock strata, and sills, which push between beds of sedimentary rock. When exposed at the surface, diabase weathers into spherical lumps.

diabetes the disease *diabetes mellitus* in which a disorder of the islets of Langerhans in the ◊pancreas prevents the body producing the hormone ◊insulin, so that sugars cannot be used properly. Treatment is by strict dietary control and oral or injected insulin.

Sugar, therefore, accumulates first in the blood, then in the urine. The patient experiences thirst, weight loss, and copious voiding, along with degenerative changes in the capillary system. Without treatment, the patient may go blind, ulcerate, lapse into diabetic coma, and die. Early-onset diabetes tends to be more severe than that developing in later years. Before the discovery of insulin by ◊Banting and ◊Best, severe diabetics did not survive. Today, it is seldom fatal. A continuous infusion of insulin can be provided via a catheter implanted under the skin, which is linked to an electric pump. This more accurately mimics the body's natural secretion of insulin than injections or oral doses, and can provide better control of diabetes. It is, however, very dangerous if the pump should malfunction.

Much rarer, *diabetes insipidus* is due to a deficiency of a hormone secreted by the ◊pituitary gland to regulate the body's water balance. It is controlled by hormone therapy. In 1989, it was estimated that 4% of the world's population had diabetes, and that there were 12 million sufferers in Canada and the US.

diagenesis or ***lithification*** in geology, the physical and chemical changes by which a sediment becomes a ◊sedimentary rock. The main processes involved include compaction of the grains, and the cementing of the grains together by the growth of new minerals deposited by percolating groundwater.

Diaghilev Sergei Pavlovich 1872–1929. Russian ballet impresario, who in 1909 founded the Ballets Russes (headquarters in Monaco), which he directed for 20 years. Through this company he brought Russian ballet to the West, introducing and encouraging a dazzling array of dancers, choreographers, and composers, such as Pavlova, Nijinsky, Fokine, Massine, Balanchine, Stravinsky, and Prokofiev.

dialect a variation of a spoken language shared by those in a particular area or a particular social group or both.

The term is used both objectively, to indicate a geographical area ("northern dialects") or social group ("black dialect"), and subjectively, in a judgmental and sometimes dismissive way. In the latter case, the standard language of a community is not seen as a dialect itself, but as the proper form of that language, dialects being considered in some way corrupt. This is a matter of social attitude, not of linguistic study.

diagenesis

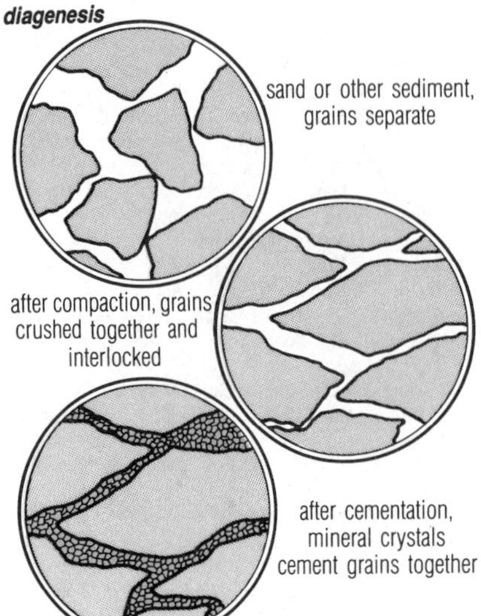
sand or other sediment, grains separate
after compaction, grains crushed together and interlocked
after cementation, mineral crystals cement grains together

dialectic a Greek term, originally associated with the philosopher Socrates' method of argument through dialogue and conversation. Hegelian dialectic refers to an interpretive method in which the contradiction between a thesis and its antithesis is resolved through synthesis.

dialectical materialism the political, philosophical, and economic theory of the 19th-century German thinkers Marx and Engels, also known as ◊Marxism.

Dial, The 1840–44 US magazine of transcendentalism, founded in Boston by several of the transcendentalist group, including Margaret Fuller (1810–1850) and Ralph Waldo Emerson, its first and second editors respectively. Publishing Thoreau and other major essayists and poets, it had great intellectual influence. Several later magazines used the same title. *The Dial* of the 1920s published modern poetry and criticism under Marianne Moore's editorship.

dialysis in medicine, the process used to mimic the effects of the kidneys. It may be life-saving in some types of poisoning. Dialysis is usually performed to compensate for failing kidneys; there are two main methods, hemodialysis and peritoneal dialysis.

In hemodialysis, the patient's blood is passed through a pump, where it is separated from sterile dialysis fluid by a semipermeable membrane. This allows any toxic substances which have built up in the blood stream, and which would normally be secreted by the kidneys, to diffuse out of the blood into the dialysis fluid. The red and white blood cells, however, are maintained in the circulation by the membrane. Hemodialysis is very expensive and requires the patient to attend a specialized unit.

Peritoneal dialysis uses one of the body's natural semipermeable membranes for the same purpose. About two liters of dialysis fluid is slowly instilled into the peritoneal cavity of the abdomen, and drained out again, over about two hours. During that time toxins from the blood diffuse into the peritoneal cavity across the peritoneal membrane. The advantage of peritoneal dialysis is that the patient can walk around while the dialysis is proceeding—this is known as continuous ambulatory peritoneal dialysis (CAPD).

In the long term dialysis is expensive and debilitating, and transplant is now the treatment of choice for patients in chronic kidney failure.

diamond a generally colorless, transparent mineral, the hard crystalline form of carbon. It is regarded as a precious gemstone, and is the hardest natural substance known (10 on the ◊Mohs' scale). Industrial diamonds are used for cutting, grinding, and polishing.

Diamond crystallizes in the cubic system as octahedral crystals, some with curved faces and striations. The high refractive index of 2.42 and the high dispersion of light, or "fire," account for the spectral displays seen in cut diamonds.

Diamonds were known before 3000 BC and until their discovery in Brazil in 1725, India was the principal source of supply. Present sources are Angola, Ghana, Guyana, Sierra Leone, South Africa, Namibia, Tanzania, and Yakut (USSR); Brazil and Zaïre are noted for industrial diamonds. In 1885 there were 42 diamond mining communities in South Africa, by 1890 only one, De Beers Consolidated.

Diamonds may be found as alluvial diamonds on or close to the Earth's surface in riverbeds or dried watercourses; on the sea bottom (off W Africa); or, more commonly, in volcanic pipes composed of "blue ground" or ◊kimberlite, where the original matrix has penetrated the Earth's crust from great depths. They are sorted from the residue of washed ground by X-ray. Natural diamonds may be exhausted by the year 2000 unless new deposits are found.

There are four chief varieties of diamond: well-crystallized transparent stones, colorless or only slightly tinted, valued as gems; bort, poorly crystallized or inferior diamonds; balas, an industrial variety, extremely hard and tough; and carbonado, or industrial diamond, also called black diamond or carbon, which is opaque, black or gray, and very tough. Industrial diamonds (20 metric tonnes per annum) are also produced synthetically from graphite.

Because diamonds act as perfectly transparent windows and do not absorb infrared radiation, they were used aboard NASA space probes to Venus in 1978. The tungsten-carbide tools used in steel mills are cut with industrial diamond tools.

Rough diamonds are dull or greasy before being cut, and only 20% are suitable as gems. Diamond gemstones are valued by weight (◊carat), cut (highlighting the stone's optical properties), color, and clarity (on a six-point scale from P or "pique," showing a flaw visible to the naked eye, to FL, or "flawless"). They are cut by the use of diamond dust. The two most frequent forms of cut gem diamonds are the brilliant, for thicker stones, and the rose, for shallower ones. By 1980 India was on the way to replacing Antwerp and Tel Aviv as the world's chief cutting and polishing centers.

Noted diamonds include the Cullinan, or Star of Africa (3,106 carats, over 17.5 oz/500 g before cutting, South Africa, 1905); Excelsior (995.2 carats, South Africa, 1893); and Star of Sierra Leone (968.9 carats, Yengema, 1972).

Diamond v Chakrabarty a US Supreme Court decision 1980 that defined human-engineered microorganisms as patentable products.

diamorphine technical term for ◊heroin.

Diana in Roman mythology, goddess of chastity, hunting, and the moon (Greek ◊Artemis), daughter of Jupiter and twin of Apollo.

Diana Princess of Wales 1961– . The daughter of the 8th Earl Spencer, she married Prince Charles at St Paul's Cathedral, London 1981, the first English bride of a royal heir since 1659. She is descended from the only sovereigns from whom Prince Charles is not descended, Charles II and James II.

DIANE (acronym from direct information access network for Europe) the collection of information suppliers or "hosts" for the European computer network.

dianetics a form of psychotherapy developed by the American science-fiction writer L Ron Hubbard (1911–1986), which formed the basis for ◊scientology. Hubbard believed that all mental illness and certain forms of physical illness are caused by "engrams," or incompletely assimilated traumatic experiences, both pre- and postnatal. These engrams can be confronted during therapy with an auditor and thus exorcised. An individual free from engrams would be a "Clear" and perfectly healthy.

Hubbard later expanded this theory: behind each mind is a nonphysical and immortal being, the Thetan, which has forgotten its true nature and is therefore trapped in a cycle of reincarnation, accumulating engrams with each lifetime. If these engrams are cleared, the individual will become an Operating Thetan, with quasi-miraculous powers.

During the 1970s and 80s the Church of Scientology was accused of having taken on a cultlike character and of financial duplicity.

diapause a period of suspended delayed development or growth that occurs in some species of insects and other invertebrates, characterized by greatly reduced metabolism. Periods of diapause are often timed to coincide with the winter months, and improve the animal's chances of surviving adverse conditions.

diaphragm a barrier contraceptive that is inserted into the vagina and fits over the cervix (neck of the uterus), preventing sperm from entering the uterus. For it to be effective, a ◊spermicide must be used and the diaphragm left in place for 6–8 hours after intercourse. This method is 97% effective if practiced correctly.

In the US, diaphragms are prescribed by physicians who fit them for size; they may then be purchased in drug stores or at clinics.

diaphragm muscular sheet separating the thorax from the abdomen in mammals. Its rhythmical movements affect the size of the thorax and cause the pressure changes within the lungs that result in breathing.

The diaphragm muscle is under both voluntary and involuntary (automatic) control. Skilled divers can voluntarily hold their breath for up to five minutes, overriding the normal breathing cycles that we barely notice in day-to-day living.

diarrhea excessive action of the bowels so that the feces are fluid or semifluid. It is caused by intestinal irritants (including some drugs and poisons), infection with harmful organisms (as in dysentery, salmonella, or cholera), or allergies.

Diarrhea is the biggest killer of children in the world. The World Health Organization estimates that 4.5 million children die each year from dehydration as a result of diarrheal disease in Third World countries. It can be treated by giving an accurately measured aqueous solution of salt and glucose by mouth in large quantities (salt water with sugar, to restore the electrolyte balance in the blood). Since most diarrhea is viral in origin, antibiotics are ineffective.

diary an informal record of day-to-day events, observations, or reflections, usually not intended for a general readership. One of the earliest diaries extant is that of a Japanese noblewoman, the *Kagerō Nikki* 954–974, and the earliest diary extant in English is that of Edward VI (ruled 1547–53). Notable diaries include those of Samuel Pepys, the writer John Evelyn, the Quaker George Fox, and in the 20th century those of Anne ◊Frank and the writers André Gide and Katherine Mansfield.

Diaspora the dispersal of the Jews, initially from Palestine after the Babylonian conquest 586 BC, and then following the Roman sack of Jerusalem AD 70 and their crushing of the Jewish revolt of 135. The term has come to refer to all the Jews living outside Israel.

diathermy the generation of heat in body tissues by the passage of high-frequency electric currents between two electrodes placed on the body, used in diathermic surgery and to relieve arthritic pain.

In diathermic surgery, one electrode is very much reduced for cutting purposes and the other correspondingly enlarged and placed at a distance on the body. The high-frequency current produces, at the tip of the cutting electrode, sufficient heat to cut tissues, or to coagulate and kill tissue cells, with a minimum of bleeding.

***diatom** Diatoms form a fundamental part of the food chain of both marine and freshwater environments.*

diatom microscopic alga of the division Bacillariophyta found in all parts of the world. They consist of single cells, sometimes grouped in colonies.

The cell wall is made up of two overlapping valves known as frustules, which are usually impregnated with silica, and which fit together like the lid and body of a pillbox. Diatomaceous earths (diatomite) are made up of the valves of fossil diatoms, and are used in the manufacture of dynamite and in the rubber and plastics industries.

diatomic molecule molecule composed of two identical atoms joined together, such as oxygen (O_2).

diatonic in music, a scale consisting of the seven notes of any major or minor key.

Diaz Bartolomeu c. 1450–1500. Portuguese explorer, the first European to reach the Cape of Good Hope 1488, and to establish a route around Africa. He drowned during an expedition with Pedro ◊Cabral.

Díaz Porfirio 1830–1915. Dictator of Mexico 1877–80 and 1884–1911. After losing the 1876 election, he overthrew the government and seized power. He was supported by conservative landowners and foreign capitalists, who invested in railroads and mines. He centralized the state at the expense of the peasants and Indians, and dismantled all local and regional leadership. He faced mounting and revolutionary opposition in his final years and was forced into exile 1911.

Diaz de Solís Juan 1471–c. 1516. Spanish explorer in South America, who reached the estuary of the River Plate and was killed and eaten by cannibals.

Dick Philip K(endred) 1928–1982. US science-fiction writer, whose works often deal with religion and the subjectivity of reality; his novels include *The Man in the High Castle* 1962 and *Do Androids Dream of Electric Sheep?* 1968.

Dickens Charles 1812–1870. English novelist, popular for his memorable characters and his portrayal of the social evils of Victorian England. In 1836 he published the first number of the *Pickwick Papers*, followed by *Oliver Twist* 1838, the first of his "reforming" novels; *Nicholas Nickleby* 1839; *Barnaby Rudge* 1840; *The Old Curiosity Shop* 1841; and *David Copperfield* 1849. Among his later books are *A Tale of Two Cities* 1859 and *Great Expectations* 1861.

Born in Portsea, Hampshire, England, the son of a clerk, Dickens received little formal education, although a short period spent working in a blacking factory in S London, while his father was imprisoned for debt in the Marshalsea prison during 1824, was followed by three years in a private school. In 1827 he became a lawyer's clerk, and then after four years a reporter for the *Morning Chronicle*, to which he contributed the *Sketches by Boz*. In 1836 he married Catherine Hogarth, three days after the publication of the first number of the *Pickwick Papers*. Originally intended merely as an accompaniment to a series of sporting illustrations, the adventures of Pickwick outgrew their setting and established Dickens' reputation.

***Dickens** English novelist Charles Dickens.*

In 1842 he visited the US, where his attack on the pirating of English books by American publishers chilled his welcome; his experiences are reflected in *American Notes* and *Martin Chuzzlewit* 1843. In 1843 he published the first of his Christmas books, *A Christmas Carol*, followed in 1844 by *The Chimes*, written in Genoa during his first long sojourn abroad, and in 1845 by the even more successful *Cricket on the Hearth*. A venture as editor of the Liberal *Daily News* in 1846 was short-lived, and *Dombey and Son* 1848 was largely written abroad. *David Copperfield*, his most popular novel, appeared 1849 and contains many autobiographical incidents and characters.

Returning to journalism, Dickens inaugurated the weekly magazine *Household Words* 1850, reorganizing it 1859 as *All the Year Round*; many of his later stories were published serially in these periodicals.

In 1857 Dickens met the actress Ellen Ternan and in 1858 agreed with his wife on a separation; his sister-in-law remained with him to care for his children. In 1858 he began giving public readings from his novels, which proved such a success that he was invited to make a second US tour 1867. Among his later novels are *Bleak House* 1853, *Hard Times* 1854, *Little Dorrit* 1857, and *Our Mutual Friend* 1864. *Edwin Drood*, a mystery story influenced by the style of his friend Wilkie ◊Collins, was left incomplete on his death.

Dickinson Emily Elizabeth 1830–1886. US poet. Dickinson wrote most of her poetry between 1850 and the late 1860s and was particularly prolific during the Civil War years, when she lived at home in Amherst, Massachusetts, in seclusion. She experimented with poetic rhythms, rhymes, and forms, as well as language and syntax. Her work is characterized by a wittiness and boldness that seem to contrast sharply with the quiet, reclusive life she led.

Born in Amherst, she lived in near seclusion there after 1862. Almost none of her many short, mystical poems were published during her lifetime, since many of those who read her poems failed to recognize their greatness, and she was discouraged from publishing. Her concentrated, brilliant work has become well known only in the 20th century. Dickinson also carried on lengthy correspondences with a number of friends and acquaintances, and many of her letters are extraordinary artistic achievements in themselves. The first collection of her poetry, *Poems by Emily Dickinson* was published 1890.

Dick-Read Grantly 1890–1959. British gynecologist. In private practice in London 1923–48, he

Dickens, major works

title	*date*	*well-known characters*
The Pickwick Papers	1837	Mr Pickwick, Sam Weller, Mr Snodgrass, Mr Jingle, Mrs Bardell
Oliver Twist	1838	Oliver Twist, Fagin, Mr Bumble, Dodger
Nicholas Nickelby	1839	Nicholas Nickelby, Mr Squeers, Madame Manatalini, Smike
The Old Curiosity Shop	1841	Dick Swiveler, Little Nell, Daniel Quilip
Barnaby Rudge	1841	Simon Tappertit (Sim), Miggs, Gashford
A Christmas Carol	1843	Ebenezer Scrooge
Martin Chuzzlewit	1844	Martin Chuzzlewit (Junior), Mr Pecksniff, Mrs Gamp, Tom Pinch
Dombey and Son	1848	Paul Dombey, Edith Dombey, Mr James Carket, Major Bagstock, Mrs Skewton, Mr Toots
David Copperfield	1850	Mr Micawber, Mr Dick, Uriah Heap, Little Em'ly, David Copperfield
Bleak House	1853	John Jarndyce, Esther Summerson, Mr Turveydrop, Lady Dedlock, Mrs Jellyby
Hard Times	1854	Gradgrind, Tom and Louisa Gradgrind, Josiah Bounderby, Bitzer, "Sissy" Jupe
Little Dorrit	1857	Amy Dorrit, Flora Finching, Mr Merille
A Tale of Two Cities	1859	Dr Manette, Charles Darnay, Sydney Carton, Jerry Cruncher, Madame Defarge
Great Expectations	1861	Pip, Estella, Miss Havisham, Joe Gargery, Wemmick, Magwitch
Our Mutual Friend	1865	Noddy, Silas Wegg, Mr Podsnap, Betty Higden, Bradley Headstone, Reginald Wilfer
The Mystery of Edward Drood (unfinished)	1870	Rosa Budd, John Jasper

developed the concept of natural childbirth: that by the elimination of fear and tension, labor pain could be minimized and anesthetics, which can be hazardous to both mother and child, rendered unnecessary.

dicotyledon a major subdivision of the ◊angiosperms, containing the great majority of flowering plants. Dicotyledons are characterized by the presence of two seed leaves, or ◊cotyledons, in the embryo, which is usually surrounded by an ◊endosperm. They generally have broad leaves with netlike veins.

Dicotyledons may be small plants such as the daisy and buttercup, shrubs such as the blueberry, or trees such as oak and birch. The other subdivision of the angiosperms is the ◊monocotyledons.

dictatorship the term or office of an absolute ruler, overriding the constitution. (In ancient Rome a dictator was a magistrate invested with emergency powers for six months.) Although dictatorships were common in Latin America during the 19th century, the only European example during this period was the rule of Napoleon III. The crises following World War I produced many dictatorships, including the regimes of Atatürk and Piłsudski (nationalist); Mussolini, Hitler, Primo de Rivera, Franco, and Salazar (all right-wing); and Stalin (Communist).

dictatorship of the proletariat Marxist term for a revolutionary dictatorship established during the transition from capitalism to ◊communism after a Socialist revolution.

dictionary book that contains a selection of the words of a language, with their pronunciations and meanings, usually arranged in alphabetical order. The term *dictionary* is also applied to any usually alphabetic work of reference containing specialized information about a particular subject, art, or science; for example, a dictionary of music. Language dictionaries provide translations of one country's language into another.

The first dictionaries of English (*glossa collectae*) served to explain difficult words, generally of Latin or Greek origin, in everyday English. Samuel Johnson's dictionary of 1755 was one of the first dictionaries of standard English, and the first to give extensive coverage to phrasal verbs. Noah Webster's *An American Dictionary of the English Language* 1828 quickly became a standard reference work throughout North America. The many-volume *Oxford English Dictionary*, begun 1884 and subject to continuous revision (and now computerization), provides a detailed historical record of each word and, therefore, the English language.

Diderot Denis 1713–1784. French philosopher. He is closely associated with the Enlightenment, the European intellectual movement for social and scientific progress, and was editor of the ◊*Encyclopédie* 1751–1780. This work exerted an enormous influence on contemporary social thinking with its materialism and anticlericalism. Its compilers were known as Encyclopédistes.

Diderot's materialism, most articulately expressed in *D'Alembert's Dream*, published after Diderot's death, sees the natural world as nothing more than matter and motion. His account of the origin and development of life is purely mechanical.

history of English dictionaries

10th century Byzantine *Lexicon* of Suidas (first A–Z).
1225 John Garland used the term *dictionarus*.
1530 The first English–English dictionary appeared (appendix to William Temple's *Pentateuch*).
1538 Thomas Elyot's *Shorte Dictionarie for Yonge Begynners* (English–Latin) was published.
16th century The first vernacular–vernacular dictionaries were prepared by William Salesbury, Welsh–English 1547, and John Florio, Italian–English 1599.
1604 Robert Cawdrey's *Table Alphabeticall of hard usuall English wordes* aimed at converting Latin to Latinate English.
1755 Samuel Johnson's dictionary of standard English appeared.
1828 Noah Webster published *An American Dictionary of the English Language.*
1852 Peter Mark Roget's *Thesaurus of English Words* was published.
1884 The *Oxford English Dictionary* was begun.

Didion Joan 1934– . US author and journalist. She is known for her terse yet eloquent views of modern American society, especially California, where she grew up. Her works include the essays *Slouching toward Bethlehem* 1968 and *The White Album* 1979 and the novels *Run River* 1963, *Play It As It Lays* 1970, *A Book of Common Prayer* 1977, and *Democracy* 1984, which depict the cultural disintegration of modern life. She reported on current events in *Salvador* 1983 and the state of affairs in the city in *Miami* 1987.

Dido Phoenician princess, legendary founder of Carthage, North Africa, who committed suicide to avoid marrying a local prince. In the Latin epic *Aeneid*, Virgil claims that it was because ◊Aeneas deserted her.

diecasting form of ◊casting in which molten metal is injected into permanent metal molds or dies.

Diefenbaker John George 1895–1979. Canadian Progressive Conservative politician, prime minister 1957–63. In 1958, seeking to increase his majority in the House of Commons, Diefenbaker called for new elections; his party won the largest majority in Canadian history. In 1963, however, Diefenbaker refused to accept atomic warheads for missiles supplied by the US, and the Progressive Conservative Party was ousted after losing a no-confidence vote in parliament.

Born in Ontario, he became head of the Progressive Conservative Party in 1956 and prime minister in 1957.

Diego Garcia island in the ◊Chagos Archipelago, named after its Portuguese discoverer in 1532. See ◊British Indian Ocean Territory.

dielectric a substance (an insulator such as ceramic, rubber, or glass) capable of supporting electric stress. The dielectric constant, or relative permittivity, of a substance is the ratio of the capacitance of a capacitor with the substance as dielectric to that of a similar capacitor in which the dielectric is replaced by a vacuum.

Diels Otto 1876–1954. German chemist. In 1950 he and his former assistant, Kurt Alder (1902–1958), were jointly awarded the Nobel Prize for Chemistry for their research into synthesis of organic chemical compounds.

Diemen Anthony van 1593–1645. Dutch admiral. In 1636 he was appointed governor general of Dutch settlements in the E Indies, and wrested Ceylon and Malacca from the Portuguese. In 1636 and 1642 he supervised expeditions to Australia, on the second of which the navigator Abel Tasman discovered land not charted by Europeans and named it Van Diemen's Land, now Tasmania.

Dien Bien Phu, Battle of decisive battle in the ◊Indochina War at a French fortress in North Vietnam, near the Laotian border. French troops were besieged March 13–May 7, 1954 by the Communist Vietminh. The fall of Dien Bien Phu resulted in the end of French control of Indochina.

Dieppe channel port at the mouth of the river Arques, Seine-Maritime *département*, N France; population (1983) 39,500. There are ferry services from its harbor to Newhaven and else-

Diderot *A portrait, by L M Loo, of the French philosopher and encyclopedist Denis Diderot. His account of the origin and nature of life anticipated evolutionary theories.*

where; industries include fishing, shipbuilding, and pharmaceuticals.

Diesel Rudolf 1858–1913. German engineer who patented the diesel engine. He began his career as a refrigerator engineer and, like many engineers of the period, sought to develop a more efficient power source than the conventional steam engine. Able to operate with greater efficiency and economy, the diesel engine soon found a ready market.

diesel engine ◊internal combustion engine that burns a lightweight fuel oil. The diesel engine operates by compressing air until it becomes sufficiently hot to ignite the fuel. They are piston-in-cylinder engines, like the ◊gasoline engine, but just air (rather than an air-and-fuel mixture) is taken into the cylinder on the first piston stroke (down). The piston moves up and compresses the air until it is at a very high temperature. The fuel oil is then injected into the hot air, where it burns, driving the piston down on its power stroke. For this reason the engine is called a compression-ignition engine.

The principle was first explained in England by Herbert Akroyd (1864–1937) in 1890, and applied practically by Rudolf Diesel in Germany 1892.

diet a particular selection of food, or the overall intake and selection of food for a particular person or people. A special diet may be recommended for medical reasons, to balance, limit, or increase certain nutrients; undertaken to lose weight, by a reduction in calorie intake or selection of specific foods; or observed on religious, moral, or emotional grounds. An adequate diet is one that fulfills the body's nutritional requirements and gives an energy intake proportional to the person's activity level (the average daily requirement is 2,400 calories for men, less for women, more for active chidren). In the Third World and in famine or poverty areas some 450 million people must subsist on fewer than 1,500 calories per day, whereas in the developed countries the average daily intake is 3,300 calories.

different types of diet

diet	*particulars*
vegetarian	eat no meat
vegan	eat no food of animal origin
Hay system	do not mix protein with starches and fruits
macrobiotic	based on unrefined cereals
fruitarian	based on fruits, nuts, and seeds
Jewish	eat ◊kosher food
Muslim	eat ◊halal food
Hindu	vegetarian

diet a meeting or convention of the princes and other dignitaries of the Holy Roman (German) Empire, for example, the Diet of Worms 1521 which met to consider the question of Luther's doctrines and the governance of the empire under Charles V.

dietetics specialized branch of human nutrition, dealing with the promotion of health through the proper kinds and quantities of food.

Therapeutic dietetics has a large part to play in the treatment of certain illnesses, such as allergies, arthritis, and diabetes; it is sometimes used alone, but often in conjunction with drugs. See ◊food.

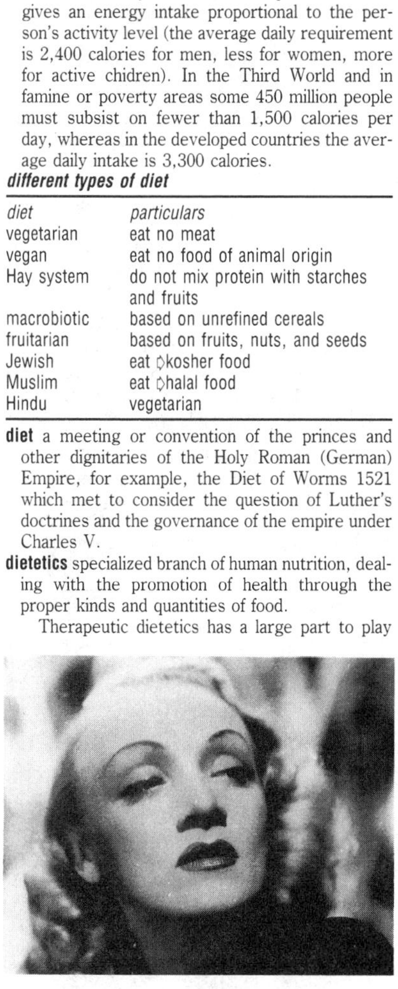

***Dietrich** Marlene Dietrich in* The Blue Angel *1930, the film that won her international fame.*

differential

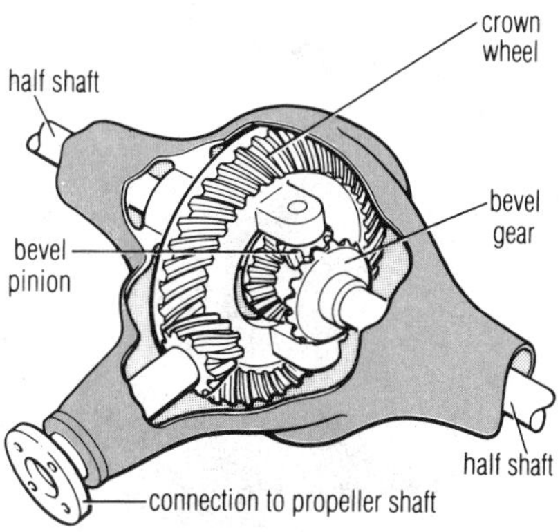
crown wheel
half shaft
bevel gear
bevel pinion
half shaft
connection to propeller shaft

Dietrich Marlene. Adopted name of Magdalene von Losch 1904– . German-born US actress and singer who first won fame by her appearance with Emil Jannings in both the German and American versions of the film *The Blue Angel* 1930. She stayed in Hollywood, becoming a US citizen in 1937. Her husky, sultry singing voice added to her appeal. Her other films include *Blonde Venus* 1932 and *Destry Rides Again* 1939, and *Just a Gigolo* 1978. She also starred in *Judgment at Nuremberg* 1961 and was the subject of Maximilian Schell's frank documentary *Marlene* 1983.

difference engine mechanical calculating machine designed, but never built, by the British mathematician Charles ◊Babbage in about 1830. It was to calculate mathematical functions by solving the differences between values given to ◊variables within equations. Babbage designed the calculator so that once the initial values for the variables were set it would produce the next few thousand values without error.

differential arrangement of gears in the final drive of a vehicle's transmission system that allows the driving wheels to turn at different speeds when cornering. The differential consists of sets of bevel gears and pinions within a cage attached to the crown wheel. When cornering, the bevel pinions rotate to allow the outer wheel to turn faster than the inner.

differential calculus a branch of ◊analysis involving the ◊differentiation of functions, with applications such as determination of maximum and minimum points and rates of change. See also ◊calculus, ◊integral calculus.

differentiation in mathematics, a procedure for determining the gradient of the tangent to a curve $f(x)$ at any point x. The first ◊derivative is usually expressed as dy/dx. Applications of this procedure are rates of change, maximum and minimum points. When a ◊function $f(x)$ is differentiated, the result is a derived function (or derivative) written $f'(x)$.

It may be regarded as the limit of the expression $[f(x + \delta x) - f(x)]/\delta x$ as δx tends to zero. Graphically, this is equivalent to the gradient (slope) of the curve represented by $y = f(x)$ at any point x.

differentiation

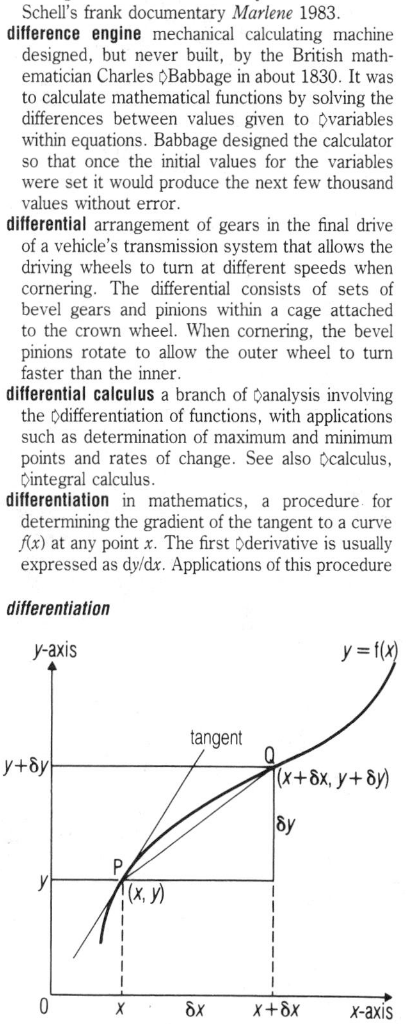
y-axis
y = f(x)
tangent
Q
y+δy
(x+δx, y+δy)
δy
P
y
(x, y)
0
x
δx
x+δx
x-axis

***diffraction** The diffraction effect is created by the use of a cross-screen filter and two polarizers.*

differentiation in embryology, the process whereby cells become increasingly different and specialized, giving rise to more complex structures that have particular functions in the adult organism. For instance, embryonic cells may develop into nerve, muscle, or bone cells.

diffraction the spreading of a wave motion (such as light or sound) as it passes an obstacle and expands into a region not exposed directly to incoming waves behind the obstacle. This accounts for interference phenomena observed at the edges of opaque objects, or discontinuities between different media in the path of a wave train. The phenomena give rise to slight spreading of light into colored bands at the shadow of a straight edge.

A diffraction grating is a plate of glass or metal ruled with close, equidistant parallel lines used for separating a wave train such as a beam of incident light into its component frequencies (white light results in a spectrum). The regular spacing of atoms in crystals are used to diffract X-rays, and in this way the structure of many substances has been elucidated, including recently that of proteins.

diffusion in physical chemistry, any of at least three processes: the spontaneous mixing of gases or liquids (classed together as fluids in scientific usage) when brought into contact without mechanical mixing or stirring; the spontaneous passage of fluids through membranes; and the spontaneous passage of dissolved materials both through the material in which they are dissolved and also through membranes.

One application is the separation of isotopes, particularly those of uranium. When uranium hexafluoride diffuses through a porous plate, the ratio of the 235 and 238 isotopes is changed slightly. With sufficient number of passages, the separation is nearly complete. There are large plants in the US and the UK for obtaining enriched fuel for fast nuclear reactors and the fissile uranium-235, originally required for the first atom bombs. Another application is the diffusion pump, used extensively in vacuum work, in which the gas to be evacuated diffuses into a chamber from which it is carried away by the vapor of a suitable medium, usually oil or mercury.

Digambara ("sky-clad") member of a sect of Jain monks (see ◊Jainism) who practice complete nudity.

digestion the process whereby food eaten by an animal is broken down physically and chemically by ◊enzymes, usually in the ◊stomach and ◊intestines, to make the nutrients available for absorption and cell metabolism.

In some single-celled organisms, such as amebas, a food particle is engulfed by the cell itself, and digested in a ◊vacuole within the cell.

digestive system the mouth, stomach, gut, and associated glands of animals, which are responsible for digesting food. The food is broken down by physical and chemical means in the ◊stomach; digestion is completed, and most nutrients are absorbed in the small intestine; what remains is stored and concentrated into feces in the large intestine. In birds, additional digestive organs are the ◊crop and ◊gizzard.

In smaller, simpler animals such as jellyfishes, the digestive system is simply a cavity (coelenteron or enteric cavity) with a "mouth" into which food is taken; the digestible portion is dissolved and absorbed in this cavity, and the remains are ejected back through the mouth.

Diggers also called true ◊Levelers. An English 17th-century radical sect that attempted to dig common land. It became prominent in April 1649 when, headed by Gerrard Winstanley (c. 1609–1660), it set up communal colonies near Cobham, Surrey, and elsewhere. These colonies were attacked by mobs and, being pacifists, the Diggers made no resistance. The support they attracted alarmed the government and they were dispersed 1650. Their ideas influenced the early ◊Quakers.

digit any of the numbers from 0 to 9. In computing, different numbering systems have different ranges of digits. For example, ◊hexadecimal has digits 0 to 9 and A to F, whereas binary has two digits (or ◊bits), 0 and 1.

digital in electronics and computing, a term meaning "coded as numbers." A digital system uses two-state, either on/off or high/low voltage pulses, to encode, receive, and transmit information. A digital display shows discrete values as numbers (as opposed to an analog signal, such as the continuous sweep of a pointer on a dial).

Digital electronics is the technology that underlies digital techniques. Low-power, miniature, integrated circuits (chips) provide the means for the coding, storage, transmission, processing, and reconstruction of information of all kinds.

digital audio tape (DAT) tape used to record sounds in digital or numerical form. During recording, the sound is sampled more than 30,000 times a second and the values recorded as numbers on the tape in a magnetic pattern. During playback, the numbers are reconverted to sounds. The system allows high-quality reproduction because unwanted noise can be eliminated electronically during recording and playback. In addition, the DAT is a compact medium, as a cassette the size of a credit card, can hold four hours of sound.

digital computer computing device that operates on a two-state system, using symbols that are internally coded as binary numbers (numbers made up of combinations of the digits 0 and 1); see ◊computer.

digital data transmission in computing, a way of sending data by converting all signals (whether pictures, sounds, or words) into numeric (normally binary) codes before transmission, then reconverting them on receipt. This virtually eliminates any distortion or degradation of the signal during transmission, storage, or processing.

digitalis plant of the genus *Digitalis* of the figwort family Scrophulariaceae, which includes the ◊foxgloves.

digitalis drug that increases the efficiency of the heart by strengthening its muscle contractions and slowing its rate. It is derived from the leaves of the common European woodland plant *Digitalis purpurea* (foxglove).

digestive system

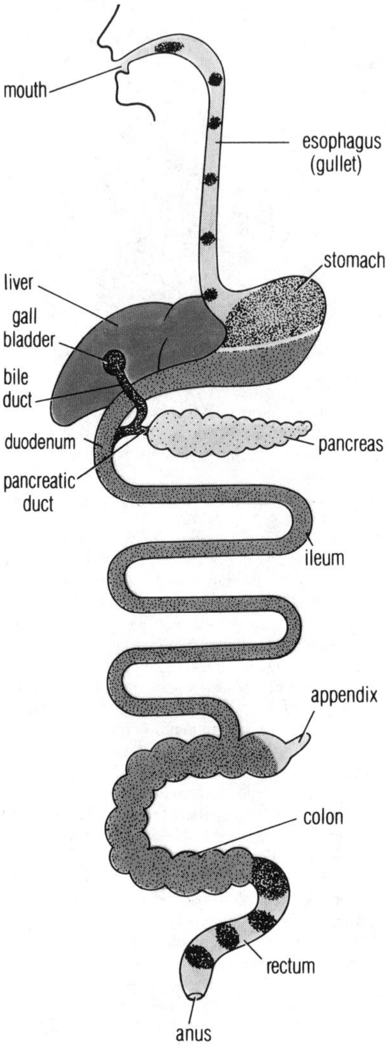
mouth
esophagus
(gullet)
stomach
liver
gall
bladder
bile
duct
duodenum
pancreas
pancreatic
duct
ileum
appendix
colon
rectum
anus

It is purified to digoxin, digitoxin, and lanatoside C, which are effective in cardiac regulation but induce the side effects of nausea, vomiting, and pulse irregularities. Pioneered in the late 1700s by William Withering, an English physician and botanist, digitalis was the first cardiac drug.

digital recording technique whereby the pressure of sound waves is sampled more than 30,000 times a second and the values recorded as numbers which, during playback, are reconverted to sound waves. This gives very high-quality reproduction. In digital recording the signals picked up by the microphone are converted into precise numerical values by computer. These values, which represent the original sound-wave form exactly, are recorded on compact disk. When this is played back by ◊laser, the exact values are retrieved. When the signal is fed via an amplifier to a loudspeaker, sound waves exactly like the original ones are reproduced.

digital sampling electronic process used in ◊telecommunications for transforming a constantly varying (analog) signal into one composed of discrete units, a digital signal. In the creation of recorded music, sampling enables the composer, producer, or remix engineer to borrow discrete vocal or instrumental parts from other recorded work (it is also possible to sample live sound).

A telephone microphone changes sound waves into an analog signal that fluctuates up and down like a wave. In the digitizing process the wave-

dik-dik

form is sampled thousands of times a second and each part of the sampled wave is given a ◊binary code number related to the height of the wave at that point, which is transmitted along the telephone line. Using digital signals, messages can be transmitted quickly, accurately and economically.

Dijon city and capital of Bourgogne (Burgundy), France; population (1983) 216,000. As well as metallurgical, chemical, and other industries, it has a wine trade and is famed for its mustard.

dik-dik any of several species of tiny antelope, genus *Madoqua*, found in Africa S of the Sahara in dry areas with scattered brush. Dik-diks are about 2 ft/60 cm long and 1.1 ft/35 cm tall, and often seen in pairs. Males have short, pointed horns. The dik-dik is so named because of its alarm call.

dilatation and curettage (D and C) common gynecological procedure in which the cervix (neck of the uterus) is widened (dilated), giving access so that the uterine lining can be scraped away (curettage). It may be carried out to terminate a pregnancy, treat an incomplete miscarriage, discover the cause of heavy menstrual bleeding, or for biopsy.

dill herb *Anethum graveolens* of the carrot family Umbelliferae, whose bitter seeds and aromatic leaves are used for culinary and medicinal purposes.

Dillinger John 1902–1934. US bank robber and murderer. In 1923 he was convicted of armed robbery and spent the next ten years in state prison. Released in 1933, he led a gang on a robbery spree throughout the Midwest, staging daring raids on police stations to obtain guns. Named "Public Enemy Number One" by the Federal Bureau of Investigation (FBI), Dillinger led the authorities on a long chase. He was finally betrayed by his mistress, the mysterious "Lady in Red," and was killed by FBI agents in Chicago as he left a movie theater.

Born in Indianapolis, Dillinger began a life of crime after deserting from the navy 1920.

Dilthey Wilhelm 1833–1911. German philosopher, a major figure in the interpretive tradition of ◊hermeneutics. He argued that the "human sciences" (*Geisteswissenschaften*) could not employ the same methods as the natural sciences but must use the procedure of "understanding" (*Verstehen*) to grasp

flower
seed
head
seed

the inner life of an alien culture or past historical period. Thus Dilthey extended the significance of hermeneutics far beyond the interpretation of texts to the whole of human history and culture.

DiMaggio Joe 1914– . US baseball player with the New York Yankees 1936–51. In 1941 he set a record by getting hits in 56 consecutive games. He was an outstanding fielder, played center field, hit 361 home runs, and had a career average of .325. He was married to the actress Marilyn Monroe. He was elected to the Baseball Hall of Fame.

dime novel melodramatic paperback novel of a series started in the US in the 1850s, published by Beadle and Adams of New York, which frequently dealt with Deadwood Dick and his frontier adventures. Authors included Edward L Wheeler, E Z C Judson, Prentiss Ingraham, and J R Coryell. The "Nick Carter" Library added detective stories to the genre. Like British "penny dreadfuls," dime novels attained massive sales and were popular with troops during the American Civil War and World War I.

Today's mass-market paperbacks continue to serve readers of Westerns, Mystery, Science Fiction, Romance, and Detective fiction that grew out of the dime-novel concept.

dimension any directly measurable physical quantity such as mass (M), length (L) and time (T) and the derived units obtainable by multiplication or division from such quantities. For example, acceleration (the rate of change of velocity) has dimensions (LT^{-2}), and is expressed in such units as km s^{-2}. A quantity that is a ratio, such as relative density or humidity, is dimensionless.

dimethyl sulfoxide (DMSO) $(CH_3)_2SO$ colorless liquid used as an industrial solvent and an antifreeze. It is obtained as a byproduct of the processing of wood to paper.

diminishing returns, law of in economics, the principle that additional application of one factor of production, such as an extra machine or employee, at first results in rapidly increasing output but then eventually yields declining returns, unless other factors are modified to sustain the increase.

Dimitrov Georgi 1882–1949. Bulgarian communist, prime minister from 1946. He was elected a deputy in 1913 and from 1919 was a member of the executive of the Comintern, an international communist organization (see the ◊International). In 1933 he was arrested in Berlin and tried with others in Leipzig for allegedly setting fire to the parliament building (see ◊Reichstag fire). Acquitted, he went to the USSR, where he became general secretary of the Comintern until its dissolution in 1943.

DIN abbreviation for *Deutsches Institut für Normung*, the West German national standards body, which has set internationally accepted standards for (among other things) paper sizes and electrical connectors.

Dinan town in Côtes-du-Nord *département*, N France, on the river Rance; population (1982) 14,150. The river is harnessed for tidal hydroelectric power.

Dinant ancient town in Namur province, Belgium, on the river Meuse; population (1982) 12,000. It is a tourist center for the Ardennes.

Dinaric Alps extension of the European ◊Alps in Western Yugoslavia and NW Albania. The highest peak is Durmitor at 8,274 ft/2,522 m.

Dine Jim 1935– . US Pop artist. He experimented with combinations of paintings and objects, such as a sink attached to a canvas.

Dine was a pioneer of happenings (art as live performance) in the 1950s and of environment art (three-dimensional works that attempt active interaction with the spectator, sometimes using sound or movement).

Dinesen Isak 1885–1962. Adopted name of Danish writer Karen ◊Blixen, born Karen Christentze Dinesen.

Dingaan died 1840. Zulu chief from 1828. He

Dinkins *The first black mayor of New York City, David Dinkins.*

obtained the throne by murdering his predecessor, Shaka, and became noted for his cruelty. In warfare with the Boer immigrants into Natal he was defeated on Dec 16, 1838 -"Dingaan's Day." He escaped to Swaziland, where he was deposed by his brother Mpande and subsequently assassinated.

Ding Ling 1904–1986. Chinese novelist. Her works include *Wei Hu* 1930 and *The Sun Shines over the Sanggan River* 1951.

She was imprisoned by the Guomindang (Chiang Kai-Shek's Nationalists) in the 1930s, wrongly labeled as rightist and expelled from the Communist Party 1957, imprisoned in the 1960s and intellectually ostracized for not keeping to Maoist literary rules; she was rehabilitated 1979. Her husband was the writer Hu Yapin, executed by Chiang Kai-Shek's police 1931.

dingo wild dog of Australia. Descended from domestic dogs brought from Asia by Aborigines thousands of years ago, it belongs to the same species *Canis familiaris* as other domestic dogs. It is reddish brown with a bushy tail, and often hunts at night. It cannot bark.

dinitrogen oxide alternate name for ◊nitrous oxide.

Dinka a member of the Dinka culture from S Sudan. The Dinka, numbering approximately 1 million, are a group of ◊Negroid tribes, primarily cattle herders, and inhabit the lands around the river system that flows into the White Nile. Their language belongs to the Chari-Nile family.

Dinkins David 1927– . Mayor of New York City from Jan 1990, a Democrat. He won a reputation as a moderate community politician and was Manhattan borough president before succeeding Edward I Koch to become New York's first black mayor.

dinosaur (Greek *deinos* "terrible," *sauros* "lizard") any of a group (sometimes considered as two separate orders) of extinct reptiles living between 215 million and 65 million years ago. Their closest living relations are crocodiles and birds, the latter perhaps descended from the dinosaurs. Many species of dinosaur evolved during the millions of years they were the dominant large land animals. Most were large (up to 90 ft/27 m, but some were as small as birds and lizards, into which some evolved. Most became extinct 65 million years ago for reasons not fully understood, although many paleontological, astronomical, and ecological theories exist. They never coexisted with the ◊human species, which began to evolve only some 6 million years ago.

Brachiosaurus, a long-necked plant-eater of the sauropod group, was about 40 ft/12.6 m to the top of its head, and weighed 80 tons. Compsognathus, a meat-eater, was only the size of a chicken, and ran on its hind legs. Stegosaurus, an armored plant-eater 20 ft/6 m long, had a brain only about 1.25 in/3 cm long. Not all dinosaurs had small brains. At the other extreme, the hunting dinosaur Stenonychosaurus, 6 ft/2 m long, had a brain size comparable to that of a mammal or bird of today, stereoscopic vision, and grasping hands. Many dinosaurs appear to have been equipped for a high level of activity.

An almost complete fossil of a dinosaur skeleton was found in 1969 in the Andean foothills, South America; it had been a two-legged carnivore 6 ft/2 m tall and weighing more than 220 lb/100 kg. More than 230 million years old, it is the oldest known dinosaur. Eggs are known of some species. In 1982 a number of nests and eggs were found in "colonies" in Montana, suggesting that some bred together like modern seabirds. In 1987 finds were made in China that may add much to the traditional knowledge of dinosaurs, chiefly gleaned from North American specimens. In 1989 and 1990 an articulated *Tyrannosaurus rex* was unearthed by a paleontological team in Montana, with a full skull, one of only six known. ◊Tyrannosaurs were huge, two-footed, meat-eating theropod dinosaurs of the Upper Cretaceous in North America and Asia.

Diocletian Gaius Valerius Diocletianus AD 245–313. Roman emperor 284–305, when he abdicated in favor of Galerius. He reorganized and subdivided the empire, with two joint and two subordinate emperors, and in 303 initiated severe persecution of Christians.

diode a cold anode and a heated cathode (or the semiconductor equivalent, which incorporates a *p–n* junction). Either device allows the passage of direct current in one direction only, and so is commonly used in a ◊rectifier to convert alternating current (AC) to direct current (DC).

dioecious describing plants that have male and female flowers borne on separate individuals of the same species. Dioecism occurs, for example, in the willows *Salix*. It is a way of avoiding self-fertilization.

Diogenes c. 412–323 BC. Ascetic Greek philosopher of the ◊Cynic school. He believed in freedom and self-sufficiency for the individual, and that the virtuous life was the simple life; he did not believe in social mores. His writings do not survive.

He was born at Sinope, captured by pirates, and sold as a slave to a Corinthian named Xeniades, who appointed Diogenes tutor to his two sons. He spent the rest of his life in Corinth. He is said to have carried a lamp during the daytime, looking for one honest man. The story of his having lived in a barrel arose when Seneca said that was where a man so crabbed ought to have lived.

Diomede two islands off the tip of the Seward peninsula, Alaska. Little Diomede (2.4 sq mi/6.2 sq km) belongs to the US and is only 3.9 km/2.4 mi from Big Diomede (11.3 sq mi/29.3 sq km), owned by the USSR. They were first sighted by Vitus Bering 1728.

Diomedes in Greek mythology, son of Tydeus, and a prominent Greek leader in ◊Homer's *Iliad*.

Dion Cassius AD 150–235. Roman historian. He wrote, in Greek, a Roman history in 80 books (of which 26 survive), covering the period from the founding of the city to AD 229, including the only surviving account of the invasion of Britain by Claudius in 43 BC.

Dionysia festivals of the god ◊Dionysus (Bacchus) celebrated in ancient Greece, especially in Athens. They included the lesser Dionysia in Dec, chiefly a rural festival, and the greater Dionysia, at the end of March, when new plays were performed.

Dionysius two tyrants of the ancient Greek city of Syracuse in Sicily. Dionysius the Elder (432–367 BC) seized power in 405. His first two wars with Carthage further extended the power of Syracuse, but in a third (383–378 BC) he was defeated. He was a patron of ◊Plato (see also ◊Damocles). He was succeeded by his son, Dionysius the Younger, who was driven out of Syracuse by Dion in 356; he was tyrant again in 353, but in 343 returned to Corinth.

Dionysus in Greek mythology, god of wine (son of Semele and Zeus), and also of orgiastic excess. He was identified with the Roman ◊Bacchus, whose rites were less savage. Attendant on him were ◊maenads.

Diophantus lived c. 250. Greek mathematician in Alexandria, whose *Arithmetica* is one of the first known works on problem solving by algebra, in which both words and symbols were used.

Dior Christian 1905–1957. French couturier. He established his own Paris salon in 1947 and made an impact with the "New Look"—long, cinch-waisted, and full-skirted—after wartime austerity.

diorite an igneous rock intermediate in composition; the coarse-grained plutonic equivalent of ◊andesite.

Dioscuri title of ◊Castor and Pollux in Classical mythology, meaning "sons of Zeus."

Diouf Abdou 1935– . Senegalese politician, president from 1980. He became prime minister 1970 under President Leopold Senghor and, on his retirement, succeeded him, being re-elected in 1983 and 1988.

Born in Louga in NW Senegal, Diouf studied at Paris University and was a civil servant before entering politics. He was chair of the Organization of African Unity 1985–86.

dioxin any of a family of over 200 organic chemicals, all of which are heterocyclic hydrocarbons (see ◊cyclic compounds), of which 2,3,7,8-tetrachlorodibenzodioxin (2,3,7,8-TCDD) is the most widespread. A highly toxic chemical, it occurred as an impurity in a defoliant (Agent Orange) used in the Vietnam war, and in the weedkiller 2,4,5-T. It has been associated with a disfiguring skin complaint (chloracne), birth defects, miscarriages, and cancer.

Disasters involving accidental release of large amounts of dioxin into the environment have occurred at Seveso in Italy and Times Beach in Missouri. Small amounts of dioxins are released by the burning of a wide range of chlorinated materials (treated wood, exhaust fumes from fuels treated with chlorinated additives, and plastics). The possibility of food becoming contaminated by dioxins in the environment has led the EC to decrease significantly dioxin emissions from incinerators. Dioxin may be produced as a byproduct in the manufacture of the bactericide ◊hexachlorophene.

dip, magnetic the angle between the horizontal and that taken up by a freely pivoted magnetic needle (the dip needle) mounted vertically in the Earth's magnetic field. It is also called the angle of inclination. The dip needle parallels the lines of force of the magnetic field at any point. Thus at the magnetic north and south poles, the needle dips vertically and the angle of dip is 90°.

diphtheria acute infectious disease in which a membrane forms in the throat (threatening death by ◊asphyxia), along with the production of a powerful neurotoxin that poisons the system. The organism responsible is a bacterium (*Corynebacterium diphtheria*). Its incidence has been reduced greatly by immunization.

diplodocus plant-eating sauropod dinosaur that lived about 145 million years ago, the fossils of which have been found in the W US. Up to 88 ft/27 m long, most of this neck and tail, it weighed about 11 tons. It walked on four elephantine legs, had nostrils on top of the skull, and peglike teeth at the front of the mouth.

diploid having two sets of ◊chromosomes in each cell. In sexually reproducing species, one set is derived from each parent, the ◊gametes, or sex cells, of each parent being ◊haploid (having only one set of chromosomes) due to ◊meiosis (reduction cell division).

diplomacy process by which states attempt to settle their differences through peaceful means such as negotiation or ◊arbitration. See ◊foreign relations.

dipper any of various passerine birds of the family Cinclidae, found in hilly and mountainous regions across Eurasia and North America, where there are clear, fast-flowing streams. It can swim, dive, or walk along the bottom using the pressure of water on its wings and tail to keep it down, while it searches for insect larvae and other small animals.

The American dipper *cinclus mexicanus* of W North America, is about 8 in/20 cm long, sooty-gray overall, and resembles a wren.

Dirac Paul Adrien Maurice 1902–1984. British physicist who worked out a version of quantum mechanics consistent with special ◊relativity. The existence of the positron (positive electron) was one of its predictions. He shared a Nobel Prize for Physics 1933.

direct current an electric current that flows in one direction, and does not reverse its flow as ◊alternating current does. The electricity produced by a battery is direct current.

directed numbers ◊integers with a positive (+) or negative (–) sign attached. On a graph, a positive sign shows a movement to the right or upward; a negative sign indicates movement downward or to the left.

Dirichlet Peter Gustav Lejeune 1805–1859. German mathematician. His most important work was on the convergence of the ◊Fourier series, which led him to the modern notion of a generalized function as represented in the form $f(x)$. He also made major contributions to number theory, producing *Dirichlet's theorem*: in every arithmetical sequence a, $a + 2d$, $a + 2d$, and so on, where a and d are relatively prime (have no common divisors other than 1), there is an infinite number of prime numbers.

Dirichlet applied his mathematical knowledge to various aspects of physics, such as an analysis of vibrating strings, and to astronomy in a critique of the ideas about the stability of the Solar System as proposed by the French mathematician Laplace.

dirigible another word for ◊airship.

Dis in Roman mythology, god of the underworld (Greek Pluto; ruler of Hades); synonym for the underworld itself..

disability limitation of a person's ability to carry out the activities of daily living, to the extent that they may need help in doing so.

Among adults the commonest disability is in walking, with almost 4.5 million adults suffering in this way in the UK in 1988. Other common disabilities are in hearing, personal care, dexterity, and continence. Most disabilities arise from debilitiating illness such as arthritis or stroke, although injury is also a leading cause. Other forms of disability are recognized in children: developmental disability is the failure to achieve a normal level of competence in some aspect of behavior during infancy, childhood, or adolescence; a learning disability in a child of normal intelligence is a difficulty in acquiring one of the basic cognitive skills of speaking, reading, writing, or calculation.

dip magnetic

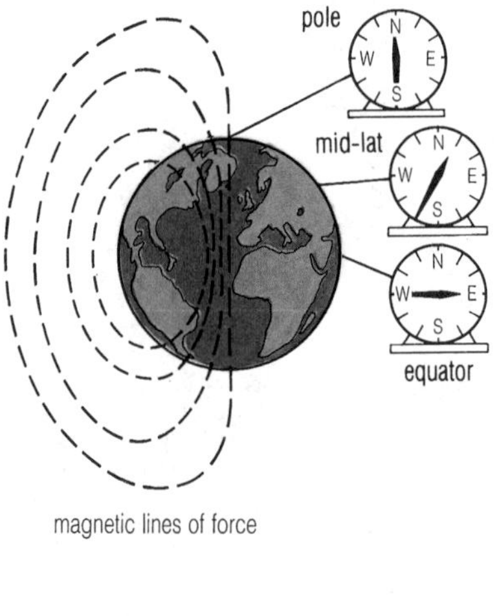
pole
N
W
E
S
mid-lat
N
W
E
S
N
W
E
S
equator

magnetic lines of force

disaccharide a ◊sugar made up of two monosaccharide units. Sucrose $C_{12}H_{22}O_{11}$, or table sugar, is a disaccharide.

disarmament the reduction of a country's weapons of war. Most disarmament talks since World War II have been concerned with nuclear-arms verification, but biological, chemical, and conventional weapons have also come under discussion at the United Nations and in other forums.

1930s League of Nations, attempts to achieve disarmament failed.

1968 US president Johnson's proposals for ◊Strategic Arms Limitation Talks (SALT) were delayed by the Soviet invasion of Czechoslovakia.

1972–77 SALT I was in effect.

1979–85 SALT II, signed by the Soviet and US leaders Brezhnev and Carter, was never ratified by the US Senate, but both countries abided by it.

1986 US president Reagan revoked this pledge, against the advice of his European NATO partners.

1987 Reagan and the Soviet leader Gorbachev agreed to reduce their nuclear arsenals by 4% by scrapping intermediate-range nuclear weapons.

1990 Conventional-arms-reductions talks continued between NATO and the Warsaw Pact for force reductions in Europe. The Ottawa meeting results in a new agreement of 195,000 Soviet troops and 225,000 US troops in Europe.

discharge tube device in which a gas conducting an electric current emits visible light. It is usually a glass tube from which virtually all the air has been removed (so that it "contains" a near vacuum), with electrodes at each end. When a high-voltage current is passed between the electrodes, the few remaining gas atoms in the tube (or some deliberately introduced ones) ionize and emit colored light as they conduct the current along the tube. The light originates as electrons change energy levels in the ionized atoms.

By coating the inside of the tube with a phosphor, invisible emitted radiation (such as ultraviolet light) can produce visible light; this is the principle of the fluorescent lamp.

disciple a follower, especially of a religious leader. The word is used in the Bible for the early followers of Jesus. They are known as the ◊apostles.

discotheque club for dancing to pop music on records (disks), originating in the 1960s. The shortened form, disco, was used for an international style of recorded dance music of the 1970s with a heavily emphasized beat, derived from funk.

discount rate the rate that banks are charged to borrow money from the ◊Federal Reserve Bank. One of the tools of ◊monetary policy, the discount rate allows the ◊Federal Reserve System to govern consumer interest rates and the amount of money in circulation.

discrimination distinction made (social, economic, political, legal) between individuals or groups such that one has the power to treat the other unfavorably. Negative discrimination, often based on ◊stereotype, includes anti-Semitism, apartheid, caste, racism, sexism, and slavery. Positive discrimination, or "affirmative action," is sometimes practiced in an attempt to counteract the effects of previous long-term discrimination. Minorities and, in some cases, majorities have been targets for discrimination.

Discrimination may be on grounds of difference of color, nationality, religion, politics, culture, class, sex, age, or a combination of such factors. Legislation has been to some degree effective in forbidding racial discrimination, against which there is a United Nations convention 1969.

National legislation in the US includes the Civil Rights Acts of 1964 and 1968, the Voting Rights Act 1965, and a movement to add an amendment to the Constitution mandating equal rights for women.

discus circular disk thrown by athletes who rotate to gain momentum from within a circle 8 ft/2.5 m in diameter. The men's discus weighs 4.4 lb/2 kg and the women's 2.2 lb/1 kg. Discus throwing was a competition in ancient Greece at gymnastic contests, especially at the Olympic Games. It is an event in modern Olympics and track and field meets.

disease any condition that impairs the normal state of an organism, and usually alters the functioning of one or more of its organs or systems. A disease is usually characterized by a set of characteristic symptoms and signs, although these may not always be apparent to the sufferer. Diseases may be inborn (see ◊congenital disease) or acquired through infection, injury, or other cause. Many diseases have unknown causes.

disinfectant agent that kills, or prevents the growth of, bacteria and other microorganisms. Chemical disinfectants include carbolic acid (phenol, used by ◊Lister in surgery in the 1870s), ethanal, methanal, chlorine, and iodine.

disinvestment the withdrawal of investments in a country for political reasons. The term is also used in economics to describe nonreplacement of stock as it wears out.

It is generally applied to the ostensive removal of funds from South Africa in recent years by such multinational companies as General Motors and to the withdrawal of private investment funds (by universities, pension funds, and other organizations) from portfolios doing business in South Africa. Disinvestment may be motivated by fear of loss of business in the home market caused by adverse publicity or by fear of loss of foreign resources if the local government changes.

disk in computing, a common medium for storing large volumes of data (an alternative is ◊magnetic tape.) A magnetic disk is rotated at high speed in a disk-drive unit as a read/write (playback or record) head passes over its surfaces to record or "read" the magnetic variations that encode the data. There are several types, including ◊floppy disks, ◊hard disks, and ◊CD-ROM.

Fixed disks provide the most storage. Up to 600 megabytes (million ◊bytes) is quite common, although the hard disks of this type used with microcomputers may hold only 10 or 20 megabytes. Fixed or hard disks are built into the drive unit, occasionally stacked one on top of another.

Removable disks are common in minicomputer systems, hold about 80 megabytes of data, and are contained in a rigid plastic case that can be taken out of the drive unit. A floppy disk (also called diskette) is very much smaller in size and capacity. Normally holding less than 1 megabyte of data, it is flexible, mounted in a card envelope or rigid plastic case, and can be removed from the drive unit.

Recently, laser disks and compact disks have been used to store computer data. These have an enormous capacity (about 600 megabytes on a compact disk and billions of bytes on a laser disk) but, once written on to the disk, data cannot be erased.

dislocation in chemistry, a fault in the atomic structure of a crystal.

Disney Walt (Walter Elias) 1901–1966. US filmmaker who became a pioneer of family entertainment. He and his brother established an animation studio in Hollywood in 1923, and his first Mickey Mouse animated cartoon (*Plane Crazy*) appeared in black and white 1928. *Steamboat Willie* 1928 was his first Mickey Mouse cartoon in color. He developed the "Silly Symphony," a type of cartoon based on the close association of music with the visual image, such as *Fantasia* 1940. His many feature-length cartoons include *Snow White and the Seven Dwarfs* 1938 (his first), *Pinocchio* 1939, *Dumbo* 1941, *Bambi* 1942, *Cinderella* 1950, *Alice in Wonderland* 1952, and *Peter Pan* 1953. Published materials such as books, magazines, comic books, and records accompanied his films and helped make his animated characters beloved throughout the world.

From 1953, when *The Living Desert* was shown, Disney made some remarkable nature-study films. Wholesome features with human casts began with *Treasure Island* 1950, *Davy Crockett* 1955, *The Swiss Family Robinson* 1960, and *Mary Poppins* 1964. Disney produced the first television series in color 1961. He also originated 1955 the concept of pleasure parks, of which Disneyland, California, was the first. Walt Disney World, near Orlando, Florida, 1971, includes the Epcot (Experimental Prototype Community of Tomorrow) Center 1982, a cross between a science museum and a theme park. There is also a park in Tokyo, Japan.

MICKEY MOUSE
STORY BOOK
By
WALT
DISNEY

Disney *Walt Disney created many beloved cartoon characters, among them the world-famous Mickey Mouse, shown here with his faithful dog Pluto and his nephews Morty and Ferdy.*

dispersion in optics, the splitting of white light into a spectrum; for example, when it passes through a prism or a diffraction grating. It occurs because the prism (or grating) bends each component wavelength to a slightly different extent. The natural dispersion of light through raindrops creates a rainbow.

displacement activity in animal behavior, an action that is performed out of its normal context, while the animal is in a state of stress, frustration, or uncertainty. Birds, for example, often peck at grass when uncertain whether to attack or flee from an opponent; similarly, humans scratch their heads when nervous.

displacement reaction chemical reaction in which a less reactive element is replaced in a compound by a more reactive one.

For example, the addition of powdered zinc to

Disraeli *One of the prime ministers during Queen Victoria's reign, Benjamin Disraeli. This portrait by John Everett Millais (1881) National Portrait Gallery, London.*

a solution of copper(II) sulfate displaces copper metal, which can be detected by its characteristic color (see ◊electrochemical series).

Disraeli Benjamin, Earl of Beaconsfield 1804–1881. British Conservative politician and novelist. Elected to Parliament 1837, he was chancellor of the Exchequer under Lord ◊Derby 1852, 1858–59, and 1866–68, and prime minister 1868 and 1874–80. His imperialist policies brought India directly under the crown, and he personally purchased control of the Suez Canal. The central Conservative Party organization is his creation. His popular, political novels reflect an interest in social reform and include *Coningsby* 1844 and *Sybil* 1845.

Entering Parliament in 1837 after four unsuccessful attempts, he was laughed at as a dandy; when his maiden speech was shouted down, he said: "The time will come when you will hear me."

Excluded from Peel's government of 1841–46, Disraeli formed his Young England group to keep a critical eye on Peel's Conservatism and gradually came to be recognized as the leader of the Conservative Party in the Commons.

During the next 20 years the Conservatives formed shortlived minority governments in 1852, 1858–59, and 1866–68, with Lord Derby as prime minister and Disraeli as chancellor of the Exchequer and leader of the Commons. On Lord Derby's retirement in 1868 Disraeli became prime minister, but a few months later he was defeated by Gladstone in a general election. In 1874 Disraeli took office for the second time. Some useful reform measures were carried, but the outstanding feature of the government's policy was its imperialism: Disraeli purchased from the Khedive of Egypt a controlling interest in the Suez Canal; conferred on the Queen the title of Empress of India; and sent the Prince of Wales on the first royal tour of that country.

Dissenter former name for a Protestant refusing to conform to the established Christian church. For example, Baptists, Presbyterians, and Independents (now known as Congregationalists) were Dissenters.

dissident in one-party states, a person intellectually dissenting from the official line. Dissidents have been sent into exile, prison, labor camps, and mental institutions, or deprived of their jobs. In the USSR the number of imprisoned dissidents declined from more than 600 in 1986 to fewer than 100 in 1990, of whom the majority were ethnic nationalists. In China the number of prisoners of conscience increased after the 1989 Tiananmen Square massacre, and in South Africa, despite the release of Nelson Mandela in 1990, numerous political dissidents remained in jail.

In the USSR before the introduction of ◊glasnost, dissidents comprised communists who advocated a more democratic and humanitarian approach; religious proselytizers; Jews wishing to emigrate; and those who supported ethnic or national separatist movements within the USSR (among them Armenians, Lithuanians, Ukrainians, and Tatars). Their views were expressed through samizdat (clandestinely distributed writings) and sometimes published abroad. In the late 1980s Gorbachev lifted censorship, accepted a degree of political pluralism, and extended tolerance to religious believers. Almost 100,000 Jews were allowed to emigrate 1985–90. Some formerly persecuted dissidents, most prominently the physicist ◊Sakharov, emerged as supporters, albeit impatient, of the new reform program.

distance ratio in a machine, the distance moved by the input force, or effort, divided by the distance moved by the output force, or load. The ratio indicates the movement magnification achieved, and is equivalent to the machine's ◊velocity ratio.

distemper any of several infectious diseases of animals characterized by catarrh, cough, and general weakness. Specifically, it refers to a virus disease in young dogs, also found in wild animals, which can now be prevented by vaccination. In 1988 an allied virus killed over 10,000 common seals in the Baltic and North seas.

distributive law in mathematics, the law that states that if there are two binary operations "×" and "+" on a set, then "×" distributes over "+" as in multiplication, so that, for example, 3 × (4 + 5) is the same as (3 × 4) + (3 x 5). See also ◊associative law.

distributor device in the ignition system of a piston engine that distributes pulses of high-voltage electricity to the ◊spark plugs in the cylinders. The electricity is passed to the plug leads by the tip of a rotor arm, driven by the engine camshaft, and current is fed to the rotor arm from the ignition coil. The distributor also houses the contact point or breaker, which opens and closes to interrupt the battery current to the coil, thus triggering the high-voltage pulses. With electronic ignition it is absent.

District of Columbia seat of the federal government of the US, conterminous with the city of ◊Washington, DC; area 69 sq mi/179 sq km. A rectangle along the Potomac River, donated by Maryland and Virginia, was selected as the federal seat of government 1791. For many years the District of Columbia included other local entities besides Washington. At the request of its residents, the portion donated by Virginia was returned to the state 1846, thus confining the District of Columbia to the E shore of the Potomac River. Residents elect a mayor and city council and a nonvoting delegate to the US Congress.

Diu island off the Kathiawar peninsular, NW India, part of the Union Territory of ◊Daman and Diu; area 15 sq mi/38 sq km; population (1981) 30,000. The main town is also called Diu, population 8,020. The economy is based on tourism, coconuts, pearl millet, and salt. Diu was captured by the Portuguese 1534.

diuretic any drug that rids the body of fluid accumulated in the tissues by increasing the output of urine by the kidneys. It may be used in the treatment of heart disease, high blood pressure, kidney or liver disease, and some endocrine disorders. A potassium supplement is prescribed where potassium loss would be dangerous.

diverticulitis inflammation of diverticula (pockets of herniation) in the large intestine. It is usually controlled by diet and antibiotics.

divertissement (French "entertainment") a dance, or group of dances, within a ballet or opera that has no connection with the plot, such as the character dances in the last act of *Coppélia* by Delibes.

dividend in business, the amount of money that company directors decide should be taken out of profits for distribution to stockholders. It is usually declared as a percentage or fixed amount per share. Most companies pay dividends quarterly; others once a year.

divination art of ascertaining future events or eliciting other hidden knowledge by supernatural or nonrational means. Divination played a large part in the ancient civilizations of the Egyptians, Greeks (see ◊oracle), Romans, and Chinese (see ◊*I Ching*), and is still practiced throughout the world.

It generally involves the intuitive interpretation of the mechanical operations of chance or natural law. Forms of divination have included omens drawn from the behavior of birds and animals; examination of the entrails of sacrificed animals; random opening of such books as the Bible; fortune-telling by cards (see ◊tarot) and palmistry; ◊dowsing; oracular trance-speaking; automatic writing; necromancy, or the supposed raising of the spirits of the dead; and dreams, often specially induced.

Divine Comedy, The an epic poem by Dante Alighieri 1307–21, describing a journey through Hell, Purgatory, and Paradise. The poet Virgil is Dante's guide through Hell and Purgatory; to each of the three realms, or circles, Dante assigns historical and contemporary personages according to their moral (and also political) worth. In Paradise Dante finds his lifelong love Beatrice. The poem makes great use of symbolism and allegory, and influenced many English writers including Milton, Byron, Shelley, and TS Eliot.

Divine Light Mission religious movement founded in India in 1960, which gained a prominent following in the US in the 1970s. It proclaims Guru Maharaj Ji as the present age's successor to the gods or religious leaders Krishna, Buddha, Jesus, and Mohammed, and who can provide his followers with the knowledge required to attain salvation.

Divine Principle sacred writings of the ◊Unification Church. The book, which offers a reinterpretation of the Bible, is also influenced by concepts from Buddhism, Islam, and Taoism.

divine right of kings Christian political doctrine that hereditary monarchy is the system approved by God, hereditary right cannot be forfeited, monarchs are accountable to God alone for their actions, and rebellion against the lawful sovereign is therefore blasphemous.

The doctrine had its origins in the anointing of Pepin in 751 by the pope after Pepin had usurped the throne of the Franks. It was at its peak in 16th- and 17th-century Europe as a weapon against the claims of the papacy—the court of Louis XIV of France pushed this to the limit—and was in 17th-century England maintained by the supporters of the Stuarts in opposition to the democratic theories of the Puritans and Whigs.

Many of the latter group migrated to the American colonies to avoid persecution.

diving the sport of entering the water either from a springboard (3 ft/1 m or 10 ft/3 m) above the water, or from a platform (33 ft/10 m) above the water. Various differing starts are adopted, facing forward or backward, and somersaults, twists and other positions or combinations thereof are performed in midair before entering the water. Pool depths of 20 ft/6 m are needed for high or platform diving, but 10 ft/3 m-deep pools may accommodate 1 or 3 meter diving. Points are awarded and the level of difficulty of each dive is used as a multiplying factor.

diving apparatus any equipment used to enable a person to spend time underwater. Diving bells were in use in the 18th century, the diver breathing air trapped in a bell-shaped chamber. This was followed by cumbersome diving suits in the early 19th century. Complete freedom of movement came with the ◊aqualung, invented by Jacques ◊Cousteau in the early 1940s. For work at greater depths the technique of saturation diving was developed in the 1970s, where divers live for a week or more breathing a mixture of helium and oxygen at the pressure existing on the seabed where they work (as in tunnel building).

The first diving suit, with a large metal helmet and supplied with air through a hose, was invented in the UK by the brothers John and Charles Deane in 1828.

Saturation diving was developed particularly for working in offshore oil-fields. Working divers are ferried down to the work site by a lock-out ◊submersible. By this technique they avoid the need for lengthy periods of decompression after every dive. Slow decompression is necessary to avoid the dangerous consequences of an attack of the bends, or ◊decompression sickness.

division of labor the separation of tasks in processing or producing goods, especially in industrial or factory settings, but also in traditional societies where males and females perform gender-related tasks (a sexual division of labor). See also ◊factory system.

divorce the legal dissolution of a lawful marriage. It is distinct from an annulment, which is a legal declaration that the marriage was invalid. The ease with which a divorce can be obtained in different countries varies considerably and is also affected by different religious practices.

In the US divorce laws differ from state to state. The grounds include adultery (in all states), cruelty, desertion, alcoholism, drug addiction, insanity, and declaration of irreconcilable differences or mutual incompatibility. Quick divorces in states with more liberal laws have been restricted by the imposition of minimum residence periods and by the right to challenge the divorce if one party has not been notified of the proceedings. Couples are increasingly negotiating prenuptial agreements that make an advance settlement of division of property and assets, including maintenance provisions. In some states, so-called no-fault divorce laws make divorces readily available to couples with no economic quarrels and with agreeable obligations to children.

The Roman Catholic Church does not permit divorce among its members, and under Pope John Paul II conditions for annulment have been tightened. Among Muslims a wife cannot divorce her husband, but he may divorce her by repeating the formula "I divorce you" three times; property settlements by careful parents make this a right infrequently exercised.

Diwali ("garland of lamps") Hindu festival in Oct/Nov celebrating Lakshmi, goddess of light and wealth. It is marked by the lighting of lamps and candles, feasting, and exchange of gifts.

Dix Dorothea Lynde 1802–1887. US educator and medical reformer. Born in Hampden, Maine, and raised in Boston, Dix began her career as a teacher at a girls' school in Worcester, Massachusetts, and opened her own school in Boston 1821. Forced by ill health to retire in 1835, she traveled in Europe and published several books. From 1841 she devoted herself to a campaign for the rights of the mentally ill, helping to improve conditions and treatment in public institutions for the insane in the US, Canada, and Japan. During the US Civil War, she served as superintendent of nurses.

Dixieland jazz name given to a jazz style that originated in New Orleans in the early 20th century and worked its way up the Mississippi. It is characterized by improvization and the playing back and forth of the cornet, trumpet, clarinet, and trombone. The steady background beat is supplied by the piano, bass, and percussion instrument players, who also have their turns to solo. It is usually played by bands of four to eight members. Noted Dixieland musicians were King ◊Oliver, Jelly Roll ◊Morton, and Louis ◊Armstrong.

Diyarbakir town in Asiatic Turkey, on the river Tigris; population (1985) 305,000. It has a trade in gold and silver filigree work, copper, wool, and mohair and manufactures textiles and leather goods.

Djakarta variant spelling of ◊Jakarta, capital of Indonesia.

Djibouti

Republic of

(Jumhouriyya Djibouti)

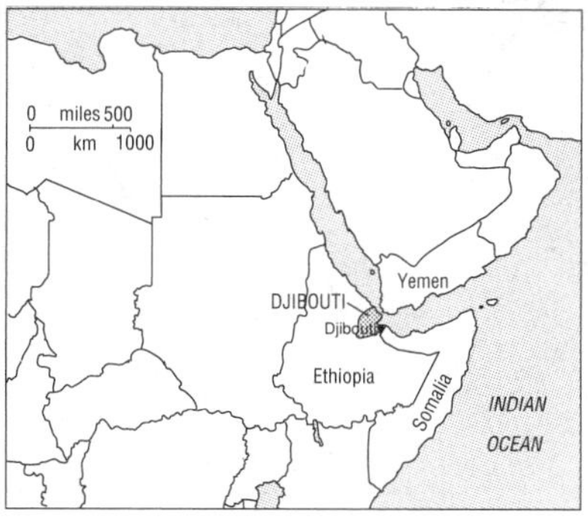
0 miles 500
0 km 1000
Yemen
DJIBOUTI
Djibouti
Ethiopia
Somalia
INDIAN
OCEAN

area 8,955 sq mi/23,200 sq km
capital (and chief port) Djibouti
cities Tadjoura, Obock, Dikhil
physical mountains divide an inland plateau from a coastal plain; hot and arid
features terminus of railroad link with Ethiopia; Lac Assal salt lake is the second lowest point on Earth (–471 ft/144 m)
head of state and government Hassan Gouled Aptidon from 1977
political system authoritarian nationalism
political parties People's Progress Assembly (RPP), nationalist
exports acts mainly as a transit port for Ethiopia
currency Djibouti franc
population (1990 est) 337,000 (Issa 47%, Afar 37%, European 8%, Arab 6%); growth rate 3.4% p.a.
life expectancy 50
language Somali, Afar, French (official), Arabic
religion Sunni Muslim
literacy 20% (1988)
GDP $378 million (1987); $1,016 per head
chronology
1896–1945 Part of French Somaliland.
1967 French Somaliland became the French Territory of the Afars and the Issas.
1977 Independence achieved from France; Hassan Gouled elected president.
1979 All political parties combined to form the People's Progress Assembly (RPP).
1981 New constitution made RPP the only legal party.
Gouled reelected. Treaties of friendship signed with Ethiopia, Somalia, Kenya, and Sudan.
1984 Policy of neutrality reaffirmed.
1987 Gouled reelected for a final term.

Djibouti country on E coast of Africa, at the S end of the Red Sea, bounded E by the Gulf of Aden, SE by the Somali Republic, and S, W, and N by Ethiopia.

government The 1981 constitution made Djibouti a one-party state, the only legal party being the People's Progress Assembly (RPP). The constitution also provides for a single-chamber legislature, the 65-member chamber of deputies, elected by universal suffrage for a five-year term, and a president, nominated by the party, who is elected for six years and may not serve more than two terms.

history During the 9th century missionaries from Arabia converted the Afars inhabiting the area to Islam. A series of wars were fought by the Afar Islamic states and Christian Ethiopia from the 13th to 17th centuries. The French arrived in 1862, and in 1884 annexed Djibouti and the neighboring region as the colony of French Somaliland. In 1967 it was renamed the French Territory of the Afars and the Issas. Opposition to French rule grew during the 1970s, and calls for independence were frequent, sometimes violent.

Independence as the Republic of Djibouti was achieved 1977, with Hassan Gouled as president. In 1979 all political parties combined to form the People's Progress Assembly (RPP) and the government embarked on the task of uniting the two main ethnic groups, the Issas, who traditionally had strong links with Somalia, and the Afars, who had been linked with Ethiopia.

In 1981 a new constitution was adopted, making RPP the only party and providing for the election of a president after nomination by RPP. President Gouled was re-elected, and in 1982 a chamber of deputies was elected from a list of RPP nominees. Under Gouled, Djibouti pursued a largely successful policy of amicable neutralism with its neighbors, concluding treaties of friendship with Ethiopia, Somalia, Kenya, and Sudan, and tried to assist the peace process in East Africa. Although affected by the 1984–85 droughts, it managed to maintain stability with EC aid. In 1987 Gouled was re-elected for his final term with 98.71% of the popular vote.

Djibouti chief port and capital of the Republic of Djibouti, on a peninsula 149 mi/240 km SW of Aden and 351 mi/565 km NE of Addis Ababa; population (1988) 290,000.

The city succeeded Obock as capital of French Somaliland 1896 and was the official port of Ethiopia from 1897.

Djilas Milovan 1911– . Yugoslav political writer and dissident. A former close wartime colleague of Marshal Tito, in 1953 he was dismissed from high office and subsequently imprisoned because of his advocacy of greater political pluralism. He was released in 1966 and formally rehabilitated in 1989.

Djilas was born in Montenegro and was a partisan during World War II. He rose to a senior position in Yugoslavia's postwar communist government before being ousted in 1953. His writings, including the books *The New Class* 1957 and *The Undivided Society* 1969, were banned until May 1989.

DM abbreviation for Deutschmark, the unit of currency in Germany.

DMus abbreviation for Doctor of Music.

DNA deoxyribonucleic acid. A complex two-stranded molecule that contains, in chemically coded form, all the information needed to build, control, and maintain a living organism. DNA is a ladderlike double-stranded ◊nucleic acid that forms the basis of genetic inheritance in all organisms, except for a few viruses that have only ◊RNA. In ◊eukaryotic organisms, it is organized into ◊chromosomes and contained in the cell nucleus.

Dneprodzerzhinsk port in Ukraine, USSR, on the river Dnieper, 30 mi/48 km NW of Dnepropetrovsk; population (1987) 279,000. It produces chemicals, iron, and steel.

Dnepropetrovsk city in Ukraine, USSR, on the right bank of the river Dnieper; population (1987) 1,182,000. It is the center of a major industrial region, with iron, steel, chemical, and engineering industries. It is linked with the Dnieper Dam, 37 mi/60 km downstream.

Dnieper or ***Dnepr*** Russian river rising in the Smolensk region and flowing south past Kiev, Dnepropetrovsk, and Zaporozhe, to enter the Black Sea E of Odessa. Total length 1,400 mi/2,250 km.

do. abbreviation for ditto.

Dobermann or ***Dobermann Pinscher*** smooth-coated dog with a docked tail, much used as a guard dog. It stands up to 2.2 ft/70 cm tall, has a long head with a flat, smooth skull, and is often black with brown markings. It takes its name from the man who bred it in 19th-century Germany.

Döblin Alfred 1878–1957. German novelist. His *Berlin-Alexanderplatz* 1929 owes much to James

DNA

how a cell divides

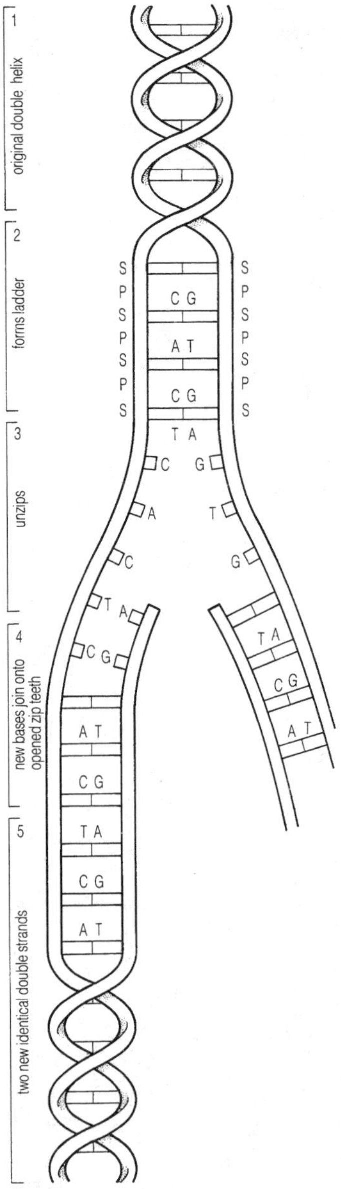
1
original double helix
2
forms ladder
3
unzips
4
new bases join onto opened zip teeth
5
two new identical double strands

Key

S sugars
P phosphates
C cytosine
G guanine
A adenine
T thymine

Joyce in its minutely detailed depiction of the inner lives of a city's inhabitants, and is considered by many to be the finest 20th-century German novel. Other works include *November 1918: Eine deutsche Revolution/A German Revolution* 1939–50 (published in four parts) about the formation of the Weimar Republic.

He practiced as a doctor in Berlin until 1933 when his books were banned and he was exiled; he moved first to France and from 1941 lived in the US.

Dobruja district in the Balkans, bounded to the N and W by the Danube and to the E by the Black Sea. It is low-lying, partly marshland, partly fertile steppe land. Constanta is the chief town. Dobruja was divided between Romania and Bulgaria in 1878. In 1913, after the second Balkan War, Bulgaria ceded its part to Romania but received it back in 1940, a cession confirmed by the peace treaty of 1947.

Dnieper River

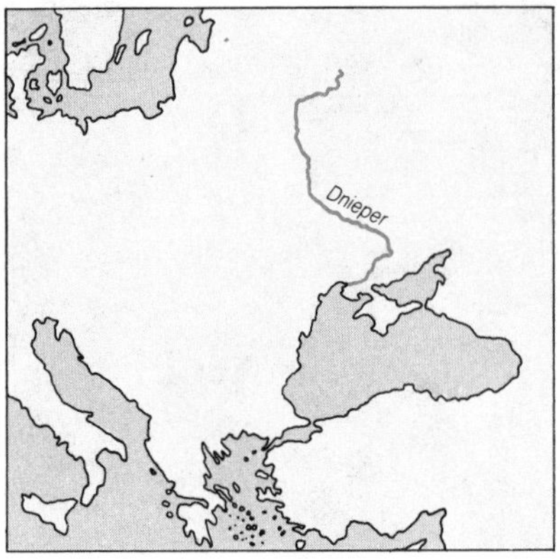
Dnieper

Dobrynin Anataloy Fedorovich 1919– . Soviet diplomat, ambassador to the US 1962–86, emerging during the 1970s as a warm supporter of ◊detente.

Dobrynin joined the Soviet diplomatic service in 1941. He served as counselor at the Soviet embassy in Washington, DC 1952–55, assistant to the minister for foreign affairs 1955–57, undersecretary at the United Nations 1957–59, and head of the USSR's American department 1959–61, before being appointed Soviet ambassador to Washington in 1962. He remained at this post for 25 years. Brought back to Moscow by the new Soviet leader Mikhail Gorbachev, he was appointed to the Communist Party's Secretariat as head of the International Department, before retiring in 1988.

Dobzhansky Theodosius 1900–1975. Ukrainian-born US geneticist. A pioneer of modern genetics and evolutionary theory, he showed that genetic variability between individuals of the same species is very high and that this diversity is vital to the process of evolution. His book *Genetics and the Origin of Species* was published in 1937.

dock or ***sorrel*** in botany, a number of plants of the genus *Rumex* of the buckwheat family Polygonaceae. They are tall, annual or perennial herbs, often with lance-shaped leaves and small, greenish flowers.

Doctorow E(dgar) L(awrence) 1931– . US writer. He is noted for novels in which he weaves history and fiction together. His first novel, *The Book of Daniel* 1971, about the ◊Rosenbergs' trial and execution, won him instant fame. His other works include *Ragtime* 1975, *Loon Lake* 1980, *Lives of the Poets* 1984, *World's Fair* 1985, and *Billy Bathgate* 1989.

dodder parasitic plant, genus *Cuscuta*, of the morning-glory family Convolvulaceae, without leaves or roots. The thin stem twines around the host, and penetrating suckers withdraw nourishment.

Dodds Johnny 1892–1940. US clarinetist, generally ranked among the top New Orleans jazz clarinetists. He played with the New Orleans Wanderers and was acclaimed for his warmth of tone and improvisation.

Dodecanese (Greek *Dhodhekánisos*, "twelve islands") group of islands in the Aegean sea; area 1,028 sq m/2,663 sq km. Once Turkish, the islands were Italian from 1912 to 1947, when they were ceded to Greece. They include ◊Rhodes and ◊Kos. Chief products include fruit, olives, and sponges.

dodecaphonic in music, the ◊twelve-tone system of composition.

Dodge City city in SW Kansas, on the Arkansas River; population (1990) 21,129. It was a noted frontier cattle town in the days of the Wild West. Founded 1872 with the arrival of the railroad, it became the terminus for cattle drives from the Santa Fe Trail. Wyatt Earp and Bat Masterson were law officials here, and Boot Hill Cemetery has been preserved. Farm and livestock-handling machinery are manufactured here.

Dodecanese Islands

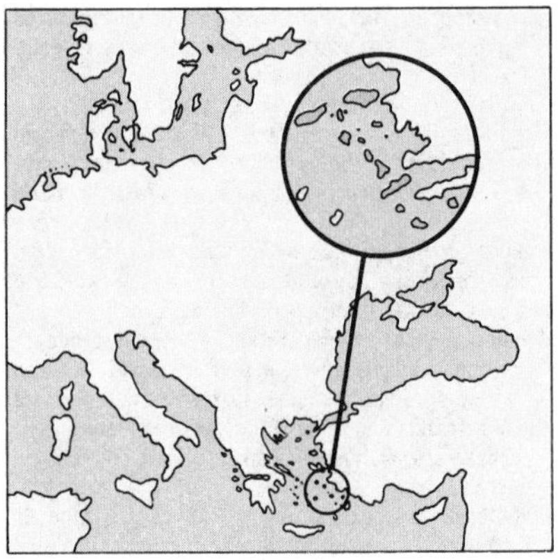

Dodgson Charles Lutwidge. Real name of writer Lewis ◊Carroll.

dodo extinct bird *Raphus cucullatus* formerly found on the island of Mauritius, but exterminated before the end of the 17th century. Related to the pigeons, it was larger than a turkey, with a bulky body and very short wings and tail. Flightless and trusting, it was easy prey to humans.

Dodoma capital (replacing Dar-es-Salaam in 1974) of Tanzania; 3,713 ft/1,132 m above sea level; population (1984) 180,000. Center of communications, linked by rail with Dar-es-Salaam and Kigoma on Lake Tanganyika, and by road with Kenya to the N and Zambia and Malawi to the S.

Doe Samuel Kenyon 1950–1990. Liberian politician and soldier, head of state 1980–90. He seized power in a coup. Having successfully put down an uprising April 1990, Doe was later deposed and killed by rebel forces in Sept 1990.

Doe joined the army in 1969 and rose to the rank of master sergeant ten years later. He led a coup in which President Tolbert was killed 1980. Doe replaced him as head of state, then had 13 cabinet members shot in front of reporters. In 1981 he made himself general and army commander in chief. In 1985 he was narrowly elected president, as leader of the newly formed National Democratic Party of Liberia. His human-rights record was poor.

dog any carnivorous mammal of the family Canidae, including wild dogs, wolves, jackals, coyotes, and foxes. Specifically, the domestic dog *Canis familiaris*, the earliest animal (perhaps as early as 60,000 years ago, when Upper Paleolithic hunters used them to stalk game), descended from the wolf or jackal, and migrated with humans to all the continents. They have been selectively bred into many different varieties for use as working animals and pets.

Of the wild dogs, some are solitary, such as the long-legged maned wolf *Chrysocyon brachurus* of South America, but others hunt in groups, such as the African hunting dog *Lycaon pictus* (classified as a vulnerable species) and the ◊wolf. ◊Jackals scavenge for food, and the raccoon dog *Nyctereutes procyonoides* of E Asia includes plant food as well as meat in the diet. The Australian wild dog is the ◊dingo

In the US, the American Kennel Club sets standards for about 200 registered breeds.

dogbane any sometimes poisonous herbaceous plant of the genus *Apocynum*, with opposite leaves, small white or pink flowers, and milky juice. The term also is used to designate any member of the dogbane family Apocynaceae, which includes various herbaceous plants, shrubs, and trees such as oleander and periwinkle.

doge the chief magistrate in the ancient constitutions of Venice and Genoa. The first doge of Venice was appointed 697 with absolute power (modified 1297), and from his accession dates

dog

Foxhound
Pekinese
Pug
Cocker spaniel
working collie
Labrador retriever
Egyptian greyhound
Jack Russell terrier
Chihuahua
Dobermann pinscher
bloodhound
Old English sheepdog

Venice's prominence in history. The last Venetian doge, Lodovico Manin, retired 1797 and the last Genoese doge in 1804.

Dōgen 1200–1253. Japanese Buddhist monk, pupil of Eisai; founder of the Sōtō school of Zen. He did not reject study, but stressed the importance of *zazen*, seated meditation, for its own sake.

dogfish any of several small sharks found in the NE Atlantic, Pacific, and Mediterranean.

The spiny dogfish *Squalus acanthius* of the Pacific and Atlantic, grows to about 4 ft/1.2 m long. It is a common subject for dissection in biology laboratories.

Dogger Bank submerged sandbank in the North Sea, about 70 mi/115 km off the coast of Yorkshire, England. In places the water is only 36 ft/11 m deep, but the general depth is 60–120 ft/18–36 m; it is a well-known fishing ground.

Dogon member of the W African Dogon culture from E Mali and NW Burkina Faso. The Dogon number approximately 250,000 and their language belongs to the Voltaic (Gur) branch of the Niger-Congo family.

dogwood any of a genus *Cornus* of trees and shrubs of the dogwood family (Cornaceae), native to temperate regions of North America and Eurasia. The flowering dogwood *Cornus florida* of E US is often cultivated as an ornamental for its beautiful blooms consisting of clusters of small greenish flowers surrounded by four large white or pink petallike ◊bracts.

Heads of small white flowers, each with four petals joined as a tube, are produced in midsummer, followed by black berries. The dogwood is characteristic of lime soils in the S of England, and is found over much of S Europe. Various other species of dogwood are planted in gardens.

Doha (Arabic *Ad Dawḥah*) capital and chief port of Qatar; population (1986) 217,000. Industries include oil refining, refrigeration plants, engineering, and food processing. It is the center of vocational training for all the Persian Gulf states.

Doi Takako 1929– . Japanese Socialist politician, leader of the Japan Socialist Party (JSP) from 1986 and responsible for much of its recent revival. She is the country's first female major party leader.

Doi was a law lecturer before being elected to the House of Representatives in 1969. She assumed leadership of the JSP at a low point in the party's fortunes and proceeded to moderate and modernize its image. With the help of "housewife volunteers" she established herself as a charismatic political leader, and at a time when the ruling Liberal Democrats were beset by scandals, the JSP vote increased to make Doi the leader of an effective opposition.

Doi Inthanon highest mountain in Thailand, rising to 8,513 ft/2,595 m SW of Chiang Mai in NW Thailand.

Doisy Edward 1893–1986. US biochemist. In 1939 Doisy succeeded in synthesizing vitamin K, a compound earlier discovered by Carl ◊Dam, with whom he shared the 1943 Nobel Prize for Medicine.

Dolci Carlo 1616–1686. Italian painter of the late Baroque period, active in Florence. He created intensely emotional versions of religious subjects, such as *The Last Communion of St Jerome*.

Dolci was the foremost painter in Florence in his time and continued to be much admired in the 18th century. He was also a portraitist, and was sent to Austria in 1675 to paint the Medici wife of the emperor Leopold I.

doldrums area of low atmospheric pressure along the equator, largely applied to oceans at the convergence of the NE and SE ◊trade winds. To some extent the area affected moves N and S with seasonal changes.

The doldrums are characterized by calm or very light westerly winds, during which there may be sudden squalls and stormy weather. For this reason the areas are avoided as far as possible by sailing ships.

dolerite an igneous rock formed below the Earth's surface, a form of basalt, containing relatively little silica (basic in composition).

Dolerite is a medium-grained (hypabyssal) basalt and forms in minor intrusions, such as dykes, which cut across the rock strata, and sills, which push between beds of sedimentary rock. When exposed at the surface, dolerite weathers into spherical lumps.

Dolin Anton. Adopted name of Patrick Healey-Kay 1904–1983. British dancer and choreographer, a pioneer of UK ballet. After studying under Nijinsky, he was a leading member of Diaghilev's company 1924–27. He formed the Markova–Dolin Ballet with Alicia Markova 1935–38, and was a guest soloist with the American Ballet Theater 1940–46.

dollar the monetary unit of several countries. In the US the dollar, which contains 100 cents, was adopted 1785 and is represented by the symbol "$." US dollars originally were issued as gold or

dolphin

silver coins; today both metal and paper dollars circulate, but paper predominates. Australia, Canada, and Hong Kong are among the other countries that use the dollar unit, but none of these dollars is equivalent in value to the US dollar.

The US dollar emerged from World War II as the standard currency for international trade. Commodities, even if priced in other currencies, were valued at the prevailing dollar exchange rate. Rising US imports, especially of oil, and government spending resulted in large numbers of dollars held in foreign hands with the resultant devaluation of the dollar by the 1980s. The German mark and the Japanese yen are increasingly important as trading currencies. See also ◊Eurodollar; ◊petrodollars.

Dollfuss Engelbert 1892–1934. Austrian Christian Socialist politician. He was appointed chancellor in 1932, and in 1933 suppressed parliament and ruled by decree. In Feb 1934 he crushed a protest by the Socialist workers by force, and in May Austria was declared a "corporative" state. The Nazis attempted a coup d'état on July 25; the Chancellery was seized and Dollfuss murdered.

Doll's House, The a play by Henrik Ibsen, first produced in Norway 1879. It describes the blackmail of Nora, the sheltered wife of a successful lawyer, the revelation of her guilty secret to her husband, and subsequent marital breakdown.

dolmen prehistoric monument in the form of a chamber built of large stone slabs, roofed over by a flat stone that they support. Dolmens are grave chambers of the Neolithic period, found in Europe and Africa, and occasionally in Asia as far east as Japan.

dolomite in geology, a sedimentary rock containing a high proportion of the mineral dolomite; a variety of limestone, or marble (if metamorphosed). The magnesian limestone of Northern England is a dolomite.

dolomite in mineralogy, calcium magnesium carbonate, $CaMg(Co_{32})$. It is similar to calcite but often forms rhombohedral crystals with curved faces. Dolomite occurs with ore minerals in veins; it can form by replacement of other carbonates in rocks, and can also precipitate from seawater.

dolphin any of various highly intelligent aquatic mammals of the family Delphinidae, which also includes porpoises. There are about 60 species. The name "dolphin" is generally applied to species having a beaklike snout and slender body, whereas the name "porpoise" is reserved for those with a blunt snout and stocky body. Dolphins use sound (echolocation) to navigate, to find prey, and for communication.

The common dolphin *Delphinus delphis* is found in all temperate and tropical seas. It is up to 8 ft/2.5 m long, and is dark above and white below, with bands of gray, white, and yellow on the sides. It has up to 100 teeth in its jaws, which make the 6 in/15 cm "beak" protrude forward from the rounded head. The corners of its mouth are permanently upturned, giving the appearance of a smile, though dolphins cannot actually smile. Dolphins feed on fish and squid.

The river dolphins, of which there are only five species, belong to the family Platanistidae. All river dolphins are threatened by dams and pollution, and some, such as the whitefin dolphin *Lipotes vexillifer* of the Chiang Jiang river, China, are in danger of extinction. As a result of living in muddy water, river dolphins' eyes have become very small. They rely on echolocation to navigate and find food.

Some species can swim at up to 35 mph/56 kph, helped by special streamlining modifications of the skin. All power themselves by beating the tail up and down, and use the flippers to steer and stabilize. The flippers betray dolphins' land-mammal ancestry with their typical five-toed limb-bone structure. The smallest dolphins are ◊porpoises.

Dolphins are popular performers in oceanaria. The species most frequently seen is the bottle-nosed dolphin *Tursiops truncatus*, found in all warm seas, mainly gray in color and growing to a maximum 14 ft/4.2 m. The US Navy began training dolphins for military purposes in 1962, and in 1987 six dolphins were sent to detect mines in the Persian Gulf.

Marine dolphins are endangered by fishing nets, speedboats, and pollution. In 1990 the North Sea states agreed to introduce legislation to protect dolphins.

Also known as dolphin is the totally unrelated true fish *Coryphaena hippurus*, up to 5 ft/1.5 m long.

Domagk Gerhard 1895–1964. German pathologist, discoverer of antibacterial sulfonamide drugs. He found in 1932 that a coal-tar dye called Prontosil red contains chemicals with powerful antibacterial properties. Sulfanilamide became the first of the sulfonamide drugs, used before ◊antibiotics were discovered to treat a wide range of conditions, including pneumonia and septic wounds. Nobel Prize for Physiology and Medicine 1939.

domain a small area in a magnetic field that behaves like a tiny magnet. Its magnetism is due to the movement of electrons in the atoms of the domain. In an unmagnetized sample, the domains point in random directions, or form closed loops, so that there is no overall magnetization of the sample. In a magnetized sample, the domains are aligned so that their magnetic effects combine to produce a strong overall magnetism.

dome a geologic feature that is the reverse of a basin. It consists of anticlinally folded rocks that dip in all directions from a central high point, like an inverted but usually irregular cup.

Such structural domes are the result of pressure acting upward from below to produce an uplifted portion of the crust. Domes are often formed by the upwelling of plastic materials such as salt or magma. The salt domes along the North American Gulf Coast were produced by upwelling ancient sea salt deposits, while the Black Hills of South Dakota are the result of structural domes pushed up by intruding igneous masses.

Domenichino real name Domenico Zampieri 1582–1641. Italian Baroque painter and architect, active in Bologna, Naples, and Rome. He began as an assistant to the ◊Carracci family of painters and continued its early Baroque style in, for example, frescoes 1624–28 in the choir of S Andrea della Valle, Rome.

This style was superseded by High Baroque, and Domenichino retreated to Naples. He is considered a pioneer of landscape painting in the Baroque period.

Domenico Veneziano c. 1400–1461. Italian painter, active in Florence. His few surviving frescoes and altarpieces show a remarkably delicate use of color and light (which recurs in the work of Piero della Francesca, who worked with him).

He worked in Sta Egidio, Florence, on frescoes now lost. Remaining works include the *Carnesecchi Madonna and Two Saints* and the St Lucy altarpiece, now divided between Florence (Uffizi), Berlin, Cambridge (Fitzwilliam), and Washington, DC (National Gallery).

Dome of the Rock building in Jerusalem dating from the 7th century AD that enshrines the rock from which, in Muslim tradition, Mohammed ascended to heaven on his ◊Night Journey. It stands on the site of the Jewish national Temple and is visited by pilgrims.

Domingo *Opera singer Placido Domingo, the noted tenor.*

Domesday Book record of the survey of England carried out 1086 by officials of William the Conqueror in order to assess land tax and other dues, ascertain the value of the crown lands, and enable the king to estimate the power of his vassal barons.

Northumberland and Durham were omitted, and also London, Winchester, and certain other towns. The Domesday Book is preserved in two volumes at the Public Record Office, London. The name is derived from the belief that its judgment was as final as that of Doomsday.

dominance in genetics, the masking of one ◊allele by another allele. For example, if a ◊heterozygous person has one allele for blue eyes and one for brown eyes, their eye color will be brown. The allele for blue eyes is described as ◊recessive and the allele for brown eyes as dominant.

Domingo Placido 1937– . Spanish tenor who excels in romantic operatic roles. A member of a musical family, he emigrated with them to Mexico in 1950. He made his debut in 1960 as Alfredo in Verdi's *La Traviata*, then spent four years with the Israel National Opera. He sang at the New York City Opera in 1965 and has since performed diverse roles in opera houses worldwide. In 1986 he starred in the film version of *Otello*.

Dominica island in E Caribbean, between Guadeloupe and Martinique, the largest of the Windward Islands, with the Atlantic to the E and the Caribbean to the W.

government Dominica is an independent republic within the ◊Commonwealth. The constitution dates from independence in 1978 and provides for a single-chamber, 30-member house of assembly. Twenty-one are representatives elected by universal suffrage, and nine are appointed senators, five on the advice of the prime minister and four on the advice of the leader of the opposition. The assembly serves a five-year term, as does the president, who is elected by it and acts as constitutional head of state, appointing the prime minister on the basis of assembly support. The prime minister chooses the cabinet, and all are responsible to the assembly. The two main political parties are the Dominica Freedom Party (DFP) and the Labor Party of Dominica.

history The island was inhabited by the Amerindian Carib tribe at the time Christopher ◊Columbus visited it in 1493 (as Columbus discovered the island on a Sunday, he named it Dominica). It became a British possession in the 18th century and was part of the Leeward Islands federation until 1939. In 1940 it was transferred to the Wind-

Dominica
Commonwealth of

USA
DOMINICA
ATLANTIC
OCEAN
Roseau
Mexico
Cuba
CARIBBEAN
SEA
Guadaloupe
Martinique
Venezuela
PACIFIC
OCEAN
0 miles 500
0 km 1000

area 290 sq mi/751 sq km
capital Roseau, with a deepwater port
cities Portsmouth, Marigot
physical second largest of the Windward Islands, mountainous central ridge with tropical rainforest
features of great beauty, it has mountains of volcanic origin rising to 5,317 ft/1,620 m; Boiling Lake (an effect produced by escaping subterranean gas)
head of state Clarence Seignoret from 1983
head of government Eugenia Charles from 1980
political system liberal democracy
political parties Dominica Freedom Party (DFP), centrist; Labor Party of Dominica (LPD), left-of-center coalition
exports bananas, coconuts, citrus, lime, bay oil
currency E Caribbean dollar
population (1990 est) 94,200 (mainly black African in origin, but with a small Carib reserve of some 500); growth rate 1.3% p.a.
life expectancy men 57, women 59
language English (official), but the Dominican *patois* still reflects earlier periods of French rule
religion Roman Catholic 80%
literacy 80%
GDP $91 million (1985); $1,090 per head
chronology
1763 Became British possession.
1978 Independence achieved from Britain. Patrick John, leader of DLP, elected prime minister.
1980 DFP, led by Eugenia Charles, won convincing victory in general election.
1981 Patrick John implicated in plot to overthrow government.
1982 John tried and acquitted.
1985 John retried and found guilty. Regrouping of left-of-center parties resulted in new Labor Party of Dominica (LPD). DFP, led by Eugenia Charles, reelected.

ward Islands and remained attached to that group until 1960, when it was given separate status, with a chief minister and legislative council.

In 1961 the leader of the Dominica Labor Party (DLP), Edward le Blanc, became chief minister; after 13 years in office he retired and was succeeded as prime minister by Patrick John. The DLP held office until full independence was achieved in 1978, at which time its leader, John, became the first prime minister under the new constitution. Opposition to John's increasingly authoritarian style of government soon developed, and in the 1980 elections the Dominica Freedom Party (DFP) won a convincing victory on a free enterprise policy program. Its leader, Eugenia Charles, became the Caribbean's first woman prime minister.

In 1981 John was thought to be implicated in a plot against the government, and a state of emergency was imposed. The next year he was tried and acquitted. He was retried in 1985, found guilty and given a 12-year prison sentence. Left-of-center parties regrouped, making the Labor Party of Dominica (LPD) the main opposition to the DFP. In the 1985 elections Eugenia Charles was reelected. Under her leadership, Dominica has developed links with France and the US and in 1983 sent a small force to participate in the US-backed invasion of ◊Grenada. Although Charles was elected to a third term in 1990, her party's legislative majority was reduced.

Dominican order Roman Catholic order of friars founded 1215 by St Dominic; they are also known as Friars Preachers, Black Friars, or Jacobins. The order is worldwide and there is also an order of contemplative nuns; the habit is black and white.

The first house was established in Toulouse in 1215; in 1216 the order received papal recognition, and their rule was drawn up in 1220–21. They soon spread all over Europe. Dominicans have included Thomas Aquinas, Savonarola, and Las Casas.

Dominican Republic country in the West Indies (E Caribbean), occupying eastern part of the island of Hispaniola, with Haiti covering western end.

government Although not a federal state, the Dominican Republic has a highly devolved system of 27 provinces (each administered by an appointed governor), and a national district, which includes the capital, Santo Domingo. The 1966 constitution provides for a popularly elected president and a two-chamber congress, comprising a senate and a chamber of deputies, all elected for a four-year term. The senate has 28 members, one for each province and one for the national district, and the chamber of deputies 120 members, one per 50,000 inhabitants. The president is head of both government and state and chooses the cabinet. Most significant among a wide range of political parties are the left-wing Dominican Revolutionary Party (PRD) and the centrist Christian Social Reform Party (PRSC).

history The island was inhabited by Arawak and Carib Indians when Christopher ◊Columbus arrived in 1492, the first European to visit the island. He named it Hispaniola ("Little Spain"). It was divided between France and Spain in 1697, and in 1795 the Spanish part (Santo Domingo) was ceded to France. After a revolt it was retaken by Spain in 1808. Following a brief period of independence in 1821 it was occupied by Haiti until a successful revolt resulted in the establishment of the Dominican Republic in 1844.

Spain occupied the country again 1861–65, and after independence was restored, it was in such financial difficulties that in 1904 the US took over its debts and intervened militarily 1916–24.

In 1930 the elected president was overthrown in a military coup, and General Rafael Trujillo Molina became dictator. He was assassinated in 1961, and in 1963 Dr Juan Bosch, founder and leader of the left-wing PRD and who had been in exile for over 30 years, won the country's first free elections. Within a year he was overthrown by the military, who set up their own three-man ruling junta.

An attempt to reestablish Bosch in 1965 was defeated with the intervention of US forces, and in 1966 Joaquín Balaguer, a protégé of Trujillo and leader of the PRSC, won the presidency. A more democratic constitution was adopted, and Balaguer, despite his links with Trujillo, proved a popular leader, being reelected in 1970 and 1974.

The 1978 election was won by the PRD candidate, Silvestre Antonio Guzmán. The PRD was again successful in the 1982 election, and Salvador Jorge Blanco, the party's left-wing nominee, became president-designate. After allegations of fraud by his family, Guzmán committed suicide before he had finished his term, and an interim president was chosen before the start of Blanco's term.

Blanco steered a restrained course in foreign policy, maintaining good relations with the US and avoiding too close an association with Cuba. The economy deteriorated, and in 1985 the Blanco administration was forced to adopt harsh austerity measures in return for ◊IMF help. The PRD became increasingly unpopular, and the PRSC, under Joaquín Balaguer, returned to power in 1986. He was reelected in 1990, but by a paper-thin margin, and his party lost its legislative majority.

Dominic, St 1170–1221. Founder of the Roman Catholic Dominican order of preaching friars. Feast day Aug 7.

Born in Old Castile, Dominic was sent by Pope Innocent III in 1205 to preach among the heretic Albigensian sect in Provence. In 1208 the pope instigated the Albigensian crusade to suppress the heretics by force, and this was supported by Dominic. In 1215 the Dominican order was given premises at Toulouse; during the following years Dominic established friaries at Bologna and elsewhere in Italy, and by the time of his death the order was established all over W Europe.

Domino "Fats" (Antoine) 1928– . US rock-and-roll pianist, singer, and songwriter, exponent of the New Orleans style. His hits include "Ain't That A Shame" 1955 and "Blueberry Hill" 1956.

domino theory idea popularized by US President Eisenhower in 1954 that if one country comes under communist rule, adjacent countries are likely to become communist as well. Initially used to justify US intervention in SE Asia, the domino theory has also been invoked in reference to Central America.

Domitian Titus Flavius Domitianus AD 51–96. Roman emperor from AD 81. He finalized the conquest of Britain (see ◊Agricola), strengthened the Rhine–Danube frontier, and suppressed immorality as well as freedom of thought (see ◊Epictetus) in philosophy and religion (Christians were persecuted). His reign of terror led to his assassination.

Don river in the USSR, rising to the S of Moscow and entering the NE extremity of the Sea of Azov; length 1,180 mi/1,900 km. In its lower reaches the Don is 1 mi/1.5 km wide, and for about four months of the year it is closed by ice. Its upper course is linked with the river Volga by a canal.

Donald Ian 1910–1987. English obstetrician who introduced ultrasound (very high-frequency sound waves) scanning. He pioneered its use in obstetrics as a means of scanning the growing fetus without exposure to the danger of X rays. Donald's experience of using radar in World War II suggested to him the use of ultrasound for medical purposes.

Donaldson Stephen 1947– . US fantasy writer, author of two Thomas Covenant trilogies 1978–83.

Donat Robert 1905–1958. English actor. He started out in the theater and made one film in Hollywood (*The Count of Monte Cristo* 1934). His other films include Alfred Hitchcock's *The Thirty-Nine Steps* 1935, *Goodbye, Mr Chips* 1939 for which he won an Academy Award, and *The Winslow Boy* 1948.

Donatello (Donato di Niccolo) 1386–1466. Italian sculptor of the early Renaissance, born in Florence. He was instrumental in reviving the Classical style, as in his graceful bronze statue of the youthful *David* (Bargello, Florence) and his equestrian statue of the general *Gattamelata* 1443 (Padua). The course of Florentine art in the 15th century was strongly influenced by his style.

Donatello introduced true perspective in his relief sculptures, like the panel of *St George Slaying the Dragon* about 1415–17 (Or San Michele, Florence). During a stay in Rome 1430–32 he absorbed Classical influences, and *David* is said

Dominican Republic
(República Dominicana)

USA
DOMINICAN REPUBLIC
Santo Domingo
Mexico
ATLANTIC OCEAN
Cuba
Haiti
Puerto Rico
CARIBBEAN SEA
Venezuela
PACIFIC OCEAN
0 miles 500
0 km 1000

area 18,700 sq mi/48,442 sq km
capital Santo Domingo
cities Santiago de los Caballeros, San Pedro de Macoris
physical comprises eastern two-thirds of island of Hispaniola; central mountain range with fertile valleys
features Pico Duarte 10,417 ft/3,174 m, highest point in Caribbean islands; Santo Domingo is the oldest European city in the western hemisphere
head of state and government Joaquín Ricardo Balaguer from 1986
political system democratic republic
political parties Dominican Revolutionary Party (PRD), moderate left-of-center; Christian Social Reform Party (PRSC), independent Socialist; Dominican Liberation Party (PLD), nationalist
exports sugar, gold, silver, tobacco, coffee, nickel
currency peso
population (1989 est) 7,307,000; growth rate 2.3% p.a.
life expectancy men 61, women 65
language Spanish (official)
religion Roman Catholic 95%
literacy men 78%/women 77% (1985 est)
GDP $4.9 bn (1987); $731 per head
chronology
1844 Dominican Republic established.
1930 Military coup established dictatorship of Rafael Trujillo.
1961 Trujillo assassinated.
1962 First democratic elections resulted in Juan Bosch, founder of PRD, becoming president.
1963 Bosch overthrown in military coup.
1965 US Marines intervened to restore order and protect foreign nationals.
1966 New constitution adopted. Joaquín Balaguer, leader of the PRSC, became president.
1978 PRD returned to power, with Silvestre Antonio Guzmán as president.
1982 PRD re-elected, with Jorge Blanco as president.
1985 Blanco forced by International Monetary Fund to adopt austerity measures to save the economy.
1986 PRSC returned to power, with Balaguer re-elected president.

to be the first free-standing nude since antiquity. In his later work, such as his wood-carving of the aged *Mary Magdalene* about 1456 (Baptistry, Florence), he sought dramatic expression through a distorted, emaciated figure style.

Donation of Constantine a forged 8th-century document purporting to record the Roman emperor Constantine's surrender of temporal sovereignty in W Europe to Pope Sylvester I (314–25).

In the Middle Ages, this document was used as papal propaganda in the struggle between pope and emperor, which was at its most heated during the ◊Investiture Contest. It was finally exposed as forged by ◊Nicholas of Cusa and Lorenzo Valla in the 15th century.

Donatist a member of a puritanical Christian movement in 4th and 5th-century N Africa, named after Donatus of Casae Nigrae, a 3rd-century bishop, later known as Donatus of Carthage.

The Donatists became for a time the major Christian movement in N Africa; following the tradition of ◊Montanism, their faith stressed the social revolutionary aspects of Christianity, the separation of church from state, and a belief in martyrdom and suffering. Their influence was ended by Bishop Augustine of Hippo; they were formally condemned 412.

Donau German name for the ◊Danube.

Donbas acronym for ◊Donets Basin, a coal-rich area in the USSR.

Doncaster town in South Yorkshire, England, on the river Don; population (1981) 81,600. It has a racecourse; famous races here are the St Leger (1776) in Sept and the Lincolnshire Handicap in Mar.

Donegal mountainous county in Ulster province in the NW of the Republic of Ireland, surrounded on three sides by the Atlantic; area 1,864 sq mi/4,830 sq km; population (1986) 130,000. The county town is Lifford; the market town and port of Donegal is at the head of Donegal Bay in the SW. Commercial activities include sheep and cattle raising, tweed and linen manufacture, and some deep-sea fishing. The river Erne hydroelectric project (1952) involved the building of large power stations at Ballyshannon.

Donellan Declan 1953– . British theater director, cofounder of Cheek by Jowl theater company 1981, and associate director of the National Theatre from 1989. His irreverent and audacious productions include many classics, such as Racine's *Andromaque*.

Donen Stanley 1924– . US film director, formerly a dancer, who codirected two of Gene Kelly's best musicals, *On the Town* 1949 and *Singin' in the Rain* 1952. His other films include *Charade* 1963 and *Two for the Road* 1968.

Donets river of the USSR rising in Kursk region and flowing 670 mi/1,080 km through Ukraine to join the river Don 60 mi/100 km E of Rostov; see also ◊Donets Basin.

Donets Basin abbreviated *Donbas* area in the bend formed by the rivers Don and Donets, which holds one of Europe's richest coalfields, together with salt, mercury, and lead, so that the Donbas is one of the greatest industrial regions of the USSR.

Donetsk city in Ukraine, USSR; capital of Donetsk region, situated in the Donets Basin, a major coal mining area, 372 mi/600 km SE of Kiev; population (1987) 1,090,000. It has blast furnaces, rolling mills, and other heavy industries.

It developed from 1871 when a Welshman, John Hughes, established a metallurgical factory, and the town was first called Yuzovka after him; renamed Stalino 1924, and Donetsk 1961.

Dongola town in the Northern Province of the Sudan, above the third cataract on the river Nile. It was founded about 1812 to replace Old Dongola, 75 mi/120 km up river, which was destroyed by the ◊Mamelukes. The latter, a trading center on a caravan route, was the capital of the Christian kingdom of ◊Nubia between the 6th and 14th centuries.

Dongting lake in Hunan province, China; area 4,000 sq mi/10,000 sq km.

Dönitz Karl 1891–1980. German admiral, originator of the wolf-pack submarine technique, which sank 15 million tons of Allied shipping in World War II. He succeeded Hitler in 1945, capitulated, and was imprisoned 1946–56.

Donizetti Gaetano 1797–1848. Italian composer who created more than 60 operas, including *Lucrezia Borgia* 1833, *Lucia di Lammermoor* 1835, *La Fille du régiment* 1840, *La Favorite* 1840, and *Don Pasquale* 1843. They show the influence of Rossini and Bellini, and are characterized by a flow of expressive melodies.

Don Juan character of Spanish legend, Don Juan Tenorio, supposed to have lived in the 14th century and notorious for his debauchery. Tirso de Molina, Molière, Mozart, Byron, and George Bernard Shaw have featured the legend in their works.

donkey another name for ◊ass.

Donne John 1571–1631. English metaphysical poet whose work is characterized by subtle imagery and figurative language. In 1615 Donne took orders in the Church of England and as dean of St Paul's Cathedral, London, was noted for his sermons. His poetry includes the sonnets "Batter my heart, three person'd God" and "Death be not proud," elegies, and satires.

Donne was brought up in the Roman Catholic faith and matriculated early at Oxford to avoid taking the oath of supremacy. Before becoming a law student 1592 he traveled in Europe. During his four years at the law courts he was notorious for his wit and reckless living. In 1596 he sailed as a volunteer with Essex and Raleigh, and on his return became private secretary to Sir Thomas Egerton, Keeper of the Seal. This appointment was ended by his secret marriage to Ann More (died 1617), niece of Egerton's wife, and they endured many years of poverty. The more passionate and tender of his love poems were probably written to her.

From 1621 to his death Donne was dean of St Paul's. His sermons rank him with the century's greatest orators, and his fervent poems of love and hate, violent, tender, or abusive, give him a unique position among English poets. His verse was not published in collected form until after his death, and was long out of favor, but he is now recognized as one of the greatest English poets.

Donnybrook former village, now part of Dublin, Republic of Ireland, notorious until 1855 for riotous fairs.

Donovan William Joseph 1883–1959. US military leader and public official. Donovan served as US district attorney 1922–24 and as assistant to the US attorney general 1925–29. He was national security adviser to both presidents Hoover and F D Roosevelt and founded the Office of Strategic Services (OSS) 1942. As OSS director 1942–45, Donovan coordinated US intelligence during World War II. When the OSS became the CIA 1947, President Truman passed over Donovan as its first director. President Eisenhower, however, appointed Donovan ambassador to Thailand 1953–54, calling him America's "last hero."

Born in Buffalo, New York, Donovan was educated at Columbia University and was admitted to the bar 1907. He saw action along the Mexican border 1912 and was decorated for bravery during World War I, gaining the nickname "Wild Bill."

Don Pacifico Affair incident in 1850 in which British foreign secretary Lord Palmerston was criticized in Parliament and elsewhere in Europe for using British naval superiority to impose his foreign policy. Palmerston sent gunboats to blockade the Greek coast in support of the claim of a Portugese merchant, David Pacifico, who was born on Gibraltar (and thus a British subject), for compensation from the Greek government after his house was burned down in anti-Semitic riots.

This action brought diplomatic protests from the governments of France and Russia, who had also guaranteed Greek independence. Palmerston successfully defended his action in Parliament, but fell from power the following year, 1851.

Don Quixote de la Mancha a satirical romance by Cervantes, published in two parts 1605 and 1615.

Don Quixote, a self-styled knight, embarks on a series of chivalric adventures accompanied by his servant Sancho Panza. Quixote's imagination leads him to see harmless objects as enemies to be fought, as in his tilting at windmills.

doodlebug another name for ◊ant lion.

Dooley Thomas Anthony 1927–1961. US medical missionary. Born in St Louis, Dooley attended Notre Dame University, joined the navy, and received an MD degree from St Louis University 1953. As a naval physician, he was sent to Vietnam 1954 to tend to the refugees streaming S after the partition of the country. This assignment aroused Dooley's compassion, and he was involved in medical work in SE Asia for the rest of his life. He founded Medico, an international welfare organization 1957, as well as medical clinics in Cambodia, Laos, and Vietnam.

Doolittle Hilda. Adopted name HD 1886–1961. US poet. She went to Europe in 1911, and was associated with Ezra Pound and the British writer Richard Aldington (to whom she was married 1913–37) in founding the ◊Imagist school of poetry, advocating simplicity, precision, and brevity. Her work includes the *Sea Garden* 1916 and *Helen in Egypt* 1916.

Doolittle James Harold 1896– . US aviation pioneer. Born in Alameda, California, Doolittle attended the University of California and served as an army flying instructor during World War I. Later, in the Army Air Corps, he became an aviation specialist, earning an engineering degree from the Massachusetts Institute of Technology (MIT). He helped develop new aircraft designs and more efficient aircraft fuel. With the approach of World War II, he returned to active service and in 1942 led a daring bombing raid over Tokyo. Later in the war he participated in the invasion of North Africa and the intensive bombing of Germany.

Doomsday Book variant spelling of ◊Domesday Book, English survey of 1086.

Doors, the US psychedelic rock group formed 1965 in Los Angeles by Jim Morrison (1943–1971, vocals), Ray Manzarek (1935– , keyboards), Robby Krieger (1946– , guitar), and John Densmore (1944– , drums). Their first hit was "Light My Fire" from their debut album *The Doors* 1967. They were noted for Morrison's poetic lyrics and flamboyant performance.

dopamine a neurotransmitter, hydroxytyramine $C_8H_{11}NO_2$, an intermediate in the formation of epinephrine. There are special neurones in the brain that use dopamine for the transmission of nervous impulses. One such area of dopamine neurones lies in the basal ganglia, a region that controls movement. Patients suffering from the tremors of Parkinson's disease show nerve degeneration in this region. Another dopamine brain area lies in the limbic system, a region closely involved with emotional responses. It has been found that schizophrenic patients respond well to drugs that act on limbic dopamine receptors in the brain.

doppelgänger (German "double-goer") a ghostly apparition identical to a living person; a twin soul.

Doppler Christian Johann 1803–1853. Austrian physicist. He became professor of experimental physics at Vienna. He described the Doppler effect.

Doppler effect change in observed frequency (or wavelength) of waves due to relative motion between wave source and observer. It is responsible for the perceived change in pitch of a siren as it approaches and then recedes, and for the ◊red shift of light from distant stars. It is named after the Austrian physicist Christian Doppler.

Dorado constellation of the southern hemisphere, represented as a goldfish. It is easy to locate because the Large ◊Magellanic Cloud marks its southern border. Its brightest star is Alpha Doradus, just under 200 light-years from Earth.

Dorati Antal 1906–1988. US conductor, born in Hungary. He toured with ballet companies 1933–45 and went on to conduct orchestras in the US and Europe in a career spanning more than half a century. Dorati gave many first performances of Bartók's music and recorded all Haydn's symphonies with the Philharmonia Hungarica.

Dordogne river in SW France, rising in Puy-de-Dôme *département* and flowing 300 mi/490 km to join the river Garonne, 14 mi/23 km N of Bordeaux. It gives its name to a *département* and is a major source of hydroelectric power.

The valley of the Dordogne is a popular tourist area, and the caves of the wooded valleys of its tributary, the Vézère, have signs of early human occupation. Famous sites include Cro Magnon, Moustier, and the Lascaux caves, discovered in 1940, which have the earliest known examples of cave art. Images of bulls, bison, and deer were painted by the CroMagnon people (named after skeletons found 1868 in Cro Magnon Cave, near Les Eyzies). The opening of the Lascaux caves to tourists led to deterioration of the paintings; the caves were closed in 1963 and a facsimile opened in 1983.

Dordrecht or ***Dort*** river port on an island in the Maas, South Holland, the Netherlands, 12 mi/ 19 km SE of Rotterdam; population (1988) 108,000, metropolitan area of Dordrecht-Zwijndrecht 203,000. It is an inland port with shipbuilding yards and makes heavy machinery, plastics, and chemicals.

Doré Gustave 1832–1883. French artist, chiefly known as a prolific illustrator, and also active as a painter, etcher, and sculptor. He produced closely worked engravings of scenes from, for example, Rabelais, Dante, Cervantes, the Bible, Milton, and Poe.

Doré was born in Strasbourg. His views of Victorian London 1869–71, concentrating on desperate poverty and overcrowding in the swollen city, were admired by van Gogh.

Dorian a people of ancient Greece. They entered Greece from the north and conquered most of the Peloponnese from the Achaeans, destroying the ◊Mycenean civilization; this invasion appears to have been completed before 1000 BC. Their chief cities were Sparta, Argos, and Corinth.

Doric in Classical architecture, one of the five types of column; see ◊order.

dormancy in botany, a phase of reduced physiological activity exhibited by certain buds, seeds, and spores. Dormancy can help a plant to survive unfavorable conditions, as in annual plants that pass the cold winter season as dormant seeds, and plants that form dormant buds.

For various reasons many seeds exhibit a period of dormancy even when conditions are favorable for growth. Sometimes this dormancy can be broken by artificial methods, such as penetrating the seed coat to facilitate the uptake of water (chitting) or exposing the seed to light. See ◊after-ripening.

dormouse small rodent, of the family Gliridae, with a hairy tail. There are about ten species, living in Europe, Asia, and Africa. They are arboreal (live in trees) and nocturnal, and they hibernate during winter in cold regions.

The fat or edible dormouse *Glis glis* lives in continental Europe and is 12 in/30 cm long including its tail. It was a delicacy at Roman feasts.

Dornier Claude 1884–1969. German pioneer aircraft designer who invented the flying boat (◊seaplane). During World War II he designed many of Germany's military aircraft.

Dorset county in SW England

area 1,023 sq mi/2,650 sq km

cities Dorchester (administrative headquarters), Poole, Shaftesbury, Sherborne; resorts: Bournemouth, Lyme Regis, Weymouth

features Chesil Bank, a shingle bank along the coast 11 mi/19 km long; Isle of Purbeck, a peninsula where kaolinite and Purbeck "marble" are quarried, and which includes Corfe Castle and the vacation resort of Swanage; Dorset Downs; Cranborne Chase; rivers Frome and Stour; Maiden Castle; Tank Museum at Royal Armoured Corps Centre, Bovington, where the cottage of T E ◊Lawrence is a museum

products Wytch Farm is the largest onshore oilfield in the UK

population (1987) 649,000

famous people Thomas Hardy, the novelist, born at Higher Bockhampton (Dorchester is "Casterbridge," the heart of Hardy's Wessex).

Dostoievsky *Author of* Crime and Punishment *and* The Brothers Karamazov, *Russian novelist Fyodor Dostoievsky.*

Dort another name for ◊Dordrecht, a port in the Netherlands.

Dortmund industrial center in the ◊Ruhr, Germany, 36 mi/58 km NE of Düsseldorf; population (1988) 568,000. It is the largest mining town of the Westphalian coalfield and the southern terminus of the Dortmund-Ems canal. Industries include iron, steel, construction machinery, engineering, and brewing.

dory any of several marine fishes of the order Zeiformes. The American John Dory *Zenopsis ocellata*, to 2 ft/60 cm long, is deep-bodied with long spines on the dorsal and ventral fins. It lives in depths of 300 ft/90 m to 1,200 ft/365 m.

DOS (acronym for disk operating system) in computing, an ◊operating system specifically designed for use with disk storage; also used as an alternate name for a particular operating system, ◊MS-DOS.

Dos Passos John 1896–1970. US author. He made his reputation with the war novels *One Man's Initiation* 1919 and *Three Soldiers* 1921. His major work is the trilogy *U.S.A.* 1930–36, which gives a panoramic view of US life through the device of placing fictitious characters against the setting of real newspaper headlines and contemporary events.

Born in Chicago, Dos Passos was a member of the post–World War I "lost generation," and his writing was shaped by his radical sympathies. He also wrote a second, less ambitious trilogy, *District of Columbia* 1939–49. Other works include *One Man's Initiation - 1917* 1919 and *Midcentury* 1961.

Dos Santos Jose Eduardo 1942– . Angolan left-wing politician, president from 1979, a member of the People's Movement for the Liberation of Angola (MPLA).

Dos Santos joined the MPLA in 1961 and went into exile the same year during the struggle for independence and the civil war between nationalist movements—the MPLA and the National Union for the Total Independence of Angola (UNITA)—backed by foreign powers. He returned to Angola in 1970 and rejoined the war, which continued after independence in 1975. He held key positions under President Agostinho Neto, and succeeded him on his death. By 1989, he had negotiated the withdrawal of South African and Cuban forces, and a ceasefire between MPLA and UNITA.

Dostoievsky Fyodor Mihailovich 1821–1881. Russian novelist. Remarkable for their profound psychological insight, Dostoievsky's novels have greatly influenced Russian writers, and since the beginning of the 20th century have been increasingly influential abroad. In 1849 he was sentenced to four years' hard labor in Siberia, followed by army service, for printing Socialist propaganda. *The House of the Dead* 1861 recalls his prison experiences, followed by his major works *Crime and Punishment* 1866, *The Idiot* 1868–69, and *The Brothers Karamazov* 1880.

Born in Moscow, the son of a physician, he was for a short time an army officer. His first novel, *Poor Folk*, appeared in 1846. In 1849, during a period of intense tsarist censorship, Dostoievsky was arrested as a member of a free-thinking literary circle and sentenced to death. After a last-minute reprieve he was sent to the penal settlement at Omsk for four years, where the terrible conditions increased his epileptic tendency. Finally pardoned in 1859, he published the humorous *Village of Stepanchikovo*, *The House of the Dead*, and *The Insulted and the Injured* 1862. Meanwhile he had launched two unsuccessful liberal periodicals, in the second of which his *Letters from the Underworld* 1864 appeared. Compelled to work by pressure of debt, he quickly produced *Crime and Punishment* 1866 and *The Gambler* 1867, before fleeing the country to escape from his creditors. He then wrote *The Idiot* (in which the hero is an epileptic like himself), *The Eternal Husband* 1870, and *The Possessed* 1871–72.

Returning to Russia in 1871, he again entered journalism and issued the personal miscellany *Journal of an Author*, in which he discussed contemporary problems. In 1875 he published *A Raw Youth*, but the great work of his last years is *The Brothers Karamazov*.

Dothan city in the SE corner of Alabama, SE of Montgomery; seat of Houston county. Its industries include fertilizer, clothing, furniture, vegetable oils, and hosiery. It is an agricultural and livestock marketing center; population (1990) 53,589.

Dou Gerard 1613–1675. Dutch genre painter, a pupil of Rembrandt. He is known for small domestic interiors, minutely observed. He was born in Leiden, where he founded a painters' guild with Jan Steen. He had many pupils, including Metsu.

Douai town in the Nord *département*, France, on the river Scarpe; population (1982) 44,515, conurbation 202,000. It has coal mines, iron foundries, and breweries. An English Roman Catholic college was founded here 1568 by English Catholics in exile. The Douai-Reims Bible, published 1582–1610, influenced the translators of the King James Version.

Douala or *Duala* chief port and industrial center (aluminum, chemicals, textiles, pulp) of Cameroon, on the Wouri river estuary; population (1981) 637,000. Known as Kamerunstadt until 1907, it was capital of German Cameroon 1885–1901.

double bass a large bowed four-stringed musical instrument, the bass of the ◊violin family, tuned in fourths, and descended from the violone of the ◊viol family.

double bond two covalent bonds between adjacent atoms, as in the ◊alkenes (–C=C–) and ◊ketones (–C=O–).

double coconut treelike ◊palm plant *Lodoicea maldivica*, also known as *coco de mer*, of the Seychelles. It produces a two-lobed edible nut, one of the largest known fruits.

Doubleday Abner 1819–1893. Military leader and reputed inventor of baseball. Born in Ballston Spa, New York, Doubleday graduated from West Point 1842 and saw action in the Mexican War. He was present at Fort Sumter at the outbreak of the Civil War and was eventually promoted to the rank of major general, serving in the Shenandoah Valley and at Bull Run, Antietam, and Gettysburg. He retired from active service 1873. In 1907 Doubleday's name surfaced during a baseball committee's investigation into the origins of the major-league sport. According to testimony given at the time, Doubleday invented the game of baseball 1839 in Cooperstown, New York, a claim refuted by sports historians ever since.

double decomposition reaction between two chemical substances (usually ◊salts in solution) that results in the exchange of a constituent from each compound to create two different compounds.

For example, if silver nitrate solution is added to a solution of sodium chloride, there is an exchange of ions yielding sodium nitrate and silver chloride.

double jeopardy in law, the principle that a person cannot be prosecuted twice for the same offense. It is contained in the Fifth Amendment of the US Constitution.

double star two stars that appear close together. Most double stars attract each other due to gravity and orbit each other, forming a genuine ◊binary star, but other double stars are at different distances from Earth, and lie in the same line of sight only by chance. Through a telescope both types of double star will look the same.

Doubs river in France and Switzerland, rising in the Jura mountains and flowing 265 mi/430 km to join the river Saône. It gives its name to a *département*.

dough a mixture consisting primarily of flour, water, and yeast, which is used in the manufacture of bread.

The preparation of dough involves thorough mixing (kneading) and standing in a warm place to "prove" (increase in volume) so that the ◊enzymes in the dough can break down the starch from the flour into smaller sugar molecues, which are then fermented by the yeast. This releases carbon dioxide, which causes the dough to rise.

doughboy nickname for a US infantry soldier in the two world wars, especially World War I.

Douglas Kirk. Adopted name of Issur Danielovitch Demsky 1916– . US film actor. Usually cast as a dynamic and intelligent hero, as in *Spartacus* 1960, he was a major star of the 1950s and 1960s in such films as *Ace in the Hole* 1951, *The Bad and the Beautiful* 1953, *Lust for Life* 1956, *The Vikings* 1958, and *Seven Days in May* 1964. He continues to act and to produce, along with his son Michael Douglas.

Douglas Stephen Arnold 1813–1861. US politician. An active Democrat, he served in the Illinois state legislature 1836, as a judge of the state supreme court 1841, and in the US House of Representatives 1843–47. As a US senator 1847–61, he gained the nickname "Little Giant" for his support for westward expansion. Urging a compromise on slavery, he debated Lincoln during the 1858 Senate race and won that election. After losing the 1860 presidential race to Lincoln, Douglas pledged his loyal support to the Lincoln administration.

Born in Brandon, Vermont, Douglas moved west, settling in Illinois, where he studied law and was admitted to the bar 1834.

Douglass Frederick 1817–1895. US antislavery campaigner, especially through speeches and his newspaper *North Star*. He issued a call to blacks to take up arms against the South and helped organize two black regiments. After the Civil War, he held several US government posts, including minister to Haiti 1889–91. He published appeals for full civil rights for blacks and also campaigned for women's suffrage.

Born a slave in Maryland, he escaped 1838 and fled to Britain to avoid reenslavement, returning to the US after he had secured sufficient funds to purchase his freedom. His autobiographical *Narrative of the Life of Frederick Douglass* 1845 aroused support for the abolition of slavery.

Doukhobor member of a Christian sect of Russian origin, now mainly found in Canada, also known as "Christians of the Universal Brotherhood." Some of the Doukhobor teachings resemble those of the Quakers.

They were long persecuted, mainly for refusing military service—the writer Tolstoy organized a relief fund for them—but in 1898 were permitted to emigrate and settled in Canada, where they number about 13,000, mainly in British Columbia and Saskatchewan. An extremist group, "the Sons of Freedom," staged demonstrations and guerrilla acts in the 1960s, leading to the imprisonment of about 100 of them.

Doulton Henry 1820–1897. English ceramicist. He developed special wares for the chemical, electrical, and building industries, and established the world's first stoneware drainpipe factory 1846. From 1870 he created art pottery and domestic tablewares in Lambeth, S London, and Burslem, near Stoke-on-Trent.

Dounreay an experimental nuclear reactor site on the north coast of Scotland, 7 mi/12 km W of Thurso. Development started in 1974 and continued until a decision was made in 1988 to decommission the site by 1994.

Douro (Spanish *Duero*) river rising in N central Spain and flowing through N Portugal to the Atlantic at Porto; length 500 mi/800 km. Navigation at the river mouth is hindered by sand bars. There are hydroelectric installations.

dove another name for ◊pigeon.

Dover market town and seaport on the SE coast of Kent, England; population (1981) 33,000. It is Britain's nearest point to mainland Europe, being only 21 mi/34 km from Calais, France. Dover's development has been chiefly due to the cross-Channel traffic, which includes train, ferry, hovercraft, and other services. It was one of the ◊Cinque Ports.

history Under Roman rule, Dover (Portus Dubris) was the terminus of Watling Street, and the beacon or "lighthouse" in the grounds of the Norman castle dates from about AD 50, making it one of the oldest buildings in Britain.

Dover city in SE New Hampshire on the Cocheco river, NW of Portsmouth; seat of Strafford county. Industries include lumber, electronics, rubber, and aluminum products; population (1990) 25,042.

Dover capital of Delaware, located in the central part of the state, on the St Jones river, S of Wilmington. Industries include synthetic materials, adhesives, latex, resins, chemicals, food products, and space equipment; population (1990) 27,630.

Dover, Strait of (French *Pas-de-Calais*) stretch of water separating England from France, and connecting the English Channel with the North Sea. It is about 22 mi/35 km long and 21 mi/34 km wide at its narrowest part. It is one of the world's busiest sea lanes.

Dowding Hugh Caswall Tremenheere, 1st Baron Dowding 1882–1970. British air chief marshal. He was chief of Fighter Command at the outbreak of World War II in 1939, a post he held through the Battle of Britain. He wrote works on spiritualism.

Dowell Anthony 1943– . British ballet dancer in

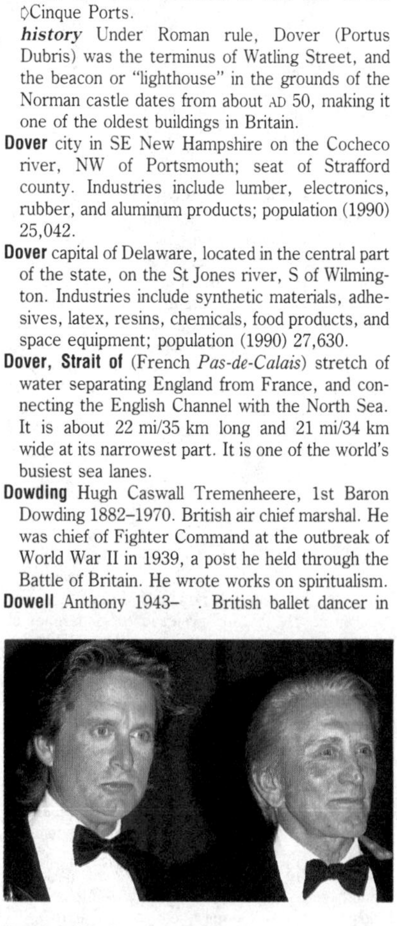

Douglas *Kirk Douglas accompanied by his son Michael Douglas. Both men are leading actors who portray characters of intelligence and virility.*

the Classical style. He was principal dancer with the Royal Ballet 1966–86, and director 1986–89.

He was guest principal dancer with the American Ballet Theater 1978–80.

Dow Jones average a daily index of prices on the New York Stock Exchange, based on 30 industrial stocks. Also known as the Dow (Jones) Industrials or the Dow (not to be confused with Dow Chemical Co.).

Down county in SE Northern Ireland, facing the Irish Sea on the E; area 953 sq mi/2,470 sq km; population (1981) 53,000. In the S are the Mourne mountains, in the E Strangford sea lough. The county town is Downpatrick; the main industry is dairying.

Downs, North and South two lines of chalk hills in SE England. They form two scarps that face each other across the Weald of Kent and Sussex and are much used for sheep pasture. The North Downs run from Salisbury Plain across Hampshire, Surrey, and Kent to the cliffs of south Foreland. The South Downs run across Sussex to Beachy Head.

Down's syndrome condition caused by a chromosomal abnormality (the presence of an extra chromosome) which in humans produces mental retardation; a flattened face; coarse, straight hair; and a fold of skin at the inner edge of the eye (hence the former name "mongolism"). Those afflicted are usually born to mothers over 40 (one in 100); they are good-natured and teachable with special education but never learn above grade-school levels. The syndrome is named after J L H Down (1828–1896), an English physician who studied it.

dowry property or money given by the bride's family to the groom or his family as part of the marriage agreement; the opposite of ◊bridewealth.

dowsing ascertaining the presence of water or minerals beneath the ground with a forked twig or pendulum. Unconscious muscular action by the dowser is thought to move the twig, usually held with one fork in each hand, possibly in response to a local change in the pattern of electrical forces. The ability has been known since at least the 16th century and, though not widely recognized by science, it has been used commercially.

Doxiadis Constantinos 1913–1975. Greek architect and town planner; designer of ◊Islamabad.

Doyle Arthur Conan 1859–1930. British writer, creator of the detective Sherlock Holmes and his assistant Dr Watson, who featured in a number of stories, including *The Hound of the Baskervilles* 1902.

Born in Edinburgh, he qualified as a doctor, and during the Boer War was senior physician of a field hospital. The first of his books, *A Study in Scarlet*, appeared in 1887 and introduced Sherlock Holmes and his ingenuous companion, Dr Watson. Other books featuring the same characters followed, including *The Sign of Four* 1889 and *The Valley of Fear* 1915, as well as several volumes of short stories, first published in the *Strand Magazine*. Conan Doyle also wrote historical romances (*Micah Clarke* 1889 and *The White Company* 1891) and the scientific romance *The Lost World* 1912. In his later years he became a spiritualist.

Doyle Creator of the popular fictional duo of Sherlock Holmes and Dr Watson, Arthur Conan Doyle.

D'Oyly Carte Richard 1844–1901. British producer of the Gilbert and Sullivan operas at the Savoy Theatre, London, which he built. The old D'Oyly Carte Opera Company founded 1876 was disbanded 1982, but a new one opened its first season 1988.

Drabble Margaret 1939– . British writer. Her novels include *The Millstone* 1966 (filmed as *The Touch of Love*), *The Middle Ground* 1980, and *The Radiant Way* 1987. She edited the 1985 edition of the *Oxford Companion to English Literature*.

Draco 7th century BC. Athenian politician, the first to codify the laws of the Athenian city-state. These were notorious for their severity; hence draconian, meaning particularly harsh.

Draco in astronomy, a large but faint constellation, representing a dragon coiled around the north celestial pole. The star Alpha Draconis (Thuban) was the pole star 4,800 years ago.

Dracula in the novel *Dracula* 1897 by Bram ◊Stoker, the caped count who, as a ◊vampire, drinks the blood of beautiful women.

draft compulsory military service; also known as ◊conscription.

drag the resistance to motion a body experiences when passing through a fluid—gas or liquid. The aerodynamic drag aircraft experience when traveling through the air represents a great waste of power, so they must be carefully shaped, or streamlined, to reduce drag to a minimum. Cars benefit from streamlining, and aerodynamic drag is used to slow down spacecraft returning from space. Boats traveling through water experience hydrodynamic drag on their hulls, and the fastest vessels are ◊hydrofoils, whose hulls lift out of the water while cruising.

dragon Euro-Asian mythical reptilian beast, often portrayed as breathing fire. The name is popularly given to various sorts of lizard. These include the ◊flying dragon *Draco volans* of SE Asia; the komodo dragon *Varanus komodoensis* of Indonesia, at over 10 ft/3 m the largest living lizard; and some Australian lizards with bizarre spines or frills.

dragonfly any of numerous insects of the order Odonata, including ◊damselflies. They all have a long narrow body, two pairs of almost equal-sized, glassy wings with a network of veins; short, bristlelike antennae; powerful, "toothed" mouthparts; and very large compound eyes which may have up to 30,000 facets. They hunt other insects by sight, both as adults and as aquatic nymphs. The largest species have a wingspan of 7 in/18 cm, but fossils related to dragonflies, with wings up to 2.3 ft/70 cm across, have been found.

dragoon a mounted soldier who carried an infantry weapon such as a "dragon," or short musket, as used by the French army in the 16th century. The name was retained by some later regiments after the original meaning became obsolete.

drag racing automobile racing sport popular in the US. High-powered single-seat automobiles with large rear and small front wheels are timed over a quarter-mile strip. Speeds of up to 280 mph/450 kph have been attained.

Drake Francis c. 1545–1596. English buccaneer and explorer. Having enriched himself as a pirate against Spanish interests in the Caribbean 1567–72, he was sponsored by Elizabeth I for an expedition to the Pacific, sailing around the world 1577–80 in the *Golden Hind*, robbing Spanish ships as he went. It was the second circumnavigation of the globe (the first was by the Portuguese explorer Magellan).

Drake suggested to Queen Elizabeth I an expedition to the Pacific, and it was granted; in Dec 1577 he sailed in the *Pelican* with four other ships and 166 men toward South America. In Aug 1578 the fleet passed through the Straits of Magellan and was then blown south to Cape Horn. The ships became separated and returned to England, all but the *Pelican*, now renamed the *Golden Hind*. Drake sailed north along the coast of Chile and Peru, robbing Spanish ships as far north as California, and then, in July 1579, traveled southwest across the Pacific. He rounded the South African Cape June 1580, and reached England Sept 1580, thus completing the second voyage around the world. When the Spanish ambassador demanded Drake's punishment, the Queen knighted him on the deck of the *Golden Hind* in London.

Drake Portrait of Sir Francis Drake by an unknown artist (1580–85), National Portrait Gallery, London.

In a raid on Cádiz 1587 he burned 10,000 tons of shipping and delayed the Spanish Armada for a year. Drake sailed on his last expedition to the West Indies 1595, and in Jan 1596 died on his ship.

Drakensberg (Afrikaans "dragon's mountain") mountain range in South Africa (Sesuto name *Quathlamba*), on the boundary of Lesotho and the Orange Free State with Natal. Its highest point is Thaban Ntlenyana, 10,988 ft/3,350 m, near which is Natal National Park.

drama in theater, any play performed by actors for an audience. The term is also used collectively to group plays into historical or stylistic periods—for example, Greek drama, Restoration drama—as well as referring to the whole body of work written by a dramatist for performance. Drama is distinct from literature in that it is a performing art open to infinite interpretation, the product not merely of the playwright but also of the collaboration of director, designer, actors, and technical staff. See also ◊comedy, ◊tragedy, ◊mime, and ◊pantomime.

dramatis personae (Latin) the characters in a play.

Dravidian a group of non-Indo-European peoples of the Deccan region of India and in N Sri Lanka. The Dravidian language family is large, with about 20 languages spoken in S India; the main ones are Tamil, which has a literary tradition 2,000 years old; Kanarese; Telugu; Malayalam; and Tulu.

Dreadnought class of battleships built for the British navy after 1905 and far superior in speed and armaments to anything then afloat. It was first launched Feb 18, 1906, with armaments consisting entirely of big guns. The German Nassau class was begun in 1907, and by 1914, the US, France, Japan and Austria-Hungary all had battleships of a similar class to the Dreadnought. German plans to build similar craft led to the naval race that contributed to Anglo-German antagonism and the origins of World War II.

dream a series of events or images perceived through the mind during sleep. For the purposes of (allegedly) foretelling the future, dreams fell into disrepute in the scientific atmosphere of the 18th century, but were given importance by Sigmund ◊Freud who saw them as wish fulfillment (nightmares being failed dreams prompted by fears of "repressed" impulses). Dreams occur in periods of rapid eye movement (REM) by the sleeper, when the cortex of the brain is approximately as active as in waking hours. Dreams occupy about a fifth of sleeping time.

If a high level of acetylcholine is present (see under ◊brain), dreams occur too early in sleep, causing wakefulness, confusion, and ◊depression, which suggests that a form of memory search is involved. Prevention of dreaming, by taking sleeping pills, for example, has similar unpleasant results.

Dred Scott Decision a US Supreme Court decision 1857 dealing with citizenship and legal rights of slaves. Dred Scott, a slave from Missouri, sued for his freedom from his owner John Sanford in the Missouri courts, arguing that he had lived with his owner in Illinois, a free state, and the Wisconsin Territory, where slavery had been outlawed by the Missouri Compromise. After a series of reversals the case reached the Supreme Court, which ruled (1) black people were not US citizens, (2) slaves did not become free by entering a free state; and (3) the Missouri Compromise was illegal as it interfered with the right to own slaves, guaranteed by the Constitution (this was only the second Congressional act overturned by the Supreme Court). The decision heightened regional tensions as the Civil War neared.

Drees Willem 1886–1988. Dutch Socialist politician, prime minister 1948–58. Chair of the Socialist Democratic Workers' Party from 1911 until the German invasion of 1940, he returned to politics in 1947, after being active in the resistance movement. In 1947, as the responsible minister, he introduced a state pension plan.

Dreikaiserbund (German "Three Emperors" League") an informal alliance from 1872 between the emperors of Russia, Germany, and Austria-Hungary. It was effectively at an end by 1879.

Dreiser Theodore 1871–1945. US writer who wrote the naturalist novels *Sister Carrie* 1900 and *An American Tragedy* 1925, based on the real-life crime of a young man, who in his drive to "make good," drowns a shop assistant he has made pregnant. It was filmed as *A Place in the Sun* 1951.

Born in Terre Haute, Indiana, Dreiser was a journalist 1889–90 in Chicago and was editor of several magazines. His other novels include *The Financier* 1912, *The Titan* 1914, and *The Genius* 1915. *An American Tragedy* finally won him great popularity after years of publishing works that largely had been ignored. His other works range from autobiographical pieces to poems and short stories. Although his work is criticized for being technically unpolished, it is praised for its powerful realism and sincerity. In the 1930s he devoted much of his energy to the radical reform movement.

Drenthe low-lying northern province of the Netherlands

area 1,027 sq mi/2,660 sq km

population (1988) 437,000

cities capital Assen; Emmen, Hoogeveen

physical fenland and moors; well-drained clay and peat soils

products livestock, arable crops, horticulture, petroleum

history governed in the Middle Ages by provincial nobles and by bishops of Utrecht, Drenthe was eventually acquired by Charles V of Spain in 1536. It developed following land drainage initiated in the mid-18th century and was established as a separate province of the Netherlands in 1796.

Dresden capital of the state of Saxony, Federal Republic of Germany; population (1990) 520,000. Industries include chemicals, machinery, glassware, and musical instruments. It was one of the most beautiful German cities prior to its devastation by Allied fire-bombing 1945. Dresden county has an area of 2,602 sq mi/6,740 sq km and a populaton of 1,772,000.

history Under the elector Augustus II the Strong (1694–1733), it became a center of art and culture. The manufacture of Dresden china, started at Dresden 1709, was transferred to Meissen

Dresden *Following the devastating bombing of Dresden in 1945, some ruins remain among the rebuilt quarters.*

1710. The city was bombed by the Allies on the night Feb 13–14, 1945, 6 sq mi/15.5 sq km of the inner town being destroyed, and deaths being estimated at 35,000–135,000. Following the reunification of Germany in 1990 Dresden once again became capital of Saxony.

dressage (French "the training of horses") a method of training a horse to carry out a predetermined routine of specified movements. Points are awarded for discipline and style.

Dreyer Carl Theodor 1889–1968. Danish director. His wide range of films include the silent classic *La Passion de Jeanne d'Arc/The Passion of Joan of Arc* 1928 and the Expressionist horror film *Vampyr* 1932, after the failure of which Dreyer made no full-length films until *Vredens Dag/Day of Wrath* 1943.

Dreyfus Alfred 1859–1935. French army officer, victim of miscarriage of justice, anti-Semitism, and cover-up. Employed in the War Ministry, in 1894 he was accused of betraying military secrets to Germany, court-martialed, and sent to the penal colony on ◊Devil's Island. When his innocence was discovered 1896 the military establishment tried to conceal it, and the implications of the Dreyfus affair were passionately discussed in the press until he was exonerated in 1906.

Dreyfus was born in Mulhouse, E France, of a Jewish family. He had been a prisoner in the French Guiana penal colony for two years when it emerged that the real criminal was a Maj Esterhazy; the high command nevertheless attempted to suppress the facts and used forged documents to strengthen their case. After a violent controversy, in which the future prime minister ◊Clemenceau and the novelist ◊Zola championed Dreyfus, he was brought back for a retrial 1899, found guilty with extenuating circumstances, and received a pardon. In 1906 the court of appeal declared him innocent, and he was reinstated in his military rank.

drill large baboonlike Old World monkey *Mandrillus leucophaeus*, in the same genus as the ◊mandrill, living in forests of W Africa. Brownish-coated, black-faced, and stoutly built, with a very short tail, the male can have a head and body up to 2.5 ft/75 cm long, although females are smaller.

Dreyfus *Victim of anti-Semitism in late 19th-century France, Alfred Dreyfus was championed by influential journalist and novelist Emile Zola.*

dromedary

drilling common woodworking and metal machinery process that involves boring holes with a drill ◊bit. The commonest kind of drill bit is the fluted drill, which has spiral grooves around it to allow the cut material to escape. In the oil industry, rotary drilling is used to bore oil wells. The drill bit usually consists of a number of toothed cutting wheels, which grind their way through the rock as the drill pipe is turned, and mud is pumped through the pipe to lubricate the bit and flush the ground-up rock to the surface.

In rotary drilling, a drill bit is fixed to the end of a length of drill pipe and rotated by a turning mechanism, the rotary table. More lengths of pipe are added as the hole deepens. The long drill pipes are handled by lifting gear in a steel tower ◊derrick.

Drogheda seaport near the mouth of the river Boyne, county Louth, Republic of Ireland. The port trades in cattle and textiles; chemicals and foodstuffs are produced. In 1649 the town was stormed by Oliver ◊Cromwell, who massacred most of the garrison, and in 1690 it surrendered to William III after the battle of the Boyne.

Drôme river in France, rising in Dauphiné Pre-Alps and flowing NW for 63 mi/101 km to join the river Rhône below Livron. It gives its name to Drôme *département*.

dromedary variety of Arabian ◊camel.

drone in music, an accompanying tone or harmony that never varies. It is heard in folk music and reproduced by many instruments, including the jew's harp, bagpipe, and hurdy-gurdy.

Drosera Latin name for the ◊sundew plant.

drought period of prolonged dry weather. The area of the world subject to serious droughts, such as the Sahara, is increasing because of destruction of forests, overgrazing, and poor agricultural practices.

drug abuse the abuse of narcotic and hallucinogenic substances and stimulants.

They are classified generally as (1) most harmful: heroin, morphine, opium, and other narcotics; cocaine, a powerful, dangerous stimulant and its relative, crack; hallucinogens, such as mescalin and LSD; and injectable amphetamines, such as methedrine; (2) less harmful: narcotics such as codeine and cannabis (marijuana); stimulants of the amphetamine type, such as Benzedrine; and barbiturate sedatives; and (3) least harmful: milder drugs of the amphetamine type. "Designer drugs," for example ecstasy, are usually modifications of the amphetamine molecule, altered in order to evade the law as well as for different effects, and may be many times more powerful and dangerous. Crack, for example, became available to drug users in the 1980s. Sources of traditional drugs include the "Golden Triangle" (where Myanmar, Laos, and Thailand meet), Mexico, Colombia, China, Pakistan, and the Middle East.

drug and alcohol dependence physical or psychological craving for addictive drugs such as alcohol, nicotine (in cigarettes), tranquilizers, heroin, or stimulants (for example, amphetamines). Such substances can alter mood or behavior. When dependence is established, sudden withdrawal from the drug can cause unpleasant physical and/or psychological reactions, which may be dangerous.

drug, generic any drug produced without a brand name that is identical to a branded product. Usually generic drugs are produced when the patent on a branded drug has expired, and are cheaper than their branded equivalents.

Druidism religion of the Celtic peoples of the pre-Christian British Isles and Gaul. The word is derived from Greek *drus* "oak." The Druids regarded this tree as sacred; one of their chief rites was the cutting of mistletoe from it with a golden sickle. They taught the immortality of the soul and a reincarnation doctrine, and were expert in astronomy. The Druids are thought to have offered human sacrifices.

Druidism was stamped out in Gaul and most of Britain after the Roman conquest. They existed in Scotland and Ireland until the coming of the Christian missionaries. What are often termed Druidic monuments—cromlechs and stone circles—are of Neolithic origin, although they may later have been used for religious purposes by the Druids.

drum percussion instrument, essentially a piece of skin (parchment, plastic, or nylon) stretched over a resonator and struck with a stick or the hands, one of the oldest instruments. Electronic drums, first marketed in 1980, are highly touch-and force-sensitive and can also be controlled by computer.

drumlin a geologic feature formed in formerly glaciated areas. It consists of long, streamlined hills formed from glacial till or unstratified glacial drift of clay, sand, boulders, and gravel. A drumlin's long axis is oriented in the direction of glacial flow, and its blunt nose points upstream, with the gentler slope trailing off downstream. Drumlins range from 25 ft/8 m to 200 ft/60 m in height. In length, they vary from 0.3 mi/0.5 km to 0.6 mi/1 km and are generally several times narrower than long.

Drummond de Andrade Carlos 1902–1987. Brazilian writer, generally considered the greatest modern Brazilian poet, and a prominent member of the Modernist school. His verse, often seemingly casual, continually confounds the reader's expectations of the "poetical."

drupe a fleshy ◊fruit containing one or more seeds which are surrounded by a hard, protective layer—for example cherry, almond, and plum. The wall of the fruit (◊pericarp) is differentiated into the outer skin (exocarp), the fleshy layer of tissues (mesocarp), and the hard layer surrounding the seed (endocarp). The coconut is a drupe, but here the pericarp becomes dry and fibrous at maturity. Blackberries are an aggregate fruit composed of a cluster of small drupes.

Druse or ***Druze*** a religious sect in the Middle East of some 500,000 people. They are monotheists, preaching that the Fatimid caliph al-Hakim (996–1021) is God; their scriptures are drawn from the Christian gospels, the Torah (the first five books of the Old Testament), the Koran, and Sufi allegories. Druse militia groups form one of the three main factions involved in the Lebanese civil war (the others are Amal Shi'ite Muslims and Christian Maronites). The Druse military leader (from the time of his father's assassination 1977) is Walid Jumblatt.

The Druse sect was founded in Egypt in the 11th century, and then fled to Palestine to avoid persecution; they today occupy areas of Syria, Lebanon, and Israel.

Druze alternate spelling of ◊Druse, Lebanese religious sect.

dryad in Greek mythology, a forest nymph or tree spirit.

dryas any arctic or alpine herbaceous plant of the genus *Dryas* of the rose family, with simple leaves and white or yellow flowers. The white-flowered mountain avens *Dryas octopetata* is a common plant of northern regions.

Dryden *English poet, satirist, dramatist, and biographer John Dryden, painted in 1693 by Kneller.*

Dryden John 1631–1700. English poet and dramatist, noted for his satirical verse and for his use of the heroic couplet. His poetry includes the verse satire *Absalom and Achitophel* 1681, *Annus Mirabilis* 1667, and "St Cecilia's Day" 1687. Plays include the comedy *Marriage à la Mode* 1671 and *All for Love* 1678, a reworking of Shakespeare's *Antony and Cleopatra*.

dry ice solid carbon dioxide (CO_2), used as a refrigerant. At temperatures above –110.2°F/–79°C, it sublimes to gaseous carbon dioxide.

dry point in printmaking, a technique of engraving on copper, using a hard, sharp tool. The resulting lines tend to be fine and angular, with a strong furry edge created by the metal shavings.

dry rot infection of timber in damp conditions by fungi, such as *Merulius lacrymans*, that form a threadlike surface. Whitish at first, the fungus later reddens as reproductive spores are formed. Fungoid tentacles also enter the fabric of the timber, rendering it dry-looking and brittle. Dry rot spreads rapidly through a building.

Dr Zhivago a novel by Boris Pasternak, published (in Italy) 1957. The novel, which describes a scientist's disillusionment with the Russian revolution, was banned in the USSR as a "hostile act" and only published there in magazine form 1988.

Dual Entente an alliance between France and Russia that lasted from 1893 until the Bolshevik Revolution of 1917.

dualism in philosophy, the belief that reality is essentially dual in nature. ◊Descartes, for example, refers to thinking and material substance. These entities interact but are fundamentally separate and distinct. Dualism is contrasted with ◊monism.

Duarte José Napoleon 1925–1990. El Salvadorean politican, president 1980–82 and 1984–88. He was mayor of San Salvador 1964–70, and was elected president 1972, but exiled by the army in 1982. On becoming president again in 1984, he sought a negotiated settlement with the left-wing guerrillas 1986, but resigned on health grounds.

Dubai one of the ◊United Arab Emirates.

Du Barry Marie Jeanne Bécu, Comtesse 1743–1793. Mistress of ◊Louis XV of France from 1768. At his death in 1774 she was banished to a convent, and during the Revolution fled to London. Returning to Paris in 1793, she was guillotined.

Dubček Alexander 1921– . Czechoslovak politician, chair of the federal assembly from 1989. He was a member of the ◊resistance movement and after World War II became first secretary of the Communist Party 1967–69. He launched a liberalization campaign (called the Prague Spring) that was opposed by the USSR and led to the Soviet invasion of Czechoslovakia in 1968. He was arrested by Soviet troops and expelled from the party 1970.

In 1989 he gave speeches at pro-democracy rallies, and in Dec, after the fall of the hardline regime, he was elected speaker of the Czechoslovak parliament, a position to which he was reelected in 1990.

Dubček *Czechoslovak politician Alexander Dubček 1968.*

Dublin (Gaelic *Baile Atha Cliath*) capital and port on the E coast of the Republic of Ireland, at the mouth of the river Liffey, facing the Irish Sea; population (1981) 526,000, Greater Dublin (including Dún Laoghaire) 921,000. It is the site of one of the world's largest breweries (Guinness); other industries include textiles, pharmaceuticals, electrical goods, and machine tools. It was the center of English rule from 1171 (exercised from Dublin Castle 1220) until 1922.

history The city was founded 840 by the invading Danes, who were finally defeated 1014 at Clontarf, now a N suburb of the city. In the Georgian period many fine squares were laid out, and the Custom House (damaged in the 1921 uprising but later restored) survives. There is a Roman Catholic pro-Cathedral, St Mary's (1816); two Protestant cathedrals; and two universities, the University of Dublin and the National University of Ireland. Trinity College library contains the Book of Kells, a splendidly illuminated 8th-century gospel book produced at the monastery of Kells in county Meath, founded by St Columba. Other buildings are the City Hall (1779), the Four Courts (1796), the National Gallery, Dublin Municipal Gallery, National Museum, Leinster House (where the *Dáil Eireann* sits), and the Abbey and Gate theaters.

Dubna town in USSR, 25 mi/40 km W of Tula; population (1985) 61,000. It is a metal-working center, and has the Volga Nuclear Physics Center.

Du Bois W(illiam) E(dward) B(urghardt) 1868–1963. US educator and social critic. Born in Great Barrington, Massachusetts, Du Bois earned a PhD from Harvard 1895 and was appointed to the faculty of Atlanta University. As an uncompromising advocate of black American rights, he came into conflict with the more accommodationist Booker T ◊Washington.

Du Bois was one of the early leaders of the ◊National Association for the Advancement of Colored People (NAACP), the editor of its journal *Crisis* 1909–32, and organizer of several Pan-African conferences. In 1962 he established his home in Accra, Ghana.

Dubos René Jules 1901–1981. French-US microbiologist who studied soil microorganisms and became interested in their antibacterial properties.

The antibacterials he discovered had limited therapeutic use since they were toxic. However, he opened up a new field of research that eventually led to the discovery of such major drugs as ◊penicillin and ◊streptomycin.

Dubrovnik (Italian *Ragusa*) port in Yugoslavia on the Adriatic sea; population (1985) 35,000. It manufactures cheese, liqueurs, silk, and leather. Once a Roman station, it was for a long time an independent republic but passed to Austrian rule 1814–1919. The city was damaged during the Yugoslav civil war 1991.

Dubuffet Jean 1901–1985. French artist. He originated *l'art brut*, "raw or brutal art," in the 1940s.

duck

pink headed duck

Dufy Deauville: Drying the Sails *(1933), Tate Gallery, London.*

He used a variety of materials in his paintings and sculptures—plaster, steel wool, straw, and so on, inspired by graffiti and children's drawings.

L'art brut emerged in 1945 with an exhibition of Dubuffet's own work and of paintings by psychiatric patients and naive or untrained artists. His own paintings and sculptural works have a similar quality, primitive and expressive.

Dubuque city in E central Iowa, NE of Iowa City, just across the Mississippi river from the Wisconsin–Illinois border. An important port, it has shipbuilding and agricultural marketing facilities; industries include meatpacking, lumber, metals, and machinery; population (1990) 57,546.

Duccio di Buoninsegna c. 1255–1319. Italian painter, a major figure in the Sienese school. His greatest work is his altarpiece for Siena Cathedral, the *Maestà* 1308–11; the figure of the Virgin is Byzantine in style, with much gold detail, but Duccio also created a graceful linear harmony in drapery hems, for example, and this proved a lasting characteristic of Sienese style.

Duce (Italian "leader") title bestowed on the fascist dictator Benito ◊Mussolini by his followers and later adopted as his official title.

Duchamp Marcel 1887–1968. US artist, born in France. He achieved notoriety with his *Nude Descending a Staircase* 1912 (Philadelphia Museum of Art), influenced by Cubism and Futurism. An active exponent of ◊Dadaism, he invented "ready-mades," everyday items like a bicycle wheel on a kitchen stool, which he displayed as works of art.

A major early work that focuses on mechanical objects endowed with mysterious significance is *La Mariée mise à nu par ses célibataires, même/ The Bride Stripped Bare by Her Bachelors, Even* 1915–23 (Philadelphia Museum of Art). Duchamp continued to experiment with collage, mechanical imagery, and abstract sculpture throughout his career. He lived mostly in New York and became a US citizen in 1954.

duck any of several shortlegged waterbirds with webbed feet and flattened bills, of the family Anatidae, which also includes the larger geese and swans. Ducks were domesticated for eggs, meat, and feathers by the ancient Chinese and the ancient Maya (see ◊poultry). Ducks have the three front toes in a web, the hind toe free, and a skin-covered bill with a horny tip provided with little plates (lamellae) through which the birds are able to strain their food from water and mud. Most ducks live in fresh water, feeding on worms and insects as well as vegetable matter. They are generally divided into dabbling ducks and diving ducks.

A typical species is the mallard *Anas platyrhynchos*, 1.9 ft/58 cm, found over most of the N hemisphere. The male (drake) has a glossy green head, brown breast, gray body, and yellow bill. The female (duck) is speckled brown, with a duller bill. The male molts and resembles the female for a while just after the breeding season. There are many other species of duck including ◊teal, ◊eider, ◊merganser, ◊shelduck, and ◊shoveler. They have different-shaped bills according to their diet and habitat; for example, the shoveler has a wide spade-shaped bill for scooping insects off the surface of water.

The main threat to the survival of ducks in the wild is hunting by humans. The pink-headed duck of India and Nepal is believed to be extinct, no wild specimens having been seen since 1936.

duckweed any of a family of tiny plants Lemnaceae, especially of the genus *Lemna*, found floating on the surface of still water throughout most of the world, except the polar regions and tropics. Each plant consists of a flat, circular, leaflike structure 0.15 in/0.4 cm or less across, with a single thin root up to 6 in/15 cm long below.

The plants bud off new individuals and soon cover the surface of the water. Flowers rarely appear, but when they do, they are minute and located in a pocket at the edge of the plant.

ductless gland alternate name for an ◊endocrine gland.

Dudintsev Vladimir Dmitriyevich 1918– . Soviet novelist, author of the remarkably frank *Not by Bread Alone* 1956, a depiction of Soviet bureaucracy and inefficiency.

Dudley town NW of Birmingham, West Midlands, England; population (1981) 187,000. Industries include light engineering and clothing manufacture.

duel a fight between two people armed with weapons. A duel is usually fought according to prearranged rules with the aim of settling a private quarrel.

In medieval Europe duels were a legal method of settling disputes. By the 16th century the practice had largely ceased but dueling with swords or pistols, often with elaborate ritual, continued unofficially in aristocratic and military circles until the 20th century. In some German universities exclusive dueling clubs continue to this day.

due process of law a legal principle, dating back to the ◊Magna Carta 1215, and now stated in the Fifth and Fourteenth amendments of the US Constitution, that no person shall be deprived of life, liberty, or property without due process of law (a fair legal procedure). In the US, the provisions have been given a wide interpretation, to include, for example, the right to representation by an attorney.

Dufay Guillaume 1400–1474. Flemish composer. He is recognized as the foremost composer of his time, of both secular songs and sacred music (including 84 songs and eight masses). His work marks a transition between the music of the Middle Ages and that of the Renaissance and is characterized by expressive melodies and rich harmonies.

Dufourspitze second highest of the alpine peaks, 15,203 ft/4,634 m high. It is the highest peak in the Monte Rosa group of the Pennine alps on the Swiss–Italian frontier.

Du Fu another name for the Chinese poet ◊Tu Fu.

Dufy Raoul 1877–1953. French painter and designer. He originated a fluent, brightly colored style in watercolor and oils, painting scenes of gaiety and leisure, such as horse racing, yachting, and life on the beach.

dugong a marine mammal *Dugong dugong* of the order Sirenia (sea cows), found in the Red Sea, the Indian Ocean and W Pacific. It can grow to 11 ft/3.6 m long, and has a tapering body with a notched tail and two fore-flippers. It is herbivorous, feeding on sea grasses and seaweeds.

It may have given rise to the mermaid myth.

duiker (Afrikaans *diver*) any of several antelopes of the family Bovidae, common in Africa. Duikers are shy and nocturnal, and grow to 12–28 in/ 30–70 cm tall.

Duisburg river port and industrial city in North Rhine–Westphalia, Federal Republic of Germany, at the confluence of the Rhine and Ruhr rivers; population (1987) 515,000. It is the largest inland river port in Europe. Heavy industries include oil refining and the production of steel, copper, zinc, plastics, and machinery.

Dukakis Michael 1933– . US Democrat politician, governor of Massachusetts 1974–78 and from 1982, presiding over a high-tech economic boom, the "Massachusetts miracle." He was a presidential candidate in 1988.

Dukakis was born in Boston, Massachusetts, the son of Greek immigrants. After studying law at Harvard and serving in Korea (1955–57), he concentrated on a political career in his home state.

Elected to the Massachusetts legislature in 1962, he became state governor in 1974. After an unsuccessful first term, marred by his unwillingness to compromise, he was defeated in 1978. He returned as governor in 1982, committed to working in a more consensual manner, was re-elected in 1986, and captured the Democratic Party's presidential nomination in 1988. After a harrowing campaign, Dukakis was defeated by the incumbent vice-president George Bush. His standing in Massachusetts dropped and he announced that he would not seek a new term.

Dukas Paul (Abraham) 1865–1935. French composer. His orchestral scherzo *L'Apprenti Sorcier/ The Sorcerer's Apprentice* 1897 is full of the color and energy that characterizes much of his work.

He was professor of composition at the Paris Conservatoire and composed the opera *Ariane et Barbe-Bleue/Ariane and Bluebeard* 1907, and the ballet *La Péri* 1912.

duke highest title in the English peerage. It originated in England in 1337, when Edward III created his son Edward, Duke of Cornwall.

dulcimer musical instrument consisting of a shallow sound-box strung with many wires that are struck with small wooden hammers. In Hungary it is called a ◊cimbalom.

Also an oval-shaped stringed instrument of the Appalachian Mountains that is played in the lap or on a surface by plucking the strings with a quill or plectrum.

Dulles Alan 1893–1969. US lawyer, director of the

Central Intelligence Agency (CIA) 1953–61. He was the brother of John Foster Dulles.

He helped found the CIA 1950 but was embroiled in the ◊Bay of Pigs controversy, among others, which forced his resignation.

Dulles John Foster 1888–1959. US lawyer and politician. Senior US adviser at the founding of the United Nations, he largely drafted the Japanese peace treaty of 1951. As secretary of state 1952–59 he was critical of Britain in the ◊Suez Crisis. He was the architect of US ◊Cold War foreign policy, securing ◊SEATO and US intervention in support of South Vietnam following the expulsion of the French in 1954.

Born in Washington, DC, he was educated at Princeton, the University of Paris, and George Washington University. His specialty as a lawyer was international law. He sought to go beyond the "containment" policy of the time, considering communism as a moral evil with which there could be no compromise. Even so, during his term as secretary of state, he was limited to giving moral support to the Hungarians 1956 when they rose against the Soviets, and Cuba and North Vietnam fell to the Communists during his tenure.

Dulong Pierre 1785–1838. French chemist and physicist who, along with Petit, discovered in 1819 the law that, for many elements solid at room temperature, the product of the ◊atomic weight and ◊specific heat capacity is approximately constant. He had earlier, in 1811, and at the cost of an eye, discovered the explosive nitrogen trichloride.

dulse edible red seaweeds, especially *Rhodymenia palmata*, found on middle and lower shores of the N Atlantic. They may have a single broad blade up to 12 in/30 cm long rising directly from the holdfast, or be palmate or fan-shaped. The frond is tough and dark red, sometimes with additional small leaflets at the edge.

Duluth port on Lake Superior; by the mouth of the St Louis River, Minnesota; population (1990) 85,493. It manufactures steel, flour, timber, and dairy products. The westernmost port on the St Lawrence Seaway, Duluth ships iron ore, grain, coal, oil, and timber. Permanent settlement on what had been a fur-trading post began 1852.

Duma in Russia, before 1917, an elected assembly that met four times following the short-lived 1905 revolution. With progressive demands the government could not accept, the Duma was largely powerless. After the abdication of Nicholas II, the Duma directed the formation of a provisional government.

Dumas Alexandre 1802–1870. French author, known as Dumas *père* (the father). His play *Henri III et sa cour/Henry III and His Court* 1829 established French romantic historical drama, but today he is remembered for his romances, the reworked output of a "fiction-factory" of collaborators. They include *Les trois mousquetaires/The Three Musketeers* 1844 and its sequels. Dumas *fils* was his illegitimate son.

Dumas *French dramatist and novelist Alexandre Dumas.*

Dumas Alexandre 1824–1895. French author, known as Dumas *fils* (the son of Dumas *père*) and remembered for the play *La Dame aux camélias/The Lady of the Camellias* 1852, based on his own novel and source of Verdi's opera *La Traviata*.

Du Maurier Daphne 1907–1989. British novelist whose romantic fiction includes *Jamaica Inn* 1936, *Rebecca* 1938, and *My Cousin Rachel* 1951. *Jamaica Inn*, *Rebecca*, and her short story "The Birds" were made into films by Alfred Hitchcock. She is the granddaughter of George Du Maurier.

Dumbarton Oaks 18th-century mansion near Washington, DC, used for conferences and seminars. It was the scene of a conference held in 1944 that led to the foundation of the United Nations.

Dumont D'Urville Jean 1780–1842. French explorer in Australasia and the Pacific. In 1838–40 he sailed around Cape Horn on a voyage to study terrestrial magnetism and reached Adélie Land in Antarctica.

Dumoriez Charles François du Périer 1739–1823. French general during the Revolution. In 1792 he was appointed foreign minister, supported the declaration of war against Austria, and after the fall of the monarchy was given command of the army defending Paris. After intriguing with the royalists he had to flee for his life, and from 1804 he lived in England.

dumping in international trade, when one country sells goods to another at below marginal cost or at a price below that in its own country. Countries dump to sell off surplus produce or to improve their competitive positions in the recipient country. The practice is deplored by ◊free-trade advocates because of the artificial, unfair advantage it yields. Dumping is also used by protectionists to justify retaliatory measures.

Dumyat (English *Damietta*) town in Egypt at the mouth of the Nile; population (1986) 121,200.

Duna Hungarian name for the ◊Danube.

Dunant Jean Henri 1828–1910. Swiss philanthropist; the originator of the Red Cross. At the Battle of Solferino 1859 he helped tend the wounded, and in *Un Souvenir de Solferino* 1862 he proposed the establishment of an international body for the aid of the wounded—an idea that was realized in the Geneva Convention 1864. He shared the Nobel Peace Prize 1901.

Dunarea Romanian and Bulgarian name for the ◊Danube.

Dunaway Faye 1941– . US actress whose first starring role was in *Bonnie and Clyde* 1967. Her subsequent films, including *Network* 1976 (for which she won an Academy Award) and *Mommie Dearest* 1981, received a varying critical reception. She also starred in Roman Polanski's celebrated *Chinatown* 1974, and *The Handmaid's Tale* 1990.

Dunbartonshire former county of Scotland, bordering the N bank of the Clyde estuary, on which stand Dunbarton (the former county town), Clydebank, and Helensburgh. It was merged 1975 in the region of Strathclyde.

Duncan Isadora 1878–1927. US dancer and teacher. An influential pioneer of modern dance, she adopted an expressive, free form, dancing barefoot and wearing a loose tunic, inspired by the ideal of Hellenic beauty. She toured extensively, often returning to Russia after her initial success there 1905. She died in an accident when her long scarf caught in the wheel of the car in which she was traveling.

Dundee city and fishing port, administrative headquarters of Tayside, Scotland, on the N side of the Firth of Tay; population (1981) 175,000. Important shipping and rail center with marine engineering, watch and clock, and textile industries.

The city developed around the jute industry in the 19th century, and has benefited from the North Sea oil discoveries of the 1970s. There is a university (1967) derived from Queen's College (founded 1881), and other notable buildings include the Albert Institute (1867) and Caird Hall.

dune a mound or ridge of wind-drifted sand. Loose sand is blown and bounced along by the wind, up the windward side of a dune. The sand particles then fall to rest on the lee side, while more are blown up from the windward side. In this way a dune moves gradually downwind.

Dunes are features of sandy deserts and beach fronts. The typical crescent-shaped dune is called a barchan. Seif dunes are longitudinal and lie parallel to the wind direction, and star-shaped dunes are formed by irregular winds.

Dunedin port on Otago harbor, South Island, New Zealand; population (1986) 106,864. Also a road, rail and air center, with engineering and textile industries. The city was founded in 1848 by members of the Free Church of Scotland and the university established 1869.

Dunfermline industrial town near the Firth of Forth in Fife region, Scotland; population (1981) 52,000. Site of the naval base of Rosyth; industries include engineering, shipbuilding, electronics, and textiles. Many Scottish kings, including Robert the Bruce, are buried in Dunfermline Abbey. Birthplace of the industrialist Andrew Carnegie.

Dunham Katherine 1912– . US dancer and choreographer. She was noted for a free, strongly emotional method. She used her extensive knowledge of anthropology as a basis for her dance techniques and choreography. Her interests lay in primitive and ethnic dance. In 1940 Dunham established an all-black dance company, which toured extensively. She also choreographed for and appeared in Hollywood films.

Dunkirk (French *Dunkerque*) seaport on the N coast of France, in Nord *département*, on the Strait of Dover; population (1983) 83,760, conurbation 196,000. Its harbor is one of the foremost in France, and it has widespread canal links with the rest of France and Belgium; ferry service to Ramsgate, England. Industries include oil refining, fishing, and the manufacture of textiles, machinery, and soap.

dune

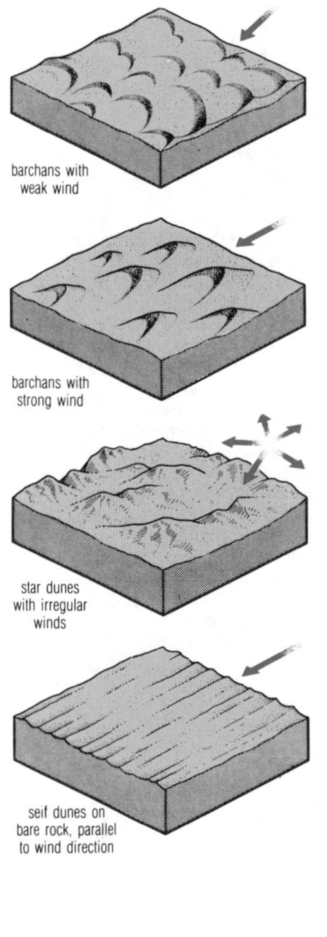
barchans with weak wind
barchans with strong wind
star dunes with irregular winds
seif dunes on bare rock, parallel to wind direction

It was close to the front line during much of World War I, and in World War II, 337,131 Allied troops, including about 110,000 French, were evacuated from the beaches as German forces approached.

dunlin small shore bird *Calidris alpina* of the sandpiper family Scolopacidae, about 7 in/18 cm long, nesting on moors and marshes in the far N regions of Eurasia and North America. Chestnut above and black below in summer, it is greyish in winter.

Dunne Finley Peter 1867–1936. US humorist and social critic. Born in Chicago, Dunne wrote humor pieces for local newspapers before becoming editor in chief of the *Chicago Journal* 1897. His best-remembered fictional character is the Irish saloonkeeper and sage Martin Dooley, better known as "Mr Dooley" to readers all over the country. Written in dialect, Mr Dooley's humorous yet pointed reflections on politics and society appeared 1892–1915. From 1900 the Mr Dooley columns appeared in such national magazines as *Collier's* and *Metropolitan*.

Duns Scotus John c. 1265–c. 1308. Scottish monk, a leading figure of medieval ◊scholasticism. On many points he turned against the orthodoxy of ◊Aquinas; for example, he rejected the idea of a necessary world, favoring a concept of God as absolute freedom capable of spontaneous activity. The church rejected his ideas, hence the word dunce. In the medieval controversy over universals he advocated nominalism. He belonged to the Franciscan order, and was known as Doctor Subtilis.

Dunstan, St c. 924–988. English priest and politician, archbishop of Canterbury from 960. As abbot of Glastonbury from 945, he made it a center of learning. Feast day May 19.

duodecimal system system of arithmetic notation using twelve as a base, at one time considered superior to the decimal system in that 12 has more factors (2,3,4,6) than 10 (2, 5).

It is now superseded by the universally accepted decimal system.

duodenum in vertebrates, a short length of alimentary canal found between the stomach and the small intestine. Its role is in digesting carbohydrates, fats, and proteins. The smaller molecules formed are then absorbed, either by the duodenum or the ileum.

Entry to the duodenum is controlled by the pyloric sphincter, a muscular ring at the base of the stomach. Once food has passed into the duodenum it is mixed with bile from the liver and with a range of enzymes secreted from the pancreas, a digestive gland near the top of the intestine. The bile neutralizes the acidity of the gastric juices passing out of the stomach and aids fat digestion.

Duparc (Marie Eugène) Henri Fouques 1848–1933. French composer. He studied under César ◊Franck. His songs, though only 15 in number, are memorable for their craft and for their place in the history of French songwriting.

Du Pré Jacqueline 1945–1987. English cellist. Celebrated for her proficient technique and powerful interpretations of the Classical cello repertory, particularly of Edward ◊Elgar. She had an international concert career while still in her teens and made many recordings.

She married Daniel ◊Barenboim in 1967 and worked with him in concerts, as a duo, and in a conductor-soloist relationship until her playing career was ended by multiple sclerosis. Although confined to a wheelchair for the last 14 years of her life, she continued to work as a teacher and to campaign on behalf of other sufferers of the disease.

duralumin lightweight aluminum ◊alloy widely used in aircraft construction, containing copper, magnesium, and manganese.

Durand Asher Brown 1796–1886. US painter and engraver. His paintings expressed communion with nature, as in *Kindred Spirits* 1849, a tribute to Thomas Cole, William Cullen Bryant, and the Catskill mountains. The founding of the Hudson River school of landscape art is ascribed to Cole and Durand.

Born in Jefferson Village, New Jersey, Durand began as an engraver of portraits, landscapes, and banknotes but, influenced by Cole, turned to painting. Having studied in Europe 1840–41, he returned a master of landscapes. Durand was president 1840–61 of the National Academy of Design.

Duras Marguerite 1914– French writer. Her works include short stories (*Des Journées entières dans les arbres*), plays (*La Musica*), film scripts (*Hiroshima mon amour* 1960), and novels such as *Le Vice-Consul* 1966, evoking an existentialist world from the setting of Calcutta, and *Emily L.* 1989. *La vie materielle* (published in France 1987) appeared in England as *Practicalities* 1990. Her autobiographical novel, *La Douleur*, is set in Paris in 1945.

Durazzo Italian form of ◊Durrës, Albanian port.

Durban principal port of Natal, South Africa, and second port of the republic; population (1985) 634,000, urban area 982,000. It exports coal, grain, and wool; imports heavy machinery and mining equipment; and is also a vacation resort.

Founded 1824 as Port Natal, it was renamed 1835 after Gen Benjamin d'Urban (1777–1849), lieutenant-governor of the E district of Cape Colony 1834–37. Natal university 1949 is divided between Durban and Pietermaritzburg.

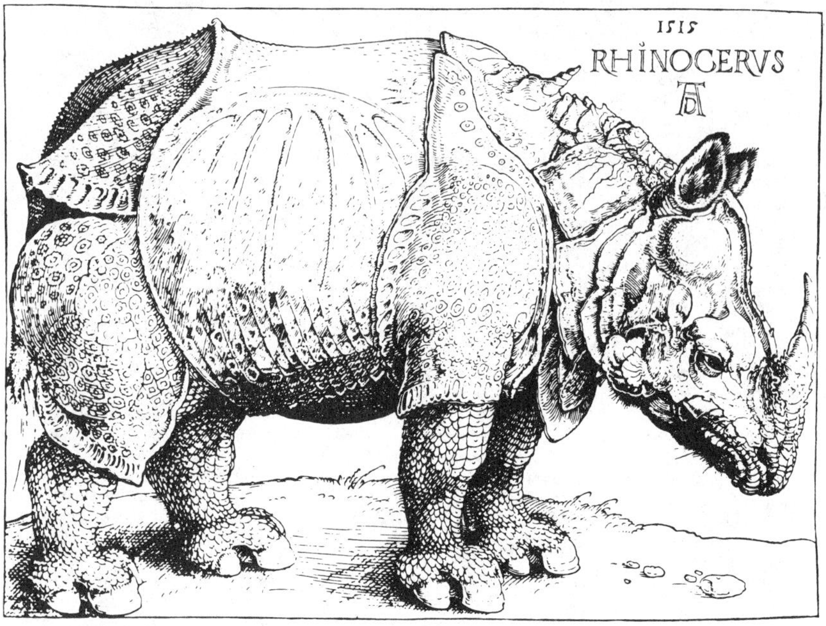
1515
RHINOCERVS
AD
Dürer Woodcut of a rhinoceros by Albrecht Dürer. The rhinoceros was described to him by a Portuguese artist in 1515.

Dürer Albrecht 1471–1528. German artist, the leading figure of the northern Renaissance. Highly skilled in drawing and a keen student of nature, he perfected the technique of woodcut and engraving, producing woodcut series such as the *Apocalypse* 1498 and copperplate engravings such as *The Knight, Death, and the Devil* 1513 and *Melancholia* 1514; he may also have invented etching. His paintings include altarpieces and meticulously observed portraits (including many self-portraits).

He was apprenticed first to his father, a goldsmith, then in 1486 to Michael Wolgemut, a painter, woodcut artist, and master of a large workshop in Nuremberg. From 1490 he traveled widely in Europe, studying Netherlandish and Italian art, then visited Colmar, Basel, and Strasbourg and returned to Nuremberg in 1495. Other notable journeys were to Venice 1505–07, where he met Giovanni Bellini, and to Antwerp 1520, where he was made court painter to Charles V of Spain and the Netherlands (recorded in detail in his diary).

Durga Hindu goddess; one of the many names for ◊Mahadevi.

Durham city and administrative headquarters of the county of Durham, England; population (1983) 88,600. Founded in 995, it has a Norman cathedral dating from 1093, where the remains of ◊Bede were transferred in 1370; the castle was built by William I in 1072 and the university founded in 1832. Textiles, engineering, and coal mining are the chief industries.

Durham city in N central North Carolina, NW of Raleigh; seat of Durham county. Tobacco is the main industry, and other manufactures include precision instruments, textiles, furniture, and lumber. Duke University is here; population (1990) 136,611.

Durkheim Emile 1858–1917. French sociologist, one of the founders of modern sociology, who also influenced social anthropology.

He was the first lecturer in social science at Bordeaux University 1887–1902, professor of education at the Sorbonne in Paris from 1902 and the first professor of sociology there in 1913. He examined the bases of social order and the effects of industrialization on traditional social and moral order; he attempted to establish sociology as a respectable and scientific discipline, capable of diagnosing social ills and recommending possible cures.

His four key works are *The Division of Labor in Society* 1893, comparing social order in small-scale societies with that in industrial ones; *The Rules of Sociological Method/Les Régles de la méthode* 1895, outlining his own brand of functionalism and proclaiming ◊positivism as the way forward for sociology as a science; *Suicide* 1897, showing social causes of this apparently individual act; and *Les Formes élémentaires de la vie religieuse/The Elementary Forms of Religion* 1912, a study of the beliefs of Australian Aborigines, showing the place of religion in social solidarity.

durra or ***doura*** grass of the genus *Sorghum*, also known as Indian millet, grown as cereal in parts of Asia and Africa. *Sorghum vulgare* is the chief cereal in many parts of Africa. See also ◊sorghum.

Durrell Lawrence (George) 1912–1990. British novelist and poet. Born in India, he joined the foreign service and lived mainly in the E Mediterranean, the setting of his novels, including the Alexandria Quartet: *Justine*, *Balthazar*, *Mountolive*, and *Clea* 1957–60; he also wrote travel books. He was the brother of the naturalist Gerald Durrell.

Dürrenmatt Friedrich 1921–1991. Swiss dramatist, author of grotesquely farcical tragicomedies, for example *The Visit* 1956 and *The Physicists* 1962.

Durrës chief port of Albania; population (1983) 72,000. It is a commercial and communications center, with flour mills, soap and cigarette factories, distilleries, and an electronics plant. It was the capital of Albania 1912–21.

Duse Eleonora 1859–1924. Italian actress. She was the mistress of the poet ◊D'Annunzio from 1897, as recorded in his novel *Il Fuoco/The Flame of Life*.

Dushanbe formerly (1929–69) *Stalinabad* capital of Tadzhik Republic, USSR, 100 mi/160 km N of the Afghan frontier; population (1987) 582,000. It is a road, rail, and air center. Industries include cotton mills, tanneries, meatpacking factories, and printing works. It is the seat of Tadzhik state university.

Düsseldorf industrial city of Germany, on the right bank of the river Rhine, 16 mi/26 km NW of Cologne, capital of North Rhine–Westphalia; population (1988) 561,000. It is a river port and the commercial and financial center of the Ruhr area, with food processing, brewing, agricultural machinery, textile, and chemical industries.

dust bowl area in the Great Plains region of North America (Texas to Kansas) that suffered extensive wind erosion as the result of drought and poor farming practice in once fertile soil. Much of the topsoil was blown away in the droughts of the 1930s.

Similar dust bowls are being formed in many areas today, noticeably across Africa, because of the same overcropping and overgrazing, resulting in ◊desert conditions.

Dutch art painting and sculpture of the Netherlands. With the rise of the Dutch nation in the second half of the 16th century came the full emergence of Dutch art with Frans Hals; Pieter Lastman (1585–1633), the teacher of Rembrandt; and Gerard van Honthorst.

Among the many masters of the 17th century are Rembrandt and his pupil Gerard Douw (1613–1675); Adriaen van Ostade (1610–1684), who painted Flemish peasant scenes; Gerard Ter Borch the Younger (1617–1681), first painter of characteristic Dutch interiors; Albert Cuyp; Jan Steen; Jakob van Ruysdael, greatest of the landscapists; Pieter de Hooch; Jan Vermeer van Delft; Willem van de Velde, sea painter to Charles II of England; Jan van der Heyden (1637–1712); and Meindert Hobbema. The houses, markets, and town halls of this period were also a consummate expression of the Dutch genius.

In the 18th and 19th centuries there was a marked decline, except for the genre painters Cornelis Troost (1697–1750) and Jozef Israels (1824–1911) and the outstanding genius of Vincent van Gogh.

Dutch East Indies former Dutch colony, which in 1945 became independent as ◊Indonesia.

Dutch elm disease a disease of elm trees *Ulmus*, principally Dutch, English, and American elm, caused by the fungus *Certocystis ulmi*. The fungus is usually spread from tree to tree by the elm-bark beetle, which lays its eggs beneath the bark. The disease has no cure and control methods involve injecting insecticide into the trees annually to prevent infection, or the destruction of all elms in a broad band around an infected area, to keep the beetles out.

It was first described in the Netherlands and by the early 1930s had spread across Britain and continental Europe, as well as North America.

Dutch Guiana former Dutch colony, which in 1975 became independent as ◊Suriname.

Dutch language member of the Germanic branch of the Indo-European language family, often referred to by scholars as Netherlandic and taken to include the standard language and dialects of the Netherlands (excluding Frisian) as well as Flemish (in Belgium and N France) and, more remotely, its offshoot Afrikaans in South Africa.

Dutch literature the earliest known poet to use the Dutch dialect was Henric van Veldeke in the 12th century, but the finest example of early Gothic literature is *Van Den Vos Reinaarde* (About Reynard the Fox) by a poet known as "Willem-who-made-the-Madoc." To the golden age belong Pieter C Hooft (1581–1647), lyricist, playwright, and historian; Constantijn Huygens (1596–1687); Gerbrand A Bredero (1585–1618); the great lyric, satiric, and dramatic poet Joost van den Vondel (1587–1679); and the moralizing poet Father Jacob Cats (1577–1660).

As in art, the 18th century was a period of decline for Dutch literature, although the epic poet Willem Bilderdijk (1756–1831) ranks highly. The Romantic movement found its fullest expression in the nationalist periodical *De Gids* (The Guide) founded 1837. Other writers of the period were Nicolas Beets (1814–1903) and Eduard Douwes Dekker (1820–87), who wrote novels under the pen name "Multatuli." Among writers of the late 19th-century revival were poets Herman Gorter (1864–1927), Albert Verwey (1865–1937), the poet, playwright, and novelists Frederick van Eeden (1860–1932), Louis Couperus (1863–1923), and Arthur van Schendel (1874–1946).

After World War I Hendrik Marsman (1899–1940), a rhetorical "vitalist" influenced by German Expressionism, led a school counterbalanced by the more sober *Forum* group of critic Menno Ter Braak (1902–40). See also ◊Flemish literature.

Duvalier François 1907–1971. Right-wing president of Haiti 1957–71. Known as Papa Doc, he ruled as a dictator, organizing the Tontons Macoutes ("bogeymen") as a private security force to intimidate and assassinate opponents of his regime. He rigged the 1961 elections in order to have his term of office extended until 1967, and in 1964 declared himself president for life. He was excommunicated by the Vatican for harassing the church, and was succeeded on his death by his son Jean-Claude Duvalier.

Duvalier Jean-Claude 1951– . Right-wing president of Haiti 1971–86. Known as Baby Doc, he succeeded his father François Duvalier, becoming, at the age of 19, the youngest president in the world. He continued to receive support from the US but was pressured into moderating some elements of his father's regime, yet still tolerated no opposition. In 1986, with Haiti's economy stagnating and with increasing civil disorder, Duvalier fled to France, taking much of the Haitian treasury with him.

Duve Christian de 1917– . Belgian scientist, who shared the Nobel Prize for Medicine in 1974 for his work on the structural and functional organization of the biological cell.

Duvivier Julien 1896–1967. French film director whose work includes *La Belle Equipe* 1936, *Un Carnet de bal* 1937 and *La Fin du jour* 1938.

Dvořák Antonin (Leopold) 1841–1904. Czech composer. International recognition came with his series of Slavonic Dances 1877–86, and he was director of the National Conservatory, New York, 1892–95. Works such as his *New World Symphony* 1893 reflect his interest in American folk themes, including black and Native American. He wrote nine symphonies; tone poems; operas; including *Rusalka* 1901; large-scale choral works; the *Carnival* and other overtures; violin and cello concertos; chamber music; piano pieces; and songs. His Romantic music extends the Classical tradition of Beethoven and Brahms and displays the influence of Czech folk music.

dwarf star a ◊main-sequence star as plotted on the ◊Hertzsprung–Russell diagram. A cool dwarf star is a ◊red dwarf and a hot one is a ◊white dwarf.

***Dvořák** Czech composer Antonin Dvořák.*

Dyak or ***Dayak*** several indigenous peoples of Indonesian Borneo and Sarawak, including the Bahau of central and E Borneo, the Land Dyak of SW Borneo, and the Iban of Sarawak. Their language belongs to the Austronesian family. Some anthropologists now call all Dyak peoples Iban.

dybbuk (Hebrew "a clinging thing") in Jewish folklore, the soul of a dead sinner which has entered the body of a living person.

Dyck Anthony van 1599–1641. Flemish painter. Born in Antwerp, van Dyck was an assistant to Rubens 1618–20, then briefly worked in England at the court of James I, and moved to Italy in 1622. In 1626 he returned to Antwerp, where he continued to paint religious works and portraits. From 1632 he lived in England and produced numerous portraits of royalty and aristocrats, such as *Charles I on Horseback* c. 1638 (National Gallery, London).

dye substance that, applied in solution to fabrics, imparts a color resistant to washing. Direct dyes combine with the material of the fabric, yielding a colored compound; indirect dyes require the presence of another substance (a mordant), with which the fabric must first be treated; vat dyes are colorless soluble substances that on exposure to air yield an insoluble colored compound.

Naturally occurring dyes include indigo, madder (alizarin), logwood, and cochineal, but industrial dyes (introduced in the 19th century) are usually synthetic: acid green was developed 1835 and bright purple 1856. Industrial dyes include azo-dyestuffs, acridine, anthracene, and aniline.

Dylan Bob. Adopted name of Robert Allen Zimmerman 1941– . US singer and songwriter, whose work in the 1960s, with its emphasis on socially conscious lyrics, first in the folk music tradition and, beginning in 1965, in an individualistic rock style, had great influence on the development of Western popular music.

Dylan's early songs, on his albums *Freewheelin'* 1963 and *The Times They Are A-Changin'* 1964, were associated with the US civil-rights movement and antiwar protest. When he first used an electric rock band he was criticized by purists, but his electric albums, *Highway 61 Revisited* 1965 and *Blonde on Blonde* 1966, are often cited as his best work. His meaningful (but increasingly obscure) lyrics provided catchphrases for a generation and influenced innumerable songwriters.

dynamics or ***kinetics*** in mechanics, the mathematical and physical study of the behavior of bodies under the action of forces that produce changes of motion in them.

dynamite an explosive consisting of a mixture of nitroglycerine and diatomaceous earth (diatomite, an absorbent, chalklike material). It was first devised by Alfred Nobel.

dynamo former name for ◊generator.

dyne unit (abbreviation dyn) of force. 10^5 dynes make one newton. The dyne is defined as the

Dylan *US singer and songwriter Bob Dylan wrote influential popular protest songs in the 1960s.*

force that will accelerate a mass of one gram by one centimeter per second per second.

dysentery infection of the large intestine causing abdominal cramps and painful ◊diarrhea with blood.

There are two kinds of dysentery: amoebic (caused by a protozoan), common in the tropics, which may lead to liver damage; and bacterial, the kind most often seen in the temperate zones. Both forms are successfully treated with antibacterials and fluids to prevent dehydration.

dyslexia (Greek "bad," "pertaining to words") a malfunction in the brain's synthesis and interpretation of sensory information, popularly "word blindness." It results in poor ability to read and write, though the person may otherwise excel, for example, in mathematics. A similar disability with figures is called dyscalculus.

dyspepsia synonym for ◊indigestion.

dysphagia difficulty in swallowing. It may be due to infection, obstruction, or spasm in the throat or esophagus (gullet).

dyspnea difficulty in breathing, or shortness of breath disproportionate to effort. It occurs if the supply of oxygen is inadequate or if carbon dioxide accumulates. It can be caused by circulatory or respiratory diseases.

dysprosium silver-white, metallic element of the ◊lanthanide series, symbol Dy, atomic number 66, atomic weight 162.50. It is among the most magnetic of all known substances and has a great capacity to absorb neutrons.

It was discovered in 1886 by French chemist Paul Lecoq de Boisbaudran (1838–1912) and was named after Greek *dysprositos* "difficult to get near."

dystopia an imaginary society whose evil qualities are meant to serve as a moral or political warning. The term was coined in the 19th century by John Stuart ◊Mill, and is the opposite of a ◊Utopia. George Orwell's *1984* 1949 and Aldous Huxley's *Brave New World* 1932 are examples. Dystopias are common in science fiction.

Dzerzhinsk city in central USSR, on the Oka river, 20 mi/32 km W of Gorky; population (1987) 281,000. There are engineering, chemical, and timber industries.

Dzhambul city in S Kazakhstan, USSR, in a fruit-growing area NE of Tashkent. Industries include fruit canning, sugar refining, and the manufacture of phosphate fertilizers. Population (1985) 303,000.

Dzo a river in central Portugal that flows 50 mi/80 km through a region noted for its wine.

Dzungarian Gates ancient route in central Asia on the border of Kazakhstan, USSR, and Xinjiang Uygur region of China, 290 mi/470 km NW of Urumqi. The route was used by the Mongol hordes on their way to Europe.

E abbreviation for east.

eagle several genera of large birds of prey of the family Accipitridae. The golden eagle *Aquila chrysaetos* of Eurasia and North America. It has a 6 ft/2 m wingspan and is dark brown.

The white-headed bald eagle *H. leukocephalus* is the symbol of the US; rendered infertile through the ingestion of agricultural chemicals, it is now very rare, except in Alaska. Another endangered species is the Philippine eagle, sometimes called the Philippine monkey-eating eagle (although its main prey is flying lemurs). Loss of large tracts of forest, coupled with hunting by humans, have greatly reduced its numbers.

In North America the golden eagle is found throughout most of the US, Canada, and N Mexico, with the exception of the SE. The larger spotted eagle *A. clanga* lives in Central Europe and Asia. The sea eagles *Haliaetus* include Steller's sea eagle *H. pelagicus*, mainly a carrion-feeder, it breeds on sea cliffs.

Eagling Wayne 1950– . Canadian dancer. He joined the Royal Ballet in London, appearing in *Gloria* 1980, and other productions.

Eakins Thomas 1844–1916. US artist. Born in Philadelphia, Eakins attended the Pennsylvania Academy of the Fine Arts and the École des Beaux-Arts in Paris, later becoming an instructor at the Pennsylvania Academy. As a trained observer of human anatomy and a devotee of photography, Eakins attempted to achieve a sense of visual realism in his work.

The most memorable motifs for his paintings were medical and sporting scenes. Among his larger-than-life-size sculptures commissioned for public monuments are the war memorials in Trenton, New Jersey, and Brooklyn, New York.

eagle

bald eagle

Ealing Studios film studios in W London, England, headed by Michael Balcon. They produced a number of George Formby and Will Hay war-related films in the 1940s, then a series of more genteel and occasionally satirical comedies, often written by T E B Clarke and starring Alec Guinness.

Titles produced at Ealing include *Passport to Pimlico* 1948, *Kind Hearts and Coronets* 1949, *The Man in the White Suit* 1951, and *The Ladykillers* 1955.

Eanes António dos Santos Ramalho 1935– . Portuguese politician. He helped plan the 1974 coup that ended the Caetano regime, and as army chief of staff put down a left-wing revolt in Nov 1975. He was president 1976–86.

ear the organ of hearing in animals. It responds to the vibrations that constitute sound, and these are translated into nerve signals and passed to the brain. A mammal's ear consists of three parts: outer ear, middle ear, and inner ear. The outer ear is a funnel that collects sound, directing it down a tube to the ear drum (tympanic membrane), which separates the outer and middle ear. Sounds vibrate this membrane, the mechanical movement of which is transferred to a smaller membrane leading to the inner ear by three small bones, the auditory ossicles. Vibrations of the inner ear membrane move fluid contained in the snail-shaped cochlea, which vibrates hair cells that stimulate the auditory nerve, connected to the brain. Three fluid-filled canals of the inner ear detect changes of position; this mechanism, with other sensory inputs, is responsible for the sense of balance.

When a loud noise occurs, muscles behind the eardrum contract automatically, suppressing the noise to enhance perception of sound and prevent injury.

Earhart Amelia Mary 1898–1937. US aviation pioneer. Born in Atchison, Kansas, Earhart had a varied early career as an army nurse and social worker, before discovering that her true calling lay in aviation. In 1928 she became the first woman to fly across the Atlantic as a passenger and in 1932 completed a solo transatlantic flight. Earhart gained national recognition as both an aviator and a popular author. She worked briefly as an airline executive 1930–31. With copilot Frederick Noonan, she attempted a round-the-world flight 1937. Somewhere over the Pacific their plane disappeared.

earl in the British peerage, the third title in order of rank, coming between marquess and viscount; it is the oldest of British titles, being of Scandinavian origin. An earl's wife is a countess.

Early Jubal Anderson 1816–1894. American Confederate military leader. Born in Franklin County, Virginia, Early graduated from West Point 1837 and saw action in the Seminole War. After studying law, he was admitted to the bar 1840 and later served in the Virginia legislature. Although long in favor of preserving the Union, Early joined the Confederate army at the outbreak of the Civil War. After Bull Run he was named general in the Army of Northern Virginia and led campaigns in the Shenandoah Valley, threatening Washington, DC 1864. After a brief period of exile after the war, he resumed his Virginia law practice.

Earp Wyatt 1848–1929. US frontier law officer. In 1876 Earp was appointed assistant marshal in Dodge City, Kansas. Known also as a gambler and brawler, Earp's closest friends were the legendary Bat Masterson and Doc Holliday. With them and his brothers Virgil and Morgan he participated in the famous gunfight at the OK Corral on Oct 26, 1881, in Tombstone, Arizona. He left Tombstone 1882, traveled, and operated saloons before he settled in Los Angeles.

ear

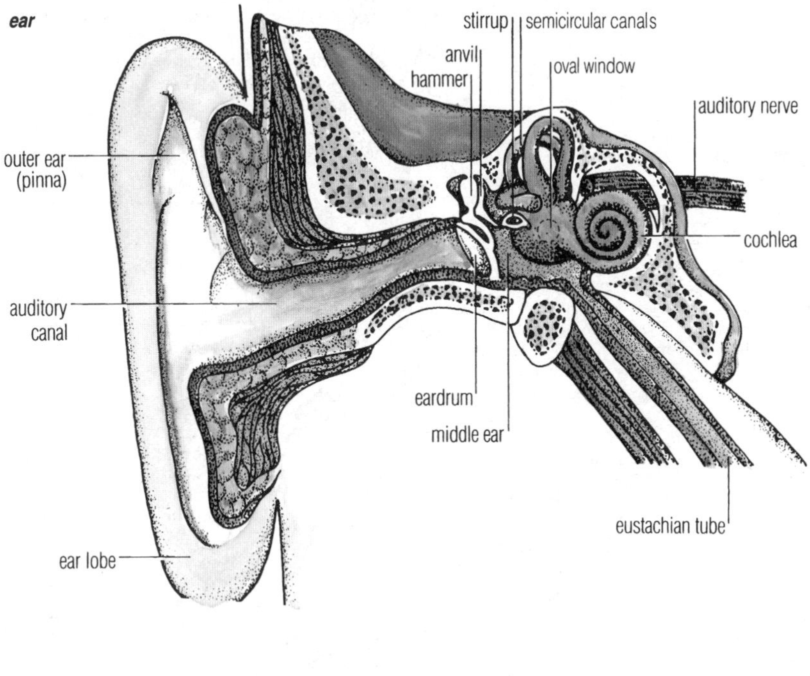
stirrup
semicircular canals
anvil
hammer
oval window
auditory nerve
outer ear (pinna)
cochlea
auditory canal
eardrum
middle ear
eustachian tube
ear lobe

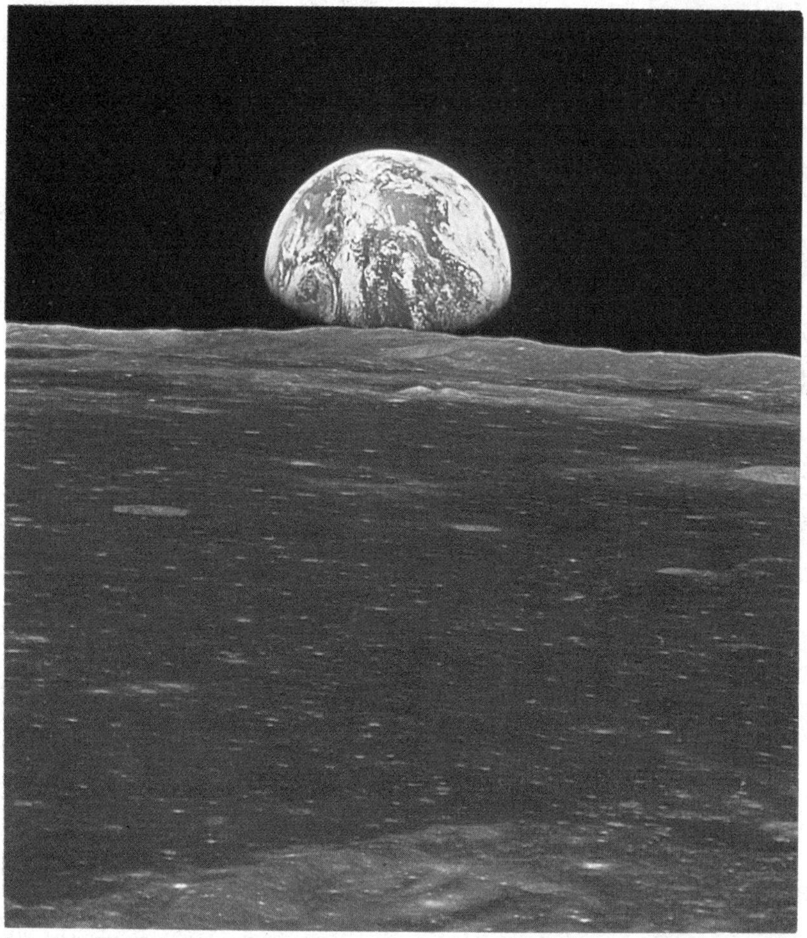

Earth View of the Earth rising above the surface of the Moon, taken by the Apollo 11 spacecraft.

earthquake *Mexico City, Sept 19, 1985. In the space of a few minutes, 10,000 people lost their lives and more than 200 buildings were razed.*

Born in Monmouth, Illinois, Earp moved with his family to Iowa, finally settling in California 1864. Later gaining fame as a scout and buffalo hunter, he moved to Wichita, Kansas, 1874, where he was occasionally employed by the US marshal.

Earth the third planet from the Sun. It is almost spherical, flattened slightly at the poles, and is composed of three concentric layers: the ◊core, the ◊mantle, and the ◊crust. As much as 70% of the surface (including the north and south polar icecaps) is covered with water. The Earth is surrounded by a life-supporting atmosphere and is the only planet on which life is known to exist.

mean distance from the Sun 92,860,000 mi/149,500,000 km.

equatorial diameter 7,923 mi/12,756 km.

circumference 24,900 mi/40,070 km.

rotation period 23 hr 56 min 4.1 sec.

year (complete orbit, or sidereal period) 365 days 5 hr 48 min 46 sec. Earth's average speed around the Sun is 18.5 mps/30 kps; the plane of its orbit is inclined to its equatorial plane at an angle of 23.5°, the reason for the changing seasons.

atmosphere nitrogen 78.09%; oxygen 20.95%; argon 0.93%; carbon dioxide 0.03%; and less than 0.0001% neon, helium, krypton, hydrogen, xenon, ozone, radon.

surface land surface 57,500,000 sq mi/150,000,000 sq km (greatest height above sea level 29,108 ft/8,872 m Mount Everest); water surface 139,400,000 sq mi/361,000,000 sq km (greatest depth 36,201 ft/11,034 m ◊Mariana Trench in the Pacific). The interior is thought to be an inner core about 1,600 mi/2,600 km in diameter, of solid iron and nickel; an outer core about 1,400 mi/2,250 km thick, of molten iron and nickel; and a mantle of mostly solid rock about 1,800 mi/2,900 km thick, separated by the ◊Mohorovičić discontinuity from the Earth's crust. The crust and the topmost layer of the mantle form about 12 major moving plates, some of which carry the continents. The plates are in constant, slow motion, called tectonic drift.

satellite the ◊Moon.

age 4.6 billion years. The Earth was formed with the rest of the ◊Solar System by consolidation of interstellar dust. Life began about 3.5 billion years ago; human life 5–6 million years ago.

earthenware pottery made of porous clay and fired, whether unglazed (flowerpots, winecoolers) or glazed (rustic tableware).

major 20th-century earthquakes

date	*place*	*magnitude (Richter scale)*	*number of deaths*
1906	San Francisco	8.3	3,000
1908	Messina, Italy	7.5	83,000
1915	Avezzano, Italy	7.5	29,980
1920	Gansu, China	8.6	100,000
1923	Tokyo, Japan	8.3	99,330
1927	Nan-Shan, China	8.3	200,000
1932	Gansu, China	7.6	70,000
1935	Quetta, India	7.5	30,000
1939	Erzincan, Turkey	7.9	30,000
1939	Chillan, Chile	8.3	28,000
1948	USSR	7.3	110,000
1970	N Peru	7.7	66,794
1976	Tangshan, China	8.2	242,000
1978	NE Iran	7.7	25,000
1985	Mexico	8.1	25,000
1988	Armenia, USSR	6.9	25,000
1989	San Francisco	7.1	300

earthquake a shaking or convulsion of the Earth's surface, the scientific study of which is called ◊seismology. Earthquakes result from a buildup of stresses within rocks until strained to fracturing point. Most occur along ◊faults (fractures or breaks) in the Earth's crust. Plate tectonic movements generate the major proportion of all earthquakes; as two plates move past each other, they can become jammed and deformed, and earthquakes occur when they spring free. Most earthquakes happen under the sea. Their force is measured on the ◊Richter scale.

The point at which an earthquake originates is the seismic focus. The point on Earth's surface directly above this is the epicenter. In 1987 a California earthquake was successfully predicted by measurement of underground pressure waves; prediction attempts have also involved the study of such phenomena as the change in gases issuing from the ◊crust, the level of water in wells, and the behavior of animals. The possibility of earthquake prevention is remote. However, rock slippage might be slowed at movement points or promoted at stoppage points by the extraction or injection of large quantities of water underground, since water serves as a lubricant. This would ease overall pressure.

earth sciences the scientific study of the planet

earth

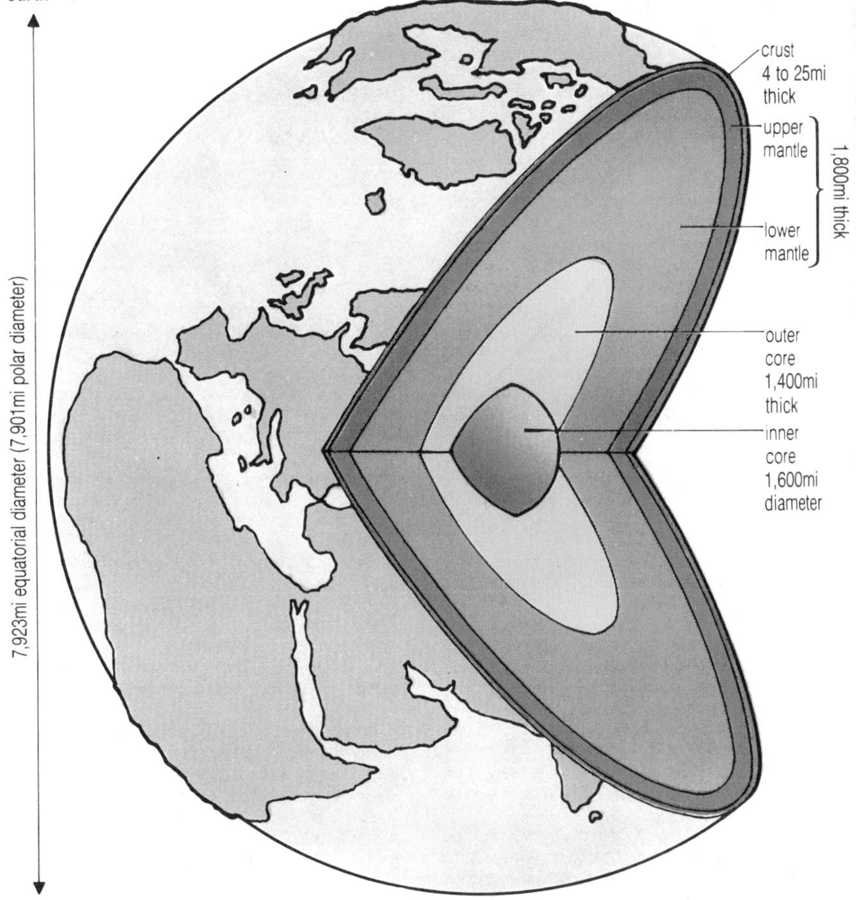
crust
4 to 25mi
thick
upper
mantle
lower
mantle
1,800mi thick
outer
core
1,400mi
thick
inner
core
1,600mi
diameter
7,923mi equatorial diameter (7,901mi polar diameter)

Earth as a whole, a synthesis of several traditional subjects such as ◊geology, ◊meteorology, oceanography, ◊geophysics, ◊geochemistry, and ◊paleontology.

The mining and extraction of minerals and gems, the prediction of weather and earthquakes, the pollution of the atmosphere, and the forces that shape the physical world all fall within its scope of study. The emergence of the discipline reflects scientists' concern that an understanding of the global aspects of the Earth's structure and its past will hold the key to how humans affect its future, ensuring that its resources are used in a sustainable way.

earthworm ◊annelid worm of the class Oligochaeta. Earthworms are hermaphroditic, and deposit their eggs in cocoons. They live by burrowing in the soil, feeding on the organic matter it contains. They are vital to the formation of humus, by aerating the soil and leveling it by transferring earth from the deeper levels to the surface as castings.

Most North American earthworms belong to the genus *Lumbricus*. These are comparatively small, but some tropical forms reach over 3 ft/1 m in length. *Megascolides australis*, of Queensland, for instance, can be over 11 ft/3 m long.

earwig nocturnal insect of the order Dermaptera. The fore-wings are short and leathery and serve to protect the hind-wings, which are large and are folded like a fan when at rest; the insects seldom fly. They have a pincer-like appendage in the rear. Earwigs are regarded as pests because they feed on flowers and fruit, but they also eat other insects, dead or alive. Eggs are laid beneath the soil, and the female cares for the young even after they have hatched.

Forficula is the common genus in North America.

earthworm

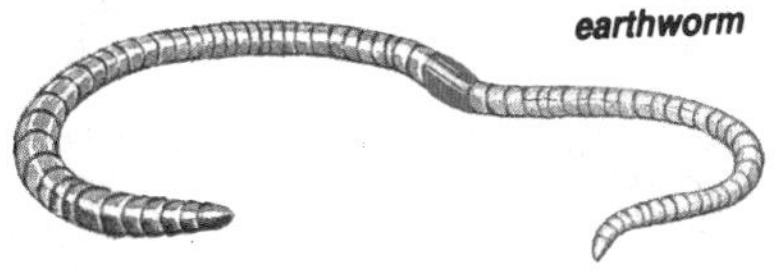

easement in law, rights that a person may have over the land of another. A common example is a right of way; others are the right to bring water over another's land and the right to an uninterrupted flow of light to windows.

east one of the four cardinal points of the compass, indicating that part of the horizon where the Sun rises; when facing north, east is to the right.

The Sun, and hence the east, has held a significant place in various religions; ancient temples had their altars at the east end so that sacrifices and other rituals could be made facing the rising Sun. In the 2nd century it became customary for Christians to worship facing the east, and also to bury the dead with their feet toward the east, so that on the morning of the Resurrection they would be facing the direction from which Christ was to come in glory.

East Anglia region of E England, formerly a Saxon kingdom, including Norfolk, Suffolk, and parts of Essex and Cambridgeshire. Norwich is the principal city of East Anglia. The University of East Anglia was founded in Norwich 1962, and includes the Sainsbury Centre for the Visual Arts, opened 1978, which has a collection of ethnographic art and sculpture. East Anglian ports such as Harwich and Felixstowe have greatly developed as trade with the rest of Europe increases.

Eastbourne English seaside resort in East Sussex, 64 mi/103 km SE of London; population (1981) 77,500. The old town was developed in the early 19th century as a model of town planning, largely caused by the 7th duke of Devonshire. The modern town extends along the coast for 3 mi/5 km.

Easter spring feast of the Christian church, commemorating the Resurrection of Jesus.

The English name derives from Eostre, Anglo-Saxon goddess of spring, who was honored in April. Dyed easter eggs, and pieces of candy shaped like eggs, young chickens, ducklings, lambs or rabbits—all symbolizing new life—are given to young children.

Easter Island or ***Rapa Nui*** Chilean island in the S Pacific Ocean, part of the Polynesian group, about 2,200 mi/3,500 km W of Chile; area about 64 sq mi/166 sq km; population (1985) 2,000. It was first reached by Europeans on Easter Sunday 1722. On it stand huge carved statues and stone houses, the work of neolithic peoples of unknown origin. The chief center is Hanga-Roa.

Easter Rising or ***Easter Rebellion*** in Irish history, a republican insurrection that began on Easter Monday, April 1916, in Dublin. It was inspired by the Irish Republican Brotherhood (IRB) in an unsuccessful attempt to overthrow British rule in Ireland. It was led by Patrick Pearce of the IRB and James Conolly of Sinn Féin.

East India Company, Dutch (VOC, or Vereenigde Oost-Indische Compagnie) a trading company chartered by the States General (parliament) of the Netherlands, and established in N Netherlands 1602. It was given a monopoly on Dutch trade in the Indonesian archipelago, and certain sovereign rights such as the creation of an army and a fleet. In the 17th century some 100 ships were regularly trading between the Netherlands and the East Indies. The company's main base was Batavia in Java (Indonesia); ships sailed there via the Cape of Good Hope, a colony founded by the company 1652 as a staging post. During the 17th and 18th centuries the company used its monopoly of East Indian trade to pay out high dividends, but wars with England and widespread corruption led to a suspension of payments 1781 and a takeover of the company by the Dutch government 1798.

East London port and resort on the SE coast of Cape Province, South Africa. Population (1980) 160,582. Founded 1846 as Port Rex, its name was changed to East London 1848. It has a good harbor, is the terminus of a railroad from the interior, and is a leading wool-exporting port.

Eastman George 1854–1932. US entrepreneur and inventor who founded the Eastman Kodak photographic company in 1892. From 1888 he marketed his patented daylight-loading flexible roll films (to replace the glass plates used previously) and portable cameras. By 1900 his company was selling a pocket camera for as little as one dollar.

The films first worked with chemicals fixed to a paper base 1884 and later on celluloid 1889. In 1928 he perfected a film process for color photography and development, an important ser-

Eastman *Founder of the Kodak photographic company, inventor and entrepreneur, George Eastman.*

Eastwood *Film actor and director Clint Eastwood 1970.*

vice offered on fine papers. He was known for his contributions to education and music.

East Pakistan a province of ◊Pakistan, now Bangladesh.

East River tidal strait 16 mi/26 km long, between Manhattan and the Bronx, and Long Island, in New York. It links Long Island Sound with New York Bay and is also connected, via the Harlem River, with the Hudson. There are docks; most famous of its many bridges is the Brooklyn.

East Siberian Sea part of the ◊Arctic Ocean, off the N coast of USSR, between the New Siberian Islands and Chukchi Sea. The world's widest continental shelf, with an average width of nearly 404 mi/650 km, lies in the East Siberian Sea.

East St Louis city in SW Illinois on the Mississippi River, across from St Louis, Missouri. A center for the processing of livestock; its other industries include steel, paint materials, and machinery; population (1990) 40,944.

East Sussex county in SE England

area 695 sq mi/1,800 sq km

towns Lewes (adminstrative headquarters), Newhaven (cross-channel port), Brighton, Eastbourne, Hastings, Bexhill, Winchelsea, Rye

features Beachy Head, highest headland in the S coast at 590 ft/180 m, the E end of the South ◊Downs; the Weald (including Ashdown Forest; rivers: Ouse, Cuckmere, East Rother; Romney March; the "Long Man" chalk hill figure at Wilmington, near Eastbourne; Herstmonceux, with a 15th-century castle (conference and exhibition center) and adjacent modern buildings, site of the Greenwich Royal Observatory 1958–90; other castles at Hastings, Lewes, Pevensey, and Bodiam; Battle Abbey and the site of the Battle of Hastings; Michelham Priory; Sheffield Park garden; University of Sussex at Falmer, near Brighton, founded in 1961

products electronics, gypsum, timber

population (1987) 698,000.

East Timor disputed territory on the island of ◊Timor in the Malay Archipelago; prior to 1975, a Portuguese colony for almost 460 years

area 5,706 sq mi/14,874 sq km

capital Dili

products coffee

population (1980) 555,000

history Following Portugal's withdrawal 1975, the left-wing Revolutionary Front of Independent East Timor (Fretilin) occupied the capital, Dili, calling for independence. In opposition, troops from neighboring Indonesia invaded the territory, declaring East Timor (Loro Sae) the 17th province of Indonesia July 1976. This claim is not recognized by the United Nations.

The Portuguese colonizers left behind a literacy rate of under 10% and no infrastructure. A brief civil war followed their departure and, after the nationalist guerrillas' calls for independence, the invading Indonesian troops bombed villages and carried out mass executions of suspected Fretilin sympathizers. The war and its attendant famine are thought to have caused more than 100,000 deaths, but starvation had been alleviated by the mid-1980s, and the Indonesian government has built schools, roads, and hospitals. Fretilin guerrillas remained active claiming to have the support of the population.

Eastwood Clint 1930– . US film actor and director. As the "man with no name" in *A Fistful of Dollars* 1964, he started the vogue for "spaghetti Westerns." Later Westerns include *The Good, the Bad, and the Ugly* 1966 and *High Plains Drifter* 1973. He also starred in the "Dirty Harry" police series and directed *Bird* 1988.

Eau Claire city in W central Wisconsin, N of LaCrosse, on the Chippewa river; seat of Eau Claire county. It is a processing and marketing center for the region's dairy farmers. Industries include machine parts, electronics, printing, and brewing. Tourism is important to the economy; population (1990) 56,856.

eau de cologne refreshing toilet water (weaker than perfume), made of alcohol and aromatic oils, whose invention is ascribed to Giovanni Maria Farina (1685–1766). He moved from Italy to Cologne in 1709 to manufacture it.

Eban Abba 1915– . Israeli diplomat and politician, Israeli ambassador in Washington 1950–59 and foreign minister 1966–74.

Eban was born in Cape Town, South Africa, and educated in England; he taught at Cambridge University before serving at Allied HQ during World War II. He subsequently settled in Israel.

EBCDIC (abbreviation of extended binary coded decimal interchange code) in computing, a code used for storing and communicating alphabetic and numeric characters. It is an 8-bit code, capable of holding 256 different characters, although only 85 of these are defined in the standard version. It is still used in many mainframe computers, but almost all mini- and microcomputers now use ◊ASCII code.

ebony any of a group of hardwood trees of the ebony family Ebenaceae, especially some tropical persimmons, genus *Diospyros*, native to Africa and Asia. Their very heavy, hard black timber polishes well and is used in cabinetmaking, inlaying, and also for piano keys, violin fingerboards, chinrests, and pegs, and for sculpture.

Eboracum Roman name for ◊York, English city. The archbishop of York signs himself "Ebor."

Ebro river in NE Spain, which rises in the Cantabrian mountains and flows some 500 mi/800 km SE to meet the Mediterranean sea SW of Barcelona. Zaragoza is on its course, and ocean-going ships can sail as far as Tortosa, 22 mi/35 km from its mouth. It is a major source of hydroelectric power.

EC abbreviation for ◊European Community.

eccentricity in geometry, a property of a ◊conic section (circle, ellipse, parabola, or hyperbola). It is the distance of any point on the curve from a fixed point (the focus) divided by the distance of that point from a fixed line (the directrix). A circle has an eccentricity of zero; for an ellipse it is less than one; for a parabola it is equal to one; and for a hyperbola it is greater than one.

Eccles John Carew 1903– . Australian physiologist who shared (with Alan Hodgkin and Andrew Huxley) the 1963 Nobel Prize for medicine for work on conduction in the central nervous system. In some of his later works, he argued that the mind has an existence independent of the brain.

Ecclesiastes also known as "The Preacher," a book of the Old Testament, traditionally attributed to ◊Solomon, on the theme of the vanity of human life.

ecdysis the periodic shedding of the ◊exoskeleton by insects and other arthropods to allow growth. Prior to shedding, a new soft and expandable layer is first laid down underneath the existing one. The old layer then splits, the animal moves free of it, and the new layer expands and hardens.

ECG abbreviation for ◊electrocardiogram.

Echegaray José 1832–1916. Spanish dramatist. His dramas include *O locura o santidad/Madman or Saint* 1877, and *El gran Galeoto/The World and his Wife* 1881. Nobel Prize 1904.

echidna or spiny ant-eater any of several species of toothless, egg-laying, spiny mammals of the genera *Tachyglossus* and *Zaglossus*, in the order Monotremata, found in Australia and New Guinea. They feed entirely upon ants and termites, which they dig out with their powerful claws and lick up with their prehensile tongues. When attacked, an echidna rolls itself into a ball, or tries to hide by burrowing in the earth.

echinoderm marine invertebrate of the phylum Echinodermata ("spiny-skinned"), with a basic body structure divided into five sectors. Included are starfishes (or sea stars), brittlestars, sea-lilies, sea-urchins, and sea-cucumbers. The skeleton is external, made of a series of limy plates, and echinoderms generally move by using tube-feet, small water-filled sacs that can be protruded or pulled back to the body.

echo the repetition of a sound wave, or of a ◊radar or ◊sonar signal, by reflection from a surface. By accurately measuring the time taken for an echo to return to the transmitter, and by knowing the speed of a radar signal (the speed of light) or a sonar signal (the speed of sound in water), it is possible to calculate the range of the object causing the echo (◊echolocation).

A similar technique is used in echo sounders to estimate the depth of water under a ship's keel or the depth of a school of fish.

Echo in Greek mythology, a nymph who pined away until only her voice remained, after being rejected by Narcissus.

echolocation method used by certain animals, notably bats and dolphins, to detect the positions of objects by using sound. The animal emits a stream of high-pitched sounds, generally at ultrasonic frequencies (beyond the range of human hearing), and listens for the returning echoes reflected off objects to determine their exact location.

The location of an object can be established by the time difference between the emitted sound and its differential return as an echo to the two ears. Echolocation is of particular value under conditions when normal vision is poor (at night in the case of bats, in murky water for dolphins). A few species of bird can also echolocate.

echo sounder alternate name for a ***sonar device*** device that detects objects under water by means of ◊sonar—by using reflected sound waves. Most boats are equipped with echo sounders to measure the water depth beneath them. An echo sounder consists of a transmitter, which emits an ultrasonic pulse (see ◊ultrasound), and a receiver, which detects the pulse after reflection from the seabed. The time between transmission and receipt of the reflected signal is a measure of the depth of water.

Eckert John Presper Jr 1919– . US mathematician who collaborated with John ◊Mauchly on the development of the early ENIAC and Univac 1 computers.

Eckhart Johannes, called Meister Eckhart c. 1260–1327. German theologian and leader of a popular mystical movement. In 1326 he was accused of heresy, and in 1329 a number of his doctrines were condemned by the pope as heretical. His theology stressed the absolute transcendence of God, and the internal spiritual development through which union with the divine could be attained.

eclampsia convulsions occurring due to ◊toxemia of pregnancy.

eclipse the passage of an astronomical body through the shadow of another. The term is usually used for solar and lunar eclipses, which may be either partial or total, but also, for example, for eclipses by Jupiter of its satellites. An eclipse of a star by a body in the Solar System is called an ◊occultation.

A solar eclipse occurs when the Moon passes in front of the Sun as seen from Earth, and can happen only at new Moon. During a total eclipse

eclipse

lunar eclipse

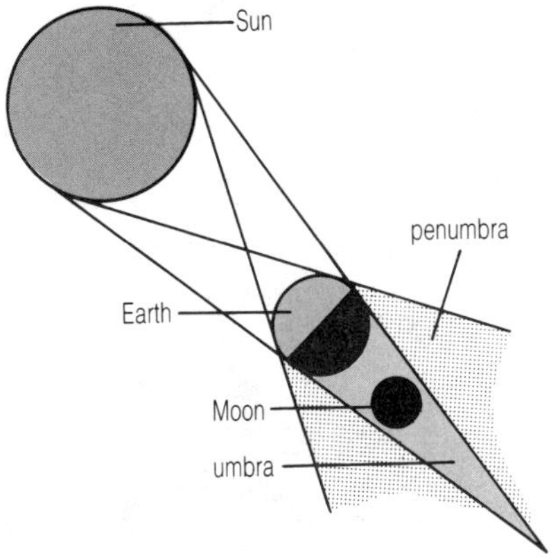
Sun
penumbra
Earth
Moon
umbra

solar eclipse

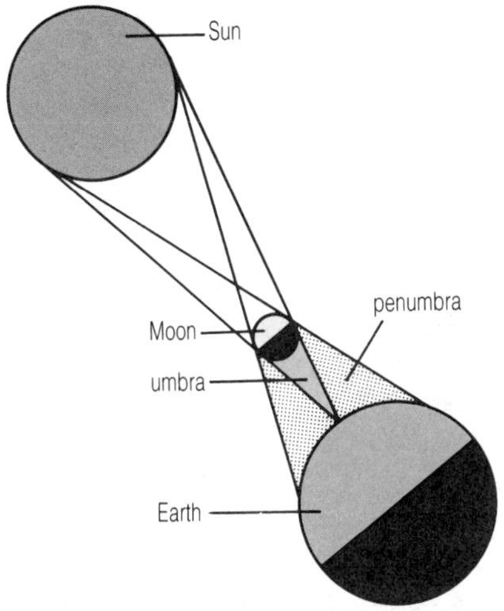
Sun
penumbra
Moon
umbra
Earth

the Sun's ◊corona can be seen. A total solar eclipse can last up to 7.5 minutes. When the Moon is at its farthest from Earth it does not completely cover the face of the Sun, leaving a ring of sunlight visible. This is an annular eclipse (from the Latin word *annulus*, "ring"). Between two and five solar eclipses occur each year.

A lunar eclipse occurs when the Moon passes into the shadow of the Earth, becoming dim until emerging from the shadow. Lunar eclipses may be partial or total, and they can happen only at full Moon. Total lunar eclipses last for up to 100 minutes; the maximum number each year is three.

eclipsing binary binary star in which the two stars periodically pass in front of each other as seen from Earth.

When one star crosses in front of the other the total light received on Earth from the two stars declines. The first eclipsing binary to be noticed was ◊Algol.

ecliptic the path, against the background of stars, that the Sun appears to follow each year as the Earth orbits the Sun. It can be thought of as marking the intersection of the plane of the Earth's orbit with the ◊celestial sphere (imaginary sphere around the Earth).

The ecliptic is tilted at about 23.5° with respect to the celestial equator, a result of the actual tilt of the Earth's axis with respect to the plane of its orbit around the Sun.

Eco Umberto 1932– . Italian writer, semiologist and literary critic. His works include *The Role of the Reader* 1979, the "philosophical thriller" *The Name of the Rose* 1983, and *Foucault's Pendulum* 1988.

ecology (Greek *oikos* "house") the study of relationships among organisms and the environments in which they live, including all living and nonliving components. The term was coined by the biologist Ernst Haeckel 1866.

Ecology may be concerned with individual organisms (for example, behavioral ecology, foraging strategies), with populations or species (for example, population dynamics), or with entire communities (for example, competition between species for access to resources in an ecosystem, or predator–prey relationships). Applied ecology is concerned with the management and conservation of habitats and the consequences and control of pollution.

econometrics the application of mathematical and statistical analysis to the study of economic relationships, including testing economic theories and making quantitative predictions.

economic community or ***common market*** an organization of autonomous countries formed to promote trade. Examples include the Caribbean Community (Caricom) 1973, Central African Economic Community 1985, European Community (EC) 1957, and Latin American Economic System 1975.

economic recovery an upturn in economic activity, usually accompanied by a fall in unemployment.

economics (Greek "household management") social science devoted to studying the production, distribution, and consumption of wealth (based on goods and services). It consists of the disciplines of ◊microeconomics, the study of individual producers, consumers, or markets, and ◊macroeconomics, the study of whole economies or systems (in particular, areas such as taxation and public spending).

Economics is the study of how, in a given society, choices are made on the allocation of resources to produce goods and services for consumption, and the mechanisms and principles that govern this process. Economics seeks to apply scientific method to construct theories about the processes involved and to test them against what actually happens. Its two central concerns are the efficient allocation of available resources and the problem of reconciling finite resources with a virtually infinite desire for goods and services. Economics analyzes the ingredients of economic efficiency in the production process, and the implications for practical policies, and examines conflicting demands or resources and the consequences of whatever choices are made, whether by individuals, enterprises, or governments.

Microeconomics and macroeconomics frequently overlap. They include the subdiscipline of econometrics, which analyzes economic relationships using mathematical and statistical techniques. Increasingly sophisticated econometric methods are today being used for such topics as economic forecasting. Pioneers in this field include ◊Frisch and ◊Kantorovich.

Economics aims to be either positive, presenting objective and scientific explanations of how an economy works, or normative, offering prescriptions and recommendations on what should be done to cure perceived ills. However, almost inevitably, value judgments are involved in all economists' formulations.

Economics came of age as a separate area of study with the publication of Adam Smith's *The Wealth of Nations* 1776; the economist Alfred Marshall (1842–1924) established the orthodox position of "Neo-Classical" economics, which, as modified by John Maynard Keynes, remains the standard today. Major economic thinkers include David Ricardo, Thomas Malthus, John Stuart Mill, Karl Marx, Vilfredo Pareto, and Milton Friedman.

economies of scale in economics, when production capacity is increased at a financial cost that is more than compensated for by the greater volume of output. In a dress factory, for example, a reduction in the unit cost may be possible only by the addition of new machinery, which would be worthwhile only if the volume of dresses produced were increased and there were sufficient market demand for them.

In business, economies of scale are usually considered in relation to specific areas of the production process, which may be technical, managerial, marketing, finance, and risk. In achieving economies of scale, many factors must be considered, not least of which is the demand for a particular product.

ecosystem in ◊ecology, an integrated unit consisting of the ◊community of living organisms and the physical environment in a particular area. The relationships among species in an ecosystem are usually complex and finely balanced, and removal of any one species may be disastrous. The removal of a major predator, for example, can result in the destruction of the ecosystem through overgrazing by herbivores.

Energy and nutrients pass through organisms in an ecosystem in a particular sequence (see ◊food chain): energy is captured through ◊photosynthesis, and nutrients are taken up from the soil or water by plants; both are passed to herbivores that eat the plants and then to carnivores that feed on herbivores. These nutrients are returned to the soil through the ◊decomposition of excrement and dead organisms, thus completing a cycle that is crucial to the stabililty and survival of the ecosystem.

ecstasy or MDMA (3,4-methylenedioxymethamphetamine) illegal drug in increasing use from the 1980s. It is a modified amphetamine with mild psychedelic effects, and works by depleting serotonin (a neurotransmitter) in the brain.

ECT abbreviation for ◊electroconvulsive therapy.

ectoparasite a ◊parasite that lives on the outer surface of its host.

ectopic in medicine, term applied to an anatomical feature that is displaced or found in an abnormal position. An ectopic pregnancy is one occurring outside the womb, usually in a Fallopian tube.

ectoplasm outer layer of a cell's ◊cytoplasm.

ectotherm "coldblooded" animal (see ◊poikilothermy), such as a lizard, that relies on external warmth (ultimately from the Sun) to raise its body temperature so that it can become active. To cool the body, ectotherms seek out a cooler environment.

ECU abbreviation for European Currency Unit, official monetary unit of the EC. It is based on the value of the different currencies used in the European Monetary System.

Ecuador country in South America, bounded N by Colombia, E and S by Peru, and W by the Pacific Ocean.

government Ecuador is not a fully federal state but has a devolved system of 20 provinces, each administered by an appointed governor. The 1979 constitution provides for a president and a single-chamber national congress—the 72-member chamber of representatives—both popularly elected for a four-year term. The president is not eligible for re-election. Seven of the 16 political parties formed a left-wing coalition 1984.

Ecuador *Once an active volcano, the snow-capped peak of Mt Chimborazo rises to a height of 20,561 ft/ 6,310 m in the Cordillera Real of the South American Andes. It is the highest mountain in Ecuador.*

Ecuador
Republic of
(República del Ecuador)

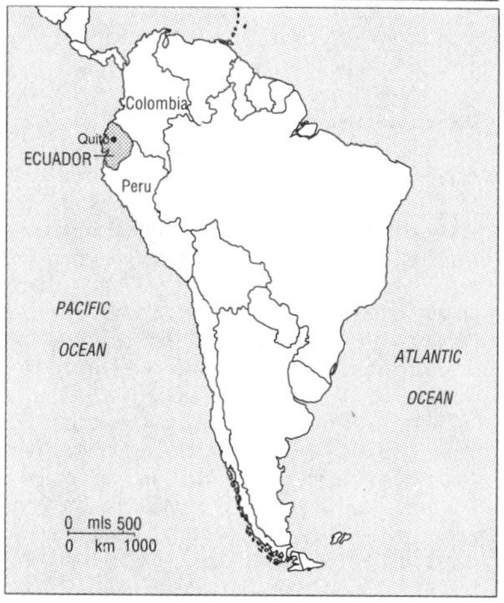
Colombia
Quito
ECUADOR
Peru
PACIFIC
OCEAN
ATLANTIC
OCEAN
0 mls 500
0 km 1000

area 104,479 sq mi/270,670 sq km
capital Quito
cities Cuenca; chief port Guayaquil
physical coastal plain rises sharply to Andes Mountains which are divided into a series of cultivated valleys; flat, low-lying rainforest in the E
features Ecuador is crossed by the equator, from which it derives its name; Galapagos Islands; Cotopaxi is world's highest active volcano; rich wildlife in rainforest of Amazon basin
head of state and government Rodrigo Borja Cevallos from 1988
political system emergent democracy
political parties Progressive Democratic Front coalition, left-of-center (composed of six individual parties); Concentration of Popular Forces (CFP), right-of-center; Social Christian Party (PSC), right-wing; Conservative Party (PC), right-wing; others
exports bananas, cocoa, coffee, sugar, rice, fruit, balsa wood, fish, petroleum
currency sucre
population (1989 est) 10,490,000; (25% Indian, 55% Mestizo, 10% European, 10% black African); growth rate 2.9% p.a.
life expectancy men 62, women 66
language Spanish (official); Quechuan, Jivaroan, and other Indian languages
religion Roman Catholic 95%
literacy men 85%/women 80% (1985 est)
GDP $10.6 bn (1987); $1,069 per head
chronology
1830 Independence achieved from Spain.
1925–48 Great political instability; no president completed his term of office.
1948–55 Liberals in power.
1956 First conservative president in 60 years.
1960 Liberals returned, with José Velasco as president.
1961 Velasco deposed and replaced by the vice-president.
1963 Military junta installed.
1968 Velasco returned as president.
1972 A coup put the military back in power.
1978 New democratic constitution adopted.
1979 Liberals in power but opposed by right- and left-wing parties.
1982 Deteriorating economy provoked strikes, demonstrations, and a state of emergency.
1983 Austerity measures introduced.
1985 No party with a clear majority in the national congress; Febres Cordero narrowly won the presidency for the conservatives.
1988 Roderigo Borja elected president for moderate left-wing coalition.
1989 Guerrilla left-wing group, numbering about 1,000, lays down arms after nine years.

history The tribes of N highland Ecuador formed the Kingdom of Quito c. AD 1000, and it was conquered by the ◊Inca in the 15th century. Ecuador was invaded and colonized by Spain from 1532. It joined Venezuela, Colombia and Panama in the confederacy of Gran Colombia 1819. After joining other South American colonies in a revolt against Spain, Ecuador was liberated 1822 by Antonio José de ◊Sucre and became fully independent 1830. Since independence, Peru has repeatedly invaded Ecuador because of boundary disputes, which remain unresolved.

From independence onward the political pendulum has swung from the conservatives to the liberals, from civilian to military rule, and from democracy to dictatorship. By 1948 some stability was evident, and eight years of liberal government ensued. In 1956, Dr Camilo Ponce became the first conservative president for 60 years. Four years later a liberal, Dr José Maria Velasco (president 1933–35, 1944–47, and 1952–56), was re-elected. He was deposed 1961 by the vice-president, who was himself replaced by a military junta the following year. In 1968 Velasco returned from exile and took up the presidency again. Another coup 1972 put the military back in power until, in 1978 (when it seemed as if Ecuador had returned permanently to its pre-1948 political pattern), a new, democratic constitution was adopted.

The 1979 constitution has survived, though economic deterioration has caused strikes, demonstrations, and, in 1982, a state of emergency. In the 1984 elections there was no clear majority in the national congress, and the conservative León Febres Cordero became president on a promise of "bread, roofs, and jobs." With no immediate support in congress, his policies seemed likely to be blocked, but in 1985 he won a majority when five opposition members shifted their allegiance to him. He was succeeded in Aug 1988 by Rodrigo Borja of the Democratic left party, who tried to steer a course between business and labor interests while negotiating foreign debt and dealing with domestic unrest.

ecumenical council (Greek *oikoumenikos* "of the whole world") a meeting of church leaders worldwide to determine Christian doctrine; their results are binding on all church members. Seven such councils are accepted as ecumenical by both Eastern and Western churches, while the Roman Catholic Church accepts a further 14 as ecumenical.

ecumenical movement movement for reunification of the various branches of the Christian church. It began in the 19th century with the extension of missionary work to Africa and Asia, where the divisions created in Europe were incomprehensible; the movement gathered momentum from the need for unity in the face of growing secularism in Christian countries and of the challenge posed by such faiths as Islam. The World Council of Churches was founded 1948.

ecumenical patriarch the head of the Eastern Orthodox Church, the patriarch of Istanbul (Constantinople). The Bishop of Constantinople was recognized as having equal rights with the Bishop of Rome 451, and first termed "patriarch" in the 6th century. The office survives today but with only limited authority, mainly confined to the Greek and Turkish Orthodox churches.

eczema inflammatory skin condition, a form of dermatitis, marked by dryness, rashes, itching, the formation of blisters, and the exudation of fluid. It may be allergic in origin and is sometimes complicated by infection.

Edam town in the Netherlands on the river Ij, North Holland province; population (1987) 24,200. It is famous for its round cheeses covered in red wax.

***Eddy** In 1876, Mary Baker Eddy founded the Christian Science Association, a faith based on divine healing.*

Edda two collections of early Icelandic literature that together constitute our chief source for Old Norse mythology. The term strictly applies to the Younger or Prose Edda, compiled by Snorri Sturluson, a priest, c. 1230.

The Elder or Poetic Edda is the collection of poems discovered by Brynjólfr Sveinsson c. 1643, written by unknown Norwegian poets of the 9th to 12th centuries.

Eddington Arthur Stanley 1882–1944. British astrophysicist who studied the motions, equilibrium, luminosity, and atomic structure of the stars and became a leading exponent of Einstein's relativity theory. In 1919 his observation of stars during an ◊eclipse confirmed Einstein's prediction that light is bent when passing near the Sun. His book *The Nature of the Physical World* 1928 is a popularization of science; in *The Expanding Universe* 1933 he expressed the theory that in the spherical universe the outer galaxies or spiral nebulae are receding from one another.

Eddy Mary Baker 1821–1910. US founder of the Christian Science movement.

She was born in New Hampshire and brought up as a Congregationalist. Her pamphlet *Science of Man* 1869 was followed by *Science and Health with Key to the Scriptures* in 1875, which systematically set forth the basis of Christian Science. In 1876 she founded the Christian Science Association. In 1879 the Church of Christ, Scientist, was established, and although living in retirement after 1892 she continued to direct the activities of the movement until her death.

Separated from her husband and in poor health, she discovered in 1862 the work of a faith healer named Phineas Quimby, who decisively influenced her belief in healing through divine grace, a belief enhanced by her own recovery.

eddy current an electric current induced, in accordance with ◊Faraday's laws, in a conductor located in a changing magnetic field. Eddy currents can cause much wasted energy in the cores of transformers and other electrical machines.

Edelman Gerald 1929– . US biochemist. The structure of the antibody gamma globulin (one of the body's defenses) was worked out by Rodney ◊Porter by 1962. Edelman tackled the related problem of working out the sequence of 1330 amino acids that compose the antibody. The task was completed by 1969 and won for Edelman a share of the 1972 Nobel Prize for Medicine with Porter.

edelweiss perennial alpine plant *Leontopodium alpi-*

Eden *Sir Anthony Eden was British prime minister 1955–1957.*

num, family Compositae, with a white, woolly, star-shaped bloom, found in high mountains of Eurasia.

edema any abnormal accumulation of fluid in tissues or cavities of the body; waterlogging of the tissues due to excessive loss of ◊plasma through the capillary walls. It may be generalized (the condition once known as dropsy) or confined to one area, such as the ankles.

Edema may be mechanical—the result of obstructed veins or heart failure—or it may be due to increased permeability of the capillary walls, as in liver or kidney disease or malnutrition. Accumulation of fluid in the abdomen, a complication of cirrhosis, is known as ascites.

Eden Anthony, 1st Earl of Avon 1897–1977. British Conservative politician, foreign secretary 1935–38, 1940–45, and 1951–55; prime minister 1955–57, when he resigned after the failure of the Anglo-French military intervention in the ◊Suez Crisis.

Upset by his prime minister's rejection of a peace plan secretly proposed by Roosevelt in Jan 1938, Eden resigned as foreign secretary in Feb 1938 in protest against Chamberlain's decision to open conversations with the Fascist dictator Mussolini, but was foreign secretary again in the wartime coalition formed Dec 1940 and in the Conservative government elected 1951. With the Soviets, he negotiated an interim peace in Vietnam 1954. In April 1955 he succeeded Churchill as prime minister. His use of force in the Suez Crisis led to his resignation in Jan 1957, but he continued to maintain that his action was justified.

Eden, Garden of in the Old Testament book of Genesis and in the Koran, the "garden" in which Adam and Eve lived after their creation, and from which they were expelled for disobedience.

Its location has often been identified with the Fertile Crescent in Mesopotamia (now in Iraq) and two of its rivers with the Euphrates and the Tigris.

Edgar known as the *Atheling* ("of royal blood") c. 1050–c. 1130. English prince, born in Hungary. Grandson of Edmund Ironside, he was supplanted as heir to Edward the Confessor by William the Conqueror. He led two rebellions against William 1068 and 1069, but made peace 1074.

Edgar the Peaceful 944–975. King of all England from 959. He was the younger son of Edmund I, and strove successfully to unite English and Danes as fellow subjects.

Edgehill, Battle of the first battle of the English Civil War. It took place 1642, on a ridge in S Warwickshire, between Royalists under Charles I and Parliamentarians under the Earl of Essex. The result was indecisive.

Edinburg city in SE Texas, NW of Brownsville; seat of Hidalgo county. It is a shipping center for the area's citrus fruit crops; population (1990) 29,885.

Edinburgh capital of Scotland and administrative center of the region of Lothian, near the southern shores of the Firth of Forth; population (1985) 440,000. A cultural center, it holds an annual festival of music and the arts; the university was established 1583. Industries include printing, publishing, banking, insurance, chemical manufactures, distilling, brewing, and some shipbuilding.

features Edinburgh Castle contains the 12th-century St Margaret's chapel, the oldest building in Edinburgh. The palace of Holyrood House was built in the 15th and 16th centuries on the site of a 12th-century abbey; it is the British sovereign's official Scottish residence. ◊Rizzio was murdered here 1566, in the apartments of Mary Queen of Scots. The Parliament House, begun 1632, is now the seat of the supreme courts. The Royal Scottish Academy and the National Gallery of Scotland (renovated 1989) in Classical style are by William Henry Playfair (1789–1857). The episcopal cathedral of St Mary, opened 1879, and St Giles parish church (mostly 15th-century) are the principal churches. The Royal Observatory has been at Blackford Hill since 1896. The two best-known thoroughfares are Princes Street and the Royal Mile. The university has a famous medical school and the Koestler chair of parapsychology (instituted 1985), the only such professorship in the UK. The Heriot-Watt University (established 1885; university status 1966) is mainly a technical institution.

history In Roman times the site was occupied by Celtic peoples and about 617 was captured by Edwin of Northumbria, from whom the town took its name. The early settlement grew up around a castle on Castle Rock, while about a mile to the E another burgh, Canongate, developed around the abbey of Holyrood, founded 1128 by David I. It remained separate from Edinburgh until 1856. Robert Bruce made Edinburgh a burgh 1329, and established its port at Leith. In 1544 the town was destroyed by the English. After the union with England 1707, Edinburgh lost its political importance but remained culturally pre-eminent.

Edirne town in European Turkey, on the river Maritsa, about 140 mi/225 km NW of Istanbul. Population (1985) 86,700. Founded on the site of ancient Uscadama, it was formerly known as Adrianople, named after the Emperor Hadrian about AD 125.

Edison Thomas Alva 1847–1931. US scientist and inventor, with over 1,000 patents. In Menlo Park, New Jersey, 1876–87, he produced his most important inventions, including the electric lightbulb 1879. He constructed a system of electric power distribution for consumers, the telephone transmitter, and the phonograph.

Edison *Pioneering scientist and inventor Thomas Edison. His many inventions included the dictating machine with which he is photographed. In founding the General Electric Co, he provided service and appliances to consumers, thus establishing daily use of his inventions.*

In 1869 he invented an automatic vote recorder and the improved stock ticker in 1871, which earned him enough to found his manufacturing plant in Newark, New Jersey. He moved to Menlo Park in 1876 and from there to West Orange, New Jersey, where he invented the movie camera, mimeograph, fluoroscope, and an improved battery. In 1889 he began the Edison Light Co., which became the General Electric Co.

Edmonton capital of Alberta, Canada, on the North Saskatchewan river; population (1986) 576,249. It is the center of an oil and mining area to the N and also an agricultural and dairying region. Petroleum pipelines link Edmonton with Superior, Wisconsin, and Vancouver, British Columbia.

The city is on the Alaska Highway. Manufactured goods include processed foods, petrochemicals, plastic and metal products, lumber, and clothing. The University of Alberta, Athabasca University, and the Provincial Museum of Alberta are here. Fort Edmonton, a Hudson's Bay Company fur-trading post, was built in 1795. It was incorporated as a town soon after the arrival of the Canadian Pacific Railroad in 1891. It flourished as an outfitting point for prospectors seeking gold in the Klondike region of the Yukon in the late 1890s. Edmonton grew rapidly as a center for the rapidly growing Alberta oil industry after 1950.

Edmund II Ironside c. 989–1016. King of England 1016, the son of Ethelred II the Unready. He led the resistance to ◊Canute's invasion 1015, and on Ethelred's death 1016 was chosen king by the citizens of London, whereas the Witan (the king's council) elected Canute. In the struggle for the throne, Edmund was defeated by Canute at Assandun (Ashington), Essex, and they divided the kingdom between them; when Edmund died the same year, Canute ruled the whole kingdom.

Edo or Yedo former name of ◊Tokyo, Japan, until 1868.

Edom in the Old Testament, a mountainous area of S Palestine, which stretched from the Dead Sea to the Gulf of Aqaba. Its people, said to be descendants of Esau, were enemies of the Israelites.

education the process, beginning at birth, of developing intellectual capacity, manual skill, and social awareness, especially through instruction. In its more restricted sense, the term refers to the process of imparting literacy, numeracy, and a generally accepted body of knowledge.

history of education The earliest known European educational systems were those of ancient Greece, based on those of the early civilizations of the Near East and Egypt. In Sparta the process was devoted mainly to the development of military skills; in Athens, to politics, philosophy, and public speaking, but both were accorded only to the privileged few.

In ancient China, formalized education received impetus from the imperial decree of 165 BC, which established open competitive examinations for the recruitment of members of the civil service, based mainly on a detailed study of literature.

The Romans adopted the Greek system of education, and imposed it on the conquered peoples of Europe. Following the fall of the Roman Empire, widespread education vanished from Europe, although Christian monasteries preserved both learning and Latin, Hebrew schools preserved Biblical studies and Judaic philosophy, and the Moors taught advanced science, mathematics and medicine. In the Middle Ages, Charlemagne's monastic schools taught the "seven liberal arts"; grammar, logic, rhetoric, arithmetic, geometry, music, and astronomy. These schools and the Jewish philosophers produced the theological philosophers of the ◊Scholastic Movement, which in the 11th–13th centuries led to the foundation of the universities of Paris (◊Sorbonne), Bologna, Padua, ◊Oxford and ◊Cambridge. The capture of Constantinople, capital of the E Roman Empire, by the Turks in 1453 sent the Christian scholars there into exile across Europe, thus reviving European interest in learning and fueling the Renaissance.

Compulsory attendance at European primary schools was first established in the mid-18th century in Prussia, and has since spread almost worldwide. Compulsory schooling in industrialized countries is typically from around age 6 to around age 15.

education today In the US, public education is paid for by property taxes and is mainly the responsibility of the states and local school boards, but the Department of Education, headed by a secretary who is a member of the president's cabinet, is responsible for federal aspects, including the administration of federal monies to state and local school systems. In the US, private schools may be church-affiliated or secular, and both must meet minimum local standards to be accredited.

Education is usually divided into optional nursery or kindergarten (to age 6), compulsory elementary or grammar school (grades 1–6), junior high school (grades 7–9) or middle school (grades 6–8), and high school (grades 10–12 or 9–12). Upon graduation, students receive a high-school diploma, awarded by the individual school or local school district on successful completion of a broad secondary school curriculum authorized by the state. High schools give specialized programs to prepare students for technical and commercial careers, as well as academic programs aimed at preparation for college. In their senior year of high school, some students take the ◊Scholastic Aptitude Test (SAT), since many private colleges and universities require certain minimum SAT schores for admission. A large proportion of US high-school graduates go on to higher education at two-year junior colleges or four-year state-funded or private colleges or universities.

educational psychology the work of psychologists primarily in schools, including the assessment of children with achievement problems and advising on problem behavior in the classroom.

Edward the Black Prince 1330–1376. Prince of Wales, eldest son of Edward III of England. The epithet (probably posthumous) may refer to his black armor. During the Hundred Years' War he fought at the Battle of Crécy 1346 and captured the French king at Poitiers 1356. He ruled Aquitaine 1360–71; during the revolt that eventually ousted him, he caused the massacre of Limoges 1370.

Edward (full name Edward Antony Richard Louis) 1964– . Prince of the UK, third son of Queen Elizabeth II. He is seventh in line to the throne after Charles, Charles's two sons, Andrew, and Andrew's two daughters.

Edward eight kings of England or the UK:

Edward I 1239–1307. King of England from 1272, son of Henry III. Edward led the royal forces against Simon de Montfort in the ◊Barons' War 1264–67, and was on a crusade when he succeeded to the throne. He established English rule over all Wales 1282–84, and secured recognition of his overlordship from the Scottish king, though the Scots (under Wallace and Bruce) fiercely resisted actual conquest. In his reign Parliament took its approximate modern form with the ◊Model Parliament 1295. He was succeeded by his son Edward II.

Edward II 1284–1327. King of England from 1307. Son of Edward I and born at Caernarvon Castle, he was created the first Prince of Wales 1301. His invasion of Scotland 1314 to suppress revolt resulted in defeat at ◊Bannockburn. He was deposed 1327 by his wife Isabella (1292–1358), daughter of Philip IV of France, and her lover Roger de ◊Mortimer, and murdered. He was succeeded by his son Edward III.

In addition to military disasters, his reign was troubled by his extravagance and the unpopularity of his favorites.

Edward III 1312–1377. King of England from 1327, son of Edward II. He assumed the government 1330 from his mother, through whom in 1337 he laid claim to the French throne and thus began the ◊Hundred Years' War. He was succeeded by Richard II.

At 18 Edward imprisoned his mother Isabella of France and executed her lover Roger de Mortimer. In 1360 he surrendered his claim to the French throne, but the war resumed 1369, and his son John of Gaunt dominated the government in his later years.

Edward IV 1442–1483. King of England 1461–70 and from 1471. He was the son of Richard, Duke of York, and succeeded Henry VI in the Wars of the ◊Roses, temporarily losing the throne to Henry when Edward fell out with his adviser ◊Warwick, but regaining it at the Battle of Barnet. He was succeeded by his son Edward V.

Edward V 1470–1483. King of England 1483. Son of Edward IV, he was deposed three months after his accession in favor of his uncle (◊Richard III), and is traditionally believed to have been murdered (with his brother) in the Tower of London on Richard's orders.

Edward VI 1537–1553. King of England from 1547, son of Henry VIII and Jane Seymour. The government was entrusted to his uncle the Duke of Somerset (who fell 1549), and then to the Earl of Warwick, later created Duke of Northumberland. He was succeeded by his sister, Mary I.

Jane Seymour was Henry VIII's third wife, and Edward was his only son. Edward became a staunch Protestant and during his reign the Reformation progressed. He died from tuberculosis.

Edward VII 1841–1910. King of Great Britain and Ireland from 1901. As Prince of Wales he was a prominent social figure, but his mother Queen Victoria considered him too frivolous to take part in political life. In 1860 he made the first tour of Canada and the US ever undertaken by a British prince.

He took a close interest in politics and was on good terms with party leaders. He succeeded to the throne 1901 and was crowned 1902. Although he overrated his political influence, he contributed to the Entente Cordiale 1904 with France and the Anglo-Russian agreement 1907.

Edward VIII 1894–1972. King of Great Britain and Northern Ireland Jan–Dec 1936, when he renounced the throne to marry Wallis Warfield ◊Simpson (see ◊abdication crisis). He was created Duke of Windsor and was governor of the Bahamas 1940–45, subsequently settling in France.

***Edward VIII** The Duke and Duchess of Windsor in a Sussex village, Sept 1939.*

Edward was extremely popular as prince of Wales, and he made fashion statements that changed the way men dressed throughout the 20th century in the Western world—soft collars, tweed sport jackets, cuffed trousers, low shoes, the Windsor knotted tie, and V-necked sweaters freed men from the starched look that characterized the turn of the century. He succeeded his father George V on Jan 20, 1936, and on Dec 10 he abdicated. A divorcee, Mrs Simpson was not acceptable constitutionally as queen. They were married in France in May 1937.

Edward, Lake lake in Uganda, area 830 sq mi/2,150 sq km, at about 3,000 ft/900 m above sea level in the Albertine rift valley. From 1973 to 1979 it was known as Lake Idi Amin Dada, after President Amin of Uganda.

Edwards Blake. Adopted name of William Blake McEdwards 1922– . US film director and writer, formerly an actor. Specializing in comedies, he directed the series of *Pink Panther* films 1963–78, starring Peter Sellers. His other work includes *Breakfast at Tiffany's* 1961 and *Blind Date* 1986.

Edwards Jonathan 1703–1758. US theologian who took a Calvinist view of predestination and initiated a religious revival, the "Great Awakening." His *The Freedom of the Will* 1754 (defending ◊determinism) received renewed attention in the 20th century.

Born in East Windsor, Connecticut, Edwards graduated 1720 from Yale and began his ministry two years later in Northampton, Massachusetts. Other well-known works include *A Faithful Narrative of the Surprising Works of God* 1737.

Edward the Confessor c. 1003–1066. King of England from 1042, the son of Ethelred II. He lived in Normandy until shortly before his accession. During his reign power was held by Earl ◊Godwin and his son ◊Harold, while the king devoted himself to religion, including the rebuilding of Westminster Abbey (consecrated 1065), where he is buried. His childlessness led ultimately to the Norman Conquest 1066. He was canonized 1161.

Edward the Elder c. 870–924. King of the West Saxons. He succeeded his father ◊Alfred the Great 899. He reconquered SE England and the Midlands from the Danes, uniting Wessex and ◊Mercia with the help of his sister, Athelflad. By the time Edward died, his kingdom was the most powerful in the British Isles. He was succeeded by his son ◊Athelstan.

Edward the Martyr c. 963–978. King of England from 975. Son of King Edgar, he was murdered at Corfe Castle, Dorset, probably at his stepmother

Edward the Confessor *A coin stamped with the head of the English king Edward the Confessor. His death in 1066 triggered off the events leading to the Norman Conquest; William the Conqueror claimed the English throne had been bequeathed him by Edward.*

Aelfthryth's instigation (she wished to secure the crown for her son, Ethelred). He was canonized 1001.

EEC abbreviation for European Economic Community; see ◊European Community.

EEG abbreviation for ◊electroencephalogram.

eel any fish of the order Anguilliformes. Eels are snakelike, with elongated dorsal and anal fins. They include the freshwater eels of Europe and North America (which breed in the Atlantic), the marine conger eels, and the morays of tropical coral reefs.

eelgrass also known as tape grass or glass wrack. Flowering plant *Zostera marina* of the pondweed family Zosteraceae, found in tidal mud flats. It is one of the few flowering plants to adapt to marine conditions, being completely submerged at high tide.

efficiency the output of a machine (work done by the machine) divided by the input (work put into the machine), usually expressed as a percentage. Because of losses caused by friction, efficiency is always less than 100%, although it can approach this for electrical machines with no moving parts (such as a transformer).

Since the mechanical advantage, or force ratio, is the ratio of the load (the output force) to the effort (the input force), and the velocity ratio is the distance moved by the effort divided by the distance moved by the load, for certain machines the efficiency can also be defined as the mechanical advantage divided by the velocity ratio.

EFTA acronym for ◊European Free Trade Association

EFTPOS (abbreviation of electronic funds transfer at point of sale) the transfer of funds from one bank account to another by electronic means. For example, a bank customer inserts a plastic card in a point-of-sale computer terminal in a supermarket, and telephone lines are used to make an automatic debit from the customer's bank account to settle the bill. See also ◊credit card.

e.g. abbreviation for exempli gratia (Latin "for the sake of example").

Egbert died 839. King of the West Saxons from 802, the son of Ealhmund, an under-king of Kent. By 829 he had united England for the first time under one king.

egg in animals, the ovum, or female ◊gamete (reproductive cell). After fertilization by a sperm cell, it begins to divide to form an embryo. Eggs may be deposited by the female (◊ovipary) or they may develop within her body (◊vivipary and ◊ovovivipary). In the oviparous reptiles and birds, the egg is protected by a shell, and well supplied with nutrients in the form of yolk.

eggplant perennial plant, *Solanum melongena*, a member of the nightshade family (Solanaceae), originally native to tropical Asia. Its purple-skinned fruits are eaten as a vegetable.

egg

section through an egg

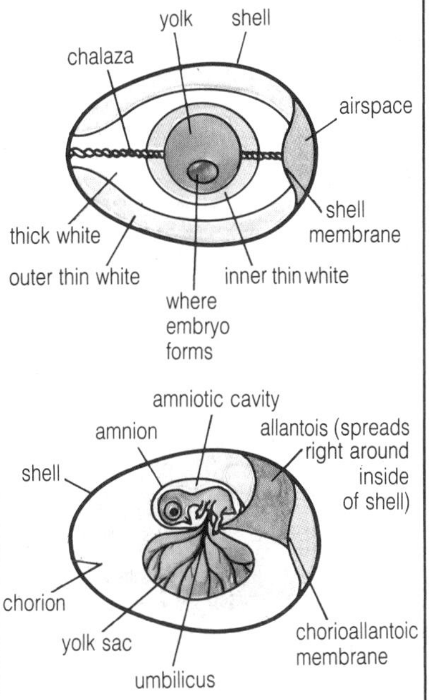

yolk
shell
chalaza
airspace
shell membrane
thick white
outer thin white
inner thin white
where embryo forms
amniotic cavity
amnion
allantois (spreads right around inside of shell)
shell
chorion
yolk sac
chorioallantoic membrane
umbilicus

Egmont Lamoral, Graaf von 1522–1568. Flemish nobleman, born in Hainault. As a servant of the Spanish crown, he defeated the French at St Quentin 1557 and Gravelines 1558, and became stadholder (chief magistrate) of Flanders and Artois. From 1561 he opposed Philip II's religious policy in the Netherlands of persecuting Protestants, but in 1567 the duke of Alva was sent to crush the resistance, and Egmont was beheaded.

Egmont, Mount (Maori *Taranaki*) symmetrical extinct volcano in North Island, New Zealand; situated S of New Plymouth; 8,260 ft/2,517 m high.

ego (Latin "I") in psychology, a general term for the processes concerned with the self and a person's conception of himself or herself, encompassing values and attitudes. In Freudian psychology, the term refers specifically to the element of the human mind that represents the conscious processes, concerned with reality, in conflict with the ◊id and the ◊superego.

egret any of several herons with long feathers on the head or neck.

The snowy egret *Egretta thula* of North America, about 2 ft/60 cm long, was almost hunted to extinction for its graceful plumes before the practice was made illegal. The little egret *E. garzetta* 2 ft/60 cm long, is found in Asia, Africa, S Europe, and Australia.

Egypt country in NE Africa, bounded N by the Mediterranean, E by the Suez Canal and Red Sea, S by Sudan, and W by Libya.

government The 1971 constitution provides for a single-chamber people's assembly of 458, ten nominated by the president and 448 elected for a five-year term by 48 constituencies. The president is nominated by the assembly and then elected by popular referendum for a six-year term, and is eligible for re-election. At least one vice-president and a council of ministers are appointed by the president. There is also a 210-member consultative council (*Shura*), with advisory powers.

history For early history see ◊Egypt, ancient. After its conquest by ◊Augustus 30 BC Egypt passed under the rule of Roman, and later Byzantine, governors, and Christianity superseded the ancient religion. The Arabs conquered Egypt AD 639–42, introducing ◊Islam and ◊Arabic to the area, and the country was ruled by successive Arab dynasties until 1250, when the ◊Mamelukes seized power. Mameluke rule lasted until 1517, when Egypt became part of the Turkish ◊Ottoman Empire.

Contact with Europe began with ◊Napoleon's invasion and the French occupation 1798–1801. A period of anarchy followed, until in 1805 an Albanian officer, Mehemet Ali, was appointed pasha, a title that later became hereditary in his family. Under his successors Egypt met with economic difficulties over the building of the ◊Suez Canal (1859–69), to the extent that an Anglo-French commission was placed in charge of its finances. After subduing a nationalist revolt 1881–82, Britain occupied Egypt, and the government was from then on mainly in the hands of British civilian agents who directed their efforts to the improvement of the Egyptian economy. On the outbreak of World War I 1914, nominal Turkish suzerainty was abolished, and the country was declared a British protectorate.

Postwar agitation by the nationalist Wafd party led to the granting of nominal independence 1922, under King Fuad I. He was succeeded by King Farouk 1936, and Britain agreed to recognize Egypt's full independence, announcing a phased withdrawal of its forces, except from the Suez Canal, Alexandria, and Port Said, where it had naval bases. The start of World War II delayed the British departure, as did the consequent campaign in Libya that ended in the defeat of the German and Italian forces that had threatened the Canal Zone.

In 1946 all British troops except the Suez Canal garrison were withdrawn. In the immediate postwar years a radical movement developed, calling for an end to the British presence and opposing Farouk for his extravagant lifestyle and his failure to prevent the creation of ◊Israel. This led, in 1952, to a bloodless coup by a group of army officers, led by Col Gamal ◊Nasser, who replaced Farouk with a military junta. The 1923 constitution was suspended, and all political parties banned. The following year Egypt declared itself a republic, with General Mohammad Neguib as president and prime minister. In 1954 Nasser became prime minister, and an agreement was signed for the withdrawal of British troops from the Canal Zone by 1956.

After a dispute with Neguib, Nasser took over as head of state and embarked on a program of social reform. He became a major force for the creation of Arab unity and a leader of the ◊nonaligned movement. In 1956 the presidency was strengthened by a new constitution, and Nasser was elected president, unopposed. Later that year, British forces were withdrawn, in accordance with the 1954 agreement.

When the US and Britain canceled their offers of financial aid for the ◊Aswan High Dam 1956, Nasser responded by nationalizing the Suez Canal. In a contrived operation, Britain, France, and Israel invaded the Sinai Peninsula Oct 31, 1956, and two days later Egypt was attacked. US pressure brought a cease-fire and an Anglo-French withdrawal 1957. The effect of the abortive Anglo-French operation was to push Egypt toward the USSR and to enhance Nasser's reputation in the Arab world.

In 1958 Egypt and Syria merged to become the United Arab Republic (UAR), with Nasser as president, but three years later Syria withdrew, though Egypt retained the title of UAR until 1971. The 1960s saw several unsuccessful attempts to federate Egypt, Syria, and Iraq. Despite these failures Nasser's prestige among his neighbors grew, while at home, in 1962, he founded the

Egypt
Arab Republic of
(Jumhuriyat Misr al-Arabiya)

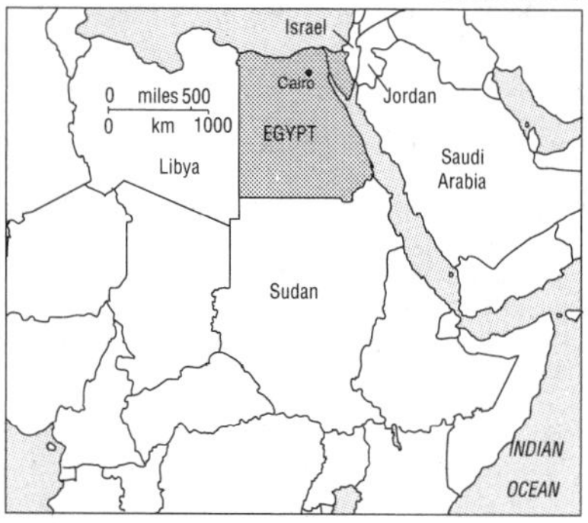
Israel
Cairo
Jordan
0 miles 500
0 km 1000
EGYPT
Libya
Saudi
Arabia
Sudan
INDIAN
OCEAN

area 386,990 sq mi/1,001,450 sq km
capital Cairo
cities Gîza; ports Alexandria, Port Said, Suez, Damietta
physical mostly desert; hills in E; fertile land along Nile valley and delta; cultivated and settled area is about 13,700 sq mi/35,500 sq km
features Aswan High Dam and Lake Nasser; Sinai; remains of ancient Egypt (Pyramids, Sphinx, Luxor, Karnak, Abu Simbel, El Faiyum)
head of state and government Hosni Mubarak from 1981
political system democratic republic
political parties National Democratic Party (NDP), moderate left-of-center; Socialist Labor Party, right-of-center; Socialist Liberal Party, free-enterprise; New Wafd Party, nationalist
exports cotton and textiles, petroleum, fruit and vegetables
currency Egyptian pound
population (1989 est) 54,779,000; growth rate 2.4% p.a.
life expectancy men 57, women 60
language Arabic (official) (ancient Egyptian survives to some extent in Coptic)
religion Sunni Muslim 95%, Coptic Christian 5%
literacy men 59%/women 30% (1985 est)
GDP $34.5 bn (1987); $679 per head

chronology
1914 Egypt became a British protectorate.
1936 Independence achieved from Britain. King Fuad succeeded by his son Farouk.
1946 Withdrawal of British troops except from Suez Canal Zone.
1952 Farouk overthrown by army in bloodless coup.
1953 Egypt declared a republic, with Gen Neguib as president.
1956 Neguib replaced by Col Gamal Nasser. Nasser announced nationalization of Suez Canal; Egypt attacked by Britain, France, and Israel. Ceasefire agreed because of US intervention.
1958 Short-lived merger of Egypt and Syria as United Arab Republic (UAR). Subsequent attempts to federate Egypt, Syria, and Iraq failed.
1967 Six-Day War with Israel ended in Egypt's defeat and Israeli occupation of Sinai and Gaza Strip.
1970 Nasser died suddenly, succeeded by Anwar Sadat.
1973 Attempt to regain territory lost to Israel led to fighting; ceasefire arranged by US secretary of state Henry Kissinger.
1977 Sadat's visit to Israel to address the Israeli parliament was criticized by Egypt's Arab neighbors.
1978–79 Camp David talks resulted in a treaty between Egypt and Israel. Egypt expelled from the Arab League.
1981 Sadat assassinated, succeeded by Hosni Mubarak.
1983 Improved relations between Egypt and the Arab world; only Libya and Syria maintained a trade boycott.
1984 Mubarak's party victorious in the people's assembly elections.
1987 Mubarak reelected. Egypt readmitted to Arab League.
1988 Full diplomatic relations with Algeria restored.
1989 Improved relations with Libya; Syrian air links restored; Mubarak proposed a peace plan.
1990 Gains for independents in general election.
1991 Participation in Gulf War on US-led side. Major force in convening Middle East conference in Spain.

Arab Socialist Union (ASU) as Egypt's only recognized political organization.

In 1967 Egypt led an attack on Israel that developed into the "Six Day War," in which Israel defeated all its opponents, including Egypt. One result of the conflict was the blocking of the Suez Canal, which was not reopened until 1975. After Egypt's defeat, Nasser offered to resign but was persuaded to stay on. In 1969, aged 52, he died of a heart attack and was succeeded by Vice-President Col Anwar ◊Sadat.

In 1971 a new constitution was approved, and the title Arab Republic of Egypt adopted. Sadat continued Nasser's policy of promoting Arab unity, but proposals to create a federation of Egypt, Libya, and Syria again failed.

In 1973 an attempt was made to regain territory from Israel. After 18 days' fighting, US Secretary of State Henry ◊Kissinger arranged a cease-fire, resulting in Israel's evacuation of parts of Sinai, with a UN buffer zone separating the rival armies. This US intervention strengthened ties between the two countries while relations with the USSR cooled.

In 1977 Sadat went to Israel to address the Israeli parliament and plead for peace. Other Arab states were dismayed by this move, and diplomatic relations with Syria, Libya, Algeria, and the Yemen, as well as the Palestine Liberation Organization (PLO), were severed and Egypt was expelled from the ◊Arab League 1979. Despite this opposition, Sadat pursued his peace initiative, and at the ◊Camp David talks in the US, he and the Israeli prime minister, Menachem ◊Begin, signed two agreements. The first laid a framework for peace in the Middle East, and the second, a framework for a treaty between the two countries. In 1979 a treaty was signed and Israel began a phased withdrawal from Sinai. As a consequence, Egypt's isolation from the Arab world grew, and the economy suffered from the withdrawal of Saudi subsidies. US aid became vital to Egypt's survival, and links between the two governments steadily grew closer.

After acceding to the presidency, Sadat had begun to introduce a more liberal regime. In 1981 he was assassinated by a group of Muslim fundamentalists who opposed him and was succeeded by Lt-Gen Hosni ◊Mubarak, who had been vice-president since 1975.

Just as Sadat had continued the policies of his predecessor, so did Mubarak. In the 1984 elections the National Democratic Party, formed by Sadat 1948, won an overwhelming victory in the assembly, strengthening Mubarak's position. Although Egypt's treaty with Israel remained intact, relations between the two countries became strained, mainly because of Israel's pre-emptive activities in Lebanon and the disputed territories. Egypt's relations with other Arab nations improved, and only Libya maintained its trade boycott; the restoration of diplomatic relations with Syria in 1989 paved the way for Egypt's resumption of its leadership of the Arab world.

Mubarak has played a growing role in the search for Middle East peace, proposing a ten-point program to bring about elections in the occupied territories. At home, problems with Muslim fundamentalists have increased Mubarak's dependence on military support. In Oct 1987 President Mubarak was re-elected, by referendum, for a second term.

Despite the success of the ruling party in the Dec 1990 general election, independents did well in many areas. Egypt was a member of the UN coalition forces that sought an economic embargo against Iraq 1990 for annexing Kuwait, and its armed forces joined in the military action against Iraq 1991. In Nov 1991, Egypt attended the historic Middle East peace conference in Spain.

Egypt, ancient ***5000 BC*** Egyptian culture already well established in the Nile Valley, with Neolithic farming villages.
3200 BC Menes united Lower Egypt (the delta) with his own kingdom of Upper Egypt.
2800 BC The architect Imhotep built the step pyramid at Sakkara.
c. 2600 BC Old Kingdom reached the height of its power and the kings of the 4th dynasty built the pyramids at Gîza.
c. 2200–1800 BC Middle Kingdom, under which the unity lost toward the end of the Old Kingdom was restored.
1730 BC Invading Asian Hyksos people established their kingdom in the Nile Delta.
c. 1580 BC New Kingdom established by the 18th dynasty, following the eviction of the Hyksos, with its capital at Thebes. High point of ancient Egyptian civilization under pharaohs Thothmes, Hatshepsut, Amenhotep, Ikhnaton (who moved the capital to Akhetaton), and Tutankhamen.
c. 1321 BC 19th dynasty: Ramses I built a temple at Karnak, Ramses II the temple at Abu Simbel.
1191 BC Ramses III defeated the Indo-European Sea Peoples, but after him there was decline, and power within the country passed from the pharaohs to the priests of Ammon.
1090–663 BC Late New Kingdom Egypt was often divided between two or more dynasties; the nobles became virtually independent.
8th–7th centuries BC Brief interlude of rule by kings from Nubia.
666 BC The Assyrians under Ashurbanipal occupied Thebes.
663–609 BC Psammetichus I restored Egypt's independence and unity.
525 BC Egypt was conquered by Cambyses and became a Persian province.
c. 405–340 BC A period of independence.
332 BC Conquest by Alexander the Great. On the division of his empire, Egypt went to one of his generals, Ptolemy I, and his descendants, the Macedonian dynasty.
30 BC Death of Cleopatra, last of the Macedonians, and conquest by the Roman emperor Augustus; Egypt became a province of the Roman and Byzantine empires.
AD 641 BC Conquest by the Arabs; the Christianity of later Roman rule was for the most part replaced by Islam.
For later history, see ◊Egypt.

Egyptian art see ◊ancient art.

Egyptian religion in the civilization of ancient Egypt, the worship of totemic animals believed to be the ancestors of the clan. Totems later developed into gods, represented as having animal heads. One of the main cults was that of ◊Osiris. Immortality, conferred by the magical rite of mummification, was originally the sole prerogative of the king, but was extended under the New Kingdom to all

Egypt, ancient *The Banquet, a fragment of wall painting, is in the British Museum, London. Dating from c. 1400 BC, it comes from the ancient Egyptian city of Thebes and shows two rows of guests waited on by serving maids.*

who could afford it; they were buried with the ◊Book of the Dead.

The hawk was sacred to Ra and Horus, the ibis to Thoth, the jackal to Anubis. The story of Osiris, who was murdered, mourned by his sister and wife Isis, and then rose again, was enacted in a fertility ritual similar to that of Tammuz; by a natural development Osiris became the god of the underworld. Under the 18th Dynasty a local deity of Thebes, Ammon, came to be regarded as supreme, a reflection of rediscovered national unity. Ikhnaton attempted, without success, to establish the monotheistic cult of Aton, the solar disk, as the one national god.

Egyptology the study of ancient Egypt. Interest in the subject was aroused by the Napoleonic expedition's discovery of the ◊Rosetta Stone 1799. Various excavations continued throughout the 19th century and gradually assumed a more scientific character, largely as a result of the work of the British archeologist Flinders ◊Petrie from 1880 onward and the formation of the Egyptian Exploration Fund 1892. In 1922 another British archeologist, Howard Carter, discovered the tomb of Tutankhamen, the only royal tomb with all its treasures intact.

Special branches of Egyptology include the study of prehistoric Egypt and the search for papyri (ancient documents) preserved by the dryness of the climate; besides ancient Egyptian writings, many lost Greek and early Christian works have been recovered.

Egyptian mask from the Ptolemeic period, 3rd–2nd centures BC.

Ehrenburg Ilya Grigorievich 1891–1967. Soviet writer, born in Kiev. His controversial work *The Thaw* 1954 depicts artistic circles in the USSR and contributed to the growing literary freedom of the 1950s.

Ehrlich Paul 1854–1915. German bacteriologist and immunologist who developed the first cure for ◊syphilis. He developed the arsenic compounds, in particular ◊Salvarsan, used in the treatment of syphilis before the discovery of antibiotics. He shared the 1908 Nobel Prize for Medicine with Ilya Mechnikov (1845–1916) for his work on immunity.

Eichendorff Joseph Freiherr von 1788–1857. German lyric poet and romantic novelist, born in Upper Silesia. His work was set to music by Schumann, Mendelssohn, and Wolf. He held various judicial posts.

Eichmann (Karl) Adolf 1906–1962. Austrian Nazi. As an ◊SS official during Hitler's regime (1933–45), he was responsible for atrocities against Jews and others, including the implementation of genocide. He managed to escape at the fall of Germany 1945, but was discovered in Argentina 1960, abducted by Israeli agents, tried in Israel 1961 for ◊war crimes, and executed.

eider large marine ◊duck, *Somateria mollissima*, highly valued for its soft down, which is used in quilts and cushions for warmth. It is found on N coasts of the Atlantic and Pacific oceans.

Eid ul-Adha Muslim festival that takes place during the *hajj*, or pilgrimage to Mecca, and commemorates Abraham's willingness to sacrifice his son ◊Ishmael at the command of Allah.

Eid ul-Fitr Muslim festival celebrating the end of Ramadan, the month of fasting.

Eiffel (Alexandre) Gustave 1832–1923. French engineer who constructed the Eiffel Tower for the 1889 Paris exhibition.

He set up his own business in Paris and quickly established his reputation with the construction of a series of ambitious railroad bridges, of which the 525 ft/160 m span across the Douro at Oporto, Portugal, was the longest. In 1881 he provided the iron skeleton for the Statue of Liberty.

Einstein *Physicist Albert Einstein formulated the theories of relativity and his unified field theory.*

Eiffel Tower iron tower 1,050 ft/320 m high, designed by Gustave Eiffel for the Paris Exhibition 1889. It stands in the Champ de Mars, Paris, where sightseers ride to the top for the view.

Eiger mountain peak in the Swiss ◊Alps.

Eijkman Christiaan 1858–1930. Dutch bacteriologist. He identified vitamin B_1 deficiency as the cause of the disease beriberi, and pioneered the recognition of vitamins as essential to health. He shared the 1929 Nobel Prize for Medicine with Frederick Hopkins.

Eilat alternate spelling of ◊Elat, a port in Israel.

Eindhoven town in North Brabant province, the Netherlands, on the river Dommel; population (1988) 381,000. Industries include electrical and electronic equipment.

Einstein Albert 1879–1955. German-born US physicist who formulated the theories of ◊relativity, and worked on radiation physics and thermodynamics. In 1905 he published the special theory of relativity, and in 1915 issued his general theory of relativity. His latest conception of the basic laws governing the universe was outlined in his ◊unified field theory, made public 1953; his "relativistic theory of the nonsymmetric field," was completed 1955. Einstein wrote that this simplified the derivations as well as the form of the field equations and thus made the whole theory more transparent, without changing its content.

Born at Ulm, in Württemberg, West Germany, he lived with his parents in Munich and then in Italy. After teaching at the polytechnic school at Zürich, he became a Swiss citizen and was appointed an inspector of patents in Berne. In his spare time, he took his PhD at Zürich. In 1909 he was given a chairmanship of theoretical physics at the university. After holding a similar post at Prague 1911, he returned to teach at Zürich 1912, and in 1913 took up a specially created post as director of the Kaiser Wilhelm Institute for Physics, Berlin. He received the Nobel Prize for Physics 1921. After being deprived of his position at Berlin by the Nazis, he emigrated to the US 1933, and became professor of mathematics and a permanent member of the Institute for Advanced Study at Princeton, New Jersey. During World War II he worked for the US Navy Ordnance Bureau.

einsteinium synthesized, radioactive, metallic element of the ◊actinide series, symbol Es, atomic number 99, atomic weight 254.

It was produced by the first thermonuclear explosion, in 1952, and discovered in fallout debris (the isotope Es-253 with a half-life of 20 days). Its longest-lived isotope, Es-254, with a half-life

Eisenhower *The 34th president of the United States of America, Dwight D Eisenhower, a Republican. 1953–1961.*

of 276 days, allowed the element to be studied. It is now synthesized by bombarding lower-numbered ◊transuranics in particle accelerators. It was named in 1955 by A Ghiorso and his team—who first identified it—for Albert ◊Einstein, German-born US physicist, in honor of his theoretical studies of mass and energy.

Einthoven Willem 1860–1927. Dutch physiologist and inventor of the electrocardiograph. He was able to show that certain disorders of the heart alter its electrical activity in characteristic ways.

Eire Gaelic name for the Republic of ◊Ireland.

Eisai 1141–1215. Japanese Buddhist monk who introduced Zen and tea from China to Japan and founded the ◊Rinzai school.

Eisenach industrial town (pottery, vehicles, machinery) in the state of Thuringia, Federal Republic of Germany; population (1981) 50,700. Martin ◊Luther made the first translation of the Bible into German in Wartburg Castle and the composer J S Bach was born here.

Eisenhower Dwight David ("Ike") 1890–1969. the 34th president of the US 1953–60, a Republican. A general in World War II, he commanded the Allied forces in Italy 1943, then the Allied invasion of Europe, and from Oct 1944 all the Allied armies in the West. As president he promoted business interests at home and conducted the ◊Cold War abroad. His vice-president was Richard Nixon.

Eisenhower was born in Texas. A graduate of West Point military academy in 1915, he served in a variety of staff and command posts before World War II. He became commander in chief of the US and British forces for the invasion of N Africa Nov 1942; commanded the Allied invasion of Sicily July 1943, and announced the surrender of Italy Sept 8, 1943. In Dec he became commander of the Allied Expeditionary Force. He served as president of Columbia University and chair of the joint chiefs of staff between 1949 and 1950. He resigned from the army 1952 to campaign for the presidency; he was elected and re-elected by a wide margin in 1956. A popular politician, Eisenhower held office during a period of domestic and international tension, with the growing civil rights movement at home and the Cold War dominating international politics, although the US was experiencing an era of postwar prosperity and growth.

He was well liked and had a talent for administration.

Eisenhower, Mount Rocky Mountain peak in Alberta, Canada, included in Banff National Park, 9,390 ft/2,862 m.

Eisenstein Sergei Mikhailovich 1898–1948. Latvian-born Soviet film director. He pioneered the use of film montage (a technique of deliberately juxtaposing shots to create a particular meaning) as a means of propaganda, as in *The Battleship Potemkin* 1925. His *Alexander Nevsky* 1938 was the first part of an uncompleted trilogy, the second part, *Ivan the Terrible* 1944, being banned in the USSR.

eisteddfod (Welsh "sitting") traditional Welsh gathering lasting 3–4 days dedicated to the encouragement of the bardic arts of music, poetry, and literature, which traditionally dates from pre-Christian times.

ejector seat device for propelling an aircraft pilot out of the plane to parachute to safety in an emergency, invented by the British engineer James Martin (1893–1981). The first seats of 1945 were powered by a compressed spring; later seats used an explosive charge. By the early 1980s, 35,000 seats had been fitted worldwide.

A major breakthrough in the 1980s are seats that can be ejected on takeoff and landing or at low altitude that are as effective as those originally designed for parachuting from high altitudes.

Ekaterinburg pre-revolutionary name of ◊Sverdlovsk, a town in the western USSR, the site of the assassination of Tsar Nikolai II and his family in 1918.

Ekaterinodar pre-revolutionary name of ◊Krasnodar, industrial town in the USSR.

Ekaterinoslav pre-revolutionary name of ◊Dnepropetrovsk, center of an industrial region in Ukraine, USSR.

EKG abbreviation for ◊electrocardiogram.

Ekman spiral effect an application of the ◊Coriolis effect to ocean currents, whereby the currents flow at an angle to the winds that drive them. It derives its name from the Swedish oceanographer Vagn Ekman (1874–1954).

In the northern hemisphere, surface currents are deflected to the right of the wind direction. The surface current then drives the subsurface layer at an angle to its original deflection. Consequent subsurface layers are similarly affected, so that the effect decreases with increasing depth. The result is that most water is transported at about right angles to the wind direction. Directions are reversed in the southern hemisphere.

El Aaiún Arabic name of ◊La'Youn.

eland largest species of ◊antelope, *Taurotragus oryx*. Pale fawn in color, it is about 6 ft/2 m high, and both sexes have spiral horns about 18 in/45 cm long. It is found in central and S Africa.

elasticity in economics, the measure of response of one variable to changes in another. If the price of butter is reduced by 10% and the demand increases by 20%, the elasticity measure is 2. Such measures are used to test the effects of changes in prices, incomes, and supply and demand. Inelasticity may exist in the demand for necessities such as water, the demand for which will remain the same even if the price changes considerably.

elasticity in physics, the ability of a solid to recover its shape once deforming forces (stresses modifying its dimensions or shape) are removed. An elastic material obeys ◊Hooke's law: that is, its deformation is proportional to the applied stress up to a certain point, called the elastic limit, beyond which additional stress will deform it permanently. Elastic materials include metals and rubber; however, all materials have some degree of elasticity.

Elat or *Eilat* port at the head of the Gulf of Aqaba, Israel's only outlet to the Red Sea; population (1982) 19,500. Founded in 1948, on the site of the Biblical Elath, it is linked by road with Beersheba. There are copper mines and granite quarries nearby, and a major geophysical observatory opened in 1968 is 10 mi/16 km to the N.

E layer (formerly called the Kennelly–Heaviside layer) the lower regions of the ◊ionosphere, which refract radio waves allowing their reception around the surface of the Earth. The E layer approaches the Earth by day and recedes from it at night.

Elba island in the Mediterranean, 6 mi/10 km off the

W coast of Italy; population (1981) 35,000; area 86 sq mi/223 sq km. Iron ore is exported from the capital, Portoferraio, to the Italian mainland, and there is a fishing industry. The small uninhabited island of Monte Cristo, 25 mi/40 km to the S, supplied the title of Alexandre Dumas's hero in *The Count of Monte Cristo*. Elba was Napoleon's place of exile 1814–15.

Elbe one of the principal rivers of the Federal Republic of Germany, 725 mi/1,166 km long, rising on the southern slopes of the Riesengebirge, Czechoslovakia, and flowing NW across the German plain to the North Sea.

Elberfeld German industrial city, merged with ◊Wuppertal in 1929.

Elbing German name for Elbląg, a Polish port.

Elbląg Polish port 7 mi/11 km from the mouth of the river Elbląg, which flows into the Vistula Lagoon, an inlet of the Baltic; population (1983) 115,900. It has shipyards, engineering works, and car and tractor factories.

Elbruz or ***Elbrus*** highest mountain (18,517 ft/5,642 m) on the continent of Europe, in the Caucasus, Georgian Republic, USSR.

Elburz volcanic mountain range in NW Iran, close to the southern shore of the Caspian Sea; the highest point is Mount Damavand at 18,602 ft/5,670 m.

Eldem Sedad Hakki 1908– . Turkish architect whose work is inspired by the spatial harmony and regular rhythms of the traditional Turkish house. These qualities are reinterpreted in modern forms with great sensitivity to context, as in the Social Security Agency Complex, Zeyrek, Istanbul (1962–64), and the Ataturk Library, Istanbul (1973).

elder in botany, small tree or shrub of the genus *Sambucus*, of the honeysuckle family (Caprifoliaceae), native to North America, Eurasia, and N Africa. Some are grown as ornamentals for their showy yellow or white flower clusters and their colorful black or scarlet berries. The American elder *Sambucus canadensis* attains tree size and has blue berries.

elder in the Presbyterian church, a lay member who assists the minister (or teaching elder) in running the church.

El Dorado fabled city of gold believed by the 16th-century Spanish and other Europeans to exist somewhere in the area of the Orinoco and Amazon rivers.

Eleanor of Aquitaine c. 1122–1204. Queen of France 1137–51 as wife of Louis VII, and of England from 1154 as wife of Henry II.

She was the daughter of William X, Duke of Aquitaine, and was married 1137–52 to Louis VII of France, but the marriage was annulled. The same year she married Henry of Anjou, who became king of England 1154. Henry imprisoned her 1174–89 for supporting their sons, the future Richard I and King John, in revolt against him.

Eleanor of Castile c. 1245–1290. Queen of Edward I of England, the daughter of Ferdinand III of Castile. She married Prince Edward 1254, and accompanied him on his crusade 1270. She died at Harby, Nottinghamshire, and Edward erected stone crosses in towns where her body rested on the funeral journey to London. Several Eleanor Crosses are still standing, for example at Northampton.

elector (German *Kurfürst*) any of originally seven (later ten) princes of the Holy Roman Empire who had the prerogative of electing the emperor (in effect, the king of Germany). The electors were the archbishops of Mainz, Trier, and Cologne, the court palatine of the Rhine, the Duke of Saxony, the Margrave of Brandenburg, and the king of Bohemia (in force to 1806). Their constitutional status was formalized 1356 in the document known as the Golden Bull, which granted them extensive powers within their own domains, to act as judges, issue coins, and impose tolls.

electoral college in US government, the indirect system by which the president and vice-president of the US are elected. The people of each state officially vote not for the presidential candidate but for an assembly of electors nominated by each party. The whole electoral-college vote of the state then usually goes to the winning party (and candidate). A majority is required for election.

The US has as many electors as it has senators and representatives in Congress, so that the electoral college numbers 538 (535 state electors and 3 from the District of Columbia), and a majority of 270 electoral votes is needed to win. The system can lead to a presidential candidate being elected with a minority of the total vote over the whole country (as happened when Benjamin Harrison was elected over Grover Cleveland 1888). It has been proposed, for example by President Carter in 1977, to substitute a direct popular vote. A constitutional amendment to this effect failed in 1979, partly because minority groups argued that this would deprive them of their politically influential block vote in key states.

electoral system see ◊vote and ◊proportional representation.

Electra in Greek mythology, daughter of ◊Agamemnon and ◊Clytemnestra, and sister of ◊Orestes and ◊Iphigenia. Her hatred of her mother for murdering her father and her desire for revenge, fulfilled by the return of her brother Orestes, made her the subject of tragedies by ◊Aeschylus, ◊Sophocles, and ◊Euripides.

Electra plays by Sophocles and Euripides, produced in Greece about 418–410 BC and 417 BC, respectively. Both plays explore Electra's role in the complex family tragedy that involved the deaths of her sister Chrysothemis, her parents King Agamemnon and Clytemnestra, and her brother Orestes.

electrical relay an electromagnetic device, such as a switch, activated by a change in one electric circuit and controlling a larger circuit or activating other devices.

electric arc a continuous electric discharge of high current between two electrodes, giving out a brilliant light and heat. The phenomenon is exploited in the carbon-arc lamp, once widely used in film projectors. In the electric-arc furnace an arc struck between very large carbon electrodes and the metal charge provides the heating. In arc ◊welding an electric arc provides the heat to fuse the metal. The discharges in low-pressure gases, as in neon and sodium lights, can also be broadly considered as electric arcs.

electric bell a bell that makes use of electromagnetism. At its heart is a wire-wound coil on an iron core (an electromagnet) that, when a direct current (from a battery) flows through it, attracts an iron ◊armature. The armature acts as a switch, whose movement causes contact with an adjustable contact point to be broken, so breaking the circuit. A spring rapidly returns the armature to the contact point, once again closing the circuit, so bringing about the oscillation. The armature oscillates back and forth, and the clapper or hammer fixed to the armature strikes the bell.

electric charge property of some bodies that causes them to exert forces on each other. Two bodies both with positive or both with negative charges repel each other, whereas bodies with opposite or "unlike" charges attract each other, since each is in the ◊electric field of the other. In atoms, ◊electrons possess a negative charge, and ◊protons an equal positive charge. The unit of electric charge is the coulomb (symbol C).

Electric charge can be generated by friction induction or chemical change and shows itself as an accumulation of electrons (negative charge) or loss of electrons (positive charge) on an atom or body. Atoms have no charge but can sometimes gain electrons to become negative ions or lose them to become positive ions. So-called ◊static electricity, seen in such phenomena as the charging of nylon shirts when they are pulled on or off, or in brushing hair, is in fact the gain or loss of electrons from the surface atoms. A flow of charge (such as electrons through a copper wire) constitutes an electric current; the flow of current is measured in amperes (symbol A).

electric current rate of flow of electric charge. It is measured in amperes (coulombs per second).

electric energy in physics, the ◊energy of a body that is due to its position in an electric field (generated by an electric charge).

electric field in physics, the electrically charged region of space surrounding an electrically charged body. In this region, an electric charge experiences a force caused by the presence of another electric charge.

electric fish any of several unrelated fishes that have electricity-producing powers, including the South American "electric eel" *Electrophorus electricus*, which is not a true eel, and in which the lateral tail muscles are modified to form electric organs capable of generating 650 volts; the current passing from tail to head is strong enough to stun another animal. Not all electric fishes produce such strong discharges; most use weak electric fields to navigate and detect nearby objects.

electricity all phenomena caused by ◊electric charge, whether static or in motion. Electric charge is caused by an excess or deficit of electrons in the charged substance, and an electric current by the movement of electrons around a circuit. Substances may be electrical conductors, such as metals, which allow the passage of electricity through them, or insulators, such as rubber, which are extremely poor conductors. Substances with relatively poor conductivities that can be improved by the addition of heat or light are known as ◊semiconductors.

Electricity generated on a commercial scale was available from the early 1880s and used for electric motors driving all kinds of machinery, and for lighting, first by carbon arc, but later by incandescent filaments, first of carbon and then of tungsten, enclosed in glass bulbs partially filled with inert gas under vacuum. Light is also produced by passing electricity through a gas or metal vapour or a fluorescent lamp. Other practical applications include telephone, radio, television, X-ray machines, and many other applications in ◊electronics.

The fact that amber has the power, after being rubbed, of attracting light objects, such as bits of straw and feathers, is said to have been known to Thales of Miletus and to the Roman naturalist Pliny. William Gilbert, Queen Elizabeth I's physician, found that many substances possessed this power, and he called it "electric" after the Greek word meaning "amber."

In the early 1700s it was recognized that there are two types of electricity and that unlike kinds attract each other and like kinds repel. The charge on glass rubbed with silk came to be known as positive electricity, and the charge on amber rubbed with wool as negative electricity. These two charges were found to cancel each other when brought together.

In 1800 Alessandro Volta found that a series of cells containing brine, in which were dipped plates of zinc and copper, gave an electric current, which later in the same year was shown to evolve hydrogen and oxygen when passed through water (◊electrolysis). Humphry Davy, in 1807, decomposed soda and potash (both thought to be elements) and isolated the metals sodium and potassium, a discovery that led the way to ◊electroplating. Other properties of electric currents discovered were the heating effect, now used in lighting and central heating, and the deflection of a magnetic needle, described by Hans Oersted 1820 and elaborated by André Ampère 1825. This work made possible the electric telegraph.

For Michael Faraday, the fact that an electric current passing through a wire caused a magnet to move suggested that moving a wire or coil of wire rapidly between the poles of a magnet would induce an electric current. He demonstrated this 1831, producing the first ◊dynamo, which became

electricity generation and supply

coal-fired power station (highly simplified)

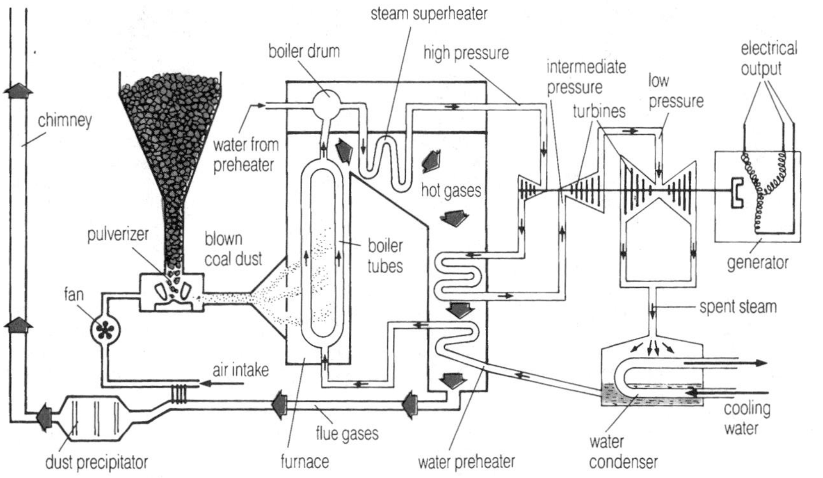
steam superheater
boiler drum
high pressure
intermediate pressure
low pressure
turbines
electrical output
chimney
water from preheater
hot gases
pulverizer
blown coal dust
boiler tubes
generator
fan
spent steam
air intake
cooling water
flue gases
water condenser
dust precipitator
furnace
water preheater

the basis of electrical engineering. The characteristics of currents were crystallized about 1827 by Georg Ohm, who showed that the current passing along a wire was equal to the electromotive force (emf) across the wire multiplied by a constant, which was the conductivity of the wire. The unit of resistance (ohm) is named after Ohm, the unit of emf is named after Volta (volt), and the unit of current after Ampère (amp).

The work of the late 1800s indicated the wide interconnections of electricity (with magnetism, heat, and light), and about 1855 James Clerk Maxwell formulated a single electromagnetic theory. The universal importance of electricity was decisively proved by the discovery that the atom, up until then thought to be the ultimate particle of matter, is composed of a positively charged central core, the nucleus, about which negatively charged electrons rotate in various orbits.

Electricity is the most useful and most convenient form of energy, readily convertible into heat and light and used to power machines. Electricity can be generated in one place and distributed anywhere because it readily flows through wires. It is generated at power stations where a suitable energy source is harnessed to drive ◊turbines that spin electricity generators. Current energy sources are coal, oil, water power (hydroelectricity), natural gas, and ◊nuclear power. Research is under way to increase the contribution of wind, tidal, and geothermal power. Nuclear fuel has proved a more expensive source of electricity than initially anticipated and worldwide concern over radioactivity may limit its future development.

Electricity is generated at power stations at a voltage of about 25,000 volts, which is not a suitable voltage for long-distance transmission. For minimal power loss, transmission must take place at very high voltage (400,000 volts or more). The generated voltage is therefore increased ("stepped up") by a ◊transformer. The resulting high-voltage electricity is then fed into the main arteries of the ◊grid system, an interconnected network of power stations and distribution centers covering a large area. After transmission to a local substation, the line voltage is reduced by a step-down transformer and distributed to consumers.

Among specialized power units that convert energy directly to electrical energy without the intervention of any moving mechanisms, the most promising are thermionic converters. These use conventional fuels such as propane gas, as in portable military power packs, or, if refueling is to be avoided, radioactive fuels, as in unscrewed navigational aids and spacecraft.

electric motor a machine that converts electrical energy into mechanical energy. There are various types, including direct-current and induction motors, most of which produce rotary motion. A linear induction motor produces linear (sideways) rather than rotary motion.

A simple ***direct-current motor*** consists of a horseshoe-shaped permanent ◊magnet with a wire-wound coil (◊armature) mounted so that it can rotate between the poles of the magnet. A ◊commutator reverses the current (from a battery) fed to the coil on each half-turn, which rotates because of the mechanical force exerted on a conductor carrying a current in a magnetic field.

An induction motor employs ◊alternating current. It comprises a stationary current-carrying coil (stator) surrounding another coil (rotor), which rotates because of the current induced in it by the magnetic field created by the stator; it thus requires no commutator.

electric power the rate at which an electrical machine uses electrical ◊energy or converts it into other forms of energy—for example, light, heat, mechanical energy. Usually measured in watts (equivalent to joules per second), it is equal to the product of the voltage and the current flowing.

An electric lamp that passes a current of 0.4 amps at 250 volts uses 100 watts of electrical power and converts it into light—in ordinary terms it is a 100-watt lamp. An electric motor that requires 6 amps at the same voltage consumes 1,500 watts (1.5 kilowatts), equivalent to delivering about 2 horsepower of mechanical energy (1 horsepower equals 756 watts).

electric ray another name for the ◊torpedo.

electrocardiogram (***ECG*** or ***EKG***) graphic recording of the electrical changes in the heart muscle, as detected by electrodes placed on the chest. Electrocardiography is used in the diagnosis of heart disease.

electrochemical series a list of chemical elements arranged in descending order of the ease with which they can lose electrons to form cations (positive ions). An element can be displaced (◊displacement reaction) from a compound by any element above it in the series.

electrochemistry the branch of science that studies chemical reactions involving electricity. The use of electricity to produce chemical effects, ◊electrolysis, is employed in many industrial processes, such as the manufacture of chlorine and the extraction of aluminum. The use of chemical reactions to produce electricity is the basis of

ectrolysis

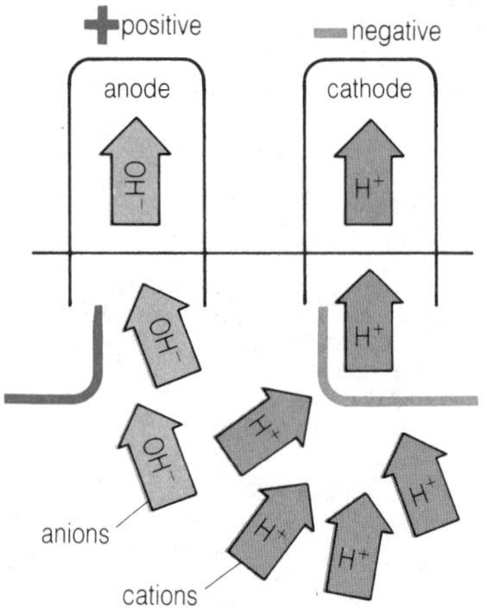
positive
negative
anode
cathode
OH⁻
H⁺
anions
cations

batteries, such as the dry cell and the ◊Leclanché cell.

Since all chemical reactions involve changes to the electron structure of atoms, all reactions are now recognized as electrochemical in nature. Oxidation, for example, was once defined as a process in which oxygen was combined with a substance, or hydrogen was removed from a compound; it is now defined as a process in which electrons are lost.

electroconvulsive therapy (ECT) or ***electroshock therapy*** a treatment for ◊schizophrenia and ◊depression, given under anesthesia and with a muscle relaxant. An electric current is passed through the brain to induce alterations in the brain's electrical activity. Although often successful, the treatment can cause distress and loss of concentration and memory, and so there is much controversy about its use and effectiveness.

electrocution death caused by electric current. It is used as a method of execution in some US states. The condemned person is strapped into a special electric chair and an electric shock of 1,800–2,000 volts is administered. See ◊capital punishment.

electrode any terminal by which an electric current passes in or out of a conducting substance; for example, the anode or cathode in a battery or the carbons in an arc lamp. The terminals that emit and collect the flow of electrons in electron tubes are also called electrodes; for example, cathodes, plates, and grids.

electrodynamics the branch of physics dealing with electric currents and associated magnetic forces. Quantum electrodynamics (QED) studies the interaction between charged particles and their emission and absorption of electromagnetic radiation. This field combines quantum ◊mechanics and ◊relativity theory, making accurate predictions about subatomic processes involving charged particles such as electrons and protons.

electroencephalogram (EEG) graphic record of the electrical discharges of the brain, as detected by electrodes placed on the scalp. The pattern of electrical activity revealed by electroencephalography is helpful in the diagnosis of some brain disorders, such as epilepsy.

electrolysis the production of chemical changes by passing an electric current through a solution (the electrolyte), resulting in the migration of the ions to the electrodes: positive ions (cations) to the negative electrode (cathode) and negative ions (anions) to the positive electrode (anode).

During electrolysis, the ions react with the electrode, either receiving or giving up electrons. The resultant atoms may be liberated as a gas, or deposited as a solid on the electrode, in amounts that are proportional to the amount of current passed, as discovered by Michael Faraday.

When acidified water is electrolyzed, the

chemical changes that occur at the electrodes are as follows:

negative electrode:

$4H^+ + 4e = 2H_2$ (reduction)

positive electrode:

$4OH^- - 4e = 2H_2O + O_2$ (oxidation)

One application of electrolysis is electroplating, in which a solution of a salt, such as silver nitrate ($AgNO_3$), is used and the object to be plated acts as the negative electrode, thus attracting silver ions (Ag^+). Electrolysis is used in many industrial processes, such as coating metals for vehicles and ships, and refining bauxite into aluminum.

electrolyte a molten substance or solution in which an electric current is made to flow by the movement and discharge of ions in accordance with ◊Faraday's laws of electrolysis.

The term "electrolyte" is frequently used to denote a substance that, when dissolved in a specified solvent, usually water, produces an electrically conducting medium.

electromagnet an iron bar with coils or wire around it, which acts as a magnet when an electric current flows through the wire. Electromagnets have many uses: in switches, electric bells, solenoids, and metal-lifting cranes.

electromagnetic field in physics, the agency by which a particle with an ◊electric charge experiences a force in a particular region of space. If it does so only when moving, it is in a pure magnetic field; if it does so when stationary, it is in an electric field. Both can be present simultaneously.

electromagnetic force one of the four ◊fundamental forces of nature, the other three being the gravitational force, the strong force, and the weak force. The ◊elementary particle that is the carrier for the electromagnetic (em) force is the photon.

electromagnetic induction in physics, the production of an ◊electromotive force (emf) in a circuit by a change of ◊magnetic flux through the circuit. The emf so produced is known as an induced emf, and any current that may result is known as an induced current. The phenomenon is applied in the induction coil.

If the change of magnetic flux is due to a variation in the current flowing in the same circuit, the phenomenon is known as self-induction; if it is due to a change of current flowing in another circuit it is known as mutual induction.

electromagnetic spectrum the complete range, over all wavelengths from the lowest to the highest, of ◊electromagnetic waves.

electromagnetic system of units former system of absolute electromagnetic units (emu) based on the ◊c.g.s. system and having, as its primary electrical unit, the unit magnetic pole. It was replaced by ◊SI units.

electromagnetic waves oscillating electric and magnetic fields traveling together through space at a speed of nearly 186,000 mi/300,000 km per second. The (limitless) range of possible wavelengths or ◊frequencies of electromagnetic waves, which can be thought of as making up the electromagnetic spectrum, includes radio waves, infrared radiation, visible light, ultraviolet radiation, X-rays, and gamma rays.

electromotive force (emf) in physics, the greatest potential difference that can be generated by a source of current. This is always greater than the measured potential difference generated, due to the resistance of the wires and components in the circuit.

electron an ◊elementary particle of negative charge (the positron is its antiparticle), which cannot be subdivided, a constituent of all ◊atoms, and a member of the class of particles known as ◊leptons. The electrons in each atom surround the nucleus in shells, the number being equal to the atom's atomic number (the number of protons in the nucleus). This electron structure is responsible for the chemical properties of the atom (see ◊element). The beta particles emitted from radioactive atoms during ◊beta decay are either electrons or positrons (electrons during beta-minus decay; positrons during beta-plus decay).

electromagnetic waves

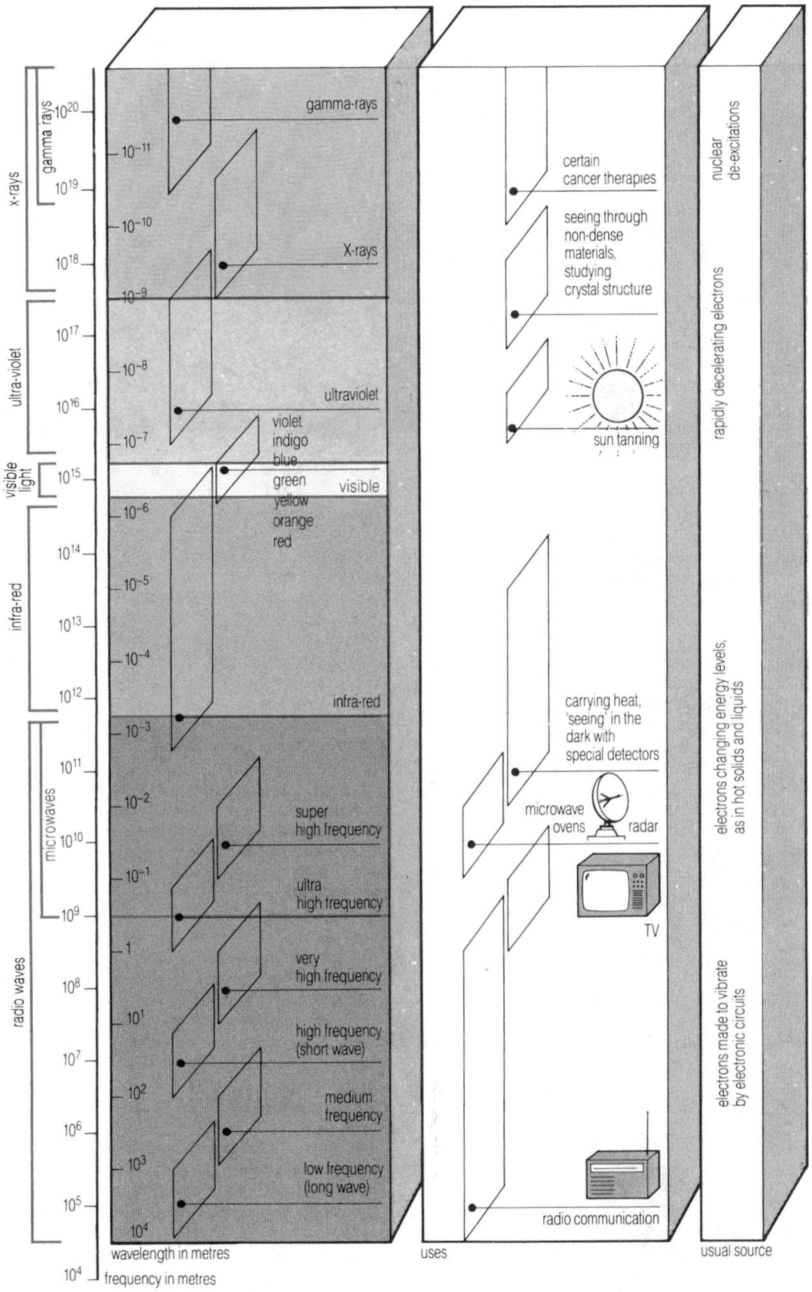
x-rays
gamma rays
ultra-violet
visible light
infra-red
microwaves
radio waves
10^{20}
10^{19}
10^{18}
10^{17}
10^{16}
10^{15}
10^{14}
10^{13}
10^{12}
10^{11}
10^{10}
10^{9}
10^{8}
10^{7}
10^{6}
10^{5}
10^{4}
10^{-11}
10^{-10}
10^{-9}
10^{-8}
10^{-7}
10^{-6}
10^{-5}
10^{-4}
10^{-3}
10^{-2}
10^{-1}
1
10^{1}
10^{2}
10^{3}
10^{4}
gamma-rays
X-rays
ultraviolet
violet
indigo
blue
green
yellow
orange
red
visible
infra-red
super high frequency
ultra high frequency
very high frequency
high frequency (short wave)
medium frequency
low frequency (long wave)
wavelength in metres
frequency in metres
certain cancer therapies
seeing through non-dense materials, studying crystal structure
sun tanning
carrying heat, 'seeing' in the dark with special detectors
microwave ovens
radar
TV
radio communication
uses
nuclear de-excitations
rapidly decelerating electrons
electrons changing energy levels, as in hot solids and liquids
electrons made to vibrate by electronic circuits
usual source

electronegativity the ease with which an atom can attract electrons to itself. Electronegative elements attract electrons, so forming negative ions.

Linus Pauling devised an electronegativity scale to indicate the relative power of attraction of elements for electrons. Fluorine, the most nonmetallic element, has a value of 4.0 on this scale; oxygen, the next most nonmetallic, has a value of 3.5.

In a covalent bond between two atoms of different electronegativities, the bonding electrons will be located close to the more electronegative atom, creating a ◊dipole.

electron gun a part in many electronic devices consisting of a series of ◊electrodes, including a cathode for producing an electron beam. It plays an essential role in ◊cathode-ray tubes (television tubes) and ◊electron microscopes.

electronic flash discharge tube that produces a high-intensity flash of light, used for photography in dim conditions. The tube contains an inert gas such as krypton. The flash lasts only a few thousandths of a second.

electronic mail ◊telecommunications system that sends messages to people or machines (such as computers) via computers and the telephone network rather than by letter.

Subscribers to an electronic mail system type messages in ordinary letter form on a word processor, or microcomputer, and "drop" the letters into a central computer's memory bank by means of a computer/telephone connector (a modem). The recipient "collects" the letter by calling up the central computer and feeding a unique password into the system.

electronic music a form of studio-based serial music composed entirely of electronically generated and modified tones, as opposed to concrete music, which arranges pre-recorded sounds by intuition. The term was later broadened to include pre-recorded vocal and instrumental sounds, although always implying a serial basis. ◊Maderna, ◊Stockhausen, and ◊Babbit were among the pioneers of electronic music in the 1950s.

After 1960, with the arrival of the purpose-built synthesizer developed by Robert Moog, Peter Zinovieff, and others, interest switched to computer-aided synthesis, culminating in the 4X system installed at ◊IRCAM.

electronics the branch of science that deals with the emission of ◊electrons from conductors and ◊semiconductors, with the subsequent manipulation of these electrons, and with the construction of electronic devices. The first electronic device was the ◊thermionic valve, or vacuum tube, in which electrons moved in a vacuum, and led to such inventions as ◊radio, ◊television, ◊radar, and the digital ◊computer. Replacement of valves with the comparatively tiny and reliable transistor in 1948 revolutionized electronic development. Modern electronic devices are based on minute integrated circuits and ◊silicon chips, wafer-thin crystal slices holding tens of thousands of electronic components.

By using solid-state devices such as silicon chips and integrated circuits, extremely complex electronic circuits can be constructed, leading to ◊digital watches, pocket ◊calculators, powerful ◊microcomputers, and ◊word processors.

electron microscope instrument that produces a magnified image by using a beam of ◊electrons instead of light rays, as in an optical ◊microscope. An electron lens is an arrangement of electromagnetic coils that control and focus the beam. Electrons are not visible to the eye, so instead of an eyepiece there is a fluorescent screen or a photographic plate on which the electrons form an image. The wavelength of the electron beam is much shorter than that of light, so much greater magnification and resolution (ability to distinguish detail) can be achieved.

A high-resolution electron microscope (HREM) can produce a magnification of 7 million times (7,000,000 £m3). The development of the electron microscope has made possible the observation of very minute organisms, viruses, and even large molecules. A transmission electron microscope passes the electron beam through a very thin slice of a specimen. A scanning electron microscope looks at the exterior of a specimen.

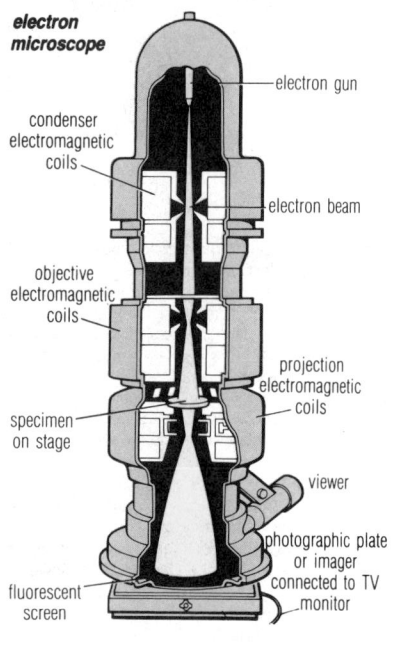

electron microscope

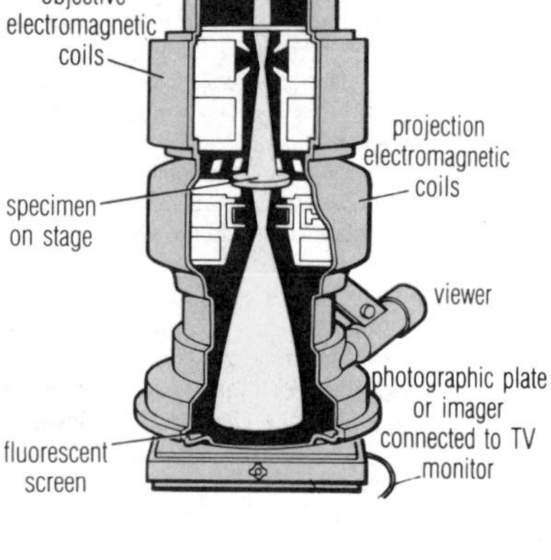
electron gun
condenser electromagnetic coils
electron beam
objective electromagnetic coils
projection electromagnetic coils
specimen on stage
viewer
photographic plate or imager connected to TV monitor
fluorescent screen

electroscope

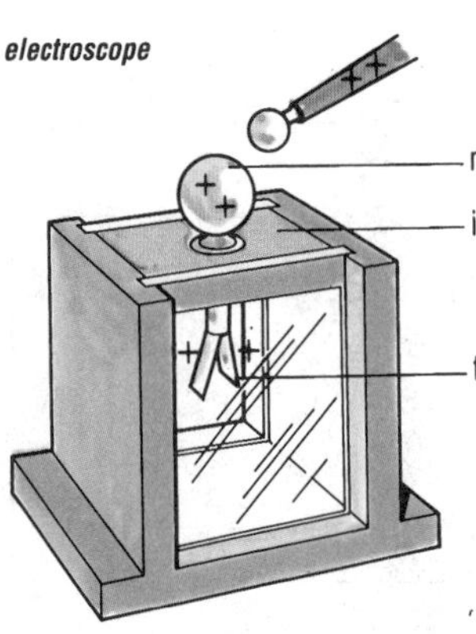
metal sphere
insulator
foil leaves

electrons, delocalized ◊electrons that are not associated with individual atoms or identifiable chemical bonds, but are shared collectively by all the constituent atoms or ions of some chemical substances (such as metals, graphite, and ◊aromatic compounds).

A metallic solid consists of a three-dimensional arrangement of metal ions through which the delocalized electrons are free to travel. Aromatic compounds are characterized by the sharing of delocalized electrons by several atoms within the molecule.

electrons, localized pair of electrons in a single covalent bond that are located between the nuclei of the two contributing atoms. Such electrons cannot move beyond this area.

electron volt unit (abbreviation eV) for measuring the energy of a charged particle (◊ion or ◊electron) in terms of the energy of motion an electron would gain from a potential difference of one volt. Because it is so small, more usual units are mega- (million) and giga- (billion) electron volts (MeV and GeV).

electrophoresis the ◊diffusion of charged particles through a fluid under the influence of an electric field. It can be used in the biological sciences to separate ◊molecules of different sizes, which diffuse at different rates. In industry, electrophoresis is used in paint-dipping operations to ensure that paint reaches awkward corners.

electroplating deposition of metals upon metallic surfaces by electrolysis for decorative and/or protective purposes. It is used in the preparation of printers' blocks, "master" audio disks, and in many other processes.

A current is passed through a bath containing a solution of a salt of the plating metal, the object to be plated being the cathode (negative terminal); the anode (positive terminal) is either an inert substance or the plating metal. Among the metals most commonly used for plating are zinc, nickel, chromium, cadmium, copper, silver, and gold.

In ***electropolishing***, the object to be polished is made the anode in an electrolytic solution and by carefully controlling the conditions the high spots on the surface are dissolved away, leaving a high-quality stain-free surface. This technique is useful in polishing irregular stainless-steel articles.

electropositivity measure of the ability of elements (mainly metals) that donate electrons to form positive ions. The greater the metallic character, the more electropositive the element.

electroscope an apparatus for detecting ◊electric charge. The simple gold-leaf electroscope consists of a vertical conducting (metal) rod ending in a pair of rectangular pieces of gold foil, mounted inside and insulated from an earthed metal case. An electric charge applied to the end of the metal rod makes the gold leaves diverge, because they each receive a similar charge (positive or negative) and so repel each other.

The polarity of the charge can be found by bringing up another charge of known polarity and applying it to the metal rod. A like charge has no effect on the gold leaves, whereas an opposite charge neutralizes the charge on the leaves and causes them to collapse.

electrostatics the study of electric charges from stationary sources (not currents).

electrovalent bond chemical ◊bond in which the combining atoms lose or gain electrons to form ions. It is also called an ionic bond.

electrum naturally occurring alloy of gold and silver used by early civilizations to make the first coins, about the 6th century BC.

element substance that cannot be split chemically into simpler substances. The atoms of a particular element all have the same number of protons in their nuclei (their atomic number). Elements are classified in the ◊periodic table. Of the 109 known elements, 95 are known to occur in nature (those with atomic numbers 1–95). Eighty-one of the elements are stable; all the others, which include atomic numbers 43, 61, and from 84 up, are radioactive. Those from 96 to 109 do not occur in nature and are synthesized elements only, produced in particle accelerators.

Elements are classified as ◊metals, nonmetals, or semimetals (see ◊metalloid) depending on a combination of their physical and chemical properties; about 75% are metallic. Some elements occur abundantly (oxygen, aluminum); others occur moderately (chromium) or rarely (neon); some, in particular the radioactive ones, are found in minute (neptunium, plutonium) or extremely minute (technetium, promethium) amounts.

Symbols (devised by Jöns Berzelius) are used to denote the elements; the symbol is usually the first letter or letters of the English or Latinized name (for example, C for carbon, Ca for calcium, Fe for iron, *ferrum*). The symbol represents one atom of the element.

According to current theories, hydrogen and helium were produced in the ◊Big Bang at the beginning of the universe. Of the other elements, those up to atomic number 26 (iron) are made by nuclear fusion within the stars. The more massive elements, such as lead and uranium, are produced when an old star explodes; as its center collapses, the gravitational energy squashes nuclei together and makes new, heavier elements, even those superheavy elements beyond atomic number 109 (as yet to be synthesized by physicists).

elementary particle or fundamental particle any of those particles that combine to form ◊atoms and all ◊matter, the most familiar being the electron, proton, and neutron. More than 200 particles have now been identified by physicists, categorized into several classes as characterized by their mass, electric charge, spin, magnetic moment, and interaction. Although many particles were thought to be nondivisible and permanent, now most are known to be combinations of a small number of basic particles.

Since the 1890s, inquiry has progressed from the atom to its nucleus to the ◊hadrons that make up the nucleus to the ◊quarks that make up the hadrons. Since the 1960s, the main interest of particle physicists has been the elucidation of hadron structure. Only a small number of the 200 known particles are nondivisible—basic and stable—those that cannot be subdivided. They include eight of the 12 ◊leptons (the electron, the positron, and six kinds of neutrinos); the quarks (36 varieties); and the ◊gauge bosons—the particles that carry the four fundamental forces (the photon, the graviton, eight kinds of gluons, and three kinds of weakons). All matter in the universe is now seen as being made up of various combinations and interactions of these particles.

elephant the two surviving species of the order Proboscidea: the Asian elephant *Elephas maximus* and the African *Loxodonta africana* elephant. Elephants can grow to 13 ft/4 m and weigh up to 8 tons; they have a thick, gray, wrinkled skin, a large head, a long trunk used to obtain food and

Asiatic Elephant

African Elephant

water, and upper incisors or tusks, which grow to a considerable length. The African elephant has very large ears and a flattened forehead, and the Asian species has smaller ears and a convex forehead. In India, Myanmar (Burma), and Thailand, Asiatic elephants are widely used for transport and logging.

Elephants are herbivorous, highly intelligent, and extremely social, living in matriarchal herds. The period of gestation is about 19–22 months (the longest among mammals), and the life span is about 60–70 years. Elephants have one of the lowest metabolic rates among placental mammals. They are slaughtered needlessly for the ivory of their tusks, and this, coupled with the fact that they reproduce slowly and do not breed readily in captivity, is leading to their extinction. In Africa there were 1.3 million in 1981; fewer than 700,000 in 1988, and about 600,000 in 1990. They were placed on the list of most endangered species in 1989, and a world ban on trade in ivory was imposed.

Elephanta island in Bombay harbor, Maharashtra, India, some 5 mi/8 km from Bombay. The Temple Caves (6th century), cut out of solid rock, have sculptures of many Hindu deities executed 450–740. There was formerly a large stone elephant near the island's landing place.

elephant bird another name for extinct members of the genus ◊Aepyornis.

elephantiasis in the human body, a condition of local enlargement and deformity, most often of a leg, the scrotum, a labium of the vulva, or a breast, caused by the blocking of lymph channels.

The commonest form of elephantiasis is the tropical variety (filariasis) caused by the infestation of parasitic roundworms (filaria); the enlargement is due to chronic blocking of the lymph channels by the worms and consequent overgrowth of the skin and tissues.

Eleusinian Mysteries ceremonies in honor of the Greek deities ◊Demeter, ◊Persephone, and ◊Dionysus, celebrated in the remains of the temple of Demeter at Eleusis, Greece. Worshipers saw visions in the darkened temple, supposedly connected with the underworld.

elevator any mechanical device for raising or lowering people or materials. It usually consists of a platform or boxlike structure suspended by motor-driven cables with safety ratchets along the sides of the shaft. US inventor Elisha Graves ◊Otis developed the first passenger safety elevator 1852, installed 1857. This invention permitted the development of skyscrapers from the

Elgar *The composer Edward Elgar.*

1880s. At first steam powered the movement, but hydraulic and then electric elevators were common from the early 1900s. Elevator operators worked controls and gates within the cab until the automatic, or self-starter, was introduced.

El Faiyûm city in N Egypt, 56 mi/90 km SW of Cairo; population (1985) 218,500. It was a center of prehistoric culture; the crocodile god Sobek was worshiped nearby, and realistic mummy portraits dating from the 1st–4th centuries AD were found in the area.

El Ferrol full name El Ferrol del Caudillo, city and port in La Coruña province, on the NW coast of Spain; population (1986) 88,000. It is a naval base and has a deep, sheltered harbor and shipbuilding industries. It is the birthplace of Francisco Franco.

Elgar Edward (William) 1857–1934. English composer. His *Enigma Variations* appeared 1899, and although his celebrated choral work, the oratorio setting of Newman's *The Dream of Gerontius*, was initially a failure, it was well received at Düsseldorf in 1902. Many of his earlier works were then performed, including the *Pomp and Circumstance* marches.

Among his later works are oratorios, two symphonies, a violin concerto, a cello concerto, chamber music, songs, and the tone-poem *Falstaff* 1913.

Elgin city in NE Illinois, NW of Chicago, on the Fox river. Industries include electrical machinery and dairy products; population (1990) 77,010. The city was once the home of Elgin watches.

Elgin marbles collection of ancient Greek sculptures mainly from the Parthenon at Athens, assembled by the 7th Earl of Elgin. Sent to England 1812, and bought for the nation 1816 for £35,000, they are now in the British Museum. Greece has asked for them to be returned to Athens.

Eli in the Old Testament, a priest and childhood teacher of the first prophet, Samuel.

Elijah c. mid-9th century BC. In the Old Testament, a Hebrew prophet during the reigns of the Israelite kings Ahab and Ahaziah. He came from Gilead. He defeated the prophets of ◊Baal, and was said to have been carried up to heaven in a fiery chariot in a whirlwind. In Jewish belief, Elijah will return to Earth to herald the coming of the Messiah.

Eliot Charles William 1834–1926. US educator. Born in Boston and educated at Harvard, Eliot specialized in mathematics and chemistry, teaching briefly at Harvard and being appointed professor at the Massachusetts Institute of Technology (MIT) 1865. After extended travel in Europe, he took up the cause of educational reform and was named president of Harvard 1869. Under Eliot's administration, the college and its graduate and professional schools were reorganized and the curriculum and admission requirements standardized. Eliot, credited with having established the standards of modern American higher education, retired 1909.

Eliot George. Adopted name of Mary Ann Evans

Eliot *Mary Ann Evans, otherwise known as the English novelist George Eliot.*

1819–1880. English novelist who portrayed Victorian society, including its intellectual hypocrisy, with realism and irony. In 1857 she published the story "Amos Barton," the first of the *Scenes of Clerical Life*. This was followed by the novels *Adam Bede* 1859, *The Mill on the Floss* 1860, and *Silas Marner* 1861. *Middlemarch* 1872 is now considered one of the greatest novels of the 19th century. Her final book *Daniel Deronda* 1876 was concerned with anti-Semitism. She also wrote poetry.

Born at Chilvers Coton, Warwickshire, she had a strict evangelical upbringing. In 1841 she was converted to free thinking (see ◊free thought). As assistant editor of the *Westminster Review* under John Chapman 1851–53, she made the acquaintance of Carlyle, Harriet Martineau, Herbert Spencer, and the philosopher and critic George Henry Lewes (1817–1878). Lewes was married but separated from his wife, and from 1854 he and Eliot lived together in a relationship that she regarded as a true marriage and that continued until his death. In 1880 she married John Cross (1840–1924).

Eliot T(homas) S(tearns) 1888–1965. US poet, playwright, and critic who lived in London from 1915. His first volume of poetry, *Prufrock and Other Observations* 1917, introduced new verse forms and rhythms; further collections include *The Waste Land* 1922, *The Hollow Men* 1925, and *Old Possum's Book of Practical Cats* 1939. *Four Quartets* 1943 revealed his religious vision. His plays include *Murder in the Cathedral* 1935 and *The Cocktail Party* 1949. His critical works

Eliot *Anglo-American poet T S Eliot, whose reputation was made by his poem* The Waste Land, *published 1922.*

include *The Sacred Wood* 1920. He was awarded the Nobel Prize for Literature in 1948.

Eliot was born in St Louis, Missouri, and was educated at Harvard, the Sorbonne, and Oxford. He settled in London 1915 and became a British subject 1927. He was for a time a bank clerk, later lecturing and entering publishing at Faber & Faber. As editor of *The Criterion* 1922–39, he exercised an influence on the thought of his generation.

Prufrock and Other Observations expressed the disillusionment of the generation affected by World War I and caused a sensation with its experimental form and rhythms. His reputation was established by the desolate modernity of *The Waste Land*. *The Hollow Men* continued on the same note, but *Ash Wednesday* 1930 revealed the change in religious attitude that led him to become a Catholic. Among his other works are *Four Quartets* 1943, a religious sequence in which he seeks the eternal reality, and the poetic dramas *Murder in the Cathedral* (about Thomas à Becket); *The Cocktail Party*; *The Confidential Clerk* 1953; and *The Elder Statesman* 1958. His collection *Old Possum's Book of Practical Cats* was used for the popular British composer Andrew Lloyd Webber's musical *Cats* 1981. His critical works include *Notes toward the Definition of Culture* 1949.

Elisabethville former name of ◊Lubumbashi, a town in Zaïre.

Elisha mid-9th century BC. In the Old Testament, a Hebrew prophet, successor to Elijah.

elite a small group with power in a society, having privileges, and status above others. An elite may be cultural, educational, religious, political, or social. Sociological interest has centered on how such minorities get, use, and hold on to power, and on what distinguishes elites from the rest of society.

Elizabeth city in NE New Jersey; population (1990) 110,002. Established 1664, it was the first English settlement in New Jersey. It has automobile, sewing machine, and tool factories; oil refineries, and chemical works.

Elizabeth in the New Testament, mother of John the Baptist. She was a cousin of Jesus' mother Mary, who came to see her shortly after the Annunciation; on this visit (called the Visitation), Mary sang the hymn of praise later to be known as "the Magnificat."

Elizabeth the Queen Mother 1900– . Wife of King George VI of England. She was born Lady Elizabeth Angela Marguerite Bowes-Lyon, and on April 26, 1923 she married Albert, Duke of York. Their children are Queen Elizabeth II and Princess Margaret.

Elizabeth two queens of England or the UK:

Elizabeth I 1533–1603. Queen of England 1558–1603, the daughter of Henry VIII and Anne Boleyn. Through her Religious Settlement of 1559 she enforced the Protestant religion by law and she had ◊Mary Queen of Scots executed 1587. Her conflict with Catholic Spain led to the defeat of the ◊Spanish Armada 1588. The Elizabethan age was expansionist in commerce and geographical exploration, and arts and literature flourished. The rulers of many European states made unsuccessful bids to marry Elizabeth, and she used these bids to strengthen her power. She was succeeded by James I.

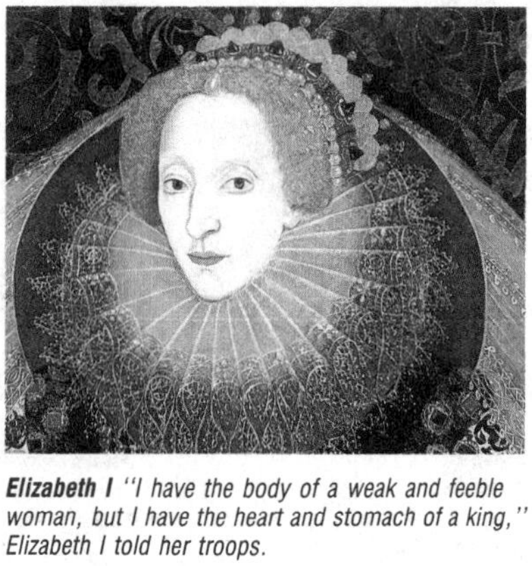

***Elizabeth I** "I have the body of a weak and feeble woman, but I have the heart and stomach of a king," Elizabeth I told her troops.*

***Elizabeth II** Queen Elizabeth II of the United Kingdom and head of the Commonwealth. This portrait was taken during her tour of Australia in 1988.*

Her mother was Henry VIII's second wife, the woman for whom he started the ◊Reformation. On the death of her Catholic half-sister Mary I, Elizabeth became queen. Mary Queen of Scots, also a Catholic, was her cousin. The colonization of the New World began during Elizabeth's reign. Although the courtiers ◊Leicester, Sir Walter ◊Raleigh, and ◊Essex were favored, Elizabeth was known as the Virgin Queen and never married. She was astute, well-educated, and shrewd in both personal and political affairs; she is considered one of England's greatest monarchs.

Elizabeth II 1926– . Queen of Great Britain and Northern Ireland from 1952, the elder daughter of George VI. She married her third cousin, Philip, the Duke of Edinburgh, 1947. They have four children: Charles, Anne, Andrew, and Edward.

Princess Elizabeth Alexandra Mary was born in London April 21, 1926, educated privately, and assumed official duties at 16. During World War II she served in the Auxiliary Territorial Service, and by an amendment to the Regency Act she became a state counselor on her 18th birthday. On the death of George VI she succeeded to the throne while in Kenya with her husband. She is the richest woman in the world, with an estimated wealth of £5.3 billion.

Elizabeth 1709–1762. Empress of Russia from 1741, daughter of Peter the Great. She carried through a palace revolution and supplanted her cousin, the infant Ivan VI (1730–1764), on the throne. She continued the policy of westernization begun by Peter and allied herself with Austria against Prussia.

Elizabethan literature literature produced during the reign of Elizabeth I of England (1558–1603). This period saw a remarkable florescence of the arts in England, and the literature of the time is characterized by a new energy, richness, and confidence. Renaissance humanism, Protestant zeal, and geographical discovery all contributed to this upsurge of creative power. Drama was the dominant form of the age, and ◊Shakespeare and ◊Marlowe were popular with all levels of society. Other writers of the period include Edmund Spenser, Philip Sidney, Frances Bacon, Thomas Lodge, Robert Greene, and John Lyly.

elk

During this period, the resources of English were increased by the free adoption of words from Latin. This was accompanied by a growing belief that English was capable of all the requirements of great literature. There was a balance between the university and courtly elements and the coarse gusto of popular culture. Music was closely related to literature, and competence in singing and musical composition was seen as a normal social skill. Successive editions of the Bible were produced during these years, written with dignity, vividness, and the deliberate intention of reaching a universal audience.

Elizavetpol former name of ◊Kirovabad, industrial town in Azerbaijan Republic, USSR.

elk or ***wapiti*** North American deer *Cervus canadensis*, closely related to the red ◊deer of Eurasia. Head and body length is about 8 ft/2.5 m, and shoulder height is about 5 ft/1.5 m. They are greyish-brown with a yellow rump patch. Males carry magnificent antlers up to 5.8 ft/1.8 m along the beam. In Europe, moose are called elk.

Elkhart city in N Indiana, E of South Bend, where the Elkhart river meets the St Joseph river. Its factories produce mobile homes, firefighting apparatus, recreational vehicles, pharmaceuticals, and musical instruments; population (1990) 43,627.

Ellesmere second-largest island of the Canadian Arctic archipelago, Northwest Territories; area 82,097 sq mi/212,687 sq km. It is for the most part barren or glacier-covered.

Ellesmere Port oil port and industrial town in Cheshire, England, on the river Mersey and the Manchester Ship Canal; population (1983) 81,900.

Ellice Islands former name of ◊Tuvalu, a group of islands in the W Pacific Ocean.

Ellington Duke (Edward Kennedy) 1899–1974. US pianist, who had an outstanding career as a composer and arranger of jazz. He wrote numerous pieces for his own jazz orchestra, accentuating the strengths of individual virtuoso instrumentalists, and became one of the leading figures in jazz over a 55-year span. Some of his most popular compositions include "Mood Indigo," "Sophisticated Lady," "Solitude," and "Black and Tan Fantasy." He was one of the founders of big band jazz.

ellipse a curve joining all points (loci) around two fixed points (foci) such that the sum of the distances from those points is always constant. The diameter passing through the foci is the major axis, and the diameter bisecting this at right angles is the minor axis. An ellipse is one of a series of curves known as ◊conic sections. A slice across a cone that is not made parallel to, or does not pass through, the base will produce an ellipse.

Ellington *Jazz musician, composer, and conductor Duke Ellington advised us to "Take the A Train," to hear the music of Harlem.*

Ellis (Henry) Havelock 1859–1939. English psychologist and writer of many works on the psychology of sex, including *Studies in the Psychology of Sex* (seven volumes) 1898–1928.

Ellis Island island in New York Harbor; area 27 acres/11 hectares; former reception center for steerage-class immigrants during the immigration waves between 1892 to 1943. It was later used as a detention center for nonresidents without documentation, or for those who were being deported. No longer used, it was declared a National Historic Site 1964 by President Lyndon Johnson.

In 1989 the Museum of Immigration was established on Ellis Island.

Ellison Ralph 1914– . US novelist. His *Invisible Man* 1952 portrays with humor and energy the plight of a black man whom postwar American society cannot acknowledge; it is regarded as one of the most impressive novels published in the US in the 1950s.

Its success encouraged the development of black literature in the 1950s and 1960s.

Ellora archeological site in Maharashtra State, India, with 35 sculpted and decorated temple caves—◊Buddhist, ◊Hindu, and ◊Jainist—dating from the late 6th century to the 10th century.

Ellsworth Oliver 1745–1807. US jurist and chief justice of the US Supreme Court 1796–1800. He was a Connecticut delegate 1787 to the Constitutional Convention, where he was instrumental in effecting the "Connecticut Compromise," which balanced large and small state interests. He was selected to be a US senator from Connecticut in 1787. He was appointed chief justice 1796 by President Washington. His opinions as chief justice shaped admiralty law and treaty law.

Born in Windsor, Connecticut, he attended Yale College and graduated from Princeton 1766. After establishing himself as a lawyer, he became a

ellipse

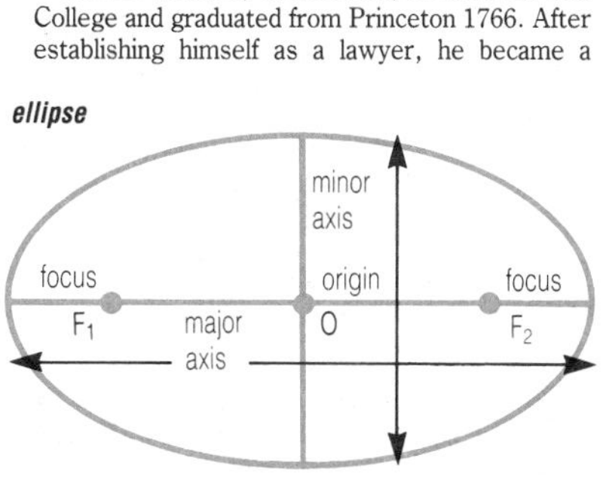
minor
axis
focus
origin
focus
F_1
major
axis
O
F_2

elm

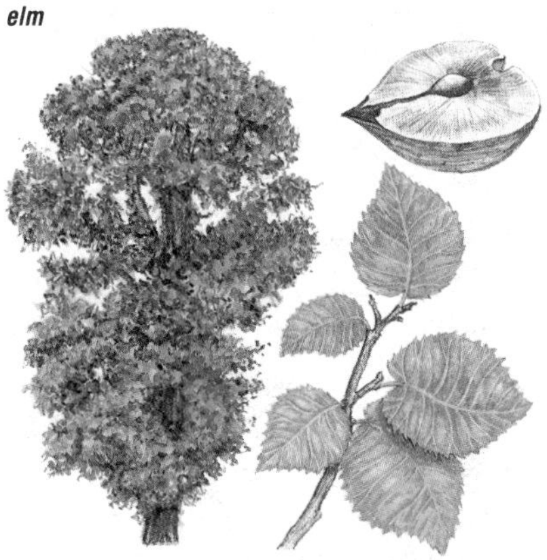

delegate from Connecticut to the Continental Congress in 1777, serving for seven years. He served concurrently in a number of political posts in Connecticut, becoming a judge of the new state court of appeals in 1785, and then moved to the new state superior court as a judge the same year.

elm tree of the genus *Ulmus* of the family Ulmaceae, found in temperate regions of the N hemisphere and in mountainous parts of the tropics. All have doubly-toothed leaf margins and bear clusters of small flowers. The American elm *U. americana* and slippery elm *U. rubra* are native to E North America.

Other species are the wych elm *Ulmacaceae glabra*, indigenous to Britain, the North American white elm *Ulmacaeae americana*, and the red or slippery elm *Ulmacaeae fulva*. Most elms (apart from the wych elm) reproduce not by seed but by suckering (new shoots arising from the root system). This nonsexual reproduction results in an enormous variety of forms.

The fungus disease *Ceratocystis ulmi*, known as Dutch elm disease because of a severe outbreak in the Netherlands 1924, has reduced the numbers of elm trees in Europe and North America. It is carried from tree to tree by beetles. Elms were widespread throughout Europe to about 4,000 BC, when they suddenly disappeared and were not again common until the 12th century. This may have been the fault of an earlier epidemic of Dutch elm disease.

Elmira city in S central New York, on the Chemung river, W of Binghamton, just below the Finger Lakes region; seat of Chemung county. It is the processing and marketing center for the area's dairy and poultry farms. Other industries include business machinery, machine parts, airplanes, and fire engines. Elmira College 1853 is located here; population (1990) 33,724.

El Niño (Spanish "the child") warm ocean surge of the ◊Peru (Humboldt) Current, so called because it tends to occur at Christmas, recurring about every ten years or so in the E Pacific off South America.

El Niño causes the trade winds to cease, so that the cool ocean currents driven by them stops and there is an influx of warm water from the west. It can disrupt the climate of the area disastrously, and has played a part in causing famine in Indonesia 1983, bush fires in Australia because of drought, rainstorms in California and South America, and the destruction of Peru's anchovy harvest and wildlife 1982–83.

El Obeid capital of Kordofan province, Sudan; population (1984) 140,025. Linked by rail with Khartoum, it is a market for cattle, gum arabic, and durra (Indian millet).

elongation in astronomy, the angular distance between a planet or other Solar System object and the Sun. This angle is 0° at either inferior ◊conjunction or superior conjunction. Quadrature occurs when the elongation angle is 90° and ◊opposition (opposite the Sun in the sky) when the angle is 180°.

El Paso city in Texas, situated at the base of the Franklin mountains, on the Rio Grande, opposite the Mexican city of Ciudad Juárez; population (1990) 515,342. It is the center of an agricultural and cattle-raising area, and there are electronics, food processing, packing, and leather industries, as well as oil refineries and industries based on local iron and copper mines.

There are several military installations in the area.

El Salvador country in Central America, bounded N and E by Honduras, S and SW by the Pacific Ocean, and NW by Guatemala.

government The 1983 constitution, amended 1985, provides for a president elected by universal suffrage for a five-year term, assisted by an appointed vice-president and a council of ministers. There is a single-chamber national assembly of 60, elected by universal suffrage for a three-year term.

history The original inhabitants of the area were Indians, who arrived from Mexico around 3000 BC. From the period of the Maya Indians AD 100 to 1000 remain huge limestone pyramids built by them in western El Salvador. The Pipil tribe were in control of the area at the time of the Spanish conquest 1525. El Salvador and other Central American Spanish colonies broke away from Spanish rule in 1821, and became part of the federation of Central American states until 1838. Since then there have been frequent coups and political violence.

After a coup 1961 the conservative Party of National Conciliation (PCN) was established, winning all the seats in the national assembly. PCN stayed in power, with reports of widespread human rights violations, until challenged 1979 by a Socialist guerrilla movement, the ◊Farabundo Martí Liberation Front. A civilian-military junta deposed the president and promised to introduce democracy and free elections, though these were postponed as the violence continued.

In 1980 the archbishop of San Salvador, Oscar Romero, a well-known champion of human rights, was shot dead in his cathedral. The murder of three US nuns and a social worker prompted US president ◊Carter to suspend economic and military aid. In 1980 José Napoléon Duarté, leader of a moderately left-of-center coalition, returned from exile and became president. The ◊Reagan administration supported him, as an anti-communist, and encouraged him to call elections 1982. The left-wing parties refused to participate, and the elections were held amid great violence, at least 40 people being killed on election day. Although Duarté's Christian Democrats won the largest number of assembly seats, a coalition of right-wing parties blocked his continuation as president. A provisional chief executive was selected from a list of candidates acceptable to the military, serving until the 1984 elections, which Duarté won following a run-off against Roberto d'Aubuisson, a rightist suspected in the death of Archibishop Romero.

During 1982 some 1,600 Salvadorean troops were trained in the US and US military advisers were said to be actively involved in the country's internal conflict. It was estimated that about 35,000 people were killed 1979–82.

Despite the new constitution 1983, guerrilla activity continued. In 1985 the anti-imperialist PDC won a convincing victory in the assembly, with 33 seats. The right-wing groups ARENA and PCN won 13 and 12 seats respectively, fighting the election on a joint platform. In 1984 the president's daughter was abducted by guerrillas, forcing him to negotiate with them, in the face of criticism from opposition parties and the military. The guerrilla war continued, Duarte again attempting, in 1986, to negotiate a settlement with the rebels. In Aug 1987 they agreed to meet and discuss the Regional Peace Plan of the ◊Con-

El Salvador
Republic of
(República de El Salvador)

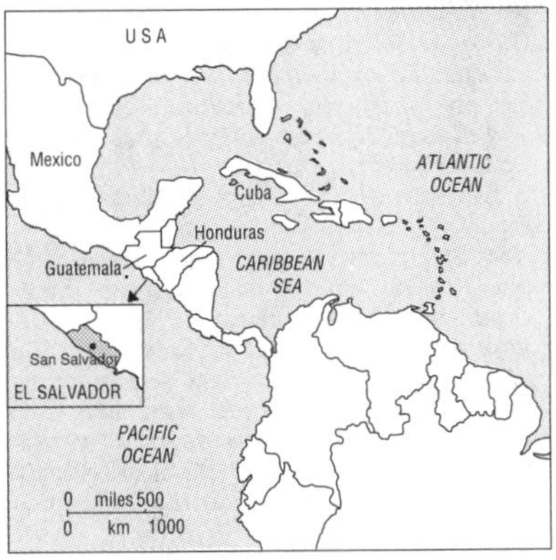
USA
Mexico
Cuba
ATLANTIC OCEAN
Honduras
Guatemala
CARIBBEAN SEA
San Salvador
EL SALVADOR
PACIFIC OCEAN
0 miles 500
0 km 1000

area 8,258 sq mi/21,393 sq km
capital San Salvador
cities Santa Ana, San Miguel
physical narrow coastal plain, rising to mountains in N with central plateau
features smallest and most densely populated Central American country; Mayan archeological remains
head of state and government Alfredo Cristiani from 1989
political system emergent democracy
political parties Christian Democrats (PDC), anti-imperialist; National Republican Alliance (ARENA), right-wing; National Conciliation Party (PCN), right-wing
exports coffee, cotton, sugar
currency colón
population (1989 est) 5,900,000 (mainly of mixed Spanish and Indian ancestry; 10% Indian); growth rate 2.9% p.a.
life expectancy men 63, women 66
language Spanish and Nahua
religion Roman Catholic 97%
literacy men 75%/women 69% (1985 est)
GDP $4.7 bn (1987); $790 per head
chronology
1821 Independence achieved from Spain.
1931 Peasant unrest followed by a military coup.
1969 "Soccer" war with Honduras.
1972 Allegations of human-rights violations and growth of left-wing guerrilla activities. Gen Carlos Romero elected president.
1979 A coup replaced Romero with a military-civilian junta.
1980 Archbishop Oscar Romero assassinated; country on verge of civil war. José Duarte became first civilian president since 1931.
1981 Mexico and France recognized the guerrillas as a legitimate political force, but the US actively assisted the government in its battle against them.
1982 Assembly elections boycotted by left-wing parties and held amid considerable violence.
1986 Duarte sought a negotiated settlement with the guerrillas.
1988 Duarte resigned following diagnosis of terminal cancer.
1989 Alfredo Cristiani (ARENA) elected president, amid allegations of ballot rigging; rebel attacks intensified; right-wing death-squad activity resurgent.
1991 UN-sponsored peace talks with the Farabundo Martí Liberation Front (FMLN) began.

tadora group with him. In 1989, the election of Alfredo Cristiani of D'Aubuisson's ARENA party appeared to herald a return to a hard line against the FMLN rebels. Although Cristiani called for a cease-fire and negotiations with the rebels, death-squad activity increased, harassment of church groups grew (including the killing of six Jesuit priests by unknown gunmen Dec 1989), and the rebels mounted a surprisingly effective offensive in the wealthy suburbs of San Salvador.

The peace initiative eventually collapsed and in the March 1989 elections the right-wing Alfredo Cristiani became president, taking up office in June. In Sept the Socialist guerrilla movement agreed to hold peace talks. The civil war 1980–90 claimed some 70,000 lives. In 1990 a consistently high level of "disappearances" was denounced by the country's Human Rights Commission.

Elsheimer Adam 1578–1610. German painter and etcher, active in Rome from 1600. His small paintings, nearly all on copper, depict landscapes darkened by storm or night, with figures picked out by beams of light, as in *The Rest on the Flight into Egypt* 1609 (Alte Pinakothek, Munich).

Elsinore another form of ◊Helsingør, a port on the NE coast of Denmark.

Elton Charles 1900– . British ecologist, a pioneer of the study of animal and plant forms in their natural environments, and of animal behavior as part of the complex pattern of life. Elton published *Animal Ecology and Evolution* 1930 and *The Pattern of Animal Communities* 1966.

Eluard Paul. Adopted name of Eugène Grindel 1895–1952. French poet, born in Paris. He expressed the suffering of poverty in his verse, and was a leader of the Surrealists. He fought in World War I, which inspired his *Poèmes pour la paix/Poems for Peace* 1918, and was a member of the Resistance in World War II. His books include *Poésie et vérité/Poetry and Truth* 1942 and *Au Rendezvous allemand/To the German Rendezvous* 1944.

Ely Richard Theodore 1854–1943. US economist. Born in Ripley, New York, he was educated at Columbia University and received his PhD from the University of Heidelberg 1879. Appointed professor of political economy at Johns Hopkins University 1881, Ely was an early advocate of government economic intervention, central planning, and the organization of the labor force. In 1885 he founded the American Economic Association and in 1892 became chairman of the department of economics at the University of Wisconsin. He joined the faculty of Northwestern University 1925 and retired from teaching 1933.

Elyria city in N Ohio, on the Black River, W of Cleveland; seat of Lorain county. Industries include tools, electric motors, chromium hardware, chemicals, and automotive parts; population (1990) 56,746.

Elysée Palace (*Palais de l'Elysée*) building in Paris erected 1718 for Louis d'Auvergne, Count of Evreux. It was later the home of Mme de Pompadour, Napoleon I, and Napoleon III, and became the official residence of the presidents of France 1870.

Elysium the Isles of the Blessed in Greek mythology, situated at the western end of the Earth, to which favored heroes are sent by the gods to enjoy a life after death. Later a region in ◊Hades.

Elysium or ***Elysian Fields*** in Classical mythology, an afterworld or paradise (sometimes called the Islands of the Blessed) for the souls of those who found favor with the gods; it was situated near the river Oceanus.

Elytis Odysseus. Adopted name of Odysseus Alepoudelis 1911– . Greek poet, born in Crete. His verse celebrates the importance of the people's attempts to shape an individual existence in freedom. His major work *To Axion Esti/Worthy It Is* 1959 is a lyric cycle, parts of which have been set to music by Theodorakis. He was awarded the Nobel Prize for Literature in 1979.

Elzevir Louis 1540–1617. Founder of the Dutch printing house Elzevir in the the 17th century. Among the firm's publications were editions of Latin, Greek, and Hebrew works, as well as French and Italian classics.

Born at Louvain, Elzevir was obliged to leave Belgium in 1580 because of his Protestant and political views. He settled at Leyden as a bookseller and printer.

emancipation term used to describe the state of being liberated, of being set free from servitude or subjection of any kind. For example, the 1829 Catholic Emancipation Act freed Roman Catholics from the civil disabilities imposed on them by English law. In 1861 the emancipation of the Russian serfs was proclaimed. In 1865 President Abraham Lincoln issued an edict freeing all slaves. The Thirteenth Amendment of the Constitution declared the abolition of slavery throughout the US. The changing role of women in social, economic, but particularly politcal terms in the 19th and 20th centuries, is sometimes referred to as the "emancipation of women" (see ◊women's movement).

Emancipation Proclamation, the in US history, President Lincoln's Civil War announcement, Sept 22, 1862, stating that from the beginning of 1863 all black slaves in states still engaged in rebellion against the federal government would be emancipated. Slaves in border states still remaining loyal to the Union were excluded.

Lincoln had read a preliminary proclamation to his cabinet, who urged him to wait until a major Union victory before delivering it publicly.

Emba river 380 mi/612 km long in the Kazakh Republic, USSR, draining into the N part of the Caspian sea.

embargo the legal prohibition by a government of trade with another country, forbidding foreign ships to leave or enter its ports. Trade embargoes may be imposed on a country seen to be violating international laws.

They also may be used as a tool of bilateral (political) policy, such as the embargo of sensitive technology from the US to the USSR.

embezzlement in law, theft by an employee of property entrusted to him or her by an employer.

embolism blockage of a blood vessel by an obstruction called an embolus (usually a blood clot, fat particle, or bubble of air).

embroidery the art of decorating cloth with colored threads by needle. It includes ◊broderie anglaise, ◊gros point, and ◊petit point; all of which have been used for the adornment of costumes, gloves, book covers, curtains, and ecclesiastical vestments, especially in Europe and Asia.

embryo early development stage of an animal or a plant following fertilization of an ovum (egg cell), or activation of an ovum by ◊parthenogenesis.

In animals the embryo exists either within an egg (where it is nourished by food contained in the yolk), or in mammals, in the ◊uterus of the mother. In mammals (except marsupials) the embryo is fed through the ◊placenta. In humans the term embryo describes the fertilized egg during its first seven weeks of existence; from the eighth week onward it is referred to as a fetus. The plant embryo is found within the seed in higher plants. It sometimes consists of only a few cells, but usually includes a root; a shoot (or primary bud); and one or two ◊cotyledons, which nourish the growing seedling.

embryology the study of the changes undergone by an organism from its conception as a fertilized ovum (egg) to its emergence into the world at hatching or birth. It is mainly concerned with the changes in cell organization in the embryo and the way in which these lead to the structures and organs of the adult (the process of ◊differentiation).

Applications of embryology include embryo transplants, both in commercial applications (for example, in building up a prize dairy-cow herd quickly at low cost) and in obstetric medicine (as a method for helping couples with fertility prob-

embryo

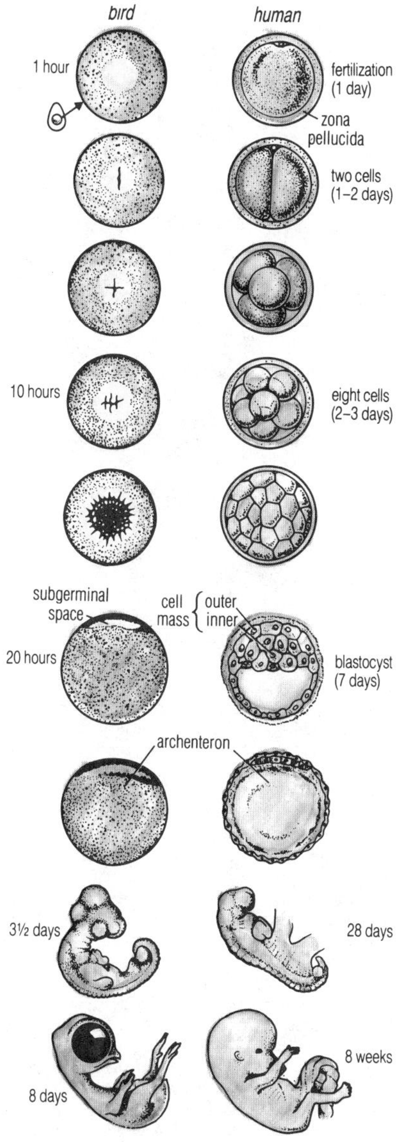
bird
human
1 hour
fertilization
(1 day)
zona
pellucida
two cells
(1–2 days)
10 hours
eight cells
(2–3 days)
subgerminal
space
cell
mass
outer
inner
20 hours
blastocyst
(7 days)
archenteron
3½ days
28 days
8 days
8 weeks

lems to have children). This usually involves the surgical removal of eggs from a female; their fertilization under laboratory conditions; and, once normal development is under way, their placement in the womb.

embryo sac a large cell within the ovule of flowering plants that represents the female ◊gametophyte when fully developed. It typically contains eight nuclei. Fertilization occurs when one of these nuclei, the egg nucleus, fuses with a male ◊gamete.

Emden port in Lower Saxony, Federal Republic of Germany, at the mouth of the river Ems; population (1984) 51,000. It is a fishing port and an export outlet for the river ◊Ruhr, with which it is connected by the Dortmund–Ems canal. There are oil refineries here.

emerald a clear, green gemstone variety of the mineral ◊beryl.

emergent properties features of a system that are due to the way in which its components are structured in relation to each other, rather than to the individual properties of those components. Thus the distinctive characteristics of chemical ◊compounds are emergent properties of the way in which the constituent elements are organized, and cannot be explained by the particular properties of those elements taken in isolation. In biology, ◊ecosystem stability is an emergent property of the interaction between the constituent species, and not a property of the species themselves.

***Emerson** Transendentalist scholar Ralph Waldo Emerson was a poet and essayist in 19th-century New England.*

Emerson Ralph Waldo 1803–1882. US philosopher, essayist, and poet. He settled in Concord, Massachusetts, which he made a center of ◊transcendentalism, and wrote *Nature* 1836, which states the movement's main principles emphasizing the value of self-reliance and the Godlike nature of human souls. His two volumes of *Essays* (1841, 1844) made his reputation; "Self-Reliance" and "Compensation" are among the best known of his essays.

Born in Boston, Massachusetts, and educated at Harvard, Emerson became a Unitarian minister. In 1832 he resigned and traveled to Europe, meeting the British writers Carlyle, Coleridge, and Wordsworth. On his return to Massachusetts in 1833 he settled in Concord. He made a second visit to England 1847 and incorporated his impressions in *English Traits* 1856. Much of his verse was published in the literary magazine *The Dial*. His poems include "The Rhodora," "Threnody," and "Brahma." His later works include *Representative Men* 1850 and *The Conduct of Life* 1870.

emery a grayish-black opaque metamorphic rock consisting of ◊corundum and magnetite, together with other minerals such as hematite. It is used as an ◊abrasive.

emetic any substance administered to induce vomiting.

emf in physics, abbreviation for ◊electromotive force.

Emi Koussi highest point of the Tibesti massif in N Chad, rising to 11,204 ft/3,415 m.

Emilia-Romagna region of N central Italy including much of the Po valley; area 8,531 sq mi/ 22,100 sq km; population (1988) 3,924,000. The capital is Bologna; other towns include Reggio, Rimini, Parma, Ferrara, and Ravenna. Agricultural produce includes fruit, wine, sugar beet, beef, and dairy products; oil and natural-gas resources have been developed in the Po valley.

éminence grise a power behind a throne; that is, a manipulator of power without immediate responsibility. The nickname was originally applied (because of his gray cloak) to the French monk François Leclerc du Tremblay (1577–1638), also known as Père Joseph, who in 1612 became the close friend and behind-the-scenes adviser of Cardinal Richelieu.

eminent domain in the US, the right of federal and state government and other authorized bodies to compulsorily purchase land that is needed for public purposes. The owner is entitled to receive a fair price for the land.

Emin Pasha Mehmed. Adopted name of Eduard Schnitzer 1849–1892. German explorer, doctor, and linguist. Appointed by General Gordon as chief medical officer and then governor of the Equatorial province of S Sudan, he carried out extensive research in anthropology, botany, zoology, and meteorology.

Isolated by his remote location and cut off from the outside world by Arab slave traders, he was "rescued" by an expedition led by H M Stanley in 1889. He traveled with Stanley as far as Zanzibar but returned to continue his work near Lake Victoria. Three years later he was killed by Arabs while leading an expedition to the W coast of Africa.

Emmental district in the valley of the Emme river, Berne, Switzerland, where a hard cheese of the same name has been made since the mid-15th century.

Emmet Robert 1778–1803. Irish nationalist leader. In 1803 he led an unsuccessful revolt in Dublin against British rule and was captured, tried, and hanged. His youth and courage made him an Irish hero.

emotivism a philosophical position in the theory of ethics. Emotivists deny that moral judgments can be true or false, maintaining that they merely express an attitude or an emotional response.

The concept came to prominence during the 1930s, largely under the influence of *Language, Truth and Logic* 1936 by A J ◊Ayer.

Empedocles c. 490–430 BC. Greek philosopher and scientist. He lived at Acragas (Agrigentum) in Sicily, and proposed that the universe is composed of four elements—fire, air, earth, and water—which through the action of love and discord are eternally constructed, destroyed, and constructed anew. According to tradition, he committed suicide by throwing himself into the crater of Mount Etna.

emphysema incurable lung disease characterized by disabling breathlessness. Progressive loss of the thin walls dividing the air spaces (alveoli) in the lungs reduces the area available for the exchange of oxygen and carbon dioxide, causing the lung tissue to swell. The term "emphysema" can also refer to any abnormal swelling of body tissues caused by the accumulation of air.

empiricism (Greek *empeiria* "experience" or "experiment") in philosophy, the belief that all knowledge is ultimately derived from sense experience. It is suspicious of metaphysical schemes based on ◊a priori propositions, which are claimed to be true irrespective of experience. It is frequently contrasted with ◊rationalism.

Empiricism developed in the 17th and early 18th centuries through the work of John ◊Locke, George ◊Berkeley, and David ◊Hume, traditionally known as the British empiricist school.

employment agency agency for bringing together employers requiring labor and workers seeking employment. Employment agencies may be state run, as in state employment services, or private agencies paid either by client companies or by individuals seeking employment.

EMS abbreviation for ◊European Monetary System.

emu flightless bird *Dromaius novaehollandiae* native to Australia. It stands about 6 ft/1.8 m high and has coarse brown plumage, small rudimentary wings, short feathers on the head and neck, and powerful legs, well adapted for running and kicking. The female has a curious bag or pouch in the windpipe that enables her to emit the characteristic loud booming note.

In Western Australia emus are farmed for their meat, skins, feathers, and oil.

emulsifaction in mammals, the process in the small intestine by which bile, secreted from the liver, breaks down fat into microscopically small particles. These tiny droplets, less than 0.5

enamel *Enamel plate showing the Virgin and child.*

micrometers in diameter, are then attacked by the digestive enzyme lipase.

Fat leaves the stomach in the form of large undigested oily droplets but is then emulsified by the bile, produced by the liver, and poured into the duodenum. The products of digestion include fatty acids, and these pass into the intestine wall, accompanied by fat-soluble vitamins. The medical condition of steatorrhea, in which fat is not properly absorbed, is often accompanied by symptoms of vitamin deficiency, showing the link between fat digestion and vitamin absorption.

emulsifier a food ◊additive used to keep oils dispersed and in suspension, in products such as mayonnaise and peanut butter. Egg yolk is a naturally occurring emulsifier, but most of the emulsifiers in commercial use today are synthetic chemicals.

emulsion a type of ◊colloid, consisting of a stable dispersion of a liquid in another liquid—for example, oil and water in some cosmetic lotions.

enabling act a legislative enactment enabling or empowering a person or corporation to take certain actions. Perhaps the best known example of an enabling law was that passed in Germany in March 1933 by the Reichstag and Reichsrat. It granted Adolf Hitler dictatorial powers until April 1937 and effectively terminated parliamentary government in Germany until 1950. The law firmly established the Nazi dictatorship by giving dictatorial powers to the government.

enamel vitrified (glasslike) coating of various colors used for decorative purposes on a metallic or porcelain surface. In ◊cloisonné the various sections of the design are separated by thin metal wires or strips. In champlevé the enamel is poured into engraved cavities in the metal surface.

The ancient art of enameling is believed to be of Near Eastern origin. The Egyptians, Greeks, and Romans enameled their jewelry, and Byzantium was famed for enamels from about the 9th to 11th centuries. The enameled altarpiece at St Mark's, Venice, which was brought from Constantinople, still survives. Byzantine work was emulated in Europe, particularly in Saxony, Brunswick, and in the Rhine valley. German enamelers were later employed in France, and during the 13th and 14th centuries the art was introduced into Italy and China. The chief centers of enameling during the 15th and 16th centuries were the cities of Lorraine and Limoges, France.

encaustic painting an ancient technique of painting, commonly used by the Egyptians, Greeks, and Romans, in which colored pigments were mixed with molten wax and painted on panels.

encephalin naturally occurring chemical produced by nerve cells in the brain that has the same effect as morphine or other derivatives of opium, acting as a natural painkiller. Unlike morphine, encephalins are quickly degraded by the body, so there is no buildup of tolerance to them, and hence no "addiction." Encephalins are a variety of ◊peptides, as are ◊endorphins, which have similar effects.

encephalitis inflammation of the brain, nearly always due to virus infection but also to parasites, fungi, or malaria. It varies widely in severity, from short-lived, relatively slight effects of headache, drowsiness, and fever to paralysis, coma, and death. One such type of viral infection is also sometimes called "sleeping sickness."

Encke's comet the comet with the shortest known orbital period, 3.3 years. It is named after German mathematician and astronomer Johann Franz Encke (1791–1865) who in 1819 calculated the orbit from earlier sightings.

It was first sighted in 1786 by the French astronomer Pierre Méchain (1744–1804). It was rediscovered by ◊Herschel in 1795 and independently by Pons, Huth, and Bouvard in 1805. In 1913, it became the first comet to be observed throughout its entire orbit when it was photographed near ◊aphelion (the point in its orbit furthest from the Sun) by astronomers at Mount Wilson Observatory in California.

encyclical a letter addressed by the pope to Roman Catholic bishops for the benefit of the people. The first was issued by Benedict XIV in 1740, but encyclicals became common only in the 19th century. They may be doctrinal (condemning errors), exhortative (recommending devotional activities), or commemorative.

Recent encyclicals include *Pacem in terris* (Pope John XXIII, 1963), *Sacerdotalis celibatus* (on the celibacy of the clergy, Pope Paul VI, 1967), and *Humanae vitae* (Pope Paul VI, 1967, on methods of contraception).

encyclopedia or encyclopedia work of reference covering either all fields of knowledge or one specific subject. Although most encyclopedias are alphabetical, with cross-references, some are organized thematically with indexes, to keep related subjects together.

The earliest extant encylopedia is the *Historia Naturalis/Natural History* AD 23–79 of ◊Pliny the Elder. The first alphabetical encyclopedia in English was the *Lexicon Technicum/Technical Lexicon* 1704, compiled by John Harris. In 1728 Ephraim Chambers published his *Cyclopedia*, which coordinated scattered articles by a system of cross-references and was translated into French 1743–45. This translation formed the basis of the *Encyclopédie* edited by Diderot and d'Alembert, published 1751–72. By this time the system of engaging a body of expert compilers and editors was established, and in 1768–71 the *Encyclopaedia Britannica* appeared.

American encyclopedias include the *Encyclopedia Americana* and *Collier's Encyclopedia*, both prepared with attention to cultural and stylistic interpretations appropriate to the US.

Encyclopédie encyclopedia in 28 volumes written 1751–72 by a group of French scholars (Encyclopédistes) including D'Alembert and Diderot, inspired by the English encyclopedia produced by Ephraim Chambers 1728. Religious skepticism and ◊Enlightenment social and political views were a feature of the work.

endangered species plant or animal species whose numbers are so few that it is at risk of becoming extinct. Officially designated endangered species are listed by the International Union for the Conservation of Nature (◊IUCN).

An example of an endangered species is the Javan rhinoceros. There are only about 50 alive today and, unless active steps are taken to promote this species' survival, it will probably be extinct within a few decades.

endemic (of a disease) more or less prevalent in a given region or country all the time. It refers most often to tropical diseases, such as ◊malaria, which are hard to eradicate.

Ender Kornelia 1958– . West German swimmer. She won a record-tying four gold medals at the 1976 Olympics at freestyle, butterfly, and relay. She won a total of eight Olympic medals 1972–76.

endocrine gland

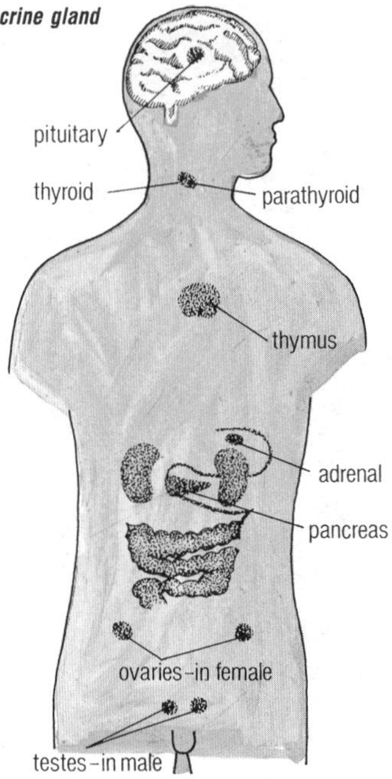
pituitary
thyroid
parathyroid
thymus
adrenal
pancreas
ovaries-in female
testes-in male

She also won a record ten world championship medals 1973 and 1975.

Enders John Franklin 1897–1985. US virologist. With Thomas Weller and Frederick Robbins, he discovered the ability of the polio virus to grow in cultures of various tissues, which led to the perfection of an effective vaccine. The three were awarded the Nobel Prize for Medicine 1954. Enders also succeeded in isolating the measles virus.

endive cultivated annual plant *Cichorium endivia*, family Compositae, the leaves of which are used in salads and cooking. One variety has narrow, curled leaves; another has wide, smooth leaves. It is related to ◊chicory.

endocrine gland gland that secretes hormones into the bloodstream to regulate body processes. Endocrine glands are most highly developed in vertebrates, but are also found in other animals, notably insects. In humans the main endocrine glands are the pituitary, thyroid, parathyroid, adrenal, pancreas, ovary, and testis.

endolymph fluid found in the inner ◊ear, filling the central passage of the cochlea as well as the semicircular canals.

Sound waves traveling into the ear pass eventually through the three small bones of the middle ear and set up vibrations in the endolymph. These are detected by receptors in the cochlea, which send nerve impulses to the hearing centers of the brain.

endometriosis common gynecological complaint in which patches of endometrium (the lining of the womb) are found outside the uterus.

This ectopic (abnormally positioned) tissue is present most often in the ovaries, although it may invade any pelvic or abdominal site, as well as the vagina and rectum. Endometriosis may be treated with analgesics, hormone preparations, or surgery.

endoparasite a ◊parasite that lives inside the body of its host.

endoplasm inner, liquid part of a cell's ◊cytoplasm.

endoplasmic reticulum (ER) a membranous system of tubes, channels and flattened sacs that form compartments within ◊eukaryotic cells. It stores and transports proteins within cells and also carries various enzymes needed for the synthesis of ◊fats. The ◊ribosomes, or the organelles that carry out protein synthesis, are attached to parts of the ER.

Under the electron microscope, ER looks like

a series of channels and vesicles, but it is in fact a large, sealed, baglike structure crumpled and folded into a convoluted mass. The interior of the "bag," the ER lumen, stores various proteins needed elsewhere in the cell, then organizes them into transport vesicles formed by a small piece of ER membrane budding from the main membrane.

endorphin natural substance (a polypeptide) that modifies the action of nerve cells. Endorphins are produced by the pituitary gland and hypothalamus of vertebrates. They lower the perception of pain by reducing the transmission of signals between nerve cells.

Endorphins not only regulate pain and hunger, but are also involved in the release of sex hormones from the pituitary gland. Opiates act in a similar way to endorphins, but are not rapidly degraded by the body, as natural endorphins are, and thus have a long-lasting effect on pain perception and mood.

endoscopy examination of internal organs or tissues by an instrument alloweing direct vision. An endoscope is equipped with an eyepiece, lenses, and its own light source to illuminate the field of vision. The endoscope that examines the alimentary canal is a flexible fiberoptic instrument swallowed by the patient.

endoskeleton the internal supporting structure of vertebrates, made up of cartilage or bone. It provides support, and acts as a system of levers to which muscles are attached to provide movement. Certain parts of the skeleton (the skull and ribs) give protection to vital body organs.

Sponges are supported by a network of rigid, or semirigid, spiky structures called spicules; a bath sponge is the proteinaceous skeleton of a sponge.

endosperm a nutritive tissue in the seeds of most flowering plants. It surrounds the embryo and is produced by an unusual process that parallels the ◊fertilization of the ovum by a male gamete. A second male gamete from the pollen grain fuses with two female nuclei within the ◊embryo sac. Thus endosperm cells are triploid (having three sets of chromosomes); they contain food reserves such as starch, fat, and protein that are utilized by the developing seedling.

In "nonendospermic" seeds, absorption of these food molecules by the embryo is completed early, so that the endosperm has disappeared by the time of germination.

endotherm "warm-blooded," or homeothermic, animal. Endotherms have internal mechanisms for regulating their body temperatures to levels different from the environmental temperature. See ◊homeothermy.

end user a user of a computer program; in particular, someone who uses a program to perform a task (such as accounting or playing a computer game), rather than someone who writes programs (a programmer).

Endymion in Greek mythology, a beautiful young man loved by Selene, the Moon goddess. He was granted eternal sleep in order to remain forever young. The English poet Keats's poem *Endymion* 1818 is an allegory of searching for perfection.

Energiya Soviet shuttle booster, launched May 15, 1987. When fully operational, the Energiya booster will be used to launch the Soviet shuttle Buran, and will be capable, with the use of strap-on boosters, of launching payloads of up to 250 tons/230 tonnes into Earth-orbit.

energy the capacity for doing ◊work. Potential energy (PE) is energy deriving from position; thus a stretched spring has elastic PE; an object raised to a height above the Earth's surface, or the water in an elevated reservoir, has gravitational PE; a lump of coal and a tank of gasoline, together with the oxygen needed for their combustion, have chemical PE (due to relative positions of atoms). Other sorts of PE include electrical and nuclear. Moving bodies possess ***kinetic energy*** (KE). Energy can be converted from one form to another, but the total quantity stays the same (in accordance with the conservation laws that govern many natural phenomena). For example, as an apple falls, it loses gravitational PE but gains KE.

So-called energy resources are stores of convertible energy. Nonrenewable resources include the fossil fuels (coal, oil, and gas) and ◊nuclear fission "fuels" -for example, uranium-235. Renewable resources, such as wind, tidal, and geothermal power, have so far been less exploited. Hydroelectric projects are well established, and wind turbines and tidal systems are being developed. All energy sources depend ultimately on the Sun's energy.

Einstein's special theory of ◊relativity 1905 correlates any gain, E, in KE with a loss, m, in "rest mass," by the equation $E = mc^2$, in which E is energy and c is the speed of light. The equation applies universally, not just to nuclear reactions, although it is only for these that the percentage change in rest mass is large enough to detect. Although energy is never lost, after a number of conversions it tends to finish up as KE of random motion of molecules (of the air, for example) at relatively low temperatures. This is "degraded" energy in that it is difficult to convert it back to other forms.

Burning fossil fuels causes ◊acid rain and is gradually increasing the carbon dioxide content in the atmosphere, with unknown consequences for future generations. Coal-fired power stations also release significant amounts of radioactive material, and the potential dangers of nuclear power stations are greater still.

The ultimate nonrenewable but almost inexhaustible energy source would be nuclear fusion (the way in which energy is generated in the Sun), but controlled fusion may never be harnessed. Harnessing resources generally implies converting their energy into electrical form, because electrical energy is easy to convert to other forms and to transmit from place to place, though not to store.

energy level or ***shell*** or ***orbital*** location of the electrons in an atom. The electrons in each level have a particular energy which is dependent upon the distance of that level from the nucleus of the atom. The levels are numbered beginning with one, the nearest to the nucleus. See ◊orbital, atomic.

energy of reaction energy released or absorbed during a chemical reaction, also called enthalpy of reaction or heat of reaction; it has the symbol ΔH. It is usually quoted in specific terms to indicate the amount of heat involved per mole of reactant in the reaction given by the chemical equation.

In a chemical reaction, the energy stored in the reacting molecules is rarely the same as that stored in the product molecules. Depending on which is the greater, energy is either released (an exothermic reaction) or absorbed (an endothermic reaction) from the surroundings (see ◊conservation of energy). The amount of energy released or absorbed by the quantities of substances represented by the chemical equation is the energy of reaction.

Engadine the upper valley of the river Inn in Switzerland, a winter sports resort.

Engels Friedrich 1820–1895. German social and political philosopher, a friend of, and collaborator with, Karl ◊Marx on *The Communist Manifesto* 1848 and other key works. His later interpretations of Marxism, and his own philosophical and historical studies such as *Origins of the Family, Private Property, and the State* 1884 (which linked patriarchy with the development of private property), developed such concepts as historical materialism. His use of positivism and Darwinian ideas gave Marxism a scientific and deterministic flavor which was to influence Soviet thinking.

In 1842 Engels's father sent him to work in the cotton factory owned by his family in Manchester, England, where he became involved with ◊Chartism. In 1844 his lifelong friendship with Karl Marx began, and together they worked out the materialist interpretation of history and in 1847–48 wrote the *Communist Manifesto.* Returning to Germany during the 1848–49 revolution, Engels worked with Marx on the *Neue Rheinische Zeitung*/New Rhineland Newspaper and fought on the barricades in Baden. After the defeat of the revolution he returned to Manchester, and for the rest of his life largely supported the Marx family.

Engels's first book was *The Condition of the Working Classes in England* 1845. The lessons of 1848 he summed up in *The Peasants' War in Germany* 1850 and *Revolution and Counter-Revolution in Germany* 1851. After Marx's death Engels was largely responsible for the wider dissemination of his ideas; he edited the second and third volumes of Marx's *Das Kapital* 1885 and 1894. Although Engels himself regarded his ideas as identical with those of Marx, discrepancies between their works are the basis of many Marxist debates.

Engel v Vitale a US Supreme Court decision 1962 dealing with the constitutionality of prayer in public schools. The case was brought against the New York Board of Regents for instituting an official daily prayer in the state's public schools. The Court ordered the regents to terminate the program, ruling that the government should not involve itself in the creation of any official religious practice, sectarian or not.

engine a device for converting stored energy into useful work or movement. Most engines use a fuel as their energy store. The fuel is burned to produce heat energy—hence the name "heat engine"—which is then converted into movement. Heat engines can be classifed according to the fuel they use (◊gasoline engine or ◊diesel engine), or according to whether the fuel is burned inside (◊internal combustion engine) or outside (◊steam engine) the engine, or according to whether they produce a reciprocating or rotary motion (◊turbine or ◊Wankel engine).

engineering the application of science to the design, construction, and maintenance of works, machinery, roads, railroads, bridges, harbor installations, engines, ships, aircraft and airports, spacecraft and space stations, and the generation, transmission and use of electrical power. The main divisions of engineering are aerospace, chemical, civil, electrical, electronic, gas, marine, materials, mechanical, mining, production, radio, and structural engineering.

engineering drawing technical drawing that forms the plans for the design and construction of engineering components and structures. Engineering drawings show different projections, or views of objects, with the relevant dimensions, and show how all the separate parts fit together.

England: history for pre-Roman history, see ◊Britain, ancient.

5th–7th centuries Anglo-Saxons overran all England except Cornwall and Cumberland, forming independent kingdoms including Northumbria, Mercia, Kent, and Wessex.

Engels *Friedrich Engels is famous for his collaboration with Karl Marx on* The Communist Manifesto *and for his work on Marx's* Das Kapital.

c. 597 England converted to Christianity by St Augustine.
829 Egbert of Wessex accepted as overlord of all England.
878 Alfred ceded N and E England to the Danish invaders but kept them out of Wessex.
1066 Norman Conquest; England passed into French hands under William the Conqueror.
1172 Henry II became king of Ireland and established a colony there.
1215 King John forced to sign Magna Carta.
1284 Conquest of Wales, begun by the Normans, completed by Edward I.
1295 Model Parliament set up.
1338–1453 Hundred Years' War with France enabled Parliament to secure control of taxation and, by impeachment, of the king's choice of ministers.
1348–49 Black Death killed about 30% of the population.
1381 Social upheaval led to the ◊Peasants' Revolt, which was brutally repressed.
1399 Richard II deposed by Parliament for absolutism.
1414 Lollard revolt repressed.
1455–85 Wars of the Roses.
1497 Henry VII ended the power of the feudal nobility with the suppression of the Yorkist revolts.
1529 Henry VIII became head of the Church of England after breaking with Rome.
1536–43 Acts of Union united England and Wales after conquest.
1547 Edward VI adopted Protestant doctrines.
1553 Reversion to Roman Catholicism under Mary I.
1558 Elizabeth I adopted a religious compromise.
1588 Attempted invasion of England by the Spanish Armada.
1603 James I united the English and Scottish crowns; parliamentary dissidence increased.
1642–52 Civil War between royalists and parliamentarians, resulting in victory for Parliament.
1649 Charles I executed and the Commonwealth set up.
1653 Oliver Cromwell appointed Lord Protector.
1660 Restoration of Charles II.
1685 Monmouth rebellion.
1688 William of Orange invited to take the throne; flight of James II.
1707 Act of Union between England and Scotland under Queen Anne, after which the countries became known as Great Britain.

For further history, see ◊United Kingdom.

English native to or an inhabitant of England, part of Britain, as well as their descendants, culture, and language. The English have a mixed cultural heritage combining Celtic, Anglo-Saxon, Norman, and Scandinavian elements.

English architecture the style of building in England. The main styles are: Saxon, Norman, Early English (of which Westminster Abbey is an example), Decorated, Perpendicular (15th century), Tudor (usually applied to domestic buildings of c. 1485–1558), Jacobean, Stuart (including the Renaissance and Queen Anne styles), Georgian, the Gothic revival of the 19th century, Modern, and Postmodern. Notable architects include Christopher Wren, Inigo Jones, John Vanbrugh, Nicholas Hawksmoor, Charles Barry, Edwin Lutyens, Hugh Casson, Basil Spence, Frederick Gibberd, Denys Lasdun, and Richard Rogers.

Roman period (55 BC–AD 410) Stretches of Hadrian's Wall remain, and excavations continue to reveal the forums, basilicas, baths, villas amd mosaic pavements spread across the country.

Anglo-Saxon period (449–1066) Much of the architecture of this period, being of timber, has disappeared. The stone church towers that remain, such as at Earls Barton, appear to imitate timber techniques with their "long and short work" and triangular arches.

Norman period (1066–1189) William the Conqueror inaugurated an enormous building program. He brought the Romanesque style of round arches, massive cylindrical columns and thick walls. At Durham Cathedral, the rib vaults (1093) were an invention of European importance in the development of the Gothic style.

Gothic architecture Early English (1189–1307) began with the very French east end of Canterbury cathedral designed in 1175 by William of Sens, and attained its English flowering in the cathedrals of Wells, Lincoln, and Salisbury. A simple elegant style of lancet windows, deeply carved moldings, and slender, contrasting shafts of Purbeck marble. Decorated (1307–77) is characterized by a growing richness in carving and a fascination with line. The double curves of the ogee arch, elaborate window tracery, and vault ribs woven into star patterns may be seen in buildings such as the Lady Chapel at Ely and the Angel Choir at Lincoln. The gridded and panelled cages of light of the Perpendicular (1377–1485) style are a dramatic contrast to the Decorated period. Lacking the richness and invention of the 14th century, they convey, however, an often impressive sense of unity, space and power. The chancel of Gloucester cathedral is early Perpendicular whereas Kings College chapel, Cambridge, is late Perpendicular.

Tudor and Elizabethan period (1485–1603) This period saw the Perpendicular style interwoven with growing Renaissance influence. Buildings develop a conscious symmetry elaborated with continental Pattenbrook details. Hybrid and exotic works result such as Burghley House and Hardwick Hall (1591–97).

Jacobean (1603–25) This period showed scarcely more sophistication.

English Renaissance: Stuart period The provincial scene was revolutionized by Inigo ◊Jones with the Queens House, Greenwich 1616, and the Banqueting House, Whitehall 1619. Strict Palladianism appeared among the half-timber and turrets of Jacobean London. With ◊Wren a more mannered classicism evolved showing French Renaissance influence, for example St Paul's cathedral (1675–1710). Under Wren's pupils Hawksmoor and ◊Vanbrugh, theatrical Baroque style emerged, as in Blenheim Palace 1705–20.

Georgian architecture Lord ◊Burlington, reacting against the Baroque, inspired a revival of the pure Palladian style of Inigo Jones. William ◊Kent, also a Palladian, invented the picturesque garden as at Rousham, Oxfordshire. Alongside the great country houses, an urban architecture evolved of plain, well-proportioned houses, defining elegant streets and squares. The second half of the century mingled Antiquarian and Neo-Classical influences, exquisitely balanced in the works of Robert ◊Adam at Kedleston Hall (1757–70). John ◊Nash carried Neo-Classicism into the new century. By the dawn of the Victorian era this had become a rather bookish Greek Revival, for example the British Museum (1823–47).

19th century Throughout the century classic and gothic engaged with Victorian earnestness in the "Battle of the Styles": Gothic for the Houses of Parliament (1840–60), Renaissance for the Foreign Office (1860–75). Meanwhile, the great developments in engineering and the needs of new types of buildings, such as railroad stations, transformed the debate. ◊Paxton's prefabricated Crystal Palace (1850–51) was the most remarkable building of the era. The Arts and Crafts architects, Philip ◊Webb and Norman ◊Shaw, brought renewal and simplicity inspired by William Morris.

20th century The early work of ◊Lutyens and the white rendered houses of ◊Voysey such as Broadleys, Windermere (1898–99), maintained the Arts and Crafts spirit of natural materials and simplicity. Norman Shaw, however, developed an Imperial Baroque style.

After World War I classicism again dominated, grandly in Lutyens' New Delhi government buildings (1912–31). There was often a clean Scandinavian influence as in the RIBA building, London (1932–34), which shows growing Modernist tendencies. Modernism arrived fully with continental refugees such as Lubetkin (1901–), the founder of the Tecton architectural team that designed London Zoo (1934–38).

The strong social dimension of English 20th-century architecture is best seen in the New Town movement. Welwyn Garden City was begun in 1919 and developed after World War II. The latest of the New Towns, Milton Keynes, was designated 1967. Recently English architects have again achieved international recognition, for example Norman ◊Foster and Richard ◊Rogers for their High-Tech innovatory Lloyds Building (1979–84). James ◊Stirling maintains a Modernist technique and planning while absorbing historicist and contextural concerns.

English art painting and sculpture of England.

painting Medieval English painting was chiefly religious and included wall paintings and illuminated manuscripts.

portrait painting Portrait painting was taken to new levels at the court of Henry VIII by the German artist Hans Holbein. At the court of Queen Elizabeth I, Nicholas Hilliard established a tradition of miniature painting. The Flemish Anthony van Dyck, employed as a court painter by Charles I from 1632, greatly influenced English portrait painters. Joshua Reynolds, Thomas Gainsborough, and Thomas Lawrence are among the best known of the late 18th and early 19th centuries. In the 20th century, Graham Sutherland, Lucian Freud, and David Hockney painted many portraits.

social satire In the 18th century William Hogarth and Thomas Rowlandson used art as a way of criticizing the customs and behavior of contemporary society in styles suggesting political cartoons.

animal painting An indigenous form is the sporting picture, George Stubbs being the great 18th-century exponent.

landscape painting Among painters specializing in landscape were Richard Wilson in the 18th century and, in the 19th, the watercolorists Samuel Palmer, John Constable, and J W M Turner. The 20th century is reflected in the war-ravaged landscapes of Paul Nash and the multifigure townscapes of L S Lowry.

the Pre-Raphaelites Millais, Holman Hunt, and Rossetti were founding members, painting literary and genre scenes in the mid-19th century.

Impressionism J M Whistler, the American who settled in London and introduced the doctrine of "art for art's sake," had as his disciple W R Sickert, who helped introduce Impressionism to England.

Modernism This style ranges from the scenes of British work and village life by Stanley Spencer to the tortured figures of Francis Bacon.

Pop art A movement influenced by mass media images, pop art began in the mid-1950s with the work of Richard Hamilton and Peter Blake.

sculpture: ancient Early Celtic and Roman work predominate.

medieval Some ecclesiastical stone, wood, and ivory sculptures survived the destruction of the churches and monasteries during the ◊Reformation.

17th-18th centuries The woodcarvings of Grinling Gibbons are found in stately homes and St Paul's cathedral. One of the first widely known English sculptors was the Neo-Classicist John Flaxman.

19th century Academic portraits were produced by Francis Chantrey and Frederick Leighton.

20th century The stylized stone figures of Jacob Epstein and Eric Gill led toward the abstract forms of Henry Moore and Barbara Hepworth. Anthony Caro and Eduardo Paolozzi have used industrial metals and machine components to create their diverse and dramatic styles since the 1960s.

English horn alternate name for ◊cor anglais, musical instrument of the oboe family.

English language member of the Germanic branch of the Indo-European language family. It developed through four major stages over about 1,500 years: ◊Old English or Anglo-Saxon (c. 500–1050), rooted in the dialects of settling invaders (Jutes, Saxons, Angles, and Danes); Middle English (c. 1050–1550), influenced by Norman French after the Conquest 1066 and by ecclesiastical Latin; Early Modern English (c. 1550–1700), standardization of the diverse influences of Middle English; and Late Modern English (c. 1700 onward), the development and spread of current Standard English. Through extensive exploration, colonization, and trade, English spread worldwide from the 17th century onward and remains the most important international language of trade and technology. It is used in many variations, for example, British, Australian, American, Canadian, West Indian, Indian, Singaporean, and Nigerian English, and many pidgins and creoles.

historical roots The ancestral forms of English were dialects brought from the NW coastlands of Europe to Britain by Angle, Saxon, and Jutish invaders who gained footholds in the SE in the 5th century and over the next 200 years extended and consolidated their settlements from S England to the middle of Scotland. Scholars distinguish four main early dialects: of the Jutes in Kent, the Saxons in the south, the Mercians or S Angles in the Midlands, and the Northumbrians or N Angles north of the Humber. Until the Danish invasions 9th–11th centuries, Old English was a highly inflected language but appears to have lost many of its grammatical endings in the interaction with Danish, creating a more open or analytic style of language that was further changed by the influence of Norman French after the Conquest 1066. For several centuries English was in competition with other languages: first the various Celtic languages of Britain, then Danish, then French as the language of Plantagenet England and Latin as the language of the Church. In Scotland, English was in competition with Gaelic and Welsh as well as French and Latin.

In 1362 English replaced French as the language of the law courts of England, although the records continued for some time to be kept in Latin. Geoffrey Chaucer was a court poet at this time and strongly influenced the literary style of the London dialect. When William Caxton set up his printing press in London 1477 the new hybrid language (vernacular English mixed with courtly French and scholarly Latin) became increasingly standardized, and by 1611, when the Authorized (King James) Version of the Bible was published, the educated English of the Home Counties and London had become the core of what is now called Standard English. Great dialect variation remained, and still remains, throughout Britain.

By the end of the 16th century, English was firmly established in four countries: England, Scotland, Wales, and Ireland, and with the establishment of the colonies in North America in the early 17th century was spoken in what are now the US, Canada, and the West Indies. Seafaring, exploration, commerce, and colonial expansion in due course took both the standard language and other varieties throughout the world. By the time of Johnson's dictionary 1755 and the American Declaration of Independence 1776, English was international and recognizable as the language we use today.

current usage English spelling was more or less established by 1650, and, in England in particular, a form of standard educated speech (known as Received Pronunciation) spread out in the 19th century from the major public (private) schools. This accent was adopted in the early 20th century by the BBC for its announcers and readers and is variously known as RP, BBC English, Oxford English, and the King's or Queen's English. It was the socially dominant accent of the British Empire and retains prestige as a model for those learning the language. In the UK, however, it is no longer as sought after as it once was.

Generally, Standard English today does not depend on accent but rather on shared educational experience, mainly of the printed language. Modern English is an immensely varied language, having absorbed material from many other tongues. It is spoken by more than 300 million native speakers, and between 400 and 800 million foreign users. It is the official language of air transport and shipping; the leading language of science, technology, computers, and commerce; and a major medium of education, publishing, and international negotiation. For this reason scholars frequently refer to its latest phase as World English.

English law one of the major European legal systems, ◊Roman law being the other. English law has spread to many other countries, including former English colonies such as the US, Canada, Australia, and New Zealand.

English law has a continuous history dating from the local customs of the Anglo-Saxons, traces of which survived until 1925. After the Norman Conquest there grew up, side by side with the Saxon shire courts, the feudal courts of the barons and the ecclesiastical courts. From the king's council developed the royal courts, presided over by professional judges, which gradually absorbed the jurisdictions of the baronial and ecclesiastical courts. By 1250 the royal judges had amalgamated the various local customs into the system of ◊common law—that is, law common to the whole country. A second system known as ◊equity developed in the Court of Chancery, in which the Lord Chancellor considered petitions.

In the 17th–18th centuries, common law absorbed the Law Merchant, the international code of mercantile customs. During the 19th century virtually the whole of English law was reformed by legislation; for example, the number of capital offenses was greatly reduced.

A unique feature of English law is the doctrine of judicial ◊precedents, whereby the reported decisions of the courts form a binding source of law for future decisions. A judge is bound by decisions of courts of superior jurisdiction but not necessarily by those of inferior courts.

English literature the earliest surviving English literature is in the form of Old English poems—*Beowulf* and the epic fragments *Finesburh*, *Waldhere*, *Deor*, and *Widsith*—that reflect the heroic age and Germanic legends of the 4th–6th centuries, although probably not written down until the 7th century. Heroic elements survive in elegiac lyrics, for example, *The Wanderer*, *The Seafarer*, and in many poems with a specifically Christian content, such as *The Dream of the Rood*; and the Saints' Lives, for example, *Elene*, by the 8th-century poet Cynewulf. These poems are all written in unrhymed alliterative meter. The great prose writers of the early period were the Latin scholars Bede, Aldhelm, and Alcuin. King Alfred founded the tradition of English prose with his translations and his establishment of the Anglo-Saxon Chronicle.

With the arrival of a Norman ruling class at the end of the 11th century, the ascendancy of Norman-French in cultural life began, and it was not until the 13th century that the native literature regained its strength. Prose was concerned chiefly with popular devotional use, but verse emerged typically in the metrical chronicles, such as Layamon's *Brut*, and the numerous romances based on the stories of Charlemagne, the Arthurian legends, and the Classical episodes of Troy. First of the great English poets was Chaucer, whose early work reflected the predominant French influence, but later that of Renaissance Italy. Of purely native inspiration was *The Vision of Piers Plowman* of Langland in the old alliterative verse, and the anonymous *Pearl*, *Patience*, and *Gawayne and the Grene Knight*.

Chaucer's mastery of versification was not shared by his successors, the most original of whom was Skelton. More successful were the anonymous authors of songs and carols, and of the ballads, which (for example those concerned with Robin Hood) often formed a complete cycle. Drama flowered in the form of ◊miracle and ◊morality plays, and prose, although still awkwardly handled by Wycliffe in his translation of the Bible, rose to a great height with Malory in the 15th century.

The Renaissance, which had first touched the English language through Chaucer, came to delayed fruition in the 16th century. Wyatt and Surrey used the sonnet and blank verse in typically Elizabethan forms and prepared the way for Spenser, Sidney, Daniel, Campion, and others. With Kyd and Marlowe, drama emerged into theatrical form; it reached the highest level in Shakespeare and Jonson. Elizabethan prose is represented by Hooker, North, Ascham, Holinshed, Lyly, and others, but English prose achieved full richness in the 17th century, with the King James Version of the Bible 1611, Bacon, Milton, Bunyan, Taylor, Browne, Walton, and Pepys. Most renowned of the 17th-century poets were Milton and Donne; others include the religious writers Herbert, Crashaw, Vaughan, and Traherne, and the Cavalier poets Herrick, Carew, Suckling, and Lovelace. In the Restoration period Butler and Dryden stand out as poets. Dramatists include Otway and Lee in tragedy. Comedy flourished with Congreve, Vanbrugh, and Farquhar.

The 18th century is known as the Augustan Age in English literature. Pope developed the poetic technique of Dryden; in prose Steele and Addison evolved the polite essay, Swift used satire, and Defoe exploited his journalistic ability. This century saw the development of the ◊novel, through the epistolary style of Richardson to the robust narrative of Fielding and Smollett, the comic genius of Sterne, and the Gothic "horror" of Horace Walpole. The Neo-Classical standards established by the Augustans were maintained by Johnson and his circle—Goldsmith, Burke, Reynolds, Sheridan, and others—but the romantic element present in the work of poets Thomson, Gray, Young, and Collins was soon to overturn them.

The *Lyrical Ballads* 1798 of Wordsworth and Coleridge were the manifesto of the new Romantic age. Byron, Shelley, and Keats form a second generation of Romantic poets. In fiction Scott took over the Gothic tradition from Mrs Radcliffe, to create the ◊historical novel, and Jane Austen established the novel of the comedy of manners. Criticism gained new prominence in Coleridge, Lamb, Hazlitt, and De Quincey.

During the 19th century the novel was further developed by Dickens, Thackeray, the Brontës, George Eliot, Trollope, and others. The principal poets of the reign of Victoria were Tennyson, Robert and Elizabeth Browning, Arnold, the Rossettis, Morris and Swinburne. Among the prose writers of the era are Macaulay, Newman, Mill, Carlyle, Ruskin, and Pater. The transition period at the end of the century saw the poetry and novels of Meredith and Hardy; the work of Butler and Gissing; and the plays of Pinero and Wilde.

Although a Victorian, Gerald Manley Hopkins anticipated the 20th century with the experimentation of his verse forms. Poets of World War I include Sassoon, Brooke, Owen, and Graves. A middle-class realism developed in the novels of Wells, Bennett, Forster, and Galsworthy while the novel's break with traditional narrative and exposition came through the Modernists James Joyce, D H Lawrence, Virginia Woolf, Somerset Maugham, Aldous Huxley, Christopher Isherwood, Evelyn Waugh, and Graham Greene. Writers for the stage include Shaw, Galsworthy,

J B Priestley, Coward, and Rattigan, and the writers of poetic drama, such as T S Eliot, Fry, Auden, Isherwood, and Dylan Thomas. The 1950s and 1960s produced the "kitchen sink" dramatists, including Osborne and Wesker. The following decade saw the rise of Harold Pinter, John Arden, Tom Stoppard, Peter Shaffer, Joe Orton, and Alan Ayckbourn. Poets since 1945 include Thom Gunn, Roy Fuller, Philip Larkin, Ted Hughes, and John Betjeman; novelists include William Golding, Iris Murdoch, Angus Wilson, Muriel Spark, Margaret Drabble, Kingsley Amis, Anthony Powell, Alan Sillitoe, Anthony Burgess, John Fowles, Ian McEwan, Angela Carter, Doris Lessing, and Martin Amis.

English-Speaking Union society for promoting the fellowship of the English-speaking peoples of the world, founded in 1918 by Evelyn Wrench.

engraving the art of creating a design by means of inscribing blocks of metal, wood, or some other hard material with a point. Intaglio prints are made mainly on metal by ◊dry point, and ◊etching.

enhanced radiation weapon another name for the ◊neutron bomb.

Enid city in N central Oklahoma, N of Oklahoma City, seat of Garfield county. It is a processing and marketing center for the surrounding region's poultry, cattle, dairy farms, and oil wells; population (1990) 45,309. Enid was founded 1893, when land in the Cherokee Strip region, which was originally put aside for Indian tribes, was opened to white settlement.

Eniwetok atoll in the ◊Marshall Islands, in the central Pacific Ocean; population (1980) 453. It was taken from Japan by the US 1944, which made the island a naval base; 43 atomic tests were conducted there from 1947. The inhabitants were resettled at Ujelang, but insisted on returning home in 1980. Despite the clearance of nuclear debris and radioactive soil to the islet of Runit, high radiation levels persisted.

Enlightenment a European intellectual movement that reached its high point in the 18th century. Enlightenment thinkers were believers in social progress and in the liberating possibilities of rational and scientific knowledge. They were often critical of existing society and were hostile to religion, which they saw as keeping the human mind chained down by superstition.

The American and French revolutions were justified by Enlightenment principles of human natural rights. Leading representatives of the Enlightenment were ◊Voltaire, ◊Lessing, and ◊Diderot.

enlightenment in Buddhism, the term used to translate the Sanskrit *bodhi*, awakening: perceiving the reality of the world, or the unreality of the self, and becoming liberated from suffering (Sanskrit *duhkha*). It is the gateway to nirvana.

Ennius Quintus 239–169 BC. Early Roman poet who wrote tragedies based on the Greek pattern. His epic poem *Annales* deals with Roman history.

enosis (Greek "union") the movement, developed from 1930, for the union of ◊Cyprus with Greece.

Enschede textile manufacturing center in Overijssel province, the Netherlands; population (1988) 145,000, urban area of Enschede-Hengelo 250,000.

Ensor James 1860–1949. Belgian painter and printmaker. His bold style uses strong colors to explore themes of human cruelty and the macabre, as in the *Entry of Christ into Brussels* 1888 (Musée Royale des Beaux-Arts, Brussels) and anticipated Expressionism.

ENT in medicine, an abbreviation for ear, nose, and throat. It is usually applied to a specialized clinic or hospital department.

entail in law, the settlement of land or other property on a successive line of people, usually succeeding generations of the original owner's family. An entail can be either general, in which case it simply descends to the heirs, or special, when it descends according to a specific arrangement—for example, to children by a named wife.

Entails are increasingly rare and the power to make them has often been destroyed by legislation—for example, restrictions in certain states of the US. In England entails can be easily terminated.

Entebbe town in Uganda, on the NW shore of Lake Victoria, 12 mi/20 km SW of Kampala, the capital; 3,728 ft/1,136 m above sea level; population (1983) 21,000. Founded 1893, it was the administrative center of Uganda 1894–1962.

In 1976, a French aircraft was hijacked by a Palestinian liberation group. It was flown to Entebbe airport, where the hostages on board were rescued six days later by Israeli troops.

Entente Cordiale (French "friendly understanding") the agreement reached by Britain and France 1904 recognizing British interests in Egypt and French interests in Morocco. It formed the basis for Anglo-French cooperation before the outbreak of World War I 1914.

enteric in medicine, of the intestine, an old term used to qualify infective fevers such as ◊typhoid and paratyphoid.

enterprise zone special zones designated by government to encourage industrial and commercial activity, usually in economically depressed areas. Investment is attracted by means of tax and other financial incentives.

In the US, enterprise zones were an important part of the early Reagan administration's plan to encourage private investment in inner-city and other economically depressed areas. It was also a step in the process of reducing government involvement in the economy. The plan called for the creation of up to 25 zones a year for a 3-year period. Tax incentives would reduce by as much as 75% the corporate income taxes, and capital-gains taxes would be eliminated entirely for participating businesses.

entomology the study of ◊insects.

entrechat (French "cross-caper") in ballet, criss-crossing of the legs while the dancer is in the air. There are two movements for each beat. Wayne Sleep broke ◊Nijinsky's record of an *entrechat dix* (five beats) with an *entrechat douze* (six beats) 1973.

entrepreneur in business, a person who successfully develops and manages an enterprise through personal skill and initiative. Examples include John D ◊Rockefeller and Henry ◊Ford.

entropy in ◊thermodynamics, a parameter representing the state of disorder of a system at the atomic, ionic, or molecular level; the greater disorder, the higher the entropy. Thus the fast-moving disordered molecules of water vapor have higher entropy than those of more ordered liquid water, which in turn have more entropy than the molecules in solid crystalline ice.

In a closed system undergoing change, entropy is a measure of the amount of energy unavailable for useful work. At ◊absolute zero (–459.67°F/–273°C/0K), when all molecular motion ceases and order is assumed to be complete, entropy is zero.

enucleation in medicine, surgical removal of a complete organ or tumor; for example, the eye from its socket.

Enugu town in Nigeria, capital of Anambra state; population (1983) 228,400. It is a coal-mining center, with steel and cement works, and is linked by rail with Port Harcourt.

envelope in geometry, a curve that touches all the members of a family of lines or curves. For example, a family of three equal circles all touching each other and forming a triangular pattern (like a clover leaf) has two envelopes: a small circle that fits in the space in the middle, and a large circle that encompasses all three circles.

Enver Pasha 1881–1922. Turkish politician and soldier. He led the military revolt 1908 that resulted in the Young Turk's revolution (see ◊Turkey). He was killed fighting the Bolsheviks in Turkestan.

environment in ecology, the sum of conditions affecting a particular organism, including physical surroundings, climate, and influences of other living organisms. See also ◊biosphere and ◊habitat.

In common usage, "the environment" often means the total global environment, without reference to any particular organism. In genetics, it is the external influences that affect an organism's development, and thus its ◊phenotype.

environmentalism a theory emphasizing the primary influence of the environment on the development of groups or individuals. It stresses the importance of the physical, biological, psychological or cultural environment as a factor influencing the structure or behavior of animals, including humans. In politics this has given rise to ◊Green parties, which aim to "preserve the planet and its people," in several countries.

Environmental Protection Agency US agency set up 1970 to control water and air quality, industrial and commercial wastes, pesticides, noise, and radiation. In its own words, it aims to protect "the country from being degraded, and its health threatened, by a multitude of human activities initiated without regard to long-ranging effects upon the life-supporting properties, the economic uses, and the recreational value of air, land, and water."

environment art large sculptural or spatial works that create environments that the spectator may enter. The US artists Jim ◊Dine and Cles ◊Oldenburg in the 1960s were early exponents.

environment–heredity controversy see ◊nature–nurture controversy

enzyme a biological ◊catalyst produced in cells, and capable of speeding up the chemical reactions necessary for life. Enzymes are not themselves destroyed by this process. They are large, complex ◊proteins, and are highly specific, each chemical reaction requiring its own particular enzyme. Digestive enzymes include ◊amylases (which digest starch), ◊lipases (which digest fats), and ◊proteases (which digest protein). Other enzymes play a part in the conversion of food energy into ◊ATP; the manufacture of all the molecular components of the body; the replication of ◊DNA when a cell divides; the production of hormones; and the control of movement of substances into and out of cells.

The activity and efficiency of enzymes are influenced by various factors, including temperature and pH conditions. Temperatures above 140°F/60°C damage (denature) the intricate structure of enzymes, causing reactions to cease. Each enzyme operates best within a specific pH range, and is denatured by excessive acidity or alkalinity.

Enzymes have many medical and industrial uses, from laundry products to drug manufacture, and as research tools in molecular biology. They can be extracted from bacteria and molds, and ◊genetic engineering now makes it possible to tailor the enzyme for a specific purpose, and greatly increase the rate of production.

Eocene second epoch of the Tertiary period of geologic time, 55–38 million years ago. Originally considered the earliest division of the Tertiary, the name means "early recent," referring to the early forms of mammals evolving at the time, following the extinction of the dinosaurs.

EOKA acronym for Ethnikí Organósis Kipriakóu Agónos (National Organization of Cypriot Struggle), an underground organization formed by General George ◊Grivas 1955 to fight for the independence of Cyprus from Britain and ultimately its union (*enosis*) with Greece. In 1971, 11 years after the independence of Cyprus, Grivas returned to the island to form EOKA B and to resume the fight for *enosis*, which had not been achieved by the Cypriot government.

eolian referring to sediments carried, formed, eroded, or deposited by the wind. Such sediments include desert sands and dunes as well as deposits of windblown silt, called loess, carried long distances from deserts and from stream sediments derived from the melting of glaciers.

eolith a chipped stone, once thought to have been manufactured as a primitive tool during the Old Stone Age, but now generally believed to be the result of natural processes, for the most part.

Eos in Greek mythology, the goddess of the dawn, equivalent to the Roman Aurora.

Eötvös Roland von, Baron 1848–1919. Hungarian scientist, born in Budapest, who investigated problems of gravitation, and constructed the double-armed torsion balance for determining variations of gravity.

eotvos unit unit (abbreviation E) for measuring small changes in the intensity of the Earth's ◊gravity with horizontal distance.

Epaminondas c. 420–362 BC. Theban general and politician who won a decisive victory over the Spartans at Leuctra 371. He was killed at the moment of victory at Mantinea.

Epernay town in Marne *département*, Champagne-Ardenne region, France; population (1986) 29,000. It is the center of the champagne industry.

ephedrine drug that acts like adrenaline on the sympathetic ◊nervous system (sympathomimetic). Once used to relieve bronchospasm in ◊asthma, it has been superseded by safer, more specific drugs. It is contained in some cold remedies as a decongestant. Side effects include rapid heartbeat, tremor, dry mouth, and anxiety.

Ephedrine is an alkaloid, $C_{10}H_{15}NO_1$, derived from Asian gymnosperms (genus *Ephedra*) or synthesized. It is sometimes misused; in 1990 an Australian truck driver collided with a coach after taking ephedrine to stay awake. Excess leads to mental confusion and increased confidence in one's own capabilities as they actually decline.

ephemeral plant a plant with a very short life cycle, sometimes as little as six or eight weeks. It may complete several generations in one growing season.

A number of common weeds are ephemerals—for example, many groundsels (ragworts and squaw-weeds) *Senecio* and many desert plants. The latter take advantage of short periods of rain to germinate and reproduce, passing the dry season as dormant seeds.

Ephesians ◊epistle in the New Testament attributed to ◊Paul but possibly written after his death; the earliest versions are not addressed specifically to the church at Ephesus.

Ephesus ancient Greek seaport in Asia Minor, a center of the ◊Ionian Greeks, with a temple of Artemis destroyed by the Goths AD 262.

In the 2nd century AD Ephesus had a population of 300,000. Now in Turkey, it is one of the world's largest archeological sites. St Paul visited the city, and addressed a letter (◊epistle) to the Christians there.

epic a narrative poem or cycle of poems dealing with some great deed—often the founding of a nation or the forging of national unity—and often using religious or cosmological themes. The two major epic poems in the Western tradition are *The Iliad* and *The Odyssey*, attributed to Homer, and which were probably intended to be chanted in sections at feasts.

Greek and later criticism, which considered the Homeric epic the highest form of poetry, produced the genre of secondary epic—such as the *Aeneid* of Virgil, Tasso's *Jerusalem Delivered*, and Milton's *Paradise Lost*—which attempted to emulate Homer, often for a patron or a political cause. The term is also applied to narrative poems of other traditions: the Anglo-Saxon *Beowulf* and the Finnish *Kalevala*; in India the *Ramayana* and *Mahabharata*; and the Babylonian *Gilgamesh*. All of these evolved in different societies to suit similar social needs and used similar literary techniques.

epicenter the point on the Earth's surface immediately above the seismic focus of an ◊earthquake. Most damage usually takes place at an earthquake's epicenter. The term sometimes refers to a point directly above or below a nuclear explosion ("at ground zero").

Epictetus c. AD 55–135. Greek Stoic philosopher who encouraged people to refrain from self-interest and to promote the common good of humanity. He believed that people were in the hands of an all-wise providence and that they should endeavor to do their duty in the position to which they were called.

Born at Hierapolis in Phrygia, he lived for many years in Rome as a slave but eventually secured his freedom. He was banished by the emperor ◊Domitian from Rome in AD 89.

Epicureanism system of philosophy that claims soundly based human happiness is the highest good, so that its rational pursuit should be adopted. It was named after the Greek philosopher Epicurus. The most distinguished Roman Epicurean was ◊Lucretius.

Epicurus 341–270 BC. Greek philosopher, founder of Epicureanism, who taught at Athens from 306 BC.

epicyclic gear or sun-and-planet gear gear system that consists of one or more gear wheels moving around another. Epicyclic gears are found in bicycle hub gears and in automatic gearboxes.

epicycloid in geometry, a curve resembling a series of arches traced out by a point on the circumference of a circle that rolls around another circle of a different diameter. If the two circles have the same diameter, the curve is a ◊cardioid.

If the radius of the inner circle is R and that of the rotating circle r, the epicycloid will have n cusps if $R = nr$ ($n = 1,2,3,\ldots$).

epicycloid *a seven cusped epicycloid*

Epidaurus or ***Epidavros*** ancient Greek city and port on the E coast of Argolis, in the NE Peloponnese. The site contains a well-preserved amphitheater of the 4th century BC; nearby are the ruins of the temple of Aesculapius, the god of healing.

Epidaurus *This ancient Theater at Epidaurus, Greece, was built by the architect Polycleitos and seats 14,000.*

epidemic outbreak of infectious disease affecting large numbers of people at the same time. A widespread epidemic that sweeps across many countries (such as the ◊Black Death in the late Middle Ages) is known as a ***pandemic***.

epidermis the outermost layer of ◊cells on an organism's body. In plants and many invertebrates such as insects, it consists of a single layer of cells. In vertebrates, it consists of several layers of cells. The epidermis of plants and invertebrates often has an outer noncellular ◊cuticle that protects the organism from desiccation. In vertebrates such as reptiles, birds, and mammals, the outermost layer of cells is dead, forming a tough, waterproof layer, which is sloughed off continuously or shed periodically.

epigeal seed germination in which the ◊cotyledons are borne above the soil.

epiglottis a small flap found in the throats of mammals. It moves during swallowing to prevent food from passing into the windpipe and causing choking.

The action of the epiglottis is a highly complex reflex process involving two phases. During the first stage a mouthful of chewed food is lifted by the tongue toward the top and back of the mouth. This is accompanied by the cessation of breathing and by the blocking of the nasal areas from the mouth. The second phase involves the epiglottis moving over the larynx while the food passes down into the esophagus.

epigram a short poem, originally a religious inscription but later a short, witty, and pithy saying.

The form was common among writers of ancient Rome, including Catullus and Martial. In English, the epigram has been employed by Ben Jonson, Herrick, Pope, Swift, Yeats, and Ogden Nash.

epigraphy (Greek *epigráphein* "to write on") the art of writing with a sharp instrument on hard, durable materials such as stone; also the scientific study of epigraphical writings or inscriptions.

epilepsy medical disorder characterized by a tendency to develop fits, which are convulsions or abnormal feelings caused by abnormal electrical discharges in the cerebral hemispheres of the ◊brain. Epilepsy can be controlled with a number of ◊anticonvulsant drugs.

Epileptic fits can be classified into four categories. The first two are generalized, where the abnormal discharges affect the whole of the cerebrum; the second two are focal in nature, involving a particular area of the cortex. In grand mal, a vague feeling of uneasiness leads to a phase of generalized stiffening (the tonic phase), followed by a phase of generalized jerking (the clonic phase). A brief period of unconsciousness follows, and finally drowsiness that may last several hours. Petit mal occurs almost exclusively in school-age children; the child stops, stares, and pales slightly. The attack lasts only a few seconds. About 5% of children will have a fit at some time in their lives, but most of these are isolated instances caused by feverish illnesses. Jacksonian fits begin with jerking in a small area of the body, for example the angle of the mouth or the thumb. They may spread to involve the whole of one side of the body. After the fit, the affected limbs may be paralyzed for several hours. Temporal-lobe fits result in hallucinations and feelings of unreality. They may also cause disordered speech and impaired consciousness.

Epilepsy is more common in the Third World, with up to 30 sufferers per 1,000 people in some areas; in industrialized countries the figure is 3–5 per 1,000.

Most epileptics have infrequent fits that have little impact on their daily lives. Epilepsy does not imply that the sufferer has any impairment of intellect, behavior, or personality.

Epimetheus in Greek mythology, "After-thought," the brother of ◊Prometheus and husband of ◊Pandora.

Epinal capital of Vosges *département,* on the river Moselle, France. Population (1982) 40,954. A cotton-textile center, it dates from the 10th century.

Epiphany festival of the Christian church, held Jan 6, celebrating the coming of the Magi (the three Wise Men) to Bethlehem with gifts for the infant Jesus, and symbolizing the manifestation of Jesus to the world. It is the 12th day after Christmas, and marks the end of the Christmas festivities.

In many countries the night before Epiphany, called Twelfth Night, is marked by the giving of gifts. In the Eastern Orthodox Church, the festival celebrated on this day is known as the theophany and commemorates the baptism of Jesus.

epiphyte any plant that grows on another plant or object above the surface of the ground, and has no roots in the soil.

An epiphyte does not parasitize the plant it grows on but merely uses it for support. Its nutrients are obtained from rainwater, organic debris such as leaf litter, or from the air. The greatest diversity of epiphytes is found in tropical areas and includes many orchids.

Epirus (Greek "mainland") country of ancient Greece; the N part was in Albania; the remainder, in NW Greece, was divided into four provinces—Arta, Thesprotia, Yanina, and Preveza.

Epirus (Greek *Ipiros*) region of NW Greece; area 3,551 sq mi/9,200 sq km; population (1981) 325,000. Its capital is Yannina, and it consists of the provinces (nomes) of Arta, Thesprotia, Yannina, and Preveza. There is livestock farming.

episcopacy in the Christian church, a system of government in which administrative and spiritual power over a district (diocese) is held by a bishop.

The Roman Catholic, Eastern Orthodox, Anglican, and Episcopal churches are episcopalian; episcopacy also exists in the Lutheran Church of Scandinavia and of the US, where bishops are elected for districts called "synods," and in most branches of the American Methodist Church, where bishops are supervisory officials.

Episcopalianism US term for the Anglican Communion.

episiotomy incision made in the perineum (the tissue bridging the vagina and rectum) to facilitate childbirth and prevent tearing of the vagina.

epistemology a branch of philosophy that examines the nature of knowledge and attempts to determine the limits of human understanding. Central issues include how knowledge is derived and how it is to be validated and tested.

epistle in the New Testament, any of the 21 letters to individuals or to the members of various churches written by Christian leaders, including the 13 written by St ◊Paul. The term also describes a letter with a suggestion of pomposity and literary affectation, and a letter addressed to someone in the form of a poem, as in the epistles of ◊Horace and ◊Pope.

The epistolary novel, a story told as a series of (fictitious) letters, was popularized by Samuel ◊Richardson in the 18th century.

EPLF abbreviation for Eritrean People's Liberation Front; see ◊Eritrea.

EPNS abbreviation for electroplated nickel silver; see ◊electroplating.

epoch a subdivision of a geologic period in the geologic time scale. Epochs are sometimes given their own names (such as the Paleocene, Eocene, Oligocene, Miocene, and Pliocene epochs comprising the Tertiary period), or they are referred to as the late, early, or middle portions of a given period (as the Late Cretaceous or the Middle Triassic epoch).

epoxy resin synthetic ◊resin used as an ◊adhesive and as an ingredient in paints. Household epoxy resin adhesives come in component form as two separate tubes of chemical, one tube containing resin, the other a curing agent (hardener). The two chemicals are mixed just before application, and the mix soon sets hard.

EPROM (acronym from erasable programmable read-only memory) computer memory device in the form of a chip that can record data and retain it indefinitely. The data can be erased by exposure to ultraviolet light, and new data added. Other kinds of memory are ◊ROM, ◊PROM, and ◊RAM.

Epsilon Aurigae an ◊eclipsing binary star in the constellation Auriga. One of the pair is an "ordinary" star, but the other seems to be an enormous distended object whose exact nature remains unknown. The period is 27 years, the longest of its kind. The last eclipse was 1982–84.

Epsom town in Surrey, England; population (1981) 68,535. In the 17th century it was a spa producing Epsom salts. There is a racecourse, where the Derby and the Oaks horse races are held. The site of Henry VIII's palace of Nonsuch was excavated in 1959.

Epsom salts $MgSO_4 \cdot 7H_2O$ hydrated magnesium sulfate, used as a relaxant and laxative and added to baths to soothe the skin. The name is derived from a bitter saline spring at Epsom, Surrey, England, which contains the salt in solution.

Epstein Jacob 1880–1959. British sculptor, born in New York. He experimented with abstract forms, but is chiefly known for muscular nude figures such as *Genesis* 1931 (Whitworth Art Gallery, Manchester).

EPSTEIN
14

Epstein *Sculptor Jacob Epstein is noted for his abstract forms and his muscular nudes. Here he stands near his statue* Lazarus.

In 1904 he moved to England, where most of his major work was done. An early example showing the strong influence of ancient sculptural styles is the angel over the tomb of Oscar Wilde 1912 (Père Lachaise cemetery, Paris), while *Rock Drill* 1913–14 (Tate Gallery, London) is Modernist and semiabstract. Such figures outraged public sensibilities. He was better appreciated as a portraitist (bust of Einstein, 1933), and in later years executed several monumental figures, notably the expressive bronze of *St Michael and the Devil* 1959 (Coventry Cathedral).

equal opportunities the right to be employed or considered for employment without discrimination on the grounds of age, race, gender, physical or mental handicap.

equation mathematical expression that represents the equality of two expressions involving constants and/or variables, and thus usually includes an equals sign (=). For example, the equation $A = \pi r^2$ equates the area A of a circle of radius r to the product πr^2. The algebraic equation $y = mx + c$ is the general one in coordinate geometry for a straight line.

If a mathematical equation is true for all variables in a given domain, it is sometimes called an identity and denoted by ≡. Thus $(x + y)^2 \equiv x^2 + 2xy + y^2$ for all $x, y \in R$.

An ***indeterminate equation*** is an equation for which there is an infinite set of solutions—for example, $2x = y$. A diophantine equation is an indeterminate equation in which the solution and terms must be whole numbers (after Diophantus of Alexandria, c. AD 250).

equations of motion mathematical equations that give the position and velocity of a moving object at any time. Given the mass of an object, the forces acting on it, and its initial position and velocity, the equations of motion are used to calculate its position and velocity at any later time. The equations must be based on ◊Newton's laws

Equatorial Guinea
Republic of
(República de Guinea Ecuatorial)

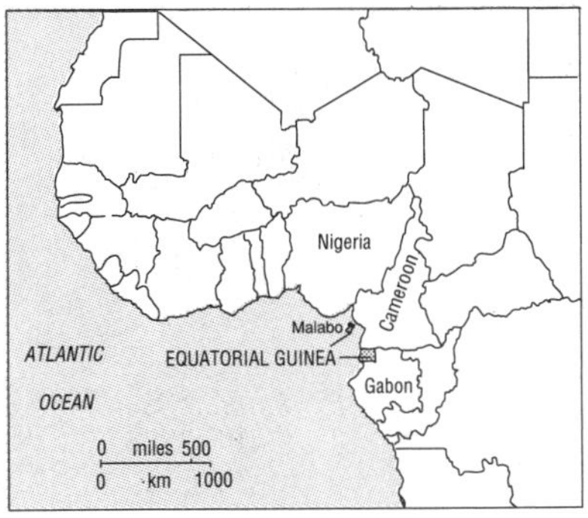
Nigeria
Cameroon
Malabo
ATLANTIC
OCEAN
EQUATORIAL GUINEA
Gabon
0 miles 500
0 km 1000

area 10,828 sq mi/28,051 sq km
capital Malabo (Bioko)
cities Bata and Mbini (Río Muni)
physical comprises mainland Río Muni, plus the small islands of Corisco, Elobey Grande and Elobey Chico, and Bioko (formerly Fernando Po) together with Annobón (formerly Pagalu)
features volcanic mountains on Bioko
head of state and government Teodoro Obiang Nguema Mbasogo from 1979
political system one-party military republic
political parties Democratic Party of Equatorial Guinea (PDGE), militarily controlled
exports cocoa, coffee, timber
currency ekuele; CFA franc
population (1988 est) 336,000 (plus 110,000 estimated to live in exile abroad); growth rate 2.2% p.a.
life expectancy men 44, women 48
language Spanish (official); pidgin English is widely spoken, and on Pagalu (whose people were formerly slaves of the Portuguese) a Portuguese dialect; Fang and other African dialects spoken on Río Muni
religion nominally Christian, mainly Catholic, but in 1978 Roman Catholicism was banned
literacy 55% (1984)
GDP $90 million (1987); $220 per head
chronology
1778 Bioko Island ceded to Spain.
1885 Mainland territory came under Spanish rule; colony known as Spanish Guinea.
1968 Independence achieved from Spain. Francisco Macias Nguema became first president, soon assuming dictatorial powers.
1979 Macias overthrown and replaced by his nephew, Teodoro Obiang Nguema Mbasogo, who established a military regime. Macias tried and executed.
1982 Obiang elected president for another seven years. New constitution adopted, promising a return to civilian government.
1989 Obiang reelected president.

of motion or, if speeds near that of light are involved, on the theory of ◊relativity.

equator the terrestrial equator is the ◊great circle whose plane is perpendicular to the Earth's axis (the line joining the poles). Its length is 24,901.8 mi/40,092 km, divided into 360 degrees of longitude. The ***celestial equator*** is the circle in which the plane of the Earth's equator intersects the ◊celestial sphere.

Equatorial Guinea country in W central Africa, bounded N by Cameroon, E and S by Gabon, and W by the Atlantic Ocean; also five offshore islands including the island of Bioko off the coast of Cameroon.

government The 1973 constitution was suspended in a military coup 1979, after which a supreme military council ruled by decree. In 1982 a new constitution was approved by referendum, providing for a president and a house of representatives of the people, elected by universal suffrage for a five-year term. The house of representatives sat for the first time 1983, its 41 members all nominated by the president and elected unopposed. The president governs with the supreme military council; a transition to civil, constitutional government is promised. All political parties have been banned.

history The area was inhabited by Pygmies before the 1200s, followed by various ethnic groups settling the mainland and islands. Reached by Portuguese explorers 1472, the islands came under Spanish rule in the mid-1800s and the mainland territory of Rio Muni (now Mbini) in 1885, the whole colony being known as Spanish Guinea. From 1959 the territory was a Spanish Overseas Province, with internal autonomy from 1963.

After 190 years of Spanish rule, Equatorial Guinea became fully independent 1968, with Francisco Macias Nguema as president with a coalition government. In 1970 he banned all political parties and replaced them with one, the United National Party (PUN). Two years later he declared himself president-for-life and established a dictatorship, controlling press and radio and forbidding citizens to leave the country. There were many arrests and executions 1976–77. He also established close relations with the Soviet bloc.

In 1979 he was overthrown in a coup by his nephew, Lt-Col Teodoro Obiang Nguema Mbasogo, with at least the tacit approval of Spain. Macias was tried and executed. Obiang expelled the Soviet advisers and technicians and renewed economic and political ties with Spain. He banned PUN and other political parties and ruled through a supreme military council. Coups against him 1981 and 1983 were unsuccessful. In 1982 a new constitution promised a return to civilian rule, but Mbasogo remained in power into the 1990s, ruling as president.

equestrianism skill in horse riding, as practiced under International Equestrian Federation rules. An Olympic sport, there are three main branches of equestrianism: show jumping, three-day eventing, and dressage.

Showjumping is horse jumping over a course of fences. The winner is usually the competitor with fewest "faults" (penalty marks given for knocking down or refusing fences), but in timed competitions it is the competitor completing the course most quickly, additional seconds being added for mistakes.

Three-Day Eventing tests the all-round abilities of a horse and rider in dressage, testing a horse's response to control; cross-country, testing speed and endurance; and showjumping, in a final modified contest.

Dressage tests the horse's obedience skills and control of the rider. Tests consist of a series of movements at walk, trot, canter, with each movement marked by judges who look for suppleness, balance and the special harmony between rider and horse. The term is derived from the French "dresser" which means training. It became an Olympic sport in 1960.

The World Championship was first held in 1953 for men, and 1965 for women; since 1978 for both concurrently.

Equiano Olaudah 1745–1797. African antislavery campaigner and writer. He traveled widely as a free man. His autobiography, *The Interesting Narrative of the Life of Olaudah Equiano, or Gustavus Vassa, the African* 1789, is one of the earliest significant works by an African written in English.

Equiano was born near the river Niger in what is now Nigeria, captured at the age of ten and sold to slavers, who transported him to the West Indies. He learned English and bought his freedom at the age of 21. He subsequently sailed to the Mediterranean and the Arctic, before being appointed commissary of stores for freed slaves returning to Sierra Leone. He was an active campaigner against slavery.

equilateral of a geometrical figure, having all sides of equal length.

For example, a rhombus is an equilateral parallelogram. An equilateral triangle is also equiangular, which means that all three angles are equal as well.

equilibrium in physics, an unchanging condition in which the forces acting on a particle or system of particles (a body) cancel out, or in which energy is distributed among the particles of a system in the most probable way; or the state in which a body is at rest or moving at constant velocity. A body is in thermal equilibrium if no heat enters or leaves it, so that all its parts are at the same temperature as its surroundings.

equinox the points in spring and autumn at which the Sun's path, the ◊ecliptic, crosses the celestial equator, so that day and night are of approximately equal length. The vernal equinox occurs about March 21 and the autumnal equinox, Sept 23.

Equity a shortened term for the American Actors' Equity Association, the labor union for professional actors in the theater.

equity a company's assets, less its liabilities, that are the property of the owner or shareholders. Popularly, equities are stocks and shares that do not pay interest at fixed rates but pay dividends based on the company's performance. The value of equities tends to rise over the long term, but in the short term they are a risk investment because of fluctuating values. Equity also is used to refer to the paid value of mortgaged real property, most commonly a house.

With changes in US tax regulations, from the late 1980s, home-equity loans (second mortgages) have become a very popular financial tool, since the interest is, like mortgage interest, tax deductible.

era any of the major divisions of geologic time, each including several periods, but smaller than an eon. The currently recognized eras all fall within the Phanerozoic eon—or the vast span of time, starting about 590 million years ago, when fossils are found to become abundant. The eras in ascending order are the Paleozoic, Mesozoic, and Cenozoic. We are living in the Recent epoch of the Quaternary period of the Cenozoic era.

Erasmus Desiderius c. 1466–1536. Dutch scholar and leading humanist of the Renaissance era, he

IMAGO·ERASMI·ROTERODAMI·AB·ALBERTO·DVRERO·AD VIVAM·EFFIGIEM·DELINIATA·
·MDXXVI·

***Erasmus** An engraving by the German artist Dürer, of Desiderius Erasmus, the Renaissance Dutch scholar and theologian.*

taught and studied all over Europe and was a prolific writer. His pioneer translation of the Greek New Testament 1516 exposed the Vulgate as a second-hand document. Although opposed to dogmatism and abuse of church power, he remained impartial during Martin ◊Luther's conflict with the pope.

Erasmus was born in Rotterdam, and as a youth he was a monk in an Augustinian monastery near Gouda. After becoming a priest, he went to study in Paris 1495. He paid the first of a number of visits to England 1499, where he met the physician Thomas Linacre, the politician Thomas More, and the Bible interpreter John Colet, and for a time was professor of divinity and Greek at Cambridge University. He edited the writings of St Jerome, and published *Colloquia* (dialogues on contemporary subjects) in 1519. In 1521 he went to Basel, Switzerland, where he edited the writings of the early Christian leaders.

Erasmus Prize prize awarded annually since 1958 to outstanding contributors to international understanding, usually in social or cultural fields. Previous winners include Martin Buber, Herbert Read, Robert Schuman, and Jan Tinbergen.

Erastianism the belief that the church should be subordinated to the state. The name is derived from Thomas Erastus (1534–1583), a German-Swiss theologian and opponent of Calvinism, who maintained in his writings that the church should not have the power of excluding people as a punishment for sin.

Eratosthenes c. 276–194 BC. Greek geographer and mathematician, whose map of the ancient world was the first to contain lines of latitude and longitude, and who calculated the Earth's circumference with an error of about 10%. His mathematical achievements include a method for duplicating the cube, and for finding ◊prime numbers (Eratosthenes" sieve).

erbium soft, lustrous, grayish, metallic element of the ◊lanthanide series, symbol Er, atomic number 68, atomic weight 167.26. It occurs with yttrium or as a minute part of various minerals. Named after the town of Ytterby, Sweden, where the rare-earth elements were first found, it was discovered in 1843 by Carl Mosander (1797–1858).

Erebus in Greek mythology, the god of darkness and the intermediate region between upper Earth and ◊Hades.

Erebus, Mount the world's southernmost active volcano, 12,452 ft/3,794 m high, on Ross Island, Antarctica.

It contains a lake of molten lava, that scientists are investigating in the belief that it can provide a "window" onto the magma beneath the Earth's crust.

Erfurt city in Federal Republic of Germany on the river Gera, capital of the state of Thuringia; population (1990) 217,000. It is in a rich horticultural area, and its industries include textiles, typewriters, and electrical goods.

ergonomics the study of the relationship between people and the furniture, tools, and machinery they use at work. The object is to improve work performance by removing sources of muscular stress and general fatigue; for example, by presenting data and control panels in easy-to-view form, making office furniture comfortable, and creating a generally pleasant environment.

ergosterol substance that, under the action of the sun's ultraviolet rays on the skin, gives rise to the production of vitamin D—a vitamin that helps in calcium and phosphorus metabolism, promotes bone-formation and in children prevents ◊rickets. ***Ergosterol*** $C_{28}H_{43}OH$ ***is a*** ◊sterol that occurs in ergot (hence the name), yeast and other fungi, and some animal fats. The principal source of commercial ergosterol is yeast.

ergot certain parasitic fungi (especially of the genus *Claviceps*), whose brown or black grainlike masses replace the kernels of rye or other cereals. *C. purpurea* attacks the rye plant. Ergot poisoning is caused by eating infected bread, resulting in burning pains, gangrene, and convulsions.

The large grains of the fungus contain the alkaloid ergotamine.

ergotamine an ◊alkaloid $C_{33}H_{35}O_5N_5$ administered to treat migraine and to induce childbirth. Isolated from ergot, a fungus that colonizes rye, it relieves symptoms by causing the cranial arteries to constrict. Its use is limited by severe side effects, including nausea and abdominal pain.

Erhard Ludwig 1897–1977. West German Christian Democrat politician, chancellor of the Federal Republic 1963–66. The "economic miracle" of West Germany's recovery after World War II is largely attributed to Erhard's policy of social free enterprise (German *Marktwirtschaft*), which he initiated during his period as federal economics minister (1949–63).

erica in botany, any plant of the genus *Erica*, family Ericaceae, including the heathers. There are about 500 species, distributed mainly in South Africa with some in Europe.

Ericsson John 1803–1889. Swedish-born US engineer who took out a patent to produce screw-propeller powered paddle-wheel ships in 1836. He built a number of such ships, including the *Monitor*, which was successfully deployed during the Civil War.

Ericsson Leif c. AD 1000. Norse explorer, son of Eric the Red, who sailed west from Greenland about 1000 to find a country first sighted by Norsemen in 986. Landing with 35 companions in North America, he called it Vinland, because he discovered grape vines growing there.

The story was confirmed 1963 when a Norwegian expedition, led by Helge Ingstad, discovered remains of a Viking settlement (dated about 1000) near the fishing village of L'Anse-aux-Meadows at the northern tip of Newfoundland.

Eric the Red 940–1010. Allegedly the first European to find Greenland. According to a 13th-century saga, he was the son of a Norwegian chieftain, who was banished from Iceland about 982 for murder and then sailed westward and discovered a land that he called Greenland.

Eridanus the sixth-largest constellation, which meanders from the celestial equator deep into the southern hemisphere of the sky. Its brilliant star, Achernar, is the ninth-brightest star in the entire sky. It represents a river.

Eridu ancient city of Mesopotamia about 5000 BC, according to tradition the cradle of Sumerian civilization. On its site is now the village of Tell Abu Shahrain, Iraq.

Erie city and port on the Pennsylvania bank of Lake Erie; population (1990) 108,718. It has heavy industries and a trade in iron, grain, and freshwater fish. A French fort was built on the site 1753, and a permanent settlement was laid out 1795.

Erie, Lake fourth largest of the Great Lakes of North America, connected to Lake Ontario by the Niagara River and bypassed by the Welland Canal; area 9,930 sq mi/25,720 sq km. It is linked to Lake Huron by Lake St Clair and the St Clair and Detroit rivers and to the Hudson River by the New York State Barge Canal. It is an important component of the St Lawrence Seaway. Lake Erie ports include Cleveland and Toledo, Ohio; Erie, Pennsylvania; and Buffalo, New York. A US naval victory near the W end of the lake on Sept 9, 1813, forced the British to evacuate Detroit. The shallowest of the Great Lakes, Lake Erie has become severely polluted from industrial and municipal waste.

Erigena Johannes Scotus 815–877. Medieval philosopher. He was probably Irish and, according to tradition, traveled in Greece and Italy. The French king Charles II (the Bald) invited him to France (before 847), where he became head of the court school. He is said to have visited Oxford, to have taught at Malmesbury, and to have been stabbed to death by his pupils. In his philosophy, he defied church orthodoxy in his

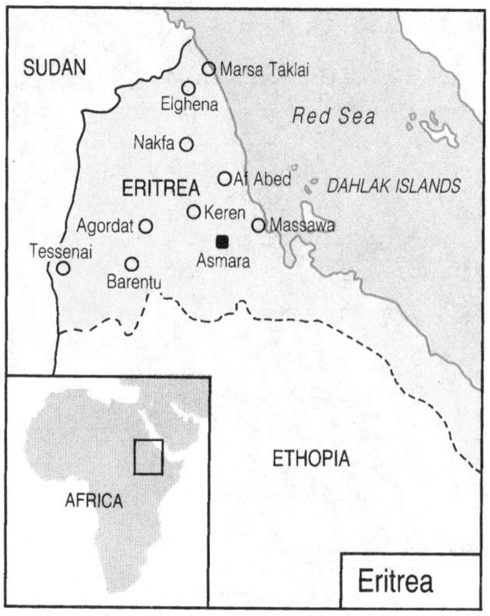
SUDAN
Marsa Taklai
Elghena
Red Sea
Nakfa
ERITREA
Af Abed
DAHLAK ISLANDS
Keren
Agordat
Massawa
Tessenai
Barentu
Asmara
ETHOPIA
AFRICA
Eritrea

writings on cosmology and predestination and tried to combine Christianity with Neo-Platonism.

Erin poetic name for Ireland, derived from the dative case Érinn of the Gaelic name Ériu, possibly derived from Sanskrit "western."

Erinyes in Greek mythology, another name for the ◊Furies.

Eritrea province of N Ethiopia
area 45,394 sq mi/117,600 sq km
capital Asmara
towns Assab and Massawa (Ethiopia's outlets to the sea)
physical coastline on the Red Sea 620 mi/1,000 km; narrow coastal plain that rises to an inland plateau
products coffee, salt, citrus fruits, grains, cotton
population (1984) 2,615,000
language Amharic (official)
religion Islam
history part of an ancient Ethiopian kingdom until the 7th century; under Ethiopian influence until it fell to the Turks mid-16th century; Italian colony 1889–1941, where it was the base for Italian invasion of Ethiopia; under British administration from 1941 to 1952, when it became an autonomous part of Ethiopia. Since 1962, when it became a region, various secessionist movements have risen. During civil war 1970s, guerrillas held most of Eritrea; Ethiopian government, backed by Soviet and Cuban forces, recaptured most towns 1978. Resistance continued throughout the 1980s, aided by conservative Gulf states, and some cooperation with guerrillas in Tigray province. The collapse of Ethiopia's government in 1991 led to the recognition of Eritrea's right to seek independence.

Erivan alternative transliteration of ◊Yerevan, capital of Armenian Republic, USSR.

Erlangen industrial city in Bavaria, Federal Republic of Germany; population (1988) 100,000.

Erl-King in Germanic folklore, the king of the elves. He inhabited the Black Forest and lured children to their deaths. The Romantic writer J W Goethe's poem "Erlkönig" was set to music by Franz Schubert 1816.

ermine short-tailed weasel *Mustela erminea*, of the N hemisphere, whose winter coat becomes white. In N latitudes the coat becomes completely white, except for a black tip to the tail, but in warmer regions the back may remain brownish. The alternate Eurasian name "stoat" is used especially during the summer, when the coat is brown. The fur is used commercially.

Ernst Max 1891–1976. German artist who worked in France 1922–38 and in the US from 1941. He was an active Dadaist, experimenting with collage, photomontage, and surreal images, and helped found the Surrealist movement 1924. His paintings are highly diverse.

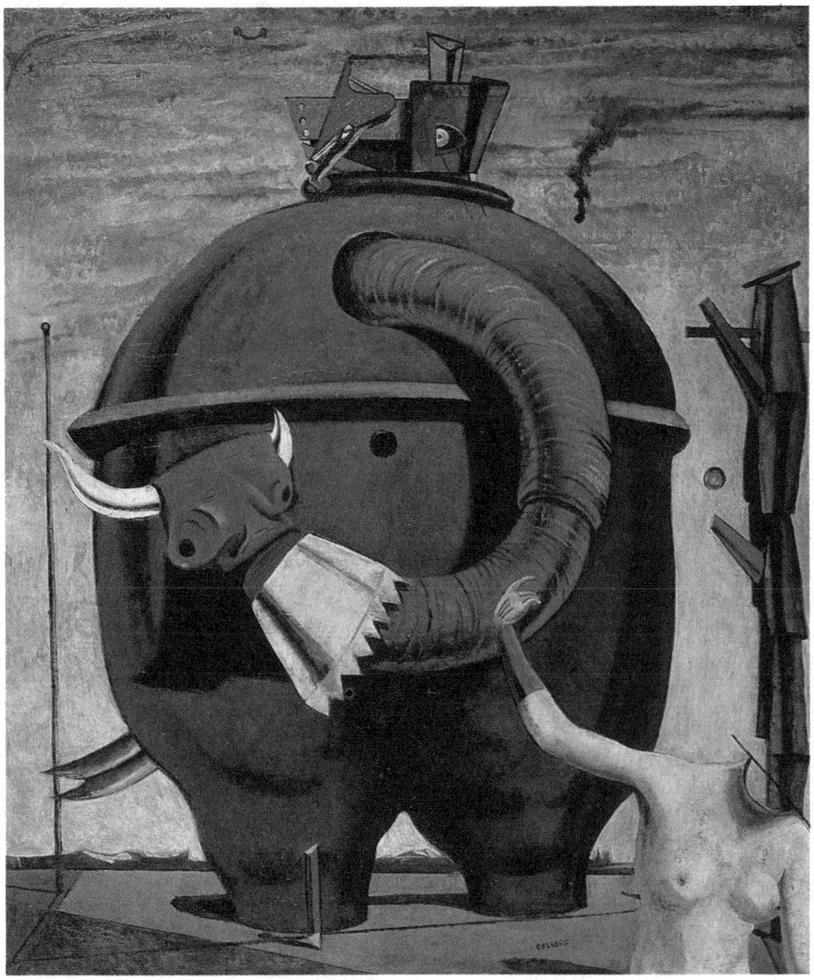

Ernst The Elephant Celébès *(1921), Tate Gallery, London.*

Ernst first exhibited in Berlin in 1916. He produced a "collage novel," *La Femme cent têtes* 1929, worked on films with Dali and Buñuel, and designed sets and costumes for Diaghilev and the Ballets Russes. His pictures range from smooth Surrealist images to highly textured emotive abstracts, from 1925 making use of frottage (rubbing over textured materials).

Eros in Greek mythology, boy-god of love, traditionally armed with bow and arrows. He was the son of Aphrodite (Roman, Venus), and fell in love with ◊Psyche. He is identified with the Roman Cupid.

Eros in astronomy, an asteroid, discovered 1898, 14 million mi/22 million km from the Earth at its nearest point. Eros was the first asteroid to be discovered that has an orbit coming within that of Mars. It is elongated, measures about 22 × 7 mi/36 × 12 km, rotates around its shortest axis every 5.3 hours, and orbits the Sun every 1.8 years.

erosion the processes whereby the rocks and soil of the Earth's surface are loosened, worn away, and transported (◊weathering does not involve transportation). There are two types, chemical and physical. Chemical erosion involves the alteration of the mineral component of the rock, by means of rainwater or the substances dissolved in it, and its subsequent movement. Physical erosion involves the breakdown and transportation of exposed rocks by physical forces. In practice the two work together. The decay of granite by the conversion of its feldspar minerals into clay by carbonic acid in rainwater, and the dissolving of limestone into caves and potholes, are examples of chemical erosion. The shattering of cliff faces in mountainous areas by the expansion of frost in the rock cracks, and the movement of boulders in an avalanche, are examples of physical erosion. Water, consisting of sea waves and currents, rivers, and rain; ice, in the form of glaciers, frost, and melting snow; and wind, hurling sand fragments against exposed rocks and moving dunes along, are the most potent forces of erosion. People also contribute to erosion by bad farming practices and the cutting down of forests, which can lead to the formation of dust bowls.

error detection in computing, the techniques that enable a program to detect incorrect data. A common method is to add a check digit to important codes, such as account numbers and product codes. The digit is chosen so that the code conforms to a rule that the program can verify. Another technique involves calculating the sum (called the ◊hash total) of each instance of a particular item of data and storing it at the end of the data.

Ershad Hussain Mohammad 1930– . Military ruler of Bangladesh 1982–90. He became chief of staff of the Bangladeshi army 1979 and assumed power in a military coup 1982. As president from 1983, Ershad introduced a successful rural-oriented economic program. He was reelected 1986 and lifted martial law, but faced continuing political opposition. Forced by unrest to resign in Dec 1990, he was convicted of weapons possession 1991.

erysipelas acute disease of the skin or mucous membranes due to infection by a streptococcus. Starting at some point where the skin is broken or injured, the infection spreads, producing a swollen red patch with small blisters and generalized fever. The condition is now rare.

erythrocyte another name for ◊red blood cell.

erythromycin an antibiotic with the chemical formula $C_{37}H_{67}NO_{13}$, isolated from a red-pigmented soil bacterium, *Streptomyces erythreus*. It is used in the treatment of a wide range of bacterial diseases and usually administered orally in the form of various salts and esters.

Erzgebirge (German "ore mountains") mountain range on the German-Czech frontier, where the rare metals uranium, cobalt, bismuth, arsenic, and antimony are mined. Some 90 mi/145 km long, its highest summit is Mount Klinovec (Keilberg), 4,080 ft/1,244 m, in Czechoslovakia.

Erzurum capital of Erzurum province, NE Turkey; population (1985) 253,000. It is a center of agricultural trade and mining and has a military base.

ESA abbreviation for ◊European Space Agency.

Esaki Leo 1925– . Japanese physicist who in 1957 noticed that electrons could sometimes "tunnel" through the barrier formed at the junctions of certain semiconductors. The effect is now widely used in the electronics industry. For this early success Esaki shared the 1973 Nobel Prize for Physics with Brian ◊Josephson and Ivar Glever (1929–).

Esarhaddon King of Assyria from 680 BC, when he succeeded his father ◊Sennacherib. He conquered Egypt 674–71 BC.

Esau in the Old Testament, the son of Isaac and Rebekah, and the hirsute elder twin brother of Jacob. Jacob tricked the blind Isaac into giving him the blessing intended for Esau by putting on goatskins for Isaac to feel. Earlier Esau had sold his birthright to Jacob for a "mess of red pottage." Esau was the ancestor of the Edomites.

Esbjerg port of Ribe county, Denmark, on the W coast of Jutland; population (1988) 81,000. It is the terminus of links with Sweden and the UK and is a base for Danish North Sea oil exploration.

escalator automatic moving staircase that carries people between floors or levels. It consists of treads linked in an endless belt arranged to form strips (steps), powered by an electric motor that moves both steps and handrails at the same speed. Toward the top and bottom the steps flatten out for ease of passage. The first escalator was exhibited in Paris 1900.

escape velocity minimum velocity with which an object must be projected for it to escape from the gravitational pull of a planetary body. In the case of the Earth, the escape velocity is 6.9 mps/11.2 kps; the Moon 1.5 mps/2.4 kps; Mars 3.1 mps/5 kps; and Jupiter 37 mps/59.6 kps.

escheat (Old French *escheir* "to fall") in feudal society, the reversion of lands to the lord in the event of the tenant dying without heirs or being convicted for treason. By the later Middle Ages in W Europe, tenants had insured against their lands escheating by granting them to trustees, or feoffees, who would pass them on to the grantor nominated in the will.

Lands held directly by the king could not legally be disposed of in this way.

Escher Maurits Cornelis 1902–1972. Dutch graphic artist. His prints are often based on mathematical concepts and contain paradoxes and illusions. The lithograph *Ascending and Descending* 1960, with interlocking staircases creating a perspective puzzle, is typical.

escrow (Old French *escroe*, "scroll") in law, a document sealed and delivered to a third party and not released or coming into effect until some condition has been fulfilled or performed, whereupon the document takes full effect.

Money deposited with a neutral third party to be delivered when conditions of a contract are fulfilled, as in real estate transactions, is commonly referred to as escrow.

Esenin or Yesenin, Sergey 1895–1925. Soviet poet, born in Konstantinovo (renamed Esenino in his honor). He went to Petrograd 1915, attached himself to the Symbolists, welcomed the Russian Revolution, revived peasant traditions and folklore, and initiated the Imaginist group of poets 1919. A selection of his poetry was translated in *Confessions of a Hooligan* 1973. He was married briefly to the US dancer Isadora Duncan 1922–23.

esker a geologic feature of formerly glaciated areas consisting of a long, steep-walled narrow ridge, often sinuous and sometimes branching. Eskers consist of stratified glacial drift and are thought to form by the deposits of streams running through tunnels underneath melting stagnant ice. When the glacier finally disappeared, the old stream deposits were left standing as a high ridge. Eskers vary in height 10–100 ft/3–30 m and can run to about 100 mi/160 km in length.

Eskilstuna town W of Stockholm, Sweden; population (1986) 88,400. It has iron foundries and steel and armament works.

Eskimo member of a group of Asian, North American, and Greenland Arctic peoples who migrated east from Siberia about 2,000 years ago, exploiting the marine coastal environment and the tundra. Eskimo languages belong to the Eskimo-Aleut family and form a continuum of dialects from Siberia east to Greenland.

Eskişehir city in Turkey, 125 mi/200 km W of Ankara; population (1985) 367,000. Products include meerschaum, chromium, magnesite, cotton goods, tiles, and aircraft.

esophagus the passage by which food travels from mouth to stomach. The human esophagus is about 9 in/23 cm long. Its upper end is at the bottom of the ◊pharynx, immediately behind the windpipe.

esparto grass *Stipa tenacissima*, native to S Spain, S Portugal, and the Balearics, but now widely grown in dry, sandy locations throughout the world. The plant is just over 3 ft/1 m high, producing greyish-green leaves, which are used for making paper, ropes, baskets, mats, and cables.

A similar grass *Lygeum spartum* from the same area and used for the same purposes is also called esparto.

Esperanto language devised 1887 by Ludwig L Zamenhof (1859–1917) as an international auxiliary language. For its structure and vocabulary it draws on Latin, the Romance languages, English, and German.

Esperanto spread from Europe to Japan, Brazil, and, especially, China. Its structure is completely regular, with consistent endings for nouns and adjectives. The spelling is phonetic, but the accent varies according to the regional background of its users.

espionage the practice of spying; a way to gather ◊intelligence.

Espronceda José de 1808–1842. Spanish poet. Originally one of the Queen's guards, he lost his commission because of his political activities, and was involved in the Republican uprisings of 1835 and 1836. His lyric poetry and life style both owed much to Byron.

Esquipulas a pilgrimage town in Chiquimula department, SE Guatemala; seat of the "Black Christ" which is a symbol of peace throughout Central America. In May 1986 five Central American presidents met here to discuss a plan for peace in the region.

Esquivel Adolfo 1932– . Argentinian sculptor and architect. As leader of the Servicio de Paz y Justicia (Peace and Justice Service), a Catholic-Protestant human-rights organization, he was awarded the 1980 Nobel Peace Prize.

essay short piece of nonfiction, often dealing from a personal point of view with some particular subject. The essay became a recognized genre with the French writer Montaigne's *Essais* 1580. Francis Bacon's *Essays* 1597 are among the most famous in English. From the 19th century the essay was increasingly used in Europe and the US as a vehicle for literary criticism.

Abraham Cowley, whose essays appeared 1668, brought a greater ease and freedom to the genre than it had possessed before in England, but it was with the development of periodical literature in the 18th century that the essay became a widely used form. The great names are Addison and Steele, with their *Tatler* and *Spectator* papers, and later Johnson and Goldsmith. In North America Benjamin Franklin was noted for his style. A new era was inaugurated by Lamb's *Essays of Elia* 1820; to the same period belong Leigh Hunt, Hazlitt, and De Quincey in England, Sainte Beuve in France, and Emerson and Thoreau in the US. Hazlitt may be regarded as the originator of the critical essay, and his successors include Arnold and Gosse. Macaulay, whose essays began to appear shortly after those of Lamb, presents a strong contrast to Lamb with his vigorous but less personal tone. There was a revival of the form during the closing years of the 19th and beginning of the 20th centuries, in the work of R L Stevenson, Oliver Wendell Holmes, Anatole France, Gautier, and Max Beerbohm. The literary journalistic tradition of the essay was continued by James Thurber, Mark Twain, H L Mencken, Edmund Wilson, Desmond MacCarthy, and others, and the critical essay by George Orwell, Cyril Connolly, F R Leavis, T S Eliot, Norman Mailer, John Updike, and others. However, its leisured approach made it a less-often used form by the mid-20th century, although its spirit survived in the radio "essays" of Alistair Cooke, and in the "opnion pieces" of newspapers and magazines.

Essen city in North Rhine–Westphalia, Federal Republic of Germany; population (1988) 615,000. It is the administrative center of the Ruhr, with textile, chemical, and electrical industries.

Essene member of an ancient Jewish religious sect located in the area near the Dead Sea c. 200 BC–AD 200, whose members lived a life of denial and asceticism, as they believed that the day of judgment was imminent.

The ◊Dead Sea Scrolls, discovered in 1947, are believed by some scholars to be the library of the community. John the Baptist may have been a member of the Essenes.

Essequibo the longest river in Guyana, South America, rising in the Guiana Highlands of S Guyana; length 630 mi/1,014 km. Part of the district of Essequibo, which lies to the west of the river, is claimed by Venezuela.

Essex county in SE England

area 1,417 sq mi/3,670 sq km

cities Chelmsford (administrative headquarters), Colchester; ports: Harwich, Tilbury; resorts: Southend, Clacton

features former royal hunting ground of Epping Forest (controlled from 1882 by the City of London); the marshy coastal headland of the Naze; since 1111 at Great Dunmow the Dunmow flitch (side of cured pork) can be claimed every four years by any couple proving to a jury they have not regretted their marriage within the year (winners are few); Stansted, London's third airport

products dairying, cereals, fruit

population (1987) 1,522,000.

Essex Robert Devereux, 2nd Earl of 1566–1601. English soldier and politician. He became a favorite with Elizabeth I from 1587, but was executed because of his policies in Ireland.

In 1599 he led an army unsuccessfully against Irish rebels under the Earl of Tyrone in Ulster, made an unauthorized truce with Tyrone, and returned without permission to England. Forbidden to return to court, he marched into the City of London at the head of a body of supporters, was promptly arrested, tried for treason, and beheaded on Tower Green.

estate in law, the rights that a person has in relation to any property. Real estate is an interest in any land; personal estate is an interest in any other kind of property.

Estate property refers to the assets of a deceased person.

Essex *Robert Devereux, 2nd Earl of Essex, a favorite of Elizabeth I. His career culminated in the capture of Cádiz 1596, but ended in imprisonment and execution.*

estate in European history, an order of society that enjoyed a specified share in government. In medieval theory, there were usually three estates—the nobility, the clergy, and the commons—with the functions of, respectively, defending society from foreign aggression and internal disorder, attending to its spiritual needs, and working to produce the base with which to support the other two orders.

When parliaments and representative assemblies developed from the 13th century, their organization reflected this theory, with separate houses for the nobility, the commons (usually burghers and gentry), and the clergy.

ester organic compound formed by the reaction between an alcohol and an acid, with the elimination of water. Unlike ◊salts, esters are covalent compounds.

Esther in the Old Testament, the wife of the Persian king Ahasuerus (Xerxes I), who prevented the extermination of her people by the king's vizier Haman. Their deliverance is celebrated in the Jewish festival of Purim. Her story is told in the Old Testament Book of Esther.

esthetics the branch of philosophy that deals with the nature of beauty, especially in art. It emerged as a distinct branch of inquiry in the mid-18th century.

The subject of esthetics was introduced by Plato and enlarged upon by Aristotle, but the term was first used by the German philosopher Baumgarten (1714–1762). Other philosophers interested in this area were Immanuel Kant,

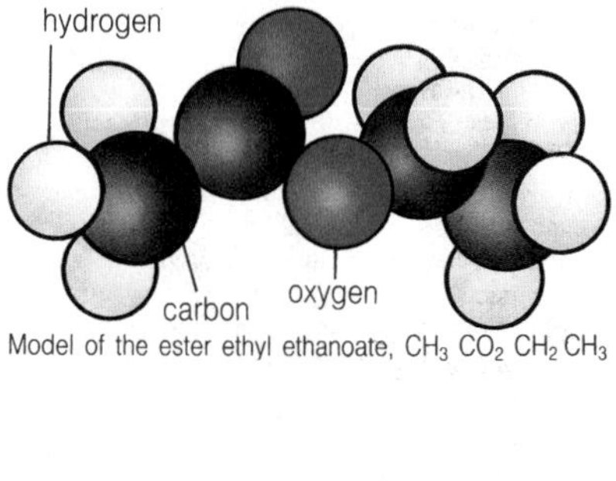
hydrogen
carbon
oxygen

Model of the ester ethyl ethanoate, $CH_3\,CO_2\,CH_2\,CH_3$

Estonia
Republic of

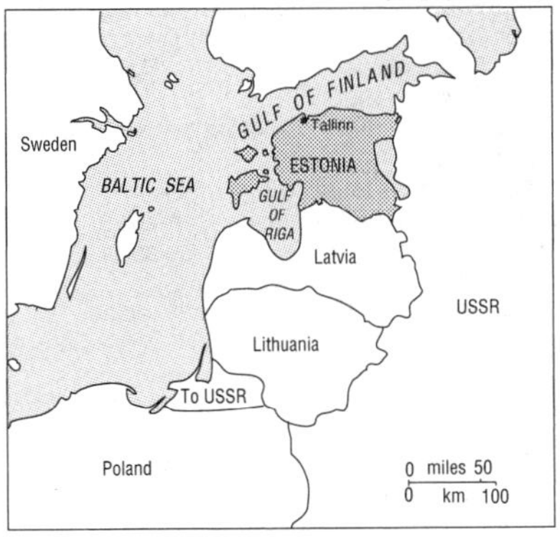
GULF OF FINLAND
Tallinn
Sweden
ESTONIA
BALTIC SEA
GULF OF RIGA
Latvia
USSR
Lithuania
To USSR
Poland
0 miles 50
0 km 100

area 17,413 sq mi/45,100 sq km
capital Tallinn
cities Tartu, Narva, Kohtla-Järve, Pärnu
physical lakes and marshes in a partly forested plain; 481 mi/774 km of coastline; mild climate
features Lake Peipus and Narva River forming boundary with Russian Soviet Federated Socialist Republic; Baltic islands, the largest of which is Saaremaa Island
head of state Arnold Rüütel from 1988
head of government Edgar Savisaar from 1990
political system emergent democratic republic
products oil (from shale), wood products, chemical fertilizers, construction materials, agricultural and mining machinery, flax, textiles, processed foods, dairy and pig products
currency ruble
population (1989 est) 1,573,000; 62% Estonian, 30% Russian, Ukrainian and Byelorussian minorities
language Estonian, allied to Finnish
religion traditionally Lutheran
chronology
1918 Estonia declared its independence. The Soviets, who had tried to regain control from occupying German forces during World War I, overthrown by German troops March; took control after German withdrawal Nov.
1919 Soviets again overthrown with help of British navy; Estonia declared a democratic republic.
1934 Fascist coup replaced government.
1939 Germany and USSR secretly agreed that Estonia should come under Russian influence.
1940 Estonia incorporated into USSR.
1941–44 German occupation in World War II.
1944 USSR regained control.
1980 Beginnings of nationalist dissent.
1988 Adopted own constitution, with power of veto on all centralized Soviet legislation. Estonian popular front (Rahvarinne) established to campaign for democratization. Estonia's supreme soviet (state assembly) voted to declare the republic "sovereign" and autonomous in all matters except military and foreign affairs; rejected by presidium of the USSR's supreme soviet as unconstitutional.
1989 Estonia's assembly denounced the 1940 incorporation of the republic into the USSR as "forced annexation." Multiparty system in place; coalition government formed. Estonian replaced Russian as main language.
1991 Aug: declared full independence at time of anti-Gorbachev coup and outlawed Communist party. Sept: independence recognized by Soviet government and Western nations; granted membership of United Nations.

David Hume, Benedetto Croce, John Dewey, and George Santayana.

estivation in zoology, a state of inactivity and reduced metabolic activity, similar to ◊hibernation, that occurs during the dry season in species such as lungfishes and snails. In botany, the term is used to describe the way in which flower petals and sepals are folded in the buds. It is an important feature in ◊plant classification.

Estonia country in N Europe, bounded E by the USSR, S by Latvia, and N and W by the Baltic Sea.

history Independent states were formed in the area now known as Estonia during the 1st century AD. In the 13th century southern Estonia came under the control of the ◊Teutonic Knights (German crusaders) who converted the inhabitants to Christianity. The Danes, who had taken control of northern Estonia, sold this area to the Teutonic Knights 1324. By the 16th century German nobles owned much of the land. In 1561 Sweden took control of the north, with Poland governing the south; from 1625 to 1710 Sweden ruled the whole country. Estonia came under Russian control 1710, but it was not until the 19th century that the Estonians started their movement for independence.

struggle for independence Estonia was occupied by German troops during World War I. The Soviets, who tried to regain power 1917, were overthrown by the Germans March 1918, restored Nov 1918, and again overthrown with the help of the British navy May 1919 when Estonia, having declared its independence 1918, was established as a democratic republic. A fascist coup 1934 replaced the government.

In 1939 the Germans and Soviets secretly agreed that Estonia should come under Russian influence and the country was incorporated into the USSR as the Estonian Soviet Socialist Republic 1940. During World War II Estonia was again occupied by the Germans 1941–44, but the Soviets subsequently regained control.

Nationalist dissent grew from 1980. In 1988 Estonia adopted its own constitution, with a power of veto on all Soviet legislation. The new constitution allowed private property and placed land and natural resources under Estonian control. An Estonian popular front (Rahvarinne) was established Oct 1988 to campaign for democratization, increased autonomy, and eventual independence, and held mass rallies. In Nov of the same year Estonia's supreme soviet (state assembly) voted to declare the republic "sovereign" and thus autonomous in all matters except military and foreign affairs, although the presidium of the USSR's supreme soviet rejected this as unconstitutional. In 1989 a law was passed replacing Russian with Estonian as the main language and in Nov of that year Estonia's assembly denounced the 1940 incorporation of the republic into the USSR as "forced annexation." A multiparty system is effectively in place in the republic, embracing the Popular Front, Christian Democrats, Independence League, and the republican Communist Party, and a coalition government was formed following the elections of Dec 1989.

A plebiscite in the spring of 1991 voted 77.8% in favor of independence. By the summer the republic had embarked on a program of privatization. On Aug 20, 1991, in the midst of the attempted anti-Gorbachev coup in the USSR, which led to Red Army troops being moved into Tallinn to seize the television transmitter and the republic's main port being blocked by the Soviet navy, Estonia declared its full independence (previously it had been in a "period of transition") and outlawed the Communist Party. In Sept 1991 this declaration was recognized by the Soviet government and Western nations and the new state was granted membership of the United Nations.

Estoril fashionable resort on the coast 13 mi/20 km W of Lisbon, Portugal; population (1981) 16,000. There is a Grand Prix motor-racing circuit.

estradiol type of ◊estrogen (female sex hormone).

estrogen any of a group of hormones produced by the ◊ovaries of vertebrates; the term is also used for various synthetic hormones that mimic their effects. (Some estrogens are also secreted by the cortex of the ◊adrenal glands.) The principal estrogen in mammals is estradiol. Estrogens promote the development of female secondary sexual characteristics; stimulate egg production; and, in mammals, prepare the lining of the uterus for pregnancy.

estrus in mammals, the period during a female's reproductive cycle (also known as the estrous cycle) when mating is most likely to occur. It usually coincides with ovulation. Only the ◊human species is free of the estrus cycle, and mates more or less at will.

estuary a river mouth widening into the sea, where fresh water mixes with salt water to form brackish water and tidal effects are felt. Estuaries are extremely rich in life forms and are breeding grounds for thousands of species. Water pollution threatens these ◊ecosystems.

Esztergom city on the Danube, NW of Budapest, Hungary; population (1986) 31,000. It was the birthplace of St Stephen and the former ecclesiastical capital of Hungary, with a fine cathedral.

et al. abbreviation for *et alii* (Latin "and others"); used in bibliography.

etc. abbreviation for et cetera (Latin "and the rest").

etching a ◊printmaking technique in which the design is made from a metal plate (usually copper or zinc), which is covered with a waxy overlayer (ground) and then drawn on with an etching needle. The exposed areas are then "etched," or bitten into, by a corrosive agent (acid), so that they will hold ink for printing. Some artists combine etching with ◊aquatint.

The method was developed in Germany about 1500, the earliest dated etched print being of 1513. Among the earliest exponents were Dürer, van Dyck, and Rembrandt.

Eteocles in Greek mythology, son of the incestuous union of ◊Oedipus and ◊Jocasta and brother of ◊Polynices. He denied his brother a share in the kingship of Thebes, thus provoking the expedition of the ◊Seven against Thebes, in which he and his brother died by each other's hands.

ethanal common name ***acetaldehyde*** CH_3CHO one of the chief members of the group of organic compounds known as ◊aldehydes. It is a colorless, inflammable liquid boiling at 69.6°F/20.8°C. Ethanal is formed by the oxidation of ethene and is used to make many other organic chemical compounds.

ethane CH_3CH_3 colorless, odorless gas, the second member of the ◊alkane series of hydrocarbons (paraffins).

ethane-1,2-diol technical name for ◊glycol.

ethanol common name ***ethyl alcohol*** C_2H_5OH alcohol found in beer, wine, cider, spirits, and other alcoholic drinks. When pure, it is a colorless liquid with a pleasant odor, miscible with water or ether, and which burns in air with a pale blue flame. The vapor forms an explosive mixture with air and may be used in high-compression internal combustion engines. It is produced naturally by the fermentation of carbohydrates by yeast cells. Industrially, it can be made by absorption of ethene and subsequent reaction with water, or by the reduction of ethanal in the presence of a catalyst, and is widely used as a solvent.

Ethanol is used as a raw material in the manufacture of ether, chloral, and iodoform. It can also be added to gasoline, where it improves the performance of the engine, or be used as a fuel in its own right. Crops such as sugar cane may be grown to provide ethanol (by fermentation) for this purpose.

Ethelred II the Unready c. 968–1016. King of England from 978. The son of King Edgar, he became king after the murder of his half brother, Edward the Martyr. He tried to buy off the Danish raiders by paying Danegeld. In 1002, he ordered the massacre of the Danish settlers, provoking an invasion by Sweyn I of Denmark. War with Sweyn and Sweyn's son, Canute, occupied the rest of Ethelred's reign. He was nicknamed the "Unready" because of his apparent lack of foresight.

ethene common name ethylene C_2H_4 colorless, flammable gas, the first member of the ◊alkene series of hydrocarbons. It is the most widely used synthetic organic chemical and is used to produce polyethylene (polythene), dichloroethane, and polyvinyl chloride (PVC). It is obtained from natural gas or coal gas, or by the dehydration of ethanol.

It also occurs naturally in plants, helping to promote growth as well as the ripening of fruit. It is applied to fruit that has been picked and shipped in an unripe state, to promote ripening.

ether any of a series of organic compounds having an oxygen atom linking the carbon atoms of two hydrocarbon radical groups (general formula R-O-R′), for example dioxyethane $C_2H_5OC_2H_5$ (also called diethyl ether). Dioxyethane is a colorless, volatile, inflammable liquid, slightly soluble in water, miscible with ethanol. It is prepared by treatment of ethanol with excess concentrated sulfuric acid at 284°F/140°C. It is used as an anesthetic by vapor inhalation and as an external cleansing agent before surgical operations. It is also used as a solvent, and in the extraction of oils, fats, waxes, resins, and alkaloids.

ether or ***aether*** in the history of science, a hypothetical medium permeating all of space. The concept originated with the Greeks, and has been revived on several occasions to explain the properties and propagation of light. It was supposed that light and other electromagnetic radiation—even in outer space—needed a medium, the ether, in which to travel. The idea was abandoned with the acceptance of relativity.

Its existence was disproved in 1887 by the classic Michelson–Morley experiment, which showed that light travels at the same speed in the direction of the Earth's motion through space as it does at right angles to the motion. This later led Einstein to formulate his special theory of ◊relativity.

Etherege George c. 1635–c. 1691. English Restoration dramatist whose play *Love in a Tub* 1664 was the first attempt at the comedy of manners (a genre further developed by Congreve and Sheridan). Later plays include *She Would if She Could* 1668 and *The Man of Mode, or Sir Fopling Flutter* 1676.

Ethical Culture Movement movement during the late 19th and early 20th centuries designed to further the moral or ethical factor as the real substance and fundamental part of religion.

It originated in the New York Society for Ethical Culture founded by Felix Adler in 1876. Mainly Jewish at first, it soon attracted adherents of Christian and skeptical backgrounds. It spread to England, Germany, and other countries by the turn of the century. In 1952 the International Humanist and Ethical Union was formed, with headquarters in Utrecht, Netherlands.

ethics area of philosophy concerned with human values, which studies the meanings of moral terms and theories of conduct and goodness; also called moral philosophy. It is one of the three main branches of contemporary philosophy.

The study of ethics began in ancient India and China, and began to be systematized by the Greek philosopher Socrates in the 5th century BC. Plato's *Republic* is an exposition of the nature of justice or righteousness, and ethical theory was advanced by Aristotle's *Nicomachean Ethics* and similar writings. The Cyrenaics, Epicureans, and Stoics advanced theories that have been many times revived.

The "Christian ethic" is mainly a combination of New Testament moral teaching with ideas drawn from Plato and Aristotle, combining hedonism and rationalism. Medieval ◊scholasticism saw God's will as the ethical standard but tempered it with Aristotelian ethics.

In the 17th–18th centuries, Thomas Hobbes and David Hume were notable British ethical philosophers. One of the greatest contributors to ethical theory was the German Immanuel Kant, an idealist, with his "categorical imperative" (the obligation to obey absolute moral law), since conscience is to ethics as intelligence is to logic.

The utilitarian ethic (for the good of society rather than the individual) was in the UK expounded in the 18th–19th centuries by Jeremy Bentham, J S Mill, and Herbert Spencer, and opposed by F H Bradley and T H Green, who linked ethics with metaphysics and emphasized the place of the individual in organized society. Utilitarianism has become the ostensible basis for law, politics, commerce, and social ethics, while conscience guides the individual.

Ethicists of the 20th century include G E Moore and C D Broad in the UK and John Dewey in the US.

Ethiopia country in E Africa, bounded NE by the Red Sea, E and SE by Somalia, S by Kenya, and W and NW by Sudan.

government A traditional monarchy until 1974, Ethiopia was then ruled by a Provisional Military Administrative Council (PMAC), chaired by the head of state, who also presided over a council of ministers and was secretary general of the only political party, the Marxist-Leninist Workers' Party of Ethiopia (WPE). Parliament was suspended 1974 when Emperor ◊Haile Selassie was deposed and Ethiopia was proclaimed a Socialist state. A new constitution in 1987 created an 835-member national assembly, elected from nominees of political parties and other economic and social organizations. When this regime was overthrown in 1991, an interim representative government was established.

history Long subject to Egypt, the area became independent about the 11th century BC. The kingdom of ◊Aksum flourished 1st–10th centuries AD, reaching its peak about the 4th century with the introduction of ◊Coptic Christianity from Egypt, and declining from the 7th century as ◊Islam expanded. The Arab conquests isolated Aksum from the rest of the Christian world.

During the 10th century there emerged a kingdom that formed the basis of Abyssinia, reinforced 1270 with the founding of a new dynasty. Although it remained independent throughout the period of European colonization of Africa, Abyssinia suffered civil unrest and several invasions from the 16th century, and was eventually reunited 1889 under ◊Menelik II, with Italian support. In 1896 Menelik put down an invasion by Italy, which claimed he had agreed to make the country an Italian protectorate, and annexed

Ethiopia

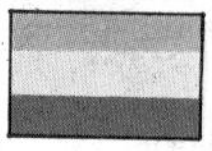

People's Democratic Republic of (*Hebretesebawit Ityopia*, formerly also known as **Abyssinia**)

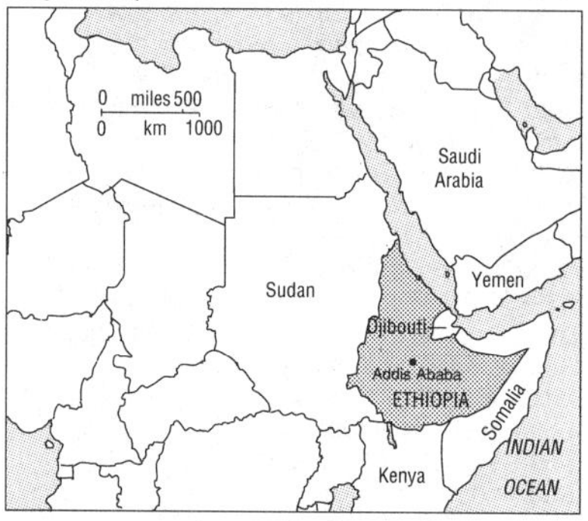
0 miles 500
0 km 1000
Saudi Arabia
Sudan
Yemen
Djibouti
Addis Ababa
ETHIOPIA
Somalia
Kenya
INDIAN OCEAN

area 471,653 sq mi/1,221,900 sq km
capital Addis Ababa
cities Asmara (capital of Eritrea), Dire Dawa; ports Massawa, Assab
physical a high plateau with central mountain range divided by Rift Valley; plains in E; source of Blue Nile River
features Danakil and Ogaden deserts; ancient remains (at Aksum, Gondar, Lalibela, among others); only African country to retain its independence during the colonial period
head of state and government Meles Zenawi from 1991
political system transition to democratic Socialist republic
political parties Workers' Party of Ethiopia (WPE), Marxist-Leninist; Eritrean People's Liberation Front (EPLE), a guerrilla army fighting for an independent Eritrea; Tigré People's Liberation Front (TPLF), fighting for regional autonomy in Tigré
exports coffee, dried legumes, oilseeds, hides, skins
currency birr
population (1989 est) 47,709,000 (Oromo 40%, Amhara 25%, Tigré 12%, Sidamo 9%); growth rate 2.5% p.a.
life expectancy 38 years
language Amharic (official); Tigrinya, Orominga, Arabic
religion Christian (Ethiopian Orthodox church, which has had its own patriarch since 1976) 40%, Sunni Muslim 45%
literacy 35% (1988)
GDP $4.8 bn (1987); $104 per head
chronology
1889 Abyssinia reunited by Menelik II.
1930 Haile Selassie became emperor.
1962 Eritrea annexed by Haile Selassie; resistance movement began.
1974 Haile Selassie deposed and replaced by a military government led by Gen Teferi Benti. Ethiopia declared a Socialist state.
1977 Teferi Benti killed and replaced by Col Mengistu Haile Mariam.
1977–79 "Red Terror" period in which Mengistu's regime killed thousands of innocent people.
1984 WPE declared the only legal political party.
1985 Worst famine in more than a decade; Western aid sent and forcible internal resettlement programs undertaken.
1987 New constitution adopted, Mengistu Mariam elected president; provisional Military Administrative Council dissolved, and elected National Assembly introduced. New famine; food aid hindered by guerrillas.
1988 Mengistu agreed to adjust his economic policies in order to secure IMF assistance. Influx of refugees from Sudan.
1989 Government forces routed from Eritrea and Tigré, rebels claimed; army accused of bombing civilian targets. Coup attempt against Mengistu foiled; another famine in N feared; peace talks mediated by former US president Carter reported some progress.
1990 Rebels captured port of Massawa. Mengistu announced new reforms.
1991 Mengistu overthrown and temporary administration set up by the Ethiopian People's Revolutionary Democratic Front (EPRDF). Independence of Eritrea agreed and access to the Red Sea guaranteed by making Assab a free port.

Ogaden in the southeast and several provinces to the west.

Ethiopia was ruled for over 50 years by Haile Selassie, who became regent 1916, king 1928, and emperor 1930. The country was occupied by Italy 1935–41, and Haile Selassie went into exile in Britain. Ogaden was returned to ◊Somalia, which was also under Italian control.

Haile Selassie returned from exile 1941 and ruled until 1974, when he was deposed by the armed forces after famine, high inflation, growing unemployment, and demands for greater democracy. His palace and estates were nationalized, parliament dissolved, and the constitution suspended. He died 1975, aged 83, in a small apartment in his former palace in Addis Ababa.

General Teferi Benti, who had led the uprising and been made head of state, was killed 1977 by fellow officers and replaced by Col Mengistu Haile Mariam. The Ethiopian empire had been built up by Haile Selassie and Menelik, and annexed regions had made frequent attempts to secede. The 1975 revolution encouraged secessionist movements to increase their efforts, and the military government had to fight to keep Eritrea and Ogaden, where Somalian troops were assisting local guerrillas.

The USSR, having adopted Ethiopia as a new ally, threatened to cut off aid to Somalia, and Cuban troops assisted Mengistu in ending the fighting there. Eritrea and its neighbor, Tigré, continued their struggle for independence.

Amid this confusion there was acute famine in the north, including Eritrea, when the rains failed for three successive seasons. In addition to a massive emergency aid program from many Western nations, the Ethiopian government tried to alleviate the problem by resettling people from the north to the more fertile south. By 1986 more than 500,000 had been forcibly resettled.

Meanwhile, the military regime had re-established normal relations with most of its neighbors, promising a return to civilian rule, and in 1986 publishing the draft of a new constitution. Tigré province was captured by Eritrean People's Liberation Front EPLF and Tigré People's Liberation Front TPLF Feb 1989, the first time the government had lost control of the entire province. In March 1989 the new constitution was adopted, ending 12 years of military rule and electing Col Mengistu Mariam as the country's first president. A coup against him in May 1989 was put down and the military high command subsequently purged. Following a mediation offer by the former US president Jimmy ◊Carter, peace talks with the Eritrean rebels began in Aug 1989. At the same time, droughts in the north threatened another widespread famine. Rebel pressure on the Mengistu government increased steadily during early 1991, and in May Mengistu fled the country, while rebels occupied Addis Ababa. An interim government was in place by July.

ethnicity (from Greek *ethnos* "a people") people's own sense of cultural identity; a social term that overlaps with such concepts as race, nation, class, and religion.

Social scientists use the term ethnic group to refer to groups or societies who feel a common sense of identity, often based on a traditional shared culture, language, religion, and customs. It may or may not include common territory, skin color, or common descent. The US, for example, is often described as a multiethnic society because many members would describe themselves as members of an ethnic group (Jewish, black, or Irish, for example) as well as their national one (American).

ethnology the branch of anthropology that deals with the comparative study of contemporary cultures, acculturation, and human ecology.

ethnomethodology the study of social order and routines used by people in their daily lives, to explain how everyday reality is created and perceived. Ethnomethodologists tend to use small-scale studies and experiments to examine the details of social life and structure (such as conversations) that people normally take for granted, rather than construct large-scale theories about society.

ethology the comparative study of animal behavior in its natural setting. Ethology is concerned with the causal mechanisms (both the stimuli that elicit behavior and the physiological mechanisms controlling it), as well as the development of behavior, its function, and its evolutionary history.

Ethology was pioneered during the 1930s by Konrad Lorenz and Karl von Frisch who, with Nikolaas Tinbergen, received the Nobel Prize in 1973. Ethologists believe that the significance of an animal's behavior can be understood only in its natural context, and emphasize the importance of field studies and an evolutionary perspective. A recent development within ethology is sociobiology, the study of the evolutionary function of ◊social behavior.

ethyl alcohol common name for ◊ethanol.

ethylene common name for ◊ethene.

ethylene glycol alternate name for ◊glycol.

ethyne common name ***acetylene*** CHCH colorless, inflammable gas produced by mixing calcium carbide and water. It is the simplest member of the ◊alkyne series of hydrocarbons. It is used in the manufacture of the synthetic rubber neoprene, and in oxyacetylene welding and cutting.

Ethyne was discovered by Edmund Davy 1836. Its combustion provides more heat, relatively, than almost any other fuel known (its calorific value is five times that of hydrogen). This means that the gas gives an intensely hot flame; hence its use in oxyacetylene welding and cutting.

etiolation in botany, a form of growth seen in plants receiving insufficient light. It is characterized by long, weak stems, small leaves, and a pale yellowish color (◊chlorosis) caused by a lack of chlorophyll. The rapid increase in height enables a plant that is surrounded by others to quickly reach a source of light, when a return to normal growth usually occurs.

Etna volcano in E central Sicily, 10,906 ft/3,323 m, the highest in Europe. About 90 eruptions have been recorded since 1800 BC, yet because of the rich soil, the cultivated zone on the lower slopes is densely populated, and includes the coastal city of Catania. Tours of this smoking volcano are conducted.

Etruscan art sculpture, painting, and design of the first known Italian civilization. Etruscan terracotta coffins (*sarcophagi*), carved with reliefs and topped with portraits of the dead reclining on one elbow, were to influence the later Romans and early Christians.

Pottery, bronzeware, and mural paintings survive. Most examples are from excavated tombs; bright colors and a vigorous style are typical and show the influence of ancient Greece and the Middle East.

etymology the study of the origin and history of words within and across languages. It has two major aspects: the study of the phonetic and written forms of words, and of the semantics or meanings of those words.

Etymological research has been successful in tracing the development of words and word elements within the Indo-European language family. Since languages are always changing and usage differs among cultures, it is important to trace words to their original sources.

Euboea (Greek *Evvoia*) mountainous island off the E coast of Greece, in the Aegean sea; area 1,450 sq mi/3,755 sq km; about 110 mi/177 km long; population (1981) 188,410. Mount Delphi reaches 5,721 ft/1,743 m. The chief town, Chalcis, is connected by a bridge to the mainland.

eucalyptus any tree of the genus *Eucalyptus* of the myrtle family Myrtaceae, native to Australia and Tasmania, where members are commonly known as gum trees. About 90% of Australian timber belongs to the eucalyptus genus, which comprises about 500 species. They are tall, aromatic, evergreen trees with pendant leaves and white, pink, or red flowers.

Eucharist chief Christian sacrament, in which bread is eaten and wine drunk in memory of the death of Jesus. Other names for it are the Lord's Supper, Holy Communion, and (among Roman Catholics, who believe that the bread and wine are transubstantiated, that is, converted to the body and blood of Christ) the Mass. The doctrine of transubstantiation was rejected by Protestant churches at the Reformation.

The word comes from the Greek for "thanksgiving," and refers to the statement in the Gospel narrative that Jesus gave thanks over the bread and the cup.

Euclid c. 330–c. 260 BC. Greek mathematician, who lived in Alexandria and wrote the *Stoicheia/Elements* in 13 books, of which nine deal with plane and solid geometry and four with number theory. His great achievement lay in the systematic arrangement of previous discoveries, based on axioms, definitions, and theorems.

Euclid's geometry texts remained in common usage for over 2,000 years.

Eugene city in W central Oregon, S of Portland, on the Willamette river. Agricultural products from the surrounding region are processed and shipped from Eugene. Wood products are also manufactured. The University of Oregon 1872 is here; population (1990) 112,669.

Eugène Prince of Savoy 1663–1736. Austrian general who had many victories against the Turkish invaders (whom he expelled from Hungary 1697 in the Battle of Zenta) and against France in the War of the ◊Spanish Succession (battles of Blenheim, Oudenaarde, and Malplaquet).

Eugene Onegin a novel in verse by Aleksandr Pushkin, published 1823–31. Eugene Onegin, bored with life but sensitive, rejects the love of Tatanya, a humble country girl; but she later rises in society and in turn rejects him. Onegin was the model for a number of Russian literary heroes.

eugenics (Greek "well-born") the study of ways in which the physical and mental quality of a people can be controlled and improved by selective breeding, and the belief that this should be done. The idea was abused by the Nazi Party in Germany during the 1930s to justify the attempted extermination of entire groups of people. Eugenics can try to control the spread of inherited genetic abnormalities by counseling prospective parents.

The term was coined by Francis ◊Galton in 1883, and the concept was originally developed in the late 19th century with a view to improving human intelligence and behavior.

In 1986 Singapore became the first democratic country to adopt an openly eugenic policy by guaranteeing pay increases to female university graduates when they give birth to a child, while offering grants toward house purchases for non-

eucalyptus

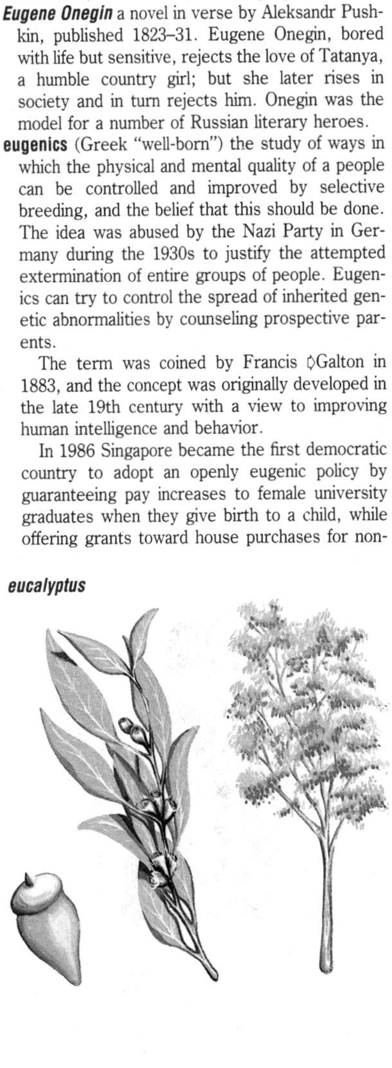

graduate married women on condition that they are sterilized after the first or second child.

Eugénie Marie Ignace Augustine de Montijo 1826–1920. Empress of France, daughter of the Spanish count of Montijo. In 1853 she married Louis Napoleon, who had become emperor as ◊Napoleon III. She encouraged court extravagance, Napoleon III's intervention in Mexico, and urged him to fight the Prussians. After his surrender to the Germans at Sedan, NE France, 1870 she fled to England.

eukaryote one of the two major groupings into which all organisms are divided. Included are all organisms, except bacteria and cyanobacteria, which belong to the ◊prokaryote grouping.

The cells of eukaryotes possess a clearly defined nucleus, bounded by a membrane, within which DNA is formed into distinct chromosomes. Their cells contain mitochondria, chloroplasts, and other structures (organelles) that, together with a defined nucleus, are lacking in the cells of prokaryotes.

Euler Leonhard 1707–1783. Swiss mathematician. He developed the theory of differential equations and the calculus of variations, and worked in astronomy and optics. He was a pupil of Johann ◊Bernoulli.

Euler became professor of physics at the University of St Petersburg in 1730. In 1741 he was invited to Berlin by Frederick the Great, where he spent 25 years before returning to Russia.

Eumenides ("kindly ones") in Greek mythology, appeasing name for the ◊Furies.

eunuch (Greek *eunoukhos* "one in charge of a bed") a castrated man. Originally eunuchs were bedchamber attendants in harems in the East, but as they were usually castrated to keep them from taking too great an interest in their charges, the term became applied more generally. Eunuchs often filled high offices of state in China, India, and Persia. Italian *castrati* were singers castrated as boys to preserve their soprano voices, a practice that ended with the accession of Pope Leo XIII 1878.

Eupen-et-Malmédy region of Belgium around the towns of Eupen and Malmédy. It was Prussian from 1814 until it became Belgian 1920 after a plebiscite; there was fierce fighting here in the German Ardennes offensive Dec 1944.

euphonium type of ◊brass instrument, like a small tuba.

Euphrates (Arabic *Furat*) river, rising in E Turkey, flowing through Syria and Iraq and joining the river Tigris above Basra to form the river Shatt-al-Arab, at the head of the Persian/Arabian Gulf; 2,240 mi/3,600 km in length. The ancient cities of Babylon, Eridu, and Ur were situated along its course.

Eurasian a person of mixed European and Asian parentage; also, native to or an inhabitant of both Europe and Asia.

Euratom acronym for ◊European Atomic Energy Commission, forming part of the ◊European Community organization.

Eure river rising in Orne *département*, France, and flowing SE, then N, to the river Seine; length 70 mi/115 km. Chartres is on its banks. It gives its name to two *départements*, Eure and Eure-et-Loire.

Europe
Arctic Circle
Reykjavik
ICELAND
NORWEGIAN SEA
NORWAY
SWEDEN
Faroe Is. (to Denmark)
Glittertind 8103ft/2470m
Oslo
Stockholm
ATLANTIC OCEAN
N IRELAND
IRELAND
Dublin
UNITED KINGDOM
NORTH SEA
DENMARK
Copenhagen
BALTIC SEA
Amsterdam
The Hague
NETHERLANDS
London
English Channel
Brussels
BELGIUM
Berlin
North
GERMANY
Elbe
Oder
Vistula
Paris
LUXEMBOURG
Prague
CZECHOSLOVAKIA
Loire
Seine
Vosges
Rhine
Danube
Vienna
Bay of Biscay
FRANCE
Bern
SWITZERLAND
LIECHT.
AUSTRIA
HUNGARY
Alps
Mt Blanc 15770ft/4807m
Cantabrian Mts
Garonne
Central Massif
Rhône
Pico de Aneto 11,168ft/3404m
Pyrenees
ANDORRA
Marseille
Ligurian Sea
MONACO
Po
SAN MARINO
YUGOSLAVIA
Dinaric Alps
PORTUGAL
Madrid
Ebro
Barcelona
Corsica
ITALY
Apennines
Gran Sasso 8620ft/2655m
ADRIATIC SEA
Lisbon
SPAIN
Rome
Tirane
Andalusia
Seville
Sardinia
Balearic Is.
Tyrrhenian Sea
Gibraltar (to UK)
Strait of Gibraltar
MEDITERRANEAN SEA
Ionian Sea
MOROCCO
ALGERIA
Sicily
TUNISIA
MALTA
0 250 500 750 1000 miles
0 500 1000 1500 km

eureka alternate name for the copper–nickel alloy ◊constantan, which is used in electrical equipment.

eurhythmics practice of coordinated bodily movement as an aid to musical development. It was founded about 1900 by the Swiss musician Emil ◊Jaques-Dalcroze, professor of harmony at the Geneva conservatoire. He devised a series of "gesture" songs, to be sung simultaneously with certain bodily actions.

Euripides c. 484–407 BC. Greek dramatist whose plays deal with the emotions and reactions of ordinary people and social issues rather than with deities and the grandiose themes of his contemporaries. He wrote more than 80 plays, of which 18 survive, including *Alcestis* 438 BC, *Medea* 431 BC, *Andromache* 426 BC, *The Trojan Women* 415 BC, *Electra* 417 BC, *Iphigenia in Tauris* 413 BC, *Iphigenia in Aulis* 405 BC, and *Bacchae* 405 BC. His influence on later drama was probably greater than that of the other two accomplished tragedians, Aeschylus and Sophocles.

A realist, he was bitterly attacked for his unorthodox "impiety" and sympathy for the despised: slaves, beggars, and women. He went into voluntary exile from Athens to Macedonia at the end of his life.

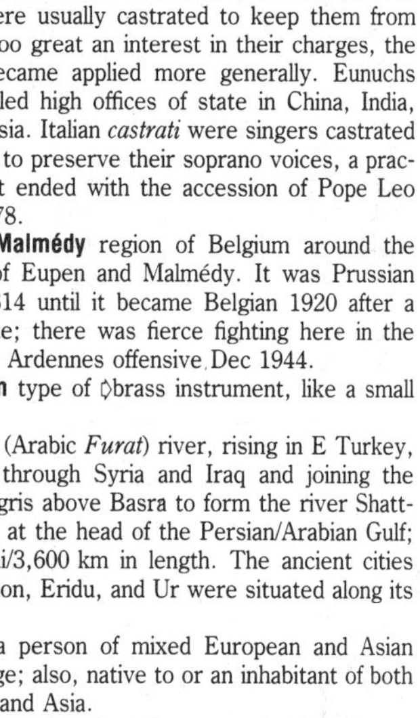

Euripides *A Roman copy of a late 4th-century BC Greek bust of the ancient Greek dramatist.*

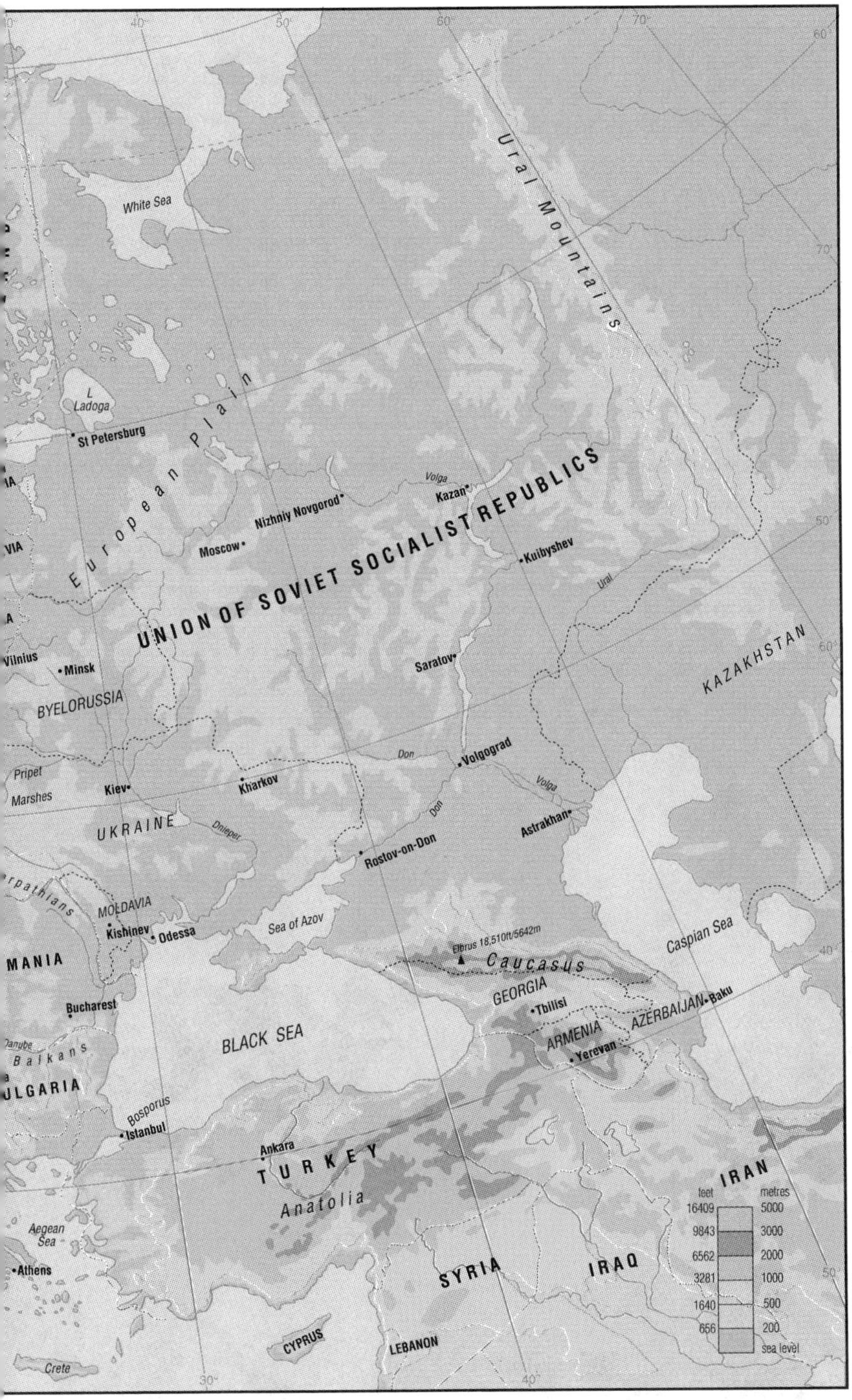
White Sea
Ural Mountains
L Ladoga
St Petersburg
European Plain
UNION OF SOVIET SOCIALIST REPUBLICS
Volga
Kazan
Nizhniy Novgorod
Moscow
Kuibyshev
Ural
Vilnius
Minsk
BYELORUSSIA
Saratov
KAZAKHSTAN
Pripet Marshes
Kiev
Kharkov
Don
Volgograd
UKRAINE
Dnieper
Astrakhan
Rostov-on-Don
MOLDAVIA
Kishinev
Odessa
Sea of Azov
Elbrus 18,510ft/5642m
Caucasus
Caspian Sea
MANIA
GEORGIA
Tbilisi
AZERBAIJAN
Baku
Bucharest
ARMENIA
Yerevan
BLACK SEA
Balkans
ULGARIA
Bosporus
Istanbul
Ankara
TURKEY
Anatolia
IRAN
Aegean Sea
Athens
SYRIA
IRAQ
CYPRUS
LEBANON
Crete
feet
metres
16409
5000
9843
3000
6562
2000
3281
1000
1640
500
656
200
sea level

Eurobond a bond underwritten by an international syndicate and sold in countries other than the country of the currency in which the issue is denominated. They provide longer-term financing than is possible with loans in Eurodollars.

Eurocommunism policy followed by communist parties in Western Europe to seek power within the framework of national political initiative rather than by revolutionary means. In addition, Eurocommunism has enabled these parties to free themselves from total reliance on the USSR.

Eurodollar US currency deposited outside the US and held by individuals and institutions, not necessarily in Europe. They originated in the 1960s when East European countries deposited their US dollars in West European banks. Banks holding Eurodollar deposits may lend in dollars, usually to finance trade, and often redeposit with other foreign banks. The practice is a means of avoiding credit controls and exploiting interest rate differentials.

Europa in astronomy, the fourth-largest moon of the planet Jupiter, diameter 1,900 mi/3,100 km, orbiting 417,000 mi/671,000 km from the planet every 3.55 days. It is covered by ice and crisscrossed by thousands of thin cracks, each some 30,000 mi/50,000 km long.

Europa in Greek mythology, the daughter of the king of Tyre, carried off by Zeus (in the form of a bull); she personifies the continent of Europe.

Europe second-smallest continent, comprising the land W of the Ural mountains; it has 8% of the Earth's surface, with 14.5% of world population
area 4,000,000 sq mi/10,400,000 sq km
largest cities (over 1.5 million) Athens, Barcelona, Berlin, Birmingham, Budapest, Hamburg, Istanbul, Kiev, Leningrad, London, Madrid, Manchester, Milan, Moscow, Paris, Rome, Vienna, Warsaw
features North European Plain on which stand London, Paris, Berlin, and Moscow; Central European Highlands (Sierra Nevada, Pyrenees, Alps, Apennines, Carpathians, Balkans); Scandinavian highland, which takes in the Scottish Highlands; highest point: Mount Elbruz in Caucasus mountains; rivers (over 1,000 mi/1,600 km): Volga, Don, Dnieper, Danube; lakes (over 2,000 sq mi/5,100 sq km): Ladoga, Onega, Vänern. The climate ranges from the variable NW, modified by the ◊Gulf Stream, through the central zone with warm summers and cold winters, becoming bitterly cold in E Europe, to the Mediterranean zone with comparatively mild winters and hot summers. The last is the richest zone for plant life, but animal species have long been reduced everywhere by the predominance of humans
population (1985) 492,000,000 (excluding Turkey and USSR)
language mostly of Indo-European origin, with a few exceptions, including Finno-Ugrian (Finnish and Hungarian) and Altaic (such as Turkish) languages, and Basque
religion Christianity (Protestantism, Roman Catholicism, Greek Orthodox), Islam, Judaism;
history see ◊Europe, history.

European native to or an inhabitant of the continent of Europe and their descendants. Europe is multicultural and, although most of its languages belong to the Indo-European family, there are also speakers of Uralic (such as Hungarian) and Altaic (such as Turkish) languages, as well as Basque.

European Atomic Energy Commission (Euratom) organization established by the second Treaty of Rome 1957, which seeks the cooperation of member states of the European Community in nuclear research and the rapid and large-scale development of nonmilitary nuclear energy.

European Coal and Steel Community (ECSC) former organization established by the treaty of Paris 1951 (ratified 1952) as a single authority for the coal and steel industries of France, West Germany, Italy, Belgium, Holland, and Luxembourg, eliminating tariffs and other restrictions; in 1967 it became part of the European Community.

The ECSC arose out of the ◊Schuman plan 1950, which proposed a union of the French and German coal and steel industries so as to make future war between the two countries impossible. The ECSC was, in effect, a prototype institution for the European Community itself, under whose authority it came 1967. Subsequent members of the EC automatically became ECSC members also.

European Community (EC) political and economic alliance consisting of the European Coal and Steel Community (1952), European Economic Community (EEC, popularly called the Common Market, 1957), and the European Atomic Energy Commission (Euratom, 1957). The original six members—Belgium, France, West Germany, Italy, Luxembourg, and the Netherlands—were joined by the UK, Denmark, and the Republic of Ireland 1974, Greece 1981, Spain and Portugal 1985. Its aims include the expansion of trade, reduction of competition, the abolition of restrictive trading practices, and the encouragement of free movement of capital and labor within the community.

From 1967 the EC has comprised the following institutions: the Commission of 13 members pledged to independence of national interests, who initiate Community action; the Council of Ministers, which makes decisions on the Com-

Europe: early history

BC	
850,000	Earliest hunter-gathering peoples arrive in Europe; Paleolithic period.
30,000	Earliest cave art.
8,300	Glaciers retreat, resulting in new animal species and flora.
6,500	Farming of cereal, sheep, and goats in Balkans and Aegean; Britain separated from Europe by rising ocean levels.
5,200	Farming spreads to Netherlands.
5,000	Gold, copper used.
4,500	Megalithic tombs.
4,000	Flint mines; farming developed in Britain.
3,500	Animals used to pull plows.
3,200	First wheeled vehicles; circles of megalithic stones.
2,000	Main phase of Stonehenge; fortified settlements; palaces in Minoan Crete.
1,900	Hieroglyphic Cretan writing.
1,450	Myceneans take control of Minoan Crete.
1,000	First hill forts in western Europe; iron industry in Aegean and central Europe.
750	Iron working in Britain.
753	Traditional foundation of Rome.

mission's proposals; the ◊European Parliament, directly elected from 1979, which is mainly a consulting body but can dismiss the Commission; and the ◊European Court of Justice, to safeguard interpretation of the Rome Treaties (1957) that established the Community.

In 1992 members became one market with the free movement of goods and capital.

European Court of Justice the court of the European Community (EC), which is responsible for interpreting Community law and ruling on breaches by member states and others of such law. It sits in Luxembourg with judges from the member states.

The European Court of Human Rights sits in Strasbourg to adjudicate on breaches of the European Convention of Human Rights.

European Economic Community (EEC) one of the organizations of the ◊European Community (EC).

European Free Trade Association (EFTA) an organization established 1960 and as of 1988 consisting of Austria, Finland, Iceland, Norway, Sweden, and Switzerland. There are no import duties between members. Of the original members, Britain and Denmark left (1972) to join the ◊European Community, as subsequently did Portugal (1985).

In 1973 the EC signed agreements with EFTA members, setting up a free-trade area of over 300 million consumers. Trade between the two groups amounts to over half of total EFTA trade.

European Monetary System (EMS) an attempt by the European Community to bring financial cooperation and monetary stability to Europe. It was established 1979 in the wake of the 1974 oil crisis, which brought growing economic disruption to European economies because of floating exchange rates. Central to the EMS is the ◊Exchange Rate Mechanism (ERM), a voluntary system of semi-fixed exchange rates based on the European Currency Unit (ECU).

European Monetary Union (EMU) the proposed European Community policy for a single currency and common economic policies. The proposal was announced by a European Community committee headed by EC Commission president Jacques Delors Apr 1989.

Three stages are envisaged for EMU. In the first stage, all controls on individual nations' capital flows would be ended, and the European System of Central Banks (ESCB) created. In stage two, the ESCB would begin to regulate money supply. Finally, exchange rates between member states would be fixed, and a single European currency created, and the ESCB would take over the function of all the nations' central banks.

European Parliament the parliament of the European Community, which meets in Strasbourg to comment on the legislative proposals of the Commission of the European Communities. Members are elected for a five-year term. The European Parliament has 518 seats, apportioned on the basis of population, of which the UK, France,

Europe

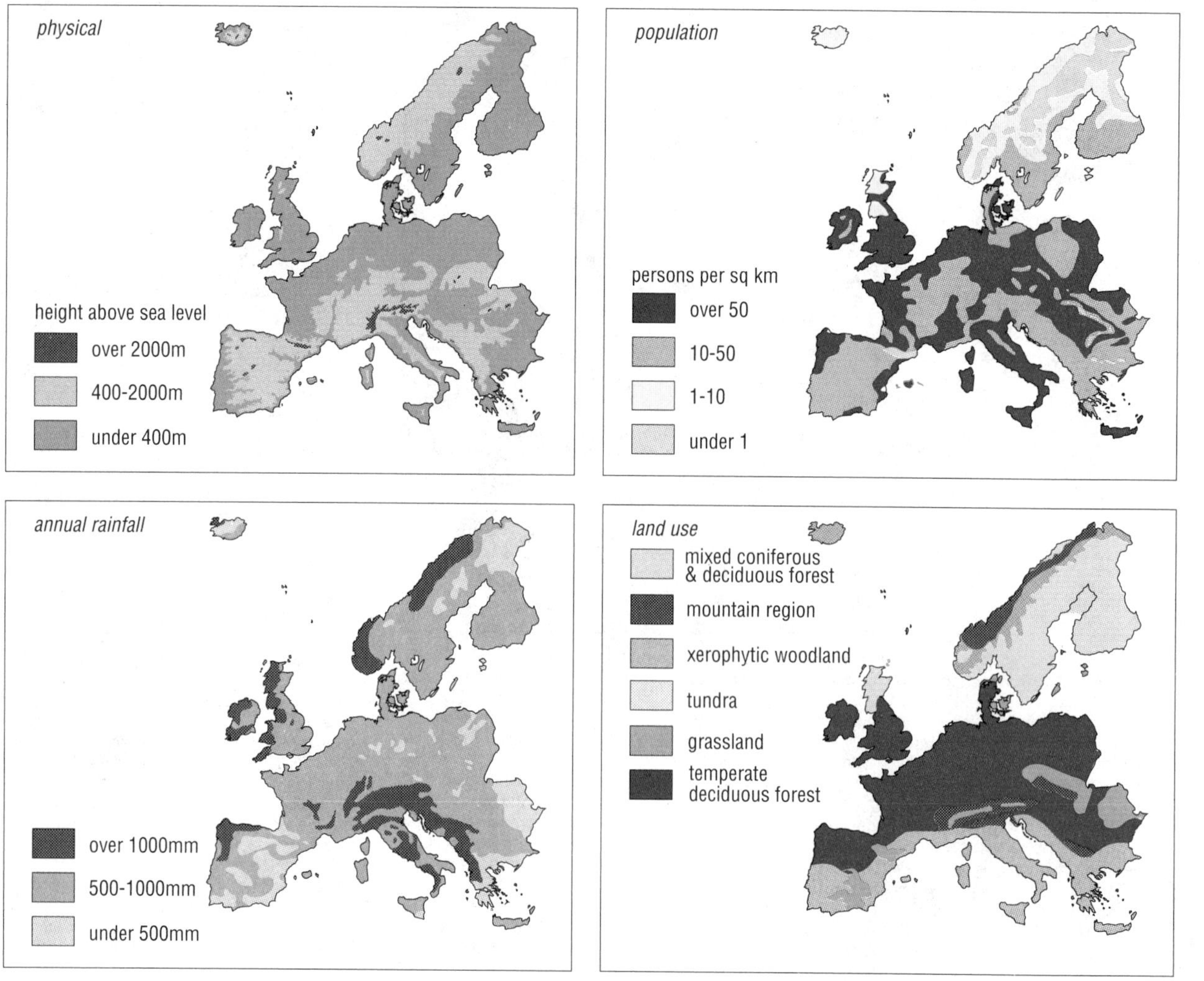
physical
height above sea level
over 2000m
400-2000m
under 400m
population
persons per sq km
over 50
10-50
1-10
under 1
annual rainfall
over 1000mm
500-1000mm
under 500mm
land use
mixed coniferous & deciduous forest
mountain region
xerophytic woodland
tundra
grassland
temperate deciduous forest

Europe: history

BC	
3000	Bronze Age civilizations: Minoan, Mycenean.
1000	Iron Age.
6th–4th centuries	Greek civilization at its height; Alexander the Great advances E to India.
3rd century	Rome in control of the Italian peninsula.
146	Greece a Roman province, and Carthage destroyed.
1st century	Augustus made the Rhine and Danube the Roman Empire's northern frontiers; see ◊Celts
AD	
1st century	Britain brought within the Roman Empire
2nd century	Roman Empire ceased to expand.
4th century	Christianity the established religion of the Roman Empire, which halved into E and W empires (see ◊Byzantine Empires).
4th–6th centuries	W Europe overrun by Anglo-Saxons, Franks, Goths, Lombards. W Roman empire fell 476. Middle Ages begin; feudalism prevails.
7th–8th centuries	Christendom threatened by the Moors (Muslim Arabs) via the Mediterranean countries.
800	Charlemagne given title of emperor by the Pope; Holy Roman empire begins.
1073	Gregory VII began 200 years of conflict between the powers of the empire and papacy.
1096–1272	Crusades to take Jerusalem.
12th century	Setting up of German, Flemish, and Italian city-states, which in the 14th–15th centuries fostered the Renaissance.
1453	Byzantine empire falls to the Turks.
16th–17th centuries	Dominated by rivalry of France and the Hapsburgs, the Protestant Reformation, and the Catholic Counter-Reformation.
17th century	Absolute monarchy came to prevail (Louis XIV) in Europe, although in Britain supremacy of Parliament established by Civil War.
18th century	War of the Austrian Succession and Seven Years' War ended in the loss of the French colonial empire to Britain and the establishment of Prussia as Europe's military power.
1789–95	French Revolution led to the Revolutionary and Napoleonic wars.
1821–29	Greek War of Independence marked the end of Turkish control of the Balkans.
1848	Year of revolutions (see ◊Louis Philippe, ◊Metternich,◊Risorgimento).
1914–1918	World War I arose from the Balkan question, Franco-German rivalry, and colonial differences; it destroyed the Austrian, Russian and Turkish empires and paved the way for the Russian Revolution and the formation of the USSR.
1933	Hitler came to power in a defeated, impoverished Germany. His geopolitical aggression caused World War II.
1939–45	World War II resulted in decline of European colonial rule in Africa and Asia; emergence of Soviet power, and most of Western Europe under the military aegis of the US (NATO); the Cold War begins.
1957	Establishment of the European Economic Community, the "Common Market."
1973	Enlargement of the European Community to include Britain, Denmark, and the Irish Republic.
1979	First direct elections to the European Parliament.
1989–90	Beginning of democratization of Eastern bloc, including USSR, Poland, Romania, Czechoslovakia, East Germany, Lithuania. Germany reunited.
1991	Baltic republics of Estonia, Latvia, and Lithuania regain independence; other Soviet republics follow.
1992	European Community becomes a single market.

West Germany, and Italy have 81 each, Spain 60, the Netherlands 25, Belgium, Greece, and Portugal 24 each, Denmark 16, the Republic of Ireland 15, and Luxembourg 6.

European Space Agency (ESA) an organization of European countries (Belgium, Denmark, France, Ireland, Italy, the Netherlands, Spain, Sweden, Switzerland, the UK, and West Germany) that engages in space research and technology. It was founded 1975, with headquarters in Paris.

The ESA has developed various scientific and communications satellites, the ◊*Giotto* space probe, and the ◊Ariane rockets. It built ◊Spacelab, plans to build its own space station, *Columbus*, for attachment to the US space station, and is working on its own shuttle project, Hermes.

europium soft, grayish, metallic element of the ◊lanthanide series, symbol Eu, atomic number 63, atomic weight 151.96. It is used in lasers and as the red phosphor in color televisions; its compounds are used to make control rods for nuclear reactors.

It was named in 1901 by French chemist Eugène Demarçay (1852–1904) for the continent of Europe, where it was first found.

Eurydice in Greek mythology, the wife of ◊Orpheus. She was a dryad, or forest nymph, and died of snake bite. Orpheus attempted unsuccessfully to fetch her back from the realm of the dead.

Eusebius c. 260–c. 340. Bishop of Caesarea (modern Qisarya, Israel); author of a history of the Christian church to 324.

Euskadi the Basque name for the ◊Basque Country.

eusociality form of social life found in insects such as honey bees and termites, in which the colony is made up of special castes (for example, workers, drones, and reproductives) whose membership is biologically determined. The worker castes do not usually reproduce. Only one mammal, the naked mole rat, has a social organization of this type. See also ◊social behavior.

eustachian tube small air-filled canal connecting the middle ◊ear with the back of the throat. It is found in all land vertebrates and equalizes the pressure on both sides of the eardrum.

Eustachio Bartolommeo 1520–1574. Italian anatomist, the discoverer of the Eustachian tube, leading from the middle ear to the pharynx, and of the Eustachian valve in the right auricles of the heart.

Eutelsat acronym for European Telecommunications Satellite Organization.

Euterpe in Greek mythology, one of the ◊Muses (nine minor divinities) who inspired lyric poetry.

euthanasia mercy killing of someone with a severe and incurable condition or illness. The Netherlands legalized voluntary euthanasia 1983, but is the only country to have done so.

eutrophication the excessive enrichment of lake waters, primarily by nitrate fertilizers, washed from the soil by rain, and by phosphates from detergents in municipal sewage. These encourage the growth of algae and bacteria which use up the oxygen in the water, thereby making it uninhabitable for fishes and other animal life.

Eutyches c. 384–c. 456. Christian theologian. An archimandrite (monastic head) in Constantinople, he held that Jesus had only one nature, the human nature being subsumed in the divine (a belief which became known as ◊Monophysitism). He was exiled after his ideas were condemned as heretical by the Council of ◊Chalcedon 451.

evangelicalism the beliefs of some Protestant Christian movements that stress biblical authority, faith, and the personal commitment of the "born again" experience.

Evangelical groups constituted the fastest-growing part of American Christianity during the 1970s and 1980s; their influence was spread through Bible colleges, Christian publishing houses and bookstores, television evangelism, and missionary efforts.

evangelist person traveling to spread the Christian gospel, in particular the authors of the four Gospels in the New Testament: Matthew, Mark, Luke, and John. See also ◊televangelist.

Evans Arthur John 1851–1941. English archeologist. His excavation of ◊Knossos on Crete resulted in the discovery of pre-Phoenician Minoan script and proved the existence of the legendary Minoan civilization.

Evans Edith 1888–1976. English character actress who performed on the London stage and on Broadway. Her many performances include the film role of Lady Bracknell in Oscar Wilde's comedy *The Importance of Being Earnest* 1952. Among her other films are *Tom Jones* 1963 and *Crooks and Coronets* 1969.

Evans Walker 1903–1975. US photographer best known for his documentary photographs of people in the rural American South during the Great Depression. Many of his photographs appeared in James Agee's book *Let Us Now Praise Famous Men* 1941.

Born in St Louis, Evans was in 1938 the first photographer to have an exhibit at the Museum of Modern Art in New York City. From 1945 to 1965 he served as an associate editor of *Fortune* magazine, in which he published several photo essays. Throughout his career, he devoted much attention to photographing architecture. He also did a renowned series of photographs of people in the New York City subways.

Evansville industrial city in SW Indiana, on the Ohio River; population (1990) 126,272. The University of Evansville is here. The community, which dates to 1812, grew as an important port for steamships on the Ohio River and as a farm market. Industries include pharmaceuticals and plastics.

evaporation a process in which a liquid turns to a vapor without its temperature reaching boiling point. A liquid left to stand in a saucer eventually evaporates because, at any time, a proportion of its molecules have sufficient energy to escape through the liquid surface into the atmosphere. The temperature of the liquid tends to fall because the evaporating molecules remove energy from the liquid. The rate of evaporation rises with an increase in temperature.

evaporite any sedimentary rock composed of minerals precipitated from solutions concentrated by evaporation of the liquid in which they were dissolved. Examples are halite (NaCl), gypsum ($CaSO_4 \cdot 2H_2O$), and anhydrite ($CaSO_4$). Most evaporite deposits were precipitated from sea water as ancient continental seas shrank and evaporated. The less highly soluble minerals are the first to drop out of solution. Thus gypsum and anhydrite are deposited first; then as evaporation progresses, the more soluble halite is precipitated.

Eve in the Old Testament, the first woman, wife of ◊Adam. She was tempted by Satan (in the form of a snake) to eat the fruit of the Tree of Knowledge of Good and Evil, and then tempted Adam to eat of the fruit as well, thus bringing about their expulsion from the Garden of Eden.

There are two versions of the creation myth

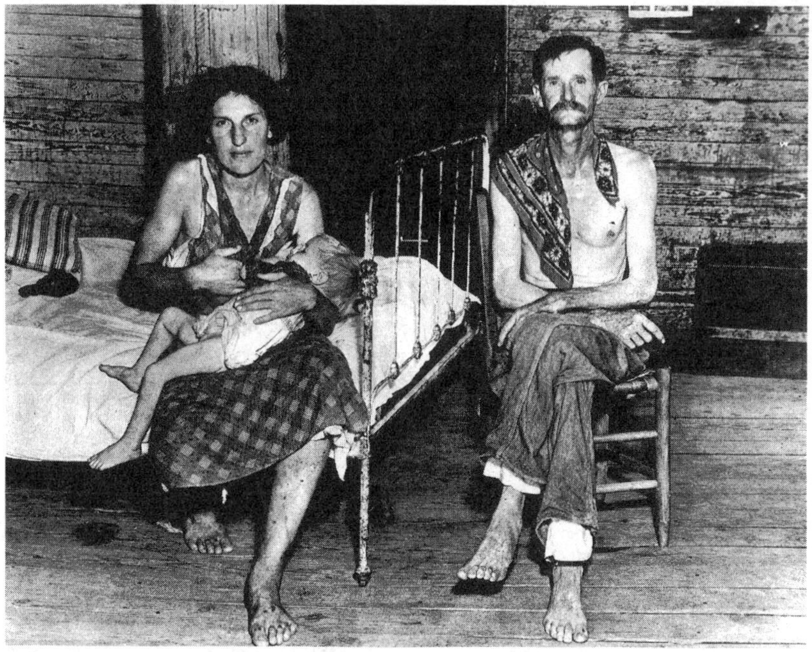

***Evans** The poverty of the Depression and the stoical dignity of its victims is sympathetically portrayed in this photograph by Walter Evans. Entitled* Depression: Bud Fields and Wife; Alabama, 1935, *it is typical of Evans's social documentary pictures of the 1930s.*

in the Bible: in one of them, Eve was created simultaneously with Adam; in the other, she was created from his rib. In the Hebrew writings known as the "Midrash," ◊Lilith was the first woman (and her children were the wives available to Eve's sons Cain and Abel).

evening primrose any plant of the genus *Oenothera*, family Onagraceae. Some 50 species are native to North America, several of which now also grow in Europe. Some are cultivated for their oil, which is used in treating eczema, premenstrual tension, and chronic fatigue syndrome.

Everest, Mount (Chinese *Qomolungma* "goddess mother of the snows/world"; Nepalese *Sagarmatha* "head of the earth") the highest mountain above sea level, in the Himalaya range, on the border of China and Nepal, height 29,108 ft/ 8,872 m (recently remeasured by satellite to this new height from the former official height of 29,028 ft/8848m). It was first climbed by Edmund Hillary and Tenzing Norgay 1953. The English name comes from George Everest (1790–1866), surveyor-general of India.

Everett Edward 1794–1865. US religious leader, educator, and public figure. Born in Dorchester, Massachusetts, and educated at Harvard, Everett was named pastor of Boston's Brattle Street Church 1814. After gaining his PhD at Göttingen 1817 and teaching at Harvard, he served in the US House of Representatives 1825–35, as Massachusetts governor 1835–39, as US minister to England 1841–45, and as president of Harvard 1846–49. His four-month role as President Fillmore's secretary of state 1852–53 was followed by a short tenure in the US Senate 1853–54. Thereafter, he spoke out as a private citizen for abolitionism and the preservation of the Union.

Everglades area of swamps, marsh, and lakes in S ◊Florida; area 5,000 sq mi/12,950 sq km. A national park covers the southern tip. Formed by overflow of Lake Okeechobee after heavy rains, it is one of the wildest areas in the US, noted for its distinctive plant and animal life. The only human residents are several hundred Seminole. Large drainage programs have reduced the flow of water from the lake southward, threatening the region's ecological balance.

evergreen plant, such as pine, spruce, or holly, that bears its leaves all year round. Most ◊conifers are evergreen. Plants that shed their leaves in autumn or a dry season are described as ◊deciduous.

everlasting flower any flower head with colored bracts that retains its color when cut and dried.

They are mostly of the composite family, including some species of *Ammobium*, *Helichrysum*, and *Xeranthemum*. The strawflower of Australia *Helichrysum bracteatum* is a popular example.

Evershed John 1864–1956. English astronomer who made solar observations. In 1909, he discovered the radial movements of gases in sunspots (the Evershed effect). He also gave his name to a spectroheliograph, the Evershed spectroscope.

Evert Chris(tine) 1954– . US tennis player. She won her first Wimbledon title 1974, and has since won 21 Grand Slam titles. She became the first woman tennis player to win $1 million in prize money.

She has an outstanding two-handed backhand and is a great exponent of baseline technique. From 1974–89 at Wimbledon she never failed to reach the quarterfinals at least.

CAREER HIGHLIGHTS

Wimbledon
singles: 1974, 1976, 1981
doubles: 1976
US Open
singles: 1975–78, 1980, 1982
French Open
singles: 1974–75, 1979–80, 1983, 1985–86
doubles: 1974–75
Australian Open
singles: 1982, 1984

evidence the testimony of witnesses and production of documents and other material in court proceedings in order to prove or disprove facts at issue in the case. Witnesses must swear or affirm that their evidence is true. In English law, giving false evidence is the crime of ◊perjury.

Documentary evidence has a wide scope including maps, soundtracks, and films, in addition to documents in writing. Objects such as weapons used in crimes may serve as evidence. Evidence obtained illegally, such as a confession under duress, may be excluded from the court.

evolution a slow process of change from one form to another, as in the evolution of the universe from its formation in the ◊Big Bang to its present state, or in the evolution of life on Earth. Some Christians and Muslims deny the theory of evolution as conflicting with the belief that God created all things (see ◊creationism).

The idea of continuous evolution in the living world can be traced as far back as ◊Lucretius in the 1st century BC, but it did not gain wide acceptance until the 19th century, following the work of Charles ◊Lyell, J B ◊Lamarck, Charles ◊Darwin, and T H ◊Huxley. Darwin assigned the major role in evolutionary change to ◊natural selection acting on randomly occurring variations. Natural selection occurs because those individuals better adapted to their particular environments reproduce more effectively, thus contributing their characteristics to future generations. The current theory of evolution, called ◊Neo-Darwinism, combines Darwin's theory with Gregor ◊Mendel's theories on genetics and Hugo de Vries' discovery of genetic mutation. Although neither the general concept of evolution nor the importance of natural selection is doubted by the vast majority of biologists, there remains dispute over other possible processes involved in evolutionary change. Besides natural selection and ◊sexual selection, chance may play a large part in deciding which genes become characteristic of a population, a phenomenon called "genetic drift." It is now also clear that evolutionary change does not always occur at a constant rate, but that the process can have long periods of relative stability interspersed with periods of rapid change. This has led to new theories, such as ◊punctuated equilibrium model. See also ◊adaptive radiation.

evolutionary stable strategy (ESS) in sociobiology, an assemblage of behavioral or physical characters (collectively termed a "strategy") of a population that is resistant to replacement by any forms bearing new traits, because the new traits will not be capable of successful reproduction.

ESS analysis is based on ◊game theory and can be applied both to genetically determined physical characters (such as horn length), and to learned behavioral responses (for example, whether to fight or retreat from an opponent). An ESS may be conditional on the context, as in the rule "fight if the opponent is smaller, but retreat if the opponent is larger."

Evreux capital of Eure *département* in NW France; population (1983) 46,250. It produces pharmaceuticals and rubber.

Evvoia Greek name for the island of ◊Euboea.

evzone member of a Greek infantry regiment whose soldiers wear distinctive white short-skirted uniform.

ex cathedra (Latin "from the throne") term describing a statement by the pope, taken to be indisputably true, and which must be accepted by Catholics.

excavator machine designed for digging in the ground, or for earth-moving in general. Diggers using hydraulically powered digging arms are widely used on building sites. They may run on wheels or on ◊caterpillar tracks. The largest excavators are the draglines used in mining to strip away earth covering the coal or mineral deposit.

exchange rate the price at which one currency is bought or sold in terms of other currencies, gold, or accounting units, such as the special drawing right (SDR) of the ◊International Monetary Fund. Exchange rates may be fixed by international agreement or by government policy; or they may be wholly or partly allowed to "float" (that is, find their own level) in world currency markets. Central banks, as large holders of foreign currency, often intervene to buy or sell particular currencies in an effort to maintain some stability in exchange rates.

Under the Reagan administration, the US dollar was allowed, even encouraged, to drop in relation to other currencies, especially the Japanese yen.

Exchange Rate Mechanism (ERM) voluntary system

evolution

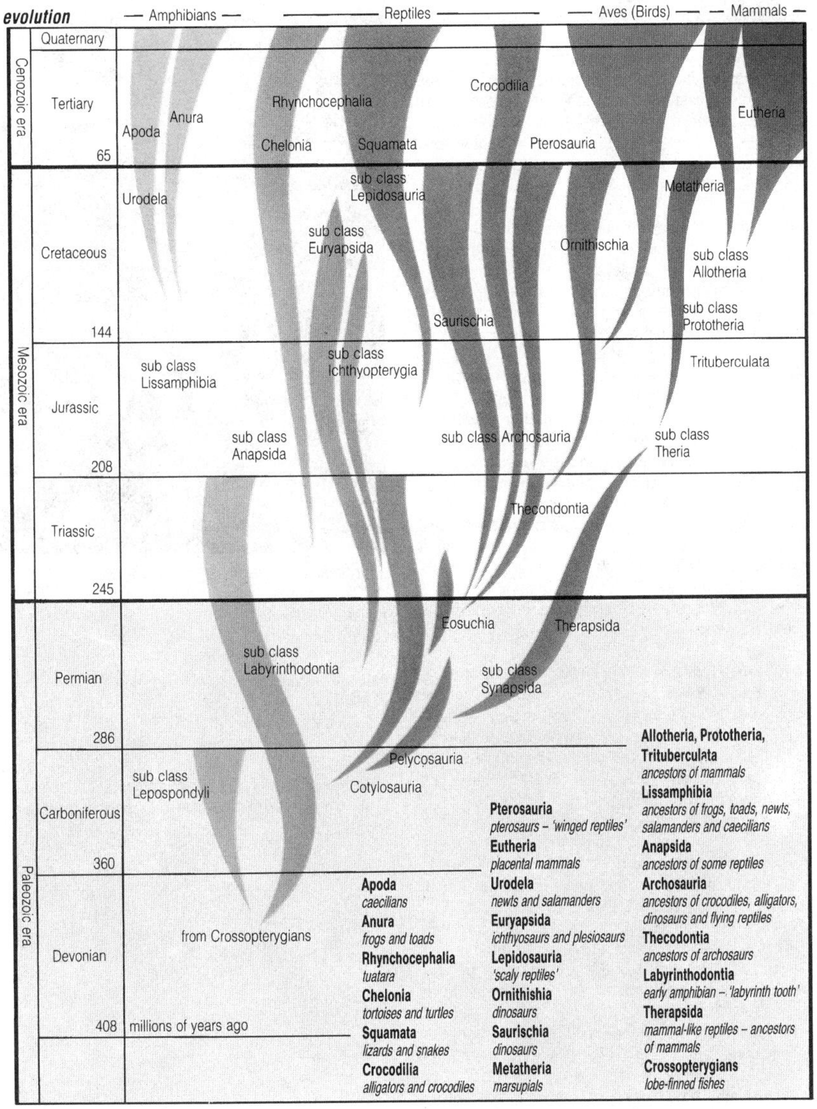

— Amphibians —
Reptiles
— Aves (Birds) —
— Mammals —
Cenozoic era
Mesozoic era
Paleozoic era
Quaternary
Tertiary
65
Cretaceous
144
Jurassic
208
Triassic
245
Permian
286
Carboniferous
360
Devonian
408
Apoda
Anura
Rhynchocephalia
Crocodilia
Eutheria
Chelonia
Squamata
Pterosauria
sub class Lepidosauria
Metatheria
Urodela
sub class Euryapsida
Ornithischia
sub class Allotheria
Saurischia
sub class Prototheria
sub class Lissamphibia
sub class Ichthyopterygia
Trituberculata
sub class Anapsida
sub class Archosauria
sub class Theria
Thecondontia
Eosuchia
Therapsida
sub class Labyrinthodontia
sub class Synapsida
Pelycosauria
sub class Lepospondyli
Cotylosauria
from Crossopterygians
millions of years ago
Apoda
caecilians
Anura
frogs and toads
Rhynchocephalia
tuatara
Chelonia
tortoises and turtles
Squamata
lizards and snakes
Crocodilia
alligators and crocodiles
Pterosauria
pterosaurs – 'winged reptiles'
Eutheria
placental mammals
Urodela
newts and salamanders
Euryapsida
ichthyosaurs and plesiosaurs
Lepidosauria
'scaly reptiles'
Ornithishia
dinosaurs
Saurischia
dinosaurs
Metatheria
marsupials
Allotheria, Prototheria, Trituberculata
ancestors of mammals
Lissamphibia
ancestors of frogs, toads, newts, salamanders and caecilians
Anapsida
ancestors of some reptiles
Archosauria
ancestors of crocodiles, alligators, dinosaurs and flying reptiles
Thecodontia
ancestors of archosaurs
Labyrinthodontia
early amphibian – 'labyrinth tooth'
Therapsida
mammal-like reptiles – ancestors of mammals
Crossopterygians
lobe-finned fishes

for controlling exchange rates within the European Community's ◊European Monetary System.

Under the ERM a central rate for each currency against the ECU (European Currency Unit) is fixed. If it moves outside specified limits, the government must take action to avert the trend. The ERM has been successful in limiting fluctuations between exchange rates of participating countries: all EC members, with the exception of Greece and Portugal. The UK entered the system in Oct 1990.

excise taxes imposed on goods, usually considered luxury items or those items quickly consumed. The taxes are paid prior to sale, the cost being passed on to the consumer.

Among the most common excise taxes in the US are those on cigarettes, gasoline, and alcohol.

exclamation point punctuation mark (!) used to indicate emphasis or strong emotion ("That's terrible!"). It is appropriate after interjections ("Rats!"), emphatic greetings ("Yo!"), and orders ("Shut up!"), as well as those sentences beginning *How* or *What* that are not questions ("How embarrassing!," "What a surprise!").

exclusion principle in physics, a principle of atomic structure originated by Wolfgang ◊Pauli. It states that no two electrons in a single atom may have the same set of ◊quantum numbers.

excommunication exclusion of an offender from the rights and privileges of the Roman Catholic Church; King John, Henry VIII, and Elizabeth I were all excommunicated.

excretion the removal of waste products from the cells of living organisms. In plants and simple animals, waste products are removed by diffusion, but in higher animals by specialized organs. In mammals, for example, carbon dioxide and water are removed via the lungs, and nitrogenous compounds and water via the liver, the kidneys, and the rest of the urinary system.

executor in law, a person appointed in a will to carry out the instructions of the deceased. A person so named has the right to refuse to act. The executor also has a duty to bury the deceased, prove the will, obtain a grant of probate (that is, establish that the will is genuine and obtain official approval of his or her actions), and pay the, liens, fees, and taxes on the estate before distributing the estate property to the heirs.

Exeter city, administrative headquarters of Devon, England, on the river Exe; population (1981) 96,000. It has medieval, Georgian, and Regency architecture, including a cathedral (1280–1369), a market center, and a university (1955). It manufactures agricultural machinery, pharmaceuticals, and textiles.

existentialism branch of philosophy based on the concept of an absurd universe where humans have free will; a pragmatic and psychological approach to reality outside religious concerns. Existentialists argue that philosophy must begin from the concrete situation of the individual in such a world, and that humans are responsible for and the sole judge of their actions as they affect others, although no one else's existence is real to the individual. The origin of existentialism is usually traced back to the Danish philosopher ◊Kierkegaard, and among its proponents were Martin Heidegger in Germany and Jean-Paul ◊Sartre in France.

exobiology the study of life forms that may possibly exist elsewhere in the universe and of the effects of extraterrestrial environments on Earth organisms.

exocrine gland gland that discharges secretions, usually through a tube or a duct, onto a surface. Examples include sweat glands which release sweat onto the skin, and digestive glands which release digestive juices onto the walls of the intestine. Some animals also have ◊endocrine glands (ductless glands) that release hormones directly into the bloodstream.

Exodus the second book of the Old Testament, which relates the departure of the Israelites from slavery in Egypt, under the leadership of ◊Moses, for the Promised Land of Canaan. The journey included the miraculous parting of the Red Sea, with Pharaoh's pursuing forces being drowned as the waters returned.

The Exodus is also recorded in the *Hagadda*, which is read at the Seder (during the Jewish festival of Passover) to commemorate the deliverance. During the 40 years of wandering in the wilderness, Moses brought the Ten Commandments down from Mt. Sinai.

exorcism rite used in a number of religions for the expulsion of so-called evil spirits. In Christianity it is employed, for example, in the Roman Catholic and Pentecostal churches.

exoskeleton the hardened external skeleton of insects, spiders, crabs, and other arthropods. It provides attachment for muscles and protection for the internal organs, as well as support. To permit growth it is periodically shed in a process called ◊ecdysis.

exosphere the uppermost layer of the ◊atmosphere. It is an ill-defined zone above the thermosphere, beginning at about 435 mi/700 km and fading off into the vacuum of space. The gases are extremely thin, with hydrogen as the main constituent.

exothermic reaction a chemical reaction during which heat is given out (see ◊energy of reaction).

expansion in physics, the increase in size of a constant mass of substance (a body) caused by, for example, increasing its temperature (◊thermal expansion) or its internal pressure. Expansivity, or coefficient of cubic (or thermal) expansion, is the expansion per unit volume per degree rise in temperature.

In mechanics, expansion refers to the increase in volume of steam in the cylinder of a steam engine after cutoff, or of gas in the cylinder of an internal-combustion engine after explosion. See also ◊Charles's law.

expansivity alternate name for coefficient of expansion. See also ◊Charles's law.

Ex parte McCardle a US Supreme Court decision 1869 dealing with the power of Congress to deprive the Supreme Court of jurisdiction over appeals. William McCardle, a Mississippi journalist convicted of sedition by a military court and refused a writ of habeas corpus by the federal circuit court, appealed his case to the Supreme Court. Afraid that the military Reconstruction governments would be found unconstitutional, Congress revoked the Court's jurisdiction over appeals. The Court ruled unanimously that this was fully within the constitutional right of Congress to make exceptions to the Supreme Court's right to hear appeals; furthermore, it was not the Court's job to discern the political motives of restrictions imposed by Congress.

Ex parte Merryman a circuit court decision 1861

dealing with the right of the US president to restrict the civilian court under martial law for secessionist activities. Merryman, a Baltimore citizen, received a writ of habeas corpus from the acting circuit court judge, Chief Justice Taney. Taney ordered that Merryman be brought to trial or released and found the military in contempt of court when, under the authority of President Lincoln, it refused to comply. Taney declared that Lincoln was in violation of the Constitution, saying only Congress had the right to suspend habeas corpus. The case never reached the US Supreme Court.

Ex parte Milligan a US Supreme Court decision 1866 that attended to the issue of the jurisdiction of military tribunals in areas where civilian courts are operating. Milligan, an Indiana citizen sentenced by a military tribunal to hang for secessionist activities, petitioned for a writ of habeas corpus on the grounds that as a civilian he was not subject to military law. The Court ruled 5–4 in favor of Milligan, holding that neither the US president nor Congress had the right to impose martial law outside of a war zone.

expectorant any substance, often added to cough mixture, intended to help expel mucus from the airways. It is debatable whether expectorants have an effect on lung secretions.

experiment in science, a practical test designed with the intention that its results will be relevant to a particular theory or set of theories. Although some experiments may be used merely for gathering more information about a topic that is already well understood, others may be of crucial importance in confirming a new theory or in undermining long-held beliefs.

The manner in which experiments are performed, and the relation between the design of an experiment and its value, are therefore of central importance. In general an experiment is of most value when the factors that might affect the results (variables) are carefully controlled; for this reason most experiments take place in a well-managed environment such as a laboratory or clinic.

experimental psychology the application of scientific methods to the study of mental processes and behavior.

This covers a wide range of fields of study including: human and animal learning, in which learning theories describe how new behaviors are acquired and modified; cognition, the study of a number of functions, such as perception, attention, memory, and language; physiological psychology, which relates the study of cognition to different regions of the brain. Artificial intelligence refers to the computer simulation of cognitive processes, such as language and problem-solving.

expert system computer program for giving advice (such as diagnosing an illness or interpreting the law) that incorporates knowledge derived from human expertise. It is a kind of ◊knowledge-based system containing rules that can be applied to find the solution to a problem. It is a form of ◊artificial intelligence.

explanation in science, an attempt to make clear the cause of any natural event, by reference to physical laws and to observations.

The extent to which any explanation can be said to be true is one of the chief concerns of philosophy, partly because observations may be wrongly interpreted, partly because explanations should help us predict how nature will behave. Although it may be reasonable to expect that a physical law will hold in the future, that expectation is problematic in that it relies on ◊induction, a much-criticized feature of human thought; in fact no explanation, however "scientific," can be held to be true for all time, and thus the difference between a scientific and a common-sense explanation remains the subject of intense philosophical debate.

Explorer series of US scientific satellites. *Explorer 1*, launched Jan 1958, was the first US satellite in orbit and discovered the Van Allen radiation belts around the Earth.

explosive any material capable of a sudden release of energy and the rapid formation of a large volume of gas, leading when compressed to the development of a high-pressure wave (blast).

exponent or index in mathematics, a number that indicates the number of times a term is multiplied by itself; for example $x^2 = x \times x$, $4^3 = 4 \times 4 \times 4$.

Exponents obey certain rules. Terms that contain them are multiplied together by adding the exponents; for example, $x^2 \times x^5 = x^7$. Division of such terms is done by subtracting the exponents; for example, $y^5 \div y^3 = y^2$. Any number with the exponent 0 is equal to 1; for example, $x^0 = 1$ and $99^0 = 1$.

exponential in mathematics, descriptive of a ◊function in which the variable quantity is an exponent (an ◊index or power to which another number or expression is raised).

Exponential functions and series involve the constant $e = 2.71828\ldots$. Napier devised natural ◊logarithms in 1614 with e as the base.

Exponential functions are basic mathematical functions, written as e^x or $\exp x$. The expression e^x has five definitions, two of which are: (i) e^x is the solution of the differential equation $dx/dt = x$ ($x = 1$ if $t = 0$); (ii) e^x is the limiting sum of the infinite series $1 + x + (x^2/2!) + (x^3/3!) + \ldots + (x^n/n!)$.

Exponential growth is not constant. It applies, for example, to population growth, where the population doubles in a short time period. A graph of population number against time is an exponential growth function and produces a curve that is characteristically rather flat at first but then shoots almost directly upward.

export goods or services produced in one country and sold to another. Exports may be visible (goods physically exported) or invisible (services provided in the exporting country but paid for in another country).

export credit loan, finance, or guarantee provided by a government or a financial institution enabling companies to export goods and services in situations where payment for them may be delayed or subject to risk.

exposure meter instrument used in photography for indicating the correct exposure—the length of time the camera shutter should be open under given light conditions. Meters use substances such as cadmium sulfide and selenium as light sensors. These materials change electrically when light strikes them, the change being proportional to the intensity of the incident light. Many cameras have a built-in exposure meter that sets the camera controls automatically as the light conditions change.

Expressionism a style of painting, sculpture, and literature that expresses inner emotions; in particular, a movement in early 20th-century art in northern and central Europe. Expressionists tended to distort or exaggerate natural appearance in order to create a reflection of an inner world; the Norwegian painter Edvard Munch's *Skriket/The Scream* 1893 is perhaps the most celebrated example. Expressionist writers include August Strindberg and Frank Wedekind.

Other leading Expressionist artists were James Ensor, Oskar Kokoschka, and Chaïm Soutine. The Blaue Reiter group was associated with this movement, and the Expressionist trend in German art emerged strongly after World War I in the work of Max Beckmann and Georg Grosz.

expressionism in music, atonal music that uses dissonance for disturbing effect.

expressway a divided highway for through traffic with controlled access and exits and with under- and overpasses at intersections. The first expressway (53 mi/85 km) ran from Milan to Varèse, Italy, and was completed 1924. The US began its development of expressways shortly after World War II.

Expressionism *Edvard Munch's* The Scream *(1893), National Gallery, Oslo. Munch's work is typically Expressionist in using color, line, and texture to create a reflection of an inner world.*

extensor a muscle that straightens a limb.

extinction in biology, the complete disappearance of a species. In the past, extinctions are believed to have occurred because species were unable to adapt quickly enough to a naturally changing environment. Today, most extinctions are due to human activity. Some species, such as the ◊dodo of Mauritius, the ◊moas of New Zealand, and the passenger ◊pigeon of North America, were exterminated by hunting. Others become extinct when their habitat is destroyed. See also ◊endangered species.

Mass extinctions are episodes during which whole groups of species have become extinct, the best known being that of the dinosaurs, other large reptiles, and various marine invertebrates about 65 million years ago. Another mass extinction occurred about 10,000 years ago when many giant species of mammal died out. This is known as the "Pleistocene overkill" because their disappearance was probably hastened by the hunting activities of prehistoric humans. The current mass extinction is largely due to human destruction of habitats, as in the tropical forests and coral reefs; it is far more serious and damaging than mass extinctions of the past because of the speed at which it occurs. Man-made climatic changes and pollution also make it less likely that the biosphere can recover and evolve new species to suit a changed environment. The rate of extinction is difficult to estimate, since most losses occur in the rich environment of the tropical rainforest, where the total number of existent species is not known. Conservative estimates put the rate of loss due to deforestation alone at 4,000 to 6,000 species a year. Overall, the rate could be as high as one species an hour, with the loss of one species putting those dependent on it at risk. Australia has the worst record for extinction: 18 mammals have disappeared since Europeans settled there, and 40 more are threatened.

extracellular matrix a strong material naturally occurring in animals and plants, made up of protein and long-chain sugars (polysaccharides) in which cells are embedded. It is often called a "biological glue," and forms part of ◊connective tissues such as bone and skin.

The cell walls of plants and bacteria, and the ◊exoskeletons of insects and other arthropods, are also formed by types of extracellular matrix.

extradition the surrender, by one state or country to another, of a person accused of a criminal

***Eyck** Jan van Eyck's* Arnolfini Wedding *(1434), National Gallery, London.*

offense in the state or country to which that person is extradited.

When two nations are involved, extradition is usually governed by a treaty between the two countries concerned. A country usually will not allow extradition for political offenses or an offense that it does not treat as a crime, even though it is a crime in the requesting country.

Extremadura autonomous region of W Spain including the provinces of Badajoz and Cáceres; area 16,058 sq mi/41,600 sq km; population (1986) 1,089,000. Irrigated land is used for growing wheat; the remainder is either oak forest or used for pig or sheep grazing.

extroversion or ***extraversion*** a personality dimension described by ◊Jung and later by Eysenck. The typical extrovert is sociable, impulsive, and carefree. The opposite of extroversion is introversion; the typical introvert is quiet and inward-looking.

extrusion common method of shaping metals, plastics, and other materials. The materials, usually hot, are forced through the hole in a metal die and take its cross-sectional shape. Rods, tubes, and sheets may be made in this way.

Eyck Jan van c. 1380–1441. Flemish painter of the early northern Renaissance, one of the first to work in oils. His paintings are technically brilliant and sumptuously rich in detail and color. Little is known of his brother Hubert van Eyck (died 1426), who is supposed to have begun the massive and complex altarpiece in St Bavo's cathedral, Ghent, *The Adoration of the Mystical Lamb*, completed by Jan 1432.

Jan van Eyck is known to have worked in The Hague 1422–24 for John of Bavaria, Count of Holland. He was court painter to Philip the Good, Duke of Burgundy, from 1425 and worked in Bruges from 1430. Philip the Good valued him not only as a painter but also as a diplomatic representative, sending him to Spain and Portugal in 1427 and 1428, and he remained in the duke's employment after he settled in Bruges.

Oil painting allowed for subtler effects of tone and color and greater command of detail than the egg-tempera technique then in common use, and van Eyck took full advantage of this. In his *Arnolfini Wedding* 1434 (National Gallery, London) the bride and groom appear in a domestic interior crammed with disguised symbols, as a kind of pictorial marriage certificate.

eye the organ of vision. The human eye is a roughly spherical structure contained in a bony socket. Light enters it through the cornea and passes through the circular opening (pupil) in the iris (the colored part of the eye). The light is focused by the combined action of the curved cornea, the internal fluids, and the lens (the rounded transparent structure behind the iris). The ciliary muscles act on the lens to change its shape, so that images of objects at different distances can be focused on the retina. This is at the back of the eye, and is packed with light-sensitive cells (rods and cones), connected to the brain by the optic nerve. In contrast, the insect eye is compound—that is, made up of many separate facets, known as ommatidia, each of which collects light and directs it separately to a receptor to build up an image. Invertebrates, such as some worms and snails, and certain bivalves, have much simpler eyes, with no lens. Among mollusks, cephalopods have complex eyes similar to those of vertebrates. The mantis shrimp's eyes contain ten color pigments with which to perceive color; some flies and fishes have five, while the human eye has only three.

eye

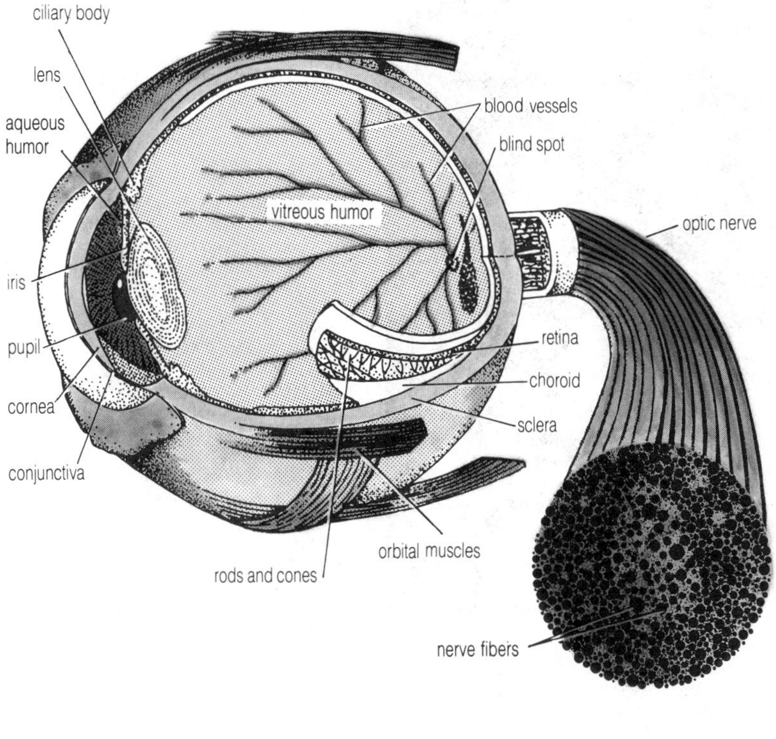

ciliary body
lens
aqueous humor
vitreous humor
blood vessels
blind spot
optic nerve
iris
pupil
cornea
conjunctiva
retina
choroid
sclera
orbital muscles
rods and cones
nerve fibers

eyebright any wild flower of the genus *Euphrasia* of the figwort family (Scrophulariaceae). *E americana* of the SE US, with pale lavender flowers in clusters, is an example.

eyeglasses pair of lenses fitted in a frame and worn in front of the eyes to correct or assist defective vision. Common defects of the eye corrected by such lenses are nearsightedness (myopia), corrected by using concave (spherical) lenses, farsightedness (hypermetropia), corrected by using convex (spherical) lenses, and astigmatism, corrected by using cylindrical lenses. Spherical and cylindrical lenses may be combined in one lens. Bifocal glasses correct vision both at a distance and for reading by combining two lenses of different curvatures in one piece of glass. Today, lightweight plastic lenses are common instead of glass.

Eyeglasses are said to have been invented in the 13th century by a Florentine monk. Few people found the need for glasses until printing was invented, when the demand for them increased rapidly. Using photosensitive glass, lenses can be produced that darken in glare and lighten in ordinary light conditions. See also ◊contact lens.

eyre in English history, one of the traveling courts set up by Henry II 1176 to enforce conformity to the king's will; they continued into the 13th century. Justices in eyre were the judges who heard pleas at these courts.

Eyre, Lake Australia's largest lake, in central South Australia, which frequently runs dry, becoming a salt marsh in dry seasons; area up to 3,500 sq mi/9,000 sq km. It is the continent's lowest point, 39 ft/12 m below sea level.

Eysenck Hans Jurgen 1916– . English psychologist. He concentrated on personality theory and testing by developing ◊behavior therapy. He is an outspoken critic of psychoanalysis as a therapeutic method.

Ezekiel lived c. 600 BC. In the Old Testament, a Hebrew prophet. Carried into captivity in Babylon by ◊Nebuchadnezzar 597, he preached that Jerusalem's fall was due to the sins of Israel. The book of Ezekiel begins with a description of a vision of supernatural beings.

Ezra in the Old Testament, a Hebrew scribe who was allowed by Artaxerxes, king of Persia (probably Artaxerxes I, 464–423 BC), to lead his people back to Jerusalem from Babylon 458 BC. He reestablished the Mosaic law (laid down by Moses) and forbade intermarriage.

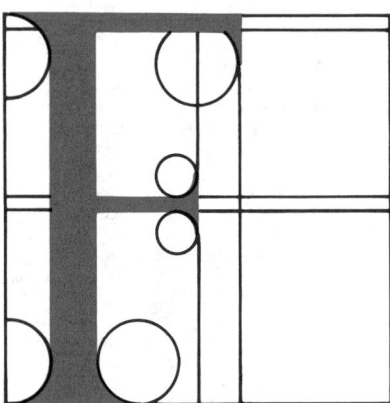

°F abbreviation for degrees ◊Fahrenheit.

Fabergé Peter Carl 1846–1920. Russian goldsmith and jeweler. His workshops in St Petersburg and Moscow were celebrated for the exquisite delicacy of their products, especially the use of gold in various shades. Among his masterpieces was a series of jeweled Easter eggs, the first of which was commissioned by Alexander III for the tsarina 1884. Fabergé died in exile in Switzerland.

Fabian Society UK Socialist organization for research, discussion, and publication, founded in London 1884. Its name is derived from the Roman commander Fabius Maximus, and refers to the evolutionary methods by which it hopes to attain socialism by a succession of gradual reforms. Early members included the playwright George Bernard Shaw and Beatrice and Sidney ◊Webb.

Fabius Laurent 1946– . French Socialist politician, prime minister 1984–86. He introduced a liberal, free-market economic program, but his career was damaged by the 1985 ◊Greenpeace sabotage scandal.

Fabius became economic adviser to the Socialist Party leader François Mitterrand in 1976, entered the National Assembly 1978, and was a member of the Socialist government from 1981. In 1984, at a time of economic crisis, he was appointed prime minister. He resigned after his party's electoral defeat in March 1986.

Fabius Maximus, Quintus c. 275–203 BC. Roman general, known as *Cunctator* or "Delayer" because of his cautious tactics against Hannibal 217–214 BC, when he continually harassed Hannibal's armies but never risked a set battle.

fable a story, either in verse or prose, in which animals or inanimate objects are endowed with the mentality and speech of human beings to point out a moral. Fabulists include Aesop, Babrius, Phaedrus, Avianus, and La Fontaine.

Fabre Jean Henri Casimir 1823–1915. French entomologist, celebrated for his vivid and intimate descriptions and paintings of the life of wasps, bees, and other insects.

Fabriano Gentile da. Italian painter, see ◊Gentile da Fabriano.

Fabricius Geronimo 1537–1619. Italian anatomist and embryologist. He made a detailed study of the veins and discovered the valves that direct the blood flow toward the heart. He also studied the development of chick embryos.

Fabricius was a professor of surgery and anatomy at Padua, where his work greatly influenced and helped his pupil William ◊Harvey. Despite many errors, he raised anatomy and embryology to a higher scientific level.

Fabritius Carel 1622–1654. Dutch painter, a pupil of Rembrandt. His own style, lighter and with more precise detail than his master's, is evident for example in *The Goldfinch* 1654. He painted religious scenes and portraits.

facies any assemblage of mineral, rock, or fossil features that reflect the environment in which rock was formed. The set of characters that distinguish one facies from another in a given-time stratigraphic unit is used to interpret local changes in simultaneously existing environments. Thus one facies in a body of rock might consist of porous limestone containing fossil reef-building organisms in their living positions. This facies might pass on the side into a reef-flank facies of steeply dipping deposits of rubble from the reef, which in turn might grade into an interreef basin composed of fine, clayey limestone. Ancient floods and migrations of the seashore up or down can also be traced by changes in facies.

facsimile transmission full name for ◊***fax*** or ***telefax***.

factor a number that divides into another number exactly. For example, the factors of 64 are 1, 2, 4, 8, 16, 32, and 64. In algebra, certain kinds of polynomials (expressions consisting of several or many terms) can be factorized. For example, the factors of $x^2 + 3x + 2$ are $x + 1$ and $x + 2$, since $x^2 + 3x + 2 = (x + 1)(x + 2)$. See also ◊prime number.

***Fabergé** One of many small, exquisite, mechanical sculptures designed and produced (usually for royalty) by the jeweler Peter Carl Fabergé.*

factorial of a positive number, the product of all the whole numbers (integers) inclusive between 1 and the number itself. A factorial is indicated by the symbol "!." Thus $6! = 1 \times 2 \times 3 \times 4 \times 5 \times 6 = 720$. Factorial zero, 0!, is defined as 1.

factory farming the intensive rearing of poultry or animals for food, usually on high-protein foodstuffs in confined quarters. Chickens for eggs and meat, and calves for veal are commonly factory farmed. Some countries restrict the use of antibiotics and growth hormones as aids to factory farming, because they can persist in the flesh of the animals after they are slaughtered. The European Commission banned steroid hormones for beef cattle at the end of 1985. Many people, particularly animal-rights activists, object to factory farming for moral as well as health reasons.

Egg-laying hens are housed in "batteries" of cages arranged in long rows. If caged singly, they lay fewer eggs, so there are often four to a cage with a floor area of only 372 sq in/2,400 sq cm. In the course of a year, battery hens average 261 eggs each, whereas for free-range chickens the figure is 199.

factory system the basis of manufacturing in the modern world. In the factory system workers are employed at a place where they carry out specific tasks that together result in a product. Usually these workers will perform their tasks with the aid of machinery. Such ◊mechanization is another feature of the modern factory system, which leads to ◊mass production.

Fadden Artie (Arthur) 1895–1973. Australian politician, born in Queensland. He was leader of the Country Party 1941–58 and prime minister Aug–Oct 1941.

Fadiman Clifton Paul 1904– . US editor. From 1938 to 1948 Fadiman served as moderator of the popular national radio program "Information Please." In 1944 he was appointed to the editorial board of the Book of the Month Club. From the 1950s, he published literary anthologies and continued to be a popular radio and television personality.

Born in Brooklyn, New York, and educated at Columbia University, Fadiman began his career as a teacher at the New York Ethical Culture School. He was hired as an editor for Simon and Schuster 1927 and published his own work as a freelance writer. In 1933 he became book reviewer for the *New Yorker*.

Faenza city on the river Lamone in Ravenna province, Emilia-Romagna, Italy; population (1985) 54,900. It has many medieval remains, including the 15th-century walls. It gave its name to "faience" pottery, a type of tin-glazed earthenware first produced there.

Faerie Queene, The a poem by Edmund Spenser, published 1590–96, dedicated to Elizabeth I. The poem, in six books, describes the adventures of six knights. Spenser used a new stanza form, later adopted by Keats, Shelley, and Byron.

Faeroe Islands or ***Faeroes*** alternate spelling of the ◊Faroe Islands, a group of islands in the N Atlantic.

Fagatogo capital of American Samoa. Situated on Pago Pago Harbor, Tutuila Island.

Fahd 1921– . King of Saudi Arabia from 1982, when he succeeded his half brother Khalid. As head of government, he has been active in trying to bring about a solution to the Middle East conflicts.

Fahrenheit Gabriel Daniel 1686–1736. German physicist who lived mainly in England and Holland. He devised the Fahrenheit temperature scale.

Fahrenheit scale a temperature scale invented 1714 by Gabriel Fahrenheit, no longer in scientific use. Intervals are measured in degrees (°F); °F = (°C × 9/5) + 32.

Fahrenheit took as the zero point the lowest temperature he could achieve anywhere in the laboratory, and, as the other fixed point, body

Fairbanks *Douglas Fairbanks Jr, actor and son of Douglas Fairbanks, the swashbuckler of silent films.*

temperature, which he set at 96°F. On this scale, water freezes at 32°F and boils at 212°F.

fainting sudden, temporary loss of consciousness caused by reduced blood supply to the brain. It may be due to emotional shock or physical factors, such as pooling of blood in the legs from standing still for long periods.

Fairbanks town in central Alaska, situated on the Chena Slough, a tributary of the Tanana River; population (1990) 30,843. Founded 1902, it became a gold-mining and fur-trading center and the terminus of the Alaska Railroad and the Pan-American Highway. It functions as a service center for the mineral development of central and N Alaska. Fort Wainwright, Eielson Air Force Base, and the main campus of the University of Alaska are outside the city limits.

Fairbanks Douglas, Sr. Adopted name of Douglas Elton Ulman 1883–1939. US actor. He played acrobatic swashbuckling heroes in silent films such as *The Mark of Zorro* 1920, *The Three Musketeers* 1921, *Robin Hood* 1922, *The Thief of Baghdad* 1924, and *Don Quixote* 1925. He was married to the film star Mary Pickford ("America's Sweetheart") from 1920 to 1933. Together with Charlie Chaplin and D W Griffith they founded United Artists in 1919.

Fairbanks Douglas, Jr 1909– . US actor who appeared in the same type of swashbuckling film roles as his father, Douglas Fairbanks; for example in *Catherine the Great* 1934 and *The Prisoner of Zenda* 1937.

fair deal name given to the policy of social improvement advocated by H S Truman, President of the US 1945–53. The Fair Deal proposals, first mooted in 1945 after the end of World War II, aimed to extend the ◊New Deal on health insurance, housing development, and the laws to maintain farming prices. Although some of the proposals were passed—for example a Housing Act, a higher minimum wage, and wider social security benefits—the main proposals were blocked by a hostile Congress.

Fairfax Thomas, 3rd Baron Fairfax of Cameron 1612–1671. English general, commander in chief of the Parliamentary army in the English Civil War. With Oliver Cromwell he formed the ◊New Model Army and defeated Charles I at Naseby. He opposed the king's execution, resigned in protest 1650 against the invasion of Scotland, and participated in the restoration of Charles II after Cromwell's death.

Fairfield city in W central California, SW of Sacramento; seat of Solano county. It is a trading center for the area's fruits, grains, and dairy products; population (1990) 77,211.

fairy tale a magical story, usually a folk tale in origin. Typically in European fairy tales, a poor, brave, and resourceful hero or heroine goes through testing adventures to eventual good fortune. The Germanic tales collected by the ◊Grimm brothers have been retold in many variants. The form may also be adapted for more individual moral and literary purposes, as was done by the Danish writer Hans Christian ◊Andersen.

Faisal Ibn Abdul Aziz 1905–1975. King of Saudi Arabia from 1964. The younger brother of King Saud, on whose accession 1953 he was declared crown prince. He was prime minister from 1953 to 1960 and from 1962 until his assassination by a nephew. In 1964 he emerged victorious from a lengthy conflict with his brother and adopted a policy of steady modernization of his country.

Faisal I 1885–1933. Arab nationalist leader during World War I and king of Iraq 1921–33. Instrumental in liberating the Near East from Ottoman control, he was declared king of Syria in 1918 but deposed by the French in 1920. The British then installed him as king in Iraq, where he continued to foster pan-Arabism.

Faisalabad city in Punjab province, Pakistan; population (1981) 1,092,000. It trades in grain, cotton, and textiles.

Faizabad town in Uttar Pradesh, N India; population (1981) 143,167. It lies at the head of navigation of the river Ghaghara and has sugar refineries and an agricultural trade.

fakir originally a Muslim mendicant of some religious order, but in India a general term for an ascetic.

Falaise town 20 mi/32 km SE of Caen, in Calvados *département*, Normandy, France; population (1982) 8,820. It is a market center and manufactures cotton and leather goods. The castle here was that of the first dukes of Normandy, and William the Conqueror was born here 1027.

Falange Española (Spanish "phalanx") former Spanish Fascist Party, founded 1933 by José Antonio de Rivera, son of the military ruler Miguel ◊Primo de Rivera. It was closely modeled in program and organization on the Italian fascists and on the Nazis. In 1937, when ◊Franco assumed leadership, it was declared the only legal party, and altered its name to Traditionalist Spanish Phalanx.

Falasha a member of a small community of black Jews in Ethiopia. They suffered discrimination there, and, after being accorded Jewish status by Israel 1975, began a gradual process of resettlement in Israel. In the early 1980s only about 30,000 Falashim remained in Ethiopia.

falcon any bird of prey of the genus *Falco*, family Falconidae, order Falconiformes. Falcons are the smallest of the hawks (6–24 in/15–60 cm). They nest in high places and kill their prey by "stooping" (swooping down at high speed). They include the peregrine and kestrel.

The peregrine falcon *F. peregrinus*, up to about 1.8 ft/50 cm long, has become re-established in North America and Britain after near extinction (by pesticides, gamekeepers, and egg collectors). When stooping on its intended prey, it is the fastest creature in the world, timed at 150 mph/240 kph.

Other hawks include the worldwide merlin or pigeon hawk *F. columbarius* and the Eurasian kestrel *F. tinnunculus*. Merlins are about 1 ft/30 cm in length, steel-blue above and reddish below, and nest on moors. Kestrels are just over 1 ft/30 cm long, with gray head and tail, light chestnut back with black spots, and an unmistakable quivering hover.

Falconet Etienne-Maurice 1716–1791. French sculptor whose works range from formal Baroque to gentle Rococo in style. He directed sculpture at the Sèvres porcelain factory 1757–66. His bronze equestrian statue *Peter the Great* in Leningrad was commissioned 1766 by Catherine II.

falconry the use of specially trained falcons and hawks to capture birds or small mammals. Practiced since ancient times in the Middle East, falconry was introduced from continental Europe to Britain in Saxon times.

Falkland Islands

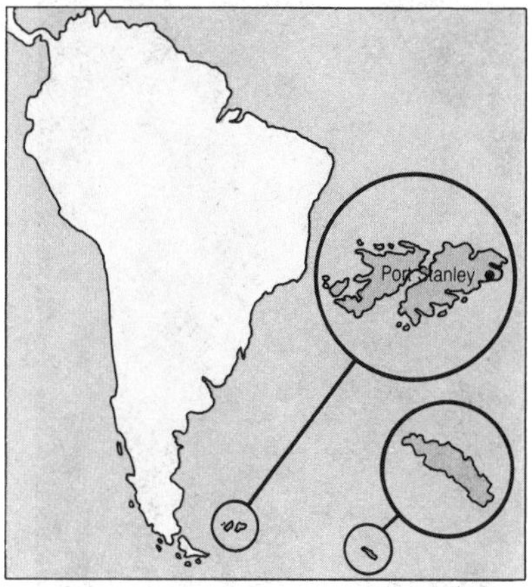

Falkland Lucius Cary, 2nd Viscount c. 1610–1643. English soldier and politician. He was elected to the ◊Long Parliament 1640 and tried hard to secure a compromise peace between royalists and parliamentarians. He was killed at the Battle of Newbury in the Civil War.

Falkland Islands British crown colony in the S Atlantic

area 4,700 sq mi/12,173 sq km, made up of two main islands: East Falkland 2,610 sq mi/6,760 sq km, and West Falkland 2,090 sq mi/5,413 sq km

capital Stanley; new port facilities opened 1984, Mount Pleasant airport 1985

features in addition to the two main islands, there are about 200 small islands, all with wild scenery and rich bird life

products wool, alginates (used as dyes and as a food additive) from seaweed beds

population (1986) 1,916

government There is a governor (Gordon Jewkes from Oct 1985) advised by an executive council, and a mainly elected legislative council. Administered with the Falklands, but separate dependencies of the UK, are South Georgia and the South ◊Sandwich Islands; see also ◊British Antarctic Territory

history The Englishman John Davis was the first European to visit the islands in 1592. At the end of the 17th century they were named after Lord Falkland, treasurer of the British navy. The first British settlers arrived 1765; Spain bought out a French settlement 1766, and the British were ejected 1770–71, but British sovereignty was never ceded and from 1833, when a few Argentines were expelled, British settlement was continuous. Argentina asserts its succession to the Spanish claim to the "Islas Malvinas," but the inhabitants oppose cession. The islands were occupied by Argentina April 1982, and recaptured by British military forces in May–June of the same year.

Falkland Islands, Battle of the British naval victory (under Admiral Sturdee) Dec 8, 1914, over the German admiral von Spee.

Falla Manuel de 1876–1946. Spanish composer. Born in Cádiz, he lived in France, where he was influenced by the Impressionist composers Claude Debussy and Maurice Ravel. His opera *La vida breve/Brief Life* 1905 (performed 1913) was followed by the ballets *El amor brujo/Love the Magician* 1915 and *El sombrero de tres picos/The Three-Cornered Hat* 1919, and his most ambitious concert work, *Noches en los jardines de España/Nights in the Gardens of Spain* 1916. The folk idiom of southern Spain is an integral part of his compositions. He also wrote songs and pieces for piano and guitar.

Fallopian tube *The auricle (trumpet-shaped ending) of the female Fallopian tube, which catches the eggs released from the ovary.*

Fallopian tube or oviduct in mammals, one of two tubes that carry eggs from the ovary to the uterus. An egg is fertilized by sperm in the Fallopian tubes, which are lined with cells whose ◊cilia move the egg toward the uterus.

Fallopius Gabriel. Latinized name of Gabriello Fallopio 1523–1562. Italian anatomist who discovered the Fallopian tubes, which in mammals carry eggs from the ovary to the uterus. Fallopius described them as "trumpets of the uterus." He studied the anatomy of the brain, eyes, and reproductive organs (he named the vagina), and gave the first accurate description of the inner ear.

Fallopius studied at Padua under Andreas ◊Vesalius, and later taught there and at Ferrara and Pisa.

fallout harmful radioactive material released into the atmosphere in the debris of a nuclear explosion and descending to Earth. Such material can enter the food chain, cause ◊radiation sickness, and last for hundreds of thousands of years (see half-life).

fallow land plowed and tilled, but left unsown for a season to allow it to recuperate. In Europe, it is associated with the medieval three-field system.

Fall River city and port in Massachusetts; population (1990) 92,703. It stands at the mouth of the Taunton River, over the Little Fall River, which gave it its name. Textiles and clothing, rubber, paper, and plastics are among the goods produced. It was founded 1656 and was one of the nation's most important textile-mill centers in the 19th century. Lizzie Borden was acquitted here of murdering her father and stepmother 1892.

false-color imagery graphic technique that displays images in false (not true-to-life) colors so as to enhance certain features. It is widely used in displaying electronic images taken by spacecraft; for example, earth-survey satellites such as *Landsat*. Any colors can be selected by a computer processing the received data.

falsificationism in philosophy of science, the belief that a scientific theory must be under constant scrutiny and that its merit lies only in how well it stands up to rigorous testing. First expounded by the philosopher Karl ◊Popper in his *Logic of Scientific Discovery* 1934.

Such thinking also implies that a theory can only be held to be scientific if it makes predictions that are clearly testable. Critics of this belief acknowledge the strict logic of this process, but doubt whether the whole of scientific method can be subsumed into so narrow a program. Philosophers and historians such as Thomas ◊Kuhn and Paul ◊Feyerabend have attempted to use the history of science to show that scientific progress has resulted from a more complicated methodology than Popper suggests.

Famagusta seaport on the E coast of Cyprus, in the Turkish Republic of Northern Cyprus; population (1985) 19,500. It was the chief port of the island prior to the Turkish invasion 1974.

family in biological classification, a group of related genera (see ◊genus). Family names are not printed in italic (unlike genus and species names), and by convention they all have the ending -idae (animals) or -aceae (plants and fungi). For example, the genera of hummingbirds are grouped in the hummingbird family, Trochilidae. Related families are grouped together in an ◊order.

family a group of people related to each other by blood or by marriage. Families are usually described as either "extended" (a large group of relations living together or in close contact with each other) or "nuclear" (a family consisting of two parents and their children).

In some societies an extended family consists of a large group of people of different generations closely or distantly related, depending on each other for economic support and security. In other societies the extended family is split into small units, with members living alone or in nuclear families. The "one-parent" family has recently emerged in the West following the divorce or separation of parents or as a result of a child born to a single woman.

family planning spacing or preventing the birth of children. Access to family-planning services (see ◊contraceptive) is a significant factor in women's health as well as in limiting population growth. If all those women who wished to avoid further childbirth were able to do so, the number of births would be reduced by 27% in Africa, 33% in Asia, and 35% in North and South America; and the number of women who die during pregnancy or childbirth would be reduced by about 50%.

The average number of pregnancies per woman is two in the industrialized countries, where 71% use family planning, as compared to six or seven pregnancies per woman in the Third World. According to a World Bank estimate, doubling the annual $2 billion spent on family planning would avert the deaths of 5.6 million infants and 250,000 mothers each year. In the face of increased populations and decreased food supplies and natural resources, family planning has become a priority for some nations.

famine a severe shortage of food affecting a large number of people. Famines arise when one group in a society loses its opportunity to exchange its labor or possessions for food. Most Western famine-relief agencies, such as the International ◊Red Cross, set out to supply food or to increase its local production, rather than becoming involved in local politics.

The food availability deficit (FAD) theory was challenged in the 1980s. Crop failures do not inevitably lead to famine; nor is it always the case that adequate food supplies are not available nearby. For example, in 1990 the Ethiopian air force bombed grain depots in a rebel-held area.

fan jet popular name for ◊***turbo fan***, the type of jet engine used by most airliners.

Fanon Frantz 1925–1961. French political writer. His experiences in Algeria during the war for liberation in the 1950s led to the writing of *Les Damnés de la terre/The Wretched of the Earth* 1964, which calls for violent revolution by the peasants of the Third World.

fantail variety of domestic pigeon, often white, with a large, widely fanning tail.

fantasia fantasy or fancy in music, a free-form instrumental composition of improvised character.

fantasy fiction nonrealistic fiction. Much of the world's fictional literature could be classified under this term, but as a commercial and literary genre fantasy started to thrive after the success of Tolkien's *Lord of the Rings* 1954–55. Earlier works by such writers as Lord Dunsany, Hope Mirrlees, E R Eddison, and Mervyn Peake, which are not classifiable in fantasy subgenres such as ◊science fiction, ◊horror, or ghost story, could be labeled fantasy.

Faraday *Pioneer in the field of electromagnetic theory, Michael Faraday.*

Much fantasy is pseudomedieval in subject matter and tone. Recent works include Ursula LeGuin's *Earthsea Trilogy*, Stephen Donaldson's *Thomas Covenant*, and, in the more urban tradition, John Crowley's *Little Big*, Michael Moorcock's *Gloriana*, and Gene Wolfe's *Free, Live Free*. Such books largely overlap in content with the ◊magic realism of writers such as Gabriel García Márquez, Angela Carter, and Isabel Allende. Well-known US fantasy authors include Thomas Pynchon (as, for example, in *V*), and Ray Bradbury, whose works are often in the science fiction genre.

Fantin-Latour Henri 1836–1904. French painter exceling in delicate still lifes, flower paintings, and portraits. *Homage à Delacroix* 1864 (Musée d'Orsay, Paris) is a portrait group with many poets, authors, and painters, including Charles Baudelaire and James Whistler.

FAO abbreviation for ◊Food and Agriculture Organization.

Fao or ***Faw*** an oil port on a peninsula at the mouth of the Shatt al-Arab in Iraq. Iran launched a major offensive against Iraq in 1986, capturing Fao for two years.

farad SI unit (abbreviation F) of electrical capacitance (how much electricity a ◊capacitor can store for a given voltage). One farad is a capacitance of one ◊coulomb per volt. For practical purposes the microfarad (one millionth of a farad) is more commonly used.

The farad is named after the British scientist Michael Faraday, and replaced the now obsolete unit the jar (so called because it represented the charge stored in a Leiden jar, the earliest electrical circuit). One farad = 9×10^8 jars.

Faraday Michael 1791–1867. English chemist and physicist. In 1821 he began experimenting with electromagnetism, and ten years later discovered the induction of electric currents and made the first dynamo. He subsequently found that a magnetic field will rotate the plane of polarization of light. Faraday also investigated electrolysis.

Faraday's laws three laws of electromagnetic induction, and two laws of electrolysis, all proposed originally by Michael Faraday:

induction (1) a changing magnetic field induces an electromagnetic force in a conductor; (2) the electromagnetic force is proportional to the rate of change of the field; (3) the direction of the induced electromagnetic force depends on the orientation of the field.

electrolysis (1) the amount of chemical change during electrolysis is proportional to the charge passing through the liquid; (2) the amount of chemical change produced in a substance by a

Fargo Founder of the Wells Fargo company, which pioneered private mail and freight delivery across 19th-century America, William George Fargo.

given amount of electricity is proportional to the electrochemical equivalent of that substance.

farandole an old French dance in six-eight time, originating in Provence. The dancers join hands in a chain and follow the leader to the accompaniment of tambourine and pipe. There is a farandole in Act II of Tchaikovsky's ballet *The Sleeping Beauty*.

farce a broad form of comedy involving stereotyped characters in complex, often improbable situations frequently revolving around extramarital relationships (hence the term "bedroom farce").

Originating in the physical knockabout comedy of Greek satyr plays and the broad humor of medieval religious drama, the farce was developed and perfected during the 19th century by Eugène Labiche (1815–1888) and Georges Feydeau (1862–1921) in France and Arthur Pinero in England.

Far East geographical term for all Asia E of the Indian subcontinent.

Fargo city in SE North Dakota, across the Red River from Moorhead, Minnesota; seat of Cass county. The largest city in the state, it is a center for processing and distributing agricultural products and farm machinery. Chemicals and building materials are also manufactured; population (1990) 74,111.

Fargo William George 1818–1881. US long-distance transport pioneer. In 1844 he established with Henry Wells (1805–1878) and Daniel Dunning the first express company to carry freight west of Buffalo. Its success led to his appointment 1850 as secretary of the newly established American Express Company, of which he was president 1868–81. He also established Wells Fargo & Company 1851, carrying goods express between New York and San Francisco via Panama.

Farmer Frances 1913–1970. US actress who starred in such films as *Come and Get It* 1936, *The Toast of New York* 1937, and *Son of Fury* 1942, before her career was ended by mental illness and frontal lobotomy. She published an autobiography *Will There Really Be a Morning?*

Farne rocky island group in the North Sea, off Northumberland, England.

The islands are a sanctuary for birds and gray seals.

Farnese an Italian family who held the duchy of Parma 1545–1731.

Faroe Islands or ***Faroes*** (Danish *Faerøerne*, "Sheep Islands") or Faeroe Islands or Faeroes island group (18 out of 22 inhabited) in the N Atlantic, between the Shetland Islands and Iceland, forming an outlying part of ◊Denmark

area 540 sq mi/1,399 sq km; largest islands are Strømø, Østerø, Vagø, Suderø, Sandø, and Bordø

capital Thorshavn on Strømø, population (1986) 15,287

products fish, crafted goods

population (1986) 46,000

language Faerøese, Danish

government since 1948 the islands have had full self-government; they do not belong to the EC

history first settled by Norsemen in the 9th century, they were a Norwegian province 1380–1709. Their parliament was restored 1852. They withdrew from the European Free Trade Association 1972.

Farouk 1920–1965. King of Egypt 1936–52. He succeeded his father ◊Fuad I. In 1952 a coup headed by General Muhammed Neguib and Colonel Gamal Nasser compelled him to abdicate, and his son Fuad II was temporarily proclaimed in his place.

Farquhar George 1677–1707. Irish dramatist. His plays *The Recruiting Officer* 1706 and *The Beaux' Stratagem* 1707 are in the tradition of the Restoration comedy of manners, although less robust.

Farragut David (Glasgow) 1801–1870. US admiral, born near Knoxville, Tennessee. During the US Civil War he took New Orleans 1862, after destroying the Confederate fleet, and in 1864 effectively put an end to blockade-running at Mobile. The ranks of vice-admiral (1864) and admiral (1866) were created for him by Congress.

It was at Mobile Bay that Farragut rallied his fleet in the face of Confederate mines (then called torpedoes) with the cry, "Damn the torpedoes: Full speed ahead!"

Farrell James T(homas) 1904–1979. US novelist and short-story writer. His naturalistic *Studs Lonigan* trilogy 1932–35, comprising *Young Lonigan*, *The Young Manhood of Studs Lonigan*, and *Judgment Day*, describes the development of a young Catholic man in Chicago after World War I, and was written from his own experience. *The Face of Time* 1953 is considered one of his finest works.

Farrow Mia 1945– . US film and television actress. Popular since the late 1960s, she has been associated with the director Woody Allen since 1982, both on- and offscreen. She starred in his films *Zelig* 1983, *Hannah and her Sisters* 1986, and *Crimes and Misdemeanors* 1990, as well as in Roman Polanski's *Rosemary's Baby* 1968.

Fars province of SW Iran, comprising fertile valleys among mountain ranges running NW–SE; population (1982) 2,035,600; area 51,487 sq mi/133,300 sq km. The capital is Shiraz, and there are imposing ruins of Cyrus the Great's city of Parargardae and of ◊Persepolis.

fasces in ancient Rome, bundles of rods carried in procession by the lictors (minor officials) in front of the chief magistrates, as a symbol of the latter's power over the lives and liberties of the people. An ax was included in the bundle. The fasces were revived in the 20th century as the symbol of ◊fascism.

Fasching period preceding Lent in German-speaking towns, particularly Munich, Cologne, and Vienna, devoted to masquerades, formal balls, and street parades.

fascism (Latin "bundle of rods") ideology that denies all rights to individuals in their relations with the state; specifically, the totalitarian nationalist movement founded in Italy 1919 by ◊Mussolini and followed by Hitler's Germany 1933.

Fascism was essentially a product of the economic and political crisis of the years after World War I. Units called *fasci di combattimento* (combat groups, from the Latin symbol ◊fasces) were originally established to oppose communism. The fascist party, the *Partitio Nazionale Fascista*, controlled Italy 1922–43. Fascism protected the existing social order by forcible suppression of the working-class movement and by providing scapegoats for popular anger such as outsiders who lived within the state: Jews, foreigners, or blacks; it also rebuilt and modernized the country's infrastructure while preparing the citizenry for the economic and psychological mobilization for war.

Fassbinder German film director Rainer Werner Fassbinder.

The atrocities committed by Nazi Germany and other fascist countries discredited fascism, but neo-fascist groups still exist in the US, Latin America, and many W European countries.

Fashoda former name (until 1905) of the town of Kodok, situated on the White Nile in SE Sudan. The capture of this town by French troops caused an international incident in 1898.

Fashoda Incident dispute 1898 in the town of Fashoda (now Kodok), Sudan, in which a clash between French and British forces nearly led the two countries into war.

Fassbinder Rainer Werner 1946–1982. German film director, who began his career as a fringe actor and founded his own "antitheater" before moving into films. His works are mainly stylized indictments of contemporary German society. He made over 30 films, including *Die bitteren Tränen der Petra von Kant/The Bitter Tears of Petra von Kant* 1972 and *Die Ehe von Maria Braun/The Marriage of Maria Braun* 1979.

fasting the practice of voluntarily going without food for a specified period. Fasts can be undertaken as a religious observance, a sign of mourning, or for slimming purposes. (Political protests called hunger strikes are theoretically unlimited, since they are meant to unseat an authoritarian position with the threat of starvation, not fasting.)

The major world religions include some form of fasting during the ceremonial year.

Prolonged fasting can be dangerous. The liver breaks up its fat stores, releasing harmful byproducts called ketones. This process results in a condition called ketosis, an early symptom of which is a smell of pear drops on the breath. Others include nausea, vomiting, fatigue, dizziness, severe depression, and irritability. Eventually the muscles and other body tissues become wasted, and death results.

fat in the broadest sense, another name for a ◊lipid: a substance that is soluble in alcohol but not water. The term is more specifically used to denote a triglyceride (a chemical containing three ◊fatty acid molecules linked to a molecule of glycerol). The three fatty acids are often of different

fat

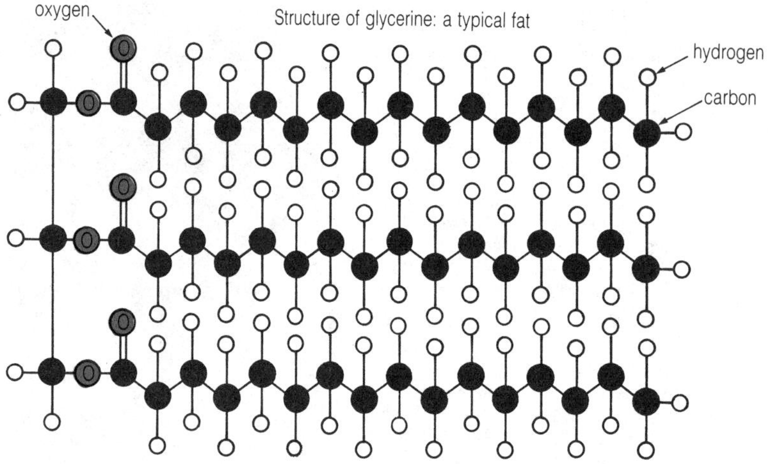
oxygen
hydrogen
carbon

Structure of glycerine: a typical fat

types. Triglycerides that are liquids at room temperature are called oils; only those that are solids are called fats.

Boiling fats in alkali forms soaps (saponification). Fats are essential constituents of food for many animals, although eating too many saturated fats has been linked with heart disease in humans.

Fatah, al- a Palestinian nationalist organization founded 1956 to bring about an independent state of Palestine. Also called the Palestine National Liberation Movement, it is the main component of the ◊Palestine Liberation Organization. Its leader is Yasser ◊Arafat.

fata morgana (Italian, Morgan the Fairy) a mirage, often seen in the Strait of Messina and traditionally attributed to the sorcery of ◊Morgan le Fay. She was believed to reside in Calabria, a region of S Italy.

Fates in Greek mythology, the three female figures, Atropos, Clotho, and Lachesis, envisaged as elderly spinners, who decided the length of human life (analogous to the Roman Parcae and Norse ◊Norns).

Father of the Church any of certain teachers and writers of the early Christian church, eminent for their learning and orthodoxy, experience, and sanctity of life. They lived between the end of the 1st and the end of the 7th century, a period divided by the Council of Nicaea 325 into the Ante-Nicene and Post-Nicene Fathers.

The Ante-Nicene Fathers include the Apostolic Fathers: Clement of Rome, Ignatius of Antioch, Polycarp of Smyrna, Barnabas, Justin Martyr, Clement of Alexandria, Origen, Tertullian, and Cyprian. Among the Post-Nicene Fathers are Cyril of Alexandria, Athanasius, John Chrysostom, Eusebius of Caesarea, Basil the Great, Ambrose of Milan, Augustine, Pope Leo I, Boethius, Jerome, Gregory of Tours, Pope Gregory the Great, and Bede.

Faulkner *US novelist William Faulkner. Spending most of his career in Mississippi, he was a pioneer of the stream-of-consciousness literary style.*

Fathers and Sons a novel by Turgenev, published in Russia 1862. Its hero, Bazarov, rejects the traditional values of his landowning family in favor of nihilistic revolutionary ideas, but his love for a noblewoman destroys his beliefs.

Father's Day a day set apart in many countries for honoring fathers, observed on the third Sunday in June in the US, UK, and Canada. The idea for a father's day originated with Sonora Louise Smart Dodd of Spokane, Washington, in 1909 (after hearing a sermon on Mother's Day), and through her efforts the first Father's Day was celebrated there in 1910.

In 1972, President Nixon made Father's Day an official national holiday.

fathom (Anglo-Saxon *faethm* "to embrace") in mining, seafaring, and handling timber, unit of depth measurement (6 ft/1.83 m) used before metrication; it approximates to the distance between an adult man's hands when the arms are outstretched.

Fatimid dynasty of Muslim Shi'ite caliphs founded 909 by Obaidallah, who claimed to be a descendant of Fatima (the prophet Mohammed's daughter) and her husband Ali, in N Africa. In 969 the Fatimids conquered Egypt, and the dynasty continued until overthrown by Saladin 1171.

fatty acid organic compound consisting of a hydrocarbon chain, up to 24 carbon atoms long, with a carboxyl group (–COOH) at one end.

The bonds may be single or double; where a double bond occurs the carbon atoms concerned carry one instead of two hydrogen atoms. Chains with only single bonds have all the hydrogen they can carry, so they are said to to be saturated with hydrogen. Chains with one or more double bonds are said to be unsaturated (see ◊polyunsaturates). Saturated fatty acids include palmitic and stearic acids; unsaturated fatty acids include oleic (one double bond), linoleic (two double bonds), and linolenic (three double bonds). Fatty acids are generally found combined with glycerol in tryglycerides or ◊fats.

fault

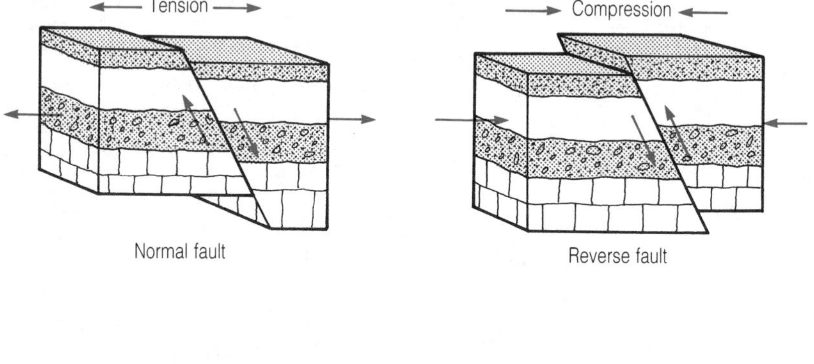
Tension
Compression
Normal fault
Reverse fault

Faulkner William 1897–1962. US novelist, often considered the finest 20th-century American writer. His works include *The Sound and the Fury* 1929, dealing with a favorite topic—the Southern family in decline; *As I Lay Dying* 1930; *Light in August* 1932, a study of segregation; *The Unvanquished* 1938, stories of the Civil War; and *The Hamlet* 1940, *The Town* 1957, and *The Mansion* 1959, a trilogy covering the rise of the materialistic Snopes family. Faulkner, a great literary technician, wrote in an experimental stream-of-consciousness style. He was awarded the Nobel Prize for Literature in 1949.

Faulkner served in World War I and his first novel, *Soldier's Pay* 1929, is about a war veteran. After the war he returned to Oxford, Mississippi, on which he was to model the town of Jefferson in the county of Yoknapatawpha, the setting of his major novels. Other of his notable novels are *Sartoris* 1929, *Intruder in the Dust* 1948, *Requiem for a Nun* 1953, dramatized 1955, and *The Reivers* 1962. He also published short stories including "A Rose for Emily" and "Barn Burning," poems, and essays.

fault in geology, a fracture in the Earth's crust along which the two sides have moved as a result of differing strains in the adjacent rock bodies. Displacement of rock masses horizontally or vertically along a fault may be microscopic, or it may be massive, causing major ◊earthquakes.

If the movement has a major vertical component, the fault is termed a normal fault, where rocks on each side have moved apart, or a reverse fault, where one side has overridden the other (a low angle reverse fault is called a ***thrust***).

Faunus in Roman mythology, god of fertility and prophecy, with goat's ears, horns, tail and hind legs, identified with the Greek Pan.

Fauré Gabriel (Urbain) 1845–1924. French composer of songs, chamber music, and *Requiem* 1888. He was a pupil of Saint-Saëns, became professor of composition at the Paris Conservatoire 1896 and was director from 1905 to 1920.

Faust legendary magician who sold his soul to the Devil. The historical Georg Faust appears to have been a wandering scholar and conjurer in Germany at the start of the 16th century.

Earlier figures such as Simon Magus (1st century AD, Middle Eastern practitioner of magic arts) contributed to the Faust legend. In 1587 the first of a series of Faust books appeared. Marlowe's tragedy, *Dr Faustus*, was acted in 1594. In the 18th century the story was a subject for pantomime in England and puppet plays in Germany. In his play *Faust* Goethe made him a symbol of humanity's striving after the infinite. Heine, Thomas Mann, and Paul Valéry also used the legend, and it inspired musical works by Schumann, Berlioz, Gounod, Boito, and Busoni.

Faust a play by Goethe, completed in two parts 1808 and 1832. Mephistopheles attempts to win over the soul of world-weary Faust but ultimately fails after helping Faust in the pursuit of good.

Fauvism style of painting with a bold use of vivid colors, a shortlived but influential art movement originating in Paris 1905 with the founding of the Salon d'Automne by Henri ◊Matisse and others. Rouault, Dufy, Marquet, Derain, and Signac were early Fauves.

CONCILIVM SEPTEM NOBILIVM ANGLORVM CONIVRANTIVM IN NECEM IACOBI · I ·
MAGNÆ BRITANNIÆ REGIS TOTIVSQ · ANGLICI CONVOCATI PARLEMENTI ·
Bates
Robert Winter
Christopher Wright
John Wright
Thomas Percy
Guido Fawkes
Robert Catesby
Thomas Winter

***Fawkes** Britain's most famous subversive, Guy Fawkes, joined the Gunpowder Plot to blow up James I and both Houses of Parliament in 1605.*

The name originated in 1905 when the critic Louis Vauxcelles called their gallery "une cage aux fauves" (a cage of wild beasts).

Fawkes Guy 1570–1606. English conspirator in the ◊Gunpowder Plot to blow up King James I and the members of both Houses of Parliament. Fawkes, a Roman Catholic convert, was arrested in the cellar underneath the House Nov 4, 1605, tortured, and executed. The event is still commemorated in Britain every Nov 5 with bonfires, fireworks, and the burning of the "guy," an effigy.

fax common name for ***facsimile transmission*** or ***telefax***: the transmission of images over a ◊telecommunications link, usually the telephone network. When placed on a fax machine, the original image is scanned by a transmitting device and converted into coded signals, which travel via the telephone lines to the receiving fax machine, where an image is created that is a copy of the original. Photographs as well as printed text and drawings can be sent.

Fayetteville city in the NW corner of Arkansas, SE of Fort Smith; seat of Washington county. It is an agricultural trading center. Its main industry is poultry processing; others include lumber, clothing, and tools. The University of Arkansas 1871 is here; population (1990) 42,099.

Fayetteville city in S central North Carolina, on the Cape Fear River, S of Durham and Chapel Hill and SW of Raleigh. Its industries include processing of the area's agricultural products, tools, textiles, and lumber; population (1990) 75,695. It was named for the Marquis de Lafayette.

FBI abbreviation for ◊Federal Bureau of Investigation, agency of the US Department of Justice.

FDN abbreviation for Nicaraguan Democratic Front.

fealty in feudalism, the loyalty and duties owed by a vassal to his lord. While in the 9th century fealty obliged the vassal not to take part in any action that would endanger the lord or his property, by the 11th century the specific duties of fealty were established and included financial obligations and military service. Following an oath of fealty, an act of allegiance and respect (homage) was made by the vassal; when a ◊fief was granted by the lord, it was formalized in the process of investiture.

feasibility study in computing, an initial study undertaken by a systems analyst investigating ways of implementing a new computer system. The likely costs and benefits of the system are estimated and used to form the basis for deciding whether or not to proceed with the implementation of the system.

feather rigid outgrowth of the outer layer of the skin of birds, made of the protein keratin. Feathers provide insulation and facilitate flight. There are several types, including long quill feathers on the wings and tail, fluffy down feathers for retaining body heat, and contour feathers covering the body. The coloring of feathers is often important in camouflage or in courtship and other displays. Feathers are replaced at least once a year.

feather star any of an unattached, free-swimming group of sea-lilies, order Comatulida. The arms are branched into numerous projections (hence "feather" star), and grow from a small cup-shaped body. Below the body are appendages that can hold on to a surface, but the feather star is not permanently attached.

February Revolution (March Western calendar) the first of the two political uprisings of the ◊Russian revolution in 1917 that led to the overthrow of the tsar and the end of the ◊Romanov dynasty.

The immediate cause of the revolution was the inability of the tsardom to manage World War I. On March 8 strikes and bread riots broke out in Petrograd (formerly St Petersburg), where the troops later mutinied and joined the rioters. A provisional government was appointed by the ◊Duma (assembly) and Tsar Nicholas II abdicated on March 15 (Feb 27 Julian calendar). The Petrograd Soviet of Workers, Peasants and Soldiers (formed originally during the Russian revolution of 1905) was revived by the Bolsheviks. The provisional government under Prince Lvov was opposed by the Petrograd Soviet, especially when Lenin returned from Switzerland in April. On 16–July 18 the Bolsheviks made an unsuccessful attempt to seize power and Lenin was forced into hiding in Finland. The provisional government tried to continue the war, but was weakened by serious misunderstandings between the prime minister, Kerensky, and the commander in chief General Kornilov, who tried unsuccessfully to gain power in Sept 1917. Shortly afterwards the Bolsheviks seized power in the ◊October Revolution.

Fécamp a seaport and resort of France, NE of Le Havre in the *département* of Seine Maritime; population (1982) 21,696. The main industries are shipbuilding and fishing. Benedictine liqueur was first produced here in the early 16th century.

feces remains of food and other debris passed out of the digestive tract of animals. Faeces consist of quantities of fibrous material, bacteria and other microorganisms, rubbed-off lining of the digestive tract, bile fluids, undigested food, minerals, and water.

Fechner Gustav 1801–1887. German psychologist. He became professor of physics at Leipzig in 1834, but in 1839 turned to the study of psychophysics (the relationship between physiology and psychology). He devised Fechner's law, a method for the exact measurement of sensation.

fecundity the rate at which an organism reproduces, as distinct from its ability to reproduce (◊fertility). In vertebrates, it is usually measured as the number of offspring produced by a female each year.

Federal Aviation Administration (FAA) agency of the US Department of Transportation that controls air traffic. Its responsibilities include regulating air transportation, aviation safety, developing and operating a system of air traffic control, requiring airports and airlines to provide antihijacking security, and conducting aviation research. The agency is also responsible for investigating airplane accidents. It was established in 1958 as the Federal Aviation Agency and was renamed upon its assignment to Transportation in 1967. It is directed by an administrator appointed directly by the President.

Federal Bureau of Investigation (FBI) agency of the US Department of Justice that reports to the US Attorney General and investigates domestic violations of federal law not specifically assigned to other agencies, being particularly concerned with internal security. The FBI was established 1908 and built up a position of powerful autonomy during the autocratic directorship of J Edgar Hoover 1924–72. It investigates espionage, sabo-

fax

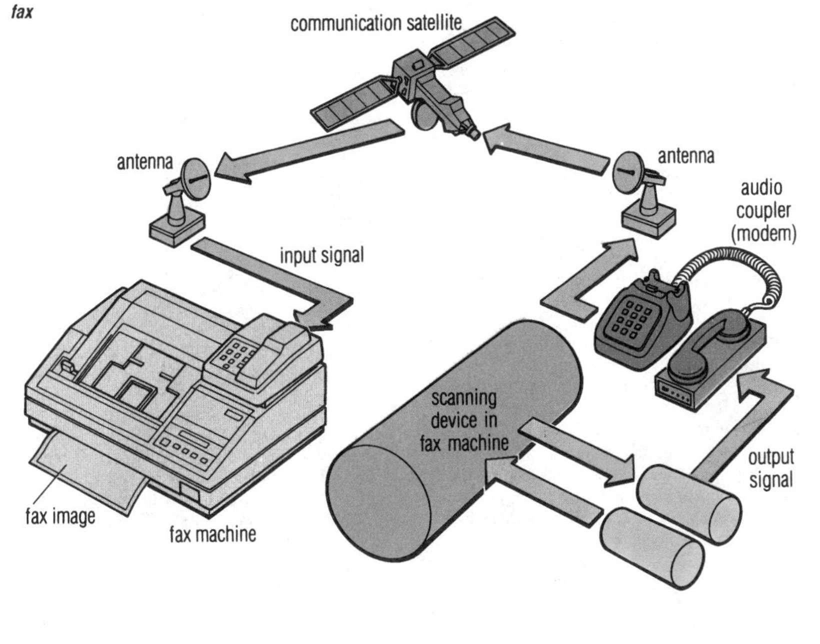
communication satellite
antenna
antenna
audio coupler (modem)
input signal
scanning device in fax machine
output signal
fax image
fax machine

feather

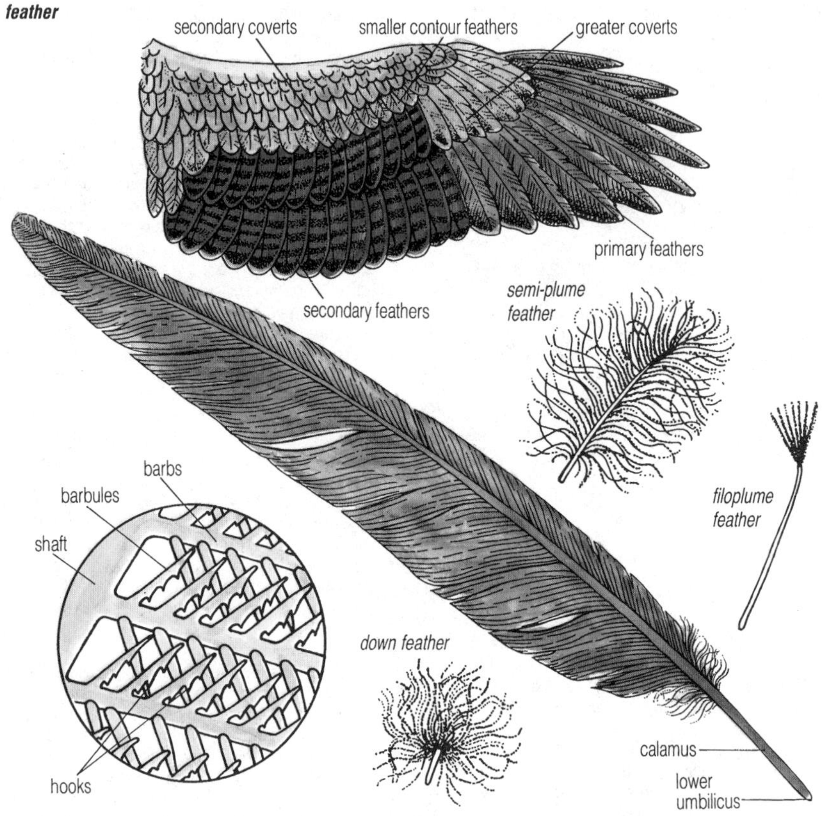
secondary coverts
smaller contour feathers
greater coverts
primary feathers
secondary feathers
semi-plume feather
barbs
barbules
shaft
filoplume feather
down feather
calamus
hooks
lower umbilicus

tage, kidnapping, bank robbery, civil-rights violations, and fraud against the government, and conducts security clearances.

Field divisions are maintained in more than 60 US cities. The FBI's special agents are qualified in law, accounting, or auditing. In 1964 the agency was criticized by the Warren Commission concerning the assassination of President Kennedy, and in 1973 L Patrick Gray, the acting director, resigned when it was revealed that he had destroyed relevant material in the ◊Watergate investigation. Through the Freedom of Information Act it became known that the FBI had kept files on many eminent citizens and that Hoover had abused his power, for example in persecuting the civil-rights leader Martin Luther King, Jr. Clarence M Kelley was director 1973–78, William Webster 1978–87, and Judge William Sessions from 1987.

Federal Deposit Insurance Corporation (FDIC) US government authority established 1933 to regulate US banks and insure them against loss.

The body was set up following the collapse of the banking sector early 1933. All members of the Federal Reserve System are required to belong to the FDIC, and many other US banks that are prepared to conform to certain regulations are also members.

federalism system of government in which two or more separate states unite under a common central government while retaining a considerable degree of local autonomy. A federation should be distinguished from a confederation, a looser union of states for mutual assistance. Switzerland, the USSR, the US, Canada, Australia, and Malaysia are all examples of federal government, and many supporters of the European Community see it as the forerunner of a federal Europe.

The US federal government is organized with an executive branch, a ◊legislature, and a judiciary; each has means to control both of the other branches, thus creating a system of checks and balances, which was considered necessary for fair governing by the framers of the US Constitution. Each of the 50 states retains rights and privileges that overlap with those of the branches of the federal government. When jurisdiction is challenged, cases are decided by the US Supreme Court of the judiciary branch, thus creating constitutional law.

Federalist in US history, one who advocated the ratification of the US Constitution 1787–88 in place of the Articles of ◊Confederation. The Federalists became in effect the ruling political party during the presidencies of George Washington and John Adams 1789–1801, legislating to strengthen the authority of the newly created federal government.

The Federalists advocated reconciliation with Britain and were urban, educated, and vaguely antidemocratic.

Federalist Papers, The in US politics, a series of 85 letters published in the newly independent USA in 1788, attempting to define the relation of the states to the nation, and making the case for a federal government. The papers were signed "Publius," which proved to be the joint pseudonym of three leading political figures, Alexander Hamilton, John Jay, and James Madison.

Federal Reserve System (the "Fed") US central banking system and note-issuing authority, established 1913 to regulate the country's credit and ◊monetary policy. The Fed consists of the 12 federal reserve banks, their 25 branches, and other facilities throughout the country; it is headed by a board of governors in Washington, DC, appointed by the president with Senate approval.

The Fed plays a major role in the formulation and implementation of monetary policy. It is independent and autonomous in its decisions. Inflation, interest rates, and overall economic activity can be governed by the Fed's decision to expand or restrict the supply of money to the economy. The ◊discount rate is the rate the Fed charges member banks to borrow money. By raising or lowering that rate, the Fed regulates credit. By requiring member banks to keep larger or smaller amounts of their deposits on hand as reserves, the Fed can apply another control. For these reasons, the chairman of the Federal Reserve is one of the most powerful figures in government. The decisions of the board of governors concerning discount and other rates are reached under exceptionally tight security and are eagerly awaited.

Federal Theater Project US arts employment scheme 1935–39 founded as part of Roosevelt's New Deal by the Works Progress Administration (WPA); it organized cheap popular theater all over the US and had long-term influence on modern US drama.

The project was directed by Hallie Flanagan, head of drama at Vassar college, and included the "Living Theater" presenting current social and economic issues, the Negro Theater (initially under John Houseman), and an experimental theater. It created many new groups and works before it was halted by Congress.

Federal Writers' Project US arts project founded in 1934 by the Works Progress Administration (WPA) to encourage and employ writers during the Depression, generate compilations of regional records and folklore, and develop a series of guides to states and regions.

feedback general principle whereby the results produced in an ongoing reaction become factors in modifying or changing the reaction; the principle used in self-regulating control systems, from a simple thermostat and steam-engine ◊governor to automatic computer-controlled machine tools. In such systems, information about what *is* happening in a system (such as level of temperature, engine speed or size of workpiece) is fed back to a controlling device, which compares it with what *should* be happening. If the two are different, the device takes suitable action (such as switching on a heater, allowing more steam to the engine, or resetting the tools).

feedback in biology, another term for ◊biofeedback.

feedback in music, a continuous tone, usually a high-pitched squeal, caused by the overloading of circuits between electric guitar and amplifier as the sound of the speakers is fed back through the guitar pickup. Deliberate feedback is much used in rock music.

The electric-guitar innovator Les Paul used feedback in recording ("How High the Moon" 1954) but it was generally regarded by producers as an unwanted noise until the Beatles introduced it on "I Feel Fine" 1964. Both live and in recording, feedback was employed especially by the Who, Jimi Hendrix, and the Velvet Underground in the 1960s, and by hardcore bands in the 1980s.

Fehling's test chemical test to determine whether an organic substance is a reducing agent (substance that donates electrons to other substances in a chemical reaction).

Feininger Lyonel 1871–1956. US abstract artist, an early Cubist. He worked at the Bauhaus, a key center of design in Germany 1919–33 and later helped to found the Bauhaus in Chicago.

While in Germany, he formed the *Blaue Vier* (Blue Four) in 1924 with the painters Alexei von Jawlensky (1864–1941), Wassily Kandinsky, and Paul Klee.

feldspar one of a group of rock-forming minerals; the chief constituents of ◊igneous rock. Feldspars all contain silicon, aluminum, and oxygen, linked together to form a framework; spaces within this structure are occupied by sodium, potassium, calcium, or occasionally barium, in various proportions. Feldspars form white, gray, or pink crystals and rank 6 on the ◊Mohs' scale of hardness.

The four components of feldspar are orthoclase, $KAlSi_3O_8$; albite, $NaAlSi_3O_8$; anorthite, $CaAl_2Si_2O_8$; and celsian, $BaAl_2Si_2O_8$. These are subdivided into plagioclase feldspars, which range from pure sodium feldspar (albite) through pure calcium feldspar (anorthite) with a negligible potassium content; and alkali feldspars, (including orthoclase), which have a high potassium content, less sodium, and little calcium.

***Fellini** Italian film director Federico Fellini was a cartoonist and journalist before he began directing films in the 1950s.* La Dolce Vita *caused a scandal at the 1960 Cannes Film Festival.*

The type known as ◊moonstone has a pearllike effect and is used in jewelry. Approximately 3,500 tons of feldspar are used in the ◊ceramics industry annually.

feldspathoid a group of silicate minerals resembling feldspars but containing less silica. Examples are nepheline ($NaAlSiO_4$) with a little potassium) and leucite ($KAlSi_{26}$). Feldspathoids occur in igneous rocks that have relatively high proportions of sodium and potassium. Such rocks may also contain alkali feldspar, but they do not generally contain quartz because any free silica would have combined with the feldspathoid to produce more feldspar instead.

felicific calculus also called hedonic calculus a term in ethics, attributed to Jeremy Bentham, that provides a technique for establishing the rightness and wrongness of an action. Using the calculus, one can attempt to work out the likely consequences of an action in terms of the pain or pleasure of those affected by the action.

fellah (plural fellahin) in Arab countries, a peasant farmer or farm laborer. In Egypt, approximately 60% of the fellah population live in rural areas, often in villages of 1,000–5,000 inhabitants.

Feller Bob (Robert William Andrew) 1918– . US baseball pitcher. Born in Van Meter, Iowa, Feller was signed by the Cleveland Indians organization while he was still in high school. He made his major-league debut 1936 and went on to a brilliant pitching career that lasted for the next 20 years, interrupted by service in the navy during World War II. Six times he led the American League by winning 20 or more games in a season; he pitched 3 no-hitters and 12 one-hitters and posted 266 career wins. Feller was famed for his powerful fastball and pinpoint control. He was elected to the Baseball Hall of Fame 1962.

Fellini Federico 1920– . Italian film director noted for his strongly subjective and dream imagery. His films include *I vitelloni/The Young and the Passionate* 1953, *La Strada/The Street* 1954 (Academy Award 1956), *Notte di Cabiria/Nights of Cabiria* 1956, *La dolce vita/The Sweet Life* 1960, *Otto e mezzo/8½ 1963, Giulietta degli Spiriti/Juliet of the Spirits* 1965, *Satyricon* 1969, *Roma/Fellini's Roma* 1972, *Amarcord* 1974, *Casanova* 1976, and *La città delle donne/City of Women* 1981.

felony former term for an offense that is more serious than a ◊misdemeanor; in the US, a felony is a crime generally punishable by imprisonment for a year or more. See also ◊criminal law.

felt matted fabric of hair fibers and/or wool, made by joining them together using pressure, heat, or chemical action.

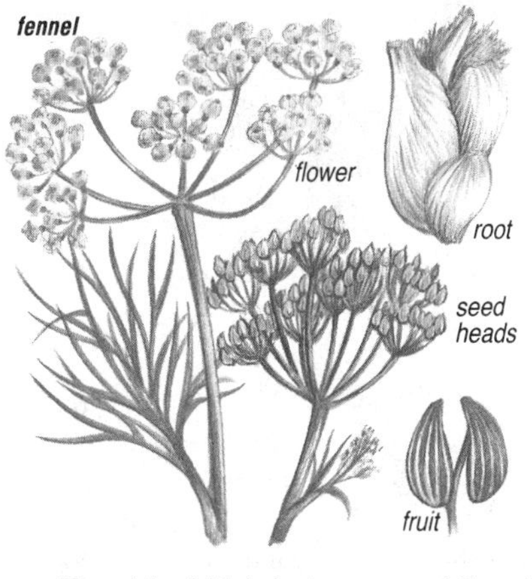
fennel
flower
root
seed heads
fruit

The origin of felt is in the steppes of Central Asia, where ◊yurts, shoes, hats, blankets, and other items were made by nomadic herding peoples.

fem. in grammar, abbreviation for feminine; see ◊gender.

feminism an active belief in equal rights and opportunities for women; see ◊women's movement.

femur the thigh-bone; also the upper bone in the hind limb of a four-limbed vertebrate.

fencing sport of fighting with swords including the foil, derived from the light weapon used in practice duels; the épée, a heavier weapon derived from the duelling sword proper; and the saber, with a curved handle and narrow V-shaped blade. In saber fighting, cuts count as well as thrusts. Masks and protective jackets are worn, and hits are registered electronically in competitions. Men's fencing has been part of every Olympic program since 1896; women started to compete in 1924 but only using the foil.

Fender pioneering series of electric guitars and bass guitars. The first solid-body electric guitar on the market was the 1948 Fender Broadcaster (renamed the Telecaster 1950), and the first electric bass guitar was the Fender Precision 1951. The Fender Stratocaster guitar dates from 1954. Their designer, Leo Fender, began manufacturing amplifiers in the US in the 1940s.

Since the traditional acoustic ◊guitar is a mellow instrument, amplification was needed to project the sound in large halls.

Fénelon François de Salignac de la Mothe 1651–1715. French writer and ecclesiastic. He entered the priesthood 1675 and in 1689 was appointed tutor to the duke of Burgundy, grandson of Louis XIV. For him he wrote his *Fables* and *Dialogues des morts/Dialogs of the Dead* 1690, *Télémaque/Telemachus* 1699, and *Plans de gouvernement/Plans of Government.*

Télémaque, with its picture of an ideal commonwealth, had the effect of a political manifesto, and Louis banished Fénelon to Cambrai, where he had been consecrated archbishop 1695. Fénelon's mystical *Maximes des Saints/Sayings of the Saints* 1697 had also led to condemnation by Pope Innocent XII and a quarrel with the Jansenists, who believed that only those chosen by God beforehand received salvation.

Fenian a member of an Irish-American republican secret society, founded 1858 and named after the ancient Irish legendary warrior band of the Fianna. The collapse of the movement began when an attempt to establish an independent Irish republic by an uprising in Ireland 1867 failed, as did raids into Canada 1866 and 1870, and England 1867.

fennec small nocturnal desert ◊fox *Fennecus zerda* found in N Africa and Arabia. It has a head and body only 1.3 ft/40 cm long, and its enormous ears act as radiators to lose excess heat. It eats insects and small animals.

fennel any of several varieties of a perennial plant *Foeniculum vulgare* with feathery green leaves, of the carrot family Umbelliferae. Fennels have an aniseed flavor, and the leaves and seeds are used in seasoning. The thickened leafstalks of sweet fennel *F. vulgare dulce* are eaten.

Fens level, low-lying tracts of land in E England, W and S of the Wash, about 70 mi/115 km N–S and 34 mi/55 km E–W. They fall within the counties of Lincolnshire, Cambridgeshire, and Norfolk, consisting of a huge area, formerly a bay of the North Sea, but now crossed by numerous drainage canals and forming some of the most productive agricultural land in Britain. The peat portion of the Fens is known as the Bedford Level.

Ferber Edna 1887–1968. US novelist and playwright. Her novel *Show Boat* 1926 was adapted as an operetta 1927 by Jerome Kern and Oscar Hammerstein II, and her plays, in which she collaborated with G S Kaufmann, include *The Royal Family* 1927, about the Barrymore theatrical family, *Dinner at Eight* 1932, and *Stage Door* 1936.

Her novels include *The Girls* 1921, *So Big* 1924, *Cimarron* 1930, *Giant* 1952, about Texas, and *Ice Palace* 1959, about Alaska.

Ferdinand 1861–1948. King of Bulgaria 1908–18. Son of Prince Augustus of Saxe-Coburg-Gotha, he was elected prince of Bulgaria 1887 and, in 1908, proclaimed Bulgaria's independence of Turkey and assumed the title of tsar. In 1915 he entered World War I as Germany's ally, and in 1918 abdicated.

Ferdinand five kings of Castile:

Ferdinand I the Great c. 1016–1065. King of Castile from 1035. He began the reconquest of Spain from the Moors and united all NW Spain under his and his brothers' rule.

Ferdinand V 1452–1516. King of Castile from 1474, Ferdinand II of Aragon from 1479, and Ferdinand III of Naples from 1504; first king of all Spain. In 1469 he married his cousin ◊Isabella I, who succeeded to the throne of Castile 1474; together they were known as the Catholic Monarchs because, as a reaction to 700 years of rule by the ◊Moors, they Catholicized Spain. When Ferdinand inherited the throne of Aragon 1479, the two great Spanish kingdoms were brought under a single government for the first time. They introduced the ◊Inquisition 1480; expelled the Jews, forced the final surrender of the Moors at Granada 1492, and financed Columbus' expedition to the Americas, 1492.

Ferdinand conquered Naples 1500–03 and Navarre 1512, completing the unification of Spain and making it one of the chief powers in Europe.

Ferdinand three Holy Roman emperors:

Ferdinand I 1503–1564. Holy Roman emperor who succeeded his brother Charles V 1558; king of Bohemia and Hungary from 1526, king of the Germans from 1531. He reformed the German monetary system and reorganized the judicial Aulic council (*Reichshofrat*). He was the son of Philip the Handsome and grandson of Maximilian I.

Ferdinand II 1578–1637. Holy Roman emperor from 1619, when he succeeded his uncle Matthias; king of Bohemia from 1617 and of Hungary from 1618. A zealous Catholic, he provoked the Bohemian revolt that led to the Thirty Years' War. He was a grandson of Ferdinand I.

Ferdinand III 1608–1657. Holy Roman emperor from 1637 when he succeeded his father Ferdinand II; king of Hungary from 1625. Although anxious to conclude the Thirty Years' War, he did not give religious liberty to Protestants.

Ferdinand 1865–1927. King of Romania from 1914, when he succeeded his uncle Charles I. In 1916 he declared war on Austria. After the Allied victory in World War I, Ferdinand acquired Transylvania and Bukovina from Austria-Hungary, and Bessarabia from Russia. In 1922 he became king of this Greater Romania. His reign saw agrarian reform and the introduction of universal suffrage.

Ferghana city in Uzbekistan, USSR, in the fertile

Fermi *Nuclear physicist Enrico Fermi.*

Ferghana valley; population (1987) 203,000. It is the capital of the major cotton- and fruit-growing Ferghana region; nearby are petroleum fields.

Fermat Pierre de 1601–1665. French mathematician who with Blaise Pascal founded the theory of ◊probability and the modern theory of numbers and who made contributions to analytical geometry.

Fermat's last theorem states that equations of the form $x^n + y^n = z^n$ where x, y, z, and n are all ◊integers have no solutions if $n < 2$. There is no general proof of this, so it constitutes a conjecture rather than a theorem.

Fermanagh county in the southern part of Northern Ireland

area 648 sq mi/1,680 sq km

towns Enniskillen (county town), Lisnaskea, Irvinestown

physical in the center is a broad trough of low-lying land, in which lie Upper and Lower Lough Erne

products mainly agricultural; livestock, tweeds, clothing

population (1981) 52,000.

fermentation the breakdown of complex carbohydrates by bacteria and fungi (yeasts) using a method of respiration without oxygen (◊anaerobic). These processes have long been utilized in baking bread; making beer and wine; and producing cheese, yogurt, soy sauce, and many other foodstuffs.

In baking and brewing, yeasts ferment carbohydrates to produce ◊ethanol and carbon dioxide; the latter makes bread rise and puts bubbles into beer.

Fermi Enrico 1901–1954. Italian-born US physicist who proved the existence of new radioactive elements produced by bombardment with neutrons; he also discovered nuclear reactions produced by slow, or low-energy, neutrons. Others realized that his work was the beginning of nuclear fission (see ◊nuclear energy). For these studies he was awarded the Nobel Prize in Physics 1938, at which time he and his family immigrated to the US directly from the award ceremony.

Born in Rome, he was professor of theoretical physics there from 1926 to 1938. He was professor at Columbia University, New York, from 1939 to 1942 and from 1946 at the University of Chicago, where he had built the first US nuclear reactor 1942. This was the basis for studies leading to the atomic bomb and nuclear energy.

Fermilab US center for ◊particle physics in Chicago, named after Enrico Fermi.

fermium synthesized, radioactive, metallic element of the ◊actinide series, symbol Fm, atomic number 100, atomic weight 257. Ten isotopes are known, the longest-lived of which, Fm-257, has a half-life of 80 days. Fermium has been produced only in minute quantities in particle accelerators. It was discovered in 1952 in the debris of the first thermonuclear explosion.

fern

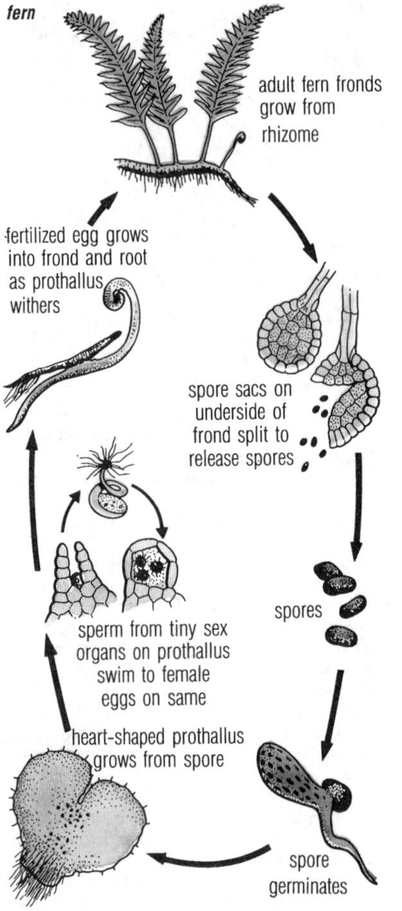
adult fern fronds grow from rhizome
fertilized egg grows into frond and root as prothallus withers
spore sacs on underside of frond split to release spores
spores
sperm from tiny sex organs on prothallus swim to female eggs on same
heart-shaped prothallus grows from spore
spore germinates

US nuclear physicist A Ghiorso and his team named it in 1955 in honor of Enrico ◊Fermi.

Fermor Patrick (Michael) Leigh 1915– . English travel writer who joined the Irish Guards in 1939 after four years travel in Central Europe and the Balkans. His publications include *The Traveller's Tree* 1950, *A Time to Keep Silence* 1953, *The Violins of Saint Jacques* 1953, *Mani* 1958, *Roumeli* 1966, *A Time of Gifts* 1977, and *Between the Woods and the Water* 1986.

fern plant of the class Filicineae, related to ◊gymnosperms and ◊angiosperms; however, ferns reproduce by spores and not seed. Most are perennial, spreading by low-growing roots. The leaves, known as fronds, vary widely in size and shape. Some taller types, such as tree-ferns, grow in the tropics. There are over 7,000 species.

Common forms include polypody (*Polypodium*); shield fern (*Polystichum*); maidenhair (*Adiantum capillus-veneris*); and bracken (*Pteridium*), a common weed.

Fernández Juan c. 1536–c. 1604. Spanish explorer and navigator. As a pilot on the Pacific coast of South America 1563, he reached the islands off the coast of Chile that now bear his name. Alexander ◊Selkirk was later marooned on one of these islands, and his life story formed the basis of Daniel Defoe's *Robinson Crusoe*.

Fernandez de Quirós Pedro 1565–1614. Spanish navigator, one of the first Europeans to search for the great southern continent that Ferdinand ◊Magellan believed lay to the south of the Magellan Strait. Despite a series of disastrous expeditions, he took part in the discovery of the Marquesas Islands and the main island of Espíritu Santo in the New Hebrides.

Fernando Pó former name (until 1973) of ◊Bioko, Equatorial Guinea.

Fernel Jean François 1497–1558. French physician who introduced the terms ◊physiology and ◊pathology into medicine.

Ferranti Sebastian de 1864–1930. British electrical engineer who electrified central London. He made and sold his first alternator 1881.

Ferrara industrial city and archbishopric in Emilia-Romagna region, N Italy, on a branch of the Po delta 32 mi/52 km W of the Adriatic Sea; population (1988) 143,000. There are chemical industries and textile manufactures.

It has the Gothic castle of its medieval rulers, the House of Este, palaces, museums, and a cathedral, consecrated 1135. The university was founded 1391. Italian religious reformer Girolamo Savonarola was born here, and the poet Torquato Tasso was confined in the asylum from 1579 to 1586.

Ferrari Enzo 1898–1988. Italian founder of the Ferrari car empire, which specializes in Grand Prix racing automobiles and high-quality sports automobiles. He was a racing driver for Alfa Romeo in the 1920s, went on to become one of their designers and in 1929 took over their racing division. In 1947 the first "true" Ferrari was seen. The Ferrari car has won more world championship Grands Prix than any other car.

Ferraro Geraldine 1935– . US Democrat politician, vice-presidential candidate in the 1984 election.

Ferraro, a lawyer, was elected to Congress in 1981 and was selected in 1984 by Walter Mondale to be the US's first female vice-presidential candidate from one of the major parties. The Democrats were defeated by the incumbent president Reagan, and Ferraro, damaged by investigations of her husband's business affairs, retired from politics.

ferret domesticated variety of the Old World ◊polecat. About 1.2 ft/35 cm long, it usually has yellowish-white fur and pink eyes, but may be the dark brown color of a wild polecat. Ferrets may breed with wild polecats. They have been used since ancient times to hunt rabbits and rats.

Ferrier Kathleen (Mary) 1912–1953. English contralto who sang oratorio and opera. In Benjamin Britten's *The Rape of Lucretia* 1946 she created the role of Lucretia, and she appeared in Gustav Mahler's *Das Lied von der Erde* 1947.

ferro-alloy alloy of iron with a high proportion of elements such as manganese, silicon, chromium, and molybdenum. Ferro-alloys are used in the manufacture of alloy steels. Each alloy is generally named after the added metal—for example, ferrochromium.

Ferrol alternate name for ◊El Ferrol, a city and port in NW Spain.

ferrous metal metal affected by magnetism. Iron, cobalt, and nickel are the three ferrous metals.

Ferry Jules François Camille 1832–1893. French republican politician, mayor of Paris during the siege of 1870–71. As a member of the republican governments of 1879–85 (prime minister 1880–81 and 1883–85). he was responsible for the law of 1882 making primary education free, compulsory, and secular. He directed French colonial expansion in Tunisia 1881 and Indochina (the acquisition of Tonkin in 1885).

fertility an organism's ability to reproduce, as distinct from the rate at which it reproduces (see ◊fecundity). Individuals become infertile (unable to reproduce) when they cannot generate gametes (eggs or sperm) or when their gametes cannot yield a viable ◊embryo after fertilization.

fertility drug any of a range of drugs taken to increase a female's fertility, developed in Sweden in the mid-1950s. They increase the chances of a multiple birth.

The most familiar is gonadotropin, which is made from hormone extracts taken from the human pituitary gland: follicle-stimulating hormone and lutenizing hormone. It stimulates ovulation in women. As a result of a fertility drug, in 1974 the first sextuplets to survive were born to Susan Rosenkowitz of South Africa.

fertilization in ◊sexual reproduction, the union of two ◊gametes (sex cells, often called egg and sperm) to produce a ◊zygote, which combines the genetic material contributed by each parent. In self-fertilization the male and female gametes come from the same plant; in cross-fertilization they come from different plants. Self-fertilization rarely occurs in animals; usually even ◊hermaphrodite animals cross-fertilize each other.

In terrestrial insects, mammals, reptiles and birds, fertilization occurs within the female's body; in the majority of fishes and amphibians, and most aquatic invertebrates, it occurs externally, when both sexes release their gametes into the water. In most fungi, gametes are not released, but the hyphae of the two parents grow toward each other and fuse to achieve fertilization. In higher plants, ◊pollination precedes fertilization.

fertilizer substance containing a range of about 20 chemical elements necessary for healthy plant growth, used to compensate the deficiencies of poor or depleted soil. Fertilizers may be organic, for example farmyard manure, composts, bonemeal, blood, and fishmeal; or inorganic, in the form of compounds, mainly of nitrogen, phosphate, and potash, which have been used on a tremendously increased scale since 1945.

Because externally applied fertilizers tend to be in excess of plant requirements and leach away to affect lakes and rivers (see ◊eutrophication), attention has turned to the modification of crop plants themselves. Plants of the pea family, including the bean, clover, and lupin, live in symbiosis with bacteria located in root nodules, which fix nitrogen from the atmosphere. Research is now directed to producing a similar relationship between such bacteria and crops such as wheat.

Fertö tó Hungarian name for the Neusiedler See.

Fès or ***Fez*** former capital of Morocco 808–1062, 1296–1548, and 1662–1912, in a valley N of the Great Atlas Mountains, 100 mi/160 km E of Rabat; population (1982) 563,000. Textiles, carpets, and leather are manufactured, and the *fez*, a brimless hat worn in S and E Mediterranean countries, is traditionally said to have originated here. Kairwan Islamic University dates from 859; the second university was founded 1961.

fescue any grass of the widely distributed genus *Festuca*. Many are used in temperate regions for lawns and pasture.

Fessenden Reginald Aubrey 1866–1932. Canadian physicist who worked in the US, first for Thomas Edison and then for George Westinghouse. Fessenden patented the modulation of radio waves (transmission of a signal using a carrier wave), an essential technique for voice transmission. At the time of his death, he held 500 patents.

Early radio communications relied on telegraphy by using bursts of single-frequency signals in Morse code. In 1900 Fessenden devised a method of making audio-frequency speech (or music) signals modulate the amplitude of a transmitted radio-frequency carrier wave—the basis of AM radio broadcasting.

fetal surgery any operation on the fetus to correct a congenital condition (for example, ◊hydrocephalus). Fetal surgery was pioneered in the US 1981. It leaves no scar tissue.

fetishism in anthropology, belief in the supernormal power of some inanimate object that is known as a fetish. Fetishism in some form is common to most cultures, and often has religio-magical significance. In psychology, the practice of associating an object with the sexual act and transferring desire to the object.

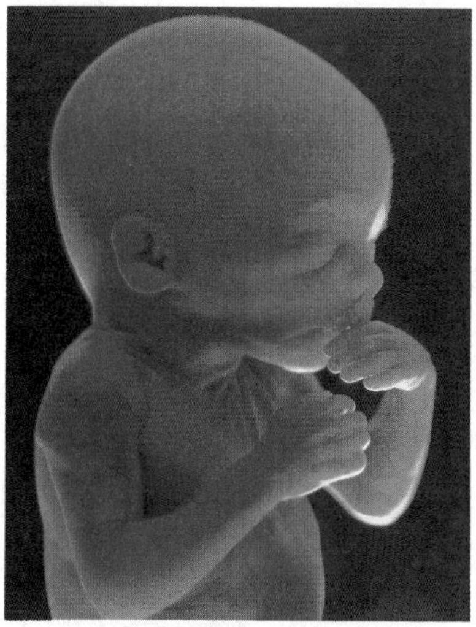

fetus *Human fetus, at about five months in development.*

fetus late stage in mammalian ◊embryo development. The human embryo is usually termed a fetus after the eighth week of development until birth.

feudalism the main form of social organization in medieval Europe. A system based primarily on land, it involved a hierarchy of authority, rights, and power that extended from the monarch downward. An intricate network of duties and obligations linked royalty, nobility, lesser gentry, free tenants, villeins, and serfs. Feudalism was reinforced by a complex legal system and supported by the Christian church. With the growth of commerce and industry from the 13th century, feudalism gradually gave way to the class system as the dominant form of social ranking.

In return for military service the monarch allowed powerful vassals to hold land, and often also to administer justice and levy taxes. They in turn "sublet" such rights. At the bottom of the system were the serfs, who worked on their lord's manor lands in return for being allowed to cultivate some for themselves, and so underpinned the system. They could not be sold as if they were slaves, but they could not leave the estate to live or work elsewhere without permission. The system declined from the 13th century, partly because of the growth of a money economy, with commerce, trade, and industry, and partly because of the many peasants' revolts 1350–1550. Serfdom ended in England in the 16th century, but lasted in France until 1789 and in the rest of Western Europe until the early 19th century. In Russia it continued until 1861.

fever condition of raised body temperature, usually due to infection but also normally caused by exercise and ovulation.

Feyerabend Paul K 1924– US philosopher of science, who rejected the attempt by certain philosophers (for instance ◊Popper) to find a methodology applicable to all scientific research. His works include *Against Method* 1975.

Although his work relies on historical evidence, Feyerabend argues that successive theories that apparently concern the same subject (for instance the motion of the planets) cannot in principle be subjected to any comparison that would aim at finding the truer explanation. According to this notion of incommensurability, there is no neutral or objective standpoint and therefore no rational way in which one theory can be chosen over another. Instead, scientific progress is claimed to be the result of a range of sociological factors working to promote politically convenient notions of how nature operates.

Feynman Richard Phillips 1918–1988. US physicist whose work provided the foundations for quantum electrodynamics. For his work on the theory of radiation he was awarded a share of the Nobel Prize for Physics 1965. As a member of the committee investigating the *Challenger* space-shuttle disaster 1986, he demonstrated the lethal faults in the rubber seals on the shuttle's booster rocket.

Toward the end of his life he became widely known for his revealing autobiography *Surely you're Joking Mr Feynman!*

Fez alternate spelling of ◊Fès, a city in Morocco.

Fezzan former province of Libya, a desert region, with many oases, and with rock paintings from about 3000 BC. It was captured from Italy 1942, and placed under French control until 1951 when it became a province of the newly-independent United Kingdom of Libya. It was split into smaller divisions 1963.

ff abbreviation for folios; and the following; used in reference citation and bibliography.

fiberglass glass that has been formed into fine fibers, either as long continuous filaments or as a fluffy, shortfiberd glass wool. Fiberglass is heat- and fire-resistant and a good electrical insulator. It has applications in the field of fiber optics and as a strengthener for plastics in ◊GRP (glass-reinforced plastics).

The long filament form is made by forcing molten glass through the holes of a spinneret, and is woven into textiles. Glass wool is made by blowing streams of molten glass in a jet of high-pressure steam, and is used for electrical, sound, and thermal insulation, especially for the roof space in houses.

Fibonacci Leonardo, also known as Leonardo of Pisa c. 1175–c. 1250. Italian mathematician. He published *Liber abaci* in Pisa 1202, which was instrumental in the introduction of Arabic notation into Europe. From 1960, interest increased in Fibonacci numbers, in their simplest form a sequence in which each number is the sum of its two predecessors (1, 1, 2, 3, 5, 8, 13, ...). They have unusual characteristics with possible applications in botany, psychology, and astronomy (for example, a more exact correspondence than is given by ◊Bode's law to the distances between the planets and the Sun).

fiber optics the branch of physics dealing with the transmission of light and images through glass or plastic fibers known as ◊optical fibers.

fibrin an insoluble blood protein used by the body to stop bleeding. When an injury occurs fibrin is deposited around the wound in the form of a mesh, which dries and hardens, so that bleeding stops. Fibrin is developed in the blood from a soluble protein, fibrinogen.

The conversion of fibrinogen to fibrin is the final stage in blood clotting. Platelets, a type of cell found in blood, release the enzyme thrombin when they come into contact with damaged tissue, and the formation of fibrin then occurs. Calcium, vitamin K, and a variety of enzymes called factors are also necessary for efficient blood clotting.

fibrositis inflammation and overgrowth of fibrous tissue, mainly of the muscle sheaths. It is also known as muscular rheumatism. Symptoms are sudden pain and stiffness, usually relieved by analgesics and rest.

fibula the rear lower bone in the hind leg of a vertebrate. It is paired and often fused with a smaller front bone, the tibia.

Fichte Johann Gottlieb 1762–1814. German philosopher who developed a comprehensive form of subjective idealism, expounded in *The Science of Knowledge* 1794. He was an admirer of Immanuel ◊Kant.

In 1792, Fichte published *Critique of Religious Revelation*, a critical study of Kant's doctrine of the "thing-in-itself." For Fichte, the absolute ego posits both the external world (the nonego) and finite self. Morality consists in the striving of this finite self to rejoin the absolute. In 1799 he was accused of atheism, and was forced to resign his

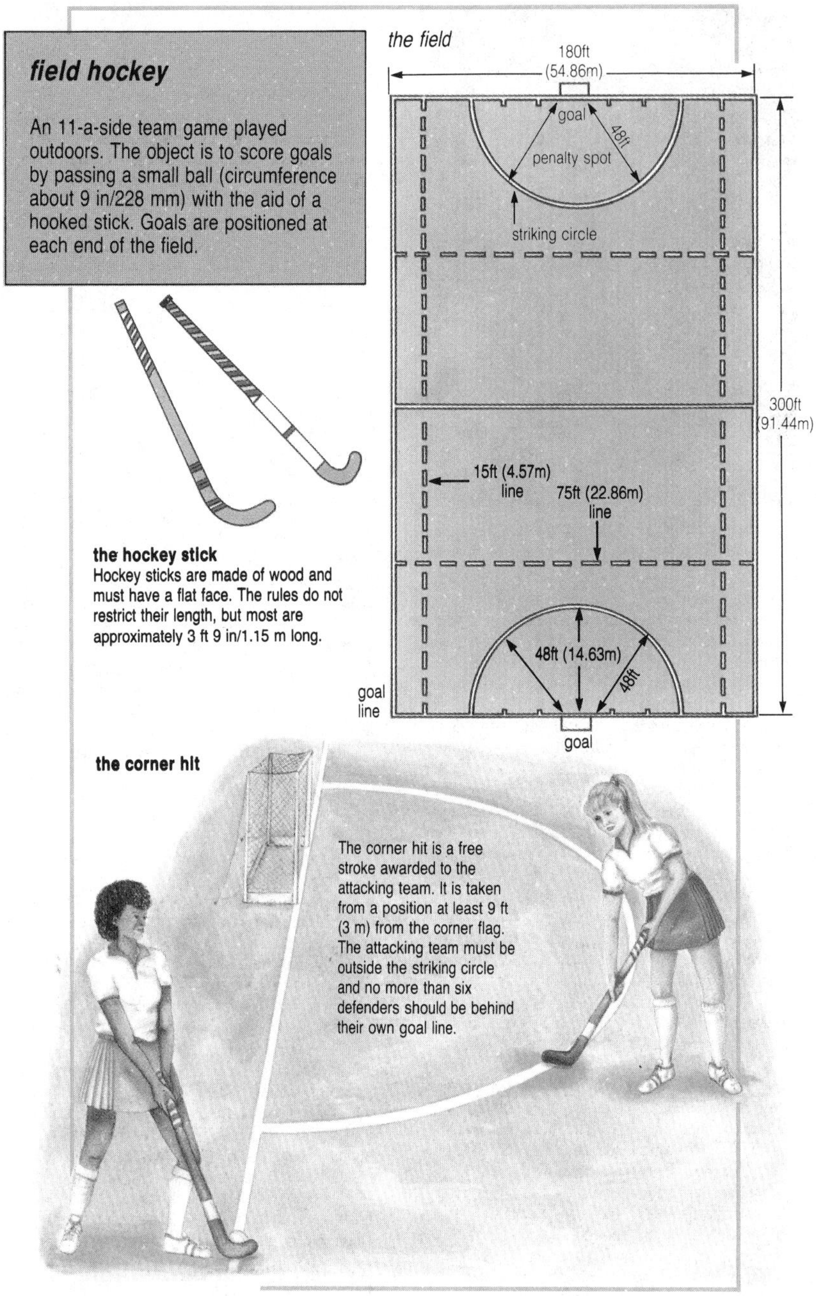
field hockey
An 11-a-side team game played outdoors. The object is to score goals by passing a small ball (circumference about 9 in/228 mm) with the aid of a hooked stick. Goals are positioned at each end of the field.
the field
180ft
(54.86m)
goal
48ft
penalty spot
striking circle
300ft
(91.44m)
15ft (4.57m) line
75ft (22.86m) line
48ft (14.63m)
48ft
goal line
goal
the hockey stick
Hockey sticks are made of wood and must have a flat face. The rules do not restrict their length, but most are approximately 3 ft 9 in/1.15 m long.
the corner hit
The corner hit is a free stroke awarded to the attacking team. It is taken from a position at least 9 ft (3 m) from the corner flag. The attacking team must be outside the striking circle and no more than six defenders should be behind their own goal line.

post as professor of philosophy at Jena. He moved to Berlin, where he devoted himself to public affairs and delivered lectures, including *Reden an die deutsche Nation/Addresses to the German People* 1807–08, which influenced contemporary liberal nationalism.

Fichtelgebirge chain of mountains in Bavaria, Federal Republic of Germany, on the Czechoslovak border. The highest peak is the Schneeberg 3,448 ft/1,051 m. There are granite quarries, uranium mining, china and glass industries, and forestry.

fiction in literature, any work in which the content is completely or largely invented. The term describes imaginative works of narrative prose (such as the novel or the short story), and is distinguished from nonfiction (such as history, biography, or works on practical subjects), and poetry.

This usage reflects the dominance in contemporary Western literature of the novel as a vehicle for imaginative literature: strictly speaking, poems can also be fictional (as opposed to factual). Genres such as the historical novel often combine a fictional plot with real events; biography may also be "fictionalized" through the use of imagined conversations or events.

Fiedler Arthur 1894–1979. US orchestra conductor. Born in Boston and trained at the Academy of Music in Berlin, Fiedler joined the Boston Symphony Orchestra 1916. Always interested in the promotion of music among the general public, he founded the Boston Sinfonetta chamber music group 1924. He reached an even wider audience with the Esplanade concerts along the Charles river from 1929. Fiedler's greatest fame came as founder and conductor of the Boston Pops Orchestra, dedicated to popularizing light Classical music through live and televised concert appearances.

fief an estate of lands held by a ◊vassal from his lord, given after the former had sworn homage, or fealty, promising to serve the lord. As a noble tenure, it carried with it rights of jurisdiction.

In the later Middle Ages, it could also refer to a grant of money, given in return for service, as part of ◊bastard feudalism.

field in physics, the region of space by which an object exerts a force on another separate object because of certain properties they both possess. For example, there is a force of attraction between any two objects that have mass, where one is in the gravitational field of the other.

Other fields of force include ◊electric fields (caused by electric charges) and ◊magnetic fields (caused by magnetic poles), either of which can involve attractive or repulsive forces.

Field Sally 1946– . US film and television actress. After years as TV's *Flying Nun*, she won an Academy Award for *Norma Rae* 1979 and again for *Places in the Heart* 1984. Her other films include *Hooper* 1978, *Absence of Malice* 1981, and *Murphy's Romance* 1985.

fieldfare thrush *Turdus pilaris* of the family Muscicapidae, breeding in Scandinavia, the N USSR, and Siberia, and a casual visitor to N North America. It has a pale-gray lower back and neck and a dark tail.

field hockey a game played with hooked sticks and a ball, the object being to hit the ball into the goal. It is played between two teams, each of not more than 11 players. Hockey has been an Olympic sport for men since 1908 and for women since 1980.

The playing field is 100 yd/91.5 m long and 60 yd/54.9 m wide. Goals 7 ft/2.1 m high and 12 ft/3.7 m wide are placed within a striking circle of 48 ft/14.6 m radius, from which all shots at goal must be made. The white ball weighs about 5.5 oz/156 g, circumference about 9 in/123 cm, and the stick must not exceed 2 in/5 cm in diameter. The game is started by a "push-back." The ball may be stopped with the hand but not held, picked-up, thrown, or kicked, except by the goalkeeper in his or her own striking circle. If the ball is sent out of bounds, it is returned to play by a "push-in." The game is divided into two 35-minute periods; it is controlled by two umpires, one for each half of the field.

A game using hooked sticks, not unlike the modern ones, was played by the ancient Greeks.

Fielding Henry 1707–1754. English novelist whose narrative power influenced the form and technique of the novel and helped to make it the most popular form of literature in England. In 1742 he parodied Richardson's novel *Pamela* in his *Joseph Andrews*, which was followed by *Jonathan Wild the Great* 1743; his masterpiece *Tom Jones* 1749, which he described as a "comic epic in prose"; and *Amelia* 1751.

field marshal the highest rank in many European armies. A British field marshal is equivalent to a US ◊general.

Field of the Cloth of Gold site between Guînes and Ardres near Calais, France, where a meeting took place between Henry VIII of England and Francis I of France June 1520, remarkable for the lavish clothes worn and tent pavilions erected. Francis hoped to gain England's support in opposing the Holy Roman emperor, Charles V, but failed.

Fields W C. Adopted name of William Claude Dukenfield 1879–1946. US actor and screenwriter. His distinctive speech and professed attitudes such as hatred of children and dogs gained him enormous popularity in films such as *David Copperfield* 1935, *My Little Chickadee* (cowritten with Mae West) and *The Bank Dick* both 1940, and *Never Give a Sucker an Even Break* 1941.

Originally a vaudeville performer, he incorporated his former stage routines, such as juggling and pool playing, into his films. He was also a popular radio performer.

field studies study of ecology, geography, geology, history, archeology, and allied subjects, in the natural environment as opposed to the laboratory.

Fiesole resort town 4 mi/6 km NE of Florence, Italy, with many Etruscan and Roman relics;

population (1971) 14,400. The Romanesque cathedral was completed 1028.

fife a type of small flute. Originally from Switzerland, it was known as the Swiss pipe and has long been played by military bands.

Fife region of E Scotland (formerly the county of Fife), facing the North Sea and Firth of Forth
area 502 sq mi/1,300 sq km
towns administrative headquarters Glenrothes; Denfermline, St Andrews, Kirkcaldy, Cupar
physical the only high land is the Lomond Hills, in the NW, chief rivers Eden and Leven
features Rosyth naval base and dockyard (used for nuclear submarine refits) on N shore of the Firth of Forth; Tentsmuir, possibly the earliest settled site in Scotland. The ancient palace of the Stuarts was at Falkland, and eight Scottish kings are buried at Dunfermline
products potatoes, cereals, electronics, petrochemicals (Mossmorran), light engineering
population (1987) 345,000.

Fifteen Rebellion one of the five ◊Jacobite rebellions 1688–1715 aimed at restoring the ◊Stuart line to the English throne. Led by the "Old Pretender," ◊James Edward Stuart in 1715, this rebellion was stopped at Sheriffmuir, Scotland. It was marked by hesitancy on the part of the plotters.

fifth column a group within a country secretly aiding an enemy attacking from without. The term originated 1936 during the Spanish Civil War, when General Mola boasted that Franco supporters were attacking Madrid with four columns and that they had a "fifth column" inside the city.

fifth-generation computer anticipated new type of computer based on emerging microelectronic technologies with high computing speeds. The development of very large-scale integration (◊VLSI), which can put many more circuits onto a ◊silicon chip than is currently possible, will enable many processors to work in parallel. Such computers will run advanced "intelligent" programs. See also ◊computer generations.

fig any tree of the genus *Ficus* of the mulberry family Moraceae, including the many cultivated varieties of *F. carica*, originally from W Asia. They produce two or three crops of fruit a year. Eaten fresh or dried, figs have a high sugar content and laxative properties.

In the wild, *F. carica* is dependent on the fig wasp for pollination, and the wasp in turn is parasitic on the flowers. The tropical banyan *F. benghalensis* has less attractive edible fruit, and roots that grow down from its branches. The bo tree under which Buddha became enlightened is the Indian peepul or wild fig *F. religiosa*.

The only native US fig is the Florida strangler fig *F. aurea*, which starts off as an ◊epiphyte before developing its own root system.

fighting fish any of a SE Asian genus *Betta* of fishes of the gourami family, especially *B. splendens*, about 2 in/6 cm long and a popular aquarium fish. It can breathe air, using an accessory breathing organ above the gill, and can live in poorly oxygenated water. The male has large fins and various colors, including shining greens, reds, and blues. The female is yellowish brown with short fins.

The male builds a nest of bubbles at the water surface and displays to a female to induce her to lay. Rival males are attacked, and in a confined space, fights may occur. In Thailand, public contests are held.

figwort any Old World plant of the genus *Scrophularia* of the figwort family, which also includes foxgloves and snapdragons. Members of the genus have square stems, opposite leaves, and open two-lipped flowers in a cluster at the top of the stem.

Fiji country comprising 844 islands and islets in the SW South Pacific Ocean, about 100 of which are inhabited.
government Fiji was a constitutional monarchy within the ◊Commonwealth, with the British monarch as head of state and represented by a resident governor general, until 1987. The constitution dates from independence in 1970. The government is modeled on the British system, with a two-chamber parliament, consisting of a senate and house of representatives, and a prime minister and cabinet drawn from and responsible to the house of representatives. The senate has 22 appointed members, eight on the advice of the great council of Fijian chiefs, seven on the advice of the prime minister, six on the advice of the leader of the opposition, and one on the advice of the council of Rotuma Island (a Fijian dependency); it has a life of six years. The house of representatives has 52 members, elected for five years through a cross-voting system that ensures all ethnic groups are represented.
history Originally inhabited by ◊Melanesian and ◊Polynesian peoples, Fiji's first European visitor was Abel ◊Tasman in 1643. Fiji became a British possession in 1874 and achieved full independence within the Commonwealth in 1970. Before independence there had been racial tension between Indians, descended from workers brought from India in the late 19th century, and Fijians, so the constitutution incorporated an electoral system that would ensure racial balance in the house of representatives.

The leader of the Alliance Party, Ratu Sir Kamisese Mara, became prime minister at the time of independence and has held office ever since. The Alliance Party has traditionally been supported by Fijians, and the National Federation Party (NFP), led by Siddiq Koya, by Indians. The main divisions between the two have centered on land ownership, with the Fijians owning more than 80% of the land and defending their traditional rights, and the Indians claiming greater security of land tenure. The Fijian Labor Party was formed in 1985 but has so far made little impact at the polls.

An attempted coup in May 1987, led by Lt-Col Sitivina Rambuka, was abandoned after intervention by the governor general and the Great Council of Chiefs. Another coup by Rambuka in Sept seemed, despite indecision by its leader, more likely to succeed. On this occasion Queen Elizabeth II, at the instigation of the governor general, condemned the coup in an unprecedented fashion. Nevertheless, the coup went ahead and in Oct 1987 the Queen accepted the resignation of the governor general, thereby relinquishing her role as head of state and making Fiji a republic. In Aug 1989 the draft of a new constitution was published, embodying an electoral law that would favor indigenous Fijians, but preventing the army from taking control.

Fiji
Republic of

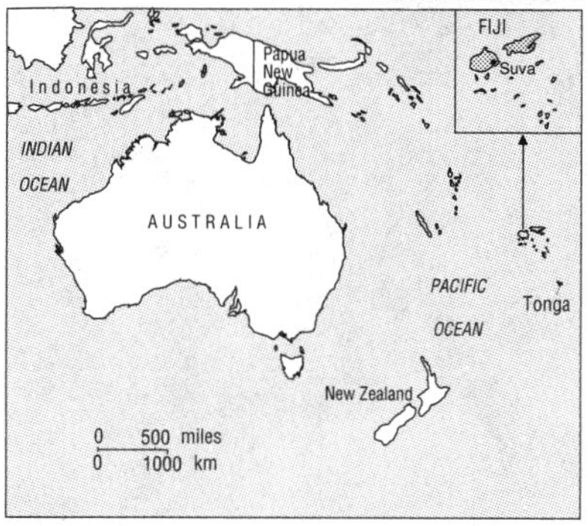
Indonesia
Papua New Guinea
FIJI
Suva
INDIAN OCEAN
AUSTRALIA
PACIFIC OCEAN
Tonga
New Zealand
0 500 miles
0 1000 km

area 7,078 sq mi/18,333 sq km
capital Suva
cities ports of Lavtoka and Levuka
physical comprises 844 Melanesian and Polynesian islands and islets (about 110 inhabited), the largest being Viti Levu (4,028 sq mi/10,429 sq km) and Vanua Levu (2,146 sq mi/5,550 sq km); mountainous, volcanic, with tropical rainforest and grasslands
features almost all islands surrounded by coral reefs; high volcanic peaks; crossroads of air and sea services between N America and Australia
head of state Ratu Sir Penaia Ganilau from 1987
head of government Ratu Sir Kamisese Mara from 1987
political system democratic republic
political parties Alliance Party (AP), moderate centrist Fijian; National Federation Party (NFP), moderate left-of-center Indian; Fijian Labor Party (FLP), left-of-center Indian; United Front, Fijian
exports sugar, coconut oil, ginger, timber, canned fish, gold; tourism is important
currency Fiji dollar
population (1989 est) 758,000 (46% Fijian, holding 80% of the land communally, and 49% Indian, introduced in the 19th century to work the sugar crop); growth rate 2.1% p.a.
life expectancy men 67, women 71
language English (official); Fijian, Hindi
religion Hindu 50%, Methodist 44%
literacy men 88%/women 77% (1980 est)
GDP $1.2 bn (1987); $1,604 per head
chronology
1874 Fiji became British crown colony.
1970 Independence achieved from Britain; Ratu Sir Kamisese Mara elected as first prime minister.
1987 April: general election brought to power an Indian-dominated coalition led by Dr Timoci Bavadra. May: military coup by Col Sitiveni Rabuka removed new government at gunpoint; Governor Gen Ratu Sir Penaia Ganilau regained control within weeks. Sept: second military coup by Rabuka proclaimed Fiji a republic and suspended the constitution. Oct: Fiji ceased to be a member of the Commonwealth. Dec: civilian government restored with Rambuka retaining control of security as minister for home affairs.
1989 New constitution proposed.

filariasis collective term for several diseases, prevalent in tropical areas, caused by certain roundworm (nematode) parasites.

Symptoms include blocked and swollen lymph vessels leading to grotesque swellings of the legs and genitals (Bancroftian filariasis, ◊elephantiasis); and blindness and dry, scaly skin (◊onchocerciasis). The disease-causing worms are spread mainly by insects, notably mosquitoes and black flies.

Filchner Wilhelm 1877–1957. German explorer who traveled extensively in Central Asia, but is remembered for his expedition into the Weddell Sea of Antarctica, where his ship became icebound for a whole winter. He landed a party and built a hut on the floating ice shelf, which eventually broke up and floated northward.

file in computing, a collection of data or a program stored in a computer's external memory, for example, on ◊disk. It might include anything from information on a company's employees to a program for an adventure game. Serial files hold information as a sequence of characters, so that to read any particular item of data, the program must read all those that precede it. Random access files allow the required data to be reached directly.

Files usually consist of a set of records, each having a number of fields for specific items of data. For example, the file for a class of schoolchildren might have five fields of information for each child: (1) family name; (2) first name; (3) house name or number; (4) street name; (5)

Fillmore The 13th president of the United States of America, Millard Fillmore, a Whig. 1850–1853.

town. To find out, for example, which children live in the same street, one would look in field 4.

Filene Edward Albert 1860–1937. US businessman. Born in Salem, Massachusetts, Filene took over his father's dry goods store in Boston, expanding it dramatically through the introduction of retailing innovations. The concern was incorporated as William Filene's Sons 1891. One of Filene's most imaginative merchandising ideas was the concept of the "bargain basement," where prices were dramatically lowered on certain goods. Filene was also committed to employee profit-sharing and for that reason was removed by his partners 1928. A political progressive, he was active in public welfare programs in Boston.

file transfer in computing, the transmission of a file (data stored on disk, for example) from one machine to another. Both machines must be physically linked (for example, by a telephone line) and both must be running appropriate communications software.

Fillmore Millard 1800–1874. the 13th president of the US 1850–53, a Whig. Born into a poor farming family in New Cayuga County, New York State, he was Zachary Taylor's vice-president from 1849, and succeeded him on Taylor's death, July 9, 1850. Fillmore supported a compromise on slavery 1850 to reconcile North and South.

This compromise pleased neither side, and it contained a harsh fugitive slave act requiring escaped slaves to be returned to their owners. He threatened to enforce this act with troops, if necessary, earning the wrath of the ◊abolitionists. Fillmore failed to be nominated for another term.

film, art of see ◊cinema.

film noir (French "dark film") a term originally used by French critics to describe any film characterized by pessimism, cynicism, and a dark, somber tone. It has been used to describe stark, grainy, black-and-white Hollywood films of the 1940s and 1950s that portrayed the seedy side of life.

Typically, the *film noir* is shot with lighting that emphasizes shadow and stark contrasts, abounds in night scenes, and contains a cynical antihero—an example is the character of Philip Marlowe as played by Humphrey Bogart in *The Big Sleep* 1946.

film, photographic strip of transparent material (usually cellulose acetate) coated with a light-sensitive emulsion, used in cameras to take pictures. The emulsion contains a mixture of light-sensitive silver halide salts (for example, bromide or iodide) in gelatin. Films differ in their sensitivities to light, this being indicated by their speeds. When the emulsion is exposed to light, the silver salts are invisibly altered, giving a latent image, which is then made visible by the process of ◊developing. Colour film consists of several layers of emulsion, each of which records a different color in the light falling on it.

In color film the front emulsion records blue light, then comes a yellow filter, followed by layers that record green and red light respectively. In the developing process the various images in the layers are dyed yellow, magenta (red), and cyan (blue), respectively. When they are viewed, either as a see-through transparency or as a color print, the colors merge to produce the true color of the original scene photographed.

film score music specially written to accompany a film on the soundtrack. Special scores were also written for some silent films and performed live as the film was shown.

Filson John c. 1747–1788. American explorer and land promoter. Filson moved W to Kentucky after the Revolutionary War. Investing heavily in land and hoping to attract a new wave of settlers to the area, he published *Discovery, Settlement, and Present State of Kentucky* 1784, the first book to popularize the personality and legend of Daniel Boone. After establishing a fur-trading outpost at Louisville, Filson moved farther west into the Illinois and Ohio territories, founding a settlement at the present site of Cincinnati.

filter in chemistry, a porous substance, such as blotting paper, through which a mixture can be passed to separate out its solid constituents. In optics, a filter is a piece of glass or transparent material that passes light of one color only.

filter in electronics, a circuit that transmits a signal of some frequencies better than others. A low-pass filter transmits signals of low frequency and direct current; a high-pass filter transmits high-frequency signals; a band-pass filter transmits signals in a band of frequencies.

filtration technique where suspended solid particles in a fluid are removed by passing the mixture through a porous barrier, usually paper or cloth. The particles are retained by the paper or cloth to form a residue and the fluid passes through to make up the filtrate. Soot is filtered from air while suspended solids are filtered from water.

final solution (to the Jewish question; German *Endlosung der Judenfrage*) phrase used by the Nazis to describe the extermination of Jews (and other unwanteds and opponents of the regime) during World War II. See ◊Holocaust.

finch any of various songbirds of the family Fringillidae, in the order Passeriformes (perching birds).

They are seed-eaters with stout conical beaks and include goldfinches, crossbills, redpolls, and canaries.

Finch Peter 1916–1977. Australian-born English film actor who began his career in Australia before going to London in 1949 to start on an international career with roles such as those in *A Town Like Alice* 1956; *The Trials of Oscar Wilde* 1960; *Sunday, Bloody, Sunday* 1971; and *Network* 1976, for which he won an Academy Award.

fin de siècle (French "end of century") the art and literature of the 1890s; decadent.

Fingal's Cave cave on the island of Staffa, Inner Hebrides, Scotland. It is lined with natural basalt columns, and is 200 ft/60 m long and 65 ft/20 m high. Fingal, based on the Irish hero Finn Mac Cumhaill, was the leading character in Macpherson's Ossianic forgeries. Visited by Mendelssohn in 1829, the cave was the inspiration of his *Hebrides* overture, otherwise known as *Fingal's Cave.*

fingerprint ridge pattern of the skin on a person's fingertips; this is constant through life and no two are exactly alike. Fingerprinting was first used as a means of identifying crime suspects in India, and was adopted by the English police 1901; it is now widely employed in police and security work.

Finistère *département* of ◊Brittany, NW France; area 7,030 sq2,714 mi/ km; population (1982) 828,500. The administrative center is Quimper.

Finisterre Cape promontory in the extreme NW of Spain.

Finland country in Scandinavia, bounded N by Norway, E by the USSR, S and W by the Baltic Sea, and NW by Sweden.

government Finland is a republic that combines a parliamentary system with a strong presidency. The single-chamber parliament, the *Eduskunta,*

Finland
Republic of
(Suomen Tasavalta)

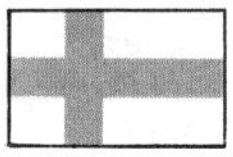

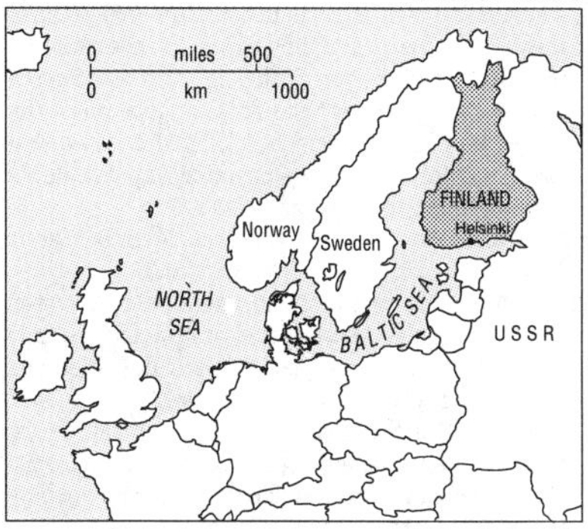
0 miles 500
0 km 1000
Norway
Sweden
FINLAND
Helsinki
NORTH SEA
BALTIC SEA
USSR

area 130,608 sq mi/338,145 sq km
capital Helsinki
cities Tampere, port Turku, Oulu, Rovaniemi, Lahti
physical most of the country is forest, with low hills and about 60,000 lakes; one-third is within the Arctic Circle; archipelago in S; includes Abland Islands
features Helsinki is the most northerly national capital on the European continent; at the 70th parallel there is constant daylight for 73 days in summer and 51 days of uninterrupted night in winter
head of state Mauno Koivisto from 1982
head of government Esko Ahoi from 1991
political system democratic republic
political parties Social Democratic Party (SDP), moderate left-of-center; National Coalition Party (KOK), moderate right-of-center; Center Party (KP), centrist, rural-orientated; Finnish People's Democratic League (SKDL), left-wing; Swedish People's Party, independent Swedish-orientated; Finnish Rural Party (SMP), farmers and small businesses; Democratic Alternative, left-wing; Green Party
exports metal, chemical and engineering products (icebreakers and oil rigs), paper, sawn wood, clothing, fine ceramics, glass, furniture
currency markka
population (1989 est) 4,990,000; growth rate 0.5% p.a.
life expectancy men 70, women 78
language Finnish 93%, Swedish 6% (both official), small Lapp and Russian-speaking minorities
religion Lutheran 97%, Eastern Orthodox 1.2%
literacy 99%
GDP $77.9 bn (1987); $15,795 per head
chronology
1809 Finland annexed by Russia.
1917 Independence achieved from Russia.
1939 Defeated by USSR in Winter War.
1941 Allowed Germany to station troops in Finland to attack USSR; USSR bombed Finland.
1944 Concluded separate armistice with USSR.
1948 Finno-Soviet Pact of Friendship, Cooperation, and Mutual Assistance signed.
1955 Finland joined the UN and the Nordic Council. 1956 Urho Kekkonen elected president; reelected 1962, 1968, 1978.
1973 Trade treaty with EEC signed.
1977 Trade agreement with USSR signed.
1982 Koivisto elected president; reelected 1988.
1989 Finland joined Council of Europe.
1991 Big swing to the center in general election. New coalition government formed.

has 200 members, elected by universal suffrage through a system of proportional representation, for a four-year term. The president is elected for six years by a 301-member electoral college, chosen by popular vote in the same way as the parliament. The president appoints a prime minister and a cabinet (called a council of state), whose members are collectively responsible to the *Eduskunta*.

The relationship between the president, prime minister, and council of state is unusual, with the nearest equivalent to be found in France. The president has supreme executive power and can ignore even a unanimous decision reached in the council of state, but the prime minister is concerned with the day-to-day operation of the government, so that to some extent they can, at times, both act as heads of government. Both the president and the *Eduskunta* can initiate legislation and the president has a right of veto, though this can be overruled by a newly appointed parliament.

Because of the system of proportional representation, there is a multiplicity of parties, and the prime minister invariably heads a coalition council of state, typically between four parties. The main parties are: the Social Democratic Party (SDP), the National Coalition Party (KOK), the Center Party (KP), the Finnish People's Democratic League (SKDL), the Finnish Rural Party (SMP), and the Swedish People's Party (SFP).

history The nomadic Lapps were the earliest-known inhabitants; from about the 1st century BC they were gradually driven north by Finnic nomads from Asia into the far northern region they occupy today. The area was conquered 12th–13th centuries by Sweden, and for much of the next 200 years the country was the scene of wars between Sweden and Russia. As a duchy of Sweden, Finland was allowed a measure of autonomy, becoming a grand duchy 1581. In 1809, during the Napoleonic Wars, Finland was invaded and annexed by Russia; nationalist feeling grew, and the country proclaimed its independence during the 1917 Russian revolution. The Soviet regime initially tried to regain control but acknowledged Finland's independence 1920.

In 1939 the USSR's request for military bases in Finland was rejected, and the two countries were involved in the "Winter War," which lasted for 15 weeks. Finland was defeated and forced to cede territory. In the hope of regaining it, in 1941 it joined Nazi Germany in attacking the USSR, but agreed to a separate armistice 1944. It was again forced to cede territory (12% of its total area) and agree to huge war reparations; in 1948 it signed the Finno-Soviet Pact of Friendship, Cooperation, and Mutual Assistance (the YYA Treaty). War reparations to the USSR were paid off in 1952 (amounting to 5% of the GDP 1945–48). In 1955 Finland joined the UN and the Nordic Council (which includes Denmark, Iceland, Norway, and Sweden).

The YYA Treaty was extended 1955, 1970, and 1983. Although the Treaty requires it to repel any attack on the USSR through Finnish territory by Germany or its allies, Finland has maintained a policy of strict neutrality. It signed a trade treaty with the EEC 1973 and a 15-year trade agreement with the USSR 1977. In 1989 it was admitted into the Council of Europe.

Finnish politics have been characterized by instability in governments, over 60 having been formed since independence, including many minority coalitions. The presidency, on the other hand, has been very stable, with only two presidents in over 30 years. Urho Kekkonen was elected president in 1956 and reelected in 1962, 1968, and 1978. In 1981 he resigned from office due to ill health and Mauno Koivisto became president in Jan 1982; he was reelected in 1988.

The Social Democratic and Center parties have dominated Finland's coalition politics for many years, but the 1987 general election resulted in the Social Democrats entering government in coalition with their archenemies, the Conservatives, while the Center Party was forced into opposition. In 1991 elections, however, the Center party scored an upset victory.

Finland, Gulf of eastern arm of the ◊Baltic Sea, separating Finland from Estonia.

Finlandization political term for the tendency of a small state to shape its foreign policy so as to accommodate a much more powerful neighbor, as in the case of Finland and the USSR.

Finney Albert 1936– . English stage and film actor. He created the title roles in Keith Waterhouse's stage play *Billy Liar* 1960 and John Osborne's *Luther* 1961, and was artistic director of the Royal Court Theatre from 1972 to 1975. His films include *Saturday Night and Sunday Morning* 1960, *Tom Jones* 1963, *Murder on the Orient Express* 1974, and *The Dresser* 1984.

Finnish architecture the earliest Finnish architecture was wooden and hence little survives, although some ecclesiastical buildings (Turku cathedral, Lohja church) date from the 15th century. Following a Classical movement in the 18th century and a Neoclassical period (typified by Helsinki's center, designed by Carl Ludvig Engel 1820), Finland developed a strongly individualistic style of architecture. The 1890s saw a fusion of Art Nouveau concepts and vernacular style, followed by a thriving Modernist stage (led by Alvar Aalto) and visionary town planning (for example, Tapiola garden suburb). The 1980s have seen the evolution of Postmodernism, or "organic" Finnish architecture.

The fusion of Art Nouveau and local Finnish style and motifs by architects, such as Lars Sonck and the Saarinen-Gesellius-Lindgren firm in the 1890s, placed Finnish architecture in a world context (since Saarinen went on to gain international reputation in the US). Later Modernist and Postmodernist developments, such as the Yhtyneet Kuvalahdet (United Magazines) building in Helsinki (by Ilmo Valjakka), have been internationally acclaimed.

Finnish language member of the Finno-Ugric language family, the national language of Finland and closely related to neighboring Estonian, Livonian, Karelian, and Ingrian languages. At the beginning of the 19th century Finnish had no official status, since Swedish was the language of education, government, and literature in Finland. The publication of the *Kalevala*, a national epic poem, in 1835, contributed greatly to the arousal of Finnish national and linguistic feeling.

Finnish literature some fragments of Finnish literature survive from the 12th century; the first book was a primer published 1544. A complete Bible in Finnish was issued in Stockholm 1642. But the predominance of the Swedes and Swedish in Finland inhibited the growth of Finnish literature until the 19th century, when it was launched with the publication in 1835 of Elias Lönnrot's epic folk verse compilation *Kalevala*. The earliest Finnish writer was Aleksis Kivi, whose classic comedy *Seitsemän veljestä/Seven Brothers* was published in 1870. The turn of the century saw the emergence of a crop of broadly realist writers, including Juhani Aho (1861–1921), Ilmari Kianto (1874–1970), and Joel Lehtonen (1881–1943) and the lyric poet Eino Leino (1878–1926). Mika Waltari (1908–79) attracted attention abroad with his *Sinuhe egyptilä inen/Sinuhe the Egyptian* 1945. Frans Emil Sillanpää (1888–1964) received a Nobel Prize in 1939. Vä inö Linna's *Tuntematon sotilas/The Unknown Soldier* is the definitive account of the Winter War of 1939. Modern writers include the poets Pentti Saarikoski (1937–83) and Paavo Haavikko (1931–), and the novelists Veijo Meri (1928–), Antti Tuuri (1944–), and Leena Krohn (1947–).

Finn Mac Cumhaill legendary Irish hero, identified with a general who organized an Irish regular army in the 3rd century. James Macpherson (1736–1796) featured him (as Fingal) and his followers in the verse of his popular epics 1762–63, which were supposedly written by a 3rd-century bard, ◊Ossian. Although challenged by the critic Dr Johnson, the poems were influential in the Romantic movement.

Finno-Ugric group or family of more than 20 languages spoken by some 22 million people in scattered communities from Norway in the west to Siberia in the east and to the Carpathian mountains in the south. Members of the family include Finnish, Lapp, and Hungarian.

Finsen Niels Ryberg 1860–1904. Danish physician, the first to use ultraviolet light treatment for skin diseases. Nobel Prize for Medicine 1903.

finsen unit unit (abbreviation FU) for measuring the intensity of ultraviolet (UV) light; for instance, UV light of 2 FUs causes sunburn in 15 minutes.

Finsteraarhorn the highest mountain, 14,020 ft/ 4,274 m, in the Bernese Alps, Switzerland.

fiord alternate spelling of ◊fjord.

fir any ◊conifers of the genus *Abies* in the pine family Pinaceae. The true firs include the balsam fir of N North America and the Eurasian silver fir *Abies alba*. Douglas firs of the genus *Pseudotsuga* are native to W North America and the Far East.

Firdausi Abdul Qasim Mansur c. 935–c. 1020. Persian poet, whose epic *Shahnama/The Book of Kings* relates the history of Persia in 60,000 verses.

firearm a weapon from which projectiles are discharged by the combustion of an explosive. Firearms are generally divided into two main sections: ◊artillery (ordnance or cannon), with a bore greater than 1 in/2.54 cm, and ◊small arms, with a bore of less than 1 in/2.54 cm. Although gunpowder was known in Europe 60 years previously, the invention of guns dates from 1300–25, and is attributed to Berthold Schwartz, a German monk.

firebrat any insect of the order Thysanura (◊bristletail).

fire clay a ◊clay with refractory characteristics (resistant to high temperatures), and hence suitable for lining furnaces (firebrick). Its chemical composition consists of a high percentage of silicon and aluminum oxides, and a low percentage of the oxides of sodium, potassium, iron, and calcium.

fire extinguisher device for putting out a fire. Fire extinguishers work by removing one of the three conditions necessary for fire to continue (heat, oxygen, and fuel), either by cooling the fire or by excluding oxygen.

The simplest fire extinguishers contain water, which when propelled onto the fire cools it down. Water extinguishers cannot be used on electrical fires, as there is a danger of electrocution, or on burning oil, as the oil will float on the water and spread the blaze.

Many domestic extinguishers contain liquid carbon dioxide under pressure. When the handle is pressed, carbon dioxide is released as a gas that blankets the burning material and prevents oxygen reaching it. Dry extinguishers spray powder, which then releases carbon dioxide gas. Wet extinguishers are often of the soda-acid type; when activated, sulfuric acid mixes with sodium bicarbonate, producing carbon dioxide. The gas pressure forces the solution out of a nozzle, and a foaming agent may be added to produce foam.

Some extinguishers contain halons (hydrocarbons with one or more hydrogens substituted for by a halogen such as chlorine, bromine or fluorine). These are very effective at smothering fires, but cause damage to the ◊ozone layer.

firefly any winged nocturnal beetle of the family Lampyridae. They all emit light through the process of ◊bioluminescence.

Firenze Italian form of ◊Florence.

fire protection methods available for fighting fires.

Industrial and commercial buildings are often protected by an automatic sprinkler system: heat or smoke opens the sprinkler heads on a network of water pipes and immediately sprays the source of the fire. In certain circumstances water is ineffective and may be dangerous; for example, for oil and gasoline storage-tank fires, foam systems are used; for industrial plants containing flammable vapours, carbon dioxide is used; where electricity is involved, vaporizing liquids create a nonflammable barrier; and for some chemicals only various dry powders can be used.

Public fire-fighting services are usually maintained by local authorities, and similar services operate in other countries. In small communities, volunteer fire departments and local government work together.

Firestone Harvey Samuel 1868–1938. US industrialist. Born in Columbiana, Ohio, and educated at local schools, Firestone entered the family buggy business and quickly recognized the advantages of rubber for wheel rims. He founded a retail tire outlet in Chicago 1896 and in 1900 established a tire-manufacturing firm, the Firestone Tire and Rubber Co., in Akron, Ohio. Firestone pioneered the principle of the detachable rim and, from 1906, was the major supplier of tires to the Ford Motor Co. A strong opponent of organized labor, he long resisted the unionization of his work force.

Firestone Shulamith 1945– . Canadian feminist writer and editor, whose book *The Dialectic of Sex: The Case for Feminist Revolution* 1970, which analyzed the limited future of feminism under Marxist and Freudian theories, exerted considerable influence on feminist thought.

She was one of the most influential early organizers of the Women's Liberation Movement in the US. Other works include *Notes from the Second Year* 1970.

firework a pyrotechnic device, originating in China, for producing a display of colored sparks (and sometimes noises) by burning chemicals. A firework consists of a container, usually cylindrical in shape and of rolled paper, enclosing a mixture capable of burning independently of the oxygen in the air. One of the ingredients holds a separate supply of oxygen that is readily given up to the other combustible ingredients.

Fireworks are often used in China, where they originated, and Japan. In Britain they are traditionally used on Nov 5, Guy Fawkes Day, and in the US on July 4, Independence Day.

firmware computer program held permanently in a computer's ◊ROM (read-only memory) chips, as opposed to a program that is read in from external memory as it is needed.

first aid action taken immediately in a medical emergency in order to save a sick or injured person's life, prevent further damage, or facilitate later treatment. See also ◊resuscitation.

First Legal Tender Case a US Supreme Court case (*Hepburn* v *Griswold*) 1870 that reviewed Congress's right to pay its debts with unbacked paper money. The case was one of numerous suits protesting the use of $450 million issued under the Legal Tender Acts (1862, 1863) to repay loans. The Court found the acts unconstitutional because they made the paper money legal tender for the payment of all debts, including ones contracted before the passage of the acts, a violation of the obligation of contracts. The Court also noted that the Constitution prohibits payment of public debts with anything but gold and silver.

First World War another name for ◊World War I, 1914–18.

fiscal policy that part of government policy devoted to achieving the desired level of revenue, notably through taxation, and deciding the priorities and purposes governing its expenditure.

US fiscal policy has been directed largely at achieving or maintaining full employment while avoiding high inflation. Raising or lowering income taxes or corporate taxes can govern the level of economic activity, and government spending can sustain activity when private funds are unavailable. The tax cuts of the early Reagan administration generated a long economic boom and brought an end to a severe recession with inflation (called a ◊stagflation), but the budget deficits incurred remain a critical economic problem.

fiscal year the financial year, which does not necessarily coincide with the calendar year.

For the US government, the budget year runs from Oct 1 to Sept 30. For businesses and financial institutions, it generally runs July 1 to June 30.

Fischer Bobby (Robert James) 1943– . US chess champion. In 1958, after proving himself in international competition, he became the youngest grand master in history. He was the author of *Games of Chess* 1959, and was also celebrated for his unorthodox psychological tactics. He won the world title from Boris Spassky in Reykjavik, Iceland, 1972.

Born in Chicago, Fischer was raised in New York and began serious involvement with chess at an early age. By 1956 he had won the US junior chess title and, within two years, had also won the US Chess Federation championship for adults.

Fischer Emil Hermann 1852–1919. German chemist who produced synthetic sugars and from these various enzymes. His descriptions of the chemistry of the carbohydrates and peptides laid the foundations for the science of biochemistry. Nobel Prize 1902.

Fischer Hans 1881–1945. German chemist awarded a Nobel Prize 1930 for his discovery of hemoglobin in blood.

Fischer-Dieskau Dietrich 1925– . German baritone, renowned for his interpretation of Franz Schubert's *lieder* (songs).

fish or ***fin fish*** aquatic vertebrate that uses gills for

fish

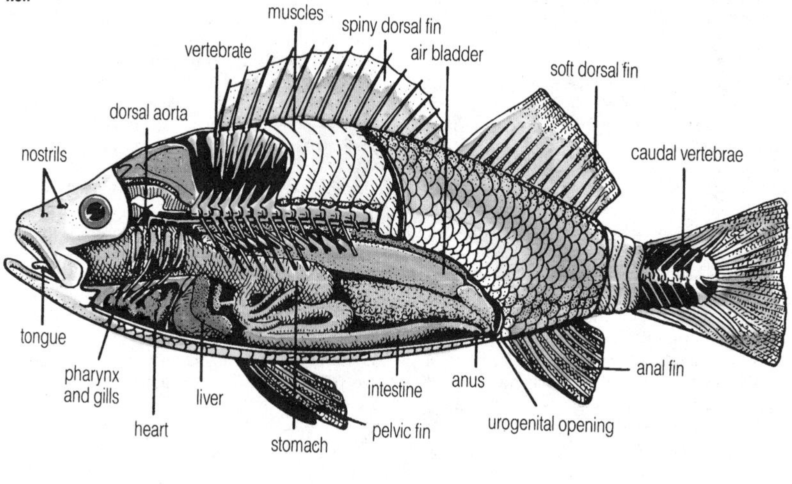
muscles
spiny dorsal fin
vertebrate
air bladder
soft dorsal fin
dorsal aorta
nostrils
caudal vertebrae
tongue
pharynx and gills
liver
intestine
anus
anal fin
heart
stomach
pelvic fin
urogenital opening

fish classification

Superclass Agnatha (jawless fishes)	Order	No of species	Examples
	Petromyzoniformes	30	lampreys
	Myxiniformes	15	hagfishes
Superclass Gnathostomata (jawed fishes)			
Class Chondrichthyes (cartilaginous fishes)			
Subclass Elasmobranchii (sharks and rays)			
	Hexanchiformes	*4*	*frilled shark, comb-toothed shark*
	Heterodontiformes	*10*	*Port Jackson sharks*
	Lamniformes	*200*	*"typical" sharks*
	Rajiformes	*300*	*skates, rays*
Subclass Holocephali (rabbitfishes)			
	'Chimaeriformes	20	chimaeras, rabbitfishes
Class Osteichthyes (bony fishes)			
Subclass Sarcopterygii (fleshy finned fishes)			
Coelacanths			
	Coelacanthiformes	*1*	*coelacanths*
Lungfishes			
	Ceratodontiformes	1	Australian lungfish
	Lepidosireniformes	4	S American and African lungfish
Subclass Actinopterygii (ray-finned fishes)			
Superorder Chondrostei			
	Polypteriormes	11	bichirs and reedfish
	Acipensiformes	25	paddlefish, sturgeons
Superorder Holostei			
	Amiiformes	8	bowfin, garpikes
Superorder Teleostei			
	Elopiformes	12	tarpons, tenpounders
	Anguilliformes	300	eels
	Notacanthiformes	20	spiny eels
	Clupeiformes	350	herrings, anchovies
	Osteoglossiformes	16	arapaima, African butterfly fish
	Mormyriformes	150	elephant-trunk fishes, featherbacks
	Salmoniformes	500	salmon, trout, smelt, pike
	Gonorhynchiformes	15	milkfish
	Cypriniformes	350	carp, barbs, characins, loaches
	Siluriformes	200	catfishes
	Myctophiformes	300	deep-sea lantern fishes, Bombay ducks
	Percopsiformes	10	pirate perches, cave-dwelling amblyopsids
	Batrachoidiformes	10	toadfishes
	Gobiesociformes	100	clingfishes
	Lophiiformes	150	anglerfishes
	Gadiformes	450	cod, pollack, pearlfish, eelpout
	Atheriniformes	600	flying fishes, toothcarps, halfbeaks
	Lampridiformes	50	opah, ribbonfish
	Beryciformes	150	squirrelfishes
	Zeiformes	60	John Dory, boarfish
	Gasterosteiforems	150	sticklebacks, pipefishes, seahorses
	Channiformes	5	snakesheads
	Synbranchiformes	7	cuchia
	Scorpaeniformes	700	gurnards, miller's thumb, stonefish
	Dactylopteriformes	6	flying gunard
	Pegasiformes	4	sea-moths
	Pleuronectiformes	500	flatfishes
	Tetraodontiformes	250	puffer fishes, trigger fishes, sun fish
	Perciformes	6500	perches, cichlids, damsel fishes, gobies, wrasses, parrotfishes, gouramis, marlin, mackerel, tuna, swordfish, spiny eels, mullets, barracudas, sea bream, croakers, ice fishes, butterfish

obtaining oxygen from fresh or sea water. There are three main groups, not closely related: the bony fishes or Osteichthyes (goldfish, cod, tuna); the cartilaginous fishes or Chondrichthyes (sharks, rays); and the jawless fishes or Agnatha (hagfishes, lampreys).

The bony fishes constitute the majority of living fishes (about 20,000 species). The skeleton is bone, movement is controlled by mobile fins, and the body is usually covered with scales. The gills are covered by a single flap. Many have a swim bladder with which the fish adjusts its buoyancy. Most lay eggs, sometimes in vast numbers; some ◊cod can produce as many as 28 million. These are laid in the open sea, and probably no more than 28 of them will survive to become adults. Those species that produce small numbers of eggs very often protect them in nests, or brood them in their mouths. Some fishes are internally fertilized and retain eggs until hatching inside the body, then giving birth to live young. Most bony fishes are ray-finned fishes, but a few, including lungfishes and coelacanths, are fleshy-finned.

The cartilaginous fishes are efficient hunters. There are fewer than 600 known species of sharks and rays. The skeleton is cartilage, the mouth is generally beneath the head, the nose is large and sensitive, and there is a series of open gill slits along the neck region. They may lay eggs ("mermaid's purses") or bear live young. Some types of cartilaginous fishes, such as sharks, retain the shape they had millions of years ago.

Jawless fishes have a body plan like that of some of the earliest vertebrates that existed before true fishes with jaws evolved. There is no true backbone but a ◊notochord. The lamprey attaches itself to the fishes on which it feeds by a suckerlike rasping mouth. Hagfishes are entirely marine, very slimy, and feed on carrion and injured fishes.

Fish Hamilton 1808–1893. US public figure and diplomat. In 1851 he was elected to the US Senate, serving until 1857, by which time he had become a member of the Republican party. Fish was appointed secretary of state by President Grant 1869. His eight years in that office were marked by moderation in his pursuit of US claims against the UK in the ◊Alabama case and in averting war with Spain over Cuba.

Born in New York and educated at Columbia University, Fish was admitted to the bar 1830. Active in Whig politics, he served as governor of New York 1849–50.

fisher North American ◊marten *Martes pennanti*, dark brown with greyish foreparts and blackish rump and tail. It is less arboreal than the smaller American marten *A. americana*.

Fisher Andrew 1862–1928. Australian Labor politician. Born in Scotland, he went to Australia 1885, and entered the Australian parliament in 1901. He was prime minister 1908–09, 1910–13, and 1914–15, and Australian high commissioner to the UK 1916–21.

Fisher Geoffrey, Baron Fisher of Lambeth 1887–1972. English priest, archbishop of Canterbury 1945–61. He was the first holder of this office to visit the pope since the 14th century.

Fisher John, St c. 1469–1535. English bishop, created bishop of Rochester 1504. He was an enthusiastic supporter of the revival in the study of Greek, and a friend of the humanists Thomas More and Desiderius Erasmus. In 1535 he was tried on a charge of denying the royal supremacy of Henry VIII and beheaded.

Fisher Ronald Aylmer 1890–1962. English statistician and geneticist. He modernized Charles Darwin's theory of evolution, thus securing the key biological concept of genetic change by natural selection. Fisher developed several new statistical techniques and, applying his methods to genetics, published *The Genetical Theory of Natural Selection* in 1930.

This classic work established that the discoveries of the geneticist Gregor Mendel could be shown to support Darwin's theory of evolution. He was appointed Head of Rothampstead Experimental Station in 1919.

fish farming or ***aquaculture*** raising under controlled conditions in tanks and ponds, sometimes in offshore pens. It has been practiced for centuries in the Far East, since ancient China, and today Japan alone produces some 100,000 tons of fish a year; the US, Norway, and Canada are also big producers. In the 1980s one-tenth of the world's consumption of fish was farmed, notably trout, Atlantic salmon, turbot, eel, mussels, and oysters.

fishing and fisheries fisheries can be classified by (1) type of water: freshwater (lake, river, pond); marine (inshore, midwater, deep sea); (2) catch: for example salmon fishing, (3) fishing method: diving, stunning or poisoning, harpooning, trawling, drifting.

marine fishing The greatest proportion of the world's catch comes from the oceans. The primary production area is the photic zone, the relatively thin surface layer (164 ft/50 m) of water that can be penetrated by light, allowing photosynthesis by plant ◊plankton to take place. Plankton-eating fish tend to be small in size and include herrings and sardines. Demersal fishes, such as haddock, halibut, and cod, live primarily near the

fishing and fisheries

drag net

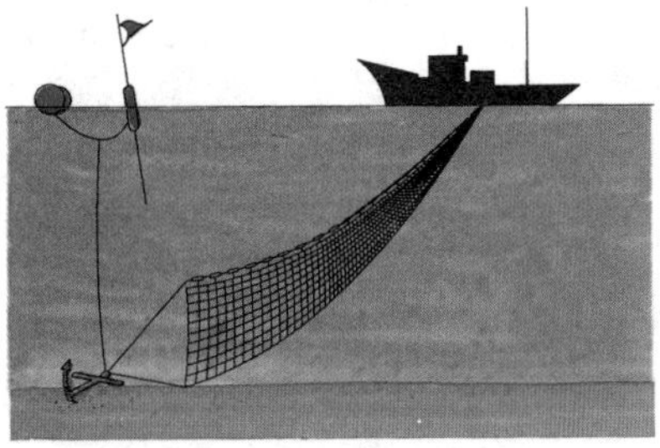

trawl net

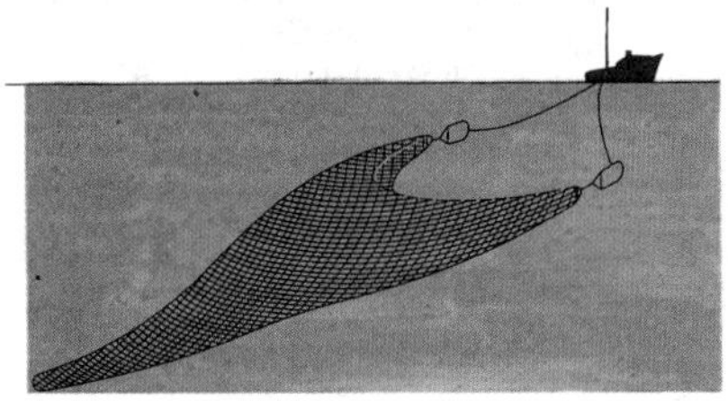

ocean floor, and feed on various invertebrate marine animals. Over 20 million tonnes of them are caught each year by trawling. Pelagic fish, such as tuna, live in the open sea, near the surface, and purse seine nets are used to catch them; the annual catch is over 30 million tonnes a year.

freshwater fishing There is large demand for salmon, trout, carp, eel, bass, pike, perch, and catfish. These inhabit ponds, lakes, rivers, or swamps, and some species have been successfully cultivated (◊fish farming).

methods Lines, seine nets, and lift nets are the common commercial methods used. Purse seine nets, which close like a purse and may be as long as 30 nautical miles, have caused a crisis in the S Pacific where Japan, Taiwan, and South Korea fish illegally in other countries' fishing zones.

history Until the introduction of refrigeration, fish was too perishable to be exported, and fishing met local needs only. Between 1950 and 1970, the global fish catch increased by an average of 7% each year. On refrigerated factory ships, filleting and processing can be done at sea. Japan evolved new techniques for locating shoals (by sonar and radar) and catching them (for example, with electrical charges and chemical baits). By the 1970s, indiscriminate overfishing had led to serious depletion of stocks, and heated confrontations between countries using the same fishing grounds. A partial solution was the extension of fishing limits to 200 mi/320 km. The North Sea countries have experimented with the artificial breeding of fish eggs and release of small fry into the sea. Overfishing of the NE Atlantic led, in 1988, to hundreds of thousands of starving seals on the N coast of Norway. Marine pollution is blamed for the increasing number (up to 30%) of diseased fish in the North Sea. United Nations resolution was passed 1989 to end drift-net fishing by June 1992.

ancillary industries These include the manufacture of nets, the processing of oil and fishmeal (nearly 25% of the fish caught annually are turned into meal for animal feed), pet food, glue, manure, and drugs such as insulin and other pharmaceutical products.

fission in physics, the splitting of the nucleus of the atom (see ◊nuclear energy).

fistula in medicine, an abnormal pathway developing between adjoining organs or tissues, or leading to the exterior of the body. A fistula developing between the bowels and the bladder, for instance, may give rise to urinary-tract infection by intestinal organisms.

Fitzgerald *Author of The Great Gatsby* 1925, F Scott Fitzgerald portrayed the Jazz Age in America.

Fitch John 1743–1798. US inventor and early experimenter with steam engines and steamships, designing in 1786 the finest steamboat to serve the Delaware river. His venture failed, so Robert ◊Fulton is erroneously considered the inventor of the steamship.

Fitchburg city in N Massachusetts, on the Nashua river, N of Worcester. Industries include paper, textiles, furniture, clothing, and foundry products; population (1990) 41,194.

fitness in genetic theory, a measure of the success with which a genetically determined character can spread in future generations. By convention, the normal character is assigned a fitness of one, and variants (determined by other ◊alleles) are then assigned fitness values relative to this. Those with fitness greater than one will spread more rapidly and will ultimately replace the normal allele; those with fitness less than one will gradually die out.

Fitzgerald Edward 1809–1883. English poet and translator. In 1859 he published his poetic version of the *Rubaiyat of Omar Khayyam*, which is generally considered more an original creation than a translation.

Fitzgerald Ella 1918– . US jazz singer, recognized as one of the finest, most lyrical voices in jazz, both in solo work and with big bands. She is celebrated for her smooth interpretations of Gershwin and Cole Porter songs.

Fitzgerald mastered the "scat" technique and was widely imitated in the 1950s and 1960s. She is among the best-selling recording artists in the history of jazz.

Fitzgerald F(rancis) Scott (Key) 1896–1940. US novelist and short-story writer. His early autobiographical novel *This Side of Paradise* 1920 made him known in the postwar society of the East Coast, and *The Great Gatsby* 1925 epitomizes the Jazz Age.

Fitzgerald was born in Minnesota. His first book, *This Side of Paradise*, reflected his experiences at Princeton University. In 1920 he married Zelda Sayre (1900–1947). His second novel, *The Beautiful and the Damned* 1922, tells of a glamorous couple (resembling the Fitzgeralds) and of their unhappy decline. In 1924 the Fitzgeralds moved to the French Riviera, where they became members of a fashionable group of expatriates. In *The Great Gatsby* 1925 the narrator resembles the author, and Gatsby, the self-made millionaire, is lost in the soulless society he enters. Zelda Fitzgerald, a schizophrenic, entered an asylum in 1930. Her descent into mental illness forms the subject of *Tender is the Night* 1934. After her confinement Fitzgerald went to Hollywood to write screenplays and earn enough to pay Zelda's medical bills. He fell in love with Sheilah Graham but declined into alcoholism. His other works include numerous short stories and his novel *The Last Tycoon*, about the film business, which was unfinished at his death but was made into a major motion picture 1976.

Fitzgerald George 1851–1901. Irish physicist known for his work on electromagnetics. In 1895 he explained the anomalous results of the ◊Michelson-Morley experiment 1887 by supposing that bodies moving through the ether contracted as their velocity increased, an effect since known as the Fitzgerald-Lorentz contraction.

Fitzherbert Maria Anne 1756–1837. Wife of the Prince of Wales, later George IV. She became Mrs Fitzherbert by her second marriage 1778 and, after her husband's death 1781, entered London society. She secretly married the Prince of Wales 1785 and finally parted from him 1803.

five pillars of Islam the five duties required of every Muslim: repeating the creed, which affirms that Allah is the one God and Mohammed is his prophet; daily prayer or ◊salat; giving alms; fasting during the month of Ramadan; and, if not prevented by ill health or poverty, the hajj, or pilgrimage to Mecca, once in a lifetime.

fixed point a temperature that can be accurately reproduced and used as the basis of a temperature scale. In the Celsius scale, the fixed points are the temperature of melting ice, which is 0°C (32°F), and the temperature of boiling water (at standard atmospheric pressure), which is 100°C (212°F).

fixed-point arithmetic form of arithmetic in which the decimal point is always in its correct position in relation to the digits. In computing, it is faster than ◊floating-point arithmetic. Fixed-point arithmetic is a system of representing numbers by a single set of digits with the decimal point in its correct position (for example, 97.8, 0.978). For very large and very small numbers this requires a lot of digits. In computing the numbers that can be handled in this form are limited by the capacity of a computer, so the slower ◊floating-point arithmetic is often preferred.

Fixx James 1932–1984. US popularizer of jogging for cardiovascular fitness with his book *The Complete Book of Running* 1978. He died of a heart attack while jogging.

fjord or ***fiord*** narrow sea inlet enclosed by high cliffs. Fjords are found in Norway and elsewhere. Fiordland is the deeply indented SW coast of South Island, New Zealand; one of the most beautiful inlets is Milford Sound.

FL abbreviation for ◊Florida.

flaccidity the loss of rigidity (turgor) in plant cells, caused by loss of water from the central vacuole so that the cytoplasm no longer pushes against the cellulose cell wall. If this condition occurs throughout the plant then wilting is seen.

Flaccidity can be induced in the laboratory by immersing the plant cell in a strong saline solution. Water leaves the cell by ◊osmosis causing the vacuole to shrink. In extreme cases the actual cytoplasm pulls away from the cell wall, a phenomenon known as plasmolysis.

flag a piece of cloth used as an emblem or symbol for nationalistic, religious, or military displays, or as a means of signaling. Flags have been used since ancient times.

The Stars and Stripes, also called Old Glory, is the flag of the US; the 50 stars on a field of blue represent the 50 states now in the Union, and the 13 red and white stripes represent the 13 original colonies. Each state also has its own flag. The US presidential standard displays the American eagle, surrounded by 50 stars.

The British national flag, the Union Jack, unites the crosses of St George, St Andrew, and St Patrick, representing England, Scotland, and Ireland.

The flag of the USSR places the crossed hammer and sickle, representing the workers of town and country, on a red field, the emblem of revolution. The flags of the Scandinavian countries bear crosses; the Danish *Dannebrog* ("strength of Denmark") is the oldest national flag, used for 700 years. The Swiss flag inspired the Red Cross flag with colors reversed. Muslim states often incorporate in their flags the crescent emblem of Islam and the color green, also associated with their faith. Similarly Israel uses the Star of David and the color blue.

The flags of Australia and New Zealand both incorporate the Union Jack, together with symbols of the Southern Cross constellation. The Canadian flag has a maple-leaf design.

As a signal, a flag is flown upside down to indicate distress; is dipped as a salute; and is flown at half-mast to show mourning. The "Blue Peter," blue with a white center, announces that a vessel is about to sail; a flag half red and half white, that a pilot is on board. Many localities and public bodies, as well as shipping lines, schools, and yacht clubs, have their own distinguishing flags.

flag in botany, another name for ◊***iris***, especially yellow flag *Iris pseudacorus*, which grows wild in damp places throughout Europe; it is a true water plant but adapts to border conditions. It has a thick rhizome, stiff, bladelike, monocotyledonous leaves, and stems up to 5 ft/150 cm high. The flowers are large and yellow.

flagellant a religious person who uses a whip on him- or herself as a means of penance. Flagellation was practiced in many religions from ancient times; notable outbreaks of this type of extremist devotion occurred in Christian Europe in the 11th–16th centuries.

flagellum small hairlike organ on the surface of certain cells. Flagella are the motile organs of certain protozoa and single-celled algae, and of the sperm cells of higher animals. Unlike ◊cilia, flagella usually occur singly or in pairs; they are also longer and have a more complex whiplike action.

Each flagellum consists of contractile filaments producing snakelike movements that propel cells through fluids, or fluids past cells. Water movement inside sponges is also produced by flagella.

Flagg James Montgomery 1877–1960. US illustrator. His World War I recruiting poster "I Want You," features a haggard image of Uncle Sam modeled on Flagg himself.

In addition to collections of humor writing, Flagg wrote numerous plays and an autobiography, *Roses and Buckshot* 1946. Born in Pelham Manor, New York, Flagg trained at the Art Students League in New York and at private studios in Paris and London. In his teens he contributed illustrations to national magazines; after his return from Europe he became a portraitist.

Flagler Henry Morrison 1830–1913. US businessman. Born in Hopewell, New York, Flagler left home at age 14, settling in Ohio, where he worked as a clerk and grain merchant. In 1862 he established a salt factory in Saginaw, Michigan, but with the failure of that concern, moved to Cleveland and entered the oil refining business with John D Rockefeller 1867. Flagler served as a director of Standard Oil 1870–1911 and invested in the Florida tourist industry, establishing the Florida East Coast Railroad 1886 and building a string of luxury hotels.

flag of convenience a flag flown by a ship registered in a country not its own in order to avoid legal or tax commitments. Flags of convenience are common in the merchant fleets of Liberia and Panama; ships registered in these countries avoid legislation governing, for example, employment of sailors and minimum rates of pay.

Flagstad Kirsten (Malfrid) 1895–1962. Norwegian soprano who specialized in Wagnerian opera.

Flaherty Robert 1884–1951. US film director; the father of documentary filmmaking. He exerted great influence through his pioneer documentary of Eskimo life, *Nanook of the North* 1922, a critical and commercial success. Later films include *Moana* 1926, a South Seas documentary; *Man of Aran* 1934; *Elephant Boy* 1936; *The Lands* 1942; and the Standard Oil-sponsored *Louisiana Story* 1948.

flamingo

flamen a sacrificial priest in ancient Rome. The office was held for life, but was terminated by the death of the flamen's wife (who assisted him at ceremonies) or by some misdemeanor. At first there were 3 flamens for each deity, but another 12 were later added.

flame test in chemistry, the use of a flame to identify metal ◊cations present in a solid.

A nichrome or platinum wire is moistened with acid, dipped in the test substance, and then held in a hot flame. The color produced in the flame is characteristic of metals present; for example, sodium burns with a yellow flame, and potassium with a lilac one.

flame tree any of various trees with brilliant red flowers, including the smooth-stemmed semideciduous tree *Sterculia acerifolia* with red or orange flowers, native to Australia, but spread throughout the tropics.

flamingo long-legged and long-necked wading bird, family Phoenicopteridae, of the stork order Ciconiiformes. Largest of the family is the greater or roseate flamingo *Phoenicopterus ruber*, found in Africa, the Caribbean, and South America, with delicate pink plumage and 4 ft/1.25 m tall. They sift the mud for food with their downbent bills, and build colonies of high, conelike mud nests, with a little hollow for the eggs at the top.

Flaminius Gaius died 217 BC. Roman consul and general. He constructed the Flaminian Way northward from Rome to Rimini 220 BC, and was killed at the battle of Lake Trasimene fighting ◊Hannibal.

Flamsteed John 1646–1719. English astronomer who began systematic observations of the positions of the stars, Moon, and planets at the Royal Observatory he founded at Greenwich, London, 1676. His observations were published 1725.

Flanders a region of the Low Countries that in the 8th and 9th centuries extended from Calais to the Scheldt and is now covered by the Belgian provinces of Oost Vlaanderen and West Vlaanderen (East and West Flanders), the French *département* of Nord, and part of the Dutch province of Zeeland. The language is Flemish. East Flanders, capital Ghent, has an area of 1,158 sq mi/3,000 sq km and a population (1987) of 1,329,000. West Flanders, capital Bruges, has an area of 1,197 sq mi/3,100 sq km and a population (1987) of 1,035,000.

It was settled by Salian Franks as Roman allies 358, and in the 6th century, became a province of the Frankish kingdom. Baldwin I (died 879), the son-in-law of Charles the Bald, became its first count 862. During the following 300 years, the county resisted Norman encroachment, expanded its territory, and became a leading center of the wool industry. In 1194, Philip II married Isabelle, the niece of Count Philip of Alsace (1143–1191), and so began a period of active French involvement in the county. In the 14th century, the long-standing friction within Flemish society between the pro-French bourgeoisie and nobility and the craftworkers in the towns who supported the English, on whom their prosperity depended as their major partners in the wool trade, erupted into violence. In 1302, the craftsmen seized power in Bruges and Ghent and defeated the French at Courtrai, but the pro-French faction regained control of the county 1328. During the Hundred Years' War, Edward III of England put a trade embargo on Flemish wool, which caused serious economic depression, and led to further popular revolts, led by Jacques (1290–1345) and Philip (1340–82) van Arteveld, which were finally defeated at the battle of Roosebeke 1382 by the French. The last count, Louis de Male, died 1384, and the county was inherited by his son-in-law, Philip the Bold of Burgundy (1342–1404), to become part of the Burgundian domains.

Flaubert *Author of Madame Bovary* 1857, French novelist Gustave Flaubert.

It underwent a decline under Austrian rule in the 17th to 19th centuries. Fierce battles were fought here in World War I. In World War II the Battle of Flanders began with the German breakthrough May 10, 1940 and ended with the British amphibious retreat from Dunkirk May 27–June 4.

flare, solar brilliant eruption on the Sun above a ◊sunspot, thought to be caused by a release of magnetic energy. Flares reach maximum brightness within a few minutes, then fade away over about an hour. They eject a burst of atomic particles into space at up to 600 mps/1,000 kps. When these particles reach Earth they can cause radio blackouts, disruptions of the Earth's magnetic field, and ◊auroras.

flash point in physics, the lowest temperature at which a liquid or volatile solid heated under standard conditions gives off sufficient vapor to ignite on the application of a small flame.

The fire point of a material is the temperature at which full combustion occurs. For safe storage of materials such as fuel or oil, conditions must be well below the flash and fire points to reduce fire risks to a minimum.

flatfish bony fishes of the order Pleuronectiformes, having a characteristically flat, asymmetrical body with both eyes (in adults) on the upper side. Species include flounders, turbots, halibuts, plaice, and the European soles.

flatworm invertebrate of the phylum *Platyhelminthes*. Some are free-living, but many are parasitic (for example, tapeworms and flukes). The body is simple and bilaterally symmetrical, with one opening to the intestine. Many are hermaphroditic (with both male and female sex organs), and practice self-fertilization.

Flaubert Gustave 1821–1880. French novelist,

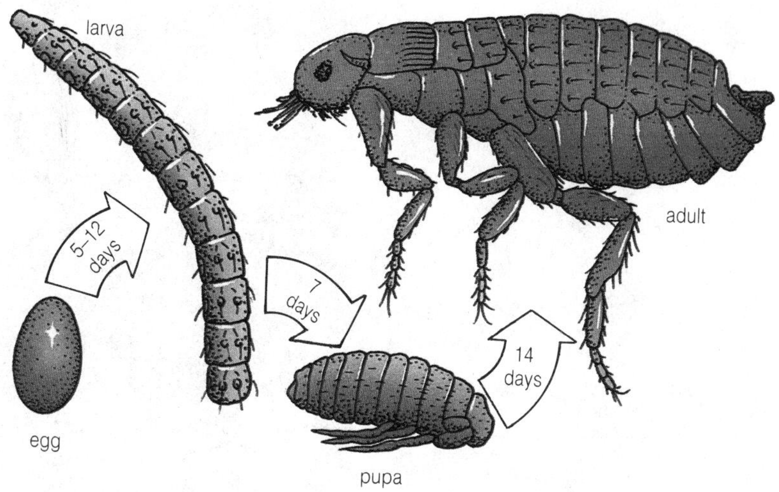
larva
adult
5–12 days
7 days
14 days
egg
pupa

author of *Madame Bovary* 1857. He entered Paris literary circles 1840, but in 1846 moved to Rouen, where he remained for the rest of his life. *Salammbô* 1862 earned him the Legion of Honor 1866, and was followed by *L'Education sentimentale/Sentimental Education* 1869, and *La Tentation de Saint Antoine/The Temptation of St Anthony* 1874. Flaubert also wrote the short stories *Trois contes/Three Tales* 1877.

flax any plant of the genus *Linum*, family Linaceae. The species *L. usitatissimum* is the cultivated strain; linen is produced from the fiber in its stems. The seeds yield linseed oil, used in paints and varnishes. The plant, of almost worldwide distribution, has a stem up to 24 in/60 cm high, small leaves, and bright blue flowers.

The residue of the seeds is fed to cattle. The stems are retted (soaked) in water after harvesting, and then dried, rolled, and scutched (pounded), separating the fiber from the central core of woody tissue. The long fibers are spun into linen thread, twice as strong as cotton, yet more delicate, and suitable for lace; shorter fibers are used to make twine or paper.

Annual world production of flax fiber amounts to approximately 60,000 tons, with the USSR accounting for half of the total. Other producers are Belgium, the Netherlands, and N Ireland.

The New Zealand flax Phormium tenax, is unrelated to the true flax. It belongs to the lily family Liliaceae, and is commercially grown for the fiber in its sword-shaped leaves, which may be up 6 ft/2 m long.

flea wingless insect of the order Siphonaptera, with blood-sucking mouthparts. Fleas are parasitic on warm-blooded animals. Some fleas can jump 130 times their own height.

Species include the human flea *Pulex irritans*; the rat flea *Xenopsylla cheopsis*, the transmitter of plague and typhus; and (fostered by central heating) the cat and dog fleas *Ctenocephalides felis* and *C. canis*.

fleabane any of several plants of the genera *Erigeron* and *Pulicaria*, of the daisy or composite family. Poor Robin's plantain *E. pulchellus* has lavender-rayed flowers on tall, slender stalks and is native to E North America.

Fleet Street street in London, England (named after the subterranean river Fleet), traditionally the center of British journalism. It runs from Temple Bar eastward to Ludgate Circus. With adjoining streets it contained the offices and printing works of many leading British newspapers until the mid-1980s, when most moved to sites farther from the center of London.

Fleming Alexander 1881–1955. Scottish bacteriologist who discovered the first antibiotic drug, ◊penicillin, in 1928 (but it did not come into use until 1941). In 1922 he had discovered lysozyme, an antibacterial enzyme present in saliva, nasal secretions, and tears. While studying this, he found an unusual mold growing on a neglected culture dish, which he isolated and grew into a pure culture; this led to his discovery of penicillin. In 1945 he won the Nobel Prize for Physiology or Medicine with Howard W Florey and Ernst B Chain, whose research had brought widespread realization of the value of penicillin.

Fleming Ian 1908–1964. English author of suspense novels featuring the ruthless, laconic James Bond, British Secret Service agent No. 007. Most of the novels were made into successful films.

Fleming Peter 1907–1971. British journalist and travel writer, remembered for his journeys up the Amazon and across the Gobi Desert recounted in *Brazilian Adventure* 1933 and *News from Tartary* 1941.

Fleming's rules memory aids for the directions of the magnetic field, current, and motion in an electric generator or motor, using one's fingers. The three directions are represented by the thu*m*b (for *m*otion), *f*orefinger (for *f*ield) and se*c*ond finger (*c*urrent), all held at right angles to each other. The right hand is used for generators and the left for motors. They were named after the English physicist John Fleming.

Flemish member of the W Germanic branch of the Indo-European language family, spoken in N Belgium and the Nord *département* of France. It is closely related to Dutch.

In opposition to the introduction of French as the official language in the Flemish provinces of Belgium after 1830, a strong Flemish movement arose. Although equality of French and Flemish was not achieved until 1898, it brought about a cultural and political revival of Flemish.

Flemish art the style of painting developed and practiced in Flanders (a county in the Lowlands of NW Europe, largely coinciding with modern Belgium). A Flemish style emerged in the early 15th century. Paintings are distinguished by keen observation, minute attention to detail, bright colors, and superb technique—oil painting was a Flemish invention. Apart from portraits, they depict religious scenes, often placed in contemporary Flemish landscapes, townscapes, and interiors. Flemish sculpture shows German and French influence.

15th century Jan van Eyck made Bruges the first center of Flemish art; other schools arose in Tournai, Ghent, and Louvain. The great names of the early period were Rogier van der Weyden, Dierick Bouts, Hugo van der Goes, Hans Memling, and Gerard David.

16th century Italian influences were strongly felt, and the center shifted to Antwerp, where Quentin Massys worked. Hieronymus Bosch painted creatures of his own wild imagination, but the pictures of Pieter Brueghel are realistic reflections of Flemish life.

17th century Peter Paul Rubens and his school created a new powerful style, which was continued by van Dyck and others. Teniers and many minor artists continued the tradition of genre painting.

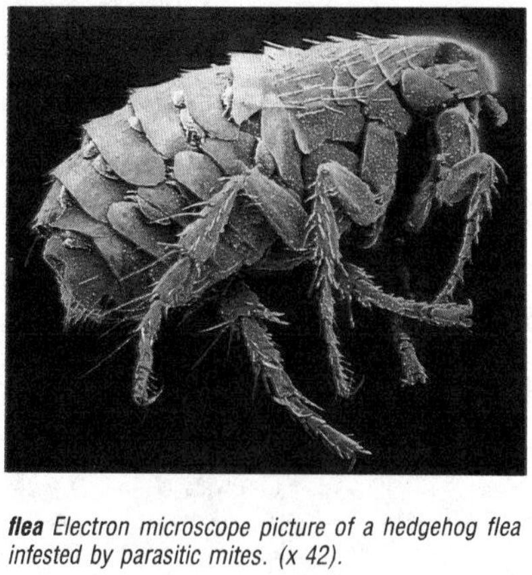

flea Electron microscope picture of a hedgehog flea infested by parasitic mites. (x 42).

Flemish literature in Belgium, Flemish literature in its written form was the same as Dutch (see ◊Flemish language) and was stimulated by the declaration, following the revolution of 1830–39, that French was the only official language in Belgium (it remained so until 1898). J F Willems (1793–1846) brought out a magazine that revived medieval Flemish works; H Conscience (1812–1883) and J T van Ryswyck (1811–1849) published novels in Flemish; K L Ledeganck (1805–1847), Prudens van Duyze (1804–1859), and Jan de Beers (1821–1888) wrote poetry. Later writers include Albrecht Rodenbach (1856–1880), Pol de Mont (1857–1931), and Cyriel Buysse (1859–1932).

Flensburg port on the E coast of Schleswig-Holstein, Federal Republic of Germany, with shipyards and breweries; population (1984) 86,700.

Fletcher John 1579–1625. English dramatist. He collaborated with ◊Beaumont, producing, most notably, *Philaster* 1609 and *The Maid's Tragedy* 1610–11. He is alleged to have collaborated with Shakespeare on *The Two Noble Kinsmen* and *Henry VIII* in 1612.

Fletcher v Peck a US Supreme Court decision 1810 dealing with the right of states to impair contracts. A complaint was filed against the Georgia state legislature, which had revoked land claims of settlers who had bought land from fraudulent land companies that had been granted the land by the corrupt legislature. In the Yazoo Land Fraud the Court ruled that the judiciary could not judge the motives of the state legislature and that Georgia could not pass a law impairing what was therefore a valid contract.

fleur-de-lis (French "flower of the lily") heraldic device in the form of a stylized iris flower, borne on coats of arms since the 12th century and adopted by the French royal house of Bourbon.

Flevoland formerly IJsselmeerpolders, a low-lying province of the Netherlands established 1986
area 544 sq mi/1,410 sq km
population (1988) 194,000
cities capital Lelystad, Dronten, Almere
history created in 1986 out of land reclaimed from the IJsselmeer 1950–68.

flexor any muscle that bends a limb. Flexors usually work in opposition to other muscles, the extensors, an arrangement known as antagonistic pairing.

flight or ***aviation*** people first took to the air in lighter-than-air craft such as balloons 1783 and began powered flight in 1852 in airships, but the history of aviation focuses on heavier-than-air craft called ◊airplanes. Developed from glider design, with wings, a tail, and a fuselage, the first

Fleming *Nobel Prizewinning Scottish bacteriologist Alexander Fleming, 1943.*

successful flight of a powered, heavier-than-air craft was in 1896 by S P ◊Langley's unmanned plane (*Model No 5*), for ¾ of a mile near the Potomac river; then, in 1903, the ◊Wright brothers flew the first piloted plane at Kitty Hawk. In 1903, Glenn ◊Curtiss publicized flight in the US and began the first flying school in 1909. A competition for the development of airplanes was inspired by a series of flights and air races in the US and Europe, and planes came into their own especially during World War I, used by both sides. Biplanes were generally succeeded by monoplanes in the 1920s and 1930s, and they used runways or water (seaplanes—floatplanes and flying boats) for takeoffs and landings at airfields that soon became airports. In these decades airlines were formed for international travel, airmail, and cargo. The first jet plane was produced in Germany in 1939, the Heinkel He-178, but conventional prop planes were used for most of the destruction and transport of World War II. The 1950s brought economical passenger air travel on turboprops and jet airliners, which by the 1970s flew transatlantic in about 6 hours. The Concorde, a supersonic jetliner, flies passengers over that route in about 3 hours.

The early development of aircraft took place in the US and Europe. In the US, after the Wright brothers' Kitty Hawk flight, Glenn Curtiss made publicity flights and founded a flight school 1909, then designed and developed 1911 planes with modern ailerons and stabilizers, for guidance control and stability; in France, Louis ◊Bleriot brought aviation much publicity by flying the Channel 1909; as did the Reims air races of that year. The flight experience of World War I (1914–18) and the subsequent rapid development of powerful gasoline engines led to planes that could maneuver at speeds of 200 mph/320 kph. Streamlining became imperative; the body, wings, and exposed parts were shaped to reduce drag and the biplane was mostly replaced by the internally braced monoplane structure. Probably the most successful plane of this type ever produced was the Douglas DC-3 and all its variants—with about 10,000 built, used for passengers and cargo in the 1930s and war duty in World War II—about 3,000 are still in daily use. Although by the 1930s planes had acquired the range for long distance flights needed in cargo, mail, and passenger service, by the 1940s new design concepts were developed especially for warplanes that later became important to peacetime aviation, such as the jet engine.

The first flight of a jet-powered aircraft was the German Heinkel He-178 in 1939, and German jets were in use during World War II by 1943; British jet fighters went into action during the last year of the war. Turboprop planes were also developed by the end of the war, and became very successful in commercial service during the interim years between propeller and jet service; in the 1960s turboprops found new operational life when they were needed for fuel economy in flying heavy loads over the short distances into small airports with difficult terrain, as in the third world. Jet airliners such as the Comet were introduced in the 1950s. The late 1960s introduced jumbo jets and the supersonic airliner, notably the Anglo-French Concorde; the former brought economical air travel and the latter a transatlantic crossing of under 3 hours with ideal conditions. Today, jet planes dominate both civilian and military aviation, although many light planes—for sport and business—use piston engines and propellers. Clubs now restore old and antique planes, which are flown in demonstrations, displayed and flown in airshows, and donated to museums. Prop planes still see use in agricultural crop dusting, in bush piloting (especially in Alaska), and for sky writing.

Fleming's rules

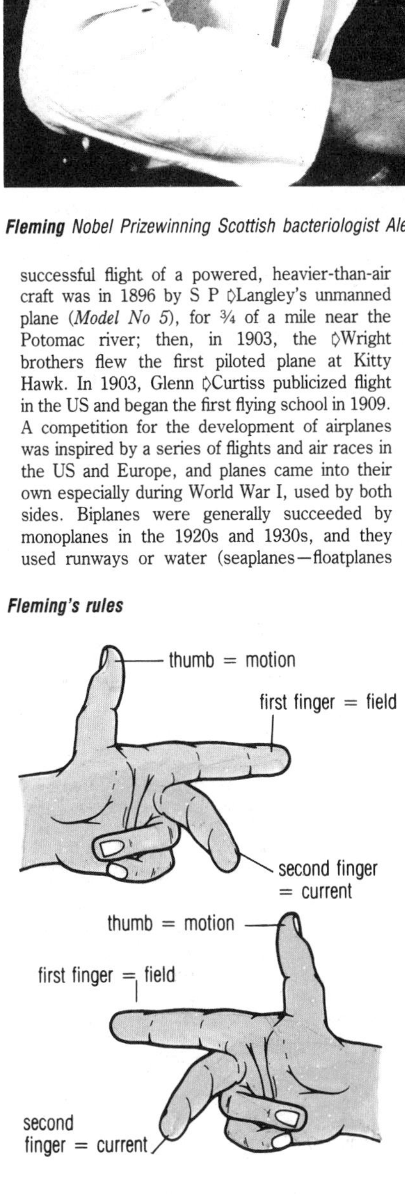
thumb = motion
first finger = field
second finger = current
thumb = motion
first finger = field
second finger = current

Flinders Matthew 1774–1814. English navigator who explored the Australian coasts 1795–99 and 1801–03.

Named after him are Flinders Island, NE of Tasmania, Australia; the Flinders Range in S Australia; and Flinders River in Queensland, Australia.

Flint city in Michigan, on the Flint River, 56 mi/90 km NW of Detroit. Automobile manufacturing is the chief industry but is declining; population (1990) 140,761.

flint a compact, hard, brittle mineral (a variety of chert), brown, black, or gray in color, found in nodules in limestone or shale deposits. It consists of fine-grained silica, SiO_2, in cryptocrystalline form (usually ◊quartz). Flint implements were widely used in prehistory and constitute the basis of all human technology.

flight

1783	First human flight, by Jean F Pilâtre de Rozier and the Marquis d'Arlandes, in Paris, using a hot-air balloon made by Joseph and Etienne Montgolfier; first ascent in a hydrogen-filled balloon by Jacques Charles and M N Robert in Paris.
1785	Jean-Pierre Blanchard and John J Jeffries made the first balloon crossing of the English Channel.
1804	George Cayley flew the first true airplane, a model glider 5 ft/1.5 m long.
1852	Henri Giffard flew the first steam-powered airship over Paris.
1891–96	Otto Lilienthal piloted a glider in flight.
1903	First powered and controlled flight of a heavier-than-air craft (airplane) by Orville Wright, at Kitty Hawk, North Carolina.
1909	Louis Bleriot flew across the English Channel from France to England by plane in 36 minutes.
1919	First E–W flight across the Atlantic by Albert C Read, using a flying boat; first nonstop flight across the Atlantic E–W by John William Alcock and Arthur Whitten Brown in 16 hours 27 minutes; first complete flight from Britain to Australia by Ross Smith and Keith Smith.
1923	Juan de la Cieva flew the first autogiro with a rotating wing.
1927	Charles Lindbergh made the first W–E solo, nonstop flight across the Atlantic from New York to Paris.
1928	First trans-Pacific flight, from San Francisco to Brisbane, by Charles Kinsford Smith and C T P Ulm.
1930	Frank Whittle patented the jet engine; Amy Johnson became the first woman to fly solo from England to Australia.
1937	The first fully pressurized aircraft, the Lockheed XC-35, came into service.
1939	Erich Warsitz flew the first Heinkel jet plane, in Germany; Igor Sikorsky designed the first helicopter, with a large main rotor and a smaller tail rotor.
1947	A rocket-powered plane, the Bell X-1, was the first aircraft to fly faster than the speed of sound.
1949	The de Havilland Comet, the first jet airliner, entered service; James Gallagher made the first nonstop round-the-world flight, in a Boeing Superfortress.
1953	The first vertical take-off aircraft, the Rolls-Royce "Flying Bedstead," was tested.
1968	The world's first supersonic airliner, the Russian TU-144, flew for the first time.
1970	The Boeing 747 jumbo jet entered service, carrying 500 passengers.
1976	A Lockheed SR-17A, piloted by Eldon W Joersz and George T Morgan, set the world air-speed record of 2,193.167 mph over Beale Air Force Base, California.
1979	First crossing of the English Channel by a human-powered aircraft, *Gossamer Albatross*, piloted by Bryan Allen.
1981	The solar-powered *Solar Challenger* flew across the English Channel, from Paris to Kent, taking 5 hours for the 163 mi journey.
1986	Dick Rutan and Jeana Yeager made the first nonstop flight around the world without refueling, piloting *Voyager*, which completed the flight in 9 days 3 minutes 44 seconds.
1987	Richard Branson made the first transatlantic crossing by hot-air balloon.
1988	*Daedelus*, a human-powered craft piloted by Kanellos Kanellopoulos, flew 74 mi/118 km across the Aegean Sea.

When chipped, the flint nodules show a shell-like fracture and a sharp cutting edge. The earliest flint implements, belonging to Paleolithic cultures and made by striking one flint against another, are simple, while those of the Neolithic are expertly chipped and formed and are often ground or polished. The best flint, used for Neolithic tools, is floorstone, a shiny black flint that occurs deep within the chalk.

Because of their hardness (7 on the ◇Mohs' scale), flint splinters are used for abrasive purposes and, when ground into powder, added to clay during pottery manufacture. Flints have been used for making fire by striking the flint against steel, which produces a spark, and for discharging guns. The so-called flints in cigarette lighters are made from cerium alloy.

floating-point arithmetic form of arithmetic in which numbers are represented as a fraction and exponent. For example, 123.45 would be represented as 0.12345 (the fraction) and 3 (because the fraction must be multiplied by 10 to the power of 3), assuming a base-10 system. In computing, it enables programs to work with very large and very small numbers, but is slower than ◇fixed-point arithmetic and suffers from small rounding errors. Floating-point arithmetic is a system of representing numbers as multiples of the appropriate base raised to some power; for example, 97.8 can be expressed as 0.0978×10^3 or 9780×10^{-2}. In computing, the number is expressed as a decimal fraction, so 97.8 becomes 0.978×10^2. See ◇fixed-point arithmetic.

In a computer, the numbers are represented by pairs; 97.8 = (.978, +2). The first number of the pair is called the mantissa and the second the exponent. The definition applies equally to numbers expressed to a different base (for example, binary fractions multiplied by 2 raised to some power).

The advantage of floating-point arithmetic is that very large and very small numbers can be expressed with a few digits. Thus (.978, +18) written out in full would require 18 digits (978 followed by 15 zeros).

flocculation in soils, the artificially-induced coupling together of particles to improve aeration and drainage. Clay soils, which have very tiny particles and are difficult to work, are often treated in this way. The method involves adding lime to the soil.

Flodden, Battle of the defeat of the Scots by the English under the Earl of Surrey Sept 9, 1513 on a site 3 mi/5 km SE of Coldstream, Northumberland, England; many Scots, including King James IV, were killed.

Flood, the in the Old Testament, the Koran, and *The Epic of Gilgamesh* (an ancient Sumerian legend), a deluge lasting 40 days and nights, a disaster alleged to have obliterated all humanity except a chosen few (in the Old Testament, the survivors were the family of ◇Noah and the pairs of animals sheltered on his ark).

The story may represent legends of a major local flood; for example, excavations at the Sumerian city of Ur in Iraq revealed 8 ft/2.5 m of water-laid clay dating before 4000 BC, over an area of about 400 mi/645 km by 100 mi/160 km.

flood plain the area bordering a stream or river over which water spreads in time of flood. When stream discharge exceeds channel capacity, water rises over the channel banks and floods the adjacent low-lying lands. A river flood plain can be regarded as part of its natural domain, statistically certain to be claimed by the river at repeated intervals. By plotting floods that have occurred and extrapolating from that data we can speak of 10-year floods, 100-year floods, 500-year floods, and so forth, based on the statistical probability of flooding across certain parts of the flood plain.

Even the most energetic flood-control plans (such as a dams, levees, dredging, and channel modification) will sometimes fail, and using flood plains as the site of towns and villages is always laden with risk. It is more judicious to use flood plains in ways compatible with flooding, such as for agriculture or a park system.

floral diagram

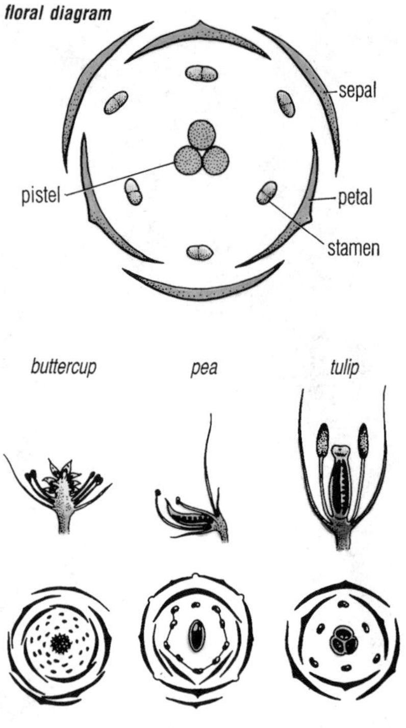
sepal
pistel
petal
stamen
buttercup
pea
tulip

floppy disk in computing, a storage device consisting of a light, flexible disk enclosed in a cardboard or plastic jacket. The disk is placed in a disk drive, where it rotates at high speed. Data are recorded magnetically on one or both surfaces.

The floppy disk was invented by IBM in 1971 as a means of loading programs into the computer. They were originally 8 in/20 cm in diameter and typically held about 240 ◇kilobytes of data. Present-day floppy disks, widely used on ◇microcomputers, are usually either 5.25 in/13.13 cm or 3.5 in/8.8 cm in diameter, and generally hold between 180 kilobytes and 1.4 ◇megabytes, depending on the disk size, recording method, and whether one or both sides are used.

Flora in Roman mythology, goddess of flowers, youth, and spring. Festivals were held in her name.

floral diagram a diagram showing the arrangement and number of parts in a flower, drawn in cross section. An ovary is drawn in the center, surrounded by representations of the other floral parts, indicating the position of each at its base. If any parts such as the petals or sepals are fused, this is also indicated. Floral diagrams allow the structure of different flowers to be compared, and are usually shown with the floral formula.

floral formula a symbolic representation of the structure of a flower. Each kind of floral part is represented by a letter (K for calyx, C for corolla, P for perianth, A for androecium, G for gynoecium) and a number to indicate the quantity of the part present, for example, C5 for a flower with five petals. The number is in brackets if the parts are fused. If the parts are arranged in distinct whorls within the flower, this is shown by two separate figures, such as A5 + 5, indicating two whorls of five stamens each.

Florence city in NW Alabama, on the Tennessee river near the Tennessee Valley Authority's Wilson Dam, NW of Birmingham; seat of Lauderdale County. Industries include agricultural and poultry products, building materials, lumber, and fertilizers; population (1990) 36,426.

Florence city in NE South Carolina, NW of Myrtle

Beach; seat of Florence County. It is a center of the trucking industry, serving as a terminus for many companies. Other industries include dairy products, fertilizers, film, furniture, machined goods, and clothing; population (1990) 29,813.

Florence (Italian *Firenze*) capital of ◊Tuscany, N Italy, 55 mi/88 km from the mouth of the river Arno; population (1988) 421,000. It has printing, engineering, and optical industries; many crafts, including leather, gold and silver work, and embroidery; and its art and architecture attract large numbers of tourists. Notable Medieval and Renaissance citizens included the writers Dante and Boccaccio, and the artists Giotto, Leonardo da Vinci, and Michelangelo.

The Roman town of Florentia was founded in the 1st century BC on the site of the Etruscan town of Faesulae. It was besieged by the Goths AD 405 and visited by Charlemagne 786.

In 1052, Florence passed to Countess Matilda of Tuscany (1046–1115), and from the 11th century onward gained increasing autonomy. In 1198 it became an independent republic, with new city walls, and governed by a body of 12 citizens. In the 13th–14th centuries, the city was the center of the struggle between the Guelphs (papal supporters) and Ghibellines (supporters of the Holy Roman emperor). Despite this, Florence became immensely prosperous and went on to reach its cultural peak during the 14th–16th centuries.

From the 15th to the 18th centuries, the ◊Medici family, originally bankers, were the predominant power, in spite of their having been twice expelled by revolutions. In the first of these, in 1493, a year after Lorenzo de' Medici's death, a republic was proclaimed (with ◊Machiavelli as secretary) that lasted until 1512. From 1494 to 1498, the city was under the control of religious reformer ◊Savonarola. In 1527, the Medicis again proclaimed a republic, which lasted through many years of gradual decline until 1737, when the city passed to Maria Theresa of Austria. From 1737 the city was ruled by the Hapsburg imperial dynasty. The city was badly damaged in World War II and by floods 1966.

features Florence's architectural treasures include the Ponte Vecchio, 1345; the Pitti and Vecchio palaces; the churches of Santa Croce and Santa Maria Novella; the cathedral of Santa Maria del Fiore, 1314; and the Uffizi Gallery, which has one of Europe's finest art collections, based on that of the Medici.

floret a small flower, usually making up part of a larger, composite flower head. There are often two different types present on one flower head: disk florets in the central area, and ray florets around the edge which usually have a single petal known as the ligule. In the common daisy, for example, the disk florets are yellow, while the ligules are white.

Florey Howard Walter, Baron Florey 1898–1968. Australian pathologist whose research into lysozyme, an antibacterial enzyme discovered by Alexander ◊Fleming, led him to study penicillin (another of Fleming's discoveries), which he and Ernst ◊Chain isolated and prepared for widespread use. With Fleming, they were awarded the Nobel Prize for Physiology or Medicine 1945.

Florianópolis seaport and resort on Santa Caterina Island, Brazil; population (1980) 153,500. It is linked to the mainland by two bridges, one of which is the largest expansion bridge in Brazil.

Florida southeasternmost state of the US; mainly a peninsula jutting into the Atlantic, which it separates from the Gulf of Mexico; nickname Sunshine State

area 58,672 sq mi/152,000 sq km

capital Tallahassee

cities Miami, Tampa, Jacksonville

population (1990) 12,937,926, one of the fastest-growing of the states; including 15% nonwhite; 10% Hispanic, (especially Cuban)

physical 50% forested; lakes (including Okeechobee 695 sq mi/1,800 sq km); Everglades National Park (1,930 sq mi/5,000 sq km), with birdlife, cypresses, alligators

features Palm Beach island resort, between the lagoon of Lake Worth and the Atlantic; Florida Keys; John F Kennedy Space Center at Cape Canaveral; Disney World theme park; beach resorts on Gulf and on Atlantic; Daytona International Speedway

products citrus fruits, melons, vegetables, fish, shellfish, phosphates, chemicals, electrical and electronic equipment, aircraft, fabricated metals;

famous people Chris Evert, Henry Flagler, James Weldon Johnson, Sidney Poitier, Philip Randolph, Joseph Stilwell

history discovered by Ponce de Leon and under Spanish rule from 1513 until its cession to England 1763; was returned to Spain 1783 and purchased by the US 1819, becoming a state 1845; grew rapidly in the early 1920s, stimulated by feverish land speculation. Despite the 1926 collapse of the boom, migration continued, especially of retirees from the North. After World War II, resorts, agriculture, and industry grew in importance. The space center at Cape Canaveral also contributed to the state economy. More recently, Florida has become a banking center, a development often partially attributed to the sizable inflow of cash derived from the traffic in illegal drugs from Latin America.

Florida

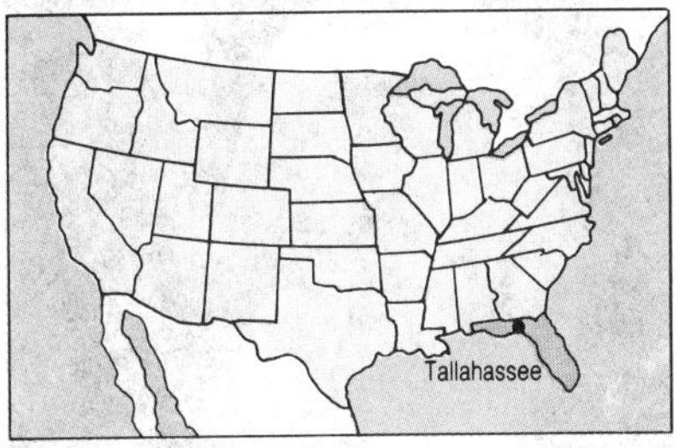
Tallahassee

Florida Keys series of small coral islands that curve over 150 mi/240 km SW from the S tip of Florida. The most important are Key Largo and Key West (with a US naval and air station); they depend on fishing and tourism. A causeway links the keys to the mainland. Key West, is the largest settlement.

flotation process common method of preparing mineral ores for subsequent processing by making use of the different wetting properties of various components. The ore is finely ground and then mixed with water and a specially selected wetting agent. Air is bubbled through the mixture, forming a froth; the desired ore particles attach themselves to the bubbles and are skimmed off, while unwanted dirt or other ores remain behind.

Flotow Friedrich (Adolf Ferdinand), Freiherr von 1812–1883. German composer who wrote 18 operas, including *Martha* 1847.

flotsam, jetsam, and lagan in law, terminology referring to goods cast from ships at sea, due usually to the event or prevention of shipwreck. Flotsam is the debris or cargo found floating; jetsam is what has been thrown overboard to lighten a sinking vessel; lagan is cargo secured, as to a buoy, for future recovery.

flounder any of a number of ◊flatfishes of several genera. A common North American species is the southern flounder *Paralichthys lethostigma*, a valuable food fish about 20 in/50 cm long.

flow chart diagram, often used in computing, to show the possible paths through a program. Different symbols are used to indicate processing, decision-making, input, and output. These are connected by arrows showing the flow of control through the program—that is, the paths the computer can take when executing the program. A flow chart is a way of visually representing an ◊algorithm.

flower the reproductive unit of an ◊angiosperm or flowering plant, typically consisting of four whorls of modified leaves: ◊sepals, ◊petals, ◊stamens, and ◊carpels. These are borne on a central axis or ◊receptacle. The many variations in size, color, number, and arrangement of parts are closely related to the method of pollination. Flowers adapted for wind pollination typically have reduced or absent petals and sepals and long, feathery ◊stigmas that hang outside the flower to trap airborne pollen. In contrast, the petals of insect-pollinated flowers are usually conspicuous and brightly colored.

The sepals and petals are collectively known as the calyx and corolla, respectively, and together comprise the perianth with the function of protecting the reproductive organs and attracting pollinators. The stamens lie within the corolla, each having a slender stalk, or filament, bearing the pollen-containing anther at the top. Collectively they are known as the androecium. The inner whorl of the flower comprises the carpels, each usually consisting of an ◊ovary in which are borne the ◊ovules, and a stigma borne at the top of a slender stalk, or style. Collectively the carpels are known as the gynoecium.

***Florence** The cathedral of Santa Maria del Fiore 1314, Florence. The spectacular dome was constructed by Filippo Brunelleschi in the 1430s.*

flow chart

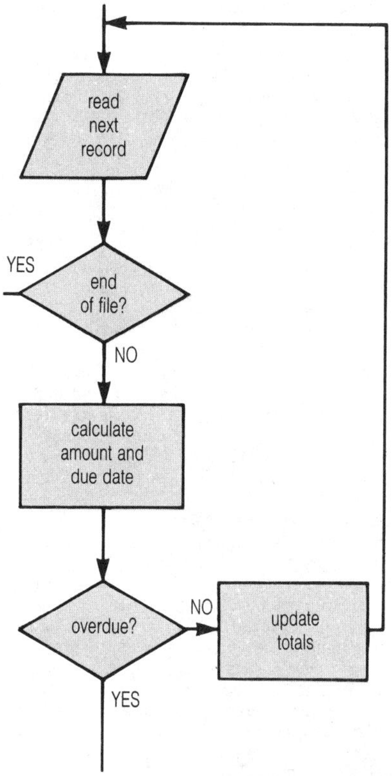
read
next
record
YES
end
of file?
NO
calculate
amount and
due date
overdue?
NO
update
totals
YES

In size, flowers range from the tiny blooms of duckweeds scarcely visible with the naked eye to the gigantic flowers of the Malaysian *Rafflesia*, which can reach over 3 ft/1 m across. Flowers may either be borne singly or grouped together in ◊inflorescences. The stalk of the whole inflorescence is termed a peduncle, and the stalk of an individual flower is termed a pedicel. A flower is termed hermaphrodite when it contains both male and female reproductive organs. When male and female organs are carried in separate flowers, they are termed monoecious; when male and female flowers are on separate plants, the term dioecious is used.

flowering plant a term generally used for ◊angiosperms, which bear flowers with various parts, including sepals, petals, stamens and carpels. Sometimes the term is used more broadly, to include both angiosperms and ◊gymnosperms, in which case the ◊cones of conifers and cycads are referred to as "flowers." Usually, however, the angiosperms and gymnosperms are referred to collectively as ◊seed plants, or spermatophytes.

flower power a youth movement of the 1960s; see ◊hippie.

flower

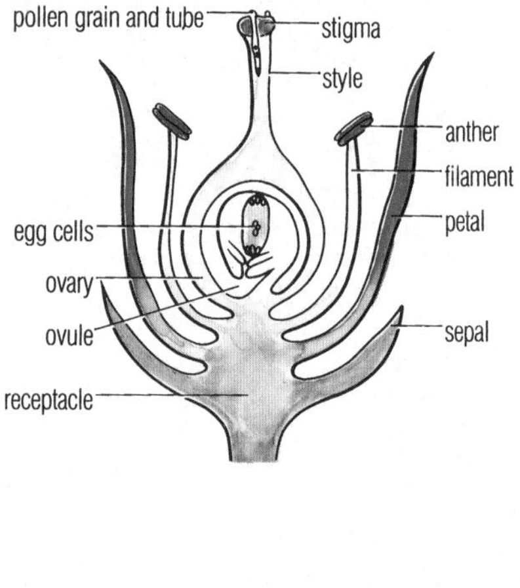
pollen grain and tube
stigma
style
anther
filament
petal
egg cells
ovary
ovule
sepal
receptacle

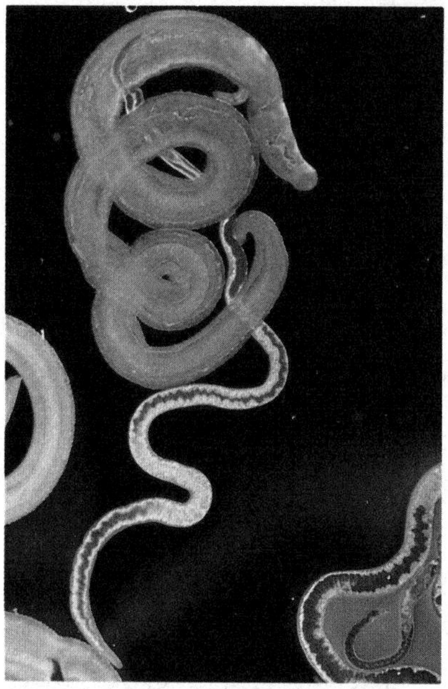

fluke *Microscope view of adult intestinal blood flukes* Schistosoma mansoni.

Flowers of Evil French *Les Fleurs du mal* a collection of poems by Baudelaire, published in France 1857, which deal with the conflict between good and evil. The work was condemned by the censor as endangering public morals, but paved the way for Rimbaud, Verlaine, and the Symbolist school.

flugelhorn an alto brass instrument, similar in appearance to the ◊cornet.

fluid any substance, either liquid or gas, in which the molecules are relatively mobile and can "flow."

fluid, supercritical fluid brought by a combination of heat and pressure to the point at which, as a near vapour, it combines the properties of a gas and a liquid. Supercritical fluids are used as solvents in chemical processes, such as the extraction of lubricating oil from refinery residues or the decaffeination of coffee, because they avoid the energy-expensive need for phase changes (from liquid to gas and back again) required in conventional distillation processes.

fluke any of various parasitic flatworms of the classes Monogenea and Digenea, that as adults live in and destroy the lives of sheep, cattle, horses, dogs, and humans. Monogenetic flukes can complete their life cycle in one host; digenetic flukes require two or more hosts, for example a snail and a human being, to complete their life cycle.

fluorescence in scientific usage, very short-lived ◊luminescence (a glow not caused by high temperature). Generally, the term is used for any luminescence regardless of the persistence. See ◊phosphorescence.

Fluorescence is used in strip and other lighting, and was developed rapidly during World War II because it was a more efficient means of illumination than the incandescent lamp. Other important applications are in fluorescent screens for television and cathode-ray tubes.

fluoridation addition of small amounts of fluoride salts to drinking water by certain water authorities to help prevent tooth decay. In areas where fluoride ions are naturally present in the water, research found that the incidence of tooth decay in children from those areas was reduced by more than 50%. A concentration of one part per million is sufficient to produce this beneficial effect.

fluoride salt of hydrofluoric acid. Fluorides occur naturally in all water to a differing extent. Experiments in Britain, the US, and elsewhere have indicated that a concentration of fluoride of 1 part per million in tap water retards the decay of teeth in children by more than 50%.

The recommended policy in Britain is to add sodium fluoride to the water to bring it up to the required amount, but implementation is up to each local authority.

fluorine pale yellow, gaseous nonmetallic element, symbol F, atomic number 9, atomic weight 18.9984. It is a member of the ◊halogen group and is pungent, poisonous, and highly reactive—the most reactive of all chemical elements, uniting directly with nearly all other elements, even the so-called nonreactive ◊inert gases. Its salts are known as fluorides.

Fluorine is a component of hydrofluoric acid, used to etch glass, and of Freon, a widespread refrigerant, which has become an environmental hazard. Combined with uranium as UF_6, it is used in the separation of uranium isotopes through the process known as gas diffusion. The name stems from Latin *flux*, "flow," originally applied to minerals used in smelting fluxes but later limited to those containing fluorine. It was discovered by the Swedish chemist Karl Scheele in 1771 and isolated by the French chemist Henri Moissan in 1886.

fluorite a glassy, brittle mineral, calcium fluoride CaF_2, forming cubes and octahedra; colorless when pure, otherwise violet.

Fluorite is used as a flux in iron and steel making; colorless fluorite is used in the manufacture of microscope lenses. It is also used for the glaze on pottery, and as a source of fluorine in the manufacture of hydrofluoric acid.

fluorocarbon compound formed by replacing the hydrogen atoms of a hydrocarbon with fluorine. Fluorocarbons are used as inert coatings, refrigerants, synthetic resins, and as propellants in aerosols.

There is concern because their release into the atmosphere depletes the ◊ozone layer, allowing more ultraviolet light from the Sun to penetrate the Earth's atmosphere, increasing the incidence of skin cancer.

Flushing (Dutch *Vlissingen*) port on Walcheren Island, Zeeland, the Netherlands; population (1987) 44,900. It stands at the entrance to the Scheldt estuary, one of the principal sea routes into Europe. Industries include fishing, shipbuilding, and petrochemicals, and there is a ferry service to Harwich. Admiral de Ruyter was born at Flushing and is commemorated in the Jacobskerk.

Flushing Meadow tennis center in the US, officially the National Tennis Center. It is situated in the borough of Queens, New York, and replaced the West Side Club at Forest Hills, Queens, as the home of the US Open championships in 1978. The main court, the Stadium Court, is one of the largest in the world.

flute a member of a group of ◊woodwind musical instruments (although usually made of metal), including the piccolo, the concert flute, and the bass or alto flute. Flutes are cylindrical in shape, with a narrowed end, containing a shaped aperture, across which the player blows. The air vibrations produce the note, which can be altered by placing fingers over lateral holes. Certain keys can be depressed to extend the range of the flute to three octaves.

The orchestral flute is at concert pitch—middle C to C sharp three octaves higher. The alto (sometimes known as the "bass") flute has a range the same as that of the concert flute, but a fourth lower. The bass flute in B flat is usually only played in fife and drum bands.

flux in smelting, a substance that combines with the unwanted components of the ore to produce a fusible slag, which can be separated from the molten metal. For example, the mineral fluorite, CaF_2, is used as a flux in iron smelting; it has a low melting point and will form a fusible mixture with substances of higher melting point such as silicates and oxides.

flux in soldering, a substance that improves the

bonding properties of solder by removing contamination form metal surfaces and preventing their oxidation, and by reducing the surface tension of the molten solder alloy. For example, with solder made of lead-tin alloys, the flux may be resin, borax, or zinc chloride.

fly any insect of the order Diptera. A fly has a single pair of wings, antennae, and compound eyes; the hind wings have become modified into knoblike projections (halteres) used to maintain equilibrium in flight. There are over 90,000 species.

The mouthparts project from the head as a proboscis used for sucking fluids, modified in some species, such as mosquitoes, to pierce a victim's skin and suck blood. Discs at the end of hairs on their feet secrete a fluid enabling them to walk up walls and across ceilings. Flies undergo complete metamorphosis; their larvae (maggots) are without true legs, and the pupae are rarely enclosed in a cocoon. The sexes are similar and coloration is rarely vivid, though some are metallic green or blue. The fruitfly, genus *Drosophila*, is much used in genetic experiments as it is easy to keep, fast-breeding, and has easily visible chromosomes.

flying dragon lizard *Draco volans* of the family Agamidae. It lives in SE Asia, and can glide on flaps of skin spread and supported by its ribs. This small (3 in/7.5 cm head and body) arboreal lizard can glide between trees for 6 m/20 ft or more.

flying fish any of a family, Exocoetidae, of marine bony fishes of the order Beloniformes, best represented in tropical waters. They have winglike pectoral fins that can be spread to glide over the water.

flying fox fruit-eating ◊bat of the suborder Megachiroptera.

flying gurnard any of various marine fishes of the order Dactylopteriformes (especially the genus *Dactylopterus*), having winglike pectoral fins and capable of gliding for short distances. They are not related to ◊flying fishes.

flying lemur commonly used, but incorrect, name for ◊colugo. It cannot fly, and it is not a lemur.

flying lizard another name for ◊flying dragon.

flying squirrel numerous species of squirrel, not closely related to the true squirrels. They are characterized by a membrane along the side of the body from forelimb to hindlimb (in some species running to neck and tail) which allows them to glide through the air. Several genera of flying squirrel are found in the Old World; the New World has the genus *Glaucomys*. Most species are E Asian. The giant flying squirrel *Petaurista* grows up to 3.5 ft/1.1 m including tail, and can glide 210 ft/65 m.

Flynn Errol. Adopted name of Leslie Thompson 1909–1959. Australian-born US film actor. He is renowned for his portrayal of swashbuckling heroes in such films as *Captain Blood* 1935, *Robin Hood* 1938, *Charge of the Light Brigade* 1938, *The Private Lives of Elizabeth and Essex* 1939, *The Sea Hawk* 1940, and *The Master of Ballantrae* 1953. In *The Sun Also Rises* 1957 he portrayed a middle-aged Hemingway roué, and in *Too Much Too Soon* 1958 he portrayed his friend, actor John Barrymore. Flynn wrote an autobiography, *My Wicked, Wicked Ways* 1959.

Flynn *Australian film actor Errol Flynn with Olivia de Havilland in* The Charge of the Light Brigade *1936.*

flywheel heavy wheel in an engine that helps keep it running and smooths its motion. The ◊crankshaft in a gasoline engine has a flywheel at one end, which keeps the crankshaft turning in between the intermittent power strokes of the pistons. It also comes into contact with the ◊clutch, serving as the connection between the engine and the car's transmission system.

FM in physics, abbreviation for frequency ◊modulation, or the variation of the frequency of a carrier wave in accordance with the signal to be transmitted. Used in radio, FM is constant in amplitude and has much better signal-to-noise ratio than AM (amplitude modulation).

FNLA abbreviation for Front National de Libération de l'Angola (French "National Front for the Liberation of Angola").

f number measure of the relative aperture of a telescope or camera lens; it indicates the light-gathering power of the lens. In photography, each successive *f* number represents a halving of exposure speed.

Fo Dario 1926– . Italian playwright. His plays are predominantly political satires combining black humor with slapstick. They include *Morte accidentale di un anarchico/Accidental Death of an Anarchist* 1970, and *Non si paga non si paga/Can't Pay? Won't Pay!* 1975/1981.

focal length or ***focal distance*** the distance from the center of a lens or curved mirror to the focal point. For a concave mirror or convex lens, it is the distance at which parallel rays of light are brought to a focus to form a real image (for a mirror, this is half the radius of curvature). For a convex mirror or concave lens, it is the distance from the center to the point at which a virtual image (an image produced by diverging rays of light) is formed.

With lenses, the greater the power (measured in diopters) of the lens the shorter its focal length.

Foch Ferdinand 1851–1929. Marshal of France during World War I. He was largely responsible for the Allied victory at the first battle of the ◊Marne Sept 1914, and commanded on the NW front Oct 1914–Sep 1916. He was appointed Commander in Chief of the Allied armies in the spring of 1918, and launched the Allied counter-offensive in July that brought about the negotiation of an armistice to end the war.

fog cloud that collects at the surface of the Earth, composed of water vapor that has condensed on particles of dust in the atmosphere. Cloud and fog are both caused by the air temperature falling below ◊dew point. The thickness of fog depends on the number of water particles it contains. Usually, fog is formed by the meeting of two currents of air, one cooler than the other, or by warm air flowing over a cold surface. Sea fogs commonly occur where warm and cold currents meet and the air above them mixes.

Fog frequently forms on calm nights as the land surface cools more rapidly than the air immediately above it. In drought areas, for example, Baja California, Canary Islands, Cape Verde islands, Namib Desert, Peru, and Chile, coastal fogs enable plant and animal life to survive without rain and are a potential source of water for human use (by means of water collectors exploiting the effect of condensation).

Officially, fog refers to a condition when visibility is reduced to 0.62 mi/1 km or less, and mist or haze to that giving a visibility of 1–2 km. A mist is produced by condensed water particles,

focal length

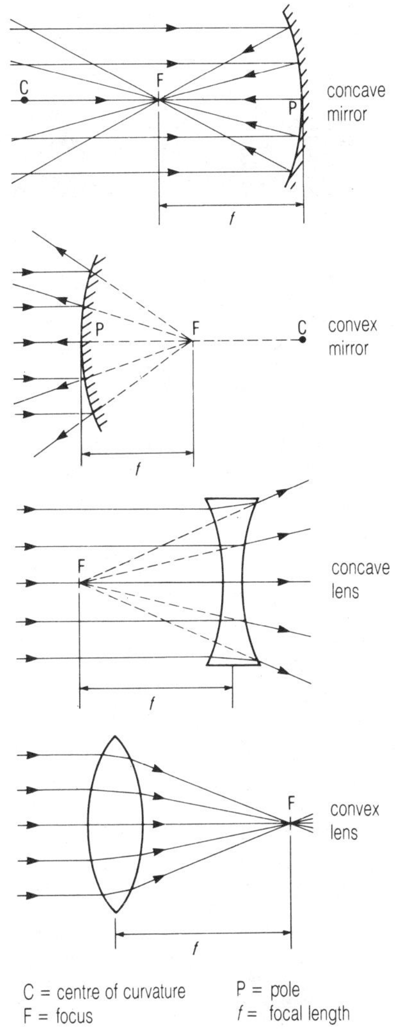

C
F
P
concave mirror
f
P
F
C
convex mirror
f
F
concave lens
f
F
convex lens
f
C = centre of curvature
F = focus
P = pole
f = focal length

and a haze by smoke or dust. Industrial areas uncontrolled by pollution laws have a continual haze of smoke over them, and if the temperature falls suddenly, a dense yellow smog forms. At some airports since 1975 it has been possible for certain aircraft to land and take off blind in fog, using radar navigation.

Foggia city of Puglia region, S Italy; population (1988) 159,000. The cathedral, dating from about 1170, was rebuilt after an earthquake 1731. Natural gas is found nearby.

föhn warm wind that blows through the valleys of the European Alps.

Fokine Mikhail 1880–1942. Russian dancer and choreographer, born in St Petersburg. He was chief choreographer to the Ballets Russes 1909–14, and with ◊Diaghilev revitalized and reformed the art of ballet, promoting the idea of artistic unity among dramatic, musical, and stylistic elements.

His creations for Diaghilev include *Les Sylphides* 1907, *Carnival* 1910, *The Firebird* 1910, *Le Spectre de la Rose* 1911, and *Petrushka* 1911.

fold in geology, a bend in rock ◊beds. If the bend is arched up in the middle it is called an anticline; if it sags downward in the middle it is called a syncline.

folic acid a ◊vitamin of the B complex. It is found in legumes, green leafy vegetables, and whole grains, and is also synthesized by intestinal bacteria. It is essential for growth, and plays many other roles in the body. Lack of folic acid causes anemia, diarrhea, and a red tongue.

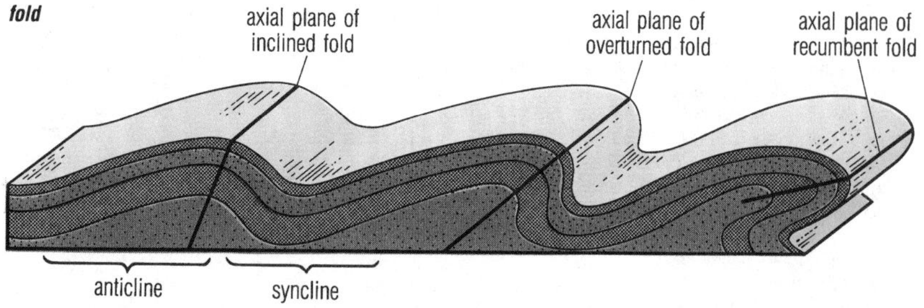
axial plane of
inclined fold
axial plane of
overturned fold
axial plane of
recumbent fold
anticline
syncline

fold

Folies-Bergère music hall in Paris, France, built 1869, named after its original proprietor and featuring lavish productions and striptease acts.

folk dance a dance characteristic of a particular people, nation, or region. Many European folk dances are derived from the dances accompanying the customs and ceremonies of pre-Christian times. Some later became ballroom dances (for example, the minuet and waltz). Once an important part of many rituals, folk dance has tended to die out in industrialized countries. Examples of folk dance are Morris dance, farandole, and jota.

folklore the oral traditions and culture of a people, expressed in legends, riddles, songs, tales, and proverbs. The term was coined 1846 by W J Thoms (1803–85), but the founder of the systematic study of the subject was Jacob ◊Grimm; see also ◊oral literature.

The approach to folklore has varied greatly: the German scholar Max Müller (1823–1900) interpreted it as evidence of nature myths; James ◊Frazer was the exponent of the comparative study of early and popular folklore as mutually explanatory; Laurence Gomme (1853–1916) adopted a historical analysis; and Bronislaw ◊Malinowski and Alfred Radcliffe-Brown (1881–1955) examined the material as an integral element of a given living culture.

folk music body of traditional music, originally transmitted orally. Many folk songs originated as a rhythmic accompaniment to manual work or to mark a specific ritual. Folk song is usually melodic, not harmonic, and the modes used are distinctive of the country of origin. See ◊roots music.

The interest in ballad poetry in the later 18th century led to the discovery of a rich body of folk song in Europe. The multiethnic background of the US has brought forth a wealth of material derived from European, African, and Latin American sources. A revival of interest in folk music began in the US in the 1950s led by the researcher Alan Lomax (1915–) and the singers Harry Belafonte (1927–), Odetta (1930–), Pete Seeger, Woody Guthrie, Joan Baez, and Bob Dylan, who wrote new material in folk-song style, dealing with contemporary topics such as nuclear weapons and racial prejudice.

follicle in botany, a dry, usually many-seeded fruit that splits along one side only to release the seeds within. It is derived from a single ◊carpel; examples include the fruits of the larkspurs *Delphinium* and columbine *Aquilegia*. It differs from a pod, which always splits open (dehisces) along both sides.

follicle in zoology, a small group of cells that surround and nourish a structure such as a hair (hair follicle) or a cell such as an egg (Graafian follicle; see ◊menstrual cycle).

follicle-stimulating hormone (FSH) a ◊hormone produced by the pituitary gland. It affects the ovaries in women, triggering the production of an egg cell. Luteinizing hormone is needed to complete the process. In men, FSH stimulates the testes to produce sperm.

Folsom site in New Mexico, where in 1926 a flint point was found embedded among the bones of an extinct type of bison, thus proving that humans had existed in the Americas in the Pleistocene period.

Fomalhaut brightest star in the southern constellation Piscis Austrinus and the 18th-brightest star in the sky; known as "the Solitary One" because it lies in a rather barren region of sky. It is a dwarf star 23 light-years from Earth, with a true luminosity 14 times that of the Sun. Fomalhaut is one of a number of stars around which the Infra-Red Astronomy Satellite (see ◊infrared astronomy) detected excess infrared radiation, presumably from a region of solid particles around the star. This material may be a planetary system in the process of formation.

Fonda Henry 1905–1982. US actor whose engaging style made him ideal in the role of the American pioneer and honorable man. His many films include the Academy Award–winning *The Grapes of Wrath* 1940, *My Darling Clementine* 1946, and *On Golden Pond* 1981, for which he won the Academy Award for best actor, appearing with his daughter Jane Fonda. He was also the father of actor and director Peter Fonda (1939–).

Fonda Jane 1937– . US actress. Her films include *Cat Ballou* 1965; *Barefoot in the Park* 1967; *Barbarella* 1968; *They Shoot Horses, Don't They?* 1969; *Julia* 1977; *The China Syndrome* 1979; *On Golden Pond* 1981, in which she appeared with her father Henry Fonda; and *Agnes of God* 1985. She won Academy Awards for *Klute* 1971 and *Coming Home* 1979. She is also active in antiwar, pro-ecology politics and in promoting physical fitness.

Fontainebleau town to the SE of Paris, in Seine-et-Marne *département*; population (1982) 18,753. The palace was built by François I in the 16th century. Mme de Montespan lived there in the reign of Louis XIV, and Mme du Barry in that of Louis XV. Napoleon signed his abdication there in 1814. Nearby is the village of Barbizon, the haunt of several 19th-century painters (see the ◊Barbizon school).

Fontainebleau school French school of Mannerist painting and sculpture. It was established at the court of Francis I, who brought Italian artists to Fontainebleau near Paris to decorate his hunting lodge: Rosso Fiorentino (1494–1540) arrived 1530, Francesco Primaticcio (1504/5–1570) came 1532. They evolved a distinctive decorative style using a combination of stucco sculpture and painting.

Their work, with its exuberant ornament and figure style, had a lasting impact on French art in the 16th century. Others associated with the school include Benvenuto ◊Cellini.

Fontana Domenico 1543–1607. Italian architect. He was employed by Pope Sixtus V, and his principal works include the Vatican library and the completion of the dome of St Peter's in Rome, and the royal palace in Naples.

Fontana Lucio 1899–1968. Italian painter and sculptor. He developed a unique abstract style, presenting bare canvases with straight parallel slashes.

Fontanne Lynn 1887–1983. US actress, one-half of the husband-and-wife acting partnership known as the "Lunts" with her husband Alfred ◊Lunt.

Fontenoy, Battle of battle in the War of the ◊Austrian Succession 1745. Marshal Saxe and the French defeated the British, Dutch, and Hanoverians under the duke of Cumberland at a village in Hainaut province, Belgium, SE of Tournai.

Fonteyn Margot. Adopted name of Margaret Hookham 1919–1991. English ballet dancer. She made her debut with the Vic-Wells Ballet in *Nutcracker* 1934 and first appeared as Giselle 1937, eventually becoming prima ballerina of the Royal Ballet,

Fonda *The Fondas at the Academy Award ceremony in Hollywood. Henry Fonda has received the Life Achievement Award and is accompanied by his famous children Jane and Peter.*

Fonteyn *One of the greatest partnerships in the history of ballet—Margot Fonteyn and Rudolf Nureyev in* Giselle.

London. Renowned for her perfect physique, musicality, and interpretive powers, she created several roles in Frederick ◊Ashton's ballets and formed a successful partnership with Rudolf ◊Nureyev.

Foochow former name of ◊Fuzhou, port and capital of Fujian province, SE China.

food anything eaten by human beings and other animals to sustain life and health. The building blocks of food are nutrients, and humans can utilize the following nutrients: carbohydrates, as starches found in cereals, potatoes, and pasta; simple sugars, as sucrose and honey; fibers, as from cereals, fruit, and vegetables; proteins, as from nuts, fish, meat, eggs, milk, and some vegetables; fats, as found in most animal products (meat, lard, dairy products, fish), also in margarine, nuts and seeds, olives, and edible oils. Vitamins are found in a wide variety of foods, except for vitamin B12, which is found mainly in animal foods; minerals are found in a wide variety of foods: calcium from broccoli and milk, for example; iodine from seafood; iron from liver and green vegetables; water is ubiquitous in nature; alcohol is found in from fermented distilled beverages, from 40% in spirits to 0.01% in low-alcohol lagers and beers.

Food is needed both for energy, measured in calories or kilojoules, and nutrients, which are converted to body tissues. Some nutrients, such as fats, carbohydrates, and alcohol, provide mainly energy; other nutrients are important in other ways; for example, fiber is an aid to metabolism. Proteins provide energy and are necessary for building cell and tissue structure.

Food and Agriculture Organization (FAO) United Nations agency that coordinates activities to improve food and timber production and levels of nutrition throughout the world. It is also concerned with investment in agriculture and dispersal of emergency food supplies. It has headquarters in Rome and was founded 1945. The US cut FAO funding in 1990 from $61.4 million to $18 million because of its alleged politicization.

food chain or ***food web*** in ecology, the sequence of organisms through which energy and other nutrients are successively transferred. Since many organisms feed at several different levels (for example, omnivores feed on both fruit and meat), the relationships often form a complex web rather than a simple chain. See also ◊ecosystem and ◊heterotroph.

The sequence of the food chain comprises the ◊autotrophs, or producers, which are principally plants and photosynthetic microorganisms, and a series of ◊heterotrophs, or consumers, which are the ◊herbivores that feed on the producers; the ◊carnivores that feed on the herbivores; and the ◊decomposers that break down the dead bodies and waste products of all four groups (including their own), ready for recycling.

food irradiation a development in ◊food technology, whereby food is exposed to low-level radiation to kill microorganisms.

Irradiation is highly effective, and does not make the food any more radioactive than it is naturally. Some vitamins are partially destroyed, such as vitamin C, and it would be unwise to eat only irradiated fruit and vegetables. The main cause for concern is that it may be used by unscrupulous traders to "clean up" consignments of food, particularly shellfish, with high bacterial counts. Bacterial toxins would remain in the food, so that it could still cause illness, although irradiation would have removed signs of live bacteria. Stringent regulations would be needed to prevent this happening. Other damaging changes may take place in the food, such as the creation of ◊free radicals, but research so far suggests that the process is relatively safe.

food poisoning any acute illness characterized by vomiting and diarrhea and caused by eating food contaminated with harmful bacteria (for example, ◊listeriosis), poisonous food (for example, certain mushrooms, puffer fish), or poisoned food (for example, lead or arsenic introduced accidentally during processing). A frequent cause of food poisoning is ◊salmonella bacteria. These come in many forms, and various strains are found in some cattle, pigs, poultry, and eggs.

Deep freezing of poultry before the birds are properly cooked is a common cause of food poisoning. Attacks of salmonella also come from contaminated eggs that have been eaten raw or cooked only lightly. Pork may carry the roundworm *Trichinella,* and rye the parasitic fungus ergot. The most dangerous food poison is the bacillus that causes ◊botulism. This is rare but leads to muscle paralysis and, often, death. ◊Food irradiation is intended to prevent food poisoning.

food technology the application of science to the commercial processing of foodstuffs. Food is processed to render it more palatable or digestible, or to preserve it from spoilage. Food spoils because of the action of ◊enzymes within the food that change its chemical composition, or because of the growth of bacteria, molds, yeasts, and other microorganisms. Fatty or oily foods also suffer oxidation of the fats, giving them a rancid flavor. Traditional forms of processing include boiling, frying, flour-milling, bread-making, yogurt- and cheese-making, brewing, and various methods of food preservation, such as salting, smoking, pickling, drying, bottling, and preserv-

food chain

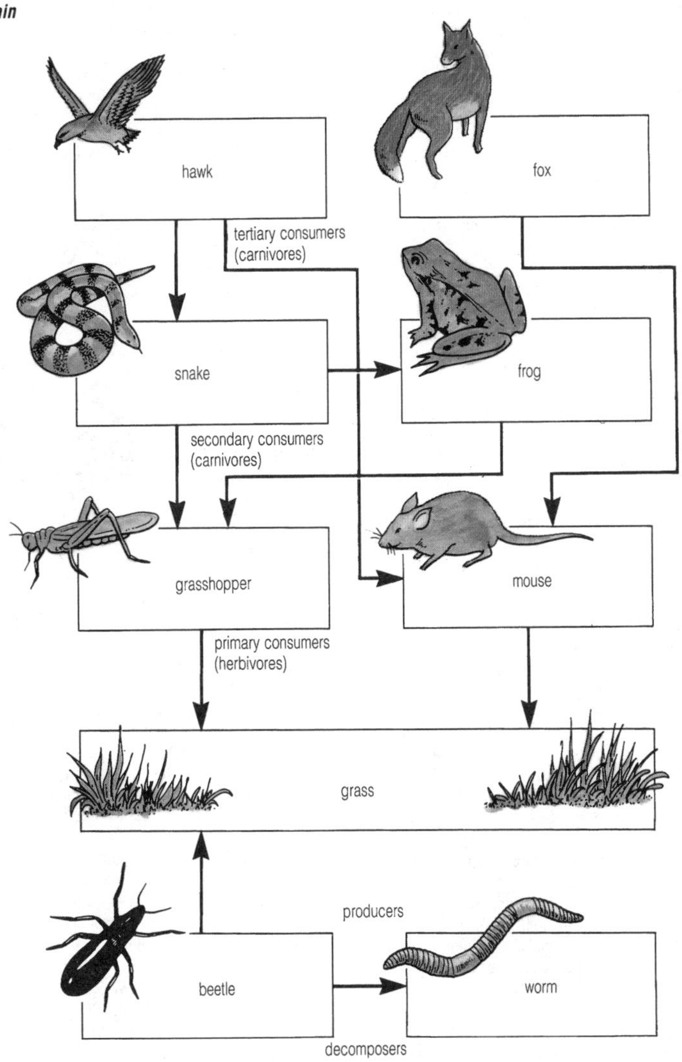
hawk
fox
tertiary consumers
(carnivores)
snake
frog
secondary consumers
(carnivores)
grasshopper
mouse
primary consumers
(herbivores)
grass
producers
beetle
worm
decomposers

ing in sugar. Modern food technology still employs traditional methods but also uses many novel processes and ◊additives, which allow a wider range of foodstuffs to be preserved.

Refrigeration below 41°F/5°C (or below 37°F/3°C for cooked foods) slows the processes of spoilage, but is less effective for foods with a high water content. Although a convenient form of preservation, this process cannot kill microorganisms, nor stop their growth completely, and a failure to realize its limitations causes many cases of food poisoning. Refrigerator temperatures should be checked as the efficiency of the machinery (see ◊refrigeration) can decline with age, and higher temperatures are dangerous.

Deep freezing (–1°F/–18°C or below) stops almost all spoilage processes, although there may be some residual enzyme activity in uncooked vegetables, which is why these are blanched (dipped in hot water to destroy the enzymes) before freezing. Microorganisms cannot grow or divide, but most remain alive and can resume activity once defrosted. Some foods are damaged by freezing, notably soft fruits and salad vegetables, whose cells are punctured by ice crystals, leading to loss of crispness. Fatty foods such as cow's milk and cream tend to separate. Various processes are used for ◊deep freezing foods commercially.

Pasteurization is used mainly for milk. By holding the milk at a high temperature, but below boiling point, for a period of time, all disease-causing bacteria can be destroyed. The milk is held at 161.6°F/72°C for 15 seconds. Other, less harmful bacteria survive, so the milk will still go sour within a few days. Boiling the milk would destroy all bacteria, but impair the flavor.

Ultra-heat treatment is used to produce UHT milk. This process uses higher temperatures than pasteurization, and kills all bacteria present, giving the milk a long shelf life but altering the flavor.

Drying is an effective method of preservation because both microorganisms and enzymes need water to be active. Products such as dried milk and instant coffee are made by spraying the liquid into a rising column of dry, heated air.

Freeze-drying is carried out under vacuum. It is less damaging to food than straight dehydration in the sense that foods reconstitute better, and is used for quality instant coffee and dried vegetables.

Canning relies on high temperatures to destroy microorganisms and enzymes. The food is sealed into a can to prevent any recontamination by bacteria. Beverages may also be canned to preserve the carbon dioxide that makes drinks fizzy.

Pickling utilizes the effect of acetic acid, found in vinegar, in stopping the growth of molds. In sauerkraut, lactic acid, produced by bacteria, has the same effect. Similar types of nonharmful, acid-generating bacteria are used to make yogurt and cheese.

Curing of meat involves soaking in salt (sodium chloride) solution, with saltpeter (sodium nitrate) added to give the meat its pink color and characteristic taste. Saltpeter (a ◊preservative) was originally included by chance because it was a natural contaminant of rock salt. The nitrates in cured meats are converted to nitrites and nitrosamines by bacteria, and these are potentially carcinogenic to humans. Of all the additives in use, the time-honored nitrates are among the most dangerous.

Irradiation is a method of preserving food by subjecting it to low-level radiation.

Puffing is a method of processing cereal grains. They are subjected to high pressures, then suddenly ejected into a normal atmospheric pressure, causing the grain to expand sharply. This type of process is used to make puffed wheat cereals and puffed rice cakes.

Chemical treatments are widely used, for example in margarine manufacture, where hydrogen is bubbled through vegetable oils in the presence of a ◊catalyst to produce a more solid, spreadable fat. The catalyst is later removed. Chemicals that are introduced in processing and remain in the food are known as food ◊additives and include flavorings, preservatives, antioxidants, emulsifiers, and colorings.

foot imperial unit of length (abbreviation ft), equivalent to 0.3048 m, in use in Britain since Anglo-Saxon times. It originally represented the length of a human foot. One foot contains 12 inches and is one-third of a yard.

foot-and-mouth disease contagious eruptive viral disease of cloven-hoofed mammals, characterized by blisters in the mouth and around the hooves. In cattle it causes deterioration of milk yield and abortions. Inoculation with a vaccine is practiced in the US as a preventive measure.

football a contact sport played between two teams of 11 players with an inflated, pointed-oval ball. It is played on a field 100 yd/91 m long from goal line to goal line, with goal posts on each of these lines, followed by a 10-yd/9-m end zone. The field is 53.3 yd/48.8 m wide. The team that scores the most points wins. Points are scored by running or passing the ball across the goal line (touchdown), by kicking it over the goal's crossbar after a touchdown (conversion or point after touchdown) or from the field during regular play (field goal), or by tackling an offensive player who has the ball in the end zone or blocking an offensive team's kick so it goes out of bounds from the end zone (safety). A touchdown counts 6 points, a field goal 3, a safety 2, and a conversion 1. Except in professional football, teams may attempt a 2-point conversion after a touchdown by running or passing the ball into the end zone. College and professional games consist of four 15-min quarters; high-school quarters are 12 min long. Players wear padded uniforms and helmets.

A game begins with one team kicking off to the other. Kickoffs also take place after each touchdown and field goal and to start the second half of the game. The team that receives the ball

football

A game played by 11 men per team. The aim is, through a series of passing or running plays, to score touchdowns which are worth six points, plus one for the "point-after" (conversion). In college and high school football, conversions of one (kicking) or two (running or passing) points may be scored. Field goals (3 points) and safeties (2 points) are other ways of scoring.

the playing field

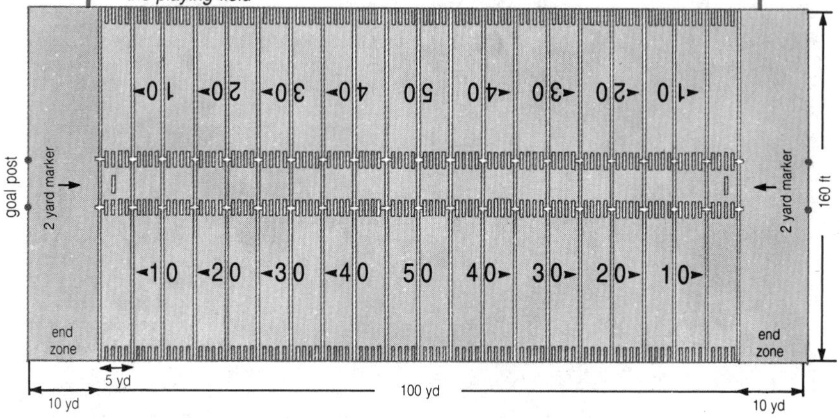
10
20
30
40
50
40
30
20
10
goal post
2 yard marker
end zone
5 yd
100 yd
10 yd
160 ft

series of plays (*downs*)

The tactics of football depend upon a series of pre-planned plays. Once in possession of the ball, the attacking side (the offense) must head for the opposing goal line by either running with the ball, or by passing the ball to upfield players. In each series of downs the offense must gain at least ten yards in four plays or it loses possession of the ball.

the snap

The snap is the first move made by the center to his quarterback, who then sets up the offensive play.

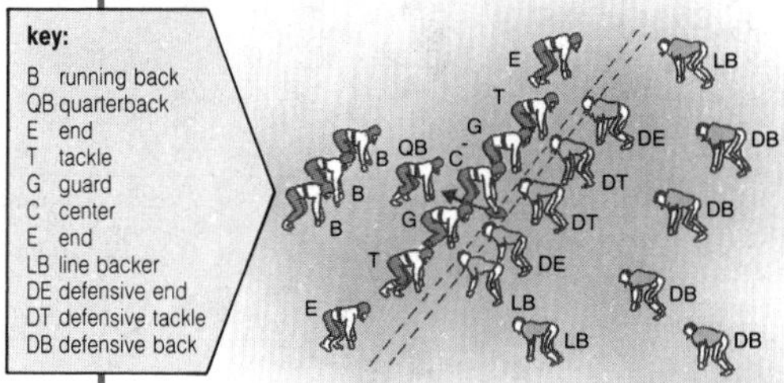
key:
B running back
QB quarterback
E end
T tackle
G guard
C center
E end
LB line backer
DE defensive end
DT defensive tackle
DB defensive back
E
T
G
QB
C
B
B
G
T
E
LB
DE
DT
DT
DE
LB
LB
DB
DB
DB
DB

the football uniform

Football is a rough game, and players need maximum protection. They wear a helmet, and underneath their outer uniform, numerous chest-, arm- and leg-pads.

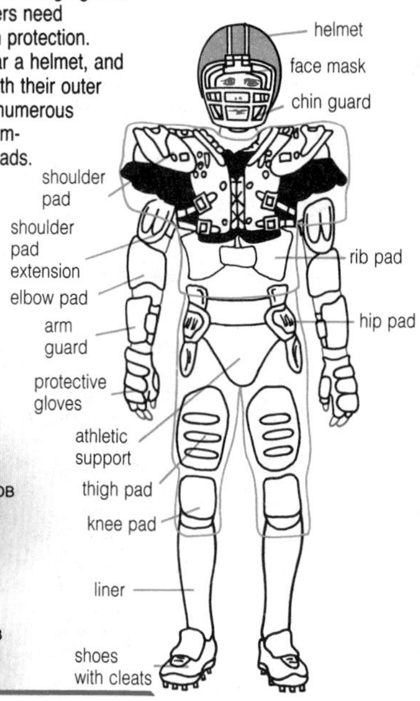
helmet
face mask
chin guard
shoulder pad
shoulder pad extension
elbow pad
arm guard
protective gloves
athletic support
thigh pad
knee pad
liner
shoes with cleats
rib pad
hip pad

becomes the offensive team; the other is the defensive team. Led by its quarterback, the offensive team tries to advance the ball by running with it or by passing it to an eligible teammate. A team must advance the ball at least 10 yd in four attempts (called downs), thereby achieving a "first down" and earning another four attempts, or surrender the ball to the other team. Each play begins with the center snapping the ball to a teammate in the offensive backfield. If a first down has not been achieved after three downs, the offensive team usually kicks (punts) the ball to the other team. The offensive team may lose the ball immediately if the player carrying the ball loses control of it (fumbles) and it is recovered by a defensive player, or if a pass is caught in the air (interception) by a defensive player.

Generally, separate groups of players on each team play offense and defense. Offensive players try to protect the person carrying or throwing the ball by blocking defensive players. The defensive players attempt to tackle the player with the ball. A play ends when the player with the ball is tackled or goes out of bounds, when a pass is incomplete, when possession of the ball changes, or when there is a score.

The game is supervised by the referee, who usually has several other officials assisting him. Infractions of the rules result in penalties against the team whose player has broken the rule. Penalties result in a loss of yards, loss of a down, or–in rare cases–expulsion of a player from the game.

history American football developed in the 19th century as a combination of soccer and rugby. The first intercollegiate game was played between Princeton and Rutgers 1869. Modern football evolved in the 1880s as eastern colleges gradually adopted rules similar to those now in use. In the early 20th century, rules were passed to reduce violence and to allow the forward pass. The popularity of college football, which has continued unabated to the present, led to the formation of professional teams from the 1890s. What is now the National Football League (NFL) was founded 1920. Although there have been other professional leagues, the NFL has remained dominant. The NFL struggled for many years but gradually established itself in large cities; explosive growth occurred after World War II as attendance rose and television broadcasts added millions of fans. Another surge of popularity followed the merger of the American Football League (AFL) into the NFL, completed 1970. There are now 28 teams in the NFL, divided into the American and National conferences. The champions of the two conferences meet in a title game called the Super Bowl.

Recent Super Bowl Winners

1981	Oakland Raiders
1982	San Francisco 49ers
1983	Washington Redskins
1984	Los Angeles Raiders
1985	San Francisco 49ers
1986	Chicago Bears
1987	New York Giants
1988	Washington Redskins
1989	San Francisco 49ers
1990	San Francisco 49ers
1991	New York Giants
1992	Washington Redskins

foot-candle unit of illuminance, now replaced by the lux. One foot-candle is the illumination received at a distance of one foot from an international candle. It is equal to 10.764 lux.

footpad thief or mugger, operating on foot, who robbed travelers on the highway in the 18th and 19th centuries in Britain. Thieves on horseback were termed highwaymen.

foot-pound imperial unit of energy (ft-lb), defined as the work done when a force of one pound moves through a distance of one foot. It has been superseded for scientific work by the joule (one foot-pound equals 1.356 joule).

***Ford** The 38th president of the United States of America, Gerald R Ford, a Republican. 1974–1977.*

foraminifera any of an order Foraminiferida of marine protozoa with shells of calcium carbonate. Their shells have pores through which filaments project. Some form part of the ◊plankton, others live on the sea bottom.

The many-chambered *Globigerina* is part of the plankton. Its shells eventually form much of the chalky ooze of the ocean floor.

Forbes Bryan (John Clarke) 1926– . British film producer, director, and screenwriter. After acting in films like *An Inspector Calls* 1954, he made his directorial debut with *Whistle Down the Wind* 1961; among his other films is *The L-Shaped Room* 1962.

force in physics, any influence that tends to change the state of rest or uniform motion in a straight line of a body. It is measured by the rate of change of momentum of the body on which it acts, that is, the mass of the body multiplied by its acceleration: $F=ma$. Force is a vector quantity, possessing both magnitude and direction; its SI unit is the newton. See also ◊Newton's laws of motion.

force ratio the magnification of a force by a machine; see ◊mechanical advantage.

forces, fundamental see ◊fundamental forces.

Ford Ford Madox. Adopted name of Ford Madox Hueffer 1873–1939. English writer of the novel *The Good Soldier* 1915 and editor of the *English Review* 1908, to which Thomas Hardy, D H Lawrence, and Joseph Conrad contributed. He was a grandson of the painter Ford Madox Brown.

Ford Gerald R(udolph) 1913– . The 38th president of the US 1974–77, a Republican. He was elected to the House of Representatives 1949, was nominated to the vice-presidency by Richard Nixon 1973 following the resignation of Spiro ◊Agnew, and in 1974, when Nixon resigned, Ford became president. He pardoned Nixon, and gave amnesty to those who had resisted the draft for the Vietnam war.

Ford was born in Omaha, Nebraska, was an All-American footballer at college, and graduated from Yale Law School. He was appointed vice-president Dec 1973, at a time when Nixon's reelection campaign was already being investigated for "dirty tricks," and became president the following Aug when the ◊Watergate scandal forced Nixon to resign. Ford's visit to Vladivostok 1974 resulted in agreement with the USSR on strategic arms limitation. He was defeated by Carter in the 1976 election by a narrow margin.

Ford Glenn (Gwyllym Samuel Newton) 1916– Canadian-born US actor, active in Hollywood films during the 1940s–1960s. Usually cast as the tough but good-natured hero, he was equally at home in Westerns, thrillers, and comedies. His films include *Gilda* 1946, *The Big Heat* 1953, and *Dear Heart* 1965.

Ford Henry 1863–1947. US automobile manufacturer, who built his first car 1893 and founded the Ford Motor Company 1903. His Model T (1908–27) was the first car to be constructed

Ford *Henry Ford in his first car, a model F Ford built in 1893.*

solely by assembly-line methods and to be mass marketed; 15 million of these automobiles were made and sold.

Born in Dearborn, Michigan, Ford was apprenticed to a Detroit machinist 1878 before he started his own company. His innovative policies, such as a $5 daily minimum wage and a 5-day work week, revolutionized employment practices. In 1928 he introduced the Model A, a stepped-up version of the Model T.

Ford was politically active and a pacifist; he opposed US intervention in both world wars and promoted his own anti-Semitic views. In 1936 he founded, with his son Edsel Ford (1893–1943), the philanthropic Ford Foundation; he retired in 1945 from the Ford Motor Co, then valued at over $1 billion.

Ford John 1586–c. 1640. English poet and dramatist. His play *'Tis Pity She's a Whore* (performed about 1626, printed 1633) is a study of incest between brother and sister.

Among his other plays are *The Witch of Edmonton* (1621, 1658), *The Broken Heart* (about 1629, 1633), *The Chronicle History of Perkin Warbeck* 1634, and *The Lady's Trial* (about 1638, 1639).

Ford John. Adopted name of Sean O'Feeney 1895–1973. US film director. Active from silent films, he was one of the original creators of the "Western," directing *The Iron Horse* 1924; *Stagecoach* 1939 became his masterpiece. He won Academy Awards for *The Informer* 1935, *The Grapes of Wrath* 1940, *How Green Was My Valley* 1941, and *The Quiet Man* 1952. Other films include *Rio Grande* 1950, *Mr. Roberts* 1955, *The Last Hurrah* 1958, and *The Man Who Shot Liberty Valance* 1962.

foreclosure in law, the transfer of title of a mortgaged property from the mortgagor (borrower, usually a home owner) to the mortgagee (loaner, for example a bank) if the mortgagor is in breach of the mortgage agreement, usually by failing to make a number of payments on the mortgage (loan).

The mortgagor may keep or sell the mortgaged property, often by auction. If the selling price is less than the mortgage, the mortgagee is responsible to the mortgagor for the difference. If the selling price is more than the worth of the mortgage, the mortgagor must give the mortgagee the difference. If the mortgage calls for installment payments, foreclosure may be warded off if the mortgagee pays all back payments and expenses incurred. Otherwise, foreclosure can be canceled only by the payment of the mortgage in full.

foredeep an elongate structural basin lying inland from an active mountain system and receiving sediment from the rising mountains. According to plate tectonic theory, a mountain chain forming behind a subduction zone along a continental margin develops a foredeep or gently sloping trough parallel to it on the landward side. Foredeeps form rapidly and usually are so deep initially that the sea floods them through gaps in the mountain range. As the mountain system evolves, sediments choke the foredeep, pushing out marine water. As marine sedimentation stops, only nonmarine deposits from the rapidly eroding mountains are formed. These consist of alluvial fans and also rivers, flood plains, and related environments inland.

Before the advent of plate tectonic theory, such foredeep deposits and changes in sediments had been interpreted as sedimentary troughs, called geosynclines, that were supposed ultimately to build upward into mountains.

foreign aid see ◊aid, foreign.

Foreign Legion a volunteer corps of foreigners within a country's army. The French Légion Etrangère, formed 1831, is one of a number of such forces. Enlisted volunteers are of any nationality (about half are now French), but the officers are usually French. Headquarters until 1962 was in Sidi Bel Abbés, Algeria; the main base is now Corsica, with reception headquarters at Aubagne, near Marseille, France.

foreign relations a country's dealings with other countries. Specialized diplomatic bodies first appeared in Europe during the 18th century. After 1818 diplomatic agents were divided into: ambassadors, papal legates, and nuncios; envoys extraordinary, ministers plenipotentiary, and other ministers accredited to the head of state; ministers resident; and chargés d'affaires, who may deputize for an ambassador or minister, or be themselves the representative accredited to a minor country. Other diplomatic staff may include counselors and attachés (military, labor, cultural, press). Consuls are state agents with commercial and political responsibilities in foreign towns.

After World War II there was an increase in the number of countries represented by a diplomat of ambassadorial rather than lower rank, although in recent years improved communications have lessened the importance of the career diplomat as the person on the spot. Professional spies (see ◊intelligence) often inflate the number of "diplomats" accredited to a country. In the USSR foreign relations are handled by the Foreign Ministry, in the US by the ◊State Department.

forensic science the use of scientific techniques to solve criminal cases. A multidisciplinary field embracing chemistry, physics, botany, zoology, and medicine, forensic science includes the identification of human bodies or traces. Traditional methods such as ◊fingerprinting are still used, assisted by computers; in addition, blood analysis, forensic dentistry, voice and speech spectograms, and ◊genetic fingerprinting are increasingly applied. Ballistics (the study of projectiles, such as bullets), another traditional forensic field, today makes use of tools such as the comparison microscope and the ◊electron microscope. Chemicals, such as poisons and drugs, are analyzed by ◊chromatography.

The first forensic laboratory was founded in France in 1910 by Edmond Locard, and the science developed as a systematic discipline in the 1930s. In 1932 the US Federal Bureau of Investigation established a forensic science laboratory in Washington, DC, and in the UK the first such laboratory was founded in London in 1935.

Forester C(ecil) S(cott) 1899–1966. English novelist, born in Egypt. He wrote a series of historical novels set in the Napoleonic era that, beginning with *The Happy Return* 1937, cover the career—from midshipman to admiral—of Horatio Hornblower.

He also wrote *Payment Deferred* 1926, a subtle crime novel, and *The African Queen* 1938, later filmed with Humphrey Bogart.

forestry the science of forest management. Recommended forestry practice aims at multipurpose crops, allowing the preservation of varied plant and animal species as well as human uses (lumbering, recreation). Forestry has often been confined to the planting of a single species, such as one of the rapid-growing conifers providing softwood for paper pulp and construction timber, for which world demand is greatest. In tropical countries, logging contributes to the destruction of the ◊rainforest, causing global environmental problems. For unplanned forests see ◊woodland and ◊forest royal.

The earliest planned forest dates from 1368 at Nuremberg, Germany; in Britain, planning of forests began in the 16th century. In the UK, Japan, and other countries, forestry practices have been criticized for concentration on softwood conifers to the neglect of native hardwoods.

A tropical forest, or rainforest, if properly preserved, yields oxygen (the bulk of the world's oxygen is provided by our dwindling rainforests); also medicinal plants, oils (from cedar, juniper, cinnamon, sandalwood), spices, gums, resins (used in inks, lacquers, linoleum), tanning and dyeing materials, forage for animals, beverages, poisons, green manure, rubber, and animal products (feathers, hides, honey).

forgery the making of a fake document, painting, or object with deliberate intention to deceive or defraud.

Financial gain is not the only motive for forgery. Han van Meegeren probably began painting in the style of Vermeer to make fools of the critics, but found such a ready market for his creations that he became a rich man before he was forced to confess. The archeological ◊Piltdown Man hoax in England in 1912 also appears to have been a practical joke.

The most common forgeries involve financial instruments such as checks or credit card transactions or money (counterfeiting). There are also literary forgeries, forged coins, forged antiques, and forged "designer" clothes and accessories.

forget-me-not any marsh plant of the genus *Myosotis* of the borage family. These plants have hairy leaves; bear clusters of small blue, white, or red flowers; and are considered a symbol of fidelity and friendship. The European true forget-me-not *Myosotis scorpioides*, 12–28 in/30–70 cm in height, now grows widely in North America.

forging one of the main methods of shaping metals, which involves hammering or a more gradual application of pressure. A blacksmith hammers red-hot metal into shape on an anvil, and the traditional place of work is called a forge. The blacksmith's mechanical equivalent is the drop forge. The metal is shaped by the blows from a falling hammer or ram, which is usually accelerated by steam or air pressure. Hydraulic presses forge by applying pressure gradually in a squeezing action.

formaldehyde common name for ◊methanal.

formalin aqueous solution of formaldehyde (methanal) used to preserve animal specimens.

Formentor, Cape northern extremity of ◊Majorca, in the Balearic Islands of the W Mediterranean sea.

Formica trademark for a heat-proof plastic laminate, widely used as a veneer on wipe-down kitchen surfaces and children's furniture. It is made from formaldehyde resins similar to ◊Bakelite.

formic acid common name for methanoic acid.

Formosa former name of ◊Taiwan.

formula in chemistry, a representation of a molecule, radical, or ion, in which chemical elements are represented by their symbols. An empirical formula indicates the simplest ratio of the elements in a compound, without indicating how many of them there are or how they are combined. A molecular formula gives the number of each type of element present in one molecule. A structural formula shows the relative positions of the atoms and the bonds between them. For example, for ethanoic acid, the empirical formula is CH_2O, the molecular formula is $C_2H_4O_2$, and the structural formula is CH_3COOH. Formula is also another name for a ◊chemical equation.

Forrest Nathan Bedford 1821–1877. American Confederate military leader and founder of the ◊Ku Klux Klan. Born in Chapel Hill, Tennessee, Forrest had little formal schooling but accumulated enough wealth through slave dealing to buy land in Mississippi and establish a cotton plantation. At the outbreak of the Civil War, Forrest led a Confederate cavalry troop and escaped from Union troops before the fall of Fort Donelson in Tennessee 1862. After the Battle of Shiloh 1862, he was promoted to the rank of brigadier general and led raids on Union forces throughout the South. After the war, while a civilian railroad executive, he founded the Klan.

Forrestal James Vincent 1892–1949. US Democratic politician. As undersecretary from 1940 and secretary of the navy from 1944, he organized its war effort, accompanying the US landings on the Japanese island Iwo Jima. He was the first secretary of the Department of Defense 1947–49, a post created to unify the three armed forces at the end of World War II.

He committed suicide after exhaustion and illness forced him to resign 1949. He wrote *The Forrestal Diaries* which were published posthumously 1951.

Forssmann Werner 1904–1979. German heart specialist. In 1929 he originated, by experiment on himself, the technique of cardiac catheterization (passing a thin tube from an arm artery up into the heart itself for diagnostic purposes). Shared Nobel Prize 1956.

Forster E(dward) M(organ) 1879–1970. English novelist, concerned with the interplay of personality and the conflict between convention and instinct. His novels include *A Room with a View* 1908, *Howard End* 1910, and *A Passage to India* 1924. He also wrote short stories, for example "The Eternal Omnibus" 1914; criticism, including *Aspects of the Novel* 1927; and essays, including *Abinger Harvest* 1936.

Forster published his first novel, *Where Angels Fear to Tread*, 1905. He enhances the superficial situations of his plots with unexpected insights in *The Longest Journey* 1907, *A Room with a View*, and *Howards End*. His many years spent in India and as secretary to the Maharajah of Dewas in 1921 provided him with the material for *A Passage to India*, which explores the relationship between the English and the Indians. *Maurice*, published 1971, has a homosexual theme.

Forsyth Frederick 1938– . English thriller writer. His books include *The Day of the Jackal* 1970, *The Dogs of War* 1974, and *The Fourth Protocol* 1984.

forsythia any temperate E Asian shrub of the genus *Forsythia* of the olive family Oleaceae, which bear yellow bell-shaped flowers in early spring before the leaves appear.

Fortaleza (also called Ceará) industrial port in NE Brazil; population (1980) 648,815. It has textile, flour-milling, and sugar-refining industries.

Fort Collins city in N Colorado, on the Cache de la Poudre River, NE of Boulder; seat of Larimer county. It is the processing and marketing center for the surrounding agricultural area. Industries include engines, cement, plastics, film, and prefabricated metal buildings; population (1990) 87,758. The city was established as a fort 1864 for the protection of travelers on the Overland Trail.

Fort-de-France capital, chief commercial center, and port of ◊Martinique, West Indies; population (1982) 99,844.

fortepiano an alternate name for ◊***pianoforte***, used to specify early pianos of the 18th and early 19th centuries.

Forth river in SE Scotland, with its headstreams rising on the NE slopes of Ben Lomond. It flows approximately 45 mi/72 km to Kincardine where the Firth of Forth begins. The firth is approximately 50 mi/80 km long, and is 16 mi/26 km wide where it joins the North Sea.

Fortin Jean 1750–1831. French physicist and instrument-maker who invented a mercury barometer that bears his name.

It measures atmospheric pressure by means of a column of mercury, formed by filling a tube, closed at one end, with mercury and upending it in a reservoir of the metal. At the upper end of the tube this leaves a gap (Torricellian vacuum), which changes size with variations in atmospheric pressure, expressed as the height of the column of mercury in millimeters. On this scale, normal atmospheric pressure is 760 mm of mercury.

Fort Knox US army post and gold depository in Kentucky, established 1917 as a training camp. The US Treasury gold-bullion vaults were built 1937.

Forster *Author of* A Passage to India *E M Forster, as photographed by Cecil Beaton.*

Fort Lamy former name of ◊N'djamena, capital of Chad.

Fort Lauderdale city in SE coastal Florida, just N of Miami; seat of Broward County, the city's main industry is tourism. Channels for boating cross the city, Atlantic Ocean beaches line it on the E, and deep-water Port Everglades to the S allows ocean-going vessels to dock; population (1990) 149,377. A fort was built here 1837 during the Seminole War.

Fort Myers city in SW Florida, on the Caloosahatchee River, SE of St Petersburg; seat of Lee County. It is a shipping center for its fish, fruit, and vegetable products. Tourism is also an important industry; population (1990) 45,206. The surrender of Holatto-Micco, the last Seminole chief, took place here 1858.

Fort Pierce city in E central Florida, where the Indian River flows into the Atlantic Ocean; seat of St Lucie County. It is an important transportation center for the fruit and vegetable crops of the surrounding area. Fishing and tourism are significant industries; population (1990) 36,830.

FORTRAN (acronym from formula translation) computer-programming language suited to mathematical and scientific computations. Developed in the mid-1950s, it is one of the earliest languages still in use.

Fort Smith city in W Arkansas, on the Arkansas River where it crosses the Oklahoma–Arkansas border, SW of Fayetteville. The site of coal and natural-gas mines, the city's industries include furniture, automobiles, paper, plastics, and metals. Fort Smith national historic site is here; population (1990) 72,798.

Fort Sumter fort in ◊Charleston Harbor, South Carolina, 4 mi/6.5 km SE of Charleston. The first shots in the American Civil War were fired here on April 12, 1861, after its commander had refused the call to surrender made by the Confederate General ◊Beauregard. The attack was successful, with the South holding the fort until 1865; it had been prompted by President Lincoln's refusal to evacuate the fort and his decision instead to send reinforcements. Southern leaders felt they must attack to lend weight to their claims of independence.

Fort Ticonderoga fort in New York State, near Lake Champlain. It was the site of battles between the British and the French 1758–59, and was captured from the British May 10, 1775 by Benedict ◊Arnold and Ethan Allen (leading the ◊Green Mountain Boys).

Fortuna in Roman mythology, goddess of chance and good fortune (Greek Tyche).

Fort Walton Beach city in NW panhandle of Florida, on the Gulf of Mexico, E of Pensacola. It is a tourist and fishing center; population (1990) 21,471.

Fort Wayne city in NE Indiana; population (1990) 173,072. Industries include electrical goods, electronics, and farm machinery. A fort was built here against the North American Indians in 1794 by General Anthony Wayne (1745–96), hero of a surprise attack on a British force at Stony Point, New York, in 1779, which earned him the nickname "Mad Anthony."

Fort Worth city in NE Texas; population (1990) 447,619. Formerly an important cattle area, it is now a grain, petroleum, aerospace, and railroad center serving the S US. Manufactured products include aerospace equipment, motor vehicles, and refined petroleum. Carswell Air Force Base, Texas Christian University, and the Kimbell Art Museum are here. Fort Worth developed from an army post 1849 and was a stop on the Chisholm cattle trail. The arrival of the railroad 1876 fostered economic development that was furthered by the discovery of oil nearby in 1920.

Forty-Five, the ◊Jacobite rebellion 1745, led by Prince ◊Charles Edward Stuart. With his army of Highlanders "Bonnie Prince Charlie" occupied Edinburgh and advanced into England as far as Derby, but then turned back. The rising was crushed by the Duke of Cumberland at Culloden 1746.

Foss Lukas 1922– . US composer and conductor. He wrote the cantata *The Prairie* 1942 and *Time Cycle* for soprano and orchestra 1960.

Born in Germany, he studied in Europe before settling in the US in 1937. A student of ◊Hindemith, his vocal music is composed in Neoclassical style; in the mid-1950s he began increasingly to employ improvisation. Foss has also written chamber and orchestral music in which the players reproduce tape-recorded effects.

Fosse Bob (Robert) ,1927–1987. US film director who entered films as a dancer and choreographer from Broadway, making his directorial debut with *Sweet Charity* 1968, his Broadway musical. He received an Academy Award for his second film as director, *Cabaret* 1972. His other work includes *All That Jazz* 1979 and several musical productions, including *Pipin* 1975.

fossil (Latin *fossilis* "dug up") remains of an animal or plant preserved in rocks and minerals. Fossils may be formed by refrigeration (for example, Arctic ◊mammoths in ice); carbonization (leaves in coal); formation of a cast (dinosaur or human footprints in mud); or mineralization of bones, more generally teeth or shells, or of plants, generally petrified wood. The study of fossils is called ◊paleontology.

fossil fuel fuel, such as coal or oil, formed from the fossilized remains of plants or other organisms that lived hundreds of millions of years ago. Fossil fuels are a ◊nonrenewable resource and will run out eventually. Extraction of coal (mining) causes considerable environmental pollution, and burning fossil fuels contributes to problems of ◊acid rain and the ◊greenhouse effect.

Fos-sur-Mer harbor and medieval township near Marseille, France, forming the southern focus of a direct Rhône–Rhine route to the North Sea.

Foster Jodie 1962– . US film actress who began as a child in a great variety of roles. Her work includes *Taxi Driver* 1976, *Bugsy Malone* 1976, *The Accused* 1988 (Academy Award), and *The Silence of the Lambs* 1991.

Foster Stephen Collins 1826–1864. US songwriter, composer of "The Old Folks at Home" 1851, "My Old Kentucky Home" 1853, and others, which mostly drew from the black minstrel style.

Born in Lawrenceville, Pennsylvania, he had no formal training in music but began to write early. Because he was not completely comfortable with the label "Ethiopian" (black minstrel) songwriter, caused by society's lack of acceptance, he also wrote sentimental popular music. Although many of his songs became very popular and profitable, he mismanaged his career and died in debt.

Foucault Jean Bernard Léon 1819–1868. French physicist who used a pendulum to demonstrate the rotation of the Earth on its axis, and invented the gyroscope.

He investigated heat and light, discovered eddy currents induced in a copper disk moving in a magnetic field, invented a polarizer, and made improvements in the electric arc.

Foster *For her leading role in* The Accused *1988, Jodie Foster won the Oscar.*

Fouché *Joseph Fouché was minister of police under Napoleon. He was also instrumental in organizing the conspiracy that overthrew Robespierre in 1794.*

Foucault Michel 1926–1984. French philosopher who rejected phenomenology and existentialism. He was concerned with how forms of knowledge and forms of human subjectivity are constructed by specific institutions and practices.

Foucault was deeply influenced by ◊Nietzsche, and developed an analysis of the operation of power in society using Nietzschean concepts.

Fouché Joseph, duke of Otranto 1759–1820. French politician. He was elected to the National Convention (the post-Revolutionary legislature), and organized the conspiracy that overthrew the ◊Jacobin leader ◊Robespierre. Napoleon employed him as police minister.

fouetté (French "whipped") in ballet, a type of ◊*pirouette* in which one leg is extended to the side and then into the knee in a whiplike action, while the dancer spins on the supporting leg. Odile performs 32 *fouettés* in Act III of *Swan Lake*.

Fou-Liang former name of ◊Jingdezhen, a town in China.

Fouquet Jean c. 1420–1481. French painter. He became court painter to Charles VIII in 1448 and to Louis XI in 1475. His *Melun diptych* about 1450 (Musées Royaux, Antwerp, and Staatliche Museen, Berlin) shows Italian Renaissance influence.

Fouquet Nicolas 1615–1680. French politician, a rival to Louis XIV's minister ◊Colbert. Fouquet became *Procureur Général* of the Paris *parlement* 1650 and *Surintendant des Finances* 1651, responsible for raising funds for the long war against Spain, a post he held until arrested and imprisoned for embezzlement (at the instigation of Colbert, who succeeded him) from 1661 until his death.

four-color process color ◊printing using four printing plates, based on the principle that any color is made up of differing proportions of the primary colors blue, red, and green. The first stage in preparing a color picture for printing is to produce separate films, one each for the blue, red, and green, respectively, in the picture (color separations). From these separations three printing plates are made, with a fourth plate for black (for shading or outlines). Ink colors used include cyan for the blue, magenta for the red, and yellow.

Four Freedoms, the the four kinds of liberty essential to human dignity as defined in an address to Congress by President F D ◊Roosevelt Jan 6, 1941: freedom of speech and expression, freedom of worship, freedom from want, freedom from fear. Before US entry into World War II, Roosevelt urged support of the democracies fighting to defend freedom, and two months later Congress passed the ◊Lend-Lease Act. The Four Freedoms were the basis for the ◊Atlantic Charter specifying Allied war aims 1941.

Fourier François Charles Marie 1772–1837. French Socialist. In *Le Nouveau monde industriel/The New Industrial World* 1829–30, he advocated that society should be organized in self-sufficient cooperative units of about 1,500 people, marriage was to be abandoned.

Fourier Jean Baptiste Joseph 1768–1830. French applied mathematician whose formulation of heat flow 1807 contains the proposal that, with certain constraints, any mathematical function can be represented by trigonometrical series. This principle forms the basis of Fourier analysis, used today in many different fields of physics. His idea, not immediately well received, gained currency and is embodied in his *Théorie analytique de la chaleur/The Analytical Theory of Heat* 1822.

Four Noble Truths in Buddhism, a summary of the basic concepts: life is suffering (Sanskrit *duhkha*); suffering has its roots in desire (*tanha*, clinging or grasping); the cessation of desire is the end of suffering, *nirvana*; and this can be reached by the Noble Eightfold Path of *dharma* (truth).

four-stroke cycle the engine-operating cycle of most gasoline and ◊diesel piston engines. The "stroke" is an upward or downward movement of a piston in a cylinder. In a gasoline engine the cycle begins with the induction of a fuel mixture as the piston goes down on its first stroke. On the second stroke (up) the piston compresses the mixture in the top of the cylinder. An electric spark then ignites the mixture, and the gases produced force the piston down on its third, power stroke. On the fourth stroke (up) the piston expels the burned gases from the cylinder into the exhaust.

Fourteen Points the terms proposed by President Wilson of the US in his address to Congress Jan 8, 1918, as a basis for the settlement of World War I. The creation of the League of Nations was one of the points.

The terms included: open diplomacy; freedom of the seas; removal of economic barriers; international disarmament; adjustment of colonial claims; German evacuation of Russian, Belgian, French, and Balkan territories; the restoration of Alsace-Lorraine to France; autonomy for the various ethnic groups in Austria, Hungary and the Ottoman Empire; an independent Poland; and a

Fourier *French Socialist François Fourier. One of his major theories was to reorganize society into self-sufficient units, living and working in cooperation.*

four-stroke cycle

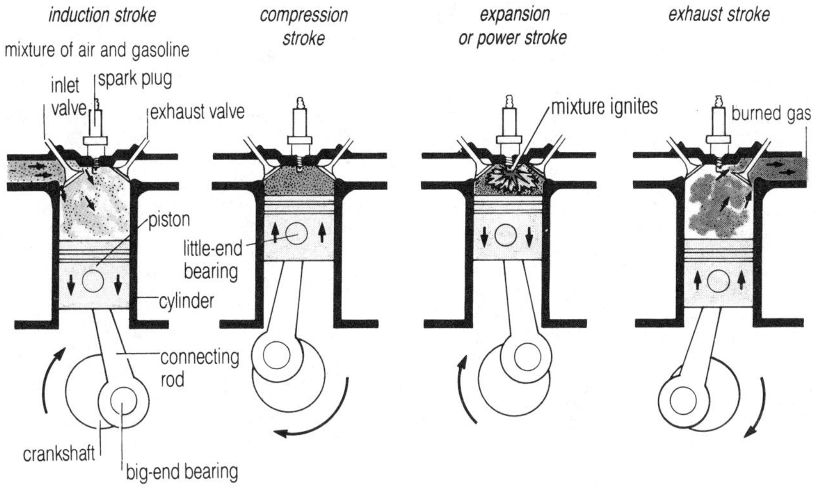
induction stroke
compression stroke
expansion or power stroke
exhaust stroke
mixture of air and gasoline
inlet valve
spark plug
exhaust valve
mixture ignites
burned gas
piston
little-end bearing
cylinder
connecting rod
crankshaft
big-end bearing

general association of nations (which was to become the League of Nations).

Wilson was obliged to compromise on many of the points in light of secret agreements concluded by several of the Allies. The Germans, having agreed to the armistice largely on the basis of the Fourteen Points, felt betrayed by subsequent decisions imposed upon them by the Treaty of ◊Versailles.

fourth estate the press. The term was coined by the British politician Edmund Burke in analogy with the traditional three ◊estates.

fourth-generation language in computing, a type of programming language designed for the rapid programming of applications but often lacking the ability to control the individual parts of the computer. Such a language typically provides easy ways of designing screens and reports, and of using databases. Other "generations" (the term implies a class of language rather than a chronological sequence) are ◊machine code (first generation), assembly code (second), and conventional high-level languages such as ◊BASIC and ◊PASCAL (third).

Fourth of July in the US, the anniversary of the day in 1776 when the ◊Declaration of Independence was adopted by the Continental Congress. It is a public vacation, officially called Independence Day, commemorating independence from Britain.

Fourth Republic the French constitutional regime that was established between 1944 and 1946 and lasted until Oct 4, 1958: from liberation after Nazi occupation during World War II to the introduction of a new constitution by Gen de Gaulle.

Foveaux Strait stretch of water between the extreme S of South Island, New Zealand, and Stewart Island, New Zealand. It is a fishing area and produces a considerable oyster catch.

fowl chicken or chickenlike bird. Sometimes the term is also used for ducks and geese. The red jungle fowl *Gallus gallus* is the ancestor of all domestic chickens. It is a forest bird of South Asia, without the size or egg-laying ability of many domestic strains. ◊Guinea fowl are of African origin.

Fowler William 1911– . US astrophysicist. In 1983 he and Subrahmanyan Chandrasekhar were awarded the Nobel Prize for Physics for their work on the life cycle of stars and the origin of chemical elements.

Fowles John 1926– . English writer whose novels, often concerned with illusion and reality and with the creative process, include *The Collector* 1963, *The Magus* 1965, *The French Lieutenant's Woman* 1969, *Daniel Martin* 1977, *Mantissa* 1982, and *A Maggot* 1985.

fox member of the smaller species of wild dog of the family Canidae, which live in Africa, Asia, Europe, North America, and South America. Foxes feed on a wide range of animals from worms to rabbits, scavenge for food, and also eat berries. They are very adaptable, maintaining high populations close to urban areas.

Most foxes are nocturnal, and make an underground den. The common or red fox *Vulpes vulpes* is about 2 ft/60 cm long plus a tail ("brush") 1.3 ft/40 cm long. The fur is reddish with black patches behind the ears and a light tip to the tail. ther foxes include the Arctic fox *Alopexlagopus*, the ◊fennec, the gray foxes genus *Urocyon* of Northand Central America, and the South American genus *Dusicyon*, to which the extinct Falkland Islands dog belonged.

Fox George 1624–1691. English founder of the Society of ◊Friends. After developing his belief in a mystical "inner light," he became a traveling preacher 1647, and in 1650 was imprisoned for blasphemy at Derby, where the name Quakers was first applied derogatorily to him and his followers, supposedly because he enjoined Judge Bennet to "quake at the word of the Lord."

He suffered further imprisonments, made a missionary journey to America in 1671–72, and wrote many evangelical and meditative works, including a *Journal*, published 1694.

Fox James 1939– . English film actor, usually cast in upper-class, refined roles but celebrated for his portrayal of a psychotic gangster in Nicolas Roeg's *Performance* 1970, which was followed by a ten-year break from acting.

Fox appeared in *The Servant* 1963 and *Isadora* 1968. He returned to acting in *A Passage to India* 1984 and *Absolute Beginners* 1985.

Fox Margaret 1833–1893. Canadian-born US spiritual medium. Raised in New York State, Fox and her younger sister Katherine claimed unusual psychic powers from an early age. Becoming famous for their ability to communicate with departed spirits, the Fox girls began to hold public demonstrations of their powers. Moving to New York City 1850, they received much favorable publicity and sparked a widespread public interest in spiritualism as a modern religious movement.

fox

foxglove

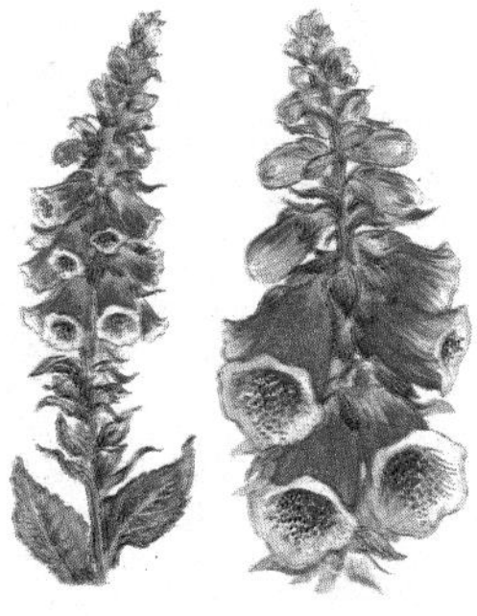

In 1888, however, Margaret publicly confessed that her "psychic powers" were a hoax.

foxglove any flowering plant of the genus *Digitalis*, family Scrophulariaceae, found in Europe and the Mediterranean region. It bears showy spikes of bell-like flowers, and grows up to 5 ft/1.5 m high.

The wild species *D. purpurea*, native to Britain, produces purple to reddish flowers. Its leaves were the original source of digitalis, a drug used for some heart problems.

foxhound a black, tan, and white, small, keen-nosed hound, up to 2 ft/60 cm tall. There are two recognized breeds: the English foxhound, bred for some 300 years to hunt foxes, and the American foxhound, not quite as stocky, used for foxes and other game.

fox-hunting the pursuit of a fox across country on horseback, aided by a pack of foxhounds, specially trained to track the fox's scent. The aim is to catch and kill the fox. In draghunting, hounds pursue a prepared trail rather than a fox.

Described by the playwright Oscar Wilde as "the unspeakable in pursuit of the uneatable," fox-hunting has met with increasing opposition. Animal-rights activists condemn it as involving excessive cruelty, and in Britain groups such as the Hunt Saboteurs disrupt it.

Fox-hunting dates from the late 17th century, when it arose as a practical method of limiting the fox population which endangered poultry farming, but by the early 19th century it was indulged in as a sport by the British aristocracy and gentry who ceremonialized it. Fox-hunting was introduced into the US by early settlers from England and continues in the S and middle Atlantic regions.

foxtrot ballroom dance originating in the US about 1914. It has alternating long and short steps, supposedly like the movements of the fox.

Fracastoro Girolamo c. 1478–1553. Italian physician known for his two medical books. He was born and worked mainly in Verona. His first book, *Syphilis sive morbus gallicus/Syphilis or the French disease* 1530, was written in verse. It was one of the earliest texts on syphilis, a disease Fracastaro named. In his second work, *De contagione/On contagion* 1546, he wrote, far ahead of his time, about "seeds of contagion."

fractal (from Latin *fractus* "broken") an irregular shape or surface produced by a procedure of repeated subdivision. Generated on a computer screen, fractals are used in creating models for geographical or biological processes (for example, the creation of a coastline by erosion or accretion, or the growth of plants).

Sets of curves with such discordant properties were developed in Germany by Georg Cantor (1845–1918) and Karl Weierstrass (1815–1897). The name was coined by the French mathematician Benoit Mandelbrod. Fractals are also used for computer art.

fraction (from Latin *fractus* "broken") in mathematics, a number that indicates one or more equal parts of a whole. Usually, the number of equal parts into which the unit is divided (denominator) is written below a horizontal line, and the number of parts comprising the fraction (numerator) is written above; thus $\frac{2}{3}$ or $\frac{3}{4}$. Such fractions are called vulgar or simple fractions. The denominator can never be zero.

A proper fraction is one in which the numerator is less than the denominator. An improper fraction has a numerator that is larger than the denominator, for example 3/2. It can therefore be expressed as a mixed number, for example, 1½. A combination such as 5/0 is not regarded as a fraction (an object cannot be divided into zero equal parts), and mathematically any number divided by 0 is equal to infinity. A decimal fraction has as its denominator a power of 10, and these are omitted by use of the decimal point and notation, for example 0.04, which is 4/100. The digits to the right of the decimal point indicate the numerators of vulgar fractions whose denominators are 10, 100, 1,000, and so on. Most fractions can be expressed exactly as decimal fractions (⅓ = 0.333...).

Fractions are also known as the rational numbers, that is numbers formed by a ratio. Integers may be expressed as fractions with a denominator of 1.

fraction in chemistry, a group of similar compounds, the boiling points of which fall within a particular range and which are separated during ◊fractionation.

crude petroleum fractions

fraction	*approximate number of carbon atoms in hydrocarbon*	*approximate boiling range (°C) at atmospheric pressure*
gases	1–4	below 25
petrol	4–12	40–100
naptha	7–14	90–150
kerosene	9–16	150–240
diesel oil	15–25	220–250
lubricating oil	20–70	250–350
bitumen residue	over 70	above 350

fractionating column device in which many separate ◊distillations can occur so that a liquid mixture can be separated into its components.

Various designs exist but the primary aim is to allow maximum contact between the hot rising vapors and the cooling descending liquid. As the vapors ascend the column the mixture becomes progressively enriched in the lower boiling components, so they separate out first.

fractionation or ***fractional distillation*** process used to split complex mixtures (such as crude oil) into their components, usually by repeated heating, boiling, and condensation.

Fra Diavolo nickname of Michele Pezza 1771–1806. Italian brigand. A renegade monk, he led a gang in the mountains of Calabria, S Italy, for many years, and was eventually executed in Naples.

Fragonard Jean Honoré 1732–1806. French painter, the leading exponent of the Rococo style (along with his master Boucher). His light-hearted subjects include *The Swing* about 1766 (Wallace Collection, London).

Frame Janet. Adopted name of Janet Paterson Frame Clutha 1924– . New Zealand novelist. After being wrongly diagnosed as schizophrenic, she reflected her experiences 1945–54 in the novel *Faces in the Water* 1961 and the autobiographical *An Angel at My Table* 1984.

franc French coin, so called from 1360 when it was a gold coin inscribed *Francorum Rex*, "King of the Franks." The franc CFA (*Communauté française d'Afrique*) is the currency of the former French territories in Africa; in France's Pacific territories the franc CFP (*Communauté française du pacifique*) is used. The currency units of Belgium, Luxembourg, and Switzerland are also called francs.

France country in W Europe, bounded NE by Belgium, E by Germany, Switzerland and Italy, S by the Mediterranean, SW by Spain and Andorra, and W by the Atlantic Ocean

government Under the 1958 Fifth Republic constitution, amended in 1962, France has a two-

France
French Republic
(République Française)

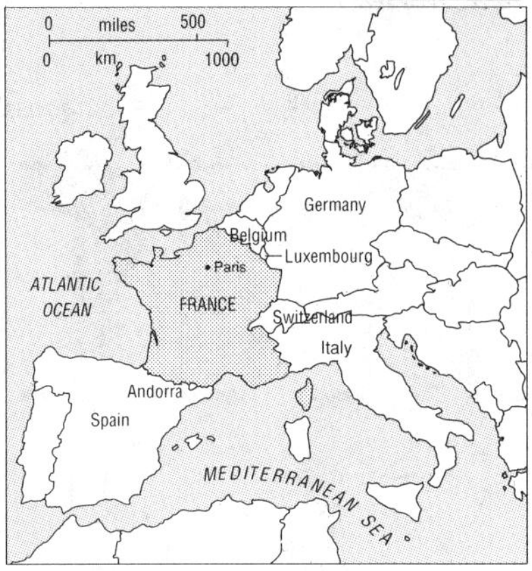
0 miles 500
0 km 1000
Germany
Belgium
Paris
Luxembourg
ATLANTIC OCEAN
FRANCE
Switzerland
Italy
Andorra
Spain
MEDITERRANEAN SEA

area (including Corsica) 209,970 sq mi/543,965 sq km
capital Paris
cities Lyons, Lille, Bordeaux, Toulouse, Nantes, Strasbourg; ports Marseilles, Nice, Le Havre
physical rivers Seine, Loire, Garonne, Rhône, Rhine; mountain ranges Alps, Massif Central, Pyrenees, Jura, Vosges, Cévennes; the island of Corsica
territories Guadeloupe, French Guiana, Martinique, Réunion, St Pierre and Miquelon, Southern and Antarctic Territories, New Caledonia, French Polynesia, Wallis and Futuna
features Ardennes forest, Auvergne mountain region, Riviera, Mont Blanc 15,781 ft/4,810 m, caves of Dordogne with relics of early humans; largest W European nation
head of state François Mitterrand from 1981
head of government Edith Cresson from 1991
political system liberal democracy
political parties Socialist Party (PS), left-of-center; Rally for the Republic (RPR), neo-Gaullist conservative; Union for French Democracy (UDF), center-right; Republican Party (RP), center-right; French Communist Party (PCF), Marxist-Leninist; National Front, far-right; Greens, environmentalist
exports fruit (especially apples), wine, cheese, wheat, automobiles, aircraft, iron and steel, petroleum products, chemicals, jewelry, silk, lace; tourism is very important
currency franc
population (1990 est) 56,184,000 (including 4,500,000 immigrants, chiefly from Portugal, Algeria, Morocco, and Tunisia); growth rate 0.3% p.a.
life expectancy men 71, women 79
language French (regional dialects include Basque, Breton, Catalan, Provençal)
religion Roman Catholic 90%, Muslim 1%, Protestant 2%
literacy 99% (1984)
GNP $568 bn (1983); $7,179 per head
chronology
1944–46 De Gaulle provisional government; start of Fourth Republic.
1954 Indochina achieved independence.
1956 Morocco and Tunisia achieved independence.
1957 Entry into EEC.
1958 Recall of de Gaulle following Algerian crisis; start of Fifth Republic.
1959 De Gaulle became president.
1962 Algeria achieved independence.
1966 France withdrew from military wing of NATO.
1968 "May events" crisis.
1969 De Gaulle resigned following referendum defeat; Pompidou became president.
1974 Giscard d'Estaing elected president.
1981 Mitterrand elected Fifth Republic's first Socialist president.
1986 "Cohabitation" experiment, with the conservative Jacques Chirac as prime minister.
1988 Mitterrand re-elected. Moderate Socialist Michel Rocard became prime minister and continued in this post despite the Socialist Party failing to obtain a secure majority in the National Assembly elections. Matignon Accord on future of New Caledonia approved by referendum.
1989 Greens gained 11% of vote in elections to European Parliament.
1991 French forces were part of the US-led coalition in the Gulf War. Edith Cresson became France's first woman prime minister.

chamber legislature and a "shared executive" government. The legislature comprises a national assembly, whose 577 deputies are elected for five-year terms from single-member constituencies following a two-ballot, "run-off" majority system (proportional representation was adopted for the 1986 elections but was later rescinded) and a senate, whose 321 members are indirectly elected, a third at a time, triennially for nine-year terms from groups of local councillors.

Twenty-two national assembly and 13 senate seats are elected by overseas *départements* and territories, and 12 senate seats by French nationals abroad. The national assembly is the dominant chamber, from whose ranks the prime minister is drawn and upon whose support the government rests. The senate can temporarily veto legislation. Its vetoes, however, can be overridden by the national assembly.

France's executive is functionally divided between the president and prime minister. The president, elected for a seven-year term by direct universal suffrage after gaining a majority in either a first or second "run-off" ballot, functions as head of state, commander-in-chief of the armed forces, and guardian of the constitution. The president selects the prime minister, presides over cabinet meetings, countersigns government bills, negotiates foreign treaties, and can call referenda and dissolve the national assembly. According to the constitution, however, ultimate control over policy making rests with the prime minister and council of ministers.

The president and prime minister work with ministers from political and technocratic backgrounds, assisted by a skilled and powerful civil service. A nine-member Constitutional Council (selected triennially in a staggered manner by the state president and the presidents of the senate and national assembly) and a *Conseil d'État*, staffed by senior civil servants, rule on the legality of legislation passed.

At the local level there are 21 regional councils concerned with economic planning. Below these are 96 *département* councils and almost 36,000 town and village councils. Corsica has its own directly elected 61-seat parliament with powers to propose amendments to national assembly legislation.

There are four overseas *départements* (◊French Guiana, ◊Guadeloupe, ◊Martinique, and ◊Réunion) with their own elected general and regional councils, two overseas "collective territories" (◊Mayotte and ◊St Pierre and Miquelon) administered by appointed commissioners, and four overseas territories (◊French Polynesia, the ◊French Southern and Antarctic Territories, ◊New Caledonia, and the ◊Wallis and Futuna Islands) governed by appointed high comissioners, which form constituent parts of the French Republic, returning deputies to the national legislature.

French politics are dominated by four parties,

English Channel
Channel Islands
Cherbourg
Le Havre
Rouen
Caen
Calais
Lille
Amiens
BELGIUM
GERMANY
LUXEMBOURG
Seine
Paris
Nancy
Strasbourg
Brest
Rennes
Troyes
Orleans
Loire
Tours
Nantes
Dijon
Saône
FRANCE
SWITZ.
Atlantic Ocean
La Rochelle
Limoges
Clermont Ferrand
Lyons
Grenoble
ITALY
Bordeaux
Dordogne
Garonne
Lot
Rhône
N
Bay of Biscay
Toulouse
Montpellier
MONACO
Nice
Marseille
Toulon
Pau
Pyrenees
0 km 50 100
0 miles 50 100
SPAIN
ANDORRA
Mediterranean Sea

divided into two broad right and left ideological and electoral coalitions. The "right coalition," which was pre-eminent 1958–81, is divided between the Rassemblement (Rally) pour la République (RPR), formed in 1976 by Jacques Chirac as the successor to ◊de Gaulle's Union pour la Nouvelle République (UNR), and the Union pour la Démocratie Française (UDF), formed by President Valéry ◊Giscard d'Estaing, Prime Minister Raymond ◊Barre, and Jean Lecanuet in 1978 to unite several center-right parties. The two major parties on the left are the pro-Moscow French Communist Party (PCF) and the Socialist Party (PS). The fifth significant party is the extreme right-wing National Front, which, although excluded from electoral coalitions, has gained ground campaigning for immigrant repatriation and the return of capital punishment.

history For history before 1945, see ◊France, history. A "united front" provisional government headed by de Gaulle, and including communists, assumed power in the re-established republic before a new constitution was framed and adopted for a Fourth Republic in Jan 1946. This provided for a weak executive and powerful national assembly that, being elected under a generous system of proportional representation, was to be divided between numerous small party groupings. With 26 impermanent governments being formed 1946–58, real power passed to the civil service, which, by introducing a new system of "indicative economic planning," engineered rapid economic reconstruction. Decolonization of French ◊Indochina 1954, Morocco and Tunisia 1956, and entry into the EEC 1957 were also effected.

The Fourth Republic was overthrown in 1958 by a political and military crisis over Algerian independence, which threatened to lead to a French army revolt. De Gaulle was recalled from retirement to head a government of national unity and supervised the framing of the new Fifth Republic constitution, which strengthened the president and prime minister.

De Gaulle, who became president in 1959, restored domestic stability and presided over the decolonization of Francophone Africa, including Algerian independence in 1962. Close economic links were maintained with former colonies. De Gaulle also initiated a new foreign policy, withdrawing France from military cooperation in ◊NATO in 1966 and developing an autonomous nuclear deterrent force. The de Gaulle era was one of economic growth and large-scale rural-urban migration. Politically, however, there was tight censorship and strong centralization, and in 1967 the public reacted against de Gaulle's paternalism by voting the "right coalition" a reduced majority.

A year later, in 1968, the nation was paralyzed by students' and workers' demonstrations in Paris that spread to the provinces and briefly threatened the government. De Gaulle called elections and won a landslide victory. In 1969, however, he was defeated in a referendum over proposed senate and local government reforms and resigned. De Gaulle's former prime minister, Georges ◊Pompidou, was elected president and pursued Gaullist policies until his death in 1974.

Pompidou's successor as president, Valéry Giscard d'Estaing, leader of the center-right Independent Republicans, introduced domestic reforms and played a more active and cooperative role in the EEC. Giscard faced opposition, however, from his "right coalition" partner, Jacques ◊Chirac, who was prime minister 1974–76, and deteriorating international economic conditions. France performed better than many of its European competitors between 1974–81, with the president launching a major nuclear power program to save on energy imports and, while Raymond ◊Barre was prime minister (1976–81), a new liberal "freer market" economic strategy. However, with 1.7 million unemployed, Giscard was defeated by the Socialist Party leader, François ◊Mitterrand, in the 1981 presidential election.

Mitterrand's victory was the first presidential success for the "left coalition" during the Fifth Republic and was immediately succeeded by a landslide victory for the PS and PCF in elections to the national assembly in 1981. The new administration, which included four communist ministers, introduced a radical program of social reform, decentralization, and nationalization, and passed a series of reflationary budgets aimed at reducing unemployment.

Financial constraints, however, forced a switch toward a more conservative policy of "rigueur" (austerity) in 1983. A U-turn in economic policy was completed in 1984 when Prime Minister Pierre ◊Mauroy was replaced by Laurent ◊Fabius, prompting the resignation of communist members of the cabinet. Unemployment rose to over 2.5 million in 1985–86, increasing racial tension in urban areas. The extreme right-wing National Front, led by Jean-Marie ◊Le Pen, benefitted from this and gained seats in the March 1986 National Assembly elections, held under a new proportional representation system. The "left coalition" lost its majority, the PCF having been in decline in recent years. The PS, however, had emerged as France's single most popular party.

From 1958 to 1986 the president and prime minister had been drawn from the same party coalition, and the president had been allowed to dominate in both home and foreign afairs. In 1986, however, Mitterrand was obliged to appoint as prime minister the leader of the opposition, Jacques Chirac, who emerged as the dominant force in the "shared executive." Chirac introduced a radical "new conservative" program of denationalization, deregulation, and "desocialization," using the executive's decree powers and the parliamentary "guillotine" to steamroller measures through. His educational and economic reforms, however, encountered serious opposition from militant students and striking workers, necessitating embarrassing policy concessions. With his national standing tarnished, Chirac was comfortably defeated by Mitterrand in the May 1988 presidential election. In the national assembly elections that followed in June 1988, the Socialists emerged as the largest single political party. Mitterrand duly appointed Michel ◊Rocard, a moderate social democrat, as prime minister heading a minority PS government that included several center party representatives. Rocard implemented a progressive program, aimed at protecting the underprivileged and improving the "quality of life." In June 1988 he negotiated the Matignon Accord, designed to solve the New Caledonia "problem," which was later approved by referendum. Between 1988 and 1990 France enjoyed a strong economic upturn and attention focused increasingly on "quality of life," with the Green Party gaining 11% of the national vote in the European Parliament elections of June 1989. The extreme right National Front continued to do well in municipal elections, forcing the government to adopt a hard line against illegal immigration and to announce new programs for the integration of Muslim immigrants into mainstream French society. Religious and cultural tensions increased with the influx of Muslims from Algeria, Tunisia, and other areas of French colonial ties.

In Sept 1990, after Iraqi violation of the French ambassador's residence in Kuwait, the French government sent 5,000 troops to Saudi Arabia.

The Rocard government narrowly survived a censure vote in the National Assembly in Nov 1990. This followed an outbreak of serious student violence in Paris and earlier antipolice race riots in the Lyons suburbs. In 1991 Rocard resigned and was replaced by Edith Cresson, the first women to hold the post.

Regions and Départements

PARIS
75
92
93
94
NORD
HAUTE NORMANDIE
PICARDIE
BASSE-NORMANDIE
BRETAGNE
ILE DE FRANCE
CHAMPAGNE-ARDENNE
LORRAINE
ALSACE
PAYS DE LA LOIRE
CENTRE
BOURGOGNE
FRANCHE-COMTE
POITOU-CHARENTES
LIMOUSIN
AUVERGNE
RHÔNE-ALPES
AQUITAINE
MIDI-PYRÉNÉES
LANGUEDOC-ROUSSILLON
PROVENCE-ALPES-COTE D'AZUR
CORSE
20B
20A
0
150 km

Départements are numbered by the standard French alphabetical system

France: regions and départements

Region and Département	*Capital*	*Area sq km*
Alsace		*8,300*
Bas-Rhin	Strasbourg	
Haut-Rhin	Colmar	
Aquitaine		*41,300*
Dordogne	Périgueux	
Gironde	Bordeaux	
Landes	Mont-de-Marsan	
Lot-et-Garonne	Agen	
Pyrénées-Atlantiques		
Auvergne		*26,000*
Allier	Moulins	
Cantal	Aurillac	
Haute-Loire	Le Puy	
Puy-de-Dôme	Clermont-Ferrand	
Basse-Normandie		*17,600*
Calvados	Caen	
Manche	Saint-Lô	
Orne	Alençon	
Bourgogne		*31,600*
Côte-d'Or	Dijon	
Nièvre	Nevers	
Saône-et-Loire	Mâcon	
Yonne	Auxerre	
Bretagne		*27,200*
Côtes-du-Nord	St Brieuc	
Finistère	Quimper	
Ille-et-Vilaine	Rennes	
Morbihan	Vannes	
Centre		*39,200*
Cher	Bourges	
Eure-et-Loire	Chartres	
Indre	Châteauroux	
Indre-et-Loire	Tours	
Loire-et-Cher	Blois	
Loiret	Orléans	
Champagne-Ardenne		*25,600*
Ardenne	Charleville-Mézières	
Aube	Troyes	
Marne	Châlons-sur-Marne	
Haute-Marne	Chaumont	
Corsica		*8,700*
Haute Corse	Bastia	
Corse du Sud	Ajaccio	
Franche-Comté		*16,200*
Doubs	Besançon	
Jura	Lons-le-Saunier	
Haute Saône	Vesoul	
Terre de Belfort	Belfort	
Haute-Normandie		*12,300*
Eure	Evreux	
Seine-Maritime	Rouen	
Île de France		*12,000*
Essonne	Évry	
Val-de-Marne	Créteil	
Val d'Oise	Cergy-Pontoise	
Ville de Paris		
Seine-et-Marne	Melun	
Hauts-de-Seine	Nanterre	
Seine-Saint-Denis	Bobigny	
Yvelines	Versailles	
Languedoc-Roussillon		*27,400*
Aude	Carcassonne	
Gard	Nimes	
Hérault	Montpellier	
Lozère	Mende	
Pyrènèes-Orientales	Perpignan	
Limousin		*16,900*
Corrèze	Tulle	
Creuse	Guéret	
Haute-Vienne	Limoges	
Lorraine		*23,600*
Meurthe-et-Moselle	Nancy	
Meuse	Bar-le-Duc	
Moselle	Metz	
Vosges	Épinal	
Midi-Pyrénées		*45,300*
Ariège	Foix	
Aveyron	Rodez	
Haute-Garonne	Toulouse	
Gers	Auch	
Lot	Cahors	
Hautes-Pyrénées	Tarbes	
Tarn	Albi	
Tarn-et-Garonne	Montauban	
Nord-Pas-de-Calais		*12,400*
Calvados	Caen	
Manche	St Lô	
Orne	Alençon	
Pays de la Loire		*32,100*
Loire Atlantique	Nantes	
Maine-et-Loire	Angers	
Mayenne	Laval	
Sarthe	Le Mans	
Vendée	La Roche-sur-Yon	
Picardie		*19,400*
Aisne	Laon	
Oise	Beauvais	
Somme	Amiens	

France, history

5th century BC France, then called Gaul (*Gallia* by the Romans) was invaded by Celtic peoples.

57–51 BC Conquest by the Roman general Julius Caesar.

1st–5th century AD During Roman rule the inhabitants of France accepted Roman civilization and the Latin language. As the empire declined, Germanic tribes overran the country and settled.

481–511 A Frankish chief, Clovis, brought the other tribes under his rule, accepted Christianity, and made Paris the capital.

511–751 Under Clovis' successors, the Merovingians, the country sank into anarchy.

741–68 Unity was restored by Pepin, founder of the Carolingian dynasty.

768–814 Charlemagne made France the center of the Holy Roman empire.

912 The province of Normandy was granted as a duchy to the Viking leader Rollo, whose invading Norsemen had settled there.

987 The first king of the House of Capet assumed the crown. Under Charlemagne's weak successors the great nobles had become semi-independent. The Capets established rule in the district around Paris but were surrounded by vassals stronger than themselves.

11th–13th centuries The power of the Capets was gradually extended, with the support of the church and the townspeople.

1337–1453 In the Hundred Years' War Charles VII expelled the English from France, aided by Joan of Arc.

1483 Burgundy and Brittany were annexed. Through the policies of Louis XI the restoration of the royal power was achieved.

1503–1697 Charles VIII's Italian wars initiated a struggle with Spain for supremacy in W Europe that lasted for two centuries.

1592–98 Protestantism (Huguenot) was adopted by a party of the nobles for political reasons; the result was a succession of civil wars, fought under religious slogans.

1589–1610 Henry IV restored peace, established religious toleration, and made the monarchy absolute.

1634–48 The ministers Richelieu and Mazarin, by their intervention in the Thirty Years' War, secured Alsace and made France the leading power in Europe.

1643–1763 Louis XIV embarked on an aggressive policy that united Europe against him; in his reign began the conflict with Britain that lost France its colonies in Canada and India in the War of the Spanish Succession (1701–14), War of the Austrian Succession (1756–58), and Seven Years' War (1756–63).

1789–99 The French Revolution abolished feudalism and absolute monarchy, but failed to establish democracy.

1799–1815 Napoleon's military dictatorship was aided by foreign wars (1792–1802, 1803–15). The Bourbon monarchy was restored 1814 with Louis XVIII.

1830 Charles X's attempt to substitute absolute for limited monarchy provoked a revolution, which placed his cousin, Louis Philippe, on the throne.

1848 In the Feb revolution Louis Philippe was overthrown and the Second Republic set up.

1852–70 The president of the republic, Louis Napoleon, Napoleon I's nephew, restored the empire 1852, with the title of Napoleon III. His expansionist foreign policy ended in defeat in the Franco-Prussian War and the foundation of the Third Republic.

1863–1946 France colonized Indochina, parts of N Africa, and the S Pacific.

1914 France entered World War I.

1936–38 A radical-Socialist-communist alliance introduced many social reforms.

1939 France entered World War II.

1940 The German invasion allowed the extreme right to set up a puppet dictatorship under Pétain in Vichy, but resistance was maintained by the *maquis* and the Free French under de Gaulle.

1944 Liberation from the Nazis.

For postwar history see ◊France.

France Anatole. Adopted name of Jacques Anatole Thibault 1844–1924. French writer, noted for the wit, urbanity, and style of his works. His earliest novel was *Le Crime de Sylvestre Bonnard/The Crime of Sylvester Bonnard* 1881; later books include the autobiographical series beginning with *Le Livre de mon ami/My Friend's Book* 1885, the satiric *L'Île des pingouins/Penguin Island* 1908, and *Les Dieux ont soif/The Gods Are Athirst* 1912. He was awarded the Nobel Prize for Literature 1921.

France was born in Paris. He published a critical study of Alfred de Vigny 1868, which was followed by several volumes of poetry and short stories. He was elected to the French Academy 1896. His other books include *Thaïs* 1890 and *Crainquebille* 1905. He was a Socialist and supporter of ◊Dreyfus.

Francesca Piero della. See ◊Piero della Francesca, Italian painter.

Franche-Comté region of E France; area 6,253 sq mi/16,200 sq km; population (1987) 1,086,000. Its capital is Besançon, and it includes the *départements* of Doubs, Jura, Haute Saône, and Territoire de Belfort. In the mountainous Jura, there is farming and forestry, and elsewhere there are engineering and plastics industries.

Once independent and ruled by its own count, it was disputed by France, Burgundy, Austria, and Spain from the 9th century until it became a French province under the Treaty of ◊Nijmegen 1678.

franchise in business, the right sold by a manufacturer to a distributor to market the manufacturer's product.

Examples of franchise operations in the US include fast-food restaurants, auto-repair shops, and speciality stores, where the owner/managers have purchased the right to operate a brand-name business using materials supplied by the manufacturer for a percentage of the profits.

Francis or ***François*** two kings of France:

Francis I 1494–1547. King of France from 1515. He succeeded his cousin Louis XII, and from 1519 European politics turned on the rivalry between him and the Holy Roman emperor Charles V, which led to war 1521–29, 1536–38, and 1542–44. In 1525 Francis was defeated and captured at Pavia and released only after signing a humiliating treaty. At home, he developed absolute monarchy.

Francis I *Unstable and vacillating as King of France, he is remembered for the brilliance of the artists and writers of his court.*

Francis II 1544–1560. King of France from 1559 when he succeeded his father, Henry II. He married Mary Queen of Scots 1558. He was completely under the influence of his mother, ◊Catherine de' Medici.

Francis II 1768–1835. Holy Roman emperor 1792–1806. He became Francis I, Emperor of Austria 1804, and abandoned the title of Holy Roman emperor 1806. During his reign Austria was five times involved in war with France, 1792–97, 1798–1801, 1805, 1809, and 1813–14. He succeeded his father Leopold II.

Franciscan order Catholic order of friars, Friars Minor or Grey Friars, founded 1209 by Francis of Assisi. Subdivisions were the strict Observants; the Conventuals, who were allowed to own property corporately; and the ◊Capuchins, founded 1529.

The Franciscan order included such scholars as the English scientist Roger Bacon. A female order, the Poor Clares, was founded by St ◊Clare 1215, and lay people who adopt a Franciscan regime without abandoning the world form a third order, Tertiaries.

Francis Ferdinand English form of ◊Franz Ferdinand, archduke of Austria.

Francis Joseph English form of ◊Franz Joseph, emperor of Austria-Hungary.

Francis of Assisi, St 1182–1226. Italian founder of the Roman Catholic Franciscan order of friars 1209 and, with St Clare, of the Poor Clares 1212. In 1224 he is said to have undergone a mystical experience during which he received the *stigmata* (five wounds of Jesus). Many stories are told of his ability to charm wild animals, and he is the patron saint of ecologists. His feast day is Oct 4.

The son of a wealthy merchant, Francis changed his life after two dreams he had during an illness following spells of military service when he was in his early twenties. He resolved to follow literally the behests of the New Testament and live a life of poverty and service while preaching a simple form of the Christian gospel. In 1219 he went to Egypt to convert the sultan, and lived for a month in his camp. Returning to Italy, he resigned his leadership of the friars.

Francis of Sales, St 1567–1622. French bishop and theologian. He became bishop of Geneva 1602, and in 1610 founded the order of the Visitation, an order of nuns. He is the patron saint of journalists and other writers. Feast day Jan 24.

Francis de Sales was born in Savoy. His writings include *Introduction à la vie dévote/Introduction to a Devout Life* 1609, written to reconcile the Christian life with living in the real world.

francium radioactive metallic element, symbol Fr, atomic number 87, atomic weight 223. It is one of the ◊alkali metals and occurs in nature in small amounts as a decay product of actinium. Its longest-lived isotope, Fr-223, has a half-life of 21 minutes. Francium was discovered and named in 1939 by Marguérite Perey (1909–) to honor her country.

Franck César Auguste 1822–1890. Belgian composer. His music, mainly religious and Romantic in style, includes the Symphony in D minor 1866–68, *Symphonic Variations* 1885 for piano and orchestra, the Violin Sonata 1886, the oratorio *Les Béatitudes/The Beatitudes* 1879, and many organ pieces.

Franck James 1882–1964. US physicist influential in atom technology. He was awarded a Nobel Prize 1925 for his experiments of 1914 on the energy transferred by colliding electrons to mercury atoms, showing that the transfer was governed by the rules of ◊quantum theory.

Born and educated in Germany, he emigrated to the US after publicly protesting against Hitler's racial policies. Franck participated in the wartime atomic-bomb project at Los Alamos but organized the "Franck petition" 1945, which argued that the bomb should not be used against Japanese cities. After World War II he turned his research to photosynthesis.

Franco Francisco (Paulino Hermenegildo Teódulo Bahamonde) 1892–1975. Spanish dictator from 1939. As a general, he led the insurgent Nationalists to victory in the Spanish ◊Civil War 1936–39, supported by Fascist Italy and Nazi Germany, and established a dictatorship. In 1942 Franco reinstated the Cortes (Spanish parliament), which in 1947 passed an act by which he became head of state for life.

Franco was born in Galicia, NW Spain. He entered the army 1910, served in Morocco 1920–26, and was appointed chief of staff 1935, but demoted to governor of the Canary Islands 1936. Dismissed from this post by the Popular Front (Republican) government, he plotted an uprising with German and Italian assistance, and on the outbreak of the Civil War organized the invasion of Spain by N African troops and foreign legionaries. After the death of Gen Sanjurjo, he took command of the Nationalists, proclaiming himself *Caudillo* (leader) of Spain. The defeat of the Republic with the surrender of Madrid 1939 brought all Spain under his government. On the outbreak of World War II, in spite of Spain's official attitude of "strictest neutrality," his pro-Axis sympathies led him to send aid, later withdrawn, to the German side.

At home, he curbed the growing power of the ◊Falange (the fascist party), and in later years slightly liberalized his regime. In 1969 he nominated ◊Juan Carlos as his successor and future king of Spain. He relinquished the premiership 1973, but remained head of state until his death.

Franco-German entente resumption of friendly relations between France and Germany, designed to erase the enmities of successive wars. It was initiated by the French president de Gaulle's visit to West Germany 1962, followed by the Franco-German Treaty of Friendship and Co-operation 1963.

François French form of ◊Francis, two kings of France.

Franco-Prussian War 1870–71. The Prussian chancellor Bismarck put forward a German candidate for the vacant Spanish throne with the deliberate, and successful, intention of provoking the French emperor Napoleon III into declaring war. The Prussians defeated the French at ◊Sedan, then besieged Paris. The Treaty of Frankfurt May 1871 gave Alsace, Lorraine, and a large French indemnity to Prussia. The war established Prussia, at the head of a newly established German empire, as Europe's leading power.

frangipani any tropical American tree of the genus *Plumeria*, especially *P. rubra*, of the dogbane family Apocynaceae. Perfume is made from the strongly scented flowers.

Franglais French language mixed with (usually unwelcome) elements of modern, especially American, English. *Le weekend, le drugstore*, and other such mixtures have prompted moves within France to limit the growth of Franglais and protect the integrity of Standard French.

Frank a member of a group of Germanic peoples prominent in Europe in the 3rd to 9th centuries. Believed to have originated in Pomerania on the Black Sea, they had settled on the Rhine by the 3rd century, spread into the Roman Empire by the 4th century, and gradually conquered most of Gaul, Italy, and Germany under the ◊Merovingian and ◊Carolingian dynasties. The kingdom of the W Franks became France; the kingdom of the E Franks became Germany.

The Salian (western) Franks conquered Roman Gaul during the 4th and 5th centuries. Their ruler, Clovis, united the Salians with the Ripuarian (eastern) Franks, and they were converted to Christianity. The agriculture of the Merovingian dynasty (named after Clovis's grandfather, Merovech) was more advanced than that of the Romans, and they introduced the three-field system (see ◊field). The Merovingians conquered most of western and central Europe, and lasted until the 8th century when the Carolingian dynasty was founded under Charlemagne. The kingdom of the W Franks was fused by the 9th century into a single people with the Gallo-Romans, speaking the modified form of Latin that became modern French.

Frank Anne 1929–1945. German diarist who fled to the Netherlands with her family 1933 to escape Nazi persecution. During the German occupation of Amsterdam, they and two other families remained in a sealed-off room, protected by Dutch sympathizers 1942–44, when betrayal resulted in their deportation and Anne's death in Belsen concentration camp. Her diary of her time in hiding was published 1947 and has been made into a play and a film publicizing the plight of millions (see ◊Holocaust).

Previously suppressed portions of her diary were published 1989. The house in which the family took refuge is preserved as a museum. Her diary sold 20 million copies in more than 50 languages.

Frank Ilya 1908– . Russian physicist known for his work on radiation. In 1934 ◊Cherenkov had noted a peculiar blue radiation sometimes emitted as electrons passed through water. It was left to Frank and his colleague at Moscow University, Igor Tamm (1895–1971), to realize that this form of radiation was produced by charged particles traveling faster through the medium than the speed of light in the same medium. Frank shared the 1958 Nobel Prize for Physics with Cherenkov and Tamm.

Frankenstein or ***The Modern Prometheus*** a Gothic horror story by Mary Shelley, published in England 1818. Frankenstein, a scientist, discovers how to bring inanimate matter to life, and creates a man-monster. When Frankenstein fails to provide a mate to satisfy the creature's human emotions, it seeks revenge by killing Frankenstein's brother and bride. Frankenstein dies in an attempt to destroy his creation.

Frankenthaler Helen 1928– . US Abstract Expressionist painter, inventor of the color-staining technique whereby the unprimed, absorbent canvas is stained or soaked with thinned-out paint, creating deep, soft veils of translucent color.

Frankfort capital of Kentucky, located in the N central part of the state, on the Kentucky River, E of Louisville. Industries include bourbon, electronic equipment, furniture, footwear; population (1990) 25,968. Frankfort became the capital of Kentucky 1786.

Frankfurt-am-Main city in Hessen, Federal Republic of Germany, 45 mi/72 km NE of Mannheim; population (1988) 592,000. It is a commercial and banking center, with electrical and machine industries, and an inland port on the river Main. An international book fair is held annually.

Frankfurt was a free imperial city from 1372 to 1806, when it was incorporated into ◊Prussia. It is the birthplace of the poet Goethe. It was the headquarters of the US zone of occupation in World War II and of the Anglo-US zone 1947–49.

Frankfurt-an-der-Oder industrial city in the state of Brandenburg, Federal Republic of Germany, 50 mi/80 km SE of Berlin; population (1990) 87,000. Former capital of the East German district of Frankfurt 1952–90. It is linked by the river Oder and its canals to the rivers Vistula and Elbe. Industries include semiconductors, chemicals, engineering, paper, and leather.

Frankfurter Felix 1882–1965. Austrian-born US jurist and Supreme Court justice. After law school he served as assistant to the US attorney for the southern district of New York and joined the faculty of Harvard Law School 1914. As a supporter of liberal causes, Frankfurter was one of the founders of the American Civil Liberties Union 1920. Appointed to the US Supreme Court 1939 by F D Roosevelt, he remained liberal yet opposed the use of the judicial veto to advance political ends. Frankfurter received the Presidential Medal of Freedom 1963.

Born in Vienna, Frankfurter immigrated with his family to the US 1894, attended the City College of New York, and received a law degree from Harvard 1906.

Frankfurt Parliament an assembly of liberal politicians and intellectuals that met for a few months in 1848 in the aftermath of the ◊revolutions of 1848 and the overthrow of monarchies in most of the German states. They discussed a constitution for a united Germany, but the restoration of the old order and the suppression of the revolutions ended the parliament.

Frankfurt School the members of the Institute of Social Research, set up at Frankfurt University, Germany, 1923 as the first Marxist research center. With the rise of Hitler, many of its members went to the US and set up the institute at Columbia University, New York. In 1969 the institute was dissolved.

In the 1930s, under its second director Max Horkheimer, a group that included Erich Fromm, Herbert Marcuse, and T W Adorno attempted to update Marxism and create a coherent and viable social theory. Drawing on a variety of disciplines as well as the writings of Marx and Freud, they produced works such as *Authority and the Family* 1936 and developed a Marxist perspective known as critical theory. After World War II the institute returned to Frankfurt, although Marcuse and some others remained in the US. The German and US branches diverged in the 1950s, and the

Franklin *The brilliant and versatile statesman of the young American republic, Benjamin Franklin, is portrayed here, after Joseph Siffred Duplessis 1783, National Portrait Gallery, London.*

institute was dissolved after Adorno's death, although Jurgen Habermas and others have since attempted to revive its theory and research program.

frankincense resin of various African and Asian trees of the genus *Boswellia*, family Burseraceae, burned as incense. Costly in ancient times, it is traditionally believed to be one of the three gifts brought by the Magi to the infant Jesus.

Franklin a district of ◊Northwest Territories, Canada; area 549,250 sq mi/1,422,550 sq km.

Franklin Benjamin 1706–1790. American printer, publisher, author, scientist, and statesman. He proved that lightning is a form of electricity, distinguished between positive and negative electricity, and invented the lightning conductor. He helped to draft the ◊Declaration of Independence and the US ◊Constitution, was the first US ambassador to France 1776–85, and negotiated peace with Britain 1783. Franklin was one of the most well-traveled of the colonial leaders, and he brought an internationalist perspective to the ◊Constitutional Convention.

Born in Boston, he moved to Philadelphia as a young man and combined a successful printing business with scientific experimentation and inventions; he authored and published the popular *Poor Richard's Almanac* 1733–58. A member of the Pennsylvania Assembly 1751–64, he was sent to Britain to lobby Parliament about tax grievances and achieved the repeal of the ◊Stamp Act; on his return to the US he was prominent in the deliberations leading to independence. As ambassador in Paris, he enlisted French help for the ◊American Revolution. As a delegate to the Continental Congress from Pennsylvania 1785–88, he helped draw up the US Constitution. He organized an effective postal system; taught himself Spanish, French, Italian, and Latin; and created a discussion group 1743 that would become the American Philosophical Society. His autobiography first appeared 1781 (in complete form, 1868).

Franklin John 1786–1847. English naval explorer who took part in expeditions to Australia, the Arctic, and N Canada, and in 1845 commanded an expedition to look for the ◊Northwest Passage from the Atlantic to the Pacific, during which he and his crew perished.

The 1845 expedition had virtually found the Passage when it became trapped in the ice. No trace of the team was discovered until 1859. In 1984, two of its members, buried on King Edward Island, were found to be perfectly preserved in the frozen ground of their graves.

Franz Ferdinand or ***Francis Ferdinand*** 1863–1914. Archduke of Austria. He became heir to his uncle, Emperor Franz Joseph, in 1884 but while visiting Sarajevo June 28, 1914, he and his wife were assassinated by Serbian nationalists. Austria used the episode to make unreasonable demands on Serbia that ultimately precipitated World War I.

Franz Josef Land (Russian *Zemlya Frantsa Iosifa*) archipelago of over 85 islands in the Arctic Ocean, E of Spitsbergen and NW of Novaya Zemlya, USSR. Area 8,000 sq mi/20,720 sq km. There are scientific stations.

Franz Joseph or ***Francis Joseph*** 1830–1916. Emperor of Austria-Hungary from 1848, when his uncle, Ferdinand I, abdicated. After the suppression of the 1848 revolution, Franz Joseph tried to establish an absolute monarchy but had to grant Austria a parliamentary constitution 1861 and Hungary equality with Austria 1867. He was defeated in the Italian War 1859 and the Prussian War 1866. In 1914 he made the assassination of his heir and nephew, Franz Ferdinand, the excuse for attacking Serbia, precipitating World War I.

Frasch process process used to extract underground deposits of sulphur. Superheated steam is piped to the sulphur deposit and melts it. Compressed air is then pumped down to force the molten sulphur to the surface. It was developed

***Franz Joseph** Emperor of the Austro-Hungarian empire 1848–1916.*

in the USA 1981 by German-born Herman Frasch (1851–1914).

Fraser river in British Columbia It rises in the Yellowhead Pass of the Rockies and flows NW, then S, then W to the Strait of Georgia. It is 850 mi/1,370 km long and rich in salmon.

Fraser Antonia 1932– . English author of biographies, including *Mary Queen of Scots* 1969; historical works, such as *The Weaker Vessel* 1984; and a series of detective novels featuring investigator Jemima Shore.

She is married to the playwright Harold Pinter, and is the daughter of Lord Longford.

Fraser Dawn 1937– . Australian swimmer. The only person to win the same swimming event at three consecutive Olympic Games: 100 meters freestyle in 1956, 1960, and 1964. The holder of 27 world records, she was the first woman to break the one-minute barrier for the 100 meters.

Fraser Peter 1884–1950. New Zealand Labor politician, born in Scotland. He held various cabinet posts 1935–40, and was prime minister 1940–49.

Fraser Simon 1776–1862. Canadian explorer and surveyor for the Hudson Bay Company who crossed the Rockies and traveled most of the way down the river that bears his name 1805–07.

fraternity and sorority student societies (fraternity for men; sorority for women) in some US and Canadian universities and colleges. Although mainly social and residential, some are purely honorary, membership being on the basis of scholastic distinction; for example, Phi Beta Kappa, earliest of the fraternities, was founded at the College of William and Mary, Virginia in 1776.

Usually named with Greek letters, they are nominally secret, with badge, dues, passwords, motto, and initiation rites. They have a central governing body and a "chapter" at participating colleges.

fraud in law, an act of deception resulting in injury to another. To establish fraud it has to be demonstrated that (1) a false representation (for example, a factually untrue statement) has been made, with the intention that it should be acted upon; (2) the person making the representation knows it is false or does not attempt to find out whether it is true or not; and (3) the person to whom the representation is made acts upon it to his or her detriment.

A contract based on fraud can be declared void, and the injured party can sue for damages.

Fraunhofer Joseph von 1787–1826. German physicist who did important work in optics. The dark lines in the solar spectrum (Fraunhofer lines), which reveal the chemical composition of the Sun's atmosphere, were accurately mapped by him.

Born in Bavaria, he was apprenticed to a glass cutter, and in 1807 founded an optical institute.

Fray Bentos river port in Uruguay; population (1985) 20,000. Linked by a bridge over the Uruguay with Puerto Unzué in Argentina (1976), it is famous for its meatpacking industry, particularly corned beef.

Frazer James George 1854–1941. Scottish anthropologist, author of *The Golden Bough* 1890, a pioneer study of the origins of religion and sociology on a comparative basis. It exerted considerable influence on writers such as T S Eliot and D H Lawrence, but by the standards of modern anthropology, many of its methods and findings are unsound.

Frederick V known as *the Winter King* 1596–1632. Elector palatine of the Rhine 1610–23 and king of Bohemia 1619–20 (for one winter, hence the name), having been chosen by the Protestant Bohemians as ruler after the deposition of Catholic emperor ◊Ferdinand II. His selection was the cause of the Thirty Years" War. Frederick was defeated at the Battle of the White Mountain, near Prague, in Nov 1620, by the army of the Catholic League and fled to Holland.

Frederick IX 1899–1972. King of Denmark from 1947. He was succeeded by his daughter who became Queen ◊Margrethe II.

Frederick two Holy Roman emperors:

Frederick I Barbarossa ("red-beard") c. 1123–1190. Holy Roman emperor from 1152. Originally duke of Swabia, he was elected emperor 1152, and was engaged in a struggle with Pope Alexander III 1159–77, which ended in his submission; the Lombard cities, headed by Milan, took advantage of this to establish their independence of imperial control. Frederick joined the Third Crusade, and was drowned in Anatolia.

Frederick II 1194–1250. Holy Roman emperor from 1212, called "the Wonder of the World." He led a crusade 1228–29 that recovered Jerusalem by treaty, without fighting. He quarrelled with the pope, who excommunicated him three times, and a feud began that lasted at intervals until the end of his reign. Frederick, who was a religious

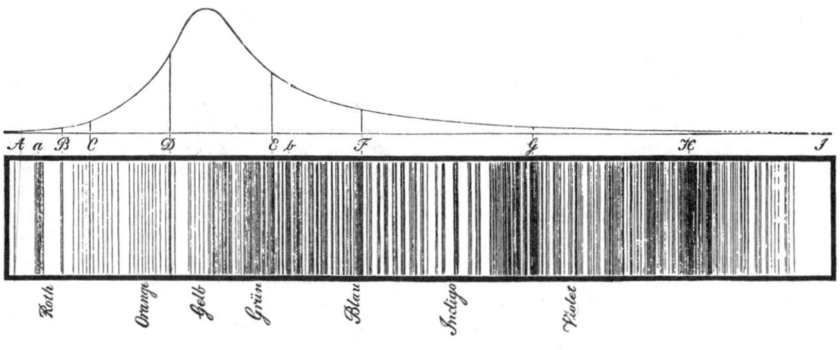

A a B C D E b F G H I
Roth
Orange
Gelb
Grün
Blau
Indigo
Violet

***Fraunhofer** Drawing of the dark lines of the solar spectrum by the German physicist Joseph von Fraunhofer, the first accurately to map the chemical composition of the Sun's atmosphere. The curve shows the intensity of sunlight in different parts of the spectrum.*

skeptic, is often considered the most cultured man of his age. He was the son of Henry VI.

Frederick three kings of Prussia:

Frederick I 1657–1713. King of Prussia from 1701. He became elector of Brandenburg 1688.

Frederick II *the Great* 1712–1786. King of Prussia from 1740, when he succeeded his father Frederick William I. In that year he started the War of the ◊Austrian Succession by his attack on Austria. In the peace of 1745 he secured Silesia. The struggle was renewed in the ◊Seven Years' War 1756–63. He acquired West Prussia in the first partition of Poland 1772 and left Prussia as Germany's foremost state. He was an efficient and just ruler in the spirit of the Enlightenment and a patron of the arts.

In his domestic policy he encouraged industry and agriculture, reformed the judicial system, fostered education, and established religious toleration. He corresponded with the French writer Voltaire, and was a talented musician.

Frederick III 1831–1888. King of Prussia and emperor of Germany 1888. The son of Wilhelm I, he married the eldest daughter (Victoria) of Queen Victoria of the UK 1858 and, as a liberal, frequently opposed Chancellor Bismarck. He died three months after his accession.

Frederick William 1620–1688. Elector of Brandenburg from 1640, "the Great Elector." By successful wars against Sweden and Poland, he prepared the way for Prussian power in the 18th century.

Frederick William 1882–1951. Last crown prince of Germany, eldest son of Wilhelm II. During World War I he commanded a group of armies on the western front. In 1918, he retired into private life.

Frederick William four kings of Prussia:

Frederick William I 1688–1740. King of Prussia from 1713, who developed Prussia's military might and commerce.

Frederick William II 1744–1797. King of Prussia from 1786. He was a nephew of Frederick II but had little of his relative's military skill. He was unsuccessful in waging war on the French 1792–95 and lost all Prussia west of the Rhine.

Frederick William III 1770–1840. King of Prussia from 1797. He was defeated by Napoleon 1806, but contributed to his final overthrow 1813–15 and profited by being allotted territory at the Congress of Vienna.

Frederick William IV 1795–1861. King of Prussia from 1840. He upheld the principle of the ◊divine right of kings, but was forced to grant a constitution 1850 after the Prussian revolution 1848. He suffered two strokes 1857 and became mentally debilitated. His brother William (later emperor) took over his duties.

Fredericton capital of New Brunswick, Canada, on the St John River; population (1986) 44,000. It was known as St Anne's Point until 1785 when it was named after Prince Frederick, second son of George III.

Fredrikstad Norwegian port at the mouth of the river Glomma, dating from 1570; population (1987) 26,650. It is a center of the timber trade and has shipyards.

Freedom, Presidential Medal of the highest peacetime civilian honor in the US. Instituted by President Kennedy 1963, it is awarded to those "who contribute significantly to the quality of American life." A list of recipients is published each Independence Day and often includes unknown individuals as well as artists, performers, and politicians.

It replaced the Medal of Freedom, instituted 1945, which had been conferred 24 times on an irregular basis.

free enterprise or ***free market*** an economic system where private capital is used in business with profits going to private companies and individuals. The term has much the same meaning as ◊capitalism.

free fall the state in which a body is falling freely under the influence of ◊gravity, as in free-fall parachuting. The term weightless is normally used to describe a body in free fall in space.

In orbit, astronauts and spacecraft are still held by gravity and are in fact falling toward the Earth. Because of their speed (orbital velocity), the amount they fall toward the Earth just equals the amount the Earth's surface curves away; in effect they remain at the same height, apparently weightless.

free-falling another name for ◊***sky diving***.

Free French in World War II, movement formed by General Charles ◊de Gaulle in the UK June 1940, consisting of French soldiers who continued to fight against the Axis after the Franco-German armistice. They took the name ***Fighting France*** 1942 and served in many campaigns, among them General Leclerc's advance from Chad to Tripolitania 1942, the Syrian campaigns 1941, the campaigns in the Western Desert, the Italian campaign, the liberation of France, and the invasion of Germany. Their emblem was the Cross of Lorraine, a cross with two bars.

freeman one who enjoys the freedom of a borough. Since the early Middle Ages, a freeman has been allowed to carry out his craft or trade within the jurisdiction of the borough and to participate in municipal government, but since the development of modern local government, such privileges have become largely honorary.

There have generally been four ways of becoming a freeman: by apprenticeship to an existing freeman; by patrimony, or being the son of a freeman; by redemption, that is, buying the privilege; or, by gift from the borough, the usual method today, when the privilege is granted in recognition of some achievement, benefaction, or special status on the part of the recipient.

Freemasonry the beliefs and practices of a group of linked national organizations open to men over the age of 21, united by a common code of morals and certain traditional "secrets." Modern Freemasonry began in 18th-century Europe. Freemasons do much charitable work, but have been criticized in recent years for their secrecy, their male exclusivity, and particularly their alleged use of influence within and between organizations (for example, the police or local government) to further each other's interests. There are approximately 6 million members.

beliefs Freemasons believe in God, whom they call the "Great Architect of the Universe."

history Freemasonry is descended from a medieval guild of itinerant masons, which existed in the 14th century and by the 16th was admitting men unconnected with the building trade. The term "freemason" may have meant a full member of the guild or one working in free-stone, that is, a mason of the highest class.

The present order of Free and Accepted Masons originated with the formation in London of the first Grand Lodge, or governing body, in 1717, and during the 18th century spread from Britain to the US, continental Europe, and elsewhere. In France and other European countries, freemasonry assumed a political and anticlerical character; it has been condemned by the papacy, and in some countries was suppressed by the state.

free port a port or sometimes a zone within a port, where cargo may be accepted for handling, processing, and reshipment without the imposition of tariffs or taxes. Duties and tax become payable only if the products are for consumption in the country to which the free port belongs.

Free ports are established to take advantage of a location with good trade links. They facilitate the quick entry and departure of ships, unhampered by lengthy customs regulations. Important free ports include Singapore, Copenhagen, New York, Gdańsk, Macao, San Francisco, and Seattle.

free radical in chemistry, an atom or molecule that has an unpaired electron and is highly reactive.

Free radicals are often produced by high temperatures and are found in flames and explosions. A very simple free radical is the methyl radical CH_3 produced by the splitting of the covalent carbon-to-carbon bond in ethane: $CH_3CH_3 = 2CH_3$. Most free radicals are very short-lived. If free radicals are produced in living organisms they can be very damaging.

freesia any plant of the South African genus *Freesia* of the iris family Iridaceae, commercially grown for their scented, funnel-shaped flowers.

free thought post-Reformation movement opposed to Christian dogma.

It included the American and British deists of the 17th and 18th centuries, the French *philosophes* of the 18th century, and such skeptics as the 19th-century American writer and orator Robert Ingersoll and the 20th-century British philosopher Bertrand Russell.

Freetown capital of Sierra Leone, W Africa; population (1988) 470,000. It has a naval station and a harbor. Industries include cement, plastics, footwear, and oil refining. Platinum, chromite, diamonds, and gold are traded. It was founded as a settlement for freed slaves in the 1790s.

free trade an economic system in which governments do not interfere in the prices or movement of goods between countries; there are thus no restrictive taxes on imports. In the modern economy, free trade tends to hold within economic groups, such as the European Community (EC), but not generally, despite such treaties as GATT (1948) and subsequent agreements to reduce tariffs. The opposite of free trade is ◊protectionism.

The case for free trade, first put forward in the 17th century, received its classic statement in Adam Smith's *Wealth of Nations* 1776. According to traditional economic theory, free trade allows nations to specialize in those commodities that can be produced most efficiently. The Ottawa Agreements 1932 marked the end of free trade until in 1948 GATT came into operation. A series of drastic international tariff reductions was agreed in the Kennedy Round Conference 1964–67, and the Tokyo Round 1974–79 gave substantial incentives to developing countries.

The 1980s recession, prompted by increased world oil prices and unemployment, swung the pendulum back toward protectionism, which discourages foreign imports by heavy duties, thus protecting home products.

Economists generally favor a system closer to free trade than now exists but recognize that developing countries might need some protection in establishing new industries and that there are health and national security reasons for some controls on trade. Among the damaging impediments to free trade, economists would cite ◊dumping of products at an unrealistically low price, subsidy by governments of export-related industries, overly strict environmental standards for imported products, and other subtle restrictions in addition to tariffs and quotas. It is feared that the EC will erect barriers against external competition after it eliminates trade restrictions within the EC in 1992.

free verse poetry without metrical form. At the beginning of the 20th century, under the very different influences of Whitman and Mallarmé, many poets believed that the 19th century had accomplished most of what could be done with regular meter, and rejected it, in much the same spirit as Milton had rejected rhyme, preferring irregular meters that made it possible to express thought clearly and without distortion.

This was true of T S ◊Eliot and the Imagists; it was also true of poets who, like the Russians Esenin and Mayakovsky, placed emphasis on public performance.

Poets including Robert Graves and Auden have criticized free verse on the ground that it lacks the difficulty of true accomplishment, but their own metrics would have been considered loose by earlier critics. The freeness of free verse is largely relative.

free will the doctrine that human beings are free to control their own actions, and that these actions are not fixed in advance by God or fate. Some Jewish and Christian theologians assert that God gave humanity free will to choose between good and evil; others that God has decided in advance the outcome of all human choices (◊predestination), as in Calvinism.

freeze-drying method of preserving food; see ◊food technology. The product to be dried is frozen and then put in a vacuum chamber that forces out the ice as water vapor, a process known as sublimation.

Many of the substances that give products such as coffee their typical flavor are volatile, and would be lost in a normal drying process because they would evaporate along with the water. In the freeze-drying process these volatile compounds do not pass into the ice that is to be sublimed, and are therefore largely retained.

freezing change from liquid to solid state, as when water becomes ice. For a given substance, freezing occurs at a definite temperature, known as the freezing point, that is invariable under similar conditions of pressure, and the temperature remains at this point until all the liquid is frozen. The amount of heat per unit mass that has to be removed to freeze a substance is a constant for any given substance, and is known as the latent heat of fusion.

Ice is less dense than water since water expands just before its freezing point is reached. If pressure is applied, expansion is retarded and the freezing point will be lowered. The presence of dissolved substances in a liquid also lowers the freezing point (depression of freezing point), the amount of lowering being proportional to the molecular concentration of the solution. Antifreeze mixtures for car radiators and the use of salt to melt ice on roads are common applications of this principle.

Animals in arctic conditions, for example insects or fish, cope with the extreme cold either by manufacturing natural "antifreeze" and staying active, or by allowing themselves to freeze in a controlled fashion; that is, they manufacture proteins to act as nuclei for the formation of ice crystals in areas that will not produce cellular damage, and so enable themselves to thaw back to life again.

freezing-point depression lowering of a solution's freezing point below that of the pure solvent; it depends on the number of molecules of solute dissolved in it. Thus for a single solvent, such as pure water, all substances in the same molecular concentration produce the same lowering of freezing point. The depression d for a molar concentration C is given by the equation $d = KC$, where K is a constant for the particular solvent (called the cryoscopic constant). Measurement of freezing-point depression is a useful method of determining molecular weights of solutes.

Frege Friedrich Ludwig Gottlob 1848–1925. German philosopher, the founder of modern mathematical logic. He created symbols for concepts like "or" and "if ... then," which are now in standard use in mathematics. His *Die Grundlagen der Arithmetik/The Foundations of Arithmetic* 1884 influenced Bertrand ◊Russell and ◊Wittgenstein.

Freiburg-im-Breisgau industrial city in Baden-Württemberg, Federal Republic of Germany; population (1988) 186,000. Pharmaceuticals and precision instruments are the most important industries. The city is the seat of a university and has a 12th-century cathedral.

Frelimo (acronym for Front for the Liberation of Mozambique) nationalist group aimed at gaining independence for Mozambique from the occupying Portuguese. It began operating from S Tanzania 1963 and continued until victory 1975.

Fremantle chief port of Western Australia, at the mouth of the Swan river, SW of ◊Perth; population (1981) 23,780. It has shipbuilding yards, lumber mills, and iron foundries and exports wheat, fruit, wool, and timber. It was founded as a penal settlement 1829.

Frémont John Charles (1813–1890) US soldier and politician who explored much of the Far West, was influential in the U.S. acquisition of California, and ultimately saw his military career overshadowed by his political ambitions.

Born in Savannah, Georgia, he became a US Army engineer and led three exploration expeditions in the West that brought him fame. He also gained political influence through his marriage to Sen. Thomas Hart Benton's daughter. Frémont came into conflict with General Kearney in California, which led to a court martial, and he resigned from the army. After a brief term representing California in the US Senate and an expedition to chart a southern railroad route, he was the Republican Party's first presidential candidate (1856), losing to Buchanan. In the Civil War, he had disagreements with Lincoln and then resigned rather than serve under Gen. John Pope. His post-war career was disappointing; railroad endeavors failed, and he was relegated to being territorial governor of Arizona (1878–83).

French native to or an inhabitant of France, as well as their descendents, culture, or primary language, which is one of the Romance languages. There are also some sociolinguistic minorities within France who speak Catalan, Breton, Flemish, German, Corsican, or Basque.

French is also spoken in the former colonies, such as in Africa and Québec, Canada, and in overseas territories such as Martinique and French Guiana.

French Daniel Chester 1850–1931. US sculptor. Trained in anatomy and sculpture in private studios in Boston, New York, and Europe, he was by far the most noted American sculptor of public monuments in the late 19th century. Among his most famous works are *The Minuteman* 1873 in Concord, Massachusetts; John Harvard 1884 at Harvard College; *Alma Mater* 1912 at Columbia University; and the imposing seated *Abraham Lincoln* 1922 in the Lincoln Memorial in Washington, DC.

Born in Exeter, New Hampshire, French briefly attended the Massachusetts Institute of Technology (MIT) before embarking on an artistic career.

French Antarctica French Southern and Antarctic Territories; territory created 1955; area 3,900 sq mi/10,100 sq km; population about 200 research scientists. It includes Adélie Land on the Antarctic continent, the Kerguelen and Crozet archipelagos, and St Paul and Nouvelle Amsterdam islands in the southern seas. It is administered from Paris, but Port-aux-Français on Kerguelen is the chief center, with several research stations. There are also research stations on Nouvelle Amsterdam and in Adélie Land and a meteorological station on Possession Island in the Crozet archipelago. St Paul is uninhabited. In 1988 French workers, who were illegally building an airstrip, thus violating a United Nations treaty on Antarctica, attacked ◊Greenpeace workers.

French art painting and sculpture of France. A number of influential styles have emerged in France over the centuries, from Gothic in the Middle Ages to Impressionism, Cubism, Surrealism, and others.

11th–14th centuries The main forms of artistic expression were manuscript painting, architecture, and sculpture. France played the leading role in creating the Gothic style.

15th century The miniatures of Jean Fouquet and the *Très riches heures* (a prayer book) of the Limbourg brothers, manuscript illuminators, show remarkable naturalism.

16th century Artists were influenced by the Italians, but the miniature tradition was kept up by the court painters such as Jean Clouet.

17th century Landscape painting became increasingly popular. Two exceptional artists in the genre were Poussin and Claude Lorrain.

18th century French painting and sculpture became dominant throughout Europe. Popular Rococo painters were Watteau, Fragonard, and Boucher. The still lifes of Chardin show Dutch influence. The Neoclassical French school was founded by David.

early-19th century Ingres was the most widely admired painter. Delacroix was the leader of the Romantic movement. Géricault exceled as a history and animal painter.

mid-19th century Courbet and Manet were the great rebels in art, breaking with age-old conventions. The Barbizon school of landscape painting was followed by the Impressionists: Monet, Renoir, Degas, and others.

late-19th century The Pointillist Seurat took the Impressionists' ideas further. The individual styles of Cézanne and Gauguin helped prepare the way for Modernism. Rodin's powerful, realistic sculptures had great influence.

1900s Fauvism, showing the influence of Gauguin with his emphasis on pure color, was introduced by Matisse and others. Cubism, deriving from Cézanne, was begun by Picasso and Braque.

1920s Paris was a center of the Surrealist movement.

1930s Abstraction-création movement started in Paris to develop a form of abstract art constructed from nonfigurative, usually geometrical elements.

1945–1990 After World War II the center of the art world shifted from France to the US.

French Canadian literature F-X Garneau's *Histoire du Canada* (1845–48) inspired a school of patriotic verse led by Octave Crémazie (1827–79) and continued by Louis Fréchette (1838–1908). A new movement began after 1900 with such poets as André Lozeau (1878–1924), Paul Morin, Robert Choquette (1862–1941), Alain Grandbois, St Denys Garneau, Eloi de Grandmont, and Pierre Trottier. Fiction reached a high point with Louis Hémon (1880–1914) whose *Maria Chapdelaine* inspired many genre works. Outstanding later novelists are Germaine Guèvremont, Gabrielle Roy, "Ringuet" (Philippe Panneton), Robert Elie, Roger Lemelin, and Yves Thériault.

French Community former association consisting of France and those overseas territories joined with it by the constitution of the Fifth Republic, following the 1958 referendum. Many of the constituent states withdrew during the 1960s, and it no longer formally exists, but in practice all former French colonies have close economic and cultural as well as linguistic links with France.

French Fourth Republic see ◊Fourth Republic.

French Guiana (French *Guyane Française*) French overseas *département* from 1946, and administrative region from 1974, on the N coast of South America, bounded to the W by Suriname and to the E and S by Brazil

area 32,230 sq mi/83,500 sq km

capital Cayenne

towns St Laurent

features Eurospace rocket launch pad at Kourou; Îles du Salut, which include ◊Devil's Island

products timber, shrimp, gold

population (1987) 89,000

language 90% Creole, French, Amerindian

famous people Alfred ◊Dreyfus

history first settled by France 1604, the territory became a French possession 1817; penal colonies, including Devil's Island, were established from 1852; by 1945, the shipments of convicts from France ceased.

French horn musical ◊brass instrument

French India former French possessions in India: Pondicherry, Chandernagore, Karikal, Mahé, and Yanam (Yanaon). They were all transferred to India by 1954.

French language member of the Romance branch of the Indo-European language family, spoken in France, Belgium, Luxembourg, Monaco, and

French Guiana

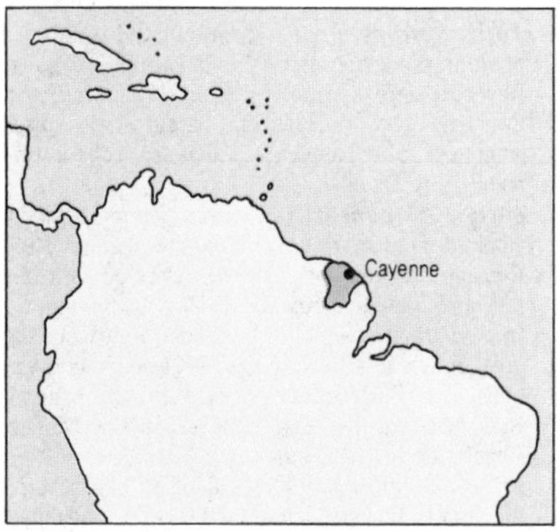
Cayenne

Switzerland in Europe; also in Canada (especially the province of Québec) in North America, and various Caribbean and Pacific Islands (overseas territories such as Martinique and French Guiana), as well as certain N and W African countries (for example, Mali and Senegal).

French developed from the medieval Latin dialect spoken in Gaul and was established as a distinct language by the 9th century. Varieties used north of the river Loire formed the *Langue d'oil* (*oui*) while those to the south formed the *Langue d'oc*, according to their word for "yes." By the 13th century the dialect of the Île de France was supreme and became the official medium of the courts and administration of France 1539. Its literary form still serves as the basis of *le bon français* ("correct French"), which is officially protected by the Academie Française (founded 1635 at the behest of Cardinal Richelieu) and by occasional legislation in both France and Québec.

French literature

The Middle Ages The *Chanson de Roland* (c. 1080) is one of the greatest of the early *chansons de geste* (epic poems about deeds of chivalry), which were superseded by the Arthurian romances (seen at their finest in the work of Chrétien de Troyes in the 12th century), and by the Classical themes of Alexander, Troy, and Thebes. Other aspects of French medieval literature are represented by the anonymous *Aucassin et Nicolette* of the early 13th century; the allegorical *Roman de la Rose/Romance of the Rose*, the first part of which was written by Guillaume de Lorris (c. 1230) and the second by Jean de Meung (c. 1275); and the satiric *Roman de Renart/Story of Renard* of the late 12th century. The period also produced the historians Villehardouin, Joinville, Froissart, and Comines, and the first great French poet, François Villon.

Renaissance to the 18th century One of the most celebrated poets of the Renaissance was Ronsard, leader of the ◊Pléiade (a group of seven writers); others included Marot at the beginning of the 16th century and Régnier at its close. In prose the period produced the broad genius of Rabelais and the essayist Montaigne. In the 17th century came the triumph of form with the great Classical dramatists Corneille, Racine, and Molière, the graceful brilliance of La Fontaine, and the poet and critic Boileau. Masters of prose in the same period include the philosophers Pascal and Descartes; the preacher Bossuet; the critics La Bruyère, Fénelon, and Malebranche; and La Rochefoucauld, Cardinal de Retz, Mme de Sévigné, and Le Sage.

The 18th century was the age of the ◊Enlightenment and an era of prose, with Montesquieu, Voltaire, and Rousseau; the scientist Buffon; the *Encyclopedist* Diderot; the ethical writer Vauvenargues; the novelists Prévost and Marivaux; and the memoir writer Saint-Simon.

19th and 20th centuries In the 19th century poetry came to the fore again with the Romantics Lamartine, Hugo, Vigny, Musset, Leconte de Lisle, and Gautier; novelists of the same school were George Sand, Stendhal, and Dumas *père*, while criticism is represented by Sainte-Beuve, and history by Thiers, Michelet, and Taine. The realist novelist Balzac was followed by the school of Naturalism, whose representatives were Flaubert, Zola, the Goncourt brothers, Alphonse Daudet, Maupassant, and Huysmans. Nineteenth-century dramatists include Hugo, Musset, and Dumas *fils*. Symbolism, a movement of experimentation and revolt against Classical verse and materialist attitudes, with the philosopher Bergson as one of its main exponents, found its first expression in the work of Gérard de Nerval, followed by Baudelaire, Verlaine, Mallarmé, Rimbaud, Corbière, and the prose writer Villiers de l'Isle Adam; later writers in the same tradition were Henri de Régnier and Laforgue.

In the late-19th and early-20th centuries drama and poetry revived with Valéry, Claudel, and Paul Fort, who advocated "pure poetry"; other writers were the novelists Gide and Proust, and the critics Thibaudet (1874–1936) and later St John Perse, also a poet. The Surrealist movement, which developed from "pure poetry" through the work of Eluard and Apollinaire, influenced writers as diverse as Giraudoux, Louis Aragon, and Cocteau. The literary reaction against the Symbolists was seen in the work of Charles Péguy, Rostand, de Noailles, and Romain Rolland. Twentieth-century novelists in the Naturalist tradition were Henri Barbusse, Jules Romains, Julian Green, François Mauriac, Francis Carco, and Georges Duhamel. Other prose writers were Maurois, Malraux, Montherlant, Anatole France, Saint-Exupéry, Alain-Fournier, Pierre Hamp, and J R Bloch, while the theater flourished with plays by J J Bernard, Anouilh, Beckett, and Ionesco. World War II had a profound effect on French writing, and distinguished postwar writers include the Existentialists Sartre and Camus, "Vercors" (pen name of Jean Bruller), Simone de Beauvoir, Alain Robbe-Grillet, Romain Gary, Nathalie Sarraute, and Marguerite Duras.

French Polynesia French Overseas Territory in the S Pacific, consisting of five archipelagos: Windward Islands, Leeward Islands (the two island groups comprising the ◊Society Islands), ◊Tuamotu Archipelago (including ◊Gambier Islands), ◊Tubuai Islands, and ◊Marquesas Islands
total area 1,521 sq mi/3,940 sq km
capital Papeete on Tahiti
products cultivated pearls, coconut oil, vanilla; tourism is important
population (1987) 185,000
language Tahitian (official), French
government a high commissioner (Alain Ohrel) and Council of Government; two deputies are returned to the National Assembly in France
history first visited by Europeans 1595; French Protectorate 1843; annexed to France 1880–82; became an Overseas Territory, changing its name from French Oceania 1958; self-governing 1977. Following demands for independence in ◊New Caledonia 1984–85, agitation increased also in Polynesia.

French Revolution the period 1789–1799 that saw the end of the French monarchy and its claim to absolute rule, and the establishment of the First Republic. Although the revolution began as an attempt to create a constitutional monarchy, by late 1792 demands for long-overdue reforms resulted in the proclamation of the republic. The violence of the revolution, attcks by other nations, and bitter factional struggles, riots, and counter-revolutionary uprisings consumed the republic. This helped bring the extremists to power, and the bloody Reign of Terror followed. French armies then succeeded in holding off their foreign enemies and one of the generals, ◊Napoleon, seized power 1799.

On May 5, 1789, after the monarchy had attempted to increase taxation and control of affairs, the ◊States General (three "estates" of nobles, clergy, and commons) met at Versailles to try to establish some constitutional controls. Divisions within the States General led to the formation of a National Assembly by the third (commons) estate June 17. Repressive measures by ◊Louis XVI led to the storming of the ◊Bastille by the Paris mob July 14, 1789.

On June 20, 1791 the royal family attempted to escape from the control of the Assembly, but Louis XVI was brought back a prisoner from Varennes and forced to accept a new constitution. War with Austria after April 20, 1792 threatened to undermine the revolution, but on Aug 10 the mob stormed the royal palace, and on Sept 21 the First French Republic was proclaimed.

On Jan 21, 1793 Louis XVI was executed. The moderate ◊Girondins were overthrown June 2 by the ◊Jacobins, and control of the country was

French Revolution 1789–99

1789	(May) Meeting of Estates-General called by Louis XIV to discuss reform of state finances. Nobility oppose reforms. (June) Third (commoners) estate demanded end to system where First (noble) estate and Second (church) estate could outvote them; rejected by Louis. Third estate declared themselves a National Assembly and "tennis court oath" pledged them to draw up new constitution. (July) Rumors of royal plans to break up the Assembly led to riots in Paris and the storming of the Bastille. Revolutionaries adopted *tricolore* as their flag. Peasant uprisings occurred throughout the country.
1789–91	National Assembly reforms included abolition of noble privileges, dissolution of religious orders, appropriation of church lands, centralization of governments, and limits on the king's power.
1791	(June) King Louis attempted to escape from Paris in order to unite opposition to the Assembly, but was recaptured. (Sept) The king agreed to a new constitution. (Oct) New Legislative Assembly met, divided between moderate Girondists and radical Jacobins.
1792	(Jan) Girondists formed a new government but their power in Paris was undermined by the Jacobins. Foreign invasion led to the breakdown of law and order. Hatred of the monarchy increased. (Aug) The king was suspended from office and the government dismissed. (Sept) National Convention elected on the basis of universal suffrage; dominated by Jacobins. A republic was proclaimed. (Dec) The king was tried and condemned to death.
1793	(Jan) The king was guillotined. (April) The National Convention delegated power to the Committee of Public Safety, dominated by Robespierre. The Reign of Terror began.
1794	(July) Robespierre became increasingly unpopular, was deposed and executed.
1795	Moderate Thermidoreans took control of the convention and created a new executive Directory of five members.
1795–99	Directory failed to solve France's internal or external problems and became increasingly unpopular.
1799	Coup d'etat overthrew the Directory and a Consulate of three was established, including Napoleon as Chief Consul with special powers.

passed to the infamous Committee of Public Safety, and ◊Robespierre. The mass executions of the Reign of Terror began Sept 5, and the excesses led to the overthrow of the Committee and Robespierre July 27, 1794. The Directory was established to hold a middle course between royalism and Jacobinism. It ruled until Napoleon seized power 1799 as dictator.

French revolutionary calendar the French Revolution 1789 was initially known as the 1st Year of Liberty. When monarchy was abolished on Sep 21 1792, the 4th year became 1st Year of the Republic. This calendar was formally adopted in Oct 1793 but its usage was backdated to Sep 22 1793, which became 1 Vendémiaire. The calendar was discarded as of Jan 1, 1806.

French revolutionary calendar

Revolutionary month (date 1–30)	*meaning*	*time period*
Vendémiaire	vintage	Sep 22–Oct 21
Brumaire	fog	Oct 22–Nov 20
Frimaire	frost	Nov 21–Dec 20
Nivôse	snow	Dec 1–Jan 19
Pluviôse	rain	Jan 20–Feb 18
Ventôse	wind	Feb 19–Mar 20
Germinal	budding	March 21–April 19
Floreal	flowers	April 20–May 19
Prairial	meadows	May 20–June 18
Messidor	harvest	June 19–July 18
Thermidor	heat	July 19–Aug 17
Fructidor	fruit	Aug 18–Sep 16
Sanculottides	festival	Sep 17–Sep 21

French Somaliland former name, until 1967, of ◊Djibouti, in E Africa.

French Sudan former name (1898–1959) of ◊Mali.

French Third Republic see ◊French history.

French West Africa group of French colonies administered from Dakar 1895–1958. They are now Senegal, Mauritania, Sudan, Burkina Faso, Guinea, Niger, Ivory Coast, and Benin.

Freneau Philip Morin 1752–1832. US poet whose *A Political Litany* 1775 was a mock prayer for deliverance from British tyranny.

His other works include *The British Prison-Ship* 1781, about his experiences as a British prisoner. He was a professional journalist, the first in the US.

frequency in physics, the number of periodic oscillations, vibrations, or waves occurring per unit of time. The unit of frequency is the hertz (Hz), one hertz being equivalent to one cycle per second. Human beings can hear sounds from objects vibrating in the range 20–15,000 Hz. Ultrasonic frequencies well above 15,000 Hz can be detected by mammals such as bats.

frequency modulation see ◊FM.

Frere John 1740–1807. English archeologist, a pioneering discoverer of Old Stone Age (Paleolithic) tools in association with large extinct animals at Hoxne, Suffolk, in 1790. He suggested (long before Charles Darwin) that they predated the conventional biblical timescale. Frere was high sheriff of Suffolk and member of Parliament for Norwich.

fresco mural painting technique using water-based paint on wet plaster.

Some of the earliest frescoes (about 1750–1400 BC) were found in Knossos, Crete (now preserved in the Heraklion Museum). Fresco reached its finest expression in Italy from the 13th to the 17th centuries. Giotto, Masaccio, Michelangelo, and many other artists worked in the medium.

Frescobaldi Girolamo 1583–1643. Italian composer of virtuoso pieces for the organ and harpsichord.

Fresnel Augustin 1788–1827. French physicist who refined the theory of ◊polarized light. Fresnel realized in 1821 that light waves do not vibrate like sound waves longitudinally, in the direction of their motion, but transversely, at right angles to the direction of the propagated wave.

Fresno city in central California, SE of San Jose, seat of Fresno County. It is the processing and marketing center for the fruits and vegetables of the San Joaquin valley. Industries include glass, machinery, fertilizers, and vending machines; population (1990) 354,202. Fresno was originally a stop on the Central Pacific Railroad.

Freud Sigmund 1865–1939. Austrian physician who pioneered the study of the subconscious and unconscious mind. He developed ◊psychoanalysis with the methods of free association and interpretation of dreams that are its basic techniques and formulated the concepts of the ◊id, ◊ego, and ◊superego. His books include *Die Traumdeutung/The Interpretation of Dreams* 1900, *Totem and Taboo* 1913, and *Das Unbehagen in der Kultur/Civilization and its Discontents* 1930.

Freud studied medicine in Vienna and was a member of the research team that discovered the local anesthetic effects of cocaine. From 1885 to 1886 he studied hypnosis in Paris under the French physiologist ◊Charcot and 1889 in Nancy under two of Charcot's opponents. From 1886 to 1938 he had a private practice in Vienna, and his theories and writings drew largely on case studies of his own patients, who were mainly upper-middle class, middle-aged women. He was also influenced by the research into hysteria of the Viennese physician ◊Breuer. In the early 1900s a group of psychoanalysts gathered around Freud. Some of these later broke away and formed their own schools: Alfred ◊Adler in 1911 and Carl ◊Jung in 1913. Following the Nazi occupation of Austria in 1938, Freud left for London, where he died.

The word "psychoanalysis" was, like much of its terminology, coined by Freud, and many terms have passed into popular usage, not without distortion. The way that subconscious and unconscious forces influence people's thoughts and actions was Freud's discovery, and his theory of the repression of infantile sexuality as the root of neuroses in the adult (as in the ◊Oedipus complex) was controversial. Later he also stressed the significance of aggressive drives. His work, long accepted as definitive by many, has been criticized from a certain section of feminist thought as well as by theorists.

Freya or ***Frigga*** in Scandinavian mythology, wife of Odin and mother of Thor, goddess of married love and the hearth. Friday is named after her.

Freyberg Bernard Cyril, Baron 1889–1963. New Zealand soldier and administrator. He fought in World War I, and during World War II he commanded the New Zealand expeditionary force. He was governor-general of New Zealand 1946–52.

friar a monk of any order, but originally the title of members of the mendicant (begging) orders, the chief of which were the Franciscans or Minors (Grey Friars), the Dominicans or Preachers (Black Friars), the Carmelites (White Friars), and Augustinians (Austin Friars).

Fribourg city in W Switzerland, on the river Sarine.

***Freud** Austrian physician who pioneered psychoanalysis, Sigmund Freud.*

capital of the canton of Fribourg; population (1980) 37,400. It is noted for its food products, particularly the cheese of the Gruyère district.

friction in physics, the force that opposes the relative motion of two bodies in contact. The coefficient of friction is the ratio of the force required to achieve this relative motion to the force pressing the two bodies together.

Friction is greatly reduced by the use of lubricants such as oil, grease, and graphite. Air bearings are now used to minimize friction in high-speed rotational machinery. In other instances friction is deliberately increased by making the surfaces rough—for example, brake linings, driving belts, soles of shoes, and tires.

Friedan Betty 1921– . US liberal feminist. Her book *The Feminine Mystique* 1963 started the contemporary women's movement, both in the US and in Britain. She was a founder of the National Organization for Women (NOW) 1966 (and its president 1966–70), the National Women's Political Caucus 1971, and the First Women's Bank 1973. Friedan also helped to organize the Women's Strike for Equality 1970 and called the First International Feminist Congress 1973.

Born in Peoria, Illinois, her other works include *It Changed My Life* 1976 and *The Second Stage* 1981, a call for a change of direction in the movement.

Friedman Milton 1912– . US economist. The foremost exponent of ◊monetarism, he argued that a country's economy, and hence inflation, can be controlled through its money supply, although most governments lack the "political will" to control inflation by cutting government spending and thereby increasing unemployment. Friedman argued for extending private choice among competing businesses into virtually all spheres of economic life. He suggested, for example, that the public school system be abolished and that parents pay to send their children to the school of their choosing. He was an influential adviser to presidents Nixon and Reagan and wrote several books. He won the Nobel Prize for Economics 1976.

Friedrich German form of ◊Frederick.

Friedrich Caspar David 1774–1840. German Romantic landscape painter, active mainly in Dresden. He imbued his subjects—mountain scenes and moonlit seas—with poetic melancholy and was later admired by Symbolist painters.

Friendly Islands another name for ◊Tonga.

Friends of the Earth (FoE or FOE) environmental pressure group, established in the UK 1971, that aims to protect the environment and to promote rational and sustainable use of the Earth's resources. It campaigns on issues such as acid rain; air, sea, river, and land pollution; recycling; disposal of toxic wastes; nuclear power and renewable energy; the destruction of rainforests; pesticides; and agriculture. FoE has branches in 30 countries.

Friends, Society of or ***Quakers*** Christian Protestant sect founded by George ◊Fox in England in the 17th century. They were persecuted for their nonviolent activism, and many emigrated to form communities elsewhere, for example in Pennsylvania and New England. They now form a worldwide movement of about 200,000. Their worship stresses meditation and the freedom of all to take an active part in the service (called a meeting, held in a meeting house). They have no priests or ministers.

The name "Quakers" may originate in Fox's injunction to "quake at the word of the Lord." Originally marked out by their sober dress and use of "thee" and "thou" to all as a sign of equality, they incurred penalties by their pacifism and refusal to take oaths or pay tithes. In the 19th century many Friends were prominent in social reform, for example, Elizabeth ◊Fry.

Quakers have exerted a profound influence on

Friedrich Winter Landscape *(c. 1811) National Gallery, London.*

American life through their pacifism and belief in social equality, education, and prison reform.

Friesland maritime province of the N Netherlands, which includes the Frisian Islands and land still being reclaimed from the former Zuyder Zee; the inhabitants of the province are called ◊Frisians
area 1,312 sq mi/3,400 sq km
population (1988) 599,000
cities capital Leeuwarden; Drachten, Harlingen, Sneek, Heerenveen
products livestock (Fresian cattle originated here), dairy products, small boats
history ruled as a county of the Holy Roman Empire during the Middle Ages, Friesland passed to Saxony in 1498 and, after a revolt, to Charles V of Spain. In 1579 it subscribed to the Treaty of Utrecht, opposing Spanish rule. In 1748 its stadholder, Prince William IV of Orange, became stadholder of all the United Provinces of the Netherlands.

frigate warship, an escort vessel smaller than a destroyer. Before 1975 the term referred to a warship larger than a destroyer but smaller than a light cruiser. In the 18th and 19th centuries a frigate was a small, fast sailing warship.

fringe benefit in employment, payment in kind over and above wages and salaries. These may include a pension, subsidized lunches, company car, favorable loan facilities, and health insurance. Fringe benefits may, in part, be subject to income tax.

fringing reef a ◊coral reef that is attached to the coast without an intervening lagoon.

Frisbee trademark for a platter-shaped, concave disk, used for toss-and-catch games. Thrown with a flick of the wrist, Frisbees spin and sail. Although primarily for recreation or fun, certain championship contests exist.

Frisch Karl von 1886–1982. German zoologist, founder with Konrad Lorenz of ◊ethology, the study of animal behavior. He specialized in bees, discovering how they communicate the location of sources of nectar by movements called "dances." He was awarded the Nobel Prize for Medicine 1973 together with Konrad Lorenz and Nikolaas ◊Tinbergen.

Frisch Max 1911– . Swiss dramatist. Inspired by ◊Brecht, his early plays such as *Als der Krieg zu Ende war/When the War Is Over* 1949 are more romantic in tone than his later symbolic dramas, such as *Andorra* 1962, dealing with questions of identity. He wrote *Biedermann und die Brandstifter/The Fire Raisers* 1958.

Frisch Otto 1904–1979. Austrian physicist who coined the term "nuclear fission." A refugee from Nazi Germany, he worked from 1943 on the atom bomb at Los Alamos, New Mexico, and later at Cambridge, England. He was the nephew of Lise ◊Meitner.

Frisch Ragnar 1895–1973. Norwegian economist, pioneer of ◊econometrics (the application of mathematical and statistical methods in economics). He shared the first Nobel Prize for Economics in 1969 with Jan ◊Tinbergen.

Frisch–Peierls memorandum a document revealing, for the first time, how small the critical mass

frog

Wallace's
flying frog

(the minimum quantity of substance required for a nuclear chain reaction to begin) of uranium needed to be if the isotope uranium-235 was separated from naturally occurring uranium; the memo thus implied the feasibility of using this isotope to make an atom bomb. It was written by Otto Frisch and Rudolf Peierls (1907–) at the University of Birmingham 1940.

Frisian or ***Friesian*** a member of a Germanic people of NW Europe (Friesland and the Frisian Islands). In Roman times they occupied the coast of Holland and may have taken part in the Anglo-Saxon invasions of Britain. Their language is closely akin to Anglo-Saxon, with which it forms the Anglo-Frisian branch of the West Germanic languages.

The Frisian language is almost extinct in the German districts of East Friesland, but it has attained some literary importance in the North Frisian Islands and Schleswig and developed a considerable literature in the West Frisian dialect of the Dutch province of Friesland.

Frisian Islands chain of low-lying islands 3–20 mi/5–32 km off the NW coasts of the Netherlands and Germany, with a northerly extension off the W coast of Denmark. They were formed by the sinking of the intervening land. Texel is the largest and westernmost island.

Frith William Powell 1819–1909. British artist who painted large contemporary scenes with numerous figures and incidental detail. *Ramsgate Sands*, bought by Queen Victoria, is a fine example, as is *Derby Day* 1856–58 (both Tate Gallery, London).

fritillary in botany, any plant of the genus *Fritillaria* of the lily family Liliaceae. Snake's head fritillary *F. meleagris* has bell-shaped flowers with purple-checkerd markings.

fritillary a large grouping of butterflies of the family Nymphalidae. Mostly medium-sized, they are generally orange and reddish with a black criss-cross pattern or spots above and with silvery spots on the underside of the hindwings.

Friuli-Venezia Giulia autonomous agricultural and wine-growing region of NE Italy, bordered on the E by Yugoslavia; area 3,011 sq mi/7,800 sq km; population (1988) 1,210,000. Cities include Udine (the capital), Gorizia, Pordenone, and Trieste.

Formed 1947 from the province of Venetian Friuli and part of Eastern Friuli, to which Trieste was added after its cession to Italy 1954, it was granted autonomy 1963. The Slav minority numbers about 100,000, and in Friuli there is a movement for complete independence.

Frobisher Martin 1535–1594. English navigator. He made his first voyage to Guinea, West Africa, 1554. In 1576 he set out in search of the Northwest Passage, and visited Labrador, and Frobisher Bay, Baffin Island. Second and third expeditions sailed 1577 and 1578.

He was vice admiral in Drake's West Indian expedition 1585. In 1588, he was knighted for helping to defeat the Armada. He was mortally wounded 1594 fighting against the Spanish off the coast of France.

Froebel Friedrich August Wilhelm 1782–1852. German educationist. He evolved a new system of education using instructive play, described in *Education of Man* 1826 and other works. In 1836 he founded the first kindergarten (German "garden for children") in Blankenburg. He was influenced by ◊Pestalozzi.

frog any amphibian of the order Anura (Greek "tailless"). There are no clear rules for distinguishing between frogs and toads. Frogs usually have squat bodies, hind legs specialized for jumping, and webbed feet for swimming. Many frogs use their long, extensible tongues to capture insects. Frogs vary in size from the tiny North American little grass frog *Limnaoedus ocularis*, 0.5 in/12 mm long, to the giant aquatic frog *Telmatobius culeus*, 20 in/50 cm long, of Lake Titicaca, South America.

In many species the males attract the females in great gatherings, usually by croaking. In some tropical species, the male's inflated vocal sac may exceed the rest of his body in size. Other courtship "lures" include thumping on the ground and "dances." Some lay eggs in large masses (spawn) in water. Some South American frogs build little mud-pool "nests," and African tree frogs make foam nests from secreted mucus. In other species, the eggs may be carried in "pockets" on the mother's back, or brooded by the male in his vocal sac, or, as with the Eurasian midwife toad *Alytes obstetricans*, carried by the male, wrapped round his hind legs until hatching. Certain species of frog have powerful skin poisons (alkaloids) to deter predators.

"True frogs" are placed in the worldwide family Ranidae, of which the genus *Rana* is the best known. The North American bullfrog *Rana catesbeiana*, with a far-reaching croak that carries for miles, is able to jump nine times its own length (annual jumping competitions are held at Calaveras, California). The flying frogs, genus *Rhacophorus*, of Malaysia, using webbed fore-and hind feet, can achieve a 40 ft/12 m glide.

froghopper or spittlebug leaping plant-bug, of the family Cercopidae, in the same order (Homoptera) as leafhoppers and aphids. Froghoppers live by sucking the juice from plants. The pale green larvae protect themselves (from drying out and from predators) by secreting froth ("cuckoo spit") from their anuses.

frogmouth nocturnal bird, related to the nightjar, of which the commonest species, the tawny frogmouth *Podargus strigoides*, is found throughout Australia, including Tasmania. Well camouflaged, it sits and awaits its prey.

Fromm Erich 1900–1980. German psychoanalyst who moved to the US 1933 to escape the Nazis. His *The Fear of Freedom* 1941 and *The Sane Society* 1955 were source books for alternative lifestyles.

Fromm stressed the role of culture in the formation of personality, a view that distinguished him from traditional psychoanalysts. He also described the authoritarian personality, an important concept in the study of personality.

frond a large leaf or leaflike structure; in ferns it is often pinnately divided. The term is also applied to the leaves of palms and less commonly to the plant bodies of certain seaweeds, liverworts, and lichens.

Fronde French revolts 1648–53 against the administration of the chief minister ◊Mazarin during Louis XIV's minority. In 1648–49 the Paris *parlement* attempted to limit the royal power, its leaders were arrested, Paris revolted, and the rising was suppressed by the royal army under Louis II Condé. In 1650 Condé led a new revolt of the nobility, but this was suppressed by 1653. The defeat of the Fronde enabled Louis to establish an absolutist monarchy in the later 17th century.

front in meteorology, the interface between two air masses of different temperature or humidity. A cold front marks the line of advance of a cold air mass from below, as it displaces a warm air mass; a warm front marks the advance of a warm air mass pushing a cold one forward.

Warm air, being lighter, tends to rise above the cold; its moisture is carried upward and usually falls as rain or snow, hence the changeable weather conditions at fronts. Fronts are rarely stable and move with the air mass. An occluded front is a composite form, where a cold front

frog

The life cycle of frogs, and of their close relatives, the toads, comprises several distinct stages. The young, or larvae, look unlike the adults and are said to undergo a complete metamorphosis "change of form." The adult common frog mates in water. From the fertilized eggs emerge the larvae, which at first breathe solely with gills and have no legs. As they grow, they become more adult-like and eventually are able to live and breathe on land.

Adult frogs breathe using their lungs, through the moist skin, and through the lining of their mouths. They feed on worms, beetles, and flies. The aquatic tadpoles at first feed on weeds and algae, but then change to a meat diet.

1
2
3

Parental care in some species of frogs and toads involves carrying the eggs or tadpoles (larvae) on the back. 1. Male stream frog with tadpoles. 2. Female Surinam toad with young. 3. Male midwife toad carrying eggs.

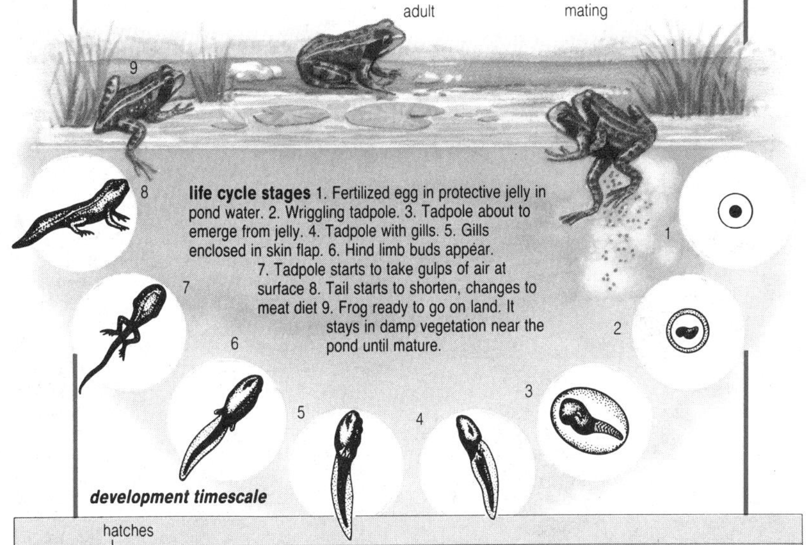
adult
mating
9
8
7
6
5
4
3
2
1

life cycle stages 1. Fertilized egg in protective jelly in pond water. 2. Wriggling tadpole. 3. Tadpole about to emerge from jelly. 4. Tadpole with gills. 5. Gills enclosed in skin flap. 6. Hind limb buds appear. 7. Tadpole starts to take gulps of air at surface 8. Tail starts to shorten, changes to meat diet 9. Frog ready to go on land. It stays in damp vegetation near the pond until mature.

development timescale

	hatches															
stage	1–2↓3 4 5		6					←7→				8				9
weeks		1	2	3	4	5	6	7	8	9	10	11	12	13	14	15	16

overtakes a warm front, lifting warm air above the Earth's surface. An inversion occurs when the normal properties get reversed; this happens when a layer of air traps another near the surface, preventing the normal rising of surface air. Warm temperatures and pollination result from inversions.

frontal lobotomy an operation on the brain. See ◊lobotomy.

Frontenac et Palluau Louis de Buade, Comte de 1622–1698. French colonial governor. He began his military career 1635, and was appointed governor of the French possessions in North America 1672. Although efficient, he quarrelled with the local bishop and his followers and was recalled 1682. After the Iroquois, supported by the English, won several military victories, Frontenac was reinstated 1689. He defended Québec against the English 1690 and defeated the Iroquois 1696.

frontier literature writing reflecting the US experience of frontier and pioneer life, long central to US literature. The category includes James Fenimore Cooper's *Leatherstocking Tales*; the frontier humor writing of Artemus Ward, Bret Harte, and Mark Twain; dime novels; westerns; the travel records of Francis Parkman; and the pioneer romances of Willa Cather. Much modern American writing has been influenced by the frontier theme.

front-line states the black nations of southern Africa in the "front line" of the struggle against the racist policies of South Africa: namely Mozambique, Tanzania, and Zambia. Botswana and Zimbabwe can also be included in this category.

frost condition of the weather when the air temperature is below freezing, 32°F/0°C. Water in the atmosphere is deposited as ice crystals on the ground or exposed objects. As cold air is heavier than warm, ground frost is more common than hoar frost, which is formed by the condensation of water particles in the same way that ◊dew collects.

Frost Robert (Lee) 1874–1963. US poet whose verse, in traditional form, is written with an individual voice and penetrating vision. His poems include "Mending Wall" ("Something there is that does not love a wall"), "The Road Not Taken," and "Stopping by Woods on a Snowy Evening."

Born in San Francisco, Frost was raised in New England, where he attended Dartmouth College and Harvard University for brief periods. His poems are collected in *A Boy's Will* 1913, *North of Boston* 1914, *New Hampshire* 1924, *Collected Poems* 1930, *A Further Range* 1936, and *A Witness Tree* 1942. He was awarded four Pulitzer prizes (1924, 1931, 1937, 1943) and in 1961 read his "The Gift Outright" at the inauguration of J F Kennedy.

frostbite the freezing of skin or flesh, with formation of ice crystals leading to tissue damage. The treatment is slow warming of the affected area; for example, by skin-to-skin contact or with lukewarm water. Frostbitten parts are extremely vulnerable to infection, with the risk of gangrene.

fructose a fruit sugar, $C_6H_{12}O_6$, which occurs naturally in honey, the nectar of flowers, and many sweet fruits, and is commercially prepared from glucose. It is a monosaccharide, whereas the more familiar cane or beet sugar is a disaccharide, made up of two monosaccharide units: fructose and glucose. It is sweeter than cane sugar.

fruit (from Latin *frui* "to enjoy") in botany, the structure that develops from the carpel of a flower and encloses one or more seeds, except in cases of ◊parthenocarpy. Its function is to protect the seeds during their development, to aid in their dispersal, and to provide material for fertilizing the soil around a germinating seed. Fruits are often edible, sweet, juicy, and colorful. They provide vitamins and minerals, but little protein. Most fruits are borne by perennial plants.

Broadly, fruits are divided into three categories on the basis of the climate in which they grow. Temperate fruits require a cold season for satisfactory growth. In order of abundance, the principal temperate fruits are apples, pears, plums, peaches, apricots, cherries, and soft fruits such as strawberries. Subtropical fruits require warm conditions but can survive light frosts; they include oranges and other citrus fruits, dates, pomegranates, and avocados. Tropical fruits succumb if temperatures drop close to freezing point; they include bananas, mangoes, pineapples, papayas, and litchis.

Fruits can also be divided into dry (such as ◊capsule, ◊follicle, ◊schizocarp, ◊nut, ◊caryopsis, ◊pod or legume, ◊lomentum, and ◊achene) and those that become fleshy (such as ◊drupe and ◊berry).

fruit

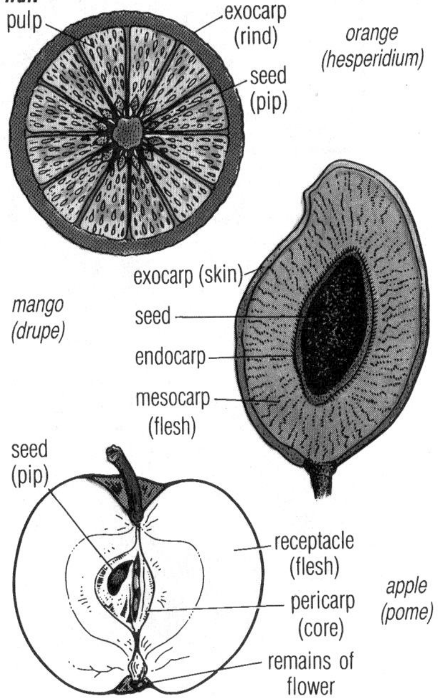
pulp
exocarp (rind)
seed (pip)
orange (hesperidium)
exocarp (skin)
seed
endocarp
mesocarp (flesh)
mango (drupe)
seed (pip)
receptacle (flesh)
pericarp (core)
remains of flower
apple (pome)

front

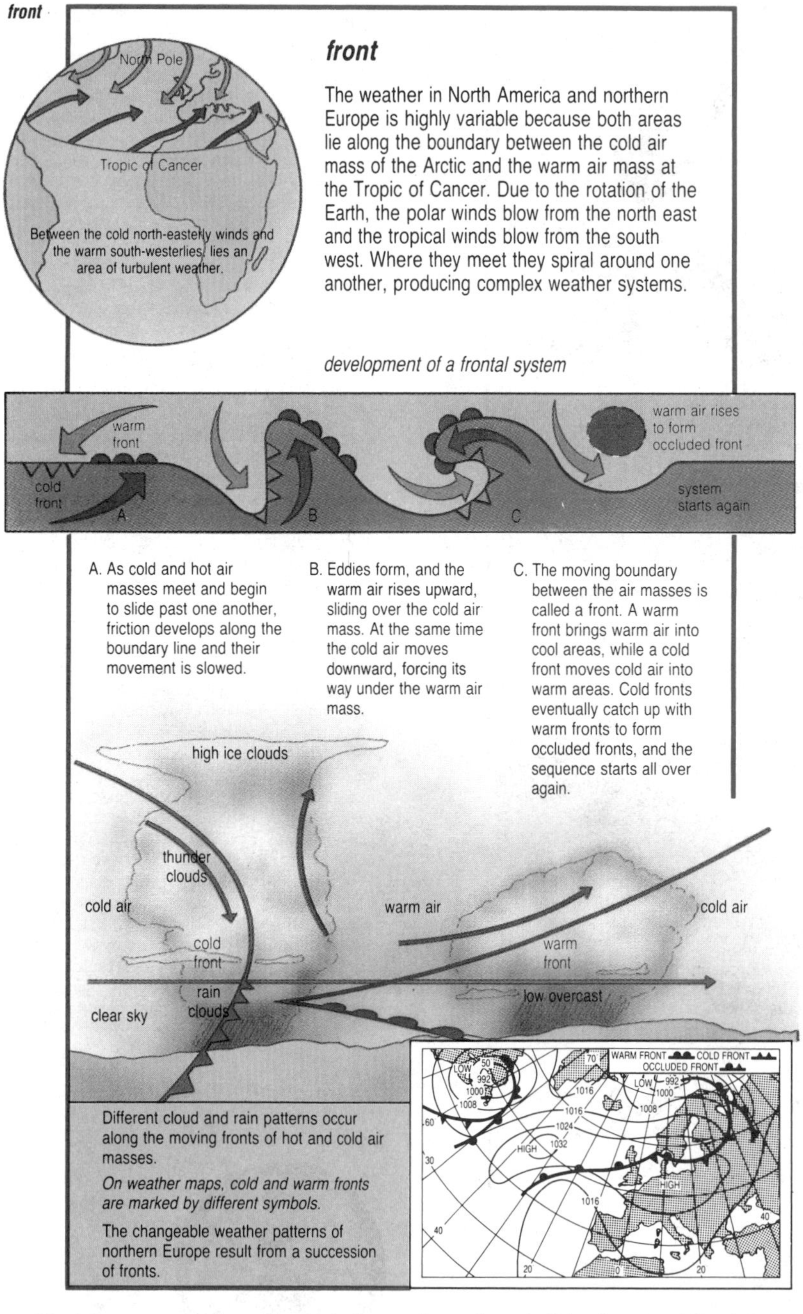
front
The weather in North America and northern Europe is highly variable because both areas lie along the boundary between the cold air mass of the Arctic and the warm air mass at the Tropic of Cancer. Due to the rotation of the Earth, the polar winds blow from the north east and the tropical winds blow from the south west. Where they meet they spiral around one another, producing complex weather systems.
North Pole
Tropic of Cancer
Between the cold north-easterly winds and the warm south-westerlies, lies an area of turbulent weather.
development of a frontal system
warm front
cold front
warm air rises to form occluded front
system starts again
A
B
C
A. As cold and hot air masses meet and begin to slide past one another, friction develops along the boundary line and their movement is slowed.
B. Eddies form, and the warm air rises upward, sliding over the cold air mass. At the same time the cold air moves downward, forcing its way under the warm air mass.
C. The moving boundary between the air masses is called a front. A warm front brings warm air into cool areas, while a cold front moves cold air into warm areas. Cold fronts eventually catch up with warm fronts to form occluded fronts, and the sequence starts all over again.
high ice clouds
thunder clouds
cold air
warm air
cold air
cold front
warm front
rain clouds
low overcast
clear sky
WARM FRONT
COLD FRONT
OCCLUDED FRONT
LOW
HIGH
Different cloud and rain patterns occur along the moving fronts of hot and cold air masses.
On weather maps, cold and warm fronts are marked by different symbols.
The changeable weather patterns of northern Europe result from a succession of fronts.

The fruit structure consists of the ◊pericarp or fruit wall, usually divided into a number of distinct layers. Sometimes parts other than the ovary are incorporated into the fruit structure, resulting in a false fruit or ◊pseudocarp, such as the apple and strawberry. Fruits may open to shed their seeds (dehiscent) or remain unopened and be dispersed as a single unit (indehiscent).

Simple fruits (for example, peaches) are derived from a single ovary, whereas composite or multiple fruits (for example, blackberries) are formed from the ovaries of a number of flowers. In ordinary usage, "fruit" includes only sweet, fleshy items; it excludes many botanical fruits such as acorns, bean pods, thistledown, and cucumbers (see ◊vegetable).

Recorded world fruit production in the mid-1980s was approximately 300 million tons per year. Technical advances in storage and transport have made tropical fruits available to consumers in temperate areas, and fresh temperate fruits available all year in major markets.

Frunze (formerly Pishpek) capital of Kirghiz Republic, USSR; population (1987) 632,000. It produces textiles, farm machinery, metal goods, and tobacco.

frustule the cell wall of a ◊diatom. Frustules are intricately patterned on the surface with spots, ridges, and furrows, each pattern being characteristic of a particular species.

frustum in geometry, a "slice" taken out of a solid figure by a pair of parallel planes. A conical frustum, for example, resembles a cone with the top cut off. The volume and area of a frustum are calculated by subtracting the volume or area of the "missing" piece from those of the whole figure.

Fry Christopher 1907– . English dramatist. He was a leader of the revival of verse drama after World War II with *The Lady's Not for Burning* 1948, *Venus Observed* 1950, and *A Sleep of Prisoners* 1951.

FSH abbreviation for ◊follicle-stimulating hormone.

f-stop in photography, one of a series of numbers on the lens barrel designating the size of the variable aperture; it stands for the focal length and follows an internationally accepted scale.

frustrum

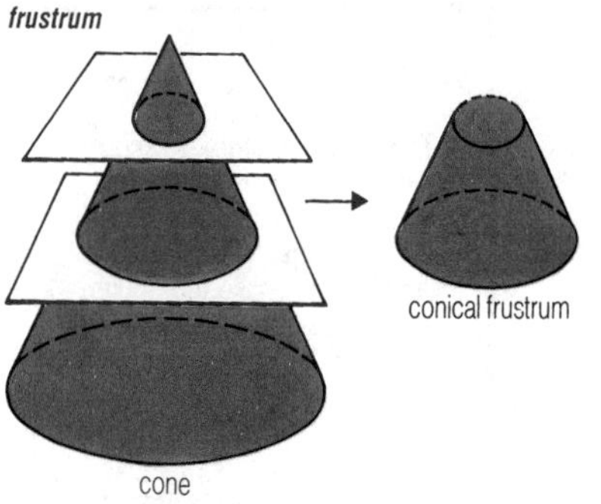
conical frustrum
cone

ft abbreviation for ◊foot, a measure of distance.

FTC abbreviation for Federal Trade Commission, US antimonopoly organization; see ◊monopoly.

Fuad two kings of Egypt:

Fuad I 1868–1936. King of Egypt from 1922. Son of the Khedive Ismail, he succeeded his elder brother Hussein Kiamil as sultan of Egypt 1917; when Egypt was declared independent 1922 he assumed the title of king.

Fuad II 1952– . King of Egypt 1952–53, between the abdication of his father ◊Farouk and the establishment of the republic. He was a grandson of Fuad I.

Fuchs Klaus (Emil Julius) 1911–1988. German spy who worked on atomic-bomb research in the UK in World War II. He was imprisoned 1950–59 for passing information to the USSR and resettled in East Germany.

Fuchs Vivian 1908– . British explorer and geologist. Before World War II, he accompanied several Cambridge University expeditions to Greenland, Africa, and Antarctica. In 1957–58, he led the Commonwealth Trans-Antarctic Expedition.

fuchsia any shrubs or herbaceous plants of the genus *Fuchsia* of the evening-primrose family Onagraceae. Species are native to South and Central America and New Zealand and bear red, purple, or pink bell-shaped flowers that hang downward.

fuel any source of heat or energy, embracing the entire range of all combustibles and including anything that burns. Nuclear fuel is any material that produces energy in a nuclear reactor.

fuel cell cell converting chemical energy directly to electrical energy. It works on the same principle as a battery but is continually fed with fuel, usually hydrogen. Fuel cells are silent and reliable (no moving parts) but expensive to produce.

Hydrogen is passed over an ◊electrode (usually nickel or platinum) containing a ◊catalyst, which strips electrons off the atoms. These pass through an external circuit while hydrogen ions (charged atoms) pass through an ◊electrolyte to another electrode, over which oxygen is passed. Water is formed at this electrode (as a by-product) in a chemical reaction involving electrons, hydrogen ions, and oxygen atoms. If the spare heat also produced is used for hot water and space heating, 80% efficiency in fuel is achieved.

fuel injection injecting fuel directly into the cylinders

fuchsia

of an internal combustion engine, instead of by way of a carburetor. It is the standard method used in ◊diesel engines, and is now becoming standard for gasoline engines. In the diesel engine oil is injected into the hot compressed air at the top of the second piston stroke and explodes to drive the piston down on its power stroke. In the gasoline engine, fuel is injected into the cylinder at the start of the first induction stroke of the ◊four-stroke cycle.

Fuentes Carlos 1928– . Mexican novelist, lawyer, and diplomat whose first novel *La región más transparente/Where the Air Is Clear* 1958 encompasses the history of the country from the Aztecs to the present day.

More than other Mexican novelists he presents the frustrated social philosophy of the failed Mexican revolution. He received international attention for *The Death of Artemeo Cruz* 1962, *Terra nostra* 1975, *El Gringo veijo/The Old Gringo* 1985, and *The Campaign* 1991.

fugue (Latin "flight") in music, a contrapuntal form (with two or more melodies) for a number of parts or "voices," which enter successively in imitation of each other. It was raised to a high art by J S ◊Bach.

Führer or ***Fuehrer*** title adopted by Adolf ◊Hitler as leader of the ◊Nazi Party.

Fujairah or ***Fujayrah*** one of the seven constituent member states of the ◊United Arab Emirates; area 450 sq mi/1,150 sq km; population (1985) 54,000.

Fujian or ***Fukien*** province of SE China, bordering Taiwan Strait, opposite Taiwan

area 47,517 sq mi/123,100 sq km

capital Fuzhou

physical dramatic mountainous coastline

features being developed for tourists; designated as pace-setting province for modernization 1980

products sugar, rice, aromatic teas, tobacco, timber, fruit

population (1986) 27,490,000.

Fujiyama or ***Mount Fuji*** Japanese volcano and highest peak, on Honshu Island; height 12,400 ft/ 3,778 m. Located near Tokyo, it has long been revered for its picturesque cone-shaped crater peak and figures prominently in Japanese art, literature, and religion.

Extinct since 1707, it has a ◊Shinto shrine and a weather station on its summit.

Fukien former name of ◊Fujian, a province of SE China.

Fukuoka formerly ***Najime*** Japanese industrial port on the NW coast of Kyushu Island; population (1987) 1,142,000. It produces chemicals, textiles, paper, and metal goods.

Fukushima city in N Honshu, Japan; population (1985) 271,000. It has a silk industry.

Fukuyama port in SW Honshu, Japan, at the mouth of the Ashida river; population (1985) 360,000. Exports include cotton and rubber.

Fula W African empire founded by people of predominantly Fulani extraction. The Fula conquered the Hausa states in the 19th century.

Fulani a member of a W African culture from the southern Sahara and Sahel. Traditionally nomadic pastoralists and traders, Fulani groups are found in Senegal, Guinea, Mali, Burkina Faso, Niger, Nigeria, Chad, and Cameroon. The Fulani language is divided into four dialects and belongs to the W Atlantic branch of the Niger-Congo family.

Fulbright (James) William 1975– . US Democratic politician. A US senator 1945–75, he was responsible for the Fulbright Act 1946, which provided grants for thousands of Americans to study abroad and for foreign students to study in the US. He chaired the Senate Foreign Relations Committee 1959–74 and was a strong internationalist.

Born in Sumner, Missouri, Fulbright studied abroad at Oxford University on a Rhodes scholarship. He served in the US House of Representatives 1942–45 before becoming a senator. He anticipated the creation of the ◊United Nations, calling for US membership in an international peacekeeping body. He was an advocate of military and economic aid to Western nations but a powerful critic of US involvement in the ◊Vietnam war.

***Fuller** US architect Buckminster Fuller invented the geodesic dome 1947.*

Fuller (Richard) Buckminster 1895–1983. US architect, engineer, and futurist social philosopher who embarked on an unorthodox career in an attempt to maximize energy resources through improved technology. He invented the lightweight geodesic dome, a half-sphere of triangular components independent of buttress or vault. He also invented a Dymaxion (a combination of the words "dynamics" and "maximum") house 1928 and car 1933 that was inexpensive and utilized his concept of using the least amount of energy output to gain maximum interior space and efficiency, respectively. Among his books are *Ideas and Integrities* 1963, *Utopia or Oblivion* 1969, and *Critical Path* 1981.

Fuller John Frederick Charles 1878–1966. British major general and military theorist who propounded the concept of armored warfare, or blitzkrieg, as adopted by the Germans 1940.

Fuller Margaret 1810–1850. US author and reformer. Born in Cambridge, Massachusetts, and tutored by her father, Fuller began adult life as a teacher and writer. From 1839 to 1844, she held public "conversations" for the edification of the women of Boston; during the same period, she became the editor of *The Dial*, the Transcendentalist magazine. Fuller was hired as the literary critic for the *New York Tribune* 1844; later, while on assignment in Italy, she met and married the Marchese Angelo Ossoli and joined Mazzini's doomed nationalist revolt. She was lost at sea while returning to the US 1850.

Fuller Melville Weston 1833–1910. US jurist and chief justice of the US Supreme Court 1888–1910. As chief justice, Fuller generally supported a conservative approach, endorsing court opinions that limited state and federal strengths to regulate private business, limiting the jurisdiction of the Supreme Court and, in *United States* v *E C Knight Co* 1895, the application of the new Sherman Antitrust Act. He sided with the majority of the Court in *Pollack* v *Farmers Loan and Trust Co* 1895, which held invalid a flat-rate US income tax and led to passage of the 16th Amendment to the Constitution in 1913, authorizing an income tax.

Fuller was born in Augusta, Maine. He followed an early career in law and Democratic politics in Maine and then continued his activities in Chicago 1856. He was a supporter of Stephen Douglas in his 1858 election as US senator and in his bid for the presidency 1860. Fuller supported Grover Cleveland in the 1884 presidential election and was appointed chief justice by Cleveland in 1888.

fuller's earth a soft, greenish-gray rock resembling clay, but without clay's plasticity. It is formed largely of clay minerals, rich in montmorillonite, but a great deal of silica is also present.

Its absorbent properties make it suitable for removing oil and grease, and it was formerly used for cleaning fleeces ("fulling"). It is still used in the textile industry, but its chief application is in the purification of oils. Beds of fuller's earth are found in the southern US, Germany, Japan, and the UK.

Fullilove v Klutznick a US Supreme Court decision 1980 dealing with the constitutionality of Congressional legislation allocating a certain percentage of public works contracts to minority-owned businesses. Fullilove, a white business owner, filed suit against the government, arguing that the Public Works Employment Act, a bill that required states to use at least 10% of federal public works funds to hire minority businesses, was racially discriminatory. The Court found that the act was not a violation of the 14th Amendment but a remedial measure intended to enforce the equal protection clause. Congress, according to a 6–3 decision, was within its rights to use control over federal funds for the legitimate goal of reversing racial discrimination.

fulmar several species of petrels of the family Procellariidae, which are similar in size and color to herring gulls. The northern fulmar *Fulmarus glacialis* is found in the N Atlantic and visits land only to nest, laying a single egg.

fulminate any salt of fulminic (cyanic) acid (HOCN), the chief ones being silver and mercury. The fulminates detonate; that is, they are exploded by a blow.

Fulton Robert 1745–1815. US gunsmith, artist, engineer, and inventor who designed steamships based on those invented by James Rumsey 1787 and John ◊Fitch 1790. He managed to acquire British steam engines to power his first vessels, although at the time the British were not selling to the newly independent US. Fulton had lived 20 years in Europe, 1786–1805, and was well known as a painter and as an engineer of naval technology and canals; with the support of the new French government 1801, he built the first submarine, the *Nautilus*. He returned to the US with a commission from Robert Livingston, who had a license to serve the Hudson by steamboat, and combined the British-built steam engine with his own design of riverboat, a sidewheeler, and registered it as the *North River Steam Boat* 1807 (now erroneously known as the *Clermont*, a stop on the river). It and others were established and maintained by Fulton, going from New York City to Albany. Fulton also designed and oversaw the building of the first steam-powered warship, the USS *Fulton*, for the new US Navy.

fumitory any plant of the genus *Fumeria*, family Fumariaceae, native to Europe and Asia. The common fumitory *F. officinalis* produces pink flowers tipped with blackish red; it was once used in medicine for stomach complaints.

Funabashi city in Kanto region, Honshu Island, E of Tokyo; population (1987) 508,000.

Funafuti atoll consisting of 30 islets in the W Pacific and capital of the state of ◊Tuvalu; area 1.1 sq mi/ 2.8 sq km; population 900.

Funchal capital and chief port of the Portuguese island of Madeira, on the south coast; population (1980) 100,000. Tourism and wine are the main industries.

function in computing, a small part of a program that supplies a specific value; for example, the square root of a specified number, or the current date. Most programming languages incorporate a number of built-in functions; some allow programmers to write their own. A function may have one or more arguments (the values on which the function operates). A function key on a keyboard is one which, when pressed, performs a designated task, such as ending a program.

function in mathematics, a function f is a nonempty set of ordered pairs $(x,f(x))$ of which no two can have the same first element. Hence, if $f(x) = x^2$, two ordered pairs are (−2,4) and (2,4). The set of all first elements in a function's ordered pairs is called the domain; the set of all second elements is the range. In the algebraic expression $y = 4x^3 + 2$, the dependent variable y is a function of the independent variable x, generally written as $f(x)$.

Functions are commonly used in all branches of mathematics, physics, and science generally; for example, the formula $t = 2\pi\sqrt{(l/g)}$ shows that for a simple pendulum the time of swing t is a function of its length l and of no other variable quantity (π and g, the acceleration due to gravity, are ◊constants).

functional group in chemistry, a small number of atoms in an arrangement that determines the chemical properties of the group and of the molecule to which it is attached (for example, the carboxylic acid group, COOH, or the amine group NH_2). Organic compounds can be considered as structural skeletons with functional groups attached.

functionalism in the social sciences, the view of society as a system made up of a number of interrelated parts, all interacting on the basis of a common value system or consensus about basic values and common goals. Every social custom and institution is seen as having a function in ensuring that society works efficiently; deviance and crime are seen as forms of social sickness.

Functionalists often describe society as an organism with a life of its own, above and beyond the sum of its members. The French sociologists Comte and ◊Durkheim and the American ◊Parsons assumed functionalist approaches for their studies.

Functionalism in architecture and design, a 20th-century school, also called Modernism or the International Style, characterized by the ideal of excluding everything that serves no practical purpose. It developed as a reaction against the 19th-century practice of imitating and combining earlier styles, and its finest achievements are in the realm of industrial architecture and office furnishings.

Its leading exponents were the German ◊Bauhaus school, the Dutch group de ◊Stijl, and the Scandinavians, especially the Swedish and Finnish designers. Prominent architects in the field were Le Corbusier and Walter ◊Gropius.

fundamental forces in physics, the four fundamental interactions believed to be at work in the physical universe. There are two long-range forces: the ◊gravitational force, which keeps the planets in orbit around the Sun and acts between all ◊particles that have mass; and the ◊electromagnetic force, which stops solids from falling apart and acts between all particles with ◊electric charge. There are two very short-range forces: the ◊weak force, responsible for radioactive decay and for other subatomic reactions; and the ◊strong force, which binds together the protons and neutrons in the nuclei of atoms.

By 1971, Steven Weinberg and Sheldon Glashow (US), Abdus Salam (UK), and others developed a theory that suggested that the weak and electromagnetic forces were linked; experimental support came from observation at ◊CERN in the 1980s. Physicists are now working on theories to unify all four forces. See ◊Superstring Theory.

fundamentalism in religion, an emphasis on basic principles or articles of faith. Christian fundamentalism emerged in the US just after World War I (as a reaction to theological modernism and the historical criticism of the Bible) and insisted on belief in the literal truth of everything in the Bible. Islamic fundamentalism insists on strict observance of Muslim Shari'a law.

Christian adherents see the virgin birth, the physical resurrection of Jesus, the atonement, and the Bible miracles as fundamental to their faith. The movement soon became more belligerent, attempting to outlaw the teaching of evolution (as

fungus

Structure of a fungus

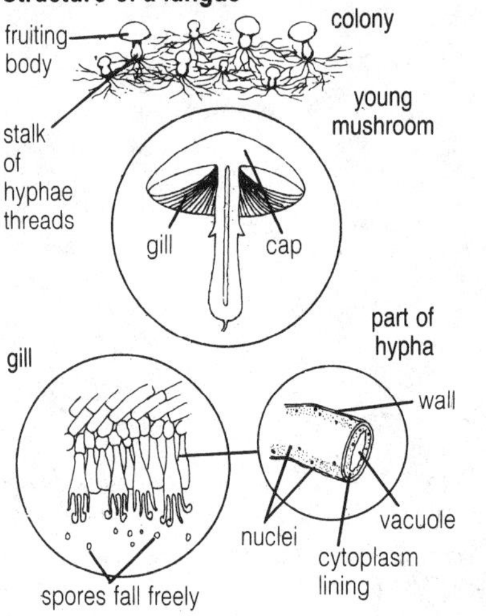
fruiting body
colony
young mushroom
stalk of hyphae threads
gill
cap
part of hypha
gill
wall
vacuole
nuclei
cytoplasm lining
spores fall freely

in ◊Dayton, Tennessee, 1925) and replace it with ◊creationism.

In the 1950s a more moderate tendency broke off to form the evangelical movement, which claims to carry on the original intentions of Fundamentalism.

fundamental particle alternate term for ◊***elementary particle***.

Fundy, Bay of Canadian Atlantic inlet between New Brunswick and Nova Scotia, with a rapid tidal rise and fall of 60 ft/18 m (harnessed for electricity since 1984). In summer, fog increases the dangers to shipping.

Fünen German form of ◊Fyn, an island forming part of Denmark.

Fünfkirchen (German "Five Churches") German name for ◊Pécs, a town in SW Hungary.

fungicide any chemical ◊pesticide used to prevent fungus diseases in plants and animals. Inorganic and organic compounds containing sulfur are widely used.

fungus (plural fungi) any of a group of organisms in the kingdom Fungi. Fungi are not considered plants. They lack leaves and roots; they contain no chlorophyll and reproduce by spores. Moulds, yeasts, rusts, smuts, mildews, and mushrooms are all types of fungus.

Because fungi have no chlorophyll, they must get food from organic substances. They are either ◊parasites, existing on living plants or animals, or ◊saprophytes, living on dead matter. Some 50,000 different species have been identified. Some are edible, but many are highly poisonous.

Before the classification Fungi came into use, they were included within the division Thallophyta, along with algae and bacteria.

funicular railroad railroad with two automobiles connected by a wire cable wound around a drum at the top of a steep incline. Funicular railroads of up to 1 mi/1.5 km exist in Switzerland.

Funk Casimir 1884–1967. US biochemist, born in Poland, who pioneered research into vitamins.

Funk proposed that certain diseases are caused by dietary deficiencies. In 1912 he demonstrated that rice extracts cure beriberi in pigeons. As the extract contains an ◊amine, he mistakenly concluded that he had discovered a class of "vital amines," a phrase soon reduced to "vitamins."

fur pelts of certain animals. Fur is used as clothing, although this is vociferously criticized by environmental groups on humane grounds, because the methods of breeding or trapping animals are often cruel. Mink, chinchilla, and sable are among the most valuable, the wild furs being finer than the farmed.

Furs have been worn since prehistoric times and have long been associated with status and luxury (ermine traditionally worn by royalty, for example), except for certain ethnic groups like the Eskimo. The fur trade had its origin in North America, exploited by the Hudson's Bay Company from the late 17th century. The chief centers of the fur trade are New York, London, Leningrad, and Kastoria. It is illegal to import furs or skins of endangered species listed by ◊CITES, for example leopard. Many synthetic fibers are widely used as substitutes.

Furies in Greek mythology, the Erinyes, appeasingly called the Eumenides ("kindly ones"). They were the daughters of Earth or of Night, represented as winged maidens with serpents twisted in their hair. They punished such crimes as filial disobedience, murder, and inhospitality.

furlong unit of measurement, originating in Anglo-Saxon England, equivalent to 220 yd (201.168 m).

A furlong consists of 40 rods, poles, or perches; 8 furlongs equal one statute ◊mile. Its literal meaning is "furrow-long," and refers to the length of a furrow in the common field characteristic of medieval farming.

Furman v Georgia (Jackson v Georgia; Branch v Texas) a US Supreme Court decision 1972 consolidating several challenges to the constitutionality of the death penalty. Three men, condemned to death by the states of Georgia and Texas, appealed their sentences, arguing that their 8th Amendment protection against cruel and unusual punishment had been violated. The Court voted 5–4 to invalidate the sentences, ruling that the death penalty not only violated the 8th Amendment but the 14th as well, since it was meted out unequally to the "poor and despised." The decision affected 600 persons already on death row.

furnace structure in which fuel such as coal, coke, gas, or oil is burned to produce heat for various purposes. Furnaces are used in conjunction with ◊boilers for heating, to produce hot water, or steam for driving turbines—in ships for propulsion and in power stations for generating electricity. The largest furnaces are those used for smelting and refining metals, such as the ◊blast furnace, electric furnace, and ◊open-hearth furnace.

Fürth city in Bavaria, Federal Republic of Germany, adjoining Nuremberg; population (1984) 98,500. It has electrical, chemical, textile, and toy industries.

Furtwängler (Gustav Heinrich Ernst Martin) Wilhelm 1886–1954. German conductor; leader of the Berlin Philharmonic Orchestra 1922–54. His interpretations of the German Romantic composers, such as Wagner, were regarded as Classically definitive. He remained in Germany during the Nazi regime.

furze another name for ◊***gorse***, a shrub.

fuse in electricity, a wire or strip of metal designed to melt when excessive current passes through. It is a safety device to stop at that point in the circuit surges of current that would otherwise damage equipment and cause fires. In explosives, a fuse is a cord impregnated with chemicals so that it burns slowly at a predetermined rate. It is used to set off a main explosive charge, sufficient length of fuse being left to allow the person lighting it to get away to safety.

fusel oil a liquid with a characteristic unpleasant smell, obtained as a by-product of the distillation of the product of any alcoholic fermentation, and used in paints, varnishes, essential oils, and plastics. Fusel oil is a mixture of fatty acids, alcohols, and esters.

Fushun coal-mining and oil-refining center in Liaoning province, China, 25 mi/40 km E of Shenyang; population (1984) 636,000. It has aluminum, steel, and chemical works.

fusion in physics, the fusing of the nuclei of light ◊elements, such as hydrogen, into those of a heavier element, such as helium. The resultant loss in the combined mass is converted into energy. Stars and thermonuclear weapons work on the principle of nuclear fusion. So far no successful fusion reactor—one able to produce the

fusion *Experiments in nuclear fusion at the first large thrmonuclear reactor at the Joint European Torus (JET), Culham, England.*

required energy and contain the reaction—has been built. See ◊energy and ◊cold fusion.

future in business, a contract to buy or sell a specific quantity of a particular commodity or currency (or even a purely notional sum, such as the value of a particular stock index) at a particular date in the future. There is usually no physical exchange between buyer and seller. It is only the difference between the ground value and the market value that changes hands. Such transactions are a function of the futures market.

futures trading buying and selling commodities (usually cereals and metals) at an agreed price for delivery several months ahead.

Futurism a literary and artistic movement 1909–14, originating in Paris. The Italian poet ◊Marinetti published the Futurist Manifesto 1909 urging Italian artists to join him in Futurism. In their works the Futurists eulogized the modern world and the "beauty of speed and energy," trying to capture the dynamism of a speeding car or train by combining the shifting geometric planes of ◊Cubism with vibrant colors. As a movement Futurism died out during World War I, but the Futurists' exultation in war and violence was seen as an early manifestation of ◊fascism.

Gino Severini (1883–1966) painted a topsy-turvy landscape as if seen from the window of a moving train, in *Suburban Train Arriving at Paris* 1915 (Tate Gallery), and Giacomo Balla (1871–1958) represented the abstract idea of speed by the moving object in such pictures as *Abstract Speed-wake of a Speeding Car* 1919 (Tate Gallery). Umberto Boccioni, a sculptor, froze his figures as if they were several frames of a film moving at once.

Fuzhou or ***Foochow*** industrial port and capital of Fujian province, SE China; population (1986) 1,190,000. It is a center for shipbuilding and steel production; rice, sugar, tea, and fruit pass through the port. There are joint foreign and Chinese factories.

The Mazu (Matsu) island group, occupied by the Nationalist Chinese, is offshore.

Fyn (German *Fünen*) island forming part of Denmark and lying between the mainland and Zealand; capital Odense; area 1,149 sq mi/ 2,976 sq km; population (1984) 454,000.

fyrd Anglo-Saxon local militia in Britain. All freemen were obliged to defend their shire but, by the 11th century, a distinction was drawn between the great fyrd, for local defense, and the select fyrd, drawn from better-equipped and experienced warriors who could serve farther afield.

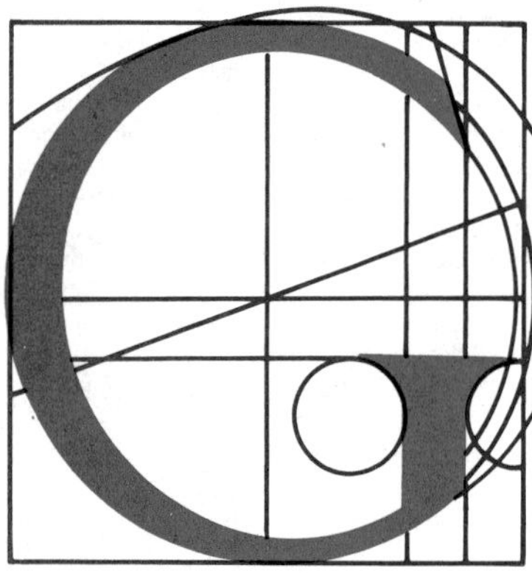

g symbol for ◊gram.

GA abbreviation for ◊Georgia (US).

gabbro a basic (low-silica) ◊igneous rock formed deep in the Earth's crust. It contains pyroxene and calcium-rich feldspar, and may contain small amounts of olivine and amphibole. Its coarse crystals of dull minerals give it a speckled appearance.

Gabbro is the plutonic version of basalt (that is, derived from magma that has solidified below the Earth's surface), and forms in large, slow-cooling intrusions.

gabelle in French history, term that originally referred to a tax on various items but came to be used exclusively for a tax on salt, first levied by Philip the Fair in 1286 and abolished 1790.

Gable Clark 1901–1960. US actor. A star for more than 30 years in 90 films, he was celebrated for his romantic, rakish nonchalance in roles such as Rhett Butler in *Gone with the Wind* 1939. Other films include *The Painted Desert* 1931 (his first), *It Happened One Night* 1934 (Academy Award), *Mutiny on the Bounty* 1935, and *The Misfits* 1960, after which he died of a heart attack. He was nicknamed the "King" of Hollywood.

Gabo Naum. Adopted name of Naum Neemia Pevsner 1890–1977. US abstract sculptor, born in Russia. One of the leading exponents of ◊Constructivism, he left the USSR in 1922 for Germany and taught at the Bauhaus in Berlin (a key center of modern design). He lived in Paris and England in the 1930s, then settled in the US in 1946. He was one of the first artists to make kinetic (moving) sculpture and often used transparent colored plastics.

Gabon country in central Africa, bounded N by Cameroon, E and S by the Congo, W by the Atlantic Ocean, and NW by Equatorial Guinea.

Gable *The career of actor Clark Gable spanned the Golden Age of Hollywood and included the role of Rhett Butler in the 1939 classic* Gone with the Wind. *This studio portrait is from the 1950s.*

government The 1961 constitution, revised in 1976, 1975, and 1981, provides for a president elected by universal suffrage for a seven-year term. As head of both state and government, the president appoints and presides over a prime minister and council of ministers and is also founder and secretary general of the Gabonese Democratic Party (PDG). There is a single-chamber legislature, the National Assembly, of 120 members, 111 elected and nine nominated for a five-year term. Gabon became a one-party state in 1968, the party being the PDG.

history Gabon was colonized by some of its present inhabitants (the Fang and the Omiéné) between the 16th and 18th centuries. Its first European visitors were the Portuguese in the late 15th century. They began a slave trade that lasted almost 400 years. In 1889 Gabon became part of the French Congo and was a province of French Equatorial Africa from 1908.

Gabon achieved full independence in 1960. There were then two main political parties, the Gabonese Democratic Bloc (BDG), led by Léon M'ba, and the Gabonese Democratic and Social Union (UDSG), led by Jean-Hilaire Aubame. Although the two parties were evenly matched in popular support, on independence M'ba became president, and Aubame, foreign minister.

In 1967 the BDG wanted the two parties to merge, but the UDSG resisted, and M'ba called a general election. Before the elections M'ba was deposed in a military coup by supporters of Aubame but was restored to office with French help. Aubame was tried and imprisoned for treason. The UDSG was outlawed, and most of its members joined the BDG.

In 1967 M'ba, although in failing health, was reelected. He died later that year and was succeeded by Albert-Bernard Bongo who, the following year, established the Gabonese Democratic Party (PDG) as the only legal party. Bongo was reelected in 1973 and was converted to Islam, changing his first name to Omar. In 1979 Bongo, as the sole presidential candidate, was reelected for a further seven years.

Gabon's reserves of uranium, manganese, and iron make it the richest country per head in Black Africa, and both M'ba and Bongo have successfully exploited these resources, gaining control of the iron-ore ventures once half-owned by the Bethlehem Steel Corporation of the US, and concluding economic and technical agreements with China as well as maintaining ties with France. Although he has operated an authoritarian regime, Gabon's prosperity has diluted any serious opposition to President Bongo. He was reelected in Nov 1986, and a coup attempt against him in 1989 was defeated by loyal troops. In Sept 1990 the first multiparty elections since 1964 were held amid claims of widespread fraud, with 553 candidates contesting 120 assembly seats.

Gabor Dennis 1900–1979. Hungarian-born British physicist. In 1947 he invented the holographic method of three-dimensional photography (see ◊holography). In 1971 he was awarded a Nobel Prize.

Gaborone capital of Botswana from 1965, mainly an administrative center; population (1988) 111,000. Light industry includes textiles.

Gabriel in the New Testament, the archangel who foretold the birth of John the Baptist to Zacharias and of Jesus to the Virgin Mary. He is also mentioned in the Old Testament in the book of Daniel. In Muslim belief, Gabriel revealed the Koran to

Gabon

Gabonese Republic
(*République Gabonaise*)

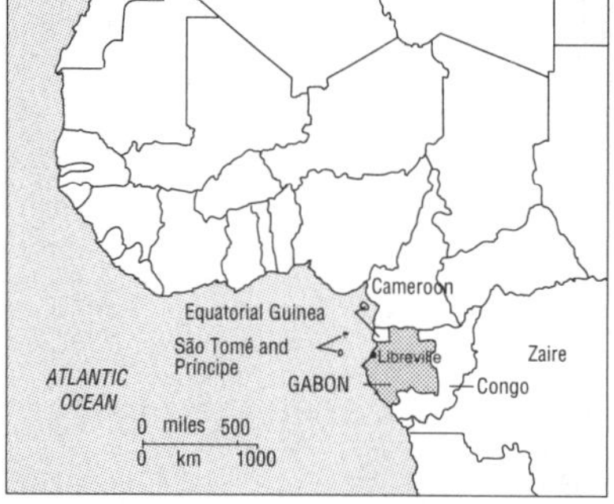
Cameroon
Equatorial Guinea
São Tomé and Príncipe
Libreville
Zaire
ATLANTIC OCEAN
GABON
Congo
0 miles 500
0 km 1000

area 103,319 sq mi/267,667 sq km
capital Libreville
cities ports Port-Gentil and Owendo; Masuku (Franceville)
physical virtually the whole country is tropical rainforest; narrow coastal plain rising to hilly interior with savanna in E and S; Ogooué River flows S–W
features Schweitzer hospital at Lambaréné; Trans-Gabonais railroad
head of state and government Omar Bongo from 1967
political system authoritarian nationalism
political parties Gabonese Democratic Party (PDG), nationalist
exports petroleum, manganese, uranium, timber
currency CFA franc
population (1988) 1,226,000 including 40 Bantu tribes; growth rate 1.6% p.a.
life expectancy men 47, women 51
language French (official), Bantu
religion 84% Christian (Roman Catholic 65%), small Muslim minority (1%), animist
literacy men 70%/women 53% (1985 est)
GDP $3.5 bn (1987); $3,308 per head
chronology
1889 Gabon became part of the French Congo.
1960 Independence from France achieved; Léon M'ba became the first president.
1967 Attempted coup by rival party foiled with French help. M'ba died; he was succeeded by his protégé, Albert-Bernard Bongo.
1968 One-party state established.
1973 Bongo reelected; converted to Islam, he changed his first name to Omar.
1986 Bongo reelected.
1989 Coup attempt against Bongo defeated.
1990 Widespread fraud alleged in first multiparty elections since 1964.

Mohammed and escorted him on his ◊Night Journey.

Gabrieli Giovanni c. 1555–1612. Italian composer and organist. Although he composed secular music and madrigals, he is best known for his motets, which are frequently dramatic and often use several choirs and groups of instruments. In 1585 he became organist at St Mark's, Venice.

Gadamer Hans-Georg 1900– . German ◊hermeneutic philosopher. In *Truth and Method* 1960, he argued that "understanding" is fundamental to human existence, and that all understanding takes place within a tradition. The relation between text and interpreter can be viewed as a dialogue, in which the interpreter must remain open to the truth of the text.

Gaddafi alternate form of ◊Khaddhafi, Libyan leader.

Gaddi family of Italian painters in Florence: Gaddo Gaddi (c. 1250–1330); his son Taddeo Gaddi (c. 1300–1366), who was inspired by Giotto and painted the fresco cycle *Life of the Virgin* in Santa Croce, Florence; and grandson Agnolo Gaddi (active 1369–96), who also painted frescoes in Santa Croce, *The Story of the Cross* 1380s, and produced panel paintings in characteristic pale pastel colors.

Gaddis William 1922– . Experimental US novelist, whose best-known novel *The Recognitions* 1955 is about artistic counterfeiting. His other novels are *JR* 1976 and *Carpenter's Gothic* 1985.

gadfly a fly that bites cattle, such as a ◊botfly, or ◊horsefly.

gadolinium silver-white metallic element of the ◊lanthanide series, symbol Gd, atomic number 64, atomic weight 157.25. It occurs in combination with other rare-earth elements in certain rare minerals. It is very magnetic at low temperatures, superconductive, and one of its isotopes has the highest neutron-absorption cross-section of any element. Gadolinium is used in electronic components, alloys, and products needing to withstand high temperatures. The name was given in 1886 in honor of the Finnish chemist J Gadolin (1760–1852) by its isolators the French chemist P-E Lecoq de Boisbaudran (1838–1912) and the Swiss chemist J-C G de Marignac (1817–1894).

Gadsden city in NE Alabama, on the Coosa River, SE of Huntsville; seat of Etowah county. It is a distribution center for the area's livestock, poultry, and dairy products. Industries include manganese, bauxite, coal, timber, steel, rubber products, electrical machinery parts, and farm equipment; population (1990) 42,523.

Gadsden James 1788–1858. US military leader and diplomat who negotiated the Gadsden Purchase for the US 1854. Born in Charleston, South Carolina, and educated at Yale, Gadsden served in the War of 1812 and in the First Seminole War. In 1823 he was appointed by President Monroe to supervise the forced resettlement of the Seminoles to S Florida and held a command in the Second Seminole War. After several years as a railroad executive, Gadsden was named US minister to Mexico 1853. In that post he negotiated for the sale of Mexican territory S of the Gila river, which became part of New Mexico and Arizona, to be used as a route to California. The Gadsden Purchase was approved by the Senate 1854.

Gadsden Purchase, the in US history, the purchase of approximately 30,000 sq mi/77,700 sq km in what is now New Mexico and Arizona by the US 1853. The land was bought from Mexico for $10 million in a treaty negotiated by James Gadsden (1788–1858) of South Carolina, to construct a transcontinental railroad route, the Southern Pacific, completed in the 1880s.

Gaelic language member of the Celtic branch of the Indo-European language family, spoken in Ireland, Scotland, and (until 1974) the Isle of Man.

It is, along with English, one of the national languages of the Republic of Ireland, with over a half million speakers, and is known there both as Irish and Irish Gaelic. In Scotland, speakers of Gaelic number around 90,000 and are concentrated in the Western Isles, in parts of the NW coast and in the city of Glasgow. Gaelic has been in decline for several centuries, discouraged until recently within the British state. There is a small Gaelic-speaking community in Nova Scotia, Canada.

Gainsborough *English painter Thomas Gainsborough's portrait of the aristocratic* Mrs. Siddons *1785 hangs in the National Gallery, London.*

Gafsa oasis town in central Tunisia, center of a phosphate-mining area; population (1984) 60,900.

Gagarin Yuri (Alexeyevich) 1934–1968. Soviet cosmonaut who in 1961 became the first human in space aboard the spacecraft *Vostok 1*.

Born in the Smolensk region, the son of a farmer, he qualified as a foundryman. He became a pilot 1957, and on Apr 12 1961 completed one orbit of the Earth, taking 108 minutes from launch to landing. He died in a plane crash while training for the *Soyuz 3* mission.

Gaia or ***Ge*** in Greek mythology, the goddess of the Earth. She sprang from primordial Chaos and herself produced Uranus, by whom she was the mother of the Cyclopes and Titans.

Gaia hypothesis theory that the Earth's living and nonliving systems form an inseparable whole that is regulated and kept adapted for life by living organisms themselves. Since life and environment are so closely linked, there is a need for humans to understand and maintain the physical environment and living things around them. The Gaia hypothesis was elaborated by the British scientist James Lovelock in the 1970s.

Gainesville city in N Florida, SW of Jacksonville; seat of Alachua County. Its industries include electronic parts, concrete, and wooden products. The University of Florida 1853 is here; population (1990) 84,770.

Gainsborough Thomas 1727–1788. English landscape and portrait painter. He was born in Suffolk; in 1760 he settled in Bath and painted society portraits. In 1774 he went to London and became one of the original members of the Royal Academy. He was one of the first British artists to follow the Dutch style of painting realistic landscapes rather than imaginative Italianate scenery.

Gainsborough began to paint while still at school and in 1741 went to London, where he learned etching and studied at the Academy of Arts, but remained largely self-taught.

gal symbol for ◊gallon.

Galahad in Arthurian legend, one of the knights of the Round Table. Galahad succeeded in the quest for the ◊Holy Grail because of his virtue. He was the son of ◊Lancelot of the Lake.

Galápagos Islands (official name Archipeliégo de Colón) group of 15 islands in the Pacific, belonging to Ecuador; area 3,000 sq mi/7,800 sq km; population (1982) 6,120. The capital is San Cristóbal on the island of the same name. The islands are a nature preserve. Their unique fauna (including giant tortoises, iguanas, penguins, flightless cormorants, and Darwin's finches), which inspired Charles ◊Darwin to formulate the principle of evolution by natural selection, is under threat from introduced species.

Galatea in Greek mythology, a sea nymph who loved Acis, and when he was killed by Polyphemus transformed his blood into the river Acis. Pygmalion, a king of Cyprus, made a statue (later named Galatea) that he married after it was brought to life by Aphrodite.

Galaţi (German Galatz) port on the river Danube in Romania; population (1985) 293,000. Industries include shipbuilding, iron, steel, textiles, food processing, and cosmetics.

Galatia ancient province of Asia Minor. It was occupied in the 3rd century BC by the ◊Gauls, and became a Roman province 25 BC.

Galatians ◊epistle in the ◊New Testament to the churches in Galatia; attributed to St Paul.

galaxy congregation of millions or billions of stars, held together by gravity. Spiral galaxies, such as the ◊Milky Way, are flattened in shape, with a central bulge of old stars surrounded by a disk of younger stars, arranged in spiral arms like a Catherine wheel. They are classified from Sa to Sc depending on how tightly the arms are wound. Barred spirals are spiral galaxies that have a straight bar of stars across their center, from the ends of which the spiral arms emerge. The arms of spiral galaxies contain gas and dust from which new stars are still forming. They are classified SBa to SBc. Elliptical galaxies contain old stars and very little gas. They include the most massive galaxies known, containing a trillion stars, classified from E0 to E7 depending on the degree of flatness. There are also irregular galaxies. Most galaxies occur in clusters, containing anything from a few to thousands of members. The largest galaxy ever discovered is an LSBG (low surface-brightness galaxy) measuring 300,000 light-years across.

Our own galaxy, the Milky Way, is about 100,000 light-years in diameter and contains at least 100 billion stars. It is a member of a small cluster, the ◊Local Group. The Sun lies in one of its spiral arms, about 25,000 light-years from the center.

Galbraith John Kenneth 1908– . Canadian-born US economist. He became a US citizen 1937. One of his major works, the *Affluent Society* 1958, documents the tendency of the "invisible hand" of free-market capitalism to create private splendor and public squalor.

He was a professor of economics at Harvard, worked for the Office of Price Administration during World War II, and served the Kennedy administration as ambassador to India. He was an adviser to presidential candidates Adlai Stevenson, Eugene McCarthy, and George McGovern and believed strongly in a governmental role in economic planning.

Galen c. 130–c. 200. Greek physician whose ideas dominated Western medicine for almost 1,500 years. Central to his thinking were the theories of ◊humors and the threefold circulation of the blood.

Galen was born in Pergamum in Asia Minor. He attended the Roman emperor Marcus Aurelius. Although he made relatively few discoveries and relied heavily on the teachings of ◊Hippocrates, he wrote a large number of books, over 100 of which are known. He remained the highest medical authority until Andreas Vesalius and William Harvey exposed the fundamental errors of his system.

galena chief ore of lead, consisting of lead sulfide, PbS. It is lead-gray in color, has a high metallic

galaxy
Hubble classification of galaxies

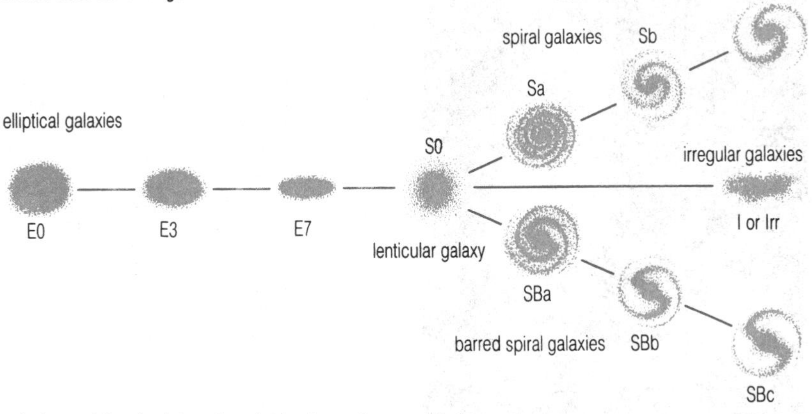
elliptical galaxies
E0
E3
E7
S0
lenticular galaxy
spiral galaxies
Sa
Sb
Sc
irregular galaxies
I or Irr
SBa
SBb
SBc
barred spiral galaxies

luster and breaks into cubes due to its perfect cubic cleavage. It may contain up to 1% silver, and so the ore is sometimes mined for both metals.

Galena occurs mainly among limestone deposits in Australia, Mexico, the USSR, the UK, and the US.

Galicia mountainous but fertile autonomous region of NW Spain, formerly an independent kingdom; area 11,348 sq mi/29,400 sq km; population (1986) 2,785,000. It includes La Coruña, Lugo, Orense, and Pontevedra. Industries include fishing and the mining of tungsten and tin. The language is similar to Portuguese.

Galicia former province of central Europe, extending from the northern slopes of the Carpathians to the Czechoslovak-Romanian border. Once part of the Austrian Empire, it was included in Poland after World War I and divided in 1945 between Poland and the USSR.

Galilee region of N Israel (once a province in Roman Palestine) which includes Nazareth and Tiberias, frequently mentioned in the Gospels of the New Testament.

Galilee, Sea of alternate name for Lake ◊Tiberias in N Israel.

Galileo spacecraft launched from the Space Shuttle *Atlantis* in Oct 1989, on a six-year journey to Jupiter.

Galileo properly Galileo Galilei 1564–1642. Italian mathematician, astronomer, and physicist. He developed the astronomical telescope and was the first to see sunspots, the four main satellites of Jupiter, mountains and craters on the Moon, and the appearance of Venus going through "phases," thus proving it was orbiting the Sun. In mechanics, Galileo discovered that freely falling bodies, heavy or light, had the same, constant acceleration (although the story of his dropping cannonballs from the Leaning Tower of Pisa is questionable) and that a body moving on a perfectly smooth horizontal surface would neither speed up nor slow down.

He discovered in 1583 that each oscillation of a pendulum takes the same amount of time despite the difference in amplitude. He invented a hydrostatic balance, and discovered that the path of a projectile is a parabola.

Galileo was born in Pisa, and in 1589 became professor of mathematics at the university there; in 1592 he became a professor at Padua, and in 1610 was appointed chief mathematician to the Grand Duke of Tuscany, Florence. Galileo's observations and arguments were an unwelcome refutation of the ideas of ◊Aristotle taught at the (Church-run) universities, largely because they made plausible for the first time the heliocentric (Sun-centered) theory of ◊Copernicus. Galileo's persuasive *Dialogues on the Two Chief Systems of the World* 1632 was banned by the Church authorities at Rome; he was made to recant by the ◊Inquisition and put under house arrest for his last years.

gall abnormal outgrowth on a plant which develops as a result of attack by insects or, less commonly, by bacteria, fungi, mites, or nematodes. The attack causes an increase in the number of cells or an enlargement of existing cells in the plant. Gall-forming insects generally pass the early stages of their life inside the gall. Gall wasps are responsible for the conspicuous bud galls forming on oak tree, 1 in/2.5 cm to 1.5 in/4 cm across, popularly known as "oak apples."

Gall c. 1840–1894. Sioux leader. Born along the Moreau river in the Dakota Territory, Gall became a noted warrior of the Hunkpapa Sioux and a protégé of Sitting Bull.

After participating in raids against the US Army along the Bozeman Trail, he opposed the Treaty of Fort Laramie 1868, which established the reservation system in the N plains. Gall accompanied Sitting Bull to Montana 1876 and led the encirclement and annihilation of Custer's force at the Little Bighorn. Escaping to Canada with Sitting Bull, he later settled on a reservation and became an Indian judge, opposing the Ghost Dance Uprising of 1890.

Gall Franz Joseph 1758–1828. Austrian anatomist, instigator of the discredited theory of ◊phrenology.

Gallatin Albert 1761–1849. Swiss-born US political leader and diplomat. He served in the Pennsylvania state legislature 1790–94 and the US House of Representatives 1795–1801. A critic of the Federalists, Gallatin helped establish the fiscal power of the House. He served as secretary of the treasury 1801–13 under presidents Jefferson and Madison and was sent to negotiate the treaty ending the War of 1812. Gallatin served as US Minister to France 1815–22 and to England 1826–27. In later years, he devoted himself to banking and American Indian ethnology.

gall bladder small muscular sac attached to the underside of the liver and connected to the small intestine by the bile duct. It stores bile from the liver.

Gallé Emile 1846–1904. French ◊Art Nouveau glassmaker. He produced glass in sinuous forms or rounded, solid-looking shapes almost as heavy as stone, typically decorated with flowers or leaves in color on color.

After training in various parts of Europe, he worked at his father's glass factory and eventually took it over. A founder of the Ecole de Nancy, he designed furniture as well as achieving significant developments in the techniques of glassmaking.

Galle Johann Gottfried 1812–1910. German astron-

Galileo
NASA
USA

Galileo *The Galileo spacecraft about to be detached from the Earth-orbiting Space Shuttle* Atlantis *at the beginning of its six-year journey to Jupiter.*

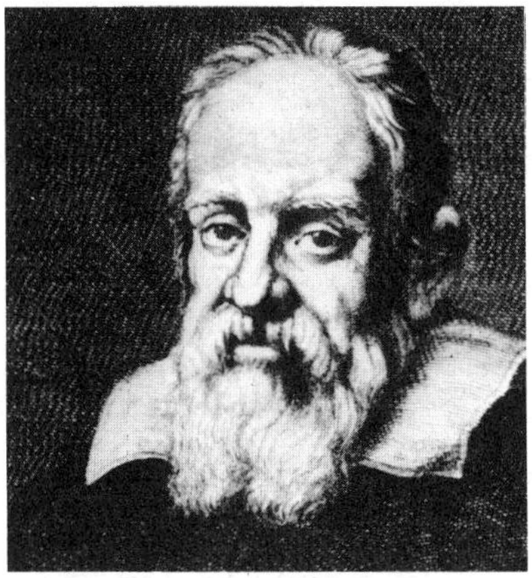

Galileo *Italian mathematician, astronomer, and physicist Galileo Galilei, whose theories aroused opposition from religious authorities.*

omer who located the planet Neptune 1846, close to the position predicted by French mathematician Urbain Leverrier, and one month later Triton, Neptune's largest moon.

Gallegos Rómulo 1884–1969. Venezuelan politican and writer. He was Venezuela's first democratically elected president in 1948 before being overthrown by a military coup the same year. He was also a professor of philosophy and literature. His novels include *La trepadora/The Climber* 1925 and *Doña Barbara* 1929.

galley ship powered by oars, and usually also with sails. Galleys typically had a crew of hundreds of oarsmen arranged in rows; they were used in warfare in the Mediterranean from antiquity until the 18th century.

France maintained a fleet of some 40 galleys, crewed by over 10,000 convicts, until 1748. The maximum speed of a galley is estimated to have been only four knots (4.5 mph/7.5 kph), while only 20% of the oarsmen's effort was effective, and galleys could not be used in stormy weather because of their very low waterline.

Gallico Paul (William) 1897–1976. US author. Originally a sports columnist, he began writing fiction in 1936. His many books include *The Snow Goose* 1941.

Gallipoli port in European Turkey, giving its name to the peninsula (ancient name Chersonesus) on which it stands. In World War I, at the instigation of Winston Churchill, an unsuccessful attempt was made Feb 1915–Jan 1916 by Allied troops to force their way through the Dardanelles and link up with Russia. The campaign was fought mainly by Australian and New Zealand (◊ANZAC) forces, who suffered heavy losses. An estimated 36,000 Commonwealth troops died during the nine-month campaign.

gallium gray-white metallic element, symbol Ga, atomic number 31, atomic weight 69.72. It is similar to mercury with a melting point somewhat above room temperature (85.6°F/29.78°C) and thus used in semiconductors, LEDs, lasers, and as a substitution for mercury in high-temperature thermometers. Gallium arsenide crystals are used in microelectronics, since electrons travel a thousand times faster through them than through silicon. The element was named in 1875 by the French chemist P-E Lecoq de Boisbaudran (1838–1912) for the old Latin name for France, *Gallia*, and as a pun on his own name Lecoq (Latin *gallus*, "cock").

Gallo Robert Charles 1937– . US scientist who, with French scientist Luc Montagnier (1932–), discovered the ◊AIDS virus. The Montagnier virus was isolated in 1983 at the Pasteur Institute, Paris. The Gallo virus, discovered in the US in 1984, has been alleged to have been accidentally contaminated by samples of the virus discovered by Montagnier, who gave them to Gallo for research at the National Cancer Institute, near Washington, DC.

gallon unit of liquid measure, equal to 3.785 liters, and subdivided into four quarts or eight pints. The UK and Canadian imperial gallon is equivalent to 4.546 liters.

gallstone pebblelike, insoluble accretion formed in the human gall bladder or bile ducts from cholesterol or calcium salts present in bile. Gallstones may be symptomless or they may cause pain, indigestion, or jaundice. They can be dissolved with medication or removed, along with the gall bladder, in an operation known as cholecystectomy.

Gallup George Horace 1901–1984. US journalist and statistician, who founded in 1935 the American Institute of Public Opinion and devised the Gallup Poll, in which public opinion is sampled by questioning a number of representative individuals.

Galois Evariste 1811–1832. French mathematician who originated the theory of groups. His attempts to gain recognition for his work were largely thwarted by the French mathematical establishment, critical of his lack of formal qualifications. Galois was killed in a duel before he was 21. The night before, he had hurriedly written out his unpublished discoveries on group theory, the importance of which would come to be appreciated more and more as the 19th century progressed.

Galsworthy John 1867–1933. British novelist and dramatist whose work examines the social issues of the Victorian period. He is best known for *The Forsyte Saga* 1922 and its sequel *A Modern Comedy* 1929. Other novels include *The Country House* 1907 and *Fraternity* 1909; plays include *The Silver Box* 1906.

Born in Kingston, Surrey, Galsworthy first achieved success with *The Man of Property* 1906, the first installment of the *Forsyte* series, which included *In Chancery* and *To Let.* Soames Forsyte, the central character, is the embodiment of Victorian values and feeling for property, and the wife whom he also "owns"—Irene—was based on Galsworthy's wife. Later additions to the series are *A Modern Comedy* 1929, which contained *The White Monkey, The Silver Spoon*, and *Swan Song*, and the short stories *On Forsyte Change* 1930.

Galtieri Leopoldo 1926– . Argentinian general, leading member of the right-wing military junta that ordered the seizure 1982 of the Falkland Islands (Malvinas), a UK colony in the SW Atlantic claimed by Argentina. He and his fellow junta members were tried for abuse of human rights and court-martialed for their conduct of the war; he was sentenced to 12 years in prison in 1986.

Galton Francis 1822–1911. English scientist who studied the inheritance of physical and mental attributes in humans, with the aim of improving the human species. He discovered that no two sets of human fingerprints are the same, and is considered the founder of ◊eugenics.

Galvani Luigi 1737–1798. Italian physiologist. Born in Bologna, where he taught anatomy, he discovered galvanic, or voltaic, electricity in 1762, when investigating the contractions produced in the muscles of dead frogs by contact with pairs of different metals. His work led quickly to Alessandro ◊Volta's invention of the electric battery, and later to an understanding of how nerves control muscles.

galvanizing process for rendering iron rust-proof, by plunging it into molten zinc (the dipping method), or by electroplating it with zinc.

galvanometer instrument for detecting small electric currents by their magnetic effect.

Galveston Gulf of Mexico port on Galveston Island, Texas; population (1990) 59,070. It exports cotton, petroleum, wheat, and timber and has chemical works and petroleum refineries. Fishing is also important, and the city has long been a resort for the island's sandy beaches. The city dates from an 1817 settlement by the pirate Jean Lafitte. In 1900, some 8,000 people died in one of the hurricanes that periodically hit the region.

Gama *An engraving of the Portuguese navigator Vasco da Gama, whose 1497 voyage around the Cape of Good Hope opened a sea route to India.*

Galway county on the W coast of the Republic of Ireland, in the province of Connacht; area 2,293 sq mi/5,940 sq km; population (1986) 178,000. Towns include Galway (county town), Ballinasloe, Tuam, Clifden, and Loughrea (near which deposits of lead, zinc, and copper were found 1959).

The E is low-lying. In the S are the Slieve Aughty mountains and Galway Bay, with the Aran islands. West of Lough Corrib is Connemara, a wild area of moors, hills, lakes, and bogs. The Shannon is the principal river.

Galway fishing port and county town of county Galway, Republic of Ireland; population (1986) 47,000. It produces textiles and chemicals. University College is part of the national university, and Galway Theatre stages Irish Gaelic plays.

Galway James 1939– . Irish flutist, born in Belfast. He was a member of the Berlin Philharmonic Orchestra 1969–75, before taking up a solo career.

Gama Vasco da 1460–1524. Portuguese navigator, who commanded an expedition in 1497 to discover the route to India around the Cape of Good Hope in modern South Africa. He reached land on Christmas Day 1497, which he named Natal. He then crossed the Indian Ocean, arriving at Calicut May 1498, and returning to Portugal Sept 1499. In 1502 he founded a Portuguese colony at Mozambique.

Gambetta Léon Michel 1838–1882. French politician, organizer of resistance during the Franco-Prussian War, and founder in 1871 of the Third Republic. In 1881–82 he was prime minister for a few weeks.

Gambia river in W Africa, which gives its name to the country ◊Gambia; 620 mi/1,000 km long.

Gambia country in W Africa, surrounded to the N, E, and S by Senegal and bordered to the W by the Atlantic Ocean

government Gambia is an independent republic within the ◊Commonwealth. Its constitution dates from 1970 and provides for a single-chamber legislature, the house of representatives, consisting of 49 members, 35 directly elected by universal suffrage, five elected by the chiefs, eight nonvoting nominated members; and the attorney general, ex-officio. It serves a five-year term, as does the president, who is elected by direct universal suffrage and appoints a vice-president

Gambia
Republic of The

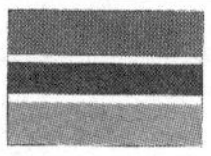

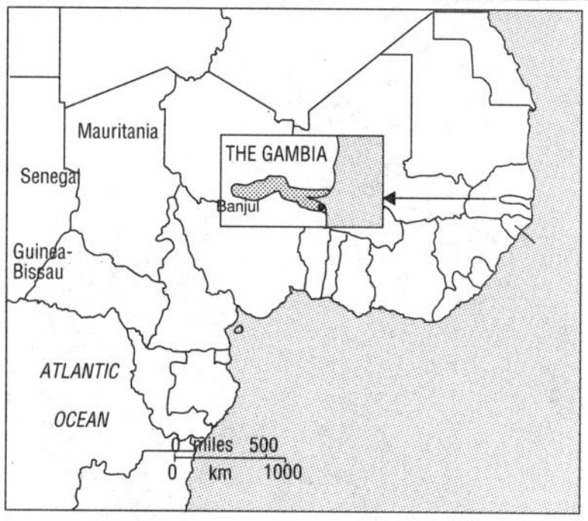
Mauritania
Senegal
THE GAMBIA
Banjul
Guinea-Bissau
ATLANTIC
OCEAN
0 miles 500
0 km 1000

area 4,018 sq mi/10,402 sq km
capital Banjul
cities Serekunda, Bakau, Georgetown
physical banks of the river Gambia flanked by low hills
features smallest state in black Africa; stone circles; Karantaba obelisk marking spot where Mungo Park began his journey to the Niger
head of state and government Dawda Kairaba Jawara from 1970
political system liberal democracy
political parties Progressive People's Party (PPP), moderate centrist; National Convention Party (NCP), left-of-center
exports groundnuts, palm oil, fish
currency dalasi
population (1990 est) 820,000; growth rate 1.9% p.a.
life expectancy 42 (1988 est)
language English (official); Mandinka, Fula and other native tongues
religion Muslim 90%, with animist and Christian minorities
literacy men 36%/women 15% (1985 est)
GDP $189 million (1987); $236 per head
chronology
1843 Gambia became a crown colony.
1965 Independence achieved from Britain as a constitutional monarchy within the Commonwealth, with Dawda K Jawara as prime minister.
1970 Declared itself a republic, with Jawara as president.
1972 Jawara reelected.
1981 Attempted coup foiled with the help of Senegal.
1982 Formed with Senegal the Confederation of Senegambia; Jawara reelected.
1987 Jawara reelected.
1989 Confederation of Senegambia dissolved.

(who also leads the house of representatives) and a cabinet. There are two main political parties, the Progressive People's Party (PPP) and the National Convention Party.

history Gambia was formerly part of the ◊Mali empire, a Muslim gold-trading empire that flourished in W Africa between the 7th and 15th centuries, and declined at the time of the Portuguese arrival 1455. In the late 16th century commerce was taken over from Portugal by England, and trading posts established on Gambia River were controlled from Sierra Leone. In 1843 Gambia was made a crown colony, becoming an independent British colony 1888.

Political parties were formed in the 1950s, internal self-government granted 1963, and full independence within the Commonwealth achieved 1965, with Dawda K Jawara as prime minister. It declared itself a republic 1970, with Jawara as president, replacing the British monarch as head of state. He was reelected 1972 and 1977.

With the PPP the dominant political force, there was pressure to make Gambia a one-party state, but Jawara resisted this. When an attempted coup against him 1981 was thwarted with Senegalese military aid, ties between the two countries were strengthened to the extent that plans were announced for their merger into a confederation of Senegambia. However, Senegal had doubts about the idea, and in economic terms Gambia had more to gain. In Sept 1989 it was announced that Gambia had formally agreed to end the confederation. In 1982 Jawara was reelected for another five-year term, with over 60% of the popular vote and over 70% of the seats; he was again reelected in 1987. In 1990, Gambia contributed troops to the multi-nation force attempting to stabilize Liberia.

Gambier Islands island group, part of ◊French Polynesia, administered with the ◊Tuamotu Archipelago; area 14 sq mi/36 sq km; population (1983) 582. It includes four coral islands and many small islets. The main island is Mangareva, with its town Rikitea.

gambling or ***gaming*** staking of money or anything else of value on the outcome of a competition. Forms of gambling include legal or illegal betting on the outcome of sports results, casino games like blackjack and roulette, card games like poker, slot machines, or lotteries. Horse racing attracts gambling through either off- or on-track ◊betting.

For many years certain forms of gambling were illegal in the US, but recent revenue needs in state and local governments have legalized some gambling operations, such as casinos, state-wide lotteries, and off-track betting parlors. Gambling is a multibillion dollar operation worldwide and can be addictive. Gamblers Anonymous was set up in the US 1957 to help compulsive gamblers overcome their addiction.

game farming protected rearing of gamebirds such as pheasants, partridges, and grouse for subsequent shooting. Game farms provide plenty of woodland and brush, which the birds require for cover, and may also plant special crops for them to feed on.

gamelan orchestra Asian orchestra, common in Indonesia and Thailand, using tuned metal percussion instruments (mainly gongs and bells), the music of which has inspired Western composers, such as Philip ◊Glass.

Gamelin Maurice Gustave 1872–1958. French commander in chief of the Allied armies in France at the outset of World War II 1939. Replaced by Maxime Weygand after the German breakthrough at Sedan 1940, he was tried by the ◊Vichy government as a scapegoat before the Riom "war guilt" court 1942. He refused to defend himself and was detained in Germany until released by the Allies 1945.

gamete a cell that functions in sexual reproduction by merging with another gamete to form a ◊zygote. Examples of gametes include sperm and egg cells. In most organisms, the gametes are ◊haploid (they contain half the number of chromosomes of the parent), caused by reduction division or ◊meiosis.

In higher organisms, gametes are of two distinct types: large immobile ones known as eggs or egg cells (see ◊ovum) and small ones known as ◊sperm. They come together at ◊fertilization. In some lower organisms the gametes are all the same, or they may belong to different mating strains but have no obvious differences in size or appearance.

game theory a group of mathematical theories, developed in 1944 by Oscar Morgenstern (1902–1977) and John von ◊Neumann, that seeks to abstract from invented game-playing scenarios and their outcome the essence of situations of conflict and/or cooperation in the real political, business, and social world.

A feature of such games is that the rationality of a decision by one player will depend on what the others do; hence game theory has particular application to the study of ◊oligopoly (a market largely controlled by a few producers).

gametophyte the ◊haploid generation in the life cycle of a plant that produces gametes; see ◊alternation of generations.

gamma radiation very high-frequency ◊electromagnetic radiation, similar in nature to X-rays but of shorter wavelength, emitted by the nuclei of ◊radioactive substances during decay or by the interactions of high-energy electrons with matter. Cosmic gamma rays have been identified as coming from pulsars, radio galaxies, and quasars, although they cannot penetrate the Earth's atmosphere.

gamma-ray astronomy the study of gamma rays produced within our Galaxy, the Milky Way. They may be due to collisions between hydrogen gas and cosmic rays. Some sources have been identified, including the Crab nebula and the Vela pulsar (the most powerful gamma-ray source detected). Gamma rays are not plentiful and only about a million gamma-ray photons have been collected. This is equivalent to the number of photons of visible light received from a star such as Sirius in about a second.

Gamma rays are difficult to detect and are generally studied by use of balloon-borne detectors and artificial satellites. The first gamma-ray satellites were *SAS II* (1972) and *COS B* (1975), although gamma-ray detectors were carried on the *Apollo 15* and *16* missions. *SAS II* failed after only a few months, but *COS B*, carrying a single gamma-ray experiment and intended to be operational for only two years, was finally switched off 1982 after a mission in which it carried out a complete survey of the galactic disk.

Gamow George 1904–1968. Russian-born US cosmologist, nuclear physicist, and popularizer of science. His work in astrophysics included a study of the structure and evolution of stars and the creation of the elements. He also explained how the collision of nuclei in the solar interior could produce the nuclear reactions that power the Sun.

Gamow was also an early supporter of the ◊Big Bang theory of the origin of the universe. He predicted that the electromagnetic radiation left over from the universe's formation, should, after having cooled down during the subsequent expansion of the universe, manifest itself as a microwave background radiation with a temperature of 10K (–442°F/–263°C). In 1965 Arno Allan Penzias (1933–) and Robert Woodrow Wilson (1936–) discovered the microwave background, which had a temperature of 3K (–454°F/–270°C), or 3°C above ◊absolute zero.

Gance Abel 1889–1981. French film director whose *Napoléon* 1927 was one of the most ambitious silent epic films. It features color and triple-screen sequences, as well as multiple-exposure shots.

Gandhi Indira (born Nehru) 1917–1984. Indian politician. Prime minister of India 1966–77 and 1980–84, and leader of the ◊Congress Party 1966–77 and subsequently of the Congress (I) party. She was assassinated 1984 by members of her Sikh bodyguard, resentful of her use of troops to clear malcontents from the Sikh temple at ◊Amritsar.

Her father, Jawaharlat Nehru, was India's first prime minister. She married Feroze Gandhi in 1942 (died 1960, not related to Mahatma Gandhi) and had two sons, Sanjay Gandhi (1946–80), who died in an airplane crash, and Rajiv ◊Gandhi who was assassinated May 21, 1991. In 1975 the validity of her re-election to parliament was questioned, and she declared a state of emergency. During this time her son Sanjay was implementing a social and economic program (including an unpopular family-planning policy) which led to her

Gandhi *Indira Gandhi, Nehru's daughter, had a controversial political career, during which she was twice prime minister of India.*

defeat in 1977, although he masterminded her return to power in 1980.

Gandhi Mohandas Karamchand, called Mahatma ("Great Soul") 1869–1948. Indian Nationalist leader. A pacifist, he led the struggle for Indian independence from the UK by advocating non-violent noncooperation (*satyagraha*, defense of and by truth) from 1915. He was imprisoned several times by the British authorities and was influential in the Nationalist ◊Congress Party and in the independence negotiations 1947. He was assassinated by a Hindu nationalist in the violence that followed the partition of British India into India and Pakistan.

Gandhi was born in Porbandar and studied law in London, later practicing as a lawyer. He settled in South Africa where until 1914 he led the Indian community in opposition to racial discrimination. Returning to India, he emerged as leader of the Indian National Congress. He organized hunger strikes and events of civil disobedience, and campaigned for social reform, including religious tolerance and an end to discrimination against the so-called untouchable ◊caste. In 1947, following World War II, he played a significant role in negotiations for an autonomous Indian State. He was assassinated by a Hindu nationalist in the violence that followed partition.

Gandhi Rajiv 1944–1991. Indian politician, prime minister from 1984, following his mother Indira Gandhi's assassination, to Nov 1989. As prime minister, he faced growing discontent with his party's elitism and lack of concern for social issues.

Rajiv Gandhi initially displayed little interest in politics and became an airline pilot. But after the death in a plane crash of his brother Sanjay (1946–1980), he was elected to his brother's Amethi parliamentary seat 1981. In the Dec 1984 parliamentary elections he won a record majority. In 1985 he reached a temporary settlement with the moderate Sikhs, which failed, however, to

Gandhi *Mahatma Gandhi with his granddaughters.*

Gandhi *Rajiv Gandhi succeeded (1984–89) his assassinated mother and was himself assassinated in a 1991 election campaign.*

hold. His reputation was tarnished by a scandal concerning alleged kickbacks to senior officials from an arms deal with the Swedish munitions firm Bofors and, following his party's defeat in the general election of Nov 1989, Gandhi was forced to resign as prime minister. He was attempting to regain office in May 1991 when he was assassinated while campaigning.

Ganesh Hindu god, son of Siva and Parvati; he is represented as elephant-headed and is worshiped as a remover of obstacles.

Ganges (Hindi *Ganga*) major river of India and Bangladesh; length 1,560 mi/2,510 km. It is the most sacred river for Hindus.

Its chief tributary is the Jumna (Yamuna length 860 mi/1,385 km), which joins the Ganges near Allahabad, where there is a sacred bathing place. The Ganges is joined in its delta in Bangladesh by the river ◊Brahmaputra, and its most commercially important and westernmost channel to the Bay of Bengal is the Hooghly. The political leaders M K Gandhi, Nehru, and Indira Gandhi were all cremated on the banks of the Jumna at Delhi.

The area regularly flooded in the wet season has almost doubled, and the annual cost of flood damage has risen to $1 billion as a consequence of deforestation of the Ganges watershed, which has also decreased the river's flow in the dry season by 20%.

ganglion (plural ganglia) a solid cluster of nervous tissue containing many cell bodies and ◊synapses, usually enclosed in a tissue sheath; found in invertebrates and vertebrates.

In many invertebrates, the central nervous system consists mainly of ganglia connected by nerve cords. The ganglia in the head (cerebral ganglia) are usually well developed and are analogous to the brain in vertebrates. In vertebrates, most ganglia occur outside the central nervous system.

Gang of Four chief members of the radical faction that tried to seize power in China after the death of Mao Zedong 1976. It included his widow, ◊Jiang Qing; the other members were Zhang Chunjao, Wang Hungwen, and Yao Wenyuan. The coup failed, and they were soon arrested.

gangrene death and decay of body tissue (often of a limb) due to bacterial action; the affected part gradually turns black and causes blood poisoning.

Gangrene sets in as a result of loss of blood supply to the area. This may be due to disease (diabetes, atherosclerosis), an obstruction of a major blood vessel (as in ◊thrombosis), injury, or frostbite. Bacteria colonize the site unopposed, and a strong risk of blood poisoning often leads to surgical removal of the tissue or the affected part (amputation).

gangsterism a term popularized in relation to organized crime, particularly in the US. One result of the 18th Amendment (Prohibition) in 1919 was an increase in organized crime. The prohibition law was difficult to enforce; illicit liquor could be brought into the US over the long land borders or coastline, and illegal distilleries were soon established. Bootlegging activities (importing or making illegal liquor) and "speakeasies" (where alcohol could be illegally purchased) gave rise to rivalry which resulted in hired gangs of criminals (gangsters) and gun battles. Social unrest and a widening gap between rich and poor also created a climate in which crime flourished. One of the most notorious gangsters was Al ◊Capone, who had his headquarters in Chicago. In 1933 the 21st Amendment was passed repealing Prohibition. This, and the actions of the Federal Bureau of Investigation (FBI) under J. Edgar Hoover, limited the opportunities for the "gangster" and contributed to some reduction in crime.

gangue the part of an ore deposit which is itself economically valuable, for example, calcite might occur as a gangue mineral with galena.

gannet a sea-bird *Sula bassana* in the same family (Sulidae) as the boobies. Gannets are found in the N Atlantic. When fully grown, it is white with black-tipped wings having a span of 5.6 ft/1.7 m. The young are speckled. It breeds on cliffs in nests made of grass and seaweed. Only one (white) egg is laid.

Gannet Peak the highest peak in Wyoming, rising to 13,804 ft/4,207 m.

Gansu or ***Kansu*** province of NW China

area 204,580 sq mi/530,000 sq km

capital Lanzhou

features subject to earthquakes; the "Silk Road" (now a motor road) passed through it in the Middle Ages, carrying trade to central Asia

products coal, oil, hydroelectric power from the Huang He (Yellow) river

population (1986) 20,710,000, including many Muslims.

Ganymede in Greek mythology, a youth so beautiful he was chosen as cupbearer to Zeus.

Ganymede in astronomy, the largest moon of the planet Jupiter and the largest moon in the Solar System, 3,300 mi/5,300 km in diameter (larger than the planet Mercury). It orbits Jupiter every 7.2 days at a distance of 700,000 mi/1.1 million km. Its surface is a mixture of cratered and grooved terrain.

Gaoxiong mainland Chinese form of Kaohsiung, a port in W Taiwan.

gar primitive bony fish of the order Semionotiformes, which also includes ◊sturgeons. Gar have long, beaklike snouts and elongated bodies covered in heavy, bony scales. All four species of gar inhabit freshwater rivers and lakes of the Mississippi drainage. See also ◊needlefish.

Garbo Greta. Adopted name of Greta Lovisa Gustafsson 1905–1990. Swedish-born US film actress. She emigrated to the US in 1925, and her leading role in *The Torrent* 1926 made her

Garbo *The Swedish-born actress Greta Garbo enjoyed great success in Hollywood and then became a near recluse. She is shown in* Anna Christie *1930, her first "talkie."*

García Márquez The Colombian writer Gabriel García Márquez, whose novels have become widely known since he was awarded the Nobel Prize for Literature in 1982.

one of Hollywood's first "stars" in silent films. Her later films include *Mata Hari* 1931, *Grand Hotel* 1932, *Queen Christina* 1933, *Anna Karenina* 1935, *Camille* 1937, and *Ninotchka* 1939. She was noted for her reclusiveness after her retirement from films.

García Lorca Federico, Spanish poet. See ◊Lorca, Federico García.

García Márquez Gabriel 1928– . Colombian novelist. His sweeping novel *Cien años de soledad/One Hundred Years of Solitude* 1967 (which tells the story of a family over a period of six generations) is an example of magic realism, a technique used to heighten the intensity of realistic portrayal of social and political issues by introducing grotesque or fanciful material. His other books include *El amor en los tiempos del cólera/Love in the Time of Cholera* 1985. Nobel Prize for Literature 1982.

García Perez Alan 1949– . Peruvian politician, leader of the moderate, left-wing APRA party; president 1985–90.

He was born in Lima and educated in Peru, Guatemala, Spain, and France. He became APRA's secretary-general 1982. In 1985 he succeeded Fernando Belaúnde Terry as president, becoming the first civilian president democratically elected. He inherited an ailing economy and was forced to trim his Socialist program.

Garcia v San Antonio Metropolitan Transit Authority a US Supreme Court decision 1985 dealing with the imposition of federal labor regulations on the states as employers. Prior to this decision, the states had enjoyed immunity from the Federal Labor Standards Act under the 10th-Amendment provision that all rights not explicitly reserved for the federal government belong to the states. The Court ruled, however, that state employees are protected by federal minimum-wage and maximum-hours laws, deciding on the grounds that the judiciary is not responsible for safeguarding state sovereignty.

Garcilaso de la Vega 1503–1536. Spanish poet. A soldier, he was a member of Charles V's expedition in 1535 to Tunis; he was killed in battle at Nice. His verse, some of the greatest of the Spanish Renaissance, includes sonnets, songs, and elegies, often on the model of Petrarch.

Garcilaso de la Vega 1539–1616. Spanish writer, called el Inca. Son of a Spanish conquistador and an Inca princess, he wrote an account of the conquest of Florida and *Commentarios* on the history of Peru.

Gard French river, 83 mi/133 km long, a tributary of the Rhône, which it joins above Beaucaire. It gives its name to Gard *département* in Languedoc-Roussillon region.

Garda, Lake largest lake in Italy; situated on the border between the regions of Lombardia and Veneto; area 143 sq mi/370 sq km.

garden a plot of land, usually belonging to a householder. It can be cultivated to produce food or to create pleasant surroundings.

Pleasure gardens were common in all ancient civilizations. In medieval Europe gardens were devoted to growing medicinal plants and herbs but in the 16th century formal recreational gardens became a feature of larger town and country houses. The taste for formality continued into the 19th century, when a more natural look became fashionable. Most 18th-century rural workers had vegetable gardens and the practice was continued wherever possible in the new industrial towns. The miniature landscaped garden with lawns and flowerbeds became a feature of 20th-century housing estates in Europe and the US.

garden city a town built in a rural area and designed to combine town and country advantages, with its own industries, controlled developments, private and public gardens, and cultural center. The idea was proposed by Sir Ebenezer Howard (1850–1928), who in 1899 founded the Garden City Association, which established the first garden city, Letchworth (in Hertfordshire).

Based on the British model, the first garden city in the US was begun in Jackson Heights, Queens, New York 1904; it was emulated by the nearby Sunnyside Gardens community, which attracted Lewis ◊Mumford and his family, as well as Forest Hills Gardens, also in Queens, New York. Although neighboring communities have surrounded these, still an aura of gentility exists in these urban, gardened streets.

gardenia any subtropical and tropical trees and shrubs of Africa and Asia, genus *Gardenia*, of the madder family Rubiaceae, with evergreen foliage and flattened rosettes of fragrant waxen-looking blooms, often white in color.

garderobe a medieval lavatory. Garderobes were often built into the thickness of a castle wall, with an open drop to the moat below.

Gardner Ava 1922–1990. US actress who starred in the 1940s and 1950s in such films as *The Killers* 1946, *Pandora and the Flying Dutchman* 1951, and *The Barefoot Contessa* 1954. She remained active in films until the 1980s.

Gardner Erle Stanley 1889–1970. US author of crime fiction. He created the character of the lawyer-detective Perry Mason, who was later featured in film and on television. Originally a lawyer, he gave up his practice with the success of the first Perry Mason stories.

Gardner Isabella Stewart 1840–1924. US art collector and founder of the Isabella Stewart Gardner Museum in Boston. Born in New York and educated in Paris, she married prominent Boston manufacturer John Gardner 1860. A tireless world traveler, socialite, and local celebrity, she scandalized proper Bostonians with her lavish parties and public appearances. Gardner was a patron of the Boston Symphony Orchestra and participant

Garfield The 20th president of the United States of America, James A Garfield, a Republican. 1881.

Garibaldi *Italian hero of the Risorgimento, Giuseppe Garibaldi.*

in the intellectual life of the city. As an art collector, she specialized in the works of the Renaissance and of the Dutch masters. Her private art gallery in Boston was opened as a public museum 1903.

Gardner John 1917– . English composer. Professor at the Royal Academy of Music from 1956, he has produced a symphony 1951; the opera *The Moon and Sixpence* 1957, based on a Somerset Maugham novel; and other works, including film music.

Garfield James A(bram) 1831–1881. The 20th president of the US 1881, a Republican. He was born in a log cabin in Ohio, and served in the Civil War with the Union forces. He was elected president but held office for only four months before being assassinated in Washington, DC railroad station by a disappointed office-seeker.

He had been a compromise candidate for president, and his short tenure was marked primarily by struggles within the Republican party over influence and cabinet posts.

gargoyle spout projecting from the roof gutter of a building with the purpose of directing water away from the wall. The term is usually applied to the ornamental forms found in Gothic architecture; these were carved in stone in the form of fantastic animals, angels, or human heads.

Garibaldi Giuseppe 1807–1882. Italian soldier who played a central role in the unification of Italy by conquering Sicily and Naples 1860. From 1834 a member of the nationalist Mazzini's ◊Young Italy society, he was forced into exile until 1848 and again 1849–54. He fought against Austria 1848–49, 1859, and 1866, and led two unsuccessful expeditions to liberate Rome from papal rule in 1862 and 1867.

Born in Nice, he became a sailor and then joined the nationalist movement ◊Risorgimento. Condemned to death for treason, he escaped to South America where he became a mercenary. He returned to Italy during the 1848 revolution, served with the Sardinian army against the Austrians, and commanded the army of the Roman republic in its defense of the city against the French. He subsequently lived in exile until 1854, when he settled on the island of Caprera. In 1860, at the head of his 1,000 redshirts, he won Sicily and Naples for the new kingdom of Italy. He served in the Austrian War of 1866 and fought for France in the Franco-Prussian War 1870–71.

Garland Judy. Adopted name of Frances Gumm 1922–1969. US singer and actress. Her films include *The Wizard of Oz* (which featured the tune

garlic

that was to become her theme song, "Over the Rainbow"), *Babes in Arms* 1939, *Strike Up the Band* 1940, *Meet Me in St Louis* 1944, *Easter Parade* 1948, *A Star is Born* 1954, and *Judgment at Nuremberg* 1961.

She began her acting career 1935 in the Andy Hardy series. She was the mother of actress-singer Liza Minnelli.

garlic perennial plant *Allium sativum* of the lily family Liliaceae, with white flowers. The bulb, made of small segments, or cloves, is used in cooking, and its pungent essence has an active medical ingredient, allyl methyl trisulfide, which prevents blood clotting.

Garner John Nance 1868–1967. US political leader and vice-president of the US. Garner was appointed county judge 1895 and embarked on a career in Democratic party politics, serving in the state legislature 1898–1902 and the US House of Representatives 1903–33. A Democratic leader in the House, he was chosen as Speaker 1931. He later served as vice-president during Franklin Roosevelt's first two terms 1933–41. Opposing Roosevelt's reelection in 1940, Garner retired from public life.

Born in Red River County, Texas, Garner briefly attended Vanderbilt University. After privately studying law in Clarksville, Texas, he was admitted to the bar 1890.

garnet a group of silicate minerals with the formula $X_3Y_2(SiO_4)_3$, when X is calcium, magnesium, iron, or manganese, and Y is iron, aluminum, or chromium. They are used as semiprecious gems (usually pink to deep red) and as abrasives. Garnets occur in metamorphic rocks such as gneiss and schist.

Garonne river in SW France, rising on the Spanish side of the Pyrenees and flowing to the ◊Gironde estuary; length 350 mi/560 km.

Garret Almeida 1799–1854. Portuguese poet, novelist, and dramatist. As a liberal, in 1823 he was forced into 14 years of exile. His works, which he saw as a singlehanded attempt to create a national literature, include the prose *Viagens na Minha Terra/Travels in My Homeland* 1843–46 and the tragedy *Frei Luis de Sousa* 1843.

Garrick David 1717–1779. British actor and theater manager. He was a pupil of Samuel ◊Johnson. From 1747 he became joint licensee of the Drury Lane theater with his own company, and instituted a number of significant theatrical conventions including concealed stage lighting and banishing spectators from the stage. He performed Shakespeare characters such as Richard III, King Lear, Hamlet, and Benedick, and collaborated with George Colman (1732–94) in writing the play *The Clandestine Marriage* 1766. He retired from the stage 1766, but continued as a manager.

Garrison William Lloyd 1805–1879. US editor and reformer who was an uncompromising opponent of slavery. He founded the abolitionist journal *The Liberator* 1831 and became a leader of the American Anti-Slavery Society. Although initially opposed to violence, he supported the Union cause in the Civil War. After the Emancipation Proclamation, he disbanded the Anti-Slavery Society and devoted his energies to prohibition, feminism, and Indian rights.

Born in Newburyport, Massachusetts, and trained as a printer, Garrison later worked as an editor of various publications in Boston, Vermont, and Baltimore.

Garter, Order of the senior British order of knighthood, founded by Edward III in about 1347. Its distinctive badge is a garter of dark blue velvet, with the motto of the order, *Honi soit qui mal y pense* ("Shame be to him who thinks evil of it") in gold letters.

Garvey Marcus (Moziah) 1887–1940. Jamaican political thinker and activist, an early advocate of black nationalism. He founded the UNIA (Universal Negro Improvement Association) in 1914, and moved to the US in 1916, where he established branches in New York and other northern cities. Aiming to achieve human rights and dignity for black people through black pride and economic self-sufficiency, he was considered one of the first militant black nationalists. He led a Back to Africa movement for black Americans to establish a black-governed country in Africa. ◊Rastafarianism is based largely on his ideas.

Gary city in NW Indiana; population (1990) 116,646. It contains the steel and cement works of the US Steel Corporation and was named after E H Gary (1846–1927), its chairman. Cutbacks in steel production have left the city economically depressed.

gas substance composed of molecules in constant random motion, filling any size or shape of container into which the gas is put. Gases can be liquefied by cooling, which lowers the speed of the molecules and enables attractive forces between them to bind them together. Several of the chemical elements are gases—for example, hydrogen, helium, oxygen, and neon. Air is the mixture of gases that surrounds Earth; it consists chiefly of nitrogen and oxygen, along with argon, carbon dioxide, water vapor, hydrogen, neon, helium, radon, and other ◊inert gases.

gas constant in physics, the constant R that appears in the equation $PV = nRT$, which describes how the pressure P, volume V and temperature T of an ideal gas are related (n is the amount of gas in the specimen). This equation combines ◊Boyle's law and ◊Charles's law.

R has a value of 8.314, 34 joules per kelvin per mole.

Gascony ancient province of SW France. With Guienne it formed the duchy of Aquitaine in the 12th century; Henry II of England gained possession of it through his marriage to Eleanor of Aquitaine in 1152, and it was often in English hands until 1451. It was then ruled by the king of France until it was united with the French royal domain 1607 under Henry IV.

The area is now divided into several *départements*, including Landes and Pyrénées-Atlantiques.

gas engine type of internal-combustion engine in which a gas (coal gas, producer gas, natural gas, or gas from a blast furnace) is used as the fuel. The first practical gas engine was built 1860 by Jean Etienne Lenoir, and the type was subsequently developed by Nikolaus August Otto, who introduced the ◊four-stroke cycle.

gas exchange in biology, the exchange of gases between living organisms and the atmosphere, principally oxygen and carbon dioxide.

In animals, gas exchange is only respiratory (or using oxygen to convert food to energy). In plants, gas exchange is photosynthetic (or using carbon dioxide to make food) as well as respiratory. In humans, and other tetrapods (four-limbed vertebrates), gas exchange or respiration is the absorption of oxygen into the blood when air meets blood vessels in the ◊lungs, and the exhalation of carbon dioxide with water and small quantities of ammonia and waste matter. Many adult amphibia and terrestrial invertebrates can absorb oxygen directly through the skin. The bodies of insects and some spiders contain a system of air-filled tubes known as ◊tracheae. Fish and most other aquatic organisms have ◊gills, which

Garvey *Jamaican-born Marcus Garvey, at a New York City rally in 1922. Active in the United States from 1916, he founded the "Back to Africa" movement.*

exchange gases with the surrounding water. In plants, gas exchange necessary for photosynthesis and respiration generally takes place via the ◊stomata.

gas laws physical laws concerning the behavior of gases. They include ◊Boyle's law and ◊Charles's law, which are concerned with the relationships between the pressure, temperature, and volume of an ideal (hypothetical) gas.

gasohol motor fuel that is 90% gasoline and 10% ethanol (alcohol). The ethanol is usually obtained by fermentation, followed by distillation, using corn, wheat, potatoes, or sugar cane. It was used in early automobiles before gasoline became economical, and its use was revived during the 1940s war shortage and the energy shortage of the 1970s, for example in Brazil.

gasoline a mixture of hydrocarbons derived from petroleum, whose main use is as a fuel for internal combustion engines. It is colorless and highly volatile.

gasoline engine or ***piston engine*** the most commonly used source of power for motor vehicles, introduced by the German engineers Gottlieb Daimler and Karl Benz 1885. The gasoline engine is a complex piece of machinery made up of about 150 moving parts. It is a reciprocating piston engine (see ◊internal-combustion engine), in which a number of pistons move up and down in cylinders. The motion of the pistons rotate a crankshaft, at the end of which is a heavy flywheel. From the flywheel the power is transferred to the car's driving wheels via the transmission system of clutch, gearbox, and final drive.

The parts of the gasoline engine can be subdivided into a number of systems. The fuel system pumps fuel from the gasoline tank into the carburetor. There it mixes with air and is sucked into the engine cylinders. (With electronic fuel injection, it goes directly from the tank into the cylinders by way of an electronic monitor.) The ignition system supplies the sparks to ignite the fuel mixture in the cylinders. By means of an ignition coil and contact breaker, it boosts the 12-volt battery voltage to pulses of 18,000 volts or more. These go via a ◊distributor to the ◊spark plugs in the cylinders, where they create the sparks. (Electronic ignitions replace these parts.) Ignition of the fuel in the cylinders produces temperatures of 1,300°F/700°C or more, and the engine must be cooled to prevent overheating. Most engines have a water-cooling system, in which water circulates through channels in the cylinder block, thus extracting the heat. It flows through pipes in a radiator, which are cooled by fan-blown air. A few automobiles and most motorbikes are air-cooled, the cylinders being surrounded by many fins to present a large surface area to the air. The lubrication system also reduces some heat, but its main job is to keep the moving parts coated with oil, which is pumped under pressure to the camshaft, crankshaft, and valve-operating gear.

Gaspé Peninsula mountainous peninsula in SE Québec, Canada; area 11,390 sq mi/29,500 sq km. It has fishing and lumbering industries.

Gasperi Alcide de 1881–1954. Italian politician. A founder of the Christian Democrat Party, he was prime minister 1945–53 and worked for European unification.

Gassendi Pierre 1592–1655. French physicist and philosopher who played a crucial role in the revival of atomism (the theory that the world is made of small, indivisible particles), and the rejection of Aristotelianism so characteristic of the period. He was a propagandist and critic of other views rather than an original thinker.

Gastonia city in SW North Carolina, directly W of Charlotte; seat of Gaston County. Its most important industry is textiles; population (1990) 54,732. It was the site of a violent labor strike 1929.

gastritis inflammation of the lining of the stomach. The term is a vague one, applied to a range of conditions.

gastroenteritis inflammation of the stomach and intestines, giving rise to abdominal pain, vomiting, and diarrhea. It may be caused by food or other poisoning, allergy, or infection, and is dangerous in babies.

gastroenterology the medical speciality concerned with disorders of the ◊alimentary canal.

gastropod any member of a very large class (Gastropoda) of ◊mollusks. Gastropods are single-shelled (in a spiral or modified spiral form), have eyes on stalks, and move on a flattened, muscular foot. They have well-developed heads and rough, scraping tongues called radulae. Some are marine, some freshwater, and others land creatures, but all tend to inhabit damp places.

They include land snails, snugs, abalones, conches, coneshells, and sowries.

gas turbine engine in which burning fuel supplies hot gas to spin a ◊turbine. The most widespread application of gas turbines has been in aviation. All ◊jet engines are modified gas turbines, and some locomotives and ships also use gas turbines as a power source. They are also used in industry for generating and pumping purposes.

In a typical gas turbine a multivaned compressor draws in and compresses air. The compressed air enters a combustion chamber at high pressure, and fuel is sprayed in and ignited. The hot gases produced escape through the blades of (typically) two turbines and spin them around. One of the turbines drives the compressor; the other provides the external power that can be harnessed.

gas warfare military use of gas to produce a toxic effect on the human body. See ◊chemical warfare.

Gates Horatio c. 1727–1806. British-born American military leader who won the first major battle (Saratoga) of the Revolution after several American losses and retreats.

Born in England, Gates joined the British army, serving in Nova Scotia and seeing action in the French and Indian War. After returning to England, he immigrated to America in 1772. A friend of George Washington, he was appointed brigadier general in the Continental army 1775. Gates was placed in command of the Northern Department and won a tide-turning victory against Burgoyne at Saratoga 1777. Later falling out of favor with Washington, he was dispatched to the South, where his defeat at the Battle of Camden in 1780 effectively ended his military career.

Gatling Richard Jordan 1818–1903. US inventor of a rapid-fire gun. Patented in 1862, the Gatling gun had ten barrels arranged as a cylinder rotated by a hand crank. Cartridges from an overhead hopper or drum dropped into the breech mechanism, which loaded, fired and extracted them at a rate of 320 rounds per minute.

It was used in the US Civil War and in the Indian Wars that followed the settling of the American West. It was the precursor of the ◊machine gun.

GATT acronym for ◊General Agreement on Tariffs and Trade.

Gaudí Spanish architect Antonio Gaudí worked exclusively in Barcelona. This is Casa Mila.

gaucho part Indian, part Spanish cattle herder of the Argentine and Uruguayan pampas.

Gaudí Antonio 1852–1926. Spanish architect distinguished by his flamboyant Art Nouveau style. He designed both domestic and industrial buildings. His spectacular Church of the Holy Family, Barcelona, begun 1883, is still under construction.

gauge any scientific measuring instrument—for example, a wire gauge or pressure gauge. The term is also applied to the width of a railroad or trolley track.

gauge boson any of the particles that carry the four ◊fundamental forces. They are ◊elementary particles that cannot be subdivided and include the ◊photon, the ◊graviton, the ◊gluons, and the ◊weakons.

Gauguin Paul 1848–1903. French Post-Impressionist painter. Going beyond the Impressionists' notion of reality, he sought a more direct experience of life in the magical rites of the people and rich colors of the South Sea islands. He disliked theories and rules of painting and his pictures are ◊Expressionist compositions characterized by his use of pure, unmixed colors. Among his paintings is *Le Christe Jaune* 1889 (Albright-Knox Art Gallery, Buffalo, USA).

Born in Paris, Gauguin spent his childhood in Peru. After a few years as a stockbroker, he took up full-time painting in 1881, exhibited with the Impressionists, and spent two months with van ◊Gogh in Arles 1888. On his return to Brittany he concentrated on his new style, Synthetism, based on the use of powerful, expressive colors and boldly outlined areas of flat tone. Influenced by Symbolism, he chose subjects reflecting his interest in the beliefs of other cultures.

After a visit to Martinique 1887, he went to Pont Aven in Brittany, becoming the leading artist in the Synthetic movement, and abandoning conventional perspective. He lived in Tahiti 1891–93 and 1895–1901 and from 1901 in the Marquesas Islands.

Gaul a member of the Celtic-speaking peoples who inhabited France and Belgium in Roman times; also their territory.

Gauls were divided into several groups but were united by a common religion controlled by the Druid priesthood. Certain Gauls invaded Italy around 400 BC, sacked Rome, and settled between the Alps and the Apennines; this district, known as Cisalpine Gaul, was conquered by Rome in about 225 BC. The Romans conquered S Gaul between the Mediterranean and the Cevennes in about 125 BC and the remaining Gauls up to the Rhine were conquered by Julius ◊Caesar 58–51 BC.

Gaulle Charles de French politician, see Charles ◊de Gaulle.

gaur Asiatic wild cattle *Bos gaurus*, dark gray-brown with white "socks," and 6 ft/2 m tall at the shoulders. The original range was from India to SE Asia and Malaysia, but numbers and range are now diminished.

gauss cgs unit (abbreviation Gs) of magnetic induction or magnetic flux density, replaced by the SI unit, the ◊tesla, but still commonly used. It is equal to one line of magnetic flux per square centimeter. The Earth's magnetic field is about 0.5 Gs, and changes to it over time are measured in gammas (one gamma equals 10^{-5} gauss).

Gauss Karl Friedrich 1777–1855. German mathematician who worked on the theory of numbers, non-Euclidian geometry, and the mathematical development of electric and magnetic theory. A method of neutralizing a magnetic field, used to protect ships from magnetic mines, is called "degaussing."

***Gauguin** French painter Paul Gauguin is best remembered for his Tahitian canvases.* Te Rerioa/The Dream *1897 is in the Courtauld Collection, London.*

Gautama family name of the historical ◊Buddha.

Gautier Théophile 1811–1872. French Romantic poet, whose later works emphasized the perfection of form and the "polished" beauty of language and imagery (for example, *Emaux et camées/ Enamels and Cameos* 1852). He was also a novelist (*Mlle de Maupin* 1835) and later turned to journalism.

gavial large reptile *Gavialis gangeticus* related to the crocodile. It grows to about 23 ft/7 m long, and has a very long snout with about 100 teeth in its jaws. Gavials live in rivers in N India, where they feed on fish and frogs. They have been extensively hunted for their skins, and are now extremely rare.

Gawain in Arthurian legend, one of the knights of the Round Table who participated in the quest for the ◊Holy Grail. He is the hero of the 14th-century epic poem *Sir Gawayne and the Greene Knight*.

Gay John 1685–1732. British poet and dramatist. He was the friend of Alexander ◊Pope and John Arbuthnot, and wrote *Trivia* 1716, a verse picture of 18th-century London. His *The Beggar's Opera* 1728, a "Newgate pastoral" using traditional songs and telling of the love of Polly for highwayman Captain Macheath, was an extraordinarily popular success. Its satiric political touches led to the banning of *Polly*, a sequel.

Gaya ancient city in Bihar state, NE India; population (1986) 200,000. It is a center of pilgrimage for Buddhists and Hindus with many temples and shrines. A bo tree at ◊Buddh Gaya is said to be a direct descendant of the original tree under which Buddha sat.

Gaye Marvin 1939–1984. US soul singer and songwriter whose hits, including "Stubborn Kinda Fellow" 1962, "I Heard It Through the Grapevine" 1968, and "What's Goin' On" 1971, exemplified the Detroit ◊Motown sound. He was killed by his father.

Gay-Lussac Joseph Louis 1778–1850. French physicist and chemist, who investigated the physical properties of gases, and discovered new methods of producing sulfuric and oxalic acids. In 1802 he discovered the approximate rule for the expansion of gases now known as ◊Charles's Law; see also ◊gas laws.

Gaza capital of the ◊Gaza Strip, once a Philistine city, and scene of three World War I battles; population (1980 est) 120,000.

Gazankulu ◊Black National State in Transvaal province, South Africa, with self-governing status from 1971; population (1985) 497,200.

Gaza Strip strip of Palestine under Israeli administration; capital Gaza; area 140 sq mi/363 sq km; population (1989) 645,000 of which 446,000 are refugees.

It was invaded by Israel 1956, reoccupied 1967, and retained 1973. Clashes between the Israeli authorities and the Palestinian people escalated to intifada (uprising) from 1988.

gazelle various species of lightly built, fast-running antelopes found on the open plains of Africa and S Asia, especially those of the genus *Gazella*.

Gaziantep Turkish city 115 mi/185 km NE of Adana; population (1985) 466,000. It has textile and tanning industries. Until 1922 it was known as Antep or Aintab.

GCC abbreviation for Gulf Cooperation Council.

Gdańsk (German *Danzig*) Polish port; population (1985) 467,000. Oil is refined, and textiles, televisions, and fertilizers are produced. In the 1980s there were repeated antigovernment strikes at the Lenin shipyards.

Formerly a member of the ◊Hanseatic League, it was in almost continuous Prussian possession 1793–1919, when it again became a free city

gazelle

under the protection of the League of Nations. Annexed by Germany 1939, it reverted to Poland 1945, when the churches and old merchant houses were restored.

GDP abbreviation for ◊Gross Domestic Product.

GDR abbreviation for German Democratic Republic (East Germany see ◊Germany, East).

Gdynia port in N Poland; population (1985) 243,000. It was established in 1920 to give newly constituted Poland a sea outlet to replace lost ◊Gdańsk. It has a naval base and shipyards and is now part of the "Tri-city," which includes Sopot and Gdańsk.

Ge in Greek mythology, an alternate name for ◊***Gaia***, goddess of the Earth.

gear a toothed wheel that transmits the turning movement of one shaft to another shaft. Gear wheels may be used in pairs, or in threes if both shafts are to turn in the same direction. The gear ratio, the ratio of the number of teeth on the two wheels, determines the torque ratio, the turning force on the output shaft compared with the turning shaft on the input shaft. The ratio of the angular velocities of the shafts is the inverse of the gear ratio.

The common type of gear for parallel shafts is the spur gear, with straight teeth parallel to the shaft axis. The helical gear has teeth cut along sections of a helix or corkscrew shape; the double form of the helix gear is the most efficient for energy transfer. Bevil gears, with tapering teeth set on the base of a cone, are used to connect intersecting shafts.

gecko any lizard of the family Gekkonidae. Geckos are common worldwide in warm climates, and have large heads and short, stout bodies. Many have no eyelids. Their adhesive toe pads enable them to climb vertically and walk upside down on smooth surfaces in their search for flies, spiders, and other prey.

The Texas banded gecko *Coleonyx brevis*, 4.5 in/12 cm long, is unusual in that it has no toe pads.

Geddes Patrick 1854–1932. Scottish town planner who established the importance of surveys, research work, and properly planned "diagnoses before treatment." His major work is *City Development* 1904. His protégé was Lewis ◊Mumford.

Geelong industrial port in S Victoria, Australia; population (1986) 148,300.

In addition to oil refining and trade in grain, it produces aluminum, motor vehicles, textiles, glass, and fertilizers.

gecko

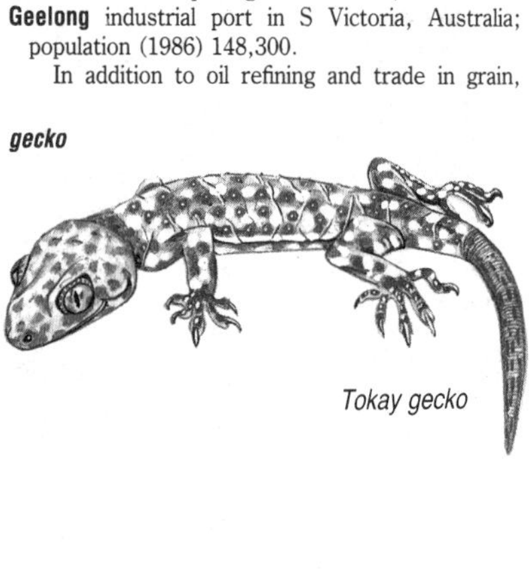

Tokay gecko

Gehenna another name for ◊***hell***; in the Old Testament, a valley S of Jerusalem where children were sacrificed to the Phoenician god Moloch and fires burned constantly.

Gehrig Lou (Henry Louis) 1903–1941. US baseball player. Nicknamed "The Iron Horse" for his incomparable stamina and strength, Gehrig was named the American League's most valuable player 1927, 1931, 1934, and 1936. Born in New York, Gehrig attended Columbia University. He was signed by the New York Yankees 1923 and went on to a 17-year career as the Yankees' first baseman and most consistent hitter.

Among his remarkable achievements as a ballplayer are his lifetime 493 home runs, his .340 lifetime batting average, and his record 2,130 consecutive games played. Diagnosed with a degenerative muscle disease (now known as "Lou Gehrig's disease"), he retired from baseball 1939 and was elected to the Baseball Hall of Fame the same year. A film biography, *Pride of the Yankees*, appeared 1942.

Gehry Frank 1929– . US architect, based in Los Angeles. His architecture approaches abstract art in its use of collage and montage techniques.

His own experimental house at Santa Monica (1977), Edgemar Shopping Center and Museum, Santa Monica (1988), and the Vitra Furniture Museum (1989)—his first building in Europe—demonstrate his vitality.

Geiger Hans 1882–1945. German physicist who produced the Geiger counter. After studying in Germany, he spent the period 1907–12 in England, working with Ernest ◊Rutherford. In 1908 they designed an instrument to detect ◊alpha particles, which was refined and made more powerful to produce the Geiger counter in the 1920s.

Geiger counter any of several devices for detecting and/or counting ionizing particles (see ◊radioactivity). They detect the momentary current that passes between ◊electrodes in a suitable gas when a nuclear particle or a radiation pulse causes ionization in the gas. The electrodes are connected to electronic devices that enable the number of particles passing to be measured. Increased frequency of measured particles indicates the intensity of radiation. It is named after Hans Geiger.

Geiger–Müller, Geiger–Klemperer, and Rutherford–Geiger counters are all devices often referred to loosely as Geiger counters. Hans Geiger studied under Ernest ◊Rutherford, and was professor of physics at Kiel, Germany.

Geisel Theodor Seuss; better known as Dr Seuss. 1904–1991. US author. His first children's book, *And to Think That I Saw It on Mulberry Street*, was published 1937. His classic *Horton Hatches the Egg* appeared 1940. After winning Academy Awards for documentary films in 1946 and 1947, Geisel returned to writing children's books in the 1950s—among them, *Horton Hears a Who* 1954, *How the Grinch Stole Christmas* 1957, *The Cat in the Hat* 1957, and *Yertle the Turtle* 1958. He later wrote books for adults, including *Oh, the Places You'll Go!* 1989.

Born in Springfield, Massachusetts, and educated at Dartmouth, Geisel began his career as a cartoonist and illustrator.

geisha female entertainer (music, singing, dancing, and conversation) in Japanese teahouses and private parties. Geishas survive mainly as a tourist attraction. They are apprenticed from childhood and highly skilled in traditional Japanese arts and graces.

Geissler tube high-voltage ◊discharge tube in which traces of gas ionize and conduct electricity. Since the electrified gas takes on a luminous color characteristic of the gas, the instrument is used in ◊spectroscopy. It was developed in 1858 by the German physicist Heinrich Geissler (1814–1879).

gel solid produced by the formation of a three-dimensional cage structure, commonly of linked

Geldof *Rock singer Bob Geldof (center) with George Michael (left) at the Live Aid fundraising concert in London, 1985.*

large-molecular-mass polymers, in which a liquid is trapped. A gel may be a jellylike mass (pectin, gelatine) or have a more rigid structure (silica gel).

gelatine water-soluble protein prepared from boiled hoofs, hide, and bone, used in cooking to set jellies, and in glues and photographic emulsions.

Gelderland (English *Guelders*) province of the E Netherlands

area 1,938 sq mi/5,020 sq km

population (1988) 1,784,000

cities capital Arnhem; Apeldoorn, Nijmegen, Ede

products livestock, textiles, electrical goods

history in the Middle Ages Gelderland was divided into Upper Gelderland (Roermond in N Limburg) and Lower Gelderland (Nijmegen, Arnhem, Zutphen). These territories were inherited by Charles V of Spain, but when the revolt against Spanish rule reached a climax in 1579, Lower Gelderland joined the United Provinces of the Netherlands.

Geldof Bob 1954– . Irish fundraiser and rock singer, leader of the group the Boomtown Rats 1975–86. In the mid-80s, Geldof instigated the charity Band Aid in partnership with fellow musician Midge Ure, which raised large sums of money for famine relief, primarily for Ethiopia.

In the 1980s he organized two simultaneous rock concerts, known as Live Aid and broadcast live worldwide, to raise money for famine relief, especially in Ethiopia.

gelignite a type of ◊dynamite.

Gell-Mann Murray 1929– . US physicist. In 1964 he formulated the theory of the ◊quark as one of the fundamental constituents of matter, which make up the ◊hadrons.

He was R A Millikan professor of theoretical physics at the California Institute of Technology from 1967. In 1969 he was awarded a Nobel Prize for his work on elementary particles and their interaction.

Gelsenkirchen industrial city in the ◊Ruhr, Federal Republic of Germany, 15 mi/25 km W of Dortmund; population (1988) 284,000. It has iron, steel, chemical, and glass industries.

gem a mineral valuable by virtue of its durability (hardness), rarity, and beauty, cut and polished for ornamental use, or engraved. Of 120 minerals known to have been used as gemstones, only about 25 are in common use in jewelry today; of these, the diamond, emerald, ruby, and sapphire are classified as precious, and all the others semi-precious, for example the topaz, amethyst, opal, and aquamarine.

Among the synthetic precious stones to have been successfully produced are rubies, sapphires, emeralds, and diamonds (first produced by General Electric in the US 1955). Pearls are not technically gems.

Gemara in Judaism, part of the ◊Talmud, the compilation of ancient Jewish law.

Gemayel Amin 1942– . Lebanese politician, a Maronite Christian; president 1982–88. He succeeded his brother, president-elect Bechir Gemayel, on his assassination on Sept 14, 1982. The Lebanese parliament was unable to agree on a successor when his term expired, so separate governments were formed under rival Christian and Muslim leaders.

Gemeinschaft and Gesellschaft German terms (roughly, "community" and "association") coined by Ferdinand ◊Tönnies 1887 to contrast social relationships in traditional rural societies with those in modern industrial societies. He saw *Gemeinschaft* (traditional) as intimate and positive, and *Gesellschaft* (modern) as impersonal and negative.

In small-scale societies where everyone knows everyone else, the social order is seen as stable and the culture homogeneous. In large urban areas life is faster and more competitive, and relationships are seen as more superficial, transitory, and anonymous.

Gemini prominent zodiac constellation in the northern hemisphere between Cancer and Taurus, and represented as the twins Castor and Pollux. Its brightest star is ◊Pollux; ◊Castor is a system of six stars. The Sun passes through Gemini from late June to late July. Each December, the Geminid meteors radiate from Gemini. In astrology, the dates for Gemini are between about May 21 and June 21 (see ◊precession).

Gemini project US space program (1965–66) in which astronauts practiced rendezvous and docking of spacecraft, and working outside their spacecraft, in preparation for the ◊Apollo Moon landings.

Gemini spacecraft carried two astronauts and were launched by Titan rockets.

gemma (plural gemmae) a unit of ◊vegetative reproduction, consisting of a small group of undifferentiated green cells. Gemmae are found in certain mosses and liverworts, forming on the surface of the plant, often in cup-shaped structures, or gemmae cups. Gemmae are dispersed by splashes of rain and can then develop into new plants. In many species, gemmation is more common than reproduction by ◊spores.

gender in grammar, one of the categories into which nouns are divided in many languages, such as masculine, feminine, and neuter (as in Latin, German, and Russian), masculine and feminine (as in French, Italian, and Spanish), or animate and inanimate (as in some North American Indian languages).

gene a unit of inherited material, encoded by a strand of ◊DNA, and transcribed by ◊RNA. In higher organisms, genes are located on the ◊chromosomes. The term "gene," coined in 1909 by the Danish geneticist Wilhelm Johannsen (1857–1927), refers to the inherited factor that consistently affects a particular character in an individual—for example the gene for eye color. Also termed a Mendelian gene, after Gregor ◊Mendel, it occurs at a particular point or ◊locus on a particular chromosome and may have several variants or ◊alleles, each specifying a particular form of that character—for example the alleles for blue or brown eyes. Some alleles show ◊dominance. These mask the effect of other alleles known as ◊recessive.

In the 1940s, it was established that a gene could be identified with a particular length of DNA, which coded for a complete protein molecule, leading to the "one-gene-one-enzyme" principle. Later it was realized that proteins can be made up of several ◊polypeptide chains, each with a separate gene, so this principle was modified to "one-gene-one-polypeptide." However, the fundamental idea remains the same, that genes produce their visible effects simply by coding for proteins; they control the structure of those proteins via the genetic code, as well as the amounts produced and the timing of production. In modern genetics, the gene is identified either with the ◊cistron (a set of ◊codons that determines a complete polypeptide) or with the unit of selection (a Mendelian gene that determines a particular character in the organism on which ◊natural selection can act). Genes undergo ◊mutation and ◊recombination to produce the variation on which natural selection operates.

genealogy the study and tracing of family histories.

In the US there are many genealogical societies that trace people's descent and some groups, such as the Daughters of the American Revolution, limit membership to those who can demonstrate a particular lineage.

gene bank collection of seeds or other forms of genetic material, such as tubers, spores, bacterial or yeast cultures, live animals and plants, frozen sperm and eggs, or frozen embryos. These are stored for possible future use in agriculture, plant and animal breeding, or in medicine, genetic engineering, or the restocking of wild habitats where species have become extinct. Gene banks will be increasingly used as the rate of extinction increases, depleting the Earth's genetic variety (biodiversity).

gene pool the total sum of ◊alleles (variants of ◊genes) possessed by all the members of a given population or species alive at a particular time.

general senior military rank, the ascending grades being major general, lieutenant general, and general. The US rank of general of the army is equivalent to the British ◊field marshal.

General Agreement on Tariffs and Trade (GATT) an organization within the United Nations founded 1948 with the aim of encouraging ◊free trade between nations through low tariffs, abolitions of quotas, and curbs on subsidies.

General Strike the term usually used to describe the cessation of work in key industries, with the intention of paralyzing the economic life of a country.

In British history, it generally refers to a nationwide strike called by the Trade Union Congress on May 3, 1926 in support of the miners' union. The immediate cause of the 1926 general strike was the report of a royal commission on the coal mining industry (Samuel Report 1926) which, among other things, recommended a cut in wages. The mine-owners wanted longer hours as well as lower wages. The miners' union under the leadership of A J Cook resisted with the slogan "not a penny off the pay, not a minute on the day." A coal strike started in early May 1926 and the miners asked the TUC to bring all major industries out on strike in support of the action; eventually it included more than 2 million workers. The conservative government under Stanley Baldwin used troops, volunteers, and special constables to maintain food supplies and essential services, and had a monopoly on the information services including BBC radio. After nine days the TUC ended the general strike, leaving the miners—who felt betrayed by the TUC—to remain on strike, unsuccessfully, until Nov 1926. The Trades Disputes Act of 1927 made general strikes illegal.

generator a machine that produces electrical energy from mechanical energy, as opposed to an ◊electric motor, which does the opposite.

A simple generator consists of a wire-wound coil (◊armature) that is rotated between the poles of a permanent magnet. The movement (of the wire in the magnetic field) induces a current in the coil by ◊electromagnetic induction, which can be fed by means of a ◊commutator as a continuous direct current into an external circuit. Slip rings instead of a commutator produce an alternating current, when the generator is called an alternator. The term dynamo is an older name for generator.

gene shears new technique in ◊genetic engineering which may have practical applications in the future. The gene shears are pieces of messenger ◊RNA that can bind to other pieces of messenger RNA, recognizing specific sequences, and cut them at that point. If a piece of ◊DNA that codes for the shears can be inserted in the chromosomes of a plant or animal cell, that cell will then destroy all messenger RNA of a particular type. Genetic shears may be used to protect plants against viruses which protect them and cause disease. They might also be useful against ◊AIDS.

Genesis first book of the Old Testament, which includes the stories of the creation of the world, Adam and Eve, the Flood, and the history of the Jewish patriarchs Abraham, Isaac, Jacob, and Joseph (who brought his people to Egypt).

gene-splicing technique for inserting a foreign gene into laboratory cultures of bacteria to generate commercial biological products, such as synthetic insulin, hepatitis-B vaccine, and interferon. It was invented 1973 by the US scientists Stanley Cohen and Herbert Boyer, and patented in the US 1984. See ◊genetic engineering.

Cohen was working at Stanford University and Boyer at the University of California. Cohen shared a 1989 Nobel Prize for Physiology or Medicine for his work in cell growth.

genet small, nocturnal, meat-eating mammal, genus *Genetta*, in the mongoose and civet family (Viverridae). Most species live in Africa, but *G. genetta* is also found in Europe and the Middle East. It is about 1.6 ft/50 cm long with a 1.5 ft/45 cm tail, and greyish yellow with rows of black spots. It climbs well.

Genet Jean 1910–1986. French dramatist, novelist, and poet, an exponent of the Theater of ◊Cruelty. His turbulent life and early years spent in prison are reflected in his drama, characterized by ritual, role-play, and illusion, in which his characters come to act out their bizarre and violent fantasies. His plays include *Les bonnes/The Maids* 1947, *Le balcon/The Balcony* 1957, and two plays dealing with the Algerian situation: *Les nègres/The Blacks* 1959, and *Les paravents/The Screens* 1961.

gene therapy a proposed medical technique for curing or alleviating inherited diseases or defects. Although not yet a practical possibility for most defects, some of the basic techniques are available as a result of intensive research in ◊genetic engineering.

Gene therapy has been used for SCID (severe combined immune deficiency) with some success. It may also be useful for diseases such as hemoglobin irregularities, where only a relatively small group of cells—those in the bone marrow, which produce the red blood cells—need to be treated. The possibility of gene therapy for reproductive cells, to prevent genetic defects being passed on to the next generation, is more remote.

In treating hemoglobin disorders, the normal gene would be cloned in bacterial cells to obtain many copies. Bone marrow cells taken from the patient would then be exposed to these cloned normal genes. Cells that had taken up the normal gene could be identified and a batch of them returned to the patient's bone marrow. The existing bone marrow cells would be destroyed beforehand, to give the introduced cells a chance to multiply.

genetic code the way in which instructions for building proteins, the basic structural molecules of living matter, are "written" in the genetic material ◊DNA. This relationship between the sequence of bases (see ◊base pair)—the subunits in a DNA molecule—and the sequence of ◊amino acids—the subunits of a protein molecule—is the basis of heredity. The code employs ◊codons of three bases each; it is the same in almost all organisms, except for a few minor differences recently discovered in some protozoa.

genetic diseases disorders caused at least partly by defective genes or chromosomes, of which in humans there are some 3,000, including cleft palate, cystic fibrosis, Down's syndrome, hemophilia, Huntington's chorea, some forms of anemia, spina bifida, and Tay-Sachs disease.

genetic engineering the deliberate manipulation of genetic material by biochemical techniques. It is often achieved by the introduction of new ◊DNA, usually by means of a virus or ◊plasmid. This can be for pure research or to breed functionally specific plants, animals or bacteria. These organisms with a foreign gene added are said to be ◊transgenic.

In genetic engineering, the splicing and reconciliation of genes is used to increase knowledge of cell function and reproduction, but it can also achieve practical ends. For example, plants grown for food could be given the ability to fix nitrogen, found in some bacteria, and so reduce the need for expensive fertilizers, or simple bacteria may be modified to produce rare drugs. Developments in genetic engineering have led to the production of human insulin, human growth hormone and a number of other bone-marrow stimulating hormones. New strains of animals have also been produced; a new strain of mouse was patented in the US 1989 (the application was rejected in the European patent office). A ◊vaccine against a sheep parasite (a larval tapeworm) has been developed by genetic engineering; most existing vaccines protect against bacteria and viruses.

There is a risk that when transplanting genes between different types of bacteria (*Escherichia coli*, which lives in the human intestine, is often used) new and harmful strains might be produced. For this reason strict safety precautions are observed, and the altered bacteria are disabled in some way so they are unable to exist outside the laboratory.

genetic fingerprinting technique used for determining the pattern of certain parts of the genetic material ◊DNA that is unique to each individual. Like skin fingerprinting, it can accurately distinguish humans from one another, with the exception of identical twins.

Genetic fingerprinting involves isolating DNA from cells, then comparing and contrasting the sequences of component chemicals between individuals. The DNA pattern can be ascertained from a sample of skin, hair, or semen. Although differences are minimal (only 0.1% between unrelated people), certain regions of DNA, known as hypervariable regions, are unique to individuals. Genetic fingerprinting was discovered by Alec Jeffreys (1950–), and is now allowed as a means of legal identification. It is used in paternity testing, forensic medicine, and inbreeding studies.

genetics the study of inheritance and of the units of inheritance (◊genes). The founder of genetics was Gregor ◊Mendel, whose experiments with plants, such as peas, showed that inheritance takes place by means of discrete "particles," which later came to be called genes.

Before Mendel, it had been assumed that the characteristics of the two parents were blended during inheritance, but Mendel showed that the genes remain intact, although their combinations change. Since Mendel, genetics has advanced greatly, first through ◊breeding experiments and light-microscope observations (Classical genetics), later by means of biochemical and electron-microscope studies (molecular genetics). An advance was the elucidation of the structure of ◊DNA by James D Watson and Francis Crick, and the subsequent cracking of the ◊genetic code. These discoveries opened up the possibility of deliberately manipulating genes, or ◊genetic engineering. See also ◊genotype, ◊phenotype or ◊monohybrid inheritance.

Geneva (French *Genève*) Swiss city, capital of Geneva canton, on the shore of Lake Geneva; population (1987) 385,000. It is a point of convergence of natural routes and is a cultural and commercial center. Industries include the manufacture of watches, scientific and optical instruments, foodstuffs, jewelry, and musical boxes.

The site on which Geneva now stands was the chief settlement of the Allobroges, a central European tribe who were annexed to Rome 121 BC; Julius Caesar built an entrenched camp here. In the Middle Ages, Geneva was controlled by the prince-bishops of Geneva and the rulers of Savoy. Under the Protestant theologian John ◊Calvin, it became a center of the Reformation 1536–64; the Academy, which he founded 1559, became a university 1892. Geneva was annexed by France 1798; it was freed 1814 and entered the Swiss Confederation 1815. In 1864 the International Red Cross Society was established in Geneva. It was the headquarters of the ◊League of Nations, whose properties in Geneva passed 1946 into the possession of the United Nations.

Geneva Convention international agreement 1864 regulating the treatment of those wounded in war, and later extended to cover the types of weapons allowed, the treatment of prisoners and the sick, and the protection of civilians in wartime. The rules were revised at conventions held 1906, 1929, and 1949, and by the 1977 Additional Protocols.

Geneva, Lake (French *Lac Léman*) largest of the central European lakes, between Switzerland and France; area 225 sq mi/580 sq km.

Geneva Protocol international agreement 1925 designed to prohibit the use of poisonous gases, chemical weapons, and bacteriological methods of warfare. It came into force 1928 but was not ratified by the US until 1974.

Genghis Khan c. 1162–1227. Mongol conqueror, ruler of all Mongol peoples from 1206. He began the conquest of N China 1213, overran the empire of the shah of Khiva 1219–25, and invaded N India, while his lieutenants advanced as far as the Crimea. When he died, his empire ranged from the Yellow Sea to the Black Sea.

The ruins of his capital Karakorum are SW of Ulaanbaatar in Mongolia; his alleged remains are preserved at Ejin Horo, Inner Mongolia.

genitalia the reproductive organs of sexually reproducing animals, particularly the external/visible organs of mammals: in males, the penis and the scrotum, which contains the testes, and in females, the clitoris and vulva.

genitive in the grammar of certain inflected languages, the form of a word used to indicate possession for nouns, pronouns, or adjectives.

Gennesaret, Lake of another name for ***Lake ◊Tiberias*** (Sea of Galilee) in N Israel.

Genoa (Italian *Genova*) historic city in NW Italy, capital of Liguria; population (1988) 722,000. It is Italy's largest port; industries include oil-refining, chemicals, engineering, and textiles.

Decline followed its conquest by the Lombards 640, but from the 10th century it established a commercial empire in the W Mediterranean, pushing back the Muslims, and founding trading posts in Corsica, Sardinia, and N Africa; during the period of the Crusades, further colonies were founded in the kingdom of Jerusalem and on the Black Sea, where Genoese merchants enjoyed the protection of the Byzantine empire. At its peak about 1300, the city had a virtual monopoly of European trade with the East. Strife between lower-class Genoese and the ruling mercantile-aristocratic oligarchy led to weakness and domination by a succession of foreign powers, including Pope John XXII (1249–1334), Robert of Anjou, king of Naples (1318–43), and Charles VI of France (1368–1422). During the 15th century, most of its trade and colonies were taken over by Venice or the Ottomans.

Rebuilt after World War II, it became the busiest port on the Mediterranean, and the first to build modern container facilities. The nationalist Giuseppe Mazzini and the explorer Columbus were born here.

genocide the deliberate and systematic extermination of a national, racial, religious, or ethnic group defined by the exterminators as undesirable.

The term is commonly applied to the policies of the Nazis during World War II (what they called the "final solution"—the extermination of all "undesirables" in occupied Europe). At the end of World War II the United Nations' indictment of 24 Nazi leaders brought the word genocide into more common usage and coined a new term in international law. In 1948 the United Nations General Assembly adopted a convention on the prevention and punishment of genocide, as well as the Universal Declaration of ◊Human Rights.

genome the full complement of ◊genes carried by a single (haploid) set of ◊chromosomes. The term may be applied to the genetic information carried by an individual or to the range of genes found in a given species.

genotype the particular set of ◊alleles (variants of genes) possessed by a given organism. The term is usually used in conjunction with ◊phenotype, which is the product of the genotype and all environmental effects. See also ◊environment–heredity controversy.

Genova Italian form of ◊Genoa, city in Italy.

genre painting (French *genre*, "kind," "type") painting scenes from everyday life. Genre paintings were common in the Netherlands and Flanders in the 17th century (Vermeer, de Hooch, and Brouwer were exponents). The term "genre" is also used more broadly to mean a category in the arts, such as landscape painting, or literary forms, such as the detective novel.

Genscher Hans-Dietrich 1927– . German politician, chair of the West German Free Democratic Party (FDP) 1974–85, foreign minister from 1974.

Born in Halle, East Germany, Genscher settled in West Germany 1952. He served as interior minister 1969–74 and then as foreign minister, committed to ◊Ostpolitik and European cooperation. As FDP leader, Genscher masterminded the party's switch of allegiance from the Social Democratic Party to the Christian Democratic Union, which resulted in the downfall of the Helmut ◊Schmidt government 1982.

Gentile da Fabriano c. 1370–1427. Italian painter of frescoes and altarpieces in the International Gothic style. Gentile was active in Venice, Florence, Siena, Orvieto, and Rome and collaborated with the artists Pisanello and Jacopo Bellini. *The Adoration of the Magi* 1423 (Uffizi, Florence) is typically detailed and crammed with courtly figures.

Gentileschi Artemisia 1593–c. 1652. Italian painter, born in Rome. She trained under her father Orazio Gentileschi, but her work is more melodramatic than his. She settled in Naples from about 1630 and focused on macabre and grisly subjects, such as *Judith Decapitating Holofernes* (Museo di Capodimonte, Naples).

Gentileschi Orazio 1563–1637. Italian painter, born in Pisa. He was a follower and friend of Caravaggio, whose influence can be seen in the dramatic treatment of light and shade in *The Annunciation* 1623 (Galleria Sabauda, Turin). From 1626 he lived in London, painting for King Charles I.

Gentili Alberico 1552–1608. Italian jurist. He practiced law in Italy but having adopted Protestantism was compelled to flee to England, where he lectured on Roman Law in Oxford. His publications, such as *De Jure Belli libri tres/On The Law Of War, Book Three* 1598, made him the first true international law writer and scholar.

Gentlemen Prefer Blondes witty 1925 novel by Anita Loos that tells the story of the classic female gold-digger Lorelei Lee, filmed 1953 with Marilyn Monroe and Jane Russell. The novel's 1928 sequel was called *But Gentlemen Marry Brunettes*.

gentry the lesser nobility, particularly in England and Wales, not entitled to sit in the House of Lords. By the later Middle Ages, it included knights, esquires, and gentlemen, and after the 17th century, baronets.

genus (plural genera) group of ◊species with many characteristics in common. Thus all doglike species (including dogs, wolves, and jackals) belong to the genus *Canis* (Latin "dog"). Species of the same genus are thought to be descended from a common ancestor species. Related genera are grouped into ◊families.

geologic time chart

Millions of years ago	Epoch	Period	Era	Eon
0.01	Holocene	Quaternary	Cenozoic	Phanerozoic
1.8	Pleistocene			
5	Pliocene	Tertiary		
25	Miocene			
38	Oligocene			
55	Eocene			
65	Paleocene			
144		Cretaceous	Mesozoic	
213		Jurassic		
248		Triassic		
286		Permian	Paleozoic	
360		Carboniferous		
408		Devonian		
438		Silurian		
505		Ordovician		
590		Cambrian		
2500		Proterozoic	Precambrian	
4600		Archaean		

geochemistry the science of chemistry as it applies to geology. It deals with the relative and absolute abundances of the chemical elements and their ◊isotopes in the Earth, and also with the chemical changes that accompany geologic processes.

geochronology the branch of geology that deals with the dating of the Earth by studying its rocks and contained fossils. The geologic time chart is a result of these studies, dividing Earth time into eons, eras, periods, and epochs determined on the basis of absolute and relative dating methods. Absolute dating methods involve the measurement of radioactive decay over time in certain chemical elements found in rocks, whereas relative dating methods establish the sequence of deposition of various rock layers by identifying and comparing their contained fossils.

geode in geology, a subspherical cavity into which crystals have grown, from the outer wall into the center. Geodes often contain very well-formed crystals of quartz (including amethyst), calcite, or other minerals .

geodesy methods of surveying the Earth for making maps and correlating geologic, gravitational, and magnetic measurements. Geodesic surveys, formerly carried out by means of various measuring techniques on the surface, are now commonly made by using radio signals and laser beams from orbiting satellites.

Geoffrey of Monmouth c. 1100–1154. Welsh writer and chronicler. While a canon at Oxford, he wrote *Historia Regum Britanniae*/*History of the Kings of Britain* c. 1139, which included accounts of the semilegendary kings Lear, Cymbeline, and Arthur, and *Vita Merlini*, a life of the legendary wizard. He was bishop-elect of St Asaph, N Wales 1151, and ordained a priest 1152.

geography the science of the Earth's surface; its topography, climate, and physical conditions, and how these factors affect civilization and society. It is usually divided into physical geography, dealing with landforms and climates; biogeography, dealing with the conditions that affect the distribution of animals and plants; and human geography, dealing with the distribution and activities of peoples on Earth.

geological time time scale embracing the history of the Earth from its physical origin to the present day. Geological time is divided into eras (Precambrian, Paleozoic, Mesozoic, Cenozoic), which in turn are divided into periods, epochs, ages, and finally chrons.

geology the science of the Earth, its origin, composition, structure, and history. It is divided into several branches: mineralogy (the minerals of Earth), petrology (rocks), stratigraphy (the deposition of successive beds of sedimentary rocks), paleontology (fossils), and tectonics (the deformation and movement of the Earth's crust).

Geology is regarded as part of earth science, a more widely embracing subject that brings in meteorology, oceanography, geophysics, and geochemistry.

geometric mean in mathematics, the *n*th root of the product of *n* positive numbers. The geometric mean *m* of two numbers *p* and *q* is such that $m^2 = p \times q$, and hence *m, p*, and *q* are in a geometric progression.

geometric progression or geometric sequence in mathematics, a sequence of terms (progression) in which each term is a constant multiple (called the common ratio) of the one preceding it. For example, 3, 12, 48, 192, 768,... is a geometric sequence with a common ratio 4, since each term is equal to the previous term multiplied by 4.

The sum of n terms of a geometric series $1 + r + r^2 + r^3 + \ldots + r^n - 1 + r^n$ is given by the formula $S^n = (1 - r^n + 1)/(1 - r)$ for all r = -3/1. For $r = 1$, the geometric series can be summed to infinity: $S\infty = 1/(1 - r)$. See ◊arithmetic sequence.

In nature, many single-celled organisms reproduce by splitting in two such that one cell gives rise to 2 then 4 then 8 cells and so on, forming a geometric sequence 1, 2, 4, 8, 16, 32, ..., in which the common ratio is 2.

geometry branch of mathematics concerned with the properties of space, usually in terms of plane (two-dimensional) and solid (three-dimensional) figures. The subject is usually divided into pure geometry, which embraces roughly the plane and solid geometry dealt with in Euclid's *Elements*, and analytical or ◊coordinate geometry, in which problems are solved using algebraic methods. A third, quite distinct, type includes the non-Euclidean geometries.

Geometry probably originated in ancient Egypt, in land measurements necessitated by the periodic inundations of the river Nile, and was soon extended into surveying and navigation. Early geometers were the Greek mathematicians Thales, Pythagoras, and Euclid. Analytical methods were introduced and developed by the French philosopher René Descartes in the 17th century. From the 19th century, various non-Euclidean geometries were devised by the Germans Karl Gauss and Georg Riemann, the Russian Nikolai Lobachevsky, and others. These proved significant in the development of the theory of relativity and in the formulation of atomic theory.

geomorphology the branch of geology that deals with the nature and origin of surface landforms such as mountains, valleys, plains, and plateaus.

At the end of the 19th century, geologist William Morris Davis advanced a unifying concept called the geomorphic cycle to this study. He believed that landforms progress from a youthful stage of high, rugged mountains to a more mature stage of rounded forms, eventually worn down to an old age of almost level plains. This kind of predictable pattern does not hold up under current insights. Any given landscape can be regarded only as the balance between whatever forces of uplift and erosion are operating at a given time. What a region is like now does not allow us to reconstruct its past or predict its future, necessarily, since mountain building is a long, drawn-out, intermittent, and uneven process. Also, even if the progression from youth to old age were an uninterrupted sequence, this progression could produce different landforms, depending on climatic variables.

geophysics branch of geology using physics to study the Earth's surface, interior, and atmosphere. Studies also include winds, weather, tides, earthquakes, volcanoes, and their effects.

George six kings of Great Britain:

George I 1600–1727. King of Great Britain from 1714. He was the son of the first elector of Hanover, Ernest Augustus (1629–1698), and his wife ◊Sophia, and a great-grandson of James I. The British Parliament, seeking to ensure a Protestant line of succession to oppose the claim of the Catholic ◊James Edward Stuart, made George third in line after Queen Anne and his mother. He was supported upon his succession by the Whigs, especially Stanhope, Townsend, and Walpole. He spoke no English and grew more and more dependent upon his advisers as scandal surrounded him; his supporters turned against him, demanding freedom of action as the price of reconciliation.

George II 1683–1760. King of Great Britain from 1727, when he succeeded his father, George I, whom he detested. He married Caroline of Anspach 1705. She supported Robert ◊Walpole's position as adviser, and Walpole rallied support for George during the ◊Jacobite rebellions against him.

George III 1738–1820. King of Great Britain from 1760, when he succeeded his grandfather George II. His rule was marked by intransigence toward the American colonies and the emancipation of Catholics in England. Possibly suffering from ◊porphyria, he had repeated attacks of insanity, permanent from 1811. He was virtually blind in his later years, giving rise to suspicions and misunderstandings concerning documents and decrees for his signature.

George IV 1762–1830. King of Great Britain and Ireland from 1820, when he succeeded his father George III, for whom he had been regent during the king's insanity 1811–20. Strictly educated, he reacted by entering into a life of debauchery and in 1785 secretly married a Catholic widow, Maria ◊Fitzherbert, but in 1795 also married Princess ◊Caroline of Brunswick, in return for payment of his debts. His prestige was undermined by his treatment of Caroline (they separated in 1796), his dissipation and extravagance. His only child, Charlotte, died in childbirth 1817. He was succeeded by his brother, the duke of Clarence, who became William IV.

George V 1865–1936. King of Great Britain from 1910, when he succeeded his father Edward VII.

He was the second son, and became heir 1892 on the death of his elder brother Albert, Duke of Clarence. In 1893, he married Princess Victoria Mary of Teck (Queen Mary), formerly engaged to his brother. During World War I he made several visits to the front. In 1917, he abandoned all German titles for himself and his family. The name of the royal house was changed from Saxe-Coburg-Gotha (popularly known as Brunswick or Hanover) to Windsor.

His mother was Princess Alexandra of Denmark, sister of Empress Marie of Russia.

George VI 1895–1952. King of Great Britain from 1936, when he succeeded after the abdication of his brother Edward VIII, who had succeeded their father George V. Created Duke of York 1920, he married in 1923 Lady Elizabeth Bowes-Lyon (1900–), and their children are Elizabeth II and Princess Margaret. During World War II, he visited the Normandy and Italian battlefields.

George two kings of Greece:

George I 1845–1913. King of Greece 1863–1913. The son of Christian IX of Denmark, he was nominated to the Greek throne and, in spite of early unpopularity, became a highly successful constitutional monarch. He was assassinated by a Greek, Schinas, at Salonika.

George II 1890–1947. King of Greece 1922–23 and 1935–47. He became king on the expulsion of his father Constantine I 1922 but was himself overthrown 1923. Restored by the military 1935, he set up a dictatorship under Joannis ◊Metaxas, and went into exile during the German occupation 1941–45.

George, St patron saint of England. The story of St George rescuing a woman by slaying a dragon, evidently derived from the ◊Perseus legend, first appears in the 6th century. The cult of St George was introduced into W Europe by the Crusaders. His feast day is Apr 23.

He is said to have been martyred at Lydda in Palestine 303, probably under the Roman emperor Diocletian, but the other elements of his legend are of doubtful historical accuracy.

George Henry 1839–1897. US economist, born in Philadelphia. His *Progress and Poverty* 1879 suggested a "single tax" on land, to replace all other taxes on earnings and savings. He hoped such a land tax would abolish poverty by ending speculation on land values. George's ideas have never been implemented thoroughly, although they have influenced taxation policy in many countries.

George Stefan 1868–1933. German poet. His early poetry was inspired by French ◊Symbolism, but his concept of himself as regenerating the German spirit first appears in *Des Teppich des Lebens/The Tapestry of Life* 1899, and later in *Der siebente Ring/The Seventh Ring* 1907.

Das neue Reich/The New Empire 1928 shows his realization that World War I had not had the right purifying effect on German culture. He rejected Nazi overtures and emigrated to Switzerland 1933.

Georgetown capital and port of Guyana; population (1983) 188,000.

Founded 1781 by the British, it was held 1784–1812 by the Dutch, who renamed it Stabroek, and ceded to Britain 1814.

Georgetown or ***Penang*** chief port of the Federation of Malaysia, and capital of Penang, on the Island of Penang; population (1980) 250,600. It produces textiles and toys.

It is named after King George III.

Georgetown, Declaration of call in 1972, at a conference in Guyana of nonaligned countries, for a multipolar system to replace the two world power blocs, and for the Mediterranean Sea and Indian Ocean to be neutral.

Georgia state in SE US; nickname Peach State/Empire State of the South
area 58,904 sq mi/152,600 sq km
capital Atlanta
cities Columbus, Savannah, Macon
features Okefenokee National Wildlife Refuge (656 sq mi/1,700 sq km), Sea Islands, historic Savannah

Georgia

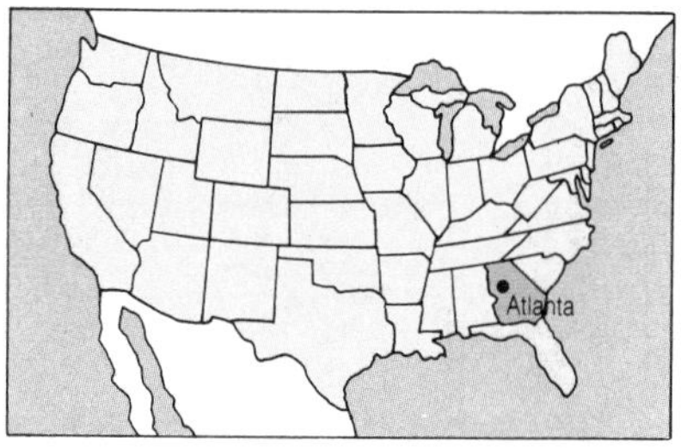
Atlanta

products poultry, livestock, tobacco, corn, peanuts, cotton, soybeans, kaolinite, crushed granite, textiles, carpets, aircraft, paper products
population (1990) 6,478,216
famous people Jim Bowie; Erskine Caldwell; Jimmy Carter; Ray Charles; Ty Cobb; Bobby Jones; Martin Luther King, Jr; Margaret Mitchell; James Oglethorpe; Jackie Robinson
history explored 1540 by Hernando de Soto; claimed by British and named after George II of England; founded 1733 as a colony for the industrious poor by James Oglethorpe, a philanthropist, and was one of the original 13 states of the US. In 1864, during the Civil War, General W T Sherman's Union troops cut a wide swath of destruction as they marched from Atlanta to the sea. The state benefited after World War II from the growth of Atlanta as the financial and transportation center of the SE US.

Georgia (Georgian Sakartvelo) republic, formerly constituent republic of the SW USSR 1936–91
area 26,911 sq mi/69,700 sq km
capital Tbilisi
features vacation resorts and spas on the Black Sea; good climate
products tea, citrus and orchard fruits, tung oil, tobacco, vines, silk, hydroelectricity
population (1987) 5,266,000; 69% Georgian, 9% Armenian, 7% Russian, 5% Azeri, 3% Ossetian, 2% Abkhazian
language Georgian
religion Georgian Church, independent of the Russian Orthodox Church since 1917
famous people Stalin
recent history independent republic 1918–21; uprising 1921 quelled by Soviet troops, who occupied Georgia; proclaimed republic 1921; linked with Armenia and Azerbaijan as the Transcaucasian Republic within the SW USSR 1922–36; increasing demands for autonomy from 1981, spearheaded from 1988 by a Georgian Popular Front. Within the republic there have been interethnic conflicts between the Osset and Abkhaz communities. Nationalist demonstrators clashed with Soviet troops in Tbilisi 1989, leaving 19 demonstrators killed by poison gas.

A huge majority supported a referendum on independence held on March 31, 1991, and on

Georgia

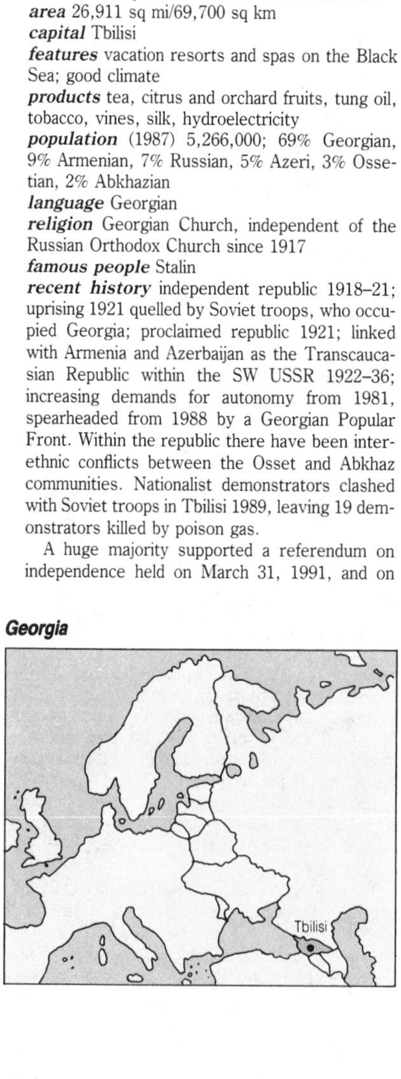
Tbilisi

April 9, 1991 the Georgian Supreme Soviet unanimously adopted a formal declaration of the "restoration of state independence." The republic's executive president, Zviad Gamsakhurdia, a former anticommunist dissident (Helsinki Watch chairman), decreed that government bodies should organize a campaign of civil disobedience against Soviet interests in support of its campaign for independence, exempt the republic's youth from service in the Soviet army, and create a Georgian National Guard. In May 1991 Gamsakhurdia was popularly elected Georgia's executive president, securing 87% of the vote, in the republic's first ever direct contest. However, his opponents, and many former allies, soon accused him of an autocratic leadership style, as opposition newspapers were closed down and the president assumed personal charge of a faction of the national guard. By September 1991 Gamsakhurdia's popularity rating had slumped and large pro-democracy crowds demanded his resignation. In Aug 1991, in the wake of the failed anti-Gorbachev coup in the USSR, the Communist Party was outlawed. In Jan 1992 he was driven from Tbilisi.

Georgian a period of English architecture, furniture making, and decorative art between 1714 and 1830. The architecture is mainly Classical in style, although external details and interiors were often rich in Rococo carving. Furniture was frequently made of mahogany and satinwood, and mass production became increasingly common; designers included Thomas Chippendale, George Hepplewhite, and Thomas Sheraton. The silver of this period is particularly fine and ranges from the earlier, simple forms to the more ornate, and from the Neo-Classical style of Robert Adam to the later, more decorated pre-Victorian taste.

geosynchronous orbit or ***geostationary orbit*** circular path 22,300 mi/35,900 km above the Earth's equator on which a ◊satellite takes 24 hours, moving from west to east, to complete an orbit, thus appearing to hang stationary over one place on the Earth's surface. Geosynchronous orbits are used for weather satellites and broadcasting and communications satellites. They were first thought of by the author Arthur C Clarke (1917–).

geothermal energy energy produced by its use of natural steam, subterranean hot water, and hot dry rock for heating and electricity generation. Hot water is pumped to the surface and converted to steam or run through a heat exchanger; or dry steam is directed through turbines to produce electricity.

geotropism the movement of part of a plant in response to gravity. Roots are positively geotropic because they move toward a gravitational attraction.

ger. in grammar, the abbreviation for gerund.

Gera an industrial city (textiles, electronics) in the state of Thuringia, Federal Republic of Germany, on the White Elster river; population (1990) 130,000. Former capital of the East German district of Gera 1952–90.

geranium or cranesbill, plant of the genus *Geranium*, family Geraniaceae, which contains about 400 species. The plants are named after the long, beaklike process attached to the seed vessels. When ripe, this splits into coiling spirals, which jerk the seeds out, assisting in their distribution.

gerbil any of numerous rodents of the family Cricetidae with elongated back legs and good hopping or jumping ability. Gerbils range from mouse- to rat-size, and have hairy tails. Many of the 13 genera live in dry, sandy, or sparsely vegetated areas of Africa and Asia.

The Mongolian jird or gerbil *Meriones unguiculatus* is a popular pet.

gerenuk antelope *Litocranius walleri* about 3 ft/1 m at the shoulder, with a greatly elongated neck. It browses on leaves, often balancing on its hind legs to do so. Sandy brown in color, it is well camouflaged in its E African habitat of dry scrub.

Gerhard Roberto 1896–1970. Spanish-born British composer. He studied with ◊Granados and ◊Schoenberg and settled in England 1939, where he composed twelve-tone works in Spanish style. He composed the *Symphony No 1* 1952–5, followed by three more symphonies and chamber music incorporating advanced techniques.

geriatrics the branch of medicine concerned with diseases and problems of the elderly.

Géricault Théodore (Jean Louis André) 1791–1824. French Romantic painter. *The Raft of the Medusa* 1819 (Louvre, Paris) was notorious for exposing a recent scandal in which shipwrecked sailors had been cut adrift and left to drown.

An avid horseman himself (he was killed in a riding accident), he painted *The Derby at Epsom* 1821 (Louvre, Paris) and pictures of cavalry. He also painted portraits.

germ colloquial term for a microorganism that causes disease, such as certain ◊bacteria and ◊viruses. Formerly, it was also used to mean something capable of developing into a complete organism (such as a fertilized egg, or the ◊embryo of a seed).

Germain Sophie 1776–1831. French mathematician, born in Paris. Although she was not allowed to study at the newly opened Ecole Polytechnique, she corresponded with ◊Lagrange and ◊Gauss. She is remembered for work she carried out in studying ◊Fermat's last theorem.

German native to or an inhabitant of Germany and their descendants, as well as their culture and language. Within E Germany the Serbs comprise a minority population who, in addition to German, speak a Slavic language. The Austrians and Swiss Germans speak German, although they are ethnically distinct. German-speaking minorities are found in France (Alsace-Lorraine), Romania (Transylvania), Czechoslovakia, the USSR, Poland, Italy (Tyrol), and in areas that once belonged to the German Empire abroad.

German art painting and sculpture in the Germanic north of Europe from the early Middle Ages to the present.

Middle Ages A revival of the arts was fostered by the emperor Charlemagne in the early 9th century. In the late 10th and early 11th centuries under the Ottoman emperors new styles emerged. German artists produced remarkable work in the Romanesque and later Gothic style. Wood carving played a major role in art.

15th century The painter Stefan Lochner, active in Cologne, exceled in the International Gothic style. Sculptors included Hans Mültscher (c. 1400–1457) and the wood carver Veit Stoss (Wit Stwosz), active in Nuremberg and Poland.

16th century The incarnation of the Renaissance in Germany was Albrecht Dürer; other painters included Hans Baldung Grien, Lucas Cranach, Albrecht Altdorfer, Grünewald, and Hans Holbein.

17th and 18th centuries Huge wall and ceiling paintings decorated new churches and princely palaces.

19th century Caspar David Friedrich was a pioneer of Romantic landscape painting in the early 19th century. At the turn of the century came Jugendstil (corresponding to French Art Nouveau).

20th century The movement known as die Brücke (the Bridge) was parallel with Fauvism. It was followed by the Munich Expressionist group Blaue Reiter (Blue Rider). After World War I, Otto Dix, George Grosz, and Max Beckmann developed satirical Expressionist styles. The Bauhaus school of design, emphasizing the dependence of form on function, had enormous impact abroad. The painter Max Ernst moved to Paris and became a founding member of Surrealism. Artists since 1945 include Joseph Beuys and Anselm Kiefer.

German expansion aggressive territorial expansion of ◊Germany during the 1930s before the outbreak of World War II.

Germanic languages branch of the Indo-European language family, divided into East Germanic (Gothic, now extinct), North Germanic (Danish, Faroese, Icelandic, Norwegian, Swedish), and West Germanic (Afrikaans, Dutch, English, Flemish, Frisian, German, Yiddish).

The Germanic languages differ from the other Indo-European languages most prominently in the consonant shift known as Grimm's law: the sounds *p, t, k* became either (as in English) *f, th, h* or (as in Old High German) *f, d, h*. Thus, the typical Indo-European of the Latin *pater* is *father* in English and *Fater* in Old High German. In addition, the Indo-European *b, d, g* moved to become *p, t, k* (in English) or (in Old High German) *f, ts, kh*; compare Latin *duo*, English *two*, and German *zwei* (pronounced tsvai).

Germanicus Caesar 15 BC–AD 19. Roman general. He was the adopted son of the emperor ◊Tiberius and married the emperor ◊Augustus' granddaughter Agrippina. Although he refused the suggestion of his troops that he claim the throne on the death of Augustus, his military victories in Germany made Tiberius jealous. Sent to the East, he died near Antioch, possibly murdered at the instigation of Tiberius. He was the father of ◊Caligula, and of Agrippina, mother of ◊Nero.

germanium brittle, gray-white semimetallic element (see ◊metalloid), symbol Ge, atomic number 32, atomic weight 72.59. It is used as a semiconductor in transistors and in infrared devices. It was discovered in 1886 by the German chemist C Winkler (1838– 1904), who named it to honor his nation.

German language member of the Germanic group of the Indo-European language family, the national language of Germany and Austria, and an official language of Switzerland. There are many spoken varieties of German, including High German (*Hochdeutsch*) and Low German (*Plattdeutsch*).

"High" and "Low" refer to dialects spoken in the highlands or the lowlands rather than to social status. Hochdeutsch originated in the central and southern highlands of Germany, Austria, and Switzerland; Plattdeutsch from the lowlands of N Germany. Standard and literary German is based on High German, in particular on the Middle German dialect used by Martin Luther for his translation of the Bible in the 16th century. Low German is closer to English in its sound system, the verb "to make" being *machen* in High German but *maken* in Low German. Such English words as *angst, blitz, frankfurter, hamburger, poltergeist*, and *sauerkraut* are borrowings from High German.

German literature the most substantial relic of the Old High German period is the fragmentary alliterative poem the *Hildebrandslied* (c. 800). In the Middle High German period there was a flowering of the vernacular, which had been forced into subservience to Latin after the early attempts at encouragement by Charlemagne. The court epics of Hartmann von Aue, Gottfried von Strassburg, and Wolfram von Eschenbach in the early 13th century were modeled on French style and material, but the folk-epic, the *Nibelungenlied*, revived the spirit of the old heroic Germanic sagas. Adopted from France and Provence, the *Minnesang* reached its height in the lyric poetry of Walther von der Vogelweide.

Modern German literature begins in the 16th century with the standard of language set by Luther's Bible. Also in this century came the climax of popular drama in the *Fastnachtsspiel* as handled by Hans Sachs. In the later 16th and early 17th centuries French influence was renewed and English influence, by troupes of players, was introduced. Martin Opitz's *Buch von der deutschen Poeterey* 1624, in which he advocates the imitation of foreign models, epitomizes the German Renaissance, which was followed by the Thirty Years' War, vividly described in Grimmelshausen's *Simplicissimus*.

In the 18th century French Classicism predominated, extolled by Gottsched but opposed by Bodmer and Breitinger, whose writings prompted the Germanic *Messias* of Klopstock. Both Lessing and Herder were admirers of Shakespeare, and Herder's enthusiasm inaugurated the *Sturm und Drang* phase which emphasized individual inspiration. His collection of folk songs was symptomatic of the feeling which inspired Bürger's ballad *Lenore*. The greatest representatives of the Classical period at the end of the century were Goethe and Schiller, but their ideals were combatted by the new Romantic school that based its theories on the work of the brothers Schlegel, and Tieck, and which included Novalis, Arnim, Brentano, Eichendorff, Chamisso, Uhland, and Hoffmann.

With Kleist and Grillparzer in the early 19th century, stress on the poetic element in drama ended, and, with Hebbel, the psychological aspect received greater emphasis. Emerging around 1830 was the "Young German" movement, led by Heine, Gutzkow, and Laube, which the authorities tried to suppress. Other 19th-century writers include Jeremias Gotthelf, who recounted stories of peasant life; the psychological novelist Friedrich Spielhagen; poets and novella writers Gottfried Keller and Theodor Storm; and the realist novelists Wilhelm Raabe and Theodor Fontane. Naturalistic drama found its chief exponents in Hauptmann and Sudermann. Influential in literature, as in politics and economics, were Marx and Nietzsche.

Outstanding writers of the early 20th century included the lyric poets Richard Dehmel, Stefan George, and Rainer Maria Rilke; the poet and dramatist von Hofmannsthal; and the novelists Thomas and Heinrich Mann, E M Remarque, and Hermann Hesse. Just before World War I Expressionism emerged in the poetry of Georg Trakl. It dominated the novels of Franz Kafka and the plays of Ernst Toller, Franz Werfel, Georg Kaiser and Karl Sternheim, and was later to influence Bertolt Brecht. Under Nazism many major writers left the country, while others were silenced or ignored. After World War II came the Swiss dramatists Max Frisch and Friedrich Dürrenmatt, the novelists Heinrich Böll, Christa Wolf, and Siegfried Lenz, the poet Paul Celan, and the poet/novelist Günter Grass.

German measles or ***rubella*** mild, communicable virus disease, usually caught by children. It is marked by a sore throat, pinkish rash, and slight fever, and has an incubation period of two to three weeks. If a woman contracts it in the first three months of pregnancy, it may cause serious damage to the unborn child.

For this reason immunization is recommended for girls.

German silver or ***nickel silver*** silvery alloy of nickel, copper, and zinc. It is widely used for cheap jewelry and the base metal for silver plating. The letters EPNS on silverware stand for electroplated nickel silver.

German Spring offensive Germany's final offensive on the Western Front during World War I. By early 1918, German forces outnumbered the Allies on the Western Front. Germany staged three separate offensives, which culminated in the Second Battle of the Marne fought between July 15 – Aug 6. It marked the turning point of World War I. After winning the battle the Allies advanced steadily, and by September, Germany had lost all the territory it had gained during Spring.

Germany, East (German Democratic Republic) formerly from the Soviet zone of occupation in the partition of Germany following World War II, East Germany was established 1949, became a sovereign state 1954, and was reunified with West Germany in Oct 1990. For history before 1949,

Germany
North Sea
Baltic Sea
0 km 50 100
0 miles 50 100
Flensburg
Heligoland
Kiel
SCHLESWIG-HOLSTEIN
Rügen
Stralsund
Rostock
Frisian Islands
Lübeck
Wismar
MECKLENBURG-WEST POMERANIA
Bremerhaven
Hamburg
Schwerin
Neubrandenburg
Groningen
Oldensburg
Bremen
Elbe
Oder
NETHERLANDS
LOWER SAXONY
POLAND
Osnabrück
Weser
Hanover
Wolfsburg
Berlin
Hildesheim
Brunswick
Brandenburg
Potsdam
Magdeburg
BRANDENBURG
NORTH RHINE-WESTPHALIA
Bielefeld
Saltzgitter
Paderborn
SAXONY-ANHALT
Hamm
Harz Mts
Spree
Bochum
Dortmund
Dessau
Cottbus
Duisburg
Hagen
Göttingen
Neisse
Düsseldorf
Wuppertal
Halle
Mönchengladbach
Kassel
Leipzig
Cologne
Meissen
Dresden
Siegen
Weimar
Marburg
Erfurt
Jena
SAXONY
Thuringian Forest
Gera
Chemnitz
BELGIUM
Giessen
Fulda
THURINGIA
Koblenz
HESSE
Wiesbaden
Frankfurt
Mosel
Mainz
LUX
Trier
RHINELAND-PALATINATE
Darmstadt
Bayreuth
Prague
Bohemian Forest
SAARLAND
Mannheim
Saarbrücken
Erlangen
Nuremberg
CZECHOSLOVAKIA
Rhine
Heilbronn
BAVARIA
Regensburg
FRANCE
Pforzheim
Stuttgart
Ingolstadt
N
Tübingen
Danube
Black Forest
BADEN-WÜRTTEMBERG
Munich
Lake Constance
Salzburg
Bavarian Alps
Zurich
AUSTRIA
SWITZERLAND

see ◊Germany, history; for history after 1949, see Federal Republic of ◊Germany.

Germany, Federal Republic of country in central Europe, bounded N by the North and Baltic Seas and Denmark, E by Poland and Czechoslovakia, S by Austria and Switzerland, and W by France, Belgium, Luxembourg, and the Netherlands.

government With reunification in 1990 the German government remained almost identical to that of former West Germany. It is based on the West German constitution (the Basic Law), drafted 1948–49 by the Allied military governors and German provincial leaders in an effort to create a stable, parliamentary form of government, diffuse authority, and safeguard liberties. It borrowed from British, American, and neighboring European constitutional models. It established, firstly, a federal system of government built around ten *Länder* (states), each with its own constitution, elected parliament, and government headed by a minister-president.

The 16 Länder have original powers in education, police, and local government, and are responsible for the administration of federal legislation through their own civil services. They have local taxation powers and are assigned shares of federal income tax and VAT revenues, being responsible for 50% of government spending.

The constitution, secondly, created a new federal parliamentary democracy, built around a two-chamber legislature comprising a directly elected 520-member lower house *Bundestag* (federal assembly), and an indirectly elected 45-member upper house *Bundesrat* (federal council). *Bundestag* representatives are elected for four-year terms by universal suffrage under a system of "personalized proportional representation" in which electors have one vote for an ordinary constituency seat and one for a *Land* party list, enabling adjustments in seats gained by each party to be made on a proportional basis.

Political parties must win at least 5% of the national vote to qualify for shares of "list seats." *Bundesrat* members are nominated and sent in blocs by *Länder* governments, each state being assigned between three and five seats depending on population size. The *Bundestag* is the dominant parliamentary chamber, electing from the ranks of its majority party or coalition a chancellor (prime minister) and cabinet to form the executive government. Once appointed, the chancellor can only be removed by a "constructive vote of no confidence" in which a majority votes positively in favor of an alternative leader.

Legislation is effected through all-party committees. The *Bundesrat* has few powers to initiate legislation, but has considerable veto authority. All legislation relating to *Länder* responsibilities requires its approval, constitutional amendments need a two-thirds *Bundesrat* (and *Bundestag*) majority, while the *Bundesrat* can temporarily block bills or force amendments in joint *Bundestag-Bundesrat* "conciliation committees." *Bundestag* members also join an equal number of representatives elected by *Länder* parliaments in a special Federal Convention *Bundesversammlung* every five years to elect a federal president as head of state. The president, however, has few powers and is primarily a titular figure.

The 1949 constitution is a written document. Adherence to it is policed by an independent federal constitutional court based at Karlsruhe which is staffed by 16 judges, who serve terms of up to 12 years. All-party committees from the *Bundestag* and *Bundesrat* select eight each. The court functions as a guarantor of civil liberties and adjudicator in Federal-*Land* disputes. (Similar courts function at the *Land* level.)

In former West Germany, politics were dominated from 1949 by two major parties, the Christian Democratic Union (CDU) and Social Democratic Party (SPD), and one minor party, the Free Democratic Party (FDP). The conservative CDU gained the most support at the national level, forming the principal party of government 1949–69 and after 1982. It is represented in Bavaria by a more right-wing sister party, the Christian Social Union (CSU). The SPD is the dominant party of the left and, after adopting a more moderate policy program, became the principal party of federal government between 1969–82. The FDP liberal party averaged 8% of the national vote since 1949, but regularly held the balance of power in the *Bundestag* and has been a coalition partner, with a 20% share of cabinet portfolios, in all but seven years (1957–61 and 1966–69) since 1949. In the 1980's a fourth significant party, the ◊Green Party, emerged, surmounting the 5% federal electoral barrier in both 1983 and 1987.

history For history before 1949, see ◊Germany, history. In 1949 Germany was divided by the Allied powers and the Soviet Union, forming the German Democratic Republic in the eastern part of the country (formerly the Soviet zone of occupation), and the Federal Republic of Germany in the west (comprising the British, US, and French occupation zones under Allied military control following Germany's surrender 1945). For the next four and a half decades West and East Germany were divided by the policies of the ◊Cold War, with West Germany becoming the strongest European NATO power, and East Germany a vital member of ◊Comecon and the ◊Warsaw Pact during the ◊Brezhnev era, stationing Soviet medium-range nuclear missiles on its soil.

In postwar West Germany, a policy of demilitarization, decentralization, and democratization was instituted by the Allied control powers and a new, intentionally provisional, constitution framed, which included eventual German reunification.

West ◊Berlin was blockaded by the Soviet Union 1948–49, but survived to form a constituent *Land* in the Federal Republic, after an airlift operation by the Allied powers. Politics during the Federal Republic's first decade were dominated by the CDU, led by the popular Konrad ◊Adenauer.

Chancellor Adenauer and his economics minister, Ludwig ◊Erhard, established a successful approach to economic management, termed the "social market economy," which combined the encouragement of free market forces with strategic state intervention on the grounds of social justice. This new approach, combined with ◊Marshall Aid and the enterprise of the labor force (many of whom were refugees from the partitioned East), brought rapid growth and reconstruction during the 1950s and 1960s, an era termed the "miracle years."

During this period, West Germany was also

Germany, Federal Republic of

Federal Republic of Germany
(Bundesrepublik Deutschland)

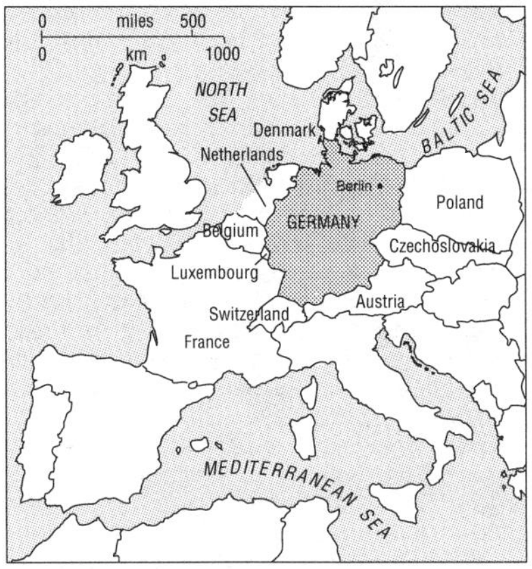
0 miles 500
0 km 1000
NORTH SEA
Denmark
Netherlands
BALTIC SEA
Berlin
Poland
Belgium
GERMANY
Czechoslovakia
Luxembourg
Austria
Switzerland
France
MEDITERRANEAN SEA

area 137,853 sq mi/357,041 sq km
capital Berlin
cities Cologne, Munich, Essen, Frankfurt-am-Main, Dortmund, Stuttgart, Düsseldorf, Leipzig, Dresden, Chemnitz, Magdeburg; ports Hamburg, Kiel, Cuxhaven, Bremerhaven, Rostock
physical flat in N, mountainous in S with Alps; rivers Rhine, Weser, Elbe flows N, Danube flows SE, Oder, Neisse flows N along Polish frontier; many lakes, including Müritz
features Black Forest, Harz Mountains, Erzgebirge (Ore Mountains), Bavarian Alps, Fichtelgebirge, Thüringer Forest
head of state Richard von Weizsäcker from 1984
head of government Helmut Kohl from 1982
political system democratic federal republic
political parties *formerly West German*: Christian Democratic Union (CDU), right-of-center; Social Democratic Party (SPD), left-of-center; Free Democratic Party (FDP), liberal; Christian Social Union (CSU), Bavarian-based conservative; Greens, environmentalist; Republicans, far-right; *formerly East German*: Socialist Union Party (SED), Marxist-Leninist; New Forum, opposition umbrella pressure group; Social Democratic Party (SPD), left-of-center; Liberal Democratic Party, Christian Democratic Union (CDU), National Democratic Party and Democratic Farmers Party, until 1989 allies of the SED; Free Democratic Party (FDP), liberal; Green Party, environmentalist
exports machine tools (world's leading exporter), automobiles, commercial vehicles, electronics, industrial goods, textiles, chemicals, iron, steel, wine, lignite (world's largest producer), uranium, coal, iron, steel, fertilizers, plastics
currency Deutschmark
population (1990 est) 77,600,000 (including nearly 5,000,000 guest workers, *Gastarbeiter*, of whom 1,600,000 are Turks; the rest are Yugoslavs, Italians, Greeks, Spanish, and Portuguese); growth rate –0.7% p.a.
life expectancy men 68, women 74
languages German, Sorbian
religion Protestant 45%, Roman Catholic 37%
literacy 99% (1985)
GNP $1,016 bn (1988); $13,000 per head
chronology
1945 Germany surrendered; country divided into four occupation zones (US, French, British, Soviet).
1948 Blockade of West Berlin.
1949 Establishment of Federal Republic under the "Basic Law" Constitution with Adenauer as chancellor; establishment of the German Democratic Republic as an independent state.
1953 Riots in East Berlin suppressed by Soviet troops.
1954 Grant of full sovereignty to West Germany.
1957 West Germany entered EC; recovery of Saarland.
1961 Construction of Berlin Wall.
1963 Retirement of Chancellor Adenauer.
1964 Treaty of Friendship and Mutual Assistance signed between East Germany and USSR.
1969 Willy Brandt became chancellor of West Germany.
1971 Erich Honecker elected Socialist Unity Party (SED) leader in East Germany.
1972 Basic Treaty between West Germany and East Germany; treaty ratified 1973, normalizing relations between the two.
1974 Resignation of Brandt; Helmut Schmidt became chancellor.
1975 East German friendship treaty with USSR renewed for 25 years.
1982 Helmut Kohl became West German chancellor.
1987 Official visit of Honecker to the Federal Republic.
1988 Death of West German Bavarian CSU leader Franz-Josef Strauss.
1989 West Germany: rising support for far right in local and European elections, and declining support for Kohl. East Germany: East German visitors to Hungary permitted to enter Austria and the West; mass exodus to West Germany began (344,000 left during 1989). Honecker replaced by Egon Krenz after mass demonstrations. New Forum opposition movement legalized; national borders opened in Nov, including Berlin Wall. Reformist Hans Modrow appointed prime minister. Krenz replaced.
1990 Jan: Secret-police (*Stasi*) headquarters in East Berlin stormed by demonstrators. Feb: Modrow called for a neutral united Germany. March: multiparty elections won by the right-wing CDU. Oct 3: official reunification of East and West Germany. Dec 2: first all-German elections since 1932, resulting in coalition government and the reelection of Chancellor Kohl.
1991 Taxes increased to finance economic development in the east, where unemployment was rising, as well as a share of the cost of the US-led Gulf War against Iraq. New Deutsche Bundesbank president: Helmut Schlesinger. Berlin voted in as the new capital.

reintegrated into the international community. It gained full sovereignty 1954, entered ◊NATO 1955, emerging as a loyal supporter of the US, and, under Adenauer's lead, joined the new ◊European Economic Community 1957. Close relations with France enabled the ◊Saarland to be transferred to German sovereignty 1957.

East Germany dissolved its five *Länder* (Brandenburg, Mecklenburg, Saxony, Saxony-Anhalt and Thuringia) in 1952, and its Chamber of States, or Upper House, in 1958, vesting local authority in 15 *Bezirke* or administrative districts. Under the 1968 constitution the supreme legislative and executive body in the German Democratic Republic was the people's chamber *Volkskammer*, whose 500 members (including 66 from East Berlin) were elected every five years by universal suffrage.

The years immediately after 1949 saw the rapid establishment of a communist regime on the Soviet model, involving the nationalization of industry, the formation of agricultural collectives, and the creation of a one-party political system. Opposition to such Sovietization led, during food shortages, to demonstrations and a general strike 1953, which was suppressed by Soviet troops.

East Germany became a sovereign state 1954, recognized at first only by the communist powers.

In 1961, East Germany's construction of the ◊Berlin Wall to prevent refugees from leaving the East created a political crisis that vaulted West Berlin's mayor, Willy ◊Brandt, to international prominence. Domestically, Brandt played a major role in shifting the SPD away from its traditional Marxist affiliation toward a more moderate position following the party's 1959 Bad Godesberg conference. Support for the SPD steadily increased after this policy switch and the party joined the CDU in a "Grand Coalition" 1966–69, before gaining power itself, with the support of the FDP, under Brandt's leadership 1969. As chancellor, Brandt introduced the foreign policy of ◊Ostpolitik, which sought reconciliation with Eastern Europe as a means of improving contacts between East and West Germany.

East Germany saw economic reforms and improved living conditions in the 1960s, and during the next decade a more moderate political stance was adopted, with the replacement of the Stalinist Socialist Unity Party (SED) leader Walter ◊Ulbricht by the pragmatic Erich ◊Honecker. Economic and diplomatic relations with the West were extended.

West German treaties 1970 normalized relations with the Soviet Union and Poland, and recognized the Oder–Neisse border line, while in 1972 a basic treaty was effected with East Germany, acknowledging East Germany's borders and separate existence and enabling both countries to enter the UN 1973. Brandt resigned as chancellor 1974, following the revelation that his personal assistant had been an East German spy. His successor, the former finance minister, Helmut ◊Schmidt, adhered to Ostpolitik and emerged as a leading advocate of European cooperation.

The West German SPD–FDP coalition only narrowly defeated the CDU–CSU in the 1976 federal election, but gained a comfortable victory 1980 when the controversial Franz-Josef ◊Strauss headed the CDU–CSU ticket. Between 1980 and 1982, however, the left wing of the SPD and the liberal FDP were divided over military policy (in particular the proposed stationing of US nuclear missiles in West Germany) and economic policy, during a period of recession.

Chancellor Schmidt fought to maintain a moderate, centrist course but the FDP eventually withdrew from the federal coalition 1982 and joined forces with the CDU, led by Dr Helmut ◊Kohl, to unseat the chancellor in a "positive vote of no confidence." Helmut Schmidt immediately retired from politics and the SPD, led by Hans-Jochen Vögel, was heavily defeated in the *Bundestag* elections 1983, losing votes on the left to the new environmentalist Green Party. The new Kohl administration, with the FDP's Hans-Dietrich ◊Genscher remaining as foreign minister, adhered closely to the external policy of the previous chancellorship.

At home, however, a freer market approach was introduced. With unemployment rising to 2.5 million in 1984, problems of social unrest emerged, while violent demonstrations greeted the installation of US nuclear missiles on German soil 1983–84. Internally, the Kohl administration was rocked by scandals over illegal party funding, which briefly touched the chancellor himself. However, a strong recovery in the German economy from 1985 enabled the CDU–CSU–FDP coalition to gain reelection in the federal election 1987, with 269 *Bundestag* seats. The opposition SPD meanwhile won 186 seats, and was divided over its future and whether or not to seek alliance with the Greens, who won 42 seats.

During 1988–89, following the death of the CSU's Franz-Josef Strauss, support for the far-right Republican party began to climb, and it secured 7% of the vote in the European Parliament elections of June 1989. In 1989–90 events in East Germany and elsewhere in Eastern Europe caused half a million economic and political refugees to enter the Federal Republic, as well as reopening the debate on reunification (*Wiedervereinigung*); this resulted in West German politics becoming more highly charged and polarized. The CDU gave strong support to swift, graduated moves toward "confederative" reunification, if desired, following free elections in East Germany; the SPD were more cautious and divided over the issue.

In East Germany Honecker had been urged by the Soviet Union since 1987 to accelerate the pace of domestic economic and political reform; his refusal to do so increased grassroots pressure for liberalization. In Sept 1989, after the violent suppression of a church and civil rights activists' demonstration in Leipzig, an umbrella dissident organization, *Neue Forum* ("New Forum"), was illegally formed. The regime was further destabilized between Aug and Oct 1989 both by the exodus of more than 30,000 of its citizens to West Germany through Hungary (which had opened its borders with Austria in May) and by Honecker's illness during the same period.

On Oct 6 and 7 the Soviet leader Mikhail ◊Gorbachev visited East Berlin, and made plain his desire to see greater reform. This catalyzed the growing reform movement, and a wave of demonstrations (the first since 1953) swept East Berlin, Dresden, Leipzig, and smaller towns. At first, under Honecker's orders, they were violently broken up by riot police. However, the security chief, Egon ◊Krenz, ordered a softer line and in Dresden the reformist Communist Party leader, Hans Modrow, actually marched with the protesters. Faced with the rising tide of protest and the increasing exodus to West Germany (between 5,000 and 10,000 people a day), which caused grave disruption to the economy, Honecker was replaced as party leader and head of state by Krenz on Oct 18–24. In an attempt to keep up with the reform movement, Krenz sanctioned far-reaching reforms in Nov 1989 that effectively ended the SED monopoly of power and laid the foundations for a pluralist system. The Politburo was purged of conservative members; Modrow became prime minister and a new cabinet was formed; New Forum was legalized, and opposition parties allowed to form; and borders with the West were opened and free travel allowed, with the Berlin Wall being effectively dismantled.

In Dec West German chancellor Kohl announced a ten-point program for reunification of the two Germanies, an idea that provoked both enthusiasm and anxiety in Europe. While the US and Soviet Union both called for a slower assessment of this idea, reunification was rapidly achieved on many administrative and economic levels as the governments cooperated on a number of cross-border issues. By mid-Dec the Communist Party had largely ceased to exist as an effective power in East Germany; following revelations of high-level corruption during the Honecker regime, Krenz was forced to resign as SED leader and head of state, being replaced by Gregor Gysi (1948–) and Manfred Gerlach (1928–) respectively. Honecker was placed under house arrest awaiting trial on charges of treason, corruption, and abuse of power, and the Politburo was again purged.

An interim SED–opposition "government of national responsibility" was formed Feb 1990. However, the political crisis continued to deepen, with the opposition divided over reunification with West Germany, while the popular reform movement showed signs of running out of control following the storming in Jan of the former security-police (*Stasi*) headquarters in East Berlin. The East German economy deteriorated further following the exodus of 344,000 people to West Germany in 1989, with a further 1,500 leaving each day, while country-wide work stoppages increased.

East German elections in March 1990 were won by the center-right Alliance for Germany, a three-party coalition led by the CDU. Talks were opened with the West German government on monetary union, concluding with a treaty unifying the economic and monetary systems in July 1990.

Official reunification came about on Oct 3, 1990, with Berlin as the capital (though the seat of government remained in Bonn). In mid-Oct new *Länder* elections were held in former East Germany, in which the conservative parties did well. The first all-German elections since 1932 took place Dec 2, 1990, resulting in victory for Chancellor Kohl and a coalition government comprised of the CDU, CSU and FDP parties, with a total of 398 seats in the new 662-member *Bundestag* (the new *Bundesrat* has 69 seats). The Green party of former West Germany lost its seats, receiving less than 5% of the vote, while the same party of former East Germany gained 8 seats (6% of the vote) in alliance with citizens' groups such as New Forum. The Communist Party of former East Germany gained seats with almost 10% of the East German vote (2.4% of entire vote). In Berlin, which became a *Land*, the ruling SPD lost control of the city council to a new coalition government. Besides the addition of Berlin as a *Land*, the former states of East Germany resumed their status as *Länder*—Brandenburg, Saxony-Anhalt, Saxony, Mecklenburg-West Pomerania, and Thuringia. During 1991, Germany struggled with the problems of integrating the systems and economics of East and West Germany, while playing a leading role in the unification movements within the European Community.

Germany: states

Republic	*Capital*	*Area sq km*
Baden-Württemberg	Stuttgart	35,800
Bavaria	Munich	70,600
Berlin	Berlin	880
Brandenburg	Potsdam	25,900
Bremen	Bremen	400
Hamburg	Hamburg	760
Hessen	Wiesbaden	21,100
Lower Saxony	Hanover	47,400
Mecklenburg-West Pomerania	Schwerin	22,900
North Rhine-Westphalia	Düsseldorf	34,100
Rhineland-Palatinate	Mainz	19,800
Saarland	Saarbrücken	2,570
Saxony-Anhalt	Magdeburg	25,900
Saxony	Dresden	17,050
Schleswig-Holstein	Kiel	15,700
Thuringia	Erfurt	15,500

Germany, history

BC–4th century AD The W Germanic peoples, originating in Scandinavia, moved into the region between the rivers Rhine, Elbe, and Danube, where they were confined by the Roman Empire.

496 The Frankish king Clovis conquered the Alemanni.

768–814 The reign of Holy Roman Emperor Charlemagne, who extended his authority over Germany and imposed Christianity on the Saxons.

814–919 After Charlemagne's death Germany was separated from France under its own kings while the local officials or dukes became virtually independent.

919–1002 Central power was restored by the Saxon dynasty. Otto I, who in 962 revived the title of emperor, began colonizing the Slav lands east of the river Elbe.

1075–1250 A feud between emperors and popes enabled the Germanic princes to recover their independence.

1493–1519 A temporary revival of imperial power took place under Maximilian I.

1521 The Diet of Worms at which Charles V confronted the Protestant Martin Luther. The Reformation increased Germany's disunity.

1618–48 The Thirty Years" War reduced the empire to a mere name and destroyed Germany's economic and cultural life.

1740–86 The rise of Brandenburg-Prussia as a military power, which had begun in the 17th century, reached its height under Frederick II.

1806 The French emperor Napoleon united W Germany in the Confederation of the Rhine and introduced the ideas and reforms of the French Revolution: his reforms were subsequently imitated in Prussia. The Holy Roman Empire was abolished.

1848 Ideas of democracy and national unity inspired the unsuccessful revolutions of 1848.

1867 The North German Confederation, under the leadership of Prussia, was formed.

1871 Under Chancellor Bismarck's leadership, the German Empire was formed after victorious wars with Austria and France. William I of Prussia became emperor.

1914–18 World War I: it was caused by Germany's political, industrial, and colonial rivalries with Britain, France, and Russia.

1918 A revolution overthrew the monarchy; the Socialists seized power and established the democratic Weimar Republic.

1922–24 Rampant inflation. In 1922 one dollar was worth 50 marks; in 1924 one dollar was worth 2.5 trillion marks.

1929–33 The economic crisis brought Germany close to revolution, until in 1933 the reaction maneuvered the Nazis into power with Adolf Hitler as chancellor.

1933–39 At home the Nazis solved the unemployment problem by a vast rearmament program; they abolished the democratic constitution and ruthlessly destroyed all opposition. Abroad, the policy of geopolitical aggression led to war.

1939–45 World War II: Germany (from 1940 in an alliance known as the Axis with Italy and Japan) attacked and occupied neighboring countries, but was defeated by the Allies (the UK and Commonwealth, France 1939–40, the USSR and the US from 1941, and China).

1945–52 Germany was divided, within its 1937 frontiers, into British, US, French, and Soviet occupation zones.

1949 Germany was partitioned into the communist German Democratic Republic (see ◊Germany, East) and the capitalist German Federal Republic (see ◊Germany, West).

1990 Reunification of East and West Germany.

Germany, West (Federal Republic of Germany) country 1949–90, formed from the British, US, and French occupation zones following World War II; reunified with East Germany in Oct 1990. For history before 1949, see ◊Germany, history; for history after 1949, see Federal Republic of ◊Germany.

germination in botany, the initial stages of growth in a seed, spore, or pollen grain. Seeds germinate when they are exposed to favorable external conditions of moisture, light, and temperature, and when any factors causing dormancy have been removed.

The process begins with the uptake of water by the seed. The embryonic root, or radicle, is normally the first organ to emerge, followed by the embryonic shoot, or plumule. Food reserves, either within the ◊endosperm or from the ◊cotyledons, are broken down to nourish the rapidly growing seedling. Germination is considered to have ended with the production of the first true leaves.

Germiston city in the Transvaal, South Africa; popu-

germination

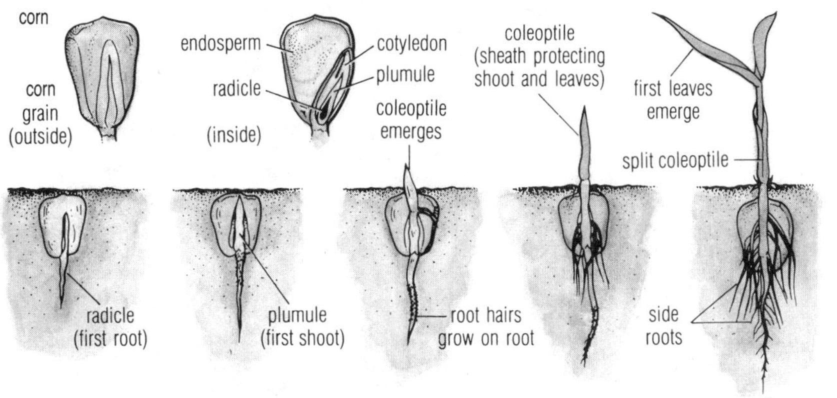
corn
corn grain (outside)
endosperm
radicle
(inside)
cotyledon
plumule
coleoptile emerges
coleoptile (sheath protecting shoot and leaves)
first leaves emerge
split coleoptile
radicle (first root)
plumule (first shoot)
root hairs grow on root
side roots

lation (1980) 155,435. Industries include gold refining, chemicals, steel, and textiles.

germ layer in ◊embryology, a layer of cells that can be distinguished during the development of a fertilized egg. Most animals have three such layers: inner, middle, and outer.

The inner layer (endoderm) gives rise to the gut, the middle one (mesoderm) develops into most of the other organs, while the outer one (ectoderm) gives rise to the skin and nervous system. Simple animals, such as sponges, lack a mesoderm.

Gerona town in Catalonia, NE Spain, capital of Gerona province; population (1986) 68,000. Industries include textiles and chemicals. There are ferry links with Ibiza, Barcelona, and Málaga.

Geronimo 1829–1909. A chief of the Chiricahua Apache and war leader. The slaughter by Mexicans of his entire family turned him away from a peaceful life. From 1875 to 1885, he fought settlers encroaching on tribal reservations in the Southwest, and federal troops, especially in SE Arizona and New Mexico. After surrendering to General George Crook in March 1886 and agreeing to go to Florida where their families were being held, Geronimo and a small band of followers escaped. Captured again Aug 1886, by 5,000 US troops, they were taken to Florida, then to Alabama. The climate proved unhealthy, and they were taken to Fort Sill, Oklahoma, where Geronimo became a farmer.

He dictated *Geronimo's Story of His Life* 1906. Geronimo fell from his horse following a drinking spree and lay on the cold ground overnight, resulting in his death from pneumonia.

gerrymander in politics, the rearranging of constituency boundaries to give an unfair advantage to the ruling party. It is now used more generally to describe various kinds of political trickery.

The term derives from US politician Elbridge Gerry (1744–1814), who, while governor of Massachusetts 1812, reorganized an electoral district (shaped like a salamander) in favor of his party.

Gers river in France, 110 mi/178 km in length; it rises in the Lannemezan Plateau and flows N to join the river Garonne 5 mi/8 km above Agen. It gives its name to a *département* in Midi-Pyrénées region.

Gershwin George 1898–1937. US composer who wrote both "serious" music, such as the tone poem *Rhapsody in Blue* 1924 and *An American in Paris* 1928, and popular musicals and songs, many with lyrics by his brother Ira Gershwin (1896–1983), including "I Got Rhythm," "'S Wonderful," and "Embraceable You." His opera *Porgy and Bess*, an ambitious work that incorporated jazz rhythms and popular song styles in an operatic format, was his masterpiece.

Of Thee I Sing 1931, a collaboration between the Gershwin brothers, was the first musical to win a Pulitzer prize. Born in Brooklyn, New York, Gershwin was a student of music all of his life. Although his scores to musicals made him famous, his "serious" work earned him much critical acclaim.

gerund in the grammar of certain languages, such as Latin, a noun formed from a verb and functioning as a noun to express an action or state. In English, gerunds end in *-ing*.

When the gerund is used as an adjective, it is called a gerundive.

Gesell Arnold Lucius 1880–1961. US psychologist and educator. Born in Alma, Wisconsin, Gesell received his PhD from Clark University 1906. Appointed to the Yale University faculty, he established the Yale Clinic of Child Development which he directed 1911–48. He received a medical degree from Yale 1915. As professor of child hygiene, he was among the first to study the stages of normal development, publishing both scholarly and popular works on child psychology. He became a consultant to The Gesell Institute of Child Development, founded to promote his educational ideas, in New Haven, Connecticut, 1950.

gestalt the concept of a unified whole that is greater than, or different from, the sum of its parts; that is, a complete structure whose nature is not explained simply by analyzing its constituent elements. A chair, for example, will generally be recognized as a chair despite great variations between individual chairs in such attributes as size, shape, and color. The term was first used in psychology in Germany about 1910. It has been adopted from German because there is no exact equivalent in English.

Gestalt psychology regards all mental phenomena as being arranged in organized, structured wholes. For example, learning is seen as a reorganizing of a whole situation (often involving insight), as opposed to the behaviorists's view that it consists of associations between stimuli and responses. Gestalt psychologists' experiments show that the brain is not a passive receiver of information, but that it structures all

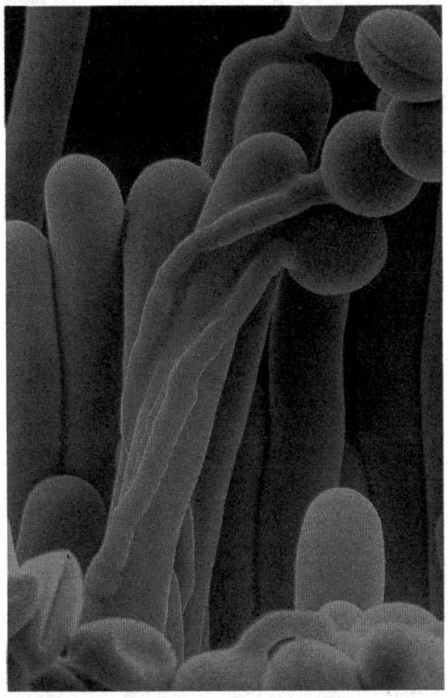

germination *False-color electron microscope view of pollen grains germinating on the stigma of the opium poppy.*

Geronimo *Chiricahua Apache chief Geronimo, who fought against encroachments on Apache lands by whites. Pictured here after his surrender, he spent his last years in Oklahoma.*

Gershwin *Jazz pianist and composer George Gershwin. He combined popular songwriting with more serious pieces, the most famous being* Rhapsody in Blue *1924.*

Getty *Oil tycoon John Paul Getty, who devoted much of his personal fortune to art collecting.*

its input in order to make sense of it, a belief that is now generally accepted.

Gestapo abbreviated form of Geheime Staatspolizei, Nazi Germany's secret police, formed 1933, and under the direction of Heinrich Himmler from 1936.

The Gestapo used torture and terrorism to stamp out anti-Nazi resistance. It was declared a criminal organization at the Nuremberg Trials 1946.

gestation in all mammals except the monotremes (duck-billed platypus and spiny anteaters), the period from the time of implantation of the embryo in the uterus to birth. This period varies among species; in humans it is about 266 days, in elephants 18–22 months, in cats about 60 days, and in some species of marsupial (such as opossum) as short as 12 days.

Gethsemane site of the garden where Judas Iscariot, according to the New Testament, betrayed Jesus. It is on the Mount of Olives, E of Jerusalem. When Jerusalem was divided between Israel and Jordan 1948, Gethsemane fell within Jordanian territory.

Getty J(ean) Paul 1892–1976. US oil billionaire, president of the Getty Oil Company from 1947 and founder of the Getty Museum (housing the world's highest-funded art gallery) in Malibu, California.

Gettysburg site in Pennsylvania of a decisive battle of the American ◊Civil War in 1863, won by the North. The site is now a national cemetery, at the dedication of which President Lincoln delivered the Gettysburg Address Nov 19, 1863, a speech in which he reiterated the principles of freedom, equality, and democracy embodied in the US Constitution.

The South's heavy losses at Gettysburg came in the same week as their defeat at Vicksburg, and the Confederacy remained on the defensive for the rest of the war. The battle ended Robert E ◊Lee's invasion of the North. The address begins with "Fourscore and seven years ago," and ends with an assertion of "government of the people, by the people, and for the people."

Getz Stan(ley) 1927– . US tenor saxophonist of the 1950s "cool jazz" school. He was the first US musician to be closely identified with the Latin American *bossa nova* sound.

geyser a natural spring that intermittently discharges an explosive column of steam and hot water into the air.

One of the most remarkable geysers is Old Faithful, in Yellowstone National Park, Wyoming.

Ghana
Republic of

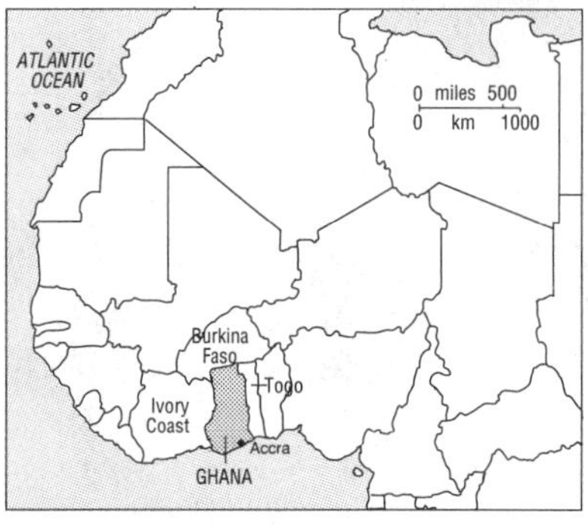
ATLANTIC OCEAN
0 miles 500
0 km 1000
Burkina Faso
Togo
Ivory Coast
Accra
GHANA

area 91,986 sq mi/238,305 sq km
capital Accra
cities Kumasi, and ports Sekondi-Takoradi, Tema
physical mostly tropical lowland plains; bisected by river Volta
features world's largest artificial lake Lake Volta; relics of traditional kingdom of Ashanti; 32,000 chiefs and kings
head of state and government Jerry Rawlings from 1981
political system military republic
political parties all political parties banned 1981
exports cocoa, coffee, timber, gold, diamonds, manganese, bauxite
currency cedi
population (1990 est) 15,310,000; growth rate 3.2% p.a.
life expectancy men 50, women 54
language English (official) and African languages
religion Christian 24%, animist 38%, Muslim 30%
literacy men 64%/women 43% (1985 est)
GNP $3.9 bn (1983); $420 per head
chronology
1957 Independence achieved, within the British Commonwealth, with Kwame Nkrumah as president.
1960 Ghana became a republic and a one-party state.
1966 Nkrumah deposed and replaced by Gen Joseph Ankrah.
1969 Ankrah replaced by Gen Akwasi Afrifa, who initiated a return to civilian government.
1970 Edward Akufo-Addo elected president.
1972 Another coup placed Col Acheampong at the head of a military government.
1978 Acheampong deposed in a bloodless coup led by Frederick Akuffo; another coup put Flight-Lt Jerry Rawlings in power.
1979 Return to civilian rule under Hilla Limann.
1981 Rawlings seized power again, citing the incompetence of previous governments.
1989 Coup attempt against Rawlings foiled.

Geysers also occur in New Zealand and Iceland.

Gezira, El plain in the Republic of Sudan, between the Blue and White Niles. The cultivation of cotton, sorghum, wheat, and groundnuts is made possible by irrigation.

G-forces the forces pilots and astronauts experience when their craft accelerate or decelerate rapidly. One G is the ordinary pull of gravity. Early astronauts were subjected to launch and re-entry forces up to six Gs or more. Pilots and astronauts wear G-suits that prevent severe G-forces stress, which can lead to unconsciousness.

Ghali Boutros Boutros 1922– , Egyptian diplomat; UN Secretary General 1992– ; first African to head United Nations. A law professor and journalist, he served as Egypt's foreign affairs minister 1977–91, before being named deputy prime minister in 1991.

geyser *Old Faithful, the most noted geyser in Yellowstone National Park, Wyoming. The time between eruptions varies from 33 to 96 minutes, depending on the length of the previous eruption.*

Ghana country in W Africa, bounded N by Burkina Faso, E by Togo, S by the Gulf of Guinea, and W by the Ivory Coast

government The 1979 constitution was suspended 1981 when Flight-Lt Jerry Rawlings seized power and set up a Provisional National Defence Council (PNDC), with himself as chair. Parliament and the council of state were abolished, and the government now rules by decree. All political parties were banned, but opposition groups still operate from outside the country. All media are government-controlled and the two daily newspapers are government-owned.

history The area now known as Ghana was once made up of several separate kingdoms, including those of the Fanti on the coast and the ◊Ashanti further inland.

The first Europeans to arrive in the region were the Portuguese 1471. Their coastal trading centers, dealing in gold and slaves, flourished alongside Dutch, Danish, British, Swedish, and French traders until about 1800, when the Ashanti, having conquered much of the interior, began to invade the coast. Denmark and the Netherlands abandoned their trading centers, and the Ashanti were defeated by Britain and the Fanti 1874. The coastal region became the British colony of The Gold Coast, and after continued fighting, the inland region to the north of Ashanti 1898, and the Ashanti kingdom 1901, were made British protectorates. After 1917 the W part of Togoland, previously governed by Germany, was administered with The Gold Coast. Britain thus controlled both coastal and inland territories, and in 1957 these, together with British Togoland, became the independent Republic of Ghana.

Dr Kwame ◊Nkrumah, a former prime minister of The Gold Coast, became president. He embarked on a policy of what he called "African socialism" and established an authoritarian regime. In 1964 he declared Ghana a one-party state, with the Convention People's Party (CPP—which he led) as the only political organization. He then dropped his stance of nonalignment and forged links with the USSR and other communist countries. In 1966, while visiting China, he was deposed in a coup led by General Joseph Ankrah, whose national liberation council released many political prisoners and purged CPP supporters.

In 1969 Ankrah was replaced by General Akwasi Afrifa, who announced plans for a return to civilian government. A new constitution established an elected national assembly and a nonexecutive presidency. The Progress Party (PP) won a big majority in the assembly, and its leader, Kofi Busia, became prime minister. In 1970 Edward Akufo-Addo became the civilian president.

Following economic problems, the army seized power again 1972. The constitution was suspended and all political institutions replaced by a National Redemption Council (NRC), under Colonel Ignatius Acheampong. In 1976 he too promised a return to civilian rule but critics doubted his sincerity and he was replaced by his deputy, Frederick Akuffo, in a bloodless coup 1978. Like his predecessors, he announced a speedy return to civilian government, but before elections could be held he, in turn, was deposed by junior officers led by Flight-Lt Jerry Rawlings, claiming that previous governments had been corrupt and had mismanaged the economy.

Civilian rule was restored 1979, but two years later Rawlings led another coup, again complaining of the government's incompetence. He established a Provisional National Defence Council (PNDC) with himself as chair, again suspending the constitution, dissolving parliament, and banning political parties. Although Rawlings' policies were initially supported by workers and students, his failure to revive the economy caused discontent, and he has had to deal with a number of demonstrations and attempted coups, including one in Oct 1989. In 1990 the country contributed troops to the multi-national force that attempted to stabilize Liberia.

Ghana, Ancient a great trading empire that flourished in NW Africa between the 5th and 13th centuries. Founded by the Soninke people, the Ghana Empire was based, like the Mali Empire that superseded it, on the Saharan gold trade. Trade consisted mainly of the exchange of gold from inland deposits for salt from the coast. At its peak in the 11th century, it occupied an area that includes parts of present-day Mali, Senegal, and Mauritania. Wars with the Berber tribes of the Sahara led to its fragmentation and collapse in the 13th century, when much of its territory was absorbed into Mali.

ghat in Hinduism, broad steps leading down to one of the sacred rivers. Some of these, known as "burning ghats," are used for cremation.

Ghats, Eastern and Western twin mountain ranges in S India, to the E and W of the central plateau; a few peaks reach about 9,800 ft/3,000 m. The name is a European misnomer, the Indian word *ghat* meaning "pass," not "mountain."

They are connected by the Nilgiri Hills.

Ghent (Flemish *Gent*, French *Gand*) city and port in East Flanders, NW Belgium; population (1982) 237,500. Industries include textiles, chemicals, electronics, and metallurgy.

The cathedral of St Bavon (12th–14th centuries) has paintings by van Eyck and Rubens, and the university was established 1816.

Gheorgiu-Dej Gheorge 1901–1965. Romanian communist politician. A member of the Romanian Communist Party from 1930, he played a leading part in establishing a communist regime in 1945. He was prime minister 1952–55 and state president 1961–65. Although retaining the support of Moscow, he adopted an increasingly independent line during his final years.

gherkin young or small green ◊cucumber, used for pickling.

ghetto (Old Venetian *gèto* "foundry") originally, the area of a town where Jews were compelled to live, decreed by a law enforced by papal bull 1555. The term first came into use in 1516 when the Jews of Venice were expelled to an island within the city that contained an iron foundary. Ghettos were abolished, except in E Europe, in the 19th century, but the concept and practice were revived by the Germans and Italians 1940–45. The term now refers to any deprived area occupied by a minority group, whether voluntarily or not.

Ghibelline in medieval Germany and Italy, a supporter of the emperor and member of a rival party to the Guelphs (see ◊Guelph and Ghibelline).

Ghiberti Lorenzo 1378–1455. Italian sculptor and goldsmith. In 1401 he won the commission for a pair of gilded bronze doors for Florence's baptistry. He produced a second pair, the *Gates of Paradise* 1425–52, which show sophisticated composition and use of perspective and are often cited as one of the masterpieces of the Italian Renaissance.

He also wrote *Commentarii/Commentaries* c. 1450, a mixture of art history, manual, and autobiography.

Ghirlandaio Domenico c. 1449–1494. Italian fresco painter, head of a large and prosperous workshop in Florence. His fresco cycle 1486–90 in Sta Maria Novella, Florence, includes portraits of many Florentines and much contemporary domestic detail. He also worked in Pisa, Rome, and San Gimignano, and painted portraits.

Ghosts a play by Henrik Ibsen, first produced 1881. Mrs Alving hides the profligacy of her late husband. The past catches up with her when her son inherits his father's syphilis and unwittingly plans to marry his half-sister.

GHQ abbreviation for general headquarters.

GI abbreviation for government issue; hence (in the US) a common soldier.

Giacometti Alberto 1901–1966. Swiss sculptor and painter who trained in Italy and Paris. In the 1930s, in his Surrealist period, he began to develop his characteristic spindly constructions. His mature style of emaciated single figures, based on wire frames, emerged in the 1940s.

Giambologna (Giovanni da Bologna or Jean de Boulogne) 1529–1608. Flemish-born sculptor active mainly in Florence and Bologna. In 1583 he completed his public commission for the Loggia dei Lanzi in Florence, *The Rape of the Sabine Women*, a dynamic group of muscular figures and a prime example of Mannerist sculpture.

Giambologna produced the *Neptune Fountain* 1563–67 in Bologna and the equestrian statues of the Medici grand dukes Cosimo and Ferdinando. There are several versions of his figure of *Mercury* on tiptoe (the one in Bargello, Florence, for example). His workshop in Florence produced small replicas of his work in bronze.

giant in many mythologies and folklore, one of a race of outsize humanoids, often characterized as stupid and aggressive. In Greek mythology the giants grew from the spilled blood of Uranus and rebelled against the gods. During the Middle Ages in many parts of Europe, wicker effigies of giants were carried in midsummer processions and sometimes burned.

Giant's Causeway stretch of columnar basalt forming a promontory on the N coast of Antrim, Northern Ireland. It was formed by an outflow of lava in Tertiary times that has solidified in polygonal columns.

gibberellin plant growth substance (see also ◊auxin) that mainly promotes stem growth but may also affect the breaking of dormancy in certain buds and seeds, and the induction of flowering. Application of gibberellin can stimulate the stems of dwarf plants to additional growth, delay the aging process in leaves, and promote the production of seedless fruit (◊parthenocarpy).

gibbon any of several small apes of the genus *Hylobates*, including the subgenus *Symphalangus*. The common or lar gibbon *H. laris* about 2 ft/60 cm tall, with a body that is hairy except for the buttocks, which distinguishes it from other types of apes. The siamang *S. syndactylus* is the largest of the gibbons, growing to 36 in/90 cm tall. It is entirely black. Gibbons have long arms and no tail. They are arboreal in habit, being very agile when swinging from branch to branch. On the ground, however, they walk upright, and are more easily caught by predators. They are found from Assam through the Malay peninsula to Borneo, but are becoming rare, with certain species classified as endangered.

Gibbon Edward 1737–1794. British historian, author of *The History of the Decline and Fall of the Roman Empire* 1776–88.

The work was a continuous narrative from the 2nd century AD to the fall of Constantinople in 1453. He began work on it while in Rome in 1764. Although immediately sucessful, he was compelled to reply to attacks on his account of the early development of Christianity by a *Vindication* 1779.

Gibbon John Heysham 1903–1974. US surgeon who invented the heart-lung machine in 1953. It has become indispensable in heart surgery, maintaining the circulation while the heart is temporarily inactivated.

Gibbons Orlando 1583–1625. English composer. A member of a family of musicians, he was appointed organist at Westminster Abbey, London in 1623. His finest works are his madrigals and motets.

Gibbons v Ogden a US Supreme Court decision 1824 dealing with states' intervention in the regulation of interstate commerce. The conflict arose when New York State issued an injunction against Gibbons prohibiting his steamboat operation between New York and New Jersey. Although Gibbons was federally licensed, his business was in violation of a state law that granted to Ogden a monopoly on all steamboat operation in New York. Gibbons appealed to the US Supreme Court, which ruled that the New York law was de facto interference with the federal regulation of interstate commerce and therefore was unconstitutional.

Gibbs Josiah Willard 1839–1903. US theoretical physicist and chemist who developed a mathematical approach to thermodynamics. His book *Vector Analysis* 1881 established vector methods in physics.

In 1863 he gained the first engineering doctorate awarded in the US, and in 1871 he became professor of mathematical physics at Yale University, where he remained until his death.

Gibbs' function in ◊thermodynamics, an expression representing part of the energy content of a system that is available to do external work, also known as the free energy G. In an equilibrium system at constant temperature and pressure, $G = H - TS$, where H is the enthalpy (heat constant), T the temperature, and S the ◊entropy (decrease in energy availability). The function was named after US physicist Josiah Willard Gibbs.

Gibraltar British dependency, situated on a narrow rocky promontory in S Spain

area 2.5 sq mi/6.5 sq km

features strategic naval and air base, with NATO underground headquarters and communications center; colony of Barbary apes; the frontier zone is adjoined by the Spanish port of La Línea

exports mainly a trading center for the import and re-export of goods

population (1988) 30,000

history captured from Spain 1704 by English admiral George Rooke (1650–1709), it was ceded to Britain under the Treaty of Utrecht 1713. A referendum 1967 confirmed the wish of the people to remain in association with the UK, but Spain continues to claim sovereignty and closed the border 1969–85. In 1989, the UK government

Gibraltar

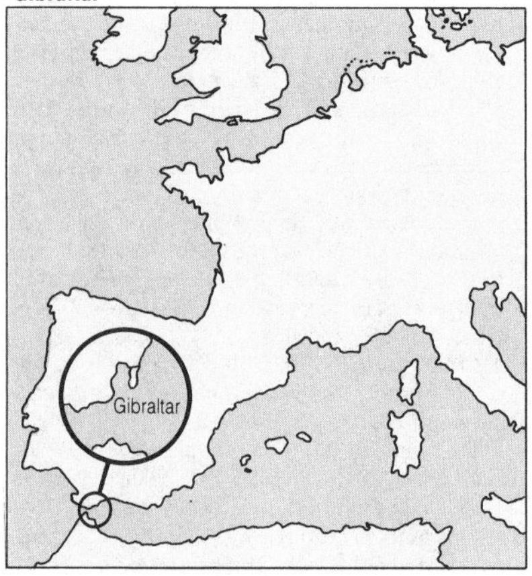
Gibraltar

announced it would reduce the military garrison by half

currency Gibraltar government notes and UK coinage

language English

religion mainly Roman Catholic

government the governor has executive authority, with the advice of the Gibraltar council, and there is an elected house of assembly (chief minister Joshua Hassan 1964–69 and from 1972).

Gibraltar, Strait of strait between N Africa and Spain, with the Rock of Gibraltar on the north side and Jebel Musa on the south, the so-called Pillars of Hercules.

Gibson Althea 1927– . US tennis player. As a student at Florida A&M University, she became the first black American woman to compete at the US Championships at Forest Hills 1950 and at Wimbledon 1951. In 1957 she took both the women's singles and doubles titles at Wimbledon and the singles at Forest Hills. In 1958 she successfully defended all three titles. She later played professional golf.

Born in Silver, South Carolina, and raised in New York, Gibson was hindered in her tennis career by racial discrimination and segregation. In 1943 she won the New York State Negro girls' singles title, and in 1948 the national Negro women's title.

Gibson Charles Dana 1867–1944. US illustrator. He portrayed an idealized type of American young woman, known as the "Gibson Girl."

Gibson was born in Roxbury, Massachusetts. He worked for *Life* magazine, eventually becoming its editor. He also illustrated books and later painted in oils.

Gide *André Gide, who received the Nobel Prize for Literature in 1947.*

Gielgud *Distinguished English actor and director John Gielgud, noted for his stage performances in Shakespearean productions.*

Gibson Desert desert in central Western Australia; area 85,000 sq mi/220,000 sq km.

Gide André 1869–1951. French novelist, born in Paris. His work is largely autobiographical and concerned with the dual themes of self-fulfillment and renunciation. It includes *L'Immoraliste/The Immoralist* 1902, *La Porte étroite/Strait Is the Gate 1909, Les Caves du Vatican/The Vatican Cellars* 1914, and *Les Faux-monnayeurs/The Counterfeiters* 1926; and an almost lifelong *Journal*. Nobel Prize for Literature 1947.

Gideon in the Old Testament, one of the Judges of Israel, who led a small band of Israelite warriors which succeeded in routing an invading Midianite army of overwhelming number in a surprise night attack.

Gideon v Wainwright a US Supreme Court decision 1963 dealing with the right of accused persons who are unable to afford legal assistance to a court-appointed lawyer. Prior to this case, only those defendants being tried for capital offenses were guaranteed counsel. Gideon, a Florida man accused only of a felony, was forced by poverty to defend himself. He was convicted but appealed his conviction, arguing that his constitutional right to a lawyer had been denied. The Court ordered a retrial, ruling that states must provide counsel for felony-case defendants who are too poor to provide their own.

Gielgud John 1904– . English actor and director. He played many Shakespearean roles, including Hamlet 1929. His film roles include Clarence in *Richard III* 1955 and the butler in *Arthur* 1981 (for which he won an Academy Award).

Gierek Edward 1913– . Polish Communist politician. He entered the Politburo of the ruling Polish United Workers" Party (PUWP) in 1956 and was party leader 1970–80. His industrialization program plunged the country heavily into debt and sparked a series of ◊Solidarity-led strikes.

Gierek, a miner's son, lived in France and Belgium for much of the period between 1923 and 1948, becoming a member of the Belgian Resistance. He served as party boss in Silesia during the 1960s. After replacing Gomulka as PUWP leader in Dec 1970, he embarked on an ambitious program of industrialization. A wave of strikes in Warsaw and Gdańsk, spearheaded by the Solidarity free trade-union movement, forced Gierek to resign in Sept 1980.

Giessen manufacturing town on the river Lahn, Hessen, Federal Republic of Germany; population (1984) 71,800. Its university was established 1605.

Giffard Henri 1825–1882. French inventor of the first passenger-carrying powered and steerable airship, called a dirigible, built 1852. The hydrogen-filled airship was 144 ft/43 m long, had a 3-hp steam engine that drove a three-bladed propeller, and was steered using a saillike rudder. It flew at an average speed of 3 mph/5 kph.

The first flight was on Sep 24th, 1852.

giga- prefix signifying multiplication by 10^9 (1,000,000,000 or 1 billion), as in gigahertz, a unit of frequency equivalent to 1 billion hertz.

gigabyte in computing, a measure of the capacity of ◊memory or storage, equal to 1,024 ◊megabytes. It is also used, less precisely, to mean 1,000 million bytes.

ginger beer a drink made with fermented ginger and bitters, for a strong taste, which creates natural carbonation.

Gigli Beniamino 1890–1957. Italian lyric tenor. Following his operatic debut in 1914 he performed roles by Puccini, Gounod, and Massenet.

Gijón port on the Bay of Biscay, Oviedo province, N Spain; population (1986) 259,000. It produces iron, steel, chemicals, and oil; is an outlet for the coal mines of Asturias; and is a major fishing and shipbuilding center.

gila monster lizard *Heloderma suspectum* of SW USA and Mexico. It is one of the only two existing venomous lizards, the other being the Mexican beaded lizard of the same genus. It has poison glands in its lower jaw, but its bite is not usually fatal to humans.

Gilbert Cass 1859–1934. US architect, major developer of the ◊skyscraper. His work includes the Woolworth Building, New York City 1913, notable for its Gothic decoration; it was the highest building in America (868 ft/265 m) when built.

Gilbert was also architect of the US Supreme Court building in Washington, DC, the Minnesota state capitol in St Paul, and the US Customs House in New York City.

Gilbert Humphrey c. 1539–1583. English soldier and navigator who claimed Newfoundland (landing at St John's) for Elizabeth I in 1583. He died when his ship sank on the return voyage.

Gilbert W(illiam) S(chwenk) 1836–1911. British humorist and dramatist who collaborated with Arthur ◊Sullivan, providing the libretti for their series of light comic operas from 1871; they include *HMS Pinafore* 1878, *The Pirates of Penzance* 1879, and *The Mikado* 1885.

Born in London, he became a lawyer in 1863, but in 1869 published a collection of his humorous verse and drawings, *Bab Ballads*—"Bab" being his own early nickname—which was followed by a second volume in 1873.

Gilbert Walter 1932– . US molecular biologist. Gilbert worked on the problem of genetic control, seeking the mechanisms which switch genes on and off. By 1966 he had established the existence of the *lac* repressor, the molecule which suppressed lactose production. Further work on the sequencing of ◊DNA nucleotides won for Gilbert a share of the 1980 Nobel Chemistry Prize with Frederick Sanger and Paul Berg.

Gilbert William 1544–1603. English scientist and physician to Elizabeth I and (briefly) James I. He

Gigli *Italian opera singer Beniamino Gigli.*

Gilbert *British humorist and dramatist W S Gilbert, best known for his collaboration with Arthur Sullivan on light comic operas.*

studied magnetism and static electricity, deducing that the Earth's magnetic field behaves as if a bar magnet joined the North and South poles. His book on magnets, published 1600, is the first printed scientific book based wholly on experimentation and observation.

He erroneously thought that the planets were held in their orbits by magnetic forces.

Gilbert and Ellice Islands former British colony in the Pacific, known since independence 1978 as ◊Tuvalu and ◊Kiribati.

Gilded Age, the in US history, a derogatory term referring to the opulence displayed in the post-Civil War decades. It borrows the title of an 1873 political satire by Mark Twain and Charles Dudley Warner (1829–1900), which highlights the respectable veneer of public life covering the many scandals of graft and corruption.

Gilgamesh hero of Sumerian, Hittite, Akkadian, and Assyrian legend. The 12 verse "books" of the *Epic of Gilgamesh* were recorded in a standard version on 12 cuneiform tablets by the Assyrian king Ashurbanipal's scholars in the 7th century BC, and the epic itself is older than Homer's *Iliad* by at least 1,500 years. One-third mortal and two-thirds divine, Gilgamesh is lord of the Sumerian city of Uruk. The *Epic*'s incident of the Flood is similar to the Old Testament account, since Abraham had been a citizen of the nearby city of Ur in Sumer.

Gilgit town and region on the NW frontier of Kashmir, under the rule of Pakistan.

gill in biology, the main respiratory organ of most fishes and immature amphibians, and of many aquatic invertebrates. In all types, water passes over the gills, and oxygen diffuses across the gill membranes into the circulatory system while, carbon dioxide passes from the system out into the water.

In aquatic insects, these gases diffuse into and out of air-filled canals called tracheae.

gill imperial unit of volume for liquid measure, equal to one-fourth of a pint or four fluid ounces (0.118 liter). It is used in selling alcoholic drinks.

Gillespie Dizzy (John Birks) 1917– . US jazz trumpeter who, with Charlie ◊Parker, was the chief creator and exponent of the ◊bebop style.

Though associated mainly with small combos, Gillespie played trumpet with a number of renowned jazz bands, such as those of Cab Calloway and Duke Ellington. Gillespie influenced many modern jazz trumpeters, including Miles Davis.

Gilman Charlotte Perkins 1860–1935. US feminist Socialist poet, novelist, and historian, author of *Women and Economics* 1898, proposing the ending of the division between "men's work" and "women's work" by abolishing housework.

From 1909 to 1916 she wrote and published a magazine *The Forerunner* in which her feminist Utopian novel *Herland* 1915 was serialized.

ginkgo

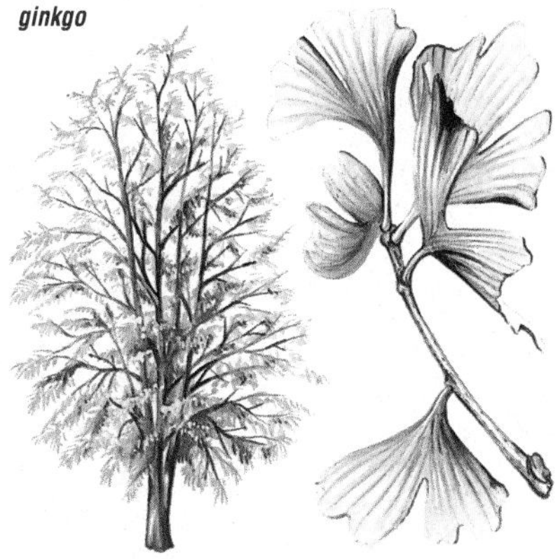

gin (Dutch *jenever* "juniper") alcoholic drink made by distilling a mash of rye and other grains with juniper flavoring. It was first produced in Holland.

ginger SE Asian reedlike perennial *Zingiber officinale*, family Zingiberaceae; the hot-tasting underground root is used as a condiment and in preserves.

ginger ale drink of sweetened carbonated water flavored with ginger.

ginkgo or maidenhair tree tree *Ginkgo biloba* of the gymnosperm (or naked-seed-bearing) division of plants. It may reach a height of 100 ft/30 m by the time it is 200 years old.

The only living member of its group (Ginkgophyta), widespread in Mesozoic times, it has been cultivated in China and Japan since ancient times, and is planted in many parts of the world. Its leaves are fan-shaped, and it bears fleshy, yellow, foul-smelling seeds enclosing nuts with delicious edible kernels, which contain immune-system boosters.

Ginsberg Allen 1926– . US poet. His "Howl" 1956, an influential poem of the ◊Beat Generation, criticizes the materialism of contemporary US society. In the 1960s Ginsberg traveled widely in Asia and was a key figure in introducing Eastern thought to students of that decade.

ginseng plant *Panax ginseng*, family Araliaceae, with thick, forked aromatic root used in medicine as a tonic.

Giolitti Giovanni 1842–1928. Italian liberal politician, born in Mondovi. He was prime minister in 1892–93, 1903–05, 1906–09, 1911–14, and 1920–21. He opposed Italian intervention in World War I and pursued a policy of broad coalitions, which proved ineffective in controlling Fascism after 1921.

Giono Jean 1895–1970. French novelist whose books are chiefly set in Provence. *Que ma joie demeure*/*Joy of Man's Desiring* 1935 is an attack on life in towns and a plea for a return to country life.

Giordano Luca 1632–1705. Italian Baroque painter, born in Naples, active in Florence in the 1680s. In 1692 he was summoned to Spain by Charles II and painted ceilings in the Escorial palace for the next ten years.

In Florence Giordano painted a ceiling in the Palazzo Riccardi-Medici 1682–83. He also produced altarpieces and frescoes for churches. His work shows a variety of influences, including Paolo ◊Veronese, and tends to be livelier than that of earlier Baroque ceiling painters.

Giorgione del Castelfranco c. 1475–1510. Italian Renaissance painter, active in Venice, probably trained by Giovanni Bellini. His work influenced Titian and other Venetian painters. His subjects are imbued with a sense of mystery and treated with a soft technique reminiscent of Leonardo da Vinci's later works, as in *The Tempest* 1504 (Accademia, Venice).

Few details of his life are certain, but Giorgione created the Renaissance poetic landscape, with rich colors and a sense of intimacy; an example is the *Madonna and Child Enthroned with Two Saints*, an alterpiece for the church of Castelfranco.

giraffe

Giotto space probe built by the European Space Agency to study ◊Halley's comet. Launched by an Ariane rocket in July 1985, *Giotto* passed within 375 mi/600 km of the comet's nucleus on March 13, 1986.

Giotto di Bondone 1267–1337. Italian painter and architect. He broke away from the conventional Gothic style of the time, and introduced a naturalistic style, painting saints as real people. He painted cycles of frescoes in churches at Assisi, Florence, and Padua.

Giotto was born in Vespignano, N of Florence. The interior of the Arena Arena Chapel, Padua, was covered by him in a fresco cycle (completed by 1306) illustrating the life of Mary and the life of Jesus. Giotto's figures occupy a definite pictorial space and there is an unusual emotional intensity and dignity in the presentation of the story. In one of the frescoes he made the Star of Bethlehem appear as a comet; ◊Halley's comet had appeared 1303, just two years before.

From 1334 he was official architect to Florence and from 1335 overseer of works at the cathedral; he collaborated with Andrea ◊Pisano in decorating the cathedral facade with statues and designing the campanile (bell tower), which was completed after his death.

giraffe tallest mammal, *Giraffa camelopardalis*, belonging to the ruminant family Giraffidae. It stands over 18 ft/5.5 m tall, the neck accounting for nearly half this amount. The giraffe has two to four small, skin-covered hornlike structures on its head and a long, tufted tail. The skin has a mottled appearance and is reddish brown and cream. Giraffes are found only in Africa, south of the Sahara Desert. Both members of the Girafidae, the giraffe and the okapi, are able to use their extremely long tongues for cleaning their eyes and ears.

Girardon François 1628–1715. French academic sculptor. His *Apollo Tended by Nymphs*, commissioned 1666, is one of several marble groups sculpted for the gardens of Louis XIV's palace at Versailles.

Giraudoux (Hippolyte) Jean 1882–1944. French playwright and novelist who wrote the plays *Amphitryon 38* 1929 and *La Folle de Chaillot*/*The Madwoman of Chaillot* 1945, and the novel *Suzanne et la Pacifique*/*Suzanne and the Pacific* 1921. His other plays include *La Guerre de Troie n'aura pas lieu*/*Tiger at the Gates* 1935.

Girgenti former name (until 1927) of ◊Agrigento, a town in Sicily, Italy.

Gironde navigable estuary 50 mi/80 km long, formed by the mouths of the ◊Garonne, length 360 mi/580 km, and ◊Dordogne rivers, in SW

Gish *Actress Lillian Gish achieved great success in the silent films of D W Griffith and later was known for her character roles.*

France. The Lot, length 300 mi/480 km, is a tributary of the Garonne.

Girondin member of the right-wing republican party in the French Revolution, so called because a number of their leaders came from the Gironde region. They were driven from power by the ◊Jacobins 1793.

Giscard d'Estaing Valéry 1926– . French conservative politician, president 1974–81. He was finance minister under de Gaulle 1962–66 and Pompidou 1969–74. As leader of the Union pour la Démocratie Française, which he formed in 1978, Giscard sought to project himself as leader of a "new center."

Giscard was active in the wartime Resistance. After a distinguished academic career, he worked in the Ministry of Finance and entered the National Assembly for Puy de Dôme in 1956 as an Independent Republican. After Pompidou's death he was narrowly elected president in 1974, in difficult economic circumstances; he was defeated by the Socialist Mitterrand in 1981. He returned to the National Assembly in 1984. In 1989 he resigned from the National Assembly to play a leading role in the European Parliament.

Gish Lillian. Adopted name of Lillian de Guiche 1896– . US film actress who began her career in silent films. Her most celebrated work was with the American director D W Griffith, including *Way Down East* 1920 and *Orphans of the Storm* 1922, playing virtuous heroines. She later made occasional appearances in character roles, starred in *The Night of The Hunter* 1955, and costarred with Bette Davis in *The Whales of August* 1987. She received a special Academy Award in 1971.

Gitlow v New York a US Supreme Court decision 1925 dealing with state legislation that restricts freedom of speech. Benjamin Gitlow, editor of the left-wing *Manifesto*, was convicted, under a New York state law, of advocating the violent overthrow of the government. The Court upheld the law, ruling that First-Amendment rights are secondary to the preservation of the state.

Giulini Carlo Maria 1914– . Italian conductor. Principal conductor at La Scala in Milan 1953–55, and musical director of the Los Angeles Philharmonic 1978–84, he is renowned as an interpreter of Verdi.

Giulio Romano c. 1499–1546. Italian painter and architect. An assistant to Raphael, he developed a Mannerist style, creating effects of exaggerated movement and using rich colors, for example the frescoes in the Palazzo del Tè 1526 (Mantua).

Gîza, El or ***al-Jizah*** site of the Great Pyramids and Sphinx; a suburb of ◊Cairo, Egypt; population (1983) 1,500,000. It has textile and film industries.

gizzard a muscular grinding organ of the digestive tract, below the ◊crop of birds, earthworms, and some insects, and forming part of the ◊stomach. The gizzard of birds is lined with a hardened horny layer of the protein keratin, preventing damage to the muscle layer during the grinding process. Most birds swallow sharp grit which aids maceration of food in the gizzard.

Glace Bay port on Cape Breton Island, Nova Scotia, Canada, center of a coal-mining area; population (1986) 20,500.

glacier a body of ice, originating in mountains in snowfields above the snowline, which traverses land surfaces (glacier flow). It moves slowly down a valley or depression, and is constantly replenished from its source. The scenery produced by the erosive action of glaciers is characteristic and includes U-shaped valleys, ◊cirques, ◊arêtes, and various features formed by the deposition of ◊moraine (rocky debris).

Glaciers form where annual snowfall exceeds annual melting and drainage. The snow compacts to ice under the weight of the layers above. When a glacier moves over an uneven surface, deep crevasses are formed in the ice mass; if it reaches the sea or a lake, it breaks up to form icebergs. A glacier that is formed by one or several valley glaciers at the base of a mountain is called a piedmont glacier. A glacier that covers a large land surface or continent, for example Greenland or Antarctica, and flows outward in all directions is called an ice sheet.

Glackens William James 1870 DOD: 1938– . American painter. Born in Philadelphia, he studied at the Pennsylvania Academy of the Fine Arts under Robert ◊Henri. He was a member of the Ashcan school and one of "The Eight," a group of realists who exhibited at New York's Macbeth Gallery 1908. Glackens's painting eventually evolved into a realism that was strongly influenced by Impressionism. He painted subjects from everyday urban life, as well as those from fashionable society.

gladiator in ancient Rome, a trained fighter, recruited mainly from slaves, criminals, and prisoners of war, who fought to the death in arenas for the entertainment of spectators. The custom, which originated in the practice of slaughtering slaves on a chieftain's grave, was introduced into Rome from Etruria in 264 BC and continued until the 5th century AD.

gladiolus any plant of the genus *Gladiolus* of S European and African cultivated perennials of the iris family Iridaceae, with brightly colored, funnel-shaped flowers, borne in a spike; the swordlike leaves spring from a corm.

glacier

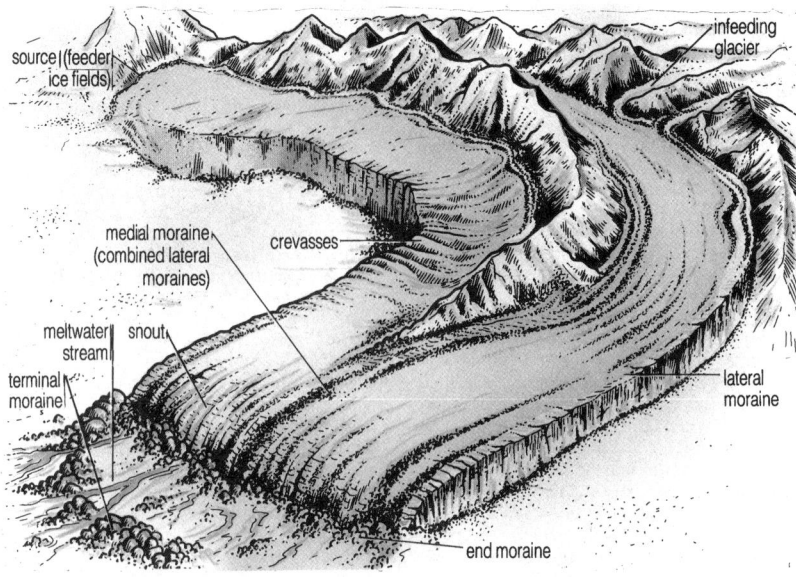

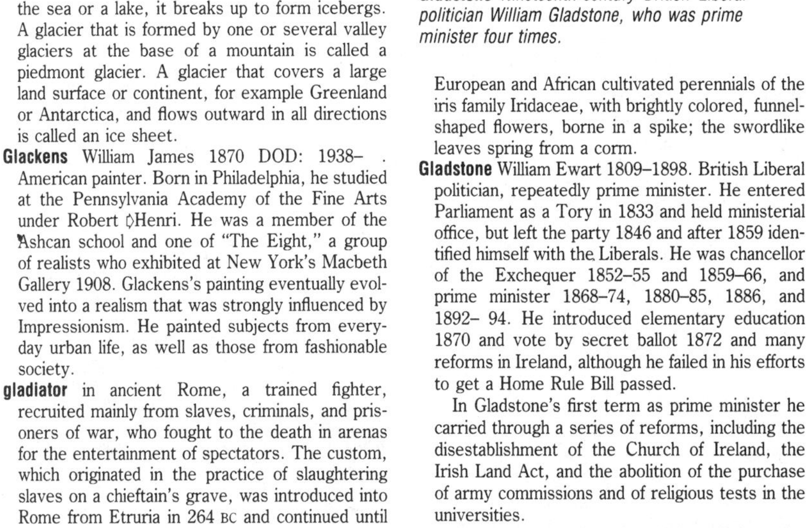
source (feeder ice fields)
infeeding glacier
medial moraine (combined lateral moraines)
crevasses
meltwater stream
snout
terminal moraine
lateral moraine
end moraine

Gladstone *Nineteenth-century British Liberal politician William Gladstone, who was prime minister four times.*

Gladstone William Ewart 1809–1898. British Liberal politician, repeatedly prime minister. He entered Parliament as a Tory in 1833 and held ministerial office, but left the party 1846 and after 1859 identified himself with the Liberals. He was chancellor of the Exchequer 1852–55 and 1859–66, and prime minister 1868–74, 1880–85, 1886, and 1892– 94. He introduced elementary education 1870 and vote by secret ballot 1872 and many reforms in Ireland, although he failed in his efforts to get a Home Rule Bill passed.

In Gladstone's first term as prime minister he carried through a series of reforms, including the disestablishment of the Church of Ireland, the Irish Land Act, and the abolition of the purchase of army commissions and of religious tests in the universities.

Gladstone strongly resisted Disraeli's imperialist and pro-Turkish policy during his government of 1874–80, not least because of Turkish violence against subject Christians; by his Midlothian campaign of 1879 he helped to overthrow Disraeli. Gladstone's second government carried the second Irish Land Act and the Reform Act 1884. Returning to office in 1886, Gladstone introduced his first Home Rule Bill, which was defeated, and he thereupon resigned. He formed his last government in 1892; his second Home Rule Bill was rejected by the Lords, and in 1894 he resigned.

Glamorgan three counties of S Wales – ◊Mid, ◊South, and ◊West Glamorgan—created in 1974 from the former county of Glamorganshire. All are on the Bristol Channel, and the administrative headquarters of Mid and South Glamorgan is Cardiff; the headquarters of West Glamorgan is Swansea. Mid Glamorgan, which also takes in a small area of the former county of Monmouthshire to the east, contains the coal-mining towns of Aberdare and Merthyr Tydfil, and the Rhondda in the valleys. The mountains are in the northern part of the county; area 394 sq mi/1,019 sq km; population (1983) 536,400. In South Glamorgan, there is mixed farming in the fertile Vale of Glamorgan, and towns include Cardiff, Penarth, and Barry; area 161 sq mi/416 sq km; population (1983) 391,700. West Glamorgan includes Swansea, with tin-plating and copper industries, Margam, with large steel rolling mills, Port Talbot, and Neath; area 315 sq mi/815 sq km; population (1983) 366,600.

gland a specialized organ of the body that manufactures and secretes enzymes, hormones, or other chemicals. In animals, glands vary in size from small (for example, tear glands) to large (for example, the pancreas), but in plants they are always small, and may consist of a single cell. Some glands discharge their products internally like ◊endocrine glands, and others such as ◊exocrine glands, externally. Lymph nodes are sometimes wrongly called glands.

glandular fever or ***infectious mononucleosis*** viral disease characterized at onset by fever and painfully swollen lymph nodes (in the neck); there may also be digestive upset, sore throat, skin rashes, and liver infection (◊hepatitis), which is sometimes fatal. Lassitude persists for months and even years, and recovery is often very slow. It is caused by the Epstein-Barr virus.

Glanville Ranalf died 1190. English ◊justiciar from 1180 and legal writer. His *Treatise on the Laws and Customs of England* 1188 was written to instruct practicing lawyers and judges and is now an important historical source on medieval common law.

Glaser Donald Arthur 1926– . US physicist, who invented the ◊bubble chamber in 1952, for which he received the Nobel Prize for Physics in 1960.

Born in Cleveland, Ohio, he was educated at the Case Institute of Technology, did research at the University of Michigan, and in 1960 became professor at the University of California.

Glasgow city and administrative headquarters of Strathclyde, Scotland; population (1985) 734,000. Industries include engineering, chemicals, printing, and distilling.

Buildings include the 12th-century cathedral of St Mungo; the Cross Steeple (part of the historic Tolbooth); the universities of Glasgow, established 1451 (19th-century buildings by Sir Gilbert Scott and Strathclyde, established 1964); the Royal Exchange; the Stock Exchange; Kelvingrove Art Gallery (Impressionist collection); the Glasgow School of Art, designed by C R Mackintosh; the Burrell Collection at Pollock Park, bequeathed by shipping magnate Sir William Burrell (1861–1958); and Mitchell Library.

Glasgow Ellen 1873–1945. US novelist. Her books, set mainly in her native Virginia, often deal with the survival of tough heroines in a world of adversity and include *Barren Ground* 1925, *The Sheltered Life* 1932, and *Vein of Iron* 1935.

Glashow Sheldon Lee 1932– . US physicist who as an elementary particle physicist at Harvard has made major contributions to our understanding of ◊quarks. In 1964 he proposed the existence of a fourth "charmed" quark, and later argued that quarks must be colored. Insights gained from these theoretical studies enabled Glashow to consider ways in which some of the ◊fundamental forces of nature (the weak and the electromagnetic) could be unified as a single force now called electroweak force. For this work he shared the Nobel Prize for Physics with Abdus ◊Salem and Steven ◊Weinberg. See ◊Superstring Theory.

glasnost (Russian "openness") Soviet leader Mikhail ◊Gorbachev's policy of liberalizing various aspects of Soviet life, such as introducing greater freedom of expression and information and opening up relations with Western countries.

Glasnost has involved the lifting of bans on books, plays, and films, the release of political ◊dissidents, the tolerance of religious worship, a reappraisal of Soviet history (destalinization), the encouragement of investigative journalism to uncover political corruption, and the sanctioning of greater candor in the reporting of social problems and disasters (such as ◊Chernobyl).

Under legislation introduced 1990, censorship of mass media is abolished; however, publication of state secrets, calls for the overthrow of the state by force, incitement of national or religious hatred, and state interference in people's private lives are prohibited. Journalists' rights to access are guaranteed, and there is a right of reply. Citizens have the right to receive information from abroad.

glass brittle, usually transparent or translucent substance which is physically neither a solid nor a liquid. Glass is made by fusing certain types of sand (silica); this fusion occurs naturally in volcanic glass (see ◊obsidian).

In the industrial production of common types of glass, the type of sand used, the particular chemicals added to it (for example, lead, potassium, barium), and refinements of technique determine the type of glass produced. Types of glass include: soda glass; flint glass, used in cut-crystal ware; optical glass; stained glass; heat-resistant glass; glasses that exclude certain ranges of the light spectrum; blown glass, which is either blown individually from molten glass using a tube 4.5 ft/1.5 m long for expensive, crafted glass, or automatically blown into a mold, for example, light bulbs and bottles; pressed glass, which is simply pressed into molds for jam jars, cheap vases, and light fittings; and sheet glass for windows, which is made by putting the molten glass through rollers to form a "ribbon" or by floating molten glass on molten tin in the "float glass" process.

Fiberglass is made from fine fiberglass. In bulk, it can be used as insulation material in construction work, or woven into material or made into glass-reinforced plastic (GRP). Fiberglass has good electrical, chemical, and weathering properties and it is also used for boat hulls, motor bodies, and aircraft components. See also ◊metallic glass.

Glass Philip 1937– . US composer. As a student of Nadia ◊Boulanger, he was strongly influenced by Indian music; his work is characterized by repeated rhythmic figures that are continually expanded and modified. His compositions include the operas *Einstein on the Beach* 1975, *Akhnaten* 1984, and *The Making of the Representative for Planet 8* 1988.

glass harmonica (or ***armonica***) is based on the principle of playing a wine glass with a wet finger. Devised by Benjamin Franklin, it consists of a graded series of glass bowls mounted on a spindle and resting in a trough part-filled with water. Rotated by a foot-pedal, it emits pure tones of unchanging intensity when touched. Mozart, Beethoven, and Schubert all wrote pieces for it.

Glasse Hannah 1708–1770. British cooking writer whose *The Art of Cookery made Plain and Easy* 1747 is regarded as the first classic recipe book in Britain.

glass lizard another name for ◊***glass snake***.

glass snake or ***glass lizard*** any of a worldwide genus *Ophisaurus* of legless lizards of the family Anguidae. Their tails are up to three times the head-body length and are easily broken off.

The eastern glass lizard *O. ventralis* grows to 36 in/1.1 m and inhabits wet grasslands in the SE US.

Glauber Johann 1604–1668. German chemist. Glauber, who made his living selling patent medicines, is remembered for his discovery of the salt known variously as "sal mirabile" and "Glauber's salt."

The salt, sodium sulfate, is produced by the action of sulfuric acid on common salt, and was used by Glauber to treat almost any complaint.

Glauber's salt in chemistry, crystalline sodium sulfate decahydrate $Na_2SO_4.10H_2O$, which melts at 87.8°F/31°C; the latent heat stored as it solidifies makes it a convenient thermal energy store. It is used in medicine.

glaucoma condition in which pressure inside the eye (intraocular pressure) is raised abnormally as excess fluid accumulates. It occurs when the normal flow of intraocular fluid out of the eye is interrupted. As pressure rises, the optic nerve suffers irreversible damage, leading to a reduction in the field of vision and, ultimately, loss of eyesight.

The most common type, chronic glaucoma, usually affects people over the age of 40, when the trabecular meshwork (the filtering tissue at the margins of the eye) gradually becomes blocked and drainage slows down. The condition cannot be cured, but, in many cases, it is controlled by drug therapy. Laser treatment to the trabecular meshwork often improves drainage for a time; surgery to create an artificial channel for fluid to leave the eye offers more long-term relief. A tiny window may be cut in the iris during the same operation.

Acute glaucoma is a medical emergency. A precipitous rise in pressure occurs when the trabecular meshwork suddenly becomes occluded (blocked). This is treated surgically to remove the cause of the obstruction. Acute glaucoma is extremely painful. Treatment is required urgently since damage to the optic nerve begins within hours of onset.

glaucophane a blue amphibole, $Na_2(Mg,Fe,Al)_5.Si_8O_{22}(OH)_2$. Its typical occurrence is in glaucophane schists (blue schists), which are formed form the ocean floor basalt under metamorphic conditions of high pressure and low temperature; these conditions are believed to exist in subduction systems associated with destructive plate boundaries (see ◊plate tectonics), and so the occurrence of glaucophane schists can indicate the location of such boundaries in geologic history.

glaze a transparent vitreous coating for pottery and porcelain, which gives the object a shining, protective finish that keeps it from leaking and chipping. Glazed pottery is first known from the mid- to late-Neolithic in Egypt, where ◊glass was first made.

Glendower Owen c. 1359–c. 1416. Welsh nationalist leader of a successful revolt against the English in N Wales, who defeated Henry IV in three campaigns 1400–02, although Wales was reconquered 1405–13. Glendower disappeared 1416 after some years of guerrilla warfare.

Glenn John Herschel, Jr 1921– . US astronaut and politician who on Feb 20, 1962 became the first American to orbit the Earth, doing so three times in the Mercury spacecraft *Friendship 7*, in a flight lasting 4 hr 55 min. After retiring from ◊NASA, he became a US senator as a Democrat from

Ohio, winning elections 1974, 1980, and 1986. He unsuccessfully sought the Democratic presidential nomination 1984. As a senator, he advocated nuclear-arms-production limitations and increased aid to education and job-skills programs.

Glens Falls city in E central New York, N of Albany and S of Lakes George and Champlain. Situated in Warren County by a waterfall in the Hudson River, its industries include clothing, paper, machinery parts, insurance, and tourism; population (1990) 15,023.

gliding the art of using air currents to fly unpowered aircraft. Technically, gliding involves the gradual loss of altitude; gliders designed for soaring flight (utilizing air rising up a cliff face or hill, warm air rising as a "thermal" above sun-heated ground, and so on) are known as sailplanes. The sport of ◊hang gliding was developed in the 1970s.

Glider pioneers include George ◊Cayley, Otto ◊Lilienthal, Octave Chanute (1832–1910), and the ◊Wright brothers, the latter perfecting gliding technique in 1902. Launching may be by rubber catapult from a hilltop, by a winch that raises the glider like a kite, or by aircraft tow. In World War II, towed troop-carrying gliders were used by the Germans in Crete and the Allies at Arnhem, because they are soundless.

Glinka Mikhail Ivanovich 1804–1857. Russian composer. He broke away from the prevailing Italian influence and turned to Russian folk music as the inspiration for his opera *A Life for the Tsar* (originally *Ivan Susanin*) 1836. His later works include another opera, *Ruslan and Lyudmila* 1842, and the orchestral *Kamarinskaya* 1848.

Glittertind the highest mountain in Norway, rising to 8,110 ft/2,470 m in the Jotunheim range.

Gliwice city in Katowice region, S Poland, formerly in German Silesia; population (1985) 213,000. It has coal-mining, iron, steel, and electrical industries. It is connected to the river Oder by the Gliwice Canal.

globefish another name for ◊***puffer fish***.

Globe Theatre a London theater, octagonal and open to the sky, near Bankside, Southwark, where many of Shakespeare's plays were performed by Richard Burbage and his company. Built 1599 by Cuthbert Burbage, it was burned down 1613 after a cannon, fired during a performance of Henry VIII, set light to the thatch. It was rebuilt in 1614 but pulled down in 1644. The site was rediscovered Oct 1989 near the remains of the contemporaneous Rose Theatre.

globular cluster spherical ◊star cluster of between 10,000 and a million stars. More than a hundred globular clusters are distributed in a spherical halo around our Galaxy. They consist of old stars, formed early in our Galaxy's history. Globular clusters are also found around other galaxies.

glockenspiel musical percussion instrument of light metal keys mounted on a carrying frame for use in military bands, or like a small xylophone for use in an orchestra.

glomerulus in the kidney, the blood capillaries responsible for forming the fluid that passes down the tubules and ultimately becomes urine. In the human kidney there are approximately one million tubules, each possessing its own glomerulus.

The structure of the glomerulus allows a wide range of substances including amino acids and sugar, as well as a large volume of water, to pass out of the blood. As the fluid moves through the tubules, most of the water and all of the sugars are reabsorbed, so that only waste remains, dissolved in a relatively small amount of water. This fluid collects in the bladder as urine.

Glomma or Glåma river in Norway, 350 mi/570 km long. The largest river in Scandinavia, it flows into the Skagerrak (an arm of the North Sea) at Frederikstad.

Glorious Revolution in British history, the events surrounding the removal of James II from the throne and his replacement by Mary (daughter of Charles I) and William of Orange as joint sovereigns in 1689. James had become increasingly unpopular on account of his unconstitutional behavior and Catholicism. Various elements in England, including seven prominent politicians, plotted to invite the Protestant William to invade. Arriving at Torbay on Nov 5, 1688, William rapidly gained support and James was allowed to flee to France after the army deserted him. William and Mary then accepted a new constitutional settlement, the Bill of Rights 1689, which assured the ascendency of parliamentary power over sovereign rule.

Gloucester city, port, and administrative headquarters of Gloucestershire, England; population (1983) 92,200. Industries include the manufacture of aircraft and agricultural machinery. Its 11th–14th-century cathedral has a Norman nucleus and additions in every style of Gothic.

Gloucester city in NE Massachusetts, on Cape Ann, NE of Boston. A famous fishing port; its industries include tourism and fish processing, especially lobster, whiting, and cod; population (1990) 28,716.

Gloucestershire county in SW England

area 1,019 sq mi/2,640 sq km

towns Gloucester (administrative headquarters), Stroud, Cheltenham, Tewkesbury, Cirencester

features Cotswold Hills; river Severn and tributaries; Berkeley Castle, where Edward II was murdered; Prinknash Abbey, famous for pottery; Cotswold Farm Park, near Stow-on-the-Wold, renowned for rare and ancient breeds of farm animals

products cereals, fruit, dairy products; engineering, coal in the Forest of Dean

population (1987) 522,000

famous people Edward Jenner.

glove box protective device used when handling toxic, radioactive, or sterile materials within an enclosure containing a window for viewing. Gloves fixed to ports in the walls of a box allow manipulation of objects within the box. The risk that the operator might inhale fine airborne particles of poisonous materials is removed by maintaining a vacuum inside the box, so that any airflow is inward.

glow-worm the wingless female of some luminous beetles (fireflies) in the family Lampyridae. The luminous organs situated under the abdomen serve to attract winged males for mating. There are about 2,000 species, distributed worldwide.

Glozel archeological site in a village near Vichy, France. A find here in 1924 was attacked as a hoax because of the disparate age of the objects. It included bones inscribed with drawings of animals 10,000 BC, axes 4000–2000 BC, inscribed clay tablets 700 BC–AD 100, and a glass kiln, possibly medieval. Thermoluminescence analysis in 1975–76 suggested the objects are genuine.

Glubb John Bagot 1897–1986. British soldier, founder of the Arab Legion (the Jordanian army), which he commanded 1939–56.

Gluck Christoph Willibald von 1714–1787. German composer who settled in Vienna as Kapellmeister to Maria Theresa in 1754. In 1762 his *Orfeo ed Euridice/Orpheus and Eurydice* revolutionized the 18th-century conception of opera by giving free scope to dramatic effect. *Orfeo* was followed by *Alceste/Alcestis* 1767 and *Paris ed Elena/Paris and Helen* 1770.

Born in Erasbach, Bavaria, he studied music at Prague, Vienna, and Milan, went to London in 1745 to compose operas for the Haymarket, but returned to Vienna in 1746 where he was knighted by the Pope. In 1762 his *Iphigénie en Aulide/Iphigenia in Aulis* 1774, produced in Paris, gave rise to controversy in which Gluck had the support of Marie Antoinette while his Italian rival Piccinni had the support of Madame Du Barry. With *Armide* 1777 and *Iphigénie en Tauride/Iphigenia in Tauris* 1779 Gluck won a complete victory over Piccinni.

glucose $C_6H_{12}O_6$ sugar or carbohydrate also known as grape-sugar or dextrose. It is present in the blood, and is found in honey and fruit juices. It is a source of energy for the body, being produced from other sugars and starches to form the "energy currency" of many biochemical reactions also involving ◊ATP.

It is usually prepared by hydrolysis from cane sugar or starch. Generally a yellowish syrup, it may be purified to a white crystalline powder. Glucose is a monosaccharide (a single sugar unit).

glue type of ◊adhesive.

glue-sniffing or ***solvent*** misuse inhalation of the fumes from organic solvents of the type found in paints, lighter fuel, and glue, for their hallucinatory effects. As well as being addictive, solvents are dangerous for their effects on the user's liver, heart, and lungs. It is believed that solvents produce hallucinations by dissolving the cell membrane of brain cells, thus altering the way the cells conduct electrical impulses.

gluon one of the ◊gauge bosons, an ◊elementary particle that cannot be subdivided and is the carrier of the ◊strong force, a component of subatomic particles that holds together ◊quarks to form the strongly interacting particles known as ◊hadrons. There are eight kinds of gluons.

glut an excess of goods in a market. A glut of agricultural produce often follows an exceptional harvest, causing prices to fall unless there is some form of intervention in the market.

glyceride an ◊ester formed between one or more acids and glycerol (propan-1,2,3-triol). A glyceride is termed mono-, di-, or triglyceride, depending on the number of hydroxyl groups from the glycerol that have reacted with the acids.

Glycerides, mainly triglycerides, occur naturally as esters of ◊fatty acids in animal and plant oils and fats.

glycerine common name for glycerol, or trihydroxypropane $HOCH_2CH(OH)CH_2OH$, a thick, colorless, odorless, sweetish liquid. It is obtained from vegetable and animal oils and fats (by treatment with acid, alkali, superheated steam, or an enzyme), or by fermentation of glucose, and is used in the manufacture of high explosives, in antifreeze solutions, to maintain moist conditions in fruits and tobacco, and in cosmetics.

glycerol another name for ◊glycerine.

glycine $CH_2(NH_2)COOH$ the simplest amino acid, and one of the main components of proteins. When purified, it is a sweet, colorless crystalline compound.

glycogen polymer (a polysaccharide) of the sugar ◊glucose made and retained in the liver as a carbohydrate store, for which reason it is sometimes called animal starch. It is a source of energy when needed by muscles, where it is converted back into glucose by the hormone ◊insulin and metabolized.

glycol (technical name dihydroxyethane) thick, colorless, odorless, sweetish liquid also called ethylene glycol or ethanediol $(CH_2OH)_2$. Glycol is used in antifreeze solutions, in the preparation of ethers and esters (used for explosives), as a solvent, and as a substitute for glycerine.

gnat any of various small flies of the order Diptera, that sometimes suck blood. In Britain, mosquitoes are often called gnats.

gneiss a coarse-grained ◊metamorphic rock, formed under conditions of increasing temperature and pressure, and often occurring in association with schists and granites. It has a foliated, laminated structure, consisting of thin bands of micas and amphiboles alternating with granular bands of quartz and feldspar. Gneisses are formed during regional metamorphism; paragneisses are derived from sedimentary rocks and orthogneisses from igneous rocks. Garnets are often found in gneiss.

gnome in fairy tales, a small, mischievous spirit of the earth. The males are bearded, wear tunics and hoods, and often guard an underground treasure.

Gnosticism esoteric cult of divine knowledge (a synthesis of Christianity, Greek philosophy, Hinduism, Buddhism, and the mystery cults of the Mediterranean), which flourished during the 2nd and 3rd centuries and was a rival to, and influence on, early Christianity. The medieval French ◊Cathar heresy and the modern *Mandean* sect (in S Iraq) descend from Gnosticism.

Gnostic 4th-century codices discovered in Egypt in the 1940s include the Gospel of St Thomas (unconnected with the disciple) and the Gospel of Mary, probably originating about AD 135. Gnosticism envisaged the world as a series of emanations from the highest of several gods. The lowest emanation was an evil god (the demiurge) who created the material world as a prison for the divine sparks that dwell in human bodies. The Gnostics identified this evil creator with the God of the Old Testament, and saw the Adam and Eve story and the ministry of Jesus as attempts to liberate humanity from his dominion, by imparting divine secret wisdom.

GNP abbreviation for ◊Gross National Product.

gnu or ***wildebeest*** either of two species of African ◊antelope, genus *Connochaetes*, with a cowlike face, a beard and mane, and heavy curved horns in both sexes. The body is up to 4.2 ft/1.3 m at the shoulder and slopes away to the hindquarters.

The brindled gnu *C. taurinus* is silver-gray with dark face, mane and tail tuft, and occurs from Kenya southward. Vast herds move together on migration. The white-tailed gnu *C. gnou* of South Africa almost became extinct, but was saved by breeding on farms.

go board game originating in China 3,000 years ago, and now the national game of Japan. It is played by placing small stones on a large grid. The object is to win territory and eventual superiority.

The board, squared off by 19 horizontal and 19 vertical lines, begins empty and gradually fills up with black and white, flattish, rounded stones, as the players win territory by surrounding areas of the board with "men" and capturing the enemy armies by surrounding them. A handicapping system enables expert and novice to play against each other.

It is far more complex and subtle than chess, the mathematical possibilities being 1×10^{720}.

Goa state of India

area 1,428 sq mi/3,700 sq km

capital Panaji

population (1981) 1,003,000

history captured by the Portuguese 1510; the inland area added in the 18th century. Goa was incorporated into India as a Union Territory with ◊Daman and ◊Diu 1961 and became a state 1987.

goat ruminant mammal of the genus *Capra* in the family Bovidae, closely related to the sheep. Both males and females have horns and beards. They are sure-footed animals, and feed on shoots and leaves more than grass.

Domestic varieties are kept for milk, or for mohair (the angora and cashmere). Wild species include the ibex *C. ibex* of the Alps, and markhor *C. falconeri* of the Himalayas, 3 ft/1 m high and with long twisted horns. The Rocky Mountain goat *Oreamnos americanus* is a "goat antelope" and is not closely related to true goats.

Gobbi Tito 1913–1984. Italian baritone singer renowned for his opera characterizations of Figaro, Scarpia, and Iago.

Gobelins French tapestry factory, originally founded as a dyeworks in Paris by Gilles and Jean Gobelin about 1450. The firm began to produce tapestries in the 16th century, and in 1662 the establishment was bought by Colbert for Louis XIV. With the support of the French government, it continues to make tapestries.

Gobi Asian desert divided between the Mongolian People's Republic and Inner Mongolia, China; 500 mi/800 km N–S, and 1,000 mi/1,600 km E–W. It is rich in fossil remains of extinct species.

Gobind Singh 1666–1708. Indian religious leader, the tenth and last guru (teacher) of Sikhism, 1675–1708, and founder of the Sikh brotherhood known as the ◊Khalsa. On his death, the Sikh holy book, the *Guru Granth Sahib*, replaced the line of human gurus as the teacher and guide of the Sikh community.

God the concept of a supreme being, a unique creative entity, basic to several monotheistic religions (for example Judaism, Christianity, Islam); in many polytheistic cultures (for example Norse, Roman, Greek), the term "god" refers to one of many supernatural beings who personifies the force behind an aspect of life (for example Neptune, Roman god of the sea).

Godard Jean-Luc 1930– . French film director, one of the leaders of ◊New Wave cinema. His works are often characterized by experimental editing techniques and an unconventional dramatic form. His films include *A bout de souffle* 1960, *Weekend* 1968, and *Je vous salue, Marie* 1985.

Godavari river in central India, flowing from the Western Ghats to the Bay of Bengal; length 900 mi/1,450 km. It is sacred to Hindus.

Goddard Robert Hutchings 1882–1945. US rocket pioneer. His first liquid-fueled rocket was launched at Auburn, Massachusetts, March 1926. By 1935 his rockets had gyroscopic control and carried cameras to record instrument readings. Two years later a Goddard rocket gained the world altitude record with an ascent of 1.9 mi/3 km.

Gödel Kurt 1906–1978. Austrian-born US mathematician and philosopher who proved that a mathematical system always contains statements that can be neither proved nor disproved within the system; in other words, as a science, mathematics can never be totally consistent and totally complete. He worked on relativity, constructing a mathematical model of the universe that made travel back through time theoretically possible.

Godfrey de Bouillon c. 1060–1100. French crusader, second son of Count Eustace II of Boulogne. He and his brothers, ◊Baldwin and Eustace, led 40,000 Germans in the First Crusade 1096. When Jerusalem was taken 1099, he was elected its ruler, but refused the title of king. After his death, Baldwin was elected king.

Godiva Lady c. 1040–1080. Wife of Leofric, earl of Mercia (died 1057). Legend has it that her husband promised to reduce the heavy taxes on the people of Coventry if she rode naked through the streets at noon. The grateful citizens remained indoors as she did so, but "Peeping Tom" bored a hole in his shutters and was struck blind.

Godkin Edwin Lawrence 1831–1902. Irish-born US editor and writer on political affairs, who founded *The Nation* magazine.

Educated in Ireland, Godkin studied law but chose a journalistic career, covering the Crimean War for the *London Daily News* and *The New York Times*. Immigrating to the US 1856, he studied law and was admitted to the bar 1858. During the American Civil War he again served as a correspondent for the *London Daily News* and in 1865 founded his own political journal, *The Nation*. In it, Godkin crusaded for national reform and progressive causes. After selling *The Nation* 1881 to the *New York Evening Post*, Godkin continued to write on national affairs.

Godthaab (Greenlandic *Nuuk*) capital and largest town of Greenland; population (1982) 9,700. It is a storage center for oil and gas, and the chief industry is fish processing.

Godunov Boris 1552–1605. Tsar of Russia from 1598. He was assassinated by a pretender to the throne. The legend that has grown up around this forms the basis of Pushkin's play *Boris Godunov* 1831 and Mussorgsky's opera of the same name 1874.

Boris Godunov was elected after the death of Fyodor I, son of Ivan the Terrible. He died during a revolt led by one who professed to be Dmitri, a brother of Fyodor and the rightful heir. The true Dmitri, however, had died in 1591 by cutting his own throat during an epileptic fit. An apocryphal story of Boris killing the true Dmitri to gain the throne was fostered by Russian historians anxious to discredit Boris because he was not descended from the main ruling families.

Godunov's rule was marked by a strengthening of the Russian church. It was also the beginning of the Time of Troubles, a period of instability.

Goebbels Paul Josef 1897–1945. German Nazi leader. He was born in the Rhineland, became a journalist, joined the Nazi party in its early days, and was given control of its propaganda 1929. As minister of propaganda from 1933, he brought all cultural and educational activities under Nazi control and built up sympathetic movements abroad to carry on the "war of nerves" against Hitler's intended victims. On the capture of Berlin by the Allies, he poisoned himself.

Goeppert-Mayer Maria 1906–1972. German-born US physicist who worked mainly on the structure of the atomic nucleus. She shared the 1963 Nobel Prize for Physics with Eugene ◊Wigner and Hans Jensen (1907–1973).

Her explanation of the stability of particular atoms 1948 envisaged atomic nuclei as shelllike layers of protons and neutrons, with the most stable atoms having completely filled outermost shells.

Goering (German *Göring*) Hermann Wilhelm 1893–1946. Nazi leader, German field marshal from 1938. He was part of Hitler's inner circle, and with Hitler's rise to power in 1933, he established the Gestapo and concentration camps. Appointed successor to Hitler in 1939, he built a vast economic empire in occupied Europe, but later lost favor and was expelled from the party in 1945. Tried at Nuremberg for war crimes, he poisoned himself before he could be executed.

Goering was born in Bavaria. He was a renowned fighter pilot in World War I, and joined the Nazi party in 1922. He was elected to the Reichstag in 1928 and became its president in 1932. As commissioner for aviation from 1933 he built up the Luftwaffe (airforce). In 1936 he took charge of the four-year plan for war preparations.

Goes Hugo van der died 1482. Flemish painter, active in Ghent. His *Portinari altarpiece* about 1475 (Uffizi, Florence) is a large oil painting of the Nativity, full of symbolism and naturalistic detail; the *Death of the Virgin* about 1480 (Musée Communale des Beaux Arts, Bruges) is remarkable for the varied expressions on the faces of the apostles.

Goethe Johann Wolfgang von 1749–1832. German poet, novelist, and dramatist, generally considered the founder of modern German literature, and leader of the Romantic ◊*Sturm und Drang* movement. His works include the autobiographical *Die Leiden des Jungen Werthers/The Sorrows of the Young Werther* 1774 and *Faust* 1808, his masterpiece. A visit to Italy 1786–88 inspired the Classical dramas *Iphigenie auf Tauris/Iphigenia in Tauris* 1787 and *Tasso* 1790.

Born at Frankfurt-am-Main, Goethe studied law. Inspired by Shakespeare, to whose work he was introduced by ◊Herder, he wrote the play *Götz von Berlichingen* 1773. His autobiographical *The Sorrows of the Young Werther* 1774, and the poetic play *Faust* 1808, brought him European reknown. Other works include the *Wilhelm Meister* novels 1796–1829. Between 1775 and 1785 he served as prime minister at the court of Weimar.

Goffman Erving 1922–1982. Canadian social scientist. He studied the ways people try to create, present, and defend a self-image within the social structures surrounding, controlling, and defining human interaction. He analyzed human interaction and the ways people behave, such as in public places. His works include *The Presentation of Self in Everyday Life* 1956, *Gender Advertisements* 1979, and *Forms of Talk* 1981.

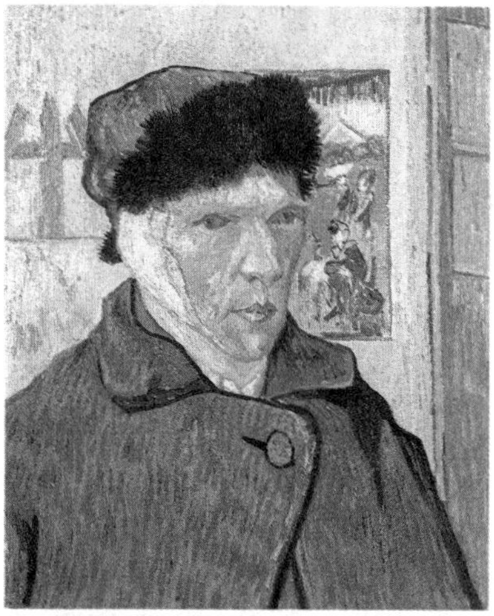

***Gogh** Dutch painter Vincent van Gogh cut off part of his own ear, as shown in* Self-Portrait with Bandaged Ear *1889, which is in the Courtauld Galleries, London.*

Gogh Vincent van 1853–1890. Dutch painter, a leading Post-Impressionist. He tried various careers, including preaching, and began painting still lifes and landscapes in the 1880s. He met Paul ◊Gauguin in Paris, and when he settled in Arles, Provence, 1888, Gauguin joined him there. After a quarrel van Gogh cut off part of his own earlobe, and in 1889 he entered a mental asylum; the following year he committed suicide. The Arles paintings vividly testify to his intense emotional involvement in his art; among them are *The Yellow Chair* 1888 and *A Cornfield with Cypresses* 1889 (National Gallery, London).

Gogol Nicolai Vasilyevich 1809–1852. Russian writer. His first success was a collection of stories, *Evenings on a Farm near Dikanka* 1831–32, followed by *Mirgorod* 1835. Later works include *Arabesques* 1835, the comedy play *The Inspector General* 1836, and the picaresque novel *Dead Souls* 1842, which satirizes Russian provincial society.

Born near Poltava, Gogol tried several careers before entering the St Petersburg Civil Service. From 1835 he traveled in Europe, and it was in Rome that he completed the earlier part of *Dead Souls* 1842. Other works include the short stories "The Overcoat" and "The Nose."

Gogra alternative transcription of river ◊Ghaghara in India.

goitre enlargement of the thyroid gland seen as a swelling on the neck. It is most pronounced in simple goitre, which is caused by iodine deficiency. Much more common is toxic goitre or ◊thyrotoxicosis, caused by overactivity of the thyroid gland.

Golan Heights (Arabic *Jawlan*) plateau on the Syrian border with Israel, bitterly contested in the ◊Arab-Israeli wars and annexed by Israel on Dec 14, 1981.

gold shiny, yellow, ductile and very malleable, metallic element, symbol Au (from Latin *aurum*, "gold"), atomic number 79, atomic weight 196.967. It occurs in nature frequently as a free metal (see ◊native metal) and is highly resistant to acids, tarnishing, and corrosion. Pure gold is the most malleable of all metals and is used as gold leaf or powder, where small amounts cover vast surfaces, such as gilded domes and statues. The elemental form is so soft that it is alloyed for strength with a number of other metals, such as silver, copper, and platinum. Its purity is then measured in ◊carats on a scale of 24 (24K = pure gold; 18K = 75% gold). It is used mainly for decorative purposes (jewelry, gilding) but also for coinage, dentistry, and conductivity in electronic devices.

Gold has been known and worked from ancient times, and currency systems were based on it in Western civilization, where mining it became an economic and imperialistic goal. In 1988 the three leading gold-producing countries were: South Africa, 563 tons; US, 186 tons; and Australia, 138 tons. In 1989 gold deposits were found in Greenland with an estimated yield of 11 tons per year.

The name is very old and derives from the Germanic form of Indo-European *ghel*, "to shine" or "to gleam."

Goldberg Rube 1883–1970. US cartoonist. Born in San Francisco and trained in engineering at the University of California, Goldberg abandoned that profession for cartooning, joining the staff of the *San Francisco Chronicle* 1904. Moving to New York City 1907, Goldberg produced several popular comic strips that were nationally syndicated from 1915. The most famous and widely read of his strips featured ridiculously complicated inventions. Goldberg also devoted time to political cartooning, winning a Pulitzer prize 1948.

Gold Coast the former name for ◊Ghana, but historically the W coast of Africa from Cape Three Points to the Volta river, where alluvial gold is washed down. Portuguese and French navigators visited this coast in the 14th century, and a British trading settlement developed into the colony of the Gold Coast 1618. With its dependencies of Ashanti and Northern Territories plus the trusteeship territory of Togoland, it became Ghana 1957. The name is also used for many coastal resort areas—for example, in Florida and in Queensland, Australia.

Gold Coast resort region on the E coast of Australia, stretching 20 mi/32 km along the coast of Queensland and New South Wales S of Brisbane; population (1986) 219,000.

Golden Ass, The or ***Metamorphoses*** a ◊picaresque adventure by the Roman writer Lucius Apuleius, written in Latin about AD 160, sometimes called the world's first novel. Lucius, turned into an ass, describes his exploits with a band of robbers, weaving into the narrative several ancient legends, including that of Cupid and Psyche.

Golden Calf in the Old Testament, image made by ◊Aaron in response to the request of the Israelites for a god, when they despaired of Moses' return from Mount Sinai, when he was receiving the Ten Commandments.

Golden Fleece in Greek mythology, fleece of the winged ram Chrysomallus, which hung on an oak tree at Colchis and was guarded by a dragon. It was stolen by Jason and the Argonauts.

Golden Gate strait in California, linking ◊San Francisco Bay with the Pacific, spanned by a bridge that was completed 1937. The longest span is 4,200 ft/1,280 m.

Golden Horde the invading Mongol-Tatar army that first terrorized Europe from 1237 under the leadership of Batu Khan, a grandson of Genghis Khan. ◊Tamerlane broke their power 1395, and ◊Ivan III ended Russia's payment of tribute to them 1480.

goldenrod one of several tall, leafy perennials of the North American genus *Solidago*, in the daisy family Compositae. Flower heads are mostly composed of yellow florets.

goldenseal a North American plant *Hydrastis canadensis* of the buttercup family whose thick yellow root is used medicinally as an astringent and a tonic. The root contains the alkaloid hydrastine, employed by herbalists to stop uterine bleeding.

golden section visually satisfying ratio, first constructed by the Greek mathematician ◊Euclid and used in art and architecture. It is found by dividing a line AB at a point O such that the rectangle produced by the whole line and one of the segments is equal to the square drawn on the other segment. The ratio of the two segments is about 8:13 or 1:1.168, and a rectangle whose sides are in this ratio is called a golden rectangle.

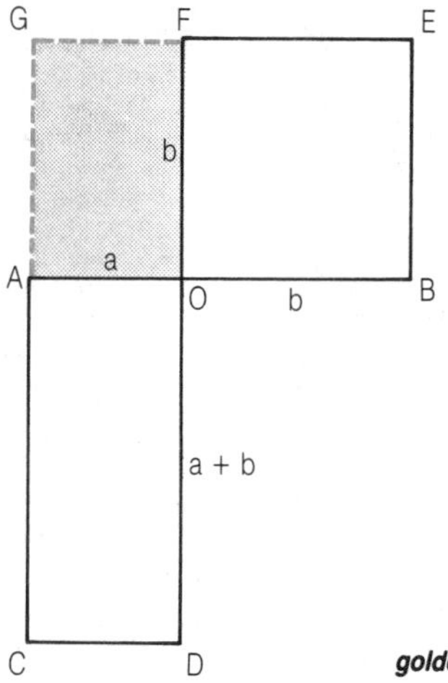
G
F
E
b
a
A
O
b
B
a + b
C
D

golden section

In van Gogh's picture *Mother and Child*, for example, the Madonna's face fits perfectly into a golden rectangle.

goldfinch songbird of the genus *Carduelis*, found in Eurasia, N Africa, and N America.

The American goldfinch *C. tristis* is about 5 in/13 cm long and golden-brownish on top and underside, with white-barred wings and tail.

goldfish fish *Carassius auratus* of the ◊carp family, found in E Asia. Greenish-brown in its natural state, it has for centuries been bred by the Chinese, taking on highly colored and sometimes freakishly shaped forms.

Goldfish can see a greater range of colors than any other animal tested.

Golding William 1911– . English novelist. His first book, *Lord of the Flies* 1954, was about savagery taking over among a group of English schoolboys marooned on a Pacific island. Later novels include *The Spire* 1964, *Rites of Passage* 1980, and *The Paper Men* 1984. He was awarded the Nobel Prize for Literature in 1983.

Goldman Emma 1869–1940. US political organizer, feminist, and anarchist. In 1893 she was jailed for inciting unemployed workers to riot; after her release she became a well-known political lecturer and was again imprisoned for opposing military conscription during World War I. With Alexander Berkman, she published the anarchist monthly *Mother Earth* 1906–17. In 1908 her citizenship was revoked, and in 1919 she was deported to Russia but broke with the Bolsheviks in 1921. She spent the rest of her life in exile. Her writings include *My Disillusionment in Russia* 1923 and *Living My Life* 1931.

Born in Lithuania and raised in Russia, Goldman immigrated to the US 1885 and worked in a clothing factory in Rochester, New York. There she became attracted to radical socialism and moved to New York City 1889, where she became part of the anarchist movement.

Goldoni Carlo 1707–1793. Italian dramatist, born in Venice. He wrote popular comedies for the Sant'Angelo theater, including *La putta onorata/The Respectable Girl* 1749, *I pettegolezzi delle donne/Women's Gossip* 1750, and *La locandiera/Mine Hostess* 1753. In 1761 he moved to Paris, where he directed the Italian theater and wrote more plays, including *L'Eventail/The Fan* 1763.

gold rush a large-scale influx of gold prospectors to an area where gold deposits have recently been discovered. The result is a dramatic increase in population. Cities such as Johannesburg, Melbourne, and San Francisco either originated or were considerably enlarged by gold rushes.

Goldsmith *Irish author Oliver Goldsmith wrote plays, novels, poems, and essays.*

famous gold rushes

1848 Sutter's Mill, California (the "Forty-niners")
1851 New South Wales and Victoria, Australia
1880s Rhodesia
1886 Fortymile Creek, Yukon, Canada; Johannesburg, Transvaal; Kimberley, West Australia
1890s Klondike River, Yukon, Canada

Goldsmith Jerry (Jerrald) 1930– . US composer of film music who originally worked in radio and television. His prolific output includes *Planet of the Apes* 1968, *The Wind and the Lion* 1975, *The Omen* 1976, and *Gremlins* 1984.

Goldsmith Oliver 1728–1774. Irish writer, whose works include the novel, *The Vicar of Wakefield* 1766; the poem, "The Deserted Village" 1770; and the play, *She Stoops to Conquer* 1773.

Goldsmith was the son of a clergyman. He was educated at Trinity College, Dublin, and Edinburgh, where he studied medicine 1752. After traveling extensively in Europe, he returned to England and became a hack writer, producing many works, including *History of England and Animated Nature* 1774. His earliest work of literary importance was *The Citizen of the World* 1762, a series of letters by an imaginary Chinese traveler. In 1761 Goldsmith met Samuel Johnson, and became a member of his "club." In 1764 he published the poem, "The Traveler," and followed it with collected essays 1765. *The Vicar of Wakefield* was sold (according to Johnson's account) to save him from imprisonment for debt.

gold standard system under which a country's currency is exchangeable for a fixed weight of gold on demand at the central bank. It was almost universally applied 1870–1914, but by 1937 no single country was on the full gold standard. Britain abandoned the gold standard 1931; the US abandoned it 1971. Holdings of gold are still retained because it is an internationally recognized commodity, which cannot be legislated upon or manipulated by interested countries.

The gold standard broke down in World War I, and attempted revivals were undermined by the Great Depression. After World War II the par values of the currency units of the ◊International Monetary Fund (which includes nearly all members of the United Nations not in the Soviet bloc) were fixed in terms of gold and the US dollar, but by 1976 floating exchange rates (already unofficially operating from 1971) were legalized.

Goldwater Barry 1909– . US Republican politician; presidential candidate in the 1964 election, when he was overwhelmingly defeated by Lyndon ◊Johnson. As a US senator 1953–86, he voiced the views of his party's right-wing conservative faction. Many of Goldwater's conservative ideas were later adopted by the Republican right, especially the Reagan administration.

Born in Phoenix, Arizona, he attended military high school in Virginia and served in the Army Air Forces during World War II. He achieved the rank of major general 1962 in the Air Force Reserve. After a stint 1949 on the Phoenix city council, he ran successfully for the US Senate. He wrote *The Conscience of a Conservative* 1960 and *Why Not Victory?* 1962.

Goldwyn Samuel. Adopted name of Samuel Goldfish 1882–1974. US film producer. Born in Warsaw, Poland, he emigrated to the US 1896. He founded the Goldwyn Pictures Corporation 1917, which eventually merged into Metro-Goldwyn-Mayer (MGM) 1924, although he was not part of the deal. He remained a producer for many years, making classics such as *Wuthering Heights* 1939, *The Little Foxes* 1941, *The Best Years of Our Lives* 1946, and *Guys and Dolls* 1955.

He was famed for his illogical aphorisms known as "goldwynisms," for example,"Include me out."

golf outdoor game in which a small rubber-cored ball is hit with a wood- or iron-faced club. The club faces have varying angles and are styled for different types of shot. On the first shot for each hole, the ball is hit from a tee, which elevates the ball slightly off the ground; subsequent strokes are played off the ground where they have come to rest. The object of the game is to sink the ball in a hole that can be anywhere between 100 yd/90 m and 500 yd/457 m away, using the least number of strokes.

Most courses consist of 18 holes (or 9 played up and back) and are approximately 6,000 yd/5,500 m in length. Each hole is made up of distinct areas: the tee, from where plays start at each hole; the green, a finely manicured area where the hole is located; the fairway, the grassed area between the tee and the green, not cut as finely as the green; and the rough, the perimeter of the fairway, which is left to grow naturally. Natural hazards such as trees, bushes, and streams make play more difficult, and there are additional artificial hazards in the form of sand-filled bunkers.

Golf is played in two principal forms: stroke play (also known as medal play) and match play. In stroke play the lowest aggregate score for a round determines the winner. Play may be more than one round, in which case the aggregate score for all rounds counts. In match play, the object is to win holes by scoring less than one's opponent(s). Golf's handicap system allows for golfers of all levels to compete on equal terms. There are three types of play (as seen in the ◊Ryder Cup): singles which has one player competing with one other; foursomes where there are two players per side alternatively playing a single ball; and four-ball, again two players per side but each plays his own ball.

The exact origin of golf is unknown, but it was played in Scotland in the 15th century. The Royal & Ancient Golf Club at St Andrews dates from 1754. Major golfing events include the British and US Opens, US Masters, US Professional Golfers Association (PGA), World Match-Play Championship, and British PGA. There are golf tours in North America, Europe, Australia, North Africa, and Japan. The major golfing events are the British Open, first held in 1860; the US Open, first held in 1895; the Masters, first held in 1934; and the United States PGA, first held in 1916.

Goldwyn *US film producer, Sam Goldwyn became one the most powerful people in Hollywood during its golden age.*

golf: recent winners

British Open
1980 Tom Watson *(US)*
1981 Bill Rogers *(US)*
1982 Tom Watson *(US)*
1983 Tom Watson *(US)*
1984 Severiano Ballesteros *(Spain)*
1985 Sandy Lyle *(UK)*
1986 Greg Norman *(Australia)*
1987 Nick Faldo *(UK)*
1988 Severiano Ballesteros *(Spain)*
1989 Mark Calcavecchia *(US)*
1990 Nick Faldo *(UK)*
1991 Ian Baker-Finch *(UK)*
US Open
1980 Jack Nicklaus *(US)*
1981 David Graham *(Australia)*
1982 Tom Watson *(US)*
1983 Larry Nelson *(US)*
1984 Fuzzy Zoeller *(US)*
1985 Andy North *(US)*
1986 Ray Floyd *US)*
1987 Scott Simpson *(US)*
1988 Curtis Strange *(US)*
1989 Curtis Strange *(US)*
1990 Hale Irwin *(US)*
1991 Payne Stewart *(US)*
Masters
1980 Severiano Ballesteros *(Spain)*
1981 Tom Watson *(US)*
1982 Craig Stadler *(US)*
1983 Severiano Ballesteros *(Spain)*
1984 Ben Crenshaw *(US)*
1985 Bernhard Langer *(West Germany)*
1986 Jack Nicklaus *(US)*
1987 Larry Mize *(US)*
1988 Sandy Lyle *(UK)*
1989 Nick Faldo *(UK)*
1990 Nick Faldo *(UK)*
1991 Ian Woosnam *(UK)*
United States PGA
1980 Jack Nicklaus *(US)*
1981 Larry Nelson *(US)*
1982 Ray Floyd *(US)*
1983 Hal Sutton *(US)*
1984 Lee Trevino *(US)*
1985 Hubert Green *(US)*
1986 Bob Tway *(US)*
1987 Larry Nelson *(US)*
1988 Jeff Sluman *(US)*
1989 Payne Stewart *(US)*
1990 Wayne Grady *(Australia)*
1991 John Daly *(US)*

Golgi Camillo 1843–1926. Italian cell biologist who with Santiago Ramon y Cajal produced the first detailed knowledge of the fine structure of the nervous system.

Golgi's use of silver salts in staining cells proved so effective in showing up the components and fine processes of nerve cells that even the synapses—tiny gaps between the cells—were visible. The Golgi body, a series of flattened membranous cavities found in the cytoplasm of cells, was first described by him in 1898. Golgi and Ramon y Cajal shared the 1906 Nobel Prize for Medicine.

Golgi apparatus or ***Golgi bodies*** a stack of flattened membranous sacs found in the cells of ◊eukaryotes. Many molecules travel through Golgi bodies on their way to other organelles or to the endoplasmic reticulum. Some are modified or asssembled inside the sacs. Named after the Italian physician Camillo Golgi (1844–1926).

Goliath in the Old Testament, champion of the ◊Philistines, who was said to have been slain by a stone from a sling by the young ◊David in single combat in front of their opposing armies.

Gomez Diego 1440–1482. Portuguese navigator who discovered the coast of Liberia during a voyage sponsored by ◊Henry the Navigator 1458–60.

Gómez Juan Vicente 1864–1935. Venezuelan dictator 1908–35. The discovery of oil during his rule attracted US, British, and Dutch oil interests and made Venezuela one of the wealthiest countries in Latin America. Gómez amassed a considerable personal fortune and used his well-equipped army to dominate the civilian population.

Gompers Samuel 1850–1924. US labor leader. His early career in the Cigarmakers' Union led him to found and lead the ◊American Federation of Labor 1882. Gompers advocated nonpolitical activity within the existing capitalist system to secure improved wages and working conditions for members.

Gomułka Władysław 1905–1982. Polish Communist politician, party leader 1943–48 and 1956–70. He introduced moderate reforms, including private farming and tolerance for Roman Catholicism.

Gomułka, born in Krosno in SE Poland, was involved in underground resistance to the Germans during World War II, taking part in the defense of Warsaw. Leader of the Communist Party in Poland from 1943, he was ousted by the Moscow-backed Bolesław Bierut (1892–1956) in 1948, but was restored to the leadership in 1956, following riots in Poznań. Gomułka was forced to resign in Dec 1970 after sudden food-price rises induced a new wave of strikes and riots.

gonad the part of an animal's body that produces the sperm or egg cells (ovules) required for sexual reproduction. The sperm-producing gonad is called a ◊testis, and the ovule-producing gonad is called an ◊ovary.

gonadotropin any hormone that supports and stimulates the function of the gonads (sex glands); some gonadotrophins are used as ◊fertility drugs.

Goncharov Ivan Alexandrovitch 1812–1891. Russian novelist. His first novel, *A Common Story* 1847, was followed in 1858 by his humorous masterpiece *Oblomov*, which satirized the indolent Russian landed gentry.

From 1852–55 he was secretary on the ship *Pallada*, which was sent to Japan by the Tsar to open it to trade. His wry description of the world cruise was published as *The Frigate "Pallada"* 1858.

Goncourt, de the brothers Edmond 1822–1896 and Jules 1830–1870. French writers. They collaborated in producing a compendium, *L'Art du XVIIIème siècle/18th-Century Art* 1859–75, historical studies, and a *Journal* 1887–96 that depicts French literary life of their day. Edmond de Goncourt founded the Académie Goncourt, opened 1903, which awards an annual prize, the Prix Goncourt, to the author of the best French novel of the year.

Gond member of a heterogeneous people of central India, about half of whom speak unwritten languages belonging to the Dravidian family. There are over 4 million Gonds, most of whom live in Madhya Pradesh, E Maharashtra, and N Andra Pradesh, although some are found in Orissa.

Gond beliefs embrace a range of gods and spirits, and there are a limited number of clans that coexist within a defined set of social and ritual relationships. The dynasties of one group, the Raj Gonds, rivaled those of neighboring Hindus until the Muslim conquests of the 16th century. Traditionally, many Gonds practiced shifting cultivation; agriculture and livestock remain the basis of the economy.

Gondar town in Ethiopia about 7,500 ft/2,300 m above sea level and 25 mi/40 km N of Lake Tana; population (1984) 69,000.

Gondwanaland land mass, including the continents of South America, Africa, Australia, and Antarctica, that formed the southern half of ◊Pangaea, the "supercontinent" or world continent that existed between 250 and 200 million years ago. The northern half was ◊Laurasia. The baobab tree of Africa and Australia is a relic of Gondwanaland.

gonorrhoea common sexually transmitted disease arising from infection with the bacterium *Neisseria gonorrhoeae*, which causes inflammation of the genito-urinary tract. After an incubation period of two to ten days, infected men experience pain while urinating and a discharge from the penis; infected women often have no external symptoms.

Untreated gonorrhea carries the threat of sterility to both sexes; there is also the risk of blindness in a baby born to an infected mother. The condition is treated with antibiotics, although ever-increasing doses are becoming necessary to combat resistant strains.

González Márquez Felipe 1942– . Spanish Socialist politician, leader of the Socialist Workers' Party (PSOE), prime minister from 1982.

After studying law in Spain and Belgium, in 1966 he opened the first labor-law office in his home city of Seville. In 1964 he had joined the PSOE, and he rose rapidly to the position of leader. In 1982 the PSOE won a sweeping electoral victory and González became prime minister.

Good Friday (probably a corruption of "God's Friday") in the Christian church, the Friday before Easter, which is observed in memory of the Crucifixion (the death of Jesus on the cross).

Goodman Benny (Benjamin David) 1909–1986. US clarinetist, nicknamed "the King of Swing" for the new jazz idiom he introduced (with arranger Fletcher Henderson). Leader of his own swing band from 1934, he is celebrated for numbers such as "Blue Skies" and "Avalon." In 1955 he organized a new band and continued touring with it throughout the world up until his death.

Goodman was also successful as a classical clarinetist; Bartók's *Contrasts* 1939 and Copland's *Clarinet Concerto* 1950 were among the pieces written for him.

It was he who introduced jazz to New York's Carnegie Hall in 1938.

Goodman Paul 1911– . US writer and social critic, whose many works (novels, plays, essays) express his anarchist, antiauthoritarian ideas. He studied youth offenders in *Growing up Absurd* 1960.

Goodyear Charles 1800–1860. US inventor who developed rubber coating 1837 and vulcanized rubber 1839, a method of curing raw rubber to make it strong and elastic, which led to many applications, especially the motor-vehicle tire.

goose aqatic birds of several genera (especially *Anser*) in the family Anatidae, which also incudes ducks and swans. Both genders are similar in appearance: they have short, webbed feet, placed nearer the front of the body than in other members of the order Anatidae, and the beak is slightly hooked. They feed entirely on grass and plants.

The greylag goose *Anser anser* is the ancestor of domesticated geese. Other species include the Canada goose *Branta canadensis*; the bean goose *A. fabalis*; the pink-footed goose *A. brachyrhynchus*; and the white-fronted goose *A. albifrons*. The goose builds a nest of grass and twigs on the ground and lays from five to nine eggs, white or cream-colored, according to the species.

***Gorbachev** President of the Soviet Union and Communist Party leader Mikhail Gorbachev. After coming to power in 1985, he embarked on a program of ambitious political and economic modernization but faced mounting domestic problems that led to his resignation in Dec 1991.*

Goose Bay a settlement at the head of Lake Melville on the Labrador coast of Newfoundland, Canada. In World War II it was used as a staging post by US and Canadian troops on their way to Europe. Until 1975 it was used by the US Air Force as a low-level-flying base.

gooseberry several prickly shrubs of the genus *Ribes* in the saxifrage family, native to Eurasia and North America, and closely related to currants in the same genus. The fleshy, red, blackish or green fruits are edible. The pasture gooseberry *R. cyanosbati* is native to North America. The European gooseberry *R. grossalaria* is cultivated in gardens.

goosefoot any plants of the genus *Chenopodium* in the goosefoot family Chenopodiaceae, closely related to spinach and beets. The seeds of white goosefoot, *C. album*, were used as food in Europe from Neolithic times, and also from early times in the Americas. White goosefoot grows to 3 ft/1 m tall and has lance- or diamond-shaped leaves and packed heads of small inconspicuous flowers. The green part is eaten as a spinach substitute.

gopher burrowing rodent of the genus *Citellus*, family Sciuridae. It is a kind of ground squirrel represented by some 20 species distributed across W North America and Eurasia. Length ranges from 6 in/15 cm to 16 in/90 cm, excluding the furry tail. coloration ranges from plain yellowish to striped and spotted species. The name "pocket gopher" is applied to the eight genera of the North American family Geomyidae.

Gorakhpur city in Uttar Pradesh, N India, situated on the Rapti river, at the center of an agricultural region producing cotton, rice, and grain; population (1981) 306,000.

Gorbachev Mikhail Sergeyevich 1931– . Soviet president, in power from 1985–91. He was a member of the Politburo from 1980 and, during the Chernenko administration 1984–85, was chair of the Foreign Affairs Commission. As general secretary of the Communist Party (CPSU) from 1985, and president of the Supreme Soviet from 1988, he introduced liberal reforms at home (◊perestroika and ◊glasnost), and attempted to halt the arms race abroad. He became head of state 1989 and in March 1990 he was formally elected to a five-year term as executive president with greater powers. At home, his plans for economic reform failed to avert a food crisis in the winter of 1990–91, and his desire to preserve a single, centrally controlled USSR met with resistance from Soviet republics seeking more independent government systems. He was awarded the Nobel Peace Prize 1990, but his international reputation suffered in the light of the harsh repression of nationalist demonstrations in the Baltic states early in 1991. His peace initiative during the ◊Gulf War Feb 1991 gained him a positve stance among Arab leaders. As the Soviet economy disintegrated during the year, his political strength declined, but Gorbachev was able to counter a short-lived coup in the summer and regained some stature by helping to convene the Middle East peace conference in Spain in Nov.

Gorbachev, born in the N Caucasus, studied law at Moscow University and joined the CPSU 1952. In 1955–62 he worked for the Komsomol (Communist Youth League) before being appointed regional agriculture secretary. As Stavropol party leader from 1970 he impressed Andropov, and was brought into the CPSU secretariat 1978.

Gorbachev was promoted into the Politburo and in 1983, when Andropov was general secretary, took broader charge of the Soviet economy. On Chernenko's death 1985 he was appointed party leader. He initiated wide-ranging reforms and broad economic restructuring, and introduced campaigns against alcoholism, corruption, and inefficiency. Gorbachev radically changed the style of Soviet leadership, but ultimately was unable to maintain control. On Dec 25, 1991, he resigned as president, yielding power to Boris ◊ Yeltsin.

Gordian knot in Greek mythology, the knot tied by King Gordius of Phrygia that an oracle revealed could be unraveled only by the future conqueror of Asia. According to tradition, Alexander the Great, unable to untie it, cut it with his sword in 334 BC.

Gordimer Nadine 1923– . South African novelist, an opponent of apartheid. Her first novel, *The Lying Days*, appeared in 1953, and other works include *The Conservationist* 1974, the volume of short stories *A Soldier's Embrace* 1980, and *July's People* 1981. She received the Nobel Prize for Literature in 1991, the year that *Jump and Other Stories* was published.

Other works include *Burger's Daughter* 1979, *A Sport of Nature* 1987, and *The Essential Gesture* 1988.

Gordon Charles (George) 1833–1885. British general sent to Khartoum in the Sudan 1884 to rescue English garrisons that were under attack by the ◊Mahdi, Mohammed Ahmed; he was himself besieged for ten months by the Mahdi's army. A relief expedition arrived Jan 28, 1885 to find that Khartoum had been captured and Gordon killed two days before.

Gordon served in the ◊Crimean War and in China 1864, where he earned his nickname "Chinese" Gordon in ending the Taiping Rebellion. In 1874 he was employed by the Khedive of Egypt to open the country and 1877–80 was British governor of the Sudan.

Gorgon in Greek mythology, any of three sisters, Stheno, Euryale, and Medusa, who had wings, claws, enormous teeth, and snakes for hair. Medusa, the only one who was mortal, was killed by ◊Perseus, but even in death her head was still so frightful that it turned the onlooker to stone.

Gorgonzola town NE of Milan, Italy, famous for cheese.

Goria Giovanni 1943– . Italian Christian Democrat (DC) politician, prime minister 1987–88. He entered the Chamber of Deputies 1976 and held a number of posts, including treasury minister, until he was asked to form a coalition government in 1987.

gorilla largest of the apes, *Gorilla gorilla*, found in the dense forests of West Africa and mountains of central Africa. The male stands about 6.5 ft/2 m, and weighs about 450 lb/200 kgs. Females are about half the size. The body is covered with

Gordon *British army general Charles Gordon, killed in the siege of Khartoum.*

blackish hair, silvered on the back in older males. Gorillas live in family groups of a senior male, several females, some younger males, and a number of infants. They are vegetarian, highly intelligent, and will attack only in self-defense. They are dwindling in numbers, being shot for food by some local people, or by poachers taking young for zoos, but protective measures are having some effect.

Gorillas construct stoutly built nests in trees for overnight use. The breast-beating movement, once thought to indicate rage, actually signifies only nervous excitement. There are three races of the one species: western lowland, eastern lowland, and mountain gorillas.

Göring Hermann Nazi leader; see ◊Goering.

Gorky Arshile 1904–1948. Armenian-born US painter who lived in the US from 1920. He painted Cubist abstracts before developing a more surreal abstract-Expressionist style, using organic shapes and bold paint strokes.

Among Gorky's major influences were Picasso, Kandinsky, Miró, and Cézanne. His works, such as *The Liver Is the Cock's Comb* 1944, are noted for their sense of fantasy.

Gorky Maxim. Adopted name of Alexei Peshkov 1868–1936. Russian writer. Born in Nizhny-Novgorod (renamed Gorky 1932 in his honor), he was exiled 1906–13 for his revolutionary principles. His works, which include the play *The Lower Depths* 1902 and the memoir *My Childhood* 1913, combine realism with optimistic faith in the potential of the industrial proletariat.

Gorky (Russian *Gor'kiy*) former name Nizhny-Novgorod until 1932 city in central USSR; population (1987) 1,425,000. Cars, locomotives, and aircraft are manufactured here.

Gorlovka industrial town (coal-mining, chemicals, engineering) on the ◊Donbas coal field, Ukraine, USSR; population (1987) 345,000.

gorse also known as ***furze*** or ***whin*** Eurasian genus of plants *Ulex*, family Leguminosae, consisting of thorny shrubs with spine-shaped leaves densely

gorilla

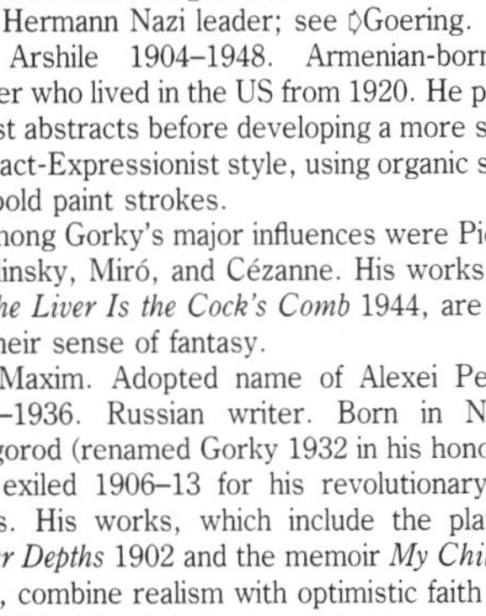

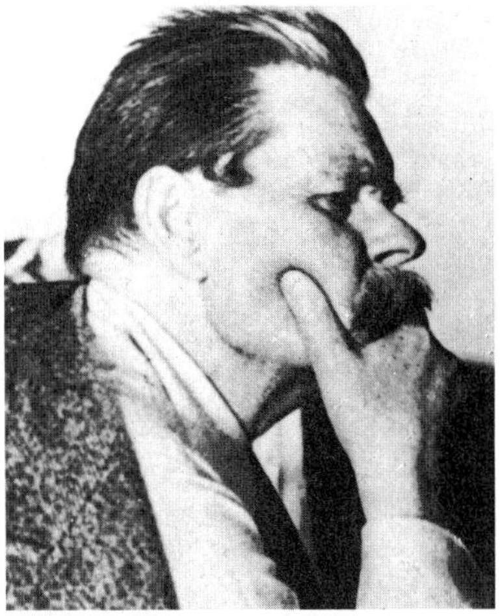

Gorky *A committed, lifelong revolutionary, Maxim Gorky attracted official disapproval both before and after the 1917 Russian Revolution.*

clustered along the stems, and bright yellow flowers.

Gorton John Grey 1911– . Australian Liberal politician. He was minister for education and science 1966–68, and prime minister 1968–71.

goshawk or northern goshawk woodland hawk *Accipiter gentilis* that is similar in appearance to the peregrine falcon, but with shorter wings and legs. It is used in falconry.

Goshen city in N Indiana, on the Elkhart River, SE of South Bend; seat of Elkhart County. It is situated in an agricultural area and serves as a market town. Industries include steel, rubber, electrical, and building products; population (1990) 23,797.

Gospel (Middle English "good news") in the New Testament generally, the message of Christian salvation; in particular the four written accounts of the life of Jesus by Matthew, Mark, Luke, and John. Although the first three give approximately the same account or synopsis (thus giving rise to the name "Synoptic Gospels"), their differences from John have raised problems for theologians.

gospel music a type of music developed in the 1920s in the black Baptist churches of the US South from spirituals, which were 18th- and 19th-century hymns joined to the old African pentatonic (five-note) scale. Outstanding among the early gospel singers was Mahalia Jackson (1911–1972), but from the 1930s to the mid-1950s male harmony groups predominated, among them the Dixie Hummingbirds, the Swan Silvertones, and the Five Blind Boys of Mississippi.

Gosport naval port opposite ◊Portsmouth, Hampshire, England; population (1981) 77,250.

Gossaert Jan, Flemish painter, known as ◊Mabuse.

Göteborg (German *Gothenburg*) port and industrial (ships, vehicles, chemicals) city (Sweden's second largest) on the W coast of Sweden, on the Göta Canal (built 1832), which links it with Stockholm; population (1988) 432,000.

Goth E Germanic people who settled near the Black Sea around AD 2nd century. There are two branches, the eastern Ostrogoths and the western Visigoths.

The Ostrogoths were conquered by the Huns 372. They regained their independence 454 and under ◊Theodoric the Great conquered Italy 488–93; they disappeared as a nation after the Byzantine emperor ◊Justinian I reconquered Italy 535–55.

The Visigoths migrated to Thrace. Under ◊Alaric they raided Greece and Italy 395–410, sacked Rome, and established a kingdom in S France. Expelled from there by the Franks, they established a Spanish kingdom which lasted until the Moorish conquest of 711.

Gotha town in Erfurt county, Federal Republic of Germany, former capital of the duchy of Saxe-Coburg-Gotha; population (1981) 57,600. It has a castle and two observatories; pottery, soap, textiles, precision instruments, and aircraft are manufactured here.

Gotha, Almanach de annual survey of the European royalty, titled aristocracy, and diplomatic ranks, published in Gotha, Germany, 1763–1944; a smaller-scale successor, *Le Petit Gotha/The Little Gotha* was revived in Paris from 1968.

Gothic architecture style of architecture that flourished in Europe from the mid-12th century to the end of the 15th century. It is characterized by vertical lines of tall pillars, spires, greater height in interior spaces, the pointed arch, rib vaulting, and the flying buttress.

Gothic architecture originated in Normandy and Burgundy in the 12th century. The term became derisory, perhaps deriving from the 16th-century critic Vasari's attribution of medieval artistic styles to the Goths, who destroyed "Classicism." The style prevailed in western Europe until the 16th century, when Classic architecture was revived.

Gothic art style of painting and sculpture that dominated European art from the late 12th century until the early Renaissance. The great Gothic church façades held hundreds of sculpted figures and profuse ornamentation, and manuscripts were lavishly decorated. Stained glass replaced mural painting in N European churches. The International Gothic style in painting emerged in the 14th century, characterized by delicate and complex ornamentation and increasing realism.

Gothic novel literary genre established by Horace Walpole's *The Castle of Otranto* 1765 and marked by mystery, violence, and horror; other exponents were Anne Radcliffe, Matthew "Monk" Lewis, Bram Stoker, Mary Shelley, and Edgar Allan Poe.

Gothic revival the resurgence of interest in Gothic style, as displayed in 19th-century architecture and design. Gothic revival buildings include the Houses of Parliament and St Pancras Station in London; the Town Hall, Vienna; and Princeton University in the US. Style elements were also used in interior furnishings to complete the theme.

The growth of Romanticism led some writers, artists, and antiquaries to embrace a fascination with Gothic forms that emphasized the supposedly bizarre and grotesque aspects of the Middle Ages. During the Victorian period, however, a far better understanding of Gothic forms was achieved, and this resulted in some impressive Neo-Gothic architecture, as well as some desecration of genuine Gothic churches in the name of "restoration" by, for example, Augustus Pugin and George Gilbert Scott.

Gotland Swedish island in the Baltic Sea; area 1,212 sq mi/3,140 sq km; population (1986) 56,200. The capital is Visby. Its products are mainly agricultural (sheep and cattle), and there is tourism. It was an area of dispute between Sweden and Denmark but became part of Sweden 1645.

Götterdämmerung (German "twilight of the gods") in Scandinavian mythology, the end of the world.

Göttingen town in Lower Saxony, Federal Republic of Germany; population (1988) 134,000. Industries include printing, publishing, precision instruments, and chemicals. Its university was founded by George II of England 1734.

Gouda town in Zuid Holland, W Netherlands; population (1987) 61,500. It produces round, flat cheeses.

Gould Elliott. Adopted name of Elliot Goldstein 1938– . US film actor. He began as a child actor and played in stage musicals before his film debut, *The Night They Raided Minsky's* 1968, led rapidly to starring roles in such films as *Bob and Carol and Ted and Alice* 1969, *M.A.S.H.* 1970, *The Long Goodbye* 1973, and *Capricorn One* 1978.

Gould Jay 1836–1892. US financier, born in New York. He is said to have caused the financial panic on "Black Friday," Sept 24, 1869, through his efforts to corner the gold market.

Gould was one of the "Robber Barons" who built the transportation and communications structures of the US while accumulating great wealth. His first major success came when he was made an associate of the Erie Railroad by Cornelius ◊Vanderbilt. Following financial and political scandals, Gould was forced to relinquish control of the Erie Railroad, but he had amassed a large fortune that he used to acquire control of western railroads, including the Union Pacific. He also controlled the Western Union Telegraph Company and elevated railroads in New York City.

Gould Stephen Jay 1941– . US paleontologist and author. In 1972 he proposed the theory of punctuated equilibrium, suggesting that the evolution of species did not occur at a steady rate but could suddenly accelerate, with rapid change occurring over a few hundred thousand years. He wrote such works as *The Panda's Thumb* 1980, *The Flamingo's Smile* 1985, and *Wonderful Life* 1989.

Gounod Charles François 1818–1893. French composer. His operas include *Sappho* 1851, *Faust* 1859, *Philémon et Baucis* 1860, and *Roméo et Juliette* 1867. He also wrote sacred songs, masses, and an oratorio, *The Redemption* 1882. His music has great lyrical appeal and emotional power and it inspired many French composers of the later 19th century.

gourd names applied to various members of the family Cucurbitaceae, including melons squashes and pumpkins. In a narrower sense, the name is applied to an inedible, ornamental variety of pumpkin *Cucurbita pepa*.

gout disease, a hereditary form of ◊arthritis, marked by an excess of uric acid crystals in the tissues, causing pain and inflammation in one or more joints (usually of the feet or hands). Acute attacks are treated with ◊anti-inflammatories.

The disease, more common in men, poses a long-term threat to the blood vessels and the kidneys, so ongoing treatment may be needed to minimize the levels of uric acid in the body fluids.

government system of political administration whereby authority is exercised. Contemporary systems of government distinguish between liberal democracies, totalitarian (one-party) states, and autocracies (authoritarian, relying on force rather than ideology). The Greek philosopher Aristotle was the first to attempt a systematic classification of governments. His main distinctions were between government by one person, by few, and by many (monarchy, oligarchy, and democracy), although the characteristics of each may vary between nations and each may degenerate into tyranny (rule by an oppressive elite in the case of oligarchy or by the mob in the case of democracy).

The French philosopher Montesquieu distinguished between constitutional governments—whether monarchies or republics—which operated under various legal and other constraints, and despotism, which was not constrained in this way.

Many of the words used (dictatorship, tyranny, totalitarian, democratic) have acquired negative or positive connotations that make it difficult to use them objectively. The term liberal democracy was coined to distinguish Western types of democracy from the many other political systems that claimed to be democratic.

Its principal characteristics are the existence of more than one political party, open processes of government and political debate, and a separation of powers.

Totalitarian has been applied to both fascist and communist states and denotes a system in which all power is centralized in the state, which in turn is controlled by a single party that derives its legitimacy from an exclusive ideology.

Goya *Spanish painter Francisco Goya often painted aristocrats in landscape settings, as in* A Picnic *1787, now in the National Gallery, London.*

Autocracy describes a form of government that has emerged in a number of Third World countries, in which state power is in the hands of either an individual or the army; ideology is not normally a central factor, individual freedoms tend to be suppressed when they may constitute a challenge to the authority of the ruling group, and when there is a reliance upon force.

Other useful distinctions are between federal governments (whose powers are dispersed among various regions which in certain respects are self-governing) and unitary governments (whose powers are concentrated in a central authority); and between presidential (in which the head of state is also the directly elected head of government, not part of the legislature) and parliamentary systems (in which the government is drawn from an elected legislature that can dismiss it).

governor in engineering, any device that controls the speed of a machine or engine, usually by regulating the intake of fuel or steam.

James ◊Watt invented the steam-engine governor in 1788. It works by means of heavy balls, which rotate on the end of linkages and move in or out because of ◊centrifugal force according to the speed of rotation. The movement of the balls closes or opens the steam valve to the engine. When the engine speed increases too much, the balls fly out, and cause the steam valve to close, so the engine slows down. The opposite happens when the engine speed drops too much.

Gowon Yakubu 1934– . Nigerian politician, head of state 1966–75. Educated at Sandhurst military college in the UK, he became chief of staff, and in the military coup of 1966 seized power. After the Biafran civil war 1967–70, he reunited the country with his policy of "no victor, no vanquished." In 1975 he was overthrown by a military coup.

Goya Francisco José de Goya y Lucientes 1746–1828. Spanish painter and engraver. He painted portraits of four successive kings of Spain, and his etchings include *The Disasters of War*, depicting the French invasion of Spain 1810–14. Among his later works are the "black paintings" (Prado, Madrid), with horrific images such as *Saturn Devouring One of His Sons* about 1822.

He was born in Aragon and was for a time a

bullfighter, the subject of some of his etchings. After studying in Italy, he returned to Spain and was employed on a number of paintings for the royal tapestry factory. In 1789 he was court painter to Charles IV.

Goyen Jan van 1596–1656. Dutch landscape painter, active in Leiden, Haarlem, and from 1631 in The Hague. A pioneer of the realist style of landscape with ◊Ruisdael, he sketched from nature and studied clouds and light effects.

Gozzoli Benozzo c. 1421–1497. Florentine painter, a late exponent of the International Gothic style. He painted frescoes 1459 in the chapel of the Palazzo Medici-Riccardi, Florence: the walls are crammed with figures, many of them portraits of the Medici family.

GP in medicine, the abbreviation for general practitioner.

GPU former name (1922–23) for ◊KGB, the Soviet security service.

Graaf Regnier de 1641–1673. Dutch physician and anatomist who discovered the ovarian follicles, which were later named Graafian follicles. He named the ovaries and gave exact descriptions of the testicles. He was also the first to isolate and collect the secretions of the pancreas and gall bladder.

Graafian follicle during the ◊menstrual cycle, a fluid-filled capsule that surrounds and protects the developing egg cell inside the ovary. After the egg cell has been released, the follicle remains and is known as a corpus luteum.

Grable Betty (Elizabeth Ruth) 1916–1973. US actress, singer, and dancer who starred in *Moon Over Miami* 1941, *I Wake Up Screaming* 1941, and *How to Marry a Millionaire* 1953. As a publicity stunt, her beautiful legs were insured for a million dollars. Her popularity peaked during World War II when GIs voted her their number one "pin-up" girl.

Gracchus the brothers Tiberius Sempronius 163–133 BC and Gaius Sempronius 153–121 BC. Roman agrarian reformers. As ◊tribune (magistrate) 133 BC, Tiberius tried to prevent the ruin of small farmers by making large slave-labor farms illegal but was murdered. Gaius, tribune 123–122 BC, revived his brother's legislation, and introduced other reforms, but was outlawed by the Senate and committed suicide.

Graces in Greek mythology, three goddesses (Aglaia, Euphrosyne, Thalia), daughters of Zeus and Hera, personifications of pleasure, charm, and beauty; the inspirers of the arts and the sciences.

CAREER HIGHLIGHTS: Steffi Graf

Wimbledon
singles: 1988–89
doubles: 1988
US Open
singles: 1988–89
French Open
singles: 1987–88
Australian Open
singles: 1988–90

Graf Steffi 1969– . German tennis player, who brought Martina ◊Navratilova's long reign as the world's number one female player to an end. She reached the semifinal of the US Open 1985 at the age of 16, and won five consecutive Grand Slam singles titles 1988–89.

graffiti (Italian "scratched drawings") inscriptions or drawings carved, scratched, or drawn on public surfaces such as walls, fences, or public transport vehicles (and which has occurred since ancient times in the Mediterranean region). Tagging is the act of writing an individual logo on surfaces with spray-paint or large felt-tip pens.

The term is derived from a traditional technique in Italian art (*sgraffito*) of scratching a design in the thin white plaster on a wall.

grafting the operation by which a piece of living tissue is removed from one organism and transplanted into the same or a different organism

Graf *German tennis star Steffi Graf, who won her first Grand Slam title in 1987.*

where it continues growing. In horticulture, it is a technique widely used for propagating plants, especially woody species. A bud or shoot on one plant, termed the scion, is inserted into another, the stock, so that they continue growing together, the tissues combining at the point of union.

Grafting is usually only successful between species that are closely related and is most commonly practiced on roses and fruit trees. Grafting of nonwoody species is more difficult but it is sometimes used to propagate tomatoes and cacti. See also ◊transplant.

Graham Billy (William Franklin) 1918– . US Protestant evangelist, who preached to millions throughout the world and on television, bringing many thousands to a "decision for Christ." He was known for the dramatic staging and charismatic eloquence of his preaching.

Born in Charlotte, North Carolina, he graduated from Wheaton College (Illinois). His first evangelical crusade was Youth for Christ 1949. From then, under the auspices of the Billy Graham Evangelistic Association 1950, he conducted worldwide crusades. Graham wrote *Peace with God* 1953, *World Aflame* 1965, and *The Challenge* 1969.

Graham Martha 1893–1991. US choreographer. An innovative exponent of American modern dance, she had a major influence on such choreographers in the contemporary dance movement as Robert

grafting

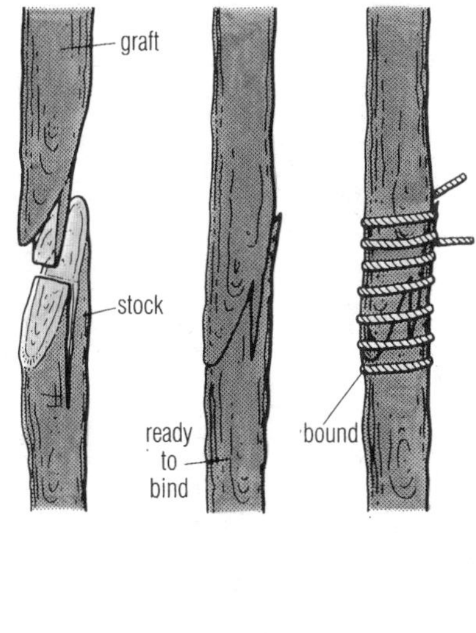
graft
stock
ready to bind
bound

Graham *Thomas Graham, one of the founders of physical chemistry and formulator of Graham's Law on the diffusion of gases.*

◊Cohan, Glen Tetley, Merce ◊Cunningham, Norman Morrice, Paul Taylor, and Robert North.

She created over 170 works, including *Appalachian Spring* 1944 (score by Aaron Copland) and *Clytemnestra* 1958 (music by Halim El-Dabh), the first full-length modern dance work. Her work was designed to reveal the "inner" person, as opposed to the more decorative traditional ballet. She danced in most of the pieces she choreographed until her retirement from performance in the 1960s.

Graham Thomas 1805–1869. Scottish chemist who laid the foundations of physical chemistry (the branch of chemistry concerned with changes in energy during a chemical transformation) by his work on the diffusion of gases and liquids. Graham's Law states that the diffusion rate of two gases varies inversely as the square root of their densities.

His work on ◊colloids (which have larger particles than true solutions) was equally fundamental; he discovered the principle of dialysis, that colloids can be separated from solutions containing smaller molecules by the differing rates at which they pass through a semipermeable membrane (a process he termed "osmosis"). The human kidney uses the principle of dialysis to extract nitrogenous waste.

Grahame Kenneth 1859–1932. Scottish author. The early volumes of sketches of childhood, *The Golden Age* 1895 and *Dream Days* 1898, were followed by his masterpiece *The Wind in the Willows* 1908, an animal fantasy created for his young son, which was dramatized by A A Milne as *Toad of Toad Hall*.

Graham Land mountainous peninsula in Antarctica, formerly a dependency of the Falkland Islands, and from 1962 part of the ◊British Antarctic Territory. It was discovered by John Biscoe in 1832 and until 1934 was thought to be an archipelago.

Grahamstown town in SE Cape Province, South Africa; population (1985) 75,000. It is the seat of Rhodes University, established 1951, founded in 1904 as Rhodes University College.

grain the smallest unit of mass in the three English

systems (avoirdupois, troy, and apothecaries' weights) used in the US and the UK, equal to 0.0648 g. It was reputedly the weight of a grain of wheat. One pound avoirdupois equals 7,000 grains; one pound troy or apothecaries' weight equals 5,760 grains.

Grainger Percy Aldridge 1882–1961. Australian-born US composer and concert pianist. He is remembered for a number of songs and short instrumental pieces drawing on folk idioms, including *Country Gardens* 1925, and for his settings of folk songs, such as *Molly on the Shore* 1921.

gram metric unit of mass; one-thousandth of a kilogram.

grammar (Greek *grammatike tekhne* "art of letters") the principles of the correct use of language, dealing with the rules of structuring words into phrases, clauses, sentences, and paragraphs in an accepted way. Emphasis on the standardizing impact of print has meant that spoken or colloquial language is often perceived as less grammatical than written language, but all forms of a language, standard or otherwise, have their own grammatical systems of differing complexity. People often acquire several overlapping grammatical systems within one language; for example, one formal system for writing and standard communication and one less formal system for everyday and peer-group communication.

Originally "grammar" was an analytical approach to writing, intended to improve the understanding and the skills of scribes, philosophers, and writers. When compared with Latin, English has been widely regarded as having less grammar or at least a simpler grammar; it would be truer, however, to say that English and Latin have different grammars, each complex in its own way. In linguistics (the contemporary study of language) grammar, or syntax, refers to the arrangement of the elements in a language for the purposes of acceptable communication in speech, writing, and print.

All forms of a language, standard or otherwise, have their grammars or grammatical systems, which children acquire through use; a child may acquire several overlapping systems within one language (especially a nonstandard form for everyday life and a standard form linked with writing, school, and national life). Not even the most comprehensive grammar book (or grammar) of a language like English, French, Arabic, or Japanese completely covers or fixes the implicit grammatical system that people use in their daily lives. The rules and tendencies of natural grammar operate largely in nonconscious ways but can, for many social and professional purposes, be studied and developed for conscious as well as inherent skills. See also ◊parts of speech.

Recent theories of the way language functions include ◊phrase structure grammar, ◊transformational grammar, and ◊case grammar.

Grampian region of Scotland
area 3,320 sq mi/8,600 sq km
city Aberdeen (administrative headquarters)
features part of the Grampian Mountains (the Cairngorms); valley of the river Spey, with its whiskey distilleries; Balmoral Castle (royal residence on the river Dee near Braemar, bought by Prince Albert 1852, and rebuilt in Scottish baronial style); Braemar Highland Games in Aug
products beef cattle (Aberdeen Angus and Beef Shorthorn), fishing, North Sea oil service industries, tourism (winter skiing)
population (1987) 503,000.

Grampian Mountains a range that separates the Highlands from the Lowlands of Scotland, running NE from Strathclyde. It takes in the S Highland region (which includes Ben Nevis, the highest mountain in the British Isles at 4,406 ft/1,340 m), northern Tayside, and the Southern border of Grampian region (the Cairngorms, which include Ben Macdhui 4,296 ft/1,309 m). The region includes Aviemore, a winter vacation and sports center.

Grampians western end of Australia's eastern highlands, in Victoria; the highest peak is Mount William 3,829 ft/1,167 m.

grampus common name for Risso's dolphin *Grampus griseus*, a slaty-gray dolphin found in tropical and temperate seas. These dolphins live in large schools and can reach 13 ft/4 m in length. They have blunt snouts with only a few teeth, and feed on squid and small fish. The name grampus is sometimes also used for the killer ◊whale.

Gramsci Antonio 1891–1937. Italian Marxist who attempted to unify social theory and political practice. He helped to found the Italian Communist Party 1921 and was elected to parliament 1924, but was imprisoned by the Fascist leader Mussolini from 1926; his *Quaderni di carcere/Prison Notebooks* were published posthumously 1947.

Granada city in the Sierra Nevada in Andalucia, S Spain; population (1986) 281,000. It produces textiles, soap, and paper
history Founded by the Moors in the 8th century, it became the capital of an independent kingdom 1236–1492, when it was the last Moorish stronghold to surrender to the Spaniards. Ferdinand and Isabella, the first sovereigns of a united Spain, are buried in the cathedral (built 1529–1703). The Alhambra, a fortified hilltop palace, was built in the 13th and 14th centuries by the Moorish kings.

Granada Nicaraguan city on the NW shore of Lake Nicaragua; population (1985) 89,000. It has shipyards and manufactures sugar, soap, clothing, and furniture. Founded 1523, it is the oldest city in Nicaragua.

Granados Enrique 1867–1916. Spanish composer-pianist. His piano-work *Goyescas* 1911, inspired by the art of ◊Goya, was converted to an opera in 1916.

Gran Chaco large lowland plain in N Argentina, W Paraguay, and SE Bolivia; area 251,000 sq mi/650,000 sq km. It consists of swamps, forests (a source of quebracho timber), and grasslands, and there is cattle-raising.

Grand Banks continental shelf in the N Atlantic off SE Newfoundland, where the shallow waters are rich fisheries, especially for cod.

Grand Canal (Chinese *Da Yune*) the world's longest canal. It is 1,000 mi/1,600 km long and runs N from Hangzhou to Tianjin, China; it is 100–200 ft/30–61 m wide, and reaches depths of over 1 mi/1.5 km. The earliest section was completed 486 BC, and the northern section was built AD 1282–92, during the reign of Kublai Khan.

Grand Canyon vast gorge of multicolored strata of rock cut by and containing the Colorado River, N Arizona. It is 217 mi/350 km long, 4–18 mi/6–29 km wide, and reaches depths of over 1.1 mi/1.7 km. John Wesley Powell and 10 companions first traveled down the river through the gorge 1869. It was made a national park 1919. Millions of tourists visit each year.

Grand Design in the early 17th century, a plan attributed by the French minister Sully to Henry IV of France (who was assassinated before he could carry it out) for a great Protestant union against the Holy Roman Empire; the term was also applied to President de Gaulle's vision of France's place in a united Europe.

Grande Dixence dam the world's highest dam, located in Switzerland, which measures 935 ft/285 m from base to crest. Completed in 1961, it contains 8 million cu yds/6 million cu m of concrete.

Grand Forks city in E central North Dakota on the Minnesota border, on the Red River, N of Fargo; seat of Grand Forks County. It serves the surrounding agricultural area; most of its industries, such as food-processing mills and fertilizer plants, are associated with agriculture. The University of North Dakota 1883 is located here; population (1990) 49,425.

Grand Guignol genre of short horror play produced at the Grand Guignol theater in Montmartre, Paris (named after the bloodthirsty character Guignol in late 18th-century marionette plays).

Grandi Dino 1895–1988. Italian politician who challenged Mussolini for leadership of the Italian Fascist Party in 1921 and was subsequently largely responsible for Mussolini's downfall in July 1943.

Grand Old Party (GOP) popular name for US ◊Republican Party.

grand opera a type of opera without any spoken dialogue (unlike the *opéra-comique*), as performed at the Paris *Opéra* 1820s–1880s. Using the enormous resources of the state-subsidized opera house, grand operas were extremely long (five acts), and included incidental music and a ballet.

Composers of grand opera include Auber, Meyerbeer, and Halevy; examples include Verdi's *Don Carlos* 1867 and Meyerbeer's *Les Huguenots* 1836.

Grand Rapids city in W Michigan on the Grand River; population (1990) 189,126. It produces furniture, motor bodies, plumbing fixtures, and electrical goods. A fur-trading post was founded here 1826, and the furniture industry developed in the 1840s. Gerald Ford, 38th president of the US, lived here.

Grand Remonstrance petition passed by the British Parliament in Nov 1641 which listed all the alleged misdeeds of Charles I and demanded Parliamentary approval for the king's ministers and the reform of the church. Charles refused to accept the Grand Remonstrance and countered by trying to arrest five leading members of the House of Commons (Pym, Hampden, Holles, Hesilrige, and Strode). The worsening of relations between king and Parliament led to the outbreak of the English Civil War in 1642.

grand slam in tennis, the four major tournaments: the Australian Open, the French Open, Wimbledon, and the US Open. In golf, it is also the four major tournaments: the US Open, the British Open, the Masters, and the PGA. In baseball, a grand slam is a home run with runners on all the bases. A grand slam in bridge is when all 13 tricks are won by one team.

Grand Teton highest point of the spectacular Teton range, NW Wyoming, rising to 13,770 ft/4,197 m. Grand Teton National Park was established 1929.

grand unified theory (GUT) in physics, a sought-for theory that would combine the successful theory of the strong nuclear force (called quantum chromodynamics) with the theory of the weak and electromagnetic forces. The search for the GUT is part of a larger program seeking a ◊unified field theory, which would combine all four ◊fundamental forces of nature (including the ◊gravitational force) within one framework.

Grange Red (Harold Edward) 1903–1991. US football player. Born in Forksville, Pennsylvania, and raised in Illinois, Grange attended the University of Illinois. In both the 1923 and 1924 seasons he was chosen All-American halfback and won the nickname "the Galloping Ghost" for his extraordinary open-field running ability. Leaving college 1925 to join the Chicago Bears professional football team, Grange became one of the first superstars of the newly founded National Football League. He became a charter member of the Football Hall of Fame 1963.

Grange Movement, the in US history, a farmers' protest in the South and Midwest states against economic hardship and exploitation. The National Grange of the Patrons of Husbandry, formed 1867, was a network of local organizations, employing cooperative practices and advocating "granger" laws. The movement petered out in the late 1870s, to be superseded by the ◊Greenbackers.

Granger Stewart. Adopted name of James Stewart 1913– . British film actor. After several leading roles in British romantic films during World War II, he moved to Hollywood in 1950 and sub-

Grand Canyon *The silt-laden Colorado River cuts through the lowest point of Arizona's Grand Canyon.*

sequently starred in adventure films, for example, *King Solomon's Mines* 1950, *Scaramouche* 1952, *The Prisoner of Zenda* 1952, and *Beau Brummell* 1954.

granite a plutonic ◊igneous rock, acidic in composition (containing a high proportion of silica). The rock is coarse-grained, the characteristic minerals being quartz, feldspars (usually alkali), and micas. It may be pink or gray, depending on the composition of the feldspars. Granites are chiefly used as building materials.

Some granites are formed by melting or partial melting of existing continental crust by heat and pressure or high-grade metamorphic conditions. Other granites are formed by igneous processes whereby ultrabasic mantle rock is partially melted and yields various magmas of more siliceous composition such as gabbro, diorite and granite.

Granites often form large intrusions in the core of mountain ranges, and they are usually surrounded by zones of thermally metamorphosed rock. Granite areas have characteristic moorland scenery and may weather along joints and cracks to produce "tors" consisting of rounded blocks that appear to have been stacked upon one another as exposed hillside.

Granite City city in SW Illinois, across the Mississippi River from St Louis, Missouri. An industrial city with its own port on the Chain of Rocks canal, it manufactures steel products, automobile frames, and building materials; population (1990) 32,862.

granite *Exposed granite "tors" can reach substantial size as in Hay Tor (1,490 ft/453 m) in England's Dartmoor region.*

Grant Cary. Adopted name of Archibald Leach 1904–1986. British-born US actor who became a US citizen 1942. His witty, debonair screen personality made him a favorite for more than three decades. He made several fims for director Alfred ◊Hitchcock, including *Suspicion* 1941, *Notorious* 1946, *To Catch a Thief* 1955, and *North by Northwest* 1959. He received a 1970 Academy Award for general excellence.

He made his US film debut in *This Is the Night* 1932. Other films include *She Done Him Wrong* 1933, *Bringing Up Baby* 1937, and *The Philadelphia Story* 1940.

Grant *Hollywood film actor Cary Grant, who was known for his witty, sophisticated comedies.*

Grant James Augustus 1827–1892. Scottish soldier and explorer who served in India and Abyssinia and, with Captain John Speke, explored the sources of the Nile 1860–63. Accounts of his travels include *A Walk Across Africa* 1864 and *Botany of the Speke and Grant Expedition*.

Grant Ulysses S(impson) 1822–1885. Noted American ◊Civil War leader and 18th president of the US 1869–77. Born Hiram Ulysses Grant, he was a Union general in the American Civil War and commander in chief from 1864. His military career nearly ended in early failure when Confederate forces surprised him at the Battle of Shiloh 1862. Abraham ◊Lincoln's support was unwavering, however, and Grant quickly redeemed himself, showing an aggressive fighting spirit. As a Republican president, he carried through a liberal ◊Reconstruction policy in the South, reformed the civil service, and ratified the Treaty of Washington with Great Britain 1871. He failed to suppress extensive political corruption within his own party and cabinet, which tarnished the reputation of his second term; he demonstrated poor judgment and political ineptness as president, placing trust in close associates who used their positions for personal gain.

Born in Point Pleasant, Ohio, he graduated from West Point 1843 and had an unsuccessful career in the army until 1854 and in business. On the outbreak of the Civil War received a commission on the Mississippi front. He took command there 1862, and by his capture of Vicksburg 1863 brought the whole Mississippi Valley under Northern control. He slowly wore down the Confederate General Robert E ◊Lee's resistance, and on April 9, 1865, received his surrender at Appomattox Courthouse, Virginia. He was elected president 1868 and reelected 1872. His two-

Grant The 18th president of the United States of America, Ulysses S Grant, a Republican. 1869–1877.

volume *Memoirs* were very successful and restored his finances.

granthi in Sikhism, the man or woman who reads from the holy book, the *Guru Granth Sahib*, during the service.

Granville-Barker Harley 1877–1946. British theater director and author. He was director and manager with J E Vedrenne at the Royal Court Theatre, London, 1904–18, producing plays by Shaw, Yeats, Ibsen, Galsworthy, and Masefield.

graph a pictorial representation of numerical data as in statistical data, or a method of showing the mathematical relationship between two or more variables by drawing a diagram.

There are often two axes or coordinates at right angles intersecting at the origin—the zero point from which values of the variables (for example, distance and time for a moving object) are assigned along the axes. Pairs of simultaneous values (the distance moved after a particular time) are plotted as points in the area between the axes, and the points then joined by a smooth curve to produce a graph.

graphic notation in music, a sign language referring to unorthodox sound effects, such as electronic sounds, for which Classical music notation is not suitable.

graphics tablet or ***bit pad*** in computing, an input device in which a stylus or cursor is moved, by hand, over a flat surface. The computer can keep track of the position of the stylus, so enabling the operator to input drawings or diagrams into the computer.

A graphics tablet is often used with a form overlaid for users to mark boxes in positions that relate to specific registers in the computer, although recent developments in handwriting recognition may increase its future versatility.

graphite blackish-gray, laminar, crystalline form of ◊carbon. It is used as a lubricant and as the active component of pencil lead.

The carbon atoms are strongly bonded together in sheets, but the bonds between the sheets are weak so that the sheets are free to slide over one another. Graphite has a very high melting point (6,332°F/3,500°C), which gives it mechanical strength and makes it a good conductor of heat and electricity. In its pure form it is used as a moderator in nuclear reactors.

grass plant of the large family Gramineae of monocotyledons, with about 9,000 species distributed worldwide except in the Arctic regions. The majority are perennial, with long, narrow leaves and jointed, hollow stems; hermaphroditic flowers are borne in spikelets; the fruits are grainlike. Included are bluegrass, wheat, rye, corn, sugarcane, and bamboo.

Grass Günter 1927– . German writer. Born in Danzig, he studied at the art academies of Düsseldorf and Berlin, worked as a writer and sculptor (first in Paris and later in Berlin), and in 1958 won the coveted "Group 47" prize. The grotesque

grass
grass flower

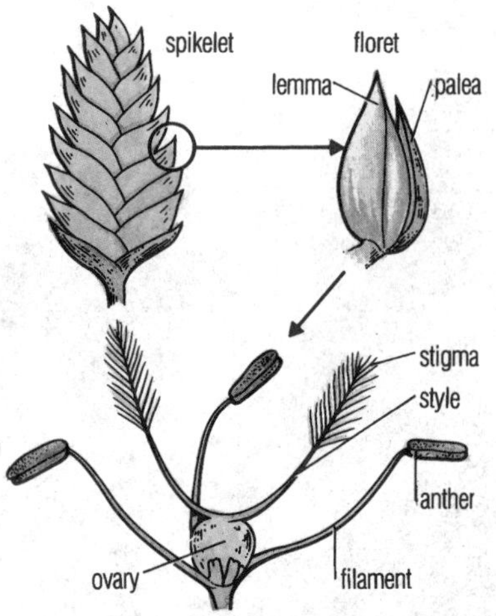
spikelet
floret
lemma
palea
stigma
style
anther
ovary
filament

humor and Socialist feeling of his novels *Die Blechtrommel/The Tin Drum* 1959 and *Der Butt/The Flounder* 1977 are also characteristic of many of his poems.

Grasse town near Cannes, SE France; population (1982) 38,360. It is the center of a perfume-manufacturing region, and flowers are grown on a large scale for this purpose.

grasshopper insect of the order Orthoptera, usually with strongly developed hind legs, enabling it to leap. Members of the order include ◊locusts, ◊crickets, and ◊katydids.

The shorthorned grasshoppers constitute the family Acrididae, and include locusts. All members of the family feed voraciously on vegetation. The femur of each hind leg in the male usually has a row of protruding joints that produce the characteristic chirping when rubbed against the hard wing veins. Eggs are laid in a small hole in the ground, and the unwinged larvae become adult after about six molts. The American grasshopper *Schistocera americana* is widespread in North America.

The long-horned grasshoppers, or katydids, form the family Tettigoniidae, and have a similar life history, but differ from the Acrididae in having long antennae and in producing their chirping by the friction of the wing covers over one another (stridulation).

grass-of-Parnassus or eastern parnassia plant (*Parnassia glauca*), unrelated to grasses, found growing in moist grasslands and thickets of North America. It is low-growing, with a rosette of heart-shaped, stalked leaves, and has five-petaled, white flowers with conspicuous green veins.

grass tree Australian plant of the genus *Xanthorrhoea*. The tall, thick stems have a grasslike tuft at the top and are surmounted by a flower spike resembling a spear.

Grattan Henry 1746–1820. Irish politician. He entered the Irish parliament in 1775, led the patriot opposition, and obtained free trade and legislative independence for Ireland 1782. He failed to prevent the Act of Union of Ireland and England in 1805, sat in the British Parliament from that year, and pressed for Catholic emancipation.

Graubünden (French ***Grisons***) Swiss canton, the largest in Switzerland; area 2,743 sq mi/ 7,106 sq km; population (1986) 167,000. The inner valleys are the highest in Europe, and the main sources of the river Rhine rise here. It also includes the resort of Davos and, in the Upper Engadine, St Moritz. The capital is Chur. Romansch is still widely spoken. Graubünden entered the Swiss Confederation 1803.

gravel a coarse ◊sediment consisting of pebbles or small fragments of rock, originating in the beds of lakes and streams or on beaches. Gravel is

gravimetry

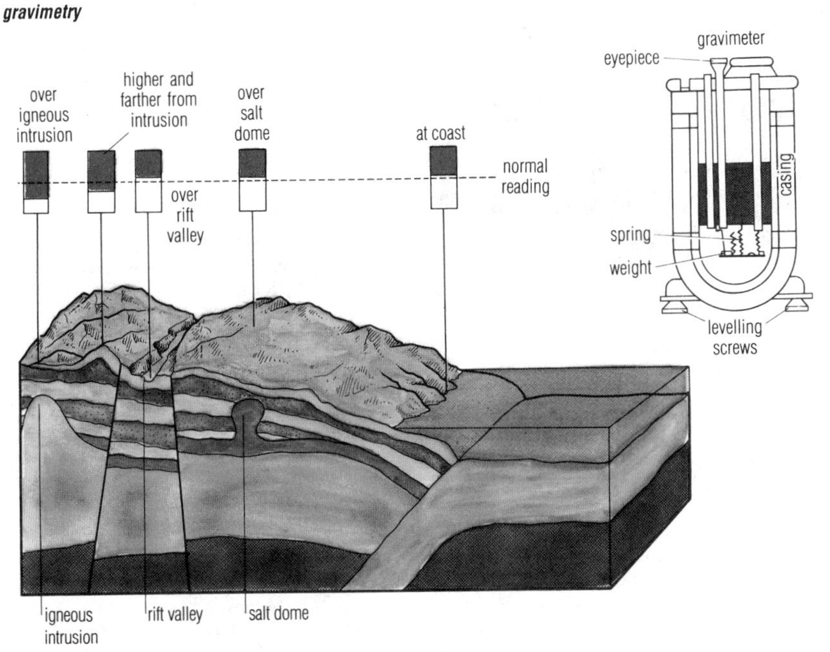
over
igneous
intrusion
higher and
farther from
intrusion
over
salt
dome
at coast
normal
reading
over
rift
valley
igneous
intrusion
rift valley
salt dome
gravimeter
eyepiece
casing
spring
weight
levelling
screws

quarried for use in road building, railroad ballast, and for an aggregate in concrete. It is obtained from quarries known as gravel pits, where it is often found mixed with sand or clay. Some gravel deposits also contain metal ores (particularly tin) or free metals (such as gold and silver).

Graves Robert (Ranke) 1895–1985. English poet and author. He was severely wounded on the Somme in World War I, and his frank autobiography *Goodbye to All That* 1929 is one of the outstanding war books. Other works include the poems *Over the Brazier* 1916; historical novels of Imperial Rome, *I Claudius* and *Claudius the God* both 1934; and books on myth, for example *The White Goddess* 1948.

Gravesend town on the river Thames, Kent, SE England, linked by ferry with Tilbury opposite; population (1981) 52,963.

gravimetry the study of the Earth's gravitational field. Small variations in the gravitational field can be caused by varying densities of rocks and structure beneath the surface, a phenomenon called the ◊Bouguer anomaly. These variations provide information about otherwise inaccessible subsurface conditions.

gravitational force one of the four ◊fundamental forces of nature, the other three being the ◊electromagnetic force, the ◊strong force, and the ◊weak force. The gravitational force is the weakest of the four forces, but it acts over great distances. The particle that is postulated as the carrier of the gravitational force is the ◊graviton.

gravitational lens the gravitational field from a very large body, such as a star, which deflects light. It was predicted by Einstein's general theory of relativity and tested successfully during the solar eclipse of 1917 when the light from stars located beyond the Sun was captured on photographs.

graviton one of the ◊gauge bosons, a particle that cannot be subdivided and is the postulated carrier of the gravitational force.

gravity the force of attraction between objects because of their masses. The force we call gravity on Earth is the force of attraction between any object in the Earth's gravitational field and the Earth itself.

According to Newton's law of gravitation, all objects fall to Earth with the same acceleration, regardless of mass. For an object of mass m_1 at a distance r from the center of the Earth (mass m_2), the gravitational force of attraction F equals Gm_1m_2/r^2, where G is the gravitational constant. However, according to Newton's second law of motion, F also equals m_1g, where g is the acceleration due to gravity; therefore $g = Gm_2/r^2$ and is independent of the mass of the object; at the Earth's surface it equals 32.174 ft/9.806 m per second per second.

Einstein's general theory of relativity treats gravitation not as a force but as a curvature of space and time around a body. Relativity predicts the bending of light and the ◊red shift of light in a gravitational field; both have been observed. Another prediction of relativity is gravitational waves, which should be produced when massive bodies are violently disturbed. These waves are so weak that they have not yet been detected with certainty, although observations of a ◊pulsar (which emits energy at regular intervals) in orbit around another star have shown that the stars are spiralling together at the rate that would be expected if they were losing energy in the form of gravitational waves.

gravure one of the three main ◊printing methods, in which printing takes place from a plate etched with a pattern of recessed cells in which the ink is held. The greater the depth of a cell, the greater the strength of the printed ink. Gravure plates are expensive to make. However, the process is economical for high-volume printing and reproduces illustrations well.

gray SI unit (abbreviation Gy) of absorbed radiation dose. One gray equals 100 ◊rads equals 100 rems, and is the dose absorbed when one kilogram of matter absorbs one joule of ionizing radiation.

Gray Asa 1810–1888. US botanist who became America's leading botanist and taxonomist, basing his revision of the Linnean system on fruit form rather than gross morphology. His *Manual of Botany* 1850 remains the standard reference work on flora E of the Rockies. In 1842 he was appointed professor of botany at Harvard and was instrumental in establishing the subject in American university curricula. A friend and supporter of Darwin, Gray was one of the founders of the National Academy of Sciences.

Born in Saquoit, New York, Gray graduated from medical school but chose botany rather than medicine as his career. Gray's major publications include *Elements of Botany* 1836 and the definitive *Flora of North America* 1838, 1843.

Gray Thomas 1716–1761. English poet whose "Elegy Written in a Country Churchyard" 1750 is one of the most quoted poems in English. Other poems include "Ode on a Distant Prospect of Eton College," "The Progress of Poesy," and "The Bard"; these poems are now seen as the precursors of Romanticism.

A close friend of Horace ◊Walpole at Eton, Gray made a continental tour with him 1739–41, an account of which is given in his vivid letters. In 1748 his first poems appeared anonymously in Dodsley's *Miscellany*.

grayling freshwater fish *Thymallus arcticus* of the family Salmonidae. It has a long, multirayed dorsal fin and exhibits a coloration shading from silver to purple. It is found in N parts of North America, Europe, and Asia. it was once common in the Great Lakes.

Graz capital of Styria province, and second-largest city in Austria; population (1981) 243,400. Industries include engineering, chemicals, iron, and steel. It has a 15th-century cathedral and a university founded in 1573. Lippizaner horses are bred near here.

Graziani Rodolfo 1882–1955. Italian general. He was commander in chief of Italian forces in N Africa during World War II but was defeated by British forces 1940, and subsequently replaced. Later, as defense minister in the new Mussolini government, he failed to reorganize a republican Fascist army, was captured by the Allies in 1945, tried by an Italian military court, and finally released in 1950.

Great Artesian Basin the largest area of artesian water in the world, it underlies much of Queensland, New South Wales and South Australia, and in prehistoric times formed a sea. It has an area of 676,250 sq mi/1,750,000 sq km.

Great Australian Bight broad bay in S Australia, notorious for storms. It was discovered by a Dutch navigator, Captain Thyssen, in 1627. The coast was charted by the English explorer Captain Matthew Flinders 1802.

Great Awakening, the a religious revival in the American colonies from the late 1730s to the 1760s, sparked off by George Whitefield (1714–1770), an itinerant English Methodist preacher whose evangelical fervor and eloquence made many converts.

A second "great awakening" occurred in the first half of the 19th century, establishing the evangelist tradition in US Protestantism.

Great Barrier Reef chain of coral reefs and islands about 1,250 mi/2,000 km long, off the E coast of Queensland, Australia, at a distance of 10–30 mi/15–45 km. It is believed to be the world's largest living organism and forms an immense natural breakwater, and the coral rock forms a structure larger than all human-made structures on Earth combined. Annually, a few nights after the full moon in Nov, 135 species of hard coral release their eggs and sperm for fertilization and the sea turns pink. The phenomenon, one of the wonders of the natural world, was discovered in 1983, and is triggered by a mechanism dependent on the moon, the tides, and water temperatures.

The reef is in danger from large numbers of starfish, which are reported to have infested 35% of the reef. Some scientists fear the entire reef will disappear within 50 years.

Great Bear popular name for the constellation ◊Ursa Major.

Great Bear Lake lake on the Arctic Circle, in the Northwest Territories, Canada; area 12,275 sq mi/31,800 sq km.

Great Britain official name for ◊England, ◊Scotland, and ◊Wales, and the adjacent islands (except the Channel Islands and the Isle of Man) from 1603, when the English and Scottish crowns were united under James I of England (James VI of Scotland). With Northern ◊Ireland it forms the ◊United Kingdom.

great circle a plane cutting through a sphere, and passing through the center point of the sphere, cuts the surface along a great circle. Thus, on the Earth, all meridians of longitude are half great

Great Barrier Reef *A collection of variously formed corals and shells from the reef.*

circles; among the parallels of latitude, only the equator is a great circle.

The shortest route between two points on the Earth's surface is along the arc of a great circle. These are used extensively as air routes although on maps, due to the distortion brought about by ◊projection, they do not appear as straight lines.

Great Dane large, shorthaired breed of dog, usually fawn in color, standing up to 36 in/92 cm tall, and weighing up to 154 lb/70 kg. It has a long head, a large nose, and small, erect ears. It was used in Europe for hunting boars and stags.

Great Dividing Range E Australian mountain range, extending 2,300 mi/3,700 km N–S from Cape York Peninsula, Queensland, to Victoria. It includes the Carnarvon Range, Queensland, which has many Aboriginal cave paintings, the Blue Mountains in New South Wales, and the Australian Alps.

Great Exhibition world's fair held in Hyde Park, London, UK, in 1851, proclaimed by its originator Prince Albert as "the Great Exhibition of the Industries of All Nations." In practice, it glorified British manufacture: over half the 100,000 exhibits were from Britain or the British Empire. Over 6 million people attended the exhibition. The exhibition hall, popularly known as the ◊Crystal Palace, was constructed of glass with a cast-iron frame, and designed by Joseph ◊Paxton.

Great Expectations a novel by Charles Dickens, published 1860–61.

Philip Pirrip ("Pip"), brought up by his sister and her husband, the blacksmith Joe Gargery, rejects his humble background and pursues wealth, which he believes comes from the elderly, eccentric Miss Havisham. Ultimately, through adversity, he recognizes the value of his origins.

Great Falls city in central Montana, on the Missouri River, NE of Helena; seat of Cascade County. Its main industries are involved with the processing of copper and zinc from nearby mines. The processing of agricultural products and oil refining is also important; population (1990) 55,097. The city is named for nearby waterfalls, first discovered in 1805 by Meriwether Lewis and William Clark.

Great Lake Australia's largest freshwater lake, 3,380 ft/1,030 m above sea level, in Tasmania; area 44 sq mi/114 sq km. It is used for hydroelectric power and is a tourist attraction.

Great Lakes series of five freshwater lakes along the US-Canada border: Lakes Superior, Michigan, Huron, Erie, and Ontario; total area 94,600 sq mi/245,000 sq km. Interconnecting canals make them navigable by large ships, and they are drained by the ◊St Lawrence River, all forming the St Lawrence Seaway. They are said to contain 20% of the world's surface fresh water.

The principal cargoes are iron ore and grain, both of which originate at Lake Superior ports. Iron ore is carried to other lake ports for transport to steel mills. Grain may be shipped to processing

Great Leap Forward *Silos on Shashiyu commune near Tangshan, China. Communes were a key feature of the policies of the Great Leap Forward.*

centers such as Buffalo, New York, or sent directly abroad.

Great Leap Forward the change in the economic policy of the People's Republic of China introduced by ◊Mao Zedong under the second 5-year plan of 1958–62. The aim was to convert China into an industrially based economy by transferring resources away from agriculture. This coincided with the creation of people's communes. The inefficient and poorly planned allocation of state resources led to the collapse of the strategy by 1960 and a return to more adequate support for agricultural production.

Great Patriotic War (1941–45) a term used to describe the war between the USSR and Germany. When Germany invaded the USSR in June 1941 the Russians retreated, carrying out a ◊scorched earth policy and relocating strategic industries beyond the Urals. Stalin remained in Moscow and the Russians, inspired to fight on by his patriotic speeches, launched a counteroffensive. The Allies tried to provide the USSR with vital supplies through Murmansk and Archangel despite German attempts to blockade the ports. In 1942 the Germans failed to take Leningrad and Moscow, and launched an attack toward the river Volga and to capture the oil wells at Baku. In August 1942 the Germans attacked Stalingrad but it was held by the Russians. The Germans were forced to surrender at Stalingrad in Jan 1943. The Red Army, under the command of Marshal Zhukov, gradually forced the Germans back and by February 1945 the Russians had reached the German border. In April 1945 the Russians, who had made tremendous sacrifices during the Great Patriotic War (20 million dead and millions more wounded) entered Berlin. In May 1945 the war ended.

Great Plains a semiarid region to the E of the Rocky Mountains, stretching as far as the 100th meridian of longitude through Oklahoma, Kansas, Nebraska and the Dakotas. The plains, which cover one-fifth of the US, extend from Texas in the S over 1,500 mi/2,400 km N to Canada. Ranching and wheat farming have resulted in over water resources to such an extent that available farmland has been reduced by erosion.

Great Power any of the major European powers of the 19th century: Russia, Austria (Austria-Hungary), France, Britain, and Prussia.

Great Red Spot prominent oval feature, 8,500 mi/14,000 km wide and some 20,000 mi/30,000 km long, in the atmosphere of the planet Jupiter, south of the equator. Observed for over a century, recent space probes showed it to be a counterclockwise vortex of cold clouds, colored possibly by phosphorus.

Great Rift Valley longest "split" in the Earth's surface, 5,000 mi/8,000 km long, running S from the Dead Sea (Israel/Jordan) to Mozambique; see ◊Rift Valley, Great.

Great Sandy Desert desert in N Western Australia; area 160,000 sq mi/415,000 sq km. It is also the name of an arid region in S Oregon.

Great Schism in European history, the period 1378–1417 in which rival popes had seats at Rome and at Avignon; it was ended by the election of Martin V during the Council of Constance 1414–17.

Great Slave Lake lake in the Northwest Territories, Canada; area 10,980 sq mi/28,450 sq km. It is the deepest lake (2,020 ft/615 m) in North America.

Great Trek in South African history, the movement of 12,000–14,000 Boer (Dutch) settlers from Cape Colony in 1835 and 1845 to escape British rule. They established republics in Natal and the Transvaal. It is seen by many white South Africans as the main event in the founding of the present republic and also as a justification for continuing whites-only rule.

Great Wall array of galaxies arranged in an almost perfect plane, discovered by astronomers in Cambridge, Massachusetts, in Nov 1989. It consists of some 2,000 galaxies (about 500 million × 200 million light-years) and is thought to be the largest structure ever discovered.

Great Wall of China continuous defensive wall stretching from W Gansu to the Gulf of Liaodong (1,450 mi/2,250 km). It was once even longer. It was built under the Qin dynasty from 214 BC to prevent incursions by the Turkish and Mongol peoples. Some 25 ft/8 m high, it consists of a

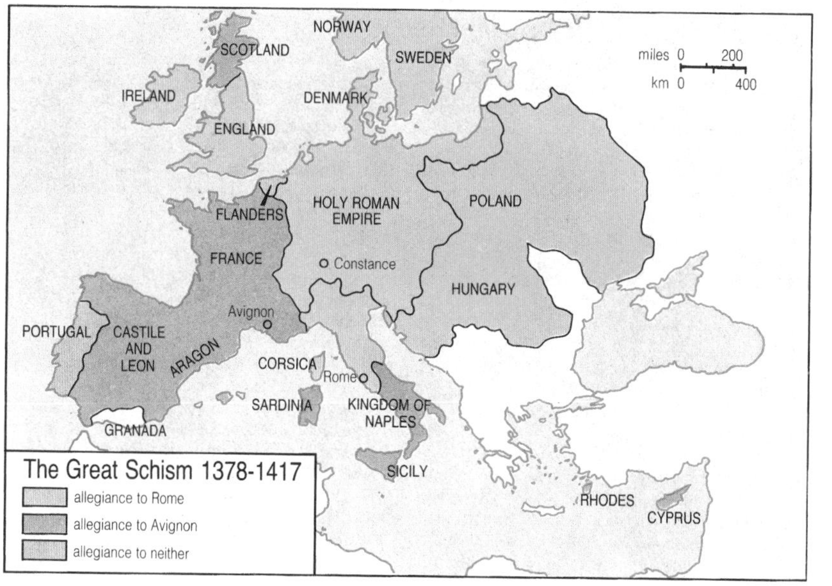
NORWAY
SCOTLAND
SWEDEN
miles 0 200
km 0 400
IRELAND
DENMARK
ENGLAND
FLANDERS
HOLY ROMAN EMPIRE
POLAND
FRANCE
Constance
HUNGARY
Avignon
PORTUGAL
CASTILE AND LEON
ARAGON
CORSICA
Rome
SARDINIA
KINGDOM OF NAPLES
GRANADA
SICILY
RHODES
CYPRUS
The Great Schism 1378-1417
allegiance to Rome
allegiance to Avignon
allegiance to neither

Great Wall of China *A section of the Great Wall of China near Badaling. Started in 214 BC, the wall was built to repel invasions by Turkish and Mongol peoples.*

brick-faced wall of earth and stone, has a series of square watchtowers, and has been carefully restored. It is the only structure built by human hand that can be seen from space.

Great War another name for ◊*World War I*.

grebe any of 19 species of water birds belonging to the family Podicipedidae. The great crested grebe *Podiceps cristatus* is the largest of the Old World grebes. It lives in ponds and marshes in Eurasia, Africa, and Australia, feeding on fish. It grows to 20 in/50 cm long and has a white breast, with chestnut and black feathers on its back and head. The head and neck feathers form a crest, especially prominent during the breeding season.

Greco, El (Doménikos Theotokopoulos) 1541–1614. Spanish painter called "the Greek" because he was born in Crete. He studied in Italy, worked in Rome from about 1570, and by 1577 had settled in Toledo. He painted elegant portraits and intensely emotional religious scenes with increasingly distorted figures and flickering light; for example, *The Burial of Count Orgaz* 1586 (Toledo).

Greece country in SE Europe, comprising the S Balkan peninsula, bounded N by Yugoslavia and Bulgaria, NW by Albania, NE by Turkey, E by the Aegean Sea, S by the Mediterranean Sea, and W by the Ionian Sea

government The 1975 constitution provides for a parliamentary system of government, with a president who is head of state, a prime minister who is head of government, and a single-chamber parliament. The president, elected by parliament for a five-year term, appoints the prime minister and cabinet. Parliament has 300 members, all elected by universal suffrage for a four-year term, and the prime minister and cabinet are collectively responsible to it. Bills passed by parliament must be ratified by the president, whose veto can be overridden by an absolute majority of the total number of members. The two main political parties are the Panhellenic Socialist Movement (PASOK) and the New Democracy Party (ND).

history For ancient history, see ◊Greece, ancient. From the 14th century Greece came under Ottoman Turkish rule, and except for the years 1686–1715, when the Peloponnese was occupied by the Venetians, it remained Turkish until the outbreak of the War of Independence 1821. British, French, and Russian intervention 1827, which brought about the destruction of the Turkish fleet at ◊Navarino, led to the establishment of Greek independence 1829. Prince Otto of Bavaria was placed on the throne 1832; his despotic rule provoked a rebellion 1843, which set up a parliamentary government, and another 1862, when he was deposed and replaced by Prince George of Denmark. Relations with Turkey were embittered by the Greeks' desire to recover Macedonia, Crete, and other Turkish territories with Greek populations. A war 1897 ended in disaster, but the ◊Balkan Wars 1912–13 won most of the disputed areas for Greece.

In a period of internal conflict from 1914, two monarchs were deposed, and there was a republic 1923–25, when a military coup restored ◊George II, who in the following year established a dictatorship under Joannis ◊Metaxas.

An Italian invasion 1940 was successfully resisted, but an intensive attack by Germany 1941 overwhelmed the Greeks. During the German occupation of Greece 1941–44, a communist-dominated resistance movement armed and trained a guerrilla army, and after World War II the National Liberation Front, as it was called, wanted to create a Socialist state. If the Greek royalist army had not had massive assistance from the US, under the provisions of the ◊Truman doctrine, this undoubtedly would have happened. The monarchy was reestablished under King Paul, who was succeeded by his son Constantine 1964.

Dissatisfaction with the government and conflicts between the king and his ministers resulted in a coup 1967, replacing the monarchy with a new regime, which, despite its democratic pretensions, was little more than a military dictatorship, with Col George Papadopoulos as its head.

grebe

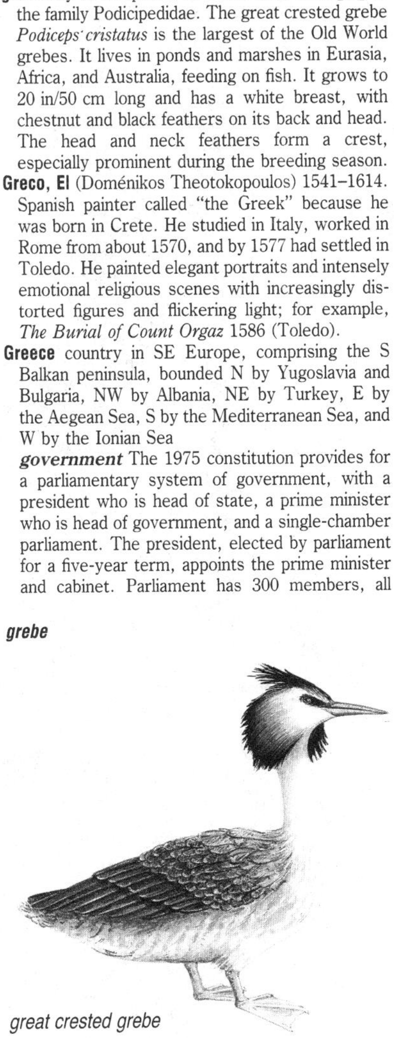

great crested grebe

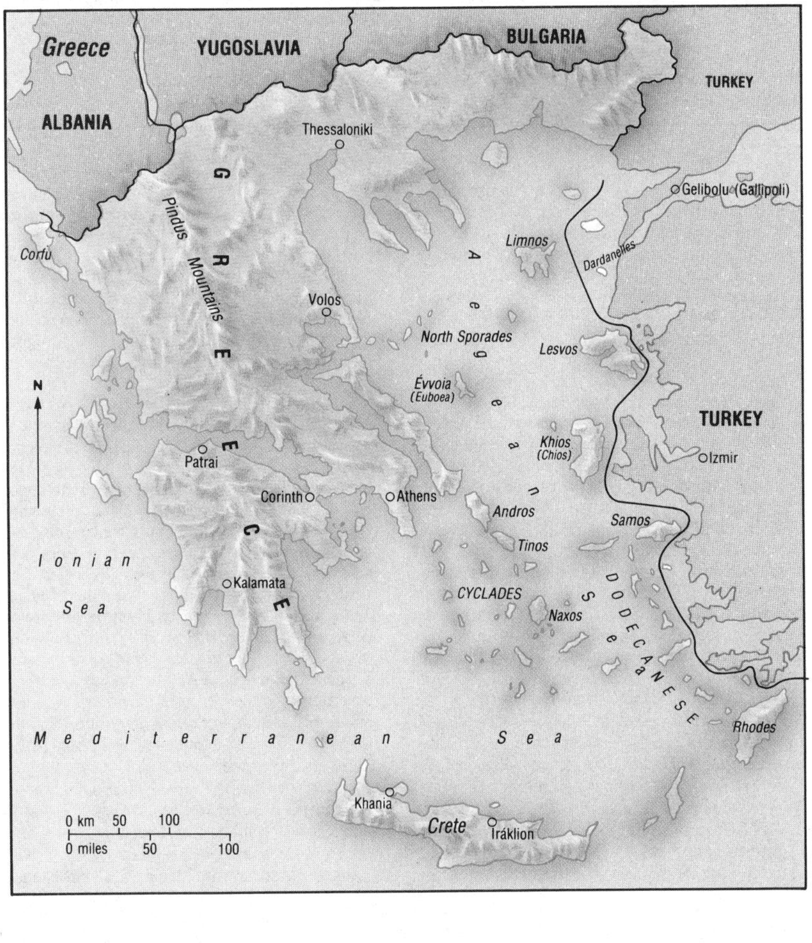
Greece
YUGOSLAVIA
BULGARIA
TURKEY
ALBANIA
Thessaloniki
Gelibolu (Gallipoli)
Pindus Mountains
G R E E C E
Limnos
Dardanelles
Corfu
Volos
A e g e a n
North Sporades
Lesvos
Évvoia
(Euboea)
N
TURKEY
Khios
(Chios)
Izmir
Patrai
Corinth
Athens
Andros
Samos
Tinos
I o n i a n
S e a
Kalamata
CYCLADES
Naxos
D O D E C A N E S E
Rhodes
M e d i t e r r a n e a n
S e a
Khania
Crete
Iráklion
0 km 50 100
0 miles 50 100

Greece
Hellenic Republic
(Elliniki Dimokratia)

0 miles 500
0 km 1000
Yugoslavia
Bulgaria
Albania
BLACK SEA
Turkey
GREECE
Athens
Crete
Cyprus
MEDITERRANEAN SEA

area 50,935 sq mi/131,957 sq km
capital Athens
cities Larisa; ports Piraeus, Thessaloniki, Patras, Iráklion
physical mountainous; a large number of islands, notably Crete, Corfu, and Rhodes
features Corinth canal; Mount Olympus; the Acropolis; many Classical archeological sites; the Aegean and Ionian Islands
head of state Christos Sartzetakis from 1985
head of government Xenophon Zolotas from 1989
political system democratic republic
political parties Panhellenic Socialist Movement (PASOK), democratic Socialist; New Democracy Party (ND), center-right; Democratic Renewal (DR); Communist Party; Greek Left Party
exports tobacco, fruit, vegetables, olives, olive oil, textiles, aluminum, iron and steel
currency drachma
population (1990 est) 10,066,000; growth rate 0.3% p.a.
life expectancy men 72, women 76
language Greek
religion Greek Orthodox 97%
literacy men 96%/women 89% (1985)
GDP $40.9 bn (1987); $4,093 per head
chronology
1829 Independence achieved from Turkish rule.
1912–13 Balkan Wars; Greece gained much land.
1941–44 German occupation of Greece.
1946 Civil war between royalists and Communists; Communists defeated.
1949 Monarchy reestablished with Paul as king.
1964 King Paul succeeded by his son Constantine.
1967 Army coup removed the king; Col George Papadopoulos became prime minister. Martial law imposed, all political activity banned.
1973 Republic proclaimed, with Papadopoulos as president.
1974 Former premier Constantine Karamanlis recalled from exile to lead government. Martial law and ban on political parties lifted; restoration of the monarchy rejected by a referendum.
1975 New constitution adopted, making Greece a republic.
1980 Karamanlis resigned as prime minister and was elected president.
1981 Greece became full member of EEC. Andreas Papandreou elected as Greece's first Socialist prime minister.
1983 Five-year defense and economic cooperation agreement signed with US; ten-year economic cooperation agreement signed with USSR.
1985 Papandreou reelected.
1988 Relations with Turkey improved. Major cabinet reshuffle after mounting criticism of Papandreou.
1989 Papandreou defeated in elections. Tzannis Tzannetakis, conservative backbencher, became prime minister, heading first all-party government (including Communists) for 15 years. This broke up and Xenophon Zolotas formed new unity government. Papandreou charged with illegal wiretapping and bribery.
1990 Siting of US bases agreed.

All political activity was banned, and opponents of the government were forced out of public life.

In 1973 Greece declared itself a republic, and Papadopoulos became president. A civilian cabinet was appointed, but before the year was out another coup brought Lt-Gen Phaidon Ghizikis to the presidency, with Adamantios Androutsopoulos as prime minister. The government's failure to prevent the Turkish invasion of ◊Cyprus led to its downfall, and a former prime minister, Constantine ◊Karamanlis, was recalled from exile to form a new Government of National Salvation. He immediately ended martial law, press censorship, and the ban on political parties, and in the 1974 general election his New Democracy Party (ND) won a decisive majority in parliament.

A referendum the same year rejected the return of the monarchy, and in 1975 a new constitution for a democratic "Hellenic Republic" was adopted, with Constantine Tsatsos as president. ND won the 1977 general election with a reduced majority, and in 1980 Karamanlis resigned as prime minister and was elected president.

The following year Greece became a full member of the EC, having been an associate since 1962. Meanwhile, the ND was faced with a growing challenge from the Panhellenic Socialist Movement (PASOK), which won an absolute majority in parliament in the 1981 general election. Its leader, Andreas ◊Papandreou, became Greece's first Socialist prime minister.

PASOK had been elected on a radical Socialist platform, which included withdrawal from the EC, the removal of US military bases, and a program of domestic reform. Important social changes, such as lowering the voting age to 18, the legalization of civil marriage and divorce, and an overhaul of the universities and the army, were carried out; but instead of withdrawing from Europe, Papandreou was content to obtain a modification of the terms of entry, and, rather than close US bases, he signed a five-year agreement on military and economic cooperation. In 1983 he also signed a ten-year economic cooperation agreement with the USSR.

Despite introducing austerity measures to deal with rising inflation, PASOK won a comfortable majority in the 1985 elections. In 1986 the constitution was amended, limiting the powers of the president in relation to those of the prime minister. Criticism of Papandreou grew in 1989 when close aides were implicated in a banking scandal; he lost the June elections, and in Sept was charged with corruption and abuse of power. Following the inconclusive general elections, Tzannis Tzannatakis, an ND backbencher, formed Greece's first all-party government. However, this soon broke up and after months of negotiation Xenophon Zolotas (PASOK) put together a government of unity, comprising communists, Socialists, conservatives, and nonpolitical figures. In July 1990 an agreement on the siting of US bases in Greece was signed.

Greece, ancient the first Greek civilization, known as Mycenean (c. 1600–1200 BC) owed much to the Minoan civilization of Crete and may have been produced by the intermarriage of Greek-speaking invaders with the original inhabitants. From the 14th century BC a new wave of invasions began. The Achaeans overran Greece and Crete, destroying the Minoan and Mycenean civilizations and penetrating Asia Minor; to this period belongs the siege of Troy (c. 1180). The latest of the invaders were the Dorians (c. 1100) who settled in the Peloponnese and founded Sparta; that great city-state arose during the obscure period that followed (1100–800). The mountainous geography of Greece hindered the cities from attaining any national unity, and led the Greeks to take to the sea. During the years 750–550 the Greeks not only became great traders, but founded colonies around the coasts of the Mediterranean and the Black Sea, in Asia Minor, Sicily, S Italy, S France, Spain, and North Africa. The main centers of Greek culture in the 6th century BC were the wealthy ◊Ionian ports of Asia Minor, where Greek philosophy, science, and lyric poetry originated.

Many Greek cities passed from monarchy to the rule of a landowning or merchant oligarchy and thence to democracy. Thus Athens passed through the democratic reforms of Solon (594), the enlightened "tyranny" of Pisistratus (560–527), and the establishment of democracy by Cleisthenes (c. 507). Sparta remained unique, a state in which a ruling race, organized on military lines, tyrannized the original population.

After 545 BC the Ionian cities fell under the dominion of the Persian Empire. Aid given them by Athens in an unsuccessful revolt in 499–494 provoked Darius of Persia to invade Greece in 490 only to be defeated by the Athenians at Marathon and forced, to withdraw. Another invasion by the Persian Emperor Xerxes, after being delayed by the heroic defense of Thermopylae by 300 Spartans, was defeated at sea off Salamis in 480 and on land at Plataea in 479. The Ionian cities were liberated and formed a naval alliance with Athens, the Confederacy of Delos. Pericles, the real ruler of Athens 461–429, attempted to convert this into an Athenian empire and to form a land empire in Greece. Mistrust of his ambitions led to the Peloponnesian War (431–404), which destroyed the political power of Athens. In 5th-century Athens, Greek tragedy, comedy, sculpture, and architecture were at their peak, and Socrates and Plato founded moral philosophy.

After the Peloponnesian War, Sparta became the leading Greek power until it was overthrown by Thebes (378–371). The constant wars between the cities gave Philip II of Macedon (358–336) the opportunity to establish his supremacy over Greece. His son ◊Alexander the Great overthrew the decadent Persian Empire, conquered Syria and Egypt, and invaded the Punjab. After his death in 323 his empire was divided among his generals, but his conquest had nevertheless spread Greek culture to the Near East.

During the 3rd century BC the cities attempted to maintain their independence against Macedon, Egypt, and Rome by forming federations; for example, the Achaean and Aetolian Leagues. Roman intervention began in 212 and ended in the annexation of Greece in 146. Under Roman rule Greece remained a cultural center, until the emperor Justinian closed the university of Athens in AD 529.

Greek native to or an inhabitant of ancient or modern Greece or person of Greek descent; also the language and culture. Modern Greek is an Indo-European language, spoken in Greece and by Greek Cypriots; also by people of Greek descent, especially in Canada, the US, and Australia.

Greek architecture the architecture of ancient Greece is the base for virtually all architectural developments in Europe. The Greeks built with post and lintels, invented the entablature, which allowed roofs to be hipped (inverted V-shape), and perfected the design of arcades with support columns. There were three styles, or orders of

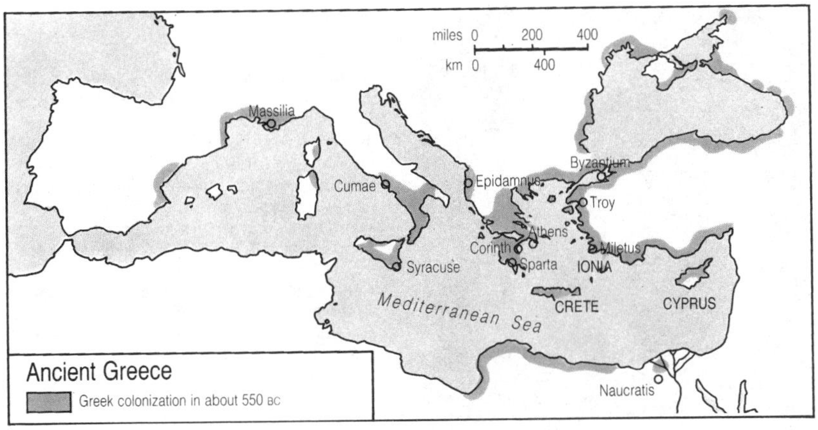
miles 0 200 400
km 0 400
Massilia
Cumae
Epidamnus
Byzantium
Troy
Athens
Corinth
Miletus
Syracuse
Sparta
IONIA
Mediterranean Sea
CRETE
CYPRUS
Naucratis
Ancient Greece
Greek colonization in about 550 BC

columns: Doric, Ionic, and Corinthian; see under ◊column and ◊order.

Of the Greek orders, the Doric is the oldest; it is said to have evolved from a former timber prototype. The finest example of a Doric temple is the Parthenon at Athens 447–438 BC. The origin of the Ionic is uncertain. The earliest building in which the Ionic capital appears is the temple of Diana at Ephesus 530 BC. The gateway to the Acropolis at Athens (known as the Propylaea) has internal columns of the Ionic order. The most perfect example is the Erechtheum in Athens. The Corinthian order belongs to a later period of Greek art. The most important example of the order is the temple of Jupiter (Zeus) Olympus in Athens 174 BC, completed under Roman influence in AD 129. The Mausoleum in Halicarnassus (353 BC) was one of the Seven Wonders of the World.

Greek art sculpture, mosaic, and crafts of ancient Greece (no large-scale painting survives). It is usually divided into three periods: Archaic (late 8th century–480 BC), showing Egyptian influence; Classical (480–323 BC), characterized by dignified realism; and Hellenistic (323–27 BC), more exuberant or dramatic. Sculptures of human figures dominate all periods, and vase painting was a focus for artistic development for many centuries.

Archaic period Statues of naked standing men (*kouroi*) and draped females (*korai*) show an Egyptian influence in their rigid frontality. By about 500 BC the figure was allowed to relax its weight onto one leg. Subjects were usually depicted smiling.

Classical period Expressions assumed a dignified serenity. Further movement was introduced in new poses, such as in Myron's bronze *Diskobolus/The Discus Thrower* 460–50 BC, and in the rhythmic Parthenon reliefs of riders and horses supervised by Phidias. Polykleitos" sculpture *Doryphoros/The Spear Carrier* 450–440 BC was of such harmony and poise that it set a standard for beautiful proportions. Praxiteles introduced the female nude into the sculptural repertory with the graceful *Aphrodite of Knidos* c. 350 BC. It was easier to express movement in bronze, hollow-cast by the lost-wax method, but relatively few bronze sculptures survive, and many are known only through Roman copies in marble.

Hellenistic period Sculptures such as the *Winged Victory of Samothrace* with its dramatic drapery, and the tortured *Laocoön* explored the effects of movement and deeply felt emotion.

vase painting Artists worked as both potters and painters until the 5th century BC, and the works they signed were exported throughout the empire. Made in several standard shapes and sizes, the pots served as functional containers for wine, water, and oil. The first decoration took the form of simple lines and circles, from which the Geometric style emerged near Athens in the 10th century BC. It consisted of precisely drawn patterns, such as the key meander. Gradually the bands of decoration multiplied and the human figure, geometrically stylized, was added. About 700 BC the potters of Corinth invented the Black Figure technique in which the unglazed red clay was painted in black with mythological scenes and battles in a narrative frieze. About 530 BC Athenian potters reversed the process and developed the sophisticated Red Figure pottery, which allowed for more detailed and elaborate painting of the figures in red against a black background. This grew increasingly naturalistic, with lively scenes of daily life; the finest examples date from the mid-6th to the mid-5th centuries BC in Athens. Later painters followed major art trends by representing spatial depth, dissipating the unique quality of their fine linear technique.

crafts The ancient Greeks exceled in carving gems and cameos and in metalwork. They also invented the pictorial mosaic, and from the 5th century BC onward floors were paved with colored pebbles depicting mythological subjects. Later, specially cut cubes of stone and glass called *tesserae* were used, and Greek artisans working for the Romans reproduced paintings, such as *Alexander at the Battle of Issus* from Pompeii, the originals of which are lost.

Greek language member of the Indo-European language family. Modern Greek, which is principally divided into the general vernacular (Demotic Greek) and the language of education and literature (Katharevousa), has a long and well-documented history: Ancient Greek from the 14th to the 12th centuries BC; Archaic Greek including Homeric epic language, until 800 BC; Classical Greek until 400 BC; Hellenistic Greek, the common language of Greece, Asia Minor, W Asia, and Egypt to 4th century AD, and Byzantine Greek, used until the 15th century and still the ecclesiastical language of the Greek Orthodox Church.

Classical Greek word forms have greatly influenced the English language, as in technical vocabulary. In its earlier phases Greek was spoken mainly in Greece, the Aegean islands, the west coast of Asia Minor, and in colonies in Sicily, the Italian mainland, S Spain, and S France. Hellenistic Greek was an important language not only in the Near East but also in the Roman Empire generally, and is the form also known as New Testament Greek (in which the Gospels and other books of the New Testament of the Bible were first written). Byzantine Greek was not only an imperial but also an ecclesiastical language, the medium of the Greek Orthodox Church; and Modern Greek, in both its forms, is spoken in Greece and in Cyprus, as well as wherever Greeks have settled throughout the world (especially Canada, the US, and Australia).

Greek art *Marble sculpture of the* Venus de Milo, *the Louvre, Paris.*

Greek literature the literature of Greece, ancient and modern.

ancient The earliest known works are those of Homer, reputed author of the epic poems the *Iliad* and the *Odyssey*, and Hesiod, whose long poem *Works and Days* deals with agricultural life. The lyric poet Pindar and the historians Herodotus and Thucydides belong to the 6th and 5th centuries BC. The 5th century BC saw the development of Athenian drama through the works of the tragic dramatists Aeschylus, Sophocles, Euripides and the comedies of Aristophanes. After the fall of Athens came a period of prose with the historian Xenophon, the idealist philosopher Plato, the orators Isocrates and Demosthenes, and the scientific teacher Aristotle.

After 323 BC Athens lost its political importance, but was still a university town with teachers such as Epicurus, Zeno, and Theophrastus, and the comic dramatist Menander. Meanwhile Alexandria had become the center of Greek culture: at the court of Philadelphus were scientists such as Euclid and the poets Callimachus, Apollonius, and Theocritus. During the 2nd century BC Rome became the new center for Greek literature, and Polybius, a historian, spent most of his life there; in the 1st century BC Rome also sheltered the poets Archias, Antipater of Sidon, Philodemus the Epicurean, and Meleager of Gadara, who compiled the first *Greek Anthology*.

In the 1st century AD Latin writers overshadowed the Greek, but there were still the geographer Strabo, the critic Dionysius of Halicarnassus (active around 10 BC), the Jewish writers Philo Judaeus and Josephus, the New Testament writers, and the biographer Plutarch. A revival came in the 2nd century with Lucian. To the 3rd century belong the historians Cassius Dio and Herodian, the Christian fathers Clement and Origen, and the neo-Platonists. For medieval Greek literature, see ◊Byzantine literature.

modern After the fall of Constantinople, the Byzantine tradition was perpetuated in the Classical Greek writing of, for example, the 15th-century chronicles of Cyprus, various historical works in the 16th and 17th centuries, and educational and theological works in the 18th century. The 17th and 18th centuries saw much controversy over whether to write in the Greek vernacular (demotic), the Classical language (*Katharevousa*), or the language of the Eastern Orthodox Church. Adamantios Korais (1748–1833), the first great modern writer, produced a compromise language; he was followed by the prose and drama writer and poet Aleksandros Rhangavis ("Rangabe") (1810–92), and many others.

The 10th-century epic of *Digenis Akritas* is usually considered to mark the beginnings of modern Greek vernacular literature, and the demotic was kept alive in the flourishing Cretan literature of the 16th and 17th centuries, in numerous popular songs, and in the Klephtic ballads of the 18th century. With independence in the 19th century the popular movement became prominent with the Ionian poet Dionysios Solomos (1798–1857), Andreas Kalvos (1796–1869), and others, and later with Iannis Psichari (1854–1929), short-story writer and dramatist, and the prose writer Alexandros Papadiamandis (1851–1911), who influenced many younger writers, for example Konstantinos Hatzopoulos (1868–1921), poet and essayist. After the 1920s, the novel began to emerge with Stratis Myrivilis (1892–1969) and Nikos Kazantzakis (1885–1957), author of *Zorba the Greek* 1946 and also a poet. There were also the Nobel Prize-winning poets George ◊Seferis and Odysseus ◊Elytis.

Greeley city in N Colorado, at the point where the Cache de Poudre River flows into the South Platte River, NE of Boulder. A distribution center for the surrounding agricultural area, its main industry is the processing of sugar beets; population (1990) 60,536. It is named for Horace Greeley, one of its founders.

Greeley Horace 1811–1872. US editor, publisher, and politician. He worked on a variety of publications before founding the *New York Tribune* 1841. A strong supporter of the Whig party, Greeley advocated many reform causes on the pages of his newspaper—among them, feminism and abolitionism. He was also an advocate of American westward expansion, as is remembered in his famous quote "Go west, young man." A founder of the Republican party 1854, Greeley was the unsuccessful presidential candidate of the breakaway Liberal Republicans 1872.

Born in Amherst, New Hampshire, Greeley was trained as a printer and moved to New York City 1831.

Green Thomas Hill 1836–1882. English philosopher. He attempted to show the limitations of Herbert ◊Spencer and John Stuart ◊Mill, and advocated the study of ◊Kant and ◊Hegel. His chief works are *Prolegomena to Ethics* 1883 and *Principles of Political Obligation* 1895. He was professor of moral philosophy at Oxford from 1878.

Greenaway Kate 1846–1901. English illustrator of children's books. In 1877 she exhibited at the Royal Academy and began her collaboration with the color-printer Edmund Evans, with whom she produced a number of children's books, including *Mother Goose*.

greenback paper money issued by the US government 1862–65 to help finance the Civil War. It was legal tender that could not be converted into gold (see ◊gold standard).

Greenbackers, the in US history, supporters of an alliance of agrarian and industrial organizations, known as the Greenback Labor Party, which campaigned for currency inflation by increasing the paper dollars "greenbacks" in circulation. In 1880 the party's presidential nominee polled only 300,000 votes; the movement was later superseded by ◊Populism.

Green Bay city in NE Wisconsin, where the Little Fox River flows into Green Bay on Lake Michigan; seat of Brown County. It is a port of entry to the US through the St Lawrence Seaway and serves as a distribution center. Industries include paper and food products; population (1990) 96,466. The Green Bay Packers team of the National Football League was organized here 1919.

green belt or ***green way*** area surrounding a large city, officially designated not to be built on but preserved as open space (for agricultural and recreational use or to be "forever wild").

greenbrier or ***catbrier*** any of several climbing woody vines of the genus *Smilax* of the lily family, having smooth, shiny green oval leaves and usually black berries. The prickly stems of these plants often form impenetrable thickets.

Greene *English author Graham Greene, whose novels often reflected his Roman Catholic beliefs.*

Greene (Henry) Graham 1904–1991. English writer, whose novels of guilt, despair, and penitence include *The Man Within* 1929, *Brighton Rock* 1938, *The Power and the Glory* 1940, *The Heart of the Matter* 1948, *The Third Man* 1950, *The Honorary Consul* 1973, *Monsignor Quixote* 1982, and *The Captain and the Enemy* 1988.

Greene Nathanel 1742–1786. American military leader. Born in Warwick, Rhode Island, Greene was a member of a Quaker family but showed an exceptional interest in military affairs. As a local militia officer, he was placed in command of the Rhode Island regiments at the outbreak of the Revolutionary War. Greene was later appointed brigadier general in the Continental army and saw action in the siege of Boston, the Battle of Long Island, and Washington's New Jersey campaigns. fter service as quartermaster general 1778–80, he commanded the successful American offensive in the South.

greenfinch songbird *Carduelis chloris*, common in Europe and N Africa. The male is green with a yellow breast, and the female is a greenish-brown.

greenfly plant-sucking insect, a type of ◊aphid.

greenhouse effect a phenomenon of the Earth's atmosphere by which solar radiation, absorbed by the Earth and reemitted from the surface, is prevented from escaping by carbon dioxide in the air. The result is a rise in the Earth's temperature; in a garden greenhouse, the glass walls have the same effect. The concentration of carbon dioxide in the atmosphere is estimated to have risen by 25% since the Industrial Revolution, and 10% since 1950; the rate of increase is now 0.5% a year. ◊Chlorofluorocarbon levels are rising by 5% a year, and nitrous oxide levels by 0.4% a year, resulting in a global warming effect of 0.5% since 1900, and a rise of about 3°F/0.1°C a year in the temperature of the world's oceans during the 1980s. Arctic ice was 20 ft/6 m to 23 ft/7 m thick in 1976 and had reduced to 13 ft/4 m to 17 ft/5 m by 1987. United Nations Environment Program estimates an increase in average world temperatures of 3.7°F/1.5°C with a consequent rise of 7.7 in/20 cm in sea level by 2025.

Greenland (Greenlandic *Kalaalit Nunaat*) world's largest island. It lies between the North Atlantic and Arctic Oceans E of North America

area 840,000 sq mi/2,175,600 sq km
capital Godthaab (Greenlandic *Nuuk*) on the W coast
features the whole of the interior is covered by a vast ice sheet (the remnant of the last glaciation, part of the N Polar icecap); the island has an important role strategically and in civil aviation, and shares military responsibilities with the US; there are lead and cryolite deposits, and offshore oil is being explored
economy fishing and fish-processing
population (1983) 51,903; Eskimo (Ammassalik), Danish, and other European US
language Greenlandic (Ammassalik Eskimoan)
history Greenland was discovered about 982 by Eric the Red, who founded colonies on the W coast soon after Eskimos from the North American Arctic had made their way to Greenland. Christianity was introduced to the Vikings about 1000. In 1261 the Viking colonies accepted Norwegian sovereignty, but early in the 15th century all communication with Europe ceased, and by the 16th century the colonies had died out, but the Eskimo had moved on to the E coast. It became a Danish colony in the 18th century, and following a referendum 1979 was granted full internal self-government 1981.

Greenland Sea area of the ◊Arctic Ocean between Spitsbergen and Greenland, and N of the Norwegian Sea.

green monkey disease another name for ◊***Marburg disease***, a virus originating in Central Africa.

Green Mountain Boys in US history, irregular troops who fought to protect the Vermont part of what was then New Hampshire colony from land claims made by neighboring New York. In the American Revolution they captured ◊Fort Ticonderoga from the British. Their leader was Ethan Allen (1738–89), who was later captured by the British. Vermont declared itself an independent republic, refusing to join the Union until 1791. It is popularly known as the Green Mountain State.

Green Party political party aiming to "preserve the planet and its people," based on the premise that incessant economic growth is unsustainable. The leaderless party structure reflects a general commitment to decentralization. Green parties were established in W Europe in the 1970s and spread in the 1980s. Parties in different countries are linked to one another but unaffiliated to any pressure group. They had a number of parliamentary seats in 1989: Austria 8, Belgium 11, Finland 4, Italy 20, Luxembourg 2, Republic of Ireland 1, Sweden 20, Switzerland 9, West Germany 42; and 24 members of the European Parliament (Belgium 3, France 9, Italy 3, Portugal 1, West Germany 8).

Greenpeace international environmental pressure group, founded 1971, with a policy of nonviolent direct action backed by scientific research. During a protest against French atmospheric nuclear testing in the S Pacific 1985, its ship *Rainbow Warrior* was sunk by French intelligence agents, killing a crew member.

green revolution in agriculture, a popular term (coined by ◊Borlaug) for the change in methods of arable farming in developing countries. The intent is to provide more and better food for their populations, albeit with a heavy reliance on chemicals and machinery. It was instigated in the 1940s and 1950s, but abandoned by some countries in the 1980s.

Measures include the increased use of tractors and other machines, artificial fertilizers and pesticides, as well as the breeding of new strains of crop plants (mainly rice, wheat, and corn) and farm animals. Much of the work is coordinated by the Food and Agriculture Organization of the United Nations.

The green revolution was initially successful in SE Asia; India doubled its wheat yield in 15 years, and the rice yield in the Philippines rose by 75%. However, yields have leveled off in many areas and some countries, which cannot afford the dams, fertilizers, and machinery required, have

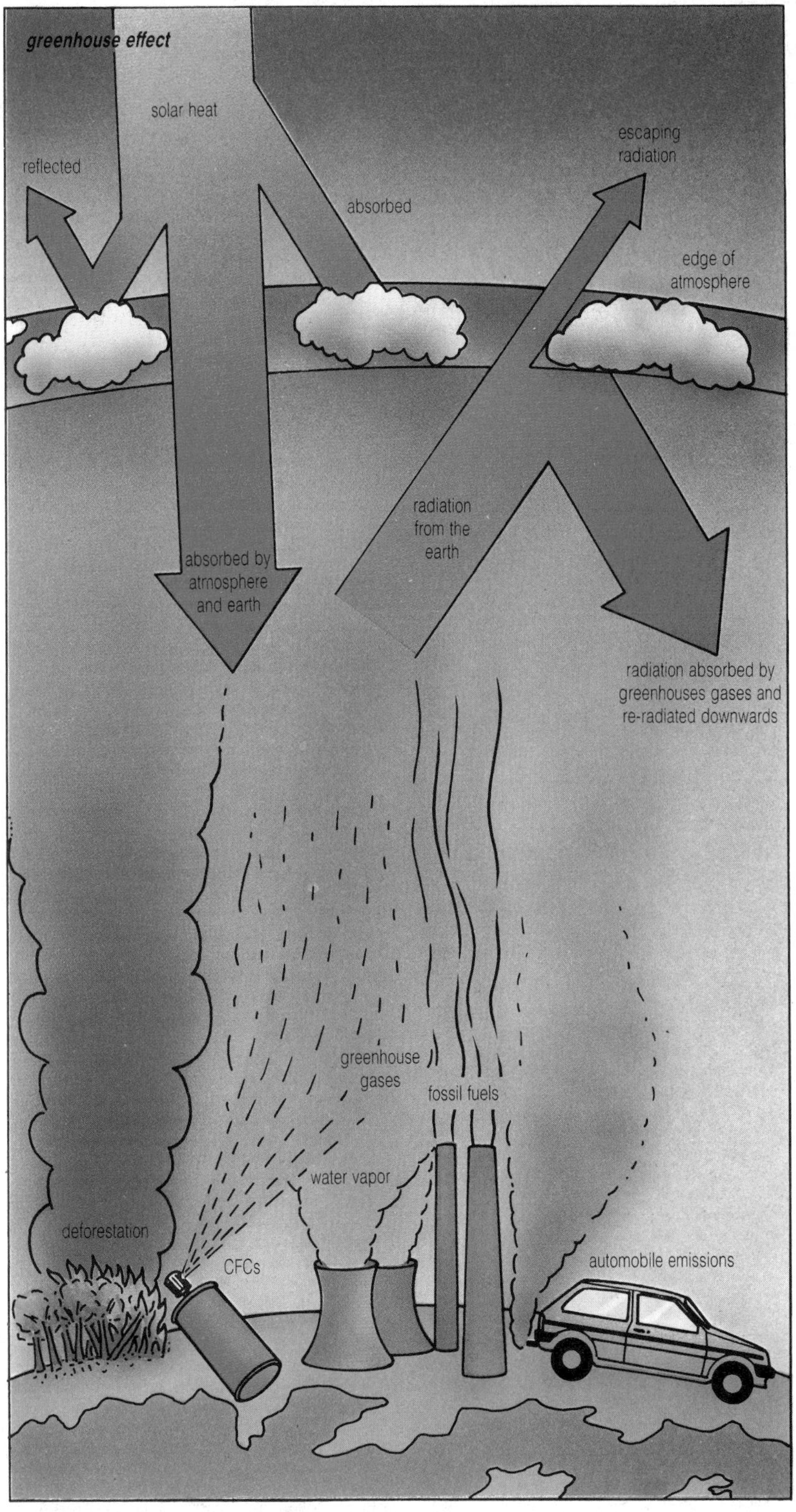
greenhouse effect
solar heat
reflected
absorbed
escaping radiation
edge of atmosphere
radiation from the earth
absorbed by atmosphere and earth
radiation absorbed by greenhouses gases and re-radiated downwards
greenhouse gases
fossil fuels
water vapor
deforestation
CFCs
automobile emissions

adopted ◊intermediate technologies. High-yield varieties of cereal plants require 154–198 lb/ 70–90 kg of nitrogen per hectare, more than is available to small farmers in developing countries. The rich farmers therefore enjoy bigger harvests, and the gap between rich and poor in the Third World has grown.

Greensboro city in N central North Carolina, W of Durham; seat of Guilford County. It is noted for its textile, chemical, and tobacco industries. Many schools are located here, including Guilford College 1834 and the University of North Carolina at Greensboro 1891; population (1990) 183,521. The Battle of Guilford Courthouse 1781 was fought nearby.

greenshank greyish shorebird *Tringa nebularia* of the sandpiper group. It has long olive-green legs and a slightly upturned bill. It breeds in N Europe and regularly migrates through the Aleutian Islands.

Greenspan Alan 1926– . US economist, who succeeded Paul ◊Volcker as head of the ◊Federal Reserve Board in 1987 and successfully pumped liquidity into the market to avert a sudden "free-fall" into recession after the stock market crash of Oct 1987.

Born in New York City and educated at Columbia University, he served as economics adviser and member of a variety of "task forces" under Republican Presidents Nixon, Ford, and Reagan.

Greenstreet Sidney 1879–1954. British character actor. He made an impressive film debut in *The Maltese Falcon* 1941 and became one of the best-known villains. His other films included *Casablanca* 1943 and *The Mask of Dimitrios* 1944.

Greenville city in NW South Carolina, on the Reedy River, near the foothills of the Blue Ridge Mountains, SW of Spartanburg; seat of Greenville County. It is known as a major textile manufacturing center. Other industries include lumber and chemicals; population (1990) 44,972.

Greenwich inner borough of Greater London, England; population (1981) 212,001.

Greenwich landmarks include the Queen's House 1637, designed by Inigo Jones, the first Palladian-style building in England; the Royal Naval College, designed by Christopher Wren in 1694; the Royal Observatory (founded here in 1675). The source of Greenwich Mean Time has been moved, but the Greenwich meridian (0°) remains unchanged. The *Cutty Sark*, one of the great tea clippers, is preserved as a museum of sail.

Greenwich Mean Time (GMT) local time on the zero line of longitude (the Greenwich meridian), which passes through the Old Royal Observatory at Greenwich, London. It was replaced 1986 by coordinated universal time (UTC); see ◊time.

Greenwich Village section of New York's City's lower Manhattan, (from 14th Street south to Houston Street and from Broadway west to the Hudson river), which from the late 19th century became the bohemian and artistic fourth of the city and, despite expensive rentals, remains so.

More generally, the term suggests the spirit of avantgardism and political radicalism in US culture; it is variously associated with left-wing causes, sexual liberation, experimental art and theater, and new magazines and movements.

This attitude caused the renaming of the adjoining section of the Lower East Side, east of Broadway, now far more outrageous than "the Village," to be called the East Village.

Greer Germaine 1939– . Australian feminist, who became widely known on the publication of her book *The Female Eunuch* 1970. Later works include *The Obstacle Race* 1979, a study of contemporary women artists, and *Sex and Destiny: The Politics of Human Fertility* 1984. She is also a speaker and activist.

Gregorian chant any of a body of plainsong choral chants associated with Pope Gregory the Great (540–604), which became standard in the Roman Catholic Church.

Gregory Isabella Augusta (born Persse) 1852–1932. Irish playwright, associated with W B Yeats in creating the ◊Abbey Theatre, Dublin, 1904. Her plays include the comedy *Spreading the News* 1904 and the tragedy *Gaol Gate* 1906. Her journals 1916–30 were published 1946.

Gregory name of 16 popes, including:

Gregory I St, the Great c. 540–604. Pope from 590, who asserted Rome's supremacy and exercised almost imperial powers. In 596 he sent St ◊Augustine to England. He introduced the choral Gregorian chant into the liturgy. Feast day March 12.

Gregory VII or Hildebrand c. 1023–1085. Chief minister to several popes before his election to the papacy 1073. In 1077 he forced the Holy Roman emperor Henry IV to wait in the snow at Canossa for four days, dressed as a penitent, before receiving pardon. He was driven from Rome and died in exile. Feast day May 25.

He claimed power to depose kings, denied lay

Grenada

USA
ATLANTIC OCEAN
Mexico
Cuba
GRENADA
St George's
CARIBBEAN SEA
Trinidad & Tobago
Venezuela
PACIFIC OCEAN
0 miles 500
0 km 1000

area (including the Grenadines, notably Carriacou) 131 sq mi/340 sq km
capital St George's
cities Grenville, Hillsborough (Carriacou)
physical southernmost of the Windward Islands; mountainous
features Grand-Anse beach; Annandale Falls; the Great Pool volcanic crater
head of state Elizabeth II from 1974 represented by governor general
head of government Ben Jones from 1989
political system emergent democracy
political parties New National Party (NNP), centrist; Grenada United Labor Party (GULP), nationalist left-of-center
exports cocoa, nutmeg, bananas, mace
currency Caribbean dollar
population (1990 est) 84,000, 84% of black African descent; growth rate –0.2% p.a.
life expectancy 69
language English (official); some French patois spoken
religion Roman Catholic
literacy 85% (1985)
GDP $139 million (1987); $1,391 per head
chronology
1974 Independence achieved from Britain; Eric Gairy elected prime minister.
1979 Gairy removed in bloodless coup led by Maurice Bishop; constitution suspended and a people's revolutionary government established.
1982 Relations with the US and Britain deteriorated as ties with Cuba and the USSR strengthened. Bishop feared impending US invasion.
1983 After Bishop's attempt to improve relations with the US, he was overthrown by left-wing opponents. A coup established the Revolutionary Military Council (RMC), and Bishop and some of his colleagues were executed. The US invaded Grenada, accompanied by troops from other E Caribbean countries; RMC overthrown, 1974 constitution reinstated.
1984 The newly formed NNP won 14 of the 15 seats in the house of representatives and its leader, Herbert Blaize, became prime minister.
1989 Herbert Blaize lost leadership of NNP, remaining as head of government; he died and was succeeded by Ben Jones.

rights to make clerical appointments, and attempted to suppress simony (the buying and selling of church preferments) and to enforce clerical celibacy, making enemies with both rulers and the church.

Gregory XIII 1502–1585. Pope from 1572, who introduced the reformed Gregorian calendar, still in use, in which a century year is not a leap year unless it is divisible by 400.

Gregory of Tours, St 538–594. French Christian bishop of Tours from 573, author of a *History of the Franks*. Feast day Nov 17.

Grenada island country in the Caribbean, the southernmost of the Windward Islands

government The constitution, which dates from full independence in 1974, provides for a system modeled on that of Britain, with a resident governor general, representing the British monarch, as the formal head of state and a prime minister and cabinet drawn from and collectively responsible to parliament. Parliament consists of two chambers, a 15-member house of representatives, elected by universal suffrage, and a senate of 13, appointed by the governor general, seven on the advice of the prime minister, three on the advice of the leader of the opposition, and three after wider consultation.

history Prior to the arrival of Christopher ◊Columbus in 1498, Grenada was inhabited by ◊Carib Indians. The island was eventually colonized by France in 1650 and ceded to Britain in 1783. Grenada remained a British colony until 1958, when it joined the Federation of the West Indies until its dissolution in 1962. Internal self-government was achieved in 1967 and full independence within the ◊Commonwealth in 1974. The early political life of the nation was dominated by two figures: Eric Gairy, a trade-union leader who founded the Grenada United Labor Party (GULP) in 1950, and Herbert Blaize, of the Grenada National Party (GNP).

On independence in 1974, Gairy was elected prime minister. He was knighted in 1977, but his rule became increasingly autocratic and corrupt, and in 1979 he was replaced in a bloodless coup by the leader of the left-wing New Jewel Movement (NJM), Maurice Bishop. Bishop suspended the 1974 constitution, established a People's Revolutionary Government (PRG), and announced the formation of a people's consultative assembly to draft a new constitution. He promised a nonaligned foreign policy but became convinced that the US was involved in a plot to destabilize his administration; this was strongly denied.

Grenada's relations with Britain and the US deteriorated while links with Cuba and the USSR grew stronger. In 1983 Bishop tried to improve relations with the US and announced the appointment of a commission to draft a new constitution. His conciliatory attitude was opposed by the more left-wing members of his regime, resulting in a military coup, during which Bishop and three of his colleagues were executed.

A Revolutionary Military Council (RMC), led by General Hudson Austin, took control. In response to the outcry caused by the executions, Austin promised a return to civilian rule as soon as possible, but on Oct 25 about 1,900 US troops, accompanied by 300 from Jamaica and Barbados, invaded the island. It was not clear whether the invasion was in response to a request from the governor general or on the initiative of the Organization of Eastern Caribbean States (OECS); in any event, concerned that Grenada might become a Cuban base, the US agreed to take part. The RMC forces were defeated and Austin and his colleagues arrested.

In Nov the governor general appointed a nonpolitical interim council, and the 1974 constitution was reinstated. Several political parties emerged from hiding, including Eric Gairy's GULP and Herbert Blaize's GNP. After considerable maneuvering, an informal coalition of center and left-of-center parties resulted in the formation of the New National Party (NNP), led by Blaize. In the 1984 general election the NNP won 14 of the 15 seats in the house of representatives and Blaize became prime minister. The US withdrew most of its forces by the end of 1983 and the remainder by July 1985. In party elections Jan 1989, Blaize lost the leadership of the NNP to the public works minister Keith Mitchell. In Dec 1989 Blaize died and was succeeded by a close colleague, Ben Jones. Elections in 1990 brought Nicholas Braithwaite of the National Democratic Congress (NDC) to power.

grenadier another name for ◊***rattail***.

Grenadines chain of about 600 small islands in the Caribbean sea, part of the group known as the Windward Islands. They are divided between ◊St Vincent and ◊Grenada.

Grendel in the Old English epic poem ◊*Beowulf*, the male monster that the hero has to kill.

He is a giant, human in shape, a descendent of Cain, living in a murky pond with his mother, among other strange and vicious sea-beasts.

Grenoble alpine town in Rhône-Alpes region, SE France; population (1982) 159,500, conurbation 392,000. Industries include engineering, nuclear research, hydroelectric power, computers, technology, chemicals, plastics, and gloves. It was the birthplace of the novelist ◊Stendhal, commemorated by a museum, and the Beaux Arts gallery has a modern collection. There is a 12th–13th-century cathedral, a university 1339, and the Institut Laue-Langevin for nuclear research. The 1968 Winter Olympics were held here.

Grenville George 1712–1770. British Whig politician, prime minister and chancellor of the Exchequer 1763–65. His government prosecuted the Radical John ◊Wilkes in 1763, and passed the Stamp Act 1765 that precipitated the American War of Independence.

Grenville Richard 1542–1591. English naval commander and adventurer, renowned for his heroic death aboard his ship *The Revenge* when attacked by Spanish warships. Grenville fought in Hungary and Ireland 1566–69, and was knighted about 1577. In 1585 he commanded the expedition that founded Virginia, for his cousin Walter ◊Raleigh. From 1586 to 1588 he organized the defense of England against the Spanish Armada.

Grenville William Wyndham, Baron 1759–1834. British Whig politician, foreign secretary from 1791; he resigned along with Prime Minister Pitt the Younger in 1801 over George III's refusal to assent to Catholic emancipation. He headed the "All the Talents" coalition of 1806–07 that abolished the slave trade.

Gresham Thomas c. 1519–1579. English merchant financier who founded and paid for the Royal Exchange and propounded Gresham's Law: that "bad money tends to drive out good money from circulation."

Gretzky Wayne 1961– . Canadian ice-hockey center with the Edmonton Oilers 1979–88 and Los Angeles Kings 1988-, noted for his ability to make or assist in making goals. In 1989 he won the Hart Trophy as the National Hockey League's most valuable player of the season for the ninth time (1980–87, 1989).

Born in Brantford, Ontario, Gretzky played hockey from a very young age. He signed with the Edmonton Oilers 1979 at the age of 18. A prolific goal scorer, he scored a record 215 points in the 1981–82 season. He went on to lead his team to the championship twice (1985, 1988) and in 1984 established the record of scoring or assisting in a score in 51 consecutive games. Traded to the Los Angeles Kings 1988, he continued to lead the league in goal points and assists during most seasons, and in 1989 he broke the all-time scoring record of 1,850 points.

Greuze Jean Baptiste 1725–1805. French painter of sentimental narrative paintings, such as *The Bible Reading* 1755 (Louvre, Paris). His works were reproduced in engravings.

Grey Beryl 1927– . British ballerina. Prima ballerina with the Sadler's Wells Company 1942–57, she then danced internationally, and was artistic director of the London Festival Ballet 1968–79.

Grey Charles, 2nd Earl 1764–1845. British Whig

politician. He entered Parliament 1786, and in 1806 became First Lord of the Admiralty, and foreign secretary soon afterwards. As prime minister 1830–34, he carried the Great Reform Bill that reshaped the parliamentary representative system 1832 and the act abolishing slavery throughout the British Empire 1833.

Grey Henry, 3rd Earl 1802–1894. British politician, son of Charles Grey. He served under his father as undersecretary for the colonies 1830–33, resigning because the cabinet would not back the immediate emancipation of slaves; he was secretary of war 1835–39 and colonial secretary 1846–52.

He was unique among politicians of the period in maintaining that the colonies should be governed for their own benefit, not that of Britain, and in his policy of granting self-government wherever possible. Yet he advocated convict transportation and was opposed to Gladstone's Home Rule policy.

He granted self-government wherever possible. Yet he advocated transport of convicts to the colonies and opposed Gladstone's Home Rule policy.

Grey Lady Jane 1537–1554. Queen of England for ten days, July 9–19, 1553, the great-granddaughter of Henry VII. She was married 1553 to Lord Guildford Dudley (died 1554), son of the Duke of ◊Northumberland. Edward VI was persuaded by Northumberland to set aside the claims to the throne of his sisters Mary and Elizabeth. When Edward died on July 6 the same year, Jane reluctantly accepted the crown and was proclaimed queen four days later. Mary, although a Roman Catholic, had the support of the populace, and the Lord Mayor of London announced that she was queen July 19. Grey was executed on Tower Green.

Grey Zane 1875–1939. US author of Westerns, such as *Riders of the Purple Sage* 1912. He wrote more than 80 books and was primarily responsible for the creation of the Western as a literary genre.

greyhound ancient breed of dog, with a long narrow muzzle, slight build, and long legs, renowned for its swiftness, it is up to 2.5 ft/75 cm tall, and can exceed 40 mph/60 kph.

greyhound racing spectator sport, invented in 1919 in the US, that has a number of greyhounds pursuing a mechanical hare around a circular or oval track. It is popular in Great Britain and Australia, attracting much on- and off-track betting.

grid the network by which electricity is generated and distributed over a region or country. It contains many power stations and switching centers and allows, for example, high demand in one area to be met by surplus power generated in another. Britain has the world's largest grid system, with over 140 power stations able to supply up to 55,000 megawatts.

The term is also used for any grating system, as in a cattle grid for controlling the movement of livestock across roads, and a conductor in a storage battery or electron gun. In trigonometry, a grid is a network of uniformly spaced vertical and horizontal lines as used to locate points on a map or to construct a graph.

grievance procedure formal arrangements with an employer, usually operating through a trade union, for settling employees' grievances.

Grieg Edward Hagerup 1843–1907. Norwegian composer. Much of his music is small scale, particularly his songs, dances, sonatas, and piano works. Among his orchestral works are the *Piano Concerto* 1869 and the incidental music for Ibsen's *Peer Gynt* 1876.

griffin mythical monster, the supposed guardian of hidden treasure, with the body, tail, and hind legs of a lion, and the head, forelegs, and wings of an eagle.

Griffith US film director D W Griffith. He pioneered many of the techniques now commonly used in filmmaking.

Griffith D(avid) W(ark) 1875–1948. US film director, one of the most influential figures in the development of cinema as an art. He made hundreds of "one reelers" (12 min) 1908–13, in which he pioneered the techniques of masking, fade-out, flashback, crosscut, close-up, and long shot. After much experimentation with photography and new techniques came his masterpiece as a director, *The Birth of a Nation* 1915, a film about the aftermath of the Civil War and the origin of the Ku Klux Klan.

Other films include the epic *Intolerance* 1916, *Broken Blossoms* 1919, *Way Down East* 1920, *Orphans of the Storm* 1921, and *The Struggle* 1931. He was a cofounder of United Artists 1919. With the advent of sound, his silent films lost money, and he lived forgotten in Hollywood until his death.

griffon small breed of dog originating in Belgium; red, black, or black and tan in color and weighing up to 11 lb/5 kg. They are square-bodied and round-headed, and there are rough) and smooth-coated varieties.

griffon vulture Old World vulture *Gyps fulvus* of the family Accipitridae found in S Europe, W and Central Asia, and parts of Africa. It has a bald head with a neck ruff, and is 3.5 ft/1.1 m long with a wingspan of up to 2.7 m/9 ft.

Grignard François Auguste-Victor 1871–1935. French chemist. The so-called Grignard reagents (compounds containing a hydrocarbon radical, magnesium, and a halogen such as chlorine) found applications as some of the most versatile reagents in organic synthesis. Grignard shared the 1912 Nobel Prize for Chemistry for his work on organometallic compounds.

Grillparzer Franz 1791–1872. Austrian poet and dramatist. His plays include the tragedy *Die Ahnfrau/The Ancestress* 1817, the Classical *Sappho* 1818, and the trilogy *Das goldene Vliess/The Golden Fleece* 1821.

Born in Vienna, Grillparzer worked for the Austrian government service 1813–56. His historical tragedies *König Ottokars Glück und Ende/King Ottocar, His Rise and Fall* 1825 and *Ein treuer Diener seines Herrn/A True Servant of His Master* 1826 both involved him with the censor. There followed his two greatest dramas, *Des Meeres und der Liebe Wellen/The Waves of Sea and Love* 1831, returning to the Hellenic world, and *Der Traum, ein Leben/A Dream Is Life* 1834. He wrote a bitter cycle of poems *Tristia ex Ponto* 1835 after an unhappy love affair.

Grimm Jakob Ludwig Karl 1785–1863. German philologist who formulated ◊Grimm's Law and collaborated with his brother Wilhelm Karl (1786–1859) in the *Fairy Tales* 1812–14, based on collected folk tales. Jakob's main work was his *Deutsche Grammatick/German Grammar* 1819, the first historical treatment of the ◊Germanic languages.

Grimm's law in linguistics, the rule (formulated 1822 by Jacob Grimm) by which certain prehistoric sound changes have occurred in the consonants of Indo-European languages: for example Latin *p* became English and German *f*, as in *pater—father, Vater*.

Such correspondences show the kinship between various native English words and those borrowed from the Classical or Romance languages.

Grimsby fishing port in Humberside, England; population (1985) 95,000. It declined in the 1970s when Icelandic waters were closed to British fishing fleets.

Gris Juan 1887–1927. Spanish abstract painter, one of the earliest Cubists. He developed a distinctive geometrical style, often strongly colored. He experimented with paper collage and made designs for Diaghilev's Ballet Russes 1922–23.

Grisons French name for the Swiss canton of ◊Graubünden.

Griswold v Connecticut a US Supreme Court decision 1965 dealing with state bans on the use of birth control. Griswold, the state director of the Planned Parenthood League, was convicted under a Connecticut anticontraceptive law for giving medical advice about birth control to a married couple. The Court overturned the conviction on appeal, ruling that the law was an illegitimate imposition of state police power on marital privacy guaranteed by the 1st, 3rd, 5th, 9th, and 14th Amendments.

Grivas George 1898–1974. Greek Cypriot general who led the underground group EOKA's attempts to secure the union (Greek ◊*enosis*) of Cyprus with Greece.

Grodno industrial city in Byelorussia, USSR, on the Sozh river; population (1987) 263,000. Part of Lithuania from 1376, it passed to Poland 1596, Russia 1795, Poland 1920, and Russia 1939.

Gromyko Andrei 1909–1989. President of the USSR 1985–88. As ambassador to the US from 1943, he took part in the Tehran, Yalta, and Potsdam conferences; as United Nations representative 1946–49, he exercised the Soviet veto 26 times. He was foreign minister 1957–85. It was Gromyko who formally nominated Mikhail Gorbachev as Communist Party leader in 1985.

Groningen most northerly province of the Netherlands

area 907 sq mi/2,350 sq km

population (1989) 555,200

cities capital Groningen; Hoogezand-Sappemeer, Stadskanaal, Veendam, Delfzijl, Winschoten

products natural gas, arable crops, dairy produce, sheep, horses

physical Ems estuary, innermost W Fresian Islands

history under the power of the bishops of Utrecht from 1040, Groningen became a member of the Hanseatic League in 1284. Taken by Spain in 1580, it was recaptured by Maurice of Nassau in 1594.

grooming in biology, the use by an animal of teeth, tongue, feet, or beak to clean fur or feathers. Grooming also helps to spread essential oils for waterproofing. In many social species, notably monkeys and apes, grooming of other individuals is used to reinforce social relationships.

Gropius Walter Adolf 1883–1969. German architect who lived in the US from 1937. An early proponent of the international modern style defined by glass curtain walls, cubic blocks, and unsupported corners—for example, the Model Factory and Office Building at the 1914 Cologne Werkbund exhibition. He found the ◊Bauhaus at Wiemar 1919–28. From 1937 he was professor of architecture at Harvard. He founded The Architects

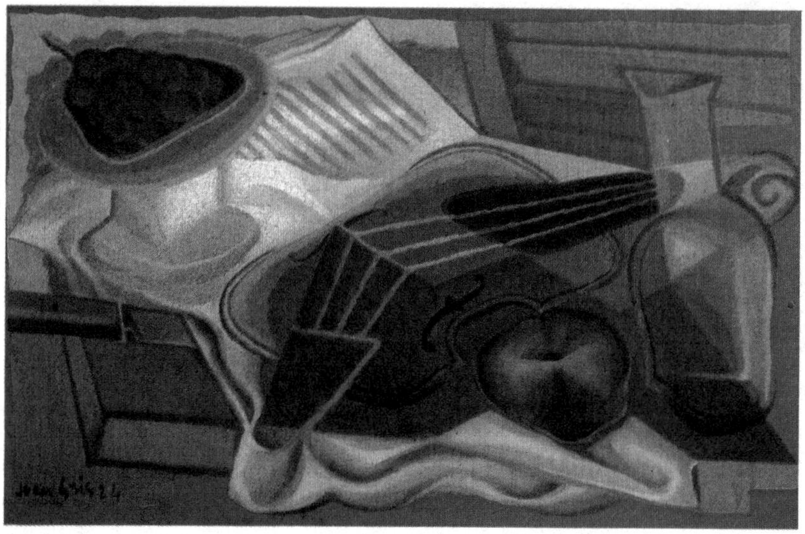

Gris *Spanish painter Juan Gris was an early Cubist. His* Violin and Fruit Dish *1924 hangs in London's Tate Gallery.*

HUGUES GROTIUS.

Grotius *A portrait of the 17th-century founder of international law Hugo Grotius by A Moro.*

Collaborative and urged teamwork in design, a product of which was the Harvard Graduate Center 1950.

grosbeak any of various thick-billed finches of the family Fringillidae. The pine grosbeak *Pinicola enucleator* breeds in Arctic forests. Its plumage is similar to that of the pine ◊crossbill.

gros point a type of embroidery, using wool to fill netting (see ◊petit point). It is normally used in colorful designs on widely spaced canvas.

Gross Domestic Product (GDP) a measure (normally annual) of the total domestic output of a country, including exports but not imports; see also ◊Gross National Product.

Grossglockner highest mountain in Austria, rising to 12,457 ft/3,797 m in the Hohe Tauern range of the Tirol alps.

Gross National Product (GNP) the most commonly used measurement of the wealth of a country. GNP is the ◊Gross Domestic Product plus income from abroad, minus income earned during the same period by foreign investors within the country; see also ◊national income.

Grosvenor Gilbert Hovey 1875–1966. US publisher. Born in Constantinople to missionary parents, Grosvenor was educated at Amherst College and named editor of *National Geographic Magazine* 1899. Its financial status was shaky, but Grosvenor soon transformed it to a mass circulation periodical through the use of color photography from 1910.

He also changed the parent body, the National Geographic Society, from a small scientific body to a national institution. As president of the Society 1920–54 and chairman of its directors 1954–66, Grosvenor sponsored scientific expeditions all over the world.

Grosz Georg 1893–1959. German Expressionist painter and illustrator, a founder of the Berlin group of the Dada movement 1918. Grosz exceled in savage satirical drawings criticizing the government and the military establishment. After numerous prosecutions he fled his native Berlin in 1932 and became a naturalized American in 1938.

Grosz Károly 1930– . Hungarian Communist politician, prime minister 1987–88. As leader of the ruling Hungarian Socialist Workers' Party (HSWP) 1988–89, he sought to establish a flexible system of "Socialist pluralism."

Grosz, a steelworker's son, was a printer and then a newspaper editor before moving to Budapest to serve as first deputy head and then head of the HSWP agitprop (agitation and propaganda) department 1968–79. He was Budapest party chief 1984–87 and briefly prime minister before succeeding János Kádár as HSWP leader in May 1988. In Oct 1989 the HSWP reconstituted itself as the Hungarian Socialist Party (HSP) and Grosz was replaced as party leader by the democrat Rezso Nyers.

Grotefend George Frederick 1775–1853. German scholar. Although a student of the Classical rather than the oriental languages, he nevertheless solved the riddle of the wedgelike ◊cuneiform script as used in ancient Persia: decipherment of Babylonian cuneiform followed from his work.

Grotius Hugo 1583–1645. Dutch jurist and politician, born in Delft. He became a lawyer, and later received political appointments. In 1618 he was arrested as a republican and sentenced to imprisonment for life. His wife contrived his escape in 1620, and he settled in France, where he composed the *De Jure Belli et Pacis/On the Law of War and Peace* 1625, the foundation of international law. He was Swedish ambassador in Paris 1634–45.

ground an electrical connection between an appliance and the ground, which becomes part of the circuit. In the event of a fault in an electrical appliance (for example, involving connection between the live part of the circuit and the outer casing) the current flows to earth, causing no harm to the user.

In most domestic installations, grounding is achieved by a connection to an underground metal water-supply pipe buried in the ground before it enters the premises.

Grosz *German painter Georg Grosz helped found the Dada movement in Berlin. His* Suicide *1916 is in the Tate Gallery, London.*

ground water the water formed underground in porous rock strata and soils and issuing as springs and streams. The ground-water table (or water table) is the boundary between two zones of rock or soil. Below the water table the pores are completely filled with water (called the saturated zone); above the water table is an unsaturated zone. Sandy or other kinds of beds that are filled with ground water are called aquifers. Most ground water near the surface moves slowly through the ground while the water table stays in the same place. The depth of the water table reflects the balance between the rate of infiltration, called recharge, and the rate of discharge at springs or rivers or pumped water wells. The force of gravity makes underground water run "downhill" underground just as it does above the surface. The greater the slope and the permeability, the greater the speed. Velocities vary from 40 in/100 cm per day to 0.2 in/0.5 cm.

Ground-water supplies vary from region to region depending on recharge rates and well use. Some areas such as W Texas and Oklahoma are in danger of depleting their ground-water supplies. In other areas, such as Long Island and New Jersey, overpumping has led to the encroachment of sea water into continental aquifers. Overall, however, the amount of usable fresh water in the ground is enormous. Recent estimates are that usable ground water amounts to more than 90% of all the fresh water on Earth, however, keeping such supplies free of pollutants entering the recharge areas is a critical environmental concern.

group in mathematics, a nonempty set of elements G, finite or infinite, that can be combined by a binary operation $*$, provided the following four conditions are satisfied: (i)G contains a unique identity element e for $G*$ (for any element a in G, $a * e = e * a = a$); (ii) within G, each element has a unique inverse element d (for any element a in G, $d * a = a * d = e$, the identity element); and (ii) $G*$ is associative (for any three, distinct or nondistinct, elements a, b and c in G, $a * (b * c) = (a * b) * c$).

Group Areas Act in South Africa, an Act of 1950, under which the different races in South Africa were assigned to separate areas. Demonstrations and interracial riots resulted from such measures of segregation.

grouper any of several species of large sea bass, especially the genera *Mycteroperca* and *Epinephelus*, found in warm waters.

group theory in mathematics, the study of the structure and applications of sets that form groups.

grouse a fowllike game bird of the subfamily Tetraonidae, in the pheasant family, Phasianidae. The subfamily also includes quail, ptarmigan, and prairie chicken. Grouse are native to North America and N Europe. They are mostly ground-living. During the mating season the males undertake elaborate courtship displays in small individual territories (◊leks).

Among the most familiar are the ruffed grouse *Bonasa umbellus*, common in woods in N and E North America, and the blue grouse *Dendragapus obscurus* of W North America.

Grove City v Bell a US Supreme Court decision 1984 dealing with sexual discrimination in publicly-funded schools. Grove City College, a private school in Pennsylvania, refused to comply officially with laws prohibiting sex discrimination. Although as a whole it was not a direct recipient of federal funds, certain programs in the school received federal scholarship money. The government moved to withhold funds from Grove City under the Education Amendments 1972. On appeal, the Court ruled 6–3 that restrictions on sex discrimination could be applied only to programs and not to the school as a whole; federal action was to be taken only on a "program-specific" basis.

growth the increase in size and weight during the development of an organism. Growth is an increase in biomass (mass of organic material, excluding water) and is associated with cell division.

All organisms grow, although the rate of growth varies over a lifetime. Typically, an organism shows an S-shaped curve, in which growth is at first slow, then fast, then, toward the end of life, nonexistent. Growth may even be negative during the period before death, with decay occurring faster than cellular replacement.

Grozny capital of the Checheno-Ingush republic, USSR; population (1987) 404,000. It is an oil-producing center.

GRP (abbreviation for glass-reinforced plastic) plastic material strengthened by fibreglass, usually erroneously known as ◊fibreglass. GRP is a favored material for boat hulls and the bodies and some structural components of performance automobiles; it is used in the manufacture of passenger cars.

Products are usually molded, mats of glass fiber being sandwiched between layers of a polyester plastic, which sets hard when mixed with a curing agent.

Grünewald (Mathias Gothardt/Neithardt) c. 1475–1528. German painter, active in Mainz, Frankfurt, and Halle. He was court painter, architect, and engineer to the archbishop of Mainz 1508–14. His few surviving paintings show an intense involvement with religious subjects.

The *Isenheim altarpiece* 1515 (Colmar Museum, France), with its tortured figure of Jesus, recalls medieval traditions.

Gruyère district in W Switzerland, famous for pale yellow cheese with large holes.

G scale scale for measuring force by comparing it with the force due to ◊gravity, *g*. Astronauts in the Space Shuttle experience over 3 *g* on liftoff.

GU abbreviation for Guam.

Guadalajara industrial (textiles, glass, soap, pottery) capital of Jalisco state, W Mexico; population (1986) 2,587,000. It is a key communications center. It has a 16th–17th-century cathedral, the Governor's Palace, and an orphanage with murals by the Mexican painter José Orozco.

Guadalcanal largest of the ◊Solomon Islands; area 2,510 sq mi/6,500 sq km; population (1987) 71,000. Gold, copra, and rubber are produced. During World War II it was the scene of a battle that was won by US forces after six months of fighting.

Guadeloupe an island group in the Leeward Islands, West Indies, an overseas *département* of France; area 658 sq mi/1,705 sq km; population (1982) 328,400. The main islands are Basse-Terre, on which is the chief town of the same name, and Grande-Terre. Sugar refining and rum distilling are the main industries.

Guam largest of the ◊Mariana Islands in the W Pacific, an unincorporated territory of the US
area 208 sq mi/540 sq km
capital Agaña
cities Apra (port)
features major US air and naval base, much used in the Vietnam war; tropical, with much rain
products sweet potatoes, fish; tourism is important
population (1984) 116,000
language English, Chamorro (basically Malay-Polynesian)
religion 96% Roman Catholic
government popularly elected governor (Ricardo Bordallo from 1985) and single-chamber legislature
recent history ceded by Spain to the US 1898; occupied by Japan 1941–44. It was granted full US citizenship and self-government from 1950. A referendum 1982 favored commonwealth status.

guan any of several large, pheasantlike birds of the family Cracidae, living in the forests of South and Central America. They are olive-green or brown.

guanaco hoofed ruminant *Lama guanacoe* of the camel family, found in South America on pampas and mountain plateaus. It grows to 4 ft/1.2 m at the shoulder, with head and body about 5 ft/1.5 m long. It is sandy-brown in color, with a blackish face, and has fine wool. It lives in small herds and is the ancestor of the domestic llama and alpaca.

Guangdong or Kwantung province of S China
area 89,320 sq mi/231,400 sq km
capital ◊Guangzhou
features tropical climate; Hainan, Leizhou peninsula, and the foreign enclaves of Hong Kong and Macao in the Pearl river delta
products rice, sugar, tobacco, minerals, fish
population (1986) 63,640,000.

Guangxi or ***Kwangsi Chuang*** autonomous region in S China
area 85,074 sq mi/220,400 sq km
capital Nanning
products rice, sugar, fruit
population (1986) 39,460,000; including the Zhuang people, allied to the Thai, who form China's largest ethnic minority.

Guangzhou or ***Kwangchow/Canton*** capital of Guangdong province, S China; population (1986) 3,290,000. Its industries include shipbuilding, engineering, chemicals, and textiles.

Sun Yat-sen Memorial Hall, a theater, commemorates the politician, who was born nearby and founded the university. There is a rail link with Beijing, and one is planned with Liuzhai.
history It was the first Chinese port opened to foreign trade, the Portuguese visiting it in 1516, and was a treaty port from 1842 until its occupation by Japan 1938.

Guantanamo capital of a province of the same name in SE Cuba; population (1986) 174,400; a trading center in a fertile agricultural region producing sugar. Iron, copper, chromium, and manganese are mined nearby. There is a US naval base.

Guanyin in Chinese Buddhism, the goddess of mercy. In Japan she is Kwannon or Kannon, an attendant of the Amida Buddha (Amitābha). Her origins were in India as the male bodhisattva Avalokiteśvara.

guarana Brazilian woody climbing plant *Paullinia cupana*, family Sapindaceae. A drink made from its roasted seeds has a high caffeine content, and it is the source of the drug known as zoom in the US. Starch, gum, and several oils are extracted from it for commercial use.

Guaraní a member of a South American Indian people who lived in the area that is now Paraguay, S Brazil, and Bolivia. About 1 million speak Guaraní, a member of the Tupian language group. Few retain the traditional ways of hunting the tropical forest, cultivation, and ritual warfare.

guard cell in plants, a specialized cell on the undersurface of leaves for controlling gas exchange and water loss. Guard cells occur in pairs and are shaped so that a pore, or ◊stomata, exists between them. They can change shape with the result that the pore disappears. During warm weather, when a plant is in danger of losing excessive water, the guard cells close, cutting down evaporation from the interior of the leaf.

Guardi Francesco 1712–1793. Italian painter. His souvenir views of Venice were commercially less successful than Canaletto's but are now considered more atmospheric, with subtler use of reflected light.

Guare John 1938– . US playwright who is particularly known for his screenplay for Louis Malle's *Atlantic City* 1980. His stage plays include *House*

Guangxi *The limestone hills near Guilin in the Chinese province of Guangxi. In the foreground is a houseboat on the river Li.*

Guatemala
Republic of
(República de Guatemala)

USA
Mexico
GUATEMALA
ATLANTIC OCEAN
Cuba
Belize
CARIBBEAN SEA
Guatemala City
El Salvador
Honduras
PACIFIC OCEAN
0 miles 500
0 km 1000

area 42,031 sq mi/108,889 sq km
capital Guatemala City
cities Quezaltenango, Puerto Barrios (naval base)
physical mountainous; narrow coastal plains; limestone tropical plateau in N; frequent earthquakes
features Mayan archeological remains, including site at Tikal
head of state and government Jorge Serrano Elias from 1991
political system democratic republic
political parties Guatemalan Christian Democratic Party (PDCG), Christian center-left; Centre Party (UCN), centrist; National Democratic Cooperation Party (PDNC), center-right; Revolutionary Party (PR), radical; Movement of National Liberation (MLN), extreme right-wing; Democratic Institutional Party (PID), moderate conservative
exports coffee, bananas, cotton, sugar, beef
currency quetzal
population (1990 est) 9,340,000 (Mayaquiche Indians 54%, mestizos 42%); growth rate 2.8% p.a. (87% of under-fives suffer from malnutrition)
life expectancy men 57, women 61
language Spanish (official); 40% speak 18 Indian dialects
religion Roman Catholic
literacy men 63%/women 47% (1985 est)
GDP $7 bn (1987); $834 per head
chronology
1839 Independence achieved from Spain.
1954 Col Carlos Castillo became president in US-backed coup, halting land reform.
1963 Military coup made Col Enrique Peralta president.
1966 Cesar Méndez elected president.
1970 Carlos Araña elected president.
1974 Gen Kjell Laugerud became president. Widespread political violence.
1978 Gen Fernando Romeo became president.
1981 Growth of antigovernment guerrilla movement.
1982 Gen Angel Anibal became president. Army coup installed Gen Ríos Montt as head of junta and then as president; political violence continued.
1983 Montt removed in coup led by Gen Mejía Victores, who declared amnesty for the guerrillas.
1985 New constitution adopted; PDCG won congressional elections; Vinicio Cerezo elected president.
1989 Coup attempt against Cerezo foiled. Over 100,000 people killed, and 40,000 reported missing since 1979.
1991 Jorge Serrano Elias of the Solidarity Action Movement (MAS) elected president.

of Blue Leaves 1971 and *Six Degrees of Separation* 1990.

Guareschi Giovanni 1909–1968. Italian author of short stories featuring the friendly feud between parish priest Don Camillo and the Communist village mayor.

Guarneri celebrated family of stringed-instrument makers of Cremona, Italy. The one known as Giuseppe "del Gesù" (1698–1744) produced the finest models.

Guatemala country in Central America, bounded N and NW by Mexico, E by Belize and the Caribbean Sea, SE by Honduras and El Salvador, and SW by the Pacific Ocean

government The 1985 constitution provides for a single-chamber national assembly of 100 deputies, 75 elected directly by universal suffrage and the rest on the basis of proportional representation; they serve a five-year term. The president, also directly elected for a similar term, appoints a cabinet and is assisted by a vice-president, and is not eligible for re-election. There is a multiplicity of political parties, the most significant being the Guatemalan Christian Democratic Party (PDCG), the Centre Party (UCN), the National Democratic Co-operation Party (PDCN), the Revolutionary Party (PR), the Movement of National Liberation (MLN), and the Democratic Institutional Party (PID).

history Formerly part of the ◊Maya empire, Guatemala became a Spanish colony 1524. Independent from Spain 1821, it then joined Mexico, becoming independent 1823. It was part of the ◊Central American Federation 1823–39 and was then ruled by a succession of dictators until the presidency of Juan José Arévalo 1944 and his successor, Col Jacobo Arbenz. Their Socialist administrations both followed programs of reform, including land appropriation, but Arbenz's nationalization of the United Fruit Company's plantations 1954 so alarmed the US government that it sponsored a revolution, led by Col Carlos Castillo Armas, who then assumed the presidency. He was assassinated 1963, and the army continued to rule until 1966. There was a brief return to constitutional government until the military returned 1970.

The next ten years saw much political violence, in which it was estimated that over 50,000 people died. In the 1982 presidential election the government candidate won, but opponents complained that the election had been rigged, and before he could take office there was a coup by a group of young right-wing officers, who installed General Rios Montt as head of a three-man junta. He soon dissolved the junta, assumed the presidency, and began fighting corruption and ending violence.

The antigovernment guerrilla movement was, however, growing and was countered by repressive measures by Montt, so that by 1983 opposition to him was widespread. After several unsuccessful attempts to remove him, a coup led by General Mejia Victores finally succeeded. Mejia Victores declared an amnesty for the guerrillas, the ending of press censorship, and the preparation of a new constitution. The latter was adopted 1985, and in the elections which followed the PDCG won a majority in the congress as well as the presidency, with Vinicio Cerezo becoming president. In 1989 an attempted coup against Cerezo was put down by the army.

The army, funded and trained by the US, destroyed 662 rural villages and killed more than 100,000 civilians since 1978, and 40,000 people disappeared between 1980 and 1989. From Jan to Nov 1989 almost 2,000 people were killed and 840 disappeared (representing a six-fold increase over the same period in the preceding year); in the first three months of 1990, there were 43 extrajudicial executions and 12 disappearances. Domestic turbulence continued through the 1990–91 election campaign, won by Jorge Serrano, an alley of Montt, in a Jan 1991 runoff.

Guatemala City capital of Guatemala; population (1983) 1,300,000. It produces textiles, tires, footwear, and cement. It was founded in 1776 when its predecessor (Antigua) was destroyed in an earthquake. It was severely damaged by another earthquake 1976.

guava tropical American tree *Psidium guajava* of the myrtle family Myrtaceae; the astringent yellow pear-shaped fruit is used to make guava jelly, or it can be stewed or canned. It has a high vitamin C content.

Guayaquil largest city and chief port of ◊Ecuador; population (1982) 1,300,868. The economic center of Ecuador, Guayaquil manufactures machinery and consumer goods, processes food, and refines petroleum. It was founded 1537 by the Spanish explorer Francisco de Orellana.

Guderian Heinz 1888–1954. German general in World War II. He created the Panzer (German "armor") divisions that formed the ground spearhead of Hitler's *Blitzkrieg* attack strategy, achieving a significant breakthrough at Sedan in Ardennes, France 1940, and leading the advance to Moscow 1941.

gudgeon any of an Old World genus *Gobio* of freshwater fishes of the carp family, especially *G. gobio* found in Europe and N Asia on the gravel bottoms of streams. It is olive-brown, spotted with black, and up to 8 in/20 cm long, and with a distinctive barbel (a sensory fleshy filament) at each side of the mouth.

guelder rose or ***snowball tree*** cultivated shrub or small tree *Viburnum opulus*, native to Europe and N Africa, with spherical clusters of white flowers and shiny red berries.

It is closely related to high-bush cranberry *V. trilobum* of North America.

Guelders another name for ◊Gelderland, a region of the Netherlands.

Guelph industrial town and agricultural center in SE Ontario, Canada, on the Speed River; population (1981) 71,250. Industries include food processing, electrical goods, and pharmaceuticals.

Guelph and Ghibelline rival parties in medieval Germany and Italy, which supported the papal party and the Holy Roman emperors respectively.

They originated in the 12th century as partisans of the rival German houses of Welf (hence Guelph or Guelf), dukes of Bavaria, and of the lords of ◊Hohenstaufen (whose castle at Waiblingen gave the Ghibellines their name), who struggled for the imperial crown after the death of Henry VI in 1197, until the Hohenstaufen dynasty died out in 1268. The Guelphs early became associated with the papacy because of their mutual Hohenstaufen enemy. In Italy, the terms were introduced about 1242, in Florence; the names seem to have been grafted on to pre-existing papal and imperial factions within the city-republics.

Guercino (Giovanni Francesco Barbieri) 1590–1666. Italian Baroque painter, active chiefly in Rome. In his ceiling painting of *Aurora* 1621–23 (Villa Ludovisi, Rome), the chariot-borne figure of dawn rides across the heavens, and the architectural framework is imitated in the painting, giving the illusion that the ceiling opens into the sky.

Guercino's use of dramatic lighting recalls ◊Caravaggio, but his brighter colors reflect a contrasting mood. His later works, produced when he had retired from Rome to Bologna, are closer in style to Guido ◊Reni.

Guérin Camille 1872–1961. French bacteriologist who, with ◊Calmette, developed the *bacille* Calmette-Guérin (◊BCG) vaccine for tuberculosis.

Guernica town in the ◊Basque provinces of Vizcaya, N Spain; population (1981) 18,000. It was where the Castilian kings formerly swore to respect the rights of the Basques. It was almost completely destroyed in 1937 by German bombers aiding Franco in the Spanish Civil War and rebuilt in

1946. The bombing inspired a painting by Picasso and a play by Fernando Arrabal.

Guernsey second largest of the ◊Channel Islands; area 24.3 sq mi/63 sq km; population (1986) 55,500. The capital is St Peter Port. From 1975 it has been a major financial center. Guernsey cattle originated here.

Products include electronics, tomatoes, flowers, and more recently butterflies. Guernsey cattle are a pale fawn color, and give rich creamy milk. Guernsey has belonged to the English Crown since 1066, but was occupied by German forces 1940–45.

guerrilla (Spanish: "little war") irregular soldier fighting in a small unofficial unit, typically against an established or occupying power, and engaging in sabotage, ambush, and the like, rather than pitched battles against an opposing army. Guerrilla tactics have been used both by resistance armies in wartime (for example, the Vietnam war) and in peacetime by national liberation groups and militant political extremists (for example, the ◊PLO; Tamil Tigers).

The term was first applied to the Spanish and Portuguese resistance to French occupation during the Peninsular war (1808–14). Guerrilla techniques were widely used against the Nazi occupying forces in World War II—for example, by the Resistance in France, Greece, and the Balkans. Political activists who resort to violence, particularly urban guerrillas, tend to be called "freedom fighters" by those who support their cause, "terrorists" by those who oppose it.

Recent efforts by postwar governments to put a stop to their activities have had only sporadic success. The Council of Europe has set up the European Convention on the Suppression of Terrorism, to which many governments are signatories. In the UK the Prevention of Terrorism Act 1984 is aimed particularly at the IRA. The Institute for the Study of Terrorism was founded in London 1986.

Violent activities (bombings, kidnappings, hijackings) by such groups as these have proliferated considerably in recent years; in 1984 there were 600 international incidents of politically motivated violence, a 20% increase on the average over the previous five years. Cooperation among the groups (for example in arms supply) has developed, as has state support (such as the US's for the Contras and Libya's for many groups, including the PLO and IRA).

Guest Edgar Albert 1881–1959. US journalist and poet. Leaving school at an early age, he worked in various jobs at the *Detroit Free Press* and from 1900 wrote "Breakfast Table Chat," a highly popular daily column of light verse and folksy wisdom, which later was syndicated nationally. Guest's best-selling collections of verse include *A Heap o' Livin'* 1916, *When Day Is Done 1921*, and *Harbor Lights of Home* 1928.

Born in Birmingham, England, Guest came to America 1891 with his parents, settling in Detroit, Michigan. From 1938 to 1942 he was the host of a popular weekly radio program.

Guevara "Che" Ernesto 1928–1967. Latin American revolutionary. He was born in Argentina and trained there as a doctor, but in 1953 left his homeland because of his opposition to the right-wing president Perón. In effecting the Cuban revolution of 1959, he was second only to Castro and Castro's brother Raúl. In 1965 he went to the Congo to fight against white mercenaries, and then to Bolivia, where he was killed in an unsuccessful attempt to lead a peasant rising. He was an orthodox Marxist, and renowned for his guerrilla techniques.

Guiana the NE part of South America, which includes ◊French Guiana, ◊Guyana, and ◊Suriname.

Guido Reni Italian painter, see ◊Reni.

Guienne ancient province of SW France which formed the duchy of Aquitaine with Gascony in the 12th century. Its capital was Bordeaux. It became English 1154 and passed to France 1453.

guild or gild medieval association, particularly of artisans or merchants, formed for mutual aid and protection and the pursuit of a common purpose, religious or economic. They became politically powerful in Europe. After the 16th century the position of the guilds was undermined by the growth of capitalism.

Guilds fulfilling charitable or religious functions, such as the maintenance of schools, roads, or bridges, the assistance of members in misfortune, or the provision of masses for the souls of dead members, flourished in western Europe from the 9th century, but were suppressed in Protestant countries at the Reformation.

The earliest form of economic guild, the guild merchant, arose during the 11th and 12th centuries; this was an organization of the traders of a town, who had been granted a practical monopoly of its trade by charter. As the merchants often strove to exclude craftworkers from the guild, and to monopolize control of local government, the craft guilds came into existence in the 12th and 13th centuries. These, which included journeymen (day workers) and apprentices as well as employers, regulated prices, wages, working conditions and apprenticeship, prevented unfair practices, and maintained high standards of craft; they also fulfilled many social, religious, and charitable functions. By the 14th century they had taken control of local government, ousting the guild merchant.

Guildford city in Surrey, S England, on the river Wey; population (1981) 56,500. It has a ruined Norman castle, a cathedral (1936–61), and the University of Surrey (1966). There is a cattle market, and industries include flour-milling, plastics, and engineering.

Guilin formerly Kweilin principal tourist city of S China, on the Li river, Guangxi province. The dramatic limestone mountains are a major attraction.

Guillaume Charles 1861–1938. Swiss physicist who studied measurement and alloy development. He discovered a nickel-steel alloy, invar, which showed negligible expansion with rising temperatures. Nobel Prize for Physics 1920.

As the son of a clockmaker, Guillaume came early in life to appreciate the value of precision in measurement. He spent most of his life at the International Bureau of Weights and Measures at Sèvres, which established the standards for the meter, liter, and kilogram.

guillemot diving seabird of the auk family that breeds in large numbers on rocky N Atlantic and Pacific coasts. The common guillemot *Uria aalge* has a sharp bill and short tail, and sooty-brown and white plumage. The black guillemot *Cepphus grylle* of N coasts is mostly black, with orange legs when breeding. Guillemots build no nest, but lay one large, almost conical egg on the rock.

guillotine beheading device consisting of a metal blade that descends between two posts. It was common in the Middle Ages but was introduced in an improved design (by physician Joseph Ignace Guillotin 1738–1814) for executions in France in 1792 during the Revolution. It is still in use in some countries.

Guinea country in W Africa, bounded N by Senegal, NE by Mali, SE by the Ivory Coast, SW by Liberia and Sierra Leone, W by the Atlantic, and NW by Guinea-Bissau

government The 1982 constitution, which provided for an elected national assembly, was suspended in 1984 after a military coup. A military committee for national recovery assumed power. The president is head of both state and government and leads an appointed council of ministers. The sole political party, the Democratic Party of Guinea (PDG), was dissolved after the coup, and opposition groups now operate from abroad.

history Formerly part of the Muslim ◊Mali empire, which flourished in the region between the 7th and 15th centuries. Guinea's first European visitors were the Portuguese in the mid-15th century, who, together with France and Britain, established the slave trade in the area. In 1849 France proclaimed the Boké region in the east a French protectorate and expanded its territory until by the late 19th century most of W Africa was united under French rule as ◊French West Africa.

French Guinea became fully independent in 1958, under the name of Guinea, after a referendum rejected a proposal to remain a self-governing colony within the French Community. The first president was Sekou Touré, who made the PDG the only political organization and embarked upon a policy of Socialist revolution. There were unsuccessful attempts to overthrow him in 1961, 1965, 1967, and 1970, and, suspicious of con-

Guinea
Republic of
(République de Guinée)

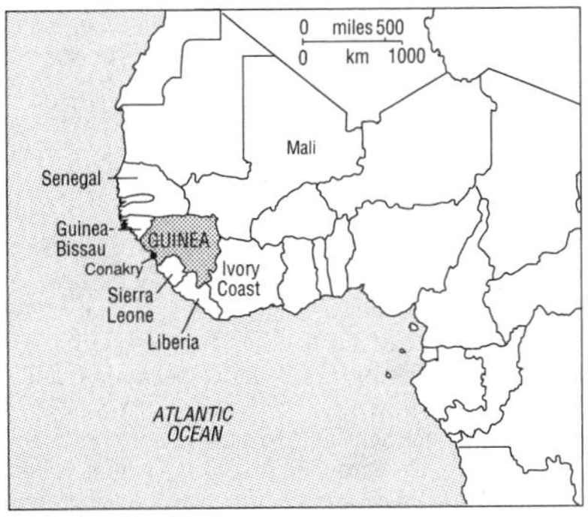
0 miles 500
0 km 1000
Mali
Senegal
Guinea-Bissau
GUINEA
Conakry
Ivory Coast
Sierra Leone
Liberia
ATLANTIC OCEAN

area 94,901 sq mi/245,857 sq km
capital Conakry
cities Labe, N'Zérékoré, Kankan
physical flat coastal plain with mountainous interior; sources of rivers Niger, Gambia, and Senegal; forest in SE
features Fouta Djallon, area of sandstone plateaus, cut by deep valleys
head of state and government Lansana Conté from 1984
political system military republic
political parties none since 1984
exports coffee, rice, palm kernels, alumina, bauxite, diamonds
currency syli or franc
population (1990 est) 7,269,000 (chief peoples are Fulani, Malinke, Susu); growth rate 2.3% p.a.
life expectancy men 39, women 42
language French (official), African languages spoken
religion Muslim 85%, Christian 10%, local 5%
literacy men 40%/women 17% (1985 est)
GNP $1.9 bn (1987); $369 per head
chronology
1958 Full independence achieved from France; Sékou Touré elected president.
1977 Strong opposition to Touré's rigid Marxist policies forced him to accept return to mixed economy.
1980 Touré returned unopposed for fourth seven-year term.
1984 Touré died. Bloodless coup established a military committee for national recovery, led by Col Lansana Conté.
1985 Attempted coup against Conté while he was out of the country was foiled by loyal troops.
1991 Antigovernment general strike.

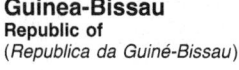

Guinea-Bissau
Republic of
(Republica da Guiné-Bissau)

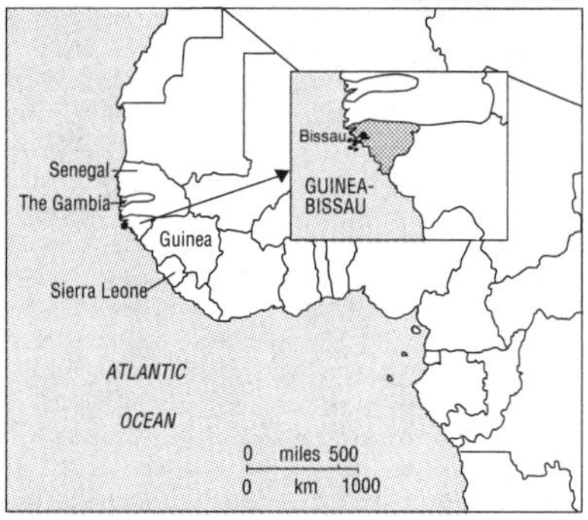
Bissau
GUINEA-BISSAU
Senegal
The Gambia
Guinea
Sierra Leone
ATLANTIC
OCEAN
0 miles 500
0 km 1000

area 13,944 sq mi/36,125 sq km
capital (and chief port) Bissau
cities Mansôa, São Domingos
physical flat coastal plain rising to savanna in E
features the archipelago of Bijagos
head of state and government João Bernardo Vieira from 1980
political system Socialist pluralist republic
political parties African Party for the Independence of Portuguese Guinea and Cape Verde (PAIGC), nationalist Socialist
exports rice, coconuts, peanuts, fish, timber
currency peso
population (1989 est) 929,000; growth rate 2.4% p.a.
life expectancy 42; 1990 infant mortality rate was 14.8%
language Portuguese (official), Crioulo (Cape Verdean dialect of Portuguese), African languages
religion Muslim 40%, Christian 4%
literacy men 46%/women 17% (1985 est)
GDP $135 million (1987); $146 per head
chronology
1956 PAIGC formed to secure independence from Portugal.
1973 Two-thirds of the country declared independent, with Luiz Cabral as president of a state council.
1974 Independence achieved from Portugal.
1980 Cape Verde decided not to join a unified state. Cabral deposed, and João Vieira became chair of a council of revolution.
1981 PAIGC confirmed as the only legal party, with Vieira as its secretary-general.
1982 Normal relations with Cape Verde restored.
1984 New constitution adopted, making Vieira head of government as well as head of state.
1989 Vieira reelected.
1991 Other parties legalized. Multiparty elections promised.

spiracies by foreign powers, he put his country into virtual diplomatic isolation. By 1975, however, relations with most of his neighbors had returned to normal.

At first rigidly Marxist, crushing all opposition to his policies, Touré gradually moved toward a mixed economy, with private enterprise becoming legal in 1979. His regime was nevertheless authoritarian and harsh. He sought closer relations with Western powers, particularly France and the US, and was re-elected unopposed in 1980. In 1984 he died while undergoing heart surgery in the US.

Before the normal machinery for electing his successor could be put into operation, the army staged a bloodless coup, suspending the constitution and setting up a military committee for national recovery, with Col Lansana Conté at its head. He pledged to restore democracy and respect human rights, releasing hundreds of political prisoners and lifting press restrictions. Conté then made efforts to restore his country's international standing through a series of overseas visits. He succeeded in persuading some 200,000 Guineans who had fled the country during the Touré regime to return. In 1985 an attempt to overthrow him while he was out of the country was foiled by loyal troops. In 1990 Guinea contributed troops to the multi-national force that attempted to stabilize Liberia.

Guinea-Bissau country in W Africa, bounded N by Senegal, E and SE by Guinea, and SW by the Atlantic

government Guinea-Bissau is a one-party state, the 1984 constitution describing the African Party for the Independence of Portuguese Guinea and Cape Verde (PAIGC) as "the leading force in society and in the nation." Although Cape Verde chose independence, the title of the original party that served the two countries was retained. The constitution provides for a 150-member national people's assembly, all nominees of PAIGC. The assembly elects the president, who is head of both state and government. Policy is determined by PAIGC, and it is there that ultimate political power lies, the president being its secretary general.

history Guinea-Bissau was first reached by Europeans when the Portuguese arrived in 1446 and it brecame a slave-trading center. Until 1879 it was administered with the Cape Verde Islands, but then became a separate colony under the name of Portuguese Guinea.

Nationalist groups began to form in the 1950s, and PAIGC was established in 1956. Portugal refused to grant independence, fighting broke out, and by 1972 PAIGC claimed to control two-thirds of the country. The following year the "liberated areas" were declared independent, and in 1973 a national people's assembly was set up and Luiz Cabral appointed president of a state council. Some 40,000 Portuguese troops were engaged in trying to put down the uprising and suffered heavy losses, but before a clear outcome was reached a coup in Portugal ended the fighting, and PAIGC negotiated independence with the new government in Lisbon.

In 1974 Portugal formally acknowledged Guinea-Bissau as a sovereign nation. PAIGC began to lay the foundations of a Socialist state, intended to include Cape Verde, but in 1980, four days before approval of the constitution, Cape Verde withdrew, feeling that Guinea-Bissau was being given preferential treatment. A coup deposed Cabral, and João Vieira became chair of a council of revolution.

At its 1981 congress, PAIGC decided to retain its name despite Cape Verde's withdrawal, and its position as the only party was confirmed, with Vieira as secretary general. Normal relations between the two countries were restored in 1982. In 1984 a new constitution made Vieira head of government as well as head of state. In June 1989 he was reelected for another five-year term.

Guinea Coast the coast of W Africa between Gambia and Cape Lopez.

guinea fowl chickenlike African bird of the family Numididae. The group includes the helmet guinea fowl *Numida meleagris*, which has a horny growth on the head, white-spotted feathers, and fleshy cheek wattles. It is the ancestor of the domestic guinea fowl.

guinea pig a species of ◊cavy, a type of rodent.

Guinevere Welsh ***Gwenhwyfar*** in British legend, the wife of King ◊Arthur. Her adulterous love affair with the knight ◊Lancelot of the Lake led ultimately to Arthur's death.

Guinness Irish brewing family who produced the dark, bitter beer of the same name. In 1752 Arthur Guinness (1725–1803) set up a brewery,

***Guinness** English actor Alec Guinness in his role as Smiley, the English intelligence operative.*

which was moved to Dublin 1759. The business grew under his son Arthur (1767–1855) and under Arthur's son Benjamin (1798–1868), who developed an export market in the US and Europe. In the 1980s the family interest in the business declined to 5% as the company expanded by taking over other beer and liquor-producing companies.

Guinness Alec 1914– . English actor. His many stage roles include Shakespeare's Hamlet 1938 and Lawrence of Arabia (in *Ross* 1960). In 1979 he gained a "lifetime achievement" Academy Award. His films include *Kind Hearts and Coronets* 1949, *The Bridge on the River Kwai* 1957, and *Star Wars* 1977.

Guise Francis, 2nd Duke of 1519–1563. French soldier and politician. He led the French victory over Germany at Metz 1552 and captured Calais from the English 1558. Along with his brother Charles (1527–1574), he was powerful in the government of France during the reign of Francis II. He was assassinated attempting to crush the ◊Huguenots.

Guise Henri, 3rd Duke of 1550–1588. French noble who persecuted the Huguenots and was partly responsible for the Massacre of ◊St Bartholomew 1572. He was assassinated.

guitar six-stringed, flat-bodied musical instrument, plucked or strummed with the fingers. The Hawaiian guitar, laid across the lap, uses a metal bar to produce a distinctive gliding tone; the solid-bodied electric guitar, developed in the 1950s, mixes and amplifies vibrations from microphone contacts at different points to produce a range of tone qualities.

Derived from a Moorish original, the guitar spread throughout Europe in medieval times, becoming firmly established in Italy, Spain, and the Spanish American colonies. Its 20th-century revival owes much to Andrés ◊Segovia, Julian ◊Bream, and John ◊Williams. The guitar's prominence in US popular music can be traced from the country traditions of the mid-West; it played a supporting harmony role in jazz and dance bands during the 1920s and adapted quickly to electric amplification.

Guiyang or ***Kweiyang*** capital and industrial city of Guizhou province, S China; population (1986) 1,380,000. Industries include metals and machinery.

Guizhou or ***Kweichow*** province of S China
area 67,164 sq mi/174,000 sq km
capital Guiyang
products rice, corn, nonferrous minerals

population (1986) 30,080,000; including many minority groups that have often been in revolt.

Guizot François Pierre Guillaume 1787–1874. French politician and historian, professor of modern history at the Sorbonne, Paris, 1812–30. He wrote histories of French and European culture and became prime minister in 1847. His resistance to all reforms led to the ◊revolution of 1848.

Gujarat state of W India
area 75,656 sq mi/196,000 sq km
capital Ahmedabad
features heavily industrialized; includes most of the Rann of Kutch; the Gir Forest (the last home of the wild Asian lion)
products cotton, petrochemicals, oil, gas, rice, textiles
population (1984) 33,961,000
language Gujarati, Hindi.

Gujarati inhabitant of Gujarat on the NW coast of India. The Gujaratis number approximately 30 million and speak their own Indo-European language, Gujurati, which has a long literary tradition. They are predominantly Hindu (90%), with Muslim (8%) and Jain (2%) minorities.

Gujarati language member of the Indo-Iranian branch of the Indo-European language family, spoken in and around the state of Gujarat in W India. It is written in its own script, a variant of the Devanagari script used for Sanskrit and Hindi.

Gujranwala city in Punjab province, Pakistan; population (1981) 597,000. It is a center of grain trading. It is a former Sikh capital and the birthplace of Sikh leader Ranjit Singh (1780–1839).

gulag Russian term for the system of prisons and labor camps used to silence dissidents and opponents of the Soviet regime.

In the Stalin era, thousands of prisoners died from the harsh conditions of these remote camps.

Gulfport city in SE Mississippi, on the Gulf of Mexico, W of Biloxi and E of New Orleans, Louisiana; seat of Harrison County and a port of entry to the US. It is a major shipping point for lumber, cotton, and food products; population (1990) 40,775.

Gulf States oil-rich countries sharing the coastline of the ◊Persian Gulf (Bahrain, Iran, Iraq, Kuwait, Oman, Qatar, Saudi Arabia, and the United Arab Emirates). In the US, the term refers to those states bordering the Gulf of Mexico (Alabama, Florida, Louisiana, Mississippi, and Texas).

Gulf Stream ocean ◊current branching from the warm waters of the equatorial current, which flows N from the Gulf of Mexico. It slows to a widening "drift" off Newfoundland, splitting as it flows E across the Atlantic, and warms what would otherwise be a colder climate in the British Isles and Western Europe.

Gulf War hostilities between the United Nations Security Forces and Iraq. In Aug 1990, Saddam Hussein's Iraqi troops invaded and annexed neighboring Kuwait. Resolutions made by the UN Security Council for his immediate withdrawal went unheeded and, in response to requests for help from King Fahd of Saudi Arabia, a large multinational force was assembled near the Saudi-Kuwait border. Efforts to avert war by negotiation and the enforcement of sanctions were unsuccessful and war began soon after Iraq's failure to respond to the UN deadline for withdrawal by Jan 15, 1991.

Within 24 hours of the deadline, American and allied forces launched massive air bombardments against Baghdad, hitting strategic targets such as military air bases and communications systems. Saddam Hussein replied by launching Scud missiles against the Israeli cities of Tel Aviv and Haifa (by which tactic he hoped to bring Israel into the war and thus break up the Arab alliance against him), as well as cities in Saudi Arabia.

On Feb 23, UN forces launched a ground assault against the Iraqis. Its overwhelming force soon broke the Iraqis, who agreed to a cease-fire Feb 28, after suffering perhaps 100,000 casualties. In April, Iraq accepted the UN's permanent cease-fire terms. Kuwait was devastated by the war, and the departing Iraqis set fire to more than 600 oil wells.

The Gulf diplomatic crisis accelerated when Iraq annexed Kuwait and moved Iraqi troops toward the Saudi Arabian border. King Fahd sought direct help from the US and UK and alerted the UN Security Council, which demanded Iraq's total withdrawal and imposed a total trade ban on Iraq. Meanwhile a build-up of a multinational force took place in Saudi Arabia as efforts were made to find a peaceful solution. In Dec 1990 the UN Security Council authorized the use of force after the deadline of Jan 15, 1991. With the failure of last-ditch peace initiatives by the UN and France war became inevitable.

It is also another name for the ◊Iran–Iraq War.

gull seabird of the family Laridae, especially the genus *Larus*. Gulls are usually 10–30 in/25–75 cm long, white with gray or black on the back and wings, and have large beaks.

The common black-headed gull *L. ridibundus*, common on both sides of the Atlantic, is gray and white with (in summer) dark brown head and red beak; it breeds in large colonies on wetlands, making a nest of dead rushes. It lays, on average, three eggs. The great black-headed gull *L. ichthyaetus* is native to Asia. The larger laughing gull and herring gull *L. argentatus* live in North America. The latter has white and pearl-gray plumage and a yellow beak. The oceanic great black-backed gull *L. marinus*, found in the Atlantic, is over 75 cm/2.5 ft long.

Gulliver's Travels satirical novel by the Irish writer Jonathan ◊Swift published 1726. The four countries visited by the narrator Gulliver ridicule different aspects of human nature, customs, and politics.

gum complex polysaccharides (carbohydrates) formed by many plants and trees, particularly by those from dry regions. They form four main groups: plant exudates (gum arabic); marine plant extracts (agar); seed extracts; and fruit and vegetable extracts. Some are made synthetically.

Gums are tasteless and odorless, insoluble in alcohol and ether but generally soluble in water. They are used for adhesives, fabric sizing, in confectionery, medicine, and calico printing. Gum is also a common name for the ◊eucalyptus tree.

gum in mammals, the soft tissues surrounding the base of the teeth. Gums are liable to inflammation (gingivitis) or to infection by microbes from food deposits (periodontal disease).

gum arabic substance obtained from certain species of ◊acacia, with uses in medicine, confectionery, and adhesive manufacture.

gun general name for any kind of firearm or any instrument consisting of a metal tube from which a projectile is discharged; see also ◊artillery, ◊machine gun, ◊pistol, and ◊small arms.

gun metal type of ◊bronze, an alloy high in copper (88%), also containing tin and zinc, so called because it was once used to cast cannons. It is tough, hard-wearing, and resists corrosion.

gunpowder or ***black powder*** the oldest known ◊explosive, a mixture of 75% potassium nitrate (saltpeter), 15% charcoal, and 10% sulfur. Sulfur ignites at a low temperature, charcoal burns readily, and the potassium nitrate provides oxygen for the explosion. Although progressively replaced since the late 19th century by high explosives, gunpowder is still widely used for quarry blasting, fuses, and fireworks.

Gunpowder Plot in British history, the Catholic conspiracy to blow up James I and his parliament on Nov 5, 1605. It was discovered through an anonymous letter. Guy ◊Fawkes was found in the cellar beneath the Palace of Westminster, ready to fire a store of explosives. Several of the conspirators were killed, and Fawkes and seven others were executed.

The event is commemorated annually in England on Nov 5 by fireworks and burning "guys" on bonfires. The searching of the vaults of Parliament before the opening of each new session, however, was not instituted until the "Popish Plot" of 1678.

Gunter Edmund 1581–1626. English mathematician who became professor of astronomy at Gresham College, London, in 1619. He is reputed to have invented a number of surveying instruments as well as the trigonometrical terms "cosine" and "cotangent."

Guomindang Chinese National People's Party, founded 1894 by ◊Sun Yat-sen (Sun Zhong Shan), which overthrew the Manchu Empire 1912. By 1927 the right wing, led by ◊Chiang Kai-shek (Jiang Jie Shi), was in conflict with the left, led by Mao Zedong until the Communist victory 1949 (except for the period of the Japanese invasion 1937–45). It survives as the sole political party of Taiwan, where it is still spelled Kuomintang.

Gurdjieff George Ivanovitch 1877–1949. Russian occultist and mystic who influenced the modern human-potential movement. His famous text is *Meetings with Remarkable Men* (Eng. trans. 1963). The mystic ◊Ouspensky was a disciple who expanded his ideas.

After years of wandering in central Asia, in 1912 Gurdjieff founded in Moscow the Institute for the Harmonious Development of Man, based on a system of raising consciousness (involving learning, group movement, manual labor, dance, and a minimum of sleep) known as the Fourth Way. After the 1917 Revolution he established similar schools in parts of Europe.

gurdwara Sikh place of worship and meeting. As well as a room housing the *Guru Granth Sahib*, the holy book, the gurdwara contains a kitchen and eating area for the *langar*, or communal meal.

Gurkha member of a people living in the mountains of Nepal, whose young men have been recruited since 1815 for the British army. They are predominantly Tibeto-Mongolians, but their language is Khas, a dialect of a N Indic language.

guru (Hindi *gurū*) a Hindu or Sikh leader, or religious teacher.

Gush Emunim (Hebrew "bloc of the faithful") Israeli religious fundamentalist group, founded 1973, which claims divine right to settlement of the West Bank, Gaza Strip, and Golan Heights as part of Israel. The claim is sometimes extended to the Euphrates.

Gustaf or Gustavus six kings of Sweden, including:

Gustavus Adolphus 1594–1632. King of Sweden from 1611, when he succeeded his father Charles IX. He waged successful wars with Denmark, Russia, and Poland, and in the Thirty Years' War became a champion of the Protestant cause. anding in Germany in 1630, he defeated the German general Wallenstein at Lützen, SW of Leipzig, on Nov 6, 1632, but was killed in the battle. He was known as the "Lion of the North."

Gustavus Vasa 1496–1560. King of Sweden from 1523, when he was elected after leading the Swedish revolt against Danish rule. He united and pacified the country and established Lutheranism as the state religion.

Gustavus I king of Sweden, better known as ◊Gustavus Vasa.

Gustavus II king of Sweden, better known as ◊Gustavus Adolphus.

Gustaf V 1858–1950. King of Sweden from 1907, when he succeeded his father Oscar II. He married Princess Victoria, daughter of the Grand Duke of Baden, in 1881, thus uniting the reigning Bernadotte dynasty with the former royal house of Vasa.

Gustaf VI 1882–1973. King of Sweden from 1950, when he succeeded his father Gustaf V. He was an archeologist and expert on Chinese art. He was succeeded by his grandson ◊Carl XVI Gustaf.

Gustavus or ◊Gustaf, kings of Sweden.

Gutenberg Johann c. 1400–1468. German printer, the inventor of printing from moveable metal type, based on the Chinese wood-block-type method (although Laurens Janszoon ◊Coster has

Gutenberg *The earliest illustration of a printing press, as invented by Johann Gutenberg. It is from the* Danse Macabre *printed by Mathias Lyons, 1499.*

a rival claim). Gutenberg began work on the process in the 1430s and in 1440 set up a printing business in Mainz with Johann Fust (c. 1400–1466) as a backer. By 1455 he produced the first printed Bible (known as the Gutenberg Bible). Fust seized the press for nonpayment of the loan, but Gutenberg is believed to have printed the Mazarin and Bamberg bibles.

Guthrie Edwin R 1886–1959. American behaviorist, who attempted to develop a theory of learning that was independent of the traditional principles of reward or reinforcement. His ideas served as a basis for later statistical models.

Guthrie Tyrone 1900–1971. British theater director, noted for his experimental approach. Administrator of the ◊Old Vic and Sadler's Wells theaters 1939–45, he helped found the Ontario (Stratford) Shakespeare Festival in 1953 and the Minneapolis theater now named after him.

Guthrie Woody (Woodrow Wilson) 1912–1967. US folk singer and songwriter, whose left-wing protest songs, "dustbowl ballads," and "talking blues" influenced, among others, Bob Dylan; they include "Deportees," "Hard Travelin'," and "This Land Is Your Land."

gutta-percha juice of various tropical trees of the sapodilla family (such as the Malaysian *Palaquium gutta*), which can be hardened to form a flexible, rubbery substance used for electrical insulation, dentistry, and golf balls; it has now been largely replaced by synthetics.

guttation the secretion of water onto the surface of leaves through specialized pores, or ◊hydathodes. The process occurs most frequently during conditions of high humidity when the rate of transpiration is low. Drops of water found on grass in early morning are often the result of guttation, rather than dew. Sometimes the water contains minerals in solution, such as calcium, which leaves a white crust on the leaf surface as it dries.

Guyana country in South America, bounded N by the Atlantic Ocean, E by Suriname, S and SW by Brazil, and NW by Venezuela.

government Guyana is a sovereign republic within the ◊Commonwealth. The 1980 constitution provides for a single-chamber national assembly of 65 members, 53 elected by universal suffrage and 12 elected by the regions, for a five-year term. The president is the nominee of the party winning most votes in the national assembly elections and serves for the life of the assembly, appointing a cabinet that is collectively responsible to it. The main political parties are the People's National Congress (PNC), and the People's Progressive Party (PPP).

history Settled by Arawak, Carib, and Warrau Indians when the first Europeans arrived in the late 1500's, the area now known as Guyana was a Dutch colony 1621–1796, when it was seized by Britain. Ceded to Britain in 1814, it was made a British colony 1831 under the name of British Guiana and became part of the Commonwealth until full independence 1966.

The transition from colonial to republican status was gradual and not entirely smooth. In 1953 a constitution providing for free elections to an assembly was introduced, and the left-wing PPP, led by Dr Cheddi Jagan, won the popular vote. Within months, however, the UK government suspended the constitution and put in its own interim administration, claiming that the PPP threatened to become a communist dictatorship.

In 1957 a breakaway group from the PPP founded a new party, the PNC, which was supported mainly by Guyanans of African descent, while PPP followers were mainly of Indian descent. Fresh elections, under a revised constitution, were held 1957, and PPP won again, with Jagan becoming chief minister. Internal self-government was granted 1961 and, with PPP again the successful party, Jagan became prime minister. Proportional representation was introduced 1963, and in the 1964 elections (under the new voting procedures) the PPP, although winning most votes, did not have an overall majority, resulting in the formation of a PPP–PNC coalition with PNC leader Forbes Burnham as prime minister.

This coalition took the country through to full independence 1966. The PNC won the 1968 and 1973 elections, and in 1970 Guyana became a republic within the Commonwealth. In 1980 a new constitution was adopted, making the president head of both state and government, and as a result of the 1981 elections—which opposition parties claimed were fraudulent—Burnham became executive president. The rest of his administration was marked by economic deterioration (necessitating austerity measures) and cool relations with the Western powers, particularly the US, whose invasion of Grenada he condemned. He died 1985 and was succeeded by Prime Minister Desmond Hoyte.

guyot a truncated or flat-topped seamount. Such undersea mountains are found throughout the abyssal plains of major ocean basins, and most of them are covered by an appreciable depth of water. They are believed to have started as volcanic cones formed near midoceanic ridges, in relatively shallow water, and to have been truncated by wave action as their tops emerged above the surface. They were then transported to deeper waters as the ocean floor moved away on either side of the ridge.

Guzmán Blanco Antonio 1829–1899. Venezuelan dictator and military leader (*caudillo*). He seized power in 1870 and remained absolute ruler until 1889. He modernized Caracas to become the po-

Guyana
Cooperative Republic of

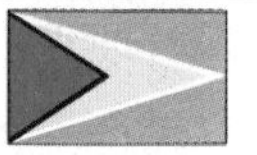

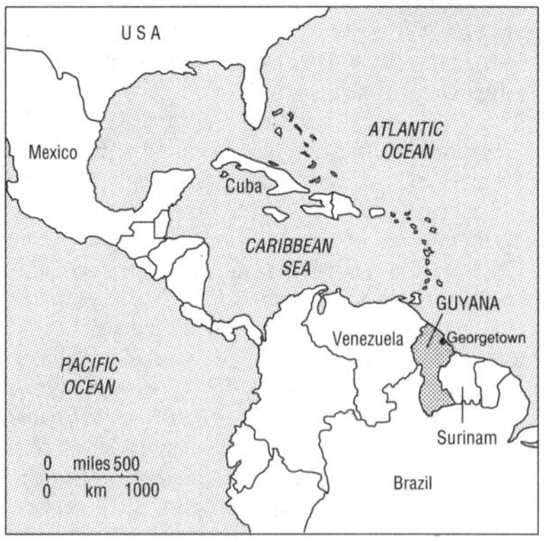
USA
Mexico
ATLANTIC
OCEAN
Cuba
CARIBBEAN
SEA
GUYANA
Georgetown
Venezuela
PACIFIC
OCEAN
Surinam
Brazil
0 miles 500
0 km 1000

area 82,978 sq mi/214,969 sq km
capital (and port) Georgetown
cities New Amsterdam, Mabaruma
physical coastal plain rises into rolling highlands with savanna in S; mostly tropical rainforest
features Mount Roraima; Kaietur National Park, including Kaietur Fall on the Potaro (tributary of Essequibo) 821 ft/250 m
head of state and government Desmond Hoyte from 1985
political system democratic republic
political parties People's National Congress (PNC), Indian nationalist Socialist; People's Progressive Party (PPP), Afro-Indian Marxist-Leninist
exports sugar, rice, rum, timber, diamonds, bauxite, shrimps, molasses
currency Guyanese dollar
population (1989 est) 846,000 (51% E Indians, introduced to work the sugar plantations after the abolition of slavery, 30% black, 5% Amerindian); growth rate 2% p.a.
life expectancy men 66, women 71
language English (official), Hindi, Amerindian
religion Christian 57%, Hindu 33%, Sunni Muslim 9%
literacy men 97%/women 95% (1985 est)
GNP $359 million (1987); $445 per head
chronology
1831 Became British colony under name of British Guiana.
1953 Assembly elections won by left-wing PPP; Britain suspended constitution and installed interim administration, fearing Communist takeover.
1961 Internal self-government granted.
1966 Independence achieved from Britain.
1970 Guyana became a republic within the Commonwealth.
1980 Forbes Burnham became first executive president under new constitution.
1985 Burnham died; succeeded by Desmond Hoyte.

litical capital; committed resources to education, communications, and agriculture; and encouraged foreign trade.

Gwalior city in Madhya Pradesh, India; population (1981) 543,862. It was formerly a small princely state and has Jain and Hindu monuments.

Gwent county in S Wales
area 533 sq mi/1,380 sq km
towns Cwmbran (administrative headquarters), Abergavenny, Newport, Tredegar
features Wye Valley; Tintern Abbey; Legionary Museum of Caerleon, and Roman amphitheater; Chepstow and Raglan castles
products salmon and trout on the Wye and Usk rivers; iron and steel at Llanwern
population (1987) 443,000
language 2.5% Welsh, English.

Gwyn Nell (Eleanor) 1651–1687. English comedy actress from 1665, formerly an orange-seller at Drury Lane Theatre, London. The poet Dryden wrote parts for her, and from 1669 she was the mistress of Charles II.

Gwynedd county in NW Wales
area 1,494 sq mi/3,870 sq km
towns Caernarvon (administrative headquarters), Bangor
products cattle, sheep, gold (at Dolgellau), textiles, electronics, slate
population (1987) 236,000
language 61% Welsh, English
features Snowdinia National Park including Snowdon, the highest mountain in Wales 3,561 ft/1,085 m, and the largest Welsh lake, Llyn Tegid (Bala); Caernarvon Castle.

gymnastics physical exercises, originally for health and training (so called from the way in which men of ancient Greece trained: *gymnos*, "naked"). The *gymnasia* were schools for training competitors for public games.

Men's gymnastics includes high bar, parallel bars, horse vault, rings, pommel horse, and floor exercises. Women's gymnastics includes asymmetrical bars, side horse vault, balance beam, and floor exercises. Also popular are sports acrobatics, performed by gymnasts in pairs, trios, or fours to music, with an emphasis on dance, balance, and timing; and rhythmic gymnastics, choreographed to music and performed by individuals or six-girl teams, with a small hand apparatus such as a ribbon, ball, or hoop.

Gymnastics was first revived in 19th-century Germany as an aid to military strength, and was also taken up by educationists including ◊Froebel and ◊Pestalozzi, becoming a recognized part of the school curriculum. Today it is a popular sport.

gymnosperm (Greek "naked seed") in botany, any plant whose seeds are exposed, as opposed to the structurally more advanced ◊angiosperms, where they are inside an ovary. The group includes conifers and related plants such as cycads and ginkgos, whose seeds develop in ◊cones. Fossil gymnosperms have been found in rocks about 350 million years old.

gynecology medical speciality concerned with disorders of the female reproductive system.

gynoecium or ***gynecium*** the collective term for the female reproductive organs of a flower, consisting of one or more ◊carpels, either free or fused together.

Györ industrial city (steel, vehicles, textiles, foodstuffs) in NW Hungary, near the frontier with Czechoslovakia; population (1988) 131,000.

gypsum a common ◊mineral, composed of hydrous calcium sulfate, $CaSO_4.2H_2O$. It ranks 2 on the Mohs' scale of hardness. Gypsum is used for making casts and molds, and for blackboard chalk.

A fine-grained gypsum, called alabaster, is used for ornamental work. Burned gypsum is known as plaster of Paris, because for a long time it was obtained from the gypsum quarries of the Montmartre district of Paris.

Gypsy English name for a member of the wandering ◊Romany people.

gyre the circular surface rotation of ocean water in each major sea (a type of ◊current). Gyres are large and permanent, and occupy the N and S halves of the three major oceans. Their movements are dictated by the prevailing winds and the ◊Coriolis effect. Gums move clockwise in the northern hemisphere and counterclockwise in the southern hemisphere.

gyroscope *High-speed photograph of a gyroscope in motion. The gyroscope is used as a stabilizing device, and in automatic pilots and gyrocompasses.*

gyroscope mechanical instrument, used as a stabilizing device and consisting, in its simplest form, of a heavy wheel mounted on an axis fixed in a ring that can be rotated about another axis, which is also fixed in a ring capable of rotation about a third axis. Important applications of the gyroscope principle include the gyrocompass, the gyropilot for automatic steering, and gyro-directed torpedoes.

The components of the gyroscope are arranged so that the three axes of rotation in any position pass through the wheel's center of gravity. The wheel is thus capable of rotation about three mutually perpendicular axes, and its axis may take up any direction. If the axis of the spinning wheel is displaced, a restoring movement develops, returning it to its initial direction.

Haakon seven kings of Norway, including:

Haakon I the Good c. 915–961. King of Norway from about 935. The son of Harald Hárfagri ("Finehair") (c. 850–930), king of Norway, he was raised in England. He seized the Norwegian throne and tried unsuccessfully to introduce Christianity there. His capital was at Trondheim.

Haakon IV 1204–1263. King of Norway from 1217, the son of Haakon III. Under his rule, Norway flourished both militarily and culturally; he took control of the Faroe Islands, Greenland 1261, and Iceland 1262–64. His court was famed throughout N Europe.

Haakon VII 1872–1957. King of Norway from 1905. Born Prince Charles, the second son of Frederick VIII of Denmark, he was elected king of Norway on separation from Sweden, and in 1906 he took the name Haakon. In World War II he carried on the resistance from Britain during the Nazi occupation of his country. He returned 1945.

Haarlem industrial city and capital of North Holland, the Netherlands, 12 mi/20 km W of Amsterdam; population (1988) 214,000. At Velsea to the N a road-rail tunnel runs under the North Sea Canal, linking N and S Holland. Industries include chemicals, pharmaceuticals, textiles, and printing. Haarlem is famous for flowering bulbs and has a 15th–16th-century cathedral and a Frans Hals museum.

Habakkuk a prophet in, and a book of, the Old Testament.

habanera or ***havanaise*** a slow dance in two-four time, originating in Havana, Cuba, which was introduced into Spain during the 19th century.- There is a celebrated example of this dance in Bizet's opera *Carmen*.

habeas corpus (Latin "you have the body") in law, a writ directed to someone who has custody of a prisoner, ordering him to bring the prisoner before the court issuing the writ and to justify why the prisoner is detained in custody. Traditional rights to habeas corpus were embodied in law mainly caused by Lord ◊Shaftesbury, in the English Habeas Corpus Act 1679. The main principles were adopted in the US Constitution.

Haber Fritz 1868–1934. German chemist whose conversion of atmospheric nitrogen to ammonia opened the way for the synthetic fertilizer industry. His study of the combustion of hydrocarbons led to the commercial "cracking" or fractionating of natural oil (petroleum) into its components (for example, diesel, gasoline, and paraffin). In electrochemistry, he was the first to demonstrate that oxidation and reduction take place at the electrodes; from this he developed a general electrochemical theory.

In World War I he worked on poison gas and devised gas masks, hence there were protests against his Nobel Prize in 1918.

Haber process industrial process in which ammonia is manufactured by direct combination of its elements, nitrogen and hydrogen. The reaction is carried out at 752–932°F/400–500°C and at 200 atmospheric pressure. The two gases, in the proportions of 1:3 by volume, are passed over a ◊catalyst of finely divided iron. Around 10% of the reactants combine, and the unused gases are recycled. The ammonia is separated by either dissolving in water or cooling to liquid $(N_2+3H_2=2NH_3)$.

habitat in ecology, the localized ◊environment in which an organism lives. Habitats are often described by the dominant plant type or physical feature, such as a grassland habitat or rocky seashore habitat.

Habsburg European royal family, see ◊Hapsburg.

hacking unauthorized access to a computer, either for fun or for malicious or fraudulent purposes. Hackers generally use microcomputers and telephone lines to obtain access. In computing, the term is used in a wider sense to mean using software for enjoyment or self-education, not necessarily involving unauthorized access. See also computer ◊virus.

Hackman Gene 1931– . US actor. He became a star as "Popeye" Doyle in *The French Connection* 1971 and continued to play major roles in films such as *The Conversation* 1974, *The French Connection II* 1975, and *Mississippi Burning* 1988.

haddock marine fish *Melanogrammus aeglefinus* of the cod family found off the N Atlantic coasts. It is brown with silvery underparts and black markings above the pectoral fins. It can grow to a length of 3 ft/1 m. Haddock are important food fish; about 100 million lb/45 million kg are taken annually off the New England fishing banks alone.

Hades in Greek mythology, the underworld where spirits went after death, usually depicted as a cavern or pit underneath the Earth. It was presided over by the god Hades or Pluto (Roman Dis).

He was the brother of Zeus and married Persephone, daughter of Demeter and Zeus. Persephone was allowed to return to the upper world for part of the year, bringing spring with her. The entrance to Hades was guarded by the three-headed dog Cerberus. Tartarus was the section where the wicked were punished, for example Tantalus.

Hadhramaut district of the People's Democratic Republic of Yemen, which was formerly ruled by Arab chiefs in protective relations with Britain. A remote plateau region at 4,500 ft/1,400 m, it was for a long time unknown to westerners and later attracted such travelers as Harry St John Philby and Freya Stark. Cereals, tobacco, and dates are grown by settled farmers, and there are nomadic Bedouin. The chief town is Mukalla.

Hadrian's Wall *A section of Hadrian's Wall, built by the Romans to mark their northern boundary in England.*

Hadith a collection of the teachings of ◊Mohammed and stories about his life, regarded by Muslims as a guide to living second only to the ◊Koran.

The teachings were at first transmitted orally, but this led to a large number of Hadiths whose origin was in doubt; later, scholars such as Mohammed al-Bukhari (810–870) collected together those believed to be authentic, and these collections form the Hadith accepted by Muslims today.

Hadrian AD 76–138. Roman emperor from 117. Born in Spain, he was adopted by his relative, the emperor Trajan, whom he succeeded. He abandoned Trajan's conquests in Mesopotamia and adopted a defensive policy, which included the building of Hadrian's Wall in Britain.

Hadrian's Wall Roman fortification built AD 122–126 to mark England's northern boundary and abandoned about 383; its ruins run 115 mi/185 km from Wallsend on the river Tyne to Maryport, W Cumbria. In some parts, the wall was covered with a glistening, white coat of mortar. The fort at South Shields, Arbeia, built to defend the eastern end, is being reconstructed.

hadron any of a class of strongly interacting ◊elementary particles, grouped into the ◊baryons (protons, neutrons, and hyperons) and the ◊mesons. All hadrons' internal structures are made up of ◊quarks. The baryons are composed of three quarks and the mesons of a quark and its antiquark. Since the 1960s, particle physicists' main interest has been the elucidation of hadron structure.

Haeckel Ernst Heinrich 1834–1919. German scientist and philosopher. His theory of "recapitulation," expressed as "ontogeny repeats phylogeny" (or that embryonic stages represent past stages in the organism's evolution), has been superseded, but it stimulated research in ◊embryology.

Hâfiz Shams al-Din Mohammed c. 1326–1390. Persian lyric poet, who was born in Shiraz and taught in a Dervish college there. His *Diwan*, a collection of short odes, extols the pleasures of life and satirizes his fellow Dervishes.

hafnium silvery, metallic element, symbol Hf, atomic number 72, atomic weight 178.49. It occurs in nature in ores of zirconium, the properties of which it resembles. Hafnium absorbs neutrons better than most metals, so it is used for control rods in nuclear reactors; it is also used for light-bulb filaments.

It was named in 1923 by Dutch physicist Dirk Coster (1889–1950) and Hungarian chemist Georg von Hevesy after *Hafnia*, Latin for Copenhagen, where the element was discovered.

Haganah Zionist military organization in Palestine. It originated under the Turkish rule of the Ottoman Empire before World War I to protect Jewish settlements, and many of its members served in the British forces in both world wars. After World War II it condemned guerrilla activity, opposing the British authorities only passively. It formed the basis of the Israeli army after Israel was established in 1948.

Hagen industrial city in the Ruhr, North Rhine–Westphalia, Federal Republic of Germany; population (1988) 206,000. It produces iron, steel, and textiles.

Hagenbeck Carl 1844–1913. German zoo proprietor. In 1907 he founded Hagenbeck's Zoo, near his native Hamburg. He was a pioneer in the display of animals against a natural setting, rather than in restrictive cages.

Hagerstown city in NW Maryland, on Antietam Creek, NW of Baltimore and just S of the Pennsylvania border. Industries include engine and missile parts and furniture; population (1980) 34,132.

Haggadah in Judaism, the part of the Talmudic literature not concerned with religious law (the *Halakah*), but devoted to folklore and legends of heroes.

Haggai minor Old Testament prophet (lived c. 520 BC), who promoted the rebuilding of the Temple in Jerusalem.

Haggard H(enry) Rider 1856–1925. English novelist. He used his experience in the South African colonial service in his romantic adventure tales, including *King Solomon's Mines* 1885 and *She* 1887.

haggis Scottish dish made from a sheep's or calf's heart, liver, and lungs, minced with onion, oatmeal, suet, spices, and salt, mixed with stock, and traditionally boiled in the animal's stomach for several hours.

Hague, The (Dutch *Gravenhage* or *Den Haag*) capital of South Holland and seat of the Netherlands government, linked by canal with Rotterdam and Amsterdam; population (1988) 680,000. It is also the seat of the United Nations International Court of Justice.

The seaside resort of Scheveningen (patronized by Wilhelm II and Churchill), with its Kurhaus, is virtually incorporated.

Hahn Otto 1879–1968. West German physical chemist, who discovered ◊nuclear fission. Nobel Prize 1944.

He worked with Ernest Rutherford and William Ramsay, and became director of the Kaiser Wilhelm Institute for Chemistry in 1928. In 1938 with Fritz Strassmann (1902–1980), he discovered that uranium nuclei split when bombarded with neutrons, which led to the development of the atomic bomb.

hahnium name proposed by US scientists for the element currently known as ◊unnilpentium (atomic number 105), to honor German nuclear physicist Otto Hahn (1879–1968). The symbol is Ha.

Haifa port in NE Israel; population (1987) 223,000. Industries include oil refining and chemicals.

Haig Alexander (Meigs) 1924– US general and Republican politician. He became President Nixon's White House chief of staff at the height of the ◊Watergate scandal, was NATO commander 1974–79, and was secretary of state to President Reagan 1981–82.

haiku seventeen-syllable Japanese verse form, usually divided into three lines of five, seven, and five syllables. ◊Bashō popularized the form in the 17th century. It evolved from the 31-syllable *tanka* form dominant from the 8th century.

hail precipitation in the form of pellets of ice (hailstones). It is caused by the circulation of moisture in strong convection currents, usually within cumulonimbus ◊clouds.

Water droplets freeze as they are carried upward. As the circulation continues, layers of ice are deposited around the droplets until they become too heavy to be supported by the currents and they fall as a hailstorm.

Haile Selassie Ras (Prince) Tafari ("the Lion of Judah") 1892–1975. Emperor of Ethiopia 1930–74. He pleaded unsuccessfully to the League of Nations against Italian conquest of his country 1935–36, and lived in the UK until his restoration in 1941. He was deposed by a military coup in 1974 and died in captivity the following year. Followers of the ◊Rastafarian religion believe that he was the Messiah, the incarnation of God (Jah).

Haile Selassie *Haile Selassie was emperor of Ethiopia until he was deposed in a military coup in 1974.*

Hainan island in the South China Sea; area 13,124 sq mi/34,000 sq km; population (1986) 6,000,000. The capital is Haikou. In 1987 Hainan was designated a Special Economic Zone; in 1988 it was separated from Guangdong and made a new province. It is China's second-largest island.

Hainaut industrial province of SW Belgium; capital Mons; area 1,467 sq mi/3,800 sq km; population (1987) 1,272,000. It produces coal, iron, and steel.

Haiphong industrial port in N Vietnam; population (1980) 1,305,000. Among its industries are shipbuilding and the making of cement, plastics, phosphates, and textiles.

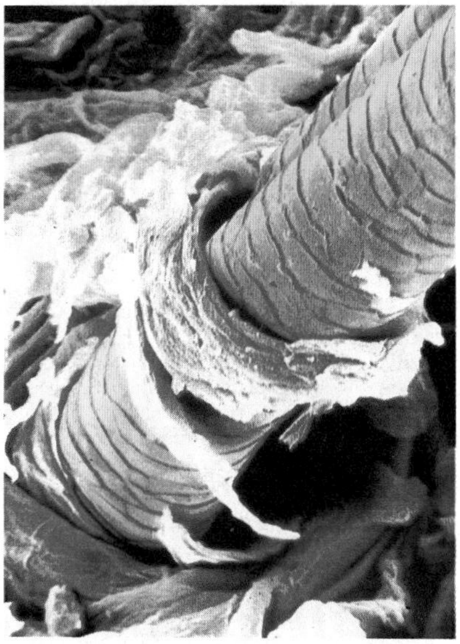

hair *False-color electron microscope view of a human hair, showing the layer of highly flattened and partly overlapping cells that covers the hair surface.*

hair threadlike structure growing from mammalian skin. Each hair grows from a pit-shaped follicle of the outer skin layer (epidermal cells). Hair consists of dead cells impregnated with the protein keratin.

There are about a million hairs on the average person's head. Each grows at the rate of 5–10 mm per month, lengthening for about three years before being replaced by a new one. A coat of hair helps to insulate mammals by trapping air next to the body. It also aids in camouflage, and its coloring or erection may be used for communication.

hairstreak any of a group of butterflies, belonging to the family Lycaenidae, to which blues and coppers also belong. Hairstreaks live in both temperate and tropical regions. Most of them are brownish or greyish-blue with hairlike tips at the end of their hind wings.

Haiti country in the Caribbean, occupying the W part of the island of Hispaniola; to the E is the Dominican Republic.

government The 1950 constitution was revised 1957, 1964, 1971, 1983, 1985, and 1987. Although it provides for an elected national assembly, under the rule of the Duvaliers (1957–86) it became a façade for their own dictatorships. In the 1984 elections about 300 government candidates contested the 59 seats, with no opposition at all. In 1985 political parties were legalized, provided they conformed to strict guidelines, but only one party registered, the National Progressive Party (PNP), which supported Duvalier's policies. The leader of the 1986 coup, Lt-Gen Henri Namphy, established a governing council, with himself as its head. The 1987 constitution provides for a 27-member senate and 77-member chamber of deputies, all popularly elected, as well as a "dual executive" of a president and prime minister sharing power; but the future of democracy in Haiti remained under test even after free elections in Dec 1990.

history The island of Hispaniola was once inhabited by ◊Arawak Indians. They were driven out in the 14th century by ◊Caribs, 300,000 of whom were wiped out by Europeans in the 50 years following the arrival of Christopher Columbus 1492. The island was made a Spanish colony under the name of Santo Domingo, but the western part was colonized by France from the mid-16th century. In 1697 it was divided between France and Spain, and in 1795 the eastern end of the island was ceded to France by Spain.

The period 1790–1804 was fraught with rebellions against France; tension between blacks, whites, and mulattos; and military intervention by France and Britain. In one such rebellion 1791 the island was taken over by slaves, under ◊Toussaint L'Ouverture, and slavery was abolished, but it was then reinstated after he was killed by the French. After independence in 1804 the instability continued, with Santo Domingo repossessed by Spain and then by Haiti, and self-proclaimed kings ruling Haiti. In 1844 Haiti and the Dominican Republic became separate states.

Friction between Haitians of African descent and mulattos, and the country's political instability, brought a period of US rule 1915–34. In the 1940s and 1950s there were several coups, the last occurring 1956, which resulted in Dr François Duvalier, a physician, being elected president. After an encouraging start, his administration degenerated into a personal dictatorship, maintained by a private army. In 1964 "Papa Doc" Duvalier made himself president for life, with the power to nominate his son as his successor.

On his father's death 1971 Jean-Claude ◊Duvalier came to the presidency at the age of 19 and soon acquired the name of "Baby Doc." Although the young Duvalier repeatedly promised a return to democracy, and his rule was judged to be less despotic than his father's, there was little change. In 1985 he announced further reform of the constitution, including the legalization of political

Haiti
Republic of
(République d'Haïti)

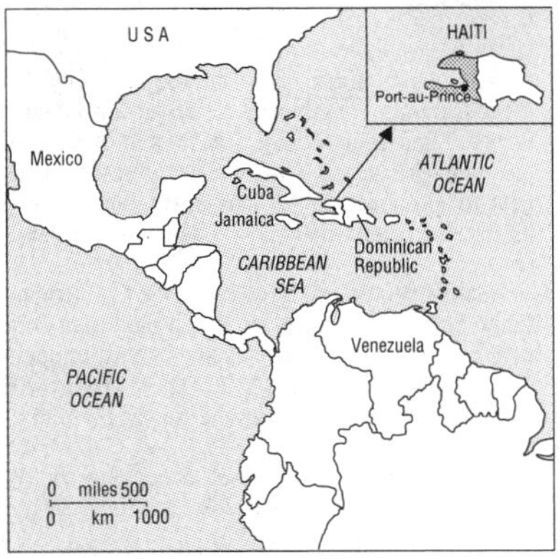
USA
HAITI
Port-au-Prince
Mexico
ATLANTIC OCEAN
Cuba
Jamaica
Dominican Republic
CARIBBEAN SEA
Venezuela
PACIFIC OCEAN
0 miles 500
0 km 1000

area 10,712 sq mi/27,750 sq km
capital Port-au-Prince
cities Cap-Haïtien, Gonaïves, Les Cayes
physical mainly mountainous and tropical; occupies W third of Hispaniola Island in Caribbean Sea; seriously deforested
features oldest black republic in the world; only French-speaking republic in the Americas; island of La Tortuga off N coast was formerly a pirate lair
head of state and government Jean-Bertrand Aristide from 1991
political system transitional
political parties National Progressive Party (PNP), right-wing military
exports coffee, sugar, sisal, cotton, cocoa, bauxite
currency gourde
population (1990 est) 6,409,000; growth rate 1.7% p.a.; one of highest population densities in the world; about 1.5 million Haitians live outside Haiti (in US and Canada); about 400,000 live in virtual slavery in the Dominican Republic, where they went or were sent to cut sugar cane
life expectancy men 51, women 54
language French (official, spoken by literate 10% minority), creole (spoken by 90% black majority)
religion voodoo; also Christianity
literacy men 40%/women 35% (1985 est)
GDP $2.2 bn (1987); $414 per head
chronology
1804 Independence achieved from France.
1915 Haiti invaded by US; remained under US control until 1934.
1957 Dr François Duvalier (Papa Doc) elected president.
1964 Duvalier pronounced himself president for life.
1971 Constitution amended to allow president to nominate his successor. Duvalier died, succeeded by his son, Jean-Claude (Baby Doc); thousands murdered during Duvalier era.
1986 Duvalier deposed; replaced by Lt Gen Henri Namphy as head of a governing council.
1988 Leslie Manigat became president in Feb despite allegations of fraudulent elections. Namphy staged a military coup in June, but another coup in Sept led by Prosper Avril replaced him with a civilian government under military control.
1989 Coup attempt against Avril foiled; US aid resumed.
1990 Opposition elements expelled; Pascal-Trouillot acting president.
1991 Newly elected president Aristide dismissed the army high command. President Aristide tightened grip on army but officers responded with a coup that forced him to flee.

parties and the eventual appointment of a prime minister, but these were not enough to prevent his overthrow and exile to France 1986. The task of establishing democratic government fell to the new military regime led by Lt-Gen Henri Namphy. The regime offered no protection to the electoral council, however, and the US government withdrew aid. Elections Nov 30, 1987 were sabotaged by armed gangs of Duvalierists who massacred voters and set fire to polling stations and to vehicles delivering ballot papers in the country.

Leslie Manigat, with army support, was made president early in 1988 but eight months later was ousted in a coup led by General Prosper Avril. Although Avril installed a largely civilian government, the army was still in control and a coup attempt in April 1989 was quickly put down. Early in 1990 opposition to Avril grew, but was quickly suppressed. Although his regime continued to be criticized by human rights organizations, the US government resumed food aid Aug 1989. In Aug and Sept 1990 Acting-President Pascal-Trouillot defied calls for her resignation and the holding of elections but in Dec 1990, Haiti held its first truly free elections. A former priest, Jean-Bertrand Aristide, won in a landslide. Discontent with his regime grew during 1991, however, and he was overthrown in a Sept 1991 coup that left Haiti's politics confused.

Haitink Bernard 1929– . Dutch conductor of the Concertgebouw Orchestra, Amsterdam, from 1964, and music director of the Royal Opera House, Covent Garden, London, from 1986.

hajj the pilgrimage to ◊Mecca that should be undertaken by every Muslim at least once in a lifetime, unless he or she is prevented by financial or health difficulties. A Muslim who has been on hajj may take the additional name Hajji. Many of the pilgrims on hajj also visit Medina, where the prophet Mohammed is buried.

hake any of various marine fishes of the cod family, found in N European, African, and American waters. They have silvery, elongated bodies and attain a length of 3 ft/1 m. They have two dorsal fins and one long anal fin. The silver hake *Merluccius bilineari s* is an important food fish.

Hakluyt Richard 1553–1616. English geographer whose chief work is *The Principal Navigations, Voyages and Discoveries of the English Nation* 1598–1600. He was assisted by Sir Walter Raleigh.

He lectured on cartography at Oxford, became geographical adviser to the East India Company, and was an original member of the Virginia Company.

Hakodate port in Hokkaido, Japan; population (1985) 319,000. It was the earliest port opened to the West, in 1854.

Halab Arabic name of ◊Aleppo, a city in Syria.

Halabja Kurdish town near the Iran border in Sulaymaniyah province, NE Iraq.

In Aug 1988 international attention was focused on the town when Iraqi planes dropped poison gas, killing 5,000 of its inhabitants.

halal (Arabic "lawful") conforming to the rules laid down by Islam. The term can be applied to all aspects of life, but usually refers to food permissible under Muslim dietary laws, including meat from animals that have been slaughtered in the correct ritual fashion.

Halas George Stanley 1895–1983. US athlete and sports promoter. He devoted himself to professional football from 1921. He was the founder of the Chicago Bears of the National Football League and was an active player until 1929. As coach until retirement 1967, Halas introduced the T-formation and laid special emphasis on the passing offense. He became a charter member of the Football Hall of Fame 1963.

Born in Chicago and educated at the University of Illinois, where he was an exceptional athlete, Halas worked briefly as a railroad engineer and in 1919 briefly played professional baseball for the New York Yankees.

Haldane J(ohn) B(urdon) S(anderson) 1892–1964. English scientist and writer. A geneticist, Haldane was better known as a popular science writer of such books as *The Causes of Evolution* 1933 and *New Paths in Genetics* 1941.

Hale George Ellery 1868–1938. US astronomer who made pioneer studies of the Sun and founded three major observatories. In 1889 he invented the spectroheliograph, a device for photographing the Sun at particular wavelengths.

In 1897 he founded the Yerkes Observatory in Wisconsin, with the largest refractor, 40 in/102 cm, ever built at that time. In 1917 he established on Mount Wilson, California a 100-in/2.5-m reflector, the world's largest telescope until superseded 1948 by the 200-in/5-m reflector on Mount Palomar, which Hale had had planned just before he died.

Hale Nathan 1755–1776. American Revolutionary War hero, hanged by the British as a spy. He crossed British lines disguised as a teacher and told George ◊Washington that he wished "to be useful." He was sent behind enemy lines on Long Island to gather information about the British army. Captured, he was hanged. Reputedly his final words were "I only regret that I have but one life to lose for my country."

Born in Coventry, Connecticut, Hale graduated from Yale 1773 and became a schoolteacher. He fought with the Connecticut militia in the American Revolution.

Hale Sarah Josepha Buell 1788–1879. US poet, author of "Mary had a Little Lamb" 1830.

Hales Stephen 1677–1761. English priest and scientist who gave accurate accounts of water movement in plants. His work laid emphasis on measurement and experimentation.

Hales demonstrated that plants absorb air, and that some part of that air is involved in their nutrition. He also measured plant growth and water loss, relating this to the upward movement of water from plants to leaves (transpiration).

Halévy Ludovic 1834–1908. French novelist and librettist. He collaborated with Hector Crémieux in the libretto for Offenbach's *Orpheus in the Underworld*; and with Henri Meilhac on librettos for Offenbach's *La Belle Hélène* and *La Vie Parisienne*, as well as for Bizet's *Carmen*.

Haley Bill 1927–1981. US pioneer of rock and roll who was originally a western-swing musician. His songs "Rock Around the Clock" 1954 (recorded with his group the Comets and featured in the 1955 film *Blackboard Jungle*) and "Shake, Rattle

***Haley** Rock-and-roll pioneer Bill Haley, best known for his hit song "Rock Around the Clock" 1954.*

and Roll" 1955 became the anthems of the early rock-and-roll era.

half-life during radioactive decay, the length of time it takes for half of any number of unstable nuclei of an isotope to disintegrate. This may vary from millionths of a second to billions of years, even among different isotopes of the same element. After the first half of the material has decayed, then half the remaining unstable nuclei disintegrate over an equivalent amount of time; then half of that half; and so on through time. For example, carbon-14 takes about 5,730 years for half the material to decay; another 5,730 for half of the remaining half to decay; then 5,730 years for half of that remaining half to decay, and so on. In the case of carbon, which exists in all organic matter, measuring the amount left (◊radiocarbon dating) helps date archeological organic matter, such as bones. In the case of extremely radioactive isotopes that are used commercially for the production of energy and weapons, the half-lives are much longer than carbon's. Plutonium-239, one of the most toxic of all radioactive substances, has a half-life of about 24,000 years—only half a given amount will decay during the first 24,000 years, leaving the second half to decay over several 24,000-year periods that stretch into the future.

halftone process technique used in printing to reproduce the full range of tones in a photograph or other illustration. The intensity of the printed color is varied from full strength to the lightest shades, even if one color of ink is used. The picture to be reproduced is photographed through a screen ruled with a rectangular mesh of fine lines, which breaks up the tones of the original into areas of dots that vary in frequency according to the intensity of the tone. In the darker areas the dots run together; in the lighter areas they have more space between them.

halibut any of several large flatfishes of the genus *Hippoglossus*, in the family Pleuronectidae, found in the Atlantic and Pacific. Largest of the flatfishes, they may grow to 6 ft/2 m and weigh 200–300 lb/90-135 kg. They are very dark mottled brown or green above and pure white beneath. The Atlantic halibut *H. hippoglossus* is caught offshore at depths from 100 to 400 fathoms.

Halicarnassus ancient city in Asia Minor (now Bodrum in Turkey), where the tomb of Mausolus, built about 350 BC by widowed Queen Artemisia, was one of the Seven Wonders of the World. The Greek historian Herodotus was born there.

halide the family name for a compound produced by combination of a ◊halogen, such as chlorine or iodine, with a less electronegative element (see ◊electronegativity). Halides may be formed by ionic or ◊covalent bonds.

Halifax capital of Nova Scotia, E Canada's main port; population (1986) 296,000. Its industries include oil refining and food processing. There are six military bases in Halifax and it is a major center of oceanography. It was founded by British settlers in 1749.

Halifax woolen textile town in W Yorkshire, England; population (1981) 87,500.

St John's parish church is Perpendicular Gothic; All Souls' is by Gilbert Scott (built for a mill owner named Ackroyd, whose home, Bankfield, is now a museum); the Town Hall is by Charles Barry; and the Piece Hall of 1779 (former cloth market) has been adapted to modern use; the surviving gibbet (predecessor of the guillotine) was used to behead cloth stealers 1541–1650.

Halifax Charles Montagu, Earl of Halifax 1661–1715. British financier. Appointed commissioner of the Treasury in 1692, he raised money for the French war by instituting the National Debt and in 1694 carried out William Paterson's plan for a national bank (the Bank of England) and became chancellor of the Excheckr.

Halifax Edward Frederick Lindley Wood, Earl of 1881–1959. British Conservative politician, viceroy of India 1926–31. As foreign secretary 1938–40 he was associated with Chamberlain's "appeasement" policy. He received an earldom 1944 for services to the Allied cause while ambassador to the US 1941–46.

halite the mineral sodium chloride, NaCl, or common ◊salt. When pure it is colorless and transparent, but it is often pink, red or yellow. It is soft and has a low density.

Halite occurs naturally in evaporite deposits that have precipitated on evaporation of bodies of salt water. As rock salt, it forms beds within a sedimentary sequence; it can also migrate upward through surrounding rocks to form salt domes. It crystallizes in the cubic system.

halitosis another name for bad breath. It may be caused by poor oral hygiene; disease of the mouth, throat, nose, or lungs; or disturbance of the digestion.

Hall Charles 1863–1914. US chemist who developed a process for the commercial production of aluminum in 1886.

He found that when mixed with cryolite (sodium aluminum fluoride), the melting point of aluminum was lowered and electrolysis became commercially viable. It had previously been as costly as gold. By 1890, Hall was in charge of the Aluminum company of the US and aluminum utensils began to spread throughout the world.

Hall Peter (Reginald Frederick) 1930– . English theater, opera, and film director. He was director of the Royal Shakespeare Theatre in Stratford-on-Avon 1960–68 and developed the Royal Shakespeare Company as director 1968–73 until appointed director of the National Theatre 1973–88, succeeding Laurence Olivier.

Hall (Marguerite) Radcliffe 1883–1943. English novelist, author of *The Well of Loneliness* 1928, whose lesbian theme brought it considerable notoriety.

Halle industrial city (salt, chemicals, lignite) on the river Saale, in the state of Saxony-Anhalt, Federal Republic of Germany; population (1990) 240,000. Former capital of the East German district of Halle 1952–90.

Hall effect production of a voltage across a conductor or semiconductor carrying a current at a right angle to a surrounding magnetic field. It was discovered 1897 by the US physicist Edwin Hall (1855–1938). It is used in the Hall probe for measuring the strengths of magnetic fields and in magnetic switches.

Haller Albrecht von 1708–1777. Swiss physician and scientist, founder of ◊neurology. He studied the muscles and nerves, and concluded that nerves provide the stimulus that triggers muscle contraction. He also showed that it is the nerves, not muscle or skin, that receive sensation.

Halley Edmond 1656–1742. English scientist. In 1682 he observed the comet named after him, predicting that it would return 1759.

Halley's other astronomical achievements include the discovery that stars have their own ◊proper motion. He was a pioneer geophysicist and meteorologist and worked in many other fields including mathematics. He was a friend of Isaac ◊Newton, whose *Principia* he financed.

Halley's comet comet that orbits the Sun about every 76 years, named after Edmond Halley. It is the brightest and most conspicuous of the periodical comets. Recorded sightings go back over 2,000 years. It travels around the Sun in the opposite direction to the planets. Its orbit is inclined at almost 20° to the main plane of the Solar System and ranges between the orbits of Venus and Neptune. It will next reappear 2061.

The comet's appearance was studied by space probes 1986, when it passed close to the Earth. The European probe *Giotto* showed that the nucleus of Halley's comet is a tiny and irregularly shaped chunk of ice, measuring some 10 m/15 km long by 5 m/8 km wide, coated by a layer of very dark material, thought to be composed of carbon-rich compounds. This surface coating has a very low ◊albedo, reflecting just 4% of the light it receives from the Sun. Although the comet is one of the darkest objects known, it has a glowing head and tail produced by jets of gas from fissures in the outer dust layer. These vents cover 10% of the total surface area and become active only when exposed to the Sun. The force of these jets affects the speed of the comet's travel in its orbit.

hallmark an official mark stamped on British gold, silver, and (from 1913) platinum, instituted in 1327 (royal charter of London Goldsmiths) in order to prevent fraud. After 1363, personal marks of identification were added. Now tests of metal content are carried out at authorized assay offices in London, Birmingham, Sheffield, and Edinburgh; each assay office has its distinguishing mark, to which is added a maker's mark, date letter, and mark guaranteeing standard.

Halloween the evening of Oct 31, immediately preceding the Christian feast of Hallowmas or All Saints' Day. Customs associated with Halloween in the US and the UK include children wearing masks or costumes, and "trick or treating"—going from house to house collecting candy, fruit, or money.

Hallstatt archeological site in Upper Austria, SW of Salzburg. The salt workings date from prehistoric times. In 1846 over 3,000 graves were discovered belonging to a 9th–5th century BC Celtic civilization transitional between the Bronze and Iron ages.

hallucinogen any substance that acts on the ◊central nervous system to produce changes in perception and mood and often hallucinations. Hallucinogens include ◊LSD, ◊peyote, and ◊mescaline. Their effects are unpredictable and they are illegal in most countries.

In some circumstances hallucinogens may produce panic or even suicidal feelings, which can recur without warning several days or months after taking the drug. In rare cases they produce an irreversible psychotic state mimicking schizophrenia. Spiritual or religious experiences are common, hence the ritual use of hallucinogens in some cultures. They work by chemical interference with the normal action of neurotransmitters in the brain.

halogen any of a group of five nonmetallic elements with similar chemical bonding properties: fluorine, chlorine, bromine, iodine, and astatine. They form a linked group in the ◊periodic table of the elements, with fluorine the most reactive and descending to astatine, the least reactive. They combine directly with most metals to form salts, for example, common salt (NaCl). Each halogen has seven electrons in its valence shell, which accounts for the chemical similarities displayed by the group.

halophyte a plant adapted to live where there is a high concentration of salt in the soil, for example, in salt marshes and mud flats.

Halophytes contain a high percentage of salts in their root cells, so that, despite the salt in the soil, water can still be taken up by the process of ◊osmosis. Some species also have fleshy leaves for storing water, such as the salt marsh *Spartina* and the salt-primrose *Glauk maritima*.

halothane anesthetic agent (a liquid, $CF_3CHBrCl$) that produces a deep level of unconsciousness when inhaled.

Hals Frans c. 1581–1666. Flemish-born painter of lively portraits, such as the *Laughing Cavalier* 1624 (Wallace Collection, London), and large groups of military companies, governors of charities, and others (many examples in the Frans Hals Museum, Haarlem, Holland). In the 1620s he experimented with genre (domestic) scenes.

Halsey William Frederick 1882–1959. US admiral, known as "Bull." Commander of the Third Fleet in the S Pacific from 1942 during World War II. The Japanese signed the surrender document ending World War II on his flagship, the battleship *Missouri*.

Hamadán city in NW Iran on the site of the ancient

Ecbatana, capital of the Medes; population (1986) 274,300.

Hamamatsu industrial city (textiles, chemicals, motorcycles) in Chubu region, central Honshu island, Japan; population (1987) 518,000.

Hamburg largest port of Europe, in Federal Republic of Germany, on the river Elbe; population (1988) 1,571,000. Industries include oil, chemicals, electronics, and cosmetics.

It is capital of the *Land* of Hamburg, and an archbishopric from 834. In alliance with Lübeck, it founded the ◊Hanseatic League.

Hamburg *Land* of Federal Republic of Germany
area 293 sq mi/760 sq km
capital Hamburg
features comprises the city and surrounding districts
products refined oil, chemicals, electrical goods, ships, processed food
population (1988) 1,570,000
religion 74% Protestant, 8% Roman Catholic
history in 1510 the emperor Maximilian I made Hamburg a free imperial city, and in 1871 it became a state of the German Empire. There is a university, established 1919, and the Hamburg Schauspielhaus is one of the republic's leading theaters.

The hamburger, a fried and seasoned patty of chopped beef, said to have been invented by medieval Tatar invaders of this Baltic area, was taken to the US in the 19th century, from where it was reintroduced to Europe in the 1960s.

Hameln English form *Hamelin* town in Lower Saxony, Federal Republic of Germany; population (1984) 56,300. Old buildings include the *Rattenhaus* (rat-catcher's house). Hameln is the setting for the Pied Piper legend.

Hamilcar Barca c. 270–228 BC. Carthaginian general, father of ◊Hannibal. From 247 to 241 he harassed the Romans in Italy and then led an expedition to Spain, where he died in battle.

Hamilton capital (since 1815) of Bermuda, on Bermuda Island; population (1980) 1,617. It was founded in 1612.

Hamilton port in Ontario, Canada; population (1986) 557,000. Linked with Lake Ontario by the Burlington Canal, it has a hydroelectric plant and steel, heavy machinery, electrical, chemical, and textile industries.

Hamilton industrial and university town on North Island, New Zealand, on the Waikato river; population (1986) 101,800. It trades in forestry, horticulture, and dairy-farming products. Waikato University was established here in 1964.

Hamilton city in the SW corner of Ohio, on the Great Miami River, NW of Cincinnati; seat of Butler county. Its industries include livestock processing, metal products, paper, and building materials; population (1990) 61,368. The city was built on the site of Fort Hamilton, constructed 1791 by Gen Arthur St Clair and used as a headquarters by Gen Anthony Wayne during his campaign in the Northwest Territory 1792–93.

Hamilton Alexander 1757–1804. US politician who influenced the adoption of a constitution with a strong central government and was the first secretary of the treasury 1789–95. He led the Federalist Party, and incurred the bitter hatred of Aaron ◊Burr when he voted against Burr and in favor of Thomas Jefferson for the presidency in 1801.

Hamilton, born in the West Indies, served during the American Revolution as captain and 1777–81 was George ◊Washington's secretary and aide-de-camp. After the war he practiced as a lawyer. He was a member of the Constitutional Convention of 1787, and in the *Federalist* influenced public opinion in favor of the ratification of the constitution. He was a strong advocate of the wealthy urban sector of American life and encouraged renewed ties with Britain, remaining distrustful of revolutionary France. As the first secretary of the treasury, he proved an able controller of the national finances. Challenged to a duel by Aaron ◊Burr, Hamilton was wounded, and died the next day.

Hamilton Edith 1867–1963. German born-US educator and Classical scholar. Born in Dresden and raised in Fort Wayne, Indiana, Hamilton was educated at Bryn Mawr. She was the headmistress of the Bryn Mawr School in Baltimore 1896–1922, later devoting her energies to the study of Greek and Roman civilization. Among her most important works are *The Greek Way* 1930 and *The Roman Way* 1932. Hamilton is best remembered as a collector and translator of ancient myths. Her anthologies *Mythology* 1942 and *The Great Age of Greek Literature* 1943 were, for many years, standard textbooks.

Hamilton Emma (born Amy Lyon), Lady 1765–1815. wife of Sir William Hamilton (1730–1803) from 1791, envoy to the court of Naples, and mistress of Admiral Horatio ◊Nelson, whom she met in Naples in 1793. After his return from the Nile battle 1798, during the Napoleonic Wars, she became his mistress and their daughter, Horatia, was born 1801. After Nelson's death in battle 1805, Lady Hamilton spent her inheritance and died in debtor's prison in Calais. She had been a great beauty and had posed for the great artists of her youth, especially George ◊Romney.

Hamilton Richard 1922– . English artist, a pioneer of Pop art. His collage *Just What Is It That Makes Today's Homes So Different, So Appealing?* 1956 (Kunsthalle, Tübingen) is often cited as the first Pop art work.

Hamilton William Rowan 1805–1865. Irish mathematician whose formulation of Isaac Newton's dynamics proved adaptable to quantum theory, and whose "quarternion" theory was a forerunner of the branch of mathematics known as vector analysis.

Hamite a person regarded as a descendant of Ham, son of ◊Noah in the Bible; anthropologically, a member of any of several dark-skinned Caucasoid peoples of N and E Africa, including the ancient Egyptians and the Berbers. Their languages belong to the Hamitic branch of the Hamito-Semitic (Afro-Asiatic) family.

Hamito-Semitic languages family of languages spoken throughout the world. It has two main branches, the Hamitic languages of N Africa and the Semitic languages originating in Syria, Mesopotamia, Palestine, and Arabia, but now found from Morocco in the west to the Persian Gulf in the east.

The Hamitic languages include ancient Egyptian, Coptic, and Berber, while the Semitic languages include the largest number of speakers—modern Arabic—as well as Hebrew, Aramaic, and Syriac. The scripts of Arabic and Hebrew are written from right to left.

Hamlet tragedy by William ◊Shakespeare, first performed 1602. Hamlet, after much hesitation, avenges the murder of his father, the king of Denmark, by the king's brother Claudius, who has married Hamlet's mother. The play ends with the death of all three.

Hamlet's agonized indecision, real or feigned mental disorder, and awareness of role playing have been said to make him the first protagonist in English literature. He is haunted by his father's ghost demanding revenge, is torn between love and loathing for his mother, and becomes responsible for the deaths of his lover Ophelia, her father and brother, and his student companions Rosencrantz and Guildenstern. In the monologue beginning "To be, or not to be" he contemplates suicide.

Hamlin Hannibal 1809–1891. US political leader and vice-president 1861–65. He entered politics as a Democrat and served in the Maine state legislature 1836–41, the US House of Representatives 1843–47, and the US Senate 1848–61 (he was briefly governor of Maine 1857). His opposition to slavery led him to join the Republican party 1856. Hamlin served as Lincoln's vice-president during his first term 1861–65.

hammerhead

Born in Paris Hill, Maine, Hamlin worked at a succession of jobs before studying law and being admitted to the bar 1833. Returning to the senate as a Radical Republican 1868–80, he later served as US minister to Spain 1881–82.

Hamm industrial town in North Rhine–Westphalia, Federal Republic of Germany; population (1988) 166,000. There are coal mines and chemical and engineering industries.

Hammarskjöld Dag 1905–1961. Swedish secretary-general of the United Nations 1953–61. Over the ◊Suez Crisis 1956 he opposed Britain. His attempts to solve the problem of the Congo (now Zaïre), where he was killed in a plane crash, were criticized by the USSR. Nobel Peace Prize 1961.

hammer in track and field athletics, a throwing event in which only men compete. The hammer is a spherical weight attached to a chain with a handle. The competitor turns with the hammer over his head to gain momentum within the confines of a circle and throws it as far as he can. The hammer weighs 16 lb/7.26 kg, and may originally have been a blacksmith's hammer.

Hammerfest fishing port in NW Norway, northernmost town of Europe; population (1985) 7,500.

hammerhead several species of shark in the genus *Sphyrna*, found in tropical seas, characterized by having eyes at the ends of flattened extensions of the skull. They can grow to 13 ft/4 m.

Hammerstein Oscar II 1895–1960. lyricist and librettist who collaborated with Richard ◊Rodgers on some of the best-known American musicals, including *Oklahoma* 1943 (Pulitzer prize), *Carousel* 1945, *South Pacific* 1949 (Pulitzer prize), *The King and I* 1951, and *The Sound of Music* 1959.

Grandson of opera impresario Oscar Hammerstein, he earned his first successes with *Rose Marie* 1924, music by Rudolf Friml; *Desert Song* 1926, music by Sigmund Romberg; and *Show Boat* 1927, music by Jerome Kern. *Show Boat* represented a major step forward in musical theater in terms of integrated plot and character. After a moderate success at film scoring, he joined Rodgers and launched their 16-year monumentally successful collaboration.

Hammer v Dagenhart a US Supreme Court decision 1918 dealing with Congress's power to regulate labor practices in the manufacture of goods for interstate trade. The father of a child who worked in a North Carolina cotton mill sued the mill for an infraction of the Child Labor Law 1916, which prohibited the interstate sale of products of child labor. The Court held that the law was invalid because it regulated local manufacturing under the guise of interstate commerce regulations. ◊*US* v *Darby Lumber Co* overturned *Hammer*.

Hammett (Samuel) Dashiell 1894–1961. US crime novelist. His works, *The Maltese Falcon* 1930, *The Glass Key* 1931, and the *The Thin Man* 1932, introduced the "hard-boiled" detective character into fiction.

Hammett was a former Pinkerton detective agent. In 1951 he was imprisoned for contempt of court for refusing to testify during the McCarthy era of anticommunist witch hunts. He lived with the playwright Lillian ◊Hellman for the latter half of his life.

Hammond city in the NW corner of Indiana, on the Calumet River, just S of Chicago, Illinois. It is a major transportation center, connecting to Lake

Michigan via the Calumet canal. Industries include soap, cereal products, publishing, railroad equipment, and transportation facilities for the city's surrounding steel plants and oil refineries; population (1990) 84,236.

Hammond Joan 1912– . Australian soprano, known in oratorio and opera, for example, *Madame Butterfly*, *Tosca*, and *Martha*.

Hammond organ an electric organ invented in the US by Laurens Hammond 1934 and widely used in gospel music. A precursor of the synthesizer.

Hammurabi king of Babylon from c. 1792 BC. He united his country and took it to the height of its power, although his consolidation of the legal code listed bloodthirsty punishments.

Hampshire county of S England
area 1,455 sq mi/3,770 sq km
cities Winchester (administrative headquarters), Southampton, Portsmouth, Gosport
features New Forest, area 144 sq mi/373 sq km, a Saxon royal hunting ground
famous people Jane Austen, Charles Dickens, Gilbert White.

Hampton Wade 1818–1902. US politician and Confederate military leader. At the outbreak of the American Civil War, he raised and led a regiment of Confederate volunteers, seeing action at the First Battle of Bull Run. In 1862 Hampton was appointed brigadier general in the cavalry and in 1864 became the commander of the entire Confederate cavalry corps. After the war he returned to South Carolina. He later served as governor 1876–79 and US senator 1879–91.

Born in Charleston, South Carolina, Hampton was educated at Carolina College and later administered his family's plantation.

hamster rodent of the family Cricetidae with a thickset body, short tail, and cheek pouches to carry food. Several genera are found across Asia and in SE Europe. Hamsters are often kept as pets.

Species include the Eurasian black-bellied or common hamster *Cricetus cricetus*, about 10 in/25 cm long, which can be a crop pest and stores up to 200 lb/90 kg of seeds in its burrow. The golden hamster *Mesocricetus auratus* lives in W Asia and SE Europe. All golden hamsters now kept as pets originated from one female and 12 young captured in Syria in 1930.

Hamsun Knut 1859–1952. Norwegian novelist whose first novel *Sult/Hunger* 1890 was largely autobiographical. Other works include *Pan* 1894 and *The Growth of the Soil* 1917, which won him a Nobel Prize in 1920. His hatred of capitalism made him sympathize with Nazism, and he was fined in 1946 for collaboration.

Hancock John 1737–1793. US revolutionary politician. As president of the Continental Congress 1775–77, he was the first to sign the Declaration of Independence in 1776. Because he signed it in a large, bold hand (in popular belief, so that it would be big enough for George III to see), his name became a colloquial term for a signature in the US. He coveted command of the Continental Army, deeply resenting the selection of George ◊Washington. He was governor of Massachusetts 1780–85 and 1787–93.

Hand Learned Billings 1872–1961. US jurist. Born in Albany, New York, and educated at Harvard, Hand received his law degree 1896. Appointed federal district judge by President Taft 1909, Hand was named to the Second Circuit Court of Appeals by President Coolidge 1924. He became chief judge of that court in 1939. Serving there until 1951, he handed down opinions in landmark copyright, antitrust, and First-Amendment cases.

Although never named to the US Supreme Court, Hand was considered a leading jurist of his day. A collection of his essays, *The Spirit of Liberty*, was published 1952.

Handel Georg Friedrich (George Frederick) 1685–1759. German composer, who became a British subject 1726. His first opera, *Almira*, was performed in Hamburg 1705. In 1710 he was appointed Kapellmeister to the elector of Hanover (the future George I of England). In 1712 he settled in England, where he established his popularity with works such as the *Water Music* 1717 (written for George I). His great choral works include the *Messiah* 1742 and the later oratorios *Samson* 1743, *Belshazzar* 1745, *Judas Maccabaeus* 1747, and *Jephtha* 1752.

Handel *Portrait by Thomas Hudson (1756) National Portrait Gallery, London.*

Born in Halle, he abandoned the study of law 1703 to become a violinist at Keiser's Opera House in Hamburg. Visits to Italy (1706–10) inspired a number of operas and oratorios, and in 1711 his opera *Rinaldo* was performed in London. *Saul* and *Israel in Egypt* (both 1739) were unsuccessful, but his masterpiece the *Messiah* was acclaimed on its first performance in Dublin 1742. Other works include the pastoral *Acis and Galatea* 1718 and a set of variations for harpsichord that were later nicknamed "The Harmonious Blacksmith." In 1751 he became totally blind.

Handke Peter 1942– . Austrian novelist and playwright whose first play *Insulting the Audience* 1966 was an example of "antitheater writing." His novels include *Die Hornissen/The Hornets* 1966 and *The Goalie's Anxiety at the Penalty Kick* 1970. He wrote and directed the film *The Left-handed Woman* 1979.

Hangchow former name for ◊***Hangzhou***, port in Zhejiang province, China.

hang-gliding technique of unpowered sport flight using air currents, perfected by a US engineer named Rogallo in the 1970s. The aeronaut is strapped into a carrier, attached to a sail wing of nylon stretched on an aluminum frame like a paper dart, and jumps into the air from a high place, where updrafts of warm air allow soaring on the "thermals." See ◊gliding.

hanging execution by suspension, usually with a drop of 2–6 ft/0.6–2 m, so that the powerful jerk of the tightened rope breaks the neck. This was once a common form of ◊capital punishment in Europe and is still practiced in some states in the US.

Hangzhou or ***Hangchow*** port and capital of Zhejiang province, China; population (1986) 1,250,000. It has jute, steel, chemical, tea, and silk industries.

Hangzhou has fine landscaped gardens and was the capital of China 1127–1278 under the Sung dynasty.

Hanna Mark 1837–1904. US businessman and political leader. As a businessman naturally sympathetic to the Republican party, he was a supporter of Garfield in 1880 and became McKinley's closest adviser. Named chairman of the Republican National Committee, Hanna engineered McKinley's victories in 1896 and 1900. He served in the US Senate from 1896 until his death.

Born in New Lisbon, Ohio, Hanna attended Case Western Reserve College before joining his father in business. He later became one of Cleveland's civil leaders, founding the Union National Bank and buying the *Cleveland Herald*.

Hannibal 247–182 BC. Carthaginian general from 221 BC, son of Hamilcar Barca. His siege of Saguntum (now Sagunto, near Valencia) precipitated the 2nd ◊Punic War with Rome. Following a campaign in Italy (after crossing the Alps in 218 with 57 elephants), Hannibal was the victor at Trasimene in 217 and Cannae in 216, but he failed to take Rome. In 203 he returned to Carthage to meet a Roman invasion but was defeated at Zama in 202 and exiled in 196 at Rome's insistence.

Hannibal town in Missouri, population (1990) 18,004. Mark Twain lived here as a boy and made it the setting of *The Adventures of Huckleberry Finn*.

Hanoi capital of Vietnam, on the Red river; population (1979) 2,571,000. Industries include textiles, paper, and engineering.

Captured by the French in 1873, it was the capital of French Indochina 1887–1946. It was the capital of North Vietnam 1954–76. Hanoi University was founded 1918.

Hanover industrial city, capital of Lower Saxony, Federal Republic of Germany; population (1988) 506,000. Industries include machinery, vehicles, electrical goods, rubber, textiles, and oil refining.

From 1386, it was a member of the ◊Hanseatic League, and from 1692 capital of the electorate of Hanover (created a kingdom 1815). ◊George I of England was also Elector of Hanover, and the two countries shared the same monarch until the accession of Victoria 1837. Since Salic Law meant a woman could not rule in Hanover, the throne passed to her uncle, Ernest, Duke of Cumberland. His son was forced by ◊Bismarck to abdicate 1866, and Hanover became a Prussian province. In 1946, Hanover was merged with Brunswick and Oldenburg to form the *Land* of Lower Saxony.

Hanover German royal dynasty that ruled Great Britain and Ireland 1714–1901. Under the Act of ◊Settlement 1701, the succession passed to the ruling family of Hanover, Germany, on the death of Queen Anne. On the death of Queen Victoria, the crown passed to Edward VII of the house of Saxe-Coburg.

Hanseatic League (German *Hanse* "group, society") a confederation of N European trading cities from the 12th century to 1669. At its height in the late 14th century the Hanseatic League included over 160 cities and towns, among them Lübeck, Hamburg, Cologne, Breslau, and Cracow. The basis of the league's power was its monopoly of the Baltic trade and its relations with Flanders and England. The decline of the Hanseatic League from the 15th century was caused by the closing and moving of trade routes and the development of nation states.

The earliest association had its headquarters in Visby, Sweden; it included over 30 cities, but was gradually supplanted by that headed by Lübeck. Hamburg and Lübeck established their own trading stations in London in 1266 and 1267 respectively, which coalesced in 1282 with that of Cologne to form the so-called Steelyard. There were three other such stations: Bruges, Bergen, and Novgorod. The last general assembly 1669 marked the end of the league.

Hansel and Gretel fairy tale, collected by the Grimm brothers. Hansel and Gretel are children (brother and sister) abandoned in the forest by their poor parents. They find a cottage made of gingerbread and are captured by the child-eating witch who lives there, but escape by wit and ingenuity. The happy ending reunites them with their parents. The story was made into a children's opera by ◊Humperdinck in 1893.

Hanukah or ***Chanukah*** Jewish festival of lights, which lasts eight days in December and celebrates the recapture of the Temple in Jerusalem by Judas Maccabaeus and his men in 164 BC, and the "miracle" of one day's oil lasting for eight days when the Eternal Light was relit.

Hanuman in the Sanskrit epic ◊*Rāmāyana*, the Hindu monkey god and king of Hindustan (N India). He helped Rama (an incarnation of the god Vishnu) to retrieve his wife Sita, abducted by Ravana of Lanka (now Sri Lanka).

Hanyang former Chinese city, now merged in ◊Wuhan, in Hubei province.

haploid having a single set of ◊chromosomes in each cell. Most higher organisms are ◊diploid—that is, they have two sets—but some plants, such as mosses, liverworts, and many seaweeds, are haploid. Male honey bees are haploid because they develop from eggs that have not been fertilized. See also ◊meiosis.

Hapsburg or ***Habsburg*** European royal family, former imperial house of Austria-Hungary. The name comes from the family castle in Switzerland. The Hapsburgs held the title Holy Roman emperor 1273–91, 1298–1308, 1438–1740, and 1745–1806. They ruled Austria from 1278, under the title emperor 1806–1918.

hara-kiri ritual suicide of the Japanese samurai (military caste) since the 12th century. Today it is illegal. It was carried out to avoid dishonor or to demonstrate sincerity, either voluntarily or on the order of a feudal lord. The correct japanese term is *seppuku* and, traditionally, the ritual involved cutting open one's stomach with a dagger before one's head was struck off by another samurai's sword.

Harappa ruined city in the Punjab, NW Pakistan, of a prehistoric culture in India, the ◊Indus Valley civilization, which flourished from 2500 to 1700 BC. It is one of two such great cities known; the other is ◊Mohenjo Daro.

Harare capital of Zimbabwe, on the Mashonaland plateau, about 5,000 ft/1,525 m above sea level; population (1982) 656,000. It is the center of a rich farming area (tobacco and corn), with metallurgical and food processing industries.

The British occupied the site in 1890 and named it Fort Salisbury in honor of Lord Salisbury, then prime minister of the UK. It was capital of the Federation of Rhodesia and Nyasaland 1953–63.

Harbin or ***Haerhpin*** or ***Pinkiang*** port on the Songhua river, NE China; capital of Heilongjiang province; population (1986) 2,630,000. Industries include metallurgy, machinery, paper, food processing, and sugar refining, and it is a major rail junction. Harbin was developed by Russian settlers after Russia was granted trading rights there 1896, and more Russians arrived as refugees after the October Revolution 1917.

hard disks in computing, a storage device consisting of a rigid magnetic disk permanently housed in a sealed case. Hard disks are the same sizes as ◊floppy discs but are much faster and have far greater memory capacities, typically between 20 and 150 ◊megabytes.

Hardenberg Karl August von 1750–1822. Prussian politician, foreign minister to King Frederick William III of Prussia during the Napoleonic Wars. He later became chancellor. His military and civic reforms were restrained by the reactionary tendencies of the king.

Hardicanute c. 1019–1042. King of England from 1040. Son of Canute, he was king of Denmark from 1028. In England he was considered a harsh ruler.

Hardie (James) Keir 1856–1915. Scottish Socialist, member of Parliament 1892–95 and 1900–15. He worked in the mines as a boy and in 1886 became secretary of the Scottish Miners' Federation. In 1888 he was the first Labour candidate to stand for Parliament; he entered Parliament independently as a Labor member in 1892 and was a chief founder of the ◊Independent Labor Party in 1893.

Harding Warren G(amaliel) 1865–1923. 29th president of the US 1921–23, a Republican whose administration was known for its corruption. Harding entered the US Senate in 1914. As president he concluded the peace treaties with Germany, Austria, and Hungary, and in the same year called the ◊Washington Conference. He opposed US membership in the ◊League of Nations, thus reinforcing the traditional US position of neutrality. There were charges of corruption among members of his cabinet (the ◊Teapot Dome Scandal), and Harding generally turned a benign eye to the activities of his close associates.

Harding was born in Corsica, Ohio, and graduated from Ohio Central College 1882. Before entering politics, he was a newspaper editor and publisher. He was an Ohio state senator 1898–1904 and lieutenant governor 1904–05. During his presidential administration, the various treaties stemming from the Washington Conference, providing for naval disarmament, and ostensibly stabilizing international relations between the great power signatories, were considered at the time a diplomatic coup for the US and Harding. He died in office shortly after undeniable evidence of corruption in his administration began to surface. He was succeeded by Calvin ◊Coolidge.

Harding *The 29th president of the United States of America, Warren G Harding, a Republican. 1921–1923.*

hardness physical property of materials that governs their use. Methods of heat treatment can increase the hardness of metals. A scale of hardness was devised by Friedrich ◊Mohs in the 1800s, based upon the hardness of certain minerals from soft talc (Mohs hardness 1) to diamond (10), the hardest of all materials. See also ◊Brinell hardness test.

The hardness of water refers to the presence of dissolved minerals in it that prevent soap lathering, particularly compounds of calcium and magnesium. Treatment with a water softener may remove or neutralize them.

Hardouin-Mansart Jules 1646–1708. French architect to Louis XIV from 1675. He designed the lavish Baroque extensions to the palace of Versailles (from 1678) and Grand Trianon. Other works include the Invalides Chapel in Paris 1680–91, the Place de Vendome, and the Place des Victoires in Paris.

Hardwar town in Uttar Pradesh, India, on the right bank of the river Ganges; population (1981) 115,513. The name means "door of Hari" (or *Vishnu*). It is one of the holy places of the Hindu religion and a pilgrimage center. The *Kumbhmela* festival, held every 12th year in honor of the god Siva, attracts about 1 million pilgrims.

hardware in computing, the mechanical, electrical, and electronic components of a computer system, as opposed to the various programs, which constitute ◊software.

In a microcomputer, hardware might include the circuit boards, the power supply and housing of the processor unit, the VDT (screen), external memory devices such as disk drives, a printer, the keyboard, and so on.

Hardy Oliver 1892–1957. US film comedian, member of the duo ◊Laurel and Hardy.

Hardy Thomas 1840–1928. English novelist and poet. His novels, set in rural "Wessex" (his native West Country), portray intense human relation-

Hardy *English novelist and poet Thomas Hardy, whose late-19th-century novels caused great controversy.*

ships played out in a harshly indifferent natural world. They include *Far From the Madding Crowd* 1874, *The Return of the Native* 1878, *The Mayor of Casterbridge* 1886, *The Woodlanders* 1887, *Tess of the D'Urbervilles* 1891, and *Jude the Obscure* 1895. His poetry includes the *Wessex Poems* 1898, the blank-verse epic of the Napoleonic Wars *The Dynasts* 1904–08, and several volumes of lyrics.

Born in Dorset, Hardy was trained as an architect. His first success was *Far From the Madding Crowd*. *Tess of the D'Urbervilles*, subtitled "A Pure Woman," outraged public opinion by portraying as its heroine a woman who had been seduced. The even greater outcry that followed *Jude the Obscure* 1895 reinforced Hardy's decision to confine himself to verse.

Hardy-Weinberg equilibrium in population genetics, the theoretical relative frequency of different ◊alleles within a given population of a species, when the stable endpoint of evolution in an undisturbed environment is reached.

hare mammal of the genus *Lepus* of the family Leporidae (which also includes rabbits) in the order Lagomorpha. Hares are larger than rabbits, with very long black-tipped ears, long hind legs, and short, upturned tails.

Throughout the long breeding season Jun–Aug, there are chases and "boxing matches" among males and females; the expression "mad as a March hare" arises from this behavior.

Unlike rabbits, hares do not burrow. Their furred, open-eyed young (leverets) are cared for in a shallow depression rather than a specially prepared nest cavity. Jack rabbits and snowshoe rabbits are actually hares.

harebell perennial plant *Campanula rotundifolia* of the ◊bellflower family, with bell-shaped blue flowers, found on dry grassland and heaths. It is known in Scotland as the ***bluebell***.

Hare Krishna popular name for a member of the ◊International Society for Krishna Consciousness, derived from their chant.

harelip congenital facial deformity, a cleft in the upper lip and jaw, which may extend back into the palate (cleft palate). It can be remedied by surgery.

Hare's apparatus

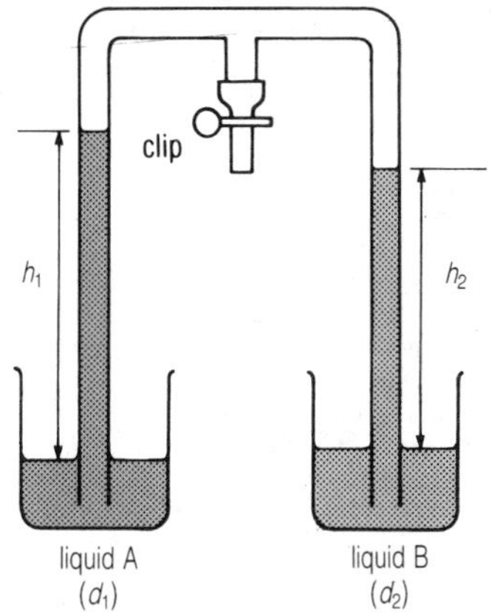
clip
h_1
h_2
liquid A
(d_1)
liquid B
(d_2)

Hare's apparatus in physics, a specific kind of ◊hydrometer used to compare the relative densities of two liquids, or to find the density of one if the other is known. It was invented by US chemist Robert Hare (1781–1858).

It consists of a vertical E-shaped glass tube, with the long limbs dipping into the two liquids and a tap on the short limb. Operating the tap removes air, pushing the liquids up the tubes by atmospheric pressure. When the tap is closed, the heights of the liquids are inversely proportional to their relative densities.

Harfleur port in NW France; population (1985) 9,700. Important in medieval times, it was superseded by ◊Le Havre.

Hargeisa trading center in NW Somalia; population (1988) 400,000.

Hargobind 1595–1644. Indian religious leader, sixth guru (teacher) of Sikhism 1606–44. He encouraged Sikhs to develop military skills in response to growing persecution. At the festival of ◊Diwali, Sikhs celebrate his release from prison.

Hargraves Edward Hammond 1816–1891. Australian prospector, born in England. In 1851 he found gold in the Blue Mountains of New South Wales, thus beginning the first Australian gold rush.

Hargreaves James died 1778. English inventor who coinvented a carding machine for combing wool in 1760. About 1764 he invented his "spinning-jenny," which enabled a number of threads to be spun simultaneously by one person.

Harijan (Hindi "children of god") member of the Indian ◊caste of untouchables. The compassionate term was introduced by Mahatma Gandhi during the independence movement.

harijan see ◊untouchable.

Har Krishen 1656–1664. Indian religious leader, eighth guru (teacher) of Sikhism 1661–64, who died at the age of eight.

Harlan John Marshall 1833–1911. US jurist and associate justice of the US Supreme Court 1877–1911. After practicing law and politics in Kentucky, Harlan supported the Union during the Civil War, serving as colonel in the 10th Kentucky Volunteer Infantry and being elected Kentucky attorney general 1863. He was defeated as Republican candidate for governor of Kentucky 1871, 1875. After service on a federal Reconstruction Commission in Louisiana, Harlan was appointed associate justice by President Hayes 1877.

Harlan John Marshall 1899–1971. US jurist and Supreme Court justice. After service in the US attorney's office 1925–27 he joined the staff of the state attorney general 1928–30. Harlan later established a private practice but returned to public life as chief counsel for the New York Crime Commission 1951–53. In 1954 President Eisenhower appointed Harlan to the US Supreme

Harlow *Hollywood film star Jean Harlow, known as the "blonde bombshell."*

Court. As associate justice, he was a conservative, especially in the areas of free speech and civil and criminal rights.

Born in Chicago and educated at Princeton and Oxford, Harlan studied law at New York University and was admitted to the bar 1925.

Harlem commercial and residential district of Manhattan, New York City. The principal thoroughfare, 125th Street, runs E-W between the Hudson River and the East river. It was a Dutch settlement in 1658; it developed as a black population center from World War I. Harlem's heyday was the 1920s, when it established its reputation as the intellectual, cultural, and entertainment center of black America. Once noted for its music clubs and theaters, it retained the famed Apollo Theatre; the Dance Theater and Theater of Harlem also are here.

Harlem Globetrotters US touring basketball team that plays exhibition matches worldwide. Comedy routines as well as their great manual skills with the ball are features of the games. They were founded by Abraham Saperstein (1903–1966) in 1927.

Harlem Renaissance a movement in US literature in the 1920s that used African-American life and black culture as its subject matter; it was an early manifestation of black pride in the US. The center of the movement was the Harlem section of New York City.

Harlem was the place where aspects of African-American culture, including jazz, flourished from the early 20th century, and attracted a new white audience. The magazine *Crisis*, edited by W E B DuBois, was a forum for the new black consciousness; writers associated with the movement include Langston Hughes, Zora Neale Hurston, James Weldon Johnson, and Countee Cullen.

Harley Robert, 1st Earl of Oxford 1661–1724. British Tory politician, chief minister to Queen Anne 1711–14, when he negotiated the Treaty of Utrecht in 1713. Accused of treason as a ◊Jacobite after the accession of George I, he was imprisoned 1714–17.

Harlingen city in the SE corner of Texas, S of Corpus Christi and just N of the Mexican border. Connected to the Rio Grande by an intracoastal waterway, it serves as the processing and marketing area for the lower Rio Grande valley. Industries include citrus-fruit processing and cotton products; population (1990) 48,735.

Harlow Jean. Adopted name of Harlean Carpenter 1911–1937. US film actress, the first "platinum blonde," and the wisecracking sex symbol of the 1930s. Her films include *Hell's Angels* 1930, *Red Dust* 1932, *Platinum Blonde* 1932, *Dinner at Eight* 1933, *China Seas* 1935, and *Saratoga* 1937, during the filming of which she died (her part was completed by a double—with rear and long shots).

harmattan in meteorology, a dry and dusty NE wind that blows over W Africa.

harmonica or ***mouth organ*** a pocket-sized reed organ blown directly from the mouth; invented by Charles Wheatstone 1829.

harmonics in music, a series of componential vibrations that combine to form a musical tone. The number and relative prominence of harmonics produced determines an instrument's tone color (timbre). An oboe is rich in harmonics, the flute has few. Harmonics conform to successive divisions of the sounding air column or string: their pitches are harmonious.

harmonium a keyboard reed organ of the 19th century, powered by foot-operated bellows.

Widely adopted in the US as a home and church instrument, in France and Germany the harmonium flourished as a concert solo and orchestral instrument, being written for by Karg-Elert, Schoenberg, and Saint-Saëns.

harmony in music, any simultaneous combination of sounds, as opposed to melody, which is a succession of sounds. Although the term suggests a pleasant or agreeable sound, it is applied to any combination of notes, whether consonant or dissonant. Harmony deals with the formation of chords and their interrelation and logical progression.

The founder of harmonic theory was Jean-Philippe ◊Rameau. In his *Traité de l'harmonie/Treatise on Harmony* 1722, he established a system of chord classification on which subsequent methods of harmony have been based.

Harold two kings of England:

Harold I died 1040. King of England from 1035. The illegitimate son of Canute, known as Harefoot, he claimed the throne 1035 when the legitimate heir Hardicanute was in Denmark. In 1037 he was elected king.

Harold II c. 1020–1066. King of England from Jan 1066. He succeeded his father Earl ◊Godwin 1053 as earl of Wessex. In 1063 William of Normandy (◊William I) tricked him into swearing to support his claim to the English throne, and when the Witan (a council of high-ranking religious and secular men) elected Harold to succeed Edward the Confessor, William prepared to invade. Meanwhile, Harold's treacherous brother Tostig (died 1066) joined the king of Norway, Harald III Hardrada (1015–1066), in invading Northumbria. Harold routed and killed them at Stamford Bridge Sept 25. Three days later William landed at Pevensey, Sussex, and Harold was killed at the Battle of Hastings Oct 14, 1066.

harp a plucked musical string instrument, with the strings stretched vertically within a wooden frame, normally triangular. The concert harp is now the largest musical instrument to be plucked by hand. It has up to 47 strings, and seven pedals set into the soundbox at the base to alter pitch.

The harp existed in the West as early as the 9th century, and it was common among medieval minstrels. At that time it was quite small, and was normally placed on the knees. It evolved in size caused by a need for increased volume following its introduction into the orchestra in the 19th century. The harp has also been used in folk music, as both a solo and accompanying instrument, and is associated with Wales and Ireland.

Harper's Ferry village in W Virginia, where the Potomac River meets the Shenandoah. It is famous for the incident in 1859 when antislavery leader John ◊Brown seized the federal government's arsenal here, an action that helped precipitate the Civil War. During the war the strategically located settlement was the site of several engagements. In commemoration, Harper's Ferry National Historical Park is here.

Harpies in early Greek mythology, wind spirits; in later legend they have horrific women's faces and the bodies of vultures.

harpsichord keyboard musical instrument common in the 16th–18th centuries, until superseded by the piano. The strings are plucked by quills. It was revived in the 20th century for the authentic performance of early music.

Har Rai 1630–1661. Indian religious leader, seventh guru (teacher) of Sikhism 1644–61.

harrier bird of prey of the genus *Circus* of the family Accipitridae. Harriers have long wings and legs, short beaks and soft plumage. They are found throughout the world.

The northern harrier or marsh hawk *C. cyaneus* is native to North America.

harrier breed of dog, a small hound originally used for hare-hunting.

Harriman (William) Averell 1891–1986. US diplomat. He was administrator of ◊lend-lease in World War II and warned of the Soviet Union's aggressive intentions from his post as ambassador to the USSR 1943–46. He became Democratic secretary of commerce 1946–48 in Truman's administration, governor of New York 1955–58, and negotiator of the Nuclear Test Ban Treaty with the USSR 1963. He served the L Johnson administration 1968–69 in the opening rounds of the Vietnam war peace talks at which he was chief negotiator.

Harris southern part of ◊Lewis with Harris, in the Outer ◊Hebrides; area 193 sq mi/500 sq km; population (1971) 2,900. It is joined to Lewis by a narrow isthmus. Harris tweeds are produced here.

Harris Arthur Travers 1892–1984. British marshal of the Royal Air Force in World War II. Known as "Bomber Harris," he was Commander in Chief of Bomber Command 1942–45.

He was an autocratic and single-minded leader, and was criticized for his policy of civilian-bombing of selected cities in Germany; he authorized the fire-bombing raids on Dresden, in which more than 100,000 died.

Harris Frank 1856–1931. Irish journalist who wrote colorful biographies of Oscar Wilde and and George Bernard Shaw, and an autobiography, *My Life and Loves* 1926, originally banned in the UK and the US for its sexual contents.

Harris Joel Chandler 1848–1908. US author, born in Georgia. He wrote tales narrated by the former slave "Uncle Remus," based on black folklore, and involving the characters Br'er Rabbit and the Tar Baby.

Harris Louis 1921– US pollster. He joined the Roper polling organization 1947 and became a partner in that firm 1954. Developing his own research techniques, he founded Louis Harris and Associates 1956. Hired by the 1960 Kennedy presidential campaign, Harris gained a national reputation and later served as a consultant to the CBS television network and as a political columnist.

Born in New Haven, Connecticut, he was educated at the University of North Carolina. After World War II, Harris gained his first experience in testing public opinion in his work for the American Veteran's Committee.

Harris Paul P 1878–1947. US lawyer, who founded the first ◊Rotary Club in Chicago 1905.

Harris Richard 1932– . Irish film actor known for playing rebel characters in such films as *This Sporting Life* 1963. His other films include *Camelot* 1967, *A Man Called Horse* 1970, *Robin and Marian* 1976, and *Tarzan the Ape Man* 1981. He won the 1990 Evening Standard Award for best actor in Pirandello's *Henry IV*.

Harris Roy 1898–1979. US composer, born in Oklahoma, who used American folk tunes. Among his works are the 10th symphony 1965 (known as "Abraham Lincoln") and the orchestral *When Johnny Comes Marching Home* 1935.

Harrisburg capital city of Pennsylvania, located in the S central part of the state, on the Susquehanna River; seat of Dauphin County. Industries include steel, railroad equipment, food processing, printing and publishing, and clothing; population (1990) 52,376.

Harrison William Henry 1773–1841. 9th president of the US 1841. Elected 1840 as a Whig, he died one month after taking office. His political career was based largely on his reputation as an Indian fighter, and his campaign was constructed to give the impression that he was a man of the people with simple tastes and that the New Yorker, Martin ◊Van Buren, his opponent, was a "foppish" sophisticate.

Born in Charles City County, Virginia, he joined the army 1791 at the age of 18. He resigned from the army 1798 and served as secretary of the Northwest Territory 1798–1800 and governor of the Indiana Territory 1801–12, where he drove off a minor Indian attack at Tippecanoe Creek, which was reported as a rout. Recalled to the army during the War of 1812, Harrison led his troops in the recapture of Detroit and was victorious at the Battle of the Thames River in Ontario He served in the US House of Representatives 1816–19 and the Senate 1825–28. Benjamin ◊Harrison was his grandson.

harrow agricultural implement used to break up the furrows left by the ◊plow and reduce the soil to a fine consistency or tilth, and to cover the seeds after sowing. The traditional harrow consists of spikes set in a frame; modern harrows use sets of disks.

Hart Gary 1936– . US Democrat politician, senator for Colorado from 1974. In 1980 he contested the Democratic nomination for the presidency and stepped down from his Senate seat in 1986 to run, again unsuccessfully, in the 1988 presidential campaign.

Early in 1987 he withdrew because of a scandal involving an alleged affair with a model; in Dec 1987 he briefly resumed his campaign and once more withdrew.

Hart Moss 1904–1961. US playwright. Born in New York City, Hart had his first play produced in 1922. After working for an independent producer and at Catskill resorts in New York State, he gained Broadway success with *Once in a Lifetime*, written with George S Kaufman 1930. He later collaborated with such major figures as Irving Berlin, Cole Porter, Kurt Weill, and Ira Gershwin. Among Hart's most famous works are *The Man Who Came to Dinner* 1939 and the films *Gentlemen's Agreement* 1947 and *A Star is Born* 1954.

Late in his career he became one of Broadway's most successful directors. His autobiography, *Act One*, appeared 1959.

Harte (Francis) Bret 1839–1902. US writer and humorist of the American West. He was born in Albany, New York, and became a California gold miner at 18, before founding *The Overland Monthly* 1868, in which he wrote short stories of the pioneer West, such as "The Outcasts of Poker Flat" and "The Luck of Roaring Camp," and poetry. In 1871, with his popularity at its height, he went East and signed a contract with *The Atlantic Monthly* for $10,000 for 12 stories a year, the most money then offered to a US writer. He entered a creative slump, however, and from 1878 to 1885 served as US consul in Germany and Scotland, where he entertained the literary circles. He then settled permanently in England.

hartebeest large African antelope *Alcelaphus buselaphus* with lyre-shaped horns set close on top of the head in both sexes. It may grow to 5 ft/1.5 m at the rather humped shoulders and up to 6 ft/2 m long. Clumsy-looking runners, hartebeest can still reach 40 mph/65 kph.

Hartford capital city of Connecticut, located in the N central part of the state, on the Connecticut River, NE of Waterbury. Industries include insurance, firearms, business office equipment, and tools; population (1990) 139,739. The Fundamental Orders of Connecticut, the first constitution that created a democratic government, were signed here 1639.

Hartford Convention in US history, a meeting of ◊Federalist party delegates from Dec 1814 to Jan

Harrison *The 9th president of the United States of America, William Henry Harrison, a Whig. 1841.*

1815 (at the end of the War of ◊1812) in Hartford, Connecticut. The meeting considered amendments to the US Constitution and the possibility of secession from the union in response to the adverse economic effects of the war on New England. The end of the war forestalled further action.

Hartly Marsden 1877–1943. US avant-garde painter. Born in Lewiston, Maine, he traveled in Europe to study art and was influenced by the Expressionist painters of the time. Hartly returned from Paris and Berlin with an original style that resembled the painting of the *Blaue Reiter* (Blue Rider) school. His paintings range from abstract, brightly colored representations of German soldiers and German military symbols, such as *Military* 1913, to New England landscapes, such as *Log Jam, Penobscot Bay* 1940–41.

hart's-tongue fern *Phyllitis scolopendrium* whose straplike undivided fronds, up to 24 in/60 cm long, have prominent brown spore-bearing organs on the undersides. The plant is native to Eurasia and E North America.

Hartz Mountains range running N to S in Tasmania, Australia, with two remarkable peaks: Hartz Mountain (4,113 ft/1,254 m) and Adamsons Peak (4,017 ft/1,224 m).

Harvard University oldest educational institution in the US, founded in 1636 at New Towne (later Cambridge), Massachusetts, and named after John Harvard (1607–38), who bequeathed half his estate and his library to it. Women were first admitted in 1969; the women's college of the university is Radcliffe College.

harvestman arachnid of the order Opiliones, with very long, thin legs and small bodies. They are distinguished from true spiders by the absence of a waist or constriction in the oval body. They are carnivorous and found from the Arctic to the tropics.

harvest mite another name for ◊***chigger***.

Harvey Laurence. Adopted name of Lauruska Mischa Skikne 1928–1973. British film actor of Lithuanian descent who worked both in England (*Room at the Top* 1958) and in Hollywood (*The Alamo* 1960; *The Manchurian Candidate* 1962).

Harvey William 1578–1657. English physician who discovered the circulation of blood. In 1628 he published his great book *De Motu Cordis/On the Motion of the Heart.*

After studying at Padua, Italy, under ◊Fabricius, he set out to question ◊Galen's account of the action of the heart. Later, Harvey explored the development of chick and deer embryos. He was court physician to James I and Charles I.

Haryana state of NW India
area 17,061 sq mi/44,200 sq km
capital Chandigarh
features part of the Ganges plain; a center of Hinduism
products sugar, cotton, oilseed, textiles, cement, iron ore

Harvey *English physician William Harvey published his theory of the circulation of the blood in 1628.*

population (1981) 12,851,000
language Hindi.

Hasdrubal Barca Carthaginian general, son of Hamilcar Barca and brother of Hannibal. He remained in command in Spain when Hannibal invaded Italy and, after fighting there against Scipio until 208, marched to Hannibal's relief. He was defeated and killed in the Metaurus valley, NE Italy.

Hašek Jaroslav 1883–1923. Czech writer. His masterpiece is the antiauthoritarian comic satire on military life under Austro-Hungarian rule, *The Good Soldier Schweik* 1923. During World War I he deserted to Russia, and eventually joined the Bolsheviks.

hashish drug made from the resin contained in the female flowering tops of hemp (◊cannabis).

hash total in computing, an arithmetic total of a set of arbitrary numeric values, such as account numbers. Although the total is meaningless, it is stored along with the data to which it refers. On subsequent occasions, the program recalculates the hash total and compares it with the one stored to ensure that the original numbers are still correct.

Hasid or ***Hassid, Chasid*** (plural Hasidim, Chasidim) a sect of Orthodox Jews, founded in 18th-century Poland, which stressed intense emotion as a part of worship. Many of their ideas are based on the ◊kabbala.

See ◊Hasidism.

Hasidism or ***Chasidism*** religious sect of Orthodox Judaism, founded by the Ba'al Shem Tov, based on study of ◊kabbala and popular piety. It spread against strong opposition throughout E Europe during the 18th and 19th centuries, led by charismatic leaders, the *zaddikim*. They stressed piety and ecstatic prayer, denouncing the academic approach of ◊talmudic academies. A later, more intellectual approach was instituted by the Lubavitch rabbi of Russia, now based in New York City. Hasidic men dress in the black suits and broad-brimmed hats of 18th-century European society, which they conservatively maintain.

Hassam Childe 1859–1935. US Impressionist painter and printmaker. He studied in Paris 1886–89. He became one of the members of The Ten, a group of American Impressionists who exhibited together until World War I.

Hassan II 1930– . King of Morocco from 1961; from 1976 he undertook the occupation of the Western Sahara when it was ceded by Spain.

The result was a long and damaging guerilla war against the Polisario fighters. Hassan is a moderate Arab leader, having met with Israeli leaders.

Hastings resort in East Sussex, England; population

(1981) 74,803. The chief of the ◊Cinque Ports, it has ruins of a Norman castle.

Hastings Warren 1732–1818. British colonial administrator. A protégé of Lord Clive, who established British rule in India, Hastings carried out major reforms, and became governor of Bengal in 1772 and governor general of India in 1774. Impeached for corruption on his return to England in 1785, he was acquitted in 1795.

Hastings, Battle of battle Oct 14, 1066 at which William the Conqueror, Duke of Normandy, defeated Harold, king of England. The site is 6 mi/10 km inland of Hastings, at Senlac, Sussex; it is marked by Battle Abbey.

William, having laid a claim to the English throne, dominated the battle with archers supported by cavalry, breaking through ranks of infantry. Both sides suffered heavy losses but the death of Harold allowed William to conquer and become England's king.

Hathor in ancient Egyptian mythology, the sky-goddess, identified with ◊Isis.

Hatshepsut c. 1540–c. 1481 BC. Queen of Egypt during the 18th dynasty. She was the daughter of Thothmes I, with whom she ruled until the accession to the throne of her husband and half brother Thotmes II. Throughout his reign real power lay with Hatshepsut, and she continued to rule after his death, as regent for her nephew Thotmes III.

Her reign was a peaceful and prosperous time in a period when Egypt was developing its armies and expanding its territories. The ruins of her magnificent temple at Deir el-Bahri survive.

Hatteras cape on the coast of N Carolina, where the waters of the N Atlantic meet the Gulf Stream, causing great turbulence; it therefore is noted for shipwrecks (more than 700 are said to have occurred here). Cape Hatteras National Seashore has both natural and historical interest, including a lighthouse and sea life typical of both the temperate and tropical zones.

Haughey Charles 1925– . Irish Fianna Fáil politician of Ulster descent. Dismissed in 1970 from Jack Lynch's cabinet for alleged complicity in IRA gun-running, he was afterward acquitted. Prime minister 1979–81, March–Nov 1982, and 1986– .

Hausa member of an agricultural Muslim people of NW Nigeria, numbering 9 million, whose Afro-Asiatic language is used as a trade language throughout W Africa.

Haussmann Georges Eugène, Baron Haussmann 1809–1891. French administrator who replanned medieval Paris 1853–70 to achieve the current city plan, with wide boulevards and parks. The cost of his scheme and his authoritarianism caused opposition, and he was made to resign.

haustorium (plural haustoria) a specialized organ produced by a parasitic plant or fungus that penetrates the cells of its host to absorb nutrients. It may be either an outgrowth of ◊hyphae, as in the case of parasitic fungi, or of the stems of flowering parasitic plants, as in dodders *Cuscuta*. The suckerlike haustoria of a dodder penetrate the vascular tissue of the host plant without killing the cells.

Haute-Normandie or Upper Normandy coastal region of NW France lying between Basse-Normandie and Picardy and bisected by the Seine; area 4,757 sq mi/12,300 sq km; population (1986) 1,693,000. It comprises the *départements* of Eure and Seine-Maritime; its capital is Rouen. Major ports include Dieppe and Fécamp. The area has many beech forests.

Havana capital and port of Cuba; population (1986) 2,015,000. Products include cigars and tobacco.

The palace of the Spanish governors and the stronghold of La Fuerza (1583) survive. In 1898 the blowing up of the US battleship *Maine* in the harbor began the ◊Spanish-American War.

Havel Vaclav 1936– . Czech playwright and politician, president from Dec 1989. His plays include *The Garden Party* 1963 and *Largo Desolato* 1985, about a dissident intellectual. Havel became

Havel *After several prison terms for his political ideals, playwright Vaclav Havel became president of Czechoslovakia 1989.*

widely known as a human-rights activist. He was imprisoned 1979–83 and again 1989 for support of Charter 77 (see ◊Czechoslovakia).

Haverhill city in NE Massachusetts on the Merrimac River, N of Boston. Manufactures include paints, chemicals, machine tools, and shoes; population (1990) 51,418.

Havre, Le see ◊Le Havre, port in France.

Hawaii Pacific state of the US; nickname Aloha State

area 6,485 sq mi/16,800 sq km

capital Honolulu, on Oahu

cities Hilo

physical consists of a chain of some 20 volcanic islands, of which 5 are chief: (1) Hawaii, noted for Mauna Kea (13,796 ft/4,205 m), the world's highest island mountain, and Mauna Loa (13,686 ft/4,170 m), the world's largest active volcanic crater; (2) Maui, the second largest of the islands; (3) Oahu, third largest, with the greatest concentration of population and tourist attractions–for example, Waikiki beach and the Pearl Harbor naval base; (4) Kauai; (5) Molokai, site of a historic leper colony

products sugar, coffee, pineapples, flowers, women's clothing

population (1990) 1,108,229; 34% European,

Hawaii

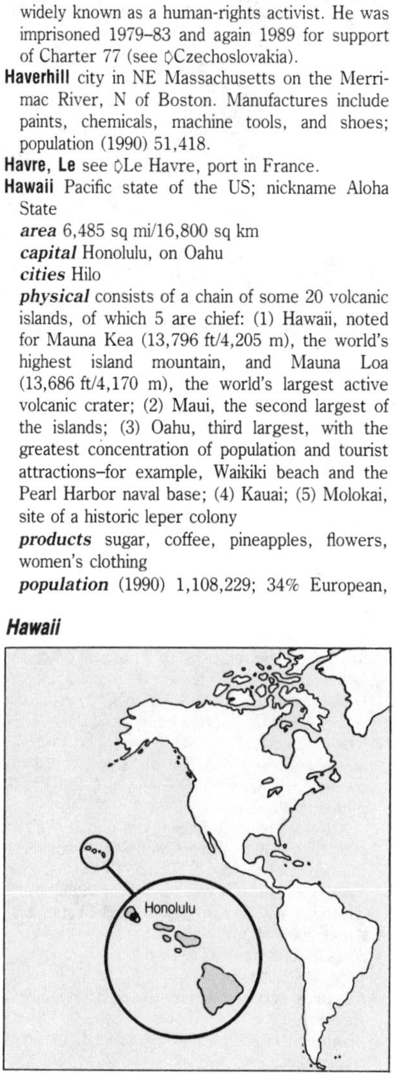
Honolulu

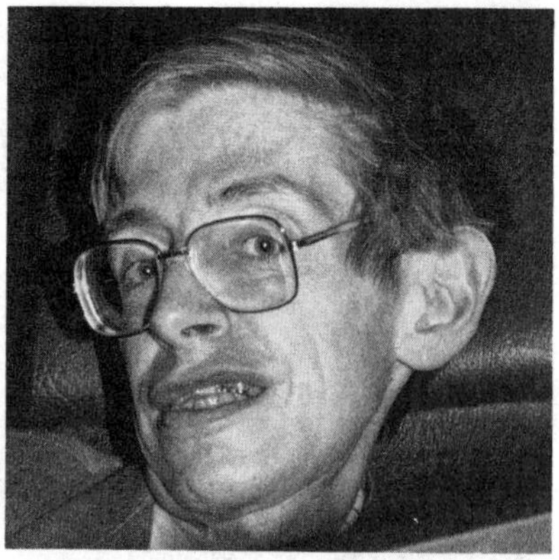

Hawking *British physicist and mathematician Stephen Hawking wrote the popular* A Brief History of Time.

25% Japanese, 14% Filipino, 12% Hawaiian, 6% Chinese

famous people Father Joseph Damien, Kamehameha I, Queen Liliuokalani, Sanford Dole

history a Polynesian kingdom from the 6th century until 1893; became a republic 1894; ceded itself to the US 1898, and became a US territory 1900. Japan's air attack on Pearl Harbor Dec 7, 1941, crippled the US Pacific fleet and turned the territory into an armed camp, under martial law, for the remainder of the war. Hawaii became a state 1959. Tourism is the chief source of income.

Captain Cook, who called Hawaii the Sandwich Islands, was the first known European visitor 1778.

hawfinch European finch *Coccothraustes coccothraustes* about 7 in/18 cm long. It feeds on berries and seeds, and can crack cherry stones with its large and powerful bill.

hawk any of various small- to medium-sized birds of prey of the family Accipitridae, other than eagles, kites, ospreys, and vultures. The name is used especially to describe the genera *Accipiter* and Buteo. Hawks have short, rounded wings compared with falcons, and keen eyesight.

The term "hawk" is also applied metaphorically to people with aggressive ideas on foreign policy, in contrast to moderate doves; it was originally used for US advocates of continuation and escalation of the Vietnam war.

Hawke Bob (Robert) 1929– . Australian Labor politician, on the right wing of the party. He was president of the Australian Council of Trade Unions 1970–80 and became prime minister 1983.

Hawkesbury river in New South Wales, Australia; length 300 mi/480 km. It is a major source of Sydney's water.

Hawking Stephen 1942– . English physicist who has researched ◊black holes and gravitational field theory. His books include *A Brief History of Time* 1988.

Professor of gravitational physics at Cambridge from 1977, he discovered that the strong gravitational field around a black hole can radiate particles of matter. Commenting on Einstein's remark, "God does not play dice with the universe," Hawking said: "God not only plays dice, he throws them where they can't be seen."

Hawkins Coleman (Randolph) 1904–1969. US virtuoso tenor saxophonist. He was, until 1934, a soloist in the swing band led by Fletcher Henderson (1898–1952), and was an influential figure in bringing the jazz saxophone to prominence as a solo instrument.

Hawkins Jack 1910–1973. British film actor, usually cast in authoritarian roles. His films include *The Cruel Sea* 1953, *The League of Gentlemen* 1959, *Zulu* 1963, *Waterloo* 1970. After 1966 his voice had to be dubbed following an operation for throat cancer that removed his vocal chords.

Hawthorne *Nathaniel Hawthorne counted fellow American novelist Herman Melville among his early supporters.*

hawk moth or sphinx moth any of a family, Sphingidae, of moths with thick bodies and narrow wings. Some 1,000 species are distributed throughout the world, but they are mainly tropical. The large hawk-moth larva usually has a "horn" at the end of its body—for example, the bright-green tomato hornworm *Protoparcequinquemaculata*.

Hawks Howard 1896–1977. US director and producer of a wide range of classic films, including *Scarface* 1932, *Bringing Up Baby* 1938, *The Big Sleep* 1946, and *Gentlemen Prefer Blondes* 1953.

Haworth Norman 1883–1950. English organic chemist who was the first to synthesize a vitamin (vitamin C), in 1933, for which he shared a Nobel Prize in 1937.

hawthorn shrub or tree of the genus *Crataegus* of the rose family Rosaceae. Species are most abundant in E North America, but many are also in Eurasia. All have alternate, toothed leaves and bear clusters of showy white, pink, or red flowers. Small applelike fruits can be red, orange, blue, or black. Hawthorns are popular as ornamentals.

Hawthorne Nathaniel 1804–1864. US author, who wrote about Puritan New England and won fame with *The Scarlet Letter* 1850, a powerful novel set in Boston 200 years earlier. He wrote three other novels (*The House of the Seven Gables* 1851, *The Blithedale Romance* 1852, and *The Marble Faun* 1860), many volumes of short stories, and *Tanglewood Tales* 1853, classic Greek legends retold for children. His short stories, which include "My Kinsman, Major Molineux" and "Young Goodman Brown," helped to establish the short story as an art form.

Born in Salem, Massachusetts, Hawthorne graduated from Bowdoin College and worked as a customs official. He was the US consul 1853–57 in Liverpool, England, and then lived in Italy until 1860. Hawthorne's fiction is marked by its haunting symbolism and its exploration of guilt, sin, and other complex moral and psychological issues. It had a profound effect on writers of his own time, notably his friend Herman Melville, and continues to influence writers.

hay preserved grass used for winter livestock feed. The grass is cut and allowed to dry in the field before being removed for storage in a barn.

The optimum period for cutting is when the grass has just come into flower and contains most feed value. During the natural drying process, the moisture content is reduced from 70–80% down to a safe level of 20%. In normal weather conditions, this takes from two to five days during which time the hay is turned by machine to ensure even drying. Hay is normally baled before removal from the field. One hectare of grass can produce up to 7.3 tons/7.5 tonnes of hay.

Hayden Sterling. Adopted name of John Hamilton 1916–1986. US film actor who played leading roles in Hollywood in the 1940s and early 1950s. Although later seen in some impressive character roles, his career as a whole failed to do justice to his talent. His work includes *The Asphalt Jungle* 1950, *Johnny Guitar* 1954, *Dr Strangelove* 1964, and *The Godfather* 1972.

Haydn Franz Joseph 1732–1809. Austrian composer. A teacher of Mozart and Beethoven, he was a major exponent of the Classical sonata form in his numerous chamber and orchestral works (he wrote more than 100 symphonies). He also composed choral music, including the oratorios *The Creation* 1798 and *The Seasons* 1801. He was the first great master of the string quartet.

Born in Lower Austria, he was Kapellmeister 1761–90 to Prince Esterházy. His work also includes operas, church music, and songs, and the "Emperor's Hymn," adopted as the Austrian, and later the German, national anthem.

Haydon Benjamin Robert 1786–1846. British historical painter. His attempts at "high art" include many gigantic canvasses such as *Christ's Entry into Jerusalem* 1820 (Philadelphia). His genre pictures include *The Mock Election* and *Chairing the Member*. He published *Autobiography and Memoirs* 1853, a lively account of the contemporary art scene and his own tragi-comic life.

Hayek Friedrich August von 1899– . Austrian economist. Born in Vienna, he taught at the London School of Economics 1931–50. His *The Road to Serfdom* 1944 was a critical study of Socialist trends in Britain. He won the 1974 Nobel Prize for Economics with Gunnar Myrdal.

He was professor of social and moral science at the University of Chicago 1950–62.

Hayes Rutherford Birchard 1822–1893. The 19th president of the US 1877–81, a Republican. Born in Ohio, he was a major general on the Union side in the Civil War. During his presidency federal troops (see ◊Reconstruction) were withdrawn from the Southern states and the Civil Service reformed.

He was noted for his honesty, and his integrity was viewed by many as a way to overcome the aura of corruption that had surrounded the ◊Grant administration. Under Hayes, the political role of federal employees was curtailed.

Hayes Office film-regulation body in the US. Officially known as the Motion Picture Producers and Distributors of America, it was created 1922 by the major film companies to improve the industry's image and provide internal regulation, including a strict moral code. It terminated in 1945.

The office was headed by Will H Hayes (1879–1954). A Production Code, listing all the subjects forbidden to films, was begun in 1930 and lasted until 1966, when it was replaced by a ratings system.

hay fever allergic reaction to pollen, causing sneezing, inflammation of the eyes, and asthmatic symptoms. Sufferers experience irritation caused by powerful body chemicals related to ◊histamine produced at the site of entry. Treatment is by antihistamine drugs.

Haywood William Dudley 1869–1928. US labor leader. Born in Salt Lake City, Utah, and having worked in the mines, Haywood joined the Western Federation of Miners (WFM) 1896. By 1899 he had become a national leader of the WFM and, in his tireless and forceful speaking tours throughout the country, had won the nickname "Big Bill." One of the founders of the Industrial Workers of the World (IWW, "Wobblies") 1905, Haywood was arrested for conspiracy to murder an antiunion politician. is acquittal in 1907 made him a labor hero. Arrested again for sedition during World War I, he spent his later years in exile in the Soviet Union.

Hayworth Rita. Adopted name of Margarita Carmen Cansino 1918–1987. US dancer and film actress who gave vivacious performances in 1940s musicals and steamy, erotic roles in *Gilda* 1946 and *Affair in Trinidad* 1952. She was known as Hollywood's "Goddess" during the height of her career. She was married to Orson Welles 1943–1948 and appeared in his films, including *The Lady From Shanghai* 1948. She was perfectly cast in *Pal Joey* 1957 and *Separate Tables* 1958. Her later appearances were intermittent and she retired in 1972, a victim of Alzheimer's disease.

hazardous substances waste substances, usually generated by industry, which represent a hazard to the environment or to people living or working nearby. Examples include radioactive wastes, acidic resins, arsenic residues, residual hardening salts, lead, mercury, nonferrous sludges, organic solvents, and pesticides. Their economic disposal or recycling is the subject of research.

hazel shrub or tree of the genus *Corylus*, family Corylaceae, including European common hazel or cob *C. avelana*, of which the filbert is the cultivated variety. North American species include the American hazel *C. americana*.

Hazlitt William 1778–1830. English essayist and critic whose work is characterized by invective, scathing irony, and a gift for epigram. His critical essays include *Characters of Shakespeare's Plays* 1817–18, *Lectures on the English Poets* 1818–19, *English Comic Writers* 1819, and *Dramatic Literature of the Age of Elizabeth* 1820. Other works are *Table Talk* 1821–22, *The Spirit of the Age* 1825, and *Liber Amoris* 1823.

H-bomb abbreviated for ◊hydrogen bomb.

Head Bessie 1937– . South African writer living in exile in Botswana. Her novels include *When Rain Clouds Gather* 1969, *Maru* 1971, and *A Question of Power* 1973.

Head Edith 1900–1981. US costume designer for Hollywood films who won eight Academy Awards for her designs in such films as *The Heiress* 1949, *All About Eve* 1950, and *The Sting* 1973.

headache pain in the head, caused by minor eye strain, stress, neck- or jaw-muscle strain, allergies, or physical illness such as infectious disease or brain tumor. It is marked by dilation of the cerebral blood vessels and irritation of the brain linings (meninges) and nerves.

health care implementation of the proper regimen to ensure long-lasting good health. Life expectancy is determined by overall efficiency of the body's vital organs and the rate at which these organs deteriorate. Fundamental health-care concerns are:

smoking This is strongly linked to heart disease, stroke, bronchitis, lung cancer, and other serious diseases.

exercise Regular physical exercise improves fitness, slows down the gradual decline in efficiency of the heart and lungs, and so helps to prolong life.

diet A healthy diet contains plenty of vegetable fiber, complex carbohydrates, vitamins, minerals, and enzymes, and polyunsaturated fats (which keep the level of blood cholesterol low), not saturated (animal) fats (which contribute to cholesterol storage in blood vessels).

weight Obesity (defined as generally being 20% or more above the desirable weight for age, sex, build, and height) is associated with many potentially dangerous conditions, such as coronary heart disease, diabetes, and stroke, as well as muscular and joint problems, and breathing difficulties.

alcohol Recommended maximum intake is no more than 21 units of alcohol a week for men, no more than 14 for women. (One glass of beer or wine or a single ounce of liquor is equivalent to one unit.) Doctors recommend at least two alcohol-free days a week. Excessive alcohol intake may lead to dependence and causes liver damage, which suppresses the immune system and may be fatal (see ◊cirrhosis).

health education teaching and advice on healthy living, including hygiene, nutrition, sex education, and advice on alcohol and drug abuse, smoking, and other threats to health. Health education in

Hayes *The 19th president of the United States of America, Rutherford B Hayes, a Republican. 1877–1881.*

Hearst *Newspaper owner William Randolph Hearst introduced sensationalist "yellow journalism," to increase sales.*

most secondary schools is also included within a course of personal and social education, or integrated into subjects such as biology, home economics, or physical education.

health psychology a new development within ◊clinical psychology that applies psychological principles to promote physical well-being. For example, people with high blood pressure can learn methods such as relaxation, meditation, and lifestyle changes.

health service government provision of medical care on a national scale.

State and local governments provide some public health services. The US provides care through private physicians and hospitals who are paid by the federally subsidized schemes Medicare and Medicaid. The Medicare health-insurance plan provides outpatient care for the elderly and disabled (toward which patients pay a share), and since 1985, fees for Medicare patients to join health-maintenance organizations (HMOs, covering visits to a group of doctors and hospital fees). The Medicaid state plan is paid to the state by the federal government for people unable to afford private care. US private health schemes include Blue Cross (established 1929) and Blue Shield (established 1917), as well as other insurance companies' plans.

Heard Island and McDonald Islands group of islands forming an Australian external territory in the S Indian Ocean, about 2,500 mi/4,000 km SW of Fremantle; area 158 sq mi/410 sq km. They were discovered 1833, annexed by Britain 1910, and transferred to Australia 1947. Heard Island, 26 mi/42 km by 12 mi/19 km, is glacier-covered, although the volcanic mountain Big Ben (9,000 ft/2,742 m), is still active. A weather station was built 1947. Shag Island is 5 mi/8 km to the N and the craggy McDonalds are 26 mi/42 km to the W.

hearing aid any device to improve the hearing of partially deaf people. Hearing aids usually consist of a battery-powered transistorized microphone/amplifier unit and earpiece. Some miniaturized aids are compact enough to fit in the ear or be concealed in the frame of eyeglasses.

hearsay evidence evidence given by a witness based on information passed to that person by others rather than evidence experienced at first-hand by the witness. It is usually not admissible as evidence in criminal proceedings.

Hearst William Randolph 1863–1951. US newspaper publisher, celebrated for his introduction of banner headlines, lavish illustration, and the sensationalist approach known as "yellow journalism."

He was also a Hollywood film maker (promoting the career of his long-time mistress Marian Davies) as well as an unsuccessful presidential candidate.

A campaigner in numerous controversies, and a strong isolationist, he was said to be the model for Citizen Kane in the 1941 film of that name by Orson Welles. He collected art treasures, antiques, zoo animals, and castles—one of which, San Simeon (Hearst Castle) in California, is a state museum and zoo.

heart muscular organ that contracts rhythmically to force blood around the body of an animal with a circulatory system. Annelid worms and some other invertebrates have simple hearts consisting of thickened sections of main blood vessels that pulse regularly. An earthworm has ten such hearts. Vertebrates have one heart. A fish heart has two chambers—the thin-walled atrium (once called the auricle) that expands to receive blood, and the thick-walled ventricle that pumps it out. Amphibians and most reptiles have two atria and one ventricle; birds and mammals have two atria and two ventricles. The beating of the heart is controlled by the autonomic nervous systems and an internal control center or pacemaker, the sinoatrial node.

heart beat the regular contraction and relaxation of the heart, and the accompanying sounds. As blood passes through the heart a double beat is heard. The first is produced by the sudden closure of the valves between the atria and the ventricles. The second, slightly delayed sound, is caused by the closure of the valves found at the entrance to the major arteries leaving the heart. Diseased valves may make unusual sounds, known as heart murmurs.

heartburn burning sensation below the breastbone (sternum). It results from irritation of the lower esophagus (gullet) by excessively acid stomach contents, as sometimes happens during pregnancy and in cases of duodenal ulcer or obesity. It is often due to a weak valve at the entrance to the stomach that allows its contents to well up into the esophagus.

heart-lung machine apparatus used during heart surgery to take over the functions of the heart and the lungs temporarily. It has a pump to circulate the blood around the body and is able to add oxygen to the blood and remove carbon dioxide from it. A heart-lung machine was first used for open-heart surgery in the US 1953.

Heart of Atlanta Motel Inc v US a US Supreme Court decision 1964 dealing with the constitutionality of certain Congressional measures designed to eliminate racial discrimination. The owner of the Heart of Atlanta Motel filed suit in protest of the

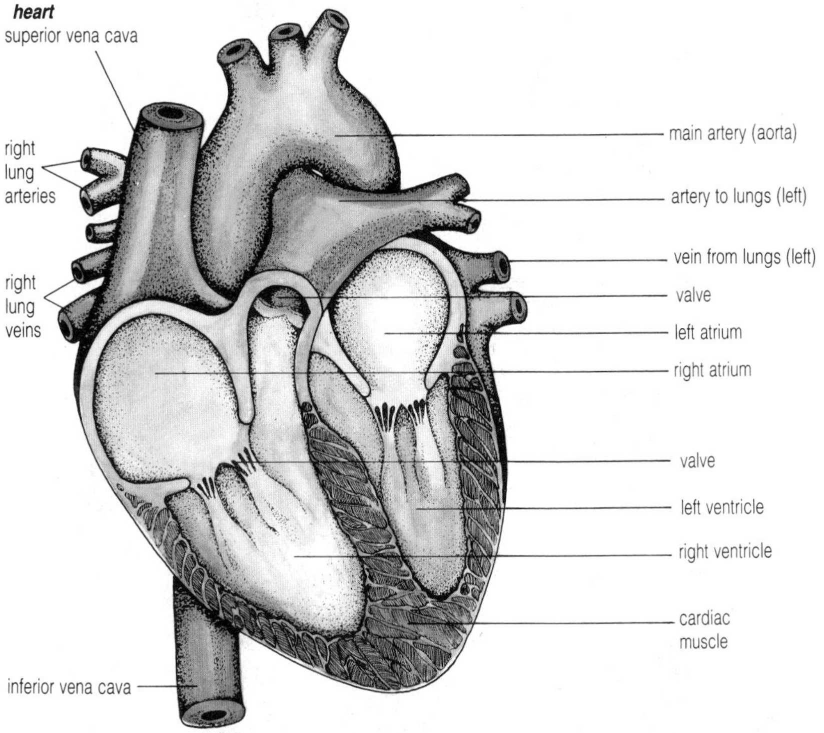
heart
superior vena cava
right lung arteries
right lung veins
inferior vena cava
main artery (aorta)
artery to lungs (left)
vein from lungs (left)
valve
left atrium
right atrium
valve
left ventricle
right ventricle
cardiac muscle

Civil Rights Act 1964, which prevented him from racially discriminating against his customers. The Court upheld the Civil Rights Act, ruling that since the motel was a business involved in interstate travel, it was subject to federal regulation. This reversed the decision in the ◊Civil Rights Cases 1883 that the government could not proscribe discrimination by private citizens.

Heart of Darkness a short novel by Joseph Conrad, published in 1902. Marlow, the narrator, tells of his journey by boat into the African interior to meet a company agent, Kurtz, who has adopted local customs and uses barbaric methods to exercise power over the indigenous people.

heat a form of internal energy of a substance due to the kinetic energy in the motion of its molecules or atoms. It is measured by ◊temperature. Heat energy is transferred by conduction, convection, and radiation. Heat always flows from a region of higher temperature to one of lower temperature. Its effect on a substance may be simply to raise its temperature, cause it to expand, melt it if a solid, vaporize it if a liquid, or increase its pressure if a confined gas.

Quantities of heat are usually measured in units of energy, such as joules (J) or calories (C).

The specific heat of a substance is the ratio of the quantity of heat required to raise the temperature of a given mass of the substance through a given range of temperature to the heat required to raise the temperature of an equal mass of water through the same range. It is measured by a ◊calorimeter.

Convection is the transmission of heat through a fluid (liquid or gas) on currents—for example, when the air in a room is warmed by a fire or radiator.

Conduction is the passing of heat along a medium to neighboring parts with no visible motion accompanying the transfer of heat—for example, when the whole length of a metal rod is heated when one end is held in a fire.

Radiation is heat transfer by infrared rays. It can pass through a vacuum, travels at the same speed as light, can be reflected and refracted, and does not affect the medium through which it passes. For example, heat reaches the Earth from the Sun by radiation.

heath in botany, any woody, mostly evergreen shrub of the family Ericaceae, native to Europe, Africa, and North America. Many heaths have bell-shaped pendant flowers. In the Old World the genera *Erica* and *Calluna* are the most common heaths, and include ◊heather.

Included among the heaths are North American blueberries, rhododendrons, mountain laurel, and Labrador tea.

Heath Edward (Richard George) 1916– . British Conservative politician, party leader 1965–75. As prime minister 1970–74 he took the UK into the European Community but was brought down by economic and industrial relations crises at home. In 1990 he undertook a mission to Iraq in an attempt to secure the release of British hostages.

heather low-growing evergreen shrub of the heath family, common on sandy or acid soil. The common heather *Calluna vulgaris* is a carpet-forming shrub, growing up to 24 in/60 cm high, bearing pale pink-purple flowers. It is found over much of Europe and has been introduced to North America.

heat pump machine, run by electricity or other power source, that cools the interior of a building by removing heat from interior air and pumping it out or, conversely, heats the inside by extracting energy from the atmosphere or from a hot-water source and pumping it in.

heat shield any heat-protecting coating or system; especially the coating (for example, tiles) used in spacecraft to protect the astronauts and equipment inside from the heat of re-entry when returning to Earth. Air friction can generate temperatures of up to 2,700°F/1,500°C on re-entry into the atmosphere.

heat storage any means of storing heat for release later. It is usually achieved by using materials that undergo phase changes; for example, ◊Glauber's salt and sodium pyrophosphate, which melts at 158°F/70°C. The latter is used to store off-peak heat in the home: the salt is liquefied by cheap heat during the night and then freezes to give off heat during the day.

Other developments include the use of plastic crystals, which change their structure rather than melting when they are heated. They could be incorporated in curtains or clothing.

heatstroke or ***sunstroke*** rise in body temperature caused by excessive exposure to heat. Mild heatstroke is experienced as feverish lassitude, sometimes with simple fainting; recovery is prompt following rest and replenishment of salt lost in sweat. Severe heatstroke causes collapse akin to that seen in acute ◊shock, and is potentially lethal without prompt treatment of cooling the body carefully and giving fluids to relieve dehydration.

In severe heatstroke, the brain swells, resulting in confusion of thought; the body becomes feverish and dehydrated, blood circulation slows, and organs, such as the kidneys, fail to function. Coma may ensue and, possibly, cardiac arrest.

heat treatment in industry, the subjection of metals and alloys to controlled heating and cooling after fabrication to relieve internal stresses and improve their physical properties. Methods include ◊annealing, quenching, and ◊tempering.

heaven in Christianity and some other religions, the abode of God and the destination of the virtuous after death. Theologians now usually describe it as a place or state in which the soul experiences the full reality of God.

Heaviside Oliver 1850–1925. British physicist. In 1902 he predicted the existence of an ionized layer of air in the upper atmosphere, which was known as the Kennelly-Heaviside layer but is now called the ◊E layer of the ◊ionosphere. Deflection from it makes possible the transmission of radio signals around the world, which would otherwise be lost in outer space.

heavy metal in music, a style of rock characterized by loudness, sex-and-violence imagery, and guitar solos. Heavy metal developed out of the hard rock of the late 1960s and early 1970s, was performed by such groups as Led Zeppelin and Deep Purple, and enjoyed a resurgence in the late 1980s. Bands of recent years include Van Halen, Def Leppard, AC/DC, and Guns n' Roses.

heavy metal metallic element of high atomic weight, for instance platinum, gold, and lead. Heavy metals are poisonous and tend to accumulate and persist in living systems, causing, for example, high levels of mercury (from industrial waste and toxic dumping) in shellfish and fish, which are in turn eaten by humans. Treatment of heavy-metal poisoning is difficult because available drugs are not able to distinguish between the heavy metals that are essential to living cells (zinc, copper) and those that are poisonous.

Various detoxification programs combining nutrition, herbs, fasts, and intestinal irrigation are often successful.

heavy water D_2O (technical name deuterium oxide) water containing the isotope deuterium instead of hydrogen (molecular weight 20 as opposed to 18 for ordinary water).

Its chemical properties are identical with those of ordinary water, while its physical properties differ slightly. It occurs in ordinary water in the ratio of about one part by mass of deuterium to 5,000 parts by mass of hydrogen and can be concentrated by electrolysis, the ordinary water being more readily decomposed by this means than the heavy water. It has been used in the nuclear industry.

Hebe in Greek mythology, the goddess of youth, daughter of Zeus and Hera.

Hebei or ***Hopei*** or ***Hupei*** province of N China
area 78,242 sq mi/202,700 sq km
capital Shijiazhuang
features includes special municipalities of Beijing and Tianjin
products cereals, textiles, iron, steel
population (1986) 56,170,000.

Hebrew a member of the Semitic people who lived in Palestine at the time of the Old Testament and who traced their ancestry to ◊Abraham of Ur, a city of Sumer.

Also the language of the Old Testament and Judaic literature, as well as the official language (since 1948) of the state of Israel, one of the Semitic languages of the Hamito-Semitic (Afro-

Asiatic) family. The Hebrew people were widely dispersed during the Roman Empire and learned the languages and cultures of those they lived among in Europe, the Near East, Asia, and (after 1492) the Americas, but continued using liturgical Hebrew in prayer, as well as the ancient Hebrew ◊alphabet to write both sacred works in Hebrew and secular works in ◊Yiddish, a 13th-century High German dialect. In the late 19th century, Hebrew was revived as a modern language, by the European Haskala movement, in both spoken and written forms.

Hebrew Bible the sacred writings of Judaism (some dating from as early as 1200 BC), called by Christians the ◊Old Testament. It includes the Torah (the first five books, ascribed to Moses), historical and prophetic books, and psalms. Originally written in Hebrew, it was later translated into Greek (◊Pentateuch) and other languages.

Hebrew language member of the ◊Hamito-Semitic language family spoken in SW Asia by the ancient Hebrews, sustained for many centuries in the Diaspora as the liturgical language of Judaism, revived by the late-19th century Haskala movement, and developed in the 20th century as Israeli Hebrew, the national language of the State of Israel. It is the original language of the Old Testament of the Bible.

Such English words as *cherub, chutzpah, Jehovah/Yahweh, kosher, rabbi, sabbath, seraph,* and *shibboleth* are borrowings from Hebrew. The Hebrew alphabet (called the *aleph-beth*) is written from right to left.

Hebrews an epistle in the New Testament, probably written to the Hebrew converts to Christianity. It is no longer attributed to Paul, but its authorship is unknown.

Hebrides group of more than 500 islands (fewer than 100 inhabited) off W Scotland; total area 1,120 sq mi/2,900 sq km. The Hebrides were settled by Scandinavians during the 6th–9th centuries and passed under Norwegian rule from about 890 to 1266.

The Inner Hebrides are divided between Highland and Strathclyde regions, and include ◊Skye, ◊Mull, ◊Jura, ◊Islay, ◊Iona, ◊Rum, Raasay, Coll, Tiree, Colonsay, Muck, and uninhabited Staffa.

The Outer Hebrides form the islands area of the ◊Western Isles administrative area, separated from the Inner Hebrides by the Little Minch. They include ◊Lewis with Harris, North Uist, South Uist, ◊Barra, and ◊St Kilda.

Hebron (Arabic *El Khalil*) town on the West Bank of the Jordan, occupied by Israel in 1967; population (1967) 43,000, including 4,000 Jews. It is a front-line position in the confrontation between Israelis and Arabs in the ◊Intifada. Within the mosque is the traditional site of the tombs of Abraham, Isaac, and Jacob.

Heb-Sed royal festival in ancient Egypt, apparently commemorating Menes's union of Upper and Lower Egypt.

Hecate in Greek mythology, the goddess of witchcraft and magic, sometimes identified with ◊Artemis and the Moon.

Hecht Ben 1894–1964. US journalist, author, and playwright. A collection of his newspaper feature stories, *1001 Nights in Chicago*, appeared 1922. Hecht's greatest success came in his 1928 collaboration with Charles MacArthur on the popular play *The Front Page*. He then went to Hollywood and wrote many successful screenplays, including *Twentieth Century* 1934 and *Wuthering Heights* 1939, and became known as a script-doctor for others' screenplays. Hecht's autobiography, *Child of the Century*, was published 1954.

Born in New York City and raised in Racine, Wisconsin, Hecht began his writing career as a reporter for the *Chicago Journal* and as a foreign corespondent for the *Chicago Daily News*. Also interested in fiction writing, he published his first novel, *Erik Dorn*, 1921.

hectare metric unit of area equal to 10,000 square meters (2.47 acres).

hedgerow

In Northern Europe, and especially in Britain, hedgerows are a traditional feature of the landscape. Hawthorn, blackthorn, elm and beech bushes were grown around the edges of farms and grazing land to define boundaries and to enclose cattle and sheep. With mechanized agriculture came the destruction of many hedgerows, along with the wildlife they support.

The dense growth and tough, thorny branches of hawthorn bushes are effective barriers to large mammals. But their foliage and flowers, and, those of the plants that grow around and beneath them, provide food for many caterpillars, butterflies, aphids and bees. The fruits are eaten by many birds and by voles and wood mice. Carniverous birds feed on the insects and other small animals.

Life in the hedgerow
1. Peacock butterfly 2. Blackbird's nest
3. Seven-spot ladybird 4. Hollybush
5. Comma butterfly 6. Tiger moth
7. Field mouse 8. Warbler 9. Dog rose
10. Nettle 11. Orange-tip butterfly
12. Hawthorn 13. Wren
14. Hogweed 15. Bramble bush
16. Hawfinch 17. Wood mouse
18. Hedgehog 19. Primrose
20. Chickweed

Hector in Greek mythology, a Trojan prince, son of King Priam who, in the siege of Troy, was the foremost warrior on the Trojan side until he was killed by ◊Achilles.

Hecuba in Greek mythology, the wife of King Priam and mother of ◊Hector and ◊Paris. She was captured by the Greeks after the fall of Troy.

Hedda Gabler a play by Henrik Ibsen, first produced 1891. Trapped in small-town society, Hedda Gabler takes out her spiritual and sexual frustrations on everyone from her ineffectual academic husband to the reformed alcoholic writer Lövborg. When her mean-spirited revenge backfires, she commits suicide.

hedge or ***hedgerow*** a row of closely planted shrubs or low trees. It generally acts as a land division and windbreak; it also serves as a source of food and as a refuge for wildlife. Generally, the older a hedge, the more plant species grow in a given length, roughly one species per century for a 30 yd length. About 309 species of plant occur only in hedgerows. Hedges are part of the landscape in Britain, N France, Ireland, and New England, but many have been destroyed to accommodate altered farming practices and larger machinery.

hedgehog insectivorous mammal of the genus *Erinaceus*, native to Europe, Asia, and Africa. The body, including the tail, is 1 ft/30 cm long. It is greyish-brown in color, has a piglike snout, and is covered with sharp spines. When alarmed it can roll itself into a ball. Hedgehogs feed on insects, slugs, and carrion. Long-eared hedgehogs and desert hedghogs are placed in different genera.

Hedin Sven Anders 1865–1952. Swedish archeologist, geographer, and explorer in central Asia and China. Between 1891 and 1908 he explored routes across the Himalayas and produced the first maps of Tibet. During 1928–33 he traveled with a Sino-Swedish expedition which crossed the Gobi Desert. His publications include *My Life as Explorer* 1925 and *Across the Gobi Desert* 1928.

hedonism ethical theory that pleasure or happiness is, or should be, the main goal in life. Hedonist sects in ancient Greece were the ◊Cyrenaics, who held that the pleasure of the moment is the only human good, and the ◊Epicureans, who advocated the pursuit of pleasure under the direction of reason. Modern hedonistic philosophies, such as those of the British philosophers Jeremy Bentham and J S Mill, regard the happiness of society, rather than that of the individual, as the aim.

Hefei or ***Hofei*** capital of Anhui province, China; population (1984) 853,000. Products include textiles, chemicals, and steel.

Hefner Hugh Marston 1926– . US publisher, founder of *Playboy* magazine 1953. With its distinctive rabbit logo, monthly "Playmate" centerfolds of nude women, and columns and interviews of opinion, fashion, and personal advice on sex and other topics, *Playboy* helped reshape the social attitudes of the postwar generation. In the early 1960s, the magazine's huge success led to the creation of a national chain of Playboy clubs and resorts.

Hefner, who was born in Chicago and educated at the University of Illinois, also saw *Playboy*'s readership drop steeply in the 1980s, due to the rise of competing men's magazines and feminist protest.

Hegel Georg Wilhelm Friedrich 1770–1831. German philosopher who conceived of consciousness and the external object as forming a unity in which neither factor can exist independently, mind and nature being two abstractions of one indivisible whole. He believed development took place through dialectic: thesis and antithesis (contradiction) and synthesis, the resolution of contradiction. For Hegel, the task of philosophy was to comprehend the rationality of what already exists; leftist followers, including Karl Marx, used Hegel's dialectic to attempt to show the inevitability of radical change and to attack both religion and the social order of the European Industrial Revolution.

He wrote *The Phenomenology of Spirit* 1807, *Encyclopedia of the Philosophical Sciences* 1817, and *Philosophy of Right* 1821. He was professor of philosophy at Heidelberg 1817–18 and at Berlin 1818–31. As a rightist, Hegel championed religion, the Prussian state, and the existing order.

hegemony (Greek *hegemonia*, "authority") political dominance of one power over others in a group in which all are supposedly equal. The term was first used for the dominance of Athens over the other Greek city-states, later applied to Prussia within Germany, and, in recent times, to the US and USSR throughout the world.

Hegira Arabic "flight"; see ◊Hijrah.

Heidegger Martin 1889–1976. German philosopher. In *Being and Time* 1927, he used the methods of ◊Husserl's phenomenology to explore the structures of human existence. His later writings meditated on the fate of a world dominated by science and technology.

He believed that Western philosophy had "forgotten" the fundamental question of the "meaning of Being." Although one of his major concerns was the angst of human existence, he denied that he was an existentialist. His support for Nazism and his unwillingness or inability to defend his position damaged his reputation.

Heidelberg city on the south bank of the river Neckar, 12 mi/19 km SE of Mannheim, in Baden-Württemberg, Federal Republic of Germany; population (1988) 136,000. Heidelberg University, the oldest in Germany, was established 1386. The city is overlooked by the ruins of its 13th–17th century castle, 330 ft/100 m above the river.

Heidelberg village near Melbourne, Australia, that gave its name to the Heidelberg School—a group of Impressionist artists (including Roberts, Streeton, and Conder) working in teaching camps in the neighborhood.

Heidi novel for children by the Swiss writer Johanna Spyri (1827–1901), published in 1881. Heidi, an orphan girl, shares a simple life with her grandfather high on a mountain, bringing happiness to those around her. Three years spent in Frankfurt as companion to a crippled girl, Clara, convince Heidi that city life is not for her and she returns to her mountain home.

Heifetz Jascha 1901–1987. Russian-born US violinist, one of the great virtuosos of the 20th century. He first performed at the age of five, and before he was 17 had played in most European capitals, and in the US, where he settled 1917. His style of playing was calm and objective.

He appeared in several Hollywood movies and played in a trio with Artur ◊Rubenstein and Gregor Piatigorsky. After retiring from the concert stage he taught several violinists, including Eugene ◊Fodor.

Heike monogatari (Japanese "tales of the Heike") Japanese chronicle, written down in the 14th century but based on oral legend describing events that took place 200 years earlier, recounting the struggle for control of the country between the rival Genji (Minamoto) and Heike (Taira) dynasties. The conflict resulted in the end of the Heian period, and the introduction of the first shogunate (military dictatorship). Many subsequent Japanese dramas are based on material from the chronicle.

Heilbronn river port in Baden-Württemberg, Federal Republic of Germany, on the river Neckar, N of Stuttgart; population (1988) 112,000. It trades extensively in wine.

Heilongjiang or ***Heilungkiang*** province of NE China, in ◊Manchuria

area 178,950 sq mi/463,600 sq km

capital Harbin

features China's largest oil-field, near Anda

products cereals, gold, coal, copper, zinc, lead, cobalt

population (1986) 33,320,000.

Heilungkiang former name of ◊Heilongjiang, a province of NE China.

Heine Heinrich 1797–1856. German romantic poet and journalist, who wrote *Reisebilder* 1826 and *Buch der Lieder/Book of Songs* 1827. From 1831 he lived mainly in Paris, working as a correspondent for German newspapers. Schubert and Schumann set many of his lyrics to music.

In 1835, he headed a list of writers forbidden to publish in Germany. He contracted a spinal disease 1845 that confined him to his bed from 1848 until his death.

Heinkel Ernst 1888–1958. German aircraft designer who pioneered jet aircraft. He founded his firm 1922 and built the first jet aircraft 1939. During World War II his company produced many military aircraft.

Heinlein Robert A(nson) 1907– . US science-fiction writer, associated with the pulp magazines of the 1940s, who wrote the militaristic novel *Starship Troopers* 1959 and the utopian cult novel *Stranger in a Strange Land* 1961. His work helped to increase the legitimacy of science fiction as a literary genre.

Heinz Henry John 1844–1919. US industrialist. Born in Pittsburgh, Heinz entered his family's brick business but became interested in the possibilities of wholesale food marketing, founding a firm for that purpose in 1876. The firm, renamed the H.J. Heinz Co. in 1888, specialized in the manufacture of prepared foods and condiments. Heinz popularized the use of ketchup and made famous his company's slogan "57 Varieties."

As president, Heinz oversaw every phase of production, from farming to advertising. Unlike some of his competitors, he was a strong supporter of the 1906 US Pure Food and Drug Act.

Heisenberg Werner Carl 1901–1976. German physicist. He was an originator of ◊quantum theory and the formulator of the ◊uncertainty principle, which concerns matter, radiation and their reactions, and places absolute limits on the achievable accuracy of measurement. Nobel Prize 1932.

Hejaz former independent kingdom, merged in 1932 with Nejd to form ◊Saudi Arabia; population (1970) 2,000,000; the capital is Mecca.

Hekmatyar Gulbuddin 1949– . Afghani Islamic fundamentalist guerrilla leader. He became a mujaheddin guerrilla in the 1980s, leading the fundamentalist faction of the Hizb-i Islami (Islamic Party), dedicated to the overthrow of the Soviet-backed communist regime in Kabul. He has refused to countenance participation in any interim "national unity" government which includes Afghani communists.

Hel or ***Hela*** in Norse mythology, the goddess of the underworld.

Helen in Greek mythology, the daughter of Zeus and Leda, and the most beautiful of women. She married Menelaus, king of Sparta, but during his absence, was abducted by Paris, prince of Troy. This precipitated the Trojan War. Afterwards she returned to Sparta with her husband.

Helena capital of Montana, located in the W central part of the state, near the Big Belt Mountains, S of the Missouri River. It was settled after gold was discovered 1864. Industries include agricultural

helicopter

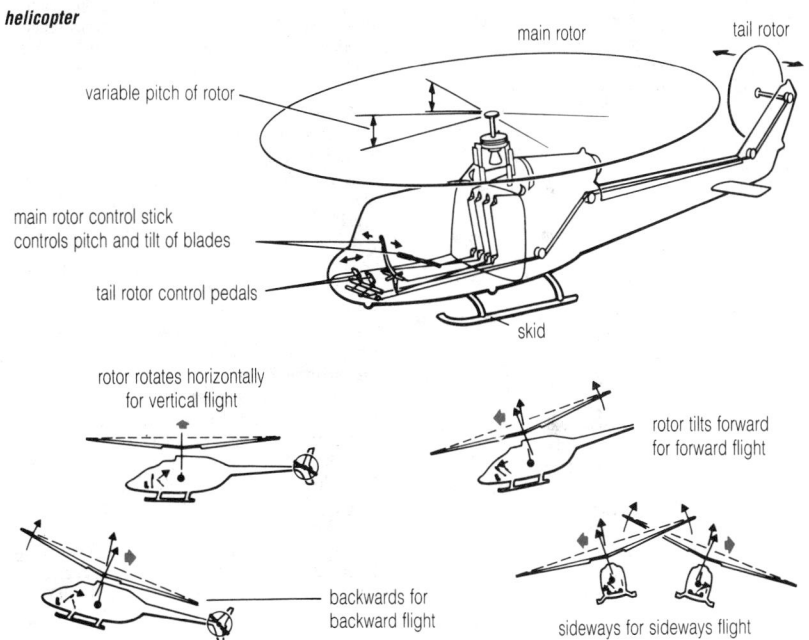

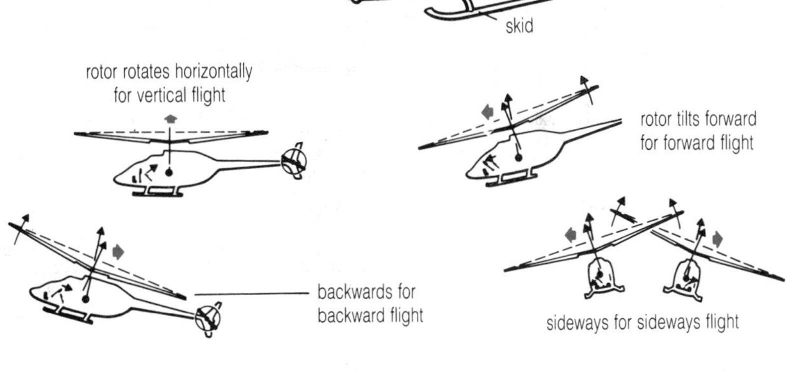
main rotor
tail rotor
variable pitch of rotor
main rotor control stick
controls pitch and tilt of blades
tail rotor control pedals
skid
rotor rotates horizontally
for vertical flight
rotor tilts forward
for forward flight
backwards for
backward flight
sideways for sideways flight

products, machine parts, ceramics, paints, sheet metal, and chemicals; population (1990) 24,569.

Helena, St c. 248–328. Roman empress, mother of Constantine the Great, and a convert to Christianity. According to legend, she discovered the true cross of Jesus in Jerusalem. Her feast day is Aug 18.

Helicon a mountain in central Greece, on which was situated a spring and a sanctuary sacred to the ◊Muses.

helicopter powered aircraft that achieves both lift and propulsion by means of a rotary wing, or rotor, on top of the fuselage. It can take off and land vertically, move in any direction, or remain stationary in the air. It can be powered by piston or jet engine.

The rotor of a helicopter has two or more blades of airfoil cross-section like an airplane's wings. Lift and propulsion are achieved by angling the blades as they rotate. Experiments using the concept of helicopter flight date from the early 1900s, with the first successful lift-off and short flight in 1907. Igor ◊Sikorsky built the first practical single-rotor craft in the US 1939. A single-rotor helicopter must have a small tail rotor to counter the torque, or tendency of the body to spin in the opposite direction to the main rotor. Twin-rotor helicopters, like the Boeing Chinook, have their rotors turning in opposite directions to prevent the body from spinning.

Helicopters are now widely used in passenger service, rescue missions on land and sea, police pursuits and traffic control, firefighting, and agriculture. In war they carry troops and equipment into difficult terrain, make aerial reconnaissance and attacks, and carry the wounded to aid stations.

Heligoland island in the North Sea, one of the North Frisian Islands; area 0.2 sq mi/0.6 sq km. It is administered by the state of Schleswig-Holstein, Federal Republic of Germany, having been ceded to Germany by Britain 1890 in exchange for ◊Zanzibar. It was used as a naval base in both world wars.

heliography old method of signaling, used by armies in the late 19th century, which employed sunlight reflected from a mirror to pass messages in ◊Morse code. On a clear day, a heliograph could send over distances in excess of 30 mi/50 km. Also, an early photographic process by which a permanent image was formed on a glass plate.

Heliopolis ancient Egyptian center (the biblical On) of the worship of the Sun-god Ra, NE of Cairo and near the village of Matariah.

Helios in Greek mythology, the Sun-god and father of ◊Phaethon, thought to make his daily journey across the sky in a chariot.

heliotrope decorative plant of the genus *Heliotropium* of the borage family Boraginaceae, with distinctive spikes of blue, lilac, or white flowers, including the Peruvian or cherry pie heliotrope *H. peruvianum*.

helium (Greek *helios* "Sun") colorless, odorless, gaseous, nonmetallic element, symbol He, atomic number 2, atomic weight 4.0026. It is grouped with the ◊inert gases, is nonreactive, and forms no compounds. It is the second most abundant element (after hydrogen) in the universe, with the lowest boiling (–452°F/–268.9°C) and melting points (–458°F/–272.2°C) of all the elements. It is present in small quantities in the Earth's atmosphere from gases issuing from radioactive elements (from ◊alpha decay) in the Earth's crust; after hydrogen it is the second lightest element.

Helium is a component of most stars, including the Sun, where the nuclear-fusion process converts hydrogen into helium with the production of heat and light. It is obtained by compression and fractionation of naturally occurring gases. It is used for inflating balloons and as a dilutant for oxygen in deep-sea breathing systems. Liquid helium is used extensively in low-temperature physics (cryogenics).

helix in mathematics, a three-dimensional curve resembling a spring, corkscrew, or screw thread. It is generated by a line that encircles a cylinder or cone at a constant angle.

hell *Stone carving of a medieval version of hell.*

hell in various religions, a place of posthumous punishment. In Hinduism, Buddhism, and Jainism, hell is a transitory stage in the progress of the soul, but in Christianity and Islam it is eternal (◊purgatory is transitory). Judaism does not postulate such punishment.

In the Bible, the word "hell" is used to translate Hebrew and Greek words all meaning "the place of departed spirits, the abode of the dead." In medieval Christian theology, hell is the place where unrepentant sinners suffer the torments of the damned, but the 20th-century tendency has been to regard hell as a state of damnation (that is, everlasting banishment from the sight of God) rather than a place.

Helle in Greek mythology, the daughter of Athamas, king of Thessaly, and sister of Phrixus. With her brother she ran away from Ino, their cruel stepmother, on a ram with a ◊Golden Fleece. Helle fell into the sea and drowned, thus giving her name to the Hellespont ("sea of Helle").

hellebore poisonous European herbaceous plant of the genus *Helleborus* of the buttercup family Ranunculaceae. The stinking hellebore *H. foetidus* has greenish flowers early in the spring.

The white, or false, hellebore *Veratrum viride* of North America is a poisonous member of the lily family Liliaceae.

helleborine temperate Old World orchid of the genera *Epipactis* and *Cephalanthera*, including the marsh helleborine *E. palustris* and the hellebore orchid *E. helleborine* introduced to North America.

The rattlesnake orchids (genus *Goodyera*) of North America are sometimes placed in the genus *Epipactis*.

Hellene (Greek *Hellas* "Greece") alternate name for a ◊Greek.

Hellenic period (from *Hellas*, Greek name for Greece) the Classical period of ancient Greek civilization, from the first Olympic Games 776 BC until the death of Alexander the Great 323 BC.

Hellenistic period the period in Greek civilization from the death of Alexander 323 BC until the accession of the Roman emperor Augustus 27 BC. Alexandria in Egypt was the center of culture and commerce during this period, and Greek culture spread throughout the Mediterranean region.

Heller Joseph 1923– . US novelist. He drew on his experiences in the US airforce in World War II to write ◊*Catch-22* 1961, satirizing war and bureaucratic methods. A film based on the book appeared in 1970.

After serving in the air force, he entered advertising. His other works include the novels *Something Happened* 1974 and *Good As Gold* 1979, and the plays *We Bombed In New Haven* 1968 and *Clevinger's Trial* 1974.

Hellespont former name of the ◊Dardanelles, the strait that separates Europe from Asia.

Hellman Lillian 1907–1984. US playwright whose work is concerned with contemporary political and social issues. *The Children's Hour* 1934, *The Little Foxes* 1939, and *Toys in the Attic* 1960 are all examples of the "well-made play."

She lived 31 years with the writer Dashiell Hammett, and in her will set up a fund to promote Marxist doctrine. Since her death there has been dispute over the accuracy of her memoirs, for example *Pentimento* 1973.

Helmand the longest river in Afghanistan. Rising in the Hindu Kush, W of Kabul, it flows SW for 703 mi/1,125 km before entering the marshland surrounding Lake Saberi on the Iranian frontier.

Helmholtz Hermann Ludwig Ferdinand von 1821–1894. German physiologist, physicist, and inventor of the ophthalmoscope for examining the inside of the eye. He was the first to explain how the cochlea of the inner ear works, and the first to measure the speed of nerve impulses. In physics he formulated the law of conservation of energy, and worked in thermodynamics.

The ophthalmoscope made possible the examination of the inside of the eye. This was a great advance in ophthalmic medicine, as was his ophthalmometer for measuring the curvature of the eye. He also studied magnetism, electricity, and the physiology of hearing.

Helmont Jean Baptiste van 1577–1644. Belgian doctor. He was the first to realize that there are gases other than air, and claimed to have coined the word "gas" (from Greek *cháos*).

Helms Richard 1913– . US director of the Central Intelligence Agency 1966–73, when he was dismissed by President Nixon. In 1977 he was convicted of lying before a congressional committee because his oath as chief of intelligence compelled him to keep secrets from the public. He was originally with the Office of Strategic Services, before it developed into the CIA 1947.

Héloïse 1101–1164. Abbess of Paraclete in Champagne, France, correspondent and lover of ◊Abelard. She became deeply interested in intellectual study in her youth and was impressed by the brilliance of Abelard, her teacher, whom she secretly married. After her affair with Abelard, and the birth of a son, Astrolabe, she became a

***Helsingør** Denmark's Kronborg Castle in Helsingør (English name Elsinore), 28 mi/45 km north of Copenhagen, was the setting for Shakespeare's* Hamlet.

nun 1129, and with Abelard's assistance, founded a nunnery at Paraclete. Her letters show her strong and pious character and her devotion to Abelard.

helot a class of slaves in ancient Sparta who were probably the indigenous inhabitants. Their cruel treatment by the Spartans became proverbial.

Helpmann Robert 1909–1986. Australian dancer, choreographer, and actor. The leading male dancer with the Sadler's Wells Ballet, London 1933–50, he partnered Margot ◊Fonteyn in the 1940s.

Helsingborg (Swedish *Hälsingborg*) port in SW Sweden, linked by ferry with Helsingør across Ore Sound; population (1986) 106,300. Industries include copper smelting, rubber and chemical manufacture, and sugar refining.

Helsingfors Swedish name for ◊Helsinki.

Helsingør (English *Elsinore*) port in NE Denmark; population (1987) 57,000. It is linked by ferry with Helsingborg across the Sound; Shakespeare made it the scene of *Hamlet*.

Helsinki (Swedish *Helsingfors*) capital and port of Finland; population (1988) 490,000, metropolitan area 978,000. Industries include shipbuilding, engineering, and textiles. The homes of the architect Eliel Saarinen and the composer Jean Sibelius outside the city are museums.

Helsinki Conference international conference 1975 at which 35 countries, including the USSR and the US, attempted to reach agreement on cooperation in security, economics, science, technology, and human rights.

Some regarded the conference as marking the beginning of ◊détente and the end of the ◊Cold War. Others felt it legitimized the division of Europe, which had been a fact since the end of World War II. Human-rights groups contended that there were many violations of the provisions of the accords. Its full title is the Helsinki Conference on Security and Cooperation in Europe (CSCE).

Helvetia region, corresponding to W Switzerland, occupied by the Celtic Helvetii 1st century BC–5th century AD. In 58 BC Caesar repulsed their invasion of southern Gaul at Bibracte (near Autun) and Helvetia became subject to Rome.

Helvetius Claude Adrien 1715–1771. French philosopher. In *De l'Esprit* 1758 he argued, following David ◊Hume, that self-interest, however disguised, is the mainspring of all human action and that since conceptions of good and evil vary according to period and locality there is no absolute good or evil. He also believed that intellectual differences are only a matter of education.

Helvetius's principle of artificial identity of interests (those manipulated by governments) influenced the utilitarian philosopher Jeremy Bentham. *De l'Esprit* was denounced and burned by the public hangman.

hematite the principal ore of iron, consisting mainly of iron(III) ferric oxide, Fe_2O_3. It occurs as specular hematite (dark, metallic luster), kidney ore (reddish radiating fibers terminating in smooth, rounded surfaces), and as a red earthy deposit.

hematology branch of medicine concerned with disorders of the blood.

Hemel Hempstead "new" town in Hertfordshire, England; population (1981) 80,000. Industries include manufacture of paper, electrical goods, and office equipment.

Hemingway Ernest 1898–1961. US writer. War, bullfighting, and fishing were used symbolically in his writings to represent honor, dignity, and primitivism—prominent themes in his short stories and novels, which included *A Farewell to Arms* 1929, *For Whom the Bell Tolls* 1940, and *The Old Man and the Sea* 1952. His deceptively simple writing styles attracted many imitators. He received the Nobel Prize for Literature in 1954.

He was born in Oak Park, Illinois and in his youth developed a passion for hunting and adventure. He became a journalist and was wounded while serving on a volunteer ambulance crew in Italy in World War I. His style was influenced by Gertrude ◊Stein, who also introduced him to bullfighting, a theme in his first novel *The Sun Also Rises* 1926 and the memoir *Death in the Afternoon* 1932. *A Farewell to Arms* deals with wartime experiences on the Italian front, and *For Whom the Bell Tolls* has a Spanish Civil War setting. He served as war correspondent both in that conflict and in Europe during World War II. After a full life, physical weakness, age, and depression contributed to his suicide.

hemlock plant *Conium maculatum* of the carrot family Umbelliferae, native to Europe, W Asia, and N Africa. Reaching up to 6 ft/2 m high, it bears umbels of small white flowers. The whole plant, especially the root and fruit, is poisonous, causing paralysis of the nervous system. The name hemlock is also applied to members of the genus *Tsuga* of North American and Asiatic conifers of the pine family.

hemoglobin protein that carries oxygen. In vertebrates it occurs in red blood cells, giving them their color. Oxygen attaches to hemoglobin in the lungs or gills where the amount dissolved in the blood is high. This process effectively increases the amount of oxygen that can be carried in the bloodstream. The oxygen is later released in the body tissues where it is at low concentration. Hemoglobin also works in carrying carbon dioxide away from tissues to the lungs or gills.

***Hemingway** Nobel Prize–winning American author Ernest Hemingway.*

hemolymph the circulatory fluid of those mollusks and insects that have an "open" circulatory system. Hemolymph contains water, amino acids, sugars, salts, and white cells like those of blood. Circulated by a contractile heart, its main functions are to transport digestive and excretory products around the body. In mollusks, it also transports oxygen and carbon dioxide.

hemolysis destruction of red blood cells. Aged cells are constantly being lyzed (broken down), but increased wastage of red cells is seen in some infections and blood disorders. It may result in ◊jaundice (through the release of too much hemoglobin) and in ◊anemia.

hemophilia any of several inherited diseases in which normal blood clotting is impaired. The sufferer experiences prolonged bleeding from the slightest wound, as well as painful internal bleeding without apparent cause.

Hemophilias are nearly always sex-linked, transmitted through the female line only to male infants; it has afflicted a number of European royal households. Males affected by the most common form are unable to synthesize Factor VIII, a protein involved in the clotting of blood. Treatment is primarily with Factor VIII (now mass-produced from donated blood), but the hemophiliac remains at risk from the slightest incident of bleeding. The disease is a painful one that causes deformities of joints.

hemorrhage loss of blood from the circulatory system. It is "manifest" when the blood can be seen, as when it flows from a wound, and "occult" when the bleeding is internal, as from an ulcer or internal injury.

Rapid, profuse hemorrhage causes ◊shock and may prove fatal if the circulating volume cannot be replaced in time. Slow, sustained bleeding may lead to ◊anemia. Arterial bleeding is potentially more serious than blood lost from a vein. It may be stemmed by pressure above the wound, as by tourniquet.

hemorrhagic fever any of several virus diseases of the tropics, in which high temperatures over several days end in hemorrhage from nose, throat, and intestines, with up to 90% mortality. The causative organism of W African ◊Lassa fever lives in rats (which betray no symptoms), but in ◊Marburg disease and Ebola fever, the host animal is unknown.

hemorrhoids distended blood vessels (◊varicose veins) in the area of the anus, popularly called piles.

hemostasis the natural or surgical stoppage of bleeding. In the natural mechanism, the damaged vessel contracts, restricting the flow, and blood ◊platelets plug the opening, releasing chemicals essential to clotting.

hemp annual plant *Cannabis sativa*, family Cannabaceae. Originally from Asia, it is cultivated in most temperate countries for its fibers, produced in the outer layer of the stem, and used in ropes, twines, and, occasionally, in a type of linen or lace. ◊Cannabis is obtained from certain varieties of hemp.

The name "hemp" is extended to similar types of fiber: sisal hemp and henequen obtained from the leaves of *Agave* species native to Yucatán and cultivated in many tropical countries, and manila hemp obtained from *Musa textilis*, a plant native to the Philippines and the Moluccas.

Henan or ***honan*** province of E central China
area 64,462 sq mi/167,000 sq km
capital Zhengzhou
features comprises river plains of the Huang He (Yellow river); in the 1980s the ruins of Xibo, capital of the Shang dynasty in the 16th-century BC, were discovered here
products cereals, cotton
population (1986) 78,080,000.

henbane poisonous plant *Hyoscyamus niger* of the nightshade family Solanaceae, found on waste ground through most of Europe and W Asia. A branching plant, up to 31 in/80 cm high, it has

hemophilia

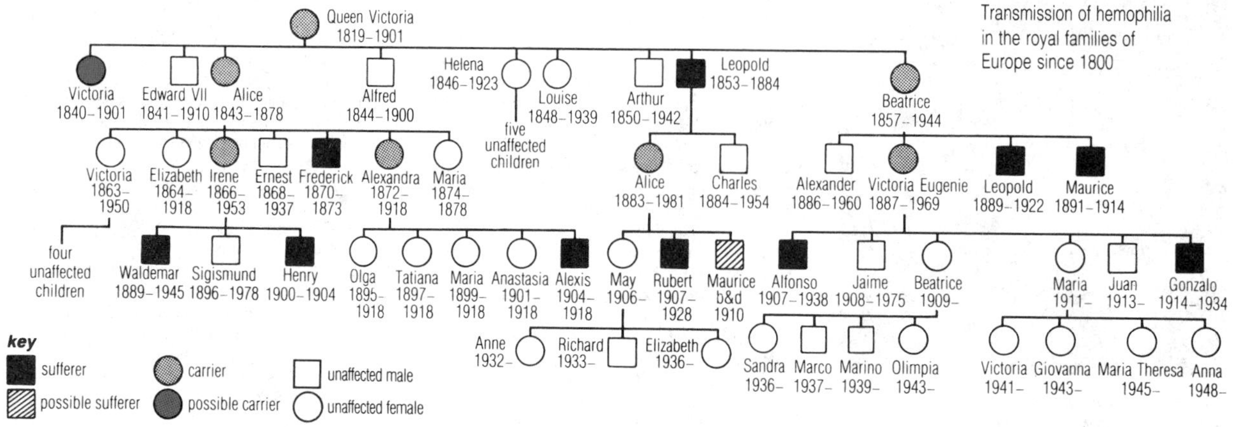
Transmission of hemophilia in the royal families of Europe since 1800
Queen Victoria 1819–1901
Victoria 1840–1901
Edward VII 1841–1910
Alice 1843–1878
Alfred 1844–1900
Helena 1846–1923
Louise 1848–1939
five unaffected children
Arthur 1850–1942
Leopold 1853–1884
Beatrice 1857–1944
Victoria 1863–1950
Elizabeth 1864–1918
Irene 1866–1953
Ernest 1868–1937
Frederick 1870–1873
Alexandra 1872–1918
Maria 1874–1878
Alice 1883–1981
Charles 1884–1954
Alexander 1886–1960
Victoria Eugenie 1887–1969
Leopold 1889–1922
Maurice 1891–1914
four unaffected children
Waldemar 1889–1945
Sigismund 1896–1978
Henry 1900–1904
Olga 1895–1918
Tatiana 1897–1918
Maria 1899–1918
Anastasia 1901–1918
Alexis 1904–1918
May 1906–
Rubert 1907–1928
Maurice b&d 1910
Alfonso 1907–1938
Jaime 1908–1975
Beatrice 1909–
Maria 1911–
Juan 1913–
Gonzalo 1914–1934
Anne 1932–
Richard 1933–
Elizabeth 1936–
Sandra 1936–
Marco 1937–
Marino 1939–
Olimpia 1943–
Victoria 1941–
Giovanna 1943–
Maria Theresa 1945–
Anna 1948–
key
sufferer
possible sufferer
carrier
possible carrier
unaffected male
unaffected female

hairy leaves and a nauseous smell. The yellow flowers are bell-shaped. Henbane is used in medicine as a source of hyoscyamine and scopolamine.

Hench Philip Showalter 1896–1965. US physician who introduced cortisone treatment for rheumatoid arthritis.

He noticed that arthritic patients improved greatly during pregnancy or an attack of jaundice and concluded that a ◊hormone secreted in increased quantity during both these conditions caused the improvement. This turned out to be cortisol, a ◊steroid converted to cortisone in the liver.

Henderson Arthur 1863–1935. British Labor politician, foreign secretary 1929–31, when he accorded the Soviet government full recognition. Nobel Peace Prize 1934.

Hendrix Jimi (James Marshall) 1942–1970. US rock guitarist, songwriter, and singer, legendary for his virtuoso experimental technique and flamboyance.

Hendrix moved to the UK 1966 and formed a trio, the Jimi Hendrix Experience, which produced hit singles with their first recorded songs ("Hey Joe" and "Purple Haze," both 1967), and attracted notice in the US when Hendrix burned his guitar at the 1967 Monterey Pop Festival. His performance at the 1969 Woodstock festival is recorded in the celebrated film *Woodstock*. The group disbanded early 1969 after three albums; Hendrix continued to record and occasionally perform until his death the following year. He greatly expanded the vocabulary of the electric guitar and influenced both rock and jazz musicians.

Heng Samrin 1934– . Cambodian politician. A former Khmer Rouge commander 1976–78, who had become disillusioned with its brutal tactics, he led an unsuccessful coup against ◊Pol Pot 1978 and established the Kampuchean People's Revolutionary Party (KPRP) in Vietnam, before returning 1979 to head the new Vietnamese-backed government.

***Hendrix** Rock performer Jimi Hendrix, known for his innovative electric-guitar performances.*

Henie Sonja 1912–1969. Norwegian skater. Norwegian champion at 11, she won ten world championships and three Olympic titles. She turned professional 1936 and went on to make numerous films in Hollywood.

CAREER HIGHLIGHTS

Olympic champion: 1928, 1932, 1936 (record 3 wins)
World champion: 1927–36 (record 10 wins)

Henlein Konrad 1898–1945. Sudeten-German leader of the Sudeten Nazi Party in Czechoslovakia, and closely allied with Hitler's Nazis. He was partly responsible for the destabilization of the Czechoslovak state 1938, which led to the ◊Munich Agreement and secession of the Sudetenland to Germany.

henna small shrub *Lawsonia inermis* of the loosestrife family Lythraceae, found in Iran, India, Egypt, and N Africa. The leaves and young twigs are ground to a powder, mixed to a paste with hot water, and applied to fingernails and hair, giving an orange-red hue. The color may then be changed to black by applying a preparation of indigo.

Henotikon declaration published by Byzantine emperor Zeno 482, aimed at reconciling warring theological factions within the early Christian Church. It refuted the Council of Chalcedon 451, and reaffirmed the heretical idea that Jesus was one person, not two. The declaration, not accepted by Rome, led to a complete split between Rome and Constantinople 484–519.

Henri Robert. Adopted name of Robert Henry Cozad 1865–1929. US landscape and portrait painter. Born in Cincinnati, Ohio, he was trained at the Pennsylvania Academy of the Fine Arts, after which he studied in Europe before returning to the US. Although he executed a number of noted works, such as *Himself* and *Herself* 1913, he is best known as a teacher, profoundly influencing such artists as George ◊Bellows, William ◊Glackens, Edward ◊Hopper, Rockwell ◊Kent, and George ◊Luks.

Henrietta Maria 1609–1669. Queen of England 1625–49. The daughter of Henry IV of France, she married Charles I of England 1625. By encouraging him to aid Roman Catholics and make himself an absolute ruler, she became highly unpopular and was exiled during the period 1644–60. She returned to England at the Restoration but retired to France 1665.

henry SI unit (abbreviation H) of ◊inductance (the reaction of an electric current against the magnetic field that surrounds it). One henry is the inductance of a circuit that produces an opposing voltage of one volt when the current changes at one ampere per second.

It is named after the US physicist Joseph Henry.

Henry eight kings of England:

Henry I 1068–1135. King of England from 1100. Youngest son of William I, he succeeded his brother William II. He won the support of the Saxons by granting them a charter and marrying a Saxon princess. An able administrator, he established a professional bureaucracy and a system of traveling judges. He was succeeded by Stephen.

Henry II 1133–1189. King of England from 1154, when he succeeded ◊Stephen. He was the son of ◊Matilda and Geoffrey of Anjou (1113–1151). He curbed the power of the barons, but his attempt to bring the church courts under control had to be abandoned after the murder of Thomas à ◊Becket. During his reign the English conquest of Ireland began. He was succeeded by his son Richard I.

He was lord of Scotland, Ireland, and Wales, and count of Anjou, Brittany, Poitou, Normandy, Maine, Gascony, and Aquitaine. He was married to Eleanor of Aquitaine.

Henry III 1207–1272. King of England from 1216, when he succeeded John, but he did not rule until 1227. His financial commitments to the papacy and his foreign favorites led to de ◊Montfort's revolt 1264. Henry was defeated at Lewes, Sussex, and imprisoned. He was restored to the throne after the royalist victory at Evesham 1265. He was succeeded by his son Edward I.

The royal powers were exercised by a regency until 1232 and by two French nobles, Peter des Roches and Peter des Rivaux, until the barons forced their expulsion 1234, marking the start of Henry's personal rule. While he was in prison, Montfort ruled in his name. On his release Henry was weak and senile and his eldest son, Edward, took charge of the government.

Henry IV (Bolingbroke) 1367–1413. King of England from 1399, the son of ◊John of Gaunt. In 1398 he was banished by ◊Richard II for political activity but returned 1399 to head a revolt and be accepted as king by Parliament. He was succeeded by his son Henry V.

He had difficulty in keeping the support of Parliament and the clergy. To win support he had to conciliate the church by a law for the burning of heretics and to make many concessions to Parliament.

Henry V 1387–1422. King of England from 1413, son of Henry IV. Invading Normandy 1415 (during the Hundred Years' War), he captured Harfleur and defeated the French at ◊Agincourt. He invaded again 1417–19, capturing Rouen. He married ◊Catherine of Valois 1420 to gain recognition as heir to the French throne by his father-in-law Charles VI. He was succeeded by his son Henry VI.

Henry VI 1421–1471. King of England from 1422, son of Henry V. He assumed royal power 1442 and sided with the party opposed to the continuation of the Hundred Years' War with France. After his marriage 1445, he was dominated by his

Henry VIII *Portrait c. 1542 of Henry VIII, who married six times and broke England's ties to the Roman Catholic Church, hangs in the National Portrait Gallery, London.*

wife, ◊Margaret of Anjou. The unpopularity of the government, especially after the loss of the English conquests in France, encouraged Richard, Duke of ◊York, to claim the throne, and though York was killed 1460, his son Edward IV proclaimed himself king 1461 (see Wars of the ◊Roses). Henry was captured 1465, temporarily restored 1470, but again imprisoned 1471 and then murdered.

Henry VII 1457–1509. King of England from 1485, son of Edmund Tudor, Earl of Richmond (c. 1430–56), and a descendant of ◊John of Gaunt. He spent his early life in Brittany until 1485, when he landed in Britain to lead the rebellion against Richard III which ended with Richard's defeat and death at ◊Bosworth. Yorkist revolts continued until 1497, but Henry restored order after the Wars of the ◊Roses by the ◊Star Chamber and achieved independence from Parliament by amassing a private fortune through confiscations. He was succeeded by his son Henry VIII.

Henry VIII 1491–1547. King of England from 1509, when he succeeded his father Henry VII and married Catherine of Aragon, the widow of his brother. His Lord Chancellor, Cardinal Wolsey, was replaced by Thomas More 1529 for failing to persuade the pope to grant Henry a divorce. After 1532 Henry broke with papal authority, proclaimed himself head of the church, dissolved the monasteries, and divorced Catherine. His subsequent wives were Anne Boleyn, Jane Seymour, Anne of Cleves, Catherine Howard, and Catherine Parr. He was succeeded by his son Edward VI.

Wolsey shared Henry's desire to make England a notable nation. Henry demanded his first divorce because his wife had become too old to bear him a (male) heir and he was taken with Anne ◊Boleyn. Thomas ◊Cromwell initiated legislation that made Henry head of the Church of England, allowing him to marry Anne 1533, who later that year gave birth to Elizabeth I. (Jane Seymour was the mother of Edward VI.) Henry's last years were devoted to war with France and Scotland, consequent economic problems, and attempts to hold back the ◊Reformation, which his own interests had unleashed in his nation.

Henry four kings of France:

Henry I 1005–1060. King of France from 1031. He spent much of his reign in conflict with ◊William I the Conqueror, then duke of Normandy.

Henry II 1519–1559. King of France from 1547. He captured the fortresses of Metz and Verdun from the Holy Roman emperor Charles V and Calais from the English. He was killed in a tournament.

In 1526 he was sent with his brother to Spain as a hostage, being returned when there was peace 1530. He married Catherine de' Medici 1533, and from then on was dominated by her, Diane de Poitiers, and Duke Montmorency. Three of his sons, Francis II, Charles IX, and Henry III, became kings of France.

Henry III 1551–1589. King of France from 1574. He fought both the ◊Huguenots (headed by his successor, Henry of Navarre) and the Catholic League (headed by the Duke of Guise). Guise expelled Henry from Paris 1588 but was assassinated. Henry allied with the Huguenots under Henry of Navarre to besiege the city, but was assassinated by a monk.

Henry IV 1553–1610. King of France from 1589. Son of Antoine de Bourbon and Jeanne, queen of Navarre, he was brought up as a Protestant and from 1576 led the ◊Huguenots. On his accession he settled the religious question by adopting Catholicism while tolerating Protestantism. He restored peace and strong government to France and brought back prosperity by measures for the promotion of industry and agriculture and the improvement of communications. He was assassinated by a Catholic extremist.

Henry seven Holy Roman emperors:

Henry I the Fowler c. 876–936. King of Germany from 919, and duke of Saxony from 912. He secured the frontiers of Saxony, ruled in harmony with its nobles, and extended German influence over the Danes, the Hungarians, and the Slavonic tribes. He was about to claim the imperial crown when he died.

Henry II the Saint 973–1024. King of Germany from 1002, Holy Roman emperor from 1014, when he recognized Benedict VIII as pope. He was canonized 1146.

Henry III the Black 1017–1056. King of Germany from 1028, Holy Roman emperor from 1039. He raised the empire to the height of its power, and extended its authority over Poland, Bohemia, and Hungary.

Henry IV 1050–1106. Holy Roman emperor from 1056, who was involved from 1075 in a struggle with the papacy (see ◊Gregory VII).

Henry V 1081–1125. Holy Roman emperor from 1106. He continued the struggle with the church until the settlement of the ◊investiture contest 1122.

Henry VI 1165–1197. Holy Roman emperor from 1190. As part of his plan for making the empire universal, he captured and imprisoned Richard I of England and compelled him to do homage.

Henry VII 1269–1313. Holy Roman emperor from 1308. He attempted unsuccessfully to revive the imperial supremacy in Italy.

Henry Joseph 1797–1878. US physicist, inventor of the electromagnetic motor 1829 and of a telegraphic apparatus. He also discovered the principle of electromagnetic induction, roughly at the same time as Michael ◊Faraday, and the phenomenon of self-induction. A unit of inductance (henry) is named after him.

Henry, O see William Sydney ◊Porter.

Henry Patrick 1736–1799. US politician, who in 1775 supported the arming of the Virginia militia against the British by a speech ending, "Give me liberty or give me death!" He was governor of Virginia 1776–79 and 1784–86.

He assisted in the creation of the ◊Continental Congress of which he was a member. He opposed ratification of the US ◊Constitution, contending that it posed a danger to state sovereignty. His influence, however, helped to ensure the passage of the first ten amendments (see the ◊Bill of Rights).

Henry William 1774–1836. British chemist. In 1803 he formulated Henry's law: when a gas is dissolved in a liquid at a given temperature, the mass that dissolves is in direct proportion to the gas pressure.

Henry of Blois died 1171. Brother of King Stephen of England, he was bishop of Winchester from 1129, and Pope Innocent II's legate to England from 1139. While remaining loyal to Henry II, he tried to effect a compromise between ◊Becket and the king.

Henryson Robert 1430–1505. Scottish poet. His works include versions of Aesop and the *Testament of Cresseid*, a continuation of Chaucer.

Henry the Navigator 1394–1460. Portuguese prince, the fourth son of John I. He set up a school for navigators 1419 and under his patronage, Portuguese seamen explored and colonized Madeira, the Cape Verde Islands, and the Azores; they sailed down the African coast almost to Sierra Leone.

Henzada city in S central Myanmar (Burma), on the Irrawaddy river; population 284,000.

Henze Hans Werner 1926– . German composer whose large and varied output includes orchestral, vocal, and chamber music. He uses traditional symphony and concerto forms, and incorporates a wide range of styles including jazz.

heparin anticoagulant substance produced by cells of the liver, lungs, and intestines. It normally inhibits the clotting of blood by interfering with the production of thrombin, which is necessary for clot formation. Heparin obtained from animals is used medically after surgery to limit the risk of ◊thrombosis, or following pulmonary ◊embolism to ensure that no further clots form.

hepatic of or pertaining to the liver.

hepatitis any inflammatory disease of the liver, usually caused by a virus. Other causes include ◊lupus erythematosus and amoebic dysentery. Symptoms include weakness, nausea, and jaundice.

The viral disease hepatitis A (infectious or viral hepatitis) is spread by contaminated food, often seafood, and via the oro-fecal route. Incubation is about four weeks. Temporary immunity is conferred by injections of normal ◊immunoglobulin (gamma globulin).

The virus causing hepatitis B (serum hepatitis) was isolated in the 1960s. Contained in all body fluids, it is very easily transmitted. Some people become ◊carriers. Those with the disease may be sick for weeks or months. The illness may be mild, or it may result in death from liver failure. Liver cancer is now recognized as a long-term complication of the disease. A successful vaccine was developed in the late 1970s.

Hepburn Audrey (Audrey Hepburn-Rushton) 1929– . British actress of Anglo-Dutch descent who often played innocent, childlike characters. Slender and doe-eyed, she set a different style from the more ample women stars of the 1950s. After playing minor parts in British films in the early 1950s, she became a Hollywood star in such films as *Funny Face* 1957, *My Fair Lady* 1964, *Wait Until Dark* 1968, and *Robin and Marian* 1976.

Hepburn Katharine 1909– . US actress who appeared in such films as *Morning Glory* 1933 (Academy Award), *Little Women* 1933, *Bringing Up Baby* 1938, *The Philadelphia Story* 1940, *Woman of the Year* 1942, *The African Queen* 1951, *Pat and Mike* 1952, *Guess Who's Coming to Dinner* 1967 (Academy Award), *Lion in Winter* 1968 (Academy Award), and *On Golden Pond* 1981 (Academy Award). She also had a distinguished stage career.

Hephaestus in Greek mythology, the god of fire and metalcraft (Roman Vulcan), son of Zeus and Hera, husband of Aphrodite. He was lame.

Hepplewhite George died 1786. English furniture maker. He developed a simple, elegant style, working mainly in mahogany or satinwood, adding delicately inlaid or painted decorations of feathers, shells, or wheat-ears. His book of designs, *The Cabinetmaker and Upholsterer's Guide* 1788, was published posthumously.

heptarchy the seven Saxon kingdoms thought to have existed in England before AD 800: Northumbria, Mercia, East Anglia, Essex, Kent, Sussex, and Wessex. The term was coined by 16th-century historians.

heptathlon a multievent athletics discipline for

women that consists of seven events over two days: 100 meters hurdles, high jump, shot put, 200 meters (day one); long jump, javelin, 800 meters (day two). Points are awarded for performances in each event in the same way as the ◊decathlon. It replaced the pentathlon (five events) in international competition in 1981.

Hera in Greek mythology, a goddess (Roman Juno), sister-consort of Zeus, mother of Hephaestus, Hebe, and Ares; protector of women and marriage.

Heracles in Greek mythology, a hero (Roman Hercules), son of Zeus and Alcmene, famed for strength. While serving Eurystheus, king of Argos, he performed 12 labors, including the cleansing of the Augean stables.

Heraclitus c. 544–483 BC. Greek philosopher who believed that the cosmos is in a ceaseless state of flux and motion, fire being the fundamental material that accounts for all change and motion in the world. Nothing in the world ever stays the same, hence the dictum, "one cannot step in the same river twice."

Wisdom came from understanding this eternal dynamic, which unified the diversity of nature, as he wrote in *On Nature*. Heraclitus was born in Ephesus.

Heraclius c. 575–641. Byzantine emperor from 610. His reign marked a turning point in the empire's fortunes. Of Armenian descent, he recaptured Armenia 622, and other provinces 622–28 from the Persians, but lost them to the Muslims 629–41.

Heraklion alternate name for ◊Iráklion.

heraldry the insignia and symbols representing a person, family, or dynasty. Heraldry originated with simple symbols used on banners and shields for recognition in battle. By the 14th century, it had become a complex pictorial language with its own regulatory bodies (courts of chivalry), used by noble families, corporations, cities, and realms.

Herapath John 1790–1868. English mathematician. His work into the behavior of gases, though seriously flawed, was acknowledged by the physicist James Joule in his own more successful investigations.

Herat capital of Herat province, and the largest city in W Afghanistan, on the N banks of the Hari Rud; population (1980) 160,000. A principal road junction, it was a great city in ancient and medieval times.

Herault river in S France, 100 mi/160 km long, rising in the Cévennes and flowing into the Gulf of Lyons near Agde. It gives its name to a *département*.

herb any plant (usually a flowering plant) tasting sweet, bitter, aromatic, or pungent, used in cooking, medicine, or perfumery; technically, any plant whose aerial parts do not remain above ground at the end of the growing season.

herbaceous plant a plant with very little or no wood, dying back at the end of every summer. The herbaceous perennials survive winters as underground storage organs such as bulbs and tubers.

herbarium a collection of dried, pressed plants used as an aid to identification of unknown plants and by taxonomists in the ◊classification of plants. The plant specimens are accompanied by information, such as the date and place of collection, by whom collected, details of habitat, flower color, and local names.

Herbaria range from small collections containing plants of a limited region, to the large university and national herbaria (some at ◊botanical gardens) containing millions of specimens from all parts of the world.

Herbert Frank (Patrick) 1920–1986. US science-fiction writer, author of the *Dune* series from 1965 (filmed by David Lynch 1984), large-scale adventure stories containing serious ideas about ecology and religion.

Herbert Victor 1859–1924. Irish-born US conductor and composer. He immigrated to the US in 1886 and played with the New York Metropolitan Opera and Philharmonic Orchestra. In 1893 he was named conductor of the 22nd Regiment Band, also composing light operettas for the New York stage. After serving as conductor of the Pittsburgh Philharmonic 1898–1904, he returned to New York and helped found the American Society of Composers, Authors, and Publishers (ASCAP) 1914.

Born in Dublin and trained as a cellist at the Stuttgart Conservatory, Herbert began his professional musical career in Vienna.

herbicide any chemical used to destroy plants or check their growth; see ◊weedkiller.

herbivore animal that feeds on green plants (or photosynthetic single-celled organisms) or their products, including seeds, fruit, and nectar. Herbivores are more numerous than other animals because their food is the most abundant. They form a vital link in the food chain between plants and carnivores.

Herblock popular name of US cartoonist Herbert Lawrence Block 1909– . He was born in Chicago and joined the staff of the *Chicago Daily News* 1929 as an editorial cartoonist. After winning a Pulitzer Prize in 1942 and serving in the army during World War II, he joined the staff of the *Washington Post* 1946. During the 1950's, he gained a national reputation through his syndicated cartoons. He won another Pulitzer Prize 1952, published several collections of his work, and took a leading role in the public campaign against the communist witch-hunting tactics of Sen Joseph ◊McCarthy.

herb Robert wild ◊geranium *Geranium robertianum* found throughout Europe and central Asia and naturalized in North America. About 12 in/30 cm high, it bears hairy leaves and small pinkish to purplish flowers.

Herculaneum ancient city of Italy between Naples and Pompeii. Along with Pompeii, it was buried when Vesuvius erupted AD 79. It was excavated from the 18th century onward.

Hercules Roman form of ◊Heracles.

Hercules in astronomy, the fifth-largest constellation, visible in the northern hemisphere. Despite its size it contains no prominent stars. Its most important feature is a ◊globular cluster of stars 22,500 light-years from Earth, one of the best examples in the sky.

Hercules, Pillars of rocks (at Gibraltar and Ceuta) which guard the western entrance to the Mediterranean.

Herder Johann Gottfried von 1744–1803. German poet, critic, and philosopher. Herder's critical writings indicated his intuitive rather than reasoning trend of thought. He collected folk songs of all nations 1778, and in the *Ideen zur Philosophie der Geschichte der Menschheit/Outlines of a Philosophy of the History of Man* 1784–91 he outlined the stages of human cultural development.

Born in East Prussia, Herder studied at Königsberg where he was influenced by Kant, became pastor at Riga, and in 1776 was called to Weimar as court preacher. He gave considerable impetus to the ◊*Sturm und Drang/Storm and Stress* Romantic movement in German literature.

heredity in biology, the transmission of traits from parent to offspring. See also ◊genetics.

Hereford city in the county of Hereford and Worcester, on the river Wye, England; population (1981) 630,000. Products include cider, beer, and metal goods.

The cathedral, which was begun 1079, contains a *Mappa Mundi*, a medieval map of the world.

Hereford and Worcester county in W central England

area 1,517 sq mi/3,930 sq km

cities Worcester (administrative headquarters), Hereford, Kidderminster, Evesham, Ross-on-Wye, Ledbury

features rivers: Wye, Severn; Malvern Hills (high point Worcester Beacon 1,395 ft/425 m) and Black Mountains; fertile Vale of Evesham.

Herero member of a nomadic Bantu-speaking people living in Namibia, SW Africa.

heresy (Greek *hairesis*, "parties" of believers) doctrine opposed to orthodox belief, especially in religion. Those holding ideas considered heretical by the Christian church have included Gnostics, Arians, Pelagians, Montanists, Albigenses, Waldenses, Lollards, and Anabaptists.

Herman Woody (Woodrow) 1913–1987. US band leader and clarinetist. A child prodigy, he was leader of his own orchestra at 23, and after 1945 formed his famous Thundering Herd band. Soloists in this or later versions of the band included Lester ◊Young and Stan ◊Getz.

hermaphrodite an organism that has both male and female sex organs. Hermaphroditism is the norm in species such as earthworms and snails, and is common in flowering plants. Cross-fertilization is the rule among hermaphrodites, with the parents functioning as male and female simultaneously, or as one or the other sex at different stages in their development.

Hermaphroditus in Greek mythology, the son of Hermes and Aphrodite. He was loved by a nymph who prayed for eternal union with him, so that they became one body with dual sexual characteristics, hence the term hermaphrodite.

hermeneutics a philosophical tradition concerned with the nature of understanding and interpretation of human behavior and social traditions.

From its origins in problems of biblical interpretation, hermeneutics has expanded to cover many fields of inquiry, including esthetics, literary theory, and science. ◊Dilthey, ◊Heidegger, and ◊Gadamer are influential contributors to this tradition.

Hermes in Greek mythology, a god, son of Zeus and ◊Maia; messenger of the gods; he wore winged sandals, a wide-brimmed hat, and carried a staff around which serpents coiled. Identified with the Roman Mercury and ancient Egyptian Thoth, he protects thieves, travelers, and merchants.

Hermes Trismegistus supposed author of the *Hermetica* (2nd–3rd centuries AD), a body of writings expounding a Hellenistic mystical philosophy in which the sun is regarded as the visible manifestation of God. In the Renaissance these writings were thought to be by an Egyptian priest contemporary with Moses, and it is possible they contain some Egyptian material.

Hermione in Greek mythology, daughter of ◊Menelaus and ◊Helen, and wife either to ◊Neoptolemos or to ◊Orestes.

hermit religious ascetic living in seclusion, often practicing extremes of mortification (such as the Stylites, early Christians who lived on top of pillars).

The monastic movement developed as a way of organizing into communities the ascetic hermits living in the deserts of ancient Egypt and the Middle East.

hermit crab a kind of ◊crab.

Hermon (Arabic Jebel esh-Sheikh) snow-topped mountain, 9,232 ft/2,814 m high, on the Syria-Lebanon border. According to tradition, Jesus was transfigured here.

Herndon v Lowry a US Supreme Court decision 1937 dealing with state restriction of First-Amendment rights in sedition cases. Herndon, a Communist organizer convicted of sedition under a Georgia law, appealed to the US Supreme Court for protection of his right to free speech. The Court reversed Herndon's conviction, ruling that a tendency to incite violent revolt was not sufficient grounds to revoke First-Amendment rights without evidence of a "clear and present danger" to society.

Herne industrial city in North Rhine–Westphalia, Federal Republic of Germany; population (1988) 171,000.

hernia or ***rupture*** protrusion of part of an internal organ through a weakness in the surrounding muscular wall, usually in the groin or navel. The appearance is that of a rounded soft lump or swelling.

Hero and Leander in Greek mythology, a pair of

lovers. Hero was a priestess of Aphrodite at Sestos on the Hellespont, in love with Leander on the opposite shore at Abydos. When he was drowned while swimming across during a storm, she threw herself into the sea.

Herod the Great 74–4 BC. King of the Roman province of Judea, S Palestine, from 40 BC. With the aid of Mark Antony he established his government in Jerusalem 37 BC. He rebuilt the Temple in Jerusalem, but his Hellenizing tendencies made him suspect to orthodox Jewry. His last years were a reign of terror, and in the New Testament Matthew alleges that he ordered the slaughter of all the infants in Bethlehem to ensure the death of Jesus, whom he foresaw as a rival. He was the father of Herod Antipas.

Herod Agrippa I 10 BC–AD 44. Ruler of Palestine from AD 41. His real name was Marcus Julius Agrippa, erroneously called "Herod" in the Bible. Grandson of Herod the Great, he was made tetrarch (governor) of Palestine by the Roman emperor Caligula and king by Emperor Claudius AD 41. He put the apostle James to death and imprisoned the apostle Peter. His son was Herod Agrippa II.

Herod Agrippa II c. 40–AD 93. King of Chalcis (now S Lebanon), son of Herod Agrippa I. He was appointed by the Roman emperor Claudius about AD 50, and in AD 60 tried the apostle Paul. He helped the Roman emperor Titus take Jerusalem AD 70, then went to Rome, where he died.

Herod Antipas 21 BC–AD 39. Tetrarch (governor) of the Roman province of Galilee, N Palestine, 4 BC–AD 9, son of Herod the Great. He divorced his wife to marry his niece Herodias, who persuaded her daughter Salome to ask for John the Baptist's head when he reproved Herod's action. Jesus was brought before him on Pontius Pilate's discovery that he was a Galilean and hence of Herod's jurisdiction, but Herod returned him without giving any verdict. In AD 38 Herod Antipas went to Rome to try to get Emperor Caligula to give him the title of king, but was instead banished.

Herodotus c. 484–424 BC. Greek historian. After four years in Athens, he traveled widely in Egypt, Asia, and eastern Europe, before settling at Thurii in S Italy 443 BC. He wrote a nine-book history of the Greek–Persian struggle that culminated in the defeat of the Persian invasion attempts 490 and 480 BC. Herodotus was the first historian to apply critical evaluation to his material.

heroin or ***diamorphine*** powerful ◊opiate analgesic, an acetyl derivative of ◊morphine. It is more addictive than morphine but causes less nausea and is one of the most abused drugs in the US. Because of its powerful habit-forming qualities, its manufacture and import are forbidden in the US, even for medical use.

heron large- to medium-sized wading bird of the family Ardeidae, which also includes bitterns, egrets, night-herons, and boatbills. Herons have sharp bills, broad wings, long legs, and soft plumage. They are found mostly in tropical and subtropical regions, but also in temperate zones.

The great blue heron *Ardea herodias* is native to North America. Gray-blue overall, breeding adults have yellowish bills and ornate plumes on head, neck and back. A wader, it feeds mainly on fish and frogs.

Hero of Alexandria Greek mathematician and engineer, probably of the 1st century AD, who invented an automatic fountain and a kind of stationary steam-engine, described in his book *Pneumatica*.

herpes any of several infectious diseases caused by viruses of the herpes group. Herpes simplex I is the causative agent of a common inflammation, the cold sore. Herpes simplex II is responsible for genital herpes, a highly contagious, sexually transmitted disease characterized by painful blisters in the genital area. It can be transmitted in the birth canal from mother to newborn. Herpes zoster causes ◊shingles; another herpes virus causes chickenpox.

A number of ◊antivirals treat these infections, which are particularly troublesome in patients whose immune system has been suppressed medically; for example, after a transplant operation.

The Epstein-Barr virus of infectious ◊mononucleosis also belongs to this group.

Herrera Francisco de, El Mozo (the younger) 1622–1685. Spanish still-life painter. He studied in Rome and worked in Seville and Madrid where he was court painter and architect. His paintings reflect Murillo's influence.

Herrera Francisco de, El Viejo (the elder) 1576–1656. Spanish painter, active in Seville. He painted genre and religious scenes, with bold effects of light and shade.

Herrick Robert 1591–1674. English poet and cleric, born in Cheapside, London. He published *Hesperides* in 1648, a collection of sacred and pastoral poetry admired for its lyric quality, including "Gather ye rosebuds" and "Cherry ripe."

herring any of various marine fishes of the herring family (Clupeidae), but especially the important food fish *Clupea harengus*. A silvered greenish-blue, it swims close to the surface, and may be 10–16 in/25–40 cm long. Herring travel in schools several miles long and wide. They are found in large quantities off the E coast of North America, and the shores of NE Europe. Overfishing and pollution have reduced their numbers.

Herriot Édouard 1872–1957. French Radical Socialist politician. An opponent of Poincaré, who as prime minister carried out the French occupation of the Ruhr, Germany, he was briefly prime minister 1924–25, 1926, and 1932. As president of the chamber of deputies 1940, he opposed the policies of the right-wing Vichy government and was arrested and later taken to Germany; he was released 1945 by the Soviets.

Herriot James. Adopted name of James Alfred Wight 1916– . English writer. A practicing veterinary surgeon in Yorkshire from 1940, he wrote of his experiences in a series of books including *If Only They Could Talk* 1970, *All Creatures Great and Small* 1972, and *The Lord God Made Them All* 1981.

Herrmann Bernard 1911–1975. US composer of film music. He worked for Alfred Hitchcock on several films, and wrote the chilling score for *Psycho* 1960.

Herschel Caroline Lucretia 1750–1848. German-born English astronomer, sister of William ◊Herschel, and from 1772 his assistant in England. She discovered eight comets and was awarded the Royal Astronomical Society's gold medal for her work on her brother's catalog of star clusters and nebulae.

Herschel John Frederick William 1792–1871. English scientist and astronomer, son of William Herschel. He discovered thousands of close ◊double stars, clusters, and ◊nebulae, reported 1847. His inventions include astronomical instruments, as well as sensitized photographic paper and the use of sodium thiosulfite to fix it.

He became director of the Cape of Good Hope observatory in South Africa 1834.

Herschel William 1738–1822. German-born English astronomer. He was a skilled telescope maker and pioneered the study of binary stars and nebulae. He discovered the planet Uranus in 1781 and infrared solar rays in 1801.

Born in Hanover, Germany, he went to England 1757 and became a professional musician and composer while instructing himself in mathematics and astronomy and constructing his own reflecting telescopes (his 40-ft/12-m telescope was the largest in the world at the time). While searching for ◊double stars, he found Uranus, and later several of its satellites. This brought him instant fame and, in 1782, the post of private astronomer to George III. He discovered the motion of double stars around one another and recorded it in his *Motion of the Solar System in Space* 1783. In 1789 he built a 4-ft/1.2-m telescope with a focal length of 40 ft/12 m, but he made most use of a more satisfactory 18-in/46-cm instrument. He cataloged over 800 double stars and found over 2,500 nebulae, cataloged by his sister Caroline Herschel; this work was continued by his son John Herschel. By studying the distribution of stars, William Herschel established the basic form of our Galaxy, the Milky Way.

Hertfordshire county in SE England

area 629 sq mi/1,630 sq km

cities Hertford (administrative headquarters), St Albans, Watford, Hatfield, Hemel Hempstead, Bishop's Stortford, Letchworth (the first ◊garden city, followed by Welwyn 1919 and Stevenage 1947)

features rivers: Lea, Stort, Colne; part of the Chiltern Hills; Hatfield House; Knebworth House (home of Lord Lytton); Brocket Hall (home of Palmerston and Melbourne); home of G B ◊Shaw at Ayot St Lawrence; Berkhamsted Castle (Norman); Rothamsted agricultural experimental station

products engineering, aircraft, electrical goods, paper and printing; general agricultural goods

population (1987) 987,000

famous people Graham Greene was born at Berkhamsted.

Hertling Count Georg von 1843–1919. German politician who was appointed imperial chancellor in Nov 1917. He maintained a degree of support in the *Reichstag* (parliament) but was powerless to control the military leadership under ◊Ludendorff.

Hertogenbosch see ◊'s-Hertogenbosch, capital of North Brabant, the Netherlands.

hertz SI unit (abbreviation Hz) of frequency (the number of repetitions of a regular occurrence in one second). Radio waves are often measured in megahertz (MHz), millions of hertz. It is named after Heinrich Hertz.

Hertz Heinrich 1857–1894. German physicist who studied electromagnetic waves, showing that their behavior resembles that of light and heat waves.

He confirmed ◊Maxwell's theory of electromagnetic waves. The unit of frequency, the hertz, is named after him.

Hertzog James Barry Munnik 1866–1942. South African politician, prime minister 1924–39, founder of the Nationalist Party 1913 (the United South African National Party from 1933). He opposed South Africa's entry into both world wars.

Hertzsprung–Russell diagram in astronomy, a graph on which the surface temperatures of stars are plotted against their luminosities. Most stars, including the Sun, fall into a narrow band called the ◊main sequence. When a star grows old it moves from the main sequence to the upper right part of the graph, into the area of the giants and supergiants. At the end of its life, as the star shrinks to become a white dwarf, it moves again, to the bottom left area. It is named after the Dane Ejnar Hertzsprung (1873–1967) and the American Henry Norris Russell (1877–1957), who independently devised it in the years 1911–13.

Herzegovina or ***Hercegovina*** part of Yugoslavia; see ◊Bosnia and Herzegovina.

Herzl Theodor 1860–1904. Austrian founder of the Zionist movement. He was born in Budapest and became a successful playwright and journalist, mainly in Vienna. The ◊Dreyfus case convinced him that the only solution to the problem of anti-Semitism was the resettlement of the Jews in a state of their own. His book *Jewish State* 1896 launched political ◊Zionism, and he became the first president of the World Zionist Organization 1897.

Herzog Werner 1942– . German film director whose highly original and visually splendid films, often shot in exotic and impractical locations, include *Aguirre der Zorn Gottes/Aguirre Wrath of God* 1972, *Nosferatu Phantom der Nacht* 1979, and *Fitzcarraldo* 1982.

Hertzsprung–Russell diagram

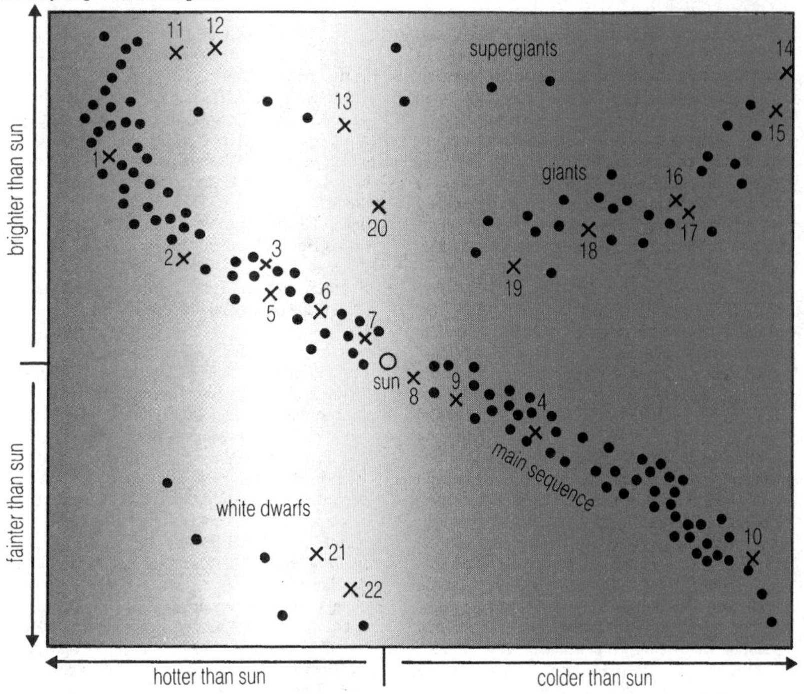
brighter than sun
fainter than sun
hotter than sun
colder than sun
supergiants
giants
main sequence
white dwarfs
sun
1
2
3
4
5
6
7
8
9
10
11
12
13
14
15
16
17
18
19
20
21
22

1	Spica	7	Procyon A	13	Polaris	18	Arcturus
2	Regulus	8	Tau Ceti	14	Betelgeuse	19	Pollux
3	Vega	9	61 Cygni A	15	Antares	20	Capella
4	61 Cygni B	10	Proxima Centauri	16	Mira	21	Sirius B
5	Sirius A	11	Rigel	17	Aldebaran	22	Procyon B
6	Altair	12	Deneb				

Heseltine Michael (Ray Dibdin) 1933– . English Conservative politician, member of Parliament for Henley, and secretary of state for the environment from 1990. He was minister of the Environment 1979–83, when he succeeded John Nott as minister of Defence Jan 1983 but resigned Jan 1986 over the Westland affair and was then seen as a major rival to Margaret Thatcher. On Nov 14, 1990, Heseltine announced his decision to challenge Thatcher's leadership of the Conservative Party.

Foreign secretary Douglas Hurd and chancellor of the Excheckr John Major then joined the contest against Heseltine. In the election Nov 27th, with Major two votes short of an absolute majority, both Hurd and Heseltine conceded defeat. On Nov 28 Heseltine rejoined the cabinet as secretary of state for the environment.

Hesiod lived c. 700 BC. Greek poet. He is supposed to have lived a little later than Homer, and according to his own account he was born in Boeotia. He is the author of "Works and Days," a poem that tells of the country life, and the *Theogony*, an account of the origin of the world and of the gods.

Hesperides in Greek mythology, the Greek maidens who guarded a tree bearing golden apples in the Islands of the Blessed (also known as the Hesperides).

Hess (Walter Richard) Rudolf 1894–1987. German Nazi leader. Imprisoned with Hitler 1923–25, he became his private secretary, taking down *Mein Kampf* from his dictation. In 1932 he was appointed deputy Führer to Hitler. On May 10, 1941 he landed by air in the UK with compromise peace proposals and was held a prisoner of war until 1945, when he was tried at Nuremberg as a war criminal and sentenced to life imprisonment. He died in ◊Spandau prison, Berlin.

He was effectively in charge of Nazi party organizations until his flight in 1941. For the last years of his life he was the only prisoner left in Spandau.

Hess Victor 1883–1964. Austrian physicist, who emigrated to the US shortly after sharing a Nobel Prize in 1936 for the discovery of cosmic radiation.

He was professor at Fordham University, New York, from 1938.

Hesse Hermann 1877–1962. German writer who became a Swiss citizen 1923. A conscientious objector in World War I and a pacifist opponent of Hitler, he published short stories, poetry, and novels, including *Peter Camenzind* 1904, *Siddhartha* 1922, and ◊*Steppenwolf* 1927. Later works, such as *Das Glasperlenspiel/The Glass Bead Game* 1943, tend toward the mystical. He was awarded the Nobel Prize for Literature 1946.

Hesse *German novelist Hermann Hesse. The main themes of his work are self-knowledge and the opposition of emotion and intellect.*

Hessen administrative region (German *Land*) of Federal Republic of Germany
area 8,145 sq mi/21,100 sq km
capital Wiesbaden
cities Frankfurt-am-Main, Kassel, Darmstadt, Offenbach am Main
features valleys of the rivers Rhine and Main; Taunus mountains, rich in mineral springs, as at Homburg and Wiesbaden; see also ◊Swabia
products wine, timber, chemicals, automobiles, electrical engineering, optical instruments
population (1988) 5,550,000
religion Protestant 61%, Roman Catholic 33%
history until 1945, Hessen was divided in two by a strip of Prussian territory, the southern portion consisting of the valleys of the rivers Rhine and the Main, the northern being dominated by the Vogelsberg mountains (2,442 ft/744 m). Its capital was Darmstadt.

Hestia in Greek mythology, the goddess (Roman Vesta) of the hearth, daughter of ◊Cronus (Roman Saturn) and Rhea.

Heston Charlton. Adopted name of Charles Carter 1924– . US film actor who often starred in biblical and historical epics (as Moses, for example, in *The Ten Commandments* 1956, and in the title role in *Ben-Hur* 1959).

heterophony a form of choral melody singing and playing, found in folk music around the world, in which individual players have some freedom to improvise.

heterosexuality sexual preference for, or attraction to, persons of the opposite sex.

heterosis or ***hybrid vigor*** an improvement in physical capacities that sometimes occurs in the ◊hybrid produced by mating two genetically different parents.

The parents may be of different strains or varieties within a species, or of different species, as in the mule, which is stronger and has a longer life span than either of its parents (donkey and horse). Heterosis is also exploited in hybrid varieties of corn, tomatoes, and other crops.

heterostyly in botany, having ◊styles of different lengths. Certain flowers, such as primroses (*Primula vulgaris*), have different-sized ◊anthers and ◊styles to ensure cross-fertilization (through ◊pollination) by visiting insects.

heterotroph any living organism that obtains its energy from organic substances produced by other organisms. All animals and fungi are heterotrophs, and they include herbivores, carnivores, and saprotrophs (those that feed on dead animal and plant material).

heterozygous in a living organism, having two different ◊alleles for a given trait. In ◊homozygous organisms, by contrast, both chromosomes carry the same allele. In an outbreeding population an individual organism will generally be heterozygous for some genes but homozygous for others. For example, in humans, alleles for both blue- and brown-pigmented eyes exist, but the "blue" allele is ◊recessive to the dominant "brown" allele. Only individuals with blue eyes are predictably homozygous for this trait; brown-eyed people can be either homozygous or heterozygous.

heuristics in computing, a process by which a program attempts to improve its performance by learning from its own experience.

Hevesy Georg von 1885–1966. Swedish chemist, discoverer of the element hafnium. He was the first to use radioactive isotope (radioactive form of an element) to follow the steps of a biological process, for which he won the Nobel Prize for Chemistry 1943.

Hewish Antony 1924– . British radio astronomer who was awarded, with Martin ◊Ryle, the Nobel Prize for Physics 1974 for his work on ◊pulsars,

heterostyly

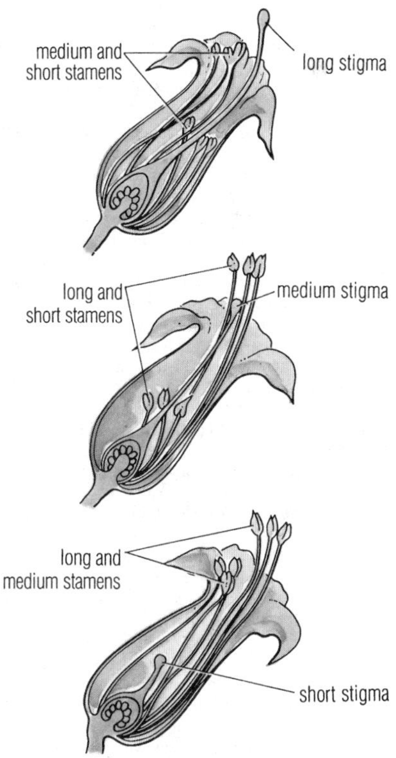
medium and short stamens
long stigma
long and short stamens
medium stigma
long and medium stamens
short stigma

rapidly rotating neutron stars that emit pulses of energy.

hexachlorophene $(C_6HCl_3OH)_2CH_2$ white, odorless bactericide, used in minute quantities in soaps and surgical disinfectants.

Trichlorophenol is used in its preparation, and, without precise temperature control, the highly toxic TCDD (tetrachlorodibenzodioxin; see ◊dioxin) may form as a by-product.

hexadecimal number system a number system to the base 16, used in computing. In hex (as it is commonly known) the decimal numbers 0–15 are represented by the characters 0, 1, 2, 3, 4, 5, 6, 7, 8, 9, A, B, C, D, E, F. Hexadecimal numbers are easy to convert to the computer's internal ◊binary code and are more compact than binary numbers.

Each place in a number increases in value by a power of 16 going from right to left; for instance, 8F is equal to $15 + (8 \times 16) = 143$ in decimal.

Heydrich Reinhard 1904–1942. German Nazi, head of the party's security service and Heinrich ◊Himmler's deputy. He was instrumental in organizing the ◊final solution, the policy of genocide used against Jews and others. While deputy "protector" of Bohemia and Moravia from 1941, he was ambushed and killed by three members of the Czechoslovak forces in Britain, who had landed by parachute. Reprisals followed, including several hundred executions and the massacre in ◊Lidice.

Heyerdahl Thor 1914– . Norwegian ethnologist. He sailed on the ancient-Peruvian-style raft *Kon Tiki* from Peru to the Tuamotu Islands along the Humboldt Current 1947, and in 1969–70 used ancient-Egyptian-style papyrus reed boats to cross the Atlantic. His expeditions proved that ancient civilizations could have traveled the oceans in similar fashion.

His voyages are described in *Kon Tiki*, translated 1950, and *The Ra Expeditions*, translated 1971. He also crossed the Persian Gulf 1977, written about in *The Tigris Expedition*, translated 1981.

Hezekiah in the Old Testament, king of Judah from 719 BC. Against the advice of the prophet Isaiah he rebelled against Assyrian suzerainty in alliance with Egypt, but was defeated by ◊Sennacherib and had to pay out large amounts in indemnities. He carried out religious reforms.

HF in physics, the abbreviation for high ◊frequency.

HI abbreviation for ◊Hawaii.

Hialeah city in SE Florida just NW of Miami. Manufactures include clothing, furniture, plastics, and chemicals. Hialeah Park racetrack is a center for horse racing; population (1990) 188,004.

Hiawatha 16th-century North American Indian teacher and Onondaga chieftain. He is said to have welded the Five Nations (later joined by a sixth) of the ◊Iroquois into the league of the Long House, as the confederacy was known in what is now upper New York State. Hiawatha is the hero of Longfellow's epic poem *The Song of Hiawatha*.

Hiawatha, The Song of poem written by H W Longfellow 1855. It is an Indian legend told in the lilting meter of the Finnish national epic *Kalevala*. It was based on data collected by Henry R Schoolcraft (1793–1864).

hibernation a state of ◊dormancy in which certain animals spend the winter. It is associated with a dramatic reduction in all metabolic processes, including body temperature, breathing, and heart rate. It is a fallacy that animals sleep throughout the winter.

The body temperature of the arctic ground squirrel falls to below 32°F/0°C during hibernation.

hibiscus any plant of the genus *Hibiscus* of the mallow family. Hibiscuses range from large herbaceous plants to trees. Popular as ornamental plants because of their brilliantly colored, red to white, bell-shaped flowers, they include *H. syriacus* and *H. rosa-sinensis* of Asia and the rose mallow *H. palustris* of North America.

Some tropical species provide fruit and timber: *H. tiliaceus* supplies timber and fibrous bark to South Pacific islanders; *H. sabdariffa* is cultivated in the West Indies and elsewhere for its fruit.

hiccup sharp noise caused by a sudden spasm of the ◊diaphragm with closing of the windpipe, commonly caused by digestive disorder.

Hickok "Wild Bill" (James Butler) 1837–1876. US pioneer and law enforcer, a legendary figure in the West. In the Civil War he was a sharpshooter and scout for the Union army. He then served as marshal in Kansas, killing as many as 27 men. He established his reputation as a gunfighter when he killed a fellow scout, turned traitor. He was a prodigious gambler and was fatally shot from behind while playing poker in Deadwood, South Dakota.

hickory tree of the genus *Carya* of the walnut family, native to North America and Asia. It provides a valuable timber, and all species produce nuts, although some are inedible. The pecan *C. illinoensis* is widely cultivated in the southern USA, and the shagbark *C. ovata* in the northern USA.

***Hickok** Legendary lawman "Wild Bill" Hickok served as a Union scout in the Civil War.*

Hickory city in W central North Carolina, in the foothills of the Blue Ridge Mountains, NW of Charlotte. Its main industry is hosiery manufacture. Other products include rope, cotton, and wagons; population (1990) 28,301.

Hidalgo y Costilla Miguel 1753–1811. Catholic priest, known as "the Father of Mexican Independence." A symbol of the opposition to Spain, he rang the church bell in Sept 1810 to announce to his parishioners in Dolores that the revolution against the Spanish had begun. He was captured and shot the following year.

hieroglyphic Egyptian writing system of the mid-4th millennium BC–3rd century AD, which combines picture signs with those indicating letters. The direction of writing is normally from right to left, the signs facing the beginning of the line. It was deciphered 1822 by the French Egyptologist J F Champollion (1790–1832) with the aid of the ◊Rosetta Stone, which has the same inscription carved in hieroglyphic, demotic, and Greek.

hi-fi (abbreviation of high-fidelity) the faithful reproduction of sound from a machine that plays recorded music or speech. A typical hi-fi system includes a turntable for playing vinyl records, a cassette tape deck to play magnetic tape recordings, a tuner to pick up radio broadcasts, an amplifier to serve all the equipment, possibly a compact-disk player, and two or more loudspeakers.

Advances in mechanical equipment and electronics, such as digital recording techniques and compact disks, have made it possible to eliminate many distortions in sound-reproduction processes.

Higashi-Osaka industrial city (textiles, chemicals, engineering), an eastern suburb of Osaka, Kinki region, Honshu Island, Japan; population (1987) 503,000.

Higgins George V 1939– . US novelist who wrote many detective and underworld novels, often set in Boston, including *The Friends of Eddie Coyle* 1972 and *The Imposters* 1986.

High Church a group in the ◊Church of England that emphasizes aspects of Christianity usually associated with Catholics, such as ceremony and hierarchy. The term was first used in 1703 to describe those who opposed Dissenters, and later for groups such as the 19th-century ◊Oxford Movement.

higher education in most countries, education beyond the age of 18 leading to a university or college degree or similar qualification.

Highland Games traditional Scottish outdoor gathering that includes tossing the caber, shot put, running, dancing, and bagpipe playing.

Highland Region administrative region of Scotland
area 10,077 sq mi/26,100 sq km
cities Inverness (administrative headquarters), Thurso, Wick
features comprises almost half the country; Grampian mountains; Ben Nevis (highest peak in the UK); Loch Ness, Caledonian Canal; Inner Hebrides; the Queen Mother's castle of Mey at Caithness; John O'Groats' House; Dounreay (with Atomic Energy Authority's prototype fast reactor, and a nuclear processing plant)
products oil services, winter sports, timber, livestock, grouse and deer hunting, salmon fishing
population (1987) 201,000.

High Point city in N central North Carolina, SW of Greensboro. The furniture industry is very important to the economy; the Southern Furniture market is held four times a year. Hosiery is also manufactured; population (1990) 69,496.

Highsmith Patricia 1921– . US crime novelist. Her first book, *Strangers on a Train* 1950, was filmed by Alfred Hitchcock. She excels in tension and psychological exploration of character.

high tech (abbreviation for high technology) in architecture, buildings that display technical innovation of a high order and celebrate structure and services to create exciting forms and spaces. The Hong Kong and Shanghai Bank, Hong Kong, is a masterpiece of this approach.

highway any road used for automobile traffic open to the public, especially a main road or thoroughfare.

hijacking the illegal seizure or taking control of a vehicle and/or its passengers or goods. The term dates from 1923 and originally referred to the robbing of freight trucks. In recent times it (and its derivative, "skyjacking") has been applied to the seizure of aircraft, usually in flight, by an individual or group, often with some political aim. International treaties (Tokyo 1963, The Hague 1970, and Montréal 1971) encourage international cooperation against hijackers and make severe penalties compulsory.

Hijrah or ***Hegira*** the trip from Mecca to Medina of the prophet Mohammed, which took place AD 622 as a result of the persecution of the prophet and his followers. The Muslim calendar dates from this event, and the day of the Hijrah is celebrated as the Muslim New Year.

Hilbert David 1862–1943. German mathematician who founded the formalist school with the publication of *Grundlagen der Geometrie/Foundations of Geometry* in 1899, which was based on his idea of postulates. He attempted to put mathematics on a logical foundation through defining it in terms of a number of basic principles, which ◊Gödel later showed to be impossible; nonetheless, his attempt greatly influenced 20th-century mathematicians.

Hildebrand Benedictine monk who became Pope ◊Gregory VII.

Hildegard of Bingen 1098–1179. Scientific writer, abbess of the Benedictine convent of St Disibode, near the Rhine, from 1136. She wrote a mystical treatise, *Liber Scivias* 1141, and an encyclopedia of natural history, *Liber Simplicis Medicinae* 1150–60, giving both Latin and German names for the species described, as well as their medicinal uses; it is the earliest surviving scientific book by a woman.

Hildesheim industrial city in Lower Saxony, Federal Republic of Germany, linked to the Mittelland Canal; population (1988) 101,000. Products include electronics and hardware. A bishopric from the 9th century, Hildesheim became a free city of the ◊Holy Roman Empire in the 13th century. It was under Prussian rule 1866–1945.

Hill Joe c. 1872–1915. Swedish-born US labor organizer. He immigrated to the US 1901 and, as a member of the Industrial Workers of the World (IWW, "Wobblies"), was a leader of a dockworkers' strike in San Pedro, California. A frequent contributor to the IWW's periodicals *Solidarity* and *Industrial Worker*, Hill is best remembered for his many popular pro-union songs. He was arrested and convicted of murder on circumstantial evidence in Salt Lake City, Utah, 1914. Despite calls by President Wilson and the Swedish government for a retrial, Hill was executed 1915, becoming a martyr for the labor movement.

Hill's original name is given variously as Joel Emmanuel Haaglund (or Hagglund) or Joseph Hillstrom.

Hillary Edmund 1919– . New Zealand mountaineer. In 1953, with Nepalese Sherpa mountaineer Tenzing Norgay, he reached the summit of Mount Everest, the first the climb the world's highest peak. As a member of the Commonwealth Transantarctic Expedition 1957–58, he was the first person since Scott to reach the South Pole overland, on Jan 3, 1958.

Hillel 1st century BC Hebrew scholar, lawyer, and teacher; member of the Pharisaic movement (see ◊Pharisee). His work was accepted by later rabbinic Judaism and is noted for its tolerance.

Hiller Wendy 1912– . British stage and film actress. Her many roles include Catherine Sloper in *The Heiress* 1947 and Eliza in the film version of Shaw's *Pygmalion* 1938.

Hilton Conrad Nicholson 1887–1979. US hotel developer. At first successful in banking, Hilton entered the hotel business after World War I. Through the 1930s he steadily expanded his chain of luxury hotels and resorts, reorganizing it as the Hilton Hotel Corporation 1946. Basing his firm's marketing appeal on its recognizable name and high-quality standardized service, Hilton retired 1966. His autobiography, *Be My Guest*, was published 1957.

Born in San Antonio, New Mexico, Hilton attended the New Mexico School of Mines and joined his father in various business ventures after graduation 1909.

Hilton James 1900–1954. English novelist. He settled in Hollywood as one of its most successful scriptwriters of, for example, *Mrs Miniver*. His books include *Lost Horizon* 1933, envisaging Shangri-la, a remote district of Tibet where time stands still; *Goodbye, Mr Chips* 1934, a portrait of an old schoolmaster; and *Random Harvest* 1941.

Hilversum city in North Holland province of the Netherlands, 17 mi/27 km SE of Amsterdam; population (1988) 103,000. Besides being a summer resort, Hilversum is the main center of Dutch broadcasting.

Himachal Pradesh state of NW India

area 21,500 sq mi/55,700 sq km

capital Simla

features mainly agricultural state, one third forested, with softwood timber industry

products timber, grain, rice, fruit

population (1981) 4,238,000; mainly Hindu

language Pahari

history created as a Union Territory 1948, it became a full state 1971.

Certain hill areas were transferred to Himachal Pradesh from the Punjab 1966.

Himalayas vast mountain system of central Asia, extending from the Indian states of Kashmir in the west to Assam in the east, covering the southern part of Tibet, Nepal, Sikkim, and Bhutan. It is the highest mountain range in the world. The two highest peaks are Mount ◊Everest and Kangchenjunga. Other major peaks include Makalu, Annapurna, and Nanga Parbat, all over 26,000 ft/8,000 m.

Himes Chester 1909–1984. US novelist. After serving seven years in prison for armed robbery, he published his first novel *If He Hollers Let Him Go* 1945, a depiction of the drudgery and racism in a Californian shipyard.

Hillary *New Zealand mountaineer and explorer Edmund Hillary, the first to climb Mount Everest.*

Himmler Heinrich 1900–1945. German Nazi leader, head of the ◊SS elite corps from 1929, the police and the ◊Gestapo secret police from 1936, and supervisor of the extermination of the Jews in E Europe. During World War II he replaced Goering as Hitler's second-in-command. He was captured May 1945 and committed suicide.

Born in Munich, he joined the Nazi Party in 1925 and became chief of the Bavarian police 1933. His accumulation of offices meant he had command of all German police forces by 1936, which made him one of the most powerful people in Germany. In April 1945 he made a proposal to the Allies that Germany should surrender to the US and Britain but not to the USSR, which was rejected.

Hīnayāna (Sanskrit "lesser vehicle") Mahāyāna Buddhist name for ◊Theravāda Buddhism.

Hindemith Paul 1895–1963. German composer. His Neoclassical, contrapuntal works include chamber ensemble and orchestral pieces, such as the *Symphonic Metamorphosis on Themes of Carl Maria von Weber* 1944, and the operas *Cardillac* 1926, revised 1952, and *Mathis der Maler/Mathis the Painter* 1938.

A fine viola player, he led the Frankfurt Opera Orchestra at 20, and taught at the Berlin Hochschule for music 1927–33. The modernity of his work, such as the *Philharmonic Concerto* 1932, led to a Nazi ban. In 1939 he went to the US, where he taught at Yale University and in 1951 he became professor of musical theory at Zürich.

Hindenburg Paul Ludwig Hans von Beneckendorf und Hindenburg 1847–1934. German field marshal and right-wing politician. During World War I he was supreme commander and, with Ludendorff, practically directed Germany's policy until the end of the war. He was president of Germany 1925–33.

Born in Posen of a Prussian Junker (aristocratic landowner) family, he was commissioned 1866, served in the Austro-Prussian and Franco-German wars, and retired 1911. Given the command in East Prussia Aug 1914, he received the credit for the defeat of the Russians at ◊Tannenberg and was promoted to supreme commander and field marshal. Re-elected president 1932, he was compelled to invite Hitler to assume the chancellorship Jan 1933.

Hindenburg German name 1915–45 of the Polish city of ◊Zabrze, in honor of General Hindenburg.

Hindenburg Line German western line of World War I fortifications built 1916–17.

Hindi language member of the Indo-Iranian branch of the Indo-European language family, the official language of the Republic of India, although resisted as such by the Dravidian-speaking states of the south. Hindi proper is used by some 30% of Indians, in such northern states as Uttar Pradesh and Madhya Pradesh.

Hindi has close historical and cultural links with Sanskrit, the Classical language of Hinduism, and is written (from left to right) in Devanagari script. Bihari, Punjabi, and Rajasthani, the dominant language varieties in the states of Bihar, Punjab, and Rajasthan, are claimed by some to be varieties of Hindi (dialects), by others to be distinct languages.

Hinduism religion originating in N India about 4,000 years ago, which is superficially and in some of its forms polytheistic, but has a concept of the supreme spirit, ◊Brahman, above the many divine manifestations. These include the triad of chief gods (the Trimurti): Brahma, Vishnu, and Siva (creator, preserver, and destroyer). Central to Hinduism are the beliefs in reincarnation and ◊karma; the oldest scriptures are the *Vedas*. Temple worship is almost universally observed and there are many festivals. There are over 805 million Hindus worldwide. Women are not

***Hinduism** Prambanan, on Indonesia's island of Java, was completed about AD 900; the three principal Hindu temples are dedicated to Brahma, Siva, and Vishnu.*

regarded as the equals of men but should be treated with kindness and respect. Muslim influence in N India led to the veiling of women and the restriction of their movements from about the end of the 12th century.

scriptures The *Veda* collection of hymns was followed by the philosophical *Upanishads*, centering on the doctrine of Brahman, and the epics *Rāmāyana* and *Mahābhārata* (which includes the *Bhagavad-Gītā*), all from before the Christian era.

beliefs The cosmos is seen as both real and an illusion (*maya*), since its reality is not lasting; the cosmos is itself personified as the goddess Maya. In addition to the various guises of the Trimurti, there are numerous lesser divinities—for example Ganesa, Hanuman, and Lakshmi—and demons, ghosts, and spirits who are also revered.

practice Hinduism has a complex of rites and ceremonies performed within the framework of the caste system under the supervision of the Brahman priests and teachers.

Hindu Kush mountain range in central Asia; length 500 mi/800 km; greatest height Tirich Mir 25,239 ft/7,690 m, in Pakistan. The narrow Khyber Pass, (33 mi/53 km long) separates Pakistan from Afghanistan and was used by ◊Zahir and other invaders of India.

The present road was built by the British in the Afghan Wars.

Hindustan ("land of the Hindus") the whole of India, but more specifically the plain of the Ganges and Jumna rivers, or that part of India north of the Deccan.

Hindustani member of the Indo-Iranian branch of the Indo-European language family, closely related to Hindi and Urdu and originating in the bazaars of Delhi. It is a ◊lingua franca in many parts of the Republic of India.

Hine Lewis 1874–1940. US photographer. His dramatic photographs of child labor conditions in US factories at the beginning of the 20th century led to changes in state and local labor laws.

Trained as a sociologist at the University of Chicago and New York University, Hine began to document social conditions by photographing the immigrants coming into the US at New York's Ellis Island 1904–08, as well as their tenement homes and the places and sweatshops in which they worked. His publication of those photos 1908 is considered the first "photo story." The National Child Labor Committee hired him to travel extensively in the US, photographing child labor conditions 1911–16. In later years, Hine photographed various government projects and construction of the Empire State Building, published 1930 in his *Men at Work*.

Hines Duncan 1880–1959. US travel author and publisher. Born in Bowling Green, Kentucky, Hines worked as a traveling salesman, compiling notes on the many hotels and restaurants he encountered in his trips. Encouraged by friends, he published his restaurant reviews as *Adventures in Good Eating* in 1936. His hotel notes appeared as *Lodging for a Night* in 1939.

Hines later founded his own publishing house for cookbooks and entertainment and travel guides. A pioneer travel critic, he helped raise the standard of travel accommodation in the US. He later licensed his name to a line of prepackaged cake mixes.

hinge joint in vertebrates, a joint where movement occurs in one plane only. Examples are the elbow and knee, which are controlled by pairs of muscles, the ◊flexors and ◊extensors.

Hinshelwood Cyril Norman 1897–1967. English chemist. He shared the 1956 Nobel Prize for Chemistry with Nikolai Semenov for his work on chemical chain reactions. He also studied the chemistry of bacterial growth.

hip-hop a style of popular music originating in New York in the early 1980s. It uses scratching (a percussive effect obtained by manually rotating a vinyl record) and heavily accented electronic drums behind a ◊rap vocal. The term "hip-hop" also comprises break dancing and graffiti.

Hipparchos acronym for the high precision parallax collecting satellite launched by the European Space Agency in Aug 1989. Named after the Greek astronomer Hipparchus, it is the world's first ◊astrometry satellite, designed to provide the first measurements of the positions and apparent motions of stars from space. The accuracy of these measurements will be far greater than from ground-based telescopes. However, because of engine failure, *Hipparchos* is making more limited orbits than had been planned, which may restrict the data it is able to provide.

Hipparchus c. 555–514 BC. Greek tyrant. Son of ◊Pisistratus, he was associated with his elder brother Hippias as ruler of Athens 527–514 BC. His affection being spurned by Harmodius, he insulted her sister, and was assassinated by Harmodius and Aristogiton.

Hipparchus c. 190–c. 120 BC. Greek astronomer who invented trigonometry, calculated the lengths of the solar year and the lunar month, discovered the precession of the equinoxes, made a catalog of 800 fixed stars, and advanced Eratosthenes' method of determining the situation of places on the Earth's surface by lines of latitude and longitude.

A native of Nicaea in Bithynia, he lived in Rhodes, and possibly in Alexandria.

hippie a member of a youth movement of the mid-1960s to mid-1970s, also known as flower power, which originated in San Francisco, California, and was characterized by nonviolent anarchy, concern for the environment, and rejection of Western materialism. The hippies formed a politically outspoken, antiwar, artistically prolific counterculture in North America and Europe. Their colorful psychedelic style, inspired by drugs such as ◊LSD, emerged in fabric design, graphic art, and music by bands such as Love (1965–71), the Grateful Dead (1965–), Jefferson Airplane (1965–74), and ◊Pink Floyd.

Hippocrates c. 460–c. 370 BC. Greek physician, often called the father of medicine. Important Hippocratic ideas include cleanliness (for patients and physicians), moderation in eating and drinking, letting nature take its course, and living where the air is good.

He was born and practiced on the island of

hippopotamus

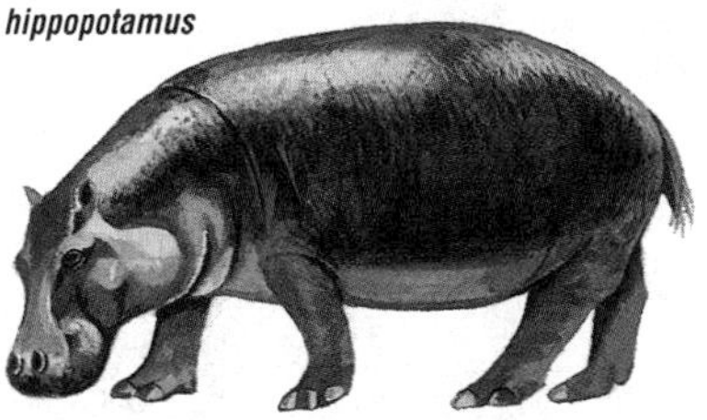

Kos and died at Larissa. He is known to have discovered aspirin in willow bark. The *Corpus Hippocraticum*, a group of some 70 works, is attributed to him but was probably not written by him, although the works outline his approach to medicine. They include *Aphorisms* and the *Hippocratic Oath*, which embodies the essence of medical ethics. He believed that health was the result of the "humors" of the body being in balance; imbalance caused disease. These ideas were later adopted by ◊Galen.

Hippolytus in Greek mythology, the son of Theseus. When he rejected the love of his stepmother, Phaedra, she falsely accused him of making advances to her and turned Theseus against him. Killed by Poseidon at Theseus' request, he was restored to life when his innocence was proven.

hippopotamus (Greek "river-horse") large herbivorous, even-toed hoofed mammal of the family Hippopotamidae. The common hippopotamus *Hippopotamus amphibius* is found in Africa. It averages over 13 ft/4 m long, 5 ft/1.5 m high, weighs about 5 tons/4,500 kg, and has a brown or slate-gray skin. It is an endangered species.

A social and gregarious animal, the hippopotamus spends the day wallowing in rivers or waterholes only emerging at night to graze. The pygmy hippopotamus *Choeropsis liberiensis* inhabits W Africa. To the ancient Egyptians, the hippopotamus symbolized both evil and female fertility.

Hirabayashi v US a US Supreme Court decision 1943 dealing with wartime legislation restricting the rights of citizens based on national origin. The case was brought in response to special curfews for Japanese-Americans on the US west coast. Hirabayashi charged that this and the forced relocation of Japanese-Americans during World War II was a violation of Fifth-Amendment rights. The Court refused to rule on relocation measures (◊*Korematsu* v *US* 1944) but upheld Congress's curfew, judging that danger of internal sabotage

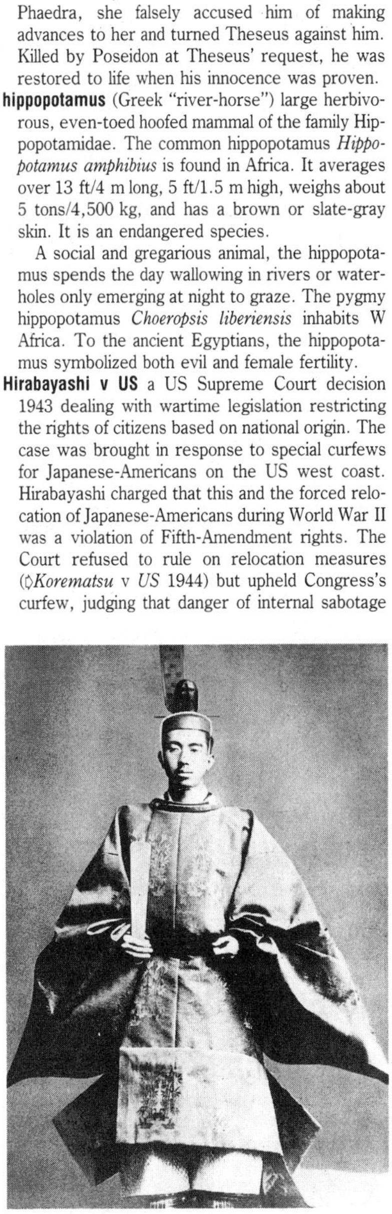

***Hirohito** Emperor Hirohito of Japan in ceremonial robes.*

***Hiroshima** The total devastation caused by the atom bomb on Hiroshima toward the end of World War II.*

in the war with Japan warranted this extraordinary measure.

Hirohito 1901–1989. Emperor of Japan from 1926. He succeeded his father Yoshihito. After the defeat of Japan in World War II 1945, he was stripped of his divine powers and made constitutional monarch by the US-backed 1946 constitution. He was believed to have played a reluctant role in ◊Tojo's prewar expansion plans. Hirohito ruled postwar occupied Japan with dignity. He was a scholar of botany and zoology and the author of books on marine biology. He was succeeded by his son ◊Akihito.

Hiroshige Andō 1797–1858. Japanese artist whose landscape prints, often using snow or rain to create atmosphere, include *Tōkaidō gojūsan-tsugi/53 Stations on the Tokaido Highway* 1833.

Hiroshige was born in Edo (now Tokyo), and his last series was *Meisho Edo Hyakkei/100 Famous Views of Edo* 1856–58, uncompleted before his death. He is thought to have made over 5,000 different prints. Whistler and van Gogh were among Western painters influenced by him.

Hiroshima industrial city and port on the S coast of Honshu, Japan, destroyed by the first wartime use of an atomic bomb Aug 6, 1945. The city has largely been rebuilt since the war; population (1987) 1,034,000.

Toward the end of World War II the city was utterly devastated by the US atomic bomb. More than 4 sq mi/10 sq km was obliterated, with very heavy fire damage outside that area. Casualties totalled at least 137,000 out of a population of 343,000: 78,150 were found dead, others died later.

Hispanic a person of Latin American descent from the Spanish-speaking nations, either native-born or an immigrant.

Hispaniola (Spanish *"little Spain"*) West Indian island, first landing place of Columbus in the New World, Dec 6, 1492; now divided into ◊Haiti and the ◊Dominican Republic.

Hiss Alger 1904– . US diplomat and liberal Democrat, a former State Department official, controversially imprisoned 1950 for allegedly having spied for the USSR.

Hiss, president of the Carnegie Endowment for International Peace and one of President Roosevelt's advisers at the 1945 ◊Yalta Conference, was accused 1948 by a former Soviet agent, Whittaker Chambers (1901–61), of having passed information to the USSR during the period 1926–37. He was convicted of perjury for swearing before the House Un-American Activities Committee that he had not spied for the USSR (under the statute of limitations he could not be tried for the original crime). Richard ◊Nixon was a prominent member of the committee, which inspired the subsequent anticommunist witch-hunts of Senator Joseph ◊McCarthy. There are doubts about the justice of Hiss's conviction.

histamine inflammatory substance normally released in damaged tissues, which also accounts for many of the symptoms of ◊allergy. Substances that neutralize its activity are known as ◊antihistamines.

It is an amine, $C_5H_9N_3$.

histochemistry the study of plant and animal tissue by visual examination, usually with a ◊microscope.

Stains are often used to highlight structural characteristics such as the presence of starch or distribution of fats.

histogram in statistics, a graph with the horizontal axis having discrete units or class boundaries with contiguous end points, and the vertical axis representing the frequency. Blocks are drawn such that their areas are proportional to the frequencies within a class or across several class boundaries. There are no spaces between blocks.

histology in medicine, the laboratory study of cells and tissues.

historical novel a fictional prose narrative set in the past. Literature set in the historic rather than the immediate past has always abounded, but in the West Walter Scott began the modern tradition by setting imaginative romances of love, impersonation, and betrayal in a past based on known fact; his use of historical detail, and subsequent imitations of this technique by European writers such as Manzoni, gave rise to the genre.

Some historical novels of the 19th century were overtly nationalistic, but most were merely novels set in the past to heighten melodrama while providing an informative framework; the genre was used by Victor Hugo, Charles Dickens, and James Fenimore Cooper, among many others. In the 20th century the historical novel also became concerned with exploring psychological states and the question of differences in outlook and mentality in past periods. Examples of this are Robert Graves' novels about the Roman emperor *I, Claudius* and *Claudius the God*, and Margaret Yourcenar's *Memoirs of Hadrian*.

The less serious possibilities of the historical novel were exploited by writers including Kenneth Roberts, James Michener, Jeffery Farnol, Stanley Weyman, and Rafael Sabatini in the early 20th century in the form of the historical romance; Dorothy Dunnett and George MacDonald Fraser revived the historical romance with some success in the late 1960s. Sub-genres of the historical novel have developed, with their own conventions. Examples include the Western, many of which draw on Owen Wister's classic *The Virginian*; and the novels of the South in the period of the Civil War, notably Margaret Mitchell's *Gone With the Wind*. In the late 20th century, generational series of novels about families, often industrialists of the early 19th century, became popular.

history the record of the events of human societies. The earliest surviving historical records are the inscriptions denoting the achievements of Egyptian and Babylonian kings. As a literary form in the Western world, historical writing or historiography began with the Greek Herodotus in the 4th century BC, who was first to pass beyond the limits of a purely national outlook. Contemporary historians make extensive use of statistics, population figures, and primary records to justify historical arguments.

Herodotus's contemporary Thucydides brought to history not only literary gifts but the interests of a scientific investigator and political philosopher. Later Greek history and Roman history tended toward rhetoric; Sallust preserved the scientific spirit of Thucydides, but Livy and Tacitus, in spite of their insight and literary distinction, tended to subordinate factual accuracy to patriotic or party considerations. Medieval history was dominated by a religious philosophy imposed by the church. English chroniclers of this period are Bede, William of Malmesbury, and Matthew Paris. France produced great chroniclers of contemporary events in Froissart and Comines.

The Renaissance revived historical writing and the study of history both by restoring Classical models and by creating the science of textual criticism. A product of the new secular spirit was Machiavelli's *History of Florence* 1520–23. This critical approach continued into the 17th century but the 18th-century ◊Enlightenment disposed of the attempt to explain history in theological terms and an interpretive masterpiece was produced by by Gibbon: *The Decline and Fall of the Roman Empire* 1776–88. An attempt to formulate a historical method and a philosophy of history, that of the Italian Vico, remained almost unknown until the 19th century. Romanticism left its mark on 19th-century historical writing in the tendency to exalt the contribution of the individual "hero," and in the introduction of a more colorful and dramatic style and treatment, variously illustrated in the works of the French historian Jules Michelet (1798–1874), and the British writers Carlyle and Macaulay.

During the 20th century the study of history has been revolutionized, partly through the contributions of other disciplines, such as the sciences and anthropology. The deciphering of the Egyptian and Babylonian inscriptions was of great importance. Researchers and archeologists have traced the development of prehistoric human beings, and have revealed forgotten civilizations such as that of Crete. Anthropological studies of primitive society and religion, which began with Frazer's *Golden Bough* 1890, have attempted to analyze the bases of later forms of social organization and belief. The changes brought about by the Industrial Revolution and the accompanying perception of economics as a science forced historians to turn their attention to economic questions. Marx's attempt to find in economic development the most significant, although by not the only determining factor in social change, an argument partly paralleled in *History of Civilization in England* 1857 by Henry Thomas Buckle (1821–1862), has influenced historians since. A comparative study of civilizations is offered in A J Toynbee's *Study of History* 1934–54, and on a smaller scale by J M Roberts' *History of the World* 1976. Contemporary historians make a distinction between historical evidence or records, historical writing, and historical method or approaches to the study of history.

history of ideas the discipline that studies the history and development of ideas and theories in terms of their origins and influences. The historian of ideas seeks to understand their significance in their original contexts.

Hitachi city on Honshu, Japan; population 204,000. The chief industry is the manufacture of electrical goods.

Hitchcock Alfred 1899–1980. British film director who became a US citizen in 1955. A master of the suspense thriller, he was noted for his artistically

Hitchcock *Suspense, melodrama, and fleeting personal appearances are the hallmarks of Alfred Hitchcock's films.*

drawn storyboards that determined his camera angles and for his hallmark of cameo "walk-ons" in his own films. He directed his first film 1925. His *Blackmail* 1929 was the first successful British talking film; *The Thirty-Nine Steps* 1935 and *The Lady Vanishes* 1939 are British suspense classics. He went to Hollywood 1940, where he made *Rebecca* 1940, *Notorious* 1946, *Strangers on a Train* 1951, *Rear Window* 1954, *Vertigo* 1958, *Psycho* 1960, and *The Birds* 1963. He also hosted two US television mystery series, "Alfred Hitchcock Presents" 1955–62 and "The Alfred Hitchcock Hour" 1963–65.

Hitler Adolf 1889–1945. German Nazi dictator, born in Austria. Führer (leader) of the Nazi party from 1921, author of *Mein Kampf/My Struggle* 1925–27. As chancellor of Germany from 1933 and head of state from 1934, he created a dictatorship by playing party and state institutions against each other and continually creating new offices and appointments. His position was not seriously challenged until the "Bomb Plot" July 20, 1944 (See ◊July plot) to assassinate him. In foreign affairs, he reoccupied the Rhineland and formed an alliance with the Italian Fascist Mussolini 1936, annexed Austria 1938, and occupied the Sudetenland under the ◊Munich Agreement. The rest of Czechoslovakia was annexed March 1939. The ◊Nazi-Soviet pact was followed in Sept by the invasion of Poland and the declaration of war by Britain and France (see ◊World War II). He committed suicide as Berlin fell.

Hitler *German Nazi leader Adolf Hitler at Berchtesgaden, Bavaria.*

Born at Braunau-am-Inn, the son of a customs official, he spent his early years in poverty in Vienna and Munich. After serving as a volunteer in the German army during World War I, he was employed as a spy by the military authorities in Munich and in 1919 joined, in this capacity, the German Workers' Party. By 1921 he had assumed its leadership, renamed it the National Socialist German Workers' Party (Nazi Party for short), and provided it with a program that mixed nationalism with ◊anti-Semitism. Having led an unsuccessful uprising in Munich 1923, he was sentenced to nine months' imprisonment during which he wrote his political testament, *Mein Kampf*. The party did not achieve national importance until the elections of 1930; by 1932, although Field Marshal Hindenburg defeated Hitler in the presidential elections, it formed the largest group in the Reichstag (parliament). As the result of an intrigue directed by Chancellor Franz von Papen, Hitler became chancellor in a Nazi–Nationalist coalition Jan 30, 1933.

The opposition was rapidly suppressed, the Nationalists removed from the government, and the Nazis declared the only legal party. In 1934 Hitler succeeded Hindenburg as head of state. Meanwhile, the drive to war began; Germany left the League of Nations, conscription was reintroduced, and in 1936 the Rhineland was reoccupied. Hitler and Mussolini, who were already both involved in Spain, formed an alliance (the Axis) 1936, joined by Japan 1940. Hitler conducted the war in a ruthless but idiosyncratic way, took and ruled most of the neighboring countries with repressive occupation forces, and had millions of Slavs, Jews, Gypsies, homosexuals, and political enemies killed in concentration camps and massacres. He narrowly escaped death 1944 from a bomb explosion at a staff meeting, prepared by high-ranking officers. On April 29, 1945, when Berlin was largely in Soviet hands, he married his mistress Eva Braun in his bunker under the chancellory building and on the following day committed suicide with her.

Hitler–Stalin pact see ◊Nazi-Soviet pact.

Hittite member of a group of people who inhabited Anatolia and N Syria from the 3rd millennium to the 1st millennium BC. The city of Hattusas (now Boğazköy in central Turkey) became the capital of a strong kingdom which overthrew the Babylonian empire. After a period of eclipse the Hittite New Empire became a great power (about 1400–1200 BC), which successfully waged war with Egypt. The Hittite language is an Indo-European language.

The original Hittites, a people of Armenian/Anatolian type, inhabited a number of city-states in E Anatolia, one of which, Hatti, gained supremacy over the others. An Indo-European people invaded the country about 2000 BC, made themselves the ruling class, and intermarried with the original inhabitants. The Hittites developed advanced military, political, and legal systems. The New Empire concluded a peace treaty with Egypt 1269 BC, but was eventually overthrown by the Sea Peoples. Small Hittite states then arose in N Syria, the most important of which was ◊Carchemish; these were conquered by the Assyrians in the 8th century BC. Carchemish was conquered 717.

The Hittites used a cuneiform script, modeled on the Babylonian, for ordinary purposes, and a hieroglyphic script for inscriptions on monuments. The Hittite royal archives were discovered at Hattusas 1906–07 and deciphered 1915.

HIV abbreviation for Human Immunodeficiency Virus, the infectious agent that causes ◊AIDS.

Hoare–Laval Pact plan for a peaceful settlement to the Italian invasion of Ethiopia in Oct 1935. It was devised by Samuel Hoare (1880–1959), British foreign secretary, and Pierre ◊Laval, French premier, at the request of the ◊League of Nations. Realizing no European country was willing to go to war over Ethiopia, Hoare and Laval proposed official recognition of Italian claims. Public outcry in Britain against the pact's seeming approval of Italian aggression was so great that the pact had to be disowned and Hoare was forced to resign.

Hobbes *English political philosopher Thomas Hobbes believed that absolutist government was the only means of ensuring order and security.*

hoatzin tropical bird *Opisthocomus hoatzin* found only in the Amazon, resembling a small pheasant in size and appearance. The bill is thick and the facial skin blue. Adults are olive with white markings above and red-brown below.

The young are hatched naked, with claws on their wings, which they use to crawl reptilian-fashion about the tree—a possible reminder of their ancestry; these claws later fall off. They fly only reluctantly and prefer to climb among branches using their wings. They cannot grip with their feet.

Hoban James C 1762–1831. Irish-born architect who emigrated to the US. He designed the White House, Washington, DC; he also worked on the Capitol and other public buildings.

Hobart capital and port of Tasmania, Australia; population (1986) 180,000. Products include zinc, textiles, and paper. Founded 1804 as a penal colony, it was named after Lord Hobart, then secretary of state for the colonies.

The University of Tasmania, established 1890, is at Hobart.

Hobbema Meindert 1638–1709. Dutch landscape painter; a pupil of Ruisdael. His early work is derivative, but later works are characteristically realistic and unsentimental.

Hobbes Thomas 1588–1679. English political philosopher and the first thinker since Aristotle to attempt to develop a comprehensive theory of nature, including human behavior. In *The Leviathan* 1651, he advocates absolutist government as the only means of ensuring order and security; he saw this as deriving from the ◊social contract.

Hobbit, The or ***There and Back Again*** a fantasy for children by J R R ◊Tolkien, published in the UK 1937. It describes the adventures of Bilbo Baggins, a "hobbit" (small humanoid) in an ancient world, Middle-Earth, populated by dragons, dwarves, elves, and other mythical creatures, including the wizard Gandalf. *The Hobbit*, together with Tolkien's later trilogy *The Lord of the Rings* 1954–55, achieved cult status in the 1960s.

hobby small falcon *Falco subbuteo* found across Europe and N Asia. It is about 1 ft/30 cm long, with gray back, streaked front and chestnut thighs. It is found in open woods and heaths, and feeds on insects and small birds.

Hoboken city and port in NE New Jersey, on the Hudson River; population (1990) 33,397.

Ho Chi Minh *President Ho Chi Minh of North Vietnam led resistance to French colonialists and then campaigned against South Vietnam in his efforts to unify Vietnam under Communist rule.*

Hochhuth Rolf 1931– . Swiss dramatist, whose controversial play *Soldaten/Soldiers* 1968 implied that the British politician Churchill was involved in a plot to assassinate the Polish general ◊Sikorski.

Ho Chi Minh adopted name of Nguyen That Tan 1890–1969. North Vietnamese Communist politician, premier and president 1954–69. Having trained in Moscow shortly after the ◊Russian Revolution, he headed the communist Vietminh from 1941 and fought against the French during the Indochina War 1946–54, becoming president and prime minister of the republic at the armistice. Aided by the Communist bloc, he did much to develop industrial potential. He relinquished the premiership 1955, but continued as president. In the years before his death, Ho successfully led his country's fight against US-aided South Vietnam in the Vietnam war 1954–75.

Ho Chi Minh City (until 1976 ***Saigon***) chief port and industrial city of S Vietnam; population (1985) 3,500,000. Industries include shipbuilding, textiles, rubber, and food products. Saigon was the capital of the Republic of Vietnam (South Vietnam) from 1954 to 1976, when it was renamed.

Ho Chi Minh Trails North Vietnamese troop and supply routes to South Vietnam via Laos during the Vietnam war, 1954–75.

Hockney David 1937– English painter, printmaker, and designer, resident in California. He exhibited at the Young Contemporaries Show of 1961 and contributed to the Pop art movement. He developed an individual figurative style, as in his portrait *Mr and Mrs Clark and Percy* 1971, Tate Gallery, London, and has prolifically experimented with technique. His views of swimming pools reflect a preoccupation with surface pattern and effects of light. He has also produced drawings, etchings, photo collages, and sets for opera.

Hockney *The work of English painter David Hockney is deliberately childlike and characterized by a gentle wit. This painting,* Peter Getting out of Nick's Pool, *is typical of his California style: flat and shadowless and showing his interest in depicting moving water.*

Hodeida or Al Hudaydah Red Sea port of Yemen; population (1986) 155,000. It trades in coffee and spices.

Hodgkin Dorothy Crowfoot 1910– . English biochemist who analyzed the structure of penicillin, insulin, and vitamin B12. Hodgkin was the first to use a computer to analyze the molecular structure of complex chemicals, and this enabled her to produce three-dimensional models. Nobel Prize for Chemistry 1964.

Hodgkin *Nobel Prize-winner in chemistry Dorothy Crowfoot Hodgkin.*

Hodgkin Thomas 1798–1856. British physician who first recognized Hodgkin's disease (lymphoadenoma), a cancerlike enlargement of the lymph nodes and other lymphoid tissues.

Hodgkin's disease rare form of cancer (also known as lymphoadenoma), mainly affecting the lymph nodes and spleen. It undermines the immune system, leaving the sufferer susceptible to infection. However, it responds well to radiotherapy and ◊cytotoxic drugs, and long-term survival is usual.

Hodler Ferdinand 1853–1918. Swiss painter. His dramatic Art Nouveau paintings of allegorical, historical, and mythological subjects include large murals with dreamy Symbolist female figures, such as *Day* c. 1900 (Kunsthaus, Zürich).

Hodza Milan 1878–1944. Czechoslovak politician, prime minister from Feb 1936. He and President Beneš were forced to agree to the secession of the Sudeten areas of Czechoslovakia to Germany before resigning Sept 22, 1938 (see ◊Munich Agreement).

Hoess Rudolf 1900–1947. German commandant of Auschwitz concentration camp 1940–43. Under his control, more than 2.5 million people were exterminated. Arrested by Allied military police in 1946, he was handed over to the Polish authorities, who tried and executed him in 1947.

Hofei former name of ◊Hefei, a city in China.

Hoffa (James Riddle) "Jimmy" 1913–1975. Notorious US labor union leader. A member of the Teamsters (trucking) Union since 1931, he became its ruthless president in 1957. In 1964 he effected the first national contract for the truckers but was also convicted in two trials of fraud and jury tampering. He went to prison in 1967 and retained his presidency until 1971, when President Nixon commuted his sentence on condition that he not engage in union activity until 1980. Hoffa disappeared in 1975, however, and is considered to have been murdered.

Hoffman Abbie (Abbot) 1936–1989. US left-wing political activist, founder of the Yippies (Youth International Party), a political offshoot of the ◊hippies. He was a member of the Chicago Seven, a radical group tried for attempting to disrupt the 1968 Democratic convention.

Hoffman was arrested 52 times and was a fugitive from justice 1973–80. He specialized in imaginative political gestures to gain media attention, for example throwing dollar bills to the floor of the New York Stock Exchange 1967. His books include *Revolution for the Hell of It* 1969. He campaigned against the Vietnam war and, later, for the environment. He committed suicide.

Hoffman Dustin 1937– . US actor who portrayed the antihero in the 1960s and 1970s in lead character roles. He won Academy Awards for his performances in *Kramer vs Kramer* 1979 and *Rain Man* 1988.

His other films include *The Graduate* 1967, *Midnight Cowboy* 1969, *Little Big Man* 1970, *All the President's Men* 1976, *Tootsie* 1982, and *Hook* 1991. He appeared on Broadway in the 1984 revival of *Death of a Salesman*, which also was produced for television 1985.

Hoffmann E(rnst) T(heodor) A(madeus) 1776–1822. German composer and writer. He composed the opera *Undine* 1816 and many fairy stories, includ-

Hoffman *Actor Dustin Hoffman won his first best-actor Oscar for his role in* Kramer vs. Kramer *1979.*

ing *Nüssknacker/Nutcracker* 1816. His stories inspired ◊Offenbach's *Tales of Hoffmann*.

Hoffmann Josef 1870–1956. Austrian architect, one of the founders of the Wiener Werkstätte (a modern design cooperative of early 20th-century Vienna), and a pupil of Otto ◊Wagner.

Hoffman's voltameter apparatus for collecting gases produced by the electrolysis of a liquid.

It consists of a vertical E-shaped glass tube with taps at the upper ends of the outer limbs and a reservoir at the top of the central limb. Platinum electrodes fused into the lower ends of the outer limbs are connected to a source of direct current. At the beginning of an experiment, the outer limbs are completely filled with electrolyte by opening the taps. The taps are then closed and the current switched on. Gases evolved at the electrodes bubble up the outer limbs and collect at the top, where they can be measured.

Hofman August 1818–1892. German chemist who studied the extraction and exploitation of coal tar derivatives. Hofmann taught chemistry in London from 1845 until his return to Berlin in 1865.

Hofmann Hans 1880–1966. German-born Abstract Expressionist painter, active in Paris and Munich from 1915 until 1932, when he moved to the US. In addition to bold brushwork (he experimented with dribbling and dripping painting techniques in the 1940s) he used strong expressive colors. In the 1960s he moved toward a hard-edged abstract style.

He opened two art schools, in New York City and Provincetown, Massachusetts, and was influential among New York artists in the 1930s.

Hofmeister Wilhelm 1824–1877. German botanist. He studied plant development and determined how a plant embryo, lying within a seed, is itself formed out of a single fertilized egg (ovule).

Hofmeister also discovered that mosses and ferns display an alternation of generations, in which the plant has two forms, spore-forming and gamete-forming.

Hofstadter Robert 1915– US high-energy physicist who revealed the structure of the atomic nucleus. He demonstrated that the nucleus is composed of a high-energy core and a surrounding area of decreasing density. He shared the 1961 Nobel Prize for Physics with Rudolf Mössbauer.

Educated in New York and Princeton, Hofstadter did his research in California after 1950. He helped to construct a new high-energy accelerator at Stanford University, with which he showed that the proton and the neutron have complex structures and cannot be considered elementary particles. See also ◊quark.

hog a member of the ◊pig family.

The river hog *Potamochoerus porcus* lives in Africa S of the Sahara. Reddish or black, up to 4.2 ft/1.3 m long plus tail, and 3 ft/90 cm at the shoulder, these gregarious animals root for food in many types of habitat. The ***giant forest hog*** *Hylochoerus meinerzthageni* lives in thick forests of central Africa and grows up to 6 ft/1.9 m long.

ET PLURIMA MORTIS IMAGO
The Company of Undertakers
Beareth Sable, an Urinal proper, between 12 Quack-Heads of the Second & 12 Cane Heads Or, Consultant. On a Chief Nebulæ, Ermine, One Compleat Doctor issuant, checkie Sustaining on his Right Hand a Baton of the Second. On his Dexter & Sinister sides two Demi-Doctors, issuant of the second, & two Cane Heads issuant of the third; The first having One Eye conchant, towards the Dexter Side of the Escocheon; the Second Faced per pale proper & Gules, Guardent. —
With this Motto — Et Plurima Mortis Imago.
Price Six pence

Hogarth *English painter and engraver William Hogarth revived the art of medieval morality pictures with series such as* A Rake's Progress *1733. He published his own engravings; this one is a bitter attack on the medical men of his time.*

Hogarth William 1697–1764. English painter and engraver who produced portraits and moralizing genre scenes, such as the series *A Rake's Progress* 1735. His portraits are remarkably direct and full of character, for example *Heads of Six of Hogarth's Servants* c. 1750–55 (Tate Gallery, London).

Hogarth was born in London and apprenticed to an engraver. He published *A Harlot's Progress* 1732, a series of six engravings, in 1732. Other series followed, including *Marriage à la Mode* 1745, *Industry and Idleness* 1749, and *The Four Stages of Cruelty* 1751. In his book *The Analysis of Beauty* 1753 he proposed a double curved line as a key to successful composition.

hogback a geologic formation consisting of a ridge with a short crest and abruptly sloping sides. Hogbacks are the result of differential erosion on steeply dipping rock strata composed of alternating resistant and soft beds. Exposed, almost vertical beds provide the sharp crests.

Hoggar alternate spelling of ◊***Ahaggar***, a plateau in the Sahara.

Hohenlinden, Battle of in the French ◊Revolutionary Wars, a defeat of the Austrians by the French Dec 1800. Coming after the defeat at ◊Marengo, it led the Austrians to make peace at the Treaty of Lunéville 1801.

Hohenlohe-Schilingsfürst Prince Chlodwig von 1819–1901. German imperial chancellor from Oct 1894 until his replacement by Prince von Bülow in Oct 1900.

Hohenstaufen German family of princes, several members of which were Holy Roman emperors 1138–1208 and 1214–54. They were the first German emperors to make use of associations with Roman law and tradition to aggrandize their office, and included Conrad III; Frederick I (Barbarossa), the first to use the title Holy Roman emperor; Henry VI; and Frederick II. The last of the line, Conradin, was executed 1268 with the approval of Pope Clement IV while attempting to gain his Sicilian inheritance.

Hohenzollern German family, originating in Württemberg, the main branch of which held the titles of ◊elector of Brandenburg from 1415, king of

Prussia from 1701, and German emperor from 1871. The last emperor, Wilhelm II, was dethroned 1918 after the disastrous course of World War I. Another branch of the family were kings of Romania 1881–1947.

Hohhot formerly Huhehot city and capital of Inner Mongolia (*Nei Mongol*) autonomous region, China; population (1984) 778,000. Industries include textiles, electronics, and dairy products. There are Lamaist monasteries and temples here.

Hokkaido northernmost of the four main islands of Japan, separated from Honshu to the south by Tsugaru Strait and from Sakhalin to the north by Soya Strait; area 32,231 sq mi/83,500 sq km; population (1986) 5,678,000, including 16,000 ◊Ainus. The capital is Sapporo. Natural resources include coal, mercury, manganese, oil and natural gas, timber, and fisheries. Coal mining and agriculture are the main industries.

Snow-covered for half the year, Hokkaido was little developed until the Meiji Restoration 1868 when disbanded samurai were settled here. Intensive exploitation followed World War II, including heavy and chemical industrial plants, development of electric power, and dairy farming. An artificial harbor has been constructed at Tomakomai, and an undersea rail tunnel links Hakodate with Aomori (Honshu) but remains as yet closed to public transport.

Hokusai Katsushika 1760–1849. Japanese artist, a leading printmaker of his time. He published *Fugaku Sanjū-rokkei/36 Views of Mount Fuji* c. 1823–29, but he produced outstanding pictures of almost every kind of subject—birds, flowers, courtesans, and scenes from legend and everyday life.

Hokusai was born in Edo (now Tokyo) and studied wood engraving and book illustration. He was interested in Western painting and perspective and introduced landscape as a woodblock-print genre. His *Manga*, a book crammed with inventive sketches, was published in 13 volumes from 1814.

Holbein Hans, the Elder c. 1464–1524. German painter, active in Augsburg. His works include altarpieces, such as that of *St Sebastian* 1516 (Alte Pinakothek, Munich). He also painted portraits and designed stained glass.

Holbein Hans, the Younger 1497/98–1543. German painter and woodcut artist; the son and pupil of Hans Holbein the Elder. Holbein was born in Augsburg. In 1515 he went to Basel, where he became friendly with Erasmus; he painted three ortraits of him in 1523, which were strongly influenced by Quentin Massys. He traveled widely in Europe and was court painter to England's Henry VIII from 1536. He also painted portraits of Thomas More and Thomas Cromwell; a notable woodcut series is *Dance of Death* c. 1525. He also designed title pages for Luther's New Testament and More's *Utopia*.

Holden William. Adopted name of William Franklin Beedle 1918–1981. US film actor, a star in the late 1940s and 1950s. He played leading roles in *The Wild Bunch* 1969, *Sunset Boulevard* 1950, *Stalag 17* 1953, and *Network* 1976.

holdfast an organ found at the base of many seaweeds, attaching them to the sea bed. It may be a flattened, suckerlike structure, or dissected and fingerlike, growing into rock crevices and firmly anchoring the plant.

holding company a company with a controlling stockholding in one or more subsidiaries.

holiday a period of allowed absence from work. The word derives from medieval holy days, which were saints' days when no work was done.

Holidays have become significant events in the US and many Western countries, where major religious festivals and national days are celebrated by gathering with family and friends, feasting, and occasionly gift giving.

Holiday Billie. Adopted name of Eleanora Gough

Holiday *Acknowledged as the supreme jazz singer of her day, Billie Holiday brought an individual blues sound to all her songs.*

McKay 1915–1959. US jazz singer, also known as "Lady Day." She made her debut in Harlem clubs and became known for her emotionally charged delivery and idiosyncratic phrasing; she brought a blues feel to performances with swing bands. Songs she made her own include "Strange Fruit" and "I Cover the Waterfront."

Holinshed Ralph c. 1520–c. 1580. English historian who published two volumes of the *Chronicles of England, Scotland and Ireland* 1578, on which Shakespeare based his history plays.

holism in philosophy, the concept that the whole is greater than the sum of its parts. In medicine, the idea that physical and mental well-being are inextricably linked, so that all aspects of a patient's life must be taken into account.

Holkeri Harri 1937– . Finnish politician, prime minister 1987–91. Joining the centrist National Coalition Party (KOK) at an early age, he eventually became its national secretary.

Holland alternate name for the ◊***Netherlands*** also two provinces of the Netherlands: see ◊North Holland and ◊South Holland.

Holland John Philip 1840–1914. Irish engineer who developed some of the first submarines. He began work in Ireland in the late 1860s and emigrated to the US 1873. His first successful boat was launched 1881 and, after several failures, he built the *Holland* 1893, which was bought by the US Navy two years later.

The first submarine, the *Fenian Ram* 1881, was built with financial support from the Irish Fenian society, who hoped to use it against England. Holland continued after 1895 to build submarines for various navies but died in poverty after his company became embroiled in litigation with backers.

Holland Sidney George 1893–1961. New Zealand politician, leader of the National Party 1940–57 and prime minister 1949–57.

Hollerith Herman 1860–1929. US inventor of a mechanical tabulating machine, the first device for data processing. Hollerith's tabulator was widely publicized after being successfully used in the 1890 census. The firm he established, the Tabulating Machine Company, was later one of the founding companies of ◊IBM.

After attending the Columbia University School of Mines, Hollerith worked on the 1880 US census and witnessed the huge task of processing so much information. In 1882 he became an instructor at the Massachusetts Institute of Technology, where he developed his machine for counting and collating census data.

Holly *Rock-and-roll singer Buddy Holly created such hits as "Peggy Sue" and "That'll Be the Day" before his tragic death in an airplane crash.*

holly tree or shrub of the genus *Ilex*, family Aquifoliaceae, generally with glossy, sharp-pointed leaves and red berries. American holly (*I. opaca*) of the E US is used for Christmas decorations. Leaves of the Brazilian holly *I. paraguayensis* are used to make the tea yerba maté.

Holly Buddy. Adopted name of Charles Hardin Holley 1936–1959. US rock-and-roll singer, guitarist, and songwriter, born in Lubbock, Texas. Holly had a distinctive, hiccuping vocal style and was an early experimenter with recording techniques. Many of his hits with his band, the Crickets, such as "That'll Be the Day" 1957, "Peggy Sue" 1957, and "Maybe Baby" 1958, have become classics. He died in a plane crash.

hollyhock plant of the genus *Althaea* of the mallow family Malvaceae. *A. rosea*, originally a native of Asia, produces spikes of large white, yellow, or red flowers, 10 ft/3 m high when cultivated as a biennial.

Hollywood district in the city of Los Angeles, California; the center of the US film industry from 1911. Home of the legendary film studios such as 20th Century-Fox, MGM, Paramount, Columbia Pictures, United Artists, Disney, and Warner Brothers. Although Hollywood lost its commanding position with the decline of the studio system in the late 1950s, the rise of independent producers and the needs of television studios made use of the soundstage and backlot facilities there. MGM Studios has become a major theme park and tourist attraction. Many film stars' homes are situated nearby in Beverly Hills and other communities adjacent to Hollywood.

Hollywood city in SE Florida, on the Atlantic Ocean, S of Fort Lauderdale and N of Miami. Its principal industry is tourism; population (1990) 121,697.

Holmes, Sherlock fictitious private detective, created by the English writer Arthur Conan ◊Doyle in *A Study in Scarlet* 1887 and recurring in novels and stories until 1914. Holmes's ability to make inferences from slight clues always astonishes the narrator, Dr Watson.

The criminal mastermind against whom Holmes repeatedly pits his wits is Professor James Moriarty. Holmes is regularly portrayed at his home, 221b Baker Street, London, where he plays the violin and has bouts of determined action interspersed by lethargy and drug-taking. His characteristic pipe and deerstalker hat were the addition of an illustrator.

Holmes Oliver Wendell 1809–1894. US writer and physician. In 1857 he founded *The Atlantic Monthly* with J R Lowell, in which were published the essays and verse collected in 1858 as *The Autocrat of the Breakfast-Table*, a record of the imaginary conversation of boarding-house guests.

This was followed by *The Professor at the Breakfast-Table* 1860 and other "Breakfast-Table" collections, and the novel *Elsie Venner* 1861. "The Chambered Nautilus" is among his best-known poems.

Holmes Oliver Wendell 1841–1935. US jurist and

holography

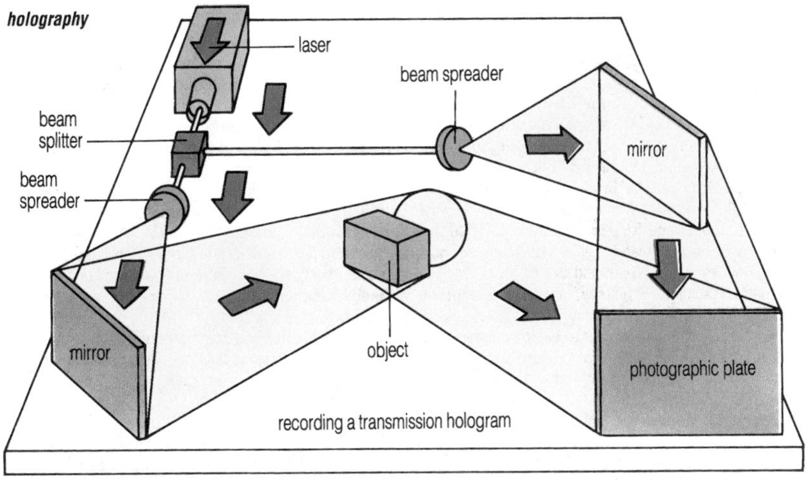
laser
beam spreader
beam splitter
beam spreader
mirror
mirror
object
photographic plate
recording a transmission hologram

Supreme Court justice noted for the elegance of his written opinions. Holmes established a private practice in Boston and gained a reputation as an author and lecturer on legal subjects. Appointed to the Massachusetts Supreme Court 1882 and to the US Supreme Court by President T Roosevelt 1902, Holmes handed down landmark decisions in a number of antitrust, First Amendment, and labor law cases. He retired from the Court 1932.

Son of the writer and physician of the same name, he was born in Boston and educated at Harvard. After service in the US Civil War, he studied law and was admitted to the bar 1867.

holmium silvery, metallic element of the ◊lanthanide series, symbol Ho, atomic number 67, atomic weight 164.93. It occurs in combination with other rare-earths and in various minerals such as gadolinite. Its compounds are highly magnetic.

The element was discovered in 1878, spectroscopically, by the Swiss chemists L Soret and Delafontaine, and independently in 1879 by the Swedish chemist Per Cleve (1840–1905), who named it for *Holmia*, Latin for Stockholm, near where it was found.

Holocaust, the the annihilation of more than 16 million people by the Hitler regime 1933–45 in the numerous extermination and ◊concentration camps, most notably Auschwitz, Sobibor, Treblinka, and Maidanek in Poland, and Belsen, Buchenwald, and Dachau in Germany. Of the victims, more than 6 million were Jews (over 67% of European Jewry); 10 million Ukrainian, Polish, and Russian civilians and prisoners-of-war, Gypsies, Socialists, homosexuals, and others (labeled "defectives") were also imprisoned and/or exterminated. Victims were variously starved, tortured, experimented on, worked to death, and executed in gas chambers, shot, and hanged.

Holocaust museums and memorial sites have been established in Israel and in other countries.

Holocene epoch of geological time that began 10,000 years ago, the second epoch of the Quaternary period. The glaciers retreated, the climate became warmer, and humans developed significantly.

holography method of producing three-dimensional (3-D) images by means of ◊laser light. Although the possibility of holography was suggested as early as 1947, it could not be demonstrated until a pure coherent light source, the laser, became available 1963. Holography uses a photographic technique (involving the splitting of a laser beam into two beams) to produce a picture, or hologram, that contains 3-D information about the object photographed. Some holograms show meaningless patterns in ordinary light and produce a 3-D image only when laser light is projected through them, but reflection holograms produce images when ordinary light is reflected from them (as found on credit cards).

The technique of holography is also applicable to sound, and bats may navigate by ultrasonic holography. Holographic techniques also have applications in storing dental records, detecting stresses and strains in construction and in retail goods, and detecting forged paintings and documents.

Holst Gustav(us Theodore von) 1874–1934. English composer. He wrote operas, including *Savitri* 1916 and *At the Boar's Head* 1925; ballets; choral works, including *Hymns from the Rig Veda* 1911 and *The Hymn of Jesus* 1920; orchestral suites, including *The Planets* 1918; and songs. He was a lifelong friend of Ralph ◊Vaughan Williams, with whom he shared an enthusiasm for English folk music. His musical style, although tonal and drawing on folk song, tends to be severe.

Holt Harold Edward 1908–1967. Australian Liberal politician, prime minister 1966–67.

He was minister of labor 1940–41 and 1949–58, and federal treasurer 1958–66, when he succeeded Menzies as prime minister.

Holy Alliance a "Christian Union of Charity, Peace, and Love" initiated by Alexander I of Russia 1815 and signed by every crowned head in Europe. The alliance became associated with Russian attempts to preserve autocratic monarchies at any price, and an excuse to meddle in the internal affairs of other states.

Ideas of an international army acting in the name of the alliance were rejected by Britain and Austria 1818 and 1820.

Holy Communion another name for the ◊***Eucharist***, a Christian sacrament.

Holy Grail in medieval Christian legend, the dish or cup having supernatural powers, used by Jesus at the Last Supper. Together with the spear with which he was wounded at the Crucifixion, it was an object of quest by King Arthur's knights in certain stories incorporated in the Arthurian legend.

According to one story, the blood of Jesus was collected in the Holy Grail by ◊Joseph of Arimathaea at the Crucifixion, and he brought it to Britain where he allegedly built the first church, at Glastonbury. At least three churches in Europe possess vessels claimed to be the Holy Grail.

Holy Island or ***Lindisfarne*** island in the North Sea; area 4 sq mi/10 sq km; 2 mi/3 km off Northumberland, England, with which it is connected by a causeway. St ◊Aidan founded a monastery here in 635.

Holy Land Christian term for ◊Israel, because of its association with Jesus and the Old Testament.

Holyoake Keith Jacka 1904–1983. New Zealand National Party politician, prime minister 1957 (for two months) and 1960–72.

Holy Office tribunal of the Roman Catholic church that deals with ecclesiastical discipline; see ◊Inquisition.

holy orders Christian priesthood, as conferred by the laying on of hands by a bishop. It is held by the Roman Catholic, Eastern Orthodox, and Anglican churches to have originated in Jesus' choosing of the Apostles.

The Roman Catholic Church includes among holy orders bishop, priest, deacon, subdeacon, acolyte, exorcist, reader, and door-keepers, and, outside the priesthood, ◊tertiary.

Holy Roman Emperors

Emperor	*Dates of reign*
Carolingian Kings and Emperors	
Charlemagne (Charles the Great)	800–14
Louis I, the Pious	814–40
Lothair I	840–55
Louis II	855–75
Charles II, the Bald	875–77
Charles III, the Fat	881–87
Guido of Spoleto	891–94
Lambert of Spoleto (co-emperor)	892–98
Arnulf (rival)	896–901
Louis III of Provence	901–05
Berengar	905–24
Conrad I of Franconia (rival)	911–18
Saxon Kings and Emperors	
Henry I, the Fowler	918–36
Otto I, the Great	936–73
Otto II	973–83
Otto III	983–1002
Henry III, the Saint	1002–24
Franconian (Salian) Emperors	
Conrad II	1024–39
Henry III, the Black	1039–56
Henry IV	1056–1106
Rudolf of Swabia (rival)	1077–80
Hermann of Luxembourg (rival)	1081–93
Conrad of Franconia (rival)	1093–1101
Henry V	1106–25
Lothair II	1126–37
Hohenstaufen Kings and Emperors	
Conrad III	1138–52
Frederick I Barbarossa	1152–90
Henry VI	1190–97
Otto IV	1198–1215
Philip of Swabia (rival)	1198–1208
Frederick II	1215–50
Henry Raspe of Thuringia (rival)	1246–47
William of Holland (rival)	1246–47
Conrad IV	1250–54
The Great Interregnum	1254–73
Rulers from Noble Families	
Richard of Cornwall (rival)	1257–72
Alfonso X of Castile (rival)	1257–73
Rudolf I (Hapsburg)	1273–91
Adolph I of Nassau	1292–98
Albert I (Hapsburg)	1298–1303
Henry VII (Luxembourg)	1308–13
Louis IV of Bavaria	1314–47
Frederick of Hapsburg (co-regent)	1314–25
Charles IV (Luxembourg)	1347–78
Wenceslas of Bohemia	1378–1400
Frederick III of Brunswick	1400
Rupert of the Palatinate	1400–10
Sigismund (Luxembourg)	1411–37
Hapsburg Emperors	
Albert II	1438–39
Frederick III	1440–93
Maximillian I	1493–1519
Charles V	1519–56
Ferdinand II	1556–64
Maximillian II	1564–76
Rudolf II	1576–1612
Mathias	1612–19
Ferdinand III	1619–57
Leopold I	1658–1705
Joseph I	1705–11
Charles VI	1711–40
Charles VII of Bavaria	1742–45
Hapsburg-Lorraine Emperors	
Francis I of Lorraine	1745–65
Joseph II	1765–90
Leopold II	1790–92
Francis II	1792–1806

Holy Roman Empire the empire of ◊Charlemagne and his successors, and the German empire 962–1806, both being regarded as the Christian (hence "holy") revival of the Roman Empire. At its height it comprised much of western and central Europe. See ◊Germany, history and ◊Hapsburg.

Holy See the diocese of the ◊pope.

Holy Shroud Christian name for the shroud of ◊Turin.

Holy Spirit the third person of the Christian ◊Trinity, also known as the ***Holy Ghost*** or the ***Paraclete***. Usually depicted as a white dove.

Holy Week in the Christian church, the last week of ◊Lent, when Christians commemorate the events that led up to the crucifixion of Jesus. Holy Week begins on Palm Sunday and includes Maundy Thursday, which commemorates the Last Supper.

Homburg or ***Bad Homburg*** town and spa at the foot of the Taunus mountains, Federal Republic of Germany; population (1984) 41,800. It has given its name to a soft felt hat for men, made fashionable by Edward VII of England.

Home Alec Douglas-Home, Baron Home of the Hirsel, British Conservative politician; see Alec ◊Douglas-Home.

Homelands Policy South Africa's apartheid policy, which set aside ◊Black National States for black Africans.

homeopathy or homoeopathy system of medicine based on the treatment of a given disease by administering minute quantities of a substance that produces the symptoms of that disease in a healthy person. It was introduced by the German physician Samuel Hahnemann (1755–1843), and is contrasted with ◊allopathy.

homeostasis the maintenance of a constant state in an organism's internal environment, particularly with regard to pH, salt concentration, temperature, and blood sugar levels. Stable conditions are important for the efficient functioning of the ◊enzyme reactions within the cells, which affect the performance of the entire organism.

homeothermy the maintenance of a constant body temperature in endothermic (warm-blooded) animals, by the use of chemical body processes to compensate for heat loss or gain when external temperatures change. Such processes include generation of heat by the breakdown of food and the contraction of muscles, and loss of heat by sweating, panting, and other means.

Mammals and birds are homeotherms, whereas invertebrates, fish, amphibians, and reptiles are coldblooded or poikilotherms. Homeotherms generally have a layer of insulating material to retain heat, such as fur, feathers, or fat (see ◊blubber). Their metabolism functions more efficiently due to homeothermy, enabling them to remain active under most climatic conditions.

Homer lived c. 8th century BC. Legendary Greek epic poet. According to tradition he was a blind minstrel and the author of the ◊*Iliad* and the ◊*Odyssey*, which are probably based on much older stories, passed on orally, concerning war with Troy in the 12th century BC.

Homer Winslow 1836–1910. US painter and lithographer, known for his seascapes, both oils and watercolors, which date from the 1880s and 1890s.

Homer, born in Boston, made his reputation as a realist painter with *Prisoners from the Front* 1866 (Metropolitan Museum of Art, New York), recording miseries of the American Civil War. After a visit to Paris he turned to lighter subjects, studies of country life, which reflect early Impressionist influence. He stayed in Britain for two years, then settled in Maine, but continued to travel to Canada, the West Indies, and elsewhere.

Home Rule, Irish the movement to repeal of the Act of ◊Union 1801 that joined Ireland to Britain and to establish an Irish parliament responsible for internal affairs. In 1870 Isaac Butt (1813–1879) formed the Home Rule Association and the movement was led in Parliament from 1880 by Charles ◊Parnell. After 1918 the demand for an independent Irish republic replaced that for home rule.

Gladstone's Home Rule bills 1886 and 1893 were both defeated. A third bill was introduced by the Liberals in 1912, which aroused opposition in Ireland where the Protestant minority in Ulster feared domination by the Catholic majority. Ireland appeared on the brink of civil war but the outbreak of World War I rendered further consideration of Home Rule inopportune. In 1920 the Government of Ireland Act introduced separate parliaments in the North and South.

Homestead Act in US history, an act of Congress 1862 to encourage settlement of land in the west by offering 160-acre/65-hectare plots cheaply or even free to those willing to cultivate and improve the land for a stipulated amount of time. By 1900 about 80,000 acres/32,400,000 hectares had been distributed. Homestead lands are available to this day.

homicide in law, the killing of a human being. This may be unlawful, lawful, or excusable, depending on the circumstances. Unlawful homicides include ◊murder, ◊manslaughter, ◊infanticide, and causing death by dangerous driving (vehicular homicide). Lawful homicide occurs where, for example, a police officer is justified in killing a criminal in the course of apprehension. Excusable homicide occurs when a person is killed in self-defense or by accident.

homologous in biology, a term describing an organ or structure possessed by members of different taxonomic groups (for example, species, genera, families, orders) that originally derived from the same structure in a common ancestor. The wing of a bat, the arm of a monkey, and the flipper of a seal are homologous because they all derive from the forelimb of an ancestral mammal.

homologous series any of a number of series of organic chemicals whose members differ by a constant molecular weight.

Alkanes (paraffins), alkenes (olefins), and alkynes (acetylenes) form such series whose members differ in mass by 14, 12, and 10 atomic mass units, respectively. For example, the alkane homologous series begins with methane (CH_4), ethane (C_2H_6), propane (C_3H_8), butane (C_4H_{10}), and pentane (C_5H_{12})—each member differing from the previous one by a CH_2 group (or 14 atomic mass units).

homonymy aspect of language in which two or more words may sound and look alike (homonymy proper; for example, a farmer's *bull* and a papal *bull*), may sound the same but look different (homophony; for example, *air* and *heir*; *gilt* and *guilt*), and may look the same but sound different (homography; for example the *wind* in the trees and roads that *wind*).

Homonyms, homophones, and homographs seldom pose problems of comprehension, because they usually belong in different contexts. Even when brought into the same context for effect ("The *heir* to the throne had an *air* of self-satisfaction"), they are entirely clear. They may, however, be used to make puns (for example, "a papal bull in a china shop").

homophony in music, a melody lead and accompanying harmony, as distinct from heterophony and polyphony in which different melody lines are combined.

homosexuality sexual preference for, or attraction to, persons of one's own sex; in women it is referred to as ◊lesbianism. Both sexes use the term "gay." Men and women who are attracted to both sexes are referred to as bisexual.

homozygous in a living organism, having two identical ◊alleles for a given trait. Individuals homozygous for a trait always breed true; that is, they produce offspring that resemble them in appearance when bred with a genetically similar individual; inbred varieties or species are homozygous for almost all traits. ◊Recessive alleles are only expressed in the homozygous condition. See also ◊heterozygous.

Homs or ***Hums city***, capital of Homs district, W Syria, near the Orontes River; population (1981) 355,000. Silk, cereals, and fruit are produced in the area, and industries include silk textiles, oil refining, and jewelry. ◊Zenobia, queen of Palmyra, was defeated at Homs by the Roman emperor ◊Aurelian 272.

Honan former name of ◊Henan, a province of China.

Hondecoeter Melchior 1636–1695. Dutch artist who painted large pictures of birds (both domestic fowl and exotic species) in grandiose settings.

Hondo another name for ◊***Honshu***, an island of Japan.

Honduras country in Central America, bounded N by the Caribbean, SE by Nicaragua, S by the Pacific, SW by El Salvador, and W and NW by Guatemala.

government The 1982 constitution, which underwent a major revision 1985, provides for the election of a president, who is head of both state and government, by universal suffrage for a four-year term, and may not serve two terms in succession. A single-chamber national assembly of 134 members is elected in the same way for a similar term.

There is a range of political parties that sometimes unite to form broad alliances for election purposes. The most significant are the Liberal Party of Honduras (PLH) and the National Party (PN).

history Originally part of the ◊Maya civilization, it was reached by Christopher Columbus 1502, and the area was colonized by Spain from 1526. Independent from Spain 1821, Honduras was part of the ◊United Provinces of Central America until 1838, when it achieved full independence. From 1939 to 1949 it was a dictatorship under the leader of the PN.

The government changed in a series of military coups, until the return of civilian rule 1980. The army, however, controlled security and was able to veto cabinet appointments, and although the 1981 general election was won by the PLH and its leader, Dr Roberto Suazo, became president, power remained in the hands of General Gustavo Alvarez, the Commander in Chief of the army. In 1982 Alvarez secured an amendment to the constitution, reducing government control over the armed forces, and was virtually in charge of foreign policy, agreeing 1983 to the establishment of US military bases in the country. The US Central Intelligence Agency was also active in assisting Nicaraguan "contra" rebels based in Honduras.

In 1984 Alvarez was ousted by a group of junior officers and the country's close relationship with the US came under review. In the same year divisions arose in the PLH over selection of presidential candidates and in 1985 the electoral law was changed. Suazo was not eligible to stand in the 1985 presidential elections, and the main PLH candidate was José Azcona. Although the PN nominee won most votes, the revised constitution made Azcona the eventual winner. In the Nov 1989 presidential election, the PN candidate, Rafael Callejas, was elected. The presence of Contras on Honduran territory provoked tensions with Nicaragua, which filed a suit against Honduras in the International Court of Justice. The Sandinista government agreed to drop the suit if Contra bases were dismantled and the fighters demobilized, in keeping with the regional peace plan adopted Feb 1989. Thus, the presence of the rebels became a distinct political liability for Honduras.

Honecker Erich 1912– . German communist politician, in power 1973–89, elected chair of the council of state (head of state) 1976. He governed in an outwardly austere and efficient manner and, while favoring East–West détente, was a loyal ally of the USSR. In Oct 1989, following a wave of pro-democracy demonstrations, he was

Honduras
Republic of
(República de Honduras)

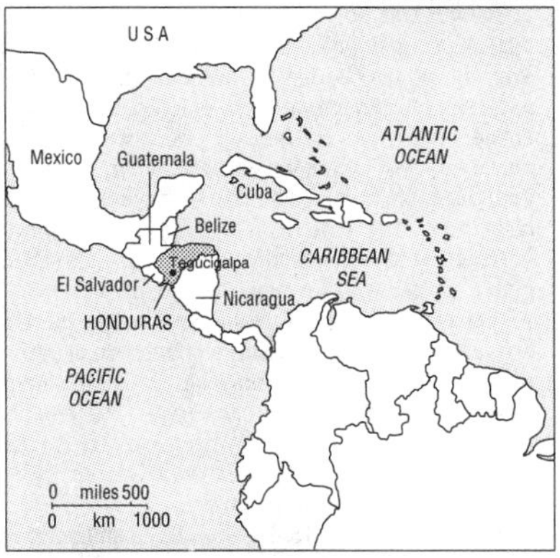
USA
Mexico
Guatemala
Cuba
Belize
ATLANTIC OCEAN
Tegucigalpa
CARIBBEAN SEA
El Salvador
Nicaragua
HONDURAS
PACIFIC OCEAN
0 miles 500
0 km 1000

area 43,282 sq mi/112,100 sq km
capital Tegucigalpa
cities San Pedro Sula; ports Henecan (on Pacific), La Ceiba, Puerto Cortés
physical narrow tropical coastal plain with mountainous interior, Bay Islands
features archeological sites; Mayan ruins at Copán
head of state and government Rafael Leonardo Callejas from 1990
political system democratic republic
political parties Liberal Party of Honduras (PLH), center-left; National Party (PN), right-wing
exports coffee, bananas, meat, sugar, timber (including mahogany, rosewood)
currency lempira
population (1989 est) 5,106,000 (90% mestizo, 10% Indians and Europeans); growth rate 3.1% p.a.
life expectancy men 58, women 62
language Spanish, Indian dialects
religion Roman Catholic 97%
literacy men 61%/women 58% (1985 est)
GDP $3.5 bn (1987); $758 per head
chronology
1838 Independence achieved from Spain.
1980 After more than a century of mostly military rule, a civilian government was elected, with Dr Roberto Suazo as president; the commander in chief of the army, Gen Gustavo Alvarez, retained considerable power.
1983 Close involvement with the US in providing naval and air bases and allowing Nicaraguan counter-revolutionaries ("contras") to operate from Honduras.
1984 Alvares ousted in coup led by junior officers, resulting in policy review toward US and Nicaragua.
1985 José Azcona elected president after electoral law changed, making Suazo ineligible for presidency.
1989 Government and opposition declared support for Central American peace plan to demobilize Nicaraguan Contras based in Honduras; Contras and their dependents in Honduras in 1989 thought to number about 55,000.
1990 Rafael Callejas (PN) elected president.

replaced as leader of the Socialist Unity Party (SED) and head of state by Egon ◊Krenz, and in Dec expelled from the Communist Party.

Honecker, the son of a miner, joined the German Communist Party 1929 and was imprisoned for antifascist activity 1935–45. He was elected to the East German parliament (*Volkskammer*) 1949 and became a member of the SED Politburo during the 1950s. A security specialist, during the 1960s he served as a secretary of the National Defence Council before being appointed first secretary of the SED 1971. After Ulbricht's death 1973, Honecker became leader of East Germany. He was replaced Oct 1989 by his protégé Egon Krenz following large-scale civil disturbances. In Feb 1990 he was arrested and charged with high treason, misuse of office, and corruption, but he was able to flee to the USSR, in Mar 1991, before trial.

Honegger Arthur 1892–1955. Swiss composer, one of ◊Les Six. His work was varied in form, for example, the opera *Antigone* 1927, the ballet *Skating Rink* 1922, the oratorio *Le Roi David/King David* 1921, program music (*Pacific 231* 1923), and the *Symphonie liturgique/Liturgical Symphony* 1946.

Hōnen 1133–1212. Japanese Buddhist monk who founded the ◊Pure Land school of Buddhism.

honey a sweet syrup produced by honey ◊bees from the nectar of flowers. It is stored in honeycombs and made in excess of their needs as food for the winter. Honey comprises various sugars, mainly levulose and dextrose, with enzymes, coloring matter, acids, and pollen grains. It has antibacterial properties and was widely used in ancient Egypt, Greece, and Rome as a wound salve. It is still popular for sore throats, in hot drinks, or in lozenges.

honey-eater or ***honey-sucker*** small, brightly colored bird of the family Meliphagidae. Honeyeaters have long, curved beaks and long tails, and they use their long tongues to sip nectar from flowers. They are native to Australia.

Honey-eaters from Australasia colonized Hawaii and four species evolved there of which only one, the Kauai O-o, survives; thought to be extinct, it was rediscovered 1960.

honey guides in botany, lines or spots on the petals of a flower that indicate to pollinating insects the position of the nectaries (see ◊nectar) within the flower. The orange dot on the lower lip of the butter-and-eggs flower *Linaria vulgaris* is an example. Sometimes the markings reflect only ultraviolet light, which can be seen by many insects although it is not visible to the human eye.

honeysuckle vine or shrub of the genus *Lonicera*, family Caprifoliaceae. The commmon honeysuckle or woodbine *L. periclymenum* of Europe is a climbing plant with sweet-scented flowers, reddish and yellow-tinted outside and creamy-white inside; it now grows in the NE US.

The North American trumpet honeysuckle *L. sempervirens* has unusual, vaselike flowers and includes scarlet and yellow varieties.

Hong Kong British crown colony SE of China, in the South China Sea, comprising Hong Kong island, the Kowloon peninsula, and the mainland New Territories. It is due to revert to Chinese control 1997.
area 413 sq mi/1,070 sq km
capital Victoria (Hong Kong City)

honey-eater

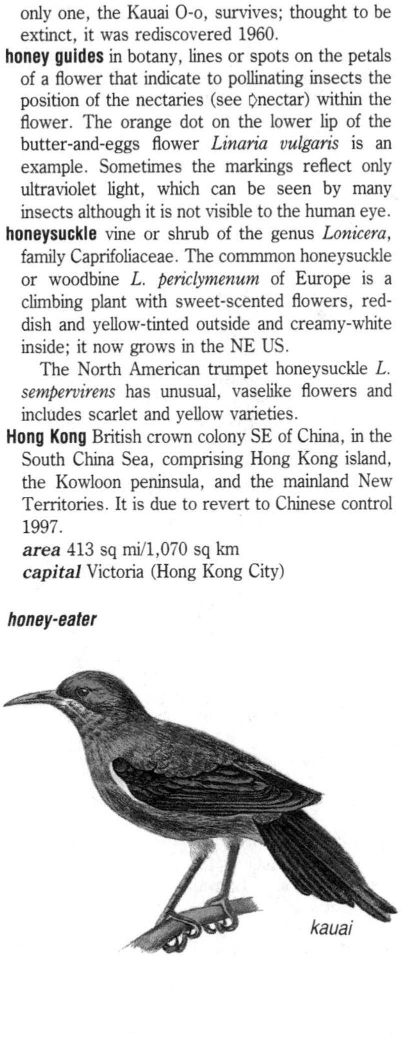
kauai

honeysuckle

cities Kowloon, Tsuen Wan (in the New Territories)
features an enclave of Kwantung province, China, it has one of the world's finest natural harbors; Hong Kong Island is connected with Kowloon by undersea railway and ferries; a world financial center, its stock market has four exchanges; across the border of the New Territories in China itself is the Shenzhen special economic zone
exports textiles, clothing, electronic goods, clocks, watches, cameras, plastic products; a large proportion of the exports and imports of S China are transshipped here; tourism is important
currency Hong Kong dollar
population (1986) 5,431,000; 57% Hong Kong Chinese, most of the remainder refugees from the mainland
languages English, Chinese
religion Confucianist, Buddhist, Taoist, with Muslim and Christian minorities
government Hong Kong is a British dependency administered by a Crown-appointed governor who presides over an unelected executive council, composed of four ex-officio and 11 nominated members, and a legislative council composed of three ex-officio members, 29 appointees, and 24 indirectly elected members
history formerly part of China, Hong Kong island was occupied by Britain 1841, during the first of the ◊Opium Wars, and ceded by China under the 1842 Treaty of Nanking. The Kowloon Peninsula was acquired under the 1860 Peking (Beijing) Convention and the New Territories secured on a 99-year lease from 1898.

The colony, which developed into a major *entrepôt* for Sino-British trade during the late 19th and early 20th centuries, was occupied by Japan 1941–45. The restored British administration promised, after 1946, to increase self-government. These plans were shelved, however, after the 1949 Communist revolution in China. During the 1950s almost 1 million Chinese (predominantly Cantonese) refugees fled to Hong Kong. Immigration continued during the 1960s and 1970s, raising the colony's population from 1 million in

Hong Kong

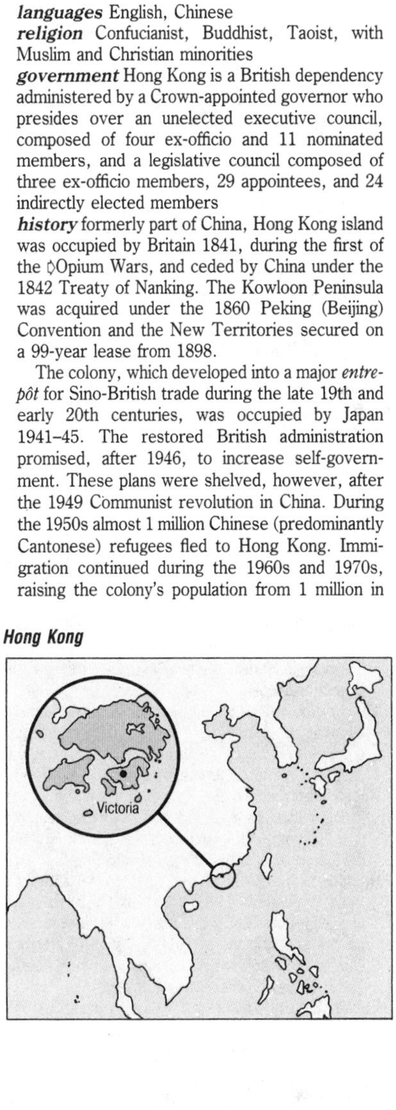
Victoria

1946 to 5 million in 1980, and forcing the imposition of strict border controls during the 1980s. Since 1975, 160,000 Vietnamese "boat people" have fled to Hong Kong; in 1989, 50,000 remained, and the UK government began forced repatriation (51 forced, 630 voluntary by Dec 1989).

Hong Kong's economy expanded rapidly during the corresponding period, however, and the colony became one of Asia's major commercial, financial, and industrial centers. As the date (1997) for the termination of the New Territories' lease approached, negotiations on Hong Kong's future were opened between Britain and China 1982. These culminated in a unique agreement, signed in Beijing 1984, in which Britain agreed to transfer full sovereignty of the Islands and New Territories to China 1997 in return for Chinese assurance that Hong Kong's social and economic freedom and capitalist lifestyle would be preserved for at least 50 years.

Under this "one country, two systems" agreement, in 1997 Hong Kong would become a special administrative region within China, with its own laws, currency, budget, and tax system, and would retain its free-port status and authority to negotiate separate international trade agreements. In preparation for its withdrawal from the colony, the British government introduced indirect elections to select a portion of the new legislative council 1984, and direct elections for seats on lower-tier local councils 1985. A Sino-British joint liaison group was also established to monitor the functioning of the new agreement, and a 59-member committee (including 25 representatives from Hong Kong) formed in Beijing 1985 to draft a new constitution. In Mar 1990 the committee agreed to a "Basic Law" with 18 directly-elected members of the legislative council from 1991, rising to 30 in 2003 (out of a total of 60). In Dec 1989 the UK government granted British citizenship to 225,000 Hong Kong residents, beginning 1997.

Honiara port and capital of the Solomon Islands, on the NW coast of Guadalcanal island; population (1985) 26,000.

Honolulu (Hawaiian "sheltered bay") capital city and port of Hawaii, on the S coast of Oahu; population (1990) 365,272. It is a vacation resort, noted for its beauty and tropical vegetation, with some industry. The University of Hawaii's main campus is here, and there is an innovative state capitol building, dating from 1959. Pearl Harbor and Hickam Air Force Base are 7 mi/11 km to the NW. William Brown, a British sea captain, was the first European to see Honolulu, in 1794. It became the Hawaiian royal capital in the 19th century.

Honshu principal island of Japan. It lies between Hokkaido to the NE and Kyushu to the SW; area 89,205 sq mi/231,100 sq km, including 382 smaller islands; population (1986) 97,283,000. A chain of volcanic mountains runs along the island, which is subject to frequent earthquakes. The main cities are Tokyo, Yokohama, Osaka, Kobe, Nagoya, and Hiroshima.

Honthorst Gerrit van 1590–1656. Dutch painter who used extremes of light and shade, influenced by Caravaggio; with Terbrugghen he formed the Utrecht school.

Around 1610–12 he was in Rome, studying Caravaggio. Later he visited England, painting *Charles I* 1628 (National Portrait Gallery, London) and became court painter in The Hague.

Hooch Pieter de 1629–1684. Dutch painter, active in Delft and, later, Amsterdam. The harmonious domestic interiors and courtyards of his Delft period were influenced by Vermeer.

Hooghly or ***Hugli*** river and town in West Bengal, India; population (1981) 125,193. The river is the western stream of the Ganges delta. The town is on the site of a factory set up by the East India Company 1640, which was moved to Calcutta, 25 mi/40 km downstream, 1686–90.

Hooke Robert 1635–1703. English scientist and inventor, originator of ◊Hooke's law, and considered the foremost mechanic of his time. His inventions included a telegraph system, the spirit-level, marine barometer, and sea gauge. He coined the term "cell" in biology.

Hooke studied elasticity, furthered the sciences of mechanics and microscopy, and helped improve such scientific instruments as watches, microscopes, telescopes, and barometers. He was elected to the Royal Society 1663, and became its curator for the rest of his life. He was professor of geometry at Gresham College, London, and designed several buildings, including the College of Physicians, London.

Hooker Joseph Dalton 1817–1911. English botanist who traveled to the Antarctic and made many botanical discoveries. His works include *Flora Antarctica* 1844–47, *Genera Plantarum* 1862–83, and *Flora of British India* 1875–97.

Hooker Thomas 1586–1647. Colonial American religious leader. In 1633 he immigrated to the Massachusetts Bay Colony, settling in Cambridge. As an opponent of the strong religious leadership of the colony, he led a group of his followers westward to the Connecticut Valley in 1636, founding Hartford. Hooker became the de facto leader of the colony and in 1639 helped to formulate Connecticut's first constitution, the Fundamental Orders.

Born in England and educated as a minister at Cambridge, Hooker served at parishes in England before fleeing to Holland in 1630 because of his Puritan beliefs.

Hooke's law in physics, law stating that the tension in a lightly stretched spring is proportional to its extension from its natural length. It was discovered by Robert Hooke 1676.

hookworm parasitic roundworm (see ◊worm), of the genus *Necator*, with hooks around the mouth. It lives mainly in tropic and subtropic regions, but also in humid areas in temperate climates. The eggs are hatched in damp soil, and the larvae bore into the host's skin, usually through the soles of the feet. They make their way to the small intestine, where they live by sucking blood. The eggs are expelled with feces, and the cycle starts again. The human hookworm causes anemia, weakness, and abdomonal pain. It is common in areas where defecation occurs outdoors.

hoopoe bird *Upupa epops* in the order Coraciiformes, slightly larger than a thrush, with a long, thin bill and a bright, buff-colored crest that expands into a fan shape. The wings are banded with black and white, and the rest of the plumage is black, white, and buff. This bird is the "lapwing" mentioned in the Old Testament.

Hoover Herbert Clark 1874–1964. 31st president of the US 1929–33, a Republican. Secretary of commerce 1921–28. He lost public confidence after the stock-market crash of 1929, when he opposed direct government aid for the unemployed in the Depression that followed.

As a mining engineer, Hoover traveled widely before World War I. After the war he organized relief work in occupied Europe; a talented administrator, he was subsequently associated with numerous international relief organizations, and became food administrator for the US 1917–19. He defeated the Democratic candidate for the presidency, Al Smith (1873–1944) by a wide margin. The shantytowns or ◊Hoovervilles of the homeless that sprang up around large cities were evidence of his failure to cope with the effects of the Depression. He was severely criticized for his adamant opposition to federal relief for the unemployed, even after the funds of states, cities, and charities were exhausted. In 1933, he was succeeded by F D Roosevelt.

Hoover was called upon to administer the European Food Program 1947, and in the late 1950s he headed two Hoover Commissions that recommended reforms in government structure and operations.

Hoover J(ohn) Edgar 1895–1972. US lawyer and director of the Federal Bureau of Investigation (FBI) from its start 1924, where he built a powerful network for the detection of organized crime, including a national fingerprint collection.

Hoover was born in Washington, DC. His drive against alleged Communist activities after World War II, and his opposition to the Kennedy administration and others, brought much criticism over abuse of power. He served under eight presidents, none of whom would dismiss him, since he kept files on them and their associates. During his tenure, the FBI (named 1935) grew from a corrupt Bureau of Investigation to a respected and highly professional national police agency, with responsibility for counterespionage within the US as well as counterterrorism. Hoover was accused of waging a personal campaign of harassment against leaders of the civil-rights movement, notably Dr Martin Luther ◊King, Jr. He wrote *Persons in Hiding* 1938, *Masters of Deceit* 1958, and *A Study of Communism* 1962.

Hoover William Henry 1849–1932. US manufacturer who developed the ◊vacuum cleaner. "Hoover" soon became a generic name for vacuum cleaner.

Hoover Dam the highest concrete dam in the US, 726 ft/221 m, on the Colorado River at the Arizona–Nevada border. It was begun during the Hoover Administration, built 1931–36. Known as Boulder Dam 1933–47, under the Roosevelt Administration, its name was restored by President Truman since President Hoover was serving the Truman Administration in postwar organization. The dam created Lake Meade, and and has a hydroelectric power capacity of 1,300 megawatts.

Hooverville colloquial term for any shantytown built by the unemployed and destitute in the US during the Depression 1929–40, named after US president Herbert ◊Hoover, whose policies were blamed for the plight of millions.

Hope Anthony. Adopted name of Anthony Hope Hawkins 1863–1933. English novelist whose romance *The Prisoner of Zenda* 1894, and its sequel *Rupert of Hentzau* 1898, introduced the imaginary Balkan state of Ruritania.

Hope Bob. Adopted name of Leslie Towne Hope. 1904– . British-born US comedian, brought to the US in 1907. His earliest success was on Broadway and as a radio star in the 1930s. His film appearances include seven "Road" films made from 1940 with Bing Crosby and Dorothy Lamour. These include *The Road to Singapore* 1940, *The Road to Zanzibar* 1941, *The Road to Morocco* 1942, *The Road to Utopia* 1946, *The Road to Rio* 1946, *The Road to Bali* 1952, and *The Road to Hong Kong* 1953. He made other films, such as *Paleface* 1948, a comic Western.

He has entertained the troops since World War II. He was a perennial star on radio and television (since 1950) in his own comedy series and specials. He has received several special ◊Academy Awards.

Hopei former name of ◊Hebei, a province of China.

Hope's apparatus in physics, an apparatus used to demonstrate the temperature at which water has its maximum density. It is named after Thomas Charles Hope (1766–1844).

It consists of a vertical cylindrical vessel fitted with horizontal thermometers through its sides near the top and bottom, and surrounded at the center by a ledge that holds a freezing mixture (ice and salt). When the cylinder is filled with water, this gradually cools, the denser water sinking to the bottom; eventually the upper thermometer records 32°F/0°C (the freezing point of water) and the lower one has a constant reading of 39°F/4°C (the temperature at which water is most dense).

Hopewell North American Indian agricultural culture of the central US, dated about AD 200 and notable for burial mounds up to 40 ft/12 m high and structures such as Serpent Mound in Ohio; see also ◊moundbuilder.

Hopi a member of a North American Indian people,

Hoover *The 31st president of the United States of America, Herbert Hoover, a Republican. 1929–1933.*

Hopkins *English poet Gerard Manley Hopkins who experienced a life-long tension between being a poet and a Jesuit priest.*

presently numbering approximately 9,000, who live mainly in pueblos in the SW US, especially NE Arizona. They live in stone and adobe houses, forming small towns on rocky plateaus, farm, and herd sheep. Their language belongs to the Uto-Aztecan family.

Hopkins Anthony 1937– . Welsh actor. Among his stage appearances are *Equus*, *Macbeth*, *Pravda*, and the title role in *King Lear*. His films include *The Lion in Winter* 1968, *A Bridge Too Far* 1977, *The Elephant Man* 1983, and *The Silence of the Lambs* 1991.

Hopkins Frederick Gowland 1861–1947. English biochemist whose research into diets revealed the existence of trace substances, now known as vitamins. Hopkins shared the 1929 Nobel Prize for Medicine with Christiaan Eijkman, who had arrived at similar conclusions.

Hopkins Gerard Manley 1844–1889. English poet and Jesuit priest. His work, marked by its religious themes and use of natural imagery, includes "The Wreck of the Deutschland" 1876 and "The Windhover" 1877. His employment of "sprung rhythm" greatly influenced later 20th-century poetry. His poetry was written in secret, and published 30 years after his death by his friend Robert Bridges.

Hopkins Harry Lloyd 1890–1946. US government official. Originally a social worker, in 1935 he became head of the WPA (Works Progress Administration), which was concerned with Depression relief work. After a period as secretary of commerce 1938–40, he was appointed supervisor of the ◊Lend-Lease program 1941, and undertook missions to Britain and the USSR during World War II.

Hopkins Mark 1802–1887. US educator and religious leader. Born in Stockbridge, Massachusetts, Hopkins was educated at Williams College and received an MD degree from Berkshire College 1829. In 1830 he was appointed professor of philosophy at Williams, serving as its president 1836–72. Becoming increasingly involved in religious affairs, Hopkins was ordained a Congregationalist minister 1836 and served as president of the American Board of Commissioners for Foreign Missions 1857–87. He was also known as a popular lecturer and author on religious subjects.

Hopkinsville city in SW Kentucky, SW of Louisville. It is a marketplace for tobacco and livestock; population (1990) 29,809.

hoplite in ancient Greece, a heavily armed infantry soldier.

Hopper Dennis 1936– US film actor and director who caused a sensation with *Easy Rider* 1969, the archetypal "road" film, but whose *The Last Movie* 1971 was poorly received by the critics. He made a comeback in the 1980s. His work as an actor includes *Rebel Without a Cause* 1955, *The American Friend/Der amerikanische Freund* 1977, and *Blue Velvet* 1986.

Hopper Edward 1882–1967. US painter and etcher. His views of New England and New York in the 1930s and 1940s captured the loneliness and superficial glamor of both rural and urban life, as in *Nighthawks* 1942 (Art Institute, Chicago).

Hopper's teacher Robert Henri (1865–1929), associated with the ◊Ashcan school, was a formative influence. Hopper was a realist who never followed avant-garde trends.

Hopper Hedda 1890–1966. US actress and celebrity reporter. From 1915 she appeared in many silent films and after a brief retirement was hired as a radio gossip reporter in 1936. From 1938 Hopper wrote a syndicated newspaper column about the private lives of the Hollywood stars. She carried on a widely publicized feud with rival columnist Louella Parsons.

Born Elda Furry in Hollidaysburg, Pennsylvania, she left home as a teenager to begin a theatrical career. First appearing on the Broadway stage in 1909, she adopted her professional name after marrying actor DeWolf Hopper.

hops female fruit-heads of the hop plant *Humulus lupulus*, family Cannabiaceae; these are dried and used as a tonic and in flavoring beer. In designated areas in Europe, no male hops may be grown, since seedless hops produced by the unpollinated female plant contain a greater proportion of the alpha acid that gives beer its bitter taste.

Horace 65–8 BC. Roman lyric poet and satirist. He became a leading poet under the patronage of Emperor Augustus. His works include *Satires* 35–30 BC; the four books of *Odes* c. 25–24 BC; *Epistles*, a series of verse letters; and a critical work, *Ars poetica*.

Born at Venusia, S Italy, the son of a freedman, Horace fought under Brutus at Philippi, lost his estate, and was reduced to poverty. In about 38 Virgil introduced him to Maecenas, who gave him a farm in the Sabine hills and recommended him to the patronage of Augustus. Horace's works are distinguished by their style, wit, and good sense.

horehound any plant of the genus *Marrubium* of the mint family Labiatae. The white horehound *M. vulgare*, found in Europe, N Africa, and W Asia and naturalized in North America, has a thick, hairy stem and clusters of dull white flowers; it has medicinal uses.

horizon the limit to which one can see across the surface of the sea or a level plain, that is, about 3 mi/5 km at 5 ft/1.5 m above sea level, and about 40 mi/65 km at 1,000 ft/300 m.

hormone product of the ◊endocrine glands, concerned with control of body functions. The main glands are the thyroid, parathyroid, pituitary, adrenal, pancreas, uterus, ovary, and testis. Hormones bring about changes in the functions of various organs according to the body's requirements. The pituitary gland, at the base of the brain, is a center for overall coordination of hormone secretion; the thyroid hormones determine the rate of general body chemistry; the adrenal hormones prepare the organism during stress for "fight or flight"; and the sexual hormones such as estrogen govern reproductive functions.

Many diseases due to hormone deficiency can be relieved with hormone preparations.

hormone-replacement therapy (HRT) the use of oral estrogen to help limit the thinning of bone that occurs in women after menopause. The treatment was first used in the 1970s.

At the menopause, the ovaries cease to secrete natural estrogen, resulting in osteoporosis, or a thinning of bone, which is associated with an increased incidence of fractures, frequently of the hip, in older women. Oral estrogens, taken to replace the decline in natural hormone levels, combined with regular exercise can help to maintain bone strength in women.

Hormuz or Ormuz small island, 16 sq mi/41 sq km, in the Strait of Hormuz, belonging to Iran. It is strategically important because oil tankers leaving the Persian Gulf for Japan and the West have to pass through the strait to reach the Arabian Sea.

It was occupied by the Portuguese 1515–1622.

horn one of a family of wind instruments, of which the French horn is the most widely used. See ◊brass instrument.

Horn Philip de Montmorency, Count of 1518–1568. Flemish politician. He held high offices under the Holy Roman emperor Charles V and his son Philip II. From 1563 he was one of the leaders of the opposition to the rule of Cardinal Granvella (1517–1586) and to the introduction of the Inquisition. In 1567 he was arrested, together with the Resistance leader Egmont, and both were beheaded in Brussels.

hornbeam any tree of the genus *Carpinus* of the birch family Betulaceae. They have oval, serrated leaves and bear pendant clusters of flowers, each with a nutlike seed attached to the base. The trunk is usually twisted, with smooth gray bark.

The American hornbeam *C. caroliniana* is native to the E US. The European hornbeam *C. betulus* is sometimes planted as an ornamental.

hornbill bird of the family of Bucerotidae, found in Africa, India, and Malaysia. Omnivorous, it is about 3 ft/1 m long, and has a powerful bill, usually surmounted by a bony growth or casque. During the breeding season, the female walls herself into a hole in a tree, and does not emerge until the young are hatched.

hornblende a green or black rock-forming mineral, one of the ◊amphiboles; it is a hydrous silicate of calcium, iron, magnesium, and aluminum. Hornblende is found in both igneous and metamorphic rocks.

hornet a kind of ◊wasp.

hornfels a ◊metamorphic rock formed by rocks heated by contact with a hot igneous body. It is fine-grained and brittle, without foliation.

Hornfels may contain minerals only formed under conditions of great heat, such as andalusite, Al_2SiO_5, and cordierite, $(Mg,Fe)_2Al_4Si_5O_{18}$. This rock, originating from sedimentary rock strata, is found in contact with large igneous ◊intrusions where it represents the heat-altered equivalent of the surrounding clays. Its hardness makes it suitable for road building and railroad ballast.

Hornsby Rajah (Rogers) 1896–1963. US baseball player. He won the National League batting title six consecutive seasons 1920–25; his .424 batting average 1924 is the highest ever achieved in the National League. In 1925 he was named the Cardinals' player-manager and won the National League's most valuable player award. In that same year, he had become the first player to win baseball's Triple Crown twice. He was traded to the New York Giants 1927 and served variously as player/player-manager for the Boston Braves 1928, the Chicago Cubs 1929–32, the Cardinals 1933, and the St Louis Browns 1933–37. After retiring as a player—with the second-highest lifetime batting average (.358) in history—he became a manager. Hornsby was elected to the Baseball Hall of Fame 1942.

Born in Winters, Texas, Hornsby was signed by the St Louis Cardinals and broke into the major leagues 1915.

Horowitz *Vladimir Horowitz enjoyed world acclaim as a virtuoso pianist, particularly with his interpretations of the Romantic repertoire.*

hornwort underwater aquatic plant, family Ceratophyllaceae. It has whorls of finely divided leaves and is found in slow-moving water. Hornwort may be up to 7 ft/2 m long.

horoscope in Western astrology, a chart of the position of the Sun, Moon, and planets relative to the ◊zodiac at the moment of birth, used to assess a person's character and forecast future influences.

In casting a horoscope, the astrologer draws a circular diagram divided into 12 sections, or houses, showing the 12 signs of the zodiac around the perimeter and the Sun, Moon, and planets as they were at the subject's time and place of birth. These heavenly bodies are supposed to represent different character traits and influences, and by observing their positions and interrelations the astrologer may gain insight into the subject's personality and foretell the main outlines of his or her career.

horse *Przewalski's horse, the only surviving species of wild horse.*

Horowitz Vladimir 1904–1989. Russian-born US pianist. He made his debut in the US 1928 with the New York Philharmonic Orchestra. Noted for his commanding virtuoso style, he was a leading interpreter of ◊Liszt, ◊Schumann, and ◊Rachmaninov.

Horowitz married Arturo ◊Toscanini's daughter, Wanda, in 1933. He toured worldwide until the early 1950s, when nervous disorders forced him to withdraw completely from the stage; he kept recording, however. After a triumphal return at Carnegie Hall 1965, in which it was clear that he had lost none of his ability, he toured briefly in the 1970s and 1980s. In 1986 Horowitz made a pilgrimage to his homeland, giving a brilliant performance at the Moscow Conservatory of Music.

horror a genre of fiction and film, devoted primarily to scaring the reader, but often also aiming to be cathartic through their exaggeration of the bizarre and grotesque. Dominant figures in the horror tradition are Mary Shelley (*Frankenstein* 1818), Edgar Allan Poe, Bram Stoker, H P Lovecraft and, among contemporary writers, Stephen King and Clive Barker.

Horror is derived from the Gothic novel, which dealt in shock effects, as well as from folk tales and ghost stories throughout the ages. Horror writing tends to use motifs such as vampirism, the eruption of ancient evil, and monstrous transformation, which often derive from folk traditions, as well as more recent concerns such as psychopathology.

horse hoofed, odd-toed, grazing mammal, *Equus caballus* of the family Equidae, which also includes zebras and asses. The many breeds of domestic horse of Euro-Asian origin range in color from white to gray, brown, and black. The yellow-brown Mongolian wild horse or Przewalski's horse *E. przewalskii*, named after its Polish "discoverer" about 1880, is the only surviving species

horse

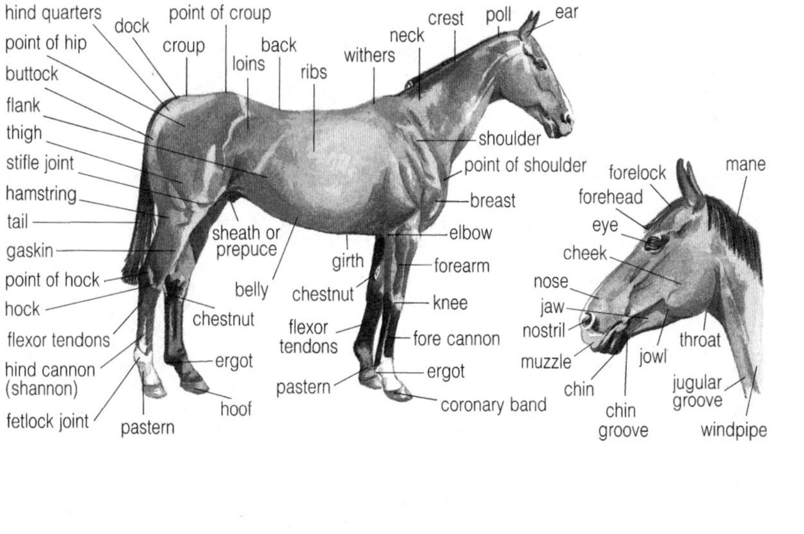
hind quarters
dock
point of croup
point of hip
croup
back
loins
ribs
withers
neck
crest
poll
ear
buttock
flank
thigh
stifle joint
hamstring
tail
gaskin
point of hock
hock
flexor tendons
hind cannon (shannon)
fetlock joint
pastern
hoof
ergot
chestnut
belly
sheath or prepuce
girth
chestnut
flexor tendons
pastern
shoulder
point of shoulder
breast
elbow
forearm
knee
fore cannon
ergot
coronary band
forelock
mane
forehead
eye
cheek
nose
jaw
nostril
muzzle
chin
chin groove
jowl
throat
jugular groove
windpipe

of wild horse. It has become extinct in the wild because of hunting and competition with domestic animals for food; about 800 survive in captivity, and there are plans to reintroduce them to Mongolia.

Breeds include the Arab, small and agile; thoroughbred, derived from the Arab via English mares, used in horse racing for its speed (the present stock is descended from three Arab horses introduced to Britain in the 18th century); quarter horse, used by cowboys for herding; Lippizaner, pure white horses, named after their place of origin in Yugoslavia; shire, the largest draft horse in the world at 17 hands (1 hand = 4 in/10.2 cm), descended from the medieval war horses that carried knights in armor. Ponies combine the qualities of various types of horses with a smaller build (under 14.2 hands, or 58 in/1.47 m). The smallest is the hardy Shetland, about 10.5 hands, or 27 in/70 cm high. The mule, a hardy pack-animal, is the usually sterile offspring of a female horse and a male ass; the hinny is a similarly sterile offspring of a male horse and a female ass, but less useful as a beast of burden.

horsefly any of over 2,500 species of fly, belonging to the family Tabanidae. The females suck blood from horses, cattle, and humans; males live on plants and suck nectar. The larvae are carnivorous.

horsepower imperial unit (abbreviation hp) of power, now replaced by the ◊watt. It was first used by the engineer James ◊Watt, who employed it to compare the power of steam engines with that of horses. In the UK, one horsepower is equal to 550 foot-pounds per second or 745.7 watts. In the US this figure has been rounded to 746 watts, and in the metric system it is 735.5 watts.

horse racing the sport of racing mounted or driven (hitched) horses. Two popular forms in the US are *flat racing*, in which thoroughbred horses are guided over a flat course by a rider called a jockey, and *harness racing*, in which a driver in a two-wheeled cart called a sulky drives a horse in one of two gaits: pacing (both legs on the same side are off the ground at the same time); trotting (diagonal legs are off the ground at the same time).

Flat racing has been popular in the Americas since the early colonial era. Thoroughbreds were introduced to North America from England during the 18th century, and the first thoroughbred course was opened on Long Island 1821. Today, the most famous races in the US for three-year-old horses are the Kentucky Derby, the Preakness, and the Belmont Stakes, collectively known as the Triple Crown. Winning all three races is a major feat. There are race tracks throughout the US, and betting on races is a major attraction for spectators and off-track betters.

Harness racing horses, called standardbreds, usually race on 0.5-mi/0.8-km oval tracks. Harness racing became popular in the early 19th century; the introduction of parimutuel betting and night racing increased its popularity in the mid-20th century.

Other types of horse racing include the *steeplechase*, in which horses race around a course that has numerous obstacles over which the horse must jump. These may include fences, barred jumps, hedges, stone walls, and water.

Triple Crown Winners

1919	Sir Barton
1930	Gallant Fox
1935	Omaha
1937	War Admiral
1941	Whirlaway
1943	Count Fleet
1946	Assault
1948	Citation
1973	Secretariat
1977	Seattle Slew
1978	Affirmed

horseradish hardy perennial *Armoracia rusticana*, native to SE Europe but naturalized elsewhere, family Cruciferae. The thick, cream-colored root is strong-tasting and is often made into a condiment.

horseradish

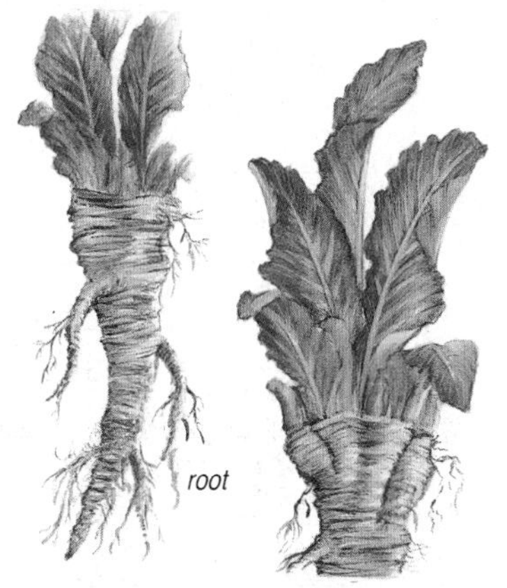
root

horseshoe crab marine arthropod of the order Xiphosura, class Merostomata, distantly related to spiders, which lives on the Atlantic coast of North America and the coasts of Asia. The upper side of the body is entirely covered with a rounded shell, and it has a long, spine-like tail. Horseshoe crabs grow upto 2 ft/60 cm long. They crawl along the bottom in coastal waters and lay their eggs in the sand at the high water mark.

horsetail plant of the genus *Equisetum*, related to ferns and club mosses; some species are also called scouring rush. There are about 35 living species, bearing their spores on cones at the stem tip. The upright stems are ribbed and often have spaced whorls of branches. Today they are of modest size, but hundreds of millions of years ago giant treelike forms existed.

Horst-Wessel-Lied song introduced by the Nazis as a second German national anthem. The text was written to a traditional tune by Horst Wessel (1907–1930), a Nazi "martyr."

Horthy de Nagybánya Nicholas 1868–1957. Hungarian politician and admiral. Leader of the counterrevolutionary White government, he became regent 1920 on the overthrow of the communist Bela Kun regime by Romanian and Czechoslovak intervention. He represented the conservative and military class, and retained power until World War II, trying (although allied to Hitler) to retain independence of action. In 1944 he tried to negotiate a surrender to the USSR but Hungary was taken over by the Nazis and he was deported to Germany.

horticulture the art and science of growing flowers, fruit, and vegetables. Horticulture is practiced in gardens and orchards, along with millions of acres of land devoted to vegetable farming. Some areas, like California, have specialized in horticulture because they have the mild climate and light fertile soil most suited to these crops.

horsetail

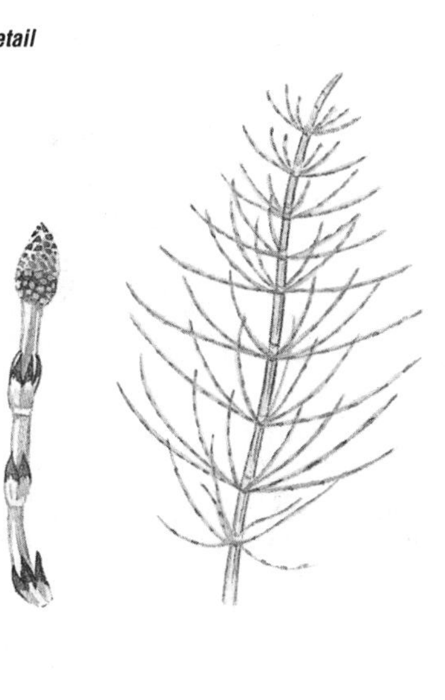

Horus in ancient Egyptian mythology, the hawk-headed Sun-god, son of Isis and Osiris, of whom the pharaohs were declared to be the incarnation.

Hosea 8th century BC. prophet in the Old Testament. His prophecy draws parallels between his own marriage and the relationship between God and Israel.

Hoskins Bob 1942–. British character actor who progressed to fame from a series of supporting roles. Films include *The Long Good Friday* 1980, *The Cotton Club* 1984, *Mona Lisa* 1985, *A Prayer for the Dying* 1987, and *Who Framed Roger Rabbit?* 1988.

hospice residential facility specializing in the care of the terminally ill.

hospital facility for the care of the sick, injured, and incapacitated.

In ancient times, temples of deities such as ◊Aesculapius offered facilities for treatment and by the 4th century, the Christian church had founded hospitals for lepers, cripples, the blind, the sick, and the poor. The oldest surviving hospital in Europe is the 7th-century Hôtel Dieu, Paris; in Britain, the most ancient are St Bartholomew's 1123 and St Thomas's 1200; and in the Americas the Hospital of Jesus of Nazareth, Mexico, 1524. Medical knowledge advanced during the Renaissance, and hospitals became increasingly secularized after the Reformation. In the 19th century, further progress was made in hospital design, administration, and staffing (Florence ◊Nightingale played a significant role in this). In the 20th century there has been an increasing trend toward specialization and the inclusion of maternity wards.

Hospitaller a member of the Order of ◊St John.

host an organism that is parasitized by another. In ◊commensalism, the partner that does not benefit may also be called the host.

hostage person taken prisoner as a means of exerting pressure on a third party, usually with threats of death or injury. In 1979, 63 staff members of the US embassy in Tehran were taken hostage by the Iranians. Most significant internationally were about 9,000 Westerners held in Kuwait and Iraq following the Iraqi invasion of Kuwait Aug 1990.

HOTOL (acronym for horizontal takeoff and landing) British concept for a hypersonic transport and satellite launcher, which could be operational before the end of the century. It will be a single-stage vehicle with no boosters and will take off and land on a runway. It will feature a revolutionary air-breathing rocket engine that will require it to carry much less oxygen than a conventional space plane. The US has a similar development under way called the Orient Express.

hot spot in geology, a hypothetical region of high thermal activity in the Earth's ◊mantle. It is believed to be the origin of many chains of ocean islands, such as Polynesia and the Galàpagos.

A volcano forms on the ocean crust immediately above the hot spot, is carried away by ◊plate tectonic movement, and becomes extinct. A new volcano forms beside it, above the hot spot. The result is an active volcano and a chain of increasingly old and eroded volcanic stumps stretching away along the line of plate movement.

Hottentot South African nomadic, pastoral people inhabiting the SW corner of the continent when Europeans first settled there. Their Khoisan language resembles that of the Kung (Bushmen), with mainly monosyllabic roots and explosive consonants that produce clicking sounds.

Houdini Harry. Adopted name of Erich Weiss 1874–1926. US escapologist and conjurer. He was renowned for his escapes from ropes and handcuffs, from trunks under water, from straitjackets and prison cells.

He also campaigned against fraudulent mind-readers and mediums.

Houdon Jean-Antoine 1741–1828. French sculptor, a portraitist who made characterful studies of Voltaire and a Neo-Classical statue of George Washington, commissioned 1785.

His other subjects included the philosophers Diderot and Rousseau, the composer Gluck, the emperor Napoleon, and the American politician Benjamin Franklin. Houdon also produced popular mythological figures, such as *Diana* and *Minerva*.

Houma city in S Louisiana, on the gulf intracoastal waterway, SW of New Orleans. The seat of Terrebonne Parish, it is a supply center for offshore oil rigs in the Gulf of Mexico. Industries include shellfish processing and sugar refining; population (1990) 30,495.

Hounsfield Godfrey 1919– . British engineer, a pioneer of ◊tomography, the application of computer techniques to X-raying the human body. He shared the Nobel Prize for Medicine 1979 with the South African physicist Allan Cormack (1924–).

Houphouët-Boigny Felix 1905– . Ivory Coast right-wing politician. He held posts in French ministries, and became president of the Republic of the Ivory Coast on independence 1960. He was re-elected for a sixth term 1985 representing the sole legal party.

hour period of time comprising 60 minutes; 24 hours make one calendar day.

Hours, Book of in medieval Europe, a collection of liturgical prayers for the use of the faithful.

Books of Hours contained short prayers and illustrations, with each prayer suitable for a different hour of the day, in honor of the Virgin Mary. The enormous demand for Books of Hours was a stimulus for the development of Gothic illumination. A celebrated example is the *Très Riches Heures du Duc de Berry*, illustrated in the early 15th century by the ◊Limbourg brothers.

House Edward Mandell 1858–1938. US politician and diplomat. Born in Houston, Texas, House attended Cornell University and, after working for many years on his family's holdings, became active in state Democratic politics. As personal adviser to a succession of Texas governors 1892–1904, he was awarded the honorary title of colonel. "Colonel" House was instrumental in obtaining the presidential nomination for Woodrow Wilson 1912 and later served as Wilson's closest adviser. During World War I, House served as US liaison with Great Britain and was an important behind-the-scenes participant in the 1919 Versailles Peace Conference.

housefly flies of the genus *Musca*, found in and around dwellings, especially *M. domestica*, a common worldwide species. They are gray, and have mouthparts adapted for drinking liquids and sucking moisture from food and manure.

Houseman John 1902–1988. US theater, film, and television producer and actor, born in Romania. He co-founded the Mercury Theatre with Orson Welles, and collaborated with Welles and Nicholas Ray as directors. He won an Academy Award for his acting debut in *The Paper Chase* 1973, and recreated his role in the subsequent TV series.

house music a type of dance music of the 1980s originating in the inner-city clubs of Chicago, combining funk with European high-tech pop, and using dub, digital sampling, and cross-fading. Acid house has minimal vocals and melody, instead surrounding the mechanically emphasized 4/4 beat with found noises, stripped-down synthesizer riffs, and a wandering bass line.

House of Commons the lower chamber of the UK Parliament. It consists of 650 elected members of Parliament, each of whom represents a constituency. Its functions are to debate, legislate, and to scrutinize the activities of government. Constituencies are kept under continuous review by the Parliamentary Boundary Commissions 1944. The House of Commons is presided over by the Speaker. Proceedings in the House of Commons were televised from Nov 1989.

House of Lords the upper chamber of the UK Parliament. Its members are unelected and comprise the temporal peers: all hereditary peers of England created to 1707, all hereditary peers of Great Britain created 1707–1800, and all hereditary peers of the UK from 1801 onward; all hereditary Scottish peers (under the Peerage Act 1963); all peeresses in their own right (under the same act); all life peers (both the law lords and those created under the Life Peerages Act 1958); and the spiritual peers: the two archbishops and 24 of the bishops (London, Durham, and Winchester by right, and the rest by seniority). Since the Parliament Act 1911 the powers of the Lords have been restricted in that they may delay a bill passed by the Commons but not reject it. The Lords are presided over by the Lord Chancellor.

House of Representatives, US, the lower chamber of the Congress. Revenue bills and impeachment charges must originate in the House, which also elects the president (as it did in 1800 and 1824) if there is no majority in the electoral college. Once bills are passed in the House, they are sent to the Senate for consideration.

The House started with fewer than 70 members, but grew as new states joined the Union and the US population increased. Since 1910 the number of members has been fixed at 435. States are represented in proportion to their population. In order to serve in the House a person must be 25 years of age, a resident of the state represented, and a US citizen. The term of office is two years. The Speaker of the House is the majority party's leader. In the late 20th century the Democrats controlled the House almost all of the time.

House Un-American Activities Committee (HUAC), Congressional committee, established 1938, noted for its public investigating into alleged subversion, particularly of Communists. First headed by Martin Dies, it achieved its greatest notoriety during the 1950s through its hearings on Communism in the movie industry. It was later renamed the House Internal Security Committee.

Housman A(lfred) E(dward) 1859–1936. English poet and Classical scholar. His *A Shropshire Lad* 1896, a series of deceptively simple, nostalgic, balladlike poems, was popular during World War I. This was followed by *Last Poems* 1922 and *More Poems* 1936.

Houston port in Texas; population (1990) 1,630,553; linked by canal to the Gulf of Mexico. It is a major center of the petroleum industry and of finance and commerce. It is also one of the busiest US ports. Industrial products include refined petroleum, oil-field equipment, and petrochemicals, chief of which are synthetic rubber, plastics, insecticides, and fertilizers. Other products include iron and steel, electrical and electronic machinery, paper products, and milled rice. The Lyndon B Johnson Space Center, the University of Houston, and Rice University are here, as is the Astrodome, the world's first all-purpose, air-conditioned domed stadium. The Texas Medical Center is one of the world's finest, and there are major museums and performing-arts groups. Houston was first settled 1826. Its modern growth dates from the discovery of oil nearby 1901 and the completion of the Houston Ship Channel 1914.

Houston Sam 1793–1863. US general who won Texas' independence from Mexico 1836 and was president of the Republic of Texas 1836–45. Houston, Texas, is named after him.

Houston was governor of the state of Tennessee and later US senator for and governor of the state of Texas. He took Indian citizenship when he married a Cherokee.

Hove seaside resort in East Sussex, England, adjoining Brighton; population (1981) 66,612.

hovercraft vehicle that rides on a cushion of high-pressure air, free from all contact with the surface beneath, invented by British engineer Christopher Cockerell 1959. Hovercraft need a smooth terrain when operating overland and are best adapted to use on waterways. They are useful in places where harbors have not been established.

Large hovercraft (SR-N4) operate a swift car-ferry service across the English Channel, taking only about 35 minutes between Dover and Calais. They are fitted with a flexible "skirt" that helps maintain the air cushion.

Howard Catherine c. 1520–1542. Queen consort of ◊Henry VIII of England from 1540. In 1541 the archbishop of Canterbury, Thomas Cranmer, accused her of being unchaste before marriage to Henry and she was beheaded 1542 after Cranmer made further charges of adultery.

Howard Charles, 2nd Baron Howard of Effingham and 1st Earl of Nottingham 1536–1624. English

hovercraft

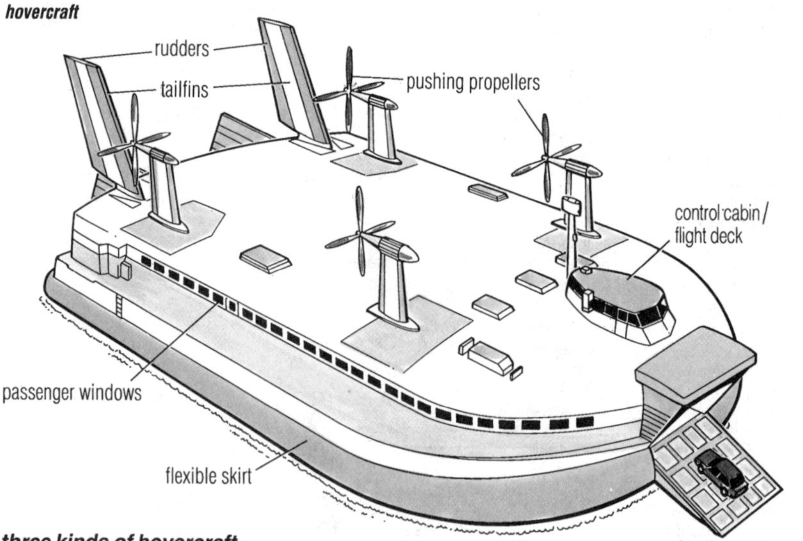
rudders
tailfins
pushing propellers
control cabin/
flight deck
passenger windows
flexible skirt
loading ramp

three kinds of hovercraft

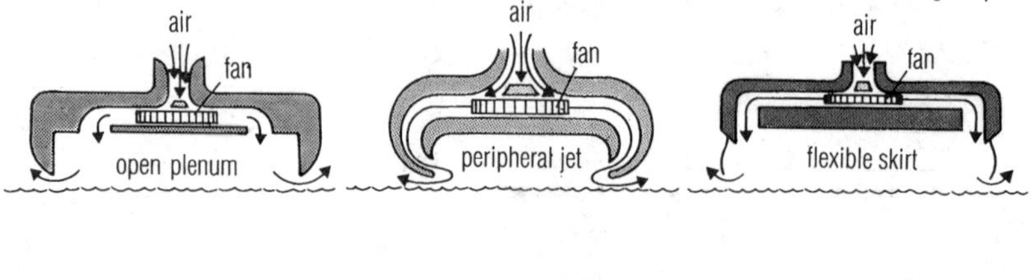
air
fan
open plenum
air
fan
peripheral jet
air
fan
flexible skirt

admiral, a cousin of Queen Elizabeth I. He commanded the fleet against the Spanish Armada while Lord High Admiral 1585–1618.

Howard Leslie. Adopted name of Leslie Stainer 1893–1943. English actor whose films include *The Scarlet Pimpernel* 1935, *The Petrified Forest* 1936, *Pygmalion* 1938, and *Gone with the Wind* 1939.

Howard Trevor (Wallace) 1916–1989. English actor whose films include *Brief Encounter* 1946, *Sons and Lovers* 1960, *Mutiny on the Bounty* 1962, *Ryan's Daughter* 1970, and *Conduct Unbecoming* 1975.

Howe Elias 1819–1867. US inventor, in 1846, of a ◊sewing machine using two threads, thus producing a lockstitch.

Born in Spencer, Massachusetts, Howe worked on several types of sewing machines before arriving at his invention that he marketed successfully in England. Eventually he manufactured the machine in Bridgeport, Connecticut, and marketed it successfully in the US.

Howe James Wong. Adopted name of Wong Tung Jim 1899–1976. Chinese-born director of film photography who lived in the US from childhood. One of Hollywood's best camera operators, he is credited with introducing the use of hand-held cameras and deep focus. His work ranges from *The Alaskan* 1924 to *Funny Lady* 1975.

Howe Julia Ward 1819–1910. US feminist and abolitionist who in 1862 wrote the poem "The Battle Hymn of the Republic"; sung to the tune of "John Brown's Body," it became associated with the Union side during the Civil War.

Born in New York City, she was an editor of *Commonwealth*, a Boston newspaper on which she worked with her husband, Samuel Gridley Howe. The couple was also active in the abolition movement. She wrote a biography 1883 of Margaret Fuller, a prominent literary figure and a member of Ralph Waldo Emerson's Transcendentalists.

Howe Richard Earl 1726–1799. British admiral. He cooperated with his brother William against the colonists during the American War of Independence, and in the French Revolutionary Wars commanded the Channel fleets 1792–96.

Howe Samuel Gridley 1801–1876. US educational reformer. Born in Boston, Howe was educated at Brown University and received an MD degree from Harvard 1824. A Philhellene, he spent seven years in Greece during its War of Independence. Returning to Boston in 1831, Howe became director of a school for the blind, developing innovative educational techniques that were widely emulated. A close associate of Horace Mann and Dorothea Dix, Howe also campaigned for expanded public education and better mental health facilities. He served as chairman of the Massachusetts Board of State Charities 1865–74.

Howe William, 5th Viscount Howe 1729–1814. British general. During the Revolutionary War he won the Battle of Bunker Hill 1775, and as Commander in Chief in America 1776–78 captured New York and defeated Washington at Brandywine and Germantown. He resigned in protest at lack of home government support.

Howells William Dean 1837–1920. US novelist and editor. The "dean" of US letters in the post-Civil War era, and editor of *The Atlantic Monthly*, he championed the realist movement in fiction and encouraged many younger authors. He wrote 35 novels, 35 plays, and many books of poetry, essays, and commentary.

His novels, filled with vivid social detail, include *A Modern Instance* 1882 and *The Rise of Silas Lapham* 1885, about the social fall and moral rise of a New England paint manufacturer, a central fable of the "Gilded Age."

howitzer a cannon, in use since the 16th century, with a particularly steep angle of fire. It was much developed in World War I for demolishing the fortresses of the trench system. The multinational NATO FH70 field howitzer is mobile and fires, under computer control, three 95 lb/43 kg shells at 20 mi/32 km range in 15 seconds.

Howrah or Haora city of West Bengal, India, on the right bank of the river Hooghly, opposite Calcutta; population (1981) 742,298. The capital of Howrah district, it has jute and cotton factories; rice, flour, and saw mills; chemical factories; and engineering works. Howrah suspension bridge, opened 1943, spans the river.

Hoxha Enver 1908–1985. Albanian Communist politician, the country's leader from 1954. He founded the Albanian Communist Party 1941, and headed the liberation movement 1939–44. He was prime minister 1944–54, combining with foreign affairs 1946–53, and from 1954 was first secretary of the Albanian Party of Labor. In policy he was a Stalinist and independent of both Chinese and Soviet communism.

Hoyle Fred(erick) 1915– . English astronomer and writer. In 1948 he joined with Hermann Bondi and Thomas Gold (1920–) in developing the ◊steady-state theory. In 1957, with Geoffrey and Margaret Burbidge (1925– and 1919–) and William Fowler, he showed that chemical elements heavier than hydrogen and helium are built up by nuclear reactions inside stars. He has suggested that life originates in the gas clouds of space and is delivered to the Earth by passing comets. His science fiction novels include *The Black Cloud* 1957.

hp symbol for ◊horsepower.

HQ abbreviation for headquarters.

Hsuan Tung name adopted by Henry ◊P'u-i on becoming emperor of China 1908.

ht abbreviation for height.

Hua Guofeng or Hua Kuofeng 1920– . Chinese politician, leader of the Chinese Communist Party (CCP) 1976–81, premier 1976–80. He dominated Chinese politics 1976–77, seeking economic modernization without major structural reform. From 1978 he was gradually eclipsed by Deng Xiaoping. Hua was ousted from the Politburo Sept 1982 but remained a member of the CCP Central Committee.

Hua, born in Shanxi into a peasant family, fought under Zhu De, the Red Army leader, during the liberation war 1937–49. He entered the CCP Central Committee 1969 and the Politburo 1973. An orthodox, loyal Maoist, Hua was selected to succeed Zhou Enlai as prime minister Jan 1976 and became party leader on Mao Zedong's death Sept 1976. He was replaced as prime minister by Zhao Ziyang Sept 1980 and as CCP chair by Hu Yaobang June 1981.

Huallaga River a tributary of the Marayon in NE Peru. The upper reaches of the river valley are used for growing coca, a major source of the drug cocaine.

Huambo town in central Angola; population (1970) 61,885. Founded 1912, it was known as Nova Lisboa ("New Lisbon") 1928–78, when it was designated by the Portuguese as the future capital. It is an agricultural center.

Huang He formerly Hwang-ho river in China; length 3,395 mi/5,464 km. It gains its name (meaning "yellow river") from its muddy waters. Formerly known as "China's sorrow" because of disastrous floods, it is now largely controlled through hydroelectric works and flood barriers.

The flood barriers, however, are ceasing to work because the silt that gives the river its name is continually raising the riverbed.

Huáscar c. 1495–1532. King of the Incas. He shared the throne with his half brother Atahualpa from 1525, but the latter overthrew and murdered him during the Spanish conquest.

Huáscaran extinct volcano in the Andes; the highest mountain in Peru, 22,205 ft/6,768 m.

Hubbard L(afayette) Ron(ald) 1911–1986. US science-fiction writer of the 1930s and 40s, founder in 1954 of ◊Scientology.

Hubble Edwin Powell 1889–1953. US astronomer who discovered the existence of other ◊galaxies outside our own and classified them according to their shape. His theory that the universe is expanding is now generally accepted.

Born in Marshfield, Missouri, Hubble originally studied law before joining ◊Yerkes Observatory 1914, subsequently moving to Mount Wilson, where in 1923 he discovered ◊Cepheid variable stars outside our own Galaxy. In 1925 he introduced the classification of galaxies as spirals, barred spirals, and ellipticals. In 1929 he announced Hubble's law, which states that the galaxies are moving apart at a rate that increases with their distance.

Hubble's constant in astronomy, a measure of the rate at which the universe is expanding, named after Edwin Hubble. Observations suggest that galaxies are moving apart at a rate of 30–60 mps/50–100 kps for every million ◊parsecs of distance. This means that the universe, which began at one point according to the ◊Big Bang theory, is between 10 billion and 20 billion years old (closer to 20).

Hubei formerly Hupei province of central China, through which flow the river Chang Jiang and its tributary the Han Shui

area 72,375 sq mi/187,500 sq km

capital Wuhan

features high land in the W, the river Chang breaking through from Sichuan in gorges; elsewhere low-lying, fertile land; many lakes

products beans, cereals, cotton, rice, vegetables, copper, gypsum, iron ore, phosphorous, salt

population (1986) 49,890,000.

hubris overweening pride. In ancient Greek tragedy, hubris was a defiance of the gods and invariably led to the downfall of the hubristic character.

Huc Abbé 1813–1860. French missionary in China. In 1845 he traveled to the border of Tibet, where he stopped for eight months to study the Tibetan language and Buddhist literature before moving on to the city of Lhasa.

huckleberry berry-bearing bush of the genus *Gaylussacia*; closely related to the genus *Vaccinium*, which includes ◊blueberry in the US and bilberry in Britain. Huckleberry bushes have edible dark-blue berries.

Huddersfield industrial town in West Yorkshire, on the river Colne, linked by canal with Manchester and other N England centers; population (1981) 123,888. A village in Anglo-Saxon times, it was a thriving center of woolen manufacture by the end of the 18th century; industries now include dyestuffs, chemicals, and electrical and mechanical engineering.

Hudson river of the NE US; length 300 mi/485 km. It rises in the Adirondack Mountains and flows S, emptying into a bay of the Atlantic Ocean at New York City. It is navigable by small ocean-going vessels as far upstream as Albany and Troy, about

Hudson *Historic sailing ships on the Hudson River at New York City.*

Hudson *Film star Rock Hudson, noted for comedies he made with Doris Day.*

150 mi/240 km from its mouth. On its W shore are the Catskill Mountains, and near its mouth, the Palisades, a vertical rock face. The New York Barge Canal system links the Hudson to Lake Champlain, Lake Erie, and the St Lawrence River. The Hudson forms the boundary between New Jersey and New York, and the states are linked by bridges and tunnels. The Hudson River valley is known for scenery that inspired a school of landscape painters in the 19th century. First sighted at its mouth by the Italian navigator Giovanni da Verrazano in 1524, the river was explored upstream as far as modern Albany in 1609 by Henry Hudson, for whom it is named.

Hudson Henry c. 1565–c. 1611. English explorer. Under the auspices of the Muscovy Company 1607–08, he made two unsuccessful attempts to find the Northeast passage to China. In Sept 1609, commissioned by the Dutch East India Company, he reached New York Bay and sailed 150 mi/240 km up the river that now bears his name, establishing Dutch claims to the area. In 1610, he sailed from London in the *Discovery* and entered what is now the Hudson Strait. After an icebound winter, he was turned adrift by a mutinous crew in what is now Hudson Bay.

Hudson had heard reports of two possible channels to the Pacific Ocean across North America. One of these had been described by English soldier and colonist John Smith. Since Hudson's search for the Northeast passage proved unsuccessful, he chose to pursue Smith's suggestion.

Hudson Rock. Adopted name of Roy Scherer Jr 1925–1985. US film actor, a star from the mid-1950s to the mid-1960s, who appeared in several melodramas directed by Douglas Sirk and in three comedies costarring Doris Day (including *Pillow Talk* 1959). He went on to have a successful TV career in the 1970s.

Hudson W(illiam) H(enry) 1841–1922. British author, born of US parents in Argentina. He was inspired by recollections of early days in Argentina to write the romances *The Purple Land* 1885 and *Green Mansions* 1904, and his autobiographical *Far Away and Long Ago* 1918. He wrote several books on birds, and on the English countryside, for example, *Nature in Down-Land* 1900 and *A Shepherd's Life* 1910.

Hudson Bay inland sea of NE Canada, linked with the Atlantic Ocean by Hudson Strait and with the Arctic Ocean by Foxe Channel; area 476,000 sq mi/1,233 sq km. It is named for Henry Hudson, who discovered it 1610. Several rivers empty into the bay, including the Churchill, Nelson, and Severn. It is ice-free and navigable during the summer, when grain is shipped from Churchill, Manitoba. The bay abounds in fish, and whales, dolphins, seals, and walruses also inhabit its waters and coastline. The Hudson Bay area is sparsely settled, chiefly by trappers, Indians, and Eskimos (Inuit).

Hudson River school group of US landscape painters of the early 19th century, inspired by the dramatic scenery of the Hudson River Valley and the Catskill mountains in New York State.

The first artist to depict the region was Thomas Cole. The group also included Asher B ◊Durand, Martin Joseph Heade, and Frederick Edwin ◊Church.

Their works, often in a Romantic vein, elevated landscape painting in importance in the US.

Hudson's Bay Company a chartered company founded by Prince ◊Rupert 1670 to trade in furs with North American Indians. In 1783 the rival North West Company was formed, but in 1851 this became amalgamated with the Hudson's Bay Company. It is still Canada's biggest fur company, but today also sells general merchandise through department stores and has oil and natural gas interests.

Hué town in central Vietnam, formerly capital of Annam, 8 mi/13 km from the China Sea; population (1973) 209,043. The Citadel, within which is the Imperial City enclosing the palace of the former emperor, lies to the west of the Old City on the north bank of the Huong (Perfume) river; the New City is on the south bank. Hué was once an architecturally beautiful cultural and religious center, but large areas were devastated, with many casualties, during the Battle of Hué Jan 31–Feb 24, 1968, when US and South Vietnamese forces retook the city after Vietcong occupation.

Huelva port and capital of Huelva province, Andalusia, SW Spain, near the mouth of the river Odiel; population (1986) 135,000. Industries include shipbuilding, oil refining, fisheries, and trade in ores from Rio Tinto. Columbus began and ended his voyage to America at nearby Palos de la Frontera.

Huesca capital of Huesca province in Aragón, northern Spain; population (1981) 41,455. Industries include engineering and food processing. Among its buldings are a fine 13th-century cathedral and the former palace of the kings of Aragón.

Hughes Charles Evans 1862–1948. US Supreme Court justice and public official. Hughes was named to the US Supreme Court by President Taft 1910 but resigned to accept the Republican nomination for president 1916. He lost narrowly to the incumbent Wilson and returned to his law practice. He served as secretary of state under Harding 1921–25. Appointed Supreme Court chief justice by Hoover 1930, Hughes presided over the constitutional tests of New Deal legislation. He retired from the Court 1941.

Born in Glens Falls, New York, Hughes received his law degree from Columbia 1884. After joining the Columbia law faculty 1891–93, he directed a state investigation of public utilities 1905 and served two terms as New York governor 1906–10.

Hughes David 1831–1900. British-born US inventor who patented an early form of telex in 1855, a type-printing instrument for use with the telegraph. He brought the instrument to Europe in 1857 where it became widely used.

Hughes Howard R 1905–1976. US aviator, aircraft designer, film producer, and entrepreneur. He founded the Hughes Aircraft Company and broke the air speed record in a craft of his own design in 1935, reaching a speed of 352 mph/566 kph. His financial empire was based on his inheritance of the Hughes Tool Co, founded by his father. In the 1920s he formed the Hughes film studio and produced *Hell's Angels* 1930, *Scarface* 1932, and *The Outlaw* 1944 (which he also directed). A billionaire for most of his later years, he invested in Las Vegas real estate, airlines, and motion picture studios but lived like a hermit, protected by his staff.

Hughes *The Australian prime minister William Morris Hughes (right), seen here with P G Stewart.*

Hughes Langston 1902–1967. US author. After graduation from Lincoln University, Hughes published a collection of his poems, *The Weary Blues* 1926. As one of the foremost black American literary figures, he became known as "the Poet Laureate of Harlem." In addition to his poetry he wrote a series of novels, short stories, and essays. His autobiography, *The Big Sea*, was published 1940.

Born in Joplin, Missouri, and raised in Cleveland, Ohio, Hughes had a poem published while still in high school. After briefly attending Columbia University, he traveled widely and continued to write.

Hughes Richard (Arthur Warren) 1900–1976. English writer. His study of childhood, *A High Wind in Jamaica*, was published 1929, and the trilogy *The Human Predicament* 1961–73.

Hughes Ted 1930– . English poet, poet laureate from 1984. His work includes *The Hawk in the Rain* 1957, *Lupercal* 1960, *Wodwo* 1967, and *River* 1983, and is characterized by its harsh portrayal of the crueller aspects of nature. In 1956 he married the poet Sylvia Plath.

Hughes William Morris 1864–1952. Australian politician, prime minister 1915–23; originally Labor, he headed a national cabinet. After resigning as prime minister 1923, he held many other cabinet posts 1934–41.

Hugo Victor (Marie) 1802–1885. French poet, novelist, and dramatist. The *Odes et poésies diverses* appeared 1822, and his verse play *Hernani* 1830 established him as the leader of French Romanticism. More volumes of verse followed between his series of dramatic novels, which included *The Hunchback of Notre Dame* 1831 and Les Misérables 1862.

Born at Besançon, Hugo was the son of one of Napoleon's generals. Originally a monarchist, his support of republican ideals in the 1840s led to his banishment 1851 for opposing Louis Napoleon's coup d'état. He lived in exile in Guernsey until the fall of the empire 1870, later becoming a senator under the Third Republic. He died a national hero and is buried in the ◊Panthéon, Paris.

Huguenot French Protestant in the 16th century; the term referred mainly to Calvinists. Severely persecuted under Francis I and Henry II, the Huguenots survived both an attempt to exterminate them (the Massacre of ◊St Bartholomew Aug 24, 1572) and the religious wars of the next 30 years. In 1598 Henry IV (himself formerly a Huguenot) granted them toleration under the ◊Edict of Nantes. Louis XIV revoked the edict 1685, attempting their forcible conversion, and 400,000 emigrated.

Provoked by Louis XIV they left, taking their industrial skills with them; many settled in North America, where they founded such towns as New Rochelle and New Paltz, NY. Only in 1802 was the Huguenot church again legalized in France.

Huhehot former name of ◊Hohhot, a city in Inner Mongolia.

Hull Cordell 1871–1955. US Democratic politician, born in Tennessee. He was a member of Congress 1907–33, and, as F D Roosevelt's secretary of state 1933–44, he opposed German and Japanese aggression. He was identified with the Good Neighbor Policy of nonintervention in Latin America.

In his last months of office he paved the way for a system of collective security, for which he was called "father" of the United Nations. He was awarded the Nobel Prize for Peace 1945.

Hull officially ***Kingston-upon-Hull*** city and port on the river Humber, administrative headquarters of Humberside, England; population (1986) 258,000. It is linked with the S bank of the estuary by the Humber Bridge. Industries include fish processing, vegetable oils, flour milling, electricals, textiles, paint, pharmaceuticals, chemicals, caravans, and aircraft.

Notable buildings include 13th-century Holy Trinity Church, Guildhall, Ferens Art Gallery (1927), and the university (1954).

Hulme Keri 1947– . New Zealand novelist. She won Britain's Booker Prize with her first novel *The Bone People* 1985.

human body the physical structure of the human being. It develops from the single cell of the fertilized ovum, is born at 40 weeks, and usually reaches sexual maturity between 11 and 18 years of age. The bony framework (skeleton) consists of more than 200 bones, over half of which are in the hands and feet. Bones are held together by joints, some of which allow movement. The circulatory system supplies muscles and organs with blood, which provides oxygen and food and removes carbon dioxide and other waste products. Body functions are controlled by the nervous system and hormones. In the upper part of the trunk is the thorax, which contains the lungs and heart. Below this is the abdomen, containing the digestive system (stomach and intestines); the liver, spleen, and pancreas; the urinary system (kidneys, ureters, and bladder); and in women, the reproductive organs (ovaries, uterus, and vagina). In men, the prostate gland and seminal vesicles only of the reproductive system are situated in the abdomen, the testes being in the scrotum, which, with the penis, is suspended in front of and below the abdomen. The bladder empties through a small channel (urethra); in the female this opens in the upper end of the vulval cleft, which also contains the opening of the vagina, or birth canal; in the male, the urethra is continued into the penis. In both sexes, the lower bowel terminates in the anus, a ring of strong muscle situated between the buttocks.

skeleton The skull is mounted on the spinal column, or spine, a chain of 24 vertebrae. The ribs, 12 on each side, are articulated to the spinal column behind, and the upper seven meet the breastbone (sternum) in front. The lower end of the spine rests on the pelvic girdle, composed of the triangular sacrum, to which are attached the hipbones (ilia), which are fused in front. Below

human body

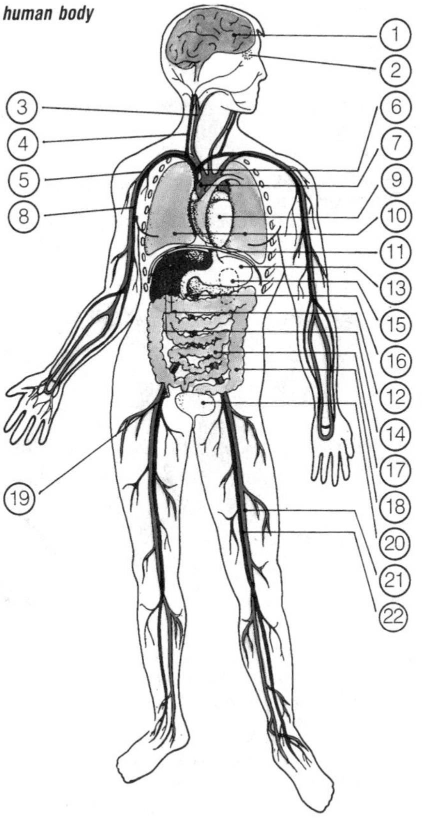
1
2
3
4
5
6
7
8
9
10
11
12
13
14
15
16
17
18
19
20
21
22

Key
1. brain
2. eye
3. carotid artery
4. jugular vein
5. subclavian artery
6. superior vena cava
7. aorta
8. subclavian vein
9. heart
10. lungs
11. diaphragm
12. liver
13. stomach
14. gall bladder
15. kidney
16. pancreas
17. small intestine
18. large intestine
19. appendix
20. bladder
21. femoral artery
22. femoral vein

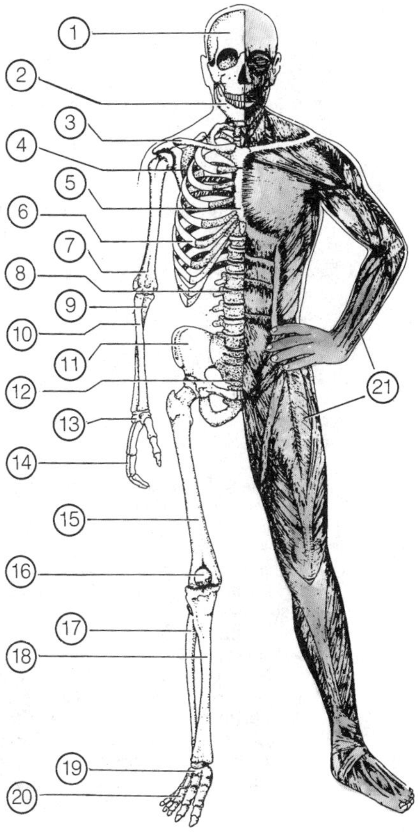
1
2
3
4
5
6
7
8
9
10
11
12
13
14
15
16
17
18
19
20
21

Key
1. cranium (skull)
2. mandible
3. clavicle
4. scapula
5. sternum
6. rib cage
7. humerus
8. vertebra
9. ulna
10. radius
11. pelvis
12. coccyx
13. metacarpals
14. phalanges
15. femur
16. patella
17. fibula
18. tibia
19. metatarsals
20. phalanges
21. superficial (upper) layer of muscles

the sacrum is the tailbone (coccyx). The shoulder blades (scapulae) are held in place behind the upper ribs by muscles, and connected in front to the breastbone by the two collarbones (clavicles). Each shoulder blade carries a cup (glenoid cavity) into which fits the upper end of the armbone (humerus). This articulates below with the two forearm bones (radius and ulna). These are articulated at the wrist (carpals) to the bones of the hand (metacarpals and phalanges). The upper end of each thighbone (femur) fits into a depression (acetabulum) in the hipbone; its lower end is articulated at the knee to the shinbone (tibia) and calf bone (fibula), which are articulated at the ankle (tarsals) to the bones of the foot (metatarsals and phalanges). At a moving joint, the end of each bone is formed of tough, smooth cartilage, lubricated by ◊synovial fluid. Points of special stress are reinforced by bands of fibrous tissue (ligaments).

Muscles are bundles of fibers wrapped in thin, tough layers of connective tissue (fascia); these are usually prolonged at the ends into strong, white cords (tendons, sinews) or sheets (aponeuroses), which connect the muscles to bones and organs, and by way of which the muscles do their work. Membranes of connective tissue also wrap the organs and line the interior cavities of the body. The blood vessels of the circulatory system, branching into multitudes of very fine tubes (capillaries), supply all parts of the muscles and organs with blood, which carries oxygen and food necessary for life. The food passes out of the blood to the cells in a clear fluid (lymph); this is returned with waste matter through a system of lymphatic vessels that converge into collecting ducts that drain into large veins in the region of the lower neck. Capillaries join together to form veins which return blood, depleted of oxygen, to the heart. A finely branching nervous system regulates the function of the muscles and organs, and makes their needs known to the controlling centers in the central nervous system, which consists of the brain and spinal cord. The inner spaces of the brain and the cord contain cerebrospinal fluid. The body processes are regulated both by the nervous system and by hormones secreted by the endocrine glands.

The thorax has a stout muscular floor, the diaphragm, which expands and contracts the lungs in the act of breathing.

Cavities of the body that open onto the surface are coated with mucous membranes, which secrete a lubricating fluid (mucus). The exterior suface of the body is coated with skin. Within the skin are the sebaceous glands, which secrete sebum, an oily fluid that makes the skin soft and pliable, and the sweat glands, which secrete water and various salts. From the skin grow hair, chiefly on the head, in the armpits, and around the sexual organs; and nails shielding the tips of the fingers and toes; both hair and nail structures are modifications of skin tissue. The skin also contains ◊nerves of touch, pain, heat, and cold.

The human digestive system is nonspecialized and can break down a wide variety of foodstuffs. Food is mixed with saliva in the mouth by chewing and is swallowed. It enters the stomach, where it is gently churned for some time and mixed with acidic gastric juice. It then passes into the small intestine. In the first part of this, the duodenum, it is broken down further by the juice of the pancreas and duodenal glands, and mixed with bile from the liver, which splits up the fat. The jejunum and ileum continue the work of digestion and absorb most of the nutritive substances from the food. The large intestine completes the process, reabsorbing water into the body, and ejecting the useless residue as feces.

The body, to be healthy, must maintain water and various salts in the right proportions; the process is called osmoregulation. The blood is filtered in the two kidneys, which remove excess water, salts, and metabolic wastes. Together these form urine, which has a yellow pigment derived from bile, and passes down through two fine tubes (ureters) into the bladder, a reservoir from which the urine is emptied at intervals (micturition) through the urethra.

Heat is constantly generated by the combustion of food in the muscles and glands, and by the activity of nerve cells and fibers. It is dissipated through the skin by conduction and evaporation of sweat, through the lungs in the expired air, and in other excreted substances. Average body temperature is about 100°F/38°C (98.6°F/37°C in the mouth).

composition of the human body by weight

Class	*Chemical element or substance*	*Body weight (%)*
pure elements	oxygen	65
	carbon	18
	hydrogen	10
	nitrogen	3
	calcium	2
	phosphorus	1.1
	potassium	0.35
	sulfur	0.25
	sodium	0.15
	chlorine	0.15
	magnesium, iron, manganese, copper, iodine, cobalt, zinc	traces
water and solid matter	water	60–80
	total solid material	20–40
organic molecules	protein	15–20
	lipid	3–20
	carbohydrate	1–15
	small organic molecules	0–1

Human Comedy, The French *La Comédie humaine* a series of novels by Balzac, published 1842–48, which aimed to depict every aspect of 19th-century French life. Of the 143 planned, only 80 were completed. These include studies of human folly and vice, as in *Le Recherche de l'absolu/The Search for the Absolute*, and analyses of professions or ranks, as in *L'Illustre Gaudissart/The Famous Gaudissart* and *Le Curé de village/The Village Parson*.

human–computer interaction the exchange of information between a person and a computer, through the medium of a ◊user interface, studied as a branch of ergonomics.

human rights civil and political rights of the individual in relation to the state.

Human Rights, Universal Declaration of charter of civil and political rights drawn up by the United Nations 1948. They include the right to life, liberty, education, and equality before the law; to freedom of movement, religion, association, and information; and to a nationality. Under the European Convention of Human Rights 1950, the Council of Europe established the European Commission of Human Rights (headquarters in Strasbourg, France), which investigates complaints by states or individuals, and its findings are examined by the European Court of Human Rights (established 1959), whose compulsory jurisdiction has been recognized by a number of states, including the UK.

Human Rights Day is Dec 10, commemorating the adoption of the Universal Declaration of Human Rights by the UN General Assembly.

The declaration is not legally binding, and the frequent contraventions are monitored by organizations such as ◊Amnesty International. Human rights were also an issue at the ◊Helsinki Conference.

human species, origins of

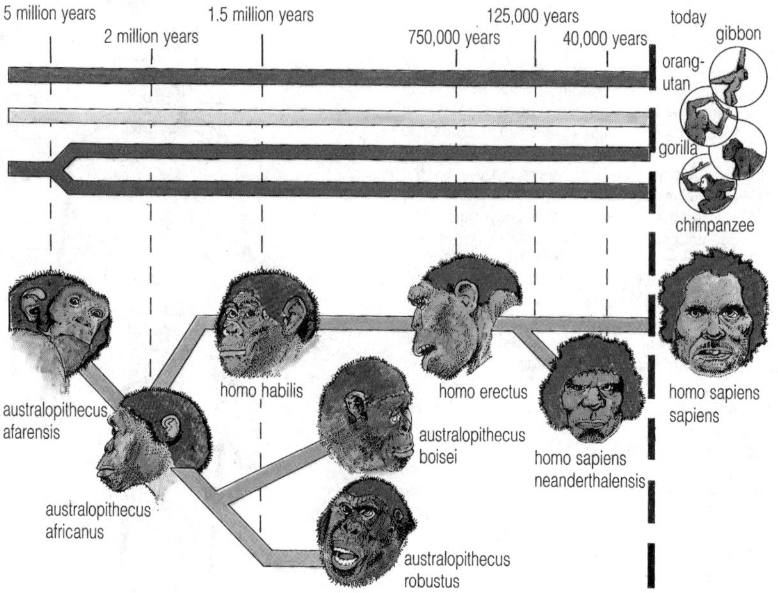

5 million years
2 million years
1.5 million years
750,000 years
125,000 years
40,000 years
today
gibbon
orang-utan
gorilla
chimpanzee
australopithecus afarensis
australopithecus africanus
homo habilis
australopithecus boisei
australopithecus robustus
homo erectus
homo sapiens neanderthalensis
homo sapiens sapiens

human species, origins of evolution of humans from ancestral ◊primates. The African apes (gorilla and chimpanzee) are shown by anatomical and molecular comparisons to be the closest living relatives of humans. Molecular studies put the date of the split between the human and African ape lines at 5–10 million years ago. There are no ape or hominid (of the human group) fossils from this period; the oldest known hominids, found in Ethiopia and Tanzania, date from 5.5 to 3.5 million years ago. These creatures are known as *Australopithecus afarensis*, and they walked upright. They were either direct ancestors or an offshoot of the line that led to modern humans. They might have been the ancestors of *Homo habilis* (considered by some to be a species of *Australopithecus*), who appeared about a million years later, had slightly larger bodies and brains, and were probably the first to use stone tools. *Australopithecus robustus* and *A. gracilis* also lived in Africa at the same time, but these are not generally considered to be our ancestors. See also Louis and Mary ◊Leakey and Raymond ◊Dart.

Over 1.5 million years ago, *Homo erectus*, believed by some to be descended from *H. habilis*, appeared in Africa. The *erectus* people had much larger brains, and were probably the first to use fire and the first to move out of Africa. Their remains are found as far afield as China, Java, Spain, Germany, and England. Modern humans, *H. sapiens sapiens*, and the Neanderthals, *H. sapiens neanderthalensis*, are probably descended from *H. erectus*. Neanderthals were large-brained and sturdily built, probably adapted to the cold conditions of the ◊ice ages. They lived in Europe and the Middle East, and died out about 40,000 years ago, leaving *H. sapiens sapiens* as the only remaining species of the hominid group. Modern humans evolved and migrated from that time to people the continents of the Earth as *H. sapiens sapiens*. See ◊race and ◊civilization.

Humberside county of NE England
area 1,355 sq mi/3,510 sq km
cities Hull (administrative headquarters), Grimsby, Scunthorpe, Goole, Cleethorpes
features Humber Bridge; fertile Holderness peninsula; Isle of Axholme, bounded by rivers Trent, Don, Idle, and Torne, where medieval open-field strip farming is still practiced
products petrochemicals, refined oil, processed fish, cereals, root crops, cattle
population (1987) 847,000
famous people Amy Johnson, Andrew Marvell, John Wesley.

Humbert anglicized form of ◊Umberto, two kings of Italy.

Humboldt Friedrich Heinrich Alexander, Baron von 1769–1859. German botanist and geologist who, with the French botanist Aimé Bonpland (1773–1858), explored the regions of the Orinoco and the Amazon rivers in South America 1800–04, and gathered 60,000 plant specimens. On his return, Humboldt devoted 21 years to writing an account of his travels.

One of the first popularizers of science, he gave a series of lectures later published as *Cosmos* 1845–62, an account of the physical sciences.

Humboldt Wilhelm von 1767–1835. German philologist, whose stress on the identity of thought and language influenced ◊Chomsky. He was the brother of Friedrich Humboldt.

Humboldt Current former name of the ◊Peru Current.

Hume David 1711–1776. Scottish philosopher. *A Treatise of Human Nature* 1740 is a central text of British empiricism. Hume denies the possibility of going beyond the subjective experiences of "ideas" and "impressions." The effect of this position is to invalidate metaphysics.

His *History of Great Britain* 1754–62 was popular within his own lifetime but *A Treatise of Human Nature* was indifferently received. He shared many of the beliefs of the British empiricist school (see ◊empiricism), including those of ◊Locke. Hume's Law in moral philosophy states that it is never possible to deduce evaluative conclusions from factual premises; this has come to be known as the "is/ought problem."

hum, environmental a disturbing sound of frequency about 40 Hz, heard by individuals sensitive to this range, but inaudible to the rest of the population. It may be caused by industrial noise pollution or have a more exotic origin, such as the jet stream, a fast-flowing high-altitude (about 50,000 ft/ 15,000 m) mass of air.

humerus the upper bone of the forelimb of tetrapods. In humans the humerous is the bone above the elbow.

humidity the quantity of water vapor in a given volume of the atmosphere (absolute humidity), or the ratio of the amount of water vapor in the atmosphere to the saturation value at the same temperature (relative humidity); at ◊dew point the latter is 100%. Relative humidity is measured by various types of ◊hygrometer.

hummingbird any of various birds of the family Trochilidae, found in the Americas. The name is derived from the sound produced by the rapid vibration of their wings, and they are the only birds able to fly backwards. Hummingbirds are brilliantly colored, and have long, needlelike bills and tongues to obtain nectar from flowers and capture insects. The Cuban bee hummingbird *Mellisuga helenae*, the world's smallest bird, is 2 in/ 5.5 cm long, and weighs less than 2.5 g/0.1 oz.

humors, theory of theory prevalent in Classical and medieval times that the human body was composed of four kinds of fluid: phlegm, blood, choler or yellow bile, and melancholy or black bile. Physical and mental characteristics were explained by different proportions of humors in individuals.

Humperdinck Engelbert 1854–1921. German composer. He studied music in Munich and in Italy and assisted Richard ◊Wagner at the Bayreuth Festival Theatre. He wrote the musical fairy operas *Hänsel und Gretel* 1893, and *Königskinder/ King's Children* 1910.

Humphrey Hubert Horatio 1911–1978. US political leader and vice-president 1965–69. In 1948 he was elected to the US Senate, where for three terms he distinguished himself as an eloquent and effective promoter of key legislation. An unsuccessful presidential candidate in 1960, he strongly supported the 1964 Civil Rights Act. He served as vice-president under L B Johnson 1965–69 and made another unsuccessful run for the presidency 1968. Briefly professor at the University of Minnesota, Humphrey was re-elected to the Senate in 1970 and 1976.

Born in Wallace, South Dakota, Humphrey was trained as a pharmacist.

Settling in Minnesota, he became active in Democratic party politics and was elected mayor of Minneapolis 1945.

humus component of ◊soil consisting of decomposed or partly decomposed organic matter, dark in color and usually richer toward the surface. It has a higher carbon content than the original material and a lower nitrogen content, and is an important source of minerals in soil fertility.

Hun member of any of a number of nomad Mongol peoples who were first recorded historically in the 2nd century BC, raiding across the Great Wall into China. They entered Europe about AD 372, settled in the area that is now Hungary, and imposed their supremacy on the Ostrogoths and other Germanic peoples. Under the leadership of Attila they attacked the Byzantine Empire, invaded Gaul, and threatened Rome. After Attila's death in 453 their power was broken by a revolt of their subject peoples. The White Huns, or Ephthalites, a kindred people, raided Persia and N India in the 5th and 6th centuries.

Hunan province of S central China

area 81,253 sq mi/210,500 sq km

capital Changsha

features Dongting Lake; farmhouse in Shaoshan village, where Mao Zedong was born

products rice, tea, tobacco, cotton; nonferrous minerals

population (1986) 56,960,000.

hundred a subdivision of a shire in England, Ireland, and parts of the US. The term was originally used by Germanic peoples to denote a group of 100 warriors, also the area occupied by 100 families or equaling 100 hides (one hide being the amount of land necessary to support a peasant family). When the Germanic peoples settled in England, the hundred remained the basic military and administrative division of England until its abolition 1867.

hundred days, the in European history, the period March 20–June 28, 1815, marking the French emperor Napoleon's escape from imprisonment on Elba to his departure from Paris after losing the battle of Waterloo June 18.

The phrase also describes other periods of new administration. In 1898 Emperor Te Tsung of China attempted 100 days of reform (June 11–Sept 16), under the guidance of K'ang Yu-wei. In 1931 Mussolini and G Forzano wrote *The 100 Days*. It is also applied to the reform period in the administration of US President F D Roosevelt from his inauguration on March 4, 1933 when much of the legislation for his New Deal program was initiated. English prime minister Harold Wilson used the phrase in *Purpose and Power* 1966.

hundredweight unit (abbreviation cwt) of mass, equal to 100 lb (45.36 kg) in the US. In the UK and Canada, it equals 112 lb (50.8 kg), and is sometimes called the long hundredweight.

Hundred Years' War the series of conflicts between England and France 1337–1453. Its origins lay with the English kings' possession of Gascony (SW France), which the French kings claimed as their ◊fief, and with trade rivalries over ◊Flanders.

The two kingdoms had a long history of strife before 1337, and the Hundred Years' war has sometimes been interpreted as merely an intensification of these struggles. It was caused by fears of French intervention in Scotland, which the English were trying to subdue, and by the claim of England's ◊Edward III (through his mother Isabel, daughter of Charles IV) to the crown of France.

After the war, domestic problems, such as the War of the ◊Roses, prevented England (which kept Calais until 1558) from attempting to conquer France again. It gave up continental aspirations and began to develop as a sea power. France was ravaged by the Black Death, famine, and gangs of bandits, in addition to the devastation caused by the war. In both countries, the decline of the feudal nobility and the rise of the middle class allowed the monarchies gradually to become established.

chronology: Hundred Years' War

1340	The English were victorious at the naval battle of Sluys.
1346	Battle of Crécy, another English victory.
1347	The English took Calais.
1356	Battle of Poitiers, where Edward the Black Prince defeated the French. King John of France was captured.
late 1350s–early 1360s	France had civil wars, brigandage, and the popular uprising of the ◊Jacquerie.
1360	Treaty of Brétigny-Calais. France accepted English possession of Calais, and of a greatly enlarged duchy of Gascony. John was ransomed for £500,000.
1369–1414	The tide turned in favor of the French, and when there was another truce in 1388, only Calais, Bordeaux, and Bayonne were in English hands. A state of half-war continued for many years.
1415	Henry V invaded France and won a victory at Agincourt, followed by conquest of Normandy.
1419	In the Treaty of Toyes, Charles VI of France was forced to disinherit his son, the Dauphin, in favor of Henry V, who was to marry Catherine, Charles's daughter. Most of N France was in English hands.
1422–28	After the death of Henry V his brother Bedford was generally successful.
1429	Joan of Arc raised the siege of Orléans, and the Dauphin was crowned Charles VII at Rheims.
1430–53	Even after Joan's capture and death the French continued their successful counteroffensive, and in 1453 only Calais was left in English hands.

Hungarian or ***Magyar*** member of the majority population of Hungary or a person of Hungarian descent; also, their culture and language. Hungarian minorities are found in Czechoslovakia, Yugoslavia, and Romania, where the Székely of Transylvania regard themselves as ethnically distinct but speak Hungarian, as do the Csángó of Moldavia. Hungarian is part of the Finno-Ugric family of languages.

Hungarian language member of the Finno-Ugric language group, spoken principally in Hungary but also in parts of Czechoslovakia, Romania, and Yugoslavia. Hungarian is known as Magyar among its speakers. It is written in a form of the Roman alphabet in which *s* corresponds to English *sh*, and *sz* to *s*.

Like the Turks, the Magyars originated in NE Asia; the term "Hungarian" appears to derive from the Turkish *on ogur* ("ten arrows"), describing their ten tribes; this may also be the origin of the English "ogre."

Hungarian uprising national uprising against Soviet dominance of ◊Hungary in 1956.

Hungary country in central Europe, bounded N by Czechoslovakia, NE by the USSR, E by Romania, S by Yugoslavia, and W by Austria.

government Under the terms of the "transitional constitution" adopted Oct 1989, Hungary is a unitary state with a one-chamber, 386-member legislature, the national assembly (*Orszaggyules*). Its members are elected for five-year terms under a mixed system of proportional and direct representation: 176 are directly elected (on a potential two-ballot run-off basis) from local constituencies; 152 are from county and metropolitan lists on a proportional basis; and 58 are elected indirectly from party-nominated national "compensation" lists designed to favor smaller parties. Free competition is allowed in these elections. The national assembly elects a president to serve as head of state and chief executive, and a council of ministers (cabinet) headed by a prime minister. Since 1989 opposition parties have been able to register freely and receive partial state funding. A constitutional court has also been appointed to serve as a watchdog.

history Inhabited by Celts and Slavs, the region became a Roman province. After the Roman era it was overrun by Germanic invaders and by Asians who established a ◊Magyar kingdom in the late 9th century, under a chief named Árpád. St Stephen (997–1038) became Hungary's first king; he established a kingdom 1001 and converted the inhabitants to Christianity.

After the Árpádian line died out, Hungary was ruled 1308–86 by the ◊Angevins, and sub-

Hungary
Republic of
(Magyar Köztársaság)

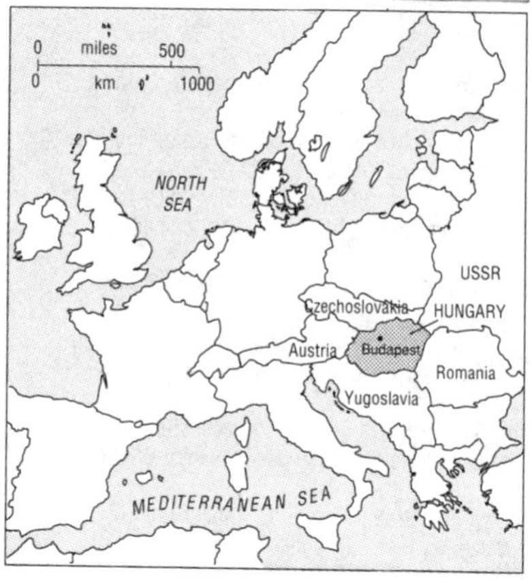
0 miles 500
0 km 1000
NORTH SEA
USSR
Czechoslovakia
HUNGARY
Austria
Budapest
Romania
Yugoslavia
MEDITERRANEAN SEA

area 35,910 sq mi/93,032 sq km
capital Budapest
cities Miskolc, Debrecen, Szeged, Pécs
physical Great Hungarian Plain covers E half of country; Bakony Forest, Lake Balaton, and Transdanubian Highlands in the W; rivers Danube, Tisza, and Raba
features more than 500 thermal springs; Hortobágy National Park; Tokay wine area
head of state Matyas Szuros (acting) from 1989
head of government Károly Grosz from 1988
political system emergent democracy
political parties over 50, including Hungarian Socialist Party (HSP), left-of-center; Hungarian Democratic Forum (MDF), umbrella prodemocracy grouping; Alliance of Free Democrats (SzDSz), radical free-market opposition group heading coalition with Alliance of Young Democrats, Social Democrats, and Smallholders Party, right-wing
exports machinery, vehicles, iron and steel, chemicals, fruit and vegetables
currency forint
population (1990 est) 10,546,000 (Magyar 92%, Romany 3%, German 2.5%; Hungarian minority in Romania has caused some friction between the two countries); growth rate 0.2% p.a.
life expectancy men 67, women 74
language Hungarian (or Magyar), one of the few languages of Europe with non-Indo-European origins; it is grouped with Finnish and Estonian in the Finno-Ugric family
religion Roman Catholic 67%, other Christian denominations 25%
literacy men 99.3%/women 98.5% (1980)
GDP $26.1 bn (1987); $2,455 per head
chronology
1918 Independence achieved from Austro-Hungarian Empire.
1919 A Communist state formed for 133 days.
1920–44 Regency formed under Admiral Hartley, who joined Hitler's attack on the USSR.
1945 Liberated by USSR.
1946 Republic proclaimed; Stalinist regime imposed.
1949 Soviet-style constitution adopted.
1956 Hungarian national uprising; workers' demonstrations in Budapest; democratization reforms by Imre Nagy overturned by Soviet tanks, Kádár installed as party leader.
1968 Economic decentralization reforms.
1983 Competition introduced into elections.
1987 VAT and income tax introduced.
1988 Kádár replaced by Károly Grosz. First free labor union recognized; rival political parties legalized.
1989 May: border with Austria opened. July: new four-man collective leadership of HSWP. Oct: new "transitional constitution" adopted, founded on multiparty democracy and new presidentialist executive. HSWP changed name to Hungarian Socialist Party, with Nyers as new leader. Kádár "retired," later died; Nagy rehabilitated.
1990 HSP reputation damaged by "Danubegate" bugging scandal.
1991 Devaluation of currency. June: legislation approved to compensate owners of land and property expropriated under Communist regime. Last Soviet troops departed.

sequently by other foreign princes. From 1396, successive rulers fought to keep out Turkish invaders but were finally defeated at Mohács 1526, and the south and center of the country came under Turkish rule for 150 years, while the east was ruled by semi-independent Hungarian princes. By the end of the 17th century the Turks had been driven out by the ◊Hapsburgs, bringing Hungary under Austrian rule.

After 1815 a national renaissance began, under the leadership of Louis ◊Kossuth. The revolution of 1848–49 proclaimed a Hungarian republic and abolished serfdom, but Austria suppressed the revolt with Russian help. In 1867 the ◊Austro-Hungarian empire was established, giving Hungary self-government.

During World War I, Hungary fought on the German side, and after the collapse of the Austro-Hungarian empire, became an independent state 1918. For 133 days in 1919, Hungary was a communist republic under Béla ◊Kun, but this was brought to an end by intervention from Romania and Czechoslovakia. From 1920–44, Hungary was ruled by Admiral ◊Horthy, acting as regent for an unnamed king. After 1933, he fell more and more under German influence, and, having joined Hitler in the invasion of the USSR 1941, Hungary was overrun by communist forces 1944–45.

Horthy fled, and a provisional government, including the communist agriculture minister, Imre ◊Nagy, was formed, distributing land to the peasants. An elected assembly inaugurated a republic 1946, but it soon fell under Soviet domination, although only 70 communists had been returned out of a total of 409 deputies.

Under Communist Party leader Matyas Rakosi (1892–1971), a Stalinist regime was imposed 1946–53, with a Soviet-style constitution being adopted 1949, industry nationalized, land collectivized, and a wave of secret-police terror launched.

Liberalization in the economic sphere was experienced 1953–55 when Imre Nagy, supported by Soviet premier Malenkov, replaced Rákosi as prime minister. Nagy was removed from office 1955, after the fall of Malenkov, but in 1956, in the wake of ◊Khrushchev's denunciation of Stalin in his "secret speech," pressure for democratization mounted. Rakosi stepped down as Communist Party leader and, following student and worker demonstrations in Budapest, Nagy was recalled as prime minister, and János ◊Kádár appointed general secretary of the renamed Hungarian Socialist Workers' Party (HSWP).

Nagy lifted restrictions on the formation of political parties, released the anticommunist primate Cardinal ◊Mindszenty, and announced plans for Hungary to withdraw from the ◊Warsaw Pact and become a neutral power. These changes were, however, opposed by Kádár, who set up a counter-government in E Hungary before returning to Budapest with Soviet tanks to overthrow the Nagy government Nov 4. Some two hundred thousand fled to the West during the 1956 "Hungarian National Uprising."

After a period of strict repression, Kádár proceeded to introduce pragmatic liberalizing reforms after 1960. Hungary remained, however, a loyal member of the Warsaw Pact and ◊Comecon. Its relations with Moscow significantly improved during the post-Brezhnev era, with Hungary's "market socialism" experiment influencing Mikhail Gorbachev's ◊perestroika program. Further reforms introduced 1987–88 included additional price deregulation, the establishment of "enterprise councils," the introduction of value-added tax (VAT), and the creation of a stock market.

As elsewhere in Eastern Europe, change came quickly to Hungary from 1988. Kádár, who had become an obstacle to reform, was ousted as general secretary of the ruling HSWP party, and was named to a new post, that of party president, replaced as general secretary by Karoly ◊Grosz. Two radical reformers, Rezso Nyers and Imre Pozsgay, were brought into the Politburo. The Hungarian Democratic Forum was formed Sept 1988 as an umbrella movement for opposition groups, and several dozen other political parties were formed 1989–90.

There then began a period of far-reaching political reform in which the rights to demonstrate freely and to form rival political parties and labor unions were ceded. The official verdict on the 1956 events was revised radically, with Nagy being posthumously rehabilitated and cleared of alleged past crimes by the Supreme Court in July 1989; in June, the remains of Imre Nagy, who had been hanged for treason 1958, were exhumed and reburied with state honors. A new "Socialist pluralist" constitution was outlined.

In May 1989 the border with Austria was opened, with adverse effects for East Germany as thousands of East Germans escaped to the West through Hungary. Two months later Grosz was forced to cede power to the more radical reformist troika of Nyers (party president), Pozsgay, and Miklos Nemeth (prime minister since Nov 1988), who joined Grosz in a new four-person ruling presidium.

In Oct 1989 a series of constitutional changes, the result of round-table talks held through the summer, were approved by the national assembly. These included the adoption of a new set of electoral rules, the banning of workplace party cells, and the change of the country's name from "People's Republic" to simply "Republic." Also in Oct the HSWP changed its name to the Hungarian Socialist Party (HSP), and adopted Poszgay as its presidential candidate. Conservatives, including Grosz, refused to play an active role in the new party, which had become essentially a social democratic party committed to multiparty democracy. Despite these changes, the HSP's standing was seriously damaged in the "Danubegate" scandal of Jan 1990, when it was revealed that the secret police had bugged opposition parties and passed the information obtained to the HSP. In Feb 1990 talks were held with the USSR to discuss the withdrawal of Soviet troops stationed in Hungary, and by June 1991, all Soviet forces were gone.

In June 1990 the Hungarian government announced the country's decision to no longer participate in Warsaw Pact military exercises and its intention to withdraw altogether from the Pact. As the Warsaw Pact and Comecon had disbanded by July 1991, the country was able to move toward the West more directly.

Hun Sen 1950– . Cambodian political leader, prime minister from 1985. Originally a member of the Khmer Rouge army, he defected in 1977 to join Vietnam-based anti-Khmer Cambodian forces.

Born into a poor peasant family in the eastern province of Kampang-Cham, Hun Sen joined the Khmer Rouge in 1970. He rose to become a regiment commander, but, disillusioned, defected to the anti-Khmer Cambodian forces in 1977. On his return to Cambodia, following the Vietnamese-backed communist takeover, he served as foreign minister 1979, and then as prime minister 1985, promoting economic liberalization and a thawing in relations with exiled, non-Khmer, opposition forces as a prelude to a compromise political settlement.

Hunt John, Baron Hunt 1910– . British mountaineer, leader of the successful Everest expedition 1953 (with ◊Hillary and ◊Tenzing).

Hunt (James Henry) Leigh 1784–1859. English poet and essayist. The appearance in his Liberal newspaper *The Examiner* of an unfavorable article that he had written about the Prince Regent caused him to be convicted for libel and imprisoned 1813. The friend and later enemy of Byron, he also knew Keats and Shelley.

His verse is little appreciated today, but he influenced the Romantics, and his book on London *The Town* 1848 and his *Autobiography* 1850 survive. The character of Harold Skimpole in Dickens' *Bleak House* was allegedly based on him.

Hunt William Holman 1827–1910. English painter, one of the founders of the ◊Pre-Raphaelite Brotherhood 1848. Obsessed with realistic detail, he traveled from 1854 onward to Syria and Palestine to paint biblical subjects. His works include *The Awakening Conscience* 1853 (Tate Gallery, London) and *The Light of the World* 1854 (Keble College, Oxford).

Hunter river in New South Wales, Australia, which rises in the Mount Royal Range and flows into the Pacific Ocean near Newcastle, after a course of about 290 mi/465 km. Although the river is liable to flooding, the Hunter Valley has dairying and market gardening, and produces wines.

Huntington city in W West Virginia, across the Ohio River from Ohio, NW of Charleston; seat of Cabell County. It is an important transportation center for coal mined to the S. Other industries include chemicals; metal, wood, and glass products; tobacco; and fruit processing; population (1990) 54,844.

Huntington's chorea rare hereditary disease that begins in middle age. It is characterized by involuntary movements and rapid mental degeneration progressing to ◊dementia. There is no known cure.

Huntsville city in NE Alabama; population (1990) 159,789. Manufactured products include textiles, electrical and electronic goods, metal products, chemicals, machinery, and cosmetics. Just outside the city is the Redstone Arsenal, which includes an army missile center and the George C Marshall Space Flight Center. A branch of the University of Alabama and a space and rocket museum are here. Huntsville was settled 1805. During the Civil War, it was occupied and burned by Union troops.

Hunyadi János Corvinus 1387–1456. Hungarian politician and general. Born in Transylvania, reputedly the son of the emperor ◊Sigismund, he won battles against the Turks from the 1440s. In 1456 he defeated them at Belgrade, but died shortly afterwards of the plague.

Hunza small state on the NW frontier of Kashmir, under the rule of Pakistan.

Hupei former name of ◊Hebei, province of China.

hurdy-gurdy musical stringed instrument resembling a violin in tone but using a form of keyboard to play a melody and drone strings to provide a continuous harmony. An inbuilt wheel turned by a handle, acts as a bow.

Hurok Sol (Solomon) 1888–1974. Russian-born US theatrical producer. Hurok immigrated to the US 1906. As a lifelong devotee of music, Hurok began to organize concerts for New York unions and social groups. In 1914 he began to produce musical and theatrical events professionally and over the years arranged US appearances for the most prominent figures in European music and dance.

His Russian contacts proved especially valuable, and in later years he worked with the NBC television network producing television specials.

hurricane *Hurricane Elena, photographed on Sept 2, 1985, from the space shuttle* Discovery.

His autobiographical *Impresario* and *S Hurok Presents* appeared 1946 and 1953, respectively.

Huron (French *hure* "head of pig") nickname for a member of a confederation of North American Indian peoples speaking an Iroquoian language and living near lakes Huron, Erie, and Ontario in the 16th and 17th centuries. They were almost wiped out by the Iroquois. In the 17th century, surviving Hurons formed a group called Wyandot, some of whose descendants now live in Québec and Oklahoma.

Huron second largest of the Great Lakes of North America, on the US-Canadian border; area 23,160 sq mi/60,000 sq km. It includes Georgian Bay, Saginaw Bay, and Manitoulin Island. There are a number of small Michigan and Ontario ports on its shores. Jesuit missionaries established the first European settlement, on Georgian Bay, in 1638.

It receives Lake Superior's waters through the Sault Ste Marie River, and Lake Michigan's through the Straits of Mackinac. It drains S into Lake Erie through the St Clair River-Lake St Clair-Detroit River system.

hurricane a revolving storm in tropical regions, called *typhoon* in the N Pacific. It originates between 5° and 20° N or S of the equator, when the surface temperature of the ocean is above 80°F/27°C. A central calm area, called the eye, is surrounded by inwardly spiralling winds (counterclockwise in the N hemisphere) of up to 200 mph/320 kph. A hurricane is accompanied by lightning and torrential rain, and can cause extensive damage. In meteorology, a hurricane is a wind of force 12 or more on the ◊Beaufort scale. The most intense hurricane recorded in the Caribbean/Atlantic sector was Hurricane Gilbert in 1988, with sustained winds of 175 mph/280 kph and gusts of over 200 mph/320 kph.

Hurston Zora Neale 1901–1960. US novelist and short-story writer, associated with the ◊Harlem Renaissance. She collected traditional African-American folk tales in *Mules and Men* 1935; her novels include *Their Eyes Were Watching God* 1937.

Hurt William 1950– . US actor whose films include *Altered States* 1980, *The Big Chill* 1983, *Kiss of the Spider Woman* 1985, and *Broadcast News* 1987.

Husák Gustáv 1913– . Leader of the Communist Party of Czechoslovakia (CCP) 1969–87 and president 1975–89. After the 1968 Prague Spring of liberalization, his task was to restore control, purge the CCP, and oversee the implementation of a new, federalist constitution. He was deposed in the popular uprising of Nov–Dec 1989 and expelled from the Communist Party in Feb 1990.

Husák, a lawyer, was active in the Resistance movement during World War II, and afterwards in the Slovak Communist Party (SCP), and was imprisoned on political grounds 1951–60. Rehabilitated, he was appointed first secretary of the SCP 1968 and CCP leader 1969–87. As titular state president he pursued a policy of cautious reform. He stepped down as party leader 1987, and was replaced as state president by Vaclav ◊Havel in Dec 1989 following the "gentle revolution."

Huscarls Anglo-Danish warriors, in 10th-century Denmark and early 11th-century England. They formed the bulk of English royal armies until the Norman Conquest.

husky any of several breeds of sled dog used in Arctic regions, growing to 2 ft/70 cm high, and weighing about 110 lb/50 kgs, with pricked ears, thick fur, and a bushy tail. The Siberian husky is the best known.

Huss John c. 1373–1415. Bohemian church

Hurt *Actor William Hurt, who was first acclaimed for his role in* The Big Chill *1983.*

***Hussein** Iraq's President Saddam Hussein, who directed his country's invasion of Kuwait in 1990, retained power after Iraq's defeat in 1991.*

reformer, rector of Prague University from 1402, who was excommunicated for attacks on ecclesiastical abuses. He was summoned before the Council of Constance 1414, defended the English reformer Wycliffe, rejected the pope's authority, and was burned at the stake. His followers were called Hussites.

Hussein ibn Ali c. 1854–1931. Leader of the Arab revolt 1916–18 against the Turks. He proclaimed himself king of the Hejaz 1916, accepted the caliphate 1924, but was unable to retain it due to internal fighting. He was deposed 1924 by Ibn Saud.

Hussein ibn Talal 1935– . King of Jordan from 1952. Great-grandson of Hussein ibn Ali, he became king after the mental incapacity of his father, Talal. By 1967 he had lost all his kingdom west of the river Jordan in the ◊Arab-Israeli Wars, and in 1970 suppressed the ◊Palestine Liberation Organization acting as a guerrilla force against his rule on the remaining East Bank territories. In recent years, he has become a moderating force in Middle Eastern politics. After Iraq's annexation of Kuwait in 1990 he attempted to mediate between the opposing sides.

Hussein Saddam 1937– . Iraqi left-wing politician, in power from 1968, president from 1979.

Ruthless in the pursuit of his objectives, he fought a bitter war against Iran 1980–88 and dealt harshly with Kurdish rebels seeking a degree of independence. In 1990 he ordered the invasion and annexation of Kuwait, provoking an international crisis, a United Nations embargo, and a UN-coalition military action (see ◊Gulf War) 1991. Even though his forces were badly defeated in the war, Saddam retained power and later in 1991 moved against the Kurds and other opponents in Iraq.

Hussein joined the Arab Ba'th Socialist Party as a young man and soon became involved in revolutionary activities. In 1959 he was sentenced to death and took refuge in Egypt, but a coup in 1963 made his return possible, although in the following year he was imprisoned for plotting to overthrow the regime he had helped to install. After his release he took a leading part in the 1968 revolution, removing the civilian government and establishing a Revolutionary Command Council (RCC). At first discreetly, and then more openly, Hussein strengthened his position and in 1979 became RCC chair and state president.

In 1977 Saddam Hussein al-Tikriti abolished the use of surnames in Iraq to conceal the fact that a large number of people in the government and ruling party all came from the village of Tikrit and therefore bore the same surname.

The 1990 Kuwait annexation followed a long-running border dispute and was prompted by alleged slant drilling by Kuwait under the border and Iraq's perceived need to protect oil resources after the expensive war against Iran. Saddam, who had enjoyed US support for being the enemy of Iran and had used poison gas against his own people in Kurdistan without any falling-off in trade with the West, suddenly found himself almost universally condemned.

Husserl Edmund (Gustav Albrecht) 1859–1938. German philosopher, regarded as the founder of ◊phenomenology, a philosophy concentrating on what is consciously experienced.

He hoped phenomenology would become the science of all sciences. His main works are *Logical Investigations* 1900, *Phenomenological Philosophy* 1913, and *The Crisis of the European Sciences* 1936. He influenced ◊Heidegger and affected sociology through the work of Alfred Schütz (1899–1959).

Hussite a follower of John ◊Huss. Opposed to both German and papal influence in Bohemia, the Hussites waged successful war against the Holy Roman Empire from 1419, but Roman Catholicism was finally re-established 1620.

Huston John 1906–1987. US film director, screenwriter, and actor. An impulsive and individualistic filmmaker, he often dealt with the themes of greed, treachery in human relationships, and the loner. His works as a director include *The Maltese Falcon* 1941 (his debut), *The Treasure of the Sierra Madre* 1948 (for which he won an Academy Award) *The African Queen* 1951, and his last, *The Dead* 1987.

He was the son of the actor Walter Huston and the father of the actress Anjelica Huston. His other films include *Key Largo* 1948, *Moby Dick* 1956, *The Misfits* 1961, and *Fat City* 1972.

Huston Walter 1884–1950. Canadian-born US actor. The father of director John Huston, he was born in Toronto and trained as an engineer. After a succession of engineering jobs, he chose a theatrical career, appearing in a vaudeville musical act. Turning to legitimate acting, he won critical acclaim for his Broadway performance in *Desire Under the Elms* 1924. For the rest of his career, Huston alternated between stage acting and appearances in feature films. In 1948 he won the Academy Award as best supporting actor for his role in *The Treasure of Sierra Madre*, a film written and directed by his son.

Hutchinson Anne Marbury 1591–1643. Colonial American religious leader. Born in England, Hutchinson was a follower of Puritan leader John Cotton and followed him to Massachusetts Bay Colony 1634 with her husband and children. Noted for her intellect and forceful personality, she developed a following in Boston, preaching a unique theology that emphasized the role of faith. The colony's leaders felt threatened by Hutchinson, and the "Antinomian Controversy" ensued. In 1637 Hutchinson was banished and excommunicated; having found asylum in nearby Rhode Island, she later moved to Long Island, where she and her family were killed by Indians.

Hutterian Brethren a Christian sect; see ◊Mennonite.

Hutton James 1726–1797. Scottish geologist, known as the "founder of geology," who formulated the concept of ◊uniformitarianism. In 1785 he developed a theory of the igneous origin of many rocks.

His *Theory of the Earth* 1788 proposed that the Earth was indefinitely old. Uniformitarianism suggests that past events could be explained in terms of processes that work today. For example, the kind of river current that produces a certain settling pattern in a bed of sand today must have been operating many millions of years ago, if that same pattern is visible in ancient sandstones.

***Huxley** English novelist and writer Aldous Huxley, whose* Brave New World *1932 depicted an emotionless society of the future.*

Huxley Aldous (Leonard) 1894–1963. English writer. The satirical disillusionment of his first novel, *Crome Yellow* 1921, continued throughout *Antic Hay* 1923, *Those Barren Leaves* 1925, *Point Counter Point* 1928, and *Brave New World* 1932, in which human beings are mass produced in the laboratory under the control of the omnipotent "Big Brother."

He was the grandson of Thomas Henry Huxley and brother of Julian Huxley. Huxley's later devotion to mysticism led to his experiments with the hallucinogenic drug mescaline, recorded in *The Doors of Perception* 1954. He also wrote the novel *Eyeless in Gaza* 1936, and two historical studies, *Grey Eminence* 1941 and *The Devils of Loudun* 1952.

Huxley Julian 1887–1975. English biologist, first director-general of UNESCO, and a founder of the World Wildlife Fund (now the World Wide Fund for Nature).

Huxley Thomas Henry 1825–1895. English scientist and humanist. Following the publication of Charles Darwin's *On the Origin of Species* 1859, he became known as "Darwin's bulldog," and for many years was a prominent champion of evolution. He is considered the founder of scientific ◊humanism.

Hu Yaobang 1915–1989. Chinese politician, Communist Party (CCP) chair 1981–87. A protégé of the communist leader Deng Xiaoping, Hu presided over a radical overhaul of the party structure and personnel 1982–86. His death ignited the pro-democracy movement, which was eventually crushed in Tiananmen Square in June 1989.

Hu, born into a peasant family in Hunan province, joined the Red Army at the age of 14 and was a political commissar during the 1934–36 Long March. In 1941 he served under Deng and later worked under him in provincial and central government. Hu was purged as a "capitalist roader" during the 1966–69 Cultural Revolution and sent into the countryside for "re-education." He was rehabilitated 1975 but disgraced again when Deng fell from prominence 1976. In Dec 1978, with Deng established in power, Hu was inducted into the CCP Politburo and became head of the revived secretariat 1980 and CCP chair 1981. He attempted to quicken reaction against Mao. He was dismissed Jan 1987 for his relaxed handling of a wave of student unrest Dec 1986.

Huygens Christiaan 1629–1695. Dutch mathematical physicist and astronomer, who proposed the wave theory of light. He developed the pendulum clock, discovered polarization, and observed Saturn's rings.

Huysmans J(oris) K(arl) 1848–1907. French novelist of Dutch ancestry. His novel *Marthe* 1876, the story of a courtesan, was followed by other realistic novels, including *À rebors/Against Nature*

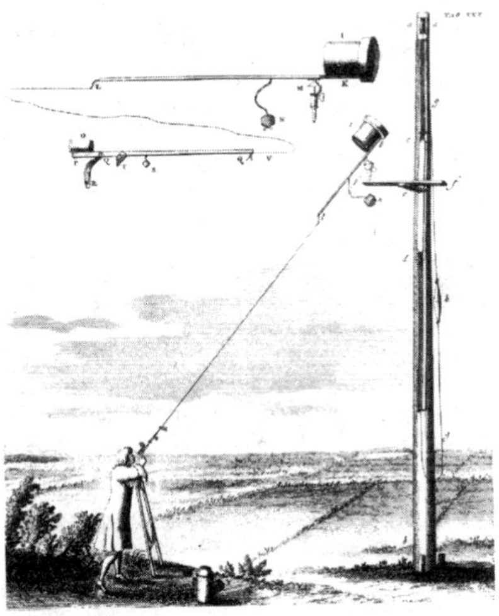

Huygens *Dutch physicist Christaan Huygens published a design for an "aerial" telescope in* Opera Varia *in 1724. The tubeless telescope works by refracting light.*

1884, a novel of self-absorbed estheticism that symbolized the "decadent" movement.

Hvannadalshnjukur highest peak in Iceland, rising to 6,952 ft/2,119 m in SE Iceland.

Hwang-Ho former name of the ◊Huang He, a river in China.

HWM abbreviation for high water mark.

hyacinth any bulb-producing plant of the genus *Hyacinthus* of the lily family Liliaceae, native to the E Mediterranean and Africa. The cultivated hyacinth *H. orientalis* has large, scented, cylindrical heads of pink, white, or blue flowers. The ◊water hyacinth, genus *Eichhornia,* is unrelated, a floating plant from South America.

Hyades V-shaped cluster of stars that forms the face of the bull in the constellation Taurus. It is 130 light-years away and contains over 200 stars, although only about 12 are visible to the naked eye.

hyaline membrane disease former name for ◊***respiratory distress syndrome***.

hybrid the offspring from a cross between individuals of the same species or of two different species. In many cases the former results in hybrid vigor, much desired in selective breeding. Hybrids from two different species are usually infertile and unable to reproduce sexually. In plants, however, doubling of the chromosomes (see ◊polyploid) can restore the fertility of such hybrids.

Hybrids between different genera are extremely rare; an example is the *leylandii* cypress which, like some hybrids, shows exceptional vigor, or ◊heterosis. In the wild, a "hybrid zone" may occur where the ranges of two related species meet.

Hydaspes Classical name of river ◊Jhelum, a river in Pakistan and Kashmir.

hydathode a specialized pore, or less commonly, a hair, through which water is secreted by hydrostatic pressure from the interior of a plant leaf onto the surface. Hydathodes are found on many different plants and are usually situated around the leaf margin at vein endings. Each pore is surrounded by two crescent-shaped cells and resembles an open ◊stoma, but the size of the opening cannot be varied as in a stoma. The process of water secretion through hydathodes is known as ◊guttation.

Hyde Douglas 1860–1949. Irish scholar and politician. Founder-president of the Gaelic League 1893–1915, he was president of Eire 1938–45. His works include *Love Songs of Connacht* 1894.

Hyderabad capital city of the S central Indian state of Andhra Pradesh, on the river Musi; population (1981) 2,528,000. Products include carpets, silks, and metal inlay work. It was formerly the capital of the state of Hyderabad. Buildings include the Jama Masjid mosque and Golconda fort.

Hyderabad city in Sind province, SE Pakistan; population (1981) 795,000. It produces gold, pottery, glass, and furniture. The third-largest city of Pakistan, it was founded 1768.

hydra in zoology, any member of the family Hydridae, or freshwater polyps, of the phylum Cnidaria (coelenterates). The body is a double-layered tube (with 6–10 hollow tentacles around the mouth), 0.5 in/1.25 cm long when extended, but capable of contracting to a small knob. Usually fixed to waterweed, hydras feed on minute animals, that are caught and paralyzed by stinging cells on the tentacles. Hydras reproduce asexually in the summer and sexually in the winter. They have no specialized organs except those of reproduction.

Hydra in astronomy, the longest constellation, winding across more than a fourth of the sky between Cancer and Libra in the southern hemisphere. Hydra represents the multiheaded monster slain by Hercules. Despite its size, it is not prominent; its brightest star is second-magnitude Alphard, about 85 light-years from Earth.

Hydra in Greek mythology, a huge monster with nine heads. If one were cut off, two would grow in its place. One of the 12 labors of Heracles was to kill it.

hydrangea any flowering shrub of the genus *Hydrangea* of the saxifrage family Hydrangeaceae, native to Japan. Cultivated varieties of *H. macrophylla* normally produce round heads of pink flowers, but these may be blue if certain chemicals, such as alum or iron, are in the soil. The name is from the Greek for "water vessel," after the cuplike seed capsules.

hydraulics the field of study concerned with utilizing the properties of water and other liquids, in particular the way they flow and transmit pressure, and with the application of these properties in engineering. It applies the principles of ◊hydrostatics and hydrodynamics. The oldest type of hydraulic machine is the hydraulic press, invented by Joseph Bramah in England 1795. The hydraulic principle of pressurized liquid increasing mechanical efficiency is commonly used on vehicle braking systems, the forging press, and the hydraulic systems of aircraft and excavators.

A hydraulic press consists of two liquid-connected pistons in cylinders, one of narrow bore, one of large bore. A force applied to the narrow piston applies a certain pressure (force per unit area) to the liquid, which is transmitted to the larger piston. Because the area of this piston is larger, the force exerted on it is larger. Thus the original force has been magnified, although the smaller piston must move a great distance to move the larger piston only a little, hence mechanical efficiency is gained in force but lost in movement.

hydraulics

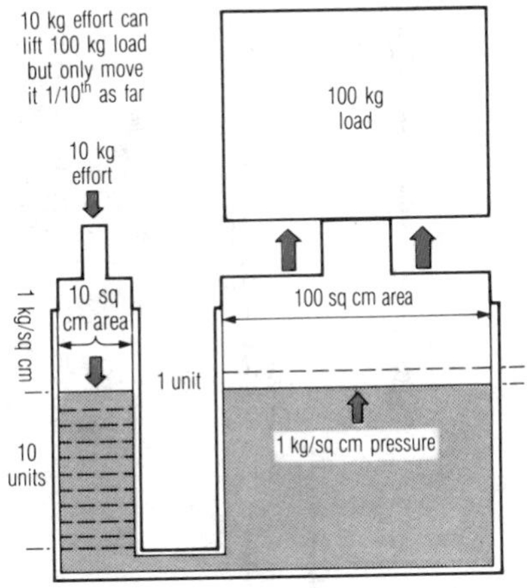
10 kg effort can lift 100 kg load but only move it 1/10th as far
100 kg load
10 kg effort
10 sq cm area
100 sq cm area
1 kg/sq cm
1 unit
10 units
1 kg/sq cm pressure

hydrocarbon any of a class of chemical compounds containing only hydrogen and carbon (for example, paraffin). Hydrocarbons are obtained industrially principally from petroleum and coal tar.

hydrocephalus potentially serious increase in the volume of cerebrospinal fluid (CSF) within the ventricles of the brain. In infants, since their skull plates have not fused, it causes enlargement of the head, and there is a risk of brain damage from CSF pressure on the developing brain.

Hydrocephalus may be due to mechanical obstruction of the outflow of CSF from the ventricles or to faulty reabsorption. Treatment usually involves surgical placement of a shunt system to drain the fluid into the abdominal cavity. In infants, the condition is often seen in association with ◊spina bifida.

hydrochloric acid highly corrosive aqueous solution of hydrogen chloride (HCl, a colorless, corrosive gas). It has many industrial uses, including recovery of zinc from galvanized scrap iron and the production of chlorides and chlorine. It is also produced in the stomachs of animals for the purposes of digestion.

hydrocyanic acid or prussic acid solution of hydrogen cyanide gas (HCN) in water. It is a colorless, highly poisonous, volatile liquid, smelling of bitter almonds.

hydrodynamics the science of nonviscous liquids (for example water, alcohol, ether) in motion.

hydroelectric power electricity generated by moving water. In a typical hydroelectric power (HEP) scheme, water stored in a reservoir, often created by damming a river, is piped into water ◊turbines, coupled to electricity generators. In ◊pumped storage plants, water flowing through the turbines is recycled. A ◊tidal power station exploits the rise and fall of the tides. About one-fifth of the world's electricity comes from hydroelectric power.

HEP plants have prodigious generating capacities. The Grand Coulee plant in Washington State, has a power output of some 10,000 megawatts. The Itaipu power station on the Paraná river (Brazil/Paraguay) has a potential capacity of 12,000 megawatts.

hydrofoil wing that develops lift in the water in much the same way that an airplane wing develops lift in the air. A hydrofoil boat is one whose hull rises out of the water due to the lift, and the boat skims along on the hydrofoils. The first hydrofoil was fitted to a boat 1906. The first commercial hydrofoil went into operation 1956. One of the most advanced hydrofoil boats is the Boeing ◊jetfoil.

hydrogen colorless, odorless, gaseous, nonmetallic element, symbol H, atomic number 1, atomic weight 1.00797. It is the lightest of all the elements and occurs on Earth chiefly in combination with oxygen as water. Hydrogen is the most abundant element in the universe, where it accounts for 93% of the total number of atoms and 76% total mass. It is a component of most stars, including the Sun, whose heat and light are produced through the nuclear-fusion process, which converts hydrogen into helium. When subjected to a pressure 500,000 times greater than that of the Earth's atmosphere, hydrogen becomes a solid metal, as in one of the inner zones of the planet Jupiter. Its common and industrial uses include the hardening of fats and oils by hydrogenation and the creation of high-temperature flames for welding.

Its isotopes ◊deuterium and ◊tritium (half-life 12.5 years) are used in nuclear weapons, and deuterons (deuterium neuclei) are used in synthesizing elements. The name derives from reference to the generation of water from the combustion of hydrogen; the element was named in 1787 from Greek *hydro* + *gen*, "water generator," by the French chemist Louis Guyton de Morveau (1737–1816).

hydrogenation the addition of hydrogen to an unsaturated organic molecule (one that contains ◊double bonds or triple bonds).

It is widely used in the manufacture of margarine and low-fat spreads by the addition of hydrogen to vegetable oils.

hydrogen bomb bomb that works on the principle of nuclear ◊fusion. Large-scale explosion results from the thermonuclear release of energy when hydrogen nuclei are condensed to helium nuclei. The first hydrogen bomb was exploded at Eniwetok Atoll by the US 1952.

The constant release of energy through nuclear fusion is the continuing reaction in the Sun and other stars; it can be duplicated by the triggering of tritium (hydrogen isotope of atomic weight 3.0170) by an ordinary atomic bomb.

hydrogen cyanide HCN poisonous gas formed by the reaction of sodium cyanide with dilute sulfuric acid, used for fumigation.

The salts formed from it are cyanides—for example sodium cyanide, used in hardening steel and extracting gold and silver from their ores. If dissolved in water, hydrogen cyanide gives hydrocyanic acid.

hydrography study and charting of Earth's surface waters in seas, lakes, and rivers.

hydrology study of the location and movement of inland water, both frozen and liquid, above and below ground. It is applied to major civil engineering projects such as irrigation schemes, dams and hydroelectric power, and in planning water supply.

hydrolysis chemical reaction in which the action of water or its ions breaks down a substance into smaller molecules. Hydrolysis occurs in certain inorganic salts in solution, in nearly all nonmetallic chlorides, in esters, and in other organic substances. It is one of the mechanisms for the breakdown of food by the body, as in the conversion of starch to glucose.

hydrometer in physics, an instrument used to measure the density of liquids compared with that of water, usually expressed in grams per cubic centimeter. It consists of a thin glass tube ending in a sphere that leads into a smaller sphere, the latter being weighted so that the hydrometer floats upright, sinking deeper into lighter liquids than into heavier liquids. It is used in brewing.

The hydrometer is based on ◊Archimedes' principle.

hydrophily a form of ◊pollination in which the pollen is carried by water.

Hydrophily is very rare but occurs in a few aquatic species. In Canadian pondweed *Elodea* and tape grass *Vallisneria*, the male flowers break off whole and rise to the water surface where they encounter the female flowers, which are borne on long stalks. In eel grasses *Zostera*, which are coastal plants growing totally submerged, the filamentous pollen grains are released into the water and carried by currents to the female flowers where they become wrapped around the stigmas.

hydrophobia another name for the disease ◊***rabies***.

hydrophone underwater ◊microphone and ancillary equipment capable of picking up waterborne sounds. It was originally developed to detect enemy submarines but is now also used, for example, for listening to the sounds made by whales.

hydrophyte a plant adapted to live in water, or in waterlogged soil.

Hydrophytes may have leaves with a very reduced or absent ◊cuticle and no ◊stomata (since there is no need to conserve water), a reduced root and water-conducting system, and less supporting tissue since water buoys plants up. There are often numerous spaces between the cells in their stems and roots to make ◊gas exchange with all parts of the plant body possible. Many have highly divided leaves, which lessens resistance to flowing water; an example is spiked water milfoil *Myriophyllum spicatum*.

hydroplane on a submarine, a moveable horizontal fin angled downward or upward when the vessel is descending or ascending. It is also a highly maneuverable motorboat with its bottom rising in steps to the stern, or a ◊hydrofoil boat that skims over the surface of the water when driven at high speed.

hydroponics the cultivation of plants without soil, using specially prepared solutions of mineral salts. Beginning in the 1930s, large crops were grown by hydroponic methods, at first in California, but since then in many other parts of the world.

J von Sachs (1832–1897) 1860 and W Knop 1865 developed a system of plant culture in water whereby the relation of mineral salts to plant growth could be determined, but it was not until about 1930 that large crops could be grown. The term was coined by W F Gericke, a US scientist.

hydrosphere the water component of the Earth, usually encompassing the oceans, seas, rivers, streams, swamps, lakes, ground water, and atmospheric water vapor.

hydrostatics in physics, the branch of ◊statics dealing with the mechanical problems of liquids in equilibrium, that is, in a static condition. Practical applications include shipbuilding and dam design.

hydrothermal in geology, pertaining to a fluid whose principal component is hot water, or to a mineral deposit believed to be precipitated from such a fluid.

hydrothermal vein an open space in rock containing a cluster of minerals precipitated through the action of circulating high-temperature fluids. Igneous activity often gives rise to the circulation of heated fluids that migrate outward and move through the surrounding rock. When such solutions carry metallic ions, mineral deposition occurs in the new surroundings on cooling.

hydroxides inorganic compounds containing one or more hydroxyl (OH) groups and generally combined with a metal. They include caustic soda (sodium hydroxide, NaOH), caustic potash (potassium hydroxide, KOH), and slaked lime (calcium hydroxide, $Ca(OH)_2$).

hydroxypropanoic acid technical name for ◊lactic acid.

hyena three species of carnivorous mammals in the family Hyaenidae, living in Africa and Asia. Hyenas have extremely powerful jaws. They are scavengers, although they will also attack and kill live prey.

There are three species: the striped hyena *Hyaena hyaena* found from Asia Minor to India; the brown hyena *H. brunnea* found in S Africa; and the spotted hyena *Crocuta crocuta*, common S of the Sahara. The ◊aardwolf also belongs to the hyena family.

hygrometer

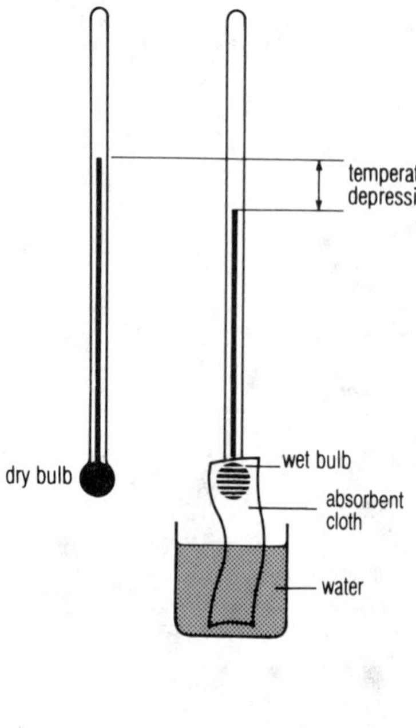
temperature depression
dry bulb
wet bulb
absorbent cloth
water

Hygieia in Greek mythology, the goddess of health (Roman Salus), daughter of Aesculapius.

hygiene the science of the preservation of health and prevention of disease. It is chiefly concerned with such external conditions as the purity of air and water; bodily cleanliness; cleanliness in the home and workplace; and good nutrition, exercise, and sex habits.

hygrometer in physics, any instrument for measuring the humidity, or water vapor content, of a gas (usually air). A wet and dry bulb hygrometer consists of two vertical thermometers, with one of the bulbs covered in absorbent cloth dipped into water. As the water evaporates, the bulb cools producing a temperature difference between the two thermometers. The amount of evaporation, and hence cooling of the wet bulb, depends on the relative humidity of the air.

Other hygrometers work on the basis of a length of natural fiber, such as hair or a fine strand of gut, changing with variations in humidity. In a dew-point hygrometer, a polished metal mirror gradually cools until a fine mist of water (dew) forms on it. This gives a measure of the ◊dew point, from which the air's relative humidity can be calculated.

hygroscopic term used to describe a substance that can absorb moisture from the air without becoming wet.

Hyksos ("Shepherd Kings" or "Princes of the Desert") a nomadic, probably Semitic people who invaded Egypt in the 18th century BC and established their own dynasty in the Nile delta, which lasted until 1580 BC. They introduced bronze metallurgy, the wheel, and the use of the horse-drawn chariot.

Hylton v US a US Supreme Court decision 1796 in which the Court, for the first time, reviewed the constitutionality of an act of Congress. The suit was a protest of a carriage tax imposed by Congress in 1794. The plaintiff argued that this tax was unconstitutional because, although it was a direct tax, it was not applied to states proportionally, according to population. The Court upheld the tax, voting 3 to 0 that a carriage tax was not a direct tax, like a head or land tax, but an impost on a consumer good.

Hymen in Greek mythology, either the son of Apollo and one of the Muses, or of Dionysus and Aphrodite. He was the god of marriage, and in painting he is represented as a youth carrying a bridal torch.

hymn song in praise of a deity. Examples include Ikhnaton's hymn to the Aton in ancient Egypt, the ancient Greek Orphic hymns, Old Testament psalms, extracts from the New Testament (such as "Ave Maria"), and hymns by the British writers John Bunyan ("Who would true valour see") and Charles Wesley ("Hark the herald angels sing"). ◊Gospel music and carols are forms of Christian hymn-singing.

hyoscine or ***scopolamine*** drug that acts on the autonomic nervous system and is frequently included in ◊premedication to dry up lung secretions and as a postoperative sedative. It is an alkaloid $C_{17}H_{21}NO_2$ obtained from various plants of the nightshade family (such as ◊belladonna).

Hypatia c. 370–c. 415. Greek philosopher, born in Alexandria. She studied Neo-Platonism in Athens, and succeeded her father Theon as professor of philosophy at Alexandria. She was murdered, it is thought by Christian fanatics.

hyperactivity condition of excessive activity in young children, combined with inability to concentrate and difficulty in learning. The cause is not known, although some ◊food additives have come under suspicion. Modification of the diet may help, and in the majority of cases there is improvement at puberty.

hyperbola

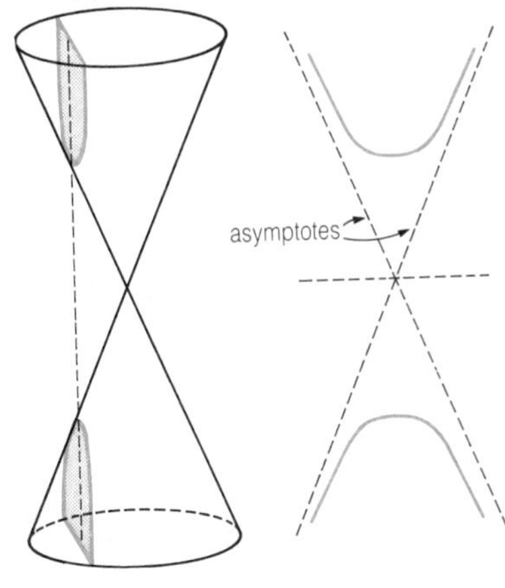
asymptotes

hyperbola in geometry, a curve formed by cutting a right circular cone with a plane so that the angle between the plane and the base is greater than the angle between the base and the side of the cone. All hyperbolae are bounded by two ◊asymptotes.

A member of the family of curves known as ◊conic sections, a hyperbola can also be defined as a path traced by a point that moves such that the ratio of its distance from a fixed point (focus) and a fixed straight line (directrix) is a constant and greater than 1; that is, it has an ◊eccentricity greater than 1.

hyperbole a figure of speech whose Greek name suggests "going over the top." When people use hyperbole, they exaggerate, usually to emphasize a point ("If I've told you once I've told you a thousand times not to do that").

hypercharge in physics, a property of certain ◊elementary particles, analogous to electric charge, that accounts for the absence of some expected behavior (such as decay) in terms of the short-range strong interaction force, which holds atomic nuclei together.

It is a number equal to twice the average charge of the particles concerned, divided by the elementary charge. ◊Protons and ◊neutrons, for example, have a hypercharge of +1, whereas a pion has a hypercharge of zero.

hyperinflation rapid and uncontrolled ◊inflation, or increases in prices, usually associated with political and/or social instability (as in Germany in the 1920s).

hypermarket a very large ◊supermarket.

hyperon a ◊***hadron***; any of a group of highly unstable ◊elementary particles that includes all the ◊baryons with a mass greater than the ◊neutron. They are all composed of three quarks.

hypertension abnormally high ◊blood pressure due to a variety of causes, leading to excessive contraction of the smooth muscle cells of the walls of the arteries. It increases the risk of kidney disease, stroke, and heart attack.

hyperthyroidism or ***thyrotoxicosis*** overactivity of the thyroid gland due to enlargement or tumor. Symptoms include accelerated heart rate, sweating, anxiety, tremor, and weight loss. Treatment is by drugs or surgery.

hypertrophy abnormal increase in size of a body organ or tissue.

hypha (plural hyphae) a delicate, usually branching filament, many of which collectively form the mycelium and fruiting bodies of a ◊fungus. Food molecules and other substances are transported along hyphae by the movement of the cytoplasm, known as "cytoplasmic streaming."

Typically hyphae grow by increasing in length from the tips and by the formation of side branches. Hyphae of the higher fungi (the ascomycetes and basidiomycetes) are divided by cross walls or septa at intervals, whereas those of lower fungi (for example, bread mold) are undivided. However, even the higher fungi are not truly cellular, as each septum is pierced by a central pore, through which cytoplasm, and even nuclei, can flow. The hyphal walls contain ◊chitin, a polysaccharide.

Hyphasis Classical name of the river ◊Beas, in India.

hyphen punctuation mark (-) with two functions: to join words, parts of words, syllables, and so on, as an aid to sense; and to mark a word break at the end of a line. Adjectival compounds (see ◊adjective) are hyphenated because they modify the noun jointly rather than separately ("a small-town boy" is a boy from a small town; "a small town boy" is a small boy from a town). The use of hyphens with adverbs is redundant unless an identical adjective exists (*well, late, long*).

Phrasal verbs are not hyphenated ("things *turned out* well," "it *washed up* on the beach") unless used adjectivally ("a well-*turned-out* crowd," "a *washed-up* athlete"). Nouns formed from phrasal verbs are hyphenated or joined together ("a good *turnout* tonight," "please do the *washing-up*"). In the use of certain prefixes, modern style is moving toward omitting the hyphen (*noncooperation*).

hypnosis an artificially induced state of relaxation in which suggestibility is heightened. The subject may carry out orders after being awakened, and may be made insensitive to pain. Hypnosis is sometimes used to treat addictions to tobacco or overeating, or to assist amnesia victims.

hypnotic any substance (such as ◊barbiturate, ◊benzodiazepine, alcohol) that depresses brain function, inducing sleep. Prolonged use may lead to physical or psychological addiction.

hypo in photography, a term for sodium thiosulfate, discovered 1819 by John ◊Herschel, and used as a fixative for photographic images since 1837.

hypocaust a floor raised on tile piers, heated by hot air circulating beneath it. It was first used by the Romans for baths about 100 BC, and was later introduced to private houses.

Hypocausts were a common feature of stone houses in the colder parts of the Roman Empire, but could not be used in timber-framed buildings. Typically the house of a wealthy person would have one furnace heating several rooms. In large houses there might be several such furnaces, and during the 1st century AD channels were built into walls and roofs in order to distribute heat more evenly around the building.

hypocycloid in geometry, a cusped curve traced by a point on the circumference of a circle that rolls around the inside of another larger circle. (Compare ◊epicycloid).

hypodermic instrument used for injecting fluids beneath the skin into either muscles or blood vessels. It consists of a small graduated tube with a close-fitting piston and a nozzle on to which a hollow needle can be fitted.

hypogeal a type of seed germination in which the ◊cotyledons remain below ground. The term can refer to fruits that develop underground, such as peanuts *Arachis hypogea*.

hypoglycemia condition of abnormally low level of sugar (glucose) in the blood, which starves the brain. It causes weakness, the shakes, and perspiration, sometimes fainting. Untreated victims have suffered paranoia and extreme anxiety. Treatment is by special diet.

Hypoglycemia is rare in combination with other diseases, but in diabetics, low blood sugar occurs when the diabetic has taken too much insulin.

hyponymy in semantics, a relationship in meaning between two words such that one (for example, *sport*) includes the other (for example, *football*), but not vice versa.

hypothalamus the region of the brain below the ◊cerebrum which regulates rhythmic activity and physiological stability within the body, including water balance and temperature. It regulates the production of the pituitary gland's hormones and controls that part of the ◊nervous system regulating the involuntary muscles.

hyssop

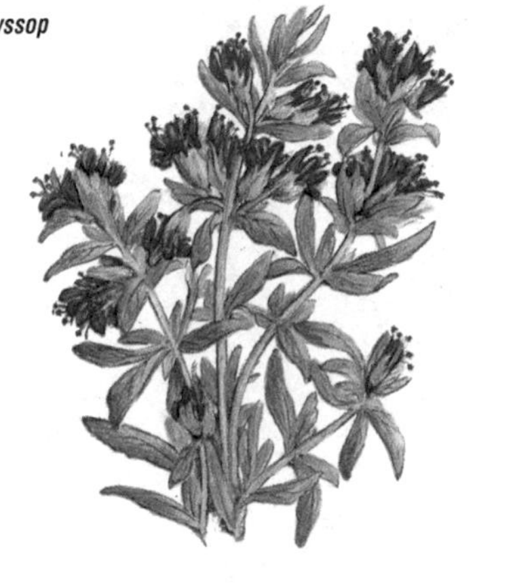

hypothermia condition in which the deep (core) temperature of the body spontaneously drops. If it is not discovered, coma and death ensue. Most at risk are the aged and babies (particularly if premature).

hypothesis in science, an idea concerning an event and its possible explanation. The term is one favored by the followers of the philosopher ◊Popper, who argue that the merit of a scientific hypothesis lies in its ability to make testable predictions.

hypothyroidism or ***myxedema*** deficient functioning of the thyroid gland, causing slowed mental and physical performance, sensitivity to cold, and susceptibility to infection.

This may be due to lack of iodine in the diet or a defect of the thyroid gland, both being productive of ◊goitre; or to the pituitary gland providing insufficient stimulus to the thyroid gland. Treatment of thyroid deficiency is by the hormone thyroxine (either synthetic or from animal thyroid glands).

hypsometer (Greek *hypsos* "height") instrument for testing the accuracy of a thermometer at the boiling point of water. It was originally used for determining altitude by comparing changes in the boiling point with changes in atmospheric pressure.

The name is also used for any of several instruments for measuring the heights of trees by ◊triangulation.

hyrax small mammal, forming the order Hyracoidea, that lives among rocks, in deserts, and in forests in Africa, Arabia, and Syria. It is about the size of a rabbit, with a plump body, short legs, short ears, brownish fur, and long, curved front teeth.

There are four toes on the front limbs, and three on the hind, each of which has a tiny hoof. There are nine species. They are related to elephants.

hyssop aromatic herb *Hyssopus officinalis* of the mint family Labiatae, found in Asia, S Europe, and around the Mediterranean. It has blue flowers, oblong leaves, and stems that are woody near the ground but herbaceous above.

hysterectomy surgical removal of all or part of the uterus (womb).

hysteresis phenomenon seen in the elastic and electromagnetic behavior of materials, in which a lag occurs between the application or removal of a force or field and its effect.

If the magnetic field applied to a magnetic material is increased and then decreased back to its original value, the magnetic field inside the material does not return to its original value. The internal field "lags" behind the external field. This behavior results in a loss of energy, called the hysteresis loss, when a sample is repeatedly magnetized and demagnetized. Hence the materials used in transformer cores and electromagnets should have a low hysteresis loss.

Similar behavior is seen in some materials when varying electric fields are applied (electric hysteresis). Elastic hysteresis occurs when a varying force repeatedly deforms an elastic material. The deformation produced does not completely disappear when the force is removed, and this results in energy loss on repeated deformations.

hysteria according to the work of ◊Freud, the conversion of a psychological conflict or anxiety feeling into a physical symptom, such as paralysis, blindness, recurrent cough, vomiting, and general malaise. The term is little used today in diagnosis.

Hz in physics, the symbol for ◊hertz.

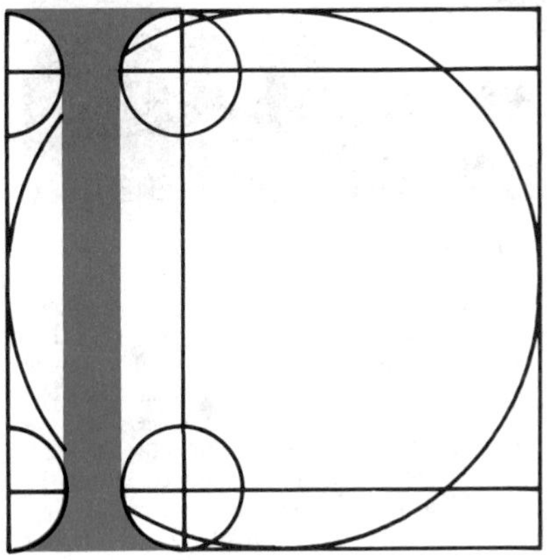

IA abbreviation for ◊Iowa.

Iaşi (German *Jassy*) city in NE Romania, capital of Moldavia; population (1985) 314,000. It has chemical, machinery, electronic, and textile industries.

iatrogenic caused by medical treatment; the term "iatrogenic disease" may be applied to any pathological condition or complication that is caused by the treatment, the facility, or the staff.

Ibadan city in SW Nigeria and capital of Oyo state; population (1981) 2,100,000. Industries include chemicals, electronics, plastics, and vehicles.

Ibague capital of Tolima department, W central Colombia; population (1985) 293,000.

Iban recent replacement term for ◊Dyak.

Ibáñez Vincente Blasco 1867–1928. Spanish novelist and politician, born in Valencia. He was actively involved in revolutionary politics. His novels include *La barraca/The Cabin* 1898, the best of his regional works; *Sangre y arena/Blood and Sand* 1908, the story of a famous bullfighter; and *Los cuatro jinetes del Apocalipsis/The Four Horsemen of the Apocalypse* 1916, a product of the effects of World War I.

Ibarruri Dolores, known as *La Pasionaria* ("the passion flower") 1895–1989. Spanish Basque politician, journalist, and orator; she was first elected to the *Cortes* in 1936. She helped to establish the Popular Front government and was a Loyalist leader in the Civil War. When Franco came to power in 1939 she left Spain for the USSR, where she was active in the Communist Party. She returned to Spain in 1977 after Franco's death and was reelected to the *Cortes* (at the age of 81) in the first parliamentary elections for 40 years.

She joined the Spanish Socialist Party in 1917 and wrote for a workers' newspaper under the pen name *La Pasionaria*.

ibis

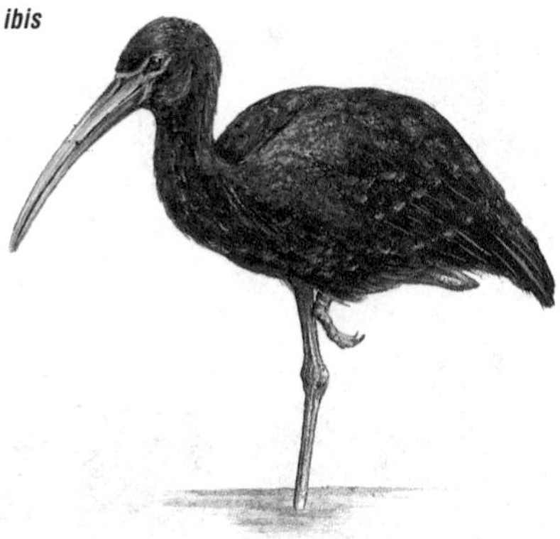

Iberia name given by ancient Greek navigators to the Spanish peninsula, derived from the river Iberus (Ebro). Anthropologists have given the name "Iberian" to a Neolithic people, traces of whom are found in the Spanish peninsula, southern France, the Canary Isles, Corsica, and part of North Africa.

Iberville Pierre Le Moyne, Sieur d' 1661–1706. French colonial administrator and explorer. Born in Montreal, Iberville joined the French navy and saw action against the English in the struggle for Canada 1686–97. After the conclusion of war, he and his brother, the Sieur de Bienville, led an expedition from France to establish a colony at the mouth of the Mississippi River. In 1699–1700 they explored the river and established settlements at the later sites of Biloxi and New Orleans. Iberville ended his military career as commander of French naval forces in the Caribbean.

ibex any of various wild goats found in mountainous areas of Europe, NE Africa, and Central Asia. They grow to 3.5 ft/100 cm, and have brown or gray coats and heavy horns. They are herbivorous and live in small groups.

ibid. abbreviation for ibidem (Latin "in the same place"); used in reference citation.

ibis any of various wading birds, about 2 ft/60 cm tall, in the same family, Threskiornidae, as spoonbills. Ibises have long legs and necks, and long, curved beaks. Various species occur in the warmer regions of the world.

The glossy ibis *Plegadis falcinellus* occurs in the SE US and on all continents except South America. The sacred ibis *Threskiornis aethiopica* of ancient Egypt is still found in the Nile basin. The Japanese ibis is in danger of extinction because of loss of its habitat; fewer than 25 birds remain.

Ibiza one of the ◊Balearic Islands, a popular tourist resort; area 230 sq mi/596 sq km; population (1986) 45,000. The capital and port, also called Ibiza, has a cathedral.

Iblis the Muslim name for the ◊devil.

IBM (abbreviation of International Business Machines) a multinational company, the largest manufacturer of computers. The company is a descendant of the Tabulating Machine Company, formed 1896 by Herman ◊Hollerith to exploit his punched-card machines. It adopted its present name in 1924. By 1988 it had an annual turnover of $60 billion and employed about 387,000 people.

Ibn Battuta 1304–1368. Arab traveler born in Tangiers. In 1325, he went on an extraordinary 75,000 mi/120,675 km journey via Mecca to Egypt, E Africa, India, and China, returning some 30 years later. During this journey he also visited Spain and crossed the Sahara to Timbuktu. The narrative of his travels, *The Adventures of Ibn Battuta*, was written with an assistant, Ibn Juzayy.

Ibn Saud 1880–1953. First king of Saudi Arabia from 1932. His father was the son of the sultan of Nejd, at whose capital, Riyadh, Ibn Saud was born. In 1891 a rival group seized Riyadh, and Ibn Saud went into exile with his father, who resigned his claim to the throne in his son's favor. In 1902 Ibn Saud recaptured Riyadh and recovered the kingdom, and by 1921 he had brought all central Arabia under his rule. In 1924 he invaded the Hejaz, of which he was proclaimed king in 1926.

Nejd and the Hejaz were united in 1932 in the kingdom of Saudi Arabia. Ibn Saud introduced programs for modernization with revenue from oil, which was discovered in 1936.

Ibn Sina Arabic name of ◊Avicenna, scholar and translator.

Ibo or ***Ebo*** member of the W African Ibo culture group occupying SE Nigeria. Primarily cultivators, they inhabit the richly forested tableland, bound by the river Niger to the west and the river Cross to the east. They are divided into five main divisions, and their languages belong to the Kwa branch of the Niger-Congo family.

Ibrahim Abdullah 1934–1990. South African pianist and composer, formerly known as "Dollar" Brand. He first performed in the US in 1965 and has had a great influence on the fusion of African rhythms with American jazz. His compositions range from songs to large works for orchestra.

Ibsen Henrik (Johan) 1828–1906. Norwegian playwright and poet, whose realistic and often controversial plays revolutionized European theater. Driven into exile 1864–91 by opposition to the satirical *Love's Comedy* 1862, he wrote the verse dramas *Brand* 1866 and *Peer Gynt* 1867, followed by realistic plays dealing with social issues, including *Pillars of Society* 1877, *The Doll's House* 1879, ◊*Ghosts* 1881, *An Enemy of the People* 1882, and ◊*Hedda Gabler* 1891. By the time of his return to Norway, he was recognized as the country's greatest living writer.

His later plays, which are more symbolic, include *The Master Builder* 1892, *Little Eyolf* 1894, *John Gabriel Borkman* 1896, and *When We Dead Awaken* 1899.

Icarus in Greek mythology, the son of ◊Daedalus, who with his father escaped from the labyrinth in Crete by making wings of feathers fastened with wax. Icarus plunged to his death when he flew too near the Sun and the wax melted.

Icarus in astronomy, an ◊Apollo asteroid 1 mi/1.5 km in diameter, discovered 1949. It orbits the Sun every 409 days at a distance of 18 million–186 million mi/28 million–300 million km (0.19–2.0 astronomical units). It is the only asteroid known to approach the Sun closer than does the planet Mercury. In 1968 it passed 4 million mi/6 million km from the Earth.

ICBM abbreviation for intercontinental ballistic missile; see ◊nuclear warfare.

ice solid formed by water when it freezes. It is colorless and its crystals are hexagonal. The water molecules are held together by ◊hydrogen bonds.

The freezing point, used as a standard for mea-

Ibsen *Norwegian dramatist Henrik Ibsen.*

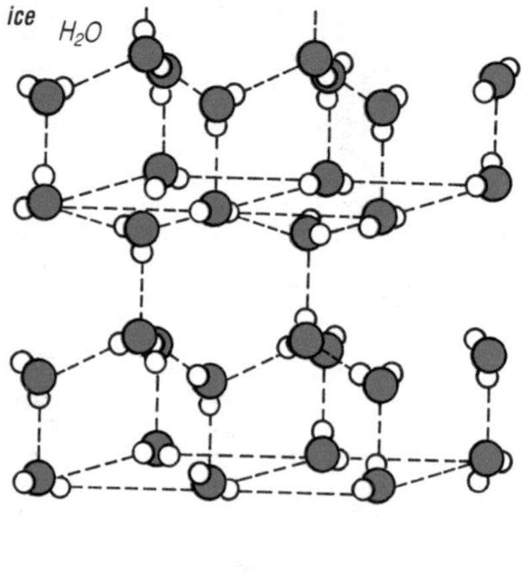
ice
H_2O

ice The crystal structrure of ice in which water molecules are held together by hydrogen bonds.

iceberg Icebergs aground in the Biscoe Islands, Antarctic Peninsula.

suring temperature, is 0° for the Celsius and Réaumur scales and 32° for the Fahrenheit. Ice expands in the act of freezing (hence burst pipes), becoming less dense than water (0.9175 at 41°F/5°C).

ice form of methamphetamine that is smoked to give a high; in illegal use in the US from 1989. Its effect may be followed by a period of depression and psychosis.

Ice Age any period of glaciation occurring in the Earth's history, but particularly that in the Pleistocene epoch, immediately preceding historic times. On the North American continent, ◊glaciers reached as far south as the Great Lakes, and an ice sheet spread over N Europe, leaving its remains as far south as Switzerland. There were several glacial advances separated by interglacial stages during which the ice melted and temperatures were higher than today.

Formerly there were thought to have been only three or four glacial advances, but recent research has shown about 20 major incidences. For example, ocean-bed cores record the absence or presence in their various layers of such coldloving small marine animals as radiolaria, which indicate a fall in ocean temperature at regular intervals. Other ice ages have occurred throughout geologic time: there were three in the Precambrian era, one in the Ordovician, and one at the end of the the Carboniferous and beginning of the Permian. The occurrence of an ice age is governed by a combination of factors (the Milankovitch hypothesis): (1) the Earth's change of attitude in relation to the Sun, that is, the way it tilts in a 41,000-year cycle and at the same time wobbles on its axis in a 22,000-year cycle, making the time of its closest approach to the Sun come at different seasons; and (2) the 92,000-year cycle of eccentricity in its orbit round the Sun, changing it from an elliptical to a near circular orbit, the severest period of an ice age coinciding with the approach to circularity. There is a possibility that the ice age is not yet over. It may reach another maximum in another 60,000 years.

Major Ice Ages

Name (European/US)	*date (years ago)*
Pleistocene:	
Riss and Wurm/Wisconsin	80,000–10,000
Mindel/Illinoian	550,000–400,000
Gunz/Kansan	900,000–700,000
Danube/Nebraskan	1.7–1.3 million
Permo-Carboniferous	330–250 million
Ordovician	440–430 million
Vérangian	615–570 million
Sturtian	820–770 million
Gnejso	940–880 million
Huronian	2,700–1,800 million

Ice Age, Little period of particularly severe winters that gripped N Europe between the 13th and 17th centuries. Contemporary writings and paintings show that Alpine glaciers were much more extensive than at present, and rivers such as the Thames, which do not ice over today, were so frozen that festivals could be held on them.

iceberg a floating mass of ice, about 80% of which is submerged, rising sometimes to 300 ft/100 m above sea level. Glaciers that reach the coast become extended into a broad foot; as this enters the sea, masses break off and drift toward temperate latitudes, becoming a danger to shipping.

ice cream a rich, creamy, frozen confection, made commercially from the early 20th century from various milk products, sugar, fruits and nuts, usually with additives to improve keeping qualities and ease of serving. Sherbet is also a frozen confection of watered fruit juice, egg white, and sugar, like an ice, but with gelatin and milk added.

ice hockey a game played on ice between two teams of six, developed in Canada from field hockey or bandy. Players, who wear skates and protective clothing, use a curved stick to advance the puck (a rubber disk) and shoot it at the opponents' goal, a netted cage, guarded by the goalie. The other positions are the left and right defensemen and the left wing, center, and right wing. The latter three are offensive players. The team with the most goals scored at the end of the three 20-minute periods wins; an overtime period may be played if a game ends in a tie.

ice hockey

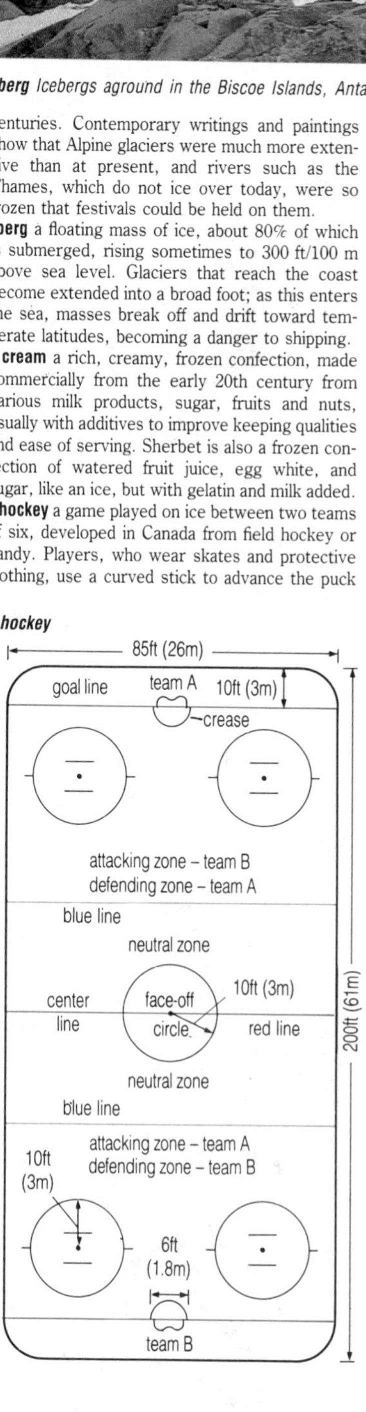
85ft (26m)
goal line
team A
10ft (3m)
crease
attacking zone – team B
defending zone – team A
blue line
neutral zone
10ft (3m)
center line
face-off circle
red line
200ft (61m)
neutral zone
blue line
attacking zone – team A
defending zone – team B
10ft (3m)
6ft (1.8m)
team B

The standard hockey rink is 200 ft/61 m long and 85 ft/26 m wide, with rounded corners and enclosed by a board wall 4 ft/1.3 m high. The goals are centered on a red line that crosses the rink 10 ft/3 m from each end of the rink. In front of each goal is a rectangular area called the crease, in which the goalie can operate freely, since other players cannot score from that area.

Each period in a game starts with a face-off at the center of the rink (in a face-off the referee drops the puck to the ice, and a player from each team tries with his stick to gain control of the puck). Other players must be at least 10 ft away from the two facing off. Face-offs at center ice (as after a goal) and at other designated spots on the ice are used to restart the game at various times during play.

During a game, substitutions are made frequently, except for the goalie. Substitutions are usually done in groups, such as all three offensive players (the "front line") or both defensemen. Serious rules infractions result in removal from the game to the penalty box for varying amounts of time (usually 2 or 5 min) or, in extreme cases, expulsion from the game.

history ice hockey is believed to have been first introduced in Canada in the 1850s, the first game being played in Kingston, Ontario. The first rules were drawn up at McGill University, Montreal. The governing body is the International Ice Hockey Federation (IIHF) founded 1908.

Canada's first hockey league, the Amateur Hockey Association, was formed 1885. In 1893, Lord Stanley, Canada's governor-general, gave a cup to be awarded to Canada's champion amateur team. By 1912, there were various professional

Recent Stanley Cup Winners

1980	New York Islanders
1981	New York Islanders
1982	New York Islanders
1983	New York Islanders
1984	Edmonton Oilers
1985	Edmonton Oilers
1986	Montreal Canadiens
1987	Edmonton Oilers
1988	Edmonton Oilers
1989	Calgary Flames
1990	Edmonton Oilers
1991	Pittsburgh Penguins

Iceland
Republic of
(Lýðveldið Ísland)

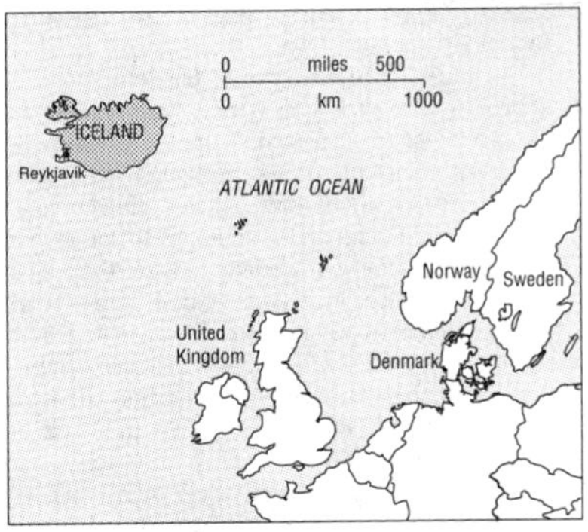

0 miles 500
0 km 1000
ICELAND
Reykjavik
ATLANTIC OCEAN
Norway
Sweden
United Kingdom
Denmark

area 39,758 sq mi/103,000 sq km
capital Reykjavik
cities Akureyri, Akranes
physical warmed by the Gulf Stream; glaciers and lava fields cover 75% of the country; active volcanoes (Hekla was once thought the gateway to Hell), geysers, hot springs, and new islands created offshore (Surtsey in 1963); subterranean hot water heats Iceland's homes
features the most westerly European country; Thingvelir, where the oldest parliament in the world first met AD 930
head of state Vigdís Finnbogadóttir from 1980
head of government David Oddsson from 1991
political system democratic republic
political parties Independence Party (IP), right-of-center; Progressive Party (PP), radical Socialist; People's Alliance (PA), Socialist; Social Democratic Party (SDP), moderate, left-of-center; Citizen's Party, centrist; Women's Alliance, women and family orientated
exports cod and other fish products, aluminum, diatomite
currency krona
population (1990 est) 251,000; growth rate 0.8% p.a.
life expectancy men 74, women 80
language Icelandic, the most archaic Scandinavian language, in which some of the finest sagas were written
religion Evangelical Lutheran 95%
literacy 99.9% (1984)
GDP $3.9 bn (1986); $16,200 per head
chronology
1944 Independence achieved from Denmark.
1949 Joined NATO and Council of Europe.
1953 Joined Nordic Council.
1976 "Cod War" with UK.
1979 Iceland announced 200-mile exclusive fishing zone.
1983 Steingrímur Hermannsson appointed to lead a coalition government.
1985 Iceland declared itself nuclear-free zone.
1987 New coalition government formed by Thorsteinn Palsson after general election.
1988 Vigdís Finnbogadóttir reelected president for a third term; Hermannsson led new coalition.
1991 David Oddsson led new IP–SDP (Independence Party and Social Democratic Party) center-right coalition, becoming prime minister in the general election.

leagues, and a playoff for the championship was inaugurated. The winner was awarded the Stanley Cup, which has since been the symbol of professional hockey's championship. The National Hockey League (NHL), founded 1917, became the dominant professional league and now consists of two conferences, each with two divisions.

Hockey has been played in the winter Olympic Games since 1920 and enjoys wide popularity in northern and central Europe, as well as in North America, where children play on frozen surfaces for fun all winter. A world championship is held each year except during the Olympiad. Top European and North American teams play each other frequently in exhibition games.

Içel another name for ◊Mersin, a city in Turkey.

Iceland island in the N Atlantic, situated S of the Arctic Circle, between Greenland and Norway.
government The 1944 constitution provides for a president, as head of state, and a legislature, the 63-member ◊*Althing*, both elected by universal suffrage for a four-year term. Voting is by a system of proportional representation that ensures, as nearly as possible, equality between the proportions of the votes cast and seats won.

Once elected, the *Althing* divides into an upper house of 21 members and a lower house of 42. The upper-house members are chosen by the *Althing* itself, and the remainder of 42 automatically constitutes the lower house. Members may speak in either house but vote only in the one for which they have been chosen. Legislation must pass through three stages in each house before being submitted to the president for ratification. On some occasions the *Althing* sits as a single house. The president appoints the prime minister and cabinet on the basis of parliamentary support, and they are collectively responsible to the *Althing*.

The main political parties are the Independence Party, the Progressive Party, the People's Alliance, the Social Democratic Party, the Social Democratic Alliance, and the Women's Alliance.
history Iceland was first occupied in 874 by Norse settlers, who founded a republic and a parliament in 930. In 1000 the inhabitants adopted Christianity and about 1263 submitted to the authority of the king of Norway. In 1380 Norway, and with it Iceland, came under Danish rule.

Iceland remained attached to Denmark after Norway became independent in 1814. From 1918 it was independent but still recognized the Danish monarch. During World War II Iceland was occupied by British and US forces and voted in a referendum for complete independence in 1944.

In 1949 it joined ◊NATO and the ◊Council of Europe, and in 1953 the Nordic Council. Since independence it has been governed by coalitions of the leading parties, sometimes right- and sometimes left-wing groupings, but mostly moderate.

The center and right-of-center parties are the Independents and Social Democrats, while those to the left are the Progressives and the People's Alliance. More recent additions have been the Social Democratic Alliance and the Women's Alliance.

Most of Iceland's external problems have been connected with the overfishing of the waters around its coasts, while domestically governments have been faced with the recurring problem of inflation. The administration formed in 1983 is a coalition of Progressives and Independents, representing a fairly solid, centrist grouping. In 1985 the *Althing* unanimously declared the country a nuclear-free zone, banning the entry of all nuclear weapons.

The 1987 elections ended control of the *Althing* by the Independence and Progressive parties, giving more influence to the minor parties, including the Women's Alliance, which doubled its seat tally. In June 1988 Vigdis Finnbogadóttir was re-elected president for a third four-year term with 92.7 percent of the vote. Steingrimur Hermannsson became prime minister.

Icelandic language member of the N Germanic branch of the Indo-European language family, spoken only in Iceland and the most conservative in form of the Scandinavian languages. Despite seven centuries of Danish rule, lasting until 1918, Icelandic has remained virtually unchanged since the 12th century.

Since independence in 1918, Icelandic has experienced a revival, as well as governmental protection against such outside linguistic influences as English-language broadcasting. Early Icelandic literature is largely anonymous and seems to have originated in Norse colonies in the British Isles (around 9th–10th centuries). The two Eddas and several Sagas date from this period. Halldor ◊Laxness, writing about Icelandic life in the style of the Sagas, was awarded a Nobel Prize in 1955.

Iceland spar a form of ◊calcite, $CaCO_3$, originally found in Iceland. In its pure form Iceland spar is transparent and exhibits the peculiar phenomenon of producing two images of anything seen through it. It is used in optical instruments. The crystals cleave into perfect rhombohedra.

Iceni ancient people of E England, who revolted against occupying Romans under ◊Boudicca.

ice-skating see ◊skating

Ichang alternate form of ◊Yichang, a port in China.

I Ching or ***Book of Changes*** an ancient Chinese book of divination based on 64 hexagrams, or patterns of six lines. The lines may be "broken" or "whole" (yin or yang) and are generated by tossing yarrow stalks or coins. The inquirer formulates a question before throwing, and the book gives interpretations of the meaning of the hexagrams.

The *I Ching* is thought to have originated in the 2nd millennium BC, with commentaries added by Confucius and later philosophers. It is proto-Taoist in that it is not used for determining the future but for making the inquirer aware of inherent possibilities and unconscious tendencies.

ichneumon fly any parasitic wasp of the family Ichneumonidae. There are several thousand species in Europe, North America, and other regions. They have slender bodies, and females have unusually long, curved ovipositors that can pierce several inches of wood. The eggs are laid in the eggs, larvae, or pupae of other insects, usually butterflies or moths.

Ickes Harold LeClair 1874–1952. US public official. A liberal Republican, he was appointed secretary of the interior by F D Roosevelt 1933. Ickes later held other senior posts in the Roosevelt administration, including director of the Public Works Administration (PWA), where he administered New Deal development projects.

Born in Blair County, Pennsylvania, and educated at the University of Chicago, Ickes was admitted to the bar 1907. After resigning from the Truman cabinet 1946, Ickes wrote a newspaper column and published several autobiographical works. *The Secret Diary of Harold L Ickes* appeared 1953.

icon in the Greek or Eastern Orthodox Church, a representation of Jesus, Mary, an angel, or a saint, in painting, low relief, or mosaic. The painted icons were traditionally done on wood. After the 17th century in Russia, a *riza*, or gold and silver covering which leaves only the face and hands visible (and may be adorned with jewels presented by the faithful in thanksgiving), was often added as protection.

Icons were regarded as holy objects, based on the doctrine that God became visible through Christ. Icon painting originated in the Byzantine Empire, but many examples were destroyed by the ◊iconoclasts in the 8th and 9th centuries. The Byzantine style of painting predominated in the Mediterranean region and in Russia until the 12th century, when Russian, Greek, and other schools developed. Andrei Rublev (c. 1365–1430) was a renowned Russian icon painter.

icon in computing, a small picture on the VDT representing an object or function that the user may manipulate or otherwise use. Icons make computers easier to use by allowing the user to point with a ◊mouse to pictures, rather than type commands.

Idaho

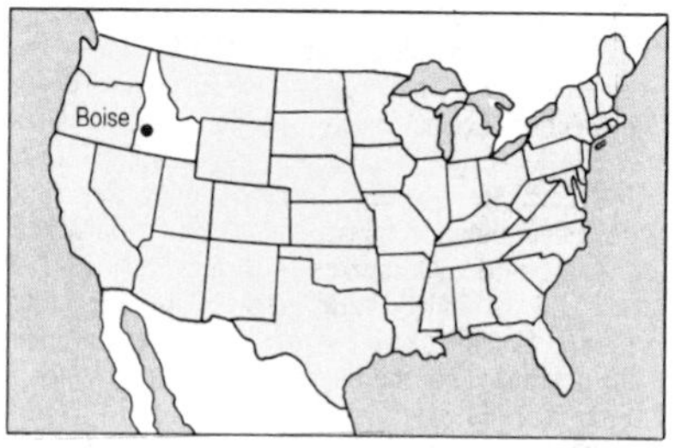
Boise

Iconium city of ancient Turkey; see ◊Konya.

iconoclast (Greek "image-breaker") literally, a person who attacks religious images, originally in obedience to the injunction of the Second Commandment not to worship "graven images." Under the influence of Islam and Judaism, an iconoclastic movement calling for the destruction of religious images developed in the Byzantine empire, and was endorsed by the Emperor Leo III in 726. Fierce persecution of those who made and venerated icons followed, until iconoclasm was declared a heresy in the 9th century.

The same name was applied to those opposing the use of images at the Reformation, when there was much destruction in churches. Figuratively, the term is used for a person who attacks established ideals or principles.

iconography in art history, significance attached to symbols that can help to identify subject matter (for example, a saint holding keys usually represents St Peter) and place a work of art in its historical context.

ICU abbreviation for ◊intensive care unit.

id in Freudian psychology, the instinctual element of the human mind, concerned with pleasure, which demands immediate satisfaction. It is regarded as the ◊unconscious element of the human psyche, and is said to be in conflict with the ◊ego and the ◊superego.

id. abbreviation for idem (Latin "the same"); used in reference citation.

ID abbreviation for ◊Idaho.

Idaho state of NW US; nickname Gem State
area 83,569 sq mi/216,500 sq km
capital Boise
cities Pocatello, Idaho Falls
features Rocky Mountains; Snake River, which runs through Hell's Canyon (7,647 ft/2,330 m), the deepest in North America, and has the National Reactor Testing Station on the plains of its upper reaches; Sun Valley ski and summer resort; Craters of the Moon National Monument; Nez Perce National Historic Park
products potatoes, wheat, livestock, timber, silver, lead, zinc, antimony
population (1990) 1,006,749
history part of the Louisiana Purchase 1803; explored by Lewis and Clark 1805–06; first permanently settled by Mormons 1860, the same year gold was discovered. Settlement in the 1870s led to a series of battles between US forces and Indian tribes. Idaho became a state in 1890. The timber industry began 1906, and by World War I agriculture was a leading enterprise.

idealism in philosophy, the theory that states that the external world is fundamentally immaterial and a dimension of the mind.

Objects in the world exist but, according to this theory, they lack substance.

identikit a set of drawings of different parts of the face used to compose a likeness of a person for identification. It was evolved by Hugh C McDonald (1913–) in the US. It has largely been replaced by ◊photofit, based on photographs, which produces a more realistic likeness.

ideology a set of ideas, beliefs, and opinions about the nature of people and society, providing a framework for a theory about how people should live, as well as how society is or should be organized.

Ides in the Roman calendar, the 15th day of March, May, July, and Oct, and the 13th day of all other months (the word originally indicated the full moon); Julius Caesar was assassinated on the Ides of March 44 BC.

Idi Amin Dada, Lake former name (1973–79) of Lake ◊Edward in Uganda/Zaïre.

i.e. abbreviation for id est (Latin "that is").

If small French island in the Mediterranean about 2 mi/3 km off Marseille, with a castle, Château d'If, built about 1529. This was used as a state prison and is the scene of the imprisonment of Dante in Dumas's *Count of Monte Cristo*.

Ifni a former Spanish overseas province in SW Morocco 1860–1969; area 740 sq mi/1,920 sq km. The chief town is Sidi Ifni.

Ifugao member of an indigenous people of N Luzon in the Philippines, numbering approximately 70,000. Their language belongs to the Austronesian family.

The Ifugao live in scattered hamlets and, traditionally, recognize a class of nobles, *kadangya*, who are obliged to provide expensive feasts on particular social occasions. Although indigenous beliefs remain important, many Ifugao have adopted Christianity. In addition to practicing shifting cultivation on highland slopes, they build elaborate terraced rice fields. Some Ifugao work as wage laborers outside their highland region.

Iglesias Pablo 1850–1925. Spanish politician, founder of the Spanish Socialist Party (Partido Socialista Obrero España, PSOE) in 1879. In 1911 he became the first Socialist deputy to be elected to the *Cortes* (Spanish parliament).

Ignatius Loyola, St 1491–1556. Spanish noble who founded the ◊Jesuit order 1540, also called the Society of Jesus.

His deep interest in the religious life began in 1521, when reading the life of Jesus while recuperating from a war wound. He visited the Holy Land in 1523, studied in Spain and Paris, where he took vows with St Francis Xavier, and was ordained in 1537. He then moved to Rome and with the approval of Pope Paul III began the Society of Jesus, sending missionaries to Brazil, India, and Japan, and founding Jesuit schools. Feast day July 31.

Ignatius of Antioch, St 1st–2nd century AD. Christian martyr. Traditionally a disciple of St John, he was bishop of Antioch, and was thrown to the wild beasts in Rome. He wrote seven epistles, important documents of the early Christian church. Feast day Feb 1.

igneous rock a rock formed from cooling magma or lava, and solidifying from a molten state. Igneous rocks are classified according to their crystal size, texture, chemical composition, or method of formation. They are largely composed of silica (SiO_2) and their silica content determines three main groups: acid (over 66% silica), intermediate (45–55%), and basic (45–55%). Igneous rocks that crystallize below the Earth's surface are called plutonic or intrusive, depending on the depth of formation. They have large crystals produced by slow cooling; examples include diabase and granite. Those extruded at the surface are called extrusive or volcanic. Rapid cooling results in small crystals; basalt is an example.

ignition coil ◊transformer that is an essential part of a gasoline engine's ignition system. It consists of two wire coils wound around an iron core. The primary coil, which is connected to the car battery, has only a few turns. The secondary coil, connected via the ◊distributor to the ◊spark plugs, has many turns. The coil takes in a low voltage (usually 12 volts) from the battery and transforms it to a high voltage (about 20,000 volts) to ignite the engine.

When the engine is running, the battery current is periodically interrupted by means of the contact breaker in the distributor. The collapsing current in the primary coil induces a current in the secondary coil, a phenomenon known as ◊electromagnetic induction. The induced current in the secondary coil is at very high voltage, typically about 15,000–20,000 volts. This passes to the spark plugs to create sparks.

ignition temperature or ***fire point*** the minimum temperature to which a substance must be heated before it will spontaneously burn independently of the source of heat; for example, ethanol has an ignition temperature of 425°C, and a ◊flash point of 12°C.

Iguaçu Falls (or Iguassú Falls) waterfall in South America, on the border between Brazil and Argentina. The falls lie 12 mi/19 km above the junction of the river Iguaç with the Paraná. The falls are divided by forested rocky islands and

ignition coil

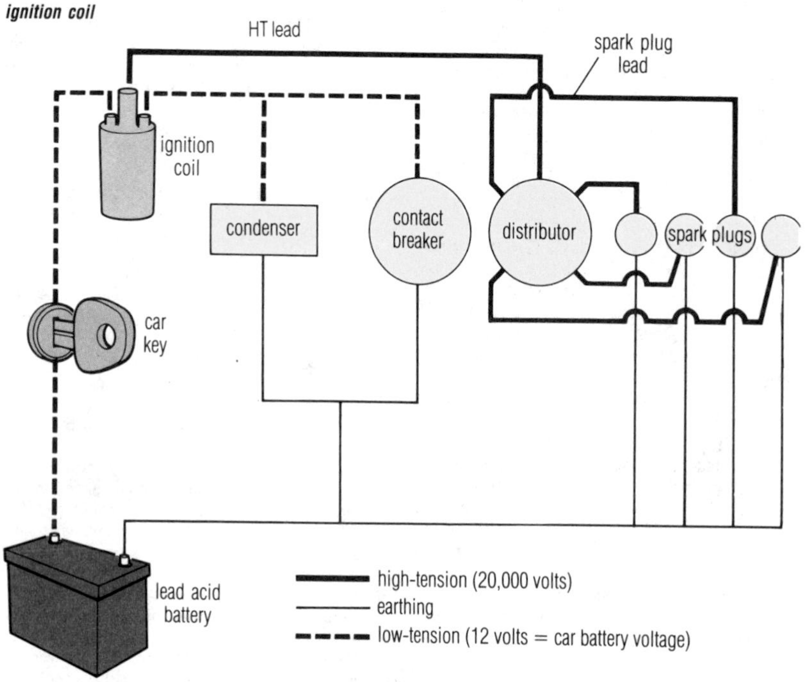
HT lead
spark plug lead
ignition coil
condenser
contact breaker
distributor
spark plugs
car key
lead acid battery
high-tension (20,000 volts)
earthing
low-tension (12 volts = car battery voltage)

Iguaçu Falls *On the Argentina-Brazil border, the horseshoe-shaped Iguacu Falls have 275 separate waterfalls.*

form a spectacular tourist attraction. The water plunges in 275 falls, many of which have separate names. They have a height of 269 ft/82 m and a width about 2.5 mi/4 km.

iguana any lizard, especially the genus *Iguana*, of the family Iguanidae, which includes about 700 species and is chiefly confined to the Americas. The common iguana *I. iguana* of Central and South America is a vegetarian and may reach 6 ft/2 m in length.

iguanodon plant-eating ◊dinosaur of the order *Ornithiscia*, whose remains are found in deposits of the Lower Cretaceous age, together with the remains of other ornithiscians such as stegosaurs and triceratops. It varied in length from 16–32 ft/5–10 m, and when standing upright was 13 ft/4 m tall. It walked on its hind legs, using its long tail to balance its body.

IJsselmeer lake in the Netherlands, formed 1932 after the Zuider Zee was cut off by a dyke from the North Sea; freshwater since 1944. Area 470 sq mi/1,217 sq km.

ikat Indonesian term for a textile that is produced by resist-printing the warp or weft before ◊weaving.

IKBS (abbreviation of intelligent knowledge-based system) in computing, an alternate name for the more usual KBS, ◊knowledge-based system.

ikebana the Japanese art of flower arrangement. It dates from the 6th–7th centuries when arrangements of flowers were placed as offerings in Buddhist temples, a practice learned from China. In the 15th century, ikebana became a favorite pastime of the nobility. Oldest of the Japanese ikebana schools is Ikenobo at Kyoto (7th century).

Ikhnaton or ***Akhenaton*** 14th century BC. King of Egypt of the 18th dynasty (c. 1379–1362 BC), who may have ruled jointly for a time with his father Amenhotep III. He developed the cult of the Sun, ◊Aton, rather than the rival cult of ◊Ammon. Some historians believe that his attention to religious reforms rather than imperial defense led to the loss of most of Egypt's possessions in Asia. His favorite wife was Nefertiti, and two of their six daughters were married to his successors Smenkhare and Tutankaton (later known as Tutankhamen).

iguana

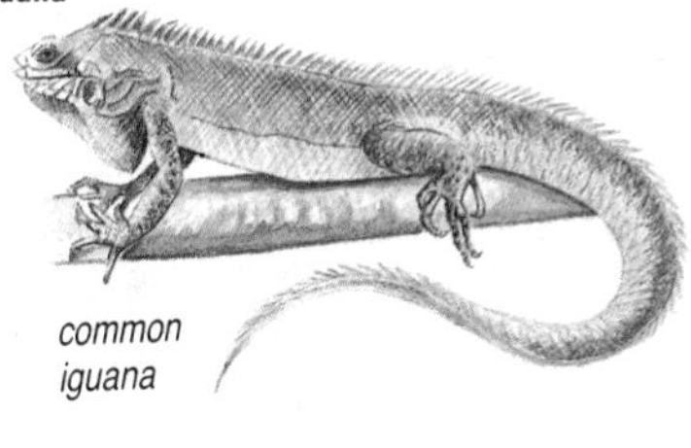
common
iguana

Illinois

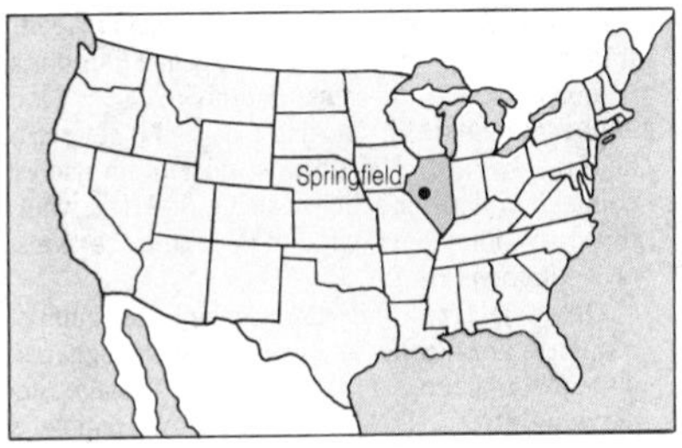
Springfield

IL abbreviation for ◊Illinois.

Île-de-France region of N France; its area is 4,632 sq mi/12,000 sq km; population (1986) 10,251,000. It includes the French capital, Paris, and the towns of Versailles, Sèvres, and St-Cloud and comprises the *départements* of Essonne, Val-de-Marne, Val d'Oise, Ville de Paris, Seine-et-Marne, Hauts-de-Seine, Seine-Saint-Denis, and Yvelines. From here the early French kings extended their authority over the whole country.

ileum part of the small intestine of the ◊digestive system, between the duodenum and the colon, that absorbs digested food. Its wall is muscular so that waves of contraction (peristalsis) can mix the food and push it forward. Numerous fingerlike projections, or villi, point inward from the wall, increasing the surface area available for absorption. The ileum has an excellent blood supply, which receives the food molecules passing through the wall and transports them to the liver via the hepatic portal vein.

Iliad Greek epic poem in 24 books, probably written before 700 BC, attributed to ◊Homer. Its title is derived from Ilion, the Greek name for Troy. Its subject is the wrath of Achilles, an incident in the 12th century BC during the tenth year of the Trojan War, when Achilles kills Hector to avenge the death of his friend Patroclus. The tragic battle scenes are described in graphic detail.

Ilium in Classical mythology, an alternate name for the city of ◊Troy, taken from its founder Ilus.

Ille French river 28 mi/45 km long, which rises in Lake Boulet and enters the Vilaine at Rennes. It gives its name to the *département* of Ille-et-Vilaine in Brittany.

illegitimacy in law, the status of a child born to a mother who is not legally married; a child may be legitimized by subsequent marriage of the parents. The nationality of the child is usually that of the mother or may depend on the place of birth.

Illegitimacy, depending on state laws, affects inheritance rights with respect to a father and may give rise to actions for judicial determination of paternity and subsequent economic responsibility toward the child.

Illich Ivan 1926– . US radical philosopher and activist, born in Austria. His works, which include *Deschooling Society* 1971, *Toward a History of Need* 1978, and *Gender* 1983, are a critique against contemporary economic development, especially in the Third World.

Illich was born in Vienna and has lived in the US and Latin America. He believes that modern technology and bureaucratic institutions are destroying peasant skills and self-sufficiency and creating a new form of dependency: on experts, professionals, and material goods. True liberation, he believes, can only be achieved by abolishing the institutions on which authority rests, such as schools and hospitals.

Illimani highest peak in the Bolivian Andes, rising to 21,004 ft/6,402 m E of La Paz.

Illinois midwest state of the US; nickname Land of Lincoln/Prairie State

area 56,395 sq mi/146,100 sq km

capital Springfield

cities Chicago, Rockford, Peoria, Decatur, Aurora

features Lake Michigan; rivers: Mississippi, Illinois, Ohio, Rock; Cahokia Mounds, the largest group of prehistoric earthworks in the US; the Lincoln Home National Historic Site, Springfield; Des Plaines, site of the first McDonald's restaurant (1955), a museum since 1985; the University of Chicago; Morman leader Joseph Smith's home, Nauvoo; the Art Institute and Field Museum, Chicago

products soybeans, cereals, meat and dairy products, machinery, electrical and electronic equipment

population (1990) 11,430,602

famous people Jane Addams, Saul Bellow, Mother Cabrini, Clarence Darrow, Enrico Fermi, Ernest Hemingway, Jesse Jackson, Edgar Lee Masters, Ronald Reagan, Louis Sullivan, Frank Lloyd Wright

history explored by Marquette and Joliet 1673; settled by the French in the 17th century; ceded to Britain by France 1763; passed to US control 1783; became a state 1818. Much settlement began 1825 following the opening of the Erie Canal. Spurred after the Civil War by the phenomenal growth of Chicago, Illinois became a major agricultural and industrial state, with heavy immigration. Labor unrest was reflected in the Haymarket Riot 1886 and Pullman strike 1894. The importance of heavy industry declined after 1950, but Chicago remained a major transport, trade, and finance center, and the state a leader in farm income; Illinois ranks first in agricultural exports and second in hog production. The enormous Fermi National Accelerator Laboratory is located at Batavia.

illumination the brightness or intensity of light falling on a surface. It depends upon the brightness, distance, and angle of any nearby light sources. The SI unit is the ◊lux.

Illyria ancient name for the eastern coastal region on the Adriatic, N of the Gulf of Corinth, conquered by Philip of Macedon. It became a Roman province AD 9. The Albanians are the survivors of its ancient peoples.

ilmenite an oxide of iron and titanium, iron titanate ($FeTiO_3$); an ore of titanium. The mineral is black, with a metallic luster. It is found in compact masses, grains, and sand.

Ilorin capital of Kwara state, Nigeria; population (1983) 344,000. It trades in tobacco and wood products.

imaginary number term often used to describe the nonreal element of a ◊complex number. For the complex number ($a + ib$), ib is the imaginary number where $i = \sqrt{-1}$, and b any real number.

Imagism a movement in Anglo-American poetry that flourished 1912–14 and affected much US and British poetry and critical thinking thereafter. A central figure was Ezra Pound, who asserted the principles of free verse, hard imagery, and poetic impersonality.

Pound encouraged Hilda Doolittle to sign her verse H D Imagiste and in 1914 edited the *Des Imagistes* anthology. Poets subsequently influenced by this movement include T S Eliot, William Carlos Williams, Wallace Stevens, and Marianne Moore. Imagism established modernism in English-language verse.

imago the sexually mature stage of an ◊insect.

imam (Arabic) in a mosque, the leader of congregational prayer, but generally any notable Islamic leader.

Imber Naphtali Herz 1856–1909. Itinerant Hebrew poet, born in Austria-Hungary. He travelled to Palestine and worked as secretary to the wife of British Gen Oilphant, then to England and the US. A Zionist and champion of restoring Hebrew as a modern spoken language, he wrote *Hatikvah/The Hope* 1878, which became the Zionist anthem 1897 until May 14, 1948, when it became the

Israeli national anthem. He wrote in Hebrew and Yiddish.

Imbros Turkish Imroz island in the Aegean; area 108 sq mi/280 sq km; population (1970) 6,786. Occupied by Greece in World War I, it became Turkish under the Treaty of ◊Lausanne 1923.

IMF abbreviation for ◊International Monetary Fund.

Imhotep c. 2800 BC. Egyptian physician and architect, adviser to King Zoser (3rd dynasty). He is thought to have designed the step pyramid at Sakkara, and his tomb (believed to be in the N Sakkara cemetery) became a center of healing. He was deified as the son of ◊Ptah and was identified with Aesculapius, the Greek god of medicine.

Immaculate Conception in the Roman Catholic Church, the belief that the Virgin Mary was, by a special act of grace, preserved free from ◊original sin from the moment she was conceived. This article of the Catholic faith was for centuries the subject of heated controversy, opposed by St Thomas Aquinas and other theologians, but generally accepted from about the 16th century. It became a dogma in 1854 under Pope Pius IX.

immigration and emigration the movement of people from one country to another. Immigration is movement to a country; emigration is movement from a country. Immigration or emigration on a large scale is often for economic reasons or because of religious, political or social persecution (which may create ◊refugees), and often prompts restrictive legislation by individual countries. The US has received immigrants on a larger scale than has any other country, more than 50 million during its history.

Immigration and Naturalization Service v Chadha a US Supreme Court decision 1983 dealing with the power of Congress to overrule decisions of the executive branch regarding immigration. Chadha, a foreign student allowed by the Immigration and Naturalization Service (INS) to remain in the country after the expiration of his visa, was deported by the House of Representatives. By the Immigration and Nationality Act, this veto of an INS ruling was within the power of either house of Congress, but Chadha appealed, challenging the constitutionality of the act. The Court ruled to invalidate the provision of the act that allowed a single house to veto INS rulings, judging one-house vetoes to be unconstitutional under any circumstance.

immiscible term describing liquids that will not mix with each other, such as oil and water. When two immiscible liquids are shaken together, a turbid mixture will be produced. This normally forms separate layers on standing.

immunity the protection that organisms have against foreign microorganisms, such as bacteria and viruses, and against cancerous cells (see ◊cancer). Immunity has been studied mostly in higher vertebrates, especially rodents, domestic animals, and primates. The cells that provide immunity are called white blood cells, or leukocytes. They include neutrophils and ◊macrophages, which can engulf invading organisms and other unwanted material, and natural killer cells that destroy cells infected by viruses and cancerous cells. Some of the most important immune cells are the ◊B cells and ◊T cells. Immune cells coordinate their activities by means of chemical messengers or ◊lymphokines, including the antiviral messenger ◊interferon. The lymph nodes play a major role in organizing the immune response.

Immunity is also provided by a range of physical barriers such as the skin, tear fluid, acid in the stomach, and mucus in the airways. ◊AIDS is one of many viral diseases in which the immune system is affected.

immunization conferring immunity to infectious disease by artificial methods. The most widely used technique is ◊vaccination.

Vaccination against smallpox was developed by Edward ◊Jenner in 1796. In the late 19th century Louis ◊Pasteur developed vaccines against cholera, typhoid, typhus, plague, and yellow fever. Immunization is now available against diptheria, whooping cough, measles, and polio.

immunocompromised lacking a fully effective immune system. The term is most often used in connection with infections such as ◊AIDS where the virus interferes with the immune response (see ◊immunity).

Other factors that can impair the immune response are alcohol and drug abuse, pregnancy, diabetes, old age, malnutrition, liver damage, and extreme stress, making someone susceptible to infections by microorganisms (such as listeria) that do not affect normal, healthy people. Some people are immunodeficient, others could be on ◊immuno suppressive drugs.

immunodeficient lacking one or more elements of a working immune system. Immune deficiency is the term generally used for patients who are born with such a defect, while those who acquire such a deficiency later in life are referred to as ◊immunocompromised or immunosuppressed.

A serious impairment of the immune system is sometimes known as SCID, or Severe Combined Immune Deficiency. At one time such children would have died in infancy. They can now be kept alive in a germ-free environment, then treated with a bone-marrow transplant from a relative, to replace the missing immune cells. At present, the success rate for this type of treatment is still fairly low.

immunoglobulin human globulin ◊protein that can be separated from blood and administered to confer immediate immunity on the recipient. It participates in the immune reaction as the antibody for a specific ◊antigen (disease-causing agent).

Normal immunoglobulin (gamma globulin) is the fraction of the blood serum that, in general, contains the most antibodies, and is obtained from plasma pooled from 1,000 donors. It is given for short-term (two to three months) protection when a person is at risk, mainly from hepatitis A (infectious hepatitis), or when a pregnant woman, not immunized against ◊German measles, is exposed to the rubella virus.

Specific immunoglobulins are injected when a susceptible (nonimmunized) person is at risk of infection from a potentially fatal disease, such as hepatitis B (serum hepatitis), rabies, or tetanus. These immunoglobulins are prepared from blood pooled from donors convalescing from the disease.

immunosuppressive any drug that suppresses the body's normal immune responses to infection or foreign tissue. It is used in the treatment of autoimmune disease (see ◊autoimmunity); as part of chemotherapy for leukemias, lymphomas, and other cancers; and to help prevent rejection following organ transplant.

impala African antelope *Aepyceros melampus* found from Kenya to South Africa in savannas and open woodlands. The body is sandy brown. Males have lyre-shaped horns up to 2.5 ft/75 cm long. Impala grow up to 5 ft/1.5 m long and 3 ft/90 cm tall. They live in herds and spring high in the air when alarmed.

impeachment a judicial procedure by which government officials are accused of wrongdoing and brought to trial before a legislative body. In the US, the House of Representatives may impeach offenders to be tried before the Senate, as in the case of President Andrew Johnson 1868. Richard ◊Nixon resigned the US presidency 1974 following the threat of impeachment.

impedance the total opposition of a circuit to the passage of electric current. It has the symbol Z. For a direct current (DC) it is the total ◊resistance R of all the components in the circuit. For an ◊alternating current (AC) it also includes the reactance X (caused by ◊capacitance or ◊inductance); the impedance can then be found using the equation $Z^2 = R^2 + X^2$.

In acoustics, impedance refers to the ratio of the force per unit area to the volume displaced by the surface across which sound is being transmitted.

imperialism the policy of extending the power and rule of a government beyond its own boundaries. A country may attempt to dominate others by direct rule or by less obvious means such as control of markets for goods or raw materials. The latter is often called ◊neo-colonialism.

impetigo any of various skin diseases marked by the eruption of pustules, such as *Staphylococcus aureus*, a contagious bacterial infection of the skin that forms yellowish crusts; it is curable with antibiotics.

Imphal capital of Manipur state on the Manipur river, India; population (1981) 156,622; a communications and trade center (tobacco, sugar, fruit). It was besieged Mar–June 1944, when Japan invaded Assam, but held out with the help of supplies dropped by air.

implantation in mammals, the process by which the developing ◊embryo attaches itself to the wall of the mother's uterus and stimulates the development of the ◊placenta.

In some species, such as seals and bats, implantation is delayed for several months, during which time the embryo does not grow; thus the interval between mating and birth may be a year, although the ◊gestation period is only seven or eight months.

import product or service that one country purchases from another for domestic consumption, or for processing and re-exporting (Hong Kong, for example, is heavily dependent on imports for its export business). If an importing country does not have a counterbalancing value of exports, it may experience balance-of-payments difficulties and accordingly consider restricting imports by some form of protectionism (such as an import tariff or imposing import quotas).

Importance of Being Earnest, The a romantic stage comedy by Oscar Wilde, first performed 1895. The courtships of two couples are comically complicated by confusions of identity and by the overpowering Lady Bracknell.

impotence in medicine, a physical inability to perform sexual intercourse (the term is not usually applied to women). Impotent men fail to achieve an erection, and this may be due to illness, the effects of certain drugs, or psychological factors.

General fatigue, stress, or lack of interest may also cause impotence. Treatment for ongoing impotence includes counseling, behavioral therapy, and surgical implants.

Impressionism movement in painting that originated in France in the 1860s and dominated European and North American painting in the late 19th century. The Impressionists wanted to depict real life, to paint straight from nature, and to capture the changing effects of light. The term was first used abusively to describe Monet's painting *Impression, Sunrise* 1872 (Musée Marmottan, Paris); other Impressionists were Renoir and Sisley, soon joined by Cézanne, Manet, Degas, and others.

The starting point of Impressionism was the *Salon des Refusés*, an exhibition in 1873 of work rejected by the official Salon. This was followed by the Impressionists' own exhibitions 1874–86, where their work aroused fierce opposition. Their styles were diverse, but many experimented with effects of light and movement created with distinct brushstrokes and fragments of color juxtaposed on the canvas rather than mixed on the palette. By the 1880s, the movement's central impulse had dispersed, and a number of new styles emerged, later described as Post-Impressionism.

Impressionism in music, a style of composition emphasizing instrumental color and texture. The term was first applied to the music of ◊Debussy.

imprinting in ◊ethology, the process whereby a young animal learns to recognize both specific individuals (for example, its mother) and its own species.

Impressionism *Claude Monet's* Impression: Sunrise *(1872), Musée Marmottan, Paris. Exhibited at the first Impressionist exhibition, this was the work that inspired the movement's name. The term was originally meant to be derogatory.*

Imprinting is characteristically an automatic response to specific stimuli at a time when the animal is especially sensitive to those stimuli (the sensitive period). Thus, goslings learn to recognize their mother by following the first moving object they see after hatching; as a result, they can easily become imprinted on other species, or even inanimate objects, if these happen to move near them at this time. In chicks, imprinting occurs only between 10 and 20 hours after hatching. In mammals, the mother's attachment to her infant may be a form of imprinting made possible by a sensitive period; this period may be as short as the first hour after giving birth.

impromptu in music, a short instrumental piece that suggests spontaneity. Composers of piano impromptus include Schubert and Chopin.

Imroz Turkish form of ◊Imbros, an island in the Aegean.

In abbreviation for ◊inch, a measure of distance.

IN abbreviation for ◊Indiana.

inbreeding in ◊genetics, the mating of closely related individuals. It is considered undesirable because it increases the risk that an offspring will inherit copies of rare deleterious ◊recessive alleles (genes) from both parents and so suffer from disabilities.

Inc. abbreviation for Incorporated.

Inca a member of an ancient Peruvian civilization of Quechua-speaking Indians that began in the Andean highlands about 1200; by the time of the Spanish Conquest in the 1530s, the Inca ruled from Ecuador in the north to Chile in the south.

The Inca empire dominated the ◊Andes region militarily and assimilated many of the conquered peoples, transplanting them into new homelands nearest their capital, Cuzco, until they had been Inca-ized, then resettling them and transporting in the newly conquered to undergo the learning process. They had an agriculturally based theocracy, with priest-rulers at the top of the hierarchy, and with "the Inca," a descendant of the Sun, (and his sister-wife) ruling over all. Their extensive road system united the empire of both highland and coastal cities but made them vulnerable to the Spanish, who conquered and enslaved the people in mining and food-producing ventures. Today's Quechua-speaking Indians are descendants of the Inca civilization; many still live in the farming villages of the highlands of Peru.

Incan art art of the Inca people of the Peruvian Andes, South America, of the 11th–16th centuries. The main sites are Cuzco, the old capital, and ◊Machu Picchu, a fortified mountain settlement. Incan artisans produced technically brilliant, highly finished ceramics, metalwork, textiles, and excellent masonry, with large blocks of stone fitted together with great precision. Stylized animal and human figures are frequent subjects.

Inca

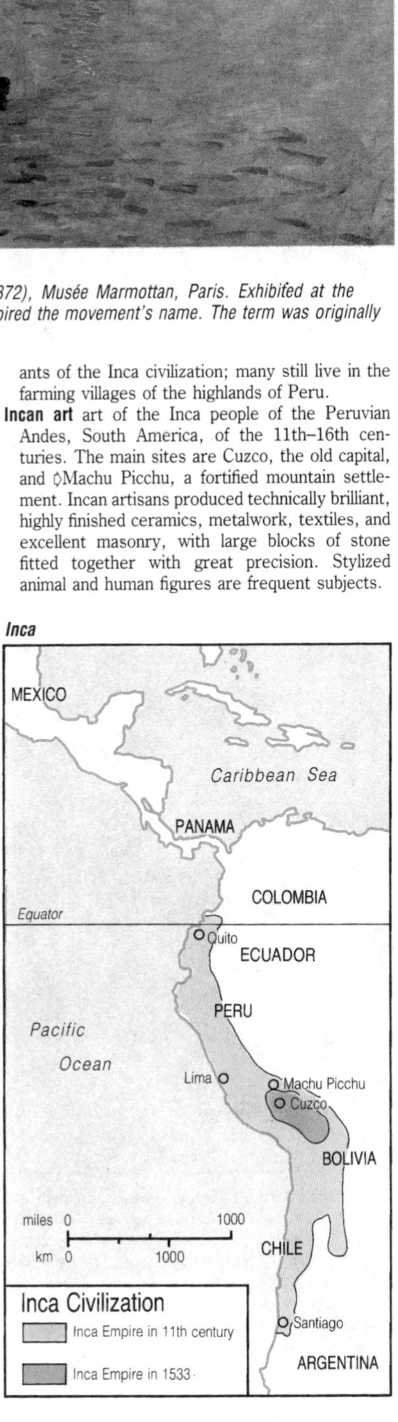
MEXICO
Caribbean Sea
PANAMA
COLOMBIA
Equator
Quito
ECUADOR
PERU
Pacific
Ocean
Lima
Machu Picchu
Cuzco
BOLIVIA
miles 0 1000
km 0 1000
CHILE
Inca Civilization
Inca Empire in 11th century
Inca Empire in 1533
Santiago
ARGENTINA

incandescence emission of light from a substance in consequence of its high temperature. The color of the emitted light from liquids or solids depends on their temperature, and for solids generally the higher the temperature the whiter the light. Gases may become incandescent through ◊ionizing radiation, as in the glowing vacuum ◊discharge tube.

The oxides of cerium and thorium are highly incandescent and for this reason are used in gas mantles. The light from an electric filament lamp is due to the incandescence of the filament, rendered white-hot when a current passes through it.

incarnation assumption of living form (plant, animal, human) by a deity, for example the gods of Greece and Rome, Hinduism, Christianity (Jesus as the second person of the Trinity).

incendiary bomb a bomb containing inflammable matter. Usually dropped by aircraft, incendiary bombs were used in World War I, and were a major weapon in attacks on cities in World War II. To hinder firefighters, delayed-action high-explosive bombs were usually dropped with them. In the Vietnam War, the US used ◊napalm in incendiary bombs.

incest sexual intercourse between persons thought to be too closely related to marry; the exact relationships that fall under the incest taboo vary widely from society to society. A biological explanation for the incest taboo is based on the necessity to avoid ◊inbreeding.

Within groups in which ritual homosexuality is practiced, for example in New Guinea, an incest taboo applies also to these relations, suggesting that the taboo is as much social as biological in origin.

inch imperial unit of linear measure, a twelfth of a foot, equal to 2.54 centimeters.

It was defined in statute by England's Edward II as the length of three barley grains laid end to end.

Inchon formerly Chemulpo chief port of Seoul, South Korea; population (1985) 1,387,000. It produces steel and textiles.

incisor sharp tooth at the front of the mammalian mouth. Incisors are used for biting or nibbling, as when a rabbit or a sheep eats grass. Rodents, such as rats and squirrels, have large continually-growing incisors, adapted for gnawing. The elephant tusk is a greatly enlarged incisor.

incomes policy see ◊wage and price controls.

Income tax a direct tax levied on corporate profits and on personal income, mainly wages and salaries, but which may include dividends, interests, rents, royalties, and the value of receipts other than in cash. It is one of the main instruments for achieving a government's income redistribution objectives.

In the US, every citizen or resident (with certain exemptions on the grounds of age or income level) must file an annual report for federal income-tax consideration. The tax rates, which are calculated on a percentage basis, and allowances (deductions) are fixed by Congress from year to year. A state income tax is also levied in many states, the amount of tax and allowances vaying from state to state; and in a few cases, such as New York City, there is a city income tax as well.

incontinence failure or inability to control evacuation of the bladder or bowel (or both in the case of double incontinence). It may arise as a result of injury, childbirth, disease, or senility.

incubus male demon who in the popular belief of the Middle Ages had sexual intercourse with women in their sleep. Supposedly the women then gave birth to witches and demons. Succubus is the female equivalent.

incunabula (Latin "swaddling clothes") the birthplace, or early stages of anything; printed books produced before 1500, when printing was in its infancy.

indemnity in law, an undertaking to compensate

another for damage, loss, trouble, or expenses, or the money paid by way of such compensation—for example, under insurance agreements.

In some laws, government officials are protected from paying indemnities and as such are "indemnified." Similarly, directors of nonprofit corporations may be indemnified or corporations may indemnify their officers and directors by the purchase of insurance.

indenture in law, a ◊deed between two or more people. Historically, an indenture was a contract between a master and apprentice. The term derives from the practice of writing the agreement twice on paper or parchment and then cutting it with a jagged edge so that both pieces fit together, proving the authenticity of each half.

Independence city in W Missouri; population (1990) 112,301. Industries include steel, Portland cement, petroleum refining, and flour milling. President Harry S Truman was raised here, and it is the site of the Truman Library and Museum.

Independence Day public vacation in the US, commemorating the adoption of the ◊Declaration of Independence July 4, 1776.

Although ties with Britain were severed, the "Fourth of July" has become one of America's most spirited vacations.

Independent Labour Party (ILP) British Socialist party, founded in Bradford 1893 by the Scottish member of Parliament Keir Hardie. In 1900 it joined with trades unions and Fabians in founding the Labour Representation Committee, the nucleus of the ◊Labour Party. Many members left the ILP to join the Communist Party 1921, and in 1932 all connections with the Labour Party were severed. After World War II the ILP dwindled, eventually becoming extinct. James Maxton (1885–1946) was its chair 1926–46.

indeterminacy principle alternate name for ◊uncertainty principle.

index in economics, an indicator of a general movement in wages and prices over a specified period.

For example, the consumer price index (CPI) records charges in the ◊cost of living. The ◊Dow Jones index indicates the general movement of the New York stock exchange.

index (Latin "sign, indicator") in mathematics, another term for ◊exponent.

Index Librorum Prohibitorum (Latin "Index of Prohibited Books") the list of books formerly officially forbidden to members of the Roman Catholic church. The process of condemning books and bringing the Index up to date was carried out by a congregation of cardinals, consultors, and examiners from the 16th century until its abolition in 1966.

India country in S Asia, bounded N by Afghanistan, China, Nepal, and Bhutan; E by Myanmar; NW by Pakistan; surrounded to the SE, S, and SW by the Indian Ocean; situated in the NE corner of India, N of the Bay of Bengal, is Bangladesh.

government India is a federal republic whose 1949 constitution contains elements from both the US and British systems of government. It comprises 25 self-governing states, administered by a governor appointed by the federal president, and a council of ministers (headed by a chief minister) drawn from a legislature (legislative assembly) that is popularly elected for a five-year term. Eight of the larger states have a second chamber (legislative council). The states have primary control over education, health, police, and local government and work in consultation with the center in the economic sphere. In times of crisis, central rule ("president's rule") can be imposed. There are also seven union territories, administered by a lieutenant-governor appointed by the federal president. The central (federal) government has sole responsibility in military and foreign affairs and plays a key role in economic affairs.

The titular, executive head of the federal government is the president, who is elected for five-year terms by an electoral college composed

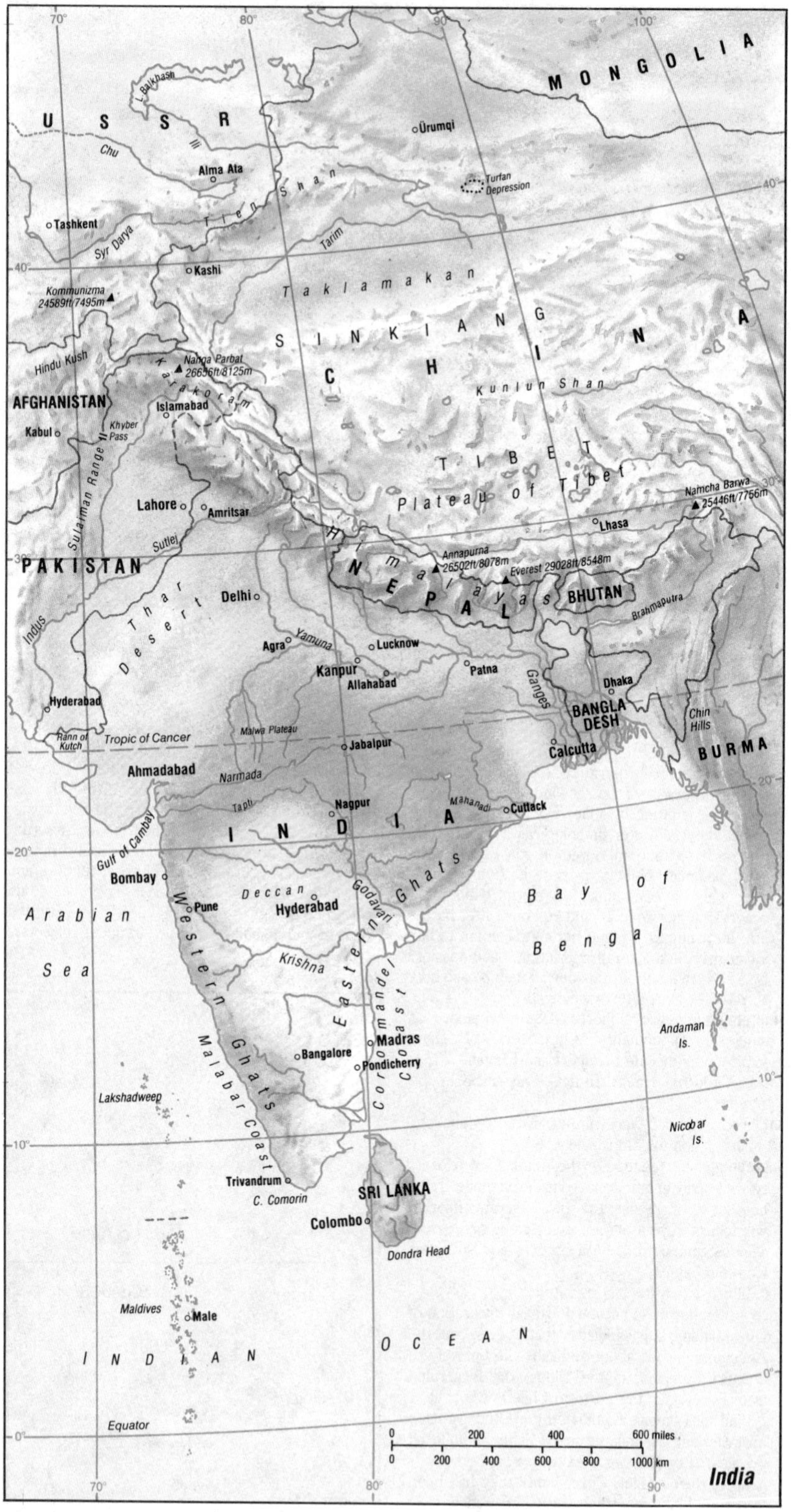
U S S R
MONGOLIA
CHINA
Alma Ata
Ürumqi
Turfan Depression
Tashkent
Syr Darya
Chu
Tien Shan
Tarim
Kashi
Kommunizma 24589ft/7495m
Taklamakan
SINKIANG
Hindu Kush
Nanga Parbat 26656ft/8125m
Karakoram
Kunlun Shan
AFGHANISTAN
Islamabad
Kabul
Khyber Pass
Sulaiman Range
TIBET
Plateau of Tibet
Namcha Barwa 25446ft/7756m
Lahore
Amritsar
Sutlej
Lhasa
PAKISTAN
Annapurna 26502ft/8078m
Everest 29028ft/8848m
Himalayas
NEPAL
BHUTAN
Brahmaputra
Delhi
Thar Desert
Indus
Agra
Yamuna
Lucknow
Kanpur
Allahabad
Patna
Ganges
Dhaka
BANGLADESH
Hyderabad
Rann of Kutch
Tropic of Cancer
Malwa Plateau
Jabalpur
Calcutta
Chin Hills
BURMA
Ahmadabad
Narmada
Mahanadi
Cuttack
Tapti
Nagpur
INDIA
Gulf of Cambay
Bombay
Deccan
Pune
Hyderabad
Godavari
Eastern Ghats
Arabian Sea
Bay of Bengal
Western Ghats
Krishna
Coromandel Coast
Madras
Bangalore
Pondicherry
Andaman Is.
Malabar Coast
Lakshadweep
Nicobar Is.
Trivandrum
C. Comorin
SRI LANKA
Colombo
Dondra Head
Maldives
Male
INDIAN OCEAN
Equator
0 200 400 600 miles
0 200 400 600 800 1000 km
India

of members from both the federal parliament and the state legislatures. However, real executive power is held by a prime minister and cabinet drawn from the majority party or coalition within the federal parliament.

The two-chamber federal parliament has a 545-member lower house, *Lok Sabha* (house of the people), which has final authority over financial matters and whose members are directly elected for terms of a maximum of five years from single-member constituencies by universal suffrage, and a 245-member upper house, *Rajya Sabha* (council of states), whose members are indirectly elected, a third at a time for six-year terms, by state legislatures on a regional quota basis. (Two seats in the *Lok Sabha* are reserved for Anglo-Indians, while the president nominates eight representatives of the *Rajya Sabha*.) Bills to become law must be approved by both chambers of parliament and receive the president's assent.

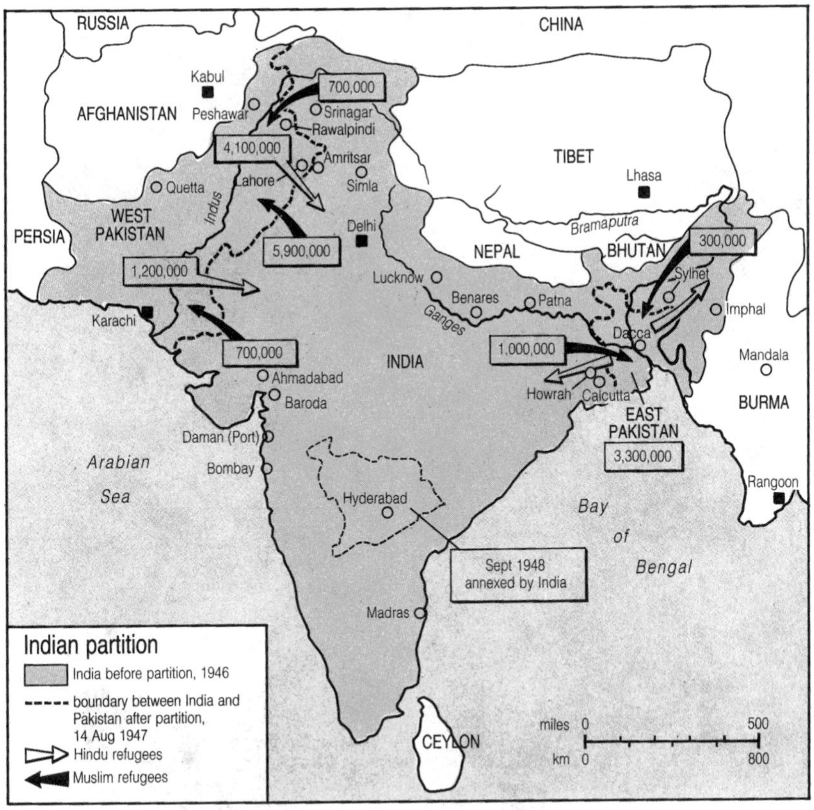
RUSSIA
CHINA
Kabul
AFGHANISTAN
Peshawar
700,000
Srinagar
Rawalpindi
4,100,000
Amritsar
Simla
TIBET
Lhasa
Quetta
Lahore
Indus
WEST PAKISTAN
PERSIA
Delhi
5,900,000
Bramaputra
NEPAL
BHUTAN
300,000
1,200,000
Lucknow
Sylhet
Benares
Patna
Imphal
Karachi
Ganges
Dacca
700,000
1,000,000
Mandala
INDIA
Ahmadabad
Baroda
Howrah
Calcutta
BURMA
EAST PAKISTAN
Daman (Port)
3,300,000
Arabian Sea
Bombay
Rangoon
Hyderabad
Bay of Bengal
Sept 1948 annexed by India
Madras
India before partition, 1946
boundary between India and Pakistan after partition, 14 Aug 1947
Hindu refugees
Muslim refugees
miles 0 500
km 0 800
CEYLON
Indian partition

India: states and union territories

State	*Capital*	*Area sq km*
Andhra Pradesh	Hyderabad	276,800
Arunachal Pradesh	Itanagar	83,600
Assam	Dispur	78,400
Bihar	Patna	173,900
Goa	Panaji	3,700
Gujarat	Gandhinagar	196,000
Haryana	Chandigarh	44,200
Himachal Pradesh	Simla	55,700
Jammu and Kashmir	Srinagar	101,300
Karnataka	Bangalore	191,800
Kerala	Trivandrum	38,900
Madhya Pradesh	Bhopal	442,800
Maharashtra	Bombay	307,800
Manipur	Imphal	22,400
Meghalaya	Shillong	22,500
Mizoram	Aizawl	21,100
Nagaland	Kohima	16,500
Orissa	Bhubaneswar	155,800
Punjab	Chandigarh	50,400
Rajasthan	Jaipur	342,200
Sikkim	Gangtok	7,300
Tamil Nadu	Madras	130,100
Tripura	Agartala	10,500
Uttar Pradesh	Lucknow	294,400
West Bengal	Calcutta	87,900
Union territory		
Andaman and Nicobar Islands	Port Blair	8,300
Chandigarh	Chandigarh	114
Dadra and Nagar Haveli	Silvassa	490
Daman and Diu	Panaji	110
Delhi	Delhi	1,500
Lakshadweep	Kavaratti Island	32
Pondicherry	Pondicherry	480

The dominant national-level party in India, which until 1989 had held power for all but three years (1977–79) since independence, is the ◊Congress Party. After splits 1969, 1978, 1981, and 1987, the main body of the party is today termed Indian National Congress (I or Indira). It is a broad, secular-based, cross-caste and religion coalition that advocates a moderate Socialist approach and is based most strongly in northern and central India. The principal national-level opposition parties are the Janata (People's) Party; the Bharatiya Janata Party (a conservative Hindu grouping); the Communist Party of India (CPI); and the Communist Party of India–Marxist (CPI-M). There are also numerous regional-level parties, the most important of which are the Dravida Munnetra Kazhagam in Tamil Nadu, the Telugu Desam in Andhra Pradesh, the Jammu and Kashmir National Conference Party, and the Shiromani Akali Dal in Punjab.

history For history before 1947, see ◊India, history. Between 1947 and 1949 India temporarily remained under the supervision of a governor-general appointed by the British monarch while a new constitution was framed and approved. Former princely states (see ◊India of the Princes; ◊Kashmir) were integrated, and the old British provinces restructured into new states; in 1950 India was proclaimed a fully independent federal republic.

During its early years the republic faced the problem of resettling refugees from Pakistan and was involved in border skirmishes over ◊Kashmir. Under the leadership of Prime Minister ◊Nehru, land reforms and a new Socialist economic program (involving protectionism), and an emphasis on heavy industries and government planning, were introduced, while sovereignty of parts of India held by France and Portugal was recovered 1950–61.

In foreign affairs, India remained within the ◊Commonwealth, was involved in border clashes with China 1962, and played a leading role in the formation of the ◊nonaligned movement 1961. In 1964, Nehru died and was succeeded as prime minister by Lal Bahadur ◊Shastri. There was a second war with Pakistan over Kashmir 1964. The new prime minister, Indira ◊Gandhi (Nehru's daughter), came to power on Shastri's death 1966 and kept broadly to her father's policy program, but drew closer to the Soviet Union with the signing of a 15-year economic and military assistance agreement 1973. In 1971 Indian troops invaded East Pakistan in support of separatist groups. They defeated Pakistan's troops and oversaw the creation of independent ◊Bangladesh.

In 1975, having been found guilty of electoral malpractice during the 1971 election by the Allahabad Court, and banned from holding elective office for six years, Indira Gandhi imposed a "state of emergency" and imprisoned almost 1,000 political opponents. She was cleared of malpractice by the Supreme Court Nov 1975, but the "emergency" continued for two years, during which period a harsh compulsory birth control program was introduced under the supervision of Sanjay Gandhi (Indira's youngest son).

The "state of emergency" was lifted March 1977 for elections in which the Janata opposition party was swept to power, its leader Morarji ◊Desai defeating Indira Gandhi in her home constituency. The new government was undermined by economic difficulties and internal factional strife, which led to the defection of many members to a new party, the *Lok Dal*, led by Raj Narain and Charan Singh. Desai was toppled as prime minister 1979, and a coalition, under Charan Singh, assumed power. After only 24 days in Aug 1979 Singh's government was overthrown, and in Jan 1980 the Congress (I) Party, led by Indira Gandhi and promising firmer government, was returned to power with a landslide victory.

The new Gandhi administration was economically successful, but the problems of intercaste violence and regional unrest, centered in Gujerat (caste strife), Muslim Kashmir, S India, and Assam (aimed against Bangladeshi immigrants), were such that the Congress (I) Party lost control of a number of states. The greatest unrest was in Punjab, where ◊Sikh demands for greater religious recognition and for resolution of water and land disputes with neighboring states escalated into calls for the creation of a separate state of "Khalistan." In 1984, troops were sent into the Sikh's most holy shrine, the Golden Temple at Amritsar, to dislodge the armed Sikh extremist leader Sant Jarnail Singh Bhindranwale, resulting in the deaths of Bhindranwale and hundreds of his supporters. The ensuing Sikh backlash brought troop mutinies, culminating in the assassination of Indira Gandhi by her Sikh bodyguards Oct 1984. In Delhi, retaliating Hindus massacred 3,000 Sikhs before the new prime minister, Rajiv ◊Gandhi (Indira's eldest son), restored order.

In the elections of Dec 1984, Congress (I), benefiting from a wave of public sympathy, gained a record victory. As prime minister, Rajiv Gandhi pledged to modernize and inject greater market efficiency into the Indian economy (vowing to "bring India into the 21st century") and to resolve the Punjab, Assam, and Kashmir disputes. Early reforms and the spread of technology, with India launching its first space satellite, promised to give substance to the former vision, while progress was made toward resolving the ethnic disputes in Assam and the hill areas, with 25 years of tribal rebellion ended in Mizoram, which was made a new state of the Indian Union. However, Gandhi was unable to resolve the Punjab problem, with Sikh-Hindu ethnic conflict continuing, while in N India Hindi-Muslim relations deteriorated. Gandhi's enthusiasm for economic reform also waned from 1986 and his personal reputation was sullied by the uncovering of the "Bofors scandal," by finance minister V P ◊Singh, involving alleged financial kickbacks received by government-connected organizations from a $1,400 million contract for the supply of howitzers to the Indian army by the Swedish Bofors Corporation.

Gandhi's standing improved in 1989 following a successful intervention by the Indian army in the Maldives in Nov 1988 to defeat a coup attempt. However, in N Sri Lanka, where an Indian Peacekeeping Force (IPKF) had been sent July 1987

India

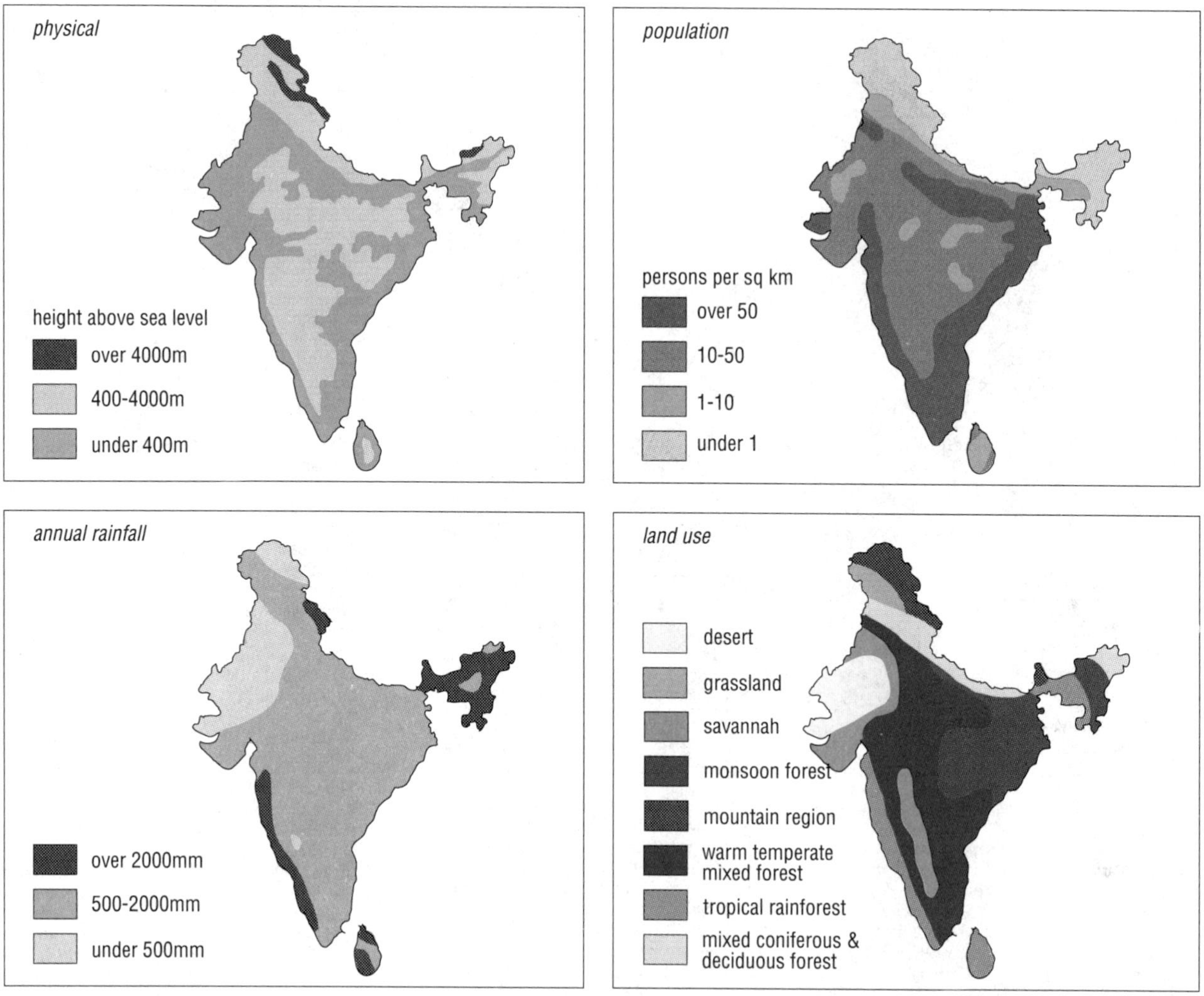
physical
height above sea level
over 4000m
400-4000m
under 400m
population
persons per sq km
over 50
10-50
1-10
under 1
annual rainfall
over 2000mm
500-2000mm
under 500mm
land use
desert
grassland
savannah
monsoon forest
mountain region
warm temperate mixed forest
tropical rainforest
mixed coniferous & deciduous forest

as part of an ambitious peace settlement, Indian troops became bogged down in a civil war.

Despite bumper harvests 1988–89, Gandhi's popularity continued to fall. V P Singh, who was dismissed from Congress (I) in 1987, attacked his increasingly dictatorial style and became the recognized leader of the opposition forces, which united under the Janata Dal umbrella Oct 1988. In the general election of Nov 1989 a broad anti-Congress electoral pact was forged, embracing the Janata Dal, BJP, Communist Party, and Teluga Desam. This ensured that Congress (I), although emerging as the largest single party in the new parliament, failed to secure a working majority. Gandhi resigned from office and V P Singh, widely respected for his incorruptibility, took over at the head of a minority "National Front" coalition.

Singh announced that his first objective was the lowering of racial tensions; he appointed a Muslim, Mufti Mohammad Sayeed, as home affairs minister, and visited the strife-torn city of Amritsar as a gesture of conciliation with the Sikhs. However, in Jan 1990 Muslim separatist violence erupted in Kashmir, forcing the imposition of direct rule and leading to a deterioration of relations with Pakistan. Relations were improved with the neighboring states of Bhutan, Nepal (which had been subject to a partial border blockade by India during 1989), and Sri Lanka, with whom a date (March 31, 1990) for the withdrawal of the IPKF was agreed. President's rule was imposed over Jammu and Kashmir in July 1990 and over Assam in Nov 1990, as a result of the rising tide of separatist violence. Punjab, where inter-ethnic murders climbed to record heights from Nov, was already under president's rule.

During the summer and early autumn of 1990 the Janata Dal government of V P Singh was rocked by a series of events, including the prime minister's decision to employ more low-caste workers in government and public sector jobs, which resulted in protests by high-caste students and a split in the Janata Dal. Chandra Shekar, a long-time Singh opponent, emerged as the leader of a rebel faction. Hindu militants (the Vishwa Hindu Parishad) announced that on Oct 30, 1990 they would begin to build a birthplace temple dedicated to the warrior god Ram in the northern city of Ajodhya. This precipitated serious communal tensions, which the government was unable to quell.

On Nov 7, after troops had fired on Hindu fanatics who were attempting to storm the the Ajodhya mosque, the Singh government was voted out of office. A new minority government was formed by Chandra Shekar, who led a tiny Janata Dal Socialist faction comprising 56 deputies, and who was assured of outside support by the Congress Party of Rajiv Gandhi (Gandhi having declined the president's invitation to head a government of his own). With the economy badly hit by the Gulf Crisis' impact upon oil prices, and caste communalist and separatist violence continuing, the minority government was insecure. Shekar's government fell in the spring of 1991, and during the ensuing election campaign, Rajiv Gandhi, who was the favorite, was assassinated. However, the Congress (I) Party won a plurality of the votes, and party leader P V Rao became prime minister in June.

India: history

c. 2500–c. 1600 *BC* The earliest Indian civilization evolved in the Indus Valley; two major city states are known, ◊Harappa and ◊Mohenjo Daro. They exhibit permanent architecture with plumbing, city planning, artisans' quarters, granaries, and evidences of basic Hindu religion. Many other sites developed along the rivers from the Himalayas to the Arabian sea, some 1,000 mi/ 1,609 km, forming the largest unitary civilization of the ancient world.

c. 1500 Aryans, militant nomadic horsemen, began to invade from the NW. They gradually overran the north and the Deccan plateau, intermarrying with the Dravidians, the majority people of the Indian subcontinent. From their religious beliefs developed Brahmanism (an early stage of ◊Hinduism).

c. 500 ◊Buddhism and ◊Jainism developed.

321–184 The subcontinent, except the far south, was first unified under the Mauryan emperors.

AD ***c. 300–500*** The north was again united under the Gupta dynasty; its rule was ended by the raids of the White Huns, which plunged India into anarchy.

11th–12th centuries Raids on India were made by Muslim adventurers, Turks, Arabs, and Afghans, and in 1206 the first Muslim dynasty was set up at Delhi.

14th–16th centuries Islam was established throughout the north and the Deccan, although the south maintained its independence under the

India
Republic of
(Hindi *Bharat*)

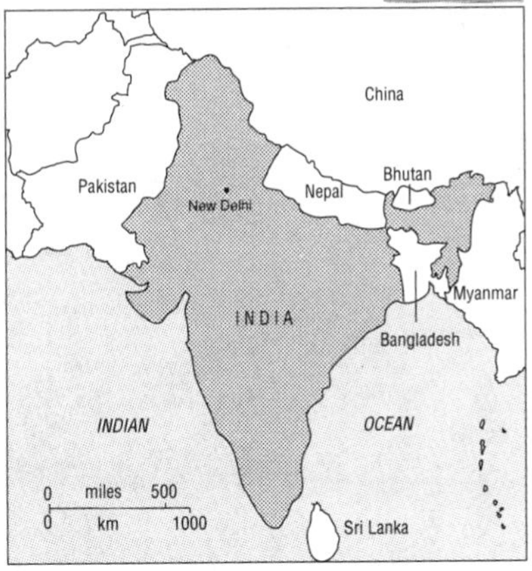
China
Pakistan
New Delhi
Nepal
Bhutan
Myanmar
INDIA
Bangladesh
INDIAN
OCEAN
0 miles 500
0 km 1000
Sri Lanka

area 1,222,396 sq mi/3,166,829 sq km
capital New Delhi
cities Bangalore, Hyderabad, Ahmedabad, Kanpur, Pune, Nagpur; ports Calcutta, Bombay, Madras
physical Himalaya mountains on N border; plains around rivers Ganges, Indus, Brahmaputra; Deccan peninsula S of the Narmada River forms plateau between W and E Ghats mountain ranges; desert in W; Andaman and Nicobar Islands, Lakshadweep (Laccadive Islands)
features Taj Mahal monument; Golden Temple, Amritsar; archeological sites and cave paintings (Ajanta); world's second most populous country
head of state R Venkataraman
head of government P V Narasimha Rao from 1991
political system federal democratic republic
political parties Janata Dal, left-of-center; All India Congress Committee (I), or Congress (I), cross-caste and religion left-of-center; Bharatiya Janata Party (BJP), conservative Hindu-chauvinist; Communist Party of India (CPI), pro-Moscow Marxist-Leninist; Communist Party of India–Marxist (CPI–M), West Bengal-based moderate Socialist
exports tea (world's largest producer), coffee, fish, iron and steel, leather, textiles, clothing, polished diamonds
currency rupee
population (1991 est) 844,000,000 (920 women to every 1,000 men); growth rate 2.0% p.a.
life expectancy men 56, women 55
language Hindi (widely spoken in N India), English, and 14 other official languages: Assamese, Bengali, Gujarati, Kannada, Kashmiri, Malayalam, Marathi, Oriya, Punjabi, Sanskrit, Sindhi, Tamil, Telugu, Urdu
religion Hindu 80%, Sunni Muslim 10%, Christian 2.5%, Sikh 2%
literacy men 57%/women 29% (1985 est)
GDP $220.8 bn (1987); $283 per head
chronology
1947 Independence achieved from Britain.
1950 Federal republic proclaimed.
1962 Border skirmishes with China.
1964 Death of Prime Minister Nehru. Border war with Pakistan over Kashmir.
1966 Indira Gandhi became prime minister.
1971 War with Pakistan leading to creation of Bangladesh.
1975–77 State of emergency proclaimed.
1977–79 Janata party government in power.
1980 Indira Gandhi returned in landslide victory.
1984 Indira Gandhi assassinated; Rajiv Gandhi elected with record majority.
1987 Signing of "Tamil" Colombo peace accord with Sri Lanka; Indian Peacekeeping Force (IPKF) sent there. Public revelation of Bofors scandal.
1988 New opposition party, Janata Dal, established by former finance minister V P Singh. Indian paratroopers foiled attempted coup in Maldives. Voting age lowered from 21 to 18.
1989 Congress (I) lost majority in general election, after Gandhi associates implicated in financial misconduct, and Janata Dal minority government formed, with V P Singh prime minister.
1990 Central rule imposed in Jammu and Kashmir following Muslim separatist violence. V P Singh resigned; new minority Janata Dal government formed by Chandra Shekhar.
1991 Central rule imposed in Tamil Nadu. Interethnic and religious violence in Punjab, Andhra Pradesh, and elsewhere. Shekhar resigned; elections called for May. Rajiv Gandhi assassinated in May. Elections resumed in June, resulting in a Congress (I) minority government led by P V Narasimha Rao.

Hindu Vijayanagar dynasty. In the 16th century Portuguese, Dutch, French, and English traders established trading bases on the coast.

1527–1858 The Mogul emperors included Babur (◊Zahir ud-din Mohammed) and his grandson Akbar. After 1707 the Mogul Empire fell into decline.

1756–63 During the Seven Years' War the ◊British East India Company overcame their French rivals and made themselves rulers of Bengal and the Carnatic.

1857–58 The ◊Sepoy Rebellion ended the rule of the East India Company, which was established all over India, and rule was transferred to the British government.

1885 The India National Congress was founded (see ◊Congress Party) as a focus for nationalism.

1915–47 Resistance to UK rule was organized under the leadership of Mohandas ◊Gandhi.

1947 British India was divided into the independent dominions of ◊India (predominantly Hindu) and ◊Pakistan (predominantly Muslim). For subsequent history, see ◊India.

Indiana state of the midwest US; nickname Hoosier State

area 36,168 sq mi/93,700 sq km

capital Indianapolis

cities Fort Wayne, Gary, Evansville, South Bend

features Wabash River; Wyandotte Cavern; Indiana Dunes National Lakeshore; Indianapolis Motor Speedway and Museum; George Rogers National Historic Park, Vincennes; Robert Owen's utopian commune, New Harmony; Lincoln Boyhood National Memorial

products corn, hogs, soybeans, limestone, machinery, electrical goods, coal, steel, iron, chemicals

population (1990) 5,544,159

famous people Eugene V Debs, Theodore Dreiser, Cole Porter

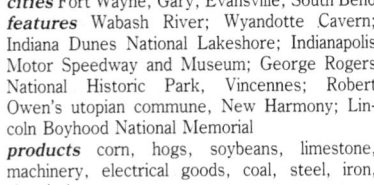

Indiana

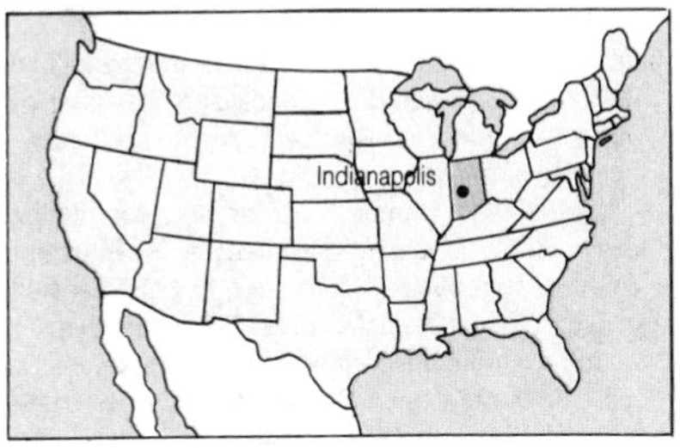
Indianapolis

history explored for France by La Salle 1679–80; first colonial settlements established 1731–35 by French traders; ceded to Britain by France 1763; passed to US control 1783; became a state 1816. Indiana became an important industrial state in the early 20th century, with steel mills, oil refineries, and factories producing automobiles and auto parts. However, the state remained one-third rural in the mid-1980s, and agriculture retained much of its former importance.

Indianapolis capital and largest city of Indiana, on the White River; population (1990) 731,327. It is an industrial center and venue of the "Indianapolis 500" automobile race. To end its heavy reliance on recession-prone auto manufacturing, the city has exploited its central location to become a warehouse, distribution, and convention center. Educational facilities include the Indiana University Medical Center, and there is a 60,000-seat domed stadium. Indianapolis was settled 1820. In 1967 surrounding Marion County was annexed to the city.

Indianapolis Raceway US auto race track and stadium, built 1910. The Indianapolis 500, a Formula One Grand Prix event, is staged here at the end of May each year as part of the Memorial Day weekend.

The circuit is 2.5 mi/4 km long and is basically rectangular, with the four corners joined with banking. The original track was paved with bricks, hence its nickname the "Brick Yard."

Indian art the painting, sculpture, and architecture of India. Indian art dates from the ancient Indus Valley civilization (see ◊Harappa and ◊Mohenjo Daro) of c. 3000 BC. Sophisticated artistic styles emerged from the 1st century AD. Buddhist art includes sculptures and murals. Hindu artists created sculptural schemes in caves and large temple complexes; the Hindu style is lively, with voluptuous nude figures. The Islamic Mogul Empire of the 16th–17th centuries created an exquisite style of miniature painting, inspired by Persian examples.

Buddhist art In NW India the Gandhara kingdom produced the first known images of the Buddha in a monumental soft and rounded style that was exported, with the Buddhist religion, to China, Korea, and Japan. The Gupta kingdom, which emerged around the 4th century AD in the Ganges plain, continued to develop Buddhist art. Its sites include Sarnath and the caves of Ajanta, which

Indian art *A party of elephant hunters traveling through a landscape (c. 1615) Victoria and Albert Museum, London.*

have extensive remains of murals of the 5th and 6th centuries as well as sculpture.

Hindu art Hinduism advanced further in central and S India. Influenced by Buddhist art, Hindu artists created brilliant sculptural schemes in rock-cut caves at Mamallapuram, and huge temple complexes: for example, in Orissa, Konarak, and Khajuraho. The caves at Ellora are known for their ensemble of religious art, Buddhist, Hindu, and Jain, dating from the 6th and 7th centuries.

Mogul art Mogul art dates from the Muslim invasion of NW India in the Middle Ages. The invaders destroyed Buddhist and Hindu temple art and introduced their own styles (see ◊Islamic art). An early example of their work is the Q'utb mosque c. 1200 in Delhi. By the 16th century the Moguls had established an extensive empire. Court artists excelled in miniature painting, particularly in the reigns of Jehangir and Shah Jehan (c. 1566–1658). Their subjects ranged from portraiture and histories to birds, animals, and flowers.

Indian corn an alternate name for ◊corn.

Indian languages traditionally, the languages of the subcontinent of India; since 1947, the languages of the Republic of India. These number some 200, depending on whether a variety is classified as a language or a dialect. They fall into five main groups, the two most widespread of which are the Indo-European languages (mainly in the north) and the Dravidian languages (mainly in the south).

The Indo-European languages include two Classical languages, Sanskrit and Pali, and such modern languages as Bengali, Hindi, Gujarati, Marathi, Oriya, Punjabi, and Urdu. The Dravidian languages include Kannada, Malayalam, Tamil, and Telugu. A wide range of scripts are used, including Devanagari for Hindi, Arabic for Urdu, and distinct scripts for the various Dravidian languages. The Sino-Tibetan group of languages is used widely in Assam and along the Himalayas.

Indian literature for the literature of ancient India see ◊Sanskrit, ◊Veda, ◊Pali, and ◊Prakrit. In the 19th century Bengali emerged as a literary language, for example in the work of philologist Ram Mohan Roy, founder of Brahma Samaj, who paved the way for such writers as Bankim Chandra Chatterji and Romesh Chunder Dutt (1848–1909). Rabindranath Tagore's Nobel Prize 1913 confirmed the reputation of Bengali in world literature. Subsequent writers include the poets Buddhadeva Bose (1908–) and Amiya Chakravarty. Other literary languages are Urdu (used by the novelist Prem Chand and poet-philosopher Iqbal) and Gujarati (used by the poet Nanalal Devi and in the writings of Gandhi). The long association with Britain established English as a literary language, and writers in English—whose work is nonetheless wholly Indian in character—include the novelist Dhan Gopal Mukerji, the poet Sarojini Naidu (1879–1949), Sri Aurobindo (1872–1950), Dom Moraes (1938–), and Nehru. Tagore did little creative writing in English, but translated many of his own works. V S Naipaul is among overseas writers of Indian descent.

Indian Mutiny see ◊Sepoy Rebellion or Mutiny.

Indian National Congress (INC) the official name for the ◊Congress Party of India.

Indian Ocean ocean between Africa and Australia, with India to the N, and the S boundary being an arbitrary line from Cape Agulhas to S Tasmania; area 28,371,000 sq mi/73,500,000 sq km; average depth 12,708 ft/3,872 m. The greatest depth is the Java Trench 25,353 ft/7,725 m.

India of the Princes the 562 Indian states ruled by princes during the period of British control. They occupied an area of 715,964 sq mi/1,854,347 sq km (45% of the total area of prepartition India) and had a population of over 93 million. At the partition of British India in 1947 the princes were given independence by the British government but were advised to adhere to either India or Pakistan. Between 1947 and 1950 all except ◊Kashmir were incorporated in either country.

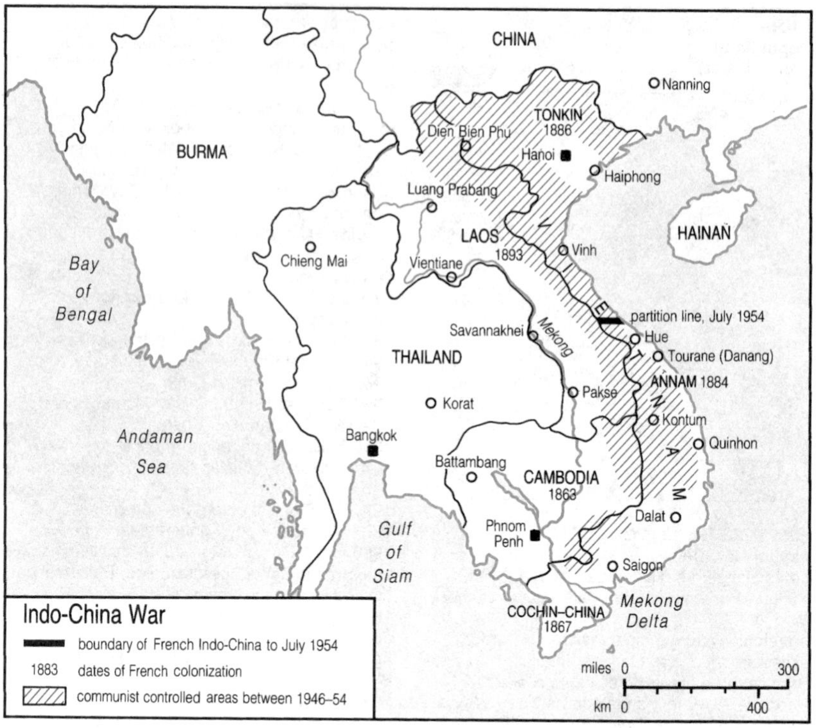
CHINA
Nanning
TONKIN
1886
Dien Bien Phu
Hanoi
Haiphong
BURMA
Luang Prabang
LAOS
1893
Vinh
HAINAN
Bay
of
Bengal
Chieng Mai
Vientiane
partition line, July 1954
Savannakhei
Mekong
Hue
Tourane (Danang)
THAILAND
ANNAM 1884
Pakse
Korat
Kontum
Quinhon
Andaman
Sea
Bangkok
Battambang
CAMBODIA
1863
Dalat
Gulf
of
Siam
Phnom
Penh
Saigon
Mekong
Delta
COCHIN-CHINA
1867
boundary of French Indo-China to July 1954
1883 dates of French colonization
communist controlled areas between 1946–54
miles 0 300
km 0 400
Indo-China War

indicator species a plant or animal whose presence or absence in an area indicates certain environmental conditions, such as soil type, high levels of pollution, or, in rivers, low levels of dissolved oxygen. Many plants show a preference for either alkaline or acid soil conditions, while certain trees require aluminum, and are found only in soils where it is present. Some lichens are sensitive to sulfur dioxide in the air, and absence of these species indicates atmospheric pollution.

indigenous the people, animals, and plants that are native to a region. Examples of indigenous peoples include Africans, Australian Aborigines, the Pacific Islanders, and American Indians. A World Council of Indigenous Peoples is based in Canada.

indigestion any pain or discomfort in the stomach or abdomen due to problems in the ◊digestive system.

indigo violet-blue vegetable dye obtained from plants of the genus *Indigofera*, family Leguminosae, but now replaced by a synthetic product. It was once a major export crop of India.

indium soft, ductile, silver-white, metallic element, symbol In, atomic number 49, atomic weight 114.82. It occurs in nature in some zinc ores, is resistant to abrasion, and is used as a coating on metal parts. It was discovered and named in 1863 by German metallurgists Ferdinand Reich (1799–1882) and H T Richter (1824–1898), so named because of the two indigo lines of its spectrum, from the Latin *indicum*.

Indo-Aryan languages another name for the ◊Indo-European languages.

Indochina French former collective name for ◊Cambodia, ◊Laos, and ◊Vietnam, which became independent after World War II.

Indochina War successful war of independence 1946–1954 between the Nationalist forces of what was to become Vietnam and France, the occupying colonial power.

In 1945 Vietnamese Nationalist communist leader Ho Chi Minh proclaimed an independent Vietnamese republic, which soon began an armed struggle against French forces. France in turn set up a noncommunist state four years later. In 1954, after the siege of ◊Dien Bien Phu, a cease-fire was agreed between France and China that resulted in the establishment of two separate Vietnamese states, North and South Vietnam, divided by the 17th parallel. Attempts at reunification of the country led subsequently to the ◊Vietnam War.

Indo-European languages family of languages that includes some of the world's major Classical languages (Sanskrit and Pali in India, Zend Avestan in Iran, Greek and Latin in Europe), as well as several of the most widely spoken languages (English worldwide; Spanish in Iberia, Latin America, and elsewhere; and the Hindi group of languages in N India). Indo-European languages were once located only along a geographical band from India through Iran into NW Asia, E Europe, the northern Mediterranean lands, N and W Europe and the British Isles.

When first discussed and described in the 19th century, this family was known as the Aryan and then the Indo-Germanic language family. Because of unwelcome associations with the Nazi idea of "Aryan" racial purity and superiority, both titles have been abandoned by scholars in favor of the neutral "Indo-European."

In general terms, many Indo-European languages (such as English, French, and Hindi) have tended to evolve from the highly inflected to a more open or analytic grammatical style that does not greatly depend on complex grammatical endings to nouns, verbs, and adjectives. Eastern Indo-European languages are often called the *satem* group (Zend "a hundred") while western Indo-European languages are the *centum* group (Latin "a hundred"); this illustrates a split that occurred over 3,000 years ago, between those that had an *s*-sound in certain words and those that had a *k*-sound. Scholars have reconstructed a Proto-Indo-European ancestral language by comparing the sound systems and historical changes within the family, but continue to dispute the original homeland of this ancient form, some arguing for N Europe, others for Russia N of the Black Sea.

Indo-Germanic languages former name for the ◊Indo-European languages.

Indonesia country in SE Asia, made up of over 13,000 islands situated on the equator, between the Indian and Pacific oceans.

government Under the 1945 constitution,

Indonesia
Republic of
(Republik Indonesia)

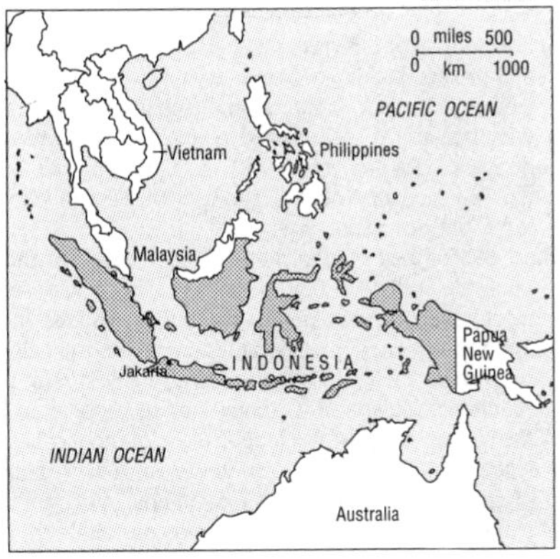
0 miles 500
0 km 1000
PACIFIC OCEAN
Vietnam
Philippines
Malaysia
Papua New Guinea
Jakarta
INDONESIA
INDIAN OCEAN
Australia

area 740,905 sq mi/1,919,443 sq km
capital Jakarta
cities Bandung; ports Surabaya, Semarang, Tanjung Priok
physical comprises 13,677 tropical islands, of the Greater Sunda group (including Java and Madura, part of Kalimantan/Borneo, Sumatra, Sulawesi and Belitung), and the Lesser Sundas/Nusa Tenggara (including Bali, Lombok, Sumba, Timor), as well as Malaku/Moluccas and part of New Guinea (Irian Jaya)
features world's largest Islamic population; Java is one of the world's most densely populated areas
head of state and government T N J Suharto from 1967
political system authoritarian nationalist republic
political parties Golkar, military-bureaucrat-farmers ruling party; United Development Party (PPP), moderate Islamic; Indonesian Democratic Party (PDI), nationalist Christian
exports coffee, rubber, timber, palm oil, coconuts, tin, tea, tobacco, oil, liquid natural gas
currency rupiah
population (1989 est) 187,726,000 (including 300 ethnic groups); growth rate 2% p.a.
life expectancy men 52, women 55
language Indonesian (official), closely allied to Malay; Javanese is the most widely spoken local dialect
religion Muslim 88%; Buddhist, Hindu, and Pancasila (a secular official ideology); Christian 9%
literacy men 83%/women 65% (1985 est)
GDP $69.7 bn (1987); $409 per head
chronology
17th century Dutch colonial rule established.
1942 Occupied by Japan; nationalist government established.
1945 Japanese surrender; nationalists declared independence under Sukarno.
1949 Formal transfer of Dutch sovereignty.
1950 Unitary constitution established.
1963 Western New Guinea (Irian Jaya) ceded by the Netherlands.
1965–66 Attempted Communist coup; Gen Suharto imposed emergency administration, carried out massacre of hundreds of thousands.
1967 Sukarno replaced as president by Suharto.
1975 Terrorists seeking independence for S Molucca seized train and Dutch Embassy, held Western hostages.
1976 Forced annexation of former Portuguese colony of East Timor.
1986 Institution of "transmigration program" to settle large numbers of Javanese on sparsely populated outer islands, particularly Irian Jaya.
1988 Partial easing of travel restrictions to East Timor. Suharto reelected for fifth term.
1989 Foreign debt reaches $50 billion; Western creditors offer aid on condition that concessions are made to foreign companies and that austerity measures are introduced.
1991 Democracy Forum launched to promote political dialogue.

amended 1950 and 1969, the supreme political body in Indonesia is, in theory, the 1,000-member people's consultative council (*Majelis Permusyawaratan Rakyat*). This comprises the 500 members of the legislature (house of representatives) as well as 500 appointed representatives from regional assemblies and functional groups (including 200 from the armed forces). It sits at least once every five years to elect an executive president and vice president, and determines the constitution.

The house of representatives *Dewan Perwakilan Rakyat* functions as a single-chamber legislature, comprising 400 directly elected members and 100 presidential appointees (of whom three quarters represent the armed forces). It meets at least once a year, with elections every five years. At the head of the executive, and the most powerful political figure in Indonesia, is the president, elected by the people's consultative council for five-year terms. The president works with an appointed cabinet, exercises the right of veto over house of representatives bills and appoints governors to supervise local government in each of Indonesia's 27 provinces.

Indonesia's dominant political party is the Golkar. The Islamic Party Persatuan Pembangunan and the Christian-oriented Party Demokrasi Indonesia also operate, holding seats in the house of representatives and People's Consultative Assembly. Parties opposed to the secular state philosophy, *Pancasila*, and that are regionally based are prohibited from functioning.

history Between 3000 and 500 BC, immigrants from S China displaced the original Melanesian population of Indonesia. Between AD 700 and 1450 , two Hindu empires developed, to be superseded by Islam from the 13th century. During the 16th century English and Portuguese traders were active in Indonesia, but in 1595 Holland took over trade in the area. In the 17th century the Dutch had only managed to establish trading centers, while Indonesian kingdoms dominated the region, but by the 18th–19th centuries Dutch control was complete and the islands were proclaimed a Dutch colony 1816.

A nationalist movement developed during the 1920s under the pro-communist Indonesian Nationalist Party (PNI), headed by Achmed ◊Sukarno. This was suppressed by the Dutch, but in 1942, after Japan's occupation of the islands, the PNI was installed in power as an anti-Western puppet government. When Japan surrendered to the Allies 1945, President Sukarno proclaimed Indonesia's independence. The Dutch challenged this by launching military expeditions before agreeing to transfer sovereignty 1949. A "special union" was established between the two countries but was abrogated by Indonesia 1956.

The new republic was planned as a federation of 16 constituent regions but was made unitary 1950. This led to dominance by Java (which has two-thirds of Indonesia's population), provoking revolts in Sumatra and the predominantly Christian South Moluccas. The paramount political figure in the new republic was President Sukarno, who ruled in an authoritarian manner and pursued an ambitious and expansionist foreign policy. He effected the transfer of Netherlands New Guinea (Irian Jaya) to Indonesia 1963 but failed in a confrontation with Malaysia over claims to Sabah and Sarawak.

With the economy deteriorating, in 1965 an attempted coup against Sukarno by groups connected with the Indonesian Communist Party was firmly put down by army Chief of Staff General ◊Suharto, who then assumed power as emergency ruler 1966. Suharto coordinated the massacre by the army of between 200,000 and 700,000 people in 1965; it was later revealed that US intelligence was directly linked to this massacre as it had provided the Indonesian military with lists of around 5,000 members of the Indonesian Communist Party.

Suharto ended hostility over Sabah and Sarawak and formally replaced Sukarno as president 1967. He proceeded to institute what was termed a "New Order." This involved the concentration of political power in the hands of a coterie of army and security-force officers, the propagation of *Pancasila*, which stressed unity and social justice, the pursuit of a liberal economic program, and the fierce suppression of communist activity.

Rising oil exports brought significant industrial and agricultural growth to Indonesia during the 1970s, and self-sufficiency in rice production was attained by the 1980s. In addition, its borders were extended by the forcible annexation of the former Portuguese colony of East Timor 1976. Suharto's authoritarian approach met with opposition from left-wing groups, from radical Muslims, from separatist groups in outlying islands (most especially in Irian Jaya), and S Moluccas. In Irian Jaya, following the supression of a rebellion organized by the Free Papua Movement (OPM), a "transmigration" program was instituted by the Suharto government, with the aim of resettling 65 million Javanese there and on other sparsely populated "outer islands" by 2006. This encountered strong opposition from native Melanesians, prompting the emigration of more than 10,000 refugees to neighboring Papua New Guinea. In East Timor, tens of thousands died from famine and continuing warfare; although travel restrictions were partly eased 1988, the UN refused to recognize Indonesia's sovereignty over the area.

In recent years, economic problems have mounted as a result of the fall in world prices of oil, which provides 70% of Indonesia's foreign exchange earnings. Indonesia has long pursued a ◊nonaligned foreign policy, hosting the ◊Bandung Conference of Third World nations 1955, and is a member of ◊ASEAN. Under General Suharto, its relations with the West have become closer.

Indore city in Madhya Pradesh, India; population (1981) 829,327. A former capital of the princely state of Indore, it now produces cotton, chemicals, and furniture.

Indra Hindu god of the sky, shown as a four-armed man on a white elephant, carrying a thunderbolt. The intoxicating drink ◊soma is associated with him.

Indre river rising in the Auvergne mountains, France, and flowing NW for 165 mi/260 km to join the Loire below Tours. It gives its name to the *départements* of Indre and Indre-et-Loire.

indri largest living lemur *Indri indri* of Madagascar. Black and white, almost tailless, it has long arms and legs. It grows to 2.3 ft/70 cm long. It is diurnal and arboreal. Its howl is doglike or human in tone. Like all lemurs, its survival is threatened by the widespread deforestation of Madagascar.

inductance in physics, the measure of the capability of an electronic circuit or circuit component to form a magnetic field or store magnetic energy when carrying a current. Its symbol is *L*, and its unit of measure is the ◊henry.

The magnetic field produced induces voltages in the same ciruit or a nearby circuit.

induction in philosophy, the process of observing particular instances of things in order to derive general statements and laws of nature. It is the opposite of ◊deduction, which moves from general statements and principles to the particular.

Induction was criticized by the Scottish philosopher David ◊Hume because it relied upon belief rather than valid reasoning. In the philosophy of science, the "problem of induction" is a crucial area of debate: however much evidence there is for a proposition, there is the possibility of a future counter-instance that will invalidate the explanation. Therefore, it is argued, no scientific statement can be said to be true.

induction in obstetrics, deliberate intervention to initiate labor before it starts naturally; then it usually proceeds normally. Induction involves rupture of the fetal membranes (amniotomy) and the use of the hormone oxytocin to stimulate contractions of the womb. In biology, induction is a term used for various processes, including the production of an ◊enzyme in response to a particular chemical in the cell, and the ◊differentiation of cells in an ◊embryo in response to the presence of neighboring tissues.

In obstetrics, induction is recommended as a medical necessity where there is risk to the mother or baby in waiting for labor to begin of its own accord.

induction coil type of electrical transformer, similar to an ◊ignition coil, that produces an intermittent high-voltage alternating current from a low-voltage direct current supply.

It has a primary coil consisting of a few turns of thick wire wound around an iron core and passing a low voltage (usually from a battery). Wound on top of this is a secondary coil made up of many turns of thin wire. An iron armature and make-and-break mechanism (similar to that in an ◊electric bell) repeatedly interrupts the current to the primary coil, producing a high, rapidly alternating current in the secondary circuit.

inductor an element possessing the characteristic of inductance (electromagnetic property).

indulgence in the Roman Catholic church, the total or partial remission of temporal punishment for sins which remain to be expiated after penitence and confession have secured exemption from eternal punishment. The doctrine of indulgence began as the commutation of church penances in exchange for suitable works of charity or money gifts to the church, and became a great source of church revenue. This trade in indulgences roused Luther in 1517 to initiate the Reformation. The Council of Trent in 1563 recommended moderate retention of indulgences, and they continue, notably in "Holy Years."

Indus river in Asia, rising in Tibet and flowing 1,975 mi/3,180 km to the Arabian Sea. In 1960 the use of its waters, including those of its five tributaries, was divided between India (rivers Ravi, Beas, Sutlej) and Pakistan (rivers Indus, Jhelum, Chenab).

industrialization a policy usually associated with modernization of developing countries where the process normally starts with the manufacture of simple goods that can replace imports. It is essential for economic development and largely responsible for the growth of cities.

industrial law or ***labor law*** the body of law relating to relationships between employers (and their representatives), employees (and their representatives), and government.

industrial relations relationship between employers and employees, and their dealings with each other. In most industries, wages and conditions are determined by free collective bargaining between employers and ◊trade unions. Some European and American countries have worker participation through profit-sharing and industrial democracy. Another solution is coownership, in which a company is entirely owned by its employees. The aim of good industrial relations is to achieve a motivated, capable work force that sees its work as creative and fulfilling.

Another approach to industrial relations is that of the Japanese and Israelis, who encourage in their workers a feeling of belonging amounting almost to family membership.

When agreement cannot be reached by collective bargaining, outside arbitration is often sought. In the US, there is a highly developed system for private, third-party arbitration. Unions have long sought such provisions, but employers resisted, agreeing generally only in return for "no-strike" clauses in contracts. Working conditions, unfair treatment, and specific complaints are usually handled through the union grievance system, which requires written complaints from workers. New issues are becoming important in the US workplace, such as provision of day care, parental leave, and flexible working hours.

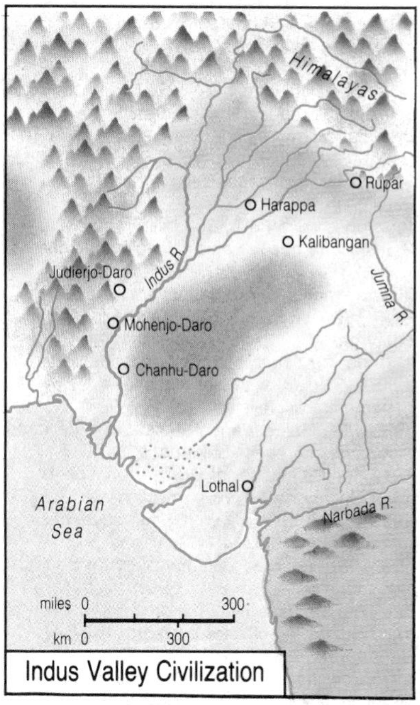
Himalayas
Rupar
Harappa
Kalibangan
Judeirjo-Daro
Indus R.
Jumna R.
Mohenjo-Daro
Chanhu-Daro
Lothal
Arabian Sea
Narbada R.
miles 0 300
km 0 300
Indus Valley Civilization

Industrial Revolution the sudden acceleration of technical and economic development that began in Britain in the second half of the 18th century. The traditional agrarian economy was replaced by one dominated by machinery and manufacturing, made possible through technical advances such as the steam engine. This transferred the balance of political power from the landowner to the industrial capitalist and created an urban working class. From 1830 to the early 20th century, the Industrial Revolution spread throughout Europe and the US to Japan and SE Asia as well as to the various colonial empires.

Industrial Workers of the World (IWW) US labor movement founded 1905, the members of which were popularly known as the Wobblies. The IWW was dedicated to the overthrow of capitalism but divided on tactics and gradually declined in popularity after 1917. At its peak, (1912–15), the organization claimed to have 100,000 members, mainly in western mining and lumber areas, and in the textile mills of New England. Demonstrations were violently suppressed by the authorities. See also ◊syndicalism.

industry the extraction and conversion of raw materials, the manufacture of goods, and the provision of services. Industry can be either low technology, unspecialized and labor-intensive as in the less developed countries, or highly automated, mechanized, and specialized, using advanced technology, as in the "industrialized" countries. Major trends in industrial activity 1960–90 were the growth of electronic, robotic, and microelectronic technologies, the expansion of the offshore oil industry, and the prominence of Japan and the Pacific region countries in manufacturing and distributing electronics, computers, and motor vehicles.

Indus Valley civilization one of the four earliest ancient civilizations of the Old World (the other three being ◊Sumer 3500 BC; ◊Egypt 3000 BC; and ◊China 2200 BC), developing in the NW of the Indian subcontinent about 2500 BC. ◊Mohenjo-Daro and ◊Harappa were the two main city complexes, but many more existed along the Indus valley, now in Pakistan. Remains include grid-planned streets with municipal drainage, public and private buildings, baths, temples, a standardized system of weights and measures—all of which testify to centralized political control. Evidence exists for trade with Sumer and Akkad. The ◊Aryan invasion of about 1500 BC probably led to its downfall.

inert gas or ***noble gas*** member of group 0 in the ◊periodic table of the elements. There are six inert gases: helium, neon, argon, krypton, xenon, and radon. They are so named because originally they were thought not to enter into any chemical reactions. This is now known not to be true and the term inert is no longer strictly applicable, since it is possible to form compounds with four of the group: argon, krypton, xenon, and radon combine with fluorine and/or oxygen. Still, they are essentially not readily reactive and, as a group, form few chemical compounds. The fact that each has a complete valence shell of eight electrons accounts for the almost total nonreactivity.

inertia in physics, the tendency of an object to remain in a state of rest or uniform motion until an external force is applied, as stated by Isaac Newton's first law of motion (see ◊Newton's laws of motion).

INF abbreviation for intermediate nuclear forces, as in the ◊Intermediate Nuclear Forces Treaty.

infant a child below full legal age; see ◊minor.

infante and ***infanta*** title given in Spain and Portugal to the sons (other than the heir apparent) and daughters, respectively, of the sovereign. The heir apparent in Spain bears the title of prince of Asturias.

infanticide killing of offspring, usually as a method of population control and most frequently of girls (as in historic India and China), although boys are killed in countries where bride prices are high. In the West, where birth control or abortion is not available, infanticide is also practiced.

infantile paralysis former term for poliomyelitis. See ◊polio.

infant mortality rate measure of the number of infants dying under one year of age. Improved sanitation, nutrition, and medical care have considerably lowered figures throughout much of the world; for example in the 18th century in the US and UK infant mortality was about 50%, compared with under 2% in 1971. In much of the Third World, however, the infant mortality rate remains high.

infarct or infarction death and scarring of a portion of the tissue in an organ, as a result of congestion or blockage of a vessel serving it. Myocardial infarct is the technical term for a heart attack.

infection invasion of the body by disease-causing organisms (pathogens, or germs) that overwhelm the immune system, become established, multiply, and produce symptoms. Bacteria and viruses cause most diseases, but there are other microorganisms, protozoans, and other parasites.

Most pathogens enter and leave the body through the digestive or respiratory tracts. Polio, dysentery, and typhoid are examples of diseases contracted by ingestion of contaminated foods or fluids. Organisms present in the saliva or nasal mucus are spread by airborne or droplet infection; fine droplets or dried particles are inhaled by others when the affected individual talks, coughs, or sneezes. Diseases such as measles, mumps, and tuberculosis are passed on in this way. The common cold is passed from hand to hand, which then touches the eye or nose.

A less common route of entry is through the skin, either by contamination of an open wound (as in tetanus) or by penetration of the intact skin surface, as in a bite from a malaria-carrying mosquito. Relatively few diseases are transmissible by skin-to-skin contact. Glandular fever and herpes simplex (cold sore) may be passed on by kissing, and the group now officially bracketed as sexually transmitted diseases (◊STDs) are mostly spread by intimate contact.

inferiority complex in psychology, a ◊complex described by ◊Adler based on physical inferiority; the term has been popularly used to describe general feelings of inferiority and the overcompensation that often ensues.

inferior planet a planet (Mercury or Venus) whose orbit lies between that of the Earth and the Sun.

inferno in astrophysics, a unit for describing the temperature inside a star. One inferno is 1 billion K, or approximately 1 billion°C.

infinite series in mathematics, a series of numbers consisting of a denumerably infinite sequence of terms. The sequence n, n^2, n^3, ... gives the series $n + n^2 + n^3 + \ldots$. For example, $1 + 2 + 3 + \ldots$ is a divergent infinite arithmetic series, and $8 + 4 + 2 + 1 + \frac{1}{2} + \ldots$ is a convergent infinite geometric series whose sum to infinity is 16.

infinity mathematical quantity that is larger than any fixed assignable quantity; symbol ∞. By convention, the result of dividing any number by zero is regarded as infinity.

inflammation defensive reaction of the body tissues to disease or damage, including redness, swelling, and heat. Denoted by the suffix *-itis* (as in appendicitis), it may be acute or chronic, and may be accompanied by the formation of pus. This is an essential part of the healing process.

Modern research has established that inflammation occurs when damaged cells release a substance (◊histamine) that causes blood vessels to widen and leak into the surrounding tissues. This phenomenon accounts for the redness, swelling, and heat. Pain is due partly to the pressure of swelling and also to irritation of nerve endings. Defensive white blood cells congregate within an area of inflammation to engulf and remove foreign matter and dead tissue.

inflation in economics, a rise in the general level of prices. The many causes include cost-push inflation that occurred in 1973 as a result of the increase in OPEC oil prices, in many industries, thus increasing production costs in many industries. Demand-pull inflation results when overall demand exceeds supply. Suppressed inflation occurs in controlled economies and is reflected in rationing, shortages, and black market prices. Deflation, a fall in the general level of prices, is the reverse of inflation.

inflation accounting a method of accounting that allows for the changing purchasing power of money due to inflation.

inflection in grammatical analysis, an ending or other element in a word that indicates its grammatical function (whether plural or singular, masculine or feminine, subject or object, and so on).

In a highly inflected language like Latin, nouns, verbs, and adjectives have many inflectional endings (for example, in the word *amabunt* the base *am* means "love" and the complex *abunt* indicates the kind of verb, the future tense, indicative mood, active voice, third person, and plurality). English has inflections only for plural and for certain forms of the verb (for example, the *s* in "He runs" indicates the third person singular, whereas in "the books" it indicates plurality).

inflorescence a flower-bearing branch, or system of branches, in plants. Inflorescences can be divided into two main types: *cymose* and *racemose*. In a cymose inflorescence, the terminal growing point produces a single flower and subsequent flowers arise on lower lateral branches, as in forget-me-not *Myosotis* and chickweed *Stellaria*; the oldest flowers are found at the apex. A racemose inflorescence consists of a main axis, bearing flowers along its length, with an active growing region at the apex, as in hyacinth and lupin; the oldest flowers are found near the base, or, in cases where the inflorescence has become flattened, toward the outside.

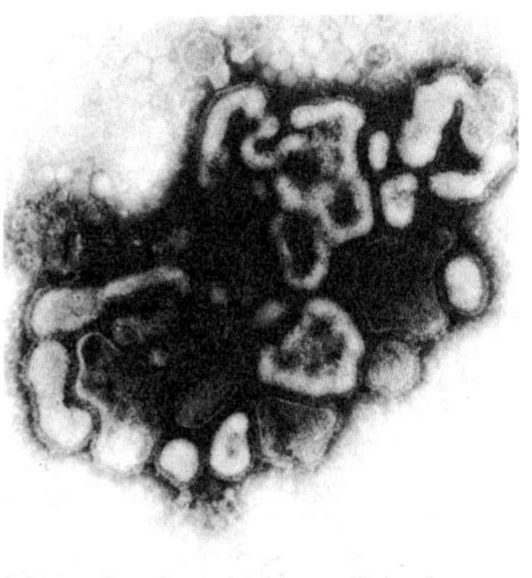

***influenza** An influenza virus, magnified under an electron microscope.*

An inflorescence is usually separated from the leaves by a stalk or peduncle and comprises two, three, or more individual flowers. The stalk of each individual flower is called a pedicel.

Types of racemose inflorescence include the raceme as seen in lupins, a spike which is similar but has stalkless flowers, for example, plantain *Plantago*; and a corymb, which is rounded or flat-topped, as in candytuft *Iberis*. A panicle is a branched inflorescence comprising a number of racemes, as seen in many grasses, for example, oats *Avena*.

An umbel, as in members of the carrot family (Umbelliferae), is a special type of racemose inflorescence with all the flower stalks arising from the same point on the main stem. Other types of racemose inflorescence include the ◊catkin, ◊spadix, and ◊capitulum.

influenza any of various virus infections primarily affecting the air passages, accompanied by ◊systemic effects such as fever, chills, headache, joint and muscle pains, and lassitude.

Depending on the virus strain, influenza varies in virulence and duration, and there is always the risk of secondary (bacterial) infection of the lungs (pneumonia). Treatment is with bed rest and analgesic drugs such as aspirin and paracetamol. Vaccines are effective against known strains but will not give protection against newly evolving viruses. The 1918–19 influenza pandemic (see ◊epidemic) killed about 20 million people worldwide.

information technology collective term for the various technologies involved in the processing and transmission of information. They include computing, telecommunications, and microelectronics.

infrared astronomy study of infrared radiation produced by relatively cool gas and dust in space, such as in the areas around forming stars. In 1983, the Infra-Red Astronomy Satellite (IRAS) surveyed the entire sky at infrared wavelengths. It found five new comets, thousands of galaxies undergoing bursts of star formation, and the possibility of planetary systems forming around several dozen stars.

infrared radiation invisible electromagnetic radiation of wavelength between about 0.75 micrometers and 1 millimeter, that is, between the limit of the red end of the visible spectrum and the shortest microwaves. All bodies above the ◊absolute zero of temperature absorb and radiate infrared radiation. Infrared radiation is used in medical photography and treatment, and in industry, astronomy, and criminology.

Infrared absorption spectra are also used in chemical analysis, particularly for organic compounds; objects that radiate infrared radiation can be photographed or made visible in the dark, or through mist or fog, on specially sensitized emulsions. This is important for military purposes and in detecting people buried under rubble. The strong absorption by many substances of infrared radiation is a useful method of applying heat, as in baking and toasting.

Ingenhousz Jan 1730–1799. Dutch physician and plant physiologist who established that in the light plants absorb carbon dioxide and give off oxygen.

ingestion the process of taking food into the mouth. The method of ◊food capture varies but may involve biting, sucking, or filtering. Many single-celled organisms have a region of their cell wall that acts as a mouth. In these cases surrounding tiny hairs (cilia) sweep food particles together, ready for ingestion.

Ingres Jean Auguste Dominique 1780–1867. French painter, a student of David and leading exponent of the Neoclassical style. From 1807 to 1820 he studied and worked in Rome, where he began the *Odalisque* series of sensuous female nudes, then went to Florence, and returned to France 1824. His portraits painted in the 1840s and 1850s are meticulously detailed and highly polished.

Ingres's style developed in opposition to the Romanticism of Delacroix. His early works include portraits of Napoleon; later he painted ceilings for the Louvre and for Autun Cathedral.

Inhambane seaport on the SE coast of Mozambique, 231 mi/370 km NE of Maputo. Population (1980) 56,000.

inhibition, neural in biology, the process in which activity in one ◊nerve cell suppresses activity in another. Neural inhibition in networks of nerve cells leading from sensory organs, or to muscles, plays an important role in allowing an animal to make fine sensory discriminations and to exercise fine control over movements.

inhibitor or ***negative catalyst*** ◊catalyst that reduces the rate of a reaction. Inhibitors are widely used in foods, medicines, and toiletries.

initiative see ◊initiative, referendum, and recall.

initiative, referendum, and recall processes used by voters to directly affect law making and the removal of elected representatives. An initiative petition for the origination of a law or constitutional amendment, which is then either voted on in special or general election or acted on by the legislature. Referendum is a final approval vote on a law or policy. Recall is a petition metod to remove an elected representative, by special election, before the term of office expires.

injunction a court order that forbids a person from doing something, or orders him or her to take certain action. Breach of an injunction is ◊contempt of court.

ink pigmented liquid used for writing, drawing, and printing. Traditional ink (blue, but later a permanent black) was produced from gallic acid and tannic acid, but inks are now based on synthetic dyes.

Inkatha South African political organization formed 1975 by Chief Gatsha ◊Buthelezi, leader of 6 million Zulus, the country's biggest ethnic group. Inkatha aims to create a nonracial democratic political situation. Because Inkatha has tried to work with the white regime, Buthelezi has been regarded as a collaborator by blacks and the United Democratic Front. Fighting between Inkatha and African National Congress members cost more than 1,000 lives in the first five months of 1990. The term Inkatha is from the grass coil worn by Zulu women for carrying head loads; its many strands give it strength.

Inkerman, Battle of a battle of the Crimean War, fought on Nov 5, 1854, during which an attack by the Russians on Inkerman Ridge, occupied by the British army besieging Sevastopol, was repulsed.

Inland Sea (Japanese Seto Naikai) an arm of the Pacific Ocean, 240 mi/390 km long, almost enclosed by the Japanese islands of Honshu, Kyushu, and Shikoku. It has about 300 small islands.

Inn river in S central Europe, tributary of the

infrared radiation *An aerial infrared photograph shows the Mississippi River (blue). Healthy vegetation appears in shades of red.*

Danube. Rising in the Swiss Alps, it flows 317 mi/507 km NE through Austria and into Bavaria, West Germany, where it meets the Danube at Passau.

Inness George 1825–1894. US landscape painter influenced by the ◊Hudson River school. His early works, such as *The Delaware Valley* 1865 (Metropolitan Museum of Art, New York), are on a grand scale and show a concern for natural effects of light. Later he moved toward Impressionism.

Innocent thirteen popes including:

Innocent III 1161–1216. Pope from 1198 who asserted papal power over secular princes, especially over the succession of Holy Roman emperors. He also made King ◊John of England his vassal, compelling him to accept ◊Langton as archbishop of Canterbury. He promoted the fourth Crusade and crusades against the non-Christian Livonians and Letts, and Albigensian heretics of S France.

Innocents' Day or ***Childermas*** festival of the Roman Catholic church, celebrated on Dec 28 in memory of the Massacre of the Innocents, the children of Bethlehem who were allegedly slaughtered by King ◊Herod after the birth of Jesus.

Innsbruck capital of Tirol state, W Austria; population (1981) 117,000. It is a tourist and winter sports center and a route junction for the Brenner Pass. The 1964 and 1976 Winter Olympics were held here.

inoculation injection into the body of dead or weakened disease-carrying organisms or their toxins to produce immunity by inducing a mild form of a disease. See also ◊vaccination.

inorganic chemistry the branch of chemistry dealing with the elements and their compounds, excluding the more complex carbon compounds which are considered in ◊organic chemistry.

The oldest known groups of inorganic compunds are ◊acids, ◊bases and ◊salts. One major group is the oxides, in which oxygen is combined with another element. Other groups are the compounds of metals with halogens (fluorine, chlorine, bromine, astatine, and iodine), which are called halides (fluorides, chlorides, and so on), and the compounds with sulfur (sulfides). The basis of the description of the elements is the ◊periodic table of elements.

All acids contain hydrogen. Acids containing one, two, or three atoms of replaceable hydrogen are called mono-, di-, or tri-basic, respectively. Salts are formed by the replacement of the acidic hydrogen by a metal or radical. If only part of the hydrogen is replaced, an acid salt is formed.

Oxides are classified into: *acidic oxides*, forming acids with water; *basic oxides*, forming bases (containing the hydroxyl group OH) with water; *neutral oxidesc*; and *peroxides* (containing more oxygen than the usual oxide). Acidic and basic oxides combine to form salts.

input device appliance for entering information into a computer. Input devices include keyboards, joysticks, touch-sensitive screens, ◊graphics tablets, speech-recognition devices, and vision systems.

inquest an inquiry held by a ◊coroner into an unexplained death.

Inquisition tribunal of the Roman Catholic church established 1233 to suppress heresy (dissenting views), originally by excommunication. Sentence was pronounced during a religious ceremony, the ◊auto-da-fé. The Inquisition operated in France, Italy, Spain, and the Holy Roman Empire, and was especially active following the ◊Reformation; it was later extended to the Americas. Its trials were conducted in secret, under torture, and penalties ranged from fines, through flogging and imprisonment, to death by burning.

The Roman Inquisition was established 1542, to combat the growth of Protestantism. The Inquisition or Holy Office (renamed Sacred Congregation for the Doctrine of the Faith 1965) still deals with ecclesiastical discipline.

In re Debs a US Supreme Court decision 1895 dealing with the right of the federal government to suppress labor movements. Eugene Debs, a well-known labor leader, was imprisoned for refusing to comply with a federal injunction against a boycott. Debs had helped organize the boycott of all Pullman carriers in support of the Pullman strike against pay cuts. The government arrested him under the Sherman Antitrust Act. Debs's lawyers petitioned for a writ of habeas corpus, arguing that the matter was outside of federal jurisdiction. The Court denied the writ, ruling that the government's actions were legal under its right to regulate interstate commerce and mail transportation.

In re Gault a US Supreme Court decision 1967 that established the right of minors to due process under the 14th Amendment. The parents of Gerald Gault, a 15-year-old sentenced to reform school by the Arizona juvenile court, filed for a writ of habeas corpus on the grounds that their son's detention after only a summary hearing violated his rights to counsel, notice of hearings, and cross examination and his protection against self-incrimination. The Supreme Court found that the juvenile court was in violation of the 14th Amendment, setting a clear precedent that minors were to be guaranteed due process of law.

insanity popular and legal term for mental disorder. In medicine the corresponding term is ◊psychosis.

insect any member of the class Insecta among the ◊arthropods or jointed-legged animals. An insect's body is divided into head, thorax, and abdomen. The head bears a pair of feelers or antennae, and attached to the thorax are three pairs of legs and

insect

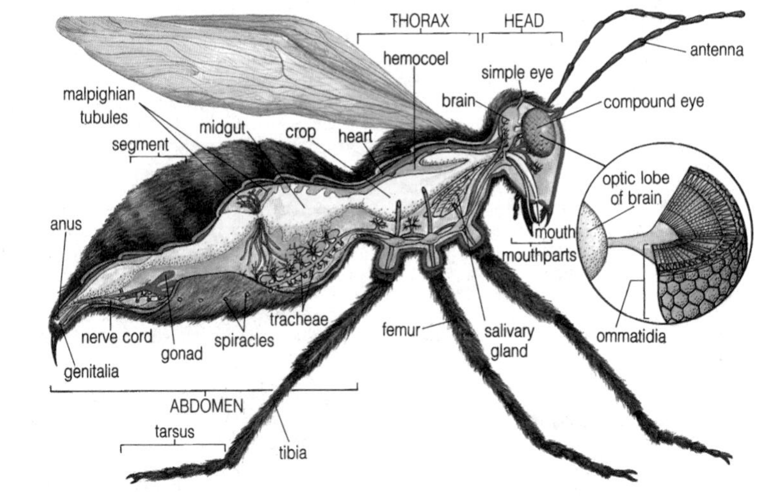
THORAX
HEAD
hemocoel
simple eye
antenna
malpighian tubules
brain
compound eye
midgut
crop
heart
segment
optic lobe of brain
anus
mouth
mouthparts
tracheae
nerve cord
spiracles
gonad
femur
salivary gland
ommatidia
genitalia
ABDOMEN
tarsus
tibia

usually two pairs of wings. The scientific study of insects is termed entomology. More than one million species are known, and several thousand new ones are discovered every year. Insects vary in size from 0.007 in/0.02 cm to 13.5 in/35 cm in length.

anatomy The skeleton is external and is composed of chitin. It is membranous at the joints, but elsewhere is hard. The head is the feeding and sensory center. It bears the antennae, eyes, and mouthparts. By means of the antennae, the insect detects odors and experiences the sense of touch. The eyes include compound eyes and simple eyes (ocelli). Compound eyes are formed of a large number of individual facets or lenses; there are about 4,000 lenses to each compound eye in the housefly. The mouthparts include a labrum, or upper lip; a pair of principal jaws, or mandibles; a pair of accessory jaws, or maxillae; and a labium, or lower lip. These mouthparts are modified in the various insect groups, depending on the diet.

The thorax is the locomotory center, and is made up of three segments: the pro-, meso-, and metathorax. Each bears a pair of legs, and, in flying insects, the second and third of these segments also each bear a pair of wings.

Wings are composed of an upper and a lower membrane, and between these two layers they are strengthened by a framework of chitinous tubes known as veins. The abdomen is the metabolic and reproductive center, where digestion, excretion, and the sexual functions take place. In the female, there is very commonly an egg-laying instrument, or ovipositor, and many insects have a pair of tail feelers, or cerci. Most insects breathe by means of fine airtubes called tracheae, which open to the exterior by a pair of breathing pores, or spiracles. Reproduction is by diverse means. In most insects, mating occurs once only, and death soon follows.

When ready to hatch from the egg, the young insect forces its way through the chorion, or eggshell, and growth takes place in cycles that are interrupted by successive molts. After molting, the new cuticle is soft and pliable, and is able to adapt itself to increase in size and change of form.

Most of the lower orders of insects pass through a direct or incomplete metamorphosis. The young closely resemble the parents and are known as nymphs.

The higher groups of insects undergo indirect or complete metamorphosis. They hatch at an earlier stage of growth than nymphs and are termed larvae. The life of the insect is interrupted by a resting pupal stage when no food is taken. During this stage, the larval organs and tissues are transformed into those of the imago, or adult. Before pupating, the insect protects itself by selecting a suitable hiding place, or making a cocoon of some material which will merge in with its surroundings. When an insect is about to emerge from the pupa, or protective sheath, it undergoes its final molt, which consists of shedding the pupal cuticle.

Many insects are seen as pests. They may be controlled by chemical insecticides (these may also kill useful insects), by importation of natural predators (that may themselves become pests), or, more recently, by the use of artificially reared sterile insects, either the males only, or in "population flushing" both sexes, so sharply reducing succeeding generations.

The classification of insects is largely based upon characters of the mouthparts, wings, and metamorphosis. Insects are divided into 2 subclasses (1 with 2 divisions), and 29 orders.

insecticide any chemical pesticide used to kill insects. Among the most effective insecticides are synthetic organic chemicals such as ◊DDT and dieldrin, which are chlorinated hydrocarbons. These chemicals, however, have proved persistent in the environment and are also poisonous to all animal life, including humans, and are consequently banned in many countries. Other synthetic insecticides include organic phosphorus, compounds such as malathion. Insecticides prepared from plants, such as derris and pyrethrum, are safer to use but need to be applied frequently and carefully.

insectivore any animal whose diet is made up largely or exclusively of insects. In particular, the name is applied to mammals of the order Insectivora, which includes the shrews, hedgehogs, moles, and tenrecs.

insectivorous plant a plant that can capture and digest animals, to obtain nitrogen compounds that are lacking in its usual marshy habitat. Some are passive traps, for example, pitcher plants *Nepenthes*. One pitcher-plant species has container-traps holding 3.5 pt/1.6 l of the liquid that "digests" its food, mostly insects but occasionally even rodents. Others, for example, sundews *Drosera*, butterworts *Pinguicula* and Venus's-flytrap *Dionea muscipula*, have an active trapping mechanism; see ◊leaf.

inselberg a prominent steep-sided hill of resistant solid rock, such as granite, rising out of a plain, usually in a tropical area. Its rounded appearance is caused by so-called onion-skin ◊weathering, in which the surface is eroded in successive layers.

The Sugar Loaf in Rio de Janeiro harbor in Brazil, and Ayers Rock in Northern Territory, Australia, are famous examples. The word is German, "island mountain."

insemination, artificial introduction by instrument of semen from a sperm bank or donor into the female reproductive tract to bring about fertili-

insect classification

Class Insecta *Subclass*	*Order*	*Number of species*	*Common names*
Apterytgota (wingless insects)	Thysanura	350	Three-pronged bristletails, silverfish
	Diplura	400	Two-pronged bristletails, campodeids, japygids
	Protura	50	Minute insects living in soil
	Collembola	1500	Springtails
Pterygota (winged insects or forms secondarily wingless)			
Exopterygota (young resemble adults but have externally developing wings)	Ephemeroptera	1,000	Mayflies
	Odonata	5,000	Dragonflies, damselflies
	Plecoptera	3,000	Stoneflies
	Grylloblattodea	12	Wingless soil-living insects of North America
	Orthoptera	20,000	Crickets, grasshoppers, locusts, mantids, roaches
	Phasmida	2,000	Stick insects, leaf insects
	Dermaptera	1,000	Earwigs
	Embioptera	150	Web-spinners
	Dictyoptera	5,000	Cockroaches, praying mantises
	Isoptera	2,000	Termites
	Zoraptera	16	Tiny insects living in decaying plants
	Psocoptera	1,600	Booklice, barklice, psocids
	Mallophaga	2,500	Biting lice, mainly parasitic on birds
	Anoplura	250	Sucking lice, mainly parasitic on mammals
	Hemiptera	55,000	True bugs, including aphids, shield and bedbugs, froghoppers, pond skaters, water boatmen
	Thysanoptera	5,000	Thrips
Endopterygota (young unlike adults, undergo sudden metamorphosis)	Neuroptera	4,500	Lacewings, alder flies, snake flies, ant lions
	Mecoptera	300	Scorpion flies
	Lepidoptera	165,000	Butterflies, moths
	Trichoptera	3,000	Caddis flies
	Diptera	70,000	True flies, including bluebeetles, mosquitoes, leather jackets, midges
	Siphonaptera	1,400	Fleas
	Hymenoptera	100,000	Bees, wasps, ants, sawflies
	Coloeoptera	350,000	Beetles, including weevils, ladybirds, glow-worms, wood-worms, chafers

zation. Originally used by animal breeders to improve stock with sperm from high-quality males, in the 20th century it has been developed for use in humans, to help the infertile. In ◊in vitro fertilization, the egg is fertilized in a test tube and then implanted in the womb.

The sperm for artificial insemination may come from the husband (AIH) or a donor (AID).

insider trading illegal use of privileged information in dealing on the stock exchanges—for example, when a company takeover bid is imminent. Insider trading is in theory detected by the Securities and Exchange Commission (SEC), and in 1988 the commission was authorized to offer bounties of up to 10% of the civil penalties to those who turned in inside traders. As one New York investment firm pleaded guilty to insider trading and paid more than $500 million in penalties, other stock markets, notably the French Bourse, suffered major inside-trading scandals.

instinct in ◊ethology, behavior found in all equivalent members of a given species (for example, all the males, or all the females with young) that is presumed to be genetically determined.

Examples include a male robin's tendency to attack other male robins intruding on its territory and the tendency of many female mammals to care for their offspring. Instincts differ from ◊reflexes in that they involve very much more complex actions, and learning often plays an important part in their development.

Institute for Advanced Study a department of Princeton University in New Jersey, established 1933, to encourage gifted scientists to further their research uninterrupted by teaching duties or an imposed research scheme. Its first professor was Albert Einstein.

instrument landing system landing aid for aircraft that uses radio beacons on the ground and instruments on the flight deck. One beacon (localizer) sends out a vertical radio beam along the center line of the runway. Another beacon (glide slope) transmits a beam in the plane at right angles to the localizer beam at the ideal approach-path angle. The pilot can tell from the instruments how to maneuver to attain the correct approach path.

insulator any poor ◊conductor of heat, sound, or electricity. Most substances lacking free (mobile) ◊electrons, such as nonmetals, are electrical or thermal insulators.

Usually, devices of glass or porcelain, called insulators, are used for insulating and supporting overhead wires.

insulin protein ◊hormone, produced by specialized cells in the islets of Langerhans in the ◊pancreas, that regulates the ◊metabolism (rate of activity) of glucose, fats, and proteins. Insulin was discovered by Canadian physician Frederick ◊Banting, who pioneered its use in treating ◊diabetes.

Normally, insulin is secreted in response to rising blood sugar levels (after a meal, for example), stimulating the body's cells to store the excess. Failure of this regulatory mechanism in ◊diabetes mellitus requires treatment with insulin injections or capsules taken by mouth. Types vary from pig and beef insulins to synthetic and bioengineered ones. They may be combined with other substances to make them longer- or shorter-acting. Implanted, battery-powered insulin pumps deliver the hormone at a preset rate, to eliminate the unnatural rises and falls that result from conventional, subcutaneous (under the skin) delivery. Human insulin has now been produced from bacteria by ◊genetic engineering techniques, but may increase the chance of sudden, unpredictable hypoglycemia, or low blood sugar. In 1990 the Medical College of Ohio developed gelatine capsules and an aspirinlike drug which helps the insulin pass into the bloodstream.

insurance contract guaranteeing compensation to the payer of periodic premiums against loss (under stipulated conditions) by fire, death, accident, and the like. Various consumer policies also insure legal or health services, paying bills or portions thereof, within the contracted conditions. Insurance is a major component of business activity, covering replacement costs of property, inventory, or goods in transit.

During the war between Iran and Iraq 1987–88, it was the refusal of insurance companies to cover losses sustained by acts of war that dissuaded oil tankers from passing through the zone of hostilities.

integer a whole number—for example, 3. Integers may be positive or negative; 0 is an integer, and is often considered positive. Formally, integers are members of the set $Z = (\ldots -3, -2, -1, 0, 1, 2, 3, \ldots)$. Fractions, such as ½ and 0.35, are known as nonintegral numbers ("not integers").

integral calculus branch of mathematics using the process of ◊integration. It is concerned with finding volumes and areas and summing infinitesimally small quantities.

integrated circuit complete electronic circuit produced on a single crystal of a ◊semiconductor (intermediate between an insulator and a conductor of electricity) such as silicon. The circuit might contain more than 1 million transistors, resistors, and capacitors, and yet measure only 0.3 in/8 mm across. See also ◊silicon chip.

The discovery in the early 1970s of the means to produce such circuits, superseding the printed circuit, began the so-called computer revolution.

integration in mathematics, a method in ◊calculus of evaluating definite or indefinite integrals. An example of a definite integral can be thought of as finding the area under a curve (as represented by an algebraic expression or function) between particular values of the function's variable. In practice, integral calculus provides scientists with a powerful tool for doing calculations that involve a continually varying quantity (such as determining the position at any given instant of a space rocket that is accelerating away from Earth). Its basic principles were discovered in the late 1660s independently by the German philosopher ◊Leibniz and the British scientist ◊Newton.

intelligence in psychology, a general concept that summarizes the abilities of an individual in reasoning and problem solving, particularly in novel situations. These consist of a wide range of verbal and nonverbal skills and therefore some psychologists dispute a unitary concept of intelligence. See ◊intelligence test.

intelligence in military and political affairs, information, often secretly or illegally obtained, about other countries. Counter-intelligence is information on the activities of hostile agents. Much intelligence is gained by technical means, such as satellites and the electronic interception of data.

The Central Intelligence Agency is responsible for gathering foreign intelligence and for coordinating the reports of the several government intelligence agencies. These include military intelligence branches within each armed service; the National Security Agency, responsible for technical intelligence gathering; and intelligence officers within the State Department and other executive-branch agencies. Domestic intelligence is the responsibility of the ◊Federal Bureau of Investigation. Double agents are those motivated by money, ideology, or dissatisfaction to provide information to the ostensible enemy, often doing great damage. Moles are double agents who betray their own security services. Sleepers are agents who assume a normal life in the target country, often inactive for years until needed.

intelligence test test that attempts to measure innate intellectual ability, rather than acquired ability.

It is now generally believed that a child's ability in an intelligence test can be affected by his or her environment, cultural background, and teaching. There is skepticism about the accuracy of intelligence tests, but they are still widely used as a diagnostic tool when children display learning difficulties.

"Sight and sound" intelligence tests, developed by Christopher Brand in 1981, avoid cultural bias and the pitfalls of improvement by practice. Subjects are shown a series of lines being flashed on a screen at increasing speed, and are asked to identify in each case the shorter of a pair; and when two notes are relayed over headphones, they are asked to identify which is the higher. There is a close correlation between these results and other intelligence test scores.

The French psychologist Alfred Binet (1857–1911) devised the first intelligence test in 1905. The concept of intelligence quotient (IQ) was adopted by US psychologist Lewis Terman in 1915. The IQ is calculated according to the formula: $IQ = MA/CA \times 100$ in which MA is "mental age" (the age at which an average child is able to perform given tasks) and CA is "chronological age," hence an average person has an IQ of 100 ± 10.

Intelligence tests were first used on a large scale in the US in 1917 during World War I for two million drafted men, and their subsequent widespread use for education and employment decisions has provoked protests from minority groups who contend the tests are culturally biased and discriminatory.

Intelsat International Telecommunications Satellite Organization, established 1964 to operate a worldwide system of ◊communications satellites. More than 100 countries are members of Intelsat, with headquarters in Washington, DC. Intelsat satellites are stationed in geosynchronous orbit (maintaining their positions relative to the Earth) over the Atlantic, Pacific, and Indian Oceans. The first Intelsat satellite was *Early Bird*, launched 1965.

intendant official appointed by the French crown under Louis XIV to administer a territorial *département*. Their powers were extensive but counteracted to some extent by other local officials. The term was also used for certain administrators in Spain, Portugal, and Latin America.

intensity the concentration of a force or energy over a given area or time. For example, the intensity or loudness of a sound is related to the energy per unit area carried by the sound wave. Likewise, the intensity or brightness of a light source is measured by the energy per unit area carried by the light.

intensive care unit (ICU) high-technology medical facility for treating the critically ill or injured.

intentionality in philosophy, the property of consciousness whereby it is directed toward an object, even when this object does not exist in reality (such as "the golden mountain"). Intentionality is a key concept in the German phenomenologist ◊Husserl's philosophy.

intercostal muscle muscle found between the ribs, responsible for producing the rib cage movements involved in some types of breathing.

When the intercostal muscles contract the ribs move upward and outward, enlarging the thorax and causing air to rush into the lungs. On relaxation the ribs move downward under their own weight, and air is pushed out of the lungs. This type of breathing complements the more gentle contractions of the ◊diaphragm, and occurs for instance during exercise.

interdict ecclesiastical punishment that excludes an individual, community, or realm from participation in spiritual activities except for communion. It was usually employed against heretics or realms whose ruler was an excommunicant.

interest in finance, a sum of money paid by a borrower to a lender as a premium for the loan, usually expressed as a percentage per annum. It is paid on savings accounts, bank certificates of deposit, and on government and corporate bonds; it is usually taxable income. Simple interest is calculated as a straight percentage of the amount loaned or invested. Compound interest is computed by reinvesting the previous interest payment before interest is calculated on that new total.

A sum of $100 invested at 10% per annum simple interest for five years earns $10 a year, giving a total of $50 interest (and at the end of the period the investor receives a total of $150). The same sum of $100 invested for five years at 10% compound interest earns a total of $61.05 interest (with $161.05 returned at the end of the period). The difference arises from adding the previous period's interest to the capital before calculating the next payment.

interface in computing, the point of contact between two programs or pieces of equipment. The term is most often used for the physical connection between the computer and a ◊peripheral device. For example, a printer interface is the cabling and circuitry used to transfer data from the computer to the printer and to compensate for differences in speed and coding systems.

interference in physics, the phenomenon of two or more wave motions interacting and combining to produce a resultant wave of larger or smaller amplitude (depending on whether the combining waves are in or out of ◊phase with each other).

Interference of white light (multiwavelength) results in spectral colored fringes, for example, the iridescent colors of oil films seen on water or soap bubbles (demonstrated by ◊Newton's rings). Interference of sound waves of similar frequency produces the phenomenon of beats, often used by musicians when tuning an instrument. With monochromatic light (of a single wavelength), interference produces patterns of light and dark bands. This is the basis of ◊holography, for example. Interferometry can also be applied to radio waves, and is a powerful tool in modern astronomy.

interferometer in physics, a device that splits a beam of light into two parts, the parts being recombined after traveling different paths to form an interference pattern of light and dark bands. Interferometers are used in many branches of science and industry where accurate measurements of distances and angles are needed.

In the Michelson interferometer, a light beam is split into two by a semisilvered mirror. The two beams are then reflected off fully silvered mirrors and recombined. The pattern of dark and light bands is sensitive to small alterations in the placing of the mirrors, so the interferometer can detect changes in their position to within one ten-millionth of a meter. Using lasers, compact devices of this kind can be built to measure distances, for example to check the accuracy of machine tools.

In radio astronomy, interferometers consist of separate radio telescopes, each observing the same distant object, such as a galaxy, in the sky. The signal received by each telescope is fed into a computer. Because the telescopes are in different places, the distance traveled by the signal to reach each differs and the overall signal is akin to the interference pattern in the Michelson interferometer. Computer analysis of the overall signal can build up a detailed picture of the source of the radio waves.

In space technology, interferometers are used in radio and radar systems. These include space-vehicle guidance systems, in which the position of the spacecraft is determined by combining the signals received by two precisely spaced antennae mounted on it.

interferon naturally occurring cellular protein that makes up part of the body's defenses against viral disease. Three types (alpha, beta, and gamma) are produced by infected cells and enter the bloodstream and uninfected cells, making them immune to virus attack.

Interferon was discovered in 1957 by Scottish virologist Alick Isaacs. At present, only alpha interferon has any proven therapeutic value, and may be used to treat a rare type of ◊leukemia.

interior decoration design, decoration, and furnishing of the inside of a building. In recent times the trend has been to a less ornate and more functional style, fostered by the interaction of architects and designers working in teams, whether to remodel existing interiors (for example Misha Black and Hugh Casson) or in new buildings (for example Gio Ponti's Pirelli building in Milan, Oscar ◊Niemeyer's capital city of Brasilia; and the many works of ◊Le Corbusier, Eero ◊Saarinen, and Skidmore Owings and Merrill). Frank Lloyd ◊Wright was instrumental in promoting a design that was free of the historic past and in keeping with modern industrial production. International style furniture—light, geometric, simple, and functional—was designed, often by architects, to complement modern architecture.

intermediate technology

windpump

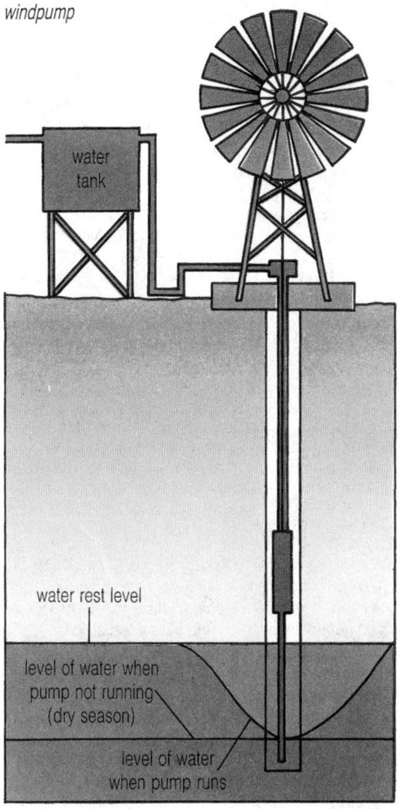
water tank
water rest level
level of water when pump not running (dry season)
level of water when pump runs

Interlaken chief town of the Bernese Oberland, on the river Aar between lakes Brienz and Thun, Switzerland; population (1985) 13,000. The site was first occupied in 1130 by a monastery, suppressed in 1528.

Intermediate Nuclear Forces Treaty agreement signed Dec 8, 1987 between the US and the USSR to eliminate all ground-based nuclear missiles in Europe that were capable of hitting only European targets (including European Russia). It reduced the countries's nuclear arsenals by some 2,000 (4% of the total). The treaty included provisions for each country to inspect the other's bases. A total of 1,269 weapons (945 Soviet, 234 US) was destroyed in the first year of the treaty.

intermediate technology the application of mechanics, electrical engineering, and other technologies, based on inventions and designs developed in scientifically sophisticated cultures, but utilizing materials, assembly, and maintenance methods found in technologically less advanced regions (known as the ◊Third World).

Intermediate technologies aim to allow developing countries to benefit from new techniques and inventions of the "First World," without the burdens of costly maintenance and supply of fuels and spare parts that in the Third World would represent an enormous and probably uneconomic overhead.

intermezzo in music, a short orchestral interlude often used between the acts of an opera to denote the passage of time; by extension, a short piece for an instrument to be played between other more substantial works.

intermolecular force or ***van der Waals' force*** force of attraction between molecules. Intermolecular forces are relatively weak, hence simple molecular compounds are gases, liquids, or low-melting-point solids.

internal-combustion engine heat engine in which fuel is burned inside the engine, contrasting with an external combustion engine (such as the steam engine) in which fuel is burned in a separate unit. The diesel and ◊gasoline are both internal-combustion engines. Gas turbines and jet and rocket engines are sometimes also considered to be internal-combustion engines because they burn their fuel inside their combustion chambers.

International, the coordinating body established by labor and Socialist organizations, including:

First International or International Working Men's Association 1864–72, formed in London under Karl ◊Marx.

Second International 1889–1940, founded in Paris.

Third (Socialist) International or Comintern 1919–43, formed in Moscow by the Soviet leader Lenin, advocating from 1933 a popular front (communist, Socialist, liberal) against the German dictator Hitler.

Fourth International or Trotskyist International 1936, somewhat indeterminate, anti-Stalinist.

Revived Socialist International 1951, formed in Frankfurt, West Germany, a largely anti-communist association of social democrats.

International Atomic Energy Agency (IAEA) agency of the United Nations established 1957 to advise and assist member countries in the development and application of nuclear power and to guard against its misuse. It has its headquarters in Vienna and is responsible for research centers in Austria, Monaco, and the International Center for Theoretical Physics, Trieste, established 1964.

International Bank for Reconstruction and Development official name of the ◊World Bank.

international biological standards drugs (such as penicillin and insulin) whose activity for a specific mass (called the international unit, or IU), prepared and stored under specific conditions, serves as a standard for measuring doses. For ◊penicillin, one IU is the activity of 0.0006 mg of the sodium salt of penicillin, so a dose of a million units would be 0.6 g.

International Brigade international volunteer force on the Republican side in the Spanish ◊Civil War 1936–39.

International Civil Aviation Organization agency of the ◊United Nations, established 1947 to regulate safety and efficiency and air law; headquarters Montreal, Canada.

International Court of Justice the main judicial organ of the ◊United Nations, at The Hague, the Netherlands.

International Date Line (IDL) a modification of the 180th meridian that marks the difference in time between E and W. The date is put forward a day when crossing the line going W, and back a day when going E. The IDL was chosen at the International Meridian Conference in 1884.

International Development Association (IDA) an agency of the United Nations, established in 1960 and affiliated to the ◊World Bank.

Internationale international revolutionary Socialist anthem; composed 1870 and first sung 1888. The words by Eugène Pottier (1816–1887) were written shortly after Napoleon III's surrender to Prussia; the music is by Pierre Degeyter. It was the Soviet national anthem 1917–44.

International Finance Corporation United Nations agency affiliated to the ◊World Bank. It was set up in 1956 to facilitate loans for private investment to developing countries.

International Fund for Agricultural Development agency of the ◊United Nations, established 1977, to provide funds for benefiting the poor in developing countries.

International Gothic a late ◊Gothic style of painting prevalent in Europe in the 14th and 15th centuries.

International Labor Organization (ILO) an agency of the United Nations, established in 1919, which formulates standards for labor and social conditions. Its headquarters are in Geneva. It was awarded the Nobel Peace Prize 1969.

international law body of rules generally accepted as governing the relations between countries, pioneered by Hugo ◊Grotius, especially in matters of human rights, territory, and war. Neither the League of Nations nor the United Nations proved able to enforce it, successes being achieved only when the law coincided with the aims of a predominant major power—for example, the ◊Korean War. The scope of the law is now extended to space—for example, the 1967 treaty that (among other things) banned nuclear weapons from space.

International Maritime Organization agency of the ◊United Nations concerned with world shipping. Established in 1958; headquarters in London, England.

International Monetary Fund (IMF) specialized agency of the United Nations, headquarters Washington, DC, established under the 1944 ◊Bretton Woods agreement and operational since 1947. It seeks to promote international monetary cooperation and the growth of world trade, and to smooth multilateral payment arrangements among member states. IMF stand-by loans are available to members in balance of payments difficulties (the amount being governed by the member's quota), usually on the basis of acceptance of instruction on stipulated corrective measures.

The Fund also operates other drawing facilities, including several designed to provide preferential credit to developing countries with liquidity problems. Having previously operated in US dollars linked to gold, since 1972 the IMF has used the ◊special drawing right (SDR) as its standard unit of account, valued in terms of a weighted "basket" of major currencies. Since the 1971 Smithsonian agreement permitting wider fluctuations from specified currency parities, IMF rules have been progressively adapted to the increasing prevalence of fully floating exchange rates.

International Settlements, Bank for (BIS) forum for European central banks, established 1930, which acts as a bank to the central banks, to prevent currency speculation. It has been superseded in some of its major functions by the ◊International Monetary Fund.

International Society for Krishna Consciousness (ISKCON) a Hindu sect based on the demonstration of intense love for Krishna (an incarnation of the god Vishnu), especially by chanting the mantra "Hare Krishna." Members wear distinctive yellow robes, and men often have their heads partly shaven. Their holy books are the Hindu scriptures and particularly the *Bhagavad-Gītā*, which they study daily.

The sect was introduced to the West by Swami Prabhupada (1896–1977). Members believe that by chanting the mantra and meditating on it they may achieve enlightenment and so remove themselves from the cycle of reincarnation. They are expected to live ascetic lives, avoiding meat, eggs, alcohol, tea, coffee, and other drugs, and gambling; sexual relationships should only take place within marriage and solely for procreation.

International Standards Organization international organization founded 1947 to standardize technical terms, units, and so on. Its headquarters are in Geneva.

International Telecommunication Union body belonging to the Economic and Social Council of the ◊United Nations.

International Union for Conservation of Nature see ◊IUCN.

internment the detention of suspected criminals without trial. Foreign citizens are often interned during times of war or civil unrest.

interplanetary matter gas and dust thinly spread through the Solar System. The gas flows outward from the Sun as the ◊solar wind. Fine dust lies in the plane of the Solar System, scattering sunlight to cause the zodiacal light. Swarms of dust shed by comets enter the Earth's atmosphere to cause ◊meteor showers.

Interpol (acronym for *Inter*national Criminal *Pol*ice Organization) agency founded following the Second International Judicial Police Conference 1923 with its headquarters in Vienna, and reconstituted after World War II with its headquarters in Paris. It has an international criminal register, fingerprint file, and methods index.

interpreter computer program that translates statements from a ◊programming language into ◊machine code and causes them to be executed. Unlike a ◊compiler, which translates the whole program at once to produce an executable program in machine code, an interpreter translates the programming language each time the program is run.

intersex an individual that is intermediate between a normal male and a normal female in its appearance (for example, a genetic male that lacks external genitalia and so resembles a female).

Intersexes are usually the result of an abnormal hormone balance during development (especially during ◊gestation) or of a failure of the ◊genes controlling sex determination. The term ◊hermaphrodite is sometimes erroneously used for intersexes.

Interstate Commerce Act in US history, an act of Congress in 1887 responding to public concern regarding profiteering and malpractice by railroad companies. It required all charges to be reasonable and fair, and established the Interstate Commerce Commission to investigate railroad management. The act proved difficult to enforce.

interstellar molecules over 50 different types of molecules existing in gas clouds in our Galaxy. Most have been detected by their radio emissions, but some have been found by the absorption lines they produce in the spectra of starlight. The most complex molecules, many of them based on ◊carbon, are found in the dense clouds where stars are forming. They may be significant for the origin of life elsewhere in space.

intestacy the absence of a will at a person's death. In law, special legal rules apply on intestacy for appointing administrators to deal with the deceased person's affairs, and for disposing of the deceased person's property in accordance with statutory provisions.

intestine in vertebrates, the digestive tract from the stomach outlet to the anus. The human small intestine is 20 ft/6 m long, 1.5 in/4 cm in diameter, and consists of the duodenum, jejunum, and ileum; the large intestine is 5 ft/1.5 m long, 2.5 in/6 cm in diameter, and includes the cecum, colon, and rectum. Both are muscular tubes comprising an inner lining that secretes alkaline digestive juice, a submucous coat containing fine blood vessels and nerves, a muscular coat, and a serous coat covering all, supported by a strong peritoneum, which carries the blood and lymph vessels, and the nerves. The contents are passed along slowly by ◊peristalsis. The term intestine is also applied to the lower digestive tract of invertebrates.

Intifada (Arabic "resurgence" or "throwing off") Palestinian uprising; also the title of the involved ***Liberation Army of Palestine***, a loosely organized group of adult and teenage Palestinians active since 1987 in attacks on Israeli troops in the occupied territories of Palestine. Their campaign for self-determination includes stone-throwing and gasoline bombing.

The uprising began in Dec 1987 in Gaza. Rumors that a fatal traffic collision had been caused by Israeli security service agents in retaliation for the stabbing of an Israeli the previous week led to demonstrations by teenagers armed with slingshots. It subsequently spread despite attempts at repression. Some 600 Palestinians and 45 Jews were killed in the uprising to the end of 1989. Over 157 Palestinian private homes have been dynamited by military order, under a still-valid British emergency regulation promulgated 1946 to put down Jewish guerrillas. The number of soldiers on duty on the West Bank at the beginning of 1989 was said to be more than three times the number needed to conquer it during the Six-Day War.

intrauterine device IUD or coil, a contraceptive device that is inserted into the uterus. It is a tiny plastic object, sometimes containing copper. By causing a mild inflammation of the lining of the uterus it prevents fertilized eggs from becoming implanted.

They are generally very reliable, as long as they stay in place, with a success rate of about 98%. Some women experience heavier and more painful periods, and there is a very small risk of a pelvic infection leading to infertility.

intravenous delivery of a substance directly into a vein.

intrusion a mass of ◊igneous rock that has formed by "injection" of molten rock into existing cracks beneath the surface of the Earth, as distinct from

intrusion

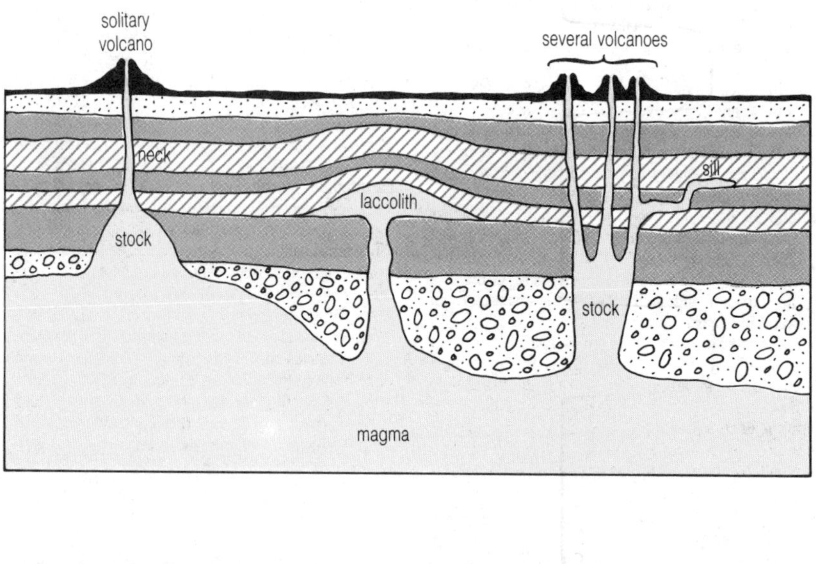

solitary volcano
several volcanoes
neck
sill
laccolith
stock
stock
magma

Invalides *The Hôtel des Invalides in Paris, established by Louis XIV in 1670 for disabled soldiers. Napoleon was buried beneath the dome of its church in 1840.*

a volcanic rock mass which has erupted from the surface.

intuition a rapid, unconscious thought process. In philosophy, intuition is that knowledge of a concept which does not derive directly from the senses. Thus, we may be said to have an intuitive idea of God, beauty, or justice. The concept of intuition is similar to Bertrand ◊Russell's theory of knowledge by acquaintance. In both cases, it is contrasted with empirical knowledge See ◊empiricism.

intuitionism in mathematics, the theory that propositions can be built up only from intuitive concepts that we all recognize easily, such as unity or plurality. The concept of ◊infinity, of which we have no intuitive experience, is thus not allowed.

Invalides, Hôtel des building in Paris, S of the Seine, founded in 1670 as a home for disabled soldiers. The church Dôme des Invalides contains the tomb of Napoleon I.

Invar trademark for an alloy of iron containing 36% nickel, which expands or contracts very little when the temperature changes. It is used to make precision instruments (such as pendulums and tuning forks) whose dimensions must not alter.

Invercargill city on the S coast of South Island, New Zealand; population (1986) 52,800. It has lumber mills and meatpacking and aluminum-smelting plants.

Inverness town in Highland region, Scotland, lying in a sheltered site at the mouth of the river Ness; population (1985) 58,000. It is a tourist center with tweed, tanning, engineering, and distilling industries.

inverse square law in physics, the statement that the magnitude of an effect (usually a force) at a point is inversely proportional to the square of the distance between that point and the point location of its cause.

Light, sound, electrostatic force (Coulomb's law), gravitational force (Newton's law) and magnetic force (see ◊magnetism) all obey the inverse square law.

invertebrate an animal without a backbone. The invertebrates form all of the major divisions of the animal kingdom called phyla, with the exception of vertebrates. Invertebrates include the sponges, coelenterates, flatworms, nematodes, annelids, arthropods, mollusks, and echinoderms. Primitive aquatic chordates such as sea-squirts and lancelets, which only have notochords and do not possess a vertebral column of cartilage or bone, are sometimes called invertebrate chordates, but this is misleading, since the notochord is the precursor of the backbone in advanced chordates.

investiture contest the conflict between the papacy and the Holy Roman Empire 1075–1122, which centered on the right of lay rulers to appoint prelates (investiture).

It began with the decree of 1075 in which Pope Gregory VII (1021–85) forbade lay investiture and with Henry IV's excommunication the following year after he refused to accept the ruling. There was a lull in the conflict after Henry's death in 1106, but in 1111, Henry V captured Paschal II (c. 1050–1118), and forced him to concede that only lay rulers could endow prelates with their temporalities (lands and other possessions). When this was overturned by the Lateran Council of 1112, the church split between pro-papal and pro-imperial factions, and fighting broke out in Germany and Italy. Settlement was reached in 1122 at the Diet of Worms, when it was agreed that lay rulers could not appoint prelates but could continue to invest them with their temporalities.

investment in economics, the purchase of any asset with the potential to yield future financial benefit to the purchaser (such as a house, a work of art, stocks and bonds, or even a private education).

investment trust a public company that makes investments in other companies on behalf of its stockholders. It may issue shares to raise capital and issue fixed interest securities. See ◊mutual fund.

Invisible Man 1952 novel by US writer Ralph Ellison about an unnamed hero who discovers that because of his blackness he lacks all social identity in postwar US society.

in vitro fertilization (IVF) literally, "fertilization in glass," that is, allowing eggs and sperm to unite in a laboratory to form embryos. The embryos produced may then either be implanted into the womb of the otherwise infertile mother (an extension of artificial ◊insemination), or used for research. The first baby to be produced by this method, Louise Brown, was born in 1978 in the UK. In cases where the fallopian tubes are blocked, fertilization may be carried out by intravaginal culture, in which egg and sperm are incubated (in a plastic tube) in the mother's vagina, then transferred surgically into the uterus.

Recent extensions of the in vitro technique have included the birth of a baby from a frozen embryo (Australia 1984) and from a frozen egg (Australia 1986). British doctors were pioneers in the field. The technique is now common in the US. As yet the success rate is relatively low; only 15–20% of in vitro fertilizations result in babies.

involute (Latin "rolled in") of a circle, a ◊spiral that can be thought of as being traced by a point at the end of a taut nonelastic thread being wound onto or unwound from a spool.

Inyangani highest peak in Zimbabwe, rising to 8,507 ft/2,593 m near the Mozambique frontier in NE Zimbabwe.

Inyokern village in the Mohave desert, California, 45 mi/72 km NW of Mohave. It is the site of a US naval ordnance test station, founded in 1944, carrying out research in rocket flight and propulsion.

Io in Greek mythology, a princess loved by ◊Zeus, who transformed her into a heifer to hide her from the jealousy of ◊Hera.

Io in astronomy, the third largest moon of the planet Jupiter, 2,240 mi/3,600 km in diameter, orbiting in 1.77 days at a distance of 257,000 mi/413,000 km. It is the most volcanically active body in the Solar System, covered by hundreds of vents that erupt not lava but sulfur, giving Io an orange-colored surface.

iodine a grayish-black nonmetallic element, symbol I, atomic number 53, atomic weight 126.9044. It is a member of the ◊halogen group. Its crystals give off, when heated, a violet vapor with an irritating odor resembling that of chlorine. It only occurs in combination with other elements. Its salts are known as iodides, which are found in sea water. As a mineral nutrient it is vital to the proper functioning of the thyroid gland, where it occurs in trace amounts as part of the hormone thyroxine. Fluorine is used in photography, in medicine as an antiseptic, and in making dyes.

Its radioactive isotope I-131 (half-life of eight days) is a dangerous fission product from nuclear explosions and from the nuclear reactors in power plants, since, if ingested, it can be taken up by the thyroid and damage it. The element was discovered in 1811 by French chemist B Courtois (1777–1838). The name derives from Greek *iodes*, violet.

ion an atom that is either positively charged (cation) or negatively charged (anion), as a result of the loss or gain of electrons during chemical reactions or from exposure to certain forms of radiation.

Ion in Greek mythology, son of Apollo, ancestor of the Ionian or eastern Greeks, and subject of a play by ◊Euripides.

Iona an island in the Inner Hebrides; area 2,100 acres/850 hectares. A center of early Christianity, it is the site of a monastery founded 563 by St ◊Columba. It later became a burial ground for Irish, Scottish, and Norwegian kings. It has a 13th-century abbey.

ion engine rocket engine that uses ◊ions (charged particles) rather than hot gas for propulsion. Ion engines have been successfully tested in space, where they will eventually be used for gradual rather than sudden velocity changes. In an ion engine, atoms of mercury, for example, are ionized (given an electric charge by an electric field) and then accelerated at high speed by a more powerful electric field.

Ionesco Eugène 1912– . Romanian-born French dramatist, a leading exponent of the Theater of the ◊Absurd. Most of his plays are in one act and concern the futility of language as a means of communication. These include *La Cantatrice chauve/The Bald Prima Donna* 1950 and *La Leçon/The Lesson* 1951.

Later full-length plays include *Rhinocéros* 1958 and *Le Roi se meurt/Exit the King* 1961. He has also written memoirs and a novel, *Le Solitaire/The Hermit* 1973.

ion exchange process whereby the ions in one compound replace the ions in another. The exchange occurs because one of the products is insoluble in water. For example, when hard water is passed over an ion-exchange resin, the dissolved calcium and magnesium ions are replaced by either sodium or hydrogen ions, so the hardness is removed. Commercial water softeners use ion-exchange resins. The addition of ◊washing-soda crystals to hard water is also an example of ion exchange.

$$\boldsymbol{Na_2CO_{3\,(aq)}} + \boldsymbol{CaSO_{4\,(aq)}} \rightarrow CaCO_{3\,(s)} + Na_2SO_{4\,(aq)}$$

Ionia in Classical times the W coast of Asia Minor, settled about 1000 BC by the Ionians; it included the cities of Ephesus, Miletus, and later Smyrna.

Ionian member of a Hellenic people from beyond the Black Sea who crossed the Balkans around 1980 BC and invaded Asia Minor. Driven back by the ◊Hittites, they settled all over mainland Greece, later being supplanted by the ◊Achaeans.

Ionian Islands (Greek *Ionioi Nisoi*) island group off the W coast of Greece; area 332 sq mi/860 sq km. A British protectorate from 1815 until their cession to Greece 1864, they include Cephalonia (Greek *Kefallínia*); Corfu (*Kérkyra*), a Venetian possession 1386–1797; Cythera (*Kíthira*); Ithaca (*Itháki*), the traditional home of ◊Odysseus; Leukas (*Levkás*); Paxos (*Paxoí*); and Zante (*Zákynthos*).

Ionian Sea the part of the Mediterranean that lies

between Italy and Greece, to the S of the Adriatic, and containing the Ionian Islands.

Ionic in Classical architecture, one of the five types of column; see ◊order.

ionic bond or ***electrovalent bond*** bond produced when atoms of one element donate electrons to another element that accepts the electrons, forming positively and negatively charged ◊ions respectively. The electrostatic attraction between the oppositely charged ions constitutes the bond. Sodium chloride (Na^+Cl^-) is a typical ionic compound.

Each ion has the electronic structure of an inert gas (see ◊noble gas structure). The maximum number of electrons that can be gained is usually two.

ionic compound substance composed of oppositely charged ions. All salts, most bases, and some acids are examples of ionic compounds. They possess the following general properties: they are crystalline solids with a high melting point; are soluble in water and insoluble in organic solvents; and always conduct electricity when molten or in aqueous solution. A typical ionic compound is sodium chloride (Na^+Cl^-).

ionization chamber any device for measuring the amount of ionizing radiation. The radiation ionizes gas in the chamber and the ions are collected and measured as an electric charge.

Ionization chambers are used for determining the intensity of X-rays or the disintegration rate of radioactive materials.

ionizing radiation radiation that knocks electrons from atoms during its passage, thereby leaving ions in its path. Alpha and beta particles are far more ionizing in their effect than are neutrons or gamma radiation.

ionosphere ionized layer of Earth's outer ◊atmosphere (38–620 mi/60–1,000 km) that contains sufficient free electrons to modify the way in which radio waves are propagated, for instance by reflecting them back to Earth. The ionosphere is thought to be produced by absorption of the Sun's ultraviolet radiation.

ion plating method of applying corrosion-resistant metal coatings. The article is placed in argon gas, together with some coating metal, which vaporizes on heating and becomes ionized (acquires charged atoms) as it diffuses through the gas to form the coating. It has important applications in the aerospace industry.

IOU short for "I owe you"; written acknowledgment of debt, signed by the debtor; see also ◊Bill of Exchange.

Iowa state of the midwest US; nickname Hawkeye State

area 56,279 sq mi/145,800 sq km

capital Des Moines

cities Cedar Rapids, Davenport, Sioux City

features Grant Wood Gallery, Davenport; Herbert Hoover birthplace, library, and museum near West Branch; "Little Switzerland" region in the NE, overlooking the Mississippi River; Effigy Mounds National Monument, near Marquette, a prehistoric Indian burial site

products corn, soybeans, hogs and cattle, chemicals, farm machinery, electrical goods, hardwood lumber, minerals

population (1990) 2,776,755

famous people "Bix" Beiderbecke, "Buffalo Bill" Cody, Herbert Hoover, Glenn Miller, Lillian Russell, Grant Wood

history Sauk and Fox Indians were forced to cede their lands 1832 in what is now E Iowa. Blessed with rich topsoil, Iowa quickly attracted settlers, and it became a state 1846. The economy remains based on agriculture; the state usually leads all others in the production of corn, soybeans, and hogs.

Iowa

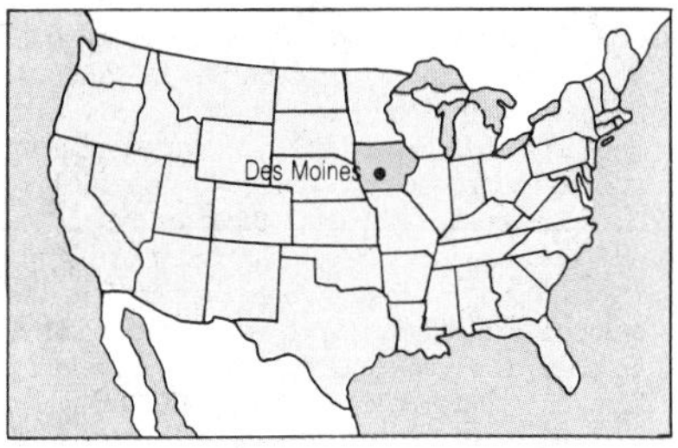
Des Moines

Iowa City city in E Iowa, on the Iowa river, S of Cedar Rapids, seat of Johnson county. It is a distribution center for the area's agricultural products. Other industries include printed matter and building materials. The University of Iowa 1847 is here; population (1990) 59,738.

ipecacuanha or ***ipecac*** South American plant *Psychotria ipecacuanha* of the madder family Rubiaceae, the dried roots of which are used as an emetic and in treating amoebic dysentery.

Iphigenia in Greek mythology, a daughter of ◊Agamemnon and Clytemnestra.

Ipoh capital of Perak state, Peninsular Malaysia; population (1980) 301,000. The economy is based on tin mining.

Ipswich river port on the Orwell estuary, administrative headquarters of Suffolk, England; population (1981) 120,500. Industries include engineering and the manufacture of textiles, plastics, and electrical goods.

IQ intelligence quotient. It is the ratio between a subject's "mental" and chronological ages, multiplied by 100. A score of 100 ± 10 is considered average. See ◊intelligence test.

Iqbāl Mohammed 1875–1938. Islamic poet and thinker. His literary works, in Urdu and Persian, were mostly verse in the Classical style, suitable for public recitation. He sought through his writings to arouse Muslims to take their place in the modern world.

His most celebrated work, the Persian *Asrā-e khūdī/Secrets of the Self* 1915, put forward a theory of the self that was opposite to the traditional abnegation found in Islam. He was an influence on the movement that led to the creation of Pakistan.

Iquique city and seaport in N Chile, capital of the province of Tarapaca; population (1985) 120,700. It exports nitrate of soda from its desert region.

Iquitos river port on the Amazon, in Peru, also a tourist center for the rainforest; population (1988) 248,000.

ir in physics, abbreviation for infrared.

IRA abbreviation for ◊Irish Republican Army.

Iráklion or ***Heraklion*** largest city and capital (since 1971) of Crete, Greece; population (1981) 102,000.

Iran country in SW Asia, bounded N by the USSR and the Caspian Sea, E by Afghanistan and Pakistan, S and SW by the Gulf of Oman, W by Iraq, and NW by Turkey

government The constitution, which came into effect on the overthrow of the shah in 1979, provides for a president elected by universal suffrage and a single-chamber legislature, the Islamic Consultative Assembly *Majlis*, consisting of 270 members, similarly elected. The president and the assembly serve a four-year term. All legislation passed by the assembly must be sent to the council for the protection of the constitution, consisting of six religious and six secular lawyers, to ensure that it complies with Islamic precepts. The president is the executive head of government but, like the assembly, ultimately subject to

Iran

Islamic Republic of
(Jomhori-e-Islami-e-Irân;
until 1935 Persia)

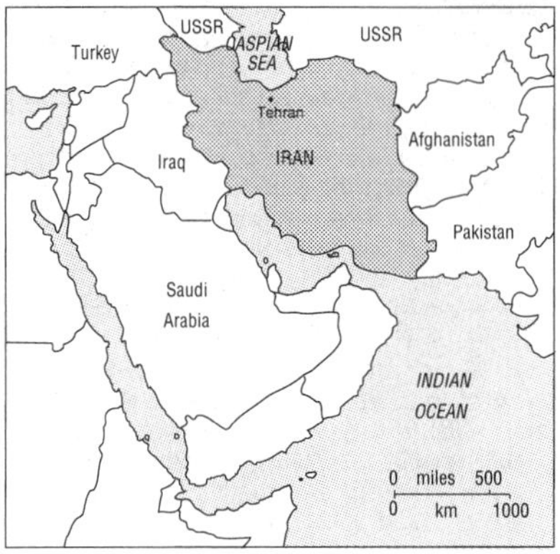
Turkey
USSR
CASPIAN SEA
USSR
Tehran
IRAN
Afghanistan
Iraq
Pakistan
Saudi Arabia
INDIAN OCEAN
0 miles 500
0 km 1000

area 636,128 sq mi/1,648,000 sq km
capital Tehran
cities Isfahan, Mashhad, Tabriz, Shiraz, Ahvaz; chief port Abadan
physical plateau surrounded by mountains, including Elburz and Zagros; Lake Rezayeh; Dasht-Ekavir Desert; occupies islands of Abu Musa, Greater Tunb and Lesser Tunb in the Gulf
features ruins of Persepolis; Mt Demavend 18,603 ft/5,670 m
Leader of the Revolution Ali Khamenei from 1989
head of government Ali Akbar Rafsanjani from 1989
political system authoritarian Islamic republic
political parties Islamic Republican Party (IRP), fundamentalist Islamic
exports carpets, cotton textiles, metalwork, leather goods, oil, petrochemicals, fruit
currency rial
population (1989 est) 51,005,000 (including minorities in Azerbaijan, Baluchistan, Khuzestan/Arabistan, and Kurdistan); growth rate 3.2% p.a.
life expectancy men 57, women 57
language Farsi, Kurdish, Turkish, Arabic, English, French
religion Shiite Muslim 93% (official), Sunni Muslim 5%, Zoroastrian 2%, Jewish, Baha'i and Christian
literacy men 62%/women 39% (1985 est)
GDP $86.4 bn (1987); $1,756 per head
chronology
1946 British, US, and Soviet forces left Iran.
1951 Oilfields nationalized by Prime Minister Mohammad Mossadegh.
1953 Mossadegh deposed and the US-backed shah took full control of the government.
1975 The shah introduced single-party system.
1978 Opposition to the shah organized from France by Ayatollah Khomeini.
1979 Shah left the country, Khomeini returned to create Islamic state. Revolutionaries seized US hostages at embassy in Tehran; US economic boycott.
1980 Start of Iran–Iraq War.
1981 US hostages released.
1984 Egyptian peace proposals rejected.
1985 Fighting intensified in Iran–Iraq War; UN secretary-general's peace moves unsuccessful.
1988 Ceasefire; talks with Iraq began.
1989 Khomeini called for the death of British writer Salman Rushdie. June: Khomeini died; Ali Khamenei elected interim Leader of the Revolution; speaker of Iranian parliament Ali Akbar Rafsanjani elected president. Secret oil deal with Israel revealed.
1990 Generous peace terms with Iraq accepted.
1991 Normal relations with UK restored; US still includes among nations that support terrorism.

the will of the religious leader. Although a number of political parties exist, Iran is fundamentally a one-party state, the Islamic Republican Party having been founded in 1978 to bring about the Islamic revolution.

history The name Iran is derived from the Aryan tribes, including the Medes and Persians, who overran Persia (see ◊Persia, ancient) from 1600 BC. ◊Cyrus the Great, who seized the Median throne 550, formed an empire including Babylonia, Syria, and Asia Minor, to which Egypt, Thrace, and Macedonia were later added. It was conquered by Alexander the Great 334–328, then passed to his general Seleucus (c. 358–280) and his descendants, until overrun in the 3rd century BC by the Parthians. The Parthian dynasty was overthrown AD 226 by Ardashir, founder of the ◊Sassanian Empire.

During 633–41 Persia was conquered for Islam by the Arabs and then in 1037–55 came under the ◊Seljuk Turks. Their empire broke up 12th century and was conquered in the 13th by the ◊Mongols. After 1334 Persia was again divided until its conquest by ◊Tamerlane in the 1380s. A period of violent disorder in the later 15th century was ended by the accession of the Safavi dynasty, who ruled 1499–1736 but were deposed by the great warrior Nadir Shah (ruled 1736–47), whose death was followed by instability until the accession of the Qajar dynasty (1794–1925).

During the 18th century Persia was threatened by Russian expansion, culminating in the loss of Georgia 1801 and a large part of Armenia 1828. Persian claims on Herat, Afghanistan, led to war with Britain 1856–57. Revolutions in 1905 and 1909 resulted in the establishment of a parliamentary regime. During World War I the country was occupied by British and Russian forces. An officer, Col Reza Khan, seized power 1921, and a coup 1925 made him the shah, allowing him to carry out a massive program of modernization to bring Persia, as it was then called, into the 20th century.

During World War II, Iran, as it had become known, was occupied by British, US, and Soviet troops until 1946. Anti-British and anti-American feeling grew, and in 1951 the newly elected prime minister, Dr Mohammed Mossadegh, obtained legislative approval for the nationalization of Iran's largely foreign-owned petroleum industry. With US connivance, he was deposed in a 1953 coup, and the dispute over nationalization was settled the following year when oil-drilling concessions were granted to a consortium of eight companies. The shah took complete control of the government, and during 1965–1977 Iran enjoyed a period of political stability and economic growth, based on oil revenue.

By 1975 the shah had introduced a one-party system, based on the Iran National Resurgence Party *Rastakhis*, but opposition to his regime was growing. The most effective opposition came from the religious leader, Ayatollah Khomeini, who campaigned from exile in France. He demanded a return to the principles of Islam, and pressure on the shah became so great that in 1979 he left the country, leaving the way open for Khomeini's return. He appointed a provisional government, but power was placed essentially in the hands of the 15-member Islamic Revolutionary Council, controlled by Khomeini.

Iran was declared an Islamic republic, and a new constitution, based on Islamic principles, was adopted. Relations with the US were badly affected when a group of Iranian students took 63 Americans hostage at the US embassy in Tehran, demanding that the shah return to face trial. Even the death of the shah, in Egypt 1980, did little to resolve the crisis, which ended when all the hostages were released Jan 1981.

In its early years several rifts developed within the new Islamic government, and although by 1982 some stability had been attained, disputes between factions developed again in the years that followed. Externally, the war with Iraq, that broke out 1980 after a border dispute, continued with considerable loss of life on both sides. Meanwhile, Islamic law was becoming stricter, with amputation as the penalty for theft and flogging for minor sexual offenses. By 1985 the failure to end the Iran-Iraq War and the harshness of the Islamic codes were increasing opposition to Khomeini's regime but his position remained secure. The intervention of the US Navy to conduct convoys through the Gulf 1987–88 resulted in confrontations that proved costly for Iranian forces. Iraq gained the initiative on the battlefield, aided by its use of chemical weapons. By 1987 both sides in the war had increased the scale of their operations, each apparently believing that outright victory was possible. In Aug 1988, under heavy domestic and international pressure, Iran accepted the provisions for a UN-sponsored ceasefire. The peace talks made little progress on territorial issues, and mistrust remained high. Full diplomatic relations with the UK were restored Dec 1988, but the issuing of a death threat to the author Salman ◊Rushdie caused a severance March 1989. Khomeini's death in June 1989 provoked a power struggle between hardline revolutionaries and so-called pragmatists who recognized a need for trade and cooperation with the West. Revelations in 1989 that Iran had negotiated secret oil sales to Israel reflected Iran's need for hard currency to rebuild its economy as well as a desire to counter Iraq. Struggle for succession began, ending with the confirmation of the former Speaker of the *Majlis*, Hoshemi Rafsanjani, as president with increased powers. Despite his reputation for moderation and pragmatism, Iran's relations with the West were slow to improve. In Aug 1990 Iran accepted Iraq's generous peace terms, which virtually gave back everything it had claimed at the start of the Iran-Iraq War. Iran's official neutrality during the Gulf War that followed Iraq's invasion of Kuwait in 1990 and its role in hostage releases in Fall 1991 led to improved relations with the West. Iran condemned, however, the Middle East peace conference held in Spain in Nov 1991.

Irangate US political scandal involving senior members of the Reagan administration (called this to echo the Nixon administration's ◊Watergate).

Arms, including Hawk missiles, were sold to Iran via Israel (at a time when the US was publicly calling for a worldwide ban on sending arms to Iran), violating the law prohibiting the sale of US weapons for resale to a third country listed as a "terrorist nation," as well as the law requiring sales above $14 million to be reported to Congress. The negotiator in the field was Lt Col Oliver North, a military aide to the National Security Council, reporting in the White House to the national security adviser (first Robert McFarlane, then John Poindexter). North and his associates were also channeling donations to the Contras from individuals and from other countries, including $2 million from Taiwan, $10 million from the sultan of Brunei, and $32 million from Saudi Arabia.

The Congressional Joint Investigative Committee reported, in Nov 1987, that the president bore "ultimate responsibility" for allowing a "cabal of zealots" to seize control of the administration's policy, but found no firm evidence that President Reagan had actually been aware of the Contra diversion. Reagan persistently claimed to have no recall of events, and some evidence was withheld on grounds of "national security." North was tried and convicted in May 1989 on charges of obstructing Congress and unlawfully destroying government documents. Poindexter was found guilty on all counts in 1990.

Congressional hearings 1986–87 revealed that the US government had secretly sold weapons to Iran in 1985 and traded them for hostages held in Lebanon by pro-Iranian militias, using the profits to supply right-wing Contra guerrillas in Nicaragua with arms. This attempt to get around the law (Boland amendment 1984) specifically prohibiting military assistance to the Contras also broke other laws in the process. The hearings were criticized for finding that the president was not responsible for the actions of his subordinates.

TURKEY
Caspian Sea
KURDISTAN
Mosul
SYRIA
Kirkuk
IRAN
Tehran
Qasr-e-Shirin
Kermanshah
Baghdad
IRAQ
Dezful
Tigris
Euphrates
Ahvaz
Shatt al-Arab
SAUDI ARABIA
Basra
Abadan
KUWAIT
Faw
Kharg Island
miles 0 200
km 0 300
The Gulf
area seized, then lost by Iraq (1980-82)
capitals
area seized, then lost by Iran (1986-88)
Iran–Iraq War

Iranian language the main language of Iran, more commonly known as ◊Persian or Farsi.

Iran-Iraq War or ***Gulf War*** war between Iran and Iraq 1980–88, claimed by the former to have begun with the Iraq offensive Sept 21, 1980, and by the latter with the Iranian shelling of border posts Sept 4, 1980. Occasioned by a boundary dispute over the ◊Shatt-al-Arab waterway, it fundamentally arose because of Iran's encouragement of the Shiite majority in Iraq to rise against the Sunni government of Saddam Hussein. An estimated 1 million people died in the war.

The war's course was marked by offensive and counter-offensive, interspersed with extended periods of stalemate. Chemical weapons were used, cities and the important oil installations of the area were the target for bombing raids and rocket attacks, and international shipping came under fire in the Persian Gulf (including in 1987 the US frigate *Stark*, which was attacked by the Iraqi airforce). Among Arab states, Iran was supported by Libya and Syria, the remainder supporting Iraq. Iran also benefited from secret US arms shipments, the disclosure of which in 1986 led to considerable scandal in the US, ◊Irangate. The intervention of the US 1987, ostensibly to keep the sea lanes open, but seen by Iran as support for Iraq, heightened, rather than reduced, tension in the Gulf, and United Nations attempts to obtain a ceasefire failed. The war ended in Aug 1988 after ceasefire talks in Geneva.

Iraq country in SW Asia, bounded N by Turkey, E by Iran; S by the Persian Gulf, Kuwait, and Saudi Arabia; SW by Jordan; and W by Syria.

government The 1970 constitution, amended in 1973, 1974, and 1980, provides for a president who is head of state, prime minister, and chair of a Revolutionary Command Council (RCC). Day-to-day administration is under the control of a council of ministers over which the president also presides. The president is also regional secretary of the Arab Ba'ath Socialist Party that, although not the only political party in Iraq, so dominates the country's institutions as to make it virtually a one-party state. In 1980 elections took place for the first 250-member national assembly. Elections for a second assembly were held 1984. On both occasions the Ba'ath Party dominated the results. In effect, therefore, Iraq is ruled by the Arab Ba'ath Socialist Party through its regional secretary and other leading members.

history The area now occupied by Iraq was for-

Iraq

Republic of
(al Jumhouriya al "Iraqia)

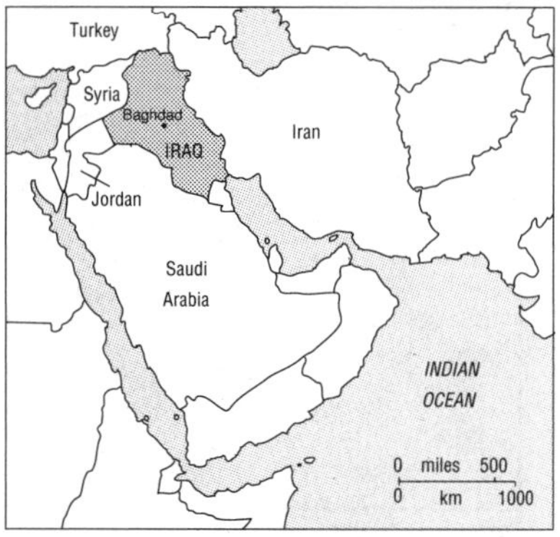
Turkey
Syria
Baghdad
IRAQ
Iran
Jordan
Saudi
Arabia
INDIAN
OCEAN
0 miles 500
0 km 1000

area 167,881 sq mi/434,924 sq km
capital Baghdad
cities Mosul and port of Basra
physical mountains in N, desert in W; wide valley of rivers Tigris and Euphrates NW–SE
features reed architecture of the marsh Arabs; ancient sites of Eridu, Babylon, Nineveh, Ur, Ctesiphon
head of state and government Saddam Hussein al-Takriti from 1979
political system one-party Socialist republic
political parties Arab Ba'ath Socialist Party, nationalist Socialist
exports dates (80% of world supply), wool, oil (prior to UN sanctions)
currency Iraqi dinar
population (1989 est) 17,610,000; growth rate 3.6% p.a.
life expectancy men 62, women 63
language Arabic (official), Kurdish, Assyrian, Armenian
religion Shiite Muslim 60%, Sunni Muslim 37%, Christian 3%
literacy men 68%/women 32% (1980 est)
GDP $42.3 bn (1987); $3,000 per head
chronology
1920 Iraq became a British League of Nations protectorate.
1921 Hashemite dynasty established, with Faisal I as king.
1932 Independence achieved from British protectorate status.
1958 Monarchy overthrown; Iraq became a republic.
1968 Military coup put Gen al-Bakr in power.
1979 Al-Bakr replaced by Saddam Hussein.
1980 War between Iraq and Iran broke out.
1985 Fighting intensified.
1988 Ceasefire; talks began with Iran. Iraq used chemical weapons against Kurdish rebels seeking greater autonomy.
1989 Unsuccessful coup against President Hussein; Iraq launched ballistic missile in successful test.
1990 Generous peace treaty with Iran agreed. Aug: Iraq invaded and annexed Kuwait, precipitating another Gulf crisis. US forces massed in Saudi Arabia at request of King Fahd. UN resolutions ordered Iraqi withdrawal from Kuwait and imposed total trade ban on Iraq; UN resolution sanctioning force approved. All foreign hostages released.
1991 Jan 16: US-led forces began aerial assault on Iraq; Iraq's infrastructure destroyed by bombing. Feb 23–28: land-sea-air offensive to free Kuwait successful. Uprisings of Kurds and Shias brutally suppressed by surviving Iraqi troops. Talks between Kurdish leaders and Saddam Hussein about Turkish autonomy. Allied troops withdrew after establishing "safe havens" for Kurds in the north. A rapid reaction force left near the Turkish border. Allies threatened to bomb strategic targets in Iraq if full information about nuclear facilities denied to United Nations.

merly ancient ◊Mesopotamia and was the center of the Sumerian, Babylonian, and Assyrian civilizations 6000 BC–AD 100. It was conquered 114 by the Romans and was ruled 266–632 by the native Sassanids before being invaded 633 by the Arabs. In 1065 the country was taken over by the Turks and was invaded by the Mongols 1258; Baghdad was destroyed 1401 by ◊Tamerlane. Annexed by Suleiman the Magnificent 1533, Iraq became part of the Turkish Ottoman Empire 1638.

Occupied by Britain in World War I, Iraq was placed under British administration by the League of Nations 1920. In 1932 Iraq became a fully independent kingdom, and in 1933 the reigning king, Faisal I, died and was succeeded by his son, Ghazi. The leading figure behind the throne was the strongly pro-Western General Nuri-el-Said, who was prime minister 1930–58. In 1939 King Ghazi was killed in an automobile accident, and Faisal II became king at the age of three, his uncle Prince Abdul Ilah acting as regent until 1953 when the king assumed full powers.

In 1955 Iraq signed the ◊Baghdad Pact, a regional collective security agreement, with the USSR seen as the main potential threat, and in 1958 joined Jordan in an Arab Federation, with King Faisal as head of state. In July of that year, a revolution overthrew the monarchy, and King Faisal, Prince Abdul Ilah, and General Nuri were all killed. The constitution was suspended, and Iraq was declared a republic, with Brig Abdul Karim Kassem as head of a left-wing military regime. He withdrew from the Baghdad Pact 1959 and, after tenuously holding power for five years, was killed 1963 in a coup led by Col Salem Aref, who established a new government, ended martial law, and within two years had introduced a civilian administration. He died in an airplane crash 1966, and his brother, who succeeded him, was ousted 1968 and replaced by Maj-Gen al-Bakr. He concentrated power in the hands of a Revolutionary Command Council (RCC) and made himself head of state, head of government, and chair of the RCC. In 1979 Saddam Hussein, who for several years had been the real power in Iraq, replaced al-Bakr as RCC chair and state president. In 1980 he introduced a National Charter, reaffirming a policy of ◊nonalignment and a constitution that provided for an elected national assembly. The first elections took place that year.

Iraq had, since 1970, enjoyed a fluctuating relationship with Syria, sometimes distant and sometimes close enough to contemplate a complete political and economic union. By 1980, however, the atmosphere was cool. Relations between Iraq and Iran had been tense for some years, with disagreement over their shared border, which runs down the Shatt-al-Arab waterway. The 1979 Iranian revolution made Iraq more suspicious of Iran's intentions, and in 1980 a full-scale war broke out. Despite Iraq's inferior military strength, Iran gained little territory, and by 1986 it seemed as if a stalemate might have been reached. The fighting intensified again in late 1986 and early 1987, by which time hundreds of thousands of lives had been lost on both sides and incalculable damage to industry and property sustained. Following Iranian acceptance of UN ceasefire provisions, the war came to an end 1988. Peace talks made little progress on fundamental issues of territory or prisoner-of-war repatriation. Hussein took advantage of the end of hostilities to turn his combat-hardened army against Kurdish separatists, many of whom had sided with Iran. Since the war's end, Iraq moved to support Christian forces in Lebanon against Syrian- and Iranian-backed Muslims. The Iraqis also launched a ballistic missile on a successful test, causing concern about Iraq's suspected nuclear weapons' development. In 1989 an unsuccessful coup attempt against President Hussein was reported.

In 1990 Hussein reopened a long-standing territorial dispute with neighboring Kuwait while seeking to assume leadership of the Arab world. Following increasing diplomatic pressure, on Aug 2 Iraqi troops invaded and annexed Kuwait, installing a puppet government and declaring it part of Iraq. As Iraqi troops massed on his borders, King Fahd of Saudi Arabia requested help from the US and the UK and a rapid buildup of US ground and air power and British aircraft began. Meanwhile the UN Security Council condemned the invasion, demanded Iraq's withdrawal, and imposed comprehensive sanctions including an embargo. These were to be enforced by a multinational naval force led by the US. To make its substantial presence in Saudi Arabia seem more legitimate, the US sought contributions from other UN members but with only limited success. Unsuccessful attempts to find a peaceful solution to the dispute were made by Egypt, Jordan, France, the US, the UK, and the United Nations.

To ensure the safety of his border, President Hussein hastily concluded a permanent peace treaty with Iran, under which he conceded virtually everything for which he had fought the Iran-Iraq war and both countries agreed to release all detained prisoners.

Refusing to withdraw from Kuwait, President Hussein sought to prevent a military strike against him by compelling thousands of non-Iraqi adult males, mainly British and American, living in Iraq to remain there, moving some to unknown strategic locations. Meanwhile, a mass exodus of foreign workers who were allowed to leave created enormous refugee problems in neighboring Jordan.

In December 1990 the UN Security Council set a January 15, 1991 deadline for Iraq's withdrawl from Kuwait, after which force could be used. Soon afterward US president Bush offered talks with Iraq and proposed a UN-sponsored international conference to discuss the Middle East's problems. President Saddam Hussein then announced that all foreign hostages in Kuwait and Iraq would be allowed to return home. Nevertheless, Iraqi troops were not removed from Kuwait by the deadline and on Jan 16 the US-led Allied forces began the aerial bombardment of Baghdad as the first phase of operation "Desert Storm," the military campaign to liberate Kuwait; the Iraqi military response during the air campaign was largely limited to the firing of "Scud" missiles into Israel and Saudi Arabia. A last-minute peace initiative by the Soviet Union to avoid a land battle failed, and on Feb 23 the Allied land offensive began, with thousands of Iraqi troops immediately surrendering without a fight to the advancing Allied armies. By March, Iraq had conceded to peace negotiations. Various factions in Iraq began uprisings against the government; these were soon queled by government forces, leading to an immense refugee problem as Kurds in the N and Shi'ites in the S fled from their homes in fear of reprisals. In the aftermath of the war Saddam Hussein remained obdurate toward the UN and the West. See ◊Gulf War.

IRCAM abbreviation of the French *Institut de Recherche et de Coordination Acoustique-Musique* organization in Paris for research into electronic music, using computers, synthesizers, and so on; founded 1976. Its director is Pierre ◊Boulez.

Ireland one of the British Isles, lying to the west of Great Britain, from which it is separated by the Irish Sea. It comprises the provinces of Ulster, Leinster, Munster, and Connacht, and is divided into the Republic of Ireland (which occupies the south, center, and northwest of the island) and

Ireland, Republic of
(Irish *Éire*)

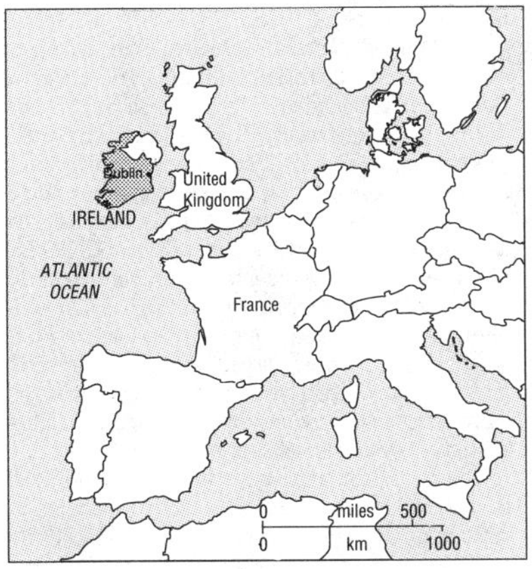
Dublin
IRELAND
United Kingdom
ATLANTIC OCEAN
France
0 miles 500
0 km 1000

area 27,146 sq mi/70,282 sq km
capital Dublin
cities ports Cork, Dún Laoghaire, Limerick, Waterford
physical central plateau surrounded by hills; rivers Shannon, Liffey, Boyne
features Bog of Allen, source of domestic and national power; Magillicuddy's Reeks, Wicklow Mountains; Lough Corrib, lakes of Killarney; Galway Bay and Aran Islands
head of state Mary Robinson from 1990
head of government Charles Haughey from 1987
political system democratic republic
political parties Fianna Fail (Soldiers of Destiny), moderate center-right; Fine Gael (Irish Tribe), moderate center-left; Labor Party, moderate left-of-center; Progressive Democrats, radical free-enterprise
exports livestock, dairy products, Irish whiskey, microelectronic components and assemblies, mining and engineering products, chemicals, clothing; tourism is important
currency punt
population (1989 est) 3,734,000; growth rate 0.1% p.a.
life expectancy men 70, women 76
language Irish and English (both official)
religion Roman Catholic 94%
literacy 99% (1984)
GDP $21.9 bn (1987); $6,184 per head
chronology
1916 Easter Rising: nationalists against British rule seized the Dublin general post office and proclaimed a republic; the revolt was suppressed by the British army and most of the leaders executed.
1918–21 Guerrilla warfare against British army led to split in rebel forces.
1921 Anglo-Irish Treaty resulted in creation of the Irish Free State (Southern Ireland).
1937 Independence achieved from Britain.
1949 Eire left the Commonwealth and became the Republic of Ireland.
1973 Fianna Fáil defeated after 40 years in office; Liam Cosgrave formed a coalition government.
1977 Fianna Fáil returned to power, with Jack Lynch as prime minister.
1979 Lynch resigned, succeeded by Charles Haughey. 1981 Garret FitzGerald formed a coalition.
1983 New Ireland Forum formed, but rejected by the British government.
1985 Anglo-Irish Agreement signed.
1986 Protests by Ulster Unionists against the agreement.
1987 General election won by Charles Haughey.
1988 Relations with UK at low ebb because of disagreement over extradition decisions.
1989 Haughey failed to win majority in general election. Progressive Democrats (a breakaway party of Fianna Fáil) given cabinet positions in coalition government.
1990 Mary Robinson elected president; John Bruton became Fine Gael leader.

Northern Ireland (which occupies the northeast corner and forms part of the United Kingdom).

The center of Ireland is a lowland, about 200–400 ft/60–120 m above sea level; hills are mainly around the coasts, although there are a few peaks over 3,000 ft/1,000 m high, the highest being Carrantuohill ("the inverted reaping hook"), 3,415 ft/1,040 m, in Macgillicuddy's Reeks, County Kerry. The entire western coastline is an intricate alternation of bays and estuaries. Several of the rivers flow in sluggish courses through the central lowland and then cut through fjordlike valleys to the sea. The ◊Shannon in particular falls 100 ft/30 m in its last 16 mi/26 km above Limerick, and is used to produce hydroelectric power.

The lowland bogs that cover parts of central Ireland are intermingled with fertile limestone country where dairy farming is the chief occupation. The bogs are an important source of fuel in the form of ◊peat, Ireland being poorly supplied with coal.

Ireland: counties

County	*Administrative headquarters*	*Area sq km*
Ulster province		
Antrim	Belfast	2,830
Armagh	Armagh	1,250
Down	Downpatrick	2,470
Fermanagh	Enniskillen	1,680
Londonderry	Derry	2,070
Tyrone	Omagh	3,160
	NORTHERN IRELAND	13,460
Cavan	Cavan	1,890
Donegal	Lifford	4,830
Monaghan	Monaghan	1,290
Munster province		
Clare	Ennis	3,190
Cork	Cork	7,460
Kerry	Tralee	4,700
Limerick	Limerick	2,690
Tipperary (N)	Nenagh	2,000
Tipperary (S)	Clonmel	2,260
Waterford	Waterford	1,840
Leinster province		
Carlow	Carlow	900
Dublin	Dublin	920
Kildare	Naas	1,690
Kilkenny	Kilkenny	2,060
Laois	Portlaoise	1,720
Longford	Longford	1,040
Louth	Dundalk	820
Meath	Trim	2,340
Offaly	Tullamore	2,000
Westmeath	Mullingar	1,760
Wexford	Wexford	2,350
Wicklow	Wicklow	2,030
Connacht province		
Galway	Galway	5,940
Leitrim	Carrick-on-Shannon	1,530
Mayo	Castlebar	5,400
Roscommon	Roscommon	2,460
Sligo	Sligo	1,800
	REPUBLIC OF IRELAND	68,910

The climate is mild, moist, and changeable. The annual rainfall on the lowlands varies from 30 in/76 cm in the east to 80 in/203 cm in some western districts, but much higher falls are recorded in the hills.

Ireland: history in prehistoric times Ireland underwent a number of invasions from Europe, the most important of which was that of the Gaels in the 3rd century BC. Gaelic Ireland was divided into kingdoms, nominally subject to an *Ardri* or High King; the chiefs were elected under the tribal or Brehon law, and were usually at war with one another. Christianity was introduced by St ◊Patrick about 432, and during the 5th and 6th centuries Ireland became the home of a civilization which sent out missionaries to Britain and Europe. From about 800 the Danes began to raid Ireland, and later founded Dublin and other coastal towns, until they were defeated by Brian Boru (king from 976) at Clontarf 1014.

Anglo-Norman adventurers invaded Ireland 1167, but by the end of the medieval period English rule was still confined to the Pale, the territory around Dublin. The Tudors adopted a policy of conquest, confiscation of Irish land, and plantation by English settlers, and further imposed the ◊Reformation and English law on Ireland. The most important of the plantations was that of Ulster, carried out under James I 1610. In 1641 the Irish took advantage of the developing struggle in England between king and parliament to begin a revolt which was crushed by Oliver ◊Cromwell 1649, the estates of all "rebels" being confiscated. Another revolt 1689–91 was also defeated, and the Roman Catholic majority held down by penal laws. In 1739–41 a famine killed one-third of the population of 1.5 million. The subordination of the Irish parliament to that of England, and of Irish economic interests to English, led to the rise of a Protestant patriot party, which in 1782 forced the British government to remove many commercial restrictions and grant the Irish parliament its independence. This did not satisfy the population, who in 1798, influenced by French revolutionary ideas, rose in rebellion, but were again defeated; and in 1800 William ◊Pitt induced the Irish parliament to vote itself out of existence by the Act of ◊Union, effective Jan 1, 1801, which gave Ireland parliamentary representation at Westminster. During another famine 1845–46, 1.5 million people emigrated, mostly to the US. By the 1880s there was a strong movement for home rule for Ireland; Gladstone supported it but was defeated by the British parliament. By 1914, home rule was conceded but World War I delayed implementation. The Easter Rising took place in April 1916, when nationalists seized the Dublin general post office and proclaimed a republic. After a week of fighting, the revolt was suppressed by the British army and most of the leaders executed. From 1918 to 1921 there was guerrilla warfare against the British army, especially by the Irish Republican Army (◊IRA), formed by Michael Collins 1919. This led to a split in the rebel forces, but in 1921 the Anglo-Irish Treaty resulted in partition and the creation of the Irish Free State in S Ireland. For history since that date, see ◊Ireland, Republic of; ◊Ireland, Northern.

Ireland John (Nicholson) 1879–1962. English composer. His works include the mystic orchestral prelude *The Forgotten Rite* 1917 and the piano solo *Sarnia* 1941. Benjamin ◊Britten was his pupil.

Ireland, Northern constituent part of the UK
area 5,196 sq mi/13,460 sq km
capital Belfast
cities Londonderry, Armagh
features Mourne mountains, Belfast Lough and Lough Neagh; Giant's Causeway; comprises the six counties (Antrim, Armagh, Down, Fermanagh, Londonderry, and Tyrone) that form part of Ireland's northernmost province of Ulster
exports engineering, especially shipbuilding, textile machinery, aircraft components; linen and synthetic textiles; processed foods, especially

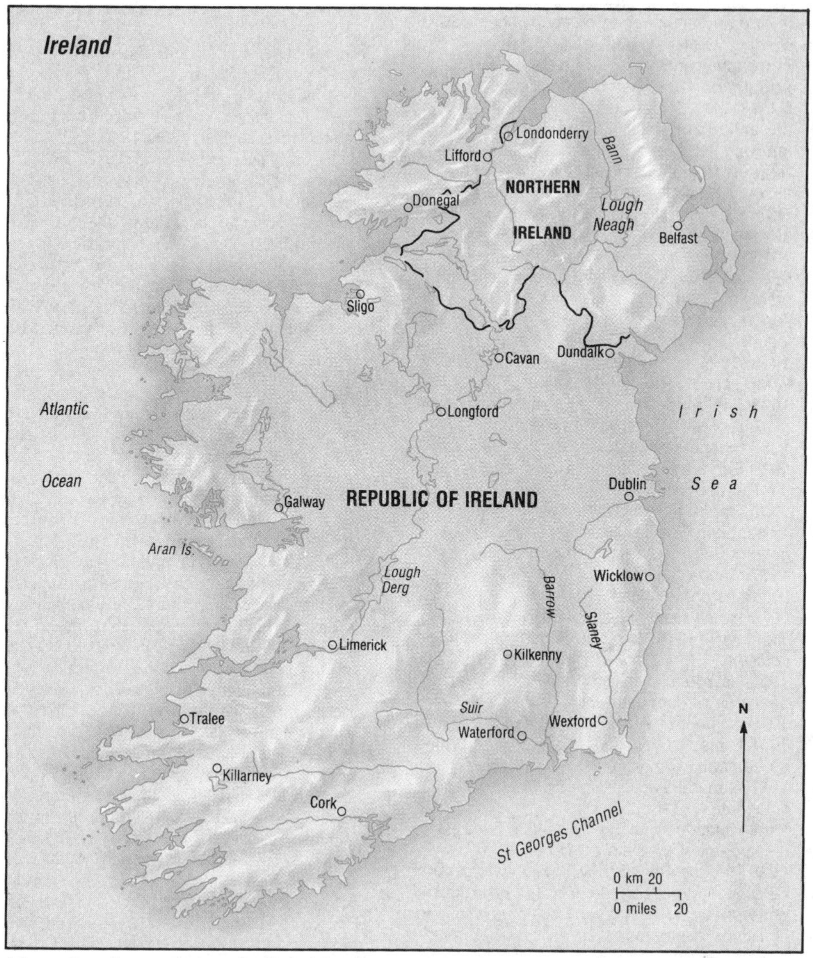
Ireland
Londonderry
Bann
Lifford
NORTHERN
IRELAND
Lough
Neagh
Donegal
Belfast
Sligo
Cavan
Dundalk
Atlantic
Ocean
Longford
Irish
Sea
Galway
REPUBLIC OF IRELAND
Dublin
Aran Is.
Lough
Derg
Barrow
Wicklow
Slaney
Limerick
Kilkenny
Suir
Tralee
Waterford
Wexford
N
Killarney
Cork
St Georges Channel
0 km 20
0 miles 20

dairy and poultry products—all affected by the 1980s depression and political unrest
currency pound sterling
population (1986) 1,567,000
language English
religion Protestant 54%, Roman Catholic 31%
famous people Montgomery, Alanbrooke
government because of the outbreak of violence, there has been direct rule from the UK since 1972. Northern Ireland is entitled to send 12 members to the Westminster Parliament.

Under the Anglo-Irish Agreement 1985, the Republic of Ireland was given a consultative role (via an Anglo-Irish conference) in the government of Northern Ireland, but agreed that there should be no change in its status except by majority consent and that there should be greater cooperation against terrorism. The agreement was approved by Parliament, but all 12 Ulster members gave up their seats, so that by-elections could be fought as a form of "referendum" on the views of the province itself. A similar boycotting of the Northern Ireland Assembly since the Anglo-Irish agreement led to its dissolution 1986 by the UK government.
history for history pre-1921, see ◊Ireland, history. The creation of Northern Ireland dates from 1921 when the mainly Protestant counties of Ulster withdrew from the newly established Irish Free State. Spasmodic outbreaks of violence by the ◊IRA continued, but only in 1968–69 were there serious disturbances arising from Protestant political dominance and discrimination against the Roman Catholic minority in employment and housing. British troops were sent to restore peace and protect Catholics, but disturbances continued, and in 1972 the parliament at Stormont was prorogued and superseded by direct rule from Westminster. Job discrimination was outlawed under the Fair Employment Act 1975, but in 1987 Catholics were two and a half times more likely to be unemployed than their Protestant counterparts—a differential that had not improved since 1971.

Ireland, Republic of country occupying the main part of the island of Ireland, off the NW coast of Europe. It is bounded E by the Irish Sea, S and W by the Atlantic, and NE by Northern Ireland.
government The 1937 constitution provides for a president, elected by universal suffrage for a seven-year term, and a two-chamber national parliament, consisting of a senate, *Seanad Eireann*, and a house of representatives, *Dail Eireann*, serving a five-year term. The senate has 60 members, 11 nominated by the prime minister (*Taoiseach*) and 49 elected by panels representative of most aspects of Irish life. The *Dail* consists of 166 members elected by universal suffrage through a system of proportional representation.

The president appoints a prime minister who is nominated by the *Dail*, which is subject to dissolution by the president if the cabinet loses its confidence within the five-year term. Proportional representation encourages the existence of several parties, the most significant being ◊Fianna Fáil, Fine Gael (United Ireland Party), the Labour Party, and the Progressive Democrats.
history For history pre-1921, see ◊Ireland, history. In 1921 a treaty gave Southern Ireland dominion status within the ◊Commonwealth, while six out of the nine counties of Ulster remained part of the UK, with limited self-government. The Irish Free State, as Southern Ireland was formally called 1922, was accepted by IRA leader Michael Collins but not by many of his colleagues, who shifted their allegiance to Fianna Fáil leader, Eamonn ◊de Valera; the latter eventually acknowledged the partition as well in 1937 when a new constitution established the country as a sovereign state under the name of Eire.

The IRA continued its fight for an independent, unified Ireland through a campaign of violence, mainly in Northern Ireland but also on the British mainland and, to a lesser extent, in the Irish

Ireland 1801–1916: chronology

1800	Act of Union established United Kingdom of Great Britain and Ireland.
1823	Catholic Association founded by Daniel O'Connell to campaign for Catholic political rights.
1828	O'Connell elected for County Clare; forces granting of rights for Catholics to sit in Parliament.
1829	Catholic Emancipation Act.
1838	Tithe Act (abolishing payment) removed a major source of discontent.
1840	Franchise in Ireland reformed. "Young Ireland" formed.
1845–50	Potato famine resulted in widespread death and emigration. Population reduced by 20%.
1850	Irish Franchise Act extended voters from 61,000 to 165,000.
1858	Fenian Brotherhood formed.
1867	Fenian insurrection failed.
1869	Church of Ireland disestablished.
1870	Land Act provided greater security for tenants but failed to halt agrarian disorders. Protestant Isaac Butt formed Home Government Association (Home Rule League).
1874	Home Rule League won 59 Parliamentary seats and adopted a policy of obstruction.
1880	Charles Stuart Parnell became leader of Home Rulers, dominated by Catholic groups. "Boycotts" against landlords unwilling to agree to fair rents.
1881	Land Act greeted with hostility. Parnell imprisoned. "No Rent" movement began.
1882	"Kilmainham Treaty" between government and Parnell agreed conciliation. Chief Secretary Cavendish and Under Secretary Burke murdered in Phoenix Park, Dublin.
1885	Franchise Reform gave Home Rulers 85 seats in new parliament and balance between Liberals and Tories. Home Rule Bill rejected.
1886	Home Rule Bill rejected again.
1890	Parnell cited in divorce case, which split Home Rule movement.
1893	Second Home Rule Bill defeated in House of Lords; Gaelic League founded.
1900	Irish Nationalists reunited under Redmond. 82 MPs elected.
1902	Sinn Féin founded by Arthur Griffith.
1906	Bill for devolution of power to Ireland rejected by Nationalists.
1910	Sir Edward Carson led Unionist opposition to Home Rule.
1912	Home Rule Bill for whole of Ireland introduced. (Protestant) Ulster Volunteers formed to resist.
1913	Home Rule Bill defeated in House of Lords but overridden. (Catholic) Irish Volunteers founded in the South.
1914	Nationalists persuaded to exclude Ulster from Bill for six years but Carson rejected it. Curragh "mutiny" cast doubt on reliability of British troops against Protestants. Extensive gun-running by both sides. World War I deferred implementation.
1916	Easter Rising by members of Irish Republican Brotherhood. Suppressed by troops and leaders executed.

Northern Ireland 1967– : chronology

1967	Northern Ireland Civil Rights Association set up to press for equal treatment for Catholics in the provinces.
1968	Series of civil rights marches sparked off rioting and violence, especially in Londonderry.
1969	Election results weakened Terence O'Neil's Unionist government. Further rioting led to call-up of (Protestant based) B-Specials to Royal Ulster Constabulary. Chichester-Clark replaced O'Neil. IRA split into "official" and "provisional" wings. RUC disarmed and B-Specials replaced by nonsectarian Ulster Defence Regiment (UDR). British Army deployed in Belfast and Londonderry.
1971	First British soldier killed. Faulkner replaced Chichester-Clark. IRA stepped up bombing campaign.
1972	"Bloody Sunday" in Londonderry when British Army killed 13 demonstrators. Direct rule from Westminster introduced.
1974	"Power sharing" between Protestant and Catholic groups tried but failed. IRA extended bombing campaign to UK mainland. Bombs in Guildford and Birmingham caused a substantial number of fatalities.
1976	British Ambassador in Dublin, Christopher Ewart Biggs, assassinated. Peace Movement founded by Betty Williams and Mairead Corrigan.
1978	British MP Airey Neave assassinated by INLA at the House of Commons.
1980	Meeting of Margaret Thatcher and Irish premier Charles Haughey on a peaceful settlement to the Irish question. Hunger strikes and "dirty protests" started by Republican prisoners in pursuit of political status.
1981	Hunger strikes led to deaths of Bobby Sands and Francis Hughes; Anglo-Irish Intergovernmental Council formed.
1982	Northern Ireland Assembly created to devolve legislative and executive powers back to the province. SDLP (19%) and Sinn Féin (10%) boycotted the assembly.
1984	Series of reports from various groups on the future of the province. IRA bomb at Conservative Party conference in Brighton killed five people. Second Anglo-Irish Intergovernmental Council summit meeting agreed to oppose violence and cooperate on security; Britain rejected ideas of confederation or joint sovereignty.
1985	Meeting of Margaret Thatcher and Irish premier Garrett Fitzgerald at Hillsborough produced Anglo-Irish Agreement on the future of Ulster; regarded as a sell-out by Unionists.
1986	Unionist opposition to Anglo-Irish Agreement included protests and strikes. Loyalist violence against police and Unionist MPs boycotted Westminster.
1987	IRA bombed British Army base in West Germany. Unionist boycott of Westminster ended. Extradition clauses of Anglo-Irish Agreement approved in Eire. IRA bombed Remembrance Day service at Enniskillen—later admitted it to be a "mistake."
1988	Three IRA bombers killed by security forces on Gibraltar.
1989	After serving fourteen years in prison, the "Guildford Four" were released when their convictions were ruled unsound by the Court of Appeal.
1990	Anglo-Irish Agreement threatened when Eire refused extraditions. Convictions of "Birmingham Six" also called into question and sent to the Court of Appeal.
1991	IRA renewed bombing campaign on British mainland, targetting a meeting of the cabinet in Downing Street and mainline railroad stations.

republic. Eire remained part of the Commonwealth until 1949, when it left, declaring itself the Republic of Ireland, while Northern Ireland remained a constituent part of the UK.

In 1973 Fianna Fáil, having held office for over 40 years, was defeated, and Liam Cosgrave formed a coalition of the Fine Gael and Labour parties. In 1977 Fianna Fáil returned to power, with Jack Lynch as prime minister. In 1979 IRA violence intensified with the killing of Earl Mountbatten in Ireland and 18 British soldiers in Northern Ireland. Lynch resigned later the same year, and was succeeded by Charles Haughey.

Atlantic Ocean
KINTYRE
Londonderry
ANTRIM
LONDONDERRY
Ballymena
TYRONE
Omagh
Belfast
L. Neagh
Armagh
Enniskillen
DOWN
Downpatrick
FERMANAGH
ARMAGH
IRELAND
Irish Sea
Northern Ireland
Protestant majority
R. Catholic majority

His aim was a united Ireland, with considerable independence for the six northern counties. After the 1981 election Garrett FitzGerald, leader of Fine Gael, formed another coalition with Labour but was defeated the following year on budget proposals and resigned. Haughey returned to office with a minority government, but he, too, had to resign later that year, resulting in the return of FitzGerald.

In 1983 all the main Irish and Northern Irish political parties initiated the New Ireland Forum as a vehicle for discussion. Its report was rejected by Margaret Thatcher's conservative government in the UK, but discussions between London and Dublin resulted in the signing of the Anglo-Irish Agreement 1985, providing for regular consultation and exchange of information on political, legal, security, and cross-border matters. The agreement also said that the status of Northern Ireland would not be changed without the consent of a majority of the people. The agreement was criticized by the Unionist parties of Northern Ireland, who asked that it be rescinded.

FitzGerald's coalition ended 1986, and the Feb 1987 election again returned Fianna Fáil and Charles Haughey. In 1988 relations between the Republic of Ireland and the UK were at a low ebb because of disagreements over extradition decisions. In 1989, Haughey failed to win a majority at the election and entered into a coalition with the Progressive Democrats (a breakaway party from Fianna Fáil), putting two of their members into the cabinet.

In Nov 1990, after being dismissed as deputy prime minister, Brian Leniham was defeated in the presidential election by the left-wing backed Mary Robinson. In the same month Alan Dukes resigned the leadership of the Fine Gael, to be replaced by the right-winger John Bruton.

Irene in Greek mythology, goddess of peace (Roman Pax).

Irene, St c. 752–c. 803. Byzantine emperor 797–802. The wife of Leo IV (750–80), she became regent for their son Constantine (771–805) on Leo's death. In 797 she deposed her son, had his eyes put out, and assumed full title of *basileus* ("emperor"), ruling in her own right until deposed and exiled to Lesvos by a revolt in 802. She was made a saint by the Greek Orthodox church for her attacks on iconoclasts.

Ireton Henry 1611–1651. English Civil War general. He joined the Parliamentary forces and fought at ◊Edgehill 1642, Gainsborough 1643, and ◊Naseby 1645. After the Battle of Naseby, Ireton, who was opposed to both the extreme republicans and ◊Levelers, strove for a compromise with Charles I, but then played a leading role in his trial and execution. He married his leader Cromwell's daughter in 1646. Lord Deputy in Ireland from 1650, he died after the capture of Limerick.

Irgun short for Irgun Zvai Leumi (National Military Society), a Jewish guerrilla group active against the British administration in Palestine 1946–48. Their bombing of the King David Hotel in Jerusalem July 22, 1946 resulted in 91 fatalities.

Irian Jaya the western portion of the island of New Guinea, part of Indonesia
area 162,000 sq mi/420,000 sq km
capital Jayapura
population (1980) 1,174,000
history part of the Dutch East Indies 1828 as Western New Guinea; retained by the Netherlands after Indonesian independence 1949 but ceded to Indonesia 1963 by the United Nations and remained part of Indonesia by an "Act of Free Choice" 1969. In the 1980s 700,000 acres/283,500 hectares were given over to Indonesia's controversial transmigration program for the resettlement of farming families from overcrowded Java, causing destruction of rainforests and displacing indigenous people.

iridium hard, brittle, silver-white, metallic element, symbol Ir, atomic number 77, atomic weight 192.2. It is twice as heavy as lead and is resistant to tarnish and corrosion. It is one of the so-called platinum group of metals; it occurs in platinum ores and as a free metal (◊native metal) with osmium in osmiridium, a natural alloy that includes platinum, ruthenium, and rhodium.

It is alloyed with platinum for jewelry and used for watch bearings and in scientific instruments. It was named in 1804 by the English chemist Smithson Tennant (1761–1815) from Latin *iridis*, rainbow, for its irridescence in solution.

iris in anatomy, the colored muscular diaphragm that controls the size of the pupil in the vertebrate eye. It contains radial muscle that increases the pupil diameter and circular muscle that constricts the pupil diameter. Both types of muscle respond involuntarily to light intensity.

iris in botany, perennial northern temperate flowering plants of the genus *Iris*, family Iridaceae. The leaves are usually sword-shaped; the purple, white, or yellow flowers have three upright inner petals and three outward- and downward-curving sepals. The wild yellow iris is called ◊flag.

iris

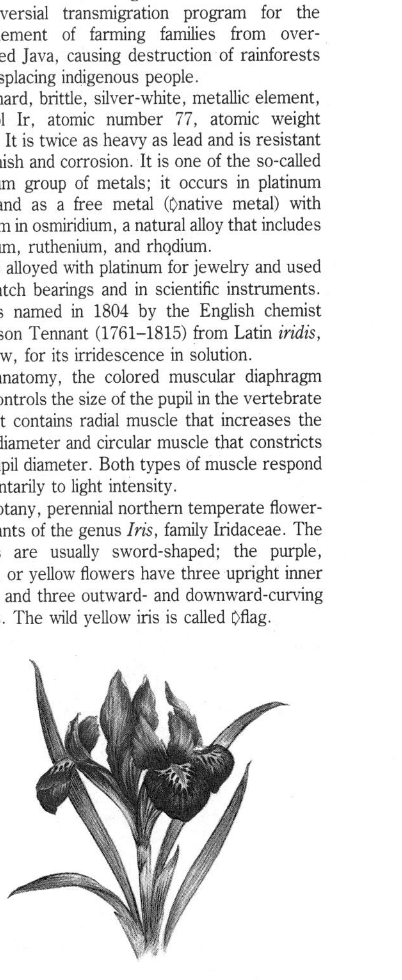

Irish Gaelic first official language of the Irish Republic, but much less widely used than the second official language, English. See ◊Gaelic language.

Irish language common name for Irish ◊Gaelic. At one time, especially in the form "Erse," also a name for the Gaelic of Scotland.

Irish literature early Irish literature, in Gaelic, consists of the sagas, which are mainly in prose, and a considerable body of verse. The chief cycles are that of Ulster, which deals with the mythological ◊Conchobar and his followers, and the Ossianic, which has influenced European literature through MacPherson's version.

Early Irish poetry has a unique lyric quality and consists mainly of religious verse and nature poetry, for example, St Patrick's hymn and Ultán's hymn to St Brigit. Much pseudo-historical verse is also extant, ascribed to such poets as Mael Mura (9th century), Mac Liac (10th century), and Flann Mainistrech (11th century). Religious literature in prose includes sermons, saints' lives (for example, those in the *Book of Lismore* and in the writings of Michael O'Clery), and visions. History is represented by annals and by isolated texts like the *Cogad Gaedel re Gallaib*, an account of the Viking invasions by an eyewitness. The "official" or "court" verse of the 13th to 17th centuries was produced by a succession of professional poets, notably Tadhg Dall O' Huiginn (died about 1617), Donnchadh Mór O'Dálaigh (died 1244), and Geoffrey Keating (died 1646), who wrote in both verse and prose.

The bardic schools ceased to exist by the end of the 17th century. Meter became accentual, rather than syllabic. The greatest exponents of the new school were Egan O'Rahilly (early 18th century) and the religious poet Tadhg Gaelach O'Súilleabháin.

Irish nationalism see ◊Ireland, history and ◊Ireland, Northern.

Irish Republican Army (IRA) militant Irish nationalist organization whose aim is to create a united Irish Socialist republic including Ulster. The paramilitary wing of ◊Sinn Féin, it was founded 1919 by Michael ◊Collins and fought a successful war against Britain 1919–21. It came to the fore again 1939 with a bombing campaign in Britain, and was declared illegal in Eire. Its activities intensified from 1968 onward, as the civil-rights disorders ("the Troubles") in Northern Ireland developed. In 1970 a group in the north broke away to become the Provisional IRA; their commitment is to the expulsion of the British from Northern Ireland.

The IRA is committed to the use of force in trying to achieve its objectives, and it regularly carries out bombings and shootings. In 1979 it murdered Louis ◊Mountbatten, and its bomb attacks in Britain have included an attempt to kill members of the UK cabinet during the Conservative Party conference in Brighton 1984. Several attacks have been carried out against British military personnel serving outside the UK, especially in Germany.

Irkutsk city in S USSR; population (1987) 609,000. It produces coal, iron, steel, and machine tools. Founded 1652, it began to grow after the Trans-Siberian railroad reached it 1898.

iron hard, malleable and ductile, silver-gray metallic element, symbol Fe (from Latin *ferrum*), atomic number 26, atomic weight 55.847. It is the fourth most abundant element (the second most abundant metal, after aluminum) in the Earth's crust. The central core of the Earth, the radius of which is believed to be 2,200 mi/3,540 km, is held to consist principally of iron with some nickel. When the amounts in the crust and core are combined, iron is probably the most abundant constituent element of the planet.

Although it almost always occurs in ores or as compounds, it sometimes occurs as a free metal (◊native metal), occasionally as fragments of iron or iron-nickel meteorites. Iron is the most common and most useful of all metals; it is strongly magnetic and is noted for becoming oxydized (rusted) in moist air. Iron is an essential component of hemoglobin, the molecule in the red blood cells, where it serves to transport oxygen to all parts of the body.

Iron is the basis for steel, an alloy with carbon and other elements. Iron has been worked into tools by early peoples in both the Old World and the New and its use has persisted since the ◊Iron Age of prehistory. The name is very old and is derived from the Germanic base of the Indo-European *eis*, strong.

Iron Age the developmental stage of human technology when weapons and tools were made from iron. Iron was produced in Thailand as early as 1600 BC but was considered inferior in strength to bronze until about 1000 when metallurgical techniques improved and the alloy steel was produced by adding carbon during the smelting process.

ironbark any species of ◊eucalyptus tree with hard, tough bark.

ironclad a wooden warship covered with armor plate. The first to be constructed was the French *Gloire* 1858, but the first to be launched was the British HMS *Warrior* 1859. The first battle between ironclads took place during the American Civil War, when the Union *Monitor* fought the Confederate *Virginia* (formerly the *Merrimack*) March 9, 1862. The design was replaced by battleships of all-metal construction in the 1890s.

The US Navy's Great White Fleet was especially well known.

Iron Cross medal awarded for valor in the German armed forces. Instituted in Prussia 1813, it consists of a Maltese cross of iron, edged with silver.

Iron Curtain in Europe after World War II, the symbolic boundary of the ◊Cold War between capitalist West and communist East. The term was popularized by the UK prime minister Winston Churchill from 1945.

An English traveler to Bolshevik Russia, Mrs Snowden, used the term with reference to the Soviet border in 1920. The Nazi minister Goebbels used it a few months before Churchill in 1945 to describe the divide between Soviet-dominated and other nations that would follow German capitulation.

Iron Gate (Romanian Porţile de Fier) narrow gorge, interrupted by rapids, in Romania. A hydroelectric scheme undertaken 1964–70 by Romania and Yugoslavia transformed this section of the river Danube into a 90 mi/145 km long lake and eliminated the rapids as a navigation hazard. Before flooding, in 1965, an archeological survey revealed Europe's oldest urban settlement, ◊Lepenski Vir.

Iron Guard pro-fascist group controlling Romania in the 1930s. To counter its influence, King Carol II established a dictatorship 1938 but the Iron Guard forced him to abdicate 1940.

iron ore any mineral from which iron is extracted. The chief iron ores are ◊magnetite, a black oxide; ◊hematite, or kidney ore, a reddish oxide; ◊limonite, a black hydro-oxide; and siderite, a brownish carbonate.

Iron ores are found in a number of different forms, including distinct layers in igneous intrusions, as components of contact metamorphic rocks, and as sedimentary beds. Much of the world's iron is extracted in the USSR. Other important producers are the US, Australia, France, Brazil, and Canada; over 40 countries produce significant quantities of ore.

iron pyrites or ***pyrite*** FeS_2 common iron ore. Brassy yellow, and occurring in cubic crystals, it is often called "fool's gold," since only those who have never seen native gold would mistake it.

irony a literary technique that achieves the effect of "saying one thing and meaning another," through the use of humor or mild sarcasm. It can be traced through all periods of literature, from Classical Greek and Roman epics and dramas to the good-humored and subtle irony of ◊Chaucer to the 20th-century writer's method for dealing with nihilism and despair, as in Samuel Beckett's *Waiting for Godot*.

The Greek philosopher Plato used irony in his dialogs, in which Socrates elicits truth through a pretence of naivety. Sophocles' use of dramatic irony also has a high seriousness, as in *Oedipus Rex*, where Oedipus prays for the discovery and punishment of the city's polluter, little knowing that it is himself. Eighteenth-century skepticism provided a natural environment for irony, with ◊Swift using the device as a powerful weapon in *Gulliver's Travels* and elsewhere.

Iroquois member of a confederation of NE North American Indians, the Six Nations (Cayuga, Mohawk, Oneida, Onondaga, and Seneca, with the Tuscarora after 1723), traditionally formed by Hiawatha (actually a priestly title) 1570.

The Iroquois lived in upstate New York, and their descendants live in New York, Ontario, Québec, and Oklahoma, on reservations and among the general public. The Mohawk steelworkers are famous for constructing the girders of skyscrapers such as the Empire State Building.

irradiation in technology, subjecting anything to radiation. Food can be sterilized by bombarding it with low-strength ◊gamma rays. Although the process is now legal in several countries, uncertainty remains about possible long-term effects on consumers from irradiated food. The process does not make the food radioactive, but many molecular changes take place including the initiation of free radicals, which may be further changed into a range of unknown and unstable chemicals. It is claimed that chemicals produced in food by irradiation are potentially carcinogenic. Irradiation also eradicates the smell, taste and poor appearance of bad or aging food products.

In optics, the term refers to the apparent enlargement of a brightly lit object when seen against a dark background.

irrationalism a feature of many philosophies rather than a philosophical movement. Irrationalists deny that the world can be comprehended by conceptual thought, and often see the human mind as determined by unconscious forces.

irrational number a number that cannot be expressed as an exact ◊fraction. Irrational numbers include some square roots (for example, $\sqrt{2}$, $\sqrt{3}$ and $\sqrt{5}$ are irrational) and numbers such as π (the ratio of the circumference of a circle to its diameter, which is approximately equal to 3.14159) and e (the base of ◊natural logarithms, approximately 2.71828).

Irrawaddy (Myanmar Ayeryarwady) chief river of Myanmar (Burma), flowing roughly N to S for 1,300 mi/2,090 km across the center of the country into the Bay of Bengal. Its sources are the Mali and N'mai rivers; its chief tributaries are the Chindwin and Shweli.

irredentist person who wishes to reclaim the lost territories of a state. The term derives from an Italian political party founded about 1878 intending to incorporate Italian-speaking areas into the newly formed state.

irrigation artificial water supply for dry agricultural areas by means of dams and channels. Irrigation has been practiced for thousands of years, in Eurasia as well the Americas.

An example is the channeling of the annual Nile flood in Egypt, which has been done from earliest times to its present control by the Aswan High Dam. Drawbacks to irrigation are that it tends to concentrate salts, ultimately causing infertility, and rich river silt is retained at dams, to the impoverishment of the land and fisheries below them.

Irving Washington 1783–1859. US essayist and short-story writer. He published a mock-heroic *History of New York* in 1809, supposedly written by the Dutchman "Diedrich Knickerbocker." In 1815 he went to England where he published *The Sketch Book of Geoffrey Crayon, Gent.* 1820, which contained such stories as "Rip van Winkle" and "The Legend of Sleepy Hollow."

His other works include *The Alhambra* 1832, sketches about Spanish subjects, and *Tour of the Prairies* 1835, about the American West. His essays and tales remain popular.

Isaac in the Old Testament, Hebrew patriarch, son of ◊Abraham and Sarah, and father of Esau and Jacob.

Isaacs Alick 1921–1967. Scottish virologist who, with Jean Lindemann, in 1957 discovered ◊interferon, a naturally occurring antiviral substance produced by cells infected with viruses. The full implications of this discovery are still being investigated.

Isabella two Spanish queens:

Isabella I the Catholic 1451–1504. Queen of Castile from 1474, after the death of her brother Henry IV. By her marriage with Ferdinand of Aragon 1469, the crowns of two of the Christian states in the Moorish-held Spanish peninsula were united. In her reign, during 1492, the Moors were driven out of Spain; she introduced the ◊Inquisition into Castile, expelled the Jews, and gave financial encouragement to ◊Columbus. Her youngest daughter was Catherine of Aragon, first wife of Henry VIII of England.

Isabella II 1830–1904. Queen of Spain from 1833, when she succeeded her father Ferdinand VII (1784–1833). The Salic Law banning a female sovereign had been repealed by the *Cortes* (parliament), but her succession was disputed by her uncle Don Carlos de Bourbon (1788–1855). After seven years of civil war, the ◊Carlists were defeated. She abdicated in favor of her son Alfonso XII in 1868.

Isabella of France 1292–1358. Daughter of King Philip IV of France, wife of King Edward II of England; she intrigued with her lover, Roger Mortimer, to have the king deposed and murdered.

Isaiah 8th century BC. In the Old Testament, the first major Hebrew prophet. The son of Amos, he was probably of high rank, and lived largely in Jerusalem.

He was influential in the court of ancient Judah until the Assyrian invasion of 701 BC.

Isaurian an 8th-century Byzantine imperial dynasty, originating in Asia Minor.

Members of the family had been employed as military leaders by the Byzantines, and they gained great influence and prestige as a result. Leo III acceded in 717 as the first Isaurian emperor, and was followed by Constantine V (718–75), Leo IV (750–80), and Leo's widow Irene, who acted as regent for their son before deposing him 797 and assuming the title of emperor herself. She was deposed 802. The Isaurian rulers maintained the integrity of the empire's borders. With the exception of Irene, they attempted to suppress the use of religious icons.

ISBN abbreviation for International Standard Book Number, used for ordering or classifying book titles.

ischemia reduction of blood supply to any part of the body.

Ischia volcanic island about 16 mi/26 km SW of Naples, Italy, in the Tyrrhenian Sea; population (1985) 26,000. It has mineral springs (known to the Romans), has beautiful scenery, and is a vacation resort.

Ise city SE of Kyoto, on Honshu, Japan. It is the site of the most sacred Shinto shrine, dedicated to sun-goddess Amaterasu. It has been rebuilt every 20 years in the form of a perfect thatched house of the 7th century BC and contains the octagonal mirror of the goddess.

Isère river in SE France, 180 mi/290 km long, a tributary of the Rhône. It gives its name to the *département* of Isère.

Isfahan or Eşfahan industrial (steel, textiles, carpets) city in central Iran; population (1986) 1,001,000. It was the ancient capital (1598–1722) of ◊Abbas I, and its features include the Great Square, Grand Mosque, and Hall of Forty Pillars.

Isherwood *Lifelong friend of W H Auden, English novelist Christopher Isherwood was a leading intellectual of the 1930s.*

Isherwood Christopher (William Bradshaw) 1904–1986. English novelist. Educated at Cambridge, he lived in Germany 1929–33 just before Hitler's rise to power, a period that inspired *Mr Norris Changes Trains* 1935 and *Goodbye to Berlin* 1939, creating the character of Sally Bowles (the basis of the musical *Cabaret* 1968). Returning to England, he collaborated with ◊Auden in three verse plays.

Ishiguro Kazuo 1954– . Japanese-born British novelist. His novel *An Artist of the Floating World* won the 1986 Whitbread Prize, and *The Remains of the Day* won the 1989 Booker Prize.

Ishmael in the Old Testament, son of ◊Abraham and his wife Sarah's Egyptian maid Hagar; traditional ancestor of Mohammed and the Arab people. He and his mother were driven away by Sarah's jealousy. Muslims believe that it was Ishmael, not Isaac, whom God commanded Abraham to sacrifice, and that Ishmael helped Abraham build the ◊Kaaba in Mecca.

Ishtar goddess of love and war, worshiped by the Babylonians and Assyrians, and personified as the legendary queen Semiramis.

Isidore of Seville c. 560–636. Writer and missionary. His *Ethymologiae* was the model for later medieval encyclopedias and helped to preserve Classical thought during the Middle Ages; his *Chronica Maiora* remains an important source for the history of Visigothic Spain. As bishop of Seville from 600, he strengthened the church in Spain and converted many Jews and Aryan Visigoths.

isinglass pure form of gelatin obtained from the internal membranes of the swim bladder of various fishes, particularly the sturgeon. Isinglass is used in the clarification of wines and beer, and in cooking.

Isis the upper stretches of the river Thames, England, above Oxford.

Isis the principal goddess of ancient Egypt. She was the daughter of Geb and Nut (earth and sky), and as the sister-wife of Osiris searched for his body after his death at the hands of his brother, Set. Her son Horus then defeated and captured Set but cut off his mother's head because she would not allow Set to be killed. She was later identified with ◊Hathor. The cult of Isis ultimately spread to Greece and Rome.

Iskandariya Arabic name for ◊Alexandria, Egypt.

Iskenderun port, naval base, and steel-manufacturing town in Turkey; population (1980) 125,000. It was founded by Alexander the Great in 333 BC and called Alexandretta until 1939.

Islam (Arabic "submission," that is, to the will of Allah) religion founded in the Arabian peninsula in the early 7th century AD. It emphasizes the oneness of God, his omnipotence, benificence, and inscrutability. The sacred book is the ◊Koran of the prophet ◊Mohammed, the Prophet or Messenger of Allah. There are two main Muslim sects: ◊Sunni and ◊Shiite. Other schools include Sufism, a mystical movement originating in the 8th century.

beliefs Creation, Fall of Adam, angels and ◊jinns, heaven and hell, Day of Judgment, God's predestination of good and evil, and the succession of scriptures revealed to the prophets, including Moses and Jesus, but of which the perfect, final form is the Koran or Quran, divided into 114 suras or chapters, said to have been divinely revealed to Mohammed; the original is said to be preserved beside the throne of Allah in heaven.

Islamic law Islam embodies a secular law (the Shari'a or "Highway"), which is clarified for Shiites by reference to their own version of the sunna, "practice" of the Prophet as transmitted by his companions; the Sunni sect also take into account ijma', the endorsement by universal consent of practices and beliefs among the faithful. A mufti is a legal expert who guides the courts in their interpretation. (In Turkey until the establish-

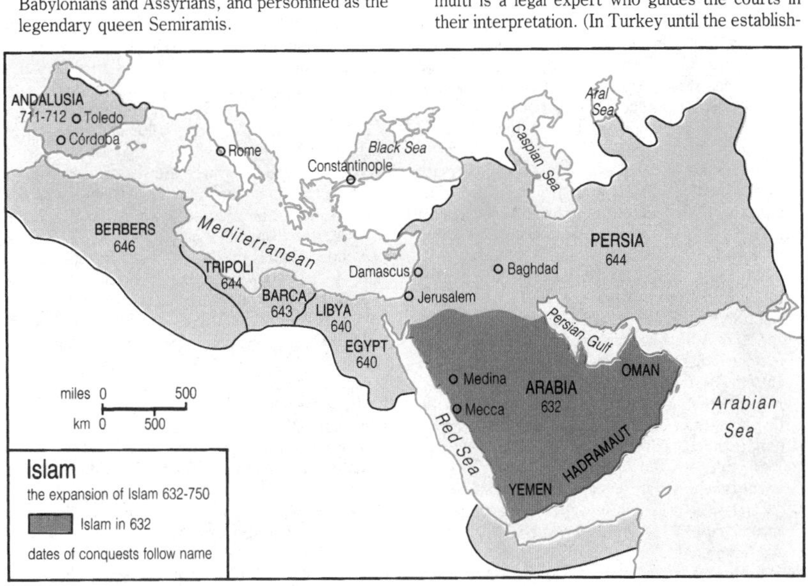
ANDALUSIA
711-712
Toledo
Córdoba
Rome
Black Sea
Constantinople
Aral Sea
Caspian Sea
BERBERS
646
Mediterranean
TRIPOLI
644
BARCA
643
LIBYA
640
EGYPT
640
Damascus
Jerusalem
Baghdad
PERSIA
644
Persian Gulf
Medina
Mecca
ARABIA
632
OMAN
Red Sea
HADRAMAUT
YEMEN
Arabian Sea
miles 0 500
km 0 500
Islam in 632
dates of conquests follow name

Islam
the expansion of Islam 632-750

ment of the republic 1924 the mufti had supreme spiritual authority.)

organization There is no organized church or priesthood, although Mohammed's descendants (the Hashim family) and popularly recognized holy men, mullahs, and ayatollahs are accorded respect.

observances The ◊"Five Pillars of the Faith" are: recitation of the creed; worship (salat) five times a day facing the holy city of ◊Mecca (the call to prayer is given by a muezzin, usually from the minaret or tower of a mosque); almsgiving; fasting sunrise to sunset through Ramadan (ninth month of the year, which varies with the calendar); and the pilgrimage to Mecca at least once in a lifetime.

history Islam began as a militant and missionary religion, and between 711 and 1492 spread east into India, west over N Africa, then north across Gibraltar into the Iberian peninsula. During the Middle Ages, Islamic scholars preserved ancient Greco-Roman learning, while the Dark Ages prevailed in Christian Europe. Islam was seen as an enemy of Christianity by European countries during the Crusades, and Christian states united against a Muslim nation as late as the Battle of Lepanto 1571. Driven from Europe, Islam remained established in N Africa and the Middle East.

Islam is a major force in the Arab world and is a focus for nationalism among the peoples of Soviet Central Asia. It is also a significant factor in Pakistan, Indonesia, Malaysia, and parts of Africa. It is the second largest religion in the UK. Since World War II there has been a resurgence of fundamentalist Islam (often passionately opposed to the ideas of the West) in Iran, Libya, Afghanistan, and elsewhere. In the UK 1987 the manifesto *The Muslim Voice* demanded rights for Muslim views on education (such as single-sex teaching) and on the avoidance of dancing, mixed bathing, and sex education.

Islamabad capital of Pakistan from 1967, in the Potwar district, at the foot of the Margala Hills and immediately NW of Rawalpindi; population (1981) 201,000. The city was designed by Constantinos Doxiadis in the 1960s. The Federal Capital Territory of Islamabad has an area of 350 sq mi/907 sq km and a population (1985) of 379,000.

Islam, five pillars of see ◊five pillows of Islam.

Islamic art art, architecture, and design of Muslim nations and territories. Because the Koran forbids representation in art, Islamic artistry was channeled into calligraphy and ornament. Despite this, there was naturalistic Persian painting, which inspired painters in the Mogul and Ottoman empires. Ceramic tiles decorated mosques and palaces from Spain (Alhambra, Granada) to S Russia and Mogul India (Taj Mahal, Agra). Wood, stone, and stucco sculpture ornamented buildings. Islamic artists produced intricate metalwork and, in Persia in the 16th and 17th centuries, woven textiles and carpets.

Islamic art is found from NW Africa and much of Spain to NW India and Anatolia. Interlacing patterns based on geometry and stylized plant motifs (including the swirling arabesque) swarm over surfaces.

calligraphy From about the 8th century the Arabic script was increasingly elaborate. The cursive script with extended flourishes (Nashki script) was widely adopted, and calligraphy was used to ornament textiles, metalwork, tiles, and pottery.

miniatures Miniature painting flourished in Persia, in cities such as Isfahan, Herat, and Shiraz during the Safavid period 1502–1736 and after 1526 under the Mogul Empire in India.

carpets The royal Persian carpet factories produced luxurious compositions featuring human and animal figures as well as calligraphic, geometrical, and floral motifs.

island area of land that is above the surrounding water level, whether seawater or freshwater. Islands protrude above ocean levels as well as lake and river waters. Australia is classed as a continent rather than an island, because of its size.

Islands have been formed in many ways. Continental islands were once part of the mainland, but became isolated (by tectonic movement, erosion, or a rise in sea level, for example). Volcanic islands, such as Japan, were formed by the explosion of underwater volcanoes. Coral islands consist mainly of ◊coral, built up over many years. An atoll is a circular coral reef surrounding a lagoon; atolls were formed when a coral reef grew up around a volcanic island that was submerged by a rise in sea level. Barrier islands are found by the shore in shallow water, formed by the deposition of sediment eroded from the shoreline.

major islands

Name and location	*sq km*	*sq mi*
Greenland (North Atlantic)	2,175,600	840,000
New Guinea (SW Pacific)	800,000	309,000
Borneo (SW Pacific)	744,100	287,300
Madagascar (Indian Ocean)	587,000	227,000
Baffin (Canadian Arctic)	507,258	195,928
Sumatra (Indian Ocean)	473,600	182,860
Honshu (NW Pacific)	230,966	89,176
Great Britain (N Atlantic)	229,978	88,795
Victoria (Canadian Arctic)	217,206	83,896
Ellesmere (Canadian Arctic)	196,160	75,767
Sulawesi (Indian Ocean)	189,216	73,057
South Island, New Zealand (SW Pacific)	149,883	57,870
Java (Indian Ocean)	126,602	48,900
Seram (W Pacific)	118,625	45,800
North Island, New Zealand (SW Pacific)	114,669	44,274
Cuba (Caribbean Sea)	110,800	44,800
Newfoundland (NW Atlantic)	108,860	42,030
Luzon (W Pacific)	104,688	40,420
Iceland (N Atlantic)	103,000	39,800
Mindanao (W Pacific)	94,630	36,537
Ireland (N Atlantic)	84,400	32,600
Hokkaido (NW Pacific)	83,515	32,245
Sakhalin (NW Pacific)	76,400	29,500
Hispaniola—Dominican Republic and Haiti (Caribbean Sea)	76,000	29,300
Banks (Canadian Arctic)	70,000	27,038
Tasmania (SW Pacific)	67,800	26,200
Sri Lanka (Indian Ocean)	64,600	24,900
Devon (Canadian Arctic)	55,247	21,331

island arc an arcuate chain of islands (◊archipelago) produced by volcanic activity caused by rising magma behind the deep-sea trench formed by one tectonic plate sliding beneath another. In such areas (called subductive zones) the lithosphere of the descending plate does so along a curved path, because of the spherical shape of the Earth. Lithosphere depressed into the less rigid asthenosphere of the mantle tends to bend downward along a curved line much in the way a circular dent forms in a ping-pong ball when pressed with the thumb.

Such island arcs are often later incorporated into continental margins during mountain-building episodes. Island arcs are common in the Pacific where they ring the ocean on both sides; the Aleutian Islands of Alaska are an example.

Islay southernmost island of the Inner Hebrides, Scotland, in Strathclyde region, separated from Jura by the Sound of Islay; area 235 sq mi/610 sq km; population (1981) 3,800. The principal towns are Bowmore and Port Ellen. It produces malt whiskey, and its wildlife includes eagles and rare wintering geese.

Isles of the Blessed an alternative title for ◊Elysium in Greek mythology.

islets of Langerhans group of cells within the pancreas responsible for the secretion of the hormone insulin. They are sensitive to the blood sugar, producing more hormone when glucose levels rise.

Ismail 1830–1895. Khedive (governor) of Egypt 1866–79. A grandson of Mehemet Ali, he became viceroy of Egypt in 1863 and in 1866 received the title of khedive from the Ottoman sultan. He amassed huge foreign debts and in 1875 Britain, at Prime Minister Disraeli's suggestion, bought the khedive's Suez Canal shares for nearly £4 million, establishing Anglo-French control of Egypt's finances. In 1879 the UK and France persuaded the sultan to appoint Tewfik, his son, khedive in his place.

isobar

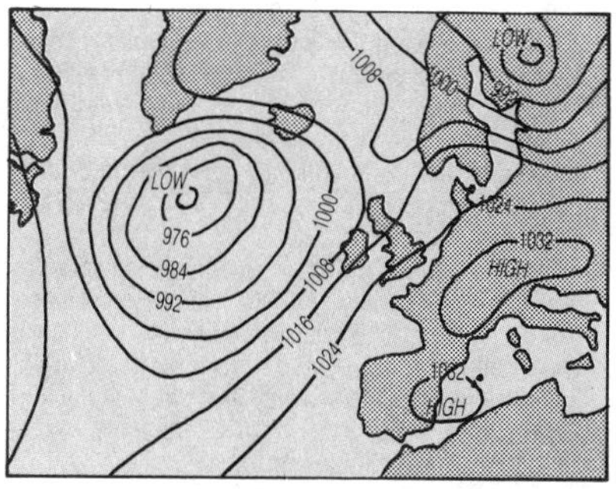
LOW
LOW
976
984
992
1000
1008
1016
1024
1032
HIGH
HIGH

Ismail I 1486–1524. Shah of Persia from 1501, founder of the Safavi dynasty, who established the first national government since the Arab conquest and Shi'ite Islam as the national religion.

Ismaili a sect of ◊Shi'ite Muslims.

Ismailia city in NE Egypt; population (1985) 191,700. It was founded in 1863 as the headquarters for construction of the Suez Canal and was named after the Khedive Ismail.

ISO in photography, a numbering system for rating the speed of films, devised by the International Standards Organization.

isobar a line drawn on maps and weather charts linking all places with the same atmospheric pressure (usually measured in millibars). When used in weather forecasting, the distance between the isobars is an indication of the barometric gradient.

Where the isobars are close together, cyclonic weather is indicated, bringing strong winds and a depression, and where far apart anticyclonic, bringing calmer, settled conditions.

Isocrates 436–338 BC. Athenian orator, a pupil of the philosopher Socrates. He was a professional speechwriter and teacher of rhetoric.

isolation in medicine, the segregation of patients to prevent the spread of infection. Today, isolation is most often required for patients who are at unusual risk, mainly those whose immune systems have been undermined by disease or suppressed by antirejection or ◊cytotoxic drugs. Strict isolation is also practiced to prevent infection due to antibiotic-resistant microbes (see ◊nosocomial infection).

isolationism in politics, concentration on domestic rather than foreign affairs; a foreign policy having no interest in international affairs that do not affect the country's own interests. In the US, isolationism is as old as George Washington, who warned against "entangling alliances." Today it is usually associated with the Republican Party, especially politicians of the Midwest (for example, the Neutrality Acts 1935–39). Intervention by the US in both World Wars was initially resisted. In the 1960s some Republicans demanded the removal of the United Nations from American soil.

There has been resistance to use of official US military forces without clearly defined objectives in pursuit of an important national interest. This so-called Vietnam Syndrome was largely dissipated during the presidencies of Ronald Reagan and George Bush, who reasserted international involvements and military action.

Isolde or ***Iseult*** in Celtic legend, the wife of King Mark of Cornwall who was brought from Ireland by his nephew ◊Tristan. She and Tristan accidentally drank the aphrodisiac given to her by her

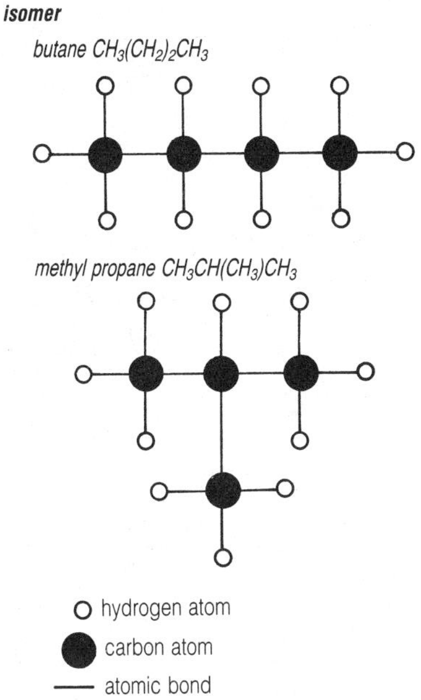
isomer
butane $CH_3(CH_2)_2CH_3$
methyl propane $CH_3CH(CH_3)CH_3$
hydrogen atom
carbon atom
atomic bond

mother for her marriage, were separated, and finally died together.

isomer chemical compound having the same molecular composition and mass as another, but with different physical or chemical properties because of the different structural arrangement of the atoms in the molecules. For example, butane and 2-methylpropane have the same formula, but different molecular structures. Optical isomers are "mirror images" of each other.

isometrics system of muscular exercises without apparatus—for example, by contracting particular sets of muscles. These exercises, some of which can be performed without visible movement, have been recommended to sedentary workers as a way of getting fit, but can be damaging when practiced by the unskilled.

isomorphism the existence of substances of different chemical composition but with similar crystalline form.

isorhythm in music, a form in which a given rhythm constantly repeats, although the notes may change. Used in European medieval music, and still practiced in Classical Indian music.

isostasy the theoretical balance in buoyancy of all parts of the Earth's ◊crust, as though they were floating on a denser layer beneath. High mountains, for example, have very deep roots, just as an iceberg floats with most of its mass submerged.

Similarly, during an ◊ice age the weight of the ice sheet pushes that continent into the earth's mantle; once the ice has melted, the continent rises again. This accounts for shoreline features being found some way inland in regions that were heavily glaciated during the Pleistocene period.

isotherm a line on a map linking all places having the same temperature at a given time.

isotope one of two or more atoms that have the same atomic number (same number of protons), but which contain a different number of neutrons, thus differing in their atomic weights. They may be stable or radioactive, naturally occurring or synthesized. The term was coined by English chemist Frederick Soddy, pioneer researcher in atomic disintegration.

Isozaki Arata 1931– . Japanese architect. One of Kenzo ◊Tange's team 1954–63, his Post-Modernist works include Ochanomizu Square, Tokyo (retaining the existing façades), and buildings for the 1992 Barcelona Olympics.

Israel ancient kingdom of N ◊Palestine, formed after the death of Solomon by Jewish peoples seceding from the rule of his son Rehoboam and electing Jeroboam in his place.

Israel country in SW Asia, bounded N by Lebanon, E by Syria and Jordan, S by the Gulf of Aqaba, and W by Egypt and the Mediterranean

government Israel has no written constitution. In 1950 the single-chamber legislature, the *Knesset*, voted to adopt a state constitution by evolution over an unspecifed period of time. As in the UK, certain laws are considered to have particular constitutional significance and could, at some time, be codified into a single written document.

Supreme authority rests with the *Knesset*, whose 120 members are elected by universal suffrage, through a system of proportional representation, for a four-year term. It is subject to dissolution within that period. The president is constitutional head of state and is elected by the *Knesset* for a five-year term. The prime minister and cabinet are mostly drawn from, and collectively responsible to, the *Knesset*, but occasionally a cabinet member may be chosen from outside. There are several political parties, the two most significant being the Israel Labour Party and the Consolidation Party (Likud).

history The Zionist movement, calling for an independent community for Jews in their historic homeland of Palestine, began in the 19th century, and in 1917 Britain declared its support for the idea. In 1920 the League of Nations placed Palestine under British administration, and the British government was immediately faced with the rival claims of Jews who wished to settle there and the indigenous Arabs who opposed them. In 1937 Britain proposed separate Arab and Jewish communities; this was accepted by the Jews but not by the Arabs, and fighting broke out between them. In Europe, the Nazi Holocaust killed about 6 million Jews, and hundreds of thousands tried to get to Palestine before, during, and after World War II 1939–45. Many survivors could no longer live in Europe.

In 1947 the British plan for partition was supported by the UN, and when Britain ended its Palestinian mandate 1948, an independent State of Israel was proclaimed, with David ◊Ben-Gurion as prime minister. Neighboring Arab states sent forces to crush Israel but failed, and when a cease-fire agreement was reached in 1949, Israel controlled more land than had been originally allocated to it. The non-Jewish-occupied remainder of Palestine, known as the West Bank, was occupied by ◊Jordan. The creation of Israel encouraged Jewish immigration on a large scale, about 2 million having arrived from all over the world by 1962. Hundreds of thousands of Arab residents had fled from Israel to neigboring countries, such as Jordan and Lebanon. In 1964 a number of Palestinian Arabs in exile founded the ◊Palestine Liberation Organization (PLO), aiming to overthrow Israel.

During the 1960s there was considerable tension between Israel and Egypt, which, under President ◊Nasser, had become a leader in the Arab world. His nationalization of the ◊Suez Canal in 1956 provided an opportunity for Israel, with Britain and France, to attack Egypt and occupy a part of Palestine that Egypt had controlled since 1949, the Gaza Strip, from which Israel was forced by UN and US pressure to withdraw in 1957. Ten years later, in the Six-Day War, Israel gained the whole of Jerusalem, the West Bank area of Jordan, the Sinai Peninsula in Egypt, and the Golan Heights in Syria. All were placed under Israeli law, although the Sinai was returned to Egypt under the terms of the ◊Camp David agreements. Ben-Gurion resigned in 1963 and was succeeded by Levi Eshkol, leading a coalition government; in 1968 three of the coalition parties combined to form the Israel Labor Party. In 1969 Golda Meir became Labor Party prime minister. Toward the end of her administration another Arab-Israeli war broke out, on ◊Yom Kippur, the holiest day of the Jewish year. Israel was attacked by Egypt and Syria, and after nearly three weeks of fighting, with heavy losses, a ceasefire was agreed. Golda Meir resigned in 1974 and was succeeded by General Itzhak Rabin, heading a Labor-led coalition.

In the 1977 elections the Consolidation (Likud) bloc, led by Menachem ◊Begin, won an unexpected victory, and Begin became prime minister. Within five months relations between Egypt and Israel changed dramatically, mainly caused by initiatives by President ◊Sadat of Egypt, encouraged by US president Jimmy ◊Carter. Setting a historical precedent for an Arab leader, Sadat visited Israel to address the *Knesset* 1977, and the following year the Egyptian and Israeli leaders met at Camp David, in the US, to sign agreements for peace in the Middle East. A treaty was signed in 1979, and in 1980 Egypt and Israel exchanged ambassadors, to the dismay of most of the Arab world.

Israel withdrew from Sinai by 1982 but continued to occupy the Golan Heights. In the same year Israel, without consulting Egypt, entered Lebanon and surrounded W Beirut, in pursuit of 6,000 PLO fighters who were trapped there. A split between Egypt and Israel was avoided by the efforts of the US special negotiator, Philip Habib, who secured the evacuation from Beirut to other Arab countries of about 15,000 PLO and Syrian fighters in Aug 1982.

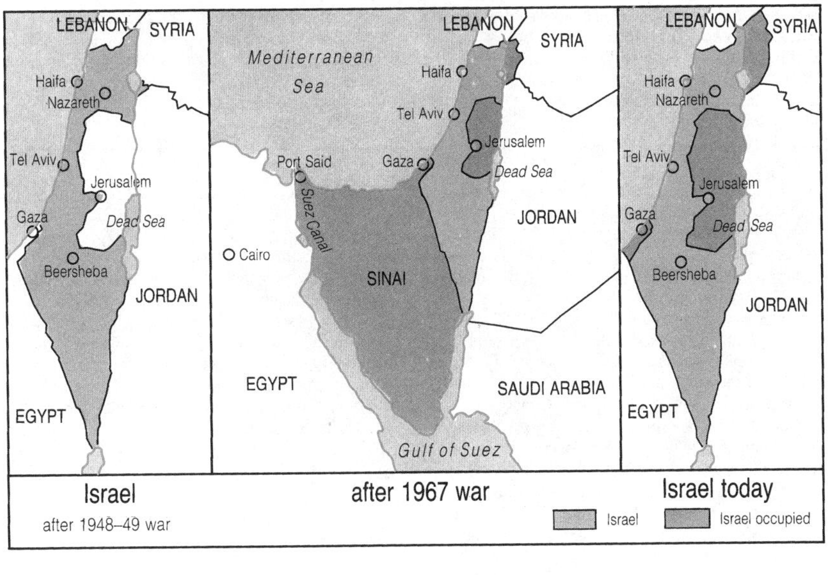
LEBANON
SYRIA
Haifa
Nazareth
Tel Aviv
Jerusalem
Gaza
Dead Sea
Beersheba
JORDAN
EGYPT
Mediterranean Sea
Port Said
Suez Canal
Cairo
SINAI
SAUDI ARABIA
Gulf of Suez
Israel
after 1948–49 war
after 1967 war
Israel today
Israel
Israel occupied

Israel
State of
(Medinat Israel)

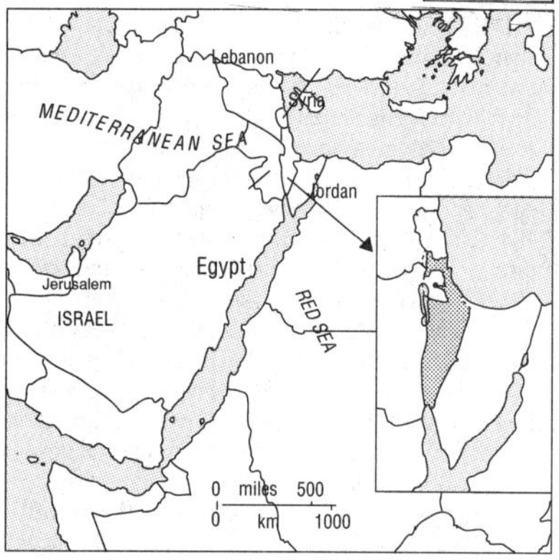
MEDITERRANEAN SEA
Egypt
Jerusalem
ISRAEL
RED SEA
0 miles 500
0 km 1000

area 8,029 sq mi/20,800 sq km (as at 1949 armistice)
capital Jerusalem (not recognized by the United Nations)
cities ports Tel Aviv/Jaffa, Haifa, Acre, Eilat; Bat-Yam, Holon, Ramat Gan, Petach Tikva, Beersheba
physical coastal plain of Sharon between Haifa and Tel Aviv noted since ancient times for fertility; central mountains of Galilee, Samariq, and Judea; Dead Sea, Lake Tiberias, and river Jordan Rift Valley along the E are below sea level; Negev Desert in the S; Israel occupies Golan Heights, West Bank, and Gaza
features historic sites: Jerusalem, Bethlehem, Nazareth, Masada, Megiddo, Jericho; caves of the Dead Sea scrolls
head of state Chaim Herzog from 1983
head of government Itzhak Shamir from 1986
political system democratic republic
political parties Israel Labor Party, moderate left-of-center; Consolidation Party (Likud), right-of-center
exports citrus and other fruit, avocados, Chinese leaves, fertilizers, diamonds, plastics, petrochemicals, textiles, electronics (military, medical, scientific, industrial), electro-optics, precision instruments, aircraft and missiles
currency shekel
population (1989 est) 4,477,000 (including 750,000 Arab Israeli citizens and over 1 million Arabs in the occupied territories); under the Law of Return 1950, "every Jew shall be entitled to come to Israel as an immigrant"; those from the East and E Europe are *Ashkenazim*, and from Mediterranean Europe (Spain, Portugal, Italy, France, Greece) and Arab N Africa are *Sephardim* (over 50% of the population is now of Sephardic descent). An Israeli-born Jew is a *Sabra*; about 500,000 Israeli Jews are resident in the US. Growth rate 1.8% p.a.
life expectancy men 73, women 76
language Hebrew and Arabic (official); Yiddish, European and W Asian languages
religion Israel is a secular state, but the predominant faith is Judaism 83%; also Sunni Muslim, Christian, and Druse
literacy Jewish 88%, Arab 70%
GDP $35 bn (1987); $8,011 per head
chronology
1948 Independent State of Israel proclaimed with Ben-Gurion as prime minister; attacked by Arab nations, Israel won the War of Independence. Many displaced Arabs settled in refugee camps in the Gaza Strip and West Bank.
1952 Col Gamal Nasser of Egypt stepped up blockade of Israeli ports and support of Arab guerrillas in Gaza.
1956 Israel invaded Gaza and Sinai.
1959 Egypt renewed blockade of Israeli trade through Suez Canal.
1963 Ben-Gurion resigned, succeeded by Levi Eshkol.
1964 Palestine Liberation Organization (PLO) founded with the aim of overthrowing the state of Israel.
1967 Israel victorious in the Six-Day War. Gaza, West Bank, E Jerusalem, Sinai, and Golan Heights captured.
1968 Israel Labor Party formed, led by Golda Meir.
1969 Golda Meir became prime minister.
1973–74 Yom Kippur War: Israel attacked by Egypt and Syria. Golda Meir succeeded by Itzhak Rabin.
1975 Suez Canal reopened.
1977 Menachem Begin elected prime minister. Egyptian president addressed the Knesset.
1978 Camp David talks.
1979 Egyptian-Israeli agreement signed. Israel agreed to withdraw from Sinai.
1980 Jerusalem declared capital of Israel.
1981 Golan Heights formally annexed.
1982 Israel pursued PLO fighters into Lebanon.
1983 Agreement reached for withdrawal from Lebanon.
1985 Israeli prime minister Shimon Peres had secret talks with King Hussein of Jordan.
1986 Itzhak Shamir took over from Peres under power-sharing agreement.
1988 Criticism of Israel's handling of Palestinian uprising in occupied territories; PLO acknowledged Israel's right to exist.
1989 New Likud–Labor coalition government formed under Shamir. Limited progress achieved on proposals for negotiations leading to elections in occupied territories.
1990 Coalition threatened by differences over peace process.
1991 Shamir gave cautious response to US Middle East peace proposals. Israel attends conference in Madrid.
1992 Israelis and Palestinians hold first direct negotiations.

Israel's alleged complicity in massacres in two Palestinian refugee camps increased Arab hostility. Talks between Israel and Lebanon, between Dec 1982 and May 1983, resulted in an agreement, drawn up by US secretary of state George Shultz, calling for the withdrawal of all foreign forces from Lebanon within three months. Syria refused to acknowledge the agreement, and left some 30,000 troops, with about 7,000 PLO members, in the northeast; Israel retaliated by refusing to withdraw its forces from the south.

During this time Begin faced growing domestic problems, including rapidly rising inflation and opposition to his foreign policies. In 1983 he resigned, and Itzhak Shamir formed a shaky coalition. Elections in July 1984 proved inconclusive, with the Labor Alignment, led by Shimon Peres, winning 44 seats in the *Knesset*, and Likud, led by Shamir, 41. Neither leader was able to form a viable coalition, so after weeks of negotiation, it was agreed that a government of national unity would be formed, with Peres as prime minister for the first 25 months, until Oct 1986, and Shamir as his deputy, and then a reversal of the positions.

Meanwhile, the problems in Lebanon continued. In 1984, under pressure from Syria, President Gemayel of Lebanon abrogated the 1983 treaty with Israel, but the government of national unity in Tel Aviv continued to plan the withdrawal of its forces, although it might lead to outright civil war in S Lebanon. Guerrilla groups of the Shi'ite community of S Lebanon took advantage of the situation by attacking the departing Israeli troops. Israel retaliated by attacking Shiite villages. Most of the withdrawal was complete by June 1985. Several peace initiatives by King Hussein of Jordan failed, largely because of Israeli and US suspicions about the PLO, some of whose supporters were alleged to have been involved in terrorism in the Mediterranean area. There were, however, signs of improvement in 1985. Prime Minister Peres met King Hussein secretly in the south of France, and later, in a speech to the UN, Peres said he would not rule out the possibility of an international conference on the Middle East. PLO leader Yasser ◊Arafat also had talks with Hussein and later, in Cairo, renounced PLO guerrilla activity outside Israeli-occupied territory. Domestically, the government of national unity was having some success with its economic policies, inflation falling in 1986 to manageable levels.

The Nov 1988 general election resulted in a hung parliament; after lengthy negotiations, Shamir formed another coalition with Peres and the Labor Party. Shamir's harsh handling of Palestinian protests, and differences over dealings with the PLO, broke the partnership in March 1990 when the coalition fell after a vote of no confidence. Egyptian president Hosini ◊Mubarak proposed a 10-point program for elections in the occupied territories leading toward an unspecified form of autonomous self-rule. Labor quickly agreed to the provisions, and the US approved the plan. In 1989 Likud accepted some of the provisions but remained opposed to any PLO role in the negotiations. In Oct 1990 the killing of at least 19 Palestinians by Israeli troops on Jerusalem's Temple Mount drew widespread international condemnation.

In Jan 1991 the Gulf War erupted with UN-coalition air raids against Iraq. In retaliation, SCUD missiles were launched against Israel. In return for Israel's restraint, the UN worked to stabilize the Middle East, and in Nov 1991 Israel and several Arab nations, as well as the Palestinians, met in Spain in an initial effort at resolving their historic differences.

Israels Jozef 1824–1911. Dutch painter. In 1870 he settled in The Hague and became a leading member of the Hague school of landscape painters, who shared some of their ideals with the ◊Barbizon school in France. His somber and sentimental scenes of peasant life recall the work of ◊Millet.

Istanbul city and chief seaport of Turkey; population (1985) 5,495,000. It produces textiles, tobacco, cement, glass, and leather. Founded as Byzantium about 660 BC, it was renamed Constantinople AD 330 and was the capital of the ◊Byzantine Empire until captured by the Turks 1453. As Istamboul it was capital of the Ottoman Empire until 1922.

Its features include the harbor of the Golden Horn; Hagia Sophia (Emperor Justinian's church of the Holy Wisdom, 537, now a mosque); Sultan Ahmet Mosque, known as the Blue Mosque, from its tiles; Topkapi Palace of the Sultans (with a harem of 400 rooms), now a museum. The Selimye Barracks in the suburb of Usküdar (Scutari) was used as a hospital in the Crimean War; the rooms used by Florence Nightingale, with her personal possessions, are preserved as a museum.

isthmus a narrow strip of land joining two larger land masses. The Isthmus of Panama joins North and South America.

Itagaki Taisuke 1837–1919. Japanese military and political leader, the founder of Japan's first political party, the (Liberal) Jiyuto 1875–81. Involved in the overthrow of the Tokugawa shogunate and the Meiji restoration 1866–68 (see ◊Mutsuhito), Itagaki became a champion of democratic principles while continuing to serve in the government for short periods.

Itaipu the world's largest dam, situated on the Parań River, SW Brazil. A joint Brazilian-Paraguayan venture, it started in 1973; it supplies hydroelectricity to a wide area.

Istanbul *The Hagia Sophia in Istanbul, formerly a Christian place of worship, was converted to a mosque in 1453.*

Italian native to or an inhabitant of Italy and their descendants, culture, and language. The language belongs to the Romance group of Indo-European languages and is spoken in S Switzerland and in areas of Italian settlement in the US, Argentina, the UK, Canada, and Australia.

Italian architecture architecture of the Italian peninsula after the fall of the Roman Empire. In the earliest styles—Byzantine, Romanesque, and Gothic—the surviving buildings are mostly churches. From the Renaissance and Baroque periods there are also palaces, town halls, and so on.

Byzantine (5th–11th centuries) Italy is rich in examples of this style of architecture, which is a mixture of oriental and Classical elements; examples are the monuments of Justinian in Ravenna and the basilica of S Marco, Venice, about 1063.

Romanesque (10th–13th centuries) In N Italy buildings in this style are often striped in dark and light marble, for example the baptistery, cathedral, and Leaning Tower of Pisa; Sicily has Romanesque churches.

Gothic (13th–15th centuries) Italian Gothic differs a great deal from that of N Europe. Façades were elaborately decorated: mosaics and colored marble were used, and sculpture placed around windows and doors. The enormous cathedral of Milan, 15th century, was built in the N European style.

Renaissance (15th–16th centuries) The style was developed by the Florentine Brunelleschi and his contemporaries, inspired by Classical models. The sculptor Michelangelo is associated with the basilica of St Peter's, Rome. In Venice the villas of Palladio continued the purity of the High Renaissance.

Baroque (17th century) The Baroque style flourished with the oval spaces of Bernini (for example, the church of S Andrea al Quirinale, Rome) and Boromini, and the fantasies of Guarini in Turin (such as the church of S Lorenzo).

Neo-Classicism (18th–19th centuries) In the 18th century a dry Classical revival prevailed. In the 19th century Neo-Classicism was the norm, as in much of Europe.

20th century The Futurist visions of Sant'Elia opened the century. Between World Wars I and II, pure Modernism was explored (under the influence of Fascism), together with a stripped Classicism. Nervi's work showed the expressive potential of structural concrete. Rationalism and a related concern with the study of the traditional types of European cities have exerted great influence, led by the work and writings of Aldo Rossi.

Italian art painting and sculpture of Italy from the early Middle Ages to the present. Schools of painting arose in many of the city-states; Florence and Venice were major centers of the Renaissance, and Rome was the focus of the High Renaissance and Baroque styles.

13th century (Italian *Duecento*) The painter Cimabue was said by the poet Dante to be the greatest painter of his day. Already there was a strong tradition of fresco painting and monumental painted altarpieces, often reflecting Byzantine art. A type of Gothic Classicism was developed by the sculptors Nicola and Giovanni Pisano.

14th century (*Trecento*) The Florentine painter Giotto broke with prevailing styles. Sienese painting remained decoratively stylized but became less somber, as exemplified by the work of Simone Martini and the Lorenzetti brothers.

Renaissance (15th and 16th centuries) The style was seen as a "rebirth" of the Classical spirit. The earliest artists of the Renaissance were based in Florence. The sculptor Ghiberti worked on the baptistery there; Donatello set new standards in naturalistic and Classically inspired sculpture. Masaccio and Uccello employed scientific perspective in painting. In the middle and later part of the century dozens of sculptors and painters were at work in Florence: Verrocchio, Pollaiuolo, Botticelli, Fra Angelico, Fra Filippo Lippi, and Filippino Lippi, among others. In Venice the Bellini family of painters influenced their successors Giorgione and Titian. Tintoretto was a pupil of Titian. The High Renaissance was dominated by the genius of Leonardo da Vinci, the forceful sculptures and frescoes of Michelangelo, and the harmonious paintings of Raphael.

Baroque (17th century) This dramatic style was developed by, among others, the sculptor and architect Bernini, and in painting by Caravaggio, who made effective use of light and shade to create high drama.

Neo-Classicism (18th and early 19th centuries) The style was inspired by the rediscovery of Classical Roman works. The sculptor Canova was an exponent. Piranesi produced engravings.

20th century The Futurist movement, founded 1910, tried to portray phenomena such as speed and electricity in painting and sculpture. The dreamlike Metaphysical paintings of de Chirico date from the same period. Modigliani moved to Paris; his paintings were characterized by elongated figures. The sculptures of Marino Marini and Giacometti created new styles in bronze.

Italian language member of the Romance branch of the Indo-European language family, the most direct descendant of the Roman form of Latin. Broadcasting and films have standardized the Italian national tongue, but most Italians speak a regional dialect as well as Standard Italian. The Italian language is also spoken in Switzerland and by people of Italian descent, especially in the US, Canada, Australia, the UK, and Argentina.

The standard language originates in the Tuscan dialect of the Middle Ages, particularly as used for literary purposes by ◊Dante Alighieri. With a strong infusion of Latin for religious, academic, and educational purposes, written Standard Italian has tended to be highly formal and divorced from the many regional dialects, which are often mutually unintelligible.

Italian literature originated in the 13th century with the Sicilian school, which imitated Provençal poetry. The works of St Francis of Assisi and Jacopone da Todi reflect the religious faith of that time. Guido Guinicelli (1230–c. 1275) and Guido Cavalcanti (c. 1250–1300) developed the spiritual conception of love and influenced Dante Alighieri, whose *Divina commedia/Divine Comedy* 1307–21 is generally recognized as the greatest work of Italian literature. Petrarch was a humanist and a poet, celebrated for his sonnets, while Boccaccio is principally known for his tales.

The Divina commedia marked the beginning of the Renaissance. Boiardo dealt with the Carolingian epics in his *Orlando Innamorato/Roland in Love* 1480–94, which was completed and transformed by Lodovico Ariosto as *Orlando furioso/The Frenzy of Roland* 1516. Their contemporaries Niccolò Machiavelli and Francesco Guicciardini (1483–1540) are historians of note. Torquato Tasso wrote his epic *Gerusalemme liberata/The Liberation of Jerusalem* 1575 in the spirit of the Counter-Reformation.

The 17th century was characterized by the exaggeration of the poets Giovanni Battista Marini (1569–1625) and Gabriello Chiabrera (1552–1638). In 1690 the "Academy of Arcadia" was formed, including among its members Innocenzo Frugoni (1692–1768) and Metastasio. Other writers include Salvator Rosa, the satirist.

During the 18th century Giuseppe Parini (1729–99) ridiculed the abuses of his day, while Vittorio Alfieri attacked tyranny in his dramas. Carlo Goldoni wrote comedies, and Ugo Foscolo (1778–1827) is chiefly remembered for his patriotic verse. Giacomo Leopardi is not only the greatest lyrical poet since Dante but also a master of Italian prose. The Romantic, Alessandro Manzoni, is best known as a novelist, and influenced among others the novelist Antonio Fogazzaro. A later outstanding literary figure, Giosuè Carducci, was followed by the verbose Gabriele d'Annunzio, writing of sensuality and violence, and Benedetto Croce, historian and philosopher, who between them dominated Italian literature at the turn of the century.

Twentieth-century writers include the realist novelists Giovanni Verga and Grazia Deledda, winner of the Nobel Prize 1926, the dramatist Luigi Pirandello, and the novelists Ignazio Silone and Italo Svevo. Poets of the period include Dino Campana and Giuseppe Ungaretti; and among the modern school are Nobel Prizewinners Eugenio Montale and Salvatore Quasimodo. Novelists of the post-Fascist period include Alberto Moravia, Carlo Levi, Cesare Pavese (1908–50), Vasco Pratolini (1913–), Elsa Morante (1916–), Natalia Ginsburg (1916–), Giuseppe Tomasi, Prince of Lampedusa, and the writers Italo Calvino, Leonardo Sciascia, and Primo Levi.

Italian Somaliland former Italian Trust Territory on the Somali coast of Africa extending to 194,999 sq mi/502,300 sq km. Established in 1892, it was extended in 1925 with the acquisition of Jubaland from Kenya; administered from Moga-

Italy
Republic of
(Repubblica Italiana)

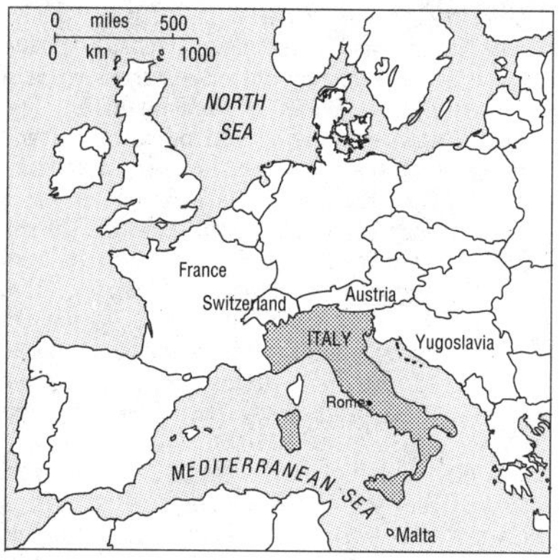
0 miles 500
0 km 1000
NORTH SEA
France
Switzerland
Austria
ITALY
Yugoslavia
Rome
MEDITERRANEAN SEA
Malta

area 116,332 sq mi/301,300 sq km
capital Rome
cities Milan, Turin; ports Naples, Genoa, Palermo, Bari, Catania, Trieste
physical mountainous (Maritime Alps, Dolomites, Apennines) with narrow coastal lowlands; rivers Po, Adige, Arno, Tiber, Rubicon; islands of Sicily, Sardinia, Elba, Capri, Ischia, Lipari, Pantelleria; lakes Como, Maggiore, Garda
features continental Europe's only active volcanoes: Vesuvius, Etna, Stromboli; historic towns include Venice, Florence, Siena, Rome; Greek, Roman, Etruscan archeological sites
political parties Christian Democratic Party (DC), Christian, centrist; Democratic Party of the Left (PDS), pro-European Socialist; Italian Socialist Party (PSI), moderate Socialist; Italian Social Movement–National Right (MSI–DN), neo-fascist; Italian Republican Party (PRI), social democratic, left-of-center; Italian Social Democratic Party (PSDI), moderate left-of-center; Liberals (PLI), right-of-center
exports wine (world's largest producer), fruit, vegetables, textiles (Europe's largest silk producer), clothing, leather goods, motor vehicles, electrical goods, chemicals, marble (Carrara), sulfur, mercury, iron, steel
head of state Francesco Cossiga from 1985
head of government Giulio Andreotti from 1989
political system democratic republic
currency lira
population (1990 est) 57,657,000; growth rate 0.1% p.a.
life expectancy men 73, women 80 (1989)
language Italian; German, French, Slovene minorities
religion Roman Catholic 100% (state religion)
literacy 97% (1989)
GDP $748 bn; $13,052 per head (1988)
chronology
1946 Monarchy replaced by a republic.
1948 New constitution adopted.
1954 Trieste returned to Italy.
1976 Communists proposed establishment of broad-based, left–right government, the "historic compromise"; rejected by Christian Democrats.
1978 Christian Democrat Aldo Moro, architect of the historic compromise, kidnapped and murdered by Red Brigade guerrillas.
1983 Bettino Craxi, a Socialist, became leader of broad coalition government.
1987 Craxi resigned; succeeding coalition fell within months.
1988 Christian Democrats leader Ciriaco de Mita, established a five-party coalition that included the Socialists.
1989 De Mita resigned after disagreements within his coalition government; succeeded by Giulio Andreotti. De Mita lost leadership of Christian Democrats; Communists formed "shadow government."
1991 Referendum approved electoral reform.

dishu; under British rule 1941–50. Thereafter it reverted to Italian authority before uniting with British Somaliland in 1960 to form the independent state of Somalia.

italic style of printing in which the letters slope to the right *like this*, introduced by the printer Aldus Manutius of Venice in 1501. It is usually used side by side with the erect Roman type, for purposes of emphasis and citation. The term is also used for the handwriting style developed for popular use in 1522 by Vatican chancery scribe Ludovico degli Arrighi, becoming the basis for modern italic script.

Italy country in S Europe, bounded N by Switzerland and Austria, E by Yugoslavia and the Adriatic Sea, S by the Ionian and Mediterranean seas, and W by the Tyrrhenian Sea and France. It includes the Mediterranean islands of Sardinia and Sicily.

government The 1948 constitution provides for a two-chamber parliament consisting of a senate and a 630-member chamber of deputies. Both are elected for a five-year term by universal suffrage, through a system of proportional representation, and have equal powers. The senate's 315 elected members are regionally representative, and there are also seven life senators. The president is constitutional head of state and is elected for a seven-year term by an electoral college consisting of both houses of parliament and 58 regional representatives. The president appoints the prime minister and cabinet (council of ministers), and they are collectively responsible to parliament.

Although Italy is not a federal state, each of its 20 regions enjoys a high degree of autonomy, with a regional council elected for a five-year term by universal suffrage. The voting system encourages a multiplicity of political parties, the most significant being the Christian Democrats (DC), the Communists (PCI), the Socialists (PSI), the Italian Social Movement–National Right (MSI-DN), the Republicans (PRI), the Social Democrats (PSDI), and the Liberals (PLI).

history The varying peoples inhabiting Italy—Etruscans in Tuscany, Latins and Sabines in middle Italy, Greek colonies in the south and Sicily, and Gauls in the north—were united under Roman rule during the 4th–3rd centuries BC. With the decline of the Roman Empire, and its final extinction in AD 476, Italy became exposed to barbarian attacks and passed in turn under the rule of the Ostrogoths and the Lombards.

The 8th century witnessed the rise of the papacy as a territorial power, the annexation of the Lombard kingdom by Charlemagne, and his coronation as emperor of the West in 800. From then until 1250 the main issue in Italian history is the relations, at first friendly and later hostile, between the papacy and the Holy Roman Empire. During this struggle the Italian cities seized the opportunity to convert themselves into self-governing republics.

By 1300 five major powers existed in Italy: the city-republics of Milan, Florence, and Venice; the papal states; and the kingdom of Naples. Their mutual rivalries and constant wars laid Italy open 1494–1559 to invasions from France and Spain; as a result Naples and Milan passed under Spanish rule. After 1700 Austria secured Milan and replaced Spain as the dominating power, while Naples passed to a Spanish Bourbon dynasty and Sardinia to the dukes of Savoy.

The period of French rule 1796–1814 temporarily unified Italy and introduced the principles of the French Revolution, but after Napoleon's fall Italy was again divided between Austria, the pope, the kingdoms of Sardinia and Naples, and four smaller duchies. Nationalist and democratic ideals nevertheless remained alive and inspired attempts at revolution in 1820, 1831, and 1848–49. After this last failure the Sardinian monarchy assumed the leadership of the national movement. With the help of Napoleon III, the Austrians were expelled from Lombardy in 1859; the duchies joined the Italian kingdom; ◊Garibaldi overthrew the Neapolitan monarchy; and Victor Emmanuel II of Sardinia was proclaimed king of Italy at Turin in 1861. Venice and part of Venetia were secured by another war with Austria in 1866; in 1870 Italian forces occupied Rome, thus completing the unification of Italy, and the pope ceased to be a temporal ruler until 1929 (see ◊Vatican City State).

In 1878 Victor Emmanuel II died and was succeeded by Humbert (Umberto) I, his son, who was assassinated in 1900. The formation of a colonial empire began in 1869 with the purchase of land on the Bay of Assab, on the Red Sea, from the local sultan. In the next 20 years the Italians occupied all ◊Eritrea, which was made a colony in 1889. An attempt to seize Ethiopia was decisively defeated at Adowa in 1896. War with Turkey 1911–12 gave Italy Tripoli and Cyrenaica. Italy's intervention on the Allied side in World War I secured it Trieste, the Trentino, and S Tirol.

Italy: regions

Region	*Capital*	*Area sq km*
Abruzzi	Aquila	10,800
Basilicata	Potenza	10,000
Calabria	Catanzaro	15,100
Campania	Naples	13,600
Emilia-Romagna	Bologna	22,100
Friuli-Venezia Giulia*	Udine	7,800
Lazio	Rome	17,200
Liguria	Genoa	5,400
Lombardy	Milan	23,900
Marche	Ancona	9,700
Molise	Campobasso	4,400
Piedmont	Turin	25,400
Puglia	Bari	19,300
Sardinia*	Cagliari	24,100
Sicily*	Palermo	25,700
Trentino-Alto Adige*	Trento**	13,600
Tuscany	Florence	23,000
Umbria	Perugia	8,500
Valle d'Aosta*	Aosta	3,300
Veneto	Venice	18,400
		301,300

*special autonomous regions
**also Bolzano-Bozen

The postwar period was marked by intense political and industrial unrest, culminating in 1922 in the establishment of ◊Mussolini's Fascist dictatorship. The regime embraced a policy of aggression with the conquest of Ethiopia 1935–36 and Albania 1939, and Italy entered World War II in 1940 as an ally of Germany. Defeat in Africa 1941–43 and the Allied conquest of Sicily 1943 resulted in Mussolini's downfall; the new government declared war on Germany, and until 1945 Italy was a battlefield of German occupying forces, the Italian underground (partisans), and the advancing Allies.

In 1946 Victor Emmanuel III, who had been king since 1900, abdicated in favor of his son Humbert (Umberto) II. The monarchy was abolished after a referendum in 1946, and the country became a republic, adopting a new constitution in 1948. Between 1946 and 1986 there were nine parliaments and 45 administrations.

The Christian Democrats were dominant until 1963 and after this participated in most coalition governments. In 1976 the Communists became a significant force, winning over a third of the votes for the chamber of deputies and pressing for what they called the "historic compromise," a broad-

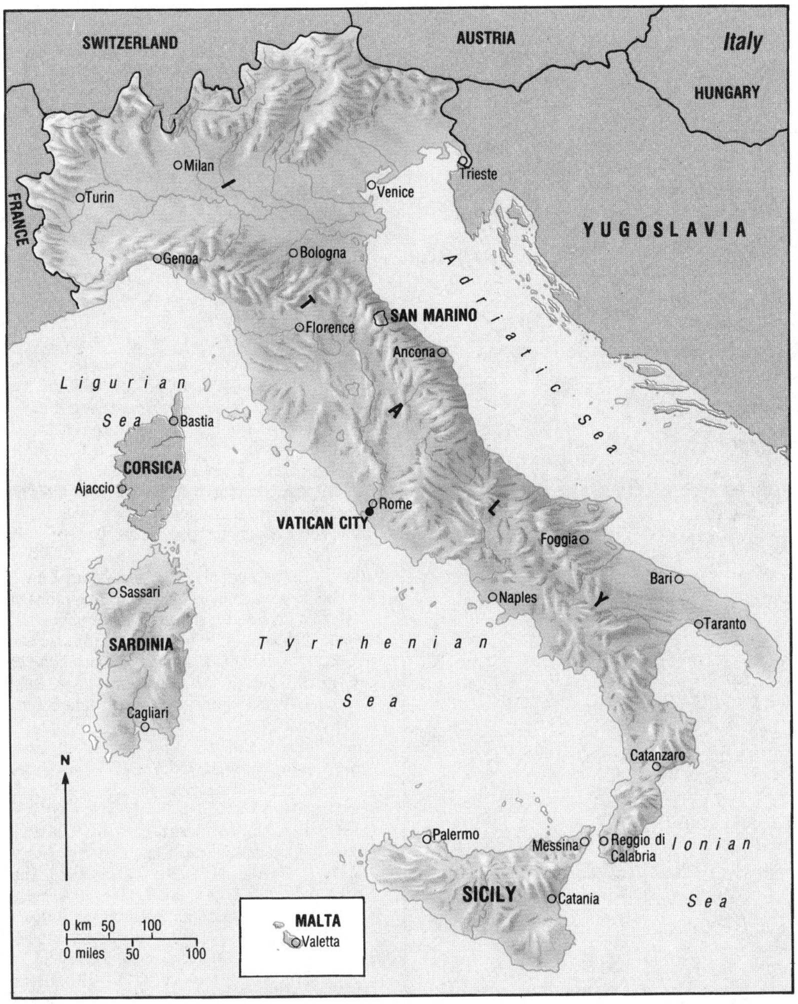
Italy
SWITZERLAND
AUSTRIA
HUNGARY
FRANCE
YUGOSLAVIA
Milan
Turin
Venice
Trieste
Genoa
Bologna
Florence
SAN MARINO
Ancona
Adriatic Sea
Ligurian Sea
Bastia
CORSICA
Ajaccio
Rome
VATICAN CITY
Foggia
Bari
Naples
Taranto
Sassari
SARDINIA
Tyrrhenian Sea
Cagliari
Catanzaro
Palermo
Messina
Reggio di Calabria
Ionian Sea
SICILY
Catania
ITALY
N
0 km 50 100
0 miles 50 100
MALTA
Valetta

based government with representatives from the Christian Democratic, Socialist, and Communist parties, which would, in effect, be an alliance between Communism and Roman Catholicism. The Christian Democrats rejected this. Apart from a brief period 1977–78, the other parties excluded the Communists from power-sharing, forcing them to join the opposition. In 1980 the Socialists returned to share power with the Christian Democrats and Republicans and participated in a number of subsequent coalitions.

In 1983, the leader of the Socialist Party, Bettino Craxi, became the republic's first Socialist prime minister, leading a coalition of Christian Democrats, Socialists, Republicans, Social Democrats, and Liberals. Despite criticism of Craxi's strong-willed style of leadership, the coalition parties could find no acceptable alternative and so continued to support him.

Under Craxi's government the state of the economy improved, although the N–S divide in productivity and prosperity persists, despite attempts to increase investment in the S. In foreign affairs Italy has demonstrated its commitment to the EC, NATO, and the UN, and in 1983 played an important part in the multinational peace-keeping force in Beirut. In 1987 the Christian Democrat Giovanni Goria formed a coalition government, that fell when the Liberal Party withdrew some three months later. He was succeeded by Ciriaco De Mita, who formed a new Christian Democrat–Socialist–Liberal coalition, but De Mita resigned a few months later after disagreements within the government. After lengthy negotiations the veteran Giulio Andreotti put together a new coalition of Christian Democrats, Socialists, and minor parties.

itch irritation of nerve endings in skin or mucous membrane that provokes the desire to scratch; also a popular name for the parasitic disorder ◊scabies.

iteration in computing, a method of solving a problem by performing the same steps repeatedly until a certain condition is satisfied. For example, in one method of sorting, adjacent items are repeatedly exchanged until the data are in the required sequence.

iteroparity in biology, the repeated production of offspring at intervals throughout the life cycle. It is usually contrasted with ◊semelparity, where each individual reproduces only once during its life. Most vertebrates are iteroparous.

Ithaca (Greek *Ithaki*) Greek island in the Ionian Sea, area 36 sq mi/93 sq km. Important in pre-Classical Greece, Ithaca was (in Homer's *Odyssey*) the birthplace of Odysseus.

Ito Hirobumi, Prince 1841–1909. Japanese politician, prime minister 1892–96, 1898, 1900–01. He was a key figure in the modernization of Japan and was involved in the Meiji restoration under ◊Mutsuhito 1866–68 and in government missions to the US and Europe in the 1870s. As minister for home affairs, he helped draft the Meiji constitution in 1889 and oversaw its implementation as prime minister the following year. While resident-general in Korea, he was assassinated by a Korean Nationalist, which led to Japan's annexation of that country.

Iturbide Agustín de 1783–1824. Mexican military leader (*caudillo*) who led the conservative faction in the nation's struggle for independence from Spain. In 1822 he crowned himself Emperor Agustín I. His extravagance and failure to restore order led all other parties to turn against him, and he reigned for less than a year (see ◊Mexican Empire).

IUCN (International Union for the Conservation of Nature) an organization established by the United Nations to promote the conservation of wildlife and habitats as part of the national policies of member states.

It has formulated guidelines and established research programs (for example, International Biological Program, IBP) and set up advisory bodies (such as Survival Services Commissions, SSC). In 1980, it launched the World Conservation Strategy to highlight particular problems, designating a small number of areas as World Heritage Sites to ensure their survival as unspoilt habitats (for example, Yosemite National Park in California, and the Simen Mountains in Ethiopia).

IUPAC abbreviation for International Union of Pure and Applied Chemistry, organization that recommends the nomenclature to be used for naming substances, the units to be used, and which conventions are to be adopted when describing particular changes.

Ivan six rulers of Russia, including:

Ivan III Ivan the Great 1440–1505. Grand duke of Muscovy from 1462, who revolted against Tatar overlordship by refusing tribute to Grand Khan Ahmed 1480. He claimed the title of tsar, and used the double-headed eagle as the Russian state emblem.

Ivan IV the Terrible 1530–1584. Grand duke of Muscovy from 1533; he assumed power 1544 and was crowned as first tsar of Russia 1547. He conquered Kazan 1552, Astrakhan 1556, and Siberia 1581. He reformed the legal code and local administration 1555 and established trade relations with England. In his last years he alternated between debauchery and religious austerities, executing thousands and, in rage, his own son.

Ivanovo capital of Ivanovo region, USSR, 150 mi/240 km NE of Moscow; population (1987) 479,000. Industries include textiles, chemicals, and engineering.

Ives Charles (Edward) 1874–1954. US composer who experimented with ◊atonality, quarter tones, clashing time signatures, and quotations from popular music of the time. He wrote five symphonies, including *Holidays Symphony* 1904–13, chamber music, including the *Concord Sonata*, and the orchestral *Three Places in New England* 1903–14 and *The Unanswered Question* 1908.

Ives Frederic Eugene 1856–1937. US inventor who developed the ◊halftone process of printing photographs in 1878. The process uses a screen to break up light and dark areas into dots. By 1886 he had evolved the halftone process now generally in use. Among his many other inventions was a three-color printing process (similar to the ◊four-color process.

IVF abbreviation for ◊in vitro fertilization.

Iviza alternate spelling of ◊Ibiza, one of the ◊Balearic Islands.

ivory the hard white substance of which the teeth and tusks of certain mammals are composed. Most valuable are elephants' tusks, which are of unusual hardness and density. Ivory is used in carving and other decorative work, and is so valuable that poachers continue to destroy the remaining wild elephant herds in Africa to obtain it illegally. Trade in ivory was halted by Kenya 1989, but Zimbabwe continued its policy of controlled culling to enable the elephant population to thrive and to release ivory for export. China and Hong Kong have refused to obey an international ban on ivory trading.

Vegetable ivory is used for buttons, toys, and cheap ivory goods. It consists of the hard albumen of the seeds of a tropical palm *Phytelephas macrocarpa*, and is imported from Colombia.

Ivory James 1928– . US film director best known for his collaboration with Indian producer Ismael ◊Merchant.

Ivory Coast (French Côte d'Ivoire) country in W Africa, bounded N by Mali and Burkina Faso, E

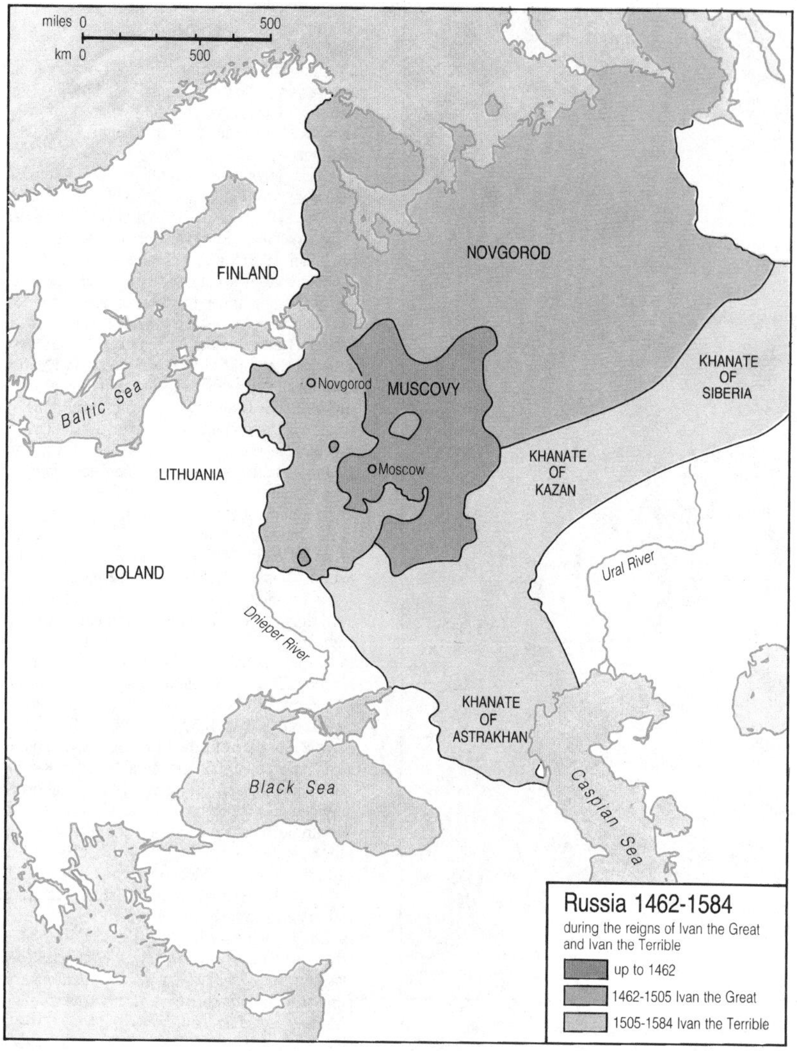
miles 0
500
km 0
500
FINLAND
NOVGOROD
Baltic Sea
Novgorod
MUSCOVY
KHANATE OF SIBERIA
LITHUANIA
Moscow
KHANATE OF KAZAN
POLAND
Ural River
Dnieper River
KHANATE OF ASTRAKHAN
Black Sea
Caspian Sea
Russia 1462-1584
during the reigns of Ivan the Great and Ivan the Terrible
up to 1462
1462-1505 Ivan the Great
1505-1584 Ivan the Terrible

by Ghana, S by the Gulf of Guinea, and W by Liberia and Guinea

government The 1960 constitution, amended 1971, 1975, 1980, and 1985, provides for a president who is head of both state and government, elected by universal suffrage for a five-year term, and a single-chamber national assembly of 175 members, also popularly elected and serving a five-year term. The president chooses and heads a council of ministers. The only political party is the Democratic Party of the Ivory Coast (PDCI), and its chair is the state president.

history The area now known as Côte d'Ivoire was once made up of several indigenous kingdoms. From the 16th century the Portuguese, French, and British established trading centers along the coast, dealing in slaves and ivory. During the 19th century France acquired the region by means of treaties with local leaders, eventually incorporating it into ◊French West Africa in 1904.

It was given self-government within the French Community in 1958 and full independence in 1960, when a new constitution was adopted. Félix ◊Houphouët-Boigny has been the country's only president. He has maintained close links with France since independence, and this support, combined with a good economic growth rate, has given his country a high degree of political stability. He has been criticized by some other African leaders for maintaining links with South Africa but has argued that a dialogue between blacks and whites is essential. He has denounced Communist intervention in African affairs and has traveled extensively to improve relations with Western powers.

In the Oct and Nov 1990 multiparty elections Houphouët-Boigny and the PDCI were re-elected amid widespread criticisms of ballot rigging and political pressurizing.

ivy any tree or shrub of the genus *Hedera* of the ginseng family Araliaceae. English or European ivy *H. helix* has shiny, evergreen, triangular or oval-shaped leaves, and clusters of small, yellowish-green flowers, followed by black berries. It climbs by means of rootlike suckers put out from its stem, and is injurious to trees.

Ground ivy *Glechoma hederacea* is a small, originally European creeping plant of the mint family Labiatae; the North American poison ivy *Rhus radicans* belongs to the cashew family Anacardiaceae.

Ivy League a collective term for eight long-established universities in the US. The term arose from the pronunciation of IV, the Roman numeral for 4—being the first four East Coast private universities: Harvard, Yale, Columbia, and Brown. The universities of Princeton, Pennsylvania, Dartmouth, and Cornell joined the league later to compete in intercollegiate athletics.

Iwo Jima largest of the Japanese Volcano Islands in the W Pacific Ocean, 760 mi/1,222 km S of Tokyo; area 8 sq mi/21 sq km. Annexed by Japan 1891, it was captured by the US 1945 after fierce fighting. It was returned to Japan 1968.

IWW abbreviation for ◊Industrial Workers of the World.

Ixion in Greek mythology, a king whom Zeus punished for his crimes by binding him to a fiery wheel rolling endlessly through the underworld.

Izhevsk industrial city in the E USSR, capital of Udmurt Autonomous Republic; population (1987) 631,000. Industries include steel, agricultural machinery, machine tools, and armaments. It was founded 1760.

Izmir formerly Smyrna port and naval base in Turkey; population (1985) 1,490,000. Products include steel, electronics, and plastics. The largest annual trade fair in the Middle East is held here. It is the headquarters of ◊North Atlantic Treaty Organization SE Command.

history Originally Greek (founded about 1000 BC), it was of considerable importance in ancient times, vying with Ephesus and Pergamum as the first city of Asia. It was destroyed by ◊Tamerlane in 1402 and became Turkish in 1424. It was occupied by the Greeks in 1919 but retaken by the Turks in 1922; in the same year it was largely destroyed by fire.

Iznik modern name of ancient ◊Nicaea, a town in Turkey noted for the richly decorated pottery and tiles produced there in the 15th and 16th centuries.

Ivory Coast

Republic of

(*République de la Côte d'Ivoire*)

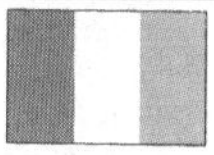

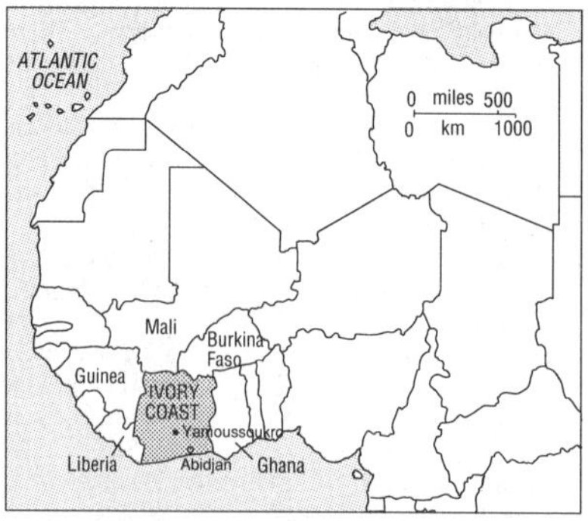
ATLANTIC OCEAN
0 miles 500
0 km 1000
Mali
Burkina Faso
Guinea
IVORY COAST
Yamoussoukro
Liberia
Abidjan
Ghana

area 124,471 sq mi/322,463 sq km
capital Abidjan; capital designate Yamoussoukro
cities Bouaké, Daloa, Man; port San Pedro
physical tropical rainforest (diminishing) in S; savanna and low mountains in N
features Vridi canal, Kossou dam, Mounts du Toura
head of state and government Félix Houphouët-Boigny from 1960
political system one-party presidential republic (since 1960)
political parties Democratic Party of the Ivory Coast (PDCI), nationalist, free-enterprise
exports coffee, cocoa, timber, petroleum products
currency franc CFA
population (1990 est) 12,070,000; growth rate 3.3% p.a.
life expectancy men 52, women 55 (1989)
language French (official), over 60 native dialects
religion animist 65%, Muslim 24%, Christian 11%
literacy 35% (1988)
GDP $7.6 bn (1987); $687 per head
chronology
1904 Became part of French West Africa.
1958 Achieved internal self-government.
1960 Independence achieved from France, with Félix Houphouët-Boigny as president of a one-party state.
1985 Houphouët-Boigny reelected, running unopposed.
1986 Name changed officially to Côte d'Ivoire.
1990 Houphouët-Boigny and PDCI reelected.

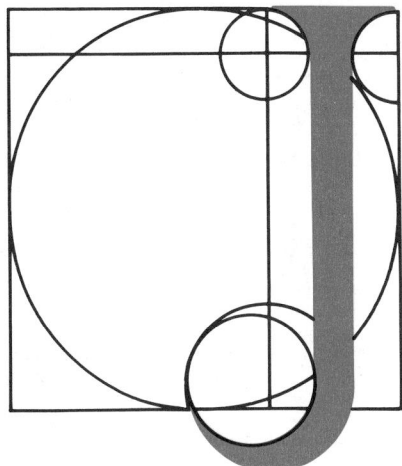

J in physics, the symbol for joule, the SI unit of energy.

Jabalpur industrial city on the Narbarda River in Madhya Pradesh, India; population (1981) 758,000. Products include textiles, oil, bauxite, and armaments.

jabiru stork *Jabiru mycteria* found in Central and South America. It is 5 ft/1.5 m high with white plumage. The head is black and red.

Jablonec town in Czechoslovakia, on the river Neisse, NE of Prague; population (1984) 45,000. It has had a glass industry since the 14th century.

jaborandi plant *Pilocarpus microphyllus* of the rue family Rutaceae, native to South America. It is the source of pilocarpine, used to contract the pupil of the eye.

jacamar insect-eating bird of the family Galbulidae, in the same order as woodpeckers. Jacamars are found in Central and South America. They have long, sharp-pointed bills, long tails, and paired toes. The plumage is brilliantly colored. The largest species grows to 12 in/30 cm.

jacana one of seven species of wading birds, family Jacanidae, with very long toes and claws enabling it to walk on the flat leaves of river plants, hence the name "lily trotter." Jacanas are found in Mexico, Central America, South America, Africa, S Asia, and Australia.

The female pheasant-tailed jacana *Hydrophasianus chirurgus* of Asia has a "harem" of two to four males.

jacaranda any tropical American tree of the genus *Jacaranda* of the bignonia family Bignoniaceae, with fragrant wood and showy blue or violet flowers, commonly cultivated in the southern US.

jacinth or ***hyacinth*** red or yellowish-red gem, a variety of zircon.

jack tool or machine for lifting, hoisting, or moving heavy weights, such as motor vehicles. A screw jack uses the principle of the screw to magnify an applied effort; in a car jack, for example, turning the handle many times causes the lifting screw to rise slightly, and the effort is magnified to lift heavy weights. A hydraulic jack uses a succession of piston strokes to increase pressure in a liquid and force up a lifting ram.

jackal any of several wild dogs of the genus *Canis*, found in S Asia, S Europe, and N Africa. It can grow to 2.7 ft/80 cm long, and has grayish-brown fur and a bushy tail.

The golden jackal *C. aureus* of S Asia, S Europe, and N Africa is 1.5 ft/45 cm high and 2 ft/60 cm long. It is grayish-yellow, darker on the back. Nocturnal, it preys on smaller mammals and poultry, although packs will attack larger animals. It will also scavenge. The side-striped jackal *C. adustus* is found over much of Africa; the black-backed jackal *C. mesomelas* occurs only in the S of Africa.

Jack and the Beanstalk English fairy tale. Jack is the lazy son of a poor widow. When he exchanges their cow for some magic beans, the beans grow into a beanstalk that Jack climbs to a realm above the clouds. There he tricks a giant out of various magical treasures before finally killing him by cutting down the beanstalk.

jackdaw Eurasian bird *Corvus monedula* of the crow family. It is mainly black, but greyish on sides and back of head, and about 1.1 ft/33 cm long. It nests in tree holes or on buildings.

jackknife clam see ◊razor clam.

Jackson city in S Michigan, on the Grand River, S of Lansing; seat of Jackson County. Its industries include automobile and airplane parts, tools, plastics, and air-conditioning equipment; population (1990) 37,446. The Republican Party was formed here 1854.

Jackson largest city and capital of Mississippi, on the Pearl River; population (1990) 196,637. It produces furniture, cottonseed oil, and iron and steel castings and owes its prosperity to the discovery of gas fields to the S in the 1930s. Educational institutions include Jackson State University, Millsaps College, and the University of Mississippi Medical Center. Named after Andrew Jackson, later president, it dates from 1821 and was virtually destroyed by Union troops 1863, during the American Civil War.

Jackson Alexander Young 1882–1974. Canadian landscape painter, a leading member of the Group of Seven, who aimed to create a specifically Canadian school of landscape art.

Jackson Andrew 1767–1845. The 7th president of the US 1829–37, a Democrat. Born in South Carolina, he spent his early life in poverty. He defeated a British force during the War of 1812 at New Orleans in 1815 (after the official end of the war in 1814) and was involved in the war which led to the purchase of Florida in 1819. After

Jackson *The 7th president of the United States of America, Andrew Jackson, a Democrat. 1829–1837.*

Jackson *British actress Glenda Jackson also took an active interest in politics.*

an unsuccessful attempt in 1824, he was elected president in 1828. This was the first election in which electors were chosen directly by voters rather than state legislators. The political organization he built, with Martin ◊Van Buren, served as the basis for the modern ◊Democratic party. He demanded and received absolute loyalty from his cabinet members and made wide use of his executive powers. In 1832 he vetoed the renewal of the US bank charter and was reelected, whereupon he continued his struggle against the power of finance.

Jackson Glenda 1936– . English actress. She has made many stage appearances, including *Marat/Sade* 1966, and her films include the Oscar-winning *Women in Love* 1971. On television she played Queen Elizabeth I in *Elizabeth R* 1971. In 1990 she was chosen as a Labour candidate for the House of Commons.

Jackson Howell Edmunds 1832–1895. US jurist. Born in Paris, Tennessee, Jackson received his law degree from Cumberland University 1856. During the US Civil War, he served as an official in Tennessee's Confederate government. He returned to private practice after the war, was elected to the state legislature 1880, and immediately thereafter was chosen for the US Senate. He was named federal district judge 1886 by Grover Cleveland and chief judge of the circuit court of appeals 1891 by Benjamin Harrison. In 1893 Jackson was appointed to the US Supreme Court by Harrison, but illness prevented him from carrying out his duties.

Jackson Jesse 1941– . US clergyman and Democrat politician, campaigner for minority rights. He contested his party's 1984 and 1988 presidential nominations in an effort to increase voter registration and to put black issues on the national agenda. He is a notable but sometimes controversial public speaker.

Born in North Carolina and educated in Chicago, Jackson emerged as a powerful Baptist preacher and black activist politician, working first with the civil-rights leader Martin Luther King, Jr, then on building the political machine that gave Chicago a black mayor 1983.

He sought to construct what he called a rainbow coalition of ethnic-minority and socially deprived groups. He took the lead in successfully campaigning for US disinvestment in South Africa 1986.

Jackson John Hughlings 1835–1911. English neurologist and neurophysiologist. As a result of his studies of ◊epilepsy, Jackson demonstrated that specific areas of the cerebral cortex (outer mantle of the brain) control the functioning of particular organs and limbs.

Jackson Mahalia 1911–1972. US gospel singer. She made her first recording in 1934, and her version of the gospel song "Move on Up a Little Higher"

Jackson *US rock singer and songwriter Michael Jackson, whose success and popularity soared with the release of the* Thriller *1982 and* Bad *1987 albums.*

was a commercial success 1945. Jackson became a well-known radio and television performer in the 1950s and was invited to sing at the inauguration of John Kennedy.

Born in New Orleans and brought up in a religious home, Jackson began singing religious music in the choir of her local church. In 1927 she left home for Chicago and became a member of the Greater Salem Baptist Church choir, where she distinguished herself as an outstanding soloist.

Jackson Michael 1958– . US rock singer and songwriter, known for his androgynous appearance and his single sequinned glove used during his meticulously choreographed performances. His first solo hit was "Got to Be There" 1971, but worldwide popularity was achieved with the albums *Thriller* 1982 and *Bad* 1987.

He turned professional in 1969 as the youngest member of the Jackson Five, who had several hits on Motown Records beginning with first single, "I Want You Back." The group left Motown in 1975 and changed its name to the Jacksons. Michael was the lead singer, but soon surpassed his brothers in popularity as a solo performer. His 1980s albums, produced by Quincy Jones (1933–), yielded an unprecedented number of hit singles, among them "Billie Jean" 1983.

Jackson Thomas Jonathan "Stonewall" 1824–1863. US Confederate general in the American Civil War. He acquired his nickname and his reputation at the Battle of Bull Run, from the firmness with which his brigade resisted the Northern attack. In 1862 he organized the Shenandoah Valley campaign and assisted Robert E ◊Lee's invasion of Maryland. He helped to defeat Gen Joseph E Hooker's Union army at the battle of Chancellorsville, Virginia, but was fatally wounded by one of his own men in the confusion of battle.

Jackson *Confederate general "Stonewall" Jackson, who earned his nickname for holding against Union forces at the Battle of Bull Run.*

A West Point graduate, after serving in the Mexican War 1846–48, he became professor of military tactics at the Virginia military institute.

Jacksonian Democracy in US history, the populist, egalitarian spirit pervading the presidencies of Andrew Jackson and Martin Van Buren 1829–1841, which encouraged greater participation in the democratic process. Recent studies have questioned the professed commitment to popular control, emphasizing Jackson's alleged cult of personality.

Jacksonville port, resort, and commercial center in Florida; population (1990) 635,230. The port has naval installations and ship-repair yards. To the N the Cross-Florida Barge Canal links the Atlantic with the Gulf of Mexico. Manufactured goods include wood and paper products, chemicals, and processed food. Among the educational institutions are Jacksonville University and the University of North Florida. French Huguenots built a shortlived settlement 1564, but the site of the present city was not settled until 1816. Much of the city was destroyed by Union troops in the American Civil War 1861–65, and there was a destructive fire in 1901. The city absorbed most of Duval County 1968, greatly increasing its area and population.

Jack the Ripper popular name for the unidentified mutilator and murderer of at least five women prostitutes in the Whitechapel area of London in 1888.

Several suspects have been suggested in extensive studies of the case, including members of the royal household.

Jacob in the Old Testament, Hebrew patriarch, son of Isaac and Rebecca, who obtained the rights of seniority from his twin brother Esau by trickery. He married his cousins Leah and Rachel, serving their father Laban seven years for each, and at the time of famine in Canaan joined his son Joseph in Egypt. His 12 sons were the traditional ancestors of the 12 tribes of Israel.

Jacob François 1920– . French biochemist who, with Jacques Monod, pioneered research into molecular genetics and showed how the production of proteins from ◊DNA is controlled. He shared the Nobel Prize for Medicine in 1965.

Jacob Joseph 1854–1916. Australian-born US folklorist and collector of fairy tales. He published collections of vividly retold fairy stories such as *English Fairy Tales* 1890, *Celtic Fairy Tales* 1892 and 1894, and *Indian Fairy Tales* 1892.

Jacobabad city in Sind province, SE Pakistan, 250 mi/400 km NE of Karachi; population (1981) 80,000. Founded by General John Jacob as a frontier post, the city now trades in wheat, rice, and millet. It has a low annual rainfall (about 2 in/5 cm) and temperatures are among the highest in the Indian subcontinent—up to 127°F/53°C.

Jacobin member of an extremist republican club of the French Revolution founded at Versailles 1789, which later used a former Jacobin (Dominican) friary as its headquarters in Paris. Helped by ◊Danton's speeches, they proclaimed the French republic, had the king executed, and overthrew the moderate ◊Girondins 1792–93. Through the Committee of Public Safety, they began the Reign of Terror, led by ◊Robespierre. After his execution 1794, the club was abandoned and the name "Jacobin" passed into general use for any left-wing extremist.

Jacobite in Britain, a supporter of the royal house of Stuart after the deposition of James II in 1688. They included the Scottish Highlanders, who rose unsuccessfully under ◊Claverhouse in 1689; and those who rose in Scotland and N England under the leadership of ◊James Edward Stuart, the Old

***Jacquard** The Jacquard loom revolutionized the art of weaving, but was originally faced with violent opposition from silk weavers. On one occasion its French inventor, Joseph Marie Jacquard, narrowly escaped with his life.*

Pretender, in 1715, and followed his son ◊Charles Edward Stuart in an invasion of England that reached Derby in 1745–46. After the defeat at ◊Culloden, Jacobitism disappeared as a political force.

Jacquard Joseph Marie 1752–1834. French textile manufacturer who invented a punched-card system for programming designs on a carpet-making loom. In 1804 he constructed looms that used a series of punched cards to control the pattern of longitudinal warp threads depressed before each sideways passage of the shuttle. On later machines the punched cards were joined to form an endless loop that represented the "program" for the repeating pattern of a carpet.

Jacquard-style punched cards were used in the early computers of the 1940s–1960s.

Jacquerie French peasant uprising 1358, caused by the ravages of the English army and French nobility during the Hundred Years' War, which reduced the rural population to destitution. The word derives from the nickname for French peasants, Jacques Bonhomme.

Jacuzzi Candido 1903–1986. Italian-born US inventor and engineer who invented the Jacuzzi, a pump that produces a whirlpool effect in a bathtub. He developed it for his 15-month-old son, a sufferer from rheumatoid arthritis.

jade a semiprecious stone consisting of either jadeite, $NaAlSi_2O_6$ (a pyroxene), or nephrite, $Ca_2(Mg,Fe)_5Si_8O_{22}(OH,F)_2$ (an amphibole), ranging from colorless through shades of green to black according to the iron content. Jade ranks 5.5–6.5 on the Mohs' scale of hardness.

The early Chinese civilization discovered jade, bringing it from E Turkestan, and carried the art of jade-carving to its peak. The Olmecs, Aztecs, Maya, and the Maoris have also carved jade for ornaments, ceremony, and utensils.

Jade Emperor in Chinese religion, the supreme god, Yu Huang, of pantheistic Taoism, who watches over human actions and is the ruler of life and death.

Jaén capital of Jaén province, S Spain, on the Guadalbullon river; population (1986) 103,000. It has remains of its Moorish walls and citadel.

jaguar

Jaffa (biblical name Joppa) port in W Israel, part of ◊Tel Aviv from 1950.

It was captured during the ◊Crusades in the 12th century, by the French emperor Napoleon in 1799, and by the British field marshall Allenby 1917.

Jaffna capital of Jaffna district, Northern Province, Sri Lanka. The focal point of Hindu Tamil nationalism and the scene of recurring riots during the 1980s.

Jagan Cheddi Berrat 1918– . Guyanese left-wing politician. Educated in British Guyana and the US, he led the People's Progressive Party from 1950, and in 1961 he became the first prime minister of British Guyana.

jaguar largest species of ◊cat *Panthera onca* in the Americas, formerly ranging from the SW US to S South America, but now extinct in most of North America. It can grow up to 8 ft/2.5 m long including the tail. The background color of the fur varies from creamy white to brown or black, and is covered with black spots. The jaguar is usually solitary.

jaguarundi wild cat *Felis yaguoaroundi* found in forests in Central and South America. Up to 3.5 ft/1.1 m long, it is very slim with rather short legs and short rounded ears. It is uniformly colored dark brown or chestnut. A good climber, it feeds on birds and small mammals and, unusually for a cat, has been reported to eat fruit.

Jahangir "Conqueror of the World." Adopted name of Salim 1569–1627. Mogul emperor of India 1605–27, succeeding his father ◊Akbar the Great. He designed the Shalimar Gardens in Kashmir and buildings and gardens in Lahore.

Jahweh or ***Yahwah*** another spelling of ◊Jehovah, the Lord (meaning God) in the Hebrew Bible, used by some writers instead of *Adonai* (Lord) or *Hashem* (the Name)—all names used to avoid the representation of God in any form.

jai alai or ***pelota*** very fast ball game of Basque derivation, popular in Latin American countries and in the US where it is a betting sport. It is played by two, four, or six players, in a walled court, or *cancha*, and resembles squash, but each player uses a long, curved, wickerwork basket, or *cesta*, strapped to the hand, to hurl the ball, or pelota (about the size of a baseball), against the walls.

Jainism Indian religion, sometimes regarded as an offshoot of Hinduism. Jains believe that noninjury to living beings is the highest religion, and their code of ethics is based on sympathy and compassion. They also believe in ◊karma. In Jainism there is no deity and, like Buddhism, it is a monastic, ascetic religion. Jains number about 3.3 million. There are two main sects: the Digambaras, who originally went about naked, and the Swetambaras. Jainism practices the most extreme form of nonviolence (*ahimsā*) of all Indian sects, and influenced the philosophy of Mahātmā Gāndhī.

Jainism's sacred books record the teachings of Mahavira (c. 540–468 BC), the last in a line of 24 great masters called Tirthankaras (or *jinas*, "those who overcome"). Mahavira was born in Vessali (now Bihar), E India. He became an ascetic at the age of 30, achieved enlightenment at 42, and preached for 30 years.

Jaipur capital of Rajasthan, India; population (1981) 1,005,000. Formerly the capital of the state of

***Jainism** The statue of Lord Bahufali (Gomateshvera) at Sravanabelagola, in the state of Tamil Nadu, is one of India's oldest and most important Jain pilgrimage centers.*

Jaipur, which was merged with Rajasthan in 1949. Products include textiles and metal products.

Jakarta or ***Djakarta*** capital of Indonesia on the NW coast of Java; population (1980) 6,504,000. Industries include textiles, chemicals, and plastics; a canal links it with its port of Tanjung Priok where rubber, oil, tin, coffee, tea, and palm oil are among its exports; also a tourist center.

Founded by the Dutch in 1619, and known as Batavia until 1949, it has the president's palace and government offices.

Jakeš Miloš 1922– . Czech communist politician, a member of the Politburo from 1981 and party leader 1987–89. A conservative, he supported the Soviet invasion of Czechoslovakia in 1968. He was forced to resign in Nov 1989 following a series of pro-democracy mass rallies.

Jakeš, an electrical engineer, joined the Communist Party of Czechoslovakia (CCP) in 1945 and studied in Moscow 1955–58. As head of the CCP's central control commission, he oversaw the purge of reformist personnel after the suppression of the 1968 ◊Prague Spring. In Dec 1987 he replaced Gustáv Husák as CCP leader.

Jalalabad capital of Nangarhar province, E Afghanistan, on the road from Kabul to Peshawar in Pakistan. The city was beseiged by mujaheddin rebels in 1989 after the withdrawal of Soviet troops from Afghanistan.

Jalgava formerly Mitau (until 1917) town in Latvian republic, USSR, 30 mi/48 km south of Riga; population about 57,000. Industries include textiles and sugar-refining. The town was founded in 1265 by Teutonic knights.

Jamaica island in the Caribbean, S of Cuba and W of Haiti

government The 1962 constitution follows closely the unwritten British model, with a resident constitutional head of state, the governor-general, representing the British monarch and appointing a prime minister and cabinet, collectively responsible to the legislature. This consists of two chambers, an appointed 21-member senate and a 60-member elected house of representatives. Normally 13 of the senators are appointed on the advice of the prime minister and 8 on the advice of the leader of the opposition. However, as the Jamaica Labour Party won all the seats in the 1983 general election, there was no opposition

Jamaica

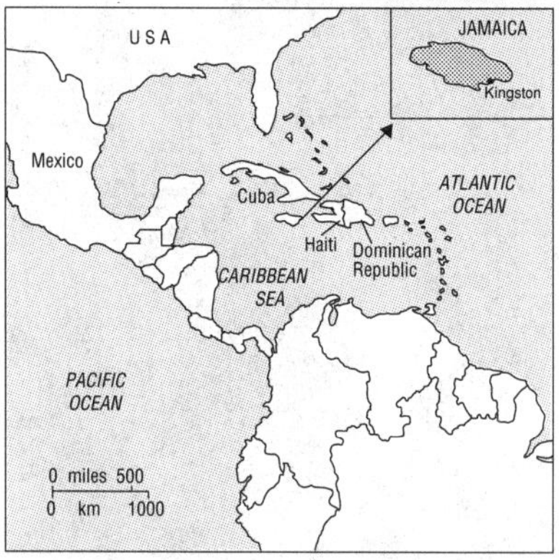
USA
JAMAICA
Kingston
Mexico
Cuba
ATLANTIC OCEAN
Haiti
Dominican Republic
CARIBBEAN SEA
PACIFIC OCEAN
0 miles 500
0 km 1000

area 4,230 sq mi/10,957 sq km
capital Kingston
cities Montego Bay, Spanish Town, St Andrew
physical mountainous tropical island
features Blue Mountains (so called because of the haze over them; renowned for their coffee); partly undersea ruins of pirate city of Port Royal, destroyed by an earthquake 1692
head of state Elizabeth II from 1962 represented by governor general
head of government Michael Manley from 1989
political system constitutional monarchy
political parties Jamaica Labor Party (JLP), moderate, centrist; People's National Party (PNP), left-of-center
exports sugar, bananas, bauxite, rum, cocoa, coconuts, liqueurs, cigars, citrus
currency Jamaican dollar (J$16.16 = ££July 1, 1991) population (1990 est) 2,513,000 (African 76%, mixed 15%, Chinese, Caucasian, East Indian); growth rate 2.2% p.a.
life expectancy men 75, women 78 (1989)
language English, Jamaican creole
religion Protestant 70%, Rastafarian
literacy 82% (1988)
GDP $2.9 bn; $1,187 per head (1989)
chronology
1655 Captured by British.
1959 Granted internal self-government.
1962 Independence achieved from Britain, with Alexander Bustamente of the JLP as prime minister.
1967 JLP reelected under Hugh Shearer.
1972 Michael Manley of the PNP became prime minister.
1980 JLP elected, with Edward Seaga as prime minister.
1983 JLP reelected, winning all 60 seats.
1988 Island badly damaged by Hurricane Gilbert.
1989 PNP won a decisive victory with Michael Manley returning as prime minister.

leader, so all 21 senators were nominated by the prime minister. Members of the house are elected by universal suffrage for a five-year term, but it is subject to dissolution within that period. The main political parties are the Jamaica Labour Party (JLP) and the People's National Party (PNP).

history Before the arrival of Christopher ◊Columbus in 1494, the island was inhabited by ◊Arawak Indians. From 1509 to 1655 it was a Spanish colony, and after this was in British hands until 1959, when it was granted internal self-government, achieving full independence within the ◊Commonwealth in 1962.

The two leading political figures in the early days of independence were Alexander Bustamante, leader of the JLP, and Norman Manley, leader of the PNP. The JLP won the 1962 and 1967 elections, led by Bustamante's successor, Hugh Shearer, but the PNP, under Norman Manley's son Michael, was successful in 1972. He advocated social reform and economic independence from the developed world. Despite high unemployment, Manley was returned to power in 1976 with an increased majority, but by 1980 the economy had deteriorated, and, rejecting the conditions attached to an ◊IMF loan, Manley sought support for his policies of economic self-reliance.

The 1980 general election campaign was extremely violent, despite calls by Manley and the leader of the JLP, Edward Seaga, for moderation. The outcome was a decisive victory for the JLP, with 51 of the 60 seats in the house of representatives. Seaga thus received a mandate for a return to a renewal of links with the US and an emphasis on free enterprise. He severed diplomatic links with Cuba in 1981. In 1983 Seaga called an early, snap election, with the opposition claiming they had been given insufficient time to nominate their candidates. The JLP won all 60 seats. There were violent demonstrations when the new parliament was inaugurated, and the PNP said it would continue its opposition outside the parliamentary arena. In 1989 Manley and the PNP were elected. The new prime minister pledged to pursue moderate economic policies and improve relations with the US.

James Henry 1843–1916. US novelist who lived in Europe from 1875 and became a naturalized British subject 1915. His novels deal with the impact of sophisticated European culture on the innocent American. They include *The Portrait of a Lady* 1881, *Washington Square* 1881, *The Bostonians* 1886, *The Ambassadors* 1903, and *The Golden Bowl* 1904. He also wrote more than a hundred shorter works of fiction, notably the supernatural tale *The Turn of the Screw* 1898.

He is assessed, both in the US and Europe, as one of the most significant and influential American writers. His career spanned more than half a century. Other major works include *Roderick Hudson* 1876, *The American* 1877, *The Tragic Muse* 1890, *The Spoils of Poynton* 1897, *The Awkward Age* 1899, *The Wings of the Dove* 1902. His mastery of the novel set the standard for many 20th-century writers.

James Jesse 1847–1882. US bank and train robber, born in Missouri and a leader (with his brother Frank) of the Quantrill raiders, a Confederate guerilla band in the Civil War. Frank later led his own gang. Jesse was killed by Bob Ford,

James *US author Henry James, who explored the effects of European culture on Americans in such novels as* Daisy Miller *and* The Ambassadors.

James *Outlaw Jesse James, who became a frontier legend for his daring robberies, was betrayed by a member of his own gang.*

an accomplice; Frank remained unconvicted and became a farmer.

James P(hyllis) D(orothy) 1920– . British detective novelist, creator of the characters Superintendent Adam Dalgliesh and private investigator Cordelia Gray. She was a tax official, hospital administrator, and civil servant before turning to writing. Her books include *Death of an Expert Witness* 1977, *The Skull Beneath the Skin* 1982, and *A Taste for Death* 1986. She was made a Baroness in 1991.

James William 1842–1910. US psychologist and philosopher, brother of the novelist Henry James. He turned from medicine to psychology and taught at Harvard 1872–1907. His books include *Principles of Psychology* 1890, *The Will to Believe* 1897, and *Varieties of Religious Experience* 1902, one of the most important works on the psychology of religion.

James I the Conqueror 1208–1276. King of Aragon from 1213, when he succeeded his father. He conquered the Balearic Islands and took Valencia from the ◊Moors, dividing it with Alfonso X of Castile by a treaty of 1244. Both these exploits are recorded in his autobiography *Llibre deis feyts*. He largely established Aragon as the dominant power in the Mediterranean.

James two kings of Britain:

James I 1566–1625. King of England from 1603 and Scotland (as James VI) from 1567. The son of Mary Queen of Scots and Lord Darnley, he succeeded on his mother's abdication from the Scottish throne, assumed power 1583, established a

James I *The son of Mary Queen of Scots, James I of England was already king of Scotland when he came to the throne in England in 1603.*

strong centralized authority, and in 1589 married Anne of Denmark (1574–1619). As successor to Elizabeth I in England, he alienated the Puritans by his High Church views and Parliament by his assertion of ◊divine right, and was generally unpopular because of his favorites, such as ◊Buckingham, and because of his schemes for an alliance with Spain. He was succeeded by his son Charles I.

James II 1633–1701. King of England and Scotland (as James VII) from 1685, second son of Charles I. He succeeded Charles II. James married Anne Hyde 1659 (1637–71, mother of Mary II and Anne) and ◊Mary of Modena 1673 (mother of James Edward Stuart). He became a Catholic 1671, which led first to attempts to exclude him from the succession, then to the rebellions of ◊Monmouth and ◊Argyll, and finally to the Whig and Tory leaders' invitation to William of Orange to take the throne in 1688. James fled to France, then led an uprising in Ireland 1689, but after defeat at the Battle of the ◊Boyne 1690 remained in exile in France.

James seven kings of Scotland:

James I 1394–1437. King of Scotland 1406–37, who assumed power 1424. He was a cultured and strong monarch whose improvements in the administration of justice brought him popularity among the common people. He was assassinated by a group of conspirators led by the Earl of Atholl.

James II 1430–1460. King of Scotland from 1437, who assumed power 1449. The only surviving son of James I, he was supported by most of the nobles and parliament. He sympathized with the Lancastrians during the Wars of the ◊Roses, and attacked English possessions in S Scotland. He was killed while besieging Roxburgh Castle.

James III 1451–1488. King of Scotland from 1460, who assumed power 1469. His reign was marked by rebellions by the nobles, including his brother Alexander, duke of Albany. He was murdered during a rebellion.

James IV 1473–1513. King of Scotland from 1488, who married Margaret (1489–1541, daughter of Henry VII) in 1503. His reign was internally peaceful, but he allied himself with France against England, invaded 1513 and was defeated and killed at the Battle of ◊Flodden.

James V 1512–1542. King of Scotland from 1513, who assumed power 1528. During the long period of James's minority, he was caught in a struggle between pro-French and pro-English factions. When he assumed power, he allied himself with France and upheld Catholicism against the Protestants. Following an attack on Scottish territory by Henry VIII's forces, he was defeated near the border at Solway Moss 1542.

James VI of Scotland. See ◊James I of England.

James VII of Scotland. See ◊James II of England.

James Edward Stuart 1688–1766. British prince, known as the Old Pretender (for the ◊Jacobites, he was James III). Son of James II, he was born at St James's Palace and after the revolution of 1688 was taken to France. He landed in Scotland in 1715 to head a Jacobite rebellion but withdrew for lack of support. In his later years he settled in Rome.

Jameson Leander Starr 1853–1917. British colonial administrator. In South Africa, early in 1896, he led the Jameson Raid from Mafeking into Transvaal to support the non-Boer colonists there, in an attempt to overthrow the government, for which he served some months in prison. Returning to South Africa, he succeeded Cecil ◊Rhodes as leader of the Progressive Party of Cape Colony, where he was prime minister 1904–08.

James, St several Christian saints, incuding:

James, St ***the Great*** died AD 44. A New Testament apostle, originally a Galilean fisherman, he was the son of Zebedee and brother of the apostle John. He was put to death by ◊Herod Agrippa. Patron saint of Spain. Feast day July 25.

James, St the Just 1st century AD. The New Testament brother of Jesus, to whom Jesus appeared after the Resurrection. Leader of the Christian church in Jerusalem, he was the author of the biblical Epistle of James.

James, St the Little 1st century AD. In the New Testament, a disciple of Christ, son of Alphaeus. Feast day May 3.

Jamestown first permanent British settlement in North America, established by Captain John Smith 1607. It was capital of Virginia 1624–99.

The colony initiated the first representative government in North America; it also brought the first slaves and built the first Anglican church there. Subject to a high mortality rate, the population remained small, and the settlement burned 1608. It was about to be abandoned when Lord De La Warr arrived with new supplies.

In the nearby Jamestown Festival Park there is a replica of the original Fort James, and models of the ships (*Discovery*, *Godspeed*, and *Constant*) that carried the 105 pioneers.

Jammu winter capital of the state of Jammu and Kashmir, India; population (1981) 206,100. It stands on the river Tavi and was linked to India's rail system in 1972.

Jammu and Kashmir state of N India

area 39,102 sq mi/101,300 sq km; another 30,455 sq mi/78,900 sq km is occupied by Pakistan, 16,482 sq mi/42,700 sq km by China

capital Jammu (winter); Srinagar (summer)

towns Leh

products timber, grain, rice, fruit, silk, carpets

population (1981) 5,982,000 (Indian-occupied territory)

history part of the Mogul Empire from 1586, Jammu came under the control of Gulab Singh 1820. In 1947 Jammu was attacked by Pakistan and chose to become part of the new state of India. Dispute over the area caused further hostilities 1971 between India and Pakistan (ended by the Simla agreement 1972).

Jamnagar city in Gujarat, India, on the Gulf of Kutch, SW of Ahmedabad; population (1981) 317,000. Its port is at Bedi.

Jamshedpur city in Bihar, India; population (1981) 439,000. It was built in 1909 and takes its name from the industrialist Jamsheedji Tata, who founded the Tata iron and steel works here and in Bombay.

Janáček Leoš 1854–1928. Czech composer. He became director of the Conservatoire at Brno in 1919 and professor at the Prague Conservatoire in 1920. His music, highly original and influenced by Moravian folk music, includes arrangements of folk songs, operas (*Jenůfa* 1904, *The Cunning Little Vixen* 1924), and the choral *Glagolitic Mass* 1927.

Janam Sakhis a collection of stories about the life of Nanak, the first guru (teacher) of Sikhism.

Janata alliance of political parties in India formed 1971 to oppose Indira Gandhi's Congress Party. Victory in the election brought Morarji Desai to power as prime minister but he was unable to control the various groups within the alliance and resigned 1979. His successors fared little better, and the elections of 1980 overwhelmingly returned Indira Gandhi to office.

Janata Dal (People's Party) Indian center-left coalition, formed Oct 1988 under the leadership of V P ◊Singh and comprising the Janata, Lok Dal (B), Congress (S), and Jan Morcha parties. In a loose alliance with the Hindu fundamentalist Bharatiya Janata Party and the Communist Party of India, the Janata Dal was victorious in the Nov 1989 general election, taking power out of the hands of the Congress (I) Party for the first time since 1947. Its minority government fell in Nov 1990.

Jane Eyre a novel by Charlotte Brontë, published 1847. Jane, an orphan, is engaged as governess to Mr Rochester's ward Adèle. Rochester and Jane fall in love, but their wedding is prevented by the revelation that Rochester already has a wife. Jane flees, but later returns to find the house destroyed by fire and Rochester blinded in a vain attempt to save his wife. Jane and Rochester marry.

Janesville city in S Wisconsin, on the Rock River, SE of Madison; seat of Rock County. It is a processing and marketing center for the area's agricultural products. Industries include automobiles and automobile parts, building materials, and electronic equipment; population (1990) 52,133.

janissary (Turkish *yeniçeri*, "new force") bodyguard of the Ottoman sultan, the Turkish standing army 1330–1826. Until the 16th century janissaries were Christian boys forcibly converted to Islam; after this time they were allowed to marry and recruit their own children. The bodyguard ceased to exist when it revolted against the decision of the sultan in 1826 to raise a regular force.

Jan Mayen Norwegian volcanic island in the Arctic, between Greenland and Norway; area 147 sq mi/ 380 sq km. It is named after a Dutchman who visited it about 1610, and was annexed by Norway 1929.

Jannequin Clament c. 1472–c. 1560. French composer. He studied with Josquin ◊Desprez and is remembered for choral works that incorporate images from real life, such as birdsong and the cries of street vendors.

Jannings Emil. Adopted name of Theodor Emil Jarenz 1882–1950. German actor in silent films of the 1920s, such as *The Last Command* 1928. In *Der Blaue Engel/The Blue Angel* 1930 he played a schoolteacher who becomes infatuated with Marlene Dietrich.

Jansen Cornelius 1585–1638. Dutch Roman Catholic theologian, founder of ◊Jansenism with his book *Augustinus* 1640.

Jansenism Christian teaching of Cornelius Jansen, which divided the Roman Catholic Church in France in the mid-17th century. Emphasizing the more predestinatory approach of Augustine's teaching, as opposed to that of the Jesuits, Jansenism was supported by the philosopher Pascal and Antoine Arnauld (a theologian linked with the abbey of ◊Port Royal). Jansenists were excommunicated 1719.

In 1713 a Jansenist work by Pasquier Quesnel (1634–1719), the leader of the Jansenist party, was condemned by Pope Clement XI as heretical, and after Quesnel's death Jansenism as an organized movement in France disappeared. It survived in the Netherlands, where in 1723 a regular Jansenist church was established under the bishop of Utrecht.

jansky unit of radiation received from outer space, used in radio astronomy, named after K G Jansky.

Jansky Karl Guthe 1905–1950. US radio engineer who discovered that the Milky Way galaxy emanates radio waves.

Born in Norman, Oklahoma, he joined Bell Telephone Laboratories, New Jersey 1928, where he investigated causes of static that created interference on radio telephone calls. Jansky found that the center of the Milky Way was giving out radio waves; he did not follow up his discovery, but it marked the birth of radio astronomy. The unit of signal strength in radio astronomy, the jansky (Jy), is equal to 10^{-26} watts per square meter per hertz.

Januarius, St or ***San Gennaro*** died c. 305. Patron saint of Naples, Italy. Traditionally, he suffered martyrdom under the Roman emperor Diocletian. Two phials of his blood preserved in the cathedral at Napels are alleged by the faithful to liquefy miraculously at regular intervals. Feast day Sept 19.

Janus in Roman mythology, god of doorways and passageways, the patron of the beginning of the day, month, and year, after whom January is named; he is represented as having two faces, one looking forward and one back.

Japan country in E Asia, occupying a group of islands of which the four main ones are Hokkaido, Honshu, Kyushu, and Shikoku. Japan is situated in the N Pacific, E of North and South Korea.

Japan
(Nippon)

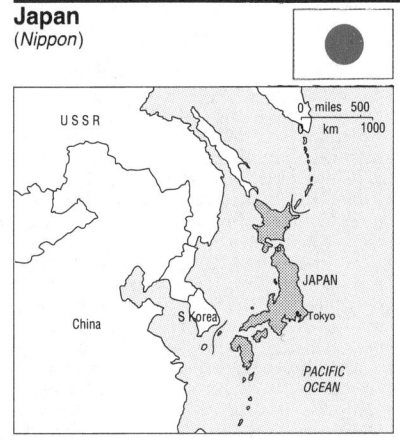

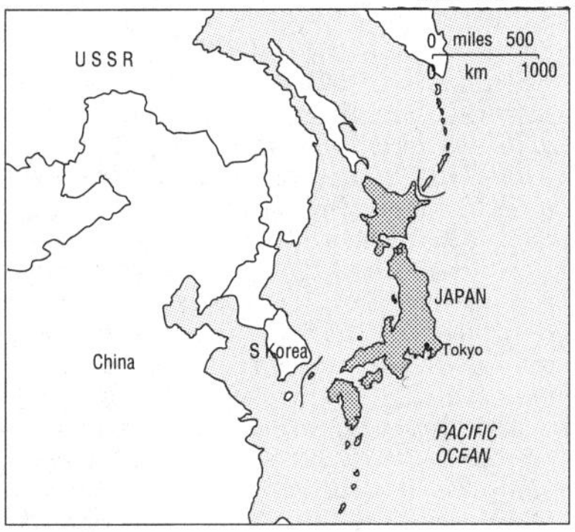
USSR
0 miles 500
km 1000
JAPAN
Tokyo
China
S Korea
PACIFIC OCEAN

area 145,822 sq mi/377,535 sq km
capital Tokyo
cities Fukuoka, Kitakyushu, Kyoto, Sapporo; ports Osaka, Nagoya, Yokohama, Kobe, Kawasaki
physical mountainous, volcanic; comprises over 1,000 islands, the longest of which are Hokkaido, Honshu, Shikoku, and Kyushu
features Mount Fuji, Mount Aso (volcanic)
head of state (figurehead) Emperor Akihito from 1989
head of government Toshiki Kaifu from 1989
political system constitutional monarchy
political parties Liberal Democratic Party (LDP), right-of-center; Japan Socialist Party (JSP), left-of-center; Komeito (Clean Government Party), Buddhist-centrist; Democratic Socialist Party, centrist; Japanese Communist Party (JCP), Socialist
exports televisions, cassette and video recorders, radios, cameras, computers, robots, other electronic and electrical equipment, motor vehicles, ships, iron, steel, chemicals, textiles
currency yen
population (1990 est) 123,778,000; growth rate 0.5% p.a.
life expectancy men 76, women 82 (1989)
language Japanese
religion Shinto, Buddhist (often combined), Christian; 30% claim a personal religious faith
literacy 99% (1989)
GDP $2.4 tri; $19,464 per head (1989)
chronology
1871 Feudal system abolished.
1894–95 War with China; Taiwan gained.
1904–05 War with Russia; Russia ceded southern half of Sakhalin.
1910 Japan anexed Korea.
1902 Formed alliance with Britain; joined Allies in World War I.
1918 Received German Pacific islands as mandates.
1931–32 War with China; renewed 1937.
1941 Japan attacked US fleet at Pearl Harbor Dec 7.
1945 World War II ended with Japanese surrender. Allied control commission took power.
1946 Framing of "peace constitution."
1952 Full sovereignty regained.
1958 Joined United Nations.
1972 Ryukyu Islands regained.
1974 Prime Minister Tanaka resigned over Lockheed bribes scandal.
1982 Yasuhiro Nakasone elected prime minister.
1987 Noboru Takeshita chosen to succeed Nakasone.
1988 Recruit corporation insider-trading scandal cast shadow over government and opposition parties.
1989 Emperor Hirohito died; succeeded by his son Akihito. Two cabinet ministers resigned over Recruit, many more implicated. Takeshita resigned because of Recruit scandal; succeeded by Sosuke Uno in June. Uno resigned Aug after sex scandal; succeeded by Toshiki Kaifu.
1990 New house of councillors' elections (Feb) won by LDP. Public-works budget increased by 50% to encourage imports.
1991 Japan contributed billions of dollars to the Gulf War. Kaifu succeeded by Kiichi Miyazawa.
1992 Miyazawa hosts President Bush and US delegation seeking trade concessions.

government Japan's 1946 constitution was framed by the occupying Allied forces with the intention of creating a consensual, parliamentary form of government and avoiding an overconcentration of executive authority. The emperor, whose functions are purely ceremonial, is head of state. The Japanese parliament is a two-chamber body composed of a 252-member house of councillors and a 512-member house of representatives. The former chamber comprises 152 representatives elected from 47 prefectural constituencies by the "limited-vote" system and 100 elected nationally by proportional representation. Each member serves a six-year term, the chamber being elected half at a time every three years. Representatives to the lower house are elected by universal suffrage for four-year terms in multimember constituencies. The house of representatives is the most powerful chamber, able to override (if a two-thirds majority is gained) vetoes on bills imposed by the house of councillors, and enjoying paramountcy on financial questions. Legislative business is effected through a system of standing committees. Executive administration is entrusted to a prime minister, chosen by parliament, who selects a cabinet that is collectively responsible to parliament.

The major political parties are: on the right, the Liberal Democratic Party (LDP); in the center, the Democratic Socialist Party and the Komeito (Clean Government) Party; and on the left, the Japan Socialist Party and the Japan Communist Party.

The LDP has dominated postwar Japanese politics, monopolizing government power. It is divided into five powerful, clanlike factions—the Takeshita, Abe, Miyazawa, Watanabe, and Komoto—that compete and bargain for cabinet portfolios. The ultimate prize is the position of prime minister, which each faction seeks to capture by succeeding in the biennial contests for presidency of the LDP.

history Evidence of early human occupation on the Japanese islands exists in the form of 30,000-year-old tools, but the Japanese nation probably arose from the fusion of two peoples, one from the Malay Peninsula or Polynesia, the other from Asia, who conquered the original inhabitants, the ◊Ainu, and forced them into the most northern islands. Japanese history remains legendary until the leadership of the first emperor Jimmu was recorded about 660 BC. From 300 BC, agriculture (rice-growing) was introduced, together with bronze, iron, and textile production. During the 4th century AD, the Yamato dynasty unified warring classes in the central Honshu and built huge tombs (the largest being nearly 1,641 ft/500 m). Gradually a feudal society was established. By the 5th century AD, the art of writing had been introduced from Korea. After the introduction of Buddhism, also from Korea, in the 6th century, Chinese culture became generally accepted, but although attempts were made in the 7th century to diminish the power of the nobles and set up a strong centralized monarchy on the Chinese model, real power remained in the hands of the great feudal families until recent times.

A group of warrior families organized local affairs, and the 12th century saw the creation of a military government (shogunate) – a form that persisted until 1867. During the Kamakura shogunate (1192–1333), the Mongol invasions from Korea were repulsed. For the next three centuries the country remained riven by factions, and it was not until the battle of Sekigahara 1600, that Tokugawa Ieyasu defeated his rivals and established the Tokugawa shogunate (1603–1867).

Contact with Europe began 1542 when Portuguese traders arrived; they were followed by the Spanish and in 1609 by the Dutch. Christianity was introduced by Francis ◊Xavier 1549. During the 15th–16th centuries Japan sank into a state of feudal anarchy, until order was restored 1570–1615 by three great rulers, Nobunaga, Hideyoshi, and Iyeyasu; the family of the latter, the Tokugawa, held power until the abolition of the shogunate 1867.

The fear that Roman Catholic propaganda was intended as a preparation for Spanish conquest led to the expulsion of the Spanish 1624 and the Portuguese 1639 and to the almost total extermination of Christianity by persecution; only the Dutch were allowed to trade with Japan, under irksome restrictions, while Japanese subjects were forbidden to leave the country. This isolation continued until 1853, when the US insisted on opening trade relations; during the next few years this example was followed by various European powers. Consequently the isolationist party compelled the shogun to abdicate 1867, and executive power was restored to the emperor. During the next 30 years the privileges of the feudal nobility were abolished, a uniform code of law was introduced, and a constitution was established 1889. The army was modernized, and a powerful navy founded. Industry developed steadily, and a considerable export trade was built up.

In 1894 a war with China secured Japanese control of Formosa and S Manchuria, as well as Korea, which was formally annexed 1910. A victory over Russia 1904–05 gave Japan the southern half of Sakhalin and compelled the Russians to evacuate Manchuria. Japan formed an alliance with Britain 1902 and joined the Allies in World War I. At the peace settlement it received the German islands in the N Pacific as mandates. The 1920s saw an advance toward democracy and party government, but after 1932 the government assumed a semi-Fascist form. As a result of successful aggression against China 1931–32, a Japanese puppet monarchy under P'u-i, the last emperor of China, was established in Manchuria (see ◊Manchukuo); war with China was renewed 1937 and continued in Asia until the attack on the US territory of Pearl Harbor Dec 7, 1941. Japan at first won a succession of victories in the Philip-

Japan *Space is at a premium in crowded Japan's housing developments.*

pines, the Malay Peninsula, Burma (now Myanmar), and the Dutch West Indies. US, Australian, and New Zealand troops retook many of the Pacific islands in battles that resulted in heavy casualties; US, French, and UK troops reclaimed much of SE Asia. Japan was compelled to surrender Aug 15, 1945, following the detonation of atomic bombs by the US at ◊Hiroshima and ◊Nagasaki. An Allied control commission took charge, and Japan was placed under military occupation by Allied (chiefly US) troops under General Douglas ◊MacArthur until 1952, when the Japanese Peace Treaty came into force and full sovereignty was regained.

After Japan's defeat, Korea was made independent; Manchuria and Formosa (◊Taiwan) were returned to China; and the islands mandated to Japan after World War I were placed by the United Nations under US trusteeship. Japan regained the ◊Ryukyu Islands 1972 and the ◊Bonin and Volcano Islands 1968 from the US, and continues to agitate for the return of the Northern Territories (the islands of the Shikotan and Habomai Group) and the southernmost ◊Kurils (Kunashiri and Etorofu).

During Allied rule, Aug 1945–April 1952, a major "democratization campaign" was launched, involving radical land, social, and educational reform and the framing of a new "Peace Constitution" 1946 in which Emperor ◊Hirohito renounced his claims to divinity and became a powerless figurehead ruler and the nation committed itself to a pacific foreign policy. Japan concentrated during the early postwar years on economic reconstruction, tending toward neutralism in foreign affairs under the protection provided by the 1951 Security Pact.

Postwar politics in Japan were dominated by the LDP, formed 1955 from the merger of existing conservative parties and providing a regular succession of prime ministers. Real decision-making, however, centered around a broader, consensual grouping of politicians, senior civil servants, and directors of the major *zaibatsu* (finance and industrial houses). Through a paternalist, guided approach to economic development, epitomized by the operations of the Ministry for International Trade and Industry (MITI), the Japanese economy expanded dramatically during the 1950s and 1960s, with gross national product (GNP) increasing by 10% per year.

During this period, Japan was rehabilitated within the international community, entering the UN 1958 and establishing diplomatic relations with Western nations and, following the lead taken by the Nixon presidency, with Communist China 1972. Japan's internal politics were rocked 1960 and 1968–69 by violent attacks by the anarchic Red Army guerrilla organization protesting US domination and in 1974 by the resignation of Prime Minister Kakuei Tanaka after a bribery scandal involving the US Lockheed Corporation. This scandal tarnished the image of the LDP and led to the loss of its majority in the house of representatives 1976 and the formation of the New Liberal Club as a breakaway grouping. The LDP remained in power, however, as the largest single party in parliament.

Japanese economic growth was maintained during the 1970s, though at a reduced annual rate of 4.5%, and the country made a major impact in the markets of North America and Europe as an exporter of electronics, machinery, and motor vehicles. This created resentment overseas as economic recession began to grip Europe and the US during the later 1970s and led to calls for Japan to open up its internal market to foreign exporters and to assume a greater share of the defense burden for the Asia-Pacific region. Prime ministers Miki, Fukuda, Ohira, and Suzuki resisted these pressures, and the Japanese government, in 1976, placed a rigid 1% of GNP limit on military spending.

A review of policy was instituted by Prime Minister Yasuhiro ◊Nakasone, who assumed power 1982. He favored a strengthening of Japan's military capability, a reevaluation of attitudes toward the country's past, and the introduction of a more liberal, open-market economic strategy at home. His policy departures were controversial and only partly implemented. However, he gained a landslide victory in the 1986 elections, and became the first prime minister since Sato (1964–72) to be reelected by the LDP for more than one term. During 1987 his plans for tax reform, including the introduction of a 5% value-added tax (VAT), were overturned by the Diet (parliament). Despite this defeat Nakasone remained popular and was able, following factional deadlock within the LDP, to select Noboru ◊Takeshita as his successor.

Takeshita continued Nakasone's domestic and foreign policies, introducing a 3% sales tax 1988 and lowering income-tax levels to boost domestic consumption. The new sales tax was electorally unpopular, and the government's standing during 1988–89 was further undermined by the Recruit-Cosmos insider share-dealing scandal (see ◊Recruit scandal), in which more than 40 senior LDP and opposition figures, including Takeshita, Nakasone, the deputy prime minister, and the finance and justice ministers, were implicated. The last three were forced to resign, as, eventually, was Takeshita in June 1989. This marked an inauspicious start to the new *Heisei* ("achievement of universal peace") era proclaimed on the death Jan 1989 of Hirohito (Showa) and the accession of his son ◊Akihito as emperor.

The new prime minister, Sosuke Uno, the former foreign minister, was soon dogged by a geisha sex scandal. His standing was further undermined by the LDP's unprecedented loss of its majority in the house of councillors, following elections July 1989, and after only 53 days in office he resigned Aug 1989. He was replaced by Toshiki Kaifu, a former education minister and member of the LDP's small scandal-free Komoto faction. Kaifu formed a new cabinet whose members were comparatively young and which, in an attempt to counter the growing appeal to women of the Japanese Socialist Party, led by Ms Takako Doi, included two women. Kaifu having partly repaired the damage done to the LDP by the Recruit scandal, parliament was dissolved Jan 1990 and elections called for Feb. They were won by the LDP, but with large gains for the JSP. Kaifu's government was weakened when, in Nov 1990, it failed to secure parliamentary approval for the despatch of (unarmed) Japanese Self Defense Forces to the Gulf. On Nov 12 Akihito was enthroned as Japan's 125th emperor. In the fall of 1991, Kaifu announced that he would not seek another term as prime minister. He was succeeded by Kiichi Miyazawa.

Japan Current or ***Kuroshio*** warm ocean ◊current flowing from Japan to North America.

Japanese native to or an inhabitant of Japan; also their descendants, culture, and language.

Although Japan has a highly distinctive culture, Korean and Chinese influences were apparent during the early centuries AD. In addition to the art of writing, from the Chinese the Japanese learned skills in the arts, public finance, administration, horticulture, and animal husbandry. Confucian philosophy and Buddhism were also introduced from China, although there was some opposition to Buddhism by the adherents of Shinto, the principal religion. Chinese influence in Japan waned during the decline of the Tang Dynasty (AD 618–907).

The 12th century saw the rise of the code of warriors. Making up approximately 8% of the population, the ◊samurai had the right to wear two swords and were the retainers of the daimyos, the hereditary feudal nobles. Merchants, although often wealthier than the samurai, belonged to a lower social order. Some highly skilled craftsmen were allowed to bear family names, a privilege usually reserved for the highest social tier. The lowest social group comprised the burakunin or eta, responsible for slaughtering animals and engaging in such trades as tanning leather and shoemaking.

Japanese art *Bando Hikozqburo (c. 1850) by Kunisada Utagawa, private collection.*

During the late 19th century the privileges of the feudal nobility were abolished and Japan began to develop its Westernized military and industrial base. After their defeat in World War II, the US-financed economic expansion of the postwar years caused the decline of the extended family, in which three or more generations lived under the same roof. Today, large corporations provide a way of life for many Japanese, although this appears to be less the case with the younger generation. The descendants of Japanese migrants are found in Hawaii and North and South America, and Japanese business communities now exist in the cities of most industrial nations.

Japanese art the painting, sculpture, and design of Japan. Early Japanese art was influenced by China. With the spread of Zen Buddhism in the 12th century, painting developed a distinct Japanese character, bolder and more angular. Ink painting and calligraphy flourished, followed by book illustration and decorative screens. Japanese prints developed in the 17th century, with multicolor prints invented around 1765. Buddhist sculpture proliferated from 580 and Japanese sculptors excelled at portraits. Japanese pottery stresses simplicity.

Japanese art is divided into the following periods:

Jōmon (10,000–300 BC) A period characterized by cord-marked pottery.

Yayoi (300 BC–AD 300) Elegant pottery was produced with geometric designs and *dōtaku*, bronze bells decorated with engravings.

Kofun (300–552) Burial mounds held *haniwa*, clay figures, some of which show Chinese influence.

Asuka (552–646) Buddhist art, introduced from Korea 552, flourished in sculpture, metalwork, and embroidered silk banners. Painters' guilds were formed.

Nara (646–794) Religious and portrait sculptures were made of bronze, clay, or dry lacquer. A few painted scrolls, screens, and murals survive. Textiles were decorated with batik, tie-dye, stencils, embroidery, and brocade.

Heian (794–1185) Buddhist statues became formalized and were usually made of wood. Shinto images emerged. A native style of secular painting

(*Yamato-e*) developed, especially in scroll painting, with a strong emphasis on surface design. Lacquerware was also decoratively stylized.

Kamakura (1185–1392) Sculpture and painting became vigorously realistic. Portraits were important, as were landscapes and religious, narrative, and humorous picture scrolls.

Ashikaga or ***Muromachi*** (1392–1568) The rapid ink sketch in line and wash introduced by Zen priests from China became popular. Pottery gained in importance from the spread of the tea ceremony. Masks and costumes were made for Nō theater.

Momoyama (1568–1615) Artists produced beautiful screens to decorate palaces and castles. The arrival of Korean potters inspired new styles.

Tokugawa or ***Edo*** (1615–1867) The print (*ukiyo-e*) originated in genre paintings of 16th- and 17th-century kabuki actors and teahouse women. It developed into the woodcut and after 1740 the true color print, while its range of subject matter expanded. *Ukiyo-e* artists include Utamaro and Hokusai. Lacquer and textiles became more sumptuous. Tiny *netsuke* figures were mostly carved from ivory or wood.

Meiji (1868–1912) Painting was influenced by styles of Western art, for example by Impressionism.

Shōwa (1926–89) Attempts were made to revive the traditional Japanese painting style and to combine traditional and foreign styles.

Japanese language language of E Asia, spoken almost exclusively in the islands of Japan. Traditionally isolated, but possibly related to Korean, Japanese was influenced by Mandarin Chinese in the 6th–9th centuries and is written in Chinese-derived ideograms supplemented by two syllabic alphabets.

Japanese has a syllabic structure; words end with a vowel or *n* (*futon, jūdō, ninja, kimono, shōgun, sumō, tōfu*). It has a pitch accent (high or low) but no stress accent. The distinction between long and short vowels affects meaning (long ones are usually, as in this volume, indicated by a macron, or line over the letter); adjacent vowels are pronounced separately and do not form diphthongs.

Japanese is written in a triple system: its *kanji* ideograms are close to their Chinese originals; *hiragana* is a syllabary for the general language; and *katakana* is a syllabary for foreign names and borrowings. In print, the three systems blend on the page much as when italic type is used together with roman.

Many English words have been adapted into Japanese (*fairu* "file," *ereganto* "elegant"), and are often shortened in the process (*fainda* "viewfinder," *remikon* "ready-mixed concrete," *wapuro* "word-processor").

Japanese literature earliest surviving works include the 8th-century *Collection of a Myriad Leaves*, with poems by Hitomaro and Akahito (the principal form being the *tanka*, a five-line stanza of 5, 7, 5, 7, 7 syllables), and the prose *Record of Ancient Matters*. The late 10th and early 11th centuries produced the writers Sei Shōnagon and Murasaki Shikibu. During the 14th century the Nō drama developed from ceremonial religious dances, combined with monologues and dialogues. The 17th century brought such scholars of Chinese studies as Fujiwara Seikwa (1560–1619) and Arai Hakuseki (1657–1725). This period also saw the beginnings of *kabuki*, the popular drama of Japan, of which Chikamatsu Monzaemon (1653–1724) is the chief exponent; of *haiku* (the stanza of three lines of 5, 7, and 5 syllables), popularized by Bashō; and of the modern novel, as represented by Ibara Saikaku (1642–93). Among those reacting against Chinese influence was the poet-historian Motoori Norinaga (1730–1801). The late 19th and early 20th centuries saw the replacement of the obsolete *Tokugawa* style as a literary medium with the modern colloquial language; the influence of Western and Russian literature, producing writers such as the "Realist" Tsubouchi Shōyo (1859–1935), was followed by the "Naturalist" and "Idealistic" novelists, whose romantic preoccupation with self-expression gave rise to the still popular "I-novels" of, for example, Dazai Osamu (1909–48).

A reaction against the autobiographical school came from Natsume Sōseki (1867–1916), Nagai Kafū (1879–1959), and Junichirō Tanizaki (1886–1965), who found inspiration in past traditions or in self-sublimation; later novelists include Yasunari Kawabata (1899–1972) and Yukio Mishima (1925–1970). Shimazaki Tōson (1872–1943) introduced Western-style poetic trends, including "Symbolism," but the traditional forms of *haiku* and *tanka* are still widely used. Western-style modern drama, inspired by Ibsen and Strindberg, has been growing since the turn of the century (as seen in the work of Shingeki, for example).

Japan, Sea of sea separating Japan from the mainland of Asia.

Japji Sikh morning hymn which consists of verses from the beginning of the holy book *Guru Granth Sahib*.

Jaques-Dalcroze Emile 1865–1950. Swiss composer and teacher. He is remembered for his system of physical training by rhythmical movement to music (◊eurhythmics), and founded the Institut Jaques-Dalcroze in Geneva, in 1915.

jargon language usage that is highly technical or occupational or designed to confuse on purpose. In writing, jargon may be highly formal, whereas in speech it often contains ◊slang expressions.

Jargon is often used to disguise unimportant information in complicated language, to mystify certain information, or to make information inaccessible to those who do not know the jargon. Jargon is often also known as *gobbledygook/gobbledegook* and is subcategorized as, for example, *bureaucratese* and *officialese* (the usage of bureaucrats and officials), *journalese* (the languages of newspapers), and *medicalese* (the often impenetrable usage of doctors), and so on.

Järnefelt (Edvard) Armas 1869–1958. Finnish composer who is chiefly known for his "Praeludium" and the lyrical "Berceuse."

jarrah type of ◊eucalyptus tree of W Australia, with durable timber.

Jarrett Keith 1945– . US jazz pianist and composer, an eccentric innovator who performs both alone and with small groups. Jarrett was a member of the rock-influenced Charles Lloyd Quartet 1966–67, and played with Miles Davis 1970–71. *The Köln Concert* 1975 is a characteristic solo live recording.

Jarry Alfred 1873–1907. French satiric dramatist, whose *Ubu Roi* 1896 foreshadowed the Theater of the Absurd and the French Surrealist movement.

Jaruzelski Wojciech 1923– . Polish general, communist leader from 1981, president from 1985. He imposed martial law for the first year of his rule, suppressed the opposition, and banned trade-union activity, but later released many political prisoners. In 1989, elections in favor of the free labor union Solidarity forced Jaruzelski to speed up democratic reforms, overseeing a transition to a new form of "Socialist pluralist" democracy, stepping down as president 1990.

Jaruzelski, who served with the Soviet army 1939–43, was defense minister 1968–83 and entered the Politburo 1971. At the height of the crisis of 1980–81 he assumed power as prime minister and PUWP first secretary; in 1985 he resigned as prime minister to become president, but remained the dominant political figure in Poland. His attempts to solve Poland's economic problems were unsuccessful.

Jarvik 7 the first successful artificial heart intended for permanent implantation in a human being. Made from polyurethane plastic and aluminum, it is powered by compressed air. Barney Clark became the first person to receive a Jarvik 7, in Salt Lake City, Utah, in Dec 1982; it kept him alive for 112 days.

Recently the US Food and Drug Administration withdrew approval for artificial heart transplants because of evidence of adverse reactions.

jasmine any subtropical plant of the genus *Jasminium* of the olive family Oleaceae, with fragrant white or yellow flowers, and yielding jasmine oil, used in perfumes. The common jasmine *J. officinale* has pure white flowers; the Chinese winter jasmine *J. nudiflorum* has bright yellow flowers that appear before the leaves.

Jason in Greek mythology, leader of the Argonauts who sailed in the *Argo* to Colchis in search of the ◊Golden Fleece.

jasper a hard, compact variety of ◊chalcedony SiO_2, usually colored red, brown, or yellow. Jasper can be used as a gem.

Jaspers Karl 1883–1969. German philosopher whose works include *General Psychopathology* 1913 and *Philosophy* 1932. He studied medicine and psychology, and in 1921 became professor of philosophy at Heidelberg.

Jassy German name for the Romanian city of ◊Iaşi.

Jataka collections of Buddhist legends compiled at various dates in several countries; the oldest and most complete has 547 stories. They were collected before AD 400.

They give an account of previous incarnations of the Buddha, and the verse sections of the text form part of the Buddhist canon. The Jataka stories were one of the sources of inspiration for the fables of Aesop.

jaundice yellow discoloration of the skin and whites of the eyes caused by an excess of bile pigment in the bloodstream.

Bile pigment is normally produced by the liver from the breakdown of red blood cells, then excreted into the intestines. A buildup in the blood is due to abnormal destruction of red cells (as in some cases of ◊anemia), impaired liver function (as in ◊hepatitis), or blockage in the excretory channels (as in gallstones or ◊cirrhosis). The jaundice gradually recedes following treatment of the underlying cause, unless coma and death follow (as in hepatitis or cirrhosis). Mild jaundice is common in newborns, but a serious form occurs in rhesus disease (see ◊rhesus factor).

Java or ***Jawa*** the most important island of Indonesia, situated between Sumatra and Bali

area (with the island of Madura) 51,000 sq mi/ 132,000 sq km

capital Jakarta (also capital of Indonesia)

towns ports include Surabaja and Semarang

physical about half the island is under cultivation, the rest being thickly forested. Mountains and sea breezes keep temperatures down, but humidity is high, with heavy rainfall from Dec to Mar

features a chain of mountains, some of which are volcanic, runs along the center, rising to 9,000 ft/ 2,750 m. The highest mountain, Semeru (12,060 ft/3,676 m) is in the E

products rice, coffee, cocoa, tea, sugar, rubber, quinine, teak, petroleum

population (with Madura; 1980) 91,270,000; including people of Javanese, Sundanese, and Madurese origin, with differing languages

religion predominantly Muslim

history fossilized early human remains (*Homo erectus*) were discovered 1891–92. In central Java there are ruins of magnificent Buddhist monuments and of the Sivaite temple in Prambanan. The island's last Hindu kingdom, Majapahit, was destroyed about 1520 and followed by a number of shortlived Javanese kingdoms. The Dutch East India company founded a factory in 1610. Britain took over during the Napoleonic period, 1811–16, and Java then reverted to Dutch control. Occupied by Japan 1942–45 while under Dutch control, Java then became part of the republic of ◊Indonesia.

Javanese inhabitant of Java, in particular one of the indigenous peoples occupying most of the island. The Javanese speak several related languages belonging to the Austronesian family.

jay

In preindependence Indonesia, Javanese society was divided into hierarchical classes ruled by Sultans, and differences in status were reflected by strict codes of dress. Java is known for the quality of its court arts, especially batik textiles and elaborate kris (traditional daggers).

Although the majority of Javanese depend on the cultivation of rice in irrigated fields, there are many large urban centers with developing industries. To relieve the pressure on the land, farmers have been moved under Indonesia's controversial transmigration scheme to less populated islands such as Sulawesi (Celebes) and Irian Jaya (W New Guinea).

javelin a type of spear used in athletics events. The men's javelin is about 8.5 ft/260 cm long, weighing 28 oz/800 g; the women's 7.5 ft/230 cm long, weighing 21 oz/600 g. The athlete runs up to a foul line to gain momentum before releasing it. The center of gravity on the men's javelin was altered 1986 to reduce the vast distances (100 yd/90 m) that were being achieved.

jaw one of two bony structures that form the framework of the mouth in all vertebrates except lampreys and hagfishes (the agnathous or jawless vertebrates). They consist of the upper jawbone (maxilla), which is fused to the skull, and the lower jawbone (mandible), which is hinged at each side to the bones of the temple by ◊ligaments.

jay any of several birds of the crow family Corvidae, generally brightly colored and native to Eurasia and the Americas.

In the Eurasian common jay *Garrulus glandarius*, the body is fawn with patches of white, blue, and black on the wings and tail. The blue jay *Cyanocitta cristata*, of the E and central US, has a crest and is very noisy and bold.

Jay John 1745–1829. US diplomat and jurist. He served as president of the Continental Congress 1779 and US minister to Spain 1779–82. With Benjamin Franklin and John Adams, he negotiated the Peace of Paris 1783, which concluded the Revolutionary War. Jay later served as foreign secretary for the Continental Congress 1783–89. A strong supporter of the federal Constitution, he collaborated with Alexander Hamilton and James Madison on the *Federalist Papers* 1787–88, which helped sway opinion in favor of its ratification. President Washington named him first chief justice of the US in 1789. He negotiated Jay's Treaty with England 1795 (which averted another war), then left the Supreme Court to serve as governor of New York 1795–1801.

Born in New York City, Jay was admitted to the bar 1768. He was a member of the Continental Congress 1774–76 and became the first chief justice of New York 1778.

Jayawardene Junius Richard 1906– . Sri Lankan politician. Leader of the United Nationalist Party from 1973, he became prime minister 1977 and the country's first president 1978–88.

jazz polyphonic, syncopated music characterized by the "blue" note and solo virtuosic improvisation, which developed in the US at the turn of the 20th century. It had its roots in African, Caribbean, and Southern black music as well as other indigenous popular music from the Mississippi River region and evolved various distinct vocal and instrumental forms.

jazz chronology

1880–1900 Dixieland originated chiefly in New Orleans from ragtime.

1920s During Prohibition, the center of jazz moved up the Mississippi to Kansas City and then to St Louis and Chicago (Louis Armstrong, Bix Beiderbecke). By the end of the decade the focus had shifted to New York City (Art Tatum, Fletcher Henderson), to radio, and recordings.

1930s The swing bands used call-and-response arrangements with improvised solos of voice and instruments (Paul Whiteman, Benny Goodman).

1940s Swing grew into the big band era with jazz composed as well as arranged (Glenn Miller, Duke Ellington); the rise of West Coast jazz (Stan Kenton) and rhythmically complex, highly improvisational bebop (Charlie Parker, Dizzy Gillespie, Thelonius Monk).

1950s Jazz had ceased to be dance music; cool jazz (Stan Getz, Miles Davis, Lionel Hampton, Modern Jazz Quartet) developed in reaction to the insistent, "hot" bebop and hard bop.

1960s Free-form or free jazz (Ornette Coleman, John Coltrane).

1970s Jazz rock (US group Weather Report, formed 1970; British guitarist John McLaughlin, 1942–); jazz funk (US saxophonist Grover Washington, Jr, 1943–); more eclectic free jazz (US pianist Keith Jarrett, 1945–).

1980s Resurgence of tradition (US trumpeter Wynton Marsalis, 1962– ; British saxophonist Courtney Pine, 1965–) and avant-garde (US chamber-music Cronus Quartet, formed 1978; anarchic British group Loose Tubes, formed 1983).

Jazz Age phrase attributed to the novelist F Scott Fitzgerald, describing the hectic and exciting 1920s in the US, when "hot jazz" became fashionable as part of the general rage for spontaneity and generational freedom.

jazz dance dance that combines African and US techniques and rhythms and was introduced into modern dance by choreographers such as Matt Mattox, Jerome ◊Robbins and Alvin Ailey.

J-curve in economics, a graphic illustration of the likely effect of a currency devaluation on the balance of payments. Initially, there will be a deterioration as import prices increase and export prices decline, followed by a decline in import volume and upsurge of export volume.

jeans denim trousers, traditionally blue, originally cut from jean cloth (*jene fustian*), a heavy canvas made in Genoa, Italy. Levi Strauss (1830–1902), a Bavarian immigrant to the US, made sturdy trousers for goldminers in San Francisco out of jean material intended for wagon covers. Hence they became known as "Levis." Later a French

Jefferson *The 3rd president of the United States of America, Thomas Jefferson, a Democratic Republican. 1801–1809.*

fabric, *serge de Nîmes* (corrupted to "denim"), was used.

Jeans James Hopwood 1877–1946. British mathematician and scientist. In physics he worked on the kinetic theory of gases, and on forms of energy radiation; in astronomy, his work focused on giant and dwarf stars, the nature of spiral nebulae, and the origin of the cosmos. He did much to popularize astronomy.

Jedda alternate spelling for the Saudi Arabian port ◊Jiddah.

Jeffers (John) Robinson 1887–1962. US poet. He wrote free verse and demonstrated an antagonism to human society. His collected volumes include *Tamar and Other Poems* 1924, *The Double Axe* 1948, and *Hungerfield and Other Poems* 1954.

Jefferson Thomas 1743–1826. The 3rd president of the US 1801–09, founder of the Democratic Republican party. He was born in Virginia into a wealthy family. He published *A Summary View of the Rights of America* 1774 and as a member of the Continental Congresses of 1775–76 was largely responsible for the drafting of the ◊Declaration of Independence. He was governor of Virginia 1779–81, ambassador to Paris 1785–89, secretary of state 1789–93, and vice-president 1797–1801.

Jefferson's interests also included music, painting, architecture, and the natural sciences; he was very much a product of the 18th-century enlightenment. His political philosophy of "agrarian democracy" placed responsibility for upholding a virtuous American republic mainly upon a citizenry of independent yeoman farmers. Ironically, his two terms as president saw the adoption of some of the ideas of his political opponents, the ◊Federalists.

He was supportive of the French Revolution and spent four years in France while dispatching advice through his ally James ◊Madison on the proposals for a Constitutional Convention. Upon his return to the political scene, he carried on his battle with Alexander ◊Hamilton, who held views of America directly opposed to his own agrarian, democratic inclinations.

Jefferson City capital of Missouri, located in the central part of the state, W of St Louis, on the Mississippi River. Industries include agricultural products, shoes, electrical appliances, and cosmetics; population (1990) 35,481.

Jeffreys Alec John 1950– . British geneticist who discovered the DNA probes necessary for accurate ◊genetic fingerprinting so that a murderer or rapist could be identified by, for example, traces of blood, tissue, or semen.

Jehol former name for the city of Chengale in NE Hebei province, N China.

Jehosophat 4th king of Judah c. 873–849 BC; he allied himself with Ahab, king of Israel, in the war against Syria.

Jehovah also ***Jahweh*** in the Old Testament the name of God, revealed to Moses; in Hebrew texts of the Old Testament the name was represented by the letters YHVH (without the vowels "a o a") and it was regarded as too sacred to be pronounced.

Jehovah's Witness member of a religious organization originating in the US 1872 under Charles Taze Russell (1852–1916). Jehovah's Witnesses attach great importance to Christ's second coming, which Russell predicted would occur 1914, and which Witnesses still believe is imminent. All Witnesses are expected to take part in house-to-house preaching; there are no clergy.

Witnesses believe that after the second coming the ensuing Armageddon and Last Judgment, which entail the destruction of all except the faithful, are to give way to the Theocratic Kingdom. Earth will continue to exist as the home of humanity, apart from 144,000 chosen believers who will reign with Christ in heaven. Witnesses believe that they should not become involved in the affairs of this world, and their tenets, involving rejection of obligations such as military service, have often brought them into conflict with authority. Because of a biblical injunction against eating blood, they will not give or receive blood transfusions. Adults are baptized by total immersion.

The Watch Tower Bible and Tract Society and the Watch Tower Students' Association form part of the movement, which numbered about one million members in the 1980s.

Jehu king of Israel c. 842–815 BC. He led a successful rebellion against the family of ◊Ahab and was responsible for the death of Jezebel.

Jekyll and Hyde two conflicting sides of a personality, as in the novel by the Scottish writer R L Stevenson, *The Strange Case of Dr Jekyll and Mr Hyde* 1886, where the good Jekyll by means of a potion periodically transforms himself into the evil Hyde.

jellyfish marine invertebrate of the phylum Cnidaria (coelenterates) with an umbrella-shaped body composed of a semitransparent gelatinous substance, with a fringe of stinging tentacles. Most adult jellyfishes move freely, but during parts of their life cycle many are polyplike and attached. They feed on small animals that are paralyzed by stinging cells in the jellyfishes' tentacles.

Jena town SE of Weimar, in the State of Thuringia, Federal Republic of Germany, population (1990) 110,000. Industries include the Zeiss firm of optical-instrument makers, founded 1846. Here in 1806 Napoleon defeated the Prussians, and Schiller and Hegel taught at the university, which dates from 1558.

Jencks Charles 1939– . US architectural theorist and furniture designer. He coined the term "Post-Modern Architecture" and wrote *The Language of Post-Modern Architecture* 1984.

Jenkins's Ear, War of war 1739 between Britain and Spain, arising from Britain's illicit trade in Spanish America; it merged into the War of the ◊Austrian Succession 1740–48. The name derives from the claim of Robert Jenkins, a merchant captain, that his ear had been cut off by Spanish coastguards near Jamaica. The incident was seized on by opponents of Robert ◊Walpole who wanted to embarrass his government's antiwar policy and force war with Spain.

Jenner Edward 1749–1823. English physician who pioneered vaccination. In Jenner's day, smallpox was a major killer. His discovery that inoculation with cowpox gives immunity to smallpox was a great medical breakthrough. He coined the word "vaccination" from the Latin word for cowpox, *vaccina*.

Jenner observed that people who worked with cattle and contracted cowpox from them never subsequently caught smallpox. In 1798 he published his findings that a child inoculated with cowpox, then two months later with smallpox, did not get smallpox.

Jennings Humphrey 1907–1950. British documentary filmmaker, active in the GPO Film Unit from 1934. His wartime films provide a vivid portrayal of London in the Blitz. His films include *Post Haste* 1934, *London Can Take It* 1940, *This is England* 1941, and *Fires Were Started* 1943.

Jerablus ancient Syrian city, adjacent to Carchemish on the Euphrates River.

erboa small, nocturnal, leaping rodent belonging to the family Dipodidae. There are about 25 species of jerboa, native to N Africa and SW Asia. Typical is the common N African jerboa *Jaculus orientalis* with a body about 6 in/15 cm long and a 10 in/25 cm tail with a tuft at the tip. At speed it moves in a series of long jumps with its forefeet held close to its body.

Jeremiah 7th–6th century BC. Old Testament Hebrew prophet, whose ministry continued 626–586 BC. He was imprisoned during ◊Nebuchadnezzar's siege of Jerusalem on suspicion of intending to desert to the enemy. On the city's fall, he retired to Egypt.

Jerez de la Frontera city in Andalusia, SW Spain; population (1986) 180,000. It is famed for sherry, the fortified wine to which it gave its name.

Jericho Israeli-administered town in Jordan, north of the Dead Sea. It was settled by 8000 BC, and by 6000 BC had become a walled city with 2,000 inhabitants. In the Old Testament it was the first Canaanite stronghold captured by the Israelites, and its walls, according to the Book of ◊Joshua, fell to the blast of Joshua's trumpets. Successive archeological excavations since 1907 show that the walls of the city were destroyed many times.

Jeroboam 10th century BC. First king of Israel c. 922–901 BC after it split away from the kingdom of Judah.

Jerome, St c. 340–420. One of the early Christian leaders and scholars known as the Fathers of the Church. His Latin versions of the Old and New Testaments form the basis of the Roman Catholic Vulgate. He is usually depicted with a lion. Feast day Sept 30.

Born in Strido, Italy, he was baptized at Rome in 360, and subsequently traveled in Gaul, Anatolia, and Syria. Summoned to Rome as adviser to Pope Damasus, he revised the Latin translation of the New Testament and the Latin psalter. On the death of Damasus in 384 he traveled to the east and settled in Bethlehem, where he translated the Old Testament from Hebrew into Latin.

Jersey largest of the ◊Channel Islands; capital St Helier; area 45 sq mi/117 sq km; population (1986) 80,000. It is governed by a lieutenant-governor representing the English crown and an assembly. Jersey cattle were originally bred here; it gave its name to a woolen garment.

Jersey zoo (founded 1959 by Gerald Durrell) is actively engaged in boosting populations of some of the world's endangered species.

Jersey City city of NE New Jersey; population (1990) 228,537. It faces Manhattan Island, to which it is connected by tunnels. A former port, it is now an industrial center.

Jerusalem capital of Israel and an ancient city of Palestine, divided 1948 between Jordan and the new republic of Israel; area (pre-1967) 14.5 sq mi/37.5 sq km, (post-1967) 42 sq mi/108 sq km, including areas of the West Bank; population (1989) 500,000, about 350,000 Israelis and 150,000 Palestinians. In 1950 the western New City was proclaimed as the Israeli capital, and, having captured from Jordan the eastern Old City 1967, Israel affirmed 1980 that the united city was the country's capital; the United Nations does not recognize the claim.

features seven gates into the Old City through the walls built by Selim I (1467–1520); notable buildings: the Church of the Holy Sepulchre (built by Emperor Constantine 335) and the mosque of the Dome of the Rock. The latter stands on the site of the ◊Temple built by King Solomon in the 10th century BC, and the Western ("wailing") Wall, held sacred by Jews, is part of the walled platform on which the Temple once stood. The Hebrew University of Jerusalem opened 1925.

religions Christian, Jewish, and Muslim, with Roman Catholic, Anglican, Eastern Orthodox, and a Coptic bishop. In 1967 Israel guaranteed freedom of access of all faiths to their holy places.

history 1400 BC Jerusalem was ruled by a king subject to Egypt.

c. 1000 BC David made it the capital of a united Jewish kingdom.

586 BC The city was destroyed by Nebuchadnezzar, king of Babylonia, who deported its inhabitants.

539–529 BC Under Cyrus the Great of Persia the exiled Jews were allowed to return to Jerusalem and a new settlement was made.

c. 445 BC The city walls were rebuilt.

333 BC Conquered by Alexander the Great.

63 BC Conquered by the Roman general Pompey.

AD 29 or 30 Under the Roman governor Pontius Pilate, Jesus was executed here.

70 A Jewish revolt led to the complete destruction of the city by the Roman emperor Titus.

135 On its site the emperor Hadrian founded the Roman city of Aelia Capitolina.

615 The city was pillaged by the Persian Chosroës II while under Byzantine rule.

637 It was first conquered by Islam.

1099 Jerusalem captured by the Crusaders and made the Kingdom of Jerusalem.

1187 Recaptured by Saladin, sultan of Egypt.

1516 Became part of the Ottoman Empire.

1917 Britain occupied Palestine.

1922–1948 Jerusalem was the capital of the British mandate.

Jerusalem artichoke a variety of ◊artichoke.

Jervis Bay deep bay on the coast of New South Wales, Australia, 90 mi/145 km SW of Sydney. The federal government in 1915 acquired 28 sq mi/73 sq km here to create a port for ◊Canberra. It forms part of the Australian Capital Territory and is the site of the Royal Australian Naval College.

Jessop William 1745–1814. British canal engineer, who built the first canal in England entirely dependent on reservoirs for its water supply (the Grantham Canal 1793–97), and who designed (with Thomas Telford) the 1,000 ft/300 m long Pontcysyllte aqueduct over the river Dee.

Jesuit a member of the largest and most influential Roman Catholic religious order (also known as the Society of Jesus) founded by Ignatius ◊Loyola 1534, with the aims of protecting Catholicism against the Reformation and carrying out missionary work. During the 16th and 17th centuries Jesuits were missionaries in Japan, China, Paraguay, and among the North American Indians. The order now has about 29,000 members (15,000 priests plus students and lay members), and their schools and universities are renowned.

history The Society of Jesus received papal approval 1540. Its main objects were defined as educational work, the suppression of heresy, and missionary work among nonbelievers (its members were not confined to monasteries). Loyola infused into the order a spirit of military discipline, with long and arduous training. Their political influence resulted in their expulsion during 1759–68 from Portugal, France, and Spain, and suppression by Pope Clement XIV 1773. The order was revived by Pius VII 1814, but has since been expelled from many of the countries of Europe and the Americas, and John Paul II criticized the Jesuits 1981 for supporting revolution in South America.

Their head (general) is known as the "Black Pope" from the color of his cassock; the general from 1983 was Pieter-Hans Kolvenbach.

Jesus c. 4 BC–AD 29 or 30. Hebrew preacher on whose teachings Christianity was founded. According to the accounts of his life in the four Gospels of the New Testament, he was born in Bethlehem, Palestine, son of God and the Virgin Mary, and brought up by Mary and her husband Joseph as a carpenter in Nazareth. After adult baptism, he gathered 12 disciples, but his preaching antagonized the Roman authorities and he was executed by crucifixion. Three days later there came reports of his resurrection and, later, his ascension to heaven.

Through his legal father Joseph, Jesus belonged to the tribe of Judah and the family of David, the second king of Israel, a heritage needed by the Messiah for whom the Hebrew people were waiting. In AD 26/27 his cousin John the Baptist proclaimed the coming of the promised Messiah and baptized Jesus, who then made two missionary journeys through the district of Galilee. His teaching, summarized in the Sermon on the Mount, aroused both religious opposition from the ◊Pharisees and secular opposition from the party supporting the Roman governor, ◊Herod Antipas. When Jesus returned to Jerusalem (probably in AD 29), a week before the Passover festival, he was greeted by the people as the Messiah, and the Hebrew authorities (aided by the apostle Judas) had him arrested and condemned to death, after a hurried trial by the Sanhedrin (supreme Jewish court). The Roman procurator, Pontius Pilate, confirmed the sentence, stressing the threat posed to imperial authority by Jesus' teaching.

jet propulsion

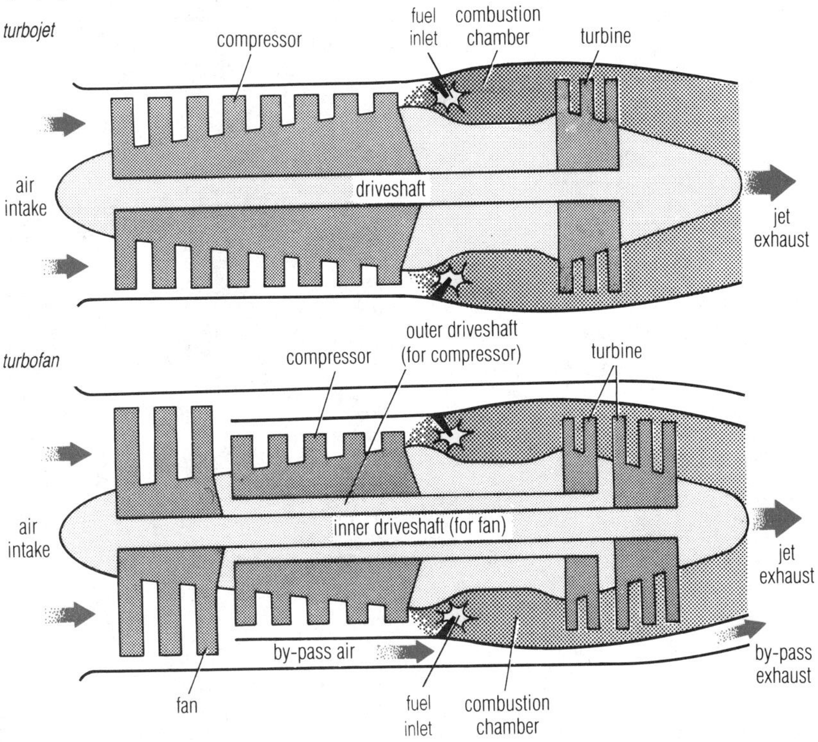

turbojet
compressor
fuel inlet
combustion chamber
turbine
air intake
driveshaft
jet exhaust
turbofan
compressor
outer driveshaft (for compressor)
turbine
air intake
inner driveshaft (for fan)
jet exhaust
by-pass air
by-pass exhaust
fan
fuel inlet
combustion chamber

jet a hard, black variety of lignite, a type of coal. It is cut and polished for use in jewelry and ornaments. Articles made of jet have been found in Bronze Age tombs.

jeté (French "thrown") in dance, a jump from one foot to the other. A *grand jeté* is a big jump in which the dancer pushes off on one foot, holds a brief pose in midair, and lands lightly on the other foot.

jetfoil advanced type of ◊hydrofoil boat built by Boeing, propelled by water jets. It features horizontal, fully submerged hydrofoils fore and aft and has a sophisticated computerized control system to maintain its stability in all waters.

Jetfoils have been in service worldwide since 1975. A jetfoil service operates across the English Channel between Dover and Ostend, Belgium, with a passage time of about 1.5 hours. Cruising speed of the jetfoil is about 50 mph/80 kph.

jet lag the effect of a sudden switch of time zones in air travel, resulting in tiredness and feeling "out of step" with day and night. In 1989 it was suggested that use of the hormone melatonin helped to lessen the effect of jet lag by resetting the body clock. See also ◊circadian rhythm.

jet propulsion method of propulsion in which an object is propelled in one direction by a jet, or stream of gases, moving in the other. This follows from ◊Newton's celebrated third law of motion "to every action, there is an equal and opposite reaction." The most widespread application of the jet principle is in the jet engine (see ◊turbojet; ◊turboprop; ◊turbofan), the most common kind of aircraft engine.

jetsam goods deliberately sunk in the sea to lighten a vessel in a storm, or wreck. See ◊flotsam, jetsam, and lagan.

jet stream a narrow band of very fast wind (velocities of over 95 mph/150 kph) found at altitudes of 6–10 mi/10–16 km in the upper troposphere or lower stratosphere. Jet streams usually occur about the latitudes of the Westerlies (35°–60°).

Jevons William Stanley 1835–1882. British economist who introduced the concept of marginal utility: the increase in total utility (satisfaction or pleasure of consumption) relative to a unit increase of the goods consumed.

Jew a follower of ◊Judaism, the Jewish religion. The term is also used to refer to those who claim descent from the ancient Hebrews, a Semitic people of the Near East. Today, many recognize their ethnic heritage but do not practice the religious or cultural traditions. The term came into use in medieval Europe, based on the Latin name for Judeans, the people of Judah. Prejudice against Jews is termed ◊anti-Semitism.

jewelweed or ***touch-me-not*** any of various North American annual herbaceous plants of the genus *Impatiens* of the balsam family, usually growing in wet soil and having yellowish-orange, sometimes spotted flowers with short spurs. Their mature seed pods burst at the slightest touch.

Jewish Agency administrative body created by the British mandate power in Palestine 1929 to oversee the Jewish population and immigration. In 1948 it took over as the government of an independent Israel.

Jewish-American writing US writing in English shaped by the Jewish experience. It was produced by the children of Eastern European immigrants who had come to the US at the close of the 19th century, and by the 1940s, second- and third-generation Jewish-American writers had become central to US literary and intellectual life. Nobel Prize-winning authors include Saul Bellow 1976 and Isaac Bashevis Singer 1978.

The first significant Jewish-American novel was Abraham Cahan's *The Rise of David Levinsky* 1917. During the 1920s many writers, including Ludwig Lewisohn and Mary Antin, signaled the Jewish presence in US culture. In the 1930s Mike Gold's *Jews Without Money* and Henry Roth's *Call It Sleep* showed in fiction the immigrant Jewish struggle to adapt to the US experience. Novelists such as Bernard Malamud, Philip Roth, and Norman Mailer, poets such as Karl Shapiro, Delmore Schwartz (1913–1966), and Muriel Rukeyser (1913–1980), playwrights and screenwriters such as Arthur Miller, S N Behrman, Neil Simon, and Woody Allen, and critics such as Lionel Trilling (1905–1975) and Irving Howe made the Jewish experience known and a genre of American letters. In the 1950s the Jewish-American novel, shaped by awareness of the Holocaust, expressed themes of human responsibility. Many subsequent writers, including Stanley Elkin, Joseph Heller, Chaim Potok, Denize Levertov, Grace Paley, and Cynthia Ozick, have extended the tradition.

Jewish Autonomous Region part of the Khabarovsk Territory, USSR, on the river Amur; capital Birobidzhan; area 13,900 sq mi/36,000 sq km; population (1986) 211,000. Industries include textiles, leather, metallurgy, light engineering, agriculture, and timber. It was established as a Jewish National District 1928 and became an Autonomous Region 1934 but became only nominally Jewish after the Stalinist purges 1936–47 and 1948–49.

Jew's harp musical instrument consisting of a two-pronged metal frame inserted between the teeth, and a springlike tongue plucked with the finger.

The resulting drone excites resonances in the mouth that can be varied in pitch to produce a melody.

Jezebel in the Old Testament, daughter of the king of Sidon. She married King Ahab of Israel, and was brought into conflict with the prophet Elijah by her introduction of the worship of Baal.

Jhansi city in Uttar Pradesh, NE India, 178 mi/286 km SW of Lucknow; population (1981) 281,000. It is a railroad and road junction and a market center. It was founded 1613, and was the scene of a massacre of British civilians 1857.

Jhelum river rising in Kashmir and flowing into Pakistan; length about 450 mi/720 km. The Mangla Dam 1967, one of the world's largest earth-filled dams, stores flood waters for irrigation and hydroelectricity. The Jhelum is one of the five rivers that give Punjab its name and was known in the ancient world as the Hydaspes, on whose banks Alexander the Great won a battle in 326 BC.

Jiang Jie Shi alternate transcription of ◊Chiang Kai-shek.

Jiang Qing or Chiang Ching 1913– . Chinese communist politician, wife of the party leader Mao Zedong. In 1960 she became minister for culture, and played a key role in the 1966–69 Cultural Revolution as the leading member of the Shanghai-based Gang of Four, who attempted to seize power 1976. Jiang was imprisoned 1981.

Jiang was a Shanghai actress when in 1937 she met Mao Zedong at the communist headquarters in Yan'an; she became his third wife 1939. She emerged as a radical, egalitarian Maoist. Her influence waned during the early 1970s and her relationship with Mao became embittered. On Mao's death Sept 1976, the ◊Gang of Four, with Jiang as a leading figure, sought to seize power by organizing military coups in Shanghai and Beijing. They were arrested for treason by Mao's successor Hua Guofeng and tried 1980–81. The Gang were blamed for the excesses of the Cultural Revolution, but Jiang asserted during her trial that she had only followed Mao's orders as an obedient wife. This was rejected, and Jiang received a death sentence Jan 1981, which was subsequently commuted to life imprisonment.

Jiangsu or ***Kiangsu*** province on the coast of E China
area 39,449 sq mi/102,200 sq km
capital Nanjing
features the swampy mouth of the Chang Jiang; the special municipality of Shanghai
products cereals, rice, tea, cotton, soybeans, fish, silk, ceramics, textiles, coal, iron, copper, cement
population (1986) 62,130,000.

Jiangxi or ***Kiangsi*** province of SE China
area 63,613 sq mi/164,800 sq km
capital Nanchang
products rice, tea, cotton, tobacco, porcelain, coal, tungsten, uranium
population (1986) 35,090,000
history the province was Mao Zedong's original

Jiangsu Massed silkworm cocoons are gathered from the cut branches by members of a commune, who are striving to diversify the local economy.

base in the first phase of the Communist struggle against the Nationalists.

Jiang Zemin 1926– . Chinese political leader. The son-in-law of ◊Li Xiannian, he joined the Chinese Communist Party's politburo in 1967 after serving in the Moscow embassy and as mayor of Shanghai. He succeeded ◊Zhao Ziyang as party leader after the Tiananmen Square massacre of 1989. A cautious proponent of economic reform coupled with unswerving adherence to the party's "political line," he subsequently replaced ◊Deng Xiaoping as head of the influential central military commission.

Jiddah or ***Jedda*** port in Hejaz, Saudi Arabia, on the E shore of the Red Sea; population (1986) 1,000,000. Industries include cement, steel, and oil refining. Pilgrims pass through here on their way to Mecca.

jihad (Arabic "conflict") a holy war undertaken by Muslims against nonbelievers. In the Mecca Declaration 1981, the Islamic powers pledged a jihad

Jiang Zemin Jiang Zemin became China's political leader after the Tiananmen Square massacre of June 1989.

Jinnah Muslim leader Mohammed Ali Jinnah, first governor-general of the state of Pakistan.

against Israel, though not necessarily military attack.

Jilin or ***Kirin*** province of NE China in central ◊Manchuria
area 72,182 sq mi/187,000 sq km
capital Changchun
population (1986) 23,150,000.

Jim Crow originally a derogatory term Americans used for a black person, it refers to the systematic practice of segregating black Americans, which was common in the South until the 1960s. "Jim Crow laws" are laws designed to deny civil rights to blacks or to enforce the policy of segregation, which existed until Supreme Court decisions and civil-rights legislation of the 1950s and 1960s (Civil Rights Act 1964, Voting Rights Act 1965) denied their legality.

See also ◊black.

Jiménez Juan Ramón 1881–1958. Spanish lyric poet. Born in Andalusia, he left Spain during the civil war to live in exile in Puerto Rico. He was awarded the Nobel Prize 1956.

Jinan or ***Tsinan*** city and capital of Shandong province, China; population (1986) 1,430,000. It has food-processing and textile industries.

Jingdezhen or ***Chingtechen*** or ***Fou-liang*** town in Jiangxi, China. Ming blue-and-white china was produced here, the name of the clay kaolin coming from Kaoling, a hill E of Jingdezhen; some of the best Chinese porcelain is still made here.

jingoism blinkered, warmongering patriotism. The term originated in 1878, when the British prime minister Disraeli developed a pro-Turkish policy, which nearly involved the UK in war with Russia. His supporters' war song included the line "We don't want to fight, but by jingo if we do … ."

jinn in Muslim mythology, a spirit able to assume human or animal shape.

Jinnah Mohammed Ali 1876–1948. Indian politician, Pakistan's first governor-general from 1947. He was president of the Muslim League from 1934, and by 1940 was advocating the need for a separate state of Pakistan; at the 1946 conferences in London he insisted on the partition of British India into Hindu and Muslim states.

Jinsha Jiang river of China, which rises in SW China and forms the Chang Jiang (Yangtze) at Yibin.

Jivaro member of a South American Indian people of the tropical forests of SE Ecuador and NE Peru. They live by farming, hunting, fishing, and weaving; the Jivaro language belongs to the Andean-Equatorial family. They were formerly notorious for preserving the hair and shrunken skin of the heads of their enemies as battle trophies.

jive an energetic American dance that evolved from the jitterbug, popular in the 1940s and 1950s; a forerunner of rock and roll.

Joachim Joseph 1831–1907. Austro-Hungarian violinist and composer. He studied under Mendelssohn and founded the Joachim Quartet (1869–1907). Joachim played and conducted the music of his friend ◊Brahms. His own compositions include pieces for violin and orchestra, chamber, and orchestral works.

Joachim of Fiore c. 1132–1202. Italian mystic, born in Calabria. In his mystical writings he interpreted history as a sequence of three ages, that of the Father, Son, and Holy Spirit, the last of which, the age of perfect spirituality, was to begin in 1260. His Messianic views were taken up enthusiastically by many followers.

Joan mythical Englishwoman supposed to have become pope in 855, as John VIII, and to have given birth to a child during a papal procession. The myth was exposed in the 17th century.

Joannitius Hunayn ibn Ishaq al Ibadi 809–873. Arabic translator, a Nestorian Christian, who translated Greek learning—including Ptolemy, Euclid, Hippocrates, Plato, and Aristotle—into Arabic or Syrian for the Abbasid court in Baghdad.

Joan of Arc, St 1412–1431. French military leader. In 1429 at Chinon, NW France, she persuaded Charles VII that she had a divine mission to expel the occupying English from N France (see ◊Hundred Years' War) and secure his coronation. She raised the siege of Orléans, defeated the English at Patay, north of Orléans, and Charles was crowned in Reims. However, she failed to take Paris and was captured May 1430 by the Burgundians, who sold her to the English. She was found guilty of witchcraft and heresy by a tribunal of French ecclesiastics who supported the English. She was burned to death at the stake in Rouen May 30, 1431. In 1920 she was canonized.

Job c. 5th century BC. In the Old Testament, Hebrew leader who in the Book of Job questioned God's infliction of suffering on the righteous while enduring great sufferings himself.

Although Job comes to no final conclusion, his book is one of the first attempts to explain the problem of human suffering in a world believed to be created and governed by a God who is all powerful and all good.

Jocasta in Greek mythology, wife of Laius, sister of ◊Creon, and mother and wife of ◊Oedipus, by whom she was mother to ◊Antigone, ◊Eteoclesz, ◊Polynices, and Ismene. She married Oedipus in ignorance, as his reward for killing the ◊Sphinx. She committed suicide on discovering his identity (◊Sophocles) or at the death of her sons (◊Euripides and Statius).

Jodhpur city in Rajasthan, India, formerly capital of Jodhpur princely state, founded in 1459 by Rao Jodha; population (1981) 493,600. It is a market center and has the training college of the Indian air force, an 18th-century Mogul palace, and a red sandstone fort. A style of riding breeches is named after it.

Jodl Alfred 1892–1946. German general. In World War II he drew up the Nazi government's plan for the attack on Yugoslavia, Greece, and the USSR. In Jan 1945 he became Chief of Staff and headed the delegation that signed Germany's surrender in Reims May 7, 1945. He was tried for war crimes in Nuremberg 1945–46 and hanged.

Jodrell Bank site in Cheshire, England, of the Nuffield Radio Astronomy Laboratories of the University of Manchester. Its largest instrument is the 250-ft/76-m radio dish, completed 1957 and modified 1970. An elliptical radio dish capable of working at shorter wavelengths and measuring 125 × 82 ft/38 × 25 m was introduced 1964. These radio telescopes are used in conjunction with six smaller dishes to produce detailed maps of radio sources.

Joel in the Old Testament, prophet of Judah who predicts punishments for Judah's sins, to be followed by a restoration of God's grace and the nation's triumph over its enemies.

Joffre Joseph Jacques Césaire 1852–1931. Marshal of France during World War I. He was chief of general staff 1911. The German invasion of Belgium 1914 took him by surprise, but his stand at the Battle of the ◊Marne resulted in his appointment as supreme commander of all the French armies 1915. His failure to make adequate preparations at Verdun 1916 and the military disasters on the ◊Somme led to his replacement by Nivelle in Dec 1916.

Jogjakarta alternate spelling of ◊Yogyakarta, a city in Indonesia.

Johannesburg largest city of South Africa, situated on the Witwatersrand River in Transvaal; population (1985) 1,609,000. It is the center of a large gold-mining industry; other industries include engineering works, meat-chilling plants, and clothing factories.

Notable buildings include the law courts, Escom House (Electricity Supply Commission), the South African Railways Administration Building, the City Hall, Chamber of Mines and Stock Exchange, the Witwatersrand (1921) and Rand Afrikaans (1966) universities, and the Union Observatory. Johannesburg was founded after the discovery of gold 1886 and was probably named after Jan (Johannes) Meyer, the first mining commissioner.

John Augustus (Edwin) 1878–1961. British painter of landscapes and portraits, including *The Smiling Woman* 1910 (Tate Gallery, London) of his second wife, Dorelia.

John Elton. Adopted name of Reginald Kenneth Dwight 1947– . English pop singer, pianist, and composer, noted for his melodies and elaborate costumes and glasses.

John Lackland 1167–1216. King of England from 1199 and acting king from 1189 during his brother Richard I (the Lionheart)'s absence on the third Crusade. He lost Normandy and almost all the other English possessions in France to Philip II of France by 1205. His repressive policies and excessive taxation brought him into conflict with his barons, and he was forced to seal the ◊Magna Carta 1215. Later repudiation of it led to the first Barons' War 1215–17, during which he died.

John two kings of France, including:

John II 1319–1364. King of France from 1350. He was defeated and captured by the Black Prince at Poitiers 1356 and imprisoned in England. Released 1360, he failed to raise the money for his ransom and returned to England 1364, where he died.

John name of 23 popes, including:

John XXII 1249–1334. Pope 1316–34. He spent his papacy in Avignon, France, engaged in a long conflict with the Holy Roman emperor, Louis of Bavaria, and the Spiritual Franciscans, a monastic order who preached the absolute poverty of the clergy.

John XXIII Angelo Giuseppe Roncalli 1881–1963. Pope from 1958. He improved relations with the USSR in line with his encyclical *Pacem in Terris/Peace on Earth* 1963, established Roman Catholic hierarchies in newly emergent states, and summoned the Second Vatican Council, which reformed church liturgy and backed the ecumenical movement.

'John XXIII' Baldassare Costa died 1419. Anti-pope 1410–15. In an attempt to end the ◊Great Schism he was elected pope by a council of cardinals in Bologna, but was deposed by the Council of Constance 1415, together with the popes of Avignon and Rome. His papacy is not recognized by the church.

John three kings of Poland, including:

John III Sobieski 1624–1696. King of Poland from 1674. He became commander-in-chief of the army 1668 after victories over the Cossacks and Tatars. A victory over the Turks 1673 helped to get him elected to the Polish throne, and he saved Vienna from the besieging Turks 1683.

John six kings of Portugal, including:

John I 1357–1433. King of Portugal from 1385. An illegitimate son of Pedro I, he was elected by the *Cortes* (parliament). His claim was supported by an English army against the rival king of Castile, thus establishing the Anglo-Portuguese Alliance 1386. He married Philippa of Lancaster, daughter of ◊John of Gaunt.

John IV 1603–1656. King of Portugal from 1640. Originally Duke of Braganza, he was elected king when the Portuguese rebelled against Spanish rule. His reign was marked by a long war against Spain, which did not end until 1668.

John VI 1769–1826. King of Portugal and regent for his insane mother Maria I from 1799 until her death 1816. He fled to Brazil when the French invaded Portugal 1807 and did not return until 1822. On his return Brazil declared its independence, with John's elder son Pedro as emperor.

John Bull an imaginary figure who is a personification of England, similar to the American Uncle Sam. The name was popularized by Dr ◊Arbuthnot's *History of John Bull* 1712. He is represented as a prosperous farmer of the 18th century.

John Chrysostom, St 345–407. Christian scholar, hermit, preacher, and Eastern Orthodox bishop of Constantinople 398–404. He was born in Antioch (now Antakya, Turkey). Feast day Sept 13.

John of Austria Don 1545–1578. Spanish soldier, the illegitimate son of the Holy Roman emperor Charles V. He defeated the Turks at the Battle of ◊Lepanto 1571.

He captured Tunis 1573 but quickly lost it. He was appointed governor-general of the Netherlands 1576 but discovered that real power lay in the hands of William of Orange. John withdrew 1577 and then attacked and defeated the patriot army at Gemblors Jan 31, 1578 with the support of reinforcements from Philip II of Spain. Lack of money stopped him from going any farther. He died of fever.

John of Damascus, St c. 676–c. 754. Eastern Orthodox theologian and hymn writer, a defender of image worship against the iconoclasts (image-breakers). Contained in his *The Fountain of Knowledge* is *An Accurate Exposition of the Orthodox Faith*, an important chronicle of theology from the 4th–7th centuries. He was born in Damascus, Syria. Feast day Dec 4.

John of Gaunt 1340–1399. English politician, born in Ghent, fourth son of Edward III, duke of Lancaster from 1362. He distinguished himself during the Hundred Years' War. During Edward's last years, and the years before Richard II attained the age of majority, he acted as head of government, and Parliament protested against his corrupt rule.

John of the Cross, St 1542–1591. Spanish Roman Catholic Carmelite friar from 1564, who was imprisoned several times for attempting to impose the reforms laid down by St Teresa. His verse describes spiritual ecstasy. Feast day Nov 24.

He was beatified 1674 and canonized 1726.

John o' Groats village in NE Highland region, Scotland, about 2 mi/3 km west of Duncansby Head, proverbially Britain's northernmost point. It is named after the Dutchman John de Groot, who built a house there in the 16th century.

John Paul two popes:

John Paul I Albino Luciani 1912–1978. Pope Aug 26–Sept 28, 1978. His name was chosen as the combination of his two immediate predecessors.

John Paul II Karol Wojtyla 1920– . Pope 1978– , the first non-Italian to be elected pope since 1522. He was born near Kraków, Poland. He has upheld the tradition of papal infallibility, condemned artificial contraception, women priests, married priests, and modern dress for monks and nuns, measures that have aroused criticism from liberalizing elements in the Church. He has warned against involvement of priests in political activity.

In 1939, at the beginning of World War II, Wojtyla was conscripted for forced labor by the Germans, working in quarries and a chemical factory, but from 1942 studied for the priesthood illegally in Kraków. After the war he taught ethics and theology at the universities of Lublin and Kraków, becoming archbishop of Kraków 1964. He was made a cardinal 1967. He was shot and wounded by a Turk in an attempt on his life 1981.

John Paul II The first pope to come from Poland, John Paul II is an accomplished linguist and author.

Johns Jasper 1930– US painter and printmaker who rejected the abstract in favor of such simple subjects as flags, maps, and numbers. He uses pigments mixed with wax (encaustic) to create a rich surface with unexpected delicacies of color. He has also created collages and lithographs.

Born in Augusta, Georgia, he moved to New York City in 1952. In the 1960s his works became more abstract before veering toward abstract expressionism in the mid-1970s. He was influenced by Marcel ◊Duchamp.

John, St AD 1st century. New Testament apostle. Traditionally, he wrote the fourth Gospel and the Johannine Epistles (when he was bishop of Ephesus), and the Book of Revelation (while exiled to the Greek island of Patmos). His emblem is an eagle; his feast day Dec 27.

St John is identified with the unnamed "disciple whom Jesus loved." Son of Zebedee, born in Judea, he and his brother James were Galilean fishermen. Jesus entrusted his mother to John at the Crucifixion, where John is often shown dressed in red, with curly hair. Another of his symbols is a chalice with a little snake in it.

Johnson Alvin Saunders 1874–1971. US social scientist and educator. After teaching at several universities, he helped found and became editor of the *New Republic* 1917. Joining with some of America's greatest scholars, Johnson was one of the founders of the New School for Social Research in New York City, serving as its director 1923–45. Johnson's memoir, *Progress: An Autobiography*, was published 1952.

Born near Homer, Nebraska, Johnson was educated at the University of Nebraska, saw service in the Spanish-American War, and received a PhD in economics from Columbia 1902.

Johns American painter Jasper Johns often incorporates numbers in his work, as in Zero Through Nine *1961 in London's Tate Gallery.*

Johnson The 17th president of the United States of America, Andrew Johnson, a Unionist. 1865–1869.

Johnson Andrew 1808–1875. The 17th president of the US 1865–69, a Democrat. He was born in Raleigh, North Carolina, and was a congressman from Tennessee 1843–53, governor of Tennessee 1853–57, senator 1857–62, and vice-president 1865. He succeeded to the presidency on Lincoln's assassination (Apr 15, 1865). His conciliatory policy to the defeated South after the Civil War involved him in a feud with the Radical Republicans. When he tried to dismiss Edwin Stanton, a cabinet secretary, his political opponents seized on the opportunity to charge him with "high crimes and misdemeanors" and attempted to remove him from office. This battle culminated with his impeachment before the Senate 1868, which failed to convict him by one vote.

Among his achievements was the purchase of Alaska from Russia 1867. He was returned to the Senate from Tennessee 1875, but died shortly afterwards.

His tenure as president was characterized by his frustration and political stalemate. He presided over the reentry of the Southern states into the Union.

Johnson Celia 1908–1982. British actress who starred with Trevor Howard in the romantic film *Brief Encounter* 1946.

Johnson Eastman 1824–1906. US painter born in Germany, trained in Düsseldorf, The Hague, and Paris. Painting in the open air, he developed a fresh and luminous landscape style.

Johnson had his first success with a nostalgic naturalist scene, *Old Kentucky Home* 1859 (New York Historical Society).

Johnson Hiram Warren 1866–1945. US politician. He was the "Bull Moose" party candidate for vice-president in Theodore Roosevelt's unsuccessful bid to regain the presidency 1912. Elected to the US Senate 1917, Johnson served there until his death. He was an unyielding isolationist, opposing US involvement in the European war and, when World War I was over, membership in the League of Nations and World Court.

Born in Sacramento, California, Johnson attended the University of California and was admitted to the bar 1888. Moving in 1902 to San Francisco, where he established a law practice, Johnson entered politics and served as governor of California 1911–17.

Johnson Jack 1878–1968. US heavyweight boxer. He overcame severe racial prejudice to become the first black heavyweight champion of the world 1908 when he traveled to Australia to challenge Tommy Burns. The US authorities wanted Johnson "dethroned" because of his color but could not find suitable challengers until 1915, when he lost the title in a dubious fight decision to the giant Jess Willard.

Johnson The 36th president of the United States of America, Lyndon B Johnson, a Democrat. 1963–1969.

CAREER HIGHLIGHTS: Jack Johnson

fights: 107
wins: 86
draws: 11
defeats: 10

Johnson James Weldon 1871–1938. US author and social critic. Born in Jacksonville, Florida, and educated at Atlanta University, Johnson became, in 1897, the first black American admitted to the Florida bar. He was a strong supporter of Theodore Roosevelt and served him and Taft as US consul in Venezuela and Nicaragua 1906–12. He was editor of *New York Age* 1912–22 and was active in the National Association for the Advancement of Colored People (NAACP). As poet and anthropologist, he became one of the chief figures of the Harlem Renaissance of the 1920s. His autobiography, *Along This Way*, was published 1933.

Johnson Lyndon Baines 1908–1973. The 36th president of the US 1963–69, a Democrat. He was born in Stonewall, Texas, elected to Congress 1937–49 and the Senate 1949–60. His persuasive powers and hard work on domestic issues led J F Kennedy to ask him to be his vice-presidential running mate 1960. Johnson brought critical Southern support which won a narrow victory.

After the ◊Tonkin Gulf Incident, the escalation of US involvement in the ◊Vietnam War eventually dissipated the support won by his Great Society legislation (civil rights, education, alleviation of poverty), and he declined to run for reelection 1968.

Following Kennedy's assassination, Johnson pushed many pieces of civil rights legislation through Congress. His foreign policy met with considerably less success, however.

Johnson Philip Cortelyou 1906– . US architect who coined the term "international style." Originally designing in the style of ◊Mies van der Rohe, he later became an exponent of ◊Postmodernism. He designed the giant AT&T building in New York City 1978, a pink skyscraper with a Chippendale-style cabinet top.

He was director of architecture and design at the Museum of Modern Art, New York City 1932–54, where he built the annex and sculpture court.

Johnson The Crystal Cathedral, Los Angeles, by Johnson and Burgee.

Johnson Portrait c. 1777 by James Barry of English author and critic Samuel Johnson, in London's National Portrait Gallery.

Johnson Samuel, known as "Dr Johnson," 1709–1784. English lexicographer, author, and critic, also a brilliant conversationalist and the dominant figure in 18th-century London literary society. His *Dictionary*, published 1755, remained authoritative for over a century, and is still remarkable for the vigour of its definitions. In 1764 he founded the "Literary Club," whose members included Reynolds, Burke, Goldsmith, Garrick, and ◊Boswell, Johnson's biographer.

Born in Lichfield, Staffordshire, Johnson became first an usher and then a literary hack. In 1735 he married Elizabeth Porter and opened a private school. When this proved unsuccessful he went to London with his pupil David Garrick, becoming a regular contributor to the *Gentleman's Magazine* and publishing the poem *London* 1738. Other works include the satire imitating Juvenal, *Vanity of Human Wishes* 1749, the philosophical romance *Rasselas* 1759, an edition of Shakespeare 1765, and the classic *Lives of the Most Eminent English Poets* 1779–81. His first meeting with ◊Boswell was 1763. A visit with Boswell to Scotland and the Hebrides 1773 was recorded in *Journey to the Western Isles of Scotland* 1775. He was buried in Westminster Abbey and his house, in Gough Square, London, is preserved as a museum; his wit and humanity are documented in Boswell's classic biography *Life of Samuel Johnson* 1791.

Johnson Uwe 1934– . German novelist who left East Germany for West Berlin 1959, and wrote of the division of Germany in, for example, *Anniversaries* 1977.

Johnson City city in NE Tennessee, just below the Virginia border, in the Appalachian Mountains NE of Knoxville. Industries include tobacco, furniture, building materials, metals, textiles, and food processing; population (1990) 49,381.

Johnston Joseph Eggleston 1807–1891. US military leader. At the outbreak of the US Civil War, he was quartermaster general of the US Army. Joining the Confederacy, Johnston was given command of the Shenandoah. In 1862 he was sent West and in 1863 commanded the Army of Tennessee. After the war, Johnston returned to private life, later serving in the US House of Representatives 1879–81 and as federal railroad commissioner 1887–91.

Born near Farmville, Virginia, Johnston graduated from West Point 1829 and saw action in the Seminole War. As a military engineer, he served with distinction during the Mexican War.

Johnstown city in SW Pennsylvania, on the Conemaugh River, E of Pittsburgh. Industries include

joint

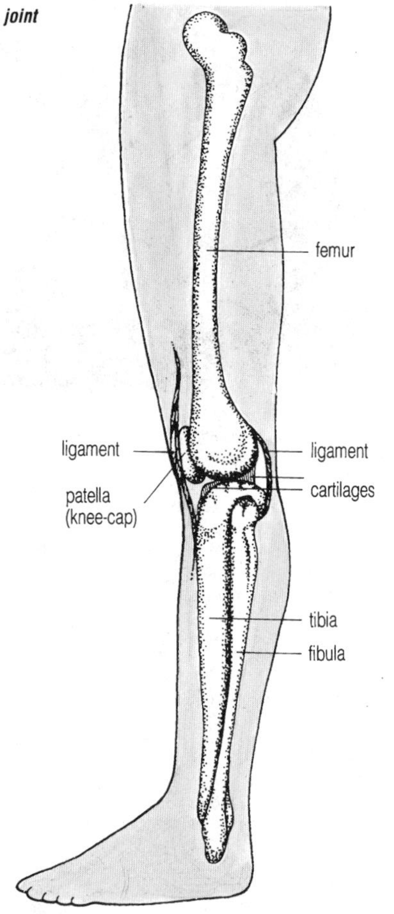
femur
ligament
ligament
patella
(knee-cap)
cartilages
tibia
fibula

steel, coal and coal by-products, chemicals, building materials, and clothing; population (1990) 28,134. Johnstown was the victim of disastrous floods 1889.

John the Baptist, St c. 12 BC–c. AD 27. In the New Testament, an itinerant preacher. After preparation in the wilderness, he proclaimed the coming of the Messiah and baptized Jesus in the River Jordan. He was later executed by ◊Herod Antiplas at the request of Salome, who demanded that his head be brought to her on a platter.

John was the son of Zacharias and Elizabeth (a cousin of Jesus' mother), born in Nazareth, Galilee. He and Jesus are often shown together as children.

Johor state in S Peninsular Malaysia; capital Johor Baharu; area 7,334 sq mi/19,000 sq km; population (1980) 1,638,000. The southernmost point of mainland Asia, it is joined to Singapore by a causeway. It is mainly forested, with swamps. There is bauxite and iron.

joint in any animal with a skeleton, a point of movement or articulation. In invertebrates with an ◊exoskeleton, the joints are places where the exoskeleton is replaced by a more flexible outer covering, the arthrodial membrane, which allows the limb (or other body part) to bend at that point. In vertebrates, it is the point where two bones meet.

Some joints allow no motion (the sutures of the skull), others allow a very small motion (the sacroiliac joints in the lower back), but most allow a relatively free motion. Of these, some allow a gliding motion (one vertebra of the spine on another), some have a hinge action (elbow and knee), and others allow motion in all directions (hip and shoulder joints), by means of a ball-and-socket arrangement.

The ends of the bones at a moving joint are covered with cartilage for greater elasticity and smoothness, and enclosed in an envelope (capsule) of tough white fibrous tissue lined with a membrane which secretes a lubricating and cushioning ◊synovial fluid. The joint is further strengthened by ligaments.

joint venture in business, an undertaking in which an individual or legal entity of one country forms a company with those of another country, with risks being shared.

Joliet city in NE Illinois, on the Des Plaines River, SW of Chicago; seat of Will county. It is a center for barge traffic. Industries include building materials, chemicals, oil refining, heavy construction machinery, and paper; population (1990) 76,836.

Joliet (or Jolliet) Louis 1645–1700. French Canadian explorer. Born in Quebec, Joliet was sent by the governor of Canada to undertake an extensive exploration of the Great Lakes 1669. Later, in response to reports that the Mississippi River flowed into the Pacific (and might thereby serve as a trade route to Asia), he and the Jesuit missionary Jacques Marquette were sent to explore the river. Joliet charted the Mississippi down to its junction with the Arkansas River and returned to Canada by way of the Illinois territory. He later explored Labrador and the Hudson Bay. The city of Joliet, Illinois, is named in his honor.

Joliot-Curie Irène 1897–1956. and Frédéric (born Frèdèric Joliot) 1900–1958. French physicists who made the discovery of artificial radioactivity for which they were jointly awarded the 1935 Nobel Prize for Chemistry.

Irène was the daughter of Marie and Pierre Curie and began work at her mother's Radium Institute in 1921. In 1926 she married Frédéric, a pupil of her mother, and they began a long and fruitful collaboration. In 1934 they found that certain elements exposed to radiation themselves become radioactive.

Jolson Al. Adopted name of Asa Yoelson 1886–1950. Russian-born US singer and entertainer. Formerly a Broadway and vaudeville star, he gained instant film immortality as the star of the first talking picture, *The Jazz Singer* 1927.

Jolson, who got his start in vaudeville, was also a popular recording star.

Jonah 7th century BC. Hebrew prophet whose name is given to a book in the Old Testament. According to this, he fled by ship to evade his mission to prophesy the destruction of Nineveh. The crew threw him overboard in a storm, as a bringer of ill fortune, and he spent three days and nights in the belly of a whale before coming to land.

Jonathan Chief (Joseph) Leabua 1914–1987. Lesotho politician. A leader in the drive for independence, Jonathan became prime minister of Lesotho in 1965. His rule was ended by a coup in 1986.

CBS

Jolson *Singer and film star Al Jolson. Originally a stage performer, he successfully made the transition to star in early talking films such as* The Jazz Singer.

Jones *A drawing after Robert Van Voerst of English architect Inigo Jones, National Portrait Gallery, London.*

Jones Bobby (Robert Tyre) 1902–1971. US golfer. He was the game's greatest amateur player, who never turned professional but won 13 major amateur and professional tournaments, including the Grand Slam of the amateur and professional opens of both the US and Britain 1930.

Born in Atlanta, Georgia, Jones finished playing competitive golf 1930 and concentrated on his law practice. He maintained his contacts with the sport and was largely responsible for inaugurating the US Masters.

CAREER HIGHLIGHTS

British Open: 1926–27, 1930
US Open: 1923, 1926, 1929–30
British Amateur: 1930
US Amateur: 1924–25, 1927–28, 1930
US Walker Cup team: 1922, 1924, 1926, 1928*, 1930*
*indicates playing captain

Jones Charles Martin (Chuck) 1912– . US film animator and cartoon director who worked at Warner Brothers with characters such as Bugs Bunny, Daffy Duck, Wile E. Coyote, and Elmer Fudd.

Jones Gwyneth 1936– . Welsh soprano who has performed as Sieglinde in *Die Walküre* and Desdemona in *Otello*.

Jones Henry Arthur 1851–1929. British playwright. Among some 60 of his melodramas, *Mrs Dane's Defence* 1900 is most notable as an early realist problem play.

Jones Inigo 1573–c. 1652. English architect. Born in London, he studied in Italy and was influenced by the works of Palladio. He was employed by James I to design scenery for Ben Jonson's masques. In 1619 he designed his English Renaissance masterpiece, the banqueting room at Whitehall, London.

Jones John Luther "Casey" 1864–1900. US railroad engineer and folk hero. Born in Cayce, Kentucky, Jones gained his nickname from the name of his hometown. Hired by the railroad 1880, he became an engineer for the Illinois Central Railroad 1890. His death at the throttle of a locomotive became the subject of popular legend. Having volunteered for an overnight run on the "Cannonball Express" in April 1900, Jones collided with a stalled freight train. Ordering his fireman to jump to safety, he rode the "Cannonball" to his death. The folk song "Casey Jones," written by Wallace Sanders, is an account of the event.

Jonestown commune of the People's Temple Sect, NW of Georgetown, Guyana, established 1974 by the American Jim Jones (1933–1978), who originally founded the sect among San Francisco's black community. After a visiting US congress-

Jonson Poet and dramatist Ben Jonson. He narrowly escaped the gallows after killing a man in a duel.

man was shot dead, Jones enforced mass suicide on his followers by instructing them to drink cyanide; 914 died, including over 240 children.

Jongkind Johan Bartold 1819–1891. Dutch painter active mainly in France. His studies of the Normandy coast show a keen observation of the natural effects of light. He influenced the Impressionist painter ◊Monet.

Jönköping city at the south end of Lake Vättern, Sweden; population (1985) 107,362. It is an industrial center in an agricultural and forestry region.

jonquil species of small daffodil *Narcissus jonquilla*, family Amaryllidaceae, with yellow flowers. Native to Spain and Portugal, it is cultivated elsewhere.

Jonson Ben(jamin) 1572–1637. English dramatist, poet, and critic. *Every Man in his Humour* 1598 established the English "comedy of humors," in which each character embodies a "humor," or vice, such as greed, lust, or avarice. This was followed by *Cynthia's Revels* 1600 and *Poetaster* 1601. His first extant tragedy is *Sejanus* 1603, with Burbage and Shakespeare as members of the original cast. The plays of his middle years include *Volpone, or The Fox* 1606, *The Alchemist* 1610, and *Bartholomew Fair* 1614.

Joplin city in SW Missouri, W of Springfield. Industries include zinc and lead smelting, leather goods, and furniture; population (1990) 40,961.

DEDICATED TO JAMES BROWN AND HIS MANDOLIN CLUB
THE ENTERTAINER
A RAG TIME TWO-STEP
BY
SCOTT JOPLIN
COMPOSER OF
MAPLE LEAF RAG
SUNFLOWER SLOW DRAG
PEACHERINE RAG
SWIPESY CAKE WALK
THE STRENUOUS LIFE (RAG)
THE RAGTIME DANCE (SONG)
ETC., ETC.
50
JOHN STARK & SON
SHEET MUSIC PUBLISHERS
ST. LOUIS

Joplin Scott Joplin's popularity was revived when his ragtime "The Entertainer" became a film theme song in 1973.

Joplin Janis 1943–1970. US blues and rock singer, born in Texas. She was lead singer with the San Francisco group Big Brother and the Holding Company 1966–68. Her biggest hit, Kris Kristofferson's "Me and Bobby McGee," was released on the posthumous *Pearl* LP 1971.

She died of a drug overdose.

Joplin Scott 1868–1917. US ◊ragtime pianist and composer active in Chicago. His "Maple Leaf Rag" 1899 was the first instrumental sheet music to sell a million copies, and "The Entertainer," as the theme tune of the film *The Sting* 1973, revived his popularity. He was an influence on Jelly Roll Morton and other early jazz musicians.

Joppa ancient name of ◊Jaffa, a port in W Israel.

Jordaens Jacob 1593–1678. Flemish painter, born in Antwerp. His style follows Rubens, whom he assisted in various commissions. Much of his work is exuberant and on a large scale, including scenes of peasant life, altarpieces, portraits, and mythological subjects.

Jordan river rising on Mount Hermon, Syria, at 1,800 ft/550 m above sea level and flowing south for about 200 mi/320 km via the Sea of Galilee to the Dead Sea, 1,290 ft/390 m below sea level. It occupies the northern part of the Great Rift Valley; its upper course forms the boundary of Israel with Syria and the kingdom of Jordan; its lower course runs through Jordan; the West Bank has been occupied by Israel since 1967.

Jordan country in SW Asia, bordered N by Syria, NE by Iraq, E and SE by Saudi Arabia, S by the Gulf of Aqaba, and W by Israel

government Jordan is not a typical constitutional monarchy on the Western model, since the king is effectively head of both state and government. The 1952 constitution, amended in 1974, 1976, and 1984, provides for a two-chamber national assembly comprising a senate (house of notables) of 30, appointed by the king for an eight-year term, and a 142-member house of representatives (house of deputies), elected by universal suffrage for a four-year term. The house is subject to dissolution within that period. In each chamber there is equal representation for the east and west (occupied) banks of the river Jordan. Three of Jordan's eight administrative provinces have been occupied by Israel since 1967.

The king governs with the help of a council of ministers whom he appoints and who are responsible to the assembly. Political parties were banned in 1963, partially restored in 1971, and then banned again in 1976.

history The area forming the kingdom of Jordan was occupied by the independent Nabataeans from the 4th century BC and perhaps earlier, until AD 106 when it became part of the Roman province of Arabia. It was included in the Crusaders' kingdom of Jerusalem 1099–1187. Palestine (the West Bank of present-day Jordan) and Transjordan (the present-day East Bank) were part of the Turkish Ottoman Empire until its dissolution after World War I. Both were then placed under British administration by the League of Nations.

Transjordan acquired greater control of its own affairs than Palestine and separated from it in 1923, achieving full independence when the British mandate expired in 1946. The mandate for Palestine ran out in 1948, whereupon Jewish leaders claimed it for a new state of Israel. Israel was attacked by Arab nations and fought until a cease-fire was agreed in 1949. By then Transjordan forces had occupied part of Palestine to add to what they called the new state of Jordan. The following year they annexed the West Bank. In 1953 Hussein ibn Talai came to the Jordanian

Jordan

Hashemite Kingdom of
(*Al Mamlaka al Urduniya al Hashemiyah*)

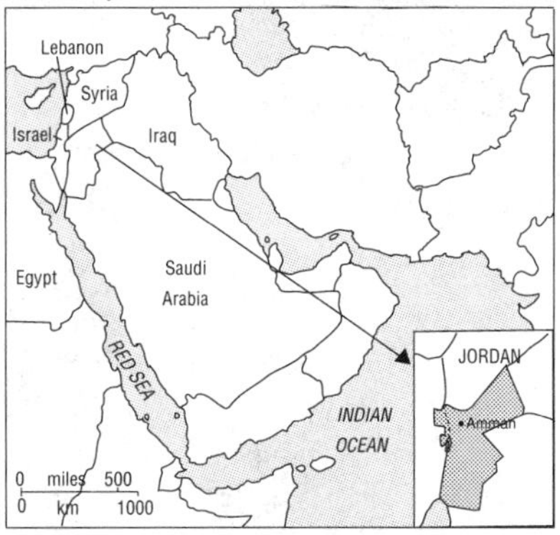
Lebanon
Syria
Israel
Iraq
Egypt
Saudi Arabia
RED SEA
INDIAN OCEAN
JORDAN
Amman
0 miles 500
0 km 1000

area 34,434 sq mi/89,206 sq km (West Bank, incorporated into Jordan 1950 but occupied by Israel since 1967, area 2,269 sq mi/5,879 sq km)
capital Amman
cities Zarqa, Irbid, Aqaba (the only port)
physical desert plateau in E; Rift valley separates E and W banks of the river Jordan
features lowest point on Earth below sea level in the Dead Sea (–1,299 ft/–396 m); archeological sites at Jerash and Petra
head of state King Hussein ibn Talai from 1952
head of government Mudar Badran from 1989
political system constitutional monarchy
political parties none (banned 1976)
exports potash, phosphates, citrus, vegetables
currency Jordanian dinar
population (1990 est) 3,065,000 (including Palestinian refugees); West Bank (1988) 866,000; growth rate 3.6% p.a.
life expectancy men 67, women 71
language Arabic (official); English
religion Sunni Muslim 92%, Christian 8%
literacy 71% (1988)
GDP $4.3 bn (1987); $1,127 per head (1988)
chronology
1946 Independence achieved from Britain as Transjordan.
1949 New state of Jordan declared.
1953 Hussein ibn Talai became king of Jordan.
1958 Jordan and Iraq formed Arab Federation that ended when the Iraqi monarchy was deposed.
1976 Lower house dissolved, elections postponed until further notice.
1982 Hussein tried to mediate in Arab-Israeli conflict.
1984 Women voted for the first time.
1985 Hussein put forward framework for Middle East peace settlement. Secret meeting between Hussein and Israeli prime minister.
1988 Hussein announced a decision to cease administering the West Bank as part of Jordan, passing responsibility to Palestine Liberation Organization, and the suspension of parliament.
1989 Prime minister Zaid al-Rifai resigned; Hussein promised new parliamentary elections following criticism of economic policies. Riots over price increases up to 50% following fall in oil revenues. 80-member parliament elected and Mudar Badran appointed prime minister. First parliamentary elections for 22 years; Muslim Brotherhood won 25 of 80 seats but exiled from government; martial law provisions lifted.
1990 Hussein unsuccessfully tried to mediate after Iraq's invasion of Kuwait. Massive refugee problems as thousands fled to Jordan from Kuwait and Iraq.
1991 Ban on political parties removed. 24 years of martial law lifted.

throne at the age of 17 upon the mental incapacity of his father. In 1958 Jordan and Iraq formed an Arab Federation, which ended five months later when the Iraqi monarchy was overthrown.

King Hussein has survived many upheavals in his own country and neighboring states, including attempts on his life, and has kept control of Jordan's affairs as well as playing a central role in Middle East affairs. Relations with his neighbors have fluctuated, but he has generally been a moderating influence. After Israel's invasion of Lebanon in 1982, Hussein played a key role in attempts to bring peace to the area, establishing a relationship with ◊Palestine Liberation Organization (PLO) leader, Yasser ◊Arafat. By 1984 the Arab world was split into two camps, with the moderates represented by Jordan, Egypt, and Arafat's PLO, and the militant radicals by Syria, Libya, and the rebel wing of the PLO. In 1985 Hussein and Arafat put together a framework for a Middle East peace settlement. It would involve bringing together all interested parties, including the PLO, but Israel objected to the PLO representation. Further progress was hampered by the PLO's alleged complicity in a number of guerrilla operations in that year. Hussein tried to revive the search for peace by secretly meeting the Israeli prime minister in France and persuading Yasser Arafat to renounce publicly PLO violence in territories not occupied by Israel. The role of Jordan, through King Hussein, could be vital in any future peacemaking moves. Jordan attended the historic Middle East peace conference in Spain in Nov 1991.

In response to mounting unrest within Jordan in 1989, Hussein promised greater democratization and in Nov elections to an 80-member parliament were held. Soon afterward the veteran politician Mudar Badran was made prime minister; he announced the lifting of martial law Dec 1989.

Following the Iraqi invasion and annexation of Kuwait in Aug 1990, under popular pressure from his own country, Hussein unsuccessfully attempted to act as a mediator. Meanwhile the UN trade embargo on Iraq and the exodus of thousands of refugees into Jordan strained Jordan's resources. Jordan attended the historic Middle East peace conference in Spain in Nov 1991.

Jörgensen Jörgen 1779–1845. Danish sailor who in 1809 seized control of Iceland, announcing it was under the protection of England. His brief reign of corruption ended later the same year when he was captured by an English naval ship and taken to London, where he was imprisoned.

Joseph in the New Testament, the husband of the Virgin Mary, a descendant of King David of the Tribe of Judah, and a carpenter by trade. Although Jesus was not the son of Joseph, Joseph was his legal father. According to Roman Catholic tradition, he had a family by a previous wife and was an elderly man when he married Mary.

Joseph in the Old Testament, the 11th and favorite son of ◊Jacob, sold into Egypt by his jealous half-brothers. After he had risen to power there, they and his father joined him to escape from famine in Canaan.

Joseph Chief c. 1840–1904. Nez Percé leader. Born in the Wallowa Valley of Oregon, Joseph was the son of a Nez Percé leader who resisted territorial encroachment by the US government. At his father's death in 1873, Joseph assumed the title of chief. Although he advocated passive resistance, initially agreeing to leave tribal lands 1877, Joseph later led his people in armed resistance to General Oliver Howard. After a defeat in Idaho, Joseph ordered a mass retreat to Canada, but the Nez Percé were soon caught by General Nelson Miles. Sent at first to the Indian Territory in Oklahoma, they were transferred to the Colville Reservation in Washington 1885.

Joseph Père. Religious name of Francis Le Clerc du Tremblay 1577–1638. French Catholic Capuchin monk. He was the influential secretary and agent to Louis XIII's chief minister Cardinal Richelieu, and nicknamed *"L'Eminence Grise"* (The Gray Eminence) in reference to his gray habit.

Josephine *A portrait of France's Empress Josephine at La Malmaison, her favorite residence, which Napoleon gave her after their divorce.*

Joseph two Holy Roman emperors:

Joseph I 1678–1711. Holy Roman emperor from 1705 and king of Austria, of the house of Hapsburg. He spent most of his reign involved in fighting the War of the ◊Spanish Succession.

Joseph II 1741–1790. Holy Roman emperor from 1765, son of Francis I (1708–1765). The reforms he carried out after the death of his mother, ◊Maria Theresa, in 1780, provoked revolts from those who lost privileges.

Josephine Marie Josèphe Rose Tascher de la Pagerie 1763–1814. As wife of ◊Napoleon Bonaparte, she was empress of France 1796–1809. Born on Martinique, she married in 1779 Alexandre de ◊Beauharnais, who played a part in the French Revolution, and in 1796 Napoleon, who divorced her in 1809 because she had not produced children.

Joseph of Arimathaea, St 1st century AD. In the New Testament, a wealthy Hebrew, member of the Sanhedrin (supreme court), and secret supporter of Jesus. On the evening of the Crucifixion he asked the Roman procurator Pilate for Jesus' body and buried it in his own tomb. Feast day Mar 17.

Josephson Brian 1940– . British physicist, a leading authority on superconductivity. In 1973 he shared a Nobel Prize for his theoretical predictions of the properties of a supercurrent through a tunnel barrier.

Josephson junction a device used in "superchips" (large and complex integrated circuits) to speed the passage of signals by a phenomenon called "electron tunneling." Although these superchips respond a thousand times faster than the ◊silicon chip, they have the disadvantage that the components of the Josephson junctions operate only at temperatures close to ◊absolute zero. They are named after Brian Josephson.

Josephus Flavius AD 37–c. 100. Jewish historian and general, born in Jerusalem. He became a Pharisee and commanded the Jewish forces in Galilee in their revolt against Rome from AD 66 (which ended with the mass suicide at Masada). When captured, he gained the favor of the Roman emperor Vespasian and settled in Rome as a citizen. He wrote *Antiquities of the Jews*, an early history to AD 66; *The Jewish War*; and an autobiography.

Joshua 13th century BC. In the Old Testament, successor of Moses, who led the Jews in their return to and conquest of the land of Canaan. The city of Jericho was the first to fall: according to the Book of Joshua, the walls crumbled to the blast of his trumpets.

Josiah c. 647–609 BC. King of Judah. Grandson of Manasseh and son of Amon, he succeeded to the throne at the age of eight. The discovery of a Book of Instruction (probably Deuteronomy, a book of the Old Testament) during repairs of the Temple in 621 BC stimulated thorough reform, which included the removal of all sanctuaries except that of Jerusalem. He was killed in a clash at ◊Megiddo with Pharaoh-nechoh, king of Egypt.

Josquin Desprez or des Prés 1440–1521. Franco-Flemish composer. His music combines a technical mastery with the feeling for words that became a hallmark of Renaissance vocal music. His works, which include 18 masses, over 100 motets, and secular vocal works, are characterized by their vitality and depth of feeling.

jota a traditional northern Spanish dance in lively triple time for one or more couples who play the castanets, accompanied by guitar and singing. There is a *jota* in de ◊Falla's *The Three-Cornered Hat.*

Jotunheim mountainous region of S Norway, containing the highest mountains in Scandinavia, Glittertind (8,048 ft/2,453 m) and Galdhöpiggen (8,097 ft/2,468 m). In Norse mythology it is the home of the giants.

Joubert Petrus Jacobus 1831–1900. Boer general in South Africa. He opposed British annexation of the Transvaal 1877, proclaimed its independence 1880, led the Boer forces in the First ◊South African War against the British 1880–81, defeated ◊Jameson 1896, and fought in the Boer War.

joule SI unit (abbreviation J) of work and energy, replacing the ◊calorie (one joule equals 4.2 calories).

It is defined as the work done (energy transferred) by a force of one newton acting over one meter and equal to 10^7 ergs. It can also be expressed as the work done in one second by a current of one ampere at a potential difference of one volt. One ◊watt is equal to one joule per second.

Joule James Prescott 1818–1889. British physicist whose work on the relations among electrical, mechanical, and chemical effects led to the discovery of the first law of ◊thermodynamics.

He determined the mechanical equivalent of heat (Joule's equivalent), and the SI unit of energy, the ◊joule, is named after him.

Joule–Thomson effect in physics, the fall in temperature of a gas as it expands adiabatically (without loss or gain of heat to the system) through a narrow jet. It can be felt when, for example, compressed air escapes through the valve of an inflated bicycle tire. Only hydrogen does not exhibit the effect. It is the basic principle of most refrigerators.

Jounieh a port on the Mediterranean coast of Lebanon, 9 mi/15 km north of Beirut. The center of an anti-Syrian Christian enclave.

journalism the profession of reporting, photographing, or editing news events for the mass media: newspapers, magazines, radio, television, documentary films, and newsreels.

Professional bodies include the ANG (American Newspaper Group) in the US and the NUJ (National Union of Journalists) in the UK. Standards are set by awards, such as those founded by J ◊Pulitzer.

journeyman in Britain, a man who served his apprenticeship in a trade and worked as a fully qualified employee. The term originated in the regulations of the medieval trade ◊guilds; it derives from the French *journée* (a day) because journeymen were paid daily.

Each guild normally recognised three grades of worker—apprentices, journeymen, and masters. As a qualified tradesman, a journeyman might have become a master with his own business but most remained employees.

Jovian 331–364. Roman emperor from 363. Captain

Joyce *Irish writer James Joyce, whose "stream of consciousness" technique revolutionized the novel.*

of the imperial bodyguard, he was chosen as emperor by the troops after ◊Julian's death in battle with the Persians. He concluded an unpopular peace and restored Christianity as the state religion.

Joyce James (Augustine Aloysius) 1882–1941. Irish writer, born in Dublin, who revolutionized the form of the English novel with his "stream of consciousness" technique. His works include *Dubliners* 1914 (short stories), *Portrait of the Artist as a Young Man* 1916, *Ulysses* 1922, and *Finnegans Wake* 1939.

Ulysses, which records the events of a single Dublin day, experiments with language and mingles direct narrative with the unspoken and unconscious reactions of the characters. Banned at first for obscenity in the US and England, it enjoyed great impact. *Finnegans Wake* continued Joyce's experiments with language, attempting a synthesis of all existence.

joystick in computing, an input device that signals to a computer the direction and extent of displacement of a hand-held lever. It is similar to the joystick used to control the flight of an aircraft.

Often used to control the movement of a cursor (marker) on a ◊VDT, joysticks allow fast and direct input for moving predetermined specific shapes or icons in computer games.

JP abbreviation for ◊justice of the peace.

Juan Carlos 1938– . King of Spain. The son of Don Juan, pretender to the Spanish throne, he married in 1962 Princess Sofia, eldest daughter of King Paul of Greece. In 1969 he was nominated by ◊Franco to succeed on the restoration of the monarchy intended to follow Franco's death; his father was excluded because of his known liberal views. Juan Carlos became king in 1975 and has sought to steer his country from dictatorship to democracy.

Juan Carlos *King of Spain Juan Carlos, who succeeded General Franco in 1975 and has since supervised the country's return to democracy and membership of the European Community.*

Juan Fernández Islands three small volcanic Pacific islands belonging to Chile; almost uninhabited. The largest is Más-a-Tierra (also sometimes called Juan Fernández Island), where Alexander Selkirk was marooned 1704–09. The islands were named after the Spanish navigator who reached them in 1563.

Juárez Benito 1806–1872. Mexican politician, president 1861–64 and 1867–72. In 1861 he suspended repayments of Mexico's foreign debts, which prompted a joint French, British, and Spanish expedition to exert pressure. French forces invaded and created an empire for ◊Maximilian, brother of the Austrian emperor. After their withdrawal in 1867, Maximilian was executed, and Juárez returned to the presidency.

He won popularity for nationalizing church property in his first year in office. He was the first Indian (non-Spanish) president of Mexico.

Juba river in E Africa, formed at Dolo, Ethiopia, by the junction of the Ganale Dorya and Dawa rivers. It flows south for about 550 mi/885 km through the Somali Republic (of which its valley is the most productive area) into the Indian Ocean.

Juba capital of Equatoria province, Sudan Republic; situated on the left bank of the White Nile, at the head of navigation above Khartoum, 750 mi/1,200 km to the north; population (1973) 56,700.

Jubbulpore alternate name for the city of ◊Jabalpur in India.

Judah or ***Judea*** district of S Palestine. After the death of King Solomon 937 BC, Judah adhered to his son Rehoboam and the Davidic line, whereas the rest of Israel elected Jeroboam as ruler of the northern kingdom. In New Testament times, Judah was the Roman province of Judea, and in current Israeli usage it refers to the southern area of the West Bank.

Judah Ha-Nasi "the Prince" c. AD 135–c. 220. Jewish scholar who with a number of colleagues edited the collection of writings known as the *Mishna*, which formed the basis of the ◊*Talmud*, in the 2nd century AD.

Judaism the religion of the ancient Hebrews and their descendants, the Jews, based, according to the Old Testament, on a covenant between God and Abraham about 2000 BC, and the renewal of the covenant with Moses about 1200 BC. It rests on the concept of one eternal invisible God, whose will is revealed in the *Torah* and who has a special relationship with the Jewish people. The Torah comprises the first five books of the Bible (the Pentateuch), which contains the history, laws, and guide to life for correct behavior. Besides those living in Israel, there are large Jewish populations today in the US, the USSR, the UK and Commonwealth nations, and in Jewish communities throughout the world. There are approximately 18 million Jews, with about 9 million in the Americas, 5 million in Europe, and 4 million in Asia, Africa, and the Pacific.

scriptures The *Talmud* combines the *Mishna*, rabbinical commentary on the law handed down orally from AD 70 and put in writing about 200, and the *Gemara*, legal discussions in the schools of Palestine and Babylon from the 3rd and 4th centuries. The *Haggadah* is a part of the Talmud dealing with stories of heroes. The *Midrash* is a collection of commentaries on the scriptures written AD 400–1200, mainly in Palestine.

observances The *synagogue* (in US non-Orthodox usage, temple) is the local building for congregational worship (originally simply the place where the Torah was read and expounded); its characteristic feature is the Ark, the enclosure where the Torah scrolls are kept. *Rabbis* are ordained teachers schooled in the Jewish law and ritual who act as spiritual leaders and pastors of their communities; some devote themselves to study. Religious practices include: circumcision, daily services in Hebrew, observance of the *Sabbath* (sunset on Friday to sunset Saturday) as a day of rest, and, among Orthodox Jews, strict dietary laws (see ◊kosher). High holy days include *Rosh Hashanah* marking the Jewish New Year (first new moon after the autumn equinox) and, a week later, the religious fast *Yom Kippur* (Day of Atonement). Other vacations are celebrated throughout the year to commemorate various events of Biblical history.

divisions There are a number of groups within Judaism. Orthodox Jews assert the supreme authority of the Torah and adhere to all the traditions of Judaism, including the strict dietary laws (see ◊kosher) and the segregation of women in the synagogue. Reform Judaism rejects the idea that Jews are the chosen people, has a liberal interpretation of the dietary laws, and takes a critical attitude toward the Torah. Conservative Judaism is a compromise between Orthodox and Reform in its acceptance of the traditional law, making some allowances for modern conditions, although its services and ceremonies are closer to Orthodox than to Reform. Liberal Judaism, or Recontructionism, goes further than Reform in attempting to adapt Judaism to the needs of the modern world and to interpret the Torah in the light of current scholarship. In all the groups except Orthodox, women are not segregated in the synagogue, and there are female rabbis in both Reform and Liberal Judaism. In the 20th century many people who call themselves Jews prefer to identify Judaism with a historical and cultural tradition rather than with strict religious observance, and a contemporary debate (complicated by the history of non-Jewish attitudes toward Jews) centers on the question of how to define a Jew. As in other religions, fundamentalist movements have emerged, for example, Gush Emunim.

history

c. 2000 BC Led by Abraham of Ur, the ancient Hebrews emigrated from Mesopotamia to Canaan (Palestine).

18th century–1580 Some settled on the borders of Egypt and were put to forced labor in Egypt.

13th century They were rescued by Moses, who aimed at their return to Palestine. Moses received the Ten Commandments from God and brought them to the people. The main invasion of Canaan was led by Joshua about 1274.

12th–11th centuries During the period of Judges, ascendancy was established over the Canaanites.

c. 1000 Complete conquest of Palestine and the union of all Judea was achieved under David, and Jerusalem became the capital.

10th century Solomon succeeded David and enjoyed a reputation for great wealth and wisdom; but his lack of a constructive policy led, after his death, to the secession of the north of Judea (Israel) under Jeroboam, with only the tribe of Judah remaining under the house of David as the southern kingdom of Judah.

9th–8th centuries Assyria became the dominant power in the Near East. Israel purchased safety by tribute, but the basis of the society had become corrupt, and prophets such as Amos, Isaiah, and Micah predicted destruction. At the hands of Tiglathpileser and his successor Shalmaneser IV, the northern kingdom (Israel) was made into Assyrian provinces after the fall of Samaria 721, although the southern kingdom of Judah was spared as an ally.

586–458 Nebuchadnezzar took Jerusalem and carried off the major part of the population to Babylon. Judaism was retained during exile, and was reconstituted by Ezra on the return to Jerusalem.

520 The Temple, originally built by Solomon, was restored.

c. 444 Ezra promulgated the legal code that was

to govern the future of the Jewish people.

4th–3rd centuries After the conquest of the Persian Empire by Alexander the Great, the Syrian Seleucid rulers and the Egyptian Ptolemaic dynasty struggled for Palestine, which came under the government of Egypt, although with a large measure of freedom.

2nd century With the advance of Syrian power, Antiochus IV attempted intervention in the internal quarrels of the Hebrews, even desecrating the Temple, and a revolt broke out 165 led by the Maccabee family.

63 Judea's near-independence ended when internal dissension caused the Roman general Pompey to intervene, and Roman suzerainty was established.

1st century AD A revolt led to the destruction of the Temple 66–70 by the Roman emperor Titus. Judean national sentiment was encouraged by the work of Rabbi Johanan ben Zakkai (c. 20–90), and following him the president of the Sanhedrin (supreme court) was recognized as the patriarch of Palestinian Jewry.

2nd–3rd centuries AD Greatest of the Sanhedrin presidents was Rabbi Judah (c. 135–220), who codified the traditional law in the *Mishna*. The Palestinian Talmud (c. 375) added the *Gemara* to the *Mishna*.

4th–5th centuries The intellectual leadership of Judaism passed to the descendants of the 6th-century exiles in Babylonia, who compiled the Babylonian Talmud.

8th–13th centuries Judaism enjoyed a golden era, producing the philosopher Saadiah, the poet Jehudah Ha-levi (c. 1075–1141), the codifier Moses Maimonides, and others.

14th–17th centuries Where Christianity became the dominant or state religion, the Jews were increasingly segregated from mainstream life and trade by the Inquisition, anti-Semitic legislation, or by explusion. The Protestant and Islamic states, and their colonies, allowed for refuge. Persecution led to messianic hopes strengthened by the 16-century revival of Kabbalism, culminating in the messianic movement of Shabbatai Sevi in the 17th century.

18th–19th centuries Outbreaks of persecution increased with the rise of European nationalism. Reform Judaism, a rejection of religious orthodoxy and an attempt to interpret it for modern times, began in Germany 1810 and soon was established in England and the US. In the late 19th century, large numbers of Jews fleeing persecution (◊pogrom) in Russia and E Europe emigrated to the US, leading to the development of large Orthodox, Conservative, and Reform communities there. Many became Americanized and lost interest in religion. The European Zionist movement convened the first World Zionist Congress 1897, in Basel, Switzerland.

20th century Zionism became dedicated to achieving a secure homeland where Jewish people would be free from persecution; this led to the establishment of the State of Israel 1948. Liberal Judaism (more radical than Reform) developed in the US. In 1911 the first synagogue in the UK was founded.

Although the Nazi German regime 1933–45 exterminated 6 million European Jews, hundreds of thousands of survivors went to Palestine to form the nucleus of the new State of Israel, to the US, and to other nations. Although most Israeli and American Jews were not affiliated with synagogues after the 1950s, they continued to affirm their Jewish heritage. Both Orthodox and Hasidic Judaism, however, flourished in their new homes and grew rapidly in the 1970s and 1980s.

Judas Iscariot 1st century AD. In the New Testament, the disciple who betrayed Jesus Christ. Judas was the treasurer of the group. At the last Passover supper, which was a Passover seder, he arranged, for 30 pieces of silver, to point out Jesus to the chief priests so that they could arrest him. Afterward, Judas was overcome with remorse and committed suicide.

Jude, St 1st century AD. Supposed half-brother of Jesus and writer of the Epistle of Jude in the New Testament; patron saint of lost causes. Feast day Oct 28.

Judea southern division of ancient Palestine, see ◊Judah.

judge a person invested with power to hear and determine legal disputes.

In the US, the federal judiciary is chosen by executive appointments. It consists of Supreme Court justices, judges of the US district courts, magistrates, and administrative law judges. Similar offices exist at the state level with judges elected or appointed. There are also county and municipal judges elected to office.

Judges a book of the Old Testament, describing the history of the Israelites from the death of Joshua to the reign of Saul, under the command of several leaders known as Judges (who deliver the people from repeated oppression).

judicial review in the US, the power of a court to decide whether legislative acts or executive actions are constitutional. The ultimate authority for judicial review is the Supreme Court, which established its right to review executive and legislative actions in the ◊Marbury v Madison decision.

judicial separation an action in a court by either husband or wife, in which it is not necessary to prove an irreconcilable breakdown of a marriage, but in which the grounds are otherwise the same as for divorce. It does not end a marriage, but a declaration may be obtained that the complainant need no longer cohabit with the defendant. The court can make similar orders to a divorce court in relation to custody and support of children and maintenance.

Judith in Biblical legend, a Jewish widow, the heroine of Bethulia, who saved her community from a Babylonian siege by killing the enemy general, Holofernes. The Book of Judith is part of the Apocrypha, a section of the Old Testament.

Judith approached Holofernes on the pretext of betraying the besieged Jews. Charming him with her beauty and wit, she made him drunk and cut his head off. Showing it to her countrymen incited them to attack and rout the army of ◊Nebuchadnezzar.

Judith of Bavaria 800–843. Empress of the French. The wife of ◊Louis the Pious (Louis I of France) from 819, she exercised power over her husband to the benefit of their son Charles the Bold.

judo (Japanese *jū do*, "gentle way") a type of wrestling of Japanese origin. The two combatants wear loose-fitting, belted jackets and trousers to facilitate holds, and falls are broken by a square mat; when one has established a painful hold that the other cannot break, the latter signifies surrender by slapping the ground with a free hand. Degrees of proficiency are indicated by the color of the belt: for novices white; after examination brown (three degrees); and finally black (nine degrees).

Judo is a synthesis of the most valuable methods from the many forms of jujitsu, the traditional Japanese skill of self-defense and offense without weapons, which was originally practiced as a secret art by the feudal samurai. Today, judo has been adopted throughout the world in the armed forces, the police, and in many schools. It became an Olympic sport 1964. The world championships were first held in 1956 and are now contested biennially.

Judson Edward Zane Carroll 1823–1886. US author. Better known by his pen name "Ned Buntline," Judson was born in Stamford, New York, served in the US Navy, and became an editor and writer in Cincinnati. Specializing in short adventure stories, he developed a stereotyped frontier hero in the pages of his own periodical, *Ned Buntline's Magazine*. Moving to New York, he established *Buntline's Own* and continued in the same literary vein.

A violent racist, Judson was one of the founders of the antiforeign "Know-Nothing" party in the 1850s. In his dime novels in the 1870s, he immortalized Buffalo Bill Cody.

Juggernaut or ***Jagannath*** a name for Vishnu, the Hindu god, meaning "Lord of the World." His temple is in Puri, Orissa, India. A statue of the god, dating from about 318, is annually carried in procession on a large vehicle (hence the word "juggernaut"). Devotees formerly threw themselves beneath its wheels.

Jugoslavia alternate spelling of ◊Yugoslavia.

jugular vein one of two veins in the necks of vertebrates; they return blood from the head to the superior (or anterior) vena cava and thence to the heart.

Jugurtha died 104 BC. King of Numidia, N Africa, who, after a long resistance, was betrayed to the Romans in 107 BC, and put to death.

jujitsu or ***jiujitsu*** traditional Japanese form of self-defense; see ◊judo.

jujube tree of the genus *Zizyphus* of the buckthorn family Thamnaceae, with berrylike fruits.

The common jujube *Z. jujuba* of Asia, Africa, and Australia, cultivated in S Europe and California, has fruit the size of small plums, known as Chinese dates when preserved in syrup.

Julian the Apostate c. 331–363. Roman emperor. Born in Constantinople, the nephew of Constantine the Great, he was brought up as a Christian but early in life became a convert to paganism. Sent by Constantius to govern Gaul in 355, he was proclaimed emperor by his troops in 360, and in 361 was marching on Constantinople when the death of Constantius allowed a peaceful succession. He revived pagan worship and refused to persecute heretics. He was killed in battle against the Persians.

Juliana 1909– . Queen of the Netherlands. The daughter of Queen Wilhelmina (1880–1962), she married Prince Bernhard of Lippe-Biesterfeld in 1937 and ruled 1948–80, when she abdicated and was succeeded by her daughter ◊Beatrix.

Julius II 1443–1513. Pope 1503–13. A politician who wanted to make the Papal States the leading power in Italy, he formed international alliances first against Venice and then against France. He began the building of St Peter's Church in Rome 1506 and was the patron of the artists Michelangelo and Raphael.

July Revolution uprising July 27–29, 1830 in France that overthrew the restored Bourbon monarchy of Charles X and substituted the constitutional monarchy of Louis Philippe, whose rule (1830–48) is sometimes referred to as the July Monarchy.

jumbo jet popular name for a generation of huge wide-bodied airliners including the Boeing 747, which is 232 ft/71 m long, has a wingspan of 196 ft/60 m, a maximum takeoff weight of nearly 400 tons/380 tonnes, and can carry more than 400 passengers.

Jumna or ***Yamuna*** river in India, 860 mi/1,385 km

***Jung** Swiss psychiatrist and pioneer psychoanalyst Carl Jung.*

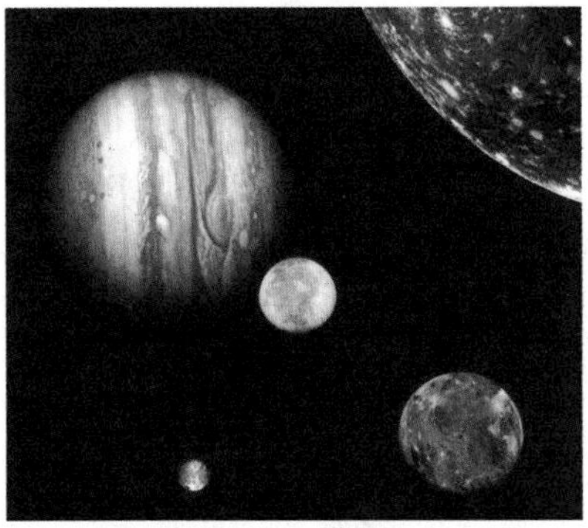

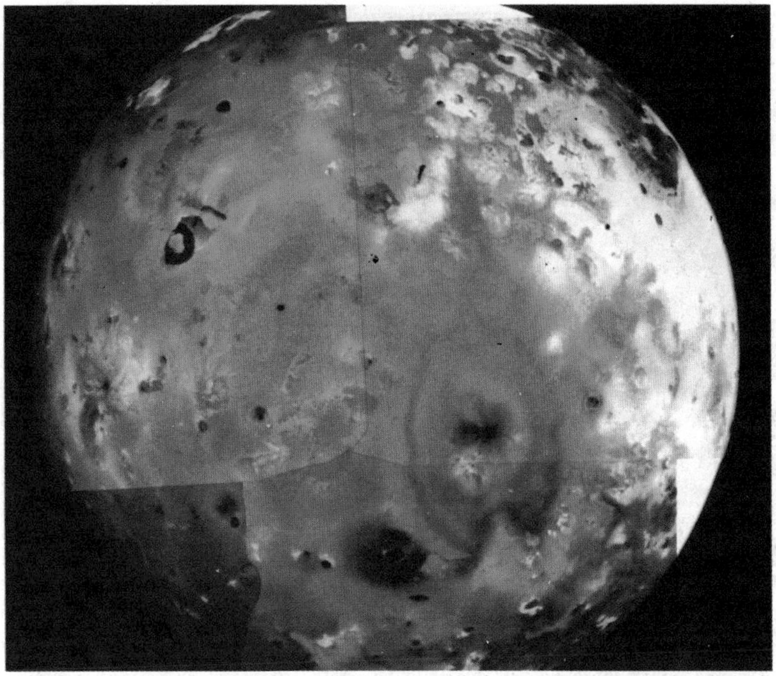

Jupiter *(Above) Jupiter, the largest planet in the solar system, together with four of its moons: Io, Europa, Ganymede, and Calisto. (Right) False-color mosaic of Io, the innermost satellite of Jupiter, from the Voyager probes. A range of colors and much volcanic activity can be seen on the surface.*

in length, rising in the Himalayas, in Uttar Pradesh, and joining the river Ganges near Allahabad, where it forms a sacred bathing place. Agra and Delhi are also on its course.

jumping hare or ***springhare*** either of two African species of long-eared rodents of the only genus (*Pedetes*) in the family Pedetidae. The springhare *P. capensis* is about 16 in/40 cm long and resembles a small kangaroo with a bushy tail. It inhabits dry sandy country in E central Africa.

Juneau ice-free port and state capital of Alaska, on Gastineau Channel in the S Alaska panhandle; population (1980) 19,528. Juneau is the commercial and distribution center for the fur-trading and mining industries of the Panhandle region; also important are salmon fishing, fish processing, and lumbering. A campus of the University of Alaska is here. Settled in 1880 by gold prospectors, Juneau was named the capital in 1900. In 1970 its boundaries were extended to cover 2,406 sq mi/ 6,232 sq km.

juneberry or ***serviceberry*** any tree or shrub of the genus *Amelanchier* of the rose family, having simple leaves, showy white flowers, and purple-black fruits. The Allegheny serviceberry *Amelanchier lavis*, native to the NE US, grows to a height of 40 ft/12 m and has edible fruit. Several species are grown as ornamentals.

Jung Carl Gustav 1875–1961. Swiss psychiatrist who collaborated with Sigmund ◊Freud until their disagreement in 1912 over the importance of sexuality in causing psychological problems. Jung studied religion and dream symbolism, saw the unconscious as a source of spiritual insight, and distinguished between introversion and extroversion. His books include *Modern Man in Search of a Soul* 1933.

Jungfrau (German "maiden") mountain in the Bernese Oberland, Switzerland; 13,669 ft/ 4,166 m high. A railroad ascends to the plateau of the Jungfraujoch, 11,340 ft/3,456 m, where there is a winter sports center.

jungle popular name for ◊rainforest.

juniper aromatic evergreen tree or shrub of the genus *Juniperus* of the cypress family Cupressaceae, found throughout temperate regions. Its berries are used to flavor gin. Some junipers are erroneously called ◊cedars.

junk bond derogatory term for a type of security that is officially rated as "below investment grade." Such bonds are issued to raise large amounts of capital in a short period, typically to finance a takeover. Junk bonds have a high yield, but are a high-risk investment. In the US securities market, junk bonds probably diminish since they must now pay an average of more than 5% more than the prevailing treasury bond rate in order to attract investors. Studies suggest that more than 35% of junk-bond issues may default.

Junker member of the landed aristocracy in Prussia; favored by Frederick the Great and ◊Bismarck, they controlled land, industry, trade, and the army, and exhibited privilege and arrogance. From the 15th century until the 1930s they were the source of most of the Prussian civil service and officer corps.

Junkers Hugo 1859–1935. German airplane designer. In 1919 he founded in Dessau the aircraft works named after him. Junkers planes, including dive bombers, night fighters, and troop carriers, were used by the Germans in World War II.

Juno principal goddess in Roman mythology (identified with the Greek Hera). The wife of Jupiter, the queen of heaven, she was concerned with all aspects of women's lives.

Jupiter the fifth planet from the Sun and the largest in the Solar System (equatorial diameter 88,700 mi/142,800 km), with a mass more than twice that of all the other planets combined, 318 times that of the Earth's. It takes 11.86 years to orbit the Sun, at an average distance of 484 million mi/778 million km, and has at least 16 moons. It is largely composed of hydrogen and helium, liquefied by pressure in its interior, and probably with a rocky core larger than the Earth. Its main feature is the Great Red Spot, a cloud of rising gases, revolving counterclockwise, 8,500 mi/ 14,000 km wide and some 20,000 mi/30,000 km long.

Its visible surface consists of clouds of white ammonia crystals, drawn out into belts by the planet's high speed of rotation (9 hr 51 min at the equator, the fastest of any planet). Darker orange and brown clouds at lower levels may contain sulfur, as well as simple organic compounds. Further down still, temperatures are warm, a result of heat left over from Jupiter's formation, and it is this heat that drives the turbulent weather patterns of the planet. The Great Red Spot was first observed 1664. Its top is higher than the surrounding clouds; its color is thought to be due to red phosphorus. Jupiter's strong magnetic field gives rise to a large surrounding magnetic "shell," or magnetosphere, from which bursts of radio waves are detected. The Southern Equatorial Belt in which the Great Red Spot occurs is subject to unexplained fluctuation. In 1989 it sustained a dramatic and sudden fading. The four largest moons, Io, Europa, Ganymede, and Callisto, are the Galilean satellites, discovered in 1610 by Galileo (Ganymede is the largest moon in the Solar System). Three small moons were discovered in 1979 by the Voyager space probes, as was a faint ring of dust around Jupiter's equator, 34,000 mi/55,000 km above the cloud tops.

Jupiter or ***Jove*** in mythology, chief god of the Romans, identified with the Greek ◊Zeus. He was god of the sky, associated with lightning and thunderbolt; protector in battle; and bestower of victory. The son of Saturn, he married his sister Juno, and reigned on Mount Olympus as lord of heaven.

Jura island of the Inner Hebrides; area 147 sq mi/ 380 sq km; population (with Colonsay, 1971) 343. It is separated from Scotland by the Sound of Jura. The whirlpool Corryvreckan (Gaelic "Brecan's cauldron") is off the N coast.

Jura mountains series of parallel mountain ranges running SW–NE along the French-Swiss frontier between the rivers Rhône and Rhine, a distance of 156 mi/250 km. The highest peak is Crête de la Neige, 5,650 ft/1,723 m.

The mountains give their name to a *département* of France, and in 1979 a Jura canton was established in Switzerland, formed from the French-speaking areas of Berne.

Jurassic period of geologic time 213–144 million years ago; the middle period of the Mesozoic era. Climates worldwide were equable, creating forests of conifers and ferns, dinosaurs were abundant, birds evolved, and limestones and iron ores were deposited.

The name comes from the Jura mountains in France and Switzerland, where the rocks formed during this period were first studied.

In North America, the Nevadan ◊orogeny marked the beginning of the Sierra Nevadas and other mountains.

Jurgens Curt (Curd Jürgens) 1912–1982. German film and stage actor who was well established in his native country before moving into French and then Hollywood films in the 1960s. His films include *Operette/Operetta* 1940, *Et Dieu Créa la Femme/And God Created Woman* 1956, *Lord Jim* 1965, and *The Spy Who Loved Me* 1977.

jurisprudence the science of law in the abstract—that is, not the study of any particular laws or legal system, but of the principles upon which legal systems are founded.

jury a body of lay people (usually 12, sometimes 6)

Jurassic *Contorted Jurassic limestone strata in Jura, Switzerland.*

sworn to reach a verdict in a court of law. Juries, used mainly in English-speaking countries, are implemented primarily in criminal cases, but also sometimes in civil cases. The members of the jury are carefully selected by both prosecution and defense attorneys.

The British jury derived from Germanic custom. It was introduced into England by the Normans. Originally it was a body of neighbors who gave their opinion on the basis of being familiar with the protagonists and background of a case. Eventually it developed into an impartial panel, giving a verdict based solely on evidence heard in court. The jury's duty is to decide the facts of a case: the judge directs them on matters of law.

The basic principles of the British system have been adopted in the US, most Commonwealth countries, and some European countries (for example, France). Grand juries are still used in the US at both state and federal levels to decide whether there is a case to be referred for trial.

justice of the peace in some states, a public officer (magistrate), usually elected, with limited jurisdiction over a small district or part of a county. This includes the authority to try minor criminal cases, administer oaths, and officiate marriages.

justiciar the chief justice minister of Norman and early Angevin kings, second in power only to the king. By 1265, the government had been divided into various departments, such as the Exchequer and Chancery, which meant that it was no longer desirable to have one official in charge of all.

Justinian I 483–565. Byzantine emperor from 527. He recovered N Africa from the Vandals, SE Spain from the Visigoths, and Italy from the Ostrogoths, largely owing to his great general Belisarius. He ordered the codification of Roman law, which has influenced European jurisprudence.

Justinian, born in Illyria, was associated with his uncle, Justin I, in the government from 518. He married the actress Theodora, and succeeded Justin in 527. Much of his reign was taken up by an indecisive struggle with the Persians. He built the church of Sta Sophia in Constantinople and closed the university in Athens in 529.

Justin St c. 100–c. 163. One of the early Christian leaders and writers known as the Fathers of the Church. Born in Palestine of a Greek family, he was converted to Christianity and wrote two *Apologies* in its defense. He spent the rest of his life as an itinerant missionary, and was martyred in Rome. Feast day June 1.

Jute member of a Germanic people who originated in Jutland but later settled in Frankish territory. They occupied Kent, SE England, about 450, according to tradition under Hengist and Horsa, and conquered the Isle of Wight and the opposite coast of Hampshire in the early 6th century.

jute fiber obtained from two plants of the genus *Corchorus* of the linden family: *C. capsularis* and *C. olitorius*. Jute is used for sacks and sacking, upholstery, webbing, twine, and stage canvas.

In the fabrication of bulk packaging and tufted carpet backing, it is now often replaced by synthetic polypropylene. The world's largest producer of jute is Bangladesh.

Jutland (Danish ***Jylland***) a peninsula of N Europe; area 11,400 sq mi/29,500 sq km. It is separated from Norway by the Skagerrak and from Sweden by the Kattegat, with the North Sea to the W. The larger northern part belongs to Denmark, the southern part to Germany.

Jutland, Battle of naval battle of World War I, fought between England and Germany on May 31, 1916, off the W coast of Jutland. Its outcome was indecisive, but the German fleet remained in port for the rest of the war.

Juvenal c. AD 60–140. Roman satirist and poet. His genius for satire brought him to the unfavorable notice of the emperor Domitian. Juvenal's 16 extant satires give an explicit and sometimes brutal picture of the decadent Roman society of his time.

juvenile delinquency offenses against the law that are committed by young people.

The American judicial system provides special status and treatment for juvenile offenders (the age limit varies according to jurisdiction). Their identities are protected and their records barred from public view. Judicial proceedings are less formal than those of criminal courts. Incarceration may not extend beyond a defendant's majority. Sentencing is tailored to the developmental needs of defendants and may consist of probation, counseling, community service, supervision, or placement in homes for youthful offenders.

Jylland Danish name for the mainland of Denmark, the N section of the Jutland peninsula. The chief towns are Aalborg, Aarhus, Esbjerg, Fredericia, Horsens, Kolding, Randers, and Vejle.

K2 or ***Chogori*** the second highest mountain above sea level, in the Karakoram range, on the border of China and Pakistan, height 29,061 ft/8,858 m (recently remeasured by satellite, significantly increasing its height from the former official height of 28,250 ft/8,611 m. When K2's new height was found to be higher than Everest's, ◊Everest was also remeasured and found to remain the world's highest at 29,108 ft/8,872 m). K2 was first climbed 1954 by an Italian expedition. The Godwin-Austen glacier near its base has caused K2 to be called, erroneously, Mount Godwin-Austen; it is named K2 since it was the second peak in the Karakorams to be surveyed (K1, K2, etc) and mapped.

Kaaba (Arabic "chamber") in Mecca, Saudi Arabia, the oblong building in the quadrangle of the Great Mosque, into the NE corner of which is built the Black Stone declared by the prophet Mohammed to have been given to Abraham by the archangel Gabriel, and revered by Muslims.

Kabardino-Balkar autonomous republic of the USSR, capital Nalchik; area 4,825 sq mi/12,500 sq km; population (1986) 724,000. Under Russian control from 1557, it was annexed 1827; it became an autonomous republic 1936.

kabbala or ***cabbala*** (Hebrew "tradition") ancient esoteric Jewish mystical tradition of philosophy containing strong elements of pantheism yet akin to neo-Platonism. Kabbalistic writing reached its peak between the 13th and 16th centuries. It is largely rejected by current Judaic thought as medieval superstition, but is basic to the ◊Hassid sect.

Among its earliest documents are the *Sefir Jezirah/The Book of Creation*, attributed to Rabbi Akiba (died 120). The *Zohar/Book of Light* was written in Aramaic in about the 13th century.

Kabinda part of Angola. See ◊Cabinda.

kabuki (Japanese "music, dance, skill") drama originating in late 16th-century Japan, drawing on ◊Nō, puppet plays, and folk dance. Its colorful, lively spectacle became popular in the 17th and 18th centuries. Kabuki actors specialize in particular characters, female impersonators being the biggest stars.

Kabuki was first popularized in Kyoto 1603 by the dancer Izumo Okuni who gave performances with a chiefly female troupe; from 1629 only men were allowed to act, in the interests of propriety. Unlike Nō actors, kabuki actors do not wear masks. The art was modernized and its following revived in the 1980s by Ennosuke III (1940–).

Kabul capital of Afghanistan, 6,900 ft/2,100 m above sea level, on the river Kabul; population (1984) 1,179,300. Products include textiles, plastics, leather, and glass. It commands the strategic routes to Pakistan via the ◊Khyber Pass.

Kabwe town in central Zambia (formerly Broken Hill); a mining industry (copper, cadmium, lead, and zinc); population (1980) 143,635.

Kabyle a member of a group of Berber tribes of Algeria and Tunisia. As ◊Zouave they served in the colonial French forces, although many were notable in the fight for Algerian independence.

Kádár János 1912–1989. Hungarian Communist leader, in power 1956–88, after suppressing the national uprising. As Hungarian Socialist Workers' Party (HSWP) leader and prime minister 1956–58 and 1961–65, Kádár introduced a series of market-Socialist economic reforms, while retaining cordial political relations with the USSR.

He was ousted as party general secretary May 1988 and forced into retirement May 1989.

Kaduna town in N Nigeria, on the Kaduna River; population (1983) 247,000. A market center for grain and cotton; industries include textiles, automobiles, timber, pottery, and oil refining.

Kaffir (Arabic *kāfir* "infidel") a South African English term, usually regarded as offensive, for a black person. It derives from the former designation used by various Bantu-speaking peoples, including the Xhosa and Pondo of Cape Province, living in much of SE Africa.

Kafka Franz 1883–1924. Czech novelist, born in Prague, who wrote in German. His three unfinished allegorical novels *Der Prozess/The Trial* 1925, *Der Schloss/The Castle* 1926, and *Amerika/America* 1927 were posthumously published despite his instructions that they should be destroyed. His short stories include "Die Verwandlung/The Metamorphosis" 1915, in which a man turns into a huge insect.

Kagoshima industrial city (Satsumayaki porcelain)

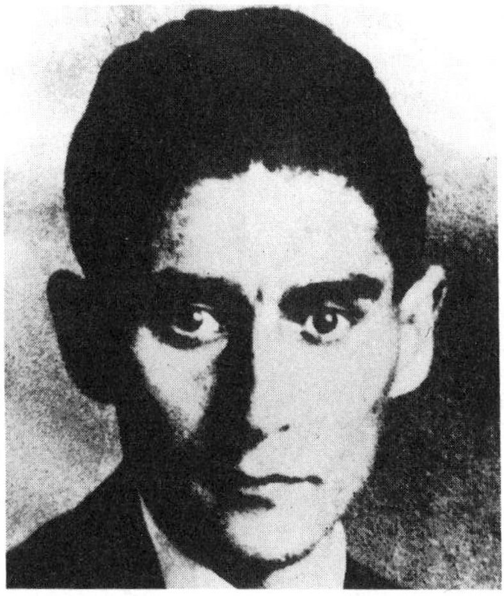

Kafka *Czech novelist Franz Kafka.*

Kaifu *Japanese conservative politician, prime minister from 1989, Toshiki Kaifu.*

and port on Kyushu Island, SW Japan; population (1987) 525,000.

kagu crested bird *Rhynochetos jubatus*, the only member of its family that is placed in the crane order (Gruiformes). It is found in New Caledonia. About 1.6 ft/50 cm long, it is virtually flightless and nests on the ground. The introduction of cats and dogs has endangered its survival.

Kahlo Frida 1907–1954. Mexican painter who mingled folk art with Classical and modern styles.

Kahn Aga, Islamic leader, see ◊Aga Kahn.

Kahn Louis 1901–1974. US architect, born in Estonia. A follower of Mies van der Rohe, he developed a Classically romantic style, in which functional "servant" areas, such as stairwells and air ducts, featured prominently, often as towerlike structures surrounding the main living and working, or "served," areas. His projects are characterized by an imaginative use of concrete and brick and include the Salk Institute for Biological Studies, La Jolla, California, and the British Art Center at Yale University.

Kaieteur waterfall on the river Potaro, a tributary of the Essequibo, Guyana. At 822 ft/250 m, it is five times as high as Niagara Falls.

Kaifeng former capital of China, 907–1127, and of Honan province; population (1984) 619,200. It has lost its importance because of the silting-up of the nearby Huang He river.

Kaifu Toshiki 1932– . Japanese conservative politician, prime minister 1989–91. A protégé of former premier Takeo Miki, he was selected as a compromise choice as Liberal Democratic Party president and prime minister in Aug 1989, following the resignation of Sosuke Uno.

Kaifu entered politics 1961, was deputy chief secretary 1974–76 in the Miki cabinet, and was education minister under Nakasone. He is a member of the minor Komoto faction. In 1987 he received what he claimed were legitimate political donations amounting to about $75,000 from a company later accused of bribing a number of LDP politicians (see ◊Recruit scandal). His popularity was dented by the unconstitutional proposal, defeated in the Diet, to contribute Japanese forces to the UN-coalition forces in the Persian Gulf area after Iraq's annexation of Kuwait 1990. His lack of power led to his replacement as prime minister 1991.

Kaikouras double range of mountains in the NE of South Island, New Zealand, separated by the Clarence River, and reaching 9,465 ft/2,885 m.

Kaingaroa forest NE of Lake Taupo in North Island, New Zealand, one of the world's largest planted forests.

Kairos in Greek mythology, the personification of Opportunity. He is portrayed in Greek art as bald at the back, but with long hair at the front.

Kairouan Muslim holy city in Tunisia, N Africa, S of Tunis; population (1984) 72,200. It is a center of carpet production. The city, said to have been founded AD 617, ranks after Mecca and Medina as a place of pilgrimage.

Kaiser title formerly used by the Holy Roman emperors, Austrian emperors 1806–1918, and German emperors 1871–1918. The word, like the Russian "tsar," is derived from the Latin *Caesar*.

Kaiser Georg 1878–1945. German playwright, the principal exponent of German ◊Expressionism. His large output includes *Die Bürger von Calais/The Burghers of Calais* 1914 and *Gas* 1918–20.

Kaiser Henry J 1882–1967. US industrialist. He developed steel and motor industries, and his shipbuilding firms became known for the mass production of vessels, including the "Liberty ships"—cheap, quickly produced, transport ships—built for the UK in World War II.

Kaiserslautern industrial town (textiles, cars) in Germany, in the Rhineland-Palatinate, 30 mi/48 km W of Mannheim; population (1978) 98,700. It dates from 882; the castle from which it gets its name was built by Frederick Barbarossa 1152 and destroyed by the French 1703.

Kakadu a national park E of Darwin in the Alligator Rivers Region of Arnhem Land, Northern Territory, Australia. Established in 1979, it overlies one of the richest uranium deposits in the world. As a result of this, it has become the focal point of controversy between conservationists and mining interests.

kakapo a nocturnal, flightless parrot *Strigops habroptilus* that lives in burrows in New Zealand. It is green, yellow, and brown and weighs up to 7.5 lb/3.5 kg. When in danger, its main defense is to keep quite still. Because of the introduction of predators such as dogs, cats, rats, and ferrets, it is in danger of extinction, there being only about 40 birds left.

Kalahari Desert semidesert area forming most of Botswana and extending into Namibia, Zimbabwe, and South Africa; area about 347,400 sq mi/900,000 sq km. The only permanent river, the Okavango, flows into a delta in the NW forming marshes rich in wildlife. Its inhabitants are the nomadic Bushmen.

Kalamazoo city in SW Michigan, on the Kalamazoo River, SW of Lansing; seat of Kalamazoo County. Its industries include the processing of the area's agricultural products, automobile and transportation machinery parts, chemicals, and metal and paper products; population (1990) 80,277. Kalamazoo is an Indian word for "boiling pot."

kale a type of ◊cabbage.

kaleidoscope optical toy invented by the British physicist David Brewster 1816. It usually consists of a pair of long mirrors at an angle to each other, and arranged inside a triangular tube containing pieces of colored glass, paper, or plastic. An axially symmetrical (hexagonal) pattern is seen by looking along the tube, which can be varied infinitely by rotating or shaking the tube.

Kalevala Finnish national epic poem compiled from legends and ballads by Elias Lönnrot in 1835; its hero is Väinamöinen, god of music and poetry.

Kalf Willem 1619–1693. Dutch painter, active in Amsterdam from 1653. He specialized in still lifes set off against a dark background.

These feature arrangements of glassware, polished metalwork, decorated porcelain, and fine carpets, with the occasional half-peeled lemon (a Dutch still-life motif).

Kalgan city in NE China, now known as ◊Zhangjiakou.

Kali in Hindu mythology, the goddess of destruction and death. She is the wife of ◊Siva.

Kālidāsa lived 5th century AD. Indian epic poet and dramatist. His works, in Sanskrit, include the classic drama *Sakuntala*, the love story of King Dushyanta and the nymph Sakuntala.

Kalimantan province of the republic of Indonesia occupying part of the island of Borneo
area 210,000 sq mi/543,900 sq km
cities Banjermasin and Balikpapan
physical mostly low-lying, with mountains in the North
products petroleum, rubber, coffee, copra, pepper, timber
population (1980) 6,723,086.

Kalinin formerly (until 1933) ***Tver*** city of the USSR, capital of Kalinin region, a transport center on the river Volga, 100 mi/160 km NW of Moscow; population (1987) 447,000. It was renamed in honor of President Kalinin.

Kalinin Mikhail Ivanovich 1875–1946. Soviet politician, founder of the newspaper *Pravda*. He was prominent in the 1917 October Revolution, and in 1919 became head of state (president of the Central Executive Committee of the Soviet government until 1937, then president of the Presidium of the Supreme Soviet until 1946).

Kaliningrad formerly ***Königsberg*** Baltic naval base in the USSR; population (1987) 394,000. Industries include engineering and paper. It was the capital of East Prussia until the latter was divided between the USSR and Poland 1945 under the Potsdam Agreement, when it was renamed in honor of President Kalinin.

Kali-Yuga in Hinduism, the last of the four *yugas* (ages) that make up one cycle of creation. The *Kali-Yuga*, in which Hindus believe we are now living, is characterized by wickedness and disaster, and leads up to the destruction of this world in preparation for a new creation and a new cycle of *yugas*.

Kalki in Hinduism, the last avatar (manifestation) of Vishnu, who will appear at the end of the Kali-Yuga, or final age of the world, to destroy it in readiness for a new creation.

Kalmar port on the SE coast of Sweden; population (1986) 55,000. Industries include paper, matches, and the Orrefors glassworks.

Kalmyk or ***Kalmuck*** autonomous republic in central USSR, on the Caspian Sea; area 29,300 sq mi/75,900 sq km; population (1986) 325,000; capital Elista. Industry is mainly agricultural. It was settled by migrants from China in the 17th century, and the autonomous republic was abolished 1943–57 because of alleged collaboration of the people with the Germans during the siege of Stalingrad but restored 1958.

Kaltenbrunner Ernst 1901–1946. Austrian Nazi leader. After the annexation of Austria 1938 he joined police chief Himmler's staff, and as head of the Security Police (SD) from 1943 was responsible for the murder of millions of Jews (see ◊Holocaust) and Allied soldiers in World War II. After the war, he was tried at Nuremberg for war crimes and hanged.

Kaluga town in the USSR, on the river Oka, 100 mi/160 km SW of Moscow, capital of Kaluga region; population (1987) 307,000. Industries include hydroelectric installations and engineering works, telephone equipment, chemicals, and measuring devices.

Kamakura city on Honshu Island, Japan; population 175,000. It was the seat of the first shogunate 1192–1333, which established the rule of the samurai class, and the Hachimangu Shrine is dedicated to the gods of war; the 13th-century statue of Buddha (Daibutsu) is 43 ft/13 m high. From the 19th century, artists and writers (for example, the novelist Kawabata) settled here.

Kamara'n island in the Red Sea, formerly belonging to South Yemen, but occupied by North Yemen 1972; area 70 sq mi/180 sq km.

Kamchatka mountainous peninsula separating the Bering Sea and Sea of Okhotsk, forming (together with the Chukchi and Koryak national districts) a region of the USSR. Its capital, Petropavlovsk, is the only town; agriculture is possible only in the S. Most of the inhabitants are fishers and hunters.

Kamenev Lev Borisovich 1883–1936. Russian leader of the Bolshevik movement after 1917 who, with Stalin and Zinoviev, formed a ruling triumvirate in the USSR after Lenin's death 1924. His alignment with the Trotskyists led to his dismissal from office and from the Communist Party by Stalin 1926. Tried for plotting to murder Stalin, he was condemned and shot 1936.

kamikaze (Japanese "wind of the gods") the pilots of the Japanese air force in World War II who deliberately crash-dived their planes, loaded with bombs, usually onto ships of the US Navy.

Kampala capital of Uganda; population (1983) 455,000. It is linked by rail with Mombasa. Products include tea, coffee, textiles, fruit, and vegetables.

Kampuchea former name (1975–89) of ◊Cambodia.

Kanaka Hawaiian word for a person; applied to the indigenous people of the South Sea islands.

Kananga chief city of Kasai Occidental region, W central Zaïre, on the Lulua river; population (1984) 291,000. It was known as Luluabourg until 1966.

Kanazawa industrial city (textiles and porcelain) on Honshu island, in Chubu region, Japan, 100 mi/

Kandinsky *Russian painter Wassily Kandinsky, a pioneer in abstract art, as in* Battle/Cossacks *1910.*

kangaroo

160 km NNW of Nagoya; population (1985) 430,000. Kanazawa was a feudal castle town from the 16th century and has a number of old samurai residencies.

Kandahar city in Afghanistan, 280 mi/450 km SW of Kabul, capital of Kandahar province and a trading center, with wool and cotton factories; population (1984) 203,200. It is surrounded by a mud wall 25 ft/8 m high. When Afghanistan became independent in 1747, Kandahar was its first capital.

Kandinsky Wassily 1866–1944. Russian painter, a pioneer of abstract art. Born in Moscow, he traveled widely, settling in Munich 1896. He was an originator of the ◊*Blaue Reiter* movement 1911–12. From 1921 he taught at the ◊Bauhaus school of design. He moved to Paris 1933, becoming a French citizen 1939.

Kandinsky originally experimented with Post-Impressionist styles and Fauvism. Around 1910 he produced the first known examples of purely abstract work in 20th-century art. His highly colored style had few imitators, but his theories on composition, *Concerning the Spiritual in Art* 1912, were taken up by the early abstract movement.

Kandy city in central Sri Lanka, former capital of the kingdom of Kandy 1480–1815; population (1985) 140,000. Products include tea. One of the most sacred Buddhist shrines is situated at Kandy, and the chief campus of the University of Sri Lanka (1942) is at Peradenia, 3 mi/5 km away.

kangaroo any marsupial of the family Macropodidae found in Australia, Tasmania, and New Guinea. Kangaroos are plant-eaters and most live in groups. They are adapted to hopping, the vast majority of species having very large back legs and feet compared with the small forelimbs. The larger types can jump 30 ft/9 m at a single bound. Most are nocturnal. Species vary from small rat kangaroos, only 1 ft/30 cm long, through the medium-sized wallabies, to the large red and great gray kangaroos, which are the largest living marsupials. These may be 5.2 ft/1.6 m long with 3.5 ft/1.1 m tails.

In New Guinea and N Queensland, tree kangaroos (genus *Dendrolagus*) occur. These have comparatively short hind limbs. The great gray kangaroo *Macropus giganteus* produces a single young ("joey") about 1 in/2 cm long after a very short gestation, usually in early summer. At birth the young kangaroo is too young even to suck. It remains in its mother's pouch, attached to a nipple from which milk is squirted into its mouth at intervals. It stays in the pouch, with excursions as it matures, for about 280 days.

kangaroo paw bulbous plant *Anigozanthos manglesii*, family Hameodoraceae, with a row of small white flowers emerging from velvety green tubes with red bases. It is the floral emblem of Western Australia.

Ka Ngwane black homeland in Natal province, South Africa; achieved self-governing status 1971; population (1985) 392,800.

Kankakee city in NE Illinois, on the Kankakee River, S of Chicago; seat of Kankakee County. It is a distribution center for corn. Industries also

Kano *A gateway into the walled city of Kano, Nigeria.*

include building materials, furniture, pharmaceuticals, and farm machinery; population (1990) 27,575.

Kano capital of Kano state in N Nigeria, trade center of an irrigated area; population (1983) 487,100. Products include bicycles, glass, furniture, textiles, and chemicals. Founded about 1000 BC, Kano is a walled city, with New Kano extending beyond the walls. Goods still arrive by camel train to a marketplace holding 20,000 people.

Kanpur formerly ***Cawnpore*** capital of Kanpur district, Uttar Pradesh, India, SW of Lucknow, on the river Ganges; a commercial and industrial center (cotton, wool, jute, chemicals, plastics, iron, steel); population (1981) 1,688,000.

Kansas state in central US; nickname Sunflower State

area 82,296 sq mi/213,200 sq km

capital Topeka

cities Kansas City, Wichita, Overland Park

features Dodge City, once "cowboy capital of the world"; Eisenhower Center, Abilene; Fort Larned and Fort Scott; Pony Express station, Hanover; Menninger Foundation, Topeka; Wichita Cowtown, a frontier-era reproduction

products wheat, cattle, coal, petroleum, natural gas, aircraft, minerals

population (1990) 2,477,574

famous people Amelia Earhart; Dwight D Eisenhower; William Inge; Buster Keaton; C F William and Karl Menninger; Carry Nation; Charlie Parker; Gordon Parks; William Allen White

history explored by Francisco de Coronado for Spain 1541 and La Salle for France 1682; ceded to the US 1803 as part of the Louisiana Purchase. The first permanent settlements were Forts Leavenworth 1827, Scott 1842, and Riley 1853, outposts to protect the Santa Fe and Oregon trails. In the 1850s it was the scene of bloody warfare between pro- and antislavery settlers. It became a state 1861. By 1872 two railroads had crossed Kansas, and such towns as Dodge City and Abilene filled with cowboys driving cattle from Texas. Hardy winter wheat was brought to the state by Russian Mennonites. Kansas was hard hit by the Great Depression and dust-bowl soil erosion of the 1930s, but aircraft, oil, and gas industries provided the basis for economic recovery and expansion.

Kansas City city in Kansas, at the confluence of the Kansas and Missouri rivers, adjacent to Kansas City, Missouri; population (1990) 149,767. Food-processing, electronics, and automobile-assembly

Kansas

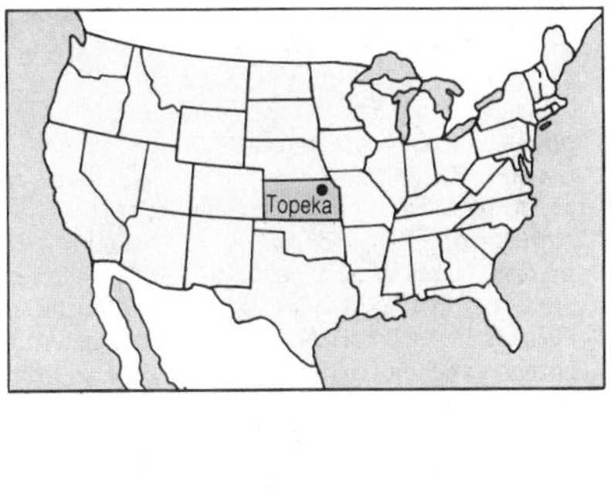
Topeka

Kant *An 1812 engraving of the German philosopher Immanuel Kant. A moral philosopher, he believed that feelings and inclinations were not a basis for ethical decisions.*

plants are here, as well as the University of Kansas Medical Center. It was laid out in 1857 as Wyandotte and expanded in 1886.

Kansas City city in Missouri, at the confluence of the Kansas and Missouri rivers, adjacent to Kansas City, Kansas; population (1990) 435,146. Industries include steel and electronics manufactures, motor-vehicle assembly, and oil refining, and it is the financial, marketing, and distribution center of the region. The University of Missouri-Kansas City and the Kansas City Art Institute are among the schools here. The site was settled as a trading post by French fur trappers in 1821. It was dominated by boss Tom Pendergast (Democrat) in the 1920s and 1930s, and under his "protection" jazz musicians such as Lester Young, Count Basie, and Charlie Parker performed. Crown Center, a gigantic office, condominium, and shopping complex was completed in the 1970s.

Kansu alternate spelling for the Chinese province ◊Gansu.

Kant Immanuel 1724–1804. German philosopher who believed that knowledge is not merely an aggregate of sense impressions but is dependent on the conceptual apparatus of the human understanding, which is itself not derived from experience. In ethics, Kant argued that right action cannot be based on feelings or inclinations but conforms to a law given by reason, the categorical imperative.

Born in Königsberg (in what was then East Prussia), he attended the university there, and was appointed professor of logic and metaphysics 1770. His first book, *Gedanken von der wahren Schätzung der lebendigen Kräfte/Thoughts on the True Estimates of Living Forces*, appeared in 1747 and the *Theorie des Himmels/Theory of the Heavens* in 1755. In the latter he combined physics and theology in an argument for the existence of God. In *Kritik der reinen Vernunft/Critique of Pure Reason* 1781, he argued that God's existence could not be proved theoretically. Other works include *Prolegomena* 1783, *Metaphysik der Sitten/Metaphysic of Ethics* 1785, *Metaphysische Anfangsgründe der Naturwissenschaft/Metaphysic of Nature* 1786, *Kritik der praktischen Vernunft/Critique of Practical Reason* 1788, and *Kritik der Urteilskraft/Critique of Judgment* 1790. In 1797 ill health led to his retirement.

Kanto flat, densely populated region of E Honshu island, Japan; population (1986) 37,156,000; area 12,505 sq mi/32,377 sq km. Chief city is Tokyo.

Kanton and Enderbury two atolls in the Phoenix group, which forms part of the Republic of ◊Kiribati. They were a UK–USA condominium (joint rule 1939–80). There are US aviation, radar, and tracking stations here.

Kantorovich Leonid 1912–1986. Russian mathematical economist whose theory that decentralization of decisions in a planned economy could only be made with a rational price system earned him a share (with Tjalling C Koopmans) of the 1975 Nobel Prize for Economics.

KANU (acronym for Kenya African National Union) political party founded 1944 and led by Jomo ◊Kenyatta from 1947, when it was the Kenya African Union; it became KANU on independence. The party formed Kenyatta's political power base in 1963 when he became prime minister; in 1964 he became the first president of Kenya.

Kaohsiung city and port on the W coast of Taiwan; population (1988) 1,300,000.

Industries include aluminum ware, fertilizers, cement, oil refineries, iron and steel works, shipyards, and food processing. Kaohsiung began to develop as a commercial port after 1858; its industrial development came about while it was occupied by Japan 1895–1945.

kaoliang variety of ◊sorghum.

kaolinite or ***kaolin*** a ◊clay mineral, hydrous aluminum silicate, $Al_2Si_2O_5(OH)_4$, formed mainly by the chemical weathering of ◊feldspar. It is important in the manufacture of porcelain and other ceramics, paper, rubber, paint, textiles, and medicines. It is mined in France, the UK, Germany, China, and the US.

Kapitza Peter 1894–1984. Soviet physicist who in 1978 shared a Nobel Prize for his work on magnetism and low-temperature physics. He was assistant director of magnetic research at the Cavendish Laboratory, Cambridge, England 1924–32, before returning to the USSR to work at the Russian Academy of Science.

Kaplan Viktor 1876–1934. Austrian engineer who invented a water turbine with adjustable rotor blades. In the machine, patented in 1920, the rotor was on a vertical shaft and could be adjusted to suit any rate of flow of water.

Horizontal Kaplan turbines are used at the installation on the estuary of the river Rance in France, the world's first tidal power station.

kapok silky hairs that surround the seeds of certain trees, particularly the kapok tree *Bombax ceiba* of India and Malaysia, and the silk-cotton tree *Ceiba pentandra*, a native of tropical America. Kapok is used for stuffing cushions and mattresses and for sound insulation; oil obtained from the seeds is used in food and soap preparation.

Kara Bogaz Gol shallow gulf of the Caspian Sea, USSR; area 8,000 sq mi/20,000 sq km. Rich deposits of sodium chloride, sulfates, and other salts have formed by evaporation.

Karachi largest city and chief seaport of Pakistan, and capital of Sind province, NW of the Indus delta; population (1981) 5,208,000. Industries include engineering, chemicals, plastics, and textiles. It was the capital of Pakistan 1947–59.

Karafuto Japanese name for ◊Sakhalin island.

Karaganda industrial town (coal, copper, tungsten, manganese) in Kazakh republic of the USSR, linked by canal with the Irtysh River; capital of Karaganda region; population (1987) 633,000.

Karaikal small port in India, 155 mi/250 km S of Madras, at the mouth of the right branch of the Cauvery delta. On a tract of land acquired by the French in 1739, it was transferred to India in 1954, confirmed by treaty in 1956. See also ◊Pondicherry.

Karaite member of an 8th-century sect of Judaism that denied the authority of rabbinic tradition, recognizing only the authority of the scriptures.

Karajan Herbert von 1908–1989. Austrian conductor. He was conductor of the Berlin Philharmonic Orchestra 1955–89. He directed the Salzburg Festival from 1964 and became director of the Vienna State Opera in 1976. He is associated with the Classical and Romantic repertoire—Beethoven, Brahms, Mahler, and Richard Strauss.

Kara-Kalpak Autonomous republic within Uzbekistan, USSR

area 61,000 sq mi/158,000 sq km

karate *A type of unarmed combat, karate became popular as a sport from the 1930s.*

capital Nukus

cities Munyak

products cotton, rice, wheat, fish

population (1986) 1,108,000

history named after the Kara-Kalpak ("black hood") people who live S of the Sea of Aral and were conquered by Russia 1867. An autonomous Kara-Kalpak region was formed 1926 within Kazakhstan, transferred to the Soviet republic 1930, made a republic 1932, and attached to Uzbekistan 1936.

Karakoram mountain range in central Asia, divided among China, Pakistan, and India. Peaks include K2, Masharbrum, Gasharbrum, and Mustagh Tower. ***Ladakh*** subsidiary range is in NE Kashmir on the Tibetan border.

Karakoram highway road constructed by China and Pakistan and completed 1978; runs 500 mi/800 km from Havelian (NW of Rawalpindi), via ◊Gilgit in Kashmir and the Khunjerab Pass (16,000 ft/4,800 m) to ◊Kashi in China.

Karakorum ruined capital of ◊Genghis Khan, SW of Ulaanbaatar in Mongolia.

Kara-Kum sandy desert occupying most of ◊Turkmenistan, USSR; area about 120,000 sq mi/310,800 sq km. It is crossed by the Caspian railroad.

Karamanlis Constantinos 1907– . Greek politician of the New Democracy Party. A lawyer and an anticommunist, he was prime minister Oct 1955–March 1958, May 1958–Sept 1961, and Nov 1961–June 1963 (when he went into self-imposed exile because of a military coup). He was recalled as prime minister on the fall of the regime of the "colonels" in July 1974, and was president 1980–85.

Kara Sea (Russian *Kavaskoye More*) part of the Arctic Ocean off the N coast of the USSR, bounded to the NW by the island of Novaya Zemlya and to the NE by Severnaya Zemlya.

Novy Port on the Gulf of Ob is the chief port, and the Yenisei also flows into it.

karat or ***carat*** the unit of purity in gold in the US. Pure gold is 24-karat; 22-karat (the purest used in jewelry) is 22 parts gold and two parts alloy (to give greater strength).

karate one of the ◊martial arts. Karate is a type of unarmed combat derived from kempo, a form of the Chinese Shaolin boxing. It became popular in the 1930s.

Karbala alternate spelling for ◊Kerbela, holy city in Iraq.

Karelia autonomous republic of the Russian Soviet Republic (RSFSR), in NW USSR

area 66,550 sq mi/172,400 sq km

capital Petrozavodsk

cities Vyborg

physical mainly forested

features Lake Ladoga

products fishing, timber, chemicals, coal

population (1986) 787,000

history Karelia was annexed to Russia by Peter the Great in 1721 as part of the grand duchy of Finland. In 1917 part of Karelia was retained by Finland when it gained its independence from Russia. The remainder became an autonomous region 1920 and an autonomous republic 1923 of the USSR. Following the wars of 1939–40 and 1941–44, Finland ceded 18,000 sq mi/46,000 sq km to the USSR. Part of this territory was incorporated in the Russian Soviet Republic and part in the Karelian autonomous republic. 400,000 Karelians were evacuated to Finland on Soviet annexation in 1940. In 1946 the Karelo-Finnish Soviet Socialist Republic was set up, but in 1956 the greater part of the republic returned to its former status as an autonomous Soviet Socialist republic.

Karelian bear dog medium-sized dog, about 2 ft/60 cm high, used to protect Russian settlements from bears. Rather like a husky, the dog is a "national treasure." It was not exported until 1989 when some were sent to Yellowstone Park, to keep bears away from tourists.

Karelian Isthmus strip of land between Lake Ladoga and the Gulf of Finland, USSR, with Leningrad at the S extremity and Vyborg at the N. Finland ceded it to the USSR 1940–41 and from 1947.

Karen member of a group of SE Asian peoples, numbering 1.9 million. They live in E Myanmar (formerly Burma), Thailand, and the Irrawaddy delta. Their language belongs to the Thai division of the Sino-Tibetan family. In 1984 the Burmese government began a large-scale military campaign against the Karen National Liberation Army (KNLA), the armed wing of the Karen National Union (KNU).

Kariba dam concrete dam on the Zambia–Zimbabwe border, about 240 mi/386 km downstream from the Victoria Falls, constructed 1955–60 to supply power to both countries. The dam crosses Kariba Gorge, and the reservoir, Lake Kariba, has important fisheries.

Karl-Marx-Stadt formerly (until 1954) ***Chemnitz*** city in the Federal Republic of Germany, capital of Karl-Marx-Stadt state, on the river Chemnitz, 40 mi/65 km SSE of Leipzig. It is an industrial center (engineering, textiles, chemicals); population (1986) 314,000. It came within the Soviet zone of occupation after World War II and was part of East Germany until 1990. Karl-Marx-Stadt county has an area of 2,320 sq mi/6,010 sq km and a population of 1,870,000.

Karloff Boris 1887–1969. British-born US actor best known for his work in the US. Born William Henry Pratt in London, he immigrated to Canada around 1911 in search of a theatrical career. Joining a touring stage company and frequently given the role of the play's villain, he adopted the sinister-sounding name Boris Karloff for professional use. Karloff later worked in Hollywood, achieving stardom with his role as the monster in the film *Frankenstein* 1931.

Several popular sequels followed as well as starring appearances in other horror films. In 1941 Karloff gained acclaim on Broadway in

Karloff *US film actor Boris Karloff, whose many horror movie roles included the monster in* Frankenstein.

Arsenic and Old Lace. He continued in television and films until the 1967 *Targets*, where he appeared as himself.

Karlovy Vary (German *Karlsbad*) spa in the Bohemian Forest, W Czechoslovakia, celebrated from the 14th century for its alkaline thermal springs; population (1983) 59,696.

Karlsbad German name of ◊Karlovy Vary, town in Czechoslovakia.

Karlsruhe industrial city in Baden-Württemberg, Federal Republic of Germany; population (1988) 268,000. Industries include nuclear research and oil refining.

karma (Sanskrit "fate") in Hinduism, the sum of a human being's actions, carried forward from one life to the next, resulting in an improved or worsened fate. Buddhism has a similar belief, except that no permanent personality is envisaged, the karma relating only to the physical and mental elements carried on from birth to birth, until the power holding them together disperses in the attainment of Nirvana.

Karmal Babrak 1929– . Afghani communist politician. In 1965 he formed what became the banned People's Democratic Party of Afghanistan (PDPA) 1977. As president 1979–86, with Soviet backing, he sought to broaden the appeal of the PDPA but encountered wide resistance from the ◊Mujaheddin Muslim guerrillas.

Karmal was imprisoned for antigovernment activity in the early 1950s. He was a member of the government 1957–62 and of the national assembly 1965–72. In Dec 1979 he returned from brief exile in E Europe with Soviet support to overthrow President Hafizullah Amin and was installed as the new head of state. Karmal was persuaded to step down as president and PDPA leader May 1986 as the USSR began to search for a compromise settlement with opposition groupings and to withdraw troops.

Karnak village of modern Egypt, on the E bank of the Nile, that gives its name to the temple of Ammon (constructed by Seti I and Ramses I) around which the major part of the city of ◊Thebes was built. An avenue of rams leads to ◊Luxor.

Karnataka formerly (until 1973) Mysore state in SW India

area 74,035 sq mi/191,800 sq km

capital Bangalore

products mainly agricultural; minerals include manganese, chromite, and India's only sources of gold and silver

population (1981) 37,043,000

language Kannada

famous people Hyder Ali, Tippu Sultan.

Kärnten German name for ◊Carinthia, province of Austria.

Karpov Anatoly 1951– . Soviet chess player. He succeeded Bobby Fischer of the US as world champion 1975, and held the title until losing to Gary Kasparov 1985.

karri giant ◊eucalyptus tree *Eucalyptus diversifolia*, found in the extreme SW of Australia. It may reach over 400 ft/120 m. Its exceptionally strong timber is used for girders.

Karroo two areas of semidesert in Cape Province, South Africa, divided into the Great Karroo and Little Karroo by the Swartberg mountains. The two Karroos together have an area of about 100,000 sq mi/260,000 sq km.

karst a landscape characterized by remarkable surface and underground forms, created as a result of the action of water on porous limestone. The feature takes its name from the Karst region on the Adriatic coast of Yugoslavia, but the name is applied to limestone landscapes throughout the world, the most dramatic of which is found near the city of Guilin in the Guangxi province of China.

karyotype in biology, the set of ◊chromosomes characteristic of a given species. It is described as the number, shape, and size of the chromosomes in a single cell of an organism. In humans for

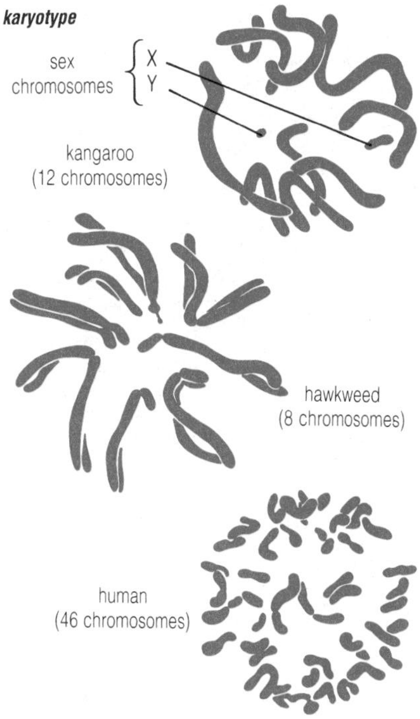
karyotype
sex chromosomes
X
Y
kangaroo
(12 chromosomes)
hawkweed
(8 chromosomes)
human
(46 chromosomes)

example, the karyotype consists of 46 chromosomes, in mice 40, crayfish 200, and in fruit flies 8.

The diagrammatic representation of a complete chromosome set is called a karyogram.

Kasai river that rises in Angola and forms the frontier with Zaïre before entering Zaïre and joining the Zaïre River, of which it is the chief tributary. It is rich in alluvial diamonds. Length 1,300 mi/2,100 km.

Kashgar former name of ◊Kashi in China.

Kashi formerly ***Kashgar*** oasis town in Xinjiang Uyghur autonomous region, China, on the river Kaxgar He; capital of Kashi district, which adjoins the Kirghiz and Tadzic republics, Afghanistan, and Jammu and Kashmir; population (1973) 180,000. It is a trading center, the Chinese terminus of the ◊Karakoram highway, and a focus of Muslim culture.

Kashmir former part of Jammu state in the N of British India with a largely Muslim population, ruled by a Hindu maharajah, who joined it to the republic of India 1947. There was fighting between pro-India and pro-Pakistan factions, the former being the Hindu ruling class and the latter the Muslim majority, and open war between the two countries 1965–66 and 1971. It remains divided: the NW is occupied by Pakistan, and the rest by India.

Kashmir Pakistan-occupied area, 30,445 sq mi/78,900 sq km, in the NW of the former state of Kashmir, now ◊Jammu and Kashmir. Azad ("free") Kashmir in the W has its own legislative assembly based in Muzaffarabad while Gilgit and Baltistan regions to the N and E are governed directly by Pakistan. The ◊Northern Areas are claimed by India and Pakistan

population 1,500,000

cities Gilgit, Skardu

features W Himalayan peak Nanga Parbat 26,660 ft/8,126 m, Karakoram Pass, Indus River, Baltoro Glacier.

Kashmiri inhabitant of or native to the state of Jammu and Kashmir, a disputed territory divided between India and Pakistan. There are approximately 6 million Kashmiris, 4 million of whom live on the Indian side of the cease-fire line.

Kashmir had been under the sway of Hindu India for many centuries when Muslim rule was established by the 14th century. Moghul rule began in the 16th century but was brought to a halt by the Afghan invasion of 1753. This was followed by a period of Sikh overlordship.

LONDON 86
KASPAROV KARPOV

Kasparov *Soviet chess players Anatoly Karpov (right) and Gary Kasparov (left).*

Kasparov Gary 1963– . Soviet chess player. When he beat his compatriot Anatoly Karpov to win the world title 1985, he was the youngest ever champion at 22 years 210 days.

Kassel industrial city in Hessen, Federal Republic of Germany, on the river Fulda; population (1988) 185,000. Industries include engineering, chemicals, and electronics. There is the spectacular Wilhelmshöhe mountain park, and the ◊Grimm Museum commemorates the compilers of fairy tales who lived here.

Kassem Abdul Karim 1914–1963. Iraqi politician, prime minister from 1958; he adopted a pro-Soviet policy. He pardoned the leaders of the pro-Egyptian party who tried to assassinate him 1959. He was executed after the 1963 coup.

Katanga former name of the ◊Shaba region in Zaïre.

Kathiawar peninsula on the W coast of India. Formerly occupied by a number of princely states, all Kathiawar (23,445 sq mi/60,723 sq km) had been included in Bombay state by 1956 but was transferred to Gujarat in 1960. Mahatma Gandhi was born in Kathiawar at Porbandar.

Katmai active volcano in Alaska, 6,715 ft/2,046 m. Its major eruption in 1912 created the "Valley of Ten Thousand Smokes." The lake-filled crater formed from the eruption is lined with glaciers. Katmai National Park, area 6,922 sq mi/17,928 sq km, was designated in 1980.

Katmandu or ***Kathmandu*** capital of Nepal; population (1981) 235,000. Founded in the 8th century on an ancient pilgrim and trade route from India to Tibet and China, it has a royal palace, Buddhist shrines, and monasteries.

Kato Kiyomasa 1562–1611. Japanese warrior and politician who was instrumental in the unification of Japan and the banning of Christianity in the country. He led the invasion of Korea 1592, and helped Toyotomi Hideyoshi and Tokugawa Ieyaso in their efforts to unify Japan.

Katō Taka-akira 1860–1926. Japanese politician and prime minister 1924–26. After a long political career with several terms as foreign minister, Katō led probably the most democratic and liberal regime of the Japanese Empire.

Katowice industrial city (anthracite, iron and coal mining, iron foundries, smelting works, machine shops) in Upper Silesia, S Poland; population (1985) 363,000.

Katsura Tarō 1847–1913. Prince of Japan, army officer, politician, and prime minister. He was responsible for the Anglo-Japanese treaty of 1902, the successful prosecution of the Russo-Japanese war 1904–05, and the annexation of Korea 1910.

Having assisted in the Meiji restoration (see ◊Mutsuhito) 1866–68, Katsura became increasingly involved in politics. His support for rearmament, distaste for political parties, and oligarchic rule created unrest; his third ministry Dec 1912–Jan 1913 lasted only seven weeks.

Kattegat sea passage between Denmark and Sweden. It is about 150 mi/240 km long and 85 mi/135 km wide at its broadest point.

Katyn village NE of Minsk, USSR, with a memorial to the many Byelorussian villages destroyed by

***Kaunda** Kenneth Kaunda was the first prime minister of Northern Rhodesia, the former name for Zambia, before becoming president when Zambia gained independence in 1964.*

the Germans in World War II, of which Katyn was one. See also ◊Katyn Forest.

Katyn Forest forest near Smolensk, USSR, where 4,500 Polish officer prisoners of war (captured in the German-Soviet partition of Poland 1940) were shot; 10,000 others were killed elsewhere. In 1989 the USSR accepted responsibility for the massacre.

Katz Bernard 1911– . British biophysicist. In 1970 he shared the 1970 Nobel Prize for Medicine with Ulf von Euler and Julius Axelrod for work on the biochemistry of the transmission and control of signals in the nervous system, vital in the search for remedies for nervous and mental disorders.

Kauffmann Angelica 1741–1807. Swiss Neo-Classical painter who worked extensively in England. She was in great demand as a portraitist, but also painted mythological scenes for large country houses.

Kaufman George S(imon) 1889–1961. US playwright. Author (often in collaboration with others) of many Broadway hits, including *Of Thee I Sing* 1932, a Pulitzer Prize-winning satire on US politics; *You Can't Take It with You* 1936; *The Man Who Came to Dinner* 1939; and *The Solid Gold Cadillac* 1952. Many of his plays became classic Hollywood films.

Kaunas formerly (until 1917) ***Kovno*** industrial river port (textiles, chemicals, agricultural machinery) in Lithuania, on the Niemen River; population (1987) 417,000. It was the capital of independent Lithuania 1910–40.

Kaunda Kenneth (David) 1924– Zambian politician. Imprisoned in 1958–60 as founder of the Zambia African National Congress, he became in 1964 first prime minister of Northern Rhodesia, then first president of Zambia. In 1973 he introduced one-party rule. He supported the nationalist movement in Southern Rhodesia, now Zimbabwe, and survived a coup attempt 1980 thought to have been promoted by South Africa. He was elected chair of the Organization of African Unity 1987. In 1990 his popularity fell and he was faced with wide antigovernment demonstrations. In 1991 he was overwhelmingly voted out of office.

kauri pine New Zealand timber conifer *Agathis australis*, family Araucariaceae, whose fossilized gum deposits are valued in varnishes; the wood is used for carving and handicrafts.

kava narcotic, intoxicating beverage prepared from the roots or leaves of a variety of pepper plant, *Piper methysticum*, found in the South Pacific islands.

Kawabata Yasunari 1899–1972. Japanese novelist, translator of Lady ◊Murasaki, and author of *Snow Country* 1947 and *A Thousand Cranes* 1952. His novels are characterized by melancholy and loneliness. He was the first Japanese to win the Nobel Prize for Literature 1968.

Kawasaki industrial city (iron, steel, shipbuilding, chemicals, textiles) on Honshu island, Japan; population (1987) 1,096,000.

Kay John 1704–c. 1764. British inventor who developed the flying shuttle, a machine to speed up the work of hand-loom weaving. In 1733 he patented his invention but was ruined by the litigation necessary for its defense.

Kayah State division of Myanmar (formerly Burma), area 4,600 sq mi/11,900 sq km, formed 1954 from the Karenni states (Kantarrawaddy, Bawlake and Kyebogyi) and inhabited mainly by the ◊Karen people. Kayah State has a measure of autonomy.

kayak long, narrow, sealskin-covered boat with a small opening in the middle for the paddler, used by Eskimo fishers and sealers, and now adapted for recreational use.

Kaye Danny. Stage-name of David Daniel Kaminski 1913–1987. US actor, comedian and singer. He appeared in many films, including *Wonder Man* 1944, *The Secret Life of Walter Mitty* 1946, and *Hans Christian Andersen* 1952.

He achieved stage success in *Lady in the Dark* 1940 and *Let's Face It* 1941 before going to Hollywood. He also starred on TV, toured for UNICEF, and guest-conducted major symphony orchestras in later years.

kayser a unit of wave number (number of waves in a unit length), used in spectroscopy. It is expressed as waves per centimeter, and is the reciprocal of the wavelength. A wavelength of 0.1 cm has a wave number of 10 kaysers.

Kayseri (ancient name *Caesarea Mazaca*) capital of Kayseri province, central Turkey; population (1985) 378,000. It produces textiles, carpets, and tiles. In Roman times it was capital of the province of Cappadocia.

Kazakh a member of a pastoral Kirghiz people of Kazakhstan, now a republic of the USSR. The Kazakhs speak a Turkic language belonging to the Altaic family.

The Kazakhs are predominantly Muslim, although pre-Islamic customs have survived. Kazakhs herd horses and make use of camels; they also keep cattle. Traditionally the Kazakhs embarked on seasonal migrations in search of fresh pastures. Collectivized herds were established in the 1920s and 1930s but Soviet economic programs have had to adapt to local circumstances.

Kazakhstan republic; formerly constituent republic of the USSR 1936–91, part of Soviet Central Asia

area 1,049,150 sq mi/2,717,300 sq km

Kazakhstan

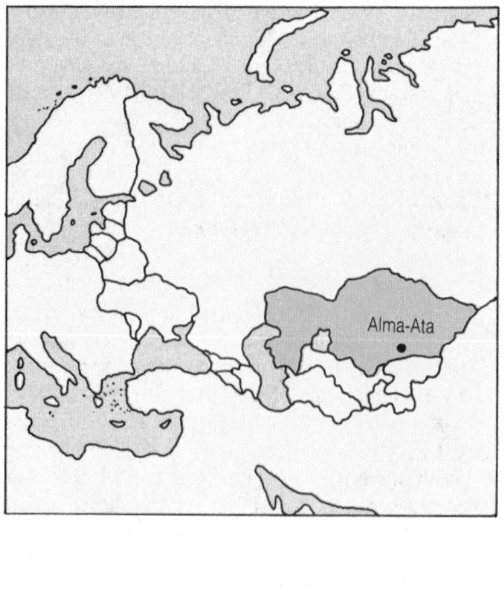
Alma-Ata

capital Alma-Ata

cities Karaganda, Semipalatinsk, Petropavlovsk

physical Caspian and Aral seas, Lake Balkhash; Steppe region

features the Baikonur Cosmodrome (official name for the Soviet space launch site at Tyuratam, near the coal-mining town of Baikonur); a weapons-testing area near the Chinese border

products grain (second only to Ukraine in production), copper, lead, zinc, manganese, coal, oil

population (1987) 16,244,000; 41% Russian, 36% Kazakh, 6% Ukrainian

language Russian; Kazakh, related to Turkish

history ruled by the Mongols from the 13th century, the region came under Russian control in the 18th century. Inhabited by the traditionally nomadic, but now largely settled, Kazakh people, it joined the USSR and became a full union republic in 1936. It was the site of ◊Khrushchev's ambitious "Virgin Lands" agricultural extension program during the 1950s, which led to overcropping and harvest failures during the early 1960s, but also to a large influx of Russian settlers, turning the Kazakhs into a minority in their own republic. There were riots in the capital 1986 from nationalist anti-Russian sentiment. In June 1989 four died in inter-ethnic violence in the oil town of Novy Uzen.

Market-centered economic reforms, including the privatization of housing and the services sector, are being instituted in the republic by Nursultan Nazerbayev, a pragmatic communist who was elected president in 1990 and has drawn on advice from economists from South Korea and Singapore. Nazerbayev resigned from the USSR Communist Party's Politburo and Central Committee after the August 1991 failed anti-Gorbachev coup and the Communist Party was abolished within the republic. A pact was signed with the Russian Republic to respect common borders and work to prevent the "uncontrolled disintegration" of the USSR.

Kazan capital of the Tatar autonomous republic in central USSR, on the river Volga; population (1987) 1,068,000. It a transport, commercial, and industrial center (engineering, oil refining, petrochemicals, textiles, large fur trade). Formerly capital of a Tatar khanate, Kazan was captured by Ivan IV "the Terrible" 1552.

The "Black Virgin of Kazan," an icon so called because blackened with age, was removed to Moscow (1612–1917), where the great Kazan Cathedral was built to house it 1631; it is now in the US. Among miracles attributed to its presence were the defeat of Poland 1612 and of Napoleon at Moscow 1812.

Kazan Elia 1909– . US stage and film director, a founder of the ◊Actors Studio 1947. Plays he directed include *The Skin of Our Teeth* 1942, *A Streetcar Named Desire* 1947, and *Cat on a Hot Tin Roof* 1955; films include *Gentlemen's Agreement* 1948, *East of Eden* 1954, and *The Visitors* 1972.

Kazantzakis Nikos 1885–1957. Greek writer, whose works include the poem *I Odysseia/The Odyssey* 1938 (which continues Homer's *Odyssey*), and the celebrated novels *Zorba the Greek* 1946, *The Greek Passion*, and *The Last Temptation of Christ*, both 1951.

kazoo a simple wind instrument adding a buzzing quality to the singing voice on the principle of "comb and paper" music.

kcal abbreviation for kilocalorie (see ◊calorie).

kea a hawklike greenish parrot *Nestor notabilis* found in New Zealand, which eats insects, fruits, and sheep offal. The Maori name imitates its cry.

Kean Edmund 1787–1833. British tragic actor, noted for his portrayal of villainy in the Shakespearean roles of Shylock, Richard III, and Iago.

Kearny Philip 1814–1862. US military leader. In 1859 Kearny served in the army of Napoleon III in Italy and received the French Croix de Guerre for his actions. With the outbreak of the US Civil

***Keaton** US comedy star Buster Keaton in a scene from* The General *1927.*

War, Kearny returned to the US, was named brigadier general of the New Jersey militia, and was killed in action near Chantilly, Virginia. He was the nephew of Stephen W ◊Kearny.

Born in New York, Kearny received a law degree from Columbia 1833. Choosing a career in the military, he obtained a commission in the US Dragoons 1837. He was trained in cavalry techniques in France and saw action in the Mexican War, where he lost an arm.

Kearny Stephen Watts 1794–1848. US military leader. Born in Newark, New Jersey, Kearny attended Columbia University and saw action in the War of 1812. Later serving on the frontier, he was promoted to the rank of brigadier general and given command of the Army of the West 1846. During the Mexican War he was the military governor of New Mexico and joined in the conquest of California 1847. After a dispute with John C Fremont over the priority of conquest, Kearny was named military governor.

In 1848 he served as governor-general of occupied Veracruz and Mexico City. He died of a tropical fever acquired there.

Keaton Buster. Adopted name of Joseph Frank Keaton 1896–1966. US comedian, actor and film director. After being a star in vaudeville, he took up a career in "Fatty" Arbuckle comedies, and became one of the great comedians of the silent film era, with an inimitable deadpan expression ("The Great Stone Face") masking a sophisticated acting ability. His films include *One Week* 1920, *The Navigator* 1924, *The General* 1927, and *The Cameraman* 1928.

He rivalled Charlie Chaplin in popularity until studio problems ended his creative career. He then made only shorts and guest appearances, as in Chaplin's *Limelight* 1952 and *A Funny Thing Happened on the Way to the Forum* 1966.

Keats John 1795–1821. English poet, a leading figure of the Romantic movement. He published his first volume of poetry 1817; this was followed by *Endymion*, *Isabella*, and *Hyperion* 1818, "The Eve of St Agnes," his odes "To Autumn," "On a Grecian Urn," and "To a Nightingale," and "Lamia" 1819. His final volume of poems appeared in 1820.

Born in London, Keats studied at Guy's Hospital 1815–17, but then abandoned medicine for poetry. *Endymion* 1818 was harshly reviewed by the Tory *Blackwood's Magazine* and *Quarterly Review*, largely because of Keats's friendship with the radical writer Leigh Hunt (1800–65). In 1819 he fell in love with Fanny Brawne. Suffering from tuberculosis, he sailed to Italy in 1820 in an attempt to regain his health, but died in Rome; the house he died in is now a museum. Valuable insight into Keats's poetic development is provided by his *Letters*, published 1848.

Keble John 1792–1866. Anglican priest and religious poet. His sermon on the decline of religious faith in Britain, preached in 1833, heralded the start of the ◊Oxford Movement, a Catholic revival in the Church of England. Keble College, Oxford, was founded in 1870 in his memory.

Kebnekaise highest peak in Sweden, rising to 6,926 ft/2,111 m in the Kolen range, W of Kiruna.

Kecskemét city in Hungary, situated on the Hungarian plain SE of Budapest; population (1988) 105,000. It is a trading center of an agricultural region.

***Keats** British Romantic poet John Keats, who abandoned the study of medicine for poetry.*

Kedah state in NW Peninsular Malaysia; capital Alor Setar; area 3,628 sq mi/9,400 sq km; population (1980) 1,116,000. Products include rice, rubber, tapioca, tin, and tungsten. Kedah was transferred by Thailand to Britain 1909, and was one of the Unfederated Malay States until 1948.

Keeling Islands another name for the ◊Cocos Islands, an Australian territory.

Keelung or ***Chi-lung*** industrial port (shipbuilding, chemicals, fertilizer) on the N coast of Taiwan, 15 mi/24 km NE of Taipei; population (1985) 351,904.

Keewatin eastern district of Northwest Territories, Canada, including the islands in Hudson and James Bays

area 228,160 sq mi/590,935 sq km

cities (trading posts) Chesterfield Inlet, Eskimo Point, and Coral Harbor (site of an air base set up during World War II)

physical upland plateau in the N, the S low and level, covering the greater part of the Arctic prairies of Canada; numerous lakes

products furs (trapping is main occupation)

history Keewatin District formed 1876, under the administration of Manitoba; it was transferred to Northwest Territories 1905, and in 1912 lost land S of 60° N to Manitoba and Ontario.

Kefallinia (English *Cephalonia*) largest of the Ionian Islands off the W coast of Greece; area 360 sq mi/935 sq km; population (1981) 31,300. It was devastated by an earthquake 1953 that destroyed the capital Argostolion.

Kefauver (Carey) Estes 1903–1963. US Democratic politician. Having established a private law practice in Chattanooga, Tennessee, he was elected to the US House of Representatives 1939, serving there until his election to the US Senate 1948. As chairman of the Senate Judiciary Committee, Kefauver held widely publicized early televised hearings on organized crime 1950–51. An unsuccessful candidate for the Democratic presidential nomination 1952 and 1956, he served in the Senate until his death.

Born near Madisonville, Tennessee, Kefauver was educated at the University of Tennessee and received a law degree from Yale 1927.

Keflavik fishing port in Iceland, 22 mi/35 km SW of Reykjavik; population (1986) 7,500. Its international airport was built during World War II by US forces (who called it Meeks Field). Keflavik became a NATO base in 1951.

Keillor Garrison 1942– . US writer and humorist. His hometown is Anoka, Minnesota, in the American Midwest. It inspired his stories about Lake Wobegon, including *Lake Wobegon Days* 1985 and *Leaving Home* 1987, which often started as radio monologues about "the town that time forgot, that the decades cannot improve."

He first achieved prominence on National Public Radio's "Prairie Home Companion."

Keitel Wilhelm 1882–1946. German field marshal in World War II, chief of the supreme command from 1938 and Hitler's chief military adviser. He signed Germany's unconditional surrender in Berlin May 8, 1945. Tried at Nuremberg for war crimes, he was hanged.

Kekulé von Stradonitz Friedrich August 1829–1896. German chemist whose theory 1858 of molecular structure revolutionized organic chemistry. He proposed two resonant forms of the ◊benzene ring.

Kelantan state in NE Peninsular Malaysia; capital Kota Baharu; area 5,751 sq mi/14,900 sq km; population (1980) 894,000. It produces rice, rubber, copra, tin, manganese, and gold. Kelantan was transferred by Siam to Britain 1909 and until 1948 was one of the Unfederated Malay States.

Keller Gottfried 1819–1890. Swiss poet and novelist, whose books include *Der Grüne Heinrich/Green Henry* 1854–55. He also wrote short stories, of which the collection "Die Leute von Seldwyla/The People of Seldwyla" 1856–74, describes small-town life.

Keller Helen (Adams) 1880–1968. US author. Born

in Alabama, she became blind and deaf after an illness when she was only 19 months old. The teaching of Anne Sullivan, her lifelong companion, enabled her to learn the names of objects and eventually to speak. She graduated with honors from Radcliffe College in 1904; published several books, including *The Story of My Life* 1902; and toured the world, lecturing to raise money for the blind.

Kellogg Frank Billings 1856–1937. US political leader and diplomat. Born in Potsdam, New York, Kellogg studied law in Minnesota and was admitted to the bar 1877. After service as a prosecutor of federal antitrust cases, he was elected to the US Senate 1916. Kellogg was named US ambassador to Great Britain by President Harding 1922 and secretary of state 1925. His greatest achievement was the formulation of the international antiwar resolution, the Kellogg–Briand Pact, for which he was awarded the Nobel Peace Prize 1929. Kellogg later served as judge on the World Court 1930–35.

Kellogg–Briand pact agreement 1927 between the US and France to renounce war and seek settlement of disputes by peaceful means. It took its name from the US secretary of state Frank B Kellogg (1856–1937) and the French foreign minister Aristide Briand. Other powers signed in Aug 1928, making a total of 67 signatories. Some successes were achieved in settling South American disputes, but the pact made no provision for measures against aggressors and became ineffective in the 1930s, with Japan in Manchuria, Italy in Ethiopia, and Hitler in central Europe.

Kells, Book of 8th-century illuminated manuscript of the Gospels produced at the monastery of Kells in County Meath, Ireland. It is now in Trinity College library, Dublin.

Kelly Emmett 1898–1979. US clown and circus performer. Drifting from circus to circus, Kelly finally unveiled his "Weary Willie" clown character while with the Hagenbeck-Wallace circus 1931. Gaining widespread popularity, he joined the Ringling Brothers and Barnum and Bailey Circus 1942 and made Weary Willie one of the most famous clowns in the world. Kelly later became a familiar film and television personality.

Born in Sedan, Kansas, Kelly had early aspirations to be a cartoonist and moved to Kansas City 1917. There he created the hobo character "Weary Willie" that was later to become the inspiration for his circus persona.

Kelly Gene (Eugene Curran) 1912– . US film actor, dancer, choreographer, and director. He was a major star of the 1940s and 1950s in a series of MGM musicals, including *On the Town* 1949, *An American in Paris* 1951, and *Singin' in the Rain* 1952. He also acted in nonmusicals, such as *Marjorie Morningstar* 1958 and *Inherit the Wind* 1960.

Kelly Grace (Patricia) 1928–1982. US film actress who retired from acting after marrying Prince Rainier III of Monaco 1956. She starred in *High Noon* 1952, *The Country Girl* 1954, for which she received an Academy Award, and *High Society* 1955. She also made three classic films for Hitchcock, *Dial M for Murder* 1954, *Rear Window* 1954, and *To Catch a Thief* 1955.

After her marriage she devoted herself to the principality, raised three children, and was active in charities until she died in a car accident.

Kelly Ned (Edward) 1854–1880. Australian ◊bushranger. The son of an Irish convict, he wounded a police officer in 1878 while resisting the arrest of his brother Daniel for horse-stealing. The two brothers escaped and carried out bank robberies. Kelly wore a distinctive home-made armor. In 1880 he was captured and hanged.

keloid in medicine, overgrowth of fibrous tissue, usually produced at the site of a scar. Black skin produces more keloid than does white skin; it has a puckered appearance caused by clawlike offshoots. Surgical removal is often unsuccessful, because the keloid returns.

Kelly *US film actress Grace Kelly retired from her career after her marriage to Prince Ranier of Monaco in 1956.*

kelp collective name for large brown seaweeds, such as those of the Fucaceae and Laminariaceae families. Kelp is also a term for the powdery ash of burned seaweeds, a source of iodine.

The brown kelp *Macrocystis pyrifera*, abundant in Antarctic and sub-Antarctic waters, is one of the fastest-growing organisms known, reaching 320 ft/100 m. It is farmed for the alginate industry, its rapid surface growth allowing cropping several times a year, but it is an alien pest in N Atlantic waters.

Kelvin William Thomson, 1st Baron Kelvin 1824–1907. Irish physicist who introduced the kelvin scale, the absolute scale of temperature. His work on the conservation of energy 1851 led to the second law of ◊thermodynamics.

Popularly known for his contributions to telegraphy, he greatly improved transatlantic communications. Maritime endeavors led to a tide gauge and predictor, an improved compass, and simpler methods for fixing a ship's position at sea.

kelvin scale temperature scale used by scientists. It begins at ◊absolute zero (–273.16°C) and increases by the same degree intervals as the Celsius scale; that is, 0°C is the same as 273 K and 100°C is 373 K.

Kelvin *Irish physicist William Kelvin pioneered the kelvin scale of temperature used by scientists.*

Kemal Atatürk Mustafa. Turkish politician; see ◊Atatürk.

Kemble (John) Philip 1757–1823. English actor and theater manager. He excelled in tragedy, including the Shakespearean roles of Hamlet and Coriolanus. As manager of Drury Lane 1788–1803 and Covent Garden 1803–17 in London, he introduced many innovations in theatrical management, costume, and scenery.

Kemerovo coal-mining town in W Siberia, USSR, center of Kuznetz coal basin; population (1987) 520,000. It has chemical and metallurgical industries. The town, which was formed out of the villages of Kemerovo and Shcheglovisk, was known as Shcheglovisk 1918–32.

Kempe Rudolf 1910–1976. German conductor. Renowned for the clarity and fidelity of his interpretations of the works of Richard Strauss and ◊Wagner's *Ring* cycle, he conducted Britain's Royal Philharmonic Orchestra 1961–75 and was musical director of the Munich Philharmonic from 1967.

Kempis Thomas à. Medieval German monk and religious writer; see ◊Thomas à Kempis.

Kendall Edward 1886–1972. US biochemist. In 1914 he isolated the hormone thyroxin, the active compound of the thyroid gland. He went on to work on secretions from the adrenal gland, among which he discovered a compound E, which was in fact the steroid cortisone. For this Kendall shared the 1950 Nobel Prize for Medicine with Philip Hench (1896–1965) and Tadeus ◊Reichstein.

kendo (Japanese "the way of the sword") Japanese armed ◊martial art in which combatants fence with bamboo replicas of samurai swords. Masks and padding are worn for protection. The earliest recorded reference to kendo is AD 789.

Kendrew John 1917– . British biochemist. Kendrew began, in 1946, the ambitious task of determining the three-dimensional structure of the major muscle protein myoglobin. This was completed in 1959 and won for Kendrew a share of the 1962 Nobel Prize for Chemistry with Max Perutz.

Keneally Thomas Michael 1935– . Australian novelist who won Britain's Booker Prize with *Schindler's Ark* 1982, a novel based on the true account of Polish Jews saved from the gas chambers in World War II by a German industrialist.

Other works include *Confederates* 1980, *A Family Madness* 1986, *The Playmaker* 1987, and *To Asmara* 1989.

Kenilworth castle and town in Warwickshire, England. The Norman castle became a royal residence and was enlarged by John of Gaunt and later by the Earl of Leicester, who entertained Elizabeth I here in 1575. It was dismantled after the Civil War.

Kennedy Anthony 1936– . US jurist and associate justice of the US Supreme Court 1988– . A conservative, he wrote the majority opinion in *Saffle* v *Parks* 1990 that a writ of habeas corpus may be obtained only according to the laws in force at the time of a prisoner's conviction and in *Washington* v *Harper* 1990 that the administration of medication for mentally ill prisoners, without the prisoner's consent, is permissible. He supported the majority opinion in the 1989 case, *Texas* v *Johnson*, that ruled that the burning of the US flag in protest was protected by the First Amendment.

Born in Sacramento, California, he attended Stanford University (spending his fourth year at the London School of Economics) and the Harvard Law School. Kennedy practiced law in private practice in California 1962–75. He taught constitutional law at McGeorge School of Law of the University of the Pacific 1965–88. He was appointed judge of the US Court of Appeals for the Seventh Circuit 1976. In 1988 President Reagan appointed him to the Supreme Court.

Kennedy Edward (Moore) "Ted" 1932– . US Democratic politician. He aided his brothers John and Robert Kennedy in the presidential campaign

Kennedy *The 35th president of the US, John F Kennedy, a Democrat. 1961– 1963.*

of 1960 and entered politics as a US Senator from Massachusetts 1962. He is a spokesman for liberal causes including national health and gun control. He failed to gain the presidential nomination 1980, largely because of questions about his delay in reporting an auto accident at Chappaquiddick Island, near Martha's Vineyard, Massachusetts, in 1969, in which his passenger, Mary Jo Kopechne, was drowned.

Kennedy John Fitzgerald "Jack" 1917–1963. 35th president of the US 1961–63, a Democrat; the first Roman Catholic and the youngest person to be elected president. In foreign policy he carried through the unsuccessful ◊Bay of Pigs invasion of Cuba and in 1963 secured the withdrawal of Soviet missiles from the island. He created the Peace Corps, volunteers who give various types of health, agricultural, and educational aid overseas, and he proposed the Alliance for Progress for aid to Latin America. In the view of many, style was more important than substance in the Kennedy White House, but he inspired a generation of idealists and created an aura of positive activism. His wit and charisma combined with political shrewdness to disarm many critics. His program for reforms at home, called the New Frontier, was largely executed by Lyndon ◊Johnson's Great Society. Kennedy was assassinated during a visit to Dallas, Texas, on Nov 22, 1963, by Lee Harvey Oswald (1939–63), who was within a few days shot dead by Jack Ruby.

Son of successful financier Joseph Kennedy, John was born in Brookline, Massachusetts, educated at Harvard, and served in the navy in the Pacific during World War II. In 1946 he was elected to the House of Representatives and in 1952 to the Senate from Massachusetts. In 1953 he married socialite Jacqueline Lee Bouvier (1929–). In 1960 he defeated Richard ◊Nixon for the presidency, partly as a result of televised debates, and brought academics and intellectuals to Washington as advisers.

A number of conspiracy theories have developed around the Kennedy assassination, which was investigated by a special commission headed by Chief Justice Earl ◊Warren. The commission determined that Oswald acted alone. Oswald was a malcontent who had gone to live in the USSR in 1959 and later returned. Ruby was a Dallas nightclub owner.

Kennedy Joseph Patrick 1888–1969. US industrialist and diplomat; ambassador to the UK 1937–40. A self-made millionaire, he ventured into the film industry, then set up the Securities and Exchange Commission (SEC) for F D Roosevelt. He groomed each of his four sons—Joseph Patrick Kennedy Jr, John Fitzgerald ◊Kennedy, Robert Francis ◊Kennedy, Edward Moore ◊Kennedy—for a career in politics. His eldest son, Joseph (1915–44), was killed in action with the naval air force in World War II.

Kennedy Robert Francis 1925–1968. US Democratic politician and lawyer. He was presidential campaign manager for his brother John F ◊Kennedy 1960, and as attorney general 1961–64 pursued a racket-busting policy and promoted the Civil Rights Act of 1964. He was also a key aid to his brother. When John Kennedy's successor, Lyndon Johnson, preferred Hubert H Humphrey for the 1964 vice-presidential nomination, Kennedy resigned and was elected senator for New York. In 1968 he campaigned for the Democratic party's presidential nomination, but during a campaign stop in California was assassinated by Sirhan Bissara Sirhan (1944–), a Jordanian.

Kennedy William 1928– . US novelist, author of the *Albany Trilogy* consisting of *Legs* 1976, about the gangster "Legs" Diamond; *Billy Phelan's Greatest Game* 1983, about a pool player; and *Ironweed* 1984, about a baseball player's return to the city of Albany, NY. He also wrote *Quinn's Book* 1988.

Kennedy Space Center the ◊NASA launch site on Merritt Island, near Cape Canaveral, Florida, used for Apollo and Space Shuttle launches.

The first flight to land on the Moon 1969 and *Skylab*, the first orbiting laboratory 1973, were launched here. The Center is dominated by the Vehicle Assembly Building, 525 ft/160 m tall, used for assembly of ◊Saturn rockets and Space Shuttles. It is named for Pres John F Kennedy.

Kennelly Arthur Edwin 1861–1939. US engineer, who gave his name to the Kennelly–Heaviside layer (now the ◊E layer) of the ◊ionosphere. He verified in 1902 the existence of an ionized layer in the upper atmosphere, predicted by ◊Heaviside.

Kennelly–Heaviside layer former term for the ◊E layer.

Kenneth two kings of Scotland:

Kenneth I MacAlpin died 858. King of Scotland from c. 844. Traditionally, he is regarded as the founder of the Scottish kingdom (Alba) by virtue of his final defeat of the Picts about 844. He invaded Northumbria six times, and drove the Angles and the Britons over the river Tweed.

Kenneth II died 995. King of Scotland from 971, son of Malcolm I. He invaded Northumbria several times, and his chiefs were in constant conflict with Sigurd the Norwegian over the area of Scotland north of the river Spey. He is believed to have been murdered by his subjects.

Kennewick city in SE Washington, on the Columbia River, SE of Seattle. Dams built on the Columbia and Snake Rivers provide irrigation for the area's grape, sugar beet, alfalfa, and corn crops; population (1990) 42,155.

Kenosha city in the SE corner of Wisconsin, on Lake Michigan, SE of Milwaukee, seat of Kenosha county. Its industries include food-processing equipment, fertilizers, automobiles, textiles and clothing, and food products; population (1980) 77,685. Kenosha is an Indian word for "pike" or "pickerel."

Kent county in SE England, nicknamed the "garden of England"

area 1,440 sq mi/3,730 sq km

cities Maidstone (administrative headquarters), Canterbury, Chatham, Rochester, Tunbridge Wells; resorts: Folkestone, Margate, Ramsgate

features traditionally, a "man of Kent" comes from east of the Medway and a "Kentish man" from W Kent; New Ash Green, a new town; Romney Marsh; the Isles of Grain, Sheppey (on which is the resort of Sheerness, formerly a royal dockyard) and Thanet; Weald (agricultural area); rivers: Darent, Medway, Stour; Leeds Castle (converted to a palace by Henry VIII); Hever Castle (where Henry VIII courted Anne Boleyn); Chartwell (Churchill's country home), Knole, Sissinghurst Castle and gardens

products hops, apples, soft fruit, coal, cement, paper

population (1987) 1,511,000

famous people Charles Dickens, Christopher Marlowe.

Kent William 1685–1748. British architect, land-

Kentucky

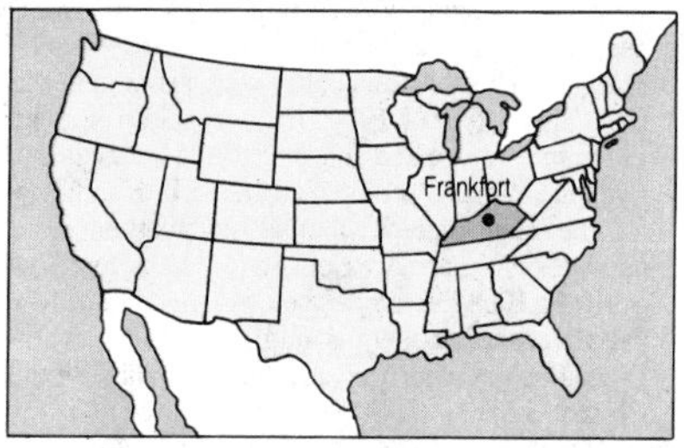
Frankfort

Kenya
Republic of
(Jamhuri ya Kenya)

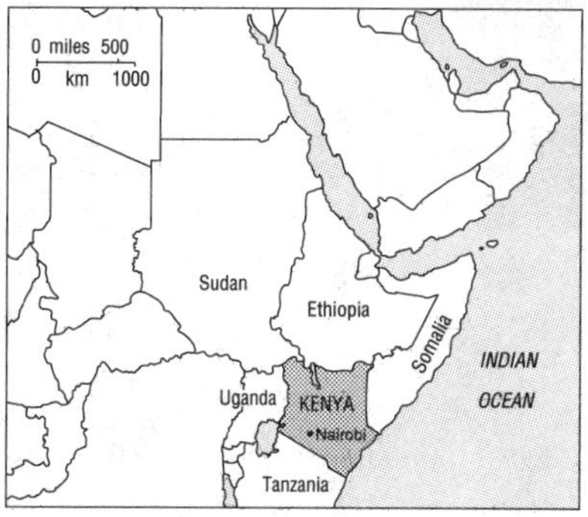
0 miles 500
0 km 1000
Sudan
Ethiopia
Somalia
INDIAN
OCEAN
Uganda
KENYA
•Nairobi
Tanzania

area 224,884 sq mi/582,600 sq km
capital Nairobi
cities Kisumu, port Mombasa
physical mountains and highlands in W and center; coastal plain in S; arid interior and tropical coast
features Great Rift Valley, Mount Kenya, Lake Nakuru (salt lake with world's largest colony of flamingos), Lake Turkana (Rudolf), national parks with wildlife, Malindini Marine Reserve, Olduvai Gorge
head of state and government Daniel arap Moi from 1978
political system authoritarian nationalism
political parties Kenya African National Union (KANU), nationalist, centrist; National Democratic Party (NDP), centrist
exports coffee, tea, pineapples, petroleum products
currency Kenya shilling
population (1990 est) 25,393,000 (Kikuyu 21%, Luo 13%, Luhya 14%, Kelenjin 11%; Asian, Arab, European); growth rate 4.2% p.a.
life expectancy men 59, women 63 (1989)
language Kiswahili (official); English, and many local dialects
religion Protestant 38%, Roman Catholic 28%, Muslim 6%; indigenous beliefs 26%
literacy 50% (1988)
GDP $6.9 bn (1987); $302 per head (1988)
chronology
1895 British East African protectorate established.
1920 Kenya became a British colony.
1944 African participation in politics began.
1950 Mau Mau campaign began.
1953 Nationalist leader Jomo Kenyatta imprisoned.
1956 Mau Mau campaign defeated, Kenyatta released. 1963 Achieved internal self-government, with Kenyatta as prime minister.
1964 Independence achieved from Britain as a republic, within the Commonwealth, with Kenyatta as president.
1978 Death of Kenyatta. Succeeded by Daniel arap Moi.
1982 Attempted coup against Moi foiled.
1983 Moi reelected.
1984 Over 2,000 people massacred by government forces at Wajir.
1985–86 Thousands of forest villagers evicted by army and police and their homes destroyed to make way for cash crops.
1988 Moi reelected. 150,000 evicted from state-owned forests.
1989 Moi announced the release of all known political prisoners. Confiscated ivory burned in attempt to stop elephant poaching.
1990 Despite antigovernment riots, Moi refused multiparty politics.
1991 Opposition National Democratic Party launched by Oginga Odinga in the face of Moi's refusal to accept it.

scape gardener, and interior designer. In architecture he was foremost in introducing the Palladian style into Britain from Italy.

Kenton Stan 1912–1979. US exponent of progressive jazz, who broke into West Coast jazz in 1941 with his "wall of brass" sound. He helped introduce Afro-Cuban rhythms to US jazz, and combined jazz and Classical music in compositions such as "Artistry in Rhythm" 1943.

Kentucky state in S central US; nickname Bluegrass State
area 40,414 sq mi/104,700 sq km
capital Frankfort
cities Louisville, Lexington, Owensboro, Covington, Bowling Green
features bluegrass country; horse racing at Louisville (Kentucky Derby); Mammoth Cave National Park (main cave 4 mi/6.5 km long, up to 125 ft/38 m high, where Indian councils were once held); Abraham Lincoln's birthplace at Hodgenville; Fort Knox, US gold bullion depository
products tobacco, cereals, textiles, coal, whiskey, horses, transport vehicles
population (1990) 3,685,296
famous people Mohammed Ali, Daniel Boone, Louis D Brandeis, Kit Carson, Henry Clay, D W Griffith, Thomas Hunt Morgan, Harland "Colonel" Sanders, Robert Penn Warren
history the first region west of the Alleghenies settled by American pioneers. James Harrod founded Harrodsburg 1774; in 1775 Daniel Boone, who blazed his Wilderness Trail 1767, founded Boonesboro. Originally part of Virginia, it became a state 1792. Badly divided over the slavery question, the state was wracked by guerrilla warfare and partisan feuds during the Civil War. In 1900, Kentucky ranked first among Southern states in per-capita income, but wealth was divided unevenly, and the Great Depression of the 1930s hit hard; by 1940, Kentucky was last among states in per-capita income. Although it remains one of the poorest states, better roads, education, television, and government programs have relieved the isolation of its rural communities.

Kenya country in E Africa, bordered N by Sudan and Ethiopia, E by Somalia, SE by the Indian Ocean, SW by Tanzania, and W by Uganda.
government The 1963 constitution, amended 1964, 1969, and 1982, provides for a president, elected by universal suffrage for a five-year term, and a single-chamber national assembly, serving a similar term. The assembly has 202 members, 188 elected by universal suffrage, 12 nominated by the president, and the attorney-general and speaker as members by virtue of their office. From 1969 to 1982 Kenya was a one-party state in fact, and since then it has become one in law, the only legitimate party being the Kenya African National Union (KANU), whose leader is the state president.
history Archeological evidence shows that the area now known as Kenya was first inhabited at least 5 million years ago by early humans. African tribal groups inhabited the area when, in the 8th century, the coast was settled by Arabs, and during the 15th–18th centuries the region was under Portuguese rule.

Kenya was a British colony 1895–1964, when it achieved full independence within the ◊Commonwealth. There was near civil war during the 20 years before independence, as nationalist groups carried out a campaign of violence. The Kenya African Union (KAU) was founded in 1944, and in 1947 Jomo ◊Kenyatta, a member of Kenya's largest ethnic group, the Kikuyu, became its president. Three years later a secret society of young Kikuyu militants was formed, called Mau Mau, that had the same aims as KAU but sought to achieve them by violent means. Although Kenyatta dissociated himself from Mau Mau, the British authorities distrusted him and imprisoned him in 1953. By 1956 the guerrilla campaign had largely ended, the state of emergency was lifted and Kenyatta was released.

Kenya was granted internal self-government in 1963, and Kenyatta, who had become leader of the Kenya African National Union (KANU), became prime minister and then president after full independence in 1964. Kenyatta continued as president until his death in 1978, during which time the country achieved considerable stability. He was succeeded by Vice-President Daniel arap Moi, who built on Kenyatta's achievements, launching an impressive four-year development plan.

An attempted coup by junior air force officers in 1982 was foiled and resulted in political detentions and press censorship. The air force and Nairobi University were temporarily dissolved. In the same year the national assembly declared Kenya a one-party state. President Moi was reelected in 1983, and his position seems secure. He has had some success in tackling corruption and inefficiency in the public services and, externally, has reestablished good relations with most of his E African neighbors. He was reelected unopposed for a third successive presidential term Feb 1988. In June 1989 Moi unexpectedly announced the release of all known political detainees. Kenya led the effort 1989 to ban trading in ivory after poaching became uncontrollable. The deaths of several US tourists on safari provoked President Moi to declare a war against poachers.

In July 1990 there were widespread antigovernment riots while more moderate elements called for a multiparty system; this has been resisted by President Moi.

Kenya, Mount or ***Kirinyaga*** extinct volcano from which Kenya takes its name, 17,058 ft/5,200 m; the first European to climb it was Halford Mackinder in 1899.

Kenyatta Jomo. Assumed name of Kamau Ngengi c. 1894–1978. Kenyan nationalist politician, prime minister from 1963, as well as first president of Kenya from 1964 until his death. He led the Kenya African Union from 1947 (◊KANU from 1963) and was active in liberating Kenya from British rule.

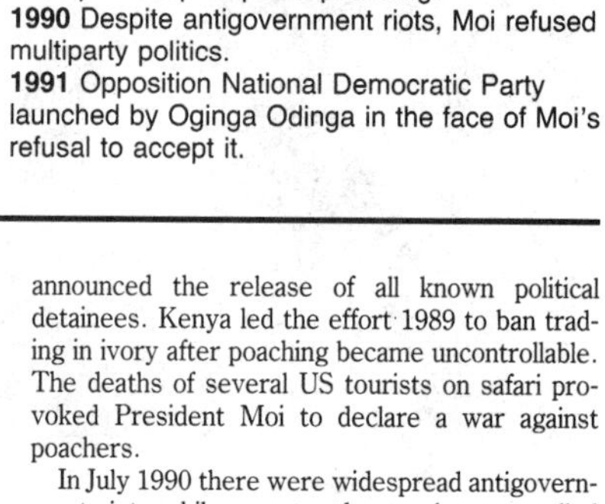

Kenyatta *The first president of independent Kenya, Jomo Kenyatta.*

Kepler's second law

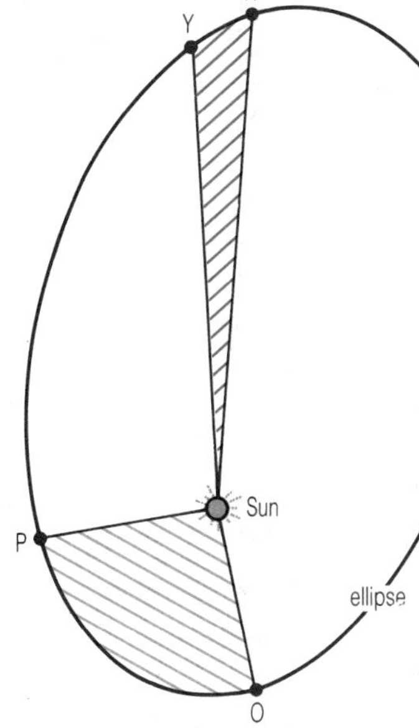
X
Y
Sun
P
ellipse
O

Kenyon Kathleen 1906–1978. British archeologist whose all-female dig in ◊Jericho uncovered remains of a New Stone Age (Neolithic) settlement dated to about 6800 BC.

Kepler Johann 1571–1630. German mathematician and astronomer. He formulated what are now called Kepler's laws of planetary motion: (1) the orbit of each planet is an ellipse with the Sun at one of the foci; (2) the radius vector of each planet sweeps out equal areas in equal times; (3) the squares of the periods of the planets are proportional to the cubes of their mean distances from the Sun.

Born in Württemberg, Kepler became assistant to Tycho ◊Brahe 1600 and succeeded him as imperial mathematician 1601. His analysis of Brahe's observations of the planets led him to discover his three laws, the first two of which he published in *Astronomia Nova* 1609 and the third in *Harmonices Mundi* 1619.

Kerala state of SW India, formed 1956 from the former princely states of Travancore and Cochin
area 15,015 sq mi/38,900 sq km
capital Trivandrum
features most densely populated, and most literate (60%), state of India; strong religious and caste divisions making it politically unstable
products tea, coffee, rice, oilseed, rubber, textiles, chemicals, electrical goods
population (1981) 25,403,000
language Kannada, Malayalam, Tamil.

keratin fibrous protein found in the ◊skin of vertebrates and also in hair, nails, claws, hooves, feathers, and the outer coating of horns in animals such as cows and sheep.

If pressure is put on some parts of the skin, more keratin is produced, forming thick callouses that protect the layers of skin beneath.

Kerbela or Karbala holy city of the Shi'ite Muslims, 60 mi/96 km SW of Baghdad, Iraq; population (1985) 184,600. Kerbela is built on the site of the battlefield where Husein, son of Ali and Fatima, was killed in 680 while defending his succession to the khalifate; his tomb in the city is visited every year by many pilgrims.

Kerch port in the Crimea, Ukraine, USSR, at the eastern end of Kerch peninsula, an iron-producing area; population (1987) 173,000. Built on the site of an ancient Greek settlement, Kerch became Russian 1783.

Kerekou Mathieu (Ahmed) 1933– . Benin Socialist politician and soldier, president from 1980. In 1972, when deputy head of the Dahomey army, he led a coup to oust the ruling president and establish his own military government. He embarked on a program of "scientific socialism," changing his country's name to Benin to mark this change of direction. Re-elected president 1984, in 1987 he resigned from the army and confirmed a civilian administration.

Kerensky Alexandr Feodorovich 1881–1970. Russian revolutionary politician, prime minister of the second provisional government before its collapse Nov 1917, during the ◊Russian Revolution. He was overthrown by the Bolshevik revolution, since he insisted on staying in World War I and mismanaged internal economic affairs. He fled to France 1918 and to the US 1940.

Kerguelen Islands or ***Desolation Islands*** volcanic archipelago in the Indian Ocean, part of the French Southern and Antarctic Territories; area 2,787 sq mi/7,215 sq km. It was discovered in 1772 by the Breton navigator Yves de Kerguelen and annexed by France in 1949. Uninhabited except for scientists (center for joint study of geomagnetism with the USSR), the islands support a unique wild cabbage containing a pungent oil.

Kerkira Greek form of ◊Corfu, an island in the Ionian Sea.

Kerman city in Kerman province SE Iran; population (1986) 254,800. It is a center for the mining of copper and precious metals.

Kermanshah former name (until 1980) of the town of ◊Bakhtaran in NW Iran.

Kern Jerome (David) 1885–1945. US composer. He wrote the popular musical *Show Boat* 1927, which includes the song "Ol' Man River." Based on Edna Ferber's novel, it was the first example of serious musical theater in the US. Many of Kern's songs have become classics, notably "Smoke Gets in Your Eyes" from his musical *Roberta* 1933.

He wrote dozens of hit songs and musicals from 1904 and Hollywood movies from the beginning of the sound era 1927. He worked mainly with lyricist Otto Harbach but also with Ira Gershwin, Oscar Hammerstein II, Dorothy Fields, and Johnny Mercer.

kernel the inner, softer part of a ◊nut, or of a seed within a hard shell.

kerosene thin oil obtained from the distillation of petroleum; a highly refined form is used in jet aircraft fuel. Kerosene is a mixture of hydrocarbons of the ◊paraffin series.

Kerouac Jack 1923–1969. US novelist who named and epitomized the ◊Beat generation of the 1950s. His books, all autobiographical, include *On the Road* 1957, *Big Sur* 1963, and *Desolation Angel* 1965.

On the Road, written in three weeks in a formless, unpolished style, awoke the nation to the attitudes of a group of young people in pursuit of love, beauty, and new experiences, who were contemptuous of staid American values.

Kerr Deborah 1921– . British actress who often played genteel, ladylike roles. Her performance in British films such as *Major Barbara* 1940 and *Black Narcissus* 1946 led to starring parts in Hollywood films such as *Quo Vadis* 1951, *From Here to Eternity* 1953, and *The King and I* 1956.

Kerry county of Munster province, Republic of Ireland, E of Cork
area 1,814 sq mi/4,700 sq km
county town Tralee
physical W coastline deeply indented; N part low-lying, but in the S are the highest mountains in Ireland including Carrantuohill 3,417 ft/1,041 m, the highest peak in Ireland; many rivers and lakes
features Macgillycuddy's Reeks, Lakes of Killarney
products engineering, woolens, shoes, cutlery; tourism is important
population (1986) 124,000.

Kertész André 1894–1986. Hungarian-born US photographer whose spontaneity had a great impact on photojournalism. A master of the 35-mm format camera, he recorded his immediate environment with wit and style.

He lived in Paris 1925–36, where he befriended and photographed many avant-garde artists and writers, and in New York City 1936–86, where he did commercial photography for major American magazines as well as creative photography.

Kesselring Albert 1885–1960. German field marshal in World War II, commander of the Luftwaffe (air force) 1939–40, during the invasions of Poland and the Low Countries and the early stages of the Battle of Britain. He later served under Field Marshal Rommel in N Africa, took command in Italy 1943, and was commander in chief on the western front March 1945. His death sentence for war crimes at the Nuremberg trials 1947 was commuted to life imprisonment, but he was released 1952.

kestrel either of two small species of ◊falcon (genus *Falco*): the Eurasian kestrel *F. tinnunculus*, about 13.5 in/35 cm long, which occasionally visits E North America and the Aleutians; and the American kestrel or sparrowhawk *F. sparverius*, somewhat smaller, of most of North America. Both species are russet, gray, and tan in color, with the male American kestrel having more gray on its wings. They hunt mainly by hovering in midair while watching for grasshoppers and small mammals.

ketone member of the group of organic compounds containing the carbonyl group (CO) bonded to two atoms of carbon (instead of one carbon and one hydrogen as in ◊aldehydes). Ketones are liquids or low-melting-point solids, slightly soluble in water.

An example is acetone (technical name propanone), CH_3COCH_3, used as a solvent.

kettle a glacial geologic feature, formed when a block of stagnant ice from a receding glacier becomes isolated and buried in glacial outwash or drift before it finally melts. When the block disappears, it leaves a pit or depression called a kettle, in the drift. These depressions range from 15 ft/5 m to 8 mi/13 km in diameter, and some exceed 100 ft/33 m in depth.

As time passes, water sometimes fills the kettles to form lakes or swamps, features found throughout much of N North America. Lake Ronkonkoma, the largest lake on Long Island, New York, is an example.

Kew Gardens popular name for the Royal Botanic Gardens, Kew, England. They were founded 1759 by the mother of King George III as a small garden and then passed to the nation by Queen Victoria 1840, when they had grown to 368 acres/149 hectares. They contain a collection of over 25,000 living plant species and many fine buildings. The gardens are also a center for botanical research.

key in music, the ◊diatonic scale around which a piece of music is written; for example, a passage in the key of C major will mainly use the notes of the C major scale. The term is also used for the lever activated by a keyboard player, such as a piano key.

Key Francis Scott 1779–1843. US lawyer and poet who wrote the song "The Star-Spangled Banner," while Fort McHenry was besieged by the British in 1814; since 1931 it has been the national anthem of the US.

Key served as US attorney for the District of Columbia 1833–41.

keyboard in computing, an input device resembling a typewriter keyboard, used to enter instructions and data.

There are many variations on the layout and labeling of keys for different purposes. Extra numeric keys may be added, as can special-purpose function keys, such as LOAD, SAVE, and PRINT, whose effects can be defined by programs in the computer.

Keynes John Maynard, 1st Baron Keynes 1883–1946. English economist whose *The General Theory of Employment, Interest, and Money*

Khaddhafi *Libyan leader Colonel Moamer al Khaddhafi.*

1936 proposed the prevention of financial crises and unemployment by adjusting demand through government control of credit and currency. He is responsible for that part of economics now known as ◊macroeconomics.

Keynes led the British delegation at the Bretton Woods Conference 1944, which set up the International Monetary Fund. His theories were widely accepted in the aftermath of World War II, and he was one of the most influential economists of the 20th century. His ideas are today often contrasted with those of ◊monetarism.

Keynesian economics the economic theory of J M Keynes, which argues that a fall in national income, lack of demand for goods, and rising unemployment should be countered by increased government expenditure to stimulate the economy. It is opposed by monetarists (see ◊monetarism).

Key West city at the tip of the Florida peninsula; population (1990) 24,832. As a tourist resort, it was popularized by the novelist Ernest Hemingway and the playwright Tennessee Williams. In 1967 it became the first US town to take all its fresh water from the sea. It was incorporated 1828 and is the southernmost city in the continental US.

kg abbreviation for ◊kilogram.

KGB the Soviet secret police, the Komitet Gosudarstvennoye Bezhopaznosti/"Committee of State Security," in control of frontier and general security and the forced-labor system. KGB officers hold key appointments in all fields of daily life, reporting to administration offices in every major town.

Many KGB officers are also said to hold diplomatic posts in embassies abroad. The headquarters are in Dzerzhinsky Square, Moscow, and the Lubyanka Prison is located behind it. Earlier names for the secret police were Okhrana under the tsars; ◊Cheka 1918–23; GPU or OGPU (*Obedinyonnoye Gosudarstvennoye Polititcheskoye Upravleniye*/Unified State Political Administration) 1923–34; NKVD (*Narodny Komisariat Vnutrennykh Del*/People's Commissariat of Internal Affairs) 1934–46; and MVD (Ministry of Internal Affairs) 1946–53. ◊Smersh was a subsection.

Khabarovsk industrial city (oil refining, lumber milling, meat packing) in SE Siberia, USSR; population (1987) 591,000.

Khabarovsk territory of the SE USSR bordering the Sea of Okhotsk and drained by the Amur; area 318,501 sq mi/824,600 sq km; population (1985) 1,728,000. The capital is Khabarovsk. Mineral resources include gold, coal and iron ore.

Khachaturian Aram Il'yich 1903–1978. Armenian composer. His use of folk themes is shown in the ballets *Gayaneh* 1942, which includes the "Saber Dance," and *Spartacus* 1956.

Khaddhafi (or Gaddafi or Qaddafi), Moamer al 1942– Libyan revolutionary leader. Overthrowing King Idris 1969, he became virtual president of a republic, although he nominally gave up all except an ideological role 1974. He favors territorial expansion in N Africa reaching as far as Zaïre, has supported rebels in Chad, and proposed mergers with a number of countries. His theories, based on those of the Chinese communist leader Mao Zedong, are contained in a *Green Book*.

Khajurāho town in Madhya Pradesh, central India, the former capital of the Candella monarchs. It has 35 sandstone temples—Jain, Buddhist, and Hindu—built in the 10th and 11th centuries. The temples are covered inside and out with erotic sculpture symbolizing mystic union with the deity.

khaki the dust-colored uniform of British and Indian troops in India from about 1850, adopted as camouflage during the Boer War 1899–1902, and later standard for military uniforms worldwide.

Khalifa Sudanese leader ◊Abd Allah.

Khalistan projected independent Sikh state. See ◊Sikhism.

Khalsa the brotherhood of the Sikhs, created by Guru Gobind Singh at the festival of Baisakhi in 1699. The Khalsa was originally founded as a militant group to defend the Sikh community from persecution.

Khama Seretse 1921–1980. Botswanan politician, prime minister of Bechuanaland 1965, and first president of Botswana from 1966 until his death.

khamsin a hot wind that blows from the Sahara desert over Egypt from late March to early May.

Khan Liaquat Ali 1895–1951. Indian politician, deputy leader of the Muslim League 1941–47, first prime minister of Pakistan from 1947. He was assassinated by a Muslim fanatic.

Khardungla Pass road linking the Indian town of Leh with the high-altitude military outpost on the Siachen Glacier at an altitude of 1,744 ft/5,662 m in the Karakoram range, Kashmir. It is thought to be the highest road in the world.

Kharga or ***Kharijah*** oasis in the Western Desert of Egypt, known to the Romans, and from 1960 headquarters of the New Valley irrigation project. An area twice the size of Italy is watered from natural underground reservoirs.

Kharg Island a small island in the Persian Gulf used by Iran as a deepwater oil terminal. Between 1982 and 1988 Kharg Island came under frequent attack during the Iran–Iraq War.

Kharkov capital of the Kharkov region, Ukraine, USSR, 250 mi/400 km E of Kiev; population (1987) 1,587,000. It is a railroad junction and industrial city (engineering, tractors), close to the Donets Basin coalfield and Krivoy Rog iron mines. Kharkov was founded 1654 as a fortress town. Its university dates from 1805.

Khartoum capital and trading center of Sudan, at the junction of the Blue and White Nile; population (1983) 476,000, and of Khartoum North, across the Blue Nile, 341,000. ◊Omdurman is also a suburb of Khartoum, giving the urban area a population of over 1.3 million.

It was founded 1830 by ◊Mehemet Ali. General ◊Gordon was killed at Khartoum by the Mahdist rebels 1885. A new city was built after the site was recaptured by British troops under Kitchener 1898.

Khazar member of a people of Turkish origin from the lower Volga basin of Central Asia, who formed a commercial link and a buffer state in the 7th–12th centuries between the Arabs and the Byzantine empire, and later between the Byzantine empire and the Baltic. Their ruler adopted Judaism as the state religion in the 8th century. In the 11th century, Slavonic and nomadic Turks invaded, and by the 13th century the Khazar empire had been absorbed by its neighbors. It has been suggested that the Khazars were the ancestors of some of the Jews living in E European countries and now throughout the world.

khedive title granted by the Turkish sultan to his Egyptian viceroy 1867, retained by succeeding rulers until 1914.

Kherson port in Ukraine, USSR, on the Dnieper river, capital of Kherson region; population (1987) 358,000. Industries include shipbuilding, soap, and tobacco manufacture. It was founded 1778 by army commander ◊Potemkin as the first Russian naval base on the Black Sea.

Khe Sanh in the Vietnam War, US Marine outpost near the Laotian border and just south of the demilitarized zone between North and South Vietnam. Garrisoned by 4,000 Marines, it was attacked unsuccessfully by 20,000 North Vietnamese troops Jan 21–Apr 7, 1968.

Khirbet Qumran archeological site in Jordan; see ◊Qumran.

Khmer or ***Kmer*** a member of the largest ethnic group in Cambodia living mainly in agricultural and fishing villages under a chief. Khmer minorities also live in E Thailand and S Vietnam. The Khmer language belongs to the Mon-Khmer family of Austro-Asiatic languages.

The Khmer empire, an early SE Asian civilization, was founded AD 616 and came under Indian cultural influence as part of the SE Asian kingdom of Funan. The earliest inscriptions in the Khmer language date from the 7th century AD. The Khmer empire reached its zenith in the 9th–13th centuries, with the building of the capital city and temple complex at Angkor. The Khmers were eventually pushed back by the Thais into the territory they occupy today. The anti-French nationalists of Cambodia adopted the name Khmer Republic 1971–75, and the name continues in use by the communist movement called the ◊Khmer Rouge.

The Khmers practice Theravāda Buddhism and trace descent through both male and female lines. Traditionally, Khmer society was divided into six groups: the royal family, the Brahmans (who officiated at royal festivals), Buddhist monks, officials, commoners, and slaves.

Khmer Republic former name of ◊Cambodia.

Khmer Rouge Communist movement in Cambodia (Kampuchea) that formed the largest opposition group to the US-backed regime led by Lon Nol 1970–75. By 1974 the Khmer Rouge controlled the countryside, and in 1975 the capital, Phnom Penh, was captured and Sihanouk installed as head of state. Internal disagreements led to the creation of the Pol Pot government 1976 and mass deportations and executions. From 1978, when Vietnam invaded the country, the Khmer Rouge conducted a guerrilla campaign against the Vietnamese forces. Pol Pot retired as military leader 1985 and was succeeded by the more moderate Khieu Samphan. Following the withdrawal of Viet-

Khomeini *The Shi'ite Muslim leader Ayatollah Khomeini, who made Islam the driving force in Iran's government.*

Khrushchev *Soviet leader Nikita Khrushchev during a state visit to France.*

namese forces in 1989, the Khmer Rouge continued its warfare against the Vietnamese-backed government making substantial advances during 1990. Its future, however, seemed imperiled by the possibility of the withdrawal of Chinese support.

Khomeini Ayatollah Ruhollah 1900–1989. Iranian Shi'ite Muslim leader, born in Khomein, central Iran. Exiled for opposition to the Shah from 1964, he returned when the Shah left the country 1979, and established a fundamentalist Islamic republic. His rule was marked by a protracted war with Iraq, and suppression of opposition within Iran, executing thousands of opponents.

Khomeini was hostile toward both superpowers, held US embassy hostages 1979–81, and supported terrorist groups.

Khorana Har Gobind 1922– . Indian biochemist who in 1976 led the team that first synthesized a biologically active gene.

Khorramshahr former port and oil-refining center in Iran, on the Shatt-al-Arab river and linked by bridge to the island of Abadan. It was completely destroyed in the 1980s by enemy action in the Iran–Iraq War.

Khrushchev Nikita Sergeyevich 1894–1971. Soviet politician, secretary general of the Communist Party 1953–64, premier 1958–64. He emerged as leader from the power struggle following Stalin's death and was the first official to denounce Stalin, in 1956. His de-Stalinization program gave rise to revolts in Poland and Hungary 1956. Because of problems with the economy and foreign affairs (a breach with China 1960; conflict with the US in the ◊Cuban missile crisis 1962), he was ousted by Leonid Breszhnev and Alexei Kosygin.

Born near Kursk, the son of a miner, Khrushchev fought in the post-Revolutionary civil war 1917–20, and in World War II organized the guerrilla defense of his native Ukraine. He denounced Stalinism in a secret session of the party Feb 1956. Many victims of the purges of the 1930s were either released or posthumously rehabilitated, but when Hungary revolted in Oct against Soviet domination, there was immediate Soviet intervention. In 1958 Khrushchev succeeded Bulganin as chair of the council of ministers (prime minister). His policy of competition with capitalism was successful in the space program, which launched the world's first satellite (◊*Sputnik*). Because of the Cuban crisis and the personal feud with Mao Zedong that led to the Sino-Soviet split, he was compelled to resign 1964, although by 1965 his reputation was to some extent officially restored. In Apr 1989 his Feb 1956 "secret speech" against Stalin was officially published for the first time.

Khufu c. 3000 BC. Egyptian king of Memphis, who built the largest of the pyramids, known to the Greeks as the pyramid of Cheops (the Greek form of Khufu).

Khulna capital of Khulna region, SW Bangladesh, situated close to the Ganges delta; population (1981) 646,000. Industry includes shipbuilding and textiles; it trades in jute, rice, salt, sugar, and oilseed.

Khuzestan SW province of Iran, which includes the chief Iranian oil resources; population (1986) 2,702,533. Towns include Ahvaz (capital) and the ports of Abadan and Khuninshahr. There have been calls for Sunni Muslim autonomy, under the name ◊Arabistan.

Khwārizmī, al- Mohammed ibn-Mūsā c. 780–c. 850. Persian mathematician from Khwarizm (now Khiva, USSR), who lived and worked in Baghdad. He wrote a book on algebra, from part of whose title (*al-jabr*) comes the word "algebra," and a book in which he introduced to the West the Hindu-Arabic decimal number system. The word "algorithm" is a corruption of his name.

He also compiled astronomical tables and was responsible for introducing the concept of zero into Arab mathematics.

Khyber Pass pass 33 mi/53 km long through the mountain range that separates Pakistan from Afghanistan. The Khyber Pass was used by invaders of India. The present road was constructed by the British during the Afghan Wars.

Kiangsi former spelling of ◊Jiangxi, province of China.

Kiangsu former spelling of ◊Jiangsu, province of China.

kibbutz Israeli communal collective settlement with collective ownership of all property and earnings, collective organization of work and decision making, and communal housing for children. A modified version, the *Moshav Shitufi*, is similar to the ◊collective farms of the USSR. Other Israeli cooperative rural settlements include the *Moshav Ovdim*, which has equal opportunity, and the similar but less strict *Moshav* settlement.

Kidd "Captain" (William) c. 1645–1701. Scottish pirate. He spent his youth privateering for the British against the French off the North American coast, and in 1695 was given a royal commission to suppress piracy in the Indian Ocean. Instead, he joined a group of pirates in Madagascar. On his way to Boston, Massachusetts, he was arrested 1699, taken to England, and hanged.

His execution marked the end of some 200 years of semiofficial condoning of piracy by the British government.

kidnapping the abduction of a person against his or her will. It often involves holding persons for ransom.

It may also occur in divorce situations with child custody disputes or involve psychosexual motives.

kidney in vertebrates, one of a pair of organs responsible for water regulation, excretion of waste products, and maintaining the ionic composition of the blood. The kidneys are situated on the rear wall of the abdomen. Each one consists of a number of long tubules; the outer parts filter the aqueous components of blood, and the inner parts selectively reabsorb vital salts, leaving waste products in the remaining fluid (urine), which is passed through the ureter to the bladder.

The action of the kidneys is vital, although if one is removed, the other enlarges to take over its function. A patient with two defective kidneys may continue near-normal life with the aid of a kidney machine or continuous ambulatory peritoneal ◊dialysis (CAPD).

Kiefer Anselm 1945– . German painter. He studied under Joseph ◊Beuys and his works include monumental landscapes on varied surfaces, often with the paint built up into relief with other substances. Much of his highly Expressionist work deals with recent German history.

Kiel Baltic port in the Federal Republic of Germany; capital of Schleswig-Holstein; population (1988) 244,000. Industries include fishing, shipbuilding and electronics engineering. Kiel Week in June is a yachting meeting.

Kiel Canal formerly ***Kaiser Wilhelm Canal*** waterway 61 mi/98.7 km long, that connects the Baltic with the North Sea. Built by Germany in the years before World War I, the canal allowed the German navy to move from Baltic bases to the open sea without traveling through international waters.

Kielce city in central Poland, NE of Kraków; population (1985) 201,000; industrial rail junction (chemicals, metals).

Kierkegaard Søren (Aabye) 1813–1855. Danish philosopher considered to be the founder of ◊existentialism. Disagreeing with the German dialectical philosopher ◊Hegel, he argued that no system of thought could explain the unique experience of the individual. He defended Christianity, suggesting that God cannot be known through reason, but only through a "leap of faith." He believed that God and exceptional individuals were above moral laws.

Kierkegaard was born in Copenhagen, where he spent most of his life. The son of a Jewish merchant, he converted to Christianity in 1838, although he became hostile to the established church and his beliefs caused much controversy. A prolific author, his works include *Enten-Eller/Either-Or* 1843, *Begrebet Angest/Concept of Dread* 1844, and *Efterskrift/Postscript* 1846, which summed up much of his earlier writings.

Kiev capital of Ukraine, industrial center (chemicals, clothing, leatherwork) and third largest city of the USSR, on the confluence of the Desna and Dnieper rivers; population (1987) 2,554,000.

history Founded in the 5th century by Vikings, Kiev replaced ◊Novgorod as the capital of Slav-dominated Russia 882 and was the original center of the Orthodox Christian faith 988. The city was occupied by Germany 1941. The Slav domination of Russia began with the rise of Kiev (see also under ◊Vikings), the "mother of Russian cities."

features St Sophia cathedral (11th century) and Kiev-Pechersky Monastery (both now museums) survive, and also remains of the Golden Gate. The Kiev ballet and opera are renowned.

Kigali capital of Rwanda, central Africa; population (1981) 157,000. Products include coffee and minerals.

Kikuyu a member of an E African agricultural people. They are Kenya's dominant ethnic group, primarily cultivators, although many are highly educated and have entered the professions. Their language belongs to the Bantu branch of the Niger-Congo family.

Kildare county of Leinster province, Republic of Ireland, S of Meath
area 652 sq mi/1,690 sq km
county town Naas
physical wet and boggy in the N
features part of the Bog of Allen; the village of Maynooth, with a training college for Roman Catholic priests; the Curragh, a plain that is the site of the national stud and headquarters of Irish horse racing
products oats, barley, potatoes, cattle
population (1986) 116,000.

Kilimanjaro volcano in ◊Tanzania, the highest mountain in Africa, 19,364 ft/5,900 m.

Kilkenny county of Leinster province, Republic of Ireland, E of Tipperary
area 795 sq mi/2,060 sq km
county town Kilkenny
features river Nore
products agricultural, coal
population (1986) 73,000.

Killarney market town in County Kerry, Republic of Ireland; population (1981) 7,693. A famous beauty spot in Ireland, it has Macgillycuddy's Reeks (a range of mountains) and the Lakes of Killarney to the SW.

Killeen city in central Texas, S of Fort Worth and N of Austin. Although some concrete is produced here, the economy relies heavily on nearby army base Fort Hood; population (1990) 63,535.

kidney

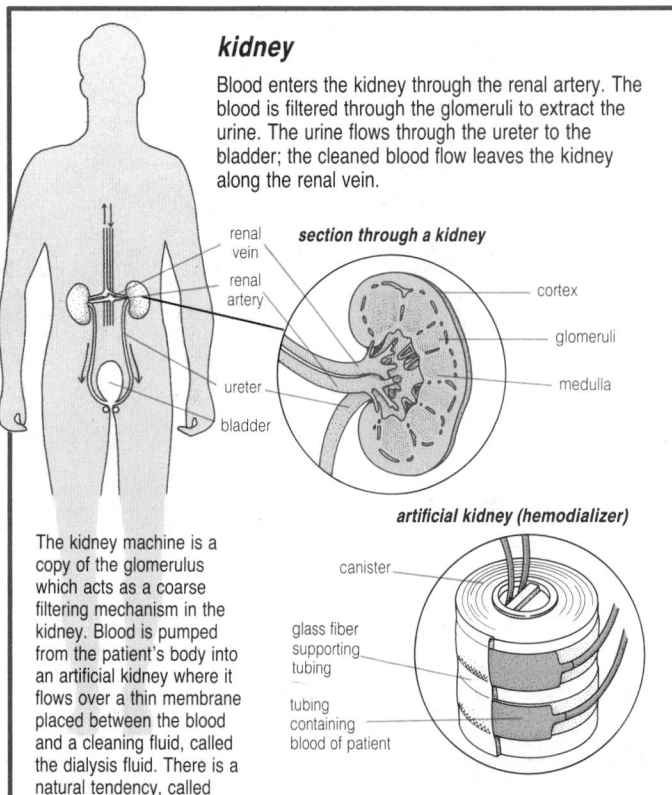

Blood enters the kidney through the renal artery. The blood is filtered through the glomeruli to extract the urine. The urine flows through the ureter to the bladder; the cleaned blood flow leaves the kidney along the renal vein.

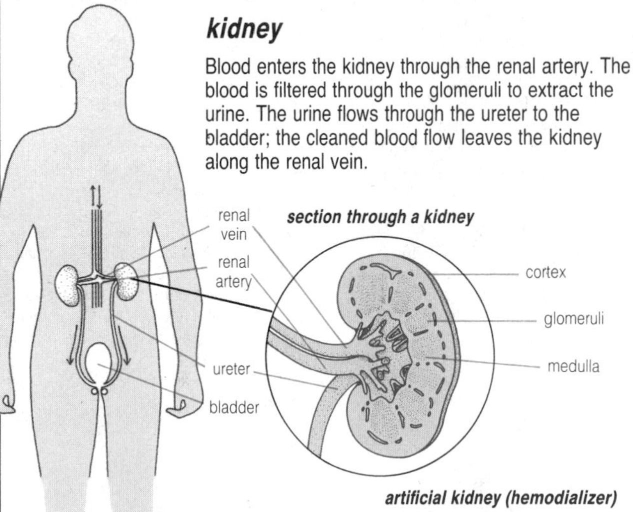

section through a kidney
renal vein
renal artery
ureter
bladder
cortex
glomeruli
medulla

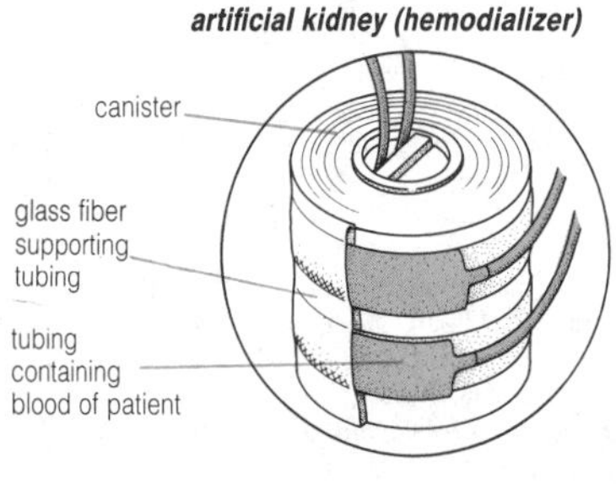

artificial kidney (hemodializer)
canister
glass fiber supporting tubing
tubing containing blood of patient

The kidney machine is a copy of the glomerulus which acts as a coarse filtering mechanism in the kidney. Blood is pumped from the patient's body into an artificial kidney where it flows over a thin membrane placed between the blood and a cleaning fluid, called the dialysis fluid. There is a natural tendency, called dialysis, for impurities in the blood to flow across the membrane into the dialysis fluid.

A man undergoing continuous ambulatory peritoneal dialysis, allowing a membrane inside the body to take over the kidney's function.▼

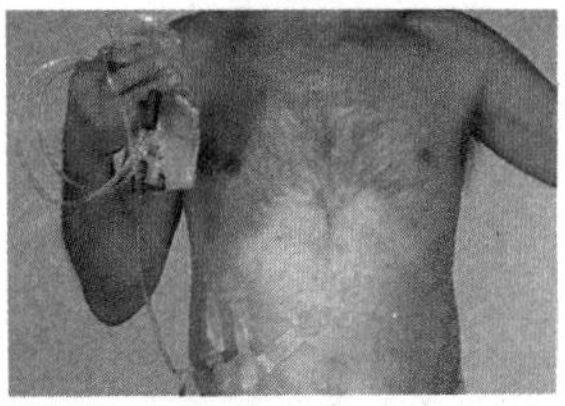

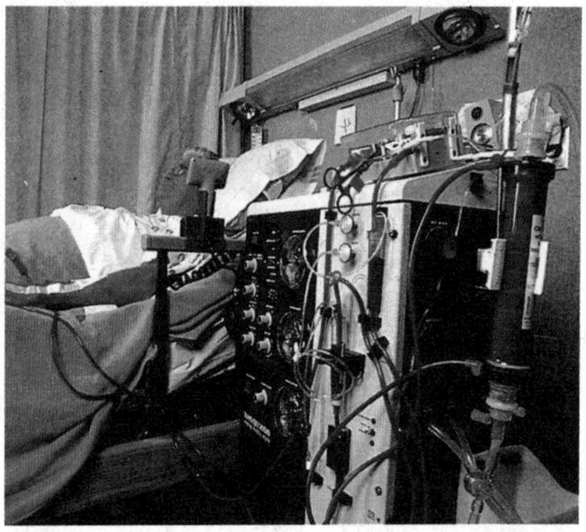

Elderly man undergoing renal dialysis on a kidney machine.

killer whale or ***orca*** toothed whale *Orcinus orca* of the dolphin family, found in all seas of the world. It is black on top, white below, and grows up to 30 ft/9 m long. It is the only whale that has been observed to prey on other whales, as well as on seals and seabirds. It has been tamed and trained to perform in sea circuses and has proved to be gentle, friendly, intelligent, and hard working, thus prompting use of its alternate name orca in the US.

Killy Jean-Claude 1943– . French skier. He won all three gold medals (slalom, giant slalom, and downhill) at the 1968 Winter Olympics in Grenoble. The first World Cup winner 1967, he retained the title 1968 and also won three world titles. He was a major force behind's France's hosting of the 1992 Winter Olympics.

CAREER HIGHLIGHTS: Jean-Claude Killy

Olympic champion
downhill: 1968
slalom: 1968
giant slalom: 1968
world champion
combined: 1966, 1968
downhill: 1966
World Cup
overall: 1967–68
downhill: 1967
giant slalom: 1967–68
slalom: 1967

Kilmer Joyce 1886–1918. US poet. His first collection of poems, *Summer of Love*, was published 1911. Kilmer later gained an international reputation with the title work of *Trees and Other Poems* 1914. At the outbreak of World War I, he joined the 165th Regiment and was killed in action in France.

Born in New Brunswick, New Jersey, Kilmer was educated at Rutgers and Columbia universities. Working briefly as a high school teacher, he moved to New York and worked in a variety of publishing jobs while pursuing his own literary career.

Kierkegaard *A portrait of the Danish philosopher Soren Kierkegaard sketched by his cousin Christian Kierkegaard.*

kiln high-temperature furnace used commercially for drying timber, roasting metal ores, or for making cement, bricks, and pottery. Oil-or gas-fired kilns are used to bake ceramics at up to 13,200°F/760°C; electric kilns do not generally reach such high temperatures.

kilobyte (KB) in computing, a unit of memory equal to 1024 ◊bytes.

kilogram SI unit (abbreviation kg) of mass equal to 1,000 grams (2.2 lb).

kilometer unit (abbreviation km) of length equal to 1,000 meters (3,280.89 ft).

kilowatt unit (abbreviation kW) of power equal to 1,000 watts or about 1.34 horsepower.

kilowatt-hour commercial unit of electrical energy (abbreviation kWh), defined as the work done by a power of 1,000 watts in one hour. It is used to calculate the cost of electrical energy taken from utility-company supply.

Kimberley diamond-mining town in Cape Province, South Africa, 95 mi/153 km NW of Bloemfontein; population (1980) 144,923. Its mines have been controlled by De Beers Consolidated Mines since 1887.

Kimberley diamond site in Western Australia, found in 1978–79, estimated to have 5% of the world's known gem-quality stones and 50% of its industrial diamonds.

kimberlite an igneous rock that is ultrabasic (containing very little silica); a type of alkaline peridotite (see ◊peridot) containing mica in addition to olivine and other minerals. Kimberlite represents the world's principal source of diamonds.

Kimberlite is found in carrot-shaped pipelike ◊intrusions called diatremes, where mobile material from very deep in the Earth's crust has forced itself upward, expanding in its ascent. The material, brought upward from near the boundary between crust and mantle, often altered and frag-

kiln *Brick kilns near Lahore in Pakistan.*

mented, includes diamonds. Diatremes are found principally near Kimberley, South Africa, from which the name of the rock is derived, and in the Yakut area of Siberia, USSR.

Kim Dae Jung 1924– . South Korean social-democratic politician. As a committed opponent of the regime of General Park Chung Hee, he suffered imprisonment and exile. He was a presidential candidate in 1971 and 1987.

Kim Il Sung 1912– . North Korean Communist politician and marshal. He became prime minister 1948 and president 1972, retaining the presidency of the Communist Workers' party. He likes to be known as the "Great Leader" and has campaigned constantly for the reunification of Korea. His son Kim Jong Il (1942–), known as the "Dear Leader," has been named as his successor.

kimono traditional Japanese costume. Already worn in the Heian period (794–1185), it is still used by women for formal wear and informally by men.

For the finest kimonos a rectangular piece of silk (about 36 ft/11 m × 1.5 ft/0.5 m) is cut into seven pieces for tailoring. The design (which must match perfectly over the seams and for which flowers are the usual motif) is then painted by hand and enhanced by embroidery or gilding. The accompanying *obi*, or sash, is also embroidered.

Kim Young Sam 1927– . South Korean democratic politician. A member of the National Assembly from 1954 and president of the New Democratic Party (NDP) from 1974, he lost his seat and was later placed under house arrest because of his opposition to President Park Chung Hee. In 1983 he led a pro-democracy hunger strike but in 1987 failed to defeat Roh Tae Woo in the presidential election. In 1990 he merged the NDP with the ruling party to form the new Democratic Liberal Party (DLP).

kinetic energy the energy of a body resulting from motion. It is contrasted with ◊potential energy.

kinetics the branch of chemistry that investigates the rates of chemical reactions.

kinetics alternate name for ◊dynamics. It is distinguished from kinematics, which deals with motion without reference to force or mass.

kinetic theory theory describing the physical properties of matter in terms of the behavior—principally movement—of its component atoms or molecules. The temperature of a substance is dependent on the velocity of movement of its constituent particles, increased temperature being accompanied by increased movement. A gas consists of rapidly moving atoms or molecules and, according to kinetic theory, it is their continual impact on the walls of the containing vessel that accounts for the pressure of the gas. The slowing of molecular motion as temperature falls, according to kinetic theory, accounts for the physical properties of liquids and solids, culminating in the concept of no molecular motion at ◊absolute zero (0 K/–273°C). By making various assumptions about the nature of gas molecules, it is possible to derive from the kinetic theory the various gas laws (such as ◊Avogadro's, ◊Boyle's, and ◊Charles's laws).

King Billie Jean (born Moffitt) 1943– . US lawn tennis player. She won a record 20 Wimbledon titles 1961–79 and 39 Grand Slam titles.

Her first Wimbledon title was the doubles with Karen Hantze 1961, and her last, also doubles, with Martina Navratilova 1979. She won the Wimbledon singles title six times, the US Open singles title four times, the French Open once, and the Australian Open once. Her 39 Grand Slam events at singles and doubles are third only to Navratilova and Margaret Court.

King Martin Luther Jr 1929–1968. US civil-rights campaigner, black leader, and Baptist minister. He first came to national attention as leader of the ◊Montgomery, Alabama, bus boycott 1955, and was one of the organizers of the massive (200,000 people) march on Washington, DC 1963

***King** Civil-rights leader Martin Luther King, Jr, marching in 1965, was assassinated in Memphis, Tennessee, in 1968.*

to demand racial equality. An advocate of ◊nonviolence, he was awarded the Nobel Peace Prize 1964. He was assassinated in Memphis, Tennessee by James Earl Ray. King's birthday (Jan 15) is observed on the third Monday in Jan as a public vacation in the US.

Born in Atlanta, Georgia, son of a Baptist minister, King founded the ◊Southern Christian Leadership Conference 1957. A brilliant and moving speaker, he was the symbol of, and leading figure in, the campaign for integration and equal rights in the late 1950s and early 1960s. In the mid-1960s his moderate approach was criticized by black militants. He was the target of intensive investigation by the federal authorities, especially the FBI under J Edgar ◊Hoover. His personal life was scrutinized and criticized by those opposed to his policies.

King Stephen 1946– . US writer of best-selling horror novels with small-town or rural settings. Many of his works have been filmed, including *Carrie* 1974, *The Shining* 1978, and *Christine* 1983.

His recent novels include *It* and *The Tommyknockers* (both 1987), *The Dark Half* 1989, and *Needful Things* 1991. He has also published three volumes of short stories, several screenplays, and a number of novels under the pseudonym Richard Bachman.

King William Lyon Mackenzie 1874–1950. Canadian Liberal prime minister 1921–26, 1926–30, and 1935–48. He maintained the unity of the English- and French-speaking populations, and was instrumental in establishing equal status for Canada with Britain.

CAREER HIGHLIGHTS: Billie Jean King

Wimbledon
singles: 1966–68, 1972–73, 1975
doubles: 1961–62, 1965, 1967–68, 1970–73, 1979
mixed: 1967, 1971, 1973–74
US Open
singles: 1967, 1971–72, 1974
doubles: 1964, 1967, 1974, 1978, 1980
mixed: 1967, 1971, 1973, 1976
French Open
singles: 1972
doubles: 1972
mixed: 1967, 1970
Australian Open
singles: 1968
mixed: 1968

king crab or ***Alaskan king crab*** large, edible crab

king crab

Paralithodescamtschatica, of the N Pacific. The term "king crab" is sometimes used as another name for the ◊horseshoe crab.

kingdom the primary division in biological ◊classification. At one time, only two kingdoms were recognized: animals and plants. Today most biologists prefer a five-kingdom system, even though it still involves grouping together organisms that are probably unrelated. One widely accepted scheme is as follows: Kingdom Animalia (all multicellular animals); Kingdom Plantae (all plants, all seaweeds and other algae, including unicellular algae); Kingdom Fungi (all fungi, including the unicellular yeasts, but not slime molds); Kingdom Protista or Protoctista (protozoa, diatoms, dinoflagellates, slime molds, and various other lower organisms with eukaryotic cells); and Kingdom Monera (all prokaryotes—the bacteria and cyanobacteria). The first four of these kingdoms make up the eukaryotes.

When only two kingdoms were recognized, any organism with a rigid cell wall was a plant, and so bacteria and fungi were considered plants, despite their many differences. Other organisms, such as the photosynthetic flagellates (euglenoids), were claimed by both kingdoms. The unsatisfactory nature of the two-kingdom system became evident during the 19th century, and the biologist Ernst ◊Haeckel was among the first to try to reform it. High-power microscopes have revealed more about the structure of cells; it has become clear that there is a fundamental difference between cells without a nucleus (◊prokaryotes) and those with a nucleus (◊eukaryotes). However, these differences are larger than those between animals and higher plants, and are unsuitable for use as kingdoms. At present there is no agreement on how many kingdoms there are in the natural world. Although the five-kingdom system is widely favored; some schemes have as many as 20.

kingfisher heavy-billed bird of the worldwide family Alcedinidae, found near streams, ponds, and coastal areas. They plunge-dive for fish and aquatic insects. The nest is usually a burrow in a river bank.

There are about 90 species of kingfishers, the largest being the Australian ◊kookaburra.

The North American belted kingfisher *Ceryle alcyon* is about 13 in/33 cm long, slate gray and white (the female has a rust-colored band on the belly), and crested in both sexes.

King Lear tragedy by William Shakespeare, first performed 1605–06. Lear, king of Britain, favors his grasping daughters, Goneril and Regan, with shares of his kingdom but refuses his third, honest daughter, Cordelia, a share. Rejected by Goneril and Regan, the old and unbalanced Lear is

kingfisher

reunited with Cordelia but dies of grief when she is murdered.

King's Council in medieval England, a court that carried out much of the monarch's daily administration. It was established in the reign of Edward I, and became the Privy Council 1534–36.

Kingsley Ben (Krishna Banji) 1944– . British film actor of Indian descent who usually plays character parts. He played the title role of *Gandhi* 1982 and appeared in *Betrayal* 1982, *Testimony* 1987, and *Pascali's Island* 1988.

Kingsport city in NE Tennessee, on the Holston River, NE of Knoxville, near the Virginia border. Manufactures include plastics, chemicals, textiles, paper and printing, and cement; population (1990) 36,365. Fort Patrick Henry, built here 1776, protected the Wilderness Road.

Kingston capital and principal port of Jamaica, West Indies, the cultural and commercial center of the island; population (1983) 101,000, metropolitan area 525,000. Founded 1693, Kingston became the capital of Jamaica 1872.

Kingston town in E Ontario, Canada, on Lake Ontario; population (1981) 60,313. Industries include shipbuilding yards, engineering works, and grain elevators. It grew from 1782 around the French Fort Frontenac, was captured by the English 1748, and renamed in honor of George III.

Kingston-upon-Hull official name of ◊Hull, city in Humberside in NE England.

Kingstown capital and principal port of St Vincent and the Grenadines, West Indies, in the SW of the island of St Vincent; population (1987) 29,000.

King-Te-Chen alternate spelling of ◊Jingdezhen, town in China.

kinkajou Central and South American carnivore *Potos flavus* of the raccoon family. Yellowish-brown, with a rounded face and slim body, the kinkajou grows to 1.8 ft/55 cm with a 1.6 ft/50 cm tail, and has short legs with sharp claws. It spends its time in trees and has a prehensile tail. It feeds largely on fruit.

Kinki region of S Honshu Island, Japan; population (1986) 21,932,000; area 12,773 sq mi/33,070 sq km. The chief city is Osaka.

Kino Eusebio Francisco c. 1644–1711. Italian-born Jesuit missionary. Kino entered the Jesuit order 1665. After teaching at the University of Ingolstadt, he was sent as a missionary to New Spain 1678. Kino arrived in Mexico City 1681 and soon joined a shortlived colony in Baja California. In 1687 he began exploration of Pimería Alta, now modern Sonora, Mexico, and S Arizona. There he established the missions of Tumacacori and San Xavier del Bac near modern Tucson. Kino later explored the Colorado Valley and discovered the massive prehistoric Indian ruins of Casa Grande.

kin selection in biology, the idea that ◊altruism shown to genetic relatives can be worthwhile, because those relatives share some genes with the individual that is behaving altruistically and may continue to reproduce.

Alarm-calling in response to predators is an example of a behavior that may have evolved through kin selection: relatives that are warned of danger can escape and continue to breed, even if the alarm caller is caught.

Kinsey Alfred 1894–1956. US researcher, whose studies of male and female sexual behavior 1948–53, based on questionnaires, were the first serious published research on this topic.

The Institute for Sex Research at Indiana University, founded 1947, continues the objective study of human sexual behavior. Many misconceptions, social class differences, and wide variations in practice and expectations have been discovered as a result of Kinsey's work.

Kinshasa formerly ***Léopoldville*** capital of Zaïre on the river Zaïre, 250 mi/400 km inland from Matadi; population (1984) 2,654,000. Industries include chemicals, textiles, engineering, food pro-

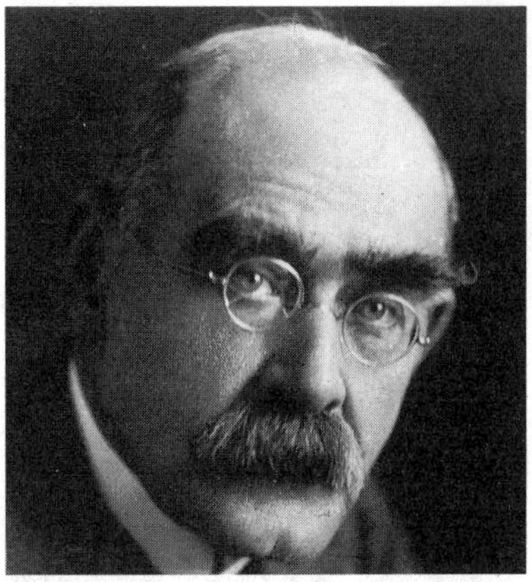

Kipling *English short-story writer, novelist, and poet Rudyard Kipling.*

cessing, and furniture. It was founded by the explorer Henry Stanley 1887.

kinship in anthropology, human relationship based on descent or marriage, and sanctified by law and custom. Kinship forms the basis for most human societies and for such social groupings as the family, clan, or tribe.

The social significance of kinship varies from society to society. Most human societies have evolved strict social rules, customs, and taboos regarding kinship and sexual behavior (such as the prohibition of incest), marriage, and inheritance.

Kinski Klaus 1926–1991. German actor who has appeared in several Werner Herzog films such as *Aguirre Wrath of God* 1972, *Nosferatu* 1978, and *Fitzcarraldo* 1982. His other film appearances include *For a Few Dollars More* 1965, *Dr Zhivago* 1965 and *Venom* 1982. He is the father of actress Nastasia Kinski.

Kipling (Joseph) Rudyard 1865–1936. English writer, born in India. His stories for children include the *Jungle Books* 1894–1895, *Stalky and Co* 1899, and the *Just So Stories* 1902. Other works include the novel *Kim* 1901, the short story "His Gift," poetry, and the unfinished autobiography *Something of Myself* 1937. In his heyday he enjoyed enormous popularity, and although subsequently denigrated for alleged "jingoist imperialism," his work is increasingly valued for its complex characterization and subtle moral viewpoints. He was awarded the Nobel Prize 1907.

Born in Bombay, Kipling was educated at the United Services College at Westward Ho!, England, which provided the background for *Stalky and Co.* He worked as a journalist in India 1882–89; during these years he wrote *Plain Tales from the Hills* 1888, *Soldiers Three* 1890, *Wee Willie Winkie* 1890, and others. Returning to London he published *The Light that Failed* 1890 and *Barrack-Room Ballads* 1892. He lived largely in the US 1892–96, where he produced the two *Jungle Books* and *Captains Courageous* 1897. Settling in Sussex, SE England, he published *Kim* (set in India), the *Just So Stories*, *Puck of Pook's Hill* 1906, and *Rewards and Fairies* 1910.

Kirchhoff Gustav Robert 1824–1887. German physicist who with ◊Bunsen used the spectroscope to show that all elements, heated to incandescence, have their individual spectra.

Kirchner Ernst Ludwig 1880–1938. German Expressionist artist, a leading member of the group *Die ◊Brücke* in Dresden from 1905 and in Berlin from 1911. He suffered a breakdown during World War I and settled in Switzerland, where he committed suicide.

His Dresden work, which includes woodcuts, shows the influence of African art. In Berlin he turned to city scenes and portraits, using lurid colors and bold diagonal paint strokes recalling woodcut technique.

Kirchner *German Expressionist painter Ernst Kirchner's* Self-Portrait with a Model *1907, Kunsthalle, Hamburg.*

Kirghiz a member of a pastoral people who inhabit the Central Asian region bounded by the Hindu Kush, the Himalayas, and the Tian Shan mountains. The Kirghiz are Sunni Muslims, and their Turkic language belongs to the Altaic family.

There are approximately 1.5 million Kirghiz divided among the USSR (Tadzhikstan, Uzbekistan, and Kirghizia), China (Xinjiang), and Afghanistan (Wakhan corridor). The most isolated group, because of its geographical situation and its international border problems, is found in Afghanistan. During the winter the Kirghiz live in individual family yurts (tents made of felt). In summer they come together in larger settlements of up to 20 yurts. They herd sheep, goats, and yaks, and use Bactrian camels for transporting their possessions. The highest political authority is traditionally entitled khan.

Kirghizia republic; formerly constituent republic of the USSR 1936–91, part of Soviet Central Asia
area 76,641 sq mi/198,500 sq km
capital Frunze
physical mountainous, an extension of the Tian Shan range
products cereals, sugar, cotton, coal, oil, sheep, yaks, horses
population (1987) 4,143,000; 48% Kirghiz of

Kirghizia

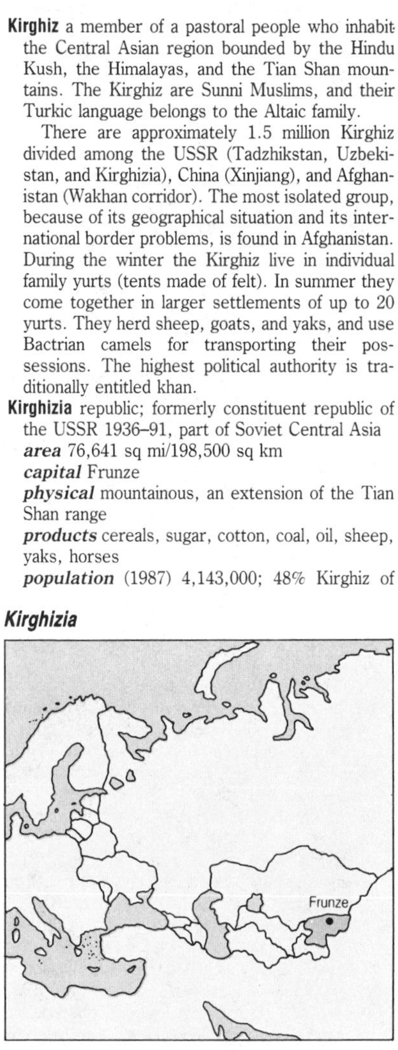
Frunze

Kiribati
Republic of

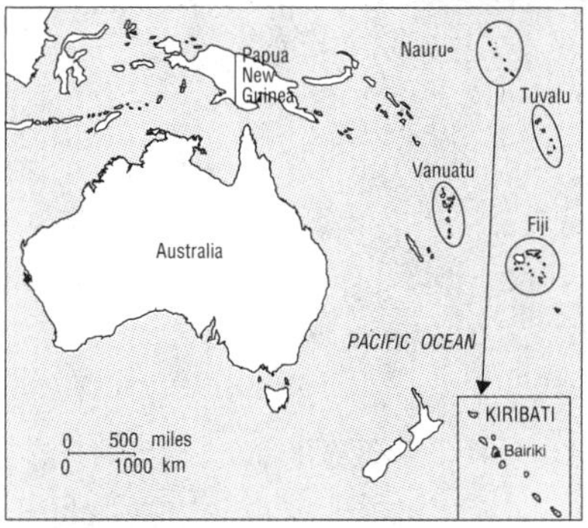
Papua New Guinea
Nauru
Tuvalu
Vanuatu
Fiji
Australia
PACIFIC OCEAN
KIRIBATI
Bairiki
0 500 miles
0 1000 km

area 277 sq mi/717 sq km
capital (and port) Bairiki (on Tarawa Atoll)
physical comprises 33 Pacific coral islands: the Kiribati (Gilbert), Rawaki (Phoenix), and Line Islands, Banaba (Ocean Island), and Kiritimati (Christmas Island)
features island groups crossed by equator and International Date Line
head of state and government Ieremia Tabai from 1979
political system liberal democracy
political parties Christian Democratic Party, opposition faction within assembly; National Party, governing faction
exports copra, fish
currency Australian dollar
population (1990 est) 65,600 (Micronesian); growth rate 1.7% p.a.
language English (official), Gilbertese
religion Roman Catholic 48%, Protestant 45%
literacy 90% (1985)
GDP $26 mn (1987); $430 per head (1988)
chronology
1892 Gilbert and Ellice Islands proclaimed a British protectorate.
1937 Phoenix Islands added to colony.
1975 Ellice Islands separated to become Tuvalu.
1977 Gilbert Islands granted internal self-government.
1979 Independence achieved from Britain, within the Commonwealth, as the Republic of Kiribati, with Ieremia Tabai as president.
1983 Tabai reelected.
1985 Fishing agreement with Soviet state-owned company negotiated, prompted formation of Kiribati's first political party, the opposition Christian Democrats.
1987 Tabai reelected.

Mongol–Tatar origin (and related to the Kazakhs), 26% Russian, 12% Uzbek, 3% Ukrainian, 2% Tatar
language Kirghiz
religion Sunni Islam
history annexed by Russia 1864, it was part of an independent Turkestan republic from 1917 to 1924, when it was reincorporated in the USSR.

Kiribati republic in the central Pacific, comprising three groups of coral atolls: the 16 Gilbert Islands, 8 uninhabited Phoenix Islands, 8 of the 11 Line Islands, and the volcanic island of Banaba.
government Kiribati's 1979 constitution provides for a president, the *Beretitenti*, who is head of both state and government, and is elected by universal suffrage for a four-year term, and a single-chamber legislature, the *Maneaba ni Maungatabu*. The president may not serve more than three terms. The *Maneaba* has 40 members: 38 popularly elected, 1 elected to represent Banaba, and the attorney-general. It also serves a four-year term. The president governs with the help of a vice-president and cabinet chosen from and responsible to the *Maneaba*. There are no formal political parties, all candidates for the *Maneaba* fighting as independents, although government and opposition factions are subsequently formed within the assembly.
history The first Europeans to visit the area were the Spanish in 1606. The 16 predominantly Micronesian-peopled Gilbert Islands and 9 predominantly Melanesian-peopled Ellice Islands became a British protectorate in 1892, and then the Gilbert and Ellice Islands Colony (GEIC) in 1916. The colony was occupied by Japan 1942–43 and was the scene of fierce fighting between Japanese and US forces. In preparation for self-government, a legislative council was set up in 1963, and in 1972 a governor took over from the British high commissioner. In 1974 the legislative council was replaced by an elected house of assembly, and in 1975, when the Ellice Islands separated and became Tuvalu, GEIC was renamed the Gilbert Islands. The islands achieved internal self-government in 1977 and full independence within the ◊Commonwealth in 1979, under the name of Kiribati, with Ieremia Tabai as their first president. He was reelected 1982 and 1983.
The once phosphate-rich island of Banaba campaigned for independence or unification with Fiji in the mid-1970s. However, its environment has been ruined by overmining and its people have been forced to resettle on Rabi Island, 2,600 mi/4,160 km away in the Fiji group.

Kirin alternate name for ◊Jilin, Chinese province.

Kirk Norman 1923–1974. New Zealand Labor politician, prime minister 1972–74.

Kirkpatrick Jeane 1926– . US politician and professor of political science. She served as US ambassador to the United Nations 1981–85.
Born in Duncan, Oklahoma, she graduated from Barnard College and Columbia University. She taught at Georgetown University 1967–81 and helped to form the Coalition for a Democratic Majority 1972. Originally a Democrat, she often spoke out against Communism and left-wing causes. She joined the Republican Party 1985.

Kirkuk city in NE Iraq; population (1985) 208,000. It is the center of a major oil-field. Formerly it was served by several pipelines providing outlets to Lebanon, Syria, and other countries, but closures caused by the Iran–Iraq War left only the pipeline to Turkey operational.

Kirov formerly (until 1934) ***Vyatka*** town NE of Gorky, on the Vyatka river, USSR; population (1987) 421,000. It is a rail and industrial center for rolling stock, tires, clothing, toys, and machine tools.

Kirov Sergei Mironovich 1886–1934. Russian Bolshevik leader who joined the party 1904 and played a prominent part in the 1917–20 civil war. As one of ◊Stalin's closest associates, he became first secretary of the Leningrad Communist Party. His assassination 1934, possibly engineered by Stalin, led to the political trials held during the next four years as part of the ◊purge.

Kirovabad city in Azerbaijan republic, USSR, known since 1989 as Gandzhe.

Kirovograd city in Ukrainian republic, USSR; population (1987) 269,000. Manufacturing includes agricultural machinery and food processing. The city is on a lignite field. It was known as Yelizavetgrad until 1924 and Zinovyevsk 1924–36.

Kirriemuir market town of Tayside, Scotland, called "Thrums" in James Barrie's novels, and his birthplace.

Kisangani formerly (until 1966) ***Stanleyville*** town in NE Zaïre, on the upper Zaïre river, below Stanley Falls; population (1984) 283,000. It is a communications center.

Kissinger *Henry Kissinger at a White House press conference in 1972, while he was national security adviser. He became secretary of state in 1973.*

Kishi Nobusuke 1896–1987. Japanese politician and prime minister 1957–60. A government minister during World War II and imprisoned 1945, he was never put on trial and returned to politics 1953. During his premiership, Japan began a substantial rearmament program and signed a new treaty with the US that gave greater equality in the relationship between the two states.

Kishinev capital of the Moldavian republic, USSR; population (1987) 663,000. Industries include cement, food processing, tobacco, and textiles.
Founded 1436, it became Russian 1812. It was taken by Romania 1918, by the USSR 1940, and by Germany 1941, when it was totally destroyed. The USSR recaptured the site 1944, and rebuilding soon began. Nationalist demonstrations were held in the city during 1989.

Kissinger Henry 1923– . German-born US diplomat. Following a brilliant academic career at Harvard University, he was appointed assistant for National Security Affairs in 1969 by President Nixon, and was secretary of state 1973–77. His missions to the USSR and China improved US relations with both countries, and he took part in negotiating US withdrawal from Vietnam 1973 and in Arab-Israeli peace negotiations 1973–75. He was awarded the Nobel Peace Prize 1973.
Born in Bavaria, Kissinger emigrated to the US in 1938. After work in Germany for army counterintelligence, he won a scholarship to Harvard, and subsequently became a government consultant. His secret trips to Beijing and Moscow led to Nixon's visits to both countries and a general détente. In 1973 he shared a Nobel Peace Prize with Le Duc Tho, the North Vietnamese Politburo member, for his part in the Vietnamese peace negotiations, and in 1976 he was involved in the negotiations in Africa arising from the Angola and Rhodesia crises. In 1983, President Reagan appointed him to head a bipartisan commission on Central America. He was widely regarded as the most powerful member of Nixon's administration.

Kiswahili another name for the ◊Swahili language.

Kitaj Ron B 1932– . US painter and printmaker, active in Britain. His work is mainly figurative, and his distinctive decorative pale palette was in part inspired by studies of the Impressionist painter Degas.
Much of Kitaj's work is outside the predominant avant-garde trend and inspired by diverse historical styles. Some compositions are in triptych form.

Kitakyushu industrial port city (coal, steel, chemicals, cotton thread, plate glass, alcohol) port city in Japan, on the Hibiki Sea, N Kyushu, formed 1963 by the amalgamation of Moji, Kokura, Tobata, Yawata, and Wakamatsu; population (1987) 1,042,000. A tunnel 1942 links it with Honshu.

Kitasato Shibasaburo 1852–1931. Japanese bacteri-

kiwi

little spotted kiwi

ologist who discovered the ◊plague bacillus while investigating an outbreak of plague in Hong Kong. Kitasato was the first to grow the tetanus bacillus in pure culture. He and the German bacteriologist Behring discovered that increasing nonlethal doses of tetanus toxin give immunity to the disease.

He founded the Tokyo Institute for Infectious Diseases 1914, and was a friend and one-time student of Robert ◊Koch.

Kitchener city in SW Ontario, Canada; population (1986) 151,000, metropolitan area (with Waterloo) 311,000. Manufacturing includes agricultural machinery and tires. Settled by Germans from Pennsylvania in the 1800s, it was known as Berlin until 1916.

Kitchener Horatio Herbert, Earl Kitchener of Khartoum 1850–1916. British soldier and administrator. He defeated the Sudanese dervishes at Omdurman 1898 and reoccupied Khartoum. In South Africa, he was Chief of Staff 1900–02 during the Boer War, and commanded the forces in India 1902–09. He was appointed war minister on the outbreak of World War I, and drowned when his ship was sunk on the way to Russia.

He was appointed to the Egyptian army 1882 and made commander in chief 1892. He was governor general of the Sudan 1898–1900. In the Boer War he conducted war by scorched-earth policy and created the earliest ◊concentration camps for civilians.

kite one of about 20 birds of prey in the family Accipitridae, found in all parts of the world.

Kites have long, pointed wings and, usually, a forked tail. North America has five species, including the American swallow-tailed kite *Elanoides forficartus* of the SE US, which catches insects in flight as well as dropping down on snakes and lizards.

Kitimat port near Prince Rupert, British Columbia, Canada; population (1981) 4,300. Founded 1955, it has one of the world's largest aluminum smelters, powered by the Kemano hydroelectric scheme.

Kitwe commercial center for the Zambian copperbelt; population (1987) 450,000. To the S are Zambia's emerald mines.

Kivu lake in the Great Rift Valley between Zaïre and Rwanda, about 65 mi/105 km long. The chief port is Bukavu.

kiwi flightless bird *Apteryx australis* found only in New Zealand. It has long, hairlike brown plumage and a very long beak with nostrils at the tip. It is nocturnal and insectivorous. The egg is larger in relation to the bird's size (similar to a domestic chicken) than that of any other bird.

All kiwi species have declined since European settlement of New Zealand, and the little spotted kiwi is most at risk. It survives only on one small island reservation, which was stocked with birds from the mainland.

kiwi fruit or ***Chinese gooseberry*** fruit of a vinelike plant *Actinidithia chinensis*, family Actinidiaceae, commercially grown on a large scale in New Zealand and Calfornia. Kiwi fruit is egg-sized, oval, and of similar color and flavor to a gooseberry, with a fuzzy brown skin. Bright-green fuzzless varieties are now available.

Klee *Swiss painter Paul Klee's* They're Biting *1920 is in London's Tate Gallery.*

Klaipeda formerly ***Memel*** port in Lithuania, on the Baltic coast at the mouth of the Dange river; population (1987) 201,000. Industries include shipbuilding and iron foundries. It was founded 1252 as the castle of Memelburg by the Teutonic Knights, joined the ◊Hanseatic League soon after, and has changed hands among Sweden, Russia, and Germany. Lithuania annexed Klaipeda 1923, and after German occupation 1939–45 it was restored to Lithuania.

Klaproth Martin Heinrich 1743–1817. German chemist who first identified the elements uranium, zirconium, cerium, and titanium.

At sixteen he was apprenticed to an apothecary; he began research in 1780. The first professor of chemistry at the University of Berlin, he is sometimes called "the father of analytical chemistry."

Klee Paul 1879–1940. Swiss painter. He settled in Munich 1906, joined the ◊*Blaue Reiter* group 1912, and worked at the Bauhaus school of art and design 1920–31, returning to Switzerland 1933. His style in the 1920s and 1930s was dominated by humorous linear fantasies.

Klee traveled with the painter August Macke to Tunisia in 1914, a trip that transformed his sense of color. The Klee Foundation, Berne, has a large collection of his work.

Klein Melanie 1882–1960. Austrian child psychoanalyst. She pioneered child psychoanalysis and play studies, and was influenced by Sigmund ◊Freud's theories. She published *The Psychoanalysis of Children* in 1960.

Klein analyzed the behavior of children through the use of play techniques; this practice was later adopted in child guidance clinics. Her research into the origins of mental disorder psychosis, schizophrenia, and depression extended the range of patients who can usefully undergo psychoanalysis.

Klein Yves 1928–1962. French painter of bold abstracts and provocative experimental works, including imprints of nude bodies.

Kleist (Bernd) Heinrich (Wilhelm) von 1777–1811. German dramatist, whose comedy *Der zerbrochene Krug/The Broken Pitcher* 1808, and drama *Prinz Friedrich von Homburg/The Prince of Homburg* 1811, achieved success only after his suicide.

Klemperer Otto 1885–1973. German conductor who is celebrated for his interpretation of contemporary and Classical music (especially ◊Beethoven and ◊Brahms). He conducted the Los Angeles Orchestra 1933–39 and the Philharmonia Orchestra, London, from 1959.

kleptomania (Greek *kleptēs* "thief") a behavioral disorder characterized by an overpowering desire to

Knossos *The palace of Minos in Knossos, Crete, showing the grand staircase in the east wing (the domestic quarter).*

possess articles for which one has no need. In kleptomania, as opposed to ordinary theft, there is no obvious need or use for what is stolen and sometimes the sufferer has no memory of the theft.

Kliegl John H 1869–1959 and Anton T 1872–1927. German-born US brothers who in 1911 invented the brilliant carbon-arc (klieg) lights used in television and films. They also created scenic effects for theater and film.

Klimt Gustav 1862–1918. Austrian painter, influenced by Jugendstil ("Youth Style," a form of Art Nouveau); a founding member of the Vienna ◊Sezession group 1897. His paintings have a jeweled effect similar to mosaics, for example *The Kiss* 1909 (Musée des Beaux-Arts, Strasbourg). His many portraits include *Judith I* 1901 (Österreichische Galerie, Vienna).

Kline Franz 1910–1962. US Abstract Expressionist painter. He created large, graphic compositions in monochrome using angular forms, like magnified calligraphic brushstrokes.

He did not introduce color into his work until the late 1950s.

Klondike former gold-mining area in ◊Yukon, Canada, named after the river valley where gold was found 1896. About 30,000 people moved there during the following 15 years. Silver is still mined there.

Klopstock Friedrich Gottlieb 1724–1803. German poet, whose religious epic *Der Messias/The Messiah* 1748–73 and *Oden/Odes* 1771 anticipated Romanticism.

Klosters alpine skiing resort NE of Davos in E Switzerland.

km abbreviation for ◊kilometer.

knapweed any of several weedy plants of the genus *Centaurea*, family Compositae. In *C. nigra*, also known as hardhead, the hard bract-covered buds break into purple composite heads. It is native to Europe and has been introduced to North America.

Kneller Godfrey 1646–1723. German-born portrait painter who lived in England from 1674. He was court painter to Charles II, James II, William III, and George I.

Knesset the Israeli parliament, consisting of a single chamber of 120 deputies elected for a period of four years.

Knickerbocker School group of US writers working in New York State in the early 19th century, which included Washington Irving, James Kirke Paulding (1779–1860), and Fitz-Greene Halleck (1790–1867).

knifefish any fish of the genus *Gymnotus* and allied genera of fishes (family Gymnotidae), in which the body is deep at the front, drawn to a narrow or pointed tail at the rear, the main fin being the well-developed long ventral that completes the knifelike shape. The ventral fin is rippled for forward or backward locomotion. Knifefishes produce electrical fields, which they use for navigation.

knighthood, order of fraternity carrying with it the rank of knight, admission to which is granted as a mark of royal favor or as a reward for public services. During the Middle Ages such fraternities fell into two classes, religious and secular. The first class, including the ◊Templars and the Knights of ◊St John, consisted of knights who had taken religious vows and devoted themselves to military service against the Saracens (Arabs) or other non-Christians. The secular orders probably arose from bands of knights engaged in the service of a prince or great noble.

knitting method of making fabric by looping and knotting yarn with two needles. Knitting may have developed from ◊crochet, which uses a single hooked needle, or from netting, using a shuttle.

A mechanized process for making stockings was developed in the 16th century, but it was not until after World War II that machine knitting was revolutionized with the introduction of synthetic yarns, colored dyes, and methods of texturing and elasticizing.

Knossos the chief city of ◊Minoan Crete, near present-day Iráklion, 4 mi/6 km SE of Candia. The archeological site excavated by Arthur ◊Evans 1899–1935, dates from about 2000 BC, and includes the palace throne room and a labyrinth, legendary home of the ◊Minotaur.

Excavation of the palace of the legendary King Minos showed that the story of Theseus's encounter with the Minotaur in a labyrinth was possibly derived from the ritual "bull-leaping" by youths and girls depicted in the palace frescoes and from the mazelike layout of the palace.

knot wading bird *Calidris canutus* of the sandpiper family. It is about 10 in/25 cm long. In the winter, it is gray above and white below, but in the breeding season, it is brick-red on the head and chest and black on its wings and back. It feeds on insects and mollusks. Breeding in North American and Eurasian arctic regions, knots travel widely in winter, to be found as far S as South Africa, Australasia, and S parts of South America.

knot unit by which a ship's speed is measured, equivalent to one ◊nautical mile per hour (one knot equals about 1.15 miles per hour). It is also sometimes used in aviation.

knot an intertwinement of parts of one or more ropes, cords, or strings, to bind them together or to other objects. It is constructed so that the strain on the knot will draw it tighter. Bends or hitches are knots used to fasten ropes together or to other objects; when two ropes are joined

knot

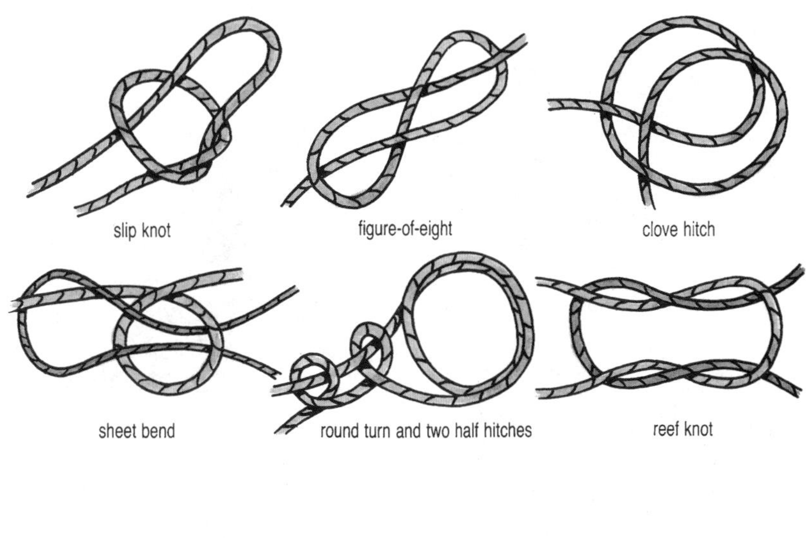
slip knot
figure-of-eight
clove hitch
sheet bend
round turn and two half hitches
reef knot

Knox An engraving of the 16th-century Scottish Protestant reformer John Knox.

end to end, they are spliced. The craft of ◊macramé uses knots to form decorative pieces and fringes.

knotgrass annual plant *Polygonum aviculare* of the dock family. The small lance-shaped leaves have bases that sheathe the slender stems, giving a superficial resemblance to grass. Small pinkish flowers are followed by seeds that are a delicacy for birds. Knotgrass grows worldwide except in the polar regions.

The creeping grass *Paspalum distichum* of North America is sometimes also called knotgrass.

knowledge-based system (KBS) computer program that uses an encoding of human knowledge to help solve problems. It was first discovered in research into ◊artificial intelligence that adding heuristics (rules of thumb) enabled programs to tackle problems that were otherwise difficult to solve by the usual techniques of computer science.

Chess-playing programs have been strengthened by including knowledge of what makes a good position, or about overall strategies, rather than relying solely on the computer's ability to calculate variations.

Knox John c. 1505–1572. Scottish Protestant reformer, founder of the Church of Scotland. He spent several years in exile for his beliefs, including a period in Geneva where he met John ◊Calvin. He returned to Scotland 1559 to promote Presbyterianism.

Originally a Roman Catholic priest, Knox is thought to have been converted by the reformer George Wishart. When Wishart was burned for heresy, Knox went into hiding, but later preached the reformed doctrines.

Knox Ronald Arbuthnott 1888–1957. British Roman Catholic scholar, whose translation of the Bible (1945–49) was officially approved by the Roman Catholic Church.

Knoxville city in E Tennessee; population (1990) 165,121. It is the center of a mining and agricultural region, and the administrative headquarters of the ◊Tennessee Valley Authority. The University of Tennessee, founded 1794, is here, and Oak Ridge National Laboratory, one of the world's largest nuclear research facilities, is nearby. Settlement began 1786, and it was the first state capital (1796–1812; 1817–19). Union troops captured the city 1863, during the Civil War. A world's fair was held here 1982.

koala marsupial *Phascolarctos cinereus* of the family Phalangeridae, found only in E Australia. It feeds almost entirely on eucalyptus shoots. It is about 2 ft/60 cm long, and resembles a bear. The popularity of its grayish fur led to its almost complete extermination by hunters. Under protection since 1936, it has rapidly increased in numbers.

kōan in Zen Buddhism, a superficially nonsensical question or riddle used by a Zen master to help a pupil achieve satori (◊enlightenment). It is used in the Rinzai school of Zen.

A *kōan* supposedly cannot be understood through the processes of logic; its solution requires attainment of a higher level of insight. An often repeated example is "What is the sound of one hand clapping?" An answer would be that the word "clapping" by definition involves two hands, and therefore this particular *kōan* is unanswerable.

Kobarid formerly ***Caporetto*** village on the Isonzo river, in Slovenia, NW Yugoslavia. Originally in Hungary, it was in Italy from 1918, and in 1947 became Kobarid. During World War I, German-Austrian troops defeated Italian forces there 1917.

Kobe deep-water port in S Honshu, Japan; population (1987) 1,413,000. Port Island, created 1960–68 from the rock of nearby mountains, area 2 sq mi/5 sq km, is one of the world's largest construction projects.

København Danish name for ◊Copenhagen, capital of Denmark.

Koblenz city in the Rhineland-Palatinate, Germany, at the junction of the rivers Rhine and Mosel; population (1988) 110,000. The city dates from Roman times. It is a center of communications and the wine trade, with industries (shoes, cigars, paper).

Koch Robert 1843–1910. German bacteriologist. Koch and his assistants devised the techniques to culture bacteria outside the body, and formulated the rules for showing whether or not a bacterium is the cause of a disease. He was awarded the Nobel Prize for Medicine 1905.

His techniques enabled him to identify the bacteria responsible for diseases like anthrax, cholera, and tuberculosis. This was a crucial first step to the later discovery of cures for these diseases. Koch was a great teacher, and many of his pupils, such as ◊Kitasato, ◊Ehrlich, and ◊Behring, became outstanding scientists.

Kodály Zoltán 1882–1967. Hungarian composer. With ◊Bartók, he recorded and transcribed Magyar folk music, the scales and rhythm of which he incorporated in a deliberately nationalist style. His works include the cantata *Psalmus Hungaricus* 1923, a comic opera *Háry János* 1925–27, and orchestral dances and variations.

Kodiak island off the S coast of Alaska, site of a US naval base; area 3,670 sq mi/9,505 sq km. It is the home of the Kodiak bear, the world's largest ◊bear. The town of Kodiak is one of the largest US fishing ports (mainly salmon).

Koestler Arthur 1905–1983. Hungarian author. Imprisoned by the Nazis in France 1940, he escaped to England. His novel *Darkness at Noon* 1941, regarded as his masterpiece, is a fictional account of the Stalinist purges, and draws on his experiences as a prisoner under sentence of death during the Spanish Civil War. He also wrote extensively about creativity, parapsychology, politics, and culture. He endowed Britain's first chair of parapsychology at Edinburgh, established in 1984.

Born in Budapest, and educated as an engineer

koala

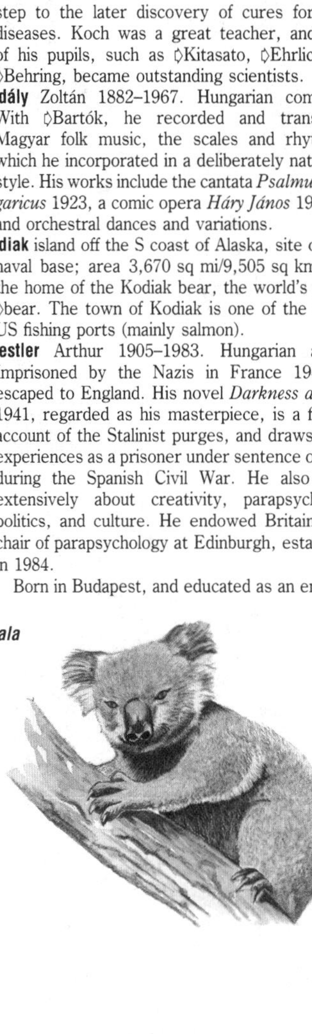

Koestler Hungarian-born writer Arthur Koestler was imprisoned in Spain by Franco, in France by the Nazis, and briefly in Britain, where he later settled.

in Vienna, he became a journalist in Palestine and the USSR. He joined the Communist party in Berlin 1931, but left it 1938 (he recounts his disillusionment with communism in *The God That Failed* 1950). His account of being held by the Nazis is contained in *Scum of the Earth* 1941.

Koh-i-noor (Persian "mountain of light") a fabulous diamond, originally part of the Aurangzeb treasure, seized in 1739 by the shah of Iran from the Moguls in India, taken back by Sikhs, and acquired by Britain in 1849 when the Punjab was annexed.

kohl (Arabic) powdered antimony sulfide, used in Asia and the Middle East to darken the area around the eyes. Commonly used eyeliners also contain carbon (bone black, lamp black, carbon black) or black iron oxide.

Kohl Helmut 1930– . German conservative politician, leader of the Christian Democratic Union (CDU) from 1976, West German chancellor 1982–90 and chancellor of the newly united Germany from 1990.

Kohl studied law and history before entering the chemical industry. Elected to the Rhineland-Palatinate *Land* (state) parliament 1959, he became state premier 1969. After the 1976 Bundestag (federal parliament) elections Kohl led the CDU in opposition. He became federal chancellor (prime minister) 1982, when the Free Democratic Party (FDP) withdrew support from the Socialist Schmidt government, and was elected at the head of a new coalition that included the FDP. From 1984 Kohl was implicated in the Flick bribes scandal over the illegal business funding of political parties, but he was cleared of all charges in 1986, and was reelected chancellor Jan 1987. During 1989–90 he oversaw the reunification of Germany. In 1990 he won a resounding victory and became the first chancellor of a reunited Germany.

kohlrabi variety of kale *Brassica oleracea*. Leaves

Kohl German chancellor Helmut Kohl at the first meeting of the European Community Emergency Summit in Brussels, Feb 1988.

shoot from a globular swelling on the main stem; it is used for food and resembles a turnip.

Kokand oasis town in the Uzbek republic of the USSR; population (1981) 156,000. It was the capital of Kokand khanate when annexed by Russia 1876. Industries include fertilizers, cotton, and silk.

Kokhba Bar. Name adopted by Simeon bar Koziba, Hebrew leader of the revolt against the Hellenization campaign of Emperor Hadrian 132–35, when Palestine was a province of the Roman Empire. The uprising resulted in the razing of Jerusalem and Kokhba's death in battle.

Kokomo city in N central Indiana, on Wildcat Creek, N of Indianapolis and SW of Fort Wayne; seat of Howard County. The city's industries produce automobile, radio, and plumbing parts; steel and wire; and electrical machinery; population (1990) 44,962. The first automobile to use gasoline was invented and tested here 1893.

Koko Nor Mongolian form of ◊Qinghai, province of China.

Kokoschka Oskar 1886–1980. Austrian Expressionist painter and writer who lived in England from 1938. Initially influenced by the Vienna ◊Sezession painters, he developed a disturbingly expressive portrait style. His writings include several plays.

After World War I Kokoschka worked in Dresden, then in Prague, and fled from the Nazis to England, taking British citizenship 1947. To portraiture he added panoramic landscapes and townscapes in the 1920s and 1930s, and political allegories in the 1950s.

kola alternate spelling of ◊cola, genus of tropical tree.

Kola (Russian ***Kol'skiy Poluostrov***) peninsula in N USSR, bounded by the White Sea on the S and E and by the Barents Sea on the N; area 50,000 sq mi/129,500 sq km; coterminous with Murmansk region. Apatite and other minerals are exported. To the NW the low-lying granite plateau adjoins Norway's thinly populated county of Finnmark, and Soviet troops are heavily concentrated here.

Kolchak Alexander Vasilievich 1875–1920. Russian admiral, commander of the White forces in Siberia after the Russian Revolution. He proclaimed himself Supreme Ruler of Russia 1918, but was later handed over to the Bolsheviks by his own men and shot.

Kolchugino former name (to 1925) of ◊Leninsk-Kuznetsky, town in USSR.

Kolhapur industrial city and film production center in Maharashtra, India; population (1981) 346,000.

kolkhoz Russian term for a ◊collective farm, as opposed to a ◊sovkhoz or state-owned farm.

Koller Carl 1857–1944. Austrian ophthalmologist who introduced local anesthesia 1884.

Kollontai Alexandra 1872–1952. Russian revolutionary, politician, and writer. In 1905 she published *On the Question of the Class Struggle*, and, as Commissar for Public Welfare, was the only female member of the first Bolshevik government. She campaigned for domestic reforms such as acceptance of free love, simplification of divorce laws, and collective childcare.

In 1896, while on a tour of a large textile factory with her husband, she saw the appalling conditions endured by factory workers in Russia. Thereafter she devoted herself to improving conditions for working women. She was harassed by the police for her views and in 1914 went into exile in Germany. On her return to the Soviet Union in 1917 she joined the Bolsheviks. She was sent abroad by Stalin, first as trade minister, then as ambassador to Sweden 1943.

Kollwitz Käthe 1867–1945. German sculptor and printmaker. Her early series of etchings depicting workers and their environment are realistic and harshly expressive. Later themes include war, death, and maternal love.

Köln German form of ◊Cologne, city in Germany.

Kolwezi mining town (copper and cobalt) in Shaba province, SE Zaïre; population (1985) 82,000. In 1978 former police of the province invaded from Angola and massacred some 650 of the inhabitants.

DIE LEBENDEN DEM TOTEN . ERINNERUNG AN DEN 15.JANUAR 1919

Kollwitz *One of a series of large lithographs called* Death *1934–35, by German artist Käthe Kollwitz.*

Komi autonomous republic in N central USSR; area 160,580 sq mi/415,900 sq km; population (1986) 1,200,000. Its capital is Syktyvkar.

Komi a member of a Finnish people living mainly in the tundra and coniferous forests of the Soviet republic of Komi in the NW Urals. They raise livestock, timber, and mine coal and oil. Their language is Zyrian, one of the Finno-Ugric family.

Kommunizma, Pik the highest mountain in the USSR, in the Akademiya Nauk range of the Pamirs, in Tadzhikistan. Communism Peak (24,590 ft/7,495 m) was formerly known as Stalin Peak (1933–62) and Garmo Peak (until 1933).

Komsomol Russian name for the USSR's All-Union Leninist Communist Youth League. Founded in 1918, it acts as the youth section of the Communist Party.

Kongur Shan mountain peak in China, 25,325 ft/7,719 m high, part of the Pamir range (see ◊Pamirs). The expedition that first reached the summit 1981 was led by British climber Chris Bonington.

Kong Zi Pinyin form of ◊Confucius, Chinese philosopher.

Koniev Ivan Stepanovich 1898–1973. Soviet marshal who in World War II liberated Ukraine from the invading German forces 1943 and advanced from the south on Berlin to link up with the British-US forces. He commanded all Warsaw Pact forces 1955–60.

Königsberg German name of ◊Kaliningrad, port in USSR.

Konoe Fumimaro, Prince 1891–1946. Japanese politician and prime minister 1937–39 and 1940–41. Entering politics in the 1920s, Konoe was active in trying to curb the power of the army in government and preventing an escalation of the war with China. He helped to engineer the fall of the ◊Tojo government 1944 but committed suicide after being suspected of war crimes.

Konstanz German form of the town of ◊Constance.

Kon-Tiki legendary creator god of Peru (Viracocha) and Sun King who was supposed to have migrated out into the Pacific. The name was used by explorer Thor ◊Heyerdahl for his raft (made of nine balsawood logs) that he sailed from Peru to the Tuamotu Islands, near Tahiti, on the Humboldt current of the Pacific, in an attempt to show that ancient South Americans might have reached Polynesia. He sailed from April 28 to August 7, 1947, with five companions, about 5,000 mi/8,000 km.

Konya (Roman *Iconium*) city in SW central Turkey; population (1985) 439,000. Carpets and silks are made here, and the city contains the monastery of the dancing ◊dervishes.

kookaburra or ***laughing jackass*** the largest of the world's ◊kingfishers *Dacelo novaeguineae*, found in Australia, with an extraordinary laughing call. It feeds on insects and other small creatures. The body and tail measure 18 in/45 cm, the head is grayish with a dark eye stripe, and the back and wings are flecked brown with gray underparts. Its laugh is one of the most familiar sounds of the bush of E Australia.

kora 21-string instrument of W African origin made from gourds, with a harplike sound.

Koran (alternatively transliterated as Quran) the sacred book of Islam. Written in the purest Arabic, it contains 114 suras (chapters), and is stated to have been divinely revealed to the prophet Mohammed about 616.

Korda Alexander 1893–1956. Hungarian-born British film producer and director, a dominant figure during the 1930s and 1940s. His films include *The Private Life of Henry VIII* 1933, *The Third Man* 1950, and *Richard III* 1956.

Kordofan province of central Sudan, that is known as the "White Land"; area 56,752 sq mi/146,990 sq km; population (1983) 3,093,300. Although never an independent state, it has a character of its own. It is mainly undulating plain, with acacia scrub producing gum arabic, marketed in the chief town ◊El Obeid. Formerly a rich agricultural region, it has been overtaken by desertification.

Korea: history

2000 BC The foundation of the Korean state traditionally dates back to the Tangun dynasty.

1122–4th century The Chinese Kija dynasty.

AD 10th century After centuries of internal war and invasion, Korea was united within its present boundaries.

16th century Japan invaded Korea for the first time, later withdrawing from a country it had devastated.

1905 Japan began to treat Korea as a protectorate.

1910 It was annexed by Japan. Many Japanese colonists settled in Korea, introducing both industrial and agricultural development.

1945 At the end of World War II, the Japanese in

Korea, North
Democratic People's Republic of
(*Chosun Minchu-chui Inmin Konghwa-guk*)

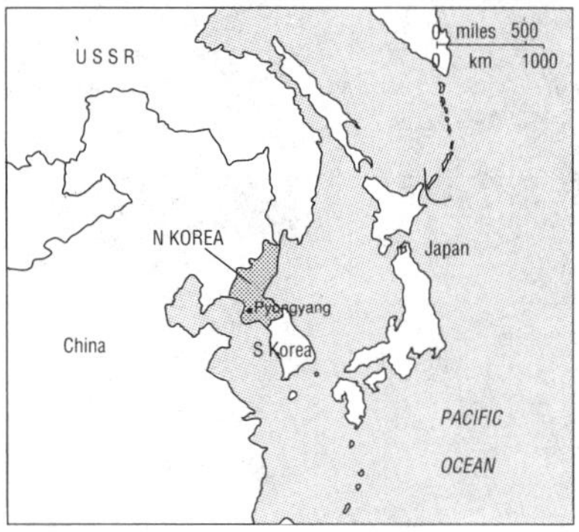
miles 500
km 1000
USSR
N KOREA
Pyongyang
China
S Korea
Japan
PACIFIC
OCEAN

area 46,528 sq mi/120,538 sq km
capital Pyongyang
cities Chongjin, Nampo, Wonsan
physical wide coastal plain in W rising to mountains cut by deep valleys in the interior
features separated from South Korea by a military demarcation line; the richer of the two Koreas in mineral resources (copper, iron ore, graphite, tungsten, zinc, lead, magnesite, gold, phosphor, phosphates)
head of state Kim Il Sung from 1972 (also head of Communist Party)
head of government Yon Hyong Muk from 1988
political system communism
political parties Korean Workers' Party (KWP), Marxist-Leninist-Kim Il Sungist
exports coal, iron, copper, textiles, chemicals
currency won
population (1990 est) 23,059,000; growth rate 2.5% p.a.
life expectancy men 67, women 73 (1989)
language Korean
religion traditionally Buddhist, Confucian, but religious activity now curtailed by the state
literacy 99% (1989)
GNP $20 bn; $3,450 per head (1988)
chronology
1910 Korea formally annexed by Japan.
1945 Russian and US troops entered Korea, forced surrender of Japanese, and divided the country in two.
1948 Democratic People's Republic of Korea declared.
1950 North Korea invaded South Korea to unite the nation, beginning the Korean war.
1953 Armistice agreed to end Korean war.
1961 Friendship and mutual assistance treaty signed with China.
1972 New constitution, with executive president, adopted. Talks took place with South Korea about possible reunification.
1980 Reunification talks broke down.
1983 Four South Korean cabinet ministers assassinated in Rangoon, Burma (Myanmar), by North Korean army officers.
1985 Increased relations with the USSR.
1989 Increasing evidence of nuclear-weapons development.
1990 Diplomatic contacts with South Korea and Japan suggested the beginning of a thaw in North Korea's international relations.
1991 Agreements with South Korea signed.

***Korean War** US infantrymen entrenched at the top of "Old Baldy," Korea, in Sept 1952.*

Korea surrendered, but the occupying forces at the ceasefire—the USSR north of the ◊38th parallel, and the US south of it—resulted in a lasting division of the country as North and South Korea (see ◊Korea, North, and ◊Korea, South, for history since 1945).

Korean native to or inhabitant of Korea; also the language and culture. There are approximately 33 million Koreans in South Korea, 15 million in North Korea, and 3 million elsewhere, principally in Japan, China (Manchuria), the USSR, and the US.

Korean language the language of Korea, written from the 5th century AD in Chinese characters until the invention of an alphabet by King Sejong 1443. The linguistic affiliations of Korean are unclear, but it may be distantly related to Japanese.

The alphabet was discouraged as "vulgar letters" (*onmun*) and banned by the colonizing Japanese of the early 20th century. After World War II it was revived and called "top letters" (*hangul*).

Korea, North country in E Asia, bounded N by China, E by the Sea of Japan, S by South Korea, and W by the Yellow Sea.

government Under the 1972 constitution, which replaced the 1948 Soviet-type constitution, the leading political figure is the president, who is head of the armed forces and executive head of government. The president is appointed for four-year terms by the 615-member supreme people's assembly, which is directly elected by universal suffrage. The assembly meets for brief sessions once or twice a year, its regular legislative business being carried out by a smaller permanent standing committee (Presidium). The president works with and presides over a powerful policy-making and supervisory central people's committee (which is responsible to the assembly for its activities) and an administrative and executive cabinet (Administration Council).

The controlling force in North Korea is the Communist Party (Workers' Party of Korea), headed since 1945 by ◊Kim Il Sung. It leads the broader Democratic Front for the Reunification of the Fatherland (which includes the minor North Korean Democratic Party and the Religious Chungwoo Party) in putting forward single slates of candidates for election contests.

history For early history, see ◊Korea, history. The Democratic People's Republic of Korea was formed from the zone north of the 38th parallel of latitude, occupied by Soviet troops after Japan's surrender in 1945. The USSR installed in power an "Executive Committee of the Korean People," staffed by Soviet-trained Korean Communists, before North Korea was declared a People's Republic in 1948 under the leadership of the Workers' Party, with ◊Kim Il Sung as president. The remaining Soviet forces withdrew in 1949.

In 1950 North Korea, seeking unification of the Korean peninsula, launched a large-scale invasion of South Korea. This began the three-year-long ◊Korean war which, after intervention by United Nations forces supported by the US (on the side of the South) and by China (on the side of the North), ended in stalemate. The 38th parallel border between north and south was re-established by the armistice agreement of July 1953, and a UN-patrolled demilitarized buffer zone was created. North Korea has never accepted this agreement and remains committed to reunification.

Relations with the South have remained tense and hostile, despite the establishment in 1972 of a North–South coordinating committee to promote peaceful unification. Border incidents have been frequent, and in Oct 1983 four South Korean cabinet ministers were assassinated in Rangoon, Myanmar (Burma), in a bombing incident organized by two North Korean army officers.

Domestically, the years since 1948 have seen economic development in a planned Socialist manner. Factories were nationalized and agriculture collectivized in the 1950s, and priority in investment programs has been given to heavy industry and rural mechanization. North Korean economic growth has, however, lagged behind that of its richer and more populous southern neighbor. In foreign affairs, North Korea adopted a neutral stance in the Sino-Soviet dispute, signing a friendship and mutual assistance treaty with China in 1961 while at the same time receiving economic and military aid from the Soviet Union. North Korea remained largely immune from the pluralist or market-Socialist wave of reform that swept other communist nations in 1989–90, making only minor adjustments. Relations with the South have, however, showed signs of improving.

In recent years, North Korean politics have been dominated by the succession question, with Kim Il Sung seeking to establish his son, Kim Jong-Il (1941–), as sole heir designate. Kim Jong-Il has accompanied Kim Il Sung on diplomatic and factory tours, been designated Armed Forces Supreme Commander, begun to preside over key party and state government meetings, and his portrait has been placed on public display across the country. Elements within the Workers' Party and armed forces appear, however, to oppose Kim's succession aims.

In Sept 1990 prime minister Yon Hyong Muk made an unprecedented three day official visit to South Korea, the highest level official contact since 1948. Talks with South Korea and Japan have been seen as evidence of a "thawing" to the outside world that has become necessary because of mounting economic shortages at home.

Korean War war 1950–53 between North Korea (supported by China) and South Korea, aided by the United Nations (the troops were mainly US). North Korean forces invaded the South June 25, 1950, and the Security Council of the United Nations, caused by a walk-out by the USSR, voted to oppose them. To begin with the North Koreans held most of the south but US reinforcements arrived Sept 1950 and forced their way through to the North Korean border with China. The Chinese retaliated, pushing them back to the original boundary Oct 1950; truce negotiations began 1951, although the war did not end until 1953.

By Sept 1950 the North Koreans had overrun most of the south, with the UN forces holding a small area, the Pusan perimeter, in the southeast. The course of the war changed after the surprise landing of American troops later the same month at Inchon on South Korea's NW coast. The troops, led by General Douglas ◊MacArthur, fought their way through North Korea to the Chinese border in little over a month. On Oct 25, 1950 Chinese troops attacked across the Yalu River, driving the UN forces below the 38th parallel. Truce talks began in July 1951, and the war ended two years later, with the restoration of the original boundary on the 38th parallel.

Korea, South country in E Asia, bordered N by

Korea, South

Republic of Korea

(Daehan Minguk)

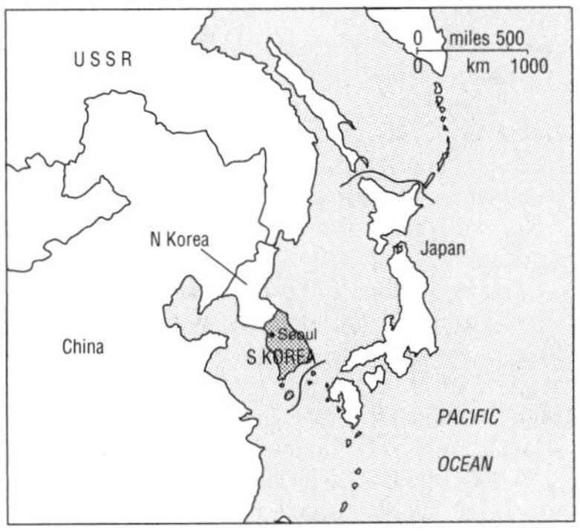
USSR
0 miles 500
0 km 1000
N Korea
Japan
China
Seoul
S KOREA
PACIFIC
OCEAN

area 38,161 sq mi/98,799 sq km
capital Seoul
cities Taegu, ports Pusan, Inchon
physical southern end of a mountainous peninsula separating the Sea of Japan from the Yellow Sea
features Chomsongdae (world's earliest observatory); giant Popchusa Buddha; granite peaks of Soraksan National Park
head of state Roh Tae-Woo from 1988
head of government Ro Jai Bong from 1990
political system emergent democracy
political parties Democratic Liberal Party (DLP), right-of-center; New Democratic Union (NDU), left-of-center
exports steel, ships, chemicals, electronics, textiles and clothing, plywood, fish
currency won
population (1990 est) 43,919,000; growth rate 1.4% p.a.
life expectancy men 66, women 73 (1989)
language Korean
religion traditionally Buddhist, Confucian, and Chondokyo; Christian 28%
literacy 92% (1989)
GNP $171bn (1988); $2,180 per head (1986)
chronology
1910 Korea formally annexed by Japan.
1945 Russian and US troops entered Korea, forced surrender of Japanese, and divided the country in two.
1948 Republic proclaimed.
1950–53 War with North Korea.
1960 President Syngman Rhee resigned amid unrest.
1961 Military coup by Gen Park Chung-Hee. Industrial growth program.
1979 Assassination of President Park.
1980 Military coup by Gen Chun Doo-Hwan.
1987 Adoption of more democratic constitution following student unrest. Roh Tae Woo elected president.
1988 Former president Chun, accused of corruption, publicly apologized and agreed to hand over his financial assets to the state. Seoul hosted Summer Olympic Games.
1989 Roh reshuffled cabinet, threatened crackdown on protesters.
1990 Two minor opposition parties united with Democratic Justice Party to form ruling Democratic Liberal Party. Diplomatic relations established with the USSR.
1991 Violent mass demonstrations against the government. New opposition grouping, New Democratic Union (NDU) formed. Agreements with North Korea signed.

North Korea, E by the Sea of Japan, S by the Korea Strait, and W by the Yellow Sea.

government Under the 1987 constitution, executive power is held by the president, who is elected directly by popular vote. The president is restricted to one five-year term of office and governs with a cabinet (state council) headed by a prime minister. Legislative authority resides in the single-chamber, 299-deputy national assembly *Kuk Hoe*, 224 of whose members are directly elected for four-year terms by universal suffrage in single-member constituencies, and the remainder of whom are appointed in accordance with a formula designed to reward the largest single assembly party. The assembly has the authority to impeach the president and to override presidential vetoes. There is also a nine-member constitutional court, and guarantees of freedom of speech, press, assembly, and association are written into the constitution.

The dominant party is the Democratic Liberal Party (DLP), which has strong support among the business community and the military. The main opposition party is the Party for Peace and Democracy (PPD) led by ◊Kim Dae Jung and based mainly in the underdeveloped SW region of Cholla.

history For early history, see ◊Korea, history. The Republic of Korea was formed out of the zone south of the 38th parallel of latitude that was occupied by US troops after Japan's surrender 1945. The US military government controlled the country until, following national elections, an independent republic was declared 1948. Dr Syngman ◊Rhee, leader of the right-wing Liberal Party, was the nation's first president in a constitution based on the US model. To begin with, the republic had to cope with a massive influx of refugees fleeing the Communist regime in the North; then came the 1950–53 ◊Korean war.

President Syngman Rhee, whose regime had been accused of corruption, resigned 1960 as a result of student-led disorder. A new parliamentary-style constitution gave greater power to the legislature, and the ensuing political instability precipitated a military coup led by General ◊Park Chung-Hee 1961. A presidential system of government was re-established, with Gen Park elected president 1963, and a major program of industrial development began, involving government planning and financial support. This program, utilizing the nation's plentiful supply of well-educated and industrious workers, was remarkably successful, with rapid industrial growth during the 1960s and 1970s as South Korea became a major exporter of light and heavy industrial goods.

Opposition to the repressive Park regime mounted during the 1970s. In response, martial law was imposed, and in 1972 a new constitution strengthened the president's powers. A clampdown on political dissent, launched 1975, was partially relaxed for the 1978 elections, but brought protests 1979 as economic conditions briefly deteriorated. President Park was assassinated later that year by the chief of the South Korean Central Intelligence Agency, and martial law was reimposed.

An interim government, led by former prime minister Choi Kyu-Hah, introduced liberalizing reforms, releasing opposition leader Kim Dae Jung 1980. However, as antigovernment demonstrations developed, a new dissident clampdown began, involving the arrest of 30 political leaders, including Kim Dae Jung. After riots in Kim's home city of Kwangju, President Choi resigned 1980 and was replaced by the leader of the army, General Chun Doo-Hwan. A new constitution was adopted, and, after Chun Doo-Hwan was re-elected president 1981, the new Fifth Republic was proclaimed.

Under President Chun economic growth resumed, but internal and external criticism of the suppression of civil liberties continued. Cautious liberalization was seen prior to the 1985 assembly elections, with the release of many political prisoners and the return from exile of Kim Dae Jung. The opposition parties emerged in a strengthened position after the 1985 election but they could not agree on a single candidate. They proceeded to launch a campaign for genuine democratization that forced the Chun regime to frame a new, more liberal constitution, which was adopted after a referendum Oct 1987. The ensuing presidential election was won by the ruling party's candidate, Roh Tae Woo, amid opposition charges of fraud. He took over Feb 1988, but in the national assembly elections April 1988 the ruling Democratic Justice Party (DJP) fell well short of an overall majority. Only in Feb 1990, when the DJP merged with two minor opposition parties to form the Democratic Liberal Party (DLP), was a stable governing majority secured. The new coalition declared its intention of amending the constitution to replace the presidential executive system with a parliamentary one, led by a powerful prime minister drawn from the majority grouping within the national assembly, moving South Korea's political system closer to Japan's model.

Since 1953 the constant threat of invasion from the North has been a key factor in South Korean politics, helping to justify stern rule (there were over 800 political prisoners in Aug 1989). South Korea has devoted large resources to modernizing its armed forces, which are supported by 40,000 US troops, whose role is to act as a "tripwire," assuring US intervention in the event of an invasion from the North. For South Korea the country's economic success and growing world stature was symbolized by Seoul's hosting the 1988 Summer Olympic Games.

In July 1990 the 80-member opposition group of the Party for Peace and Democracy (PPD), led by Kim Dae Jung, all resigned from the National Assembly in protest at what they viewed as government attempts to push through new legislation and demanded the calling of a general election. This followed an outbreak of violence within the Assembly itself. The Assembly's speaker refused to accept the resignations, but the opposition deputies continued to boycott parliament when it reconvened in Sept. In the same month full diplomatic relations were established with the USSR.

In Dec 1990 the government launched a "purification" campaign designed to improve public morals and reduce the society's materialism.

Korematsu v US a US Supreme Court decision 1944 dealing with congressional measures forcing the relocation of citizens of certain national origins. Korematsu, a Japanese-American, filed suit to challenge a 1942 law excluding Americans of Japanese descent from living on the US W coast. Those Japanese-Americans already living on the coast were removed to inland internment camps. This, Korematsu argued, was a discriminatory violation of Fifth-Amendment rights. Citing the danger of domestic sabotage in the war against Japan, the Court ruled against Korematsu 6–3. The decision to uphold exclusion and relocation laws as legitimate exercises of war powers stood until 1983, when the Korematsu decision was reversed.

Korinthos Greek form of ◊Corinth.

Kornberg Arthur 1918– . US biochemist. In 1956, while working on enzymes at Washington University, Kornberg discovered the enzyme DNA-polymerase, which enabled molecules of ◊DNA to be synthesized for the first time. For this work Kornberg shared the 1959 Nobel Prize for Medicine with Severo ◊Ochoa.

Korngold Erich Wolfgang 1897–1957. Austrian-born composer. He began composing operas while still in his teens and is known for his violin concerto. In 1934 he moved to Hollywood to become a composer for Warner Brothers. His film scores combine a richly orchestrated and romantic style, reflecting the rapid changes of mood characteristic of screen action.

Korolev Sergei Pavlovich 1906–1966. Soviet

designer of the first Soviet intercontinental missile, used Oct 4, 1957 to launch the first ◊Sputnik satellite, and Aug 6, 1961 to launch the ◊Vostok crewed Earth-orbiting spacecraft (also designed by Korolev).

Born in Zhitomir, Ukraine, Korolev became an aircraft designer before turning to rocketry.

Kortrijk Flemish form of ◊Courtrai, town in Belgium.

Kos or ***Cos*** fertile Greek island, one of the Dodecanese, in the Aegean Sea; area 111 sq mi/ 287 sq km. It gives its name to the Cos lettuce.

Kosciusko highest mountain in Australia (7,316 ft/ 2,229 m), in New South Wales.

Paul Strzelecki, who was born in Prussian Poland, named the mountain 1839 after the Polish revolutionary hero.

Kościuszko Tadeusz 1746–1817. Polish general and nationalist who served with George Washington in the American Revolution (1776–83). He returned to Poland 1784, fought against the Russian invasion that ended in the partition of Poland, and withdrew to Saxony. He returned in 1794 to lead the revolt against the occupation, but was defeated by combined Russian and Prussian forces and imprisoned until 1796.

kosher (Hebrew "appropriate") conforming to religious law with regard to the preparation and consumption of food; in Judaism, conforming to the Mosaic law of the Book of Deuteronomy. For example, only the front end of animals that chew the cud and have cloven hooves (cows and sheep, but not pigs) may be eaten. There are rules governing their humane slaughter and their preparation (such as complete draining of blood), which also apply to fowl. Only fish with scales and fins may be eaten; shellfish may not. Milk products may not be cooked or eaten with meat or poultry, or until four hours after eating them. Utensils for meat must be kept separate from those for milk as well.

Kosiče town in SE Czechoslovakia; population (1986) 222,000 (92% Magyar-speaking). It has a textile industry and is a road center. Kosiče was in Hungary until 1920 and 1938–45.

Kosinski Jerzy 1933–1991. Polish-born US novelist, author of *The Painted Bird* 1965, about a strange boy brutally treated during World War II; *Being There* 1971, about a retarded gardener who is thought to be a wise man because his gardening tips are taken as metaphors for life; and *Passion Play* 1979.

He was born in Lodz, and escaped from Poland through the USSR during World War II. He was then educated as a sociologist at the university in Lodz but eventually went to the US in 1957. He taught himself English, the language in which he writes.

Kosovo autonomous region (since 1974) in S Serbia, Yugoslavia; capital Priština; area 4,207 sq mi/ 10,900 sq km; population (1986) 1,900,000 consisting of about 200,000 Serbs and about 1.7 million Albanians. Products include wine, nickel, lead, and zinc. Since it is largely inhabited by Albanians and bordering on Albania, there are demands for unification with that country, while in the late 1980s Serbians were agitating for Kosovo to be merged with the rest of Serbia. A state of emergency was declared Feb 1990 after fighting broke out between ethnic Albanians, police, and the Slavic minority.

Kossuth Lajos 1802–1894. Hungarian nationalist and leader of the revolution of 1848. He proclaimed Hungarian independence of Hapsburg rule, became governor of a Hungarian republic 1849, and, when it was defeated by Austria and Russia, fled first to Turkey and then to exile in Britain and Italy.

Kosygin Alexei Nikolaievich 1904–1980. Soviet politician, prime minister 1964–80. He was elected to the Supreme Soviet 1938, became a member of the Politburo 1946, deputy prime minister 1960, and succeeded Khrushchev as premier (while Brezhnev succeeded him as party secretary). In the late 1960s Kosygin's influence declined.

***Kosygin** Soviet politician and prime minister Alexei Kosygin at a press conference in Denmark 1971.*

Kota Bharu capital of Kelantan, Malaysia; population (1980) 170,600.

Kota Kinabalu formerly ***Jesselton*** (until 1968) capital and port in Sabah, Malaysia; population (1980) 59,500. Exports include rubber and timber.

koto Japanese musical instrument; a long zither of ancient Chinese origin, having 13 silk strings supported by movable bridges. It rests on the floor and the strings are plucked with ivory plectra, producing a brittle sound.

Kottbus alternate spelling of ◊Cottbus, town in East Germany.

kouprey wild cattle *Bos sauveli* native to the forests of N Cambodia. Only known to science since 1937, it is in great danger of extinction. They have cylindrical, widely separated horns and grow to 6 ft/1.9 m in height.

Kourou river and second-largest town of French Guiana, NW of Cayenne, site of the Guiana Space Center of the European Space Agency. Situated near the equator, it is an ideal site for launches of satellites into ◊geosynchronous orbit.

Koussevitsky Serge 1874–1951. Russian musician and conductor, well known for his work in the US. He was trained at a conservatory in Moscow and became recognized as a virtuoso on the double bass. First appearing as a conductor in Berlin 1908, he established his own orchestra in Moscow in the following year and introduced works of Prokofiev, Rachmaninoff, and Stravinsky. Although named director of the State Symphony after the Bolshevik Revolution, Koussevitsky left the USSR, becoming director of the Boston Symphony Orchestra 1924. In 1934 he founded the annual Tanglewood summer music festival in W Massachusetts.

Kovalevsky Sonja Vasilevna 1850–1891. Russian mathematician, who received a doctorate from Göttingen University 1874 for her dissertation on partial differential equations. She was professor of mathematics at the University of Stockholm from 1884. In 1886 she won the Prix Bordin of the French Academy of Sciences for a paper on the rotation of a rigid body about a point, a problem the 18th-century mathematicians Euler and Lagrange had both failed to solve.

Kovno Russian form of ◊Kaunas, port in Lithuania, USSR.

Kowloon peninsula on the Chinese coast forming part of the British crown colony of Hong Kong; the town of Kowloon is a residential area.

kph or km/h abbreviation for kilometers per hour.

Krafft-Ebing Baron Richard von 1840–1902. German pioneer psychiatrist and neurologist. He published *Psychopathia Sexualis* 1886.

Kragujevac garrison town and former capital (1818–39) of Serbia, Yugoslavia; population (1981) 165,000.

Krakatoa (Indonesian *Krakatau*) volcanic island in Sunda strait, Indonesia, that erupted in 1883, causing 36,000 deaths on Java and Sumatra by the tidal waves that followed. The island is now uninhabited.

Kraków or ***Cracow*** city in Poland, on the river Vistula; population (1985) 716,000. It is an industrial center producing freight cars, paper, chemicals, and tobacco. It was capital of Poland c. 1300–1595.

Founded about 1400, its university, at which the astronomer ◊Copernicus was a student, is one of the oldest in central Europe. There is a 14th-century Gothic cathedral.

Kramatorsk industrial town in Ukraine, USSR, in the Donbas, N of Donetsk; population (1987) 198,000. Industries include coal-mining machinery, steel, ceramics, and railroad repairs.

Krasnodar territory of the Russian Soviet Federal Socialist Republic in the N Caucasus, adjacent to the Black Sea; area 32,290 sq mi/83,600 sq km; population (1985) 4,992,000. The capital is Krasnodar. In addition to stock rearing and the production of grain, rice, fruit, and tobacco, oil is refined.

Krasnodar formerly ***Ekaterinodar*** (until 1920) industrial town at the head of navigation of the Kuban river, in SW USSR; population (1987) 623,000. It is linked by pipeline with the Caspian oil fields.

Krasnoyarsk industrial city in central USSR; population (1987) 899,000. Industries include locomotives, paper, timber, cement, gold refining, and a large hydroelectric works. There is an early-warning and space-tracking radar phased array device at nearby Abalakova. See also ◊Novosibirsk.

Krasnoyarsk territory of the USSR in central Siberia stretching N to the Arctic Ocean; area 927,617 sq mi/2,401,600 sq km; population (1985) 3,430,000. The capital is Krasnoyarsk. It is drained by the Yenisei river. Mineral resources include gold, graphite, coal, iron ore, and uranium.

Krebs Hans 1900–1981. German-born British biochemist who discovered the citric acid cycle, also known as the Krebs cycle, by which food is converted into energy in living tissues. For this work he shared with Fritz Lipmann the 1953 Nobel Prize for Medicine.

Krebs cycle or ***citric acid cycle*** part of the chain of biochemical reactions through which organisms break down food using oxygen (respiration) to release energy. It breaks down food molecules in a series of small steps, producing energy-rich molecules of ◊ATP.

Krefeld industrial town near the river Rhine; 32 mi/ 52 km NW of Cologne, Germany; population (1988) 217,000. Industries include chemicals, textiles, and machinery. It is situated on the Westphalian coalfield.

Kreisler Fritz 1875–1962. Austrian violinist and composer, renowned as an interpreter of Brahms and Beethoven. From 1911 he was one of the earliest recording artists of Classical music, including records of his own compositions.

Kremenchug industrial town on the river Dnieper, in Ukraine republic, USSR; population (1987) 230,000. Manufacturing includes road-building machinery, rail wagons, and processed food.

kremlin citadel or fortress of Russian cities. The Moscow kremlin dates from the 12th century, and the name "the Kremlin" became synonymous with the Soviet government.

Krenek Ernst 1900– . Austrian-born composer. His jazz opera *Jonny spielt auf/Johnny plays up* 1927 received international acclaim.

He moved to the US 1939 and explored the implications of contemporary and Renaissance musical theories in a succession of works and theoretical writings.

Krenz Egon 1937– . German communist politician.

Kraków *Kraków's 14th-century Gothic cathedral.*

A member of the East German Socialist Unity Party (SED) from 1955, he joined its politburo in 1983 and was a hardline protégé of Erich ◊Honecker, succeeding him as party leader and head of state in 1989 after widespread pro-democracy demonstrations. Pledging a "new course," Krenz opened the country's western border and promised more open elections, but his conversion to pluralism proved weak in the face of popular protest and he resigned after a few weeks in Dec 1989, as party general secretary and head of state. He was replaced by Gregor Gysi and Manfred Gerlach respectively.

Kreutzer Rodolphe 1766–1831. French violinist and composer of German descent to whom Beethoven dedicated his violin sonata Opus 47, known as the *Kreutzer Sonata*.

krill any of several Antarctic crustaceans of the order Euphausiacea, the most common species being *Euphausia superba*. Shrimplike, it is about 2.5 in/6 cm long, with two antennae, five pairs of legs, seven pairs of light organs along the body, and is colored orange above and green beneath.

Moving in enormous swarms, krill constitute the chief food of the baleen whales, and have been used to produce a protein concentrate for human consumption and meal for animal feed.

Krishna incarnation of the Hindu god ◊Vishnu. The devotion of the ◊bhakti movement is usually directed toward Krishna; an example of this is the ◊International Society for Krishna Consciousness. Many stories are told of Krishna's mischievous youth, and he is the charioteer of Arjuna in the *Bhagavad-Gītā*.

Krishna Menon Vengalil Krishnan 1897–1974. Indian politician, who was a leading light in the Indian nationalist movement. He represented India at the United Nations 1952–62, and was defense minister 1957–62, when he was dismissed by Nehru following China's invasion of N India.

Kristallnacht the "night of (broken) glass" Nov 9–10, 1938 when the Nazi Sturmabteilung (SA) militia in Germany and Austria mounted a concerted attack on Jews, their synagogues, homes, and shops. It followed the assassination of a German embassy official in Paris by a Polish-Jewish youth. Subsequent measures included German legislation against Jews owning businesses or property, and restrictions on their going to school or leaving Germany. It was part of the ◊Holocaust.

Krivoi Rog town in Ukraine, USSR, 80 mi/130 km SW of Dnepropetrovsk; population (1987) 698,000. The surrounding district is rich in iron ore, and there is a metallurgical industry. The name means "crooked horn."

Kroeber Alfred Louis 1876–1960. US anthropologist. After establishing a department of anthropology at the University of California at Berkeley, he led archeological expeditions to New Mexico beginning 1915. In 1917 he became president of the American Anthropological Association, a group he helped found. At Berkeley, Kroeber served as professor 1919–46 and anthropology museum director 1925–46. His extensive research into and analysis of the culture of the California, the Plains, Mexican, and South American Indians dramatically broadened the scope of anthropological studies. His textbook *Anthropology* 1923; 1948 remains a classic and influential work.

Born in Hoboken, New Jersey, Kroeber was the first student of Franz ◊Boas to receive a PhD from Columbia University 1901.

Kronstadt Russian naval base, founded by Peter the Great 1703, on Kotlin island, Gulf of Finland, commanding the sea approach to Leningrad, whose defense under siege was aided by its guns 1941–43.

Kronstadt uprising revolt in March 1921 by sailors of the Russian Baltic Fleet at their headquarters in Kronstadt, outside Petrograd (now Leningrad). On the orders of the leading Bolshevik Trotsky, Red Army troops, dressed in white camouflage, crossed the ice to the naval base and captured it on March 18. The leaders were subsequently shot.

Kropotkin Peter Alexeivich, Prince Kropotkin 1842–1921. Russian anarchist. Imprisoned for revolutionary activities 1874, he escaped to the UK in 1876 and later moved to Switzerland. Expelled from Switzerland, he went to France, where he was imprisoned 1883–86. He lived in Britain until 1917, when he returned to Moscow, but, unsympathetic to the Bolsheviks, he retired from politics. Among his works are *Memoirs of a Revolutionist* 1899, *Mutual Aid* 1902, and *Modern Science and Anarchism* 1903.

He was a noted geologist and geographer.

Kruger Stephanus Johannes Paulus 1825–1904. President of the Transvaal 1883–1900. He refused to remedy the grievances of the uitlanders (English and other non-Boer white residents) and so precipitated the Second ◊South African War.

Kruger National Park game reserve in NE Transvaal, South Africa, between the Limpopo and Crocodile rivers; it is the largest in the world (about 8,000 sq mi/20,720 sq km). The Sabie Game Reserve was established 1898 by President Kruger, and the park declared in 1926.

Krugersdorp mining town in the Witwatersrand district, Transvaal, South Africa; population (1980) 103,000. Manganese, uranium, and gold are mined.

Kruger telegram message sent by Kaiser Wilhelm II of Germany to President Kruger of the Transvaal Jan 3, 1896 congratulating him on defeating the ◊Jameson raid of 1895. The text of the telegram provoked indignation in Britain and elsewhere, and represented a worsening of Anglo-German relations, in spite of a German government retraction.

Krupp German steelmaking armaments firm founded 1811 by Friedrich Krupp (1787–1826) and developed by Alfred Krupp (1812–1887) by pioneering the Bessemer steelmaking process. Krupp developed the long-distance artillery used in World War I, and supported Hitler's regime in preparation for World War II, after which the head of the firm was imprisoned and his property confiscated until 1951 when he was granted an amnesty.

krypton colorless, odorless, gaseous, nonmetallic element, symbol Kr, atomic number 36, atomic weight 83.80. It is grouped with the ◊inert gases and was long believed not to enter into reactions, but it is now known to combine with fluorine under certain conditions; it remains inert to all other reagents. It is present in very small quantities in the air (about 114 parts per million). It is used chiefly in fluorescent lamps, lasers and gas-filled electronic valves.

Krypton was discovered in 1898 in the residue from liquid air by British chemists William Ramsay and Morris Travers (1872–1961) and named by them for Greek *kryptos*, hidden; the name refers to their difficulty in isolating it.

Kryukov Fyodor 1870–1920. Russian writer, alleged by Solzhenitsyn to be the real author of *And Quiet Flows the Don* by ◊Sholokhov.

KS abbreviation for ◊Kansas.

Kuala Lumpur capital of the Federation of Malaysia; area 93 sq mi/240 sq km; population (1980) 938,000. The city developed after 1873 with the expansion of tin and rubber trading; these are now its major industries. Formerly within the state of Selangor, of which it was also the capital, it was created a federal territory 1974.

Kuanyin transliteration of ◊Guanyin, goddess of mercy in Chinese Buddhism.

Kuban river in the USSR, rising in Georgia (see ◊Krasnodar) and flowing to the Sea of Azov; length 563 mi/906 km.

Kubelik Jan 1880–1940. Czech violinist and composer. He performed in Prague at the age of

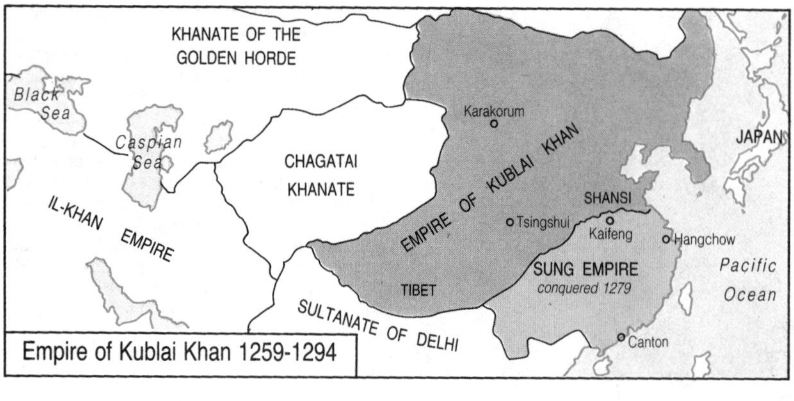
KHANATE OF THE
GOLDEN HORDE
Black Sea
Caspian Sea
CHAGATAI
KHANATE
IL-KHAN EMPIRE
Karakorum
EMPIRE OF KUBLAI KHAN
JAPAN
SHANSI
Tsingshui
Kaifeng
Hangchow
SUNG EMPIRE
conquered 1279
TIBET
Pacific
Ocean
SULTANATE OF DELHI
Canton
Empire of Kublai Khan 1259-1294

eight, and was one of the world's greatest virtuosos; he also wrote six violin concertos.

Kubelik Rafael 1914– . Czech conductor and composer, son of violinist Jan Kubelik. His works include symphonies and operas, such as *Veronika* 1947. He was musical director of the Royal Opera House, Covent Garden, London 1955–58.

Kublai Khan 1216–1294. Mongol emperor of China from 1259. He completed his grandfather ◊Genghis Khan's conquest of N China from 1240, and on his brother Mungo's death 1259 established himself as emperor of China. He moved the capital to Beijing and founded the Yuan dynasty, successfully expanding his empire into Indochina, but was defeated in an attempt to conquer Japan 1281.

Kubrick Stanley 1928– . US-born British director, producer, and screenwriter. His films include *Paths of Glory* 1957, *Dr Strangelove* 1964, *2001: A Space Odyssey* 1968, *A Clockwork Orange* 1971, and *The Shining* 1979.

Kuching capital and port of Sarawak state, E Malaysia; on the Sarawak river; population (1980) 74,200.

kudu two species of African antelope of the genus *Tragelaphus*. The greater kudu *Tragelaphus strepsiceros* is fawn-colored with thin white vertical stripes, and stands 4.2 ft/1.3 m at the shoulder, with head and body 8 ft/2.4 m long. Males have long spiral horns. The greater kudu is found S Africa in bush country from Angola to Ethiopia.

The similar lesser kudu *Tragelaphus imberbis* lives in E Africa and is 3 ft/1 m at the shoulder.

kudzu Japanese creeper *Pueraria lobata*, family Leguminosae, which helps fix nitrogen (see ◊nitrogen cycle) and can be used as fodder, but became a pest in the southern USA when introduced to check soil erosion.

Kufra group of oases in the Libyan Desert, N Africa, SE of Tripoli. By the 1970s the vast underground reservoirs were being used for irrigation.

Kuhn Richard 1900–1967. Austrian chemist. Working at Heidelberg University in the 1930s, Kuhn succeeded in determining the structures of vitamins A, B_2, and B_6. He was awarded the 1938 Nobel Prize for Chemistry, but was unable to receive it until after World War II.

Kuhn Thomas S 1922– . US historian and philosopher of science, who showed that social and cultural conditions affect the directions of science. *The Structure of Scientific Revolutions* 1962 argued that even scientific knowledge is relative, dependent on the ◊paradigm (theoretical framework) that dominates a scientific field at the time.

Such paradigms (for example, Darwinism and Newtonian theory) are so dominant that they are uncritically accepted as true, until a "scientific revolution" creates a new orthodoxy. Kuhn's ideas have also influenced ideas in the social sciences.

Kuibyshev or ***Kuybyshev*** capital of Kuibyshev region, USSR, and port at the junction of the rivers Samara and Volga, situated in the center of the fertile middle Volga plain; population (1987) 1,280,000. Industries include aircraft, locomotives, cables, synthetic rubber, textiles, fertilizers, petroleum refining, and quarrying.

Founded as Samara, the city was renamed Kuibyshev 1935. It was provisional capital of the USSR 1941–43. The Kuibyshev Sea is an artificial lake about 300 mi/480 km long, created in the 1950s by damming the river Volga.

Kuiper Gerard Peter 1905–1973. Dutch-born US astronomer who made extensive studies of the Solar System. His discoveries included the atmosphere of the planet Mars and that of Titan, the largest moon of the planet Saturn.

Kuiper was adviser to many NASA exploratory missions and pioneered the use of telescopes on high-flying aircraft. The Kuiper Airborne Observatory, one such telescope, is named after him.

Ku Klux Klan US secret society dedicated to white supremacy, founded 1866 in the Southern US states to oppose ◊Reconstruction after the American ◊Civil War and to deny political rights to the black population. Members wore hooded white robes to hide their identities and burned crosses as a symbol. It was publicized in the 1960s for terrorizing civil-rights activists and organizing racist demonstrations.

It was originally headed by former Confederate general Nathan Bedford ◊Forrest and was disbanded in 1869 under pressure from members who opposed violence. Scattered groups continued a campaign of lynching and flogging, prompting anti-Klan laws in 1871. The group reemerged in 1915 as an antiblack, anti-Semitic, anti-Catholic, right-wing group that portrayed itself as fervently patriotic. Today the Klan has evolved into a paramilitary extremist group that has forged loose ties with other white supremacist groups.

Ku Klux Klan Case a US Supreme Court decision (*Ex parte Yarbrough*) 1884 dealing with federal enforcement of the 15th Amendment. Jasper Yarbrough, a Georgia Klansman, was convicted under the Enforcement Act 1870 of harassing a black voter. He appealed to the US Supreme Court on the grounds that the 15th Amendment grants only the right to vote; it does not give Congress the power to protect that right. The Court unanimously upheld the Enforcement Act, ruling that the federal government had legitimate power to protect citizens from racial discrimination in all circumstances surrounding voting in federal elections.

kulak Russian term for a peasant who could afford to hire labor and often acted as village usurer. The kulaks resisted the Soviet government's policy of collectivization, and in 1930 they were "liquidated as a class," with up to 5 million being either killed or deported to Siberia.

Kulturkampf German word for policy introduced by Chancellor Bismarck in Germany in 1873 that isolated the Catholic interest and attempted to reduce its power to create a political coalition of liberals and agrarian conservatives. The alienation of such a large section of the German population as the Catholics could not be sustained, and the policy was abandoned after 1876 to be replaced by an anti-Socialist policy.

Kumamoto city on Kyushu Island, Japan, 50 mi/ 80 km E of Nagasaki; population (1987) 550,000. A military stronghold until the 19th century, the city is now a center for fishing, food processing, and textile industries.

Kumasi the second-largest city in Ghana, W Africa, capital of Ashanti region, with trade in cocoa, rubber, and cattle; population (1984) 376,200.

history From the late 17th century until 1901, when it was absorbed into the British Gold Coast Colony, Kumasi was capital of the Ashanti confederation.

Kun Béla 1885–1938. Hungarian politician who created a Soviet republic in Hungary March 1919, which was overthrown Aug 1919 by a Western blockade and Romanian military actions. The succeeding regime under Admiral Horthy effectively liquidated both socialism and liberalism in Hungary.

Kundera Milan 1929– . Czech writer, born in Brno. His first novel *The Joke* 1967 brought him into official disfavor in Prague, and, unable to publish further works, he moved to France. His novels include *The Book of Laughter and Forgetting* 1979 and *The Unbearable Lightness of Being* 1984.

Kung see ◊Bushman.

kung fu the Chinese art of unarmed combat (Mandarin *ch'üan fa*), one of the ◊martial arts. It is practiced in many forms, the most popular being *wing chun*, "beautiful springtime." The basic principle is to use attack as a form of defense.

Kuniyoshi Utagawa 1797–1861. Japanese printmaker. His series *108 Heroes of the Suikoden*, depicts heroes of the Chinese classic *The Water Margin*. Kuniyoshi's dramatic, innovative style lent itself to warriors and fantasy, but his subjects also include landscapes and cats.

Kunlunshan mountain range on the edge of the great Tibetan plateau, China; 2,500 mi/4,000 km from E to W; highest peak Muztag (23,900 ft/7,282 m).

Kunming formerly ***Yunnan*** capital of Yunnan province, China, on Lake Dian Chi, about 6,500 ft/ 2,000 m above sea level; population (1986) 1,490,000. Industries include chemicals, textiles, and copper smelted with nearby hydroelectric power.

Kuomintang original spelling of the Chinese nationalist party, now known (outside Taiwan) as ◊Guomindang.

kurchatovium name proposed by Soviet scientists for the element currently known as ◊unnilquadium (atomic number 104), to honor Soviet nuclear physicist Igor Kurchatov (1903–1960).

Kurd a member of an Iranian people, living mostly in the region called Kurdistan. Although divided among more powerful states, the Kurds have nationalist aspirations; there are approximately 8 million in Turkey, 5 million in Iran, 4 million in Iraq, 500,000 in Syria, and 100,000 in the USSR. Some 1 million Kurds were made homeless and 25,000 killed as a result of chemical weapon attacks by Iraq 1984–89. The Kurdish language is a member of the Iranian branch of the Indo-European family and the Kurds are a non-Arab ethnic group.

Kurdistan or ***Kordestan*** hilly region in SW Asia near Mount Ararat, where the borders of Iran, Iraq, Syria, Turkey, and the USSR meet; area 74,600 sq mi/193,000 sq km; total population around 18 million.

Kure naval base and port 20 mi/32 km SE of Hiroshima, on the S coast of Honshu, Japan; population (1980) 234,500. Industries include shipyards and engineering works.

Kuria Muria group of five islands in the Arabian Sea, off the S coast of Oman; area 28 sq mi/72 sq km.

Kuril Islands chain of about 50 small islands stretching from the NE of Hokkaido, Japan, to the S of Kamchatka peninsula, USSR; area 5,700 sq mi/ 14,765 sq km; population (1970) 15,000. Some of

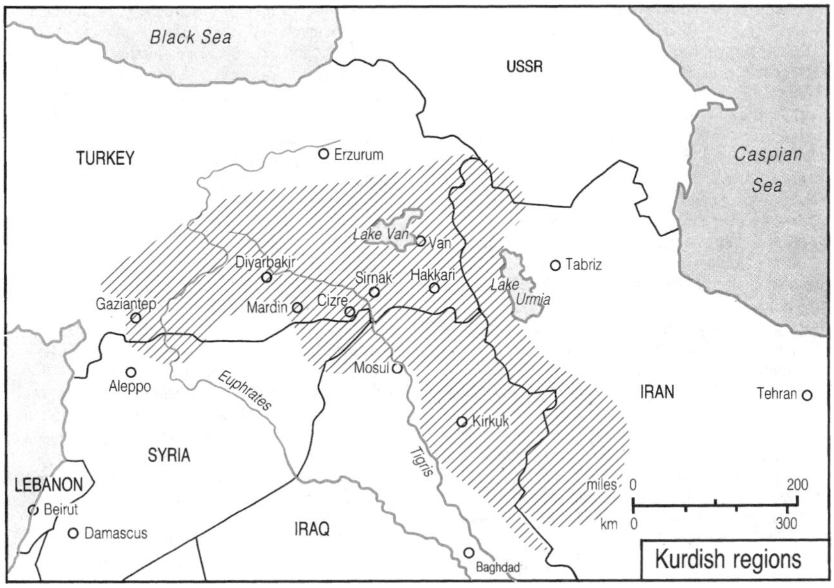
Black Sea
USSR
TURKEY
Erzurum
Caspian Sea
Lake Van
Van
Diyarbakir
Sirnak
Hakkari
Tabriz
Lake Urmia
Gaziantep
Mardin
Cizre
Mosul
Aleppo
Euphrates
IRAN
Tehran
Kirkuk
SYRIA
Tigris
LEBANON
Beirut
Damascus
IRAQ
Baghdad
miles 0 200
km 0 300
Kurdish regions

them are of volcanic origin. Two of the Kurils are claimed by both Japan and the USSR.

The Kurils were discovered 1634 by a Russian navigator and were settled by Russians. Japan seized them 1875 and held them until 1945, when under the Yalta agreement they were returned to the USSR. Japan still claims the southernmost (Etorou and Kunashiri) and also the nearby small islands of Habomai and Shikotan (not part of the Kurils). The USSR agreed to the latter 1972, but the question of Etorofu and Kunashiri prevents signature of a Japan-Soviet peace treaty.

Kuropatkin Alexei Nikolaievich 1848–1921. Russian general. He distinguished himself as chief of staff during the Russo-Turkish War 1877–78, was commander in chief in Manchuria 1903, and resigned after his defeat at Mukden in the ◊Russo-Japanese War. During World War I he commanded the armies on the northern front until 1916.

Kurosawa Akira 1910– . Japanese director whose film *Rashomon* 1950 introduced Western audiences to Japanese cinema. Epics such as *Seven Samurai* 1954 combine spectacle with intimate human drama. His other films include *Drunken Angel* 1948, *Yojimbo* 1961, *Kagemusha* 1981, and *Ran* 1985.

Kuroshio or ***Japan Current*** a warm ocean ◊current flowing from Japan to North America.

Kursk capital city of Kursk region of the USSR; population (1987) 434,000. It dates from the 9th century. Industries include chemicals, machinery, alcohol, and tobacco.

Kūt-al-Imāra or ***al Kūt*** city in Iraq, on the river Tigris; population (1985) 58,600. It is a grain market and carpet-manufacturing center. In World War I it was under siege by Turkish forces from Dec 1915 to April 1916, when the British garrison surrendered.

Kutch, Rann of salt-marsh area in Gujarat state, India, that forms two shallow lakes (the Great Rann and the Little Rann) in the wet season and is a salt-covered desert in the dry. It takes its name from the former princely state of Kutch, which it adjoined. An international tribunal 1968 awarded 90% of the Rann of Kutch to India and 10% (about 300 sq mi/800 sq km) to Pakistan, the latter comprising almost all the elevated area above water the year round.

Kutuzov Mikhail Larionovich, Prince of Smolensk 1745–1813. Commander of the Russian forces in the Napoleonic Wars. He commanded an army corps at ◊Austerlitz and the retreating army 1812. After the burning of Moscow, he harried the French throughout their retreat and later took command of the united Prussian armies.

Kuwait country in SW Asia, bordered N and NW by Iraq, E by the Persian Gulf, and S and SW by Saudi Arabia

government The 1962 constitution was partly suspended by the emir 1976 and reinstated 1980. It vests executive power in the hands of the emir, who governs through an appointed prime minister and council of ministers. The current prime minister is the emir's eldest son, the crown prince. There is a single-chamber national assembly of 50 members, elected on a restricted suffrage for a four-year term. Political parties are not permitted and, despite the appearance of constitutional government, Kuwait is, in effect, a personal monarchy.

history The region was part of the Turkish ◊Ottoman Empire from the 16th century; the ruling family founded the sheikdom of Kuwait 1756. The ruler made a treaty with Britain 1899 enabling it to become a self-governing protectorate until it achieved full independence 1961.

Oil was first discovered 1938, and its large-scale exploitation began after 1945, transforming Kuwait City from a small fishing port into a thriving commercial center. The oil revenues have enabled ambitious public works and education programs to be undertaken. Sheik Abdullah al-Salem al-Sabah took the title of emir 1961 when he assumed full executive powers. He died 1965 and was succeeded by his brother, Sheik Sabah al-Salem al-Sabah. He, in turn, died 1977 and was succeeded by Crown Prince Jabir, who appointed Sheik Saad al-Abdullah al-Salem al-Sabah as his heir apparent. In Jan 1990 pro-democracy demonstrations were dispersed by the police.

Kuwait has used its considerable wealth not only to improve its infrastructure and social services but also to secure its borders, making, for example, substantial donations to Iraq, which in the past had made territorial claims on it. It has also been a strong supporter of the Arab cause generally.

During the 1980–88 Iran–Iraq War, Kuwait was the target of destabilization efforts by the revolutionary Iranian government. Shi'ite terrorists conducted a bombing campaign as part of an effort to incite the Shi'ite minority in Kuwait. Seventeen were arrested 1983 and their freedom was the demand in several hijacking incidents that followed. In 1987 Kuwait sought US protection for its tankers in the wake of attacks on Gulf shipping. Several Kuwaiti tankers were "reflagged," and the US Navy conducted convoys through the Gulf. Iranian missiles also struck Kuwaiti installations, provoking fears of an expansion of the conflict. Kuwait released two of the convicted bombers Feb 1989.

On Aug 2, 1990 President Hussein of Iraq reactivated a long-standing territorial dispute and invaded and occupied the country. The emir and most of his family escaped to Saudi Arabia. With more assets outside than in Kuwait, the government in exile was able to provide virtually un-

Kuwait
State of
(Dowlat al Kuwait)

Iraq
Iran
Kuwait
KUWAIT
THE GULF
Saudi Arabia
Oman
RED SEA
YEMEN
INDIAN OCEAN
Djibouti
Ethiopia
0 miles 500
0 km 1000

area 6,878 sq mi/17,819 sq km
capital (and chief port) Kuwait
cities Jahra, Ahmadi, Fahaheel
physical hot desert and islands of Failaka, Bubiyan, and Warba at NE corner of Arabian Peninsula
features there are no rivers and rain is light; the world's largest desalination plants built in the 1950s
head of state and government Jabir al-Ahmad al-Jabir al-Sabah from 1977
political system absolute monarchy
political parties none
exports oil
currency Kuwaiti dinar
population (1990 est) 2,080,000 (Kuwaitis 40%, Palestinians 30%); growth rate 5.5% p.a.
life expectancy men 72, women 76 (1989)
language Arabic 78%, Kurdish 10%, Farsi 4%
religion Sunni Muslim 45%, Shi'ite minority 30%
literacy 71% (1988)
GNP $19.1 bn; $10,410 per head (1988)
chronology
1914 Britain recognized Kuwait as an independent sovereign state.
1961 Full independence achieved from Britain, with Sheik Abdullah al-Salem al-Sabah as emir.
1965 Sheik Abdullah died; succeeded by his brother, Sheik Sabah.
1977 Sheik Sabah died; succeeded by Crown Prince Jabir.
1983 Shi'ite terrorists bombed targets in Kuwait; 17 arrested.
1984 Shi'ite terrorists convicted.
1987 Kuwaiti oil tankers reflagged, received US Navy protection; missile attacks by Iran.
1988 Aircraft hijacked by pro-Iranian Shi'ites demanding release of convicted bombers; Kuwait refused.
1990 Prodemocracy demonstrations suppressed. Kuwait annexed by Iraq. Emir set up government in exile in Saudi Arabia.
1991 Feb: Kuwait liberated by US-led coalition forces; extensive damage to property and environment. Emir returned to Kuwait. New government omits any opposition representatives. Trials of alleged Iraqi collaborators criticized. Promised elections postponed.

limited finance to support Kuwaitis who had fled and to countries willing to help it regain its territory. By March 1991, UN-coalition forces had liberated Kuwait and peace negotiations began as part of the effort to restabilize the entire Middle East.

Not until Nov 1991 was Kuwait able to extinguish all the oil-well fires set by the retreating Iraqis.

Kuwait City (Arabic ***Al Kuwayt***) formerly ***Qurein*** chief port and capital of the state of Kuwait, on the S shore of Kuwait Bay; population (1985) 44,300, plus the suburbs of Hawalli, population (1985) 145,100, Jahrą, population (1985) 111,200, and as-Salimiya, population (1985) 153,400. Kuwait is a banking and investment center.

Kuzbas industrial area in Kemerovo region, S USSR, lying on the Tom River N of the Altai mountains. Development began in the 1930s. It takes its name from the old town of Kuznetsk.

Kuznets Simon 1901–1985. Russian-born economist who emigrated to the US 1922. He developed theories of national income and economic growth, used to forecast the future, in *Economic Growth of Nations* 1971. He won the Nobel Prize in economics 1971.

Kuznetsk Basin industrial area in Kemorovo region, S USSR. It is abbreviated to ◊Kuzbas.

Kuznetsov Anatoli 1930–1979. Russian writer. His novels *Babi Yar* 1966, describing the wartime execution of Jews at Babi Yar, near Kiev, and *The Fire* 1969, about workers in a large metallurgical factory, were seen as anti-Soviet. He lived in Britain from 1969.

Kwakiutl or ***Kwa-Gulth*** a member of a North American Indian people who live on both sides of the northern entrance to the Queen Charlotte Strait in British Columbia. Their language belongs to the Wakashan family. They are one of the NW coast tribes famed for their potlatches, status festivals involving a lavish consumption, even destruction, of goods.

kW abbreviation for ◊kilowatt.

Kwa Ndebele black homeland in Transvaal province, South Africa; achieved self-governing status 1981; population (1985) 235,800.

Kwangchow alternate name of ◊Guangzhou, city in China.

Kwangchu or ***Kwangju*** capital of South Cholla province, SW South Korea; population (1985) 906,000. It is at the center of a rice-growing region. A museum in the city houses a large collection of Chinese porcelain dredged up 1976 after lying for over 600 years on the ocean floor.

Kwangsi-Chuang alternate name of ◊Guanxi Zhuang, region of China.

Kwangtung alternate name of ◊Guangdong, province of China.

Kwannon or ***Kannon*** in Japanese Buddhism, a female form (known to the West as "goddess of mercy") of the bodhisattva ◊Avalokiteśvara. Sometimes depicted with many arms extending compassion.

kwashiorkor severe protein deficiency in children under five years, resulting in retarded growth and a swollen abdomen.

Kwa Zulu black homeland in Natal province, South Africa; population (1985) 3,747,000. It achieved self-governing status 1971.

Kweichow alternate name of ◊Guizhou, province of China.

Kweilin alternate name of ◊Guilin in China.

KY abbreviation for ◊Kentucky.

kyanite aluminum silicate, Al_2SiO_5, a pale blue mineral occurring as blade-shaped crystals. It is an indicator of high pressure conditions in metamorphic rocks formed from clay sediments. Andalusite, Kyanite, and sillimanite are all polymorphs.

Kyd Thomas c. 1557–1595. English dramatist, author in about 1588 of a bloody revenge tragedy, *The Spanish Tragedy*, that anticipated elements present in Shakespeare's *Hamlet*.

Kyoga lake in central Uganda; area 1,709 sq mi/4,425 sq km. The Victoria Nile River passes through it.

Kyoto former capital of Japan 794–1868 (when the capital was changed to Tokyo) on Honshu island, linked by canal with Biwa Lake; population (1987) 1,469,000. Industries include electrical, chemical, and machinery plants; silk weaving; and the manufacture of porcelain, bronze, and lacquerware.

kyphosis exaggerated outward curve of the upper spine, resulting in a lump. It is usually due to spinal disease, arthritis, or bad posture.

Kyprianou Spyros 1932– Cypriot politician. Foreign minister 1961–72, he founded the Democratic Front (DIKO) in 1976. He was president 1977–88.

Educated in Cyprus and the UK, he was called to the English Bar in 1954. He became secretary to Archbishop Makarios in London in 1952 and returned with him to Cyprus in 1959. On the death of Makarios in 1977 he became acting president and was then elected.

Kyushu southernmost of the main islands of Japan, separated from Shikoku and Honshu by Bungo Channel and Suo Bay, but connected to Honshu by bridge and rail tunnel

area 16,270 sq mi/42,150 sq km, including about 370 small islands

capital Nagasaki

cities Fukuoka, Kumamoto, Kagoshima

physical mountainous, volcanic, with subtropical climate

features the active volcano Aso-take (5,225 ft/1,592 m), with the world's largest crater

products coal, gold, silver, iron, tin, rice, tea, timber

population (1986) 13,295,000.

Kyustendil town with hot springs in SW Bulgaria, SW of Sofia; population about 25,000.

Kyzyl-Kum desert in Kazakhstan and Uzbekistan, USSR, between the Sur-Darya and Amu-Darya rivers; area about 116,000 sq mi/300,000 sq km. It is being reclaimed for cultivation by irrigation and protective tree-planting.

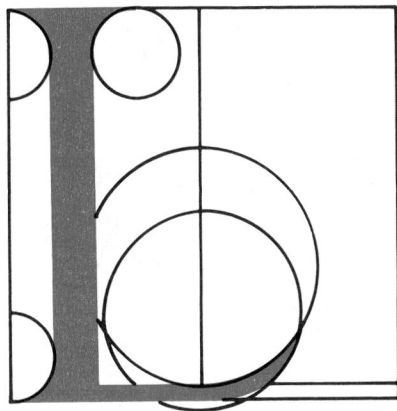

L Roman numeral for 50.

LA abbreviation for ◊Louisiana; Los Angeles.

Labanotation a comprehensive system of accurate dance notation (*Kinetographie Laban*) devised 1928 by Rudolf von Laban (1879–1958), dancer, choreographer, and dance theorist.

labeled compound or ***tagged compound*** chemical compound in which a radioactive isotope is substituted for a stable one. Thus labeled, the path taken by the compound through a system can be followed, for example by measuring the radiation emitted.

This powerful and sensitive technique is used in medicine, chemistry, biochemistry, and industry.

labellum the lower petal of an orchid flower, which is a different shape from the two other lateral petals and gives the orchid its characteristic appearance.

The labellum is more elaborate and usually larger than the other petals. It often has distinctive patterning to encourage ◊pollination by insects; sometimes it is extended backwards to form a hollow spur containing nectar.

Labor, Knights of in US history, a national labor organization founded by Philadelphia tailor Uriah Stephens 1869 and committed to cooperative enterprise, equal pay for both sexes, and an eight-hour day. The Knights grew rapidly in the mid-1880s under Terence V Powderly (1849–1924) but gave way to the ◊American Federation of Labor after 1886.

Labor Day legal vacation in honor of workers. In Canada and the US, Labor Day is celebrated on the first Monday in September. In many countries it coincides with ◊May Day.

labor market the market that determines the cost and conditions of the work force. This will depend on the demand of employers, the levels and availability of skills, and social conditions.

Labor Party in Australia, political party based on Socialist principles. It was founded 1891 and first held office 1904. It formed governments 1929–31 and 1939–49, but in the intervening periods internal discord provoked splits, and reduced its effectiveness. It returned to power under Gough Whitlam 1972–75, and again under Bob Hawke from 1983.

labor theory of value in Classical economics, the theory that the price (value) of a product directly reflects the amount of labor it involves. According to theory, if the price of a product falls, either the share of labor in that product has declined or that expended in the production of other goods has risen.

◊Marx adopted and developed the theory but it was not supported by all Classical economists. ◊Malthus was a dissenter.

Labour Party UK political party based on Socialist principles, originally formed to represent workers. It was founded 1900 and first held office 1924. The first majority Labour government 1945–51 introduced ◊nationalization and the National Health Service, and expanded ◊social security. Labour was again in power 1964–70 and 1974–79. The party leader is elected by Labour members of Parliament. Neil Kinnock became leader 1983.

labor union organization of employed workers formed to undertake collective bargaining with employers and to try to achieve improved working conditions for its members. Attitudes of government to unions and of unions to management vary greatly from country to country. Probably the most effective trade-union system is that of Sweden, and the most internationally known is the Polish ◊Solidarity.

history Trade unions of a kind existed in the Middle Ages as artisans' guilds, and combinations of wage earners were formed at the time of industrialization in the 18th century; but labor unions did not formally (or legally) come into existence in Britain until the Industrial Revolution in the 19th century. The early history of labor unions is one of illegality and of legislation to prevent their existence.

history, US The great growth of US labor unionism, apart from the abortive Knights of Labor 1869–86 (see also ◊American Federation of Labor), came in the post-Depression years. Employers and the US government have historically been more opposed to labor unionism than those in Britain, often using police and armed guards to harass pickets and protect strike breakers, which has led to episodes of violence and bitter confrontation. US legislation includes the Taft–Hartley Act 1947, which among other measures outlaws the closed shop.

international In the present day, US unions have the reputation of being open to the acceptance of new techniques, taking a broad view of these as conducive to greater eventual prosperity. In Sweden, for example, conflicts of unions within an industry (demarcation disputes) are largely eliminated, and unions and employers cooperate freely.

labor unionism, international worldwide cooperation between unions. In 1973 a European Trade Union Confederation was established, membership 29 million, and there is an International Labor Organization, established 1919 and affiliated to the United Nations from 1945, which formulates standards for labor and social conditions. Other organizations are the International Confederation of Free Trade Unions (1949), including the American Federation of Labor and Congress of Industrial Organizations and the UK Trades Union Congress, and the World Federation of Trade Unions (1945).

Labrador area of NE Canada, part of the province of Newfoundland, lying between Ungava Bay on the NW, the Atlantic Ocean on the E, and the Strait of Belle Isle on the SE; area 102,699 sq mi/ 266,060 sq km; population (1986) 28,741. It consists primarily of a gently sloping plateau with an irregular coastline of numerous bays, fjords, inlets, and cliffs 200 ft/60 m to 400 ft/120 m high. Industries include fisheries, timber and pulp, and many minerals. Hydroelectric resources include Churchill Falls on Churchill River, where one of the world's largest underground power houses is situated. The Canadian Air Force base in Goose Bay is on land claimed by the Innu (or Montagnais-Naskapi) Indian people, who call themselves a sovereign nation (in 1989 numbering 9,500).

La Bruyère Jean de 1645–1696. French essayist. He was born in Paris, studied law, took a post in the revenue office, and in 1684 entered the service of the house of Condé. His *Caractères* 1688, satirical portraits of his contemporaries, made him many enemies.

Labuan a flat, wooded island off NW Borneo, a Federal Territory of East Malaysia; area 39 sq mi/100 sq km; population (1980) 12,000. Its chief port city is Victoria, population 3,200. Labuan was ceded to Great Britain 1846, and from 1963 included in Sabah, Federation of Malaysia.

laburnum any flowering tree or shrub of the genus *Laburnum* of the pea family Leguminosae. The seeds are poisonous. *L. anagyroides*, native to the mountainous parts of central Europe, is often grown as an ornamental.

Labyrinth in Greek mythology, the maze designed by ◊Daedalus at ◊Knossos in Crete for King ◊Minos as a home for the ◊Minotaur. After killing the Minotaur, ◊Theseus was guided out of the Labyrinth by a thread given to him by the king's daughter, Ariadne.

lac resinous incrustation exuded by the female of the lac insect *Laccifer lacca*, which eventually covers the twigs of trees in India and the Far East. The gathered twigs are known as stick lac, and yield a useful crimson dye; shellac is manufactured commercially by melting the separated resin and spreading it into thin layers or flakes.

Laccadive, Minicoy, and Amindivi Islands former name of Indian island group ◊Lakshadweep.

laccolith an intruded mass of igneous rock that forces apart two strata and forms a round lens-shaped mass many times wider than thick. The overlying layers are often pushed upward to form a dome. A classic development of laccoliths is illustrated in the Henry La Sal and Abajo mountains of SE Utah, found on the Colorado plateau.

lace a delicate, decorative openwork textile fabric. Needlepoint or point laces (a development of embroidery) originated in Italy in the late 15th or early 16th centuries. Lace was first made from linen thread and sometimes also with gold, silver, or silk; cotton, wool, and synthetic fibers have been used more recently. The other chief variety of lace is bobbin or pillow ("true") lace, made by twisting threads together in pairs or groups, according to a pattern marked out by pins set in a cushion. It is said to have been invented by Barbara Uttmann (born 1514) of Saxony; elaborate patterns may require over a thousand bobbins. Lace is a European craft, with centers in Germany, France, Belgium, Italy, and England, such as Venice, Alençon, and Argentan for point lace, and Mechlin, Valenciennes, and Honiton for bobbin lace; both types are made at Brussels.

La Ceiba chief Atlantic port of Honduras; population (1985) 61,900.

lacewing insect of the families Hemerobiidae (the brown lacewings) and Chrysopidae (the green lacewings) of the order Neuroptera. Found throughout the world, they are so called because of the intricate veining of their two pairs of semi-transparent wings. They have narrow bodies and long thin antennae. The larvae (called aphid lions) are predators, especially on aphids. The eggs of the golden-eye lacewing *Chrysopa aculata* are laid on the ends of stalks.

Lachish ancient city SW of Jerusalem, destroyed 589 BC. Inscribed pottery fragments found there have thrown light on Hebrew manuscripts and the early development of the alphabet.

Lachlan river that rises in the Blue Mountains, Australia; a tributary of the Murrumbidgee; length 920 mi/1,485 km.

Laclos Pierre Choderlos de 1741–1803. French author. An army officer, he wrote a single novel in letter form, *Les Liaisons dangereuses/Dangerous Liaisons* 1782, an analysis of moral corruption.

La Condamine Charles Marie de 1701–1774. French soldier and geographer who was sent by the French Academy of Sciences to Peru to measure the length of an arc of the meridian 1735–43. On his return journey he traveled the length of the Amazon, writing about the use of the nerve toxin curare, india rubber, and the advantages of inoculation.

lacquer a clear or colored resinous varnish obtained from Oriental trees (*Toxicodendron verniciflua*), and used for decorating furniture and art objects. It was developed in China, probably as early as the 4th century BC, and was later adopted in Japan.

lacrosse Canadian ball game, adopted from the North American Indians, and named after a fancied resemblance of the lacrosse stick (crosse) to a bishop's crosier. Thongs across the curved end of the crosse form a pocket to carry the small rubber ball.

The field is approximately 110 yd/100 m long and a minimum 60 yd/55 m wide in the men's game, which is played with ten players per side; the women's field is larger, and there are twelve players per side. The goals are just under 6 ft/2 m square, with loose nets. The world championships were first held in 1967 for men, and in 1969 for women.

La Crosse city in SW Wisconsin, at the confluence of the Black, La Crosse, and Mississippi rivers, NW of Madison; seat of La Crosse County. The processing and marketing center for the area's agricultural products, it also manufactures plastics, rubber products, and electrical machinery; population (1990) 51,003. The city began as a French trading post and grew as a lumber town.

lactation the secretion of milk from the mammary glands of mammals. In late pregnancy, the cells lining the lobules inside the mammary glands begin extracting substances from the blood to produce milk. The supply of milk starts shortly after birth with the production of colostrum, a clear fluid consisting largely of water, protein, antibodies, and vitamins. The production of milk continues practically as long as the infant continues to suck.

lacteal small vessel responsible for absorbing fat in the small intestine. Occurring in the fingerlike villi of the ileum, lacteals have a milky appearance and drain into the lymphatic system.

Before fat can pass into the lacteal, bile from the liver causes its emulsification into droplets small enough for attack by the enzyme lipase. The products of this digestion form into even smaller droplets, which diffuse into the villi. Large droplets re-form before entering the lacteal and this causes the milky appearance.

lactic acid $CH_3CHOHCOOH$ (technical name hydroxypropanoic acid) organic acid, a colorless, almost odorless syrup, produced by certain bacteria during fermentation. It occurs in yogurt, buttermilk, sour cream, wine, and certain plant extracts; it is present in muscles when they are exercised hard, and also in the stomach. It is used in food preservation and in the preparation of pharmaceuticals.

lactose white sugar, found in solution in milk; it forms 5% of cow's milk. It is commercially prepared from the whey obtained in cheese-making.

Like table sugar (sucrose), it is a disaccharide, consisting of two basic sugar units (monosaccharides), in this case, glucose and galactose. Unlike sucrose, it is tasteless.

Ladakh subsidiary range of the ◊Karakoram and district of NE Kashmir, India, on the border of Tibet; chief town Leh. After China occupied Tibet in 1951, it made claims on the area.

Ladd Alan 1913–1964. US actor whose first leading role, as the professional killer in *This Gun for Hire* 1942, made him a star. His career declined after the mid-1950s although his last role, in *The Carpetbaggers* 1964, was one of his best. His other films include *The Blue Dahlia* 1946 and his greatest success, *Shane* 1953.

Ladin a member of an ethnic community (about 16,000) in the Dolomites, S Tyrol, whose language (Ladin) derives directly from Latin; they may be descended from the Etruscans and other early Italian tribes and have links with the speakers of ◊Romansch in Switzerland.

Ladoga (Russian *Ladozhskoye*) largest lake on the continent of Europe, in the USSR, just NE of St Petersburg; area 7,100 sq mi/18,400 sq km. It receives the waters of several rivers, including the Svir, which drains lake Onega and runs to the Gulf of Finland by the river Neva.

Ladrones Spanish name (meaning "thieves") of the ◊Marianas archipelago.

Lady in the UK, the formal title of the daughter of an earl, marquis, or duke; and of any woman whose husband is above the rank of baronet or knight, as well as (by courtesy only) the wives of these latter ranks.

ladybird or ladybug beetle of the family Coccinellidae, generally red or yellow in color, with black spots. There are numerous species which, as larvae and adults, feed on aphids and scale-insect pests.

Laënnec René Théophile Hyacinthe 1781–1826. French physician, inventor of the ◊stethoscope 1814. He introduced the new diagnostic technique of auscultation (evaluating internal organs by listening with a stethoscope) in his book *Traité de l'auscultation médiaté* 1819, which quickly became a medical classic.

Laetrile patent name for an extract from the seeds of apricots, which was claimed as a cancer cure on no accepted evidence. In 1981 it was found to be of no effect against cancer.

Laetrile is banned in the US.

Lafarge John 1835–1910. US painter and ecclesiastical designer. He is credited with the revival of stained glass in America and also created woodcuts, watercolors, and murals.

He visited Europe in 1856 and the Far East in 1886. In the 1870s Lafarge turned from landscape painting (inspired by ◊Corot) to religious and still-life painting. Decorating the newly built Trinity Church in Boston, Massachusetts, he worked alongside the sculptor ◊Saint-Gaudens.

Lafayette city in W central Indiana, on the Wabash River, NW of Indianapolis, seat of Tippecanoe County. A distribution center for the area's agricultural products, its industries also include building materials, chemicals, wire, pharmaceuticals, and automobile parts. Purdue University 1865 is nearby; population (1990) 43,764. The Battle of Tippecanoe 1811 was fought here.

Lafayette city in S Louisiana, on the Vermilion River, W of New Orleans and SW of Baton Rouge; seat of Lafayette Parish. Its economy centers around the area's oil industry; population (1990) 94,440. Settled by Acadians from Nova Scotia in the late 1700s, Lafayette is in the heart of the area of Louisiana that is associated with French-speaking "Cajuns."

Lafayette Marie Joseph Gilbert de Motier, Marquis de 1757–1834. French soldier and politician. He fought against Britain in the American Revolution 1777–79 and 1780–82. During the French Revolution he sat in the National Assembly as a constitutional royalist and in 1789 presented the Declaration of the Rights of Man. After the storming of the ◊Bastille, he was given command of the National Guard. In 1792 he fled the country after attempting to restore the monarchy and was imprisoned by the Austrians until 1797. He supported Napoleon in 1815, sat in the chamber of deputies as a Liberal from 1818, and played a leading part in the revolution of 1830.

He was a popular hero in the US, and the cities of Lafayette in Louisiana and Indiana are named after him, as was the Lafayette Escadrille—American aviators flying for France during World War I, before the US entered 1917.

Lafayette Marie-Madeleine, Comtesse de Lafayette 1634–1693. French author. Her *Mémoires* of the French court are keenly observed, and her *La Princesse de Clèves* 1678 is the first French psychological novel and *roman à clef* ("novel with a key"), in that real-life characters (including ◊La Rochefoucauld, who was for many years her lover) are presented under fictitious names.

Lafitte Jean c. 1780–c. 1825. Pirate. Reportedly born in France, Lafitte settled in New Orleans, where he became a smuggler and privateer. Gathering a band of followers around him, he set up headquarters in nearby Barataria Bay. After several years of raiding Spanish shipping in the Gulf of Mexico, he was suspected of complicity with the British and was attacked by American forces soon after the outbreak of the War of 1812. He proved his loyalty to General Andrew Jackson in 1815 by his heroic participation in the Battle of New Orleans. After the war Lafitte established headquarters in Galveston Bay.

La Follette Robert Marion 1855–1925. US political leader. As a US senator 1906–25, La Follette became a leader of the national progressive movement, running for president on the Progressive ticket 1924. His memoirs, *Autobiography, A Personal Narrative of Political Experiences*, appeared in 1913.

Born in Primrose, Wisconsin, La Follette was educated at the state university and was admitted to the bar 1880. Entering politics, he served as district attorney 1880–94 and as a member of the US House of Representatives 1885–91. He was defeated for reelection to Congress 1890 and was elected Wisconsin governor 1900.

La Fontaine Jean de 1621–1695. French poet. He was born at Château-Thierry, and from 1656 lived largely in Paris, the friend of Molière, Racine, and Boileau. His works include *Fables* 1668–94 and *Contes* 1665–74, a series of witty and bawdy tales in verse.

Lafontaine Oskar 1943– . German Socialist politician, federal deputy chair of the Social Democrat Party (SPD) from 1987. Leader of the Saar regional branch of the SPD from 1977 and former mayor of Saarbrucken, West Germany, he was dubbed "Red Oskar" because of his radical views on military and environmental issues. His attitude became more conservative once he had become minister-president of Saarland in 1985.

Laforgue Jules 1860–1887. French poet who pioneered ◊free verse and who inspired later French and English writers.

lagan the legal term for wreckage lying on the ocean floor. See ◊flotsam, jetsam, and lagan.

Lagash Sumerian city north of Shatra, Iraq, under independent and semi-independent rulers from about 3000 to 2700 BC. Besides objects of high artistic value, it has provided about 30,000 clay tablets giving detailed information on temple administration. It was discovered 1877 and excavated by Ernest de Sarzec, then French consul in Basra.

lager a type of ◊beer.

Lagerkvist Pär 1891–1974. Swedish author of lyric poetry, dramas (including *The Hangman* 1935), and novels, such as *Barabbas* 1950. He was awarded the Nobel Prize for Literature 1951.

Lagerlöf Selma 1858–1940. Swedish novelist. She was originally a schoolteacher, and in 1891 published a collection of stories of peasant life, *Gösta Berling's Saga*. She was the first woman to receive a Nobel Prize, in 1909.

lagoon a coastal body of shallow salt water, usually

Lahore The Lahore Fort was largely reconstructed by the Mogul emperor Akbar, who reigned 1556–1605. The city of Lahore, capital of Pakistan's Punjab province, is now the country's second largest.

with limited access to the sea. The term is normally used to describe the shallow sea area cut off by a ◊coral reef or barrier islands.

Lagos chief port and former capital of Nigeria, located at the W end of an island in a lagoon and linked by bridges with the mainland via Iddo Island; population (1983) 1,097,000. Industries include chemicals, metal products, and fish. ◊Abuja was established as the new capital 1982.

Lagrange Joseph Louis 1736–1813. French mathematician. His *Mécanique analytique* 1788 applied mathematical analysis, using principles established by Newton, to such problems as the movements of planets when affected by each other's gravitational force. He presided over the commission that introduced the metric system 1793.

Lagrangian points the five locations in space where the centrifugal and gravitational forces of two bodies neutralize each other; a third, less massive body located at any one of these points will be held in equilibrium with respect to the other two. Three of the points, L1–L3, lie on a line joining the two large bodies. The other two points, L4 and L5, which are the most stable, lie on either side of this line. Their existence was predicted 1772 by Joseph Louis Lagrange.

The Trojan asteroids lie at Lagrangian points L4 and L5 in Jupiter's orbit around the Sun. Clouds of dust and debris may lie at the Lagrangian points of the Moon's orbit around the Earth.

La Guardia Fiorello (Henrico) 1882–1947. US Republican politician; congressman 1917, 1919, 1923–33; mayor of New York 1933–45. Elected against the opposition of the powerful Tammany Hall Democratic Party organization, he cleaned up the administration, suppressed racketeering, and organized unemployment relief, slum-clearance schemes, and social services. Although nominally a Republican, he strongly supported F D ◊Roosevelt's New Deal. La Guardia Airport, in New York City, is named after him.

Lahore capital of the province of Punjab and second city of Pakistan; population (1981) 2,920,000. Industries include engineering, textiles, carpets, and chemicals. It is associated with Mogul rulers Akbar, Jahangir, and Aurangzeb, whose capital it was in the 16th and 17th centuries.

Laibach German name of ◊Ljubljana, a city in Yugoslavia.

Lailat ul-Barah Muslim festival, the Night of Forgiveness, that takes place two weeks before the beginning of the fast of Ramadan (the ninth month of the Islamic year) and is a time for asking and granting forgiveness.

Lailat ul-Isra Wal Mi'raj Muslim festival that celebrates the prophet Mohammed's ◊Night Journey.

Lailat ul-Qadr Muslim festival, the Night of Power, that celebrates the giving of the Koran to Mohammed. It usually falls at the end of Ramadan.

Laing R(onald) D(avid) 1927–1989. Scottish psychoanalyst, originator of the "social theory" of mental illness, for example that ◊schizophrenia is promoted by family pressure for its members to conform to standards alien to themselves. His books include *The Divided Self* 1960 and *The Politics of the Family* 1971.

laissez faire theory that government should refrain from all intervention in economic affairs, unless it becomes necessary to break up a monopoly. The phrase originated with Physiocrats, 18th-century French economists whose maxim was *laissez faire et laissez passer* (literally, "let go and let pass"—that is, leave the individual alone and let commodities circulate freely). The amount of acceptable intervention remains one of the chief problems of modern economics, in both capitalist and Communist regimes. See also Adam ◊Smith.

Before the 17th century, control by the guild, local authorities, or the state, of wages, prices, employment, and the training of workmen, was taken for granted. As capitalist enterprises developed in the 16th and 17th centuries, entrepreneurs shook off the control of the guilds and local authorities. By the 18th century this process was complete.

The reaction against laissez faire began in the mid-19th century and found expression in the factory acts and elsewhere. This reaction was inspired partly by humanitarian protests against the social conditions created by the ◊Industrial Revolution and partly by the wish to counter the political and popular unrest of the 1830s and 1840s by removing some of its causes. In general the 20th century has shown an increasing degree of state intervention to promote social goals. Environmental, safety, and antidiscrimination regulations have been imposed on businesses in some countries, in addition to campaigns to foster corporate responsibility.

A far-reaching program of ◊deregulation was instituted from 1980 by President Reagan as part of an effort to return to a more laissez-faire system.

lake body of still water lying in depressed ground without direct communication with the sea. Lakes are common in formerly glaciated regions, along the courses of slow rivers, and in low land near the sea. The main classifications are by origin: glacial lakes, formed by glacial scouring; barrier lakes, formed by landslides and glacial moraines; crater lakes, found in volcanoes; and tectonic lakes, occurring in natural fissures.

Most lakes are freshwater, such as the Great Lakes in North America, but in hot regions where evaporation is excessive they may contain many salts, for example the Dead Sea. In the 20th century large artificial lakes have been created in connection with hydroelectric and other works. Some lakes have become polluted as a result of human activity. Sometimes ◊eutrophication (a state of overnourishment) occurs, when agricultural fertilizers leaching into lakes cause an explosion of aquatic life, which then depletes the lake's oxygen supply until it is no longer able to support life.

major lakes

Name and location	*sq km*	*sq mi*
Caspian Sea (USSR/Iran)	370,990	143,240
Superior (USA/Canada)	82,071	31,700
Victoria (Tanzania/Kenya/Uganda)	69,463	26,820
Aral Sea (USSR)	64,500	24,904
Huron (USA/Canada)	59,547	23,000
Michigan (USA)	57,735	22,300
Tanganyika (Malawi/Zaire/Zambia/Burundi)	32,880	12,700
Baikal (USSR)	31,456	12,150
Great Bear (Canada)	31,316	12,096
Malawi (Tanzania/Malawi/Mozambique)	28,867	11,150
Great Slave (Canada)	28,560	11,031
Erie (USA/Canada)	25,657	9,910
Winnipeg (Canada)	25,380	9,417
Ontario (USA/Canada)	19,547	7,550
Balkhash (USSR)	18,421	7,115
Ladoga (USSR)	17,695	6,835
Chad (Chad/Niger/Nigeria)	16,310	6,300
Maracaibo (Venezuela)	13,507	5,217

Lake Charles city in SW Louisiana, on the Calcasieu River, SW of Baton Rouge, seat of Calcasieu Parish. It is a port of entry on the Gulf of Mexico via a deep-water channel in the Calcasieu River. Most of the city's industries are related to the area's oil and gas resources and major crop, rice; population (1990) 70,580.

Lake District region in Cumbria, England; area 700 sq mi/1,800 sq km. It embraces the principal English lakes separated by wild uplands rising to many peaks, including Scafell Pike (3,210 ft/978 m).

The Lake District has associations with the writers Wordsworth, Coleridge, Southey, De Quincey, Ruskin, and Beatrix Potter and was made a national park in 1951.

lake dwelling prehistoric village built on piles driven into the bottom of a lake. Such villages are found throughout Europe, in W Africa, South America, Borneo, and New Guinea.

Lake Havasu City town in Arizona, developed as a tourist resort. Old London Bridge was transported and reconstructed there in 1971.

Lakeland city in W central Florida, NE of Tampa and SW of Orlando, in the lake region and citrus belt. It serves as a center for the area's citrus products, but its economy depends mainly on its reputation as a winter resort; population (1990) 70,576.

Lake Veronica. Adopted name of Constance Frances Marie Ockelman 1919–1973. US film actress who was almost as celebrated for her much imitated "peekaboo" hairstyle as acting. She costarred with Alan Ladd in several films during the 1940s, including *This Gun for Hire* and *The Glass Key* both 1942, and *The Blue Dahlia* 1946. She also appeared in *Sullivan's Travels* 1942 and *I Married a Witch* 1942.

Lakshadweep group of 36 coral islands, 10 inhabited, in the Indian Ocean, 200 mi/320 km off the Malabar coast; area 12 sq mi/32 sq km; population (1981) 40,000. The administrative headquarters is on Kavaratti Island. Products include coir, copra, and fish. The religion is Muslim. The first Western visitor was Vasco da Gama 1499. They were British from 1877 until Indian independence and were created a Union Territory of India 1956. Formerly known as the Laccadive, Minicoy, and Amindivi Islands, they were renamed Lakshadweep 1973.

Lakshmi Hindu goddess of wealth and beauty, consort of Vishnu; her festival is ◊Diwali.

Lalande Michel de 1657–1726. French organist and composer of church music for the court at Versailles.

La Línea port city on the isthmus of Algeciras Bay, S Spain, adjoining the frontier zone with Gibraltar; population (1981) 56,300.

Lalique René 1860–1945. French designer and manufacturer of ◊Art Nouveau glass, jewelry, and house interiors.

Lalo (Victor Antoine) Edouard 1823–1892. French composer. His Spanish ancestry and violin training are evident in the *Symphonie Espagnole* 1873 for violin and orchestra, and *Concerto for cello and orchestra* 1877. He also wrote an opera, *Le Roi d'Ys* 1887.

Lam Wilfredo 1902–1982. Cuban abstract painter. Influenced by Surrealism in the 1930s (he lived in Paris 1937–41), he created a semiabstract style using mysterious and sometimes menacing images and symbols, mainly taken from Caribbean tradition. His *Jungle* series, for example, contains voodoo elements.

Lamaism the religion of Tibet and Mongolia, a form of Mahāyāna Buddhism. Buddhism was introduced into Tibet AD 640, but the real founder of Lamaism was the Indian missionary Padma Sambhava who began his activity about 750. The head of the church is the ◊Dalai Lama, who is considered an incarnation of the Bodhisattva Avalokiteśvara. On the death of the Dalai Lama great care is taken in finding the infant in whom he has been reincarnated.

In the 15th century Tsongkhapa founded the sect of Geluk-Pa (virtuous), which has remained the most powerful organization in the country. The Dalai Lama, residing at the palace of Potala in Lhasa, exercised both spiritual and temporal authority as head of the Tibetan state until 1959, aided by the ◊Panchen Lama.

Before Chinese Communist rule, it was estimated that one in four of Tibet's male population was a Lamaist monk, but now their numbers are greatly reduced. Prayer-wheels and prayer-flags, on which were inscribed prayers, were formerly a common sight in the Tibetan countryside; when these were turned by hand or moved by the wind, great spiritual benefit was supposed to accrue.

La Mancha (Arabic *al mansha* "the dry land"), former province of Spain now part of the autonomous region of ◊Castilla-La Mancha. The fictional travels of Cervantes's *Don Quixote de la Mancha* 1605 begin there.

Lamar Lucius Quintus Cincinnatus 1825–1893. US public official and Supreme Court justice. After teaching at the University of Mississippi, he was elected to the US House of Representatives, serving 1857–60. During the American Civil War he served briefly in the Confederate army and was named Confederate envoy to Russia. After the war he returned to the University of Mississippi and sat in the US House of Representatives 1873–77. Lamar was a member of the US Senate 1877–85, served as President Cleveland's secretary of the interior 1885–87, and sat on the US Supreme Court 1888–93.

Born in Elbert County, Georgia, and educated at Emory College, Lamar was admitted to the bar 1847.

Lamarck Jean Baptiste de 1744–1829. French naturalist, whose theory of evolution, known as Lamarckism, was based on the idea that acquired characteristics (changes aquired in an individual's lifetime) are inherited, and that organisms have an intrinsic urge to evolve into better-adapted forms. His works include *Philosophie Zoologique/Zoological Philosophy* 1809 and *Histoire naturelle des animaux sans vertèbres/Natural History of Invertebrate Animals* 1815–22.

***Lamb** The English essayist and critic Charles Lamb collaborated with his sister Mary in* Tales from Shakespeare. *His portrait is by fellow essayist William Hazlitt.*

Lamarckism a theory of evolution advocated during the early 19th century by Lamarck. It differed from modern theory of evolution (formulated by Darwin). According to Lamarck, organisms have an urge to "improve" rather than being shaped by natural selection acting on random variations. Later, Lamarckism just came to mean a belief in the inheritance of acquired characteristics—a now discarded opinion shared by most biologists before the discovery of genetics.

Lamartine Alphonse de 1790–1869. French poet. He wrote romantic poems, including *Méditations* 1820, followed by *Nouveles méditations/New Meditations* 1823, and *Harmonies* 1830. His *Histoire des Girondins/History of the Girondins* 1847 helped to inspire the revolution of 1848.

Lamb Charles 1775–1834. English essayist and critic. He collaborated with his sister Mary Lamb (1764–1847) on *Tales from Shakespeare* 1807, and his *Specimens of English Dramatic Poets* 1808 helped to revive interest in Elizabethan plays. As "Elia" he contributed essays to the *London Magazine* from 1820 (collected 1823 and 1833).

Born in London, Lamb was educated at Christ's Hospital. He was a contemporary of ◊Coleridge, with whom he published some poetry in 1796. He was a clerk at India House 1792–1825, when he retired to Enfield. His sister Mary stabbed their mother to death in a fit of insanity 1796, and Charles cared for her between her periodic returns to an asylum.

Lamb Willis 1913– . US physicist who revised the quantum theory of Paul ◊Dirac. The hydrogen atom was thought to exist in either of two distinct states carrying equal energies. More sophisticated measurements by Lamb in 1947 demonstrated that the two energy levels were not equal. This discrepancy, since known as the Lamb shift, won for him the 1955 Nobel Prize for Physics.

lambert unit of luminance (the light shining from a surface), equal to one ◊lumen per square centimeter. In scientific work the ◊candela per square meter is preferred.

lamina in flowering plants (◊angiosperms), the blade of the ◊leaf on either side of the midrib. The lamina is generally thin and flattened, and is usually the primary organ of ◊photosynthesis. It has a network of veins through which water and nutrients are conducted. More generally, a lamina is any thin, flat plant structure, such as the ◊thallus of many seaweeds.

lammergeier Old World vulture *Gypaetus barbatus*, also known as the bearded vulture, with a wingspan of 9 ft/2.7 m. It ranges over S Europe, N Africa, and Asia, in wild mountainous areas. It feeds on offal and carrion and drops bones onto rocks to get at the marrow.

Lampedusa Giuseppe Tomasi di 1896–1957. Italian aristocrat, author of *The Leopard* 1958, a novel set in his native Sicily during the period following its annexation by Garibaldi in 1860. It chronicles the reactions of an aristocratic family to social and political upheavals.

lamprey any of various eel-shaped jawless fishes belonging to the family Petromyzontidae. A lamprey feeds on other fish by fixing itself by the round mouth to its host and boring into the flesh with its toothed tongue.

Lamu island off the E coast of Kenya.

Lanarkshire former inland county of Scotland, merged 1975 in the region of Strathclyde. The county town was Lanark.

Lancashire county in NW England
area 1,173 sq mi/3,040 sq km
cities Preston (administrative headquarters), which forms part of Central Lancashire New Town (together with Fulwood, Bamber Bridge, Leyland, and Chorley); Lancaster, Accrington, Blackburn, Burnley; ports Fleetwood and Heysham; seaside resorts Blackpool, Morecambe, and Southport
features river: Ribble; mountains: Pennines; Forest of Bowland (moors and farming valleys); Pendle Hill
products formerly a world center of cotton manufacture, now replaced with high-technology aerospace and electronics industries
population (1987) 1,381,000

Lancaster city in Lancashire, England, on the river Lune; population (1983) 126,400. It was the former county town of Lancashire (now Preston).

The university was founded in 1964. Industries include paper, furniture, plastics, and chemicals. A castle here, which incorporates Roman work, was captured by Cromwell during the Civil War.

Lancaster city in Pennsylvania, 70 mi/115 km W of Philadelphia; population (1990) 55,551. It produces textiles and electrical goods. It was capital of the US briefly in 1777, and was the state capital 1799–1812.

Lancaster Burt (Burton Stephen) 1913– . US film actor who was formerly an acrobat. A star from his first film, *The Killers* 1946, he proved himself adept both at action roles and more complex character parts in such films as *From Here to Eternity* 1953, *The Rose Tattoo* 1955, *Elmer Gantry* 1960, and *The Leopard/Il Gattopardo* 1963.

He was one of the first stars to produce, forming Hecht-Hill-Lancaster. His later films include *The Swimmer* 1968 and *Atlantic City* 1980.

Lancaster House Agreement accord reached at a conference Sept 1979 at Lancaster House, London, between Britain and representative groups of Rhodesia, including the Rhodesian government under Ian Smith and black nationalist groups. The Agreement enabled a smooth transition to the independent state of Zimbabwe 1980.

Lancaster, House of English royal house, branch of the Plantagenets.

It originated 1267 when Edmund (died 1296), the younger son of Henry III, was granted the earldom of Lancaster. Converted to a duchy for Henry of Grosmont (died 1361), it passed to John of Gaunt 1362 by his marriage to Blanche, Henry's daughter. John's son, Henry IV, established the royal dynasty of Lancaster 1399, and he was followed by two more Lancastrian kings, Henry V and Henry VI.

lancelet any of various marine animals of the subphylum cephalocordates (see ◊chordate), genus *Amphioxus*, about 1 in/2.5 cm long. It has no skull, brain, eyes, heart, vertebral column, centralized brain, nor paired limbs, but there is a notochord (a supportive rod) which runs from end to end of the body, a tail, and a number of gill slits. Found in all seas, it burrows in the sand but when disturbed swims freely.

Lancelot of the Lake in British legend, the most celebrated of King Arthur's knights, the lover of Queen Guinevere. Originally a folk-hero, he first appeared in the Arthurian cycle of tales in the 12th century.

Lanchow former name of ◊Lanzhou, city in China.

Lancret Nicolas 1690–1743. French painter. His graceful *fêtes galantes* (festive groups of courtly figures in fancy dress) followed a theme made popular by Watteau. He also illustrated amorous scenes from the *Fables* of La Fontaine.

Land federal state (plural *Länder*) of Germany or Austria.

Landau Lev Davidovich 1908–1968. Russian theoretical physicist. He was awarded the 1962 Nobel Prize for Physics for his work on liquid helium.

Land Edwin Herbert 1909–1991. US inventor of the Polaroid Land camera 1947, which developed the film in one minute inside the camera and produced an "instant" photograph.

While a student at Harvard, Land became interested in polarized light and invented the sheet polarizer, which imbedded lined-up crystals in a clear plastic sheet. This tremendous advance had implications for camera filters, sunglasses and other optical equipment, and related products. Land dropped out of school and set up a laboratory 1932, then established the Polaroid Corporation 1937–80. His research also led to a process for 3-D pictures, "instant" color film, "instant" motion pictures, and a new theory of color perception, the "retinex" theory 1977.

Landes sandy, low-lying area in SW France, along the Bay of Biscay, about 5,000 sq mi/ 12,950 sq km in extent. Formerly covered with furze and heath, it has in many parts been planted with pine and oak forests. It gives its name to a *département* and extends into the *départements* of Gironde and Lot-et-Garonne. There is a testing range for rockets and missiles at Biscarosse, 45 mi/72 km SW of Bordeaux. There is an oil field in Parentis-en-Born.

Landis Kenesaw Mountain 1866–1944. US judge and baseball commissioner. Born in Millville, Ohio, Landis received his law degree 1891. He was appointed federal district judge in Chicago 1905 and presided in important antitrust and labor relations cases. Having served as judge in the fraud trial of the nine members of the infamous "Black Sox" who had conspired to throw the 1919 World Series, Landis was named the first commissioner of major-league baseball 1921. In that position he restored the integrity of the game by establishing strict standards against players' involvement with gamblers.

Land League Irish peasant-rights organization, formed by Michael ◊Davitt and Charles ◊Parnell 1879 to fight against tenant evictions. Through its skillful use of the boycott against anyone who took a farm from which another had been evicted, it forced Gladstone's government to introduce a law 1881 restricting rents and granting tenants security of tenure.

landlord and tenant in law, the relationship that exists when an owner (the landlord) of land or buildings gives to another (the tenant) the exclusive right of occupation for a definite limited period, such as a year, a term of years, a week, or a month. The relationship is known as lessor and lessee, and the lease agreement gives both parties legal rights and obligations.

In the US, there is traditionally a free market in rent prices. Under some circumstances—a wartime housing shortage, for example—the government may impose rent controls. These have been applied at the local level and used in instances, such as in New York City, where the market value of housing would have gone beyond the reach of most wage-earners. Such controls specify allowable increases in rents and may have the unintended effect of reducing available housing stock as landlords sell or withdraw unprofitable units.

Landon Alfred Mossman "Alf" 1887–1987. US public official. After a successful career in business, he entered politics and was elected governor of Kansas 1932. As a popular liberal Republican, Landon ran for president against incumbent F D Roosevelt 1936 but was overwhelmingly defeated. He later accepted a presidential appointment as US delegate to the 1938 Pan-American Conference. After World War II, Landon became a spokesman for the elimination of trade barriers and for international development.

Born in West Middlesex, Pennsylvania, Landon was raised in Kansas and received a law degree from the University of Kansas 1908.

Landowska Wanda 1877–1959. Polish harpsichordist and scholar. She founded a school near Paris for the study of early music, and was for many years one of the few artists regularly performing on the harpsichord. In 1941 she moved to the US.

land reform theory that ownership of land should be shared among the workers, the peasants, and the agricultural workers.

Landseer Edwin Henry 1802–1873. English painter, sculptor, and engraver of animal studies. Much of his work reflects the Victorian taste for sentimental and moralistic pictures, for example *Dignity and Impudence* 1839 (Tate Gallery, London).

The *Monarch of the Glen* (John Dewar and Sons Ltd) 1850, depicting a highland stag, was painted for the House of Lords. His sculptures include the lions at the base of Nelson's Column in Trafalgar Square, London, 1857–67.

Land's End promontory of W Cornwall, 9 mi/15 km WSW of Penzance, the westernmost point of England.

An extension of Land's End is a group of dangerous rocks, the Longships, a mile out, marked by a lighthouse.

Landskrona port city in Sweden, on the ◊Sound, 20 mi/32 km N of Malmö; population (1983) 36,500. Industries include shipyards, machinery, chemicals, and sugar refining. Carl XI defeated the Danes off Landskrona in 1677.

landslide a sudden downward movement of a mass of soil or rocks from a cliff or steep slope. Landslides happen when a slope becomes unstable, usually because the base has been undercut or certain boundaries of materials within the mass have become wet and slippery.

A mudflow happens when soil or loose material is soaked so that it no longer adheres to the slope; it forms a tongue of mud that reaches downhill from a semicircular hollow. A slump occurs when the material stays together as a large mass, or several smaller masses, and these may form a tilted steplike structure as they slide. A landslip is formed when ◊beds of rock dipping toward a cliff slide along a lower bed. Earthquakes may precipitate landslides.

Landsteiner Karl 1868–1943. Austrian immunologist who discovered the ABO ◊blood group system 1900–02, and aided in the discovery of the Rhesus blood factors 1940. He also discovered the polio virus. He was awarded the Nobel Prize 1930.

He worked at the Vienna Pathology Laboratory, and the Rockefeller Institute for Medical Research, New York, where he was involved in the discovery of the MN blood groups in 1927. In 1936 he wrote *The Specificity of Serological Reactions*, which helped establish the science of immunology. He also developed a test for syphilis.

Landtag legislature of each of the *Länder* (states) that form the federal republics of Germany and Austria.

Lanfranc c. 1010–1089. Italian archbishop of Canterbury from 1070; he rebuilt the cathedral, replaced English clergy by Normans, enforced clerical celibacy, and separated the ecclesiastical from the secular courts.

His skill in theological controversy did much to secure the church's adoption of the doctrine of transubstantiation. He came over to England with William the Conqueror, whose adviser he was.

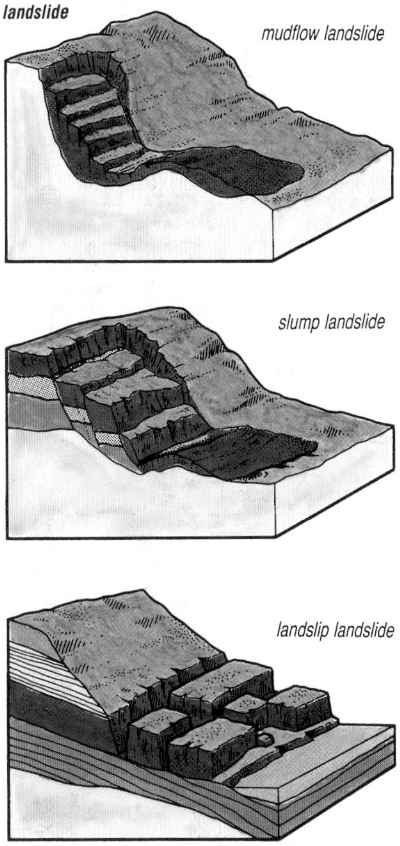
landslide
mudflow landslide
slump landslide
landslip landslide

Lang Fritz 1890–1976. Austrian film director whose films are characterized by a strong sense of social realism. His German movies include *Metropolis* 1927, the sensational *M* 1931 in which Peter Lorre starred as a child-killer, and the series of Dr Mabuse films, after which he fled from the Nazis to Hollywood 1936. His US films include *Fury* 1936, *You Only Live Once* 1937, *Scarlet Street* 1945, *Rancho Notorious* 1952, and *The Big Heat* 1953. He returned to Germany and directed a third picture in the *Dr Mabuse* series 1960.

Lange David (Russell) 1942–. New Zealand Labour Party prime minister 1983–89. Lange, a lawyer, was elected to the House of Representatives in 1977. Labour had a decisive win in the 1984 general election on a nonnuclear military policy, which Lange immediately put into effect, despite criticism from the US. He introduced a free-market economic policy and was reelected 1987. He resigned Aug 1989 over a disagreement with his finance minister.

Lange Dorothea 1895–1965. US photographer. After establishing a private studio in San Francisco, she was hired in 1935 by the federal Farm Security Administration to document the westward migration of farm families from the Dust Bowl of the S central US. She won national acclaim for the gritty realism of her photographs, which were widely exhibited and subsequently published as *An American Exodus: A Record of Human Erosion* 1939.

Born in Hoboken, New Jersey, Lange attended a teachers' college before receiving professional training in photography from Clarence White in New York.

Langevin Paul 1872–1946. French physicist who contributed to the studies of magnetism and X-ray emissions. During World War I he invented an apparatus for locating enemy submarines. The nuclear institute at ◊Grenoble is named after him.

Langland William c. 1332–c. 1400. English poet. His alliterative *Vision Concerning Piers Plowman* appeared in three versions between about 1362 and 1398, but some critics believe he was only responsible for the first of these. The poem forms a series of allegorical visions, in which Piers develops from the typical poor peasant to a symbol of Jesus, and condemns the social and moral evils of 14th-century England.

Langley Samuel Pierpoint 1834–1906. US astronomer, scientist, and inventor of the ◊bolometer; from 1887 he was secretary of the Smithsonian Institution in Washington, DC. He founded the Smithsonian Astrophysical Observatory in 1890 and turned to pioneering work in aerodynamics, contributing greatly to the design of early aircraft. He built and tested the first successful (but unmanned) heavier-than-air craft (airplane), which he launched by catapult and which flew over the Potomac River in 1896. The subsequent catapult-launched flights of the ◊Wright brothers at Kitty Hawk owe much Langley's principles and to the more powerful engines available by the early 1900s, capable of lifting and sustaining piloted craft in flight. The Langley design, now on view at the Smithsonian, was tested in later years by using a model with a modern engine; it flew successfully with a pilot aboard.

Langmuir Irving 1881–1957. US scientist who invented the mercury vapor pump for producing a high vacuum, and the atomic hydrogen welding process; he was also a pioneer of the thermionic valve. In 1932 he was awarded a Nobel Prize for his work on surface chemistry.

Langobard alternate name for ◊Lombard, member of a Germanic people.

Langton Stephen c. 1150–1228. English priest. He studied in Paris, where he became chancellor of the university, and in 1206 was created a cardinal. When in 1207 Pope Innocent III secured Langton's election as archbishop of Canterbury, King John refused to recognize him, and he was not allowed to enter England until 1213. He supported the barons in their struggle against John and was mainly responsible for drafting the charter of rights, the ◊Magna Carta.

He continued to work for revisions to both church and state policies, which could only begin to go into effect after the death of John.

Langtry Lillie. Adopted name of Emilie Charlotte le Breton 1853–1929. English actress, mistress of the future Edward VII. She was known as the "Jersey Lily" from her birthplace and considered to be one of the most beautiful women of her time.

language human communication through speech, writing, or both. "A language" is any expression of language used by one or more communities for everyday purposes (the English language, the European languages, the Indo-European language family, and so on). One language may have various ◊dialects, which may be seen by those who use them as languages in their own right. The term is also used for systems of communication with languagelike qualities, such as animal language (the way animals communicate), body language (gestures and expressions used to communicate ideas), sign language (gestures for the deaf or for use as a ◊lingua franca, as among American Indians), and computer languages (such as BASIC and COBOL).

Natural human language has a neurological basis centered on the left hemisphere of the brain and is expressed through two distinct media in most present-day societies: mouth and ear (the medium of sound, or phonic medium), and hand and eye (the medium of writing, or graphic medium). Language appears to develop in children under normal circumstances, either as a unilingual or multilingual skill, crucially between the ages of one and five, and as a necessary interplay of innate and environmental factors. Any human child can learn any human language, under the appropriate conditions.

When forms of language are as distinct as Dutch and Arabic, it is obvious that they are different languages. When, however, they are mutually intelligible, as are Dutch and Flemish, a categorical distinction is harder to make. Rather than say that Dutch and Flemish are dialects of a common Netherlandic language, Dutch and Flemish speakers may, for traditional reasons that include ethnic pride and political distinctness, prefer to talk about two distinct languages. To strengthen the differences among similar languages, groups may emphasize those differences (for example, the historical distancing of Portuguese from Castillian Spanish) or adopt different scripts (Urdu is written in Arabic script, its relative Hindi in Devanagari script). From outside, Italian appears to be a single language; inside Italy, it is a standard variety resting on a base of many very distinct dialects. The terms "language" and "dialect" are not therefore easily defined and distinguished. English is today the most widespread world language, but it has so many varieties (often mutually unintelligible) that scholars now talk about "Englishes" and even "the English languages"—all, however, united for international purposes by Standard English.

Languedoc former province of S France, bounded by the Rhône river, the Mediterranean sea, and the regions of Guienne and Gascony.

Languedoc-Roussillon region of S France, comprising the *départements* of Aude, Gard, Hérault, Lozère, and Pyrénées-Orientales; area 10,576 sq mi/27,400 sq km; population (1986) 2,012,000. Its capital is Montpellier, and products include fruit, vegetables, wine, and cheese.

langur any of various leaf-eating Old World monkeys of several genera, especially the genus Presbytis, that lives in trees in S Asia. There are about 20 species. It is related to the colobus monkey of Africa.

lanolin a sticky, purified wax obtained from sheep's wool and used in cosmetics, soap, and leather preparation.

Lansing capital of Michigan, at the confluence of the Grand and Red Cedar rivers; population (1990) 127,321. Manufacturing includes motor vehicles, diesel engines, and pumps. General Motors automobile plants are here, and Michigan State University is the adjoining city of East Lansing. Lansing was settled in the 1840s and has been the state capital since 1847.

lanthanide any of a series of 15 metallic elements (also known as rare earths) with atomic numbers 57 (lanthanum) to 71 (lutetium). One of its members, promethium, is radioactive. All occur in nature. Lanthanides are grouped because of their chemical similarities (they are all bivalent), their properties differing only slightly with atomic number.

They were called rare earths originally because they were not widespread and were difficult to identify and separate from their ores by their discoverers. The series is set out in a band in the ◊periodic table of the elements, as are the ◊actinides.

lanthanum (Greek *lanthanein* "to be hidden") soft, silvery, ductile and malleable, metallic element, symbol La, atomic number 57, atomic weight 138.91, the first of the ◊lanthanide series. It is used in making alloys. It was named in 1839 by Swedish chemist Carl Mosander (1797–1858).

Lanzhou formerly ***Lanchow*** capital of Gansu province, China, on the river Huang He, 120 mi/190 km S of the Great Wall; population (1986) 1,350,000. Industries include oil refining, chemicals, fertilizers, and synthetic rubber.

Laocoon in Classical mythology, a Trojan, brother of ◊Anchises, priest of ◊Apollo and a visionary. He and his sons were killed by serpents when he foresaw disaster for ◊Troy in the ◊Trojan horse left by the Greeks.

The scene of their death is the subject of a Classical marble group, rediscovered in the ◊Renaissance, and forms an episode in ◊Virgil's *Aeneid*.

Laos
Lao People's Democratic Republic
(*Saathiaranagroat Prachhathippatay Prachhachhon Lao*)

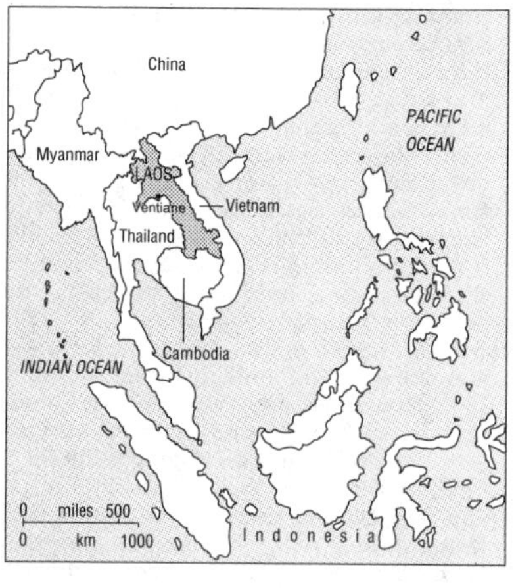
China
PACIFIC OCEAN
Myanmar
LAOS
Vientiane
Vietnam
Thailand
Cambodia
INDIAN OCEAN
Indonesia
0 miles 500
0 km 1000

area 91,400 sq mi/236,790 sq km
capital Vientiane
cities Luang Prabang (the former royal capital), Pakse, Savannakhet
physical landlocked state with high mountains in E; Mekong River in W; jungle covers nearly 60% of land
features hydroelectric power from the Mekong is exported to Thailand; Plain of Jars, where prehistoric people carved stone jars large enough to hold a person; formerly known as the Land of a Million Elephants
head of state Prince Souphanouvong from 1975; Phoumi Vongvichit acting president from 1986
head of government Kaysone Phomvihane from 1975
political system communism, one-party state
political parties Lao People's Revolutionary Party (only legal party)
exports timber, teak, coffee, electricity
currency new kip
population (1990 est) 4,024,000 (Lao 48%, Thai 14%, Khmer 25%, Chinese 13%); growth rate 2.2% p.a.
life expectancy men 48, women 51 (1989)
language Lao (official), French
religion Theravab1da Buddhist 85%, animist beliefs among mountain tribes
literacy 45% (1991)
GNP $500 mn (1987); $180 per head (1988)
chronology
1893–1945 Laos a French protectorate.
1945 Temporarily occupied by Japan.
1946 Retaken by France.
1950 Granted semiautonomy in French Union.
1954 Independence achieved from France.
1960 Right-wing government seized power.
1962 Coalition government established; civil war continued.
1973 Vientiane ceasefire agreement.
1975 Communist-dominated republic proclaimed with Prince Souphanouvong as head of state.
1987 Phoumi Vongvichit became acting president.
1988 Plans announced to withdraw 40% of Vietnamese forces stationed in the country.
1989 First assembly elections since communist takeover.
1990 Draft constitution published.

Laois or ***Laoighis*** county in Leinster province, Republic of Ireland
area 664 sq mi/1,720 sq km
county town Portlaoise
physical flat except for the Slieve Bloom mountains in the NW
products sugarbeets, dairy products, woolens, agricultural machinery
population (1986) 53,000

Laon capital of Aisne *département*, Picardie, N France; 75 mi/120 km NE of Paris; population (1982) 29,000. It was the capital of France and a royal residence until the 10th century. It has a 12th-century cathedral.

Laos landlocked country in SE Asia, bordered N by China, E by Vietnam, S by Cambodia, and W by Thailand
government Laos became a republic Dec 1975 when the monarchy was abolished. The indirectly elected 264-member national congress of people's representatives appointed Prince Souphanouvong (1909–) as executive head of state (president) to be served by a cabinet (council of ministers) led by a prime minister. A 45-member supreme people's assembly (SPA), chaired by the president, was established to frame a new constitution. By 1986 a draft document had ben completed, but remained the subject of government discussion. In the meantime, elections were finally held to the SPA, which was expanded to comprise 79 deputies elected for five-year terms and accorded the task of framing the economic plan and overseeing the work of state ministries. The controlling force and only political party in Laos is the Communist party (Lao People's Revolutionary Party), which is dominated by its 11-member Political Bureau and heads the broader Lao Front for National Reconstruction.
history The original SE Asian tribal groups saw a migration from the 4th–5th centuries of peoples from China. Laos came under Indian influence and adopted Buddhism during the 7th–11th centuries. As part of the ◊Khmer empire from the 11th–13th centuries, it experienced much artistic and architectural activity. From the 12th century, the country was invaded by the Lao from Thailand, who established small independent kingdoms and became Buddhists. Laos became an independent kingdom in the 14th century and was first visited by Europeans in the 17th century, becoming a French protectorate 1893–1945. After a brief period of Japanese occupation, France re-established control 1946 despite opposition from the Chinese-backed Lao Issara (Free Laos) nationalist movement. The country became semiautonomous 1950, when, under the constitutional monarchy of the king of ◊Luang Prabang, it became an associated state of the French Union.

In 1954, after the Geneva Agreements, Laos gained full independence. Civil war broke out between two factions of former Lao Issara supporters: a moderate, royalist-neutralist group led by Prince Souvanna Phouma, which had supported the 1950 French compromise and was the recognized government for most of the country; and a more extreme Communist resistance group, the Pathet Lao (Land of the Lao), led by ex-Prince Souphanouvong (the half-brother of Prince Souvanna) and supported by China and the ◊Vietminh, which controlled much of N Laos.

A coalition government was established after the 1957 Vientiane Agreement. This soon collapsed, and in 1960 a third, right-wing force emerged when General Phoumi Nosavan, backed by the royal army, overthrew Souvanna Phouma and set up a pro-Western government headed by Prince Boun Gum. A new Geneva Agreement 1962 established a tripartite (right-left-neutral) government under the leadership of Prince Souvanna Phouma. Fighting continued, however, between the North Vietnamese–backed Pathet Lao and the US-backed neutralists and right wing, until the 1973 Vientiane Agreement established a ceasefire line dividing the country NW to SE, giving the Communists two-thirds of the country, including the Plain of Jars and the Bolovens Plateau in the south, but giving the Souvanna Phouma government two-thirds of the population. All foreign forces (North Vietnamese, Thai, and US) were to be withdrawn, and both sides received equal representation in Souvanna Phouma's provisional government 1974.

In 1975 the Communist Pathet Lao (renamed the Lao People's Front) seized power. King Savang Vatthana (1908–80), who had succeeded 1959, abdicated, and Laos became a People's Democratic Republic under the presidency of Prince Souphanouvong. Prince Souvanna Phouma remained as an "adviser" to the government, but the real controlling force was now the prime minister and communist party leader, Kaysone Phomvihane.

The new administration, which inherited a poor, war-ravaged economy, attempted to reorganize the country along Socialist lines, nationalizing businesses and industries and collectivizing agriculture. Faced with a food shortage and the flight of more than 250,000 refugees to Thailand, it modified its approach in 1979, introducing production incentives and allowing greater scope for the private sector. Further "liberalization" followed from 1985 under the prompting of the Soviet leader Michail Gorbachev, with a new profit-related "Socialist business accounting system" being adopted. National elections were held in March 1989. Laos, now closely tied to the USSR and Vietnam (which has 40,000 troops stationed in Laos), still suffers from border skirmishes with rebels backed by Thailand in the south and China in the north. There have been attempts to improve relations with Thailand and China for economic reasons. In March 1989, multiparty elections were held for the first time since the Communists came to power 1975, with the Communists retaining political control. In Aug 1989 party-to-party relations were established with China after a ten-year break. A draft constitution was published June 1990.

Laotian member of an Indochinese people who live along the Mekong river system. There are approximately 9 million Laotians in Thailand and 2 million in Laos. The Laotian language is a Thai member of the Sino-Tibetan family.

Lao Zi c. 604–531 BC. Chinese philosopher, commonly regarded as the founder of ◊Taoism. Nothing certain is known of his life, and he is variously said to have lived in the 6th or the 4th century BC. The *Tao Tê Ching*, the Taoist scripture, is attributed to him but apparently dates from the 3rd century BC.

La Palma see under La ◊Palma, one of the Spanish Canary Islands.

La Pampa see under ◊Pampas, province in Argentina.

laparotomy exploratory surgical procedure involving incision into the abdomen, especially when done at the flanks. The use of laparotomy, as of other exploratory surgery, has decreased sharply with technical advances in scanning and the direct-viewing technique known as ◊endoscopy.

La Paz capital city of Bolivia, in Murillo province, 12,400 ft/3,800 m above sea level; population (1985) 992,600. Products include textiles and copper. Founded by the Spanish 1548, it has been the seat of government since 1900.

lapis lazuli a rock containing the blue mineral lazurite in a matrix of white calcite with small amounts of other minerals. It occurs in silica-poor igneous rocks and metamorphic limestones found in Afghanistan, Siberia, Iran, and Chile.

Lapis lazuli was a valuable pigment of the Middle Ages, also used as a gemstone and in inlaying and ornamental work.

Lapiths in Greek mythology, a people of Thessaly in northern Greece, often represented in Greek

La Paz *The seat of government in Bolivia, La Paz is situated high in the Andes.*

lapis lazuli *The deep blue mineral lapis lazuli, a complex mixture of lazurite (sodium aluminum silicate) with other minerals, is the source of the pigment ultramarine.*

art in a battle with their neighbors the ◊Centaurs at the wedding of their king, Pirithous.

Laplace Pierre Simon, Marquis de Laplace 1749–1827. French astronomer and mathematician. In 1796, he theorized that the Solar System originated from a cloud of gas (the nebular hypothesis). He studied the motion of the Moon and planets, and published a five-volume survey of ◊celestial mechanics, *Traité de méchanique céleste* 1799–1825. Among his mathematical achievements was the development of probability theory.

Lapland region of Europe within the Arctic Circle in Norway, Sweden, Finland, and the USSR, without political definition. Its chief resources are chromium, copper, iron, timber, hydroelectric power, and tourism. There are about 20,000 Lapps, who live by hunting, fishing, reindeer herding, and handicrafts.

La Plata capital of Buenos Aires province, Argentina; population (1980) 560,300. Industries include meat packing and petroleum refining. It was founded 1882.

La Plata, Río de or ***River Plate*** estuary in South America into which the rivers Paraná and Uruguay flow; length 200 mi/320 km and width up to 150 mi/240 km. The basin drains much of Argentina, Bolivia, Brazil, Uruguay, and Paraguay, who all cooperate in its development.

Laptev Sea part of the Arctic Ocean off the N coast of the USSR between Taimyr Peninsula and New Siberian Island.

laptop computer portable ◊microcomputer, small enough to be used on the operator's lap. It consists of a single unit, incorporating a keyboard, ◊floppy disk or ◊hard disk drives, and a screen. The screen often forms a lid that folds back in use. It uses a liquid crystal or gas plasma display, rather than the bulkier and heavier cathode ray tubes found in most ◊VDTs. A typical laptop computer measures about 14 in/360 mm × 15 in/380 mm × 4 in/100 mm, and weighs between 6 lb 9 oz/3 kg and 14 lb 2 oz/7 kg.

Laplace *Pierre Simon Laplace was called "the French Newton" for his work on planetary orbits.*

lapwing Eurasian bird *Vanellus vanellus* of the plover family, also known as the green plover, and from its call, as the peewit. Bottle-green above and white below, with a long thin crest and rounded wings, it is about 1 ft/30 cm long. It inhabits moorland in Europe and Asia, making a nest scratched out of the ground.

It is an occasional visitor to NE North America.

Laramie town in Wyoming, on the Laramie Plains, a plateau 7,500 ft/2,300 m above sea level, bounded to the N and E by the Laramie Mountains; population (1990) 26,687. The Laramie River, on which it stands, is linked with the Missouri via the Platte. It is a commercial and transport center for a ranching and lumber-producing area; its manufactures include cement and wood products. On the overland trail and Pony Express route, Fort Laramie, built 1834, features in western legend. A rail line came through 1868, and Laramie was incorporated 1874.

larceny in the US, the taking of personal property without consent and with the intention of permanently depriving the owner of it; ◊theft.

In some US states, larceny in which the value of the property exceeds a specified amount is grand larceny; larceny involving lesser amounts is petty larceny.

larch any tree of the genus *Larix*, of the family Pinaceae. The common larch *L. decidua* grows to 130 ft/40 m. It is one of the few ◊conifer trees to shed its leaves annually. The small needlelike leaves are replaced every year by new bright-green foliage, which later darkens.

Closely resembling it is the North American tamarack *L. laricina*, and both are timber trees. The golden larch *Pseudolarix amabilis*, a native of China, turns golden in autumn.

lard the melted and clarified edible fat of pigs. It is used in cooking and in the manufacture of cooking fats, soaps, and ointments.

Larderello site in the Tuscan hills, NE Italy, where the sulfur springs were used by the Romans for baths and exploited for boric acid in the 18th–19th centuries. Since 1904 they have been used to generate electricity; the water reaches 220°F.

Lardner Ring 1885–1933. US short-story writer. A sports reporter, he based his characters on the people he met professionally. His collected volumes of short stories include *You Know Me, Al* 1916, *Round Up* 1929, and *Ring Lardner's Best Short Stories* 1938, all written in colloquial language.

Laredo city on the Rio Grande, Texas; population (1990) 122,899. It was founded 1755. Industries include oil refining and metal processing. Laredo State University is here. Nuevo Laredo, Mexico, on the opposite bank, is a textile center; population (1980) 203,300. It was considered part of Laredo until the international border was established 1848. There is much cross-border trade.

lares and penates in Roman mythology, spirits of the farm and of the store cupboard, often identified with the family ancestors, whose shrine was the center of family worship in Roman homes.

Large Electron–Positron Collider (LEP) the world's largest particle ◊accelerator, in operation from 1989 at the CERN laboratories near Geneva. It occupies a tunnel 12.5 ft/3.8 m wide and 16.7 mi/27 km long, which is buried 590 ft/180 m underground and forms a ring consisting of eight curved and eight straight sections. In 1989 the LEP was used to measure the mass and lifetime of the Z particle, carrier of the weak nuclear force.

Electrons and positrons enter the ring after passing through the Super Proton Synchrotron accelerator. They travel in opposite directions around the ring, guided by 3,328 bending magnets and kept within tight beams by 1,272 focusing magnets. As they pass through the straight sections, the particles are accelerated by a pulse of radio energy. Once sufficient energy is accumulated, the beams are allowed to collide. Four giant detectors are used to study the resulting shower of particles.

large intestine in the ◊digestive system, the lower gut or bowels, made up of the colon, the cecum, and the rectum. No absorption of food takes place in the large intestine but the colon removes water from the undigested material, which is then stored as feces in the rectum.

Approximately eight and a half liters of liquid enter the human gut every day, derived from intestinal juices and dietary fluid. Only 2% of this remains in the feces.

La Rioja region of N Spain; area 1,930 sq mi/5,000 sq km; population (1986) 263,000.

Larionov Mikhail Fedorovich 1881–1964. Russian painter, active in Paris from 1919. He pioneered a semiabstract style known as Rayonnism with his wife Natalia Goncharova, in which subjects appear to be deconstructed by rays of light from various sources.

Larionov also produced stage sets for Diaghilev's *Ballets Russes* from 1915. In Paris he continued to work as a theatrical designer and book illustrator.

Larisa town in Thessaly, Greece, S of Mount Olympus; population (1981) 102,000. Products include textiles and agriculture.

lark songbird of the family Alaudidae, found mainly in the Old World, but also in North America. They are brownish-tan in color and usually about 7 in/18 cm long, and nest on the ground in the open. The skylark *Alauda arvensis* sings as it rises almost vertically in the air.

The skylark has been introduced to Vancouver Island. The North American horned lark *Eremophila alpestris* has black "horns" and only a weak, twittering song.

Larkin Philip 1922–1985. English poet. His perfectionist, pessimistic verse includes *The North Ship* 1945, *The Whitsun Weddings* 1964, and *High Windows* 1974. He edited *The Oxford Book of 20th-Century English Verse* 1973.

larkspur plant of the genus ◊delphinium.

La Rochefoucauld François, duc de La Rochefoucauld 1613–1680. French writer. His *Réflexions, ou sentences et maximes morales/Reflections, or Moral Maxims* 1665 is a collection of brief, epigrammatic, and cynical observations on life and society, with the epigraph "Our virtues are mostly our vices in disguise." He was a lover of Mme de ◊Lafayette.

Born in Paris, he became a soldier, and took part in the ◊*Fronde*. His later years were divided between the court and literary society.

La Rochelle fishing port in W France; population (1982) 102,000. It is the capital of Charente-Maritime *département*. Industries include shipbuilding, chemicals, and motor vehicles. A Huguenot stronghold, it was taken by Cardinal Richelieu in the siege of 1627–28.

Larousse Pierre 1817–1875. French grammarian and lexicographer. His encyclopedic dictionary, the *Grand dictionnaire universel du XIXème siècle/Great Universal 19th-Century Dictionary* 1865–76 was an influential work and continues to be published in revised form.

Larsson Carl 1853–1919. Swedish painter, engraver, and illustrator. His watercolors of domestic life, delicately colored and full of detail, were painted for his book *Ett Hem/A Home* 1899.

Lartigue Jacques-Henri 1894–1986. French photographer. He began taking photographs of his family at the age of seven, and went on to make ◊autochrome color prints of women. During his lifetime he made over 40,000 photographs, documenting everyday people and situations.

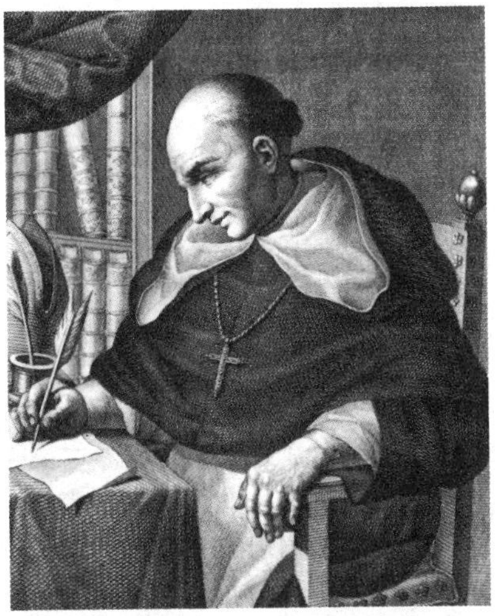

Las Casas *Las Casas, Spanish missionary in the Americas who called for the abolition of Indian slavery.*

laser

laser
The laser was invented by US scientist, Theodore Maiman, who followed up a suggestion made by Charles Townes.

Technician working with a laser at an optical bench.

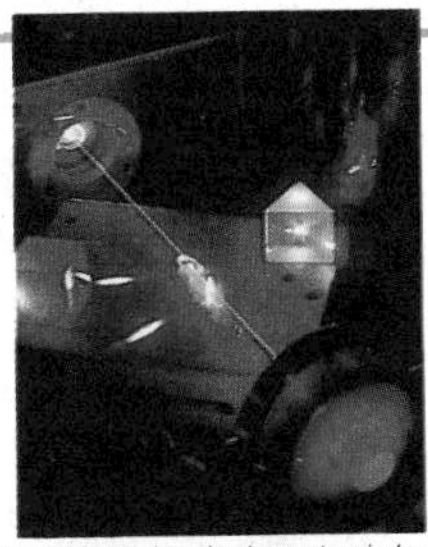

A laser beam is used to check quartz windows (center) for cleanliness, used in electro-optical technology.

Mirrors reflecting the beam of an argon ion laser.

Gas laser

(1) In a gas laser, electrons moving between the electrodes pass energy to gas atoms. An energised atom emits a ray of light.

(2) The ray hits another energised atom causing it to emit a further ray of light.

(3) The rays bounce between the mirrors at each end causing a build-up of light. Eventually the beam becomes strong enough to pass through the half-silvered mirror at one end, producing a laser beam.

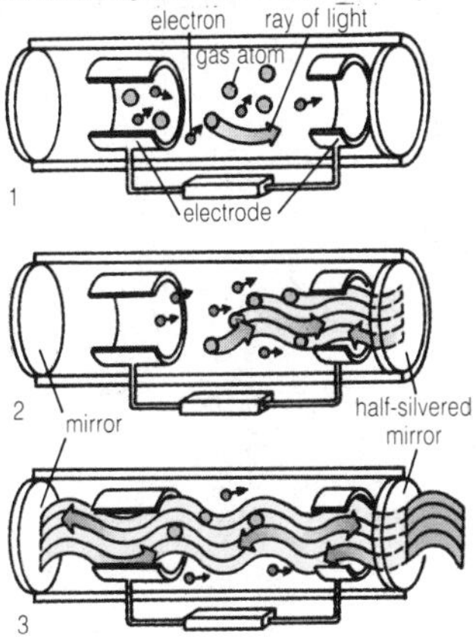
electron
ray of light
gas atom
1
electrode
2
mirror
half-silvered mirror
3

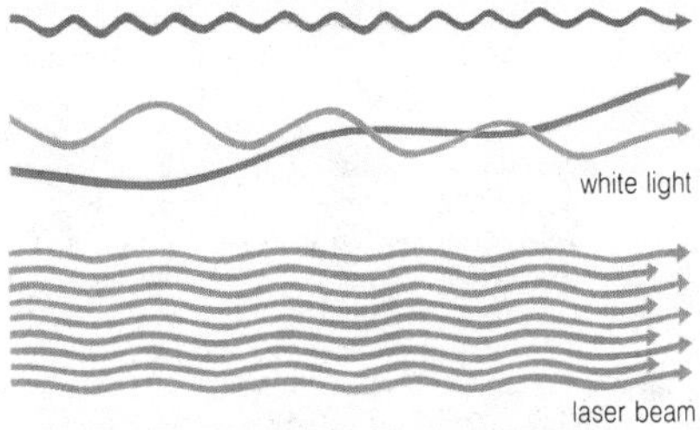
white light
laser beam

White light is a mixture of light waves of different wavelengths, corresponding to different colors. In a beam of white light, all the waves are out of step.

In a laser beam, all the waves are of the same wavelength, so the beam is a pure color. All the waves in a laser beam are in step.

larva the stage between hatching and adulthood in those species in which the young have a different appearance and way of life from the adults. Examples include tadpoles (frogs) and caterpillars (butterflies and moths). Larvae are typical of the invertebrates, and some (for example, shrimps) have two or more distinct larval stages. Among vertebrates, it is only the amphibians and some fishes that have a larval stage.

The process whereby the larva changes into another stage, such as a pupa (chrysalis) or adult, is known as ◊metamorphosis.

laryngitis inflammation of the larynx, causing soreness of the throat, dry cough, and hoarseness. The acute form is due to a virus or other infection, excessive use of the voice, or inhalation of irritating smoke, and may cause the voice to be completely lost. With rest, the inflammation usually subsides in a few days.

larynx in mammals, a cavity at the upper end of the trachea (windpipe), containing the vocal cords. It is stiffened with cartilage and lined with mucous membrane. Amphibians and reptiles have much simpler larynxes, with no vocal cords. Birds have a similar cavity, called the syrinx, found lower down the trachea, where it branches to form the bronchi. It is very complex, with well-developed vocal cords.

la Salle René Robert Cavelier, Sieur de la Salle 1643–1687. French explorer. He made an epic voyage through North America, exploring the Mississippi River down to its mouth, and in 1682 founded Louisiana.

When he returned with colonists, he failed to find the river mouth again, and was eventually murdered by his mutinous men.

lascar East Indian seaman. The word derives from the Persian *lashkar* ("army"), and lascars were originally a class of ◊sepoy.

Las Casas Bartolomé de 1474–1566. Spanish missionary, historian, and colonial reformer, known as the Apostle of the Indies. He was the first European to call for the abolition of Indian slavery in Latin America. He took part in the conquest of Cuba 1513, but subsequently worked for American Indian freedom in the Spanish colonies. *Apologética historia de las Indias* (first published 1875–76) is his account of Indian traditions and his witnessing of Spanish oppression of the Indians.

Las Casas sailed to Hispaniola in the West Indies 1502 and was ordained priest there 1512. From Cuba he returned to Spain 1515 to plead for the Indian cause, winning the support of the Holy Roman emperor Charles V. In what is now Venezuela he unsuccessfully attempted to found a settlement of free Indians. In 1530, shortly before the conquest of Peru, he persuaded the Spanish government to forbid slavery there. In 1542 he became bishop of Chiapas in S Mexico. He returned finally to Spain 1547.

Lascaux cave system in SW France with prehistoric wall paintings. It is richly decorated with realistic and symbolic paintings of buffalos, horses, and red deer of the Upper Paleolithic period, about 18,000 BC. The caves, near Montignac in the Dordogne, were discovered 1940. Similar paintings are found in ◊Altamira, Spain.

Las Cruces city in S New Mexico, on the Rio Grande, N of the Mexican border. It is a processing center for the area's crops, such as pecans, cotton, and vegetables. White Sands Missile Range is nearby; population (1990) 62,126.

laser (acronym for light amplification by stimulated emission of radiation) a device for producing a narrow beam of light, capable of traveling over vast distances without dispersion, of being focused to give enormous power densities (10^8 watts per cm^2 for high-energy lasers), and operating on a principle similar to that of the ◊maser. Uses of lasers include communications (a laser beam can carry much more information than radio waves), cutting, drilling, welding, satellite tracking, medical and biological research, and surgery.

A blue shortwave laser was developed in Japan 1988. Its expected application is in random access memory (◊RAM) and CD phonograph recording, where its shorter wavelength will allow a greater concentration of digital information to be stored and read. A gallium arsenide chip, produced by IBM 1989, contains the world's smallest lasers in the form of cylinders of ◊semiconductor roughly one tenth of the thickness of a human hair; a million lasers can fit on a chip 2.5 in/1 cm square.

Sound wave vibrations from the window glass of a room can be picked up by a reflected laser beam. Lasers are also used as entertainment in theaters, concerts, and light shows.

Any substance the majority of whose atoms or molecules can be put into an excited energy state can be used as laser material. Many solid, liquid, and gaseous substances have been used, including synthetic ruby crystal (used for the first extraction of laser light 1960, and giving a high-power pulsed output) and a helium–neon gas mixture, capable of continuous operation, but at a lower power.

laser printer computer printer in which an image is formed by the action of a laser on a light-sensitive drum, then transferred to paper by means of an electrostatic charge. The image, which can be text or pictures, is made up of tiny dots, usually 300 per in/120 per cm.

laser surgery the use of intense light sources to cut, coagulate, and vaporize tissue. Less invasive than normal surgery, it destroys diseased tissue gently and allows quicker, more natural healing. It can be used with a flexible endoscope, to enable the surgeon to see the diseased area at which the laser needs to be aimed.

Lashio town in N Myanmar, about 125 mi/200 km NE of Mandalay; beginning of the Burma Road, constructed in 1938, to Kunming in China.

Laski Harold 1893–1950. British political theorist. Professor of political science at the London School of Economics from 1926, he taught a modified Marxism and published *A Grammar of Politics* 1925 and *The American Presidency* 1940. He was chairman of the Labour Party 1945–46.

Las Palmas or ***Las Palmas de Gran Canaria*** tourist resort on the NE coast of Gran Canaria, Canary Islands; population (1986) 372,000. Products include sugar and bananas.

La Spezia port in NW Italy, chief Italian naval base; population (1988) 107,000. Industries include shipbuilding, engineering, electrical goods, and textiles. The poet Shelley drowned in the Gulf of Spezia.

Lassa fever acute disease caused by a virus, first detected 1969, and spread by a species of rat found only in W Africa. It is characterized by high fever and inflammation of various organs. There is no known cure, the survival rate being less than 50%.

Lassalle Ferdinand 1825–1864. German Socialist. He was imprisoned for his part in the ◊revolution of 1848, during which he met ◊Marx, and in 1863 founded the General Association of German Workers (later the Social-Democratic Party). His publications include *The Working Man's Program* 1862 and *The Open Letter* 1863. He was killed in a duel arising from a love affair.

Lasseter's Reef legendary location of a rich gold-bearing area in Rawlinson Range, Western Australia, discovered by H B Lasseter 1897, but which he could never find again.

Lassus Roland de. Also known as Orlando di Lasso c. 1532–1594. Franco-Flemish composer. His works include polyphonic sacred music, songs, and madrigals, including settings of poems by his friend ◊Ronsard.

Las Vegas city in Nevada, known for its nightclubs and gambling casinos; population (1990) 258,295. Las Vegas entertains millions of visitors and is an important convention center. The University of Nevada-Las Vegas is here, and Nellis Air Force Base, Hoover Dam, and Lake Mead National Recreation Area are nearby. An army base was established here 1864, and the modern community developed with the coming of the railroad 1905. Las Vegas's growth dates from the first casino-hotel 1947, helped by its proximity to S California population centers and the development of air conditioning.

Latakia port with tobacco industries in NW Syria; population (1981) 197,000.

La Tène prehistoric settlement at the east end of Lake Neuchâtel, Switzerland, which has given its name to a culture of the Iron Age. The culture lasted from the 5th century BC to the Roman conquest.

latent heat in physics, the heat absorbed or radiated by a substance as it changes phase (for example,

lateral line system

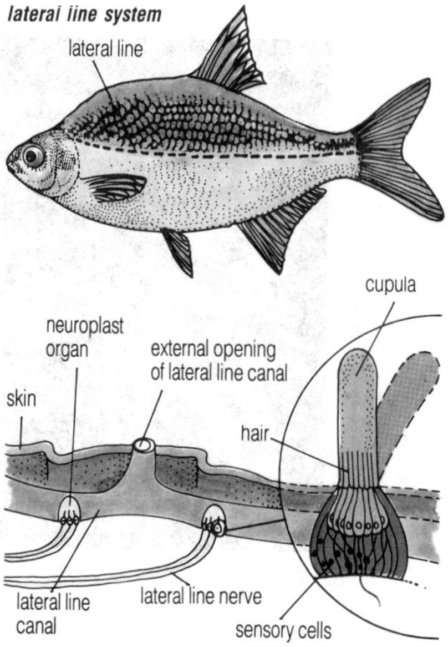
lateral line
cupula
neuroplast organ
external opening of lateral line canal
skin
hair
lateral line canal
lateral line nerve
sensory cells

from solid to liquid) at constant temperature and pressure.

lateral line system a system of sense organs in fishes and larval amphibians (tadpoles) that detects water movement. It usually consists of a row of interconnected pores on either side of the body that divide into a system of canals across the head.

Lateran Treaties series of agreements that marked the reconciliation of the Italian state with the papacy 1929. They were hailed as a propaganda victory for the Fascist regime. The treaties involved recognition of the sovereignty of the ◊Vatican City State, the payment of an indemnity for papal possessions lost during unification in 1870, and agreement on the role of the Catholic church within the Italian state in the form of a concordat between Pope Pius XI and the dictator Mussolini.

laterite a red residual soil characteristic of tropical rain forests. It is formed by the weathering of basalts, granites, and shales and contains a high percentage of aluminum and iron hydroxides.

latex (Latin "liquid") fluid of some ◊angiosperm plants (such as rubber tree and poppy), an emulsion of resins, proteins, and other organic substances. It is used as the basis for making rubber. The name is also applied to a suspension in water of natural or synthetic rubber (or plastic) particles used in rubber goods, paints, and adhesives.

lathe machine tool, used for turning. The workpiece to be machined, usually wood or metal, is held and rotated while cutting tools are moved against it. Modern lathes are driven by electric motors, which can drive the spindle carrying the workpiece at various speeds.

latifundium (Latin "broad" + "farm") in ancient Rome, a large agricultural estate designed to make maximum use of cheap labor, whether free workmen or slaves.

In present-day Italy, Spain, and South America, the terms *latifondo* or *latifundio* refer to a large agricultural estate worked by low-paid casual or semiservile labor in the interests of absentee landlords.

Latimer Hugh 1490–1555. English Christian church reformer and bishop. After his conversion to Protestantism 1524 he was imprisoned several times but was protected by Cardinal Wolsey and Henry VIII. He was burned for heresy.

Latimer was appointed bishop of Worcester 1535, but resigned 1539. Under Edward VI his sermons denouncing social injustice won him great influence, but after the accession of Mary he was arrested 1553 and two years later burned at the stake in Oxford.

Latin Indo-European language of ancient Italy. Latin has passed through four influential phases: as the language of (1) republican Rome, (2) the Roman Empire, (3) the Roman Catholic Church, and (4) W European culture, science, philosophy, and law during the Middle Ages and the Renaissance. During the third and fourth phases, much Latin vocabulary entered the English language. It is the parent form of the ◊Romance languages, noted for its highly inflected grammar and conciseness of expression.

The direct influence of Latin in Europe has decreased since Renaissance times but is still considerable, and indirectly both the language and its Classical literature still affect many modern languages and literatures. The insistence of Renaissance scholars upon an exact Classical purity, together with the rise of the European nation-states, contributed to the decline of Latin as an international cultural medium.

Latin vocabulary has entered English in two major waves: as religious vocabulary from Anglo-Saxon times until the Reformation, and as the vocabulary of science, scholarship, and the law from the Middle Ages onward. In the 17th century the makers of English dictionaries deliberately converted Latin words into English, enlarging the already powerful French component of English vocabulary into the language of education and refinement, placing *fraternity* alongside "brotherhood," *comprehend* beside "understand," *feline* beside "catlike," and so on. Many "Latin tags" are in regular use in English: *habeas corpus* ("you may have the body"), *ipse dixit* ("he said it himself"), *non sequitur* ("it does not follow"), and so on. English that consists of many Latin elements is "Latinate" and often has a grandiose and even pompous quality.

Today, with fewer students studying Latin in schools and universities, there is a tendency to make Latin words more conventionally English; for example, "cactuses" rather than *cacti* as the plural of "cactus." This tendency is accompanied by some uncertainty about usage, for example whether words like *data* and *media* are singular or plural. They are technically plural and are so treated by scholars, writers, and editors.

Latin America countries of South and Central America (also including Mexico) in which Spanish, Portuguese, and French are spoken.

Latin literature only a few hymns and inscriptions survive from the earliest period of Latin literature before the 3rd century BC. Greek influence began with the work of Livius Andronicus (c. 284–204 BC), who translated the *Odyssey* and Greek plays into Latin. Naevius and Ennius both attempted epics on patriotic themes; the former used the native "Saturnian" meter, but the latter introduced the Greek hexameter. Plautus and Terence successfully adapted Greek comedy to the Latin stage. Lucilius (190–103 BC) founded Latin verse satire, while the writings of Cato were the first important works in Latin prose.

In the *De Rerum natura* of Lucretius, and the passionate lyrics of Catullus, Latin verse reached maturity. Cicero set a standard for Latin prose, in his orations, philosophical essays, and letters. To the same period of the Roman republic belong the histories of Caesar.

The Augustan age (43 BC–AD 17) is called the golden age of Latin literature. There is strong patriotic feeling in the work of the poets Virgil and Horace and the historian Livy, who belonged to the emperor Augustus's court circle. Virgil produced the one great Latin epic, the *Aeneid*, while Horace brought charm and polish to both lyric and satire. Younger poets of the period were Ovid, who dealt with themes of love, and the elegiac poets Tibullus and Propertius.

The silver age of the empire begins with the writers of Nero's reign: the Stoic philosopher Seneca; Lucan, author of the epic *Pharsalia*; the satirist Persius; and, by far the greatest, the realistic novelist Petronius. Around the end of the

latitude and longitude

Point X lies on longitude 60°W

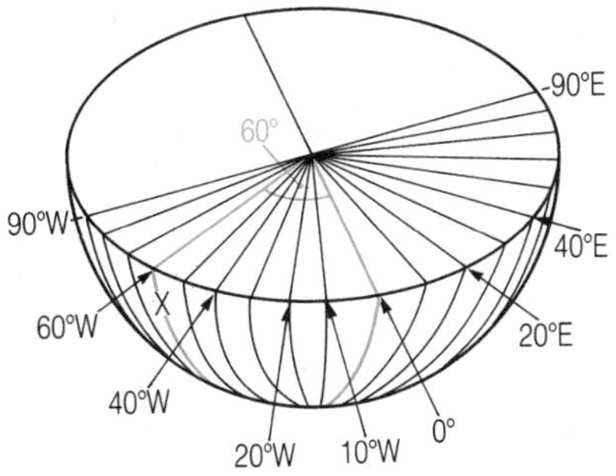
90°E
60°
90°W
40°E
60°W
X
20°E
40°W
20°W
10°W
0°

Point X lies on latitude 20°S

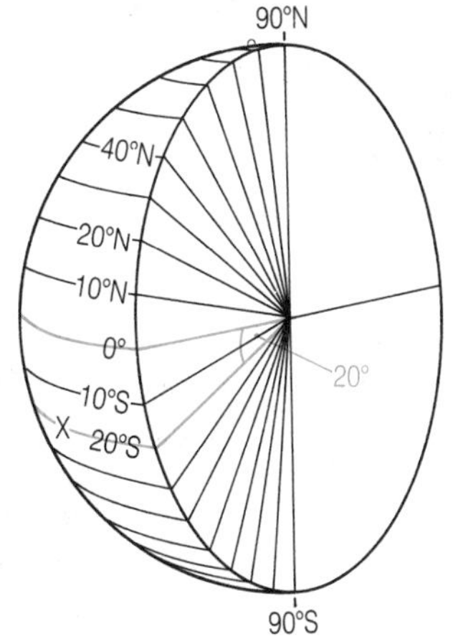
90°N
40°N
20°N
10°N
0°
20°
10°S
X
20°S
90°S

1st century and and at the beginning of the 2nd came the historian Tacitus and the satirist Juvenal; other writers of the period were the epigrammatist Martial, the scientist Pliny the Elder, the letter-writer Pliny the Younger, the critic Quintilian, the historian Suetonius, and the epic poet Statius.

The 2nd and 3rd centuries produced only one pagan writer of importance, the romancer Apuleius, but there were several able Christian writers, such as Tertullian, Cyprian, Arnobius (died 327), and Lactantius (died 325). In the 4th century there was something of a poetic revival, with Ausonius, Claudian, and the Christian poets Prudentius and St Ambrose. The Classical period ends, and the Middle Ages begin, with St Augustine's *City of God* and St Jerome's translation of the Bible.

Throughout the Middle Ages, Latin remained the language of the church and was normally employed for theology, philosophy, histories, and other learned works. Latin verse, adapted to rhyme and non-Classical meters, was used both for hymns and the secular songs of the wandering scholars. Even after the Reformation, Latin retained its prestige as the international language of scholars and was used as such by the English writers Thomas More, Francis Bacon, John Milton, and many others. Medieval Latin vernacular evolved into the Romance languages.

latitude and longitude angular distances defining position on the globe. Latitude (abbreviation lat.) is the angular distance of any point from the ◊equator, measured N or S along the Earth's curved surface, equaling the angle between the respective horizontal planes. It is measured in degrees, minutes, and seconds, each minute equaling one nautical mile (1.15 mi/1.85 km) in length. Longitude (abbreviation long.) is the angle between the terrestrial meridian through a place, and a standard meridian now taken at Greenwich, England. At the equator one degree of longitude measures approximately 70 mi/113 km.

For map making, latitude is based on the supposition that the Earth is an oblate spheroid. The difference between this (the geographical) and astronomical latitude is the correction necessary for local deviation of plumb line. All determinations of longitude are based on the Earth turning through 360° in 24 hours, or the Sun reaching 15° W each hour.

Latium Latin name for ◊Lazio, a region of W central Italy.

La Tour Georges de 1593–1652. French painter active in Lorraine. He was patronized by the duke of Lorraine and perhaps also by Louis XIII. Many of his pictures are illuminated by a single source of light, with deep contrasts of light and shade. They range from religious paintings to domestic genre scenes.

La Tour's style suggests a connection with the Dutch painters Honthorst and Terbrugghen, who were followers of Caravaggio, but it is distinctive, with fire or candlelight creating warm and glowing tones. His subjects include solitary women in domestic interiors.

Lattakia alternate form of ◊Latakia in Syria.

Latter-day Saint member of the Christian sect, the ◊Mormons.

Latvia country in N Europe, bounded E by the USSR, N by Estonia, N and NW by the Baltic Sea, and S by Lithuania and the USSR

history The Vikings invaded the area now known as Latvia in the 9th century, and the Russians attacked in the 10th century. The invasion of the ◊Teutonic Knights (German crusaders) in the 13th century was resisted in a lengthy struggle, but Latvia eventually came under their control 1230, converted to Christianity, and was governed by them for more than 200 years. By 1562 Poland and Lithuania had taken over most of the country. Sweden conquered the north 1621 and Russia took over control of this area 1710. By 1800 all of Latvia had come under Russian control. The Latvian independence movement began to emerge in the late 1800s and continued to grow in the early 20th century.

struggle for independence Latvia was partially occupied by the Germans during World War I. The Soviets reclaimed control 1917 but were overthrown by the Germans Feb 1918, when Latvia declared its independence. Soviet rule was restored when the Germans withdrew Dec 1918, but the Soviets were again overthrown by British naval and German forces May–Dec 1919, and democratic rule was established. A coup 1934 replaced the established government. In 1939 a secret German–Soviet agreement assigned Latvia to Russian rule, and in 1940 Latvia was incorporated as a constituent republic of the USSR. During World War II Latvia was again occupied by the Germans 1941–44, but the USSR regained control 1944.

As in the other Baltic republics, nationalist dissent grew from 1980, influenced by the Polish example and prompted by an influx of Russian workers and officials. A Latvian popular front was established Oct 1988 to campaign for independence, and in the same month the prewar flag was readopted and official status given to the Latvian language. A multiparty system was put in place, with, following the republic's elections of Dec 1989, a coalition government. In Jan 1990 the Latvian Communist Party broke its links with Moscow, and in May Latvia followed the lead taken by Lithuania when it unilaterally declared its independence from the USSR, subject to a transition period for negotiation. In Jan 1991 Soviet paratroopers seized key installations in Riga, but began to withdraw later that month after protests both within and outside the USSR.

On Aug 20, 1991, in the midst of the failed anti-

Latvia
Republic of

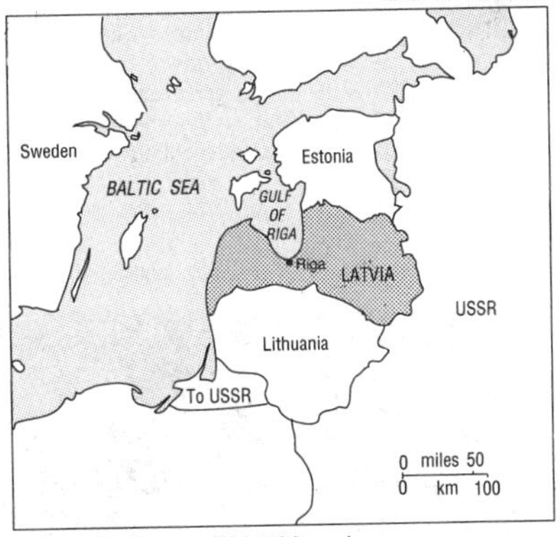
Sweden
Estonia
BALTIC SEA
GULF OF RIGA
Riga
LATVIA
USSR
Lithuania
To USSR
0 miles 50
0 km 100

area 24,595 sq mi/63,700 sq km
capital Riga
cities Daugavpils, Liepab1ja, Jurmala, Jelgava, Ventspils
physical wooded lowland (highest point 1,024 ft/312 m), marshes, lakes; 293 mi/472 km of coastline; mild climate
features Western Dvina River; Riga is largest port on the Baltic after Leningrad
head of state Anatolijs Gorbunovs from 1988
head of government Ivacs Godmanis from 1990
political system emergent democracy
products electronic and communications equipment, electric railroad carriages, motorcycles, consumer durables, timber, paper and woolen goods, meat and dairy products
currency ruble
population (1989 est) 2,681,000; 54% Latvian, 33% Russian
language Latvian
religion mostly Lutheran Protestant, with a Roman Catholic minority
chronology
1917 Soviets reclaimed power in partially German-occupied Latvia.
1918 Feb: Soviets overthrown by Germans. Nov: Latvia declared its independence. Dec: Soviet rule restored after German withdrawal.
1919 Soviet rule overthrown by British naval and German forces May–Dec; democracy established.
1934 Coup replaced established government.
1939 German–Soviet secret agreement placed Latvia under Russian influence.
1940 Incorporated into USSR as constituent republic.
1941 During World War II, Germans invaded and occupied Latvia.
1944 USSR regained control.
1980 Nationalist dissent began to grow.
1988 Latvian popular front established to campaign for independence. Prewar flag readopted; official status given to Latvian language.
1989 Dec elections led to a coalition government.
1990 Jan: Latvian Communist Party broke links with Moscow. May: unilateral declaration of independence from the USSR, subject to transition period for negotiation.
1991 Jan: Soviet paratroopers seized key installations in Riga, but began to withdraw after protests within and outside the USSR. Aug: full independence declared at time of anti-Gorbachev coup; Communist Party outlawed. Sept: independence recognized by Soviet government and Western nations and membership of the United Nations granted.

CHARLES LAUGHTON

Laughton *An actor with a wide dramatic range, Charles Laughton won an Academy Award for his performance in the film* The Private Life of Henry VIII *1933.*

Gorbachev coup in the USSR that led to Red Army troops seizing the radio and television station in Riga, the republic declared its full independence (previously it had been in a "period of transition") and outlawed the Communist Party. This declaration was recognized by the Soviet government and Western nations Sept 1991, and the new state was granted membership in the United Nations.

Latvian language the language of Latvia; with Lithuanian it is one of the two surviving members of the Baltic branch of the Indo-European language family.

Laud William 1573–1645. English priest. As archbishop of Canterbury from 1633, his High Church policy, support for Charles I's unparliamentary rule, censorship of the press, and persecution of the Puritans all aroused bitter opposition, while his strict enforcement of the statutes against enclosures and of laws regulating wages and prices alienated the propertied classes. His attempt to impose the use of the Prayer Book on the Scots precipitated the English ◊Civil War. Impeached by Parliament 1640, he was imprisoned in the Tower of London, summarily condemned to death and beheaded.

laudanum alcoholic solution (tincture) of ◊opium. Used formerly as a narcotic and painkiller, it was available in the 19th century from pharmacists on demand in most of Europe and the US.

Lauder Harry. Adopted name of Hugh MacLennan 1870–1950. Scottish music-hall comedian and singer, who began his career as an "Irish" comedian.

Laue Max Theodor Felix von 1879–1960. German physicist who was a pioneer in measuring the wavelength of X-rays by their diffraction through the closely spaced atoms in a crystal. His work led to the powerful technique now used to elucidate the structure of complex biological materials such as ◊DNA. He was awarded a Nobel Prize 1914.

laughing gas popular name for ◊nitrous oxide, an anesthetic.

laughing jackass another name for ◊kookaburra.

Laughton Charles 1899–1962. British actor who became a US citizen 1950. Initially a Classical stage actor, he joined the Old Vic 1933. His films were made in Hollywood and include such roles as the king in *The Private Life of Henry VIII* 1933, for which he won an Academy Award; *The Hunchback of Notre Dame* 1939; *Ruggles of Red Gap* 1935; and Captain Bligh in *Mutiny on the Bounty* 1935. In 1955 he directed *Night of the Hunter* and in 1961 appeared in *Judgment at Nuremberg*.

Launceston port in NE Tasmania, Australia, on the Tamar River; population (1986) 88,500. Founded in 1805, its industries include woolen blankets, lumber milling, engineering, furniture and pottery making, and railroad workshops.

Laurel and Hardy *The popular duo Laurel and Hardy, one of the most successful comedy teams in cinema history.*

Laurasia former land mass or supercontinent, formed by the fusion of North America, Greenland, Europe, and Asia. It made up the northern half of ◊Pangaea, the "world continent" that is thought to have existed between 250 and 200 million years ago. The southern half was ◊Gondwanaland.

laurel any evergreen tree of the European genus *Laurus*, family Lauraceae, with glossy, aromatic leaves, yellowish flowers, and black berries. The leaves of sweet bay or poet's laurel *L. nobilis* are used in cooking. Several species are cultivated worldwide.

California laurel *Umbellularia californica* of the W US belongs to a different genus in the laurel family.

Laurel and Hardy Stan Laurel (adopted name of Arthur Stanley Jefferson) 1890–1965 and Oliver Hardy 1892–1957. US film comedians who were the most successful comedy team in film history (Stan was slim; Oliver, rotund). Their unique partnership began in 1927, survived the transition from silent films to sound, and resulted in more than 200 short and feature-length films, which were revived as a worldwide cult in the 1970s. Among these are *Pack Up Your Troubles* 1932, *Our Relations* 1936, and *A Chump at Oxford* 1940.

Laurel, a former music-hall comedian, conceived the gags and directed their feature films *Babes in Toyland* 1934, *Way Out West* 1937, and *Swiss Miss* 1938. In 1940 they formed a production company and made films until 1945.

Laurence Margaret 1926–1987. Canadian writer whose novels include *A Jest of God* 1966 and *The Diviners* 1974. She also wrote short stories set in Africa, where she lived for a time.

Laurier Wilfrid 1841–1919. Canadian politician, leader of the Liberal Party 1887–1919 and prime minister 1896–1911. The first French-Canadian to hold the office, he encouraged immigration into Canada from Europe and the US, established a separate Canadian navy, and sent troops to help Britain in the Boer War.

Lausanne resort and capital of Vaud canton, W Switzerland, above the north shore of Lake Geneva; population (1987) 262,000. Industries include chocolate, scientific instruments, and publishing.

Lausanne, Treaty of peace settlement 1923 between Greece and Turkey after Turkey refused to accept the terms of the Treaty of Sèvres 1920, which would have made peace with the western Allies. It involved the surrender by Greece of Smyrna (now Izmir) to Turkey and the enforced exchange of the Greek population of Smyrna for the Turkish population of Greece.

lava molten material that erupts from a ◊volcano and cools to form extrusive ◊igneous rock. A lava high in silica is viscous and sticky and does not flow far, wheras low-silica lava can flow for long distances.

Lava differs from its parent ◊magma in that the fluid "fractionates" on its way to the surface of the Earth; that is, certain heavy or high-temperature minerals settle out and the constituent gases form bubbles and boil away into the atmosphere.

Laval Pierre 1883–1945. French right-wing politician. He was prime minister and foreign secretary 1931–32, and again 1935–36. In World War II he joined Pétain's ◊Vichy government as vice-premier June 1940; dismissed Dec 1940, he was reinstated by Hitler's orders as head of the government and foreign minister 1942. After the war he was executed.

Laval, born near Vichy, entered the chamber of deputies 1914 as a Socialist, but after World War I moved toward the right. His second period as prime minister was marked by the ◊Hoare–Laval Pact for concessions to Italy in Abyssinia. His part in the deportation of French labor to Germany during World War II made him universally hated. When the Allies invaded, he fled

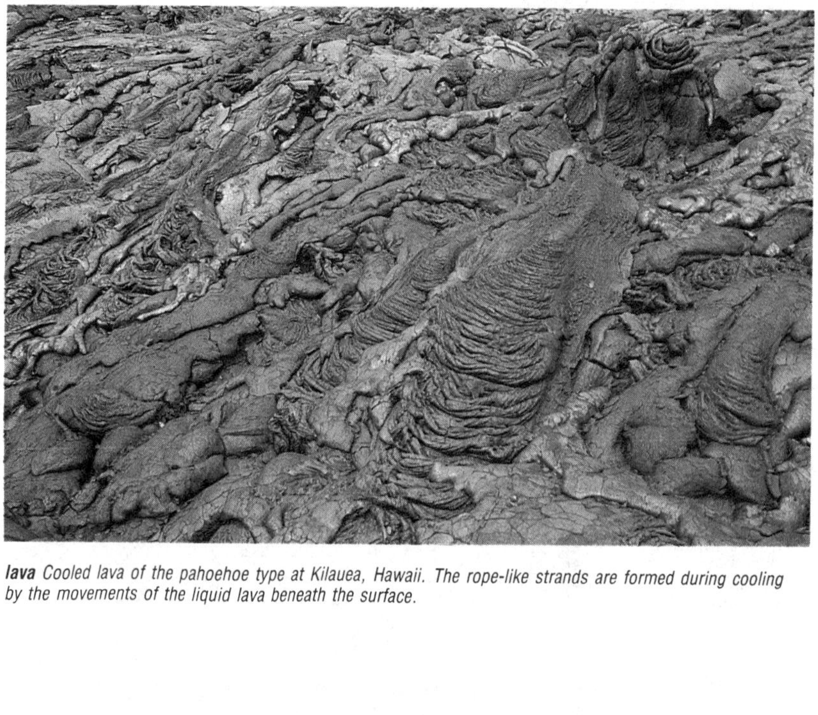

lava *Cooled lava of the pahoehoe type at Kilauea, Hawaii. The rope-like strands are formed during cooling by the movements of the liquid lava beneath the surface.*

Lavoisier French chemist Antoine Lavoisier.

the country but was arrested in Austria, tried for treason, and shot after trying to poison himself.

La Vallière Louise de la Baume le Blance, Duchesse de 1644–1710. Mistress of the French king Louis XIV; she gave birth to four children 1661–74. She retired to a convent when superseded in his affections by the Marquise de Montespan.

La Vendée see ◊Vendée, La.

lavender sweet-smelling herb, genus *Lavandula*, of the mint family Labiatae, native to W Mediterranean countries. The bushy low-growing *L. angustifolia* has long, narrow, erect leaves of a silver-green color. The flowers, borne on a terminal spike, vary in color from lilac to deep purple and are covered with small fragrant oil glands. The oil is extensively used in pharmacy and the manufacture of perfumes.

laver any of several edible red seaweeds, including *Porphyra umbicalis*. Growing on the shore and below, attached to rocks and stones, it forms thin, flat, irregularly rounded sheets of tissue up to 8 in/20 cm across. It becomes almost black when dry.

Laver Rod(ney George) 1938– . Australian tennis player. He was one of the greatest left-handed players, and the only player to achieve the Grand Slam twice (1962 and 1969).

He won four Wimbledon singles titles, the Australian title three times, the US Open twice, and the French Open twice. He turned professional after winning Wimbledon 1962 but returned when the championships were opened to professionals in 1968.

CAREER HIGHLIGHTS

Wimbledon
singles: 1961–62, 1968–69
doubles: 1971
mixed: 1959–60
US Open
singles: 1962, 1969
French Open
singles: 1962, 1969
doubles: 1961
mixed: 1961
Australian Open
singles: 1960, 1962, 1969
doubles: 1959–61, 1969

Lavoisier Antoine Laurent 1743–1794. French chemist. He proved that combustion needed only a part of the air, which he called oxygen, thereby destroying the theory of phlogiston (an imaginary "fire element" released during combustion).

With Pierre Laplace (1749–1827), he showed that water was a compound of oxygen and hydrogen. In this way he established the basic rules of chemical combination.

law the body of rules and principles under which justice is administered or order enforced in a state or nation. In Western Europe there are two main systems: ◊Roman law and ◊English law. US law is a modified form of English law.

Roman law, first codified 450 BC and finalized under Justinian AD 528–534, advanced to a system of international law (*jus gentium*), applied in disputes between Romans and foreigners or provincials, or between provincials of different states. Church influence led to the adoption of Roman law throughout western continental Europe, and it was spread to Eastern Europe and parts of Asia by the French *Code Napoléon* in the 19th century. Scotland and Québec (because of their French links) and South Africa (because of its link with Holland) also have it as the basis of their legal systems.

English law derives from Anglo-Saxon customs, which were too entrenched to be broken by the Norman Conquest and still form the basis of the ◊common law, which by 1250 had been systematized by the royal judges. Unique to English law are the judicial ◊precedents whereby the reported decisions of the courts form a binding source of law for future decisions. These two concepts are the basis for US law.

law courts the bodies that adjudicate in legal disputes. Civil and criminal cases are usually dealt with by separate courts. In many countries there is a hierarchy of courts that provide an appeal system.

In the US, the head of the federal judiciary is the Supreme Court, which also hears appeals from the inferior federal courts and from the decisions of the highest state courts. The US Courts of Appeal—organized in circuits—deal with appeals from the US district courts in which civil and criminal cases are heard. State courts deal with civil and criminal cases involving state laws and usually consist of a Supreme Court or appeals court and courts in judicial districts.

Many counties and municipalities also have courts, usually limited to minor offenses. There are also a number of federal and state specialized judicial and quasi-judicial bodies dealing with ◊administrative law.

Lawrence town in Massachusetts; population (1990) 70,207. Industries include textiles, clothing, paper, and radio equipment. The town was established in 1845 to utilize power from the Merrimack Rapids on a site first settled in 1655.

Lawrence city in NE Kansas, on the Kansas River between Topeka to the W and Kansas City to the E; seat of Douglas County. Its main industries are food processing and chemicals. The University of Kansas 1863 is here; population (1990) 65,608. Lawrence was terrorized by Quantrill's Raiders 1863.

Lawrence D(avid) H(erbert) 1885–1930. English writer whose work expresses his belief in emotion and the sexual impulse as creative and true to human nature. His novels include *Sons and Lovers* 1913, *The Rainbow* 1915, *Women in Love* 1921, and *Lady Chatterley's Lover* 1928. Lawrence also wrote short stories (for example "The Woman Who Rode Away") and poetry.

Son of a Nottinghamshire miner, Lawrence studied at University College, Nottingham, and became a teacher. His writing first received attention after the publication of the semiautobiographical *Sons and Lovers*, which includes a portrayal of his mother (died 1911). In 1914 he married Frieda von Richthofen, ex-wife of his university professor, with whom he had run away 1912. Frieda was the model for Ursula Brangwen in *The Rainbow*, suppressed for obscenity, and its sequel, *Women in Love*. His travels in search of health (he suffered from tuberculosis, from which he eventually died near Nice) prompted books such as *Mornings in Mexico* 1927. *Lady Chatterley's Lover* 1928 was banned as obscene in the UK until 1960.

Lawrence Ernest O(rlando) 1901–1958. US physicist. His invention of the cyclotron pioneered the production of synthesized radioisotopes.

He was professor of physics at the University of California, Berkeley, from 1930 and director of the Radiation Laboratory from 1936, which he built into a major research center for nuclear physics. He was awarded a Nobel Prize in 1939.

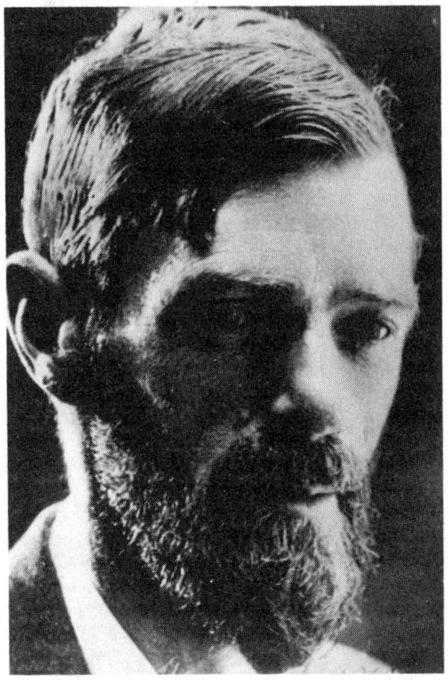

Lawrence English novelist and poet D H Lawrence, whose works long caused controversy because of their sexual explicitness.

Lawrence Gertrude 1898–1952. English actress who began as a dancer in the 1920s and later took leading roles in musical comedies. Her greatest successes were *Private Lives* 1930–31, written especially for her by Noël Coward, with whom she costarred, and *The King and I* 1951.

Lawrence T(homas) E(dward), known as Lawrence of Arabia 1888–1935. British soldier and writer. Appointed to the military intelligence department in Cairo, Egypt, during World War I, he took part in negotiations for an Arab revolt against the Ottoman Turks, and in 1916 attached himself to the emir Faisal. He became a guerrilla leader of genius, combining raids on Turkish communications with the organization of a joint Arab revolt, described in *The Seven Pillars of Wisdom* 1935.

Lawrence English soldier T E Lawrence, known as Lawrence of Arabia for his exploits as a guerrilla leader during World War I.

In 1918 he led his successful Arabs into Damascus. His account of his exploits (published privately 1926) brought legendary fame. Disappointed by the Paris Peace Conference's failure to establish Arab independence, he rejoined the military under assumed names and died in a motorcycle accident.

Lawrence Thomas 1769–1830. British painter, the leading portraitist of his day. He became painter to George III 1792 and president of the Royal Academy 1820.

Lawrence, St Christian martyr. Probably born in Spain, he became a deacon of Rome under Pope Sixtus II and, when summoned to deliver the treasures of the church, displayed the beggars in his charge, for which he was broiled on a gridiron. Feast day Aug 10.

lawrencium synthesized, radioactive, metallic element, the last of the ◊actinide series, symbol Lr, atomic number 103, atomic weight 262. It has a half-life of about a minute and was originally synthesized at the University of California at Berkeley in 1961 by bombarding californium with boron nuclei. The original symbol, Lw, was officially changed in 1963. It was named after Ernest Lawrence (1901–1958), the US physicist and inventor of the cyclotron.

law, rule of the principle that law (as administered by the ordinary courts) is supreme and that all citizens (including members of the government) are equally subject to it and equally entitled to its protection.

Lawton city in SW Oklahoma, on Cache Creek, SW of Oklahoma City, seat of Comanche County. Processing the area's agricultural products is the city's main industry. Fort Sill, an army base, is to the N; population (1990) 80,561.

lawyer a member of the legal profession who provides counsel to clients on matters of civil or criminal law and who represents clients on such matters in negotiations with others, before government agencies, and in civil and criminal counts. An ◊attorney.

Activities of lawyers include business advice, ◊conveyancing of property, making ◊wills and settling estates, ◊divorce, litigation and criminal prosecution or defense. A lawyer usually obtains a postgraduate Juris Doctor (JD) degree and must pass a state bar examination and be admitted to the bar before he or she may practice within a state court's jurisdiction. A federal bar examination permits the trying of cases in federal courts, including the US Supreme Court.

laxative substance used to relieve constipation (infrequent bowel movement). Current medical opinion discourages regular or prolonged use. Regular exercise and a diet high in vegetable fiber is believed to be the best means of preventing and treating constipation.

Laxness Halldor 1902– . Icelandic novelist who wrote about Icelandic life in the style of the early sagas. He was awarded the Nobel Prize 1955.

La'youn (Arabic *El Aaiún*) capital of Western Sahara; population (1982) 97,000. The city has expanded from a population of 25,000 in 1970 as a result of Moroccan investment (Morocco lays claim to Western Sahara).

Lazarus in the New Testament, the brother of Martha, a friend of Jesus, raised by him from the dead. Lazarus is also the name of a beggar in a parable told by Jesus (Luke 16).

Lazarus Emma 1849–1887. US poet, author of the poem on the base of the Statue of Liberty that begins: "Give me your tired, your poor/Your huddled masses yearning to breathe free."

Lazio (Roman *Latium*) region of W central Italy; area 6,639 sq mi/17,200 sq km; capital Rome; population (1988) 5,137,000. Products include olives, wine, chemicals, pharmaceuticals, and textiles. Home of the Latins from the 10th century BC, it was dominated by the Romans from the 4th century BC.

LCD abbreviation for ◊liquid crystal display.

L-dopa chemical, normally produced by the body, which is converted by an enzyme in the bloodstream to dopamine in the brain. It is essential for integrated movement of localized muscle groups.

L-dopa is a left-handed isomer of an amino acid $C_9H_{11}NO_2$. As a treatment, it relieves the tremor and rigidity of ◊Parkinson's disease but may have significant side effects, such as extreme mood changes, hallucinations, and uncontrolled writhing movements. It is often given in combination with other drugs to improve its effectiveness at lower doses.

LDR abbreviation for light-dependent resistor, a resistor that conducts electricity better when light falls on it. LDRs are made from ◊semiconductors, such as cadmium sulfide, and are used in electric-eye burglar alarms and light meters.

Lea river that rises in Bedfordshire, England, and joins the river Thames at Blackwall.

leaching process by which substances are washed out of the ◊soil. Fertilizers leached out of the soil drain into rivers, lakes, and ponds and cause water ◊pollution. In tropical areas, leaching of the soil after ◊deforestation removes scarce nutrients and leads to a dramatic loss of soil fertility.

The leaching of soluble minerals with soils can lead to the formation of distinct soil horizons as different minerals are deposited at successive levels.

Leacock Stephen Butler 1869–1944. Canadian humorist whose writings include *Literary Lapses* 1910, *Sunshine Sketches of a Little Town* 1912, and *Frenzied Fiction* 1918.

Born in Hampshire, Leacock lived in Canada from 1876 and was head of the department of economics at McGill University, Montreal, 1908–36. He published works on politics and economics, and studies of Mark Twain and Charles Dickens.

lead heavy, soft, malleable, gray, metallic element, symbol Pb (from Latin *plumbum*), atomic number 82, atomic weight 207.19. Usually found as an ore (most often in galena), it occasionally occurs as a free metal (◊native metal). It is the final stable product of the decay of uranium. It is the softest and weakest of the commonly used metals, with a low melting point, is a poor conductor of electricity, and resists acid corrosion. Lead is a cumulative poison that enters the body from lead water pipes, lead-based paints, and leaded gasoline. It is an effective shield against radiation and is used in batteries, glass, ceramics, and alloys, such as pewter and solder. The name is very old and derives from an Indo-European base, *pleu*, to flow or pour.

lead–acid cell a type of ◊battery (storage battery).

lead ore any of several minerals from which lead is extracted. The main primary ore is galena or lead sulfite PbS. This is unstable, and on prolonged exposure to the atmosphere it oxidizes into the minerals cerussite, $PbCO_3$ and anglesite, $PbSO_4$. Lead ores are usually associated with other metals, particularly silver—which can be mined at the same time—and zinc, which can cause problems during smelting.

Most commercial deposits of lead ore are in the form of veins, where hot fluids have leached the ore from cooling ◊igneous masses and deposited it in cracks in the surrounding country rock, and in thermal ◊metamorphic zones, where the heat of igneous intrusions has altered the minerals of surrounding rocks. Lead is mined in over 40 countries, but half of the world's output

leaf

leaf margins

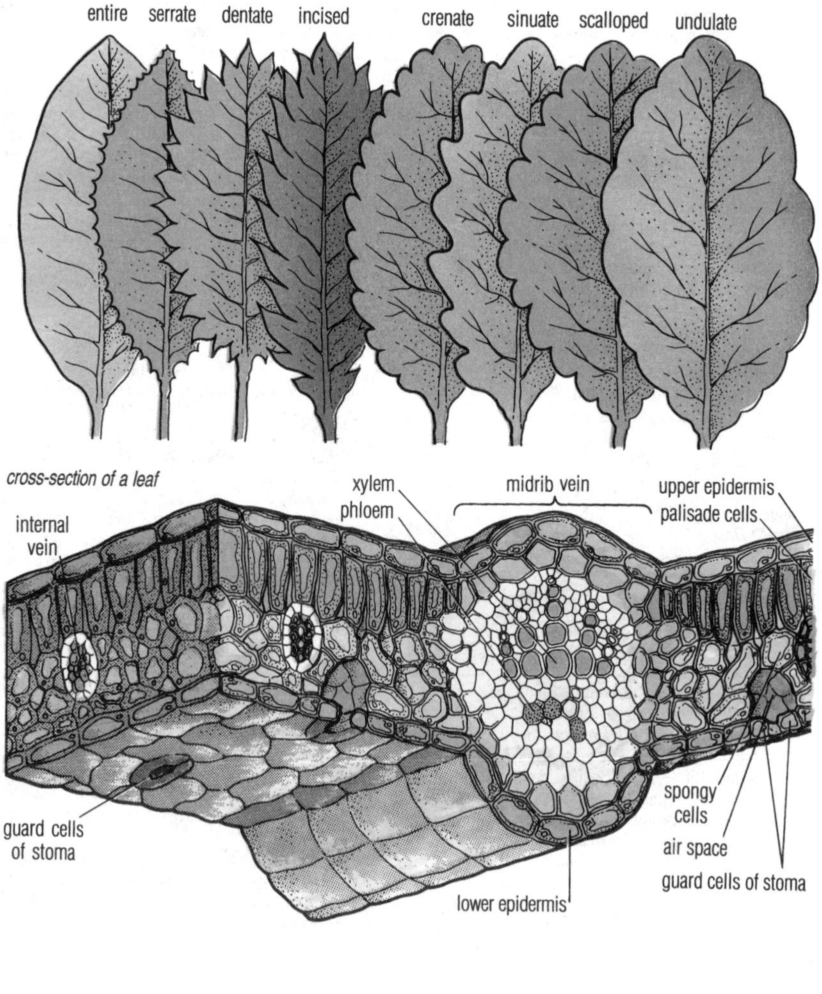
entire
serrate
dentate
incised
crenate
sinuate
scalloped
undulate
cross-section of a leaf
xylem
phloem
midrib vein
upper epidermis
palisade cells
internal vein
spongy cells
air space
guard cells of stoma
guard cells of stoma
lower epidermis

comes from the US, the USSR, Canada, and Australia.

leaf lateral outgrowth on the stem of a plant, and in most species the primary organ of ◊photosynthesis. The chief leaf types are ◊cotyledons (seed leaves), scale leaves (on underground stems), foliage leaves, and ◊bracts (in the axil of which a flower is produced).

Typically leaves are composed of three parts: the sheath or leaf base, the petiole or stalk, and the ◊lamina or blade. The lamina has a network of veins through which water and nutrients are conducted. Structurally the leaf is made up of ◊mesophyll cells surrounded by the epidermis and usually, in addition, a waxy layer, termed the ◊cuticle, which prevents excessive evaporation of water from the leaf tissues by ◊transpiration. The epidermis is interrupted by small pores, or ◊stomata, through which ◊gas exchange occurs.

A simple leaf is undivided, as in the maple or oak. A compound leaf is composed of several leaflets, as in the blackberry, horse chestnut, or ash (the latter being a ◊pinnate leaf). Leaves that fall in the autumn are termed deciduous, while evergreens are persistent.

leaf-hopper any of numerous species of plant-sucking insects (order Homoptera) of the family Cicadellidae. They feed on the sap of leaves. Each species feeds on a limited range of plants.

leaf insect insect of the order Phasmida, about 4 in/10 cm long, with a green, flattened body, remarkable for closely resembling the foliage on which it lives. It is most common in SE Asia.

Leaf insects are related to walking sticks and ◊mantises.

League of Nations international organization formed after World War I to solve international disputes by arbitration. Established in Geneva, Switzerland, 1920, the league included representatives from states throughout the world, but was severely weakened by the US decision not to become a member, and had no power to enforce its decisions. It was dissolved 1946. Its subsidiaries included the International Labor Organization and the Permanent Court of International Justice in The Hague, Netherlands, both now under the auspices of the ◊United Nations.

The formation of the league was first suggested by President ◊Wilson in his Fourteen Points as part of the peace settlement for World War I. The US did not become a member since it did not ratify the the Treaty of ◊Versailles. Although the league organized conferences, settled minor disputes, and did humanitarian work, it failed to handle the aggression of the 1930s—of Japan against China, Italy in Ethiopia, and Germany against neighboring countries.

Leakey Louis (Seymour Bazett) 1903–1972. British archeologist, born in Kenya. In 1958, with his wife Mary Leakey, he discovered gigantic extinct-animal fossils in ◊Olduvai Gorge, as well as many remains of early humans.

Leakey Mary 1913– . British archeologist. In 1948 she discovered, on Rusinga Island, Lake Victoria, E Africa, the prehistoric ape skull known as ◊*Proconsul*, about 20 million years old; and human remains at Laetolil, to the south, about 3,750,000 years old.

Leakey Richard 1944– . British archeologist, son of Louis and Mary Leakey. In 1972 he discovered at Lake Turkana, Kenya, an apelike skull, estimated to be about 2.9 million years old; it had some human characteristics and a brain capacity of 800 cu cm. In 1984 his team found an almost complete skeleton of *Homo erectus* some 1.6 million years old.

Lean David 1908–1991. British film director. His films, noted for their atmospheric quality, include early codirection with Noel ◊Coward. On his own, Lean directed *Blithe Spirit* 1945, *Brief Encounter* 1946, *Great Expectations* 1946, and *Oliver Twist* 1948. His later films included such expensive extravaganzas as *The Bridge on the River Kwai* 1957 (Academy Award), *Lawrence of Arabia* 1962 (Academy Award), *Dr Zhivago* 1965, *Ryan's Daughter* 1970, and *A Passage to India* 1985.

Lear Edward 1812–1888. English artist and humorist. His *Book of Nonsense* 1846 popularized the limerick. He first attracted attention by his paintings of birds, and later turned to landscapes. He traveled to Italy, Greece, Egypt, and India, publishing books on his travels with his own illustrations, and spent most of his later life in Italy.

learning theory in psychology, a theory about how an organism acquires new behaviors. Two main theories are Classical and operant ◊conditioning.

leasehold in law, land or property held by a tenant (lessee) for a specified period, (unlike freehold, outright ownership) usually at a rent from the landlord (lessor).

least action principle in science, the principle that nature "chooses" the easiest path for moving objects, rays of light, and so on; also known in biology as the principle of parsimony.

leather material prepared from the hides and skins of animals, by tanning with vegetable tannins and chromium salts. Leather is a durable and water-resistant material, and is used for bags, shoes, clothing, and upholstery. There are three main stages in the process of converting animal skin into leather: cleaning, tanning, and dressing.

The skin, usually cattle hide, is dehydrated after removal to arrest decay. Re-soaking is necessary before tanning in order to replace the lost water with something that will bind the fibers together. The earliest practice, at least 7,000 years old, was to pound grease into the skin. In about 400 BC the Egyptians began to use vegetable extracts containing tannic acid, a method adopted in medieval Europe. Chemical tanning using mineral salts was introduced in the late 19th century.

Leatherstocking Tales, The five US novels by James Fenimore Cooper, describing the ideal frontiersman, Natty Bumppo, also known as Leatherstocking or the Deerslayer: *The Pioneers* 1823, *The Last of the Mohicans* 1826, *The Prairie* 1827, *The Pathfinder* 1840, and *The Deerslayer* 1841.

The novels follow (though not in order of publication) Natty's life from his youth before the American Revolution to his death after the Louisiana Purchase.

Leaves of Grass collection of poems by US writer Walt Whitman, published anonymously in 1855 and augmented through many editions up to 1892. With its open and "barbaric yawp" meter, the book influenced subsequent US verse.

Leavitt Henrietta Swan 1868–1921. US astronomer who in 1912 discovered the period–luminosity law that links the brightness of a ◊Cepheid variable star to its period of variation. This law allows astronomers to use Cepheid variables as "standard candles" for measuring distances in space. She joined the Harvard College Observatory 1902.

Lebanon country in W Asia, bordered N and E by Syria, S by Israel, and W by the Mediterranean

government Under the 1926 constitution, amended 1927, 1929, 1943, 1947, and 1989, legislative power is held by the national assembly, whose 99 members are elected by universal adult suffrage, through a system of proportional representation, in order to give a fair reflection of all the country's religious groups. The assembly serves a four-year term. The president is elected by the assembly for a six-year term and appoints a prime minister and cabinet who are collectively responsible to the assembly. Elections to the assembly were last held 1972. Civil war prevented elections thereafter, and its life has been extended at least six times until 1988. There are several political parties but membership of the national assembly is more easily recognized in terms of religious groupings. Under the agreement 1943 the president is Christian, the prime minister is Sunni Muslim, and the speaker of the national assembly is Shi'ite Muslim. In 1989 the legislators met in Taif, Saudi Arabia, and created a constitution that reflects the Muslim majority that has emerged since 1947. The powers of the president have been much diminished, although the post is still reserved for a Maronite Christian.

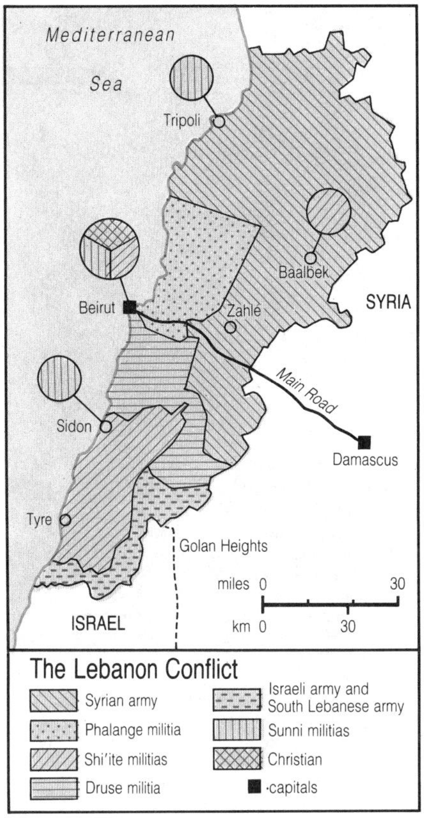
Mediterranean
Sea
Tripoli
Baalbek
Beirut
Zahle
SYRIA
Main Road
Sidon
Damascus
Tyre
Golan Heights
miles 0
30
km 0
30
ISRAEL
Syrian army
Israeli army and South Lebanese army
Phalange militia
Sunni militias
Shi'ite militias
Christian
Druse militia
·capitals

The Lebanon Conflict

history The area now known as Lebanon was once occupied by ◊Phoenicia, an empire that flourished from the 5th century BC–1st century AD, when it came under Roman rule. Christianity was introduced during the Roman occupation, and Islam arrived with the Arabs 635. Lebanon was part of the Turkish Ottoman Empire from the 16th century, until administered by France under a League of Nations mandate 1920–41. It was declared independent 1941, became a republic 1943, and achieved full autonomy 1944.

Lebanon has a wide variety of religions, including Christianity and many Islamic sects. For many years these coexisted peacefully, giving Lebanon a stability that enabled it, until the mid-1970s, to be a commercial and financial center. Beirut's thriving business district was largely destroyed 1975–76, and Lebanon's role as an international trader has been greatly diminished.

After the establishment of Israel 1948, thousands of Palestinian refugees fled to Lebanon, and the ◊Palestine Liberation Organization (PLO) was founded in Beirut 1964 (its headquarters moved to Tunis 1982). The PLO presence in Lebanon has been the main reason for Israeli invasions and much of the subsequent civil strife. Fighting has been largely between left-wing Muslims, led by Kamul Joumblatt of the Progressive Socialist Party, and conservative Christian groups, mainly members of the Phalangist Party. There have also been differences between pro-Iranian traditional Muslims, such as the ◊Shi'ites, and Syrian-backed deviationist Muslims, such as the ◊Druse.

In 1975 the fighting developed into full-scale civil war. A ceasefire was agreed 1976, but fighting began again 1978, when Israeli forces invaded Lebanon in search of PLO guerrillas. The United Nations secured Israel's agreement to a withdrawal and set up an international peacekeeping force, but to little avail. In 1979 Maj Saad Haddad,

Lebanon
Republic of
(al-Jumhouria al-Lubnaniya)

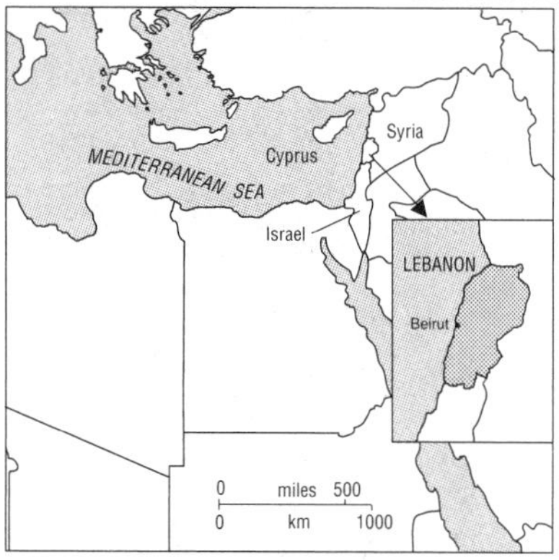
Syria
MEDITERRANEAN SEA
Cyprus
Israel
LEBANON
Beirut
0 miles 500
0 km 1000

area 4,034 sq mi/10,452 sq km
capital (and port) Beirut
cities ports Tripoli, Tyre, Sidon
physical narrow coastal plain; Bekka valley N–S between Lebanon and Antilebanon mountain ranges
features few of the cedars of Lebanon remain; Mount Hermon; Chouf Mountains; archeological sites at Baalbeck, Byblos, Tyre; until the civil war, the financial center of the Middle East
head of state Elias Hrawi from 1989
head of government Umar Karami from 1990
political system emergent democratic republic
political parties Phalangist Party, Christian, radical, right-wing; Progressive Socialist Party (PSP), Druze, moderate, Socialist; National Liberal Party (NLP), Maronite, center-left; Parliamentary Democratic Front, Sunni Muslim, centrist; Lebanese Communist Party (PCL), nationalist, communist
exports citrus and other fruit, vegetables; industrial products to Arab neighbors
currency Lebanese pound
population (1990 est) 3,340,000 (Lebanese 82%, Palestinian 9%, Armenian 5%); growth rate −0.1% p.a.
life expectancy men 65, women 70 (1989)
language Arabic, French (both official); Armenian, English
religion Muslim 57% (Shi'ite 33%, Sunni 24%), Christian (Maronite and Orthodox) 40%, Druse 3%
literacy 75% (1989)
GNP $1.8 bn; $690 per head (1986)

chronology
1920–41 Administered under French mandate.
1944 Independence achieved.
1948–49 Lebanon joined first Arab war against Israel. Palestinian refugees settled in the south.
1964 Palestine Liberation Organization (PLO) founded in Beirut.
1967 More Palestinian refugees settled in Lebanon.
1970 PLO expelled from Jordan; established headquarters in Lebanon.
1975 Outbreak of civil war between Christians and Muslims.
1976 Ceasefire agreed; Syrian-dominated Arab deterrent force formed to keep the peace but considered by Christians as an occupying force.
1978 Israel invaded S Lebanon in search of PLO fighters. International peacekeeping force established. Fighting broke out again.
1979 Part of S Lebanon declared an "independent free Lebanon."
1982 Bachir Gemayel became president but was assassinated before he could assume office; succeeded by his brother Amin Gemayel. Israel invaded Lebanon. Palestinians withdrew from Beirut under supervision of international peacekeeping force.
1983 Agreement reached for the withdrawal of Syrian and Israeli troops but abrogated under Syrian pressure.
1984 Most of international peacekeeping force withdrawn. Muslim militia took control of W Beirut.
1985 Lebanon in chaos; many foreigners taken hostage.
1987 Syrian troops sent into Beirut.
1988 Agreement on a Christian successor to Gemayel failed; he established a military government; Selim al-Hoss set up rival government; threat of partition hung over the country.
1989 Christian leader, Gen Aoun declared "war of liberation" against Syrian occupation; Saudis and Arab League sponsored talks resulting in new constitution recognizing Muslim majority; Muawad named president, assassinated after 17 days in office; Elias Hrawi named successor; Aoun occupied presidential palace, rejected constitution; Amal battled Party of God.
1990 Irish hostage Brian Keenan released. Gen Aoun surrendered and legitimate government restored, with Umar Karami as prime minister.
1991 Government extended control to the whole country. Treaty of cooperation with Syria signed. US and British hostages released.

a right-wing Lebanese army officer, with Israeli encouragement, declared an area of about 700 sq mi/1,800 sq km in S Lebanon an "independent free Lebanon," and the following year Christian Phalangist soldiers took over an area N of Beirut. Throughout this turmoil the Lebanese government was virtually powerless. In 1982 Bachir Gemayel, youngest son of Pierre Gemayel the founder of the Phalangist Party, became president. He was assassinated before he could assume office and his brother Amin took his place.

In 1983, after exhaustive talks between Lebanon and Israel, under US auspices, an agreement declared an end to hostilities and called for the withdrawal of all foreign forces from the country within three months. Syria refused to recognize the agreement and left about 40,000 troops, with about 7,000 PLO fighters, in N Lebanon. Israel responded by refusing to take its forces from the south. Meanwhile, a full-scale war began between Phalangist and Druse soldiers in the Chouf mountains, ending in a Christian defeat and the creation of a Druse-controlled mini-state. The multinational force was drawn gradually but unwillingly into the conflict until it was withdrawn in the spring of 1984. Attempts were made 1985 and 1986 to end the civil war but rifts within both Muslim and Christian groups have so far prevented it. Meanwhile Lebanon, and particularly Beirut, has seen its infrastructure and earlier prosperity virtually destroyed as it continues to be a battlefield for the rival factions.

The civil war in Beirut long pitted the E Beirut "administration" of General Michel Aoun, backed by Christian army units and Lebanese militia forces (although 30% of them are Muslim), against the W Beirut "administration" (Muslim) of Premier Salim al-Hoss, supported by Syrian army and Muslim militia allies, including Walid Jumblatt's Progressive Socialist Party (Druse).

In May 1989 the Arab League secured agreement to a ceasefire between Christians and Muslims and in Sept a peace plan was agreed by all except General Aoun, who dissolved the national assembly. The assembly ignored him and in Nov elected the Maronite-Christian René Muawad as president instead of Aoun, but within days he was killed by a car bomb. Elias Hrawi was made his successor and he immediately confirmed the acting prime minister, Salim al-Hoss, in that post. Despite being replaced as army Commander in Chief, Aoun continued to defy the constituted government.

In 1990 it was estimated that 18 Westerners, including eight Americans, were held hostage in Lebanon by pro-Iranian Shi'ite Muslim groups. In Aug the Irish hostage Brian Keenan was released. In Oct government troops, backed by Syria, stormed the presidential palace occupied by General Aoun, who surrendered and took refuge in the French embassy. By Nov the government of President Elias Hrawi and Prime Minister Salim al-Hoss had regained control of Beirut. Aoun left the county for exile in France in Aug 1991.

Lebanon city in SE Pennsylvania, NE of Harrisburg, seat of Lebanon County. Industries include iron and steel products, textiles, clothing, and chemicals; population (1990) 24,800.

Lebda former name of ◊Homs, a city in Syria near the river Orontes.

Lebedev Peter Nikolaievich 1866–1912. Russian physicist. He proved by experiment, and then measured, the minute pressure that light exerts upon a physical body.

Lebedev was professor at Moscow university 1892–1911, and his work confirmed ◊Maxwell's theoretical determination.

Lebensraum (German "living space") theory developed by Hitler for the expansion of Germany into E Europe, and in the 1930s used by the Nazis to justify their annexation of neighboring states on the grounds that Germany was overpopulated.

Leblanc Nicolas 1742–1806. French chemist who in 1790 developed a process for making soda ash (sodium carbonate, Na_2CO_3) from common salt (sodium chloride, NaCl).

In the Leblanc process, salt was first converted into sodium sulfate by the action of sulfuric acid, which was then roasted with chalk or limestone (calcium carbonate) and coal to produce a mixture of sodium carbonate and sulfide. The carbonate was leached out with water and the solution crystallized. Leblanc devised this method of producing soda ash (for use in making glass, paper, soap, and various other chemicals) to win a prize offered in 1775 by the French Academy of Sciences, but the Revolutionary government granted him only a patent (1791), which they seized along with his factory three years later. A broken man, Leblanc committed suicide.

Lebowa black homeland in Transvaal province, South Africa; it achieved self-governing status 1972; population (1985) 1,836,000.

Lebrun Albert 1871–1950. French politician. He became president of the senate in 1931 and in 1932 was chosen as president of the republic. In 1940 he handed his powers over to Marshal Pétain.

Le Brun Charles 1619–1690. French artist, painter to Louis XIV from 1662. In 1663 he became director of the French Academy and of the Gobelin factory, which produced art, tapestries, and furnishings for the new palace of Versailles.

In the 1640s he studied under the painter Poussin in Rome. Returning to Paris in 1646, he worked on large decorative schemes including the *Galerie des glaces* (Hall of Mirrors) at Versailles. He also painted portraits.

Le Carré John. Pseudonym of David John Cornwell 1931– . English writer of thrillers. His low-key realistic accounts of complex espionage include *The Spy Who Came in from the Cold* 1963, *Tinker Tailor Soldier Spy* 1974, *Smiley's People* 1980, and *The Russia House* 1989. He was a member of the Foreign Service 1960–64.

Le Chatelier's principle or ***Le Chatelier-Braun principle*** in science, the principle that if a change in conditions is imposed on a system in equilibrium, the system will react to counteract that change and restore the equilibrium.

First stated 1884 by French chemist Henri le Chatelier (1850–1936), it has been found to apply widely outside the field of chemistry.

lecithin a type of lipid (fat), containing nitrogen and

Le Carré English thriller writer John Le Carré spent four years in the British Foreign Service and used his experiences in The Spy Who Came in from the Cold *1963 and other novels of international espionage.*

phosphorus, that forms a vital part of the cell membranes of plant and animal cells. The name is from the Greek *lekithos* "egg yolk," eggs being a major source of lecithin.

Leclair Jean-Marie 1697–1764. French violinist and composer. Originally a dancer and ballet-master, he composed ballet music, an opera (*Scilla et Glaucus*), and violin concertos.

Leclanché Georges 1839–1882. French engineer. In 1866 he invented a primary electrical ◊cell, the Leclanché cell, which is still the basis of most dry batteries.

A Leclanché cell consists of a carbon rod (the ◊anode) inserted into a mixture of powdered carbon and manganese dioxide contained in a porous pot, which sits in a glass jar containing an ◊electrolyte (conducting medium) of ammonium chloride solution, into which a zinc ◊cathode is inserted. The cell produces a continuous current, the carbon mixture acting as a depolarizer; that is, it prevents hydrogen bubbles from forming on the anode and increasing resistance. In a dry battery, the electrolyte is made in the form of a paste with starch.

Leconte de Lisle Charles Marie René 1818–1894. French poet. He was born on Réunion, settled in Paris 1846, and headed the anti-Romantic group Les ◊Parnassiens 1866–76. His work drew inspiration from the ancient world, as in *Poèmes antiques/Antique Poems* 1852, *Poèmes barbares/ Barbaric Poems* 1862, and *Poèmes tragiques/ Tragic Poems* 1884.

Le Corbusier Assumed name of Charles-Édouard Jeanneret 1887–1965. Swiss architect. His functionalist approach to town and urban planning in industrial society was based on the interrelationship between machine forms and the techniques of modern architecture. His concept, *La Ville Radieuse*, developed in Marseille, France (1945–50) and Chandigarh, India, placed buildings and open spaces with related functions in a circular formation, with buildings based on standard-sized units mathematically calculated according to the proportions of the human figure (see ◊Fibonacci, ◊golden section).

He was originally a painter and engraver, but turned his attention to the problems of contemporary industrial society. His books *Vers une architecture* 1923 and *Le Modulor* 1948 have had worldwide significance for town planning and building design.

Lecouvreur Adrienne 1692–1730. French actress. She performed at the ◊Comédie Française national theater, where she first appeared 1717. Her many admirers included the philosopher Voltaire and the army officer Maurice de Saxe; a rival mistress of the latter, the Duchesse de Bouillon, is thought to have poisoned her.

LED abbreviation for ◊light-emitting diode.

Leda in Greek mythology, wife of Tyndareus, and mother of Clytemnestra. Zeus, who came to her as a swan, was the father of her children Helen of Troy, and the twins Castor and Pollux.

Ledbetter Huddie, "Leadbelly" c. 1888–1949. US musician. Better known by his nickname, he was born in Mooringsport, Louisiana, and spent his early years as a farmhand. Drawn to music at an early age, he traveled throughout the South and became well known for his blues guitar playing. In 1934 he was "discovered" by visiting folklorists John and Alan Lomax, who helped him begin a professional concert and recording career. Ledbetter was an important source of inspiration for the urban folk movement of the 1950s. His rendition of "Good Night, Irene" became a folk classic.

Lederberg Joshua 1925– . US geneticist who showed that bacteria can reproduce sexually, combining genetic material so that offspring possess characteristics of both parent organisms.

Lederberg is considered a pioneer of genetic engineering, a science that relies on the possibility of artificially shuffling genes from cell to cell. He realized that bacteriophages, viruses which invade bacteria, can transfer genes from one bacterium to another, a discovery that led to the deliberate insertion by scientists of foreign genes into bacterial cells.

Le Duc Tho 1911–1990. North Vietnamese diplomat who was joint winner (with US Secretary of State Kissinger) of the Nobel Peace Prize 1973 for his part in the negotiations to end the Vietnam War. He indefinitely postponed receiving the award.

Ledyard John 1751–1789. American explorer and adventurer. Born in Groton, Connecticut, Ledyard briefly attended Dartmouth but left school for a life at sea. In 1776, in London, he signed on with Captain Cook for a voyage around the Cape of Good Hope. As a British marine, Ledyard was sent to Long Island during the American Revolution, but, refusing to fight against his own countrymen, he deserted in 1782. Always scheming, he devised a plan for opening the fur trade with China but could not raise the necessary capital. After an ill-fated journey through Siberia, he died in Cairo on his way to find the source of the Niger river.

Lee Bruce. Adopted name of Lee Yuen Kam 1941–1973. US "Chinese Western" film actor, an expert in ◊kung fu, who popularized the oriental martial arts in the West with pictures made in Hong Kong, such as *Fists of Fury* 1972 and *Enter the Dragon* 1973, his last film.

Lee Christopher 1922– . English film actor whose tall, gaunt figure was memorable in the title role of *Dracula* 1958 and its sequels. He has not lost his sinister image in subsequent Hollywood productions. His other films include *Hamlet* 1948, *The Mummy* 1959, *Julius Caesar* 1970, and *The Man with the Golden Gun* 1974.

Lee Gyspy Rose 1914–1970. US entertainer. In her teenage years Lee learned the art of the striptease in New York and began performing as an "elegant lady" in burlesque reviews. Unique in her intelligence and friendship with leading literary figures of her time, Lee was herself a published author, writing magazine articles and, after her retirement from stripping, two popular mystery novels, *The G-String Murders* 1941 and *Mother Finds a Body* 1942. Later appearing on Broadway and television, she became a national celebrity. Her autobiography, *Gypsy: A Memoir* 1957, was adapted for stage 1959 and film 1962.

Born Rose Louise Hovick in Seattle, Washington, she began, at about age four, performing song and dance routines with her sister, actress June Havoc.

Lee Confederate general Robert E Lee, remembered for his daring tactics and tenacious defense and for epitomizing the Southern gentleman.

Lee Henry 1756–1818. American military and political leader. Born in Leesylvania, Virginia, Lee was educated at Princeton and served in the cavalry in the American Revolution. Rising to the rank of major, he won the nickname "Light-Horse Harry" for his lightning attacks. After the war, he entered politics, serving in the Continental Congress 1785–88 and as governor of Virginia 1792–95.

He was a close friend of George Washington and helped suppress the Whiskey Rebellion 1794. Lee was a member of the US House of Representatives 1799–1801 and eventually lost his fortune through bad investments. He was the father of Robert E ◊Lee.

Lee Robert E(dward) 1807–1870. US military leader, Confederate commander in the American ◊Civil War, and military strategist. In 1859 he suppressed John ◊Brown's raid on Harper's Ferry. Lee had freed his own slaves long before the war began, and he was opposed to secession, however his devotion to his native Virginia led him to join the Confederacy.

At the outbreak of war he became military adviser to Jefferson ◊Davis, president of the Confederacy, and in 1862 commander of the Army of Northern Virginia. Lee actually had been offered command of the Union armies, but he resigned his commission to return to Virginia. During 1862–63 he made several raids into Northern territory but after his defeat at Gettysburg was compelled to take the defensive; he surrendered 1865 at Appomattox.

Lee graduated from West Point and distinguished himself in the Mexican War 1846–48. In 1861 he joined the army of the Confederacy of Southern states; in 1862 he received the command of the Army of Northern Virginia and won the Seven Days' Battle defending Richmond, Virginia, the Confederate capital, against General McClellan's Union forces. In 1863 Lee won victories at Fredericksburg and Chancellorsville, both in Virginia, and in 1864 at Cold Harbor, Virginia, but was besieged in Petersburg, Virginia, June 1864–April 1865. He surrendered to General ◊Grant on April 9, 1865, at Appomattox courthouse. Following the war he was paroled and served as president of Washington College (now Washington and Lee University). His home had been seized by Union forces and now is part of Arlington National Cemetery.

Lee and Yang Lee Tsung Dao (1926–) and Yang Chen Ning (1922–) Chinese physicists who studied how parity operates at the nuclear level. They found no proof for the claim, made by ◊Wigner, that nuclear processes were indis-

***Lee Kuan Yew** Singapore politician and premier Lee Kuan Yew, 1972.*

tinguishable from their mirror images, and that elementary particles made no distinction between left and right. In 1956 they predicted that parity was not conserved in weak interactions. They shared a Nobel Prize 1957.

leech annelid worm forming the class Hirudinea. Leeches inhabit fresh water, and in tropical countries infest damp forests. As bloodsucking animals they are injurious to people and animals, to whom they attach themselves by means of a strong mouth adapted to sucking.

Formerly, the medicinal leech *Hirudo medicinalis* was used extensively for "bleeding" for a variety of ills. It still has some medicinal use and is cultivated as the source of the anticoagulant hirudin.

Leeds city in W Yorkshire, England, on the river Aire; population (1984) 712,200. Industries include engineering, printing, chemicals, glass, and woolens.

Notable buildings include the Town Hall designed by Cuthbert Brodrick, Leeds University 1904, the Art Gallery 1844, Temple Newsam (birthplace of Henry Darnley in 1545, now a museum), and the Cistercian Abbey of Kirkstall 1147. It is a center of communications where road, rail, and canal (to Liverpool and Goole) meet. Opera North is based here, and the Leeds International Pianoforte Competition is held here every three years.

leek onionlike plant of the genus *Allium* of the lily family Liliaceae. The cultivated leek is a variety of the wild *A. ampeloprasum* of the Mediterranean area and Atlantic islands. The lower leaf parts form the bulb, which is eaten as a vegetable.

Lee Kuan Yew 1923– . Singapore politician, prime minister 1959–1990. Lee founded the anti-communist Socialist People's Action Party 1954 and entered the Singapore legislative assembly 1955. He was elected the country's first prime minister 1959, and took Singapore out of the Malaysian federation 1965. He retired 1990 but continued to exert considerable power.

He was trained as a lawyer in London. His son, Brig-Gen Lee Hsien Loong (1952–), already deputy prime minister, is viewed as a possible successor.

Lee Teng-hui 1923– . Taiwanese right-wing politician, vice-president 1984–88, president and Kuomintang (see ◊Guomindang) party leader from 1988. Lee, the country's first island-born leader, is viewed as a reforming technocrat.

Born in Tamsui, Taiwan, Lee taught for two decades as professor of economics at the National Taiwan University before becoming mayor of Taipei 1979. A member of the Kuomintang party and a protégé of Chiang Ching-kuo, he became vice-president of Taiwan 1984 and succeeded to both the state presidency and Kuomintang leadership on Chiang's death Jan 1988. He has significantly accelerated the pace of liberalization and Taiwanization in the political sphere.

Leeuwarden city in the Netherlands, on the Ee river; population (1987) 85,200. It is the capital of Friesland province. A marketing center, it also makes gold and silver ware. After the draining of the Middelzee fenlands, the town changed from being a port to an agricultural market town. Notable buildings include the palace of the stadholders of Friesland and the church of St Jacob.

Leeuwenhoek Anton van 1632–1723. Dutch pioneer of microscopic research. He ground his own lenses, some of which magnified up to 200 times. With these he was able to see individual red blood cells, sperm, and bacteria, achievements not repeated for more than a century.

Leeward Islands (1) group of islands, part of the ◊Society Islands, in ◊French Polynesia, S Pacific; (2) general term for the northern half of the Lesser ◊Antilles in the West Indies; (3) former British colony in the West Indies (1871–1956) comprising Antigua, Montserrat, St Christopher/St Kitts-Nevis, Anguilla, and the Virgin Islands.

Lefebvre Marcel 1905– . French Catholic priest in open conflict with the Roman Catholic Church. In 1976, he was suspended by Pope Paul VI for the unauthorized ordination of priests at his Swiss headquarters. He continued and in June 1988 he was excommunicated by Pope John Paul II, in the first formal schism within the church since 1870.

Ordained in 1929, Lefebvre was a missionary and an archbishop in West Africa until 1962. He opposed the liberalizing reforms of the Second Vatican Council 1962–65 and formed the "Priestly Cofraternity of Pius X."

left-handedness in humans, using the left hand more skillfully and in preference to the right hand for most actions. It occurs in about 9% of the population, predominantly males. It is caused by dominance of the right side of the brain.

left-hand rule rule used to recall which way a wire connected to a source of electricity will move when near a magnet. The thumb and first two fingers of the left hand are placed at right angles to each other. If the first finger is pointed in the direction of the magnetic field (from the N to the S pole of the magnet) and the second finger is pointed in the direction of the electric current (from the positive terminal to the negative terminal of the electric source), the thumb will point in the direction in which the wire will move.

left wing in politics, the Socialist parties. The term originated in the French National Assembly 1789, where the nobles sat in the place of honor to the right of the president, and the commons sat to the left. It is also usual to speak of the right, left, and center, when referring to the different elements composing a single party.

legacy in law, a gift of personal property made by a testator in a ◊will and transferred on the testator's death to the legatee. Specific legacies are definite named objects; a general legacy is a sum of money or item not specially identified; a residuary legacy is all the remainder of the deceased's personal estate after debts have been paid and the other legacies have been distributed.

legal tender currency that must be accepted in payment of debt. Checks and money orders are not included. In most countries, limits are set on the amount of coinage, particularly of small denominations, that must legally be accepted.

legend (Latin *legere* "to read") a traditional or undocumented story about famous people. The term was originally applied to the books of readings designed for use in Divine Service, and afterward extended to the stories of saints read in monasteries.

A collection of such stories was the 13th-century *Legenda Aurea* by Jacobus de Voragine.

Léger Fernand 1881–1955. French painter, associated with ◊Cubism. From around 1909 he evolved a characteristic style, composing abstract and semiabstract works with cylindrical forms, reducing the human figure to constructions of pure shape.

Mechanical forms are constant themes in his work, including his designs for the Swedish Ballet 1921–22, murals, and the abstract film *Ballet mécanique/Mechanical Ballet.*

Leghorn former English name for the Italian port ◊Livorno.

Legionnaire's disease pneumonialike disease, so called because it was first identified when it broke out at a convention of the American Legion in Philadelphia 1976.

It is caused by the bacterium *Legionella pneumophila*, which breeds in warm water (for example, in the cooling towers of air-conditioning systems). It is spread in minute water droplets, which may be inhaled.

legislature assembly of elected representatives empowered to enact statute law and levy taxes. Some are bicameral (and some are called diets); for example, the US Congress has two houses, the House of Represenatives and the Senate, based on the British model (see ◊parliament). Others are unicameral, such as Israel's Knesset.

Legitimist the party in France that continued to support the claims of the house of ◊Bourbon after the revolution of 1830. When the direct line became extinct 1883, the majority of the party transferred their allegiance to the house of Orléans.

Legnano, Battle of defeat of Holy Roman emperor Frederick I Barbarossa by members of the Lombard League 1176 at Legnano, NW of Milan. It was a major setback to the emperor's plans for imperial domination over Italy and showed for the first time the power of infantry against feudal cavalry.

Le Guin Ursula K(roeber) 1929– . US writer of science fiction and fantasy. Her novels include *The Left Hand of Darkness* 1969, which questions sex roles; the *Earthsea* trilogy 1968–72; *The Dispossessed* 1974, which compares an anarchist and a capitalist society; *Orsinian Tales* 1976; and *Always Coming Home* 1985.

legume plant of the family Leguminosae (pea family), which has a pod containing dry fruits. Legumes are important in agriculture because of their specialized roots, used to fix nitrogen in the soil.

Leh capital of Ladakh region, E Kashmir, India, situated E of the Indus, 150 mi/240 km E of Srinagar. Leh is the nearest supply base to the Indian army outpost on the Siachen Glacier.

Lehár Franz 1870–1948. Hungarian composer. He wrote many operettas, among them *The Merry Widow* 1905, *The Count of Luxembourg* 1909, *Gypsy Love* 1910, and *The Land of Smiles* 1929. He also composed songs, marches, and a violin concerto.

Le Havre industrial port (engineering, chemicals, oil refining) in Normandy, NW France, on the river Seine; population (1982) 255,000. It is the largest port in Europe, and has transatlantic passenger links.

Lehman Herbert Henry 1878–1963. US political leader. In 1932 he became governor of New York, and his subsequent support of F D Roosevelt's policies caused his own administration to be called the "Little New Deal." In 1942 Lehman was appointed director of the federal Office of Foreign Relief and Rehabilitation. He served in the US Senate 1949–57.

Born in New York and educated at Williams College, Lehman joined his family's banking business and served in the army during World War I. Later entering politics, he was an adviser to Al Smith and was elected New York's lieutenant governor 1928.

Lehmann Lotte 1888–1976. German soprano. She excelled in Wagnerian operas and was an outstanding Marschallin in Richard ◊Strauss's *Der Rosenkavalier*.

Leibniz Gottfried Wilhelm 1646–1716. German mathematician and philosopher. Independently of, but concurrently with, the British scientist Isaac Newton he developed ◊calculus. In his metaphysical works, such as *The Monadology* 1714, he argued that everything consisted of innumerable units, monads, whose individual properties determined each thing's past, present, and future.

Monads, although independent of each other, interacted predictably; this meant that Christian faith and scientific reason need not be in conflict and that "this is the best of all possible worlds." His optimism is satirized in Voltaire's *Candide*.

Leicester industrial city (food processing, hosiery, footwear, engineering, electronics, printing, plastics) and administrative headquarters of Leicestershire, England, on the river Soar; population (1983) 282,300.

Leicester Robert Dudley, Earl of c. 1532–1588. English courtier. Son of the Duke of Northumberland, he was created earl of Leicester 1564. Queen Elizabeth I gave him command of the army sent to the Netherlands 1585–87 and of the forces prepared to resist the threat of Spanish invasion 1588.

His good looks attracted Queen Elizabeth, who made him Master of the Horse 1558 and a privy councillor 1559. But his poor performance in the army led to recall and the end of any chance of marrying the queen. He was a staunch supporter of the Protestant cause and retained Elizabeth's favor until his death.

Leicestershire county in central England
area 984 sq mi/2,550 sq km
cities Leicester (administrative headquarters), Loughborough, Melton Mowbray, Market Harborough
features Rutland district (formerly England's smallest county, with Oakham as its county town); Rutland Water, one of Europe's largest reservoirs; Charnwood Forest; Vale of Belvoir (under which are large coal deposits)
products horses, cattle, sheep, dairy products, coal
population (1987) 879,000
famous people C P Snow.

Leichhardt Friedrich 1813–1848. Prussian-born Australian explorer. In 1843, he walked 600 mi/965 km from Sydney to Moreton Bay, Queensland, and in 1844 walked from Brisbane to Arnhem Land. He disappeared during a further expedition from Queensland 1848.

Leiden or ***Leyden*** city in South Holland province, the Netherlands; population (1988) 183,000. Industries include textiles and cigars. It has been a printing center since 1580, with a university established 1575. It is linked by canal to Haarlem, Amsterdam, and Rotterdam. The painters Rembrandt and Jan Steen were born here.

Leif Ericsson see ◇Ericsson, Leif.

Leigh Vivien. Adopted name of Vivian Mary Hartley 1913–1967. English actress, born in Darjeeling, India. She appeared on the stage in London and New York and won Academy Awards for her performances as Scarlett O'Hara in *Gone With the Wind* 1939 and as Blanche du Bois in *A Streetcar Named Desire* 1951. She was married to Laurence Olivier 1940–60 and starred with him in the plays *Romeo and Juliet* 1940 and *Antony and Cleopatra* 1951, as well as in films such as *That Hamilton Women* 1941. She continued acting into the 1960s, until illness ended her career.

Leigh-Mallory Trafford 1892–1944. British air chief marshal in World War II. He took part in the Battle of Britain and was Commander in Chief of Allied air forces during the invasion of France.

Leinster SE province of the Republic of Ireland, comprising the counties of Carlow, Dublin, Kildare, Kilkenny, Laois, Longford, Louth, Meath, Offaly, Westmeath, Wexford, and Wicklow; area 7,577 sq mi/19,630 sq km; capital Dublin; population (1986) 1,850,000.

Leipzig capital of Leipzig county, Federal Republic of Germany, 90 mi/145 km SW of Berlin; population (1986) 552,000. Products include furs, leather goods, cloth, glass, automobiles, and musical instruments. The county of Leipzig has an area of 1,918 sq mi/4,970 sq km and a population of 1,374,000.

leishmaniasis any of several parasitic diseases caused by microscopic protozoans of the genus *Leishmania*, identified by William Leishman (1865–1926), and transmitted by sandflies. Either localized infection or dangerous fever can be a symptom. They are prevalent in NE Africa and S Asia.

Kala-azar, characterized by an enlarged spleen and liver, fever, and anemia, is an example.

Leisler Jacob 1640–1691. Public figure in colonial New York. Born in Frankfurt, Germany, Leisler came to New Amsterdam as a mercenary for the Dutch West India Company 1660. He became a successful merchant when the colony passed to English rule and was one of the leaders of a local party that took advantage of the political instability caused by England's Glorious Revolution of 1688. As an officer in the militia, Leisler ousted the royal authorities and assumed command of New York in the name of William and Mary. Deposed in 1691 by troops dispatched from England, Leisler was tried and hanged for treason.

Leitrim county in Connacht province, Republic of Ireland, bounded on the NW by Donegal Bay
area 591 sq mi/1,530 sq km
county town Carrick-on-Shannon
features rivers: Shannon, Bonet, Drowes and Duff
products potatoes, cattle, linen, woolens, pottery, coal, iron, lead
population (1986) 27,000.

lek in biology, a closely spaced set of very small ◇territories each occupied by a single male during the mating season. Leks are found in the mating systems of several ground-dwelling birds (such as grouse) and a few antelopes.

The lek is a traditional site where both males and females congregate during the breeding season. The males display to passing females in the hope of attracting them to mate. Once mated, the females go elsewhere to lay their eggs or to complete gestation.

Lely Peter. Adopted name of Pieter van der Faes 1618–1680. Dutch painter, active in England from 1641, who painted fashionable portraits in Baroque style. His subjects included Charles I, Cromwell, and Charles II.

He painted a series of admirals, *Flagmen* (National Maritime Museum, Greenwich), and one of *The Windsor Beauties* (Hampton Court, Richmond), fashionable women of Charles II's court.

Lemaître Georges Edouard 1894–1966. Belgian cosmologist who proposed the ◇Big Bang theory of the origin of the universe 1927. Lemaître predicted that the entire universe was expanding, which ◇Hubble confirmed, and suggested that the expansion had been started by an initial explosion, the Big Bang, a theory that is now generally accepted.

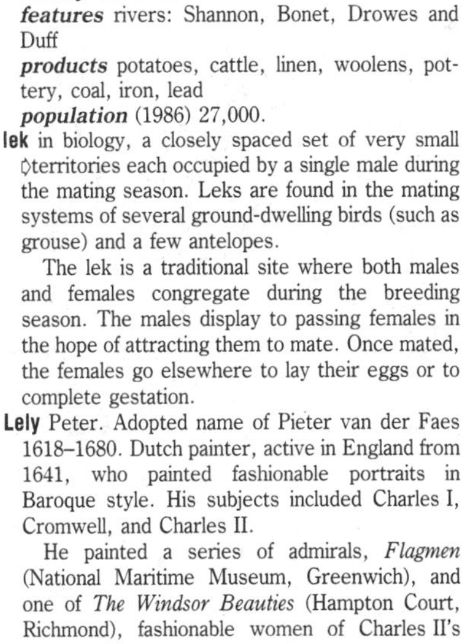

Leigh *English actress Vivien Leigh won an Academy Award for the role of Scarlett O'Hara in the Hollywood epic* Gone With the Wind *1939. She and Laurence Olivier were married in 1940 amid a blaze of publicity.*

lemon

Léman, Lac French name for Lake ◇Geneva.

Le Mans industrial city in and capital of Sarthe, France; population (1982) 150,000, conurbation 191,000. It has an automobile circuit where the annual 24-hour endurance race (established 1923) for sports automobiles and their prototypes is held.

Lemberg German name of ◇Lvov, city in USSR.

lemming small rodent of the family Cricetidae, especially the genus *Lemmus*, comprising four species worldwide in N latitudes. It is about 5 in/12 cm long, with thick brownish fur, small head, and short tail. Periodically, when their population exceeds the available food supply, lemmings undertake mass migrations.

Lemmon Jack (John Uhler III) 1925– . US actor, often cast as the lead in comedy films, such as *Some Like It Hot* 1959 and *The Apartment* 1960 but equally skilled at straight drama, as in *Save The Tiger* 1973 (Academy Award), *The China Syndrome* 1979, and *Dad* 1990.

Lemnos (Greek *Límnos)* Greek island in the N of the Aegean Sea
area 184 sq mi/476 sq km
cities Kastron, Mudros
physical of volcanic origin, rising to 1,411 ft/430 m
products mulberries and other fruit, tobacco, sheep
population (1981) 15,700.

lemon sour fruit of the small, evergreen, semitropical lemon tree *Citrus limon*. It may have originated in NW India, and was introduced into Europe by the Spanish Moors in the 12th or 13th century. It is now grown in Italy, Spain, California, Florida, South Africa, and Australia.

lemon balm perennial herb *Melissa officinalis* of the mint family Labiatae, with lemon-scented leaves. It is widely used in teas, liqueurs, and medicines.

LeMond Greg 1961– . US racing cyclist, the first American to win the Tour de France 1986.

Although his career received a setback in 1987 through injury, he recovered sufficiently to regain his Tour de France title in 1989 by seven seconds, the smallest margin ever. He won it again in 1990. He also won the World Professional Road Race in 1983 and 1989.

lemur prosimian ◇primate of the family Lemuridae, inhabiting Madagascar and the Comoro Islands. There are about 16 species, ranging from mouse-sized to dog-sized animals. They are arboreal animals, and some species are nocturnal. They have long, bushy tails. They feed on fruit, insects, and small animals. Many are threatened with extinction caused by loss of their forest habitat and, in some cases, from hunting.

Lena longest river in Asiatic Russia, 2,730 mi/4,400 km, with numerous tributaries. Its source is near Lake Baikal, and it empties into the Arctic

LeMond US cyclist Greg LeMond in the Tour de France, *1989.*

Ocean through a delta 240 mi/400 km wide. It is ice-covered for half the year.

Le Nain family of French painters, the brothers Antoine (1588–1648), Louis (1593–1648), and Mathieu (1607–1677). They were born in Laon, settled in Paris, and were among the original members of the French Academy in 1648. Attribution of works among them is uncertain. They chiefly painted somber and dignified scenes of peasant life.

Lenard Phillip 1862–1947. German physicist who investigated the ◊photoelectric effect (light causes metals to emit electrons) and cathode rays (the stream of electrodes emitted from the cathode in a vacuum tube). He was awarded the Nobel Prize 1905.

In later life he became obsessed with the idea of producing a purely "Aryan" physics free from the influence of ◊Einstein and other Jewish physicists.

Lendl Ivan 1960– . Czech lawn tennis player. He has won seven Grand Slam singles titles, including the US and French titles three times each. He has won more than $15 million in prize money.

CAREER HIGHLIGHTS

US Championship 1985–87
French Championship 1984, 1986–87
Australian Championship 1989–90
Grand Prix Masters 1982–83, 1986–87.

lemur

fork-marked

***Lendl** Czech tennis star Ivan Lendl had his greatest success after he settled in the US.*

lend-lease an act of the US congress March 1941 that gave the president power to order "any defense article for the government of any country whose defense the president deemed vital to the defense of the US." During World War II, the USA negotiated many lend-lease agreements, most notably with Britain and the Soviet Union.

The aim of such agreements was to ignore trade balances among the participating countries during the war effort and to aid the Allied war effort without fanning isolationist sentiments. Lend-lease was officially stopped Aug 1945, by which time goods and services to the value of $42 billion had been supplied in this way, of which the British Empire had received 65% and the Soviet Union 23%.

Lenin Vladimir Ilyich. Adopted name of Vladimir Ilyich Ulyanov 1870–1924. Russian revolutionary, first leader of the USSR, and communist theoretician. Active in the 1905 Revolution, Lenin had to leave Russia when it failed, settling in Switzerland 1914. He returned to Russia after the February revolution of 1917 (see ◊Russian Revolution). He led the Bolshevik revolution in Nov 1917 and became leader of a Soviet government, concluded peace with Germany, and organized a successful resistance to White Russian (pro-tsarist) uprisings and foreign intervention 1918–20. His modification of traditional Marxist doctrine to fit conditions prevailing in Russia became known as Marxism-Leninism, the basis of communist ideology.

Lenin was born April 22 in Simbirsk (now

***Lenin** Communist political theorist and leader Lenin with his family in 1922.*

renamed Ulyanovsk), on the river Volga, and became a lawyer in St Petersburg (later Leningrad). His brother was executed in 1887 for attempting to assassinate Tsar Alexander III. A Marxist from 1889, Lenin was sent to Siberia for spreading revolutionary propaganda 1895–1900. He then edited the political paper *Iskra* ("The Spark") from abroad, and visited London several times. In *What Is to Be Done?* 1902 he advocated a professional core of Social Democratic Party activists to spearhead the revolution in Russia, a suggestion accepted by the majority (*bolsheviki*) at the London party congress 1903. From Switzerland he attacked Socialist support for World War I as aiding an "imperialist' struggle, and wrote *Imperialism* 1917. After the renewed outbreak of revolution in Feb/March 1917, he returned to Russia in April and called for the transfer of power to the soviets (workers' councils). From the overthrow of the provisional government Nov 1917 until his death, Lenin effectively controlled the Soviet Union, although an assassination attempt 1918 injured his health. He founded the Third (Communist) ◊International in 1919. Communism proving inadequate to put the country on its feet, in 1921 he introduced the private-enterprise ◊New Economic Policy. His embalmed body is in a mausoleum in Red Square, Moscow.

In 1898 he married Nadezhda Konstantinova Krupskaya (1869–1939), who shared his work and wrote *Memories of Lenin.*

Leninakan city in the Armenian republic, USSR, 25 mi/40 km NW of Yerevan; population (1987) 228,000. Industries include textiles and engineering. It was founded 1837 as a fortress called Alexandropol. The city was virtually destroyed by an earthquake 1926 and again 1988.

Leningrad former name of the city of ◊St Petersburg, USSR.

Leninsk-Kuznetsky city in Kemerovo region, S USSR, on the Inya river, 200 mi/320 km SSE of Tomsk; population (1985) 110,000. It is a mining center in the Kuzbas, with a large iron and steel works; coal, iron, manganese, other metals, and precious stones are mined in the area. Formerly Kolchugino, the town was renamed Leninsk-Kuznetsky in 1925.

Lennon John 1940–1980. UK rock singer and songwriter, a former member of the ◊Beatles.

Le Nôtre André 1613–1700. French landscape gardener, creator of the gardens at Versailles and Les Tuileries, Paris.

Lens coal-mining town in Pas-de-Calais *département*, France; population (1982) 38,300, conurbation 327,000. During World War I it was in German occupation and close to the front line Oct 1914–Oct 1918, when the town and its mines were severely damaged. In World War II it was occupied by the Germans, May 1940–Sept 1944, but suffered less physical damage.

lens in optics, a piece of a transparent material such as glass with two polished surfaces—one concave or convex, and the other plane, concave or convex—to modify rays of light. A convex lens brings rays of light together; a concave lens makes the rays diverge. Lenses are essential to glasses, microscopes, telescopes, cameras, and almost all optical instruments.

The image formed by a single lens suffers from several defects or aberrations, notably spherical aberration in which a straight line becomes a curved image, and chromatic aberration in which an image in white light tends to have colored edges. Aberrations are corrected by the use of compound lenses, which are built up from two or more lenses of different refractive index.

lens, gravitational see ◊gravitational lens.

Lent in the Christian church, the 40-day period of fasting that precedes Easter, beginning on Ash Wednesday, but omitting Sundays.

lenticel a small pore on the stems of woody plants or the trunks of trees. Lenticels are means of ◊gas exchange between the stem interior and the

lens

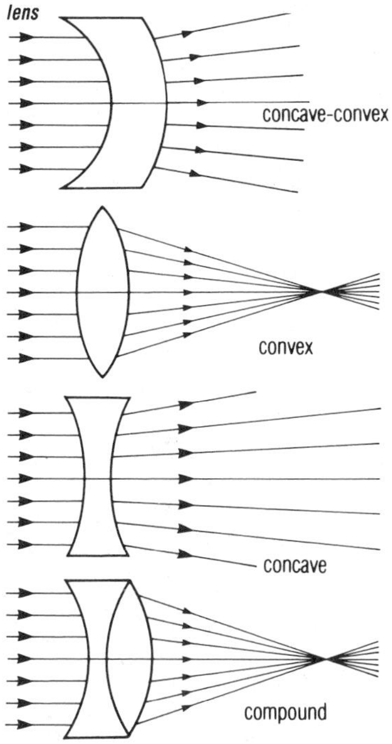
concave-convex
convex
concave
compound

atmosphere. They consist of loosely packed cells with many air spaces in between, and are easily seen on smooth-barked trees such as cherries, where they form horizontal lines on the trunk.

lentil annual Old World plant *Lens culinaris* of the pea family Leguminosae. The plant, which resembles vetch, grows 6–18 in/15–45 cm high and has white, blue, or purplish flowers. The seeds, contained in pods about 0.6 in/1.6 cm long, are widely used as food.

The most common varieties are the grayish French lentil and the red Egyptian lentil.

Lenya Lotte. Adopted name of Karoline Blamauer 1905–1981. Austrian actress and singer. She married Kurt ◊Weill in 1926 and appeared in several of the Brecht-Weill operas, notably *The Threepenny Opera* 1928.

Lenz's law in physics, law stating that the direction of an electromagnetically induced current (generated by moving a magnet near a wire or a wire in a magnetic field) will oppose the motion producing it.

It is named after the German physicist Heinrich Friedrich Lenz (1804–1865), who announced it in 1833.

Leo zodiac constellation in the northern hemisphere between Cancer and Virgo, near Ursa Major, and represented as a lion. The Sun passes through Leo from mid-Aug to mid-Sept. Its brightest star is first-magnitude Regulus (Alpha Leo), a blue-white star 85 light-years away; Regulus is at the base of a cluster of stars called the Sickle. In astrology, the dates for Leo are between about July 23 and Aug 22 (see ◊precession).

Leo III the Isaurian c. 680–740. Byzantine emperor and soldier. He seized the throne 717, successfully defended Constantinople against the Saracens 717–18, and attempted to suppress the use of images in church worship (see ◊iconoclast).

Leo thirteen popes, including:

Leo I St (the Great) c. 390–461. Pope from 440 who helped to establish the Christian liturgy. Leo summoned the Chalcedon Council where his Dogmatical Letter was accepted as the voice of St Peter. Acting as ambassador for the emperor Valentinian III (425–455), Leo saved Rome from devastation by the Huns by buying off their king, Attila.

Leo III c. 750–816. Pope from 795. After the withdrawal of the Byzantine emperors, the popes had become the real rulers of Rome. Leo III was forced to flee because of a conspiracy in Rome and took refuge at the court of ◊Charlemagne. He returned to Rome 799 and crowned Charlemagne emperor on Christmas Day 800, establishing the secular sovereignty of the pope over Rome under the suzereignty of the emperor (who became the Holy Roman emperor).

Leo X Giovanni de Medici 1475–1521. Pope from 1513. The son of Lorenzo the Magnificent of Florence, he was created a cardinal at 13. He bestowed on Henry VIII of England the title of Defender of the Faith. A patron of the arts, he sponsored the rebuilding of St Peter's Church, Rome. He raised funds for this by selling indulgences (remissions of punishment for sin), a sale that led the religious reformer Martin Luther to rebel against papal authority. Leo X condemned Luther in the bull *Exsurge domine* 1520 and excommunicated him 1521.

Leo XIII Gioacchino Pecci 1810–1903. Pope from 1878. After a successful career as a papal diplomat, he established good relations between the papacy and European powers, the US, and Japan. He remained intransigent in negotiations with the Italian government over the status of Rome, insisting that he keep control over part of it.

He was the first pope to emphasize the duty of the church in matters of social justice. His encyclical *Rerum novarum* 1891 pointed out the moral duties of employers toward workers.

Leominster city in N central Massachusetts, on the Nashua River, NE of Worcester. Industries include plastics, paper products, clothing, and chemicals; population (1990) 38,145.

León city in W Nicaragua; population (1985) 101,000. Industries include textiles and food processing. Founded 1524, it was the capital of Nicaragua until 1855.

León city in Castilla-León, Spain; population (1986) 137,000. It was the capital of the kingdom of León from 10th century until 1230, when it was merged with Castile.

Leonard Elmore (John, Jr) 1925– . US author of westerns and thrillers, marked by vivid dialogue, as in *City Primeval* 1980, *La Brava* 1983, *Stick* 1983, *Glitz* 1985, *Freaky Deaky* 1988, and *Get Shorty* 1990.

Born in New Orleans, Leonard received a PhD in English from the University of Detroit and worked for an advertising agency while he churned out westerns for pulp magazines. His *Hombre* 1961 is considered among the top westerns of all time; it became a motion picture 1967. In the late 1960s Leonard changed genre, writing about city life and crime. His other works include *The Bounty Hunters* 1953, *The Big Bounce* 1969, *The Moonshine War* 1969, *Unknown Man No. 89* 1977, *Split Images* 1982, and *Cat Chaser* 1982. Many of his works were made into motion pictures.

Leonard Sugar Ray 1956– . US boxer. In 1988 he became the first man to have won world titles at five officially recognized weights. In 1976 he was Olympic light-welterweight champion; he won his first professional title in 1979 when he beat Wilfred Benitez for the WBC welterweight title. He later won titles at junior-middleweight (WBA version) 1981, middleweight (WBC) 1987, light-heavyweight (WBC) 1988, and super-middleweight (WBC) 1988. In 1989 he drew with Thomas Hearns.

Leonardo da Vinci 1452–1519. Italian painter, sculptor, architect, engineer, and scientist, one of the greatest figures of the Italian Renaissance, active in Florence, Milan, and from 1516 France. As state engineer and court painter to the duke of Milan, he painted the *Last Supper* mural about 1495 (Sta Maria delle Grazie, Milan), and on his return to Florence painted the *Mona Lisa* c. 1503–06 (Louvre, Paris). His notebooks and drawings show an immensely inventive and inquiring mind, studying aspects of the natural world from anatomy to aerodynamics.

Leonardo was born at Vinci in Tuscany and studied under ◊Verrocchio in Florence in the 1470s. His earliest dated work is a sketch of the Tuscan countryside 1473 (Uffizi, Florence); his early works include drawings, portraits, and religious scenes, such as the unfinished *Adoration of the Magi* (Uffizi). About 1482 he went to the court of Lodovico Sforza in Milan. In 1500 he returned to Florence (where he was architect and engineer to Cesare Borgia in 1502), and then to Milan 1506. He went to France 1516 and died at Château Cloux, near Amboise, on the Loire.

Leonardo da Vinci The Virgin and Child with St Anne and St John the Baptist *(mid-1490s) National Gallery, London.*

Apart from portraits, religious themes, and historical paintings, Leonardo's greatest legacies were his notebooks and drawings. He influenced many of his contemporary artists, including Michelangelo, Raphael, and Giorgione.

Leoncavallo Ruggiero 1857–1919. Italian operatic composer, born in Naples. He played in restaurants, composing in his spare time, until the success of *Pagliacci* in 1892. His other operas include *La Bohème* 1897 (contemporary with Puccini's version) and *Zaza* 1900.

León de los Aldamas industrial city (leather goods, footwear) in central Mexico; population (1986) 947,000.

Leone Sergio 1928–1989. Italian film director, responsible for popularizing "spaghetti" Westerns (Westerns made in Italy and Spain, usually with a US leading actor and a European supporting cast and film crew) and making a world star of Clint Eastwood. His films include *A Fistful of Dollars* 1964, *Once upon a Time in the West* 1968, and *Once Upon a Time in America* 1984.

Leonidas died 480 BC. King of Sparta. He was killed while defending the pass of ◊Thermopylae with 300 Spartans, 700 Thespians, and 400 Thebans against a huge Persian army.

Leonov Aleksei Arkhipovich 1934– . Soviet cosmonaut. In 1965 he was the first person to walk in space, from the spacecraft *Voskhod 2*.

Leonov Leonid 1899– . Russian novelist and playwright, author of the novels *The Badgers* 1925 and *The Thief* 1927, and the drama *The Orchards of Polovchansk* 1938.

leopard or ***panther*** cat *Panthera pardus*, found in Africa and Asia. The background color of the coat is golden, and the black spots form rosettes, that differ according to the variety; black panthers are simply a color variation and retain the patterning as a "watered-silk" effect. The leopard is 5–8 ft/1.5–2.5 m long, including the tail, which may measure 3 ft/1 m.

The snow leopard or ounce *P. uncia*, which has irregular rosettes of much larger black spots

leopard

on a light cream or gray background, is a native of mountains in central Asia. The clouded leopard *Neofelis nebulosa* is rather smaller, about 5.8 ft/ 1.75 m overall, with large blotchy markings rather than rosettes, and found in SE Asia. There are seven subspecies, of which six are in danger of extinction, including the Amur leopard and the South Arabian leopard. One subspecies, the Zanzibar leopard, may already be extinct.

Leopardi Giacomo, Count Leopardi 1798–1837. Italian romantic poet. The first collection of his uniquely pessimistic poems, *I Versi/Verses*, appeared in 1824, and was followed by his philosophical *Operette morali/Minor Moral Works* 1827, in prose, and *I Canti/Lyrics* 1831.

Born at Recanati of a noble family, Leopardi wrote many of his finest poems, including his great patriotic odes, before he was 21. Throughout his life he was tormented by ill health, by the consciousness of his deformity (he was hunchbacked), by loneliness and a succession of unhappy love affairs, and by his "cosmic pessimism" and failure to find consolation in any philosophy.

Leopold three kings of Belgium:

Leopold I 1790–1865. King of Belgium from 1831, having been elected to the throne on the creation of an independent Belgium. Through his marriage, when prince of Saxe-Coburg, to Princess Charlotte Augusta, he was the uncle of Queen ◊Victoria of Britain and had considerable influence over her.

Leopold II 1835–1909. King of Belgium from 1865, son of Leopold I. He financed the journalist Stanley's explorations in Africa, which resulted in the foundation of the Congo Free State (now Zaïre), from which he extracted a huge fortune by ruthless exploitation.

Leopold III 1901–1983. King of Belgium from 1934. He surrendered to the German army in 1940. Postwar charges against his conduct led to a regency by his brother Charles and his eventual abdication 1951 in favor of his son ◊Baudouin.

Leopold two Holy Roman emperors:

Leopold I 1640–1705. Holy Roman emperor from 1658, in succession to his father Ferdinand III. He warred against Louis XIV of France and the Ottoman Empire.

Leopold II 1747–1792. Holy Roman emperor in succession to his brother Joseph II, he was the son of Empress Maria Theresa. His hostility to the French Revolution led to the outbreak of war a few weeks after his death.

Léopoldville former name (until 1966) of ◊Kinshasa, city in Zaïre.

Lepanto, Battle of sea battle Oct 7, 1571, fought in the Mediterranean Gulf of Corinth off Lepanto (Italian name of the Greek port of Naupaktos), then in Turkish possession, between the Ottoman Empire and forces from Spain, Venice, Genoa, and the Papal States, jointly commanded by Don ◊John of Austria. The combined western fleets delivered a crushing blow to Muslim sea power. The Spanish writer Cervantes was wounded in the battle.

Le Pen Jean-Marie 1928– . French extreme right-wing politician. In 1972 he formed the French National Front, supporting immigrant repatriation and capital punishment; the party gained 14% of the national vote in the 1986 election. Le Pen was elected to the European Parliament 1984.

Lepenski Vir the site of Europe's oldest urban settlement (6th millennium BC), now submerged by an artificial lake on the river Danube.

lepidoptera an order of insects, including ◊butterflies and ◊moths; the order consists of some 165,000 species. Butterflies and moths have overlapping scales on their wings.

leprosy or Hansen's disease chronic, progressive disease caused by a bacterium (*Mycobacterium leprae*) closely related to that of tuberculosis. The infection attacks skin and nerves. Once common in many countries, leprosy is now confined almost entirely to the tropics. It is controlled with drugs.

There are two principal manifestations. Lepromatous leprosy is a contagious, progressive form distinguished by the appearance of raised blotches and lumps on the skin and thickening of the skin and nerves, with numbness, weakness, paralysis, and ultimately deformity of the affected parts. In tuberculoid leprosy, sensation is lost in some areas of the skin; sometimes there is loss of pigmentation and hair. The visible effects of long-standing leprosy (joint damage, paralysis, loss of fingers or toes) are due to nerve damage and injuries of which the sufferer may be unaware. Damage to the nerves remains, and the technique of using the patient's muscle material to encourage nerve regrowth is being explored.

Leptis Magna ruined city in Libya, 75 mi/120 km E of Tripoli. It was founded by the Phoenicians, then came under Carthage, and in 47 BC under Rome. Excavation in the 20th century revealed remains of fine Roman buildings.

lepton any of a class of 12 ◊elementary particles that do not interact strongly with other particles or nuclei. They include six particles and their antiparticles: the ◊electron; the three types of ◊neutrinos (electron neutrino, muon neutrino, and tauon neutrino); the muon; and the tauon.

leptospirosis any of several infectious diseases of domestic animals and humans caused by spirochetes of the genus *Leptospira* found in sewage and natural waters. One such disease in cattle causes abortion; in humans, eyes, liver, and kidneys may be affected; meningitis is another symptom.

Le Puy capital of Haute-Loire *département*, Auvergne, SE France; population (1982) 26,000. It is dramatically situated on a rocky plateau, and has a 12th-century cathedral.

Lérida (Catalan *Lleida*) capital of Lérida province, N Spain, on the river Segre; 82 mi/132 km W of Barcelona; population (1986) 112,000. Industries include leather, paper, glass, and cloth. Lérida was captured by Caesar 49 BC. It has a palace of the kings of Aragon.

Lermontov Mikhail Yurevich 1814–1841. Russian Romantic poet and novelist. In 1837 he was sent into active military service in the Caucasus for writing a revolutionary poem on the death of Pushkin, which criticized Court values, and for participating in a duel. Among his works are the psychological novel *A Hero of Our Time* 1840 and a volume of poems *October* 1840.

Lerner Alan Jay 1918–1986. US lyricist, collaborator with Frederick ◊Loewe on musicals including *Brigadoon* 1947, *Paint Your Wagon* 1951, *My Fair Lady* 1956, *Gigi* 1958, and *Camelot* 1960.

Le Sage Alan René 1668–1747. French novelist and dramatist. Born in Brittany, he abandoned law for literature. His novels include *Le Diable boîteux/The Devil upon Two Sticks* 1707 and his picaresque masterpiece *Gil Blas* 1715–1735, much indebted to Spanish originals.

lesbianism ◊homosexuality between women, so called from the Greek island of Lesbos (now Lesvos), the home of ◊Sappho the poet and her followers to whom the behavior was attributed.

Lesbos alternate spelling of ◊Lesvos, an island in the Aegean Sea.

lesion any change in a body tissue that is a manifestation of disease or injury.

Lesotho landlocked country in southern Africa, an enclave within South Africa.

government Lesotho is an independent monarchy within the ◊Commonwealth. Its 1966 constitution was suspended, reinstated, and then suspended again, and all executive and legislative powers are now vested in the hereditary king, assisted by a six-member military council and a council of ministers. The constitution provides for a 99-member, single-chamber elected national assembly. The last elections were in 1973, when the Basotho National Party (BNP) won a majority of the seats. Elections due in 1985 were canceled by the king because no candidates opposed the BNP, all of whose nominees were deemed to have been returned unopposed.

history The area now known as Lesotho was originally inhabited by the San, or Bushmen. During the 18th–19th centuries they were superseded by the Sotho, who were being driven southward by the Mfecane ("the shaking-up of peoples") caused by the rise of the Zulu nation. Under the name of Basutoland, the Sotho nation was founded by Moshoeshoe I (1790–1870) from 1827, and at his request it became a British protectorate in 1868. It achieved internal self-government in 1965, with the paramount chief Moshoeshoe II, as king and was given full independence as Lesotho in 1966.

The BNP, a conservative group favoring limited cooperation with South Africa, held power from independence until 1986. Its leader, Chief Leabua Jonathan, became prime minister in 1966 and after 1970, when the king's powers were severely curtailed, the country was effectively under the prime minister's control. Since 1975 an organization called the Lesotho Liberation Army (LLA) has carried out a number of attacks on BNP members, with alleged South African support. South Africa, while denying complicity, has pointed out that Lesotho was allowing the then (until 1990) banned South African nationalist movement, the ◊African National Congress (ANC), to use it as a base.

Economically, Lesotho is dependent on South Africa but has openly rejected the policy of apartheid. In retaliation, South Africa has tightened its border controls, causing food shortages in Lesotho. It has been alleged that South Africa has encouraged BNP dissenters to form a new party, the Basotho Democratic Alliance (BDA), and plotted with the BDA to overthrow the Lesotho government. Lesotho has also been under pressure from South Africa to sign a nonaggression pact, similar to the Nkomati accord between South Africa and Mozambique, but the Lesotho government has refused to do so.

In 1986 South Africa imposed a border blockade, cutting off food and fuel supplies to Lesotho, and the government of Chief Jonathan was ousted and replaced in a coup led by General Justin Lekhanya. He announced that all executive and legislative powers would be vested in the king, ruling through a military council chaired by General Lekhanya, and a council of ministers. A week after the coup about 60 ANC members were deported to Zambia, and on the same day the South African blockade was lifted. Although South Africa has denied playing any part in the coup, it is clear that it will find the new government more acceptable than the old.

In Nov 1990 the son of the exiled King Moshoeshoe was sworn in as King Letsie III.

less developed country (ldc) any country late in developing an industrial base, and dependent on cash crops and unprocessed minerals. The Group of 77 was established 1964 to pressure industrialized countries into giving greater aid to less developed countries.

The terms "less developed" and "developing" imply that industrial development is desirable or inevitable; many writers prefer to use ◊Third World as opposed to "industrialized countries."

Lesseps Ferdinand, Vicomte de 1805–1894. French

Lesotho
Kingdom of

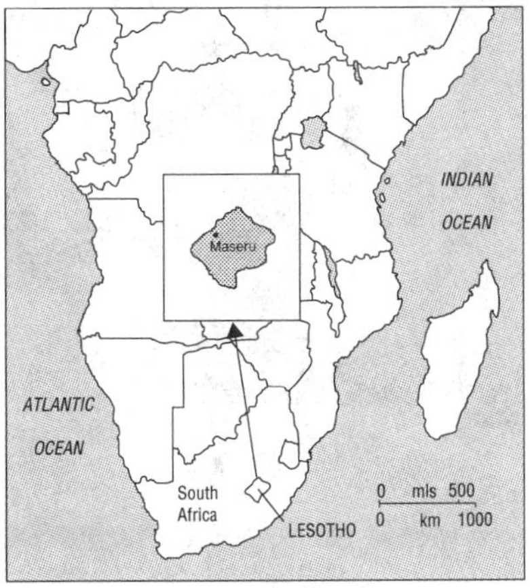
INDIAN
OCEAN
Maseru
ATLANTIC
OCEAN
South
Africa
LESOTHO
0 mls 500
0 km 1000

area 11,717 sq mi/30,355 sq km
capital Maseru
cities Teyateyaneng, Mafeteng, Roma, Quthing
physical mountainous with plateaus, forming part of South Africa's chief watershed
features Lesotho is an enclave within South Africa **political system** military-controlled monarchy
head of state King Letsie I from 1990
head of government Elias Tutsoane Ramaema from 1991
political parties Basotho National Party (BNP), traditionalist, nationalist, Basutoland Congress Party (BCP) **exports** wool, mohair, diamonds, cattle, wheat, vegetables
currency maluti
population (1990 est) 1,757,000; growth rate 2.7% p.a.
life expectancy men 59, women 62 (1989)
language Sesotho, English (official); Zulu, Xhosa
religion Protestant 42%, Roman Catholic 38%
literacy 59% (1988)
GNP $408 mn; $410 per head (1988)
chronology
1966 Independence achieved from Britain, within the Commonwealth, as the Kingdom of Lesotho, with Chief Leabua Jonathan as prime minister.
1970 State of emergency declared and constitution suspended.
1973 Pro-government interim assembly established.
1975 Members of the ruling party attacked by guerrillas backed by South Africa.
1986 South Africa imposed border blockade, forcing deportation of 60 African National Congress members. Gen Lekhanya ousted Chief Jonathan in coup. National Assembly abolished. Highlands Water Project agreement signed with South Africa.
1990 Moshoeshoe II dethroned by military council; replaced by his son Mohato.
1991 Lekhanya ousted in military coup led by Col Elias Tutsoane Ramaema. Political parties permitted to operate.

engineer, constructor of the ◊Suez Canal 1859–69; he began the ◊Panama Canal 1879, but withdrew after failing to construct it without locks.

Lessing Doris (May) (née Taylor) 1919– . British novelist, born in Iran. Concerned with social and political themes, particularly the place of women in society, her work includes *The Grass is Singing* 1950, *The Golden Notebook* 1962, the five-novel series *Children of Violence* 1952–69, *The Good Terrorist* 1985, and *The Fifth Child* 1988. She has also written an "inner space fiction" series *Canopus in Argus Archives* 1979–83, and under the pen name "Jane Somers," *The Diary of a Good Neighbor* 1981.

Lessing Gotthold Ephraim 1729–1781. German dramatist and critic. His plays include *Miss Sara Sampson* 1755, *Minna von Barnhelm* 1767, *Emilia Galotti* 1772, and the verse play *Nathan der Weise* 1779. His works of criticism *Laokoon* 1766 and *Hamburgische Dramaturgie* 1767–68 influenced German literature. He also produced many theological and philosophical writings.

Lessing *Political and social themes predominate in the works of British novelist Doris Lessing.*

Les Six (French "the six") a group of French composers: Georges ◊Auric, Louis Durey (1888–1979), Arthur ◊Honegger, Darius ◊Milhaud, Francis ◊Poulenc, and Germaine Tailleferre (1892–1983). Formed in 1917, they were dedicated to producing works free from foreign influences and reflecting the contemporary world. They split up in the early 1920s.

Lesvos Greek island in the Aegean Sea, near the coast of Turkey
area 831 sq mi/2,154 sq km
capital Mytilene
products olives, wine, grain
population (1981) 104,620
history ancient name Lesbos; an Aeolian settlement, the home of the poets ◊Alcaeus and ◊Sappho; conquered by the Turks from Genoa 1462; annexed to Greece 1913.

Lethe in Greek mythology, a river of the underworld whose waters, when drunk, brought forgetfulness of the past.

Leto in Greek mythology, a goddess, mother by ◊Zeus of ◊Artemis and ◊Apollo, to whom she gave birth on the Aegean island of ◊Delos, which became their sanctuary.

Le Touquet resort in N France, at the mouth of the river Canche; fashionable in the 1920s–30s.

letter a written or printed message, chiefly a personal communication. Letters are valuable as reflections of social conditions and of literary and political life. Legally, ownership of a letter (as a document) passes to the recipient, but the copyright remains with the writer.

Outstanding examples include:
ancient Cicero, Pliny the Younger, and St Paul;
medieval Abelard and Héloïse (12th-century France), the Paston letters (15th-century England);
16th century Erasmus (the Netherlands), Luther, Melanchthon (Germany), Spenser, Sidney (England);
17th century Donne, Milton, Cromwell, Dorothy Osborne, Wotton (England); Pascal, Mme de Sévigné (France);
18th century Pope, Walpole, Swift, Mary Wortley Montagu, Chesterfield, Cowper, Gray (England); Bossuet, Voltaire, Rousseau (France);
19th century Emerson, J R Lowell (US); Byron, Lamb, Keats, Fitzgerald, Stevenson (England); George Sand, Saint-Beuve, Goncourt brothers (France); Schiller, Goethe (Germany); Gottfried Keller (Switzerland);
20th century T E Lawrence, G B Shaw, Ellen Terry, Katherine Mansfield (England); Rilke (Germany).

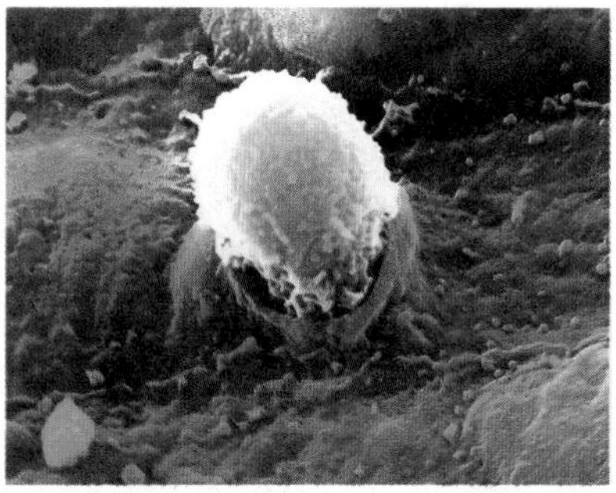

leukocyte *False-color electron-microscope view of a leukocyte passing through the thin layer of tissue that lines blood vessels.*

letterpress the method of printing from raised type, pioneered by Johannes ◊Gutenberg in Europe in the 1450s.

lettuce annual edible plant *Lactuca sativa*, family Compositae, believed to have been derived from the wild species *L. serriola*. There are many varieties, including the cabbage lettuce, with round or loose heads, and the Cos lettuce, with long, upright heads. Iceberg and Romaine are the two salad varieties grown especially for US supermarkets, but Boston and Redleaf are sometimes shipped to markets.

leucite a silicate mineral, $KAlSi_2O_6$, occurring frequently in some potassium-rich volcanic rocks. It is dull white to gray, and usually opaque. It is used as a source of potassium for fertilizer.

leucotomy another term for frontal ◊lobotomy, a brain operation.

leukemia any one of a group of cancerlike diseases of the blood cells, with widespread involvement of the bone marrow and other blood-forming tissue.

The central feature is runaway production of white blood cells that are immature or in some way abnormal. These rogue cells, which lack the defensive capacity of healthy white cells, overwhelm the normal ones, leaving the victim vulnerable to infection. Abnormal functioning of the bone marrow also suppresses production of red blood cells and blood ◊platelets, resulting in ◊anemia and a failure of the blood to clot.

Leukemias are classified into acute or chronic, depending on their known rates of progression. They are also grouped according to the type of white cell involved. Treatment is with radiotherapy and ◊cytotoxic drugs to suppress replication of abnormal cells, or by bone-marrow transplant.

leukocyte a white blood cell. Leukocytes are part of the body's defenses and give immunity against disease. There are several different types. Some (◊phagocytes and ◊macrophages) engulf invading microorganisms, others kill infected cells, while ◊lymphocytes produce more specific immune responses. Human blood contains about 11,000 leukocytes to the cubic millimeter—about one to every 500 red cells.

Leukocyte numbers may be reduced (leukopenia) by starvation, pernicious anemia, and certain infections, such as typhoid and malaria. An increase in the numbers (leukocytosis) is a reaction to normal events such as digestion, exertion,

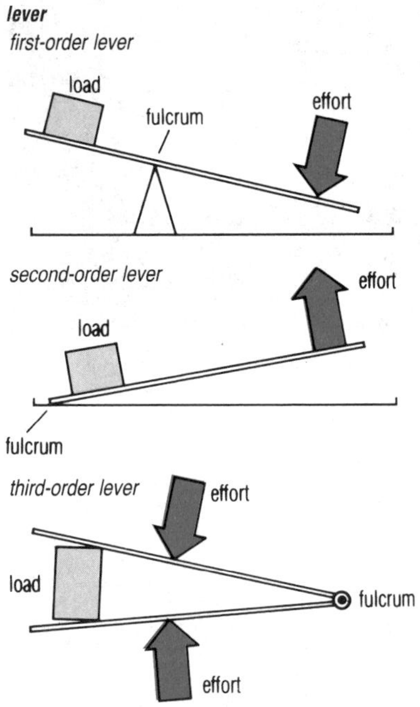
lever
first-order lever
load
fulcrum
effort
second-order lever
effort
load
fulcrum
third-order lever
effort
load
fulcrum
effort

and pregnancy, and to abnormal ones such as loss of blood, cancer, and most infections.

Levant the E Mediterranean region, or more specifically, the coastal regions of Turkey-in-Asia, Syria, Lebanon, and Israel.

Le Vau Louis 1612–1670. French architect who drafted the plan of Versailles, rebuilt the Louvre, and built Les Tuileries in Paris.

levee a naturally formed raised bank along the side of a river. When a river overflows its banks, the rate of flow in the flooded area is less than that in the channel, and silt is deposited. After the waters have withdrawn the silt is left as a bank that grows with successive floods. Eventually the river, contained by the levee, may be above the surface of the surrounding flood plain. Notable levees are found on the lower reaches of the Mississippi in the US and the Po in Italy.

level or ***spirit level*** instrument for finding horizontal level, or adjusting a surface to an even level, used in surveying, building construction, and archeology. It has a glass tube of colored liquid, in which a bubble is trapped, mounted in an elongated frame. When the tube is horizontal, the bubble moves to the center.

Levellers the democratic party in the English Civil War. They found wide support among Cromwell's New Model Army and the yeoman farmers, artisans, and small traders, and proved a powerful political force 1647–49. Their program included the establishment of a republic, government by a parliament of one house elected by male suffrage, religious toleration, and sweeping social reforms.

Cromwell's refusal to implement this program led to mutinies by Levellers in the army, which, when suppressed by Cromwell in 1649, ended the movement. They were led by John ◊Lilburne.

lever a simple machine consisting of a rigid rod pivoted at a fixed point called the fulcrum, used for shifting or raising a heavy load or applying force in a similar way. Levers are classified into orders according to where the effort is applied, and the load-moving force developed, in relation to the position of the fulcrum.

A first-order lever has the load and the effort on opposite sides of the fulcrum—for example, a see-saw or pair of scissors. A second-order lever has the load and the effort on the same side of the fulcrum, with the load nearer the fulcrum—for example, nutcrackers or a wheelbarrow. A third-order lever has the effort nearer the fulcrum than the load with both on the same side of it—for example, a pair of tweezers or tongs. The mechanical advantage of a lever is the ratio of load to effort, equal to the perpendicular distance of the effort's line of action from the fulcrum divided by the distance to the load's line of action. Thus tweezers, for instance, have a mechanical advantage of less than one.

leveraged buyout in business, the purchase of a controlling proportion of the shares of a company by its own management, financed almost exclusively by borrowing. It is so called because the ratio of a company's long-term debt to its equity (capital assets) is known as its "leverage."

Leverkusen river port in North Rhine–Westphalia, Federal Republic of Germany, 5 mi/8 km N of Cologne; population (1988) 155,000. It has iron, steel, and chemical industries.

Leverrier Urbain Jean Joseph 1811–1877. French astronomer who predicted the existence and position of the planet Neptune, discovered in 1846.

Lévesque René 1922–1987. French-Canadian politician. In 1968 he founded the Parti Québecois, with the aim of an independent Québec, but a referendum rejected the proposal 1980. He was premier of Québec 1976–85.

Levi Primò 1919–1987. Italian novelist. He joined the anti-Fascist resistance during World War II, was captured, and sent to the concentration camp at Auschwitz. He wrote of these experiences in *Se questo è un uomo/If This Is a Man* 1947.

leviathan in the Old Testament, a mythical evil sea monster, identified by later commentators with the whale.

Levi-Montalcini Rita 1909– . Italian neurologist who discovered nerve-growth factor, a substance that controls how many cells make up the adult nervous system. She was awarded the Nobel Prize 1986.

Levi-Montalcini studied at Turin and worked there until the Fascist anti-Semitic laws forced her to go into hiding. She continued research into the nervous systems of chick embryos. After World War II she moved to the US.

Lévi-Strauss Claude 1908–1990. French anthropologist who sought to find a universal structure governing all societies, as reflected in the way their myths are constructed. His works include *Tristes Tropiques* 1955 and *Mythologiques/Mythologies* 1964–71.

levitation counteraction of gravitational forces on a body. As claimed by medieval mystics, spiritualist mediums, and practitioners of transcendental meditation, it is unproven. In the laboratory it can be produced scientifically; for example, electrostatic force and acoustical waves have been used to suspend water drops for microscopic study. It is also used in technology, for example, in magnetic levitation as in ◊maglev trains.

Levite in the Old Testament, a member of one of the 12 tribes of Israel, descended from Levi, a son of ◊Jacob. The Levites performed the lesser services of the Temple; the high priesthood was confined to the descendants of Aaron, the brother of Moses.

Lewes George Henry 1817–1878. English philosopher and critic. From acting he turned to literature and philosophy; his works include a *Biographical History of Philosophy* 1845–46, and *Life and Works of Goethe* 1855. He married in 1840, but left his wife in 1854 to form a life-long union with the writer Mary Ann Evans (George ◊Eliot), whom he had met in 1851.

Lewes, Battle of battle 1264 caused by the baronial opposition to England's Henry III, led by Simon de Montfort, earl of Leicester (1208–1265). The king was defeated and captured at the battle.

The barons objected to Henry's patronage of French nobles in the English court, his weak foreign policy, and his support for the papacy against the Holy Roman Empire. In 1258, they forced him to issue the ◊Provisions of Oxford, and when he later refused to implement them, they revolted. They defeated and captured the king at Lewes in Sussex. Their revolt was broken by de Montfort's death and defeat at Evesham 1265.

***Lewis** US track and field athlete Carl Lewis excelled in the sprints and the long jump.*

Lewis (William) Arthur 1915– . British economist born on St Lucia, West Indies. He specialized in the economic problems of developing countries and created a model relating the terms of trade between less developed and more developed nations to their respective levels of labor productivity in agriculture. He shared the Nobel Prize for Economics with an American, Theodore Schultz, 1979. He wrote many books, including the *Theory of Economic Growth* 1955.

Lewis Carl (Frederick Carleton) 1961– . US track and field athlete. At the 1984 Olympic Games he equaled the performance of Jesse ◊Owens, winning gold medals in the 100 and 200 meters, sprint relay, and long jump. In the 1988 Olympics, he repeated his golds in the 100 meters and long jump, and won a silver in the 200 meters.

CAREER HIGHLIGHTS

Olympic Games
gold:
100 meters 1984, 1988
200 meters 1984
4 × 100 meters relay 1984
long jump 1984, 1988
silver:
200 meters 1988

Lewis Cecil Day see ◊Day Lewis.

Lewis C(live) S(taples) 1898–1963. British academic and writer, born in Belfast. His books include the medieval study, *The Allegory of Love* 1936, and the space fiction, *Out of the Silent Planet* 1938. He was a committed Christian and wrote essays in popular theology such as *The Screwtape Letters* 1942 and *Mere Christianity* 1952; the autobiographical *Surprised by Joy* 1955; and a series of books of Christian allegory for children, set in the magic land of Narnia, including *The Lion, the Witch, and the Wardrobe* 1950.

Lewis Jerry. Adopted name of Joseph Levitch 1926– . US comic actor and director, formerly in partnership with Dean Martin (1946–1956); their film debut was in *My Friend Irma* 1949. Lewis enjoyed great commercial success as a solo performer and was revered by French critics, but films that he directed such as *The Nutty Professor* 1963 were less well received in the US. He gave a strong performance with Robert de Niro in *King of Comedy* 1982.

Lewis US singer Jerry Lee Lewis "crossed over" from country to rock-and-roll music and remained popular with both groups of fans.

Lewis Jerry Lee 1935– . US rock-and-roll and country singer and pianist. His trademark was the "pumping piano" style in hits such as "Whole Lotta Shakin' Going On" and "Great Balls of Fire" 1957; later recordings include "What Made Milwaukee Famous" 1968.

Lewis John L(lewellyn) 1880–1969. US labor leader. Born in Lucas, Iowa, Lewis worked in the coal mines from an early age. He became a regional officer of the United Mine Workers (UMW) and served as its liaison with the American Federation of Labor (AFL) 1911. Elected president of the UMW 1920–60, he helped found the Congress of Industrial Organizations 1935, the AFL offshoot that unionized workers in mass-production industries. Campaigning for the unionization of workers in heavy industry, he eventually came into conflict with F D Roosevelt. Lewis's militancy led to miners' strikes during and after World War II, and thus to Truman's nationalization of the mines in 1946. His concerns, however, led to the adoption of national mining safety standards.

Lewis Meriwether 1774–1809. US explorer. He was commissioned by President Thomas Jefferson to find a land route to the Pacific with William Clark (1770–1838). They followed the Missouri River to its source, crossed the Rocky Mountains (aided by an Indian girl, Sacajawea) and followed the Columbia River to the Pacific, then returned overland to St Louis 1804–06.

The detailed journals kept of the expedition added to an understanding of the region and facilitated westward expansion.

Formerly private secretary to President Jefferson, he was rewarded for his expedition with the governorship of the Louisiana Territory. His death, near Nashville, Tennessee, has been ascribed to suicide, but was more probably murder.

Lewis (Harry) Sinclair 1885–1951. US novelist. He made a reputation with satirical novels: *Main Street* 1920, depicting American small-town life; *Babbitt* 1922, the story of a real-estate dealer of the Midwest caught in the conventions of his milieu; *Arrowsmith* 1925, a study of the pettiness in medical science; and *Elmer Gantry* 1927, a satiric portrayal of evangelical religion. *Dodsworth*, a gentler novel of a US industrialist, was published 1929. He was the first American to be awarded the Nobel Prize for Literature 1930.

Born in Sauk Centre, Minnesota, Lewis graduated from Yale University. He stayed for a time at Upton Sinclair's Socialist colony in New Jersey, then became a freelance journalist. His other works include *It Can't Happen Here* 1935, *Cass Timberlane* 1945, *Kingsblood Royal* 1947, and *The God-Seeker* 1949.

Lewis US novelist Sinclair Lewis' depictions of small-town American life won him a Nobel prize 1930.

Lewis (Percy) Wyndham 1886–1957. English writer and artist who pioneered Vorticism, which with its feeling of movement sought to reflect the age of industry. He had a hard and aggressive style in both his writing and his painting. His literary works include the novels *Tarr* 1918 and *The Childermass* 1928, the essay *Time and Western Man* 1927, and autobiographies.

Born off Maine, in his father's yacht, he was educated at the Slade art school and in Paris. On returning to England he pioneered the new spirit of art that his friend Ezra Pound called Vorticism; he also edited *Blast*, a literary and artistic magazine proclaiming its principles. Of his paintings, his portraits are memorable, such as those of Edith Sitwell and T S Eliot. Although he has been assessed by some as a leading force of the early 20th century, his support in the 1930s of Fascist principles and Adolph Hitler alienated most critics.

Lewiston city in SW Maine, across the Androscoggin River from Auburn. It is known for its textile, shoe, and clothing industries. Bates College 1855 is here; population (1990) 39,757.

Lewis with Harris largest island in the Outer Hebrides; area 857 sq mi/2,220 sq km; population (1981) 23,400. Its main town is Stornoway. It is separated from NW Scotland by the Minch. There are many lakes and peat moors. Harris is famous for its tweeds.

Lewton Val. Adopted name of Vladimir Ivan Leventon 1904–1951. Russian-born US film producer, responsible for a series of atmospheric "B" horror films made for RKO in the 1940s, including *Cat People* 1942 and *The Body Snatcher* 1946. He cowrote several of his films under the adopted name of Carlos Keith.

Lexington town in Massachusetts; population (1990) 28,974. Industries include printing and publishing. The Battle of Lexington and Concord, April 19, 1775, opened the American Revolution. See also Paul ◊Revere.

Lexington or ***Lexington–Fayette*** city in Kentucky, center of the bluegrass country; population (1990) 225,366. Racehorses are bred in the area, and races and shows are held. There is a tobacco market and the University of Kentucky (1865).

ley an area of temporary grassland, sown to produce grazing and hay or silage for a period of one to ten years before being plowed and cropped. Short-term leys are often incorporated in systems of crop rotation.

A simple seven-year rotation, for example, might include a three-year ley followed by two years of wheat and then two years of barley, before returning the land to temporary grass once more. In this way, the cereal crops can take advantage of the buildup of soil fertility that occurs during the period under grass.

Leyden alternate form of ◊Leiden, city in the Netherlands.

Leyden Lucas van; see ◊Lucas van Leyden, Dutch painter.

LH abbreviation for ◊luteinizing hormone.

Lhasa ("the Forbidden City") capital of the autonomous region of Tibet, China, at 16,400 ft/5,000 m; population (1982) 105,000. Products include handicrafts and light industry.

The holy city of ◊Lamaism, Lhasa was closed to Westerners until the early 20th century. It was annexed with the rest of Tibet 1950–51 by China, and the Dalai Lama fled 1959 after a popular uprising against Chinese rule. Monasteries have been destroyed and monks killed, and an influx of Chinese settlers has generated resentment. In 1988 and 1989 nationalist demonstrators were shot by Chinese soldiers.

Lhote André 1885–1962. French painter, art teacher, and critic. He opened the Académie Montparnasse 1922 and founded a South American branch of the school in Rio de Janeiro 1952. He also wrote treatises on painting techniques. His own paintings are complicated compositions of geometrical forms painted in pure colors, for example *Rugby* (Musée d'Art Moderne, Paris).

liability in accounting, a financial obligation. Liabilities are placed alongside assets on a balance sheet to show the wealth of the entity at a given date.

liana a woody, perennial climbing plant with very long stems, which grows around trees up to the canopy, where there is more sunlight. Lianas are common in tropical rainforests, where individual stems may grow up to 255 ft/78 m long. They have an unusual stem structure that allows them to retain some flexibility, despite being woody.

Liao river in NE China, frozen Dec–Mar; the main headstream rises in the mountains of Inner Mongolia and flows E, then S to the Gulf of Liaodong; length 900 mi/1,450 km.

Liaoning province of NE China
area 58,300 sq mi/151,000 sq km
capital Shenyang
towns Anshan, Fushun, Liaoyang
featuresone of China's most heavily industrialized areas
products cereals, coal, iron, salt, oil
population (1986) 37,260,000
history developed by Japan 1905–45, including the Liaodong Peninsula, whose ports had been conquered from the Russians.

Liaoyang industrial city (engineering, textiles) in Liaoning province; population (1970) 250,000. In 1904 Russia was defeated by Japan here.

Libau German name of Latvian port ◊Liepablja.

Libby Willard Frank 1908–1980. US chemist, whose development in 1947 of ◊radiocarbon dating as a means of determining the age of organic or fossilized material won him a Nobel Prize 1960.

liberalism political and social theory that favors representative government, freedom of the press, speech, and worship, the moderation and regulation of class privileges, the use of state resources to protect the welfare of the individual, and international ◊free trade. It is historically associated with the Liberal Party in the UK and the Democratic Party in the US.

Liberalism developed during the 17th–19th centuries as the distinctive theory of the industrial and commercial classes in their struggle against the power of the monarchy, the church, and the feudal landowners. Economically it was associated with ◊laissez faire, or nonintervention. In the late 19th and early 20th centuries its ideas were modified by the acceptance of universal suffrage and a certain amount of state intervention in economic affairs, to ensure a minimum standard of living and to remove extremes of poverty and wealth. The Classical statement of liberal principles is found in *On Liberty* and other works of the British philosopher J S Mill.

Liberal Party in the UK, a political party, the successor to the ◊Whig Party, with an ideology of liberalism. In the 19th century it was the party of the left, representing the interests of commerce and industry. Its outstanding leaders were Palmerston, Gladstone, and Lloyd George. From 1914 it declined, and the rise of the Labour Party pushed the Liberals into the middle ground. The Liberals joined forces with the Social Democratic Party (SDP) as the Alliance for the 1983 and 1987 elections. In 1988, a majority of the SDP voted to merge with the Liberals to form the Social and ◊Liberal Democrats.

The term "Liberal," used officially from about 1840 and unofficially from about 1815, marked the transfer of control from aristocrats to the more progressive industrialists, backed by supporters of the utilitarian reformer ◊Bentham, Nonconformists, and the middle classes. During the Liberals' first period of power 1830–41, they promoted parliamentary and municipal government reform and the abolition of slavery, but their ◊*laissez-faire* theories led to the harsh Poor Law of 1834. Except for two short periods the Liberals were in power 1846–66, but the only major change was the general adoption of ◊free trade. Liberal pressure forced Peel to repeal the Corn Laws 1846, thereby splitting the Tory party.

Extended franchise in 1867 and Gladstone's emergence as leader began a new phase, dominated by the Manchester school with a program of "peace, retrenchment, and reform." Gladstone's 1868–74 government introduced many important reforms, including elementary education and vote by ballot. The party's left, mainly composed of working-class ◊Radicals led by Charles Bradlaugh and Joseph ◊Chamberlain, repudiated laissez faire and inclined toward republicanism, but the Liberals were split over Home Rule 1886 and many became Liberal Unionists or joined the Conservatives. Except for 1892–95, the Liberals remained out of power until 1906, when, reinforced by Labour and Irish support, they returned with a huge majority. Old-age pensions, National Insurance, limitation of the powers of the Lords, and the Irish Home Rule Bill followed.

Lloyd George's alliance with the Conservatives 1916–22 divided them between him and his predecessor Asquith, and although reunited 1923 the Liberals continued to lose votes. They briefly joined the National Government 1931–32. After World War II they were reduced to a handful of members of Parliament. A revival began under the leadership 1956–67 of Jo Grimond and continued under Jeremy Thorpe, who resigned after a period of controversy within the party 1976.

After a caretaker return by Grimond, David Steel became the first party leader in British politics to be elected by party members who were not MPs. In 1977–78 Steel entered into an agreement to support Labour in any vote of confidence in return for consultation on measures undertaken. He resigned 1988 and was replaced by Paddy Ashdown.

Liberal Party, Australian political party established 1944 by Robert Menzies, after a Labor landslide, and derived from the former United Australia Party. After the voters rejected Labor's extensive nationalization plans, the Liberals were in power 1949–72 and 1975–83 and were led in succession by Harold Holt, John Gorton, William McMahon (1908–), Billy Snedden (1926–), and Malcolm Fraser.

liberation theology a Christian theory of Jesus' primary importance as the "Liberator," personifying the poor and devoted to freeing them from oppression (Matthew 19:21, 25:35, 40). Initiated by the Peruvian priest Gustavo Gutierrez in *The Theology of Liberation* 1969, and enthusiastically (and sometimes violently) adopted in Latin America, it embodies a Marxist interpretation of the class struggle, especially by Third World nations. It has been criticized by some Roman Catholic authorities including Pope John Paul II.

Liberator, the another name for Simón ◊Bolívar and Bernardo ◊O'Higgins, South American revolutionary leaders.

Liberia
Republic of

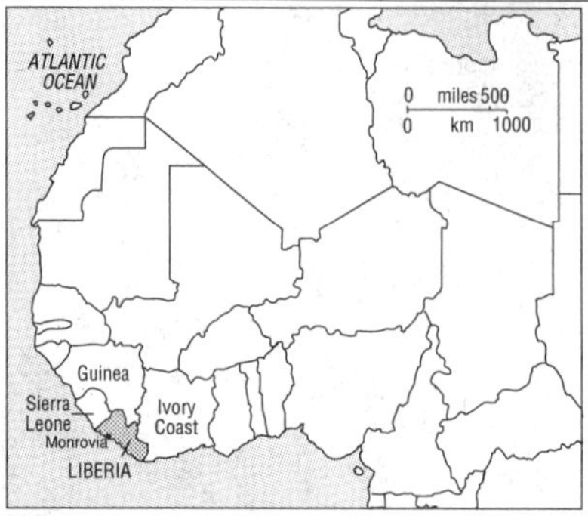
ATLANTIC OCEAN
0 miles 500
0 km 1000
Guinea
Sierra Leone
Monrovia
Ivory Coast
LIBERIA

area 42,989 sq mi/111,370 sq km
capital (and port) Monrovia
cities ports Buchanan, Greenville
physical forested highlands; swampy tropical coast where six rivers enter the sea
features nominally the world's largest merchant marine as minimal registration controls make Liberia's a flag of convenience; the world's largest rubber plantations
head of state and government Amos Sawyer from 1990 political parties National Democratic party of Liberia (NDLP), nationalist; Liberian Action Party; Liberian Unity Party; United People's Party; Unity Party
political system emergent democratic republic
exports iron ore, rubber (Africa's largest producer), timber, diamonds, coffee, cocoa, palm oil
currency Liberian dollar
population (1990 est) 2,644,000 (95% indigenous); growth rate 3% p.a.
life expectancy men 53, women 56 (1989)
language English (official); over 20 Niger-Congo languages
religion Muslim 20%, Christian 15%, traditional 65%
literacy 47% male/23% female (1985 est)
GNP $973 mn; $410 per head (1987)
chronology
1847 Founded as an independent republic.
1944 William Tubman elected president.
1971 Tubman died and was succeeded by William Tolbert.
1980 Tolbert assassinated in coup led by Samuel Doe, who suspended the constitution and ruled through a People's Redemption Council.
1984 New constitution approved. National Democratic Party of Liberia (NDPL) founded by Doe.
1985 NDPL won decisive victory in general election. Unsuccessful coup against Doe.
1990 Rebels under former government minister Charles Taylor controlled nearly entire country by July. Doe killed during a bloody civil war between rival rebel factions. Amos Sawyer became interim head of government.
1991 Amos Sawyer re-elected president. Rebel leader Charles Taylor agreed to work together.

Liberia country in W Africa, bounded N and NE by Guinea, E by the Ivory Coast, S and SW by the Atlantic, and NW by Sierra Leone.

government The 1984 constitution provides for a two-chamber national assembly consisting of a 26-member senate and a 64-member house of representatives, elected, like the president, by universal suffrage for a six-year term.

history The area now known as Liberia was bought by the American Colonization Society, a philanthropic organization active in the first half of the 19th century. The society's aim was to establish a settlement for liberated black slaves from the southern US. The first settlers arrived in 1822, and Liberia was declared an independent republic in 1847. The new state suffered from financial difficulties, bankruptcy in 1909 bringing reorganization by US army officers. For almost 160 years the country's leaders were descended from the black American settlers, but the 1980 coup put Africans in power.

William Tubman was president from 1944 until his death in 1971 and was succeeded by Vice-President William R Tolbert (1913–1980), who was re-elected in 1975. In 1980 Tolbert was assassinated in a coup led by Master Sgt Samuel Doe (1952–), who suspended the constitution, banned all political parties and ruled through the People's Redemption Council (PRC). He proceeded to stamp out corruption in the public service, encountering considerable opposition and making enemies who were later to threaten his position.

A new constitution was approved by the PRC in 1983 and by national referendum in 1984. Political parties were again permitted, provided they registered with the Special Electoral Commission (SECOM). In 1984 Doe founded the National Democratic Party of Liberia (NDPL) and announced his intention to stand for the presidency. By 1985 there were 11 political parties, but they complained about the difficulties of the registration process, and only three registered in time for the elections. Doe's party won clear majorities in both chambers, despite alleged election fraud, and he was pronounced president with 51% of the vote. In 1985 there was an unsuccessful attempt to unseat him. Doe alleged complicity by neighboring Sierra Leone and dealt harshly with the coup leaders. There has been a gradual movement toward a pluralist political system, with a number of parties registering in opposition to the ruling NDPL, which, with growing economic problems, has threatened the stability of the Doe regime. In July 1990 rebel forces under Charles Taylor and a breakaway faction led by Prince Johnson laid seige to Doe in the presidential palace. Doe refused an offer of assistance by the US to leave the country. In Sept 1990 President Doe was captured and killed by rebel forces and in Nov the rebel leader was forced to sign a ceasefire agreement. Amos Sawyer became the head of an interim government.

liberty in its medieval sense, a franchise, or collection of privileges, granted to an individual or community by the king, and the area over which this franchise extended.

Liberty Arthur Lasenby 1843–1917. English shopkeeper and founder of a shop of the same name in London, 1875. Originally importing oriental goods, it gradually started selling British Arts and Crafts and Art Nouveau furniture, tableware, and fabrics.

Libra faint zodiac constellation in the southern hemisphere near Scorpius, and represented as the scales of justice. The Sun passes through Libra during Nov. The constellation was once considered to be a part of Scorpius, representing its claws. Its brightest star, Zubeneschamali (or Beta Libra), is about 120 light-years from Earth. In astrology, the dates for Libra are between about Sept 23 and Oct 23 (see ◊precession).

library a collection of information (usually in the form of books) held for common use. The earliest was at Nineveh in Babylonian times. The first public library was opened in Athens 330 BC. All ancient libraries were reference libraries; books could be consulted but not borrowed.

Books are now usually classified by two major systems: Dewey Decimal Classification (now

Libya
Great Socialist People's Libyan Arab Jamahiriya
(*al-Jamahiriya al-Arabiya al-Libya al-Shabiya al-Ishtirakiya al-Uzma*)

MEDITERRANEAN SEA
Tunisia
Tripoli
Algeria
LIBYA
Egypt
Niger
Chad
Sudan
0 miles 500
0 km 1000

area 679,182 sq mi/1,759,540 sq km
capital Tripoli
cities ports Benghazi, Misurata, Tobruk
physical flat to undulating plains with plateaus and depressions stretch S from the Mediterranean coast to an extremely dry desert interior
features Gulf of Sirte; rock paintings of about 3000 BC in the Fezzan; Roman city sites include Leptis Magna, Sabratha
political system one-party, Socialist state
head of state and government Moamer Khaddhafi from 1969
political parties Arab Socialist Union (ASU), radical, left-wing
exports oil, natural gas
currency Libyan dinar
population (1990 est) 4,280,000 (including 500,000 foreign workers); growth rate 3.1% p.a.
life expectancy men 64, women 69 (1989)
language Arabic
religion Sunni Muslim 97%
literacy 60% (1989)
GNP $20 bn; $5,410 per head (1988)
chronology
1911 Conquered by Italy.
1934 Colony named Libya.
1942 Divided into 3 provinces: Fezzan (under French control); Cyrenaica, Tripolitana (under British control).
1951 Achieved independence as the United Kingdom of Libya, under King Idris.
1969 King deposed in a coup led by Col Moamer Khaddhafi. Revolution Command Council set up and the Arab Socialist Union (ASU) proclaimed the only legal party.
1972 Proposed federation of Libya, Syria, and Egypt abandoned.
1980 Proposed merger with Syria abandoned. Libyan troops began fighting in Chad.
1981 Proposed merger with Chad abandoned.
1986 US bombing of Khaddhafi's headquarters, following allegations of his complicity in terrorist activities.
1988 Diplomatic relations with Chad restored.
1989 US accused Libya of building a chemical-weapons factory and shot down two Libyan planes; reconciliation with Egypt.

known as Universal Decimal Classification), invented by Melvil Dewey (1851–1931), and the Library of Congress system. Library cataloging systems range from cards to microfiche to computer databases with on-line terminals.

major world libraries with date founded

Alexandrian library 284
Vatican Library, Rome 4th century
Bibliothèque nationale, Paris 1520
Bodleian Library, Oxford 1598
British Library, London 1757
Library of Congress, Washington, DC 1800
The New York Public Library, New York City 1895

libretto (Italian "little book") the text of an opera or other dramatic vocal work, or the scenario of a ballet.

Libreville capital of Gabon, on the estuary of the river Gabon; population (1985) 350,000. Products include timber, oil, and minerals. It was founded 1849 as a refuge for slaves freed by the French.

Libya country in N Africa, bordered N by the Mediterranean, E by Egypt, SE by Sudan, S by Chad and Niger, and W by Algeria and Tunisia

government The 1977 constitution created an Islamic Socialist state, and the government is designed to allow the greatest possible popular involvement, through a large congress and smaller secretariats and committees. There is a General People's Congress (GPC) of 1,112 members that elects a secretary general who was intended to be head of state. The GPC is serviced by a general secretariat, which is Libya's nearest equivalent to a legislature. The executive organ of the state is the General People's Committee, which replaces the structure of ministries that operated before the 1969 revolution. The Arab Socialist Union (ASU) is the only political party, and, despite Libya's elaborately democratic structure, ultimate power rests with the party and the revolutionary leader, Colonel Khaddhafi.

history The area now known as Libya was inhabited by N African nomads until it came successively under the domination of Phoenicia, Greece, Rome, the Vandals, Byzantium, and Islam, and from the 16th century was part of the Turkish Ottoman Empire. In 1911 it was conquered by Italy, becoming known as Libya from 1934. After being the scene of much fighting during World War II, in 1942 it was divided into three provinces: Fezzan, which was placed under French control; Cyrenaica; and Tripolitania, which was placed under British control. In 1951 it achieved independence as the United Kingdom of Libya, Mohammed Idris-as-Sanusi becoming King Idris.

The country enjoyed internal and external stability until a bloodless revolution 1969, led by young nationalist officers, deposed the king and proclaimed a Libyan Arab Republic. Power was vested in a Revolution Command Council (RCC), chaired by Col Moamer al-Khaddhafi, with the Arab Socialist Union (ASU) as the only political party. Khaddhafi soon began proposing schemes for Arab unity, none of which was permanently adopted. In 1972 he planned a federation of Libya, Syria, and Egypt and later that year a merger between Libya and Egypt. In 1980 he proposed a union with Syria and in 1981 with Chad.

Khaddhafi tried to run the country on Socialist Islamic lines, with people's committees pledged to socialism and the teachings of the Koran. The 1977 constitution made him secretary general of the general secretariat of the GPC, but in 1979 he resigned the post in order to devote more time to "preserving the revolution." His attempts to establish himself as a leader of the Arab world have brought him into conflict with Western powers, particularly the US. The Reagan administration objected to Libya's presence in Chad and its attempts to unseat the French-US-sponsored government of President Habré. The US has linked Khaddhafi to worldwide terrorist activities, despite his denials of complicity, and the killing of a US soldier in a bomb attack in Berlin 1986 by an unidentified guerrilla group prompted a raid by US aircraft, some of them British-based, on Khaddhafi's personal headquarters, killing a number of civilians.

In Jan 1989 Khaddaffi resisted the urge to respond to the shooting-down of two of his fighters off the Libyan coast by the US navy and has worked steadily at improving external relations, particularly in the Arab world, effecting a reconciliation with Egypt in Oct 1989. For the US and other Western nations, Khaddhafi remains suspect, and US intelligence official released evidence that Libya intended to produce chemical weapons.

license document issued by a government or other recognized authority conveying permission to the holder to do something otherwise prohibited and designed to facilitate accurate records, the maintenance of order, and collection of revenue.

Examples are licenses required for marriage, driving, keeping a handgun or pistol, and for sale of alcohol.

Also permission (in writing or not) granted by a private person or corporation for use of that person's or corporation's property such as a design, written material, computer software, artistic production, and manufacturing process, product, or likeness.

lichen any organism of the group Lichenes, which consists of a specific fungus and a specific alga existing in a mutually beneficial relationship. Found as colored patches or spongelike masses adhering to trees, rocks, and other substrates, lichens flourish under very adverse conditions.

Some lichens have food value; for example, reindeer moss and Iceland moss; others give dyes, such as litmus, or are used in medicine. They are sensitive to atmospheric pollution (see ◊indicator species).

Lichtenstein Roy 1923– . US Pop artist. He uses advertising imagery and comic-strip techniques, often focusing on popular ideals of romance and heroism, as in *Whaam!* 1963 (Tate Gallery, London). He has also produced sculptures in brass, plastic, and enameled metal.

Lichtenstein's reputation was made with an exhibition in New York 1962. His controversial work is a commentary on American culture.

licorice perennial European herb *Glycyrrhiza glabra*, of the pea family Leguminosae. The long, sweet root yields an extract which, made into a hard black paste, is used in confectionery and medicines.

Lidice Czechoslovak mining village, replacing one destroyed by the Nazis June 10, 1942 as a reprisal for the assassination of ◊Heydrich. The men were shot, the women sent to concentration camps, and the children taken to Germany. The officer responsible was hanged 1946.

Lie Trygve (Halvdan) 1896–1968. Norwegian Labor politician and diplomat. He became secretary of the Labor Party 1926. During the German occupation of Norway in World War II he was foreign minister in the exiled government 1941–46, when he helped retain the Norwegian fleet for the Allies. He became the first secretary general of the United Nations 1946–53, but resigned over Soviet opposition to his handling of the Korean War.

Liebig Justus, Baron von 1803–1873. German chemist, a major contributor to agricultural chemistry. He introduced the theory of ◊radicals and discovered chloroform and chloral.

Liebknecht Karl 1871–1919. German Socialist, son of Wilhelm Liebknecht. A founder of the German Communist Party, originally known as the Spartacus League (see ◊Spartacist) 1918, he was one of the few Socialists who refused to support World War I. He led an unsuccessful revolt with Rosa ◊Luxemburg in Berlin 1919 and both were murdered by army officers.

Liebknecht Wilhelm 1826–1900. German Socialist. A friend of the communist theoretician Marx, with whom he took part in the ◊revolution of 1848, he was imprisoned for opposition to the Franco-

Liechtenstein
Principality of
(Fürstentum Liechtenstein)

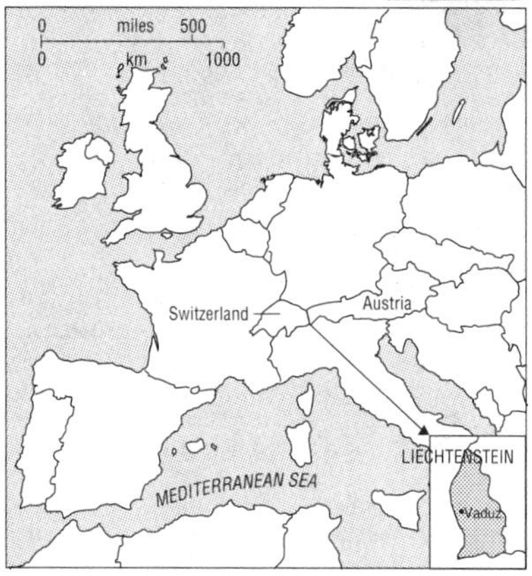
0 miles 500
0 km 1000
Switzerland
Austria
LIECHTENSTEIN
MEDITERRANEAN SEA
Vaduz

area 62 sq mi/160 sq km
capital Vaduz
cities Balzers, Schaan, Ruggell
physical landlocked alpine; includes part of Rhine Valley in W
features only country in the world to take its name from its reigning family; easy tax laws make it an international haven for foreign companies and banks
head of state Prince Hans Adam II from 1989
head of government Hans Brunhart from 1978
political system constitutional monarchy
political parties Fatherland Union (VU); Progressive Citizens' Party (FBP)
exports microchips, dental products, small machinery, processed foods, postage stamps
currency Swiss franc
population (1990 est) 30,000 (33% foreign); growth rate 1.4% p.a.
life expectancy men 78, women 83 (1989)
language German (official), Alemannic dialect
religion Roman Catholic 87%, Protestant 8%
literacy 100% (1989)
GDP $1 bn (1987); $32,000 per head
chronology
1342 Became a sovereign state.
1434 Present boundaries established.
1719 Former counties of Schellenberg and Vaduz constituted as the Principality of Liechtenstein.
1923 United with Switzerland in a customs union.
1938 Prince Franz Josef II came to power.
1984 Vote extended to women in national elections.
1989 Prince Franz Joseph II died; Hans Adam II succeeded him as prince. Liechtenstein sought admission to UN.

Prussian War 1870–71. He was one of the founders of the Social Democratic Party 1875. He was the father of Karl Liebknecht.

Liechtenstein landlocked country in W central Europe, bounded E by Austria and W by Switzerland

government The 1921 constitution established a hereditary principality with a single-chamber parliament, the *Landtag*. The prince is formal and constitutional head of state. The *Landtag* has 25 members, 15 from the Upper Country and 10 from the Lower Country, elected for a four-year term through a system of proportional representation. The *Landtag* elects five people to form the government for its duration.

history Liechtenstein's history as a sovereign state began in 1342; its boundaries have been unchanged since 1434, and it has been known by its present name since 1719. Because of its small population of fewer than 30,000, it has found it convenient to associate itself with larger nations in international matters. For example, since 1923 it has shared a customs union with Switzerland, which since 1919 represents it abroad. Before this Austria undertook its diplomatic representation.

Liechtenstein is one of the world's richest countries, with an income per head of population greater than that of the US, nearly twice that of the UK, and only slightly less than that of Switzerland. It is not a full member of the United Nations but is represented in some UN specialist agencies. Prince Franz Josef II came to power in 1938, and although he retained the title, he passed the duties of prince to his heir, Hans Adam, in 1984. Franz Joseph II died in Oct 1989 and Hans Adam II immediately began to press strongly for the country to consider applying for full membership of the UN.

Despite the growing indications of change, Liechtenstein's political system remains innately conservative. Women did not achieve the right to vote in national elections until 1984 and were debarred from voting in three of the principality's 11 communes until April 1986.

Lied (German "song") a musical setting of a poem, usually for solo voice and piano; referring to Romantic songs of Schubert, Schumann, Brahms, and Hugo Wolf.

lie detector popular name for a ◊polygraph.

liege in the feudal system, the allegiance owed by a vassal to his or her lord.

Liège (German *Luik*) industrial city (weapons, textiles, paper, chemicals), capital of Liège province in Belgium, SE of Brussels, on the river Meuse; population (1988) 200,000. The province of Liège has an area of 1,505 sq mi/3,900 sq km and a population (1987) of 992,000.

lien in law, a claim on the property of another as security for the payment of a just debt.

Liepāja (German *Libau*) naval and industrial port in Latvia; population (1985) 112,000. The Knights of Livonia founded Liepāja in the 13th century. Industries include steel, engineering, textiles, and chemicals.

Lifar Serge 1905–1986. Russian dancer and choreographer. Born in Kiev, he studied under ◊Nijinsky, joined the Diaghilev company 1923, and was *maître de ballet* at the Paris Opéra 1930–44 and 1947–59.

A great experimenter, he produced his first ballet without music, *Icare*, in 1935, and published the same year the controversial *Le Manifeste du choréographie*. He developed the importance of the male dancer in his *Prometheus* 1929 and *Romeo and Juliet* (music by Prokofiev) 1955.

life the ability to grow, reproduce, and respond to such stimuli as light, heat, and sound. It is thought that life on Earth began about 4 billion years ago. The earliest fossil evidence of life is threadlike chains of cells discovered 1980 in deposits in NW Australia that have been dated as 3.5 billion years old.

It seems probable that the original atmosphere of Earth consisted of carbon dioxide, nitrogen, and water, and that complex organic molecules, such as ◊amino acids, were created when the then oxygen- (and ozone-) free atmosphere was bombarded by ultraviolet radiation or by lightning. Attempts to replicate these conditions in the laboratory have successfully shown that amino acids, purine and pyrimidine bases (◊base pairs in DNA), and other vital molecules can be created in this way. It has also been suggested that life could have reached Earth from elsewhere in the universe in the form of complex organic molecules present in meteors or comets, but others argue that this is not really an alternative explanation because these primitive life forms must then have been created elsewhere by much the same process. Once the atmosphere changed to its present composition, life could only be created by living organisms (a process called ◊biogenesis).

Life US weekly magazine of photo journalism, which recorded US and world events pictorially from 1936. It was founded by Henry Luce, owner of Time Inc., who bought the title of an older magazine.

lifeboat a small land-based vessel specially built for rescuing swimmers in danger of drowning, or a boat carried aboard a larger ship in case of a need to abandon ship.

life cycle in biology, the sequence of developmental stages through which members of a given species pass. Most vertebrates have a simple life cycle consisting of ◊fertilization of sex cells or ◊gametes, a period of development as an ◊embryo, a period of juvenile growth after hatching or birth, an adulthood including ◊sexual reproduction, and finally death. Invertebrate life cycles are generally more complex and may involve major reconstitution of the individual's appearance (◊metamorphosis) and completely different styles of life. Plants have a special type of life cycle with two distinct phases, known as ◊alternation of generations.

Thus dragonflies live an aquatic life as larvae and an aerial life during the adult phase. In many invertebrates and protozoa there is a sequence of stages in the life cycle, and in parasites different stages often occur in different host organisms.

life expectancy the average life span of a person at birth. It depends on nutrition, disease control, environmental contaminants, war, stress, and living standards in general.

There is a marked difference between First World countries, which generally have an aging population, and Third World countries, where life expectancy is much shorter. In Bangladesh, life expectancy is currently 48; in Nigeria 49. In famine-prone Ethiopia it is only 41.

life insurance an insurance policy that pays money on the death of the insured. Policies are available in many forms, the most common being term life insurance, in which a policyholder pays equal premiums each year for coverage in the event of death before the end of the contract. The premium rates are higher for the entire term for policyholders in succeeding age brackets. A whole life policy requires higher annual payments than term life but remains in effect until the death of the holder. The premiums add up and earn dividends so that at the end of a specified number of years the policy pays for itself and an actual cash value exists, against which the policyholder can borrow.

life sciences scientific study of the living world as a whole, a new synthesis of several traditional scientific disciplines including ◊biology, ◊zoology, and ◊botany, and newer, more specialized areas of study such as ◊biophysics and sociobiology.

This approach has led to many new ideas and discoveries as well as to an emphasis on ◊ecology, the study of living organisms in their natural environments.

life table a way of summarizing the probability that an individual will give birth or die during successive periods of life. From this, the proportion of individuals who survive from birth to any given age (survivorship) and the mean number of offspring produced (net reproductive rate) can be determined.

Insurance companies use life tables to estimate risks of death in order to set their premiums and governments use them to determine future needs for education and health services.

Liffey river in E Ireland, flowing from the Wicklow mountains to Dublin Bay; length 50 mi/80 km.

Ligachev Egor (Kuzmich) 1920– . Soviet politician. He joined the Communist Party 1944, and became a member of the Politburo 1985. He was replaced as the party ideologist 1988 by Vadim Medvedev.

ligament strong flexible connective tissue, made of

life table

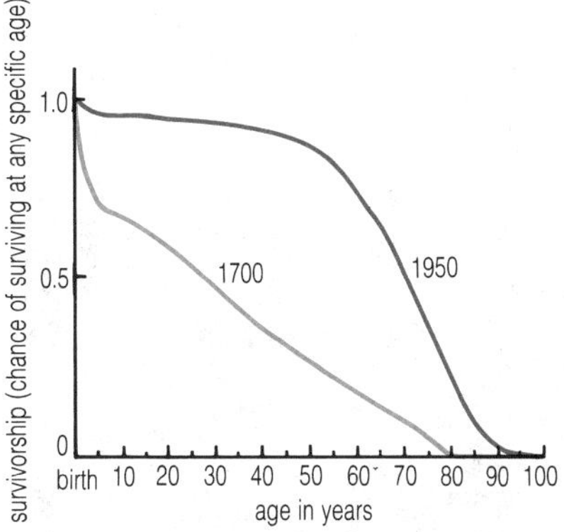
survivorship (chance of surviving at any specific age)
1.0
0.5
0
1700
1950
birth 10 20 30 40 50 60 70 80 90 100
age in years

the protein collagen, which joins bone to bone at moveable joints. Ligaments prevent bone dislocation (under normal circumstances) but permit joint flexion.

ligature any surgical device (nylon, gut, wire) for tying a blood vessel, limb, or base of a tumor, used to stop the flow of blood or other fluid through it.

Ligeti György (Sándor) 1923– . Hungarian-born Austrian composer who developed a dense, highly chromatic, polyphonic style in which melody and rhythm are sometimes lost in shifting blocks of sound. He achieved international prominence with *Atmosphères* 1961 and *Requiem* 1965, which were used for Kubrick's film epic *2001: A Space Odyssey*. Other works include an opera *Le Grand Macabre* 1978, and *Poème symphonique* 1962, for 100 metronomes.

light ◊electromagnetic radiation in the visible range, having a wavelength from about 400 nanometers in the extreme violet to about 770 nanometers in the extreme red. Light is considered to exhibit both particle and wave properties, and the fundamental particle or quantum of light is called the photon. The speed of light (and of all electromagnetic radiation) in a vacuum is approximately 186,000 mi/300,000 km per second, and is a universal constant denoted by *c*.

Newton was the first to discover, in 1666, that sunlight is composed of a mixture of light of different colors in certain proportions and that it could be separated into its components by dispersion. Before his time it was supposed that dispersion of light produced color instead of separating already existing colors.

The speed of light is allegedly the fastest speed in nature, but in 1971 a jet from the galaxy 3 273 was calculated as traveling at three times this speed, which should be impossible.

light bulb incandescent filament lamp, first demonstrated by Joseph Swan in the UK 1878 and Thomas Edison in the US 1879. The present-day light bulb is a thin glass bulb filled with an inert mixture of nitrogen and argon gas. It contains a filament made of fine tungsten wire. When electricity is passed through the wire, it glows white hot, producing light.

light-emitting diode (LED) means of displaying symbols in electronic instruments and devices. An LED is made of ◊semiconductor material, such as gallium arsenide phosphide, that glows when electricity is passed through it. The first digital watches and calculators had LED displays, but many later models use ◊liquid crystal displays.

Lighthill James 1924– . British mathematician who specialized in the application of mathematics to high-speed aerodynamics and jet propulsion.

He was Lucasian professor at Cambridge 1969–79 and provost of University College, London (1979–). He received a knighthood 1971.

lighthouse structure carrying a powerful light to warn ships or airplanes that they are approaching

lightning *A household light bulb would have to shine for 10,000 years to release the same amount of energy as a lightning bolt.*

a place (usually land) dangerous or important to navigation. The light is magnified and directed out to the horizon or up to the zenith by a series of mirrors or prisms. Increasingly lighthouses are powered by electricity and automated rather than staffed; the more recent models also emit radio signals. Only a minority of the remaining staffed lighthouses still use dissolved acetylene as a source of power.

Lights may be either flashing (the dark period exceeding the light) or rotating (the dark period being equal or less); fixed lights are liable to cause confusion. The pattern of lighting is individually varied so that ships or aircraft can identify the lighthouse.

Among early lighthouses were the Pharos of Alexandria (about 280 BC) and those built by the Romans at Ostia, Ravenna, Boulogne, and Dover.

In the US, the supervisory authority is the Coast Guard.

lightning high-voltage electrical discharge between two charged rainclouds or between a cloud and the Earth, caused by the buildup of electrical charges. Air in the path of lightning ionizes (becomes conducting), and expands; the accompanying noise is heard as thunder. Currents of 20,000 amps and temperatures of 54,000°F/30,000°C are common.

light pen in computing, an ◊input device resembling an ordinary pen, used to indicate locations on a computer screen. With certain computer-aided design (◊CAD) programs, the light pen can be used to instruct the computer to change the shape, size, position, and colors of sections of a screen image.

At its tip, the pen has a photoreceptor that emits signals as light from the screen passes beneath it. From the timing of this signal and a gridlike representation of the screen in the computer's memory, a computer program can calculate the position of the light pen.

light reaction the first stage of ◊photosynthesis, in which light energy splits water into oxygen and hydrogen ions. The second stage does not require light and results in the formation of carbohydrates.

light second unit of length, equal to the distance traveled by light in one second. It is equal to 9.835592×10^8 ft/2.997925×10^8 m. See ◊light-year.

light watt unit of radiant power (brightness of light). One light watt is the power required to produce a perceived brightness equal to that of light at a wavelength of 550 nanometers and 680 lumens.

light-year in astronomy, the distance traveled by a beam of light in a vacuum in one year, approximately 5.88 trillion (million million) miles/9.45 trillion km.

lignin a naturally occurring substance produced by plants to strengthen their tissues. It is difficult for ◊enzymes to attack lignin, so living organisms cannot digest wood, with the exception of a few specialized fungi and bacteria. It is the essential ingredient of all wood and is, therefore, of great commercial importance.

Chemically, lignin is made up of thousands of rings of carbon atoms joined together in a long chain. The way in which they are linked up varies along the chain.

lignite a type of ◊coal that is brown and fibrous, with a relatively low carbon content. In Scandinavia it is burned to generate power.

lignocaine short-term local anesthetic injected into tissues or applied to skin. It is effective for brief, invasive procedures such as dental care or insertion of a cannula (small tube) into a vein. Temporary paralysis (to prevent involuntary movement during eye surgery, for example) can be achieved by injection directly into the nerve serving the region.

Rapidly absorbed by mucous membranes (lining tissues), lignocaine may be sprayed into the nose or throat to allow comfortable insertion of a viewing instrument during ◊endoscopy. Its action makes it a potent antiarrhythmia drug as well: given intravenously during or following a heart attack, it reduces the risk of irregular contractions of the ventricles.

Liguria coastal region of NW Italy, which includes the resorts of the Italian Riviera, lying between the western Alps and the Mediterranean Gulf of Genoa. The region comprises the provinces of Genova, La Spezia, Imperia, and Savona, with a population (1988) of 1,750,000 and an area of 2,093 sq mi/5,418 sq km. Genoa is the chief port and city.

Likud alliance of right-wing Israeli political parties that defeated the Labor Party coalition in the May 1977 election and brought Menachem Begin to power. In 1987 Likud became part of an uneasy national coalition with Labor, formed to solve Israel's economic crisis. In 1989, another coalition was formed under Shamir.

lilac any flowering Old World shrub of the genus *Syringa* (such as *S. vulgaris*) of the olive family Oleaceae, bearing panicles (clusters) of small, sweetly scented, white or purplish flowers. The smaller Persian lilac is also popular in gardens.

Lilburne John 1614–1657. English republican agitator. He was imprisoned 1638–40 for circulating Puritan pamphlets, fought in the Parliamentary army in the Civil War, and by his advocacy of a democratic republic won the leadership of the ◊Levellers.

Lilienthal Otto 1848–1896. German aviation pioneer who inspired the ◊Wright brothers. He made and successfully flew many gliders before he was killed in a glider crash.

Lilith in the Old Testament, Assyrian female demon of the night. According to the ◊Talmud, she was the wife of Adam before Eve's creation.

Lille (Flemish *Ryssel*) industrial city (textiles, chemicals, engineering, distilling), capital of Nord-Pas-de-Calais, France; population (1982) 174,000, metropolitan area 936,000. The world's first entirely automatic underground system was opened here 1982.

Lilongwe capital of Malawi since 1975; population (1985) 187,000. Products include tobacco and textiles.

lily plant of the genus *Lilium*, family Liliaceae, of which there are some 80 species, most with showy, trumpet-shaped flowers growing from bulbs. The lily family includes hyacinths, tulips,

***limestone** Carboniferous limestone pavement near Ballynahowan, Ireland, showing the patterns caused by rain wearing away joints in the rock.*

asparagus, and plants of the onion genus. The term "lily" is also applied to many lilylike plants of allied genera and families.

lily of the valley plant *Convallaria majalis* of the lily family Liliaceae, growing in woods in Europe, N Asia, and North America. The small, pendant, white flowers are strongly scented. The plant is often cultivated.

Lima capital of Peru, an industrial city (textiles, chemicals, glass, cement) with its port at Callao; population (1988) 418,000, metropolitan area 4,605,000. Founded by the conquistador Pizarro 1535, it was rebuilt after destruction by an earthquake 1746.

Survivals of the colonial period are the university 1551, cathedral 1746, government palace (the rebuilt palace of the viceroys), and the senate house (once the headquarters of the Inquisition).

Lima city in NW Ohio, on the Ottawa River, N of Dayton; seat of Allen County. Industries include automobile and airplane parts, heavy machinery, electrical products, and oil processing; population (1990) 45,549.

Liman von Sanders Otto 1855–1929. German general assigned to the Turkish army to become inspector-general and a Turkish field marshal in Dec 1913. This link between the Turks and the Germans caused great suspicion on the part of the French and Russians.

Limassol port in S Cyprus in Akrotiri Bay; population (1985) 120,000. Products include cigarettes and wine. Richard I married Berengaria of Navarre here 1191. The town's population increased rapidly with the influx of Greek Cypriot refugees after the Turkish invasion 1974.

limbo a West Indian dance in which the performer leans backwards from the knees to pass under a pole, which is lowered closer to the ground with each attempt. The world record has been unchanged since 1973 at 6⅛ in/15.5 cm, although on roller skates the record is 5¼ in/13.3 cm.

limbo in Christian theology, a region for the souls of those who were not admitted to the divine vision. *Limbus infantum* was a place where unbaptized infants enjoyed inferior blessedness, and *limbus patrum* was where the prophets of the Old Testament dwelt. The word was first used in this sense in the 13th century by St Thomas Aquinas.

Limbourg province of Belgium; capital Hasselt; area 926 sq mi/2,400 sq km; population (1987) 737,000.

Limbourg brothers Franco-Flemish painters, Pol, Herman, and Jan (Hennequin, Janneken), active in the late 14th and early 15th centuries, first in Paris, then at the ducal court of Burgundy. They produced richly detailed manuscript illuminations, including two Books of ◊Hours.

Patronized by Jean de Berri, duke of Burgundy, from about 1404, they illustrated two Books of Hours that are masterpieces of the International Gothic style, the *Belles Heures* about 1408 (Metropolitan Museum of Art, New York), and *Les très riches Heures du Duc de Berri* about 1413–15 (Musée Condé, Chantilly). Their miniature paintings include a series of scenes representing the months, presenting almost a fairy-tale world of pinnacled castles with lords and ladies, full of detail and brilliant decorative effects. All three brothers were dead by 1416.

Limburg southernmost province of the Netherlands in the plain of the Maas (Meuse); area 838 sq mi/2,170 sq km; population (1988) 1,095,000. Its capital is Maastricht, the oldest city in the Netherlands. Manufacture of chemicals has now replaced coal mining but the coal industry is still remembered at Kerkrade, alleged site of the first European coal mine. The marl soils of S Limburg are used in the manufacture of cement and fertilizer. Mixed arable farming and horticulture are also important.

lime small thorny bush *Citrus aurantifolia* of the rue family Rutaceae, native to India. The white flowers are succeeded by light green or yellow fruits, limes, which resemble lemons but are more globular in shape.

lime or ***quicklime*** CaO (technical name calcium oxide quicklime white powdery substance used in making mortar and cement and to reduce soil acidity. It is made commercially by heating calcium carbonate ($CaCO_3$) obtained from limestone or chalk.

Quicklime readily absorbs water to become calcium hydroxide (CaOH), known as slaked lime.

Limerick county town of Limerick, Republic of Ireland, the main port of W Ireland, on the Shannon estuary; population (1986) 77,000. It was founded in the 12th century.

Limerick county in SW Republic of Ireland, in Munster province

area 1,038 sq mi/2,690 sq km

county town Limerick

physical fertile, with hills in the S

products dairy products

population (1986) 164,000.

limestone sedimentary rock composed chiefly of calcium carbonate $CaCO_3$, either derived from the shells of marine organisms or precipitated from solution, mostly in the ocean. Various types of limestone are used as building stone.

◊Marble is metamorphosed limestone. Certain so-called marbles are not marbles but fine-grained fossiliferous limestones that take an attractive polish. Caves commonly occur in limestone. ◊Karst is a type of limestone landscape.

limiting factor any factor affecting the rate of a metabolic reaction. Levels of light or of carbon dioxide are limiting factors in ◊photosynthesis because both are necessary for the production of carbohydrates. In experiments, photosynthesis is observed to slow down and eventually stop as the levels of light decrease.

It is believed that the increased concentrations of carbon dioxide building up in the atmosphere through burning of fossil fuels will allow faster plant growth.

limnology study of lakes and other bodies of open fresh water, in terms of their plant and animal biology, and their physical properties.

Limoges city and capital of Limousin, France; population (1982) 172,000. Fine enamels were made here in the medieval period, and it is the center of the modern French porcelain industry. Other industries include textiles, electrical equipment, and metal goods. The city was sacked by the Black Prince 1370.

limonite an iron ore, mostly poorly crystalline iron oxyhydroxide, but usually mixed with ◊hematite and other iron oxides. Also known as brown iron ore, it is often found in bog deposits.

Limousin former province and modern region of central France; area 6,544 sq mi/16,900 sq km; population (1986) 736,000. It consists of the *départements* of Corréze, Creuse, and Haute-Vienne. Chief town is Limoges. A thinly populated and largely unfertile region, it is crossed by the mountains of the Massif Central. Fruit and vegetables are produced in the more fertile lowlands. Kaolin is mined.

limpet any of various marine ◊snails belonging to several families and genera, especially *Acmaea* and *Patella*. A limpet has a conical shell and adheres firmly to rocks by the disclike foot. Limpets leave their fixed positions only to graze on seaweeds, always returning to the same spot. They are found in the Atlantic and Pacific.

Limpopo river in SE Africa, rising in the Transvaal and reaching the Indian Ocean in Mozambique; length 1,000 mi/1,600 km.

Lin Biao 1907–1971. Chinese politician and general. He joined the Communists 1927, became a commander of ◊Mao Zedong's Red Army, and led the Northeast People's Liberation Army in the civil war after 1945. He became defense minister 1959, and as vice chairman of the party in 1969

Lincoln *The 16th president of the United States of America, Abraham Lincoln, a Republican. 1861–1865.*

he was expected to be Mao's successor. But in 1972 the government announced that Lin had been killed in an airplane crash in Mongolia Sept 17, 1971 while fleeing to the USSR following an abortive coup attempt.

Lincoln industrial city in Lincolnshire, England; population (1981) 76,200. Manufacturing includes excavators, cranes, gas turbines, power units for oil platforms, and cosmetics. It was the flourishing Roman colony of Lindum, and had a big medieval wool trade. Paulinus built a church here in the 7th century, and the 11th–15th-century cathedral has the earliest Gothic work in Britain. The 12th-century High Bridge is the oldest in Britain still to have buildings on it.

Lincoln industrial city and capital of Nebraska; population (1990) 191,972. Industries include engineering, pharmaceuticals, electronic and electrical equipment, and food processing. Educational institutions include the main campus of the University of Nebraska and Nebraska Wesleyan University. It was known as Lancaster until 1867, when it was renamed after Abraham Lincoln and designated the state capital.

Lincoln Abraham 1809–1865. 16th president of the US 1861–65. In the American ◊Civil War, his chief concern was the preservation of the Union from which the Confederate (Southern) slave states had seceded on his election. In 1863 he announced the freedom of the slaves with the Emancipation Proclamation. He was reelected 1864 with victory for the North in sight, but assassinated just after the end of the war.

Lincoln was born in a log cabin in Kentucky, raised in Indiana, then settled in Illinois as a storekeeper. Self-educated, he practiced law from 1837 in Springfield, Illinois. He was a member of the state legislature 1832–42 and was known as Honest Abe. He joined the new Republican party 1856, when the ◊Whig party split over the slavery issue, and was elected president 1860 on a minority vote. Although his antislavery views were limited to a desire to keep the institution from spreading to the new territories, he was seen by Southerners as a dangerous enemy. His refusal to concede to Confederate demands for the evacuation of the federal garrison at Fort Sumter, South Carolina, precipitated the first hostilities of the Civil War. The Emancipation Proclamation was more a political than a moral document, with Lincoln acknowledging that he held as his first priority the preservation of the Union; the proclamation, however, largely ended European sympathies for the Confederacy. In his Gettysburg Address 1863, he declared the aims of preserving a "nation conceived in liberty, and dedicated to the proposition that all men are created equal." Reelected with a large majority 1864 on a National Union ticket, he advocated a reconciliatory policy toward the South "with malice toward none, with charity for all." Five days after General Lee's surrender, Lincoln was shot in a Washington, DC theater audience by an actor and Confederate sympathizer, John Wilkes ◊Booth.

Lincoln Benjamin 1733–1810. American military and political leader. Born in Hingham, Massachusetts, Lincoln served in the legislature and provincial congress prior to the American Revolution. With the outbreak of hostilities, he was named brigadier general in the Continental army and placed in command of troops in New York. After helping to win victory at Saratoga, Lincoln was sent to the South but he had to surrender to the British at Charleston 1780. Lincoln served as secretary of war for the Continental Congress 1781–83, and he led the Massachusetts militia in the suppression of Shays' Rebellion 1787.

Lincolnshire county in E England

area 2,274 sq mi/5,890 sq km

towns Lincoln (administrative headquarters), Skegness

physical Lincoln Wolds; marshy coastline; the Fens in the SE; rivers: Witham, Welland

features 16th-century Burghley House; Belton House, a Restoration mansion

products cattle, sheep, horses, cereals, flower bulbs, oil

population (1987) 575,000

famous people Isaac Newton, Alfred Tennyson, Margaret Thatcher.

Lind Jenny 1820–1887. Swedish soprano of remarkable range, nicknamed the "Swedish nightingale."

She toured the US from 1850–52 under the management of P T ◊Barnum.

Lindbergh Charles A(ugustus) 1902–1974. US aviator who made the first solo nonstop flight in 33.5 hr across the Atlantic (Roosevelt Field, Long Island, New York to Le Bourget airport, Paris) 1927 in the *Spirit of St Louis*, a Ryan monoplane designed by him.

Born in Detroit, Michigan, Lindbergh was a barnstorming pilot before attending the US Army School in Texas 1924 and becoming an officer in the Army Air Service Reserve 1925. His son, Charles, Jr (1930–32), was kidnapped and killed, a crime for which Bruno Hauptmann was convicted and executed. Ensuing legislation against kidnapping was called the Lindbergh Act. Although he admired the Nazi air force and championed US neutrality in the late 1930s, he flew 50 combat missions in the Pacific theater in World War II. He wrote *The Spirit of St Louis* 1953 (Pulitzer prize).

Lindbergh *Pioneer US aviator, Charles Lindbergh. He was the first person to fly solo non-stop across the Atlantic.*

Lindisfarne site of monastery off the coast of Northumberland, England; see under ◊Holy Island.

Lindsay (Nicholas) Vachel 1879–1931. US poet. He wandered the country, living by reciting his ballad-like verse, collected in volumes including *General William Booth Enters into Heaven* 1913, *The Congo* 1914, and *Johnny Appleseed* 1928.

linear accelerator see ◊accelerator.

linear equation in mathematics, an equation involving two variables (x,y) of the general form $y = mx + b$, where m is the slope of the line represented by the equation and b is the y-intercept, or the value of y where the line crosses the y-axis in the ◊Cartesian coordinate system. Linear equations can be used to describe the behavior of buildings, bridges, trusses, and other static structures.

linear motor type of electric motor, an induction motor in which the fixed stator and moving armature are straight and parallel to each other (rather than being circular and one inside the other as in an ordinary induction motor). Linear motors are used, for example, to power sliding doors. There is a magnetic force between the stator and armature; this force has been used to support a vehicle, as in the experimental ◊maglev linear motor train.

linear programming in mathematics and economics, a set of techniques for finding the maxima or minima of certain variables governed by linear equations or inequalities. These maxima and minima are used to represent "best" solutions in terms of goals such as maximizing profit or minimizing cost.

Line Islands coral-island group in the Pacific ocean; population (1985) 2,500. Products include coconut and guano. Eight of the islands belong to Kiribati, and two (Palmyra and Jarvis) are administered by the US.

linen the yarn spun and the textile woven from ◊flax.

To get the longest possible fibers, flax is pulled, rather than cut by hand or machine, just as the seed bolls are beginning to set. After preliminary drying, it is steeped in water so that the fiber can be more easily separated from the wood of the stem, then hackled (combed), classified, drawn into continuous fibers, and spun. Bleaching, weaving, and finishing processes vary according to the final product, which can be sailcloth, canvas, sacking, cambric, or lawn. Because of the length of its fiber, linen yarn has twice the strength of cotton, and yet is superior in delicacy, so that it is suitable for lace making. It mixes well with synthetics.

line of force a line in a field of magnetic or electrical force indicating the direction of the force at any point.

ling any of several deepwater long-bodied fishes of the cod family found in the N Atlantic.

lingam in Hinduism, phallic emblem of ◊Siva, the yoni being the female equivalent.

lingua franca (Italian "Frankish tongue") any language that is used as a means of communication by groups who do not themselves normally speak that language; for example, English is a lingua franca used by Japanese doing business in Finland, or by Swedes in Saudi Arabia. The term comes from the mixture of French, Italian, Spanish, Greek, Turkish, and Arabic that was spoken around the Mediterranean from the time of the Crusades until the 18th century.

Many of the world's lingua francas are ◊pidgin languages; for example, Bazaar Hindi (Hindustani), Bazaar Malay, and Neo-Melanesian (also known as Tok Pisin), which became the official language of Papua New Guinea.

linguistics the scientific study of language, from its origins (historical linguistics) to the changing way it is pronounced (phonetics), derivation of words through various languages (etymology), development of meanings (semantics), and the arrangement and modifications of words to convey a message (grammar).

linkage in genetics, the association between two or more genes that tend to be inherited together because they are on the same chromosome. The closer together they are on the chromosome, the less likely they are to be separated by crossing over (one of the processes of ◊recombination) and they are then described as being "tightly linked."

Linköping industrial town in SE Sweden; 107 mi/172 km SW of Stockholm; population (1986) 117,800. Industries include hosiery, aircraft and engines, and tobacco. It has a 12th-century cathedral.

Linlithgow tourist center in Lothian region, Scotland; population (1981) 9,600.

Linlithgow Palace, now in ruins, was once a royal residence, and Mary Queen of Scots was born there.

Linnaeus Carolus 1707–1778. Swedish naturalist and physician. His botanical work *Systema naturae* 1758 contained his system for classifying plants into groups depending on shared characteristics (such as the number of stamens in flowers), providing a much-needed framework for identification. He also devised the concise and precise system for naming plants and animals, using one Latin (or Latinized) word to represent the genus and a second to distinguish the species.

For example, in the Latin name of the daisy, *Bellis perennis*, *Bellis* is the name of the genus to which the plant belongs, and *perennis* distinguishes the species from others of the same genus. By tradition the generic name always begins with a capital letter. The author who first described a particular species is often indicated after the name, for example, *Bellis perennis* Linnaeus, showing that the author was Linnaeus. See also ◊binomial classification, ◊taxonomy.

linnet Old World finch *Acanthis cannabina*. Mainly brown, the males, noted for their song, have a crimson crown and breast in summer.

Linotype trademark for a typesetting machine once universally used for newspaper work, which sets complete lines (slugs) of hot-metal type as operators type the copy at a keyboard. It was invented in the US 1884 by German-born Ottmar ◊Mergenthaler. It has been replaced by phototypesetting.

Lin Piao alternate form of ◊Lin Biao.

linsang nocturnal, tree-dwelling, carnivorous mammal of the civet family, about 2.5 ft/75 cm long. It is native to Africa and SE Asia.

The African linsang *Poiana richardsoni* is a long, low and lithe spotted animal about 1.1 ft/33 cm long with a 1.25 ft/38 cm tail. The two species of oriental linsang, genus *Prionodon*, of Asia are slightly bigger.

linseed seeds of the flax plant *Linum usitatissimum*, from which linseed oil is expressed, the residue being used as cattle feed. The oil is used in paint, wood treatments and varnishes, and in the manufacture of linoleum.

Linz industrial port (iron, steel, metalworking) on the river Danube in N Austria; population (1981) 199,900.

lion cat *Panthera leo*, now found only in Africa and NW India. The coat is tawny, the young having darker spot markings that usually disappear in the adult. The male has a heavy mane and a tuft at the end of the tail. Head and body measure about 6 ft/2 m, plus 3 ft/1 m of tail, the lioness being slightly smaller.

Lions produce litters of two to six cubs, and often live in prides of several adult males and females with several young. Capable of short bursts of speed, they skillfully collaborate in stalking herbivorous animals. Old lions whose teeth and strength are failing may resort to eating humans. "Mountain lion" is a name for the ◊puma.

In zoos, a *liger* is the offspring of a male lion and female tiger; a *tigon* of a male tiger and female lion.

Lipari Islands or ***Aeolian Islands*** volcanic group of seven islands off NE Sicily, including Lipari (on which is the capital of the same name), Stromboli (active volcano 3,038 ft/926 m high), and Vulcano (also with an active volcano); area 44 sq mi/114 sq km. In Greek mythology, the god Aeolus kept the winds imprisoned in a cave on the Lipari Islands.

lipase the enzyme responsible for breaking down fats into fatty acids and glycerol. It is produced by the ◊pancreas and requires a slightly alkaline environment. The products of fat digestion are absorbed by the intestinal wall.

Lipatti Dinu 1917–1950. Romanian pianist, who perfected a small repertoire, notably Chopin. He died of leukemia at 33.

Lipchitz Jacques 1891–1973. Lithuanian-born sculptor, active in Paris from 1909; he emigrated to the US 1941. He was one of the first Cubist sculptors.

The Barnes Foundation, Philadelphia, has many of his early works.

Li Peng 1928– . Chinese communist politician, a member of the Politburo from 1985, and head of government from 1987. During the prodemocracy demonstrations 1989 he supported the massacre of students by Chinese troops and the subsequent executions of others. He favors maintaining firm central and party control over the economy and seeks improved relations with the USSR.

Li was born at Chengdu in Sichuan province, the son of the writer Li Shouxun (who took part in the Nanchang rising 1927 and was executed 1930), and was adopted by the communist leader Zhou Enlai. He studied at the communist headquarters of Yanan 1941–47 and trained as a hydroelectric engineer at the Moscow Power Institute from 1948. He was appointed minister of the electric power industry 1981, a vice premier 1983, and prime minister 1987. In 1989 he launched the crackdown on demonstrators in Beijing that led to the massacre in ◊Tiananmen Square.

lipid any of a group of organic compounds soluble in solvents such as ethanol (alcohol), but not in water. They include oils, fats, waxes, steroids, carotenoids, and other fatty substances.

Lipmann Fritz 1899–1986. US biochemist. He investigated the means by which the cell acquires energy and highlighted the crucial role played by the energy-rich phosphate molecule, adenosine triphosphate (ATP). For this and further work on metabolism, Lipmann shared the 1953 Nobel Prize for Medicine with Hans Krebs.

Li Po 705–762. Chinese poet. He used traditional literary forms, but his exuberance, the boldness of his imagination, and the intensity of his feeling have won him recognition as perhaps the greatest of all Chinese poets. Although he was mostly concerned with higher themes, he is also remembered for his celebratory verses on drinking.

Lippe river of N Germany flowing into the river Rhine; length 147 mi/230 km; also a former German state, now part of North Rhine–Westphalia.

Lippershey Hans c. 1570–1619. Dutch lens maker, credited with inventing the telescope 1608.

Lippi Filippino 1457–1504. Italian painter of the Florentine school, trained by Botticelli. He produced altarpieces and several fresco cycles, full of detail and drama, elegant and finely drawn. He was the son of Filippo Lippi.

His frescoes, typical of late 15th-century Florentine work, can be found in Sta Maria sopra Minerva, Rome, in Sta Maria Novella, Florence, and elsewhere.

Lippi Fra Filippo 1406–1469. Italian painter, born in Florence and patronized by the Medici family. His works include frescoes depicting the lives of St Stephen and St John the Baptist in Prato Cathedral 1452–66. He also painted many altarpieces of Madonnas and groups of saints.

The painter and biographer Giorgio ◊Vasari gave a colorful account of his life including how, as a monk, he was tried in the 1450s for abducting a nun (the mother of his son Filippino).

Lippizaner pure white horse, named after its place of origin in Lippiza, Yugoslavia. They are trained at the Spanish Riding School of Vienna.

Lippmann Gabriel 1845–1921. French doctor who invented the direct color process in photography. He won the Nobel Prize for Physics in 1908.

Lippmann Walter 1889–1974. US political commentator. From 1921 Lippmann was the chief editorial writer for the *New York World* and from 1931 wrote the daily column "Today and Tomorrow," which was widely syndicated through the *New York Herald Tribune*. Among his books are *A Preface to Morals* 1922, *The Good Society* 1937, and *Essays in the Public Philosophy* 1955.

Born in New York and educated at Harvard, Lippmann was one of the founders of the *New Republic* 1914. After service in army intelligence during World War I, he became an adviser to President Wilson at the Versailles Peace Conference.

liquefied petroleum gas (LPG) liquid form of butane, propane, or pentane, produced by the distillation of petroleum during oil refining. At room temperature these substances are gases, although they can be easily liquefied and stored under pressure in metal containers. They are used for heating and cooking where other fuels are not available: camping stoves and cigarette lighters, for instance, often use liquefied butane as fuel.

liquid state of matter between a ◊solid and a ◊gas. A liquid forms a level surface and assumes the shape of its container. Its atoms do not occupy fixed positions as in a crystalline solid, nor do they have freedom of movement as in a gas. Unlike a gas, a liquid is difficult to compress since pressure applied at one point is equally transmitted throughout (Pascal's principle). ◊Hydraulics makes use of this property.

liquid air air that has been cooled so much that it has liquefied. This happens at temperatures below about −321°F/−196°C. The various constituent gases, including nitrogen, oxygen, argon, and neon, can be separated from liquid air by the technique of ◊fractionation.

liquid crystal display

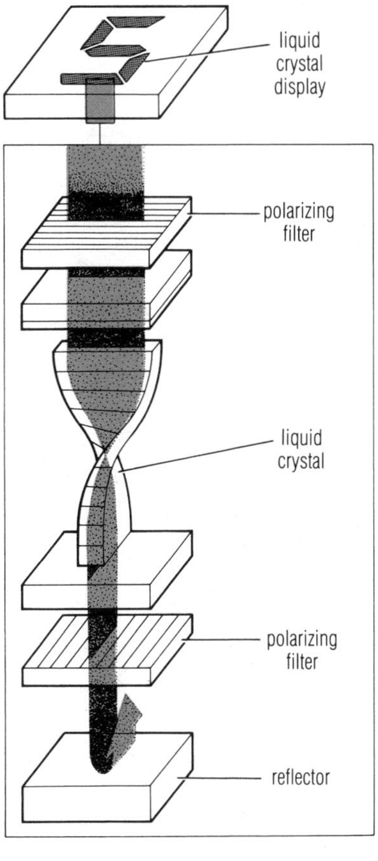
liquid
crystal
display
polarizing
filter
liquid
crystal
polarizing
filter
reflector

***Lisbon** The Bélem Tower, a fortress built in the 16th century by King Manuel I to protect the approaches to Lisbon.*

Air is liquefied by the Linde process, in which air is alternately compressed, cooled, and expanded, the expansion resulting each time in a considerable reduction in temperature.

liquidation in economics, the termination of a company by converting all its assets into cash to pay off its liabilities.

liquid crystal display (LCD) display of numbers (for example, in a calculator) or picture (such as on a pocket television screen) produced by molecules of a substance in a semiliquid state with some crystalline properties, in that clusters of molecules align in parallel formations. The display is a blank until the application of an electric field, which "twists" the molecules so that they reflect or transmit light falling on them.

liquidity in economics, the state of possessing sufficient money and/or assets to be able to pay off all liabilities. Liquid assets are those that may be converted quickly into cash, such as stock shares, as opposed to property.

Lisbon (Portuguese ***Lisboa***) city and capital of Portugal, in the SW on the tidal lake and estuary formed by the river Tagus; population (1984) 808,000. Industries include steel, textiles, chemicals, pottery, shipbuilding, and fishing. It has been capital since 1260 and reached its peak of prosperity in the period of Portugal's empire during the 16th century.

Lisburn cathedral city and market town in Antrim, N Ireland, on the river Lagan; population (1985) 87,900. It produces linen and furniture.

Lisieux town in Calvados *département*, France, to the SE of Caen; population (1982) 25,823. St Thérèse of Lisieux spent her religious life in the Carmelite convent here, and her tomb attracts pilgrims.

LISP (acronym from list processing) computer-programming language for list processing used primarily in research into artificial intelligence (AI).

Developed in the 1960s, and until recently common only in university laboratories, LISP is more popular in the US than in Europe, where the language ◊PROLOG is often preferred for AI work.

Lister Joseph, 1st Baron Lister 1827–1912. English surgeon and founder of antiseptic surgery, influenced by Louis ◊Pasteur's work on bacteria. He introduced dressings soaked in carbolic acid and strict rules of hygiene to combat wound sepsis in hospitals.

The number of surgical operations had greatly increased since the introduction of anesthetics, and death rates had been more than 40%. Under Lister's regime they fell dramatically.

listeriosis disease of animals that may occasionally infect humans, caused by the bacterium *Listeria monocytogenes*. The bacteria multiply at temperatures close to 32°F/0°C, which means they may flourish in precooked frozen meals if the cooking has not been thorough. Listeriosis causes inflammation of the brain and its surrounding membranes, but can be treated with penicillin.

Liszt Franz 1811–1886. Hungarian pianist and composer. An outstanding virtuoso of the piano, he was an established concert artist by the age of

***Liszt** Hungarian Franz Liszt, Romantic composer and pianist who championed the work of Berlioz and Wagner.*

12. His expressive, romantic, and frequently chromatic works include piano music (*Transcendental Studies* 1851), symphonies, piano concertos, and organ music. Much of his music is programmatic; he also originated the symphonic poem.

Liszt was taught by his father, then by Carl Czerny (1791–1857). He traveled widely in Europe, producing an opera *Don Sanche* in Paris at the age of 14. As musical director and conductor at Weimar 1848–59, he was a champion of the music of Berlioz and Wagner.

Retiring to Rome, he turned again to his early love of religion, and in 1865 became a secular priest (adopting the title Abbé), but he continued to teach and give concert tours. Many of his compositions are lyrical, often technically difficult, piano works, including the *Liebesträume* and the *Hungarian Rhapsodies*, based on folk music. He also wrote an opera and a symphony; masses and oratorios; songs; and piano arrangements of works by Beethoven, Schubert, and Wagner among others. He died at Bayreuth.

Litani river rising near Baalbek in the Anti-Lebanon mountains of E Lebanon. It flows NE–SW through the Beqa'a Valley then E to the Mediterranean 5 mi/8 km N of Tyre. The Israelis invaded Lebanon as far as the Litani River in 1978.

litany in the Christian church, a form of prayer or supplication led by a priest with set responses by the congregation.

litchi or ***lychee*** evergreen tree *Litchi chinensis* of the soapberry family Sapindaceae. The delicately flavored ovate fruit is encased in a brownish rough outer skin and has a hard seed. The litchi is native to S China, where it has been cultivated for 2,000 years.

liter metric unit of volume (abbreviation l), equal since 1964 to one cubic decimeter (61.025 cu in, 1.057 liquid qt, or 0.91 dry qt). It was formerly defined as the volume occupied by one kilogram of pure water at 4°C at standard pressure, but this is slightly larger than one cubic decimeter.

literacy the ability to read and write. The level at which functional literacy is set rises as society becomes more complex, and it becomes increasingly difficult for an illiterate person to find work and cope with the other demands of everyday life.

Literacy classes and tutorials are available in both day and evening sessions to help adults learn to read. Children are taught to read beginning with the first grade.

literary criticism the establishment of principles governing literary composition, and the assessment and interpretation of literary works. Contemporary criticism offers analyses of literary works from structuralist, semiological, feminist, Marxist, and psychoanalytical perspectives, whereas earlier criticism tended to deal with moral or political ideas, or with a literary work as a formal object independent of its creator.

The earliest systematic literary criticism was the *Poetics* of Aristotle; a later Greek critic was the author of the treatise *On the Sublime*, usually attributed to Longinus. Horace and Quintilian were influential Latin critics. The Italian Renaissance introduced humanist criticism, and the revival of Classical scholarship exalted the authority of Aristotle and Horace. Like literature itself, European criticism then applied Neo-Classical, Romantic, and modern approaches.

literature words set apart in some way from ordinary everyday communication. In the ancient oral traditions, before stories and poems were written down, literature had a mainly public function—mythic and religious. As literary works came to be preserved in writing, and, eventually, printed, their role became more private, serving as a vehicle for the exploration and expression of emotion and the human situation.

In the development of literature, esthetic criteria have come increasingly to the fore. The English poet and critic Coleridge defined *prose* as words in their best order, and *poetry* as the "best" words in the best order. The distinction between ◊verse and ◊prose is not always clear-cut, but in practice ◊poetry tends to be metrically formal (making it easier to memorize), whereas prose corresponds more closely to the patterns of ordinary speech. Poetry therefore had an early advantage over prose in the days before printing, which it did not relinquish until comparatively recently. Over the centuries poetry has taken on a wide range of forms, from the lengthy narrative such as the ◊epic, to the lyric, expressing personal emotion in songlike form; from the ◊ballad, and the 14-line ◊sonnet, to the extreme conciseness of the 17-syllable Japanese ◊haiku. Prose came into its own in the West as a vehicle for imaginative literature with the rise of the ◊novel in the 18th century, and ◊fiction has since been divided into various genres such as the ◊historical novel, ◊detective fiction, ◊fantasy, and ◊science fiction.

See also the literature of particular countries, under ◊American literature, ◊English literature, ◊French literature, and so on.

lithification another term for ◊diagenesis.

lithium soft, ductile, silver-white, metallic element, symbol Li, atomic number 3, atomic weight 6.941. It is one of the ◊alkali metals, has a very low density (far less than most woods), and floats on water (specific gravity 0.57); it is the lightest of all metals. Lithium is used to harden alloys, in batteries, and its compounds are used in medication to treat manic depression.

It was named in 1818 by Swedish chemist Jöns Berzelius for the element discovered the previous year by his student Johan A Arfwedson (1792–1841), for Greek *lithos*, stone, since it is found in most igneous rocks and many mineral springs.

lithography ◊printmaking technique originated by Aloys Senefelder 1798, based on the antipathy of grease and water. A drawing is made with greasy crayon on an absorbent stone, which is then wetted. The wet stone repels ink (which is greasy) applied to the surface and the crayon attracts it, so that the drawing can be printed. Lithographic ◊printing is used for color printing, posters, and in book production and has developed this basic principle into complex processes.

lithosphere the topmost layer of the Earth's structure, forming the jigsaw of plates that take part in the movements of ◊plate tectonics. The lithosphere comprises the ◊crust and a portion of the upper ◊mantle. It is regarded as being rigid and moves about on the semimolten ◊asthenosphere. The lithosphere is about 47 mi/75 km thick.

Lithuania country in N Europe, bounded E and S by the USSR; W by Poland, the Kaliningrad area of the Russian Soviet Federative Socialist Republic, and the Baltic Sea; N by Latvia.

Lithuania
Republic of

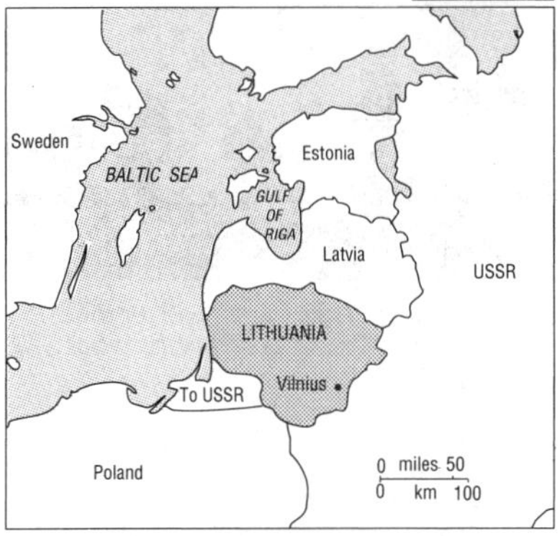
Sweden
BALTIC SEA
Estonia
GULF OF RIGA
Latvia
USSR
LITHUANIA
Vilnius
To USSR
Poland
0 miles 50
0 km 100

area 25,174 sq mi/65,200 sq km
capital Vilnius
cities Kaunas, Klaipeda, Klaipeda, Siauliai, Panevezys
physical central lowlands with gentle hills in W and higher terrain in SE; 25% forested; some 3,000 small lakes, marshes, and complex sandy coastline
features river Nemen; white sand dunes on Kursiu Marios lagoon
head of state Vytautas Landsbergis from 1990
head of government Albertas Shiminas from 1991
political system emergent democratic republic
products heavy engineering, electrical goods, shipbuilding, cement, food processing, bacon, dairy products, cereals, potatoes
currency ruble
population (1989 est) 3,690,000; 80% Lithuanian, 9% Russian, 8% Polish, Byelorussian and Ukrainian minorities
language Lithuanian
religion predominantly Roman Catholic
chronology
1918 Independence declared following withdrawal of German occupying troops at end of World War I; Soviets attempted to regain power.
1919 Soviets overthrown by Germans, Poles, and nationalist Lithuanians; democratic republic established.
1920-39 Province and city of Vilnius occupied by Poles.
1926 Coup overthrew established government; Antanas Smetona became president.
1939 Secret German–Soviet agreement brought most of Lithuania under Soviet influence.
1940 Incorporated into USSR as constituent republic.
1941 Lithuania revolted against USSR and established own government. During World War II Germans again occupied the country.
1944 USSR resumed rule.
1944-52 Lithuanian guerrillas fought USSR.
1972 Demonstrations against Soviet government.
1980 Nationalist dissent, influenced by Polish example.
1988 Popular front formed, the Lithuanian Restructuring Movement (Sajudis) to campaign for increased autonomy.
1989 Lithuanian declared the state language and flag of independent interwar republic readopted. Communist Party split into two, with the majority formally breaking away from the Communist Party of the USSR and establishing itself as a social-democratic, Lithuanian-nationalist body.
1990 March: unilateral declaration of independence.
1991 Jan: Prime Minister Kazimiera Prunskiene resigned and went into exile; replaced by Albertas Shiminas. Soviet paratroopers seized political and communications buildings in Vilnius, killing 13 civilians, but quickly began to withdraw. July: four Lithuanian policemen and two customs officers killed at border post with Byelorussia. Sept: independence recognized by Soviet government and Western nations; membership of the United Nations granted. Communist Party outlawed.

history Lithuania became a single nation at the end of the 12th century. The ◊Teutonic Knights (German crusaders) who attempted to invade in the 13th century were successfully driven back, and Lithuania extended its boundaries in the 14th century to reach almost as far as Moscow and the Black Sea. In 1386 Lithuania was joined with Poland in a mutually beneficial confederation. The two eventually became a single state 1569, and passed into the control of the Russian tsar 1795. Revolts 1831 and 1863 failed to win independence for the state, and a more organized movement for the independence of Lithuania emerged in the 1880s. When self-government was demanded 1905 this was denied by the Russians.

struggle for independence During World War I Lithuania was occupied by German troops. After the war, it declared its independence, but the Soviets claimed Lithuania as a Soviet republic 1918. The Soviets were overthrown by the Germans, Poles, and nationalist Lithuanians 1919, and a democratic republic was established. This was in turn overthrown by a coup 1926, and the new president, Antanas Smetona, assumed increasing authority. In 1939 Germany took control of part of Lithuania, handing it over to the USSR later the same year. In 1940 Lithuania was incorporated as a constituent republic of the USSR, being designated the Lithuanian Soviet Socialist Republic. In 1941, when the Germans had invaded the USSR, Lithuania revolted against Soviet rule and established its own government. The Germans occupied Lithuania 1941–44, after which Soviet rule was restored.

As in the other Baltic republics, there was strong nationalist dissent from 1980, influenced by the Polish example and prompted by the influx of Russian workers and officials. A popular front, the Lithuanian Restructuring Movement (Sajudis), was formed Oct 1988 to campaign for increased autonomy, and in Nov 1989 the republic's supreme soviet (state assembly), to the chagrin of Russian immigrants, decreed Lithuanian the state language and readopted the flag of the independent interwar republic. A month later, the republic's Communist Party split into two, with the majority wing formally breaking away from the Communist Party of the USSR and establishing itself as a social-democratic, Lithuanian-nationalist body. A multiparty system is effectively in place in the republic. In March 1990 Lithuania unilaterally declared its independence.

Criticized by militant nationalists as being too conciliatory toward Moscow, Prime Minister Kazimiera Prunskiene resigned Jan 1991 and went into exile. She was replaced by Albertas Shiminas. Also in Jan, Soviet paratroopers seized political and communications buildings in Vilnius, killing 13 civilians, but began to withdraw the same month. On July 31 four Lithuanian policemen and two customs officers were killed at a border post with Byelorussia in what was the worst bloodshed in the Baltics since Jan. The OMON black beret troops of the Soviet Interior Ministry and KGB were suspected.

In the wake of the overthrow of the Aug 1991 anti-Gorbachev coup in the USSR, Lithuania's declaration of independence was recognized by the Soviet government and Western nations Sept 1991 and the new state was granted membership of the United Nations.

Lithuanian language Indo-European language spoken by the people of Lithuania, which through its geographical isolation has retained many ancient features of the Indo-European language family. It acquired a written form in the 16th century, using the Latin alphabet, and is currently spoken by some 3–4 million people.

litmus dye obtained from various lichens and used as an indicator to test the acidic or alkaline nature of aqueous solutions; it turns red in the presence of acid, and blue in the presence of alkali.

Little Bighorn, Battle of the engagement in Montana; Lieutenant Colonel George ◊Custer's defeat by the ◊Sioux Indians, June 25, 1876, under Chiefs ◊Crazy Horse and Sitting Bull, known as Custer's Last Stand. The battle was precipitated by the discovery of gold in the Black Hills and the subsequent violations of the 1868 treaty with the Sioux, which had granted them "sole use" of the area. Custer ignored scouting reports of an overwhelming Indian force and led a column of 265 soldiers into a ravine where thousands of Indian warriors lay in wait. Custer and every one of his command were killed. US reprisals against the Indians followed, abrogating the treaty, ending their rights, and driving them from the area.

Little Dipper alternate name for ◊Ursa Minor, the Little Bear. The name has also been applied to the stars in the ◊Pleiades open star cluster, the overall shape of the cluster being similar to that of the ◊Big Dipper.

Little Entente series of alliances between Czechoslovakia, Romania, and Yugoslavia 1920–21 for mutual security and the maintenance of existing frontiers. Reinforced by the Treaty of Belgrade 1929, the entente collapsed upon Yugoslav cooperation with Germany 1935–38 and the Anglo-French abandonment of Czechoslovakia 1938.

Little Red Book, The book written by ◊Mao Zedong, in which he adapted Marxist theory to Chinese conditions.

Little Review, The 1914–29 US literary magazine founded in Chicago by Margaret Anderson. It published many experimental figures including W B Yeats, Ezra Pound, T S Eliot, and William Carlos Williams, and was banned for publishing part of James Joyce's *Ulysses*. The *Little Review* was variously published in New York, Paris, and elsewhere.

Little Rock largest city and capital of Arkansas; population (1990) 175,795. Products include metal goods, oil-field and electronic equipment, chemicals, clothing, and processed food. Educational institutions include the University of Arkansas at Little Rock. A French trading post was built here 1722, and in 1821 it became the territorial capital. Union forces captured the city 1863, during the Civil War. Federal troops were sent here 1957 to enforce the integration of all-white Central High School.

Little Women a novel for children by Louisa M ◊Alcott published in 1868. It describes the daily life of a New England family of reduced circumstances, and the tensions and harmony between the four teenage daughters, Meg, Jo, Beth, and Amy. One of the most popular children's books ever written, it was followed by a sequel in 1869, entitled in England *Good Wives*.

liturgy in the Christian church, any service for public worship; the term was originally limited to the celebration of the ◊Eucharist.

Litvinov Maxim 1876–1951. Soviet politician, commissioner for foreign affairs under Stalin from Jan 1931 until his removal from office in May 1939.

Litvinov believed in cooperation with the West and obtained US recognition of the USSR in 1934. In the League of Nations he advocated action against the ◊Axis; he was therefore dismissed just before the signing of the Hitler–Stalin nonaggression pact 1939. After the German invasion of the USSR, he was ambassador to the US 1941–43.

Liu Shaoqi or Liu Shao-chi 1898–1969. Chinese communist politician, in effective control of government 1960–65. A labor organizer, he was a firm proponent of the Soviet style of government based around disciplined one-party control, the use of incentive gradings, and priority for industry over agriculture. This was opposed by Mao Zedong, but began to be implemented by Liu while he was state president 1960–65. Liu was brought down during the ◊Cultural Revolution.

The son of a Hunan peasant farmer, Liu attended the same local school as Mao. As a member of the Chinese Communist Party (CCP), he was sent to Moscow to study communism, and returned to Shanghai 1922. Mao yielded the title of president to him 1960, and after the failure of the Great Leap Forward to create effective agricultural communes, Liu introduced a recovery program. This was successful, but was seen as a return to capitalism. He was stripped of his post and expelled from the CCP April 1969 and banished to Kaifeng in Henan province, where he died Nov 1969 after being locked in a disused bank vault. He was rehabilitated ten years later.

liver large organ of vertebrates, which has many regulatory and storage functions. The human liver is situated in the upper abdomen, and weighs about 4.5 lb/2 kg. It receives the products of digestion, converts glucose to glycogen (a long-chain carbohydrate used for storage), and breaks down fats. It removes excess amino acids from the blood, converting them to urea, which is excreted by the kidneys. The liver also synthesizes vitamins, produces bile and blood-clotting factors, and removes damaged red cells and toxins such as alcohol from the blood.

Liverpool city, seaport, and administrative headquarters of Merseyside, NW England; population (1984) 497,300. In the 19th and early 20th centuries it exported the textiles of Lancashire and Yorkshire, it is the UK's chief Atlantic port with miles of specialized, mechanized quays on the river Mersey.

liverwort plant of the class Hepaticae, of the bryophyte division of nonvascular plants, related to mosses, found growing in damp places.

The main sexual generation consists of a ◊thallus, which may be flat, green, and lobed, like a small leaf, or leafy and mosslike. The spore-bearing generation is smaller, typically parasitic on the thallus, and throws up a capsule from which spores are spread.

Livia Drusilla 58 BC–AD 29. Roman empress, wife of ◊Augustus from 39 BC, she was the mother by her first husband of ◊Tiberius and engaged in intrigue to secure his succession to the imperial crown. She remained politically active to the end of her life.

Livingston Robert R 1746–1813. American public official and diplomat who, after service in the Continental Congress 1775, helped write the New York Constitution and served as state chancellor 1776–1801. He returned to the Continental Congress 1779 and was named secretary for foreign affairs 1781 and directed negotiations for the Paris Peace Treaty. In 1801 he was named minister to France by Jefferson. With James Monroe, Livingston secured the purchase of the Louisiana Territory 1803.

Born in New York and educated at King's College (now Columbia), Livingston was admitted to the bar 1770.

Livingstone David 1813–1873. Scottish missionary explorer. In 1841 he went to Africa, reached Lake Ngami 1849, followed the Zambezi to its mouth, saw the Victoria Falls 1855, and went to East and Central Africa 1858–64, reaching Lakes Shirwa and Malawi. From 1866, he tried to find the source of the river Nile, and reached Ujiji Oct 1871.

British explorer Henry Stanley joined Livingstone in Ujiji, and the two explored Africa together. Livingstone not only mapped a great deal of the continent but also helped to end the slave trade by Arabs.

***Livingstone** Scottish doctor and missionary David Livingstone was the first European to explore many parts of Central and East Africa.*

Livingstone formerly ***Maramba*** town in Zambia; population (1987) 95,000. Founded 1905, it was named after explorer David Livingstone, and was capital of N Rhodesia 1907–35. Victoria Falls is nearby.

Living Theater experimental US theater group founded in 1951 by Judith Malina and Julian Beck, which mounted avant-garde plays by Jack Gelber, John Ashbery, and others. The group production *Paradise Now* 1968 was considered to have expressed the spirit of the sixties.

Livonia former region in Europe on the E coast of the Baltic Sea comprising most of present-day Latvia and Estonia. Conquered and converted to Christianity in the early 13th century by the Livonian Knights, a crusading order, Livonia was independent until 1583, when it was divided between Poland and Sweden. In 1710 it was occupied by Russia, and in 1721 was ceded to Peter the Great, Tsar of Russia.

Livorno (English, ***Leghorn***) industrial port in W Italy; population (1988) 173,000. Industries include shipbuilding, distilling, and motor vehicles. A fortress town since the 12th century, it was developed by the Medici family. It has a naval academy and is also a resort.

Livy Titus Livius 59 BC–AD 17. Roman historian, author of a *History of Rome* from the city's foundation to 9 BC, based partly on legend. It was composed of 142 books, of which 35 survive, covering the periods from the arrival of Aeneas in Italy to 293 BC and from 218 to 167 BC.

Li Xiannian 1905– . Chinese politician, member of the Chinese Communist Party (CCP) Politburo from 1956. He fell from favor during the 1966–69 Cultural Revolution, but was rehabilitated as finance minister 1973, supporting cautious economic reform. He was state president 1983–88.

Li, born into a poor peasant family in Hubei province, joined the CCP 1927 and served as a political commissar during the Long March of 1934–36. During the 1950s and early 1960s Li was vice premier to the State Council and minister for finance and was inducted into the CCP Politburo and secretariat in 1956 and 1958 respectively. He retains a seat on the Politburo's standing committee and chairs the Chinese People's Political Consultative Conference.

lizard reptile of the suborder Lacertilia, which together with snakes constitute the order Squamata. Lizards are generally distinguishable from snakes by having four legs, movable eyelids, ear-

lizard

frilled
lizard

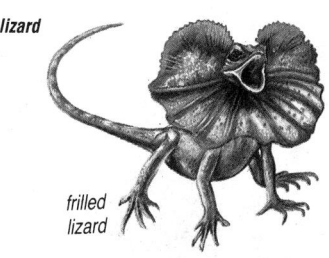

drums, and a fleshy tongue, but some lizards are legless and snakelike in appearance. There are over 3,000 species of lizard worldwide.

Like other reptiles, they are abundant in the tropics, although some species live as far N as the Arctic circle. There are some 20 families of lizards, including ◊geckos, ◊chameleons, ◊skinks, ◊monitors, ◊agamas and ◊iguanas. The frilled lizard *Chlamydosaurus kingi* of Australia has an erectile collar to frighten its enemies. For flying lizard see ◊flying dragon.

Lizard Point southernmost point of England in Cornwall. The coast is broken into small bays overlooked by two cliff lighthouses.

Ljubljana (German ***Laibach***) capital and industrial city (textiles, chemicals, paper, leather goods) of Slovenia, Yugoslavia; population (1981) 305,200. It has a nuclear research center and is linked with S Austria by the Karawanken road tunnel under the Alps (1979–83).

llama South American even-toed hoofed mammal *Lama peruana* of the camel family, about 4 ft/1.2 m high at the shoulder. Llamas can be white, brown, or dark, sometimes with spots or patches. They are very hardy, and require little food or water. They spit profusely when annoyed.

Llamas are used in Peru as beasts of burden, and also for their wool, milk, and meat. Llamas and ◊alpacas are both domesticated forms of the ◊guanaco.

Llewellyn Richard. Adopted name of Richard Vivian Llewellyn Lloyd 1907–1983. Welsh writer. *How Green Was My Valley* 1939, a novel about a S Wales mining family, was made into a play and a film.

Llewelyn two kings of Wales:

Llewelyn I 1173–1240. King of Wales from 1194, who extended his rule to all Wales not in Norman hands, driving the English from N Wales 1212, and taking Shrewsbury 1215. During the early part of Henry III's reign, he was several times attacked by English armies. He was married to Joanna, illegitimate daughter of King John.

Llewelyn II c. 1225–1282. King of Wales from 1246, grandson of Llewelyn I. In 1277 Edward I of England compelled Llewelyn to acknowledge him as overlord and to surrender S Wales. His death while leading a national uprising ended Welsh independence.

Lloyd Harold 1893–1971. US film comedian, noted for his "trademark" of thick horn-rim glasses and a straw hat, who invented the bumbling cliff-hanger and dangler. He appeared from 1913 in silent and talking films. His silent films include *Grandma's Boy* 1922, *Safety Last* 1923, and *The Freshman* 1925. His first talkie was *Movie Crazy* 1932. He produced films after 1938, including the reissued *Harold Lloyd's World of Comedy* 1962 and *Funny Side of Life* 1964.

Lloyd John lived 15th century. Welsh sailor, known as John Scoluus, "the skillful," who carried out an illegal trade with Greenland and is claimed to have reached North America, sailing as far south as Maryland, in 1477 (15 years before the voyage of Columbus).

Lloyd George David 1863–1945. Welsh Liberal politician, prime minister 1916–22. A pioneer of social reform, as chancellor of the Exchequer 1908–15 he introduced old-age pensions 1908 and health and unemployment insurance 1911. High unemployment, intervention in the Russian Civil War, and use of the military police force the ◊Black and Tans in Ireland eroded his support as prime minister, and creation of the Irish Free State 1921 and his pro-Greek policy against the Turks caused the collapse of his coalition government.

Lloyd George was born in Manchester, became a lawyer, and was member of Parliament for Caernarvon Boroughs from 1890. During the Boer War, he was prominent as a pro-Boer. His 1909 budget (with graduated direct taxes and taxing land values) provoked the Lords to reject it, and resulted in the Act of 1911 limiting their powers. He held ministerial posts during World War I until 1916 when there was an open breach between him and Prime Minister ◊Asquith, and he became prime minister of a coalition government. Securing a unified Allied command, he enabled the Allies to withstand the last German offensive and achieve victory. After World War I he had a major role in the Versailles peace treaty.

In the 1918 elections, he achieved a huge majority over Labor and Asquith's followers. He had become largely distrusted within his own party by 1922, and never regained power.

Lloyd Webber Andrew 1948– . English composer. His early musicals, with lyrics by Tim Rice, include *Joseph and the Amazing Technicolor Dreamcoat* 1968; *Jesus Christ Superstar* 1970; and *Evita* 1978, based on the life of the Argentinian leader Eva Perón. He also wrote *Cats* 1981 and *The Phantom of the Opera* 1986.

Llull Ramon 1232–1316. Catalan scholar and mystic. He began his career at the court of James I of Aragon (1212–76) in Majorca. He produced treatises on theology, mysticism, and chivalry in Catalan, Latin, and Arabic. His *Ars magna* was a mechanical device, a kind of prototype computer, by which all problems could be solved by manipulating fundamental Aristotelian categories.

He also wrote the prose romance *Blanquerna*, in his native Catalan, the first novel written in a Romance language. In later life he became a Franciscan, and died a martyr at Bugia, Algeria.

loa a spirit in voodoo. They may be male or female, and include Maman Brigitte, the loa of death and cemeteries, and Aida-Wedo, the rainbow snake. Believers may be under the protection of one particular loa.

loach carplike freshwater fish, family Cobitidae, with long narrow body, and no teeth in the small, downward-pointing mouth, which is surrounded by barbels. They are native to Asian and European waters.

Lobachevsky Nikolai Ivanovich 1792–1856. Russian mathematician who concurrently with, but independently of, Karl ◊Gauss and the Hungarian János Bolyai (1802–1860), founded non-Euclidean geometry. Lobachevsky published the first account of the subject in 1829, but his work went unrecognized until Georg ◊Riemann's system was published.

Lloyd George *British prime minister David Lloyd George, who played a leading role at the Versailles peace conference after World War I, in a portrait by William Orpen 1927.*

lobby individual or ◊pressure group that sets out to influence government action. Lobbying is prevalent in the US, where the term originated in the 1830s from the practice of those wishing to influence state policy waiting for elected representatives in the lobby of the Capitol.

lobelia any temperate and tropical plant of the genus *Lobelia* of the bellflower family Lobeliaceae, with white to mauve flowers. They may grow to shrub size but are mostly small annual plants.

The cardinal lobelia *L. cardinalis* of E North America has large bright red flowers.

Lobengula 1836–1894. King of Matabeleland (now part of Zimbabwe) 1870–93. He was overthrown 1893 by a military expedition organized by Cecil ◊Rhodes' South African Company.

Lobito port in Angola; population (1970) 60,000. It is linked by rail with Beira in Mozambique, via the Zaïre and Zambia copperbelt.

lobotomy in medicine, the cutting of a lobe. The term usually refers to the operation of frontal lobotomy (or leucotomy), where the frontal lobes are disconnected from the rest of the brain by cutting the white matter that joins them. This may alleviate the condition of patients with severe depression, anxiety states, or obsessive-compulsive disorders, but it is now rarely performed, and only on patients who have proved resistant to all other forms of treatment. See also ◊psychosurgery.

It was pioneered by A E Moniz (1874–1955), who shared the 1949 Nobel Prize for Medicine for his work in brain surgery.

lobster large marine crustacean of the order Decapoda. Lobsters are grouped with freshwater ◊crayfish in the suborder Reptantia ("walking"), although both lobsters and crayfish can also swim, using their fanlike tails. All have eyes on stalks and long antennae, and are mainly nocturnal. They scavenge and eat dead or dying fish.

True lobsters, family Homaridae, are distinguished by having very large "claws" or pincers on their first pair of legs, and smaller ones on their second and third pairs.

Spiny lobsters, family Palinuridae, have no large pincers. They communicate by means of a serrated pad at the base of their antennae, the "sound" being picked up by sensory nerves located on hairlike outgrowths on their fellow lobsters up to 180 ft/60 ft away.

Species include the American lobster *Homarus americanus*; and the Norwegian lobster *Nephrops norvegicus*, a small orange species.

local government that part of government dealing mainly with matters concerning the inhabitants of a county, city, township, town, or village, usually financed at least in part by local taxes. The US system was built on the early type of settlement (for example, in New England the town is the unit of local government, in the South the county, and in the N central states the combined county and township).

Local Group in astronomy, a cluster of about 36 galaxies that includes our own, the Milky Way. Like other groups of galaxies, the Local Group is held together by the gravitational attraction among its members and does not expand with the expanding universe. Its two largest galaxies are the Milky Way and the ◊Andromeda galaxy; most of the others are small and faint.

Locarno health resort in the Ticino canton of Switzerland on the N shore of Lago Maggiore, W of Bellinzona; population (1983) 15,300. Formerly in the duchy of Milan, it was captured by the Swiss in 1803.

Locarno, Pact of series of diplomatic documents initialed in Locarno Oct 16, 1925 and formally signed in London Dec 1, 1925. The pact settled the question of French security, and the signatories—Britain, France, Belgium, Italy, and Germany—guaranteed Germany's existing frontiers with France and Belgium. Following the signing of the pact, Germany was admitted to the League of Nations.

lock

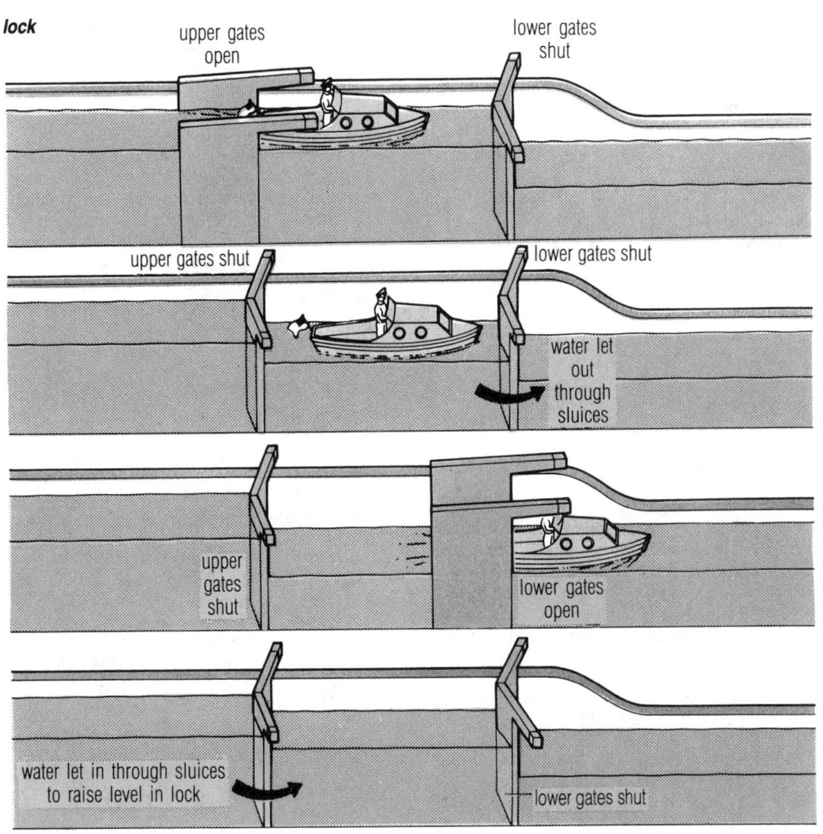
upper gates open
lower gates shut
upper gates shut
lower gates shut
water let out through sluices
upper gates shut
lower gates open
water let in through sluices to raise level in lock
lower gates shut

loc. cit. abbreviation for loco citato (Latin "at the place cited"); used in reference citation.

Lochner Stephan died 1451. German painter, active in Cologne from 1442, a master of the International ◊Gothic style. Most of his work is still in Cologne: for example, the *Virgin in the Rose Garden* (Wallraf-Richartz Museum) and *Adoration of the Magi* (Cologne Cathedral).

Lochner v New York a US Supreme Court decision 1905 dealing with the use of state police power to regulate working conditions. Lochner, an owner of a bakery convicted of violating a New York law that set maximum working hours for bakery workers, filed suit against the state. The US Supreme Court voted narrowly to overrule the New York law, ruling it an excessive use of state police power that violated the 14th-Amendment right to freedom of contract. Dissenting, Justice Holmes criticized the majority ruling for making its decision because of a belief in laissez-faire economics.

Loch Ness lake in Highland region, Scotland, forming part of the Caledonian Canal; 22.5 mi/36 km long, 229 m/754 ft deep. There have been unconfirmed reports of a Loch Ness monster since the 15th century.

lock gated chamber installed in canals, rivers, and seaways that allows boats or ships to ascend or descend when the topography is not level. This is important to shipping where canals link oceans of differing levels, such as the Panama Canal, or where falls or rapids are replaced by these adjustable water "steps." A lock has gates at each end, and a boat sails in through one gate when the levels are the same. Then water is allowed in (or out of) the lock until the level rises (or falls) to the new level outside the next gate.

lock and key devices that provide security, usually fitted to a door of some kind. In 1778 English locksmith Robert Barron made the forerunner of the mortise lock, which contains levers that the key must raise to an exact height before the bolt can be moved. The Yale lock, a pin-tumbler cylinder design, was invented by US locksmith Linus Yale, Jr, 1865. More secure locks include combination locks, whose dial mechanism must be turned certain distances backwards and forwards to open, and time locks, which are set to be opened only at specific times.

Locks originated in the Far East over 4,000 years ago. The Romans developed the warded lock, which contains obstacles (wards) that the key must pass to turn.

Locke John 1632–1704. English philosopher. His *Essay Concerning Human Understanding* 1690 maintained that experience was the only source of knowledge (empiricism), and that "we can have knowlege no farther than we have ideas" prompted by such experience. *Two Treatises on Government* 1690 helped to form contemporary ideas of liberal democracy.

Locke studied at Oxford, practiced medicine, and in 1667 became secretary to the Earl of Shaftesbury. He consequently fell under suspicion as a Whig and in 1683 fled to Holland, where he lived until the 1688 revolution. In later life he published many works on philosophy, politics, theology, and economics; these include *Letters on Toleration* 1689–92 and *Some Thoughts Concerning Education* 1693. His *Two Treatises on Government* supplied the Classical statement of Whig theory and enjoyed great influence in America and France. It supposed that governments derive their authority from popular consent (regarded as a "contract"), so that a government may be rightly overthrown if it infringes such fundamental rights of the people as religious freedom. He believed that, at birth, the mind was a blank, and that all ideas came from sense impressions.

Locke *English philosopher John Locke wrote* Two Treatises on Government *and* Essay Concerning Human Understanding. *The painting is by Dutch artist Herman Verelst (c. 1689).*

lockjaw former name for ◊tetanus, a type of infection.

locomotive engine for hauling railroad trains. In 1804 Richard ◊Trevithick built the first locomotive, a steam engine on wheels. Locomotive design did not radically improve until George ◊Stephenson built the *Rocket* 1829, which featured a multitube boiler and blastpipe, standard in all following steam locomotives. Today most locomotives are diesel or electric: diesel locomotives have a powerful diesel engine, and electric locomotives draw their power either from an overhead cable or from a third rail alongside the ordinary track.

In a steam locomotive, fuel (usually coal, sometimes wood) is burned in a furnace. The hot gases and flames produced are drawn through tubes running through a huge water-filled boiler and heat up the water to steam. The steam is then fed to the cylinders, where it forces the pistons back and forth. Movement of the pistons is conveyed to the wheels by cranks and connecting rods.

Diesel locomotives have a powerful diesel engine, burning oil. The engine may drive a generator to produce electricity to power electric motors that turn the wheels, or the engine drives the wheels mechanically or through a hydraulic link. A number of gas-turbine locomotives are in use, in which a turbine spun by hot gases provides the power to drive the wheels.

locus (Latin "place") in mathematics, traditionally the path traced out by a moving point, but now defined as the set of all points on a curve satisfying given conditions. For example, the locus of a point that moves so that it is always at the same distance from another fixed point is a circle; the locus of a point that is always at the same distance from two fixed points is a straight line that perpendicularly bisects the line joining them.

locus the point on a ◊chromosome where a particular ◊gene occurs.

locust swarming grasshopper, with short antennae and auditory organs on the abdomen, in the family Acrididae. As winged adults, flying in swarms, they may be carried by the wind hundreds of miles from their breeding grounds, and on landing devour all vegetation. Locusts occur in nearly every continent.

The migratory locust *Locusta migratoria* ranges from Europe to China, and even small swarms may cover several square kilometers, and weigh thousands of tons. Control by spreading poisoned food among the bands is very effective, but it is cheapest to spray concentrated insecticide solutions from aircraft over the insects or the vegetation on which they feed. They eat the equivalent of their own weight in a day, and, flying at night with the wind, may cover some 300 mi/500 km. The largest known swarm covered 400 sq mi/1,036 sq km, comprising approximately 40 billion insects.

locust tree in botany, any of several trees of the genera *Robinia* and *Gleditsia* of the legume family, with primate compound leaves and many-seeded pods, of E US. The black locust *R. pseudoacacia* and the honeylocust *G. triacanthos* are examples. The name locust tree is also applied to the ◊carob, a small European tree.

lode a distinct geologic deposit rich in certain minerals, generally consisting of a large vein or set

locomotive

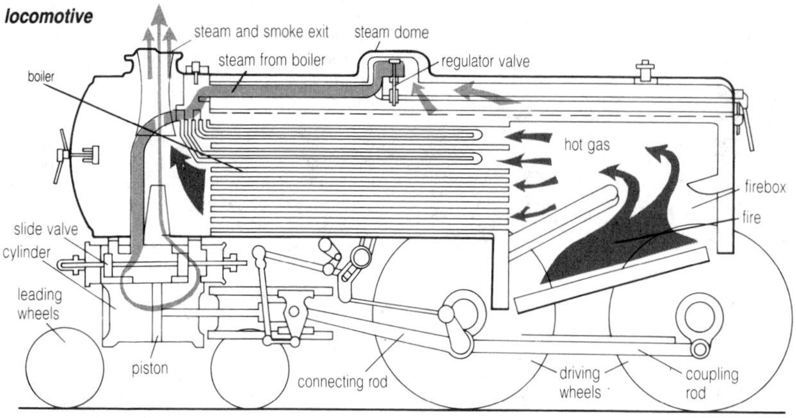
steam and smoke exit
steam dome
steam from boiler
regulator valve
boiler
hot gas
firebox
fire
slide valve
cylinder
leading wheels
piston
connecting rod
driving wheels
coupling rod

of veins containing ore minerals. A system of veins that can be mined directly forms a lode, like the famous mother lode of the California gold rush.

They form because hot liquids and gases from magmas penetrate surrounding rocks, especially when these are limestones; on cooling, veins of ores formed from the magma then extend from the igneous mass into the local rock.

lodestar a star used in navigation or astronomy, often ◊Polaris, the Pole Star.

Lodge Henry Cabot 1850–1924. US politician, Republican senator from 1893, and chairman of the Senate Foreign Relations Committee after World War I, who supported conservative economic legislation at home but expansionist policies abroad. Nevertheless, he influenced the US to stay out of the ◊League of Nations 1920 as a threat to US sovereignty.

As an advocate of American pursuit of empire, he joined President T ◊Roosevelt in calling for war against Spain 1898. He insisted on modifications to the Treaty of ◊Versailles with its provisions for the League of Nations. President ◊Wilson refused to accede, and the Senate was deadlocked, finally refusing to ratify the treaty.

Lodge Henry Cabot, II 1902–1985. US diplomat. He was Eisenhower's presidential campaign manager and the US representative at the UN 1953–60. Ambassador to South Vietnam 1963–64 and 1965–67, he replaced W A ◊Harriman as President Nixon's negotiator in the Vietnam peace talks 1969.

Born in Nahant, Massachusetts, Lodge served in the US Senate 1937–44, 1947–53. He was a grandson of Henry Cabot ◊Lodge.

Lodi town in Italy, 18 mi/30 km SE of Milan; population (1980) 46,000. It is a market center for agricultural produce; fertilizers, agricultural machinery, and textiles are produced. Napoleon's defeat of Austria at the battle of Lodi in 1796 gave him control of Lombardy.

Łódź industrial town (textiles, machinery, dyes) in central Poland, 75 mi/120 km SW of Warsaw; population (1984) 849,000.

Loeb James 1867–1933. German banker, born in New York, who financed the Loeb Classical Library of Greek and Latin authors, which gives original text with parallel translation.

loess a yellow loam, derived from glacial meltwater deposits and accumulated by wind in periglacial regions during the ◊ice ages. It usually attains considerable depths, and the soil derived from it is very fertile. There are large deposits in central Europe (Hungary), China, and North America. Loess was first described 1821 in the Rhine area, and takes its name from a village in Alsace.

Loewe Frederick 1901–1988. US composer of musicals, born in Berlin. Son of an operatic tenor, he studied under Busoni, and in 1924 went with his father to the US. In 1942 he joined forces with the lyricist Alan Jay Lerner (1918–86), and their joint successes include *Brigadoon* 1947, *Paint Your Wagon* 1951, *My Fair Lady* 1956, *Gigi* 1958, and *Camelot* 1960.

Loewi Otto 1873–1961. German physiologist whose work on the nervous system established that a chemical substance is responsible for the stimulation of one neuron by another.

The substance was shown by the physiologist Henry Dale to be acetylcholine, now known to be one of the most vital neurotransmitters. For this work Loewi and Dale were jointly awarded the 1936 Nobel Prize for Medicine.

Lofoten and Vesterålen island group off NW Norway; area 1,750 sq mi/4,530 sq km. Hinnoy, in the Vesterålens, is the largest island of Norway. The surrounding waters are rich in cod and herring. The Maelström, a large whirlpool hazardous to ships, which gives its name to similar features elsewhere, occurs in one of the island channels.

log any apparatus for measuring the speed of a ship; also the daily record of events on board a ship or aircraft.

It originally consisted of a piece of weighted wood (log chip) attached to a line with knots at equal intervals that was cast from the rear of a ship. The vessel's speed was estimated by timing the passage of the knots with a sandglass (like an egg timer). Today logs use electromagnetism and sonar.

log in mathematics, abbreviation for ◊logarithm.

loganberry hybrid between ◊blackberry and ◊raspberry with large, tart, dull-red fruit. It was developed by US judge James H Logan in 1881.

logarithm or ***log*** the ◊exponent or index of a number to a specified base. If $b^a = x$, then a is the logarithm of x to the base b. Before the advent of cheap electronic calculators, multiplication and division could be simplified by being replaced with the addition and subtraction of logarithms.

For any two numbers x and y (where $x = b^a$ and $y = b^c$) $x \times y = b^a \times b^c = b^{a+c}$; hence we would add the logarithms of x and y, and look up this answer in antilogarithm tables. Tables of logarithms and antilogarithms are available (usually to the base ten) that show conversions of numbers into logarithms, and vice versa. For example, to multiply 6,560 by 980, one looks up their logarithms (3.8169 and 2.9912), adds them together (6.8081), then looks up the antilogarithm of this to get the answer (6,428,800). Natural or Napierian logarithms are to the base e, an ◊irrational number equal to approximately 2.7183.

The principle of logarithms is also the basis of the slide rule. With the general availability of the electronic pocket calculator, the need for logarithms has been reduced. The first log tables (to base e) were published by the Scottish mathematician John Napier in 1614. Base-ten logs were introduced by the Englishman Henry Briggs (1561–1631) and Dutch mathematician Adriaen Vlacq (1600–1667).

logic branch of philosophy that studies valid reasoning and argument. It is also the way in which one thing may be said to follow from, or be a consequence of, another (deductive logic). Logic is generally divided into the traditional formal logic of Aristotle and the symbolic logic derived from Gottlob ◊Frege and Bertrand ◊Russell.

Aristotle's *Organon* is the founding work on logic, and Aristotelian methods as revived in the medieval church by Abelard in the 12th century were used in the synthesis of ideas aimed at scholasticism. As befitted the spirit of the Renaissance, Bacon considered many of the general principles used as premises by the scholastics to be groundless; he envisaged that in natural philosophy principles worthy of investigation would emerge by "inductive" logic, which works backward from the accumulated facts to the principle that accounts for them.

logical positivism doctrine that the only meaningful propositions are those that can be verified empirically. Metaphysics, religion, and esthetics are therefore meaningless.

It was characteristic of the Vienna Circle in the 1920s and 1930s, and was influenced by Gottlob Frege, Bertrand Russell, and Ludwig Wittgenstein.

logic gate the basic component of digital electronics, from which more complex circuits are built. There are seven main types of gate: Not, And, Or, Equivalence, Non-Equivalence (also called Exclusive Or, or Xor), Nand, and Nor. The type of gate determines how signals are processed. The process has close parallels in computer programming, where it forms the basis of binary logic.

LOGO (from the Greek *logos* meaning "word") computer-programming language designed to teach mathematical concepts. Developed about 1970 at the Massachusetts Institute of Technology, it became popular in schools and with home computer users because of its "turtle graphics" feature. This allows the user to write programs that create line drawings on a computer screen, or drive a small mobile robot (a "turtle" or a "buggy") around the floor.

It encourages the use of languages in a logical and structured way, leading to "microworlds," in which problems can be solved by using a few standard solutions.

logos (Greek "word") a term in Greek, Hebrew, and Christian philosophy and theology. It was used by Greek philosophers as the embodiment of "reason" in the universe. Under Greek influence the Jews came to conceive of "wisdom" as an aspect of God's activity. The Jewish philosopher ◊Philo (1st century AD) attempted to reconcile Platonic, Stoic, and Hebrew philosophy by identifying the logos with the Jewish idea of "wisdom." Several of the New Testament writers took over Philo's conception of the logos, which they identified with Christ and hence the second person of the Trinity.

Logroño market town in La Rioja, N Spain, on the river Ebro; population (1986) 119,000. It is the center of a wine region.

Lohengrin son of ◊Parsifal, hero of a late 13th-century Germanic legend, on which Wagner based his German opera *Lohengrin* 1847. Lohengrin married Princess Elsa, who broke his condition that she never ask his origin, and he returned to the temple of the ◊Holy Grail.

Loir French river, rising N of Illiers in the *département* of Eure-et-Loir and flowing SE, then SW to join the Sarthe near Angers; 500 mi/310 km. It gives its name to the *départements* of Loir-et-Cher and Eure-et-Loir.

Loire the longest river in France, rising in the Cévennes mountain, at 4,430 ft/1,350 m and flowing for 650 mi/1,050 km first N then W until it reaches the Bay of Biscay at St Nazaire, passing Nevers, Orléans, Tours, and Nantes. It gives its name to the *départements* of Loire, Haute-Loire, Loire-Atlantique, Indre-et-Loire, Maine-et-Loire, and Saône-et-Loire. There are many chateaux and vineyards along its banks.

Loki in Norse mythology, one of the ◊Aesir, but the

cause of dissension among the gods, and the slayer of ◊Balder. His children are the Midgard serpent Jörmungander, which girdles the Earth, the wolf Fenris, and Hela, goddess of death.

Lolita a novel by Nabokov, published 1955. It describes the infatuation of a middle-aged man for a precocious 12-year-old girl, and added the word "nymphet" to the English language.

Lollard follower of the English religious reformer John ◊Wycliffe in the 14th century. The Lollards condemned transubstantiation, advocated the diversion of ecclesiastical property to charitable uses, and denounced war and capital punishment. They were active from about 1377; after the passing of the statute *De heretico comburendo* ("The Necessity of Burning Heretics") 1401 many Lollards were burned, and in 1414 they raised an unsuccessful revolt in London.

The movement began at Oxford University, where Wycliffe taught, but thereafter included nonacademics, merchants, lesser clergy, and a few members of Richard II's court. Repression began in Henry IV's reign. The 1414 revolt was known as Oldcastle's rebellion, and the Lollards subsequently went underground; much of their policy was advocated by the early Protestants.

Lombard Carole. Adopted name of Jane Alice Peters 1908–1942. US comedy film actress. Her successful career, which included starring roles in some of the best screwball comedies of the 1930s, was cut short by her death in a plane crash; her films include *Twentieth Century* 1934, *My Man Godfrey* 1936, and *To Be or Not To Be* 1942. She was married to Clark Gable in 1939.

Lombard or ***Langobard*** member of a Germanic people who invaded Italy 568 and occupied Lombardy (named after them) and central Italy. Their capital was Monza. They were conquered by the Frankish ruler Charlemagne 774.

Lombardi Vince(nt Thomas) 1913–1970. US football coach. He accepted a job as offensive coach with the New York Giants 1954 and remained in professional football for the rest of his career. Lombardi became head coach of the Green Bay Packers 1959 and transformed a losing team into a major power, winning the first two Super Bowls 1967 and 1968. His last coaching position was with the Washington Redskins 1969–70.

Born in Brooklyn, New York, and educated at Fordham University, Lombardi became a successful high school coach, breaking into the college level as an assistant coach at Fordham 1947–48 and West Point 1949–54.

Lombard league an association of N Italian communes established 1164 to maintain their independence against the Holy Roman emperors' claims of sovereignty (Lombard had been conquered by ◊Charlemagne in 774).

Supported by Milan and Pope Alexander III (1105–81), it defeated Frederick I Barbarossa at Legnano in N Italy 1179 and effectively resisted Otto IV (1175–1218) and Frederick II, becoming the most powerful champion of the ◊Guelph cause. Internal rivalries led to its dissolution in 1250.

Lombardy (Italian *Lombardia*) region of N Italy, including Lake Como; capital Milan; area 9,225 sq mi/23,900 sq km; population (1988) 8,886,000. It is the country's chief industrial area (chemical, pharmaceuticals, engineering, textiles).

Lombok (Javanese "chili pepper") island of Indonesia, E of Java, one of the Sunda Islands; area 1,826 sq mi/4,730 sq km; population (1980) 1,957,000. The chief town is Mataram. It has a fertile plain between N and S mountain ranges.

Lombroso Cesare 1836–1909. Italian criminologist. His major work is *L'uomo delinquente/The Delinquent Man* 1889. He held the now discredited idea that there was a physically distinguishable "criminal type."

Lomé capital and port of Togo; population (1983) 366,000. It is a center for gold, silver, and marble crafts; major industries include steel production and oil refining.

ENTRY TO THE TRAITORS GATE

London *The imposing keep of the Tower of London was built by Gundulf, William the Conqueror's bishop-architect.*

Lomé Convention convention 1975 that established economic cooperation between the European Community and African, Caribbean, and Pacific countries. It was renewed 1979 and 1985.

lomentum a type of ◊fruit, similar to a pod but constricted between the seeds. When ripe, it splits into one-seeded units, as seen, for example, in the fruit of sainfoin *Onobrychis viciifolia* and radish *Raphanus raphanistrum*. It is a type of ◊schizocarp.

Lomond, Loch largest freshwater Scottish lake, 21 mi/37 km long, area 27 sq mi/70 sq km, divided between Strathclyde and Central regions. It is overlooked by the mountain Ben Lomond (973 ft/297 m) and linked to the Clyde estuary.

Lompoc city in SW California, near the Pacific Ocean, W of Santa Barbara. Industries include the processing of oil from the city's oil wells; population (1990) 37,649.

London city in SW Ontario, Canada, on the river Thames, 100 mi/160 km SW of Toronto; population (1986) 342,000. The center of a farming district, it has tanneries, breweries, and factories making hosiery, radio and electrical equipment, leather, and shoes. It dates from 1826 and is the seat of the University of Western Ontario.

London the capital of England and the UK, on the river Thames; area 610 sq mi/1,580 sq km; population (1987) 6,770,000, larger metropolitan area about 9 million. The City of London, known as the "square mile," area 677 acres/274 hectares, is the financial and commercial center of the UK. Greater London from 1965 comprises the City of London and 32 boroughs. Popular tourist attractions include the Tower of London, St Paul's Cathedral, Buckingham Palace, and Westminster Abbey.

Roman Londinium was established soon after the Roman invasion AD 43; in the 2nd century London became a walled city; by the 11th century, it was the main city of England and gradually extended beyond the walls to link with the originally separate Westminster. The Monument (a column designed by Wren) marks the site in Pudding Lane where the Great Fire of 1666 began.

features The Tower of London, built by William the Conqueror on a Roman site, houses the crown jewels and the royal armories; 15th-century Guildhall; Mansion House (residence of the lord mayor); Barbican arts and conference center; Central Criminal Court (Old Bailey) and the Inner and Middle Temples; Spitalfields market (fruit and vegetables); Covent Garden market is now a tourist shopping and entertainment area.

architecture Contains buildings in all styles of English architecture since the 11th century. Norman: the White Tower, Tower of London; St Bartholomew's, Smithfield; the Temple Church. Gothic: Westminster Abbey; Westminster Hall; Lambeth Palace; Southwark Cathedral. Tudor: St James's Palace; Staple Inn. 17th century: Banqueting Hall, Whitehall (Inigo Jones); St Paul's, Kensington Palace; many City churches (Wren). 18th century: Somerset House (Chambers); St Martin-in-the-Fields; Buckingham Palace. 19th century: British Museum (Neo-Classical); Houses of Parliament; Law Courts (Neo-Gothic); Westminster Cathedral (Byzantine style). 20th century: Lloyd's of London.

commerce and industry From Saxon times the Port of London dominated the Thames from Tower Bridge to Tilbury; its activity is now centered outside the metropolitan area, and downstream Tilbury has been extended to cope with container traffic. The prime economic importance of modern London is as a financial center. There are various industries, mainly on the outskirts. There are also recording, broadcasting, television, and film studios; publishing companies; and the works and offices of the national press. Tourism is important. Some of the docks in the East End of London, once the busiest in the world, have been sold to the Docklands Development Corporation, which has built houses, factories, and a railroad. Canary Wharf is now the site of the world's largest office development project.

education and entertainment Museums: British, Victoria and Albert, Natural History, Science museums; galleries: National and Tate. London University is the largest in Britain, while the Inns of Court have been the training school for lawyers since the 13th century. London has been the center of English drama ever since its first theater was built by Burbage in 1576.

government There has since 1986 been no central authority for Greater London; responsibility is divided between individual boroughs and central government. The City of London has been governed by a corporation from the 12th century. Its structure and the electoral procedures for its common councillors and aldermen are medievally complex, and it is headed by the lord mayor (who is, broadly speaking, nominated by the former and elected annually by the latter).

London Jack (John Griffith) 1876–1916. US novelist, author of the adventure stories *The Call of the Wild* 1903, *The Sea Wolf* 1904, and *White Fang* 1906.

By 1906 he was the most widely read writer in the US and had been translated into 68 languages.

Born in San Francisco, London was an adventurer himself, at various times a sailor, a hobo riding freight trains, and a gold prospector in the Klondike. Many of his works, which are uneven in quality, concern the human struggle against extreme natural forces for survival. His many short stories are collected in *The Son of the Wolf* 1900, *The God of His Fathers* 1901, *Children of the Frost* 1902, *Love of Life* 1907, and *Smoke Bellew* 1912. Among his other novels are *The People of the Abyss* 1903, *The Road* 1907, *The Iron Heel* 1907, and *Martin Eden* 1909.

Londonderry former name (until 1984) of the county and city of ◊Derry in Northern Ireland.

London, Greater the metropolitan area of ◊London, England, comprising the City of London, which forms a self-governing enclave and 32 surrounding boroughs; area 610 sq mi/1,580 sq km; population (1987) 6,770,000. Certain powers were exercised over this whole area by the Greater London Council (GLC) until its abolition 1986.

London University university originated in 1826 with the founding of University College, to provide higher education free from religious tests. In 1836 a charter set up an examining body with power to grant degrees. London University opened all its degrees to women in 1878, the first British university to do so.

Long Huey Pierce 1893–1935. US Democratic politician, nicknamed "the Kingfish," governor of Louisiana 1928–31, US senator from Louisiana 1930–35, legendary as a demagogue. He was popular with poor white voters for his program of social and economic reform, which he called the "Share Our Wealth" program and which represented a significant challenge to F D Roosevelt's ◊New Deal. Long's scheme called for massive redistribution of wealth through high inheritance taxes and confiscatory taxes on high incomes.

Born in Winnfield, Louisiana, he graduated from Tulane University with a law degree. Although he became virtual dictator in the state, his slogan was "Every man a king, but no man wears a crown." His own extravagance, including the state capitol building at Baton Rouge built of bronze and marble, was widely criticized. Long was assassinated by a young physician.

Long Beach city in SW California; population (1990) 429,433. A port and industrial city, it also has oil wells and a naval shipyard. Manufactured goods include aircraft, ships, petroleum products, chemicals, fabricated metals, electronic equipment, and processed food. It is also a convention center. Long Beach forms part of Greater Los Angeles and adjoins the San Pedro harbor of Los Angeles. California State University-Long Beach is here, and the retired ocean liner *Queen Mary* is a tourist attraction. Long Beach was laid out in the 1880s; the port was opened 1909. Oil was discovered 1921, and the aircraft industry dates from World War II.

Longchamp pleasure resort and racecourse in Paris, France, in the Bois de Boulogne. It is on the site of a former nunnery founded in 1260, suppressed 1790. Most of the major races in France are run at Longchamp including the most prestigous open-age group race in Europe, the *Prix de L'Arc de Triomphe*, which attracts a top-quality field every Oct.

Long Day's Journey into Night US play by Eugene O'Neill, the harrowing tragedy of the theatrical Tyrone family, based on the author's own family. Written 1941 and published posthumously 1956, it has been repeatedly performed on stage and made into a film.

Longfellow *US poet Henry Wadsworth Longfellow, author of* The Song of Hiawatha, *photographed shortly before he died in 1882.*

Longfellow Henry Wadsworth 1807–1882. US poet, remembered for ballads ("Excelsior," "The Village Blacksmith," "The Wreck of the Hesperus") and the mythic narrative epics *Evangeline* 1847, *The Song of ◊Hiawatha* 1855, and *The Courtship of Miles Standish* 1858.

Born in Portland, Maine, Longfellow graduated from Bowdoin College and taught modern languages there and at Harvard University 1835–54, after which he traveled widely. The most popular US poet of the 19th century, Longfellow was also an adept translator. His other works include six sonnets on Dante, a translation of Dante's *Divine Comedy*, and *Tales of a Wayside Inn* 1863, which includes the popular poem "Paul Revere's Ride."

Longford county of Leinster province, Republic of Ireland

area 401 sq mi/1,040 sq km

county town Longford

features rivers: Camlin, Inny, Shannon (the W boundary); several lakes

population (1986) 31,000.

Longinus Cassius AD 213–273. Greek philosopher. He taught in Athens for many years. Adviser to ◊Zenobia of Palmyra, he instigated her revolt against Rome and was put to death when she was captured.

Longinus Dionysius lived 1st century AD. Greek critic, author of the treatise *On the Sublime*, which influenced the English poets John Dryden and Alexander Pope.

Long Island island E of Manhattan and SE of Connecticut, separated from the mainland by Long Island Sound and the East River; 120 mi/193 km long by about 30 mi/48 km wide; area 1,400 sq mi/3,627 sq km; population (1984) 6,818,482. The two New York City boroughs of Queens and Brooklyn are the western eighth of the island with a combined population of 4,165,093 (1984). East of them are the counties of Nassau and Suffolk. Along the N shore, facing the sound, are the wealthy Gold Coast communities, such as Great Neck and Oyster Bay. On the S shore, facing the Atlantic, are the popular summer-resort communities of the sandy barrier beaches, Coney Island, the Rockaways, Long Beach, Fire Island, and the Hamptons. The last glaciation of the ◊Ice Age came as far south as Long Island, leaving its rocky moraine to distinguish the cliffed and rolling north shore from the flat and sandy south; the westernmost extent of the moraine is in Jamaica, Queens.

Educational institutions include Adelphi, Hofstra, C W Post, Farmingdale and Stony Brook-SUNY, and various branches of the City University. La Guardia, Kennedy, and MacArthur airports service the region, and several bridges and tunnels connect the island to Manhattan and the Bronx. The island's many public and private facilities include museums, parks, parkways, beaches, marinas, nature preserves, golf, tennis, and country clubs; Jones Beach State Park, Shea Stadium, and Belmont and Aquaduct raceways are here.

The largest employer is Grumman Aircraft, a major military contractor. Vegetable farms, orchards, vineyards, dairies, poultry and horse raising, fishing and shellfishing exist but are losing ground to suburban developments and pollution. Henry Hudson discovered the island 1609, and it was settled by the Dutch from New Amsterdam (in the W) and the English from New England (in the E) from the 1640s.

longitude see ◊latitude and longitude.

Long March, the in Chinese history, the 6,000 mi/10,000 km trek undertaken 1934–35 by ◊Mao Zedong and his Communist forces from SE to NW China, under harassment from the Nationalist army.

Some 100,000 Communists left Jiangxi, Mao's first headquarters, in Oct 1934 and only 8,000 lasted the journey to arrive about a year later in Shanxi, which became their new base. The march cemented Mao Zedong's control of the movement.

The New Long March is China's plan to achieve world leadership in science and technology by the year 2000.

Longmont city in N central Colorado, in the Rocky Mountain foothills, S of Fort Collins and NE of Boulder. Industries include business machinery, sugar-beet refining, and recreational vehicles; population (1990) 51,555.

Long Parliament the English Parliament 1640–53 and 1659–60, which continued through the Civil War. After the Royalists withdrew in 1642 and the Presbyterian right was excluded in 1648, the remaining ◊Rump ruled England until expelled by Oliver Cromwell in 1653. Reassembled 1659–60, the Long Parliament initiated the negotiations for the restoration of the monarchy.

Longview city in E Texas, E of Dallas; seat of Gregg County. In the heart of the oil fields of E Texas, Longview's industries are mainly oil and natural-gas processing; population (1990) 70,311.

loofah or ***luffa*** fibrous skeleton of the cylindrical fruit of the dishcloth gourd *Luffa cylindrica*, family Cucurbitaceae, used as a bath sponge.

loom any machine for weaving yarn or thread into cloth. The first looms were used to weave sheep's wool about 5,000 BC. A loom is a frame on which a set of lengthwise threads (warp) is strung. Then a second set of threads (weft), carried in a shuttle, is inserted at right angles over and under the warp. In practice the warp threads are separated as appropriate, to create a gap, or shed, through which the shuttle can be passed in a straight line. The warp threads are moved by means of a harness. A device called a reed presses each new line of weave tight against the previous ones.

All looms have similar features, but on the power loom, weaving takes place automatically at great speed. Mechanization of weaving began 1733 when John Kay invented the flying shuttle. In 1785 Edmund Cartwright introduced a steam-powered loom. Among recent developments are shuttleless looms, which work at very high speed, passing the weft through the warp by means of "rapiers," and jets of air or water.

loon any of various birds of the genus *Gavia*, family Gavidae, found in N regions of the N hemisphere. Loons are specialized for swimming and diving. Their legs are set so far back that walking is almost impossible, and they come to land only to nest, but loons are powerful swimmers and good flyers. They have straight bills and long bodies and feed on fish, crustaceans, and some water plants. There are just five species, the largest, the yellow-billed loon *G. adamsii*, being an Arctic species 2.5 ft/75 cm long.

Loos Adolf 1870–1933. Austrian architect and author of the article *Ornament and Crime* 1908, in which he rejected the ornamentation and curved lines of the Viennese *Jugendstil* movement (see ◊Art Nouveau). His buildings include private houses on Lake Geneva 1904 and the Steiner House in Vienna 1910.

Loos Anita 1888–1981. US writer, author of the humorous fictitious diary ◊*Gentlemen Prefer Blondes* 1925.

She became a screenwriter 1912 and worked on more than 60 films including D W ◊Griffith's *Intolerance* 1916.

loosestrife genus *Lysimachia* of plants of the primrose family (Primulaceae) including swampcandles *Lysimachia terrestris* of North America, with yellow and purple-streaked flowers on a spike. The name is also applied to members of the genus *Lythrum* of the loosestrife family, such as the European willow loosestrife *L. salicaria*, now a weed in NE US.

Lope de Vega (Carpio) Felix 1562–1635. Spanish poet and dramatist, one of the founders of modern Spanish drama. He was born in Madrid, served with the Armada 1588, and in 1613 took holy orders. He wrote epics, pastorals, odes, sonnets, novels, and, reputedly, over 1,500 plays (of which 426 are still in existence), mostly tragicomedies. He set out his views on drama in *Arte nuevo de hacer comedias/The New Art of Writing Plays* 1609, while reaffirming the Classical form. *Fuenteovejuna* 1614 has been acclaimed as the first proletarian drama.

Lopes Fernão c. 1380–1460. Portuguese historian whose *Crónicas/Chronicles* (begun 1434) relate vividly the history of the Portuguese monarchy between 1357 and 1411.

López Carlos Antonio 1790–1862. Paraguayan dictator (in succession to his uncle José Francia) from 1840. He achieved some economic improvement; he was succeeded by his son Francisco López.

López Francisco Solano 1827–1870. Paraguayan dictator in succession to his father Carlos López. He involved the country in a war with Brazil, Uruguay, and Argentina, during which approximately 80% of Paraguay's population died.

Lop Nor series of shallow salt lakes with shifting boundaries in the Taklimakan Shamo (desert) in Xinjiang Uyghur, NW China. Marco Polo visited Lop Nor, then a single lake of considerable extent, about 1273. The area is used for atomic tests.

loquat evergreen tree *Eriobotrya japonica* of the family Rosaceae, native to China and Japan and also known as the *Japan medlar*. The golden pear-shaped fruit has a delicate sweet-sour taste.

Lorain city in N central Ohio, on lake Erie, NW of Akron and SW of Cleveland. An important Great Lakes port, it has shipbuilding yards and manufactures automobiles and heavy construction equipment; population (1990) 71,245.

Lorca Federico García 1898–1936. Spanish poet and playwright, born in Granada. *Romancero gitano/Gipsy Ballad-book* 1928 shows the influence of the Andalusian songs of the area. In 1929–30 Lorca visited New York, and his experiences are reflected in *Poeta en Nuevo York* 1940. He returned to Spain, founded a touring theatrical company, and wrote plays such as *Bodas de sangre/Blood Wedding* 1933 and *La casa de Bernarda Alba/The House of Bernarda Alba* 1936. His poems include *Lament*, written for the bullfighter Mejías. He was shot by the Falangists during the Spanish Civil War.

Lord in the UK, prefix used informally as alternative to the full title of a marquess, earl, or viscount; normally also in speaking of a baron, and as a courtesy title before the forename and surname of younger sons of dukes and marquesses.

Lord Howe Island volcanic island and dependency of New South Wales, Australia, 435 mi/700 km NE of Sydney; area 6 sq mi/15 sq km; population (1984) 300. It is a tourist resort and heritage area because of its scenery and wildlife. The woodhen is a bird found only here.

Lorenz Austrian zoologist and biologist Konrad Lorenz shared the Nobel Prize for Medicine in 1973.

Lords, House of the upper house of the UK ◊Parliament; see ◊House of Lords.

Lord's Prayer in the New Testament, prayer taught by Jesus to his disciples. It is sometimes called "Our Father" or "Paternoster" from the opening words in English and Latin respectively.

Lord's Supper in the Christian church, another name for the ◊Eucharist.

Lorelei in Germanic folklore, a river nymph of the Rhine who lures sailors on to the rock where she sits combing her hair; a ◊siren. She features in several poems, including "Die Lorelei" by the Romantic writer Heine. The Lurlei rock S of Koblenz is 430 ft/130 m high.

Loren Sophia. Adopted name of Sofia Scicolone 1934– . Italian film actress who achieved fame under the guidance of her husband, producer Carlo Ponti. She is known for her beauty, her adeptness for comedy, and also her serious roles. Her work includes *Aida* 1953, *The Key* 1958, *La ciociara/Two Women* 1961, *Marriage Italian Style* 1964, *Judith* 1965, *A Special Day* 1977, and *Firepower* 1979.

Lorentz Hendrik Antoon 1853–1928. Dutch physicist, winner (with his pupil Pieter ◊Zeeman) of the Nobel Prize 1902 for his work on the Zeeman effect.

Lorentz spent most of his career trying to develop and improve James ◊Maxwell's electromagnetic theory. He also attempted to account for the anomalies of the ◊Michelson–Morley experiment by proposing, independently of George Fitzgerald, that moving bodies contracted in their direction of motion. He took the matter further with his method of transforming space and time coordinates, later known as Lorentz transformations, which prepared the way for Einstein's theory of ◊relativity.

Lorenz Konrad 1903–1989. Austrian ethologist. Director of the Max Planck Institute for the Physiology of Behavior in Bavaria 1955–73, he is best known for his popular works on animal behavior, *King Solomon's Ring* 1952 and *On Aggression* 1966. In 1973 he shared the Nobel Prize for Medicine with Nikolaas Tinbergen and Karl von Frisch.

Lorenz Ludwig Valentine 1829–1891. Danish mathematician and physicist. He developed mathematical formulae to describe phenomena such as the relation between the refraction of light and the density of a pure transparent substance, and the relation between a metal's electrical and thermal conductivity and temperature.

Lorenzetti Ambrogio c. 1319–1347. Italian painter active in Siena and Florence. His allegorical frescoes *Good and Bad Government* 1337–39 (Town Hall, Siena) include a detailed panoramic landscape and a view of the city of Siena that shows an unusual mastery of spatial effects.

Lorenzetti Pietro c. 1306–1345. Italian painter of the Sienese school, active in Assisi. His frescoes in the Franciscan basilica, Assisi, reflect ◊Giotto's concern with mass and weight. He was the brother of Ambrogio Lorenzetti.

Lorestan alternate form of ◊Luristan, Iran.

Loreto town in the Marche region of central Italy; population (1981) 10,600. The town allegedly holds the Virgin Mary's house, carried there by angels from Nazareth; hence Our Lady of Loreto is the patron saint of aviators.

Lorient commercial and naval port in Brittany, NW France; population (1983) 104,000. Industries include fishing and shipbuilding.

lorikeet any of various small, brightly colored parrots, found in SE Asia and Australasia.

loris any of various small prosimian primates of the family Lorisidae. Lorises are slow-moving, arboreal, and nocturnal. They have very large eyes; true lorises have no tails. They climb without leaping, gripping branches tightly and moving on or hanging below them.

The slender loris *Loris tardigradus* of S India and Sri Lanka is about 8 in/20 cm long. The tubbier slow loris *Nycticebus coucang* of SE Asia is 1 ft/30 cm. The angwantibo (genus *Arctocebus*), potto (genus *Perodicticus*), and galagos are similar African forms.

Lorrain Claude French painter; see ◊Claude Lorrain.

Lorraine region of NE France in the upper reaches of the Meuse and Moselle rivers; bounded to the N by Belgium, Luxembourg, and Germany and to the E by Alsace; area 9,095 sq mi/23,600 sq km; population (1986) 2,313,000. It comprises the *départements* of Meurthe-et-Moselle, Meuse, Moselle, and Vosges, and its capital is Nancy. There are deposits of coal, iron ore, and salt; grain, fruit, and livestock are farmed. In 1871 the region was ceded to Germany as part of Alsace-Lorraine.

Lorraine, Cross of heraldic cross with double crossbars, emblem of the medieval French nationalist Joan of Arc. It was adopted by the ◊Free French forces in World War II.

Lorre Peter. Adopted name of Lazlo Löwenstein 1904–1964. Hungarian-born US actor whose bulging eyes and sinister voice made him one of film's most memorable performers. He made several films in Germany (*M* 1931) before moving to London, where he made two films for Alfred Hitchcock, *The Man Who Knew Too Much* 1934 and *The Secret Agent* 1936. He then moved to Hollywood, where he made eight Mr Moto films and appeared in *The Maltese Falcon* 1941, *Casablanca* 1942, *Beat the Devil* 1953, and *The Raven* 1963. His last film was *The Patsy* 1964.

lory any of various Australasian, honey-eating, brilliantly colored ◊parrot.

Los Alamos town in New Mexico, which has had a center for atomic and space research since 1942. In World War II the first atomic (nuclear fission) bombs (2) were built there (under Robert ◊Oppenheimer), based on data from other research stations; the ◊hydrogen bomb was also developed there.

Los Angeles city and port in SW California; population (1990) 3,485,398, the metropolitan area of Los Angeles-Long Beach (1990) 14,531,529. Industries include aerospace, electronics, motor vehicles, chemicals, clothing, printing, and food processing. Features include Hollywood, center of the US film industry since 1911; the Hollywood Bowl concert arena; the Los Angeles Music Center; and the Los Angeles County Museum of Art. Educational institutions include the University of California at Los Angeles and the University of Southern California.

Los Angeles was established as a Spanish settlement 1781, but it was a farming region with orange groves until the early 20th century, when it annexed neighboring communities and acquired distant water supplies, a deepwater port, and the film industry. In the 1920s large petroleum deposits were found in the area. The aircraft industry, with its need for year-round flying wea-

Losey *Early in his career, US film director Joseph Losey was influenced by Brecht and worked with him.*

ther, developed here soon after and grew rapidly with the advent of World War II.

Los Angeles Victoria de 1923– . Spanish soprano. She is renowned for her interpretations of Spanish songs and for the roles of Manon and Madame Butterfly in Puccini's operas.

Losey, Joseph 1909–1984. US film director. Blacklisted as a former communist in the ◊McCarthy era, he settled in England, where his films included *The Servant* 1963 and *The Go-Between* 1971.

Lost Generation, the the disillusioned US literary generation of the 1920s who went to live in Paris. The phrase is attributed to the writer Gertrude Stein in Ernest Hemingway's early novel of 1920s Paris, *The Sun Also Rises* 1926.

Lot French river; see under ◊Gironde.

Lot in the Old Testament, Abraham's nephew, who escaped the destruction of Sodom. Lot's wife disobeyed the condition of not looking back at Sodom and was punished by being turned into a pillar of salt.

Lothair 825–869. King of Lotharingia (called after him, and later corrupted to Lorraine, now part of Alsace-Lorraine) from 855, when he inherited from his father, the Holy Roman emperor Lothair I, a district west of the Rhine, between the Jura mountains and the North Sea.

Lothair two Holy Roman emperors:

Lothair I 795–855. Holy Roman emperor from 817 in association with his father Louis I. On Louis's death in 840, the empire was divided between Lothair and his brothers; Lothair took N Italy and the valleys of the rivers Rhône and Rhine.

Lothair II c. 1070–1137. Holy Roman emperor from 1133 and German king from 1125. His election as emperor, opposed by the ◊Hohenstaufens, was the start of the feud between the ◊Guelph and Ghibelline factions, who supported the papal party and the Hohenstaufens' claim to the imperial throne respectively.

Lothian region of Scotland
area 695 sq mi/1,800 sq km
cities Edinburgh (administrative headquarters), Livingston
features hills: Lammermuir, Moorfoot, Pentland; Bass Rock in the Firth of Forth, noted for seabirds
products bacon, vegetables, coal, whiskey, engineering, electronics
population (1987) 744,000
famous people R L Stevenson.

lottery game of chance in which tickets sold may win a prize.

In state-sponsored lotteries the players choose numbers which, if selected in a random drawing, can bring the winner millions of dollars. State-sponsored lotteries are a means of raising revenue, especially for education and other public needs.

Lottery Case popular name for the US Supreme Court decision ◊*Champion* v *Ames* 1903.

Lotto Lorenzo c. 1480–1556. Italian painter, born in Venice, active in Bergamo, Treviso, Venice, Ancona, and Rome. His early works were influenced by Giovanni Bellini; his mature style belongs to the High Renaissance. He painted dignified portraits, altarpieces, and frescoes.

lotus several different plants: those of the genus *Lotus*, family Leguminosae, including the bird's foot trefoil *Lotus corniculatus*; the ◊jujube shrub *Zizyphus lotus*, known to the ancient Greeks who used its fruit to make a type of bread and also a wine supposed to induce happy oblivion—hence lotus-eaters; the water lily *Nymphaea lotus*, frequent in Egyptian art; *Nelumbo nucifera*, the pink Asiatic lotus, a sacred symbol in Hinduism and Buddhism, which floats, its flowerhead erect above the water; and the American lotus *Nelumbo lutea*, a pale yellow water lily of southern USA.

Lotus 1–2–3 ◊spreadsheet computer program, produced by Lotus Development Corporation. It first appeared in 1982 and is credited with being one of the main reasons for the widespread acceptance of the IBM Personal Computer in businesses.

Lotus-Eaters in ◊Homer's *Odyssey* a mythical people living on the lotus plant, which induced travelers to forget their journey home.

Lotus Sūtra a scripture of Mahāyāna Buddhism. It is Buddha Śākyamuni's final teaching, emphasizing that everyone can attain Buddhahood with the help of bodhisattvas. The original is in Sanskrit (*Saddharmapuṇḍarīka Sūtra*) and is thought to date to some time after 100 BC.

loudspeaker electromechanical device that converts electrical signals into sound waves that are radiated into the air. It is used in all sound-reproducing systems such as radios, record players, tape recorders, and televisions.

The most common type is the moving-coil speaker. Electrical signals from, for example, a radio are fed to a coil of fine wire wound around the top of a cone. The coil is surrounded by a magnet. When signals pass through it, the coil becomes an electromagnet, which by moving causes the cone to vibrate, setting up sound waves.

Louis, Prince of Battenberg 1854–1921. German-born British admiral, who took British nationality 1917 and translated his name to Mountbatten.

loudspeaker

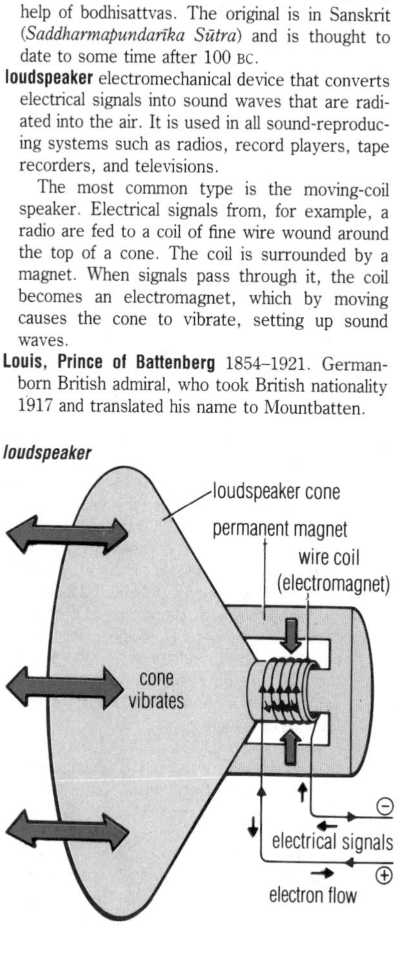
loudspeaker cone
permanent magnet
wire coil
(electromagnet)
cone
vibrates
electrical signals
electron flow

Mountbatten is also the surname of Prince Philip and the hyphenated version, Mountbatten-Windsor, the surname of his children.

Louis Joe. Assumed name of Joseph Louis Barrow 1914–1981. US boxer, nicknamed "the Brown Bomber." He was world heavyweight champion between 1937 and 1949 and made a record 25 successful defenses (a record for any weight class).

Louis was the longest-reigning world heavyweight champion at 11 years and 252 days before announcing his retirement 1949. He subsequently made a comeback and lost to Ezzard Charles in a world title fight 1950.

CAREER HIGHLIGHTS

Professional fights: 66
wins: 63
knockouts: 49
defeats: 3
1st professional fight:
July 4, 1934 v. Jack Kracken *(US)*
last professional fight:
Oct 26, 1951 v. Rocky Marciano *(US)*

Louis Morris 1912–1962. US abstract painter. From Abstract Expressionism he turned to the color-staining technique developed by Helen ◊Frankenthaler, using thinned-out acrylic paints poured on rough canvas to create the illusion of vaporous layers of color. The *Veil* paintings of the 1950s are examples.

Louis 18 kings of France:

Louis I the Pious 788–840. Holy Roman emperor from 814, when he succeeded his father Charlemagne.

Louis II the Stammerer 846–879. King of France from 877, son of Charles II the Bald. He was dominated by the clergy and nobility, who exacted many concessions from him.

Louis III 863–882. King of N France from 879, while his brother Carloman (866–84) ruled S France. He was the son of Louis II. Louis countered a revolt of the nobility at the beginning of his reign, and his resistance to the Normans made him a hero of epic poems.

Louis IV (d'Outremer) 921–954. King of France from 936. His reign was marked by the rebellion of nobles who refused to recognize his authority. As a result of his liberality they were able to build powerful feudal lordships.

He was raised in England after his father Charles III, the Simple, had been overthrown 922 by Robert I. After the death of Raoul, Robert's brother-in-law and successor, Louis was chosen by the nobles to be king. He had difficulties with his vassal Hugh the Great, and skirmishes with the Hungarians, who had invaded S France.

Louis V 966–987. King of France from 986, last of the ◊Carolingian dynasty (descendants of Charlemagne).

Louis VI the Fat 1081–1137. King of France from 1108. He led his army against feudal brigands, the English (under Henry I), and the Holy Roman Empire, temporarily consolidating his realm and extending it into Flanders. He was a benefactor to the church, and his advisers included Abbot ◊Suger.

Louis VII c. 1120–1180. King of France from 1137, who led the Second ◊Crusade.

Louis VIII 1187–1226. King of France from 1223, who was invited to become king of England in place of ◊John by the English barons, and unsuccessfully invaded England 1215–17.

Louis IX St 1214–1270. King of France from 1226, leader of the 7th and 8th ◊Crusades. He was defeated in the former by the Muslims, spending four years in captivity. He died in Tunis. He was canonized 1297.

Louis X the Stubborn 1289–1316. King of France who succeeded his father Philip IV 1314. His reign saw widespread discontent among the nobles that he countered by granting charters guaranteeing seignorial rights, although some his-

Louis XIV *A marble bust of the "Sun King" Louis XIV of France, by Italian sculptor Bernini.*

torians claim that by using evasive tactics, he gave up nothing.

Louis XI 1423–1483. King of France from 1461. He broke the power of the nobility (headed by ◊Charles the Bold) by intrigue and military power.

Louis XII 1462–1515. King of France from 1499. He was duke of Orléans until he succeeded his cousin Charles VIII to the throne. His reign was devoted to Italian wars.

Louis XIII 1601–1643. King of France from 1610 (in succession to his father Henry IV), he assumed royal power in 1617. He was under the political control of ◊Richelieu 1624–42.

Louis XIV the Sun King 1638–1715. King of France from 1643, when he succeeded his father Louis XIII; his mother was Anne of Austria. Until 1661 France was ruled by the chief minister, Mazarin, but later Louis took absolute power, summed up in his saying *L'Etat c'est moi* ("I am the State"). Throughout his reign he was engaged in unsuccessful expansionist wars—1667–68, 1672–78, 1688–97, and 1701–13 (the War of the ◊Spanish Succession)—against various European alliances, always including Britain and the Netherlands. He was a patron of the arts.

In 1660 Louis married the Infanta Maria Theresa of Spain, but he was greatly influenced by his mistresses, including Louise de ◊La Vallière, Madame de ◊Montespan, and Madame de ◊Maintenon.

Louis XV 1710–1774. King of France from 1715, with the Duke of Orléans as regent until 1723. He was the great-grandson of Louis XIV. Indolent and frivolous, Louis left government in the hands of his ministers, the Duke of Bourbon and Cardinal Fleury (1653–1743). On the latter's death he attempted to rule alone but became entirely dominated by his mistresses, Madame de ◊Pompador and Madame ◊Du Barry. His foreign policy led to Canada and India being lost to England.

Louis XVI 1754–1793. King of France from 1774, grandson of Louis XV, and son of Louis the Dauphin. He was dominated by his queen, ◊Marie Antoinette, and the finances fell into such confusion that in 1789 the ◊States General (parliament) had to be summoned, and the ◊French Revolution began. Louis lost his personal popularity June 1791 when he attempted to flee the country (the Flight to Varennes), and in Aug 1792 the Parisians stormed the Tuileries palace and took the royal family prisoner. Deposed Sept 1792, Louis was tried in Dec, sentenced for treason Jan 1793, and guillotined.

Louis XVII 1785–1795. Nominal king of France, the son of Louis XVI. During the French Revolution he was imprisoned with his parents 1792 and probably died in prison.

Louis XVIII 1755–1824. King of France 1814–24, the younger brother of Louis XVI. He assumed the title of king 1795, having fled into exile 1791 during the French Revolution, but became king only on the fall of Napoleon I Apr 1814. Expelled

Louisiana

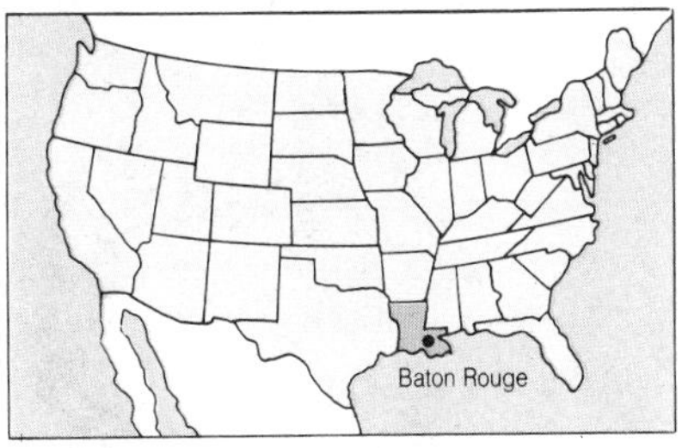
Baton Rouge

during Napoleon's brief return (the "hundred days") 1815, he resumed power after Napoleon's final defeat at Waterloo, pursuing a policy of calculated liberalism until ultra-royalist pressure became dominant after 1820.

Louisiana state in S US; nickname Pelican State

area 52,457 sq mi/135,900 sq km

capital Baton Rouge

cities New Orleans, Shreveport, Lafayette, Lake Charles

features New Orleans French Quarter: jazz, restaurants, Mardi Gras; Çajun country and the Mississippi River delta; Jean Lafitte National Park and Chalmette National Historical Park; plantation homes near Natchitoches

products rice, cotton, sugar, oil, natural gas, chemicals, sulfur, fish and shellfish, salt, processed foods, petroleum products, lumber, paper

population (1990) 4,219,973; including Cajuns, descendants of 18th-century religious exiles from Canada, who speak a French dialect

famous people Louis Armstrong, P G T Beauregard, Huey Long

history explored by the Spanish Piñeda 1519, Cabeza de Vaca 1528, and de Soto 1541 and by the French explorer La Salle 1862, who named it after Louis XIV and claimed it for France. It became Spanish 1762–1800, then French, then passed to the US 1803 under the ◊Louisiana Purchase. Statehood came 1812. The Civil War destroyed the plantation economy. Recovery was slow, but in the 1930s Louisiana became one of the world's major centers of petrochemical manufacturing, based on oil wells in the Gulf of Mexico.

Louisiana Purchase the purchase by the US from France 1803 of an area covering about 828,000 sq mi/2,144,000 sq km, including the present-day states of Louisiana, Missouri, Arkansas, Iowa, Nebraska, North Dakota, South Dakota, and Oklahoma. The purchase, which doubled the size of the US, marked the end of Napoleon's plans for a colonial empire and ensured free navigation on the Mississippi River for the US. President Thomas ◊Jefferson, fearing that the French (having just acquired New Orleans from the Spanish) might restrict American access to the Mississippi, offered $10 million for the area to Napoleon, who initially refused. Faced with an impending war with Britain and reverses in his colonial campaigns, the French emperor then offered to sell the entire territory for $15 million. Jefferson's special emissary, James ◊Monroe, agreed to the purchase, but Jefferson was concerned that he lacked the authority, under the US Constitution, for such an agreement. Although he was eager to seek Congressional assent, Jefferson was forced to act on his own initiative since Napoleon grew impatient, and Secretary of State James ◊Madison completed the negotiation 1803.

Louis Philippe 1773–1850. King of France 1830–48. Son of Louis Philippe Joseph, Duke of Orléans 1747–93; both were known as Philippe Egalité from their support of the 1792 Revolution. He fled into exile 1793–1814, but became king after the 1830 revolution with the backing of the rich bourgeoisie. Corruption discredited his regime, and after his overthrow, he escaped to the UK and died there.

Louisville industrial city and river port on the Ohio River, Kentucky; population (1990) 269,063. Products include electrical goods, agricultural machinery, motor vehicles, tobacco, and whiskey. It is noted for its Kentucky Fair and Exposition Center and for the Kentucky Derby. The University of Louisville and the Actors Theatre of Louisville are here. Louisville was founded 1778.

Lourdes town in SW France, population (1982) 18,000. Its Christian shrine to St ◊Bernadette has a reputation for miraculous cures.

Lourenço Marques former name of ◊Maputo, capital of Mozambique.

louse parasitic insect of the order Anoplura, which lives on mammals. It has a flat, segmented body without wings, and a tube attached to the head, used for sucking blood from its host.

Some occur on humans including the head louse *Pediculus capitis*, and the body louse *Pediculus corporis*, a typhus carrier. Most mammals have a species of lice adapted to living on them. Biting lice belong to a different order of insects, Mallophaga, and feed on the skin, feathers, or hair.

Louth smallest county of the Republic of Ireland, in Leinster province; county town Dundalk; area 317 sq mi/820 sq km; population (1986) 92,000.

Louvain (Flemish *Leuven*) industrial town in Brabant province, central Belgium; population (1985) 85,000. Manufacturing includes fertilizers and food processing. Its university dates from 1425 and there is a Science City.

Louvre French art gallery, former palace of the French kings, in Paris. It was converted by Napoleon to an art gallery 1793 and houses the sculpture *Venus de Milo* and Leonardo da Vinci's painting *Mona Lisa*.

lovebird any small bird of the ◊parrot family, especially the African genus *Agapornis*.

Lovecraft H(oward) P(hillips) 1890–1937. US writer of horror fiction whose stories of hostile, supernatural forces have lent names and material to many other writers in the genre. Much of his work on this theme was collected in *The Outsider and Others* 1939.

love-in-a-mist perennial plant of S Europe *Nigella damascena* of the buttercup family Ranunculaceae, with fernlike leaves and delicate blue or white flowers.

Lovelace Richard 1618–1658. English poet. Imprisoned 1642 for petitioning for the restoration of royal rule, he wrote "To Althea from Prison," and in a second term in jail 1648 revised his collection *Lucasta* 1649.

Loveland city in N central Colorado, S of Fort Collins. It is a processing and marketing center for the agricultural products of the area. Tourism is important to the economy, and Rocky Mountain National Park is to the W; population (1990) 37,352.

Lovell (Alfred Charles) Bernard 1913– . British radio astronomer, director (until 1981) of the ◊Jodrell Bank Experimental Station (now Nuffield Radio Astronomy Laboratories).

During World War II he worked at the Telecommunications Research Establishment (1939–45) and in 1951 became professor of radio astronomy at the University of Manchester. His books include *Radio Astronomy* 1951 and *The Exploration of Outer Space* 1961.

Loving v Virginia a US Supreme Court decision 1967 dealing with the constitutionality of state antimiscegenation laws. The case was brought by a Virginia couple convicted of violating a state law against interracial marriages. The Court sustained their challenge to the Virginia statute as a violation of the 14th Amendment. According to the 8–1 ruling, states may not prevent marriages solely because of the race of the participants.

Low David 1891–1963. New Zealand-born British political cartoonist, creator (in newspapers such as the London *Evening Standard*) of Colonel Blimp, the TUC drafthorse, and others.

Low Juliette Gordon 1860–1927. Founder of the Girl Scouts in the US. Born in Savannah, Georgia, and educated in New York, Low moved temporarily to England, where she became impressed with

Louvre *US architect I M Pei designed the glass pyramid for the Louvre art gallery in Paris 1986–88.*

the scouting organizations founded by Robert Baden-Powell. Returning to the US, she formed a troop of 16 "Girl Guides" in Savannah 1912. Establishing national headquarters in Washington, DC in the following year, she changed the name of the organization to the Girl Scouts of America (GSA).

Low served as president of the GSA 1915–20 and worked tirelessly to establish Girl Scout troops throughout the country.

Low Countries the region of Europe that consists of ◊Belgium and the ◊Netherlands, and usually includes ◊Luxembourg.

Lowell city in Massachusetts; population (1990) 103,439. Industries include electronics, plastics, and chemicals. Lowell was a textile center in the 19th century; a substantial part of the old city was designated a national park in 1978 as a birthplace of the US industrial revolution. Wang Laboratories moved its headquarters here 1978.

Lowell Amy (Lawrence) 1874–1925. US poet who began her career by publishing the conventional *A Dome of Many-Colored Glass* 1912 but eventually succeeded Ezra Pound as leader of the ◊Imagists. Her works, in free verse, include *Sword Blades and Poppy Seed* 1916.

She was a controversial figure who demonstrated her scorn for conventionality by, for example, openly smoking cigars.

Lowell Francis Cabot 1775–1817. US industrialist. Born in Newburyport, Massachusetts, and educated at Harvard, Lowell was a successful merchant. On a trip to England 1810–12, he was impressed with mechanized textile mills and, committing to memory their basic plans, became intent on bringing this technology to the US. With the cutoff of international trade during the War of 1812, Lowell established the Boston Manufacturing Co, a textile mill at Waltham, Massachusetts. After the war he campaigned for tariff protection for the US textile industry. In 1822 the mill town of Lowell, Massachusetts, was established and named for him.

Lowell J(ames) R(ussell) 1819–1891. US poet whose works range from the didactic *The Vision of Sir Launfal* 1848 to such satirical poems as *The Biglow Papers* 1848.

He was also a critic who developed a deep awareness of the US literary tradition and a diplomat who served as minister to Spain 1877–80 and England 1880–85.

Born in Cambridge, Massachusetts, Lowell graduated 1840 from Harvard Law School. He taught at Harvard and was editor 1857–61 of *The Atlantic Monthly* and coeditor 1863–72 of *The North American Review*. Among his critical works are essays on great masters, including Shakespeare, Dante, and Coleridge. Lowell was active in the abolitionist movement, publishing more than 50 antislavery articles between 1845 and 1850. Other works include *Leaves from My Italian Journal* 1854.

Lowell Percival 1855–1916. US astronomer who, by mathematical calculation, started the search for "Planet X" beyond Neptune, which led to the discovery of Pluto in 1930. In 1894 he founded the Lowell Observatory at Flagstaff, Arizona, where he reported seeing "canals" (now known to be optical artifacts) on the surface of Mars.

Lowell Robert (Traill Spence, Jr) 1917–1977. US poet whose work stressed the importance of individualism, especially during times of war. His works include *Lord Weary's Castle* 1946 and *For the Union Dead* 1964.

Lowell *US poet Robert Lowell.*

Much of his poetry is confessional. During World War II he was imprisoned for five months for conscientious objection. In several of his poems, notably "Memories of West Street and Lepke," he reflects on this experience. "Skunk Hour," included in *Life Studies* 1959, is another example of his autobiographical poetry. Other works include *Land of Unlikeness* 1944, *The Mills of the Kaanaughs* 1951, *The Old Glory* 1965, *Near the Ocean* 1967, *Notebook* 1969, *The Dolphin* 1973, and *Day by Day* 1977. In the 1960s he was again a war protester and also a civil-rights activist.

Lower Austria (German *Niederösterreich*) largest federal state of Austria; drained by the Danube; area 7,411 sq mi/19,200 sq km; population (1987) 1,426,000. Its capital is St Pölten. In addition to wine, sugar beet, and grain, there are reserves of oil. Manufactured products include textiles, chemicals, and metal goods.

Lower California English name for ◊Baja California, Mexico.

Lower Saxony (German *Niedersachsen*) administrative region (German *Land*) of N West Germany
area 18,296 sq mi/47,400 sq km
capital Hanover
towns Brunswick, Osnabrück, Oldenburg, Göttingen, Wolfsburg, Salzgitter, Hildesheim
features Lüneburg Heath
products cereals, automobiles, machinery, electrical engineering
population (1988) 7,190,000
religion 75% Protestant, 20% Roman Catholic
history formed 1946 from Hanover, Oldenburg, Brunswick, and Schaumburg-Lippe.

Loy Myrna. Adopted name of Myrna Williams 1905– . US film actress who played the blithe Nora Charles in the *Thin Man* series (1934–47) costarring William Powell and other 1930s screwball comedies. Her other films include *The Mask of Fu Manchu* 1932, *The Rains Came* 1939, *The Best Years of Our Lives* 1946, and *Cheaper by the Dozen* 1950.

Loyalist member of approximately 30% of the US population remaining loyal to Britain in the ◊American Revolution. Many went to Canada, especially E Ontario, after 1783.

Known widely as Tories, most were crown officials, Anglican clergy, and economically advantaged, although they were represented in every segment of colonial society.

Loyola founder of the Jesuits. See ◊Ignatius Loyola.

Lozère section of the Cévennes mountains, S France. It rises in Finiels to 5,584 ft/1,702 m and gives its name to a *département* in Languedoc-Roussillon region.

LSD abbreviation for lysergic acid diethylamide, a psychedelic drug and a hallucinogen, often producing states resembling those common in psychosis (for example, schizophrenia). It is derived from lysergic acid, originally extracted from poisonous ◊ergot alkaloids. Its use is illegal.

LSI (abbreviation of large-scale integration) the technology that enables whole electrical circuits to be etched into a piece of semiconducting material just a few millimeters square. Most of today's electronics industry is based on LSI.

By the late 1960s a complete computer processor could be integrated on a single ◊silicon chip, and in 1971 the US electronics company Intel produced the first commercially available ◊microprocessor. Very large-scale integration (◊VLSI) results in even smaller chips.

Ltd. abbreviation for Limited; see ◊private limited company.

Lualaba another name for the upper reaches of the river ◊Zaïre in Africa, as it flows N through Zaïre from near the Zambia border.

Luanda formerly ***Loanda*** capital and industrial port (cotton, sugar, tobacco, timber, paper, oil) of Angola; population (1988) 1,200,000. It was founded 1575 and became a Portuguese colonial administrative center as well as an outlet for slaves transported to Brazil.

Luang Prabang or ***Louangphrabang*** Buddhist religious center in Laos, on the Mekong at the head of river navigation; population (1984) 44,244. It was the capital of the kingdom of Luang Prabang, incorporated in Laos in 1946, and the royal capital of Laos 1946–75.

Lubbers Rudolph (Frans Marie) 1939– . Netherlands politician. He became minister for economic affairs 1973 and prime minister from 1982.

Lubbock city in NW Texas, S of Amarillo; seat of Lubbock County. Industries include heavy farm and construction machinery, cotton, sorghum, and mobile homes; population (1990) 186,206.

Lübeck seaport of Schleswig-Holstein, Germany, on the Baltic Sea, 37 mi/60 km NE of Hamburg; population (1988) 209,000. Founded 1143, it has five Gothic churches and a cathedral from 1173. Once head of the powerful ◊Hanseatic League, it later lost much of its trade to Hamburg and Bremen but improved canal and port facilities helped it to retain its position as a center of Baltic trade. Lübeck was a free state of both the empire and the Weimar Republic.

Lubitsch Ernst 1892–1947. German film director known for his stylish comedies, who worked in the US from 1921. Starting as an actor in silent films in Berlin, he turned to writing and directing, including *Die Augen der Mummie Ma/The Eyes of the Mummy* 1918 and *Die Austernprinzessin/The Oyster Princess* 1919. In the US he directed sophisticated films with "that Lubitsch touch," *The Marriage Circle* 1924 and *The Student Prince* 1927; his sound films include *Trouble in Paradise* 1932, *Design for Living* 1933, *Ninotchka* 1939, and *To Be or Not To Be* 1942.

Lublin city in Poland, on the Bystrzyca River, 95 mi/150 km SE of Warsaw; population (1985) 324,000. Industries include textiles, engineering, aircraft, and electrical goods. A trading center from the 10th century, it has an ancient citadel, a 16th-century cathedral, and a university (1918). A council of workers and peasants proclaimed Poland's independence at Lublin in 1918, and a Russian-sponsored committee of national liberation, which proclaimed itself the provincial government of Poland at Lublin on Dec 31, 1944, was recognized by Russia five days later.

lubricant substance used between moving surfaces to reduce friction. Carbon-based (organic) lubricants, commonly called grease and oil, are recovered from petroleum distillation.

Extensive research has been carried out on chemical additives to lubricants, which can reduce corrosive wear, prevent the accumulation of "cold sludge" (often the result of stop-start driving in city traffic jams), keep pace with the higher working temperatures of aviation gas turbines, or provide radiation-resistant greases for nuclear power plants. Silicon-based spray-on lubricants are also used; they tend to attract dust and dirt less than carbon-based ones.

A solid lubricant is graphite, an allotropic form of carbon, either flaked or emulsified (colloidal) in water or oil.

Lubumbashi formerly (until 1986) ***Elisabethville*** town in Zaïre, on the Lualaba river; population (1984) 543,000. It is chief commercial center of the Shaba copper-mining region.

Lucan (Marcus Annaeus Lucanus) AD 39–65. Latin poet, born in Cordova, a nephew of Seneca and favorite of Nero until the emperor became jealous of his verse. He then joined a republican conspiracy and committed suicide on its failure. His epic *Pharsalia* deals with the civil wars of the Roman rulers Caesar and Pompey.

Lucas George 1944– . US director and producer whose imagination was fired by the comic books in his father's store. He wrote and directed (in collaboration with Steven Spielberg) *Star Wars* 1977, *The Empire Strikes Back* 1980, and *Return of the Jedi* 1983. Other major films include *THX 1138* 1971, *American Graffiti* 1973, *Raiders of the Lost Ark* 1981, *Indiana Jones and the Temple of Doom* 1984, *Willow* 1988, and *Indiana Jones and the Last Crusade* 1989, most of which were enormous box-office hits.

Lucas Robert 1937– . US economist, leader of the University of Chicago school of "new Classical" macroeconomics, which contends that wage and price adjustment is almost instantaneous and that the level of unemployment at any time must be the natural rate (it cannot be reduced by government action except in the short term and at the cost of increasing inflation).

Lucas van Leyden 1494–1533. Dutch painter and engraver, active in Leiden and Antwerp. He was a pioneer of Netherlandish genre scenes, for example *The Chess Players* (Staatliche Museen, Berlin). His woodcuts and engravings were inspired by Albrecht Dürer, whom he met in Antwerp 1521.

Lucas's work influenced ◊Rembrandt.

Lucca city in NW Italy; population (1981) 91,246. It was an independent republic from 1160 until its absorption into Tuscany in 1847. The composer Puccini was born here.

Luce Clare Boothe 1903–1987. US journalist, playwright, and politician. She was managing editor of *Vanity Fair* magazine 1933–34, and wrote several successful plays, including *The Women* 1936 and *Margin for Error* 1939, both made into films.

She was born in New York, served as a Republican member of Congress 1943–47 and as ambassador to Italy 1953–57. She was married to Time-Life founder Henry Robinson Luce.

Luce Henry Robinson 1898–1967. US publisher, founder of Time, Inc, which publishes the weekly news magazine *Time* 1923, the business magazine *Fortune* 1930, the pictorial magazine *Life* 1936, and the sports magazine *Sports Illustrated* 1954. He married Clare Boothe ◊Luce 1935.

Born of missionary parents in Tengchow, China, Luce was educated at Yale and Oxford universities. Other publications of Time, Inc, include *House and Home*, *Architectural Forum*, and Time-Life Books.

lucerne another name for the plant ◊alfalfa.

Lucerne (German *Luzern*) capital and tourist center of Lucerne canton, Switzerland, on the river Reuss where it flows out of Lake Lucerne; population (1987) 161,000. It developed around the Benedictine monastery, established about 750, and owes its prosperity to its position on the St Gotthard road and railroad.

Lucerne, Lake (German *Luzern*) scenic lake in central Switzerland; area 44 sq mi/114 sq km.

Lucian c. 125–c. 190. Greek writer of satirical dialogues, in which he pours scorn on all religions. He was born at Samosata in Syria and for a time was an advocate at Antioch, but later traveled before settling in Athens about 165. He occupied an official post in Egypt, where he died.

Lucifer (Latin "bearer of light") in Christian theology, another name for the ◊devil, the leader of the angels that rebelled against God. Lucifer is also another name for the morning star (the planet ◊Venus).

Lucknow capital and industrial city (engineering, chemicals, textiles, many handicrafts) of the state of Uttar Pradesh, India; population (1981) 1,007,000. During the Indian Mutiny against British rule, it was besieged July 2–Nov 16, 1857.

Lucretia Roman woman, the wife of Collatinus, said to have committed suicide after being raped by Sextus, son of ◊Tarquinius Superbus. According to tradition, this incident led to the dethronement of Tarquinius and the establishment of the Roman Republic 509 BC.

Lucretius (Titus Lucretius Carus) c. 99–55 BC. Roman poet and ◊Epicurean philosopher whose *De Rerum natura/On the Nature of Things* envisaged the whole universe as a combination of atoms, and had some concept of evolutionary theory.

Animals were complex but initially quite fortuitous clusters of atoms, only certain combinations surviving to reproduce.

Lucullus Lucius Licinius 110–56 BC. Roman general and consul. As commander against ◊Mithridates of Pontus 74–66 he proved to be one of Rome's ablest generals and administrators, until superseded by Pompey. He then retired from politics. His wealth enabled him to live a life of luxury, and Lucullan feasts became legendary.

Lüda formerly ***Hüta*** industrial port (engineering, chemicals, textiles, oil refining, shipbuilding, food processing) in Liaoning, China, on Liaodong Peninsula, facing the Yellow Sea; population (1986) 4,500,000. It comprises the naval base of Lüshun (known under 19th-century Russian occupation as Port Arthur) and the commercial port of Dalien (formerly Talien/Dairen).

Both were leased to Russia (which needed an ice-free naval base) 1898, but were ceded to Japan after the ◊Russo-Japanese War; Lüshun was under Japanese siege June 1904–Jan 1905. After World War II, Lüshun was occupied by Russian airborne troops (returned to China 1955) and Russia was granted shared facilities at Dalien (ended on the deterioration of Sino-Russian relations 1955).

Luddite one of a group of people involved in machine-wrecking riots in N England 1811–16. The organizer of the Luddites was referred to as General Ludd, but may not have existed. Many Luddites were hanged or transported to penal colonies, such as Australia.

The movement, which began in Nottinghamshire and spread to Lancashire, Cheshire, Derbyshire, Leicestershire, and Yorkshire, was primarily a revolt against the unemployment caused by the introduction of machines in the Industrial Revolution.

Ludendorff Erich von 1865–1937. German general, Chief of Staff to ◊Hindenburg in World War I, and responsible for the eastern-front victory at the Battle of ◊Tannenberg 1914. After Hindenburg's appointment as chief of general staff and Ludendorff's as quartermaster-general 1916, he was also politically influential. He took part in the Nazi rising in Munich 1923 and sat in the Reichstag (parliament) as a right-wing Nationalist.

Lüderitz port on Lüderitz Bay, Nambia; population (1970) 6,500. It is a center for diamond-mining. The town, formerly a German possession, was named after a German merchant who acquired land here in 1883.

Ludwig Karl Friedrich Wilhelm 1816–1895. German physiologist who invented graphic methods of recording events within the body.

Ludwig demonstrated that the circulation of the blood is purely mechanical in nature and involves no occult vital forces. In the course of this work, he invented the kymograph, a rotating drum on which a stylus charts a continuous record of blood pressure and temperature. This was a forerunner of today's monitoring systems.

Ludwig three kings of Bavaria:

Ludwig I 1786–1868. King of Bavaria 1825–48, succeeding his father Maximilian Joseph I. He made Munich an international cultural center, but his association with the dancer Lola ◊Montez, who dictated his policies for a year, led to his abdication 1848.

Ludwig II 1845–1886. King of Bavaria from 1864, when he succeeded his father Maximilian II. He supported Austria during the Austro-Prussian War 1866, but brought Bavaria into the Franco-Prussian War as Prussia's ally and in 1871 offered the German crown to the king of Prussia. He was the composer Wagner's patron and built the Bayreuth theater for him. Declared insane 1886, he drowned himself soon after.

Ludwig III 1845–1921. King of Bavaria 1913–1918, when he abdicated upon the formation of a republic.

Ludwigshafen city and Rhine river port, Rhineland-Palatinate, Germany; population (1988) 152,000.

Industries include chemicals, dyes, fertilizers, plastics, and textiles.

Luening Otto 1900– . US composer. He studied in Zurich, and privately with Busoni. In 1949 he joined the staff at Columbia University, and in 1951 began a series of pioneering compositions for instruments and tape, some in partnership with Vladimir Ussachevsky (*Incantation* 1952, *Poem in Cycles and Bells* 1954). In 1959 he became codirector, with Milton ◊Babbitt and Vladimir Ussachevsky, of the Columbia-Princeton Electronic Music Center.

Luftwaffe German air force. In World War I and, as reorganized by the Nazi leader Goering 1933, in World War II, it also covered antiaircraft defense and the launching of the flying bombs ◊V1, V2.

Lugano resort town on Lake Lugano, Switzerland; population (1980) 28,600.

Lugano, Lake lake partly in Italy, between lakes Maggiore and Como, and partly in Switzerland; area 19 sq mi/49 sq km.

Lugansk formerly (1935–58 and 1970–89) ***Voroshilovgrad*** industrial city (locomotives, textiles, mining machinery) in the Ukraine, USSR; population (1987) 509,000.

luge a one- or two-person racing sled, on which riders lie face up. Luges are raced by both men and women in the winter Olympics.

Lugosi Bela 1884–1956. Hungarian-born US film actor. Acclaimed for his performance in *Dracula* on Broadway 1927, Lugosi began appearing in feature films in 1930. His appearance in the film version of *Dracula* 1931 marked the start of Lugosi's long career in horror films—among them, *Murders in the Rue Morgue* 1932, *The Raven* 1935, and *The Wolf Man* 1941.

Trained at the Academy of Theatrical Art in Budapest, Lugosi began his stage career with the Hungarian National Theater. After service in the Austro-Hungarian army in World War I, he immigrated to the US 1921.

lugworm any of a genus *Arenicola* of marine annelid worms that grow up to 10 in/25 cm long, and are common burrowers between tidemarks. They are useful for their cleansing and powdering of the beach sand, of which they may annually bring to the surface about 2,000 tons per acre/5,000 tons per hectare.

Lu Hsün alternative transliteration of ◊Lu Xun, Chinese writer.

Lukács Georg 1885–1971. Hungarian philosopher, one of the founders of "Western" or "Hegelian" Marxism, a philosophy opposed to the Marxism of the official communist movement.

In *History and Class Consciousness* 1923, he argued that the proletariat was the "identical subject-object" of history. Under capitalism, social relations were "reified" (turned into objective things), but the proletariat could grasp the social totality.

Lukács himself repudiated the book and spent much of the rest of his life as an orthodox communist. He also made contributions to Marxist esthetics and literary theory. He believed, as a cultural relativist, that the most important art was that which reflected the historical movement of the time: for the 20th century, ◊Socialist realism.

Luke, St 1st century AD. Traditionally the compiler of the third Gospel and of the Acts of the Apostles in the New Testament. He is the patron saint of painters; his emblem is a winged ox, and his feast day Oct 18.

Luke is supposed to have been a Greek physician born in Antioch (Antakya, Turkey) and to have accompanied Paul after the ascension of Jesus.

Luks George 1867–1933. US painter and graphic artist, a member of the ◊Ashcan School.

Born in Williamsport, Pennsylvania, he studied at the Pennsylvania Academy of the Fine Arts and worked as an illustrator and cartoonist 1894–96 for various newspapers. Robert ◊Henri convinced him to take up painting. Luks's painting captured the excitement and color of life in New York City's slums.

Luleå port in N Sweden, on the Gulf of Bothnia at the mouth of the river Luleå; population (1986) 66,500. It is the capital of Norrbotten county. Exports include iron ore and timber in ice-free months.

Lully Jean-Baptiste. Adopted name of Giovanni Battista Lulli 1632–1687. French composer of Italian origin who was court composer to Louis XIV. He composed music for the ballet, for Molière's plays, and established French opera with such works as *Alceste* 1674 and *Armide et Renaud* 1686. He was also a ballet dancer.

lumbago pain in the lower region of the back, usually due to strain or faulty posture. If it occurs with ◊sciatica, it may be due to pressure on spinal nerves by a displaced vertebra. Treatment includes rest, application of heat, and skilled manipulation (see ◊chiropractic and ◊osteopathy). Surgery may be needed in rare cases.

lumbar puncture or ***spinal tap*** the insertion of a hollow needle between two lumbar (lower back) vertebrae to withdraw a sample of cerebrospinal fluid (CSF) for testing. Normally clear and colorless, the CSF acts as a fluid buffer around the brain and spinal cord. Changes in its quantity, color, or composition may indicate neurological damage or disease.

Lumbini birthplace of ◊Buddha in the foothills of the Himalayas near the Nepalese-Indian frontier. A sacred garden and shrine were established 1970 by the Nepalese government.

lumen SI unit (abbreviation lm) of luminous flux (the amount of light passing through an area per second).

The lumen is defined in terms of the light falling on a unit area at a unit distance from a light source of luminous intensity of one ◊candela. One lumen at a wavelength of 5,550 angströms equals 0.0014706 watts.

lumen the hollow interior of the alimentary canal, and the site of digestion in many invertebrates and all vertebrates.

Lumet Sidney 1924– . US film director. His films, sometimes marked by a heavy-handed seriousness, have met with varying critical and commercial success. They include *Twelve Angry Men* 1957, *Fail Safe* 1964, *The Deadly Affair* 1967, *Network* 1976, and *Equus* 1977.

Lumière Auguste Marie 1862–1954 and Louis Jean 1864–1948. French brothers who pioneered cinematography. In 1895 they patented their cinematograph, a combined camera and projector operating at 16 frames per second, and opened the world's first cinema in Paris to show their films.

The Lumière's first films were short static shots of everyday events such as *La Sorties des Usines Lumière* 1895 about workers leaving a factory and *L'Arroseur Arrosé* 1895, the world's first fiction film. Production was abandoned in 1900.

luminescence emission of light from a body when its atoms are excited to incandescence by means other than raising its temperature. Short-lived luminescence is called fluorescence; longer-lived luminescence is called phosphorescence.

When exposed to an external source of energy, the outer electrons in atoms of a luminescent substance absorb energy and "jump" to a higher energy level. When these electrons "jump" back to their former level they emit their excess energy as light. Many different exciting mechanisms are possible: visible light or some other ◊electromagnetic radiation (ultraviolet rays or X-rays), electron bombardment, chemical reactions, friction, and ◊radioactivity. Certain living organisms produce ◊bioluminescence.

luminism a method of painting, associated with the ◊Hudson River school in the 19th century, that emphasized the effects of light on water.

Luminist painters included F H Lane, T Cole, A B Durand, M J Heade, and F E Church. They gave particular attention to the treatment of light in their paintings, stressing precision through technical accuracy.

luminous paint preparation containing a mixture of pigment, oil, and a phosphorescent sulfide, usually calcium or barium. After exposure to light it appears luminous in the dark. The luminous paint used on watch faces contains radium, is radioactive and therefore does not require exposure to light. It has become a health hazard to those working in the industry and to those living in the regions surrounding manufacturing plants (because of the disposal of radioactive wastes).

Lumpenproletariat (German "ragged proletariat") the poorest of the poor: beggars, tramps, and criminals (according to Karl Marx).

Lumumba Patrice 1926–1961. Congolese politician, prime minister of Zaïre 1960. Imprisoned by the Belgians, but released in time to attend the conference giving the Congo independence 1960, he led the National Congolese Movement to victory in the subsequent general election. He was deposed in a coup d'état, and murdered some months later.

Lund city in Malmöhus county, SW Sweden; 10 mi/16 km NE of Malmö; population (1986) 83,400. It has an 11th-century Romanesque cathedral and a university established 1666. The treaty of Lund was signed in 1676 after Carl XI had defeated the Danes.

Lüneburg town in Lower Saxony, Germany, on the river Ilmenau; population (1985) 61,000. Industries include chemicals, paper, and iron works. It is a health resort.

lung large cavity of the body, used for ◊gas exchange. It is essentially a sheet of thin, moist membrane that is folded so as to occupy less space. Lungs are found in some slugs and snails, particularly those that live on land. Some fishes (lungfish) and most ◊tetrapod vertebrates have a pair of lungs, which occupy the thorax (the upper part of the trunk). Lungs function by bringing inhaled air into close contact with the blood, so that oxygen can pass into the organism and waste carbon dioxide can be passed out; the oxygen is carried by ◊hemoglobin in red blood cells. The lung tissue, consisting of multitudes of air sacs and blood vessels, is very light and spongy.

Air is drawn into the lungs through the trachea and bronchi by the expansion of the ribs and the contraction of the diaphragm. The principal diseases of the lungs are tuberculosis, pneumonia, bronchitis, emphysema, and cancer.

lungfish three genera of fleshy-finned bony fishes of the subclass Dipnoi, found in Africa, South America, and Australia. They have elongated bodies, and grow to about 6 ft/2 m, and in addition to gills have "lungs" with which they can breathe air during periods of drought conditions.

Lungfish are related to the lobefins such as the ◊coelacanth, and were abundant 350 million years ago.

Lunt Alfred 1893–1977. US actor. He went straight from school into the theater, and in 1922 married Lynn ◊Fontanne with whom he subsequently co-starred in more than 30 successful plays. They formed a sophisticated comedy duo, and the New York Lunt-Fontanne theater was named after them. Their shows included *Design for Living* by Noël Coward 1933, *There Shall Be No Night* 1940–41, and *The Visit* 1960.

Luo Guan Zhong or ***Luo Kuan-chung*** lived 14th-century. Chinese novelist who reworked popular tales into *The Romance of the Three Kingdoms* and *The Water Margin*.

Luo Kuan-chung alternative transliteration of ◊Luo Guan Zhong, Chinese writer

Luoyang formerly ***Loyang*** industrial city in Henan province, S of the river Huang He; population 1,114,000. Formerly the capital of China, its industries include machinery and tractors.

Lupercalia Roman festival celebrated Feb 15. It took place at the Lupercal, the cave where ◊Romulus and Remus were supposedly suckled by the wolf (*lupus*). Lupercalia included feasting,

lung

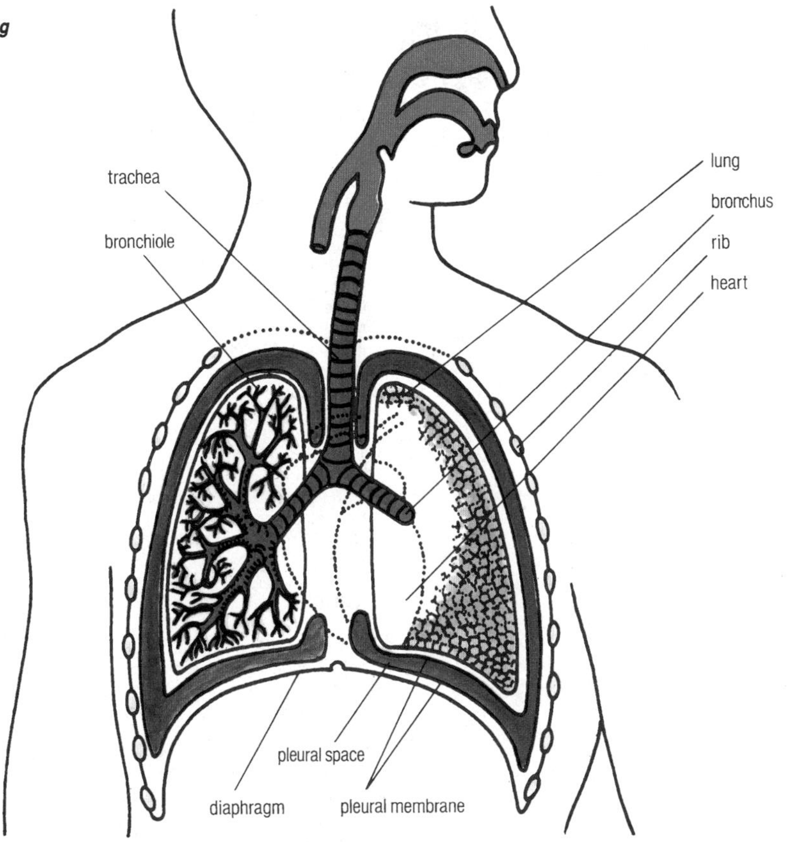
trachea
bronchiole
lung
bronchus
rib
heart
pleural space
diaphragm
pleural membrane

dancing, and sacrificing goats. Priests ran round the city carrying whips made from the hides of the sacrificed goats, a blow from which was believed to cure sterility in women.

lupin any plant of the genus *Lupinus*, of the pea family (Leguminosae), including about 300 species. They are native to Mediterranean regions and parts of N and S America. Their spikes of pealike flowers may be white, yellow, blue, or pink. The European lupin *L. albus* is cultivated in some places for cattle fodder and for manure.

lupus in medicine, any of various diseases characterized by lesions of the skin. In one form (lupus vulgaris), it is caused by the tubercle bacillus (see ◊tuberculosis). The organism produces ulcers that spread and eat away the underlying tissues. Treatment is primarily with standard antituberculous drugs, such as streptomycin, but ultraviolet light may also be used.

Lupus erythematous (LE) has two forms: discoid LE, seen as red, scaly patches on the skin, especially the face; and disseminated or systemic LE, which may affect connective tissue anywhere in the body, often involving the internal organs. The latter is much more serious. Treatment is with ◊corticosteroids.

Lurçat Jean 1892–1966. French artist, inspired by the Cubists, who revived tapestry design, as in *Le Chant du Monde*.

lupin

Lurie Alison 1926– . US novelist and critic. Her subtly written and satirical novels include *Imaginary Friends* 1967; *The War Between the Tates* 1974; *Foreign Affairs* 1985, a tale of transatlantic relations that won the Pulitzer Prize; and *The Truth About Lorin Jones* 1988.

Luristan or ***Lorestan*** mountainous province in W Iran; area 11,117 sq mi/28,800 sq km; population (1986) 1,367,000. The capital is Khorramabad. The province is inhabited by Lur tribes who live by their sheep and cattle. Excavation in the area has revealed a culture of the 8th–7th centuries BC with bronzes decorated with animal forms; its origins are uncertain.

Lusaka capital of Zambia from 1964 (of Northern Rhodesia 1935–64), 230 mi/370 km NE of Livingstone; commercial and agricultural center (flour mills, tobacco factories, vehicle assembly, plastics, printing); population (1987) 819,000.

Lüshun-Dalien see ◊Lüda, port in China.

Lusitania ancient area of the Iberian peninsula, roughly equivalent to Portugal. Conquered by Rome in 139 BC, the province of Lusitania rebelled periodically until finally conquered by Pompey 73–72 BC.

Lusitania ocean liner sunk by a German submarine May 7, 1915 with the loss of 1,200 lives, including some Americans; its destruction helped bring the US into World War I.

Lü-ta former name of ◊Lüda, port in China.

lute family of stringed musical instruments of the 14th–18th centuries, including the mandore, theorbo, and chitarrone. They are pear-shaped and plucked with the fingers. Members of the lute family were used both as solo instruments and for vocal accompaniment, and were often played in addition to, or instead of, keyboard ◊continuo instruments in larger ensembles and in opera.

luteinizing hormone a ◊hormone produced by the pituitary gland. In males, it stimulates the testes to produce ◊androgens. In the female ◊menstrual cycle, it works together with follicle stimulating hormone to initiate production of egg cells by the ovary. If fertilization of the egg cell occurs, it plays a part in maintaining the pregnancy by controlling the levels of estrogen and progesterone in the body.

lutetium silver-white, metallic element, the last of the ◊lanthanide series, symbol Lu, atomic number 71, atomic weight 174.97. It is used in the "cracking," or breakdown, of petroleum and in other chemical processes. It was named by its discoverer, French chemist Georges Urbain (1872–1938) for his native city, Paris, called *Lutetia* in Latin.

Luther Martin 1483–1546. German Christian church reformer, a founder of Protestantism. While he was a priest at the University of Wittenberg, he wrote an attack on the sale of indulgences (remissions of punishment for sin) in 95 theses which he nailed to a church door 1517, in defiance of papal condemnation. The Holy Roman emperor Charles V summoned him to the Diet of Worms 1521, where he refused to retract his objections. Originally intending reform, his protest led to schism, with the emergence, following the ◊Augsburg Confession 1530, of a new Protestant church.

Luther was born in Eisleben, the son of a miner; he studied at the University of Erfurt, spent three years as a monk in the Augustinian convent there, and in 1507 was ordained priest. Shortly afterwards he attracted attention as a teacher and preacher at the University of Wittenberg; and in 1517, after returning from a visit to Rome, he attained nationwide celebrity for his denunciation of the Dominican monk Johann Tetzel (1455–1519), one of those sent out by the Pope to sell indulgences as a means of raising funds for the rebuilding of St Peter's Basilica in Rome.

On Oct 31, 1517, Luther nailed on the church door in Wittenberg a statement of 95 theses concerning indulgences, and the following year he was summoned to Rome to defend his action. His reply was to attack the papal system even more strongly, and in 1520 he publicly burned in Wittenberg the papal bull that had been launched against him. On his way home from the imperial Diet of Worms he was taken into "protective custody" by the elector of Saxony in the castle of Wartburg. Later he became estranged from the Dutch theologian Erasmus, who had formerly supported him in his attacks on papal authority, and engaged in violent controversies with political and religious opponents. After the Augsburg Confession 1530, Luther gradually retired from the Protestant leadership.

Formerly condemned by communism, Luther had by the 1980s been rehabilitated as a revolutionary Socialist hero and was claimed as patron saint by both East and West Germany.

Lutheranism a form of Protestant Christianity derived from the life and teaching of Martin Luther; it is sometimes called Evangelical to distinguish it from the other main branch of European Protestantism, the Reformed. The most generally accepted statement of Lutheranism is that of the Augsburg Confession 1530, but Luther's Shorter Catechism also carries great weight. It is the largest Protestant body, including some 80 million persons, of whom 40 million are in Germany, 19 million in Scandinavia, 8.5 million in the US and Canada, and most of the remainder in central Europe.

It is the principal form of Protestantism in Germany and is the national faith of Denmark, Norway, Sweden, Finland, and Iceland. The organization may be episcopal (Germany, Sweden) or synodal (the Netherlands and the US); the Lutheran World Federation has its headquarters in Geneva. In the US, Lutheranism is particularly strong in the Midwest, where several churches were originally founded by German and Scandinavian immigrants. Lutheranism in the US

***Lutyens** English architect Edwin Lutyens used Renaissance and Classical elements in many of his designs, as in the Midland Bank, Manchester, England.*

is divided into three main bodies: the Lutheran Church in America, formed 1962 from the United Lutheran Church, Augustana Lutheran Church (Swedish), the Finnish Evangelical Lutheran Church, and the American Evangelical Lutheran Church (Danish); the more conservative Lutheran Church, the Missouri Synod; and the American Lutheran Church (largely Norwegian and centered in the upper Midwest).

Luthuli or ***Lutuli*** Albert 1899–1967. South African politician, president of the African National Congress from 1952. Luthuli, a Zulu tribal chief, preached nonviolence and multiracialism.

Luton industrial town in Bedfordshire, England, 33 mi/53 km SW of Cambridge; population (1985) 165,000. Luton airport is a secondary one for London. Manufacturing includes automobiles, chemicals, electrical goods, ballbearings, as well as traditionally, hats.

Lutosławski Witold 1913– . Polish composer and conductor, born in Warsaw. His early music, dissonant and powerful (*First Symphony* 1947), was criticized by the communist government, so he adopted a more popular style. With the lifting of artistic repression, he quickly adopted avant-garde techniques, including improvisatory and aleatoric forms.

He has written chamber, vocal, and orchestral music, including three symphonies, *Livre pour orchestre* 1968 and *Mi-parti* 1976.

Lutyens (Agnes) Elisabeth 1906–1983. English composer. Her works, using the 12-tone system, are expressive and tightly organized, and include a substantial amount of chamber music, stage, and orchestral works. Her choral and vocal works include a setting of ◊Wittgenstein's *Tractatus* and a cantata *The Tears of Night*.

Lutyens Edwin Landseer 1869–1944. English architect. His designs ranged from picturesque to Renaissance-style country houses and ultimately evolved into a Classical style as in the Cenotaph, London, and the Viceroy's House, New Delhi.

Lützen town in Halle county, Germany, SW of Leipzig, where in 1632 Gustavus Adolphus, king of Sweden, defeated the German commander Wallenstein in the Thirty Years' War; Gustavus was killed in the battle. Napoleon overcame the Russians and Prussians here in 1813.

lux SI unit (abbreviation lx) of illuminance or illumination (the light falling on an object). It is equivalent to one lumen per square meter or to the illuminance of a surface one meter distant from a point source of one candela.

Luxembourg
Grand Duchy of
(Grand-Duché de Luxembourg)

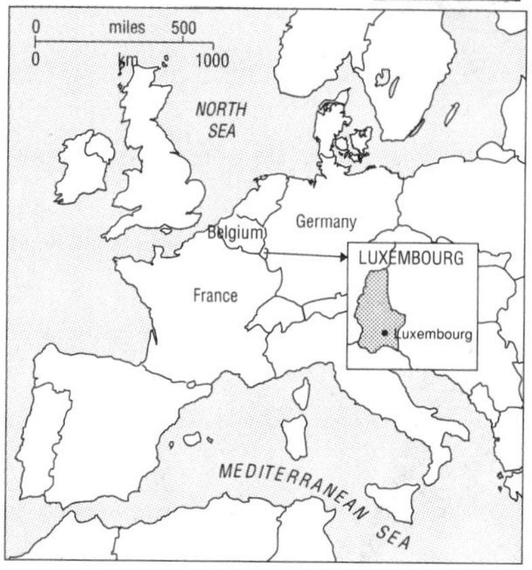
0 miles 500
0 km 1000
NORTH SEA
Belgium
Germany
France
LUXEMBOURG
Luxembourg
MEDITERRANEAN SEA

area 998 sq mi/2,586 sq km
capital Luxembourg
cities Esch-sur-Alzette, Dudelange
physical on the river Moselle; part of the Ardennes (Oesling) forest in N
features seat of the European Court of Justice, Secretariat of the European Parliament, international banking center; economically linked with Belgium
head of state Grand Duke Jean from 1964
head of government Jacques Santer from 1984
political system liberal democracy
political parties Christian Social Party (PCS), moderate, left-of-center; Luxembourg Socialist Workers' Party (POSL), moderate, Socialist; Democratic Party (PD), center-left; Communist Party of Luxembourg, pro-European left-wing
exports pharmaceuticals, synthetic textiles, steel
currency Luxembourg franc
population (1990 est) 369,000; growth rate 0% p.a.
life expectancy men 71, women 78 (1989)
language French (official); local Letzeburgesch; German
religion Roman Catholic 97%
literacy 100% (1989)
GNP $4.9 bn; $13,380 per head (1988)
chronology
1354 Became a duchy.
1482 Under Hapsburg control.
1797 Ceded, with Belgium, to France.
1815 Treaty of Vienna created Luxembourg a grand duchy, ruled by the king of the Netherlands.
1830 With Belgium, revolted against Dutch rule.
1890 Link with Netherlands ended with accession of Grand Duke Adolphe of Nassau-Weilburg.
1948 With Belgium and the Netherlands, formed the Benelux customs union.
1958 Benelux became economic union.
1961 Prince Jean became acting head of state on behalf of his mother, Grand Duchess Charlotte.
1964 Grand Duchess Charlotte abdicated, and Prince Jean became grand duke.

Luxembourg landlocked country in W Europe, bordered N and W by Belgium, E by Germany, and S by France

government Luxembourg is a hereditary and constitutional monarchy. The 1868 constitution, revised 1919 and 1956, provides for a single-chamber legislature, the 60-member chamber of deputies, elected by universal suffrage through a system of proportional representation, for a five-year term. There is also an advisory body called the Council of State, whose 21 members are appointed by the grand duke for life. Any of its decisions can be overruled by the chamber of deputies. The grand duke also appoints a prime minister and council of ministers who are collectively responsible to the chamber. The four main political parties are the Christian Social Party, the Socialist Party, the Democratic Party (or Liberals), and the Communist Party.

history Formerly part of the Holy Roman Empire, Luxembourg became a duchy 1354. From 1482 it was under ◊Hapsburg control, and in 1797 was ceded, with Belgium, to France. The 1815 ◊Treaty of Vienna made Luxembourg a grand duchy, ruled by the king of the Netherlands. In 1830 Belgium and Luxembourg revolted against Dutch rule; Belgium achieved independence 1839 and most of Luxembourg became part of it, the rest becoming independent in its own right 1848.

Although a small country, Luxembourg occupies an important position in W Europe, being a founding member of many international organizations, including the European Coal and Steel Community, the European Atomic Energy Commission, and the European Community. It formed an economic union with Belgium and the Netherlands 1948 (◊Benelux), which was the forerunner of wider European cooperation.

Grand Duchess Charlotte (1896–1985) abdicated 1964 after a reign of 45 years, and was succeeded by her son, Prince Jean. Proportional representation has resulted in a series of coalition governments. The Christian Social Party headed most of these from 1945–74 when its dominance was challenged by the Socialists. It regained preeminence 1979, and leads the current administration.

Luxembourg province of Belgium; capital Arlon; area 1,698 sq mi/4,400 sq km; population (1987) 227,000.

Luxembourg capital of Luxembourg; population (1985) 76,000. The 16th-century Grand Ducal Palace, European Court of Justice, and European Parliament secretariat are situated here, but plenary sessions of the parliament are now held only in ◊Strasbourg. Products include steel, chemicals, textiles, and processed food.

Luxembourg, Palais du palace in Paris, France, in which the Senate sits. It was built 1615 for Marie de Medici by Salomon de Brosse.

Luxembourg Accord French-initiated agreement in 1966 that a decision of the Council of Ministers of the European Community may be vetoed by a member whose national interests are at stake.

Luxemburg Rosa 1870–1919. Polish-born German communist, a leader of the left wing of the German Social Democratic Party from 1898 and collaborator with Karl Liebknecht in founding the communist Spartacus League in 1918 (see ◊Spartacist). She was murdered with him by army officers during the Jan 1919 Berlin workers' revolt.

Luxor (Arabic *al-Uqsur*) small town in Egypt on the E bank of the Nile near the ruins of ◊Thebes.

Lu Xun pen name of Chon Shu-jêu 1881–1936. Chinese short-story writer. His three volumes of satirically realistic stories, *Call to Arms, Wandering*, and *Old Tales Retold*, reveal the influence of Gogol.

He is one of the most popular of modern Chinese writers.

Luzern German name of ◊Lucerne, town and lake in Switzerland.

Luzon largest island of the ◊Philippines; area 41,750 sq mi/108,130 sq km; capital Quezon City; population (1970) 18,001,270. The chief city

Luxor *The temple of Queen Hatshepsut in Luxor, Egypt, showing a bust of the queen on one of the columns.*

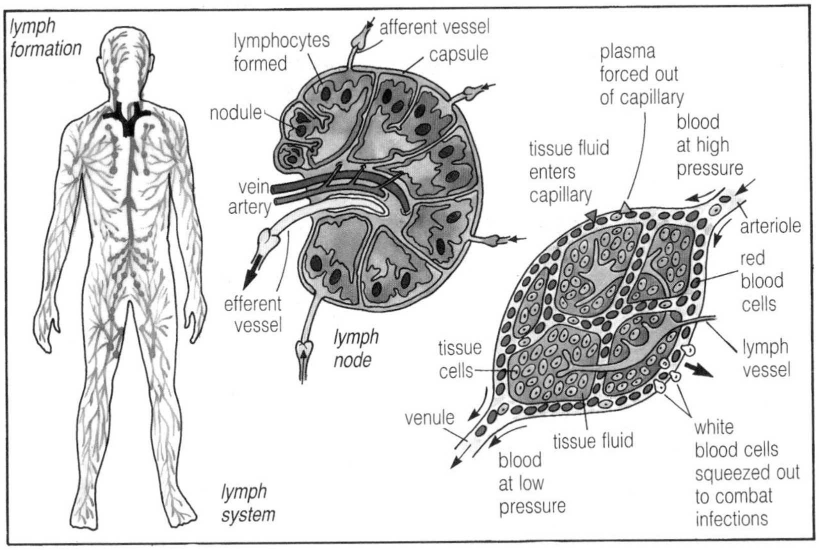
lymph formation
lymphocytes formed
afferent vessel
capsule
nodule
vein
artery
efferent vessel
lymph node
lymph system
plasma forced out of capillary
blood at high pressure
tissue fluid enters capillary
arteriole
red blood cells
tissue cells
lymph vessel
venule
tissue fluid
blood at low pressure
white blood cells squeezed out to combat infections

is Manila, capital of the Philippines. Products include rice, timber, and minerals. It has US military bases.

Lvov (Ukrainian *Lviv*) capital and major industrial city of the Lvov region in the Ukraine; population (1987) 767,000. Industries include textiles, metals, and engineering. The university was founded 1661. It was formerly a trade center on the Black Sea–Baltic route. Lvov, founded in the 13th century by a Galician prince (the name means "city of Leo" or "city of Lev"), was Polish 1340–1772, Austrian 1772–1919, Polish 1919–39, and annexed by the USSR 1945. It was the site of violent nationalist demonstrations in Oct 1989.

LW (abbreviation for long wave) radio wave with a wavelength of over 3,300 ft/1,000 m; one of the main wavebands into which radio frequency transmissions are divided.

LWM abbreviation for low water mark.

Lwów Polish form of ◊Lvov, city in Ukraine, USSR.

lycanthropy in folk belief, transformation of a human being into a ◊werewolf; or, in psychology, a delusion involving this belief.

Lyceum an ancient Athenian gymnasium and garden, with covered walks, where ◊Aristotle taught. It was SE of the city and named after the nearby temple of Apollo Lyceus.

lychee alternate spelling of ◊litchi.

Lycurgus Spartan lawgiver. He is said to have been a member of the royal house, who, while acting as regent, gave the Spartans their constitution and system of education. Many scholars believe him to be purely mythical.

Lydgate John c. 1370–c. 1450. English poet. He was a Benedictine monk and later prior. His numerous works were often translations or adaptations, such as *Troy Book* and *Falls of Princes*.

Lydia ancient kingdom in Anatolia (7th–6th centuries BC), with its capital at Sardis. The Lydians were the first Western people to use standard coinage. Their last king, Croesus, was conquered by the Persians 546 BC.

Lyell Charles 1797–1875. Scottish geologist. In his book *The Principles of Geology* 1830–33, he opposed ◊Cuvier's theory that the features of the Earth were formed by a series of catastrophes, and expounded ◊Hutton's view, known as ◊uniformitarianism, that past events were brought about by the same processes that occur today—a view that influenced Charles ◊Darwin's theory of evolution.

Lyell trained and practiced as a lawyer, but retired from the law in 1827 and devoted himself full time to geology and writing. He implied that the Earth was much older than the 6,000 years of prevalent contemporary theory, and provided the first detailed description of the ◊Tertiary period. Although it was only in old age that he accepted that species had changed through evolution, he nevertheless provided Darwin with a geologic framework within which evolutionary theories could be placed. Darwin simply applied Lyell's geologic method—explaining the past through what is observable in the present—to biology.

lyme disease disease transmitted by tick bites that affects all the systems of the body. First described in 1977 following an outbreak in children living around Lyme, Connecticut, it is caused by the microorganism *Borrelia burgdorferi*, isolated by Burgdorfer and Barbor in the US in 1982. Untreated, the disease attacks the nervous system, heart, liver, kidney, eyes and joints, but responds to the antibiotic tetracycline. The tick that carries the disease, *Iricinus*, lives on deer, while *B. burgdorferi* relies on mice during its life cycle.

lymph the fluid found in the lymphatic system of vertebrates, which returns excess, filtered tissue fluid and some proteins to the bloodstream. Lymph vessels also transport fat from the digestive tract to the blood. Lymph moves in only one direction; flaplike valves prevent backflow.

Lymph is drained from the tissues by lymph capillaries, which empty into larger lymph vessels (lymphatics). These lead to lymph nodes (small, round bodies chiefly situated in the neck, armpit, groin, thorax, and abdomen), which process the ◊lymphocytes produced by the bone marrow, and filter out harmful substances and bacteria. From the lymph nodes, vessels carry the lymph to the thoracic duct and the right lymphatic duct, which lead into the large veins in the neck. Some vertebrates, such as amphibians, have a lymph heart, which pumps lymph through the lymph vessels.

lymph nodes small masses of lymphatic tissue in the body that occur at various points along the major lymphatic vessels. Tonsils and adenoids are large lymph nodes. As the lymph passes through them it is filtered, and bacteria and other microorganisms are engulfed by cells known as macrophages.

Lymph nodes are sometimes mistakenly called "lymph glands," and the term "swollen glands" refers to swelling of the lymph nodes caused by infection.

lymphocyte a type of white blood cell with a large nucleus, produced in the bone marrow. Most occur in the ◊lymph and blood, and around sites of infection. B lymphocytes or ◊B cells are responsible for producing ◊antibodies. T lymphocytes or ◊T cells have several roles forming ◊immunity.

lymphogranuloma venerum or ***chlamydia*** a sexually transmitted disease caused by the bacterium *Chlamydia trachomatis*, the same organism that causes the eye disease trachoma. The disease is characterized by genital ulcers, inflammation of the urinary tract, and swelling of the lymph nodes in the groin. Chronic pelvic inflammatory disease can result if left untreated.

lymphokines chemical messengers produced by ◊lymphocytes that carry messages between the cells of the immune system (see ◊immunity). Examples include interferon, which initiates defensive reactions to viruses, and the interleukins, which activate specific immune cells.

Lynchburg city in S central Virginia, on the James River, NE of Roanoke. Industries include clothing, paper and rubber products, and machine parts; population (1990) 66,049.

lynching the killing of an alleged offender by an individual or group having no legal authority. In the US it originated in 1780 with creation of a "committee of vigilance" in Virginia; it is named after a member of that committee, Captain William Lynch, to whom is attributed "Lynch's Law." Later examples occurred mostly in the Southern states after the Civil War and were racially motivated. During 1882–1900 the annual number of lynchings in the US varied between 96 and 231, but today it is an exceptional occurrence.

Lynn industrial city in Massachusetts, on Massachusetts Bay; population (1990) 81,245. Founded as Saugus in 1629, it was renamed 1637 after King's Lynn, England.

Lynn Vera 1917– . British singer, the "Forces' Sweetheart" of World War II with "We'll Meet Again" and "White Cliffs of Dover," and in 1952 "Auf Wiederseh'n, Sweetheart."

lynx cat *Felis lynx* found in rocky and forested regions of North America and Europe. About 3 ft/1 m in length, it has a short tail and tufted ears, and the long, silky fur is reddish brown or gray with dark spots. The North American bobcat or bay lynx *Felix rufus* looks similar but is smaller. Some zoologists place the lynx, the bobcat, and the ◊caracal in a separate genus, *Lynx*.

Lyon (English, *Lyons*) industrial city (textiles, chemicals, machinery, printing) and capital of Rhône *département*, Rhône-Alpes region, and third largest city of France, at the confluence of the rivers Rhône and Saône, 170 mi/275 km NNW of Marseille; population (1982) 418,476, conurbation 1,221,000. Formerly a chief fortress of France, it was the ancient Lugdunum, taken by the Romans 43 BC.

Lyons English form of Lyon, a city in France.

Lyons Joseph Aloysius 1879–1939. Australian politician, founder of the United Australia Party 1931, prime minister 1931–39.

Lyra small but prominent constellation of the northern hemisphere, representing the lyre of Orpheus. Its brightest star is Vega, 27 light-years from Earth.

Epsilon Lyrae, the "double double," is a system of four gravitationally linked stars. Beta Lyrae is an eclipsing binary. The Ring nebula, M57, is a ◊planetary nebula.

lyre stringed instrument of great antiquity. It consists of a soundbox with two curved arms extended upward to a crosspiece to which four to ten strings are attached. It is played with a plectrum or the fingers.

It originated in Asia, and was used in Greece and Egypt.

lyrebird any birds of the order *Passeriformes*, forming the Australian family Menuridae. There are two species, both in the genus *Menura*. The male has a large lyre-shaped tail, brilliantly colored. They nest on the ground, and feed on insects, worms, and snails.

Lysander Spartan general. He brought the Peloponnesian War to a successful conclusion by capturing the Athenian fleet at Aegospotami 405 BC, and by starving Athens into surrender in the following year. He then aspired to make Sparta supreme in Greece and himself supreme in Sparta; he set up puppet governments in Athens and her former allies, and tried to secure for himself the Spartan kingship, but he was killed in battle with the Thebans.

Lysenko Trofim Denisovich 1898–1976. Soviet biologist who believed in the inheritance of ◊acquired characteristics (changes acquired in an individual's lifetime) and used his position under Stalin officially to exclude ◊Mendel's theory of inheritance. He was removed from office after the fall of Khrushchev 1964.

Lysippus 4th century BC. Greek sculptor. He made a series of portraits of Alexander the Great (Roman copies survive, including examples in the British Museum and the Louvre) and also sculpted the *Apoxyomenos*, an athlete (copy in the Vatican), and a colossal *Hercules* (lost).

lysis in biology, any process that destroys a cell by rupturing its membrane or cell wall (see ◊lysosome).

Lysistrata a Greek comedy by Aristophanes, produced 411 BC. The women of Athens, tired of war, refuse to make love with their husbands and occupy the Acropolis to force a peace between the Athenians and the Spartans.

lysosome a membrane-enclosed structure, or organelle, inside a ◊cell, principally found in animal cells. Lysosomes contain enzymes that can break down proteins and other biological substances. They play a part in digestion, and in the white blood cells known as phagocytes the lysosyme enzymes attack ingested bacteria.

Lytham St Annes resort in Lancashire, England, on the river Ribble; 6 mi/10 km SE of Blackpool; population (1982) 39,641. It has a championship golf course.

Lytton Edward George Earle Bulwer-Lytton, 1st Baron Lytton of Knebworth 1803–1873. English writer. His novels successfully followed every turn of the public taste and include the Byronic *Pelham* 1828, *The Last Days of Pompeii* 1834, and *Rienzi* 1835. His plays include *Richelieu* 1838.

Lytton Edward Robert Bulwer-Lytton, 1st Earl of 1831–1891. British diplomat, viceroy of India 1876–80, where he pursued a controversial "forward" policy. Only son of the novelist, he was himself a poet under the pseudonym Owen Meredith, writing "King Poppy" 1892 and other poems.

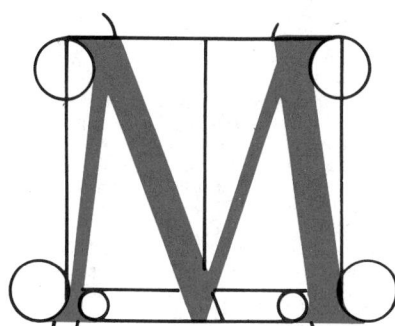

M Roman numeral for 1,000.

MA abbreviation for Master of Arts degree of education; the state of ◊Massachusetts.

Maas Dutch or Flemish name for the river ◊Meuse.

Maastricht industrial city (metallurgy, textiles, pottery) and capital of the province of Limburg, the Netherlands, on the river Maas, near the Dutch-Belgian frontier; population (1988) 160,000. Maastricht dates from Roman times.

Maazel Lorin (Varencove) 1930– . US conductor and violinist. He studied the violin and made his debut as a conductor at the age of nine. He was conductor of the Cleveland Orchestra 1972–82 and the first US director of the Vienna State Opera.

Mabuse Jan. Adopted name of Jan Gossaert c. 1478–c. 1533. Flemish painter, active chiefly in Antwerp. His common name derives from his birthplace, Maubeuge. His visit to Italy in 1508 with Philip of Burgundy started a new vogue in Flanders for Italianate ornament and Classical detail in painting, including sculptural nude figures.

McAdam John Loudon 1756–1836. Scottish engineer, inventor of the macadam road surface. It consisted of broken granite bound together with slag or gravel, raised for drainage. Today, it is bound with tar or asphalt.

macadamia edible nut from the tree *Macadamia ternifolia*, family Proteaceae, native to Australia and cultivated in Hawaii.

McAllen city in S Texas, just N of the Mexican border formed by the Rio Grande, SE of Laredo. It is a US port of entry for Mexicans, and many of the city's inhabitants are Spanish-speaking. Industries include oil refining and the processing

Maazel *US conductor Lorin Maazel made his debut as a conductor at the age of nine and as a violinist a few years later.*

of agricultural products from the Rio Grande valley; population (1990) 84,021.

Macao Portuguese possession on the south coast of China, about 40 mi/65 km west of Hong Kong, from which it is separated by the estuary of the Canton river; it consists of a peninsula and the islands of Taipa and Colôane

area 7 sq mi/17 sq km

capital Macao, on the peninsula

features the peninsula is linked to Taipa by a bridge and to Colôane by a causeway, both 1 mi/2 km long

currency pataca

population (1986) 426,000

language Cantonese; Portuguese (official)

religion Buddhist, with 6% Catholic minority

government Under the constitution ("organic statute") of 1976, Macao enjoys considerable political autonomy. The Portuguese president controls the colony's external affairs but appoints, in consultation with the local legislative assembly, a governor to exercise control over domestic matters. The governor works with a cabinet of five appointed secretaries and confers with a ten-member consultative council and a 17-member legislative council, both composed of a mixture of elected and nominated members. The legislative council frames internal legislation, but any bills passed by less than a two-thirds majority can be vetoed by the governor. A number of "civic associations" and interest groups function, sending representatives to the legislative council.

Macao

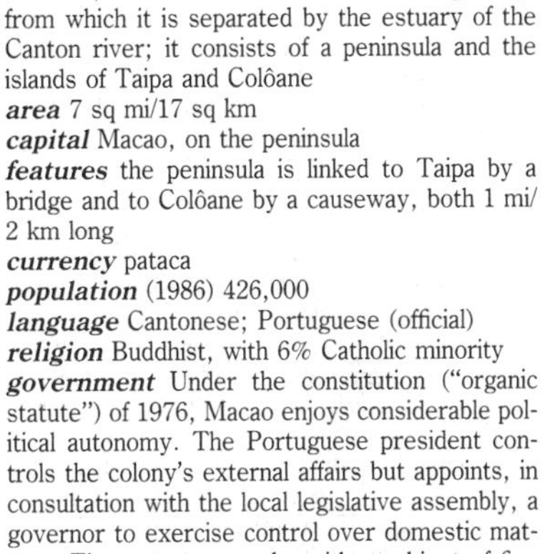
Macao

MacArthur *US general Douglas MacArthur in 1945. He had been Allied commander in the SW Pacific area since 1942 and helped mastermind the defeat of Japan in World War II.*

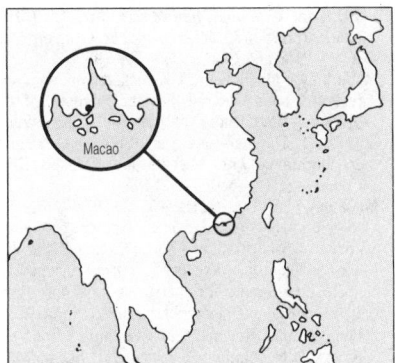

history Macao was first established as a Portuguese trading and missionary post in the Far East 1537, and was leased from China 1557. It was annexed 1849 and recognized as a Portuguese colony by the Chinese government in a treaty 1887. The port declined in prosperity during the late 19th and early 20th centuries, as its harbor silted up and international trade was diverted to Hong Kong and the new treaty ports. The colony thus concentrated instead on local "country trade" and became a center for gambling and, later, tourism.

In 1951 Macao became an overseas province of Portugal, sending an elected representative to the Lisbon parliament. After the Portuguese revolution 1974, it became a "special territory" and was granted considerable autonomy under a governor appointed by the Portuguese president.

In 1986 negotiations opened between the Portuguese and the Chinese government over the question of the return of Macao's sovereignty under similar "one country, two systems" terms to those agreed by China and the UK for ◊Hong Kong. These negotiations proved successful and were concluded April 1987 by the signing of the Macao Pact, under which Portugal agreed to hand over sovereignty to the People's Republic Dec 1999, and China agreed in return to guarantee to maintain the port's capitalist economic and social system for at least 50 years.

In May 1990 administrative, economic, and financial autonomy was secured from Portugal: this followed the approval of a new Organic Law for the territory by both Portugal's parliament and Macao's Legislative Assembly. Under the terms of this law, the Legislative Assembly was enlarged to 23 members—comprising seven government appointees, eight indirectly elected by business associations and eight directly elected by universal suffrage. Executive power is held by the governor. Sovereignty is to be transferred to China at the close of 1999.

macaque Old World monkey of the genus *Macaca*. Various species of these medium-sized monkeys live in forests from the Far East to N Africa. The ◊rhesus and the ◊Barbary ape are part of this group.

Macaques range from long-tailed to tailless types, and have well-developed cheek pouches to carry food.

MacArthur Douglas 1880–1964. US general in World War II, commander of US forces in the Far East and from March 1942 of the Allied forces in the SW Pacific. After receiving the surrender of Japan he commanded the Allied occupation forces there.

During 1950 he commanded the UN forces in Korea, but in April 1951, after expressing views contrary to US and UN policy, he was relieved of all his commands by President Truman.

Born in Little Rock, Arkansas, the son of an army officer, MacArthur graduated first in his class at West Point 1903, had a distinguished combat record in World War I, and rose to become chief of staff 1930–35. He defended the Philippines against the Japanese 1941–42 and escaped to Australia when his small force was overwhelmed and he was forced to surrender. He vowed at the time, "I shall return." He was responsible for the reconquest of New Guinea 1942–45 and of the Philippines 1944–45, being appointed General of the Army 1944. He retired from the army, but when North Korea crossed the 38th parallel and invaded South Korea 1950, he was asked to command UN forces to support the South's sovereignty. After a surprise landing at Inchon forced the North Koreans to retreat, MacArthur invaded the North until beaten back by Chinese troops. After he was removed from command, he received a hero's welcome on his return to the US.

Macassar another name for ◊Ujung Pandang, port in the Celebes, Indonesia.

Macaulay Thomas Babington, Baron 1800–1859. English historian, essayist, poet, and politician, secretary of war 1839–41. His *History of England* in five volumes 1849–61 celebrates the Glorious Revolution of 1668 as the crowning achievement of the Whig party.

His works include an essay on Milton 1825 published in the *Edinburgh Review*; a volume of verse, *Lays of Ancient Rome* 1842; and the *History of England* covering the years up to 1702.

macaw any of various large, brilliantly colored, long-tailed tropical American ◊parrots, especially the genus *Ara*.

Macbeth died 1057. King of Scotland from 1040. The son of Findlech, hereditary ruler of Moray, he was commander of the forces of Duncan I, King of Scotia, whom he killed in battle 1040. His reign was prosperous until Duncan's son Malcolm III led an invasion and killed him at Lumphanan. Shakespeare's tragedy *Macbeth* was based on the 16th-century historian ◊Holinshed's *Chronicles*.

Macbeth a tragedy by William Shakespeare, first performed 1605–06. Acting on a prophecy by three witches that he will be king of Scotland, Macbeth, egged on by Lady Macbeth, murders King Duncan and becomes king but is eventually killed by Macduff.

McCabe John 1939– . English pianist and composer. His works include three symphonies; orchestral works, including *The Chagall Windows*; and songs.

Maccabees Hebrew family, sometimes known as the Hasmoneans. It was founded by the priest Mattathias (died 166 BC) who, with his sons, led the struggle for independence against the Syrians in the 2nd century BC. Judas (died 161) reconquered Jerusalem in 164 BC, and Simon (died 135) established its independence in 142 BC. The revolt of the Maccabees lasted until the capture of Jerusalem by the Romans in 63 BC. The story is told in four books of the ◊Apocrypha.

McCarran Patrick 1876–1954. US Democrat politician. He became senator for Nevada 1932, and as an isolationist strongly opposed ◊lend-lease during World War II. He sponsored the McCarran–Walter Immigration and Nationality Act of 1952, which severely restricted entry and immigration to the US; the act was amended 1965.

McCarthy Eugene Joseph 1916– . US politician. Born in Watkins, Minnesota, McCarthy received a master's degree in economics from the University of Minnesota. Active in the Democratic-Farmer-Labor party, he was elected to the US House of Representatives 1948 and to the US Senate 1958. An early opponent of the Vietnam War, he ran for president 1968. Although his upset victory in the New Hampshire primary forced incumbent L B Johnson out of the race, McCarthy lost the presidential nomination to Hubert Humphrey.

***McCarthy** US senator Joe McCarthy of Wisconsin brandishing "evidence" during a hearing of the House Un-American Activities Committee.*

After another unsuccessful bid in 1972, he returned to private life, concentrating on writing and lecturing.

McCarthy Joe (Joseph Raymond) 1909–1957. US right-wing Republican politician, whose unsubstantiated claim 1950 that the State Department and US army had been infiltrated by Communists started a wave of anticommunist hysteria, wild accusations, and blacklists, which continued until he was discredited 1954. He was censured by the US senate for misconduct.

A lawyer, McCarthy became senator for his native Wisconsin in 1946, and in Feb 1950 caused a sensation by claiming to hold a list of about 200 Communist party members working in the State Department. This was in part inspired by the ◊Hiss case. McCarthy continued a witch-hunting campaign against, among others, members of the ◊Truman administration. When he turned his attention to the army, and it was shown that he and his aides had been falsifying evidence, then President ◊Eisenhower renounced him and his tactics. By this time, however, many people in public life and the arts had been unofficially blacklisted as suspected Communists or fellow travelers (Communist sympathizers). McCarthyism came to represent the practice of using innuendo and unsubstantiated accusations against political adversaries.

McCarthy Mary (Therese) 1912–1989. US novelist and critic. Much of her work looks probingly and scathingly at US society, including the satirical novel *The Groves of Academe* 1952, which describes the early anticommunist "witch hunts" of the era, and *The Group* 1963 (film 1966), her best-known novel, which follows the lives of eight Vassar graduates into their thirties.

Born in Seattle, Washington, McCarthy graduated from Vassar 1933 and was a book reviewer for *The Nation* and *The New Republic*. She also wrote *A Charmed Life* 1955, *Venice Observed* 1956, *The Stones of Florence* 1959, *Vietnam* 1967, *Hanoi* 1968, *Mask of State: Watergate Portraits* 1974, and *Cannibals and Missionaries* 1979. Her short stories are collected in *The Company She Keeps* 1942 and *Cast a Cold Eye* 1950.

McCartney Paul 1942– . UK rock singer, songwriter, and bass guitarist; former member of the ◊Beatles, and leader of the pop group Wings 1971–81. His subsequent solo hits have included collaborations with Michael Jackson and Elvis Costello.

McCauley Mary Ludwig Hays 1754–1832. American Revolutionary War heroine. Known to generations of Americans as "Molly Pitcher," she was born in Trenton, New Jersey. After working as a domestic servant, she married a local man, John Hays, who joined an artillery company in the 7th Pennsylvania Regiment at the outbreak of the American Revolution. Accompanying her husband to the Battle of Monmouth 1778, she faithfully brought water in a pitcher to the artillerymen during the heat of the battle, thus gaining her famous nickname. When her husband became incapacitated, she took over one of the field pieces herself. In recognition of her valor, the Pennsylvania General Assembly awarded her a lifetime annuity.

McClellan George Brinton 1826–1885. American Civil War general, the first general in chief of the Union forces 1861–62. He was dismissed twice by President Lincoln, for various delays in following up and attacking the Confederate army. Early in the Civil War he was replaced by General John Pope, but after the rout at the Second Battle of ◊Bull Run, Lincoln asked McClellan to rebuild and reorganize the Union's Army of the Potomac. He saved Washington, DC from the threatening Confederate forces but delayed his offense until the opportunity was lost. He was dismissed again at this point, ran unsuccessfully for the presidency against Lincoln on the Democratic ticket 1864, and became governor of New Jersey 1878–81.

McClellan was born in Philadelphia, went to West Point, then served with distinction in the Mexican War. He then worked surveying for the railroads moving west and as a railroad executive until the Civil War.

Macclesfield industrial city in Cheshire, NW England; population (1986) 151,800. Industries include textiles, light engineering, paper, and plastics.

McClintock Barbara 1902– . US geneticist who worked at the Carnegie Institute, Cold Spring Harbor, New York, in the early days of chromosome mapping, and made some important contributions. She was awarded a Nobel Prize 1983.

McClintock Francis Leopold 1819–1907. Irish polar explorer and admiral. He was knighted 1860 after discovering the fate of the John ◊Franklin expedition and further exploring the Canadian Arctic.

McClure Robert John le Mesurier 1807–1873. Irish-born British admiral and explorer. While on an expedition 1850–54 searching for John ◊Franklin, he was the first to pass through the Northwest Passage.

McCormick Cyrus Hall 1809–1884. US inventor of the reaping machine in 1831, which revolutionized 19th-century agriculture.

McCowen Alec 1925– . British actor. His Shakespearean roles include Richard II and the Fool in *King Lear*; he is also known for his dramatic one-man shows.

MacCready Paul 1925– . US designer of the *Gossamer Condor* aircraft, which made the first controlled flight using only human power in 1977. His *Solar Challenger* flew from Paris to London under solar power; and in 1985 he constructed a powered model of a giant pterosaur, an extinct flying animal.

McCullers Carson (Smith) 1917–1967. US novelist. Most of her writing, including her novels *The Heart is a Lonely Hunter* 1940 and *Reflections in a Golden Eye* 1941, is set in the South, where she was born, and deals with spiritual isolation, containing elements of sometimes macabre violence.

Her novel *A Member of the Wedding* 1946 was made into a successful stage play and film.

MacDermot Galt 1928– . US composer. He wrote the rock musical *Hair* 1967, with lyrics by Gerome Ragni and James Rado. It challenged conventional attitudes about sex, drugs, and the war in Vietnam.

Macdonald George 1824–1905. Scottish novelist and children's writer. *David Elginbrod* 1863 and *Robert Falconer* 1868 are characteristic novels but his children's stories, including *At the Back of the North Wind* 1871 and *The Princess and the Goblin* 1872 are now more often read. Mystical imagination pervades all his books and this inspired later writers including G K Chesterton, C S Lewis, and J R R Tolkien.

MacDonald (James) Ramsay 1866–1937. British politician, first Labour prime minister Jan–Oct 1924 and 1929–31. He joined the ◊Independent Labour Party 1894, and became first secretary of the new Labour Party 1900. In Parliament he led the party 1906–14 and 1922–31 and was prime minister of the first two Labour governments. Failing to deal with worsening economic conditions, he left the party to form a coalition government 1931, which was increasingly dominated by Conservatives, until he was replaced by Stanley Baldwin 1935.

Macdonald John Alexander 1815–1891. Canadian Conservative politician, prime minister 1867–73 and 1878–91. He was born in Glasgow but taken to Ontario as a child. In 1857 he became prime minister of Upper Canada. He took the leading part in the movement for federation, and in 1867 became the first prime minister of Canada. He was defeated 1873 but returned to office 1878 and retained it until his death.

Macdonnell Ranges mountain range in central Australia, Northern Territory, with the town of Alice Springs; highest peak Mount Zeil 4,955 ft/1,510 m.

MacDowell Edward Alexander 1861–1908. US Romantic composer, influenced by ◊Liszt. His works include the *Indian Suite* 1896 and piano concertos and sonatas.

Returning to the US after several years in Germany, he played his *Second Piano Concerto in D Minor* 1889, his most successful longer work, in New York City. He was one of the first US composers to receive international acclaim. MacDowell was at his best with short, lyrical piano pieces, such as "To a Wild Rose" from *Woodland Sketches* 1896.

McDowell Malcolm 1943– . English actor who played the rebellious hero in Lindsay Anderson's film *If* 1969 and confirmed his acting abilities in Stanley Kubrick's *A Clockwork Orange* 1971.

Macedonia ancient region of Greece, forming parts of modern Greece, Bulgaria, and Yugoslavia. Macedonia gained control of Greece after Philip II's victory at Chaeronea in 338 BC. His son, ◊Alexander the Great, conquered a vast empire. Macedonia became a Roman province in 146 BC.

Macedonia (Greek *Makedhonia*) mountainous region of N Greece, bounded to the W and N by Albania and Yugoslavia; population (1981) 2,122,000; area 13,200 sq mi/34,177 sq km. Chief city is Thessaloniki. Fertile valleys produce grain, olives, grapes, tobacco and livestock. Mt Olympus rises to 9,570 ft/2,918 m on the border with Thessaly.

Macedonia (Serbo-Croat *Makedonija*) a federal republic of Yugoslavia

area 9,920 sq mi/25,700 sq km

capital Skopje

physical mountainous; rivers: Struma, Vardar

population (1981) 2,040,000, 63% Macedonians, 19% Albanians, 4% Turks

language Macedonian, closely allied to Bulgarian and written in Cyrillic

religion Macedonian Orthodox Christian

history an ancient country of SE Europe bounded by Illyria, Thrace, and the Aegean Sea; settled by Slavs in the 6th century; conquered by Bulgars in the 7th century, by Byzantium 1014, by Serbia in the 14th century, and by the Ottoman Empire 1355; divided between Serbia, Bulgaria, and Greece after the Balkan Wars of 1912–13.

Maceió industrial town in NE Brazil, capital of Alagaos state with its port at Jaraguá; population (1980) 375,800. Industries include sugar, tobacco, textile, and timber.

Macgillycuddy's Reeks a range of mountains in SW Ireland lying W of Killarney, in County Kerry; includes Carrantuohill 3,414 ft/1,041 m, the highest peak in Ireland.

McGinley Phyllis 1905–1978. Canadian-born US writer of light verse. She became a contributor to *The New Yorker* magazine and published many collections of social satire. Her works include *One More Manhattan* 1937 and *The Love Letters of Phyllis McGinley* 1954.

McGovern George Stanley 1922– . US politician. He was elected to the US House of Representatives as a Democrat 1956 and served as an adviser to the Kennedy administration. He was elected to the US Senate 1962 and campaigned briefly for the presidential nomination 1968. Winning the Democratic nomination 1972, he was soundly defeated by incumbent Richard Nixon.

McGovern was defeated for reelection to the Senate 1980 and retired to a career of lecturing and writing.

Born in Avon, South Dakota, McGovern served as a combat pilot during World War II and received a PhD in history from Northwestern University 1953.

McGraw John Joseph 1873–1934. US baseball manager. Born in Truxton, New York, McGraw began his career 1891 as an infielder with the Baltimore Orioles. He had a successful career with the team (which joined the National League 1892) and became its manager 1899. McGraw became player-manager of the New York Giants 1902 and in this dual capacity led the team to two National League pennants and a World Series championship. After retiring as a player 1906, he managed the Giants to eight more pennants and two world championships. He was elected to the Baseball Hall of Fame 1937.

McGuffey William Holmes 1800–1873. US educator. In 1825 he joined the faculty of Miami University, where he lectured on philosophy and became interested in the issue of public-school reform. McGuffey served as the president of Cincinnati College 1836–39 and Ohio University 1839–45 and as professor at the University of Virginia 1845–73. He is best remembered for his series of reading textbooks, the *Eclectic Readers*, which became standard throughout the US in the 19th century.

Born in Claysville, Pennsylvania, and raised in Ohio, McGuffey attended Washington and Jefferson College.

Mach Ernst 1838–1916. Austrian philosopher and physicist. He was an empiricist, believing that science is a record of facts perceived by the senses, and that acceptance of a scientific law depends solely on its standing the practical test of use; he opposed concepts such as Newton's "absolute motion." He researched airflow, and ◊Mach numbers are named after him.

Machado Antonio 1875–1939. Spanish poet and dramatist. Born in Seville, he was inspired by the Castilian countryside in his lyric verse, contained in *Campos de Castilla/Countryside of Castile* 1912.

Machado de Assis Joaquim Maria 1839–1908. Brazilian writer and poet. He is regarded as the greatest Brazilian novelist. His skeptical, ironic wit is well displayed in his 30 volumes of novels and short stories, including *Epitaph for a Small Winner* 1880 and *Dom Casmurro* 1900.

Machaut Guillame de 1300–1377. French poet and composer. Born in Champagne, he was in the service of John of Bohemia for 30 years and, later, of King John the Good of France. He gave the forms of the *ballade* and *rondo* a new individuality and ensured their lasting popularity.

Machel Samora 1933–1986. Mozambique nationalist leader, president 1975–86. Machel was active in the liberation front ◊Frelimo from its conception 1962, fighting for independence from Portugal. He became Frelimo leader 1966, and Mozambique's first president from independence 1975 until his death in a plane crash near the South African border.

Machiavelli Niccolò 1469–1527. Italian politician and author whose name is synonymous with cunning and cynical statecraft. In his most celebrated political writings, *Il principe/The Prince* 1513 and *Discorsi/Discourses* 1531, he discusses ways in which rulers can advance the interests of their states (and themselves) through an often amoral and opportunistic manipulation of other people.

***Machiavelli** Florentine diplomat and writer Niccolò Machiavelli's reputation rests largely on his work* The Prince.

Machiavelli was born in Florence and was second chancellor to the republic 1498–1512. On the accession to power of the ◊Medici 1512, he was arrested and imprisoned on a charge of conspiracy, but in 1513 was released to exile in the country. *The Prince*, based on his observations of Cesare ◊Borgia, is a guide for the future prince of a unified Italian state (which did not occur until the Risorgimento in the 19th century). In *L'Arte della guerra/The Art of War* 1520 Machiavelli outlined the provision of an army for the prince, and in *Historie fiorentine/History of Florence* he analyzed the historical development of Florence until 1492. Among his later works are the comedies *La Mandragola/The Mandrake* 1524 and *Clizia*.

machine device that allows a small force (the effort) to overcome a larger one (the load). There are three basic machines: the sloping or inclined plane, the ◊lever, and the wheel and axle. All other machines are combinations of these three basic types. Simple machines derived from the inclined plane include the wedge and the screw; the spanner is derived from the lever; the pulley from the wheel.

The two principal features of a machine are its ◊mechanical advantage, which is the ratio load/effort, and its ◊efficiency, which is the work done by the load divided by the work done by the effort; the latter is expressed as a percentage. In a perfect machine, with no friction, the efficiency would be 100%. All practical machines have efficiencies of less than 100%, otherwise perpetual motion would be possible.

machine code in computing, the "language" the computer understands. In machine-code programs, instructions and storage locations are represented as binary numbers. A programmer writes programs in a high-level (easy-to-use) language and this is converted to machine code by a ◊compiler or ◊interpreter program within the computer.

machine gun a rapid-firing automatic gun.

The forerunner of the modern machine gun was the Gatling (named after its US inventor R J Gatling 1818–1903), perfected in the US in 1860 and used in the Civil War. It had a number of barrels arranged about a central axis, and the breech containing the reloading, ejection, and firing mechanism was rotated by hand, shots being fired through each barrel in turn.

The Maxim (named after its inventor, US-born British engineer H S Maxim 1840–1916) of 1884 was recoil-operated, but some later types have

Machu Picchu *Undiscovered by the Spanish, the Inca city of Machu Picchu remained hidden until the 20th century.*

been gas-operated (Bren) or recoil assisted by gas (some versions of the Browning).

The submachine-gun, exploited by Chicago gangsters in the 1920s, was widely used in World War II; for instance, the Thompson, often called the Tommy gun. See ◊small arms.

machine politics the organization of a local political party to ensure its own election by influencing the electorate, and then to retain power through patronage and the control of key committees and offices. The idea of machine politics was epitomized in the US in the late 19th century, where it was used to control individual cities, most notably Chicago and New York.

machine tool automatic or semiautomatic power-driven machine for cutting and shaping metals. Machine tools have powerful electric motors to force cutting tools into the metal. They are made from hardened steel containing heat-resistant metals such as tungsten and chromium. The use of precision machine tools in ◊mass-production assembly methods ensures that all duplicate parts produced are virtually identical.

Many machine tools now work under computer control and are employed in factory ◊automation. The most common machine tool is the ◊lathe, which shapes shafts and similar objects. A ◊milling machine cuts metal with a rotary toothed cutting wheel. Other machine tools cut, plane, grind, drill, and polish.

Mach number ratio of the speed of a body to the speed of sound in the undisturbed medium through which the body travels. Mach 1 is reached when a body (such as an aircraft) has a velocity greater than that of sound ("passes the sound barrier"), namely 1,087 ft/331 m per second at sea level. It is named after Austrian physicist Ernst Mach (1838–1916).

Machtpolitik (German) power politics.

Machu Picchu a ruined Inca city in Peru, built c. AD 1500, NW of Cuzco, discovered in 1911 by Hiram Bingham. It stands at the top of 1,000 ft/300 m high cliffs, and contains the well-preserved remains of houses and temples.

Macias Nguema former name (until 1979) of ◊Bioko, an island of Equatorial Guinea in the Bight of Bonny, W Africa.

McIndoe Archibald 1900–1960. New Zealand plastic surgeon. He became known in the UK during World War II for his remodeling of the faces of badly burned pilots.

Macintosh Charles 1766–1843. Scottish manufacturing chemist who invented a waterproof fabric lined with a rubber that was used for raincoats—hence mackintosh. Other waterproofing processes have now largely superseded this method.

Mack Connie. Adopted name of Cornelius McGillicuddy. 1862–1956. US baseball manager. Born in East Brookfield, Massachusetts, he began his professional baseball career as a catcher 1883 and became player-manager of the Pittsburgh Pirates 1894. With the establishment of the American League 1901, Mack invested his own money in the Philadelphia Athletics ("A's") and became the team's first manager. In his record 50 years with the A's, he led the team to nine American League pennants and five World Series championships. Mack was elected to the Baseball Hall of Fame 1939.

Macke August 1887–1914. German Expressionist painter, a founding member of the ◊*Blaue Reiter* group in Munich. With Franz ◊Marc he developed a semiabstract style comprising Cubist and Fauve characteristics. He was killed during World War I.

Macke visited Paris in 1907. In 1909 he met Marc, and together they went to Paris 1912, where they encountered the abstract style of Robert Delaunay. In 1914 Macke visited Tunis with Paul ◊Klee and was inspired to paint a series of brightly colored watercolors largely composed of geometrical shapes but still representational.

Mackendrick Alexander 1912– . US-born Scottish film director responsible for some of ◊Ealing studios' finest comedies, including *Whisky Galore* 1949 and *The Man in the White Suit* 1951. He made *Mandy* 1952 before leaving to work in Hollywood, where his films included *Sweet Smell of Success* 1957.

Mackenzie Alexander c. 1755–1820. British explorer and fur trader. In 1789, he was the first European to see the river, now part of N Canada, named after him. In 1792–93 he crossed the Rocky Mountains to the Pacific.

In 1793 Mackenzie crossed the Rocky Mountains to the Pacific coast of what is now British Columbia, making the first known crossing N of Mexico. He was knighted in 1807.

Mackenzie Compton 1883–1972. Scottish author. His parents were actors. He was educated at Oxford University and published his first novel *The Passionate Elopement* in 1911. Later works were *Carnival* 1912, *Sinister Street* 1913–14 (an autobiographical novel), and the comic *Whisky Galore* 1947. He published his autobiography in ten "octaves" (volumes) 1963–71.

Mackenzie William Lyon 1795–1861. Canadian politician, born in Scotland. He emigrated to Canada in 1820, and led the rebellion of 1837–38, an unsuccessful attempt to limit British rule and establish more democratic institutions in Canada. After its failure he lived in the US until 1849, and in 1851–58 sat on the Canadian legislature as a Radical. He was grandfather of W L Mackenzie King, the Liberal prime minister.

Mackenzie river in the Northwest Territories, Canada, flowing from Great Slave Lake NW to the Arctic Ocean; about 1,120 mi/1,800 km long. It is the main channel of the Finlay-Peace-Mackenzie system, 2,635 mi/4,241 km long.

It was named after the British explorer Alexander Mackenzie, who saw it 1789.

mackerel any of various fishes of the mackerel family Scombroidia, especially the common mackerel *Scomber Scombrus* found in the N Atlantic and Mediterranean. It weighs about 1.5 lb/0.7 kg, and is blue with irregular black bands down its sides, the latter and the under surface showing a metallic sheen. Like all mackerels, it has a deeply forked tail, and a sleek, streamlined body form.

The largest of the mackerels is the tuna, which weighs up to 1,550 lb/700 kgs.

McKinley, Mount or ***Denali*** peak in Alaska, the highest in North America, 20,320 ft/6,194 m; named after US president William McKinley. The summit was first reached in 1913 by the Anglo-American explorer Hudson Stuck and three others. Mount McKinley, called Denali, "the high one," by the Indians, rises in the enlarged and renamed (1980) Denali National Park. See ◊Rocky Mountains.

McKinley William 1843–1901. 25th president of the US 1897–1901, a Republican. His period as president was marked by US adoption of an imperialist policy, as exemplified by the Spanish-American War 1898 and the annexation of the Philippines.

Born in Niles, Ohio, he became a lawyer. Throughout his political life, he was a trusted friend of business interests, supporting high tariffs for fledging US industries. He sat in the House of Representatives 1877–83, 1885–91, and was governor of Ohio 1892–96. As president he presided over a period of prosperity and was drawn into foreign conflicts largely against his will. He annexed the Philippine Islands and implemented the ◊Open Door Policy with China. He was assassinated in Buffalo, New York, and was succeeded by Theodore Roosevelt.

Mackmurdo Arthur H 1851–1942. English designer and architect. He founded the Century Guild in 1882, a group of architects, artists, and designers inspired by William ◊Morris and John ◊Ruskin. His book and textile designs are forerunners of ◊Art Nouveau.

MacLaine Shirley. Adopted name of Shirley MacLean Beaty 1934– . US dancer and actress, sister of Warren Beatty. She has played in musicals, comedy, and dramatic roles. Her many off-screen interests (politics, writing) have limited her film appearances, which include her debut in Alfred Hitchcock's *The Trouble with Harry* 1955, *Some Came Running* 1958, *The Apartment* 1960, *The Turning Point* 1977, and *Terms of Endearment* 1983, for which she won an Academy Award.

Maclean Alistair 1922–1987. Scottish adventure novelist. His first novel, *HMS Ulysses* 1955, was based on wartime experience. It was followed by *The Guns of Navarone* 1957 and other adventure novels. Many of his books were made into films.

Maclean Donald 1913–1983. British spy who worked as a counterspy for the USSR while in the UK civil service. He defected to the USSR 1951 together with Guy ◊Burgess.

Maclean, brought up in a strict Presbyterian family, was educated at Cambridge, where he was recruited by the Soviet ◊KGB. He worked for the UK Foreign Office in Washington 1944 and then Cairo 1948 before returning to London, becoming head of the American Department at the Foreign Office 1950.

McLean John 1785–1861. US Supreme Court justice. Appointed postmaster general by President

McKinley *The 25th president of the United States of America, William McKinley, a Republican. 1897–1901.*

Macmillan *Britain's prime minister Harold Macmillan, a Conservative, tried to obtain UK membership in the European Economic Community in 1963.*

Monroe 1823, McLean reorganized the post office department, eliminating much corruption and waste. In 1829 he was appointed to the US Supreme Court by President Jackson. During his Court tenure, McLean was an outspoken abolitionist, writing a passionate dissent in the Dred Scott Case 1857.

Born in Morris County, New Jersey, and raised in Ohio, McLean studied law in Cincinnati and was admitted to the bar 1807. After editing a local newspaper, he served in the US Congress 1813–16 and as a judge on the Ohio Supreme Court 1816–22.

MacLeish Archibald 1892–1982. US poet. He made his name with the long narrative poem "Conquistador" 1932, which describes Cortés' march to the Aztec capital, but his later plays in verse, *Panic* 1935 and *Air Raid* 1938, deal with contemporary problems.

Born in Illinois, he went to France in 1923, and during his expatriate years there published his most personal poetry, including "Ars Poetica" 1926. He was assistant secretary of state 1944–45, and helped to draft the constitution of UNESCO. From 1949 to 1962 he was Boylston Professor of Rhetoric at Harvard, and his essays in *Poetry and Opinion* 1950 reflect his feeling that a poet should be "committed," expressing his outlook in his verse.

McLuhan (Herbert) Marshall 1911–1980. Canadian theorist of communication, famed for his views on the effects of technology on modern society. He coined the phrase "the medium is the message," meaning that the form rather than the content of information has become crucial. His works include *The Gutenberg Galaxy* 1962 (in which he coined the phrase "the global village" for the worldwide electronic society then emerging), *Understanding Media* 1964, and *The Medium is the Massage* (sic) 1967.

MacMahon Marie Edmé Patrice Maurice, Comte de 1808–1893. Marshal of France. Captured at Sedan in 1870 during the Franco-Prussian War, he suppressed the ◊Paris Commune after his release, and as president of the republic 1873–79 worked for a royalist restoration until forced to resign.

McMillan Edwin Mattison 1907–1991. US physicist. In 1940 he discovered neptunium, the first ◊transuranic element, by bombarding uranium with neutrons. In 1951 he shared a Nobel Prize with ◊Seaborg for their discovery of transuranic elements. In 1943 he developed a method of overcoming the limitations of the cyclotron, the first ◊accelerator, for which he shared, 20 years later, an Atoms for Peace award with I Veksler, director of the Soviet Joint Institute for Nuclear Research, who had come to the same discovery independently. McMillan was a professor at the University of California 1946–73.

Macmillan (Maurice) Harold, 1st Earl of Stockton 1894–1986. British prime minister 1957–63. Conservative member of Parliament 1924–29 and 1931–64. As minister of housing 1951–54 he achieved the construction of 300,000 new houses a year. He became foreign secretary 1955 and was chancellor of the Exchequer from 1955 to 1957. He became prime minister on the resignation of Anthony ◊Eden after the Suez crisis. Macmillan led the Conservative Party to victory in the 1959 elections on the slogan "You've never had it so good" (the phrase was borrowed from a US election campaign). Internationally, his realization of the "wind of change" in Africa advanced the independence of former colonies. In 1963 he attempted to negotiate British entry to the European Economic Community, but was blocked by the French president de Gaulle. Much of his career as prime minister was spent trying to maintain a UK nuclear weapon, and he was responsible for the purchase of US Polaris missiles 1962. Macmillan's nickname Supermac was coined by the cartoonist Vicky. He was awarded an earldom 1984.

Mâcon capital of the French *département* of Saône-et-Loire, on the river Saône, 45 mi/72 km N of Lyon; population (1983) 39,000. It produces wine. Mâcon dates from ancient Gaul, when it was known as Matisco. The French writer Lamartine was born here.

Macon city in central Georgia, on the Ocmulgee River, NE of Columbus; seat of Bibb County. An industrial city, Macon produces textiles, building materials, farm machinery, and chemicals; it processes fruits, pecans, and the special kaolin clay that is found nearby; population (1990) 106,612.

McPhee Colin 1900–1964. US composer. His studies of Balinese music 1934–36 produced two works, *Tabuh-tabuhan* for two pianos and orchestra 1936 and *Balinese Ceremonial Music* for two pianos 1940, which influenced ◊Cage and later generations of US composers.

McPherson Aimee Semple 1890–1944. Canadian-born US religious leader. Born in Ingersoll, Ontario, she worked as a missionary to China before becoming an itinerant evangelist in the US. Through revival tours, she gained a large following and eventually established the Church of the Four-Square Gospel in Los Angeles 1918. As a popular preacher, "Sister Aimee" reached millions through radio broadcasts of her weekly sermons, in which she emphasized the power of faith. Her brief but suspicious 1926 "disappearance" tarnished her reputation; she committed suicide 1944.

Macquarie Island outlying Australian territorial possession, a Tasmanian dependency, some 850 mi/1,370 km SE of Hobart; area 65 sq mi/170 sq km; it is uninhabited except for an Australian government research station.

McQueen Steve (Terrence Steven) 1930–1980. US actor. He was one of the most popular film stars of the 1960s and 1970s, admired for his portrayals of the strong, silent loner, and noted for perform-

McQueen US actor Steve McQueen.

ing his own stunt work. After television success in the 1950s he became a film star with *The Magnificent Seven* 1960. His films include *The Great Escape* 1963, *Bullitt* 1968, *Papillon* 1973 and *The Hunter* 1980.

macramé the art of making decorative fringes and lacework with knotted threads. The name comes from the Arabic word for "striped cloth," which is often decorated in this way.

macro in computer programming, a new command created by combining a number of existing ones. For example, if the language has separate commands for obtaining data from the keyboard and for displaying data on the screen, the programmer might create a macro that performs both these tasks with one command. A macro key is a key on the keyboard that combines the effects of several individual key presses.

macrobiotics the study of prolonging life, as by special diet, specifically one based on organically grown wholefoods.

macroeconomics the division of economics concerned with the study of whole (aggregate) economies or systems, including such aspects as government income and expenditure, the balance of payments, fiscal policy, investment, inflation, and unemployment. It seeks to understand the influence of all relevant economic factors on each other and thus to quantify and predict aggregate national income.

Modern macroeconomics takes much of its inspiration from the work of Keynes, whose *The General Theory of Employment, Interest, and Money* 1936 proposed that governments could prevent financial crises and unemployment by adjusting demand through control of credit and currency. Keynesian macroeconomics thus analyzes aggregate supply and demand and holds that markets do not continuously "clear" (quickly attain equilibrium between supply and demand) and may require intervention if objectives such as full employment are thought desirable. Keynesian macroeconomic formulations were generally accepted well into the postwar era and have been refined and extended by the neo-Keynesian school, which contends that in a recession the market will clear only very slowly and that full employment equilibrium may never return without significant demand management (by government). At the same time, however, Neo-Classical economics has experienced a recent resurgence, using tools from ◊microeconomics to challenge the central Keynesian assumption that resources may be underemployed and that full employment equilibrium requires state intervention. Another important school is new Classical economics, which seeks to show the futility of Keynesian demand management policies and stresses instead the importance of supply-side economics, believing that the principal factor influencing growth of national output is the efficient allocation and use of labor and capital. A related school is that of the Chicago monetarists, led by Milton ◊Friedman, who have revived the old idea that an increase in money supply leads inevitably to an increase in prices rather than in output; however, whereas the new Classical school contends that wage and price adjustment are almost instantaneous and so the level of employment at any time must be the natural rate, the Chicago monetarists are more gradualist, believing that such adjustment may take some years.

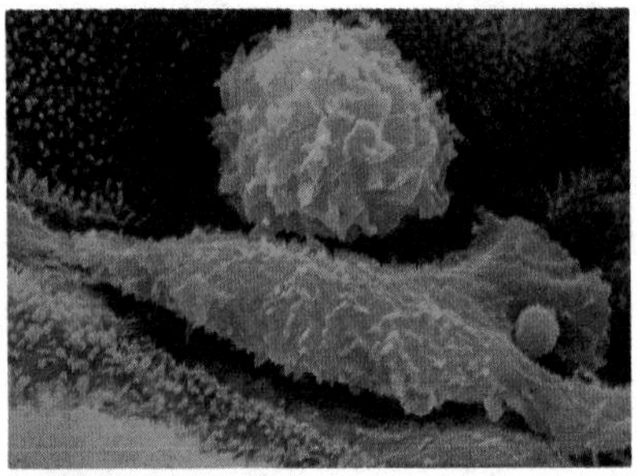

macrophage Scanning electron micrograph of two macrophages on human lung tissue. The top one is the normal shape, covered with ruffles. The one below has elongated itself to engulf the particle at left. Macrophages are essential to clear the lung of dust and bacteria.

macromolecule in chemistry, a very large molecule, generally a ◊polymer.

macrophage a type of ◊white blood cell, or leukocyte, found in all vertebrate animals. Macrophages specialize in the removal of bacteria and other microorganisms, or of cell debris after injury. Like phagocytes, they engulf foreign matter, but they are larger than phagocytes and have a longer life span. They are found throughout the body, but mainly in the lymph and connective tissues, and espcially the lungs, where they ingest dust, fibers, and other inhaled particles.

McWhirter Norris 1925– . British editor and compiler, with his twin brother, Ross McWhirter (1925–1975), of the *Guinness Book of Records* from 1955.

MAD abbreviation for mutual assured destruction; the basis of the theory of ◊deterrence by possession of nuclear weapons.

Madagascar island in the Indian Ocean, off the coast of E Africa, about 280 mi/400 km from Mozambique.

government The 1975 constitution radically changed government structure and renamed the state the Democratic Republic of Madagascar. The constitution provides for a single-chamber national people's assembly of 137 members, elected by universal suffrage for a five-year term, and a president elected in the same way for a seven-year term. The president appoints and chairs a supreme revolutionary council (SRC), which acts as "the guardian of the Malagasy Socialist Revolution." A third of its members are nominated by the assembly, and the rest are chosen by the president, who is also secretary-general of the political organization that embraces all the various party factions: the National Front for the Defence of the Malagasy Socialist Revolution (FNDR). Power therefore ultimately lies with the president's party. For day-to-day administration, the president appoints a prime minister and a council of ministers.

history Madagascar was colonized over 2,000 years ago by Africans and Indonesians. They were joined from the 12th century by Muslim traders, and, from 1500, Europeans began to visit the island. Portuguese, Dutch, and English trad-

Madagascar

Democratic Republic of
(Repoblika Demokratika n'i Madagaskar)

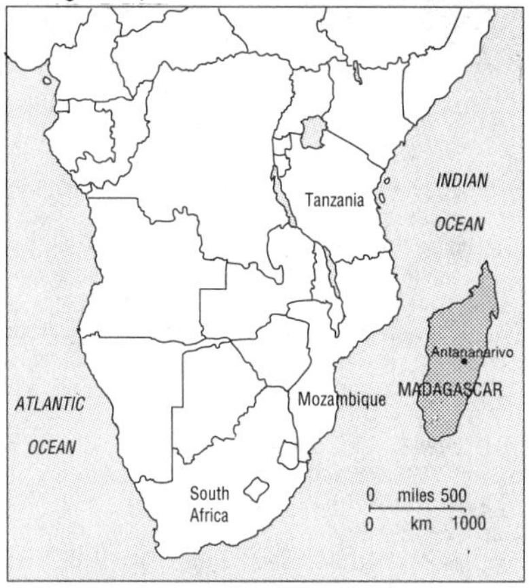
INDIAN
OCEAN
Tanzania
Antananarivo
MADAGASCAR
Mozambique
ATLANTIC
OCEAN
South Africa
0 miles 500
0 km 1000

area 226,598 sq mi/587,041 sq km
capital Antananarivo
cities (chief port) Toamasina, Antseranana, Fianarantsoa, Toliary
physical temperate central highlands; humid valleys and tropical coastal plains; arid in S
features one of the last places to be inhabited, it evolved in isolation with unique animals (such as the lemur, now under threat from deforestation)
head of state and government Didier Ratsiraka from 1975
political system one-party Socialist republic
political parties National Front for the Defence of the Malagasy Socialist Revolution (FNDR)
exports coffee, cloves, vanilla, sugar, chromite, shrimps
currency Malagasy franc (2,968.50 = ££July 1, 1991)
population (1990 est) 11,802,000, mostly of Malayo-Indonesian origin; growth rate 3.2% p.a.
life expectancy men 50, women 53 (1989)
language Malagasy (official); French, English
religion animist 50%, Christian 40%, Muslim 10%
literacy 53% (1988)
GNP $2.1 bn (1987); $280 per head (1988)
chronology
1885 Became a French protectorate.
1896 Became a French colony.
1960 Independence achieved from France, with Philibert Tsiranana as president.
1972 Army took control of the government.
1975 Martial law imposed under a national military directorate. New Marxist constitution proclaimed the Democratic Republic of Madagascar, with Didier Ratsiraka as president.
1976 Front-Line Revolutionary Organization (AREMA) formed.
1977 National Front for the Defense of the Malagasy Socialist Revolution (FNDR) became the sole legal political organization.
1980 Ratsiraka abandoned Marxist experiment.
1983 Ratsiraka reelected, despite strong opposition from radical Socialist National Movement for the Independence of Madagascar (MONIMA) under Monja Jaona.
1989 Ratsiraka reelected for third term after restricting opposition parties.
1990 Political opposition legalized; 36 new parties created.
1991 Antigovernment demonstrations; opposition to Ratsiraka led to general strike.

ers having given up, the French established a colony in the mid-17th century but fled after a massacre by local inhabitants. Madagascar was subsequently divided into small kingdoms until the late 18th century when, aided by traders and Christian missionaries, the Merina (the inhabitants of the highland area) united almost all the country under one ruler. In 1885 the country was made a French protectorate, though French control was not complete until 20 years later.

Madagascar remained loyal to ◊Vichy France during World War II, but it was taken by British forces 1942–43 and then handed over to the Free French. During the postwar period nationalist movements became active, and Madagascar became an autonomous state within the ◊French Community in 1958 and achieved full independence, as a republic, in 1960. Its history since independence has been greatly influenced by the competing interests of its two main ethnic groups, the coastal people, or *cotiers*, and the highland Merina.

The first president of the republic was Philibert Tsiranana, leader of the Social Democratic Party (PSD), which identified itself with the *cotiers*. In 1972 the army, representing the Merina, took control of the government and pursued a more nationalistic line than Tsiranana. This caused resentment among the *cotiers* and, with rising unemployment, led to a government crisis in 1975 that resulted in the imposition of martial law under a national military directorate and the banning of all political parties. Later that year a new, Socialist constitution was approved and Lt-Comdr Didier Ratsiraka, a *cotier*, was elected president of the Democratic Republic of Madagascar. Political parties were permitted again and in 1976 the Front-Line Revolutionary Organization (AREMA) was formed by Ratsiraka as the nucleus of a single party for the state. By 1977 all political activity was concentrated in FNDR, and all the candidates for the national people's assembly were FNDR nominees.

In 1977 the National Movement for the Independence of Madagascar (MONIMA), a radical Socialist party, withdrew from the FNDR and was declared illegal. MONIMA's leader, Monja Jaona, unsuccessfully challenged Ratsiraka for the presidency and, although his party did well in the capital, AREMA won 117 of the 137 assembly seats in the 1983 elections. Despite this overwhelming victory, social and political discontent has continued, particularly among the Merinas, who have openly demonstrated their opposition to the government. President Ratsiraka was reelected with a 62% popular vote in March 1989, and in May AREMA won 120 of the 137 assembly seats.

According to 1990 UN figures, 93% of the forest area has been destroyed and about 100,000 species made extinct.

Madame Bovary a novel by Flaubert, published in France 1857. It aroused controversy by its portrayal of a country doctor's wife driven to suicide by a series of unhappy love affairs.

madder any plant of the genus *Rubia* of the family Rubiaceae, bearing small funnel-shaped flowers, especially the perennial vine *Rubia tinctorum*, the red root of which yields a red dye called alizarin (now made synthetically from coal tar).

Madeira group of islands forming an autonomous region of Portugal off the NW coast of Africa, about 260 mi/420 km N of the Canary Islands. Madeira, the largest, and Porto Santo are the only inhabited islands. The Desertas and Selvagens are uninhabited islets. Their mild climate makes them year-round resorts
area 308 sq mi/796 sq km
capital Funchal, on Madeira
physical Pico Ruivo, on Madeira, its highest mountain being 6,106 ft/1,861 m
products Madeira (a fortified wine), sugar cane, fruit, fish, handicrafts
population (1986) 269,500
history Portuguese from the 15th century; occupied by Britain in 1801 and 1807–14. In 1980 Madeira gained partial autonomy but remains a Portuguese overseas territory.

Madeira river of W Brazil; length 2,020 mi/3,250 km. It is formed by the rivers Beni and Mamoré, and flows NE to join the Amazon.

Maderna Bruno 1920–1973. Italian composer and conductor. He studied with Malapiero and ◊Scherchen, and collaborated with ◊Berio in setting up an electronic studio in Milan. His compositions combine advanced techniques with an elegance of sound, and include a pioneering work for live and prerecorded flute, *Musica su due dimensioni* 1952, numerous concertos, and the aleatoric *Aura* for orchestra 1974.

Madhya Bharat state of India 1950–56. It was a union of 24 states of which Gwalior and ◊Indore were the most important. In 1956 Madhya Bharat was absorbed in ◊Madhya Pradesh.

Madhya Pradesh state of central India; the largest of the Indian states
area 170,921 sq mi/442,700 sq km
capital Bhopal
cities Indore, Jabalpur, Gwalior, Durg-Bhilainagar, Raipur, Ujjain,
products cotton, oilseed, sugar, textiles, engineering, paper, aluminum
population (1981) 52,132,000
language Hindi
history formed 1950 from the former British province of Central Provinces and Berar and the princely states of Makrai and Chattisgarh; lost some SW districts 1956, including ◊Nagpur, and absorbed Bhopal, Madhya Bharat, and Vindhya Pradesh.

Madison capital of Wisconsin, 120 mi/193 km NW of Chicago, between lakes Mendota and Monona;

Madeira

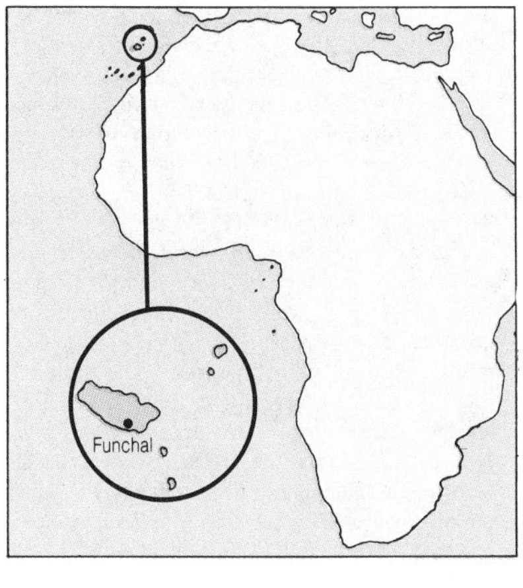
Funchal

Madison *The 4th president of the United States of America, James Madison, a Democratic Republican. 1809–1817.*

population (1990) 191,262; products include agricultural machinery and medical equipment. The main campus of the University of Wisconsin and the US Forest Products Laboratory are here. The city was founded 1836 as the territorial capital and named for James Madison, fourth president of the US.

Madison James 1751–1836. 4th president of the US 1809–17. In 1787 he became a member of the Philadelphia Constitutional Convention and took a leading part in drawing up the US Constitution and the Bill of Rights. He allied himself firmly with Thomas ◊Jefferson against Alexander ◊Hamilton in the struggle between the more democratic views of Jefferson and the aristocratic, upper-class sentiments of Hamilton. As secretary of state in Jefferson's government 1801–09, Madison's main achievement was completing the ◊Louisiana Purchase negotiated by James ◊Monroe.

Born in Port Conway, Virginia, Madison graduated from the College of New Jersey (now Princeton) 1771. During his presidential administration, the nation was unprepared for the War of 1812, and there were threats of secession by New England states. Madison had long been an articulate champion of the federal structure of government, and as president, as he had done as a member of the Constitutional Convention, he regarded promotion of the Union as his paramount task. Although the War of 1812 ended in stalemate, Madison's fortunes rose with the national expansion that followed.

Madison Square Garden an arena in New York City used for sports events, concerts, shows, and the circus. The current "Garden" is the fourth; it was built over Pennsylvania Station on 7th Avenue and 33rd Street in 1968.

The original was first P.T. Barnum's Hippodrome (a theater for spectacles), on Madison Avenue and 26th Street; it was bought by Patrick Gilmore 1875 and named Gilmore's Garden; then in 1879 it was renamed Madison Square Garden. In 1889 it was replaced by the elegant Stanford ◊White structure on Madison Square with a roof garden and restaurant. In 1925 the "Garden" was rebuilt on 8th Avenue and 49th Street.

Madras industrial port (cotton, cement, chemicals, iron, and steel) and capital of Tamil Nadu, India, on the Bay of Bengal; population (1981) 4,277,000. Fort St George 1639 remains from the East India Company when Madras was the chief port on the E coast. Madras was occupied by the French 1746–48 and shelled by the German ship *Emden* in 1914, the only place in India attacked in World War I.

Madras former name of Tamil Nadu, state of India.

Madrid industrial city (leather, chemicals, furniture, tobacco, paper) and capital of Spain and of Madrid province; population (1986) 3,124,000. Built on an elevated plateau in the center of the country, at 2,183 ft/655 m it is the highest capital city in Europe and has excesses of heat and cold. Madrid province has an area of 3,088 sq mi/8,000 sq km and a population of 4,855,000. Madrid began as a Moorish citadel captured by Castile 1083, became important in the times of Charles V and Philip II, and was designated capital 1561.

Features include the Real Academia de Bellas Artes 1752, the Prado Museum 1785, and the royal palace 1764. During the Spanish Civil War, Madrid was besieged by the Nationalists Nov 7, 1936–March 28, 1939.

madrigal a form of secular song in four or five parts, usually sung without instrumental accompaniment. It originated in 14th-century Italy. Madrigal composers include Andrea ◊Gabrieli, ◊Monteverdi, Thomas ◊Morley, and Orlando ◊Gibbons.

Madura an island in Indonesia, off Surabaya, Java; one of the Sunda Islands

area 1,762 sq mi/4,564 sq km; with offshore islands, more than 2,000 sq mi/5,000 sq km

capital Pamekasan

features central hills rising to 1,545 ft/480 m; forested

Madurai *An elaborate gateway to the Dravidian Meenakshi temple at Madurai, India.*

products rice, tobacco, salt, cattle, fish

population (1970) 2,447,000

history See ◊Java.

Madurai city in Tamil Nadu, India; site of the 16th–17th-century Hindu temple of Sundareswara, and of Madurai University 1966; cotton industry; population (1981) 904,000.

Maeander anglicized form of the ancient Greek name of the river ◊Menderes in Turkey.

Maecenas Gaius Cilnius 69–8 BC. Roman patron of the arts who encouraged the work of ◊Horace and ◊Virgil.

maelstrom whirlpool off the ◊Lofoten Islands, Norway, also known as the Moskenesstraumen, which gave its name to whirlpools in general.

maenad in Greek mythology, one of the women participants in the orgiastic rites of ◊Dionysus; maenads were also known as Bacchae.

Maestricht alternate form of ◊Maastricht, city in the Netherlands.

Maeterlinck Maurice, Count Maeterlinck 1862–1949. Belgian poet and dramatist. His plays include *Pelléas et Mélisande* 1892, *L'Oiseau bleu/ The Blue Bird* 1908, and *Le Bourgmestre de Stilmonde/The Burgomaster of Stilemonde* 1918. The latter celebrates Belgian resistance in World War I, a subject that led to his exile in the US 1940. He was awarded the Nobel Prize 1911.

Mafeking former name of Mafikeng, town in South Africa, incorporated into Bophuthatswana in 1980.

Mafia (Italian "swank") secret society reputed to control organized crime such as gambling, loan-sharking, drug traffic, prostitution, and protection. It originated in 15th-century Sicily and now operates chiefly there and in US cities; connected with the ◊Camorra of Naples.

It began as a secret society that avenged wrongs against Sicilian peasants by means of terror and ◊vendetta. In 19th-century Sicily the Mafia was employed by absentee landlords to manage their *latifundia* (landed estates), and through intimidation it soon became the unofficial ruling group. Despite the expropriation and division of the *latifundia* after World War II, the Mafia remains powerful in Sicily. The Italian government has waged periodic campaigns of suppression, notably 1927, when the Fascist leader Mussolini appointed Cesare Mori (1872–?) as prefect of Palermo. Mori's methods were, however, as suspect as those of the people he was arresting, and he was fired 1929. A further campaign was waged 1963–64.

The Mafia spread through immigration, mainly to the US, where it grew during ◊Prohibition. Main centers are New York, Las Vegas, Miami, Atlantic City, and Chicago. Organization is in "families," each with its own boss, or *capo*. A code of loyalty and secrecy, combined with intimidation of witnesses, makes it difficult to bring criminal charges against its members, although Al Capone was sentenced for federal tax evasion and Lucky Luciano was deported. Recent cases of the US government vs. the Mafia implicated Sicilian-based operators in the drug traffic that plagues much of the Western world (the "pizza connection"). The Mafia, also known in the US as La Cosa Nostra ("our affair") or the Mob, features frequently in fiction, for example in the book by Mario Puzo and film *The Godfather* 1972.

Mafikeng town (called Mafeking until 1980) in Bophuthatswana, South Africa; it was the capital of Bechuanaland, and the British officer Baden-Powell held it under Boer siege Oct 12, 1899–May 17, 1900.

Magadan port for the gold mines in East Siberia, USSR, off the N shore of the Sea of Okhotsk; population (1985) 142,000.

Magadha a kingdom of ancient NE India, roughly corresponding to the middle and southern parts of modern ◊Bihar. It was the scene of many incidents in the life of Buddha and was the seat of the Maurya dynasty, founded by Chandragupta in the 3rd century BC. Its capital Pataliputra was a great cultural and political center.

magazine a periodical publication, typically containing articles, essays, reviews, illustrations, and advertising. It is thought that the first magazine was *Le Journal des savants*, published in France 1665. The earliest illustrations were wood engravings; the halftone process was invented 1882 and photogravure was used commercially from 1895. ◊Printing and paper-manufacturing techniques made great progress during the 19th century, making larger print runs possible. Advertising began to appear in magazines around 1800; it was a moderately important factor by 1850 and crucial to most magazines' finances by 1880. Specialty magazines for various interests and hobbies appeared in the 20th century. In the US, subscriptions account for the majority of magazine sales. In Europe, distribution and sales are largely through newsdealers' shops and stands.

history Among the first magazines in the US were Benjamin ◊Franklin's *Poor Richard's Almanac* 1732–57 and the short-lived *The American Magazine* 1741 and *General Magazine* 1741. By the 1800s the magazine industry was flourishing. *North American Review* began 1815. Around the time of the Civil War, such magazines as *Harper's Weekly*, *Harper's Monthly Magazine*, and *The Atlantic Monthly* were published for the first time. At the beginning of the 1900s *The Nation* and *Illustrated Newspaper* began publication, and soon *The Ladies' Home Journal* and *The Saturday Evening Post* followed. *McClure's*, *Collier's*, and *Cosmopolitan* began as messengers of social reform, attacking government and business policies. The *Reader's Digest* was founded 1921, *Time* 1923, *The New Yorker* 1925, *Fortune* 1930, and *Life* 1936. The 1930s saw the rise of the photojournalism magazine and the introduction of color printing. The US pulp magazines of the 1930s and 1940s, specializing in crime fiction and science fiction, were breeding grounds for writers. The development of cheap offset litho printing made possible the flourishing of the underground press in much of the Western world in the 1960s, although it was limited by unorthodox distribution methods, such as street sales. Prosecutions and economic recession largely killed the underground press; the main survivor in the US is the rock-music magazine *Rolling Stone* 1968.

The *Reader's Digest*, with editions in many different countries and languages, is the world's best-selling magazine. *TV Guide* is the best-selling magazine in the US. The *Ladies' Home Journal*, first published in the late 1800s, led the way for women's magazines in the US. With magazines such as *McCall's*, *Women's Day*, *Ms*, *Good Housekeeping*, *Redbook*, *Vogue*, and *Family Circle*, women's magazines constitute the largest group.

Comic books are usually aimed at children, although in Japan, Latin America, and Europe millions of adults read them. Artistically sophisticated adult comics are produced in the US and several European countries, notably France. They developed from ◊comic strips in newspapers or, like those of Walt ◊Disney, as spinoffs from animated cartoon films. The first superhero, Superman, created 1938 by Jerome Siegel and Joseph Shuster, soon had his own monthly periodical, and others followed; the Marvel Comics group, formed 1961, was selling 50 million copies a year worldwide by the end of the 1960s and found a cult readership among college students for titles such as *Spiderman* and *The Incredible Hulk*.

Magdeburg industrial city (vehicles, paper, textiles, machinery) and capital of Saxony-Anhalt, Federal Republic of Germany, on the river Elbe; population (1990) 290,000. A former capital of Saxony, Magdeburg became capital of Saxony-Anhalt on German reunification 1990. In 1938 the city was linked by canal with the Rhine and Ruhr rivers.

Magdeburg was a member of the Hanseatic League, and has a 13th-century Gothic cathedral. Magdeburg county has an area of 4,451 sq mi/ 11,530 sq km.

Magellan Ferdinand 1480–1521. Portuguese navigator. In 1519 he set sail in the *Victoria* from Seville with the intention of reaching the East Indies by a westerly route. He sailed through the Magellan Strait at the tip of South America, crossed an ocean he named the Pacific, and in 1521 reached the Philippines, where he was killed in a battle with the islanders. His companions returned to Seville in 1522, completing the voyage under del ◊Cano.

Magellanic Clouds the two galaxies nearest to our own Galaxy. They are irregularly shaped, and appear as detached parts of the ◊Milky Way, in the southern constellations Dorado and Tucana.

The Large Magellanic Cloud is 160,000 light-years from Earth and about a third the diameter of our Galaxy; the Small Magellanic Cloud, 180,000 light-years away, is about a fifth the diameter of our Galaxy. They are named after the navigator Ferdinand Magellan, who first described them.

Magellan, Strait of channel between South America and Tierra del Fuego, named after the navigator. It is 370 mi/595 km long, and joins the Atlantic and Pacific Oceans.

Magenta town in Lombardy, Italy, 15 mi/24 km W of Milan, where France and Sardinia defeated Austria in 1859 during the struggle for Italian independence. Magenta dye was named in honor of the victory.

Maggiore, Lago lake partly in Italy, partly in Swiss canton of Ticino, with Locarno on its N shore; 39 mi/63 km long and up to 5.5 mi/9 km wide (area 82 sq mi/212 sq km), with fine scenery.

maggot the footless larvae of flies, a typical example being the larva of the blowfly which is deposited as an egg on flesh.

Maghreb name for NW Africa (Arabic "far west," "sunset"). The Maghreb powers—Algeria, Libya, Morocco, Tunisia, and Western Sahara—agreed on economic coordination 1964–65, with Mauritania cooperating from 1970. Chad and Mali are sometimes included. See also ◊Mashraq.

magi priests of the Zoroastrian religion of ancient Persia, noted for their knowledge of astrology. The term is used in the New Testament of the Latin Vulgate Bible where the King James Version gives "wise men." The magi who came to visit the infant Jesus with gifts of gold, frankincense, and myrrh (the Adoration of the Magi) were in later tradition described as "the three kings"—Caspar, Melchior, and Balthazar.

magic the art of controlling the forces of nature by supernatural means such as charms and ritual. The central ideas are that like produces like (sympathetic magic) and that influence carries by contagion or association; for example, by the former principle an enemy could be destroyed through an effigy, by the latter principle through personal items such as hair or nail clippings. See also ◊witchcraft.

It is now generally accepted that most early religious practices and much early art were rooted in beliefs in magical processes. There are similarities between magic and the use of symbolism in religious ritual. Under Christianity existing magical rites were either suppressed (although they survived in modified form in folk custom and superstition) or replaced by those of the church itself. Those still practicing the ancient rites were persecuted as witches.

magic bullet a term sometimes used for drugs that are specifically targeted on certain cells or tissues in the body, such as a small collection of cancerous cells (see ◊cancer) or cells that have been invaded by a virus. Such drugs can be made in various ways, but ◊monoclonal antibodies are increasingly being used to direct the drug to a specific target.

Magic Mountain, The a novel by Thomas Mann, published in Germany 1924. An ironic portrayal of the lives of a group of patients in a Swiss sanatorium, it shows the beauty and futility of their sheltered existence.

magic numbers in atomic physics, certain numbers of ◊neutrons or ◊protons (2, 8, 20, 28, 50, 82, 126) in the nuclei of elements of outstanding stability such as lead and helium. Such stability is the result of neutrons and protons being arranged in completed "layers" or "shells."

magic realism in literature, a fantastic situation realistically treated, as in the works of many Latin American writers such as Isabel Allende, Jorge Luis Borges, Gabriel García Márquez.

It was pioneered in Europe by E T A Hoffman and Hermann Hesse. The term was coined in the 1920s to describe German paintings.

magic square in mathematics, a square array of different numbers in which the rows, columns, and diagonals add up to the same total. A simple example employing the numbers 1 to 9, with a total of 15, is:

6	7	2
1	5	9
8	3	4

Maginot Line French fortification system along the German frontier from Switzerland to Luxembourg built 1929–36 under the direction of the war minister, André Maginot. It consisted of semiunderground forts joined by underground passages, and protected by antitank defenses; lighter fortifications continued the line to the sea. In 1940 German forces pierced the Belgian frontier line and outflanked the Maginot Line.

maglev (short for magnetic levitation) high-speed surface transport using the repellent force of superconductive magnets (see ◊superconductivity) to propel and support, for example, a train above a track. Maglev trains have been developed in Japan.

magma molten material made up of solids and gases beneath the Earth's surface from which ◊igneous rocks are formed. Magma released by volcanoes is called ◊lava.

Magna Carta (Latin "great charter") in English history, the charter granted by King John in 1215, traditionally seen as guaranteeing human rights against the excessive use of royal power. As a reply to the king's demands for excessive feudal dues and attacks on the privileges of the church, Archbishop Langton proposed to the barons the drawing-up of a binding document in 1213. John was forced to accept this at Runnymede (now in Surrey) on June 15, 1215.

The king's financial demands were caused by a disastrous foreign policy. The charter defined the barons' obligations to the monarch, confirmed the liberties of the English church, and opposed the arbitrary application of justice. Although it did not avert the first Barons' War and was annulled by the pope, it was reissued with changes in 1216, 1217, and 1225. As feudalism declined Magna Carta lost its significance, and under the Tudors was almost forgotten. During the 17th century it was rediscovered and reinterpreted by the Parliamentary party as a democratic document.

Four original copies exist, one each in Salisbury and Lincoln cathedrals and two in the British Library.

magnesia common name for ◊magnesium oxide.

magnesium lightweight, very ductile and malleable, silver-white, metallic element, symbol Mg, atomic number 12, atomic weight 24.305. It is one of the ◊alkaline-earth metals, the lightest of the commonly used metals. Magnesium silicate, carbonate, and chloride are widely distributed in nature. The metal is used in alloys and flash photography. It is a necessary trace element in the human diet, and green plants cannot grow without it since it is an essential constituent of chlorophyll ($C_{55}H_{72}MgN_4O_5$).

It was named after the ancient Greek city of Magnesia, near where it was first found. It was first recognized as an element by Joseph ◊Black in 1755 and discovered in its oxide by Humphry ◊Davy in 1808. Pure magnesium was isolated in 1828 by Antoine-Alexandre-Brutus Bussy.

magnesium oxide or ***magnesia*** MgO white powder or colorless crystals, formed when magnesium is burned in air or oxygen; a typical basic oxide. It is used to treat acidity of the stomach, and in some industrial processes – for example as a lining brick in furnaces, as it is very stable when heated (refractory oxide).

magnet any object that forms a magnetic field (displays ◊magnetism) either permanently or temporarily through induction.

magnetic field the physical field or region around a permanent magnet, or around a conductor carrying an electric current, in which a force acts on a moving charge or on a magnet placed in the field. The field can be represented by lines of force, which by convention link north and south poles and are parallel to the directions of a small com-

maglev express

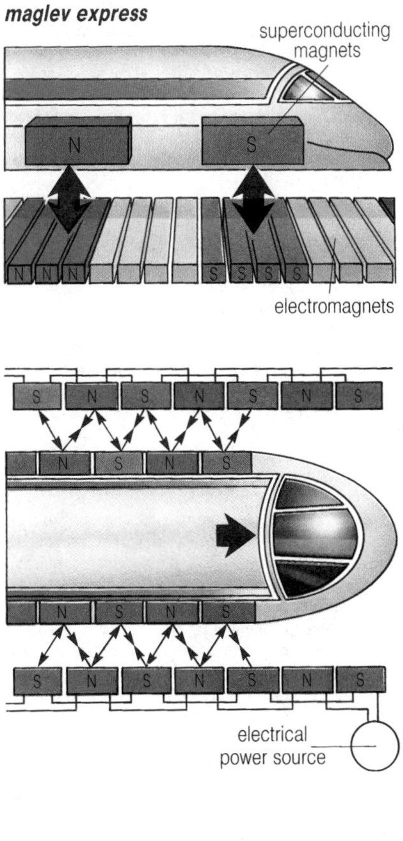

superconducting magnets
N
S
N N N
S S S S
electromagnets
S N S N S N S
N S N S
N S N S
S N S N S N S
electrical power source

magnetic field

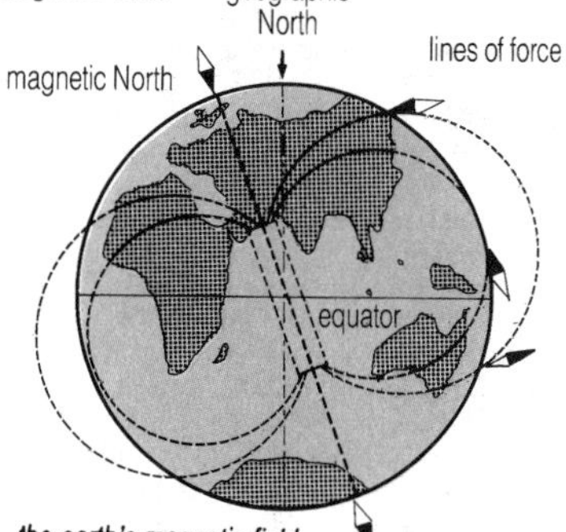
geographic North
lines of force
magnetic North
equator

the earth's magnetic field

pass needle placed on them. Its magnitude and direction are given by the ◊magnetic flux density, expressed in ◊teslas.

Experiments have confirmed that homing pigeons and some other animals rely on their perception of Earth's magnetic field for their sense of direction, and by 1979 it was suggested that humans to some extent share this sense.

magnetic flux a measurement of the strength of the magnetic field around electric currents and magnets. It is measured in ◊webers; one weber per square meter is equal to one tesla.

The amount of magnetic flux through an area equals the product of the area and the magnetic field strength at a point within that area. It is a measure of the number of magnetic field lines passing through an area.

magnetic pole the region on a magnet where its magnetic effects are strongest. Magnets (electromagnets as well as permanent magnets) always have two poles, called north and south. When a magnet is suspended freely, the north pole always points north and the south pole always points south.

Single magnetic poles, called monopoles, have never been observed, despite being searched for, although there is no theoretical reason why they could not exist. If monopoles were discovered it would have profound effects on the theory of quantum electrodynamics.

magnetic resonance imaging (MRI) diagnostic scanning system based on the principles of nuclear magnetic resonance. MRI yields finely detailed three-dimensional images of structures within the body without exposing the patient to harmful radiation. The technique is useful for imaging the soft tissues of the body, such as the brain and the spinal cord.

Claimed as the biggest breakthrough in diagnostic imaging since the discovery of X rays, MRI is a noninvasive technique using the principle that atomic nuclei in a strong magnetic field can be made to give off electromagnetic radiation, the characteristics of which depend on the environment of the nuclei.

magnetic storm in meteorology, a sudden disturbance affecting the Earth's magnetic field, causing anomalies in radio transmissions and magnetic compasses. It is probably caused by ◊sunspot activity.

magnetic tape narrow plastic ribbon coated with an easily magnetizable material on which data can be recorded. It is used in sound recording, audiovisual systems (videotape) and computing. For mass storage on commercial mainframe computers, large reel-to-reel tapes are used, but for the smaller mini- and microcomputers, tape cassettes and cartridges are more usual.

Magnetic tape was first used in sound recording in 1947, and made overdubbing possible, unlike the direct-to-disk system it replaced. Two-track (stereo) tape was introduced in the 1950s and four-track in the early 1960s; modern studios use 16–, 24–, or 3-track tape, from which the tracks are mixed down to a stereo master tape.

In computing, magnetic tape was first used to record data and programs in 1951 as part of the UNIVAC 1 system. It was very popular as a storage medium for external memory in the 1950s and 1960s. Since then it has largely been replaced by magnetic disks. Information is recorded on the tape in binary form, with two different strengths of signal representing 1 and 0. It is common for 20,000 ◊bits of information to be recorded on each ½ in/1 cm of tape. The tape drives of a mainframe or minicomputer can be capable of reading 16 ft/5 m of tape in a second.

magnetism branch of physics dealing with the properties of magnets and ◊magnetic fields. Magnetic fields are produced by moving charged particles: in electromagnets, electrons flow through a coil of wire connected to a battery; in magnets, spinning electrons within the atoms generate the field.

Substances differ in the extent to which they can be magnetized by an external field (susceptibility). Materials that can be strongly magnetized, such as iron, cobalt, and nickel, are said to be ferromagnetic. This is due to the formation of areas called domains in which atoms, weakly magnetic because of their spinning electrons, align to form areas of strong magnetism. Ferromagnetic materials lose their magnetism if heated to the Curie temperature. Most other materials are paramagnetic, being only weakly pulled toward a strong magnet. This is because their atoms have a low level of magnetism and do not form domains. Diamagnetic materials are weakly repelled by a magnet since electrons within their atoms act as electromagnets and reduce magnetism. Antiferromagnetic materials have a very low susceptibility that increases with temperature; a similar phenomenen in materials such as ferrites is called ferrimagnetism.

Apart from its universal application in generators and electric motors, magnetism is of considerable importance in advanced technology, for example in particle ◊accelerators for nuclear research, memory stores for computers, tape recorders, and ◊cryogenics.

Experiments have confirmed that homing pigeons and some other animals rely on their perception of the Earth's magnetic field for their sense of direction, and by 1979 it was suggested that humans to some extent share this sense.

magnetite a black iron ore, iron oxide (Fe_3O_4). Widely distributed, magnetite is found in nearly all igneous and metamorphic rocks. It is strongly magnetic and some deposits, called lodestone, are permanently magnetized. Lodestone has been used as a compass since the first millennium BC.

magneto simple electric generator, often used to provide the electricity for the ignition system of motorcycles and used in early automobiles. It consists of a rotating magnet that sets up an electric current in a coil, providing the spark.

magnetohydrodynamics (MHD) the field of science concerned with the behavior of ionized gases or liquid in a magnetic field. Systems have been developed that use MHD to generate electrical power.

magnetosphere the volume of space, surrounding a planet, controlled by the planet's magnetic field and acting as a magnetic "shell." The Earth's extends 40,000 mi/64,000 km toward the Sun but many times this distance on the side away from the Sun.

The extension away from the Sun is called the magnetotail. The outer edge of the magnetosphere is the magnetopause. Beyond this is a turbulent region, the magnetosheath, where the ◊solar wind is deflected around the magnetosphere. Inside the magnetosphere, atomic particles follow the Earth's lines of magnetic force. The magnetosphere contains the ◊Van Allen radiation belts. Other planets have magnetospheres, notably Jupiter.

magnetron a ◊thermionic valve (electron tube) for generating very high-frequency oscillations, used in radar and to produce microwaves in a microwave oven. The flow of electrons from the tube's cathode to one or more anodes is controlled by an applied magnetic field.

magnolia

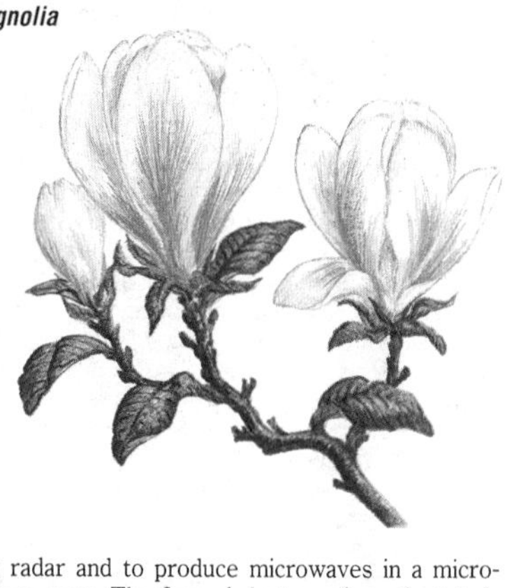

Magnificat in the New Testament, the song of praise sung by Mary, the mother of Jesus, on her visit to her cousin Elizabeth shortly after the Annunciation; it is used in the liturgy of some Christian churches.

magnification measure of the enlargement or reduction of an object in an imaging optical system. Linear magnification is the ratio of the size (height) of the image to that of the object. Angular magnification is the ratio of the angle subtended at the observer's eye by the image to the angle subtended by the object when viewed directly.

Magnitogorsk industrial city in Chelyabinsk region, USSR, on the E slopes of the Ural Mountains; population (1987) 430,000. It was developed in the 1930s to work iron, manganese, bauxite, and other metals in the district. Today the major industries are steel, motor vehicles, tractors, and railroad rolling stock.

magnitude in astronomy, measure of the brightness of a star or other celestial object. The larger the number denoting the magnitude, the fainter the object. Zero or first magnitude indicates some of the brightest stars. Still brighter are those of negative magnitude, such as Sirius, whose magnitude is −1.42. Apparent magnitude is the brightness of an object as seen from Earth; absolute magnitude is the brightness at a standard distance of 10 parsecs (32.6 light-years).

Each magnitude step is equal to a brightness difference of 2.512 times. Thus a first-magnitude star (magnitude 1) is 2.512^5 or 100 times brighter than a sixth-magnitude star just visible to the naked eye. The apparent magnitude of the Sun is −26.8, its absolute magnitude +4.8.

magnolia tree or shrub of the genus *Magnolia*, family Magnoliaceae, native to North America and E Asia. Magnolias vary in height from 2 ft/60 cm to 150 ft/30 m. The large, fragrant single flowers are white, rose, or purple. The up to 80 ft/24 m tall southern magnolia *M. grandiflora* of the US has white flowers 9 in/23 cm across.

magpie any of a genus *Pica* of birds in the crow family. It feeds on insects, snails, young birds, and carrion, and is found in Europe, Asia, N Africa, and W North America.

The black-billed magpie *P. pica* of Eurasia and Western N America, about 18 in/45 cm long, has black and white plumage, the long tail having a metallic sheen.

Magritte René 1898–1967. Belgian Surrealist painter. His paintings focus on visual paradoxes and everyday objects taken out of context. Recurring motifs include bowler hats, apples, and windows.

Magritte joined the other Surrealists in Paris 1927. Returning to Brussels in 1930, he painted murals for public buildings, and throughout his life created variations on themes of mystery treated with apparent literalism.

Magyar member of the largest ethnic group in Hungary, comprising 92% of the population. Magyars are of mixed Ugric and Turkic origin, and they arrived in Hungary toward the end of the 9th century. The Magyar language (see ◊Hungarian) belongs to the Uralic group.

Mahabad Kurdish town in Azerbaijan, W Iran, population (1983) 63,000. Occupied by Russian troops in 1941, it formed the center of a short-lived Kurdish republic (1945–46) before being reoccupied by the Iranians. In the 1980s Mahabad was the focal point of resistance by Iranian Kurds against the Islamic republic.

Mahābhārata (Sanskrit "great poem of the Bharatas") Sanskrit Hindu epic consisting of 18 books probably composed in its present form about 300 BC. It forms with the *Rāmāyana* the two great epics of the Hindus. It deals with the fortunes of the rival families of the Kauravas and the Pandavas, and contains the ◊*Bhagavad-Gītā*, or *Song of the Blessed*, an episode in the sixth book.

Mahādeva (Sanskrit "great god") a title given to the Hindu god ◊Siva.

Mahādevī (Sanskrit "great goddess") a title given to Sakti, the consort of the Hindu god Siva. She is worshiped in many forms, including her more active manifestations as Kali or Durga and her peaceful form as Parvati.

Mahan Alfred Thayer 1840–1914. US naval historian. Born in Quogue, New York, Mahan graduated from the US Naval Academy 1859. Serving in the blockade of the South during the Civil War, he published a history of the naval operations, *The Gulf and Inland Waters* 1883. In 1885 Mahan was promoted to captain and joined the faculty of the Naval War College. His lectures, published as *The Influence of Sea Power Upon History* 1890–92, deeply influenced Theodore Roosevelt and Wilhelm II of Germany to expand their respective nations' fleets. Mahan's memoirs were published as *From Sail to Steam* 1907.

Maharashtra state in W central India

area 118,811 sq mi/307,800 sq km

capital Bombay

towns Pune, Nagpur, Ulhasnagar, Sholapur, Nasik, Thana, Kolhapur, Aurangabad, Sangli, Amravati

features cave temples of Ajanta, containing 200 BC–7th century AD Buddhist murals and sculptures; Ellora cave temples 6th–9th century with Buddhist, Hindu, and Jain sculptures

products cotton, rice, groundnuts, sugar, minerals

population (1981) 62,694,000

language Marathi 50%

religion Hindu 80%, Parsee, Jain, and Sikh minorities

history formed 1960 from the southern part of the former Bombay state.

maharishi (Sanskrit *mahā* "great," *rishi* "sage") Hindu guru (teacher), or spiritual leader. The Maharishi Mahesh Yogi influenced the Beatles and other Westerners in the 1960s.

mahatma (Sanskrit "great soul") title conferred on Mohandas K ◊Gandhi by his followers as the first great national Indian leader.

Mahāyāna (Sanskrit "greater vehicle") one of the two major forms of ◊Buddhism, common in N Asia (China, Korea, Japan, and Tibet). Veneration of bodhisattvas (those who achieve enlightenment but remain on the human plane in order to help other living beings) is a fundamental belief in Mahāyāna, as is the idea that everyone has within them the seeds of Buddhahood.

A synthesis of Mahāyāna doctrines is found in the *Sūtra of the Golden Light*, stressing that people should obey reason (*prajñā*), which enables them to tell right from wrong; an act of self-sacrifice is the highest triumph of reason. The *Lotus Sūtra* describes the historical Buddha as only one manifestation of the eternal Buddha, the ultimate law (*dharma*) of the cosmos and the omnipresent and compassionate savior.

Mahdi (Arabic "he who is guided aright") in Islam, the title of a coming messiah who will establish

Mahler *Austrian composer and conductor Gustav Mahler.*

the reign of justice on Earth. The title has been assumed by many Muslim leaders, notably the Sudanese sheik Mohammed Ahmed (1848–85), who headed a revolt in 1881 against Egypt and in 1885 captured Khartoum.

His great-grandson Sadiq el Mahdi (1936–), leader of the Umma party in Sudan, was prime minister 1966–67. He was imprisoned 1969–74 for attempting to overthrow the military regime.

Mahfouz Naguib 1911– . Egyptian novelist and playwright. His novels, which deal with the urban working class, include a semiautobiographical trilogy 1957, *Children of Gebelawi* 1959 (banned in Egypt because of its treatment of religious themes), and *Respected Sir* 1988. He was awarded the Nobel Prize for literature in 1988.

mah-jong or ***mah-jongg*** (Chinese "sparrows") originally an ancient Chinese card game, dating from the Song dynasty 960–1279. It is now usually played by four people with 144 small ivory tiles, divided into six suits.

Mahler Alma (born Schindler) 1879–1964. Austrian pianist and critic. She was the daughter of the artist Anton Schindler and married the composer Gustav Mahler 1901.

Mahler Gustav 1860–1911. Austrian composer and conductor. He composed 14 symphonies, including three composed as a student and unnumbered, his nine massive repertoire symphonies, the titled symphony *Das Lied von der Erde/Song of the Earth* 1909, and the incomplete *Symphony No. 10*. He also wrote song cycles displaying a synthesis of Romanticism and new uses of chromatic harmonies and musical forms.

Mahler was born in Bohemia (now in Czechoslovakia); he studied at the Vienna Conservatoire, and conducted in Prague, Leipzig, Budapest, and Hamburg 1891–97. He was director of the Vienna Court Opera from 1897 and conducted the New York Philharmonic from 1910.

Mahmud two sultans of the Ottoman Empire:

Mahmud I 1696–1754. Ottoman sultan from 1730. After restoring order to the empire in Istanbul 1730, he suppressed the ◊Janissary rebellion 1731 and waged war against Persia 1731–46. He led successful wars against Austria and Russia, concluded by the Treaty of Belgrade 1739. He was a patron of the arts and also carried out reform of the army.

Mahmud II 1785–1839. Ottoman sultan from 1808 who attempted to westernize the declining empire, carrying out a series of far-reaching reforms in the civil service and army. In 1826 he destroyed the ◊Janissaries. Wars against Russia 1807–12 led to losses of territory. The pressure for Greek independence after 1821 led to conflict with Britain, France, and Russia, leading to the destruction of the Ottoman fleet at the Battle of Navarino in 1829 and defeat in the Russo-Turkish war 1828–29. He was forced to recognize Greek independence in 1830.

There was further disorder with the revolt in Egypt of ◊Mehemet Ali 1831–32, which in turn led to temporary Ottoman-Russian peace. Attempts to control the rebellious provinces failed in 1839, resulting in effect in the granting of Egyptian autonomy.

mahogany timber from several genera of trees found in the Americas and Africa. Mahogany is a tropical hardwood obtained chiefly by rainforest logging. It has a warm red color and takes a high polish.

True mahogany comes from trees of the genus *Swietenia*, but other types come from the Spanish and Australian cedars, the Indian redwood, and other trees of the mahogany family Meliaceae, native to Africa and the E Indies.

Mahón or ***Port Mahon*** capital and port of the Spanish island of Minorca; population (1981) 21,900. Probably founded by the Carthaginians, it was in British occupation 1708–56 and 1762–82.

Maia in Greek mythology, daughter of Atlas and mother of Hermes.

Maiden Castle prehistoric hillfort and later earthworks near Dorchester, Dorset, England. The site was inhabited from Neolithic times (about 2000 BC) and was stormed by the Romans AD 43.

maidenhair any fern of the genus *Adiantum*, especially *A. capillus-veneris* with hairlike fronds terminating in small kidney-shaped, spore-bearing pinnules. It is widely distributed in the Americas, and is sometimes found in the British Isles.

maidenhair tree another name for ◊ginkgo, a surviving member of an ancient group of gymnosperms.

Maidenhead town in Berkshire, S England, 25 mi/40 km W of London, on the river Thames. It is a boating center; major manufactures are computer software, plastics, and pharmaceuticals; and it has a printing industry. Population (1983) 48,473.

Maidstone town in Kent, SE England, on the river Medway, administrative headquarters of the county; prison, law courts; population (1986) 133,700. Industries include agricultural machinery and paper.

Maidstone has the ruins of All Saints' College 1260. The Elizabethan Chillington Manor is an art gallery and museum.

Maiduguri capital of Borno state, NE Nigeria; population (1983) 230,900.

Maikop capital of Adyge autonomous region of the USSR on the river Bielaia, with timber mills, distilleries, tanneries, and tobacco and furniture factories; population (1985) 140,000. Oilfields, discovered in 1900, are linked by pipeline with Tapse on the Black Sea.

Mailer Norman 1923– . US writer and journalist. He gained wide attention with his novel of World War II *The Naked and the Dead* 1948. A commentator on the US social, literary, and political scene, he has run for mayor of New York City and has expressed radical sexual views.

His other novels include *An American Dream* 1964, *Genius and Lust* 1976, *Ancient Evenings* 1983, *Tough Guys Don't Dance* 1984, and *Harlot's Ghost* 1991. His journalistic work includes *Armies of the Night* 1968, about protest against the Vietnam War, and *The Executioner's Song* 1979 (Pulitzer Prize), about convicted murderer Gary Gilmore. Mailer has also ventured into filmmaking.

Maillart Ella 1903– . Swiss explorer, skier, and Olympic sailor whose six-month journey into Soviet Turkestan was described in *Turkestan Solo* 1934. Her expedition across the Gobi Desert with Peter Fleming is recounted in *Forbidden Journey* 1937.

Maillol Aristide Joseph Bonaventure 1861–1944. French artist who turned to sculpture in the 1890s. His work is mainly devoted to the female nude. It shows the influence of Classical Greek art but tends toward simplified rounded forms.

Maillol was influenced by the ◊Nabis. A typical

Mailer *US novelist and journalist Norman Mailer, who received wide acclaim for his writing and caused controversy with his social and political views.*

example of his work is *Fame* for the Cézanne monument in Aix-en-Provence.

mail order a type of business in which retail organizations sell their goods by mail through catalogs.

Maimonides Moses (Moses Ben Maimon) 1135–1204. Jewish rabbi and philosopher, born in Córdoba, Spain. Known as one of the greatest Hebrew scholars, he attempted to reconcile faith and reason.

He left Spain in 1160 to escape the persecution of the Jews and settled in Fez, and later in Cairo, where he was personal physician to Sultan Saladin. His codification of Jewish law is known as the *Mishneh Torah/The Torah Reviewed* 1180; he also formulated the Thirteen Principles, which summarize the basic beliefs of Judaism. His philosophical classic *More nevukhim/The Guide to the Perplexed* 1176–91, helped to introduce Aristotelian thought into medieval philosophy.

Main river in Germany, flowing through Frankfurt to join the river Rhine at Mainz. A canal links it with the Danube. Length 320 mi/515 km.

Maine French river, 7 mi/11 km long, formed by the junction of the Mayenne and Sarthe; it enters the Loire below Angers, and gives its name to Maine-et-Loire *département*.

Maine northeasternmost state of the US, largest of the New England states; nickname Pine Tree State

area 33,273 sq mi/86,200 sq km

capital Augusta

cities Portland, Lewiston, Bangor

population (1990) 1,227,928.

features Acadia National Park, including Bar Harbor and most of Mount Desert Island; Baxter State Park, including Mount Katahadin; Roosevelt's Campobello International Park; canoeing along the Allagush Wilderness Waterway

products dairy and market garden produce, paper, pulp, timber, footwear, textiles, fish and lobster; tourism is important

famous people James G Blaine, Dorothea Dix, Henry Wadsworth Longfellow, Elijah Lovejoy, Edna St Vincent Millay, Edmund Muskie, Edward Arlington Robinson, Margaret Chase Smith

history permanently settled by the British from 1623; absorbed by Massachusetts 1691. In colonial days, white-pine masts were built for the Royal Navy at Falmouth (now Portland). Statehood was achieved in 1820. Maine produces 98% of the nation's blueberries and has the largest papermaking capacity of any of the 50 states but is generally economically depressed.

Maine

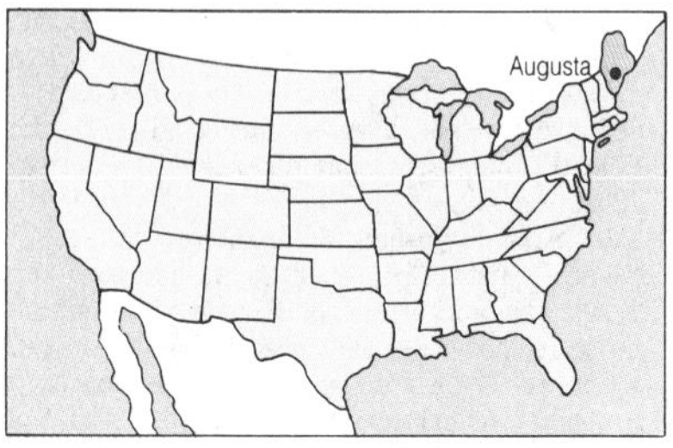
Augusta

mainframe large computer used for commercial data processing and other large-scale operations. Because of the increase in computing power, the differences between the mainframe, ◊supercomputer, ◊minicomputer, and ◊microcomputer (personal computer) are becoming less marked.

main sequence in astronomy, the part of the ◊Hertzsprung-Russell diagram that contains most of the stars, including the Sun. It runs diagonally from the top left of the diagram to the lower right. The most massive (and hence brightest) stars are at the top left, with the least massive (coolest) stars at the bottom right.

Main Street classic satirical novel by Sinclair Lewis, published in 1920, which made the American small-town Main Street the exemplification of enduring if simplistic social values.

Maintenon Françoise d'Aubigné, Marquise de 1635–1719. Second wife of Louis XIV of France from 1684, and widow of the writer Paul Scarron (1610–1660). She was governess to the children of Mme de Montespan by Louis, and his mistress from 1667. She secretly married the king after the death of Queen Marie Thérèse in 1683. Her political influence was considerable, and, as a Catholic convert from Protestantism, her religious opinions were zealous.

Mainz (French *Mayence*) capital of Rhineland-Palatinate, Federal Republic of Germany, on the Rhine, 23 mi/37 km WSW of Frankfurt-am-Main; population (1988) 189,000. In Roman times it was a fortified camp and became the capital of Germania Superior. Printing was possibly invented here about 1448 by ◊Gutenberg.

maiolica or ***majolica*** a type of enameled ◊pottery, so named after the Italian form of Majorca, the Spanish island where such ware was originally made. The term is applied to the richly decorated, multicolored enamel pottery produced in Italy in the 15th to 18th centuries.

Maitreya the Buddha to come, "the kindly one," a principal figure in all forms of Buddhism; he is known as Mi-lo-fo in China and Miroku in Japan. Buddhists believe that a Buddha appears from time to time to maintain knowledge of the true path; Maitreya is the next future Buddha.

maize see ◊corn.

Maiziere Lothar de 1940– . German conservative politician, leader of the former East German Christian Democratic Union. He became premier after East Germany's first democratic elections in Apr 1990, until German reunification in Oct 1990.

Major John 1943– . British Conservative politician, foreign secretary 1989, chancellor of the Exchequer 1989–90; he was elected prime minister in the Conservative party leadership election November 1990 following the resignation of Conservative prime minister Margaret Thatcher.

Major *British prime minister John Major.*

Makarios III *Archbishop Makarios, president of Cyprus 1960–77.*

Majorca (Spanish *Mallorca*) largest of the ◊Balearic Islands, belonging to Spain, in the W Mediterranean

area 1,405 sq mi/3,640 sq km

capital Palma

features the highest mountain is Puig Mayor 4,741 ft/1,445 m

products olives, figs, oranges, wine, brandy, timber, sheep; tourism is the mainstay of the economy

population (1981) 561,215

history captured 797 by the Moors, it became the kingdom of Majorca 1276, and was united with Aragon in 1343.

Makarios III 1913–1977. Cypriot politician, Greek Orthodox archbishop 1950–77. A leader of the Resistance organization ◊EOKA, he was exiled by the British to the Seychelles 1956–57 for supporting armed action to achieve union with Greece (*enosis*). He was president of the republic of Cyprus 1960–77 (briefly deposed by a Greek military coup July–Dec 1974).

Makarova Natalia 1940– . Russian ballerina. She danced with the Kirov Ballet 1959–70, then sought political asylum in the West. Her roles include the title role in *Giselle*, and Aurora in *The Sleeping Beauty*.

Makeyevka formerly (until 1931) ***Dmitrievsk*** city in the Donets Basin, SE Ukraine, USSR; population (1987) 455,000. Industries include coal, iron, steel, and chemicals.

Makhachkala formerly (until 1922) ***Port Petrovsk*** capital of Dagestan, USSR, on the Caspian Sea, ESE of Grozny, from which pipelines bring petroleum to Makhachkala's refineries; population (1987) 320,000. Other industries include shipbuilding, meat packing, chemicals, matches, and cotton textiles.

Malabar Coast the coastal area of Karnataka and Kerala states, India, lying between the Arabian Sea and the Western Ghats; about 40 mi/65 km W to E, 450 mi/725 km N to S. A fertile area with heavy rains, it produces food grains, coconuts, rubber, spices; teak, ebony, and other woods. Lagoons fringe the shore. A district of Tamil Nadu transferred in 1956 to Kerala was called Malabar Coast.

Malabo port and capital of Equatorial Guinea, on the island of Bioko; population (1983) 15,253. It was founded in the 1820s by the British as Port Clarence. Under Spanish rule it was known as Santa Isabel (until 1973).

Malacca or ***Melaka*** state of W Peninsular Malaysia;

malaria
life cycle of the malaria parasite, split between mosquito and human

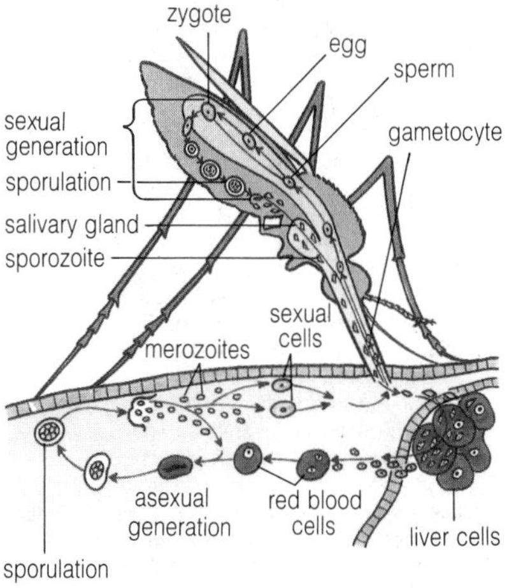
zygote
egg
sperm
sexual generation
gametocyte
sporulation
salivary gland
sporozoite
sexual cells
merozoites
asexual generation
red blood cells
liver cells
sporulation

capital Malacca; area 656 sq mi/1,700 sq km; population (1980) 465,000 (about 70% Chinese). Products include rubber, tin, and wire. The town originated in the 13th century as a fishing village frequented by pirates, and later developed into a trading port. Portuguese from 1511, then Dutch from 1641, it was ceded to Britain 1824, becoming part of the Straits Settlements.

Malacca, Strait of channel between Sumatra and the Malay Peninsula; length 600 mi/965 km; narrows to less than 24 mi/38 km wide. It carries all shipping between the Indian Ocean and the South China Sea.

malachite a common ◊copper ore, basic copper carbonate, $Cu_2CO_3(OH)_2$. It is a source of green pigment and is polished for use in jewelry, ornaments, and art objects.

Málaga industrial seaport (sugar refining, distilling, brewing, olive-oil pressing, shipbuilding) and vacation resort in Andalusia, Spain; capital of Málaga province on the Mediterranean; population (1986) 595,000. Founded by the Phoenicians and taken by the Moors 711, Málaga was capital of the Moorish kingdom of Malaga from the 13th century until captured 1487 by the Catholic Monarchs Ferdinand and Isabella.

Malagasy inhabitant of or native to Madagascar. Primarily rice farmers, the Malagasy make use of both irrigated fields and swidden (temporary plot) methods. The language belongs to the ◊Malayo-Polynesian family and, despite Madagascar's proximity to Africa, contains only a small number of Bantu and Arabic loan words.

Malagasy Republic former name (1958–75) of ◊Madagascar.

Malamud Bernard 1914–1986. US novelist and short-story writer. He first attracted attention with *The Natural* 1952, making a professional baseball player his hero. Later novels, often dealing with the Jewish immigrant tradition, include *The Assistant* 1957, *The Fixer* 1966, *Dubin's Lives* 1979, and *God's Grace* 1982.

Short-story collections include *The Magic Barrel* 1958, *Rembrandt's Hat* 1973, and *The Stories of Bernard Malamud* 1983.

malapropism an amusing slip of the tongue, arising from the confusion of similar-sounding words. The term derives from the French *mal à propos* (inappropriate); historically, it is associated with Mrs Malaprop, a character in Sheridan's play *The Rivals* 1775, who was the pineapple (pinnacle) of perfection in such matters.

malaria infectious parasitic disease of the tropics transmitted by mosquitoes, marked by periodic fever and an enlarged spleen. When a female mosquito of the *Anopheles* genus bites a human who has malaria, it takes in with the human blood one of four malaria protozoa of the genus *Plasmodium*. This matures within the insect and is then transferred when the mosquito bites a new victim. Malaria affects some 200 million people a year on a recurring basis.

Inside the human body the parasite settles first in the liver, then multiplies to attack the red blood cells, when the symptoms of malaria become evident. ◊Quinine was the first drug used against malaria, now replaced by synthetics, such as atabrine to prevent the disease and chloroquine to treat it. Tests on a vaccine were begun in 1986 in the US. In Brazil a malaria epidemic broke out among new settlers in the Amazon region, with 287,000 cases 1983 and 500,000 cases 1988.

Malatya capital of a province of the same name in E central Turkey, lying W of the river Euphrates; population (1985) 251,000.

Malawi country in SE Africa, bordered N and NE by Tanzania; E, S and W by Mozambique; and W by Zambia.

government The 1966 constitution provides for a president elected for a five-year term but was amended in 1971 to make Hastings ◊Banda president for life. Malawi is a one-party state, all adults being required to be members of the Malawi Congress Party. The single-chamber legislature, the national assembly, has 112 elected members, and the president may appoint any number of additional members. He also appoints a cabinet whose members are directly responsible to him. Hastings Banda's system of personal, paternalistic rule has not been seriously challenged in his 20 years of office. There are at least three opposition groups that operate from outside Malawi.

history During the 15th–19th centuries the Malawi empire occupied roughly the southern part of the region that makes up present-day Malawi. The Portuguese, in the 17th century, were the first Europeans to visit the area, but Britain intervened to stop them from annexing it and thereby linking the Portuguese colonies of Angola and Mozambique. The difficulty of the terrain and the warfare between the rival Yao and Ngoni groups long prevented penetration of the region by outsiders, though David ◊Livingstone reached Lake Malawi in 1859. In 1891 Britain annexed the country, making it the British protectorate of Nyasaland from 1907. Between 1953 and 1964 it was part of the Federation of Rhodesia and Nyasaland, which comprised the territory that is now Zimbabwe, Zambia, and Malawi.

Dr Hastings Banda, through the Malawi Congress Party, led a campaign for independence, and in 1963 the federation was dissolved. Nyasaland became independent as Malawi in 1964 and two years later became a republic and a one-party state, with Banda as its first president. He has governed his country in a very individual way, tolerating no opposition, and his foreign policies have at times been rather idiosyncratic. He astonished his black African colleagues in 1967 by officially recognizing the Republic of South Africa, and in 1971 became the first African head of state to visit that country. In 1976, however, he also recognized the Communist government in Angola.

Banda keeps a tight control over his government colleagues, and, as yet, no successor has emerged. In 1977 he embarked upon a policy of cautious liberalism, releasing some political detainees and allowing greater press freedom. His external policies are based on a mixture of national self-interest and practical reality and have enabled Malawi to live in reasonable harmony with its neighbors.

Malawi adopted an "open-door" policy toward refugees fleeing the civil war in neighboring Mozambique; about 70,000 refugees crossed the border Sept 1986. By 1988 one in ten of the population of eight million was a Mozambican.

Malawi, Lake or ***Lake Nyasa*** African lake, bordered by Malawi, Tanzania, and Mozambique, formed in a section of the Great ◊Rift Valley. It is about 1,650 ft/500 m above sea level and 350 mi/560 km long, with an area of 14,280 sq mi/37,000 sq km. It is intermittently drained to the south by the river Shiré into the Zambezi.

Malay a member of a large group of peoples comprising the majority population of the Malay Peninsula and Archipelago, also found in S Thailand and coastal Sumatra and Borneo. Their language belongs to the western branch of the Austronesian family.

Malay language member of the Western or Indonesian branch of the Malayo-Polynesian language family, used in the Malay peninsula and many of the islands of Malaysia and Indonesia. The Malay language can be written with either Arabic or Roman scripts.

The dialect of the S Malay peninsula is the basis of both standard Malay in Malaysia and Bahasa

Malawi
Republic of
(Malaŵi)

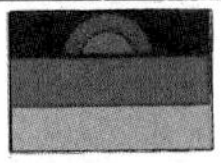

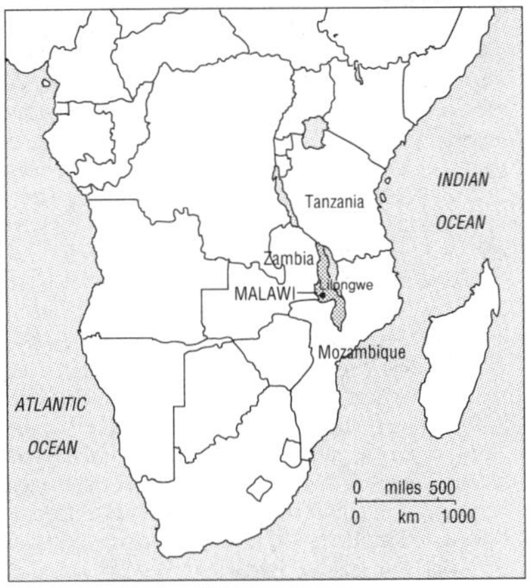
INDIAN
OCEAN
Tanzania
Zambia
MALAWI
Lilongwe
Mozambique
ATLANTIC
OCEAN
0 miles 500
0 km 1000

area 45,560 sq mi/118,000 sq km
capital Lilongwe
cities Blantire (largest city and commercial center), Mzuzu, Zomba
physical landlocked narrow plateau with rolling plains; mountainous W of Lake Malawi
features one-third is water; Great Rift Valley; Nyika, Kasungu, and Lengare national parks; Mulanje Massif; Lakes Malawi, Chilara, and Malombe; Shire River
head of state and government Hastings Kamusu Banda from 1966 for life
political system one-party republic Malawi Congress Party (MCP), multiracial, right-wing
exports tea, tobacco, cotton, peanuts, sugar
currency kwacha
population (1990 est) 9,080,000 (nearly 1 million refugees from Mozambique); growth rate 3.3% p.a.
life expectancy men 46, women 50 (1989)
language English, Chichewa (both official)
religion Christian 75%; Muslim 20%
literacy 25% (1989)
GNP $1.2 bn (1987); $160 per head (1988)
chronology
1964 Independence achieved from Britain, within the Commonwealth, as Malawi.
1966 Became a one-party republic, with Hastings Banda as president.
1971 Banda was made president for life.
1977 Banda started a program of moderate liberalization, releasing some political detainees and allowing greater freedom of the press.
1986–89 Influx of nearly 1 million refugees from Mozambique.

Malaysia

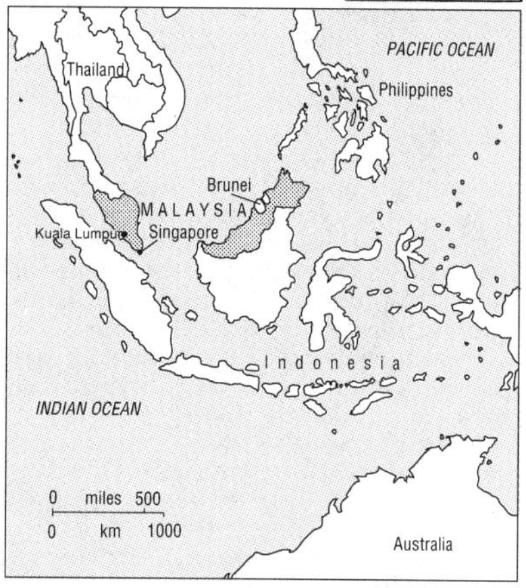
PACIFIC OCEAN
Thailand
Philippines
Brunei
MALAYSIA
Kuala Lumpur
Singapore
Indonesia
INDIAN OCEAN
0 miles 500
0 km 1000
Australia

area 127,287 sq mi/329,759 sq km
capital Kuala Lumpur
cities Johor Baharu, Ipoh, Georgetown (Penang), Kuching in Sarawak, Kota Kinabalu in Sabah
physical comprises Peninsular Malaysia (the nine Malay states—Perlis, Kedah, Johore, Selangor, Perak, Negri Sembilan, Kelantan, Trengganu, Pahang—plus Penang and Malacca); and E Malaysia (Sarawak and Sabah); 75% tropical jungle; central mountain range; swamps in E
features Mount Kinabalu (highest peak in SE Asia); Niah caves (Sarawak)
head of state Rajah Azlan Muhibuddin Shah (sultan of Perak) from 1989
head of government Mahathir bin Mohamad from 1981
political system liberal democracy
political parties New United Malay's National Organization (UMNO Baru) Malay-oriented nationalist; Malaysian Chinese Association (MCA), Chinese-oriented conservative; Gerakan, Chinese-oriented left-of-center; Malaysian Indian Congress (MIC), Indian-oriented; Democratic Action Party (DAP), left-of-center multiracial, but Chinese dominated; Pan-Malayan Islamic Party (PAS), Islamic; Semangat '46, moderate, multiracial
exports pineapples, palm oil, rubber, timber, petroleum (Sarawak), bauxite
currency ringgit
population (1990 est) 17,053,000 (Malaysian 47%, Chinese 32%, Indian 8%, others 13%); growth rate 2% p.a.
life expectancy men 65, women 70 (1989)
language Bahasa Malaysia (official); English, Chinese, Indian, and tribal languages
religion Muslim (official), Buddhist, Hindu, tribal beliefs
literacy 80% (1989)
GNP $34.3 bn; $1,870 per head (1988)
chronology
1867 Britain established control.
1963 Federation of Malaysia formed, including Malaya, Singapore, Sabah (N Borneo), and Sarawak (NW Borneo).
1965 Secession of Singapore from federation.
1969 Anti-Chinese riots in Kuala Lumpur.
1971 Launch of Bumiputra "new economic policy."
1981 Election of Dr Mahathir bin Mohamad as prime minister.
1982 Mahathir bin Mohamad reelected.
1986 Mahathir bin Mohamad reelected.
1987 Arrest of opposition leader DAP leader as Malay-Chinese relations deteriorate.
1988 Split in ruling UMNO party over Mahathir's leadership style; new UMNO formed.
1989 Semangat '46 set up by former members of UMNO inluding ex-premier Tunku Abdul Rahman.
1990 Mahathir bin Mohamad reelected.

Indonesia, the official language of Indonesia. Bazaar Malay is a widespread pidgin variety used for trading and shopping.

Malayo-Polynesian or ***Austronesian*** a family of languages spoken in Malaysia, the Indonesian archipelago, parts of the region that was formerly Indochina, Taiwan, Madagascar, Melanesia, and Polynesia (excluding Australia and most of New Guinea). The group contains some 500 distinct languages, including Malay in Malaysia, Bahasa in Indonesia, Fijian, Hawaiian, and Maori.

Malay Peninsula southern projection of the continent of Asia, lying between the Strait of Malacca, which divides it from Sumatra, and the China Sea.

The northern portion is partly in Myanmar (formerly Burma), partly in Thailand; the south forms part of Malaysia. The island of Singapore lies off its southern extremity.

Malaysia country in SE Asia, comprising the Malay Peninsula, bordered N by Thailand, and surrounded E, S, and W by the South China Sea; and the states of Sabah and Sarawak in the northern part of the island of Borneo (S Borneo is part of Indonesia).

government Malaysia is a federation of 13 states: Johore, Kedah, Kelantan, Malacca, Negri Sembilan, Pahang, Penang, Perak, Perlis, Sabah, Sarawak, Selangor, and Trengganu. Each has its own constitution, head of state, and elected assembly, led by a chief minister and cabinet, and legislates on matters outside the federal parliament's sphere.

Under the 1957 constitution, a monarch is elected for five-year terms by and from among the hereditary rulers of Johore, Kedah, Kelantan, Negri Sembilan, Pahang, Perak, Perlis, Selangor, and Trengganu. The paramount ruler's powers are similar to those of the British monarch, including discretion in the appointment of a prime minister and in granting a dissolution of parliament. Generally, the monarch acts on the advice of the prime minister and cabinet, who wield effective power.

The two-chamber federal legislature or parliament is composed of a 68-member upper house or senate, *Dewan Negara*, comprising 42 members appointed by the monarch and two members elected by each of the 13 state assemblies for six-year terms, and a house of representatives, *Dewan Rakyat*, whose 177 members are elected for five-year terms from single-member constituencies by universal suffrage. The senate can only delay bills already approved by the dominant house of representatives, whose majority party or coalition provides the prime minister, who governs with a cabinet selected from parliament.

Malaysia's principal party is the New United Malays' National Organization (UMNO Baru), which is oriented toward ethnic Malays. It leads the National Front coalition, which is composed of 12 other parties, chiefly the Chinese-oriented Malaysian Chinese Association (MCA), the Gerakan Party, and the Indian-oriented Malaysian Indian Congress (MIC). The principal opposition parties are the moderate, mainly Chinese, Democratic Action Party (DAP), the radical Muslim Pan-Malayan Islamic Party (PAS), and Spirit of 1946 (Semangat '46), a breakaway from the UMNO. Smaller regional parties operate at state level.

history The areas that comprise present-day Malaysia were part of the Buddhist Sri Vijaya empire in the 9th–14th centuries. This was overthrown by Majapahit, Java's last Hindu kingdom. After this period of Indian influence came the introduction of Islam, and a powerful Muslim empire developed in the area. Its growth was checked by the Portuguese conquest of Malacca in 1511. In 1641 the Dutch ousted the Portuguese, and the area came under British control from 1786, with a brief return to Dutch rule 1818–24. Britain succeeded in unifying its protectorates in Borneo and the Malay Peninsula after World War II, making them a crown colony under the name of the Federation of Malaya in 1948.

The Federation of Malaysia was formed 1963 by the union of the 11 states of the Federation of Malaya with the British crown colonies of N Borneo (then renamed Sabah) and Sarawak, and Singapore, which seceded from the federation in 1965. Since 1966 the 11 states on the Malay Peninsula have been known as West Malaysia, and Sabah and Sarawak, as East Malaysia. The two regions are separated by 400 miles of the South China Sea. The establishment of the federation was opposed by guerrillas backed by Sukarno of Indonesia 1963–66, while the Philippines disputed the sovereignty of East Malaysia in 1968 through their claim on Sabah.

Tunku Abdul ◊Rahman was Malaysia's first prime minister 1963–69, and his multiracial style of government was successful until anti-Chinese riots in Kuala Lumpur in 1969 prompted the formation of an emergency administration. These riots followed a fall in support for the United Malays' National Organization (UMNO) in the federal election and were indicative of Malay resentment of the economic success of the Chinese business community. They provoked the resignation of Tunku Abdul Rahman in 1970 and the creation by his successor, Tun Abdul Razak, of a broader National Front governing coalition, including previous opposition parties in its ranks. In addition, a "new economic policy" was launched in 1971, with the aim of raising the percentage of Malay-owned businesses from 4% to 30% by 1990 and to extend the use of pro-Malay "affirmative action" quota systems for university entrance and company employment. During the 1970s Malaysia enjoyed economic growth, but relations with the Chinese community became uneasy later in the decade as a result of the federal government's refusal to welcome Vietnamese refugees. Even more serious has been a revival in fundamentalist Islam in the west and north.

Dr Mahathir bin ◊Mohamad became the new leader of the UMNO and prime minister in 1981 and pursued a more narrowly Islamic and Malay strategy than his predecessors. He also launched an ambitious industrialization program, seeking to emulate Japan. He was reelected in 1982 and 1986 but has encountered opposition from his Malaysian Chinese Association coalition partners, Christian-Muslim conflict in Sabah, and slower economic growth as a result of the fall in world tin, rubber, and palm-oil prices. In 1987, in the wake of worsening Malay-Chinese relations, Mahathir ordered the arrest of more than 100 prominent opposition activists, including the DAP's leader, Lim Kit Siang, and a tightening of press censorship. These moves precipitated a rift in the UMNO, with the former premier Tunku Abdul Rahman and former trade and industry minister Razaleigh Hamzah leaving to form a new multiracial party grouping, Semangat '46, in 1989. In 1988 a reconstituted New UMNO had been set up by Mahathir following a high-court ruling that, as a result of irregularities in its 1987 leadership election, the existing UMNO was an "unlawful body." The prime minister also announced some relaxation of the 1971 ethnic Malaya (*bumiputra*) oriented "new economic policy"—Malay equity ownership having reached only 18% by 1987—as part of the more consensual "Malay unity" program.

Malaysia joined ◊ASEAN in 1967 and originally adopted a pro-Western, anti-Communist position. During recent years, while close economic links

Maldives
Republic of
(Divehi Jumhuriya)

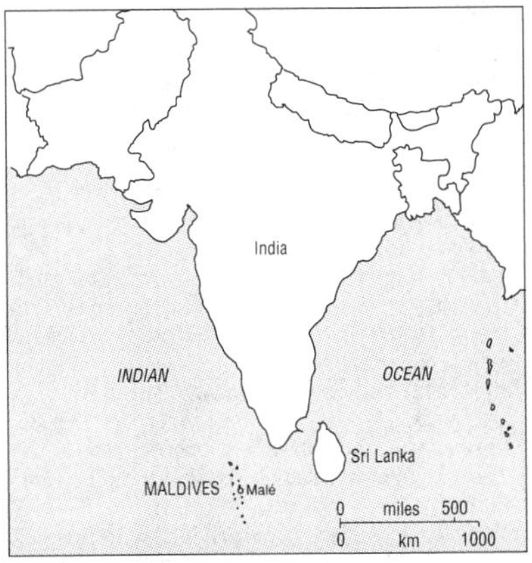
India
INDIAN
OCEAN
Sri Lanka
MALDIVES
Malé
0 miles 500
0 km 1000

area 115 sq mi/298 sq km
capital Malé
cities Seenu
physical comprises 1,200 coral islands, grouped into 12 clusters of atolls, largely flat, none bigger than 5 sq mi/13 sq km; 202 are inhabited
features tourism developed since 1972
head of state and government Maumoon Abdul Gayoom from 1978
political system authoritarian nationalism
political parties none; candidates elected on the basis of personal influence and clan loyalties
exports coconuts, copra, bonito (fish related to tuna), garments
currency Rufiya
population (1990 est) 219,000; growth rate 3.7% p.a.
life expectancy men 60, women 63 (1989)
language Divehi (Sinhalese dialect), English
religion Sunni Muslim
literacy 36% (1989)
GNP $69 mn (1987); $410 per head (1988)
chronology
1887 Became a British protectorate.
1953 Long a sultanate, the Maldive Islands became a republic within the Commonwealth.
1954 Sultanate restored.
1965 Achieved full independence outside the Commonwealth.
1968 Sultan deposed; republic reinstated with Ibrahim Nasir as president.
1978 Nasir retired; replaced by Maumoon Abdul Gayoom.
1983 Gayoom reelected.
1985 Rejoined the Commonwealth.
1988 Gayoom reelected. Coup attempt by mercenaries thought to have the backing of former president Nasir was foiled by Indian paratroops.

have been developed with Japan and joint ventures encouraged, relations with the communist powers and with Islamic nations have also become closer.

In Oct 1990 federal and state elections were held. Prime Minister Mahathir bin Mohamad's ruling National Front coalition captured 127 of the 180 National Assembly seats. The expected strong challenge from Mahathir's rival and former colleague Tunku (Prince) Razaleigh failed to materialize; his Semangat '46 party lost five of its twelve seats. However, Islamic (PAS) and Chinese (DAP) party allies polled well locally, with the opposition achieving a clean sweep (and control of the state legislature) in Tunku's home state of Kelantan.

Malcolm four kings of Scotland, including:

Malcolm III called Canmore c. 1031–1093. King of Scotland from 1054, the son of Duncan I (murdered by ◊Macbeth 1040). He was killed at Alnwick while invading Northumberland, England.

Malcolm X 1925–1965. US political leader. Born in Omaha, Nebraska, as Malcolm Little, he grew up in foster homes in Michigan, Massachusetts, and New York. Convicted of robbery 1946, he spent seven years in prison, becoming a follower of Black Muslim leader Elijah Mohammed and converting to Islam. In 1952 he officially changed his name to "Malcolm X" to signify his rootlessness in a racist society. Having become an influential national and international leader, Malcolm publicly broke with the Black Muslims 1964 and was assassinated in Harlem 1965. *The Autobiography of Malcolm X* appeared the same year.

Maldives group of 1,196 islands in the N Indian Ocean, about 400 mi/640 km SW of Sri Lanka, only 203 of which are inhabited.

government The 1968 constitution provides for a single-chamber citizens' council (*Majilis*) of 48 members and a president, nominated by the *Majilis* and elected by referendum. They all serve a five-year term. Forty of the *Majilis*'s members are elected by universal suffrage and eight are appointed by the president, who appoints and leads a cabinet that is responsible to the *Majilis*. There are no political parties and women are precluded from holding office.

history The islanders, under Muslim control from the 12th century, came under Portuguese rule in 1518. A dependency of Ceylon 1645–1948, they were under British protection 1887–1965 as the Maldive Islands and became a republic in 1953. The sultan was restored in 1954, and then, three years after achieving full independence as Maldives, the islands returned to republican status in 1968.

Maldives became fully independent as a sultanate outside the ◊Commonwealth in 1965, with Ibrahim Nasir as prime minister. Nasir became president when the sultan was deposed for the second time, in 1968, and the country became a republic. It rejoined the Commonwealth in 1982. Britain had an air-force staging post on the southern island of Gan 1956–75, and its closure meant a substantial loss of income. The president nevertheless refused a Soviet offer in 1977 to lease the former base, saying that he did not want it used for military purposes again nor leased to a superpower.

In 1978 Nasir announced that he would not stand for reelection, and the *Majilis* nominated Maumoon Abdul Gayoom, a member of Nasir's cabinet, as his successor. Nasir went to Singapore but was called back to answer charges of misusing government funds. He denied the charges, and attempts to extradite him failed. Despite rumors of a plot to overthrow him, Gayoom was reelected for a further five years in 1983. Under Gayoom economic growth accelerated, helped by an expansion in tourism. Overseas, Gayoom broadly adhered to his predecessor's policy of nonalignment, but also began to develop closer links with the Arab nations of the Middle East, and in 1985 rejoined the Commonwealth and was a founder member of the ◊South Asian Association for Regional Cooperation (SAARC). In Nov 1988, soon after being reelected for a third term, Gayoom was briefly ousted in an attempted coup led by Abdullah Luthufi, an exiled businessman from the pro-secessional atoll of Adu, who had recruited a force of 200 Tamil mercenaries in Sri Lanka. Gayoom was restored to office following the intervention of Indian paratroops; 17 of those captured, including Luthufi, were sentenced to life imprisonment in 1989.

Maldon English market town in Essex, at the mouth of the river Chelmer; population (1981) 14,750. It was the scene of a battle in which the East Saxons were defeated by the Danes in 991, commemorated in the Anglo-Saxon poem *The Battle of Maldon*.

Malé capital of the Maldives in the Indian Ocean; population (1985) 38,000. It trades in copra, breadfruit, and palm products.

Malebranche Nicolas 1638–1715. French philosopher. *De la Recherche de la Vérité/Search after Truth* 1674–78 was inspired by René ◊Descartes; he maintained that exact ideas of external objects are obtainable only through God.

Malenkov Georgi Maximilianovich 1901–1988. Soviet prime minister 1953–55, Stalin's designated successor but abruptly ousted as Communist Party secretary within two weeks of Stalin's death by ◊Khrushchev, and forced out as prime minister in 1955 by ◊Bulganin.

Malenkov subsequently occupied minor party posts. He was expelled from the Central Committee 1957 and from the Communist Party 1961.

Malevich Kasimir 1878–1935. Russian abstract painter. In 1912 he visited Paris and became a Cubist, and in 1913 he launched his own abstract movement, ◊Suprematism. Later he returned to figurative themes treated in a semiabstract style.

Malherbe François de 1555–1628. French poet and grammarian, born in Caen. He became court poet about 1605 under Henry IV and Louis XIII. He advocated reform of language and versification, and established the 12-syllable Alexandrine as the standard form of French verse.

Mali landlocked country in NW Africa, bordered to the NE by Algeria, E by Niger, SE by Burkina Faso, S by the Ivory Coast, SW by Senegal and Guinea, and W and N by Mauritania.

government The 1974 constitution, amended in 1981 and 1985, provides for a one-party state with a president elected by universal suffrage and an 82-member national assembly elected from a party list for a three-year term. The president serves for six years and may be reelected any number of times. The party is the Malian People's Democratic Union (UDPM).

history From the 7th to the 11th century part of the ◊Ghana Empire, then of the Muslim ◊Mali Empire, which flourished in NW Africa during the 7th–15th centuries, the area now known as Mali came under the rule of the ◊Songhai Empire during the 15th–16th centuries. In 1591 an invasion by Moroccan forces seeking to take over the W Sudanese gold trade destroyed the Songhai Empire and left the area divided into small kingdoms.

Because of its inland position, the region had little contact with Europeans, who were trading around the coast from the 16th century, and it was not until the 19th century that France, by means of treaties with local rulers, established colonies throughout most of NW Africa. As French Sudan, Mali was part of ◊French West Africa from 1893. In 1959, with Senegal, it formed the Federation of Mali. In 1960 Senegal left, and Mali became a fully independent republic.

Its first president, Modibo Keita, imposed an authoritarian Socialist regime, but his economic policies failed, and he was removed in an army coup in 1968. The constitution was suspended, political activity was banned, and government was placed in the hands of a Military Committee for National Liberation (CMLN) with Lt Moussa Traoré as president and head of state. In 1969 he became prime minister as well. He promised a return to civilian rule, and in 1974 a new constitution made Mali a one-party state. A new party, the UDPM, was announced in 1976. Despite student opposition to a one-party state and army objections to civilian rule, Traoré successfully made the transition so that by 1979 Mali had a constitutional government, while ultimate power lay with the party and the military establishment.

In 1983 Mali and Guinea signed an agreement for eventual economic and political integration. In 1985 a border dispute with Burkina Faso resulted in a five-day conflict that was settled by the Inter-

Mali
Republic of
(République du Mali)

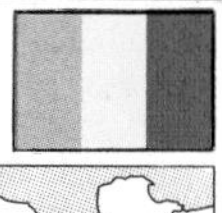

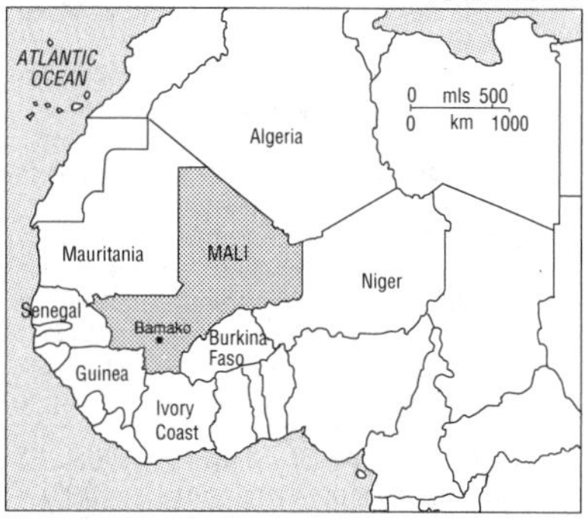
ATLANTIC
OCEAN
Algeria
0 mls 500
0 km 1000
Mauritania
MALI
Niger
Senegal
Bamako
Burkina
Faso
Guinea
Ivory
Coast

area 478,695 sq mi/1,240,142 sq km
capital Bamako
cities Mopti, Kayes, Ségou, Timbuktu
physical landlocked state with river Niger and savanna in S; part of the Sahara in N; hills in NE; Senegal River and its branches irrigate the SW
features ancient town of Timbuktu; railroad to Dakar is the only outlet to the sea
head of state and government Amadou Toumani Toure from 1991
political system one-party republic
political parties Malian People's Democratic Union (UDPM)), nationalist
exports cotton, peanuts, livestock, fish
currency franc CFA
population (1990 est) 9,182,000; growth rate 2.9% p.a.
life expectancy men 44, women 47 (1989)
language French (official), Bambara
religion Sunni Muslim 90%, animist 9%, Christian 1%
literacy 10% (1989)
GNP $1.6 bn (1987); $230 per head (1988)
chronology
1898 Came under French rule.
1959 With Senegal, formed the Federation of Mali.
1960 Became the independent Republic of Mali, with Mobido Keita as president.
1968 Keita replaced in an army coup by Moussa Traoré.
1974 New constitution made Mali a one-party state.
1976 New national party, the Malian People's Democratic Union, announced.
1983 Agreement between Mali and Guinea for eventual political and economic integration signed.
1985 War with Burkina Faso lasted 5 days, mediated by International Court of Justice.
1991 Demonstrations against one-party rule. Moussa Traore ousted in a coup led by Lt-Col Amadou Toumani Toure.

national Court of Justice. Traoré was overthrown in Mar 1991 by dissidents who installed a civilian premier and promised a multi-party democracy.

malic acid COOHCH$_2$ CH(OH)COOH an organic crystalline acid that can be extracted from apples, plums, cherries, grapes, and other fruits, but occurs in all living cells in smaller amounts, being one of the intermediates of ◊Krebs's cycle.

Mali Empire a Muslim state in NW Africa during the 7th–15th centuries. Thriving on its trade in gold, it reached its peak in the 14th century under Mansa Musa (reigned 1312–37), when it occupied an area covering present-day Senegal, Gambia, Mali, and S Mauritania. Mali's territory was similar to (though larger than) that of the ◊Ghana Empire, and gave way in turn to the ◊Songhai Empire.

Malik Yakob Alexandrovich 1906–1980. Soviet diplomat. He was permanent representative at the United Nations 1948–53 and 1968–76, and it was his walkout from the Security Council in Jan 1950 that allowed the authorization of UN intervention in Korea (see ◊Korean War).

Malines French name for ◊Mechelen, city in Belgium.

Malinovsky Rodion Yakolevich 1898–1967. Russian soldier and politician. In World War II he fought at Stalingrad, commanded in the Ukraine, and led the advance through the Balkans to capture Budapest 1945. He was minister of defense 1957–67.

Malinowski Bronislaw 1884–1942. Polish-born British anthropologist, one of the founders of the theory of ◊functionalism in the social sciences. His classic study of the peoples of the Trobriand Islands led him to see customs and practices in terms of their function in creating and maintaining social order.

Malipiero Gian Francesco 1882–1973. Italian composer and editor of ◊Monteverdi and ◊Vivaldi. His own works include operas based on Shakespeare's *Julius Caesar* 1934–35 and *Antony and Cleopatra* 1936–37 in a Neo-Classical style.

mallard common wild duck *Anas platyrhynchos*, found almost worldwide, from which domestic ducks were bred. The male, which can grow to a length of 2 ft/60 cm, usually has a green head and brown breast, while the female is mottled brown. Mallards are omnivorous, dabbling ducks.

Mallarmé Stéphane 1842–1898. French poet who founded the Symbolist school with Paul Verlaine. His belief that poetry should be evocative and suggestive was reflected in *L'Après-midi d'un faune/Afternoon of a Faun* 1876, which inspired the composer Debussy. Later works are *Poésies complètes/Complete Poems* 1887, *Vers et prose/Verse and Prose* 1893, and the prose *Divagations/Digressions* 1897.

Malle Louis 1932– . French film director. After a period as assistant to Robert Bresson, he directed *Les Amants/The Lovers* 1958, audacious for its time in its explicitness. His subsequent films, made in France and the USA, include *Zazie dans le métro* 1961, *Viva Maria* 1965, *Pretty Baby* 1978, *Atlantic City* 1980, and *Au Revoir les enfants* 1988.

mallee small trees and shrubs of the genus *Eucalyptus* with many small stems and thick underground roots that retain water. Before irrigation farming began, dense thickets of mallee characterized most of NW Victoria, Australia, known as the mallee region.

Mallorca Spanish form of ◊Majorca, an island in the Mediterranean.

mallow any plant of the family Malvaceae, especially the genus *Malva*, including the North American rose mallow *Hibiscus palustris* and the European marsh mallow *Althaea officinalis*. Most have showy pink or purple flowers. See also ◊hollyhock, ◊cotton, ◊okra, ◊hibiscus.

Malmédy town in Liège, E Belgium 25 mi/40 km S of Aachen, in the region of Eupen et Malmédy.

Malmö industrial port (shipbuilding, engineering, textiles) in SW Sweden; population (1988) 231,000.

malnutrition the physical condition resulting from dietary deficiencies. These may be caused by lack of food resources (famine) or by lack of knowledge about ◊nutrition.

When essential nutrients are missing from the diet, opportunistic infection takes hold in weakened individuals, those with deficiency disease, and may kill before starvation occurs. A high global death rate linked to malnutrition has arisen from famine situations caused by global warming, droughts, and the ◊greenhouse effect as well as by sociopolitical factors, such as alcohol and drug abuse, poverty and war.

Malory Thomas 15th century. English author of the prose romance *Le Morte d'Arthur* about 1470. It is a translation from the French, modified by material from other sources, and it deals with the exploits of King Arthur's knights of the Round Table and the quest for the ◊Holy Grail.

Malory's identity is uncertain. He is thought to have been the Warwickshire landowner of that name who was member of Parliament for Warwick in 1445 and in 1451 and 1452 was charged with rape, theft, and attempted murder. If that is so, he must have compiled *Morte d'Arthur* during his 20 years in Newgate prison.

Malpighi Marcello 1628–1694. Italian physiologist who made many anatomical discoveries (still known by his name) in his microscope studies of animal and plant tissues.

Malplaquet, Battle of victory in 1709 of the British, Dutch, and Austrian forces over the French forces during the War of the ◊Spanish Succession. The village of Malplaquet is in Nord *département*, France.

malpractice in US law, ◊negligence by a professional person, usually a doctor, that may lead to an action for damages by the client. Such legal actions result in doctors having high insurance costs that are included in the high fees charged to their patients.

Malraux André 1901–1976. French writer. An active antifascist, he gained international renown for his novel *La Condition humaine/Man's Estate* 1933, set during the Nationalist/Communist Revolution in China in the 1920s. *L'Espoir/Days of Hope* 1937 is set in Civil War Spain, where he was a bomber pilot in the International Brigade. In World War II he supported the Gaullist resistance, and was minister of cultural affairs 1960–69.

malt in brewing, grain (barley, oats, or wheat) artificially germinated and then dried in a kiln. Malts are fermented to make beers or lagers, or fermented and then distilled to produce spirits such as whiskey.

Malta island in the Mediterranean, S of Sicily, E of Tunisia, and N of Libya.

government The 1974 constitution provides for a single-chamber legislature, the 65-member House of Representatives, elected by universal suffrage, through a system of proportional representation, for a five-year term. As formal head of state the president is elected by the House for a five-year term and appoints a prime minister and cabinet, drawn from and collectively responsible to the House, which may be dissolved within its five-year term. A 1987 amendment to the constitution made provision for any party winning more than 50% of the votes in a general election to be guaranteed a majority of seats in the House of Representatives, regardless of the number of seats actually won.

history Malta was occupied in turn by Phoenicia, Greece, Carthage, and Rome, and fell to the Arabs 870. In 1090 the Norman Count Roger of Sicily conquered Malta, and it remained under Sicilian rule until the 16th century, when the Holy Roman Emperor Charles V handed it over to the Knights of ◊St John of Jerusalem 1530. After a Turkish attack 1565 the knights fortified the island and held it until 1798, when they surrendered to Napoleon. After requesting British protection, Malta was annexed by Britain 1814 and became a leading naval base. A vital link in World War II, Malta came under heavy attack and was awarded the George Cross decoration.

The island was made self-governing 1947, and in 1955 Dom Mintoff, leader of the Malta Labor Party (MLP), became prime minister. In 1956 the MLP's proposal for integration with the UK was approved by a referendum but opposed by the conservative Nationalist Party, led by Dr Giorgio Borg Olivier. In 1958 Mintoff rejected the British proposals and resigned, causing a constitutional crisis. By 1961 both parties favored indepen-

Malta
Republic of
(Repubblika Ta'Malta)

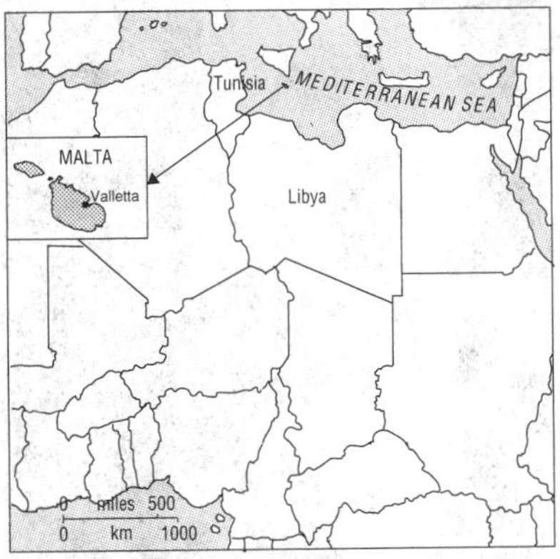
Tunisia
MEDITERRANEAN SEA
MALTA
Valletta
Libya
miles 500
km 1000

area 124 sq mi/320 sq km
capital (and port) Valletta
cities Rabat; port of Marsaxlokk
physical includes islands of Gozo 26 sq mi/67 sq km and Comino 1 sq mi/2.5 sq km
features occupies strategic location in central Mediterranean; large commercial dock facilities
head of state Vincent Tabone from 1989
head of government Edward Fenech Adami from 1987
political system liberal democracy
political parties Malta Labor Party (MLP), moderate, left-of-center; Nationalist Party, Christian, centrist, pro-European
exports vegetables, knitwear, handmade lace, plastics, electronic equipment
currency Maltese lira
population (1990 est) 373,000; growth rate 0.7% p.a.
life expectancy men 72, women 77 (1987)
language Maltese, English
religion Roman Catholic 98%
literacy 90% (1988)
GNP $1.6 bn; $4,750 per head (1988)
chronology
1814 Annexed to Britain by the Treaty of Paris.
1947 Achieved self-government.
1955 Dom Mintoff of the Malta Labor Party (MLP) became prime minister.
1956 Referendum approved proposal for integration with the UK. Proposal opposed by the Nationalist Party.
1958 MLP rejected the integration proposal.
1962 Nationalists elected, with Borg Olivier as prime minister.
1964 Independence achieved from Britain, within the Commonwealth. Ten-year defense and economic-aid treaty with UK signed.
1971 Mintoff reelected. 1964 treaty declared invalid and negotiations began for leasing the NATO base in Malta.
1972 Seven-year NATO agreement signed.
1974 Became a republic.
1979 British military base closed.
1984 Mintoff retired and was replaced by Mifsud Bonnici as prime minister and MLP leader.
1987 Edward Fenech Adami (Nationalist) elected prime minister.
1989 Vincent Tabone elected president. US–USSR summit held offshore.
1990 Formal application made for EC membership.

dence, and talks began 1962, with Borg Olivier as prime minister.

Malta became a fully independent state within the ◊Commonwealth and under the British crown in 1964, having signed a ten-year military and economic aid treaty with the UK. In 1971 Mintoff and the MLP returned to power with a policy of international nonalignment. He declared the 1964 treaty invalid and began to negotiate a new arrangement for leasing the Maltese NATO base and obtaining the maximum economic benefit from it for his country.

A seven-year agreement was signed 1972. Malta became a republic 1974, and in the 1976 general election the MLP was returned with a reduced majority. It again won a narrow majority in the House of Representatives 1981, even though the Nationalists had a bigger share of the popular vote. As a result, Nationalist MPs refused to take their seats for over a year. Relations between the two parties were also damaged by allegations of pro-government bias in the broadcasting service. At the end of 1984 Mintoff announced his retirement, and Dr Mifsud Bonnici succeeded him as MLP leader and prime minister. The Nationalist Party was elected in 1987 and its leader, Edward Fenech Adami, became prime minister. Malta was the site of the Dec 1989 summit meeting between US President Bush and Soviet President Gorbachev. In Oct 1990 Malta formally applied for EC membership.

Malta, Knights of another name for members of the military-religious order of the Hospital of ◊St John of Jerusalem.

maltase enzyme found in plants and animals that breaks down the disaccharide maltose into glucose.

Malthus Thomas Robert 1766–1834. English economist and cleric, whose *Essay on the Principle of Population* 1798 (revised 1803) argued for population control, since populations increase in geometric ratio and food supply only in arithmetic ratio.

maltose $C_{12}H_{22}O_{11}$ a ◊dissaccharide sugar in which both monosaccharide units are glucose.

It is produced by the enzymic hydrolysis of starch and is a major constituent of malt, produced in the early stages of beer and whiskey manufacture.

Maluku or ***Moluccas*** group of Indonesian islands
area 28,764 sq mi/74,500 sq km
capital Ambon, on Amboina
population (1980) 1,411,000
history as the Spice Islands, they were formerly part of the Netherlands East Indies, and the S Moluccas attempted secession from the newly created Indonesian republic from 1949; exiles continue agitation in the Netherlands.

Malvern English spa in Hereford and Worcester, on the E side of the Malvern Hills, which extend for about 10 mi/16 km, and have their high point in Worcester Beacon 1,395 ft/425 m; population (1981) 32,000. The Malvern Festival 1929–39, associated with Shaw and Elgar, was revived in 1977.

Maluku (Moluccas)

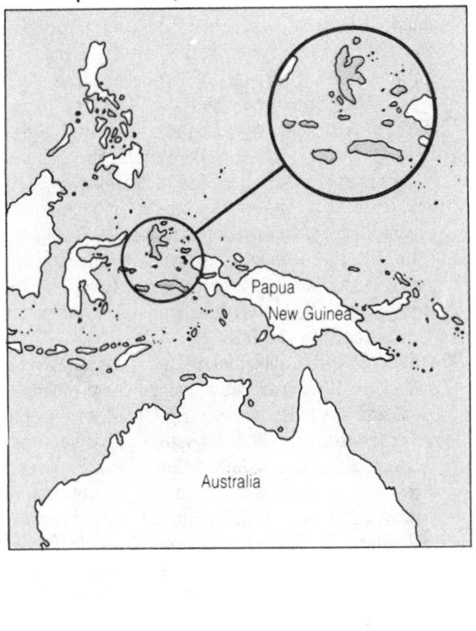
Papua
New Guinea
Australia

Malvinas Argentine name for the ◊Falkland Islands.

mamba one of two venomous snakes, genus *Dendroaspis*, of the cobra family Elapidae, found in Africa S of the Sahara. Unlike cobras they are not hooded.

The green mamba *D. angusticeps* is 5 ft/1.5 m long or more and lives in trees, feeding on birds and lizards. The black mamba *D. polylepis* is the largest venomous snake in Africa, occasionally as much as 11 ft/3.4 m long, and spends more time on the ground.

Mameluke member of a powerful political class which dominated Egypt from the 13th century until their massacre in 1811 by Mehmet Ali.

The Mamelukes were originally descended from freed Turkish slaves. They formed the royal bodyguard in the 13th century, and in 1250 placed one of their own number on the throne. Mameluke sultans ruled Egypt until the Turkish conquest of 1517, and they remained the ruling class until 1811.

Mamet David 1947– . US playwright. His plays, with their vivid, freewheeling language and sense of ordinary US life, include *American Buffalo* 1977, *Sexual Perversity in Chicago* 1978, and *Glengarry Glen Ross* 1984.

mammal any vertebrate that suckles its young and has hair including humans. Mammals maintain a constant body temperature in varied surroundings. Most mammals give birth to live young, but the platypus and echidna lay eggs. There are over 4,000 species, adapted to almost every way of life. The smallest shrew weighs only 0.07 oz/2 g, the largest whale up to 140 tons.

mammals: classification

order	*typical species*
Monotremata	kangaroo, koala, opossum
Insectivora	shrew, hedgehog, mole
Chiroptera	bat
Primates	lemur, monkey, ape, human
Edentata	anteater, armadillo, sloth
Pholidota	pangolin
Dermoptera	flying lemur
Rodentia	rat, mouse, squirrel, porcupine
Lagomorpha	rabbit, hare, pika
Cetacea	whale, dolphin
Carnivora	cat, dog, weasel, bear
Pinnipedia	seal, walrus
Artiodactyla	pig, deer, cattle, camel, giraffe
Perissodactyla	horse, rhinocerous, tapir
Sirenia	dugong, manatee
Tubulidentata	aardvark
Hyracoidea	hyrax
Proboscidea	elephant

mammary gland in female mammals, milk-producing gland derived from epithelial cells underlying the skin, active only after the production of young. In all but monotremes (egg-laying mammals), the mammary glands terminate in teats which aid infant suckling. The number of glands and their position vary between species. In humans there are two, in cows four, and in pigs between ten and fourteen.

The hatched young of monotremes simply lick milk from a specialized area of skin on the mother's abdomen.

mammography an X-ray procedure used to detect breast cancer at an early stage, before the tumors can be seen or felt.

Mammon an evil personification of wealth and greed; originally a Syrian god of riches, cited in the New Testament as being opposed to the Christian god.

mammoth extinct elephants of genus *Mammuthus*, whose remains are found worldwide. Some were 50% taller than modern elephants. The woolly mammoth *Elephas primigenius* of N zones, the size of an Indian elephant, had long fur, and large inward-curving tusks. Various species of mammoth were abundant in both the Old World and the New World in Pleistocene times, and were hunted by humans for food.

Mammoth Cave vast limestone cavern in Mammoth Cave National Park 1936, Kentucky. The main cave is 4 mi/6.5 km long, and rises to a height of 125 ft/38 m; it is known for its stalactites and stalagmites. Indian councils were once held here.

Mamoulian Rouben 1898–1987. Armenian-born US film director who lived in the US from 1923. After several years on Broadway he went to Hollywood, making the first sound version of *Dr Jekyll and Mr Hyde* 1932 and *Queen Christina* 1933. His later work includes *The Mark of Zorro* 1940 and *Silk Stockings* 1957.

Man. abbreviation for ◊Manitoba, Canadian province.

management process or technique of managing (organizing and operating) a business. Systems vary according to the size and type of organization, company, and objectives.

Since the early 1970s, there has been a growing demand for learned management skills, such as those taught in the Harvard Business School (US) and at the London Business School. By contrast, in Japan, such skills are learned on the job; employees tend to spend their careers with the same company and toward the end of it will acquire management status.

Managua capital and chief industrial city of Nicaragua, on the lake of the same name; population (1985) 682,000. It has twice been destroyed by earthquake and rebuilt, in 1931 and 1972; it was also badly damaged during the civil war in the late 1970s.

manakin any bird of the order Passeriformes, family Pipridae, found in South and Central America, about 6 in/15 cm long and often brightly colored. They feed on berries and other small fruits. The males of the genus *Manacus* clear a patch of the forest floor with a small tree as a display perch.

Manama (Arabic *Al Manamah*) capital and free trade port of Bahrain, on Bahrain Island; handles oil and entrepôt trade; population (1988) 152,000.

manatee any plant-eating aquatic mammal of the genus *Trichechus* constituting the family Trichechidae in the order Sirenia (sea cows). Manatees occur in marine bays and sluggish rivers, usually in turbid water.

The three species of Manatee are found on the E coasts of tropical North and South America, and around W Africa. All are in danger of becoming extinct. Their forelimbs are flippers; their hindlimbs are absent, but they have a short, rounded and flattened tail that is used for propulsion.

Manaus capital of Amazonas, Brazil, on the Rio Negro, near its confluence with the Amazon; population (1980) 612,000. It can be reached by sea-going vessels, although 1,000 mi/1,600 km from the Atlantic. Formerly a center of the rubber trade, it developed as a tourist center in the 1970s.

Manawatu river in North Island, New Zealand, rising in the Ruahine Range. Manawatu Plain is a rich farming area, specializing in dairying and fat lamb production.

Mancha see ◊La Mancha, former province of Spain.

Manche, La French name for the English ◊Channel. It gives its name to a French *département*.

Manchester city in NW England, on the river Irwell, 31 mi/50 km E of Liverpool

It is a manufacturing (textile machinery, chemicals, rubber, processed foods) and financial center; population (1985) 451,000. It is linked by the Manchester Ship Canal, built 1894, to the river Mersey and the sea.

features home of the Hallé Orchestra, the Northern College of Music, the Royal Exchange (built 1869, now a theater), a town hall (by Alfred Waterhouse), and a Cotton Exchange (now a leisure center).

history originally a Roman camp, Manchester is mentioned in the Domesday Book, and already by the 13th century was a center for the wool trade. Its damp climate made it ideal for cotton, introduced in the 16th century, and in the 19th century the Manchester area was a world center of manufacture, using cotton imported from North America and India. After 1945 there was a sharp decline, and many disused mills were refurbished to provide alternative industrial uses. Long a hub of ◊Radical thought, Manchester has always been a cultural and intellectual center; it was the original home of the *Guardian* (founded as the *Manchester Guardian* 1821). Pop music flourished there in the 1980s.

Manchu last ruling dynasty in China, from 1644 until their overthrow in 1912; their last emperor was the infant ◊P'u-i. Originally a nomadic people from Manchuria, they established power through a series of successful invasions from the north, then granted trading rights to the US and Europeans, which eventually brought strife and the ◊Boxer Rebellion.

Manchukuo former Japanese puppet state in Manchuria and Jehol 1932–45.

Manchuria European name for the NE region of China, comprising the provinces of Heilongjiang, Jilin, and Liaoning. It was united with China by the ◊Manchu dynasty 1644, but as the Chinese Empire declined, Japan and Russia were rivals for its control. The Russians were expelled after the ◊Russo-Japanese War 1904–05, and in 1932 Japan consolidated its position by creating a puppet state, Manchukuo, which disintegrated on the defeat of Japan in World War II.

Mandaean a member of the only surviving Gnostic sect of Christianity (see ◊Gnosticism). The Mandaeans live near the Euphrates, S Iraq, and their sacred book is the *Ginza*. The sect claims descent from John the Baptist, but its incorporation of Christian, Hebrew, and indigenous Persian traditions keeps its origins in dispute.

They are hostile to Jesus as the Christ but revere John the Baptist and see a universe where evil spirits try to keep souls from ascending to God.

mandala a symmetrical design in Hindu and Buddhist art, representing the universe; used in some forms of meditation.

Mandalay chief town of Upper Myanmar, on the river Irrawaddy, about 370 mi/495 km N of Yangon; population (1983) 533,000.

Founded by King Mindon Min in 1857, it was capital of Burma 1857–85, and has many pagodas, temples, and monasteries.

Mandarin (Sanskrit *mantrin* "counselor") the standard form of the ◊Chinese language. Historically it derives from the language spoken by mandarins, Chinese imperial officials, from the 7th century onward. It is used by 70% of the population and taught in schools of the People's Republic of China.

mandarin variety of the tangerine ◊orange *Citrus reticulata*.

mandate in history, a territory whose administration was entrusted to Allied states by the League of Nations under the Treaty of Versailles after World War I. Mandated territories were former German and Turkish possessions (including Iraq, Syria, Lebanon, and Palestine). When the United Nations replaced the League of Nations in 1945, mandates that had not achieved independence became known as ◊trust territories.

In general, mandate means any official command; in politics it is also the right (given by the electors) of an elected government to carry out its program of policies.

Mandela Nelson (Rolihlahla) 1918– . South African politician and lawyer. As organizer of the banned ◊African National Congress (ANC), he was acquitted of treason 1961, but was given a life sentence 1964 on charges of sabotage and plotting to overthrow the government. In prison he became a symbol of unity for the worldwide anti-apartheid movement. In Feb 1990 he was released, the ban on the ANC having been lifted. In July 1991 he was unopposed and was elected president of the ANC.

***Mandela** African National Congress leader Nelson Mandela, released by the South African government in 1990 after 27 years in prison, helped break down the apartheid system.*

Mandela Winnie (Nomzamo) 1934– . Civil-rights activist in South Africa and wife of Nelson Mandela. A leading spokesperson for the African National Congress during her husband's imprisonment 1964–90, she had been jailed for a year and put under house arrest several times. In 1991 a highly-controversial trial convicted her of kidnapping.

Mandelbrot Benoit B 1924– . Polish-born US scientist who coined the term fractal geometry to describe "self-similar" shape, a motif that repeats indefinitely, each time smaller. This is associated with chaos theory.

Mandelshtam Osip Emilevich 1891–1938. Russian poet. Son of a Jewish merchant, he was sent to a concentration camp by the communist authorities in the 1930s, and died there. His posthumously published work, with its classic brevity, established his reputation as one of the greatest 20th-century Russian poets. His wife Nadezhda's memoirs of her life with her husband, *Hope Against Hope*, were published in the West in 1970, but not until 1988 in the USSR.

mandolin musical instrument with four or five pairs of strings. It is descended from the ◊lute, and takes its name from its almond-shaped body (Italian *mandorla* "almond").

mandragora or ***mandrake*** plant of the Old World genus *Mandragora* of almost stemless plants with narcotic properties, of the nighshade family Solanaceae. They have large leaves, pale blue or violet flowers, and globose berries known as devil's apples.

The humanoid shape of the root of *M. officinarum* gave rise to the superstition that it shrieks when pulled from the ground.

mandrake another name for the plant mandragora.

mandrill large W African forest-living baboon *Mandrillus sphinx*, most active on the ground. The nose is bright red and the cheeks striped with blue. There are red callosities on the buttocks; the fur is brown, apart from a yellow beard, and it has large canine teeth like the drill *M. leucophaeus*, to which it is closely related.

Manes in Classical Roman religious belief, spirits of the dead worshiped as divine and associated with the gods of the underworld (◊Dis).

Manet Edouard 1832–1883. French painter, active

Manet *French painter Edouard Manet's* A Bar at the Folies-Bergère *1882.*

in Paris. Rebelling against the academic tradition, he developed a clear and unaffected Realist style. His subjects were mainly contemporary, such as *Un Bar aux Folies-Bergère/A Bar at the Folies-Bergère* 1882 (Courtauld Art Gallery, London).

Manet, born in Paris, trained under a history painter and was inspired by Goya and Velázquez and also by Courbet. His *Déjeuner sur l'herbe/Picnic on the Grass* 1863 and *Olympia* 1865 (both Musée d'Orsay, Paris) offended conservative tastes in their matter-of-fact treatment of the nude body. He never exhibited with the Impressionists, although he was associated with them from the 1870s.

mangabey any of the Old World monkeys of the tropical African genus *Cercocebus*. The four species have long tails that can be used for support, although they are not fully prehensile. They feed on shoots, leaves, fruit, and some animal food.

Mangalore industrial port at the mouth of the Netravati river in Karnataka, S India; population (1981) 306,000. Textiles, timber, and food processing are important industries.

manganese a hard, brittle, gray-white metallic element, symbol Mn, atomic number 25, atomic weight 54.9380. It resembles iron (and rusts), but it is not magnetic and is softer. It is used chiefly in making steel alloys, also alloys with aluminum and copper. It is used in fertilizers, paints, and industrial chemicals. It is a necessary trace element in human nutrition. The name is old, deriving from the French and Italian forms of Latin for *magnesia* (MgO), the white tasteless powder used as an antacid from ancient times.

manganese ore any mineral from which manganese is produced. The main ores are the oxides, such as pyrolusite, MnO_2; hausmannite, Mn_3O_4; and manganite, MnO(OH).

Manganese ores may accumulate in metamorphic rocks or as sedimentary deposits, frequently forming nodules on the sea floor (since the 1970s many schemes have been put forward to harvest deep-sea manganese nodules). The world's main producers are the USSR, South Africa, Brazil, Gabon, and India.

mangel wurzel or ***mangold*** variety of the common beet *Beta vulgaris* used chiefly as feed for cattle and sheep.

mango evergreen tree *Mangifera indica* of the cashew family Anacardiaceae, native to India but now widely cultivated for its oval fruits in other tropical and subtropical areas, for example the West Indies.

mangrove any of several shrubs and trees, especially of the mangrove family Rhizophoraceae, found in the muddy swamps of tropical coasts and estuaries. By sending down aerial roots from their branches, they rapidly form close-growing mangrove thickets. Their timber is impervious to water and resists marine worms.

Manhattan an island 12.5 mi/20 km long and 2.5 mi/4 km wide, lying between the Hudson and East rivers and forming a borough of the city of New York. It includes the Wall Street business center and Broadway theaters.

Manhattan Project code name for the development of the ◊atomic bomb in the US in World War II, to which the physicists Enrico Fermi and J Robert Oppenheimer contributed.

manic depression a mental disorder characterized by recurring periods of ◊depression which may or may not alternate with periods of inappropriate elation (mania) or overactivity. Sufferers may be genetically predisposed to the condition.

Some cases have been improved by taking prescribed doses of ◊lithium.

Manichaeism religion founded by the prophet Mani (Latinized as Manichaeus, c. 216–276). Despite persecution Manichaeism spread and flourished until about the 10th century. Based on the concept of dualism, it held that the material world is evil, an invasion of the spiritual realm of light by the powers of darkness; particles of divine light imprisoned in evil matter were to be rescued by messengers such as Jesus, and finally by Mani himself.

Mani proclaimed his creed in 241 at the Persian court. Returning from missions to China and India, he was put to death at the instigation of the Zoroastrian priesthood.

Manifest Destiny in US history, the belief that Americans had a providential mission to extend both their territory and their democratic processes westward across the continent. The phrase was coined by journalist John L O'Sullivan in 1845. Reflecting this belief, Texas and California were shortly afterwards annexed by the US. (See ◊Mexican War.)

Manila industrial port (textiles, tobacco, distilling, chemicals, shipbuilding) and capital of the Philippines, on the island of Luzon; population (1980) 1,630,000, metropolitan area (including ◊Quezon City) 5,926,000.

history Manila was founded 1571 by Spain, captured by the US 1898, and in 1945 during World War II the old city to the south of the river Pasig was reduced to rubble in fighting between US and Japanese troops. It was replaced as capital by Quezon City 1948–76.

manioc another name for the plant ◊cassava.

Manipur state of NE India

area 8,646 sq mi/22,400 sq km

capital Imphal

features Loktak Lake; original Indian home of polo

products grain, fruit, vegetables, sugar, textiles, cement

population (1981) 1,434,000

language Hindi

religion Hindu 70%

history administered from the state of Assam

mangrove *Mangrove swamp in Costa Rica. The extensive root system helps trap mud and silt. The trees are adapted to cope with the salt water that engulfs the roots at each high tide.*

Manitoba

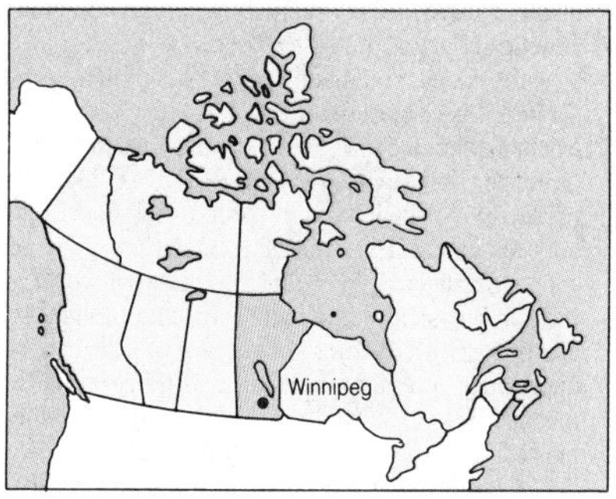
Winnipeg

until 1947 when it became a Union Territory. It became a state 1972.

Man, Isle of island in the Irish Sea, a dependency of the British crown, but not part of the UK
area 220 sq mi/570 sq km
capital Douglas
towns Ramsey, Peel, Castletown
features Snefell 2,035 ft/620 m; annual TT (Tourist Trophy) motorcycle races, gambling casinos, Britain's first free port, tax haven; tailless Manx cat; tourism, banking, and insurance are important
exports light engineering products
currency the island produces its own coins and notes in UK currency denominations
population (1986) 64,000
language English (Manx, nearer to Scottish than Irish Gaelic, has been almost extinct since the 1970s)
government crown-appointed lieutenant-governor, a legislative council, and the representative House of Keys, which together make up the Court of Tynwald, passing laws subject to the royal assent. Laws passed at Westminster only affect the island if specifically so provided
history Norwegian until 1266, when the island was ceded to Scotland; it came under UK administration 1765.

Manitoba prairie province of Canada
area 250,900 sq mi/650,000 sq km
capital Winnipeg
features lakes: Winnipeg, Winnipegosis, Manitoba; 50% forested
products grain, livestock, manufactured foods, transportation equipment, clothing and textiles, nickel, zinc, copper
population (1986) 1,071,000
history trading posts and forts built by fur traders 18th century. What came to be called the Red River settlement was first colonized 1811 by dispossessed Scottish highlanders; the colony became the Canadian province of Manitoba 1870, after the Riel Rebellion 1869 ended. The area of the province was extended 1881 and 1912.

Manitoba, Lake lake in Manitoba province, Canada, which drains into Lake Winnipeg to the NE through the river Dauphin; area 1,800 sq mi/4,700 sq km.

Manizales city in the Central Cordillera in W Colombia 7,000 ft/2,150 m above sea level, center of a coffee-growing area; population (1985) 328,000. It is linked with Mariquita by the world's longest overhead cable transport system 45 mi/72 km.

Manley Michael 1924– . Jamaican politician, prime minister 1972–80 and from 1989, adopting more moderate Socialist policies. His father, Norman Manley (1893–1969), was founder of the People's National Party and prime minister 1959–62.

Mann Anthony. Adopted name of Emil Anton Bundmann 1906–1967. US film director who made a series of violent but intelligent 1950s Westerns starring James Stewart, such as *Winchester '73* 1950. He also directed one of the best film epics, *El Cid* 1961. His other films include *The Glenn Miller Story* 1954 and *A Dandy in Aspic* 1968.

Mann Heinrich 1871–1950. German novelist who fled to the US in 1937 with his brother Thomas Mann. His books include *Im Schlaraffenland/In the Land of Cockaigne* 1901; *Professor Unrat/The Blue Angel* 1904, depicting the sensual downfall of a schoolmaster; a scathing trilogy dealing with the Kaiser's Germany *Das Kaiserreich/The Empire* 1918–25; and two volumes on the career of Henry IV of France 1935–38.

Mann Horace 1796–1859. US political leader and education reformer. He served in the Massachusetts House of Representatives 1827–33 and Massachusetts Senate 1835–37. In 1837, with the passage of a state public-school act, Mann resigned from the legislature to serve as the secretary of the state school board 1837–48. In that position he helped raise the level of funding and instruction for public education.

Born in Franklin, Massachusetts, Mann was educated at Brown University and was admitted to the bar 1823. After serving in the US House of Representatives 1848–53, Mann became president of Antioch College 1853–59.

Mann Thomas 1875–1955. German novelist and critic, concerned with the theme of the artist's relation to society. His first novel was ◊*Buddenbrooks* 1901, which, followed by *Der Zauberberg/The Magic Mountain* 1924, led to a Nobel Prize 1929. Later works include *Dr Faustus* 1947 and *Die Bekenntnisse des Hochstaplers Felix Krull/Confessions of Felix Krull* 1954. Notable among his works of short fiction is *Der Tod in Venedig/Death in Venice* 1913.

Mann worked in an insurance office in Munich and on the staff of the periodical *Simplicissimus*. His opposition to the Nazi regime forced him to leave Germany and in 1940 he became a US citizen. Among his other works are the biblical tetralogy on the theme of Joseph and his brothers 1933–44, and a number of short stories, including "Tonio Kröger" 1903.

manna a sweetish exudation obtained from many trees such as the ash and larch, and used in medicine. The manna of the Bible is thought to have been from the tamarisk tree, or a form of lichen.

Mannerheim Carl Gustav Emil von 1867–1951. Finnish general and politician, leader of the conservative forces in the civil war 1917–18 and regent 1918–19. He commanded the Finnish army 1939–40 and 1941–44, and was president of Finland 1944–46.

After the Russian Revolution 1917, a Red (Socialist) militia was formed in Finland with Russian backing, and independence was declared in Dec. The Red forces were opposed by a White (counterrevolutionary) army led by Mannerheim, who in 1918 crushed the Socialists with German assistance. In 1944, after leading the defense against Soviet invasion in two wars, he negotiated the peace settlement with the USSR and became president.

Mannerism in painting and architecture, a style characterized by a subtle but conscious breaking of the "rules" of Classical composition, for example, displaying the human body in an off-center, distorted pose, or by using harsh, nonblending colors. The term was coined by Giorgio ◊Vasari and used to describe the 16th-century reaction to the peak of Renaissance classicism as achieved by Raphael, Leonardo da Vinci, and the early Michelangelo.

The effect is to unsettle the viewer, who is expected to understand the norms that the Mannerist picture is deliberately violating. Strictly speaking, Mannerism refers to painters and architects in Italy (primarily Rome and Florence) during the years 1520 to 1575 beginning with, and largely derived from, the later works of Michelangelo in painting and architecture; it includes the works of the painters Giovanni Rosso and Parmigianino, and the architect Giulio Romano. The term has been extended, however, to cover similar ideas in other arts and in other countries.

Mannheim industrial city on the Rhine in Baden-Württemberg, Federal Republic of Germany; population (1988) 295,000. Industries include

manometer

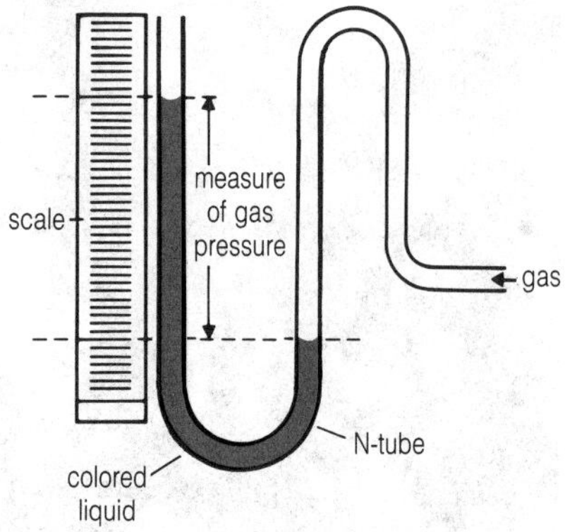
measure
of gas
pressure
scale
gas
N-tube
colored
liquid

heavy machinery, glass, earthenware, and chemicals. The modern symphony orchestra, with its balance of instruments and the vital role of the conductor, originated at Mannheim in the 18th century when the elector palatine assembled the finest players of his day.

Mannheim Karl 1893–1947. Hungarian sociologist who settled in the UK 1933. In *Ideology and Utopia* 1929 he argued that all knowledge, except in mathematics and physics, is ideological, a reflection of class interests and values; that there is therefore no such thing as objective knowledge or absolute truth.

Mannheim distinguished between ruling class ideologies and those of utopian or revolutionary groups, arguing that knowledge is thus created by a continual power struggle between rival groups and ideas. Later works such as *Man and Society* 1940 analyzed contemporary mass society in terms of its fragmentation and susceptibility to extremist ideas and totalitarian governments.

Manning Henry Edward 1808–1892. English priest, one of the leaders of the Oxford Movement. In 1851 he was converted to Roman Catholicism, and in 1865 became archbishop of Westminster. He was created a cardinal 1875.

Manoel two kings of Portugal, including:

Manoel I 1469–1521. King of Portugal from 1495, when he succeeded his uncle John II (1455–95). He was known as "the Fortunate," because his reign was distinguished by the discoveries made by Portuguese navigators and the expansion of the Portuguese empire.

manometer instrument for measuring the pressure of liquids (including human blood pressure) or gases. In its basic form, it is a U-tube partly filled with colored liquid; pressure of a gas entering at one side is measured by the level to which the liquid rises at the other.

manor basic economic unit in ◊feudalism in Europe, established in England under the Norman conquest. It consisted of the lord's house and cultivated land, land rented by free tenants, land held by villagers, common land, woodland, and waste land.

Here and there traces of the system survive in England—the common land may have become an area for public recreation—but the documents sometimes sold at auction and entitling the owner to be called "lord of the manor" seldom have any rights attached to them.

Man Ray adopted name of Emmanuel Rudnitsky 1890–1977. US photographer, painter, and sculptor, active mainly in France; associated with the Dada movement. His pictures often showed Surrealist images like the photograph *Le Violon d'Ingres* 1924.

Man Ray was born in Philadelphia, but lived mostly in Paris from 1921. He began as a painter and took up photography in 1915, the year he met the Dada artist Duchamp in New York. In 1922 he invented the rayograph, a black and white image obtained without a camera by placing objects on sensitized photographic paper and exposing them to light; he also used the technique of solarization

Mantegna *Italian Renaissance painter Andrea Mantegna's* The Agony in the Garden *c. 1455.*

(partly reversing the tones on a photograph). His photographs include portraits of many artists and writers.

Mansart Jules Hardouin 1646–1708. See ◊Hardouin-Mansart, Jules.

Mansfield industrial town (textiles, shoes, machinery, chemicals, coal) in Nottinghamshire, England, on the river Maun, 14 mi/22 km N of Nottingham; population (1981) 59,000.

Mansfield city in N central Ohio, NE of Columbus, seat of Richland County. An industrial city, its manufactures include automobile parts and steel and rubber products; population (1990) 50,627.

Mansfield Jayne. Adopted name of Vera Jayne Palmer 1933–1967. US actress who had a short career as a kind of living parody of Marilyn Monroe in films including *The Girl Can't Help It* 1956 and *Will Success Spoil Rock Hunter?* 1957.

manslaughter the unlawful killing of a human being in circumstances less culpable than ◊murder—for example, when the killer suffers extreme provocation; is in some way mentally ill (diminished responsibility); did not intend to kill but did so accidentally, or in the course of committing another crime, or by behaving with criminal recklessness; or is the survivor of a genuine suicide pact that involved killing the other person.

Mans, Le see ◊Le Mans.

Manson Patrick 1844–1922. Scottish physician who showed that insects are responsible for the spread of diseases like elephantiasis and malaria.

Manson spent many years in practice in the Far East. On his return to London, he founded the School of Tropical Medicine.

Mansûra industrial town (cotton) and capital of Dakahlia province, NE Egypt, on the Damietta branch of the Nile; population (1983) 310,900. Mansûra was founded about 1220; St Louis IX, king of France, was imprisoned in the fortress while on a Crusade, 1250.

manta another name for ◊devil ray, a large fish.

Mantegna Andrea c. 1431–1506. Italian Renaissance painter and engraver, active chiefly in Padua and Mantua, where some of his frescoes remain. Paintings such as *The Agony in the Garden* c. 1455 (National Gallery, London) reveal a dramatic linear style, mastery of perspective, and strongly Classical architectural detail.

Mantegna was born in Vicenza. Early works include frescoes for the Eremitani Church in Padua painted during the 1440s (badly damaged). From 1460 he worked for Ludovico Gonzaga in Mantua, producing an outstanding fresco series in the Ducal Palace (1470s) and later *The Triumph of Caesar* (Hampton Court, near London). He was influenced by the sculptor Donatello and in turn influenced the Venetian painter Giovanni Bellini (his brother-in-law) and the German artist Albrecht Dürer.

mantis any insect of the family Mantidae, related to cockroaches. Some species can reach a length of 8 in/20 cm. There are about 2,000 species of mantis, mainly tropical.

Mantises are often called "praying mantises" because of the way they hold their front legs,

mantis

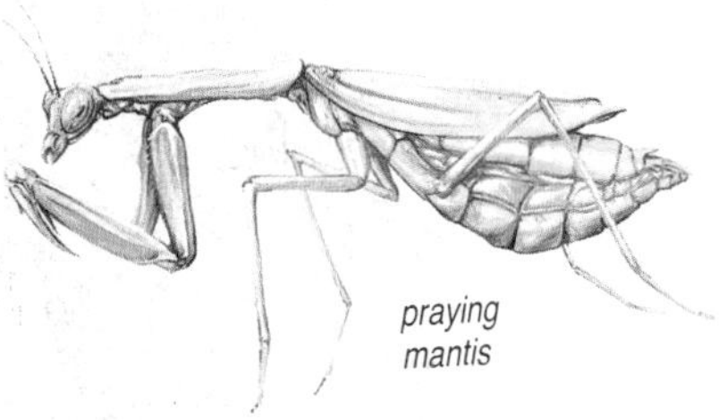
praying mantis

adapted for grasping prey, when at rest. The eggs are laid in Sept and hatch early in the following summer.

The 4 in/10 cm-long Chinese praying mantis, proficient at garden pest control, is now naturalized in North America.

mantissa in mathematics, the decimal part of a ◊logarithm. For example, the logarithm of 347.6 is 2.5411; in this case, the 0.5411 is the mantissa, and the integral (whole number) part of the logarithm, the 2, is the ◊characteristic.

mantle the intermediate zone of the Earth between the ◊crust and the ◊core. It is thought to consist of silicate minerals such as olivine and spinel.

The mantle is separated from the crust by the ◊Mohorovičić discontinuity, and from the core by the Gutenberg discontinuity. The patterns of seismic waves passing through it show that its uppermost as well as its lower layers are solid. However, from 45 mi/72 km to 155 mi/250 km in depth is a zone through which seismic waves pass more slowly (the "low-velocity zone"). The inference is that materials in this zone are close to their melting points and they are partly molten. The low-velocity zone is considered the ◊asthenosphere on which the solid lithosphere rides.

Mantle Mickey Charles 1931– . US baseball player. Signed by the New York Yankees, he broke into the major leagues 1951. A switchhitter with home-run power, Mantle also excelled as a centerfielder. In 1956 he won baseball's Triple Crown, leading the American League in batting average, home runs, and runs batted in. After playing 18 years with the Yankees, including 12 pennant-winning seasons and seven World Series championships, Mantle retired 1969 and was elected to the Baseball Hall of Fame 1974.

Born in Spavinaw, Oklahoma, Mantle was an exceptional high-school athlete in football and basketball as well as baseball.

mantra in Hindu or Buddhist belief, a word repeatedly intoned to assist concentration and develop spiritual power; for example *om*, which represents the names of Brahma, Vishnu, and Siva. Followers of a guru may receive their own individual mantra.

Mantua (Italian *Mantova*) capital of Mantua province, Lombardy, Italy, on an island of a lagoon of the river Mincio, SW of Verona; industry (chemicals, brewing, printing); population (1981) 60,866. The poet Virgil was born near Mantua, which dates from Roman times; it has Gothic palaces and a cathedral founded in the 12th century.

Manu in Hindu mythology, the founder of the human race, who was saved by ◊Brahma from a deluge.

Manuel II 1889–1932. King of Portugal 1908–10. He ascended the throne on the assassination of his father, Carlos I, but was driven out by a revolution 1910, and lived in England.

Manutius Aldus 1450–1515. Italian printer, established in Venice (which he made the publishing center of Europe) from 1490; he introduced ◊italic type and was the first to print books in Greek.

Manx Gaelic a form of ◊Gaelic language.

Manzoni Alessandro, Count Manzoni 1785–1873. Italian poet and novelist, author of the historical romance, *I promessi sposi/The Betrothed* 1825–27, set in Spanish-occupied Milan during the 17th century. Verdi's *Requiem* commemorates him.

Maoism form of communism based on the ideas and teachings of the Chinese communist leader ◊Mao Zedong. It involves an adaptation of ◊Marxism to suit conditions in China and apportions a much greater role to agriculture and the peasantry in the building of socialism, thus effectively bypassing the capitalist (industrial) stage envisaged by Marx.

Maori member of the indigenous Polynesian people of New Zealand, who numbered 294,200 in 1986, about 10% of the total population. In recent years there has been increased Maori consciousness, a demand for official status for the Maori language, and a review of the Waitangi Treaty of 1840 (under which the Maoris surrendered their lands to British sovereignty). The Maori Unity Movement/Kotahitanga was founded 1983 by Eva Rickard. The Maoris claim 70% of the country's land; they have secured a ruling that the fishing grounds of the far north belong solely to local tribes.

Maori language member of the Polynesian branch of the Malayo-Polynesian language family, spoken by the Maori people of New Zealand. Only one-third use the language today, but efforts are being made to strengthen it after a long period of decline and official indifference.

In Maori, New Zealand is *Aotearoa* ("land of the long white cloud") and European settlers are *Pakeha*, a term often used by white New Zealanders when constrasting themselves with the Maori.

Mao Zedong or ***Mao Tse-tung*** 1893–1976. Chinese political leader and Marxist theoretician. A founder of the Chinese Communist Party (CCP) 1921, Mao soon emerged as its leader. He organized the ◊Long March 1934–36 and the war of liberation 1937–49, following which he established a People's Republic and Communist rule in China; he headed the CCP and government until his death. His influence diminished with the failure of his 1958–60 ◊Great Leap Forward, but he emerged dominant again during the 1966–69 ◊Cultural Revolution. Mao adapted communism to Chinese conditions, as set out in the *Little Red Book*.

Mao, son of a peasant farmer in Hunan province, was once library assistant at Beijing University and a headmaster at Changsha. He became chief of CCP propaganda under the Guomindang (Nationalist) leader Sun Yat-sen (Sun Zhong Shan) until dismissed by Sun's successor Chiang Kai-shek (Jiang Jie Shi). In 1931–34 Mao set up a Communist republic at Jiangxi and, together with Zhu De, marshaled the Red Army and organized the Long March to Shaanxi to evade Nationalist suppressive tactics. CCP head from 1935, Mao secured an alliance with the Nationalist forces 1936–45 aimed at repelling the Japanese invaders. At Yen'an, he built up a people's republic 1936–47 and married his third wife ◊Jiang Qing 1939. Civil war with the Nationalists was renewed from 1946 until 1949 when Mao defeated them at Nanking and established the People's Republic and Communist party rule under his leadership. During the civil war, he successfully employed mobile, rural-based guerrilla tactics.

Mao served as party head until his death Sept 1976 and as state president until 1959. After the

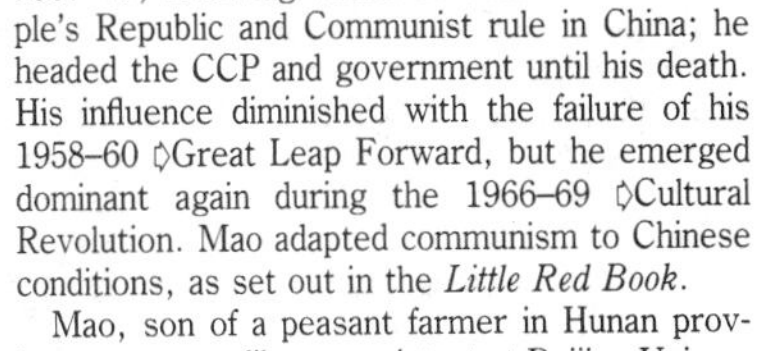

Mao Zedong *Chairman Mao with vice-chair Lin Biao, who is holding the* Little Red Book *of Mao's thoughts.*

maple

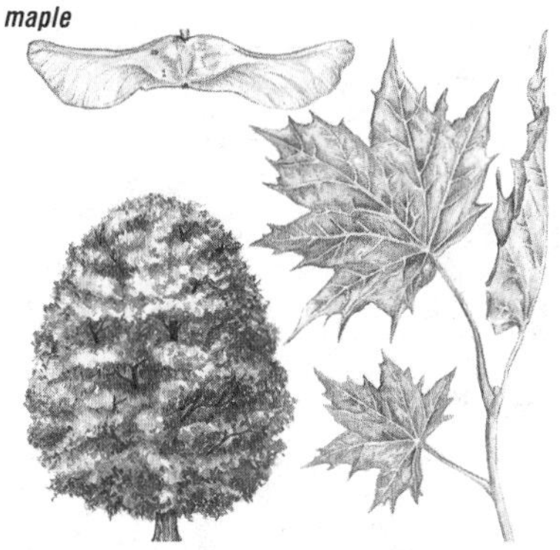

map projection

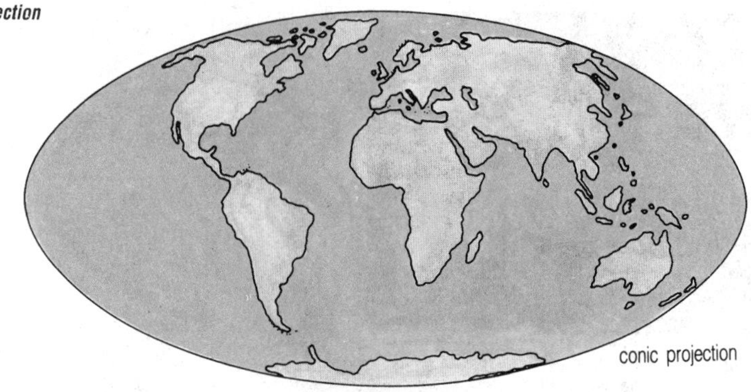

conic projection

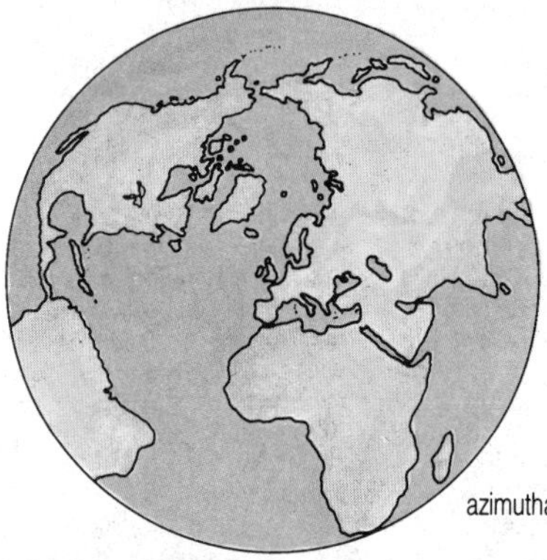

azimuthal projection

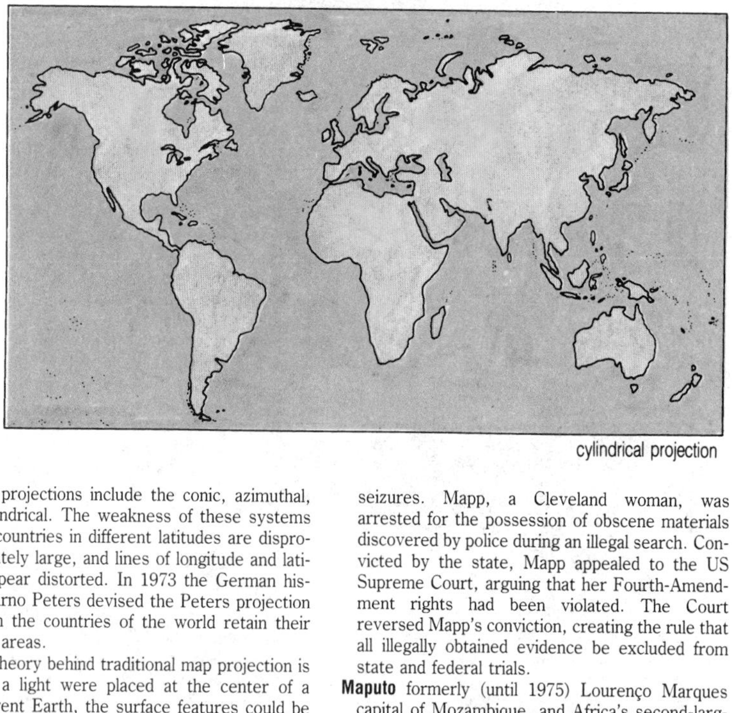

cylindrical projection

damages of the Cultural Revolution, the Great Helmsman, as he was called, working with his prime minister Zhou Enlai, oversaw a period of reconstruction from 1970 until deteriorating health weakened his political grip in the final years.

Mao's writings and thoughts dominated the functioning of the People's Republic 1949–76. He wrote some 2,300 publications, comprising 3 million words; 740 million copies of his *Quotations* have been printed. He stressed the need for rural rather than urban-based revolutions in Asia, for reducing rural-urban differences, and for perpetual revolution to prevent the emergence of new elites. Mao helped precipitate the Sino-Soviet split 1960 and was a firm advocate of a ◊nonaligned Third World strategy. Since 1978, the leadership of Deng Xiaoping has reinterpreted Maoism, and criticized its policy excesses, but many of Mao's ideas remain valued.

map a diagrammatic representation of an area, for example part of the Earth's surface, or the distribution of the stars. Modern maps of the Earth are made using aerial photography; a series of overlapping stereoscopic photographs is taken which can then be used to prepare a three-dimensional image.

Laser beams, microwaves, and infrared equipment are also used for land surveying, and satellite pictures make a valuable contribution when large areas are being mapped. Many different kinds of ◊map projection (the means by which a three-dimensional body is shown in two dimensions) are used in map-making. Detailed maps requiring constant updating are kept in digital form on computer so that minor revisions can be made without redrafting.

Map Walter c. 1140–c. 1209. Welsh cleric and satirist in the service of Henry II as an itinerant justice in England; envoy to Alexander III of Scotland. His *De Nugis Curialium* was a collection of gossip and scandal from royal and ecclesiastical courts.

Mapai (Miphlegeth Poale Israel) the Israeli Workers' Party or Labour Party, founded 1930. Its leading figure until 1965 was David Ben-Gurion. In 1968, the party allied with two other democratic Socialist parties to form the Israeli Labour Party, led initially by Levi Eshkol and later by Golda Meir.

maple deciduous tree of the genus *Acer*, family Aceraceae, with lobed leaves and green flowers, followed by two-winged fruits, or samaras. There are over 200 species, chiefly in northern temperate regions.

A. campestre and *A. pseudoplatanus*, the ◊sycamore or great maple, are native to Europe.

About 12 species are native to North America. The North American sugar maple *A. saccharum* is a source of maple syrup. The European plane tree—sometimes erroneously called sycamore—has been introduced worldwide.

map projection ways of depicting the spherical surface of the Earth on a flat piece of paper. Traditional projections include the conic, azimuthal, and cylindrical. The weakness of these systems is that countries in different latitudes are disproportionately large, and lines of longitude and latitude appear distorted. In 1973 the German historian Arno Peters devised the Peters projection in which the countries of the world retain their relative areas.

The theory behind traditional map projection is that, if a light were placed at the center of a transparent Earth, the surface features could be thrown as shadows on a piece of paper close to the surface. This paper may be flat and placed on a pole (azimuthal or zenithal), or may be rolled around the equator (cylindrical), or may be in the form of a tall cone resting on the equator (conical). The resulting maps differ from one another, distorting either area or direction, and each is suitable for a particular purpose. For example, projections distorting area the least are used for distribution maps, and those with least distortion of direction are used for navigation charts. ◊Mercator's projection dates from 1569.

Mapp v Ohio a US Supreme Court decision 1961 dealing with the admission into criminal trials of evidence procured through illegal searches and seizures. Mapp, a Cleveland woman, was arrested for the possession of obscene materials discovered by police during an illegal search. Convicted by the state, Mapp appealed to the US Supreme Court, arguing that her Fourth-Amendment rights had been violated. The Court reversed Mapp's conviction, creating the rule that all illegally obtained evidence be excluded from state and federal trials.

Maputo formerly (until 1975) Lourenço Marques capital of Mozambique, and Africa's second-largest port, on Delagoa Bay; population (1986) 883,000. Linked by rail with Zimbabwe and South Africa, it is a major outlet for minerals, steel, textiles, processed foods, and furniture.

maquis mostly evergreen vegetation common in many Mediterranean countries, consisting of scrub woodland with many low-growing tangled bushes and shrubs, typically including species of broom, gorse, and heather.

Maquis French ◊Resistance movement that fought against the German occupation during World War II.

mara one of two species of rodents, genus *Dolichotis* of the guinea-pig family, occurring in Argentina, with long back limbs and a short tail. They

Buitoni

Maradona *Argentine soccer forward Diego Maradona starred in South America and Europe.*

can grow to 2.5 ft/75 cm long and are sometimes known as "Patagonian cavies" or "hares."

Mara (Sanskrit "killing") in Buddhism, a supernatural being who attempted to distract the Buddha from the meditations that led to his enlightenment. In Hinduism, a goddess of death.

marabou stork *Leptoptilos crumeniferus* found in Africa. It is about 4 ft/120 cm tall, has a bald head, and eats snakes, lizards, insects, and carrion. It is largely dark gray and white and has an inflatable throat pouch.

Maracaibo oil-exporting port in Venezuela, on the channel connecting Lake Maracaibo with the Gulf of Venezuela; population (1981) 889,000.

Maracaibo, Lake lake in a rich oil-producing region in NW Venezuela; area 5,400 sq mi/14,000 sq km.

Maradona Diego 1960– . Argentine soccer player who helped his country to win the ◊World Cup 1986.

He left South America for Barcelona, Spain, 1982, and moved to Napoli, Italy, 1984, and contributed to their first Italian League title. In the early 1990s his drug abuse problems led to suspension from playing.

Marat Jean Paul 1743–1793. French Revolutionary leader and journalist. He was elected in 1792 to the National Convention, where he carried on a long struggle with the ◊Girondins, ending in their overthrow in May 1793. In July he was murdered by Charlotte ◊Corday.

Marat was a hero of the Paris revolutionary crowds. He was killed in his bath, where he generally worked, while treating a skin condition.

marathon athletics endurance race over 26 mi/42.195 km 385 yd. It was first included in the Olympic Games in Athens 1896. The distance varied until it was standardized in 1924. More recently, races have been opened to wider participation, including social runners as well as those competing at senior level.

The marathon derives its name from the story of Pheidippides, a Greek soldier who ran the distance of approximately 24 mi/39 km from the battlefield of Marathon to Athens with the news of a Greek victory over the Persians in 490 BC.

The current marathon distance was first used at the 1908 Olympic Games in London when the race was increased by an extra 385 yards so the race would finish in front of the royal box. The

A. MARAT
DAVID

Marat *French revolutionary Jean Paul Marat, murdered in his bath, was immortalized by painter Jacques-Louis David in* The Death of Marat *1793.*

best known US marathons are run annually in Boston, New York City, and Los Angeles.

Marathon, Battle of 490 BC. Fought between the Greeks, who were ultimately victorious, and invading Persians on the plain of Marathon, NE of Athens. Before the battle, news of the Persian destruction of the Greek city of Eretria was taken from Athens to Sparta by a courier, Pheidippides, who fell dead on arrival. His feat is commemorated by the marathon race.

marble metamorphosed ◊limestone that takes and retains a good polish; it is used in building and sculpture. In its pure form it is white and consists almost entirely of calcite $CaCO_3$. Mineral impurities give it various colors and patterns. Carrara, Italy, is known for white marble.

Marburg manufacturing town (chemicals, machinery, pottery) in Hessen, Germany, on the river Lahn, 50 mi/80 km N of Frankfurt-am-Main; population (1984) 77,300. The university 1527 was founded as a center of Protestant teaching. Luther and Zwingli disputed on religion at Marburg in 1529.

Marburg disease or ***green monkey disease*** viral disease of central Africa, first occurring in Europe in 1967 among research workers in Germany working with African green monkeys. It is characterized by hemorrhage of the mucous membranes, fever, vomiting, and diarrhea; mortality is high.

Marbury v Madison a US Supreme Court decision 1803 that affirmed the process of judicial review over Congressional acts. The plaintiff, William Marbury, had been appointed the District of Columbia's justice of the peace by President J Adams shortly before Jefferson replaced Adams in office, but the new secretary of state, James Madison, withheld the letter of appointment. Marbury appealed to the Court to force Madison to produce the letter by issuing a writ of mandamus, a power granted by Congress in the Judiciary Act of 1789. The Court ruled unanimously that Congress did not have the right to expand judiciary powers. Since writs of mandamus were not provided for in the Constitution, the Court was not empowered to issue them. This was the first time the Court nullified an act of Congress on the basis of constitutionality.

Marc Franz 1880–1916. German Expressionist painter, associated with Wassily Kandinsky in founding the ◊*Blaue Reiter* movement. Animals played an essential part in his view of the world, and bold semiabstracts of red and blue horses are characteristic of his work.

Marceau Marcel 1923– . French mime artist. He is the creator of the clown-harlequin Bip and mime sequences such as "Youth, Maturity, Old Age, and Death."

Marchais Georges 1920– . Leader of the French Communist Party (PCF) from 1972. Under his leadership, the party committed itself to a "transition to socialism" by democratic means and entered into a union of the left with the Socialist Party (PS). This was severed 1977, and the PCF returned to a more orthodox pro-Moscow line, since when its share of the vote has decreased.

Marchand Jean Baptiste 1863–1934. French general and explorer. In 1898, he headed an expedition in Africa from the French Congo, which occupied the town of Fashoda (now Kodok) on the White Nile. The subsequent arrival of British troops under Kitchener resulted in a crisis that nearly led to war between Britain and France.

Marche region of E central Italy consisting of the provinces of Ancona, Ascoli Piceno, Macerata, and Pesaro e Urbino; capital Ancona; area 3,744 sq mi/9,700 sq km; population (1988) 1,429,000.

marches the boundary areas of England with Wales, and England with Scotland. In the Middle Ages these troubled frontier regions were held by lords of the marches, sometimes called *marchiones* and later earls of March. The 1st Earl of March of the Welsh marches was Roger de Mortimer (c. 1286–1330); of the Scottish marches, Patrick Dunbar (died 1285).

Marcian 396–457. Eastern Roman emperor 450–457. He was a general who married Pulcheria, sister of Theodosius II, and became emperor at the latter's death. He convened the Council of ◊Chalcedon in 451 and refused to pay tribute to Attila the Hun.

Marciano Rocky (Rocco Francis Marchegiano) 1923–1969. US boxer, world heavyweight champion 1952–56. He retired after 49 professional fights, the only heavyweight champion to retire undefeated.

CAREER HIGHLIGHTS

Professional fights: 49
wins: 49
knockouts: 43
defeats: 0
1st professional fight: March 17, 1947 v. Lee Epperson
last professional fight: Sept 21, 1955 v. Archie Moore

Marc Blue Horse *by German Expressionist painter Franz Marc.*

Marconi Italian inventor Guglielmo Marconi whose pioneering work on radio ("wireless telegraphy") earned him a Nobel Prize in 1909.

Born in Brockton, Massachusetts, he was known as the "Brockton Blockbuster." He knocked out 43 of his 49 opponents. Marciano was killed in a plane crash.

Marconi Guglielmo 1874–1937. Italian electrical engineer and pioneer in the invention and development of radio. In 1895 he achieved radio communication over more than a mile, and in England in 1896 he conducted successful experiments that led to the formation of the company that became Marconi's Wireless Telegraph Company Ltd. He shared the Nobel Prize for Physics 1909.

After reading about radio waves, he built a device to convert them into electrical signals. He then tried to transmit and receive radio waves over increasing distances. In 1898 he successfully transmitted signals across the English Channel, and in 1901 established communication with St John's, Newfoundland, from Poldhu in Cornwall, and in 1918 with Australia.

Marco Polo bridge incident a conflict 1937 between Chinese and Japanese army troops on the border of Japanese-controlled ◊Manchukuo and China that led to full-scale war between the two states. It lasted until the Japanese surrender 1945.

Marcos Ferdinand 1917–1989. Filipino right-wing politician, president from 1965 to 1986, when he was forced into exile in Hawaii. He was backed by the US when in power, but in 1988 US authorities indicted him and his wife Imelda Marcos (1931–) for racketeering, embezzlement, and defrauding US banks; she was acquitted after his death.

Marcos was convicted while a law student 1939 of murdering a political opponent of his father, but eventually secured his own acquittal. In World War II he was a guerrilla fighter, survived the Japanese prison camps, and became president 1965. His regime became increasingly repressive, with secret pro-Marcos groups terrorizing and executing his opponents. He was overthrown and exiled 1986 by a popular front led by Corazón ◊Aquino, widow of a murdered opposition leader. A US grand jury investigating Marcos and his wife alleged that they had embezzled over $100 million from the government of the Philippines, received bribes, and defrauded US banks. Marcos was too ill to stand trial.

Marcus Aurelius Antoninus AD 121–180. Roman emperor from 161 and Stoic philosopher. Although considered one of the best of the Roman emperors, he persecuted the Christians for political reasons. He wrote the philosophical *Meditations*.

Born in Rome, he was adopted (at the same time as Lucius Aurelius Verus) by his uncle, the emperor Antoninus Pius, whom he succeeded in 161. He conceded an equal share in the rule to Lucius Verus (died 169). Marcus Aurelius spent much of his reign warring against the Germanic tribes and died in Pannonia, where he had gone to drive back the invading Marcomanni.

Marcuse Herbert 1898–1979. US political philosopher, born in Germany. His theories, combining Marxism and Freudianism, greatly influenced the radicalism of the 1960s and 1970s. He preached the overthrow of the existing social order by using the system's very tolerance to ensure its defeat, but he was not an advocate of violent revolution.

A refugee from Hitler's Germany, Marcuse came to the US 1934. He taught philosophy at several universities, including Columbia 1934–40, Brandeis 1954–65, and the University of California at San Diego 1965–79. He wrote several books, including *Eros and Civilization* 1955 and *One-Dimensional Man* 1964.

Mardi Gras (French "fat Tuesday" from the custom of using up all the fat in the household before the beginning of ◊Lent) Shrove Tuesday. A festival was traditionally held on this day in Paris, and there are carnivals in many parts of the world, including New Orleans, Louisiana; Italy; and Brazil.

Marduk in Babylonian mythology, the sun god, creator of Earth and humans.

mare (plural maria) dark lowland plain on the Moon. The name comes from Latin "sea," because these areas were once wrongly thought to be water.

Marengo, Battle of defeat of the Austrians by the French emperor Napoleon on 14 Jun 1800, as part of his Italian campaign, near the village of Marengo in Piedmont, Italy.

Margaret (Rose) 1930– . Princess of the UK, younger daughter of George VI and sister of Elizabeth II. In 1960 she married Anthony Armstrong-Jones, later created Lord Snowdon, but were divorced 1978. Their children are David, Viscount Linley (1961–) and Lady Sarah Armstrong-Jones (1964–).

Margaret the Maid of Norway 1282–1290. Queen of Scotland from 1285, the daughter of Eric II, king of Norway, and Princess Margaret of Scotland. When only two years old she became queen of Scotland on the death of her grandfather, Alexander III, but died in the Orkneys on the voyage from Norway to her kingdom.

Her great-uncle Edward I of England arranged her marriage to his son Edward, later Edward II. Edward declared himself overlord of Scotland by virtue of the marriage treaty, and 20 years of civil war and foreign intervention followed.

Margaret, St 1045–1093. Queen of Scotland, the granddaughter of King Edmund Ironside of England. She went to Scotland after the Norman Conquest, and soon after married Malcolm III. The marriage of her daughter Matilda to Henry I united the Norman and English royal houses.

Through her influence, the Lowlands, until then purely Celtic, became largely anglicized. She was canonized 1251 in recognition of her benefactions to the church.

Margaret of Anjou 1430–1482. Queen of England from 1445, wife of ◊Henry VI of England. After the outbreak of the Wars of the ◊Roses in 1455, she acted as the leader of the Lancastrians, but was defeated and captured at the battle of Tewkesbury 1471 by Edward IV.

Her one object had been to secure the succession of her son, Edward (born 1453), who was killed at Tewkesbury. After five years' imprisonment Margaret was allowed in 1476 to return to her native France, where she died in poverty.

margarine a butter substitute invented by the French chemist Hippolyte Mège-Mouries 1889. Modern margarines are usually made from vegetable oils, such as soy, corn, or sunflower oil, giving a product low in saturated fats ◊polyunsaturate and fortified with vitamins A and D.

Margate town and seaside resort on the N coast of Kent, SE England; industry (textiles, scientific instruments); population (1981) 53,280. It has a fine promenade and beach.

margay small cat *Felis wiedi* found from southern US to South America in forested areas, where it hunts birds and small mammals. It is about 2 ft/60 cm long with a 1.3 ft/40 cm tail, has a rounded head, and has black spots and blotches on a yellowish brown coat.

margin in finance, the difference between cost and selling price; also cash or collateral on deposit with a broker or lender to meet legal requirements against loss, as when stocks and other securities have been financed by funds supplied by the lender.

Margin accounts were set at 10% of the selling price before the stock market crash of 1929. Since the establishment of the ◊Securities and Exchange Commission 1934, margin was set at 50%.

marginal theory in economics, the study of the effect of increasing a factor by one more unit (known as the marginal unit). For example, if a firm's production is increased by one unit, its costs will increase also; the increase in costs is called the marginal cost of production. Marginal theory is a central tool of microeconomics.

margrave German title (equivalent of marquess) for the "counts of the march," who guarded the frontier regions of the Holy Roman Empire from Charlemagne's time. Later the title was used by other territorial princes. Chief among these were the margraves of Austria and of Brandenburg.

Margrethe II 1940– . Queen of Denmark from 1972, when she succeeded her father Frederick IX. In 1967, she married the French diplomat Count Henri de Laborde de Monpezat, who took the title Prince Hendrik. Her heir is Crown Prince Frederick (1968–).

marguerite European plant *Leucanthemum vulgare* of the daisy family Compositae. It is a shrubby perennial and bears white daisylike flowers. Marguerite is also the name of a cultivated variety of ◊chrysanthemum.

Marguerite of Navarre also known as ***Margaret d'Angoulême*** 1492–1549. Queen of Navarre from 1527, French poet, and author of the *Heptaméron* 1558, a collection of stories in imitation of Boccaccio's *Decameron*. The sister of Francis I of France, she was born in Angoulême. Her second husband 1527 was Henri d'Albret, king of Navarre.

Mari autonomous republic of the USSR, E of Gorky and W of the Urals

area 8,900 sq mi/23,200 sq km

capital Yoshkar-Ola

features the Volga flows through the SW; 60% is forested

products timber, paper; grain, flax, potatoes, fruit

population (1985) 725,000; about 43% are ethnic Mari

history the Mari were conquered by Russia in 1552. Mari was made an autonomous region 1920, an autonomous republic 1936.

Mariana Islands or ***Marianas*** archipelago in the NW Pacific E of the Philippines, divided politically into ◊Guam (an unincorporated territory of the US) and Northern Marianas (a commonwealth of the USA with its own internal government, of 16 mountainous islands, extending 350 mi/560 km N from Guam)

area 185 sq mi/480 sq km

capital Garapan on Saipan

products sugar, coconuts, coffee

currency US dollar

population (1988) 21,000, mainly Micronesian

language Chamorro 55%, English

religion mainly Roman Catholic

government own constitutionally elected government

Marianas

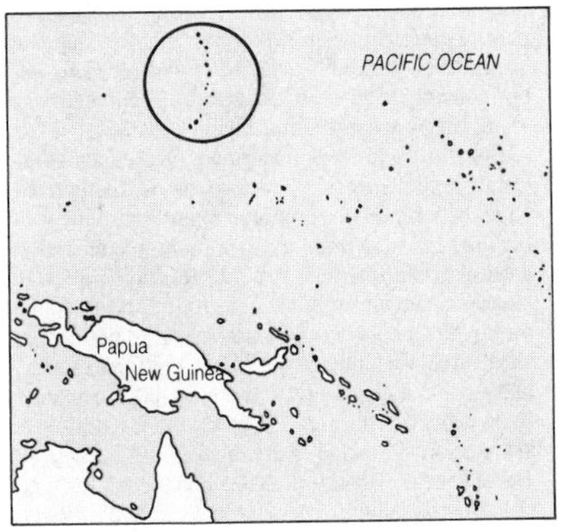
PACIFIC OCEAN
Papua
New Guinea

history sold to Germany by Spain 1899. The islands were mandated by the League of Nations to Japan 1918, and taken by US Marines 1944–45 in World War II. The islands were part of the US Trust Territory of the Pacific 1947–78. Since 1978 they are a commonwealth of the US.

Mariana Trench the lowest region on the Earth's surface; the deepest part of the sea floor. The trench is 1,500 mi/2,400 km long and is situated 200 mi/300 km E of the Mariana Islands, in the NW Pacific Ocean. Its deepest part is the gorge known as the Challenger Deep, which extends 36,201 ft/11,034 m below sea level.

Marianne symbolic figure of the French republic, dating from the Revolution. Statues of her adorn public buildings in France. Her name combines those of the Virgin Mary and St Anne.

Mariánské Lázně (German *Marienbad*) spa town in Czechoslovakia. An international reputation for its healthy waters was established before World War II; population (1981) 17,950. The water of its springs, which contains ◊Glauber's salts, has been used medicinally since the 16th century.

Maria Theresa 1717–1780. Empress of Austria from 1740, when she succeeded her father, the Holy Roman Emperor Charles VI; her claim to the throne was challenged and she became embroiled, first in the War of the ◊Austrian Succession 1740–48, then in the ◊Seven Years' War 1756–63; she remained in possession of Austria but lost Silesia. The rest of her reign was peaceful and, with her son Joseph II, she introduced social reforms.

After 1763 she pursued a consistently peaceful policy, concentrating on internal reforms; although her methods were despotic, she fostered education, codified the laws, and abolished torture. She also expelled the Jesuits. In these measures she was assisted by her son, Joseph II, who became emperor 1765, and succeeded her in the Hapsburg domains.

Maribor (German *Marburg*) resort city on the river Drave in Slovenia, Yugoslavia, with a 12th-century cathedral and some industry (boots and shoes, railroad rolling stock); population (1981) 185,500. Maribor dates from Roman times.

Marie 1875–1938. Queen of Romania. She was the daughter of the duke of Edinburgh, second son of Queen Victoria, and married Prince Ferdinand of Romania in 1893 (he was king 1922–27). She wrote a number of literary works, notably *Story of My Life* 1934–35. Her son Carol became king of Romania, and her daughters, Elisabeth and Marie, queens of Greece and Yugoslavia respectively.

Marie Antoinette 1755–1793. Queen of France from 1774. She was the daughter of Empress Maria Theresa of Austria, and married ◊Louis XVI of France in 1770. Her reputation for extravagance helped provoke the ◊French Revolution of 1789. She was tried for treason in Oct 1793 and guillotined.

Marie Antoinette influenced her husband to resist concessions in the early days of the Revolution, for example, ◊Mirabeau's plan for a constitutional settlement. She instigated the disastrous flight to Varennes, which discredited the monarchy, and welcomed foreign intervention against the Revolution, betraying French war strategy to the Austrians in 1792.

Marie de France c. 1150–1215. French poet, thought to have been the half-sister of Henry II of England, and abbess of Shaftesbury 1181–1215. She wrote *Lais* (verse tales that dealt with Celtic and Arthurian themes) and *Ysopet*, a collection of fables.

Marie de' Medici 1573–1642. Queen of France, wife of Henry IV from 1600, and regent (after his murder) for their son Louis XIII. She left the government to her favorites, the Concinis, until in 1617 Louis XIII seized power and executed them. She was banished, but after she led a revolt in 1619, ◊Richelieu effected her reconciliation with her son. When she attempted to oust him again in 1630, she was exiled.

Marie Louise 1791–1847. Queen consort of Napoleon I from 1810 (after his divorce from Josephine), mother of Napoleon II. She was the daughter of Francis I of Austria (see Emperor ◊Francis II) and on Napoleon's fall returned with their son to Austria, where she was granted the duchy of Parma 1815.

Marienbad German name of ◊Mariánské Lázně, spa town in Czechoslovakia.

Marietta city in SE Ohio, where the Muskingum River flows into the Ohio River, SE of Columbus; seat of Washington County. Marietta's industries include plastics, metal products, chemicals, and office equipment; population (1990) 15,026. It was the first permanent settlement 1788 in Ohio.

Mariette Auguste Ferdinand François 1821–1881. French Egyptologist, whose discoveries from 1850 included the "temple" between the paws of the Sphinx. He founded the Egyptian Museum in Cairo.

marigold several members of the family Compositae, especially the genus *Tagetes* including pot marigold *Calendula officinalis* and the tropical American *Tagetes patula*, commonly known as French marigold.

marijuana the dried leaves and flowers of the ◊hemp plant (*Cannabis sativa*), used as a recreational but illegal drug. It is eaten or inhaled and causes euphoria, distortion of time, and heightened sensations of sight and sound.

marimba a type of bass ◊xylophone.

Marin John 1870–1953. US painter of seascapes in watercolor and oil, influenced by Impressionism. He visited Europe 1905–11 and began his paintings of the Maine coast 1914.

Mariner spacecraft series of US space probes that explored the planets Mercury, Venus, and Mars 1962–75.

Mariner 1 (to Venus) had a failed launch. *Mariner 2* 1962 made the first fly-by of Venus, at 21,000 mi/34,000 km, confirmed the existence of ◊solar wind, and measured Venusian temperature. *Mariner 3* did not achieve its intended trajectory to Mars. *Mariner 4* 1965 passed Mars at a distance of 6,100 mi/9,800 km and took photographs, revealing a dry, cratered surface. *Mariner 5* 1967 passed Venus at 2,500 mi/4,000 km and measured Venusian temperature, atmosphere, mass, and diameter. *Mariner 6* and *7* 1969 photographed Mars' equator and southern hemisphere respectively, and also measured temperature, atmospheric pressure and composition, and diameter. *Mariner 8* (to Mars) had a failed launch. *Mariner 9* 1971 mapped the entire Martian surface and photographed Mars' moons. Its photographs revealed the changing of the polar caps and the extent of volcanism, canyons, and "canals," which suggested that there might once have been water on Mars. *Mariner 10* 1974–75 took close-up photographs of Mercury and Venus and measured temperature, radiation, and magnetic fields. *Mariner 11* and *12* were renamed *Voyager 1* and *2*; they reached Jupiter 1979, Saturn 1980–81, Uranus 1986, Neptune 1989, and continue to the present traveling beyond the Solar System.

marines a fighting force that operates both on land and at sea.

The US Marine Corps (1775) is constituted as an arm of the US Navy. It is made up of infantry and air support units trained and equipped for amphibious landings under fire.

Marinetti Filippo Tommaso 1876–1944. Italian author who in 1909 published the first manifesto of ◊Futurism, which called for a break with tradition in art, poetry, and the novel, and glorified the machine age.

Born at Alexandria, he illustrated his theories in *Mafarka le futuriste/Mafarka the Futurist* 1910, plays, and a volume on theatrical practice 1916. He recorded his World War I experiences in *Otto anime in una bomba* 1919, and welcomed Mussolini with *Futurismo e fascismo/Futurism and Fascism* 1924.

Marini Marino 1901–1980. Italian sculptor. Inspired by ancient art, he developed a distinctive horse-and-rider theme and a dancers series, reducing the forms to an elemental simplicity. He also produced fine portraits in bronze.

Marion Francis c. 1732–1795. American military leader. Born in Berkeley County, South Carolina, Marion served in the colonial militia during the Revolutionary War and saw action against the British in the battle for Charleston 1776. Following the fall of Charleston 1780, Marion, by then promoted to lieutenant colonel, waged a successful guerrilla war against the British. Establishing his field headquarters in inaccessible areas, he became popularly known as the "Swamp Fox." Marion played a major role in the American victory at Eutaw Springs 1781. After the war, he served in the South Carolina Senate.

marionette type of ◊puppet, a jointed figure controlled from above by wires or strings. Intricately crafted marionettes were used in Burma (now Myanmar) and Ceylon (now Sri Lanka) and later at the courts of Italian princes in the 16th–18th centuries.

Mariotte Edme 1620–1684. French physicist and priest known for his recognition in 1676 of ◊Boyle's law about the inverse relationship of volume and pressure in gases, formulated in 1672. He had earlier, in 1660, discovered the eye's blind spot.

Maritain Jacques 1882–1973. French philosopher. Originally a disciple of Henri ◊Bergson, as in *La philosophie bergsonienne/Bergsonian Philosophy* 1914, he later became the best known of the Neo-Thomists, applying the methods of Thomas ◊Aquinas to contemporary problems, for example *Introduction à la Philosophie/Introduction to Philosophy* 1920.

maritime law that part of the law dealing with the sea: in particular, fishing areas, ships, and navigation. Seas are divided into internal waters governed by a state's internal laws (such as harbors, inlets); ◊territorial waters (the area of sea adjoining the coast over which a state claims rights); the continental shelf (the seabed and subsoil that the coastal state is entitled to exploit beyond the territorial waters); and the high seas, where international law applies.

Maritsa (Greek *Hevros*; Turkish *Meric*) river, rising in the Rhodope Mountains, Bulgaria, which forms the Greco-Turkish frontier before entering the Aegean Sea near Enez; length 275 mi/440 km.

Mariupol former name (until 1948) of the port of ◊Zhdanov in the USSR.

Marius Gaius 155–86 BC. Roman military commander and politician, born near Arpinum. He was elected consul seven times, the first time in 107 BC. He defeated the Cimbri and the Teutons (Germanic tribes attacking Gaul and Italy) 102–101 BC. Marius tried to deprive Sulla of the command in the East against Mithridates and, as a result, civil war broke out in 88 BC. Sulla marched on Rome, and Marius fled to Africa, but

marjoram

flower
detail

later Cinna held Rome for Marius and together they created a reign of terror in Rome.

Marivaux Pierre Carlet de Chamblain de 1688–1763. French novelist and dramatist. His sophisticated comedies include *Le Jeu de l'amour et du hasard/The Game of Love and Chance* 1730 and *Les Fausses confidences/False Confidences* 1737; his novel *La Vie de Marianne/The Life of Marianne* 1731–41 has autobiographical elements. Marivaux gave the word *marivaudage* (overly-subtle lovers' conversation) to the French language.

He was born and lived for most of his life in Paris, writing for both of the major Paris theater companies: the ◊Comédie Française and the Comédie Italienne, which specialized in ◊commedia dell'arte.

marjoram aromatic herb of the mint family Labiatae. Wild marjoram *Origanum vulgare* is found both in Europe and Asia and has become naturalized in the Americas; the culinary sweet marjoram *Origanum majorana* is widely cultivated.

Mark, St 1st century AD. In the New Testament, Christian apostle and evangelist, whose name is given to the second Gospel. It was probably written AD 65–70, and used by the authors of the first and third Gospels. He is the patron saint of Venice, and his emblem is a winged lion; feast day Apr 25.

His first name was John, and his mother, Mary, was one of the first Christians in Jerusalem. He was a cousin of Barnabas, and accompanied Barnabas and Paul on their first missionary journey. He was a fellow worker with Paul in Rome, and later became Peter's interpreter after Paul's death. According to tradition he was the founder of the Christian church in Alexandria, and St Jerome says that he died and was buried there.

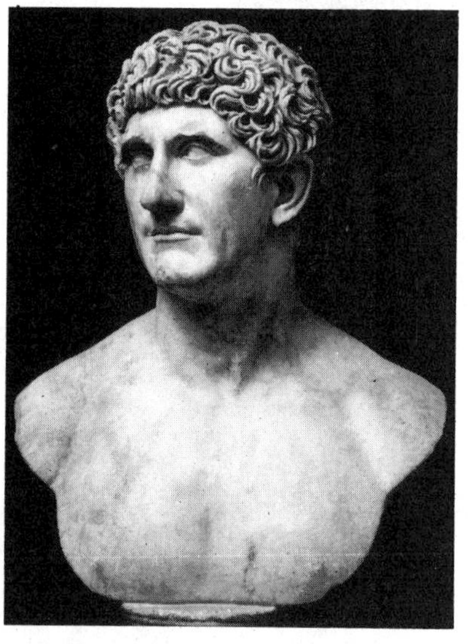

Mark Antony *A great Roman orator and soldier, Mark Antony committed suicide after his defeat at Actium by Augustus in 31 BC.*

Mark Antony Antonius, Marcus 83–30 BC. Roman politician and soldier. He was tribune and later consul under Julius Caesar, serving under him in Gaul. In 44 BC he tried to secure for Caesar the title of king. After Caesar's assassination, he formed the Second Triumvirate with Octavian (◊Augustus) and Lepidus. In 42 he defeated Brutus and Cassius at Philippi. He took Egypt as his share of the empire and formed a liaison with ◊Cleopatra. In 40 he returned to Rome to marry Octavia, the sister of Augustus. In 32 the Senate declared war on Cleopatra. Antony was defeated by Augustus at the battle of Actium 31 BC. He returned to Egypt and committed suicide.

marketing promoting goods and services to consumers. In the 20th century marketing has played an increasingly larger role in determining company policy, influencing product development, pricing, methods of distribution, advertising, and promotion techniques. Marketing skills are beginning to appear on the curriculum of some schools and colleges.

Markevich Igor 1912–1983. Russian-born composer and conductor, who settled in Paris 1927. He composed the ballet *L'Envol d'Icare* 1932, and the cantata *Le Paradis Perdu* 1933–35 to words by Milton. After World War II he concentrated on conducting.

markhor large wild goat *Capra falconeri*, with spirally twisted horns and long shaggy coat. It is found in the Himalayas.

Markov Andrei 1856–1922. Russian mathematician, formulator of the ◊Markov chain, an example of a stochastic process.

Markova Alicia. Adopted name of Lilian Alicia Marks 1910– . British ballet dancer. Trained by ◊Pavlova, she was ballerina with ◊Diaghilev's company 1925–29, was the first resident ballerina of the Vic-Wells Ballet 1933–35, partnered Anton ◊Dolin in their own Markova-Dolin Company 1935–37, and danced with the Ballets Russes de Monte Carlo 1938–41 and Ballet Theatre, 1941–46. She is associated with the great Classical ballets, such as *Giselle*.

Markov chain in statistics, an ordered sequence of discrete states (random variables) $x_1, x_2, \ldots, x_i, \ldots, x_n$ such that the probability of x_i depends only on n and/or the state $x_i - 1$ which has preceded it. If independent of n, the chain is said to be homogeneous.

marl crumbling sedimentary rock, sometimes called clayey limestone, including various types of calcareous ◊clays and argillaceous ◊limestones. Marls are often laid down in freshwater lakes and are usually soft, earthy, and of a white, gray, or brownish color. They are used in cement-making and as fertilizer.

Marlborough market town in Wiltshire, England, 76 mi/122 km W of London, site of Marlborough College 1843, a public school.

Marlborough John Churchill, 1st Duke of 1650–1722. English soldier, created a duke 1702 by Queen Anne. He was granted the Blenheim mansion in Oxfordshire in recognition of his services, which included defeating the French army outside Vienna in the Battle of Blenheim 1704, during the War of the ◊Spanish Succession.

Marley Bob (Robert Nesta) 1945–1981. Jamaican reggae singer, a Rastafarian whose songs, many of which were topical and political, popularized reggae in the 1970s. One of his greatest hit songs is "No Woman No Cry"; his albums include *Natty Dread* 1975 and *Exodus* 1977.

marlin or ***spearfish*** any of several genera of open-sea fishes known as billfishes, of the family Istiophoridae, order Perciformes. Some 7 ft/2.5 m long, they are found in warmer waters, have elongated snouts, and high-standing dorsal fins. The blue marlin *Makaira nigricans* is the best-known species.

Marlowe Christopher 1564–1593. English poet and dramatist. His work includes the blank-verse plays *Tamburlaine the Great* about 1587, *The Jew of Malta* about 1589, *Edward II* and *Dr Faustus*, both about 1592, the poem *Hero and Leander* 1598, and a translation of Ovid's *Amores*.

Born in Canterbury, Marlowe was educated at Cambridge University, where he is thought to have become a government agent. His life was turbulent, with a brief imprisonment in connection with a man's death in a brawl (of which he was cleared), and a charge of atheism (following statements by the playwright Thomas ◊Kyd under torture). He was murdered in a Deptford tavern, allegedly in a dispute over the bill, but it may have been a political killing.

Marmara small inland sea separating Turkey in Europe from Turkey in Asia, connected through the Bosporus with the Black Sea, and through the Dardanelles with the Aegean; length 170 mi/275 km, breadth up to 50 mi/80 km.

Marmontel Jean François 1723–1799. French novelist and dramatist. He wrote tragedies and libretti, and contributed to the ◊*Encyclopédie*. In 1758 he obtained control of the journal *Le Mercure/The Mercury*, in which his *Contes moraux/Moral Studies* 1761 appeared. Other works include *Bélisaire/Belisarius* 1767 and *Les Incas/The Incas* 1777.

Marmontel was appointed historiographer of France 1771, secretary to the Académie 1783, and professor of history at the Lycée 1786, but retired in 1792 to write his *Mémoires d'un père/Memoirs of a Father* 1804.

marmoset small tree-dwelling monkey in the family Callithricidae, found in South and Central America. Most species have characteristic tufted ears, clawlike nails, and a handsome tail, and some only reach a body length of 18 cm/7 in. The tail is not prehensile. Some are known as tamarins.

Best known is the common marmoset *Callithrix jacchus* of Brazil, often kept there as a pet.

marmot any of several large burrowing rodents of the genus *Marmota*, in the squirrel family Sciuridae. There are about 15 species. They eat plants and some insects. Marmots are found throughout Canada and the US, and from the Alps to the Himalayas. Marmots live in colonies, make burrows (one to each family), and hibernate. In North America they are called woodchucks or groundhogs.

Marne river in France that rises in the plateau of Langres and joins the Seine at Charenton near Paris; length 928 mi/5,251 km. It gives its name to the *départements* of Marne, Haute Marne, Seine-et-Marne, and Val de Marne; and to two battles of World War I.

Marne, Battles of the in World War I, two unsuccessful German offensives: First Battle Sept 6–9, 1914, von Moltke's advance was halted by the

Marley *Reggae artist Bob Marley.*

British Expeditionary Force and the French under Foch; Second Battle July 15–Aug 4, 1918, Ludendorff's advance was defeated by British, French, and US troops under the French general Pétain, and German morale crumbled.

Maronite member of a Christian sect deriving from refugee Monothelites (Christian heretics) of the 7th century. They were subsequently united with the Roman Catholic Church and number about 400,000 in Lebanon and Syria, with an equal number scattered in southern Europe and the Americas.

maroon (Spanish *cimarrón* "wild, untamed") in the West Indies and Suriname, a freed or escaped African slave. They were organized and armed by the Spanish in Jamaica in the late 17th century and early 18th century. They harried the British with guerrilla tactics.

Marot Clément 1496–1544. French poet, known for his translation of the *Psalms* 1539–43. His graceful, witty style became a model for later writers of light verse.

Born at Cahors, he accompanied Francis I to Italy in 1524 and was taken prisoner at Pavia; he was soon released, and by 1528 was a salaried member of the royal household. Suspected of heresy, he fled to Turin, where he died.

Marquand J(ohn) P(hillips) 1893–1960. US writer. Author of a series of stories featuring the Japanese detective Mr Moto, he later made his reputation with gently satirical novels of Boston society, including *The Late George Apley* 1937 and *H M Pulham, Esq* 1941.

Marquesas Islands (French *Îles Marquises*) island group in ◊French Polynesia, lying north of the Tuamotu Archipelago; area 490 sq mi/ 1,270 sq km; population (1983) 6,500. The administrative headquarters is Atuona on Hiva Oa. It was annexed by France 1842.

marquess or ***marquis*** title and rank of a nobleman who in the British peerage ranks below a duke and above an earl. The wife of a marquess is a marchioness.

The first English marquess was created in 1385, but the lords of the Scottish and Welsh "marches" were known as *marchiones* before this date.

Marquet Pierre Albert 1876–1947. French painter of landscapes and Parisian scenes, chiefly the river Seine and its bridges. He was associated with the ◊Fauves but soon developed a more conventional, naturalistic style.

marquetry the inlaying of various woods, bone, or ivory, usually on furniture, to create ornate patterns and pictures. Parquetry is the term used for geometrical inlaid patterns. The method is thought to have originated in Germany or Holland.

Marquette Jacques 1637–1675. French Jesuit missionary and explorer. He went to Canada in 1666, explored the upper lakes of the St Lawrence, and in 1673 with Louis Jolliet (1645–1700), set out on a voyage down the Mississippi on which they made the first accurate record of its course.

In 1674 he and two companions camped near the site of present-day Chicago, making them the first Europeans to live there.

Márquez Gabriel García see ◊García Márquez, Colombian novelist.

Marquis Don(ald Robert Perry) 1878–1937. US author. He is chiefly known for his humorous writing, including *Old Soak* 1921, which portrays a hard-drinking comic, and *archy and mehitabel* 1927, verse adventures typewritten by a literary cockroach.

Marquises, Îles French form of ◊Marquesas Islands, part of ◊French Polynesia.

Marrakesh historic town in Morocco in the foothills of the Atlas mountains, about 130 mi/210 km south of Casablanca; population (1982) 549,000. It is a tourist center, and has textile, leather, and food-processing industries. Founded 1062, it has a medieval palace and mosques, and was formerly the capital of Morocco.

marram grass coarse perennial grass *Ammophila arenaria*, flourishing on sandy areas. Because of its tough, creeping rootstocks, it is widely used to hold coastal dunes in place.

Marrano (Spanish *marrãno* "pig") a Spanish or Portuguese Jew who, during the 14th and 15th centuries, converted to Christianity to escape death or persecution at the hands of the ◊Inquisition. Many continued to adhere secretly to Judaism and carry out Jewish rites. During the Spanish Inquisition thousands were burned at the stake as "heretics."

marriage the legally or culturally sanctioned union of one man and one woman (monogamy); one man and two or more women (polygamy); one woman and two or more men (polyandry). The basis of marriage varies considerably in different societies (romantic love in the West; arranged marriages in some other societies), but most marriage ceremonies, contracts, or customs involve a set of rights and duties, such as care and protection, and there is generally an expectation that children will be born of the union to continue the family line and maintain the family property.

In different cultures and communities there are various conventions and laws that limit the choice of a marriage partner. Restrictive factors include: age limits, below which no marriage is valid; degrees of consanguinity or other special relationships within which marriage is either forbidden or enjoined; economic factors such as ability to pay a dowry; rank, caste, or religious differences or expectations; medical requirements, such as the blood tests of some US states; the necessity of obtaining parental, family, or community consent; the negotiations of a marriage broker in some cultures, as in Japan; color, for example, marriage was illegal until 1985 between "European" and "non-European" people in South Africa, and until 1967 was illegal between white and black people in some Southern US states and between white and Asian people in some western states.

rights In Western cultures, social trends have led to increased legal equality for women within marriage: in England married women were not allowed to hold property in their own name until 1882; in California community property laws entail the equal division of all assets between the partners on divorce. Other legal changes have made ◊divorce easier, notably in the US and increasingly in the UK, so that remarriage is more and more frequent for both sexes within the lifetime of the original partner.

law In most European countries and in the US civil registration of marriage, as well as (or instead of) a religious ceremony, is obligatory. Common-law marriages (that is, cohabitation as man and wife without a legal ceremony) are recognized (for inheritance purposes) in, for example, Scotland, some states of the US, and the USSR. As a step to international agreement on marriage law the United Nations in 1962 adopted a convention on consent to marriage, minimum age for marriage, and registration.

marrow any variety of elongated, smooth-skinned ◊squash, especially *Cucurbita pepo*, used as vegetables and in preserves; the young fruits of one variety are known as zucchinis.

Mars in Roman mythology, the god of war, after whom the month of March is named. He is equivalent to the Greek Ares.

Mars the fourth planet from the Sun, average distance 141.5 million mi/227.8 million km. It revolves around the Sun in 687 Earth days and has a rotation period of 24 hr 37 min. It is much smaller than Venus or Earth, with diameter 4,210 mi/6,780 km, and mass 0.11 that of Earth. Mars is slightly pear-shaped, with a low, level northern hemisphere, which is comparatively uncratered and geologicly "young," and a heavily cratered "ancient" southern hemisphere.

The landscape is a dusty, red, eroded lava plain; red atmospheric dust whipped up by winds of up to 125 mph/200 kph account for the light pink sky. Mars has white polar caps (water ice and frozen carbon dioxide) that advance and retreat with the seasons. There are four enormous volcanoes near the equator, of which the largest is Olympus Mons 15 mi/24 km high, with a base 375 mi/600 km across, and a crater 40 mi/ 65 km wide. The atmosphere is 95% carbon dioxide, 3% nitrogen, 1.5% argon, and 0.15% oxygen. Recorded temperatures vary from –148°F/–100°C to 32°F/0°C. The atmospheric pressure is 7 millibars, equivalent to the pressure 22 mi/35 km above Earth. No proof of life on Mars has been obtained.

There are two small satellites: ◊Phobos and Deimos.

Mars may approach Earth to within 34 million mi/54.7 million km. The first human-made object to orbit the planet was *Mariner 9*.

Viking 1 and *2*, which landed, also provided much information. Studies in 1985 showed that enough water might exist to sustain prolonged missions by space crews. To the east of the four volcanoes lies a high plateau cut by a system of valleys some 2,500 mi/4,000 km long, up to 120 mi/200 km wide, and 4 mi/6 km deep; these

Mars *Mars as seen by the* Viking *spacecraft on its approach to the red planet.*

features are apparently caused by faulting and wind erosion.

Marsala port in W Sicily, Italy, notable for the sweet wine of the same name; population (1980) 85,000. The nationalist leader ◊Garibaldi landed here 1860.

Marsala dry or sweet Sicilian dessert wine, with a dark amber color and a caramel flavor. It is fortified with grape juice that has been cooked and reduced to one-third of its original volume.

Marseillaise, La French national anthem; the words and music were composed in 1792 as a revolutionary song by the army officer Rouget de Lisle.

Marseille the chief seaport of France, industrial center (chemicals, oil refining, metallurgy, shipbuilding, food processing), and capital of the *département* of Bouches-du-Rhône, on the Golfe du Lion, Mediterranean Sea; population (1982) 1,111,000.

It is surrounded by hills and connected with the river Rhône by a canal, and there are several offshore islands including ◊If. Its university was founded 1409.

history Marseille was founded by mariners of Phocaea in Asia Minor in 600 BC. Under the Romans it was a free city, and then, after suffering successive waves of invaders, became in the 13th century an independent republic, until included in France in 1481. Much of the old quarter was destroyed by Germany in 1943.

Marsh Ngaio 1899–1982. New Zealand writer of detective fiction. Her first detective novel *A Man Lay Dead* 1934 introduced her protagonist Chief Inspector Roderick Alleyn.

Marsh Othniel Charles 1831–1899. US paleontologist. Born in Lockport, New York, Marsh was educated at Yale and in Germany. Named to the Yale faculty as the first professor of paleontology in the US, he mounted fossil-hunting expeditions to the West from 1870. He became official paleontologist for the US Geological Survey 1882 and identified many previously unknown fossil species. An early devotee of Darwin's theory of evolution, Marsh wrote *Odontornithes* 1880, *Dinocerata* 1884, and *Dinosaurs of North America* 1896. He served as president of the American Academy of Sciences 1883–95.

marshal highest military rank in the British Royal Air Force.

In the French army the highest officers bear the designation of *maréchal de France*/marshal of France.

Marshall city in NE Texas, SE of Dallas and across the border from Shreveport, Louisiana; seat of Harrison County. Industries include food processing, cotton, clothing, building materials, vehicle parts, and chemicals; population (1990) 23,682.

Marshall Alfred 1842–1924. English economist, professor of economics at Cambridge University 1885–1908. He was a founder of neo-Classical economics, and stressed the power of supply and demand to generate equilibrium prices in markets, introducing the concept of elasticity of demand relative to price. His *Principles of Economics* 1890 remains perhaps the chief textbook of neo-Classical economics.

Marshall George Catlett 1880–1959. US general and diplomat. He was army chief of staff in World War II, secretary of state 1947–49, and secretary of defense Sept 1950–Sept 1951. He initiated the ◊Marshall Plan 1947 and received the Nobel Peace Prize 1953.

Marshall, born in Pennsylvania, was commissioned in 1901, served in World War I, and in 1939 became chief of staff with the rank of general. Franklin ◊Roosevelt promoted him to the newly created rank of general of the army. Following Marshall's resignation from the army, President Truman recalled him to serve as a special envoy to China in Nov 1945. He attempted to secure a coalition between the Nationalist and Communist forces against Japan. As defense secretary (a post not normally held by a soldier), he backed Truman's recall of General ◊MacArthur from Korea.

Marshall Islands

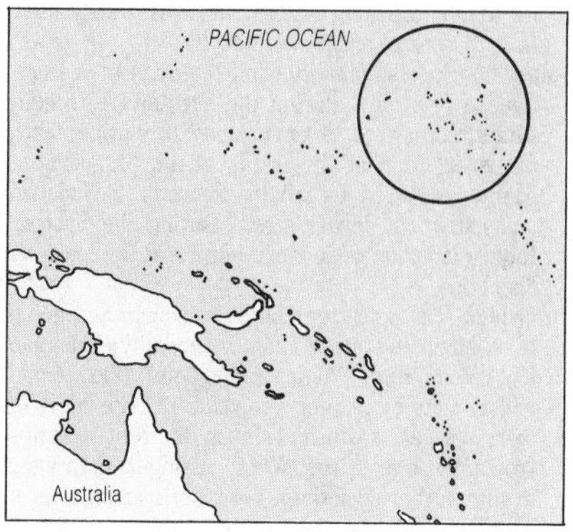
PACIFIC OCEAN
Australia

Marshall John 1755–1835. US jurist and chief justice of the US Supreme Court 1801–35. He established the independence of the Court, the supremacy of federal over state law, and laid down interpretations of the US Constitution in a series of decisions that have since become universally accepted.

Born in Prince William (now Faquier) County, Virginia, Marshall served in the Continental Army on and off until 1780 and then studied law. As a Federalist, he served in the Virginia state legislature and 1797 became a minister to France. He was in the US House of Representatives 1799–1800 and was secretary of state 1800–01. In 1801, President Adams appointed him Chief Justice. Marshall's first opinion, rendered in *Marbury* v *Madison* 1801, declared a law unconstitutional and established the principle of judicial review by the Court. He clearly defined the contract clause in the Constitution in the cases *Fletcher* v *Peck* 1810, *Dartmouth College* v *Woodward* 1819, and *Sturges* v *Crowninshield* 1819. The role of the federal government was defined in *McCulloch* v *Maryland* 1819, when Marshall wrote the opinion that when federal and state laws conflict, federal law supersedes that of the states, and in *Gibbons* v *Ogden* 1824, when he wrote that a state could not enact laws that give exclusive rights to its waters.

Marshall presided over the treason trial 1807 of Aaron Burr, in which Burr was found not guilty. Marshall died of injuries sustained in a stagecoach accident.

Marshall Thurgood 1908– . US Supreme Court justice (1967–91) and civil rights leader. Born in Baltimore, Maryland, Marshall received a law degree from Howard University 1933. Active in civil rights, he was named director of the National Association for the Advancement of Colored People (NAACP) Legal Defense and Education Fund 1940. Marshall appeared frequently before the US Supreme Court in landmark civil rights cases—among them, *Brown* v *Board of Education* 1954. He was named to the US Court of Appeals 1961 and served as US solicitor general 1965–67. In 1967 President Johnson appointed him to the US Supreme Court. The first black associate justice, he remained a strong voice for civil and individual rights until his retirement for health reasons. Clarence ◊Thomas succeeded to Marshall's seat.

Marshall Islands the Radak (13 islands) and Ralik (11 islands) chains in the W Pacific

area 69 sq mi/180 sq km

capital Majuro

features include two atolls used for US atom-bomb tests 1946–63, Eniwetok and Bikini (hence the name given to two-piece swimsuits which supposedly had an explosive impact)—radioactivity will last for 100 years, and the people have made claims for rehabilitation; and Kwajalein atoll (the

marsh marigold

largest) which has a US intercontinental missile range

products copra, phosphates, fish, tourism

population (1988) 41,000

government internally self-governing

recent history German 1906–19; administered by Japan until 1946, passed to the US as part of the Pacific Islands Trust Territory 1947. They were used for many atomic bomb tests 1946–63, and the islanders are demanding compensation. In 1986 a compact of Free Association with the US was signed, under which the islands manage their own internal and external affairs but the US controls military activities in exchange for financial support.

currency US dollar

language English (official)

religion Christian and local faiths

Marshall Plan a program of US financial aid to Europe, set up at the end of World War II, totaling $13,000 billion 1948–52. Officially known as the European Recovery Program, it was announced by Secretary of State George ◊Marshall in a speech at Harvard in June 1947, but it was in fact the work of a State Department group led by Dean ◊Acheson.

The danger of communist takeover in postwar Europe was the major motivation for the aid effort.

marsh gas a gas, consisting mostly of ◊methane. It is produced in swamps and marshes by the action of bacteria on dead vegetation.

marsh marigold plant *Caltha palustris* of the buttercup family Ranunculaceae, known as the kingcup in the UK and as the cowslip in the US. It grows in moist sheltered spots and has five-sepalled flowers of a brilliant yellow.

Marston Moor, Battle of battle fought in the English Civil War on July 2, 1644 on Marston Moor, 7 mi/11 km W of York. The Royalists were completely defeated by the Parliamentarians and Scots.

The Royalist forces were commanded by Prince Rupert and the Duke of Newcastle; their opponents by Oliver Cromwell and Lord Leven.

marsupial (Greek *marsupion*, "little purse") mammal in which the female has a pouch where she carries her young (born tiny and immature) for a considerable time after birth. Marsupials include omnivorous, herbivorous, and carnivorous species, among them kangaroo, wombat, opossum, phalanger, bandicoot, dasyure, and wallaby.

The marsupial anteater *Myrmecobius* has no pouch.

Martello tower circular tower for coastal defense. Formerly much used in Europe, many were built along the English coast, especially in Sussex and Kent, in 1804, as a defense against the threatened French invasion. The name is derived from a tower on Cape Mortella, Corsica, which was captured by the British with great difficulty in 1794, and was taken as a model. They are round towers of solid masonry, sometimes moated, with a flat roof for mounted guns.

marten any of a genus *Martes*, of carnivores belonging to the weasel family Mustelidae. Martens live in North America, Europe, and Asia.

The sable *M. zibellina* lives in E Siberia, and provides the most valued fur. The largest is the fisher *M. pennanti*, of North America, with black fur and reaching 4 ft/125 cm.

Martens Wilfried 1936– . Prime minister of Belgium from 1979, member of the Social Christian Party. He was president of the Dutch-speaking CVP 1972–79 and, as prime minister, headed several coalition governments in the period from 1979.

Martha's Vineyard island 20 mi/32 km long off the coast of Cape Cod, Massachusetts; chief town Edgartown. It is the former home of whaling captains, and now a summer resort.

Martial (Marcus Valerius Martialis) AD 41–104. Latin epigrammatist. His poetry, often bawdy, reflects contemporary Roman life.

Born in Bilbilis, Spain, Martial settled in Rome in 64, and lived by his literary and social gifts. He is renowned for correctness of diction, versification, and form.

martial arts styles of armed and unarmed combat developed in the East from ancient techniques and arts. Common martial arts include ◊aikido, ◊judo, ◊jujitsu, ◊karate, ◊kendo, and ◊kung fu.

martial law the replacement of civilian by military authorities in the maintenance of order.

In the US, martial law is usually proclaimed by the president or the government of a state in areas of the country where the civil authorities have been rendered unable to act, or to act with safety. The legal position of martial law is neither well defined in the constitution nor laid down in statutes. In effect, when war or rebellion is in progress in an area, the military authorities are recognized as having the powers to maintain order by summary means.

martin several species of birds in the swallow family, Hirundinidae.

Only one species, the purple martin *Progne subis*, is native to North America. It is a dark, glossy purplish blue and about 8 in/20 cm long with a notched tail. It winters in South America.

Martin Archer John Porter 1910– . British biochemist who received the 1952 Nobel Prize for Chemistry for work with Richard Synge on paper chromatography in 1944.

Martin John 1789–1854. British Romantic painter of grandiose landscapes and ambitious religious subjects, such as *Belshazzar's Feast* (several versions).

Other examples of his work are *The Great Day of His Wrath* and *The Plains of Heaven* 1851–53 (both Tate Gallery, London). Martin often made mezzotints (types of engraving) from his work.

Martin five popes, including:

Martin V 1368–1431. Pope from 1417. A member of the Roman family of Colonna, he was elected during the Council of Constance, and ended the Great Schism between the rival popes of Rome and Avignon.

Martin, St 316–400. Bishop of Tours, France, from about 371, and founder of the first monastery in Gaul. He is usually represented as tearing his cloak to share it with a beggar. His feast day is Martinmas, Nov 11.

Born in Pannonia, SE Europe, a soldier by profession, Martin was converted to Christianity, left the army, and lived for ten years as a recluse. After being elected bishop of Tours, he worked for the extinction of idolatry and the extension of monasticism in France.

Martin du Gard Roger 1881–1958. French novelist who realistically recorded the way of life of the bourgeoisie in the eight-volume *Les Thibault/The World of the Thibaults* 1922–40. He received the Nobel Prize 1937.

Martinet Jean. French inspector-general of infantry under Louis XIV, whose constant drilling brought the army to a high degree of efficiency—hence the use of his name to mean a strict disciplinarian.

Martinez Maria Montoya 1890–1980. Pueblo Indian potter, who revived the traditional silvery black-on-black ware (made without the wheel) at San Ildefonso Pueblo, New Mexico.

Martinique

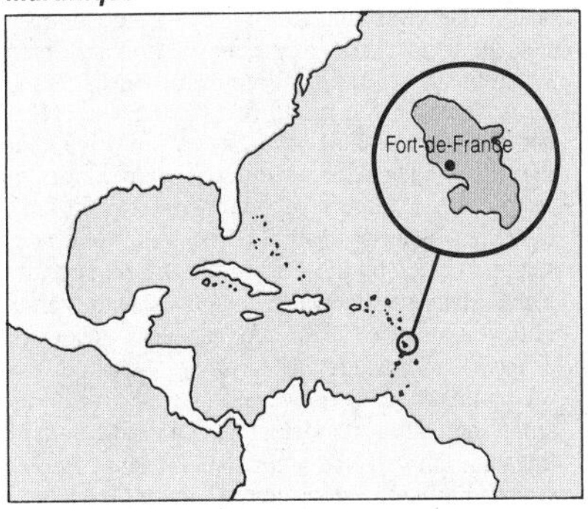
Fort-de-France

Martínez Ruiz José. Real name of ◊Azorín, Spanish author.

Martini Simone c. 1284–1344. Italian painter, a master of the Sienese school. He was a pupil of Duccio and continued the graceful linear patterns of Sienese art but introduced a fresh element of naturalism. His patrons included the city of Siena, the king of Naples, and the pope. Two of his frescoes are in the Town Hall in Siena: the *Maestà* c. 1315 and the horseback warrior *Guidoriccio da Fogliano* (the attribution of the latter is disputed).

Martinique French island in the West Indies (Lesser Antilles)

area 417 sq mi/1,079 sq km

capital Fort-de-France

features several active volcanoes; Napoleon's empress Josephine was born in Martinique, and her childhood home is a museum

products sugar, cocoa, rum, bananas, pineapples

population (1984) 327,000

history Martinique was reached by Spanish navigators in 1493, and became a French colony in 1635; since 1972 it has been a French overseas region.

Martinmas in the Christian calendar, the feast of St Martin, Nov 11.

On this day fairs were traditionally held, at which farmworkers were hired. In the Middle Ages it was also the day on which cattle were slaughtered and salted for winter consumption.

Martins Peter 1946– . Danish-born US dancer, choreographer, and director, principal dancer with the New York City Ballet from 1965 and its joint director from 1983.

Martins trained at the Royal Danish Ballet School, joining the company 1965, and the same year joined the New York City Ballet as a principal. He created roles in, among others, Robbins's *Goldberg Variations* 1971 and Balanchine's *Violin Concerto* and *Duo Concertant* both 1972, and choreographed, for example, *Calcium Night Light* 1978.

Martin's Hundred plantation town established in Virginia (1619) and eliminated by an Indian massacre three years later. Its remains, the earliest extensive trace of British colonization in America, were discovered in 1970.

Martinu Bohuslav (Jan) 1890–1959. Czech composer, who studied in Paris. He left Czechoslovakia after the Nazi occupation of 1939. The quality of his music varies but at its best it is richly expressive and has great vitality. His works include the operas *Julietta* 1937 and *The Greek Passion* 1959, symphonies, and chamber music.

Martin v Hunter's Lessee a US Supreme Court decision 1816 that established the right of the Supreme Court to overrule certain state court rulings. The Virginia state court refused to return Martin certain property confiscated by state law during the American Revolution, ignoring the treaty with the British that guaranteed that Loyalists would not be deprived of their properties. When, on appeal, the Supreme Court reversed the decision, the Virginia courts protested that land matters in states were outside of Supreme Court jurisdiction. The Court ruled that, by the Judiciary Act, such matters were within its jurisdiction.

martyr (Greek "witness") one who voluntarily suffers death for refusing to renounce a religious faith. The first recorded Christian martyr was St Stephen, who was killed in Jerusalem shortly after Jesus' alleged ascension to heaven.

Marvell Andrew 1621–1678. English metaphysical poet and satirist. His poems include "To His Coy Mistress" and "Horatian Ode upon Cromwell's Return from Ireland." He was committed to the parliamentary cause, and was member of Parliament for Hull from 1659. He devoted his last years mainly to verse satire and prose works attacking repressive aspects of government.

Marvin Lee 1924–1987. US film actor who began his career playing violent, often psychotic villains and progressed to playing violent, occasionally psychotic heroes. His work includes *The Big Heat* 1953, *The Killers* 1964, and *Cat Ballou* 1965.

Marx Karl (Heinrich) 1818–1883. German philosopher, economist, and social theorist whose account of change through conflict is known as historical, or dialectical, materialism (see ◊Marxism). His ◊*Das Kapital/Capital* 1867–95 is the fundamental text of Marxist economics, and his systematic theses on class struggle, history, and the importance of economic factors in politics have exercised an enormous influence on later thinkers and political activists.

The son of a lawyer, he was born in Trier and studied law and philosophy at Bonn and Berlin. During 1842–43, he edited the *Rheinische Zeitung/Rhineland Newspaper* until its suppression. In 1844 he began his life-long collaboration with Friedrich ◊Engels, with whom he developed the Marxist philosophy, first formulated in their joint works, *Die heilige Familie/The Holy Family* 1844 and *Die deutsche Ideologie/German Ideology* 1846 (which contains the theory demonstrating the material basis of all human activity: "Life is not determined by consciousness, but consciousness by life"), and Marx's *Misère de la philosophie/Poverty of Philosophy* 1847. Both joined the Communist League, a German refugee organization, and in 1847–48 they prepared its program, *The Communist Manifesto*. During the 1848 revolution Marx edited the *Neue Rheinische Zeitung/New Rhineland Newspaper*, until he was expelled from Prussia 1849.

He then settled in London, where he wrote *Die Klassenkämpfe in Frankreich/Class Struggles in France* 1849, *Die Achtzehnte Brumaire des Louis Bonaparte/The 18th Brumaire of Louis Bonaparte* 1852, *Zur Kritik der politischen Ökonomie/Critique of Political Economy* 1859, and his monumental work *Das Kapital/Capital*. In 1864 the International Working Men's Association was formed, whose policy Marx, as a member of the general council, largely controlled. Although he showed extraordinary tact in holding together its diverse elements, it collapsed 1872 due to Marx's disputes with the anarchists, including the Russian ◊Bakunin. The second and third volumes of *Das Kapital* were edited from his notes by Engels and published posthumously.

Marx's philosophical work owes much to the writings of ◊Hegel, though he rejected Hegel's idealism.

Marx Brothers team of US film comedians: Leonard "Chico" (from the "chicks"— girls—he chased) 1887–1961; Adolph, the silent "Harpo" (from the harp he played), 1888–1964; Julius "Groucho" 1890–1977; Milton "Gummo" (from his gumshoes) 1894–1977, who left the team before films; and Herbert "Zeppo" (born at the time of the first zeppelins) 1901–79, part of the team until 1935. They appeared in musical comedy but made their reputation on Broadway in *Coconuts* 1926 (later filmed). In Hollywood they made such films as *Monkey Business* 1931, *Animal Crackers* 1932, *Duck Soup* 1933, *A Night at the Opera* 1935, *A Day at the Races* 1937. After the team disbanded 1948, Groucho, who carried the comedy line, con-

***Marx Brothers** US film comedians (clockwise, from top left) Zeppo, Groucho, Harpo, and Chico. Through his later television shows, Groucho became the best known of the Marx Brothers.*

tinued to make films and appeared on his own television quiz show, *You Bet Your Life* 1947–62.

Marxism philosophical system, developed by the 19th-century German social theorists ◊Marx and ◊Engels, also known as dialectical materialism, under which matter gives rise to mind (materialism) and all is subject to change (from dialectic; see ◊Hegel). As applied to history, it supposes that the succession of feudalism, capitalism, socialism, and finally the classless society is inevitable. The stubborn resistance of any existing system to change necessitates its complete overthrow in the class struggle—in the case of capitalism, by the proletariat—rather than gradual modification.

Social and political institutions progressively change their nature as economic developments transform material conditions. The orthodox belief is that each successive form is "higher" than the last; perfect socialism is seen as the ultimate rational system, and it is alleged that the state would then wither away. Marxism has proved one of the most powerful and debated theories in modern history, inspiring both dedicated exponents (Lenin, Trotsky, Stalin, Mao) and bitter opponents. It is the basis of ◊communism.

Mary in the New Testament, the mother of Jesus through divine intervention (see ◊Annunciation) and the wife of ◊Joseph. The Roman Catholic Church maintains belief in her ◊Immaculate Conception and bodily assumption into heaven, and venerates her as a mediator. Feast day of the Assumption Aug 15.

Traditionally her parents were elderly and named Joachim and Anna. Mary (Hebrew Miriam) married Joseph and accompanied him to Bethlehem. Roman Catholic doctrine assumes that the brothers of Jesus were Joseph's sons by an earlier marriage, and that Mary remained a virgin. Pope Paul VI proclaimed her "Mother of the Church" in 1964.

Mary town in Turkmenistan, S USSR, on the Murghab River; population (1985) 85,000. It is situated in a cotton-growing oasis in the Kara Kum desert, near where Alexander the Great founded a city (◊Merv).

Mary Queen of Scots 1542–1587. Queen of Scotland 1542–67. Also known as Mary Stuart, she was the daughter of James V. Mary's connection with the English royal line from Henry VII made her a threat to Elizabeth I's hold on the English throne, especially as she represented a champion of the Catholic cause. She was married three times. After her forced abdication she was imprisoned but escaped 1568 to England. Elizabeth I held her prisoner, while the Roman Catholics, who regarded Mary as rightful queen of England, formed many conspiracies to place her on the throne, and for complicity in one of these she was executed.

Mary's mother was the French Mary of Guise. Born in Linlithgow (now in Lothian region, Scotland), Mary was sent to France, where she married the dauphin, later Francis II. After his death she returned in 1561 to Scotland, which, during her absence, had turned Protestant. She married her cousin, the Earl of ◊Darnley, in 1565, but they soon quarrelled, and Darnley took part in the murder of Mary's secretary, ◊Rizzio. In 1567 Darnley was assassinated as the result of a conspiracy formed by the Earl of ◊Bothwell, possibly with Mary's connivance, and shortly after Bothwell married her. A rebellion followed; defeated at Carberry Hill, Mary abdicated and was imprisoned. She escaped in 1568, raised an army, and after its defeat at Langside fled to England, only to be imprisoned again. A plot against Elizabeth I devised by Anthony Babington led to her trial and execution at Fotheringay Castle in 1587.

Mary Duchess of Burgundy 1457–1482. Daughter of Charles the Bold. She married Maximilian of Austria 1477, thus bringing the Low Countries into the possession of the Hapsburgs and, ultimately, of Spain.

Mary of Guise or ***Mary of Lorraine*** 1515–1560. French wife of James V of Scotland from 1538, and from 1554 regent of Scotland for her daughter ◊Mary Queen of Scots. A Catholic, she moved from reconciliation with Scottish Protestants to repression, and died during a Protestant rebellion in Edinburgh.

Mary two queens of England:

Mary I Bloody Mary 1516–1558. Queen of England from 1553. She was the eldest daughter of Henry VIII by Catherine of Aragon. When Edward VI died, Mary secured the crown without difficulty in spite of the conspiracy to substitute Lady Jane ◊Grey. In 1554 Mary married Philip II of Spain, and as a devout Roman Catholic obtained the restoration of papal supremacy and sanctioned the persecution of Protestants. She was succeeded by her half-sister Elizabeth I.

When Mary died, the Protestant Elizabeth I gained the throne and settled the religious question, for the time, during her long, pivotal reign.

Mary II 1662–1694. Queen of England, Scotland, and Ireland from 1688. She was the Protestant elder daughter of the Catholic ◊James II, and in 1677 was married to her cousin ◊William III of Orange. After the 1688 revolution she accepted the crown jointly with William.

During his absences from England she took charge of the government, and showed courage and resource when invasion seemed possible in 1690 and 1692.

Maryborough Australian coastal and market (grain, livestock) town in SE Queensland; industries (coal and gold-mining, iron, steel); population (1980) 21,000.

Maryborough former name of Portlaoighise, capital of County Laois in the Republic of Ireland. The name gradually went out of use during the 1950s.

***Mary** Portrait of Mary, Queen of Scots, who was a threat to Elizabeth I's hold on the throne of England.*

Maryland

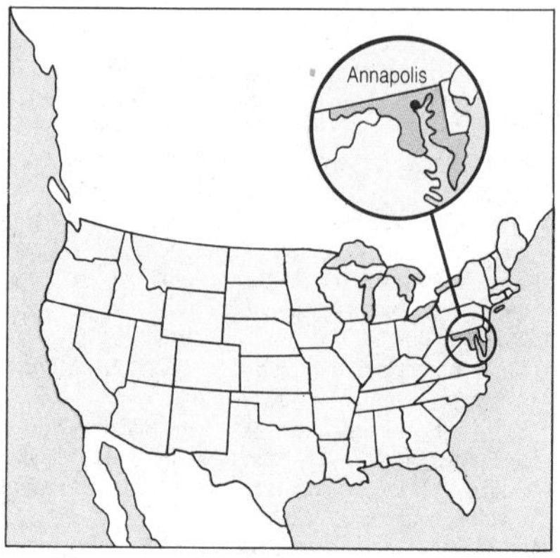
Annapolis

Maryland state E US; nickname Old Line State/Free State

area 12,198 sq mi/31,600 sq km

capital Annapolis

cities Baltimore, Silver Spring, Dundalk, Bethesda

features Chesapeake Bay, an inlet of the Atlantic; horse racing (the Preakness Stakes at Baltimore); yacht racing and the US Naval Academy at Annapolis; historic Fort McHenry, Baltimore harbor

products poultry, dairy products, machinery, steel, automobiles and parts, electric and electronic equipment, chemicals, fish and shellfish

population (1990) 4,781,468

famous people Edwin Booth, Stephen Decatur, Frederick Douglass, Billie Holliday, Francis Scott Key, H L Mencken, Edgar Allen Poe, Babe Ruth, Upton Sinclair, Harriet Tubman

history in 1608 John Smith explored Chesapeake Bay, but the colony of Maryland, awarded by royal grant 1632 to Lord Baltimore for the settlement of English Catholics, dates from 1634. It was one of the original Thirteen Colonies and ratified the federal Constitution 1788. During the British bombardment of Fort McHenry in the War of 1812, Francis Scott Key wrote the poem "The Star-Spangled Banner," which later became the lyrics to the US national anthem. Some Marylanders favored secession during the Civil War, during which the state was largely occupied by Union troops because of its strategic location near Washington, DC, and the Confederate armies three times invaded Maryland. In recent times the state has prospered from the growth of the federal government in nearby Washington and the redevelopment of Baltimore, whose port ranks second in handling foreign shipping. Between 1940 and 1980, Maryland's population more than tripled.

Mary Magdalene, St 1st century AD. In the New Testament, woman whom Jesus cured of possession by evil spirits, was present at the Crucifixion and burial, and was the first to meet the risen Jesus. She is often identified with the woman of St Luke's gospel who anointed Jesus' feet, and her symbol is a jar of ointment; feast day July 22.

Mary of Modena 1658–1718. Queen consort of England and Scotland. She was the daughter of the Duke of Modena, Italy, and married James, Duke of York, later James II, in 1673. The birth of their son James Francis Edward Stuart was the signal for the revolution of 1688 that overthrew James II. Mary fled to France.

Masaccio (Tomaso di Giovanni di Simone Guidi) 1401–1428. Florentine painter, a leader of the early Italian Renaissance. His frescoes in Sta Maria del Carmine, Florence, 1425–28, which he painted with Masolino da Panicale (c. 1384–1447), show a decisive break with Gothic conventions. He was the first painter to apply the scientific laws

Masaccio *A master of the early Italian Renaissance, Masaccio painted* The Virgin and Child *(from the Pisa polyptych) in 1426.*

of perspective, newly discovered by the architect Brunelleschi.

Masaccio's frescoes in the Brancacci Chapel of Sta Maria del Carmine include scenes from the life of St Peter (notably *The Tribute Money*) and a moving account of *Adam and Eve's Expulsion from Paradise*. They have a monumental grandeur, without trace of Gothic decorative detail, unlike the work of his colleague and teacher Masolino. Masaccio's figures have solidity and weight and are clearly set in three-dimensional space.

Other works by Masaccio are the *Trinity* c. 1428 (Sta Maria Novella, Florence) and the *Pisa polyptych* (National Gallery, London, Staatliche Museen, Berlin, and Museo di Capodimonte, Naples). Although his career marks a turning point in Italian art, he attracted few imitators (Fra Filippo Lippi's early style followed Masaccio).

Masada rock fortress 1,300 ft/396 m above the W shore of the Dead Sea, Israel. Site of the Hebrews' final stand in their revolt against the Romans (AD 66–72). After withstanding a year-long seige, the Hebrew population of 953 committed mass suicide rather than be conquered and enslaved.

The site was excavated 1963–65, including the palace of Herod, and is now an Israeli national monument.

Masai member of an E African people, whose territory is divided between Tanzania and Kenya. They were originally warriors and nomads, breeding humped zebu cattle, but are now adopting a more settled life. They speak an E Sudanic (Nilotic) language.

Masaryk Jan (Garrigue) 1886–1948. Czechoslovak politician, son of Tomáš Masaryk. He was foreign minister from 1940, when the Czechoslovak government was exiled in London in World War II. He returned in 1945, retaining the post, but as a result of political pressure by the communists committed suicide.

Masaryk Tomáš (Garrigue) 1850–1937. Czechoslovak nationalist politician. He directed the revolutionary movement against the Austrian Empire, founding with Eduard Beneš and Stefanik the Czechoslovak National Council, and in 1918 was

Masaryk *Tomáš Garrigue Masaryk, the first president of Czechoslovakia.*

elected first president of the newly formed Czechoslovak Republic. Three times reelected, he resigned in 1935 in favor of Beneš.

masc. in grammer, the abbreviation for ***masculine***; see ◊gender.

Mascagni Pietro 1863–1945. Italian composer of the one-act opera *Cavalleria rusticana/Rustic Chivalry*, first produced in Rome in 1890.

Mascara town and wine-trade center, 60 mi/96 km SE of Oran, Algeria; the headquarters of Abd-el-Kader (c. 1807–83) who fought the French invasion of Algeria 1830–47, Mascara being captured 1841.

Masekela Hugh 1939– . South African trumpet player, exiled from his homeland in 1960, who has recorded jazz, rock, and *mbaqanga*, or township jive. His albums include *Techno-Bush* 1984.

maser (acronym for microwave amplification by stimulated emission of radiation) in physics, a high-frequency microwave amplifier or oscillator in which the signal to be amplified is used to stimulate unstable atoms into emitting energy at the same frequency. Atoms or molecules are raised to a higher energy level and then allowed to lose this energy by radiation emitted at a precise frequency. The principle has been extended to other parts of the electromagnetic spectrum as, for example, in the ◊laser.

The two-level ammonia-gas maser was first suggested in 1954 by C H Townes at Columbia University, New York, and independently the same year by Basov and Prokhorov in the USSR. The solid-state three-level maser, the most sensitive amplifier known, was envisaged by Bloembergen in 1956 at Harvard. The ammonia maser is used as a frequency standard oscillator (see ◊clock), and the three-level maser as a receiver for satellite communications and radioastronomy.

Maseru capital of Lesotho, South Africa, on the Caledon river; population (1986) 289,000. It is a center for trade and diamond processing.

Mashhad or ***Meshed*** holy city of the Shi'ites, and industrial center (carpets, textiles, leather goods), in NE Iran; population (1986) 1,464,000. It is the second-largest city in Iran.

Mashonaland E Zimbabwe, the land of the Shona people, now divided into three administrative regions. Granted to the British South Africa Company in 1889, it was included in Southern Rhodesia in 1923. The ◊Zimbabwe ruins are here. Prime Minister Robert Mugabe is a Shona.

Mashraq (Arabic "east") the Arab countries of the E Mediterranean: Egypt, Sudan, Jordan, Syria, and Lebanon. The term is contrasted with ◊Maghreb, comprising the Arab countries of NW Africa.

Masire Quett Ketumile Joni 1925– . President of Botswana from 1980. In 1962, with Seretse ◊Khama, he founded the Botswana Democratic Party (BDP) and in 1965 was made deputy prime minister. After independence, in 1966, he became vice-president and, on Khama's death in 1980, president, continuing a policy of nonalignment.

Masire was a journalist before entering politics, sitting in the Bangwaketse Tribal Council and then the Legislative Council before cofounding the BDP. He has helped Botswana become one of the most stable states in Africa.

Maskelyne Nevil 1732–1811. English astronomer who accurately measured the distance from the Earth to the Sun by observing a transit of Venus across the Sun's face 1769. In 1774 he measured the mass of the Earth by noting the deflection of a plumb line near Mount Schiehallion in Scotland.

masochism a desire to subject oneself to physical or mental pain, humiliation, or punishment, for erotic pleasure, to alleviate guilt, or out of destructive impulses turned inward. The term is derived from Leopold von ◊Sacher-Masoch.

Mason James 1909–1984. English actor who portrayed romantic villains in British films of the 1940s. After *Odd Man Out* 1947 he worked in the US, playing intelligent but troubled, vulnerable men, notably in *A Star is Born* 1954. Other films include *Five Fingers* 1952 and *North by Northwest* 1959. He returned to Europe 1960 where he made *Lolita* 1962, *Georgy Girl* 1966, and *Cross of Iron* 1977. His final role was *The Shooting Party* 1984.

Mason–Dixon Line in the US, the boundary line between Maryland and Pennsylvania (latitude 39° 43′ 26.3″ N), named after Charles Mason (1730–87) and Jeremiah Dixon (died 1777), English astronomers and surveyors who surveyed it 1763–67. It was popularly seen as dividing the North from the South.

The two colonies had argued for almost a century and even fought some armed skirmishes over the boundary. In 1760, the two agreed to allow Mason and Dixon to delineate the line.

masque a spectacular and essentially aristocratic entertainment with a fantastic or mythological theme in which music, dance, and extravagant costumes and scenic design figured larger than plot. Originating in Italy, it reached its height of popularity at the English court between 1600 and 1640, with the collaboration of Ben ◊Jonson as writer and Inigo ◊Jones as stage designer.

The masque had great influence on the development of ballet and opera, and the elaborate frame in which it was performed developed into the proscenium arch.

mass in physics, the quantity of matter in a body as measured by its inertia. Mass determines the acceleration produced in a body by a given force acting on it, the acceleration being inversely proportional to the mass of the body. The mass also determines the force exerted on a body by ◊gravity on Earth, although this attraction varies slightly from place to place. In the SI system, the base unit of mass is the kilogram.

At a given place, equal masses experience equal gravitational forces, which are known as the weights of the bodies. Masses may, therefore, be compared by comparing the weights of bodies at the same place. The standard unit of mass to which all other masses are compared is a platinum-iridium cylinder of 1 kg.

Mass in Christianity, the celebration of the ◊Eucharist.

Mass in music, the setting of the invariable parts of the Christian Mass, that is *Kyrie*, *Gloria*, *Credo*, *Sanctus* with *Benedictus*, and *Agnus Dei*. A notable example is Bach's *Mass in B Minor*.

Massachusetts state of US; nickname Bay State/Old Colony State

area 8,299 sq mi/21,500 sq km

capital Boston

cities Worcester, Springfield, New Bedford, Brockton, Cambridge

Massachusetts

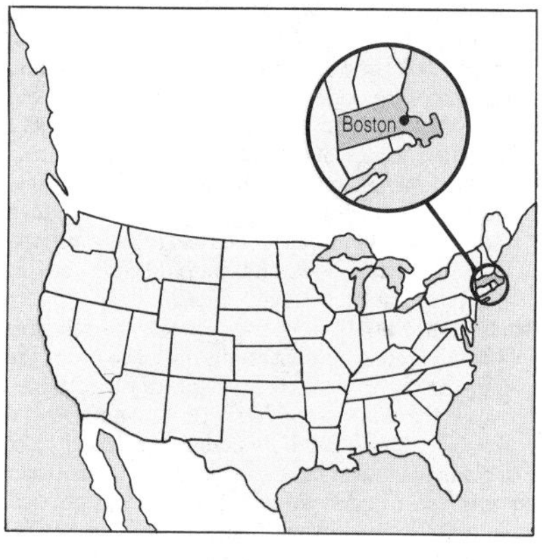
Boston

population (1990) 6,016,425
features Boston landmarks; Harvard University and the Massachusetts Institute of Technology, Cambridge; Cape Cod National Seashore; New Bedford and the islands of Nantucket and Martha's Vineyard, former major whaling ports; Berkshire Hills with Tanglewood and other performing arts centers; the battlefields of Lexington and Concord near Minute Man National Historical Park; Salem, site of witch trials; Plymouth Rock
products electronic, communications, and optical equipment; precision instruments; nonelectrical machinery; fish; cranberries; dairy products
famous people the Adamses: Abigail, Henry, John, John Quincy, Samuel; Louis Brandeis; Emily Dickinson; Ralph Waldo Emerson; Robert Goddard; Nathaniel Hawthorne; Oliver Wendell Holmes; Winslow Homer; William James; the Kennedys: Joseph, John F, Robert; Robert Lowell; Paul Revere; Henry Thoreau; Daniel Webster
history one of the original Thirteen Colonies, it was first settled 1620 by the Pilgrims at Plymouth. After the Boston Tea Party 1773, the American Revolution began at Lexington and Concord April 19, 1775, and the British evacuated Boston the following year. Massachusetts achieved statehood 1788. In the early 19th century the first large-scale factories were built here to turn out textiles. The state also prospered from whaling and shipbuilding. Heavy immigration of Irish, Germans, and Italians greatly modified the Yankee character of Massachusetts by 1900. After World War II, high technology, sophisticated services, and tourism replaced textiles, footwear, and maritime activities as the mainspring of the economy.

massage method of relieving muscle tension in the body by systematic stroking, pressing, and kneading. It is used as an aid to relaxation (sometimes in combination with ◊aromatherapy) as well as in medical treatment.

Massasoit c. 1590–1661. Wampanoag leader. Born in the area of modern Bristol, Rhode Island, he was also known as Ousamequin, or "Yellow Feather." As one of the leaders of the Wampanoag, a people inhabiting the coasts of Massachusetts Bay and Cape Cod, he officially allied himself with the Plymouth Colony 1621 as a political counterbalance against the neighboring Narragansett. In 1638 Massasoit formed an alliance with the founders of the Massachusetts Bay Colony. Upon his death, his son Metacomet, known to the English as "King ◊Philip," assumed leadership of the Wampanoag.

Massawa chief port and naval base of Ethiopia, in Eritrea, on the Red Sea, with salt production and pearl fishing; population (1980) 33,000. It is one of the hottest inhabited spots in the world, the temperature reaching 100°F/37.8°C in May. Massawa was an Italian possession 1885–1941.

Masséna André 1756–1817. Marshal of France. He served in the French Revolutionary Wars and under the emperor Napoleon was created marshal 1804, duke of Rivoli 1808, and prince of Essling 1809. He was in command in Spain 1810–11 in the Peninsular War and was defeated by British troops under Wellington.

mass–energy equation ◊Einstein's equation $E = mc^2$, denoting the equivalence of mass and energy, where E is the energy in joules, m is the mass in kilograms, and c is the speed of light, in a vacuum, in meters per second.

Massenet Jules Emile Frédéric 1842–1912. French composer of opera, ballets, oratorios, and orchestral suites.

His many operas include *Hérodiade* 1881, *Manon* 1884, *Le Cid* 1885, and *Thaïs* 1894; among other works is the orchestral suite *Scènes pittoresques* 1874.

Masses, The US left-wing magazine that published many prominent radical writers 1911–17, including John Reed and Max Eastman. It was superseded by *The Liberator* 1918–25 and then by *New Masses*, which advanced the cause of proletarian writing during the Depression years of the 1930s.

Massey Vincent 1887–1967. Canadian Liberal Party politician. He was the first Canadian to become governor-general of Canada (1952–59).

Massawa Workers processing salt at the Ethiopian port of Massawa, where water evaporates quickly in temperatures that reach 115°F/46°C.

Massif Central mountainous plateau region of S central France; area 36,000 sq mi/93,000 sq km, highest peak Puy de Sancy 6,188 ft/1,886 m. It is a source of hydroelectricity.

Massine Léonide 1895–1979. Russian choreographer and dancer with the Ballets Russes. He was a creator of comedy in ballet and also symphonic ballet using concert music.

He succeeded Mikhail ◊Fokine at the Ballets Russes and continued with the company after Sergei ◊Diaghilev's death, later working in both the US and Europe. His works include the first Cubist-inspired ballet, *Parade* 1917, *La Boutique Fantasque* 1919, and *The Three-Cornered Hat* 1919.

Massinger Philip 1583–1640. English dramatist, author of *A New Way to Pay Old Debts* about 1625. He collaborated with ◊Fletcher and ◊Dekker, and has been credited with a share in writing Shakespeare's *Two Noble Kinsmen* and *Henry VIII*.

mass number or ***nucleon number*** the sum (symbol A) of the numbers of protons and neutrons in the nucleus of an atom. It is used along with the ◊atomic number in the symbols that represent nuclear isotopes—for example, in ${}^{14}_{6}C$, the lower number is the atomic number of the carbon isotope, and the upper number is its mass number.

Masson André 1896–1987. French artist and writer, a leader of Surrealism until 1929. His interest in the unconscious led him to experiment with "automatic" drawing—simple pen and ink work, and later multitextured accretions of pigment, glue, and sand.

Masson left the Surrealist movement after a quarrel with the writer André Breton. During World War II he moved to the US, then returned to France and painted landscapes.

Massorah a collection of philological notes on the Hebrew text of the Old Testament. It was at first an oral tradition, but was committed to writing in the Aramaic language at Tiberias, Palestine, between the 6th and 9th centuries.

mass production the manufacture of goods on a large scale, a technique that aims for low unit cost and high output. In factories mass production is achieved by a variety of means, such as division and specialization of labor and ◊mechanization. These speed up production and allow the manufacture of near-identical, interchangeable parts. Such parts can then be assembled quickly into a finished product on an ◊assembly line.

Division of labor means that a job is divided into a number of steps, and then groups of workers are employed to carry each step out, specializing and therefore doing the job in a routine way, producing more than if each individually had to carry out all the stages of manufacture. However, the system has been criticized for deskilling workers and removing their involvement with the end product.

Many of the machines now used in factories are ◊robots: they work automatically under computer control. Such automation further streamlines production and raises output.

mass spectrograph or ***mass spectrometer*** in physics, an apparatus for analyzing chemical composition. Positive ions (charged particles) of a substance are separated by an electromagnetic system, designed to focus particles of equal mass to a point where they can be detected. This permits accurate measurement of the relative concentrations of the various ionic masses present, particularly isotopes.

Masters Edgar Lee 1869–1950. US poet and novelist. In his book *Spoon River Anthology* 1915, a collection of free-verse epitaphs, the people of a small town tell of their frustrated lives.

He published numerous other volumes of verse, novels, and biographies.

Masters John 1914–1983. British novelist, born in Calcutta, who served in the Indian army 1934–47.

He wrote a series of books dealing with the Savage family throughout the period of the Raj, for example, *Nightrunners of Bengal* 1951, *The Deceivers* 1952, and *Bhowani Junction* 1954.

Masterson Bat (William Barclay) 1853–1921. US marshal and sportswriter. In 1878 he succeeded his murdered brother, Edward, as marshal in Dodge City, Kansas, and gunned down his brother's killers. After a brief time in Tombstone, Arizona, where he served with Wyatt Earp 1880, Masterson returned to Kansas. He moved to New York 1902, where he became a sportswriter for the *Morning Telegraph*.

Born in Iroquois County, Illinois, and raised in Kansas, Masterson worked in his early adult years as a buffalo hunter and scout before becoming a deputy marshal in Dodge City 1876.

mastiff breed of powerful dog, usually fawn in color, that was originally bred in Britain for hunting purposes. It has a large head, wide-set eyes, and broad muzzle. It can grow up to 3 ft/90 cm at the shoulder, and weigh 220 lb/100 kg.

mastodon any of an extinct family (Mastodontidae) of mammals of the elephant order (Proboscidae). They differed from elephants and mammoths in the structure of their grinding teeth. There were numerous species, among which the American mastodon *Mastodon americanum*, about 10 ft/3 m high, of the Pleistocene era, is well known. They were hunted by humans for food.

Mastroianni Marcello 1924– . Italian film actor, most popular for his carefully understated roles as an unhappy romantic lover in such films as Antonioni's *La Notte/The Night* 1961. He starred in several films with Sophia Loren such as *A Special Day* 1977 and worked with Fellini in *La dolce vita* 1960, *8½* 1963, *Roma* 1971, and *Ginger and Fred* 1985.

Masulipatnam or ***Manchilipatnam***, also ***Bandar*** Indian seaport (its name means fish town) in Andhra, at the mouth of the northern branch of the river Kistna; population (1981) 138,500.

Masurian Lakes lakes in Poland (former East Prussia) which in 1914–15 were the scene of battles in which the Germans defeated the Russians.

Matabeleland the W portion of Zimbabwe between the Zambezi and Nimpopo rivers, inhabited by the Ndebele people

area 70,118 sq mi/181,605 sq km

cities Bulawayo

features rich plains watered by tributaries of the Zambezi and Limpopo, with mineral resources

language Matabele

famous people Joshua Nkomo

history Matabeleland was granted to the British South Africa Company 1889 and occupied 1893 after attacks on white settlements in Mashonaland; in 1923 it was included in Southern Rhodesia. It is now divided into two administrative regions. Joshua Nkomo was accused of plotting to overthrow the post-independence government of Zimbabwe and then expelled from the cabinet in 1981. Zimbabwe African People's Union (ZAPU) supporters, mostly drawn from the Ndebele people, began a loosely organized armed rebellion against the Zimbabwe African National Union (ZANU) government of Robert Mugabe. The insurgency was brought to an end in April 1988, when a unity agreement was reached between ZANU and ZAPU and Nkomo was appointed minister of state in the office of the president.

Matadi chief port of Zaïre on the river Zaïre, 70 mi/115 km from its mouth, linked by oil pipelines with Kinshasa; population (1984) 144,700.

Mata Hari stage name of Gertrud Margarete Zelle 1876–1917. Dutch courtesan, dancer, and probable spy. In World War I she had affairs with highly placed military and government officials on both sides and told Allied secrets to the Germans. She may have been a double agent, in the pay of both France and Germany. She was shot by the French on espionage charges.

matamata South American freshwater turtle or terrapin *Chelys fimbriata* with a shell up to 15 in/40 cm long.

The head is flattened, with a "snorkel" nose, and the neck has many projections of skin. The movement of these in the water may attract prey, which the matamata catches by opening its mouth suddenly to produce an inrush of water.

Matanzas industrial port (tanning, textiles, sugar) in NW Cuba; population (1986) 105,400. Founded 1693, it became a major center of coffee, tobacco, and sugar production.

Matapan southernmost cape of mainland Greece, off which, on March 28, 1941, during World War II, a British fleet under Admiral Cunningham sank an Italian squadron.

match small strip of wood or paper, tipped with combustible material for producing fire. Friction matches containing phosphorus were first made in 1816 in France by François Derosne.

A safety match is one in which the oxidizing agent and the combustible body are kept apart, the former being incorporated into the striking surface on the side of the box, the latter into the match. Safety matches were patented by a Swede, J E Lundström, 1855. Book matches were invented in the US 1892 by Joshua Pusey.

maté dried leaves of the Brazilian ◊holly *Ilex paraguensis*, an evergreen shrub that grows in Paraguay and Brazil. The roasted, powdered leaves are made into a tea.

materialism the philosophical theory that there is nothing in existence over and above matter and matter in motion. Such a theory excludes the possibility of deities. It also sees mind as an attribute of the physical, denying idealist theories that see mind as something independent of body; for example, Descartes' theory of "thinking substance."

Like most other philosophical ideas, materialism probably arose among the early Greek thinkers. The Stoics and the Epicureans were materialists, and so were the ancient Buddhists. Among later materialists have been Hobbes, Diderot, d'Holbach, Büchner, and Haeckel; Hume, J S Mill, Huxley, and Spencer showed materialist tendencies.

material product or ***social product*** system of national accounting used by Socialist countries which includes all productive services but usually does not include nonpublic services and financial activities that would be included in conventional Western national accounts to give gross national product. Gross domestic product (GDP) is a more comprehensive measure of a country's output.

mathematical induction a formal method of proof in which the proposition $P(n + 1)$ is proved true on the hypothesis that the proposition $P(n)$ is true. The proposition is then shown to be true for a particular value of n, say k, and therefore by induction the proposition must be true for $n = k + 1, k + 2, k + 3, \ldots$. In many cases $k = 1$, so then the proposition is true for all positive integers.

mathematics the science of spatial and numerical relationships. The main divisions of pure mathematics include geometry, arithmetic, algebra, calculus, and trigonometry. Mechanics, statistics, numerical analysis, computing, the mathematical theories of astronomy, electricity, optics, thermodynamics, and atomic studies come under the heading of applied mathematics.

early history Prehistoric human beings probably learned to count at least up to ten on their fingers. The Chinese, Mayans, Hindus, Babylonians, and Egyptians all devised methods of counting and measuring that were of practical importance in their everyday lives. The first theoretical mathematician is held to be Thales of Melitus (c. 580 BC) who is believed to have proposed the first theorems in plane geometry. His disciple ◊Pythagoras established geometry as a recognized science among the Greeks. The later school of Alexandrian geometers (4th and 3rd centuries BC) included ◊Euclid and ◊Archimedes. Our present decimal numerals are based on a Hindu-Arabic system that reached Europe about AD 100 from Arab mathematicians of the Middle East such as al ◊Khwarizmi.

Europe Western mathematics began to develop from the 15th century. Geometry was revitalized by the invention of coordinate geometry by Descartes 1637; Pascal and Fermat developed probability theory, Napier invented logarithms, and Newton and Leibniz developed calculus. In Russia, Lobachevsky rejected Euclid's parallelism and developed non-Euclidean geometry, a more developed form of which (by Riemann) was later utilized by Einstein in his relativity theory.

the present Higher mathematics has a powerful tool in the high-speed electronic computer, which can create and manipulate mathematical "models" of various systems in science, technology, and commerce. Modern additions to school syllabuses such as sets, group theory, matrices, and graph theory are sometimes referred to as "new" or "modern" mathematics.

Mather Cotton 1663–1728. American theologian and writer. He was a Puritan minister in Boston, a promoter of strict Congregationalism, and a man of great learning, writing over 400 works of theology, history, and science.

Born in Boston, Mather graduated from Harvard with a master's degree 1681 and was ordained a minister 1685. Mather appears to have supported the Salem witch hunts; he wrote *Memorable Providences Relating to Witchcraft and Possession* 1689 and told of the witchcraft trials in *Wonders of the Invisible World* 1693. His history of New England, *Magnalia Christi Americana* 1702, was the most extensive history of the area at the time.

Mather Increase 1639–1723. Colonial American religious leader. Born in Dorchester, Massachusetts, and educated at Harvard, Mather served as a cleric in England during the Puritan Commonwealth. He returned to Massachusetts 1661, was named teacher of Boston's Second Church 1664, and served as president of Harvard 1685–1701 As a defender of the colonial right to self-government, Mather went to England 1688 to protest revocation of the Massachusetts charter. However, his association with the new governor and his silence during the Salem witch trials of the 1690s lessened his public influence. His eldest son was Cotton ◊Mather.

Mathewson Christy (Christopher) 1880–1925. US baseball player. Born in Factoryville, Pennsylvania, Mathewson attended Bucknell University. A standout pitcher, he was signed by the New York Giants of the National League 1900. During a 17-year major-league career, Mathewson amassed an impressive record of 373 wins and 188 losses. He retired from play 1916, assuming the job of Cincinnati Reds manager 1916–18. Mathewson was elected to the Baseball Hall of Fame 1936.

Matilda 1102–1167. Claimant to the throne of England. On the death of her father, Henry I, in 1135, the barons elected her cousin Stephen to be king. Matilda invaded England 1139, and was crowned by her supporters 1141. Civil war ensued until in 1153 Stephen was finally recognized as king, with Henry II (Matilda's son) as his successor.

Matilda was recognized during the reign of Henry I as his heir. She married first the Holy Roman emperor Henry V and, after his death, Geoffrey Plantagenet, Count of Anjou (1113–1151).

Matisse Henri 1869–1954. French painter, sculptor, illustrator, and designer; one of the most original creative forces in early 20th-century art. His work concentrates on designs that emphasize curvaceous surface patterns, linear arabesques, and brilliant color. Subjects include odalisques (women of the harem), bathers, and dancers; later works include pure abstracts, as in his collages of colored paper shapes and the designs 1949–51 for the

mathematical symbols

$a \rightarrow b$	*a* implies *b*
∞	infinity
lim	limiting value
$a \sim b$	numerical difference between *a* and *b*
$a \approx b$	*a* approximately equal to *b*
$a=b$	*a* equal to *b*
$a=b$	*a* identical with *b* (for formulae only)
$a>b$	*a* greater than *b*
$a<b$	*a* smaller than *b*
$a \neq b$	*a* not equal to *b*
$b<a<c$	*a* greater than *b* and smaller than *c*, that is *a* lies between the values *b* & *c* but cannot equal either.
$a \geqslant b$	*a* equal to or greater than *b*, that is, *a* at least as great as *b*
$a \leqslant b$	*a* equal to or less than *b*, that is, *a* at most as great as *b*
$b \leqslant a \leqslant c$	*a* lies between the values *b* & *c* and could take the values *b* and *c*.
$\lvert a \rvert$	absolute value of *a*; this is always positive, for example $\lvert -5 \rvert = 5$
$+$	addition sign, positive
$-$	subtraction sign, negative
$\times$ or $\odot$	multiplication sign, times
$:$ or $\div$ or $/$	division sign, divided by
$a+b=c$	$a+b$, read as '*a* plus *b*', denotes the addition of *a* and *b*. The result of the addition, *c*, is also known as the sum.
$\int$	indefinite integral
$\int_a^b f(x)dx$	definite integral, or integral between $x=a$ and $x=b$
$a-b=c$	$a-b$, read as '*a* minus *b*', denotes subtraction of *b* from *a*. $a-b$, or *c*, is the difference. Subtraction is the opposite of addition.
$a \times b=c$, $ab=c$, $a.b=c$	$a \times b$, read as '*a* multiplied by *b*', denotes multiplication of *a* by *b*. $a \times b$, or *c*, is the product, *a* and *b* are factors of *c*.
$a:b=c$, $a \div b=c$, $a/b=c$	$a:c$, read as '*a* divided by *b*', denotes division. *a* is the dividend, *b* is the divisor; $a:b$, or *c*, is the quotient. One aspect of division – repeated subtraction, is the opposite of multiplication – repeated addition. In fractions, $\frac{a}{b}$ or a/b, *a* is the numerator (= dividend), *b* the denominator (= divisor).
$a^b=c$	a^b, read as '*a* to the power *b*'; *a* is the base, *b* the exponent.
$^b\sqrt{a}=c$	$^b\sqrt{a}$, is the *b*th root of *a*, *b* being known as the root exponent. In the special case of $^2\sqrt{a}=c$, $^2\sqrt{a}$ or *c* is known as the square root of *a*, and the root exponent is usually omitted, that is, $^2\sqrt{a} = \sqrt{a}$.
e	exponential constant and is the base of natural (napierian) logarithms = 2.7182818284........
π	ratio of the circumference of a circle to its diameter = 3.1415925535........

decoration of a chapel for the Dominican convent in Vence, near Nice.

In 1904 Matisse worked with Signac in the south of France in a Neo-Impressionist style. The following year he was the foremost of the Fauve painters exhibiting at the Salon d'Automne, painting with bold brushstrokes, thick paint, and strong colors. He soon abandoned conventional perspective in his continued experiments with color, and in 1910 an exhibition of Islamic art further influenced him toward the decorative. He settled in the south of France in 1914. His murals of *The Dance* 1932–33 (Barnes Foundation, Merion, Pennsylvania) are characteristic.

Matlock spa town with warm springs, administrative headquarters of Derbyshire, England; population (1981) 21,000.

Mato Grosso (Portuguese "dense forest") area of SW Brazil, now forming two states, with their capitals at Cuiaba and Campo Grande. The forests, now depleted, supplied rubber and rare timbers; diamonds and silver are mined.

matriarchy a form of social organization in which the mother is recognized as head of the family or group, with descent and kinship traced to the mother, and where women rule or dominate the group's organization. See also ◊matriliny.

matriliny a form of social organization, such as a clan, in which descent and relationship are calculated through the female line. In matrilineal societies, powerful positions are usually held by men but acceded to through female kin. See also ◊matriarchy.

matrix in mathematics, a square ($n \times n$) or rectangular ($m \times n$) array of elements (numbers or algebraic variables). They are a means of condensing information about mathematical systems and can be used for, among other things, solving simultaneous linear equations and transformations.

Much early matrix theory was developed by the British mathematician Arthur ◊Cayley, although the term was coined by his contemporary James Sylvester (1814–1897).

matrix in biology, usually refers to the ◊extracellular matrix.

Matsudaira Tsuneo 1877–1949. Japanese diplomat and politician who became the first chair of the Japanese Diet (parliament) after World War II.

Matsudaira negotiated for Japan at the London Naval Conference of 1930 and acted as imperial household minister 1936–45, advising the emperor, but was unsuccessful in keeping Japan out of a war with the Western powers.

Matsue city NW of Osaka on Honshu, Japan; population (1980) 135,500. It has remains of a castle, fine old tea houses, and the Izumo Grand Shrine (dating in its present form from 1744).

Matsukata Masayoshi, Prince 1835–1924. Japanese politician, premier 1891–92 and 1896–98. As minister of finance 1881–91 and 1898–1900, he paved the way for the modernization of the Japanese economy.

Matsuoka Yosuke 1880–1946. Japanese politician, foreign minister 1940–41. A fervent nationalist, Matsuoka led Japan out of the League of Nations when it condemned Japan for the seizure of Manchuria. As foreign minister, he allied Japan with Germany and Italy. At the end of World War II, he was arrested as a war criminal but died before his trial.

Matsuyama largest city on Shikoku, Japan; industries (agricultural machinery, textiles, chemicals); population (1984) 418,000. There is a feudal fortress 1634.

Matsys also ***Massys*** or ***Metsys*** Quentin c. 1464–1530. Flemish painter, born in Louvain, active in Antwerp. He painted religious subjects such as the *Lamentation* 1511 (Musées Royaux, Antwerp) and portraits set against landscapes or realistic interiors.

His works include the *St Anne Altarpiece* 1509 (Musées Royaux, Brussels) and a portrait of *Erasmus* 1517 (Museo Nazionale, Rome).

matter in physics, anything that has mass and can be detected and measured. All matter (see also ◊antimatter) is made up of ◊atoms and ◊elementary particles, and exists ordinarily as a solid, liquid, or gas. The history of science and philosophy is largely taken up with accounts of theories of matter, ranging from the hard "atoms" of Democritus to the "waves" of modern quantum theory.

Matterhorn (French *le Cervin*, Italian *il Cervino*) mountain peak in the Alps on the Swiss-Italian border; 14,690 ft/4,478 m.

It was first climbed in 1865 by English mountaineer Edward Whymper (1840–1911); four members of his party of seven were killed when the rope broke during the descent.

Matthau Walter. Adopted name of Walter Matuschanskavasky 1920– . US character actor, impressive in both comedy and dramatic roles. He gained film stardom in the 1960s after his stage success in *The Odd Couple* 1965. His many films include *Kotch* 1971, *Charley Varrick* 1973, and *The Sunshine Boys* 1975.

Matthew, St 1st century AD. Christian apostle and evangelist, the traditional author of the first Gospel. He is usually identified with Levi, who was a tax collector in the service of Herod Antipas, and was called by Jesus to be a disciple as he sat by the Lake of Galilee receiving customs dues. His emblem is a man with wings; feast day Sept 21.

Matthews Stanley 1824–1889. US jurist and associate justice of the US Supreme Court 1881–89. His most important decision, *Hurtado* v *California* 1888, was an important constitutional definition of due process of law.

Born in Cincinnati, Ohio, Matthews graduated

Matterhorn *Switzerland's Matterhorn, long a challenge to the world's best climbers, appears to be an isolated peak, but is actually the end of a ridge.*

Maugham British writer Somerset Maugham, noted particularly for his short stories and novels, in a 1931 portrait.

from Kenyon College and studied law in Cincinnati. He practiced law in Tennessee and later in Ohio. He served in the Ohio Senate 1855–57 and as a US attorney for the southern district of Ohio 1858–61. After Civil War service, Matthews sat as a judge of the Cincinnati Superior Court and then returned to private practice. He was appointed to the Supreme Court by President Garfield 1881.

Matthias Corvinus 1440–1490. King of Hungary from 1458. His aim of uniting Hungary, Austria, and Bohemia involved him in long wars with the Holy Roman emperor and the kings of Bohemia and Poland, during which he captured Vienna (1485) and made it his capital. His father was János ◊Hunyadi.

Mature Victor 1915– . US actor, film star of the 1940s and early 1950s. He gave memorable performances in, among others, *My Darling Clementine* 1946, *Kiss of Death* 1947, and *Samson and Delilah* 1949.

Mauchly John William 1907–1980. US physicist and engineer who, in 1946, constructed the first general-purpose computer, the ENIAC, in collaboration with John ◊Eckert. Their company was bought by Remington Rand in 1950, and they built the UNIVAC 1 computer in 1951 for the US census.

The idea for ENIAC grew out of work carried out by the two during World War II on ways of automating the calculation of artillery firing tables for the US Army.

Maugham (William) Somerset 1874–1965. English writer. His work includes the novels *Of Human Bondage* 1915, *The Moon and Sixpence* 1919, and *Cakes and Ale* 1930; the short-story collections *The Trembling of a Leaf* 1921 and *Ashenden* 1928; and the plays *Lady Frederick* 1907 and *Our Betters* 1923.

Born in Paris, he studied medicine at St Thomas's, London. During World War I he was a secret agent in Russia; his *Ashenden* spy stories are based on this experience.

Mau Mau a Kenyan secret guerrilla movement 1952–60, an offshoot of the Kikuyu Central Association banned in World War II. Its aim was to end British colonial rule. This was achieved in 1960 with the granting of Kenyan independence and the election of Jomo Kenyatta as Kenya's first prime minister.

A state of emergency was declared in 1952, and by 1956 colonial government forces had killed more than 11,000 Kikuyu. More than 100 Europeans and Asians and 2,000 pro-government Kikuyu were killed by the Mau Mau. The state of emergency was ended in 1960, and three years later Kenya was granted independence. Jomo Kenyatta, who was convicted of being the leader of the Mau Mau, became the country's first prime minister.

Mauna Kea astronomical observatory in Hawaii, built on a dormant volcano at 13,784 ft/4,200 m above sea level. Because of its elevation high above clouds, atmospheric moisture, and artificial lighting, Mauna Kea is ideal for infrared astronomy. The first telescope on the site was installed 1970.

Telescopes include the 88-in/2.24-m University of Hawaii Reflector 1970. In 1979 three telescopes were erected: the 150-in/3.8-m United Kingdom Infrared Telescope (UKIRT) (also used for optical observations); the 120-in/3-m NASA Infrared Telescope Facility (IRTF); and the 142-in/3.6-m Canada–France–Hawaii Telescope (CFHT), designed for optical and infrared work. The 50-ft/15-m diameter UK/Netherlands James Clerk Maxwell Telescope (JCMT) is the world's largest telescope specifically designed to observe millimeter-wave radiation from nebulae, stars, and galaxies. The JCMT is operated via satellite links by astronomers in Europe.

Work began 1986 on what will be the world's largest optical telescope, the W M Keck Telescope. It will have a primary mirror 33 ft/10 m across, unique in that it comprises 36 individual hexagonal segments joined together in a giant mosaic, each controlled and adjusted by computer to generate single images of the objects observed. The Keck Telescope will be built and operated jointly on Mauna Kea by the California Institute of Technology and the University of California.

Mauna Loa active volcano rising to a height of 13,678 ft/4,169 m on the Pacific island of Hawaii; it has numerous craters, including the second-largest active crater in the world.

Maundy Thursday in the Christian church, the Thursday before Easter. The ceremony of washing the feet of pilgrims on that day was instituted in commemoration of Jesus' washing of the apostles' feet and observed from the 4th century to 1754.

Maupassant Guy de 1850–1893. French author who established a reputation with the short story "Boule de Suif/Ball of Fat" 1880 and wrote some 300 short stories in all. His novels include *Une Vie*/*A Woman's Life* 1883 and *Bel-Ami* 1885. He was encouraged as a writer by ◊Flaubert.

Mauriac François 1885–1970. French novelist. His novel *Le Baiser au lépreux*/*A Kiss for the Leper* 1922 describes the conflict of an unhappy marriage. The irreconcilability of Christian practice and human nature are examined in *Fleuve de feu*/*River of Fire* 1923, *Le Désert de l'amour*/*The Desert of Love* 1925, and *Thérèse Desqueyroux* 1927. He received the Nobel Prize for Literature 1952.

Maurist a congregation of French Benedictine Catholic monks, established in 1621 at the monastery of St Maur-sur-Loire. Subsequently its chief house was in Paris, and there the Maurist fathers carried on literary and historical work. In 1792 the congregation was suppressed.

Mauritania country in NW Africa, bordered NE by Algeria, E and S by Mali, SW by Senegal, W by the Atlantic Ocean, and NW by Western Sahara.

government The 1961 constitution was suspended 1978 after a coup and was replaced by a charter that gave executive and legislative power to a Military Committee for National Recovery (CMRN), which in 1979 became the Military Committee for National Salvation (CMSN). The chair of the CMSN is also president of the republic, prime minister, and minister of defense. The only political party, the Mauritanian People's Party (PPM), was banned 1978, and some of its exiled supporters now operate from Paris through the Alliance for a Democratic Mauritania (AMI), or from Dakar, in Senegal, through the Organization of Nationalist Mauritanians.

Mauritania
Islamic Republic of
(*République Islamique de Mauritanie*)

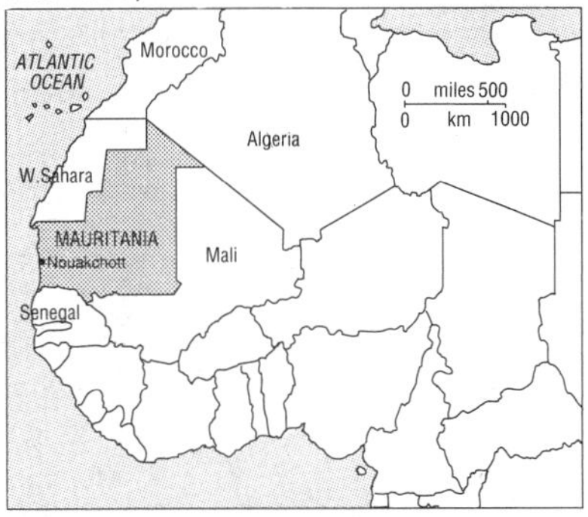

ATLANTIC OCEAN
Morocco
0 miles 500
0 km 1000
Algeria
W.Sahara
MAURITANIA
Nouakchott
Mali
Senegal

area 397,850 sq mi/1,030,700 sq km
capital Nouakchott
cities port of Nouadhibou, Kaédi, Zouérate
physical valley of river Senegal in S; remainder arid and flat
features part of the Sahara Desert; dusty sirocco wind blows in March
head of state and government Moaouia Ould Sidi Mohamed Taya from 1984
political system military republic
political parties none
exports iron ore, fish, gypsum
currency ouguiya
population (1990 est) 2,038,000 (30% Arab-Berber, 30% black Africans, 30% Haratine–descendants of black slaves, who remained slaves until 1980); growth rate 3% p.a.
life expectancy men 43, women 48 (1989)
language French (official), Hasaniya Arabic, and Black African languages
religion Sunni Muslim 99%
literacy 17% (1987)
GNP $843 mn; $480 per head (1988)
chronology
1903 Became a French protectorate.
1960 Independence achieved from France, with Moktar Ould Daddah as president.
1975 Western Sahara ceded by Spain. Mauritania occupied the southern part and Morocco the rest. Polisario Front formed in Sahara to resist the occupation by Mauritania and Morocco.
1978 Daddah deposed in bloodless coup; replaced by Mohamed Khouni Ould Haidalla. Peace agreed with Polisario Front.
1981 Diplomatic relations with Morocco broken.
1984 Haidalla overthrown by Moaouia Ould Sidi Mohamed Taya. Polisario regime formally recognized.
1985 Relations with Morocco restored.
1989 Violent clashes between Mauritanians and Senegalese in Nouakchott and Dakar over disputed border grazing rights. Arab-dominated government expelled thousands of Africans into N Senegal; governments had earlier agreed to repatriate each other's citizens (about 250,000).
1991 Amnesty for political prisoners. Multiparty elections promised. Calls for resignation of President Taya.

history Mauritania was the name of the Roman province of NW Africa, after the Mauri, a ◊Berber people who inhabited it. Berbers occupied the region during the 1st–3rd centuries AD, and it came under the control of the ◊Ghana Empire in the 7th–11th centuries. The Berbers were converted to Islam from the 8th century, and Islamic influence continued to dominate as the area was controlled by the ◊Almoravids and then the Arabs. French influence began in the 17th century, with the trade in gum arabic, and developed into colonization by the mid-18th century, when France gained control of S Mauritania.

In 1920 Mauritania became a French colony as part of ◊French West Africa. It achieved internal self-government within the French Community 1958 and full independence 1960. Moktar Ould Daddah, leader of the PPM, became president 1961.

In 1975 Spain ceded Western Sahara to Mauritania and Morocco, leaving them to decide how to share it. Without consulting the Saharan people, Mauritania occupied the south, leaving the north to Morocco. A resistance movement developed against this occupation, the Popular Front for Liberation, or the Polisario Front, with Algerian backing, and Mauritania and Morocco found themselves engaged in a guerrilla war, forcing the two former rivals into a mutual defense pact. The conflict weakened Mauritania's economy, and in 1978 President Daddah was deposed in a bloodless coup led by Col Mohamed Khouna Ould Haidalla. Peace with the Polisario was eventually agreed in Aug, allowing diplomatic relations with Algeria to be restored.

In Dec 1984, while Colonel Haidalla was attending a Franco-African summit meeting in Burundi, Col Moaouya Ould Sidi Ahmed Taya, a former prime minister, led a bloodless coup to overthrow him. Diplomatic relations with Morocco were broken 1981 and the situation worsened 1984 when Mauritania formally recognized the Polisario regime in Western Sahara. Normal relations were restored 1985. During 1989 there were a number of clashes with Senegalese in border areas, and the presidents of the two countries met to try to resolve their differences. Citizens of each country were forced to return to their native country, with nearly 50,000 people repatriating by June. In July 1991 voters approved a new constitution that increased political freedom, and opposition political parties were approved.

Mauritius island in the Indian Ocean, E of Madagascar.

government Mauritius is an independent state within the ◊Commonwealth, with a resident governor-general as head of state, representing the British monarch. Its 1968 constitution, amended in 1969, provides for a single-chamber legislative assembly of up to 71 members, 62 elected by universal adult suffrage, plus the speaker and up to 8 of the most successful nonelected candidates as "additional" members. The governor-general appoints the prime minister and a council of ministers who are collectively responsible to the assembly. Of a number of political parties, the three most significant are the Mauritius Labor Party (MLP), the Mauritius Socialist Movement (MSM), and the Mauritius Militant Movement (MMM).

history Uninhabited until the 16th century, the island was colonized on a small scale by the Dutch, who named it Mauricius after Prince Maurice of Nassau. They abandoned it in 1710, and in 1715 it was occupied by the French, who imported African slaves to work on their sugar-cane plantations. Mauritius was seized by Britain in 1810 and was formally ceded by the Treaty of ◊Paris in 1814. The abolition of slavery in 1833 brought about the importation of indentured laborers from India, whose descendants now make up about 70% of the island's population. In 1957 Mauritius achieved internal self-government, and full independence within the Commomwealth in 1968.

Mauritius
State of

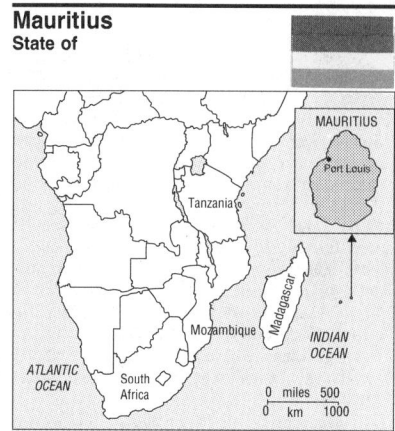

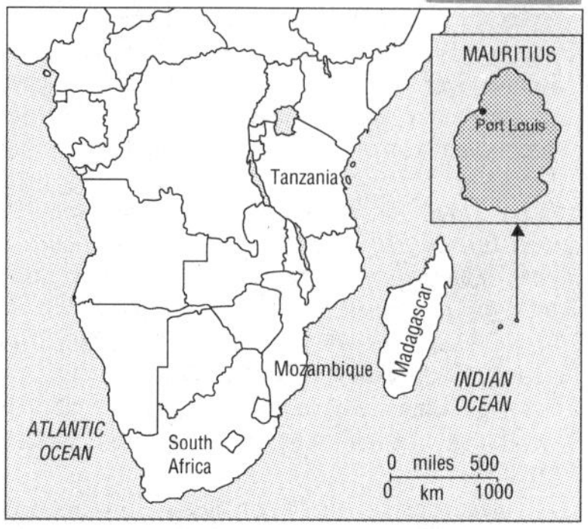
MAURITIUS
Port Louis
Tanzania
Madagascar
Mozambique
INDIAN OCEAN
ATLANTIC OCEAN
South Africa
0 miles 500
0 km 1000

area 720 sq mi/1,865 sq km; the island of Rodrigues is part of Mauritius; there are several small island dependencies
capital Port Louis
cities Beau Bassin-Rose Hill, Curepipe, Quatre Bornes
physical mountainous, volcanic island surrounded by coral reefs
features unusual wildlife includes flying fox and ostrich; it was home of the dodo (extinct from about 1680)
head of state Elizabeth II represented by governor-general
head of government Aneerood Jugnauth from 1982
political system constitutional monarchy
political parties Mauritius Socialist Movement (MSM), moderate Socialist-republican; Mauritius Labor Party (MLP), centrist Hindu-orientated; Mauritius Social Democratic Party (PMSD), conservative, Francophile; Mauritius Militant Movement (MMM), Marxist-republican
exports sugar, knitted goods, tea
currency Mauritius rupee
population (1990 est) 1,141,900, 68% of Indian origin; growth rate 1.5% p.a.
life expectancy men 64, women 71 (1989)
language English (official); French, Creole, Indian languages
religion Hindu 51%, Christian 30%, Muslim 17%
literacy 94% (1989)
GNP $1.4 bn (1987); $1,810 per head (1988)
chronology
1814 Annexed to Britain by the Treaty of Paris.
1968 Independence achieved from Britain within the Commonwealth, with Seewoosagur Ramgoolam as prime minister.
1982 Aneerood Jugnauth prime minister.
1983 Jugnauth formed a new party, the Mauritius Socialist Movement, pledged to make Mauritius a republic within the Commonwealth, but Assembly refused. Ramgoolam appointed governor-general. Jugnauth formed a new coalition government.
1985 Ramgoolam died, succeeded by Ringadoo.
1987 Jugnauth's coalition reelected.
1990 Attempt to create a republic failed.

Seewoosagur Ramgoolam, leader of the MLP, who had led the country since 1959, became its first prime minister. During the 1970s he led a succession of coalition governments, and even in 1976, when the MMM became the assembly's largest single party, Ramgoolam formed another fragile coalition. Dissatisfaction with the government's economic policies led to Ramgoolam's defeat and the formation in 1982 of an MMM-Mauritius Socialist Party (PSM) coalition government led by Aneerood Jugnauth. Strains developed within the alliance, 12 MMM ministers resigned in 1983, and the coalition was dissolved. Jugnauth then founded the MSM, and the PSM was incorporated in the new party. A general election later that year resulted in an MSM-MLP-Mauritius Social Democratic Party (PMSD) coalition, which won 37 assembly seats. Jugnauth became prime minister on the understanding that Sir Seewoosagur Ramgoolam would be president if Mauritius became a republic. When the constitutional change failed to get legislative approval, Sir Seewoosagur Ramgoolam was appointed governor-general in 1983. He died in 1985, and former finance minister, Sir Veersamy Ringadoo, replaced him.

Recent economic policies have cut inflation and unemployment, on the strength of which Aneerood Jugnauth was reelected in an early general election in Aug 1987. Mauritius, which has no standing army, has pursued a moderately nonaligned foreign policy during recent years.

In Aug 1990 an attempt by Prime Minister Jugnauth to make the country a republic was narrowly defeated in the Legislative Assembly.

Maurois André. Adopted name of Emile Herzog 1885–1967. French novelist and writer whose works include the semiautobiographical *Bernard Quesnay* 1926 and fictionalized biographies, such as *Ariel* 1923, a life of Shelley.

Mauroy Pierre 1928– . French Socialist politician, prime minister 1981–84. He oversaw the introduction of a radical reflationary program.

Mauroy worked for the FEN teachers' labor union and served as national secretary for the Young Socialists during the 1950s, rising in the ranks of the Socialist Party in the northeast region. He entered the National Assembly in 1973 and was prime minister in the Mitterrand government of 1981, but was replaced by Laurent Fabius in July 1984.

Maury Matthew Fontaine 1806–1873. US naval officer, founder of the US Naval Oceanographic Office. His system of recording oceanographic data is still used today.

Maurya dynasty Indian dynasty c. 321–c. 185 BC, founded by Chandragupta Maurya (321–c. 279 BC). Under Emperor ◊Asoka most of India was united for the first time, but after his death in 232 the empire was riven by dynastic disputes.

Mawson Douglas 1882–1958. Australian explorer, born in Britain, who reached the magnetic South Pole on Ernest ◊Shackleton's expedition of 1907–09.

Mawson led Antarctic expeditions 1911–14 and 1929–31. Australia's first permanent Antarctic base was named after him. He was professor of mineralogy at the University of Adelaide 1920–1953.

max. abbreviation for maximum.

Maxim Hiram Stevens 1840–1916. US-born (naturalized British) inventor of the first automatic machine gun, in 1884.

Maximilian 1832–1867. Emperor of Mexico 1864–67. He accepted that title when the French emperor Napoleon III's troops occupied the country, but encountered resistance from the deposed president Benito ◊Juárez. In 1866, after the French troops withdrew on the insistence of the US, Maximilian was captured by Mexican republicans and shot.

Maximilian I 1459–1519. Holy Roman emperor from 1493, the son of Emperor Frederick III. He had acquired the Low Countries through his marriage to Mary of Burgundy 1477.

He married his son Philip I (the Handsome) to the heiress to the Spanish throne, and undertook long wars with Italy and Hungary in attempts to extend Hapsburg power. He was the patron of the artist Dürer.

Maurya dynasty

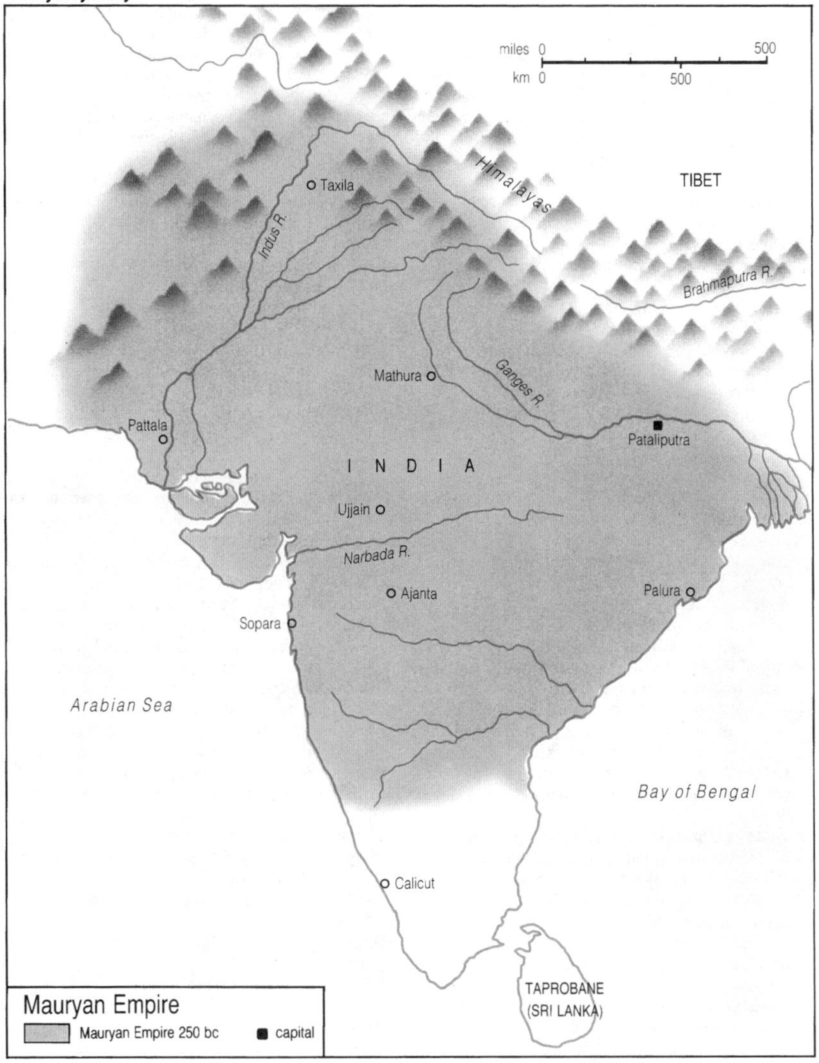

miles 0 500
km 0 500
TIBET
Himalayas
Brahmaputra R.
Taxila
Indus R.
Mathura
Ganges R.
Pattala
I N D I A
Pataliputra
Ujjain
Narbada R.
Ajanta
Palura
Sopara
Arabian Sea
Bay of Bengal
Calicut
TAPROBANE
(SRI LANKA)
Mauryan Empire
Mauryan Empire 250 bc
capital

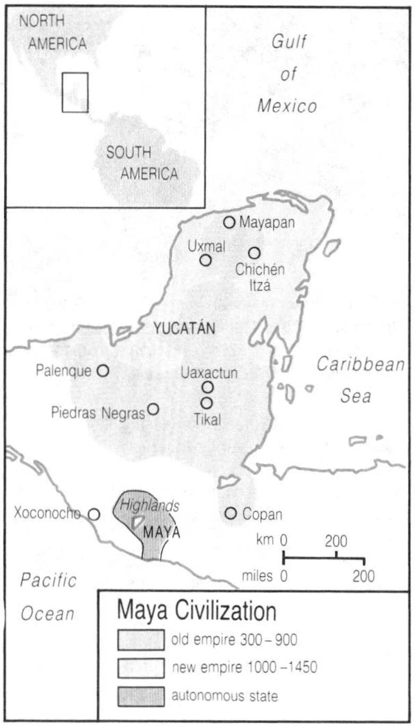

NORTH
AMERICA
SOUTH
AMERICA
Gulf
of
Mexico
Mayapan
Uxmal
Chichén
Itzá
YUCATÁN
Caribbean
Sea
Palenque
Uaxactun
Piedras Negras
Tikal
Xoconocho
Highlands
MAYA
Copan
km 0 200
miles 0 200
Pacific
Ocean
Maya Civilization
old empire 300 - 900
new empire 1000 -1450
autonomous state

maximum and minimum in mathematics, points at which the slope of a curve representing a ◊function in ◊coordinate geometry changes from positive to negative (maximum), or from negative to positive (minimum). A tangent to the curve at a maximum or minimum has zero gradient.

Maxima and minima can be found by differentiating the function for the curve and setting the differential to zero (the value of the slope at the turning point). For example, differentiating the function for the ◊parabola $y = 2x^2 - 8x$ gives $dy/dx = 4x - 8$. Setting this equal to zero gives $x = 2$, so that $y = -8$ (found by substituting $x = 2$ into the parabola equation). Thus the function has a minimum at the point (2, –8).

maximum and minimum

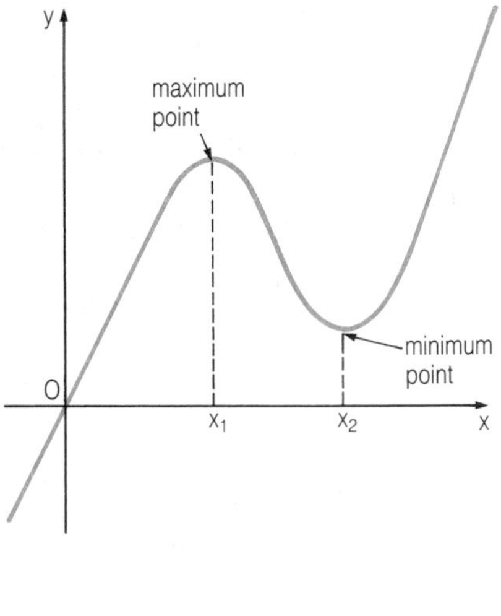

y
maximum
point
minimum
point
0
x1
x2
x

maxwell unit (abbreviation Mx) of magnetic flux (the strength of a ◊magnetic field in an area multiplied by the area). It is now replaced by the SI unit, the ◊weber (one maxwell equals 10^{-8} weber).

The maxwell is a very small unit, representing a single line of magnetic flux. It is equal to the flux through one square centimeter normal to a magnetic field with an intensity of one gauss.

Maxwell (Ian) Robert 1923–1991. Czech-born British publishing and newspaper proprietor, owner of several UK national newspapers, including the *Daily Mirror*, the Macmillan Publishing Co, and the New York *Daily News*.

Maxwell James Clerk 1831–1879. Scottish physicist. His major achievement was in the understanding of electromagnetic waves: Maxwell's equations bring together electicity, magnetism, and light in one set of relations. He contributed to every branch of physical science—gases, optics, and color sensation. His theoretical work in magnetism prepared the way for wireless telegraphy and telephony.

His principal works include *Perception of Colour* 1860, *Theory of Heat* 1871, *Electricity and Magnetism* 1873, and *Matter and Motion* 1876.

Maxwell–Boltzmann distribution basic equation concerning the distribution of velocities of the molecules of a gas.

maya (Sanskrit "illusion") in Hindu philosophy, mainly in the *Vedānta*, the cosmos which Isvara, the personal expression of Brahman, or the ◊atman, has called into being. This is real, yet also an illusion, since its reality is not everlasting.

Maya member of a group of Central American Indians who lived in agricultural villages in and around the Yucatán Peninsula and Guatemalan highlands from at least 3000 BC, and who developed a civilization of city-states that flourished from about AD 300 until about 900, when Toltecs from the Valley of Mexico moved south into the area, building new ceremonial centers of their own and dominating the local people. Nevertheless, Mayan sovereignty was maintained, for the most part, until late in the Spanish Conquest 1560s in some areas. The Maya had been ruled by a theocracy supported by taxation and tribute; they traded with their neighbors to the north and south; developed advanced mathematics, astronomy, art, and architecture; a glyph system of writing on stone, ceramics, and in book form; and they celebrated a complex religion with a calendar, many deities, and ceremonies that included a form of ball game and human sacrifice. Today they are Roman Catholic, live in farming and fishing villages, as well as the cities of Yucatán, Guatemala, Belize, and W Honduras. Many still speak Maya, a member of the Totonac-Mayan language family, as well as Spanish.

Mayagüez port in W Puerto Rico with needlework industry and a US agricultural experimental station; population (1980) 96,200.

Mayakovsky Vladimir 1893–1930. Russian futurist poet who combined revolutionary propaganda with efforts to revolutionize poetic technique in his poems "150,000,000" 1920 and "V I Lenin" 1924. His satiric play *The Bedbug* 1928 was taken in the West as an attack on philistinism in the USSR.

Mayan art art of the Central American civilization of the Maya, especially of the Classical period between about AD 300 and 900. Mayan figures have distinctive squat proportions and squared-off composition. Large, steeply inclined pyramids were built, such as those at ◊Chichén Itzá, decorated with sculpture and inscription.

Bonampak, Copan, Tikal, and Palenque were other sites of Mayan urban life amd worship. In sculpture, human heads and giant reclining figures of Mayan deities are frequent motifs. A few intri-

Mayan art A Chac Mool idol reclines at the center of a sacrificial altar in the Mayan city of Chichén Itzá, on Mexico's Yucatan Peninsula.

cately painted manuscripts (each called a ◊codex) survive (in the Museo de América, Madrid, Spain, for example).

May Day first day of May. In many countries it is a public vacation in honor of labor; see also ◊Labor Day.

Traditionally the first day of summer. In parts of England it is still celebrated as a pre-Christian magical rite; for example, the dance around the maypole (an ancient fertility symbol).

Mayence French name for the city of ◊Mainz in the Federal Republic of Germany.

Mayenne *département* of W France in Pays-de-Loire region
area 2,033 sq mi/5,212 sq km
capital Laval
features river Mayenne
products iron, slate; paper
population (1982) 271,184.

Mayenne river in W France which gives its name to the *département* of Mayenne; length 125 mi/ 200 km. It rises in Orne, flows in a generally southerly direction through Mayenne and Maine-et-Loire, and joins the river Sarthe just above Angers to form the Maine.

Mayer Julius Robert von 1814–1878. German physicist who in 1842 anticipated ◊Joule in deriving the mechanical equivalent of heat, and ◊Helmholtz in the principle of conservation of energy.

Mayer Louis B(urt). Adopted name of Eliezer Mayer. 1885–1957. Russian-born US film producer. Attracted to the entertainment industry, he became a successful theater owner in New England and in 1914 began to buy the distribution rights to feature films. Mayer soon became involved in film production, moving to Los Angeles 1918 and becoming one of the founders of Metro-Goldwyn-Mayer (MGM) studios 1924. In charge of production, Mayer instituted the Hollywood "star" system. He retired from MGM 1951.

Mayerling site near Vienna of the hunting lodge of Crown Prince ◊Rudolph of Austria, where he and his mistress were found shot dead in 1889.

Mayfair district of Westminster in London, England, vaguely defined as lying between Piccadilly and Oxford Street, and including Park Lane; formerly a fashionable residential district, but increasingly taken up by offices.

Mayflower the ship in which the ◊Pilgrims sailed 1620 from Plymouth, England, to found Plymouth plantation and Plymouth colony in present-day Massachusetts. The *Mayflower* was one of two ships scheduled for departure in 1620. The second ship, the *Speedwell*, was deemed unseaworthy, so 102 people were crowded into the 90-foot *Mayflower*, which was bound for Virginia. Tension between Pilgrim and non-Pilgrim passengers threatened to erupt into a mutiny. Blown off course, the ship reached Cape Cod, Massachusetts, in December. The Mayflower Compact was drafted to establish self-rule for the Plymouth colony and to protect the rights of all the settlers.

mayfly any insect of the order Ephemerida (Greek *ephemeros* "lasting for a day," an allusion to the very brief life of the adult). The larval stage, which can last a year or more, is passed in water, the adult form developing gradually from the nymph through successive molts. The adult has transparent, net-veined wings.

Maynard Smith John 1920– . British biologist. Using ◊game theory, he developed the concept of ◊evolutionarily stable strategy (ESS) as a mathematical technique for studying the evolution of behavior.

Maynooth village in Kildare, Republic of Ireland, with a Roman Catholic training college for priests; population (1981) 3,388.

Mayo county in Connacht province, Republic of Ireland
area 2,084 sq mi/5,400 sq km
cities administrative town Castlebar
features Lough Conn; wild Atlantic coast scenery; Achill Island; the village of Knock, where two women claimed a vision of the Virgin with two saints 1897, now a site of pilgrimage
products sheep and cattle farming; fishing
population (1986) 115,000.

Mayo William James 1861–1939. US surgeon, founder, with his brother Charles Horace Mayo (1865–1939), of the Mayo Clinic for medical treatment 1889 in Rochester, Minnesota.

mayor title of head of local administration for a town or city. Powers vary widely, although generally mayors oversee financial issues, local education, public safety, planning and zoning, taxation, and other aspects of municipal government.

Mayor of the Palace administrator of the ◊Merovingian royal court from 439 to 751. After the death of Dagobert I (605–39) and the subsequent decline of the Merovingian kings, holders of this office became, in effect, rulers of the kingdom and established a hereditary succession until 751, when the Carolingian line began with ◊Pepin the Short.

Mayotte or ***Mahore*** island group of the ◊Comoros, off the E coast of Africa, a *collectivité territoriale* of France by its own wish. The two main islands are Grande Terre and Petite Terre
area 144 sq mi/374 sq km
capital Dzaoudzi
products coffee, copra, vanilla, fishing
languages French, Swahili
population (1984) 59,000
history a French colony 1843–1914, and later, with the Comoros, an overseas territory of France. In 1974, Mayotte voted to remain a French dependency.

Mays Willie (Howard Jr) 1931– . US baseball player, born in Westfield, Alabama, who played for 22 years with the New York (later San Francisco) Giants (1951–72) and the New York Mets (1973). He hit 660 career home runs, third best in baseball history, and was also an outstanding fielder and runner. He was elected to the Baseball Hall of Fame 1979.

mayweed several species of the daisy family Compositae, including the European dog fennel or stinking daisy *Anthemis cotula*, naturalized in North America, and Eurasian pineapple mayweed *Matricaria matricarioides*. All have finely divided leaves.

Mazarin Jules 1602–1661. French politician who succeeded Richelieu as chief minister of France in 1642. His attack on the power of the nobility led to the ◊Fronde and his temporary exile, but his diplomacy achieved a successful conclusion to the Thirty Years' War, and, in alliance with Oliver Cromwell during the British protectorate, he gained victory over Spain.

Mazowiecki Tadeusz 1927– . Polish politician, founder member of ◊Solidarity, and Poland's first postwar noncommunist prime minister 1989–1990. Forced to introduce unpopular economic reforms, he was knocked out in the first round of the Nov 1990 presidential elections, resigning in favor of his former colleague, Lech ◊Wałęsa.

A former member of the Polish parliament 1961–70, he was debarred from reelection by the authorities after investigating the police massacre of Gdańsk strikers. He became legal adviser to Lech Wałęsa and, after a period of internment, edited the Solidarity newspaper *Tygodnik Solidarność*. In 1989 he became prime minister after the elections denied the communists their customary majority. A devout Catholic, he is a close friend of Pope John Paul II.

mazurka a lively national dance of Poland from the 16th century. In triple time, it is characterized by foot-stamping and heel-clicking, together with a turning movement.

Mazzini Giuseppe 1805–1872. Italian nationalist. He was a member of the revolutionary society, the ◊Carbonari, and founded in exile the nationalist movement Giovane Italia (Young Italy) 1832. Returning to Italy on the outbreak of the 1848 revolution, he headed a republican government established in Rome, but was forced into exile again on its overthrow 1849. He acted as a focus for the movement for Italian unity (see ◊Risorgimento).

Mazzini, born in Genoa, studied law. For his subversive activity with the Carbonari he was imprisoned 1830, then went to France, founding in Marseille the Young Italy movement, followed by an international revolutionary organization, Young Europe, 1834. For many years he lived in exile in France, Switzerland, and the UK, and was condemned to death in his absence by the Sardinian government, but returned to Italy for the ◊revolution of 1848. He conducted the defense of Rome against French forces and, when it failed, he refused to join in the capitulation and returned to London, where he continued to agitate until his death in Geneva, Switzerland.

Mbabane capital (since 1902) of Swaziland, 100 mi/ 160 km west of Maputo, in the Dalgeni Hills; population (1986) 38,000.

Mboma another spelling of ◊Boma, Zaïrean port.

Mboya Tom 1930–1969. Kenyan politician, a founder of the Kenya African National Union (◊KANU), and minister of economic affairs from 1964 until his assassination.

MD abbreviation for Doctor of Medicine; ◊Maryland.

MDMA psychedelic drug, also known as ◊ecstasy.

ME abbreviation for ◊Maine.

ME abbreviation for Middle English, the period of the English language from 1050 to 1550.

ME abbreviation for myalgic enkephalitis, a debilitating condition still not universally accepted as a genuine disease. The condition occurs after a flu-like attack and has a diffuse range of symptoms. These strike and recur for years and include extreme fatigue, muscular pain, weakness, and depression.

ME, sometimes known as postviral fatigue syndrome or chronic fatigue syndrome, is not a new phenomenon. Outbreaks have been documented worldwide for more than 50 years. Recent research suggests that ME may be the result of chronic viral infection, leaving the sufferer exhausted, debilitated, and with generally lowered resistance. There is no definitive treatment for ME, but with time the symptoms become less severe.

mead alcoholic drink made from honey and water fermented with yeast, often with added spices. It was known in ancient times and was drunk by the Greeks, Romans, Britons, and Norse.

Mead George Herbert 1863–1931. US philosopher and social psychologist, who helped to found the philosophy of pragmatism.

He taught at the University of Chicago during its prominence as a center of social scientific development in the early 20th century, and is regarded as the founder of ◊symbolic interactionism. His work on group interaction had a major influence on sociology, stimulating the development of role theory, ◊phenomenology, and ◊ethnomethodology.

Mead Margaret 1901–1978. US anthropologist who popularized cultural relativity and challenged the

meander *The river Cuckmere, Sussex, England, meanders over the flood plain near its mouth.*

conventions of Western society with *Coming of Age in Samoa* 1928, a study of differences in temperament between males and females in Samoan and Western societies caused by child-rearing practices. She expanded on this same subject in *Growing Up in New Guinea* 1930 and *Sex and Temperament in Three Primitive Societies* 1935.

Mead studied at Barnard College 1923 and Columbia University 1929 under Franz ◊Boas. She also wrote *And Keep Your Powder Dry* 1942, about the US national character, and *Soviet Attitudes Toward Authority* 1951. Her autobiographical works include *Blackberry Winter: My Earlier Years* 1972 and *Letters from the Field, 1925–1975* 1977. She was a popular speaker on civil liberties, ecological sanity, feminism, and population control. She wrote columns for magazines and scholarly papers for journals, appeared on television talk shows, was curator of Pacific Ethnology at the American Museum of Natural History from 1926, and was adjunct professor of anthropology at Columbia University from 1954.

Meade George Gordon 1815–1872. US military leader. At the outbreak of the American Civil War, he was placed in command of Pennsylvania volunteers and participated in the Peninsular Campaign, Bull Run, and Antietam. He led the Army of the Potomac 1863 and the Union forces at Gettysburg. After the war, Meade served as military governor of Georgia, Alabama, and Florida 1868–69.

Born in Cadiz, Spain, Meade graduated from West Point 1835. After working on private railroad and surveying projects 1836–42, he returned to the army, serving in the Mexican War.

Meade James Edward 1907– . British Keynesian economist. He shared a Nobel Prize in 1977 for his work on trade and capital movements, and published a four-volume *Principles of Political Economy* 1965–76.

mean in mathematics, a measure of the average of a number of terms or quantities. The simple arithmetic mean is the average value of the quantities, that is, the sum of the quantities divided by their number. The weighted mean takes into account the frequency of the terms that are summed; it is calculated by multiplying each term by the number of times it occurs, summing the results and dividing this total by the total number of occurrences. The geometric mean is the corresponding root of the product of the quantities. In statistics, it is a measure of central tendency of a set of data.

meander a loop-shaped curve in a river flowing across flat country. As a river flows, any curve in its course is accentuated by the current. The current is fastest on the outside of the curve where it cuts into the bank; on the curve's inside the current is slow and deposits any transported material. In this way the river changes its course across the floodplain.

A loop in a river's flow may become so accentuated that it becomes cut off from the normal course and forms an ◊oxbow lake. The word comes from the river ◊Menderes in Turkey.

mean deviation in statistics, a measure of the spread of a population from the ◊mean.

Thus, if there are n observations with a mean of m, the mean deviation is the sum of the ◊absolute values of the differences of the observation values from m, divided by n.

mean free path in physics, the average distance traveled by a particle, atom, or molecule between successive collisions. It is of importance in the ◊kinetic theory of gases.

measles acute virus disease (rubeola), spread by airborne infection. Symptoms are fever, severe catarrh, small spots inside the mouth, and a raised, blotchy red rash appearing for about a week after two weeks' incubation. Prevention is by vaccination.

In industrialized countries it is not usually a serious disease, though serious complications may develop. Third World children suffer a high mortality, as did the North and South American Indians, who died by the thousands in the 17th, 18th, and 19th centuries.

meat flesh of animals taken as food, in Western countries chiefly from domesticated herds of cattle, sheep, pigs, and poultry. Major exporters include Argentina, Australia, New Zealand, Canada, the US, and Denmark (chiefly bacon). Meat substitutes are textured vegetable protein (TVP), usually soya-based and extruded in fibers in the same way as plastics. Animals have been hunted for meat since the beginnings of human society. The domestication of animals for meat began during the ◊Neolithic in the Near East about 10,000 BC. The practice of cooking meat is at least 600,000 years old.

Meat is wasteful in production (the same area of grazing land would produce greater food value in cereal crops). Grazing lands take up more than 7.4 billion acres/3 billion hectares and produce about 140 million tons of meat per year, of which the developed nations in 1980 consumed 90 million tons, or 242 lb/110 kg per person in the US, 165 lb/75 kg in the UK, 66 lb/30 kg in Japan, 13 lb/6 kg in Nigeria, and 2.4 lb/1.1 kg in India. Research suggests that, in a healthy diet, consumption of meat (especially with a high fat content) should not exceed the Japanese level.

Meath county in the province of Leinster, Republic of Ireland.
area 903 sq mi/2,340 sq km
county town Trim
features Tara Hill, 509 ft/155 m high, was the site of a palace and coronation place of many kings of Ireland (abandoned in the 6th century) and St Patrick preached here.
products sheep, cattle
population (1986) 104,000.

meatpacking the preparation of meat for consumption, especially if it is to be transported long distances. The industry depends on refrigeration, which was invented in 1861.

The first commercial use of frozen meat was in a shipment from the US to London in 1874. Frozen meat was first despatched from Argentina to London in 1878, and from Australia in 1879. Chicago had the world's largest meatpacking plants until the stockyards closed in 1971.

Mecca or ***Makkah*** city in Saudi Arabia and, as birthplace of Mohammed, the holiest city of the Islamic world; population (1974) 367,000. In the center of Mecca is the Great Mosque, in whose courtyard is the ◊Kaaba.

It also contains the well Zam-Zam, associated by tradition with the biblical characters Hagar and Ishmael. Most pilgrims come via the port of ◊Jiddah.

mechanical advantage the amount by which a machine can magnify a force. It is the load (the weight lifted or moved by the machine) divided by the effort (the force used by the operator).

mechanical equivalent of heat in physics, a constant factor relating the calorie (the c.g.s. unit of heat) to the joule (the unit of mechanical energy), equal to 4.1868 joules per calorie. It is redundant in the SI system of units, which measures heat and all forms of energy in joules (so that the mechanical equivalent of heat is 1).

mechanics branch of physics dealing with the motions of bodies and the forces causing these motions, and also with the forces acting on bodies in ◊equilibrium. It is usually divided into ◊dynamics and ◊statics.

Quantum mechanics is the system based on the ◊quantum theory that has superseded Newtonian mechanics in the interpretation of physical phenomena on the atomic scale.

mechanization the use of machines in place of manual labor or the use of animals. Until the 1700s there were few machines available to help people in the home, on the land, or in industry. There were no factories, only cottage industries, in which people carried out work, such as weaving, in their own homes for other people. The 1700s saw a long series of inventions, initially in the textile industry, that ushered in a machine age and brought about the ◊Industrial Revolution.

Among the first inventions in the textile industry were those made by John ◊Kay (flying shuttle, 1773), James ◊Hargreaves (spinning jenny, 1767), and Richard ◊Arkwright (water frame, 1769). Arkwright pioneered the mechanized factory system by installing many of his ◊spinning machines in one building and employing people to work them.

Mechelen (French *Malines*) industrial city (furniture, carpets, textiles) and market gardening center in Antwerp province, N Belgium, which gave its name to Mechlin lace; population (1985) 76,120.

Mechnikov Elie 1845–1916. Russian scientist who discovered the function of white blood cells and ◊phagocytes. After leaving Russia and joining ◊Pasteur in Paris, he described how these "scavenger cells" can attack the body itself (autoimmune disease).

Mecklenburg–West Pomerania (German *Mecklen-*

burg-Vorpommern) administrative *Land* (state) of the Federal Republic of Germany
area 8,840 sq mi/22,887 sq km
capital Schwerin
towns Rostock, Wismar, Stralsund, Neubrandenburg
products fish, ships, diesel engines, electronics, plastics, chalk
population (1990) 2,100,000
history the state was formerly the two grand duchies of Mecklenburg-Schwerin and Mecklenburg-Strelitz, which became free states of the Weimar Republic 1918–34, and were joined 1946 with part of Pomerania to form a region of East Germany. In 1952 it was split into the districts of Rostock, Schwerin, and Neubrandenburg. Following German reunification 1990, the districts were abolished and Mecklenburg–West Pomerania was reconstructed as one of the five new states of the Federal Republic.

Medal of Honor in the US, the highest award for valor. Established by Congress originally for the navy (1861) and army (1862). Of differing design, both are bronze stars with the goddess Minerva encircled in their centers. Members of the Marine Corps receive the Navy version. The Air Force version has Liberty in its center.

medals and decorations coinlike metal pieces, struck or cast to commemorate historic events; mark distinguished service, whether civil or military (in the latter case in connection with a particular battle, or for individual feats of courage, or for service over the period of a campaign); or as a badge of membership of an order of knighthood, society, or other special group.

Armada medal issued by Elizabeth I following the defeat of the Armada; the first English commemorative medal
George Cross 1940 highest British civilian award for bravery, the medallion in the center of the cross depicting St George and the Dragon
Iron Cross German, see under ◊knighthood
Légion d'honneur French, see under ◊knighthood
Medal of Honor highest award given in the US for the navy (1861) and army (1862) for gallantry in action; of differing design, both are bronze stars with the goddess Minerva encircled in their centers
Medal for Merit US civilian, 1942; recognizes exceptional conduct in the performance of outstanding service
Ordre National du Mérite French, civil and military, 1963, replacing earlier merit awards
Order of Merit British, see ◊Merit, Order of, and ◊knighthood
Order of the Purple Heart US military, established by Washington 1782, when it was of purple cloth (now made of bronze and enamel); revived by Hoover 1932, when it was issued to those wounded in action from World War I onward
Pour le Mérite German, instituted by Frederick the Great, military in 1740, and since 1842 for science and art
Presidential Medal of Freedom US civilian, highest peacetime civilian award since 1963
USSR Gold Star Medal Soviet Union, civilian and military
Victoria Cross British military, 1856

Medan seaport and economic center of the island of Sumatra, Indonesia; population (1980) 1,379,000. It trades in rubber, tobacco, and palm oil.

Medawar Peter (Brian) 1915–1987. Brazilian-born British immunologist who, with Macfarlane ◊Burnet, discovered that the body's resistance to grafted tissue is undeveloped in the newborn child, and studied the way it is acquired.

Medawar's work has been vital in understanding the phenomenon of tissue rejection following ◊transplant. He shared the 1960 Nobel Prize for Medicine with Burnet (1899–1985), an Australian who also worked on acquired immunological tolerance.

Mede member of a people of NW Iran who in the 9th century BC were tributaries to Assyria, with their capital at Ecbatana (now Hamadán). Allying themselves with Babylon, they destroyed the Assyrian capital of ◊Nineveh 612 BC, and extended their conquests into central Anatolia. In 550 BC they were overthrown by the Persians, with whom they rapidly merged.

Medea in Greek mythology, the sorceress daughter of the king of Colchis. When ◊Jason reached the court, she fell in love with him, helped him acquire the Golden Fleece, and they fled together. When Jason married Creusa, Medea killed his bride with the gift of a poisoned garment, and then killed her own two children by Jason.

Medea Greek tragedy by Euripides, produced 431 BC. It deals with the later part of the legend of Medea: her murder of Jason's bride and of her own children.

Medellín industrial town in the Central Cordillera, Colombia, 5,048 ft/1,538 m above sea level; population (1985) 2,069,000. Industries include textiles, chemicals, engineering, coffee. It is a center of the Colombian drug trade, and there has been considerable violence in the late 1980s.

Medford city in SW Oregon, S of Eugene; seat of Jackson County. It is a summer resort, and tourism is important to the economy. Other industries include processing of the area's agricutural crops and dairy products; population (1990) 46,951.

median in mathematics, the middle number of an ordered group of numbers. If there is no middle number (because there is an even number of terms), the median is the ◊mean (average) of the two middle numbers. For example, the median of the group 2, 3, 7, 11, 12 is 7; that of 3, 4, 7, 9, 11, 13 is 8 (the average of 7 and 9).

mediation a technical term in ◊Hegel's philosophy, and in Marxist philosophy influenced by Hegel, describing the way in which an entity is defined through its relations to other entities.

Medici noble family of Florence, the city's rulers from 1434 until they died out 1737. Family members included ◊Catherine de' Medici, Pope ◊Leo X, Pope ◊Clement VII, ◊Marie de' Medici.

Medici Giovanni de' 1360–1429. Italian entrepreneur and banker, with political influence in Florence as a supporter of the popular party. He was the father of Cosimo de' Medici.

Medici Cosimo de' 1389–1464. Italian politician and banker. Regarded as the model for Machiavelli's *The Prince*, he dominated the government of Florence from 1434 and was a patron of the arts. He was succeeded by his inept son Piero de' Medici (1416–1469).

Medici Cosimo de' 1519–1574. Italian politician, ruler of Florence; duke of Florence from 1537 and 1st grand duke of Tuscany from 1569.

Medici Ferdinand de' 1549–1609. Italian politician, grand duke of Tuscany from 1587.

Medici Lorenzo de' the Magnificent 1449–1492. Italian politician, ruler of Florence from 1469. He was also a poet and a generous patron of the arts.

medicine the science of preventing, diagnosing, alleviating, or curing disease, both physical and mental; also any substance used in the treatment of disease. The basis of medicine is anatomy (the structure and form of the body) and physiology (the study of the body's functions).

In the West, medicine increasingly relies on new drugs and sophisticated surgical techniques, while diagnosis of disease is more and more by noninvasive procedures. The time and cost of Western-type medical training makes it inaccessible to many parts of the Third World; where health care of this kind is provided it is often by auxiliary medical helpers trained in hygiene and the administration of a limited number of standard drugs for the prevalent diseases of a particular region.

medicine, alternative forms of medical treatment that do not use synthetic drugs or surgery in response to the symptoms of a disease, but aim

western medicine: chronology

c. 400 BC	Hippocrates recognized that disease had natural causes.
c. AD 200	Galen, the authority of the Middle Ages, consolidated the work of the Alexandrian doctors.
1543	Andreas Versalius gave the first accurate account of the human body.
1628	William Harvey discovered the circulation of the blood.
1768	John Hunter began the foundation of experimental and surgical pathology.
1785	Digitalis was used to treat heart disease; the active ingredient was isolated 1904.
1798	Edward Jenner published his work on vaccination.
1877	Patrick Manson, Scottish parasitologist, worked on animal carriers of infectious diseases.
1882	Robert Koch isolated the tuberculosis bacillus.
1884	Edwin Klebs, German pathologist, isolated the diptheria bacillus.
1885	Louis Pasteur produced the rabies vaccine.
1890	Joseph Lister demonstrated antiseptic surgery.
1897	Martinus Beijerinck, Dutch botanist, discovered viruses.
1899	German doctor Felix Hoffman developed aspirin; Sigmund Freud founded psychiatry.
1910	Paul Ehrlich synthesized the first specific bacterial agent, salvarsan (cure for syphilis).
1922	Insulin was first used to treat diabetes.
1928	Alexander Fleming discovered the antibiotic penicillin.
1930s	Electro-convulsive therapy (ECT) was developed.
1932	Gerhard Domagk, German bacteriologist and pathologist, began work on the sulfonamide drugs, a kind of antibiotic.
1940s	Lithium treatment for depression was developed.
1950	Proof of a link between cigarette smoking and lung cancer was established.
1950s	Major development of antidepressant drugs and beta-blockers for heart disease; Medawar's work on the immune system.
1950–75	Manipulation of the molecules of synthetic chemicals, the main source of new drugs.
1953	Vaccine for polio developed by Jonas Salk.
1960s	Heart-transplant surgery began with the work of Christiaan Barnard; new generation of minor tranquilizers called benzodiazepenes developed.
1971	Viroids, disease-causing organisms even smaller than viruses, were isolated outside the living body.
1975	Nuclear medicine, for example positron-emission tomography (Hounsfield), came into practical use.
1978	Birth of the first "test-tube baby," Louise Brown, in England.
1980s	AIDS (acquired immune-deficiency syndrome) first recognized in the US; recognition of the discovery of the transposable gene by Barbara McClintock, US geneticist.
1980	Smallpox eradicated by the World Health Organization.
1984	Vaccine for leprosy developed; discovery of the human immuno-deficiency virus (HIV), responsible for AIDS, at the Institut Pasteur in Paris and in the US.
1987	World's longest-surviving heart-transplant patient died in France, 18 years after his operation.
1989	Patient with Parkinson's disease first treated by graft of fetal brain tissue.

to treat the patient as a whole (◊holism). The emphasis is on maintaining health (with diet and exercise) and on dealing with the underlying causes rather than just the symptoms of illness. It may involve the use of herbal remedies and techniques like ◊acupuncture, ◊homeopathy, and ◊chiropractic.

Some alternative treatments are increasingly accepted by orthodox medicine, but the absence of enforceable standards in some fields has led to the proliferation of eccentric or untrained practitioners.

medieval art painting and sculpture of the Middle Ages in Europe and parts of the Middle East, from about the 4th century to the emergence of the Renaissance in Italy in the 1400s. This period includes early Christian, Byzantine, Celtic, Anglo-Saxon, and Carolingian art. The Romanesque style was the first Western international style of medieval times, superseded by Gothic in the late 12th century. Religious sculpture, frescoes, and manuscript illumination proliferated; panel painting came only toward the end of the period.

early Christian art (3rd–5th centuries AD). When Christianity was made one of the official religions of the Roman state, churches were built and artistic traditions adapted to the portrayal of the new Christian saints and symbols. Roman burial chests (*sarcophagi*) were adopted by the Christians and their imagery of pagan myths gradually changed into biblical themes.

Byzantine art (4th century–1453). A style that developed in the eastern empire, centered on Constantinople. The use of mosaic associated with Byzantine art also appears in church decoration in the West: for example, in Ravenna. Churches there, built in the 5th and 6th centuries, present powerful religious images on walls and vaults in brilliant, glittering color. Byzantine art soon froze into religious stereotypes and iconlike figures. The Byzantine style continued in icon painting, a strong theme in the art of Greece and Russia.

early medieval art (4th–10th centuries). S Europe was overrun by people from the north, and their art consisted mainly of portable objects, articles for personal use or adornment. They excelled in metalwork and jewelry, often in gold with garnet or enamel inlays, ornamented with highly stylized, animal-based interlace patterns. This type of ornament was translated into manuscript illumination produced in Christian monasteries, such as the decorated pages of the Northumbrian *Lindisfarne Gospels* (British Museum, London) 7th century or the Celtic 8th-century *Book of Kells* (Trinity College, Dublin, Ireland).

Carolingian art (late 8th–early 9th centuries). Manuscript painting flourished in Charlemagne's empire, drawing its inspiration from the late Classical artistic traditions of the early Christian and Byzantine styles. Several monasteries produced richly illustrated prayer books and biblical texts.

Romanesque or ***Norman art*** (10th–12th centuries). A style chiefly evident in church sculpture, on capitals and portals, and in manuscript illumination. Romanesque art combined naturalistic elements with the fantastic, poetical, and pattern-loving Celtic and Germanic tradition. Imaginary beasts and medieval warriors mingle with biblical themes. Fine examples remain throughout Europe, from N Spain and Italy to France, the Germanic lands of the Holy Roman Empire, and England. The Romanesque style arrived in Scandinavia in the late 11th century.

Gothic art (late 12th–15th centuries). As large cathedrals were built in Europe, sculptural decoration became more monumental and stained glass filled the tall windows; as in Chartres Cathedral, France. Figures were also carved in wood. Court patronage produced exquisite small ivories, goldsmith's work, devotional books illustrated with miniatures, and tapestries depicting romantic tales. Panel painting, initially on a gold background, evolved in N Europe into the more realistic International Gothic style. In Italy fresco painting made great advances; a seminal figure in this development was the artist Giotto, whose cycle of the lives of Mary and Jesus in the Arena Chapel, Padua (completed 1306), is seen as proto-Renaissance.

Medina or ***Madinah*** Saudi Arabian city, about 220 mi/355 km N of Mecca; population (1974) 198,000. It is the second holiest city in the Islamic world, containing the tomb of Mohammed. It produces grain and fruit.

It also contains the tombs of the caliphs or Muslim leaders Abu Bakr, Omar, and Fatima, Mohammed's daughter.

meditation act of spiritual contemplation, practiced by members of many religions or as a secular exercise. It is a central practice in Buddhism. The Sanskrit term is *dhyāna*. See also ◊transcendental meditation.

Mediterranean inland sea separating Europe from N Africa, with Asia to the E; extreme length 2,300 mi/3,700 km; area 1,145,000 sq mi/2,966,000 sq km. It is linked to the Atlantic (at the Strait of Gibraltar), Red Sea, and Indian Ocean (by the Suez Canal), Black Sea (at the Dardanelles and Sea of Marmara). The main subdivisions are the Adriatic, Aegean, Ionian, and Tyrrhenian seas.

The Mediterranean is almost tideless, saltier and warmer than the Atlantic, and shallows from Sicily to Cape Bon (Africa) divide it into an E and W basin. It is endangered by human and industrial waste pollution; 100 million people live along the coast and it is regularly crossed by oil tankers. The Barcelona Convention 1976 to clean up the Mediterranean was signed by 17 countries and led to a ban on dumping of mercury, cadmium, persistent plastics, DDT, crude oil, and hydrocarbons.

Mediterranean climate a climate characterized by hot dry summers and warm wet winters. Mediterranean zones are situated in either hemisphere on the western side of continents, between latitudes of 30° and 60°.

During the winter rain is brought by the ◊westerlies; in summer Mediterranean zones are under the influence of the ◊trade winds. The regions bordering the Mediterranean Sea, California, central Chile, the Cape of Good Hope, and parts of S Australia have such climates.

medlar small shrub or tree *Mespilus germanica* of the rose family Rosaceae. Native to SE Europe, it is widely cultivated for its fruit, resembling a small brown-green pear or quince. These are palatable when decay has set in.

Médoc French district bordering the Gironde in Aquitaine region, N of Bordeaux. It is famed for its wines, Margaux and St Julien being two of the most popular varieties. Lesparre and Pauillac are the chief towns.

medulla central part of an organ. In the mammalian kidney, the medulla lies beneath the outer cortex and is responsible for the reabsorption of water from the filtrate. In plants, a region of packing tissue in the center of the stem. In the vertebrate brain, the posterior region responsible for the coordination of basic activities such as breathing and temperature control.

Mediterranean Sea

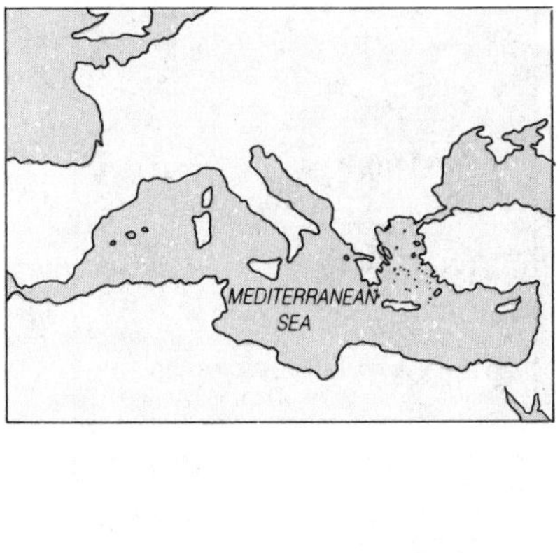
MEDITERRANEAN
SEA

Medusa in Greek mythology, a mortal woman who was transformed into a ◊Gorgon. The winged horse ◊Pegasus was supposed to have sprung from her blood.

medusa jellyfish stage in the life cycle of coelenterates (order Cnidaria).

Medvedev Vadim 1929– . Soviet communist politician. He was deputy chief of propaganda 1970–78, was in charge of party relations with communist countries 1986–88, and in 1988 was appointed by the Soviet leader Gorbachev to succeed the conservative Ligachev as head of ideology. He adheres to a firm Leninist line.

Medway river of SE England, rising in Sussex and flowing through Kent and the Medway towns (Chatham, Gillingham, Rochester) to Sheerness, where it enters the Thames; about 60 mi/96 km long. In local tradition it divides the "Men of Kent," who live to the E, from the "Kentish Men," who live to the W.

Meegeren Hans van 1889–1947. Dutch forger; mainly of Vermeer's paintings. His "Vermeer" *Christ at Emmaus* was bought for Rotterdam's Boymans Museum in 1937. He was discovered when a "Vermeer" sold to the Nazi leader Goering was traced back to him after World War II. Sentenced to a year's imprisonment, he died two months later.

meerschaum an aggregate of minerals, usually the soft white mineral, sepiolite, hydrous magnesium silicate. It floats on water and is used for making pipe bowls.

Meerut industrial city (chemicals, soap, food processing) in Uttar Pradesh, N India; population (1981) 538,000. The ◊Indian Mutiny began here in 1857.

megabyte in computing, a measure of the capacity of ◊memory or storage, equal to 1,024 ◊kilobytes. It is also used, less precisely, to mean 1 million bytes.

megalith prehistoric stone monument of the late Neolithic or early Bronze Age. Megaliths include single, large uprights (menhirs); rows; circles, generally with a central "altar stone" (for example Stonehenge); and the remains of burial chambers with the covering earth removed, looking like a hut (◊dolmens).

megamouth filter-feeding deep-sea shark *Megachasma pelagios*, first discovered 1976. It has a bulbous head with protruding jaws and blubbery lips, is 15 ft/4.5 m long, and weighs 1,650 lb/750 kg.

megapode large (up to 2.3 ft/70 cm long) chicken-like bird of the family Megapodiidae, found mainly in Australia, but also in SE Asia. They lay their eggs in a pile of rotting vegetation 13 ft/4 m across, and the warmth from this provides the heat for incubation. The male bird feels the mound with his tongue and adds or takes away vegetation to provide the correct temperature.

megatherium genus of extinct giant ground sloth of North and South America. Various species lived from about 7 million years ago until geologically recent times. They were plant-eaters, and some grew to 20 ft/6 m long.

megaton one million (10^6) tons. Used with reference to the explosive power of a nuclear weapon, it is equivalent to the explosive force of one million tons of trinitrotoluene (TNT).

Meghalaya state of NE India
area 8,685 sq mi/22,500 sq km
capital Shillong
features mainly agricultural and comprises tribal hill districts
products potatoes, cotton, jute, fruit
minerals coal, limestone, white clay, corundum, sillimanite
population (1981) 1,328,000, mainly Khasi, Jaintia, and Garo
religion Hindu 70%
language various.

Meier US architect Richard Meier's Museum für Kunsthandwerk (Museum of Arts and Crafts), Frankfurt, Germany, 1984.

Megiddo site of a fortress town in N Israel, where Thothmes III defeated the Canaanites about 1469 BC; the Old Testament figure Josiah was killed in battle about 609 BC; and in World War I the British field marshal Allenby broke the Turkish front 1918. It is identified with ◊Armageddon.

Mehemet Ali 1769–1849. Pasha (governor) of Egypt from 1805, and founder of the dynasty that ruled until 1953. An Albanian in the Ottoman service, he had originally been sent to Egypt to fight the French. As pasha, he established a European-style army and navy, fought his Turkish overlord 1831 and 1839, and conquered Sudan.

Mehta Zubin 1936– . Indian conductor who became music director of the New York Philharmonic 1978. He is known for his flamboyant style of conducting and his interpretations of the Romantic composers.

His father, Mehli Mehta, helped found the Bombay Symphony and exposed his son to Western music from an early age. Zubin Mehta's fame spread rapidly when he toured with the Royal Liverpool Philharmonic, the first orchestra that he conducted. He was appointed music director of the Montreal Symphony 1961–67 and of the Los Angeles Philharmonic 1962–78, thus becoming the first person to direct two North American symphony orchestras simultaneously.

Meier Richard 1934– . US architect whose white designs spring from the poetic Modernism of the ◊Le Corbusier villas of the 1920s. His abstract style is at its most mature in the Museum für Kunsthandwerk (Museum of Arts and Crafts), Frankfurt, Germany, which was completed 1984.

Earlier schemes are the Bronx Developmental Center, New York 1970–76 and the Athenaeum–New Harmony 1974. He is the architect for the Getty Museum, Los Angeles.

Meiji Mutsuhito 1852–1912. Emperor of Japan from 1867, when he took the title *meiji tennō* ("enlightened sovereign"). During his reign Japan became a world industrial and naval power. He abolished the feudal system and discrimination against the lowest caste, established state schools, and introduced conscription, the Western calendar, and other measures in an attempt to modernize Japan, including a constitution 1889.

The son of Emperor Komei, he took the personal name Mutsuhito when he became crown prince 1860.

Meiji era in Japanese history, the reign of Emperor ◊Meiji 1867–1912.

Meikle Andrew 1719–1811. Scottish millwright who in 1785 designed and built the first practical threshing machine for separating cereal grains from the husks.

Meinhof Ulrike 1934–1976. West German urban guerrilla, member of the ◊Baader–Meinhof gang in the 1970s.

A left-wing journalist, Meinhof was converted to the use of violence to achieve political change by the imprisoned Andreas Baader. She helped free Baader and they became joint leaders of the urban guerrilla organization the Red Army Faction. As the faction's chief ideologist, Meinhof was arrested in 1972 and, in 1974, sentenced to eight years' imprisonment. She committed suicide in 1976 in the Stammheim high-security prison.

Mein Kampf (German "my struggle") book written by Adolf ◊Hitler 1924 during his jail sentence for his part in the abortive 1923 Munich beer-hall putsch. Part autobiography, part political philosophy, the book presents Hitler's ideas of German expansion, anticommunism, and anti-Semitism.

meiosis

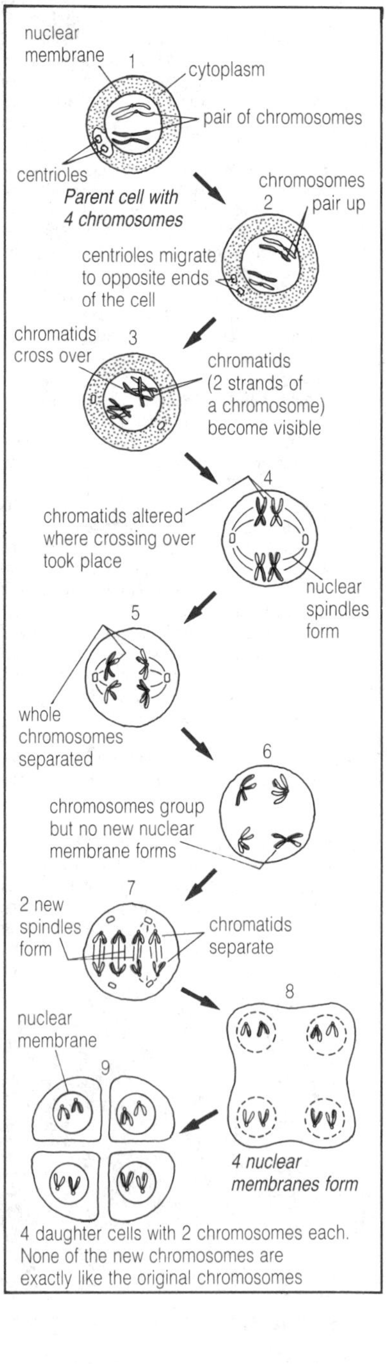
nuclear membrane
1
cytoplasm
pair of chromosomes
centrioles
Parent cell with 4 chromosomes
chromosomes pair up
2
centrioles migrate to opposite ends of the cell
chromatids cross over
3
chromatids (2 strands of a chromosome) become visible
4
chromatids altered where crossing over took place
nuclear spindles form
5
whole chromosomes separated
6
chromosomes group but no new nuclear membrane forms
7
2 new spindles form
chromatids separate
8
nuclear membrane
9
4 nuclear membranes form
4 daughter cells with 2 chromosomes each. None of the new chromosomes are exactly like the original chromosomes

Meir Israeli politician and prime minister Golda Meir, 1970.

meiosis in biology, a process of cell division in which the number of ◊chromosomes in the cell is halved. It only occurs in ◊eukaryotic cells, and is part of a life cycle that involves sexual reproduction because it allows the genes of two parents to be combined without the total number of chromosomes increasing.

In sexually reproducing ◊diploid animals (having two sets of chromosomes per cell), meiosis occurs during formation of the ◊gametes (sex cells, sperm and egg), so that the gametes are ◊haploid (having only one set of chromosomes). When the gametes unite during ◊fertilization, the diploid condition is restored. In plants, meiosis occurs just before spore formation. Thus the spores are haploid and in lower plants such as mosses they develop into a haploid plant called a gametophyte which produces the gametes (see ◊alternation of generations). See also ◊mitosis.

Meir Golda 1898–1978. Israeli Labour (*Mapai*) politician. Born in Russia, she emigrated to the US 1906, and in 1921 went to Palestine. She was foreign minister 1956–66 and prime minister 1969–74. Criticism of the Israelis' lack of preparation for the 1973 Arab-Israeli War led to election losses for Labour and, unable to form a government, she resigned.

Meissen city in the state of Saxony, Federal Republic of Germany, on the river Elbe; known for Meissen or Dresden porcelain from 1710; population (1983) 38,908.

Meistersinger (German "master singer") one of a group of German lyric poets, singers, and musicians of the 14th–16th centuries, who formed guilds for the revival of minstrelsy. Hans Sachs was a Meistersinger, and Richard Wagner's opera, *Die Meistersinger von Nürnberg* 1868, depicts the tradition.

Meitner Lise 1878–1968. Austrian physicist who worked with Otto ◊Hahn and was the first to realize that they had inadvertently achieved the fission of uranium. Driven from Nazi Germany because of her Jewish origin, she later worked in Sweden, where she published the results of their work. She refused to work on the atomic bomb.

Mekele capital of Tigray region, N Ethiopia. Population (1984) 62,000.

Meknès (Spanish *Mequinez*) city in N Morocco, known for wine and carpet-making; population (1981) 487,000. One of Morocco's four imperial cities, it was the capital until 1728, and is the site of the tomb of Sultan Moulay Ismail.

Mekong river rising as the Za Qu in Tibet and flowing to the South China Sea, through a vast delta (about 77,000 sq mi/200,000 sq km); length 2,750 mi/4,425 km. It is being developed for irrigation and hydroelectricity by Cambodia, Laos, Thailand, and Vietnam.

Melaka Malaysian form of ◊Malacca, state of Peninsular Malaysia.

melaleuca tree tropical tree, also known as the paperbark *Melaleuca leucadendron*, family Myrtaceae. The leaves produce cajuput oil, which has medicinal uses.

In favorable conditions, such as in the Florida

Mekong River

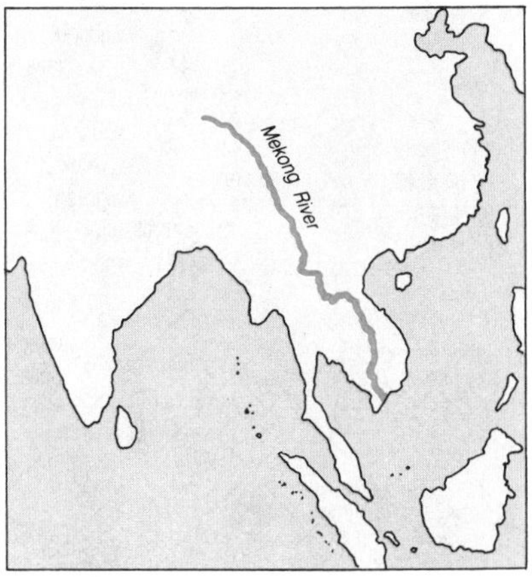
Mekong River

Everglades, the tree reproduces rapidly. Attempts are being made to extirpate it because in a forest fire its crown becomes a ball of flame, accelerating the spread of the blaze in all directions.

melamine $C_3N_6H_6$ thermosetting ◊polymer based on urea–formaldehyde. It is extremely resistant to heat and is also scratch-resistant. Its uses include synthetic resins.

Melanchthon Philip. Assumed name of Philip Schwarzerd 1497–1560. German theologian who helped Luther prepare a German translation of the New Testament. In 1521 he issued the first systematic formulation of Protestant theology, reiterated in the Confession of ◊Augsburg 1530.

Melanesia islands in the SW Pacific between Micronesia to the north and Polynesia to the east, embracing all the islands from the New Britain archipelago to Fiji.

Melanesian a member of any of the dark-skinned indigenous Pacific peoples of Melanesia, including groups from the Bismarck Archipelago to the Fiji Islands. The Melanesian languages belong to the Austronesian family.

Melanesian languages see ◊Malayo-Polynesian languages.

Melanesian pidgin English a form of ◊pidgin English.

melanism black coloration of animal bodies caused by large amounts of the pigment melanin. Melanin is of significance in insects, because melanic ones warm more rapidly in sunshine than do pale ones, and can be more active in cool weather. A fall in temperature may stimulate such insects to produce more melanin. In industrial areas, dark insects and pigeons match sooty backgrounds and escape predation, but they are at a disadvantage in rural areas where they do not match their backgrounds. This is known as industrial melanism.

melanoma mole or growth containing the dark pigment melanin. Malignant melanoma is a type of skin cancer developing in association with a pre-existing mole. Once rare, this disease is now frequent, possibly due to depletion of the ozone layer, which provides some protection against ultraviolet radiation from the Sun. Most at risk are those with fair hair and light skin.

Melanesia

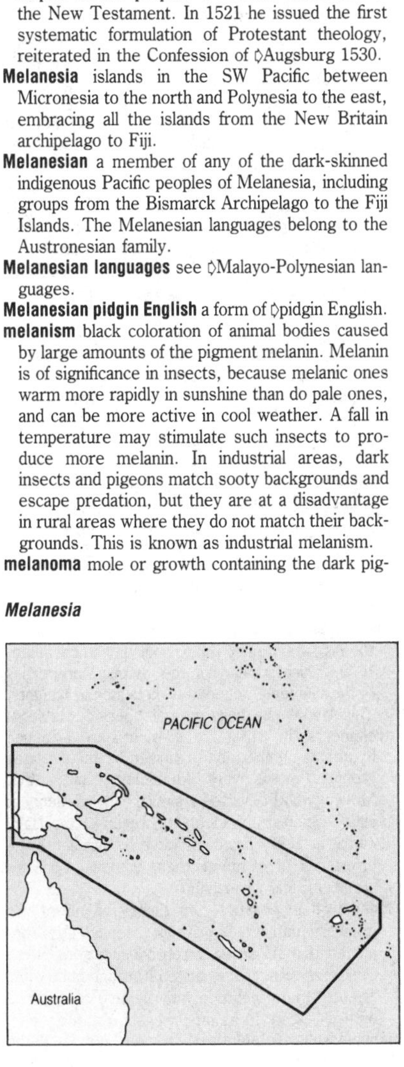
PACIFIC OCEAN
Australia

Melba Nellie, adopted name of Helen Porter Mitchell 1861–1931. Australian soprano. One of her finest roles was Donizetti's *Lucia*. Peach melba (half a peach plus vanilla ice cream and melba sauce, made from sweetened, fresh raspberries) and melba toast (crisp, thin toast) are named after her.

Melbourne capital of Victoria, Australia, near the mouth of the river Yarra; population (1986) 2,943,000. Industries include engineering, shipbuilding, electronics, chemicals, food processing, clothing, and textiles.

Founded 1835, it was named after Lord Melbourne 1837, grew in the wake of the gold rushes, and was the seat of the Commonwealth government 1901–27. It is the country's second-largest city, with three universities, and was the site of the 1956 Olympics.

Melbourne city on the E coast of Florida, on the Indian River, SE of Orlando. Industries include food processing and electronic and aviation equipment; tourism is also important to the economy; population (1990) 59,646.

Melbourne William Lamb, 2nd Viscount 1779–1848. British Whig politician. Home secretary 1830–34, he was briefly prime minister in 1834 and again 1835–41. Accused in 1836 of seducing Caroline Norton, he lost the favor of William IV.

Melchite or ***Melkite*** member of a Christian church in Syria, Egypt, Lebanon, and Israel. The Melchite Church was founded in Syria in the 6th–7th centuries and is now part of the Eastern Orthodox Church.

The Melchites accepted Byzantine rule at the council of Chalcedon 451 (unlike the ◊Maronites). In 1754 some Melchites broke away to form a ◊Uniate Church with Rome.

Méliès Georges 1861–1938. French film pioneer, born in Paris. In the period 1896 to 1912 he made over 1,000 films, mostly fantasies, such as *Le Voyage dans la Lune/A Trip to the Moon* 1902. He developed trick effects such as slow motion, double exposure, and dissolves, and in 1897 built Europe's first film studio at Montreuil.

Melilla port and military base on the NE coast of Morocco; area 5 sq mi/14 sq km; population (1986) 56,000. It was captured by Spain 1496 and is still under Spanish rule. Also administered from Melilla are three other Spanish possessions: Peña ("rock") de Velez de la Gomera, Peña d'Alhucemas, and the Chaffarine Islands.

melitin (Greek "bee") extract of honey-bee poison used as a powerful antibiotic.

Mellon Andrew William 1855–1937. US financier who donated his art collection to found the National Gallery of Art, Washington, DC in 1937. His son, Paul Mellon (1907–) was its president 1963–79. He funded Yale University's Center for British Art, New Haven, Connecticut, and donated major works of art to both collections.

Born in Pittsburgh, Mellon attended Western University of Pennsylvania and entered the family banking firm. Through farsighted investments and loans to the expanding steel and oil industries of Pennsylvania, Mellon became one of the wealthiest men in America. He founded the Mellon National Bank 1902. He was appointed secretary of the treasury by President Harding 1921 and held the post until 1932, under presidents Coolidge and Hoover.

melodrama a play or film with romantic and sensational plot elements, often unsubtly acted. Originally it meant a play accompanied by music. The early melodramas used extravagant theatrical effects to heighten violent emotions and actions artificially. By the end of the 19th century, melodrama had become a popular genre of stage play.

***Melville** US author Herman Melville, whose whaling voyages inspired the classic novel* Moby Dick *1851 and other works.*

melody in music, a sequence of notes forming a theme or tune.

melon any of several large, juicy, thick-skinned fruit of trailing plants of the gourd family Cucurbitaceae. The muskmelon *Cucumis melo* and the watermelon *Citrullus vulgaris* are two of the many edible varieties.

Melos (modern Greek *Mílos*) Greek island in the Aegean, one of the Cyclades; area 60 sq mi/155 sq km. The sculpture of *Venus de Milo* was discovered here 1820 (now in the Louvre). The capital is Plaka.

Melpomene in Greek mythology, the ◊Muse of tragedy.

Melrose town in Borders region, Scotland. The heart of King Robert the Bruce is buried here and the ruins of Melrose Abbey 1136 are commemorated in verse by Sir Walter Scott.

meltdown the melting of the core of a nuclear reactor, due to overheating. To prevent such accidents all reactors have equipment intended to flood the core with water in an emergency. The reactor is housed in a strong containment vessel, designed to prevent radiation escaping into the atmosphere. The result of a meltdown is an area radioactively contaminated for hundreds of thousands of years. See ◊half-life.

At Three Mile Island, Pennsylvania, in March 1979, a partial meltdown occurred caused by a combination of equipment failure and operator error, and radiation was released. In Apr 1986, gases in the reactor at ◊Chernobyl, near Kiev, USSR, exploded, causing a partial meltdown of the core. Radioactive ◊fallout was detected worldwide.

melting point the temperature at which a substance melts, or changes from a solid to liquid form. A pure substance under standard conditions of pressure (usually one atmosphere) has a definite melting point. If heat is supplied to a solid at its melting point, the temperature does not change until the melting process is complete. The melting point of ice is 32°F/0°C.

Melville Herman 1819–1891. US writer, whose ◊*Moby-Dick* 1851 was inspired by his whaling experiences in the South Seas. These experiences were also the basis for earlier fiction, such as *Typee* 1846 and *Omoo* 1847. He published several volumes of verse, as well as short stories (*The Piazza Tales* 1856). *Billy Budd* was completed just before his death and published 1924. Although most of his works were unappreciated during his lifetime, today he is one of the most highly regarded of US authors.

Melville was born in Albany, New York, took to the sea after his father went bankrupt, and

Memling Flemish painter Hans Memlinc's St John the Baptist and St Lawrence *hangs in London's National Gallery.*

struggled to make a literary living. He worked in the New York customs office 1866–85, writing no prose from 1857 until *Billy Budd*. A friend of Nathaniel Hawthorne, he explored the dark, troubled side of American experience in novels of unusual form and great philosophical power. He died in obscurity.

Moby-Dick was filmed by John Huston in 1956. *Billy Budd* was the basis of an opera by Benjamin Britten 1951, which was made into a film 1962.

membrane in living things, a continuous layer, made up principally of fat molecules, that encloses a ◊cell or ◊organelles within a cell. Certain small molecules can pass through the cell membrane, but most must enter or leave the cell via channels in the membrane made up of special proteins. The ◊Golgi apparatus within the cell is thought to produce certain membranes.

In cell organelles, enzymes may be attached to the membrane at specific positions, often alongside other enzymes involved in the same process, like workers at a conveyor belt. Thus membranes help to make cellular processes more efficient.

Memel German name for ◊Klaipeda, port in Lithuania.

Memling or ***Memlinc*** Hans c. 1430–1494. Flemish painter, born near Frankfurt-am-Main, Germany, but active in Bruges. He painted religious subjects and portraits. Some of his works are in the Hospital of St John, Bruges, including the *Adoration of the Magi* 1479.

Memling is said to have been a pupil of van der Weyden, but his style is calmer and softer. His portraits include *Tommaso Portinari and His Wife* (Metropolitan Museum of Art, New York), and he decorated the *Shrine of St Ursula* 1489 (Hospital of St John, Bruges).

Memorial Day in the US, a day of remembrance (formerly Decoration Day) instituted 1868 for those killed in the US Civil War. Since World War I it has been observed as a public vacation on the last Monday in May, traditionally falling on May 30, in remembrance of all Americans killed in war.

memory in computing, the part of a system used to store data and programs either permanently or temporarily. There are two main types: internal memory and external memory. Memory capacity is measured in ◊kilobytes (KB) or megabytes.

Internal memory is either read-only (stored in ◊ROM, ◊PROM, and ◊EPROM chips) or read/write (stored in ◊RAM chips). Read-only memory stores information that must be constantly available or accessed very quickly and is unlikely to be changed. It is nonvolatile: it is not lost when the computer is switched off. Read/write memory is volatile: it stores programs and data only while the computer is switched on.

External memory is permanent, nonvolatile memory employing storage devices such as magnetic ◊disks (such as floppy disks, hard disks), ◊magnetic tape (tape streamers, cassettes), laser disks (including ◊CD-ROM) and ◊bubble memory. By swapping blocks of information rapidly in and out of internal memory from external memory, the limited size of a computer's memory may be increased artificially.

memory ability to store and recall observations and sensations. Memory does not seem to be based in any particular part of the brain; it may depend on changes to the pathways followed by nerve impulses as they move through the brain. Memory can be improved by regular use as the connections between ◊nerve cells (neurons) become "well-worn paths" in the brain. Events stored in short-term memory are forgotten quickly, whereas those in long-term memory can last for many years, enabling recall of information and recognition of people and places over long periods of time. Research is just beginning to uncover the biochemical and electrical bases of the human memory.

Memphis ruined city beside the Nile, 12 mi/19 km S of Cairo, Egypt. Once the center of the worship of Ptah, it was the earliest capital of a united Egypt under King Menes about 3200 BC, but was superseded by Thebes under the new empire 1570 BC. It was later used as a stone quarry, but the "cemetery city" of Sakkara survives, with the step pyramid built for King Zoser by ◊Imhotep, probably the world's oldest stone building.

Memphis industrial port city (pharmaceuticals, food processing, cotton, timber, tobacco) on the Mississippi River, in Tennessee; population (1990) 610,337. A major historic site is Beale Street, home of the blues composer W C Handy. The French built a fort here 1739, but Memphis was not founded until 1819. During the Civil War it was captured 1862 by Union forces after a river battle. Martin Luther King, Jr, was assassinated here April 4, 1968.

It has recording studios and record companies (Sun 1953–68, Stax 1960–75); Graceland, the home of Elvis Presley, is a museum. A 1980s industry of handmade ultramodern furniture is called Memphis style and copied by Italian and French firms.

Menai Strait channel of the Irish Sea, dividing Anglesey from the Welsh mainland; about 14 mi/22 km long, up to 2 mi/3 km wide. It is crossed by Telford's suspension bridge 1826 (reconstructed 1940) and Stephenson's tubular rail bridge 1850.

Menam another name for the ◊Chao Phraya river, Thailand.

Menander c. 342–291 BC. Greek comic dramatist, born in Athens. Of his 105 plays only fragments (many used as papier-mâché for Egyptian mummy cases) and Latin adaptations were known prior to the discovery 1957 of the *Dyscholos/The Bad-Tempered Man*.

Mencius Latinized name of Mengzi c. 372–289 BC. Chinese philosopher and moralist, in the tradition of Confucius. Mencius considered human nature innately good, although this goodness required cultivation, and based his conception of morality on this conviction.

Born in Shantung (Shandong) province, he was founder of a Confucian school. After 20 years' unsuccessful search for a ruler to put into practice his enlightened political program, based on people's innate goodness, he retired. His teachings are preserved as the *Book of Mengzi*.

Mencken H(enry) L(ouis) 1880–1956. US essayist and critic, known as "the sage of Baltimore." His unconventionally phrased, satiric contributions to the periodicals *The Smart Set* and *American Mercury* (both of which he edited) aroused controversy.

His critical reviews and essays were gathered

Mendelism

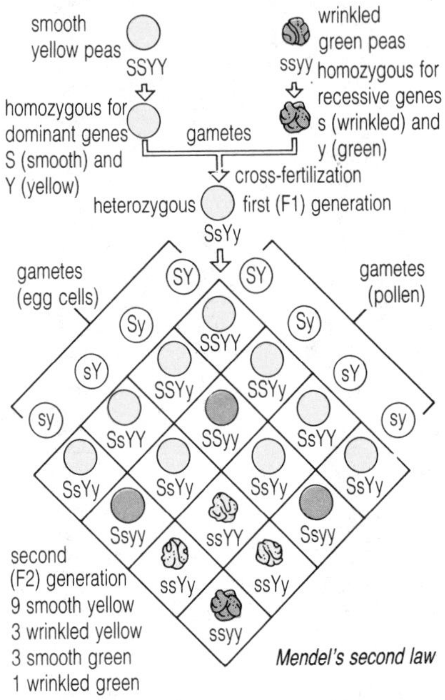
smooth yellow peas
SSYY
wrinkled green peas
ssyy homozygous for recessive genes s (wrinkled) and y (green)
homozygous for dominant genes S (smooth) and Y (yellow)
gametes
cross-fertilization
heterozygous
first (F1) generation
SsYy
gametes (egg cells)
gametes (pollen)
SY
SY
Sy
Sy
sY
sY
sy
sy
SSYY
SSYy
SSYy
SsYY
SSyy
SsYY
SsYy
SsYy
SsYy
SsYy
Ssyy
ssYY
Ssyy
ssYy
ssYy
ssyy
second (F2) generation
9 smooth yellow
3 wrinkled yellow
3 smooth green
1 wrinkled green
Mendel's second law

in *Prejudices* 1919–27, comprising six volumes. He did not restrict himself to literary criticism, but took nearly every US institution to task in his writings. His book, *The American Language* 1918, is often revised.

Mende member of a W African people from central-east Sierra Leone and W Liberia. They number approximately 1 million, and their language belongs to the Niger-Congo family.

Mendel Gregor Johann 1822–1884. Austrian biologist, founder of ◊genetics. His experiments with successive generations of peas gave the basis for his theory of particulate inheritance rather than blending, involving dominant and recessive characters. His results, published 1865–69, remained unrecognized until early this century.

Mendel was abbot of the Augustinian abbey at Brünn (now Brno, Czechoslovakia) from 1868.

mendelevium a synthesized, radioactive metallic element of the ◊actinide series, symbol Md, atomic number 101, atomic weight 258. It was first produced by bombardment of Es-253 with helium nuclei. Its longest-lived isotope, Md-258, has a half-life of about two months. The element is chemically similar to thulium. It was named by the US physicists at the University of California at Berkeley who first synthesized it in 1955 for the Russian chemist ◊Mendeleyev, who in 1869 devised the basis for the periodic table of the elements.

Mendeleyev Dmitri Ivanovich 1834–1907. Russian chemist who framed the periodic law in chemistry 1869, which states that the chemical properties of the elements depend on their atomic weights. This law is the basis of the ◊periodic table of elements, in which the elements are arranged by atomic number and organized by their related groups. For his work, Mendeleyev and Lothar Meyer (who presented a similar but independent classification of the elements) received the Davy medal in 1882. From his table he predicted the properties of elements then unknown (gallium, scandium, and germanium).

Mendelism in genetics, the theory of inheritance originally outlined by Gregor Mendel. He suggested that, in sexually reproducing species, all characteristics are inherited through indivisible "factors" (now identifed with ◊genes) contributed by each parent to its offspring.

Mendelssohn (-Bartholdy) (Jakob Ludwig) Felix

Mendelssohn (-Bartholdy) *German composer and pianist Felix Mendelssohn.*

1809–1847. German composer, also a pianist and conductor. Among his many works are *A Midsummer Night's Dream* 1827; the *Fingal's Cave* overture 1832; and five symphonies, which include the Reformation 1830, the Italian 1833, and the Scottish 1842.

As a child he composed and performed with his own orchestra and as an adult was helpful to ◊Schumann's career. Mendelssohn wrote chamber music, two violin concertos including the renowned E minor 1844; operas, including *Son and Strangers* 1829; piano works; choral works, and songs.

Menderes (Turkish *Büyük Menderes*) river in European Turkey, about 250 mi/400 km long, rising near Afyonkarahisar and flowing along a winding course into the Aegean. The word "meander" is derived from the ancient Greek name for the river.

Mendes Chico (Filho Francisco) 1944–1988. Brazilian environmentalist and labor leader. Opposed to the destruction of Brazil's rainforests, he organized itinerant rubber tappers into the Workers' Party (PT) and was assassinated by Darci Alves, a cattle rancher's son.

Born in the NW Amazonian state of Acre, Mendes became an outspoken opponent of the destruction of Brazil's rainforests for cattle-ranching purposes, and received death threats from ranchers. (Rubber-tapping is sustainable rainforest use.) Mendes was awarded the UN Global 500 Ecology Prize in 1987.

The assassination and trial attracted international attention and a Brazilian company is filming Mendes's life, having defeated several Hollywood studios in bidding for the rights.

Mendès-France Pierre 1907–1982. French prime minister and foreign minister 1954–55. He extricated France from the war in Indochina, and prepared the way for Tunisian independence.

mendicant order religious order dependent on alms. In the Roman Catholic Church there are four orders of mendicant friars: Franciscans, Dominicans, Carmelites, and Augustinians. Hinduism has similar orders.

Mendoza capital of the Argentine province of the same name; population (1980) 597,000. Founded 1561, it developed because of its position on the Trans-Andean railroad; it lies at the center of a wine-producing area.

Mendoza Antonio de c. 1490–1552. First Spanish viceroy of New Spain (Mexico) 1535–51. He attempted to develop agriculture and mining and supported the church in its attempts to convert the Indians. The system he established lasted until the 19th century. He was subsequently viceroy of Peru 1551–52.

Menelaus in Greek mythology, king of Sparta, son of Atreus, brother of Agamemnon, and husband of Helen. With his brother he was joint leader of the Greek expedition against ◊Troy.

Menelik II 1844–1913. Negus (emperor) of Abyssinia (now Ethiopia) from 1889. He defeated the Italians 1896 at ◊Aduwa and thereby retained the independence of his country.

Menem Carlos Saul 1935– . Argentine politician, president from 1989; leader of the Peronist (Justice Party) movement. As president, he improved relations with the UK concerning the future of the Falklands.

Menem, born in La Rioja province, joined the Justice Party while training to be a lawyer. In 1963 he was elected president of the party in La Rioja and in 1983 became governor. In 1989 he defeated the Radical Union Party (UCR) candidate and became president of Argentina. Despite anti-British speeches during the election campaign, President Menem soon declared a wish to resume normal diplomatic relations with the UK and to discuss the future of the Falkland Islands in a spirit of compromise.

Menéndez de Avilés Pedro 1519–1574. Spanish colonial administrator. Born in Avilés, Spain, he saw service in the navy of Charles V and was named to the vital post of captain general of the Indies fleet 1554. With the accession of Philip II, Menéndez was granted the right to establish a colony in Florida to counter French presence there. In 1565 he founded St Augustine, repulsed a French attack, and eventually destroyed their outpost at Fort Caroline. Although his later attempts to establish colonies in the Chesapeake region were unsuccessful, Menéndez established a firm Spanish claim on the Florida peninsula.

Menes c. 3200 BC. Traditionally, the first king of the first dynasty of ancient Egypt. He is said to have founded Memphis and organized worship of the gods.

Mengistu Haile Mariam 1937– . Ethiopian soldier and Socialist politician, head of state 1977–91 (president from 1987). As an officer in the Ethiopian army, he took part in the overthrow in 1974 of Emperor ◊Haile Selassie and in 1977 led another coup, becoming head of state. He was confronted with severe problems of drought and secessionist uprisings, but survived with help from the USSR and the West. In 1987 civilian rule was formally reintroduced, but with the Marxist-Leninist Workers' Party of Ethiopia the only legally permitted party. In spring 1991 two sucessionist forces closed in on the capital of Addis Ababa, and Mengistu fled the country.

Mengs Anton Raffael 1728–1779. German Neo-Classical painter, born in Bohemia. He was court painter in Dresden 1745 and in Madrid 1761; he then worked alternately in Rome and Spain. The ceiling painting *Parnassus* 1761 (Villa Albani, Rome) is an example of his work.

Mengs's father was a miniature painter at the Dresden court and encouraged his son to specialize in portraiture. In 1755 he met the art connoisseur Johann Winckelmann (1717–1768), a founder of Neo-Classicism; Mengs adopted his artistic ideals and wrote a treatise entitled *Beauty in Painting*.

menhir (Breton "long stone") a prehistoric standing stone; see ◊megalith.

Ménière's disease or ***Ménière's syndrome*** recurring condition of the inner ear affecting mechanisms of both hearing and balance. It usually develops in the middle or later years. Symptoms, which include ringing in the ears, nausea, vertigo, and loss of balance, may be relieved by drugs.

Menindee village and sheep center on the Darling River in New South Wales, Australia. It is the center of a scheme for conserving the waters of the Darling in Menindee Lake (60 sq mi/155 sq km) and other lakes nearby.

meningitis inflammation of the meninges (membranes) surrounding the brain, caused by bacterial or viral infection. The severity of the disease varies from mild to rapidly lethal, and symptoms include fever, headache, nausea, neck stiffness, delirium, and (rarely) convulsions. Many common viruses can cause the occasional case of meningitis, although not usually in its more severe form. The treatment for viral meningitis is rest. Bacterial meningitis, though treatable by antibiotics, is a much more serious threat. Diagnosis is by ◊lumbar puncture.

meniscus

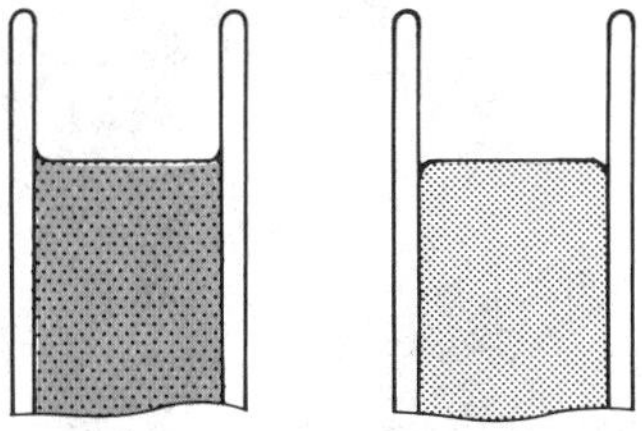
water
mercury

meniscus in physics, the curved shape of the surface of a liquid in a thin tube, caused by the cohesive effects of ◊surface tension (capillary action). When the walls of the container are made wet by the liquid, the meniscus is concave, but with highly viscous liquids (such as mercury) the meniscus is convex. Meniscus is also the name of a concavo-convex or convexo-concave ◊lens.

Menninger Karl Augustus 1893–1990. US psychiatrist. With his father, prominent psychiatrist Charles Menninger, he founded the Menninger Clinic in Topeka 1920. With his brother William, also a psychiatrist, he established the Menninger Foundation for clinical research and public education 1941. Menninger was instrumental in reforming public mental-health facilities.

Born in Topeka, Kansas, and educated at the University of Kansas, Menninger received his MD degree from Harvard 1917. Among his influential books were *The Human Mind* 1930, *Man Against Himself*, and *The Vital Balance* 1963.

Mennonite member of a Protestant Christian sect, originating as part of the ◊Anabaptist movement in Zürich, Switzerland, 1523. They were named Mennonites after Menno Simons (1496–1559), leader of a group in Holland. Persecution drove other groups to Russia and North America.

Some Swiss and German Mennonites settled in Germantown, Pennsylvania, in 1683. From there they eventually spread to the Midwest and Canada. Additional groups came to the Great Plains and to the prairie provinces of Canada after Russia began military conscription in the 1880s. Mennonites have traditionally refused to hold public office or serve in the armed forces. Of the 600,000 Mennonites in the world, some 250,000 are in the US.

menopause in women, the cessation of reproductive ability, characterized by menstruation (see ◊menstrual cycle) becoming irregular and eventually ceasing. The onset is at about the age of 50, but often varies greatly. Menopause is usually uneventful, but some women suffer from complications such as flushing, excessive bleeding, and nervous disorders. Since the 1950s, hormone replacement therapy (HRT), using ◊estrogen alone or with ◊progesterone, has been developed to counteract such effects.

Long-term use of HRT is associated with an increased risk of cancer of the uterus, and shares with the contraceptive pill a risk of clot formation in the blood vessels, leading to possible stroke (pulmonary embolism). However, without HRT there is increased risk of ◊osteoporosis leading to broken bones, which may be indirectly fatal.

The menopause is also known as the "change of life."

Menorca Spanish form of ◊Minorca, one of the Balearic Islands.

Menotti Gian Carlo 1911– . Italian-born US composer. He wrote both the music and the libretti for operas, including *The Medium* 1946, *The Telephone* 1947, *The Consul* 1950, *Amahl and the Night Visitors* 1951 (the first opera to be written for television), and *The Saint of Bleecker Street* 1954. He has also written orchestral and chamber music.

Menotti US composer Gian Carlo Menotti wrote the first opera for television, Amahl and the Night Visitors *1951.*

Menshevik member of the minority (Russian *menshinstvo* "minority") of the Russian Social Democratic Party, who split from the ◊Bolsheviks 1903. The Mensheviks believed in a large, loosely organized party and that, before Socialist revolution could occur in Russia, capitalist society had to develop further. During the Russian Revolution they had limited power and set up a government in Georgia, but were suppressed 1922.

menstrual cycle the cycle that occurs in female mammals of reproductive age, in which the body is prepared for pregnancy. At the beginning of the cycle, a Graafian (egg) follicle develops in the ovary, and the inner wall of the uterus forms a soft spongy lining. The egg is released from the ovary, and the lining of the uterus becomes vascularized (filled with blood vessels). If fertilization does not occur, the corpus luteum (remains of the Graafian follicle) degenerates, and the uterine lining breaks down, and is shed. This is what causes the loss of blood that marks menstruation. The cycle then begins again. Human menstruation takes place from puberty to menopause, occurring about every 28 days.

The cycle is controlled by a number of ◊hormones, including ◊estrogen and ◊progesterone. If fertilization occurs, the corpus luteum persists and goes on producing progesterone.

mental handicap impairment of intelligence. It can be very mild, but in more severe cases, it is associated with social problems and difficulties in living independently. A person may be born with a mental handicap or may acquire it through brain damage. There are between 90 and 130 million people in the world suffering such disabilities.

mental illness abnormal working of the mind. Since normal working cannot be defined, the borderline between mild mental illness and normality is a matter of opinion (not to be confused with normative behavior; see ◊norm). Mild forms are known as neuroses, affecting the emotions, whereas more severe forms, psychoses, distort conscious reasoning.

menthol a pungent, waxy, crystalline alcohol $C_{10}H_{19}OH$, derived from oil of peppermint and used in medicines and cosmetics.

Menton (Italian *Mentone*) resort on the French Riviera, close to the Italian frontier; population (1982) 22,234. It belonged to the princes of Monaco from the 14th century until briefly independent 1848–60, when the citizens voted to merge with France.

Mentor in Homer's ◊*Odyssey*, an old man, advisor to ◊Telemachus in the absence of his father Odysseus. His form is often taken by the goddess Athene.

menu in computing, a list of options, displayed on screen, from which the user may make a choice—for example, the choice of services offered to the customer by a bank cash dispenser: withdrawal, deposit, balance, statement.

Menuhin Yehudi 1916– . US violinist. A child prodigy, he achieved great depth of interpretation, and was often accompanied on the piano by his sister Hephzibah (1921–1981). He conducted his own chamber orchestra and founded a school in Surrey, England, 1963 for training young musicians.

Menzies Robert Gordon 1894–1978. Australian politician, leader of the United Australia (now Liberal) Party and prime minister 1939–41 and 1949–66.

Menzies William Cameron 1896–1957. US art director of films, later a film director and producer, who was one of Hollywood's most imaginative and talented designers. He was responsible for the sets of such classics as *Gone With the Wind* (Academy Award for best art direction) 1939 and *Foreign Correspondent* 1940. His films as director include *Things to Come* 1936 and *Invaders from Mars* 1953.

Meo or ***Miao*** member of a SE Asian highland people (also known as Hmong). They are predominantly hill farmers, rearing pigs and cultivating rice and grain, and many are involved in growing the opium poppy. Their language belongs to the Sino-Tibetan family.

menstrual cycle

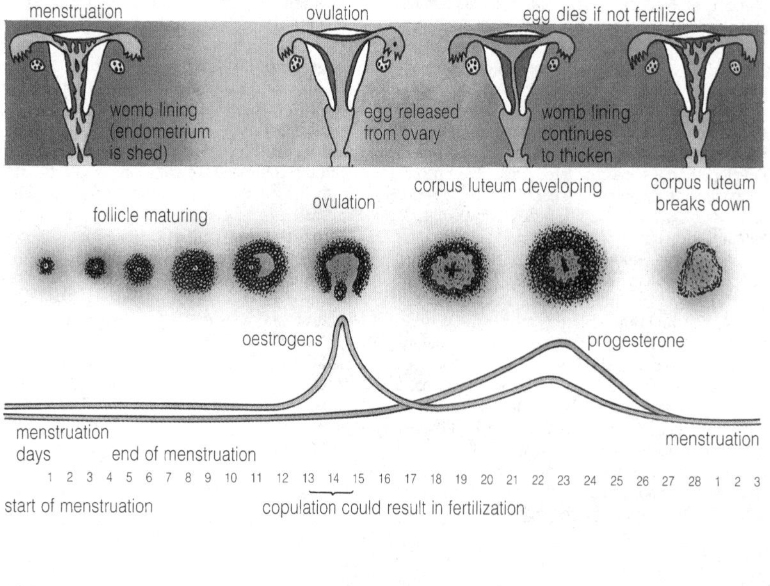
menstruation
ovulation
egg dies if not fertilized
womb lining (endometrium is shed)
egg released from ovary
womb lining continues to thicken
follicle maturing
ovulation
corpus luteum developing
corpus luteum breaks down
oestrogens
progesterone
menstruation
days
end of menstruation
menstruation
1 2 3 4 5 6 7 8 9 10 11 12 13 14 15 16 17 18 19 20 21 22 23 24 25 26 27 28 1 2 3
start of menstruation
copulation could result in fertilization

MEP abbreviation for Member of the ◊European Parliament.

Mephistopheles or ***Mephisto*** another name for the ◊devil, or an agent of the devil, associated with the ◊Faust legend.

Mequinez Spanish name for ◊Meknès, a town in Morocco.

Mercalli scale scale used to measure the intensity of an ◊earthquake. It differs from the ◊Richter scale, which measures magnitude. It is named after the Italian seismologist Giuseppe Mercalli (1850–1914).

Intensity is a subjective value, based on observed phenomena, and varies from place to place with the same earthquake.

mercantilism economic theory, held in the 16th–18th centuries, that a nation's wealth (in the form of bullion or treasure) was the key to its prosperity. To this end, foreign trade should be regulated to create a surplus of exports over imports, and the state should intervene where necessary (for example, subsidizing exports and taxing imports). The bullion theory of wealth was demolished by Adam ◊Smith in Book IV of *The Wealth of Nations* 1776.

Mercator Gerardus 1512–1594. Latinized form of the name of the Flemish map-maker Gerhard Kremer. He devised the first modern atlas, showing Mercator's projection in which the parallels and meridians on maps are drawn uniformly at 90°. It is often used for navigational charts, because compass courses can be drawn as straight lines, but the true area of countries is increasingly distorted the further north or south they are from the equator. For other types, see ◊map projection.

Mercedes-Benz German car-manufacturing company created by a merger of the Daimler and Benz factories 1926. The first automobiles to carry the Mercedes name were those built by Gottlieb ◊Daimler 1901.

In the 1930s, Mercedes-Benz dominated Grand Prix races. The W196, which made its debut 1954, was one of the finest racing automobiles of the postwar era. Following a disaster at Le Mans 1955, when 80 spectators lost their lives after an accident involving a Mercedes, the company withdrew from motor sport until 1989.

mercenary a soldier hired by the army of another country or by a private army. Mercenary military service originated in the 14th century, when cash payment on a regular basis was the only means of guaranteeing soldiers' loyalty. In the 20th century mercenaries have been common in wars and guerrilla activity in Asia, Africa, and Latin America.

Most famous of the mercenary armies was the Great Company of the 14th century, which was in effect a glorified protection racket, comprising some 10,000 knights of all nationalities and employing condottieri, or contractors, to serve the highest bidder. By the end of the 14th century, condottieri and freelances were an institutionalized aspect of warfare. In the 18th century, Swiss cantons and some German states regularly provided the French with troops for mercenary service as a means of raising money; they were regarded as the best forces in the French army. Britain employed 20,000 German mercenaries to make up its numbers during the Seven Years' War 1756–63 and used Hessian forces during the War of American Independence 1775–83.

Article 47 of the 1977 Additional Protocols to the Geneva Convention stipulates that "a mercenary shall not have the right to be a combatant or a prisoner of war" but leaves a party to the Protocols the freedom to grant such status if so wished.

Merchant Ismail 1936– . Indian film producer,

Mercalli Scale

Intensity Value	Description
I	Only detected by instrument.
II	Felt by people resting.
III	Felt indoors; hanging objects swing; feels like passing traffic.
IV	Feels like passing heavy traffic; standing automobiles rock; windows, dishes, and doors rattle; wooden frames creak.
V	Felt outdoors; sleepers are woken; liquids spill; doors swing open.
VI	Felt by everybody; people stagger; windows break; trees and bushes rustle; weak plaster cracks.
VII	Difficult to stand upright; noticed by vehicle drivers; plaster, loose bricks, tiles, and chimneys fall; bells ring.
VIII	Car steering affected; some collapse of masonry; chimney stacks and towers fall; branches break from trees; cracks in wet ground.
IX	General panic; serious damage to buildings; underground pipes break; cracks and subsidence in ground.
X	Most buildings destroyed; landslides; water thrown out of canals.
XI	Rails bent; underground pipes totally destoyed.
XII	Damage nearly total; rocks displaced; objects thrown into the air.

known for his stylish collaborations with James ◊Ivory on films including *Shakespeare Wallah* 1965, *The Europeans* 1979, *Heat and Dust* 1983, *A Room with a View* 1986, and *Maurice* 1987.

merchant bank a bank that developed from merchant houses trading in various parts of the world. As such houses became known, they found that a remunerative way to finance trade was to accept bills of exchange from lesser-known traders. Originally developed in the UK in the 19th century, merchant banks now offer many of the services provided by the commercial banks.

merchant marine the passenger and cargo ships of a country. Most are owned by private companies, but in the USSR and other communist countries they are state-owned and closely associated with the navy. To avoid strict regulations on safety, union rules on crew wages, and so on, many ships are today registered under "flags of convenience," that is, flags of countries that do not have such rules. During wartime, merchant shipping may be drafted by the national government for military purposes.

Merchant of Venice, The a comedy by William Shakespeare, first performed 1596–97. Antonio, a rich merchant, borrows money from Shylock, a Jewish moneylender, promising a pound of flesh if the sum is not repaid; when Shylock presses his claim, the heroine, Portia, disguised as a lawyer, saves Antonio's life.

Merchants Adventurers English trading company founded 1407, which controlled the export of cloth to continental Europe. It comprised guilds and traders in many N European ports. In direct opposition to the Hanseatic League, it came to control 75% of English overseas trade by 1550. In 1689 it lost its charter for furthering the traders' own interests at the expense of the English economy. The company was finally dissolved 1806.

Mercia Anglo-Saxon kingdom that emerged in the 6th century. By the late 8th century it dominated all England south of the Humber, but from about 825 came under the power of ◊Wessex. Mercia eventually came to denote an area bounded by the Welsh border, the river Humber, East Anglia, and the river Thames.

Merckx Eddie 1945– . Belgian cyclist known as "the Cannibal." He won the Tour de France a joint record five times 1969–74.

CAREER HIGHLIGHTS

Tour de France: 1969–72, 1974
Tour of Italy: 1968, 1970, 1972–74
Tour of Spain: 1973
world professional champion: 1967, 1971, 1974
world amateur champion: 1964.

Mercury Roman god, identified with the Greek Hermes, and like him represented with winged sandals and a winged staff entwined with snakes. He was the messenger of the gods.

Mercury in astronomy, the closest planet to the Sun, at an average distance of 36 million mi/58 million km. Its diameter is 3,030 mi/4,880 km, its mass 0.056 that of Earth. Mercury orbits the Sun every 88 days and spins on its axis every 59 days. On its sunward side the surface temperature reaches over 752°F/400°C, but on the "night" side it falls to –274°F/–170°C. Mercury has an atmosphere with minute traces of argon and helium. In 1974 the US space probe *Mariner 10* discovered that its surface is cratered by meteorite impacts. Mercury has no moons.

Its largest known feature is the Caloris Basin, 870 mi/1,400 km wide. There are also cliffs hundreds of miles long and up to 2.5 mi/4 km high, thought to have been formed by the cooling of the planet billions of years ago. Inside is an iron core three-quarters of the planet's diameter, which produces a magnetic field 1% the strength of the Earth's.

mercury heavy, silver-gray, metallic element, symbol Hg (from Latin *hydrargyrum*), atomic number 80, atomic weight 200.59. It is a dense, mobile liquid (popularly called quicksilver) with a low melting point (–37.96°F/–38.87°C). The chief source is the mineral cinnabar, HgS. Mercury sometimes occurs as a free metal (see ◊native metal). Its alloys with other metals are called amalgams, and dentistry uses a silver–mercury amalgam for filling teeth, which is a source of cumulative mercury poisoning to the human body. Industrial uses include drugs and chemicals, mercury-vapor lamps, arc rectifiers, power-control switches, barometers and thermometers. Industrial dumping of this toxic substance has caused global pollution of land and waters, which has contaminated the food chain.

The name is very old and derives from Latin *mercurius*, so named by the alchemists for its fluidity.

mercury fulminate highly explosive compound used in detonators and percussion caps. It is a gray, sandy powder and extremely poisonous (see ◊fulminate).

Mercury project US project to put a human in space in the one-seat Mercury spacecraft 1961–63.

The first two Mercury flights, on Redstone rockets, were short flights to the edge of space and back. The orbital flights, beginning with the third in the series (made by John ◊Glenn), were launched by Atlas rockets.

Meredith George 1828–1909. English novelist and poet. He published the first realistic psychological novel *The Ordeal of Richard Feverel* 1859. Later works include *Evan Harrington* 1861, *The Egoist* 1879, *Diana of the Crossways* 1885, and *The Amazing Marriage* 1895. His verse includes *Modern Love* 1862 and *Poems and Lyrics of the Joy of Earth* 1883.

merengue a type of Latin American dance music with a lively 2/4 beat. Accordion and saxophone are prominent instruments, with ethnic percussion. It originated in the Dominican Republic and became popular in New York in the 1980s.

merganser any of several diving ducks with long, serrated bills for catching fish. They are widely distributed in the northern hemisphere; most have crested heads.

Mergenthaler Ottmar 1854–1899. German-born American who invented a typesetting method. He went to the US in 1872 and developed the first linotype machine (for casting hot-metal type in complete lines) 1876–86.

merger the linking of two or more companies, either by creating a new organization by consolidating the original companies or by absorption by one of the others. Unlike a takeover, which is not always a voluntary fusion of the parties, a merger is the result of an agreement.

Mérida capital of Yucatán state, Mexico, a center of the sisal industry; population (1986) 580,000. It was founded 1542, and has a cathedral 1598. Its port on the Gulf of Mexico is Progreso.

Meriden city in S central Connecticut, E of Waterbury. An industrial city, its best-known products include plastics, silver, and electronics; population (1990) 59,479.

meridian half a ◊great circle drawn on the Earth's

Mercury *Mariner 10 spacecraft's photomosaic of the heavily cratered surface of the planet Mercury, taken on March 29, 1974.*

surface passing through both poles and thus through all places with the same longitude. Terrestrial longitudes are usually measured from the Greenwich Meridian.

An astronomical meridian is a great circle passing through the celestial pole and the zenith (the point immediately overhead).

Mérimée Prosper 1803–1870. French author. Among his works are the short novels *Colomba* 1841, *Carmen* 1846, and the *Lettres à une inconnue/Letters to an Unknown Girl* 1873.

Born in Paris, he entered the public service and under Napoleon III was employed on unofficial diplomatic missions.

merino breed of sheep. Its close-set, silky wool is highly valued. The merino, originally from Spain, is now found all over the world, and is the breed on which the Australian wool industry is built.

Merionethshire former county of N Wales, included in the new county of Gwynedd 1974. Dolgellau was the administrative town.

meristem a region of plant tissue containing cells that are actively dividing to produce new tissues (or have the potential to do so). Meristems found in the tip of roots and stems, the apical meristems, are responsible for the growth in length of these organs.

The ◊cambium is a lateral meristem that is responsible for increase in girth in perennial plants. Some plants also have intercalary meristems, as in the stems of grasses, for example. These are responsible for their continued growth after cutting or grazing has removed the apical meristems of the shoots.

Meristem culture involves growing meristems taken from shoots on a nutrient-containing medium, and using them to grow new plants. It is used to propagate infertile plants or hybrids that do not breed true from seed and to generate virus-free stock, since viruses rarely infect apical meristems.

meritocracy a system (of, for example, education or government) in which selection is by performance (in education, by competitive examinations), which therefore favors intelligence and ability rather than social position or wealth.

The Chinese Mandarin system was based on the testing of scholars to work for the emperor; they rose through the ranks, as do civil service employees.

Merleau-Ponty Maurice 1908–1961. French philosopher, one of the most significant contributors to ◊phenomenology after Edmund ◊Husserl. He attempted to move beyond the notion of a pure experiencing consciousness, arguing in *The Phenomenology of Perception* 1945 that perception is intertwined with bodily awareness and with language. In his posthumously published work *The Visible and the Invisible* 1964, he argued that our experience is inherently ambiguous and elusive and that the traditional concepts of philosophy are therefore inadequate to grasp it.

Merlin legendary magician and counselor to King ◊Arthur. Welsh bardic literature has a cycle of poems attributed to him, and he may have been a real person.

merlin a small ◊falcon *Falco columbarius*, of Eurasia and North America, where it is also called pigeon hawk.

mermaid mythical sea creature (the male is a merman), having a human head and torso and a fish's tail. The dugong and seal are among suggested origins for the idea.

Meroe ancient city in Sudan, on the Nile near Khartoum, capital of Nubia from about 600 BC to AD 350. Tombs and inscriptions have been excavated, and iron-smelting slag heaps have been found.

Merovingian dynasty a Frankish dynasty, named after its founder, Merovech (5th century AD). His descendants ruled France from the time of Clovis (481–511) to 751.

Mersenne Marin 1588–1648. French mathematician and philosopher who, from his base in Paris, did much to disseminate throughout Europe the main advances of French science. In mathematics he defined a particular form of ◊prime number, since referred to as a Mersenne prime.

Mersey river in NW England; length 70 mi/112 km. Formed by the confluence of the Goyt and Etherow rivers, it flows W to join the Irish Sea at Liverpool Bay. It is linked to the Manchester Ship Canal.

Mersey beat a type of pop music of the mid-1960s that originated in the NW of England. It was also known as the Liverpool sound or beat music in the UK or the British Invasion in the US. The beat groups characteristically had a simple, guitar-dominated line-up, vocal harmonies and catchy tunes. It was almost exclusively performed by all-male groups, of whom the most celebrated was the Beatles.

Mersin or ***Içel*** Turkish industrial free port (chrome, copper, textiles, oil refining); population (1985) 314,000.

Merthyr Tydfil industrial town (light engineering, electrical goods) in Mid Glamorgan, Wales, UK; population (1982) 60,000. It was formerly a center of the Welsh coal and steel industries.

Merv oasis in Soviet Turkmenistan, a center of civilization from at least 1200 BC, and site of a town founded by Alexander the Great. Old Merv was destroyed by the emir of Bokhara 1787, and the modern town of Mary, founded by the Russians in 1885, lies 18 mi/29 km to its west.

mesa (Spanish "table") a flat-topped steep-sided plateau, consisting of horizontal weak layers of rock topped by a resistant formation; in particular, those found in the desert areas of the US and Mexico. A small mesa is called a butte.

Mesa Verde (Spanish "green table") a wooded clifftop in Colorado, with Pueblo dwellings, called the Cliff Palace, built into its side. Dating from about 1000 BC, with 200 rooms and 23 circular ceremonial chambers (kivas), it had an estimated population of about 400 people and was probably a regional center.

mescaline psychedelic drug derived from a small, spineless cactus *Lophophora williamsii* of N Mexico and the SW US, known as ◊peyote. The tops (called mescal buttons), which scarcely appear above ground, are dried and chewed, or added to alcoholic drinks. Mescaline is a crystalline alkaloid $C_{11}H_{17}NO_3$. It is used by some North American Indians in religious rites.

Meshed a variant spelling of ◊Mashhad, a town in Iran.

Meskhetian member of a community of Turkish descent that formerly inhabited Meskhetia, USSR, on the Turkish-Soviet border. They were deported by Stalin 1944 to Kazakhstan and Uzbekistan, and have campaigned since then for a return to their homeland. In June 1989 at least 70 were killed in pogroms directed against their community in the Ferghana Valley of Uzbekistan by the native Uzbeks.

Mesmer Friedrich Anton 1733–1815. Austrian physician, an early experimenter in ◊hypnosis, which was formerly (and popularly) called mesmerism after him.

He claimed to reduce people to trance state by consciously exerted "animal magnetism," their willpower being entirely subordinated to his. Expelled by the police from Vienna, he created a sensation in Paris in 1778, but was denounced as a charlatan in 1785.

mesmerism former term for ◊hypnosis, after Friedrich Mesmer.

Mesolithic the Middle Stone Age developmental stage of human technology and of ◊prehistory.

meson any of a class of ◊hadron, ◊elementary particles that are composed of a quark and its antiquark, found in cosmic radiation and emitted by nuclei under bombardment by very high-energy particles. Included are kaons and pions.

Their existence was predicted in 1935 by Japanese physicist Hideki Yukawa (1907–1981).

mesophyll the tissue between the upper and lower epidermis of a leaf blade (◊lamina), consisting of parenchymalike cells containing numerous ◊chloroplasts.

In many plants, mesophyll is divided into two distinct layers. The palisade mesophyll is usually just below the upper epidermis and is composed of regular layers of elongated cells. Lying below them is the spongy mesophyll, composed of loosely arranged cells of irregular shape. This layer contains fewer chloroplasts and has many intercellular spaces for the diffusion of gases (required for ◊respiration and ◊photosynthesis), linked to the outside by means of ◊stomata.

Mesopotamia the land between the Tigris and Euphrates rivers, now part of Iraq. Here the civilizations of Sumer and Babylon flourished. Sumer (3500 BC) may have been the earliest civilization.

mesosphere layer in the Earth's ◊atmosphere above the stratosphere and below the thermosphere. It lies between about 31 mi/50 km and 50 mi/80 km above the ground.

Mesozoic era of geologic time 248–65 million years ago, consisting of the Triassic, Jurassic, and Cretaceous periods. At the beginning of the era, the continents were joined together as Pangaea, dinosaurs and other giant reptiles dominated the sea and air; and ferns, horsetails, and cycads thrived in a warm climate worldwide. By the end of the Mesozoic era, the continents had begun to assume their present positions, flowering plants were dominant and many of the large reptiles and marine fauna were becoming extinct.

Messager André Charles Prosper 1853–1929. French composer and conductor. He studied under ◊Saint-Saëns.

Messager composed light operas, such as *La Béarnaise* 1885 and *Véronique* 1898.

Messalina Valeria c. AD 22–48. Third wife of the Roman emperor ◊Claudius, whom she dominated. She was notorious for her immorality, forcing a noble to marry her in AD 48, although still married to Claudius, who then had her executed.

Messerschmitt Willy 1898–1978. German airplane designer whose Me-109 was a standard Luftwaffe fighter in World War II, and whose Me-262 (1942) was the first mass-produced jet fighter.

Messiaen Olivier 1908– . French composer and organist. His music is mystical in character, vividly colored, and incorporates transcriptions of birdsong. Among his works are the *Quartet for the End of Time* 1941, the large-scale *Turangalîla Symphony* 1949, and solo organ and piano pieces.

His theories of melody, harmony, and rhythm, drawing on medieval and oriental music, have inspired contemporary composers such as ◊Boulez and ◊Stockhausen.

Messiah (from Hebrew *māshīach* "anointed") in Judaism and Christianity, the savior or deliverer. Jews from the time of the Old Testament exile in Babylon have looked forward to the coming of the Messiah. Christians believe that the Messiah came in the person of ◊Jesus, and hence called him the Christ.

Messier Charles 1730–1817. French astronomer who discovered 15 comets and in 1781 published a list of 103 star clusters and nebulae. Objects on this list are given M (for Messier) numbers, which astronomers still use today, such as M1 (the Crab nebula) and M31 (the Andromeda galaxy).

Messina city and port in NE Sicily; population (1988) 271,000. It produces soap, olive oil, wine, and pasta. Originally an ancient Greek settlement (Zancle), it was taken first by Carthage and then by Rome. It was rebuilt after an earthquake 1908.

Messina, Strait of channel in the central Mediterranean separating Sicily from mainland Italy; in Greek legend a monster (Charybdis), who devoured ships, lived in the whirlpool on the Sicilian side, and another (Scylla), who devoured sailors, in the rock on the Italian side. The Classical hero Odysseus passed safely between them.

Messrs abbreviation for *messieurs* (French "sirs" or "gentlemen") used in formal writing to address an organization or group of people.

Meštrović Ivan 1883–1962. Yugoslav sculptor, a US citizen from 1954. His works include portrait busts of the sculptor Rodin (with whom he is often compared), President Hoover, Pope Pius XI, and many public monuments.

metabolism the chemical processes of living organisms: a constant alternation of building up (anabolism) and breaking down (catabolism). For example, green plants build up complex organic substances from water, carbon dioxide, and mineral salts (photosynthesis); by digestion animals partially break down complex organic substances, ingested as food, and subsequently resynthesize them in their own bodies.

Metacomet Wampanoag leader better known as King ◊Philip.

metal any of a class of chemical elements with certain chemical characteristics and physical properties; they are good conductors of heat and electricity; opaque but reflect light well; malleable, which enables them to be coldworked and rolled into sheets; and ductile, which permits them to be drawn into thin wires. Metallic elements comprise about 75% of the 109 elements shown in the ◊periodic table of the elements. They form alloys with each other, ◊bases with the hydroxyl radical (OH), and replace the hydrogen in an ◊acid to form a salt. The majority are found in the combined form only, as compounds or mineral ores; about 16 of them also occur in the elemental form, as ◊native metals. They have been put to many uses, both structural and decorative, since prehistoric times, and the Copper Age, Bronze Age, and Iron Age are named for the metal that formed the technological base for that stage of human evolution.

metal detector electronic device for detecting metal, usually below ground, developed from the wartime mine detector. In the head of the metal detector is a coil, which is part of an electronic circuit. The presence of metal causes the frequency of the signal in the circuit to change, setting up an audible note in the headphones worn by the user. They are used to survey areas for buried metallic objects, especially in archeology.

metal fatigue condition in which metals fail or fracture under relatively light loads, when these loads are applied repeatedly. Structures that are subject to flexing, such as the airframes of aircraft, are prone to metal fatigue.

Metalious Grace (born Repentigny) 1924–1964. US novelist. She wrote many short stories but made headlines with *Peyton Place* 1956, an exposé of life in a small New England town, which was made into a film 1957 and a long-running television series.

metallic bond the force of attraction operating in a metal that holds the atoms together. In the metal the ◊valency electrons are able to move within the crystal and these electrons are said to be delocalized (see ◊electrons, delocalized). Their movement creates short-lived, positively charged ions. The electrostatic attraction between the delocalized electrons and the ceaselessly forming ions constitutes the metallic bond.

metallic character chemical properties associated with those elements classed as metals. These properties, which arise from the element's ability to lose electrons, are: the displacement of hydrogen from dilute acids; the formation of ◊basic oxides; the formation of ionic chlorides; and their reducing reaction, as in the ◊thermite process.

In the periodic table of the elements, metallic character increases down any group and across a period from right to left.

metalloid or ***semimetal*** a chemical element having some of but not all the properties of metals; metalloids are thus usually electrically semiconducting. They comprise the elements germanium, arsenic, antimony, and tellurium.

metallurgy the science and technology of producing metals, which includes extraction, alloying, and hardening. Extractive, or process, metallurgy is concerned with the extraction of metals from their ◊ores and refining and adapting them for use. Physical metallurgy is concerned with their properties and application. Metallography establishes the microscopic structures that contribute to hardness, ductility, and strength.

Metals can be extracted from their ores in three main ways: dry processes, such as smelting, volatilization, or amalgamation (treatment with mercury); wet processes, involving chemical reactions; and electrolytic processes, which work on the principle of ◊electrolysis.

The foundations of metallurgical science were laid before 3500 BC in Mesopotamia, Egypt, China, and India, where the art of ◊smelting metals from ores was discovered, starting with the natural alloy bronze. Later, gold, silver, copper, lead, and tin were worked in various ways, although they had been cold hammered as native metals for thousands of years. The smelting of iron was discovered about 1500 BC. The Romans hardened and tempered iron into steel, using ◊heat treatment. From then until about AD 1400, advances in metallurgy came into Europe by way of Arabian chemists. ◊Cast iron began to be made in the 14th century in a crude blast furnace. The demands of the Industrial Revolution led to an enormous increase in ◊wrought iron production. The invention by Henry Bessemer of the ◊Bessemer process in 1856 made cheap steel available for the first time, leading to its present widespread use and the industrial development of many specialized steel alloys.

metamorphic rocks

Typical depth and temperature of formation	Main primary material (before metamorphosis) Shale with several minerals	Sandstone with only quartz	Limestone with only calcite
15 km/300°C	slate	quartzite	marble
20 km/400°C	schist		
25 km/500°C	gneiss		
30 km/600°C	hornfels	quartzite	marble

metamorphic rock a rock altered in structure and composition by pressure, heat, or chemically active fluids after original formation. (If heat is sufficient to melt the original rock, technically it becomes an igneous rock upon cooling.)

The mineral assemblage present in a metamorphic rock depends on the composition of the starting material (which may be sedimentary or igneous) and the temperature and pressure conditions to which it is subjected. For example, a clay rich in sediment might become a slate when metamorphozed at low temperature and pressure, a mica-schist at a higher temperature and pressure, or a gneiss if temperature and pressure are very high.

Thermal metamorphism involves mainly heat changes as in rocks adjacent to an igneous body; dynamic metamorphism occurs with changes in stress as in a fault. Regional metamorphism involves both heat and pressure and is associated with rock deformation taking place at convergent plate boundaries (see ◊plate tectonics). Most metamorphism invloves little change in bulk chemistry except for loss or gain of water and other volatiles; chemical changes may, however, occur due to the action of fluids. Very high-grade metamorphism can cause a rock to melt, and some granites appear to have been formed in this way.

metamorphism geologic term referring to the changes in rocks of the Earth's crust caused by increasing pressure and temperature.

metamorphosis a period during the life cycle of many invertebrates, most amphibians, and some fish, during which the individual's body changes from one form to another through a major reconstitution of its tissues. For example, adult frogs are produced by metamorphosis from tadpoles, and butterflies are produced from caterpillars following metamorphosis within a pupa.

In Classical thought and literature, metamorphosis is the transformation of a living being into another shape, either living or animate (for example ◊Niobe). The Roman poet ◊Ovid wrote about this theme.

metaphor (Greek "transfer") figure of speech using an analogy or close comparison between two things that are not normally treated as if they had anything in common. Metaphor is a common means of extending the uses and references of words. See also ◊simile.

If we call people cabbages or foxes, we are indicating that in our opinion they share certain qualities with those vegetables or animals: an inert quality in the case of cabbages, a cunning quality in the case of foxes, which may lead on to calling people "foxy" and saying "He really foxed them that time," meaning that he tricked them. If a scientist is doing research in the *field* of nuclear physics, the word "field" results from comparison between scientists and farmers (who literally work in fields). Such usages are metaphorical.

metaphysical poets a group of 17th-century English poets whose work is characterized by conciseness; ingenious, often highly intricate wordplay; and striking imagery. Among the exponents of this genre are John ◊Donne and George ◊Herbert.

metaphysics a branch of philosophy that deals with first principles, in particular "being" (ontology) and "knowing" (◊epistemology), and that is concerned with the ultimate nature of reality. It has been maintained that no certain knowledge of metaphysical questions is possible.

Epistemology, or the study of how we know,

metamorphosis *An adult green darner dragonfly perched on its empty larval skin after metamorphosis. The green darner is found throughout North America, on Hawaii and the E coast of Africa.*

lies at the threshold of the subject. Metaphysics is concerned with the nature and origin of existence and of mind, the interaction between them, the meaning of time and space, causation, determinism and free will, personality and the self, arguments for belief in God, and human immortality. The foundations of metaphysics were laid by ◊Plato and ◊Aristotle. St Thomas ◊Aquinas, basing himself on Aristotle, produced a metaphysical structure that is accepted by the Catholic church. The subject has been advanced by Descartes, Spinoza, Leibniz, Berkeley, Hume, Locke, Kant, Hegel, Schopenhauer, and Marx; and in the 20th century by Bergson, Bradley, Croce, McTaggart, Whitehead, and Wittgenstein.

Metastasio pen name of Pietro Trapassi 1698–1782. Italian poet and the leading librettist of his day, creating 18th-century Italian *opera seria* (serious opera).

Metaxas Ioannis 1870–1941. Greek general and politician, born in Ithaca. He restored ◊George II (1890–1947) as king of Greece, under whom he established a dictatorship as prime minister from 1936, and introduced several necessary economic and military reforms. He led resistance to the Italian invasion of Greece in 1941, refusing to abandon Greece's neutral position.

metazoa another name for animals. It reflects an earlier system of classification, in which there were two main divisions within the animal kingdom, the multicellular animals, or metazoa, and the single-celled "animals" or protozoa. The ◊protozoa are no longer included in the animal kingdom, so only the metazoa remain.

metempsychosis another name for ◊reincarnation.

meteor flash of light in the sky, popularly known as a shooting or falling star, caused by a particle of dust, a meteoroid, entering the atmosphere at speeds up to 45 mps/70 kps and burning up by friction.

Several times each year the Earth encounters swarms of dust shed by comets, which give rise to a meteor shower. This appears to radiate from one particular point in the sky, after which the shower is named; the Perseid meteor shower in August appears in the constellation Perseus. A brilliant meteor is termed a fireball. Most meteoroids are smaller than grains of sand.

meteor-burst communications technique for sending messages by bouncing radio waves off the fiery tails of ◊meteors. High-speed computer-controlled equipment is used to sense the presence of a meteor and to broadcast a signal during the short time that the meteor races across the sky.

The system, first suggested in the late 1920s, remained impracticable until data-compression techniques were developed, enabling messages to be sent in automatic high-speed bursts each time a meteor trail appeared. There are usually enough meteor trails in the sky at any time to permit continuous transmission of a message. The technique offers a communications link that is difficult to jam, undisturbed by storms on the Sun, and would not be affected by nuclear war.

meteorite piece of rock or metal from space that reaches the surface of the Earth, Moon, or other body. Most meteorites are thought to be fragments from asteroids, although some may be pieces from the heads of comets. Most are stony, although some are made of iron and a few have a mixed rock–iron composition. Meteorites provide evidence for the nature of the Solar System and may be similar to the Earth's core and mantle, neither of which can be observed directly.

Thousands of meteorites hit the Earth each year, but most fall in the sea or in remote areas and are never recovered. The largest known meteorite is one composed of iron, weighing 66 tons, which lies where it fell in prehistoric times at Grootfontein, Namibia. Meteorites are slowed down by the Earth's atmosphere, but if they are moving fast enough they can form a ◊crater on impact. Meteor Crater in Arizona, about 4,000 ft/1,200 m in diameter and 650 ft/200 m deep, is the site of a meteorite impact about 50,000 years ago.

meteoroid chunk of rock in interplanetary space. There is no official distinction between meteoroids and asteroids, except that the term asteroid is generally reserved for objects larger than 1 mi/1.6 km in diameter, whereas meteoroids can range anywhere from pebble-size up.

Meteoroids are believed to result from the fragmentation of asteroids after collisions. Some meteoroids strike the Earth's atmosphere, and their fiery trails are called meteors. If they fall to Earth, they are named meteorites.

meteorology the scientific observation and study of the ◊atmosphere, so that weather can be accurately forecasted. Data from meteorological stations and weather satellites is collated by computer at central agencies such as the Meteorological Office in Bracknell, near London, and a forecast and ◊weather maps based on current readings are issued at regular intervals.

At meteorological stations readings are taken of the factors determining weather conditions: atmospheric pressure, temperature, humidity, wind (using the ◊Beaufort scale), cloud cover (measuring both type of cloud and coverage), and precipitation such as rain, snow, and hail (measured at 12-hourly intervals). Satellites are used either to relay information transmitted from the Earth-based stations or to send pictures of cloud development, indicating wind patterns, and snow and ice cover.

meter any instrument used for measurement; the term is often compounded with a prefix to denote a specific type of meter; for example, ammeter, voltmeter, flowmeter, or pedometer.

meter SI unit (abbreviation m) of length, equivalent to 1.093 yards or 39.37 inches. It is defined by scientists as the length of the path traveled by light in a vacuum during a time interval of 1/299,792,458 of a second.

methanal (common name formaldehyde) HCHO gas at ordinary temperatures, condensing to a liquid at −5.8°F/−21°C. It has a powerful penetrating smell. Dissolved in water, it is used as a biological preservative. It is used in the manufacture of plastics, dyes, foam (for example urea-formaldehyde foam, used in insulation), and in medicine.

methane CH_4 the simplest hydrocarbon of the paraffin series. Colorless, odorless, and lighter than air, it burns with a bluish flame and explodes when mixed with air or oxygen. It is the chief constituent of natural gas and also occurs in the explosive firedamp of coal mines. In marsh gas methane forms from rotting vegetation by spontaneous combustion resulting in the pale flame seen over marshland and known as will-o'-the-wisp.

Methane is causing about 38% of the warming of the globe through the ◊greenhouse effect; the amount of methane in the air is predicted to double over the next 60 years.

methanogenic bacteria one of a group of primitive bacteria (◊archaebacteria). They give off methane gas as a by-product of their metabolism, and are common in sewage treatment plants and hot springs, where the temperature is high and oxygen is absent.

methanol (common name methyl alcohol) CH_3OH the simplest of the alcohols. It can be made by the dry distillation of wood (hence it is also known as wood alcohol), but is usually made from coal or natural gas. When pure, it is a colorless, flammable liquid with a pleasant odor, and is highly poisonous.

Methanol is used to produce formaldehyde (from which resins and plastics can be made), methyl-ter-butyl ether (MTB, a replacement for lead as an octane-booster in gasoline), vinyl acetate (largely used in paint manufacture), and gasoline.

Method the US adaptation of ◊Stanislavsky's teachings on acting and direction, in which importance is attached to the psychological building of a role rather than the technical side of its presentation. Emphasis is placed on improvisation, aiming for a spontaneous and realistic style of acting. One of the principal exponents of the Method was the US actor and director Lee Strasberg, who taught at the ◊Actors Studio in New York.

Methodism evangelical Protestant Christian movement that was founded by John ◊Wesley 1739 within the Church of England, but which became a separate body 1795. The church government is presbyterian in Britain and episcopal in the US. There were more than 50 million Methodists throughout the world in 1988.

The itinerant, open-air preaching of John and Charles Wesley and George Whitefield drew immense crowds and led to a revival of faith among members of the English working and agricultural classes who were alienated from the formalism and conservatism of the Church of England. The Methodist emphasis on emotion and the conversion experience proved equally popular in America, where the Wesleys went to preach in 1735. As the movement grew there during the Great Awakening, Wesley encouraged the formation of an independent American Methodist Church. Methodist doctrines are contained in Wesley's sermons and *Notes on the New Testament.* There are now more than 20 separate Methodist groups in the US. The largest, the Methodist Church, was formed through the merger of various Methodist groups in 1938 and 1968.

Methodius, St c. 825–884. Greek Christian bishop, who with his brother ◊Cyril translated much of the Bible into Slavonic. Feast day Feb 14.

Methuselah in the Old Testament, Hebrew patriarch who lived before the Flood; his life span of 969 years makes him a byword for longevity.

methyl alcohol common name for ◊methanol.

methylated spirit alcohol that has been rendered undrinkable, and is used for industrial purposes.

It is nevertheless drunk by some individuals, resulting eventually in death. One of the poisonous substances in it is ◊methanol, or methyl alcohol, and this gives it its name. (The "alcohol" of alcoholic drinks is ethanol.)

methyl benzene alternate name for ◊toluene.

methyl orange $C_{14}H_{14}N_3NaO_3S$ orange-yellow powder used as an acid–base indicator in chemical tests, and as a stain in the preparation of slides of biological material. Its color changes with pH; below pH 3.1 it is red, above pH 4.4 it is yellow.

metonymy (Greek "transferred title") figure of speech that works by association, naming something closely connected with what is meant; for example, calling the theatrical profession "the stage," horse racing "the turf," or journalists "the press." See also ◊synecdoche.

metric system system of weights and measures developed in France in the 18th century and recognized by other countries in the 19th century. In 1960 an international conference on weights and measures recommended the universal adoption of a revised International System (Système International d'Unités, or SI), with seven prescribed "base units": the meter (m) for length, kilogram (kg) for mass, second (s) for time, ampere (A) for electric current, kelvin (K) for thermodynamic temperature, candela (cd) for luminous intensity, and mole (mol) for quantity of matter.

Two supplementary units are included in the SI system—the radian (rad) and steradian (sr)—used to measure plane and solid angles. In addition, there are recognized derived units that can be expressed as simple products or divisions of powers of the basic units, with no other integers appearing in the expression; for example, the watt.

Some non-SI units, well established and internationally recognized, remain in use in conjunction with SI: minute, hour, and day in measuring time; multiples or submultiples of base or derived units which have long-established names, such as tonne

Metternich The architect of the 1815 Congress of Vienna, Austrian chancellor and foreign minister Prince von Metternich.

for mass, the liter for volume; and specialist measures such as the metric carat for gemstones.

Prefixes used with metric units are tera (T) million million times; giga (G) billion (thousand million) times; mega (M) million times; kilo (k) thousand times; hecto (h) hundred times; deka (da) ten times; deci (d) tenth part; centi (c) hundredth part; milli (m) thousandth part; micro (M) millionth part; nano (n) billionth part; pico (p) trillionth part; femto (f) quadrillionth part; atto (a) quintillionth part.

The metric system was made legal for most purposes in the US in the 19th century. A Metric Act was passed in the US in 1975 to promote the use, without compulsion, of the metric system.

metric ton or ***tonne*** unit of mass (abbreviation t or T) equal to 2,205 lb/1,000 kg.

metronome a clockwork device, invented by Johann Maelzel in 1814, using a sliding weight to regulate the speed of a pendulum to assist in keeping time.

metropolitan (Greek "mother-state, capital") in the Christian church generally, a bishop who has rule over other bishops (termed suffragans). In the Eastern Orthodox Church, a metropolitan has a rank between an archbishop and a ◊patriarch.

Metropolitan Opera Company foremost opera company in the US, founded 1883 in New York City. The Metropolitan Opera House (opened 1883) was demolished 1966, and the company moved to the new Metropolitan Opera House at Lincoln Center.

The first production of the Metropolitan Opera House Co, Ltd, was Gounod's *Faust*. Highlights of its history include: the "Golden Age" 1898–1903, when artists from all over the world appeared at the "Met"; the 1903 New York debut of Enrico ◊Caruso; the 1955 appearance of Marian ◊Anderson, the first black to sing in a lead role there, in Verdi's *Un Ballo in Maschera*; and the first live telecast of a Metropolitan Opera production, Puccini's *La Bohème*, featuring Renata Scotto and Luciano Pavarotti, 1977.

Metsu Gabriel 1629–1667. Dutch painter, born in Leiden, active in Amsterdam from 1657. His main subjects were genre (domestic) scenes, usually with a few well-dressed figures. He was skilled in depicting rich glossy fabrics.

Metternich Klemens (Wenzel Lothar), Prince von 1773–1859. Austrian politician, the leading figure in European diplomacy after the fall of Napoleon. As foreign minister 1809–48 (as well as chancellor from 1821), he tried to maintain the balance of power in Europe, supporting monarchy and repressing liberalism. At the Congress of Vienna 1815 he advocated cooperation by the great powers to suppress democratic movements. The ◊revolution of 1848 forced him to flee to the UK; he returned 1851 as a power behind the scenes.

Metz industrial city (shoes, metal goods, tobacco) in Lorraine region, NE France, on the Moselle river; population (1982) 186,000. Part of the Holy Roman Empire 870–1552, it became one of the great frontier fortresses of France, and was in German hands 1871–1918.

Meurthe river rising in the Vosges mountains in NE France and flowing in a NW direction to join the Moselle at Frouard, near Nancy; length 102 mi/163 km. It gives its name to the *département* of Meurthe-et-Moselle.

Meuse (Dutch *Maas*) river flowing through France, Belgium, and the Netherlands; length 560 mi/900 km. It was a line of battle in both World Wars.

Mewar another name for ◊Udaipur, a city in Rajasthan, India.

Mexicali city in NW Mexico; population (1984) 500,000. It produces soap and cottonseed oil. The availability of cheap labor attracts many US companies (Hughes Aerospace, Rockwell International, and others).

Mexican Empire short-lived empire 1822–23 following the liberation of Mexico from Spain. The empire lasted only eight months, under the revolutionary leader Agustín de ◊Iturbide.

When the French emperor Napoleon I put his brother Joseph on the Spanish throne in 1808, links between Spain and its colonies weakened and an independence movement grew in Mexico. There were several unsuccessful uprisings until, in 1821, Gen Agustín de Iturbide published a plan promising independence, protection for the church, and the establishment of a monarchy. As no European came forward, in 1822 he proclaimed himself emperor. Forced to abdicate, he went into exile; on his return to Mexico he was ordered shot by republican leaders Guadalupe Victoria and Santa Anna. Victoria became the first president of Mexico.

Mexican War war between the US and Mexico 1846–48, begun when General Zachary Taylor invaded New Mexico. By the treaty of Guadelupe Hidalgo that ended the war, the US acquired New Mexico and California, as well as clear title to Texas, in exchange for $15 million.

President James ◊Polk had dispatched Taylor after efforts to purchase what are now California and New Mexico failed. Tensions were high between the US and Mexico as a result of continuing border disputes and the annexation of Texas. Polk was determined to pursue his notion of ◊Manifest Destiny for the US and set out to add the disputed territories, by force if necessary. After repeated defeats and invasion of its home territory, a Mexican government was formed that was willing to negotiate a settlement. Presidential envoy Nicholas Trist was ordered home, but he ignored his orders and negotiated the pact ceding vast Mexican territories to the US. Polk was enraged but had little choice but to submit the exceptionally favorable treaty to the Senate, which ratified it.

Mexico country in Central America, bordered N by the US, E by the Gulf of Mexico, SE by Belize and Guatemala, and SW and W by the Pacific Ocean.

government Mexico is a federal republic of 31 states and a federal district, based in Mexico City. The constitution dates from 1917. Legislative power rests with a two-chamber national congress of senate, chamber of deputies, and directly elected president, all serving a six-year term. The president chooses the cabinet. The Senate has 64 members, each state and the federal district being represented by two senators. The Chamber has 400 members: 300 representing single-member constituencies and 100 elected by proportional representation so as to give due weight to minority parties. Members of Congress are elected by universal suffrage. Each state has an elected governor and chamber of deputies, elected for a six-year term. Political parties must register and meet certain criteria in order to operate. The main parties are the Institutional Revolutionary Party (PRI) and the National Action Party (PAN).

history Mexico was the region of the New World where many ◊civilizations developed, including the Olmec, Maya, Toltec, Mixtec, Zapotec, and the Aztec, who settled on the central plateau and whose last king, Montezuma II, was killed 1520

Mexico

United States of
(*Estados Unidos Mexicanos*)

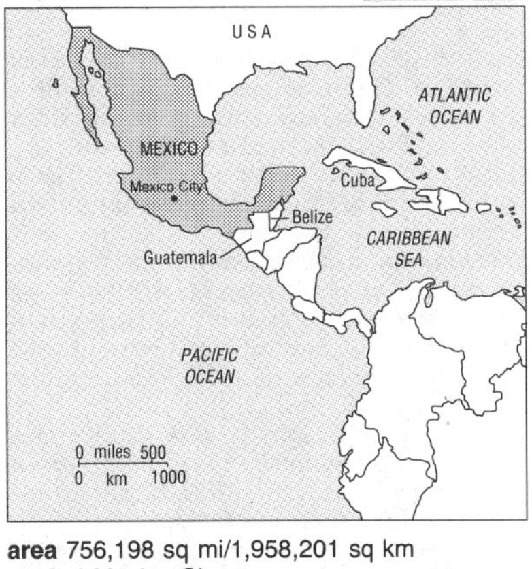

USA
ATLANTIC OCEAN
MEXICO
Mexico City
Cuba
Belize
CARIBBEAN SEA
Guatemala
PACIFIC OCEAN
0 miles 500
0 km 1000

area 756,198 sq mi/1,958,201 sq km
capital Mexico City
cities Guadalajara, Monterrey; port Veracruz
physical partly arid central highlands; Sierra Madre mountain ranges E and W; tropical coastal plains
features Rio Grande; 2,000 mi frontier with US; resorts Acapulco, Cancun, Mexicali, Tijuana; Baja California, Yucatan peninsula; volcanoes, including Popocatepetl; pre-Columbian archeological sites
head of state and government Carlos Salinas de Gortari from 1988
political system federal democratic republic
political parties Institutional Revolutionary Party (PRI), moderate, left-wing; National Action Party (PAN), moderate Christian Socialist
exports silver, gold, lead, uranium, oil, natural gas, handicrafts, fish, shellfish, fruits and vegetables, cotton, machinery
currency peso
population (1990 est) 88,335,000 (10% Spanish descent, 30% Indian, 60% mixed descent; 50% under 20 years of age); growth rate 2.6% p.a.
life expectancy men 67, women 73
language Spanish (official) 92%; Náhuatl, Maya, Mixtec
religion Roman Catholic 97%
literacy men 92%/women 88% (1989)
GNP $126 bn (1987); $2,082 per head
chronology
1821 Independence achieved from Spain.
1846–48 Mexico at war with US; loses territory.
1848 Maya Indian revolt suppressed.
1917 New constitution introduced, designed to establish permanent democracy.
1983–84 Financial crisis.
1985 Institutional Revolutionary Party (PRI) returned to power. Earthquake in Mexico City.
1986 IMF loan agreement signed to keep the country solvent until at least 1988.
1988 PRI candidate Carlos Salinas Gotari elected president, amid allegations of election fraud.
1989 Debt reduction accords negotiated with Bush administration.

during the Spanish conquest. The indigenous population was reduced from 21 million in 1519 to 1 million by 1607, with many deaths from Old World diseases to which they had no resistance.

In 1535 Mexico became the viceroyalty of New Spain. Spanish culture and Catholicism were established, and the country's natural resources were exploited. Colonial rule became increasingly oppressive; the struggle for independence began 1810, and Spanish rule was ended 1821. The ◊Mexican Empire followed 1822–23.

Mexico's early history as an independent nation was marked by civil and foreign wars and was dominated until 1855 by the dictator Antonio López de ◊Santa Anna. The US annexation of Texas 1835 brought about the ◊Mexican War 1846–48, in the course of which Mexico suffered further losses, including New Mexico and California. Santa Anna was overthrown 1855 by Benito Juárez, whose liberal reforms included many anti-clerical measures.

In 1861, enticed by the offer of 30% of the proceeds, France planned to intervene in the recovery of 79 million francs owed to a Swiss banker by former Mexican president Miramon, who was overthrown and exiled by Juárez 1860. Seeking to regain power, in 1862 Miramon appealed to Empress Eugénie, consort of Napoleon III, saying that steps must be taken against Juárez and his anti-Christian policies. Eugénie proposed ◊Maximilian, the brother of Emperor Franz-Josef of Austria. Napoleon agreed, since the plan suited his colonial ambitions, and in 1864 Maximilian accepted the crown offered him by conservative opponents of Juárez. Juárez and his supporters continued to fight against this new branch of the Hapsburg empire, and in 1867 the monarchy collapsed and Maximilian was executed.

There followed a capitalist dictatorship under General Porfirio Diaz, who gave the country stability but whose handling of the economy made him unpopular. He was overthrown 1910 by Madero, who reestablished a liberal regime but was himself assassinated 1913. The 1910 revolution brought changes in land ownership, labor legislations, and reduction in the powers of the Roman Catholic Church. After a brief period of civil war 1920, Mexico experienced gradual agricultural, political, and social reforms. In 1938 all foreign-owned oil wells were nationalized; compensation was not agreed until 1941. The years after Diaz were marked by political and military strife with the US, culminating in the unsuccesful US expedition 1916–17 to kill Pancho Villa, a revolutionary.

The broadly based PRI has dominated Mexican politics since the 1920s, pursuing moderate, left-of-center policies. Its popularity has been damaged in recent years by the country's poor economic performance and rising international debts. However, despite criticisms from vested-interest groups such as the labor unions and the church, the PRI scored a clear win in the 1985 elections. The government's problems grew worse later that year when an earthquake in Mexico City caused thousands of deaths and made hundreds of thousands homeless.

Mexico's foreign policy has been influenced by its proximity to the US. At times the Mexican government has criticized US policy in Central America, and as a member, with Colombia, Panama, and Venezuela, of the ◊Contadora Group, has argued for the withdrawal of all foreign advisers from the region. The PRI faced its strongest challenge to date in the 1988 elections. Despite claims of frauds during the elections, the PRI candidate, Carlos Salinas de Gortari, was declared president by the electoral college. He subsequently led campaigns against corrupt labor unions and drug traffickers. Opposition from both the left and the right continues to become better established. President Salinas also worked closely with the Bush administration to negotiate debt reductions.

Mexico City *The ornate Metropolitan Cathedral (1573), which stands at the center of Mexico City.*

Mexico City (Spanish *Ciudad de México*) capital, and industrial (iron, steel, chemicals, textiles) and cultural center of Mexico, 7,400 ft/2,255 m above sea level on the southern edge of the central plateau; population (1986) 18,748,000. It is thought to be the most polluted city in the world.

Notable buildings include the 16th-century cathedral, the national palace, national library, Palace of Justice, and national university; the Ministry of Education has murals 1923–27 by Diego Rivera.

The city dates from about 1325, when the Aztec capital Tenochtitlán was begun on an island in Lake Texcoco. This city was leveled 1521 by the Spaniards, who in 1522 founded a new city on the site. It was the location of the 1968 Summer Olympics. In 1984, the explosion of a liquefied gas tank caused the deaths of over 450 people, and in 1985, over 2,000 were killed by an earthquake.

Meyerbeer Giacomo. Adopted name of Jakob Liebmann Beer 1791–1864. German composer. He is renowned for his spectacular operas, including *Robert le Diable* 1831 and *Les Huguenots* 1836. From 1826 he lived mainly in Paris, returning to Berlin after 1842 as musical director of the Royal Opera.

mezuza in Judaism, a small box containing a parchment scroll inscribed with a prayer, the Shema from Deuteronomy 6:4–9; 11:13–21, which is found on the doorpost of every home and the doorway of every room in a Jewish house, except the bathroom.

mezzanine (Italian *mezzano* "middle") architectural term for a story with a lower ceiling placed between two main stories, usually between the ground and first floors of a building.

Mezzogiorno (Italian "midday") the hot, impoverished regions of S Italy.

mezzotint a print produced by a method of ◊etching in density of tone rather than line, popular in the 18th and 19th centuries. A copper or steel plate is worked with a tool that raises a burr (rough edge), which will hold ink. The burr is then scraped away to produce a range of lighter tones.

Mfecane in African history, a series of disturbances in the early 19th century among communities in what is today the eastern part of South Africa. They arose when chief ◊Shaka conquered the Nguni peoples between the Tugela and Pongola rivers, then created by conquest a centralized, militaristic Zulu kingdom from several communities, resulting in large-scale displacement of people.

mg abbreviation for milligram.

Mgr in the Roman Catholic Church, the abbreviation for Monsignor.

mi abbreviation for ◊mile.

MI abbreviation for ◊Michigan.

Miami city and port in Florida; population (1990) 358,548. It is the hub of finance, trade, and air transport for the US, Latin America, and the Caribbean. Industries include food processing and the manufacture of transportation and electronic equipment, clothing, and machinery. The first permanent non-Indian settlement dates from the 1870s. In 1896 a railroad was extended to Miami, and the city subsequently was promoted as a tourist resort, noted for its beaches. The Florida land boom of the 1920s led to rapid development. By the 1980s large amounts of illegal drugs were said to come to the US through Miami. Destructive riots by blacks in 1980 and 1982 followed charges of police misconduct.

There has been an influx of immigrants from Cuba, Haiti, Mexico, and South America since 1959. It is also a center for oceanographic research.

mica a group of silicate minerals that split easily into thin flakes along lines of weakness in their crystal structure (perfect basal cleavage). They are glossy, have a pearly luster, and are found in many igneous and metamorphic rocks. Their good thermal and electrical insulation qualities make them valuable in industry.

Their chemical composition is complicated, but they are silicates with silicon-oxygen tetrahedra arranged in continuous sheets, with weak bonding betwen the layers, resulting in perfect cleavage. A common example of mica is muscovite (white mica), $KAl_2Si_3Al_{10}(OH)_4$.

Micah 8th century BC. In the Old Testament, a Hebrew prophet whose writings denounced the oppressive ruling class of Judah and demanded justice.

Michael in the Old Testament, an archangel, referred to as the guardian angel of Israel. In the New Testament Book of Revelation he leads the hosts of heaven to battle against Satan. In paintings, he is depicted with a flaming sword and sometimes a pair of scales. Feast day Sept 29 (Michaelmas).

Michael 1921– . King of Romania 1927–30 and 1940–47. The son of Carol II, he succeeded his grandfather as king 1927 but was displaced when his father returned from exile 1930. In 1940 he was proclaimed king again on his father's abdication, overthrew 1944 the fascist dictatorship of Ion Antonescu (1882–1946), and enabled Romania to share in the victory of the Allies at the end of World War II. He abdicated and left Romania 1947.

Michael Mikhail Fyodorovich Romanov 1596–1645. Tsar of Russia from 1613. He was elected tsar by a national assembly, at a time of chaos and foreign invasion, and was the first of the Romanov dynasty, which ruled until 1917.

Michaelmas Day in Christian church tradition, the festival of St Michael and all angels, observed Sept 29.

Michelangelo Buonarroti 1475–1564. Italian sculptor, painter, architect, and poet, active in his native Florence and in Rome. His giant talent dominated the High Renaissance. The marble *David* 1501–04 (Accademia, Florence) set a new standard in nude sculpture. His massive figure style was translated into fresco in the Sistine Chapel 1508–12 and 1536–41 (Vatican). Other works in Rome include the dome of St Peter's basilica.

Born near Florence, he was a student of Ghirlandaio and trained under the patronage of Lorenzo de' Medici. His patrons later included several popes and Medici princes. In 1496 he completed the *Pietà* (St Peter's, Rome), a techni-

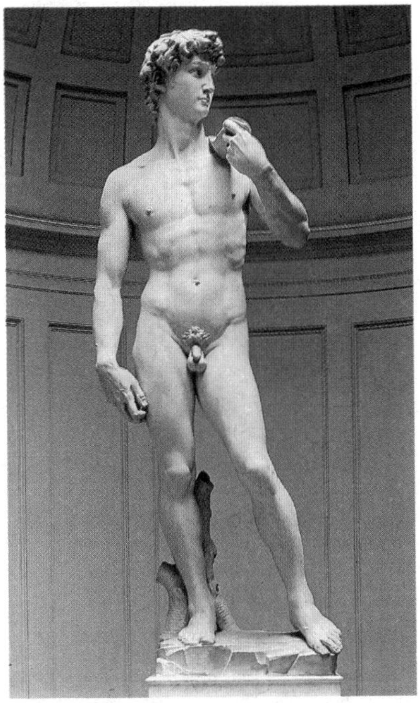

Michelangelo *The dominant talent of the High Renaissance, Michelangelo worked primarily in Rome and Florence, where his* David *1501 is in the Accademia.*

cally brilliant piece that established his reputation. Also in Rome he began the great tomb of Pope Julius II: *The Slaves* (Louvre, Paris) and *Moses* (S Pietro in Vincoli, Rome) were sculpted for this unfinished project. His grandiose scheme for the Sistine Chapel tells, on the ceiling, the Old Testament story from Genesis to the Deluge, and on the altar wall he later added a vast *Last Judgment*.

From 1516 to 1534 he was again in Florence, where his chief work was the design of the Medici sepulchral chapel in S Lorenzo. Back in Rome he became chief architect of St Peter's in 1547. His friendship with Vittoria Colonna (1492–1547), a noblewoman, inspired many of his sonnets and madrigals.

Michigan

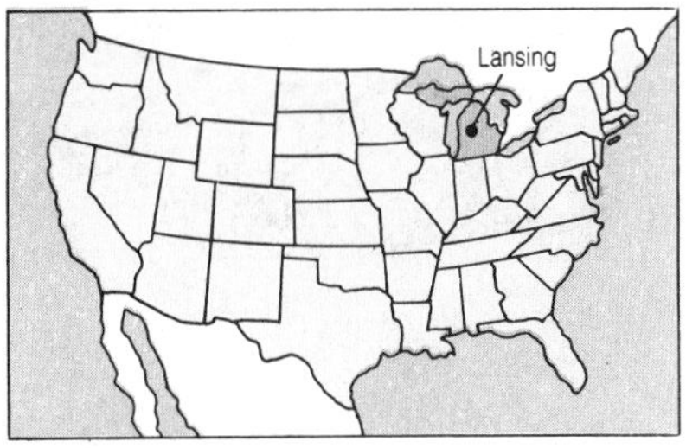
Lansing

Michels Robert 1876–1936. German social and political theorist. Originally a radical, he became a critic of socialism and Marxism, and in his last years supported Hitler and Mussolini. In *Political Parties* 1911 he propounded the Iron Law of Oligarchy, arguing that in any organization or society, even a democracy, there is a tendency toward rule by the few in the interests of the few, and that ideologies such as socialism and communism were merely propaganda to control the masses. He believed that the rise of totalitarian governments—both fascist and communist—in the 1930s confirmed his analysis and proved that the masses were incapable of asserting their own interests.

Michelson Albert Abraham 1852–1931. German-born US physicist. In conjunction with Edward Morley, he performed in 1887 the Michelson–Morley experiment to detect the motion of the Earth through the postulated ether (a medium believed to be necessary for the propagation of light). The failure of the experiment indicated the nonexistence of the ether, and led ◊Einstein to his theory of ◊relativity. Michelson was the first American to be awarded a Nobel Prize 1907.

He invented the Michelson interferometer and made precise measurement of the speed of light. From 1892 he was professor of physics at the University of Chicago.

Michigan state in N central US; nickname Wolverine State/Great Lake State
area 58,518 sq mi/151,600 sq km
capital Lansing
cities Detroit, Grand Rapids, Flint
population (1990) 9,295,297
features Great Lakes: Superior, Michigan, Huron, Erie; Isle Royale National Park; Pictured Rocks and Sleeping Bear national seashores; Detroit auto factories; Henry Ford Museum and Greenfield Village, Dearborn
products motor vehicles and equipment; nonelectrical machinery; iron and steel; chemicals; pharmaceuticals; dairy products
famous people Edna Ferber, Gerald Ford, Henry Ford, Jimmy Hoffa, Walter Reuther, Diana Ross
history temporary posts established in early 17th century by French explorers Brulé, Marquette, Joliet, and La Salle; first settled 1668 at Sault Sainte Marie; present-day Detroit settled 1701; passed to the British 1763 and to the US 1796; statehood 1837. Henry Ford's establishment of the moving assembly line in 1913–14 secured Detroit as the auto-production capital of the world. Since then the state's fortunes have been closely tied to the fortunes of the motor industry, prospering in the 1920s, 1940s, and 1950s, but badly hurt by the Great Depression of the 1930s and competition from Japanese manufacturers since the 1970s.

Michigan, Lake lake in north central USA, one of the Great Lakes; area 22,390 sq mi/58,000 sq km. Chicago and Milwaukee are its main ports.

Lake Michigan is joined to Lake Huron by the Straits of Mackinac. Green Bay is the major inlet.

Mickiewicz Adam 1798–1855. Polish revolutionary poet, whose *Pan Tadeusz* 1832–34 is Poland's national epic. He died at Constantinople while raising a Polish corps to fight against Russia in the Crimean War.

microbe another name for ◊microorganism.

microbiological warfare use of harmful microorganisms as a weapon. See ◊biological warfare.

microbiology the study of organisms that can only be seen under the microscope, mostly viruses and single-celled organisms such as bacteria, protozoa, and yeasts. The practical applications of microbiology are in medicine (since many microorganisms cause disease); in brewing, baking, and other food and beverage processes, where the microorganisms carry out fermentation; and in genetic engineering, which is creating increasing interest in the field of microbiology.

microchip popular name for the ◊silicon chip or ◊integrated circuit.

microclimate the particular climate found in a small area or locality.

microcomputer or ***micro*** small desktop or portable computer, typically designed to be used by one person at a time. Microcomputers are the smallest of the four classes of computer (the others are ◊supercomputer, ◊mainframe, and ◊minicomputer). Since the appearance in 1975 of the first commercially available microcomputer, the Altair 8800, micros have become widely accepted in commerce and industry.

microeconomics the division of economics concerned with the study of individual decision-making units within an economy: a consumer, firm, or industry. Unlike macroeconomics, it looks at how individual markets work and how individual producers and consumers make their choices and with what consequences. This is done by analyzing how relevant prices of goods are determined and the quantities that will be bought and sold.

For simplicity, microeconomics begins by analyzing a market in which there is perfect competition, a theoretical state that exists only when no individual producer or consumer can influence the market price. In the real world, there is always imperfect competition for various reasons (monopoly practices, barriers to trade, and so on), and microeconomics examines what effect these have on wages and prices.

Underlying these and other concerns of micro-

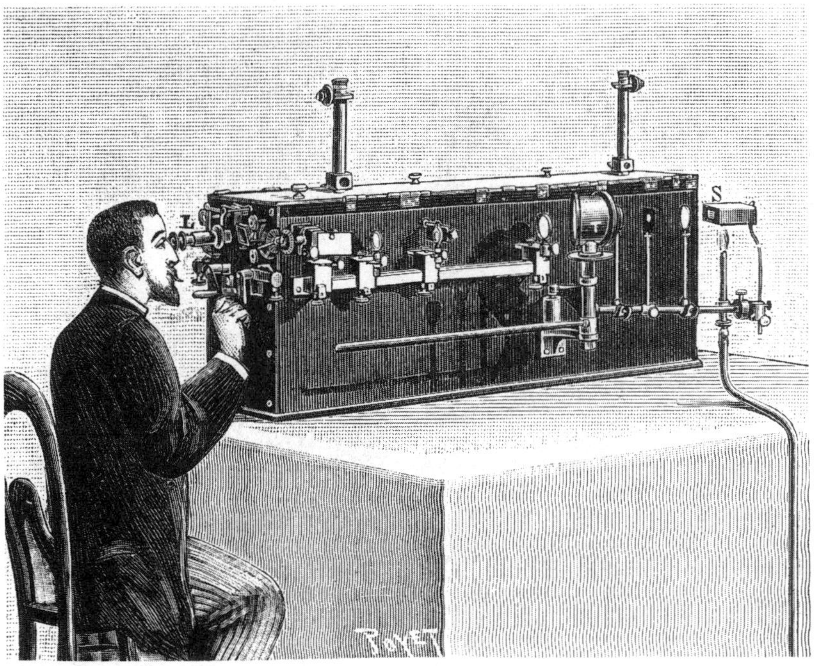
S
L

Michelson *Albert Abraham Michelson's interferometer, designed to detect a difference in the velocities of light in directions parallel to and perpendicular to the motion of the Earth.*

micrometer

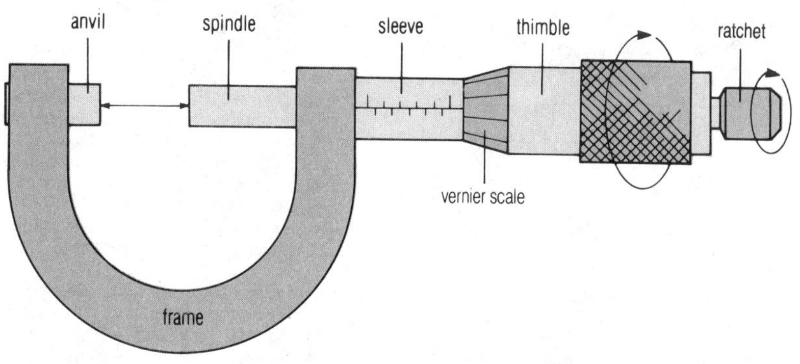
anvil
spindle
sleeve
thimble
ratchet
vernier scale
frame

economics is the concept of optimality, first advanced by Vilfredo ◊Pareto in the 19th century. Pareto's perception of the most efficient state of an economy, when there is no scope to reallocate resources without making someone worse off, has been of great influence.

microfiche sheet of film on which printed text is photographically reduced. See ◊microform.

microform generic name for media on which text or images are photographically reduced. The main examples are microfilm (similar to the film in an ordinary camera) and microfiche (flat sheets of film, generally 105 mm/4 in × 6 in/148 mm, holding the equivalent of 420 A4 sheets). Microform has the advantages of low reproduction and storage costs, but it requires special devices for reading the text. It is widely used for archiving and for storing large volumes of text, such as library catalogs.

micrometer instrument for measuring minute lengths or angles with great accuracy; different types of micrometer are used in astronomical and engineering work.

The type of micrometer used in astronomy consists of two fine wires, one fixed and the other movable, placed in the focal plane of a telescope; the movable wire is fixed on a sliding plate and can be positioned parallel to the other until the object appears between the wires. The movement is then indicated by a scale on the adjusting screw.

The micrometer caliper, of great value in engineering, has its adjustment effected by an extremely accurate fine-pitch screw (◊vernier).

micrometer or ***micron*** one-millionth of a meter.

microminiaturization the reduction in size and weight of electronic components. The first size reduction in electronics was brought about by the introduction of the ◊transistor. Further reductions were achieved with ◊integrated circuits and the ◊silicon chip.

Micronesia islands in the Pacific Ocean lying N of ◊Melanesia, including the Federated States of Micronesia, Belau, Kiribati, the Mariana and Marshall Islands, Nauru, and Tuvalu.

Micronesia, Federated States of

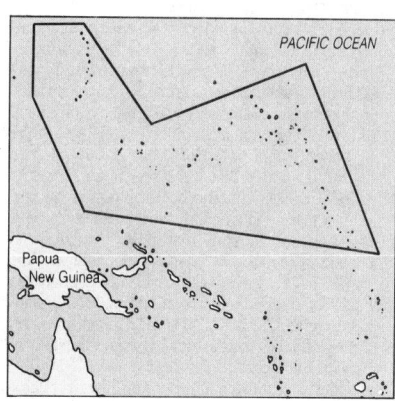

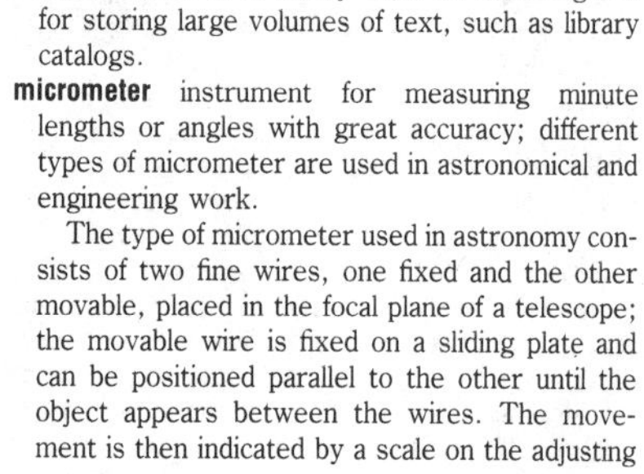
PACIFIC OCEAN
Papua
New Guinea

Micronesia, Federated States of self-governing island group (Kosrae, Ponape, Truk, and Yap) in the W Pacific; capital Kolonia, on Ponape; area 270 sq mi/700 sq km; population (1988) 86,000. It is part of the US Trust Territory. Purchased by Germany from Spain 1898, they were occupied 1914 by Japan. They were captured by the US in World War II, and became part of the US Trust Territory of the Pacific 1947. Micronesia became internally self-governing from 1979, and in free association with the US from 1986 (there is US control of military activities in return for economic aid). The people are Micronesian and Polynesian, and the main languages are Kosrean, Ponapean, Trukese, and Yapese, although the official language is English.

Micronesian member of any of the indigenous Australoid and Polynesian peoples of Micronesia, including Pacific islands N of the equator, such as the Caroline, Marshall, Mariana, and Gilbert islands. Their languages belong to the Austronesian family.

microorganism or ***microbe*** a living organism invisible to the naked eye but visible under a microscope. Microorganisms include viruses and single-celled organisms such as bacteria, protozoa, yeasts, and some algae. The term has no taxonomic significance in biology. The study of microorganisms is known as microbiology.

microphone the primary component in a sound-reproducing system, whereby the mechanical energy of sound waves is converted into electrical signals by means of a ◊transducer. One of the simplest is the telephone receiver mouthpiece, invented by Alexander Graham Bell in 1876; other types of microphone are used with broadcasting and sound-film apparatus.

Telephones have a carbon microphone, which reproduces only a narrow range of frequencies. For live music, a moving-coil microphone is often used. In it, a diaphragm that vibrates with sound waves moves a coil through a magnetic field, thus generating an electric current. The ribbon microphone combines the diaphragm and coil. The condenser microphone is most common in recording and works by a ◊capacitor.

microprocessor a computer's ◊central processing unit (CPU) contained on a single ◊integrated circuit. The appearance of the first microprocessors in 1971 heralded the introduction of the microcomputer. The microprocessor has led to a dramatic fall in the size and cost of computers and to the introduction of ◊dedicated computers in washing machines, automobiles, and so on.

micropyle in flowering plants, a small hole toward one end of the ovule. At pollination the pollen tube growing down from the ◊stigma eventually passes through this pore. The male gamete is contained within the tube and is able to travel to the egg in the interior of the ovule. Fertilization can then take place, with subsequent seed formation and dispersal.

microscope

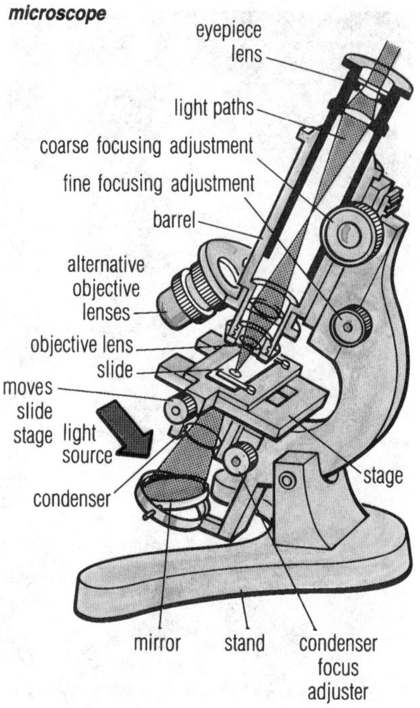
eyepiece
lens
light paths
coarse focusing adjustment
fine focusing adjustment
barrel
alternative
objective
lenses
objective lens
slide
moves
slide
stage
light
source
condenser
stage
mirror
stand
condenser
focus
adjuster

microscope instrument for magnification with high resolution for detail. Optical and electron microscopes are the ones chiefly in use; other types include acoustic and X-ray. In 1988 a scanning tunneling microscope was used to photograph a single protein molecule for the first time. Laser microscopy is under development.

The optical microscope usually has two sets of glass lenses and an eyepiece. It was invented 1609 in the Netherlands by Zacharias Janssen (1580–c. 1638).

The electron microscope, developed from 1932, passes a beam of electrons, instead of a beam of light, through a specimen and, since electrons are not visible, the eyepiece is replaced with a fluorescent screen or photographic plate; far higher magnification and resolution is possible than with the optical microscope.

The scanning electron microscope (SEM), developed in the mid-1960s, moves a fine beam of electrons over the surface of a specimen, the reflected electrons being collected to form the image. The specimen has to be in a vacuum chamber.

The acoustic microscope passes an acoustic (ultrahigh-frequency sound) wave through the specimen, the transmitted sound being used to form an image on a computer screen.

The scanned-probe microscope, developed in the late 1980s, runs a probe, with a tip so fine that it may consist only of a single atom, across the surface of the specimen, which requires no special preparation. In the scanning tunneling

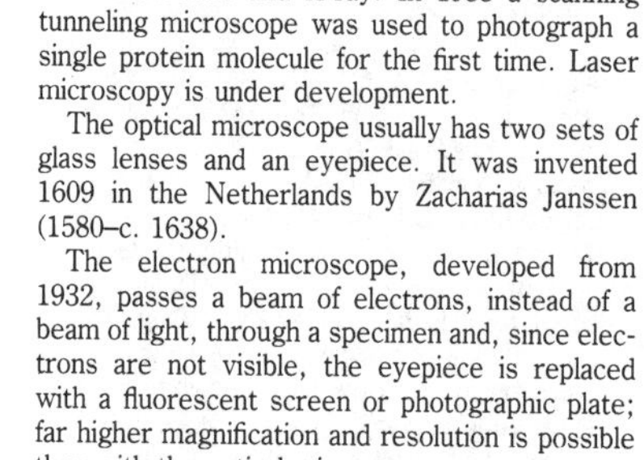

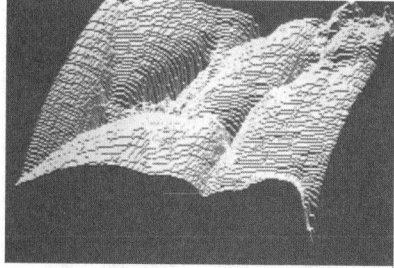

***microscope** Scanning tunneling microscope (STM) image, magnified about 250,000 times, of a high purity gold surface. Scanning tunneling microscopy is based on quantum mechanical effects and can reveal individual atoms.*

Mid-Atlantic Ridge

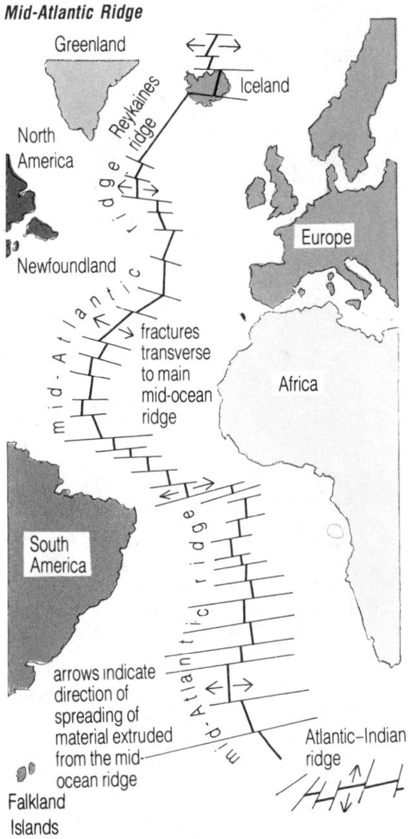
Greenland
Reykjanes ridge
Iceland
North America
Europe
Newfoundland
mid-Atlantic ridge
fractures transverse to main mid-ocean ridge
Africa
South America
arrows indicate direction of spreading of material extruded from the mid-ocean ridge
Atlantic–Indian ridge
Falkland Islands

microscope, an electric current that flows through the probe is used to construct an image of the specimen. In the atomic force microscope, the force felt by the probe is measured and used to form the image. These instruments can magnify a million times and give images of single atoms.

microsurgery surgical operation for which the surgeon uses a binocular microscope, magnifying 25 times, for example in rejoining a severed limb. Sewing of the nerves and blood vessels is done with a nylon thread so fine that it is only just visible to the naked eye. Restoration of movement and sensation may be comparatively limited.

microtubules tiny tubes found in almost all cells with a nucleus. They help to define the shape of a cell by forming scaffolding for cilia and form fibers of mitotic spindle.

microwave ◊electromagnetic radiation with a wavelength in the range 0.1 in to 12 in/0.3 to 30 cm, or 300–300,000 megahertz (between radio waves and ◊infrared radiation). They are used in radar, as carrier waves in radio broadcasting, and in microwave heating and cooking.

microwave heating heating by means of microwaves. Microwave ovens use this form of heating for the rapid cooking or reheating of foods, where heat is generated throughout the food simultaneously. If food is not heated completely, there is a danger of bacterial growth that may lead to food poisoning. Industrially, microwave heating is used for destroying insects in grain and enzymes in processed food, pasteurizing and sterilizing liquids, and drying timber and paper.

Midas in Greek legend, a king of Phrygia who was granted the gift of converting all he touched to gold, and who, for preferring the music of Pan to that of Apollo, was given ass's ears by the latter.

MIDAS acronym for Missile Defense Alarm System.

Mid-Atlantic Ridge the ◊ocean ridge, formed by the movement of plates described by ◊plate tectonics, that runs along the center of the Atlantic Ocean, parallel to its edges, for some 8,800 mi/14,000 km—almost from the Arctic to the Antarctic.

The Mid-Atlantic Ridge is central because the ocean crust beneath the Atlantic Ocean has continually grown outward from the ridge at a steady rate during the past 200 million years. Iceland straddles the ridge and was formed by volcanic outporings.

Middelburg industrial town (engineering, tobacco, furniture) in SW Netherlands, capital of Zeeland and former ◊Hanseatic town; population (1985) 38,930. The town hall dates from the 15th century.

Middle Ages the period of European history between the fall of the Roman Empire in the 5th century and the Renaissance in the 15th. Among the period's distinctive features were the unity of W Europe within the Roman Catholic church, the feudal organization of political, social, and economic relations, and the use of art for largely religious purposes.

It can be divided into three subperiods:

The early Middle Ages, 5th–11th centuries, when Europe was settled by pagan Germanic tribes who adopted the vestiges of Roman institutions and traditions, were converted to Christianity by the church (which had preserved Latin culture after the fall of Rome), and who then founded feudal kingdoms; the high Middle Ages, 12th–13th centuries, which saw the consolidation of feudal states, the expansion of European influence during the ◊Crusades, the flowering of ◊scholasticism and monasteries, and the growth of population and trade; the later Middle Ages, 14th–15th centuries, when Europe was devastated by the ◊Black Death and incessant warfare, ◊feudalism was transformed under the influence of incipient nation-states and new modes of social and economic organization, and the first voyages of discovery were made.

middle C the white note at the center of the piano keyboard, indicating the division between left and right-hand regions and corresponding to the treble and bass staves of printed music.

Middle East indeterminate area now usually taken to include the Balkan States, Egypt, and SW Asia. Until the 1940s, this area was generally called the Near East, and the term Middle East referred to the area from Iran to Burma (now Myanmar).

Middle English the period of the ◊English language from about 1050 to 1550.

Middle Kingdom a period of Egyptian history extending from the late 11th to the 13th dynasty (roughly 2040–1670 BC). Also, a Chinese term for China and its empire until 1912, describing its central position in the Far East.

Middlemarch: A Study of Provincial Life a novel by George Eliot, published in England 1871–72. Set in the fictitious provincial town of Middlemarch, the novel has several interwoven plots played out against a background of social and political upheaval.

Middle Range or ***Middleback range*** mountain range in the NE of Eyre Peninsula, South Australia, about 40 mi/65 km long, parallel with the W coast of Spencer Gulf. Iron deposits are mined at Iron Baron, Iron Knob, and Iron Monarch.

Middlesbrough industrial port city on the Tees, Cleveland, England, commercial and cultural center of the urban area formed by Stockton-on-Tees, Redcar, Billingham, Thornaby, and Eston; population (1983) 148,400. Formerly a center of heavy industry, it diversified its products in the 1960s. It is the birthplace of the navigator Captain James Cook (1728–79).

Middlesex former English county, absorbed by Greater London in 1965. Contained within the Thames basin, it provided good agricultural land before it was built over. It was settled in the 6th century by Saxons, and its name comes from its position between the kingdoms of the East and West Saxons.

Middleton Thomas c. 1570–1627. English dramatist. He produced numerous romantic plays, tragedies, and realistic comedies, both alone and in collaboration, including *A Fair Quarrel* and *The Changeling* 1622 with Rowley; *The Roaring Girl* with Dekker; and *Women Beware Women* 1621.

Middletown city in S central Connecticut, on the Connecticut River, S of Hartford. Industries include insurance, banking, automobile parts, electronics, hardware, and paper products. Wesleyan University is here; population (1990) 42,762.

Middletown city in SW Ohio, on the Miami River, N of Cincinnati. Industries include steel, paper products, and aircraft parts; population (1990) 46,022.

Middle Way the path to enlightenment, taught by Buddha, which avoids the extremes of indulgence and asceticism.

midge common name for many insects resembling ◊gnats, generally divided into biting midges (family Ceratopogonidae) that suck blood, and nonbiting midges (family Chironomidae).

The larvae of some midges are the "bloodworms" of stagnant water.

Mid Glamorgan county in S Wales

area 394 sq mi/1,020 sq km

cities administrative headquarters Cardiff; resort Porthcawl; Aberdare, Merthyr Tydfil, Bridgend, Pontypridd

features Caerphilly Castle, with its water defenses

products the north was formerly a leading coal (Rhondda) and iron and steel area; Royal Mint at Llantrisant; agriculture in the south; Caerphilly mild cheese

population (1987) 535,000

language 8% Welsh, English.

MIDI abbreviation for Musical Instrument Digital Interface, a manufacturer's standard allowing different pieces of digital music equipment used in composing and recording to be freely connected.

The information-sending device (any electronic instrument) is called a controller, and the reading device (such as a computer) the sequencer. Pitch, dynamics, decay rate, and stereo "position" may all be transmitted via the interface.

Midi-Pyrénées region of SW France, comprising the *départements* of Ariège, Aveyron, Haute-Garonne, Gers, Lot, Haute-Pyrénées, Tarn, and Tarn-et-Garonne

area 17,486 sq mi/45,300 sq km

population (1986) 2,355,000

cities capital Toulouse; Montauban, Cahors, Rodez, and Lourdes

products fruit, wine, livestock

features several spa towns, winter resorts, and prehistoric caves

history occupied by the Basques since prehistoric times, this region once formed part of the prehistoric province of Gascony that was taken by the English 1154, recaptured by the French 1453, inherited by Henry of Navarre, and reunited with France 1607.

Midland city in central Michigan, on the Tittabawassee River, NW of Saginaw. Industries include chemicals and concrete; oil and gas wells are here; population (1990) 38,053.

Midland city in W Texas, halfway betwen Fort Worth and El Paso. The city's economy depends on the oil companies located here after the discovery of oil 1923; population (1990) 89,443.

Midlands area of England corresponding roughly to the Anglo-Saxon kingdom of ◊Mercia. East Midlands Derbyshire, Leicestershire, Northamptonshire, Nottinghamshire. West Midlands the former metropolitan county created from parts of Staffordshire, Warwickshire, and Worcestershire; and (often included) South Midlands Bedfordshire, Buckinghamshire, and Oxfordshire.

In World War II, the E Midlands was worked for oil, and substantial finds were made in the 1980s; the oilbearing E Midlands Shelf extends into Yorkshire and Lincolnshire.

Midlothian former Scottish county S of the Firth of

Forth, included 1975 in the region of Lothian; Edinburgh was the administrative headquarters.

midnight sun the constant appearance of the Sun (within the Arctic and Antarctic circles) above the ◊horizon during the summer.

Midrash (Hebrew "inquiry") the medieval Hebrew commentaries on the Bible, in the form of sermons, in which allegory and legendary illustration are used. They were compiled mainly in Palestine between AD 400 and 1200.

midshipman a trainee naval officer.

In the US, a midshipman is a student in training for the rank of ensign, in particular one at the US Naval Academy at Annapolis. In the British navy, a midshipman is a junior naval officer ranking just below sublieutenant.

midsummer the time of the summer ◊solstice, about June 21. Midsummer Day, June 24, is the Christian festival of St John the Baptist.

Midsummer Night's Dream, A a comedy by William Shakespeare, first performed 1595–96. Hermia, Lysander, Demetrius, and Helena in their various romantic endeavors are subjected to the playful manipulations of the fairies Puck and Oberon in a wood near Athens. Titania, queen of the fairies, is similarly bewitched and falls in love with Bottom, a stupid weaver, whose head has been replaced with that of an ass.

Midway Islands two islands in the Pacific, 1,120 mi/1,800 km NW of Honolulu; area 2 sq mi/5 sq km; population about 500. They were annexed by the US 1867, and are now administered by the US Navy. The naval Battle of Midway June 3–6, 1942, between the US and Japan, was the turning point in the Pacific in World War II.

Midwest or ***Middle West*** a large area of the N central US. It is loosely defined, but is generally taken to comprise the states of Illinois, Iowa, Wisconsin, Minnesota, Nebraska, Kansas, Missouri, North Dakota, and South Dakota and the portions of Montana, Wyoming, and Colorado that lie E of the Rocky Mountains. Ohio, Michigan, and Indiana are often variously included, as well. The main urban Midwest center is Chicago. The majority of Midwesterners tend to be conservative socially and politically and less interested in international affairs than the general public in other parts of the country, but liberal and Socialistic ideals have a long tradition in the states that championed the Populist and Granger movements of the 19th century. The region is generally flat and well-watered, with good transportation links. Traditionally its economy is divided between agriculture and heavy industry. In its broadest sense, the Midwest has an area of 986,800 sq mi/2,556,000 sq km and a population of about 61.5 million—roughly one-fourth of the national total.

midwifery the assistance of women in childbirth. Traditionally, it was undertaken by experienced specialists; in modern medical training it is a nursing speciality for practitioners called midwives.

Mies van der Rohe Ludwig 1886–1969. German architect who practiced in the US from 1937. He succeeded ◊Gropius as director of the ◊Bauhaus 1929–33. He became professor at the Illinois Technical Institute 1938–58, for which he designed new buildings on characteristically functional lines from 1941. He also designed the bronze-and-glass Seagram building in New York City 1956–59 and numerous apartment buildings. He designed the National Gallery, Berlin 1963–68.

Mifune Toshiro 1920– . Japanese actor who appeared in many films directed by Akira ◊Kurosawa, including *Rashomon* 1950, *Seven Samurai* 1954, and *Throne of Blood* 1957. He has also appeared in European and American films.

mignonette sweet-scented plant *Reseda odorata*, native to N Africa, bearing yellowish-green flowers in racemes (along the main stem), with abundant foliage; it is widely cultivated.

migraine acute, sometimes incapacitating headache (generally only on one side), accompanied by nausea, that recurs, often with advance symptoms such as flashing lights. No cure has been discovered, but ◊ergotamine normally relieves the symptoms. Some sufferers learn to avoid certain foods, such as chocolate, which suggests an allergic factor.

In 1990 Hammersmith Hospital in London, England, reported successful treatment with goggles that turn down beta waves in the brain (associated with stress) and stimulate alpha waves (whose effect is calming).

migrant labor people who move from place to place to work or harvest seasonal crops. Economic or political pressures often cause people to leave their homelands to earn wages in this way, but some families live this way for several generations. Since the Great Depression of the 1930s, many families lost land and homes and took to the road. Since the 1960s, unions for migrant farm workers have been formed, principally by Cesar ◊Chavez.

The world's pool of legal and illegal immigrants has been exploited by business and has become an important economic and social factor. Migrants from the Caribbean and Central and South America enter this job market in the US and Canada just as South Europeans and Middle Easterners provide such labor in industrialized northern European countries. Some go home after each seasonal round, while others try to stay and become citizens if possible.

migration the movement, either seasonal or as part of a single life cycle, of certain animals, chiefly birds and fish, to distant breeding or feeding grounds.

The precise methods by which animals navigate and know where to go are still obscure. Birds have much sharper eyesight and better visual memory of ground clues than humans, but in long-distance flights appear to navigate by the Sun and stars, possibly in combination with a "reading" of the Earth's magnetic field through an inbuilt "magnetic compass," which is a tiny mass of tissue between the eye and brain in birds. Similar cells occur in "homing" honeybees and in certain bacteria that use it to determine which way is "down." Most striking, however, is the migration of young birds that have never flown a route before and are unaccompanied by adults. It is postulated that they may inherit as part of their genetic code an overall "sky chart" of their journey that is triggered into use when they become aware of how the local sky pattern above the place in which they hatch fits into it. Similar theories have been advanced in the case of fish, such as eels and salmon, with whom vision obviously plays a lesser role, but for whom currents and changes in the composition and temperature of the sea in particular locations may play a part—for example in enabling salmon to return to the precise river in which they were spawned.

migration

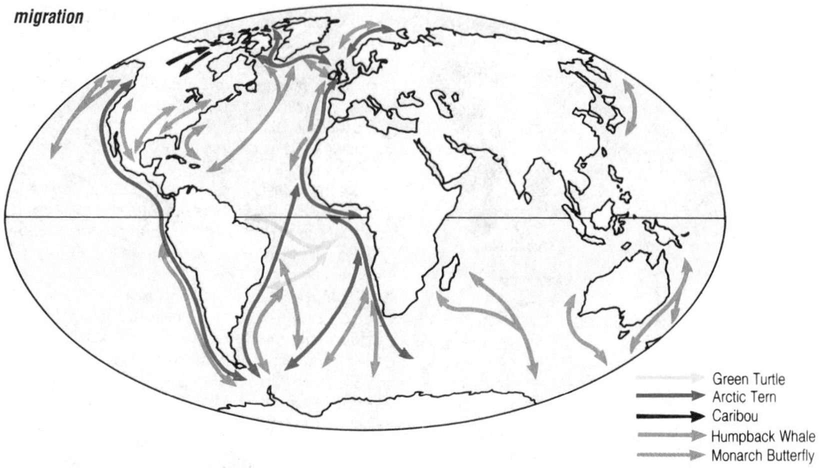
Green Turtle
Arctic Tern
Caribou
Humpback Whale
Monarch Butterfly

Migration also occurs with land animals— for example, lemmings and antelope.

Related to migration is the homing ability of pigeons, bees, and other creatures.

Mihailovič Draza 1893–1946. Yugoslav soldier, leader of the guerrilla ◊Chetniks of World War II against the German occupation. His feud with Tito's communists led to the withdrawal of Allied support and that of his own exiled government from 1943. He turned for help to the Italians and Germans, and was eventually shot for treason.

mikado (Japanese "honorable palace gate") title until 1867 of the Japanese emperor, when it was replaced by the term *tennō* (heavenly sovereign).

Milan (Italian *Milano*) industrial city (aircraft, automobiles, locomotives, textiles), financial and cultural center, capital of Lombardy, Italy; population (1988) 1,479,000

features The Gothic cathedral, built about 1450, crowned with pinnacles, can hold 40,000 worshippers; the Brera art gallery; the convent with Leonardo da Vinci's *Last Supper* 1495–97; La Scala opera house (Italian *Teatro alla Scala*) 1778; an annual trade fair

history Settled by the Gauls in the 5th century BC, it was conquered by the Roman consul Marcellus 222 BC to become the Roman city of *Mediolanum*. Under Diocletian, in AD 286 Milan was capital of the Western empire. Destroyed by Attila the Hun 452, and again by the Goths 539, the city regained its power through the political importance of its bishops. It became an autonomous commune 1045; then followed a long struggle for supremacy in Lombardy.

The city was taken by ◊Frederick I (Barbarossa) 1162; only in 1176 were his forces finally defeated, at the battle of Legnano. Milanese forces were again defeated by the emperor at the battle of Cortenuova 1237. In the Guelph-Ghibelline struggle the Visconti family emerged at the head of the Ghibelline faction; they gained power 1277, establishing a dynasty which lasted until 1450 when Francesco Sforza seized control

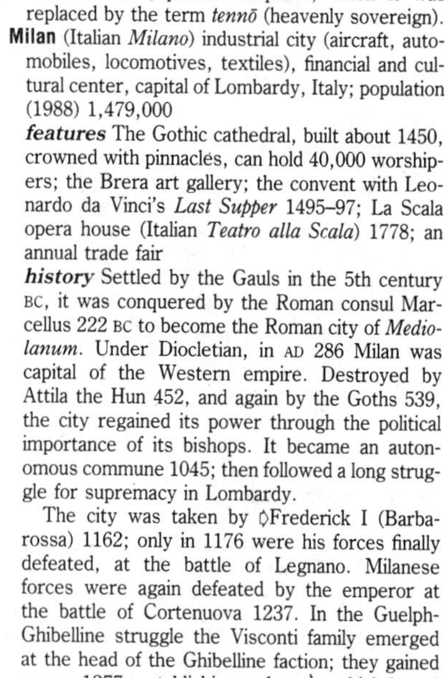

Milan *The Gothic cathedral, built about 1450, can hold up to 40,000 worshippers.*

and became duke. The Sforza court marked the highpoint of Milan as a cultural and artistic center. Control of the city passed to Louis XII of France 1499, and in 1540 it was annexed by Spain, beginning a long decline. The city was ceded to Austria by the Treaty of ◊Utrecht 1714, and in the 18th century began a period of intellectual enlightenment. Milan was in 1796 taken by Napoleon, who made it the capital of the Cisalpine Republic 1799, and in 1805 capital of the kingdom of Italy until 1814, when it reverted to the Austrians. In 1848, Milan rebelled unsuccessfully (the *Cinque Giornate/Five Days*), and in 1859 was joined to Piedmont.

Milankovitch hypothesis the combination of factors governing the occurrence of ◊ice ages proposed in 1930 by the Yugoslavian geophysicist Milankovitch (1879–1958).

mildew any fungus that appears as a destructive growth on plants, paper, leather, or wood when exposed to damp; such fungi usually form a thin white coating.

Mildura town in NW Victoria, Australia, on the Murray River, with food-processing industries; population (1985) 16,500.

mile imperial unit of linear measure. A statute mile is equal to 1,760 yards (1.60934 km), and an international nautical mile is equal to 2,026 yards (1,852 m).

Mile End area of the East End of London, in the district of Stepney, now part of the London borough of Tower Hamlets. Mile End Green (now Stepney Green) was the scene of Richard II's meeting with the rebel peasants 1381, and in later centuries was the exercise ground of the London "trained bands," or ◊militia.

Miletus ancient Greek city in SW Asia Minor, with a port that eventually silted up. It carried on an important trade with Egypt and the Black Sea.

milfoil another name for the herb ◊yarrow. Water milfoils, plants of the genus *Miriophyllum*, are unrelated; they have whorls of fine leaves and grow underwater.

Milford city in SW Connecticut, situated by the Housatonic River and Long Island Sound, W of New Haven. Industries include fabricated metal, writing pens, and electronics; population (1990) 49,938.

Milford Haven (Welsh *Aberdaugleddau*) seaport in Dyfed, SW Wales, on the estuary of the E and W Cleddau rivers; population (1985) 14,000. It has oil refineries, and a terminal for giant tankers linked by pipeline with Llandarcy, near Swansea.

Milhaud Darius 1892–1974. French composer, a member of the group of composers known as ◊*Les Six*. Among his works are the operas *Christophe Colombe* 1928 and *Bolívar* 1943, and the jazz ballet *La Création du monde* 1923. He lived in both France and the US.

He collaborated on ballets with Paul ◊Claudel. In 1940 he went to the US as professor of music at Mills College, California, and became professor of composition at the National Conservatoire in Paris 1947. Much of his later work—which includes chamber, orchestral, and choral music—is polytonal.

miliaria itchy blisters formed in the skin condition ◊prickly heat.

military-industrial complex the conjunction of the military establishment and the arms industry, both inflated by Cold War demands. The phrase was first used by US president and former general Dwight D Eisenhower in 1961 to warn Americans of the potential misplacement of power.

military law articles or regulations that apply to members of the armed forces.

militia a body of civilian soldiers, usually with some military training, who are on call in emergencies, distinct from professional soldiers. In Switzerland, the militia is the national defense force, and every able-bodied man is liable for service in it. In the UK the ◊Territorial Army and in the US the ◊National Guard have supplanted earlier voluntary militias.

After the Restoration, the militia fell into neglect, but it was reorganized in 1757, and was relied upon for home defense during the French wars. In the 19th century it extended its activities, serving in the Peninsular, Crimean, and South African wars. In 1852 it adopted a volunteer status, and in 1908 it was merged with the Territorial Army and the Special Reserve forces, to supplement the regular army, and ceased to exist as a separate force.

milk the secretion of the ◊mammary glands of female mammals, with which they suckle their young (during ◊lactation). Over 85% is water, the remainder comprising protein, fat, lactose (a sugar), calcium, phosphorus, iron, and vitamins. The milk of cows, goats, and sheep is often consumed by humans, but only Western societies drink milk after infancy; for people in most of the world, milk causes flatulence and diarrhea. Milk composition varies among species, depending on the nutritional requirements of the young; human milk contains less protein and more lactose than that of cows.

milking machine machine that uses suction to milk cows. The first milking machine was invented in the US by L O Colvjn in 1860. Later it was improved so that the suction was regularly released by a pulsating device, since it was found that continuous suction is harmful to cows.

milk teeth a child's first set of teeth. The complete group of 20 milk teeth are present after two or three years and begin to be replaced by the second permanent set after the age of six. A normal adult dentition consists of 32 teeth, the extra teeth being molars and wisdom teeth.

Milky Way the faint band of light crossing the night sky, consisting of stars in the plane of our Galaxy. The name Milky Way is often used for the Galaxy itself. It is a spiral ◊galaxy, about 100,000 light-years in diameter, containing at least 100 billion stars. The Sun is in one of its spiral arms, about 25,000 light-years from the center.

The Milky Way is a member of a small cluster, the ◊Local Group. The densest parts, toward the center, lie in the constellation Sagittarius. In places, the Milky Way is interrupted by lanes of dark dust that obscure light from the stars beyond, such as the Coalsack nebula in Crux (the Southern Cross).

Mill James 1773–1836. Scottish philosopher and political thinker who developed the theory of ◊Utilitarianism. He is remembered for his political articles, and for the rigorous education he gave his son John Stuart Mill.

Born near Montrose, Mill moved to London 1802. Associated for most of his working life with

***Mill** Educated by his father, John Stuart Mill was reading Plato and Demosthenes with ease at the age of ten. His* Autobiography *gives a painful account of the teaching methods that turned him against Utilitarianism.*

the East India Company, he wrote a vast *History of British India* 1817–18. He was one of the founders of University College, London, together with his friend and fellow utilitarian Jeremy Bentham.

Mill John Stuart 1806–1873. English philosopher and economist who wrote *On Liberty* 1859, the classic philosophical defense of liberalism, and *Utilitarianism* 1863, a version of the "greatest happiness for the greatest number" principle in ethics. His progressive views inspired *On the Subjection of Women* 1869. In his social philosophy, he gradually abandoned the Utilitarians' extreme individualism for an outlook akin to liberal socialism, while still laying great emphasis on the liberty of the individual; this change can be traced in the later editions of *Principles of Political Economy* 1848.

He was born in London, the son of James Mill. In 1822 he entered the East India Company, where he remained until retiring in 1858. In 1826, as described in his *Autobiography* 1873, he passed through a mental crisis; he found his father's bleakly intellectual Utilitarianism emotionally unsatisfying and abandoned it for a more human

***Millais** British artist John Millais painted* Christ in the House of His Parents *in 1850, while a member of the Pre-Raphaelite Brotherhood.*

***Miller** US playwright Arthur Miller's works include the classic* Death of a Salesman *1949.*

philosophy influenced by Coleridge. In *Utilitarianism*, he states that actions are right if they bring about happiness and wrong if they bring about the reverse of happiness. *On Liberty* moved away from the utilitarian notion that individual liberty was necessary for economic and governmental efficiency and advanced the Classical defense of individual freedom as a value in itself and the mark of a mature society. He sat in Parliament as a Radical 1865–68 and introduced a motion for women's suffrage. His philosophical and political writings include *A System of Logic* 1843 and *Considerations on Representative Government* 1861.

Millais John Everett 1829–1896. British painter, a founding member of the ◊Pre-Raphaelite Brotherhood (PRB) in 1848. By the late 1850s he had dropped out of the PRB and his style had become more fluent and less detailed.

One of his PRB works, *Christ in the House of His Parents* 1850 (Tate Gallery, London), caused an outcry on its first showing, since its realistic detail was considered unfitting to the sacred subject.

Millay Edna St Vincent 1892–1950. US poet who wrote romantic, emotional verse, including *Renascence and Other Poems* 1917 and *The Harp-Weaver and Other Poems* 1923 (Pulitzer prize 1924). She was a favorite of the free-spirited youth of the 1920s.

Born in Rockland, Maine, she moved to New York City's Greenwich Village and became a voice for political and social causes through such works as *A Few Figs from Thistles* 1920 and *Second April* 1921. Her other works include the sonnet sequence *Fatal Interview* 1931, *Make Bright the Arrows*, and several verse plays.

millennium a period of 1,000 years. Some Christian sects, such as Jehovah's Witnesses, believe that Jesus will return to govern the Earth in person at the next millennium, the 6001st year after the creation (as located by Archbishop Usher at 4004 BC).

This belief, millenarianism, also called chiliasm (from the Greek for 1,000), was widespread in the early days of Christianity. As hopes were disappointed, belief in the imminence of the second coming tended to fade, but millenarian views have been expressed at periods of great religious excitement, such as the Reformation.

Miller Arthur 1915– . US playwright. His plays deal with family relationships and contemporary American values, and include *Death of a Salesman* 1949 and *The Crucible* 1953, based on the Salem witch trials and reflecting the communist witch-hunts of Senator Joe ◊McCarthy. He was married 1956–61 to the film star Marilyn Monroe, for whom he wrote the film *The Misfits* 1960.

Among other plays are *All My Sons* 1947, *A View from the Bridge* 1955, and *After the Fall* 1964, based on his relationship with Monroe. He also wrote the television film *Playing for Time* 1980.

Miller Glenn 1904–1944. US trombonist and, as bandleader, exponent of the big-band swing sound from 1938. He composed his signature tune "Moonlight Serenade" (a hit 1939). Miller became leader of the US Army Air Force Band in Europe 1942, made broadcasts to troops throughout the world during the war, and disappeared without trace on a flight between England and France during World War II.

millet

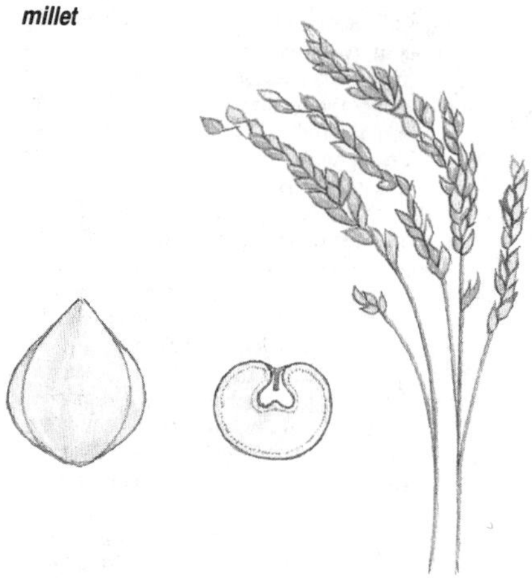

Miller Henry 1891–1980. US writer. From 1930 to 1940 he lived a bohemian life in Paris, where he wrote his novels *Tropic of Cancer* 1934 and *Tropic of Capricorn* 1938. They were so outspoken and sexually frank that they were banned in the US and England until the 1960s.

Born in New York City, Miller settled in Big Sur, California, in the 1940s and wrote the autobiographical *Rosy Crucifixion* trilogy, consisting of *Sexus* 1949, *Plexus* 1949, and *Nexus* 1957 (published as a whole in the US 1965). His bohemian image made him a favorite of the ◊Beat Generation. Other works include *The Colossus of Maroussi* 1941, *The Air-Conditioned Nightmare* 1945, and *Letters to Anaïs Nin* 1965.

Miller Stanley 1930– . US chemist. In the early 1950s, under laboratory conditions, he tried to imitate the original conditions of the Earth's atmosphere (a mixture of methane, ammonia, and hydrogen), added an electrical discharge, and waited. After a few days he found that amino acids, the ingredients of protein, had been formed.

Miller William 1801–1880. Welsh crystallographer, developer of the Miller indices, a coordinate system of mapping the shapes and surfaces of crystals.

Miller William 1782–1849. US religious leader. Born in Pittsfield, Massachusetts, and raised in New York, Miller later settled in Vermont. Convinced that the Second Coming of Jesus was imminent, he began to preach about the millennium. Ordained as a Baptist minister 1833, Miller lectured and preached about the Second Advent, which he predicted would occur 1844. As the time neared, many of Miller's followers sold their property in expectation of the end of the world. Although Miller's movement disbanded soon after, his teachings paved the way for later Adventist sects.

millet any of several grasses, family Gramineae, of which the grains are used as a cereal food and the stems as fodder.

Species include *Panicum miliaceum*, extensively cultivated in the warmer parts of Europe, and *Sorghum bicolor*, also known as ◊durra.

Millet Jean François 1814–1875. French artist, a leading member of the ◊Barbizon school, who painted scenes of peasant life and landscapes. *The Angelus* 1859 (Musée d'Orsay, Paris) was widely reproduced in his day.

Millett Kate 1934– . US radical feminist lecturer, writer, and sculptor whose book *Sexual Politics* 1970 was a landmark in feminist thinking. She was a founding member of the National Organization of Women (NOW). Later books include *Flying* 1974, *The Prostitution Papers* 1976, and *Sita* 1977.

millibar unit of pressure, equal to one-thousandth of a ◊bar.

Millikan Robert Andrews 1868–1953. US physicist, awarded a Nobel Prize 1923 for his determination of the ◊electric charge on an electron 1913.

His experiment, which took five years to perfect, involved observing oil droplets, charged by external radiation, falling under gravity between two horizontal metal plates connected to a high-voltage supply. By varying the voltage, he was able to make the electrostatic field between the plates balance the gravitational field so that some droplets became stationary and floated. If a droplet of weight W is held stationary between plates separated by a distance d and carrying a potential difference V, the charge, e, on the drop is equal to Wd/V.

milliliter one-thousandth of a liter (ml), equivalent to 1 cu cm (cc) or 0.0338 fluid ounce.

millimeter of mercury unit of pressure, used in barometers for measuring atmospheric pressure, defined as the pressure exerted by a column of mercury one millimeter high, at standard gravity and at a temperature of 32°F/0°C.

Millin Sarah Gertrude (born Liebson) 1889–1968. South African novelist, an opponent of racial discrimination, as seen in, for example, *God's Step-Children* 1924.

milling metal machining method that uses a rotating toothed cutting wheel to shape a surface. The term also applies to grinding grain, cacao, coffee, pepper, and other spices.

millipede any arthropod of the class Diplopoda. It has a segmented body, each segment usually bearing two pairs of legs, and the distinct head bears a pair of short clubbed antennae. Most are no more than 1 in/2.5 cm long; a few in the tropics are 12 in/30 cm.

Millipedes live in damp, dark places, feeding mainly on rotting vegetation. Some species injure crops by feeding on tender roots, and some produce a poisonous secretion in defense. Certain orders have silk glands.

Mills C Wright 1916–1962. US sociologist, whose concern for humanity, ethical values, and individual freedom led him to criticize the US establishment.

Originally in the liberal tradition, Mills later adopted Weberian and even Marxist ideas. He aroused considerable popular interest in sociology with such works as *White Collar* 1951; *The Power Elite* 1956, depicting the US as ruled by businessmen, military experts, and politicians; and *Listen, Yankee* 1960.

Mills John 1908– . English actor who appeared in films such as *In Which We Serve* 1942, *The Rocking Horse Winner* 1949, *The Wrong Box* 1966, and *Oh, What a Lovely War* 1969. He received an Academy Award for *Ryan's Daughter* 1971. He is the father of the actresses Hayley Mills and Juliet Mills.

Mills Brothers US vocal group who specialized in close-harmony vocal imitations of instruments, comprising Herbert Mills (1912–), Harry Mills (1913–1982), John Mills (1889–1935), and Donald Mills (1915–). Formed 1922, the group first broadcast on radio in 1925, and continued to perform until the 1950s. Their 70 hits include "Lazy River" 1948 and "You Always Hurt the One You Love" 1944.

Mills Cross type of ◊radio telescope consisting of two rows of aerials at right angles to each other, invented 1953 by the Australian radio astronomer Bernard Mills (1920–). The cross-shape produces a narrow beam useful for pinpointing the positions of radio sources.

Millville city in SW New Jersey, on the Maurice River, SE of Philadelphia. Industries include vegetables, poultry, and glass products; population (1990) 25,992.

Milne A(lan) A(lexander) 1882–1956. English

Ioannis Miltoni Effigies Ætat: 62.
1670.

Milton *The 17th-century English poet John Milton.*

writer. His books for children were based on the teddy bear and other toys of his son Christopher Robin (*Winnie-the-Pooh* 1926 and *The House at Pooh Corner* 1928). He also wrote children's verse (*When We Were Very Young* 1924 and *Now We Are Six* 1927) and plays, including an adaptation of Kenneth Grahame's *The Wind in the Willows* as *Toad of Toad Hall* 1929.

Milosevic Slobodan 1941– . Serbian communist politician. A leading figure in the Yugoslavian Communist Party (LCY) in the republic of Serbia, he became Serbian party chief and president in 1986 and campaigned to reintegrate Kosovo and Vojvodina provinces into "greater Serbia."

He was educated at Belgrade University and rapidly rose through the ranks of the LCY in his home republic of Serbia, helped by his close political and business links to Ivan Stambolic, his predecessor as local party leader. Milosevic won popular support within Serbia for his assertive nationalist stance, encouraging street demonstrations in favor of the reintegration of Kosovo and Vojvodina autonomous provinces into the Serbian republic.

Miłosz Czesław 1911– . Polish writer, born in Lithuania. He became a diplomat before defecting and becoming a US citizen. His poetry in English translation, Classical in style, includes *Selected Poems* 1973 and *Bells in Winter* 1978.

His collection of essays *The Captive Mind* 1953 concerns the impact of communism on Polish intellectuals. Among his novels are *The Seizure of Power* 1955, *The Issa Valley* 1981, and *The Land of Ulro* 1984. He was awarded the Nobel Prize for Literature in 1980.

Milstein César 1927– . Argentine molecular biologist who developed monoclonal antibodies, giving immunity against specific diseases. He shared the Nobel Prize for Medicine 1984.

Milstein and his colleagues, while working at Britain's Cambridge University, devised a means of accessing the immune system for purposes of research, diagnosis, and treatment. They developed monoclonal antibodies (MABs), cloned cells that, when introduced into the body, can be targeted to seek out sites of disease. The full potential of this breakthrough is still being investigated. However, MABs, which can be duplicated in limitless quantities, are already in use to combat disease. Milstein shared the Nobel Prize for Medicine with two colleagues, George Kohler and Niels Jerne.

Milton John 1608–1674. English poet. His early poems include the pastoral *L'allegro* and *Il penseroso* 1632, the masque *Comus* 1633, and the

mimicry

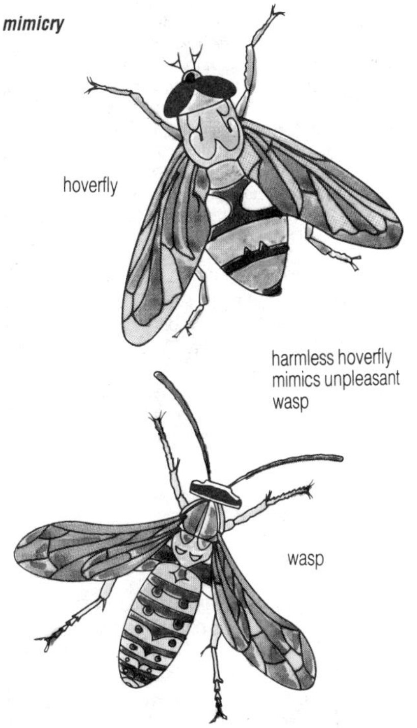
hoverfly
harmless hoverfly
mimics unpleasant
wasp
wasp

elegy *Lycidas* 1637. His later works include *Paradise Lost* 1667, *Paradise Regained* 1677, and the classic drama *Samson Agonistes* 1677.

Born in London, Milton was educated at Christ's College, Cambridge (where he was known as "the Lady of Christ's" for his fine features), and then devoted himself to study for his poetic career. His middle years were devoted to the Puritan cause and pamphleteering, including one advocating divorce, and another (*Areopagitica*) freedom of the press. From 1649 he was (Latin) secretary to the Council of State. His assistants (as his sight failed) included ◊Marvell. He married Mary Powell 1643, and their three daughters were later his somewhat unwilling scribes. After Mary's death 1652, the year of his total blindness, he married twice more, his second wife Catherine Woodcock dying in childbirth, while Elizabeth Minshull survived him for over half a century. He is buried in St Giles's, Cripplegate, London.

Milton Keynes industrial new town in ◊Buckinghamshire, England; principal industries engineering and electronics; population (1983) 146,000. It was developed 1967 around the old village of the same name, following a grid design by Richard Llewelyn-Davies; it is the headquarters of the Open University.

Milwaukee industrial (meatpacking, brewing, engineering, machinery, electronic and electrical equipment, chemicals) port in Wisconsin, on Lake Michigan; population (1990) 628,088. Educational institutions include Marquette University. The site was settled 1818 and drew a large influx of German immigrants, beginning in the 1840s.

mime a type of acting in which gestures, movements, and facial expressions replace speech. It has developed as a form of theater, particularly in France, where Marcel ◊Marceau and Jean Louis ◊Barrault have continued the traditions established in the 19th century by Deburau and the practices of the ◊commedia dell'arte in Italy. In ancient Greece, mime was a crude, realistic comedy with dialogue and exaggerated gesture.

mimicry the imitation of one species (or group of species) by another. The most common form is Batesian mimicry (named after H W ◊Bates), where the mimic resembles a model that is poisonous or unpleasant to eat, and has aposematic, or warning, coloration; the mimic thus benefits from the fact that predators have learned to avoid the model. Hoverflies that resemble bees or wasps are an example. Appearance is usually the basis for mimicry, but calls, songs, scents, and other signals can also be mimicked.

In Mullerian mimicry, two or more equally poisonous or distasteful species have a similar color pattern, thereby reinforcing the warning each gives to predators. In some cases, mimicry is not for protection, but allows the mimic to prey on, or parasitize, the model.

mimosa tree, shrub, or herb of the genus *Mimosa* of the family Leguminosae, found in tropical and subtropical regions. All bear small, fluffy, golden, balllike flowers.

Certain species, such as the sensitive plant of Brazil *M. pudica*, shrink momentarily on being touched.

min. abbreviation for minute (time); minimum.

Minangkabau member of an Indonesian people of W Sumatra. In addition to approximately 3 million Minangkabau in W Sumatra, there are sizeable communities in the major Indonesian cities. The Minangkabau language belongs to the Austronesian family.

minaret a slender turret or tower attached to a Muslim mosque or to buildings designed in that style. It has one or more balconies, from which the *muezzin* calls the people to prayer five times a day.

Minas Gerais state in SE Brazil; center of the country's iron ore, coal, diamond and gold mining industries; area 226,710 sq mi/587,172 sq km; population (1980) 13,378,500; capital Belo Horizonte.

mind in philosophy, the presumed mental or physical being or faculty that enables a person to think, will, and feel; the seat of the intelligence and of memory; sometimes only the cognitive or intellectual powers, as distinguished from the will and the emotions.

Mind may be seen as synonymous with the merely random chemical reactions within the brain, or as a function of the brain as a whole, or (more traditionally) as existing independently of the physical brain, through which it expresses itself, or even as the only reality, matter being considered the creation of intelligence. The relation of mind to matter may be variously regarded. Traditionally, materialism identifies mental and physical phenomena equally in terms of matter and motion. Dualism holds that mind and matter exist independently side by side. Idealism maintains that mind is the ultimate reality and that matter does not exist apart from it.

Mindanao the second-largest island of the Philippines

area 36,526 sq mi/94,627 sq km

towns Davao, Zamboanga

physical mountainous rainforest

features in 1971, an isolated people, the Tasaday, were reputedly first seen by others (this may be a hoax). The active volcano Apo reaches 9,600 ft/2,954 m, and Mindanao is subject to severe earthquakes. There is a Muslim guerrilla resistance movement

products pineapples, coffee, rice, coconut, rubber, hemp, timber, nickel, gold, steel, chemicals, fertilizer

population (1980) 10,905,250.

Minden industrial town of North Rhine-Westphalia, Federal Republic of Germany, on the river Weser; population (1985) 80,000. Industries include tobacco and food processing. The French were defeated here 1759 by an allied army from Britain, Hanover, and Brunswick, commanded by the duke of Brunswick.

Mindoro island of the Philippine Republic, S of Luzon

area 3,995 sq mi/10,347 sq km

cities Calapan

features Mount Halcon 8,500 ft/2,590 m

population (1980) 500,000.

Mindszenty József 1892–1975. Roman Catholic primate of Hungary. He was imprisoned by the communist government 1949, but escaped 1956 to take refuge in the US legation. The pope persuaded him to go into exile in Austria 1971, and he was "retired" when Hungary's relations with the Vatican improved 1974.

mine explosive charge on land or sea, or in the atmosphere, designed to be detonated by contact, vibration (for example from an enemy engine), magnetic influence, or a timing device. Countermeasures include metal detectors (useless for plastic types), specially equipped helicopters, and (at sea) ◊minesweepers.

mineral a naturally formed inorganic substance with a particular chemical composition and an ordered internal structure. Either in their perfect crystalline form or otherwise, minerals are the constituents of ◊rocks. Ice is also a mineral, the crystalline form of water, H_2O. In more general usage, a mineral is any substance economically valuable for mining (including coal and oil, despite their organic origins).

mineral dressing preparing a mineral ore for processing. Ore is seldom ready to be processed when it is mined; it often contains unwanted rock and dirt. Therefore it is usually crushed into uniform size and then separated from the dirt, or gangue. This may be done magnetically (some iron ores), by washing (gold), by treatment with chemicals (copper ores), or by ◊flotation.

mineralogy the study of minerals. The classification of minerals is based chiefly on their chemical composition and the kind of chemical bonding that holds these atoms together. The mineralogist also studies their crystallographic and physical characters, occurrence, and mode of formation.

mineral oil oil obtained from mineral sources, for example, coal or petroleum, as distinct from oil obtained from vegetable or animal sources.

mineral salt in nutrition, a simple inorganic chemical that is required by living organisms. Plants usually obtain their mineral salts from the soil, while animals get theirs from their food. Important mineral salts include iron salts (needed by both plants and animals), magnesium salts (needed mainly by plants, to make chlorophyll), and calcium salts (needed by animals to make bone or shell). See also ◊trace element.

mineral water water with mineral constituents gathered from the rocks with which it comes in contact, and classified by these into earthy, brine, and oil mineral waters; also water with artificially added minerals and, sometimes, carbon dioxide.

Many people believe that mineral waters have curative powers, the types of these medicinal waters being alkaline (Vichy), bitter (Seidlitz), salt (Droitwich), earthy (Bath), sulfurous (Saratoga Springs), and special varieties, such as barium (Harrogate). The most widely sold mineral water is Perrier, from the French village of Vergèze in W Provence. In 1990 minute traces of benzene, a cancer-causing chemical, were found in samples of Perrier, and 160 million bottles were recalled. Production was resumed once charcoal filters at the bottling plant had been replaced. Evian water comes from Haute-Savoie *département*, France, and Malvern water from Hereford and Worcester, England.

Minerva in Roman mythology, the goddess of intelligence, and of the handicrafts and arts, counterpart of the Greek ◊Athena. From the earliest days of ancient Rome, there was a temple to her on the Capitoline Hill, near the Temple of Jupiter.

minesweeper small naval vessel for locating and destroying mines at sea. A typical minesweeper weighs about 725 tons, and is built of reinforced plastic (immune to magnetic and acoustic mines). Remote-controlled miniature submarines may be used to lay charges next to the mines and destroy them.

Mingus Charles 1922–1979. US jazz bassist and composer. His experimentation with atonality and dissonant effects opened the way for the new style of free collective jazz improvisation of the 1960s.

Minhow name in use 1934–43 for Foochow (◊Fuzhou), a town in SE China.

miniature painting (Latin *miniare* "to paint with minium" (a red color)) painting on a very small scale, notably early manuscript paintings, and later miniature portraits, sometimes set in jeweled cases. The art of manuscript painting was developed in Classical times in the West and revived in the Middle Ages. Several Islamic countries, for example Persia and India, developed strong traditions of manuscript art. Miniature portrait painting enjoyed a vogue in France and England in the 16th–19th centuries.

Jean Clouet and Holbein the Younger both practiced the art for royal patrons. Later in the 16th century Nicholas Hilliard painted miniatures exclusively and set out the rules of this portrait style in his treatise *The Art of Limning*.

minicomputer multiuser computer with a size and processing power between those of a ◊mainframe and a ◊microcomputer.

Minicomputers are often used in medium-sized businesses and in university departments handling ◊database or other commercial programs and running scientific or graphical applications requiring much numerical computation.

Minimalism a movement beginning in the late 1960s in abstract art and music toward a severely simplified composition. In painting, it emphasized geometrical and elemental shapes. In sculpture, Carl André focused on industrial materials. In music, large-scale statements are based on layers of imperceptibly shifting repetitive patterns; its major exponents are Steve ◊Reich and Philip ◊Glass.

The idea of hypnotic repetition is a feature of US music from the Balinese transcriptions of Colin ◊McPhee and the rhythmic experiments of Nancarrow to the tape music of Terry Riley (1935–).

mining the extraction of minerals from under the land or sea for industrial or domestic uses.

mining

Since prehistoric times, humans have dug into the earth to obtain the materials needed to help sustain life. In the resources-hungry 20th century, power, mineral, and building needs are being met by an ever-increasing range of mining methods, allowing exploration and extraction wherever required.

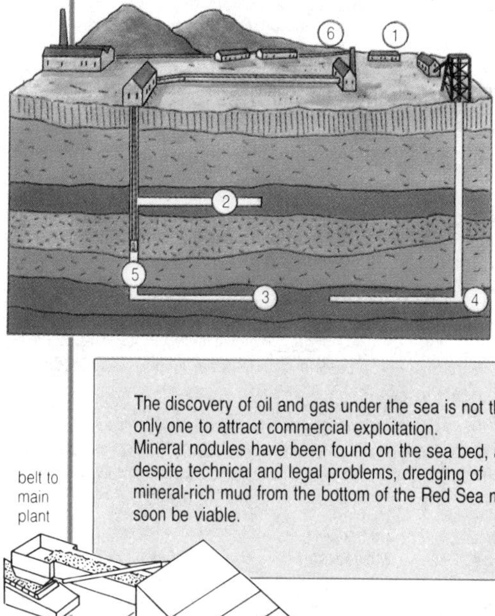

6
1
2
5
3
4

Traditional ways of raising hand-hewn coal are being replaced by safer and more efficient computer-controlled operations. (1) MINOS, the Mine-Operating System, has a control center on the surface. (2) FIDO continuously monitors underground teams. (3) MIDAS surveys seams and adjusts the shearer automatically. (4) IMPACT monitors the machinery, to save on maintenance and avoid breakdown. (5) Transport is also monitored to minimize delays. (6) Coal is graded and washed under electronic control.

The discovery of oil and gas under the sea is not the only one to attract commercial exploitation. Mineral nodules have been found on the sea bed, and despite technical and legal problems, dredging of mineral-rich mud from the bottom of the Red Sea may soon be viable.

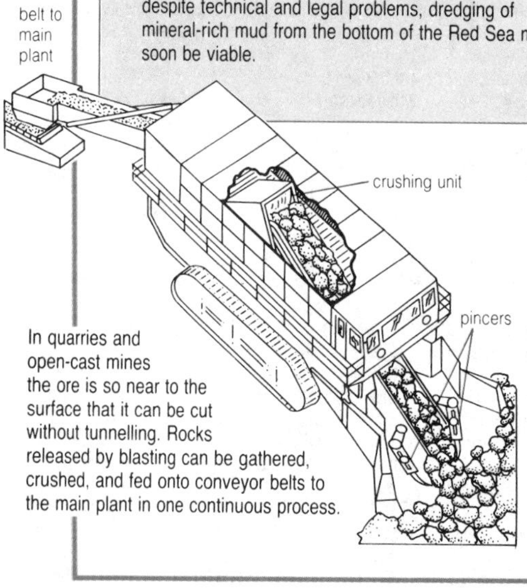

belt to main plant
crushing unit
pincers

In quarries and open-cast mines the ore is so near to the surface that it can be cut without tunnelling. Rocks released by blasting can be gathered, crushed, and fed onto conveyor belts to the main plant in one continuous process.

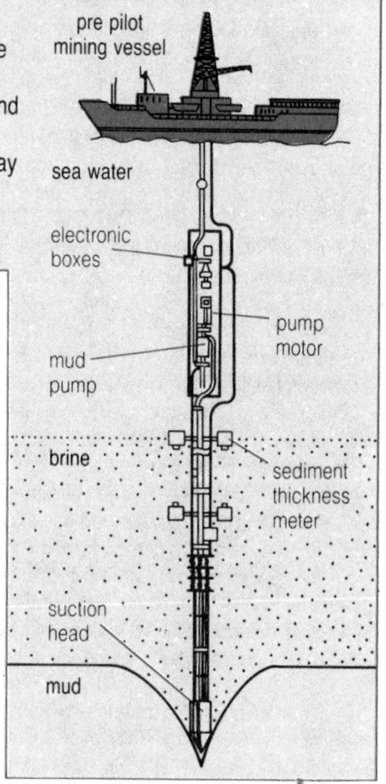

pre pilot mining vessel
sea water
electronic boxes
pump motor
mud pump
brine
sediment thickness meter
suction head
mud

Minnesota

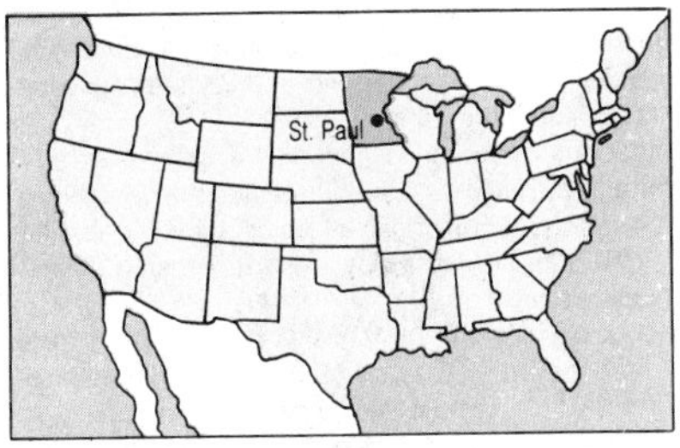
St. Paul

Exhaustion of traditionally accessible resources has led to development of new mining techniques; for example, extraction of oil from offshore deposits and from land shale reserves. Technology is also under development for the exploitation of minerals from entirely new sources such as mud deposits and mineral nodules from the sea bed.

Mud deposits are laid down by hot springs (about 660°F/350°C): sea water penetrates beneath the ocean floor and carries copper, silver, and zinc with it on its return. Such springs occur along the midocean ridges of the Atlantic and Pacific and in the geologic rift between Africa and Arabia under the Red Sea.

Mineral nodules form on the ocean bed and contain manganese, cobalt, copper, molybdenum, and nickel; they stand out on the surface, and "grow" by only a few millimeters every 100,000 years.

mink two species of carnivores of the weasel family, genus *Mustela*, usually found in or near water. They have rich, brown fur, and are up to 1.6 ft/50 cm long with bushy tails 8 in/20 cm long. They live in Eurasia (*Mustela lutreola*) and North America (*M. vison*).

They produce an annual litter of six in their riverbank burrows. The demand for their fur led to the establishment from the 1930s of mink ranches for breeding of the animals in a wide range of fur colors.

Minneapolis city in Minnesota, forming with St Paul the Twin Cities area; population (1990) 368,383, metropolitan area (1990) 2,464,124. It is at the head of navigation of the Mississippi River. Industries include food processing and the manufacture of machinery, electrical and electronic equipment, precision instruments, transport machinery, and metal and paper products. It was incorporated as a village 1855.

The powerful Cray computers are built here, used for long-range weather forecasting, spacecraft design, and code-breaking. Shopping areas of the city center are glass-covered against the difficult climate; there is an arts institute, symphony orchestra, the University of Minnesota, and Tyrone ◊Guthrie theater.

Minnelli Liza 1946– . US actress and singer, daughter of Judy ◊Garland and the director Vincente Minnelli. She achieved stardom in the Broadway musical *Flora, The Red Menace* 1965 and in the film *Cabaret* 1972. Her subsequent films include *New York, New York* 1977 and *Arthur* 1981.

Minnelli Vincente 1910–1986. US film director who specialized in musicals and occasional melodramas. His best films, such as *Meet Me in St Louis* 1944 and *The Band Wagon* 1953, display a powerful visual flair.

Minnesinger any of a group of German lyric poets of the 12th and 13th centuries who, in their songs, dealt mainly with the theme of courtly love without revealing the identity of the object of their affections. Minnesingers included Dietmar von Aist, Friedrich von Hausen, Heinrich von Morungen, Reinmar, and Walther von der Vogelweide.

Minnesota state in N midwest US; nickname Gopher State/North Star State
area 84,418 sq mi/218,700 sq km

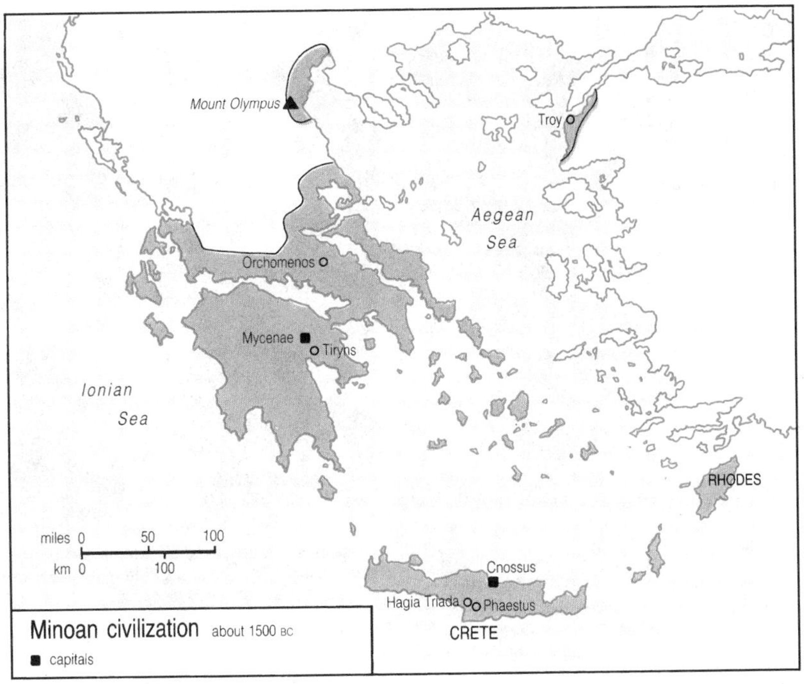
Mount Olympus
Troy
Aegean Sea
Orchomenos
Mycenae
Tiryns
Ionian Sea
RHODES
Cnossus
Hagia Triada
Phaestus
CRETE
miles 0 50 100
km 0 100

Minoan civilization about 1500 BC
■ capitals

capital St Paul
cities Minneapolis, Duluth, Bloomington, Rochester
population (1990) 4,375,099
features sources of the Mississippi River and the Red River of the North; Voyageurs National Park near the Canadian border; Minnehaha Falls at Minneapolis; Mayo Clinic at Rochester; more than 15,000 lakes
products cereals, soybeans, livestock, meat and dairy products, iron ore (about two-thirds of US output), nonelectrical machinery, electronic equipment
famous people F Scott Fitzgerald, Hubert H Humphrey, Sinclair Lewis, Charles and William Mayo
history first European exploration, by French fur traders, 17th century; region claimed for France by Daniel Greysolon, Sieur Duluth, 1679; part E of Mississippi River ceded to Britain 1763 and to the US 1783; part W of Mississippi passed to the US under the Louisiana Purchase 1803; became a territory 1849; statehood 1858. With the coming of the railroad in 1867, Minneapolis became the major US flour-milling center. Iron ore was discovered in the Mesabi, Cuyuna, and Vermilion ranges 1880s, and Duluth became a major Great Lakes port. In 1848 the value of manufactured products exceeded farm cash receipts for the first time as the state became increasingly urbanized and industrial.

minnow various small freshwater fishes of the carp family (Cyprinidae), found in streams and ponds worldwide. Most species are small and dully colored, but some are brightly colored. They feed on larvae and insects.

Red-bellied daces, genus *Chrosomus*, and cutlipped minnows, genus *Exoglossum*, are North American representatives.

Minoan civilization Bronze Age civilization on the Aegean island of Crete. The name is derived from Minos, the legendary king of Crete, reputed to be the son of the god Zeus. The civilization is divided into three main periods: early Minoan, about 3000–2200 BC, middle Minoan, about 2200–1580 BC; and late Minoan, about 1580–1100 BC. The Minoan language was deciphered by Michael ◊Ventris.

No paleolithic remains have yet been found in Crete, but in the Neolithic Age some centuries before 3000 BC the island was inhabited by people coming probably from SW Asia Minor, and akin to the early Bronze Age inhabitants of the Greek mainland. With the opening of the Bronze Age, about 3000 BC, the Minoan culture proper began. Each period was marked by cultural advances in copper and bronze weapons, pottery of increasingly intricate design, frescoes, and the construction of palaces and fine houses. About 1400 BC, in the late Minoan period, the civilization was suddenly destroyed by earthquake or war. A partial revival continued until about 1100.

In religion the Minoans seem to have worshiped principally a great mother goddess with whom was associated a young male god. The tales of Greek mythology about Rhea, the mother of Zeus, and the birth of Zeus himself in a Cretan cave seem to be based on Minoan religion.

minor the legal term for those under the age of majority, which varies from country to country but is usually between 18 and 21. In the US (from 1971 for voting, and in some states for nearly all other purposes) and certain European countries (in Britain since 1970) the age of majority is 18. Most civic and legal rights and duties only accrue at the age of majority; for example, the rights to vote, to make a will, and (usually) to make a fully binding contract, and the duty to act as a juror.

Minorca (Spanish *Menorca*) second largest of the Spanish ◊Balearic Islands in the Mediterranean
area 266 sq mi/689 sq km
towns Mahon, Ciudadela
products copper, lead, iron; tourism is an important industry
population (1985) 55,500.

minor planet another name for an ◊asteroid.

Minos in Greek mythology, a king of Crete (son of ◊Zeus and ◊Europa).

Minotaur in Greek mythology, a monster, half man and half bull, offspring of Pasiphaë, wife of King Minos of Crete, and a bull. It lived in the Labyrinth at Knossos, and its victims were seven girls and seven youths, sent in annual tribute by Athens, until ◊Theseus killed it, with the aid of Ariadne, the daughter of Minos.

Minsk industrial city (machinery, textiles, leather; center of the Soviet computer industry) and capital of Byelorussia, USSR; population (1987) 1,543,000.

Minsk dates from the 11th century and has in turn been held by Lithuania, Poland, Sweden, and Russia. The city was devastated by Napoleon

1812 and heavily damaged by German forces 1944. Mass graves from between 1937 and 1941 of more than 30,000 victims of Joseph Stalin's terror were discovered in a forest outside Minsk 1989.

minster in the UK, church formerly attached to a monastery. After dissolution of the Roman Catholic monasteries by Henry VIII, the term, which originally meant monastery, survived in the name of churches, such as Westminster Abbey or York Minster.

mint in botany, any aromatic plant, genus *Mentha*, of the family Labiatae, widely distributed in temperate regions. The plants have square stems, creeping rootstocks, and flowers, usually pink or purplish, that grow in a terminal spike. Mints include garden mint *M. spicata* and peppermint *M. piperita*.

mint in economics, a place where coins are stamped from metal under government authority.

In the US the official mint is the Bureau of the Mint, a division of the Treasury Department. The official Mint of the United States was established by the Coining Act 1792 in Philadelphia. The US Mint has general supervision of the four current coinage mints—in Denver, West Point, San Francisco, and Philadelphia—all of which are assay offices and bullion depositories. It directs the coinage of money, the manufacture of medals, and the custody of bullion.

Mintoff Dom(inic) 1916– . Labour prime minister of Malta 1971–84. He negotiated the removal of British and other foreign military bases 1971–79 and made treaties with Libya.

Minton Thomas 1765–1836. English potter. He first worked under the potter Josiah Spode, but in 1789 established himself at Stoke-on-Trent as an engraver of designs (he originated the "willow pattern") and in the 1790s founded a pottery there, producing high-quality bone china, including tableware.

minuet European courtly dance of the 17th century, used in the 18th century with the trio as the third movement in a Classical symphony.

Minuit Peter c. 1580–1638. Dutch colonial administrator. Born in Prussia, Minuit was active in the colonization activities of the Dutch West India Company and established the settlement of New Amsterdam on Manhattan Island 1626. Appointed director general of the colony, he conducted purchase negotiations with the local Indians and supervised the construction of Fort Amsterdam. Minuit was relieved of his post 1631 due to a personal conflict with the Dutch Reformed Church, and he later participated in a Swedish colonization effort, founding Fort Christina at the modern site of Wilmington, Delaware, 1638. He was lost in a hurricane in the West Indies.

minute unit of time consisting of 60 seconds; also a unit of angle equal to one sixtieth of a degree.

Minuteman in weaponry, a US three-stage intercontinental ballistic missile (ICBM) with a range of about 5,000 mi/8,000 km. In US history the term was applied to members of the citizens' militia in the 1770s. These citizen-soldiers had pledged to be available for battle at a "minute's notice" during the ◊American Revolution.

Miocene fourth epoch of the Tertiary period of geologic time, 25–5 million years ago. The name means "middle recent." At this time grasslands spread over the interior of continents, and hoofed mammals rapidly evolved.

mips (acronym from million instructions per second) in computing, a measure of the speed of a processor.

Miquelon Islands small group of islands off the S coast of Newfoundland which with St Pierre form a French overseas *département*. See ◊St Pierre and Miquelon

area 83 sq mi/216 sq km

products cod; silver fox and mink are bred

population (with St Pierre, 1982) 6,045.

Mir (Russian "peace") Soviet space station, the core of which was launched Feb 20, 1986. *Mir* is intended to be a permanently occupied space station.

Mir weighs almost 23 tons, is approximately 44 ft/13.5 m long, and has a maximum diameter of 13.6 ft/4.15 m. It carries a number of improvements over the earlier ◊Salyut series of space stations, including six docking ports; four of these can have scientific and technical modules attached to them. The first of these was the *Kvant* (quantum) *Astrophysics Module*, launched 1987. This had two main sections: a main experimental module and a service module, which would be separated in orbit. The experimental module was 19 ft/5.8 m long and had a maximum diameter matching that of *Mir*. When attached to the *Mir* core, *Kvant* added a further 1,413 cu ft/40 cu m of workspace to that already there. Among the equipment carried by *Kvant* were several X-ray telescopes and an ultraviolet telescope.

Mirabeau *As leader of the National Assembly, Honoré Gabriel Mirabeau sought to remodel rather than overthrow the French monarcy.*

mir (Russian "world") in Russia before the 1917 Revolution, a self-governing village community in which the peasants distributed land and collected taxes.

Mira or ***Omicron Ceti*** the brightest long-period pulsating ◊variable star, located in the constellation ◊Cetus. Mira was the first star discovered to vary periodically in brightness.

In 1596 Dutch astronomer David Fabricus noticed Mira as a third-magnitude object. Because it did not appear on any of the star charts available at the time, he mistook it for a ◊nova. The German astronomer Johann Bayer included it on his star atlas 1603 and designated it Omicron Ceti. The star vanished from view again, only to reappear within a year. Continued observation revealed a periodic variation between third or fourth magnitude and ninth magnitude over an average period of 331 days. Mira can sometimes reach second magnitude and once, in 1779, it almost attained first magnitude.

Mirabeau Honoré Gabriel Riqueti, Comte de 1749–1791. French politician, leader of the National Assembly in the French Revolution. He wanted to establish a parliamentary monarchy on the English model. From May 1790 he secretly acted as political adviser to the king.

Mirabeau was from a noble Provençal family. Before the French Revolution he had a stormy career, was three times imprisoned, and spent several years in exile. In 1789 he was elected to the States General. His eloquence won him the leadership of the National Assembly; nevertheless, he was out of sympathy with the majority of the deputies, whom he regarded as mere theoreticians.

miracle an event that cannot be explained by the known laws of nature and is therefore attributed to divine intervention.

miracle play another name for ◊mystery play.

mirage the illusion seen in hot climates of water on the horizon, or of distant objects being enlarged. The effect is caused by the ◊refraction, or bending, of light.

Light rays from the sky bend as they pass through the hot layers of air near the ground, so that they appear to come from the horizon. Because the light is from a blue sky, the horizon appears blue and watery. If, during the night, cold air collects near the ground, light can be bent in the opposite direction, so that objects below the horizon appear to float above it. In the same way, objects such as trees or rocks near the horizon can appear enlarged.

Miranda Carmen. Adopted name of Maria de Carmo Miranda da Cunha 1909–1955. Portuguese-born dancer and singer who lived in Brazil from childhood. Successful in Brazilian films, she went to Hollywood 1939 via Broadway and appeared in over a dozen musicals, including *Down Argentine Way* 1940 and *The Gang's All Here* 1943. A fine comedienne, her hallmarks were extravagant costumes and exotic headgear adorned by an array of tropical fruits as well as a staccato singing voice and fiery temperament.

Miranda v Arizona a US Supreme Court decision 1966 dealing with the admission into a trial of evidence obtained from suspects who are unaware of their rights. The petitioner, Ernesto Miranda, was convicted of kidnapping and rape after confessing to police interrogators. Miranda appealed the conviction, arguing that due process had been violated because he had not been informed of his rights before his confession. The Court voted 5 to 4 to overturn Miranda's conviction. The ruling mandated that in order for testimony to be admissible in criminal trials, suspects must have been informed (1) of the right to remain silent, (2) that anything they do or say will be used against them in court, (3) of the right to an attorney, and (4) of the right to a court-appointed attorney if unable to afford one.

Mirandola Italian 15th-century philosopher. See ◊Pico della Mirandola.

Miró Joan 1893–1983. Spanish Surrealist painter, born in Barcelona. In the mid-1920s he developed a distinctive abstract style with amoeba shapes, some linear, some highly colored, generally floating on a plain background.

During the 1930s his style became more somber and after World War II he produced larger abstracts. He experimented with sculpture and printmaking and produced ceramic murals (including two in the UNESCO building, Paris, 1958). He also designed stained glass and sets for the ballet director Sergei Diaghilev.

mirror any polished surface that reflects light; often made from "silvered" glass (in practice, a mercury alloy coating of glass). A plane (flat) mirror produces a same-size, erect "virtual" image located behind the mirror at the same distance from it as the object is in front of it. A spherical concave mirror produces a reduced, inverted real image in front or an enlarged, erect virtual image behind it (as with a shaving mirror), depending on how close the object is to the mirror. A spherical convex mirror produces a reduced, erect virtual image behind it (as with a car's rear-view mirror).

In a plane mirror the light rays appear to come from behind the mirror but do not actually do so. The inverted real image from a spherical concave mirror is an image in which the rays of light pass through it. The ◊focal length f of a spherical mirror is half the radius of curvature; it is related to the image distance v and object distance u by the equation $1/v + 1/u = 1/f$.

MIRV abbreviation for multiple independently targeted reentry vehicle, used in ◊nuclear warfare.

Mishima *Japanese novelist and playwright Yukio Mishima, 1970.*

Mirzapur city of Uttar Pradesh, India, on the river Ganges; a grain and cotton market, with bathing sites and temples on the river; population (1981) 127,785.

Misanthrope, The a comedy by Molière, first produced in France 1666. The play contrasts the noble ideals of Alceste with the worldliness of his lover Celimene.

miscarriage spontaneous expulsion of a fetus from the womb before it is capable of independent survival.

misdemeanor in US law, a term for an offense less serious than a ◊felony. A misdemeanor is an offense punishable by a relatively lenient penalty, such as a fine or short term in prison or a term of community service, while a felony carries more severe penalties, such as a specified term of imprisonment of a year or more up to the death penalty.

Mishawaka city in N central Indiana, E of South Bend. It is an industrial center for plastics, rubber, missiles, and automobile and aircraft parts; population (1990) 42,608.

Mishima Yukio 1925–1970. Japanese novelist whose work often deals with sexual desire and perversion, as in *Confessions of a Mask* 1949 and *The Temple of the Golden Pavilion* 1956. He committed hara-kiri (ritual suicide) as a protest against what he saw as the corruption of the nation and the loss of the samurai warrior tradition.

Mishna (Hebrew "oral instruction") a collection of commentaries on written Hebrew law, consisting of discussions between rabbis, handed down orally from their inception in AD 70 until about 200, when, with the Gemara (the main body of rabbinical debate on interpretations of the Mishna) it was committed to writing to form the Talmud.

Miskito member of an American Indian people of Central America, living mainly in the area that is now Nicaragua.

Miskolc industrial city (iron, steel, textiles, furniture, paper) in NE Hungary, on the river Sajo, 90 mi/145 km NE of Budapest; population (1988) 210,000.

Misr Egyptian name for ◊Egypt and for ◊Cairo.

missal in the Roman Catholic Church, a service book containing the complete office of Mass for the entire year. A simplified missal in the vernacular was introduced 1969 (obligatory from 1971): the first major reform since 1570.

missile rocket-propelled weapon, which may be nuclear-armed (see ◊nuclear warfare). Modern missiles are classified according to range into intercontinental ballistic missiles (ICBMs, capable of reaching targets over 3,400 mi/5,500 km), intermediate-range (680 mi to 1,700 mi/1,100 km to 2,750 km), and short-range (under 680 mi/1,100 km) missiles. The first long-range ballistic missiles used in warfare were the ◊V1 and V2

Mississippi/Missouri Rivers

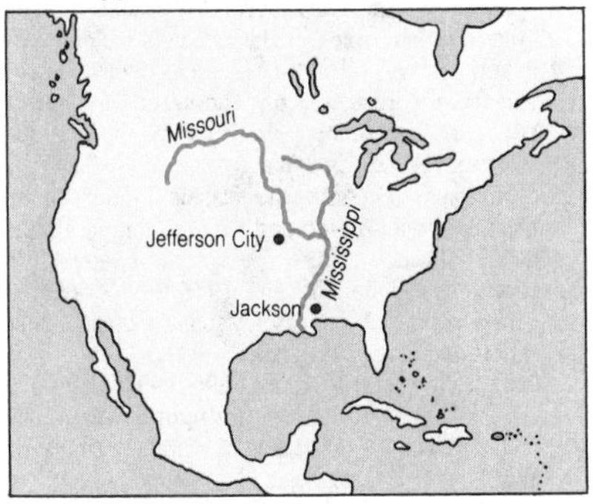
Missouri
Jefferson City
Mississippi
Jackson

launched by Germany against Britain in World War II.

Outside the industrialized countries, 22 nations had active ballistic-missile programs by 1989, and 17 had deployed these weapons: Afghanistan, Argentina, Brazil, Cuba, Egypt, India, Iran, Iraq, Israel, North Korea, South Korea, Libya, Pakistan, Saudi Arabia, South Africa, Syria, and Taiwan. Non-nuclear short-range missiles were used during the Iran–Iraq War 1980–88 against Iraqi cities. In the Falklands conflict 1982, smaller, conventionally armed sea-skimming missiles were used (the French Exocet) against British ships by the Argentine forces, and similar small missiles have been used against aircraft and ships elsewhere.

Mission city in S Texas near the Rio Grande, W of McAllen. The economy is based on processing the area's citrus fruits and vegetables, and on nearby oil wells; population (1990) 28,653.

mission an organized attempt to spread a religion. Throughout history, Christianity has been the most aggressive missionary religion; its activities during the colonization of what are now Third World nations was in some instances excessive, and it has frequently been criticized for obliterating both the beliefs and the people of some indigenous societies, as during the Spanish Conquest. During the 20th century, sects such as the Mormons and Jehovah's Witnesses proselytize regularly and systematically. Islam also has a history of militant missionizing, but in the 20th century has found ready converts in the Black Muslim movement of the US. Buddhism was spread both historically and recently by the teaching spirit of the wandering Buddha and his followers.

In developmental terms, the transition from tribal religions to the Great World Religions can be traced to the missionary movement that emerged in the ancient Near East even before the beginning of the Christian era. See, for example, ◊Mithraism.

Mississippi river in the US, the main arm of the great river-system drainage of North America, flowing S to the Gulf of Mexico between the Appalachian and Rocky mountains (an area of about 1,257,000 sq mi/3,256,000 sq km). The length of the Mississippi is 2,350 mi/3,780 km, of the Mississippi-Missouri system 3,740 mi/6,020 km. Levees extend over more than 1,600 mi/2,575 km of its course because of the potentially dangerous spring flooding. St Louis is the chief central port on its banks. Waterborne commerce consists mainly of bulk commodities such as petroleum and petroleum products, grain, and iron ore. Passenger traffic was important during the 19th century, today, excursion boats, especially paddle-wheel craft, provide day trips or longer cruises.

The Mississippi rises in the lake region of N Minnesota, with St Anthony Falls at Minneapolis. Below the tributaries Minnesota, Wisconsin, Des Moines, and Illinois, the confluence of the Missouri and Mississippi occurs at St Louis. Turning at the Ohio River junction, it passes Memphis and takes in the St Francis, Arkansas, Yazoo, and

Mississippi

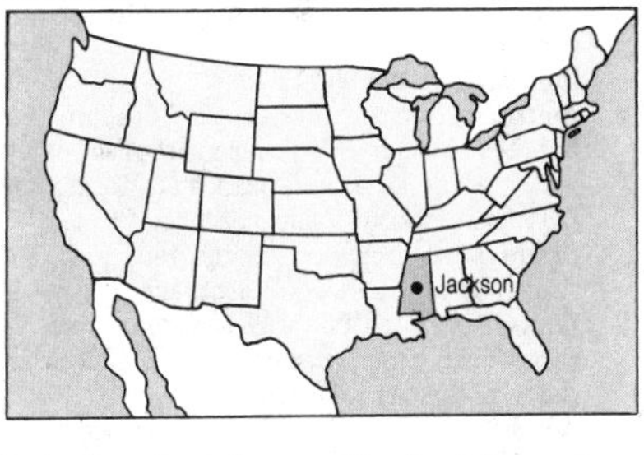
Jackson

Red tributaries before reaching its delta on the Gulf of Mexico beyond New Orleans.

In spring, warm air from the Gulf of Mexico collides with cold fronts from the N to create tornadoes along the Red River, a western tributary. The Spanish explorer Hernando de Soto reached a point on the Mississippi near present-day Memphis 1541. The Sieur de La Salle, a French explorer, reached the river's mouth 1682 after descending from the Great Lakes. Before the coming of the railroad, river commerce was of greater importance, and the securing of the Mississippi 1861–63, in the American Civil War, was a vital objective of the Union forces.

Mississippi state in SE US; nickname Magnolia State/Bayou State
area 47,710 sq mi/123,600 sq km
capital Jackson
cities Biloxi, Meridian, Hattiesburg
population (1990) 2,573,216
features rivers: Mississippi, Pearl, Big Black; Vicksburg National Military Park (Civil War site); Gulf Islands National Seashore; mansions and plantations, many in the Natchez area
products cotton, rice, soybeans, chickens, fish and shellfish, lumber and wood products, petroleum and natural gas, transportation equipment, chemicals
famous people Jefferson Davis, William Faulkner, Elvis Presley, Leontyne Price, Eudora Welty, Tennessee Williams, Richard Wright
history first explored by Hernando de Soto for Spain 1540; settled by the French 1699, the English 1763; ceded to US 1798; statehood achieved 1817. After secession from the Union during the Civil War, it was the scene of heavy fighting that left it devastated. Tenant farming replaced plantations, and only in the mid-1960s did manufacturing pass farming as a source of jobs. The legal segregation of blacks was dismantled during this period. Mississippi remains the poorest of the states in many respects, including per-capita personal income.

Mississippian US term for the lower ◊Carboniferous period of geologic time, named after the state of Mississippi.

Missolonghi (Greek *Mesolóngion*) town in W Central Greece and Eubrea region, on the N shore of the Gulf of Patras; population (1981) 10,200. It was several times under siege by the Turks in the wars of 1822–26 and it was here that the British poet Byron died.

Missouri state in central US; nickname Show Me State/Bullion State
area 69,712 sq mi/180,600 sq km

Missouri

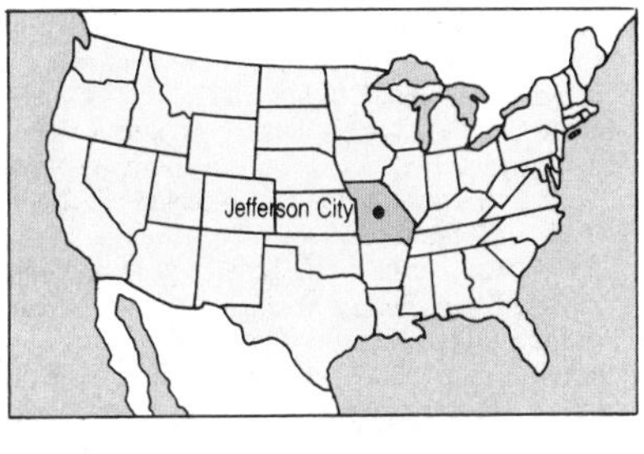
Jefferson City

capital Jefferson City
cities St Louis, Kansas City, Springfield, Independence;
population (1990) 5,117,073
features rivers: Mississippi, Missouri; Pony Express Museum at St Joseph; birthplace of Jesse James; Mark Twain and Ozark state parks; Harry S Truman Library at Independence
products meat and other processed food, aerospace and transport equipment, lead, zinc
famous people George Washington Carver, T S Eliot, Jesse James, Joseph Pulitzer, Carl Schurz, Harry S Truman, Mark Twain
history explored by de Soto 1541; acquired by the US under the Louisiana Purchase 1803; achieved statehood 1821, following the Missouri Compromise of 1820. Strong sympathy for both sides existed, but the state remained Union during the Civil War; many battles and skirmishes fostered a general lawlessness that continued in the postwar exploits of such bandits as Jesse and Frank James. While St Louis was eclipsed by Chicago as the commercial center of the Midwest, Kansas City benefited from the growth of the railroads. Increasingly urbanized and industrialized in the 20th century, Missouri is second to Michigan in auto production and ranks high in aerospace production.

Missouri major river in the central US, a tributary of the Mississippi, which it joins N of St Louis; length 2,683 mi/4,320 km. It is formed by the confluence of the Jefferson, Gallatin, and Madison rivers in SW Montana and flows SE through the states of Montana, North Dakota, and South Dakota to Sioux City, Iowa, where it turns S and forms the borders between Iowa and Nebraska and between Kansas and Missouri. Kansas City, Missouri, is the largest city on its banks. Since 1944 the muddy, turbulent river has been tamed by a series of locks and dams for irrigation and flood control.

Missouri Compromise, the in US history, the solution by Congress (1820–21) of a sectional crisis caused by the 1819 request from Missouri for admission to the union as a slave state, despite its proximity to existing nonslave states. The compromise was the simultaneous admission of Maine as a nonslave state to keep the same ratio.

Mistinguett stage name of Jeanne Bourgeois 1873–1956. French actress and dancer. A leading music-hall artist in Paris from 1899, she appeared in revues at the Folies-Bergère, Casino de Paris, and Moulin Rouge. She was known for the song "Mon Homme" and her partnership with Maurice Chevalier.

mistletoe any of several parasitic evergreen shrubs of the genera *Viscum* and *Phoradendron* of the family Loranthaceae, especially American mistletoe *Phoradendron flavescens*, parasitic on broad-leaved trees, and European mistletoe *Viscum album*. They grow on trees as branched bushes, with translucent white berries, and are used as Christmas decorations. See ◊Druidism. The seeds of the European mistletoe are dispersed by birds, but the dwarf mistletoe *Arceuthobium pusillum* of North America shoots its seeds at 60 mph/100 kph as far as 16 yd/15 m. Mistletoes lose water more than ten times as fast as other plants to draw nutrients to them, and the dwarf mistletoe causes loss of 20 million cubic meters of wood fiber a year.

mistral cold, dry, northerly wind that occasionally blows during the winter on the Mediterranean coast of France. It has been known to reach a velocity of 90 mph/145 kph.

Mistral Gabriela. Adopted name of Lucila Godoy de Alcayaga 1889–1957. Chilean poet who wrote *Sonnets of Death* 1915. She received the Nobel Prize for Literature 1945.

She was consul of Chile in Spain, and represented her country at the League of Nations and the United Nations.

Mitchell Arthur 1934– . US dancer, director of the Dance Theater of Harlem, which he founded with Karel Shook in 1968. Mitchell was a principal dancer with the New York City Ballet 1956–68, creating many roles in Balanchine's ballets.

Mitchell Margaret 1900–1949. US novelist, born in Atlanta, Georgia, which is the setting for her one book, the bestseller *Gone With the Wind* 1936, a story of the US Civil War.

It was made into the classic motion picture starring Vivien Leigh and Clark Gable in 1939.

Mitchell Peter 1920– . British chemist. He received a Nobel Prize in 1978 for work on the conservation of energy by plants during respiration and photosynthesis.

Mitchell R(eginald) J(oseph) 1895–1937. British aircraft designer whose Spitfire fighter was a major factor in winning the Battle of Britain during World War II.

Mitchum Robert 1917– . US film actor, a star for over 30 years, the big, strong but relaxed modern hero. His films include *Out of the Past* 1947, *The Night of the Hunter* 1955, and *Farewell My Lovely* 1975.

mite minute ◊arachnid of the subclass Acari.

Some mites are free-living scavengers or predators. Some are parasitic, such as the itch mite *Sarcoptes scabiei*, which burrows in human skin, or the red mite *Dermanyssus gallinae*, which sucks blood from poultry and other birds. Others parasitize plants.

miter in the Christian church, the headdress worn by bishops, cardinals, and mitered abbots at solemn services. There are miters of many different shapes, but in the Western church they usually take the form of a tall cleft cap. The miter worn by the pope is called a tiara.

Miter Bartólomé 1821–1906. Argentine president 1862–68. In 1852 he helped overthrow the dictatorial regime of Juan Manuel de Rosas, and in 1861 he helped unify Argentina. Miter encouraged immigration and favored growing commercial links with Europe. He is seen as a symbol of national unity.

Mitford sisters the six daughters of British aristocrat Lord Redesdale, including:
Nancy (1904–73), author of the semiautobiographical *The Pursuit of Love* 1945 and *Love in a Cold Climate* 1949, and editor and part author of *Noblesse Oblige* 1956 elucidating "U" (upper-class) and "non-U' behavior;
Diana (1910–), who married Oswald ◊Mosley;
Unity (1914–48), who became an admirer of Hitler; and
Jessica (1917–), author of the autobiographical *Hons and Rebels* 1960 and *The American Way of Death* 1963.

Mithraism the ancient Persian worship of Mithras. His cult was introduced into the Roman Empire in 68 BC and spread rapidly, gaining converts especially among soldiers; by about AD 250 it rivalled Christianity in strength.

Mithras in Persian mythology, the god of light. Mithras represented the power of goodness, and promised his followers compensation for present evil after death. He was said to have captured and killed the sacred bull, from whose blood all life sprang.

A bath in the blood of a sacrificed bull formed part of the initiation ceremony of the Mithraic cult, which was introduced into the Roman Empire 68 BC. By the 3rd century AD, it rivaled Christianity in strength. In 1954 remains of a Roman temple dedicated to Mithras were discovered in the City of London.

Mithridates VI Eupator known as the Great 132–63 BC. King of Pontus (NE Asia Minor, on the Black Sea) from 120 BC. He massacred 80,000 Romans in overrunning the rest of Asia Minor and went on to invade Greece. He was defeated by ◊Sulla in the First Mithridatic War 88–84; by ◊Lucullus in the Second 83–81; and by ◊Pompey in the Third 74–64. He was killed by a soldier at his own order rather than surrender.

Mitilíni modern Greek name of ◊Mytilene, town on the island of Lesvos.

Mithras This marble head wearing a Phrygian cap was found in the excavation of London's temple of Mithras.

mitochondria (singular mitochondrion) membrane-enclosed organelles within ◊eukaryotic cells, containing enzymes responsible for energy production during ◊aerobic respiration. These rodlike or spherical bodies are thought to be derived from free-living bacteria that, at a very early stage in the history of life, invaded larger cells and took up a symbiotic way of life inside. Each still contains its own small loop of DNA, and new mitochondria arise by division of existing ones.

mitosis in biology, the process of cell division. The genetic material of ◊eukaryotic cells is carried on a number of ◊chromosomes. To control their movements during cell division so that both new cells get a full complement, a system of protein tubules, known as the spindle, organizes the chromosomes into position in the middle of the cell before they replicate. The spindle then controls the movement of chromosomes as the cell goes through the stages of division: interphase, prophase, metaphase, anaphase, and telophase. See also ◊meiosis.

Mitterrand François 1916– . French Socialist politician, president from 1981. He held ministerial posts in 11 governments 1947–1958. He founded the French Socialist Party (PS) 1971. In 1985 he introduced proportional representation, allegedly to weaken the growing opposition from left and right.

Mitterrand studied law and politics in Paris. During World War II he was prominent in the Resistance. He entered the National Assembly as a center-left deputy for Nièvre. Opposed to General de Gaulle's creation of the Fifth Republic

mitosis

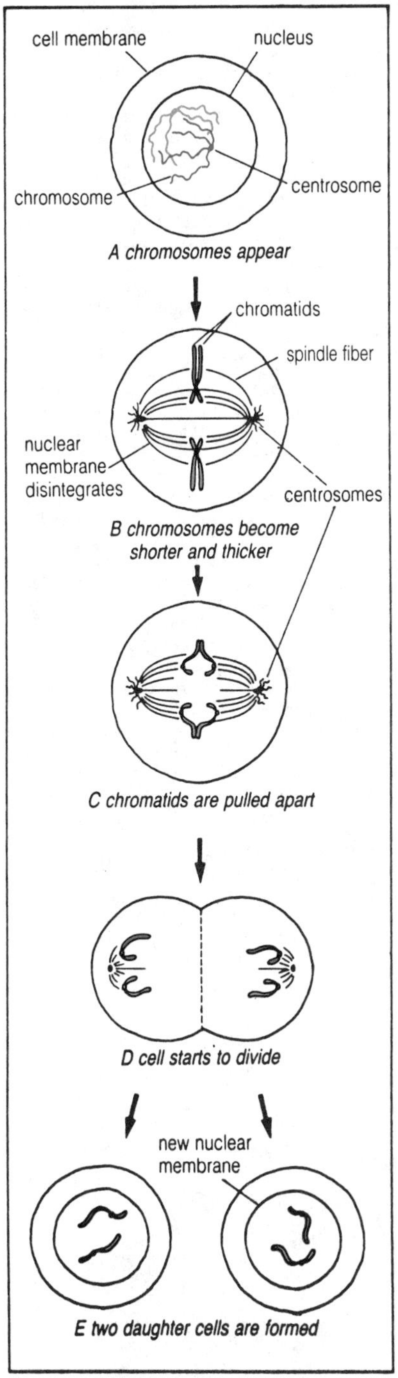
cell membrane
nucleus
chromosome
centrosome
A chromosomes appear
chromatids
spindle fiber
nuclear membrane disintegrates
centrosomes
B chromosomes become shorter and thicker
C chromatids are pulled apart
D cell starts to divide
new nuclear membrane
E two daughter cells are formed

1958, he formed the center-left anti-Gaullist Federation of the Left in the 1960s. In 1971 he became leader of the new PS. An electoral union with the Communist Party 1972–77 established the PS as the most popular party in France.

Mitterrand was elected president 1981. His program of reform was hampered by deteriorating economic conditions after 1983. When the Socialists lost their majority March 1986, he was compelled to work with a right-wing prime minister, Jacques Chirac, and grew in popularity. He defeated Chirac to secure a second term in the presidential election May 1988.

Mitylene alternate spelling of ◊Mytilene, Greek city on the island of Lesvos.

Mix Tom (Thomas) 1880–1940. US actor who was

Mitterrand *French Socialist president François Mitterrand, May 1989.*

the most colorful cowboy star of silent films. At their best his films, such as *The Range Riders* 1910 and *King Cowboy* 1928, were fast-moving and full of impressive stunts. His talkies include *Destry Rides Again* 1932 and *The Miracle Rider* 1935, a serial. After his death in an auto accident, his character lived on into the 1940s in a radio serial.

mixture in chemistry, a substance containing two or more compounds that still retain their separate physical and chemical properties. There is no chemical bonding between them and they can be separated from each other by physical means.

Mizoguchi Kenji 1898–1956. Japanese film director whose *Ugetsu Monogatari* 1953 confirmed his international reputation. He also directed *Blood and Soul* 1923, *The Poppies* 1935, and *Street of Shame* 1956.

Mizoram state of NE India
area 8,145 sq mi/21,100 sq km
capital Aizawl
products rice, hand loom weaving
population (1981) 488,000
religion 84% Christian
history made a Union Territory 1972 from the Mizo Hills District of Assam. Rebels carried on a guerrilla war 1966–76, but in 1976 acknowledged Mizoram as an integral part of India. It became a state 1986.

Mix *Film actor Tom Mix in the film* Fighting for Gold *1919. He starred in more than 60 Westerns over 30 years.*

Mobutu *The president of Zaïre.*

ml abbreviation for milliliter.

Mladenov Petar 1936– . Bulgarian Communist politician, secretary general of the Bulgarian Communist Party from Nov 1989, after the resignation of ◊Zhivkov, until Feb 1990. He was elected state president in Apr 1990 but replaced four months later.

mm abbreviation for millimeter.

mmHg abbreviation for ◊millimeter of mercury.

Mmabatho or Sun City capital of Bophuthatswana, South Africa; population (1985) 28,000. It is a casino resort frequented by many white South Africans.

MN abbreviation for ◊Minnesota.

MO abbreviation for ◊Missouri.

moa extinct flightless kiwilike bird, order Dinornithoformes, 19 species of which lived in New Zealand. They varied from 2 to 12 ft/0.5 to 3.5 m, with strong limbs, a long neck, and no wings. The last moa was killed in the 1800s.

The Maoris used them as food, and with the use of European firearms killed them in too large numbers.

Moab ancient country in Jordan east of the southern part of the river Jordan and the Dead Sea. The inhabitants were closely akin to the Hebrews in culture, language, and religion, but were often at war with them, as recorded in the Old Testament. Moab eventually fell to Arab invaders. The Moabite Stone, discovered in 1868 at Dhiban, dates from the 9th century BC and records the rising of Mesha, king of Moab, against Israel.

Mobile industrial city (meatpacking, paper, cement, clothing, chemicals) and only seaport in Alabama; population (1990) 196,278. Founded 1702 by the French a little to the north of the present city, Mobile was capital of the French colony of Louisiana until 1763. It was then British until 1780, and Spanish to 1813.

Möbius August Ferdinand 1790–1868. German mathematician, discoverer of the Möbius strip and considered one of the founders of ◊topology.

Möbius strip structure made by giving a half twist to a flat strip of paper and joining the ends together. It has certain remarkable properties, arising from the fact that it has only one edge and one side. If cut down the center of the strip, instead of two new strips of paper, only one long strip is produced. It was invented by the German mathematician August Möbius.

Mobutu Sese-Seko-Kuku-Ngbeandu-Wa-Za-Banga 1930– . Zaïrean president from 1965. He assumed the presidency by coup, and created a unitary state under his centralized government. He abolished secret voting in elections 1976 in favor of a system of acclamation at mass rallies. His personal wealth is estimated at $3–4 billion, and more money is spent on the presidency than on the entire social-services budget. The harshness of some of his policies and charges of corruption have attracted widespread international criticism. In 1991 opposition leaders forced Mobutu to agree formally to give up some of his powers.

Mobutu Sese Seko Lake lake on the border of Uganda and Zaïre in the Great ◊Rift Valley; area 1,650 sq mi/4,275 sq km. The first European to see it was the British explorer Samuel ◊Baker, who named it Lake Albert after the Prince Consort. It was renamed 1973 by Zaïre's president Mobutu after himself.

Moby-Dick or ***The Whale*** US novel by Herman Melville, published 1851. Its story of the conflict between the monomaniac Captain Ahab and the great white whale explores the mystery and the destructiveness of both man and nature's power.

Moçambique the Portuguese name for ◊Mozambique.

Moche or ***Mochica*** pre-Inca civilization on the coast of Peru AD 100–800. Remains include cities, massive platform tombs (*adobe*), and pottery that details daily and ceremonial life.

In 1988 the burial of one of their warrior-priest rulers was discovered. He was nicknamed the "Great Lord of Sipan," after the village near the site of his pyramid tomb (*huaca*). It contained a priceless treasure hoard, including a gold mask and ear pendants.

mockingbird North American songbird *Mimus polyglottos*, of the mimic thrush family, Mimidae, found in the US and Mexico. About 10 in/25 cm long, it is brownish gray, with white markings on the black wings and tail. It is remarkable for its ability to mimic the songs of other species.

mock orange or ***syringa*** deciduous shrub of the genus *Philadelphus*, of the saxifrage family. They have white, strongly scented flowers, resembling those of the orange. The common mock orange (*P. inodorus*) is native to the S US.

mode in mathematics, the element that appears most frequently in a given group. For example, the mode of the group 0,0,9,9,9,12,87,87 is 9. (Not all groups have modes.)

Model Parliament English parliament set up 1295 by Edward I; it was the first to include representatives from outside the clergy and aristocracy, and was established because Edward needed the support of the whole country against his opponents: Wales, France, and Scotland. His sole aim was to raise money for military purposes, and the parliament did not pass any legislation.

modem (acronym from modulator/demodulator) (also called an "acoustic coupler") device for transmitting data over telephone lines. The modem converts digital signals to analog, and back again. Modems are used for linking remote terminals to central computers and enable computers to communicate with each other anywhere in the world.

Modena city in Emilia, Italy, capital of the province of Modena, 23 mi/37 km NW of Bologna; population (1988) 177,000. It has a 12th-century cathedral, a 17th-century ducal palace, and a university 1683, known for its medical and legal faculties.

moderator in a nuclear reactor, a material such as graphite or heavy water used to reduce the speed of high-energy neutrons. Neutrons produced by nuclear fission are fast-moving and must be slowed to initiate further fission so that nuclear energy continues to be released at a controlled rate.

Slow neutrons are much more likely to cause ◊fission in a uranium-235 nucleus than to be captured in a U-238 (nonfissile uranium) nucleus. By using a moderator, a reactor can thus be made to work with fuel containing only a small proportion of U-235.

Modernism in the arts, a general term used to describe the 20th century's conscious attempt to break with the artistic traditions of the 19th century; it is based on a concern with form and the exploration of technique as opposed to content and narrative.

In the visual arts, direct representationalism gave way to abstraction (see ◊abstract art); in literature, writers experimented with alternatives to orthodox sequential storytelling, such as ◊stream of consciousness; in music, the traditional concept of key was challenged by ◊atonality; and in architecture, ◊Functionalism ousted decorativeness as a central objective. Critics of

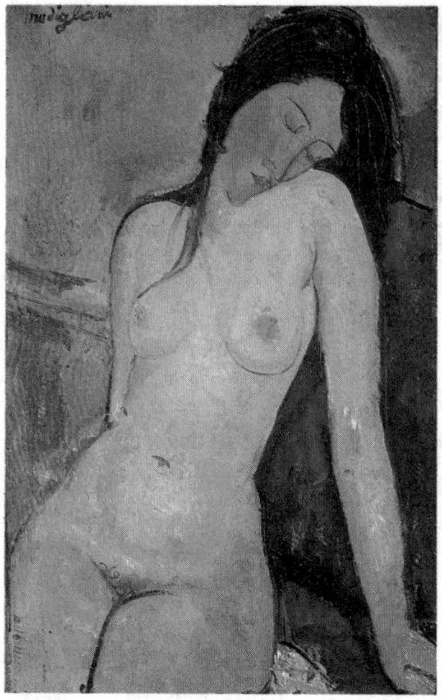

Modigliani *Nude (c. 1916), Courtauld Collection, London.*

Modernism have found in it an austerity that is seen as dehumanizing. Modernism as a movement is followed by ◊Postmodernism.

Modernism in Protestantism, liberal thought that emerged early in the 20th century and attempted to reconsider Christian beliefs in the light of modern scientific theories and historical methods, without abandoning the essential doctrines. It was against modernism that the Fundamentalist movement defined itself. The term was originally used for liberal tendencies in the Roman Catholic Church. Modernism was condemned by Pope Pius X in 1907.

Modern Jazz Quartet US jazz group specializing in group improvisation, formed 1952 (disbanded 1974 and reformed 1981).

Noted for elegance and mastery of form, the quartet has sometimes been criticized for being too "Classical."

Modesto city in central California, on the Tuolumne River, SE of San Francisco, on the fringes of the San Joaquin Valley. It is an agricultural center for wine, apricots, melons, beans, peaches, and livestock; population (1990) 164,730.

Modigliani Amedeo 1884–1920. Italian artist, active in Paris from 1906. He painted and sculpted graceful nudes and portrait studies. His paintings have a distinctive elongated, linear style. The portrait of *Jeanne Hebuterne* 1919 (Guggenheim Museum, New York) is typical.

Modigliani was born in Livorno. He was encouraged to sculpt by Constantin Brancusi, and his series of strictly simplified heads reflects a shared interest in archaic sculptural styles. He led a dissolute life and died of the combined effects of alcoholism, drug addiction, and tuberculosis.

modular course in education, a course, usually leading to a recognized qualification, which is divided into short and often optional units that are assessed as they are completed.

An accumulation of modular credits may then lead to the award of a qualification such as a degree, a BTEC diploma or a GCSE pass. Modular schemes are increasingly popular as a means of allowing students to take a wider range of subjects.

modulation in radio transmission, the intermittent change of frequency, or phase amplitude, of a radio carrier wave, in accordance with the audio characteristics of the speaking voice, music, or other signal being transmitted. See ◊pulse-code modulation, ◊AM (amplitude modulation), and ◊FM (frequency modulation).

module in construction, a standard or unit that governs the form of the rest: for example, Japanese room sizes are traditionally governed by multiples of standard tatami floor mats; today prefabricated buildings are mass-produced in a similar way. The components of a spacecraft are designed in coordination; for example, for the Apollo Moon landings the craft comprised a command module (for working, eating, sleeping), service module (electricity generators, oxygen supplies, maneuvring rocket), and lunar module (to land and return the astronauts).

modulus in mathematics, the positive value of a ◊real number, irrespective of its sign, indicated by a pair of vertical lines. Thus $|3|$ is 3; and $|-5|$ is 5.

For a ◊complex number, the modulus is its distance to the origin when it is plotted on an Argand diagram, and can be calculated (without plotting) by applying ◊Pythagorean theorem. In general, the modulus of the complex number $a + bi$ is $\sqrt{(a^2 + b^2)}$.

modulus a quantity that will yield the same remainders when two given quantities are divided by it. Also, the multiplication factor used to convert a logarithm of one base to a logarithm of another base. Also, another name for ◊absolute value.

Mogadishu or ***Mugdisho*** capital and chief port of Somalia; population (1988) 1,000,000. It is a center for oil refining, food processing, and uranium mining.

It has mosques dating back to the 13th century, and a cathedral built 1925–28.

Mogilev industrial city (tractors, clothing, chemicals, furniture) in the Byelorussian republic, USSR, on the Dneiper, 120 mi/193 km east of Minsk; population (1987) 359,000. It was annexed by Russia from Sweden 1772.

Mogok village in Myanmar (Burma), 71 mi/114 km NNE of Mandalay, known for its ruby and sapphire mines.

Mogul emperors N Indian dynasty 1526–1857, established by ◊Zahir ("Babur"). Muslim descendants of Tamerlane, the 14th-century Mongol leader, they ruled until the last Mogul emperor was dethroned and exiled by the British in 1857; they included ◊Akbar, ◊Aurangzeb, and ◊Shah Jehan.

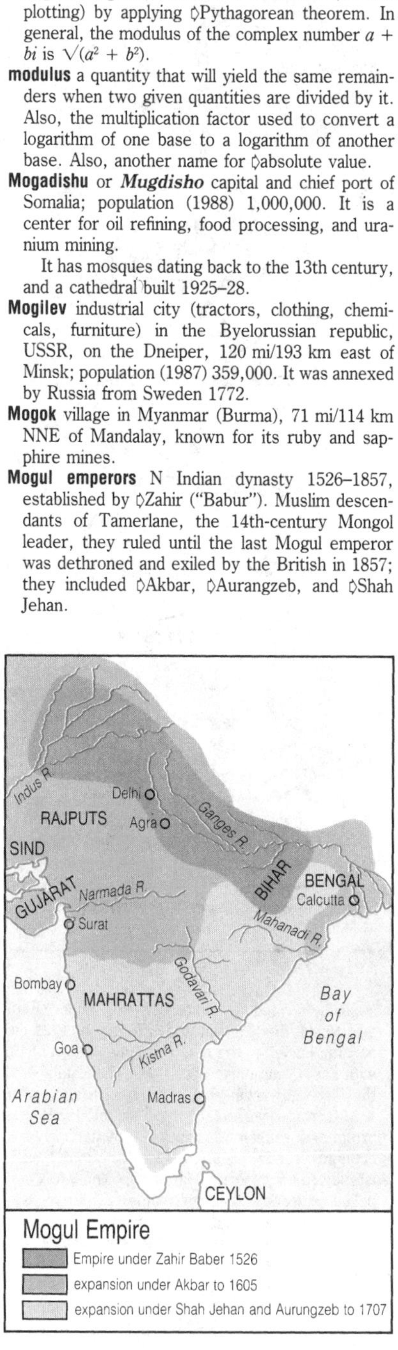
Indus R.
Delhi
RAJPUTS
Agra
Ganges R.
SIND
BIHAR
BENGAL
Calcutta
GUJARAT
Narmada R.
Mahanadi R.
Surat
Godavari R.
Bombay
MAHRATTAS
Bay of Bengal
Goa
Kistna R.
Arabian Sea
Madras
CEYLON
Mogul Empire
Empire under Zahir Baber 1526
expansion under Akbar to 1605
expansion under Shah Jehan and Aurungzeb to 1707

Mohács, Battle of Austro-Hungarian defeat of the Turks 1687, which effectively marked the end of Turkish expansion into Europe. It is also the site of a Turkish victory in 1526. Mohács is now a river port on the Danube in Hungary.

mohair hair of the Angora goat. The fine, white, lustrous fiber is manufactured into fabric. Commercial mohair is now obtained from cross-bred animals, pure-bred supplies being insufficient to demand.

Mohamad Mahathir bin 1925– . Prime minister of Malaysia from 1981 and leader of the United Malays' National Organization (UMNO). His "look east" economic policy emulates Japanese industrialization.

Mahathir bin Mohamad was elected to the House of Representatives 1964 and gained the support of the dominant UMNO's radical youth wing as an advocate of economic help to *bumiputras* (ethnic Malays) and as a proponent of a more Islamic social policy. Dr Mahathir held a number of ministerial posts from 1974 before being appointed prime minister and UMNO leader in 1981. He was reelected 1986, but has alienated sections of UMNO by his authoritarian leadership.

Mohammed or ***Muhammed, Mahomet*** c. 570–632. Founder of Islam, born in Mecca on the Arabian peninsula. In about 616 he claimed to be a prophet and that the *Koran* was revealed to him by God (it was later written down by his followers). He fled from persecution to the town now known as Medina in 622: the flight, Hegira, marks the beginning of the Islamic era.

Originally a shepherd and caravan conductor, he found leisure for meditation by his marriage with a wealthy widow in 595, and received his first revelation in 610. After some years of secret teaching, he openly declared himself the prophet of God, and, as the number of his followers increased, he was forced to flee to Medina. After the battle of Badr in 623, he was continuously victorious, entering Mecca as the recognized prophet of Arabia 630. The succession was troubled.

Mohammedanism misnomer for ◊Islam, the religion founded by Mohammed.

Mohave Desert arid region in S California; part of the Great Basin; area 15,000 sq mi/ 38,500 sq km. The US military has appropriated thousands of acres for bombing ranges and test stations, including Edwards Air Force Base, landing place for space shuttles.

Mohawk member of a North American Indian people, part of the ◊Iroquois confederation, who lived in the Mohawk Valley, New York, and now live on reservations in Ontario, Québec, and New York State, as well as among the general population.

Mohenjo Daro site of a city about 2500–1600 BC on the lower Indus river, Pakistan, where excavations from the 1920s have revealed the ◊Indus Valley civilization. The most striking artistic remains are soapstone seals of elephants and snakes. ◊Harappa in India was built by the same civilization.

Mohican and Mohegan or ***Mahican*** two closely related North American Indian peoples, speaking an Algonquian language, who formerly occupied the Hudson Valley and parts of Connecticut, respectively. The novelist James Fenimore ◊Cooper confused the two peoples in his fictional account *The Last of the Mohicans* 1826.

Mohole US project for drilling a hole through the Earth's crust, so named after the ◊Mohorovičić discontinuity that marks the transition from crust to mantle. Initial tests were made in the Pacific in 1961, but the project was subsequently abandoned.

The cores that were brought up illuminated the geologic history of the Earth and aided the development of geophysics.

Moholy-Nagy Laszlo 1895–1946. US photographer, born in Hungary. He lived in Germany 1923–29, where he was a member of the Bauhaus school, and fled from the Nazis in 1935. Through the publication of his illuminating theories and practical experiments, he had great influence on 20th-century photography and design.

Moi *Kenyan politician Daniel arap Moi became president in 1978 after the death of Jomo Kenyatta.*

Mohorovičić discontinuity also ***Moho*** or ***M-discontinuity*** boundary that separates the Earth's crust and mantle, marked by a rapid increase in the speed of earthquake waves. It follows the variations in the thickness of the crust and is found approximately 20 mi/32 km below the continents and about 6 mi/10 km below the oceans. It is named after the Yugoslav geophysicist Andrija Mohorovičić (1857–1936) who suspected its presence after analyzing seismic waves from the Kulpa Valley earthquake 1909.

Mohs' scale

Number	Defining mineral	Other substances compared
1	talc	
2	gypsum	fingernail (2½)
3	calcite	copper coin (3½)
4	fluorite	
5	apatite	steel blade (5½)
6	orthoclase	glass (5¾)
7	quartz	steel file (7)
8	topaz	
9	corundum	
10	diamond	

The scale is not regular; diamond, at number 10 the hardest natural substance, is 90 times harder in absolute terms than corundum, at number 9.

Mohs Friedrich 1773–1839. German mineralogist, who in 1812 devised Mohs' scale of minerals, classified in order of relative hardness.

Mohs' scale scale of hardness for minerals (in ascending order): 1 talc; 2 gypsum; 3 calcite; 4 fluorite; 5 apatite; 6 orthoclase; 7 quartz; 8 topaz; 9 corundum; 10 diamond.

The scale is useful in mineral identification because any mineral will scratch any other mineral lower on the scale than itself, and similarly it will be scratched by any other mineral higher on the scale.

Moi Daniel arap 1924– . Kenyan politician, president from 1978. Originally a teacher, he became minister of home affairs in 1964, vice-president in 1967, and succeeded Jomo Kenyatta as president.

Moissan Henri 1852–1907. French chemist. For his preparation of pure fluorine in 1886, Moissan was awarded the 1906 Nobel Prize for Chemistry. He also attempted to create artificial diamonds by rapidly cooling carbon heated to high temperatures. His claims of success were treated with suspicion.

Mokha or ***Mocha*** seaport of N Yemen near the mouth of the Red Sea, once famed for its coffee exports. It has declined since the USSR built a new port near Hodeida. Population about 8,000.

moksha (Sanskrit "liberation") in Hinduism, liberation from the cycle of reincarnation and from the illusion of ◊maya. In Buddhism, ◊enlightenment.

molar one of the large teeth found toward the back of the mammalian mouth. The structure of the jaw, and the relation of the muscles, allows a massive force to be applied to molars. In herbivores the molars are flat with sharp ridges of enamel and are used for grinding, an adaptation to a diet of tough plant material. Carnivores have sharp powerful molars called carnassials, which are adapted for cutting meat.

Moldavia

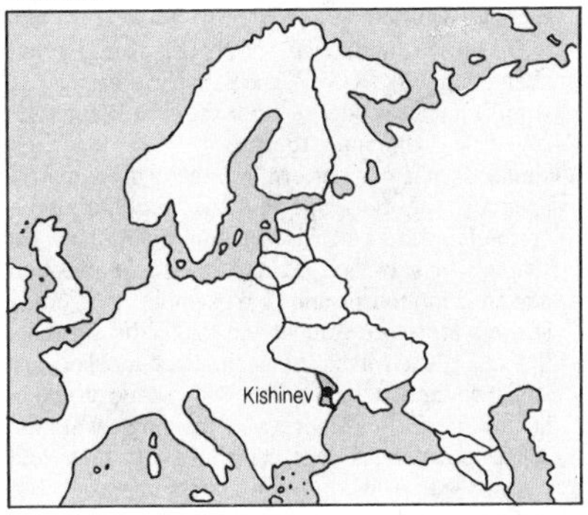
Kishinev

molar volume volume occupied by one ◊mole (the molecular mass in grams) of any gas at standard temperature and pressure, equal to 2.24136×10^{-2} m^3.

molasses thick, usually dark, syrup obtained during the refining of sugar (either cane or beet) or made from varieties of sorghum. Fermented sugar-cane molasses produces rum; fermented beet-sugar molasses yields ethyl alcohol. Unsulfured raw molasses, called Blackstrap, is a nutritious food, containing in 1 tablespoon 585 mg of potassium.

mold mainly saprophytic ◊fungi living on foodstuffs and other organic matter, a few being parasitic on plants, animals, or each other. many are of medical or industrial importance, for example penicillin.

Mold market town in Clwyd, Wales, on the river Alyn; population about 8,500. It is the administrative headquarters of Clywd and has two theaters.

Moldavia former principality in Eastern Europe, on the river Danube, occupying an area divided today between the Soviet republic of Moldavia and Romania. It was independent between the 14th and 16th centuries, when it became part of the Ottoman Empire. In 1940 the E part, Bessarabia, became part of the USSR, whereas the W part remained in Romania.

Moldavia or ***Moldova*** republic of the USSR (1940–91), voted for its independence 1991
area 13,012 sq mi/33,700 sq km
capital Kishinev
features ◊Black Earth region
products wine, tobacco, canned goods
population (1987) 4,185,000; Moldavian (a branch of the Romanian people) 64%, Ukrainian 14%, Russian 13%, Gagauzi 4%, Jewish 2%
language Moldavian, allied to Romanian
religion Russian Orthodox
recent history formed from part of the former Moldavian republic of the USSR (within Ukraine) and areas of Bessarabia ceded by Romania 1940, except the area bordering the Black Sea (added to Ukraine). In 1988 a popular front, the Democratic Movement for Perestroika, was formed, campaigning for accelerated political reform. The Moldavian language was granted official status 1989, triggering clashes between ethnic Russians and Moldavians in Kishinev. In June 1990 the Moldavian parliament declared sovereignty.

The nationalist Moldavian Popular Front progressively ousted the communists from power, forcing a change to Moldavian as the official language in 1989, and taking charge of the government in 1990. In April 1991 there was a split within the republic's communist party, and the Independent Communist Party of Moldavia was formed by radicals on a democratic platform; it was to have no relations with the Communist Party of the Soviet Union (CPSU). In May 1991 the Moldavian Supreme Soviet passed a resolution renaming the country the Moldavian republic.

On Aug 27, in the wake of the failed anti-Gorbachev coup in the USSR, the republic's parliament voted for independence from the USSR and outlawed the Communist Party.

molding the use of a pattern, hollow form, or matrix to give a specific shape to something in a plastic or molten state. Molds are commonly used for shaping plastics, clays, and glass. In injection molding, molten plastic, for example, is injected into a water-cooled mold and takes the shape of the mold when it solidifies. In blow molding, air is blown into a blob of molten plastic inside a hollow mold. In compression molding, synthetic resin powder is simultaneously heated and pressed into a mold. When metals are used, the process is called ◊casting.

mole burrowing insectivore of the family Talpidae. Moles grow to 7 in/18 cm, and have acute senses of hearing, smell, and touch, but poor vision. They have shovellike, clawed front feet for burrowing, and eat insects, grubs, and worms. Some members of the family are aquatic, such as the Russian desman *Desmana moschata* and the North American star-nosed mole *Condylura cristata*.

The eastern American mole *Scalopus aquaticus*, about 6 in/15 cm long, has blackish to coppery soft, dense fur and a long snout. Its eyes and ears are not visible externally. It excavates tunnels just under the surface, leaving raised ridges, in search of earthworms and insect larvae.

mole in construction, a mechanical device for boring horizontal holes underground without the need for digging trenches. It is used for laying pipes and cables.

mole person working subversively within an organization. The term has come to be used broadly for someone who gives out ("leaks") secret information in the public interest; it originally meant a person who spends several years working for a government department or a company with the intention of passing secrets to an enemy or a rival.

mole SI unit (abbreviation mol) of the amount of a substance. One mole of an element that exists as single atoms weighs as many grams as its ◊atomic number (so one mole of carbon weighs 12 g), and it contains 6.022137×10^{23} atoms, which is ◊Avogadro's number.

One mole of a substance is defined as the amount of that substance that contains as many elementary entities (atoms, molecules, and so on) as there are atoms in 12 g of the ◊isotope carbon-12.

molecular biology the study of the molecular basis of life, including the biochemistry of molecules such as DNA, RNA, and proteins, and the molecular structure and function of the various parts of living cells.

molecular clock the use of rates of ◊mutation in genetic material to calculate the length of time elapsed since two related species diverged from each other during evolution. The method can be based on comparisons of the DNA or of widely occurring proteins, such as hemoglobin.

Since mutations are thought to occur at a constant rate, the length of time that must have elapsed in order to produce the difference between two species can be estimated. This information can be compared with the evidence obtained from paleontology to reconstruct evolutionary events.

molecule the smallest unit of an ◊element or ◊compound that can exist and still retain the characteristics of the element or compound. A molecule of an element consists of one or more like ◊atoms; a molecule of a compound consists of two or more different atoms bonded together. Molecules vary in size and complexity from the hydrogen molecule (H_2) to the large ◊macromolecules found in polymers. They are held together by electrovalent bonds, in which the atoms gain or lose electrons to form ◊ions, or covalent bonds, where electrons from each atom are shared in a new molecular orbital.

The symbolic representation of a molecule is known as its formula. The presence of more than one atom is denoted by a subscript figure—for example, one molecule of the compound water is shown as H_2O, having two atoms of hydrogen and one atom of oxygen.

molecule

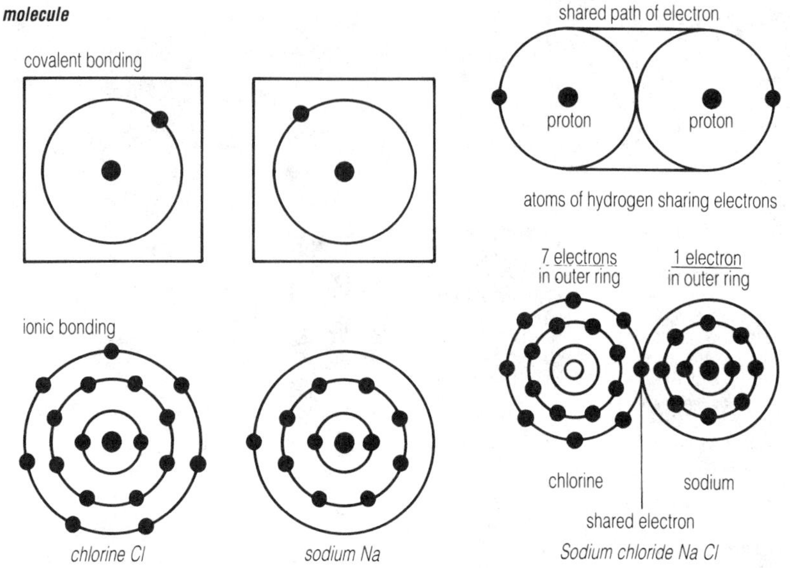
covalent bonding
shared path of electron
proton
proton
atoms of hydrogen sharing electrons
ionic bonding
7 electrons in outer ring
1 electron in outer ring
chlorine
sodium
shared electron
chlorine Cl
sodium Na
Sodium chloride Na Cl

Molière pen name of Jean Baptiste Poquelin 1622–1673. French satirical playwright from whose work modern French comedy developed. One of the founders of the Illustre Théâtre 1643, he was later its leading actor. In 1655 he wrote his first play, *L'Etourdi*, followed by *Les Précieuses ridicules* 1659. His satires include *L'École des femmes* 1662, ◊*Le Misanthrope* 1666, *Le Bourgeois gentilhomme* 1670, and *Le Malade imaginaire* 1673.

Other satiric plays include *Tartuffe* 1664 (banned until 1697 for attacking the hypocrisy of the clergy), *Le Médecin malgré lui* 1666, and *Les Femmes Savantes* 1672. Molière's comedies, based on the exposure of hypocrisy and cant, made him vulnerable to many attacks (from which he was protected by Louis XIV) and marked a new departure in the French theater away from reliance on Classical Greek themes.

Moline city in NW Illinois, on the Mississippi River, W of Chicago. Manufactures include farm implements, furniture, and metal products; population (1990) 43,202.

Molinos Miguel de 1640–1697. Spanish mystic and Roman Catholic priest. He settled in Rome and wrote several devotional works in Italian, including the *Guida spirituale/Spiritual Guide* 1675, which aroused the hostility of the Jesuits. In 1687 he was sentenced to life imprisonment. His doctrine is known as ◊quietism.

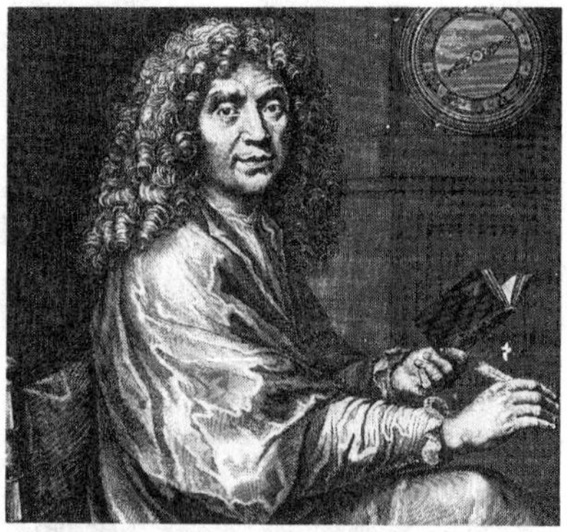

Molière *Molière died a day after performing the title role in his* Le Médecin malgré lui.

Molise mainly agricultural region of S central Italy, comprising the provinces of Campobasso and Isernia; area 1,698 sq mi/4,400 sq km; population (1988) 335,000. Its capital is Campobasso.

mollusk or ***mollusc*** any invertebrate of the phylum Mollusca. The majority of mollusks are marine animals, but some inhabit fresh water, and a few are terrestrial. They include bivalves, snails, slugs, and squids. The body is soft, limbless, and coldblooded. There is no internal skeleton, but most species have a hard shell covering the body.

Mollusks vary in diet, the carnivorous species feeding chiefly upon other members of the phylum. Some are vegetarian. Reproduction is by means of eggs and is sexual; many species are hermaphrodite.

mollusks: classification

Phylum Mollusca	
Class Monoplacophora	primitive marine forms, including Neopilina (2 species)
Class Amphineura	(1,150 species)
1 Aplacophora	wormlike marine forms
2 Polyplacophora	chitons, coat-of-mail shells
Class Gastropoda	snaillike mollusks, with single or no shell (9,000 species)
1 Prosobranchia	limpets, winkles, whelks
2 Opisthobranchia	seaslugs
3 Pulmonata	land and freshwater snails, slugs
Class Scaphopoda	tusk shells, marine burrowers (350 species)
Class Bivalvia	mollusks with a double (two-valved) shell (15,000 species); mussels, oysters, clams, cockles, scallops, tellins, razor shells, shipworms
Class Cephalopoda	mollusks with shell generally reduced, arms to capture prey, beaklike mouth, and well-developed eyes, comparable to those of vertebrates; body bilaterally symmetrical and nervous system well developed (750 species); squids, cuttlefish, octopuses, pearly nautilus, argonaut

The shells of mollusks take a variety of forms: univalve (snail), bivalve (clam), chambered (nautilus), and many other variations. In some cases (for example cuttlefish and squid) the shell is internal. Every mollusk has a fold of skin, the mantle, which covers the whole body or the back only, and secretes the calcareous substance forming the shell. The lower ventral surface forms the locomotory organ, or foot.

Molly Maguires, the in US history, a secret Irish coalminers' organization in the 1870s that staged strikes and used violence against coal-company officials and property in the anthracite fields of Pennsylvania, prefiguring a long period of turbulence in industrial relations. The movement was infiltrated by ◊Pinkerton agents (detectives), and in 1876 trials led to convictions and executions.

Molnár Ferenc 1878–1952. Hungarian novelist and playwright. His play *Liliom* 1909 is a study of a circus barker (a person who calls out to attract the attention of members of the public), adapted as the musical *Carousel*.

Moloch or ***Molech*** in the Old Testament, a Phoenician deity worshiped in Jerusalem in the 7th century BC, to whom live children were sacrificed by fire.

Molokai mountainous island of Hawaii State, SE of Oahu

area 259 sq mi/673 sq km

features Kamakou 4,960 ft/1,512 m is the highest peak

history the island was the site of a leper colony organized 1873–89 by Belgian missionary Joseph De Veuster (Father ◊Damien).

Molotov former name (1940–62) for the port of ◊Perm in the USSR.

Molotov Vyacheslav Mikhailovich. Assumed name of V M Skriabin 1890–1986. Soviet communist politician. He was chair of the Council of People's Commissars (prime minister) 1930–41 and foreign minister 1939–49 and 1953–56. He negotiated the 1939 nonaggression treaty with Germany (the ◊Hitler–Stalin pact), and, after the German invasion 1941, the Soviet partnership with the Allies. His postwar stance prolonged the Cold War and in 1957 he was expelled from the government for Stalinist activities.

Molotov cocktail or ***gasoline bomb*** home-made weapon consisting of a bottle filled with gasoline, plugged with a rag as a wick, ignited, and thrown as a grenade. Resistance groups during World War II named them after the Soviet foreign minister Molotov.

molting the periodic shedding of the hair or fur of mammals, feathers of birds, or skin of reptiles. In mammals and birds, molting is usually seasonal and is triggered by changes of day length.

The term is also often applied to the shedding of the ◊exoskeleton of arthropods, but this is more correctly called ◊ecdysis.

Moltke Helmuth Carl Bernhard, Count von 1800–1891. Prussian general. He became chief of the general staff 1857, and was responsible for the Prussian strategy in the wars with Denmark 1863–64, Austria 1866, and France 1870–71.

Moltke Helmuth Johannes Ludwig von 1848–1916. German general (nephew of Count von Moltke, the Prussian general), chief of the German general staff 1906–14. His use of General Alfred von Schlieffen's (1833–1913) plan for a rapid victory on two fronts failed and he was relieved of command after the defeat at the Marne.

Moluccas another name for ◊Maluku, Indonesia.

molybdenite molybdenum sulfide, MoS_2, the chief ore mineral of molybdenum. It possesses a hexagonal crystal structure similar to graphite, has a blue metallic luster, and is very soft (1–1.5 on Mohs' scale). The largest source of molybdenite is a deposit in Colorado.

molybdenum heavy, hard, lustrous, silver-white, metallic element, symbol Mo, atomic number 42, atomic weight 95.94. The chief ore is the mineral molybdenite. The element is highly resistant to heat and conducts electricity easily. It is used in alloys, often to harden steels. It is a necessary trace element in human nutrition. It was named in 1781 by Swedish chemist Karl Scheele, after its isolation by P J Hjelm (1746–1813), for its resemblance to lead ore from Greek *malybdos*, "lead."

Mombasa industrial port (oil refining, cement) in Kenya (serving also Uganda and Tanzania), built on Mombasa Island and adjacent mainland; population (1984) 481,000.

moment of a force in physics, measure of the turning effect, or torque, produced by a force acting on a body. It is equal to the product of the force and the perpendicular distance from its line of action to the point, or pivot, about which the body will turn. Its unit is the newton meter.

moment of inertia in physics, the sum of all the point masses of a rotating object multiplied by the squares of their respective distances from the axis of rotation. It is analogous to the ◊mass of a stationary object or one moving in a straight line.

In linear dynamics, Newton's second law of motion states that the force F on a moving object equals the products of its mass m and acceleration a ($F = ma$); the analagous equation in rotational dynamics is $T = IA$, where T is the torque (the turning effect of a force) that causes an angular acceleration A and I is the moment of inertia. For a given object, I depends on its shape and the position of its axis of rotation.

momentum in physics, the product of the mass of a body and its linear velocity. Angular momentum (of a body in rotational motion) is the product of its moment of inertia and its angular velocity. The momentum of a body does not change unless it is acted on by an external force.

The law of conservation of momentum is one of the fundamental concepts of Classical physics. It states that the total momentum of all bodies in a closed system is constant and unaffected by processes occurring within the system.

An orbiting body possesses angular momentum, this being the result of the combined effects of its orbital velocity, mass, and distance from the primary. Angular momentum is also a property of rotating bodies. The angular momentum of an object of mass m traveling at a velocity v in a circular orbit of radius R is expressed as mvR. Angular momentum is conserved, and should any of the values alter (such as the radius of orbit), the other values (such as the velocity) will compensate to preserve the value of angular momentum, and that lost by one component is passed to another. An example is a rotating gas cloud: any large contracting gas cloud undergoes an increase in its axial rotation velocity to conserve angular momentum. Another example is a spinning ice skater. With outstretched arms, the skater spins only slowly; the rate of spin increases dramatically when the arms are pulled in, redistributing the mass of the skater.

Momoh Joseph Saidu 1937– . Sierra Leone soldier and politician, president from 1985. An army officer who became commander 1983, with the rank of major-general, he succeeded Siaka Stevens as president when he retired; Momoh was endorsed by Sierra Leone's one political party, the All-People's Congress. He has dissociated himself from the policies of his predecessor, pledging to fight corruption and improve the economy.

Mona Latin name for ◊Anglesey, island in Wales.

Monaco small sovereign state forming an enclave in southern France, with the Mediterranean to the south.

government Under the 1911 constitution, modified 1917 and largely rewritten 1962, Monaco is a hereditary principality, but an earlier concept of endowing the prince with a divine right to rule has been deleted. Legislative power is shared between the prince and a single-chamber national council, with 18 members elected by universal suffrage for a five-year term. Executive power is formally vested in the prince but in practice is exercised by a four-member council of government.

There are no political parties as such, but the 1983 and 1988 National Council elections were contested by the National and Democratic Union (UND), formed in 1962, which supports the ruling monarch, Prince Rainier, and captured all the Council's seats. A rival organization, the Democratic and Socialist Union, also contested the 1983 election but has since been dormant.

history Formerly part of the Roman empire, Monaco became a Genoese possession in the 12th century and has been ruled since 1297 by the Grimaldi family. It was a Spanish protectorate 1542–1641, then came under French protection and during the French revolution was annexed by France. The ruling family was imprisoned (one was guillotined) but regained power after the 1814 ◊Treaty of Paris. In 1815 Monaco became a protectorate of Sardinia but reverted to French protection in 1861. In 1940 it was occupied by Italy and in 1943 by Germany but was liberated in 1945.

Monaco
Principality of

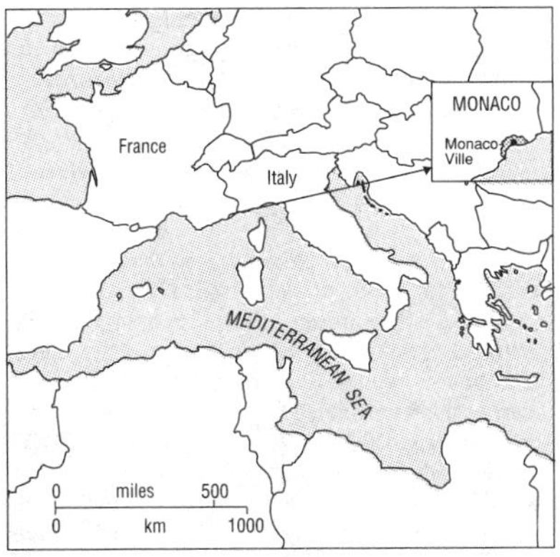
MONACO
Monaco Ville
France
Italy
MEDITERRANEAN SEA
0 miles 500
0 km 1000

area 0.75 sq mi/1.95 sq km
capital Monaco-Ville
cities Monte Carlo, La Condamine; heliport Fontvieille
physical steep and rugged; surrounded landward by French territory, being expanded by filling in the sea
features aquarium and oceanographic center; Monte Carlo film festival, motor races, and casinos; second smallest state in world
head of state Prince Rainier III from 1949
head of government Jean Ausseil from 1986
political system constitutional monarchy under French protectorate
political parties National and Democratic Union; Democratic Union Movement; Monaco Action; Monegasque Socialist Party
exports some light industry; economy dependent on tourism and gambling
currency French franc
population (1989) 29,000; growth rate –0.5% p.a.
language French (official), English, Italian
religion Roman Catholic 95%
literacy 99% (1985)
chronology
1861 Became an independent state under French protection.
1918 France given a veto over succession to the throne.
1949 Prince Rainier III ascended the throne.
1956 Prince Rainier married US actress Grace Kelly; male heir born 1958.
1959 Constitution of 1911 suspended.
1962 New constitution adopted.

Agreements between France and Monaco state that Monaco will be incorporated into France if the reigning prince dies without a male heir. France is closely involved in the government of Monaco, providing a civil servant, of the prince's choosing, to head its Council of Government.

monad philosophical term deriving from the work of Gottfried Leibniz, suggesting a soul or metaphysical unit that has a self-contained life. The monads are independent of each other but coordinated by a "preestablished harmony."

Monadnock a mountain in New Hampshire, 3,186 ft/1,063 m high. The term Monadnock is also used to mean any isolated hill or mountain.

Monaghan (Irish *Mhuineachain*) county of the NE Republic of Ireland, province of Ulster; area 498 sq mi/1,290 sq km; population (1986) 52,000. The county town is Monaghan. The county is low and rolling, and includes the rivers Finn and Blackwater. Products include cereals, linen, potatoes, and cattle.

Monarchianism a form of belief in the Christian Trinity that emphasizes the undifferentiated unity of God. It was common in the early 3rd century.

monasticism devotion to religious life under vows of poverty, chastity, and obedience, known to Judaism (for example ◊Essenes), Buddhism, and other religions, before Christianity. In Islam, the Sufis formed monastic orders from the 12th century.

history, Christian

3rd century The institution of monasticism is ascribed to St Anthony in Egypt, but the inauguration of communal life is attributed to his disciple, St Pachomius. Possibly communities for women (nuns, from Latin *nonna* "elderly woman") preceded those for men, and most male orders have their female counterpart.

6th century Full adaptation to conditions in W Europe was made by St Benedict, his "rule" being generally adopted.

10th century In 910 the founding of Cluny began the system of orders whereby each monastery was subordinated to a central institution.

11th century During the Middle Ages other forms of monasticism were established, including the hermitlike Carthusians 1084 and the Augustinian Canons, who were clerics organized under a monastic system.

12th century The military Knights Templar and Knights Hospitallers of St John were formed.

13th century The four mendicant orders of friars—Franciscans, Dominicans, Carmelites, and Augustinians—were established, and monasticism reached the height of its influence.

16th century Already weakened by the wars, plagues, and schisms of the 14th and 15th centuries, monasticism was severely affected by the Reformation. A revival came with the foundation of orders dedicated to particular missions, such as the great weapon of the Counter-Reformation, the Society of Jesus (Jesuits) 1540.

17th century The Trappist Cistercians were founded at La Trappe.

18th century The French Revolution exercised a repressive influence.

20th century Since the Vatican II Council, the trend in many orders is toward modern dress and involvement outside the monastery, despite disapproval by Pope John Paul II.

Monastir Turkish name for the town of ◊Bitolj in S Yugoslavia.

Monastir resort town on the Mediterranean coast of Tunisia, 11 mi/18 km S of Sousse. Birthplace of the former president, Habib Bourguiba, and summer residence of the president of Tunisia.

monazite a mineral, $(Ce,La,Y,Th)PO_4$, yellow to red, valued as a source of ◊lanthanides or rare earths, including cerium and europium; generally found in placer deposit (alluvial) sands.

Mönchengladbach industrial city (textiles, machinery, paper) in North Rhine-Westphalia, Federal Republic of Germany, on the river Niers near Düsseldorf; population (1988) 255,000. It is the NATO headquarters for N Europe.

Monet *French Impressionist painter Claude Monet is noted for his series of paintings of water lilies, as in* The Water Lily Pond *1899.*

Mondale Walter "Fritz" 1928– . US Democrat politician, unsuccessful presidential candidate 1984. He was a senator 1964–76 for his home state of Minnesota, and vice-president to Jimmy Carter 1977–81. After losing the 1984 presidential election to Reagan, Mondale retired from national politics to resume his law practice.

Monday the second day of the week, following Sunday. The name derives from its having been considered sacred to the Moon (Old English *Mōnandaeg* and Latin *Lunae dies*).

Mondrian Piet (Pieter Mondriaan) 1872–1944. Dutch painter, a pioneer of abstract art. He lived in Paris 1919–38, then in London, and from 1940 in New York. He was a founder member of the de ◊Stijl movement and chief exponent of Neo-Plasticism, a rigorous abstract style based on the use of simple geometric forms and pure colors.

In Paris from 1911 Mondrian was inspired by Cubism. He returned to the Netherlands during World War I, where he used a series of still lifes and landscapes to refine his ideas, ultimately developing a pure abstract style. His esthetic theories were published in the journal *De Stijl* from 1917, in *Neoplasticism* 1920, and in the essay "Plastic Art and Pure Plastic Art" 1937. From the New York period his *Broadway Boogie-Woogie* 1942–43 (Museum of Modern Art, New York) reflects a late preoccupation with jazz rhythms.

Monet Claude 1840–1926. French painter, a pioneer of Impressionism and a lifelong exponent of its ideals; his painting *Impression, Sunrise* 1872 (Musée Marmottan, Paris) gave the movement its name. In the 1870s he began painting the same subjects at different times of day to explore the effects of light on color and form; the *Haystacks* and *Rouen Cathedral* series followed in the 1890s, and from 1899 he painted a series of *Water Lilies* in the garden of his house at Giverny, Normandy (now a museum).

Monet was born in Paris. In Le Havre in the 1850s he was encouraged to paint by Boudin, and met Jongkind, whose light and airy seascapes made a lasting impact. From 1862 in Paris he shared a studio with Renoir, Sisley, and others, and they showed their work together at the First Impressionist Exhibition 1874.

Monet's work from the 1860s onward concentrates on the evanescent effects of light and color, and from the late 1860s he painted in the classic Impressionist manner, juxtaposing brushstrokes of color to create an effect of dappled, glowing light. His first series showed the Gare St Lazare in Paris with its puffing steam engines. Views of the water garden in Giverny gradually developed into large, increasingly abstract color compositions. Between 1900 and 1909 he produced a series of water-lily mural panels for the French state (the Orangerie, Paris).

monetarism an economic policy, advocated by the economist Milton ◊Friedman and others, that proposes control of a country's money supply to keep it in step with the country's ability to produce goods, with the aim of curbing inflation. Cutting government spending is advocated, and the long-term aim is to return as much of the economy as possible to the private sector, allegedly in the interests of efficiency.

Central banks—in the US, the ◊Federal Reserve Bank—use the ◊discount rate and other tools to restrict or expand the supply of money to the economy. Unemployment may result from some efforts to withdraw government "safety nets," but monetarists claim it is less than eventually occurs if the methods of ◊Keynesian economics are adopted. Monetarist policies were widely adopted in the 1980s in response to the inflation problems caused by spiraling oil prices in 1979. See also ◊deregulation, ◊privatization.

monetary policy an economic policy that sees control of both the money supply and liquidity as important determinants of the level of employment and inflation. By influencing interest rates, the policy aims to ease balance of payment problems.

money any common medium of exchange acceptable in payment for goods or services or for the settlement of debts; legal tender. Money is usually coinage (invented by the Chinese in the second millennium BC) and paper notes (used by the Chinese from about AD 800). Recent developments such as the check and credit card fulfill many of the traditional functions of money.

money market an institution that deals in gold, foreign exchange, and securities in the short term. Long-term transactions are dealt with on the capital market. There is no physical marketplace, and many deals are made by telephone or telex.

money supply the quantity of money present in an economy at a given moment. Monetarists hold that a rapid increase in money supply inevitably provokes an increase in the rate of inflation.

The money-supply classification M-1 consists of currency and demand deposits. Since the ◊Federal Reserve holds some currency, only circulating currency is included in M-1. Bank deposits, payable on demand, constitute as much as three-fourths of the money supply. Some economists consider near-money, such as time deposits or liquid assets, as part of M-1. The government can expand or restrict M-1 through ◊monetary policy.

Mongol member of any of the various Mongol (or Mongolian) ethnic groups of Central Asia. Mongols live in the Mongolian People's Republic, the USSR, Inner Mongolia, Tibet, and Nepal. The Mongol language belongs to the Altaic family; some groups of Mongol descent speak languages in the Sino-Tibetan family however.

The Mongols are primarily pastoral nomads, herding sheep, horses, cattle, and camels. Traditionally the Mongols moved with their animals in summer to the higher pastures, returning in winter to the lower steppes. The government of the Mongolian People's Republic now encourages more sedentary forms of pastoralism, and winter quarters are often more permanent. About 60% of the Mongolian population live in felt-covered domed tents known as *gers*. Many Mongols are Buddhist, although the Mongolian government has been communist since 1924. During the 13th century AD, under Genghis Khan, the Mongols conquered Central Asia and attacked Eastern Europe. Kublai Khan, the grandson of Genghis Khan, was the first emperor of the Yuan Dynasty (1279–1368) in China.

Mongol Empire empire established by Genghis Khan, who extended his domains from Russia to N China and became khan of the Mongol tribes in 1206. His grandson Kublai Khan conquered China and used foreigners such as Marco Polo as well as subjects to administer his empire. The Mongols lost China 1367 and suffered defeats in

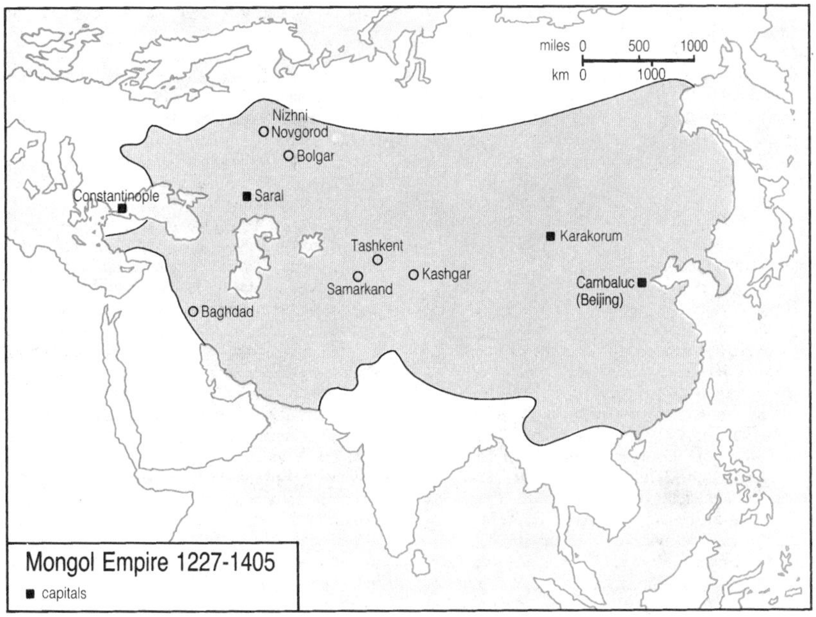
miles 0 500 1000
km 0 1000
Nizhni Novgorod
Bolgar
Constantinople
Sarai
Tashkent
Karakorum
Samarkand
Kashgar
Cambaluc (Beijing)
Baghdad

Mongol Empire 1227-1405
■ capitals

the West 1380; the empire broke up soon afterwards.

Mongolia country in E Central Asia, bounded N by the USSR and S by China.

government Under recent constitutional changes, the 430-seat Great People's Hural, formerly the dominant legislative body within the country, has been transformed into an "upper house" with reduced powers. A new 53-seat Little Hural has been created as a standing legislature with control over the budget and day-to-day running of the country. Mongolia's controlling force and sole political party is the Mongol People's Revolutionary Party (MPRP), headed by Gombojavyn Ochirbat. This is organized on Communist lines and has a Congress, Central Committee, Secretariat, and Politburo, all serving five-year terms.

history Inhabited by nomads from N Asia, the area was united under Genghis Khan in 1206 and by the end of the 13th century was part of the Mongol empire that stretched across Asia. From 1689 it was part of China.

After the revolution of 1911–12 Mongolia became autonomous under the Lamaist religious ruler Jebsten Damba Khutukhtu (the Living Buddha). From 1915 it increasingly fell under Chinese influence and not until 1921, with the support of the USSR, were Mongolian nationalists able to cast off the Chinese yoke. In 1924 it adopted the Soviet system of government and, after proclaiming itself a people's republic, launched a program of "defeudalization," involving the destruction of Lamaism. In 1931, when two provinces revolted against the Communist Party, religious buildings were destroyed and mass executions carried out on the Soviet dictator Stalin's orders. An armed uprising by antigovernment forces in 1932 was suppressed with Soviet assistance. China recognized its independence in 1946, but relations deteriorated as Mongolia took the Soviet side in the Sino-Soviet dispute. In 1966 Mongolia signed a 20-year friendship, cooperation and mutual-assistance pact with the USSR, and some 60,000 Soviet troops based in the country caused China to see it as a Russian colony.

Isolated from the outside world during the 1970s, under the leadership of Yumjaagiyn Tsedenbal—the nation's dominant figure since 1958—Mongolia underwent great economic change as urban industries developed and settled agriculture on the collective system spread, with new areas being brought under cultivation. Tsedenbal was deposed 1984. After the accession to power in the USSR of Mikhail Gorbachev, Mongolia was encouraged to broaden its outside contacts. Cultural exchanges with China increased, diplomatic relations were established with the US, and between 1987 and 1990 the number of Soviet troops stationed in the country was reduced from 80,000 to 15,000. A Mongolian nationalist revival developed, with increasing study and use of the Mongolian script, which was nationally readopted to replace the Cyrillic in 1990. Influenced by events in Eastern Europe, an opposition grouping, the Mongolian Democratic Union, was illegally formed Dec 1989 by the Moscow University–educated Sanjasuren Zorig (1962–). During 1990 it spearheaded a campaign demanding greater democratization and the return of Tsedenbal (from exile in Moscow) to face trial.

Free multiparty national elections and local municipal and people's hurals were held on July 29, 1990. The MPRP secured 83% of the seats of the central parliament and 62% of the seats in the Little Hural. The principal opposition body, the Democratic Party (MDP), led by Erdenijn Bat-Uul, captured only 5% of the seats. In Sept 1990 the new assembly elected the MPRP's Punsalmaagiyn Ochirbat as president and Dashiyn Byambasuren as prime minister.

Mongolia

Mongolian People's Republic
(*Bügd Nayramdakh Mongol Ard Uls*) (formerly Outer Mongolia)

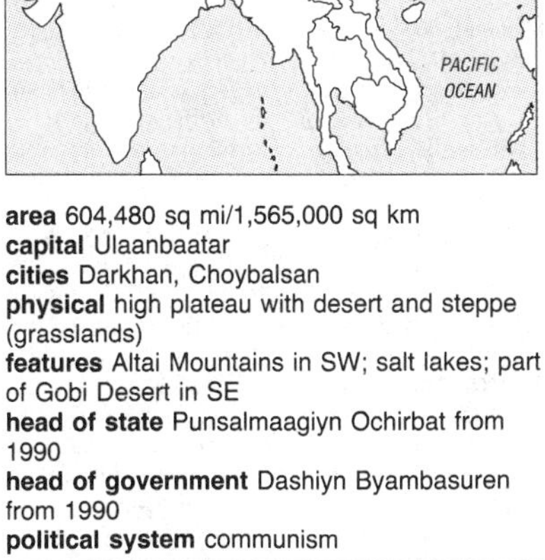
0 mls 500
0 km 1000
USSR
Ulaanbaatar
MONGOLIA
China
PACIFIC OCEAN

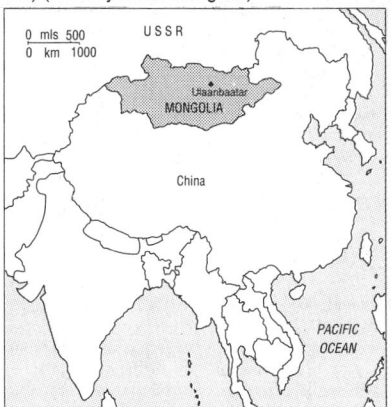

area 604,480 sq mi/1,565,000 sq km
capital Ulaanbaatar
cities Darkhan, Choybalsan
physical high plateau with desert and steppe (grasslands)
features Altai Mountains in SW; salt lakes; part of Gobi Desert in SE
head of state Punsalmaagiyn Ochirbat from 1990
head of government Dashiyn Byambasuren from 1990
political system communism
political parties Mongolian People's Revolutionary Party; Mongolian Democratic Union
exports meat and hides, minerals, wool, livestock, grain, cement, timber
currency tugrik
population (1990 est) 2,185,000; growth rate 2.8% p.a.
life expectancy men 63, women 67 (1989)
language Khalkha Mongolian (official), Chinese, Russian and Turkic languages
religion officially none (Tibetan Buddhist Lamaism suppressed 1930s)
literacy 89% (1985)
GNP $3.6 bn; $1,820 per head (1986)
chronology
1911 Mongolia gained autonomy from China.
1915 Chinese sovereignty reasserted.
1921 Chinese rule overthrown with Soviet help.
1924 People's Republic proclaimed.
1946 China recognized Mongolia's independence.
1966 20-year friendship, cooperation, and mutual-assistance pact signed with USSR. Relations deteriorated with China.
1984 Yumjaagiyn Tsedenbal, effective leader, deposed and replaced by Jambyn Batmonh.
1987 Soviet troops reduced; Mongolia's external contacts broadened.
1989 Further Soviet troop reductions.
1990 Democratization campaign launched by Mongolian Democratic Union. Ochirbat's Mongolian People's Revolutionary Party elected in free multiparty elections.
1991 Country's name changed to Mongolia. Massive privatization program launched.

Mongolia, Inner (Chinese *Nei Mongol*) autonomous region of NE China from 1947
area 173,700 sq mi/450,000 sq km
capital Hohhot
features strategic frontier area with USSR; known for Mongol herdsmen, now becoming settled farmers
physical grassland and desert
products cereals under irrigation; coal; reserves of rare earth oxides europium, and yttrium at Bayan Obo
population (1986) 20,290,000.

mongolism former name (now considered offensive) for ◊Down's syndrome.

Mongoloid referring to one of the three major varieties (see ◊races) of humans, *Homo sapiens sapiens*, including the indigenous peoples of Asia, the Indians of the Americas, Polynesians, and the Eskimos and Aleuts. General physical traits include dark eyes with epicanthic folds; straight to wavy dark hair; little beard or body hair; fair to tawny skin; low to medium-bridged noses; thin to medium lips. See also ◊Caucasoid, ◊Negroid.

mongoose any of various carnivorous mammals of the family Viverridae, especially the genus *Herpestes*. The Indian mongoose *H. mungo* is grayish in color and about 1.5 ft/50 cm long, with a long tail. It may be tamed and is often kept for its ability to kill snakes. The white-tailed mongoose *Ichneumia albicauda* of central Africa has a distinctive gray or white bushy tail.

monism in philosophy, the theory that reality is made up of only one substance. This view is usually contrasted with ◊dualism, which divides reality into two substances, matter and mind. The

monkey-puzzle tree

Dutch philosopher Baruch Spinoza saw the one substance as God or Nature.

monitor any of various lizards of the family Varanidae, found in Africa, S Asia, and Australasia. Monitors are generally large and carnivorous, with well-developed legs and claws and a long powerful tail that can be swung in defense.

Monitors include the Komodo dragon, the largest of all lizards, and also the slimmer Salvador's monitor *Varanus salvadorii* which may reach 8 ft/ 2.5 m. Several other monitors, such as the lace monitor *Varanus varius* and the perentie *Varanus giganteus* of Australia and the Nile monitor *Varanus niloticus* of Africa, are up to 6 ft/2 m long.

monk a man belonging to a religious order under the vows of poverty, chastity, and obedience, and living under a particular rule; see ◊monasticism.

Monk Thelonious 1917–1982. US jazz pianist and composer. Working in Harlem, New York, during the Depression, he took part in the development of the jazz style known as bebop or bop. He became popular in the 1950s, and is remembered for numbers such as "Round Midnight," "Blue Monk," and "Hackensack."

monkey any of the various smaller, mainly tree-dwelling anthropoid primates, not including humans and the ◊apes.

Old World monkeys, family Cercopithecidae, of tropical Africa and Asia are distinguished by their close-set nostrils and differentiated thumbs, some also having cheek pouches and rumps with bare patches (callosities) of hardened skin. They include ◊baboons, ◊langurs, ◊macaques, and guenons.

New World monkeys of Central and South America are characterized by wide-set nostrils, and some have highly sensitive prehensile tails. They include two families: (1) the family Cebidae, which includes the larger species saki, ◊capuchin, squirrel, howler, and spider monkeys; (2) the family Callithricidae, which includes the small ◊marmosets and tamarins.

monkey puzzle or ***Chilean pine*** coniferous evergreen tree *Araucaria araucana* (see ◊araucaria), native to Chile; it has whorled branches covered in prickly leaves of a leathery texture.

Monmouth market town in Gwent, Wales; Henry V was born in the now-ruined castle.

Monmouth James Scott, Duke of Monmouth 1649–1685. Claimant to the English crown, the illegitimate son of Charles II and Lucy Walter. After James II's accession in 1685, Monmouth landed in England at Lyme Regis, Dorset, claimed the crown, and raised a rebellion, which was crushed at ◊Sedgemoor in Somerset. He was executed with 320 of his accomplices.

When ◊James II converted to Catholicism, the Whig opposition attempted unsuccessfully to secure Monmouth the succession to the crown by the Exclusion Bill, and in 1684, having become implicated in a Whig conspiracy, he fled to Holland.

Monmouthshire former county of Wales, which in 1974 became, minus a small strip on the border with Mid Glamorgan, the new county of Gwent.

Monnet Jean 1888–1979. French economist. The originator of Winston Churchill's offer of union between the UK and France in 1940, he devised and took charge of the French modernization program under Charles de Gaulle in 1945. In 1950 he produced the "Shuman Plan" initiating the coordination of European coal and steel production in the European Coal and Steel Community (ECSC), which developed into the Common Market (EC).

monocarpic or ***hapaxanthic*** describing plants that flower and produce fruit only once during their lifecycle, after which they die. Most ◊annual plants and ◊biennial plants are monocarpic, but there are also a small number of monocarpic ◊perennial plants that flower just once, sometimes after as long as 90 years, dying shortly afterwards, for example, century plant *Agave* and some species of bamboo *Bambusa*. The general biological term for organisms that reproduce only once during their lifetime is ◊semelparity.

monoclonal antibodies (MABs) antibodies produced by fusing an antibody-producing lymphocyte with a cancerous myeloma (bone-marrow) cell. The resulting fused cell, called a hybridoma, is immortal and can be used to produce large quantities of a single, specific antibody. By choosing antibodies that are directed against antigens found on cancer cells, and combining them with cytotoxic drugs, it is hoped to make so-called magic bullets that will be able to pick out and kill cancers.

It is the antigens on the outer cell walls of germs entering the body that provoke the production of antibodies as a first line of defense against disease. Antibodies "recognize" these foreign antigens, and, in locking onto them, cause the release of chemical signals in the bloodstream to alert the immune system for further action. MABs are copies of these natural antibodies, with the same ability to recognize specific antigens. Introduced into the body, they can be targeted at disease sites.

The full potential of these biological missiles, developed by César ◊Milstein and others at Cambridge University, England, 1975, is still under investigation. However, they are already in use in blood-grouping, in pinpointing viruses and other sources of disease, in tracing cancer sites, and in developing vaccines.

monocotyledon angiosperm (flowering plant) having an embryo with a single cotyledon, or seed leaf (as opposed to ◊dicotyledons, which have two). Monocotyledons usually have narrow leaves with parallel veins and smooth edges, and hollow or soft stems. Their flower parts are arranged in threes. Most are small plants such as orchids, grasses, and lilies, but some are trees such as palms.

Monod Jacques 1910–1976. French biochemist who shared the 1965 Nobel Prize for Medicine (with two colleagues) for research in genetics and microbiology.

monody in music, declamation by accompanied solo voice, used at the turn of the 16th and 17th centuries.

monoecious having separate male and female flowers on the same plant. Maize (*Zea mays*), for example, has a tassel of male flowers at the top of the stalk and a group of female flowers (on the ear, or cob) lower down. Monoecism is a way of avoiding self-fertilization. ◊Dioecious plants have male and female flowers on separate plants.

monogamy the practice of having only one husband or wife at a time in ◊marriage.

monohybrid inheritance a pattern of inheritance seen in simple ◊genetics experiments, where the two animals (or two plants) being crossed are genetically identical except for one gene.

This gene may code for some obvious external features such as seed color, with one parent having green seeds and the other having yellow seeds. The offspring are monohybrids, that is, hybrids for one gene only, having received one copy of the gene from each parent. Known as the F1 generation, they are all identical, and usually resemble one parent, whose version of the gene (the dominant ◊allele) masks the effect of the other version (the recessive allele). Although the characteristic coded for by the recessive allele (for example, green seeds) completely disappears in this generation, it can reappear in offspring of the next generation if they have two recessive alleles. On average, this will occur in one out of four offspring from a cross between two of the monohybrids. The next generation (called F2) show a 3:1 ratio for the characteristic in question, 75% being like the original parent with the recessive allele. Gregor ◊Mendel first carried out experiments of this type (crossing varieties of artificially bred plants, such as peas) and they revealed the principles of genetics. The same basic mechanism underlies all inheritance, but in most plants and animals there are so many genetic differences interacting to produce the external appearance (phenotype) that such simple, clear-cut patterns of inheritance are not evident.

mononucleosis viral disease (also called "kissing disease," since it may be passed by body fluids, including saliva) characterized at onset by fever and painfully swollen lymph nodes (in the neck); there may also be digestive upset, sore throat, and skin rashes. Lassitude persists for months and even years, and recovery is often very slow. It is caused by the Epstein-Barr virus. A serious to fatal complication may be hepatitis.

Monophysite (Greek "one-nature") a member of a group of Christian heretics of the 5th–7th centuries who taught that Jesus had one nature, in opposition to the orthodox doctrine (laid down at the Council of Chalcedon in 451) that he had two natures, the human and the divine. Monophysitism developed as a reaction to ◊Nestorianism and led to the formal secession of the Coptic and Armenian churches from the rest of the Christian church. Monophysites survive today in Armenia, Syria, and Egypt.

monopoly in economics, the domination of a market for a particular product or service by a single company, which therefore has no competition and can keep prices high. In practice, a company can be said to have a monopoly when it controls a significant proportion of the market (technically an ◊oligopoly).

In the US, antitrust legislation has been used vigorously to break up and/or prevent the growth of monopolies. Even some closely regulated monopolies, such as the American Telegraph & Telephone Company, have been broken up to ensure competition. A monopsony is a situation in which there is only one buyer; for example, most governments are the only legal purchasers of military equipment inside their countries.

monorail a railroad that runs on a single rail; the cars can be balanced on it or suspended from it. It was invented in 1882 to carry light loads, and when run by electricity was called a telpher.

The Wuppertal Schwebebahn, which has been running in Germany since 1901, is a suspension monorail, where the passenger cars hang from an arm fixed to a trolley that runs along the rail. Today most monorails are of the straddle type, where the passenger cars run on top of the rail. They are used to transport passengers between terminals at some airports.

monosaccharide or ***simple sugar*** a ◊carbohydrate that cannot be hydrolyzed (split) into smaller carbohydrate units. Examples are glucose and fructose, both of which have the molecular formula $C_6H_{12}O_6$.

monosodium glutamate (MSG) $NaC_5H_8NO_4$ a white, crystalline powder, the sodium salt of glutamic acid (an ◊amino acid found in proteins that plays a role in the metabolism of plants and animals). It is used to enhance the flavor of many packaged and "fast foods," and in Chinese cooking. Ill effects may arise from its overconsumption, and

Monroe *The 5th President of the United States of America, James Monroe, a Democratic Republican. 1817–1825.*

some people are very sensitive to it, even in small amounts. It is commercially derived from vegetable protein.

monotheism the belief or doctrine that there is only one God; the opposite of polytheism.

It is the unifying theme of the Old Testament.

Monothelite member of a group of Christian heretics of the 7th century who sought to reconcile the orthodox and ◊Monophysite theologies by maintaining that, while Christ possessed two natures, he had only one will. Monothelitism was condemned as a heresy by the Third Council of Constantinople 680.

monotreme any member of the order Monotremata, the only living egg-laying mammals, found in Australasia. They include the echidnas and the platypus.

Monroe city in NE Louisiana on the Ouachita River, E of Shreveport. Industries include furniture, chemicals, paper, natural gas, and soybeans; population (1990) 54,909.

Monroe James 1758–1831. 5th president of the US 1817–25. He served in the American Revolution, studied law under his lifelong friend Thomas ◊Jefferson, was minister to France 1794–96, and in 1803 negotiated the ◊Louisiana Purchase completed by James ◊Madison. During the ◊Constitutional Convention he opposed ratification, fearing a central government with excessive power. He was secretary of state 1811–17. As president, he presided over the so-called Era of Good Feeling, a period of domestic tranquility. He took no firm stand on the question of slavery, making his mark in foreign policy. He introduced the ◊Monroe Doctrine, which proclaimed the Americas closed to further colonization by the European powers.

Born in Westmoreland County, Virginia, he attended the College of William and Mary. He served in the Virginia legislature 1782, in the US Senate 1790–94, and as governor of Virginia 1799–1802.

Monroe Marilyn. Adopted name of Norma Jean Mortenson or Baker 1926–1962. US film actress, the voluptuous blonde sex symbol of the 1950s, who made adroit comedies such as *Gentlemen Prefer Blondes* 1953, *How to Marry a Millionaire* 1953, *The Seven Year Itch* 1955, *Bus Stop* 1956, and *Some Like It Hot* 1959. Her third husband, playwright Arthur ◊Miller, wrote *The Misfits* 1961 for her, a serious film that became her last. Her second husband was baseball star Joe DiMaggio.

Monroe Doctrine the declaration by President James Monroe 1823 that any further European colonial ambitions in the W hemisphere would be threats to US peace and security, made in response to proposed European intervention against newly independent former Spanish colonies in South America. In return, the US would not interfere in European affairs.

The doctrine, subsequently broadened, has been a recurrent theme in US foreign policy, although it has no basis in US or international law. At the time of the declaration, the US was militarily incapable of enforcing its sweeping proclamations. The impetus for and the power behind the doctrine came from the British, whose commercial interests were at risk in the event of a Franco-Spanish reassertion of colonial influence. President Theodore ◊Roosevelt drew on the doctrine to proclaim a US right to intervene in the internal affairs of Latin American states.

Monrovia capital and port of Liberia; population (1985) 500,000. Industries include rubber, cement, and gasoline processing.

It was founded 1821 for slaves repatriated from the US. Originally called Christopolis, it was named after US president James Monroe.

Mons (Flemish *Bergen*) industrial city (coal-mining, textiles, sugar) and capital of the province of Hainaut, Belgium; population (1985) 90,500. The military headquarters of NATO is at nearby Chièvres-Casteau.

Monsarrat Nicholas 1910–1979. English novelist who served with the navy in the Battle of the ◊Atlantic, the subject of his book *The Cruel Sea* 1951.

monsoon (Old Dutch *monçon*) a wind system that dominates the climate of a wide region, with seasonal reversals of direction; in particular, the wind in S Asia that blows toward the sea in winter and toward the land in summer, bringing heavy rain. The monsoon may cause destructive flooding all over India and SE Asia from Apr to Sept. Thousands of people are rendered homeless each year.

monstera or ***Swiss cheese plant*** genus of evergreen climbing plants of the arum family (Araceae), native to tropical America. *Monstera deliciosa* is cultivated as a house plant. A striking feature is the drying up of areas between the veins of the leaves, creating deep marginal notches and ultimately holes.

monstrance in the Roman Catholic Church, a vessel used from the 13th century to hold the Host (bread consecrated in the Eucharist) when exposed at benediction or in processions.

Montagnard member of a group in the legislative assembly and National Convention convened after the ◊French Revolution. They supported the more extreme aims of the revolution, and were destroyed as a political force after the fall of Robespierre 1794.

Montagu Ashley 1905– . British-born US anthropologist. A strong critic of theories of racial determinism, Montagu became a forceful defender of human rights, as evidenced in writings such as *Man's Most Dangerous Myth: The Fallacy of Race* 1942. In 1950 he helped draft the definitive UNESCO "Statement on Race." Montagu served on the faculty of Rutgers University 1949–55 and became well known for popularizing social issues, such as "psychosclerosis," the so-called hardening of the psyche in *Growing Young* 1981.

Born in London and educated at the University of London, Columbia University, and the University of Florence, Montagu taught anatomy at New York University 1931–38. He became deeply

Monroe *Legendary film star Marilyn Monroe. Her vulnerability was part of her appeal.*

Montana

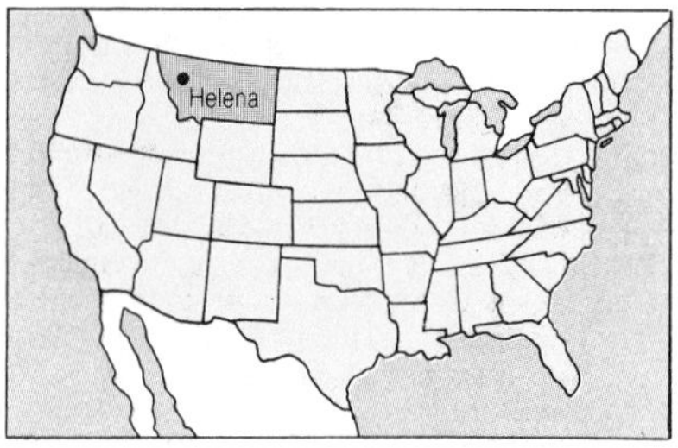
Helena

interested in anthropology and received his PhD from Columbia under Franz ◊Boas 1937.

Montaigne Michel Eyquem de 1533–1592. French writer, regarded as the creator of the essay form. In 1580 he published the first two volumes of his *Essais*; the third volume appeared in 1588. Montaigne deals with all aspects of life from an urbanely skeptical viewpoint. Through the translation by John Florio in 1603, he influenced Shakespeare and other English writers.

Born at the Château de Montaigne near Bordeaux, he studied law, and in 1554 became a counselor of the Bordeaux *parlement*. Little is known of his earlier life, except that he regularly visited Paris and the court of Francis II. In 1571 he retired to his estates, relinquishing his magistracy. He toured Germany, Switzerland, and Italy 1580–81, returning upon his election as mayor of Bordeaux, a post he held until 1585.

Montale Eugenio 1896–1981. Italian poet and writer. His pessimistic poetry, for which he was awarded a Nobel Prize in 1975, includes *Ossi di seppia/Cuttlefish bones* 1925 and *Le Occasioni/Occasions* 1939. In 1989 it was revealed that much of his literary journalism, such as his regular column in the *Corriere della Sera* newspaper, was in fact written by an American, Henry Frost.

Montana state in W US, on the Canadian border; nickname Treasure State

area 147,143 sq mi/318,100 sq km

capital Helena

cities Billings, Great Falls, Butte

population (1990) 799,065

physical mountainous forests in the West, rolling grasslands in the East

features rivers: Missouri, Yellowstone, Little Bighorn; Glacier National Park on the Continental Divide and Yellowstone National Park; Museum of the Plains Indian; Custer Battlefield National Monument; hunting and ski resorts

products wheat (under irrigation), cattle, coal, copper, oil, natural gas, lumber, wood products

famous people Gary Cooper, Myrna Loy, Michael Mansfield

history explored for France by Verendrye early 1740s; passed to the US 1803 in the Louisiana Purchase; first settled 1809; W Montana obtained from Britain in the Oregon Treaty 1846; influx of gold-seeking immigrants mid-19th century; fierce Indian wars 1867–77, which included "Custer's Last Stand" at the Little Bighorn with the Sioux; achieved statehood 1889. Energy production, in the form of oil, natural gas, and strip-mined coal, has replaced precious metals and copper in mineral exploitation. The plains area still produces grain crops, sheep, and cattle.

Montana Joe 1956– . US football player. As quarterback for the San Francisco 49ers he appeared in four winning Super Bowls 1982, 1985, 1989, and 1990, winning the most valuable player award in all but 1989, and setting a record for passing yardage 1989 and the most touchdown passes 1990.

He graduated from Notre Dame college, where he led his team to the national college championship 1978. He was the leading passer in the National Conference 1981, 1984, and 1985. He recovered from a serious back injury in 1986 to become the leading passer in the National Football League 1987, setting league records for touchdowns thrown (31), and consecutive completions (22). In the 1989 Super Bowl, he set a record for most passes without an interception (33).

Montand Yves 1921– . French actor and singer who achieved fame in the thriller *Le Salaire de la peur/The Wages of Fear* 1953 and continued to be popular in French and American films, including *Let's Make Love* 1960 (with Marilyn Monroe), *Grand Prix* 1966, *Le Sauvage/The Savage* 1976, *Jean de Florette* 1986, and *Manon des sources* 1986.

Montanism movement within the early Christian church that strove to return to the purity of primitive Christianity. It originated in Phrygia in about 156 with the teaching of a prophet named Montanus, and spread to Anatolia, Rome, Carthage, and Gaul. The theologian ◊Tertullian was a Montanist.

Montaubon industrial town (porcelain, textiles) in the Midi-Pyrénées region, SW France, on the river Tarn; population (1982) 53,147. The painter Ingres was born here.

Mont Blanc (Italian *Monte Bianco*) the highest mountain in the ◊Alps, between France and Italy; height 15,772 ft/4,807 m. It was first climbed 1786.

montbretia European plant *Tritonia crocosmiflora* of the iris family Iridaceae, with orange or reddish flowers on long stems.

Montcalm Louis-Joseph de Montcalm-Gozon, Marquis de 1712–1759. French general, appointed military commander in Canada 1756. He won a succession of victories over the British during the French and Indian War, but was defeated in 1759 by James ◊Wolfe at Québec, where both he and Wolfe were killed; this battle marked the end of French rule in Canada.

Mont Cenis pass in the Alps between Lyon, France, and Turin, Italy, at 6,831 ft/2,082 m.

Monte Bello Islands group of uninhabited islands in the Indian Ocean, off Western Australia, used by the UK for nuclear-weapons testing 1952; the largest of the group is Barrow Island.

Monte Carlo a resort city in ◊Monaco, known for its gambling; population (1982) 12,000.

Monte Cristo a small uninhabited island 25 mi/40 km to the S of Elba, in the Tyrrhenian Sea; its name supplied a title for Dumas' hero in *The Count of Monte Cristo*.

Montego Bay port and resort on the NW coast of Jamaica; population (1982) 70,200.

Montélimar town in Drôme district, France; known for the nougat to which its name is given; population (1982) 30,213.

Montenegro (Serbo-Croat *Crna Gora*) constituent republic of Yugoslavia

area 5,327 sq mi/13,800 sq km

capital Titograd

town Cetinje

features smallest of the republics; Skadarsko Jezero (Lake Scutari) shared with Albania

physical mountainous

population (1986) 620,000, including 400,000 Montenegrins, 80,000 Muslims, and 40,000 Albanians

language Serbian variant of Serbo-Croat

religion Serbian Orthodox

famous people Milovan Djilas

history part of ◊Serbia from the late 12th century, it became independent (under Venetian protection) after Serbia was defeated by the Turks 1389. It was forced to accept Turkish suzerainty in the late 15th century, but was never completely subdued by Turkey. It was ruled by bishop princes until 1851, when a monarchy was founded, and became a sovereign principality under the Treaty of Berlin 1878. The monarch used the title of king from 1910 with Nicholas I (1841–1921). Montenegro participated in the Balkan Wars 1912 and 1913. It was overrun by Austria in World War I, and in 1918 voted after the deposition of King Nicholas to become part of Serbia. In 1946 it became a republic of Yugoslavia.

In Jan 1989 the entire Communist Party leadership resigned after mass protests. Later that year the body of Nicholas I was brought back to Montenegro and ceremonially reburied in Cetinje. Montenegro is the poorest of the Yugoslav republics and had 25% unemployment 1990.

***Monteverdi** One of the great composers of operas, Claudio Monteverdi.*

Monterey fishing port on Monterey Bay in California, once the state capital; population (1990) 31,954. It is the setting for Steinbeck's novels *Cannery Row* 1945 and *Tortilla Flat* 1935 dealing with migrant fruit workers.

Monterrey industrial city (iron, steel, textiles, chemicals, food processing) in NE Mexico; population (1986) 2,335,000.

Montespan Françoise-Athénaïs de Rochechouart, Marquise de 1641–1707. Mistress of Louis XIV of France from 1667. They had seven children, for whom she engaged as governess the future Madame de ◊Maintenon, who replaced her. She retired to a convent in 1691.

Montesquieu Charles Louis de Secondat, baron de la Brède 1689–1755. French philosophical historian, author of the *Lettres persanes/Persian Letters* 1721. *De l'Esprit des lois/The Spirit of the Laws* 1748, a 31-volume philosophical disquisition on politics and sociology as well as legal matters, advocated the separation of powers within government, a doctrine that became the basis of liberal constitutions.

Born near Bordeaux, Montesquieu became adviser to the Bordeaux parliament 1714. After the success of *Lettres persanes*, he adopted a literary career, writing *Considérations sur les causes de la grandeur des Romains et de leur décadence/Considerations on the Greatness and Decadence of the Romans* 1734.

Montessori Maria 1870–1952. Italian educator. From her experience with mentally handicapped children, she developed the Montessori method, an educational system for all children based on an informal approach, incorporating instructive play and allowing children to develop at their own pace.

Monteux Pierre 1875–1964. French conductor. Ravel's *Daphnis and Chloe* and Stravinsky's *Rite of Spring* were first performed under his direction. He conducted Sergei ◊Diaghilev's Ballets Russes 1911–14 and 1917, and the San Francisco Symphony Orchestra 1935–52.

Monteverdi Claudio (Giovanni Antonio) 1567–1643. Italian composer. He contributed to the development of the opera with *Orfeo* 1607 and *The Coronation of Poppea* 1642. He also wrote madrigals, ◊motets, and sacred music, notably the *Vespers* 1610.

Montevideo capital and chief port (grain, meat prod-

***Montgomery** The British field marshal Viscount Montgomery of Alamein advances in the turret of a tank during the attack on El Alamein, Oct 1942.*

ucts, hides) of Uruguay, on Río de la Plata; population (1985) 1,250,000. It was founded 1726.

Montez Lola. Adopted name of Maria Gilbert 1818–1861. Irish actress and dancer. She appeared on the stage as a Spanish dancer, and in 1847 became the mistress of King Ludwig I of Bavaria, whose policy she dictated for a year. Her liberal sympathies led to her banishment through Jesuit influence in 1848. She died in poverty in the US.

Montezuma II 1466–1520. Aztec emperor 1502–20. When the Spanish conquistador Cortés invaded Mexico, Montezuma entertained him and his party, although he mistrusted them. He was imprisoned and killed during the Aztec attack on Cortés's forces as they tried to leave Tenochtitlán, the Aztec capital city.

Montfort Simon de Montfort, Earl of Leicester c. 1208–1265. English politician and soldier. From 1258 he led the baronial opposition to Henry III's misrule during the second ◊Barons' War and in 1264 defeated and captured the king at Lewes, Sussex. In 1265, as head of government, he summoned the first parliament in which the towns were represented; he was killed at the Battle of Evesham during the last of the Barons' Wars.

Montgolfier Joseph Michel 1740–1810 and Étienne Jacques 1745–1799. French brothers whose hot-air balloon was used for the first successful human flight Nov 21, 1783.

They were papermakers of Annonay, near Lyon, where on June 5, 1783 they first sent up a balloon filled with hot air. After further experiments with wood-fueled paper balloons, they went aloft themselves, in Paris. The Montgolfier experiments greatly stimulated scientific interest in aviation.

Montgomery market town in Powys, Wales; population about 1,000.

Montgomery state capital of Alabama; population (1990) 187,106. The "Montgomery Bus Boycott" 1955 began here when a black passenger, Rosa Parks, refused to give up her seat to a white. Led by Martin Luther King, Jr, the boycott was a landmark in the civil rights campaign. Two settlements on the site of the present-day city were consolidated 1819. Montgomery was the capital of the Confederacy in the first months of the American Civil War.

Montgomery Bernard Law, 1st Viscount Montgomery of Alamein 1887–1976. British field marshal. In World War II he commanded the 8th Army in N Africa in the Second Battle of El ◊Alamein 1942. As commander of British troops in N Europe from 1944, he received the German surrender on 1945.

At the start of World War II he commanded part of the British Expeditionary Force in France 1939–40 and took part in the evacuation from Dunkirk. In Aug 1942 he took command of the 8th Army, then barring the German advance on Cairo; the victory of El ◊Alamein in Oct turned the tide in N Africa and was followed by the expulsion of Field Marshal Rommel from Egypt and rapid Allied advance into Tunisia. In Feb 1943 Montgomery's forces came under US general Eisenhower's command, and they took part in the conquest of Tunisia and Sicily and the invasion of Italy. Montgomery was promoted to field marshal in 1944. In 1948 he became permanent military chair of the Commanders-in-Chief Committee for W European defense, and 1951–58 was deputy Supreme Commander Europe.

***Montréal** The Hotel de Ville in Montréal.*

Montgomery Robert (Henry) 1904–1981. US film actor of the 1930s and 1940s. He directed some of his later films, such as *Lady in the Lake* 1947, before leaving the screen for television and Republican politics. His other films include *Private Lives* 1931, *Night Must Fall* 1937, and *Mr and Mrs Smith* 1941. He directed James Cagney in *The Gallant Hours* 1960.

Montgomeryshire former county of N Wales, included in Powys 1974.

month unit of time based on the motion of the Moon around the Earth. The time from one new or full Moon to the next (the synodic or lunar month) is 29.53 days. The time for the Moon to complete one orbit around the Earth relative to the stars (the sidereal month) is 27.32 days. The solar month equals 30.44 days, and is exactly one-twelfth of the solar or tropical year, the time taken for the Earth to orbit the Sun. The calendar month is a human invention, devised to fit the calendar year.

Montherlant Henri Millon de 1896–1972. French author. He was a Nazi sympathizer. His novels, which are marked by an obsession with the physical, include *Aux Fontaines du désir/To the Fountains of Desire* 1927 and *Pitié pour les femmes/Pity for Women* 1936. His most critically acclaimed work is *Le Chaos et la nuit/Chaos and Night* 1963.

Montmartre district of Paris, France, dominated by the basilica of Sacré Coeur 1875. It is situated in the N of the city on a 400 ft/120 m high hill.

Montoneros left-wing guerrillas in Argentina.

Montparnasse district of Paris, France, frequented by artists and writers. The Pasteur Institute is also here.

Montpelier capital of Vermont, located in the Green Mountains in the central part of the state, on the Winooski River. Industries include granite, insurance, and tourism; population (1990) 8,247.

Montpellier industrial city (engineering, textiles, food processing, and a trade in wine and brandy), capital of ◊Languedoc-Roussillon, France; population (1982) 221,000. It is the birthplace of the philosopher Auguste Comte.

Montréal inland port, industrial city (aircraft, chemicals, oil and petrochemicals, flour, sugar, brewing, meat packing) of Québec, Canada, on Montreal island at the junction of the Ottawa and St Lawrence rivers; population (1986) 2,921,000.

features Mont Réal (Mount Royal, 753 ft/230 m) overlooks the city; an artificial island in the St Lawrence (site of the international exhibition 1967); three universities; except for Paris, the world's largest French-speaking city

history Jacques ◊Cartier reached the site 1535, Samuel de ◊Champlain established a trading post 1611, and the original Ville Marie (later renamed Montréal) was founded 1642 by Paul de Chomédy, Sieur de Maisonneuve (1612–76). It was the last town surrendered by France to Britain 1760. Nevertheless, when troops of the rebel Continental Congress occupied the city 1775–76, the citizens refused to be persuaded (even by a visit from Benjamin Franklin) to join the future US in its revolt against Britain.

Montreux winter resort in W Switzerland on Lake Geneva; population (1980) 21,000. It is the site of the island rock fortress of Chillon, where François Bonivard (commemorated by the poet Byron), prior of the Abbey of St Victor, was imprisoned 1530–36 for his opposition to the Duke of Savoy. At the annual television festival (first held 1961), the premier award is the Golden Rose of Montreux.

Montreux, Convention of international agreement 1936 allowing Turkey to remilitarize the Dardenelles.

Mont St Michel islet in NW France converted to a peninsula by an artificial causeway; it has a Benedictine monastery, founded 708.

Montserrat volcanic island in the West Indies, one of the Leeward group, a British crown colony; capital Plymouth; area 42 sq mi/110 sq km; population (1985) 12,000. Practically all buildings were destroyed by Hurricane Hugo Sept 1989.

Montserrat produces cotton, cotton-seed, coconuts, citrus and other fruits, and vegetables. Its first European visitor was Christopher ◊Columbus 1493, who named it after the mountain in Spain. It was first colonized by English and Irish settlers who moved from St Christopher 1632. The island became a British crown colony 1871.

Montserrat (Spanish *monte serrado*, "serrated mountain") mountain in NE Spain, height 4,070 ft/1,240 m, so called because its uneven outline resembles the edge of a saw.

Monza town in N Italy, known for its automobile racing circuit; population (1988) 123,000. Once the capital of the ◊Lombards, it preserves the Iron Crown of Lombardy in the 13th-century cathedral. Umberto I was assassinated here.

Moody Dwight Lyman 1837–1899. US evangelist. During the American Civil War, Moody worked with the Young Men's Christian Association (YMCA), providing medical and moral support to the troops. In the 1870s he became a popular evangelist, touring in company with organist Ira D Sankey. In Northfield, Massachusetts, Moody founded the Northfield Seminary (now School) for girls 1879 and the Mount Hermon School for boys 1881. In 1889 he founded the Chicago (later Moody) Bible Institute.

Born in East Northfield, Massachusetts, Moody moved to Boston as a young man and joined the Congregational Church 1856. Later settling in Chicago, he established a church school and devoted himself to preaching among the poor.

Moody Helen Wills. Married name of US tennis player Helen Newington ◊Wills.

Moon Sun Myung 1920– . Korean industrialist and founder of the ◊Unification Church (Moonies) 1954. From 1973 he launched a major mission in the US and elsewhere. The church has been criticized for its manipulative methods of recruiting and keeping members. He was convicted of tax fraud in the US 1982.

Moon has allegedly been associated with extreme right-wing organizations, arms manufacture, and the Korean Central Intelligence Agency.

moon in astronomy, any natural satellite that orbits a planet. Mercury and Venus are the only planets in the Solar System that do not have moons.

Moon the natural satellite of Earth, 2,160 mi/3,476 km in diameter, with a mass 0.012 (approximately one-eightieth) that of Earth. Its average distance from Earth is 238,857 mi/384,404 km, and it orbits in a west-to-east direction every 27.32 days (the sidereal month). It spins on its axis with one side permanently turned toward Earth. The Moon has no atmosphere or water. Much of our information about the Moon is derived from photographs and measurements taken by US and Soviet Moon probes; from geologic samples brought back by US Apollo astronauts and by Soviet Luna probes; and from experiments set up by the US astronauts 1969–72.

The Moon is illuminated by sunlight and goes through a cycle of phases of shadow, waxing from new (dark) via first quarter (half Moon) to full, and waning back again to new every 29.53 days (the synodic month, also known as a lunation). On its sunlit side, temperatures reach 230°F/110°C, but during the two-week lunar night the surface temperature drops to –274°F/–170°C.

The origin of the Moon is still open to debate. Scientists have suggested the following theories: that it split from the Earth; that it was a separate body captured by Earth's gravity; that it formed in orbit around Earth; or that it was formed from debris thrown off when a body the size of Mars struck Earth. Future exploration of the Moon may provide information on lunar resources, using gamma-ray spectrometers, or detect water permafrost, which might be located at the permanently shadowed lunar poles.

The Moon's composition is rocky, with a surface heavily scarred by ◊meteorite impacts that have formed craters up to 150 mi/240 km across. Rocks brought back by astronauts show the Moon is 4.6 billion years old, the same age as Earth. It differs from Earth in that most of the Moon's surface features were formed within the first billion years of its history when it was hit repeatedly by meteorites. The youngest craters are surrounded by bright rays of ejected rock. The largest scars have been filled by dark lava to produce the lowland plains called seas, or maria (plural of ◊mare). These dark patches form the so-called man-in-the-Moon pattern.

Moonie town in SE Queensland, W of Brisbane, the site of Australia's first commercial oil strike; population (1961) approximately 100.

Moonie popular name for a follower of the ◊Unification Church, a religious sect founded by Sun Myung Moon.

Moon probe crewless spacecraft used to investigate the Moon from 1959. Early probes flew past the Moon or crash-landed on it, but later ones achieved soft landings or went into orbit. Soviet probes included the Lunik/Luna series. US probes (Ranger, Surveyor, Lunar Orbiter) prepared the way for the Apollo crewed flights.

The first space probe to hit the Moon was the Soviet *Lunik 2*, on Sept 13, 1959 (*Lunik 1* had missed the Moon eight months earlier). In Oct 1959, *Lunik 3* sent back the first photographs of the Moon's far side. *Lunik 9* was the first probe to soft-land on the Moon, on Feb 3, 1966, transmitting photographs of the surface to Earth. *Lunik 16* was the first probe to return automatically to Earth carrying Moon samples, in Sept 1970, although by then Moon rocks had already been brought back by US ◊Apollo astronauts who had landed on the Moon on July 20, 1969. *Lunik 17* landed in Nov 1970 carrying a lunar rover, Lunokhod, which was driven over the Moon's surface by remote control from Earth.

The first successful US Moon probe was *Ranger 7*, which took close-up photographs before it hit the Moon on July 31, 1964. *Surveyor 1*, on June 2, 1966, was the first US probe to soft-land on the lunar surface. It took photographs, and later Surveyors analyzed the surface rocks. Between 1966 and 1967 a series of five Lunar Orbiters photographed the entire Moon in detail in preparation for the Apollo landings, when Neil Armstrong and Edwin Aldrin became the first men to walk on the Moon.

moonstone a translucent, pearly variety of potassium sodium ◊feldspar, found in Sri Lanka and Myanmar, and distinguished by a blue, silvery, or red opalescent tint. It is valued as a gem.

***Moore** British sculptor Henry Moore often interlocked forms, as in his* Family Group, *a 1949 bronze.*

Moor any of the NW African Muslims, of mixed Arab and Berber origin, who conquered Spain and ruled its southern part from 711 to 1492. The name (English form of Latin *Maurus*) was originally applied to an inhabitant of the Roman province of Mauritania, in NW Africa.

Moore Dudley 1935– . English actor, comedian and pianist, formerly teamed with comedian Peter Cook. He became a Hollywood star after appearing in *"10"* 1979, and his other films, mostly comedies, include *Bedazzled* 1968, *Arthur* 1981, and *Santa Claus* 1985. He has played Classical piano concerts, including Carnegie Hall.

Moore G(eorge) E(dward) 1873–1958. British philosopher. Educated at Trinity College, Cambridge University, he was professor of philosophy at the university 1925–39, and edited the journal *Mind*, to which he contributed 1921–47. His books include *Principia Ethica* 1903, in which he attempted to analyze the moral question "What is good?," and *Some Main Problems of Philosophy* 1953, but his chief influence was as a teacher.

Moore Henry 1898–1986. British sculptor. His subjects include the reclining nude, mother and child groups, the warrior, and interlocking abstract forms. Many of his post-World War II works are in bronze or marble, including monumental semi-abstracts such as *Reclining Figure* 1957–58 (outside the UNESCO building, Paris), and often designed to be placed in landscape settings.

Moore claimed to have learned much from archaic South and Central American sculpture, and this is reflected in his work from the 1920s. By the early 1930s most of his main themes had emerged, and the Surrealists' preoccupation with organic forms in abstract works proved a strong influence; Moore's hollowed wooden shapes strung with wires date from the late 1930s. Abstract work suggesting organic structures recurs after World War II, for example in the interwoven bonelike forms of the *Hill Arches* and the bronze *Sheep Pieces* 1970s, set in fields by his studio in Hertfordshire.

Moore Marianne 1887–1972. US poet. She edited the literary magazine *The Dial* 1925–29, and published several volumes of witty and intellectual verse, including *Observations* 1924, *What are Years* 1941, and *A Marianne Moore Reader* 1961.

She also published translations and essays. Her work is noted for its observation of detail. T S Eliot was an admirer of her poetry.

Moore Roger 1928– . English actor who starred in the television series *The Saint* 1962–70, and assumed the film role of James Bond in 1973 in *Live and Let Die*. His films include *Diane* 1955, *Gold* 1974, *The Wild Geese* 1978, and *Octopussy* 1983.

Moorhead city in W Minnesota on the Red River, opposite Fargo, North Dakota. It is a center for an agricultural region that produces sugar beets, potatoes, grain, and dairy products; population (1990) 32,295.

moorhen marsh bird *Gallinula chloropus* of the rail family, common in water of swamps, lakes, and ponds in Eurasia, Africa, and North and South America. It is about 13 in/33 cm long, and mainly brown and gray, but with a red bill and forehead, and a vivid white underside to the tail. The big feet are not webbed or lobed, but the moorhen can swim well.

moose large ◊deer *Alces alces* inhabiting N Asia and N Europe, where it is known as the elk. It is brown in color, stands about 6 ft/2 m at the shoulders, and has very large palmate antlers, a fleshy muzzle, a short neck, and long legs. It feeds on leaves and shoots.

Moose Jaw town in S Saskatchewan, Canada, with grain elevators, extensive stockyards, petroleum refineries; population (1985) 35,500.

moot a legal and administrative assembly found in nearly every community in medieval England.

Moradabad trading city in Uttar Pradesh, India, on the Ramganga river; produces textiles and engraved brassware; population (1981) 348,000. It was founded 1625 by Rustan Khan, and the Great Mosque dates from 1631.

moraine rocky debris or ◊till carried along and deposited by a ◊glacier. Material eroded from the side of a glaciated valley and carried along the glacier's edge is called lateral moraine; that worn from the valley floor and carried along the base of the glacier is called ground moraine. Rubble dropped at the foot of a melting glacier is called terminal moraine.

When two glaciers converge their lateral moraines unite to form a medial moraine. Debris that has fallen down crevasses and become embedded in the ice is termed englacial moraine; when this is exposed at the surface due to partial melting it becomes ablation moraine.

morality play didactic medieval verse drama, in part a development of the ◊mystery play (or miracle play), in which human characters are replaced by personified virtues and vices, the limited humorous elements being provided by the Devil. Morality plays, such as *Everyman*, flourished in the 15th century. They exerted an influence on the development of Elizabethan drama and comedy.

Moral Rearmament (MRA) international movement calling for "moral and spiritual renewal." Founded by the Christian evangelist F N D Buchman in the 1920s, it called itself the "Oxford Group," and based its teachings on the "Four Absolutes" (honesty, purity, unselfishness, love).

Morandi Giorgio 1890–1964. Italian still-life painter and etcher whose subtle studies of bottles and jars convey a sense of calm and repose.

Moravia (Czech *Morava*) district of central Europe, from 1960 two regions of Czechoslovakia:

South Moravia (Czech *Jihomoravský*)
area 5,802 sq mi/15,030 sq km
capital Brno
population (1986) 2,075,000.
North Moravia (Czech *Severomoravský*)
area 4,273 sq mi/11,070 sq km
capital Ostrava
population (1986) 1,957,000.
features (N and S) river Morava; 25% forested
products corn, grapes, wine in the south; wheat, barley, rye, flax, sugarbeet in the north; coal and iron
history part of the Avar territory since the 6th century; conquered by Charlemagne's Holy Roman Empire. In 874 the kingdom of Great Moravia was founded by the Slavic prince Sviatopluk, who ruled until 894. It was conquered by the Magyars 906, and became a fief of Bohemia 1029. It was passed to the Hapsburgs 1526, and

Moravia *Italian novelist Alberto Moravia, long a leading figure in Italian intellectual and cultural life.*

became an Austrian crown land 1849. It was incorporated in the new republic of Czechoslovakia 1918, forming a province until 1949.

Moravia Alberto. Adopted name of Alberto Pincherle 1907–1990. Italian novelist. His first successful novel was *Gli indifferenti/The Time of Indifference* 1929. But its criticism of Mussolini's regime led to the government censoring his work until after World War II. Later books include *La romana/Woman of Rome* 1947, *La ciociara/Two Women* 1957, and *La noia/The Empty Canvas* 1961, a study of an artist's obsession with his model.

Moravian member of a Christian Protestant sect, the Moravian Brethren. An episcopal church that grew out of the earlier Bohemian Brethren, it was established by the Lutheran Count Zinzendorf in Saxony 1722.

Persecution of the Bohemian Brethren began 1620, and they were held together mainly by the leadership of their bishop, Comenius. Driven out of Bohemia in 1722, they spread into Germany, England, and North America. In 1732 missionary work began.

It is an unworldly practice, in doctrine close to Lutheranism, with a simplified church hierarchy and liturgy. There are about 63,000 Moravians in the US.

Moray Firth North Sea inlet in Scotland, between Burghead (Grampian) and Tarbat Ness (Highland region), 15 mi/38 km wide at its entrance. The town of Inverness is situated at the head of the Firth.

Morayshire former county of NE Scotland, divided 1975 between Highland region (the SW section) and Grampian region (the NE); the county town was Elgin.

Morazán Francisco 1792–1842. Central American politician, born in Honduras. He was elected president of the United Provinces of Central America in 1830. In the face of secessions he attempted to hold the union together by force but was driven out by the Guatemalan dictator Rafael Carrera. Morazán was eventually captured and executed in 1842.

Morbihan, Gulf of seawater lake in Brittany, W France, linked by a channel with the Bay of Biscay; area 40 sq mi/104 sq km. Morbihan is a Breton word meaning "little sea" and the gulf gives its name to a *département*.

Mordovia another name for Mordvinia, republic of the USSR.

Mordred in Arthurian legend, nephew and final opponent of King ◊Arthur. What may be an early version of his name (Medraut) appears with Arthur in annals from the 10th century, listed under the year AD 537.

More *Portrait of English official Thomas More, executed for refusing to recognize Henry VIII as head of the church in England.*

Mordvinia or ***Mordovia*** autonomous republic of central USSR
area 10,100 sq mi/26,200 sq km
capital Saransk
features river Sura on the E; forested in the W
products sugar beet, grains, potatoes; sheep and dairy farming; timber, furniture, and textiles
population (1986) 964,000
history Mordvinia was conquered by Russia during the 13th century. It was made an autonomous region 1930, and an Autonomous Soviet Socialist Republic 1934.

More (St) Thomas 1478–1535. English politician and author. From 1509 he was favored by ◊Henry VIII and employed on foreign embassies. He was a member of the privy council from 1518 and Lord Chancellor from 1529 but resigned over Henry's break with the pope. For refusing to accept the king as head of the new English church (see ◊Reformation), he was imprisoned, tried, and executed. The title of his political book *Utopia* 1516 has come to mean any supposedly perfect society.

Before his execution More was imprisoned in the Tower of London for a year. He was canonized in 1935.

Moreau Gustave 1826–1898. French Symbolist painter. His works are atmospheric biblical, mythological, and literary scenes, richly colored and detailed, for example *Salome Dancing Before Herod* 1876.

In the 1890s Moreau taught at the École des Beaux-Arts in Paris, where his pupils included Matisse and Rouault. Much of his work is in the Musée Moreau, Paris.

Moreau Jeanne 1928– . French actress who has appeared in international films, often in quiet but passionate roles. Her work includes *Les Amants/The Lovers* 1958, *Jules et Jim/Jules and Jim* 1961, *Chimes at Midnight* 1966, and *Querelle* 1982.

Moreau Jean Victor Marie 1763–1813. French general in the Revolutionary Wars who won a brilliant victory over the Austrians at ◊Hohenlinden 1800; as a republican he intrigued against Napoleon and, when banished, joined the Allies and was killed at the Battle of Dresden.

Morecambe resort city in Lancashire, England, on Morecambe Bay, conjoined with the port of Heysham, which has a ferry service to Ireland; joint population (1982) 43,000.

Morecambe Bay inlet of the Irish Sea, between the Furness Peninsula (Cumbria) and Lancashire, England, with shallow sands. There are oil wells, and natural gas 30 mi/50 km offshore.

morel any edible mushroom of the genus *Morchella*. The common morel, *M. esculenta*, grows in Europe and North America. The yellowish-brown cap is pitted like a sponge and about 1 in/2.5 cm long. It is used for seasoning gravies, soups, and sauces.

mores (Latin) the customs and manners of a society.

Morgagni Giovanni Battista 1682–1771. Italian anatomist. As professor of anatomy at Padua, Morgagni carried out more than 400 autopsies, and developed the view that disease was not an imbalance of the body's humors but a result of alterations in the organs. His work *On the Seats and Causes of Diseases as Investigated by Anatomy* 1761 formed the basis of ◊pathology.

Morgan Henry c. 1635–1688. Welsh buccaneer in the Caribbean. He made war against Spain, capturing and sacking Panama 1671. In 1674 he was knighted and appointed lieutenant-governor of Jamaica.

Morgan J(ohn) P(ierpont) 1837–1913. US financier and investment banker whose company (sometimes criticized as "the money trust") became the most influential private banking house after the Civil War, being instrumental in the formation of many trusts to stifle competition. He set up the US Steel Corporation in 1901, and International Harvester in 1902.

They were powerful enough to bail out the Federal Reserve System 1895 and stabilized the economy after the crisis of 1907.

Morgan Lewis Henry 1818–1881. US anthropologist who pioneered the study of NE American Indian culture and was adopted by the Iroquois.

Morgan Thomas Hunt 1866–1945. US geneticist, awarded the 1933 Nobel Prize for Medicine for his pioneering studies in Classical genetics. He was the first to work on the fruit fly, *Drosophila*, which has since become a major subject of genetic studies. He helped establish that the genes were located on the chromosomes, discovered sex chromosomes, and invented the techniques of genetic mapping.

Morgan le Fay in the romance and legend of the English king ◊Arthur, an enchantress and healer, ruler of ◊Avalon and sister of the king, whom she tended after his final battle. In some versions of the legend she is responsible for the suspicions held by the king of his wife ◊Guinevere.

Morgenthau Plan proposals for Germany after World War II, originated by Henry Morgenthau, Jr (1891–1967), US secretary of the Treasury, calling for the elimination of war industries in the Ruhr and Saar basins and the conversion of Germany "into a country primarily agricultural and pastoral in character." The plan had already been dropped by the time the Allied leaders Churchill, Roosevelt, and Stalin met at Yalta Feb 1945.

Morisco one of the Spanish Muslims and their descendants who accepted Christian baptism. They were all expelled from Spain in 1609.

Morisot Berthe 1841–1895. French Impressionist painter who specialized in pictures of women and children.

Morland George 1763–1804. English painter whose picturesque rural subjects were widely reproduced in engravings. He was an admirer of Dutch and Flemish painters of rustic life.

Morley Edward 1838–1923. US physicist who collaborated with Albert ◊Michelson on the Michelson–Morley experiment 1887. In 1895 he established precise and accurate measurements of the densities of oxygen and hydrogen.

Morley Malcolm 1931– . British painter, active in New York from 1964. He coined the term Super-realism for his work in the 1960s.

Morley Robert 1908– . English actor and playwright, active in both Britain and the US. His film work has been mainly character roles, in movies such as *Marie Antoinette* 1938, *The African Queen* 1952, and *Oscar Wilde* 1960.

Morley Thomas 1557–1602. English composer. A student of William ◊Byrd, he became organist at St Paul's Cathedral, London, and obtained a monopoly on music printing. A composer of the English madrigal school, he also wrote sacred music, songs for Shakespeare's plays, and a musical textbook.

Mormon or ***Latter-day Saint*** member of a Christian sect, the Church of Jesus Christ of Latter-day Saints, founded at Fayette, New York, 1830 by Joseph ◊Smith. According to Smith, Mormon was an ancient prophet in North America; his *Book of Mormon* is accepted by Mormons as part of the Christian scriptures. Smith said he found the book, inscribed on golden tablets, with the help of the angel Moroni in 1827, and that he translated it from "reformed Egyptian" by using special glasses. Originally persecuted, the Mormons migrated West under Brigham ◊Young's leadership and prospered. Today the worldwide membership of the Mormon church is about 6 million.

The *Book of Mormon* describes American Indians as descendants of ancient Hebrews who came to North America across the Pacific. Christ is said to have appeared to them after his ascension to establish his church in the New World. The Mormon church claims to be a reestablishment of this pure, original Christianity by divine intervention. The church grew rapidly, especially in the Midwest, but its controversial doctrines and rumors that Smith had taken several wives (as allowed in the Old Testament) provoked persecution, and Smith was killed in Illinois. Further settlements were rapidly established despite opposition, and in 1847 Brigham Young led a westward migration of most of the church's members to the Valley of the Great Salt Lake in what is now Utah. The Mormons under Young openly practiced polygamy, but the church repudiated the practice in 1890, following Congressional pressure related to the proposed admission of Utah as a state. Mormons hold several doctrines not held by other Christians, including the belief that God has a physical body and that human beings may become gods, just as God was once a man. They advocate a strict sexual morality, large families, and respect for authority. They forbid the consumption of alcohol, coffee, tea, and tobacco.

morning glory any twining or creeping plant of the genus *Ipomoea*, especially *I. purpurea*, family Convolvulaceae, native to tropical America, with dazzling blue flowers. Small quantities of substances similar to the hallucinogenic drug ◊LSD are found in the seeds of some species.

Big-root morning glory *I. pandurata* is native to the E US.

Moro Aldo 1916–1978. Italian Christian Democrat politician. Prime minister 1963–68 and 1974–76, he was expected to become Italy's president, but he was kidnapped and shot by Red Brigade urban guerrillas.

Moroccan Crises two periods of international tension 1905 and 1911 following German objections to French expansion in Morocco. Their wider purpose was to break up the Anglo-French entente 1904, but both crises served to reinforce the entente and isolate Germany.

Morocco country in N Africa, bordered N and NW by the Mediterranean, E and SE by Algeria, and S by Western Sahara.

government Morocco is an unusual constitutional monarchy in that the king, as well as being the formal head of state, presides over his appointed cabinet and has powers, under the 1972 constitution, to dismiss the prime minister and other ministers, as well as to dissolve the legislature. This consists of a 306-member chamber of representatives, serving a six-year term; 206 are directly elected by universal suffrage, and 100 are chosen by an electoral college of local councillors and employers' and employees' representatives. There are a number of political parties including the Constitutional Union (UC), the National Rally of Independents (RNI), the Popular Movement (MP), Istiqlal, the Socialist Union of Popular Forces (USFP), and the National Democratic Party (PND).

history Originally occupied by ◊Berber tribes, the coastal regions of the area now known as Morocco were under Phoenician rule during the 10th–3rd centuries BC, became a Roman colony in the 1st century AD. It was invaded in the 5th century by the ◊Vandals, in the 6th century by the Visigoths, and in the 7th century began to be conquered by the Arabs. From the 11th century the region was united under the ◊Almoravids, who ruled a Muslim empire that included Spain, Morocco, and Algeria. They were followed by the ◊Almohads, another Muslim dynasty, whose empire included Libya and Tunisia.

In the 15th century Portugal occupied the Moroccan port of Ceuta but was defeated in 1578. Further European influence began in the 19th century and was more lasting, with Morocco being divided in 1912 into French and Spanish protectorates. It became fully independent as the Sultanate of Morocco in 1956 under Mohammed V (sultan since 1927). The former Spanish protectorate joined the new state, with Tangier, which had previously been an international zone.

The sultan was restyled king of Morocco in 1957. After his death in 1961 he was succeeded by King Hassan II, who has survived several attempted coups and assassinations. Between 1960 and 1972 several constitutions were formulated in an attempt to balance personal royal rule with demands for greater democracy.

Hassan's reign has been dominated by the dispute over ◊Western Sahara, a former Spanish colony seen as historically Moroccan. In 1975 Spain ceded it to Morocco and Mauritania, leaving them to divide it. The inhabitants, who had not been consulted, reacted violently through an independence movement, the ◊Polisario Front. Less than a year later, Morocco and Mauritania were involved in a guerrilla war.

With Algerian support, Polisario set up a government in exile in Algiers, the Sahrahwi Arab Democratic Republic (SADR). This prompted Hassan to sever diplomatic relations with Algeria in 1976. In 1979 Mauritania agreed to a peace treaty with Polisario, and Morocco annexed the part of Western Sahara that Mauritania had vacated. Polisario reacted by intensifying its operations. In 1983 the Organization of African Unity (OAU) proposed a cease-fire, direct negotiations between Morocco and Polisario, and a referendum in Western Sahara. Morocco agreed but refused to deal directly with Polisario.

Although the war was costly, it allowed Hassan to capitalize on the patriotism it generated in his country. In 1984 he unexpectedly signed an agreement with Colonel Khaddhafi of Libya, who had been helping Polisario, for economic and political cooperation and mutual defense. Meanwhile, Morocco was becoming more isolated as SADR gained wider recognition. Toward the end of 1987 the Polisario guerrillas agreed to a cease-fire and in Aug 1988 a United Nations peace plan was accepted by both sides, calling for a referendum to permit the area's inhabitants to choose independence or incorporation into Morocco. Full diplomatic relations with Algeria were restored in May 1988, and with Syria in Jan 1989. In 1990–91 Morocco opposed Iraq's invasion of Kuwait. Domestically, the surge in Islamic fundamentalism concerned the government.

Morocco
The Kingdom of
(al-Mamlaka al-Maghrebia)

0 miles 500
0 km 1000
ATLANTIC OCEAN
MEDITERRANEAN SEA
Rabat
MOROCCO
Algeria
Western Sahara

area 177,070 sq mi/458,730 sq km (excluding W Sahara)
capital Rabat
cities Marrakesh, Fez, Meknès; ports Casablanca, Tangier, Agadir
physical mountain ranges NE–SW; fertile coastal plains in W
features Atlas Mountains; the towns Ceuta (from 1580) and Melilla (from 1492) are held by Spain; tunnel crossing the Strait of Gibraltar to Spain proposed 1985
head of state Hassan II from 1961
head of government Mohamed Karim Lamrani from 1984
political system constitutional monarchy
political parties Constitutional Union (UC), right-wing; National Rally of Independents (RNI), royalist; Popular Movement (MP), moderate Socialist; Istiqual, nationalist, right-of-center; Socialist Union of Popular Forces (USFP), progressive Socialist; National Democratic Party (PND), moderate, nationalist
exports dates, figs, cork, wood pulp, canned fish, phosphates
currency dirham
population (1990 est) 26,249,000; growth rate 2.5% p.a.
life expectancy men 62, women 65 (1989)
language Arabic (official) 75%, Berber 25%, French, Spanish
religion Sunni Muslim 99%
literacy men 45%/women 22% (1985 est)
GNP $18.7 bn; $750 per head (1988)
chronology
1912 Morocco established as a French and Spanish protectorate.
1956 Independence achieved from France as the Sultanate of Morocco.
1957 Sultan restyled king of Morocco.
1961 Hassan II came to the throne.
1969 Former Spanish province of Ifni returned to Morocco.
1972 Major revision of the constitution.
1975 Western Sahara ceded by Spain to Morocco and Mauritania.
1976 Guerrilla war in the Sahara by the Polisario Front. Sahrawi Arab Democratic Republic (SADR) established in Algiers. Diplomatic relations between Morocco and Algeria broken.
1979 Mauritania signed a peace treaty with Polisario.
1983 Peace formula for the Sahara proposed by the Organization of African Unity (OAU) but not accepted by Morocco.
1984 Hassan signed an agreement for cooperation and mutual defense with Libya.
1987 Cease-fire agreed with Polisario, but fighting continued.
1988 Diplomatic relations with Algeria restored.
1989 Diplomatic relations with Syria restored.

Moroni capital of the Comoros Republic, on Njazídja (Grand Comore); population (1980) 20,000.

Morpheus in Greek and Roman mythology, the god of dreams, son of Hypnos or Somnus, god of sleep.

morphine narcotic alkaloid $C_{17}H_{19}NO_3$ derived from ◊opium and prescribed only to alleviate severe pain. Its use produces serious side effects, including nausea, constipation, tolerance, and addiction, but it is highly valued for the relief of the terminally ill.

morphogen in medicine, one of a class of substances believed to be present in the growing embryo, controlling its growth pattern. It is thought that

Morris *(left) William Morris, photographed by Abel Lewis (c. 1880). (right) The "strawberry thief" design by Morris, in printed cotton. It was patented 1883.*

variations in the concentration of morphogens in different parts of the embryo cause them to grow at different rates.

morphology in biology, the study of the physical structure and form of organisms, in particular their soft tissues.

Morrigan in Celtic mythology, a goddess of war and death who could take the shape of a crow.

Morris Robert 1734–1806. American merchant and political leader; signer of the Declaration of Independence. He became a cautious supporter of American independence, serving in the Continental Congress 1775–78 and signing the Declaration of Independence 1776. In 1781 he was appointed superintendent of finance by the Continental Congress and dealt with the pressing economic problems of the new nation. After attending the Constitutional Convention 1787, he served as one of Pennsylvania's first US senators 1789–95. Poor investments and bankruptcy plagued him in later years.

Born in Liverpool, England, Morris immigrated to America 1747, joining a merchant firm in Philadelphia.

Morris Thomas, Jr 1851–1875. British golfer. One of the first great champions, he was known as "Young Tom" to distinguish him from his father (known as "Old Tom"). Morris Jr won the British Open four times between 1868 and 1872.

Morris William 1834–1896. English designer, Socialist, and poet who shared the Pre-Raphaelite painters' fascination with medieval settings. His first book of verse was *The Defence of Guenevere* 1858. In 1862 he founded a firm for the manufacture of furniture, wallpapers, and the like, and in 1890 he set up the Kelmscott Press to print beautifully designed books. The prose romances *A Dream of John Ball* 1888 and *News from Nowhere* 1891 reflect his Socialist ideology. He also lectured on socialism.

Morris abandoned his first profession, architecture, to study painting, but had a considerable influence on such architects as William Lethaby and Philip ◊Webb. A founder of the Arts and Crafts movement, Morris did much to raise British craft standards.

morris dance an English folk dance. In early times it was usually performed by six men, one of whom wore girl's clothing while another portrayed a horse. The others wore costumes decorated with bells. Morris dancing probably originated in pre-Christian ritual dances and is still popular in the UK and the US.

Morrison Toni 1931– . US novelist whose fiction records black life in the South. Her works include *Song of Solomon* 1978, *Tar Baby* 1981, and *Beloved* 1987, based on a true story about infanticide in Kentucky, which won the Pulitzer Prize 1988.

Morse Samuel (Finley Breese) 1791–1872. US inventor. In 1835 he produced the first adequate electric ◊telegraph, and in 1843 was granted $30,000 by Congress for an experimental telegraph line between Washington, DC and Baltimore, Maryland. The first message 1844 transmitted between the two cities was "What hath God wrought!" With his assistant Alexander Bain he invented the ◊Morse code.

Born in Charlestown, Massachusetts, Morse graduated from Yale 1810 and studied art in England. He served as the first president of the National Academy of Design 1826–45, which he helped to found, and taught at New York University from 1832.

Morse *Samuel Morse invented the electric telegraph and developed a code system (Morse Code) to send messages.*

Morse code international code for transmitting messages by wire or radio using signals of short (dots) and long (dashes) duration, originated by Samuel Morse for use on his ◊telegraph.

The letters SOS (3 short, 3 long, 3 short) form the international distress signal, being distinctive and easily transmitted (popularly but erroneously save our souls). By radio telephone the distress call is "Mayday," for similar reasons (popularly alleged to derive from French *m'aidez*, help me).

Morse code

A .-	B -...	C -.-.	D -..	E .	F ..-.
G --.	H	I ..	J .---	K -.-	L .-..
M --	N -.	O ---	P .--.	Q --.-	R .-.
S ...	T -	U ..-	V ...-	W .--	X -..-
Y -.--	Z --..				
1 .----	2 ..---	3 ...--	4 ....-	5	
6 -....	7 --...	8 ---..	9 ----.	0 -----	

Morte D'Arthur, Le a series of episodes from the legendary life of King Arthur by Thomas Malory, completed 1470, regarded as the first great prose work in English literature. Only the last of the eight books composing the series is titled *Le Morte D'Arthur*.

mortgage the pledging of real property—usually a building—as security for repayment of a loan. The loan and contracted interest is repaid over a contracted period of years, at which time ownership of the property reverts to the titleholder.

Mortimer John 1923– . English lawyer and writer. His works include the plays *The Dock Brief* 1958 and *A Voyage Round My Father* 1970, the novel *Paradise Postponed* 1985, and the television series "Rumpole of the Bailey," from 1978, centered on a fictional lawyer.

Mortimer Roger de, 8th Baron of Wigmore and 1st Earl of March c. 1287–1330. English politician and adventurer. He opposed Edward II and with Edward's queen, Isabella, led a rebellion against him 1326, bringing about his abdication. From 1327 Mortimer ruled England as the queen's lover, until Edward III had him executed.

mortmain lands held by a corporate body, such as the church, in perpetual or inalienable tenure.

In the Middle Ages, alienation in mortmain, usually to a church in return for a ◊chantry foundation, deprived the feudal lord of his future incidents (payments due to him when the land changed ownership) and rights of wardship, and so attempts were often made to regulate the practice.

Morton Henry Vollam 1892–1979. English journalist and travel writer, author of the *In Search of . . .* series published during the 1950s. His earlier travel books include *The Heart of London* 1925, *In the Steps of the Master* 1934, and *Middle East* 1941.

Morton Jelly Roll. Adopted name of Ferdinand Joseph La Menthe 1885–1941. US New Orleans-style jazz pianist, singer, and composer. Influenced by Scott Joplin, he was a pioneer in the development of jazz from ragtime to swing by improvising and imposing his own personality on the music. His 1920s band was called the Red Hot Peppers.

Morton William Thomas Green 1819–1868. US dentist who in 1846, with C Thomas Jackson (1805–80), a chemist and physician, introduced ◊ether as an anesthetic. They patented the process and successfully publicized it.

mosaic a design or picture produced by inlaying small pieces of marble, glass, or other materials. Mosaic was commonly used by the Romans for decorating the floors and walls of their villas and baths (for example Hadrian's Villa at Tivoli). It was used to decorate churches by the Byzantines.

The art was revived by the Italians during the 13th century, when it was used chiefly for the decoration of churches (for example San Vitale, ◊Ravenna).

Moscow (Russian *Moskva*) capital of the USSR (to 1991) and Moskva region, on the Moskva river

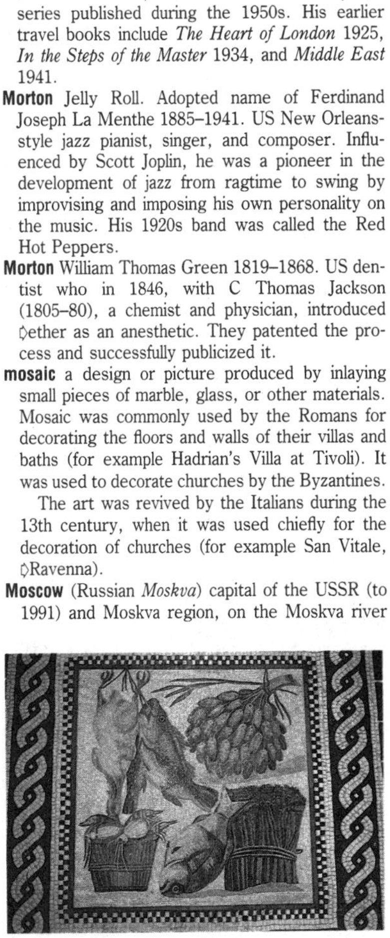

mosaic *A mosaic from the 1st or 2nd century AD from southern Italy.*

400 mi/640 km SE of Leningrad; population (1987) 8,815,000. Its industries include machinery, electrical equipment, textiles, chemicals, and many food products.

features The 12th-century Kremlin (Citadel), at the center of the city, is a walled enclosure containing a number of historic buildings, including three cathedrals, one of them the burial place of the tsars; the Ivan Veliki tower 300 ft/90 m, a famine-relief work commissioned by Boris Godunov 1600; various palaces, including the former imperial palace, museums, and the Tsar Kolokol, the world's largest bell (200 tons) 1735. The walls of the Kremlin are crowned by 18 towers and have five gates. Red Square, used for political demonstrations and processions, contains St Basil's Cathedral, the state department store GUM, and Lenin's tomb. The headquarters of the ◊KGB, with Lubyanka Prison behind it, is in Dzerzhinsky Square; the underground railroad was opened 1935. Institutions include Moscow University 1755 and People's Friendship University (for foreign students) 1953; the ◊Academy of Sciences, which moved from Leningrad 1934; Tretyakov Gallery of Russian Art 1856; Bolshoi Theatre 1780 for opera and ballet; Moscow Art Theatre 1898; Moscow State Circus. Moscow is the seat of the patriarch of the Russian Orthodox Church. On the city outskirts is Star City (Zvezdnoy Gorodok), the Soviet space center.

Moscow is the largest industrial center of the USSR, linked with Stavropol by oil pipeline 300 mi/480 km, built 1957.

history Moscow, founded as the city-state of Muscovy 1127, was destroyed by the Mongols during the 13th century, but rebuilt 1294 by Prince Daniel (died 1303) as the capital of his principality. During the 14th century, it was under the rule of ◊Alexander Nevski, Ivan I (1304–41), and Dmitri Donskai (1350–89), and became the foremost political power in Russia, and its religious capital. It was burned in 1571 by the khan of the Crimea, and ravaged by fire in 1739, 1748, and 1753; in 1812 it was burned by its own citizens to save it from Napoleon's troops, or perhaps by accident. It became capital of the Russian Soviet Federated Social Republic (RSFSR) 1918, and of the Union of Soviet Socialist Republics (USSR) 1922. In World War II Hitler's troops were within 20 mi/30 km of Moscow by Nov 1941, but failed to take the city. In the USSR's governmental disintegration 1991, Moscow lost its status as capital.

Moseley Henry Gwyn-Jeffreys 1887–1915. British physicist, a student of Ernest ◊Rutherford, who devoted his career to research on the structure of the atom. He concluded that the atomic number is equal to the charge on the nucleus, thus modernizing the ◊periodic table of the elements 1913–14, arranging it by atomic number (instead of atomic weight, as presented by ◊Mendeleyev). When the elements are so arranged, problems appearing in the Mendeleyev version are resolved. Moseley's work was widely respected; his career was cut short by serving in the Gallipoli campaign of World War I.

Moselle or ***Mosel*** a river in W Europe some 320 mi/515 km long; it rises in the Vosges, France, and is canalized from Thionville to its confluence with the ◊Rhine at Koblenz in Germany. It gives its name to the *départements* of Moselle and Meurthe-et-Moselle in France.

Moses c. 13th century BC. Hebrew lawgiver and judge who led the Hebrews out of slavery in Egypt (Exodus) and, after wandering 40 years in the desert, brought them to the border (E of the Jordan) of the promised land of Canaan. On Mount Sinai he claimed to have received from Jehovah the Ten Commandments engraved on tablets of stone. The first five books of the Old Testament—in Judaism, the ◊*Torah*—are called the *Five Books of Moses*.

According to the Torah, the infant Moses was hidden among the bulrushes on the banks of the Nile when the pharaoh commanded that all newborn male Hebrew children should be destroyed. He was found by a daughter of pharaoh, who reared him. His brother ◊Aaron helped him lead and he and his descendents are the high priests of Judaism. Moses died at the age of 120, being allowed only a view of the promised land (from Mt Pisgah).

Moses "Grandma" (born Anna Mary Robertson) 1860–1961. US painter. She was self-taught, and began full-time painting in about 1927, after many years as a farmer's wife. She painted naive and colorful scenes from rural American life.

Moses Ed(win Corley) 1955– . US track athlete and 400 meters hurdler. Between 1977 and 1987 he ran 122 races without defeat.

He first broke the world record in 1976 and set a time of 47.02 seconds in 1983. Twice Olympic champion and twice world champion.

CAREER HIGHLIGHTS

Olympic champion (400 meters hurdles) 1976, 1984
world champion (400 meters hurdles) 1983, 1987.

Moses Robert 1888–1981. US public official and urban planner. Although never elected to public office, he had tremendous power for more than 40 years and was known as a power broker. He was hired by the New York City municipal government, later headed a state redevelopment program, and served as New York secretary of state 1927–28. Moses was the unsuccessful Republican candidate for New York governor 1934. Parks commissioner for New York State 1924–64 and New York City 1934–60, he oversaw the development of bridges, highways, and public facilities. Moses served as chairman of the Triborough Bridge and Tunnel Authority 1946–68, chairman of the New York State Power Authority 1954–63, and president of the 1964–65 New York World's Fair.

Born in New Haven, Connecticut, and educated at Yale and Oxford universities, Moses received his PhD from Columbia University 1914.

Mosi-oa-tunya the African name for the ◊Victoria Falls of the Zambezi river.

Moskva the Russian name for ◊Moscow, capital of the USSR.

Moslem alternate spelling of Muslim, a follower of ◊Islam.

Mosley Oswald (Ernald) 1896–1980. British politician, founder of the British Union of Fascists (BUF). He was a member of Parliament 1918–31, then led the BUF until his internment 1940–43, when he was released on health grounds. In 1946 Mosley was denounced when it became known that Italy had funded his prewar efforts to establish ◊fascism in Britain, but in 1948 he resumed fascist propaganda with his Union Movement, the revived BUF.

mosque (Arabic *mesjid*) in Islam, a place of worship. Chief features are: the dome; the minaret, a balconied turret from which the faithful are called to prayer; the *mihrab*, or prayer niche, in one of the interior walls, showing the direction of the holy city of Mecca; and an open court surrounded by porticoes.

The earliest mosques were based on the plan of Christian basilicas, although different influences contributed toward their architectural development and various styles are now found throughout the world.

mosquito any of the family Culicidae. The female mosquito has needlelike mouthparts and sucks blood before laying eggs. Males feed on plant juices. Some mosquitoes carry diseases such as ◊malaria.

Mosquito Coast the Caribbean coast of Honduras and Nicaragua, characterized by swamp, lagoons and tropical rainforest. A largely undeveloped territory occupied by Miskito Indians, Garifunas and Zambos, many of whom speak English. Between 1823 and 1860 Britain maintained a protectorate over the Mosquito Coast which was ruled by a succession of "Mosquito Kings."

moss small nonflowering plant of the class Musci (10,000 species), forming with the ◊liverworts and the ◊hornworts the order Bryophyta. The stem of each plant bears ◊rhizoids that anchor it; there are no true roots. Leaves spirally arranged on its lower portion have sexual organs at their tips. Most mosses flourish best in damp conditions where other vegetation is thin. The peat or bog moss *Sphagnum* was formerly used for surgical dressings.

Moss gardens are popular in Japan; there is one at the Moss Temple, near Kyoto.

Mossadegh Mohammed 1880–1967. Iranian prime minister 1951–53. A dispute arose with the Anglo-Iranian Oil Company when he called for the nationalization of Iran's oil production, and when he failed in his attempt to overthrow the shah he was arrested by loyalist forces with support from the US. From 1956 he was under house arrest.

Mössbauer Rudolf 1929– . German physicist who discovered in 1958 that in certain conditions a nucleus can be stimulated to emit very sharply defined beams of gamma rays. This became known as the Mössbauer effect. Such a beam was used in 1960 to provide the first laboratory test of ◊Einstein's general theory of relativity. For his work on gamma rays Mössbauer shared the 1961 Nobel Prize for Physics with Robert ◊Hofstadter.

Mostaganem industrial port (metal and cement) in NW Algeria, linked by pipeline with the natural gas fields at Hassi Messaoud; population (1982) 169,500. It was founded in the 11th century.

Mostar industrial town (aluminum, tobacco) in Bosnia and Herzegovina, Yugoslavia, known for its grapes and wines; population (1981) 110,000.

Mostel Zero (Samuel Joel) 1915–1977. US comedian and actor, active mainly in the theater. His films include *Panic in the Streets* 1950, *A Funny Thing Happened on the Way to the Forum* 1966, *The Producers* 1967, and *The Front* 1976.

Mosul industrial city (cement, textiles) and oil center in Iraq, on the right bank of the Tigris, opposite the site of ancient ◊Nineveh; population (1985) 571,000. Once it manufactured the light cotton fabric muslin, which was named after it.

motet a form of sacred, polyphonic music for unaccompanied voices that originated in 13th-century Europe.

moth any of the various families of mainly night-flying insects of the order Lepidoptera, which also includes the butterflies. Their wings are covered with microscopic scales. The mouthparts are formed into a sucking proboscis, but certain moths have no functional mouthparts, and rely upon stores of fat and other reserves built up during the caterpillar stage. In many cases the males are smaller and more brightly colored than the females. At least 100,000 different species of moths are known.

Moths feed chiefly on the nectar of flowers, and other fluid matter; some, like the ◊hawk moths, frequent flowers and feed while hovering.

The females of some species (such as bagworm moths) have wings either absent or reduced to minute flaps. Moths vary greatly in size. The minute Nepticulidae sometimes have a wingspread less than 0.1 in/3 mm, while the giant Noctuid or owlet moth *Erebus agrippina* measures about 11 in/280 mm across.

The larvae (caterpillars) have a well-developed head and three thoracic and ten abdominal segments. Each thoracic segment bears a pair of short legs, ending in single claws; a pair of sucker-like abdominal feet is present on segments three to six and ten of the hind-body. In the family Geometridae the caterpillars bear the abdominal feet only on segments six and ten of the hind body. They move by a characteristic looping gait and are known as "loopers," "inchworms," or geometers. Projecting from the middle of the lower lip of a caterpillar is a minute tube or spinneret, through which silk is emitted to make a cocoon within which the change to the pupa or chrysalis occurs. Silk glands are especially large in the ◊silkworm moth. Many caterpillars, including the geometers, which are sought by birds, are protected by their resemblance in both form and coloration to their immediate surroundings. Others, which are distasteful to such enemies, are brightly colored or densely hairy.

The feeding caterpillars of many moths cause damage: the codling moth, for example, attacks fruit trees; and several species of clothes moth eat natural fibers.

The corn earworm moth infests corn. The largest North American moths are the cecropia moth and polyphemus moth with wingspreads up to 5.5 in/14 cm.

mother-of-pearl or ***nacre*** the smooth lustrous lining in the shells of certain mollusks—for example pearl oysters, abalones, and mussels. When this layer is especially heavy it is used commercially for jewellry and decorations. Mother-of-pearl consists of calcium carbonate. See ◊pearl.

Mother's Day a day set apart in the US, England, and many European countries for honoring mothers. It is thought to have originated in Grafton, West Virginia in 1908 when Anna Jarvis observed the anniversary of her mother's death.

In the US, Australia, and Canada Mother's Day is observed on the second Sunday in May; in the UK it is known as Mothering Sunday and observed on the fourth Sunday of Lent.

Motherwell Robert 1915–1991. US painter associated with the New York school of ◊action painting. Borrowing from Picasso, Matisse, and the Surrealists, Motherwell's style of Abstract Expressionism retained some suggestion of the figurative. His works include the "Elegies to the Spanish Republic" 1949–76, a series of over 100 paintings devoted to the Spanish Revolution.

Born in Aberdeen, Washington, Motherwell studied art in California and at Harvard and Columbia universities.

Motherwell and Wishaw industrial town (Ravenscraig iron and steel works, coal mines) in Strathclyde, Scotland, SE of Glasgow; population (1981) 68,000. The two burghs were amalgamated in 1920.

motion picture or ***moving picture*** see ◊cinema.

motion sickness nausea and vomiting caused by the motion of automobiles, boats, or aircraft. Constant vibration and movement sometimes stimulates changes in the fluid of the semicircular canals (responsible for balance) of the inner ear, to which the individual fails to adapt, and to which are added visual and psychological factors.

Space sickness is a special case where normal body movements result in unexpected and unfamiliar signals to the brain, due to the unique environment of weightlessness. Astronauts achieve some control over symptoms by wedging themselves in their bunks.

motor anything that produces or imparts motion; a machine that provides mechanical power, particularly an ◊electric motor. Machines that burn fuel (gasoline, diesel) are usually called engines, but the internal-combustion engine that propels vehicles has long been called a motor, hence "motoring" and "motorcar" were used as early automotive terms. Actually the motor is a part of the ◊automobile engine.

motorboat small, waterborne craft for pleasure cruising or racing, powered by a gasoline, diesel, or gas-turbine engine. A boat not equipped as a motorboat may be converted by a detachable outboard motor. For increased speed, such as in racing, motorboat hulls are designed to skim the water (aquaplane) and reduce frictional resistance. Plastics, steel, and light alloys are now used in construction as well as the traditional wood.

In recent designs, drag is further reduced with hydrofins and ◊hydrofoils, which enable the hull to rise clear of the water at normal speeds. Notable events in motor or "powerboat" racing include the American Gold Cup 1947 (over a 90 mi/145 km course) and the Round-Britain race 1969.

motorcycle or ***motorbike*** two-wheeled vehicle propelled by a ◊gasoline engine. The motorbike is the lightweight version, with less power than the motorcycle, which may be equipped with a sidecar. The first successful motorized bicycle was built in France 1901, and British and US manufacturers first produced motorbikes 1903.

In 1868 Ernest and Pierre Michaux in France experimented with a steam-powered bicycle, but the steam power unit was too heavy and cumbersome. Gottlieb ◊Daimler, a German engineer, created the first motorcycle when he installed his lightweight gasoline engine in a bicycle frame 1885. Daimler soon lost interest in two wheels in favor of four and went on to pioneer the ◊automobile.

The first really successful two-wheel design was devised by Michael and Eugene Werner in France 1901. They adopted the classic motorcycle layout with the engine low down between the wheels. Harley Davidson in the US and Triumph in the UK began manufacture 1903. Road races like the Isle of Man TT (Tourist Trophy), established 1907, helped improve motorcycle design and it soon evolved into more or less its present form. Until the 1970s British manufacturers predominated but today Japanese motorcycles, such as Honda, Kawasaki, Suzuki, and Yamaha, dominate the world market. They make a wide variety of machines, from mopeds (lightweights with pedal assistance) to streamlined superbikes capable of speeds up to 160 mph/250 kph. There is still a smaller but thriving Italian motorcycle industy, making more specialist bikes. Laverda, Moto Guzzi, and Ducati continue to manufacture in Italy.

The lightweight bikes are generally powered by a ◊two-stroke gasoline engine, while bikes with an engine capacity of 250 cc upward are generally ◊four-strokes, although many special-use larger bikes (such as those developed for off-road riding and racing) are two-stroke. Most motorcycles are air-cooled—their engines are surrounded by metal fins to offer a large surface area—although some have a water-cooling system similar to that of a car. Most small bikes have single-cylinder engines, but larger machines can have as many as six. The single-cylinder engine is economical and was popular in British manufacture, then the Japanese developed multiple-cylinder models, but there has recently been some return to single-cylinder engines. A revived British Norton racing motorcycle uses a Wankel (rotary) engine. In the majority of bikes a chain carries the drive from the engine to the rear wheel, though some machines are now fitted with shaft drive.

motorcycle racing speed contests on motorcycles. It has many different forms: road racing over open roads; circuit racing over purpose-built tracks; speedway over oval-shaped dirt tracks; motocross over natural terrain, incorporating hill climbs; and trials, also over natural terrain, but with the addition of artificial hazards.

For finely tuned production machines, there exists a season-long world championship Grand Prix series with various categories for machines with engine sizes 125 cc–500 cc. Important events are the world championships which have been in existence since 1949: the Blue Riband event is the 500 cc class; the Isle of Man Tourist Trophy, the principal race of which is the Senior TT.

motor effect the tendency of a wire carrying an electric current in a magnetic field to move. The direction of the movement is given by the ◊left-hand rule. This effect is used in the ◊electric motor. It also explains why streams of electrons produced, for instance, in a television tube can be directed by electromagnets.

motor nerves in anatomy, nerves that transmit impulses from the central nervous system to muscles or body organs. Motor nerves cause voluntary and involuntary muscle contractions, and stimulate glands to secrete hormones.

motor neuron disease incurable wasting disease in which the nerve cells controlling muscle action gradually die, causing progressive weakness and paralysis. It usually occurs in later life and may be caused by an abnormal protein retained within the nerve cells.

Motown the first black-owned US record company, founded in Detroit (Mo[tor] Town) 1959 by Berry Gordy, Jr (1929–). Its distinctive, upbeat sound (exemplified by the Four Tops and the ◊Supremes) was a major element in 1960s pop music.

The Motown sound was created by in-house producers and songwriters such as Smokey Robinson (1940–) and the team of Holland–Dozier–Holland; performers included Stevie Wonder, Marvin Gaye, and the Temptations. Its influence faded after the company's move to Los Angeles 1971, but it still served as a breeding ground for singers such as Lionel Richie (1950–) and Michael Jackson. Gordy sold Motown to the larger MCA company in 1988.

Mott Nevill Francis 1905– . British physicist who researched the electronic properties of metals, semiconductors, and noncrystalline materials. He shared the Nobel Prize for Physics 1977.

mouflon sheep *Ovis ammon* found wild in Cyprus, Corsica, and Sardinia. It has woolly underfur in winter, but this is covered by heavy guard hairs. The coat is brown, with white belly and rump. Males have strong curving horns. The mouflon lives in mountain areas.

mold mainly saprophytic ◊fungi living on foodstuffs and other organic matter, a few being parasitic on plants, animals, or each other. Many are of medical or industrial importance, for example penicillin.

Moulins capital of the *département* of Allier, Auvergne, central France; main industries are cutlery, textiles, and glass; population (1982) 25,500. Moulins was capital of the old province of Bourbonnais 1368–1527.

Moulmein port and capital of Mon state in SE Myanmar, on the Salween estuary; population (1983) 202,967.

Moundbuilder a member of any of the various North American Indian peoples of the Midwest and the South who built earth mounds, from about 300 BC. They were linear and pictographic in form for tombs, such as the Great Serpent Mound in Ohio, and truncated pyramids and cones for the platforms of chiefs' houses and temples. See also ◊Hopewell; ◊Natchez.

They carried out group labor projects under the rule of an elite. A major site is Monk's Mound in Mississippi. They were in decline by the time of the Spanish invasion, but traces of their culture live on in the folklore of the Choctaw and ◊Cherokee Indians.

mountain a natural upward projection of the Earth's surface, higher and steeper than a hill. The process of mountain building (orogenesis) consists of volcanism, folding, faulting, and thrusting, resulting from the collision and welding together of two tectonic plates.

mountain ash or rowan flowering tree of the genus *Sorbus*, family Rosaceae. It has pinnate leaves and large clusters of whitish flowers, followed by scarlet berries. The American mountain ash *S. americana* grows to 30 ft/9 m and is native to NE US. The European mountain ash or rowan tree *S. Aucaparia* is planted widely as an ornamental.

mountain biking recreational sport that is enjoying increasing popularity in the 1990s. Mountain bikes first appeared on the mass market in the US in 1981, in the UK in 1984, and have been used in all aspects of cycling. However, it is also a competition sport with the first world championship being held in France in 1987. The second, the 1990 world championship, was held in Mexico. National bike championships have been held in the US since 1983 and in the UK since 1984. Mountain bikes have ten or 15 gears, a toughened frame, and wider treads on the tires than ordinary bicycles.

mountain

Animals and plants that live on mountains are adapted to cope with low temperatures, strong winds, a thin, poor soil, and air with little oxygen.

With increasing altitude, the climate becomes bleaker. Temperature, for example, falls by roughly 2°F/1°C for every 500ft/150m. On high mountains near the equator, this usually produces distinct zones of vegetation (shown right) similar to those found as one travels from the tropics to the North Pole.

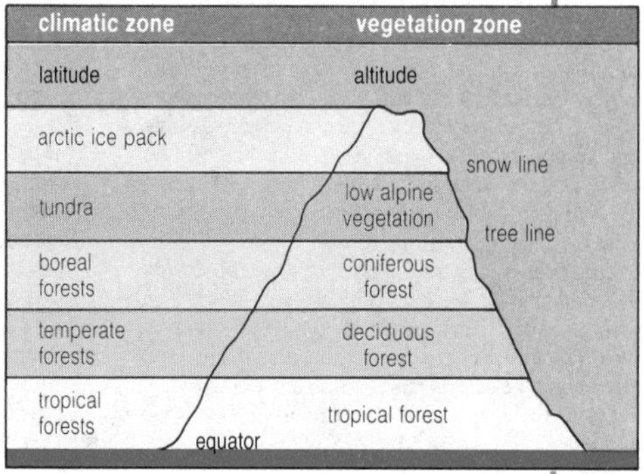
climatic zone
vegetation zone
latitude
altitude
arctic ice pack
snow line
tundra
low alpine vegetation
tree line
boreal forests
coniferous forest
temperate forests
deciduous forest
tropical forests
tropical forest
equator

Alpine wildlife 1. Brown bear 2. Alpine marmot 3. Chamois 4. Peregrine falcon 5. Golden eagle 6. Ibex.

7. Windflowers and gentians bloom in spring and last just a few weeks.

Plants of the alpine zone are small, compact and low-growing to survive the cold, strong winds. Most are perennial, continuing their growth over several years. Mountain animals tend to stay on the high slopes and peaks throughout the year. Many have a thick protective coat, and some of the hoofed mammals have soft pads on their feet that help them to cling to rocks.

1
2
3
4
5
6
7

mountaineering the art and practice of mountain climbing. For major peaks of the Himalayas it was formerly thought necessary to have elaborate support from Sherpas (local people), fixed ropes, and oxygen at high altitudes (siege-style climbing). In the 1980s the Alpine style was introduced. This dispenses with these aids, and relies on human ability to adapt, Sherpa-style, to high altitude.

In 1854 Wetterhorn, Switzerland, was climbed by Alfred Wills, thereby founding the sport; 1865 Matterhorn, Switzerland–Italy, by Edward ◊Whymper; 1897 Aconcagua, Argentina, by Zurbriggen; 1938 Eiger (north face), Switzerland, by Heinrich Harrer; 1953 Everest, Nepal–Tibet, by Edmund ◊Hillary and Norgay ◊Tenzing; 1981 Kongur, China, by Chris Bonington.

mountain lion another name for ◊puma.

Mountbatten Louis, 1st Earl Mountbatten of Burma 1900–1979. British admiral and administrator. In World War II he became chief of combined operations 1942 and commander in chief in SE Asia 1943. As last viceroy of India 1947 and first governor-general of India until 1948, he oversaw that country's transition to independence. He was killed by an Irish Republican Army bomb aboard his yacht in the Republic of Ireland.

He was a favorite relative of the royal family and counselor to Prince Charles.

Mounties popular name for the Royal Canadian Mounted Police, known for their uniform of red jacket and broad-brimmed hat. Their Security Service was established 1950, disbanded 1981, and replaced by the independent Canadian Security Intelligence Service.

Mount Isa mining town (copper, lead, silver, zinc) in NW Queensland, Australia; population (1984) 25,000.

Mount Lofty Range mountain range in SE South Australia; Mount Bryan 3,064 ft/934 m is the highest peak.

Mount Vernon village in Virginia, on the Potomac River, where George Washington lived 1752–99 and was buried on the family estate, now a national monument.

Mourning Becomes Electra 1931 trilogy of plays by

***Mountbatten** Admiral Lord Louis Mountbatten, as India's last viceroy, oversaw the transition to independence.*

Eugene O'Neill that retells the Orestes legend (see ◊Agamemnon), setting it in the world of 19th-century New England. The three are considered among the greatest of modern US plays.

mouse in computing, an input device used to control a pointer on a computer screen. It is about the size of a pack of playing cards, is connected to the computer by a wire, and incorporates one or more buttons that can be pressed. Moving the mouse across a flat surface causes a corresponding movement of the pointer. In this way, the operator can manipulate objects on the screen and make menu selections.

mouse in zoology, one of a number of small rodents with small ears and a long, thin tail, belonging largely to the Old World family Muridae. The house mouse *Mus musculus* is distributed worldwide. It is 3 in/75 mm long, with a naked tail of equal length, and has a gray-brown body.

Native New World mice all belong to the family Cricetidae that is represented worldwide. American cricitids, sometimes called mice, include ◊voles and deer mice. Jumping mice, family Zapodidae, with enlarged back legs, live across the northern hemisphere.

mousebird bird of the order Coliiformes, including a single family (Coliidae) of small crested species peculiar to Africa. They have hairlike feathers, long tails, and mouselike agility. The largest is the blue-naped mousebird *Colius macrourus*, about 14 in/35 cm long.

mouse-hare another name for ◊pika.

Moustier, Le cave in the Dordogne, SW France, with prehistoric remains, giving the name Mousterian to the flint-tool culture of Neanderthal peoples; the earliest ritual burials are linked with Mousterian settlements (150,000 years ago).

mouth the cavity forming the entrance to the digestive tract. In land vertebrates, air from the nostrils enters the mouth cavity to pass down the trachea. The mouth in mammals is enclosed by the jaws, cheeks, and palate.

mouth organ another name for ◊harmonica, a musical instrument.

movie camera or ***motion picture camera*** camera that takes a rapid sequence of still photographs—24 frames (pictures) each second. When the pictures are projected one after the other at the same speed onto a screen, they appear to show movement, because our eyes hold on to the image of one picture before the next one appears.

The cinecamera differs from an ordinary still

mouse

Mozambique
People's Republic of
(República Popular de Moçambique)

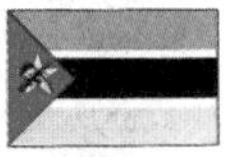

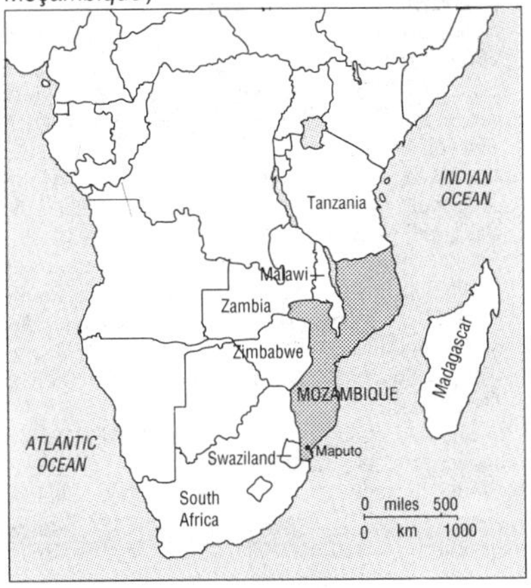
INDIAN OCEAN
Tanzania
Malawi
Zambia
Zimbabwe
MOZAMBIQUE
Madagascar
ATLANTIC OCEAN
Swaziland
Maputo
South Africa
0 miles 500
0 km 1000

area 308,561 sq mi/799,380 sq km
capital (and chief port) Maputo
cities Beira, Nampula
physical mostly flat tropical lowland; mountains in W
features rivers Zambezi, Limpopo; "Beira Corridor" rail, road, and pipeline link with Zimbabwe
head of state and government Joaquim Alberto Chissano from 1986
political system one-party Socialist republic
political parties National Front for the Liberation of Mozambique (Frelimo), Marxist-Leninist
exports shrimp, cashews, sugar, cotton, tea, petroleum products, copra
currency metical
population (1990 est) 14,718,000 (mainly indigenous Bantu peoples; Portuguese 50,000); growth rate 2.8% p.a.; nearly 1 mn refugees in Malawi
life expectancy men 45, women 48 (1989)
language Portuguese (official), 16 African languages
religion animist 60%, Roman Catholic 18%, Muslim 16%
literacy men 55%/women 22% (1985 est)
GDP $4.7 bn; $319 per head (1987)
chronology
1951 Mozambique became an overseas province of Portugal (Portuguese East Africa).
1962 Frelimo (liberation front) established.
1975 Independence achieved from Portugal as a Socialist republic, with Samora Machel as president and Frelimo as the sole legal party.
1977 Renamo resistance group formed.
1983 Reestablishment of good relations with Western powers.
1984 Nkomati Accord of nonaggression signed with South Africa.
1986 Machel killed in airplane crash and succeeded by Joaquim Chissano.
1988 Tanzania announced withdrawal of its troops. South Africa provided training to Mozambiquan forces.
1989 Frelimo offered to abandon Marxist-Leninism; Chissano reelected. Renamo continued attacks on government facilities and civilians.
1990 One-party rule ended. Partial cease-fire agreed.
1991 Peace talks resumed in Rome. Attempted antigovernment coup thwarted.

camera in having a motor that winds on the film continuously, but the film is held still by a claw mechanism while each frame is exposed. When the film is moved between frames, a semicircular disk slides between the lens and the film and prevents exposure.

moving picture see ◊cinema.

Mozambique country in SE Africa, bordered N by Zambia, Malawi, and Tanzania; E by the Indian Ocean; S by South Africa; and E by Swaziland and Zimbabwe.

government The 1975 constitution, revised 1978, provides for a one-party Socialist state, based on the National Front for the Liberation of Mozambique (Frelimo). The president heads its political bureau and central committee secretariat. There is a 250-member People's Assembly, comprising 130 members of Frelimo's central committee plus 120 others from central and provincial governments, the armed forces, and citizens' representatives. The assembly is convened by the president and meets twice a year. Its functions are performed in its absence by a 15-member inner group, called the Permanent Commission, also convened and presided over by the president. Frelimo was formed in 1962 by a merger of three nationalist parties, the Mozambique National Democratic Union (UDENAMO), the Mozambique African Nationalist Union (MANU), and the African Union of Independent Mozambique (UNAMI). Frelimo was reconstituted in 1977 as a "Marxist-Leninist vanguard party."

history Mozambique's indigenous peoples are of Bantu origin. By the 10th century the Arabs had established themselves on the coast. The first European to reach Mozambique was Vasco da ◊Gama in 1498, and the country became a Portuguese colony in 1505. Portugal exploited Mozambique's resources of gold and ivory and used it as a source of slave labor, both locally and overseas. By 1820 the slave trade accounted for 85% of all exports. The trade continued as late as 1912, and 2 million people were shipped to the sugar plantations of Brazil and Cuba; others to neighboring colonies. In 1891 Portugal leased half the country to two British companies who seized African lands and employed forced labor. In 1895 the last indigenous resistance leader was crushed. From 1926 to 1968 Portuguese were encouraged to emigrate to Mozambique, where they were given land and use of forced labor. Mozambicans were forbidden by law to trade or run their own business.

Guerrilla groups opposed Portuguese rule from the early 1960s, the various left-wing factions combining to form Frelimo. Its leader, Samora Machel, demanded complete independence, and in 1974 internal self-government was achieved, with Joaquim Chissano, a member of Frelimo's Central Committee, as prime minister.

Becoming president of an independent Mozambique in 1975, Machel was faced with the emigration of hundreds of thousands of Portuguese settlers, leaving no trained replacements in key economic positions. Two activities had been the mainstay of Mozambique's economy: transit traffic from South Africa and ◊Rhodesia and the export of labor to South African mines. Although Machel supported the African National Congress (ANC) in South Africa and the Patriotic Front in Rhodesia, he knew he must coexist and trade with his two white-governed neighbors. He put heavy pressure on the Patriotic Front for a settlement of the guerrilla war, and this eventually bore fruit in the 1979 ◊Lancaster House Agreement and the election victory in Zimbabwe of Robert Mugabe, a reliable friend of Mozambique, as leader of the newly independent Zimbabwe.

From 1980 Mozambique was faced with widespread drought, which affected most of southern Africa, and attacks by mercenaries under the banner of the Mozambique National Resistance (Renamo), also known as the MNR, who were covertly but strongly backed by South Africa. The attacks concentrated on Mozambique's transport system. MNR forces killed an estimated 100,000 Mozambiquans 1982–1987; 25% of the population were forced to become refugees. 100,000 people died in the famine between 1983 and 1984.

Machel, showing considerable diplomatic skill, had by 1983 repaired relations with the US, undertaken a successful European tour, and established himself as a respected African leader. In 1984 he signed the Nkomati accord, under which South Africa agreed to deny facilities to the MNR, and Mozambique in return agreed not to provide bases for the banned ANC. Machel took steps to honor his side of the bargain but was doubtful about South Africa's good faith. In Oct 1986 he died in an airplane crash near the South African border. Despite the suspicious circumstances, two inquiries pronounced his death an accident.

The following month Frelimo's Central Committee elected former prime minister Joaquim Chissano as his successor. Chissano immediately pledged to carry on the policies of his predecessor. He strengthened the ties forged by Machel with Zimbabwe and Britain and in 1987 took the unprecedented step of requesting permission to attend the ◊Commonwealth Heads of Government summit that year. Mozambique's economic problems were aggravated in 1987 by food shortages, after another year of drought. The MNR also continued to attack government facilities and kill civilians, by some estimates as many as 100,000. In May 1988, South Africa announced that it would provide training and nonlethal material to Mozambiquan forces to enable them to defend the Cabora Bassa dam from MNR attack. In 1988 President Chissano met South African state president Botha and later that year, as tension was reduced, Tanzanian troops were withdrawn from the country. In July 1989, at its annual conference, Frelimo offered to abandon Marxism-Leninism to achieve a national consensus and Chissano was reelected president and party leader.

In Aug 1990 one-party rule was formally ended and in Dec a partial ceasefire was agreed.

Mozart Wolfgang Amadeus 1756–1791. Austrian composer and performer who showed astonishing precocity as a child and was an adult virtuoso. He was trained by his father, Leopold Mozart (1719–1787). From an early age he composed prolifically, the total being some 835 works, including 27 piano concertos, 23 string quartets, 35 violin sonatas, and more than 50 symphonies. His operas include *Idomeneo* 1781, *Le Nozze di Figaro/The Marriage of Figaro* 1786, *Don Giovanni* 1787, *Così fan tutte/Thus Do All Women* 1790, and *Die Zauberflöte/The Magic Flute* 1791. Strongly influenced by ◊Haydn, Mozart's music marks the height of the Classical age of music in its purity of melody and form.

Mozart's career began when, with his sister, Maria Anna, he was taken on a number of tours 1762–79, visiting Vienna, the Rhineland, Holland, Paris, London, and Italy. Mozart not only gave public recitals, but had already begun to compose. In 1772 he was appointed master of the archbishop of Salzburg's court band. He found the post uncongenial, since he was treated as a servant, and in 1781 he was suddenly dismissed. From then on he lived mostly in Vienna and married Constanze Weber in 1782. He supported himself as a pianist, composer, and teacher, but his lack of business acumen often resulted in financial difficulties. His *Requiem*, unfinished at his death, was completed by a pupil. Mozart had been in failing health, and died impoverished. His works were cataloged chronologically by the musicologist Ludwig von Köchel (1800–1877) in 1862.

MP abbreviation for member of Parliament.

mpg abbreviation for miles per gallon.

mph abbreviation for miles per hour.

MPLA Portuguese *Movimento Popular de Libertaçaõ de Angola* (Popular Movement for the Liberation of Angola) Socialist organization founded in the early 1950s that sought to free Angola from Portuguese rule 1961–75 before being involved in the civil war against its former allies ◊UNITA and ◊FNLA 1975–76. The MPLA took control of the country, but UNITA guerrilla activity continues, supported by South Africa.

Mr abbreviation for mister; title used before a name to show that the person is male.

Mr was originally the abbreviation for "master," and "mister" is a corrupted pronunciation of the abbreviation.

MRBM abbreviation for medium-range ballistic missile.

Mrs title used before a name to show that the person is married and female; partly superseded by Ms, which does not indicate marital status. Pronounced "missus," Mrs was originally an abbreviation for mistress.

Ms title used before a woman's name; pronounced "miz." Unlike Miss or Mrs, it can be used by married or unmarried women, and was introduced by the women's movement in the 1970s to parallel Mr, which also does not distinguish marital status.

MS abbreviation for ◊Mississippi.

MS abbreviation for ◊multiple sclerosis.

MSc in education, abbreviation for Master of Science degree.

MS-DOS (abbreviation of Microsoft Disk Operating System) ◊operating system produced by the Microsoft Corporation, widely used on ◊microcomputers with 16-bit microprocessors. A version called PC-DOS is sold by IBM specifically for their range of personal computers. MS-DOS and PC-DOS are usually referred to as DOS. MS-DOS first appeared in the early 1980s, and was based on an earlier system for computers with 8-bit microprocessors, CP/M.

MS(S) abbreviation for manuscript(s).

MT abbreviation for ◊Montana.

Mtwara deepwater seaport in S Tanzania, on Mtwara Bay; population (1978) 48,500. It was opened 1954.

Mubarak Hosni 1928– . Egyptian politician, president from 1981. He commanded the air force 1972–75 (and was responsible for the initial victories in the Egyptian campaign of 1973 against Israel), when he became an active vice-president to Anwar Sadat, and succeeded him on his assassination. He has continued to pursue Sadat's moderate policies, and has significantly increased the freedom of the press and of political association, while trying to repress the growing Islamic fundamentalist movement. He led Egypt's opposition to Iraq's 1990 invasion of Kuwait and had an instrumental role in arranging the historic Middle East peace conference in Nov 1991.

Muckrakers, the a movement of US writers and journalists about 1880–1914 who aimed to expose political, commercial, and corporate corruption, and record frankly the age of industrialism, urban poverty and degradation, unbridled business trusts, and conspicuous consumption. Novelists included Frank Norris, Theodore Dreiser, Jack London, and Upton Sinclair.

Major figures of the earlier period include Rebecca Harding Davis, Henry George (*Progress and Poverty* 1879), and Henry Demarest Lloyd (1847–1903). Later, with the growth of journals like *McClure's Magazine*, the movement included Lincoln Steffens (1866–1936) (*The Shame of the Cities* 1904), Ida M Tarbell, and Thorstein Veblen (*The Theory of the Leisure Class* 1904). Also associated with the Progressive movement in politics, it gave to both US literature and journalism a critical role it was to maintain.

mucous membrane thin skin lining all animal body cavities and canals that come into contact with the air (for example, eyelids, breathing and digestive passages, genital tract). It secretes mucus, a moistening, lubricating, and protective fluid.

mucus a lubricating and protective fluid, secreted by mucous membranes in many different parts of the body. In the gut, mucus smooths the passage of food and keeps potentially damaging digestive enzymes away from the gut lining. In the lungs, it traps airborne particles so that they can be expelled.

mudskipper

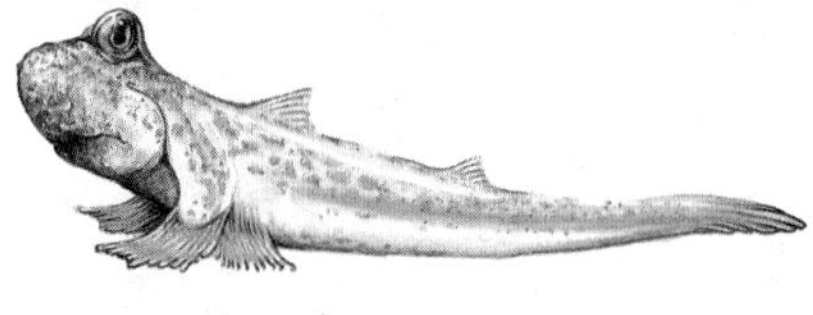

mudnesters Australian group of birds that make their nests from mud, including the apostle bird *Struthidea cinerea* (so called from its appearance in little flocks of about 12), the white-winged chough *Corcorax melanorhamphos*, and the magpie lark *Grallina cyanoleuca*.

mudpuppy brownish salamander of the genus *Necturus* in the family Proteidae. There are five species, living in fresh water in North America. They all breathe in water using external gills. *Necturus maculatus* is about 8 in/20 cm long. Mudpuppies eat fish, snails, and other invertebrates.

mudskipper fish of the goby family, genus *Periophthalmus*, found in brackish water and shores in the tropics, except for the Americas. It can walk or climb over mudflats, using its strong pectoral fins as legs, and has eyes set close together on top of the head. It grows up to 12 in/30 cm long.

mudstone a fine-grained sedimentary rock made up of clay- to silt-sized particles (up to 0.0025 in/0.0625 mm).

muezzin (Arabic) a person whose job is to perform the call to prayer five times a day from the minaret of a Muslim mosque.

muffler device in the exhaust system of cars and motorbikes. Gases leave the engine at supersonic speeds, the exhaust system and muffler are designed to slow them down, thereby silencing them.

Some mufflers use baffle plates (plates with holes, which disrupt the airflow); others use perforated tubes and an expansion box (a large chamber that slows down airflow).

Mugabe Robert (Gabriel) 1925– . Zimbabwean politician, prime minister from 1980 and president from 1987. He was in detention in Rhodesia for nationalist activities 1964–74, then carried on guerrilla warfare from Mozambique. As leader of ◊ZANU he was in an uneasy alliance with Joshua ◊Nkomo of ZAPU (Zimbabwe African People's Union) from 1976. The two parties merged 1987.

Muggeridge Malcolm 1903– . British journalist. He worked for *The Guardian* and *The Daily Telegraph*, and was editor of *Punch* 1953–57. *Chronicles of Wasted Time* 1972–73 is an autobiography.

mugwump (derived from an Indian word meaning "chief") in US political history, a colloquial name for the Republicans who voted in the 1884 presidential election for Grover Cleveland, the Democratic candidate, rather than for their Republican nominee, James G Blaine (1830–1893). Blaine was accused of financial improprieties, and the reform-minded mugwumps were partly responsible for his defeat. The term has come to mean a politician who remains neutral on divisive issues.

Muir John 1838–1914. Scottish-born US conservationist. Beginning in 1880, Muir headed a campaign that led to the establishment of Yosemite National Park. He was named adviser to the National Forestry Commission 1896 and continued to campaign for the preservation of wilderness areas for the rest of his life.

Muir came to the US with his family 1849. After attending the University of Wisconsin, he traveled widely and compiled detailed nature journals of his trips. He moved to California 1868 and later explored Glacier Bay in Alaska and mounted other expeditions to Australia and South America.

Mujaheddin (Arabic *mujahid*, "fighters," from *jihad*, "holy war") Islamic fundamentalist guerrillas of contemporary Afghanistan and Iran.

Mukalla seaport capital of the Hadhramaut coastal region of South Yemen; on the Gulf of Aden 480 km E of Aden; population (1984) 158,000.

Mukden former name of ◊Shenyang, city in China.

Mukden, Battle of the taking of Mukden (now Shenyang), NE China, from Russian occupation by the Japanese 1905, during the ◊Russo-Japanese War. Mukden was later the scene of a surprise attack Sept 18, 1931 by the Japanese on the Chinese garrison, which marked the beginning of their invasion of China.

mulberry any tree of the genus *Morus*, family Moraceae, consisting of a dozen species, including the black mulberry *M. nigra*. It is native to W Asia and has heart-shaped, toothed leaves, and spikes of whitish flowers. It is widely cultivated for its fruit, which, made up of a cluster of small drupes, resembles a raspberry. The leaves of the Asiatic white mulberry *M. alba* are those used in feeding silkworms.

The red mulberry *M. rubra* of the E US also has large edible multiple fruit.

Muldoon Robert David 1921– . New Zealand National Party politician, prime minister 1975–84.

mule hybrid animal, usually the offspring of a male ass and a female horse.

Mülheim an der Ruhr industrial city in North Rhine-Westphalia, Federal Republic of Germany, on the river Ruhr; population (1988) 170,000.

Mulhouse (German *Mülhausen*) industrial city (textiles, engineering, electrical goods) in Haut-Rhin *département*, Alsace, E France; population (1982) 221,000.

Mull second-largest island of the Inner Hebrides, Strathclyde, Scotland; area 367 sq mi/950 sq km; population (1981) 2,600. It is mountainous and is separated from the mainland by the Sound of Mull. There is only one town, Tobermory. The economy is based on fishing, forestry, tourism, and some livestock.

mullah (Arabic "master") a teacher, scholar, or religious leader of Islam. It is also a title of respect given to various other dignitaries who perform duties connected with the sacred law.

mullein any plant of the genus *Verbascum*, family Scrophulariaceae. The great mullein *Verbascum thapsus* has lance-shaped leaves 12 in/30 cm or more in length, covered in woolly down, and a large spike of yellow flowers. It is found in Europe and Asia and is naturalized in North America.

Muller Hermann Joseph 1890–1967. US geneticist who discovered the effect of radiation on genes by his work on fruit flies. He was awarded the Nobel Prize for Medicine 1946.

Müller Johannes Peter 1801–1858. German comparative anatomist whose studies of nerves and sense organs opened a new chapter in physiology by demonstrating the physical nature of sensory perception. His name is associated with a number of discoveries, including the Müllerian ducts in the mammalian fetus and the lymph heart in frogs.

Müller Paul 1899–1965. Swiss chemist awarded a Nobel Prize in 1948 for his discovery 1939 of the first synthetic contact insecticide, DDT.

Muller v Oregon a US Supreme Court decision 1908 dealing with the constitutionality of state laws regulating working conditions for women. Muller, an Oregon laundry owner, was convicted for requiring his female employees to work longer than 10 hours a day, exceeding the legal maximum for women according to state law. He appealed the conviction on the grounds that the state law violated the 14th-Amendment right to freedom of contracts. The Court upheld the conviction, ruling that the law legitimately promoted public health; since women were at greater risk in the workplace, they warranted state protection.

mullet blunt-nosed warm-water fish of the family Mugilidae, found in the Atlantic and Pacific. The striped mullet *Mugil cephalus*, about 2 ft/60 cm long, is commonly netted and smoked. The name mullet is sometimes used for goatfishes, tropical reef fishes of the family Mullidae.

Mulliken Robert Sanderson 1896–1986. US chemist and physicist, who received the 1966 Nobel Prize for Chemistry for his development of the molecular orbital theory.

He was professor at the University of Chicago 1931–61.

Mullingar county town of Westmeath, Republic of Ireland; population (1983) 7,000. It is a cattle market and trout-fishing center.

Mulroney Brian 1939– . Canadian politician. A former businessman, he replaced Joe Clark as Progressive Conservative Party leader 1983 and achieved a landslide in the 1984 election to become prime minister. He won the 1988 election on a platform of free trade with the US, and by the end of 1988 the Canada–US trade agreement was approved. Opposition within Canada to the Meech Lake agreement, a prerequisite to signing the 1982 Constitution, continued to plague Mulroney in his second term.

A compromise reached to persuade Quebec to sign the constitution, the Meech Lake agreement 1987 acknowledged Quebec's separateness and offered more powers and federal funding to all provinces. Not all provinces would agree to the compromise, however, and it collapsed in 1990, contributing to the decline in Mulroney's popularity with the electorate.

Multan industrial city (textiles, precision instruments, chemicals, pottery, jewelry) in Punjab province, central Pakistan, 190 mi/205 km SW of Lahore; population (1981) 732,000. It trades in grain, fruit, cotton, and wool. It is on a site inhabited since the time of Alexander the Great.

multilateralism trade among more than two countries without discrimination over origin or destination and regardless of whether a large trade gap is involved.

Unlike ◊bilateralism, multilateralism does not require the trade flow between countries to be of the same value.

multinational corporation company or enterprise operating in several countries, usually defined as one that has 25% or more of its output capacity located outside its country of origin.

multiple birth in humans, the production of more than two babies from one pregnancy. Multiple births can be caused by more than two eggs being produced and fertilized (often as the result of hormone therapy to assist pregnancy), or by a single fertilized egg dividing more than once before implantation.

multiple sclerosis (MS) incurable chronic disease of the central nervous system, occurring in young or middle adulthood. It is characterized by degeneration of the myelin sheath that surrounds nerves in the brain and spinal cord. It is also known as disseminated sclerosis. Its cause is unknown.

Depending on where the demyelination occurs—which nerves are affected—the symptoms of MS can mimic almost any neurological disorder. Typically seen are unsteadiness, ataxia (loss of muscular coordination), weakness, speech difficulties, and rapid involuntary movements of the eyes. The course of the disease is episodic, with frequent intervals of ◊remission.

multiplier in economics, the theoretical concept, formulated by John Maynard Keynes, of the effect on national income or employment by an adjustment in overall demand. For example, investment by a company in a new plant will stimulate new income and expenditure, which will in turn generate new investment, and so on, so that the actual increase in national income may be several times greater than the original investment.

multistage rocket rocket launch vehicle made up of several rocket stages (often three) joined end to end. The bottom stage fires first, boosting the vehicle to high speed, then it falls away. The next stage fires, thrusting the now lighter vehicle even faster. The remaining stages fire and fall away in turn, boosting the vehicle's payload (cargo) to an orbital speed that can reach 17,500 mph/28,000 kph.

multitasking or ***multiprogramming*** in computing, a system in which one processor appears to run several different programs (or different parts of the same program) at the same time. All the programs are held in memory together and each is allowed to run for a certain period, for example while other programs are waiting for a ◊peripheral device to work or for input from an operator. The ability to multitask depends on the ◊operating system rather than the type of computer.

Munch *Norwegian painter Edvard Munch often used broad areas of color in his paintings, as in* The Sick Child *1907 in Tate Gallery, London.*

Mulu mountainous region in N Borneo near the border with Sabah. Its limestone cave system, one of the largest in the world, was explored by a Royal Geographical Society Expedition 1978.

Mumford Lewis 1895–1990. US urban planner and social critic, concerned with the adverse effect of technology on contemporary society.

He was also concerned about the dehumanization of the individual as a response to a deadening environment. His writings show faith in human capacity to renew the world, however. He is noted for *The Culture of Cities* 1938 and *The City in History* 1961.

mummers' play or ***St George play*** British folk drama enacted in dumb show by a masked cast, performed on Christmas Day to celebrate the death of the old year and its rebirth as the new year. The plot usually consists of a duel between St George and an infidel knight, in which one of them is killed but later revived by a doctor. Mummers' plays are still performed in some parts of Britain.

mummy any dead body, human or animal, that has been naturally or artificially preserved. Natural mummification can occur through freezing (for example, mammoths in glacial ice from 25,000 years ago), drying, or preservation in bogs or oil seeps. Artificial mummification may be achieved by embalming (for example, the mummies of ancient Egypt) or by freeze-drying (see ◊cryonics).

mumps virus infection marked by fever and swelling of the parotid salivary glands (such as those under the ears). It is usually minor in children, although meningitis is a possible complication. In adults the symptoms are severe and it may cause sterility in adult men.

Mumps is the most common form of ◊meningitis in children, but it follows a much milder course than bacterial meningitis, and a complete recovery is usual. Rarely, mumps meningitis may lead to deafness. An effective vaccine against mumps, measles, and rubella (MMR vaccine) is now offered to children aged 18 months.

Munch Edvard 1863–1944. Norwegian painter and printmaker. He studied in Paris and Berlin, and his major works date from the period 1892–1908, when he lived mainly in Germany. His paintings often focus on neurotic emotional states. The *Frieze of Life* 1890s, a sequence of highly charged, symbolic paintings, includes some of his most characteristic images, such as *Skriket/The Scream* 1893. He later reused these in etchings, lithographs, and woodcuts.

Munch was influenced by van Gogh and Gauguin but soon developed his own expressive style, reducing his compositions to broad areas of color with sinuous contours emphasized by heavy brushstrokes, distorting faces and figures. His first show in Berlin 1892 made a great impact on young German artists. In 1908 he suffered a nervous breakdown and returned to Norway. His later works include a series of murals 1910–15 in the assembly halls of Oslo University.

München German name of ◊Munich, city in the Federal Republic of Germany.

Münchhausen Karl Friedrich, Freiherr (Baron) von 1720–1797. German soldier, born in Hanover. He served with the Russian army against the Turks, and after his retirement in 1760 told exaggerated stories of his adventures. This idiosyncrasy was utilized by the German writer Rudolph Erich Raspe (1737–94) in his extravagantly fictitious *Adventures of Baron Munchausen* 1785, which he wrote in English while living in London.

Münchhausen's syndrome emotional disorder in which a patient feigns or invents symptoms to secure medical treatment. In some cases the patient will secretly ingest substances to produce real symptoms. It was named after the exaggerated tales of Baron Münchhausen.

Muncie city in E central Indiana, NE of Indianapolis. Industries include automobile parts, livestock, dairy products, steel forgings, and wire; population (1990) 71,035. It was the subject of Robert and Helen Lynd's *Middletown*, a sociological study of a midwestern city.

Munich (German *München*) industrial city (brewing, printing, precision instruments, machinery, electrical goods, textiles), capital of Bavaria, Federal Republic of Germany, on the river Isar; population (1986) 1,269,400.

features Munich owes many of its buildings and art treasures to the kings ◊Ludwig I and Maximilian II of Bavaria. The cathedral is late 15th century. The Alte Pinakothek contains paintings by old masters, the Neue Pinakothek, modern paintings; there is the Bavarian National Museum, the Bavarian State Library, and the Deutsches Museum (science and technology). The university, founded at Ingolstadt 1472, was transferred to Munich 1826; to the NE at Garching there is a nuclear research center.

history Dating from the 12th century, Munich became the residence of the dukes of Wittelsbach in the 13th century, and the capital of independent Bavaria. It was the scene of the November revolution of 1918, the "Soviet" republic of 1919, and the Hitler putsch of 1923. It became the center of the Nazi movement, and the Munich Agreement of 1938 was signed there. When the 1972 Summer Olympics were held in Munich, a number of Israeli athletes were killed by guerrillas.

Munich Agreement pact signed on Sept 29, 1938 by the leaders of the UK (Neville ◊Chamberlain), France (Edouard ◊Daladier), Germany (Hitler), and Italy (Mussolini), under which Czechoslovakia was compelled to surrender its Sudeten-German districts (the Sudetenland) to Germany. Chamberlain claimed it would guarantee "peace in our time," but it did not prevent Hitler from seizing the rest of Czechoslovakia in March 1939.

Most districts were not given the option of a plebiscite under the agreement. After World War II the Sudetenland was returned to Czechoslovakia, and over 2 million German-speaking people were expelled from the country.

Munn v Illinois a US Supreme Court decision (one of the "Granger Cases") 1877 dealing with state regulation of industry. The owners of Illinois grain elevators filed suit against the state legislature over an 1873 law, which established maximum legal rates for grain storage. The petitioners claimed that this populist legislation interfered with federal regulation of interstate commerce and violated the due process clause. The Court

Münster *Germany's university of Münster, founded 1773 as the university of the duchy of Westphalia.*

voted 7 to 2 to uphold the Illinois law, ruling that it was a legitimate use of state police power in the public interest.

Munro H(ugh) H(ector) British author who wrote under the pen name ◊Saki.

Munster southern province of the Republic of Ireland, comprising the counties of Clare, Cork, Kerry, Limerick, North and South Tipperary, and Waterford; area 9,318 sq mi/24,140 sq km; population (1986) 1,019,000.

It was a kingdom until the 12th century, and was settled in plantations by the English from 1586.

Münster industrial city (wire, cement, iron, brewing and distilling) in North Rhine-Westphalia, Federal Republic of Germany, formerly the capital of Westphalia; population (1988) 268,000. The Treaty of Westphalia was signed simultaneously here and at Osnabrück 1648, ending the Thirty Years' War.

Its university was founded 1773. Badly damaged in World War II, its ancient buildings, including the 15th-century cathedral and town hall, have been restored or rebuilt.

Munternia Romanian name of ◊Wallachia, former province of Romania.

muntjac small deer, genus *Muntiacus*, found in SE Asia. There are about six species. Males have short spiked antlers and two sharp canine teeth forming tusks. They are sometimes called "barking deer" because of their voices.

Muntjac live mostly in dense vegetation and do not form herds.

mural painting (Latin *murus*, wall) the decoration of walls, vaults, and ceilings by means of ◊fresco, oil, ◊tempera, or ◊encaustic methods. Mural painters include Cimabue, Giotto, Masaccio, Ghirlandaio, and, in the 20th century, Diego Rivera.

Murasaki Shikibu c. 978–c. 1015. Japanese writer, a lady at the court. Her masterpiece of fiction, *The Tale of Genji*, is one of the classic works of Japanese literature, and may be the world's first novel.

She was a member of the Fujiwara clan, but her own name is not known; scholars have given her the name Murasaki after a character in the book. It deals with upper-class life in Heian Japan, centering on the affairs of Prince Genji.

Murat Joachim 1767–1815. King of Naples from 1808. An officer in the French army, he was made king by Napoleon, but deserted him in 1813 in the vain hope that Austria and Great Britain would recognize him. In 1815 he attempted unsuccessfully to make himself king of all Italy, but when he landed in Calabria in an attempt to gain the throne he was captured and shot.

Murcia industrial city (silk, metal, glass, textiles, pharmaceuticals), capital of the Spanish province of Murcia, on the river Segura; population (1986) 310,000. Murcia was founded 825 on the site of a Roman colony by 'Abd-ar-Rahman II, caliph of Córdoba. It has a university and 14th-century cathedral.

Murcia autonomous region of SE Spain; area 4,362 sq mi/11,300 sq km; population (1986) 1,014,000. It includes the cities Murcia and Cartagena, and produces esparto grass, lead, zinc, iron, and fruit.

murder unlawful killing of one person by another. If the killer can show provocation by the victim (action or words that would make a reasonable person lose self-control) or diminished responsibility (an abnormal state of mind caused by illness, injury, or mental subnormality), the charge may be reduced to a less serious one. See also ◊assassination; ◊homicide; ◊manslaughter.

Murders in the Rue Morgue, The 1841 tale by the US writer Edgar Allan Poe, acknowledged as the first detective story. Poe's detective Auguste Dupin points to the clues leading to the solution of the macabre mystery in what Poe called a "tale of ratiocination."

Murdoch Iris 1919– . British novelist, born in Dublin. Her novels combine philosophical speculation with often outrageous situations and tangled human relationships. They include *The Sandcastle* 1957, *The Sea, The Sea* 1978, and *The Message to the Planet* 1989.

Murdoch Rupert 1931– . Australian-born US media magnate, who by 1982 had interests in Australia, the UK, the US, and other countries. Among his UK newspapers are the *Sun*, the *News of the World*, and *The Times*; in the US, he has a 50% share of 20th Century Fox, six Metromedia TV stations, and newspaper and magazine publishing companies.

He became a US citizen in 1985.

Murger Henri 1822–1861. French writer, born in Paris. In 1848 he published *Scènes de la vie de bohème/Scenes of Bohemian Life* which formed the basis of Puccini's opera *La Bohème*.

Murillo Bartolomé Estebán c. 1617–1682. Spanish painter, active mainly in Seville. He painted sentimental pictures of the Immaculate Conception; he also specialized in studies of street urchins.

Murillo was born in Seville. Visiting Madrid in the 1640s, he was befriended by the court painter Velázquez. After his return to Seville he received many religious commissions. He founded the academy of painting in Seville 1660 with the help of Herrera the Younger.

Murdoch *British novelist Iris Murdoch has won numerous awards, including Britain's prestigious Booker prize for* The Sea *in 1978.*

Murmansk seaport in NW USSR, on the Barents Sea; population (1987) 432,000. It is the largest city in the Arctic, the USSR's most important fishing port, and base of the icebreakers that keep the Northeast Passage open.

It is the center of Soviet Lapland and the only port on the Soviet Arctic coast that is in use all year round. After the entry of the USSR into World War II in 1941, supplies from the UK and later from the US were unloaded there.

Murnau F W Adopted name of Friedrich Wilhelm Plumpe 1889–1931. German silent-film director, known for his expressive images and "subjective" use of a moving camera in *Der letzte Mumm/The Last Laugh* 1924. Other films include *Nosferatu* 1922, a version of the Dracula story, *Sunrise* 1927.

Murphy Audie 1924–1971. US actor who starred mainly in low-budget Western films. His work includes *The Red Badge of Courage* 1951, *The Quiet American* 1958, and *The Unforgiven* 1960. He was the most decorated soldier of World War II, and was promoted by Hollywood as such, in the film story of his war years *To Hell and Back* 1955, in which he starred.

Murray principal river of Australia, 1,600 mi/2,575 km long. It rises in the Australian Alps near Mount Kosciusko and flows west, forming the boundary between New South Wales and Victoria, and reaches the sea at Encounter Bay, South Australia. With its main tributary, the Darling, it is 2,330 mi/3,750 km long.

Its other tributaries include the Lachlan and the Murrumbidgee. The Dartmouth Dam (1979) in the Great Dividing Range supplies hydroelectric power and has drought-proofed the Murray River system, but irrigation (for grapes, citrus and stone fruits) and navigation schemes have led to soil salinization.

Murray James Augustus Henry 1837–1915. Scottish philologist. He was the first editor of the *Oxford English Dictionary* (originally the *New English Dictionary*) from 1878 until his death; the first volume was published 1884.

Murray cod Australian freshwater fish *Maccullochella macquariensis* that grows to about 6 ft/2 m. It is is named after the river in which it is found.

Murrayfield Scottish rugby ground and home of the national team. It staged its first international in 1925 when Scotland beat England 14–11. The capacity is approximately 70,000.

The ground was built on the site of the old Edinburgh Polo Ground at Murray's Field. The West Stand was added in the 1930s and the East Stand in the 1980s. Over 100,000 fans are reputed to have been in the ground for the match against Wales in 1975.

Murrow Edward R(oscoe) 1908–1965. US broadcast journalist. Hired by the Columbia Broadcasting System (CBS) 1935 to plan its educational programs, Murrow was named director of its European Bureau 1937. From London he covered the events of World War II. Murrow hosted the popular radio show "Hear It Now" 1948–51 and television shows "See It Now" 1951–58, "Person to Person" 1953–58, and "Small World" 1958–60. After leaving CBS, he served as director of the US Information Agency 1961–64.

Born in Greensboro, North Carolina, Murrow attended Washington State College and joined the staff of the Institute of International Education 1932.

Murrumbidgee river of New South Wales, Australia; length 1,050 mi/1,690 km. It rises in the Australian Alps, flows north to the Burrinjuck reservoir, and then west to meet the river ◊Murray.

Murry John Middleton 1889–1957. British writer. He produced studies of Dostoievsky, Keats, Blake, and Shakespeare, poetry, and an autobiographical novel, *Still Life* 1916. In 1913 he mar-

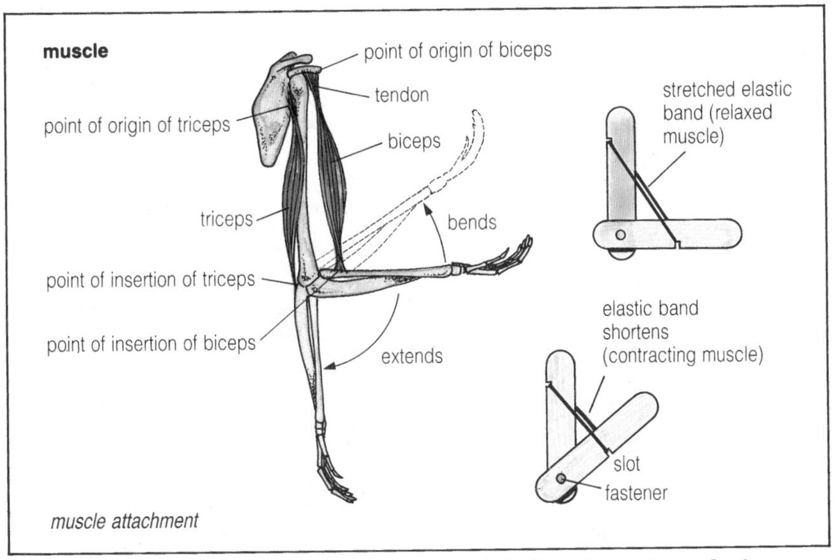
muscle
point of origin of biceps
tendon
point of origin of triceps
biceps
triceps
bends
point of insertion of triceps
point of insertion of biceps
extends
stretched elastic band (relaxed muscle)
elastic band shortens (contracting muscle)
slot
fastener
muscle attachment

ried Katherine Mansfield, whose biography he wrote. He was a friend of D H Lawrence.

Musashi Miyamato 1584–1645. Japanese exponent of the martial arts whose manual *A Book of Five Rings* on samurai strategy achieved immense popularity in the US from 1974 when it appeared in translation. it was said that Japanese businessmen used it as a guide to success.

Muscat or ***Masqat*** capital of Oman, E Arabia, adjoining the port of Matrah, which has a deepwater harbor; combined population (1982) 80,000. It produces natural gas and chemicals.

Muscat and Oman the former name of ◊Oman, country in the Middle East.

muscle contractile animal tissue that produces locomotion and maintains the movement of body substances. Muscle is made of long cells that can contract to between one-half and one-third of their relaxed length.

Striped muscles are activated by ◊motor nerves under voluntary control; their ends are usually attached via tendons to bones. Involuntary or smooth muscles are controlled by motor nerves of the ◊autonomic nervous system, and located in the gut, blood vessels, iris, and various ducts. Cardiac muscle occurs only in the heart, and is also controlled by the autonomic nervous system.

An artificial muscle fiber was developed in the US 1990. Besides replacing muscle fiber, it can be used for substitute ligaments and blood vessels and to prevent tissues sticking together after surgery.

muscovite white mica, $KAl_2(Al,Si_3O_{10}(OH,F)_2$, a common silicate mineral. It is colorless to silvery white with shiny surfaces, and like all micas it splits into thin flakes along its one perfect cleavage. Muscovite is a metamorphic mineral occurring mainly in schists; it is also found in some granites, and appears as shiny flakes on bedding planes of some sandstones.

muscular dystrophy any of a group of inherited chronic muscle disorders marked by weakening and wasting of muscle. Muscle fibers degenerate, to be replaced by fatty tissue, although the nerve supply remains unimpaired.

The commonest form, Duchenne muscular dystrophy, strikes boys, usually before the age of four. The child develops a waddling gait and an inward curvature (lordosis) of the lumbar spine. The muscles affected by dystrophy and the rate of progress vary. There is no cure, but physical treatments can minimize disability.

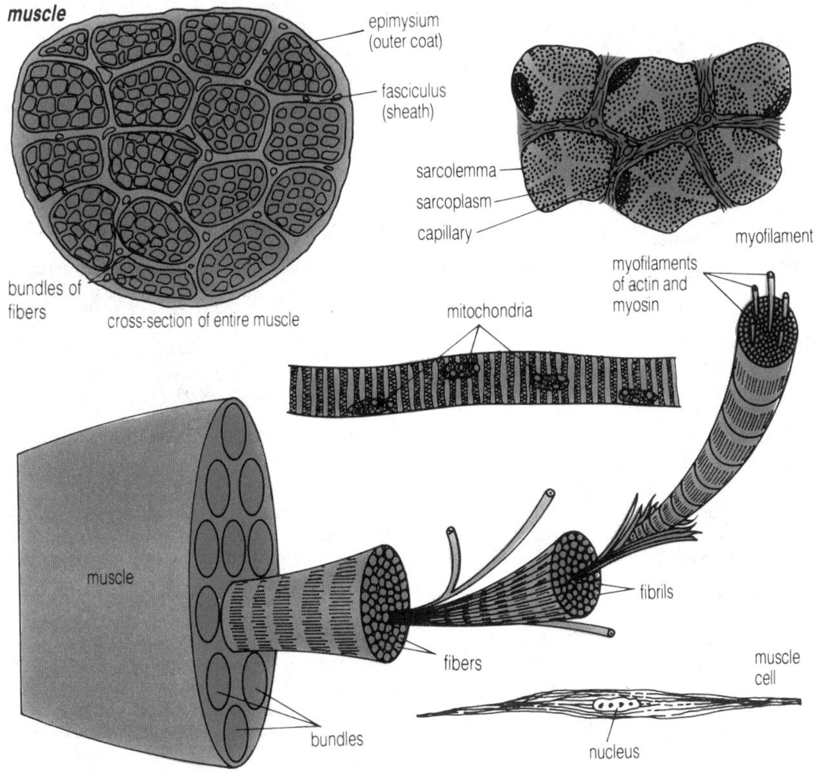
muscle
epimysium (outer coat)
fasciculus (sheath)
sarcolemma
sarcoplasm
capillary
myofilament
bundles of fibers
cross-section of entire muscle
myofilaments of actin and myosin
mitochondria
muscle
fibrils
fibers
muscle cell
bundles
nucleus

Muses in Greek mythology, the nine daughters of Zeus and Mnemosyne (goddess of memory) and inspirers of creative arts: Calliope, epic poetry; Clio, history; Erato, love poetry; Euterpe, lyric poetry; Melpomene, tragedy; Polyhymnia, hymns; Terpsichore, dance; Thalia, comedy; and Urania, astronomy.

Museveni Yoweri Kaguta 1945– . Ugandan general and politician, president from 1986. He led the opposition to Idi Amin's regime 1971–78 and was minister of defense 1979–80 but, unhappy with Milton Obote's autocratic leadership, formed the National Resistance Army (NRA), which helped to remove him. Museveni leads a broad-based coalition government.

Museveni was educated in Uganda and at the University of Dar es Salaam, Tanzania. He entered the army, eventually rising to the rank of general. Until Amin's removal Museveni led the anti-Amin Front for National Salvation. When Obote was ousted in a coup by Tito Okello 1985, Museveni entered into a brief power-sharing agreement with Okello, before taking over as president.

Musgrave Thea 1928– . Scottish composer. Her works, in a conservative modern idiom, include concertos for horn, clarinet, and viola; string quartets; and operas, including *Mary, Queen of Scots* 1977.

Musgrave Ranges Australian mountain ranges on the border between South Australia and the Northern Territory; the highest peak is Mount Woodruffe 5,000 ft/1,525 m. The area is an Aboriginal reserve.

mushroom fruiting body of certain fungi, consisting of an upright stem and a spore-producing cap with radiating gills on the undersurface. There are many edible species belonging to the genus *Agaricus*. See also ◊fungus and ◊toadstool.

Musial Stan(ley Frank). Nicknamed "Stan the Man." 1920– . US baseball player. Born in Donora, Pennsylvania, Musial was an outstanding high-school athlete and was signed by the St Louis Cardinals 1938. As a Cardinal outfielder and first baseman from 1941, Musial played 22 years, during which he led the National League 6 times in hits, 8 times in doubles, 5 times in triples, and 7 times in batting average. He played his last season 1963 and was hired by the Cardinals as an executive. Musial was elected to the Baseball Hall of Fame 1969.

music the art of combining sounds into a unified whole, typically in accordance with fixed patterns and for an esthetic purpose. Music is generally categorized as Classical, ◊jazz, ◊pop music, ◊country and western, and so on.

The Greek word *mousikē* covered all the arts presided over by the Muses. The various civilizations of the ancient and modern world developed their own musical systems. Eastern music recognizes many more subdivisions of an interval than does Western music and also differs from Western music in that the absence, until recently, of written notation ruled out the composition of major developed works; it fostered melodic and rhythmic patterns, freely interpreted (as in the Indian *raga*) by virtuosos.

Western Classical music

Middle Ages The documented history of Western music begins with the liturgical music of the medieval Catholic church, derived from Greek and Hebrew antecedents. The four scales, or modes, to which the words of the liturgy were chanted were traditionally first set in order by St Ambrose in AD 384. St Gregory the Great added four more to the original Ambrosian modes, and this system forms the basis of Gregorian ◊plainsong, still used in the Roman Catholic Church. The organ was introduced in the 8th century, and in the 9th century harmonized music began to be used in churches with notation developing toward its present form. In the 11th century counterpoint was introduced, notably at the monastery of St Martial, Limoges, France, and in the late 12th century at Nôtre Dame in Paris (by Léonin and Perotin). In the late Middle Ages the Provençal and French ◊troubadors and court composers, such as Machaut, developed a secular music, derived from church and folk music (see also ◊Minnesinger).

The 15th and 16th centuries in Europe saw the growth of contrapuntal or polyphonic music. One of the earliest composers was the English musician John Dunstable, whose works inspired the French composer Guillaume Dufay, founder of the Flemish school; its members included Dufay's pupil Joannes Okeghem and the Renaissance composer Josquin Desprez. Other composers of this era were Palestrina of Italy, Orlando di Lasso of Flanders, Victoria of Spain, and Thomas Tallis and William Byrd of England. ◊Madrigals were written during the Elizabethan age in England by such composers as Thomas Morley and Orlando Gibbons.

The 17th-century Florentine Academy, a group of artists and writers, aimed to revive the principles of Greek tragedy. This led to the invention of dramatic recitative and the beginning of opera. Monteverdi was an early operatic composer; by the end of the century the form had evolved further in the hands of Alessandro Scarlatti in Italy and Jean-Baptiste Lully in France. In England the outstanding composer of the period was Purcell.

The early 18th century was dominated by J S Bach and Handel. Bach was a master of harmony and counterpoint. Handel is renowned for his dramatic oratorios. Bach's sons, C P E Bach and J C Bach, reacted against contrapuntal forms and developed the sonata form, the basis of the Classical sonata, quartet, and symphony. In these types of composition mastery of style was achieved by the Austrian composers Haydn and Mozart. With Beethoven, music developed new dynamic and expression, which prefigured Romanticism.

19th century Romantic music, represented in its early stages by Weber, Schubert, Schumann, Mendelssohn, Paganini, and Chopin, tended to be subjectively emotional. Orchestral color was increasingly exploited—most notably by Berlioz—and harmony became more chromatic. Nationalism became prominent at this time, as evidenced by the intense Polish nationalism of Chopin; and the exploitation of Hungarian music by Liszt; the Russians Rimsky-Korsakov, Borodin, Mussorgsky, and, less typically, Tchaikovsky; and the works of the Czechs Dvŏrák, Smetana; and the Norwegian Grieg. Revolutionary changes were brought to German opera by Wagner, although traditional Italian lyricism continued in the operas of Rossini, Verdi, and Puccini. Wagner's contemporary, Brahms, composed with Classical discipline of form combined with Romantic feeling. The Belgian César Franck, with a newly chromatic idiom, also renewed the tradition of polyphonic writing.

20th century Around 1900 a reaction against Romanticism became apparent in the Impressionism of Debussy and Ravel and the chromaticism of Stravinsky and Scriabin. In Austria and Germany, the tonal tradition of Bruckner, Mahler, and Richard Strauss paralleled a disturbing new world of atonal expressionism as composed by Schoenberg, Berg, and Webern. After World War I, Neo-Classicism, represented by Stravinsky, Prokofiev, and Hindemith, attempted to restore 18th-century principles of objectivity and order while maintaining a distinctively 20th-cen-

music: chronology

AD 590	St Gregory the Great was elected pope. His enlightened leadership inspired church music to new heights, initiating Gregorian Chant.
1026	The Italian monk Guido d'Arezzo completed his treatise *Micrologus*. He founded modern notation and tonic so-fa.
1207	Walther von der Vogelweide, Tannhauser, and Wolfram von Eschenbach competed in a song contest at Wartburg Castle, as the age of the Minnesingers or German poet-musicians approached its height.
1240	The earliest known canon, *Sumer is Icumen In*, was composed around this year.
1280	*Carmina burana*, a collection of students' songs, was compiled in Benediktbuern, Bavaria.
1288	France's greatest troubador, Adam de la Halle, died in Naples.
1320	*Ars nova*, a tract by Philippe de Vitry, gave its name to a new, more graceful era in music.
1364	Music's first large-scale masterpiece, the *Notre Dame Mass* of Guillaume de Machaut, was performed in Rheims at the coronation of Charles V of France.
1453	John Dunstable, England's first composer of significance, died in London.
1473	The earliest known printed music, the *Collectorium super Magnificat* by Johannes Gerson, was published in Esslingen, near Stuttgart.
c. 1500	Early forms of the violin were designed in Italy.
1521	Josquin Desprez, the leading musician of his time, died in Condé-sur-Escaut, Burgundy.
c. 1535	The violin was brought to its classic form by Andrea Amati in Italy.
1575	Thomas Tallis and William Byrd jointly published their *Cantiones sacrae*, a collection of 34 motets.
1576	Hans Sachs, the most famous of the Meistersinger (mastersinger) poets and composers, died in Nuremberg.
1597	The first opera, *Dafne*, by Jacopo Corsi and Jacopo Peri, was staged privately at the Corsi Palazzo in Florence.
1610	Monteverdi's *Vespers* was published in Venice.
1637	The world's first opera house opened in Venice.
1644	Antonio Stradivarius was born. His Cremona workshop made more than 1100 stringed instruments (violins, violas, cellos, and guitars); more than 600 of his violins survived into the 20th century.
1672	The violinist John Banister pioneered public concerts in London.
1704	Bartolemmeo Cristofori built the first piano in Florence.
1721	Bach completed his six *Brandenburg Concertos*.
1722	Jean-Philippe Rameau's book *Traité de l'harmonie* founded modern harmonic theory.
1725	Vivaldi's *The Four Seasons* was published in Amsterdam.
1732	Covent Garden Theatre opened in London. It was later destroyed twice by fire, in 1808 and 1856, but rebuilt.
1742	Handel's *Messiah* received its world premiere in Dublin.
1757	Johann Stamitz died in Mannheim, where he had founded the world's first virtuoso orchestra.
1761	Haydn became vice Kapellmeister with the aristocratic Esterháy family, to whom he was connected until his death in 1809.
1788	Mozart completed his last three symphonies, numbers 39–41, in six weeks.
1795	The composer and inventor Thomas Wright introduced metronome markings.
1798	The *Allgemeine Musikalische Zeitung*, a journal of music criticism, was first published in Leipzig.
1805	Beethoven's *Eroica Symphony* vastly expanded the horizons of orchestral music.
1815	Schubert's output for this year included two symphonies, two masses, 20 waltzes and 145 songs.
1821	Weber's opera *Der Freischutz* introduced heroic German Romanticism to opera.
1828	The limits of violin virtuosity were redefined by Paganini's Vienna debut.
1830	Berlioz's dazzlingly avant-garde and programmatic *Symphonie Fantastique* startled Paris concertgoers.
1831	Grand opera was inaugurated with *Robert le Diable* by Meyerbeer.
1851	Jenny Lind, the singer managed by P T Barnum, earned $176,675 from nine months of concerts in the US.
1842	The Vienna Philharmonic Orchestra gave its first concerts.
1854	In Weimar, Liszt conducted the premieres of his first symphonic poems.
1855	Like most orchestras around this date, the New York Philharmonic sat down during performance for the first time (cellists were already seated).
1865	Wagner's opera *Tristan and Isolde* scaled new heights of expressiveness using unprecedented chromaticism. Schubert's *Unfinished Symphony* (1822) was premiered in Vienna.
1875	The first of a series of collaborations between Arthur Sullivan and the librettist W S Gilbert, *Trial by Jury*, was given its premiere.
1876	Wagner's *The Ring of the Nibelung* was produced in Bayreuth. Brahms's *First Symphony* was performed in Karlsruhe.
1877	Edison invented the cylindrical tin-foil phonograph, but few showed interest.
1883	The Metropolitan Opera House opened in New York with a production of Gounod's *Faust*.
1885	Liszt composed *Bagatelle without Tonality* (his *Faust Symphony* of 1857 opened with a twelve-note series).
1894	Debussy's *Prélude à l'Après-midi d'un Faune* presented the Impressionistic use of the whole-tone scale, which was much developed in the early 20th century.
1899	Scott Joplin's "Maple Leaf Rag" was published in Sedalia, Missouri.
1902	Caruso recorded ten arias in a hotel room in Milan, the success of which established the popularity of the phonograph. By the time of his death in 1921 he had earned $2 million from sales of his recordings.
1908	Saint-Saëns became the first leading composer to write a film score, for *L'Assassinat du Duc de Guise*.
1911	Irving Berlin had his first big success as a songwriter with "Alexander's Ragtime Band."
1912	Schoenberg's atonal *Pierrot Lunaire*, for reciter and chamber ensemble, foreshadowed many similar small-scale quasi-theatrical works.
1913	Stravinsky's ballet *The Rite of Spring* precipitated a riot at its premiere in Paris.
1919	Schoenberg, who was experimenting with serial technique, set up the Society for Private Musical Performances in Vienna, which lasted until 1921.

1925	Louis Armstrong made his first records with the Hot Five. Duke Ellington's Washingtonians also started recording.
1927	Jerome Kern's *Showboat*, with libretto by Oscar Hammerstein II, laid the foundations for the US musical.
1937	Arturo Toscanini, one of the greatest conductors in the history of music, began his 17-year association with the NBC Symphony Orchestra.
1938	Prokofiev's score for Eisenstein's *Alexander Nevsky* raised film music to new levels. In popular music, Big Bands were the rage.
1939	Elisabeth Lutyens was one of the first English composers to use 12-note composition in her Chamber Concerto no. 1 for nine instruments.
1940	Walt Disney's *Fantasia* introduced Classical music, conducted by Leopold Stokowski, to a worldwide audience of filmgoers.
1942	In Chicago, John Cage conducted the premiere of his *Imaginary Landscape no 3*, scored for marimbula, gongs, tin cans, buzzers, plucked coil, electric oscillator, and generator.
1945	Bebop jazz was initiated. The jazz greats Charlie Parker and Dizzy Gillespie first recorded together.
1952	The BBC Symphony Orchestra was founded in London under Sir Adrian Boult.
1954	Stockhausen's *Electronic Studies* for magnetic tape were broadcast in Cologne. Edgard Varèse's *Déserts*, the first work to combine instruments and prerecorded magnetic tape, was performed in Paris. Elvis Presley made his first rock-and-roll recordings.
1955	Boulez's *Le Marteau sans Maître*, for contralto and chamber ensemble, was performed in Baden-Baden. Its formidable serial technique and exotic orchestration was acclaimed by the avant-garde. The Miles Davis Quintet with John Coltrane united two of the most important innovators in jazz.
1956	The first annual Warsaw Autumn festival of contemporary music was held. This became important for the promotion of Polish composers such as Lutoslawksi and Penderecki.
1957	Leonard Bernstein's *West Side Story* was premiered in New York. A computer, programmed at the University of Illinois by Lejaren Hiller and Leonard Isaacson, composed the *Illiac Suite* for string quartet.
1963	Shostakovich's opera *Lady Macbeth of Mezensk*, earlier banned and condemned in the Soviet newspaper *Pravda* 1936, was produced in a revised version as *Katerina Ismailova*.
1965	Robert Moog invented a synthesizer that considerably widened the scope of electronic music. The film soundtrack of *The Sound of Music*, with music by Rodgers and lyrics by Hammerstein, was released, and stayed in the music charts for the next two years. Bob Dylan used electric instrumentation on *Highway 61 Revisited*.
1967	The Beatles' album *Sgt Pepper's Lonely Hearts Club Band*, which took over 500 hours to record, was released. The first Velvet Underground album was released. Psychedelic rock spread from San Francisco, and hard rock developed in the UK and the US.
1969	Peter Maxwell Davies's theater piece *Eight Songs for a Mad King* for vocalist and six instruments, was premiered in London by the Pierrot Players, later to become the Fires of London ensemble under Davies's direction.
1976	Philip Glass's opera *Einstein on the Beach*, using the repetitive techniques of minimalism, was given its first performance in Paris. Punk rock arrived with the Sex Pistols' "Anarchy in the UK."
1977	The Institute for Research and Coordination of Acoustics and Music (IRCAM) was founded in Paris under the direction of Pierre Boulez, for visiting composers to make use of advanced electronic equipment.
1983	Messiaen's only opera, *Saint François d'Assise*, was given its first performance in Paris. Lutoslawski's Third Symphony was premiered to worldwide acclaim by the Chicago Symphony Orchestra under Sir Georg Solti. Compact disks launched in the West.
1986	Paul Simon's *Graceland* drew on and popularized world music.
1991	Carnegie Hall celebrated its 100th anniversary.

tury dissonant tone. In Paris ◊Les Six adopted a more relaxed style, while composers further from the cosmopolitan centers of Europe, such as Ives, Elgar, Delius, and Sibelius, continued loyal to the romantic symphonic tradition. The rise of radio and recorded media created a new mass market for Classical and Romantic music, but one resistant to music by contemporary composers. Organizations such as the International Society for Contemporary Music became increasingly responsible for ensuring that music continued to be publicly performed.

The second half of the 20th century has seen dramatic changes in the nature of composition and in the instruments used to create sounds. The recording studio has facilitated the development of *musique concrète*/concrete music based on recorded natural sounds, and electronic music in which sounds are generated electrically, developments implying the creation of music as a finished object without the need for interpretation by live performers. Chance music, promoted by John Cage, introduced the notion of a music designed to provoke unforeseen results and thereby make new connections; aleatoric music, developed by Boulez, introduced performers to freedom of choice from a range of options. Since the 1960s the computer has become a focus of attention for developments in the synthesis of musical tones, and also in the automation of compositional techniques, most notably at Stanford University and MIT in the US, and at IRCAM in Paris.

musical 20th-century form of dramatic musical performance, combining elements of song, dance, and the spoken word, often characterized by lavish staging and large casts. It developed from the operettas and musical comedies of the 19th century.

The operetta is a light-hearted entertainment with extensive musical content: Jaques Offenbach, Johann Strauss, Franz Lehár, and Gilbert and Sullivan all composed operettas. The musical comedy is an anglicization of the French *opéra bouffe*, of which the first was *A Gaiety Girl* 1893, mounted by George Edwardes (1852–1915) at the Gaiety Theatre, London. Typical musical comedies of the 1920s were *Rose Marie* 1924 by Rudolf Friml (1879–1972); *The Student Prince* 1924 and *The Desert Song* 1926, both by Sigmund Romberg (1887–1951); and *No, No, Nanette* 1925 by Vincent Youmans (1898–1946). The sophisticated Jerome Kern *Show Boat* 1927 changed the concept of musicals and foreshadowed the integrated productions that dominated from the 1940s. The 1930s and 1940s were an era of sophisticated musical comedies with many filmed examples and a strong US presence (Irving Berlin, Jerome Kern, Cole Porter, and George Gershwin). In England Noël Coward and Ivor Novello wrote musicals.

In 1943 Rodgers and Hammerstein's *Oklahoma!* introduced a plot fully integrated with music, which was developed in Lerner and Loewe's *My Fair Lady* 1956 and Bernstein's *West Side Story* 1957. Sandy Wilson's *The Boy Friend* 1953 revived the British musical and was followed by hits such as Lionel Bart's *Oliver!* 1960. Musicals began to branch into religious and political themes with *Oh What a Lovely War!* 1963, produced by Joan Littlewood and Charles Chiltern, and the Andrew Lloyd Webber musicals *Jesus Christ Superstar* 1970 and *Evita* 1978. Another category of musical, substituting a theme for conventional plotting, includes Stephen Sondheim's *Company* 1970, Hamlisch and Kleban's *A Chorus Line* 1975, and Lloyd Webber's *Cats* 1981, using verses by T S Eliot. In the 1980s 19th-century melodrama was popular, for example *Phantom of the Opera* 1986 and *Les Misérables* 1987.

music hall a British light theatrical entertainment, in which singers, dancers, comedians, and acrobats perform in "turns." The music hall's heyday was at the beginning of the 20th century, with such artistes as Marie Lloyd, Harry Lauder, and George Formby. The US equivalent is ◊vaudeville.

music theater the staged performance of vocal music that deliberately sets out to get away from the grandiose style and scale of traditional opera.

Its origins can be traced to the 1920s and 1930s, to plays with music like Kurt Weill's *Mahagonny-Songspiel*, but it came into its own as a movement in the 1960s. It includes not just contemporary opera (such as Alexander Goehr's *Naboth's Vineyard* 1968) but also works like Peter Maxwell Davies's *Eight Songs for a Mad King* 1969.

Musil Robert 1880–1942. Austrian novelist, author of the unfinished *Der Mann ohne Eigenschaften*/*The Man without Qualities* (three volumes, 1930–43). Its hero shares the author's background of philosophical study and scientific and military training, and is preoccupied with the problems of the self viewed from a mystic but agnostic viewpoint.

musk in botany, perennial plant *Mimulus moschatus* of the family Scrophulariaceae; its small oblong leaves exude the musky scent from which it takes its name; it is also called monkey flower. Also any of several plants with a musky odor, including the musk mallow *Malva moschata* and the musk rose *Rosa moschata*.

musk deer small deer *Moschus moschiferus* native to mountains of central Asia. A solitary animal, it is about 20 in/50 cm high, sure-footed, and has large ears and no antlers. Males have tusk-like upper canine teeth. It is hunted and farmed for the musk secreted by an abdominal gland, which is used as medicine or perfume.

Muskegon city in W Michigan, on the Muskegon River where it enters into Lake Michigan, NW of Grand Rapids. Industries include heavy machinery, metal products, automobile parts, and sporting goods; population (1990) 40,283.

musk ox ruminant *Ovibos moschatus* of the family Bovidae, native to the Arctic regions of North America. It displays characteristics of sheep and oxen, is about the size of a small domestic cow, and has long brown hair. At certain seasons it exhales a musky odor.

Its underwool (*qiviut*) is almost as fine as vicuna, and musk-ox farms have been established in Alaska, Québec, and Norway.

muskrat rodent *Ondatra zibethicus* of the family Cricetidae, about 30 cm/12in long, living along streams, rivers, and lakes in North America. It

musk ox

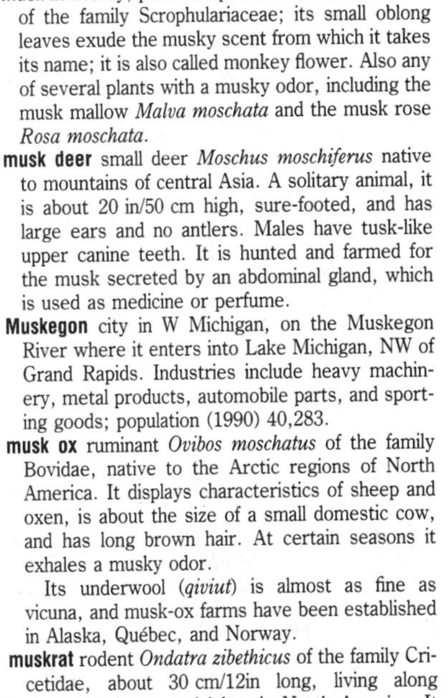

10242

***Mussolini** Italian dictator Benito Mussolini greets Germany's Adolph Hitler at the Florence railroad station in Oct 1940.*

has webbed hind feet, a side-to-side flattened tail, and shiny, light-brown fur. It builds up a store of food, plastering it over with mud, for winter consumption. It is hunted for its fur.

Muslim or ***Moslem*** a follower of ◊Islam.

Muslim Brotherhood movement founded by members of the Sunni branch of Islam in Egypt in 1928. It aims at the establishment of a theocratic Islamic state and is headed by a "supreme guide." It is also active in Jordan, Sudan, and Syria.

mussel one of a number of bivalve mollusks, some of them edible, such as *Mytilus edulis*, found in clusters attached to rocks around the N Atlantic and American coasts. It has a blue-black shell.

Freshwater pearl mussels, such as *Unio margaritiferus*, are found in some North American and European rivers. The green-lipped mussel, found only off New Zealand, produces an extract that is used in the treatment of arthritis.

Musset Alfred de 1810–1857. French poet and playwright. He achieved success with the volume of poems *Contes d'Espagne et d'Italie/Stories of Spain and Italy* 1829. His *Confession d'un enfant du siècle/Confessions of a Child of the Century* 1835 recounts his broken relationship with George Sand.

Born in Paris, he abandoned the study of law and medicine to join the circle of Victor Hugo. Typical of his work are the verse in *Les Nuits/Nights* 1835–37 and the short plays *Comédies et proverbes/Comedies and Proverbs* 1840.

Mussolini Benito 1883–1945. Italian dictator from 1925 to 1943. As founder of the Fascist Movement (see ◊fascism) 1919 and prime minister from 1922, he became known as *Il Duce* ("the leader"). He invaded Ethiopia 1935–36, intervened in the Spanish Civil War 1936–39 in support of Franco, and conquered Albania 1939. In June 1940 Italy entered World War II supporting Hitler. Forced by military and domestic setbacks to resign 1943, Mussolini established a breakaway government in N Italy 1944–45, but was killed trying to flee the country.

Mussolini was born in the Romagna, the son of a blacksmith, and worked in early life as a teacher and journalist. He became active in the Socialist movement, from which he was expelled 1914 for advocating Italian intervention in World War I. In 1919 he founded the Fascist Movement, whose program combined violent nationalism with demagogic republican and anticapitalist slogans, and launched a campaign of terrorism against the Socialists. This movement was backed by many landowners and industrialists and by the heads of the army and police, and in Oct 1922 Mussolini was in power as prime minister at the head of a coalition government. In 1925 he assumed dictatorial powers, and in 1926 all opposition parties were banned. During the years that followed, the political, legal, and education systems were remodeled on Fascist lines.

Mussolini's Blackshirt followers were the forerunners of Hitler's Brownshirts, and his career of conquest drew him into close cooperation with Nazi Germany. Italy and Germany formed the ◊Axis alliance 1936. During World War II, Italian defeats in N Africa and Greece, the Allied invasion of Sicily, and discontent at home destroyed Mussolini's prestige, and in July 1943 he was compelled to resign by his own Fascist Grand Council. He was released from prison by German parachutists in Sept 1943 and set up a "Republican Fascist" government in N Italy. In April 1945 he and his mistress, Clara Petacci, were captured by partisans at Lake Como while heading for the Swiss border, and shot. Their bodies were taken to Milan and hung upside down in a public square.

Mussorgsky Modest Petrovich 1839–1881. Russian composer, who was largely self-taught. His opera *Boris Godunov* was completed in 1869, although not produced in St Petersburg until 1874. Some of his works were "revised" by ◊Rimsky-Korsakov, and only recently has their harsh and primitive beauty been recognized.

Born at Karevo, he resigned his commission in the army in 1858 to concentrate on music while working as a government clerk. A member of the group of nationalist composers, the Five, he was influenced by both folk music and literature. Among his other works are the incomplete operas *Khovanshchina* and *Sorochintsy Fair*, the orchestral *A Night on the Bare Mountain* 1867, the suite for piano *Pictures at an Exhibition* 1874, and many songs. Mussorgsky died in poverty, from alcoholism.

Mustafa Kemal Turkish leader who assumed the name of ◊Atatürk.

mustard any of several annual plants of the family Cruciferae. The seeds of black mustard *Brassica nigra* and white mustard *Sinapis alba* are used in the preparation of table mustard.

Black and white mustard are cultivated in Europe and North America. The seedlings of white mustard are used in salads. Mustard is sometimes grown by farmers and plowed in to enrich the soil.

Mustique an island in the Caribbean. See under ◊St Vincent and the Grenadines.

mutagen any substance that makes ◊mutation of genes more likely. A mutagen is likely to also act as a ◊carcinogen.

Mutare formerly (until 1982) ***Umtali*** industrial town in E Zimbabwe; chief town of Manicaland province. Industries include vehicle assembly, engineering, tobacco, textiles, paper. Population (1982) 69,621.

mutation in biology, a change in the genes produced by a change in the ◊DNA that makes up the hereditary material of all living organisms. Mutations, the raw material of evolution, result from mistakes during replication (copying) of DNA molecules. Only a few improve the organism's performance and are therefore favored by ◊natural selection. Mutation rates are increased by certain chemicals and by radiation.

Common mutations include the omission or insertion of a base (one of the chemical subunits of DNA); these are known as point mutations. Larger-scale mutations include removal of a whole segment of DNA or its inversion within the DNA strand. Not all mutations affect the organism, because there is a certain amount of redundancy in the genetic information. If a mutation is "translated" from DNA into the protein that makes up the organism's structure, it may be in a nonfunctional part of the protein and thus have no detectable effect. This is known as a neutral mutation, and is of importance in ◊molecular-clock studies because such mutations tend to accumulate gradually as time passes. Some mutations do affect genes that control protein production or functional parts of protein, and most of these are lethal to the organism.

mute in music, any device used to dampen the vibration of an instrument and so affect the tone. Brass instruments use plugs of metal or cardboard inserted in the bell, while orchestral strings apply a form of clamp to the bridge.

A cloth applied to the skin of a kettledrum, or inserted into the bell of a saxophone or clarinet, has a similar effect.

Muti Riccardo 1941– . Italian conductor of the Philharmonia Orchestra, London, 1973–82, the Philadelphia Orchestra from 1981, and artistic director of La Scala, Milan, from 1986. He is known as a purist, devoted to carrying out a composer's intentions to the last detail.

mutiny an organized act of disobedience or defiance by two or more members of the armed services. In naval and military law, mutiny has always been regarded as one of the most serious crimes, punishable in wartime by death.

Mutsuhito personal name of the Japanese emperor ◊Meiji.

mutton bird any of various shearwaters and petrels that breed in burrows on Australasian islands. The young are very fat, and are killed for food and oil.

mutual fund a company that invests its clients' funds in other companies, equities, or securities. The owner of stock in the investment company holds a proportional interest in the investment company based on the number of shares in the portfolio holdings of the company. In this way a small investor may benefit from professional judgment and a much broader range of investments than might be possible individually.

Mutual funds are generally of two types: open-end investment, companies that issue new stock whenever they sell shares to purchasers, and closed-end investment, companies that issue a fixed number of shares that must be purchased through a stock broker. In open-end funds, the investor is not generally committed to hold the stock for a specified period. Closed-end funds are sometimes sold on a contractual basis requiring a minimum investment and holdings kept for a minimum period.

mutual induction in physics, the production of an electromotive force (emf) or voltage in an electric circuit caused by a changing ◊magnetic flux in a neighboring circuit. The two circuits are often coils of wire, as in a ◊transformer, and the size

Muzorewa Zimbabwean politician and bishop of the Methodist Church, Abel Muzorewa, 1979.

Myanmar Union of

(*Thammada Myanmar Naingngandaw*) (formerly **Burma**)

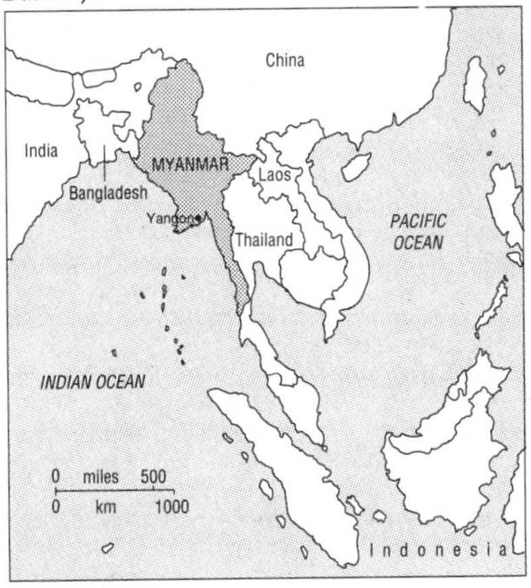
China
India
MYANMAR
Laos
Bangladesh
Yangon
Thailand
PACIFIC OCEAN
INDIAN OCEAN
0 miles 500
0 km 1000
Indonesia

area 261,228 sq mi/676,577 sq km
capital and chief port Yangon (formerly Rangoon)
cities Mandalay, Moulmein, Pegu
physical over half is rainforest; rivers Irrawaddy and Chindwin in central lowlands ringed by mountains in N, W, and E
features ruined cities of Pagan and Mingun
head of state and government Gen Saw Maung from 1988
political system military republic
political parties National Unity Party, military-Socialist ruling party; National League for Democracy (NLD), pluralist opposition grouping
exports rice, rubber, jute, teak, jade, rubies, sapphires
currency kyat
population (1990 est) 41,279,000; growth rate 1.9% p.a. (includes Shan, Karen, Raljome, Chinese, and Indian minorities)
life expectancy men 53, women 56 (1989)
language Burmese
religion Hinayana Buddhist 85%; animist, Christian literacy 66% (1989)
GNP $9.3 bn (1988); $210 per head (1989)
chronology
1886 United as province of British India.
1937 Became crown colony in the British Commonwealth.
1942–45 Occupied by Japan.
1948 Independence achieved from Britain. Left the Commonwealth.
1962 Gen Ne Win assumed power in army coup.
1973–74 Adopted presidential-style "civilian" constitution.
1975 Opposition National Democratic Front formed.
1986 Several thousand supporters of opposition leader Suu Kyi arrested.
1988 Government resigned after violent demonstrations. Gen Saw Maung seized power in military coup Sept; over 1,000 killed.
1989 Martial law declared; thousands arrested including advocates of democracy and human rights.
1990 Breakaway opposition group formed "parallel government" on rebel-held territory.
1991 Martial law and human-rights abuses continued.

of the induced emf depends largely on the numbers of turns of wire in each of the coils.

mutualism an association between two organisms of different species whereby both profit from the relationship. See also ◊symbiosis.

Muybridge Eadweard. Adopted name of Edward James Muggeridge 1830–1904. British photographer. He made a series of animal locomotion photographs in the US in the 1870s and proved that, when a horse trots, there are times when all its feet are off the ground. He also explored motion in birds and humans.

Muzorewa Abel (Tendekayi) 1925– . Zimbabwean politician and Methodist bishop. He was president of the African National Council 1971–85 and prime minister of Rhodesia/Zimbabwe 1979. He was detained for a year in 1983–84. He is leader of the minority United Africa National Council.

Muzorewa was educated at Methodist colleges in Rhodesia and Nashville, Tennessee.

MVD Soviet Ministry of Internal Affairs, name of the secret police 1946–53; now the ◊KGB.

Mwiiny Ali Hassan 1925– . Tanzanian Socialist politician, president from 1985, when he succeeded Julius Nyerere. He began a revival of private enterprise and control of state involvement and spending.

myalgic encephalomyelitis see ◊ME.

Myanmar formerly (until 1989) ***Burma*** country in SE Asia, bordered NW by India, NE by China, SE by Laos and Thailand, and SW by the Bay of Bengal.

government Under the 1974 constitution, which was temporarily suspended in Sept 1988, Myanmar is a unitary republic. The highest organ of state power is the 489-member people's assembly (*Pyithu Hluttaw*), elected by universal suffrage every four years. The people's assembly elects the nation's executive, the 30-member state council, which has a representative from each of Myanmar's 14 states and divisions and is headed by a chair who acts as president. It is the sole legislature and elects a council of ministers, headed by a prime minister, in charge of day-to-day administration. The controlling force and sole party in Myanmar is the National Unity Party (formerly the Socialist Program Party).

history The Burmese date their era from AD 638, when they had arrived from the region where China meets Tibet. By 850 they had organized a state in the center of the plain at Pagan, and in the period 1044–1287 maintained a hegemony over most of the area. In 1287 Kublai Khan's grandson Ye-su Timur occupied the region after destroying the Pagan dynasty. After he withdrew, anarchy supervened. From about 1490 to 1750 the Toungoo dynasty maintained itself, with increasing difficulty; in 1752 Alaungpaya reunited the country and founded Rangoon (now Yangon) as his capital. In a struggle with Britain 1824–26, his descendants lost the coastal strip from Chittagong to Cape Negrais. The second Burmese War 1852 resulted in the British annexation of Lower Burma, including Rangoon. Thibaw, the last Burmese king, precipitated the third Burmese War 1885, and the British seized Upper Burma 1886. The country was united as a province of India until 1937, when it was made a crown colony with a degree of self-government.

Burma was occupied 1942–45 by Japan, under a government of anti-British nationalists. The nationalists, led by Aung San and U Nu, later founded the Anti-Fascist People's Freedom League (AFPFL). Burma was liberated 1945 and achieved full independence outside the ◊Commonwealth 1948.

A parliamentary democracy was established under the Socialist AFPFL led by Prime Minister U Nu. The republic was weakened by civil war between ◊Karens, Communist guerrillas, and ethnic group separatists. Splits within the AFPFL forced the formation of an emergency caretaker government by General Ne Win (1911–) 1958–60, leading to a military coup 1962 and abolition of the parliamentary system. Ne Win became head of a revolutionary council and established a strong one-party state.

In 1974 a new presidential constitution was adopted, and the revolutionary council was dissolved. The military leaders became civilian rulers. Ne Win became president and was re-elected 1978, before stepping down to be replaced by U San Yu (1918–) 1981, although Ne Win remained head of the BSPP.

The post-1962 government adopted a foreign policy of neutralist isolationism while at home it pursued its unique, self-reliant, Buddhist-influenced "Burmese Way toward Socialism," founded upon state ownership in the commercial-industrial sector and strict agricultural price control. Internal opposition by armed separatist groups continued after 1962, causing the economy to deteriorate. The Burmese Communist Party, which received Chinese funding during the 1960s, established control over parts of the N; the Karen National Liberation Army in the SE; and the Kachin Independence Army in the NE. In 1975 the non-Communist ethnic separatist groups joined together to form the broad National Democratic Front with the aim of creating a federal union. In 1974 and 1976 worsening economic conditions prompted a wave of food riots and in Sept 1987, with rice prices spiralling, student demonstrations broke out in Yangon. Workers' riots followed in the spring of 1988. Initially they were violently supressed, at the cost of several hundred lives. In the summer of 1988 San Yu and Ne Win, the leader of the ruling party, were forced to resign, as was the newly appointed president, Brig-Gen Sein Lwin, following the murder of 3,000 unarmed demonstrators. With the government control crumbling, as a widely supported pro-democracy movement swept the nation, the more reformist Maung Maung took over as president and free multiparty elections were promised "within three months." However, in Sept 1988 a military coup was staged by General Saw Maung, with the constitution being suspended, martial law imposed, and authority transferred to a 19-member State Law and Order Restoration Council. The new regime proceeded to pursue a more liberal economic course and to legalize the formation of political parties. Popular opposition leaders, including Suu Kyi (1945– , the daughter of the late Aung San) and U Nu, were harassed and debarred from standing in the elections that were promised in May 1990. Behind the scenes, Ne Win remained in control. In June 1989 the government announced the change in the country's name; it was recognized by the UN in the same month.

Elections in May 1990 resulted in an overwhelming victory by opposition parties. Foreign observers remained cautious about whether the military would surrender power as promised. In Oct 1991, Suu Kyri was awarded the Nobel Prize for peace for her campaign for democracy in Myanmar.

myasthenia gravis in medicine, an uncommon con-

***Mycenae** The Lion Gate, the main entrance to the citadel.*

dition characterized by loss of muscle power, especially in the face and neck. The muscles tire rapidly and fail to respond to repeated nervous stimulation. ◊Autoimmunity is the cause.

mycelium an interwoven mass of threadlike filaments or ◊hyphae, forming the main body of most fungi. The reproductive structures, or "fruiting bodies," grow from the mycelium.

Mycenae ancient Greek city in the E Peloponnese, which gave its name to the Mycenean (Bronze Age) civilization. Its peak was 1400–1200 BC, when the Cyclopean walls (using close-fitting stones) were erected. The city ceased to be inhabited after about 1120 BC.

Mycenean civilization Bronze Age civilization that flourished in Crete, Cyprus, Greece, the Aegean Islands, and W Anatolia about 4000–1000 BC. During this period, magnificent architecture and sophisticated artifacts were produced.

Originating in Crete, it spread into Greece about 1600 BC, where it continued to thrive, with its center at Mycenae, after the decline of Crete in about 1400. It was finally overthrown by the Dorian invasions, about 1100. The system of government was by kings, who also monopolized priestly functions. The Myceneans have been identified with the ◊Achaeans of Homer, and were among the besiegers at ◊Troy. They may also have been the marauding ◊sea peoples of Egyptian records. They used a form of Greek deciphered by Michael ◊Ventris. Their palaces were large and luxurious, and contained highly efficient sanitary arrangements. Commercial relations were maintained with Egypt. Pottery, frescoes, and metalwork reached a high artistic level. Evidence of the civilization was brought to light by the excavations of Heinrich ◊Schliemann at Troy, Mycenae, and Tiryns (a stronghold on the plain of Argolis) from 1870 onward, and of Arthur ◊Evans in Crete from 1899.

mycorrhiza a mutually beneficial (mutualistic) association occurring between plant roots and a soil fungus. Mycorrhizal roots take up nutrients more efficiently than nonmycorrhizal roots, and the fungus benefits by obtaining carbohydrates from the tree.

An ectotrophic mycorrhiza occurs on many tree species, which usually grow much better, most noticeably in the seeding stage, as a result. Typically the roots become repeatedly branched and corallike, penetrated by hyphae of a surrounding fungal ◊mycelium. In an endotrophic mycorrhiza, the growth of the fungus is mainly inside the root, as in orchids. Such plants do not usually grow properly, and may not even germinate, unless the appropriate fungus is present.

myelin sheath the insulating layer that surrounds nerve cells in vertebrate animals. It acts to speed up the passage of nerve impulses. Myelin is made up of fats and proteins and is formed from up to a hundred layers, laid down by special cells, the Schwann cells.

My Lai massacre the killing of 109 civilians in My Lai, a village in South Vietnam, by US troops in March 1968. An investigation in 1969 was followed by the conviction of Lt William Calley, commander of the platoon.

Sentenced to life imprisonment 1971, Calley was later released on parole. His superior officer was acquitted but the trial revealed a US Army policy of punitive tactics against civilians. News of the massacre contributed to domestic pressure for the US to end its involvement in Vietnam.

The incident also focused attention on the emotional pressures faced by US forces in Vietnam. Often unable to identify the enemy, soldiers adopted a policy of firing quickly.

mynah various tropical starlings, family Sturnidae, of SE Asia. The glossy blackhill mynah *Gracula religiosa* of India is a realistic mimic ofsounds and human speech.

myoglobin globular protein, closely related to ◊hemoglobin and located in vertebrate muscle. Oxygen binds to myoglobin and is released only when the hemoglobin can no longer supply adequate oxygen to muscle cells.

myopia or ***nearsightedness*** a condition of visual impairment in which light rays from distant objects are focused in front of the retina instead of on it. This can be due to an eyeball that is too long or a lens that does not accommodate properly. Nearby objects are sharply perceived, but distance vision is blurred. Myopia can be corrected by suitable eyeglasses or contact lenses.

myopia, low-luminance poor night vision. About 20% of people have poor vision in twilight and nearly 50% in the dark. Low-luminance myopia does not show up in normal optical tests, but in 1989 a method was developed of measuring the degree of blurring by projecting images on a screen using a weak laser beam.

Myrdal Gunnar 1898–1987. Swedish economist, author of many works on development economics. He shared a Nobel Prize 1974 with F A Hayek.

myrmecophyte a plant that lives in association with a colony of ants and possesses specialized organs in which the ants live. For example, *Myrmecodia*, an epiphytic plant from Malaysia, develops root tubers containing a network of cavities inhabited by ants.

Several species of *Acacia* from tropical America have specialized hollow thorns for the same purpose. This is probably a mutualistic (mutually beneficial) relationship, with the ants helping to protect the plant from other insect pests and in return receiving shelter.

Myron c. 500–440 BC. Greek sculptor. His *Discobolus/Discus-Thrower* and *Athene and Marsyas*, much admired in his time, are known through Roman copies. They confirm his ancient reputation for brilliant composition and naturalism.

myrrh gum resin produced by small trees of the genus *Commiphora* of the bursera family, especially *C. myrrha*, found in Ethiopia and Arabia. In ancient times it was used for incense and perfume and in embalming.

myrtle evergreen shrub of the Old World genus *Myrtus*, family Myrtaceae. The commonly cultivated Mediterranean myrtle *M. communis* has oval opposite leaves and white flowers followed by purple berries, all of which are fragrant.

The Oregon myrtle or California laurel *Umbellularia california* belongs to the ◊laurel family. The wax murtles (genus *Myrica*) of the US bear wax-covered nuts collected for candle making.

Mysore or ***Maisur*** industrial city (engineering, silk) in ◊Karnataka, S India, some 80 mi/130 km SW of Bangalore; population (1981) 476,000.

mystery play or ***miracle play*** a medieval religious drama based on stories from the Bible. Mystery plays were performed around the time of church festivals, reaching their height in Europe during the 15th and 16th centuries. A whole cycle running from the Creation to the Last Judgment was performed in separate scenes on mobile wagons by various town guilds.

mystery religion any of various cults of the ancient world, open only to the initiated; for example, the cults of Demeter (see ◊Eleusinian Mysteries), Dionysus, Cybele, Isis, and Mithras. Underlying some of them is a fertility ritual, in which a deity undergoes death and resurrection and the initiates feed on the flesh and blood to attain communion with the divine and ensure their own life beyond the grave. The influence of mystery religions on early Christianity was considerable.

mysticism religious belief or spiritual experience based on direct, intuitive communion with the divine. It does not always involve an orthodox deity, though it is found in all the major religions—for example, kabbalism in Judaism, Sufism in Islam, and the bhakti movement in Hinduism. The mystical experience is often rooted in ascetism and can involve visions, trances, and ecstasies; many religious traditions prescribe meditative and contemplative techniques for achieving mystical experience. Official churches fluctuate between acceptance of mysticism as a form of special grace, and suspicion of it as a dangerous deviation, verging on the heretical.

3rd century Mysticism was first introduced to W Europe through Neo-Platonism, which was largely affected by Oriental schools of thought, and in its turn influenced the rise of Christian mysticism.

8th century Beginning of Sufism, an Islamic mystical movement.

11th–12th centuries Ramanuja, a Tamil Brahmin, taught that the way of devotion (*bhakti*) in Hinduism was superior to the way of knowledge.

13th century A kabbalistic movement in Judaism arose in S France and Spain.

14th–16th centuries Among the Christian mystics of this era, when feudalism was breaking down, were Thomas à Kempis, Jacob Boehme, and Meister Eckhart in Germany, and Julian of Norwich and the author of *The Cloud of Unknowing* in England. The Counter-Reformation produced Catholic mystics such as St Teresa and St John of the Cross.

17th century Quietism spread from Spain to France, while the Quakers (Friends) originated in England.

18th century Two great English mystics: William Law and William Blake.

19th century The scientific study of mysticism was begun by the American William James and others.

20th century A renewed interest in mysticism in the UK and the US was expressed in, for example, the works of the poet W B Yeats, the novelist Aldous Huxley (often drawing on Eastern religions and psychedelic experiences), and the Catholic monk and writer Thomas Merton.

From the 1960s an interest in Zen Buddhism, Tantric Buddhism, Taoism, and other mystical Asian religions became widespread.

mythology the study and interpretation of the stories symbolically underlying a given culture and of how they relate to similar stories told in other cultures. These stories describe gods and other supernatural beings, with whom humans may have relationships, and are intended to explain the workings of the universe and human history.

Ancient mythologies, with the names of the chief god of each, include those of Egypt (Osiris), Greece (Zeus), Rome (Jupiter), India (Brahma), and the Teutonic peoples (Odin or Woden).

Mytilene (modern Greek *Mitilíni*) port, capital of the Greek island of Lesvos (to which the name Mytilene is sometimes applied) and a center of sponge fishing; population (1981) 24,000.

myxedema thyroid-deficiency disease developing in adult life, most commonly in middle-aged women. The symptoms are loss of energy and appetite, inability to keep warm, mental dullness, and dry, puffy skin. It is completely reversed by giving the thyroid hormone known as thyroxine.

myxomatosis contagious, usually fatal, virus infection of rabbits. It has been deliberately introduced in the UK and Australia since the 1950s to reduce the rabbit population.

N

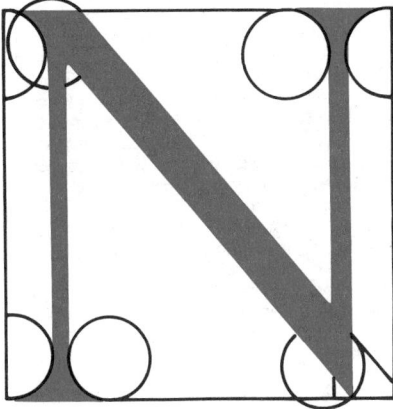

n. abbreviation for ◊noun, neuter, and, in mathematics, an indefinite number.

N abbreviation for north, ◊newton, and the chemical symbol for nitrogen.

NAACP abbreviation for ◊National Association for the Advancement of Colored People, a US civil rights organization.

Nabis, les (Hebrew "prophets") a group of French artists, active in the 1890s in Paris, united in their admiration of Gauguin—the mystic content of his work, the surface pattern and intense color. In practice their work was decorative. ◊Bonnard and ◊Vuillard were members.

Nablus market town on the West Bank of the river Jordan, N of Jerusalem; the largest Palestinian town, after E Jerusalem, in Israeli occupation; population (1971) 64,000. Formerly Shechem, it was the ancient capital of Samaria, and a few ◊Samaritans remain. The British field marshal Allenby's defeat of the Turks here 1918 completed the conquest of Palestine.

Nabokov Vladimir 1899–1977. US writer who left his native Russia 1917 and began writing in English in the 1940s. His most widely known book is *Lolita* 1955, the story of the middle-aged Humbert Humbert's infatuation with a precocious child of 12. His other books include *Laughter in the Dark* 1938, *The Real Life of Sebastian Knight* 1945, *Pnin* 1957, and his memoirs *Speak, Memory* 1947.

Born in St Petersburg, Nabokov settled in the US 1940, and became a US citizen 1945. He was professor of Russian literature at Cornell University 1948–59, producing a translation and commentary on Pushkin's *Eugene Onegin* 1963. He was also a lepidopterist (a collector of butterflies and moths), a theme used in his book *Pale Fire* 1962.

***Nabokov** Born in Russia, Vladimir Nabokov was an exile for all his adult life. The theme of alienation runs throughout his work, and his best-known novel remains the controversial* Lolita *1955.*

Nacala seaport in Nampula province, N Mozambique; a major outlet for minerals. It is linked by rail with Malawi.

Nachingwea military training base in Tanzania, about 225 mi/360 km south of Dar-es-Salaam. It was used by the guerrillas of Frelimo (Mozambique) 1964–75 and the African National Congress 1975–80.

nacre another name for ◊mother-of-pearl.

Nadar adopted name of Gaspard-Félix Tournachon 1820–1910. French portrait photographer and caricaturist. He took the first aerial photographs (from a balloon 1858) and was the first to use artificial light.

Nader Ralph 1934– . US lawyer and consumer advocate. Called the "scourge of corporate morality," he led many major consumer campaigns. His book *Unsafe at Any Speed* 1965 led to US auto-safety legislation.

The Traffic Safety Act 1966 gave the federal government the right to establish safety standards for automobiles sold in the US.

Born in Winsted, Connecticut, he graduated from Princeton and Harvard universities and practiced law in Connecticut and Washington, DC. He has investigated the lack of safety of color televisions, nuclear plants, and X-rays, as well as the procedures used by food and drug companies, overall job safety standards, and environmental pollution. The people who worked with and for him became known as "Nader's Raiders." Nader also cowrote *Who's Poisoning America: Corporate Polluters and Their Victims in the Chemical Age* 1981 and *The Big Boys: Styles of Corporate Power* 1986.

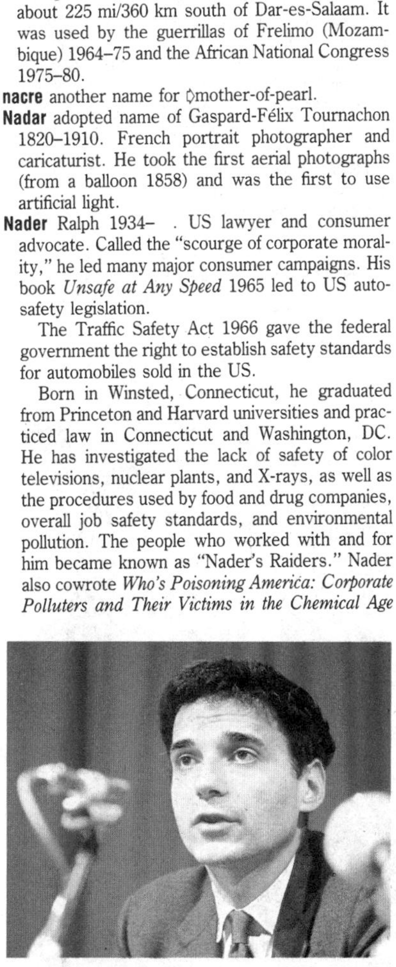

***Nader** US consumer advocate Ralph Nader has campaigned for numerous diverse causes, including safer automobiles.*

nadir the point on the celestial sphere vertically below the observer and hence diametrically opposite the ◊zenith. The term is used metaphorically to mean the low point of a person's fortunes.

Nadir Shah (Khan) c. 1880–1933. King of Afghanistan from 1929. Nadir played a key role in the 1919 Afghan War, but was subsequently forced into exile in France. He returned to Kabul in 1929 to seize the throne and embarked on an ambitious modernization program. This alienated the Muslim clergy and in 1933 he was assassinated by fundamentalists. His successor as king was his son ◊Zahir Shah.

Naemen Flemish form of ◊Namur, city in Belgium.

Nafud desert area in Saudi Arabia to the S of the Syrian Desert.

Naga member of any of the various peoples who inhabit the highland region near the Indian-Myanmar border. These peoples do not possess a common name; some of the main groups are Ao, Konyak, Sangtam, Lhota, Sema, Rengma, Chang, and Angami. Their languages belong to the Sino-Tibetan family.

Nagaland state of NE India, bordering Myanmar (Burma) on the E.
area 6,456 sq mi/16,721 sq km
capital Kohima
products rice, tea, coffee, paper, sugar
population (1981) 775,000
history formerly part of Assam, it was seized by Britain from Burma (now Myanmar) 1826. The British sent 18 expeditions against the Naga peoples in the N 1832–87. After India attained independence 1947, there was Naga guerrilla activity against the Indian government; the state of Nagaland was established 1963 in response to demands for self-government, but fighting continued sporadically.

nagana animal ◊sleeping sickness spread by the ◊tsetse fly.

Nagasaki industrial port (coal, iron, shipbuilding) on Kyushu island, Japan; population (1987) 447,000. An atom bomb was dropped on it Aug 9, 1945.

Nagasaki was the only Japanese port open to European trade from the 16th century until other ports were opened 1859. Three days after ◊Hiroshima, the second atom bomb was dropped here. Of Nagasaki's population of 212,000, 73,884 were killed and 76,796 injured, not counting the long-term victims of radiation.

Nagorno-Karabakh autonomous region (*oblast*) of the Soviet republic of ◊Azerbaijan; population (1987) 180,000 (76% Armenian, 23% Azeri), the Christian Armenians forming an enclave within the predominantly Shi'ite Muslim Azerbaijan. Since Feb 1988 the region has been the site of ethnic conflicts between the two groups and the subject of violent disputes between Azerbaijan and the neighboring republic of Armenia
area 1,700 sq mi/4,400 sq km
capital Stepanakert
history an autonomous protectorate after the Russian revolution in 1917, Nagorno-Karabakh was annexed in 1923 to Azerbaijan against the wishes of the local population. Armenians in Nagorno-Karabakh felt discriminated against by the Azerbaijan republic. Interethnic violence was provoked in 1988 by the local council voting to transfer the region's administrative control to Armenia, and in response the area was placed under direct rule from Moscow Jan–Nov 1989. During autumn 1989 the conflict within the republic escalated, with Azerbaijan first imposing an economic blockade on Armenia, and then descending into civil war and threatening secession from the USSR, which resulted in 20,000 Soviet troops being sent to the republic in Jan 1990. The Armenian parliament had voted to annex Nagorno-Karabakh in Dec 1989, and there were attacks on Armenians in Baku, the capital of Azerbaijan. There have been large-scale cross-

border migrations of Armenians from Azerbaijan and Azeris from Armenia, involving over 300,000 people. Between 1988 and Jan 1990 some 170 people were killed in clashes.

Nagoya industrial seaport (cars, textiles, clocks) on Honshu island, Japan; population (1987) 2,091,000. It has a shogun fortress 1610 and a notable Shinto shrine, *Atsuta Jingu*.

Nagpur industrial city (textiles, metals) in Maharashtra, India; population (1981) 1,298,000. The university was founded 1923.

Nagy Imre 1895–1958. Hungarian politician, prime minister 1953–55 and 1956. He led the Hungarian revolt against Soviet domination in 1956, for which he was executed.

Nagy, an Austro-Hungarian prisoner of war in Siberia during World War I, became a Soviet citizen after the Russian Revolution, and lived in the USSR 1930–44. In 1953, after Stalin's death, he became prime minister, introducing liberal measures such as encouraging the production of consumer goods, but was dismissed 1955 by hardline Stalinist premier Rákosi. Reappointed Oct 1956 during the Hungarian uprising, he began taking liberalization further than the Soviets wanted; for example, announcing Hungarian withdrawal from the Warsaw Pact. Soviet troops entered Budapest, and Nagy was dismissed Nov 1956. He was captured by the KGB and shot. In 1989 the Hungarian Supreme Court recognized his leadership of a legitimate government and quashed his conviction for treachery.

Naha chief port on Okinawa island, Japan; population (1984) 304,000.

Nahayan Sheik Zayed bin Sultan al- 1918– . Emir of Abu Dhabi from 1969, when he deposed his brother, Sheik Shakhbut. He was elected president of the supreme council of the United Arab Emirates (UAE) in 1971. Before 1969 he was governor of the eastern province of Abu Dhabi, one of seven ◊Trucial States in the Persian Gulf and Gulf of Oman, then under British protection.

He was unanimously reelected emir in 1986. In 1991 he was implicated, through his majority ownership, in the international financial scandals associated with the takeover of the Bank of Commerce and Credit International (BCCI).

Nahuatl member of any of a group of Mesoamerican Indians (Mexico and Central America), of which the best known group were the Aztecs. The Nahuatlan languages, members of the Uto-Aztecan family, are spoken by over a million people today.

Nāhum 7th century BC. In the Old Testament, a Hebrew prophet, possibly born in Galilee, who forecast the destruction of Nineveh, the Assyrian capital, by the Medes in 612 BC.

naiad in Classical mythology, a water-nymph.

nail in biology, a hard, flat, flexible outgrowth of the digits of primates (humans, monkeys, and apes). Nails are derived from the ◊claws of ancestral primates.

Naipaul V(idiadhar) S(urajprasad) 1932– . British writer, born in Trinidad of Hindu parents. His novels include *A House for Mr Biswas* 1961, *The Mimic Men* 1967, *A Bend in the River* 1979, and *Finding the Centre* 1984. His brother Shiva(dhar) Naipaul (1940–85) was also a novelist (*Fireflies* 1970) and journalist.

Nairobi capital of Kenya, in the central highlands at 5,450 ft/1,660 m; population (1985) 1,100,000. It has light industry and food processing and is the headquarters of the United Nations Environment Program (UNEP). Nairobi was founded 1899, and its university 1970. It has the International Louis Leakey Institute for African Prehistory 1977, and the International Primate Research Institute is nearby.

Naismith James 1861–1939. Canadian-born inventor of basketball. While attending the YMCA Training School in Springfield, Massachusetts, 1891, Naismith invented basketball as a game to be played indoors during the winter. He later received an

Najibullah *Afghan communist state president Najibullah Ahmadzai, who headed a military regime.*

MD degree from the University of Colorado and served on the physical education faculty of the University of Kansas 1898–1937. Among his books is *Basketball, Its Origin and Development*, published posthumously 1941.

Born in Almonte, Ontario, Naismith was educated at McGill University, where he later served as director of physical education.

Najaf a holy city near the Euphrates in Iraq, 90 mi/ 144 km S of Baghdad.

Najibullah Ahmadzai 1947– . Afghan communist politician, a member of the Politburo from 1981, and leader of the ruling People's Democratic Party of Afghanistan (PDPA) from 1986, later state president. His attempts to broaden the support of the PDPA regime had little success, but his government survived the withdrawal of Soviet troops Feb 1989.

Nakasone Yasuhiro 1917– . Japanese conservative politician, leader of the Liberal Democratic Party (LDP) and prime minister 1982–87. He stepped

Nairobi *Kimathi Street and the Hilton Hotel in Kenya's capital of Nairobi.*

up military spending and increased Japanese participation in international affairs, with closer ties to the US. He was forced to resign his party post May 1989 as a result of having profited from insider trading in the ◊Recruit scandal.

Nakasone was educated at Tokyo University. He held ministerial posts from 1967 and established his own faction within the conservative LDP. In 1982 he was elected president of the LDP and prime minister. He encouraged a less paternalist approach to economic management. Although embarrassed by the conviction of one of his supporters in the 1983 Lockheed corruption scandal, he was reelected 1986 by a landslide.

Naked and the Dead, The first novel by the US writer Norman Mailer, published 1948. Set on a Pacific island during combat in World War II, it depicts war not only as a battle with the enemy but as a psychic and political condition.

Nakhichevan autonomous republic forming part of Azerbaijan republic, USSR, even though it is entirely outside the Azerbaijan boundary, being separated from it by the Armenian republic; area 2,120 sq mi/5,500 sq km; population (1986) 272,000. Taken by Russia in 1828, it was annexed to the Azerbaijan Republic in 1924. 85% of the 278,000 population are Muslim Azeris who maintain strong links with Iran to the south. Nakhichevan has been affected by the Armenia–Azerbaijan conflict; many Azeris have fled to Azerbaijan, and in Jan 1990 frontier posts and border fences with Iran were destroyed, and Nakhichevan declared itself independent of the USSR.

Nakhodka Pacific port in E Siberia, USSR, on the sea of Japan, E of Vladivostok; population (1985) 150,000. US-caught fish, especially pollock, is processed by Soviet factory ships in a joint venture.

Nakuru, Lake a salt lake in the Great Rift Valley, Kenya.

Namaqualand or ***Namaland*** near-desert area on the SW coast of Africa divided between Namibia and South Africa. Great Namaqualand is in Namibia, N of the Orange River, area 150,000 sq mi/ 388,500 sq km; sparsely populated by the Nama, a Hottentot people. Little Namaqualand is in Cape Province, South Africa, S of the Orange River, area 20,000 sq mi/52,000 sq km; copper and diamonds are mined here.

Namath Joseph William 1943– . US football player. In 1965 Namath signed with the New York Jets of the newly established American Football League. In 1969 Namath led the Jets to a historic upset victory over the Baltimore Colts in Super Bowl III. After leaving the Jets 1977, Namath joined the Los Angeles Rams; however, knee injuries forced his retirement as a player the following year. He later became a sports broadcaster and actor.

Born in Beaver Falls, Pennsylvania, Namath played quarterback for the University of Alabama, leading his team to victory in the 1965 Orange Bowl.

Namib Desert coastal desert region in Namibia between the Kalahari Desert and the Atlantic Ocean. Its sand dunes are among the tallest in the world, reaching heights of 1,200 ft/370 m.

Namibia formerly (to 1968) ***South West Africa*** country in SW Africa, bounded N by Angola and Zambia, E by Botswana and South Africa, and W by the Atlantic Ocean. Much of the land is desert.

government A new constitution was framed by the transitional 72-member constituent assembly elected by proportional representation in Nov 1989. Unanimously approved in Feb 1990, it entrenches a multiparty system with an independent judiciary and bill of fundamental human rights. Executive authority is wielded by a president who may serve a maximum of two five-year terms.

history Originally inhabited by the Damara people, it was annexed, with the exception of the British/Cape Colony enclave of ◊Walvis Bay, by

Namibia

formerly **South West Africa**
(*Suidwes-Afrika*)

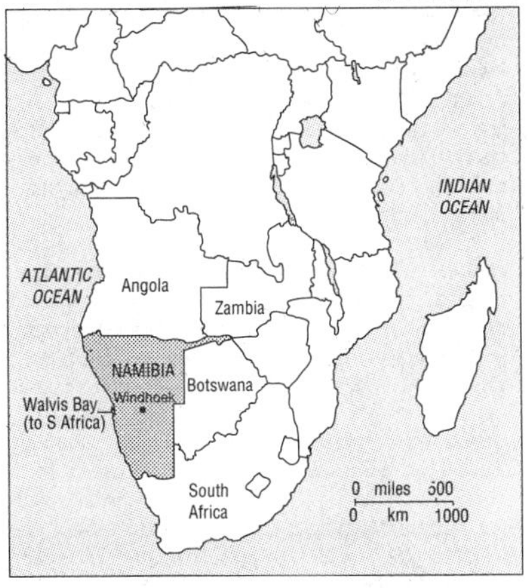
INDIAN
OCEAN
ATLANTIC
OCEAN
Angola
Zambia
NAMIBIA
Windhoek
Botswana
Walvis Bay
(to S Africa)
South
Africa
0 miles 500
0 km 1000

area 318,262 sq mi/824,300 sq km
capital Windhoek
cities Swakopmund, Rehoboth, Rundu
physical mainly desert; includes the enclave of Walvis Bay (area 432 sq mi/1,120 sq km)
features Namib and Kalahari deserts; Orange River; Caprivi Strip links Namibia to Zambezi River
head of state and government Sam Nujoma from 1989
political system democracy
political parties South West African People's Organization of Namibia (SWAPO), Socialist Ovambo-oriented; Democratic Turnhalle Alliance (DTA), moderate, multiracial coalition; United Democratic Front (UDF), disaffected ex-SWAPO members; National Christian Action (ACN), white conservative
exports diamonds, uranium, copper, lead, zinc
currency South African rand
population (1990 est) 1,372,000 (85% black African, 6% European)
life expectancy blacks 40, whites 69
language Afrikaans (spoken by 60% of white population), German, English (all official), several indigenous languages
religion 51% Lutheran, 19% Roman Catholic, 6% Dutch Reformed Church, 6% Anglican
literacy nonwhites 16%, whites 100%
GNP $1.6 bn; $1,300 per head (1988)
chronology
1884 German and British colonies established.
1915 German colony seized by South Africa.
1920 Administered by South Africa, under League of Nations mandate, as British South Africa.
1946 Full incorporation in South Africa refused by United Nations (UN).
1958 South West African People's Organization (SWAPO) set up to seek racial equality and full independence.
1966 South Africa's apartheid laws extended to the country.
1968 Redesignated Namibia by UN.
1978 UN Security Council Resolution 435 for the granting of full sovereignty accepted by South Africa and then rescinded.
1988 Peace talks between South Africa, Angola, and Cuba led to agreement on full independence for Namibia.
1989 Unexpected incursion by SWAPO guerrillas from Angola into Namibia threatened agreed timetable for independence from South Africa; transitional constitution created by elected representatives; SWAPO dominant party.
1990 Liberal multiparty "independence" constitution adopted; independence achieved from South Africa. Sam Nujoma elected president.

Germany 1884; it was occupied in World War I by South African forces under L Botha, and was mandated to South Africa 1920. South Africa did not accept the termination of the mandate by the United Nations 1966, although briefly accepting the principle of ultimate independence 1978 (UN Security Council Resolution 435); in 1968 the UN renamed the territory Namibia. South Africa's apartheid laws were extended to the colony in 1966 and in opposition to such racial discrimination Sam ◊Nujoma, an Ovambu, led a political (from 1958) and then (from mid-1960s) an armed resistance campaign for independence, forming the South-West Africa People's Organization (SWAPO) and the People's Liberation Army of Namibia (PLAN). Following harassment, he was forced into exile in 1960, establishing guerrilla bases in Angola and Zambia. Military conflict in Namibia escalated from the mid-1970s as the Pretoria regime attempted to topple the Marxist government in neighboring Angola. In 1985 South Africa installed a puppet regime in Namibia, the Transitional Government of National Unity (TGNU), a multiracial body, but including only one Ovambo minister. It attempted to reform the apartheid system but was internally divided between moderate reformist and conservative wings, and failed to secure UN recognition.

In 1988 progress was finally made toward a peace settlement in Namibia as a result of both South Africa and the USSR's (via Cuba) tiring of the cost of their proxy military involvment in the civil wars of both the colony and neighboring Angola. In Aug 1988 the South African and Angolan governments signed an agreement that provided for an immediate ceasefire, followed by the rapid withdrawal of South African forces from Angola and, during 1989, the phased withdrawal of Cuba's troops from Angola and South Africa's from Namibia. From April 1989, a UN peacekeeping force was stationed in Namibia to oversee the holding of multiparty elections in Nov. These were won by SWAPO, but its 57% share of the seats in the constituent assembly, which had the task of framing a new "independence constitution," fell short of the two-thirds majority required for it to dominate the proceedings. As a consequence, a moderate multiparty constitution was adopted in Feb 1990. Sam Nujoma was unanimously elected Namibia's first president by the assembly on Feb 16, 1990, and was formally sworn in by the UN secretary general on independence day, March 21, 1990.

Nampo formerly (until 1947) ***Chinnampo*** city on the W coast of North Korea, 25 mi/40 km SW of Pyongan; population (1984) 691,000.

Namur (Flemish *Naemen*) industrial city (cutlery, porcelain, paper, iron, steel), capital of the province of Namur, in S Belgium, at the confluence of the Sambre and Meuse rivers; population (1988) 103,000. It was a strategic location during both world wars. The province of Namur has an area of 1,428 sq mi/3,700 sq km and a population (1987) of 415,000.

Nanaimo coal-mining center of British Columbia, Canada, on the E coast of Vancouver Island; population (1985) 50,500.

Nanak 1469–c. 1539. Indian guru and founder of Sikhism, a religion based on the unity of God and the equality of all human beings. He was strongly opposed to caste divisions.

Nanchang industrial capital of Jiangxi province, China, about 160 mi/260 km SE of Wuhan. Major industries are textiles, glass, porcelain, and soap. Population (1986) 1,120,000.

Nanchang is a road and rail junction. It was originally a walled city built in the 12th century. The first Chinese Communist uprising took place here Aug 1, 1927.

Nancy capital of the *département* of Meurthe-et-Moselle and of the region of Lorraine, France, on the river Meurthe 175 mi/280 km E of Paris; population (1982) 307,000. Nancy dates from the 11th century.

Nanda Devi peak in the Himalayas, Uttar Pradesh, N India; height 25,645 ft/7,817 m. Until Kanchenjunga was absorbed into India, Nanda Devi was the country's highest mountain.

Nanga Parbat peak in the Himalayan Karakoram mountains of Kashmir; height 26,660 ft/8,126 m.

Nanjing or ***Nanking*** capital of Jiangsu province, China, 165 mi/270 km NW of Shanghai; center of industry (engineering, shipbuilding, oil refining), commerce, and communications; population (1986) 2,250,000. The bridge 1968 over the Chang Jiang river is the longest in China at 22,000 ft/6,705 m.

The city dates from the 2nd century BC, perhaps earlier. It received the name Nanjing ("southern capital") under the Ming dynasty (1368–1644) and was the capital of China 1368–1403, 1928–37, and 1946–49. Its university was founded 1888.

Nanking another spelling of ◊Nanjing, city in China.

Nanning industrial river port, capital of Guangxi Zhuang autonomous region, China, on the river You Jiang; population (1982) 866,000. It was a supply town during the Vietnam War and the Sino-Vietnamese confrontation 1979.

nano- prefix used in ◊SI units of measurement, equivalent to a one-billionth part (10^{-9}). For example, a nanosecond is one-billionth of a second.

nanotechnology the building of devices on a molecular scale. Micromachines, such as gears smaller in diameter than a human hair, have been made at the AT&T Bell laboratories in New Jersey. Building large molecules with useful shapes has been accomplished by research groups in the US. A robot small enough to travel through the bloodstream and into organs of the body, inspecting or removing diseased tissue, was under development in Japan 1990.

The scanning electron ◊microscope can be used to see and position single atoms and molecules, and to drill holes a nanometer (billionth of a meter) across in a variety of materials. The instrument can be used for ultrafine etching; the entire 28 volumes of the *Encyclopedia Britannica* could be engraved on the head of a pin. A complete electric motor has been built in the US; it is less than 0.1 mm across with a top speed of 600,000 rpm. It is etched out of silicon, using the ordinary methods of chip manufacturers.

The idea of manipulating material on a nanometer scale—atom by atom—was first discussed by Richard ◊Feynman in 1959. Nanotechnology enthusiasts say that it will eventually be possible to build computers on the molecular scale, produce ultrastrong materials, and allow the molecular correction of most diseases, even the repair of aging cells.

Nansen Fridtjof 1861–1930. Norwegian explorer and scientist. In 1893, he sailed to the Arctic in the *Fram*, which was deliberately allowed to drift north with an iceflow. Nansen, accompanied by F Hjalmar Johansen (1867–1923), continued north on foot and reached 86° 14′ N, the highest latitude then attained. After World War I, Nansen became League of Nations high commissioner for refugees. He was awarded the Nobel Peace Prize 1923.

He made his first voyage to Greenland waters in a sealing ship 1882, and in 1888–89 attempted to cross the Greenland icefield. He was professor of zoology and oceanography at the University of Christiania (now Oslo). Norwegian ambassador in London 1906–08.

Nanshan Islands Chinese name for the ◊Spratly Islands.

Nantes industrial port in W France on the river Loire, capital of Pays de la Loire region; industries include oil, sugar refining, textiles, soap, and tobacco; population (1982) 465,000. It has a cathedral 1434–1884 and a castle founded 938. It is the birthplace of the writer Jules Verne.

Nantes, Edict of decree by which Henry IV of France granted religious freedom to the ◊Huguenots 1598. It was revoked 1685 by Louis XIV.

Nantucket island and resort in Massachusetts, S of Cape Cod, 57 sq mi/148 sq km, population (1990) 5,087. In the 18th-19th centuries, Nantucket was a major whaling port; it is now a popular summer resort because of its excellent beaches. The island was discovered 1602, settled 1659 by Quakers, and became part of Massachusetts 1692.

Napa city in NW California on the Napa River, NE of San Francisco on San Pablo Bay; It is a major trading center for wine; other products include fruits and clothing; population (1990) 61,842.

napalm fuel used in flamethrowers and incendiary bombs. Produced from jellied gasoline, it is a mixture of naphthenic and palmitic acids. Napalm causes extensive burns because it sticks to the skin even when aflame. It was widely used by the US Army during the Vietnam War.

naphtha term originally applied to naturally occurring liquid hydrocarbons, now used for the mixtures of hydrocarbons obtained by destructive distillation of petroleum, coal tar, and shale oil. It is raw material for the petrochemical and plastics industries.

naphthalene $C_{10}H_8$ a solid, white, shiny, aromatic hydrocarbon obtained from coal tar. The smell of moth-balls is due to their napthalene content. It is used in making indigo and certain azo dyes, as a mild disinfectant, and an insecticide.

Napier wool port in Hawke Bay on the E coast of North Island, New Zealand; population (1986) 52,000.

Napier John 1550–1617. Scottish mathematician who invented ◊logarithms 1614 and "Napier's bones," an early mechanical calculating device for multiplication and division.

Napier Robert Cornelis, 1st Baron Napier of Magdala 1810–1890. British field marshal. Knighted for his services in relieving Lucknow during the Indian (Sepoy) Mutiny, he took part in capturing Peking (Beijing) 1860 during the war against China in 1860. He was commander in chief in India 1870–76 and governor of Gibraltar 1876–82.

Naples (Italian *Napoli*) industrial port (shipbuilding, automobiles, textiles, paper, food processing) and capital of Campania, Italy, on the Tyrrhenian Sea; population (1988) 1,201,000. To the S is the Isle of Capri, and behind the city is Mount Vesuvius, with the ruins of Pompeii at its foot.

Naples is the third-largest city of Italy, and as a port second in importance only to Genoa. Buildings include the royal palace, the San Carlo Opera House, the Castel Nuovo 1283, and the university 1224.

The city began as the Greek colony Neapolis in the 6th century BC and was taken over by Romans 326 BC; it became part of the Kingdom of the Two Sicilies 1140 and capital of the Kingdom of Naples 1282. (See ◊Sicily.)

Naples, Kingdom of the southern part of Italy, alternately independent and united with ◊Sicily in the Kingdom of the Two Sicilies.

Naples was united with Sicily 1140–1282, first under Norman rule 1130–94, then Hohenstaufen 1194–1266, then Angevin from 1268; apart from Sicily, but under continued Angevin rule to 1435; reunited with Sicily 1442–1503, under the house of Aragon to 1501; a Spanish Hapsburg possession 1504–1707 and Austrian 1707–35; under Spanish Bourbon rule 1735–99. The Neapolitan Republic was established 1799 after Napoleon had left Italy for Egypt, but fell after five months to the forces of reaction under Cardinal Ruffo, with the British admiral Nelson blockading the city by sea; many prominent citizens were massacred after the capitulation. The Spanish Bourbons were restored 1799, 1802–05, and 1815–1860, when Naples joined the Kingdom of Italy.

Napoleon I Napoleon Crossing the Alps *1800 by Jacques Louis David, celebrating one of the dramatic military campaigns of the French emperor.*

Napoleon I Bonaparte 1769–1821. Emperor of the French 1804–14 and 1814–15. A general from 1796 in the ◊Revolutionary Wars, in 1799 he overthrew the ruling Directory (see ◊French Revolution) and made himself dictator. From 1803 he conquered most of Europe (the ◊Napoleonic Wars) and installed his brothers as puppet kings (see ◊Bonaparte). After the Peninsular War and retreat from Moscow 1812, he was forced to abdicate 1814 and was banished to the island of Elba. In March 1815 he reassumed power but was defeated by British forces at the Battle of ◊Waterloo and exiled to the island of St Helena. His internal administrative reforms and laws are still evident in France.

Napoleon, born in Ajaccio, Corsica, received a commission in the artillery 1785 and first distinguished himself at the siege of ◊Toulon 1793. Having suppressed a royalist uprising in Paris 1795, he was given command against the Austrians in Italy and defeated them at Lodi, Arcole, and Rivoli 1796–97. Egypt, seen as a halfway house to India, was overrun and Syria invaded, but his fleet was destroyed by the British admiral ◊Nelson at the Battle of the Nile. Napoleon returned to France and carried out a coup against the government of the Directory to establish his own dictatorship, nominally as First Consul. The Austrians were again defeated at Marengo 1800 and the coalition against France shattered, a truce being declared 1802. A plebiscite the same year made him consul for life. In 1804 a plebiscite made him emperor.

While retaining and extending the legal and educational reforms of the Jacobins, Napoleon replaced the democratic constitution established by the Revolution with a centralized despotism, and by his ◊concordat with Pius VII conciliated the Catholic church. The Code Napoléon remains the basis of French law.

War was renewed by Britain 1803, aided by Austria and Russia from 1805 and Prussia from 1806. Prevented by the British navy from invading Britain, Napoleon drove Austria out of the war by victories at Ulm and Austerlitz 1805, and Prussia by the victory at Jena 1806. Then, after the battles of Eylau and Friedland, he formed an alliance with Russia at Tilsit 1807. Napoleon now forbade entry of British goods to Europe, attempting an economic blockade known as the ◊Continental System, occupied Portugal, and in 1808 placed his brother Joseph on the Spanish throne. Both countries revolted, with British aid, and Austria attempted to reenter the war but was defeated at Wagram. In 1796 Napoleon had married ◊Josephine de Beauharnais, but in 1809, to assert his equality with the Hapsburgs, he divorced her to marry the Austrian emperor's daughter, ◊Marie Louise.

When Russia failed to enforce the Continental System, Napoleon marched on and occupied Moscow, but his army's retreat in the bitter winter of 1812 encouraged Prussia and Austria to declare war again 1813. He was defeated at Leipzig and driven from Germany. Despite his brilliant campaign on French soil, the Allies invaded Paris and compelled him to abdicate April 1814; he was banished to the island of Elba, off the west coast of Italy. In March 1815 he escaped and took power for a hundred days, with the aid

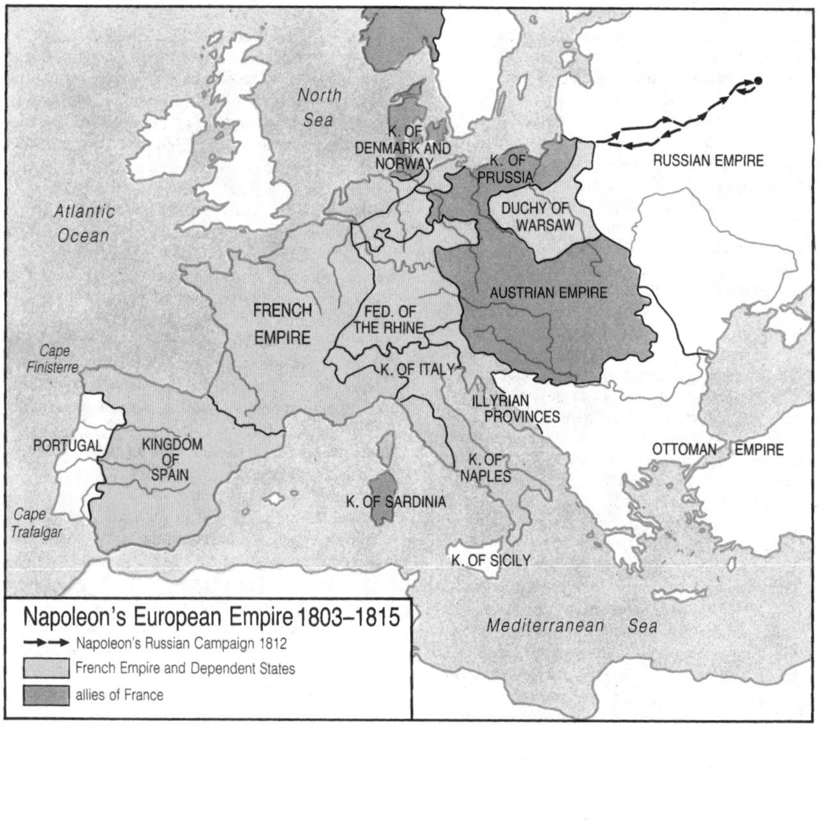
North Sea
K. OF DENMARK AND NORWAY
K. OF PRUSSIA
RUSSIAN EMPIRE
DUCHY OF WARSAW
Atlantic Ocean
AUSTRIAN EMPIRE
FRENCH EMPIRE
FED. OF THE RHINE
Cape Finisterre
K. OF ITALY
ILLYRIAN PROVINCES
PORTUGAL
KINGDOM OF SPAIN
OTTOMAN EMPIRE
K. OF NAPLES
K. OF SARDINIA
Cape Trafalgar
K. OF SICILY
Mediterranean Sea
Napoleon's Russian Campaign 1812
French Empire and Dependent States
allies of France

Napoleon's European Empire 1803–1815

of Marshal ◊Ney, but Britain and Prussia led an alliance against him at Waterloo, Belgium, in June. Surrendering to the British, he again abdicated, and was exiled to the island of St Helena, 1,200 mi/1,900 km west of Africa, where he died. His body was brought back 1840 to be interred in the Hôtel des Invalides, Paris.

Napoleon II 1811–1832. Title given by the Bonapartists to the son of Napoleon I and ◊Marie Louise; until 1814 he was known as the king of Rome and after 1818 as the duke of Reichstadt. After his father's abdication 1814 he was taken to the Austrian court, where he spent the rest of his life.

Napoleon III 1808–1873. Emperor of the French 1852–70, known as Louis-Napoleon. After two attempted coups (1836 and 1840) he was jailed, then went into exile, returning for the revolution of 1848, when he became president of the Second Republic but soon turned authoritarian. In 1870 he was maneuvered by the German chancellor Bismarck into war with Prussia (see ◊Franco-Prussian war); he was forced to surrender at Sedan, NE France, and the empire collapsed.

He fled to England.

Napoleonic Wars ***1803–15*** a series of European wars conducted by Napoleon I following the ◊Revolutionary Wars, aiming for French conquest of Europe.

1803 Britain renewed the war against France, following an appeal from the Maltese against Napoleon's 1798 seizure of the island.

1805 Napoleon's planned invasion of Britain from Boulogne ended with Nelson's victory at ◊Trafalgar. Coalition formed against France by Britain, Austria, Russia, and Sweden. Austria defeated at Ulm; Austria and Russia at ◊Austerlitz.

1806 Prussia joined the coalition and was defeated at Jena; Napoleon instituted an attempted blockade, the Continental System, to isolate Britain from Europe.

1807 Russia defeated at Eylau and Friedland and, on making peace with Napoleon under the Treaty of Tilsit, changed sides, agreeing to attack Sweden, but was forced to retreat.

1808 Napoleon's invasion of Portugal and strategy of installing his relatives as puppet kings led to the ◊Peninsular War.

1809 Revived Austrian opposition to Napoleon was ended by defeat at ◊Wagram.

1812 The Continental System finally collapsed on its rejection by Russia, and Napoleon made the fatal decision to invade; he reached Moscow but was defeated by the Russian resistance and by the bitter winter as he retreated through a countryside laid waste by the retreating Russians (380,000 French soldiers died).

1813 Britain, Prussia, Russia, Austria, and Sweden formed a new coalition, which defeated Napoleon at the Battle of the Nations, Leipzig, Germany. He abdicated and was exiled to Elba.

1814 Louis XVIII became king of France, and the Congress of Vienna met to conclude peace.

1815 Napoleon returned to Paris. June 16 the

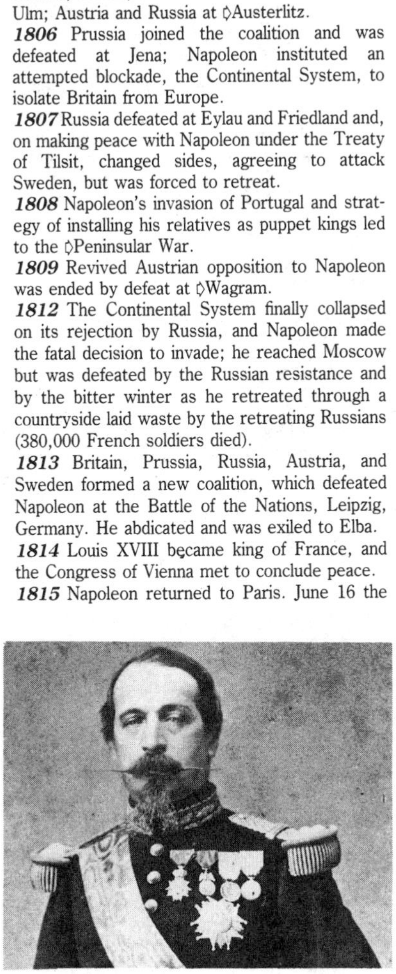

Napoleon III *Napoleon III, emperor of the French 1852–70.*

narcissus

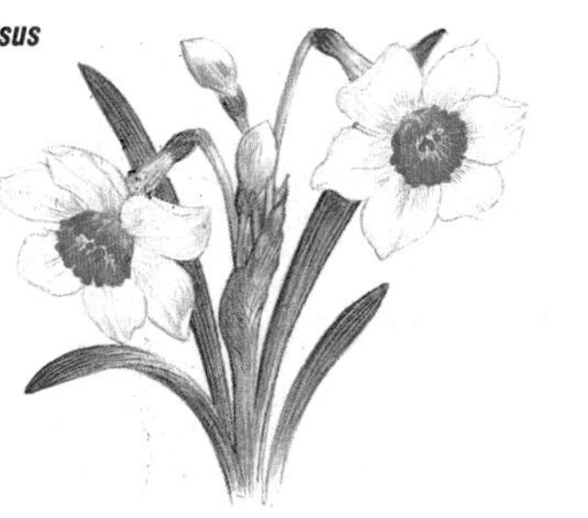

British commander Wellington defeated the French marshal Ney at Quatre Bras (in Belgium, SE of Brussels), and Napoleon was finally defeated at Waterloo, S of Brussels, June 18.

Napoli Italian form of ◊Naples, city in Italy.

Nara city in Japan, in the S of Honshu island, the capital of the country 710–94; population (1984) 316,000. It was the birthplace of Japanese art and literature and has ancient wooden temples.

Narbonne city in Aude *département*, S France; population (1983) 39,246. It was the chief town of S Gaul in Roman times and a port in medieval times.

narcissism in psychology, an exaggeration of normal self-respect and self-involvement which may amount to mental disorder when it precludes relationships with other people.

narcissus genus of bulbous plants of the family Amaryllidaceae. Species include the daffodil, jonquil, and narcissus. All have flowers with a cup projecting from the center.

Narcissus in Greek mythology, a beautiful youth who rejected the love of the nymph ◊Echo and was condemned to fall in love with his own reflection in a pool. He pined away and in the place where he died a flower sprang up that was named after him.

narcolepsy rare disorder characterized by bouts of overwhelming sleepiness and loss of muscle power. It is controlled by drugs.

narcotic pain-relieving and sleep-inducing drug. The chief narcotics induce dependency, and include opium, its derivatives and synthetic modifications (such as morphine and heroin); alcohols (for example paraldehyde and ethyl alcohol); and barbiturates.

Nares George Strong 1831–1915. Scottish vice-admiral and explorer who sailed to the Canadian Arctic on an expedition in search of John ◊Franklin 1852, and again in 1876 when he discovered the Challenger Mountains. During 1872–76 he commanded the Challenger Expedition. His Arctic explorations are recounted in *Voyage to the Polar Seas* 1878.

Narmada River a river that rises in the Maikala range in Madhya Pradesh state, central India, and flows 778 mi/1,245 km WSW to the Gulf of Khambat, an inlet of the Arabian Sea. Forming the traditional boundary between Hindustan and Deccan, the Narmada is a holy river of the Hindus. India's Narmada Valley Project is one of the largest and most controversial river development projects in the world. Between 1990 and 2040 it is planned to build 30 major dams, 135 medium-sized dams and 3,000 smaller dams in a scheme that will involve moving 1 million of the valley's population of 20 million people.

Narodnik member of a secret Russian political movement, active 1873–76 before its suppression by the tsarist authorities. Narodniks were largely university students, and their main purpose was to convert the peasantry to socialism.

Narragansett Bay Atlantic inlet, Rhode Island. Running inland for 28 mi/45 km, it encloses a number of islands. At the head of the bay is Providence, the state capital; at its mouth is the island of Aquidneck with Newport, site of the US Naval War College (1885), the America's Cup yachting races, a jazz festival, the Tennis Hall of Fame, and summer mansions of the wealthy (many open as museums).

Narses c. 478–c. 573. Byzantine general. Originally a eunuch slave, he later became an official in the imperial treasury. He was joint commander with the Roman general Belisarius in Italy 538–39, and in 552 destroyed the Ostrogoths at Taginae in the Apennines.

Narvik seaport in Nordland county, N Norway, on Ofot Fjord, exporting iron ore from Swedish mines; population (1980) 19,500. To secure this ore supply Germany seized Narvik in Apr 1940. British, French, Polish, and Norwegian forces recaptured the port but had to abandon it on June 10 to cope with the worsening Allied situation elsewhere in Europe.

narwhal toothed whale *Monodon monoceros*, found only in the Arctic Ocean. It grows to 16 ft/5 m long, has a gray and black body, a small head, and short flippers. The male has a single spirally fluted tusk that may be up to 9 ft/2.7 m long.

NASA *N*ational *A*eronautics and *S*pace *A*dministration, the US government agency, founded 1958 by the National Aeronautics and Space Act, for spaceflight and aeronautical research. Its headquarters are in Washington, DC and its main installation is at the ◊Kennedy Space Center in Florida. NASA's early planetary and lunar programs included Pioneer spacecraft from 1958, which gathered data for the later crewed missions, the most famous of which brought men to the Moon in *Apollo 11* on July 16–24, 1969.

Other installations are located in Virginia (Langley Research Center and Wallops Station); California (Ames Research Center, Flight Research Center, and the Jet Propulsion Laboratory); Ohio (Lewis Research Center); Alabama (George C Marshall Space Flight Center); Maryland (Goddard Space Flight Center); and Texas (Manned Spacecraft Center). The Office of Manned Space Flight is responsible for space missions with crews and for the space-station and Space Shuttle programs. The Office of Space Science and Applications deals with the scientific exploration of space. The Office of Advanced Research and Technology plans future flights and research. The Office of Tracking and Data Acquisition provides a network for tracking flights and accumulating data.

Naseby, Battle of decisive battle of the English Civil War June 14, 1645, when the Royalists, led by Prince Rupert, were defeated by Oliver Cromwell and General Fairfax. It is named after the nearby village of Naseby, 20 mi/32 km S of Leicester.

Nash John 1752–1835. English architect. He laid out Regent's Park, London, and its approaches. Between 1813 and 1820 he planned Regent Street (later rebuilt), repaired and enlarged Buckingham Palace (for which he designed Marble Arch), and rebuilt Brighton Pavilion in flamboyant oriental style.

Nash (Frederic) Ogden 1902–1971. US poet and wit. He published numerous volumes of humorous, quietly satirical light verse with unorthodox rhymes and puns. They include *I'm a Stranger Here Myself* 1938, *Versus* 1949, and *Bed Riddance* 1970. Most of his poems first appeared in *The New Yorker*, where he held an editorial post and did much to establish the magazine's tone.

narwhal

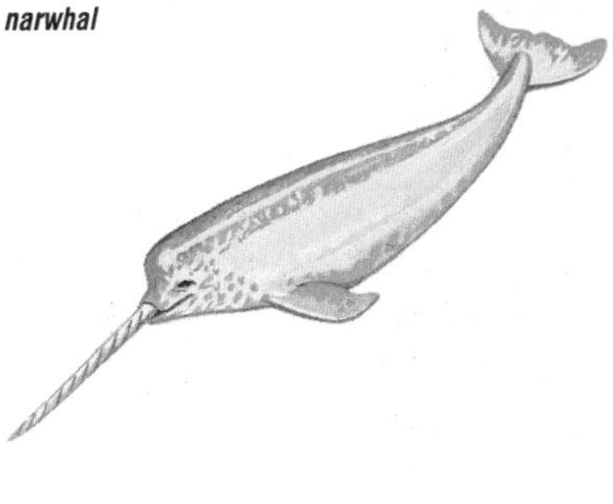

Nasser *Egyptian politician and prime minister Gamal Abdel Nasser, a heroic figure to Arabs in the Middle East.*

Born in Rye, New York, Nash also wrote children's books and lyrics for such musicals as *A Touch of Venus* 1943.

Nash Walter 1882–1968. New Zealand Labour politician. He was born in England, and emigrated to New Zealand 1909. He held ministerial posts 1935–49, was prime minister 1957–60, and leader of the Labour Party until 1963.

Nashua city in S New Hampshire on the Nashua River where it meets the Merrimack River, just N of the Massachusetts border. Industries include electronics, asbestos, chemicals, and glass products; population (1990) 79,662.

Nashville port on the Cumberland River and capital of Tennessee; population (1990) 488,374. It is a banking and commercial center and has large printing, music-publishing, and recording industries.

Most of the Bibles in the US are printed here, and it is the hub of the country-music business. It is the home of the Country Music Hall of Fame and Museum and Opryland. Educational institutions include Vanderbilt and Fisk universities. The Southern Baptist Convention is headquartered here.

Nashville dates from 1778, and the Confederate army was defeated here 1864 in the Civil War. In 1963 Nashville merged with surrounding Davidson County.

Nassau capital and port of the Bahamas, on New Providence Island; population (1980) 135,000. A tourist center, it is known for fine beaches and the resort community of Paradise Island across the harbor. The College of the Bahamas is here. English settlers founded it in the 17th century, and it was a supply base for Confederate blockade runners during the American Civil War.

Nassau agreement treaty signed Dec 18, 1962 whereby the US provided Britain with Polaris missiles, marking a strengthening in Anglo-American relations.

Nasser Gamal Abdel 1918–1970. Egyptian politician, prime minister 1954–56 and from 1956 president of Egypt (the United Arab Republic 1958–71). In 1952 he was the driving power behind the Neguib coup, which ended the monarchy. His nationalization of the Suez Canal 1956 led to an Anglo-French invasion and the ◊Suez Crisis, and his ambitions for an Egyptian-led union of Arab states led to disquiet in the Middle East (and in the West). Nasser was also an early and influential leader of the nonaligned movement.

Nast Thomas 1840–1902. German-born US illustrator and cartoonist. During the American Civil War, Nast served as a staff artist for *Harper's Weekly* and later drew its editorial cartoons. Nast's vivid caricatures helped bring down New York's Boss ◊Tweed and established the donkey and the elephant as the symbols of Democrats and Republicans, respectively.

Nast came to the US with his family in 1846. After attending the National Academy of Design in New York, he worked as an illustrator for several popular New York weeklies, eventually being sent to Europe as a foreign correspondent.

nastic movement a plant movement that is caused by an external stimulus, such as light or temperature, but which is directionally independent of its source, unlike ◊tropisms. Nastic movements occur due to changes in water pressure within specialized cells or as a result of differing rates of growth in parts of the plant. Examples include the opening and closing of crocus flowers following an increase or decrease in temperature (thermonasty), and the opening and closing of evening-primrose *Oenothera* flowers on exposure to dark and light (photonasty).

The leaf movements of Venus's-flytrap *Dionea muscipula* following a tactile stimulus, and the rapid collapse of the leaflets of the sensitive plant *Mimosa pudica* are examples of haptonasty. Sleep movements, where the leaves or flowers of some plants adopt a different position at night, are described as nyctinasty. Other movement types include hydronasty, in response to a change in the atmospheric humidity, and chemonasty, in response to a chemical stimulus.

nasturtium any plant of the genus *Nasturtium*, family Cruciferae, including watercress *N. officinale*, a perennial aquatic plant of Europe and Asia, grown as a salad crop. It also includes plants of the South American family Tropeolaceae, including the cultivated species *Tropeolum majus*, with orange or scarlet flowers, and *T. minus*, which has smaller flowers.

Natal province of South Africa, NE of Cape Province, bounded on the E by the Indian Ocean
area 35,429 sq mi/91,785 sq km
capital Pietermaritzburg
towns Durban
physical slopes from the Drakensberg to a fertile subtropical coastal plain
features St Lucia National Park extends from coral reefs of the Indian Ocean N of Umfolozi river (whales, dolphins, turtles, crayfish), over forested sandhills to inland grasslands and swamps of Lake St Lucia, 125 sq mi/324 sq km (reedbuck, buffalo, crocodile, hippopotamus, black rhino, cheetah, pelican, flamingo, stork). It is under threat from titanium mining
products sugar cane, black wattle (*Acacia mollissima*), corn, fruits, vegetables, tobacco, coal
population (1985) 2,145,000
history called Natal ("of [Christ's] birth") because Vasco da Gama reached it Christmas Day 1497; part of the British Cape Colony from 1843 until 1856, when it was made into a separate colony. Zululand was annexed to Natal 1897, and the districts of Vrijheid, Utrecht, and part of Wakkerstroom were transferred from the Transvaal to Natal 1903; the colony became a part of the Union of South Africa 1910.

Natal industrial (textiles, salt refining) seaport in Brazil, capital of the state of Rio Grande do Norte; population (1980) 376,500. Natal was founded 1599 and became a city 1822.

Nataraja ("Lord of the Dance") in Hinduism, a title of ◊Siva.

Natchez member of a North American Indian people of the Mississippi area, one of the ◊Moundbuilder group of peoples. They had a highly developed caste system unusual in North America, headed by a ruler priest (the "Great Sun"). Members of the highest caste always married members of the lowest caste. The system lasted until the French colonized the area 1731. Only a few Natchez now survive in Oklahoma. Their Muskogean language is extinct.

Natchez city in Mississippi, on the E bluffs above the Mississippi River; population (1990) 19,460. It has many houses of the antebellum period and was important in the heyday of steamboat traffic. The Natchez Trace National Parkway is a restoration of the frontier road that followed Indian pathways and linked the city to Nashville, Tennessee.

Nation Carrie Amelia Moore 1846–1911. US temperance crusader. Born in Kentucky, she briefly taught school in Missouri. After the death of her alcoholic husband, Dr Charles Gloyd, she began a campaign against the use of alcohol. Moving to Kansas, where she married David Nation, she began to protest the flagrant disregard of that state's prohibition law. Marching into illegal saloons with a hatchet, Nation would lecture the patrons and then perform a "hatchetation" on bottles and bar. As the publisher of the *Smasher's Mail*, she was the most outspoken prohibitionist in the country.

national anthem a patriotic song for official occasions. The US national anthem "The Star-Spangled Banner," was written during the war of 1812 by Francis Scott ◊Key and was adopted officially in 1931. In Britain "God Save the King/Queen" has been accepted as such since 1745, although both music and words are of much earlier origin. The German anthem "Deutschland über Alles/Germany before everything" is sung to music by Haydn. The French national anthem, the ◊"Marseillaise," dates from 1792. The ◊"Internationale," adopted as the Soviet national anthem 1917, was replaced by the song "Unbreakable Union of Freeborn Republics" 1944.

National Association for the Advancement of Colored People (NAACP) US civil-rights organization, dedicated to ending inequality and segregation for African-Americans through nonviolent protest. Founded 1910, its first aim was to eradicate lynching. The NAACP campaigned to end segregation in state schools; it funded test cases that eventually led to the Supreme Court decision 1954 outlawing school segregation, although it was only through the ◊civil-rights movement of the 1960s that de-segregation was achieved. In 1987 the NAACP had about 500,000 members, black and white.

The NAACP was founded by a group of white liberals, including William Walling, Oswald Villard, social worker Jane Addams, philosopher John Dewey, and novelist William Dean Howells. Most of the officials were white, but most of the members were drawn from the ranks of the black bourgeoisie. It merged with the Niagara Movement founded 1905 by W E B DuBois. During World War II its membership increased from 50,000 to 400,000. The organization has been criticized by militants and black separatists for its moderate stance and its commitment to integration. See also history under ◊black.

The NAACP has focused on bringing to court challenges to discriminatory practices, and many famous lawyers—among them Thurgood ◊Marshall—have argued their case. The ◊Brown v. Board of Education case was a major triumph, forcing the end of overt segregation of public schools. It has also been criticized for depending too heavily on funds from white liberals.

National Country Party former name for the Australian ◊National Party.

national debt debt incurred by the central government of a country to its own people and institutions and also to overseas creditors. If it does not wish to raise taxes to finance its activities, a government can borrow from the public by means of selling interest-bearing bonds, for example, or from abroad. Traditionally, a major cause of incurring national debt was the cost of war but in recent decades governments have borrowed heavily in order to finance development or nationalization, to support an ailing currency, or to avoid raising taxation.

Government budgets are often planned with a deficit that is funded by overseas borrowing. In the 1980s most governments adopted monetary policies designed to limit their borrowing requirements, both to reduce the cost of servicing the debt and because borrowing money tends to cause inflation.

In the US the net government debt as a proportion of gross national product rose steadily in the 1980s from only 19% in 1981 to 31% in 1988, as its borrowing increased to finance a huge influx of imported goods and to support increased defense spending.

National Endowment for Democracy US political agency founded 1983 with government backing. It has funded a range of political organizations abroad, with over 95% of its $114 million annual income coming from the US government after 1984.

Recipients of funding include the Chilean Communist Party, Solidarity in Poland, the Social Christian Party in Costa Rica, and the anti-Sandinista election campaign in Nicaragua 1990. It has been criticized for financing political activities that would be illegal under US law and for funding the pro-Noriega election campaign in Panama 1984 as well as the anti-Noriega campaign 1989. Its president is Carl Gershman.

National Guard ◊militia force recruited by each state of the US. The volunteer National Guard units are under federal orders in emergencies, are under the control of state governors in peacetime, and are now an integral part of the US Army. The National Guard has been used against demonstrators; in May 1970 at Kent State University, Ohio, they killed four students who were protesting against the bombing of Cambodia by the US.

national income the total income earned, not necessarily received, by all persons in a country over a specified time period. It consists of wages, interest, rent, profits, and the net income of the self-employed. Profits of government enterprises are not included. See ◊national income and products accounts.

national income and products accounts a detailed description of the volume, composition, and use of a nation's output of goods and services. There are two basic components: the value of all goods and services produced (product side) and the costs incurred and payments received in the course of producing all goods and services (income side). These accounts are basic tools used in analyzing current economic performance and in forecasting future developments. See also ◊Gross National Product (GNP).

nationalism in music, a 19th-century movement in which composers (such as Smetana and Grieg) included the folk material of their country in their works, projecting the national spirit and its expression.

nationalism in politics, a movement that consciously aims to unify a nation, create a state, or liberate it from foreign rule. Nationalist movements became a potent factor in European politics during the 19th century; since 1900 nationalism has become a strong force in Asia and Africa and in the late 1980s revived strongly in E Europe.

Stimulated by the French Revolution, movements arose in the 19th century in favor of national unification in Germany and Italy and national independence in Ireland, Italy, Belgium, Hungary, Bohemia, Poland, Finland, and the Balkan states. Revival of interest in the national language, history, traditions, and culture has accompanied and influenced most political movements. See also ◊African nationalism, ◊Irish nationalism.

nationalization policy of bringing a country's essential services and industries under public ownership. It was pursued, for example, by the UK Labour government 1945–51. In recent years the trend toward nationalization has slowed and in many countries (the UK, France, and Japan) reversed (◊privatization). Assets in the hands of foreign governments or companies with property in another country may also be nationalized by that country; for example, Iran's oil industry (see ◊Abadan), the ◊Suez Canal, and US-owned fruit plantations in Guatemala, were all nationalized in the 1950s.

National Labor Relations Board v Jones and Laughlin Steel Co a US Supreme Court decision 1937 dealing with federal jurisdiction over intrastate trade. Jones and Laughlin appealed an NLRB order to reinstate several employees fired for union activities. The steel company argued that as an exclusively intrastate trader, it was immune to federal regulatory measures. The Court voted 5 to 4 to uphold the NLRB ruling, judging that since the steel industry was so intrinsically an interstate business the actions of Jones and Laughlin must have affected interstate commerce. The Court ruled that the "stream of commerce" placed local steel companies within federal jurisdiction.

national park land set aside and conserved for public enjoyment. The first was Yellowstone National Park, established 1872. National parks include not only the most scenic places, but also places distinguished for their historic, prehistoric, or scientific interest, or for their superior recreational assets.

National Party, Australian Australian political party representing the interests of the farmers and people of the smaller towns. It developed from about 1860 as the National Country Party, and holds the power balance between Liberals and Labor. It gained strength following the introduction of proportional representation 1918, and has been in coalition with the Liberals since 1949.

national security adviser an appointee of the executive branch, the head of the ◊National Security Council, which, since the National Security Act 1947, coordinates the defense and foreign policy of the US; also the assistant to the US president on aspects of foreign affairs. The national security adviser appointed 1989 was Lt-Gen Brent Scowcroft, the author of a 1983 weapons report proposing MX missiles.

The office was originally a clerical post but took on greater stature when held by McGeorge Bundy 1961–66, Walt Rostow 1966–69, and Henry ◊Kissinger 1969–75, who exceeded Secretary of State William Rogers in influence with President Nixon. Zbigniew ◊Brzezinski, appointed 1977, struggled with Secretary of State Vance for influence on President Carter. President Reagan's adviser, Admiral John Poindexter, who succeeded Robert McFarlane (1937–) in 1985, was forced to resign 1986 because of his part in the illicit sale of arms to Iran (see ◊Irangate). He was succeeded by Frank Carlucci (1930–), Lt-Gen Colin Powell (1937–), and Scowcroft.

National Security Agency (NSA) the largest and most secret of US intelligence agencies. Established 1952 to intercept foreign communications as well as to safeguard US transmissions, the NSA collects and analyzes computer communications, telephone signals and other electronic data, and gathers intelligence. Known as the Puzzle Palace, its headquarters are at Fort Meade, Maryland (with a major facility at Menwith Hill, England).

The NSA was set up by a classified presidential memorandum and its very existence was not acknowledged until 1962. It operates outside normal channels of government accountability, and its budget (also secret) is thought to exceed several billion dollars. Fort Meade has several Cray supercomputers.

National Security Council US federal executive council that was established under the National Security Act of 1947. The membership includes the president, vice-president, and secretaries of state and defense. Their special advisors include the head of the Joint Chiefs of Staff and the director of the Central Intellegence Agency. The national security advisor heads the council's staff.

national security directive in the US, secret decree issued by the president that can establish national policy and commit federal funds without the knowledge of Congress, under the National Security Act 1947. The ◊National Security Council alone decides whether these directives may be made public; most are not. The directives have been criticized as unconstitutional, since they enable the executive branch of government to make laws.

history In 1950 President Truman issued a secret directive for covert operations to foment "unrest and revolt" in the Eastern bloc. J F Kennedy authorized an invasion of Cuba by this means (see ◊Bay of Pigs), and Lyndon Johnson approved military incursions into Laos during the Vietnam War. The US invasion of Grenada and the allocation of $19 million for the CIA to start arming and training Contras in Central America were also authorized by national security directives. Ronald Reagan signed some 300 such directives during his time in office, of which only about 50 have been made known.

National Socialism official name for the ◊Nazi movement in Germany; see also ◊fascism.

Native American the modern, politically conscious term used by North ◊American Indians, ◊Eskimo, and Aleuts to describe themselves as a group, although each society maintains its autonomy and its own name. See ◊Hopi, ◊Navaho, ◊Cherokee, ◊Sioux.

native companion another name for the ◊brolga, so called because these birds are often seen in pairs.

native element a nongaseous element that occurs naturally, uncombined with any other element(s). Examples include gold, silver, copper, and some platinum group metals. Examples of native nonmetals are carbon and sulfur.

native metal or ***free metal*** any of the metallic elements that occur in nature in the chemically uncombined or elemental form (in addition to any combined form). They include bismuth, cobalt, copper, gold, iridium, iron, lead, mercury, nickel, osmium, palladium, platinum, ruthenium, rhodium, tin, and silver. Some are commonly found in the free state, such as gold; others occur almost exclusively in the combined state, but under unusual conditions do occur as native metals, such as mercury.

nativity a Christian festival celebrating a birth: Christmas is celebrated Dec 25 from AD 336 in memory of the birth of Jesus in Bethlehem; Nativity of the Virgin Mary is celebrated Sept 8 by the Catholic and Eastern Orthodox churches; Nativity of John the Baptist is celebrated June 24 by the Catholic, Eastern Orthodox, and Anglican churches.

NATO abbreviation for ◊North Atlantic Treaty Organization.

Natron, Lake a salt and soda lake in the Great Rift Valley, Tanzania; length 35 mi/56 km, width 15 mi/24 km.

natural in music, a sign canceling a sharp or flat. A natural trumpet or horn is an instrument without valves.

Natural Bridge a village in Virginia, 115 mi/185 km W of Richmond. The nearby Cedar Creek is straddled by an arch of limestone 215 ft/66 m high and 90 ft/27 m wide.

natural frequency the frequency at which a mechanical system will vibrate freely. A pendulum, for example, always oscillates at the same frequency when set in motion. This natural frequency depends upon the string's weight and tension.

More complicated systems, such as bridges, also vibrate with a fixed natural frequency. If a varying force with a frequency equal to the natural frequency is applied to such an object the vibrations can become violent, a phenomenon known as ◊resonance.

natural gas mixture of flammable gases found in the

Earth's crust (often in association with petroleum), now one of the world's three main fossil fuels (with coal and oil). Natural gas is a mixture of ◊hydrocarbons, chiefly methane, with ethane, butane, and propane.

Before the gas is piped to storage tanks and on to consumers, butane and propane are removed and liquefied to form "bottled gas." Natural gas is liquefied for transport and storage, and is therefore often used where other fuels are scarce and expensive.

Test flights of the first aircraft powered by liquefied natural gas began 1989. The craft, made in the USSR, will save 8.9 tons/9 tonnes of kerosene on a journey of 125 mi/2,000 km.

natural logarithm in mathematics, the exponent of a number expressed to base *e*, where *e* represents the ◊irrational number 2.71828... .

Natural ◊logarithms are also called Napierian logarithms, after their inventor, the Scottish mathematician John Napier.

natural radioactivity radioactivity generated by those radioactive elements that exist in the Earth's crust. These include technicium (atomic number 43), promethium (atomic number 61), and all the elements from polonium (atomic number 84) to americium (atomic number 95). All elements from curium (atomic number 96) up, although radioactive, are synthesized and do not occur in nature. ◊Radioisotopes of many nonradioactive elements are also found in nature (for example, potassium-40).

natural selection the process whereby gene frequencies in a population change through certain individuals producing more descendants than others because they are better able to survive and reproduce in their environment. The accumulated effect of natural selection is to produce ◊adaptations such as the insulating coat of a polar bear or the spadelike forelimbs of a mole. The process is slow, relying firstly on random variation in the genes of an organism being produced by ◊mutation and the genetic ◊recombination of sexual reproduction. It was recognized by Charles Darwin and Alfred Russel Wallace as the main process driving ◊evolution.

nature the living world, including plants, animals, fungi, and all microorganisms, and naturally formed features of the landscape, such as mountains and rivers.

nature–nurture controversy or ***environment–heredity controversy*** a long-standing dispute among philosophers and psychologists over the relative importance of environment, that is upbringing, experience and learning ("nurture"), and heredity, that is genetic inheritance ("nature") in determining the make-up of an organism, as related to human personality and intelligence.

One area of contention is the reason for differences between individuals, for example, in performing intelligence tests. The environmentalist position assumes that individuals do not differ significantly in their inherited mental abilities and that subsequent differences are due to learning, or to differences in early experiences. Opponents insist that certain differences in the capacities of individuals (and hence their behavior) can be attributed to inherited differences in their genetic makeup.

nature preserve area set aside to protect a habitat and the wildlife that lives within it, with only restricted admission for the public. A nature preserve often provides a sanctuary for rare species, and rare habitats, such as marshlands. The world's largest is Etosha Reserve, Namibia; area 38,415 sq mi/99,520 sq km.

Many state and local preserves have been established in the US since 1970. Some are called greenbelts and some are designated "forever wild," as well as those that are administered for limited or educational access.

Nauru
Republic of
(Naoero)

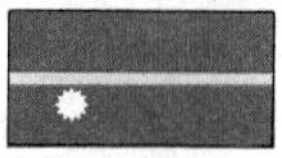

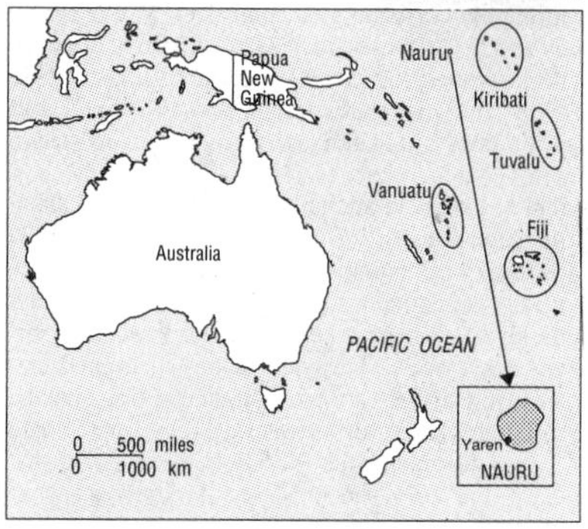
Papua
New
Guinea
Nauru
Kiribati
Tuvalu
Vanuatu
Fiji
Australia
PACIFIC OCEAN
0 500 miles
0 1000 km
Yaren
NAURU

area 8 sq mi/21 sq km
capital (seat of government) Yaren District
physical tropical island country in W Pacific; plateau circled by coral cliffs and sandy beaches
features phosphate lies just S of equator; one of three phosphate rock islands in the Pacific
head of state and government Hammer DeRoburt from 1987
political system liberal democracy
political parties Democratic Party of Nauru (DPN)
exports phosphates
currency Australian dollar
population (1990 est) 8,100 (mainly Polynesian; Chinese 8%, European 8%); growth rate 1.7% p.a.
language Nauruan (official), English
religion Protestant 66%, Roman Catholic 33%
literacy 99% (1988)
GNP $160 mn (1986); $9,091 per head (1985)
chronology
1888 Annexed by Germany.
1920 Administered by Australia, New Zealand, and UK until independence, except 1942–45, when it was occupied by Japan.
1968 Independence achieved from Australia, New Zealand, and Britain with "special member" Commonwealth status. Hammer DeRoburt elected president.
1976 Bernard Dowiyogo elected president.
1978 DeRoburt elected.
1986 DeRoburt briefly replaced as president by Kenneth Adeang.
1987 DeRoburt elected; Adeang established the Democratic Party of Nauru.
1989 DeRoburt replaced by Kensas Aroi, who was later succeeded by Bernard Dowiyogo.

Nauru island country in ◊Polynesia, SW Pacific, W of Kiribati.

government The constitution dates from independence in 1968. It provides for a single-chamber parliament of 18 members, elected by universal suffrage for a three-year term, and a president who is both head of state and head of government. The president and cabinet are elected by parliament and responsible to it. The size of the country allows an intimate style of government, with the president combining several portfolios in a cabinet of only five. Voting in parliamentary elections is compulsory. Traditionally, members of parliament have been elected as independents and then grouped themselves into pro- and antigovernment factions. In 1987, however, the Democratic Party of Nauru was formed by the then opposition leader Kennan Adeang.

history The first Europeans, Britons, arrived 1798 and called it Pleasant Island. The German empire seized it 1888. Nauru was placed under Australian administration by the League of Nations in 1920, with the UK and New Zealand as cotrustees. Japan occupied and devastated Nauru 1942–45, destroying its mining facilities and deporting two-thirds of its population to Truk Atoll in ◊Micronesia, 1,600 km to the northwest. In 1947 Nauru became a United Nations trust territory administered by Australia.

Internal self-government was granted 1966, and in 1968, on achieving full independence, Nauru became a "special member" of the ◊Commonwealth, with no direct representation at meetings of heads of government. The chief of Nauru, Hammer DeRoburt, was elected president in 1968 and reelected until 1983 with one interruption, 1976–78, when Bernard Dowiyogo was president. The Dec 1986 elections resulted in a hung parliament.

In the 1987 elections, DeRoburt secured a narrow majority. This prompted the defeated Kennan Adeang, who had briefly held power in 1986, to establish the Democratic Party of Nauru as a formal opposition grouping. In Aug 1989 Adeang secured the ousting of DeRoburt on a vote of no confidence and Kensas Aroi became president, with Adeang as finance minister in the new government. According to Australian government sources, Aroi was DeRoburt's "unaknowledged natural son." Four months later Aroi resigned on the grounds of ill health and in the subsequent election was defeated by Bernard Dowiyogo.

Nauru is attempting to sue its former trustees (New Zealand, the UK, and Australia) for removing nearly all the island's phosphate-rich soil 1922–68, leaving it barren. Nauru received $2.5 million for phosphate worth $65 million and had to pay Australia $20 million to keep the remaining soil. Nauru's residual phosphate supplies, which have earned $80 million a year, are due to run out in 1995 and an economic diversification program has been launched.

nautical mile formerly various units of distance used in navigation; since 1959, an internationally agreed-on standard equaling the average length of one minute of arc on a great circle of the Earth, or 6,076.12 ft/1,852 m.

nautilus shelled ◊cephalopod, genus *Nautilus*, found in the Indian and Pacific oceans. The pearly nautilus *N. pompilius* has a chambered spiral shell about 8 in/20 cm in diameter. Its body occupies the outer chamber. The nautilus has a large number of short, grasping tentacles surrounding a sharp beak. The living nautiluses are representatives of a group common 450 million years ago. Paper nautilus is an another name for the ◊argonaut, a type of octopus. *Nautilus* is also the name of the world's first nuclear-powered submarine, launched by the US 1954; it sailed under the icecap to the North Pole.

Navaho member of a peaceable agricultural North American Indian people, related to the ◊Apache; population about 200,000. They were attacked by Kit ◊Carson and US troops 1864, and were rounded up and exiled. Their reservation, created 1868, is the largest in the US (25,000 sq mi/65,000 sq km), and is mainly in NE Arizona, but extends into NW New Mexico and SE Utah. Many Navaho now herd sheep and earn an income from tourism, making and selling rugs, blankets, and silver and turquoise jewelry. Some uranium and natural gas is mined on their reservation. Like the Apache, they speak a Southern Athabaskan language.

Navarino, Battle of a decisive naval action Oct 20, 1827 off Pylos in the Greek war of liberation that was won by the combined fleets of the English, French, and Russians under Vice-Admiral Edward Codrington (1770–1851) over the Turkish and Egyptian fleets. Navarino is the Italian and historic name of Pylos Bay, Greece, on the SW coast of the Peloponnese.

Navarre (Spanish *Navarra*) autonomous mountain region of N Spain

area 4,014 sq mi/10,400 sq km

capital Pamplona

features Monte Adi 4,933 ft/1,503 m; rivers: Ebro, Arga

population (1986) 513,000

history part of the medieval kingdom of ◊Navarre. Estella, to the SW, where Don Carlos was proclaimed king 1833, was a center of agitation by the ◊Carlists.

Navarre, Kingdom of former kingdom comprising the Spanish province of Navarre and part of what is now the French *département* of Basses-Pyrénées. It resisted the conquest of the ◊Moors and was independent until it became French 1284 on the marriage of Philip IV to the heiress of Navarre. In 1479 Ferdinand of Aragon annexed Spanish Navarre, with French Navarre going to Catherine of Foix (1483–1512), who kept the royal title. Her grandson became Henry IV of France, and Navarre was absorbed in the French crown lands 1620.

nave in architecture, the central part of a church, between the choir and the entrance.

navel small indentation in the center of the abdomen of mammals, the remains of the site of attachment of the ◊umbilical cord, which connects the fetus to the ◊placenta.

navigation the science and technology of finding the position, course, and distance traveled by a ship, plane, or other craft. Traditional methods include the magnetic ◊compass and ◊sextant. Today the gyrocompass is usually used, together with highly sophisticated electronic methods, employing beacons of radio signals. Satellite navigation uses satellites that broadcast time and position signals.

The US Global Positioning System, when complete, will feature 18 Navstar satellites that will enable users (including eventually motorists and walkers) to triangulate their position (from any three satellites) to within 50 ft/15 m.

navigation

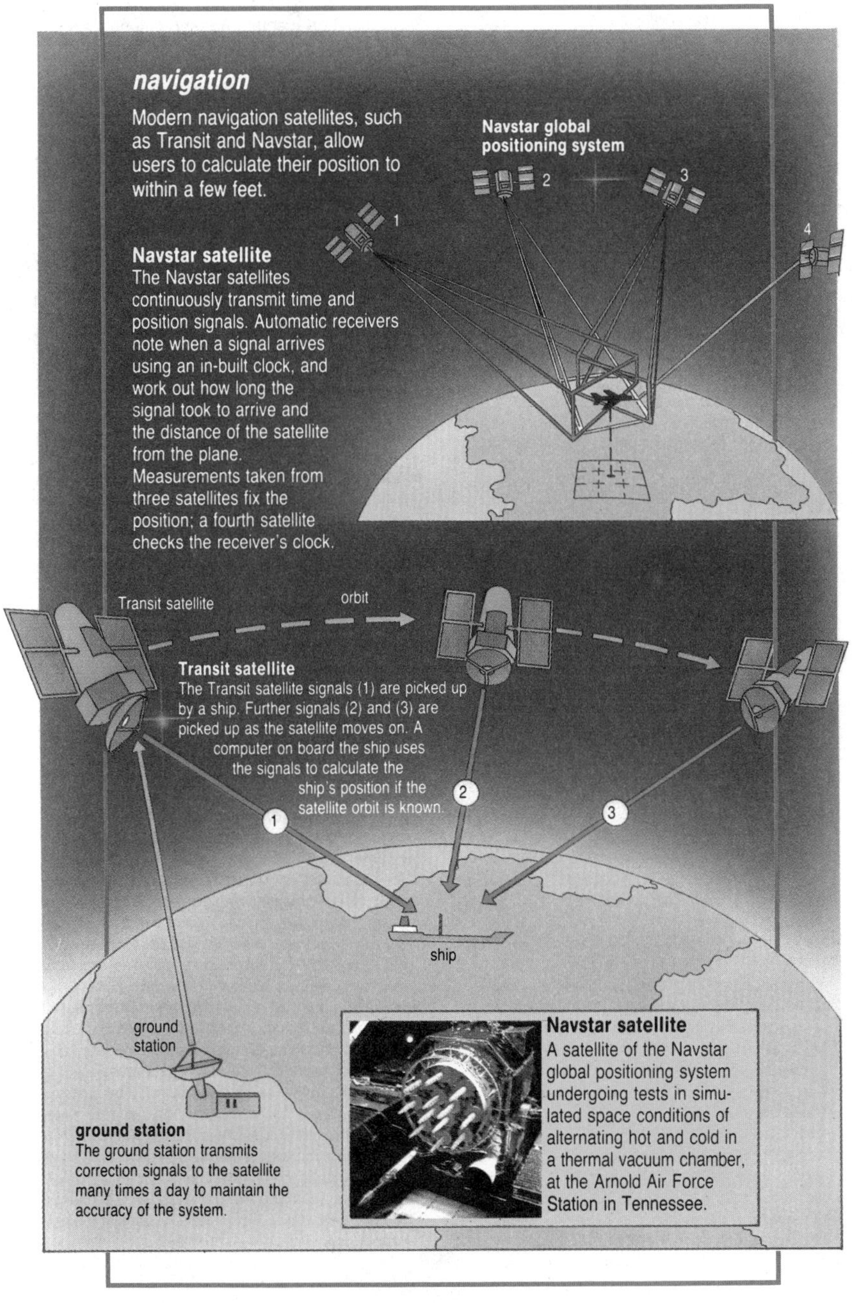
navigation
Modern navigation satellites, such as Transit and Navstar, allow users to calculate their position to within a few feet.
Navstar global positioning system
Navstar satellite
The Navstar satellites continuously transmit time and position signals. Automatic receivers note when a signal arrives using an in-built clock, and work out how long the signal took to arrive and the distance of the satellite from the plane. Measurements taken from three satellites fix the position; a fourth satellite checks the receiver's clock.
Transit satellite
orbit
Transit satellite
The Transit satellite signals (1) are picked up by a ship. Further signals (2) and (3) are picked up as the satellite moves on. A computer on board the ship uses the signals to calculate the ship's position if the satellite orbit is known.
ship
ground station
ground station
The ground station transmits correction signals to the satellite many times a day to maintain the accuracy of the system.
Navstar satellite
A satellite of the Navstar global positioning system undergoing tests in simulated space conditions of alternating hot and cold in a thermal vacuum chamber, at the Arnold Air Force Station in Tennessee.

Navigation Acts in British history, a series of acts of Parliament passed from 1381 to protect English shipping from foreign competition and to ensure monopoly trading between Britain and its colonies. The last was repealed 1849. The Navigation Acts helped to establish England as a major sea power, although they led to higher prices. They ruined the Dutch merchant fleet in the 17th century, and were one of the causes of the ◊American Revolution.

1650 "Commonwealth Ordinance" forbade foreign ships to trade in English colonies.

1651 Forbade the importation of goods except in English vessels or in vessels of the country of origin of the goods. This act led to the Anglo-Dutch War 1652–54.

1660 All colonial produce was required to be exported in English vessels.

1663 Colonies were prohibited from receiving goods in foreign (rather than English) vessels.

navigation, biological the ability of animals or insects to navigate. Although many animals navigate by following established routes or known landmarks, many animals can navigate without such aids; for example, birds can fly several thousand miles back to their nest site, over unknown terrain. Such feats may be based on compass information derived from the position of the Sun, Moon, or stars, or on the characteristic patterns of Earth's magnetic field.

Biological navigation refers to the ability to navigate both in long-distance ◊migrations and over shorter distances when foraging (for example, the honey bee finding its way from the hive to a nectar site and back). Where reliant on known landmarks, birds may home on features that can be seen from very great distances (such as the cloud caps that often form above isolated midocean islands). Even smells can act as a landmark. Aquatic species like salmon are believed to learn the characteristic taste of the river where they hatch and return to it, often many years later. Brain cells in some birds have been found to contain ◊magnetite and may therefore be sensitive to the Earth's magnetic field.

Navratilova Martina 1956– . Czech tennis player, who became a naturalized US citizen 1981. The most outstanding woman player of the 1980s, she has 52 Grand Slam victories, including 18 singles titles. She has won the Wimbledon singles title nine times, including six in succession 1982–87.

Navratilova was born in Prague, Czecho-

Navratilova *Martina Navratilova, the outstanding women's tennis player in the 1980s.*

slovakia. She won her first Wimbledon title in 1976 (doubles with Chris Evert). Between 1974 and 1988 she won 52 Grand Slam titles (singles and doubles), second only to Margaret ◊Court. Her first Grand Slam win was mixed doubles at the 1974 French Championship (with Ivan Molina, Colombia).

CAREER HIGHLIGHTS

Wimbledon
singles: 1978–79, 1982–87, 1990
doubles: 1976, 1979, 1981–84, 1986
mixed: 1985
US Open
singles: 1983–84, 1986–87
doubles: 1977–78, 1980, 1983–84, 1986–89
mixed: 1985, 1987
French Open
singles: 1982, 1984
doubles: 1975, 1982, 1984–88
mixed: 1974, 1985
Australian Open
singles: 1981, 1983, 1985
doubles: 1980, 1982–85, 1987–89

navy a fleet of ships, usually a nation's ◊warships and the organization to maintain them. The USSR has one of the world's largest merchant fleets, and the world's largest fishing, hydrographic, and oceanographic fleets, in which all ships have intelligence-gathering equipment.

navy: chronology

5th century BC	Naval power was an important factor in the struggle for supremacy in the Mediterranean; for example, the defeat of Persia by Greece at Salamis.
311 BC	The first permanent naval organization was established by the Roman Empire with the appointment of navy commissioners to safeguard trade routes from pirates and eliminate the threat of rival sea power.
878	Alfred the Great of England overcame the Danes with a few king's ships, plus ships from the shires and some privileged coastal towns.
12th century	Turkish invasions ended Byzantine dominance.
13th century	The first French royal fleet was established by Louis IX. His admirals came from Genoa.
1339–1453	During the Hundred Years' War there was a great deal of cross-Channel raiding by England and France.
16th century	Spain built a large navy for exploration and conquest in the early part of the century. In England, building on the beginnings made by his father Henry VII, Henry VIII raised a force that included a number of battleships, such as the *Mary Rose*, created the long-enduring administrative machinery of the Admiralty, and, by mounting heavy guns low on a ship's side, revolutionized strategy by the use of the "broadside." Elizabeth I encouraged Drake, Frobisher, Hawkins, Raleigh, and other navigators to enlarge the empire.
1571	The Battle of Lepanto was one of the last to be fought with galleys, or oar-propelled ships.
1588	The defeat of the Spanish Armada began the decline of the sea power of Spain.
17th century	There was a substantial development in naval power among the powers of N Europe; for example, in the Netherlands, which then founded an empire in the Americas and the East; France, where a strong fleet was built up by Richelieu and Louis XIV that maintained the links with possessions in India and North America; and England, comparatively briefly under Cromwell. In the late 17th century the British overtook the Dutch as the leading naval power.
1775–83	The US navy grew out of the coastal colonies' need to protect their harbors during the War of Independence, as well as the need to capture British war supplies. In late 1775 Washington prepared five schooners and a sloop, manned with army personnel, and sent them to prey on inbound supply vessels. By the time of the Declaration of Independence 1776 these were augmented by armed brigs and sloops from the various colonies. The hero of the period was John Paul Jones.
1805	Effectively reorganized by Pitt in time for the French Revolutionary Wars, the Royal Navy under Nelson won a victory over the French at Trafalgar, which ensured British naval supremacy for the rest of the 19th century.
19th century	The US fleet was successful in actions against pirates off Tripoli 1803–05 and the British navy 1812–14, and rapidly expanded during the Civil War and again for the Spanish-American War 1898.
World War I	Britain maintained naval supremacy in the face of German U-boat and surface threats.
1918–41	Between the wars the US fleet was developed to protect US trade routes, with an eye to the renewed German threat in the Atlantic and the danger from Japan in the Pacific.
1950s	After World War II the US fleet emerged as the world's most powerful.
1962	The Cuban missile crisis (when the US forced the removal of Soviet missiles from Cuba) demonstrated the USSR's weakness at sea and led to its development under Admiral Sergei Gorshkov.
1980s	The Soviet fleets (based in the Arctic, Baltic, Mediterranean, and Pacific) continued their expansion, becoming more powerful than the combined NATO forces. The new pattern of the Soviet navy reflected that of other fleets: over 400 submarines, many with Polaris-type missiles, and over 200 surface combat vessels (mostly of recent date) including helicopter carriers, cruisers, destroyers, and escort vessels. The US maintained aircraft-carrier battle groups and recommissioned World War II battleships to give its fleet superior firepower, as well as the smaller support vessels.

Naxalite member of an Indian extremist communist movement named after the town of Naxalbari, W Bengal, where a peasant uprising was suppressed 1967. The movement was founded by Charu Mazumdar (1915–1972).

Naxos an island of Greece, the largest of the Cyclades, area 175 sq mi/453 sq km. Known since early times for its wine, it was a center for the worship of Bacchus, who, according to Greek mythology, found the deserted Ariadne on its shore and married her.

Nazareth town in Galilee, N Israel, SE of Haifa; population (1981) 64,000. According to the New Testament, it was the boyhood home of Jesus.

Nazarite or ***Nazirite*** a Hebrew under a vow to God to observe certain rules, including not to cut his hair, drink wine, or have contact with dead bodies. Some took the vow for life, others for only a certain period. ◊Samson and ◊Samuel were Nazarites from birth.

Nazca town S of Lima, Peru, near a plateau that has geometric linear markings interspersed with giant outlines of birds and animals. The markings were made by American Indians, possibly in the 6th century AD, and their function is thought to be ritual rather than astronomical.

Nazism ideology based on racism, nationalism, and the supremacy of the state over the individual. The German Nazi party, the Nationalsozialistiche Deutsche Arbeiterpartei (National Socialist German Workers' Party), was formed from the German Workers' Party (founded 1919) and led by Adolph ◊Hitler 1921–45.

During the 1930s, many similar parties were created throughout Europe and the US, although only those of Austria, Hungary, and Sudetenland were of major importance. These parties collaborated with the German occupation of Europe 1939–45. After the Nazi atrocities of World War II (see ◊SS, ◊concentration camp, ◊Holocaust), the party was banned in Germany, but parties with Nazi or neo-Nazi ideologies still exist in Germany and many other countries.

Nazi-Soviet pact a nonaggression treaty signed by Germany and the USSR on August 23, 1939. Under the terms of the treaty both countries agreed to remain neutral and to refrain from acts of aggression against each other if either went to war. Secret clauses allowed for the partition of Poland—Hitler was to acquire western Poland, Stalin the eastern part. On Sept 1, 1939 Hitler invaded Poland. The Pact ended when Hitler invaded Russia on June 22, 1941. See also ◊World War II.

NB abbreviation for ◊New Brunswick; ◊Nebraska; *nota bene* (Latin "note well"), used in references and citations.

NBS abbreviation for National Bureau of Standards, the US federal standards organization, on whose technical standards all US weights and measures are based.

NC abbreviation for ◊North Carolina.

ND abbreviation for ◊North Dakota.

N'djamena capital of Chad, at the confluence of the Chari and Logone rivers, on the Cameroon border; population (1985) 511,700.

Founded 1900 by the French at the junction of caravan routes, it was used 1903–12 as a military center against the kingdoms of central Sudan. Its name until 1973 was Fort Lamy.

Ndola mining center and chief city of the Copperbelt province of central Zambia; population (1987) 418,000.

N'Dour Youssou 1959– . Senegalese singer, songwriter, and musician whose fusion of traditional mbalax percussion music with bluesy Arab-style vocals, accompanied by African and electronic instruments, became popular in the West in the 1980s on albums such as *Immigrés* 1984 with the band Le Super Etoile de Dakar.

Neagh, Lough lake in Northern Ireland, 15 mi/25 km W of Belfast; area 153 sq mi/396 sq km. It is the largest lake in the British Isles.

Neanderthal hominid of the Mid-Late Paleolithic, named after a skeleton found in the Neander Thal (valley) near Dusseldorf, Germany, in 1856. *Homo sapiens neanderthalensis* lived from about 100,000 to 40,000 years ago and was similar in build to present-day people, but slightly smaller, stockier, and heavier-featured with a strong jaw and prominent brow ridges on a sloping forehead.

They lived in Europe, the Near East, and Africa. They looked after their disabled and buried their dead ritualistically. Recent evidence suggests their physical capacity for the sounds of speech. They were replaced throughout Europe by, or possibly interbred with, *Homo sapiens sapiens* (Cro-Magnon Man).

Near East term used until the 1940s to describe the area of the Balkan states, Egypt and SW Asia, now known as the ◊Middle East.

nearsightedness alternate name for ◊myopia.

Near v Minnesota a US Supreme Court decision 1931 dealing with restrictions on the free press imposed by state libel laws. The Court overruled the actions of Minnesota officials who shut down Near's newspaper because it criticized law enforcement in the state. The Court found the Minnesota statute prohibiting scandalous publications unconstitutional because it allowed the

Nebraska

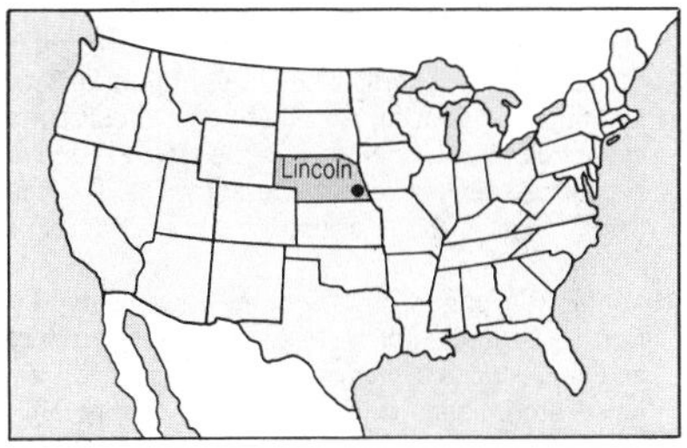
Lincoln

state to suppress material before it was written rather than prosecuting authors of scandalous material after publication.

Nebraska state in central US; nickname Cornhusker State/Blackwater State
area 77,354 sq mi/200,400 sq km
capital Lincoln
cities Omaha, Grand Island, North Platte
population (1990) 1,578,385
features Rocky Mountain foothills; tributaries of the Missouri; Boys' Town for the homeless, near Omaha; the ranch of Buffalo Bill; the only unicameral legislature
products cereals, livestock, processed foods, fertilizers, oil, natural gas
famous people Fred Astaire, William Jennings Bryan, Johnny Carson, Willa Cather, Henry Fonda, Harold Lloyd, Malcom X
history exploited by French fur traders early 1700s; ceded to Spain by France 1763; retroceded to France 1801; part of the Louisiana Purchase 1803; explored by Lewis and Clark 1804–06; first settlement at Bellevue 1823; became a territory 1854 and a state 1867 after the Union Pacific began its transcontinental railroad at Omaha 1865. Nebraska's farm economy was weakened in the 1930s by the Great Depression and dust storms, but World War II brought military airfields and war industries. Much of the industry developed since that time is related to agriculture.

Nebuchadnezzar or ***Nebuchadrezzar II*** king of Babylonia from 60 BC. Shortly before his accession he defeated the Egyptians at Carchemish and brought Palestine and Syria into his empire. Judah revolted, with Egyptian assistance, 596 and 587–586 BC; on both occasions he captured Jerusalem and took many Hebrews into captivity. He largely rebuilt Babylon and constructed the hanging gardens.

nebula cloud of gas and dust in space. Nebulae are the birthplaces of stars. An emission nebula, such as the ◊Orion nebula, glows brightly because its gas is energized by stars that have formed within it. In a reflection nebula, such as the one that surrounds the stars of the ◊Pleiades cluster, starlight reflects off grains of dust in the nebula. A dark nebula is a dense cloud, composed of molecular hydrogen, which partially or completely absorbs light behind it. Examples include the Coalsack nebula in ◊Crux and the Horsehead nebula in Orion. Some nebulae are produced by gas thrown off from dying stars (see ◊planetary nebula; ◊supernova).

***nebula** The Orion nebula is located 1,600 light-years from Earth and its fan-shaped cloud is 15 light-years across.*

neck the structure between the head and the trunk in animals. In the back of the neck are the upper seven vertebrae, and there are many powerful muscles that support and move the head. In front, the neck region contains the pharynx and trachea, and behind these the esophagus. The large arteries (carotid, temporal, maxillary) and veins (jugular) that supply the brain and head are also located in the neck.

Necker Jacques 1732–1804. French politician. As finance minister 1776–81, he attempted reforms, and was dismissed through Queen Marie Antoinette's influence. Recalled 1788, he persuaded Louis XVI to summon the States General (parliament), which earned him the hatred of the court, and in July 1789 he was banished. The outbreak of the French Revolution with the storming of the Bastille forced his reinstatement, but he resigned Sept 1790.

necrosis death or decay of tissue in a particular part of the body, usually due to bacterial poisoning or loss of local blood supply.

nectar a sugary liquid secreted by some plants from a nectary, a specialized gland usually situated near the base of the flower. Nectar often accumulates in special pouches or spurs, not always in the same location as the nectary. Nectar attracts insects, birds, bats, and other animals to the flower for ◊pollination and is the raw material used by bees in the production of honey.

nectarine smooth, shiny-skinned variety of ◊peach, usually sweeter than other peaches and with firmer flesh. It arose from a natural mutation.

Needham Joseph 1900– . British biochemist and sinologist known for his work on the history of Chinese science. He worked first as a biochemist concentrating mainly on problems in embryology. In the 1930s he learned Chinese and began to collect material. The first volume of his *Science and Civilisation in China* was published in 1954 and by 1989 fifteen volumes had appeared.

needlefish any bony fish of the marine family Belonidae, with an elongated body and long jaws lined with many sharp teeth.

Neenah city in E Wisconsin, on the Fox River near Lake Winnebago, N of Oshkosh. To its E is Menasha, with which it forms one community. It is a processing and marketing center for the area's agricultural products; population (1990) 23,219.

Nefertiti or ***Nofretète*** queen of Egypt, who ruled c. 1372–1350 BC; wife of the pharoah ◊Ikhnaton.

She disappeared from the records about 12 years after the marriage, and her name was defaced on monuments at some later date. A small gold scarab bearing her name, inscribed within the royal cartouche that marks the name of a pharaoh, was recovered in 1986 from an ancient wreck and confirms that she briefly ruled in her own right.

negative/positive in photography, a reverse image, which when printed is again reversed, restoring the original scene. It was invented by ◊Talbot about 1834.

Today the most common snapshots and photos are printed positives (on paper) made from film negatives.

Negev desert in S Israel that tapers to the port of Eilat. It is fertile under irrigation, and minerals include oil and copper.

negligence in law, negligence consists in doing some act that a "prudent and reasonable" person would not do, or omitting to do some act that such a person would do. Negligence may arise in respect of a person's duty toward an individual or toward other people in general. Contributory negligence is a defense sometimes raised where the defendant to an action for negligence claims that the plaintiff by his own negligence contributed to the cause of the action.

A person's duty toward an individual may cover parenthood, guardianship, trusteeship, or a contractual relationship; a person's duty toward other people may include the duties owed to the community, such as care upon the public highway, and the maintenance of structures in a safe condition.

Negri Sembilan state of S Peninsular Malaysia; area 2,565 sq mi/6,646 sq km; population (1980) 574,000. It is mainly mountainous; products include rice and rubber. The capital is Seremban.

Negroid referring to one of the three major varieties (see ◊races) of humans, *Homo sapiens sapiens*, mainly the indigenous peoples of Subsaharan Africa and some of the nearby islands in the Indian Ocean and the W Pacific. General physical traits include dark eyes, tightly curled dark hair, brown to very dark skin, little beard or body hair, low to medium-bridged wide noses, and wide or everted lips. See ◊Caucasoid, ◊Mongoloid.

Nehemiah Hebrew governor of Judea under Persian rule. He rebuilt Jerusalem's walls 444 BC, and made religious and social reforms.

***Nehru** Pandit Jawaharlal Nehru (left), who led India to independence as prime minister, with Mohammed Ali Jinnah, the founder of Pakistan.*

Nelson *British admiral Horatio Nelson, who was mortally wounded at the Battle of Trafalgar 1805.*

Nehru Jawaharlal 1889–1964. Indian nationalist politician, prime minister from 1947. Before the partition (the division of British India into India and Pakistan) he led the Socialist wing of the Nationalist ◊Congress Party, and was second in influence only to Mohandas ◊Gandhi. He was imprisoned nine times by the British 1921–45 for political activities. As prime minister from the creation of the dominion (later republic) of India Aug 1947, he originated the idea of ◊nonalignment (neutrality toward major powers). His daughter was Prime Minister Indira ◊Gandhi.

Neizvestny Ernst 1926– . Russian artist and sculptor who argued with Soviet leader Khrushchev in 1962 and eventually left the country 1976. His works include a vast relief in the Moscow Institute of Electronics and the Aswan monument, the tallest sculpture in the world.

Nejd region of central Arabia consisting chiefly of desert; area about 800,000 sq mi/2,072,000 sq km. It forms part of the kingdom of Saudi Arabia and is inhabited by Bedouins. The capital is Riyadh.

Nekrasov Nikolai Alekseevich 1821–1877. Russian poet and publisher. He espoused the cause of the freeing of the serfs and identified himself with the peasants in such poems as "Who Can Live Happy in Russia?" 1876.

Nelson Horatio, Viscount Nelson 1758–1805. English admiral. He joined the navy in 1770. In the Revolutionary Wars against France he lost the sight in his right eye 1794 and lost his right arm 1797. He became a national hero, and rear admiral, after the victory off Cape St Vincent, Portugal. In 1798 he tracked the French fleet to Aboukir Bay and almost entirely destroyed it in the Battle of the Nile. In 1801 he won a decisive victory over Denmark at the Battle of ◊Copenhagen, and in 1805, after two years of blockading Toulon, another over the Franco-Spanish fleet at the Battle of ◊Trafalgar, near Gibraltar.

The son of a clergyman, he was almost continuously on active service in the Mediterranean 1793–1800 and lingered at Naples for a year, during which he helped to crush a democratic uprising and fell completely under the influence of Lady ◊Hamilton. In 1800 he returned to England and soon after separated from his wife, Frances Nisbet. He was promoted to vice admiral 1801 and sent to the Baltic to operate against the Danes, nominally as second-in-command; in fact, it was Nelson who was responsible for the victory of Copenhagen and for negotiating peace with Denmark.

In 1803 he received the Mediterranean command, and for nearly two years blockaded Toulon. On Oct 21, 1805, he defeated the combined French and Spanish fleets off Cape Trafalgar, 20 of the enemy ships being captured, but Nelson himself was mortally wounded.

nematode unsegmented worm of the phylum Aschelminthes. Nematodes are pointed at both ends, with a tough, smooth outer skin. They include many free-living soil and water forms, but a large number are parasites, such as the roundworms and pinworms that live in humans, or the eelworms that attack plant roots.

Nemerov Howard 1920– . US poet, critic, and novelist. He published his poetry collection *Guide to the Ruins* 1950, a short-story collection *A Commodity of Dreams* 1959, and in 1977 his *Collected Poems* won both the National Book Award and the Pulitzer Prize.

Nemesis in Greek mythology, the goddess of retribution, who especially punished hubris (Greek *hybris*), the arrogant defiance of the gods.

nemesis theory theory of animal extinction, suggesting that a sister star to the Sun caused the extinction of groups of animals such as dinosaurs. The theory holds that the movement of this as yet undiscovered star disrupts the ◊Oort cloud of comets every 26 million years, resulting in the Earth suffering an increased bombardment from comets at these times. The theory was proposed in 1984 to explain the newly discovered layer of iridium—an element found in comets and meteorites—in rocks dating from the end of dinosaur times. However, many paleontologists deny any evidence for a 26-million-year cycle of extinctions.

Nennius c. 800. Welsh historian, believed to be the author of a Latin *Historia Britonum*, which contains the earliest reference to King Arthur's wars against the Saxons.

neo-Classical economics a school of economic thought based on the work of 19th-century economists, such as Alfred Marshall, using ◊marginal theory to modify Classical economic theories. Mathematics became extremely important, as did microeconomic theoretical systems. Neo-classicists believed competition to be the regulator of economic activity that would establish equilibrium between output and consumption. Neo-Classical economics was largely superseded from the 1930s by the work of ◊Keynes.

Neo-Classicism movement in art and architecture in Europe and North America about 1750–1850, a revival of Classical style elements that superseded the rococo style. It was partly inspired by the excavation of the Roman cities of Pompeii and Herculaneum. The architect Piranesi was an early Neo-Classicist; in sculpture ◊Canova and in painting ◊David were exponents.

Others include Thorvaldsen (sculpture), Ingres (painting), and Robert Adam (architecture).

neocolonialism disguised form of imperialism, by which a country may grant independence to another country but continue to dominate it by control of markets for goods or raw materials.

This system was analyzed in the Ghanaian leader Kwame Nkrumah's book *Neo-Colonialism, the Last Stage of Imperialism* 1965.

neo-Darwinism the modern theory of ◊evolution, built up since the 1930s by integrating ◊Darwin's theory of evolution through natural selection with the theory of genetic inheritance founded on the work of ◊Mendel.

néo-Destour (New Socialist Destour Party) an offshoot of the conservative/liberal Tunisian Destour party that has held power since independence from France after its creation in 1934. Néo-Destour rose to prominence under the leadership of Habib ◊Bourguiba after 1937 and led the rebellion of 1953 which resulted in independence in 1956. Despite party splits during the early 1950s, it has consolidated its position as the country's sole political party.

neodymium a yellowish metallic element of the ◊lanthanide series, symbol Nd, atomic number 60, atomic weight 144.24. Its rose-colored salts are used in coloring glass, and neodymium is used in lasers.

It was named in 1885 by Austrian chemist C A von Welsbach (1858–1929), who fractionated it away from didymium (originally thought to be an element but actually a mixture of rare-earth metals consisting largely of neodymium, presodymium, and cerium).

Neo-Impressionism movement in French painting in the 1880s, an extension of the Impressionists' technique of placing small strokes of different color side by side. Seurat was the chief exponent; his minute technique became known as "pointillism." Signac and Pissarro practiced the same style for a few years.

Neolithic last period of the ◊Stone Age, characterized by settled communities based on agriculture and domesticated animals, and identified by sophisticated, finely honed stone tools, and ceramic wares. The earliest neolithic communities appeared about 9000 BC in the Near East, followed by Egypt, India, and China, the four regions of the Old World where civilization first developed. In Europe farming began in about 6500 BC in the Balkans and Aegean, spreading north and east by 1000 BC.

neon colorless, odorless, nonmetallic, gaseous element, symbol Ne, atomic number 10, atomic weight 20.183. It is grouped with the ◊inert gases, is nonreactive, and forms no compounds. It occurs in small quantities in the Earth's atmosphere.

Tubes containing neon are used in electric advertising signs, giving off a fiery red glow; it is also used in lasers. Neon was discovered by Scottish chemist William Ramsay and the Englishman Morris Travers (1872–1961), and named in 1988 by Ramsay for Greek *neon*, "new."

neoplasm (Greek "new growth") any lump or tumor, which may be benign or malignant (cancerous).

neoprene synthetic rubber, developed in the US 1931 from the polymerization of chloroprene. It is much more resistant to heat, light, oxidation, and petroleum than is ordinary rubber.

Neoptolemos or ***Pyrrhus*** in Greek mythology, son of Achilles. With ◊Odysseus he conducted the Trojan hero Philoctetes to ◊Troy after the death of his father, and killed the Trojan king Priam at the altar of Zeus. He took Hector's wife Andromache as his concubine, and was killed in a quarrel at the shrine of Delphi.

Neo-Realism a movement in Italian cinema that emerged in the 1940s. It is characterized by its naturalism, social themes, and the visual authenticity achieved through location filming. Exponents included the directors de Sica, Visconti, and Rossellini.

neoteny or ***infantilism*** in biology, the retention of some juvenile characteristics in an animal that seems otherwise mature. An example is provided by the axolotl, a salamander that can reproduce sexually although still in its larval form.

It has been suggested that new species could arise in this way, and that the ◊human species evolved from its apelike ancestors by neoteny; in human fossil skulls, we see a developmental trend—that facially we resemble a young ape.

NEP abbreviation for the Soviet leader Lenin's ◊New Economic Policy.

Nepal landlocked country in the Himalayan mountain range, bounded N by Tibet, E by Sikkim, and S and W by India.

government Under the constitution of 1962, amended 1980, Nepal is ruled by a monarch. There is a tiered system of *panchayats* (councils) and a one-chamber legislature, the *Rashtriya Panchayat* (National Assembly), of whose members 112 are directly elected every five years and 28 are nominated by the monarch, who may veto its decisions. The *Panchayat* debates and passes bills and elects a prime minister, who heads and, with the monarch, selects the cabinet. Executive power is exercised by the sovereign and cabinet.

history From one of a group of small principalities, the Gurkhas emerged to unite Nepal under King Prithivi Narayan Shah in 1768. In 1816, after the year-long Anglo-Nepali "Gurkha War," a British Resident was stationed in Katmandu and the kingdom became a British-dependent "buffer-

Nepal

(Nepal Adhirajya)

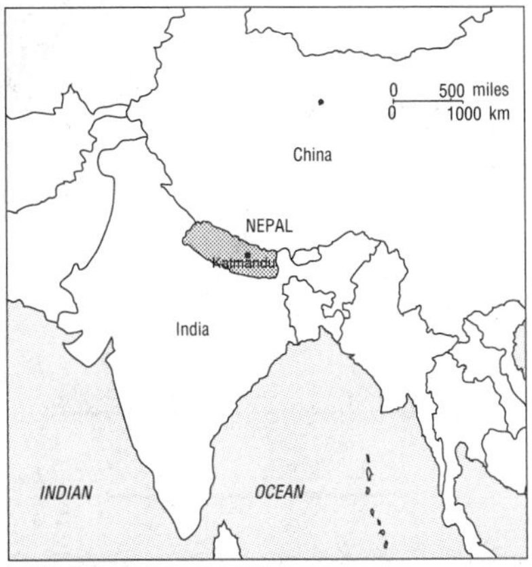
0 500 miles
0 1000 km
China
NEPAL
Kátmándu
India
INDIAN
OCEAN

area 56,850 sq mi/147,181 sq km
capital Kátmándu
cities Pátan, Moráng, Bhádgáon
physical descends from the Himalayan mountain range in N through foothills to the river Ganges plain in S
features Mount Everest, Mount Kangchenjunga, the only Hindu kingdom in the world; Lumbini, birthplace of Buddha
head of state King Birendra Bir Bikram Sháh Dev from 1972
head of government Girija Prasad Koirala from 1991
political system constitutional monarchy
political parties banned from 1961; four opposition parties function unofficially: the United Nepal Communist Party (UNCP), Marxist-Leninist-Maoist; the Nepali Congress Party (NCP), left-of-center; the United Liberation Torchbearers; the Democratic Front, radical republican
exports jute, rice, timber, oilseed
currency Nepalese rupee
population (1990 est) 19,158,000 (mainly known by name of predominant clan, the Gurkhas; the Sherpas are a Buddhist minority of NE Nepal); growth rate 2.3% p.a.
life expectancy men 50, women 49 (1989)
language Nepali (official); 20 dialects spoken
religion Hindu 90%; Buddhist, Muslim, Christian
literacy men 39%/women 12% (1985 est)
GNP $3.1 bn (1988); $160 per head (1986)
chronology
1768 Nepal emerged as unified kingdom.
1815–16 Anglo-Nepali "Gurkha War"; Nepal became a British-dependent buffer state.
1846–1951 Ruled by the Rana family.
1923 Independence achieved from Britain.
1951 Monarchy restored.
1959 Constitution created elected legislature.
1960–61 Parliament dissolved by king; political parties banned.
1980 Constitutional referendum held following popular agitation.
1981 Direct elections held to national assembly.
1983 Overthrow of monarch-supported prime minister.
1986 New assembly elections returned a majority opposed to *panchayat* system of partyless government.
1988 Strict curbs placed on opposition activity; over 100 supporters of banned opposition party arrested; censorship imposed.
1989 Border blockade imposed by India in treaty dispute.
1990 *Panchayat* system collapsed; new constitution introduced; elections set for May 1991.
1991 Nepali Congress Party, led by Girija Prasad Koirala, won the general election.

state." The country was recognized as fully independent by Britain in 1923 although it remained bound by treaty obligations until 1947, the year of India's independence. Between 1846 and 1951 Nepal was ruled by a hereditary prime minister of the Rana family. The Ranas were overthrown in a revolution led by the Nepali congress, and the monarchy, in the person of King Tribhuvan, was restored to power.

In 1959 King Mahendra Bir Bikram Shah, who had succeeded his father in 1955, promulgated the nation's first constitution and held elections. The Nepali Congress Party leader B P Koirala became prime minister and proceeded to clash with the king over policy. King Mahendra thus dissolved parliament in Dec 1960 and issued a ban on political parties in Jan 1961. In Dec 1962 he introduced the new constitution with an indirectly elected assembly.

King Mahendra died in 1972. His son Birendra (1945–), faced with mounting agitation for political reform led by B P Koriala, held a referendum on the constitution. As a result, it was amended, and the first elections to the National Assembly were held in May 1981. They led to the defeat of a third of the pro-government candidates and returned a more independently minded National Assembly, that in July 1983 unseated Prime Minister Surya Bahadur Thapa, despite his royal support, and installed in office Lokendra Bahadur Chand. Opposition to the banning of political parties has increased in recent years, with terrorist actions in Kathmandu in June 1985. In May 1986 elections to the National Assembly returned a majority of members opposed to the partyless *panchayat* system and resulted in the replacement of Prime Minister Chand. Four opposition parties function unofficially: the Communist Party of Nepal, the Nepali Congress Party, the United Liberation Torchbearers, and the Democratic Front. In April 1990 King Birendra lifted the ban on opposition parties, following mass demonstrations.

In foreign affairs, Nepal has pursued a neutral, ◊nonaligned policy, seeking to create a "zone of peace" in S Asia between India and China. In recent years commercial links with China have increased. This has been resented by India who, in March 1989, imposed a partial blockade on Nepal's borders as part of a dispute over the renegotiation of expired transit and trade duties. In June 1990 India agreed to restore the trade and transit concessions.

In Sept 1990 King Birendra approved a new draft constitution that would transfer political power from the monarchy to an elected government, transforming the state into a constitutional monarchy. The country's first multi-party elections since 1959 were held May 1991 and demonstrated strong support for communist candidates.

nepenth or ***nepenthes*** a mythical drug that makes people forget cares or worries, used by ◊Helen of Troy in ◊Homer's *Odyssey*.

neper unit used in telecommunications to express a ratio of powers and currents. It gives the attenuation of amplitudes as the natural logarithm of the ratio.

nephrectomy surgical removal of a kidney.

nephritis inflammation of the kidneys, caused by bacterial infection or, sometimes, by a body disorder that affects the kidneys, such as streptococcal infection of the throat. The degree of illness varies, and it may be acute or chronic, requiring a range of treatments from antibiotics to ◊dialysis.

nephron a microscopic unit in vertebrate kidneys that forms urine.

A human kidney is composed of over a million nephrons. Each nephron consists of a filter cup surrounding a knot of blood capillaries and a long narrow collecting tubule in close association with yet more capillaries. Waste materials and water pass from the bloodstream into the filter cup, and essential minerals and some water are reabsorbed from the tubule back into the blood. The urine that is left eventually passes out from the body.

Neptune in Roman mythology, god of the sea, the equivalent of the Greek ◊Poseidon.

Neptune in astronomy, the eighth planet in average distance from the Sun. Neptune orbits the Sun every 164.8 years at an average distance of 2.794 billion mi/4.497 billion km. It is a giant gas (hydrogen, helium, methane) planet with a diameter of 30,200 mi/48,600 km and a mass 17.2 times that of Earth. It has three narrow orbital rings enclosed in a disk of dust that may reach down to the Neptunian cloud tops. Its rotation period is 16 hours 3 minutes. Neptune has two named moons (Triton and Nereid), and six more discovered by the *Voyager 2* probe in 1989, of which 1989 N1 (diameter 260 mi/418 km) is larger than Nereid.

Neptune was located 1846 by the German astronomers Galle and Heinrich D'Arrest (1822–1875) after calculations by Adams and Le-

nephron

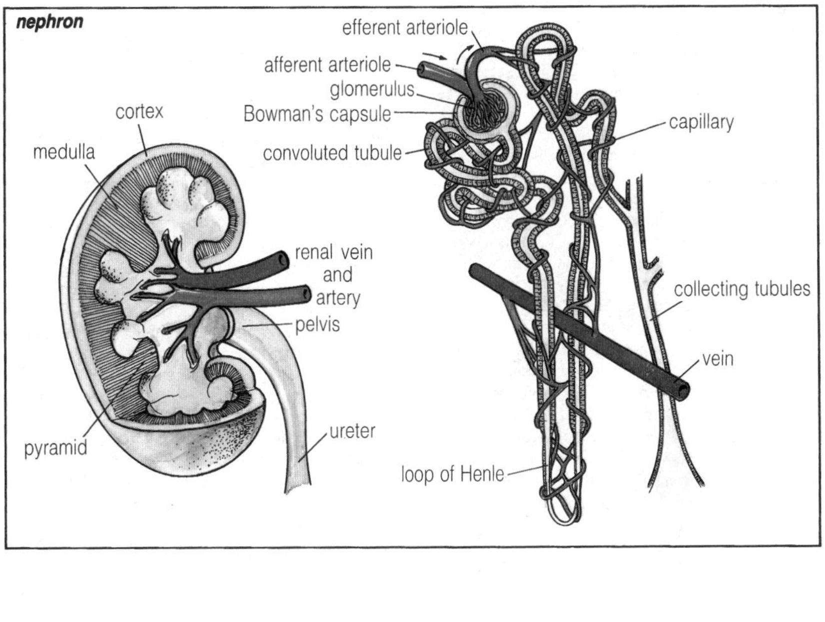
efferent arteriole
afferent arteriole
glomerulus
Bowman's capsule
cortex
capillary
medulla
convoluted tubule
renal vein
and
artery
collecting tubules
pelvis
vein
ureter
pyramid
loop of Henle

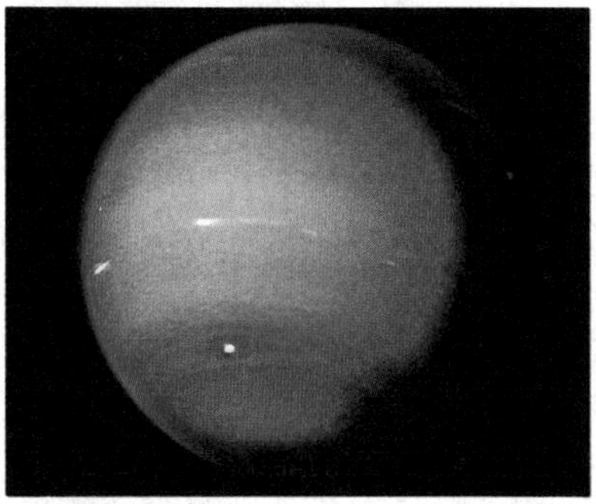

Neptune *False-color image of Neptune taken on Aug 25, 1989, when* Voyager 2 *flew within 3,000 mi/ 4,800 km of the planet.*

verrier had predicted its existence on the basis that another body must be disturbing the orbit of Uranus. The cameras of *Voyager 2*, which passed Neptune in Aug 1989, revealed a wide variety of cloud features. Notable among these were bright polar collars and broad bands in different shades of blue girdling Neptune's southern hemisphere. The blue coloring results from the absorption of red light by the methane in the atmosphere. Another cloud feature is an Earth-sized oval storm cloud, which has been named the Great Dark Spot and has been likened to the Great Red Spot on Jupiter. Above and around it, cirrus-type clouds of frozen methane are forming and taking shape, with winds of up to 1,500 mph/2,400 kph. "The Scooter" is so called because it is a cloud that travels around the planet at a faster rate than the other clouds. Neptune is believed to have a central rocky core covered by a layer of ice.

Nereid orbits every 360 days on a highly elliptical path; Triton, one of the four largest moons in the Solar System, orbits every 5.9 days in an east-to-west retrograde direction and is thought to be similar in nature to the planet Pluto.

neptunium a silvery, radioactive metallic element of the ◊actinide series, symbol Np, atomic number 93, atomic weight 237.048. It occurs in nature in minute amounts in ◊pitchblende and other uranium ores, where it is produced from the decay of neutron-bombarded uranium in these ores. The longest-lived isotope, Np-237, has a half-life of 2.2 million years. The element can be produced by bombardment of U-238 with neutrons and is chemically highly reactive.

It was first synthesized in 1940 by US physicists E McMillan (1907–) and P Abelson (1913–), who named it for the planet Neptune (since it comes after uranium as the planet Neptune comes after Uranus). Neptunium was the first ◊transuranic element to be synthesized.

Nereids in Greek mythology, 50 sea goddesses who sometimes mated with mortals. Their father was Nereus, a sea god, and their mother was Doris.

Nergal Babylonian god of the Sun, war, and pestilence, ruler of the underworld, symbolized by a winged lion.

Nernst (Walther) Hermann 1864–1941. German physical chemist. His investigations, for which he won the 1920 Nobel Prize for Chemistry, were concerned with heat changes in chemical reactions. He proposed in 1906 the principle known as the Nernst heat theorem or the third law of thermodynamics: the law states that chemical changes at the temperature of ◊absolute zero involve no change of ◊entropy (disorder).

Born in Briesen, Prussia, Nernst was professor of chemistry at Göttingen 1905, and Berlin. He suffered under the Nazi regime because two of his daughters married Jews.

Nero AD 37–68. Roman emperor from 54. Son of Domitius Ahenobarbus and Agrippina, he was adopted by Claudius, and succeeded him as emperor in 54. He was a poet, connoisseur of

Neruda *As a poet, Pablo Neruda of Chile identified with the working class from which he came, voicing the dreams and sorrows of his people.*

art, and performed publicly as an actor and singer. He is said to have murdered his stepfather ◊Claudius' son Britannicus, his own mother, his wives Octavia and Poppaea, and many others. After the great fire of Rome 64, he persecuted the Christians, who were suspected of causing it. Military revolt followed in 68; the Senate condemned Nero to death, and he committed suicide.

Neruda Pablo. Adopted name of Neftalí Ricardo Reyes y Basualto 1904–1973. Chilean poet and diplomat. His work includes lyrics and the epic poem of the American continent *Canto General* 1950. He was awarded the Nobel Prize for Literature 1971. He served as consul and ambassador to many countries.

After World War II he entered political life in Chile as a communist, and was a senator 1945–48. He went into exile in 1948 but returned in 1952; he later became consul to France 1971–72.

Nerva Marcus Cocceius Nerva c. AD 35–98. Roman emperor. He was proclaimed emperor on Domitian's death AD 96, and introduced state loans for farmers, family allowances, and allotments of land to poor citizens.

Nerval Gérard de. Adopted name of Gérard Labrunie 1808–1855. French writer and poet, precursor of French ◊Symbolism and ◊Surrealism. His writings include the travelogue *Voyage en Orient* 1851; short stories, including the collection *Les Filles du feu* 1854; poetry; a novel *Aurélia* 1855, containing episodes of visionary psychosis; and drama. He lived a wandering life, and suffered from periodic insanity, finally taking his own life.

nerve strand of nerve cells enclosed in a sheath of connective tissue joining the ◊central and the ◊autonomic nervous systems with receptor and effector organs. A single nerve may contain both ◊motor and sensory nerve cells, but they act independently.

nerve cell or ***neuron*** an elongated cell, part of the ◊nervous system, that transmits information between different parts of the body. A nerve impulse is a traveling wave of chemical and electrical changes that affects the surface membrane of the nerve fiber. Sequential changes in the permeability of the membrane to positive sodium (Na^+) ions and potassium (K^+) ions produce electrical signals called action potentials. Impulses are received by the cell body and passed, as a pulse of electric charge, along the ◊axon. At the far end of the axon, the impulse triggers the release of chemical ◊neurotransmitters across a ◊synapse (junction), thereby stimulating another nerve cell

nerve cell

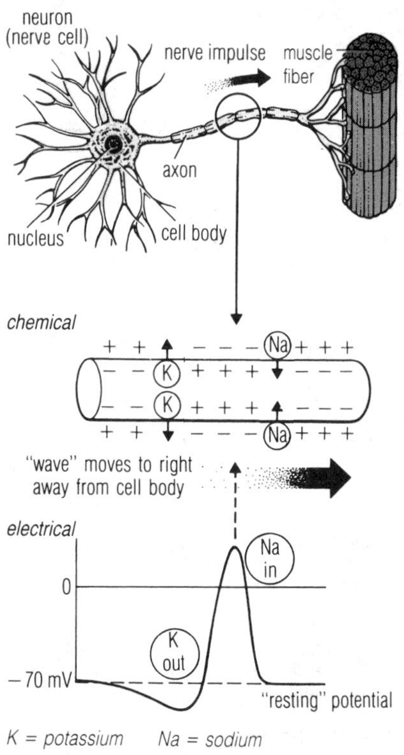

neuron (nerve cell)
nerve impulse
muscle fiber
axon
nucleus
cell body
chemical
"wave" moves to right away from cell body
electrical
Na in
0
K out
– 70 mV
"resting" potential
K = potassium
Na = sodium

or the action of an effector organ (for example, a muscle). Nerve impulses travel quickly, in humans as fast as 525 ft/160 m per second along a nerve cell.

Nervi Pier Luigi 1891–1979. Italian architect who used soft steel mesh within concrete to give it flowing form. Examples are the Turin exhibition hall 1949; the UNESCO building in Paris 1952; and the cathedral at New Norcia, near Perth, Australia 1960.

nervous system the system of interconnected ◊nerve cells of most invertebrates and all vertebrates. It is composed of the ◊central and ◊autonomic nervous systems. It may be as simple as the nerve net of coelenterates (for example, jellyfish) or as complex as the mammalian nervous system, with a central nervous system comprising brain and spinal cord, and a peripheral nervous system connecting up with sensory organs, muscles, and glands.

Ness, Loch see ◊Loch Ness.

Nestlé Henri 1814–1890. Swiss industrialist who established a milk-based baby-food factory in Vevey, Switzerland 1867, Farine Lactée Henri Nestlé. He abandoned all his interest in the business 1875.

Nestorianism Christian doctrine held by the Syrian ecclesiastic Nestorius (died c. 457), patriarch of Constantinople 428–431. He asserted that Jesus had two natures, human and divine. He was banished for maintaining that Mary was the mother of the man Jesus only, and therefore should not be called the Mother of God. His followers survived as the Assyrian church in Syria, Iraq, Iran, and as the Christians of St Thomas in S India.

Netherlands, the country in W Europe on the North Sea, bounded E by Germany and S by Belgium.

government The Netherlands is a hereditary monarchy. Its constitution 1983, based on that of 1814, provides for a two-chamber legislature called the States-General, consisting of a First Chamber of 75 and a Second Chamber of 150. Members of the First Chamber are indirectly elected by representatives of 11 provincial councils for a six-year term, half retiring every three years, and Second Chamber members are elected

Netherlands

Kingdom of the (*Koninkrijk der Nederlanden*), popularly referred to as **Holland**

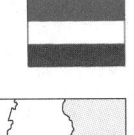

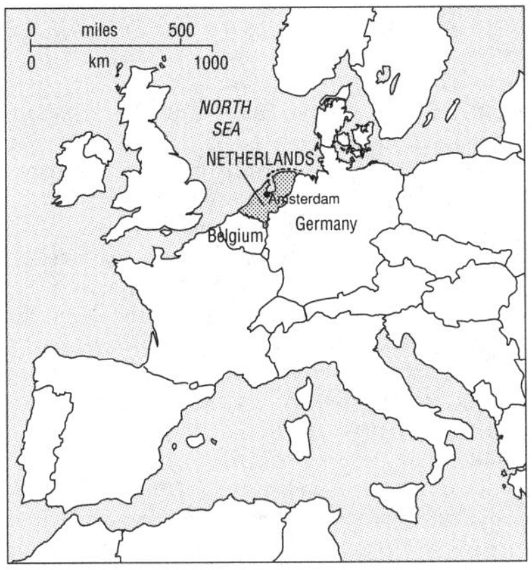
0 miles 500
0 km 1000
NORTH SEA
NETHERLANDS
Germany

area 16,169 sq mi/41,863 sq km
capital Amsterdam
cities The Hague (seat of government), Utrecht, Eindhoven, Maastricht; chief port Rotterdam
physical flat coastal lowland; rivers Rhine, Scheldt, Maas; Frisian Islands
territories Aruba, Netherlands Antilles (Caribbean)
features polders; land reclamation has turned former Zuider Zee inlet into the freshwater IJsselmeer
head of state Queen Beatrix Wilhelmina Armgard from 1980
head of government Ruud Lubbers from 1989
political system constitutional monarchy
political parties Christian Democratic Appeal (CDA), Christian, right-of-center; Labor party (PvdA), moderate, left-of-center; People's Party for Freedom and Democracy (VVD), free enterprise, centrist
exports dairy products, flower bulbs, vegetables, petrochemicals, electronics
currency guilder
population (1990 est) 14,864,000 (including 300,000 of Dutch-Indonesian origin absorbed 1949–64 from former colonial possessions); growth rate 0.4% p.a.
life expectancy men 74, women 81 (1989)
language Dutch
religion Roman Catholic 40%, Protestant 31%
literacy 99% (1989)
GNP $223 bn (1988); $13,065 per head (1987)
chronology
1940–45 Occupied by Germany during World War II.
1947 Joined Benelux Union.
1948 Queen Juliana succeeded Queen Wilhelmina to the throne.
1949 Founding member of NATO.
1953 Dykes breached by storm; nearly 2,000 people and tens of thousands of cattle died in flood.
1958 Joined European Community.
1980 Queen Juliana abdicated in favor of her daughter Beatrix.
1981 Opposition to cruise missiles averted their being sited on Dutch soil.
1989 Prime minister Lubbers resigned over environmental issue; returned to head new coalition after elections.

by universal adult suffrage, through a system of proportional representation, for a four-year term. Legislation is introduced and bills amended in the Second Chamber, while the First has the right to approve or reject.

The monarch appoints a prime minister as head of government, and the prime minister chooses the cabinet. Cabinet members are not permitted to be members of the legislature, but they may attend its meetings and take part in debates, and they are collectively responsible to it. There is also a council of state, the government's oldest advisory body, whose members are intended to represent a broad cross section of the country's life, and include former politicians, scholars, judges, and business people, all appointed for life. The sovereign is its formal president but appoints a vice-president to chair it.

Although not a federal state, the Netherlands gives considerable autonomy to its 11 provinces, each of which has an appointed governor and an elected council.

history The land south of the Rhine, inhabited by ◊Celts and Germanic peoples, was brought under Roman rule by Julius Caesar as governor of ◊Gaul 51 BC. The ◊Franks followed, and their kings subdued the ◊Frisians and Saxons north of the Rhine in the 7th–8th centuries and imposed Christianity on them. After the empire of ◊Charlemagne broke up, the local feudal lords, headed by the count of ◊Holland and the bishop of ◊Utrecht, became practically independent, although they owed nominal allegiance to the German or Holy Roman Empire. Many Dutch towns during the Middle Ages became prosperous trading centers, usually ruled by small groups of merchants. In the 15th century the Netherlands or Low Countries (Holland, Belgium, Flanders) passed to the dukes of Burgundy, and in 1504 to the Spanish Hapsburgs.

The Dutch aspired to political freedom and Protestantism and rebelled from 1568 against the tyranny of the Catholic Philip II of Spain. William the Silent, Prince of Orange, and his sons Maurice (1567–1625) and Frederick Henry (1584–1647) were the leaders of the revolt and of a confederation established in the north, the United Provinces, that repudiated Spain 1581. The south (now Belgium and Luxembourg) was reconquered by Spain, but not the north, and in 1648 its independence as the Dutch Republic was finally recognized under the Treaty of ◊Westphalia. A long struggle followed between the Orangist or popular party, which favored centralization under the Prince of Orange as chief magistrate or *stadholder*, and the oligarchical or states' rights party. The latter, headed by John de ◊Witt, seized control 1650, but ◊William of Orange (William III of England) recovered the *stadholderate* with the French invasion 1672.

Despite the long war of independence, during the early 17th century the Dutch led the world in trade, art, and science, and founded an empire in the East and West Indies. Commercial and colonial rivalries led to naval wars with England 1652–54, 1665–67, and 1672–74. Thereafter until 1713 Dutch history was dominated by a struggle with France under Louis XIV. These wars exhausted the Netherlands, which in the 18th century ceased to be a great power. The French revolutionary army was welcomed 1795 and created the Batavian Republic. In 1806 Napoleon made his brother Louis king of Holland and 1810–13 annexed the country to France. The Congress of ◊Vienna united N and S Netherlands under King William I (son of Prince William V of Orange), but the south broke away 1830 to become independent Belgium.

Under William I (reigned 1814–40), William II (1840–49), William III (1849–90), and Queen Wilhelmina (1890–1948), the Netherlands followed a path of strict neutrality, but its brutal occupation by Germany 1940–45 persuaded it to adopt a policy of cooperation with its neighbors. It became a member of the Western European Union, the North Atlantic Treaty Organization (NATO), the Benelux customs union, the European Coal and Steel Community, the European Atomic Energy Community (Euratom), and the European Community. In 1980 Queen Juliana, who had reigned since 1948, abdicated in favor of her eldest daughter, Beatrix.

The granting of independence to former colonies (Indonesia 1949, with the addition of W New Guinea 1963; Suriname 1975; see also ◊Netherlands Antilles) increased immigration and unemployment. All governments since 1945 have been coalitions, with the parties differing mainly over economic policies. The three significant parties are the Christian Democratic Appeal (CDA) the Labor Party (PvdA), and the Liberal Party. In Sept 1989 elections fought largely on environmental issues, Ruud Lubbers' Christian Democrats won the most parliamentary seats. Lubbers formed a coalition government with the leftist Labor Party.

Netherlands Antilles two groups of Caribbean islands, part of the Netherlands with full internal autonomy, comprising ◊Curaçao and Bonaire off the coast of Venezuela (◊Aruba is considered separately), and St Eustatius, Saba, and the S part of St Maarten in the Leeward Islands, 500 mi/800 km NE
area 308 sq mi/797 sq km
capital Willemstad on Curaçao
products oil from Venezuela refined here; tourism is important
language Dutch (official), Papiamento, English
population (1983) 193,000.

Netherlands East Indies former name of ◊Indonesia (1798–1945).

netsuke toggle of ivory, wood, or other materials, made to secure a purse or tobacco pouch, for men wearing Japanese traditional costume. Made especially in the Edo period in Japan 1601–1867, the miniature sculptures are now valued as works of art in their own right.

nettle any plant of the genus *Urtica*, family Urticaceae. Stinging hairs on the generally ovate leaves can penetrate the skin, causing inflammation. The common nettle *U. dioica* grows on waste ground in Europe and North America, where it was introduced.

network in computing, a method of connecting computers so that they can share data and ◊peripheral devices, such as printers. The main types are classified by the pattern of the connections—star or ring network, for example; or by the degree of geographical spread allowed—for example, local area networks (LANs) for communication within a room or building, and wide area networks (WANs) for more remote systems.

Netzahualcóyotl Mexican city lying to the S of Lake Texcoco, forming a suburb to the NE of Mexico City; population (1980) 1,341,200.

Neubrandenburg county in the Federal Republic of Germany; capital Neubrandenburg; area 4,227 sq mi/10,950 sq km; population (1986) 619,000.

Neuchâtel (German *Neuenburg*) capital of Neuchâtel

Netherlands Antilles

Willemstad on Curaçao

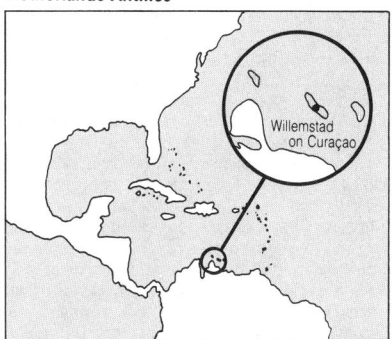

Netherlands
North Sea
Frisian Islands
Waddenzee
IJsselmeer
Leeuwarden
Groningen
Den Helder
Assen
Emmen
Alkmaar
Hoorn
Meppel
Hoogeveen
Zwolle
Haarlem
Amsterdam
Apeldoorn
IJssel
Enschede
Leiden
NETHERLANDS
Amersfoort
The Hague
Utrecht
Rotterdam
Arnhem
Dordrecht
Nijmegen
GERMANY
Breda
Tilburg
Eindhoven
Rhine
Maas
N
Antwerp
Mönchengladbach
Grote Nete
Schelde
BELGIUM
0 km 25 50
0 miles 25 50
Maastricht
4°
6°
52°

canton in NW Switzerland, on Lake Neuchâtel, W of Berne; population (1980) 34,500. It has a Horological (clock) Research Laboratory.

Neumann Balthasar 1687–1753. German Rococo architect and military engineer whose work includes the bishop's palace in Würzburg.

neuralgia sharp or burning pain originating in a nerve and spreading over its area of distribution. Trigeminal neuralgia, a common form, is a severe pain on one side of the face.

neural network artificial network of processors that attempts to mimic the structure of neurons in the human brain. Neural networks may be electronic, optical, or simulated by computer software. A basic network has three layers of processors: an input layer, an output layer, and a "hidden" layer in between. Each processor is connected to every other in the network by a system of "synapses"; every processor in the top layer connects to every one in the hidden layer, and each of these connects to every processor in the output layer. This means that each neuron in the middle and bottom layers receives input from several different sources; only when the amount of input exceeds a critical level does the neuron fire an output signal.

The chief characteristic of neural networks is their ability to sum up large amounts of imprecise data and decide whether they match a pattern or not. Networks of this type may be used in developing robot vision, matching fingerprints, and analyzing fluctuations in stock-market prices. However, it is thought unlikely by scientists that such networks will ever be able accurately to imitate the human brain, which is very much more complicated; it contains around 10 billion neurons, whereas current artificial networks contain only a hundred or so.

neurasthenia an obsolete term for nervous exhaustion, covering mild ◊depression and various symptoms of ◊neurosis. Formerly thought to be a bodily malfunction, it is now generally considered to be mental in origin.

neuritis nerve inflammation caused by injury, poisoning, or disease, and accompanied by sensory and motor changes in the area of the affected nerve.

neuroleptic alternate name for ◊antipsychotic.

neurology the branch of medicine concerned with the study and treatment of the brain, spinal cord, and peripheral nerves.

neuron another name for a ◊nerve cell.

neurosis in psychology, a general term referring to emotional disorders, such as anxiety, depression, and obsessions. The main disturbance tends to be one of mood; contact with reality is relatively unaffected, in contrast to the effects of ◊psychosis.

neuroticism a personality dimension described by ◊Eysenck. People with high neuroticism are worriers, emotional, and moody.

neurotoxin any substance that destroys nerve tissue.

neurotransmitter chemical that diffuses across a ◊synapse, and thus transmits impulses between ◊nerve cells, or between nerve cells and effector organs (for example, muscles). Common neurotransmitters are norepinephrine (which also acts as a hormone) and acetylcholine, the latter being most frequent at junctions between nerve and muscle. Nearly 50 different neurotransmitters have been identified.

Neusiedler See (Hungarian *Fertö Tó*) shallow lake in E Austria and NW Hungary, SE of Vienna; area 60 sq mi/152 sq km; the only steppe lake in Europe.

Neuss industrial city in North Rhine–Westphalia, Federal Republic of Germany; population (1988) 144,000.

Neutra Richard Joseph 1892–1970. Austrian-born architect who became a US citizen 1929. His works, often in impressive landscape settings, include Lovell Health House, Los Angeles (1929), and Mathematics Park, Princeton, New Jersey.

neutrality the legal status of a country that decides not to choose sides in a war. Certain states, notably Switzerland and Austria, have opted for permanent neutrality. Neutrality always has a legal connotation. In peacetime, neutrality toward the big power alliances is called nonalignment (see ◊nonaligned movement).

neutralization process occurring when the excess acid (or excess base) in a substance is reacted with added base (or added acid) in an amount so that the resulting substance is neither acidic nor basic. In theory neutralization involves adding acid or base as required to achieve ◊pH7. When the color of an ◊indicator is used to test for neutralization, the final pH may differ from pH7 depending upon the indicator used.

neutrino any of three uncharged ◊elementary particles (and their antiparticles) of the ◊lepton class, which cannot be subdivided and have a mass too close to zero to be measured. The most familiar type, the electron neutrino, is emitted in beta decay of a nucleus. The other two are the muon neutrino and the tauon neutrino.

neutron one of the three main ◊subatomic particles, the others being the proton and the electron. It belongs to the ◊baryon group of the ◊hadrons. It is composed of one up and two down quarks. Neutrons have about the same mass as protons but no electric charge and occur in the nuclei of all atoms except hydrogen. Neutrons contribute to the mass of atoms but do not affect their chemistry. For instance, ◊isotopes of a single element (with different masses) differ only in the number of neutrons in their nuclei but have identical chemical properties. Outside a nucleus, a free neutron is radioactive, decaying with a half-life of 11.6 minutes into a proton, an electron, and an antineutrino. The neutron was discovered by the British chemist James ◊Chadwick in 1932.

neutron beam machine a nuclear reactor or accelerator producing a stream of neutrons, which can "see" through metals. It is used in industry to check molecular changes in metal under stress.

neutron bomb small hydrogen bomb for battlefield use that kills by radiation without destroying buildings and other structures. See ◊nuclear warfare.

neutron star very small, superdense star composed mostly of ◊neutrons. Neutron stars are thought to form when massive stars explode as ◊supernovae, during which the ◊protons and ◊electrons of the star's atoms merge, due to intense gravitational collapse, to make neutrons. A neutron star may have the mass of up to three Suns, compressed into a globe only 12 mi/20 km in diameter. If its mass is any greater, its gravity will be so strong that it will shrink even further to become a ◊black hole. Being so small, neutron stars can spin very quickly. The rapidly "flashing" radio stars called ◊pulsars are believed to be neutron stars. The "flashing" is caused by a rotating beam of radio energy similar in behavior to a lighthouse beam of light.

Nevada state in W US; nickname Silver State/Sagebrush State

area 110,550 sq mi/286,400 sq km

capital Carson City

cities Las Vegas, Reno

population (1990) 1,201,833

physical Mohave desert; lakes: Tahoe, Pyramid,

Nevada

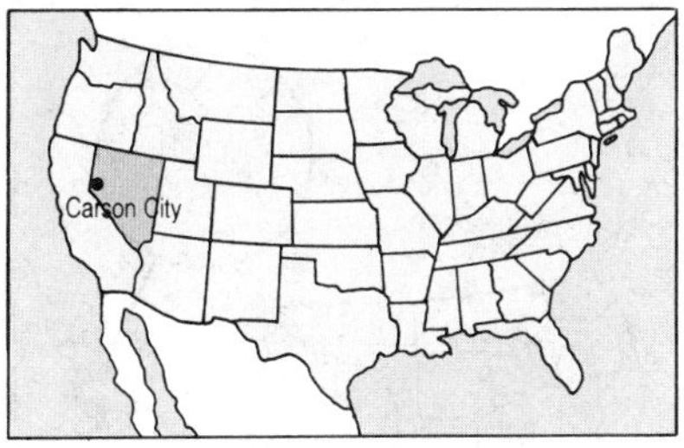
Carson City

Mead; mountains and plateaus alternating with valleys
features legal gambling and prostitution (in some counties); entertainment at Las Vegas and Reno casinos; Lehman Caves National Monument
products mercury, barite, gold
history explored by Kit Carson and John C Fremont 1843–45; ceded to the US after the Mexican War 1848; first permanent settlement a Mormon trading post 1848. The Comstock Lode 1858 led to rapid population growth and statehood 1864. The building of the Hoover Dam in the 1930s provided the water and power needed for the growth of Las Vegas. In 1931 the state created two industries, divorce (Reno) and gambling (Las Vegas). Oil was discovered 1954, but gold exceeds all other mineral production. Tourism and gambling now generate more than half of the state's income.

Nevers industrial town in Burgundy, central France, at the meeting of the Loire and Nièvre rivers; capital of the former province of Nivernais and the modern *département* of Nièvre; population (1982) 44,800.

nevus any birthmark, mole, or colored spot on the skin, especially the kind called a "port-wine mark." This is a maroon-colored area of the skin, consisting of a mass of small blood vessels.

A nevus of moderate size is harmless, and such marks are usually disguised cosmetically unless they are extremely disfiguring, when they can sometimes be treated by cutting out, by burning with an electric needle, by freezing with carbon dioxide snow, or by argon laser treatment.

New Age a type of instrumental or ambient music of the 1980s, often semiacoustic or electronic; less insistent than rock.

New Amsterdam town in Guyana, on the river Berbice, founded by the Dutch; population (1980) 25,000. Also a former name (1624–64) of ◊New York.

Newark largest city (industrial and commercial) of New Jersey; industries include electrical equipment, machinery, chemicals, paints, and canned meats; population (1990) 275,221. The city dates from 1666, when a settlement called Milford was made on the site. Since World War II, Newark has suffered from poverty and urban decay, and there was a major racial disturbance 1967. The airport was upgraded and modernized in the 1970s to serve New York City, and urban renewal projects in the 1980s have kept it a center for business and finance, especially insurance.

New Bedford city in SE Massachusetts, on the Acushnet River near Buzzards Bay, S of Boston. Industries include electronics, rubber and metal products, and fishing; population (1990) 99,922. During the 1800s it was a prosperous whaling town.

New Britain largest island in the ◊Bismarck Archipelago, part of Papua New Guinea; capital Rabaul; population (1985) 253,000.

New Britain city in central Connecticut, SW of Hartford and NE of Waterbury. Long an industrial city, its manufactures include tools, hardware, and household appliances; population (1990) 75,491.

New Brunswick maritime province of E Canada
area 28,332 sq mi/73,400 sq km

New Brunswick

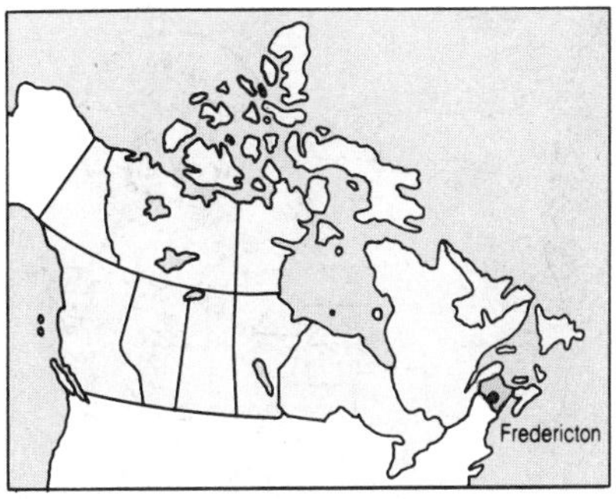
Fredericton

capital Fredericton
towns Saint John, Moncton
features Grand Lake, St John river; Bay of Fundy
products cereals, wood, paper, fish, lead, zinc, copper, oil, natural gas
population (1986) 710,000; 37% French-speaking
history first reached by Europeans (Cartier) 1534; explored by Champlain 1604; remained a French colony as part of Nova Scotia until ceded to England 1713. After the American Revolution many United Empire Loyalists settled there, and it became a province of the Dominion of Canada 1867.

New Caledonia island group in the S Pacific, a French overseas territory between Australia and the Fiji Islands
area 7,170 sq mi/18,576 sq km
capital Nouméa
physical fertile, surrounded by a barrier reef
products nickel (the world's third-largest producer), chrome, iron
currency CFP franc
population (1983) 145,300, 43% Kanak (Melanesian), 37% European, 8% Wallisian, 5% Vietnamese and Indonesian, 4% Polynesian
language French (official)
religion Roman Catholic 60%, Protestant 30%
history New Caledonia was visited by Captain Cook 1774 and became French 1853. A general strike to gain local control of nickel mines 1974 was defeated. In 1981 the French Socialist government promised moves toward independence. The 1985 elections resulted in control of most regions by Kanaks, but not the majority of seats. In 1986 the French conservative government reversed the reforms. The Kanaks boycotted a referendum Sept 1987 and a majority were in favor of remaining a French dependency. In 1989 the leader of the Socialist National Liberation front (the most prominent separatist group), Jean-Marie Tjibaou, was murdered.

Newcastle industrial port (iron, steel, chemicals, textiles, ships) in New South Wales, Australia; population (1986) 429,000. The nearby coal mines were discovered 1796. A penal settlement was founded 1804.

Newcastle Thomas Pelham-Holles, Duke of 1693–1768. British Whig politician. He was secretary of state 1724–54 and then prime minister during the Seven Years' War, until 1762, although ◊Pitt the Elder (1st Earl of Chatham) was mainly responsible for the conduct of the war.

Newcastle-under-Lyme industrial town (coal, bricks and tiles, clothing) in Staffordshire, England; population (1981) 120,100.

Newcastle-upon-Tyne industrial port (coal, shipbuilding, marine and electrical engineering, chemicals, metals), commercial and cultural center, in Tyne and Wear, NE England, administrative headquarters of Tyne and Wear and Northumberland; population (1981) 278,000.
history Chiefly known as a coaling center, Newcastle first began to trade in coal in the 13th century. In 1826 ironworks were established by George ◊Stephenson, and the first engine used on the Stockton and Darlington railroad was made in Newcastle.

Newcomen Thomas 1663–1729. English inventor of an early steam engine. He patented his "fire engine" 1705, which was used for pumping water from mines until James ◊Watt invented one with a separate condenser.

new criticism in literature, a 20th-century US movement stressing the preeminence of the text without biographical and other external interpolation, but instead using techniques such as statistical counting. The term was coined by J E Spingarn in 1910.

New Deal in US history, the program introduced by President F D ◊Roosevelt 1933 to counter the ◊Depression of 1929, including employment on public works, farm loans at low rates, and social reforms such as old-age and unemployment insurance, prevention of child labor, protection of employees against unfair practices by employers, and loans to local authorities for slum clearance. In the first 100 days of Roosevelt's administration, he introduced and pushed through Congress hundreds of programs and economic initiatives. Critics from the right called his approach too Socialistic, and the role of the federal government in the nation's economic life was strengthened to include policies that remain today. Some of his programs' provisions were declared unconstitutional by the Supreme Court 1935–36, and full employment was not established until the military-industrial needs of World War II.

The Public Works Administration (PWA) was given $3.3 billion to spend on roads, public buildings, and similar developments (the ◊Tennessee Valley Authority was a separate project). The Agricultural Adjustment Administration (AAA) raised agricultural prices by restriction of output. In 1935 Harry L ◊Hopkins was put in charge of a new agency, the Works Progress Administration (WPA), which, in addition to taking over the public works, created something of a cultural revolution with its federal theater, writers', and arts projects. When the WPA was disbanded in 1943 it had found employment for 8.5 million persons. The New Deal encouraged the growth of trade-union membership, brought previously unregulated areas of the US economy under federal control, and revitalized cultural life and community spirit. Although it did not succeed in restoring full prosperity, it did bring hope and political stability.

New Delhi see ◊Delhi, capital of India.

New Delhi city in the Union Territory of Delhi, designed by Lutyens; capital of India since 1912; population (1981) 273,000.

New Democratic Party (NDP) Canadian political party, moderately Socialist, formed 1961 by a merger of the Labor Congress and the Cooperative Commonwealth Federation.

There are also provincial and territorial New Democratic Parties, which have formed governments in British Columbia, Saskatchewan, Manitoba, and Yukon.

New Economic Policy (NEP) economic policy of the USSR 1921–29 devised by the Soviet leader Lenin. Rather than requisitioning all agricultural produce above a stated subsistence allowance, the state requisitioned only a fixed proportion of the surplus; the rest could be traded freely by the peasant. The NEP thus reinstated a limited form of free-market trading, although the state retained complete control of major industries.

The NEP was introduced in March 1921 after a series of peasant revolts and the ◊Kronstadt uprising. Aimed at reestablishing an alliance with the peasantry, it began as an agricultural measure to act as an incentive for peasants to produce more food. The policy was ended in 1928 by Stalin's first Five-Year Plan, which began the collectivization of agriculture.

New England NE region of the US, comprising the states of Maine, New Hampshire, Vermont, Massachusetts, Rhode Island, and Connecticut; originally settled by Pilgrims and Puritans from Eng-

Newfoundland and Labrador

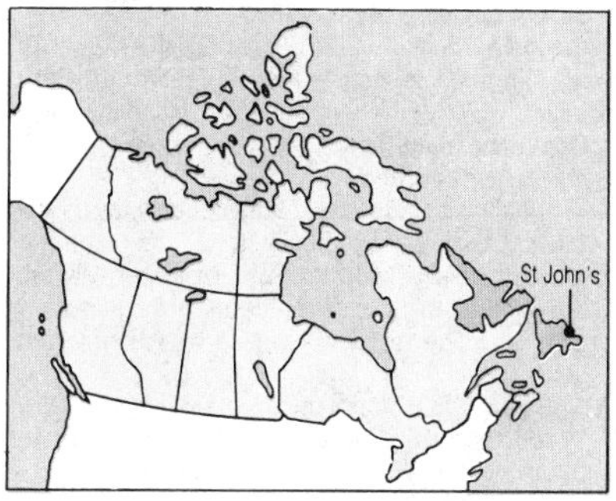
St John's

land. It has an area of 66,672 sq mi/172,681 sq km. Boston is the major urban center of the region, and Harvard and Yale its major universities.

It is a geographic region rather than a political entity. The area is still heavily forested, and the economy relies on tourism and services as well as industry. Its share of US personal income is larger than its share of population.

Newfoundland breed of dog, said to have originated in Newfoundland. Males can grow to 2.3 ft/70 cm tall, and weigh 145 lb/65 kgs; the females are slightly smaller. They are gentle in temperament, and their fur is dense, flat, and usually dull black. Newfoundlands that are black and white or brown and white are called Landseers.

Newfoundland and Labrador Canadian province on the Atlantic Ocean
area 156,600 sq mi/405,700 sq km
capital St John's
towns Corner Brook, Gander
physical Newfoundland island and ◊Labrador on the mainland on the other side of the Straits of Belle Isle; rocky
features Grand Banks section of the continental shelf rich in cod; home of the Newfoundland and Labrador dogs
products newsprint, fish products, hydroelectric power, iron, copper, zinc, uranium, offshore oil
population (1986) 568,000
history colonized by Vikings about AD 1000; Newfoundland reached by the English, under the Italian navigator Giovanni ◊Caboto, 1497. It was the first English colony, established 1583. French settlements made; British sovereignty was not recognized until 1713, although France retained the offshore islands of St Pierre and Miquelon. Internal self-government was achieved 1855. In 1934, as Newfoundland had fallen into financial difficulties, administration was vested in a governor and a special commission. A 1948 referendum favored federation with Canada and the province joined Canada 1949.

New General Catalog catalog of star clusters and nebulae compiled by the Danish astronomer John Louis Emil Dreyer (1852–1926) and published 1888. Its main aim was to revise, correct, and expand upon the *General Catalog* compiled by John Herschel, which appeared 1864.

New Guinea island in the SW Pacific, N of Australia, comprising Papua New Guinea and the Indonesian province of West Irian (Irian Jaya area); area 306,000 sq mi/792,000 sq km; population (1980) 1,174,000. Part of the Dutch East Indies from 1828, it was ceded by the United Nations to Indonesia 1963.

Tension between Papua New Guinea and Indonesia has been heightened as a result of a growing number of border incidents involving Indonesian troops and Irianese separatist guerrillas. At the same time large numbers of refugees have fled eastward into Papua New Guinea from West Irian. Its tropical rainforest and the 0.5 million hunter-gatherers who inhabit it are under threat from logging companies and resettlement schemes.

New Hampshire

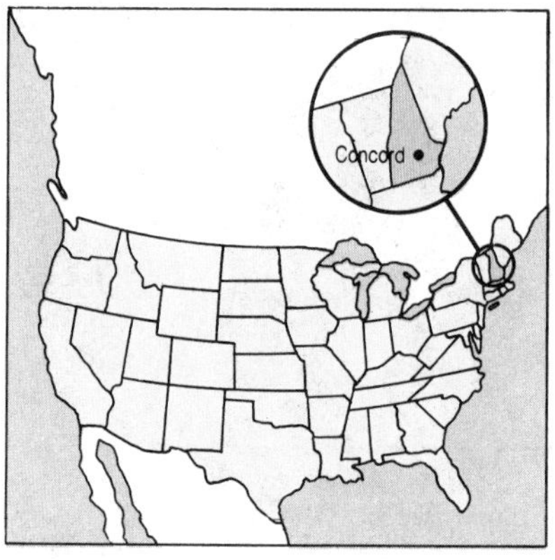
Concord

New Hampshire state in NE US; nickname Granite State
area 9,264 sq mi/24,000 sq km
capital Concord
cities Manchester, Nashua
population (1990) 1,109,252
features White Mountains, including Mount Washington the tallest peak E of the Rockies (with its cog railroad), and Mount Monadnock; the Connecticut River forms boundary with Vermont; earliest presidential-election party primaries every four years; no state income tax or sales tax; ski and tourist resorts (inns)
products dairy, poultry, fruits and vegetables; electrical and other machinery; pulp and paper
famous people Mary Baker Eddy, Robert Frost
history settled as a fishing colony near Rye and Dover 1623; separated from Massachusetts colony 1679. As leaders in the Revolutionary cause, its leaders received the honor of being the first to declare independence of Britain July 4, 1776. It became a state 1788, one of the original thirteen states. In the 19th century, abundant water power allowed textile mills to flourish, but the industry later declined. The state experienced rapid growth after 1970, as people and industry–especially high-technology businesses–moved north from the Boston area into southern New Hampshire.

New Haven port city in Connecticut, on Long Island Sound; population (1990) 130,474. Yale University, third oldest in the US, was founded here 1701 and named after Elihu Yale (1648–1721), an early benefactor. New Haven was founded in 1638 by English Protestants.

New Hebrides former name (until 1980) of ◊Vanuatu.

Ne Win Adopted name of Maung Shu Maung 1911– . Myanmar (Burmese) politician, prime minister 1958–60, ruler from 1962 to 1974, president 1974–81.

Active in the Nationalist movement during the 1930s, Ne Win joined the Allied forces in the war against Japan in 1945 and held senior military posts before becoming prime minister in 1958. After leading a coup in 1962, he ruled the country as chair of the revolutionary council until 1974, when he became state president. Although he stepped down as president 1981, he continued to dominate political affairs as chair of the ruling Burma Socialist Program Party (BSPP). His domestic "Burmese Way to Socialism" policy program brought the economy into serious decline, and Ne Win was forced to step down as BSPP leader 1988 after riots in Rangoon (now Yangon).

New Jersey state in NE US; nickname Garden State
area 7,797 sq mi/20,200 sq km
capital Trenton
cities Newark, Jersey City, Paterson, Elizabeth
population (1990) 7,730,188
features about 125 mi/200 km of seashore, including legalized gambling in Atlantic City and the Victorian beach resort of Cape May; Delaware

New Jersey

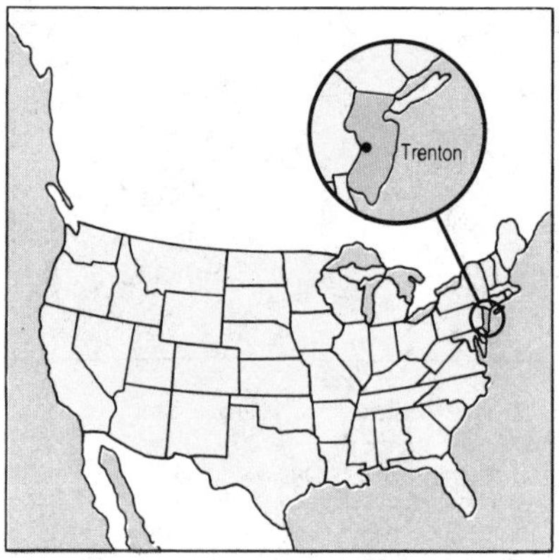
Trenton

Water Gap; Palisades along the W bank of the Hudson River; Princeton University; Morristown National Historic Park; Edison National Historic Site, Menlo Park; Walt Whitman House, Camden; Statue of Liberty National Monument (shared with New York); the Meadowlands stadium
products fruits and vegetables, fish and shellfish, chemicals, pharmaceuticals, soaps and cleansers, transport equipment, petroleum refining
famous people Stephen Crane, Thomas Edison, Thomas Paine, Paul Robeson, Frank Sinatra, Bruce Springsteen, Woodrow Wilson
history colonized in the 17th century by the Dutch (New Netherlands); ceded to England 1664; became a state 1787. It was one of the original thirteen states. Wedged between the growing cities of Philadelphia and New York, New Jersey saw much fighting during the Revolution and became increasingly urban and industrial in the 19th century. In the 20th century, much of the state remains a farming region but also has experienced much air and water pollution as well as the dumping of toxic wastes in landfills. It remains a favored site for development, however, and ranks near the top among states in per-capita income; much urban renewal has occurred in the industrial port cities along the Hudson since the 1970s.

Newlands John A 1838–1898. British chemist who worked as an industrial chemist; he prepared in 1863 the first ◊periodic table of the elements arranged in order of atomic weights, and pointed out the "Law of Octaves" whereby every eighth element has similar properties. He was ridiculed at the time, but five years later Russian chemist D I Mendeleyev published a more developed form of the table, also based on atomic weights, which forms the basis of the one used today (arranged by atomic number).

New London port city in SE Connecticut, on Long Island Sound at the mouth of the Thames River; population (1990) 28,540. It is a naval base and home of the US Coast Guard Academy and the US Submarine Officers School. Industries include submarine production, pharmaceuticals, and chemicals. Tourism is also important to the economy. Connecticut College is here. Settled 1646 as part of the Massachusetts Bay Colony, it served as a privateering base during the American Revolution, a whaling center during the 1800s, and an important base for ships during World War II.

newly industrialized country (NIC) a developing country that has in recent decades experienced a breakthrough into manufacturing and rapid export-led economic growth. The prime examples are Taiwan, Hong Kong, Singapore, and South Korea. Their economic development during the 1970s and 1980s was partly due to a rapid increase of manufactured goods in their exports.

Newman Barnett 1905–1970. US painter, sculptor, and theorist. His paintings are solid-colored canvases with a few sparse vertical stripes. They represent a mystical pursuit of simple or elemental art. His sculptures, such as *Broken Obelisk* 1963–67, consist of geometric shapes on top of each other.

Born in New York City, he was involved in the development of colorfield painting.

Newman John Henry 1801–1890. English Roman Catholic theologian. While still an Anglican, he wrote a series of *Tracts for the Times*, which gave their name to the Tractarian Movement (subsequently called the ◊Oxford Movement) for the revival of Catholicism. He became a Catholic 1845 and was made a cardinal 1879. In 1864 his autobiography, *Apologia pro vita sua*, was published.

Newman, born in London, was ordained in the Church of England in 1824, and in 1827 became vicar of St Mary's, Oxford. There he was influenced by the historian R H Froude and the Anglican priest Keble, and in 1833 published the first of the *Tracts for the Times*. His poem *The Dream of Gerontius* appeared in 1866, and *The Grammar of Assent*, an analysis of the nature of belief, in 1870.

Newman Paul 1925– . US actor and director, Hollywood's leading male star of the 1960s and 1970s. His films include *Somebody Up There Likes Me* 1956, *Cat on a Hot Tin Roof* 1958, *The Hustler* 1961, *Sweet Bird of Youth* 1962, *Hud* 1963, *Cool Hand Luke* 1967, *Butch Cassidy and the Sundance Kid* 1969, *The Sting* 1973, *The Verdict* 1983, *The Color of Money* 1986 (for which he won an Academy Award), and *Mr and Mrs Bridge* 1991.

He directed his wife Joanne Woodward in *Rachel, Rachel* 1968 and other films and was noted as a race-car driver and for his philanthropic activities. The profits from his Newman's Own specialty foods are donated to charity.

New Mexico state in SW US; nickname Land of Enchantment
area 121,590 sq mi/315,000 sq km
capital Santa Fe
cities Albuquerque, Las Cruces, Roswell
population (1990) 1,515,069
physical more than 75% of the area lies over 3,900 ft/1,200 m above sea level; plains, mountains, caverns
features Great Plains; Rocky Mountains; Rio Grande; Carlsbad Caverns, the largest known; Los Alamos atomic and space research center; White Sands Missile Range (also used by Space Shuttle); Kiowa Ranch, site of D H Lawrence's stay in the Sangre de Christos mountains; Taos art colony; Santa Fe Opera Company; Navaho and Hopi Indian reservations; White Sands and Gila Cliff Dwellings National monuments
products uranium, potash, copper, oil, natural gas, petroleum and coal products; sheep farming; cotton; pecans; vegetables
famous people William Bonney ("Billy the Kid"), Kit Carson, Georgia O'Keeffe
history explored by Francisco de Coronado for Spain 1540–42; Spanish settlement 1598 on the Rio Grande; Santa Fe founded 1610; most of New Mexico ceded to the US by Mexico 1848; became a state 1912. The first atomic bomb, a test device, was exploded in the desert near Alamogordo, July 16, 1945. Oil and gas development and tourism now contribute greatly to the state economy.

New Mexico

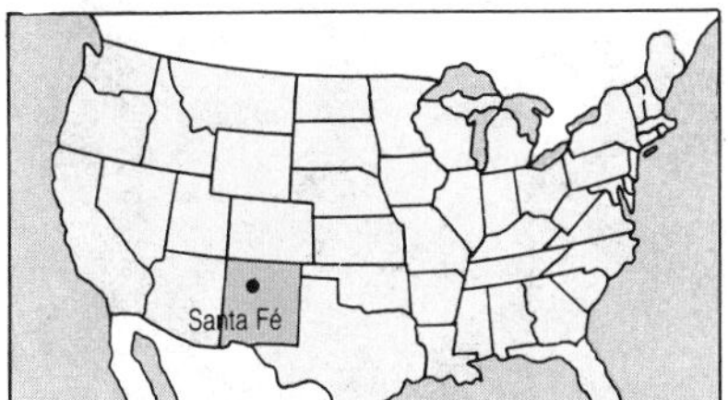
Santa Fé

New South Wales

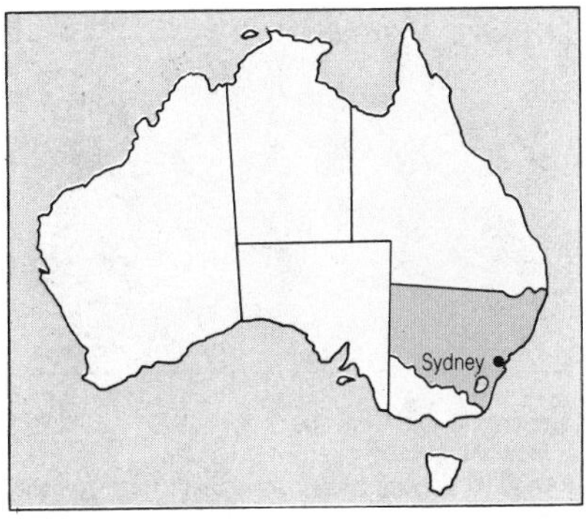
Sydney

New Model Army army created 1645 by Oliver Cromwell to support the cause of Parliament during the English ◊Civil War. It was characterized by organization and discipline. Thomas Fairfax was its first commander.

New Orleans city and Mississippi River port in Louisiana; population (1990) 496,938. With an outlet to the Gulf of Mexico, New Orleans has led all US ports in shipping tonnage handled. It is a commercial and manufacturing center, refined petroleum and petrochemicals are its major products. Educational institutions include Tulane University. In the 18th century New Orleans was the capital of Louisiana Territory. It passed to the US with the ◊Louisiana Purchase, and by 1852 it was the third-largest US city. It is the traditional birthplace of jazz.

Founded by the French in 1718, it still has a distinctive French Quarter and Mardi Gras celebrations. Dixieland jazz exponents still play at Preservation Hall. The Superdome sports palace is among the world's largest enclosed stadiums and is adaptable to various games and expected audience size.

Newport seaport and administrative headquarters in Gwent, Wales, on the river Usk, NW of Bristol; population (1983) 130,200. There is a steelworks at nearby Llanwern, and a high-tech complex at Cleppa Park.

Newport News industrial (engineering, shipbuilding) port city of SE Virginia, at the mouth of the James River; population (1990) 170,045. With neighboring Chesapeake, Norfolk, and Portsmouth, it forms the Port of Hampton Roads, one of the chief US ports. One of the world's largest shipyards is here.

The site was settled by the British around 1620. During the Civil War the first battle between ironclad ships (the *Monitor* and the *Merrimac*) 1862 took place off Newport News.

Newport Riots violent demonstrations in Newport, Wales in support of the Peoples' Charter by the ◊Chartists in 1839. It was suppressed with the loss of twenty lives.

New Rochelle residential suburb of New York on Long Island Sound; population (1990) 67,265.

news agency business handling news stories and photographs that are then sold to newspapers and magazines. Major world agencies include the Associated Press (AP), Agence France-Presse (AFP), United Press International (UPI), Telegraphic Agency of the Soviet Union (TASS), and Reuters.

Journalists write and edit their material on a VDT (visual display terminal), then press a button to transmit it to the agency headquarters. Stories are coded to arrive at the editor's desk in order of priority (such as flash or urgent) for worldwide distribution to individual newspapers. Third World countries dislike the dominance of the agencies, which they accuse of "Western bias," and have attempted to start their own system.

New South Wales state of SE Australia
area 309,418 sq mi/801,600 sq km
capital Sydney
towns Newcastle, Wollongong, Broken Hill
physical Great Dividing Range (including Blue Mountains)and part of the Australian Alps (including Snowy Mountains and Mount Kosciusko); Riverina district, irrigated by the Murray-Darling-Murrumbidgee river system
features a radio telescope at Parkes; Siding Spring Mountain 2,817 ft/859 m, NW of Sydney, with telescopes that can observe the central sector of the galaxy. ◊Canberra forms an enclave within the state, and New South Wales administers the dependency of ◊Lord Howe Island
products cereals, fruit, sugar, tobacco, wool, meat, hides and skins, gold, silver, copper, tin, zinc, coal; hydroelectric power from the Snowy River
population (1987) 5,570,000; 60% in Sydney
history convict settlement 1788–1850; opened to free settlement by 1819; received self-government 1856; became a state of the Commonwealth of Australia 1901. Since 1973 there has been decentralization to counteract the pull of Sydney, and the New England and Riverina districts have separatist movements. It was called New Wales by James ◊Cook, who landed at Botany Bay 1770 and thought that the coastline resembled that of Wales.

newspaper a daily or weekly publication in the form of folded sheets containing news, illustrations, timely comments, and advertising. Newsheets became commercial undertakings after the invention of printing and were introduced 1609 in Germany, 1616 in the Netherlands. In 1620, the first newspaper in English appeared in the Netherlands. In England, Addison and Steele published the *Tatler* 1709–11 and the *Spectator* 1711–12. The first newspaper in colonial America was *Publick Occurrences Both Forreign and Domestick*. It was planned as a monthly publication, but it was only published once, in Boston 1690. It was not until 1704 that another paper, the *News-Letter*, also published in Boston, appeared.
history One of the earliest newspapers, the Roman *Acta Diurna*, said to have been started by the emperor Julius Caesar, contained handwritten announcements of marriages, deaths, military appointments, and so on, and was posted in public places. In colonial America, small newspapers were in abundance. By the time of the Revolutionary War, newspapers were used to give opinions from both sides; Thomas Paine's first *Crisis* letters 1776 were published in the *Pennsylvania Journal*. Later, newspapers represented political parties; *The Federalist* essays were first published in the *Independent Journal*, while the *National Gazette* represented Republican views. From 1830, newspapers became more like they are today. News was presented along with human interest stories, crime and court happenings, and other things to attract readership.

Most newspapers are issued daily, but many are weeklies. There are almost 2,000 daily newspapers in the US today. The most well-known and most widely read newspapers are *The New York Times*, the *Los Angeles Times*, and the *Washington Post*. Newspapers such as the *Wall Street Journal* and *Women's Wear Daily* are aimed at special interests and are widely read.

New Style the Gregorian ◊calendar introduced in 1582 and now used throughout most of the Christian world.

newt small salamander, of the family Salamandridae, found in Eurasia, NW Africa, and North America.

newt

Newton *English physicist and mathematician Isaac Newton, in a 1702 portrait by Godfrey Kneller.*

The red spotted newt *Notophthalmus viridescens* of E North America, about 3.5 in/9 cm long, is olive green with red spots when adult. The young, called red efts, are bright orange and are terrestrial.

New Testament the second part of the ◊Bible, recognized by the Christian church from the 4th century as sacred doctrine. The New Testament includes the Gospels, which tell of the life and teachings of Jesus, the history of the early church, the teachings of St Paul, and mystical writings. It was written in Greek during the 1st and 2nd centuries AD, and the individual sections have been ascribed to various authors by Biblical scholars.

newton SI unit (abbreviation N) of ◊force. One newton is the force needed to accelerate an object with mass of one kilogram by one meter per second per second. To accelerate a car weighing 2,200 lb/1,000 kg from 0 to 60 mph in 30 seconds would take about 2.5×10^5 N.

Newton Isaac 1642–1727. English physicist and mathematician who laid the foundations of physics as a modern discipline. He discovered the law of gravity, created calculus, discovered that white light is composed of many colors, and developed the three standard laws of motion still in use today. During 1665–66, he discovered the binomial theorem and differential and integral calculus, and also began to investigate the phenomenon of gravitation. In 1685, he expounded his universal law of gravitation. His *Philosophiae naturalis principia mathematica*, usually referred to as *Principia* was published in three volumes 1686–87, with the aid of Edmund ◊Halley.

Newton's universal law of gravitation states: "Every particle of matter in the universe attracts every other particle with a force whose direction is that of the line joining the two, and whose magnitude is directly as [proportional to] the product of the masses, and inversely as [proportional to] the square of their distance from each other."

Newtonian physics ◊physics based on the concepts of Isaac ◊Newton, before the formulation of ◊quantum theory or ◊relativity theory.

Newton's laws of motion in physics, three laws that form the basis of Newtonian mechanics. (1) Unless acted upon by a net force, a body at rest stays at rest, and a moving body continues moving at the same speed in the same straight line. (2) A net force applied to a body gives it a rate of change of ◊momentum proportional to the force and in the direction of the force. (3) When a body A exerts a force on a body B, B exerts an equal and opposite force on A; that is, to every action there is an equal and opposite reaction.

Newton's rings in optics, an ◊interference phenomenon seen (using white light) as concentric rings of spectral colors where light passes through a thin film of transparent medium, such as the wedge of air between a large-radius convex lens and a flat glass plate. With monochromatic light (light of a single wavelength), the rings take the form of alternate light and dark bands. They are caused by interference (interaction) between light rays reflected from the plate and those reflected from the curved surface of the lens.

New York

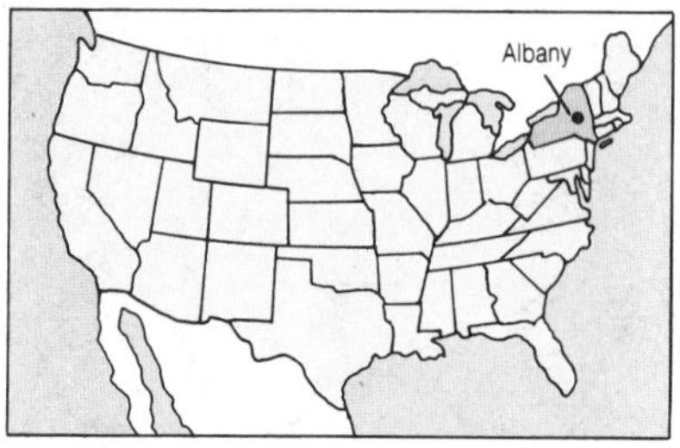
Albany

New Wave in pop music, a style that evolved parallel to punk in the second half of the 1970s. It shared the urban aggressive spirit of punk but was musically and lyrically more sophisticated; examples are the early work of Elvis Costello and Talking Heads.

New Wave (French *nouvelle vague*) French literary movement of the 1950s, a cross-fertilization of the novel (Marguerite Duras, Alain Robbe-Grillet, Nathalie Sarraute) and film (directors Jean-Luc Godard, Alain Resnais, and François Truffaut).

New World the Americas, so called by the first Europeans who reached them. The term also describes animals and plants that live in the western hemisphere.

New York state in NE US; nickname Empire State/Excelsior State

area 49,099 sq mi/127,200 sq km

capital Albany

cities New York, Buffalo, Rochester, Yonkers, Syracuse

physical mountains: Adirondacks, Catskills; lakes: Champlain, Placid, Erie, Ontario; rivers: Mohawk, Hudson, St Lawrence (with Thousand Islands); Niagara Falls; Long Island; New York Bay

features West Point, site of the US Military Academy 1801; National Baseball Hall of Fame, Cooperstown; horse racing at Belmont, Aqueduct, Saratoga Springs; colleges: Colgate, Cornell, Columbia, New York University, CUNY, SUNY, Renssalaer Polytech, Pratt, Juilliard, and Vassar; Washington Irving's home at Philipsburg Manor; Fenimore House (J F ◊Cooper), Cooperstown; home of F D Roosevelt at Hyde Park, and the Roosevelt Library; home of Theodore Roosevelt, Oyster Bay; Statue of Liberty National Monument; Erie Canal; United Nations headquarters; New York City

products dairy products, apples, clothing, periodical and book printing and publishing, electronic components and accessories, office machines and computers, communications equipment, motor vehicles and equipment, pharmaceuticals, aircraft and parts

population (1990) 17,990,455

famous people Aaron Burr, Grover Cleveland, James Fenimore Cooper, George Gershwin, Alexander Hamilton, Fiorello La Guardia, Washington Irving, Henry James, Herman Melville, Arthur Miller, Nelson Rockefeller, Franklin D Roosevelt, Theodore Roosevelt, Peter Stuyvesant, Walt Whitman

history explored by Giovanni da Verrazano for France 1524; explored by Champlain for France and Hudson for the Netherlands 1609; colonized by the Dutch from 1614; first permanent settlement at Albany (Fort Orange) 1624; Manhattan Island purchased by Peter Minuit 1625; New Amsterdam annexed by the English 1664. The first constitution was adopted 1777, when New York became one of the original thirteen states. The Battle of Saratoga 1777, following which British troops surrendered, is considered the turning point of the American Revolution. By 1810 New York was the most populous of the states, a rank it maintained until the 1960s. The Erie Canal, completed 1825, fostered commerce by providing a link between the Atlantic and the Great Lakes. After the Civil War, New York was transformed from a chiefly agricultural state to an industrial giant. By 1970, however, the state was suffering economic decline, particularly in manufacturing. But it remains an important industrial state, and in New York City it contains the commercial, financial (Wall Street) and cultural capital of the country.

New York largest city in the US; industrial port (printing, publishing, clothing) and cultural, financial, and commercial center in S New York State; at the junction of the Hudson and East rivers and including New York Bay. It comprises the boroughs of the Bronx, Brooklyn, Manhattan, Queens, and Staten Island, with the subways, bridges, and tunnels that link them; population (1990) 7,322,564.

New York is the nation's corporate, financial, and media center. Real estate is one of its biggest businesses. It remains an important manufacturing center, although a declining one. It is the nation's center for book and magazine publishing and the visual and performing arts. It also ranks first among US cities in wholesale and retail trade. The two major airports are Kennedy International

New York *The New York skyline, showing the twin towers of the World Trade Center.*

and La Guardia. The Port of New York is the nation's second-busiest harbor, although most active piers and harbors are now in New Jersey and Brooklyn. Tourism, conventions, and educational institutions are also important to the city's economy.

The Statue of Liberty stands on Liberty Island (called Bedloe's Island until 1956) in the inner harbor of New York Bay. Skyscrapers include the twin towers of the World Trade Center (1,350 ft/412 m) and the art deco Empire State Building (1,250 ft/381 m) and Chrysler Building. St Patrick's Cathedral is in 19th-century Gothic style. Notable art museums include the Frick Collection, the Metropolitan Museum of Art (with a medieval department, the ◊Cloisters), the Museum of Modern Art, the Guggenheim (designed by Frank Lloyd Wright), the Whitney, and the Morgan Library. Columbia University 1754 is the best known of a number of institutions of higher education. Other features include Central Park, Rockefeller Center, the United Nations complex, Carnegie Hall, Lincoln Center for the Performing Arts, the Broadway theater district, the New York Stock Exchange, Chinatown, Greenwich Village and South Street Seaport.

The Italian navigator Giovanni da Verrazano (?1485–?1528) reached New York Bay 1524, and Henry Hudson explored it 1609. The Dutch established a settlement on Manhattan 1624, named New Amsterdam, and on Governor's Island in New York Bay; they also settled in Brooklyn, Queens, and Staten Island by the 1640s; all this was captured by the English in 1664 and renamed New York. During the American Revolution, British troops occupied New York 1776–84. After the Revolution, New York was the capital of the US 1785–89. In the early 19th century, it passed Philadelphia to become the nation's largest city, and for the next 100 years it swelled with immigrants. In 1898 the five boroughs joined together to form the City of Greater New York. In the 1960s New York began declining in population, and its economy suffered because of high taxation (which led businesses to move to tax-free, nearby localities) and the departure of the middle class. In the 1970s a severe municipal financial crisis threatened, but in the 1980s the economy recovered, based on gains in service employment (particularly in financial services), office construction, and the cooperative real-estate market. From the late 1980s, the city's economy was once again threatened.

New Yorker, The sophisticated US weekly magazine founded 1925 by Harold Ross (1892–1951), which contains an entertainment calendar, general articles, fiction, poetry, criticism, and cartoons. It has nurtured many writers, including Dorothy Parker, James Thurber, J D Salinger, John Updike, and S J Perelman.

As editor, Ross was succeeded 1952 by William Shawn (1907–), who was replaced 1987 by Robert Gottlieb (1931–), then president of the publishing firm Knopf, *The New Yorker* having been bought 1985 by the Newhouse conglomerate, owners of Knopf.

New York Times v Sullivan a US Supreme Court decision 1964 imposing limits on the power of public officials to bring libel suits against people who criticize their actions as public servants. The case was brought by Police Commissioner Sullivan of Montgomery, Alabama, in response to a paid advertisement in the *Times* that accused Sullivan's police force of brutality and repression. The Court ruled that Sullivan's case should not be sustained, finding unanimously that public officials cannot recover damages in libel suits without proof that defamatory falsehoods have been published intentionally and with actual malice.

New Zealand or ***Aotearoa*** country in the S Pacific, SE of Australia.

government New Zealand is a constitutional monarchy. As in Britain, the constitution is the gradual product of legislation, much of it passed by Parliament in London. The governor-general represents the British monarch as formal head of state and appoints the prime minister, who chooses the cabinet. All ministers are drawn from and collectively responsible to the single-chamber legislature, the House of Representatives. This has 97 members, including four ◊Maoris, elected by universal suffrage from single-member constituencies. It has a maximum life of three years and is subject to dissolution within that period. There are seven active political parties.

history New Zealand was occupied by the Polynesian ◊Maoris some time before the 14th century. ◊Tasman reached it 1642 but the Maoris would not let him land. ◊Cook explored the coasts 1769, 1773, and 1777. British missionaries began to arrive from 1815. By the Treaty of Waitangi 1840 the Maoris accepted British sovereignty; colonization began, and large-scale sheep farming was developed. The colony was granted self-government 1853. The Maoris resented the loss of their land and rose in revolt 1845–47 and 1860–72, until concessions were made, including representation in parliament. George Grey, governor 1845–53 and 1861–70 and Radical prime minister 1877–84, was largely responsible for the conciliation of the Maoris and the introduction of male suffrage.

The Conservatives held power 1879–90 and were succeeded by a Liberal government that ruled with labor union support; this government introduced women's suffrage 1893 and old-age pensions 1898, and was a pioneer in labor legislation. After 1912 the Reform (formerly Conservative) Party regained power, and the labor unions broke with the Liberals to form the Labour Party. The Reform and Liberal parties united to become the National Party 1931. New Zealand became a dominion in the British Empire 1907 and was granted full independence 1931. New Zealand troops had served in the Boer War in South Africa, and more than 100,000 fought in World Wars I and II. Independence was formally accepted by the New Zealand legislature 1947.

The country has a record of political stability, with the centrist National Party holding office from the 1930s until it was replaced by a Labor Party administration, led by Norman Kirk, in 1972. During this period New Zealand built up a good social security system. The economy was thriving at the time Kirk took office, but growing inflation was aggravated by the 1973–74 energy crisis that resulted in a balance-of-payments deficit. The Labour government's foreign policy line was influenced by the UK's decision to join the European Community, which was likely to affect New Zealand's future exports. It began a phased withdrawal from some of the country's military commitments in SE Asia and established diplomatic relations with China. Norman Kirk died Aug 1974 and was succeeded by the finance minister, Wallace Rowling. The state of the economy worsened, and in 1975 the National Party, led by Robert ◊Muldoon, was returned to power. However, the economy failed to revive, and in 1984 Muldoon introduced controversial labor legislation. To renew his mandate, he called an early election but was swept out of office by the Labor Party.

The Labour government elected Aug 1987 (with the same majority as in the previous parlia-

New Zealand

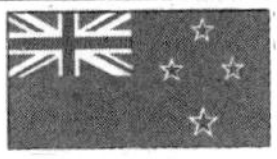

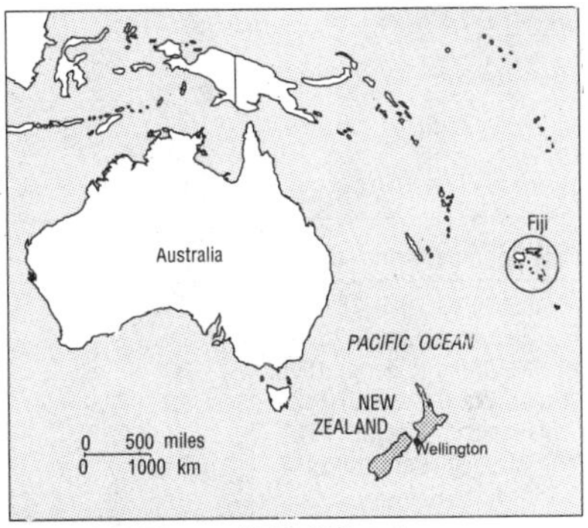
Australia
Fiji
PACIFIC OCEAN
NEW ZEALAND
Wellington
0 500 miles
0 1000 km

area 103,777 sq mi/268,680 sq km
capital Wellington
cities Hamilton, Palmerston North, Christchurch, Dunedin; ports Wellington, Auckland
physical comprises North Island, South Island, Stewart Island, Chatham Islands, and minor islands; mainly mountainous
overseas territories Tokelau (three atolls transferred 1926 from former Gilbert and Ellice Islands colony); Niue Island (one of the Cook Islands, separately administered from 1903: chief town Alafi); Cook Islands are internally self-governing but share common citizenship with New Zealand; Ross Dependency in Antarctica
features Ruapehu on North Island, 9,180 ft/2,797 m, highest of three active volcanoes; geysers and hot springs of the Rotorua district; Lake Taupo (238 sq mi/616 sq km), source of Waikato River; Kaingaroa state forest. On South Island are the Southern Alps and Canterbury Plains
head of state Elizabeth II from 1952 represented by governor-general
head of government Prime Minister Jim Bolger from 1990
political system constitutional monarchy
political parties Labour Party, moderate, left-of-center; New Zealand National Party, free enterprise, center-right
exports lamb, beef, wool, leather, dairy products, processed foods, kiwi fruit; seeds and breeding stock; timber, paper, pulp, light aircraft
currency New Zealand dollar
population (1990 est) 3,397,000 (European (mostly British) 87%; Polynesian (mostly Maori) 12%); growth rate 0.9% p.a.
life expectancy men 72, women 78 (1989)
language English (official); Maori
religion Protestant 50%, Roman Catholic 15%
literacy 99% (1989)
GNP $37 bn; $11,040 per head (1988)
chronology
1931 Granted independence from Britain.
1947 Full independence within the Commonwealth confirmed by the New Zealand parliament.
1972 National party government replaced Labour party, with Norman Kirk as prime minister.
1974 Kirk died; replaced by Wallace Rowling.
1975 National party returned, with Robert Muldoon as prime minister.
1984 Labour party returned under David Lange.
1985 Nonnuclear military policy created disagreements with France and the US.
1987 National party declared support for the Labour government's nonnuclear policy. Lange reelected. New Zealand officially became a "friendly" rather than "allied" country to the US because of its nonnuclear military policy.
1988 Free-trade agreement with Australia signed.
1989 Lange resigned over economic differences with finance minister; replaced by Geoffrey Palmer.
1990 Palmer replaced by Mike Moore. Labour party defeated by National party in general election; Jim Bolger becomes prime minister.

New Zealand

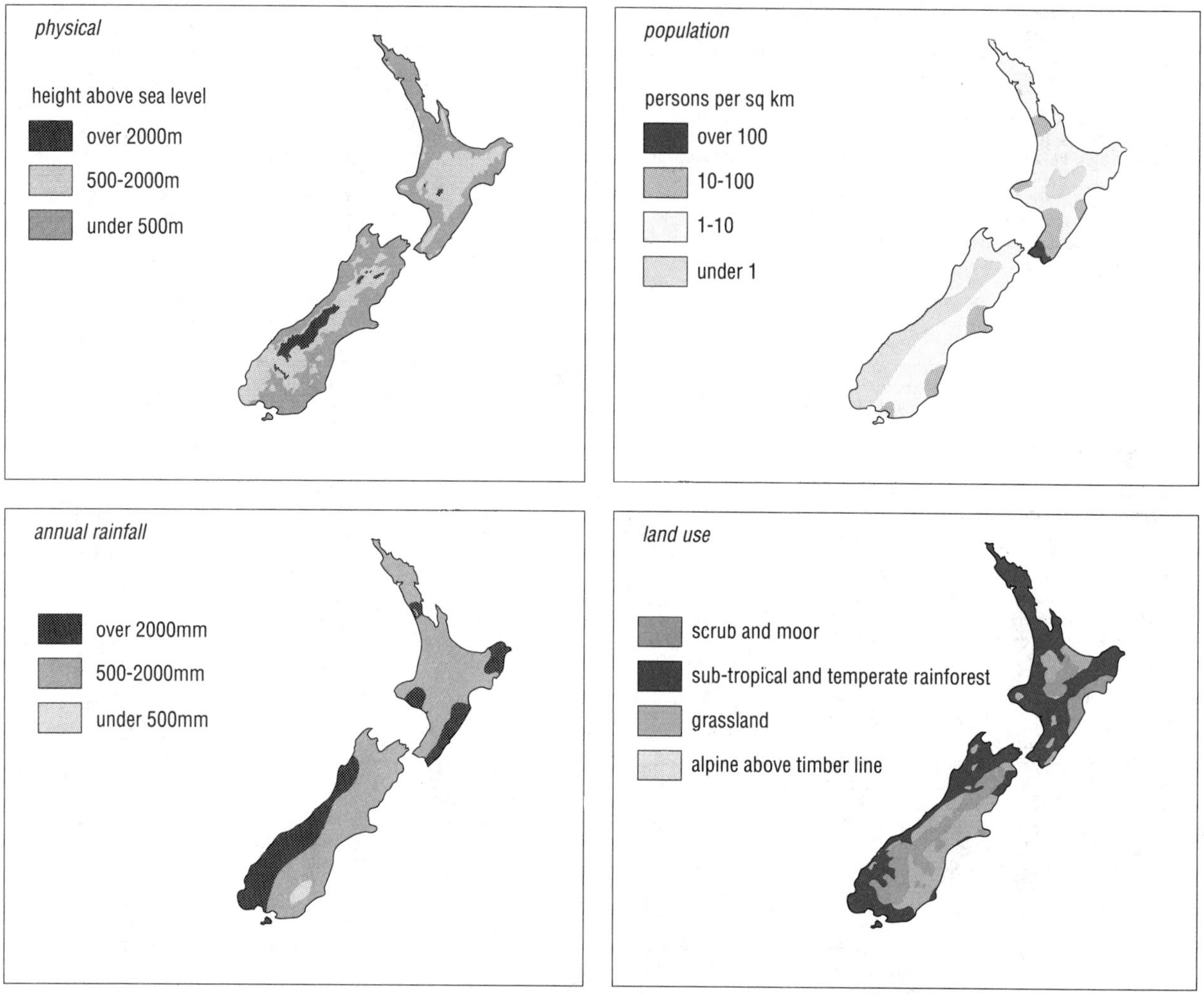
physical
height above sea level
over 2000m
500-2000m
under 500m
population
persons per sq km
over 100
10-100
1-10
under 1
annual rainfall
over 2000mm
500-2000mm
under 500mm
land use
scrub and moor
sub-tropical and temperate rainforest
grassland
alpine above timber line

ment) had fought the election on a nonnuclear defense policy, which its leader prime minister David Lange immediately put into effect, forbidding any vessels carrying nuclear weapons or powered by nuclear energy from entering New Zealand's ports. This put a strain on relations with the US, resulting in a suspension of several defense-related provisions of the ◊ANZUS pact. In 1985 the trawler *Rainbow Warrior*, the flagship of the environmentalist pressure group ◊Greenpeace, which was monitoring nuclear tests in French Polynesia, was mined in Auckland harbor by French secret service agents, killing a Portuguese photographer who had been aboard. The French prime minister eventually admitted responsibility, and New Zealand demanded compensation.

James McLay was leader of the National Party 1984–86, replaced by James Bolger. In the 1984 general election Labour won 56 seats in the House, and the National Party, 37. In July 1987 the National Party gave its support to the government in a bi-partisan nonnuclear policy, and as a result the US reclassified New Zealand as a "friendly," rather than an "allied" country. In Aug Lange was reelected with a majority of 17. In Aug 1989, Lange resigned, citing health reasons, and was replaced by Geoffrey Palmer. In Sept 1990, faced with a "no confidence" vote, Prime Minister Palmer resigned and was replaced by the former foreign affairs minister, Mike Moore. In the Oct general election the ruling Labour Party was defeated and the National Party leader, Jim Bolger, became the new prime minister.

New Zealand: prime ministers

J Ballance (Liberal) 1891
R J Seddon (Liberal) 1893
W Hall-Jones (Liberal) 1906
Joseph Ward (Liberal) 1906
T MacKenzie (Liberal) 1912
W F Massey (Reform) 1912
J G Coates (Reform) 1925
Joseph Ward (United) 1928
G W Forbes (United) 1930
M J Savage (Labour) 1935
P Fraser (Labour) 1940
S G Holland (National) 1949
K J Holyoake (National) 1957
Walter Nash (Labour) 1957
K J Holyoake (National) 1960
J Marshall (National) 1972
N Kirk (Labour) 1972
W Rowling (Labour) 1974
R Muldoon (National) 1975
D Lange (Labour) 1984
G Palmer (Labour) 1989
M Moore (Labour) 1990
J Bolger (National) 1990

New Zealand

	Area in sq km
North Island	114,700
South Island	149,800
Chatham Islands	960
Stewart Island	1,750
minor islands	823
	268,033
Island Territories	
Cook Islands	290
Niue	260
Ross Dependency	450,000
Tokelau	10

New Zealand literature prose and poetry of New Zealand. Among interesting pioneer records of the mid- to late 19th century are those of Edward Jerningham Wakefield and F E Maning; and *A First Year in Canterbury Settlement* by Samuel ◊Butler. Earliest of the popular poets was Thomas Bracken, author of the New Zealand national song, followed by native-born Jessie Mackay and W Pember Reeves, though the latter is better known as the author of the prose account of New Zealand *The Long White Cloud*; and Ursula Bethell (1874–1945). In the 20th century New Zealand literature gained an international appeal with the short stories of Katherine Mansfield, produced an exponent of detective fiction in Dame Ngaio ◊Marsh, and struck a specifically New Zealand note in *Tutira, the Story of a New Zealand Sheep Station* 1926, by W H Guthrie Smith (1861–1940). Poetry of a new quality was written by R A K Mason (1905–71) in the 1920s, and in the 1930s by a group of which A R D Fairburn (1904–57) with a witty conversational turn, and Allen Curnow (1911–), poet, critic, and anthologist, are the most striking. In fiction the 1930s were remarkable for the short stories of Frank Sargeson (1903–) and Roderick Finlayson (1904–), and the talent of John Mulgan (1911–45), who is remembered both for his novel

Man Alone, and for his posthumous factual account of World War II, in which he died, *Report on Experience* 1947. Kendrick Smithyman (1922–) struck a metaphysical note in poetry, James K Baxter (1926–72) published fluent lyrics, and Janet Frame (1924–) has a brooding depth of meaning in such novels as *The Rainbirds* 1968 and *Intensive Care* 1970. In 1985 Keri Hulme (1947–) won Britain's Booker Prize for her novel *The Bone People*.

Ney Michael, Duke of Elchingen, Prince of Ney 1769–1815. Marshal of France under ◊Napoleon I, who commanded the rearguard of the French army during the retreat from Moscow, and for his personal courage was called "the bravest of the brave." When Napoleon returned from Elba, Ney was sent to arrest him, but instead deserted to him and fought at Waterloo. He was subsequently shot for treason.

NF abbreviation for ◊Newfoundland.

Ngorongoro Crater crater in the Tanzanian section of the African Great ◊Rift Valley notable for its large numbers of wildebeest, gazelle, and zebra.

Ngugi wa Thiong'o 1938– . Kenyan writer of essays, plays, short stories, and novels. He was imprisoned after the performance of the play *Ngaahika Ndeenda/I Will Marry When I Want* 1977 and lived in exile from 1982. His novels, written in English and Gikuyu, include *The River Between*, *Petals of Blood*, and *Caitaani Muthara-ba-ini/Devil on the Cross*, and deal with colonial and post-independence oppression.

Nguyen Van Linh 1914– . Vietnamese communist politician, member of the Politburo 1976–81 and from 1985; party leader from 1986. He began economic liberalization and troop withdrawal from Cambodia and Laos.

Nguyen, born in North Vietnam, joined the anticolonial Thanh Nien, a forerunner of the current Communist Party of Vietnam (CPV), in Haiphong 1929. He spent much of his subsequent party career in the South as a pragmatic reformer. He was a member of CPV's Politburo and secretariat 1976–81, suffered a temporary setback when party conservatives gained the ascendancy, and reentered the Politburo in 1985, becoming CPV leader in Dec 1986.

NH abbreviation for ◊New Hampshire.

niacin one of the "B group" ◊vitamins, deficiency of which gives rise to ◊pellagra.

Niacin is the collective name for compounds that satisfy the dietary need for this function. Nicotinic acid ($C_5H_5N.COOH$) and nicotinamide ($C_5H_5N.CONH_2$) are both used by the body. Common natural sources are yeast, wheat, and meat.

Niagara Falls two waterfalls on the Niagara River, on the Canada-US border, between Lakes Erie and Ontario and separated by Goat Island. The American Falls are 167 ft/51 m high and 1,080 ft/330 m wide; Horseshoe Falls, in Canada, are curved 162 ft/49 m high and 2,600 ft/790 m across.

On the W bank of the river is Niagara Falls, a city in Ontario, Canada, population (1981) 71,000; on the E bank is Niagara Falls, New York State, population (1990) 61,840. They have hydroelectric generating plants, diversified industry, and tourism. The French explorer Samuel de Champlain may have seen Niagara Falls 1613, and Father Louis Hennepin viewed this natural wonder 1678. The use of hydroelectric power in North America was pioneered here 1881.

Niamey river port and capital of ◊Niger; population (1983) 399,000. It produces textiles, chemicals, pharmaceuticals, and foodstuffs.

Nibelungenlied *Song of the Nibelungs*, anonymous 12th-century German epic poem, derived from older sources. The composer Richard ◊Wagner made use of the legends in his *Ring* cycle.

◊Siegfried, possessor of the Nibelung treasure, marries Kriemhild (sister of Gunther of Worms) and wins Brunhild as a bride for Gunther. However, Gunther's vassal Hagen murders Siegfried, and Kriemhild achieves revenge by marrying Etzel (Attila) of the Huns, at whose court both Hagen and Gunther are killed.

Niagara Falls *The 1,000-ft/300-m-wide crest of the US section of Niagara Falls.*

Nicaea ruined city (modern Iznik) in Turkey, site of the Council of Nicaea AD 325.

Nicaea, Council of Christian church council held in Nicaea (now Iznik, Turkey) in 325, called by the Roman emperor Constantine. It condemned ◊Arianism as heretical and upheld the doctrine of the Trinity in the Nicene ◊Creed.

Nicaragua country in Central America, between the Pacific Ocean and the Caribbean, bounded N by Honduras and S by Costa Rica.

government The constitution dates from Jan 1987. The 96-member National Constituent Assembly is elected by universal suffrage through a system of proportional representation, and a president, also popularly elected, serves a six-year term, with the assistance of a vice-president and an appointed cabinet. The two main parties are the Sandinista National Liberation Front (FSLN) and the Democratic Conservative Party (PCD).

history For early history, see ◊American Indian. The first European to reach Nicaragua was Gil Gonzalez de Avila 1522, who brought it under Spanish rule. It remained Spanish until 1821 and was then briefly united with Mexico. Nicaragua achieved full independence 1838.

In 1912, at the Nicaraguan government's request, the US established military bases in the country. Their presence was opposed by a guerrilla group led by Augusto César Sandino. The US withdrew its forces 1933, but not before it had

Nicaragua
Republic of
(República de Nicaragua)

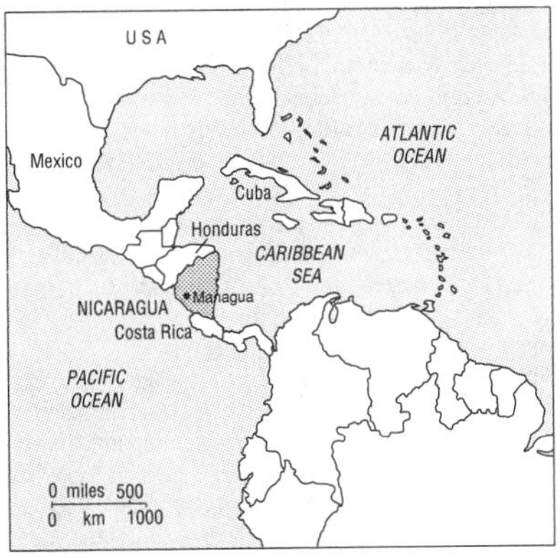
USA
ATLANTIC OCEAN
Mexico
Cuba
Honduras
CARIBBEAN SEA
NICARAGUA
Managua
Costa Rica
PACIFIC OCEAN
0 miles 500
0 km 1000

area 49,363 sq mi/127,849 sq km
capital Managua
cities León, Granada; chief ports Corinto, Puerto Cabezas, El Bluff
physical narrow Pacific coastal plain separated from broad Atlantic coastal plain by volcanic mountains and lakes Managua and Nicaragua
features largest state of Central America and most thinly populated; Mosquito Coast, Fonseca Bay, Corn Islands
head of state and government Violeta Barrios de Chamorro from April 1990
political system emergent democracy
political parties Sandinista National Liberation Front (FSLN), Marxist-Leninist; Democratic Conservative Party (PCD), centrist; National Opposition Union (UNO), loose, US-backed coalition
exports coffee, cotton, sugar, bananas, meat
currency cordoba
population (1990) 3,606,000 (70% mestizo, 15% Spanish descent, 10% Indian or black); growth rate 3.3% p.a.
life expectancy men 61, women 63 (1989)
language Spanish (official), Indian, English
religion Roman Catholic 95%
literacy 66% (1986)
GNP $2.1 bn; $610 per head (1988)
chronology
1838 Independence achieved from Spain.
1926–1933 Occupied by US marines.
1962 Sandinista National Liberation Front (FSLN) formed to fight Somoza regime.
1979 Somoza government ousted by FSLN.
1982 Subversive activity against the government promoted by the US. State of emergency declared.
1984 The US mined Nicaraguan harbors.
1985 Denunciation of Sandinista government by US president Reagan. FSLN won assembly elections.
1987 Central American peace agreement cosigned by Nicaraguan leaders.
1988 Peace agreement failed. Nicaragua held talks with Contra rebel leaders. Hurricane left 180,000 people homeless.
1989 Demobilization of rebels and release of former Somozan supporters; Ortega ended cease-fire with Contras.
1990 FSLN defeated by UNO, a US-backed coalition; Violeta Chamorro elected president. Antigovernment riots.

set up and trained a national guard, commanded by a trusted nominee, General Anastasio Somoza. Sandino was assassinated 1934, reputedly on Somoza's orders, but some of his followers continued their guerrilla activity.

The Somoza family began a near-dictatorial rule that was to last for over 40 years. During this time they developed wide business interests and amassed a huge personal fortune. General Anastasio Somoza was elected president 1936 and stayed in office until his assassination 1956, when he was succeeded by his son Luis. The left-wing FSLN, named after the former guerrilla leader, was formed 1962 with the object of overthrowing the Somozas by revolution. Luis Somoza was followed by his brother Anastasio, who headed an even more notorious regime. In 1979, after considerable violence and loss of life, Somoza was ousted, fled the country, and was assassinated 1980 in Paraguay. The FSLN established a provisional junta of national reconstruction led by Daniel Ortega Saavedra, published a guarantee of civil rights, and appointed a council of state, prior to an elected national assembly and a new constitution.

Nicaragua's relations with the US deteriorated rapidly with the election of President Reagan. He froze the package of economic assistance arranged by his predecessor, Jimmy ◊Carter, alleging that the Sandinista government was supporting attempts to overthrow the administration in El Salvador. In March 1982 the Nicaraguan government declared a state of emergency in the wake of attacks on bridges and petroleum installations. The Reagan administration embarked on a policy of destabilizing Nicaragua's government and economy by actively supporting the counter-revolutionary forces (the Contras)—known to have executed prisoners, killed civilians, and engaged in forced conscription—and by covert ◊Central Intelligence Agency operations, including the mining of Nicaraguan harbors 1984. In Feb 1985 Reagan denounced Ortega's regime, saying that his objective was to "remove it in the sense of its present structure." In May 1986 Eden Pastora, a Contra leader, gave up the fight against the Sandinistas and was granted asylum in Costa Rica. The following month the US Congress approved $100 million in overt military aid to the Contras.

Political parties have ostensibly been legalized under the terms of a regional peace plan signed by the presidents of El Salvador, Guatemala, Costa Rica, Honduras, and Nicaragua, and peace talks with the Contra rebels have had several false starts. In March 1989 1,900 members of the former National Guard of Anastasia Somoza were released. In June 1989, an electoral council was named in preparation for 1990 elections. By mid-1989, there were 17 parties cleared to participate in the balloting. Despite international concern about the viability of the promised elections, they were held Feb 1990 and brought a victory by Violeta Barrios de Chamorra of the US-backed National Opposition Union (UNO). In July 1990 violent riots occurred as people protested about land rights, inflation and unemployment. Eventually a peace agreement was reached.

Nicaragua, Lake lake in Nicaragua, the largest in Central America; area 3,185 sq mi/8,250 sq km.

Nicaraguan Revolution the revolt 1978–79 in Nicaragua, led by the Socialist Sandinistas against the US-supported right-wing dictatorship established by Anastasio ◊Somoza. His son, President Anastasio (Debayle) Somoza (1925–1980), was forced into exile 1979 and assassinated in Paraguay. The Sandinista National Liberation Front (FSLN) is named after Augusto César Sandino, a guerrilla leader killed by the US-trained National Guard 1934.

Nice city on the French Riviera; population (1982) 449,500. Founded in the 3rd century BC, it repeatedly changed hands between France and the Duchy of Savoy from the 14th to the 19th century. In 1860 it was finally transferred to France.

Nicholas II *Tsar Nicholas II of Russia in his youth.*

There is an annual Battle of Flowers, and chocolate and perfume are made. Chapels in the nearby village of Vence have been decorated by Marc Chagall and Henri Matisse, and Nice has a Chagall museum.

Nicene Creed one of the fundamental creeds of Christianity, promulgated by the Council of ◊Nicaea 325.

niche in ecology, the "place" occupied by a species in its habitat, including all chemical, physical, and biological components, such as what it eats, the time of day at which the species feeds, temperature, moisture, the parts of the habitat that it uses (for example, trees or open grassland), the way it reproduces, and how it behaves. It is believed that no two species can occupy exactly the same niche, because they would be in direct competition for the same resources at every stage of their life cycle.

Nichiren 1222–1282. Japanese Buddhist monk, founder of the sect that bears his name. It bases its beliefs on the *Lotus Sūtra*, which Nichiren held to be the only true revelation of the teachings of Buddha, and stresses the need for personal effort to attain enlightenment.

Nicholas two tsars of Russia:

Nicholas I 1796–1855. Tsar of Russia from 1825. His Balkan ambitions led to war with Turkey 1827–29 and the Crimean War 1853–56.

Nicholas II 1868–1918. Tsar of Russia 1894–1917. He was dominated by his wife, Princess Alix of Hessen (Tsarina ◊Alexandra), who was under the influence of ◊Rasputin. His mismanagement of the Russo-Japanese War and of internal affairs led to the revolution of 1905, which he suppressed, although he was forced to grant limited constitutional reforms. He took Russia into World War I in 1914, was forced to abdicate in 1917 (see ◊Rusysian Revolution) and was executed with his family.

Nicholas, St (also known as Santa Claus) 4th century AD. In the Christian church, patron saint of Russia, children, merchants, sailors, and pawnbrokers; bishop of Myra (now in Turkey). His legendary gifts of dowries to poor girls led to the custom of giving gifts to children on the eve of his feast day, Dec 6, still retained in some countries, such as the Netherlands; elsewhere the custom has been transferred to Christmas Day. His emblem is three balls.

Nicholas of Cusa 1401–1464. German philosopher, involved in the transition from scholasticism to the philosophy of modern times. He argued that knowledge is learned ignorance (*docta ignorantia*) since God, the ultimate object of knowledge, is above the opposites by which human reason grasps the objects of nature. He also asserted that the universe is boundless and has no circumference, thus breaking with medieval cosmology.

Nicholson Ben 1894–1982. English abstract artist. After early experiments influenced by Cubism and *de Stijl* (see ◊Mondrian), Nicholson developed a

Nicholson *Versatile film actor Jack Nicholson as the Joker in* Batman *1989.*

style of geometrical reliefs, notably a series of white reliefs (from 1933).

Nicholson Jack 1937– . US film actor who, in the late 1960s, captured the mood of nonconformist, uncertain young Americans in such films as *Easy Rider* 1969 and *Five Easy Pieces* 1970. He subsequently became a mainstream Hollywood star, appearing in *Chinatown* 1974, *One Flew over the Cuckoo's Nest* (Academy Award) 1975, *The Shining* 1979, *Terms of Endearment* (Academy Award) 1983, and *Batman* 1989.

nickel a hard, malleable and ductile, silver-white metallic element, symbol Ni, atomic number 28, atomic weight 58.71. It occurs in igneous rocks and as a free metal (◊native metal), occasionally occurring in fragments of iron-nickel meteorites. It is a component of the Earth's core, which is held to consist principally of iron with some nickel. It has a high melting point, low electrical and thermal conductivity, and can be magnetized. It does not tarnish and therefore is much used for alloys, electroplating, and for coinage.

It was discovered in 1751 by Swedish mineralogist A F Cronstedt and the name given as an abbreviated form of *Kopparnickel*, Swedish for false copper, since the ore in which it is found resembles copper but yields none.

nickel ore any mineral ore from which nickel is obtained. The main minerals are arsenides such as chloanthite ($NiAs_2$), and the sulfides millerite (NiS) and pentlandite $(Ni,Fe)_9S_8$, the commonest ore. The chief nickel-producing countries are Canada, the USSR, Cuba, and Australia.

Nicklaus Jack (William) 1940– . US golfer, nicknamed "the Golden Bear." He won a record 20 major titles, including 18 professional majors between 1962 and 1986.

Nicklaus played for the US Ryder Cup team six times 1969–81 and was nonplaying captain 1983 and 1987 when the event was played over the course he designed at Muirfield Village, Ohio. He was voted the "Golfer of the Century" 1988.

CAREER HIGHLIGHTS

US Amateur: 1959, 1961
US Open: 1962, 1967, 1972, 1980
British Open: 1966, 1970, 1978
US Masters: 1963, 1965–66, 1972, 1975, 1986
US PGA: 1963, 1971, 1973, 1975, 1980
US Ryder Cup team: 1969, 1971, 1973, 1975, 1977

Nicobar Islands group of Indian islands, part of the Union Territory of ◊Andaman and Nicobar Islands.

Nicolle Charles 1866–1936. French bacteriologist whose discovery in 1909 that typhus is transmitted by the body louse made the armies of World War I introduce delousing as a compulsory part of the military routine.

His original observation was that typhus victims, once admitted to hospitals, did not infect the staff; he speculated that transmission must be via the skin or clothes, which were washed as standard procedure for new admissions. The experimental evidence was provided by infecting a healthy monkey using a louse recently fed on an infected chimpanzee.

Nicolson Harold 1886–1968. British author and diplomat. His works include biographies (*Lord Carnock* 1930; *Curzon: The Last Phase* 1934; and *King George V* 1952) and studies such as *Monarchy* 1962, as well as *Diaries and Letters 1930–62*. He married Vita ◊Sackville-West in 1913.

Nicosia capital of Cyprus, with leather, textile, and pottery industries; population (1987) 165,000. Nicosia was the residence of Lusignan kings of Cyprus 1192–1475. The Venetians, who took Cyprus 1489, surrounded Nicosia with a high wall, that still exists; it fell to the Turks 1571. It was again partly taken by the Turks in the invasion 1974.

nicotine $C_{10}H_{14}N_2$ an ◊alkaloid (nitrogenous compound) obtained from the dried leaves of the tobacco plant *Nicotiana tabacum* and used as an insecticide. A colorless oil, soluble in water, it turns brown on exposure to the air.

Nicotine in its pure form is one of the most powerful poisons known. It is named after a 16th-century French diplomat, Jacques Nicot, who introduced tobacco to France. It is the component of cigarette smoke that causes physical addiction.

Niebuhr Barthold Georg 1776–1831. German historian. He was Prussian ambassador in Rome 1816–23, and professor of Roman history at Bonn until 1831. His three-volume *History of Rome* 1811–32 critically examined original sources.

Niebuhr Karsten 1733–1815. Danish map-maker, surveyor, and traveler, sent by the Danish government to explore the Arabian peninsula 1761–67.

Niebuhr Reinhold 1892–1971. US Protestant theologian. An ordained Lutheran minister, he taught for more than 30 years at the Union Theological Seminary in New York City. He was a noted pacifist, activist, and Socialist but advocated the war to stop totalitarianism in the 1940s. From 1945 he founded Americans for Democratic Action and became an adviser to the State Department.

Originally a strong exponent of Christian socialism, he became increasingly pessimistic about the possibility of achieving it, given humanity's irreducible egoistic pride, which he identified with original sin. He came to believe that liberal democracy must be sustained not because it can bring about human perfection but as a way of avoiding the systematic cruelty that comes with unrestrained power. His *Moral Man and Immoral Society* 1932 attacked depersonalized modern industrial society but denied the possibility of fulfilling religious and political utopian aspirations, a position that came to be known as Christian Realism.

Niederösterreich German name for the federal state of ◊Lower Austria.

Niedersachsen German name for the region of ◊Lower Saxony, Federal Republic of Germany.

nielsbohrium name proposed by Soviet scientists for the element currently known as ◊unnilpentium (atomic number 105), to honor Danish physicist Niels Bohr.

Nielsen Carl (August) 1865–1931. Danish composer. His works show a progressive tonality, as in his opera *Saul and David* 1902 and six symphonies.

He also composed concertos for violin 1911 and clarinet 1928, chamber music, piano works, and songs.

Niemeyer Oscar 1907– . Brazilian architect, joint designer of the United Nations headquarters in New York City, and of many buildings in Brasilia, capital of Brazil.

Niemöller Martin 1892–1984. German Christian Protestant pastor. He was imprisoned in a concentration camp 1938–45 for campaigning against Nazism in the German church. He was president of the World Council of Churches 1961–68.

Nietzsche *German author Friedrich Nietzsche's writings had considerable influence on modern literature, philosophy, psychoanalysis, and religion.*

NIEO abbreviation for New International Economic Order.

Niepce (Joseph) Nicéphore 1765–1833. French pioneer of photography. Niepce invented heliography, a precursor of photography that fixed images onto pewter plates coated with pitch and required eight-hour expòsures.

He produced the world's first photographs in the early to mid-1820s but his earliest surviving photograph dates from 1827. He later collaborated with ◊Daguerre on the faster daguerreotype process.

Nietzsche Friedrich Wilhelm 1844–1900. German philosopher who rejected the accepted absolute moral values and the "slave morality" of Christianity. He argued that "God is dead" and therefore people were free to create their own values. His ideal was the *Übermensch*, or "Superman," who would impose his will on the weak and worthless. Nietzsche claimed that knowledge is never objective but always serves some interest or unconscious purpose.

His insights into the relation between thought and language were a major influence on philosophy. Although claimed as a precursor by Nazism, many of his views are incompatible with totalitarian ideology. He is a profoundly ambivalent thinker whose philosophy can be appropriated for many purposes.

Born in Röcken, Saxony, he attended Bonn and Leipzig universities and was professor of Greek at Basel, Switzerland, 1869–80. He had abandoned theology for philology, and was influenced by the writings of Schopenhauer and the music of Wagner, of whom he became both friend and advocate. Both these attractions passed, however, and ill-health caused his resignation from the university. He spent his later years in northern Italy, in the Engadine, and in southern France. He published *Morgenröte/The Dawn* 1880–81, *Die fröhliche Wissenschaft/The Gay Science* 1881–82, *Also sprach Zarathustra/Thus Spoke Zarathustra* 1883–85, *Jenseits von Gut und Böse/Between Good and Evil* 1885–86, *Zur Genealogie der Moral/Toward a Genealogy of Morals* 1887, and *Ecce Homo* 1888. He suffered a permanent breakdown in 1889 from overwork and loneliness.

Nièvre river in central France, rising near Varzy and flowing 25 mi/40 km S to join the river Loire at Nevers; it gives its name to a *département*.

Niger third longest river in Africa, 2,600 mi/ 4,185 km from the highlands bordering Sierra Leone and Guinea NE through Mali, then SE through Niger and Nigeria to an inland delta on the Gulf of Guinea. Its flow has been badly affected by the expansion of the Sahara Desert. It is sluggish and frequently floods its banks. It was explored by Mungo Park 1795–96.

Niger landlocked country in W Africa, bounded N by Nigeria and Libya, E by Chad, S by Nigeria and Benin, and W by Burkina Faso and Mali.

government The 1960 constitution was suspended after a military coup in 1974, and Niger is now ruled by a supreme military council of army officers and a council of ministers appointed by the president, who is head of state as well as head of government and also combines the portfolios of interior and national defense. In a move toward greater democracy, the National Development Council, of 150 elected members, was reconstituted 1983 and given the task of drawing up a national charter. A new constitution was approved in Sept, and the first elections since independence in 1960 were held in Dec, with President Ali running without opposition.

Niger
Republic of
(République du Niger)

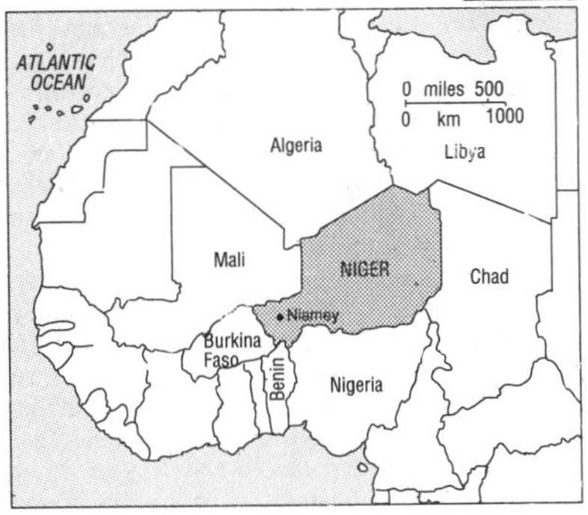
ATLANTIC OCEAN
0 miles 500
0 km 1000
Algeria
Libya
Mali
NIGER
Chad
Niamey
Burkina Faso
Benin
Nigeria

area 457,953 sq mi/1,186,408 sq km
capital Niamey
cities Zinder, Maradi, Tahoua
physical desert plains between hills in N and savanna in S; river Niger in SW, Lake Chad in SE
features part of the Sahara Desert and subject to Sahel droughts
head of state and government Mamane Oumarou from 1988
political system military republic
political parties banned from 1974
exports peanuts, livestock, gum arabic, uranium
currency franc CFA
population (1990 est) 7,691,000; growth rate 2.8% p.a.
life expectancy men 48, women 50 (1989)
language French (official), Hausa, Djerma, and other minority languages
religion Sunni Muslim 85%, animist 15%
literacy men 19%/women 9% (1985 est)
GNP $2.2 bn; $310 per head (1987)
chronology
1960 Achieved full independence from France; Hamani Diori elected president.
1974 Diori ousted in army coup led by Seyni Kountché.
1977 Cooperation agreement signed with France.
1987 Kountché died and was replaced by Col Ali Seybou.
1990 Multiparty politics promised.

Nigeria
Federal Republic of

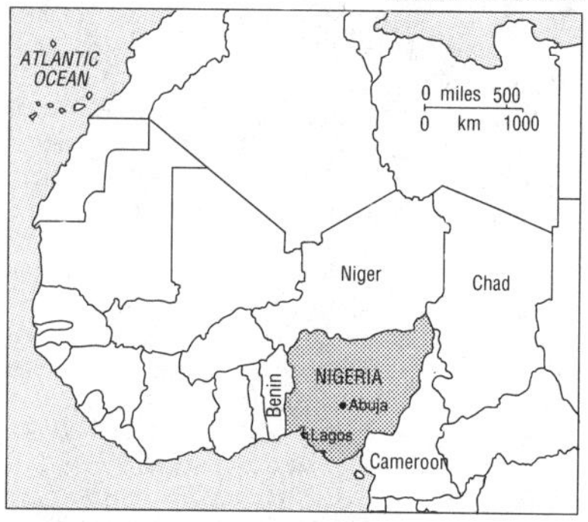
ATLANTIC OCEAN
0 miles 500
0 km 1000
Niger
Chad
Benin
NIGERIA
Abuja
Lagos
Cameroo

area 356,576 sq mi/923,773 sq km
capital (and chief port) Lagos
cities administrative headquarters Ibadan, Ogbomosho, Kano; ports Port Harcourt, Warri, Calabar
physical arid savanna in N; tropical rainforest in S, with mangrove swamps along the coast; river Niger forms wide delta; mountains in SE
features harmattan (dry wind from the Sahara); rich artistic heritage; for example, Benin bronzes
head of state and government Ibrahim Babangida from 1985
political system military authoritarianism pending promised elections
political parties Social Democratic Party (SDP), left-of-center; National Republican Convention (NRC), right-of-center
exports petroleum (largest oil resources in Africa), cocoa, peanuts, palm oil (Africa's largest producer), cotton, rubber, tin
currency naira
population (1990 est) 118,865,000 (Yoruba in W , Ibo in E, and Hausa-Fulani in N); growth rate 3.3% p.a.
life expectancy men 47, women 49 (1989)
language English (official), Hausa, Ibo, Yoruba
religion Sunni Muslim (50%) in N, Christian (40%) in S, local beliefs (10%)
literacy men 54%/women 31% (1985 est)
GNP $78 bn (1987); $790 per head (1984)
chronology
1914 N Nigeria and S Nigeria united to become Britain's largest African colony.
1954 Nigeria became a federation.
1960 Independence achieved from Britain within the Commonwealth.
1963 Became a republic, with Nnamdi Azikiwe as president.
1966 Military coup, followed by a counter-coup led by Gen Yakubu Gowon. Slaughter of many members of the Ibo tribe in N.
1967 Conflict over oil revenues led to declaration of an independent state of Biafra and outbreak of civil war.
1970 Surrender of Biafra and end of civil war.
1975 Gowon ousted in military coup; second coup puts Gen Obasanjo in power.
1979 Shehu Shagari became civilian president.
1983 Shagari's government overthrown in coup by Maj-Gen Buhari.
1985 Buhari replaced in a bloodless coup led by Maj-Gen Ibrahim Babangida.
1989 Two new parties approved. Babangida promised a return to pluralist politics; date set for 1992.

history Niger was part of ancient and medieval empires in ◊Africa. European explorers arrived in the late 18th century, and Tuareg people invaded the area from the north. France seized it from the Tuaregs 1904 and made it part of ◊French West Africa, although fighting continued until 1922. It became a French overseas territory 1946 and an autonomous republic within the French Community 1958.

Niger achieved full independence in 1960, and Hamani Diori was elected president. Maintaining close relations with France, Diori seemed to have established one of the most stable regimes in Africa, and the discovery of uranium deposits promised a sound economic future. However, a severe drought 1968–74 resulted in widespread civil disorder, and in April 1974 Diori was ousted by the army led by the chief of staff, Lt-Col Seyni Kountché. Having suspended the constitution and established a military government with himself as president, he tried to restore the economy and negotiated a more equal relationship with France through a cooperation agreement 1977.

Still threatened by possible droughts and consequential unrest, Kountché has tried to widen his popular support by liberalizing his regime and releasing political prisoners, including former President Diori. More civilians have been introduced into the government with the prospect of an eventual return to constitutional rule. When Lt-Col Seyni Kountché died in 1987, the Supreme Military Council appointed Col Ali Seybou acting president. He was elected without opposition in elections 1989.

In July 1990 the government announced plans for the introduction of a multiparty political system and in Nov these were endorsed by President Ali Saibu.

Nigeria country in W Africa on the Gulf of Guinea, bounded N by Niger, E by Chad and Cameroon, and W by Benin.

government The constitution is based on one of 1979, amended after military coups 1983 and 1985. The president is head of state, Commander in Chief of the armed forces, and chair of the 28-member Armed Forces Ruling Council (AFRC), composed of senior officers of the army and police force. The AFRC appoints the National Council of Ministers, which is also headed by the president.

Nigeria is a federal republic of 19 states. Each of the states has a military governor, appointed by the AFRC, who in turn appoints and leads a state executive council. There is also a coordinating federal body called the National Council of States, which includes the president and all the state governors.

history Nigeria has been inhabited since at least 700 BC. In the 12th–14th centuries civilizations developed in the Yoruba area and, in the Muslim north, Portuguese and British slave traders raided from the 15th century (see ◊slavery).

◊Lagos was supposedly bought from a chief by British traders in 1861; in 1886 it became the colony and protectorate of Lagos. The Niger River valley was developed by the National African Company (later the Royal Niger Company), which ceased 1899, and in 1900 two protectorates were set up: N Nigeria and S Nigeria, with Lagos joined to S Nigeria 1906. Britain's largest African colony, Nigeria, was united 1914.

Nigeria became a federation 1954 and achieved full independence, as a constitutional monarchy within the ◊Commonwealth, in 1960. In 1963 it became a republic, based on a federal structure so as to accommodate the many different ethnic groups, which included the Ibo, the Yoruba, the Aro, the Angas, and the Hausa. Nigeria's first president was Dr Nnamdi Azikiwe, a banker and proprietor of a newspaper group, who had played a leading part in the movement for independence. He came from the Ibo tribe. His chief rival was Abubakar ◊Tafawa Balewa, who was prime minister from 1957 until he was assassinated in a military coup in 1966. The coup had been led mainly by Ibo junior officers from the eastern region, which had become richer after the discovery of oil there in 1958. The offices of president and prime minister were suspended, and it was announced that the state's federal structure would be abandoned. Before this could be done, the new military government was overturned in a counter-coup by a mostly Christian group from the north, led by Col Yakubu ◊Gowon. He reestablished the federal system and appointed a military governor for each region. Soon afterwards tens of thousands of Ibos in the north were killed.

In 1967 a conflict developed between Gowon and the military governor of the eastern region, Col Chukwuemeka Odumegwu-Ojukwu, about the distribution of oil revenues, which resulted in Ojukwu's declaration of an independent Ibo state of ◊Biafra. Gowon, after failing to pacify the Ibos, ordered federal troops into the eastern region, and a civil war began, lasting until Jan 1970, when Biafra surrendered to the federal forces. It was the first war among black Africans, and it left the economy gravely weakened. Warfare and famine together took an estimated 1 million lives.

In 1975, while he was out of the country, Gowon was replaced in a bloodless coup led by Brigadier Murtala Mohammad, but he was killed within a month and replaced by Gen Olusegun Obasanjo. He announced a gradual return to civilian rule, and in 1979 the leader of the National Party of Nigeria, Shehu Shagari, became president. In Dec 1983, with the economy suffering from falling oil prices, Shagari's civilian government was deposed in another bloodless coup, led by Maj-Gen Mohammedu Buhari. In 1985 another peaceful coup replaced Buhari with a new military government, led by Maj-Gen Ibrahim Babangida, the army Chief of Staff. At the end of the year an attempted coup by rival officers was thwarted.

President Babangida promised a return to a democratic civilian government in 1992, although in an effort to end the corruption that has existed since independence, he has banned all persons who have ever held elective office from being candidates for the new civilian government. The ban on political activity was also lifted May 1989, but the government has rejected the applications of former political associations for recognition as political parties, instead creating two official parties, one to the left and one to the right of the political spectrum. An official population policy encouraging mothers to have no more than four children was ratified in 1988. Half the population is under 15. In 1990 inflation was running at 51%. Austerity measures, prescribed by the IMF in response to economic assistance, created widespread dissatisfaction with the government.

nightingale songbird of the thrush family with a song of great beauty, heard at night as well as by day. About 6.5 in/16.5 cm long, it is dull brown, lighter below, with a reddish-brown tail. It migrates to Europe and winters in Africa. It feeds on insects and small animals.

Nightingale Florence 1820–1910. English nurse, the founder of nursing as a profession. She took a team of nurses to Scutari (now Üsküdar, Turkey) in 1854 and reduced the ◊Crimean War hospital death rate from 42% to 2%. In 1856 she founded the Nightingale School and Home for Nurses in London.

nightjar any of about 65 species of night-hunting birds forming the family Caprimulgidae. They have wide, bristly mouths for catching flying insects. Their distinctive calls have earned them such names as whippoorwill and church-will's-widow. Some are called nighthawks.

The whippoorwill of North America *Caprimulgus vociferus* measures about 10 in/25 cm in length, and is mottled gray-brown.

Night Journey or ***al-Miraj*** (Arabic "the ascent") in Islam, the journey of the prophet Mohammed, guided by the archangel Gabriel, from Mecca to Jerusalem, where he met the earlier prophets, including Adam, Moses, and Jesus; he then ascended to paradise, where he experienced the majesty of Allah, and was also shown hell.

***Nightingale** A pencil drawing of British nurse Florence Nightingale.*

nightshade any of several plants in the family Solanaceae, which includes the black nightshade *Solanum nigrum*, bittersweet or woody nightshade *S. dulcamara*, and deadly nightshade or ◊belladonna.

Nihilist member of a group of Russian revolutionaries in the reign of Alexander II 1855–81. The name, popularized by the writer Turgenev, means "one who approves of nothing" (Latin *nihil*) belonging to the existing order. In 1878 the Nihilists launched a guerrilla campaign leading to the murder of the tsar 1881.

Niigata industrial port (textiles, metals, oil refining, chemicals) in Chuburegion, Honshu island, Japan; population (1984) 459,000.

Nijinsky Vaslav 1890–1950. Russian dancer and choreographer. Noted for his powerful but graceful technique, he was a legendary member of ◊Diaghilev's Ballets Russes, for whom he choreographed Debussy's *Prélude à l'Après-midi d'un faune* 1912 and *Jeux* 1913, and Stravinsky's *The Rite of Spring* 1913. He also took lead roles in ballets such as *Petrushka* 1911. He rejected conventional forms of Classical ballet in favor of free expression. His sister was the choreographer Bronislava Nijinska (1891–1972).

***Nijinsky** The great Russian dancer and choreographer Vaslav Nijinsky as "Le Dieu Blau" in 1912. He rejected the forms of Classical ballet in favor of free expression.*

Nile River

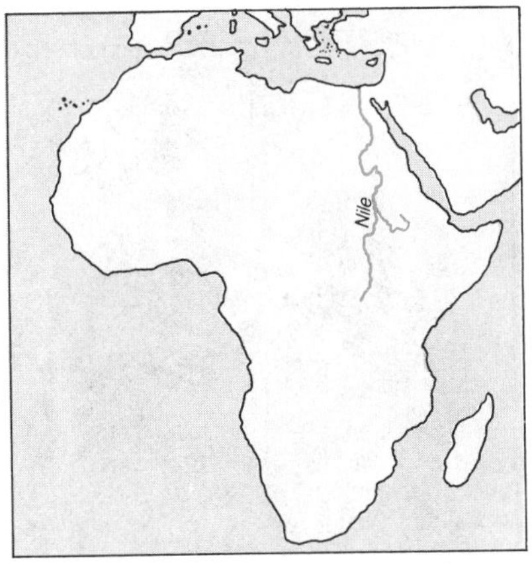
Nile

Nijmegen industrial city (brewery, electrical engineering, leather, tobacco) in E Netherlands, on the river Waal; population (1988) 241,000. The Roman Noviomagus, Nijmegen was a free city of the Holy Roman Empire and a member of the Hanseatic League.

Nijmegen, Treaties of peace treaties 1678–79 between France on the one hand and the Netherlands, Spain, and the Holy Roman Empire on the other, ending the Third Dutch War.

Nike in Greek mythology, goddess of victory, represented as "winged," as in the statue from Samothrace in the Louvre, Paris. One of the most beautiful architectural monuments of Athens was the temple of Nike Apteros.

Nikolayev port (with shipyards) and naval base on the Black Sea, Ukraine, USSR; population (1987) 501,000.

Nile river in Africa, the world's longest, 4,160 mi/6,695 km. The Blue Nile rises in Lake Tana, Ethiopia, the White Nile at Lake Victoria, and they join at Khartoum, Sudan. It enters the Mediterranean at a vast delta in N Egypt.

Its remotest headstream is the Luvironza, in Burundi. The Nile proper begins on leaving Lake Victoria above ◊Owen Falls. From Lake Victoria it flows over rocky country, and there are many cataracts and rapids, including the Murchison Falls, until it enters Lake Mobutu (Albert). From here it flows across flat country and in places spreads out to form lakes. At Lake No it is joined by the Bahr el Ghazal, and from this point to Khartoum it is called the White Nile. At Khartoum it is joined by the Blue Nile, which rises in the Ethiopian highlands, and 200 mi/320 km below Khartoum it is joined by the Atbara. From Khartoum to ◊Aswan there are six cataracts. The Nile is navigable to the second cataract, a distance of 960 mi/1,545 km. The delta of the Nile is 120 mi/190 km wide. From 1982 Nile water has been piped beneath the Suez Canal to irrigate ◊Sinai. The water level behind the Aswan Dam fell from 558 ft/170 m (1979) to 492 ft/150 m (1988), threatening Egypt's hydroelectric power generation.

Nile, Battle of the alternate name for the Battle of Aboukir Bay Aug 1, 1798, in which Nelson defeated Napoleon's fleet, thus ending the projected French conquest of the Middle East.

nilgai large antelope *Boselaphus tragocamelus* native to India. The bull has short conical horns and is bluish-gray. The female is brown.

Nîmes capital of Gard *département*, Languedoc-Roussillon, S France; population (1982) 132,500. Roman remains include an amphitheater dating from the 2nd century and the Pont du Gard (aqueduct). The city gives its name to the cloth known as denim (de Nîmes); it is the birthplace of the writer Alphonse Daudet.

Nimitz Chester William 1885–1966. US admiral, commander in chief of the US Pacific fleet. He reconquered the Solomon Islands 1942–43, Gilbert Islands 1943, the Marianas and Marshalls 1944, and signed the Japanese surrender 1945 as the US representative.

Nin Anaïs 1903–1977. US novelist and diarist. Her extensive and impressionistic diaries, published 1966–76, reflect her interest in dreams, which along with psychoanalysis are recurring themes of her gently erotic novels (such as *House of Incest* 1936 and *A Spy in the House of Love* 1954).

Born in Paris, she started out as a model and dancer, but later took up the study of psychoanalysis. She emigrated to the US in 1940, becoming a prominent member of Greenwich Village literary society in New York.

Nineteen Eighty-Four a futuristic novel by George Orwell, published 1949, which tells of an individual's battle against, and eventual surrender to, a totalitarian state where Big Brother rules. It is a dystopia (the opposite of utopia) and many of the words and concepts in it have passed into common usage (newspeak, doublethink, thought police).

Nineteen Propositions demands presented by the English Parliament to Charles I 1642. They were designed to limit the powers of the crown, and their rejection represented the beginning of the Civil War.

Nineveh capital of the Assyrian Empire from the 8th century BC until its destruction by the Medes under King Cyaxares in 612 BC, as forecast by the Old Testament prophet Nahum. It was situated on the river Tigris (opposite the present city of Mosul, Iraq) and was adorned with palaces.

Excavations from 1842 onward by Emile Botta (1802–70), French consul in Iraq, and the British archeologist Austen Layard brought to light the ruins of Nineveh (including the library of King Ashurbanipal) under the mounds, or tells, of Kuyunjik and Nebi Yunus.

Ningbo or ***Ningpo*** port and special economic zone in Zhejiang province, E China; industries (fishing, shipbuilding, high-tech); population (1984) 615,600. Already a center of foreign trade under the Tang dynasty (618–907), it was one of the original treaty ports 1842.

Ningpo former name for ◊Ningbo, port in China.

Ningxia or ***Ningxia Hui*** autonomous region (formerly Ninghsia-Hui) of NW China
area 65,620 sq mi/170,000 sq km
capital Yinchuan
physical desert plateau
products cereals and rice under irrigation; coal
population (1986) 4,240,000; including many Muslims and nomadic herders.

Niobe in Greek mythology, the daughter of Tantalus and wife of Amphion, the king of Thebes. She was contemptuous of the goddess Leto for having produced only two children, Apollo and Artemis. She died of grief when her own twelve offspring were killed by them in revenge, and was changed to stone by Zeus.

niobium soft, gray-white, somewhat ductile and malleable, metallic element, symbol Nb, atomic number 41, atomic weight 92.906. It occurs in nature with tantalum, which it resembles in chemical properties. It is used in making stainless steel and other alloys for jet engines and rockets and for making superconductor magnets.

Niobium was discovered in 1801 by English chemist Charles Hatchett (1765–1847), who named it columbium (symbol Cb), a name that is still used in metallurgy. It was renamed for Niobe in 1844 by German chemist Heinrich Rose (1795–1864) because of its similarity to tantalum (Niobe is the daughter of Tantalus in Greek mythology).

Nippon English transliteration of the Japanese name for ◊Japan.

nirvana in Buddhism, the attainment of perfect serenity by the eradication of all desires. To some Buddhists it means complete annihilation, to others it means the absorption of the self in the infinite.

Niterói or ***Nictheroy*** port and resort city in Brazil on the E shore of Guanabara Bay, linked by bridge with Rio de Janeiro; population (1980) 382,700.

nitrate any salt of nitric acid, containing the NO_3^- ion. Nitrates of various kinds are used in explosives, in the chemical industry, in curing meat (see ◊nitre), and as inorganic fertilizers.

Nitrates in the soil, whether naturally occurring or from inorganic or organic fertilizers, can be used by plants to make proteins and nucleic acids. Being soluble in water, nitrates are leached out by rain into streams and reservoirs. High levels are now found in drinking water in arable areas. These are harmful to newborn babies, and it is possible that they contribute to stomach cancer, although the evidence for this is unproven.

nitre or saltpeter, potassium nitrate, KNO_3, a mineral found on and just under the ground in desert regions; used in explosives.

Nitre occurs in Bihar, India, Iran, and Cape Province, South Africa. The salt was formerly used for the manufacture of gunpowder, but the supply of nitre for explosives is today largely met by making the salt from nitratine (also called Chile saltpeter, $NaNO_3$). Saltpeter is a ◊preservative and is widely used for curing meats.

Niter formed in limestone caverns, associated with bat guano, was used by the confederacy during the US Civil War.

nitric acid or ***aqua fortis*** HNO_3 fuming acid obtained by the oxidation of ammonia or the action of sulfuric acid on potassium nitrate. It is a strong oxidizing agent, dissolves most metals, and is used for nitration and esterification of organic substances; for explosives, plastics, and dyes; and in making sulfuric acid and nitrates.

nitrification a process that takes place in soil when bacteria oxidize ammonia, turning it into nitrates. Nitrates can be absorbed by the roots of plants, so this is a vital stage in the ◊nitrogen cycle.

nitrite salt or ester of nitrous acid, containing the nitrite ion (NO_2^-). Nitrites are used as preservatives (for example, to prevent the growth of botulism spores) and as coloring agents in cured meats such as bacon and sausages.

nitrocellulose series of esters with two to six nitrate (NO_3) groups per molecule, made by the action of concentrated nitric acid on cellulose (for example cotton waste) in the presence of concentrated sulfuric acid. Those with five or more nitrate groups are explosive (gun cotton), but those with less were once used in lacquers, rayon, and plastics, such as colored and photographic film, until replaced by nonflammable cellulose acetate.

nitrogen colorless, odorless, tasteless, gaseous, nonmetallic element, symbol N, atomic number 7, atomic weight 14.0067. It forms almost 80% of the Earth's atmosphere by volume and is a necessary part of all plant and animal tissues (in proteins and nucleic acids). For industrial uses it is obtained by liquifaction and fractional distillation of air.

Nitrogen has been recognized as a plant nutrient, found in manures and other organic matter, from early times, long before the complex cycle of ◊nitrogen fixation was understood. It was isolated in 1772 by English chemist Daniel Rutherford (1749–1819) and named in 1790 by French chemist Jean Chaptal (1756–1832) for Greek *nitron*, "native soda" (a sodium or potassium nitrate).

nitrogen cycle in ecology, the process of nitrogen passing through the ecosystem. Nitrogen, in the form of inorganic compounds (such as nitrates) in the soil, is absorbed by plants and turned into organic compounds (such as proteins) in plant tissue. A proportion of this nitrogen is eaten by ◊herbivores and used for their own biological processes, with some of this in turn being passed on to the carnivores, which feed on the herbivores. The nitrogen is ultimately returned to the soil as excrement and when organisms die and are converted back to inorganic form by bacterial ◊decomposers.

nitrogen cycle

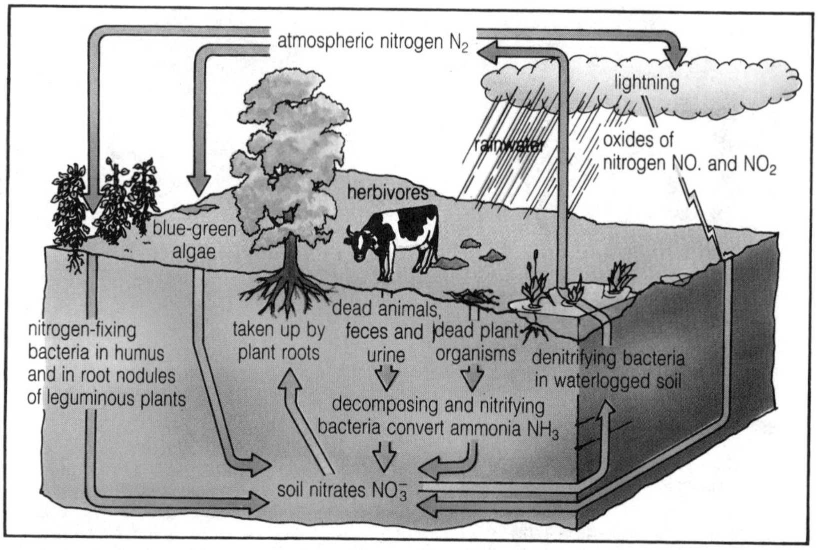
atmospheric nitrogen N_2
lightning
rainwater
oxides of nitrogen NO. and NO_2
herbivores
blue-green algae
dead animals, feces and urine
dead plant organisms
nitrogen-fixing bacteria in humus and in root nodules of leguminous plants
taken up by plant roots
denitrifying bacteria in waterlogged soil
decomposing and nitrifying bacteria convert ammonia NH_3
soil nitrates NO_3^-

Although about 78% of the atmosphere is nitrogen, this cannot be used directly by most organisms. However, certain bacteria and cyanobacteria are capable of ◊nitrogen fixation; that is, they can extract nitrogen directly from the atmosphere and convert it to compounds such as nitrates that other organisms can use. Some nitrogen-fixing bacteria live mutually with leguminous plants (peas and beans) or other plants (for example, alder), where they form characteristic nodules on the roots. The presence of such plants increases the nitrate content, and hence the fertility, of the soil.

nitrogen fixation the process by which nitrogen in the atmosphere is converted into nitrogenous compounds by the action of microorganisms, such as cyanobacteria and bacteria, in conjunction with certain ◊legumes. Several chemical processes duplicate nitrogen fixation to produce fertilizers; see ◊nitrogen cycle.

nitroglycerine $C_3H_5(ONO_2)_3$ flammable, explosive oil produced by the action of nitric and sulfuric acids on glycerol. Although poisonous, it is used in cardiac medicine. It explodes with great violence if heated in a confined space and is used in the preparation of dynamite, cordite, and other high explosives.

nitrous oxide or ***dinitrogen oxide*** N_2O colorless, nonflammable gas that reduces sensitivity to pain. In higher doses it is an anesthetic. Well-tolerated, but less potent than some other anesthetic gases, it is often combined with other drugs to allow lower doses to be used. It may be self-administered; for example, in childbirth. It is popularly known as "laughing gas."

Niue coral island in the S Pacific, W of the Cook Islands; overseas territory of New Zealand
area 100 sq mi/260 sq km
cities port Alofi
products coconuts, passion fruit, honey
population (1988) 2,200
history inhabited by warriors who stopped Capt Cook from landing 1774; British protectorate 1900; annexed by New Zealand 1901; attained self-government in free association with New Zealand (with which there is common citizenship) 1974.

Niven David 1909–1983. Scottish-born US film actor. He went to Hollywood in the 1930s, where he made *The Charge of the Light Brigade* 1936, *Bachelor Mother* 1939, and *Wuthering Heights* 1939 before serving as a British officer in World War II. When he returned to Hollywood he starred in *Around the World in 80 Days* 1956, *Separate Tables* 1958 (Academy Award), *The Guns of Navarone* 1961, and *The Pink Panther* 1964. He published two bestselling volumes of autobiography, *The Moon's a Balloon* 1972 and *Bring on the Empty Horses* 1975.

Nixon Richard (Milhous) 1913– . 37th president of the US 1969–74, a Republican. He attracted attention as a member of the Un-American Activities Committee 1948, and was vice-president to Eisenhower 1953–61. As president he was responsible for US withdrawal from Vietnam, and forged new links with China, but at home his culpability in the cover-up of the ◊Watergate scandal and the existence of a "slush fund" for political machinations during his reelection campaign 1972 led to his resignation 1974 after being threatened with ◊impeachment.

Of Quaker family, Nixon grew up in Whittier, California; he became a lawyer, entered Congress in 1947, and in 1948, as a member of the Un-American Activities Committee, pressed for the investigation of Alger ◊Hiss, accused of being a spy. Nixon was senator for California from 1951 until elected vice-president. He lost the presidential election 1960 to J F Kennedy, partly because televised electoral debates put him at a disadvantage. He did not seek presidential nomination in 1964, but in a "law and order" campaign defeated Vice-President Humphrey 1968 in one of the most closely contested elections in US history.

In 1969 he formulated the Nixon Doctrine abandoning close involvement with Asian countries, but escalated the war in Cambodia by massive bombing. Reelected 1972 in a landslide victory over George McGovern, he resigned 1974, the first US president to do so, under threat of impeachment on three counts: obstruction of the administration of justice in the investigation of Watergate; violation of constitutional rights of citizens, for example attempting to use the Internal Revenue Service, Federal Bureau of Investigation, and Central Intelligence Agency as weapons against political opponents; and failure to produce "papers and things" as ordered by the Judiciary Committee. He was granted a pardon 1974 by President Ford and turned to lecturing and writing.

Nixon Doctrine political principle formulated in 1969 by President Nixon, which called for the US to supply military aid and arms, but no troops, to Asian nations fighting communist insurgencies. It was issued during opposition to US fighting in Vietnam.

Nizhni-Novgorod former name (until 1932) of the city of ◊Gorky in central USSR.

NJ abbreviation for ◊New Jersey.

Nixon *The 37th president of the United States of America, Richard Milhaus Nixon, a Republican. 1969–1974.*

Nkomo Joshua 1917– . Zimbabwean politician, president of ZAPU (Zimbabwe African People's Union) from 1961 and a leader of the black nationalist movement against the white Rhodesian regime. He was a member of Robert ◊Mugabe's cabinet in 1980–82 and from 1987.

After completing his education in South Africa, Joshua Nkomo became a welfare officer on Rhodesian Railways and later organizing secretary of the Rhodesian African Railway Workers' Union. He entered politics 1950 and rose to become president of ZAPU. He was soon arrested, with other black African politicians, and was in detention during 1963–74. After his release he joined forces with Robert Mugabe as a joint leader of the Patriotic Front 1976, opposing the white-dominated regime of Ian Smith. Nkomo took part in the Lancaster House Conference, which led to Rhodesia's independence as the new state of Zimbabwe, and became a cabinet minister and vice-president.

Nkomo *Zimbabwean politician and cabinet member Joshua Nkomo.*

Nkrumah Kwame 1909–1972. Ghanaian nationalist politician, prime minister of the Gold Coast (Ghana's former name) 1952–57 and of newly independent Ghana 1957–60. He became Ghana's first president 1960 but was overthrown in a coup 1966. His policy of "African socialism" led to links with the Communist bloc.

Deposed from the presidency while on a visit to Beijing (Peking) 1966, he remained in exile in Guinea, where he was made cohead of state until his death, but was posthumously "rehabilitated" 1973.

NKVD (Russian "People's Commissariat of Internal Affairs") the Soviet secret police 1934–38, replaced by the ◊KGB. The NKVD was reponsible for Stalin's infamous ◊purges.

NM abbreviation for ◊New Mexico.

Nō or ***Noh*** the Classical, aristocratic Japanese drama, which developed from the 14th to the 16th centuries and is still performed. There is a repertory of some 250 pieces, of which five, one from each of the several classes devoted to different subjects, may be put on in a performance lasting a whole day. Dance, mime, music, and chanting develop the mythical or historical themes. All the actors are men, some of whom wear masks and elaborate costumes; scenery is limited. Nō influenced ◊kabuki drama.

Nkrumah *The first president of Ghana, Kwame Nkrumah.*

Nō developed from popular rural entertainments and religious performances staged at shrines and temples by traveling companies. The leader of one of these troupes, Kan'ami (1333–1384), and his son and successor Zeami (1363–1443/4) wrote a number of Nō plays and are regarded as the founders of the form. The plots often feature a ghost or demon seeking rest or revenge, but the esthetics are those of Zen Buddhism. Symbolism and suggestion take precedence over action, and the slow, stylized dance is the strongest element. Flute, drums, and chorus supply the music.

no. or ***No.*** abbreviation for number.

Noah in the Old Testament, the son of Lamech and father of Shem, Ham, and Japheth, who, according to God's instructions, built an ark so that he and his family and specimens of all existing animals might survive the ◊Flood. There is also a Babylonian version of the tale, *The Epic of Gilgamesh.*

Nobel Alfred Bernhard 1833–1896. Swedish chemist and engineer. He invented ◊dynamite in 1867 and ballistite, a smokeless gunpowder, in 1889. He amassed a large fortune from the manufacture of explosives and the exploitation of the Baku oilfields in Azerbaijan, near the Caspian Sea. He left this fortune in trust for the endowment of five ◊Nobel Prizes.

nobelium synthesized, radioactive, metallic element of the ◊actinide series, symbol No, atomic number 102, atomic weight 259. It is synthesized by bombarding curium with carbon nuclei.

It was named in 1957 for the Nobel Institute in Stockholm, Sweden, where it was claimed to have been first synthesized. Later evaluations determined that this was in fact not so, as the successful 1958 synthesis at the University of California at Berkeley produced a different set of data. The name was not, however, challenged.

Nobel Prize annual international prize, first awarded 1901 under the will of Alfred Nobel, Swedish chemist, who invented dynamite. The interest on the Nobel endowment fund is divided annually among the persons who have made the greatest contributions in the fields of physics, chemistry, medicine, literature, and world peace.

The first four are awarded by academic committees based in Sweden, while the peace prize is awarded by a committee of the Norwegian parliament. A sixth prize, for economics, financed by the Swedish National Bank, was first awarded 1969. The prizes have a large cash award and are given to organizations—such as the United Nations peacekeeping forces, which received the Nobel Peace Prize in 1988—as well as individuals.

Recent Nobel Prizewinners

Peace

1982 Alva Myrdal (Sweden) and Alfonso Garcia Robles (Mexico)
1983 Lech Wałesa (Poland)
1984 Bishop Desmond Tutu (South Africa)

1985 International Physicians for the Prevention of Nuclear War
1986 Elie Wiesel (US)
1987 President Oscar Arias Sanchez (Costa Rica)
1988 The United Nations peacekeeping forces
1989 The Dalai Lama (Tibet)
1990 President Mikhail Gorbachev (USSR)
1991 Aung San Suu Kyi (Myanmar)

Economics
1982 George J Stigler (US)
1983 Gérard Debreu (US)
1984 Richard Stone (UK)
1985 Franco Modigliani (US)
1986 James Buchanan (US)
1987 Robert Solow (US)
1988 Maurice Allais (France)
1989 Trygve Haavelmo (Norway)
1990 Harry M Markowitz (US), Merton H Miller (US), and William F Sharpe (US)
1991 George H. Coase (US)

Physiology and Medicine
1982 Sune Bergström (Sweden), Bengt I Samuelson (Sweden), and John R Vane (UK)
1983 Barbara McClintock (US)
1984 Niels K Jerne (Denmark), Georges Köhler (Germany), and Cesar Milstein (UK)
1985 Michael Brown (US) and Joseph Goldstein (US)
1986 Stanley Cohen (US) and Rita Levi-Montalcini (US)
1987 Susumu Tonegawa (Japan)
1988 Gertrude Elion (US), George Hitchins (US), and James Black (UK)
1989 Michael Bishop (US) and Harold Varmus (US)
1990 Joseph E Murray (US) and E Donnall Thomas (US)
1991 Erwin Neher (Germany) and Bert Sakmann (Germany)

Literature
1982 Gabriel García Marquez (Colombia)
1983 William Golding (UK)
1984 Jaroslav Seifert (Czechoslovakia)
1985 Claude Simon (France)
1986 Wole Soyinka (Nigeria)
1987 Joseph Brodsky (USSR/US)
1988 Naguib Mahfouz (Egypt)
1989 Camilo Jose Cela (Spain)
1990 Octavio Paz (Mexico)
1991 Nadine Gordimer (South Africa)

Chemistry
1982 Aaron Klug (UK)
1983 Henry Taube (US)
1984 Robert Bruce Merrifield (US)
1985 Herbert Hauptman (US) and Jerome Karle (US)
1986 Dudley R Herschbach (US), Yuan Lee (US), and John Polanyi (Canada)
1987 Jean-Marie Lehn (France), Charles Pedersen (US), and Donald Cram (US)
1988 Johann Deisenhofer, Robert Huber, and Hartmut Michel (Germany)
1989 Sidney Altman (US) and Thomas Cech (US)
1990 Elias James Corey (US)
1991 Richard R. Ernst (Switzerland)

Physics
1982 Kenneth G Wilson (US)
1983 Subrahmanyan Chandrasekhar (US) and William A Fowler (US)
1984 Carlo Rubbia (Italy) and Simon van der Meer (Netherlands)
1985 Klaus von Klitzing (Germany)
1986 Ernst Ruska (Germany), Gerd Binnig (Switzerland), and Heinrich Rohrer (Switzerland)
1987 Georg Bednorz (Switzerland) and Alex Müller (Germany)
1988 Leon Lederman, Melvin Schwartz, and Jack Steinberger (US)
1989 Norman Ramsey (US), Hans Dehmelt (US), and Wolfgang Paul (Germany)
1990 Richard E Taylor (Canada), Jerome I Friedman (US), and Henry W Kendall (US)
1991 Pierre-Gilles de Gennes (France)

nobility the ranks of society who originally enjoyed certain hereditary privileges. Their wealth was mainly derived from land. In many societies until the 20th century, they provided the elite personnel of government and the military.

noble gas alternate name for ◊inert gas.

noble gas structure the configuration of electrons in noble or ◊inert gases (helium, neon, argon, krypton, xenon, and radon).

This is characterized by full electron shells around the nucleus of an atom, which render the element stable. Any ion, produced by the gain or loss of electrons, that achieves an electronic configuration similar to one of the inert gases is said to have a noble gas structure.

Noble Savage, the ◊Enlightenment idea of the virtuous innocence of "savage" peoples, often embodied in the American Indian, and celebrated by the writers J J Rousseau, Chateaubriand (in *Atala* 1801), and James Fenimore Cooper.

nocturne in music, a lyrical, dreamy piece, often for piano, introduced by John Field (1782–1837) and adopted by Chopin.

node a position in a ◊standing wave pattern at which there is no vibration. Points at which there is maximum vibration are called antinodes. Stretched strings, for example, can show nodes when they vibrate.

Guitarists can produce special effects (◊harmonics) by touching a sounding string lightly to produce a node.

nodule in geology, a lump of mineral or other matter found within rocks or formed on the seabed surface; ◊mining technology is being developed to exploit them.

Nofretète alternate name for ◊Nefertiti, queen of Egypt.

Noguchi Hideyo 1876–1928. Japanese bacteriologist who studied syphilitic diseases, snake venoms, trachoma, and poliomyelitis. He discovered the parasite of yellow fever, a disease from which he died while working in British W Africa.

noise pollution unwanted and damaging sound. Permanent, incurable loss of hearing can be caused by prolonged exposure to high noise levels (above 85 decibels).

If the noise is in a narrow frequency band, temporary hearing loss can occur even though the level is below 85 decibels or exposure is only for short periods. Lower levels of noise are an irritant, but seem not to increase fatigue or affect efficiency to any great extent.

Noland Kenneth 1924– . US painter, associated with Abstract Expressionism. In the 1950s and early 1960s he painted targets, or concentric circles of color, in a clean, hard-edged style on unprimed canvas. His work centered on geometry, color, and symmetry. His later 1960s paintings experimented with the manipulation of color vision and afterimages, pioneering the field of ◊op art.

Noland was born in Asheville, North Carolina. In *Graded Exposure* 1967, he used large stripes to form a plaid.

Nolde Emil. Adopted name of Emil Hansen 1867–1956. German Expressionist painter. Nolde studied in Paris and Dachau, joined the group of artists known as *Die Brücke* 1906–07, and visited Polynesia 1913; he then became almost a recluse in NE Germany. Many of his themes were religious.

noli me tangere (Latin "touch me not") in the Bible, the words spoken by Jesus to Mary Magdalene after the Resurrection (John 20:17); in art, the title of many works depicting this scene; in botany, a plant of the genus *Impatiens*.

Nom Chinese-style characters used in writing the Vietnamese language. Nom characters were used from the 13th century for Vietnamese literature, but were replaced in the 19th century by a romanized script known as Quoc Ngu. The greatest Nom writer was the poet Nguyen Du.

nominalism trend in the medieval philosophy of scholasticism. In opposition to the Realists, who maintained that universals have a real existence, the Nominalists taught that they are mere names invented to describe the qualities of real things; that is, classes of things have no independent reality. William of ◊Occam was a leading medieval exponent of nominalism. Dispute over the issue continued at intervals from the 11th to the 15th centuries.

nominative in the grammar of some inflected languages—such as Latin, Russian, and Sanskrit—the form of a word used to indicate that a noun or pronoun is the subject of a finite verb.

nonaligned movement strategic and political position of neutrality ("nonalignment") toward major powers, specifically the US and USSR. Although originally used by poorer states, the nonaligned position was later adopted by oil-producing nations. The 1989 summit in Belgrade was attended by 102 member states.

The term was originally used by the Indian prime minister Nehru and was adopted 1961 at an international conference in Belgrade, Yugoslavia, by that country's president, Tito, in general opposition to colonialism, neocolonialism, and imperialism, and to the dominance of dangerously conflicting East and West alliances. However, many members were in receipt of aid from either East or West or both, and some went to war with one another (Vietnam– Cambodia, Ethiopia–Somalia).

Nonconformist in religion, originally a member of the Puritan section of the Church of England clergy who, in the Elizabethan age, refused to conform to certain practices, for example the wearing of the surplice and kneeling to receive Holy Communion.

After 1662 the term was confined to members of independent Protestant churches in Great Britain.

Nonjurors priests of the Church of England who, after the revolution of 1688, refused to take the oaths of allegiance to William and Mary. They continued to exist as a rival church for over a century, and consecrated their own bishops, the last of whom died 1805.

nonmetal one of a set of elements (about 23 in total) with certain physical and chemical properties opposite to those of metals. Nonmetals accept electrons (see ◊electronegativity) and are sometimes called electronegative elements.

Nono Luigi 1924–1990. Italian composer. His early vocal compositions have something of the spatial character of ◊Gabrieli, for example *Il Canto Sospeso* 1955–56. After the opera *Intolleranza* 1960 his style moved away from ◊serialism to become increasingly expressionistic. His music is frequently polemical in subject matter, and a number of works incorporate tape-recorded elements.

nonrenewable resource natural resource, such as coal or oil, that takes thousands or millions of years to form naturally and can therefore not be replaced once it is consumed. The main energy sources used by humans are nonrenewable resources.

nonsteroidal anti-inflammatory drug full name of ◊NSAID.

nonviolence the principle or practice of abstaining from the use of violence. The Indian nationalist leader Mahatma Gandhi adopted a campaign of passive resistance 1907–14 in response to the attempts by the Transvaal government to discriminate against Indians in South Africa. Later, in India, Gandhi employed nonviolent methods, including the boycotting of British goods and hunger strikes. Martin Luther ◊King, Jr, led a nonviolent civil-rights movement in the US. He organized a boycott against segregated seating on the buses in Montgomery, Alabama. In June 1963 he led a peaceful demonstration in Washington, DC, and in March 1965 led a civil-rights march from Selina to Montgomery.

Nordenskjöld Nils Adolf Erik 1832–1901. Swedish explorer. He made voyages to the Arctic with the geologist Torell and in 1878–79 discovered the Northeast Passage. He published the results of his voyages in a series of books, including *Voyage of the Vega round Asia and Europe* 1881.

He contributed to geographic research with *Periplus* 1897.

Nordic ethnic designation for any of the various Germanic peoples, especially those of Scandinavia. The physical type of Caucasoid described under that term is tall, long-headed, blue-eyed, fair of skin and hair. The term is no longer in current scientific use.

Nord-Pas-de-Calais region of N France; area 4,786 sq mi/12,400 sq km; population (1986) 3,923,000. Its capital is Lille, and it consists of the *départements* of Nord and Pas-de-Calais.

Pas-de-Calais is the French term for the Straits of Dover.

Norfolk county on E coast of England

area 2,069 sq mi/5,360 sq km

towns Norwich (administrative headquarters), King's Lynn; resorts: Great Yarmouth, Cromer, Hunstanton

physical rivers: Ouse, Yare, Bure, Waveney; the ◊Broads; Halvergate Marshes wildlife area

features traditional reed thatching; Grime's Graves (Neolithic flint mines); shrine of Our Lady of Walsingham, a medieval and present-day center of pilgrimage; Blickling Hall (Jacobean); residence of Elizabeth II at Sandringham (built 1869–71)

products cereals, turnips, sugar beets, turkeys, geese, offshore natural gas

population (1987) 736,000.

Norfolk seaport in SE Virginia, on the Atlantic Ocean at the mouth of the James and Elizabeth rivers; population (1990) 261,229. It is one of the nation's busiest ports, the headquarters of the US Navy's Atlantic fleet, and the home of 22 other Navy commands. Industries include shipbuilding, chemicals, and motor-vehicle assembly. The Chesapeake Bay Bridge-Tunnel links it to the Delmarva peninsula. Old Dominion University is here. Norfolk was laid out in 1682. It suffered heavy damage during the American Revolution, was captured by Union forces in the Civil War, and grew rapidly during both world wars.

Norfolk Broads area of some 12 interlinked freshwater lakes in E England, created about 600 years ago by the digging out of peat deposits; they are used for boating and fishing.

Norfolk Island Pacific island territory of Australia, S of New Caledonia

area 15 sq mi/40 sq km

products citrus fruit, bananas; tourist industry

population (1986) 2,000

history reached by Cook 1774: settled 1856 by descendants of the mutineers of the *Bounty* (see ◊Bligh) from ◊Pitcairn Island; Australian territory from 1914: largely self-governing from 1979.

Noriega Manuel Antonio Morena 1940– . Panamanian soldier and politician, effective ruler of Panama from 1982 until arrested by the US 1989 and detained for trial on drug-trafficking charges.

Noriega was commissioned in the National Guard 1962. He became intelligence chief 1970 and chief of staff 1982. He wielded considerable political power behind the scenes, which led to his enlistment by the US Central Intelligence Agency until charges of drug trafficking discredited him. Relations with the US deteriorated and in Dec 1989 President Bush ordered an invasion of Panama by 24,000 US troops that eventually resulted in Noriega's arrest and detention, pending trial, in the US.

Norilsk world's northernmost industrial city (nickel, cobalt, platinum, selenium, tellurium, gold, silver) in Siberia, USSR; population (1987) 181,000. The permafrost is 1,000 ft/300 m deep, and the winter temperature may be 67°F–55°C.

norm informal guideline about what is, or is not, considered normal social behavior (as opposed to rules and laws, which are formal guidelines). Such shared values and expectations may be measured by statistical sampling and vary from one society to another and from one situation to another; they range from crucial taboos such as those against

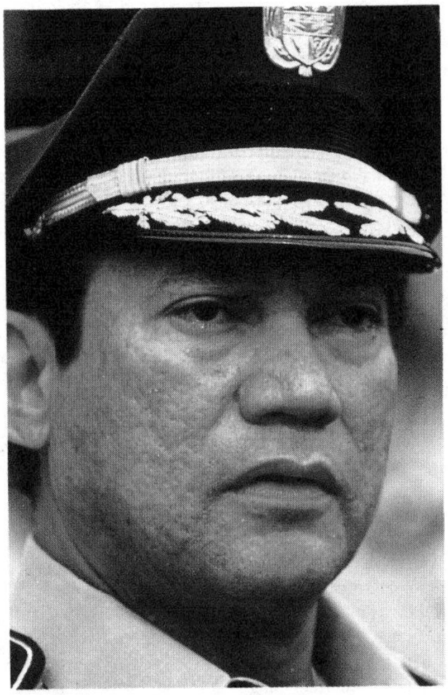

Noriega *Panama's former national strongman General Manuel Noriega. In Dec 1989 US troops overthrew his corrupt regime; he was flown to the US to be tried for drug trafficking.*

incest or cannibalism to trivial customs and traditions, such as the correct way to hold a fork. Norms play a key part in social control and social order.

Normal city in central Illinois, NE of Bloomington. It is a marketing center for the livestock and grains produced in the surrounding area. Illinois State University is here; population (1990) 40,023.

Norman any of the descendants of the Norsemen (to whose chief, Rollo, Normandy was granted by Charles III of France 911) who adopted French language and culture. During the 11th and 12th centuries they conquered England 1066 (under William the Conqueror), Scotland 1072, parts of Wales and Ireland, S Italy, Sicily, and Malta, and took a prominent part in the Crusades.

They introduced feudalism, Latin as the language of government, and Norman French as the language of literature. Church architecture and organization were also influenced by the Nor-

Norman architecture *Norman tower in Hedingham, England, begun in the late 11th century. It is 72 ft/22 m high.*

Norman *US soprano Jessye Norman, celebrated for her powerful voice in opera and solo performances.*

mans, although they ceased to exist as a distinct people after the 13th century.

Norman Greg 1955– . Australian golfer, nicknamed "the Great White Shark." After many wins in his home country, he enjoyed success on the European PGA Tour before joining the US Tour. He has won the world match-play title three times.

CAREER HIGHLIGHTS

British Open: 1986
World Match-play Championship: 1980, 1983, 1986
Dunlop Masters: 1981–82
Canadian Open: 1984

Norman Jessye 1945– . US soprano, born in Augusta, Georgia. She made her operatic debut at the Deutsche Opera, Berlin, 1969. She is acclaimed for her interpretation of *Lieder*, as well as operatic roles, and for her powerful voice.

Normandy two regions of NW France: ◊Haute-Normandie and ◊Basse-Normandie. Its main towns are Alençon, Bayeux, Caen, Cherbourg, Dieppe, Deauville, Lisieux, Le Havre, and Rouen. It was named after the Viking Northmen (Normans), the people who conquered and settled the area in the 9th century. As a French duchy it reached its peak under William the Conqueror and was renowned for its centers of learning established by Lanfranc and St Anselm. Normandy was united with England 1100–35. England and France fought over it during the Hundred Years' War, England finally losing it 1449 to Charles VII. In World War II the Normandy beaches were the site of the Allied invasion on D day, June 6, 1944. Features of Normandy include the painter Monet's restored home and garden at Giverny; Mont St Michel; Château Miromesnil, the birthplace of de Maupassant; Victor Hugo's house at Villequier; and ◊Calvados apple brandy.

Normandy landings alternate name for ◊D day.

Norman French the form of French used by the Normans in Normandy from the 10th century, and by the Norman ruling class in England after the Conquest 1066. It remained the language of the English court until the 15th century, the official language of the law courts until the 17th century, and is still used in the Channel Islands.

Norn in Scandinavian mythology, any of three goddesses of fate—the goddess of the past (Urd), the goddess of the present (Verdandi), and the goddess of the future (Skuld).

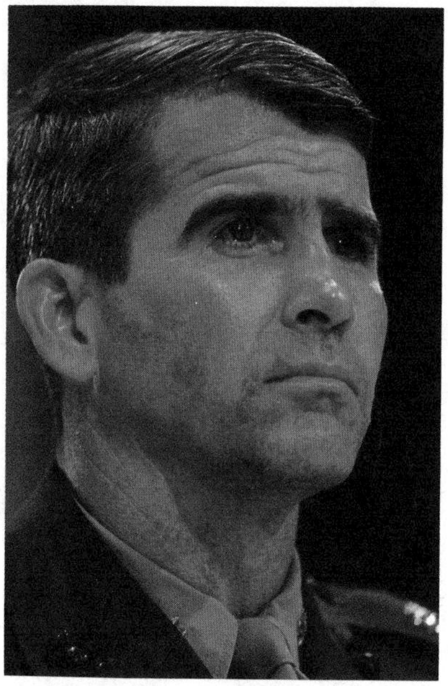

North *US Marine Lt Col Oliver North, a National Security Council official who was a central figure in the Iran-Contra Affair, in which he oversaw a clandestine foreign-policy network.*

Norris Frank 1870–1902. US novelist. A naturalist writer, he wrote *McTeague* 1899, about a brutish San Francisco dentist and the love of gold. He completed only two parts of his projected trilogy, the *Epic of Wheat*: *The Octopus* 1901, dealing with the struggles between wheat farmers, and *The Pit* 1903, describing the Chicago wheat exchange.

Norse or ***Norseman*** a member of any of the ancient Scandinavian peoples, also called ◊Vikings when they traded, explored, and raided far afield from their homelands during the 8th–11th centuries, settling in Iceland, Greenland, Russia, the British Isles, and N France. The term is sometimes used to refer specifically to W Scandinavians or just to Norwegians.

North Frederick, 8th Lord 1732–1792. British Tory politician. He entered Parliament in 1754, became chancellor of the Exchequer in 1767, and was prime minister in a government of Tories and "king's friends" from 1770. His hard line against the American colonies was supported by George III, but in 1782 he was forced to resign by the failure of his policy. In 1783 he returned to office in a coalition with ◊Fox, and after its defeat retired from politics.

North Oliver 1943– . US Marine lieutenant colonel. In 1981 he was inducted into the ◊National Security Council (NSC), where he supervised the mining of Nicaraguan harbors 1983, an air-force bombing raid on Libya 1986, and an arms-for-hostages deal with Iran 1985 which, when uncovered in 1986 (◊Irangate), forced his dismissal and conviction on felony charges. His convictions were later overturned.

He was born into a San Antonio, Texas, military family and was a graduate of the US Naval Academy, Annapolis. He led a counterinsurgency Marine platoon in the Vietnam War 1968–69, winning a Silver Star and Purple Heart. After working as a Marine instructor, as well as participating in a number of overseas secret missions, he became the NSC deputy director for political military affairs.

North America third largest of the continents (when including Central America)
area 9,500,000 sq mi/24,000,000 sq km
largest cities (population over 1 million) Mexico City, New York, Chicago, Toronto, Los Angeles, Montreal, Guadalajara, Monterrey, Philadelphia, Houston, Guatemala City, Vancouver, Detroit
population (1990 est) 395,000,000; the aboriginal American Indian, Eskimo, and Aleut peoples are now a minority within a population predominantly of European immigrant origin. Many Africans were brought in as laborers by the slave trade. Asians were also brought in as laborers, and today immigration from Asia and Latin America is on the increase
physical mountain belts to the E (Appalachians) and W (see ◊Cordilleras), the latter including the Rocky Mountains and the Sierra Madre; coastal plain on the Gulf of Mexico, into which the Mississippi River system drains from the central Great Plains; the St Lawrence River and the Great Lakes form a rough crescent with the Great Bear and Great Slave lakes and Lakes Athabasca and Winnipeg around the exposed rock of the great

North America

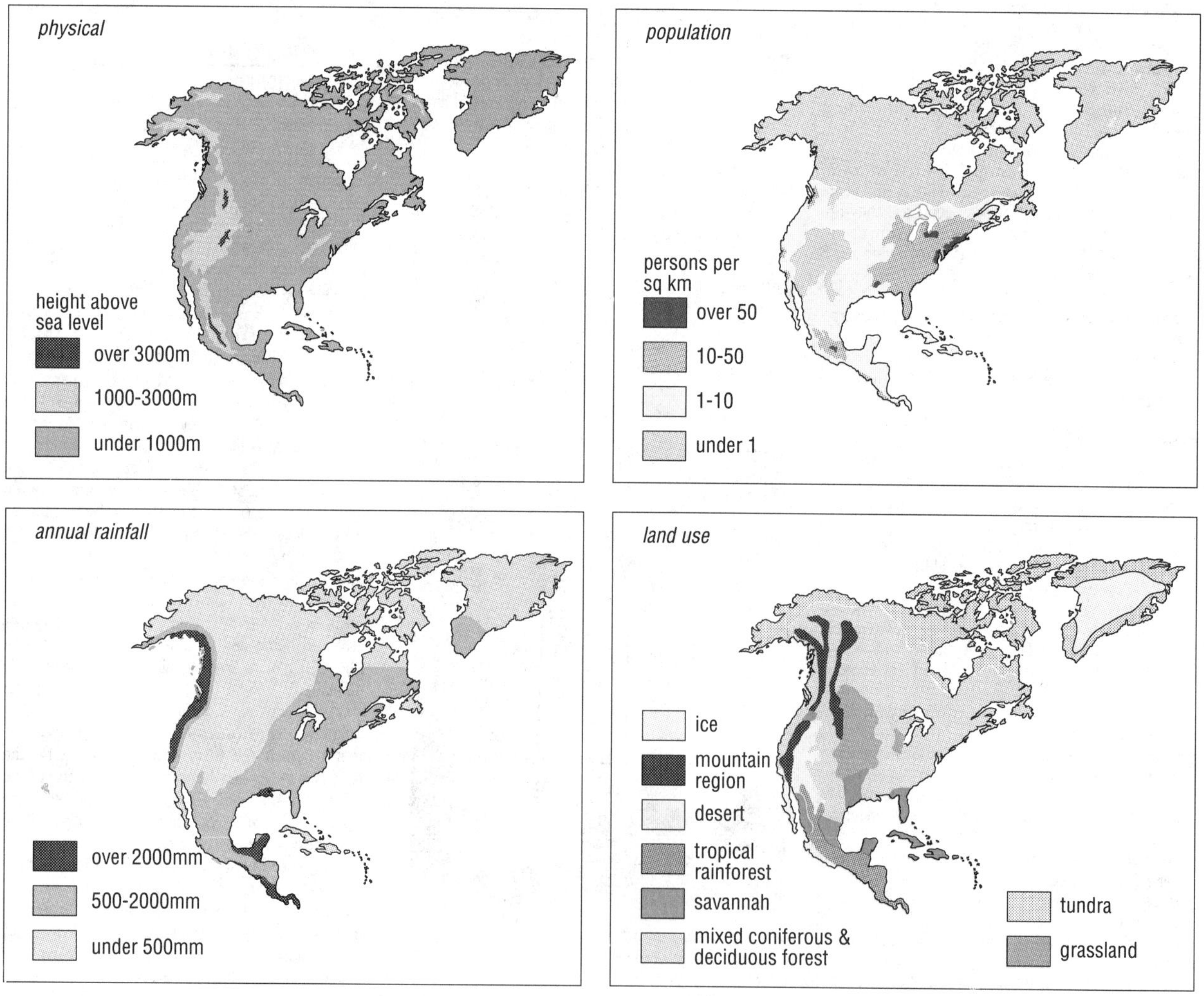
physical
height above sea level
over 3000m
1000-3000m
under 1000m
population
persons per sq km
over 50
10-50
1-10
under 1
annual rainfall
over 2000mm
500-2000mm
under 500mm
land use
ice
mountain region
desert
tropical rainforest
savannah
mixed coniferous & deciduous forest
tundra
grassland

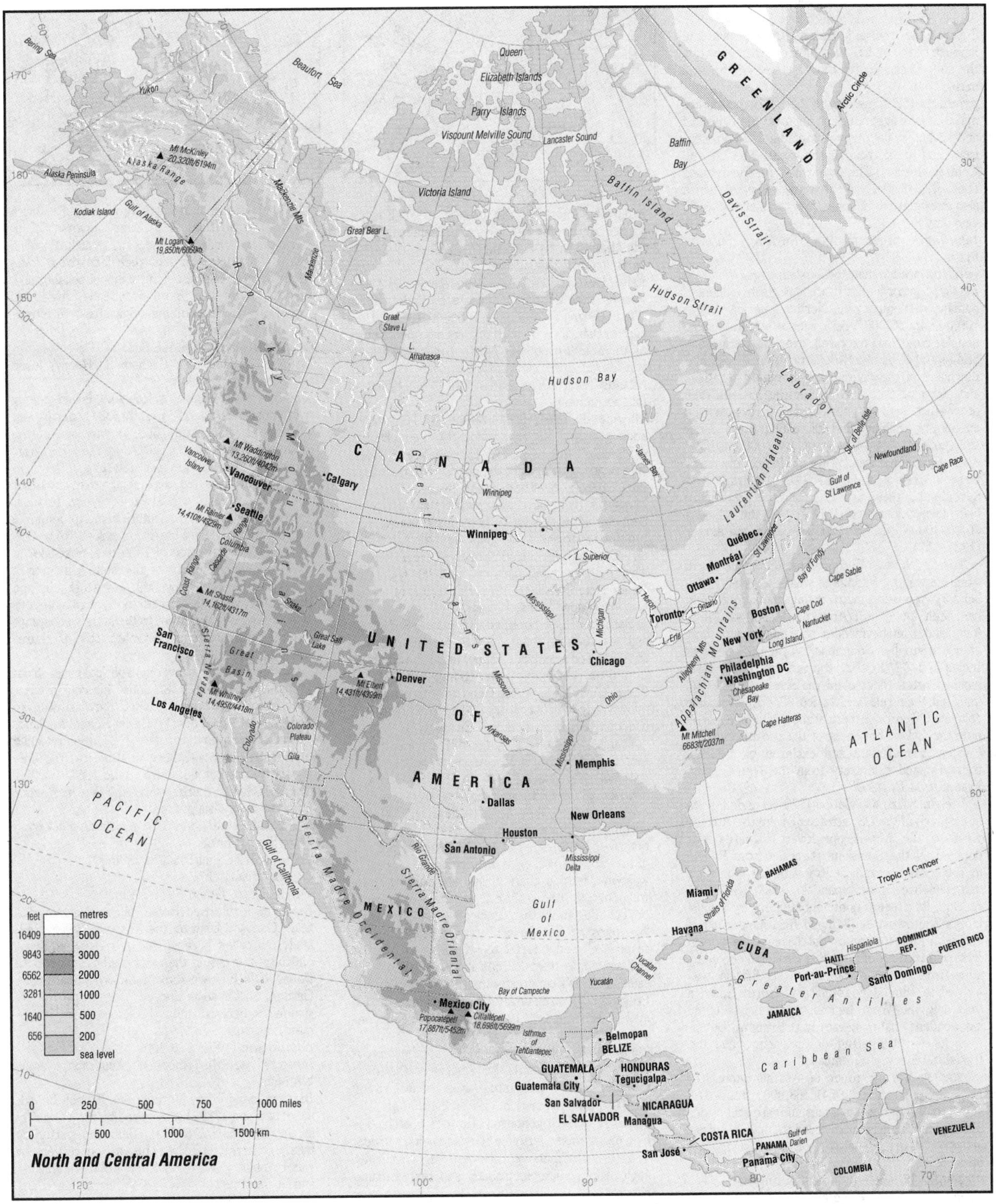
Bering Sea
Beaufort Sea
Yukon
Queen Elizabeth Islands
Parry Islands
Viscount Melville Sound
Lancaster Sound
GREENLAND
Arctic Circle
Baffin Bay
Mt McKinley 20,320ft/6194m
Alaska Range
Alaska Peninsula
Kodiak Island
Gulf of Alaska
Mackenzie Mts
Victoria Island
Baffin Island
Davis Strait
Mt Logan 19,850ft/6050m
Great Bear L.
Mackenzie
Hudson Strait
Great Slave L.
L. Athabasca
Hudson Bay
Labrador
Rocky Mountains
Mt Waddington 13,260ft/4042m
Vancouver Island
Vancouver
Calgary
CANADA
Great Plains
L. Winnipeg
James Bay
Laurentian Plateau
Str. of Belle Isle
Newfoundland
Cape Race
Gulf of St Lawrence
Mt Rainier 14,410ft/4392m
Seattle
Cascade Range
Columbia
Winnipeg
L. Superior
Québec
Montréal
St Lawrence
Ottawa
Bay of Fundy
Cape Sable
Coast Range
Mt Shasta 14,162ft/4317m
Snake
Mississippi
L. Huron
L. Michigan
Toronto
L. Ontario
Boston
Cape Cod
Nantucket
L. Erie
New York
Long Island
San Francisco
Sierra Nevada
Great Basin
Great Salt Lake
UNITED STATES OF AMERICA
Chicago
Allegheny Mts
Appalachian Mountains
Philadelphia
Washington DC
Chesapeake Bay
Mt Elbert 14,431ft/4399m
Denver
Missouri
Mt Whitney 14,495ft/4418m
Los Angeles
Ohio
Colorado Plateau
Colorado
Arkansas
Mt Mitchell 6683ft/2037m
Cape Hatteras
ATLANTIC OCEAN
Gila
Memphis
Dallas
New Orleans
PACIFIC OCEAN
Houston
San Antonio
Rio Grande
Mississippi Delta
Gulf of California
Sierra Madre Occidental
Sierra Madre Oriental
MEXICO
Gulf of Mexico
BAHAMAS
Tropic of Cancer
Miami
Straits of Florida
Havana
CUBA
Hispaniola
DOMINICAN REP.
PUERTO RICO
HAITI
Port-au-Prince
Santo Domingo
Yucatán Channel
Yucatán
Greater Antilles
JAMAICA
Bay of Campeche
Mexico City
Popocatépetl 17,887ft/5452m
Citlaltépetl 18,698ft/5699m
Isthmus of Tehuantepec
Belmopan
BELIZE
Caribbean Sea
GUATEMALA
HONDURAS
Tegucigalpa
Guatemala City
San Salvador
NICARAGUA
EL SALVADOR
Managua
COSTA RICA
San José
PANAMA
Gulf of Darien
Panama City
VENEZUELA
COLOMBIA
feet
metres
16409 5000
9843 3000
6562 2000
3281 1000
1640 500
656 200
sea level
0 250 500 750 1000 miles
0 500 1000 1500 km

North and Central America

Canadian/Laurentian Shield, into which Hudson Bay breaks from the N
features wide climatic range, from arctic in Alaska and N Canada (only above freezing June–Sept) to the tropical in Central America, and arid in much of the W US; also, great extremes within the range, caused by the vast size of the land mass
products the immensity of the US home market makes it less dependent on imports; the industrial and technological strengths of the US automatically tend to exert a pull on Canada, Mexico, and Central America. The continent is unique in being dominated in this way by a single power, which also exerts great influence over the general world economy
language predominantly English, Spanish, French
religion predominantly Christian
history according to archeological evidence, human settlement in North America began 100,000 to 40,000 years ago, when Mongoloid peoples from Asia migrated, over the Bering land bridge and E of the Brooks range in Alaska into the heart of the continent. Settlement by these ancestors of the North American Indians then proceeded S and E. These Stone Age people lived by hunting, fishing, and harvesting fruits, nuts, and the seeds of wild plants. By 7000 BC, however, agriculture was known in Mexico and upper Central America, and by 1400 BC, ◊civilization had developed in these areas. Among the pre-Columbian civilizations were those of the Olmecs (1400–400 BC), Maya (1200 BC-1521), and Aztecs (1325–1521).

The first-known European settlement in North America was by Vikings in what they called Vinland; a Norse settlement, dating from about 1000, has been found at L'Anse-aux-Meadows, Newfoundland. But permanent settlement came only after Christopher Columbus's voyage to the West Indies in 1492. In 1521 the Spanish, under Hernándo Cortés, destroyed the Aztec empire and imposed their rule on Mexico. The Spanish also colonized Central America and parts of what is now the S US, but most of the present US and Canada was claimed and explored by traders, trappers, and colonizers from the Netherlands, France, and England.

The American Revolution 1775–83 ended in the emergence of the US, stretching from the Atlantic west to the Mississippi River; its area was doubled by the Louisiana Purchase from France in 1803. Mexico and Central America won their independence from Spain in 1821. The US reached its present continental extent by acquiring its Southwest in 1848 and 1851 as a result of war with Mexico, and by purchasing Alaska from Russia in 1867. N of the US, a Canadian confederation, with continuing links to Great Britain, was formed in 1867. Geographically, North America (including the West Indies) now consists of 22 independent nations; several British, Dutch, French, and US island dependencies; and the Danish territory of Greenland.

Northampton county town of Northamptonshire, England; population (1984) 163,000. Boots and shoes (of which there is a museum) are still made, but engineering has superseded them as the chief industry; there is also food processing and brewing.

Northamptonshire county in central England
area 915 sq mi/2,370 sq km
towns Northampton (administrative headquarters), Kettering
features river Nene; Canons Ashby, Tudor house, home of the Drydens for 400 years; churches with broached spires
products cereals, cattle
population (1987) 562,000
famous people John Dryden.

North Atlantic Drift warm ocean ◊current in the N Atlantic Ocean; the continuation of the ◊Gulf Stream. It flows E across the Atlantic and has a

North Carolina

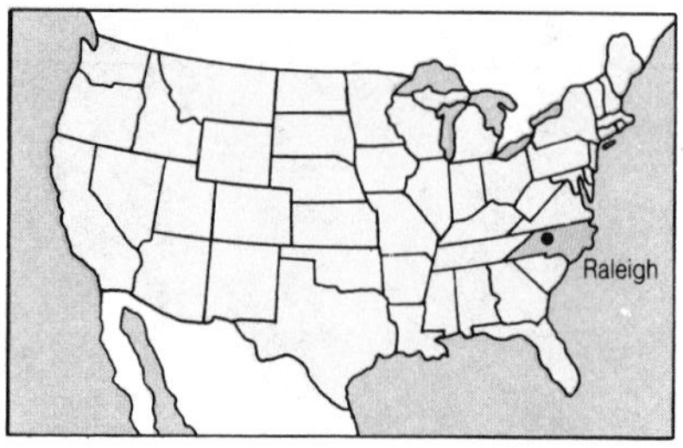
Raleigh

mellowing effect on the climate of W Europe, particularly the British Isles and Scandinavia.

North Atlantic Treaty agreement signed April 4, 1949 by Belgium, Canada, Denmark, France, Iceland, Italy, Luxembourg, the Netherlands, Norway, Portugal, the UK, the US; Greece, Turkey 1952; West Germany 1955; and Spain 1982. They agreed that "an armed attack against one or more of them in Europe or North America shall be considered an attack against them all." The North Atlantic Treaty Organization (NATO) is based on this agreement.

North Atlantic Treaty Organization (NATO) association set up 1949 to provide for the collective defense of the major W European and North American states against the perceived threat from the USSR. Its chief body is the Council of Foreign Ministers (who have representatives in permanent session), and there is an international secretariat in Brussels, Belgium, and also the Military Committee consisting of the Chiefs of Staff. The military headquarters SHAPE (Supreme Headquarters Allied Powers, Europe) is in Chièvres, near Mons, Belgium.

Both the Supreme Allied Commanders (Europe and Atlantic) are from the US, but there is also an Allied Commander, Channel (a British admiral). In 1960 a permanent multinational Allied Mobile Force (AMF) was established to move immediately to any NATO country under threat of attack; headquarters in Heidelberg, Germany.

France withdrew from the military integration (not the alliance) 1966; Greece withdrew politically but not militarily 1974. In 1980 Turkey was opposed to Greek reentry because of differences over rights in the Aegean Sea. NATO has encountered numerous problems since its inception over such issues as the hegemonial position of the US, the presence in Europe of US nuclear weapons, burden sharing, and standardization of weapons. In 1990, after a meeting in London, NATO declared that nuclear weapons were "weapons of last resort" rather than "flexible response," and offered to withdraw all nuclear artillery shells from Europe if the USSR did the same. NATO's counterpart is the ◊Warsaw Pact. President Bush's unilateral reductions in US nuclear arms in Oct 1991 resulted in reductions in NATO arms.

North Brabant (Dutch *Noordbrabant*) southern province of the Netherlands, lying between the Maas (Meuse) and Belgium; area 1,907 sq mi/4,940 sq km; population (1988) 2,156,000. The capital is 's Hertogenbosch. Former heathland is now under mixed farming. Towns such as Breda, Tilburg, and Eindhoven are centers of brewing, engineering, microelectronics, and textile manufacture.

North Cape (Norwegian *Nordkapp*) a cape in the Norwegian county of Finnmark; the most northerly point of Europe.

North Carolina state in E US; nickname Tar Heel State/Old North State
area 52,650 sq mi/136,400 sq km
capital Raleigh
cities Charlotte, Greensboro, Winston-Salem
features Appalachian Mountains (including Blue Ridge and Great Smoky mountains), site of Fort Raleigh on Roanoke Island, Wright Brothers

North Dakota

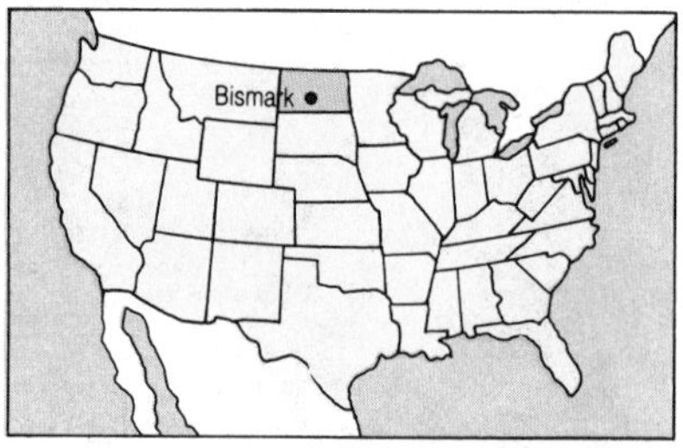
Bismark

National Memorial at Kitty Hawk, the Research Triangle established 1956 (Duke University, University of North Carolina, and North Carolina State University) for high-tech industries, Cape Hatteras and Cape Lookout national seashores
products tobacco, corn, soybeans, livestock, poultry, textiles, clothing, cigarettes, furniture, chemicals, machinery
population (1990) 6,628,637
famous people Billy Graham, O Henry, Jesse Jackson, Thomas Wolfe
history after England's Roanoke Island colony was unsuccessful 1585 and 1587, permanent settlement was made 1663; it was one of the original thirteen states 1789. In the Civil War, North Carolina was the last state to join the Confederacy but provided more troops than any other Southern state. After postwar recovery, textiles, tobacco products, and furniture came to dominate the economy. Per-capita income rose from 47% of the national average in 1930 to almost 83% in 1983. However, many of the state's industries offer predominantly low-skill, low-wage jobs and are, moreover, threatened by foreign competition. Tourism is important to the state's economy, and the mild climate has been attractive to retirement communities.

Walter Raleigh sent out 108 colonists from Plymouth, England, 1585 under his cousin Richard Grenville, who established the first English settlement in the New World on Roanoke Island; Virginia Dare was born there 1587, the first child of English parentage born in America; the survivors were taken home by Drake 1586. Further attempts failed there, since the settlers were found to have disappeared.

North Dakota state in N US; nickname Flickertail State/Sioux State
area 70,677 sq mi/183,100 sq km
capital Bismarck
cities Fargo, Grand Forks, Minot
features fertile Red River valley, Missouri Plateau; Garrison Dam on the Missouri River; Badlands, so called because the pioneers had great difficulty in crossing them (also site of Theodore Roosevelt's Elkhorn Ranch); International Peace Garden, on Canadian border
products cereals, meat products, farm equipment, oil, coal
population (1990) 638,800
famous people Maxwell Anderson, Louis L'Amour
history explored by Verendrye's French Canadian expedition 1738–40; acquired by the US partly in the Louisiana Purchase 1803 and partly by treaty with Britain 1813. The earliest settlement was Pembina 1812, by Scottish and Irish families, and it became a state 1889, attracting many German and Norwegian settlers. They and their descendants were hard hit by low prices in the 1920s and 1930s for the state's abundant wheat. Since 1950, North Dakota's oil, natural-gas, and lignite resources have contributed to a more diversified economic base, but it remains the most rural of all the states, with 90% of the land in agriculture.

North-East Frontier Agency former name (until 1972) for ◊Arunachal Pradesh, territory of India.

North-East India area of India (Meghalaya, Assam, Mizoram, Tripura, Manipur, Nagaland, and Arun-

Northern Territory

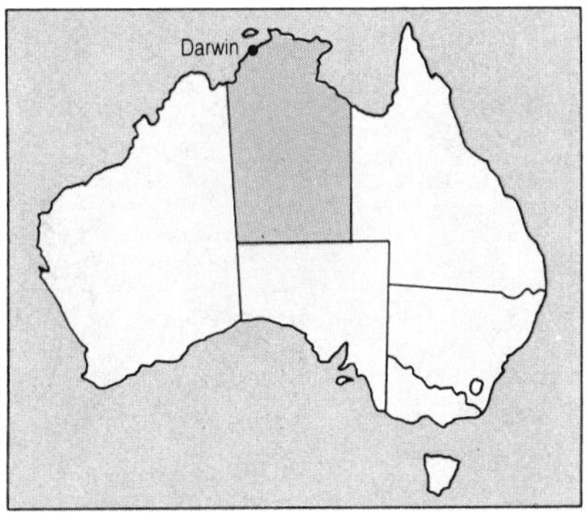
Darwin

achal Pradesh) linked with the rest of India only by a narrow corridor. There is opposition to immigration from Bangladesh and the rest of India, and demand for secession.

Northeast Passage sea route from the N Atlantic, around Asia, to the N Pacific, pioneered by ◊Nordenskjöld 1878–79 and developed by the USSR in settling N Siberia from 1935. The USSR owns offshore islands and claims it as an internal waterway; the US claims that it is international.

Northern Areas districts N of Azad Kashmir, directly administered by Pakistan but not merged with it. India and Azad Kashmir each claim them as part of disputed Kashmir. They include Baltistan, Gilgit, Skardu, and Hunza (an independent principality for 900 years until 1974).

Northern Ireland see ◊Ireland, Northern.

northern lights common name for the ◊aurora borealis.

Northern Rhodesia former name (until 1964) of ◊Zambia.

Northern Securities Co v US a US Supreme Court decision 1904 dealing with the right of the federal government to restrict monopolistic business practices. Two competitors, the Great Northern and the Northern Pacific railroad companies, joined finances to form the Northern Securities holding company. Convicted under the Sherman Antitrust Act 1890, the holding company appealed to the Supreme Court, arguing that the financial merger was not illegal because it was not intended for the restraint of trade. The Court voted 5 to 4 to uphold the conviction, rejuvenating federal authority under the antitrust laws.

Northern Territory territory of Australia
area 519,633 sq mi/1,346,200 sq km
capital Darwin (chief port)
towns Alice Springs
features mainly within the tropics, although with wide range of temperature; very low rainfall, but artesian bores are used; Macdonnell Ranges (Mt Zeil 4,956 ft/1,510 m); ◊Cocos and ◊Christmas Islands included in the territory 1984
products beef cattle, shrimps, bauxite (Gove), gold and copper (Tennant Creek), uranium (Ranger)
population (1987) 157,000
government there is an administrator and legislative assembly, and the territory is also represented in the federal parliament
history originally part of New South Wales, it was annexed 1863 to South Australia but from 1911 until 1978 (when self-government was granted) was under the control of the Commonwealth of Australia government. Mineral discoveries on land occupied by Aborigines led to a royalty agreement 1979.

North Holland (Dutch ***Noord-Holland***) low-lying coastal province of the Netherlands occupying the peninsula jutting northward between the North Sea and the IJsselmeer; area 1,031 sq mi/2,670 sq km; population (1988) 2,353,000. Most of it is below sea level, protected from the sea by a series of sand dunes and artificial dykes. The capital is Haarlem; other towns are Amsterdam, Hilversum, Den Helder, and the cheese centers Alkmaar and Edam. Famous for its bulbfields, the province also produces grain and vegetables.

North Korea see ◊Korea, North.

North Ossetian area of the Caucasus, USSR; see also ◊Ossetia.

North Pole the N point where an imaginary line penetrates the Earth's surface by the axis about which it revolves; see also ◊Poles and ◊Arctic.

North Rhine–Westphalia (German *Nordrhein-Westfalen*) administrative *Land* of the Federal Republic of Germany
area 13,163 sq mi/34,100 sq km
capital Düsseldorf
cities Cologne, Essen, Dortmund, Duisburg, Bochum, Wuppertal, Bielefeld, Bonn, Gelsenkirchen, Münster, Mönchengladbach
features valley of the Rhine; Ruhr industrial district
products iron, steel, coal, lignite, electrical goods, fertilizers, synthetic textiles
population (1988) 16,700,000
religion 53% Roman Catholic, 42% Protestant
history see ◊Westphalia.

Northrop John 1891–1987. US chemist. In the 1930s he crystallized a number of enzymes, including pepsin and trypsin, showing conclusively that they were proteins. He shared the 1946 Nobel Prize for Chemistry with Wendell ◊Stanley and James ◊Sumner.

North Sea sea to the E of Britain and bounded by the coasts of Belgium, the Netherlands, Germany, Denmark, and Norway; area 202,000 sq mi/523,000 sq km; average depth 180 ft/55 m, greatest depth 2,165 ft/660 m. In the NE it joins the Norwegian Sea, and in the S it meets the Strait of Dover. It has fisheries, oil, and gas. In 1987, Britain dumped more than 4,700 tons of sewage sludge into the North Sea: see ◊sewage disposal.

North–South divide the North–South geographical division of the world which theoretically demarcates the rich from the poor. The South includes all of Asia except Japan, Australia, and New Zealand, all of Africa, the Middle East, Central and South America. The North includes Europe, the US, Canada, and the USSR.

Many of the countries in the South, particularly the relatively newly industrialized ones such as South Korea and Taiwan could be said to have more in common with the developed than developing ◊Third World counties.

Northumberland county in N England
area 1,942 sq mi/5,030 sq km
cities Newcastle-upon-Tyne (administrative headquarters), Berwick-upon-Tweed, Hexham
features Cheviot Hills; rivers: Tweed, upper Tyne of Northumberland National Park in the W; ◊Holy Island; ◊Farne Islands; part of Hadrian's Wall and Housestead's Fort; Alnwick and Bamburgh castles; Thomas Bewick museum; large moorland areas are used for military maneuvers
products sheep
population (1986) 301,000
famous people Thomas Bewick, Jack Charlton.

Northumberland John Dudley, Duke of c. 1502–1553. English politician, son of the privy councillor Edmund Dudley (beheaded 1510) and chief minister until Edward VI's death 1553. He tried to place his daughter-in-law Lady Jane ◊Grey on the throne, and was executed on Mary I's accession.

Northumbria Anglo-Saxon kingdom that covered NE England and SE Scotland, comprising the 6th-century kingdoms of Bernicia (Forth–Tees) and Deira (Tees–Humber), united in the 7th century. It accepted the supremacy of Wessex 827 and was conquered by the Danes in the late 9th century.

North-West Frontier Province province of Pakistan; capital Peshawar; area 28,757 sq mi/74,500 sq km; population (1985) 12,287,000. It was a province of British India 1901–47. It includes the strategic Khyber Pass, the site of constant struggle between the British Raj and the ◊Pathan warriors.

Northwest Territories

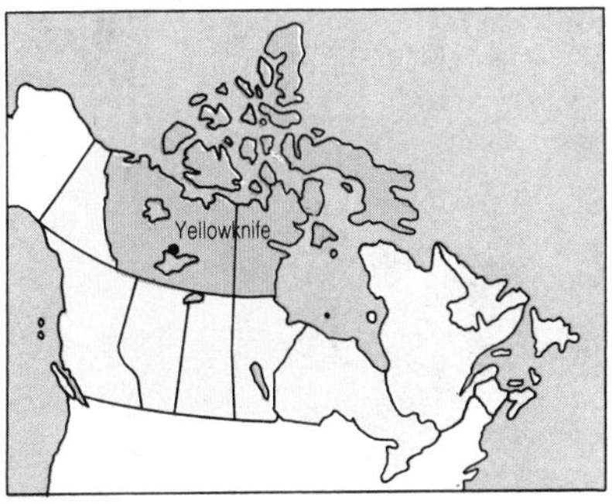
Yellowknife

In the 1980s it had to accommodate a stream of refugees from neighboring Afghanistan.

Northwest Passage Atlantic–Pacific sea route around the N of Canada. Canada, which owns offshore islands, claims it as an internal waterway; the US insists that it is an international waterway and sent an icebreaker through without permission 1985.

Early explorers included the Englishmen Martin Frobisher and, later, John Franklin, whose failure to return 1847 led to the organization of 39 expeditions in the next 10 years. R McClune explored the passage 1850–53 although he did not cover the whole route by sea. The polar explorer ◊Amundsen was the first European to sail through.

Northwest Territories territory of Canada
area 1,322,552 sq mi/3,426,300 sq km
capital Yellowknife physical extends to the North Pole, to Hudson's Bay in the east, and in the west to the edge of the Canadian Shield
features Mackenzie River; lakes: Great Slave, Great Bear; Miles Canyon
products oil, natural gas, zinc, lead, gold, tungsten, silver
population (1986) 52,000; over 50% native peoples (Indian, Eskimo)
history the area was the northern part of Rupert's Land, bought by the Canadian government from the Hudson's Bay Company 1869. An act of 1952 placed the Northwest Territories under a commissioner acting in Ottawa under the Ministry of Northern Affairs and Natural Resources. In 1990 territorial control of over 135,000 sq mi/350,000 sq km of the Northwest Territories was given to the ◊Eskimo.

North Yorkshire county in NE England
area 3,212 sq mi/8,320 sq km
cities Northallerton (administrative headquarters), York; resorts: Harrogate, Scarborough, Whitby
features England's largest county; including part of the Pennines, the Vale of York, and the Cleveland Hills and North Yorkshire Moors, which form a national park (within which is Fylingdales radar station to give early warning—4 min—of nuclear attack); and Rievaulx abbey; Yorkshire Dales National Park (including Swaledale, Wensleydale, and Bolton Abbey in Wharfedale); rivers: Derwent, Ouse; Fountains Abbey near Ripon, with Studley Royal Gardens; Castle Howard; York Minster
products cereals, wool and meat from sheep, dairy products, coal, electrical goods
population (1987) 706,000
famous people Alcuin, W H Auden.

Norwalk city in SW Connecticut, on the Norwalk River where it flows into Long Island Sound, NE of Stamford. Industries include electronic equipment, clothing, hardware, and furniture; population (1990) 78,331.

Norway country in NW Europe, on the Scandinavian peninsula, bounded E by Sweden and NE by Finland and the USSR.
government Norway's constitution dates from 1814. The hereditary monarch is the formal head of state, and the legislature consists of a single-

Norway
Kingdom of
(Kongeriket Norge)

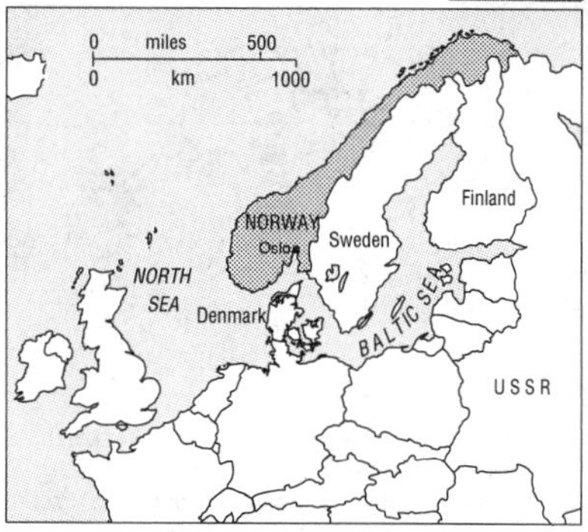
0 miles 500
0 km 1000
NORWAY
Oslo
Sweden
Finland
NORTH SEA
Denmark
BALTIC SEA
USSR

area 149,421 sq mi/387,000 sq km (includes Svalbard and Jan Mayen)
capital Oslo
cities Bergen, Trondheim, Stavanger
physical mountainous with fertile valleys and deeply indented coast; forests cover 25%; extends N of Arctic Circle
territories dependencies in the Arctic (Svalbard and Jan Mayen) and in Antarctica (Bouvet and Peter I Island, and Queen Maud Land)
features fjords, including Hardanger and Sogne, longest 115 mi/185 km, deepest 4,086 ft/1,245 m; glaciers in north; midnight sun and northern lights
head of state Harald V from 1991
head of government Prime Minister Gro Harlem Brundtland from 1990
political system constitutional monarchy
political parties Norwegian Labor Party (DNA), moderate, left-of-center; Conservative Party, progressive, right-of-center; Christian People's Party (KrF), Christian, center-left; Centre Party (SP), left-of-center, rural-oriented
exports petrochemicals from North Sea oil and gas, paper, wood pulp, furniture, iron ore and other minerals, high-tech goods, sports goods, fish
currency krone
population (1990 est) 4,214,000; growth rate 0.3% p.a.
life expectancy men 73, women 80 (1989)
language Norwegian (official); Lapp and Finnish-speaking minorities
religion Evangelical Lutheran (endowed by state) 94%
literacy 100% (1989)
GNP $89 bn (1988); $13,790 per head (1984)
chronology
1814 Became independent from Denmark.
1905 Links with Sweden ended.
1940–45 Occupied by Germany.
1949 Joined NATO.
1952 Joined Nordic Council.
1957 King Haakon VII succeeded by his son Olaf V.
1960 Joined EFTA.
1972 Accepted into membership of European Community; application withdrawn after a referendum.
1988 Gro Harlem Brundtland awarded Third World Prize.
1989 Jan P Syze became prime minister.
1990 Brundtland returned to power.
1991 King Olaf V dies and is succeeded by his son Harald V.

nose

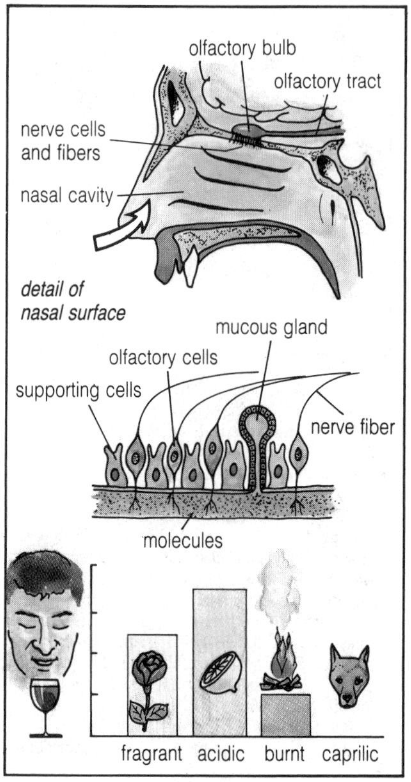
olfactory bulb
olfactory tract
nerve cells and fibers
nasal cavity
detail of nasal surface
mucous gland
olfactory cells
supporting cells
nerve fiber
molecules
fragrant
acidic
burnt
caprilic

chamber parliament, the *Storting*. The monarch appoints a prime minister and state council on the basis of support in the *Storting*, to which they are all responsible.

***The** Storting* has 157 members, elected for a four-year term by universal suffrage through a system of proportional representation. Once elected, it divides itself into two parts, a fourth of the members being chosen to form an upper house, the *Lagting*, and the remainder a lower house, the *Odelsting*. All legislation must be first introduced in the *Odelsting* and then passed to the *Lagting* for approval, amendment, or rejection. Once a bill has had parliamentary approval it must receive the royal assent.

history Norway was originally inhabited by Lapps and other nomads and was gradually invaded by ◊Goths. It was ruled by local chieftains until unified by Harald Fairhair (reigned 872–933) as a feudal country. Norway's ◊Vikings raided and settled in many parts of Europe in the 8th–11th centuries. Christianity was introduced by ◊Olaf II in the 11th century; he was defeated 1030 by rebel chiefs backed by ◊Canute, but his son Magnus I regained the throne 1035. Haakon IV (1217–63) established the authority of the crown over the nobles and the church and made the monarchy hereditary.

◊Denmark and Norway were united by marriage 1380, and in 1397 Norway, Denmark, and Sweden became united under one sovereign. Sweden broke away 1523, but Norway remained under Danish rule until 1814, when it was ceded to Sweden. Norway rebelled, Sweden invaded, and a compromise was reached whereby Norway kept its own parliament but was united with Sweden under a common monarch.

Conflict between the Norwegian parliament and the Swedish crown continued until 1905, when the parliament declared Norway completely independent. This was confirmed by plebiscite, and Prince Carl of Denmark was elected king as Haakon VII. He ruled for 52 years until his death 1957. His son ◊Olaf V is the reigning monarch.

The experience of German occupation 1940–45 persuaded the Norwegians to abandon their traditional neutral stance and join NATO 1949, the Nordic Council 1952, and the European Free Trade Area (EFTA) 1960. Norway was accepted into membership of the European Community 1972, but a referendum held that year rejected the proposal and the application was withdrawn. Its exploitation of North Sea oil and gas resources have given it a higher income per head of population than most of its European neighbors, and during the Cold War it succeeded in maintaining good relations with the USSR without damaging its commitments in the West.

Norway has enjoyed stability under a series of coalition governments. In Nov 1988 Prime Minister Gro Harlem Brundtland was awarded the annual Third World Prize for her work on environmental issues but in the Sept 1989 election her party lost seats to the far-rights and the far-left. Following a vote of no confidence, she resigned in Oct 1989 and was succeeded by the conservative Jan P Syze. In Oct 1990 the Syze coalition collapsed and Mrs Brundtland returned to power, leading a minority Labour government. In 1991, King Olav V died; his son Harald V succeeded.

Norwegian Sea part of the ◊Arctic Ocean.

Norwich cathedral city in Norfolk, E England; population (1986) 121,600. Industries include shoes, clothing, chemicals, confectionery, engineering, and printing.

It has a Norman castle (with a collection of paintings by the Norwich school; Cotman and Crome); 15th-century Guildhall, medieval churches, Tudor houses, Georgian Assembly House. The University of East Anglia 1963 has the Richard Rogers Sainsbury Art Gallery on its campus. The Sainsbury Laboratory 1987, in association with the John Innes Institute, was founded to study the molecular causes of disease.

Norwich city in SE Connecticut, at the confluence of the Yantic and Quinebaug rivers that form the Thames River, N of New London; seat of New London County. Industries include leather, paper, and metal products; electronic equipment; and clothing; population (1990) 37,391. In the 1700s it was a shipping and shipbuilding center.

nose in humans, the upper entrance of the respiratory tract; the organ of the sense of smell. The external part is divided down the middle by a septum of ◊cartilage. The nostrils contain plates of cartilage that can be moved by muscles and have a growth of stiff hairs at the margin to prevent foreign objects from entering. The whole nasal cavity is lined with a ◊mucous membrane that warms and moistens the air and ejects dirt. In the upper parts of the cavity the membrane contains 50 million olfactory receptor cells (cells sensitive to smell).

nosebleed bleeding from the nose. Although usually minor and easily controlled, the loss of blood may occasionally be so rapid as to be life-threatening, particularly in small children. Most nosebleeds can be stopped by simply squeezing the nose for a few minutes with the head tilted back, but in exceptional cases transfusion may be required and the nose may need to be packed with ribbon gauze or cauterized.

nosocomial description of any infection acquired in a hospital or other medical facility, whether its effects are seen during the patient's stay or following discharge. Widely prevalent in some hospitals, nosocomial infections threaten patients who are seriously ill or whose immune systems have been suppressed. The threat is compounded by the prevalence of drug-resistant ◊pathogens endemic to the hospital environment.

Nostradamus Latinized name of Michel de Nôtredame 1503–1566. French physician and astrologer who was consulted by Catherine de' Medici and was physician to Charles IX. His book of prophecies in rhyme, *Centuries* 1555, has had a number of interpretations.

nostril in vertebrates, the opening of the nasal cavity, in which cells sensitive to smell are located. (In fish, these cells detect water-borne chemicals, so they are effectively organs of taste.) In vertebrates with lungs (lungfish and tetrapod vertebrates), the nostrils also take in air. In humans, and most other mammals, the nostrils are located on a ◊nose.

notation in music, the use of symbols to represent individual sounds (such as the notes of the chromatic scale) so that they can be accurately interpreted and reproduced. The earliest system was developed by the ancient Sumerians; later the Greeks and Romans devised systems for their music dramas. The system in use today goes back to the Middle Ages, to the Italian monk Guido d'Arezzo 1026.

notation in dance, the recording of dances by symbols. There are several dance notation systems; prominent among them is ◊Labanotation.

note in music, the written symbol indicating pitch and duration, the sound of which is a tone.

notochord the stiff but flexible rod that lies between the gut and nerve cord of all embryonic and larval chordates, including the vertebrates. It forms the supporting structure of the adult lancelet, but in vertebrates it is replaced by the vertebral column, or spine.

Nottingham industrial city (engineering, coal-mining, bicycles, textiles, knitwear, pharmaceuticals, tobacco, lace, electronics) and administrative headquarters of Nottinghamshire, England; population (1981) 217,080.

Features include the university 1881, the Playhouse (opened 1963), and the recently refurbished Theatre Royal. Nearby are Newstead Abbey, home of Byron, and D H Lawrence's home at Eastwood.

Nottinghamshire county in central England
area 834 sq mi/2,160 sq km
towns Nottingham (administrative headquarters), Mansfield, Worksop
features river Trent; the remaining areas of Sherwood Forest (home of ◊Robin Hood), formerly a royal hunting ground, are included in the "Dukeries"; Cresswell Crags (remains of prehistoric humans); D H Lawrence commemorative walk from Eastwood (where he lived) to Old Brinsley Colliery
products cereals, cattle, sheep, light engineering, footwear, limestone, ironstone, oil
population (1987) 1,008,000
famous people D H Lawrence, Alan Sillitoe
history in World War II Nottinghamshire produced the only oil out of U-boat reach, and drilling revived in the 1980s.

Nouakchott capital of Mauritania; population (1985) 500,000. Products include salt, cement, and insecticides.

Nouméa a port on the SW coast of New Caledonia; population (1983) 60,100.

noun grammatical ◊part of speech that names a person, animal, object, quality, idea, or time. Nouns can refer to objects such as *house*, *tree* (concrete nouns); specific persons and places such as *John Alden*, the *White House* (proper nouns); ideas such as *love*, *anger* (abstract nouns). In English many simple words are both noun and verb (*jump*, *reign*, *rain*). Adjectives are sometimes used as nouns ("a *local* man," "one of the *locals*").

A common noun does not begin with a capital letter (*child*, *cat*), whereas a proper noun does, because it is the name of a particular person, animal, or place (*Jane*, *Rover*, *Norfolk*). A concrete noun refers to things that can be sensed (*dog*, *box*), whereas an abstract noun relates to generalizations abstracted from life as we observe it (*fear*, *condition*, *truth*). A countable noun can have a plural form (*book*: *books*), while an uncountable noun or mass noun cannot (*dough*). Many English nouns can be used both countably and uncountably (*wine*: "Have some *wine*; it's one of our best *wines*"). A collective noun is singular in form but refers to a group (*flock*, *group*, *committee*), and a compound noun is made up of two or more nouns (*teapot*, *baseball team*, *car-factory strike committee*). A verbal noun is formed from a

Nova Scotia

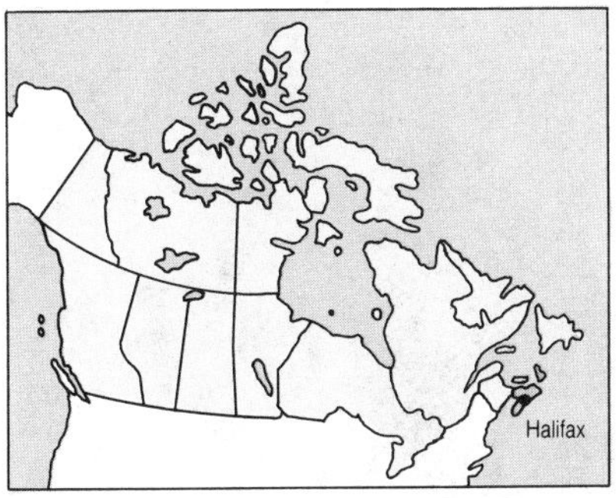
Halifax

verb as a ◊gerund or otherwise (*build: building*; *regulate*: *regulation*).

nouvelle cuisine (French "new cooking") contemporary French cooking style that avoids traditional rich sauces, emphasizing fresh ingredients, attractive presentation and small portions. The phrase was coined in the British magazine *Harpers & Queen* in June 1975.

nova (plural novae) faint star that suddenly erupts in brightness, becoming visible with binoculars or to the naked eye. Novae are believed to occur in close ◊double star systems, where gas from one star flows to a companion ◊white dwarf. The gas ignites and is thrown off in an explosion, the star increasing in brightness by 10,000 times or more. Unlike a ◊supernova, the star is not completely disrupted by the outburst.

After a few weeks or months it subsides to its previous state; it may erupt many more times. The name comes from the Latin "new," although novae are not new stars at all.

Novak Kim (Marilyn Pauline) 1933– . US film actress who charmed audiences with her roles in *The Man with The Golden Arm* 1955 and *Picnic* 1956. She also starred in such films as *Pal Joey* 1957, *Bell, Book and Candle* 1958, *Vertigo* 1958, *The Legend of Lyla Clare* 1968, and *The Mirror Crack'd* 1980.

Novalis pen name of Friedrich Leopold von Hardenberg 1772–1801. Pioneer German Romantic poet, who wrote *Hymnen an die Nacht/Hymns to the Night* 1800, prompted by the death of his fiancée Sophie von Kühn. He left two unfinished romances, *Die Lehrlinge zu Sais/The Novices of Sais* and *Heinrich von Ofterdingen*.

Nova Lisboa former name (1928–73) for ◊Huambo, in Angola.

Nova Scotia province of E Canada
area 21,423 sq mi/55,500 sq km
capital Halifax (chief port)
towns Dartmouth, Sydney
features Cabot Trail (Cape Breton Island); Alexander Graham Bell Museum; Fortress Louisbourg; Strait of Canso Superport, the largest deepwater harbor on the Atlantic coast of North America
products coal, gypsum, dairy products, poultry, fruit, forest products, fish products (including scallop and lobster)
population (1986) 873,000
history Nova Scotia was visited by the navigator Giovanni ◊Caboto 1497. A French settlement was established 1604, but expelled 1613 by English colonists from Virginia. The name of the colony was changed from Acadia to Nova Scotia 1621. England and France contended for possession of the territory until Nova Scotia (which then included present-day New Brunswick and Prince Edward Island) was ceded to Britain 1713; Cape Breton Island remained French until 1763. Nova Scotia was one of the four original provinces of the dominion of Canada.

Novaya Zemlya Arctic island group off the NE of the USSR; area 31,394 sq mi/81,279 sq km; population, a few Samoyed. It is rich in birds, seals, and walrus.

novel an extended fictional prose narrative, often including some sense of the psychological development of the central characters and of their relationship with a broader world. The European novel is said to have originated in Greece in the 2nd century BC. The modern novel took its name and inspiration from the Italian *novella*, the short tale of varied character which became popular in the late 13th century. As the main form of narrative fiction in the 20th century, the novel is frequently classified according to genres and subgenres such as the ◊historical novel, ◊detective fiction, ◊fantasy, and ◊science fiction.

Ancient Greek examples include the *Daphnis and Chloë* of Longus; almost the only surviving Latin work that could be called a novel is the *Golden Ass* of Apuleius (late 2nd century), based on a Greek model. There is a similar, but until the 19th century independent, tradition of prose narrative including psychological development in the Far East, notably in Japan, with *The Tale of Genji* by Murasaki Shikibu (978–c. 1015).

The works of the Italian writers Boccaccio and Bandello were translated into English in such collections as Painter's *Palace of Pleasure* 1566–67, and inspired the Elizabethan novelists, including Lyly, Sidney, Greene, Nash, and Lodge. In Spain, Cervantes's *Don Quixote* 1604 contributed to the development of the novel through its translation into other European languages, but the 17th century was dominated by the French romances of La Calprenède and Mlle de Scudéry, although Congreve and Aphra Behn continued the English tradition.

In the 18th century the realistic novel was established in England by the work of Defoe, Richardson, Fielding, Sterne, and Smollett. Walpole, and later Mary Shelley, developed the Gothic novel; in the early 19th century Sir Walter Scott developed the historical novel, and Jane Austen wrote "novels of manners." Celebrated novelists of the Victorian age in Britain were Dickens, Thackeray, the Brontës, George Eliot, Trollope, and Stevenson. The 19th century was also a great period for the novel in the US, with Cooper, Melville, Hawthorne, and Twain; in France, with Hugo, Balzac, the two Dumas, George Sand, and Zola; in Germany, with Goethe and Jean Paul; and in Russia, with Gogol, Turgenev, Dostoievsky, and Tolstoy.

From the end of the 19th century the US produced novelists in such schools as realism (Wharton, Crane, Howells, and Cather) and naturalism/social protest (Dreiser, Sinclair, Norris, and London). Before World War II Ferber, Lewis, Buck, Hemingway, Fitzgerald, Steinbeck, Thomas Wolfe, and Faulkner had made names for themselves; many of them continued to enjoy success after the war too.

In Britain the transition period from Victorian times to the 20th century includes Meredith, Butler, Hardy, Henry James, Kipling, Conrad, Wells, and Galsworthy. Slightly later are W Somerset Maugham, E M Forster, James Joyce, D H Lawrence, and Virginia Woolf—the last three being influential in the development of novel technique. Among those who began writing in the 1920s are J B Priestley, Aldous Huxley, Christopher Isherwood, Graham Greene, V S Pritchett, and Evelyn Waugh. The 1930s produced Joyce Cary, Lawrence Durrell, and George Orwell; more recent British writers include Anthony Powell, John Fowles, Kingsley Amis, Anthony Burgess, Iris Murdoch, Doris Lessing, and Salman Rushdie.

After World War II a new generation of US novelists reached maturity, with many of them crossing into poetry and short stories as well. This group includes Mailer, Jones, Heller, Warren, Capote, Hellman, Porter, McCullers, O'Connor, Salinger, Baldwin, Roth, Bellow, Sinter, Oates, Vonnegut, and Updike.

Twentieth-century European novelists include Lion Feuchtwanger, Thomas Mann, Franz Kafka, Ernst Wiechert, Stefan Zweig, Christa Wolff,

Novgorod *The theater, the monument to the 1,000th anniversary of the founding of the Russian state (862), and the cathedral of St Sophia (11th century) inside the Novgorod kremlin.*

Heinrich Böll, and Gunter Grass (Germany); André Gide, Marcel Proust, Jules Romains, François Mauriac, Michel Butor, Nathalie Sarraute, and Alain Robbe-Grillet (French); Gabriele d'Annunzio, Ignazio Silone, Alberto Moravia, Italo Calvino, Primo Levi, and Natalia Ginzburg (Italian); Maxim Gorky, Mikhail Sholokhov, Aleksei Tolstoi, Boris Pasternak, and Alexander Solzhenitsyn (Russian); Arturo Baréa, Pío Baroja and Ramón Pérez de Ayala (Spain). In Latin America contemporary novelists include Mario Vargas Llosa and Gabriel García Márquez. Canadians who have received acclaim include Morley Callaghan, Robertson Davies, Mordecai Richler, and Margaret Atwood.

Novello Ivor. Adopted name of Ivor Novello Davies 1893–1951. Welsh composer and actor-manager. He wrote popular songs, such as "Keep the Home Fires Burning," in World War I, and musicals in which he often appeared as the romantic lead, including *Glamorous Night* 1925, *The Dancing Years* 1939, and *Gay's the Word* 1951.

November criminals name given by right-wing nationalists in post-1918 Germany to the Socialist politicians who had taken over the government after the abdication of Kaiser Wilhelm II and had signed the armistice with the Western Allies Nov 1918.

Noverre Jean-Georges 1727–1810. French choreographer, writer, and ballet reformer. He promoted ◊*ballet d'action* (with a plot) and simple, free movement, and is often considered the creator of modern Classical ballet. *Les Petits Riens* 1778 was one of his works.

Novgorod industrial (chemicals, engineering, clothing, brewing) city on the Volkhov river, NW USSR; a major trading city in medieval times; population (1987) 228,000.

Novgorod was the original capital of the Russian state, founded at the invitation of the people of the city by the Viking (Varangian) chieftain Rurik 862. The Viking merchants who went there quickly became fully assimilated into the native Slav population. In 912 the capital of the principality moved to Kiev, but this did little to harm Novgorod. It developed a strong municipal government run by the leaders of the craft guilds and, until the 13th century, flourished as a major commercial center (with a monopoly on the Russian fur trade) for trade with Scandinavia, the Byzantine empire, and the Muslim world. It became one of the principal members of the ◊Hanseatic League, but its economy had already started to decline. This was hastened during the 15th-century rule of the boyars, nobles who had seized power from the guilds 1416. It came under the control of Ivan the Great III 1478 and was sacked by Ivan the Terrible 1570.

Novgorod school Russian school of icon and mural painters, active from the late 14th to the 16th century in Novgorod. They were inspired by the work of the refugee Byzantine artist ◊Theophanes the Greek. Russian artists imitated his linear style, but this became increasingly stilted and mannered.

Novi Sad industrial and commercial (pottery and cotton) city, capital of the autonomous province of Vojvodina, Yugoslavia, on the river Danube; population (1981) 257,700. Products include leather, textiles, and tobacco.

Novocaine trade name of procaine, the first synthetic local anesthetic, invented 1905. It has now been replaced by agents such as ◊lignocaine.

Novokuznetsk industrial city (steel, aluminum, chemicals) in the Kuzbas, S central USSR; population (1987) 589,000. It was called Stalinsk 1932–61.

Novorossiisk USSR Black Sea port and industrial (cement, metallurgy, food processing) city; population (1987) 179,000.

Novosibirsk industrial city (engineering, textiles, chemicals, food processing) in W Siberia, USSR, on the river Ob; population (1987) 1,423,000. Winter lasts eight months here.

At Akademgorodok ("Science City"), population 25,000, advanced research is carried on into Siberia's local problems.

Nowa Huta an industrial suburb of Kraków, on the Vistula river. It is the center of Poland's steel industry.

Noyes John Humphrey 1811–1886. US religious and communal leader. Founding a religious community 1836 in Putney, Vermont, he experimented with alternate forms of marriage, formulating the doctrine of free love in 1837. In 1848 he established an even larger religious society in central New York. This Oneida Community, as it was called, served for 30 years as a forum for Noyes's experiments in "complex marriage." By 1879, internal doubts and tensions had risen to such a degree that Noyes moved to Canada to avoid legal actions against him, and the community, which made silverware and steel traps, ended the social experiment and in 1881 became a joint-stock company.

Born in Brattleboro, Vermont, Noyes was educated at Dartmouth and the Andover Seminary.

nuclear warfare

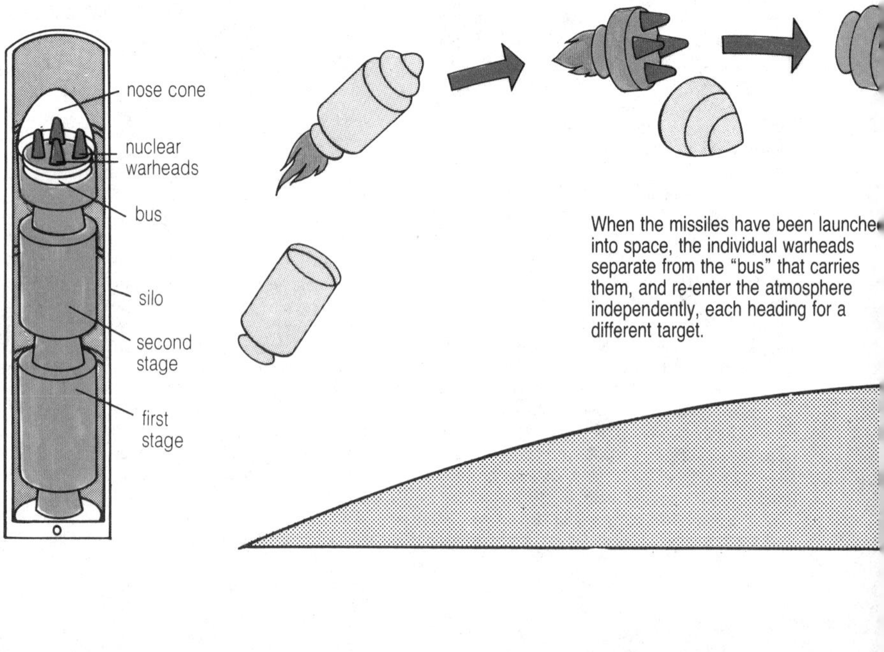
nose cone
nuclear warheads
bus
silo
second stage
first stage
When the missiles have been launched into space, the individual warheads separate from the "bus" that carries them, and re-enter the atmosphere independently, each heading for a different target.

While at Yale Divinity School, he developed ideas about the possibility of overcoming sin, and in 1834, when he announced that he had achieved human perfection, he was promptly expelled from Yale.

NPA abbreviation for New People's Army (Philippines).

NS abbreviation for ◊Nova Scotia.

NSAID abbreviation for nonsteroidal anti-inflammatory drug. There are several, and they are effective in the long-term treatment of rheumatoid ◊arthritis and osteoarthritis, and act to reduce swelling and pain in soft tissues. Bleeding into the digestive tract is a serious side effect: NSAIDs should not be taken by persons with peptic ulcers.

NT abbreviation for ◊Northern Territory, Australia.

NTP abbreviation for normal temperature and pressure, former name for ◊STP (standard temperature and pressure).

Nu U (Thakin) 1907– . Myanmar politician, prime minister of Burma (now Myanmar) for most of the period from 1948 to the military coup of 1962. Exiled from 1966, U Nu returned to the country 1980 and, in 1988, helped found the National League for Democracy opposition movement.

Formerly a teacher, U Nu joined the Dobhama Asiayone ("Our Burma") nationalist organization during the 1930s and was imprisoned by the British authorities at the start of World War II. He was released 1942, following Japan's invasion of Burma, and appointed foreign minister in a puppet government. In 1945 he fought with the British against the Japanese and on independence became Burma's first prime minister. Except for short breaks during 1956–57 and 1958–60, he remained in this post until General ◊Ne Win overthrew the parliamentary regime in 1962.

Nuba a member of the peoples of the Nuba mountains, W of the White Nile, Sudan. Their languages belong to the Nubian branch of the Chari-Nile family.

Nubia former African country now divided between Egypt and Sudan; it gives its name to the Nubian Desert S of Lake Nasser.

Ancient Egypt, which was briefly ruled by Nubian kings in the 8th–7th century BC, knew the N as Wawat and the S as Kush, with the dividing line roughly at Dongola. Egyptian building work in the area included temples at ◊Abu Simbel, Philae, and a defensive chain of forts that established the lines of development of medieval fortification. Nubia's capital about 600 BC–AD 350 was Meroe, near Khartoum. About AD 250–550 most of Nubia was occupied by the x-group people, of whom little is known; their royal mound tombs (mistaken by earlier investigations for natural mounds created by wind erosion) were excavated in the 1930s by W B Emery, and many horses and attendants were found to have been slaughtered to accompany the richly jeweled dead.

nuclear arms verification the process of checking the number and types of nuclear weapons held by a country in accordance with negotiated limits. The chief means are:

reconnaissance satellites that detect submarines or weapon silos, using angled cameras to give three-dimensional pictures of installations, penetrating camouflage by means of scanners, and partially seeing through cloud and darkness by infrared devices;

telemetry, or radio transmission of instrument readings;

interception to get information on performance of weapons under test;

on-site inspection by experts visiting bases, launch sites, storage facilities, and test sites in another country;

radar tracking of missiles in flight;

seismic monitoring of underground tests, in the same way as with earthquakes. This is not accurate and on-site inspection is needed. Tests in the atmosphere, space, or the oceans are forbidden, and the ban is accepted because explosions are not only dangerous to all but immediately detectable.

nuclear energy energy from the inner core or ◊nucleus of the atom, as opposed to energy released in chemical processes, which is derived from the electrons surrounding the nucleus.

Nuclear fission, as in an atomic bomb, is achieved by allowing a ◊neutron to strike the nucleus of an atom of fissile material (such as uranium-235 or plutonium-239), which then splits apart to release two or three other neutrons. If the uranium-235 is pure, a ◊chain reaction is set up when these neutrons in turn strike other nuclei. This happens very quickly, resulting in the tremendous release of energy seen in nuclear explosions. The process is controlled inside the reactor of a nuclear power plant by absorbing excess neutrons in control rods and slowing down their speed.

Nuclear fusion is the release of thermonuclear energy by the conversion of hydrogen nuclei to helium nuclei, a continuing reaction in the Sun and other stars. Nuclear fusion is the principle behind thermonuclear weapons (the ◊hydrogen bomb). Attempts to harness nuclear fusion for commercial power production have so far not succeeded.

nuclear physics the study of the properties of the nucleus of the ◊atom, including the structure of nuclei; nuclear forces; the interactions between particles and nuclei; and the study of ◊radioactive decay. See also ◊particle physics.

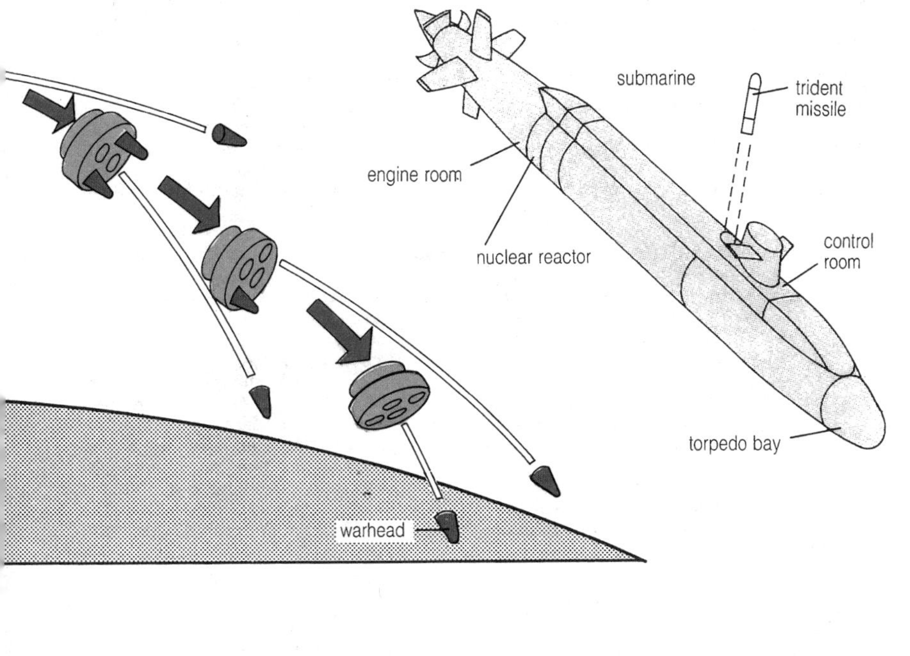
submarine
trident missile
engine room
nuclear reactor
control room
torpedo bay
warhead

nuclear reactor device for producing ◊nuclear energy in a controlled manner. There are various types of reactor in use, all using nuclear fission. In a gas-cooled reactor, a circulating gas under pressure (such as carbon dioxide) removes heat from the core of the reactor, which usually contains natural uranium. The efficiency of the fission process is increased by slowing neutrons in the core by using a ◊moderator such as carbon. The reaction is controlled with neutron-absorbing rods made of boron. An advanced gas-cooled reactor (AGR) generally has enriched uranium as its fuel. A water-cooled reactor, such as the steam-generating heavy water (deuterium oxide) reactor, has water circulating through the hot core. The water is converted to steam, which drives turbo-alternators for generating electricity. The most widely used reactor is the pressurized-water reactor, which contains a sealed system of pressurized water that is heated to form steam in heat exchangers in an external circuit. The ◊breeder reactor has no moderator and uses fast neutrons to bring about fission; it produces more fuel than it consumes.

nuclear safety the use of nuclear energy has given rise to concern over safety. Anxiety has been heightened by accidents such as those at Windscale (UK), Five Mile Island (US) and Chernobyl (USSR). There has also been mounting concern about the production and disposal of nuclear waste, the ◊radioactive and toxic by-products of the nuclear energy industry. Burial on land or at sea raises problems of safety, environmental pollution, and security. Nuclear waste has an active half-life of thousands of years and no guarantees exist for the safety of the various methods of disposal. Nuclear safety is still a controversial subject since governments will not recognize the hazards of ◊radiation and ◊radiation sickness. In 1990 a scientific study revealed an increased risk of leukemia in children whose fathers had worked at Sellafield between 1950 and 1985. Sellafield (UK) is the world's greatest discharger of radioactive waste, followed by Hanford, Washington (US).

nuclear warfare war involving the use of nuclear weapons. Nuclear-weapons research began in Britain 1940, but was transferred to the US after it entered World War II. The research program, known as the Manhattan Project, was directed by J Robert Oppenheimer. The worldwide total of nuclear weapons in 1989 was about 50,000, and the number of countries possessing nuclear weapons stood officially at five—the US, USSR, UK, France, and China—although many other nations were thought either to have a usable stockpile of these weapons (Israel, South Africa) or the ability to produce them quickly (India, Pakistan, and others).

atomic bomb The original weapons relied on use of a chemical explosion to trigger a chain reaction. The first test explosion was at Alamogordo, New Mexico, July 16, 1945; the first use in war was by the US against Japan Aug 6, 1945, over Hiroshima and three days later at Nagasaki.

hydrogen bomb A much more powerful weapon than the atomic bomb, it relies on the release of thermonuclear energy by the condensation of hydrogen nuclei to helium nuclei (as happens in the Sun). The first detonation was at Eniwetok Atoll, Pacific Ocean, 1952 by the US.

neutron bomb or enhanced radiation weapon (ERW). A very small hydrogen bomb that has relatively high radiation but relatively low blast, designed to kill (in up to six days) by a brief neutron radiation that leaves buildings and weaponry intact.

nuclear methods of attack now include aircraft bombs, rocket-propelled missiles with nuclear warheads (long- or short-range, surface-to-surface, and surface-to-air), depth charges, and high-powered landmines ("atomic demolition munitions" to blast craters in the path of an advancing enemy army).

nuclear waste the radioactive and toxic by-products of the nuclear-energy and nuclear-weapons industries. Reactor waste is of three types: high-level spent fuel, or the residue when nuclear fuel has been removed from a reactor and reprocessed; intermediate, which may be long- or short-lived; and low-level, but bulky, waste from reactors, which has only short-lived radioactivity. Disposal, by burial on land or at sea, has raised problems of safety, environmental pollution, and security. In absolute terms, nuclear waste cannot be safely relocated or disposed of.

nuclear winter an expected long-term effect of a widespread nuclear war. In the wake of the destruction caused by nuclear blasts and the subsequent radiation, it has been suggested that atmospheric pollution by dust, smoke, soot, and ash could prevent the Sun's rays from penetrating for a period of time sufficient to eradicate most plant life on which other life depends, and create a new Ice Age.

Even after it had settled, ash would still reflect the Sun's rays and delay the planet's return to normal warmth. Insects, grasses, and sea life would have the best prospects of survival, as well as microorganisms.

nucleic acid complex organic acid made up of a long chain of nucleotides. The two types, known as DNA (deoxyribonucleic acid) and RNA (ribonucleic acid), form the basis of heredity. The nucleotides are made up of a sugar (deoxyribose or ribose), a phosphate group, and one of four purine or pyrimidine bases. The order of the bases along the nucleic acid strand contains the genetic code.

nucleolus in biology, a structure found in the nucleus of ◊eukaryotic cells. It produces the RNA that makes up the ◊ribosomes, from instructions in the DNA.

nucleon either a ◊proton or a ◊neutron, a particle present in the atomic nucleus.

nucleon number alternate name for the ◊mass number of an atom.

nucleotide organic compound consisting of a purine (adenine or guanine) or a pyrimidine (thymine, uracil, or cytosine) base linked to a sugar (deoxyribose or ribose) and a phosphate group. ◊DNA and ◊RNA are made up of long chains of nucleotides.

nucleus in physics, the positively charged central part of an ◊atom, which constitutes almost all its mass. Except for hydrogen nuclei, which have only ◊protons, nuclei are composed of both protons and ◊neutrons. Surrounding the nuclei are ◊electrons, which contain a negative charge equal to the protons, thus giving the atom a neutral charge.

nucleus in biology, the central, membrane-enclosed part of a ◊eukaryotic cell, containing the chromosomes.

nugget piece of gold found as a lump of the native ore. Nuggets occur in ◊alluvial deposits where river-borne particles of the metal have adhered to one another.

nuisance in law, interference with enjoyment of, or rights over, land. There are two kinds of nuisance. Private nuisance affects a particular occupier of land, such as noise from a neighbor; the aggrieved occupier can apply for an ◊injunction and claim ◊damages. Public nuisance affects an indefinite number of members of the public, such as obstructing the highway; it is a criminal offense. In this case, individuals can claim damages only if they are affected more than the general public.

Nujoma Sam 1929– . Namibian left-wing politician, president from 1990, founder and leader of ◊SWAPO (the South-West Africa People's Organization) from 1959. He was exiled in 1960 and controlled guerrillas from Angolan bases until the first free elections were held 1989, taking office early the following year.

Nuku'alofa capital and port of Tonga on Tongatapu; population (1986) 29,000.

Nullarbor Plain (Latin *nullus arbor* "no tree") arid coastal plateau area divided between W and S Australia; there is a network of caves beneath it. Atom-bomb experiments were carried out in the 1950s at Maralinga, an area in the NE bordering on the Great Victoria Desert.

Numa Pompilius legendary king of Rome c. 716–c. 679 BC, who succeeded Romulus and was credited with the introduction of religious rites.

numbat or ***banded anteater*** Australian marsupial anteater *Myrmecobius fasciatus*. It is brown with white stripes on the back and has a long tubular tongue to gather termites and ants. The body is about 10 in/25 cm long, and the tongue can be extended 4 in/10 cm.

number a symbol used in counting or measuring. In mathematics, there are various kinds of numbers. The everyday number system is the decimal ("proceeding by tens") system, using the base ten. ◊Real numbers include all rational numbers (integers, or whole numbers, and fractions) and irrational numbers (those not expressible as fractions). ◊Complex numbers include the real and unreal numbers (real-number multiples of the square root of –1). The ◊binary number system, used in computers, has two as its base.

The ordinary numerals, 0, 1, 2, 3, 4, 5, 6, 7, 8, and 9, give a counting system that, in the decimal system, continues 10, 11, 12, 13, and so on. These are whole numbers (positive integers), with fractions represented as, for example, ¼, ½, ¾, or as decimal fractions (0.25, 0.5, 0.75). They are also rational numbers. Irrational numbers cannot be represented in this way and require symbols, such as $\sqrt{2}$, π, and e. They can be expressed numerically only as the (inexact) approximations 1.414, 3.142 and 2.718 (to three places of decimals) respectively. The symbols π and e are also examples of transcendental numbers, because they (unlike $\sqrt{2}$) cannot be derived by solving a ◊polynomial equation (an equation with one ◊variable quantity) with rational ◊coefficients (multiplying factors). Complex numbers, which include the real numbers as well as unreal numbers, take the general form $a + bi$, where $i = \sqrt{-1}$ (that is, $i^2 = -1$), and a is the real part and bi the unreal part.

history The ancient Egyptians, Greeks, Romans, and Babylonians all evolved number systems, although none had a zero, which was introduced from India by way of Arab mathematicians in about the 6th century AD and allowed a place-value system to be devised on which the decimal system is based. Other number systems have since evolved and have found applications. For example, numbers to base two (binary numbers), using only 0 and 1, are commonly used in digital computers to represent the two-state "on" or "off" pulses of electricity. Binary numbers were first developed by Gottfried Leibniz in the late 17th century.

Numidia Roman N African territory "nomads' land," now E ◊Algeria.

numismatics the study of ◊coins, and ◊medals and decorations.

nun (Latin *nonna* "elderly woman") a woman belonging to a religious order under the vows of poverty, chastity, and obedience, and living under a particular rule. Christian convents are ruled by a superior (often elected), who is subject to the authority of the bishop of the diocese or sometimes directly to the pope. See ◊monasticism.

It is possible that the institution of Christian communities for nuns preceded the establishment of monasteries. The majority of the male orders have their female counterparts.

nunatak a mountain peak protruding through an ice sheet.

nuncio (Italian "messenger") a diplomatic representative of the pope, from the 16th century, performing the functions of a papal ambassador.

Nunn Trevor 1940– . British stage director, linked with the Royal Shakespeare Company from 1968. He received a Tony award (with John Caird 1948–) for his production of *Nicholas Nickleby* 1982 and for the musical *Les Misérables* 1987.

Nuremberg (German *Nürnberg*) industrial city (electrical and other machinery, precision instruments, textiles, toys) in Bavaria, Federal Republic of Germany; population (1988) 467,000. From 1933 the Nuremberg rallies were held here, and in 1945 the Nuremberg trials of war criminals.

Created an imperial city 1219, it has an 11th–16th-century fortress and many medieval buildings (restored after destruction of 75% of the city in World War II), including the home of the 16th-century composer Hans Sachs, where the ◊Meistersingers met. The artist Dürer was born here.

Nuremberg rallies annual meetings 1933–38 of the German ◊Nazi Party. They were characterized by extensive torchlight parades, marches in party formations, and mass rallies addressed by Nazi leaders such as Hitler and Goebbels.

Nuremberg trials after World War II, the trials of the 24 chief ◊Nazi war criminals Nov 1945–Oct 1946 by an international military tribunal consisting of four judges and four prosecutors: one of each from the US, UK, USSR, and France. An appendix accused the German cabinet, general staff, high command, Nazi leadership corps, ◊SS, ◊Sturmabteilung, and ◊Gestapo of criminal behavior.

The main charges in the indictment were: (1) conspiracy to wage wars of aggression; (2) crimes against peace; (3) war crimes, for example, murder and ill-treatment of civilians and prisoners of war, deportation of civilians for slave labor, and killing of hostages; (4) crimes against humanity, for example, mass murder of the Jews and other peoples, and murder and ill-treatment of political opponents.

Of the accused, Krupp was too ill to be tried; Ley (1890–1945) committed suicide during the trial; and ◊Bormann, who had fled, was sentenced to death in his absence. Fritsche (1899–1953), Schacht (1877–1970), and ◊Papen were acquitted. The other 18 were found guilty on one or more counts. ◊Hess, Walther Funk (1890–1960), and ◊Raeder were sentenced to life imprisonment; Shirach (1907–1974) and Speer (1905–1981) to 20 years; Neurath (1873–1956) to 15 years; and Doenitz (1891–1980) to 10 years. The remaining 11 men, sentenced to death by hanging, were Hans Frank (1900–1946), Wilhelm Frick (1877–1946), ◊Goering (who committed suicide before he could be executed), ◊Jodl, ◊Kaltenbrunner, ◊Keitel, ◊Ribbentrop, ◊Rosenberg, Fritz Sauckel (1894–1946), Arthur Seyss-Inquart (1892–1946), and Julius Streicher (1885–1946). The SS and Gestapo were declared criminal organizations.

Nureyev Rudolf 1938– Russian dancer and choreographer. A soloist with the Kirov Ballet, he defected to the West during a visit to Paris in 1961. Mainly associated with the Royal Ballet (London) and as Margot ◊Fonteyn's principal partner, he was one of the most brilliant dancers of the 1960s and 1970s.

Nureyev danced in such roles as Prince Siegfried in *Swan Lake* and Armand in *Marguerite and Armand*, which was created specifically for Fonteyn and Nureyev. He also danced and acted in films and on television and choreographed several ballets.

nursery rhyme children's jingle. Usually limited to a couplet or quatrain with strongly marked rhythm and rhymes, nursery rhymes have often been handed down by oral tradition.

Some of the oldest nursery rhymes are connected with a traditional tune and were sung as accompaniment to ancient ring games, such as "Here we go round the mulberry bush," which was part of the May Day festivities. Others contain fragments of incantations and other rites; still others have a factual basis and commemorated popular figures, such as Jack Sprat and Jack Horner.

nursing care of the sick, the very young, the very old, and the disabled. Organized training originated 1836 in Germany, and was developed in Britain by the work of Florence ◊Nightingale, who, during the Crimean War, established standards of scientific, humanitarian care in military hospitals. Nurses give day-to-day care and carry out routine medical and surgical procedures under the supervision of a physician.

In ancient times very limited care was associated with some temples, and in Christian times nursing became associated with the religious orders until the Reformation brought it into secular hands in Protestant countries. Many specialities and qualifications now exist in Western countries, standards being maintained by professional bodies and boards.

In the US, although registration (RN) is the responsibility of individual states, an almost uniform standard has been established by the National League for Nursing (1952). There are a variety of degree programs.

Nusa Tenggara or ***Lesser Sunda Island*** volcanic archipelago in Indonesia, including ◊Bali, ◊Lombok, and ◊Timor; area 28,241 sq mi/ 73,144 sq km. The islands form two provinces of Indonesia: Nusu Tenggara Barat, population (1980) 2,724,500; and Nusu Tenggara Timur, population (1980) 2,737,000.

nut common name for a dry, single-seeded fruit that does not split open to release the seed. A nut is formed from more than one carpel, but only one seed becomes fully formed; the remainder is aborted. The wall of the fruit, the pericarp, becomes hard and woody, forming the outer shell. Examples are the acorn, hazelnut, and sweet chestnut. The kernels of most nuts provide a concentrated food with about 50% fat and a protein content of 10–20%, though a few, such as chestnuts, are high in carbohydrates and have only a moderate (5%) protein content. Most nuts are produced by perennial trees and bushes.

The term also describes various hard-shelled fruits and seeds, including almonds and walnuts, which are really the stones of ◊drupes, and Brazil nuts and shelled peanuts, which are both seeds. While the majority of nuts are obtained from plantations, considerable quantities of pecan and Brazil nuts are still collected from the wild. World nut production in the mid-1980s was about 4 million tons a year. Nuts also provide edible and industrial oils.

nut and bolt common method of fastening pieces of metal or wood together. The nut consists of a small block (usually metal) with a threaded hole in the center for screwing on to a threaded rod or pin (bolt or screw). The method came into use at the turn of the 19th century, following Henry Maudslay's invention of a precision screw-cutting ◊lathe.

nutation in botany, the spiral movement exhibited by the tips of certain stems during growth; it enables a climbing plant to find a suitable support. Nutation sometimes also occurs in tendrils and flower stalks.

nutation in astronomy, a slight "nodding" of the Earth in space, caused by the varying gravitational pulls of the Sun and Moon. Nutation changes the angle of the Earth's axial tilt (average 23.5°) by about 9 seconds of arc to either side of its mean position, a complete cycle taking just over 18.5 years.

nutcracker two jaylike birds of the genus *Nucifraga*, in the crow family (Corvidae).

One, *N. caryocatactes*, is native to Eurasia; the other, Clark's nutcracker *N. columbiana*, 12 in/ 30 cm long, lives in W North America and has gray and black plumage and a powerful beak.

nuthatch small bird of the family Sittidae, with a short tail and pointed beak. Nuthatches climb head first up, down, and around tree trunks and branches, foraging for insects and their larvae.

nuthatch

European nuthatch

The 5.5 in/14 cm long white-breasted nuthatch *Sitta carolinensis* of North America has a black cap, gray wings, and white underparts.

nutmeg kernel of the seed of the evergreen tree *Myristica fragrans*, native to the Moluccas. Both the nutmeg and its secondary covering, known as mace, are used as spice in cooking.

nutria or ***coypu*** South American water rodent *Myocastor coypus*, about 2 ft/60 cm long and weighing up to 20 lb/9 kg. It has a scaly, ratlike tail, webbed hind feet, a blunt, muzzled head, and large, orange incisors. The fur is reddish brown. It feeds on vegetation and lives in burrows in river and lake banks.

Taken to Europe and then to North America to be farmed for their fur, many escaped or were released and became established, often to the detriment of native species.

nutrition the science of food, and its effect on human and animal life, health, and disease. Nutrition is the study of the basic nutrients required to sustain life, their bioavailability in foods and overall diet, and the effects upon them of cooking and storage. Malnutrition can be caused by underfeeding, an imbalanced diet, and over-feeding. Nutrition is also the study of feeds for farm animals, pets, and wild animals kept in captivity.

Nuuk Greenlandic for ◊Godthaab, capital of Greenland.

NV abbreviation for ◊Nevada.

NY abbreviation for ◊New York.

nyala antelope *Tragelaphus angasi* found in the thick bush of S Africa. About 3 ft/1 m at the shoulder, it is grayish brown with thin vertical white stripes. Males have horns up to 2.6 ft/80 cm long.

Nyasa former name for Lake ◊Malawi.

Nyasaland former name (until 1964) for ◊Malawi.

Nyerere Julius (Kambarage) 1922– . Tanzanian Socialist politician, president 1964–85. Originally a teacher, he devoted himself from 1954 to the formation of the Tanganyika African National Union and subsequent campaigning for independence. He became chief minister 1960, was prime minister of Tanganyika 1961–62, president of the newly formed Tanganyika Republic 1962–64, and first president Tanzania 1964–85.

Nyerere *Julius Nyerere, president of Tanzania 1964–85.*

Nyers Rezso 1923– . Hungarian Socialist leader. As secretary of the ruling Hungarian Socialist Worker's Party's (HSWP) central committee 1962–74 and a member of its politburo 1966–74, he was the architect of Hungary's liberalizing economic reforms in 1968.

In 1940 Nyers joined the Hungarian Social Democratic Party, which in 1948 was forcibly merged with the communists. He was removed from his HSWP posts in 1974 and his career remained at a standstill until 1988, when, with a new reform initiative under way, he was brought back into the politburo. He became head of the newly formed Hungarian Socialist Party in 1989.

Nyíregyháza market town in E Hungary; population (1988) 119,000. It trades in tobacco and vegetables.

Nykvist Sven 1922– . Swedish director of photography, associated with the film director Ingmar Bergman. He worked frequently in the US from the mid-1970s onward. His films include *The Virgin Spring* 1960 (for Bergman), *Pretty Baby* 1978 (for Louis Malle), and *Fanny and Alexander* 1982 (for Bergman).

nylon synthetic long-chain polymer similar in chemical structure to protein. Nylon was the first all-synthesized fiber, made from petroleum, natural gas, air, and water by the Du Pont firm in 1938. It is used in the manufacture of molded articles, textiles, and medical sutures. Nylon fibers are stronger and more elastic than silk and are relatively insensitive to moisture and mildew. Nylon is used for hosiery and woven goods, simulating other materials such as silks and furs; it is also used for carpets.

nymph in Greek mythology, a guardian spirit of nature. Hamadryads or dryads guarded trees; naiads, springs and pools; oreads, hills and rocks; and nereids, the sea.

nymph in entomology, the immature form of insects that do not have a pupal stage—for example, grasshoppers and dragonflies. Nymphs generally resemble the adult (unlike larvae), but do not have fully formed reproductive organs or wings.

NZ abbreviation for ◊New Zealand.

Oahu island of Hawaii, in the N Pacific
area 589 sq mi/1,525 sq km
cities Honolulu (state capital)
physical formed by two extinct volcanoes
features Waikiki beach; Pearl Harbor naval base; Diamond Head; punchbowl craters
products sugar, pineapples; tourism is important
history settled by Polynesians from other Pacific islands AD 300–600. Kamehameha I, ruler 1824–54 of Hawaii, had taken Oahu by 1810; he made Honolulu the capital city of the Hawaiian kingdom.

oak any tree or shrub of the genus *Quercus* of the beech family Fagaceae, with over 300 known species widely distributed in temperate zones. Oaks are valuable for timber, the wood being durable and straight-grained. Their fruits are called acorns.

The 60 species of North American oaks are divided into two groups: white oaks and red oaks. Most white oaks have leaves with rounded lobes, and their acorns are sweet and mature in one season. Red oaks characteristically have spiny, pointed lobes on their leaves, and their bitter acorns take two years to mature. The white oak *Q. alba* of E US and the northern red oak *Q. rubra* are typical examples. The evergreen live oaks (such as *Q. virginiana*) form a subsection in the red oak group.

Oakland industrial port (vehicles, textiles, chemicals, food processing, shipbuilding) in California, on the E coast of San Francisco Bay; population (1990) 372,242. It is linked by bridge (1936) with San Francisco. An army terminal and naval air station are here. The community was laid out 1852 and became a terminus of the first transcontinental railroad 1869. A major earthquake 1989 buckled the bay bridge and an Oakland freeway section, causing more than 60 deaths.

Oakley Annie (full name, Phoebe Annie Oakley Mozee) 1860–1926. American sharpshooter, member of Buffalo Bill's Wild West Show (see William ◊Cody). Even though she was partially paralyzed in a train wreck, she continued to astound audiences with her ability virtually until her death. Kaiser Wilhelm of Germany had such faith in her talent that he allowed her to shoot a cigarette from his mouth.

Oak Ridge city in Tennessee, on the Clinch river, noted for the Oak Ridge National Laboratory 1943, which manufactures plutonium for nuclear weapons; population (1990) 27,310. Electronic equipment and scientific instruments are also manufactured here. Oak Ridge Associated Universities is a research and educational center. The community was founded 1942 as part of the Manhattan Project to develop an atomic bomb; by the end of World War II its population was more than 75,000. Ownership of the community passed to the residents in the late 1950s.

oarfish any of a family *Regalecidae* of deep-sea bony fishes, found in warm parts of the Atlantic, Pacific, and Indian oceans. They are large, up to 30 ft/9 m long, elongated, and compressed, with a fin along the back and a manelike crest behind the head. They have a small mouth, no teeth or scales, and large eyes. They are often reported as sea serpents.

oarweed any of several large, coarse, brown seaweeds (algae) found on the lower shore and below, also known as ◊kelp or tangle weed, especially *Laminaria digitata*. This species has fronds 3 to 6 ft/1 to 2 m long, a thick stalk, and a frond divided into flat fingers.

OAS abbreviation for ◊Organization of American States.

oasis area of land made fertile by the presence of water near the surface in an otherwise arid region. The occurrence of oases affects the distribution of plants, animals, and people in the desert regions of the world.

oat type of grass, genus *Avena*, a cereal food. The plant has long, narrow leaves and a stiff straw stem; the panicles of flowers, and later of grain, hang downward. The cultivated oat *Avena sativa* was an early domesticant (as a weed in the wheatfields) and survived cool temperatures where wheat had trouble growing. It is especially hardy in N Europe and is produced for human and animal food.

Oates Joyce Carol 1938– . US writer. Her novels, often containing surrealism and violence, include *A Garden of Earthly Delights* 1967, *Them* 1969, *Unholy Loves* 1979, and *A Bloodsmoor Romance* 1982, and *Because It Is Bitter, And Because It Is My Heart* 1990.

Born in Lockport, New York, Oates uses genres that range from romance to mystery to history, but most of her novels have supernatural elements. She also has written many short stories—notably, "Where Are You Going, Where

oak

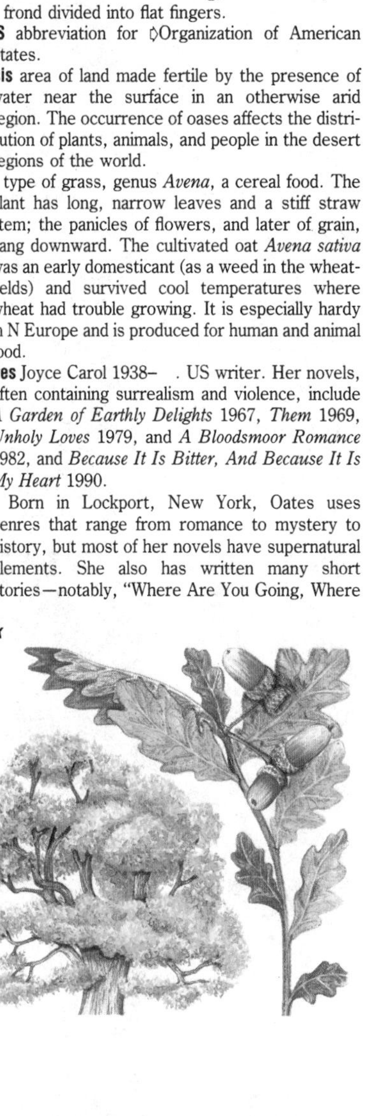

oat

Have You Been?"—poems, reviews, and critical essays. Her other works include *Goddess and Other Women* 1974, *The Assassions* 1975, *Bellefleur* 1980, *Angel of Light* 1981, *Last Days* 1984, *Marya: A Life* 1986, *You Must Remember This* 1987, *The Assignation* 1988, and *American Appetites* 1989.

oath a solemn promise to tell the truth or perform some duty, combined with an appeal to a deity or something held sacred.

OAU abbreviation for ◊Organization of African Unity.

Oaxaca capital of a state of the same name in the Sierra Madre del Sur mountain range, central Mexico; population (1980) 157,300; former hometown of presidents Benito Juárez and Porfirio Diaz; industries include food processing, textiles, and handicrafts.

Ob river in Asian USSR, flowing 2,100 mi/3,380 km from the Altai mountains through the W Siberian Plain to the Gulf of Ob in the Arctic Ocean. With its main tributary, the Irtysh, it is 3,480 mi/5,600 km.

Although frozen for half the year, and subject to flooding, it is a major transportation route. Novosobirsk and Barnaul are the main ports.

Obeid, El see ◊El Obeid, city in Sudan.

Oberammergau village in Bavaria, Germany; population (1980) 5,000. A Christian ◊passion play has been performed here every ten years since 1634 (except during the world wars) to commemorate the ending of the Black Death plague.

Oberhausen industrial (metals, machinery, plastics, chemicals) and coal-mining city in the Ruhr valley, North Rhine–Westphalia, Federal Republic of Germany; population (1988) 222,000.

Oberon in folklore, king of the elves or fairies and, according to the 13th-century French romance *Huon of Bordeaux*, an illegitimate son of Julius Caesar. Shakespeare used the character in *A Midsummer Night's Dream*.

Oberon Merle. Adopted name of Estelle Merle O'Brien Thompson 1911–1979. Born in Bombay, India (but claiming to be Tasmanian), she became a British actress who starred in several Alexander Korda (to whom she was married 1939–45) films, including *The Scarlet Pimpernel* 1935. Commuting between Hollywood and England, she starred in *These Three* 1936 and played Cathy to Laurence Olivier's Heathcliff in *Wuthering Heights* 1939. After 1940, she worked successfully in the US.

Oberösterreich German name for the federal state of ◊Upper Austria.

obesity condition of being overweight (generally, 20% or more above the desirable weight for one's sex, build, and height).

Obesity increases susceptibility to disease, strains the vital organs, and lessens life expectancy; it is remedied by healthy diet and exercise, unless caused by systemic (glandular) problems.

obi or ***obeah*** a form of witchcraft practiced in the

oat

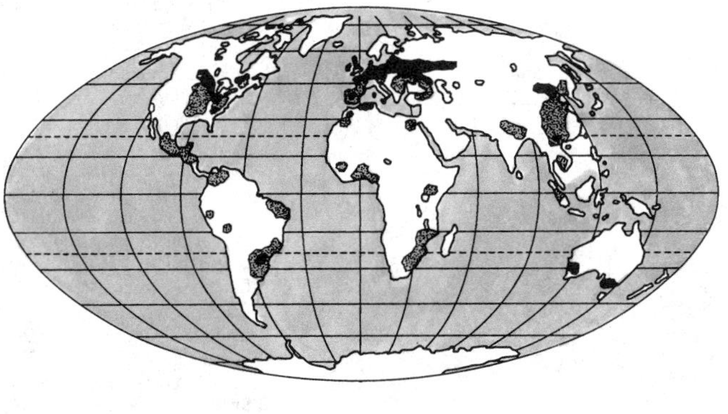

■ major areas

▩ important areas

West Indies. It combines elements of Christianity and African religions, such as snake worship.

object-oriented programming (OOP) computer programming based on "objects," in which data are closely linked to the procedures that operate on them. For example, a circle on the screen might be an object: it has data, such as a center point and a radius, as well as procedures for moving it, erasing it, changing its size, and so on.

The technique originated with the Simula and Smalltalk languages in the 1960s and early 1970s, but it has now been incorporated into many general-purpose programming languages.

oboe a musical instrument of the ◊woodwind family. Played vertically, it is a wooden tube with a bell, is double-reeded, and has a yearning, poignant tone. Its range is almost three octaves.

Obote (Apollo) Milton 1924– . Ugandan politician who led the independence movement from 1961. He became prime minister 1962 and was president 1966–71 and 1980–85, being overthrown by first Idi ◊Amin and then Lt-Gen Tito Okello.

Obrenovich Serbian dynasty that ruled 1816–42 and 1859–1903. The dynasty engaged in a feud with the rival house of Karageorgevich, which obtained the throne by the murder of the last Obrenovich 1903.

O'Brien Margaret (Angela Maxine) 1937– . US child actress, a star of the 1940s. She received a special Academy Award in 1944, but her career, including leading parts in *Lost Angel* 1943, *Meet Me in St Louis* 1944, and *The Secret Garden* 1949, did not survive into adolescence.

O'Brien Willis H 1886–1962. US film animator and special-effects creator, responsible for one of the cinema's most memorable monsters, *King Kong* 1933.

obscenity law law prohibiting the publishing of any material that tends to deprave or corrupt.

In the US the law prohibits books, films, etc., which, when judged by contemporary standards, are found to have a prurient interest in sex, be patently offensive, and have no serious artistic, scientific, or social value.

observation in science, the perception of a phenomenon—for example, examining the Moon through a telescope, watching mice to discover their mating habits, or seeing how a plant grows.

Traditionally, observation was seen as entirely separate from theory, free from preconceptions and therefore lending support to the idea of scientific objectivity. However, as the preceding examples show, observations are ordered according to a pre-existing theory; for instance, one cannot observe mating behavior without having decided what mating behavior might look like. In addition many observations actually affect the behavior of the observed (for instance, of mating mice).

observatory site or facility for observing natural phenomena. The earliest recorded observatory was at Alexandria, built by Ptolemy Soter in about 300 BC. The erection of observatories was revived in W Asia about AD 1000 and extended to Europe. The one built on the island of Hven (now Ven) in Denmark 1576 for Tycho ◊Brahe was elaborate but survived only to 1597. It was followed by those at Paris 1667, Greenwich (the ◊Royal Greenwich Observatory) 1675, and Kew, England. The modern observatory dates from the invention of the telescope. Most early observatories were near towns, but with the advent of big telescopes, clear skies with little background light, and hence high, remote sites, became essential. The most powerful optical telescopes covering the sky are at ◊Mauna Kea; Mount ◊Palomar; Kitt Peak, Arizona; La Palma, Canary Islands; and Mount Semirodniki, Caucasus, USSR. ◊Radio astronomy observatories include ◊Jodrell Bank; the Mullard, Cambridge, England; ◊Arecibo; Effelsberg, Germany; and ◊Parkes. In the 1970s optical telescopes were established at Cerro Tololo, Las Campanas, and La Silla, Chile; and at ◊Siding Spring. Observatories are also carried on aircraft or sent into orbit as satellites, in space stations, and on the Space Shuttle. The Hubble Space Telescope was launched into orbit in Apr 1990. The Very Large Telescope is under construction by the European Southern Observatory (ESO) in the mountains of N Chile and is expected to be in operation by 1997.

obsession repetitive unwanted thought or compulsive action that is often recognized by the sufferer as being irrational, but which nevertheless causes distress. It can be associated with the irresistible urge of an individual to carry out a repetitive series of actions.

For example, a person excessively troubled by fears of contamination by dirt or disease may engage in continuous hand-washing.

obsidian a black or dark-colored glassy volcanic rock, chemically similar to ◊granite, but formed by cooling rapidly on the Earth's surface at low pressure.

The glassy texture is the result of rapid cooling, which inhibits the growth of crystals. Obsidian was valued by the early civilizations of Mexico for making sharp-edged tools and ceremonial sculptures.

obstetrics medical specialty concerned with the management of pregnancy, childbirth, and the immediate postnatal period.

Ocala city in N central Florida, SE of Gainesville; seat of Marion county. It is a marketing and shipping center for the citrus, poultry, cotton, and tobacco products grown in the surrounding area. Tourism is also essential to the economy; population (1990) 42,045.

O'Casey Sean. Adopted name of John Casey 1884–1964. Irish dramatist. His early plays are tragicomedies, blending realism with symbolism and poetic with vernacular speech: *The Shadow of a Gunman* 1922, *Juno and the Paycock* 1925, and *The Plough and the Stars* 1926. Later plays include *Red Roses for Me* 1946 and *The Drums of Father Ned* 1960.

He also wrote the antiwar drama *The Silver Tassie* 1929, *The Star Turns Red* 1940, *Oak Leaves and Lavender* 1947, and a six-volume autobiography.

Occam or ***Ockham*** William of c. 1300–1349. English philosopher and scholastic logician, who revived the fundamentals of nominalism. As a Franciscan monk he defended evangelical poverty against Pope John XXII, becoming known as the Invincible Doctor. He was imprisoned in Avignon, France, on charges of heresy in 1328 but escaped to Munich, Germany, where he died. The principle of reducing assumptions to the absolute minimum is known as Occam's razor.

occultation in astronomy, the temporary obscuring of a star by a body in the Solar System. Occultations are used to provide information about changes in an orbit, and the structure of objects in space, such as radio sources.

The exact shapes and sizes of planets and asteroids can be found when they occult stars. The rings of Uranus were discovered when that planet occulted a star 1977.

occupational psychology the study of human behavior at work. It includes dealing with problems in organizations, advising on management difficulties, and investigating the relationship between humans and machines (as in the design of aircraft controls; see also ◊ergonomics). Another area is ◊psychometrics and the use of assessment to assist in selection of personnel.

ocean great mass of salt water. Strictly speaking three oceans exist—◊Atlantic, ◊Indian, and ◊Pacific—to which the Arctic is often added. They cover approximately 70% or 1.4 million sq mi/ 3.63 million sq km of the total surface area of the Earth. Water levels recorded in the world's oceans have shown an increase of 0.1 in/2.4 mm per year for the past 100 years.

depth (average) 12,000 ft/3,660 m, but shallow ledges 600 ft/180 m run out from the continents, beyond which the continental slope reaches down to the ◊abyssal zone, the largest area, ranging from 6,500–19,500 ft/2,000–6,000 m. Only the ◊deep-sea trenches go deeper, the deepest recorded being 36,201 ft/11,034 m (by the *Vityaz*, USSR) in the Mariana Trench of the W Pacific 1957

features deep trenches (off E and SE Asia, and western South America), volcanic belts (in the W Pacific and E Indian Ocean), and ocean ridges (in the mid-Atlantic, E Pacific, and Indian Ocean)

temperature varies on the surface with latitude (−2°C to +29°C); decreases rapidly to 1,200 ft/ 370 m, then more slowly to 7,200 ft/2,200 m; and hardly at all beyond that

water contents salinity averages about 3%; minerals commercially extracted include bromine, magnesium, potassium, salt; those potentially recoverable include aluminum, calcium, copper, gold, manganese, silver.

oceanarium large display tank in which aquatic animals and plants live together much as they would in their natural environment. The first oceanarium was created by the explorer and naturalist W Douglas Burden in 1938 in Florida.

Ocean Island another name for ◊Banaba, island in Kiribati.

oceanography the study of the oceans. It is a very wide science and its subdivisions deal with the individual ocean's extent and depth, the water's evolution and composition, its physics and chemistry, the bottom topography, currents and wind effects, tidal ranges, the biology, and the various aspects of human use.

ocean ridge topographical feature of the seabed indicating the presence of a constructive plate margin produced by the rise of magma to the surface, see ◊plate tectonics. It can rise many thousands of feet or meters above the surrounding abyssal plain.

Ocean ridges usually have a ◊rift valley along their crests, indicating where the flanks are being pulled apart by the growth of the plates of the ◊lithosphere beneath. The crests are generally free of sediment; increasing depths of sediment

ocean

Wildlife in oceans ultimately depends on the tiny floating plants, the phytoplankton, that live in the lighted surface waters (the euphotic zone).

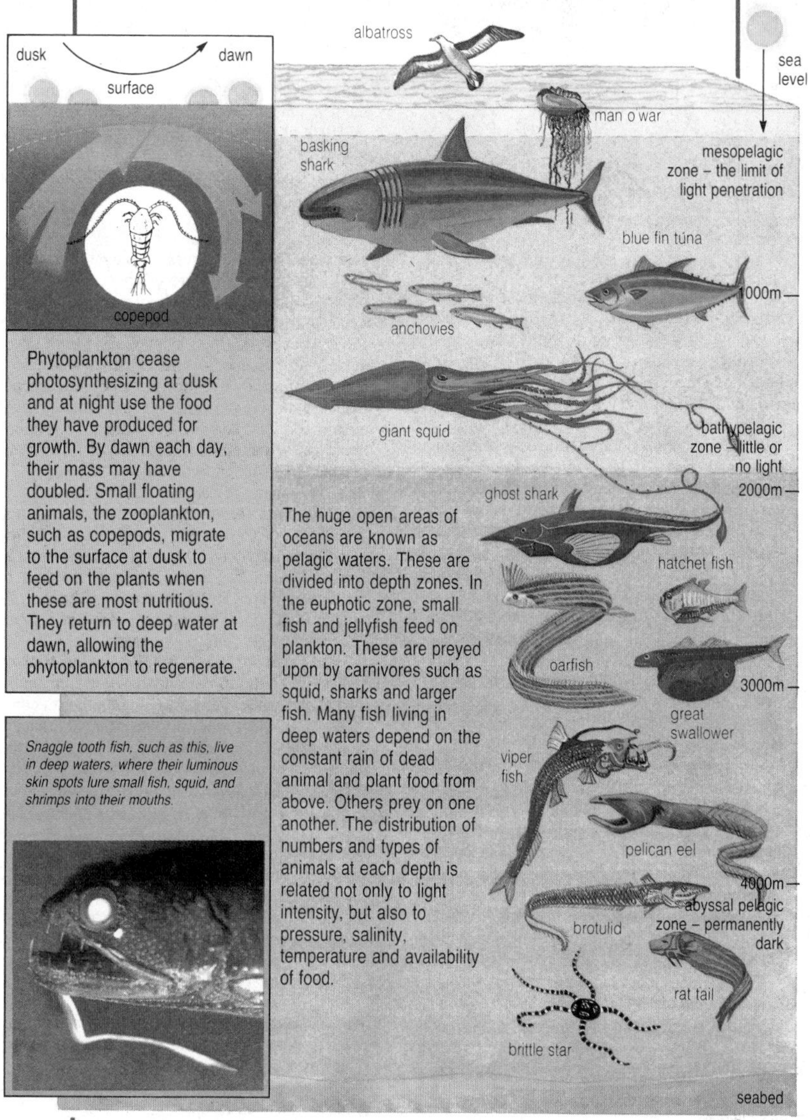
sunlight
sea level
dusk
dawn
surface
albatross
man o war
basking shark
mesopelagic zone – the limit of light penetration
blue fin tuna
1000m
anchovies
copepod
Phytoplankton cease photosynthesizing at dusk and at night use the food they have produced for growth. By dawn each day, their mass may have doubled. Small floating animals, the zooplankton, such as copepods, migrate to the surface at dusk to feed on the plants when these are most nutritious. They return to deep water at dawn, allowing the phytoplankton to regenerate.
giant squid
bathypelagic zone – little or no light
2000m
ghost shark
The huge open areas of oceans are known as pelagic waters. These are divided into depth zones. In the euphotic zone, small fish and jellyfish feed on plankton. These are preyed upon by carnivores such as squid, sharks and larger fish. Many fish living in deep waters depend on the constant rain of dead animal and plant food from above. Others prey on one another. The distribution of numbers and types of animals at each depth is related not only to light intensity, but also to pressure, salinity, temperature and availability of food.
hatchet fish
oarfish
3000m
great swallower
viper fish
pelican eel
4000m
abyssal pelagic zone – permanently dark
brotulid
rat tail
brittle star
seabed

Snaggle tooth fish, such as this, live in deep waters, where their luminous skin spots lure small fish, squid, and shrimps into their mouths.

are found with increasing distance down the flanks. Ocean ridges, such as the ◊Mid-Atlantic Ridge, consist of many segments offset along ◊faults.

ocean trench topographical feature of the seabed indicating the presence of a destructive plate margin (produced by the movements of ◊plate tectonics). The subduction or dragging downward of one plate of the ◊lithosphere beneath another means that the ocean floor is pulled down.

Ocean trenches are found around the edge of the Pacific Ocean and the NE Indian Ocean; minor ones occur in the Caribbean and near the Falkland Islands. Ocean trenches represent the deepest parts of the ocean floor, the deepest being the ◊Mariana Trench which has a depth of 36,201 ft/ 11,034 m.

Oceanus in Greek mythology, one of the ◊Titans, the god of a river supposed to encircle the Earth. He was the ancestor of other river gods and the nymphs of the seas and rivers.

ocelot wild cat *Felis pardalis* of the SW US, Mexico, and Central and South America, up to 3 ft/1 m long with a 1.5 ft/45 cm tail. It weighs about 40 lb/ 18 kg and has a pale yellowish coat marked with longitudinal stripes and blotches.

Hunted for its fur, it is close to extinction.

Ochoa Severo 1905– . US biochemist. He discovered an enzyme able to assemble units of the ◊nucleic acid RNA in 1955, while working at New York University. For his work toward the synthesis of RNA, Ochoa shared the 1959 Nobel Prize for Medicine with Arthur ◊Kornberg.

Ochs Adolph Simon 1858–1935. US newspaper publisher. Born in Cincinnati, Ohio, and raised in Tennessee, Ochs began his career in the newspaper industry as an office boy for the *Knoxville Chronicle* 1869. Moving to Chattanooga, he worked at various jobs before borrowing funds to purchase the *Chattanooga Times*. Ochs was successful with this paper and in 1891 founded the Southern Associated Press. In 1896 he gained control of the then-faltering *New York Times* and transformed it into a serious, authoritative publication. Among Ochs's innovations were a yearly index and a weekly book-review section.

Ockham William. English philosopher, see ◊Occam.

O'Connell Daniel 1775–1847. Irish politician, called "the Liberator." In 1823 he founded the Catholic Association to press Roman Catholic claims. Although ineligible, as a Roman Catholic, to take his seat, he was elected member of Parliament for County Clare 1828 and so forced the government to grant Catholic emancipation. In Parliament he cooperated with the Whigs in the hope of obtaining concessions until 1841, when he launched his campaign for repeal of the union.

O'Connor Feargus 1794–1855. Irish parliamentary follower of Daniel ◊O'Connell. He sat in parliament 1832–35, and as editor of the *Northern Star* became an influential figure of the radical working-class Chartist movement (see ◊Chartism).

O'Connor Flannery 1925–1964. US novelist and short-story writer. Her works have a great sense of evil and sin, and often explore the religious sensibility of the Deep South. Her short stories include *A Good Man Is Hard to Find* 1955, *Everything That Rises Must Converge* 1965, *The Habit of Being* 1979, and *Flannery O'Connor: Collected Works* 1988.

Her novels are *Wise Blood* 1952 and *The Violent Bear It Away* 1960. Her work exemplifies the postwar revival of the ◊Gothic novel in Southern US fiction.

O'Connor Sandra Day 1930– . US jurist and the first female associate justice of the US Supreme Court 1981– . Considered a moderate conservative, she dissented in *Texas* v *Johnson* 1990, a decision that ruled that the legality of burning the US flag in protest was protected by the First Amendment.

Born in El Paso, Texas, O'Connor attended Stanford University and Stanford University Law School. She practiced law in California, in Germany with the US Quartermaster Corps, and in Arizona, where she also became active in the Republican Party. In 1965 she became an assistant Arizona attorney general and in 1969 was appointed to a vacancy in the state senate, to which she was later elected and of which she became majority leader 1972. In 1974 she was elected a county court judge and in 1979 was appointed to the state court of appeals. In 1981 President Reagan appointed her to the US Supreme Court, where she generally espoused a conservative position.

OCR (abbreviation of optical character recognition) in computing, a technique that enables a program to understand words or figures by "reading" a printed image of the text. The image is first input from paper by ◊scanning. The program then uses its knowledge of the shapes of characters to convert the image to a set of internal codes.

Once, OCR required specially designed characters, such as the OCRA-B lettering on checks, but current devices will recognize most standard typefaces and even handwriting.

octal number system a number system to the ◊base eight, used in computing, in which all numbers are made up of the digits 0 to 7. For example, decimal 8 is represented as octal 10, and decimal 17 as octal 21. See also ◊hexadecimal number system.

octane rating a numerical classification of petroleum fuels indicating their combustion characteristics.

The efficient running of an ◊internal combustion engine depends on the ignition of a gasoline–air mixture at the correct time during the cycle of the engine. Higher-rated gasoline burns faster than lower-rated fuels. The use of the correct grade must be matched to the engine.

Octans constellation in the southern hemisphere containing the southern celestial pole. It is one of the 13 constellations conceived by the French astronomer Nicolas-Louis de Lacaille (1713–1762) in the 18th century to fill the star-poor regions near the South Pole still undelineated by his time.

octave in music, a distance of eight notes as mea-

octopus

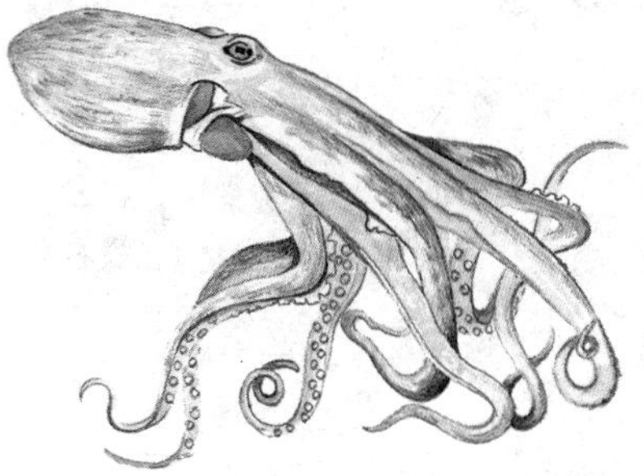

sured on the white notes of a piano keyboard. It corresponds to the consonance of first and second harmonics.

Octavian original name of ◊Augustus, the first Roman emperor.

octet rule in chemistry, rule stating that elements combine in a way that gives them the electronic structure of the nearest ◊inert gas. All the inert gases except helium (which has two) have eight electrons in their outermost shell, hence the use of the term octet.

October Revolution the second stage of the ◊Russian Revolution 1917, when, on Oct 24 (Nov 6, Western calendar), the Red Guards under Trotsky, and on orders from Lenin, seized the Winter Palace and arrested members of the Provisional Government. The following day the Second All-Russian Congress of Soviets handed over power to the Bolsheviks.

Octobrists group of Russian liberal constitutional politicians who accepted the reforming October Manifesto instituted by Tsar Nicholas II after the 1905 revolution and rejected more radical reforms.

octopus any of an order (Octopoda) of ◊cephalopods, genus *Octopus*, having a round or oval body, and eight arms with rows of suckers on each. They occur in all temperate and tropical seas, where they feed on crabs and other small animals. They can vary their coloration according to their background and can swim using their arms as well as by a type of jet propulsion by means of their funnel. They are as intelligent as some vertebrates and are not dangerous.

The common octopus *O. vulgaris* may reach 6 ft/2 m, and the rare, deep-sea giant octopus *O. apollyon* may span more than 32 ft/10 m. Octopuses are shy creatures that release clouds of ink when frightened.

Ocussi Ambeno port on the N coast of Indonesian West Timor, until 1975 an exclave of the Portuguese colony of East Timor. The port is an outlet for rice, copra, and sandalwood.

ODA abbreviation for ◊Overseas Development Adminstration.

ode lyric poem of complex form, originally chanted to a musical accompaniment. From ancient Greece exponents include Sappho, Pindar, Horace, and Catullus; and among English poets, Spenser, Milton, Dryden, and Keats.

Odense industrial port (shipbuilding, electrical goods, glass, textiles) on the island of Fyn, Denmark; population (1988) 174,000. It is the birthplace of Hans Christian Andersen.

Oder (Polish *Odra*) European river flowing N from Czechoslovakia to the Baltic Sea (the river Neisse is a tributary); length 550 mi/885 km.

Oder-Neisse Line provisional border between Poland and East Germany agreed at the Potsdam Conference in 1945 at the end of World War II, named after the two rivers that form the frontier.

Odessa seaport in Ukraine, USSR, on the Black Sea, capital of Odessa region; population (1987) 1,141,000. Products include chemicals, pharmaceuticals, and machinery. Odessa was founded by Catherine II 1795 near the site of an ancient Greek settlement.

Occupied by Germany 1941–44, Odessa suffered severe damage under the Soviet scorched-earth policy and from German destruction.

Odessa city in W Texas, SW of Big Springs; seat of Ector county. It grew up among the oil fields located here. Industries include petroleum products; it is also a livestock processing and shipping center; population (1990) 89,699.

Odets Clifford 1906–1963. US playwright, famous for his play about a taxi drivers' strike, *Waiting for Lefty* 1935. The most renowned of the Depression-era social-protest playwrights, he also wrote such plays as *Awake and Sing* 1935, perhaps his finest, and *Golden Boy* 1937. In the late 1930s he went to Hollywood and became a successful film writer and director, but he continued to write plays, including *The Country Girl* 1950.

Odin chief god of Scandinavian mythology, the Woden or Wotan of the Germanic peoples. A sky god, he lives in Asgard, at the top of the world-tree, and from the Valkyries (the divine maidens) receives the souls of heroic slain warriors, feasting with them in his great hall, Valhalla. The wife of Odin is Freya, or Frigga, and Thor is their son. Wednesday is named after Odin.

Odoacer 433–493. King of Italy from 476, when he deposed Romulus Augustulus, the last Roman emperor. He was a leader of the barbarian mercenaries employed by Rome. He was overthrown and killed by Theodoric the Great, king of the Ostrogoths.

Odoyevsky Vladimir 1804–1869. Russian writer whose works include tales of the supernatural, science fiction, satires, children's stories, and music criticism.

Odysseus the chief character of the *Odyssey*, attributed to ◊Homer, and mentioned also in the *Iliad* as one of the leaders of the Greek forces at the siege of Troy, a man of courage and ingenuity. He is said to have been the ruler of the island of Ithaca.

Odyssey Greek epic poem in 24 books, probably written before 700 BC, attributed to ◊Homer. It describes the ten-year voyage of Odysseus after the fall of Troy in the 12th century BC and the vengeance he takes on the suitors of his wife, Penelope, on his return. During his wanderings he has many adventures, including encounters with the Cyclops, Circe, Scylla and Charybdis, and the Sirens.

OE abbreviation for Old English; see ◊English language.

OECD abbreviation for ◊Organization for Economic Cooperation and Development.

Oedipus in Greek legend, king of Thebes. Left to die at birth because his father Laius had been warned by an oracle that his son would kill him, he was saved and brought up by the king of Corinth. Oedipus killed Laius in a quarrel (without recognizing him). Because Oedipus saved Thebes from the Sphinx, he was granted the Theban kingdom and Jocasta (wife of Laius and his own mother) as his wife. After four children had been born, the truth was discovered. Jocasta hanged herself, Oedipus blinded himself, and as an exiled wanderer was guided by his daughter, Antigone.

Oedipus complex in psychology, term coined by ◊Freud for the unconscious antagonism of a son to his father, whom he sees as a rival for his mother's affection. For a girl antagonistic to her mother, as a rival for her father's affection, the term is Electra complex.

Freud saw this as a universal part of childhood development, which in most children is resolved during late childhood. Contemporary theory places less importance on the Oedipus/Electra complex than did Freud and his followers.

Oedipus Tyrannus or ***Oedipus the King*** 409 BC and *Oedipus at Colonus* 401 BC, two Greek tragedies by ◊Sophocles based on the legend of Oedipus, king of Thebes.

Oersted Hans Christian 1777–1851. Danish physicist who founded the science of electromagnetism. In 1820 he discovered the ◊magnetic field associated with an electric current.

Offa died 796. King of Mercia, England, from 757. He conquered Essex, Kent, Sussex, and Surrey; defeated the Welsh and the West Saxons; and established Mercian supremacy over all England south of the river Humber.

Offaly county of the Republic of Ireland, in the province of Leinster, between Galway on the W and Kildare on the E; area 772 sq mi/2,000 sq km; population (1986) 60,000.

Towns include the county town of Tullamore. Features include the rivers Shannon (along the W boundary), Brosna, Clodagh, and Broughill and the Slieve Bloom mountains in the SE.

Offa's Dyke a defensive earthwork along the Welsh border, of which there are remains from the mouth of the river Dee to that of the river Severn.

It represents the boundary secured by ◊Offa's wars with Wales.

Offenbach Jacques 1819–1880. French composer. He wrote light opera, initially for presentation at the Bouffes Parisiens. Among his works are *Orphée aux enfers/Orpheus in the Underworld* 1858, *La belle Hélène* 1864, and *Les contes d'Hoffmann/The Tales of Hoffmann* 1881.

Offenbach am Main city in Hessen, Federal Republic of Germany; population (1988) 107,000. It faces Frankfurt on the other side of the river Main.

office automation the introduction of computers and other electronic equipment, such as fax machines, to support an office routine. Increasingly, computers have been used to support administrative tasks such as document processing, filing, mail, and schedule management; project planning and management accounting have also been computerized.

offset printing the most common method of ◊printing, which uses smooth (often rubber) printing plates. It works on the principle of ◊lithography: that grease and water repel one another. The printing plate is prepared using a photographic technique, resulting in a type image that attracts greasy printing ink. On the printing press the plate is wrapped around a cylinder and wetted and inked in turn. The ink adheres only to the type area, and this image is then transferred via an intermediate blanket cylinder to the paper.

O'Flaherty Liam 1897–1984. Irish author whose novels, set in County Mayo, include *The Neighbor's Wife* 1923, *The Informer* 1925, and *Land* 1946.

Ogaden desert region in Harar province, SE Ethiopia, that borders on Somalia. It is a desert plateau, rising to 3,280 ft/1,000 m, inhabited mainly by Somali nomads practicing arid farming. A claim to the area was made by Somalia in the 1960s, resulting in the guerrilla fighting that has continued intermittently. It is one of five new autonomous provinces created in Ethiopia 1987.

Ogallala Aquifer the largest source of groundwater in the US, stretching from southern South Dakota to NW Texas. The over-exploitation of this water resource has resulted in the loss of over 18% of the irrigated farmland of Oklahoma and Texas in the period 1940–90.

Ogbomosho city and commercial center in W Nigeria, 50 mi/80 km NE of Ibadan; population (1981) 590,600.

Ogden city in N Utah, on the Weber and Ogden rivers, N of Salt Lake City. It is a railroad, trading, and military supply center; Hill Air Force Base is nearby. Tourism is also important to the economy; population (1990) 63,909.

Ogdon John 1937–1989. English pianist, renowned for his interpretation of Chopin, Liszt, and Busoni. In 1962 he shared the Tchaikovsky award with Vladimir Ashkenazy in Moscow.

Oglethorpe James Edward 1696–1785. English soldier and colonizer of Georgia. He served in Parliament for 32 years and in 1732 obtained a charter for the colony of Georgia, intended as a refuge for debtors and for European Protestants. The colony was also intended by the British to act as

Ohio

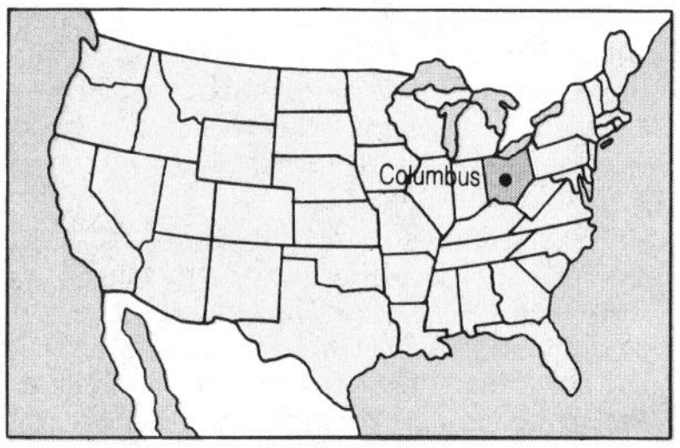
Columbus

a buffer against Spanish Florida. The colonists were selected carefully, and every aspect of life was planned and supervised.

Oglethorpe served as Georgia's first colonial governor 1733–43. In 1743, frustrated by settlers' complaints, he returned to England.

OGPU former name 1923–34 of the Soviet secret police, now the ◊KGB.

Ogun a state of SW Nigeria; population (1982) 2,473,300; area 6,474 sq mi/16,762 sq km; capital Abeokuta.

OH abbreviation for ◊Ohio.

O Henry pen name of US author William Sydney ◊Porter.

O'Higgins Bernardo 1778–1842. Chilean revolutionary, known as "the Liberator of Chile." He was a leader of the struggle for independence from Spanish rule 1810–17 and head of the first permanent national government 1817–23.

Ohio river in the US, 980 mi/1,580 km long; it is formed by the union of the Allegheny and Monongahela rivers at Pittsburgh, Pennsylvania, and flows SW until it joins the Mississippi River at Cairo, Illinois. The Ohio carries twice the freight tonnage of the Panama Canal–bulk cargos such as iron ore, oil, chemicals, metals, salt, sand, gravel, and, especially, coal from West Virginia, Indiana, Kentucky, and E Ohio fields. Cincinnati, Ohio, and Louisville, Kentucky, are the chief cities on its banks. Flooding periodically has damaged river communities, most severely in 1937.

Ohio state in N central US; nickname Buckeye State

area 41,341 sq mi/107,100 sq km

capital Columbus

cities Cleveland, Cincinnati, Dayton, Akron, Toledo, Youngstown, Canton

population (1990) 10,847,115

features Ohio River; Lake Erie; Serpent Mound, a 4-ft/1.3-m embankment, 1,330 ft/405 m long and about 18 ft/5 m across (built by ◊Hopewell Indians about 2nd–1st centuries BC)

products coal, cereals, livestock, dairy, machinery, chemicals, steel, motor vehicles, automotive and aircraft parts, rubber products, office equipment, refined petroleum

famous people Sherwood Anderson, Neil Armstrong, Hart Crane, Thomas Edison, James Garfield, John Glenn, Ulysses S Grant, Zane Grey, Warren Harding, Benjamin Harrison, William H Harrison, Rutherford B Hayes, William McKinley, Paul Newman, Jesse Owens, John D Rockefeller, William T Sherman, William H Taft, James Thurber, Orville and Wilbur Wright

history explored for France by La Salle 1669; ceded to Britain by France 1763; first settled at Marietta (capital of the Northwest Territory) by Europeans 1788; statehood 1803. By 1850 Ohio was the third most populous state. In the Civil War, Ohio gave the Union its greatest generals–U S Grant, W T Sherman, and P Sheridan. In the 1870s J D Rockefeller of Cleveland organized the Standard Oil Company, which soon controlled oil refining and distribution throughout the nation. At the same time, Akron became rubber capital of the world. For a century, Ohio remained a leader in heavy industry, but manufacturing peaked in 1969; agriculture and mining remain important. Seeking service and high-technology industries, the state needs to overcome an aging infrastructure and urban pollution and decay. Tourism continues as a valuable revenue producer.

ohmic heating *An ohmic heating system, in which liquid food is sterilized by passing an electric current through it.*

ohm SI unit (symbol Ω) of electrical ◊resistance (the property of a substance that restricts the flow of electrons through it).

It was originally defined with reference to the resistance of a column of mercury, but is now taken as the resistance between two points when a potential difference of one volt between them produces a current of one ampere.

Ohm Georg Simon 1787–1854. German physicist who studied electricity and discovered the fundamental law that bears his name. The SI unit of electrical resistance is named after him, and the unit of conductance (the reverse of resistance) was formerly called the mho, which is Ohm spelled backwards.

ohmic heating method of heating used in the food-processing industry, in which an electric current is passed through foodstuffs to sterilize them before packing. The heating effect is similar to that obtained by microwaves in that electrical energy is transformed into heat throughout the whole volume of the food, not just at the surface. This makes the method suitable for heating foods containing chunks of meat or fruit. It is an alternative to in-can sterilization and has been used to produce canned foods such as meat chunks, shrimps, baked beans, fruit, and vegetables.

Ohm's law law proposed by Georg Ohm in 1827 that states that the steady electrical current in a metallic circuit is directly proportional to the constant total ◊electromotive force in the circuit.

If a current I flows between two points in a conductor across which the ◊potential difference (voltage) is E, then E/I is a constant (which is known as the ◊resistance, R, between the two points). Hence $E/I = R$. Equations relating E, I and R are often quoted as Ohm's law, but the term "resistance" did not enter into the law as originally stated.

Ohrid, Lake a lake on the frontier between Albania and Yugoslavia; area 135 sq mi/350 sq km.

oil inflammable substance, usually insoluble in water, and chiefly composed of carbon and hydrogen. Oils may be solids (fats and waxes) or liquids. The three main types are: essential oils, obtained from plants; fixed oils, obtained from animals and plants; and mineral oils, obtained chiefly from the refining of ◊petroleum. Eight of the 14 top-earning companies in the US in 1990 (led by Exxon with $7 billion in sales) are in the global petroleum industry.

Essential oils are volatile liquids that have the odor of their plant source and are used in perfumes, flavoring essences, and in ◊aromatherapy. Fixed oils are mixtures of ◊esters of fatty acids, of varying consistency, found in both animals (for example, fish oils) and plants (in nuts and seeds). They are used as food; to make soaps, paints, and varnishes; and for lubrication.

oil crop plant from which vegetable oils are pressed from the seeds. Cool temperate areas grow rapeseed and linseed; warm temperate regions produce sunflowers, olives, and soy beans; tropical regions produce groundnuts (such as peanuts), palm oil, and coconuts. Some of the major vegetable oils, such as soy bean oil, peanut oil, and cottonseed oil, are derived from crops grown primarily for other purposes. Most vegetable oils are used both as edible oils and as ingredients in industrial products such as soaps, varnishes, printing inks, and paints.

oil palm African ◊palm tree *Eleis guineensis*, the fruit of which yields valuable oils, used as food or processed into margarine, soaps, and livestock feeds.

oil spill leakage of oil from an ocean-going tanker, a pipeline, or other source. Oil spills are frequent and may cause enormous ecological harm. In Feb 1991 Iraqi military forces opened oil pipelines to leak into the Persian Gulf as part of military tactics during the Gulf War; the coalition force operations also damaged oil facilities causing leakage. Together the largest-ever oil spill pollutes the Gulf. In March 1989 the *Exxon Valdez* went aground, covering in oil 4,800 sq mi/1,850 sq km in Prince William Sound, Alaska, and killing 34,434 sea birds, 9,994 otters, and at least nine whales. The spill left pools of oil up to 3 ft/100 cm deep on some beaches.

In Dec 1989 an Iranian tanker leaked 70,000 tons (19 million gallons) off the coast of Morocco. In Jan 1990 a broken Exxon pipeline leaked 567,000 gallons into New York harbor; in June 1990 another 260,000 gallons was spilled in New

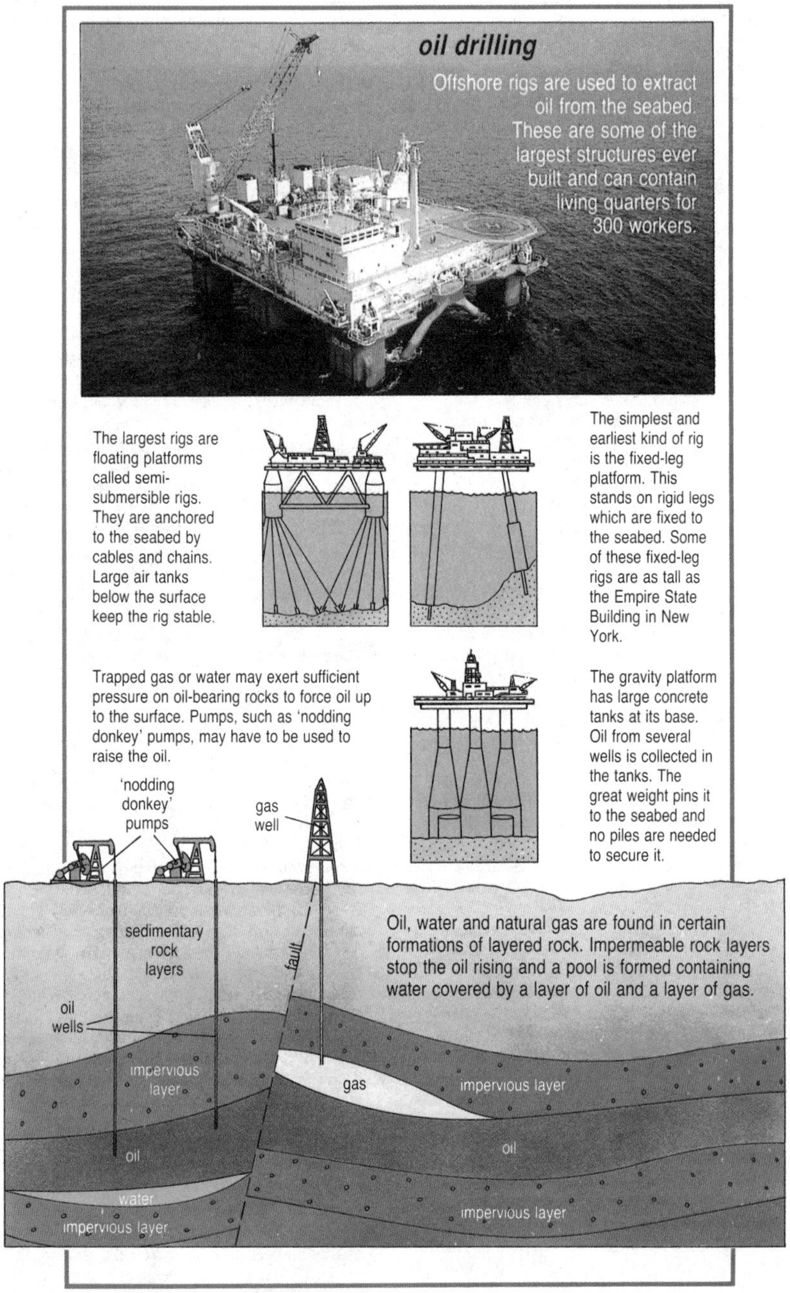
oil drilling
Offshore rigs are used to extract oil from the seabed. These are some of the largest structures ever built and can contain living quarters for 300 workers.
The largest rigs are floating platforms called semi-submersible rigs. They are anchored to the seabed by cables and chains. Large air tanks below the surface keep the rig stable.
The simplest and earliest kind of rig is the fixed-leg platform. This stands on rigid legs which are fixed to the seabed. Some of these fixed-leg rigs are as tall as the Empire State Building in New York.
Trapped gas or water may exert sufficient pressure on oil-bearing rocks to force oil up to the surface. Pumps, such as 'nodding donkey' pumps, may have to be used to raise the oil.
The gravity platform has large concrete tanks at its base. Oil from several wells is collected in the tanks. The great weight pins it to the seabed and no piles are needed to secure it.
'nodding donkey' pumps
gas well
sedimentary rock layers
fault
Oil, water and natural gas are found in certain formations of layered rock. Impermeable rock layers stop the oil rising and a pool is formed containing water covered by a layer of oil and a layer of gas.
oil wells
impervious layer
gas
impervious layer
oil
oil
water
impervious layer
impervious layer

York harbor and a tanker carrying 38 million gallons caught fire and leaked oil in the Gulf of Mexico, posing a serious threat to local shrimp nurseries and wildlife refuges. In Feb 1990 300,000 gallons leaked from a damaged tanker off Southern California, fouling miles of shoreline.

Oise European river that rises in the Ardennes plateau, Belgium, and flows through France in a SW direction for 186 mi/300 km to join the Seine about 40 mi/65 km below Paris. It gives its name to a French *département* in Picardie.

Oistrakh David Fyodorovich 1908–1974. Soviet violinist, celebrated for performances of both standard and contemporary Russian repertoire. Shostakovich wrote both his violin concertos for him.

He was born in Odessa, S Ukraine. His son Igor (1931–) is equally renowned as a violinist.

OK abbreviation for ◊Oklahoma.

okapi ruminant *Okapia johnstoni* of the giraffe family, although with much shorter legs and neck, found in the tropical rainforests of central Africa. Purplish brown with creamy face and black and white stripes on the legs and hindquarters, it is excellently camouflaged. Okapis have remained virtually unchanged for millions of years. Unknown to Europeans until 1901, only a few hundred are thought to survive.

Okavango Swamp marshy area in NW Botswana, fed by the Okavango River, which rises in Angola and flows SE about 1,000 mi/1,600 km.

Okayama industrial port (textiles, cotton) in W Honshu, Japan; population (1987) 570,000. It has three Buddhist temples.

Okeechobee lake in the N Everglades, Florida; 40 mi/65 km long and 25 mi/40 km wide. The largest lake in S US, about 700 sq mi/1,800 sq km, Okeechobee has no single outlet but flows S through the Everglades.

O'Keeffe Georgia 1887–1986. US painter, based mainly in New York and New Mexico, known for her large, semiabstract studies of flowers and skulls.

Her mature style stressed contours and subtle tonal transitions, and in paintings such as *Black Iris* 1926 (Metropolitan Museum of Art, New York) the subject is transformed into a powerful and erotic abstract image. In 1946 she settled in New Mexico, where the desert landscape inspired many of her paintings.

She was married (1924–46) to photographer and art exhibitor Alfred Stieglitz, in whose gallery her work was first shown.

okapi

female okapi

Okefenokee swamp in SE Georgia and NE Florida, rich in alligators, bears, deer, and birds. Much of its 660 sq mi/1,700 sq km forms a national wildlife refuge. It is drained by the St Marys and Suwannee rivers.

Okeghem Johannes (Jean d') c. 1420–1497. Flemish composer of church music, including masses and motets. He was court composer to Charles VII, Louis XI, and Charles VIII of France.

Okhotsk, Sea of arm of the N Pacific between the Kamchatka Peninsula and Sakhalin and bordered southward by the Kurile Islands; area 361,700 sq mi/937,000 sq km. Free of ice only in summer, it is often fogbound.

Okinawa largest of the Japanese ◊Ryukyu Islands in the W Pacific
area 869 sq mi/2,250 sq km
capital Naha
population (1986) 1,190,000
history captured by the US in the Battle of Okinawa Apr 1–June 21, 1945, with 47,000 US casualties (12,000 dead) and 60,000 Japanese (only a few hundred survived as prisoners); the island was returned to Japan 1972.

Oklahoma state in S central US; nickname Sooner State
area 69,905 sq mi/181,100 sq km
capital Oklahoma City
cities Tulsa, Lawton, Norman, Enid
population (1990) 3,145,585
features rivers: Arkansas, Red, Canadian mountains: Wichita, Ozarks; high plains, with Indian reservations (Cherokee, Chicasaw, Choctaw, Creek, Seminole); American Indian Hall of Fame, Andadarko; Chicasaw National Recreation Area
products cereals, peanuts, cotton, livestock, oil, natural gas, helium, machinery and other metal products
famous people John Berryman, Ralph Ellison,

Oklahoma

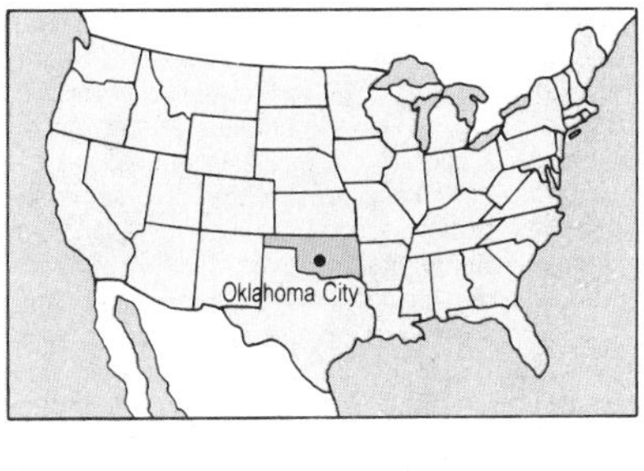
Oklahoma City

Woody Guthrie, Mickey Mantle, Will Rogers, Jim Thorpe

history explored for Spain by Francisco de Coronado 1541; most acquired by US from France with the Louisiana Purchase 1803. The W panhandle became US territory when Texas was annexed 1845. It was divided into Indian Territory and Oklahoma Territory 1890, part of which was thrown open to settlers with lotteries and other hurried distribution of land. Together with what remained of Indian Territory, it became a state 1907. Oil was struck 1897, and the state led all others in oil production until 1928. The 1930s brought drought, dust storms, and an exodus of many, especially to California. Economic growth resumed thereafter, particularly in the 1970s, when world oil prices rose.

Oklahoma City industrial city (oil refining, machinery, aircraft, telephone equipment) and capital of Oklahoma, on the Canadian River; population (1990) 444,719. On April 22, 1889, a tent city of nearly 10,000 inhabitants was set up overnight as the area was opened to settlement. In 1910 Oklahoma City had 64,000 people and became the state capital. Oil was discovered in 1928, and derricks are situated even on the state capitol grounds. A General Motors auto plant was established here 1979.

okra annual plant *Abelmoschus esculentus* of the ◊mallow family, related to ◊hibiscus, with edible fingerlike fruit.

Okubo Toshimichi 1831–1878. Japanese ◊samurai leader whose opposition to the Tokugawa shogunate made him a leader in the ◊Meiji restoration 1866–88.

Okuma Shigenobu 1838–1922. Japanese politician and prime minister 1898 and 1914–16. He presided over Japanese pressure for territorial concessions in China, before retiring 1916.

Olaf five kings of Norway, including:

Olaf I Tryggvesson 969–1000. King of Norway from 995. He began the conversion of Norway to Christianity and was killed in a sea battle against the Danes and Swedes.

Olaf II Haraldsson 995–1030. King of Norway from 1015. He offended his subjects by his centralizing policy and zeal for Christianity, and was killed in battle by Norwegian rebel chiefs backed by ◊Canute of Denmark. He was declared the patron saint of Norway 1164.

Olaf V 1903–1991. King of Norway from 1957, when he succeeded his father Haakon VII.

Olazabal Jose Maria 1966– . Spanish golfer, one of the leading players on the European circuit. After a distinguished amateur career he turned professional 1986. He was a member of the European Ryder Cup teams in 1987 and 1989.

He won the English amateur championship in 1984 and Youths title the following year. He finished second in the European money list in his second year as a professional.

Olbers Heinrich 1758–1840. German astronomer. A medical doctor, Olbers was a keen amateur astronomer and a founder member of the Celestial Police, a group of astronomers who attempted to locate a supposed "missing planet" between Mars and Jupiter. During his search he discovered two ◊asteroids, Pallas 1802 and Vesta 1807. Credited to him are a number of comet discoveries, a new method of calculating cometary orbits, and the stating of Olbers' paradox.

Olbers' paradox question put forward 1826 by Heinrich Olbers, who asked: If the universe is infinite in extent and filled with stars, why is the sky dark at night? The answer is that the stars do not live infinitely long, so there is not enough starlight to fill the universe. A wrong answer, frequently given, is that the expansion of the universe weakens the starlight.

Olbrich Joseph Maria 1867–1908. Austrian architect who worked under Otto ◊Wagner and was opposed to the over-ornamentation of Art Nouveau. His major buildings, however, remain Art Nouveau in spirit: the Vienna Sezession 1897–98, the Hochzeitsturm 1907 in Vienna, and the Tietz department store in Düsseldorf, Germany.

old age the later years of life. The causes of progressive degeneration of bodily and mental processes associated with it are still not precisely known, but every one of the phenomena of ◊aging can occur at almost any age, and the process does not take place throughout the body at an equal rate. Geriatrics is the branch of medicine dealing with old age and its diseases.

Normally, aging begins after about 30. The arteries start to lose their elasticity, so that a greater strain is placed on the heart. The resulting gradual impairment of the blood supply is responsible for many of the changes, but between 30 and 60 there is a period of maturity in which aging usually makes little progress. Research into the process of old age (gerontology) includes study of dietary factors and the mechanisms behind structural changes in arteries and bones.

Old Catholic one of various breakaway groups from Roman Catholicism—including those in Holland (such as the Church of Utrecht, who separated from Rome 1724 after accusations of ◊Jansenism) and groups in Austria, Czechoslovakia, Germany, and Switzerland—who rejected the proclamation of ◊papal infallibility of 1870. Old Catholic clergy are not celibate.

The Old Catholic Church entered full communion with the Church of England 1931. Anglican and Old Catholic bishops have joined in the consecration of new bishops so that their consecration can be traced back to the time of an undivided church.

Oldenbarneveldt Johan van 1547–1619. Dutch politician, a leading figure in the Netherlands' struggle for independence from Spain, who helped William the Silent negotiate the Union of Utrecht 1579.

He presided over the vast expansion of overseas trade and the formation of the Dutch ◊East India Company. Religious strife with Calvinists effected his downfall, and he was arrested and executed.

Oldenburg industrial city in Lower Saxony, Federal Republic of Germany, on the river Hunte; population (1988) 139,000. It is linked by river and canal to the Ems and Wieser rivers.

Oldenburg Claes 1929– . US pop artist who made "soft sculptures," gigantic replicas of everyday objects and foods, of stuffed canvas or vinyl.

One characteristic work is *Lipstick* 1969 (Yale University).

Oldenburg Henry 1615–1677. German official who founded and edited the first scientific periodical *Philosophical Transactions*, and, through his extensive correspondence, acted as a clearing house for the science of the day. He was born in Bremen and first came to London in 1652, working as a Bremen agent and then a tutor. In 1663 he was appointed to the new post of secretary to the Royal Society, a position he held until his death.

Old English another term for ◊Anglo-Saxon; see also ◊English language.

Old English general name for the range of dialects spoken by Germanic settlers in England between the 5th and 11th centuries AD. The literature of the period includes *Beowulf*, an epic in West Saxon dialect, shorter poems such as *The Wanderer* and *The Seafarer*, and prose chronicles, Bible translations, spells, and charms.

Oldfield Barney 1878–1946. US race-car driver. Born in Wauseon, Ohio, Oldfield established a reputation as a successful bicycle racer as a youth and came to the attention of Henry Ford, who was seeking a driver for his experimental race car. Oldfield accepted the job 1902 and in the following year set the world land speed record of 60 mph/96.6 kph. In 1910 Oldfield reached a speed in excess of 130 mph/209 kph.

A familiar figure at races across the country, Oldfield retired from competitive driving 1918 and spent the rest of his career as a consultant to various automobile and tire makers.

Oldfield Bruce 1950– English fashion designer, who set up his own business 1975. His evening wear has been worn by the British royal family and other personalities.

Oldham industrial city in Greater Manchester, England; population (1981) 107,800. Industries include textiles and textile machinery, plastics, electrical goods, and electronic equipment.

Old Pretender nickname of ◊James Edward Stuart, the son of James II of England.

Olds Ransom Eli 1864–1950. US automobile manufacturer. Born in Geneva, Ohio, and raised in Michigan, Olds began to experiment with steam-powered prototype automobiles 1886. He produced a gas-powered car 1895 and in the following year founded the Olds Motor Vehicle Company. He reorganized the operation as the Olds Motor Works and began producing his popular Oldsmobiles 1899 in Detroit. Olds pioneered the assembly-line method of auto production that would later be refined by Henry Ford. After selling the Olds Motor Works 1904, Olds established the Reo Motor Car Company, serving as its president 1904–24 and chairman of the board 1924–36.

Old Stone Age art see ◊ancient art.

Old Style a qualification, often abbreviated to "OS," of dates before the year 1752 in England as quoted in later writings. In that year the ◊calendar in use in England was reformed by the omission of 11 days, in order to bring it into line with the more exact Gregorian system, and the beginning of the year was put back from March 25 to Jan 1.

Old Testament Christian term for the ◊Hebrew Bible, which is the first part of the Christian ◊Bible. It contains 39 (according to Christianity) or 24 (according to Judaism) books, which include the origins of the world, the history of the ancient Hebrews and their covenant with God, prophetical writings, and religious poetry. The first five books (*The Five Books of Moses*) are traditionally ascribed to Moses and known as the Pentateuch (by Christians) or the Torah (by Jews).

The language of the original text was Hebrew, dating from the 12th–2nd centuries BC. The earliest known manuscripts containing part of the text were found among the ◊Dead Sea Scrolls. The traditional text (translated first into Greek and then other langages) was compiled by rabbinical authorities around the 2nd century AD.

Olduvai Gorge deep cleft in the Serengeti steppe, Tanzania, where the ◊Leakeys found prehistoric stone tools in the 1930s. They discovered Pleistocene remains of prehumans and gigantic animals 1958–59. The gorge has given its name to the Olduvai culture, a simple stone-tool culture of prehistoric hominids, dating from 2–0.5 million years ago.

The Pleistocene remains include sheep the size of a drafthorse, pigs as big as rhinoceroses, and a gorilla-sized baboon. The skull of an early hominid (1.75 million years old), *Australopithecus boisei* (its massive teeth earned it the nickname "Nutcracker Man") was also found here, as well as remains of *Homo habilis* and primitive types of *Homo erectus*.

Old Vic theater in S London, England, former home of the National Theatre (1963–76).

The theater was founded 1818 as the Coburg. Taken over by Emma Cons 1880 (as the Royal Victoria Hall), it became a popular center for opera and drama, and was affectionately dubbed the Old Vic. In 1898 Lilian Baylis, niece of Emma Cons, assumed the management, and in 1914 began a celebrated series of Shakespeare productions. Badly damaged in 1940 air raids, the Old Vic reopened 1950–81, becoming the temporary home of the National Theatre until the South Bank building was finished. It was completely refurbished 1985.

Old World the continents of the eastern hemisphere, so called because they were familiar to Europeans before the Americas. The term is used as an adjective to describe animals and plants that live in the eastern hemisphere.

oleander or ***rose bay*** evergreen Mediterranean shrub *Nerium oleander* of the dogbane family Apocynaceae, with pink or white flowers and aromatic leaves that secrete the poison oleandrin.

olefin common name for ◊alkene.

olfactory cell in mammals, receptor cells found high up inside the nose, associated with the sense of smell. They are stimulated by chemicals in the air and enhance the related sense of taste.

Olfactory cells can be extremely sensitive, although in humans the sense of smell is not well developed. Many mammals rely on the sense of smell for marking out their territories. Insects can respond to minute levels of airborne chemicals such as ◊pheromones.

Olga, St the wife of Igor, the Scandinavian prince of Kiev. Her baptism around 955 was a decisive step in the Christianization of Russia.

Oligocene third epoch of the Tertiary period of geologic time, 38–25 million years ago. The name, from Greek, means "a little recent," referring to the presence of the remains of some modern types of animals existing at that time.

oligopoly in economics, a situation in which a few companies control the major part of a particular market and concert their actions to perpetuate such control. This may include an agreement to fix prices (a ◊cartel).

oligosaccharide ◊carbohydrate comprising a few ◊monosaccharide units linked together. It is a general term used to indicate that a carbohydrate is larger than a simple di- or trisaccharide but not as large as a polysaccharide.

Olivares Count-Duke of (born Gaspar de Guzmán) 1587–1645. Spanish prime minister 1621–43. He overstretched Spain in foreign affairs and unsuccessfully attempted domestic reform. He committed Spain to recapturing the Netherlands and to involvement in the Thirty Years' War 1618–48, and his efforts to centralize power led to revolts in Catalonia and Portugal, which brought about his downfall.

olive evergreen tree *Olea europaea* of the family Oleaceae. Native to Asia but widely cultivated in Mediterranean and subtropical areas, it grows up to 50 ft/15 m high, with twisted branches and opposite, lance-shaped silvery leaves. The white flowers are followed by green oval fruits that ripen a bluish-black. They are preserved in brine or oil, dried, or pressed to make olive oil.

The oil, which is pale green-yellow and chiefly composed of glycerides, is widely consumed; it is also used in soaps and ointments, and as a lubricant.

olive branch an ancient symbol of peace; in the Bible (Genesis 9), an olive branch is brought back by the dove to Noah to show that the flood has abated.

olivenite basic copper arsenate, $Cu_2(AsO_4)(OH)$, occurring as a mineral in olive-green prisms.

Oliver Isaac c. 1556–1617. English painter of miniatures, originally a Huguenot refugee, who studied under Nicholas Hilliard (c. 1547–1619). He became a court artist in the reign of James I. His sitters included the poet John Donne.

Olives, Mount of a range of hills E of Jerusalem, associated with the Christian religion: a former chapel (now a mosque) marks the traditional site of Jesus' ascension to heaven, with the Garden of Gethsemane at its foot.

Olivier Laurence (Kerr), Baron Olivier 1907–1989. English actor and director. For many years associated with the Old Vic theater, he was director of the National Theatre company 1962–73. His stage roles include Henry V, Hamlet, Richard III, and Archie Rice in John Osborne's *The Entertainer*. His acting and direction of filmed versions of Shakespeare's plays received critical acclaim, for example *Henry V* 1944 and *Hamlet* 1948.

Other films in which he appeared are *Wuthering Heights* 1939, *Rebecca* 1940, *Sleuth* 1972, *Marathon Man* 1976, and *The Boys from Brazil* 1978. The Olivier Theatre (part of the National Theatre on the South Bank, London) is named after him.

olivine greenish mineral, magnesium iron silicate, $(Mg,Fe)_2SiO_4$. It is a rock-forming mineral, present in, for example, peridotite, gabbro, and basalt. Olivine is called peridot when pale green and transparent, and used in jewelry.

olm cave-dwelling aquatic salamander *Proteus anguinus*, the only European member of the family Proteidae, the other members being the North American mudpuppies. Olms are found in underground caves along the Adriatic seaboard in Italy and Yugoslavia. The adult is permanently larval in form, about 10 in/25 cm long, almost blind, with external gills and under-developed limbs. See ◊neoteny.

Olmos a small town on the edge of the Sechura Desert, NW Peru. It gives its name to the large scale Olmos Project which began in 1926 in an attempt to irrigate the desert plain and increase cotton and sugar cane production.

Olmstead v US a US Supreme Court decision 1928 dealing with the legality of telephone wiretapping in criminal investigations. The petitioner, a man convicted of selling alcohol illegally, appealed the case on the grounds that, in violation of the Fourth Amendment, the evidence against him had been obtained through telephone wiretaps. The Court upheld the conviction, ruling 5 to 4 that, since law enforcement officers made no actual entry into Olmstead's house, the surveillance was constitutional.

Olmsted Frederick Law 1822–1903. US landscape designer. Appointed superintendent of New York's Central Park 1857, Olmsted and his partner Calvert Vaux directed its design and construction. After the Civil War, he became a sought-after planner of public parks. In 1893 he designed the grounds of the World's Columbian Exposition; he also planned several garden communities and landscaped urban building complexes.

Born in Hartford, Connecticut, Olmsted became interested in scientific farming and founded a successful nursery business 1844. A keen observer of social and economic conditions, he published his travel journals of the South as *Journeys and Explorations in the Cotton Kingdom* 1861.

Olomouc industrial city in central Czechoslovakia, at the confluence of the Bystrice and Morava rivers; population (1986) 106,000. Industries include sugar refining, brewing, and metal goods.

Olson Charles 1910–1970. US poet, associated with the Black Mountain school of experimental poets and originator of the theory of "composition by field." His *Maximus* poems 1953–75 were a striking attempt to extend the American epic poem beyond Ezra Pound's *Cantos* or William Carlos Williams's *Paterson*.

Olsztyn formerly ***Allenstein*** industrial town in NE Poland at the center of the Mazurian Lakes region; population (1985) 147,000. It was founded 1334 and was formerly in East Prussia.

Olympia sanctuary in the W Peloponnese, ancient Greece, with a temple of Zeus, and the stadium (for foot races, boxing, wrestling) and hippodrome (for chariot and horse races), where the original Olympic games were held.

Olympia capital of Washington, located in the W central part of the state, on the Deschutes river near Puget Sound. It is a deep-water port; fishing and tourism are important to the economy; population (1990) 33,840.

Olympic Games sporting contests originally held in Olympia, ancient Greece, every four years during a sacred truce; records were kept from 776 BC. Women were forbidden to be present, and the male contestants were naked. The ancient Games were abolished AD 394. The present-day games have been held every four years since 1896. Since 1924 there has been a separate winter Games program. From 1994 the winter and summer Games will be held two years apart.

Olympic venues

summer games/winter games
1896 Athens, Greece
1900 Paris, France
1904 St Louis
1906 Athens, Greece
1908 London, England
1912 Stockholm, Sweden
1920 Antwerp, Belgium
1924 Paris, France/Chamonix, France
1928 Amsterdam, Holland/St Moritz, Switzerland
1932 Los Angeles/Lake Placid
1936 Berlin, Germany/Garmisch-Partenkirchen, Germany
1948 London, England/St Moritz, Switzerland
1952 Helsinki, Finland/Oslo, Norway
1956 Melbourne, Australia*/Cortina d'Ampezzo, Italy
1960 Rome, Italy/Squaw Valley
1964 Tokyo, Japan/Innsbruck, Austria
1968 Mexico City, Mexico/Grenoble, France
1972 Munich, West Germany/Sapporo, Japan
1976 Montreal, Canada/Innsbruck, Austria
1980 Moscow, USSR/Lake Placid
1984 Los Angeles/Sarajevo, Yugoslavia
1988 Seoul, South Korea/Calgary, Canada
1992 Barcelona, Spain/Albertville, France
1994 Lillehammer, Norway (winter games)
1996 Atlanta (summer games)

* Because of quarantine restrictions, equestrian events were held in Stockholm, Sweden.

The first modern Games were held in Athens, Greece. They were revived by Frenchman Pierre de Fredi, Baron de Coubertin (1863–1937), and have been held every four years with the exception of 1916, 1940, and 1944, when the two world wars intervened. Special tenth-anniversary Games were held in Athens 1906. At the first revived Games, 311 competitors represented 13 nations in nine sports. At Seoul, South Korea, in 1988, nearly 10,000 athletes represented nearly 150 nations in 23 sports, plus demonstration sports like tenpin bowling, baseball, and tae kwon

Olympic Games *Bas relief on the base of a statue c. 510 BC, now in the Athens Museum, showing a pair of wrestlers practicing, a runner in the starting position, and a javelin thrower.*

Oman
Sultanate of
(Saltanat 'Uman)

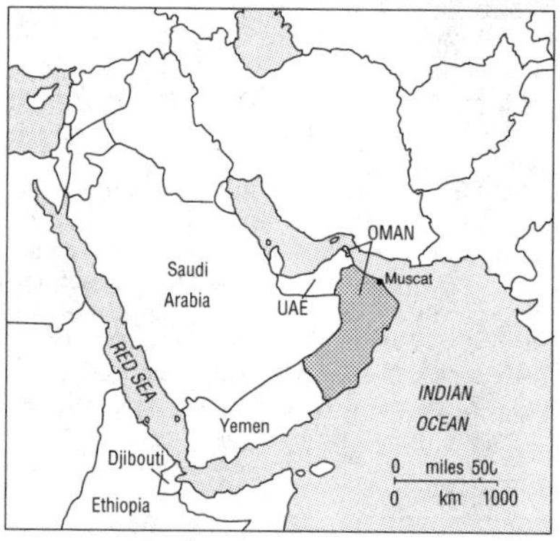
OMAN
Muscat
Saudi
Arabia
UAE
RED SEA
Yemen
INDIAN
OCEAN
Djibouti
Ethiopia
0 miles 500
0 km 1000

area 105,000 sq mi/272,000 sq km
capital Muscat
cities Salalah
physical mountains to N and S of a high arid plateau; fertile coastal strip
features Jebel Akhdar highlands; Kuria Muria islands; Masirah Island is used in aerial reconnaissance of the Arabian Sea and Indian Ocean; exclave on Musandam Peninsula controlling Strait of Hormuz
head of state and government Qaboos bin Said from 1970
political system absolute monarchy
exports oil, dates, silverware, copper
currency rial Omani
population (1990 est) 1,305,000; growth rate 3.0% p.a.
life expectancy men 55, women 58 (1989)
language Arabic (official); English, Urdu, and other Indian dialects
religion Ibadhi Muslim 75%; Sunni Muslim, Shiite Muslim, Hindu
literacy 20% (1989)
GNP $7.5 bn (1987); $5,070 per head (1988)
chronology
1951 The Sultanate of Muscat and Oman achieved full independence from Britain. Treaty of Friendship with Britain signed.
1970 After 38 years' rule, Sultan Said bin Taimur replaced in coup by his son Qaboos bin Said. Name changed to Sultanate of Oman.
1975 Left-wing rebels in S defeated.
1982 Memorandum of Understanding with UK signed, providing for regular consultation on international issues.
1985 Diplomatic ties established with USSR.

do (a form of martial arts). The Olympic flag bears the emblem of five colored rings (red, yellow, blue, black, and green) which are said to represent the five continents.

Olympus (Greek *Olimbos*) several mountains in Greece and elsewhere, one of which is Mount Olympus in N Thessaly, Greece, 9,577 ft/2,918 m high. In ancient Greece it was considered the home of the gods.

Om sacred word in Hinduism, used to begin prayers and placed at the beginning and end of books. It is composed of three syllables, symbolic of the Hindu Trimurti, or trinity of gods.

Omaha city in E Nebraska, on the Missouri River; population (1990) 335,795. It is a livestock-market center, with food-processing and meat-packing industries. Creighton University and the University of Nebraska Medical Center are here. Omaha was laid out in 1854. Its location at the E terminus of the Union Pacific Railroad (1869) spurred economic growth.

Oman country on the Arabian peninsula, bounded W by the United Arab Emirates, Saudi Arabia, and Yemen, and E by the Arabian Sea.

government Oman has no written constitution, and the sultan has absolute power, ruling by decree. There is no legislature. The sultan takes advice from an appointed cabinet. There is also a consultative assembly of 55 nominated members. There are no political parties.

history For early history, see ◊Arabia. The city of ◊Muscat has long been a trading post. The country was in Portugal's possession 1508–1658 and was then ruled by Persia until 1744. By the early 19th century, the state of Muscat and Oman was the most powerful in Arabia: it ruled Zanzibar until 1861 and also coastal parts of Persia and Pakistan.

In 1951 it became the independent sultanate of Muscat and Oman and signed a treaty of friendship with Britain. Said bin Taimur, who had been sultan since 1932, was overthrown by his son, Qaboos bin Said, in a bloodless coup 1970, and the country was renamed Oman. Qaboos embarked on a more liberal and expansionist policy than his father. The Popular Front for the Liberation of Oman has been fighting to overthrow the sultanate since 1965.

Oman's wealth is based on a few oil fields. Conflicts in neighboring countries, such as Yemen, Iran, Iraq, Kuwait, and Afghanistan, have not only emphasized the country's strategic importance but put its own security at risk. The sultan has tried to follow a path of ◊nonalignment, maintaining close ties with the US and other NATO countries but also keeping good relations with the USSR.

Omar 581–644. Adviser of the prophet Mohammed. In 634 he succeeded Abu Bakr as caliph (civic and religious leader of Islam), and conquered Syria, Palestine, Egypt, and Persia. He was assassinated by a slave. The Mosque of Omar in Jerusalem is attributed to him.

Omar Khayyam c. 1050–1123. Persian astronomer, mathematician, and poet. Born in Nishapur, he founded a school of astronomical research and assisted in reforming the calendar. The result of his observations was the *Jalālī* era, begun 1079. He wrote a study of algebra, which was known in Europe as well as in the East. In the West, Omar Khayyam is chiefly known as a poet through Edward ◊Fitzgerald's version of *The Rubaiyat of Omar Khayyam* 1859.

Omayyad dynasty Arabian dynasty of the Islamic empire who reigned as caliphs (civic and religious leaders of Islam) 661–750. They were overthrown by Abbasids, but a member of the family escaped to Spain and in 756 assumed the title of emir of Córdoba. His dynasty, which took the title of caliph in 929, ruled in Córdoba until the early 11th century.

ombudsman (Swedish "commissioner") official who acts on behalf of the private citizen in investigating complaints against the government. The post is of Scandinavian origin; it was introduced in Sweden 1809, Denmark 1954, and Norway 1962, and spread to other countries from the 1960s.

Hawaii was the first state to appoint an ombudsman 1967.

Omdurman city in Sudan, on the White Nile, a suburb of Khartoum; population (1983) 526,000. It was the residence of the Sudanese sheik known as the Mahdi 1884–98.

Omdurman, Battle of battle on Sept 2, 1898 in which the Sudanese, led by the Khalifa, were defeated by British and Egyptian troops under Gen Kitchener.

omnivore animal that feeds on both plant and animal material. Omnivores have digestive adaptations intermediate between those of ◊herbivores and ◊carnivores, with relatively unspecialized digestive systems and gut microorganisms that can digest a variety of foodstuffs.

On occasion, when regular food supplies are low, most mammals become omnivores.

Omphalos in Classical antiquity, a conical navel-stone, thought to mark the center of the world, such as that in the temple of Apollo at ◊Delphi in Greece.

Omsk industrial city (agricultural and other machinery, food processing, lumber mills, oil refining) in the USSR, capital of Omsk region, W Siberia; population (1987) 1,134,000. Its oil refineries are linked with Tuimazy in Bashkiria by a 1,000 mi/1,600 km pipeline.

onager wild ass *Equus hemionus* found in W Asia. Onagers are sandy brown, lighter underneath, and about the size of a small horse.

Onassis Aristotle (Socrates) 1906–1975. Turkish-born Greek shipowner. In 1932 he started what became the largest independent shipping line and during the 1950s he was one of the first to construct supertankers. In 1968 he married Jacqueline Kennedy, widow of US president John F Kennedy.

onchocerciasis or ***river blindness*** disease found in tropical Africa and Latin America. It is transmitted by bloodsucking black flies, which infect the victim with parasitic filarial worms (genus *Onco-cerca*), producing skin disorders and blindness.

oncogene a gene carried by a virus that induces a cell to divide abnormally, forming a ◊tumor. Oncogenes arise from mutations in genes (proto-oncogenes) found in all normal cells. They are usually also found in viruses that are capable of transforming normal cells to tumor cells. Such viruses are able to insert their oncogenes into the host cell's DNA, causing it to divide uncontrollably. More than one oncogene may be necessary to transform a cell in this way.

In 1989 US scientists J Michael Bishop and Harold Varmus were jointly awarded the Nobel Prize for Medicine for their concept of oncogenes, although credit for the discovery was claimed by a French cancer specialist, Dominique Stehelin.

oncology branch of medicine concerned with the diagnosis and treatment of ◊neoplasms, especially cancer.

ondes Martenot (French "Martenot waves") electronic musical instrument invented by Maurice Martenot and first demonstrated in 1928. A melody of considerable range and voice-like timbre is produced by sliding a contact along a conductive ribbon, the left hand controlling the tone color. In addition to inspiring works from Messiaen, Varkse, Jolivet and others, it has been in regular demand among composers of film and radio incidental music.

Onega, Lake second-largest lake in Europe, NE of St Petersburg, partly in Karelia, USSR; area 3,710 sq mi/9,600 sq km. The Onega canal, along its S shore, is part of the Mariinsk system linking St Petersburg with the river Volga.

Oneida town in New York State, named after the Oneida people (a nation of the ◊Iroquois confederacy). It became known from 1848 for the Oneida Community, a religious sect that practiced a form of "complex marriage" until its dissolution 1879.

O'Neill Eugene (Gladstone) 1888–1953. US playwright, widely regarded as the greatest US dramatist. His plays, although tragic, are characterized by a down-to-earth quality and are often experimental in form, influenced by German expressionism, Strindberg, and Freud. They were a radical departure from the romantic and melodramatic American theater entertainments. They include the Pulitzer prize-winning plays *Beyond the Horizon* 1920 and *Anna Christie* 1921, as well as *The Emperor Jones* 1920, *The Hairy Ape* 1922, *Desire Under the Elms* 1924, *The Iceman Cometh* 1946, and the posthumously produced autobiographical drama *Long Day's Journey into Night* 1956 (written 1940), also a Pulitzer-prize winner. He was awarded the Nobel Prize for Literature 1936.

O'Neill was born in New York City, the son of stage actors James O'Neill and Ella Quinlan. His

***O'Neill** Previously a sailor, gold prospector, actor, and reporter, US playwright Eugene O'Neill was awarded the Nobel Prize for Literature in 1936.*

tumultuous family relationships would later provide much material for his plays. He left Princeton University after a year to learn about life but nearly died from heavy drinking and a suicide attempt while living a derelict's lifestyle. The sailors, prostitutes, and other down-and-out people he met during this period, like the members of his family, people his plays. His other plays include *The Straw* 1921; *All God's Chillun Got Wings* 1924; *The Great God Brown* 1925; *Strange Interlude* 1928, a revolutionary five-hour drama; *Mourning Becomes Electra* 1931, a trilogy based on the story of Orestes from Greek mythology; and *A Moon for the Misbegotten* 1952. Many of his plays were first produced by the Provincetown Players in Provincetown, Massachusetts. It was largely through the work of O'Neill that the American theater became a forum for serious and significant ideas.

one-party state a state in which there is a ban, constitutional or unofficial, on the number of political parties permitted to stand for election. In some cases there may be no legal alternative parties. For example: in the USSR until the 1990s members of only one political party stood for election; in others there may be limited tolerance of a few token members of an opposition party; or one party may be permanently in power with no elections.

onion bulbous plant *Allium cepa* of the lily family Liliaceae. Cultivated from ancient times, it may have originated in Asia. The edible part is the bulb, containing an acrid volatile oil and having a strong flavor.

The onion is a biennial, the common variety producing a bulb in the first season and seeds in the second.

online system in computing, a system that allows the computer to work interactively with its users, responding to each instruction as it is given and prompting users for information when necessary, as opposed to a batch system. Since the fall in the cost of computers in the 1970s, online operation has become increasingly attractive commercially.

Onnes Kamerlingh 1853–1926. Dutch physicist, who worked mainly in the field of low-temperature physics. In 1911, he discovered the phenomenon of ◊superconductivity (enhanced electrical conductivity at very low temperatures), for which he was awarded the 1913 Nobel Prize for Physics.

onomatopoeia (Greek "name-making") a figure of speech that copies natural sounds. Thus the word or name "cuckoo" imitates the sound that the cuckoo makes.

Ontario

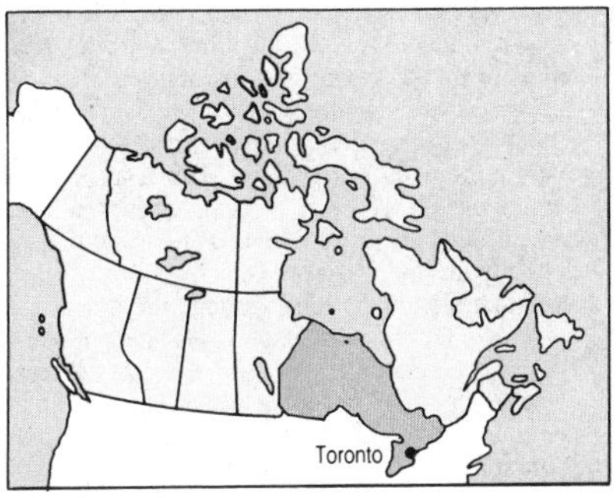
Toronto

Onsager Lars 1903–1976. Norwegian-born US physical chemist whose discovery of the "reciprocity relations of Onsager" in 1931 was vital to the production of nuclear energy. He was awarded a Nobel Prize 1968.

Ont. abbreviation for ◊Ontario.

Ontario province of central Canada

area 412,480 sq mi/1,068,600 sq km

capital Toronto

cities Hamilton, Ottawa (federal capital), London, Windsor, Kitchener, St Catherines, Oshawa, Thunder Bay, Sudbury

features Black Creek Pioneer Village; ◊Niagara Falls; lakes: Superior, Huron, Erie, Ontario; richest, chief-manufacturing, most-populated, and leading cultural province of English-speaking Canada

products nickel, iron, forest products, aircraft, motor vehicles, iron, steel, paper, chemicals, copper, uranium, gold, zinc

population (1986) 9,114,000

history an attempt 1841 to form a merged province with French-speaking Québec failed, and Ontario became a separate province of Canada 1867. Under the protectionist policies of the new federal government, Ontario gradually became industrialized and urban. Since World War II, more than 2 million immigrants, chiefly from Europe, have settled in Ontario.

First explored by the French in the 17th century, it came under British control 1763 (Treaty of Paris).

Ontario, Lake smallest and easternmost of the Great Lakes, on the US–Canadian border; area 7,400 sq mi/19,200 sq km. It is connected to Lake Erie by the Welland Canal and the Niagara River, and drains into the St Lawrence River. Its main port is Toronto.

On the Road novel by Jack Kerouac, published 1957, exploring the freewheeling life of the ◊Beat Generation in the style of "spontaneous bop prosody."

ontogeny the process of development of a living organism, including the part of development that takes place after hatching or birth. The idea that "ontogeny recapitulates phylogeny" (the development of an organism goes through the same stages as its evolutionary history), proposed by the German scientist Haeckel, has now been greatly modified.

ontology that branch of philosophy concerned with the study of being. In the 20th century, ◊Heidegger distinguished between an "ontological" inquiry (an inquiry into Being) and an "ontic" inquiry (an inquiry into a specific kind of entity).

onyx a semiprecious variety of chalcedonic ◊silica (SiO_2) in which the crystals are too fine to be detected under a microscope, a state known as cryptocrystalline. It has straight parallel bands of different colors: milk-white, black, and red.

Sardonyx, an onyx variety, has layers of brown or red carnelian alternating with lighter layers of onyx. It can be carved into cameos.

oolite a limestone made up of tiny spherical carbonate particles called ooliths. Ooliths have a concentric structure with a diameter up to 0.08 in/2 mm. They were formed by chemical precipitation and accumulation on ancient sea floors.

The surface texture of oolites is rather like that of fish roe. The late Jurassic limestones of the British Isles are mostly oolitic in nature.

Oort Jan Hendrik 1900– . Dutch astronomer. In 1927, he calculated the mass and size of our Galaxy, the Milky Way, and the Sun's distance from its center, from the observed movements of stars around the Galaxy's center. In 1950 Oort proposed that comets exist in a vast swarm, now called the Oort Cloud, at the edge of the Solar System.

In 1944 Oort's student Hendrik van de Hulst (1918–) calculated that hydrogen in space would emit radio waves at a wavelength of 8.3 in/21 cm, and in the 1950s Oort's team mapped the spiral structure of the Milky Way from the radio waves given out by interstellar hydrogen.

oosphere another name for the female gamete or ◊ovum of certain plants such as algae.

Oostende Flemish form, meaning "east end," of ◊Ostend.

ooze sediment of fine texture consisting mainly of organic matter found on the ocean floor at depths greater than 6,600 ft/2,000 m. Several kinds of ooze exist, each named after its constituents.

Siliceous ooze is composed of the ◊silica shells of tiny marine plants (diatoms) and animals (radiolarians). Calcareous ooze is formed from the ◊calcite shells of microscopic animals (foraminifera) and floating algae (coccoliths).

opal a form of ◊silica (SiO_2), often occurring as stalactites and found in many types of rock. Opal is cryptocrystalline, that is, the crystals are too fine to be detected under a microscope. The common opal is translucent, milk-white, yellow, red, blue, or green, and lustrous. Precious opal is opalescent, the characteristic play of colors being caused by close-packed silica spheres diffracting light rays within the stone.

Opals are found in Hungary, New South Wales, Australia (black opals were first discovered there in 1905), and Mexico (red fire opals).

Op art movement in modern art, popular in the 1960s. It uses scientifically based optical effects that confuse the spectator's eye. Precisely painted lines or dots are arranged in carefully regulated patterns that create an illusion of surface movement. Exponents include Victor Vasarely and Bridget Riley.

op. cit. abbreviation for opere citato (Latin "in the work cited"), used in reference citation.

OPEC abbreviation for ◊Organization of Petroleum-Exporting Countries.

open-door policy economic philosophy of equal access by all nations to another nation's markets.

The term was applied Sept 1899 by Secretary of State John Hay to the US policy toward China. Several European powers had carved out spheres of influence in China, and US and British interests were excluded from those areas. Hay called on all nations to preserve and respect China's territorial and administrative independence and integrity. The US reaffirmed its position 1931 and 1937 when Japan attacked China.

open-hearth furnace former method of steelmaking, now largely superseded by the ◊basic-oxygen process. The open-hearth furnace was developed in England by German-born William and Friedrich Siemens, and improved by Pierre and Emile Martin 1864. In the furnace, which has a wide, saucer-shaped hearth and a low roof, molten pig iron and scrap are packed into the shallow hearth and heated by overhead gas burners using preheated air.

open shop factory or other business employing men and women not belonging to labor unions, as opposed to the ◊closed shop, which employs labor union members only.

opera dramatic musical work in which singing takes the place of speech. In opera the music accompanying the action has paramount importance, although dancing and spectacular staging may also play their parts. Opera originated in late 16th-century Florence when the musical declamation, lyrical monologues, and choruses of Classical Greek drama were reproduced in current forms.

One of the earliest opera composers was Jacopo Peri (1561–1633), whose *Euridice* influenced Monteverdi. At first solely a court entertainment, opera soon became popular, and in 1637 the first public opera house was opened in Venice. In the later 17th century the elaborately conventional aria, designed to display the virtuosity of the singer, became predominant, overshadowing the dramatic element. Composers of this type of opera included Cavalli, Cesti, and Alessandro Scarlatti. In France opera was developed by Lully and Rameau, and in England by Purcell, but the Italian style retained its ascendancy, as exemplified by Handel.

Comic opera (*opera buffa*) was developed in Italy by such composers as Pergolesi, while in England *The Beggar's Opera* 1728 by John Gay started the vogue of the ballad opera, using popular tunes and spoken dialogue. Singspiel was the German equivalent (although its music was newly composed). A lessening of artificiality began with Gluck, who insisted on the pre-eminence of the dramatic over the purely vocal element. Mozart learned much from Gluck in writing his serious operas, but exceled in Italian *opera buffa*. In works such as *The Magic Flute* his librettist wrote in German, thus laying the foundations of the German-language opera, using the *Singspiel* as a basis. German librettos were then used by Beethoven in *Fidelio* and by Weber, who introduced the Romantic style for the first time in opera.

The Italian tradition, which placed the main stress on vocal display and melodic suavity (*bel canto*), continued unbroken into the 19th century in the operas of Rossini, Donizetti, and Bellini. It is in the Romantic operas of Weber and Meyerbeer that the work of Wagner has its roots. Dominating the operatic scene of his time, Wagner attempted to create, in his "music-dramas," a new art-form, and completely transformed the 19th-century conception of opera. In Italy, Verdi assimilated, in his mature work, much of the Wagnerian technique, without sacrificing the Italian virtues of vocal clarity and melody. This tradition was continued by Puccini. In French opera in the mid-19th century, represented by such composers as Delibes, Gounod, Saint-Saëns, and Massenet, the drama was subservient to the music. More serious artistic ideals were put into practice by Berlioz in *The Trojans*, but the merits of his work were largely unrecognized in his own time.

Bizet's *Carmen* began a trend toward realism in opera; his lead was followed in Italy by Mascagni, Leoncavallo, and Puccini. Debussy's *Pelléas and Melisande* represented a reaction against the over-emphatic emotionalism of Wagnerian opera. National operatic styles were developed in Russia by Glinka, Rimsky-Korsakov, Mussorgsky, Borodin, and Tchaikovsky, and in Bohemia by Smetana. Several composers of light opera emerged, including Sullivan, Lehár, Offenbach, and Johann Strauss.

In the 20th century the Viennese school produced an outstanding opera in Berg's *Wozzeck*, and the Romanticism of Wagner was revived by Richard Strauss in *Der Rosenkavalier*. Other 20th-century composers of opera include Gershwin, Bernstein, and Stravinsky in the US; Tippett, Britten, and Harrison Birtwistle in the UK; Henze in Germany; Petrassi in Italy; and Prokofiev and Shostakovich in the USSR.

opera buffa (Italian "comic opera") a type of humorous opera with characters taken from everyday life. The form began as a musical intermezzo in the 18th century and was then adopted in Italy and France for complete operas. An example is Rossini's *The Barber of Seville*.

opéra comique (French "comic opera") opera that includes text to be spoken, not sung; Bizet's *Carmen* is an example. Of the two Paris opera houses in the 18th and 19th centuries, the *Opéra* (which aimed at setting a grand style) allowed no spoken dialogue, whereas the *Opéra Comique* did.

opera seria (Italian "serious opera") a type of opera distinct from *opera buffa*, or humorous opera. Common in the 17th and 18th centuries, it tended toward formality. Examples include many of Handel's mythology-based operas.

operating system (OS) in computing, a program that controls the basic operation of a computer. A typical OS controls the ◊peripheral devices, organizes the filing system, provides a means of communicating with the operator, and runs other programs.

Some operating systems were written for specific computers, but some are accepted standards. These include CP/M (by Digital Research), widely used for computers with 8-bit microprocessors; MS-DOS (by Microsoft) for microcomputers with 16-bit microprocessors; and Unix (by Bell Laboratories) for minicomputers.

operetta a short amusing musical play, which may use spoken dialogue.

operon a group of genes that are found next to each other on a chromosome, and are turned on and off as an integrated unit. They usually produce enzymes that control different steps in the same biochemical pathway. Operons were discovered 1961 (by the French biochemists F Jacob and J Monod) in bacteria; they are less common in higher organisms where the control of metabolism is a more complex process.

Ophiuchus large constellation along the celestial equator, known as the serpent bearer because the constellation Serpens is wrapped around it. The Sun passes through Ophiuchus each Dec, but the constellation is not part of the zodiac. Ophiuchus contains ◊Barnard's Star.

ophthalmia inflammation of the eyeball or conjunctiva.

Ophthalmia neonatorum ("of the newborn") is an acute inflammation of a baby's eyes at birth with the organism of gonorrhea caught from the mother. Sympathetic ophthalmia is the diffuse inflammation of the sound eye that is apt to follow septic inflammation of the other.

ophthalmology medical specialty concerned with diseases of the eye and its surrounding tissues.

Ophuls Max. Adopted name of Max Oppenheimer 1902–1957. German film director. He moved to films from the theater, and his work used intricate camera movements. He worked in Europe and the US, attracting much critical praise for films such as *Letter from an Unknown Woman* 1948 and *Lola Montes* 1955.

opiate, endogenous a naturally produced chemical (neurotransmitter) in the body that has effects similar to morphine and other opiate drugs. These include ◊endorphins and ◊enkephalins.

opinion poll attempt to measure public opinion by taking a survey of the views of a representative sample of the electorate. The first accurately sampled opinion poll was carried out by the statistician George ◊Gallup during the US presidential election 1936. Opinion polls have encountered criticism on the grounds that their publication may influence the outcome of an election.

Rather than simply predicting how people will vote, poll results may alter voters' intentions, for example, by establishing one party as likely to win and making the voters wish to join the winning side, or by making the lead of one party seem so great that its supporters feel they need not bother to vote.

opium drug extracted from the unripe seeds of the opium poppy *Papaver somniferum* of SW Asia. An addictive narcotic, it contains several alkaloids, including morphine, one of the most powerful natural painkillers and addictive narcotics known, and codeine, a milder painkiller.

Heroin is a synthetic derivative of morphine and even more powerful as a drug. Opium is still sometimes given as a tincture, dissolved in alcohol and known as laudanum. Opium also contains the highly poisonous alkaloid thebaine.

***Oppenheimer** US physicist J Robert Oppenheimer, who led the Manhattan Project to design the first atomic bomb, but later opposed work on the hydrogen bomb.*

Opium Wars wars waged in the mid-19th century by the UK against China to enforce the opening of Chinese ports to trade in opium. Opium from British India paid for Britain's imports from China, such as porcelain, silk, and, above all, tea.

The First Opium War 1839–42, between Britain and China, resulted in the cession of Hong Kong to Britain and the opening of five treaty ports. Other European states were also subsequently given concessions.

A Second Opium War 1856–60 followed between Britain and France in alliance against China, when there was further Chinese resistance to the opium trade. China was forced to give the European states greater trading privileges, at the expense of its people.

Opole industrial town in S Poland, on the river Oder; population (1983) 121,900. It is an agricultural center; with manufactures including textiles, chemicals, and cement.

Oporto alternate form of ◊Porto in Portugal.

opossum any of a family (Didelphidae) of marsupials native to North and South America. Most opossums are tree-living, nocturnal animals, with prehensile tails, and hands and feet well adapted for grasping. They range from 4 in/10 cm to 20 in/50 cm in length and are insectivorous, carnivorous, or, more commonly, omnivorous.

The name is also popularly applied to some of the similar-looking phalangers found in Australia.

Most true opossums are confined to Central and South America, but the American opossum *Didelphis marsupialis*, with yellowish-gray fur, has spread its range into North America.

Oppenheimer J(ulius) Robert 1904–1967. US physicist. As director of the Los Alamos Science Laboratory 1943–45, he was in charge of the development of the atomic bomb (the Manhattan Project). When later he realized the dangers of radioactivity, he objected to the development of the hydrogen bomb and was alleged to be a security risk 1953 by the US Atomic Energy Commission (AEC).

Oppenheimer was the son of a German immigrant. Before World War II he worked with the physicist Ernest Rutherford in Cambridge. In 1963 the AEC, under G T Seaborg, granted him the Fermi award for accomplishments in physics.

opposition in astronomy, the moment at which the longitude of a body in the Solar System differs from that of the Sun by 180°, so that it lies

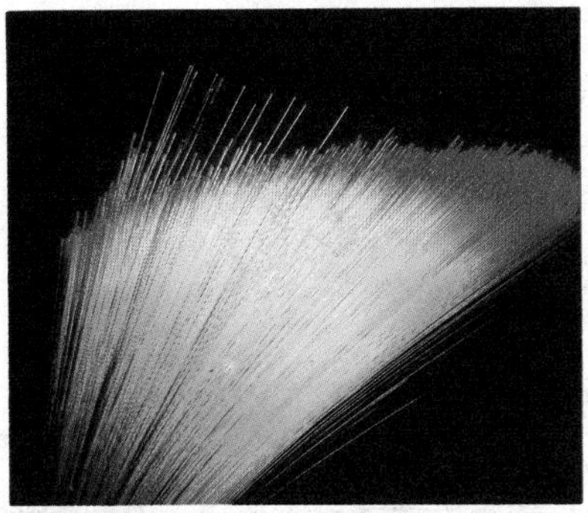

optical fiber *Spray of glass optical fibers, showing the pinpoint of light emerging at the tip of each fiber.*

opposite the Sun in the sky and crosses the ◊meridian at about midnight.

Although the ◊inferior planets cannot come to opposition, it is the best time for observing the ◊superior planets as they can then be seen all night.

optical aberration see ◊aberration, optical.

optical computer computer in which both light and electrical signals are used in the ◊CPU (central processing unit). The technology is still not fully developed, but such a computer promises to be faster and less vulnerable to outside electrical interference than one that relies solely on electricity.

optical contouring computerized monitoring of a light pattern projected onto a patient to detect discrepancies in movements during breathing.

optical fiber very fine, optically pure fiberglass through which light can be reflected to transmit an image or information from one end to the other. Bundles of such fibers are used in ◊endoscopes to inspect otherwise inaccessible parts of machines or of the living body. Optical fibers are increasingly being used to replace copper wire in telephone cables, the messages being coded as pulses of light rather than a fluctuating electric current. In 1989 a 1,690 mi/2,700 km optical-fiber link was opened between Adelaide and Perth, Australia.

optical illusion scene or picture that fools the eye. An example of a natural optical illusion is that the Moon appears bigger when it is on the horizon than when it is high in the sky, caused by the ◊refraction of light rays by the Earth's atmosphere.

optical instrument a device that uses one or more ◊lenses or ◊mirrors to produce an image. See ◊eye, ◊microscope, ◊periscope, ◊projector, and ◊telescope.

optic nerve large nerve passing from the eye to the brain, carrying visual information. In mammals it may contain up to a million nerve fibers, connecting the sensory cells of the retina to the optical centers in the brain. Embryologically, the optic nerve develops as an outgrowth of the brain.

optical illusion

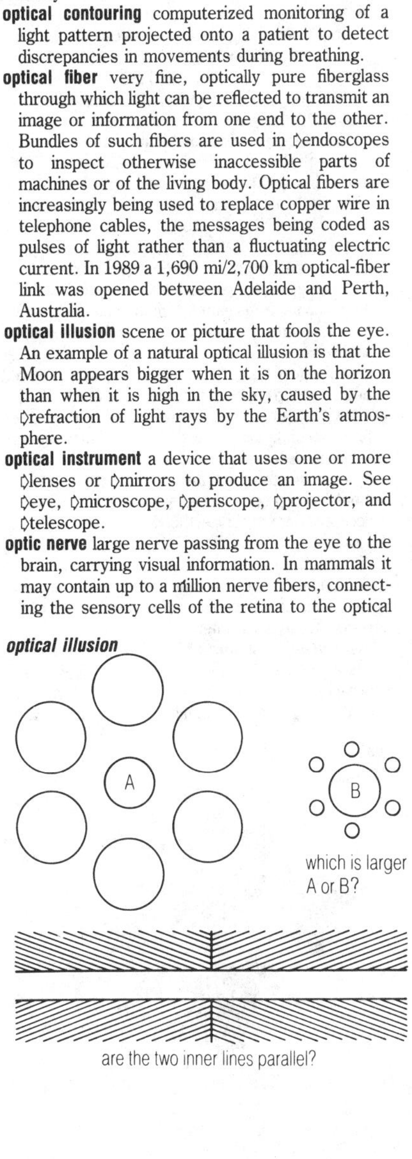
A
B
which is larger
A or B?
are the two inner lines parallel?

optics the branch of physics that deals with the study of light and vision—for example shadows and mirror images, lenses, microscopes, telescopes, and cameras. For all practical purposes light rays travel in straight lines, although ◊Einstein demonstrated that they may be "bent" by a gravitational field. On striking a surface they are reflected or refracted with some absorption of energy, and the study of this is known as geometrical optics.

option in business, a contract giving the owner the right (as opposed to the obligation, as with futures contracts; see ◊futures trading) to buy or sell a specific quantity of a particular commodity or currency at a future date and at an agreed price, in return for a premium. The buyer or seller can decide not to exercise the option if it would prove disadvantageous.

optoelectronics branch of electronics concerned with the development of devices (based on the ◊semiconductor gallium arsenide) that respond not only to the ◊electrons of electronic data transmission, but also to ◊photons.

In 1989, scientists at IBM in the US built a gallium arsenide microprocessor ("chip") containing 8,000 transistors and four photodetectors. The densest optoelectronic chip yet produced, this can detect and process data at a speed of 1 billion bits per second.

opuntia any cactus of the genus *Opuntia* of plants to which the ◊prickly pear belongs. They all have showy flowers and fleshy, jointed stems.

opus (Latin "work") in music, a term, used with a figure, to indicate the numbering of a composer's works, usually in chronological order.

Opus Dei (Latin "God's work") a Roman Catholic institution aimed at the dissemination of the ideals of Christian perfection. Founded in Madrid in 1928, and still powerful in Spain, it is now international. Its members may be of either sex, and lay or clerical.

OR abbreviation of ◊Oregon.

oracle Greek sacred site where answers (also called oracles) were given by a deity to inquirers about future events; these were usually ambivalent, so that the deity was proven right whatever happened. The earliest was probably at Dodona (in ◊Epirus), where priests interpreted the sounds made by the sacred oaks of ◊Zeus, but the most celebrated was that of Apollo at ◊Delphi.

Oradea or ***Oradea-Mare*** industrial city in Romania, on the river Koös; population (1983) 206,200. Industries include agricultural machinery, chemicals, nonferrous metallurgy, leather goods, printing, glass, textiles, clothing, and brewing. Created seat of a bishopric by St Ladislas in 1083, Oradea was destroyed by the Turks in 1241 and rebuilt. Many of its buildings date from the reign of Maria Theresa in the 18th century. It was ceded by Hungary to Romania in 1919 and held by Hungary 1940–45.

oral literature stories that are or have been transmitted in spoken form, such as public recitation, rather than through writing or printing. Most preliterate societies have had a tradition of oral literature, including short folk tales, legends, myths, proverbs, and riddles as well as longer narrative works; and most of the ancient epics—such as the Greek *Odyssey* and the Mesopotamian *Gilgamesh*—seem to have been composed and added to over many centuries before they were committed to writing.

Some ancient stories from oral traditions were not written down as literary works until the 19th century, such as the Finnish *Kalevala* (1822); many fairy tales, such as those collected in Germany by the Grimm brothers, also come into this category. Much of this sort of folk literature may have been consciously embellished and altered, for example in 19th-century Europe for nationalistic purposes.

Oran (Arabic *Wahran*) seaport in Algeria; population (1984) 663,500. Products include iron, textiles, footwear, and processed food; the port trades in grain, wool, and vegetables, and exports grass.

history Oran was part of the Ottoman Empire, except when it was under Spanish rule 1509–1708 and 1732–91. It was occupied by France in 1831. After the surrender of France to Germany in 1940, the French warships in the naval base of Mers-el-Kebir nearby were put out of action by the British navy to prevent them from falling into German hands.

orange any of several evergreen trees of the genus *Citrus*, family Rutaceae, which bear blossom and fruit at the same time. Thought to have originated in SE Asia, orange trees are commercially cultivated in Spain, Israel, the US, Brazil, South Africa, and elsewhere. The sweet orange *C. sinensis* is the one commonly eaten fresh; the Jaffa, blood, and navel orange are varieties of this species. Tangerines and mandarins belong to a related species *C. reticulata*. The sour orange or Seville *C. aurantium* is the bitter orange used in making marmalade. Oranges yield several essential oils.

Orange river in South Africa, rising on the Mont aux Sources in Lesotho and flowing W to the Atlantic; length 1,300 mi/2,100 km. It runs along the S boundary of the Orange Free State and was named 1779 after William of Orange. Water from the Orange is diverted via the Orange–Fish River Tunnel 1975 to irrigate the semiarid E Cape Province.

Orange town in France, N of Avignon; population (1982) 27,500. It has the remains of a Roman theater and arch. It was a medieval principality from which came the royal house of Orange.

Orange County metropolitan area of S California; area 801 sq mi/2,075 sq km; it adjoins Los Angeles County; population (1980) 1,932,700. Industries include aerospace and electronics. Oranges and strawberries are grown, Disneyland is here, and Santa Ana is the chief town.

Orange Free State province of the Republic of South Africa

area 49,405 sq mi/127,993 sq km

capital Bloemfontein

features plain of the High Veld; Lesotho forms an enclave on the Natal–Cape Province border

products grain, wool, cattle, gold, oil from coal, cement, pharmaceuticals

population (1987) 1,863,000; 82% ethnic Africans

history original settlements from 1810 were complemented by the ◊Great Trek, and the state was recognized by Britain as independent 1854. Following the South African, or Boer, War 1899–1902, it was annexed by Britain until it entered the union as a province 1910.

Orange, House of the royal family of the Netherlands. The title is derived from the small principality of Orange, in S France, held by the family from the 8th century to 1713. They held considerable possessions in the Netherlands, to which, after 1530, was added the German county of Nassau. From the time of William the Silent (1533–1585) the family dominated Dutch history, bearing the title of stadholder (magistrate) for the greater part of the 17th and 18th centuries. The son of Stadholder William V became King William I in 1815.

Orangeman member of the Ulster Protestant Orange Society established 1795 in opposition to the United Irishmen and the Roman Catholic secret societies. It was a revival of the Orange Institution 1688, formed in support of William (III) of Orange, whose victory over the Catholic James II at the Battle of the Boyne 1690 is commemorated annually by Protestants in parades on July 12.

orangutan ape *Pongo pygmaeus*, found solely in Borneo and Sumatra. Up to 5.5 ft/1.65 m in height, it is covered with long, red-brown hair and mainly lives a solitary, arboreal life, feeding chiefly on fruit. Now an endangered species, it is

orangutan

officially protected because its habitat is being systematically destroyed by ◊deforestation. Orangutans are slow-moving and have been hunted for food, as well as by animal collectors. They are sometimes considered the most intelligent of the apes. The name means "man of the forest."

Orasul Stalin name 1948–56 of the Romanian town ◊Braşov.

Oratorian a member of the Roman Catholic order of secular priests, called in full Congregation of the Oratory of St Philip Neri, formally constituted by Philip Neri 1575 in Rome, and characterized by the degree of freedom allowed to individual communities.

oratorio musical setting of religious texts, scored for orchestra, chorus, and solo voices, on a scale more dramatic and larger than that of a cantata.

The term derives from St Philip Neri's Oratory in Rome, where settings of the *Laudi spirituali* were performed in the 16th century. The definitive form of oratorio began in the 17th century with Cavalieri, Carissimi, Alessandro Scarlatti, and Schütz, and reached perfection in such works as J S Bach's *Christmas Oratorio*, and Handel's *Messiah*. Other examples of oratorios are Haydn's *The Creation* and *The Seasons*, Mendelssohn's *Elijah*, and Elgar's *The Dream of Gerontius*.

Orbison Roy 1936–1989. US pop singer and songwriter, composer of ballads such as "Only The Lonely" 1960 and "Running Scared" 1961. His biggest hit was the jaunty "Oh, Pretty Woman" 1964.

Born in Texas, Orbison began in the mid-1950s as a rockabilly singer on Sun Records. He soon specialized in slow, dramatic numbers. In the 1970s he turned to country material but made a pop comeback in 1988 as a member of the Travelin' Wilburys with Bob Dylan, George Harrison (ex-Beatles), Tom Petty (1952–), and Jeff Lynne (1947–).

orbit the path of one body in space around another, such as the orbit of Earth around the Sun, or of the Moon around Earth. When the two bodies are similar in mass, as in a ◊double star, both bodies move around their common center of mass. The movement of objects in orbit follows ◊Kepler's laws, which apply to artificial satellites as well as to natural bodies.

As stated by the laws, the orbit of one body around another is an ellipse. The ellipse can be highly elongated, as are comet orbits around the Sun, or it may be almost circular, as are those of some planets. The closest point of a planet's orbit to the Sun is called perihelion; the most distant point is aphelion. (For a body orbiting the Earth, the closest and furthest points of the orbit are called perigee and apogee.)

orbital, atomic the region around the nucleus of an atom (or, in a molecule, around several nuclei) in which an ◊electron is most likely to be found. According to ◊quantum theory, the position of an electron is uncertain; it may be found at any point. However, it is more likely to be found in some places than in others, and it is these that make up the orbital.

orbital, atomic

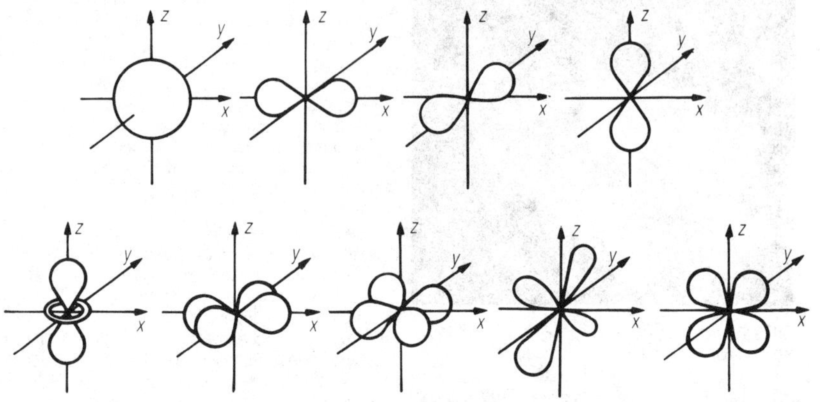
z
y
x

shapes of atomic orbitals

An atom or molecule has numerous orbitals, each of which has a fixed size and shape. An orbital is characterized by three numbers, called quantum numbers, representing its energy (and hence size), its angular momentum (and hence shape), and its orientation. Each orbital can be occupied by one or (if their spins are aligned in opposite directions) two electrons.

orca another name for ◊killer whale.

orchestra a group of musicians playing together on different instruments. In Western music, an orchestra typically contains various bowed string instruments and sections of wind, brass, and percussion. The size and format may vary according to the needs of composers.

The term was originally used in Greek theater for the semicircular space in front of the stage, and was adopted in 17th-century France to refer first to the space in front of the stage where musicians sat, and later to the musicians themselves.

The string section is commonly divided into two groups of violins (first and second), violas, cellos, and double basses. The woodwind section became standardized by the end of the 18th century, when it consisted of two each of flutes, oboes, clarinets, and bassoons, to which were later added piccolo, cor anglais, bass clarinet, and double bassoon. At that time, two timpani and two horns were also standard, and two trumpets were occasionally added. During the 19th century, the brass section was gradually expanded to include four horns, three trumpets, three trombones, and tuba. To the percussion section a third timpani was added, and from Turkey came the bass drum, side drum, cymbals, and triangle. One or more harps became common and, to maintain balance, the number of string instruments to a part also increased. Other instruments used occasionally in the orchestra include xylophone, ◊celesta, piano, and organ.

The term may also be applied to non-Western ensembles such as the Indonesian gamelan orchestra, consisting solely of percussion instruments, mainly tuned gongs and bells.

orchid any plant of the family Orchidaceae, which contains some 18,000 species, distributed throughout the world except in the coldest areas, and most numerous in damp equatorial regions. The flowers are the most evolved of the plant kingdom, have three sepals and three petals and are sometimes solitary, but more usually borne in spikes, racemes, or panicles, either erect or drooping.

ordeal, trial by in tribal societies and in Europe until the Renaissance, a method of testing the guilt of an accused person based on the belief in heaven's protection of the innocent. Examples of such ordeals are walking barefoot over heated iron, dipping the hand into boiling water, and swallowing consecrated bread (causing the guilty to choke).

order in Classical architecture, the ◊column (including capital, shaft, and base) and the entablature, considered as an architectural whole. The five orders are Doric, Ionic, Corinthian, Tuscan, and Composite.

The earliest order was the Doric (which had no base), which originated before the 5th century BC, soon followed by the Ionic, which was first found in Asia Minor. The Corinthian (with leaves in the capitals) dates from the end of the 5th century BC, while the Composite appears first on the arch of Titus in Rome AD 82. No Tuscan columns survive from antiquity, although the order was thought to originate in Etruscan times. The five orders were described in detail by the Italian Sebastiano Serlio in his treatise on architecture 1537.

order in biological classification, a group of related ◊families. For example, the horse, rhinoceros, and tapir families are grouped in the order Perissodactyla, the odd-toed ungulates, because they all have either one or three toes on each foot. The names of orders are not shown in italic (unlike genus and species names) and by convention they have the ending "-formes" in birds and fish; "-a" in mammals, amphibians, reptiles, and other animals; and "-ales" in fungi and plants. Related orders are grouped together in a ◊class.

ordinal number in mathematics, one of the series first, second, third, fourth,... . Ordinal numbers relate to order, whereas ◊cardinal numbers (1, 2, 3, 4,...) relate to quantity, or count.

ordination religious ceremony by which a person is accepted into the priesthood or monastic life in various religions. Within the Christian church, ordination authorizes a person to administer the sacraments. The Roman Catholic and Eastern Orthodox churches and the Church of England refuse to ordain women.

ordination of women Many Protestant denominations, such as the Methodists and Baptists, ordain women as ministers, as do many churches in the Anglican Communion outside the UK. In

orchid

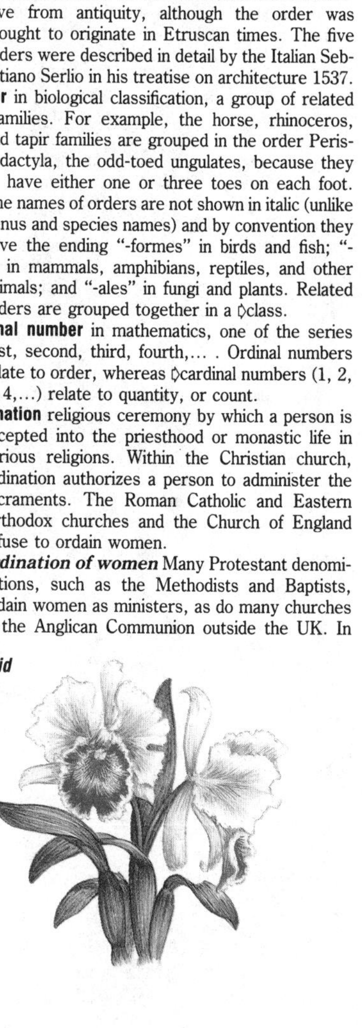

Oregon

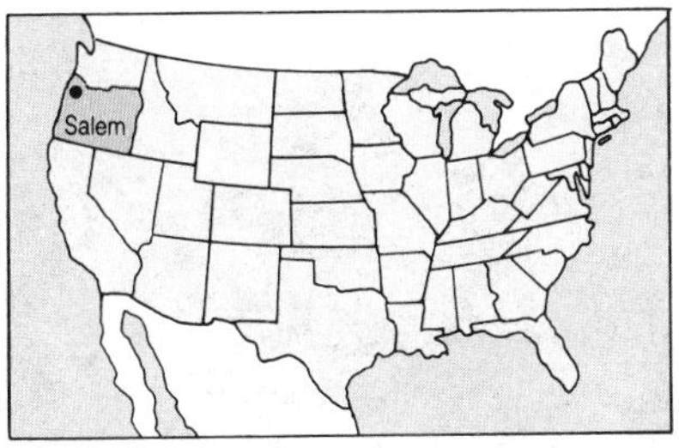
Salem

1988 the first female bishop was elected within the Anglican Communion (in Massachusetts).

Ordovician period of geologic time 505–438 million years ago; the second period of the ◊Paleozoic era. Animal life was confined to the sea: reef-building algae and the first jawless fish are characteristic.

The period is named after the Ordovices, an ancient Welsh people, because the system of rocks formed in the Ordovician period was first studied in Wales.

ore body of rock, a vein within it, or a deposit of sediment, worth mining for the economically valuable mineral it contains.

The term is usually applied to sources of metals. Hydrothermal ore deposits are formed from fluids such as saline water passing through fissures in the host rock at an elevated temperature. Examples are the "porphyry copper" deposits of Chile and Bolivia, the submarine copper–zinc–iron sulfide deposits recently discovered on the East Pacific Rise, and the limestone lead–zinc deposits that occur in the southern US and in the Pennines of Britain.

Other ores are concentrated by igneous processes, causing the ore metals to become segregated from a magma, for example, the chromite and platinum-metal-rich bands within the Bushveld, South Africa. Erosion and transportation in rivers of material from an existing rock source can lead to further concentration of heavy minerals in a deposit, for example, Malaysian tin deposits. Weathering of rocks in situ can result in residual metal-rich soils, such as the nickel-bearing laterites of New Caledonia.

Oregon state in NW US, on the Pacific; nickname Beaver State

area 97,079 sq mi/251,500 sq km

capital Salem

cities Portland, Eugene

features fertile Willamette River valley; rivers: Columbia, Snake; Crater Lake, deepest in the US (1,933 ft/589 m); mountains: Coast and Cascades; Oregon Dunes National Recreation Area, on Pacific coast; the Oregon Trail (2,000 mi/3,200 km from Independence, Missouri, to the Columbia River) was the pioneer route across the US 1804–60

products wheat, livestock, timber, electronics

population (1990) 2,842,321

famous people Chief Joseph, Ursula LeGuin, Linus Pauling, John Reed

history coast sighted by Spanish and English sailors 16th-17th centuries; part of coastline charted by James Cook 1778 on his search for the Northwest Passage; claimed for the US 1792 by Robert Gray, whose ship *Columbia* sailed into the river now named for it; explored by Lewis and Clark 1805; Astoria, John Jacob Astor's fur depot, founded at the mouth of the Columbia 1811; boundary between US settlers and the Hudson's Bay Company fixed 1846 by Oregon Treaty. Oregon Territory included Washington until 1853; Oregon achieved statehood 1859. It remained relatively isolated until the completion of the first transcontinental railroad link 1883. Improved transportation helped make it the nation's leading lumber producer and a major exporter of food products. Development also was aided by hydroelectric projects, many of them undertaken by the federal government.

Orel industrial city in the USSR, capital of Orel region, on the river Oka, 200 mi/320 km SSW of Moscow; population (1987) 335,000. Industries include engineering, textiles, and foodstuffs. It is the birthplace of the writer Ivan Turgenev.

Orellana Francisco de 1511–1546. Spanish explorer who traveled with Francesco ◊Pizarro from Guayaquil, on the Pacific coast of South America, to Quito in the Andes. He was the first person known to have navigated the full length of the Amazon from the Napo River to the Atlantic Ocean 1541–43.

Orem city in N central Utah, SE of Salt Lake City. It was settled by Mormons 1861. Industries include electronics and steel; population (1990) 67,561.

Orenburg city in S central USSR, on the Ural river; population (1987) 537,000. It is a trading and mining center and capital of Orenburg region. It dates from the early 18th century and was called Chkalov 1938–57 in honor of Soviet aviator Valeri Chkalov.

Orense town in NW Galicia, Spain, on the river Miño; population (1986) 102,000. It produces textiles, furniture, food products, and metal goods.

Oresteia trilogy of tragic Greek plays by ◊Aeschylus—*Agamemnon*, *Choephoroe*, and *The Eumenides*—which won first prize at the festival of Dionysus in 458 BC. They describe the murder of Agamemnon by his wife Clytemnestra and the consequent vengeance of his son Orestes and daughter Electra.

Orestes in Greek legend, the son of ◊Agamemnon and ◊Clytemnestra, who killed his mother because she and her lover Aegisthus had murdered his father.

Öresund strait between Sweden and Denmark; in English called the ◊Sound.

Orff Carl 1895–1982. German composer, an individual stylist whose work is characterized by sharp dissonances and percussion. Among his compositions are the cantata *Carmina Burana* 1937 and the opera *Antigone* 1949.

organ musical wind instrument of ancient origin. It produces sound from pipes of various sizes under applied pressure and has keyboard controls.

One note only is sounded by each pipe, but these are grouped into stops, which are ranks or scales of pipes prepared to "speak" by a knob. These, in turn, form part of a sectional organ, one of the tonal divisions comprising the whole organ. These separate manuals are the great, swell, choir, solo, echo, and pedal organs, controlled by the player's hands and feet. By this grouping and subdivision, extremes of tone and volume are obtained.

It developed from the Panpipe and hydraulus, and is mentioned in writings as early as the 3rd century BC. Organs were imported to France from Byzantium in the 8th and 9th centuries, after which their manufacture in Europe began. The superseding of the old drawslides by the key system dates from the 11th–13th centuries, the first chromatic keyboard from 1361. The more recent designs date from 1809 when the composition pedal was introduced.

Apart from its continued use in serious compositions and for church music, the organ has been adapted for light entertainment. The electric tone-wheel organ was invented 1934 by the US engineer Laurens Hammond (1895–1973). Other types of electric organ were developed in the 1960s. Electrically controlled organs substitute electrical impulses and relays for some of the air-pressure controls. These, such as the Hammond organs, built during the 1930s for the large cinemas of the period, include many special sound effects as well as color displays. In electronic organs the notes are produced by electronic oscillators and are amplified at will.

organ in biology, part of a living body, such as the liver or brain, that has a distinctive function or set of functions.

organic chemistry
common organic molecule groupings

formula	name	atomic bonding
CH_3	Methyl	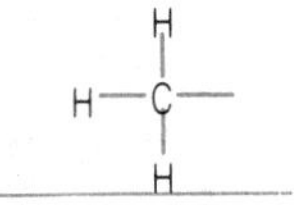
CH_2CH_3	Ethyl	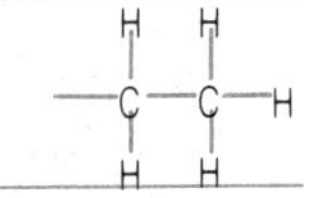
CC	Double bond	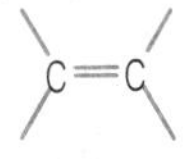
CHO	Aldehyde	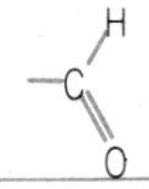
CH_2OH	Alcohol	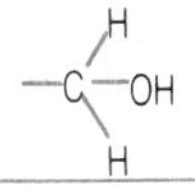
CO	Ketone	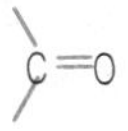
COOH	Acid	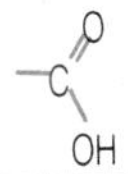
CH_2NH_2	Amine	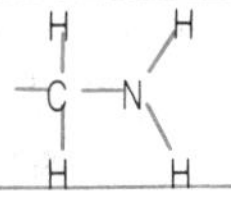
C_6H_6	Benzene ring	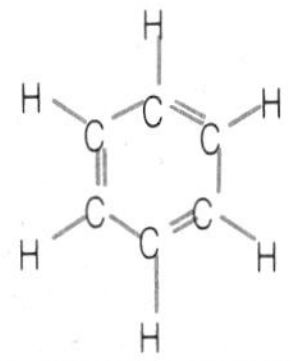

organelle a discrete and specialized structure in a living cell; organelles include mitochondria, chloroplasts, lysosomes, ribosomes, and the nucleus.

organic chemistry branch of chemistry that deals with carbon compounds, in particular the more complex ones. Organic compounds form the chemical basis of life and are more abundant than inorganic compounds. The basis of organic chemistry is the ability of carbon to form long chains of atoms, branching chains, rings, and other complex structures. In a typical organic compound, each carbon atom forms a bond with each of its neighboring carbon atoms in the chain or ring, and two more with hydrogen atoms (carbon has a valency of four). Other atoms that may be involved in organic molecules include oxygen and nitrogen. Compounds containing only carbon and hydrogen are known as hydrocarbons.

organic farming farming without the use of synthetic fertilizers (such as ◊nitrates and phosphates) or ◊pesticides (herbicides, insecticides ,and fungicides) or other agrochemicals (such as hormones, growth stimulants, or fruit regulators). The concept is based on growing clean fuel in a naturally prepared and managed soil.

In place of artificial fertilizers, compost, manure, seaweed, or other substances derived from living things are used (hence the name "organic"). Growing a crop of a nitrogen-fixing plant such as alfalfa, then plowing it back into the soil, also fertilizes the ground. Some organic farmers use naturally occurring chemicals such as nicotine or pyrethrum to kill pests, but control by nonchemical methods is preferred. Those methods include removal by hand, intercropping (planting with companion plants which deter pests), mechanical barriers to infestation, crop rotation, better cultivation methods, and ◊biological control. Weeds can be controlled by hoeing, mulching (covering with manure, straw, or black plastic), or burning off. Organic farming methods produce food without pesticide residues and greatly reduce pollution of the environment. They are more labor intensive, and therefore more expensive, but use less fossil fuel. Soil structure is greatly improved by organic methods, and recent studies show that a conventional farm can lose four times as much soil through erosion as an organic farm, although the loss may not be immediately obvious.

Organisation de l'Armée Secrète (OAS) guerrilla organization formed 1961 by French settlers devoted to perpetuating their own rule in Algeria (Algérie Française). It collapsed on the imprisonment 1962–68 of its leader, General Raoul Salan.

Organization for Economic Cooperation and Development (OECD) Paris-based international organization of 24 industrialized countries, which coordinates member states' economic policy strategies. The OECD's subsidiary bodies include the International Energy Agency 1974, set up in the face of a world oil crisis.

It superseded the Organization for European Economic Cooperation (established 1948 to promote European recovery under the ◊Marshall Plan) 1961, when the US and Canada became members and its scope was extended to include development aid. The OECD members are: Australia, Austria, Belgium, Canada, Denmark, Finland, France, Germany, Greece, Iceland, Ireland, Italy, Japan, Luxembourg, Netherlands, New Zealand, Norway, Portugal, Spain, Sweden, Switzerland, Turkey, UK, and US.

Organization of African Unity (OAU) association established 1963 to eradicate colonialism and improve economic, cultural, and political cooperation in Africa; headquarters Addis Ababa, Ethiopia. The secretary-general is Salim Ahmed Salim (deputy prime minister of Tanzania). The French-speaking Joint African and Mauritian Organization/Organisation Commune Africaine et Mauritienne (OCAM) (1962) works within the framework of the OAU for African solidarity; headquarters Yaoundé, Cameroon.

Organization of American States (OAS) association founded 1948 by a charter signed by representatives of 30 North, Central, and South American states. Canada held observer status from 1972 and became a full member 1990. It aims to maintain peace and solidarity within the hemisphere and is concerned with the social and economic development of Latin America. Its headquarters are in Washington, DC. It is based on the International Union of American Republics 1890–1910 and Pan-American Union 1910–48, set up to encourage friendly relations between countries of North and South America.

Organization of Central American States (Organización de Estados Centro Americanos: ODECA) international association promoting common economic, political, educational, and military aims in Central America. The first organization, established 1951, was superseded in 1962. Its members are Costa Rica, El Salvador, Guatemala, Honduras, and Nicaragua, provision being made for Panama to join at a later date. The permanent headquarters are in Guatemala City.

Organization of Petroleum Exporting Countries (OPEC) body established 1960 to coordinate price and supply policies of oil-producing states, and also to improve the position of Third World states by forcing Western states to open their markets to the resultant products. Its concerted action in raising prices in the 1970s triggered worldwide recession but also lessened demand so that its influence was reduced by the mid-1980s. OPEC members are: Algeria, Ecuador, Gabon, Indonesia, Iran, Iraq, Kuwait, Libya, Nigeria, Qatar, Saudi Arabia, United Arab Emirates, and Venezuela.

OPEC's importance in the world market was reflected in its ability to implement oil price increases from $3 a barrel in 1973 to $30 a barrel in 1980. In the 1980s, OPEC's dominant position was undermined by reduced demand for oil in industrialized countries, increased non-OPEC oil supplies, and production of alternative energy. These factors contributed to the dramatic fall in world oil prices to $10 a barrel in July 1986 from $28 at the beginning of the year. OPEC's efforts to stabilize oil prices through mandatory reduced production have been resisted by various members.

organizer in embryology, a part of the embryo that causes changes to occur in another part, through ◊induction, thus "organizing" development and ◊differentiation.

organum in music, a form of early medieval harmony in which voices move in parallel.

orienteering sport of cross-country running and route-finding. Competitors set off at one-minute intervals and have to find their way, using map and compass, to various checkpoints (approximately 0.5 mi/0.8 km apart), where their control cards are marked. World championships have been held since 1966. Orienteering was invented in Sweden by Major Ernst Killander in 1918.

origami the art of folding paper into forms such as dolls and birds, originating in Japan in the 10th century.

Origen c. 185–c. 254. Christian theologian, born in Alexandria, who produced a fancifully allegorical interpretation of the Bible. He castrated himself to ensure his celibacy.

original sin Christian doctrine that Adam's fall rendered humanity innately tainted and unable to achieve salvation except through divine grace.

Orinoco river in N South America, flowing for about 1,500 mi/2,400 km through Venezuela and forming for about 200 mi/320 km the boundary with Colombia; tributaries include the Guaviare, Meta, Apure, Ventuari, Caura, and Caroni. It is navigable by large steamers for 700 mi/1,125 km from its Atlantic delta; rapids obstruct the upper river.

oriole any of two families of brightly colored songbirds.

The Old World orioles of Africa and Eurasia belong to the family Oriolidae. New World orioles belong to the family Icteridae, which also includes blackbirds, bobolinks, grackles, meadowlarks, cowbirds, and tanagers. The northern oriole *Icterus galbula* of North America, has a black head and wings and bright orange underparts.

Orion in astronomy, a very prominent constellation in the equatorial region of the sky (the celestial region), near Taurus, and represented as the hunter of Greek mythology. It contains the bright stars Betelgeuse and Rigel, as well as a distinctive row of three stars that make up Orion's belt. Beneath the belt, marking the sword of Orion, is the Orion nebula; nearby is one of the most distinctive dark nebulae, the Horsehead.

Orion in Greek mythology, a giant of ◊Boeotia, famed as a hunter.

Orion nebula luminous cloud of gas and dust 1,500 light-years away, in the constellation Orion, from which stars are forming. It is about 15 light-years in diameter and contains enough gas to make a cluster of thousands of stars. At the nebula's center is a group of hot young stars, called the Trapezium, which make the surrounding gas glow. The nebula is visible to the naked eye as a misty patch below the belt of Orion.

Orissa state of NE India
area 60,139 sq mi/155,800 sq km
capital Bhubaneswar
cities Cuttack, Rourkela
features mainly agricultural; Chilka lake with fisheries and game; temple of Jagannath or Juggernaut at Puri
products rice, wheat, oilseed, sugar, timber, chromite, dolomite, graphite, iron
population (1981) 26,272,000
language Oriya (official)
religion 90% Hindu
history administered by the British 1803–1912 as a subdivision of Bengal, it joined with Bihar to become a province. In 1936 Orissa became a separate province, and in 1948–49 its area was almost doubled before its designation as a state 1950.

***Orkney Islands** The houses of the Neolithic village of Skara Brae in Scotland's Orkney Islands are of dry-stone construction.*

Orizaba industrial city (brewing, paper, and textiles) and resort in Veracruz state, Mexico; population (1980) 115,000. An earthquake in 1973 severely damaged it.

Orizaba Spanish name for ◊Citlalt petl, mountain in Mexico.

Orkney Islands island group off the NE coast of Scotland
area 375 sq mi/970 sq km
cities Kirkwall (administrative headquarters), on Mainland (Pomona)
features comprises about 71 islands and islets, low-lying and treeless; mild climate caused by the Gulf Stream; Skara Brae, a remarkably well-preserved Neolithic village on Mainland. Population, long falling, has in recent years risen as the islands' remoteness attracts new settlers. Scapa Flow, between Mainland and Hoy, was a naval base in both world wars, and the German fleet scuttled itself here June 21, 1919
products fishing and farming, wind power (Burgar Hill has the world's most productive wind generator; blades 197 ft/60 m diameter)
population (1987) 19,000
history Harald I (Fairhair) of Norway conquered the islands 876; pledged to James III of Scotland 1468 for the dowry of Margaret of Denmark and annexed by Scotland (the dowry unpaid) 1472.

Orkneys, South islands in the British Antarctic Territory; see ◊South Orkneys.

Orlando industrial city in Florida; population (1990) 164,693. It is a winter resort and tourist center, with Walt Disney World and Epcot Center nearby. Electronic and aerospace equipment are manufactured in the city, and citrus-fruit products are processed here. Educational institutions include the University of Central Florida. Orlando was settled 1843.

Orlando Vittorio Emanuele 1860–1952. Italian politician, prime minister 1917–19. He attended the Paris Peace Conference after World War I, but dissatisfaction with his handling of the Adriatic settlement led to his resignation. He initially supported Mussolini but was in retirement 1925–46, when he returned to the assembly and then the senate.

Orlando Furioso a poem by the Italian Renaissance writer Ariosto, published 1532 as a sequel to Boiardo's *Orlando innamorato* 1441–94. The poem describes the unrequited love of Orlando for Angelica, set against the war between Saracens (Arabs) and Christians during Charlemagne's reign. It influenced Shakespeare, Byron, and Milton, and is considered to be the greatest poem of the Italian Renaissance.

Orleanists French monarchist group that supported the Orléans branch of the royal family in opposition to the Bourbon Legitimists. Both groups were united in 1883 when the Bourbon line died out.

Orléans industrial city of France, on the river Loire; 70 mi/115 km SW of Paris; population (1982) 220,500. It is the capital of Loiret *département*. Industries include engineering and food processing.

Orléans, of pre-Roman origin and formerly the capital of the old province of Orléanais, is associated with Joan of Arc, who liberated it from English rule in 1429.

Orly a suburb of Paris in the *département* of Val-de-Marne; population (1982) 17,000. Orly international airport is the busiest in France.

Ormandy Eugene 1899–1985. Hungarian-born US conductor, music director of the Philadelphia Orchestra 1936–80. Originally a violin virtuoso, he championed ◊Rachmaninov and ◊Shostakovich.

ormolu (French *or moulu* "ground gold") alloy of copper, zinc, and sometimes tin, used for furniture decoration.

Ormuz alternate name for the Iranian island ◊Hormuz.

Ormuzd another name for Ahura Mazda, the good god of ◊Zoroastrianism.

Orne French river rising E of Sées and flowing NW, then NE to the English Channel below Caen; 94 mi/152 km long. A ship canal runs alongside it from Caen to the sea at Ouistreham. The Orne gives its name to a *département* in Normandy; population (1982) 295,500.

ornithology the study of birds. It covers scientific aspects relating to their structure and classification, and their habits, song, flight, and value to agriculture as destroyers of insect pests.

Interest in birds has led to the formation of societies for their protection, of which the Society for the Protection of Birds 1889 in Britain was the first. The Audubon Society 1905 in the US has similar aims. Other countries now have similar societies, and there is an International Council for Bird Preservation with its headquarters at the Natural History Museum, London. Worldwide scientific banding (or the fitting of coded rings to captured specimens) has resulted in accurate information on bird movements and distribution.

ornithophily the ◊pollination of flowers by birds. Ornithophilous flowers are typically brightly colored, often red or orange. They produce large quantities of thin, watery nectar, and are scentless because most birds do not respond well to smell. They are found mostly in tropical areas, with hummingbirds being important pollinators in North and South America, and the sunbirds in Africa and Asia.

orogeny formation of mountains, by processes of volcanism, folding, faulting, and upthrusting (by the action of ◊plate tectonics).

Oromo a member of a group of E African peoples, especially of S Ethiopia, who speak a Hamito-Semitic (Afro-Asiatic) language.

Orontes (Arabic *'Asi*) river flowing through Lebanon, Syria, and Turkey to the Mediterranean and used mainly for irrigation; length 250 mi/400 km.

Orozco José Clemente 1883–1949. Mexican painter whose murals were inspired by the Mexican revolution of 1910, such as the series in the Palace of Government, Guadalajara, 1949.

Orpheus mythical Greek poet and musician. The son of Apollo and a muse, he married Eurydice, who died from the bite of a snake. Orpheus went down to Hades to bring her back and her return to life was granted on condition that he walk ahead of her without looking back. But he did look back and Eurydice was irretrievably lost. In his grief, he offended the Maenad women of Thrace, and was torn to pieces by them.

Orphism ancient Greek mystery cult, of which the Orphic hymns formed part. Secret rites, accompanied by a harsh lifestyle, were aimed at securing immortality.

Orr Bobby (Robert) 1948– Canadian hockey player, who played for the Boston Bruins 1967–76 and the Chicago Blackhawks 1976–79 of the National Hockey League. He was voted the best defenseman every year 1967–75, and was Most Valuable Player 1970–72. He was the first defenseman to score 100 points in a season, and was leading scorer 1970 and 1975.

orris root underground stem of a species of ◊iris grown in S Europe. Violet-scented, it is used in perfumery, and herbal medicine.

Orsini Felice 1819–1858. Italian political activist, a member of the ◊Carbonari secret revolutionary group, who attempted unsuccessfully to assassinate Napoleon III in Paris Jan 1858. He was subsequently executed, but the Orsini affair awakened Napoleon's interest in Italy and led to a secret alliance with Piedmont at Plombières 1858, directed against Italy.

Orsk industrial city in the USSR, at the junction of the Or and Ural rivers; population (1987) 273,000. Industries include mining, oil refining, locomotives, and aluminum. Its refineries are fed by a pipeline from Guriev. The town was originally a fortress.

Ortega Saavedra Daniel 1945– . Nicaraguan Socialist politician, head of state 1981–90. He was a member of the Sandinista Liberation Front (FSLN), which overthrew the regime of Anastasio Somoza 1979. US-sponsored ◊Contra guerrillas opposed his government from 1982.

A participant in underground activities against the Somoza regime from an early age, Ortega was imprisoned and tortured several times.

He became a member of the national directorate of the FSLN and fought in the two-year campaign for the ◊Nicaraguan Revolution. Ortega became a member of the junta of national reconstruction, and its coordinator two years later. In Feb 1990, Ortega lost the presidency to US-backed Violeta Chamorro.

Ortega y Gasset José 1883–1955. Spanish philosopher and critic. He considered communism and fascism the cause of the downfall of Western civilization. His *Toward a Philosophy of History* 1941 contains philosophical reflections on the state and an interpretation of the meaning of human history.

orthochromatic a photographic film or paper of decreased sensitivity, that can be processed with a red safelight. Using it, blue objects appear lighter and red ones darker because of increased blue sensitivity.

orthodontics branch of ◊dentistry, mainly dealing with correction of malocclusion (faulty position of teeth).

Orthodox Church or ***Eastern Orthodox Church*** or ***Greek Orthodox Church*** a federation of self-governing Christian churches mainly found in E and SE Europe, the Soviet Union, and parts of Asia. The center of worship is the Eucharist. There is a married clergy, except for bishops; the Immaculate Conception is not accepted. The highest rank in the church is that of Ecumenical Patriarch, or Bishop of Istanbul. There are approximately 130 million adherents.

The church's teaching is based on the Bible, and the Nicene ◊Creed (as modified by the Council of Constantinople 381) is the only confession of faith used. The celebration of the Eucharist has changed little since the 6th century. The ritual is elaborate, and accompanied by singing in which both men and women take part, but no instrumental music is used. Besides the seven sacraments, the prayer book contains many other services for daily life. During the marriage service, the bride and groom are crowned.

Its adherents include Greeks, Russians, Romanians, Serbians, Bulgarians, Georgians, and Albanians. In the last 200 years the Orthodox Church has spread into China, Korea, Japan, and the US, as well as among the people of Siberia and central Asia. Some of the churches were founded by the apostles and their disciples; all conduct services in their own languages and follow their own customs and traditions, but are in full communion with one another. There are many monasteries, for example Mount Athos in Greece, which has flourished since the 10th century. The senior church of Eastern Christendom is that of Constantinople (Istanbul).

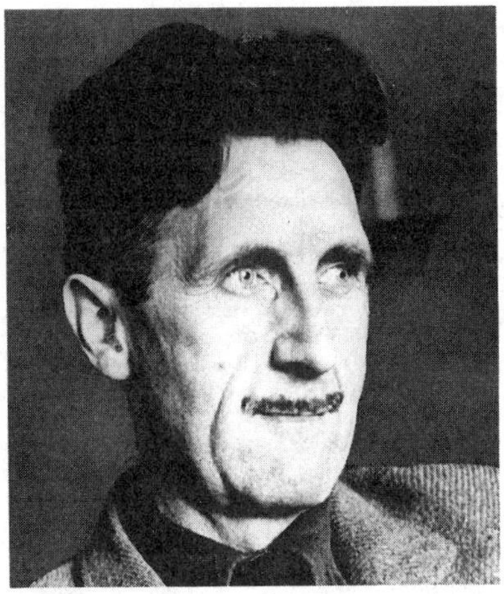

Orwell *English novelist and essayist George Orwell.*

orthopedics branch of medicine concerned with the surgery of bones and joints.

ortolan songbird *Emberiza hortulana* of the bunting family, common in Europe and W Asia, migrating to Africa in the winter. It is considered a delicacy among gourmets.

Orvieto town in Umbria, Italy, NE of Lake Bolsena, population (1981) 22,800.

Built on the site of Volsinii, an Etruscan town destroyed by the Romans 280 BC, Orvieto has many Etruscan remains. The name is from Latin *Urbs Vetus* "old town."

Orwell George. Adopted name of Eric Arthur Blair 1903–1950. English author. His books include the satire *Animal Farm* 1945, which included such sayings as "All animals are equal, but some are more equal than others," and the prophetic *Nineteen Eighty-Four* 1949, portraying the dangers of excessive state control over the individual. Other works include *Down and Out in Paris and London* 1933 and *Homage to Catalonia* 1938.

Born in India and educated in England, he served for five years in the Burmese police force, an experience reflected in the novel *Burmese Days* 1935. Life as a dishwasher and tramp were related in *Down and Out in Paris and London*, and service for the Republican cause in the Spanish Civil War in *Homage to Catalonia*. He also wrote numerous essays.

oryx any of a genus *Oryx* of large antelopes native to Africa and Asia. The Arabian oryx *O. leucoryx* was extinct in the wild, but bred in captivity, it has been successfully reintroduced into the wild.

The scimitar-horned oryx *O. tao* of the Sahara is also rare. Beisaoryx *O. beisa* in E Africa and gemsbok *O. gazella* in the Kalahari are more common. In profile the two long horns appear as one, which may have given rise to the legend of the unicorn.

OS/2 single-user computer ◊operating system produced jointly by Microsoft Corporation and IBM for use on large microcomputers. Its main features are ◊multitasking and the ability to access large amounts of internal ◊memory.

It was announced in 1987, and is partly based on an earlier system, ◊MS-DOS.

Osaka industrial port (iron, steel, shipbuilding, chemicals, textiles) on Honshu island; population (1987) 2,546,000, metropolitan area 8,000,000. It is the oldest city of Japan and was at times the seat of government in the 4th–8th centuries.

Lying on a plain sheltered by hills and opening on to Osaka Bay, Osaka is honeycombed with waterways. It is a tourist center for Kyoto and the Seto Inland Sea and is linked with Tokyo by fast electric train 124 mph/200 kph. An underground shopping and leisure center 1951 has been used as a model for others throughout Japan. It was a mercantile center in the 18th century, and in the 20th century set the pace for Japan's revolution based on light industries.

Osborn Henry Fairfield 1857–1935. US paleontologist. Born in Fairfield, Connecticut, Osborn was educated at Princeton and made his first fossil-hunting expedition to the West 1877. Appointed to the Princeton faculty 1881, he was named professor of biology at Columbia 1891. In the same year, he also began to serve as curator of vertebrate paleontology at the American Museum of Natural History.

In addition to his teaching, Osborn was a staff paleontologist with the US Geological Survey 1900–24 and president of the American Museum of Natural History 1908–33.

Osborne John (James) 1929– . English dramatist. He was one of the first ◊Angry Young Men (anti-establishment writers of the 1950s) of British theater with his debut play, *Look Back in Anger* 1956. Other plays include *The Entertainer* 1957, *Luther* 1960, and *Watch It Come Down* 1976.

Osborne House preferred residence of Queen Victoria, for whom it was built 1845, on the Isle of Wight, England. It was presented to the nation by Edward VII.

Oscar in film, popular name for ◊Academy Award.

Oscar two kings of Sweden and Norway:

Oscar I 1799–1859. King of Sweden and Norway from 1844, when he succeeded his father, Charles XIV. He established freedom of the press, and supported Denmark against Germany 1848.

Oscar II 1829–1907. King of Sweden and Norway 1872–1905, king of Sweden until 1907. He was the younger son of Oscar I, and succeeded his brother Charles XV. He tried hard to prevent the separation of his two kingdoms but relinquished the throne of Norway to Haakon VII in 1905.

oscillating universe in astronomy, a theory that states that the gravitational attraction of the mass within the universe will eventually slow down and stop the expansion of the universe. The outward motions of the galaxies will then be reversed, eventually resulting in a "Big Crunch" where all the matter in the universe would be contracted into a small volume of high density. This could undergo a further ◊Big Bang, thereby creating another expansion phase. The theory suggests that the universe would alternately expand and collapse through alternate Big Bangs and Big Crunches.

oscillator any device producing a desired oscillation (vibration). There are many types of oscillator for different purposes, involving various arrangements of electron tubes or components such as ◊transistors, ◊inductors, ◊capacitors, and ◊resistors. It is an essential part of a radio transmitter, generating the high-frequency carrier signal necessary for radio communication. The ◊frequency is often controlled by the vibrations set up in a crystal (such as quartz).

oscillograph instrument for displaying or recording the values of rapidly changing oscillations, electrical or mechanical. An oscilloscope shows variations in electrical potential on the screen of a ◊cathode-ray tube, by means of deflection of a beam of ◊electrons.

Oshima Nagisa 1932– . Japanese film director whose violent and sexually explicit *In the Realm of the Senses/Ai No Corrida* 1977 caused controversy when first released. His other work includes *Death by Hanging* 1968 and *Merry Christmas Mr Lawrence* 1983, which starred the singer David Bowie.

Oshkosh city in E central Wisconsin where the Fox river flows into Lake Winnebago, NW of Milwaukee; seat of Winnebago county. Industries include clothing, machinery, lumber, and electronics; population (1990) 55,006.

Oshogbo city and trading center on the river Niger, in W Nigeria, 125 mi/200 km NE of Lagos; population (1986) 405,000. Industries include cotton and brewing.

osier any of several trees and shrubs of the willow genus *Salix*, cultivated for basket making; in particular, *S. viminalis*.

The name is also applied to several North American ◊dogwoods.

Osijek (German *Esseg*) industrial port in Croatia, Yugoslavia, on the river Drava; population (1981) 158,800. Industries include textiles, chemicals, and electrical goods.

Osiris ancient Egyptian god, the embodiment of goodness, who ruled the underworld after being killed by ◊Set. The sister-wife of Osiris was ◊Isis or Hathor, and their son ◊Horus captured his father's murderer.

Under ◊Ptolemy I's Greco-Egyptian empire Osiris was developed (as a means of uniting his Greek and Egyptian subjects) into Serapis (Osiris+Apis, the latter being the bull-god of Memphis who carried the dead to the tomb), elements of the cults of Zeus and Hades being included, which did not please the Egyptians; the greatest temple of Serapis was the Serapeum in Alexandria. The cult of Osiris, and that of Isis, later spread to Rome.

Oslo capital and industrial port (textiles, engineering, timber) of Norway; population (1988) 454,000. The first recorded settlement was made in the 11th century by Harald III, but after a fire 1624, it was entirely replanned by Christian IV and renamed Christiania 1624–1924.

The port is built at the head of Oslo fjord, which is kept open in winter by icebreakers. There is a Viking museum, the 13th-century Akershus Castle, a 17th-century cathedral, and the National Gallery, which includes many paintings by Munch.

Osman I or ***Othman I*** 1259–1326. Turkish ruler from 1299. He began his career in the service of the ◊Seljuk Turks, but in 1299 he set up a kingdom of his own in Bithynia, NW Asia and assumed the title of sultan. He conquered a great part of Anatolia, so founding a Turkish empire. His successors were known as "sons of Osman," from which the term ◊Ottoman Empire is derived.

osmium hard, heavy, bluish-white, metallic element, symbol Os, atomic number 76, atomic weight 190.2. It is the densest of the elements and is resistant to tarnish and corrosion. It occurs in platinum ores and as a free metal (see ◊native metal) with iridium in a natural alloy called osmiridium, containing traces of platinum, ruthenium, and rhodium. Its uses include pen points and light-bulb filaments; like platinum, it is a useful catalyst.

It was discovered in 1803 and named in 1804 by English chemist Smithson Tennant (1761–1815), for Greek *osme*, "odor," relating to the irritating smell of one of its oxides.

osmoregulation the process whereby the water content of living organisms is maintained at a constant level. If the water balance is disrupted, the concentration of salts will be too high or too low, and vital functions, such as nerve conduction, will be adversely affected.

In mammals, loss of water by evaporation is

osmosis

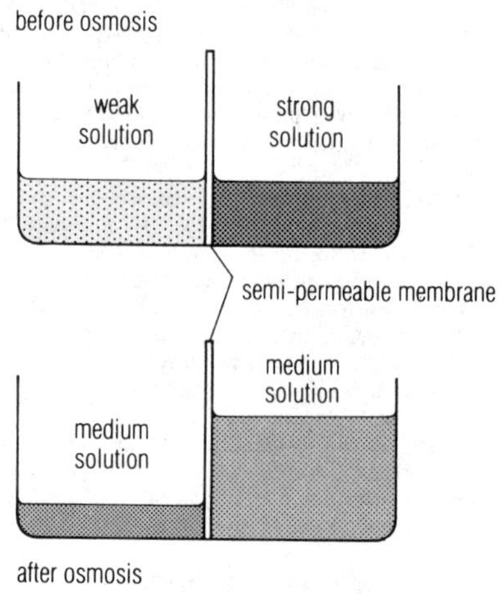
before osmosis
weak solution
strong solution
semi-permeable membrane
medium solution
medium solution
after osmosis

counteracted by increased intake and by mechanisms in the kidneys that enhance the rate at which water is resorbed before urine production. Both these responses are mediated by hormones, primarily those of the adrenal cortex (see ◊adrenal gland).

osmosis the movement of solvent (liquid) through a semipermeable membrane separating solutions of different concentrations. The solvent passes from the more dilute solution to the more concentrated solution until the two concentrations are equal. Applying external pressure to the solution on the more concentrated side arrests osmosis, and is a measure of the osmotic pressure of the solution.

Many cell membranes behave as semipermeable membranes, and osmosis is a vital mechanism in the transport of fluids in living organisms—for example, in the transport of water from the roots up the stems of plants.

Fishes have kidney mechanisms to counteract the effects of osmosis fluid transport between their bodies and the surrounding water (outward in saltwater fish, inward in freshwater fish).

Osnabrück industrial city in Lower Saxony, Federal Republic of Germany; 71 mi/115 km W of Hanover; population (1988) 154,000. Industries include engineering, iron, steel, textiles, clothing, paper, and food processing. Before World War II, Osnabrück contained fine examples of Gothic and Renaissance architecture.

Osnabrück bishopric was founded by Charlemagne 783. The Treaty of Westphalia was signed at Osnabrück and Münster 1648, ending the Thirty Years' War. A type of rough fabric, osnaburg, was originally made here.

osprey bird of prey *Pandion haliaetus*, the single member of the family Pandionidae; sometimes erroneously called "fish hawk." Its most distinguishing characteristic is one of habit: to catch fish, it plunges feet first into the water. Dark brown above and a striking white below, it measures 2 ft/60 cm with a 6 ft/2 m wingspan. Ospreys occur on all continents except Antarctica and have faced extinction in several areas of habitation. Efforts to preserve the species have been successful.

Ossa mountain in Thessaly, Greece; height 6,490 ft/1,978 m. In mythology, two of Poseidon's giant sons were said to have tried to dislodge the gods from Olympus by piling nearby Mount Pelion on top of Ossa to scale the great mountain.

Ossa, Mount the highest peak on the island of Tasmania, Australia; height 5,250 ft/1,617 m.

Ossetia region of SW USSR, in the Caucasus, on the border of the republic of Georgia. It is inhabited by the Ossets, who speak the Iranian language Ossetic, and who were conquered by the Russians in 1802. Some live in North Ossetia, an autonomous republic of the SW USSR; area

3,088 sq mi/8,000 sq km; population (1985) 613,000; capital Ordzhonikidze. The rest live in the South Ossetia autonomous region of the Georgian republic, population (1984) 98,000; capital Tshkinvali. The region has been the scene of Osset-Georgian inter-ethnic conflict from 1989. The South Ossetians, an ethnic minority in the Caucasus Mountains, want to leave Georgia, now ruled by the nationalist-minded president Zviad Gamsakhurdia, and join North Ossetia in the Russian Republic. As a preliminary to reunification they have demanded that South Ossetia be upgraded to an autonomous republic.

Inter-ethnic, Georgian versus Osset, gun battles continued in the vicinity of the beseiged, Osset-controlled regional capital of Tskhninvali during the spring of 1991. By September 1991 the death toll in this local conflict for the year 1991 had risen to 210. Only the presence of Soviet troops maintained some semblance of daylight peace.

Ossian (Celtic *Oisin*) legendary Irish hero, invented by the Scottish writer James ◊Macpherson. He is sometimes represented as the son of ◊Finn Mac Cumhaill, about 250, and as having lived to tell the tales of Finn and the Ulster heroes to St Patrick, about 400. The publication 1760 of Macpherson's poems, attributed to Ossian, made Ossian's name familiar throughout Europe.

ossification the process whereby bone is formed in vertebrate animals by special cells (osteoblasts) that secrete layers of ◊extracellular matrix on the surface of the existing ◊cartilage. Conversion to bone occurs through the deposition of calcium phosphate crystals within the matrix.

Ossory ancient kingdom, lasting until 1110, in Leinster, Ireland; the name is preserved in some Church of Ireland and Roman Catholic bishoprics.

Ostade Adriaen van 1610–1685. Dutch painter and engraver of tavern scenes and village fairs. A native of Haarlem, Ostade may have studied under Frans Hals. His brother, Isaac van Ostade (1621–49), painted winter landscapes and roadside and farmyard scenes.

Östberg Ragnar 1866–1945. Swedish architect who designed the City Hall in Stockholm, Sweden 1911–23.

Ostend (Flemish *Oostende*) seaport and pleasure resort in W Flanders, Belgium; 67 mi/108 km NW of Brussels; population (1985) 69,000. There are large docks, and the Belgian fishing fleet has its headquarters here. There are ferry links to Dover and Folkestone, England.

osteoarthritis degenerative disease of the joints in later life, sometimes resulting in disabling stiffness and wasting of muscles.

Formerly thought to be due to wear and tear, it has been shown to be less common in the physically active. It appears to be linked with crystal deposits (in the form of calcium phosphate) in cartilage, a discovery that suggests hope of eventual prevention.

osteology part of the science of ◊anatomy, dealing with the structure, function, and development of bones.

osteomalacia softening of the bones, a condition caused by lack of vitamin D in adult life. It results in pain and muscle cramps, bone deformity, and a tendency to spontaneous fracture.

osteomyelitis infection of bone, with spread of pus along the marrow cavity. Now quite rare, it may follow from a compound fracture (where broken bone protrudes through the skin), or from infectious disease elsewhere in the body.

The symptoms are high fever, severe illness, and pain over the limb. If the infection is at the surface of the bone it may quickly form an abscess; if it is deep in the bone marrow it may spread into the circulation and lead to blood poisoning. Most cases can be treated with antibiotics, but sometimes surgery is needed.

osteopathy system of alternative medical practice that relies on physical manipulation to treat mechanical stress. It claims to relieve not only postural problems and muscle pain, but asthma and other disorders.

ostrich

osteoporosis disease in which the bone substance becomes porous and brittle. It is common in older people, affecting more women than men. It may occur in women whose ovaries have been removed, unless hormone-replacement therapy (HRT) is instituted. Osteoporosis may occur as a side effect of long-term treatment with ◊corticosteroids. Early menopause in women, childlessness, small body build, lack of exercise, heavy drinking, smoking, and hereditary factors may also be contributory factors.

Osteoporosis is also seen in the bones of young people whose limb has been immobilized.

Ostia ancient Roman town near the mouth of the Tiber. Founded about 330 BC, it was the port of Rome and had become a major commercial center by the 2nd century AD. It was abandoned in the 9th century. The present-day seaside resort Ostia Mare is situated nearby.

Ostpolitik (German "eastern policy") West German chancellor ◊Brandt's policy of reconciliation with the communist bloc from 1971, pursued to a modified extent by his successors Schmidt and Kohl. The policy attained its goal with the reunification of Germany in 1990.

ostracism the deliberate exclusion of an individual, or group, from society. It was an ancient Athenian political device to preserve public order. Votes on pieces of broken pot (Greek *ostrakon*) were used to exile unpopular politicians for ten years.

Ostrava industrial city (iron works, furnaces, coal, chemicals) in Czechoslovakia, capital of Severomoravsky region, NE of Brno; population (1984) 324,000.

ostrich large flightless bird *Struthio camelus*, found in Africa. The male may be about 8 ft/2.5 m tall and weigh 300 lb/135 kg, and is the largest living bird. It has exceptionally strong legs and feet (two-toed) that enable it to run at high speed, and are also used in defense. It lives in family groups of one cock with several hens. Ostriches are bred in South Africa and elsewhere for leather and also for their tail feathers.

Ostrogoth member of a branch of the E Germanic people, the ◊Goths.

Ostrovsky Alexander Nikolaevich 1823–1886. Russian playwright, founder of the modern Russian theater. He dealt satirically with the manners of the middle class in numerous plays, for example *A Family Affair* 1850. His fairy-tale play *The Snow Maiden* 1873 inspired the composers Tchaikovsky and Rimsky-Korsakov.

Ostwald Wilhelm 1853–1932. German chemist who devised the Ostwald process (the oxidation of ammonia over a platinum catalyst to give nitric acid). His work on catalysts laid the foundations of the petrochemical industry. Nobel prize 1909.

Oswald, St c. 605–642. King of Northumbria from 634, after killing the Welsh king Cadwallon.

Oswald had become a Christian convert during exile on the Scottish island of Iona. With the help of St Aidan he furthered the spread of Christianity in N England.

Oswiecim (German ◊*Auschwitz*) town in S Poland, site of the World War II extermination and ◊concentration camp.

OT abbreviation for ◊Old Testament.

Otago a peninsula and coastal plain on South Island, New Zealand, constituting a district; area 25,220 sq mi/64,230 sq km; chief cities include Dunedin and Invercargill.

Otaru fishing port on W coast of Hokkaido, Japan; industries include fish processing, paper, sake; population (1984) 179,000.

Othello a tragedy by William Shakespeare, first performed 1604–05. Othello, a Moorish commander in the Venetian army, is persuaded by Iago that his wife Desdemona is having an affair with his friend Cassio. Othello murders Desdemona; on discovering her innocence, he kills himself.

Othman c. 574–656. third caliph (leader of the Islamic empire) from 644, a son-in-law of the prophet Mohammed. Under his rule the Arabs became a naval power and extended their rule to N Africa and Cyprus, but Othman's personal weaknesses led to his assassination. He was responsible for the compilation of the authoritative version of the Koran, the sacred book of Islam.

Othman I another name for the Turkish sultan ◊Osman I.

Otho I 1815–1867. King of Greece 1832–62. As the 17-year-old son of King Ludwig I of Bavaria, he was selected by the European powers as the first king of independent Greece. He was overthrown by a popular revolt.

Otis Elisha Graves 1811–1861. US engineer who developed an elevator that incorporated a safety device, making it acceptable for passenger use in the first skyscrapers. The device, invented 1852, consisted of vertical ratchets on the sides of the elevator shaft into which spring-loaded catches engage and "lock" the elevator into position in the event of cable failure.

otitis inflammation of the ear. *Otitis externa*, occurring in the outer ear canal, is easily treated with antibiotics. Inflamed conditions of the middle ear (*otitis media*) or inner ear (*otitis interna*) are more serious, carrying the risk of deafness and infection of the brain.

O'Toole Peter 1932– . Irish-born English actor who made his name as *Lawrence of Arabia* 1962, and who then starred in complex theatrical films such as *Beckett* 1964 and *The Lion in Winter* 1968. Subsequent appearances were few and poorly received by critics until *The Ruling Class* 1972, *The Stuntman* 1978, and *High Spirits* 1988.

otosclerosis overgrowth of bone in the middle ear causing progressive deafness. This inherited condition is gradual in onset, developing usually before middle age. It is twice as common in women as in men.

The middle ear cavity houses the sound-conduction mechanism called the ossicular chain, consisting of three tiny bones (ossicles) that magnify vibrations received at the eardrum for onward transmission to the inner ear. In otosclerosis, extraneous growth of spongy bone immobilizes the chain, preventing the conduction of sound. Surgery is necessary to remove the diseased bone and reconstruct the ossicular chain.

Otranto seaport in Puglia, Italy, on the Strait of Otranto; population (1981) 5,000. It has Greek and Roman remains, a ruined castle (the inspiration for Horace Walpole's novel *The Castle of Otranto* 1764), and a castle begun 1080. The port is linked by ferry with Corfu.

Ottawa capital of Canada, in E Ontario, on the hills overlooking the Ottawa river and divided by the Rideau Canal into the Upper (western) and Lower (eastern) towns; population (1986) 301,000, metropolitan area (with adjoining Hull, Québec)

otter

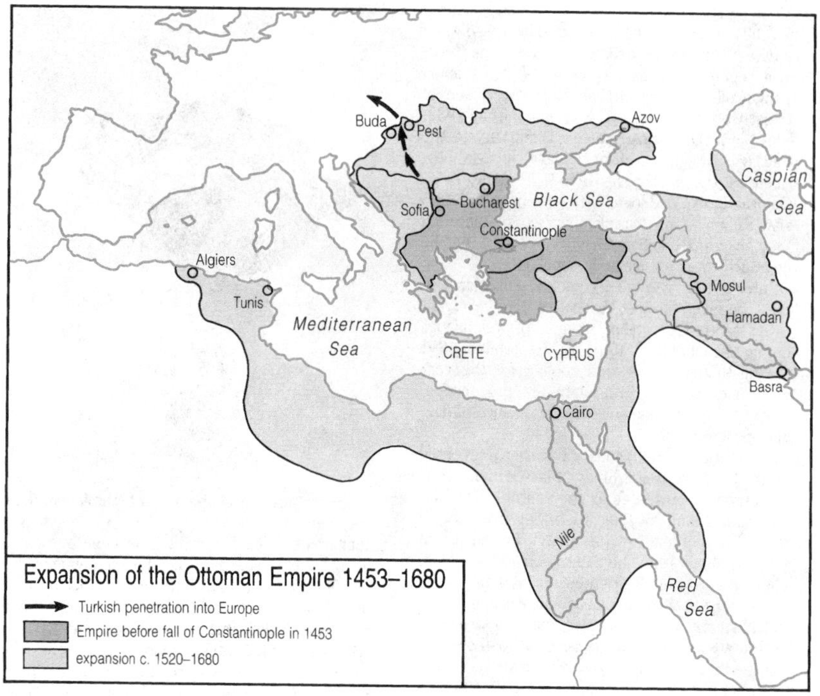
Buda
Pest
Azov
Caspian Sea
Black Sea
Sofia
Bucharest
Constantinople
Algiers
Tunis
Mediterranean Sea
CRETE
CYPRUS
Mosul
Hamadan
Basra
Cairo
Nile
Red Sea
Turkish penetration into Europe
Empire before fall of Constantinople in 1453
expansion c. 1520–1680

Expansion of the Ottoman Empire 1453–1680

819,000. Industries include timber, pulp and paper, engineering, food processing, and publishing. It was founded 1826–32 as Bytown, in honor of John By (1781–1836), whose army engineers were building the Rideau Canal. It was renamed 1854 after the Outaouac Indians.

Features include the National Museum, National Art Gallery, Observatory, Rideau Hall (the governor-general's residence), and the National Arts Centre 1969 (with an orchestra and English/French theater). In 1858 it was chosen by Queen Victoria as the country's capital.

otter any of various aquatic carnivores of the weasel family, found on all continents except Australia. Otters have thick, brown fur, short limbs, webbed toes, and long, compressed tails. They are social, playful, and agile.

The genus *Lutra* includes the river otters of North America and Eurasia, about 3.5 ft/1 m long, including the tail. The sea otter *Enhydra lutris* of the N Pacific is the most aquatic. It sometimes lies on its back in the water, resting a stone on its chest, on which it breaks shellfish. The giant otter *Pteronura brasiliensis* of South America reaches 5 ft/1.5 m plus a 2.3 ft/70 cm tail.

Otto Nikolaus August 1832–1891. German engineer who in 1876 patented an effective internal-combustion engine.

Otto four Holy Roman emperors, including:

Otto I 912–973. Holy Roman emperor from 936. He restored the power of the empire, asserted his authority over the pope and the nobles, ended the Magyar menace by his victory at the Lechfeld 955, and refounded the East Mark, or Austria, as a barrier against them.

Otto IV c. 1182–1218. Holy Roman emperor, elected 1198. He engaged in controversy with Pope Innocent III, and was defeated by the pope's ally, Philip of France, at Bouvines 1214.

Otto cycle alternate name for the ◊four-stroke cycle, introduced by the German engineer Nikolaus Otto (1832–91) in 1876. It improved on existing piston engines by compressing the fuel mixture in the cylinder before it was ignited.

Ottoman Empire Muslim empire of the Turks 1300–1920, the successor of the ◊Seljuk Empire. It was founded by ◊Osman I and reached its height with ◊Suleiman in the 16th century. Its capital was Istanbul (formerly Constantinople). At its greatest extent its boundaries were Europe as far as Hungary, part of S Russia, Iran, the Palestinian coastline, Egypt, and N Africa. From the 17th century it was in decline. There was an attempted revival and reform under the Young Turk party 1908, but the regime crumbled when Turkey sided with Germany in World War I. The sultanate was abolished by Atatürk 1922; the last sultan was Mohammed VI.

Otway Thomas 1652–1685. English dramatist. His plays include the tragedies *Alcibiades* 1675, *Don Carlos* 1676, *The Orphan* 1680, and *Venice Preserv'd* 1682.

Otztal Alps a range of the Alps in Italy and Austria, rising to 12,382 ft/3,774 m at Wildspitze, Austria's second highest peak.

Ouagadougou capital and industrial center of Burkina Faso; population (1985) 442,000. Products include textiles, vegetable oil, and soap.

Oudenaarde town of E Flanders, W Belgium, on the river Scheldt, 18 mi/28 km SSW of Ghent; population (1982) 27,200. It is a center of tapestry-making and carpet-weaving. Oudenaarde was the site of the victory by the British, Dutch, and Austrians over the French in 1708 during the War of the Spanish Succession.

Oudh region of N India, now part of Uttar Pradesh. An independent kingdom before it fell under Mughal rule, Oudh regained independence 1732–1856, when it was annexed by Britain. Its capital was Lucknow, center of the ◊Indian Mutiny 1857–58. In 1877 it was joined with Agra, from 1902 as the United Provinces of Agra and Oudh, renamed Uttar Pradesh 1950.

Oughtred William 1575–1660. English mathematician, credited as the inventor of the slide rule 1622. His major work *Clavis mathematicae/The Key to Mathematics* 1631 was a survey of the entire body of mathematical knowledge of his day. It introduced the "×" symbol for multiplication, as well as the abbreviations "sin" for sine and "cos" for cosine.

Oujda industrial and commercial city (lead and coal-mining) in N Morocco, near the border with Algeria; population (1982) 471,000. It trades in wool, grain, and fruit.

Oulu (Swedish *Uleåborg*) industrial port (lumber mills, tanneries, shipyards) in W Finland, on the Gulf of Bothnia; population (1986) 97,900. It was originally a Swedish fortress 1375.

ounce another name for the snow ◊leopard.

ounce unit of mass, one-sixteenth of a pound ◊avoirdupois, equal to 437.5 grains (28.35 g); also one-twelfth of a pound troy, equal to 480 grains.

The fluid ounce is a measure of capacity, in the US equivalent to one-sixteenth of a pint, or eight fluid drams. In the UK and Canada, it equals one-twentieth of a pint.

Ouse (Celtic "water") several British rivers: The Great Ouse rises in Northamptonshire and winds its way across 160 mi/250 km to enter the Wash N of King's Lynn. A large sluice across the Great Ouse, near King's Lynn, was built as part of extensive flood-control works 1959. The Little Ouse flows for 24 mi/38 km along part of the Norfolk/Suffolk border and is a tributary of the Great Ouse. The Yorkshire Ouse is formed by the junction of the Ure and Swale near Boroughbridge and joins the river Trent to form the Humber. The Sussex Ouse rises between Horsham and Cuckfield and flows through the South Downs to enter the English Channel at Newhaven.

Ousmane Sembene 1923– . Senegalese writer and film director. His novels, written in French, include *Le docker noir* 1956, about his experiences as a union leader in Marseille; *Les bouts de bois/God's bits of wood* 1960; *Le mandat/The money order*; and *Xala*, the last two of which he made into films.

Ouspensky Peter 1878–1947. Russian mystic. Originally a scientist, he became a disciple of ◊Gurdjieff and expanded his ideas in terms of other dimensions of space and time, for example in *Tertium Organum* 1912.

outback the immense inland region of Australia. Its main inhabitants are Aborigines, miners (including opals), and cattlemen. Its harsh beauty has been recorded by artists such as Sidney Nolan.

output device in computing, any device for displaying, in a form intelligible to the user, the results of processing carried out by a computer. The most common output devices are the ◊VDT (visual display terminal) and the printer.

Ovamboland region of N Namibia stretching along the Namibia–Angola frontier; the scene of conflict between SWAPO guerrillas and South African forces in the 1970s and 1980s.

ovary in female animals, the organ that generates the ◊ovum. In humans, the ovaries are two whitish rounded bodies about 1 in/25 mm by 1.5 in/35 mm, located in the abdomen near the ends of the ◊Fallopian tubes. Every month, from puberty to the onset of the menopause, an ovum is released from the ovary. This is called ovulation, and forms part of the ◊menstrual cycle. In botany, an ovary is the expanded basal portion of the ◊carpel of flowering plants, containing one or more ◊ovules. It is hollow with a thick wall to protect the ovules. Following fertilization of the ovum, it develops into the fruit wall or pericarp.

The ovaries of female animals secrete the hormones responsible for the secondary sexual characteristics of the female, such as smooth, hairless facial skin and enlarged breasts. An ovary in a half-grown human fetus contains 5 million eggs, and it is possible that infertile women may grow new ovaries as a result of minute cell-transplant operations from such immature eggs.

In botany, the relative position of the ovary to the other floral parts is often a distinguishing character in classification; it may be either inferior or superior, depending on whether the petals and sepals are inserted above or below.

Ovens River river in Victoria, Australia, a tributary of the Murray.

overhead in economics, fixed costs in a business that do not vary in the short term. These might include property rental, heating and lighting, insurance, and administration costs.

Overijssel province of the E central Netherlands
area 1,289 sq mi/3,340 sq km
physical it is generally flat and contains the rivers Ijssel and Vecht
cities capital Zwolle; Enschede, Hengelo, Deventer
products livestock, dairy products, textiles
population (1988) 1,010,000
history ruled by the Bishops of Utrecht during the Middle Ages, Overijssel was sold to Charles V of Spain 1527. Joining the revolt against Spanish authority, it became one of the United Provinces of the Netherlands 1579.

Overlord, Operation the Allied invasion of Normandy June 6, 1944 (D day) during World War II.

overtone a note that has a frequency or pitch that is a multiple of the fundamental frequency, the sounding body's ◊natural frequency. Each sound source produces a unique set of overtones, which gives the source its quality or timbre.

overture a piece of instrumental music, usually preceding an opera. There are also overtures to suites and plays, ballets, and "concert" overtures, such as Elgar's *Cockaigne* and John Ireland's descriptive *London Overture*.

The use of an overture in opera began during the 17th century; the "Italian" overture consisting of two quick movements separated by a slow one, and the "French" of a quick movement between two in slower tempo.

Ovid (Publius Ovidius Naso) 43–17 BC. Roman poet. His poetry deals mainly with the themes of love (*Amores* 20 BC, *Ars amatoria* 1 BC), mythology (*Metamorphoses* AD 2), and exile (*Tristia* AD 9–12).

Born at Sulmo, Ovid studied legal career, but soon turned to literature. In 8 BC he was banished by Emperor Augustus to Tomi, on the Black Sea, where he died. This punishment, supposedly for his immoral *Ars amatoria*, was probably due to some connection with Julia, the profligate daughter of Augustus.

Oviedo industrial city (textiles, metal goods, pharmaceuticals, matches, chocolate, sugar) and capital of Asturias region, Spain, 16 mi/25 km S of the Bay of Biscay; population (1986) 191,000.

ovipary method of animal reproduction in which eggs are laid by the female and develop outside her body, in contrast to ovovivipary and vivipary. It is the most common form of reproduction.

ovovivipary method of animal reproduction in which fertilized eggs develop within the female (unlike ovipary), and the embryo gains no nutritional substances from the female (unlike vivipary). It occurs in some invertebrates, fishes, and reptiles.

ovulation in female animals, the process of making and releasing egg cells. In mammals it occurs as part of the ◊menstrual cycle.

ovule a structure found in seed plants that develops into a seed after fertilization. It consists of an ◊embryo sac containing the female gamete (◊ovum or egg cell), surrounded by nutritive tissue, the nucellus. Outside this there are one or two coverings that provide protection, developing into the testa, or seed coat, following fertilization.

In flowering plants (◊angiosperms) the ovule is within an ◊ovary, but in ◊gymnosperms (conifers and their allies) the ovules are borne on the surface of an ovuliferous (ovule-bearing) scale, usually within a ◊cone, and are not enclosed by an ovary.

ovum (plural ova) the female gamete (sex cell) before fertilization. In animals it is called an egg, and is produced in the ovaries. In plants, where it is also known as an egg cell or oosphere, the ovum is produced in an ovule. The ovum is non-motile. It must be fertilized by a male gamete before it can develop further, except in cases of ◊parthenogenesis.

***Owens** US track and field athlete Jesse Owens dominated the 1936 Summer Olympics in Berlin.*

Owen Richard 1804–1892. British anatomist and paleontologist. He attacked the theory of natural selection and in 1860 published an anonymous and damaging review of Charles ◊Darwin's work. He was Director of the Natural History Museum, London, 1856–1883 and was responsible for the first public exhibition of dinosaurs.

Owen Robert 1771–1858. British Socialist, born in Wales. In 1800 he became manager of a mill at New Lanark, Scotland, where by improving working and housing conditions and providing schools he created a model community. His ideas stimulated the ◊cooperative movement.

Owen Wilfred 1893–1918. English poet. His verse, owing much to the encouragement of Siegfried ◊Sassoon, expresses his hatred of war, for example *Anthem for Doomed Youth*, published 1921.

Owen Falls waterfall in Uganda on the White Nile, 2.5 mi/4 km below the point at which the river leaves Lake Victoria. A dam, built 1949–60, provides hydroelectricity for Uganda and Kenya and helps to control the flood waters.

Owens Jesse (James Cleveland) 1913–1980. US track and field athlete who excelled in the sprints, hurdles, and the long jump. At the 1936 Berlin Olympics he won four gold medals.

The Nazi leader Hitler is said to have stormed out of the stadium at the 1936 Berlin Olympic Games, in disgust at the black man's triumph. Owens held the world long jump record for 25 years 1935–60. At Ann Arbor, Michigan, on May 25, 1935, he broke six world records in less than an hour.

Owensboro city in NW Kentucky on the Ohio river, SW of Louisville; seat of Daviess county. Industries include bourbon, electronics, tobacco, and steel; population (1990) 53,549.

CAREER HIGHLIGHTS: Jesse Owens

Olympic Games—gold:
100 meters, 200 meters, 4 × 100 meters relay, long jump: 1936
World Records:
100 meters: 1936
100 yards: 1935, 1936
200 meters: 1935
220 yards: 1935
200 meters hurdles: 1935
220 yards hurdles: 1935
4 × 100 meters relay: 1936 (US National team)
long jump: 1935

owl any bird of the order Strigiformes, found worldwide. They are mainly nocturnal birds of prey, with mobile heads, soundless flight, acute hearing, and forward-facing immobile eyes, surrounded by "facial disks" of rayed feathers. All species lay white eggs, and begin incubation as soon as the first is laid. They regurgitate indigestible remains of their prey in pellets (castings).

They comprise two families: typical owls, family Strigidae, of which there are about 120 species; and barn owls, family Tytonidae, of which there are 10 species.

The shorteared owl *Asio flammeus*, of North America, South America, and Eurasia, is a streaked tawny color, about 15 in/38 cm long; it

owl

barn owl

hunts at dawn and dusk and roosts mainly on the ground. The great horned owl *Bubo virginianus*, of North and South America, measures 22 in/56 cm, has long ear-tufts, and lives in forests, grasslands, and deserts. The snowy owl *Nyctea scandiaca* lives in the Arctic. The largest of the owls are the eagle owl *B. bubo*, of Eurasia, and the powerful owl *Ninox strenua*, of Australia, both up to 2.25 ft/0.75 m long. The worldwide common barn owl *Tyto alba* is now diminished by pesticides and loss of habitat; in Malaysia, it is used for rat control.

"Owl and the Nightingale" early Middle English poem, written about 1200, which takes the form of an argument between an owl, who may represent wisdom and respectability, and a nightingale, who may symbolize gaiety and ◊courtly love.

ox the castrated male of domestic species of cattle, used in Third World countries for plowing and other agricultural purposes. Also the extinct wild ox or ◊aurochs of Europe, and extant wild species such as buffaloes and yaks.

oxalic acid $(COOH)_2 \cdot 2H_2O$ white, poisonous solid, soluble in water, alcohol, and ether. Oxalic acid is found in rhubarb, and its salts (oxalates) occur in wood sorrel (genus *Oxalis*, family Oxalidaceae) and other plants. It is used in the leather and textile industries, in dyeing and bleaching, ink manufacture, metal polishes, and for removing rust and ink stains.

oxbow lake curved lake found on the flood plain of a river. Oxbows are caused by the loops of ◊meanders being cut off at times of flood and the river subsequently adopting a shorter course. In the US, the term ◊bayou is often used.

Oxbridge generic term for Oxford and Cambridge, the two oldest universities in the UK.

Oxenstjerna Axel Gustafsson, Count Oxenstjerna 1583–1654. Swedish politician, chancellor from 1612. He pursued Gustavus Adolphus's foreign policy, acted as regent for Queen Christina, and conducted the Thirty Years' War to a successful conclusion.

OXFAM (Oxford Committee for Famine Relief) charity established in the UK 1942 by Canon Theodore Richard Milford (1896–1987), initially to assist the starving people of Greece and subsequently to relieve poverty and famine worldwide.

Oxford Movement also known as ***Tractarian Movement*** or ***Catholic Revival*** a movement that attempted to revive Catholic religion in the Church of England. Cardinal Newman dated the movement from ◊Keble's sermon in Oxford 1833. The Oxford Movement by the turn of the century had transformed the Anglican communion, and survives today as Anglo-Catholicism.

Oxfordshire county in S central England

area 1,007 sq mi/2,610 sq km

cities Oxford (administrative headquarters), Abingdon, Banbury, Henley-on-Thames, Witney, Woodstock

features river Thames and tributaries; Cotswolds and Chiltern Hills; Vale of the White Horse (chalk hill figure 374 ft/114 m long); Oxford University; Europe's major fusion project JET (Joint European Torus), being built at the UK Atomic Energy Authority's fusion laboratories at Culham

products cereals, automobiles, paper, bricks, cement

population (1987) 578,000.

Oxford University oldest British university, established during the 12th century, the earliest existing college being founded 1249. After suffering from land confiscation during the Reformation, it was reorganized by Elizabeth I 1571. In 1985 there were 9,000 undergraduate and 3,000 postgraduate students.

oxidation in chemistry, the loss of ◊electrons, gain of oxygen, or loss of hydrogen by an atom, ion, or molecule during a chemical reaction.

Oxidation may be brought about by reaction with another compound (oxidizing agent), which simultaneously undergoes ◊reduction, or electrically at the anode (positive terminal) of an electric cell.

oxide compound of oxygen and another element, frequently produced by burning the element or a compound of it in air or oxygen.

Oxides of metals are normally ◊bases and will react with an acid to produce a ◊salt in which the metal forms the cation (positive ion). Some of them will also react with a strong alkali to produce a salt in which the metal is part of a complex anion (negative ion; see amphoteric). Most oxides of nonmetals are acidic (dissolve in water to form an ◊acid). Some oxides display no pronounced acidic or basic properties.

Oxnard city in SW California, NW of Los Angeles. Industries include paper products, aircraft parts, and oil refining; population (1990) 142,216.

oxpecker African bird, of the genus *Buphagus*, of the starling family. It clambers about the bodies of large mammals, feeding on ticks and other parasites. It may help to warn the host of approaching dangers.

Oxus ancient name of ◊Amu Darya, river in USSR.

oxygen colorless, odorless, tasteless, nonmetallic, gaseous element, symbol O, atomic number 8, atomic weight 15.9994. It is the most abundant element in the Earth's crust (almost 50% by mass), forms about 21% by volume of the atmosphere, and is present in combined form in water, carbon dioxide, silicon dioxide (quartz), iron ore, calcium carbonate (limestone), and many other substances. Life on Earth evolved using oxygen, which is a byproduct of ◊photosynthesis and the basis for ◊respiration in plants and animals. ◊Ozone is an allotrope of oxygen.

Oxygen is very reactive and combines with all other elements except the ◊inert gases and fluorine. In nature it exists as a molecule composed of two atoms (O_2). Single atoms of oxygen are very short-lived caused by their reactivity; they can be produced by electric sparks and by the Sun's ultraviolet radiation in space, where they rapidly combine with molecular oxygen to form ozone.

Oxygen was first identified by English chemist Joseph Priestley in 1774 and independently in the same year by Swedish chemist Karl Scheele (1742–86). It was named in 1777 by French chemist Antoine Lavoisier from Greek *oxys*, "acid," and *genes*, "forming."

oxygen debt a physiological state produced by vigorous exercise, in which the lungs cannot supply all the oxygen that the muscles need.

Oxygen is required for the release of energy from food molecules (aerobic ◊respiration). Instead of breaking food molecules down fully, muscle cells switch to a form of partial breakdown that does not require oxygen (anaerobic respiration) so that they can continue to generate energy. This partial breakdown produces ◊lactic acid, which results in a sensation of fatigue when it reaches certain levels in the muscles and the blood. Once the vigorous muscle movements cease, the body breaks down the lactic acid, using up extra oxygen to do so. Panting after exercise is an automatic reaction to "pay off" the oxygen debt.

oxyhemoglobin the oxygenated form of hemoglobin, the pigment found in the red blood cells. All vertebrates, and some invertebrates, use hemoglobin for oxygen transport because the two substances can combine reversibly. In mammals oxyhemoglobin forms in the lungs and is transported to the rest of the body, where the oxygen is released. The deoxygenated blood is then

Ozal *President Turgat Ozal, who in 1989 became Turkey's first civilian head of state since 1960.*

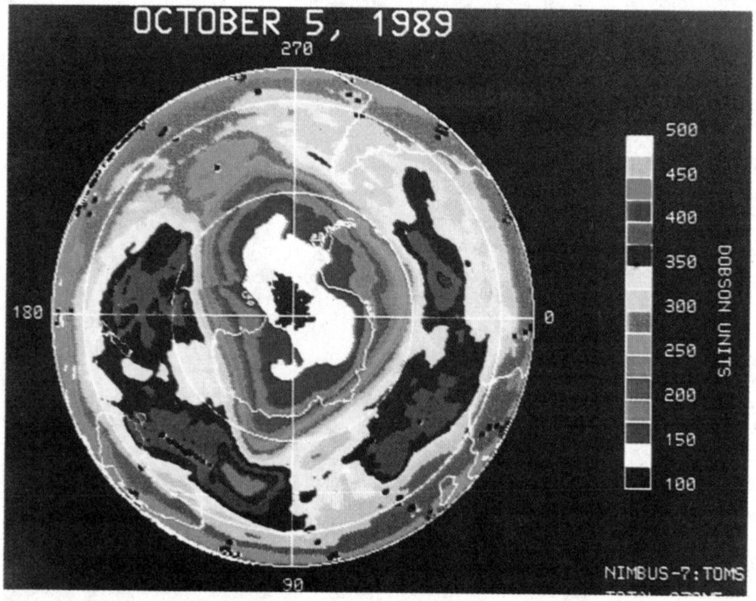
OCTOBER 5, 1989
270
180
0
90
500
450
400
350
300
250
200
150
100
DOBSON UNITS
NIMBUS-7:TOMS

ozone *Satellite map showing the "hole" in the ozone layer over Antarctica on Oct 5, 1989. The colors represent Dobson units, a measure of atmospheric ozone, as shown on the color scale at the right.*

returned to the lungs. Hemoglobin will combine also with carbon monoxide, to form carboxyhemoglobin, but in this case the reaction is irreversible. Asphyxiation can result when oxyhemoglobin cannot form in sufficient quantities.

oxymoron (Greek "sharply dull" or "pointedly foolish") a figure of speech, the combination of two or more words that are normally opposites, in order to startle. *Bittersweet* is an oxymoron, as are *cruel to be kind* and *beloved enemy*.

oxytocin hormone that stimulates the uterus in late pregnancy to initiate and sustain labor. After birth, it stimulates the uterine muscles to contract, reducing bleeding at the site where the placenta was attached.

Intravenous injections of oxytocin may be given to induce labor, improve contractions, or control hemorrhage after birth. It is also secreted during lactation. Oxytocin sprayed in the nose a few minutes before nursing improves milk production. It is secreted by the pituitary gland.

oyster bivalve ◊mollusk constituting the Ostreidae, or true oyster, family, having the upper valve flat, the lower concave, hinged by an elastic ligament. The mantle, lying against the shell, protects the inner body, which includes respiratory, digestive, and reproductive organs. Oysters commonly change their sex annually or more frequently; females may discharge up to a million eggs during a spawning period.

Among the species commercially exploited for food are the North American eastern oyster *Crassostrea virginica* of the Atlantic coast and the European oyster *Ostrea edulis*. The former is oviparous (eggs are discharged straight into the water) and the latter is larviparous (eggs and larvae remain in the mantle cavity for a period before release). Oyster farming is increasingly practiced, the beds being specially cleansed for the easy setting of the free-swimming larvae (known as "spats"), and the oysters later properly spaced for growth and fattened.

Valuable ◊pearls are not obtained from members of the true oyster family; they occur in pearl oysters (family Pteriidae). There are also tree oysters (family Isognomonidae) and thorny oysters (family Spondylidae).

oyster catcher chunky shorebird of the family Haematopodidae, with a laterally flattened, heavy bill that can pry open mollusk shells.

The black and white American oystercatcher *Haematopus palliatus* is found on the Atlantic and S Pacific coasts.

oz abbreviation for ounce.

Ozal Turgut 1927– . Turkish Islamic right-wing politician, prime minister 1983–89, president from 1989.

Ozal first entered government service, then worked for the World Bank 1971–79. In 1980 he was deputy to Prime Minister Bulent Ulusu under the military regime of Kenan Evren, and, when political pluralism returned in 1983, he founded the Islamic, right-of-center Motherland Party (ANAP) and led it to victory in the elections of that year. In the 1987 general election he retained his majority and in Nov 1989 replaced Evren as Turkey's first civilian president in 30 years.

Ozalid process trademarked copying process used to produce positive prints from drawn or printed materials or film, such as printing proofs from film images. The film is placed on top of chemically treated paper and then exposed to ultraviolet light. The image is developed dry using ammonia vapor.

Ozark Mountains area in US (shared by Arkansas, Kansas, Mississippi, and Oklahoma) of ridges, valleys, and streams; highest point 2,300 ft/700 m; area 50,000 sq mi/130,000 sq km. This heavily forested region between the Missouri and Arkansas rivers has agriculture and lead and zinc mines.

ozone O_3 highly reactive pale-blue gas with a penetrating odor. Ozone is an allotrope of oxygen (see ◊allotropy), made up of three atoms of oxygen. It is formed when the molecule of the stable form of oxygen (O_2) is split by ultraviolet radiation or electrical discharge. It forms a layer in the upper atmosphere, which protects life on Earth from ultraviolet rays, a cause of skin cancer. At lower atmospheric levels it contributes to the ◊greenhouse effect.

At ground level, ozone can cause asthma attacks, stunted growth in plants, and corrosion of certain materials. It is produced by the action of sunlight on auto exhaust fumes, and is a major air pollutant in hot summers. Ozone is a powerful oxidizing agent; it is used industrially in bleaching and air-conditioning.

Ozu Yasujiro 1903–1963. Japanese film director who became known in the West only in his last years. *Tokyo Monogatari/Tokyo Story* 1953 illustrates his typical low camera angles, and his theme of middle-class family life.

p in music, abbreviation for piano.

p(p). abbreviation for page(s).

PA abbreviation for ◊Pennsylvania.

Paarl a town on the Great Berg River, Cape Province, South Africa; population (1980) 71,300. It is the center of a noted wine-producing area, 31 mi/50 km NE of Cape Town. Nelson Mandela served the last days of his imprisonment at the Victor Vester prison near here.

Pabst G(eorg) W(ilhelm) 1885–1967. German film director whose films include *Die Büchse der Pandora/Pandora's Box* 1928, *Das Tagebuch einer Verlorenen/The Diary of a Lost Girl* 1929, both starring Louise ◊Brooks, and *Die Dreigroschenoper/The Threepenny Opera* 1931.

paca large, tailless, nocturnal, burrowing ◊rodent of the genus *Cuniculus*, in the family Dasyproctidae, which also includes the agoutis. The paca, about 2 ft/60 cm long, is native to Central and South America.

Pacaraima, Sierra mountain range along the Brazil–Venezuela frontier, extending into Guyana; length 385 mi/620 km; highest point Mount Roraima, a plateau about 20 sq mi/50 sq km, 8,625 ft/2,629 m above sea level, surrounded by 1,000-ft/300-m cliffs, at the conjunction of the three countries. Formed 300 million years ago, it has unique fauna and flora, because of its isolation, consisting only of grasses, bushes, flowers, insects, and small amphibians.

pacemaker medical device implanted in a patient whose heart beats irregularly. It delivers minute electric shocks to stimulate the heart muscles at regular intervals and restores normal heartbeat. The latest ones are powered by radioactive isotopes for long life and weigh no more than 0.5 oz/15 grams. They are implanted under the skin.

Pachomius, St 292–346. Egyptian Christian, the founder of the first Christian monastery, near Dendera on the river Nile.

Pacific Islands United Nations trust territory in the W Pacific comprising over 2,000 islands and atolls, under Japanese mandate 1919–47, and administered by the US 1947–80, when all its members, the ◊Carolines, ◊Marianas (except ◊Guam), and ◊Marshall Islands, became independent.

Pacific Ocean world's largest ocean, extending from Antarctica to the Bering Strait; area 64,170,000 sq mi/166,242,500 sq km; average depth 13,749 ft/4,188 m; greatest depth of any ocean 36,210 ft/11,034 m in the ◊Mariana Trench.

Pacific Security Treaty military alliance agreement between Australia, New Zealand, and the US, signed 1951 (see ◊ANZUS). Military cooperation between the US and New Zealand has been restricted by the latter's policy of banning ships that might be carrying nuclear weapons or nuclear power sources.

Pacific War war 1879–83 fought by an alliance of Bolivia and Peru against Chile. Chile seized Antofagasta and the coast between the mouths of the rivers Loa and Raposo, rendering Bolivia landlocked, and also annexed the southern Peruvian coastline from Arica to the mouth of the Loa, including the nitrate fields of the Atacama Desert.

Bolivia has since tried to regain Pacific access, either by a corridor across its former Antofagasta province or by a twin port with Arica at the end of the rail link from La Paz. Brazil supports the Bolivian claims, which would facilitate its own transcontinental traffic.

pacifism belief that violence, even in self-defense, is unjustifiable under any condition and that arbitration is preferable to war as a means of solving disputes.

Pacino Al(berto) 1940– . US film actor who played powerful, introverted but violent roles in films such as *The Godfather* 1972, *Serpico* 1973, and *Scarface* 1983. *Dick Tracy* 1990 added comedy to his range of acting styles, and *The Godfather Part III* 1991 added subdued style to his virtuoso performances.

pact of steel the military alliance between Nazi Germany and Fascist Italy, instituted 1939.

Padang port on the W coast of Sumatra, Indonesia; population (1980) 481,000. The Dutch secured trading rights here 1663. The port trades in copra, coffee, and rubber.

Paderborn market town in North Rhine–Westphalia, Federal Republic of Germany; population (1988) 110,000. Industries include leather goods, metal products, and precision instruments. It was the seat of a bishopric in Charlemagne's time and later became a member of the Hanseatic League.

Paderewski Ignacy Jan 1860–1941. Polish pianist, composer, and politician. After his debut in Vienna 1887 he became celebrated in Europe and the US as an exponent of Chopin. During World War I he helped organize the Polish army in France; in 1919 he became prime minister of the newly independent Poland, which he represented at the Peace Conference, but continuing opposition forced him to resign the same year. He resumed a musical career 1922, was president of the Polish National Council in Paris 1940, and died in New York.

Padua (Italian *Padova*) city in N Italy, 28 mi/45 km W of Venice; population (1988) 224,000.

The astronomer Galileo taught at the university, founded 1222.

The 13th-century Palazzo della Ragione, the basilica of S Antonio, and the botanical garden 1545 are notable. It is the birthplace of the historian Livy and the painter Andrea Mantegna.

Paestum ancient Greek city, near Salerno in S Italy. Founded about 600 BC as the Greek colony Posidonia, a number of Doric temples remain.

Pagalu former name (1973–79) of ◊Annobón, an island in Equatorial Guinea.

Pagan archeological site in Myanmar with the ruins of the former capital (founded 847, taken by Kublai Khan 1287). These include Buddhist pagodas, shrines, and temples with wall paintings of the great period of Burmese art (11th–13th centuries).

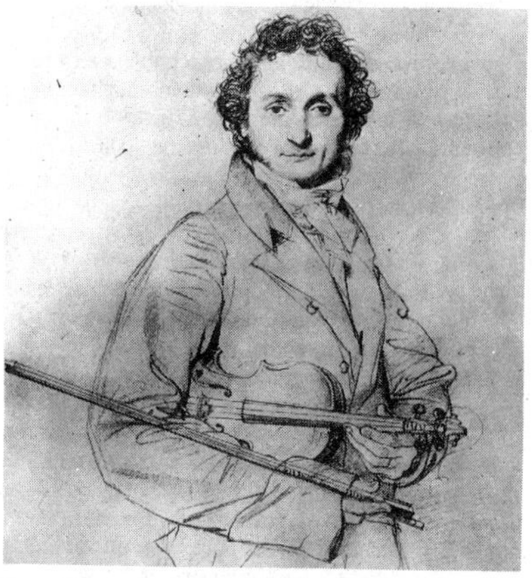

Paganini *A drawing by Ingres of the Italian violinist and composer Paganini.*

Paganini Niccolò 1782–1840. Italian violinist and composer, a virtuoso soloist from the age of nine. He invented all the virtuoso techniques that have since been included in violin composition. His works for the violin ingeniously exploit the full potential of the instrument.

Page Earle (Christmas Grafton) 1880–1961. Australian politician, leader of the Country Party 1920–39 and briefly prime minister in April 1939. He represented Australia in the British war cabinet 1941–42 and was minister of health 1949–55.

Page Frederick Handley 1885–1962. British aircraft engineer, founder of one of the earliest aircraft-manufacturing companies 1909 and designer of long-range civil airplanes and multiengined bombers in both world wars; for example, the Halifax, flown in World War II.

pageant originally the wagon on which medieval ◊mystery plays were performed. The term was later applied to the street procession of songs, dances, and historical tableaux that became fashionable during the 1920s.

paging in computing, a way of increasing a computer's apparent memory capacity. See ◊virtual memory.

Pagnol Marcel 1895–1974. French film director, author, and playwright whose work includes *Fanny* 1932 and *Manon des sources* 1953. He regarded the cinema as recorded theater; thus his films, although strong on character and background, fail to exploit the medium fully as an independent art form.

Pago Pago chief port of American Samoa on the island of Tutuila; population (1980) 3,060. Formerly a naval coaling station, it was acquired by the US under a commercial treaty with the local king 1872.

Pahang state of E Peninsular Malaysia; capital Kuantan; area 13,896 sq mi/36,000 sq km; population (1980) 799,000. It is mountainous and forested and produces rubber, tin, gold, and timber. There is a port at Tanjung Gelang. Pahang is ruled by a sultan.

Pahlavi dynasty Iranian dynasty founded by Riza Khan (1877–1944), an army officer who seized control of the government 1921 and was proclaimed shah 1925. During World War II, Britain and the USSR were nervous of his German sympathies and occupied Iran 1941–46. They compelled him to abdicate 1941 in favor of his son Mohammed Riza Shah Pahlavi, who took office in 1956, with US support, and who was deposed in the Islamic revolution 1979.

Pahsien another name for ◊Chongqing, port in SW China.

Paine English political writer Thomas Paine. Portrait after George Romney (c. 1880), National Portrait Gallery, London.

Paige Satchel (Leroy Robert) 1906–1982. US baseball player. Born in Mobile, Alabama, Paige began playing professional baseball in the Negro leagues in the 1920s and traveled extensively throughout the US and Latin America. As a pitcher, Paige established a near-legendary record, leading the Kansas City Monarchs of the Negro National League to the championship 1942. In 1948, with the end of racial segregation in the major leagues, Paige joined the Cleveland Indians. He later played with the St Louis Browns 1951–53 and was elected to the Baseball Hall of Fame 1971.

pain the sense that gives an awareness of harmful effects on or in the body. It may be triggered by stimuli such as trauma, inflammation, and heat. Pain is transmitted by specialized nerves and also has psychological component controlled by higher centers in the brain. Painkillers are also known as analgesics.

A pain message to the brain travels along the sensory nerves as electrical impulses. When these reach the gap between one nerve and another, biochemistry governs whether this gap is bridged and may also either increase or decrease the attention the message receives or modify its intensity in either direction. The main type of pain transmitter is known simply as "substance P," a neuropeptide concentrated in a certain area of the spinal cord. Substance P has been found in fish, and there is also evidence that the same substances that cause pain in humans, for example, bee venom, cause a similar reaction in insects and arachnids (for instance, spiders).

Since the sensation of pain is transmitted by separate nerves from that of fine touch, it is possible in diseases such as syringomyelia to have no sense of pain in a limb, yet maintain a normal sense of touch. Such a desensitized limb is at great risk of infection via unnoticed cuts and abrasions.

Paine Thomas 1737–1809. English left-wing political writer, active in the American and French revolutions. His pamphlet *Common Sense* 1776 ignited passions in the American Revolution; others include *The Rights of Man* 1791 and *The Age of Reason* 1793. He advocated republicanism, deism, the abolition of slavery, and the emancipation of women.

Paine, born in Thetford, Norfolk, was a friend of Benjamin Franklin and went to America 1774, where he published several republican pamphlets and fought for the colonists in the revolution. In 1787 he returned to Britain. *The Rights of Man* is an answer to the conservative theorist Burke's *Reflections on the Revolution in France*. In 1792, Paine was indicted for treason and escaped to France, to represent Calais in the National Convention. Narrowly escaping the guillotine, he regained his seat after the fall of Robespierre. Paine returned to the US 1802 and died in New York.

painkillers include ◊analgesics such as ◊aspirin and aspirin substitutes, ◊morphine, ◊codeine, paracetamol, and synthetic versions of the natural pain inhibitors, the encephalins and endorphins, which avoid the side effects of the others.

Topical nerve irritants are also used in salves, such as camphor and eucalyptus; they cause the nerve endings to react to them, bringing increased blood flow to the areas and alleviating localized and joint pain.

paint any of various materials used to give a protective and decorative finish to surfaces or for making pictures. A paint consists of a pigment suspended in a vehicle, or binder, usually with added solvents. It is the vehicle that dries and hardens to form an adhesive film of paint. Among the most common kinds are cellulose paints (or lacquers), oil-based paints, emulsion paints, and special types such as enamels and primers.

Lacquers consist of a synthetic resin (such as an acrylic resin or cellulose acetate) dissolved in a volatile organic solvent, which evaporates rapidly to give a very quick-drying paint. A typical oil-based paint has a vehicle of a natural drying oil (such as linseed oil), containing a prime pigment of iron, lead, titanium, or zinc oxide, to which colored pigments may be added. The finish—gloss, semimatte, or matte—depends on the amount of inert pigment (such as clay or silicates). Oil-based paints can be thinned, and brushes cleaned, in a solvent such as turpentine or white spirit (a petroleum product). Emulsion paints, sometimes called latex paints, consist of pigments dispersed in a water-based emulsion of a polymer (such as polyvinyl chloride [PVC] or acrylic resin). They can be thinned with water, which can also be used to wash the paint out of brushes and rollers. Enamels have little pigment, and they dry to an extremely hard, high-gloss film. Primers for the first coat on wood or metal, on the other hand, have a high pigment content (as do undercoat paints). Aluminum or bronze powder may be used for priming or finishing objects made of metal.

painting the application of color, pigment, or paint to a surface. The chief methods of painting are:
tempera emulsion painting, with a gelatinous (for example, egg yolk) rather than oil base; known in ancient Egypt
fresco watercolor painting on plaster walls; the palace of Knossos, Crete, contains examples from about 2,000 BC
ink developed in China from calligraphy in the Sung period and became highly popular in Japan from the 15th century
oil ground pigments in linseed, walnut, or other oil; spread from N to S Europe in the 15th century
watercolor pigments combined with gum arabic and glycerine, which are diluted with water; the method was developed in the 15th–17th centuries from wash drawings
acrylic synthetic pigments developed after World War II; the colors are very hard and brilliant.

For the history of painting see ◊ancient art; ◊medieval art; ◊Chinese art; and so on. Individual painters and art movements are listed alphabetically.

Pakistan country in S Asia, stretching from the Himalayas to the Arabian Sea, bounded W by Iran, NW by Afghanistan, NE by China, and E by India.
government The 1973 constitution, suspended 1977, has been restored in part and amended 1985 to make the president the dominant political figure. Primary power resides with the central government, headed by an executive president who is elected for five-year terms by a joint sitting of the federal legislature. Day-to-day administration is performed by a prime minister (drawn from the National Assembly) and cabinet appointed by the president. After the death of General Zia in 1988 and the election of Benazir Bhutto, power shifted from the president to the prime minister in what has become a dual administration.

Pakistan is a federal republic comprising four

Pakistan
Islamic Republic of

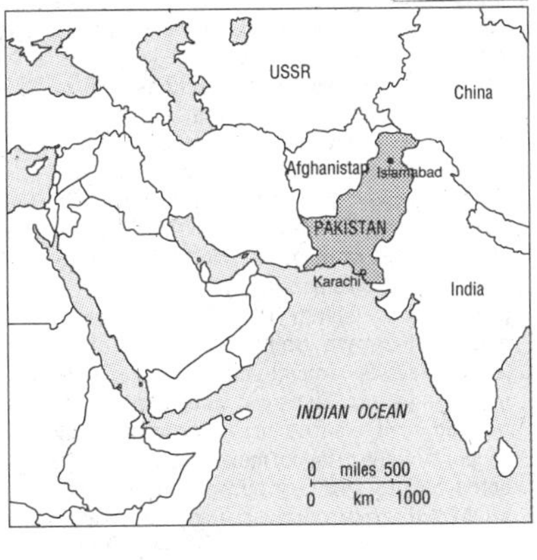

USSR
China
Afghanistan
Islamabad
PAKISTAN
Karachi
India
INDIAN OCEAN
0 miles 500
0 km 1000

area 307,295 sq mi/796,100 sq km; one-third of Kashmir under Pakistani control
capital Islamabad
cities Karachi, Lahore, Rawalpindi, Peshawar
physical fertile Indus plain in E; Baluchistan plateau in W, mountains in N and NW
features the "five rivers" (Indus, Jhelum, Chenab, Ravi, and Sutlej) feed the world's largest irrigation system; Tarbela (world's largest earthfill dam); K2 mountain; Khyber Pass; sites of the Indus Valley civilization
head of state Ghulam Ishaq Khan from 1988
head of government Nawaz Sharif from 1990
political system emergent democracy
political parties Pakistan People's Party (PPP), moderate, Islamic, Socialist; Islamic Democratic Alliance (IJI), including the Pakistan Muslim League (PML), Islamic conservative; Mohajir National Movement (MQM), Sind-based *mohajir* settlers
exports cotton textiles, rice, leather, carpets
currency Pakistan rupee
population (1990 est) 113,163,000 (66% Punjabi, 13% Sindhi); growth rate 3.1% p.a.
life expectancy men 54, women 55 (1989)
language Urdu and English (official); Punjabi, Sindhi, Pashto, Baluchi, and other local dialects
religion Sunni Muslim 75%, Shiite Muslim 20%, Hindu 4%
literacy men 40%/women 19% (1985 est)
GDP $39 bn (1988); $360 per head (1984)
chronology
1947 Independence achieved from Britain, Pakistan formed following partition of India.
1956 Proclaimed a republic.
1958 Military rule imposed by Gen Ayub Khan.
1969 Power transferred to Gen Yahya Khan.
1971 Secession of East Pakistan (Bangladesh). After civil war, power transferred to Zulfiqar Ali Bhutto.
1977 Bhutto overthrown in military coup by Gen Zia ul-haq; martial law imposed.
1979 Bhutto executed.
1981 Opposition Movement for Restoration of Democracy formed. Islamization process pushed forward.
1985 Nonparty elections held, amended constitution adopted, martial law and ban on political parties lifted.
1986 Agitation for free elections launched by Benazir Bhutto.
1988 Zia introduced Islamic legal code, the *Shariah*. He was killed in a military plane crash in Aug; Benazir Bhutto elected prime minister in Nov.
1989 Pakistan rejoined the Commonwealth.
1990 Army mobilized in support of Muslim separatists in Indian Kashmir. Bhutto dismissed.

provinces: Sind, Punjab, North-West Frontier Province, and Baluchistan, administered by appointed governors and local governments drawn from elected provincial assemblies; ◊Tribal Areas, that are administered by the central government; and the Federal Capital Territory of Islamabad. The federal legislature *Majlis i-Shura* comprises two chambers, a lower house (National Assembly) composed of 207 members directly elected for five-year terms by universal suffrage as well as 20 women and 10 minority group appointees, and an upper chamber (Senate) composed of 87 members elected, a third at a time, for six-year terms by provincial assemblies and tribal areas following a quota system. The National Assembly has sole jurisdiction over financial affairs.

history For history before 1947, see ◊Indus Valley Civilization and ◊India. The name "Pakistan" for a Muslim division of British India was put forward 1930 by Choudhary Rahmat Ali (1897–1951) from names of the Muslim parts of the subcontinent: *P*unjab, the *A*fghan NW Frontier, *K*ashmir, *S*ind, and Baluchi*stan*. *Pak* means "pure" in Urdu and *stan* means "land." Fear of domination by the Hindu majority in India led in 1940 to a serious demand for a separate Muslim state, which delayed for some years India's independence. In 1947 British India was divided into two dominions, India and Pakistan.

Ater the death of its leader ◊Jinnah 1948, Pakistan remained a dominion with the British monarch as head of state until being declared a republic March 1956. Its new constitution was abrogated Oct 1958, and military rule was imposed through a coup by General Mohammed Ayub Khan. The country experienced rapid economic growth during the 1960s, but regional tension mounted between demographically dominant East Pakistan and West Pakistan, where political and military power was concentrated.

After serious strikes and riots March 1969, General Ayub Khan stepped down and was replaced by the commander-in-chief, General Agha Mohammed Yahya Khan. Pakistan's first elections with universal suffrage were held Dec 1970 to elect an assembly to frame a new constitution. Sheik Mujib ur-Rahman's Awami League, which proposed autonomy, gained a majority of seats in East Pakistan, and the Pakistan People's Party (or PPP) in West Pakistan. East Pakistan declared its independence from the West March 1971, precipitating a civil war. India intervened on East Pakistan's side Dec 1971, and the independent republic of ◊Bangladesh emerged.

General Yahya Khan resigned, passing power in (W) Pakistan to the People's Party leader Zulfiqar Ali ◊Bhutto, who introduced a new federal parliamentary constitution (April 1973) and a Socialist economic program of land reform and nationalization. From the mid-1970s the Sind-based Bhutto faced deteriorating economic conditions and growing regional opposition, particularly from Baluchistan and from ◊Pathans campaigning for an independent Pakhtoonistan. Bhutto won a majority in the March 1977 Assembly elections but was accused of ballot rigging by the Pakistan National Alliance opposition. Riots ensued, and after four months of unrest, the Punjabi Muslim army Chief of Staff, General ◊Zia ul-Haq, seized power in a bloodless coup July 1977. Martial law was imposed; Bhutto was imprisoned for alleged murder and hanged April 1979.

After the Dec 1979 Soviet invasion of ◊Afghanistan, more than 2 million refugees poured into Pakistan, which became the recipient of massive US military and economic aid. The economy also relied on remittances from workers in the Middle East. Between 1979 and 1981 General Zia imposed severe restrictions on political activity. He introduced a broad Islamization program aimed at deepening his support base and appeasing Islamic fundamentalists. This was opposed by middle-class professionals and by the Shi'ite minority. In March 1981, nine banned opposition parties, including the People's Party of Pakistan, formed the Movement for the Restoration of Democracy alliance to campaign for a return to parliamentary government. The military government responded by arresting several hundred opposition politicians. A renewed democracy campaign 1983 resulted in considerable antigovernment violence in Sind province. From 1982, however, General Zia slowly began enlarging the civilian element in his government and in Dec 1984, he held a successful referendum on the Islamization process, which was taken to legitimize his continuing as president for a further five-year term. In Feb 1985, direct elections were held to the National and Provincial assemblies, but on a nonparty basis. The opposition boycotted the poll, as they had done in Dec, resulting in a turnout of only 53%. A new civilian cabinet was nevertheless formed and an amended constitution adopted.

In Dec 1985, martial law and the ban on political parties were lifted, military courts were abolished, and military administrators stepped down in favor of civilians. A government was formed by the Pagaro faction of the Pakistan Muslim League led by Mohammad Khan Junejo, which supported, and was subservient to General Zia. Benazir ◊Bhutto (1953–), the daughter of Zulfiqar Ali Bhutto and leader of the PPP, returned from self-exile in London April 1986 to launch a popular campaign for immediate open elections. Riots erupted in Lahore, Karachi, and rural Sind, where troops were sent in, and PPP leaders were arrested.

In May 1988, concerned with the deteriorating state of the economy and anxious to accelerate the Islamization process, president Zia dismissed the Junejo government and dissolved the National Assembly and provincial legislatures, promising fresh elections within 90 days. Ruling by ordinance, Zia decreed, in July 1988, that the Sharia, the Islamic legal code, would immediately become the country's supreme law. A month later, the president was killed, along with senior army officers, in a military airplane crash near Bahawalpur. Sabotage was suspected. Ghulam Ishaq Khan, the senate's elderly chair, succeeded as president, but in the free multiparty elections held in Nov 1988 the PPP, which had moved toward the center in its policy stance, emerged as the largest single party, with 45% of the National Assembly's elective seats. After forging a coalition with the Mohajir National Movement (MQM), Benazir Bhutto was sworn in as prime minister in Dec 1988, and Ghulam Ishaq Khan was elected as president. In March 1989 Nusrat Bhutto, the mother of Benazir Bhutto and widow of Zulfikar Ali Bhutto, was brought into the cabinet as deputy prime minsiter. The new Bhutto administration pledged itself to a free market economic program, support of the Afghan mujaheddin, and to leave untouched the military budget. In Oct 1989 the MQM withdrew from the ruling coalition and allied itself with the opposition Islamic Democratic Alliance. The Bhutto government narrowly survived a vote of no confidence a month later.

In foreign affairs, Pakistan's relations with India have been strained since independence, with border wars over Kashmir 1965 and East Pakistan 1971. It left the Commonwealth 1972, when the new state of Bangladesh was accepted, but rejoined in 1989. As a result of shared hostility to India, Pakistan has been allied with China since the 1950s; during the 1970s it developed close relations with the US, providing support for the US-backed Afghan rebels, while at the same time joining the ◊nonaligned movement (1979) and drawing closer to the Islamic states of the Middle East and Africa.

Benazir Bhutto's government was dismissed from office by president Ghulam Ishaq Khan in Aug 1990 having been accused of incompetence, corruption, and abuse of power. The National Assemblies were also dissolved. On Oct 24, 1990 the opposition was swept to victory and Nawaz Sharif, Bhutto's former chief minister of Punjab province, was sworn in as prime minister. Sharif had headed the Islamic Democratic Alliance (IDA), which incorporated Jatoi's National Party and the Muslim League (led by former premier Mohammed Khan Junejo). The IDA captured 105 of the 207 parliamentary seats contested to the 45 of Bhutto's PPP. It also secured control of three of the four provincial assemblies: Bhutto's Sind stronghold being the exception. Sharif promised to pursue a free market economic program and was supported by the military, state bureaucracy, and mullahs.

Pakula Alan J 1928– . US film director, formerly a producer, whose best films are among the finest of the 1970s and include *Klute* 1971 and *All the President's Men* 1976. His later work includes *Sophie's Choice* 1982 and *Presumed Innocent* 1990.

Palamas Kostes 1859–1943. Greek poet. He enriched the Greek vernacular by his use of it as a literary language, particularly in his poetry, such as in *Songs of My Fatherland* 1886 and *The Flute of the King* 1910, which expresses his vivid awareness of Greek history.

Palance Jack. Adopted name of Walter Jack Palahnuik 1920– . US film actor, often cast as a villain. His films include *Shane* 1953, *Contempt* 1963, and *Batman* 1989.

palate in mammals, the ceiling of the mouth. The bony front part is the hard palate, the muscular rear part the soft palate. Incomplete fusion of the two lateral halves of the palate causes interference with speech.

Technically, the mammalian palate is a secondary structure and parallel to the original mouth roof of fishes, amphibians, reptiles, and birds.

Palatinate (called the ***Pfalz*** in Germany) a historic division of Germany, dating from before the 8th century. It was ruled by a count palatine (a count with royal prerogatives) and varied in size.

When it was attached to Bavaria 1815 it consisted of two separate parts: Rhenish (or Lower) Palatinate on the Rhine (capital Heidelberg), and Upper Palatinate (capital Amberg on the Vils) 130 mi/210 km to the E. In 1946 Rhenish Palatinate became an administrative division of the *Land* (German region) of Rhineland-Palatinate with its capital at Neustadt; Upper Palatinate remained an administrative division of Bavaria with its capital at Regensburg.

Palau former name (until 1981) of the Republic of ◊Belau.

Paldiski small, ice-free port in Estonia; a Soviet naval base 25 mi/40 km W of Tallinn at the entrance to the Gulf of Finland.

Palembang oil-refining city in Indonesia, capital of S Sumatra province; population (1980) 786,000. Palembang was the capital of a sultanate when the Dutch established a trading station there 1616.

Paleocene first epoch of the Tertiary period of geologic time, 65–55 million years ago. Many types of mammals spread rapidly after the disappearance of the great reptiles of the Mesozoic. The name means "the ancient part of the early recent."

Paleolithic earliest stage of human technology and development of the Stone Age; see ◊prehistory.

paleomagnetism the science of the reconstruction of the Earth's ancient magnetic field and the former positions of the continents, from the evidence of what is called remanent magnetization in ancient rocks. Remanent magnetization is the record of magnetization acquired by igneous rocks as they cool past the point where they can be influenced by any later magnetization through the presence of the Earth's magnetic field. This permanent record of the direction of the Earth's magnetic field at the time of formation permits geologists to reconstruct the intervals at which the Earth's magnetic field has changed direction, or become reversed. Paleomagnetism shows that such events occur with some regularity—the magnetic N pole becoming the magnetic S pole, and vice versa at approximate half-million-year intervals, with shorter reversal periods in between the major spans. Starting in the 1960s, this known pattern of magnetic reversals was used to demonstrate seafloor spreading or the formation of new ocean crust on either side of midoceanic ridges. As new material hardened on either side of a ridge, it would retain the imprint of the magnetic field, furnishing datable proof that material was spreading steadily outward. Paleomagnetism is also used to demonstrate continental drift, of the movement of continents on tectonic plates, through time, by determining the direction of the magnetic field of dated rocks from different continents.

paleontology in geology, the study of ancient life that encompasses the structure of ancient organisms and their environment, evolution, and ecology, as revealed by their ◊fossils.

The practical aspects of paleontology are based on using the presence of different fossils to date particular rock strata and to identify rocks that were laid down under particular conditions, for instance giving rise to the formation of oil. The term paleontology was first used in 1834, during the period when the first ◊dinosaur remains were discovered.

Paleozoic era of geologic time 590–248 million years ago. It comprises the Cambrian, Ordovician, Silurian, Devonian, Carboniferous, and Permian periods. The Cambrian, Ordovician, and Silurian constitute the Lower Paleozoic; the Devonian, Carboniferous, and Permian make up the Upper Paleozoic. The era includes the evolution of multicellular life forms in the sea; the invasion of land by plants and animals; and the evolution of fish, amphibians, and early reptiles. The continents were very different from the present ones but, toward the end of the era, all were joined together as a single world continent called ◊Pangaea.

Palermo capital and seaport of Sicily; population (1988) 729,000. Industries include shipbuilding, steel, glass, and chemicals. It was founded by the Phoenicians in the 8th century BC.

Palestine (Arabic *Falastin* "Philistines") (also called the Holy Land because of its links with Judaism, Christianity, and Islam) the area between the Mediterranean and the river Jordan, with Lebanon to the north and Sinai to the south. It was in ancient times dominated in turn by Egypt, Assyria, Babylonia, Persia, Macedonia, the Ptolemies, the Seleucids, and the Roman and Byzantine empires. Today it forms part of Israel. The Palestinian people (about 500,000 in the West Bank, E Jerusalem, and the Gaza Strip; 1.2 million in Jordan; 1.2 million in Israel; 300,000 in Lebanon; and 100,000 in the US) are descendants of the people of ◊Canaan.

history

AD 636 Conquest by the Muslim Arabs, which made it a target for the ◊Crusades (see also ◊Jerusalem)

1516 Conquest by the Ottoman Turks

1880–1914 As a result of pogroms in Russia and Poland, Jewish immigration increased

1897 At the first Zionist Congress, Jews called for a permanent homeland in Palestine

1909 Tel Aviv, the first all-Jewish town in Palestine, was built

1917–18 Turks driven out by General ◊Allenby in World War I

1922 Britain received Palestine as a League of Nations mandate (incorporating the ◊Balfour Declaration) to administer both historic Palestine and lands across the river Jordan that were recognized 1923 as the Hashimite Kingdom of Jordan

1929 and ***1936–38*** Arab revolts fueled by Jewish immigration (300,000 during 1920–39)

1937 Pan-Arab Congress

1939 British plan for Palestine

1939–45 Both Arab and Jewish Palestinians served in the Allied forces in World War II

1947 Following Jewish guerrilla activities, prompted by restriction of Jewish immigration, Britain put the question before the United Nations, which voted for partition

1948 May 15 (eight hours before Britain's renunciation of the mandate was due) a Jewish state of ◊Israel was proclaimed. A series of ◊Arab-Israeli Wars resulted in the total loss of the Palestinian state, and the displacement of large numbers of Palestinian Arabs

1964 The ◊Palestine Liberation Organization (PLO) was formed and a guerrilla war was waged against the Jewish state

1974 The Palestine Liberation Organization became the first nongovernmental delegation to be admitted to a plenary session of the United Nations General Assembly

1987 Palestinian uprising (◊Intifada) begins in occupied territories

1988 PLO leader Yasir ◊Arafat renounces terrorism; US agrees to meetings

1989 Israeli prime minister Yitzhak Shamir proposed Palestinian elections in the West Bank/Gaza Strip

1991 Gulf War against Iraq's annexation of Kuwait caused United Nations and diplomatic reconsideration of a Palestinian state in an effort to stabilize the Middle East. Peace conference in Spain in Nov includes Israel and Arab states.

Palestine Liberation Organization (PLO) Arab organization founded 1964 to bring about an independent state of Palestine. It consists of several distinct groupings, the chief of which is al-◊Fatah, led by Yasser ◊Arafat, the president of the PLO since 1969. To achieve its ends it has pursued diplomatic initiatives but also operates as a guerrilla army. In 1988, the Palestine National Council voted to create a state of Palestine, but at the same time it endorsed United Nations resolution 242, recognizing Israel's right to exist.

Beirut, Lebanon became PLO headquarters 1970–71 after its defeat in the Jordanian civil war. In 1974 the PLO became the first nongovernmental delegation to be admitted to a session of the United Nations General Assembly. Israel invaded Lebanon 1982 so that the PLO would abandon its headquarters there; it moved on to Tunis, Tunisia, and in 1986 to Baghdad, Iraq. PLO members who remained in Lebanon after the expulsion were later drawn into the internal conflict (see ◊Arab-Israeli Wars). In 1986 Jordan suspended "political coordination" with the PLO and expelled Arafat's deputy, dealing instead directly with Palestinians in Israeli-occupied territories.

Discussions with the US government began for the first time when Arafat renounced terrorism as a policy.

Palestine wars another name for the ◊Arab-Israeli wars.

Palestrina Giovanni Pierluigi da 1525–1594. Italian composer of secular and sacred choral music. Apart from motets and madrigals, he also wrote 105 masses, including *Missa Papae Marcelli*.

Paley Grace 1922– . US short-story writer and critic. Her stories express Jewish and feminist experience with bitter humor, as in *The Little Disturbances of Man* 1960 and *Later the Same Day* 1985.

Pali ancient Indo-European language of N India, related to Sanskrit, and a Classical language of Buddhism.

palisade cell cylindrical cell lying immediately beneath the upper epidermis of a leaf. Palisade cells normally exist as one closely packed row and contain many chloroplasts. During the hours of daylight palisade cells are photosynthetic, using the energy of the sun to create carbohydrates from water and carbon dioxide.

Palk Strait a channel separating SE India from the island of Sri Lanka; 33 mi/53 km at its widest point.

Palladio Andrea 1518–1580. Italian Renaissance architect noted for his harmonious and balanced Classical structures. He designed numerous country houses in and around Vicenza, Italy, making use of Roman Classical forms, symmetry, and proportion. He also designed churches in Venice and published his studies of Classical form in several illustrated books. His ideas were revived in England in the early 17th century by Inigo Jones and in the 18th century by Lord Burlington and later by architects in Italy, Holland, Germany, Russia, and the US, where his ideas were introduced by Thomas Jefferson and had wide influence on Federal-period architecture.

palladium in Greek mythology, an image of Pallas ◊Athene, a gift from Zeus to the city of Troy. According to legend, the city could not be captured while the image remained there. It was stolen by Odysseus and Diomedes and was later alleged to have been taken to Rome by Aeneas.

palladium lightweight, ductile and malleable, silver-white, metallic element, symbol Pd, atomic number 46, atomic weight 106.4. It is one of the so-called platinum group of metals, and is resistant to tarnish and corrosion. It often occurs in nature as a free metal (see ◊native metal) in a natural alloy with platinum. Palladium is used as a catalyst, in alloys of gold (to make white gold) and silver, in electroplating, and in dentistry.

It was discovered 1803 by British physicist William Wollaston (1766–1828) and named for the then recently discovered asteroid Pallas (found in 1802).

Pallas in Greek mythology, a title of the goddess ◊Athene.

palliative in medicine, any treatment given to relieve symptoms rather than to cure the underlying cause.

In conditions that will resolve of their own accord (for instance, the common cold) or that are incurable, the entire treatment may be palliative.

pallium a woven vestment worn by the pope and by Catholic primates and archbishops. It is Y-shaped, falling across the shoulders, back and front.

palm plant of the family Palmae, characterized by a single tall stem bearing a thick cluster of large palmate or pinnate leaves at the top. The majority of the numerous species are tropical or subtropical. Some, such as the coconut, date, sago, and oil palms, are important economically.

Several plams are native to Florida.

Palma (Spanish Palma de Mallorca) industrial port (textiles, cement, paper, pottery), resort, and capital of the Balearic Islands, Spain, on Majorca; population (1986) 321,000. Palma was founded 276 BC as a Roman colony.

Palma, La one of the ◊Canary Islands, Spain
area 282 sq mi/730 sq km
capital Santa Cruz de la Palma
features forested
products wine, fruit, honey, silk; tourism is important
population (1981) 77,000.

Palmas, Las port in the Canary Islands; see ◊Las Palmas.

Palm Beach luxurious winter resort in Florida, on an island between Lake Worth and the Atlantic; population (1990) 9,814. Henry Flagler first developed the community as a resort in the 1890s, when he built the Royal Poinciana Hotel. It now has mansions, clubs, and large estates as well as resort hotels.

Palme (Sven) Olof 1927–1986. Swedish social-democratic politician, prime minister 1969–76 and 1982–86. He entered government 1963, holding several posts before becoming leader of the Social Democratic Labor Party (SAP) 1969. He was assassinated Feb 1986.

Palme, educated in Sweden and the US, joined the SAP 1949 and became secretary to the prime minister 1954. He led the SAP youth movement 1955–61. As prime minister he carried out constitutional reforms, turning the Riksdag into a single-chamber parliament and stripping the monarch of power.

Palmer A(lexander) Mitchell 1872–1936. US public official. After establishing a private legal practice in Stroudsburg, Pennsylvania, he became active in state Democratic politics and sat in the US House of Representatives 1909–15. Owing to his Quaker beliefs, Palmer declined an appointment as secretary of war by President Wilson, serving instead as custodian of alien property during World War I. As US attorney general 1919–21, he led the controversial "Palmer Raids" against alleged political radicals.

Born in Moosehead, Pennsylvania, Palmer was educated at Swarthmore College and was admitted to the bar 1893.

Palmer Arnold (Daniel) 1929– . US golfer, who helped to popularize the professional sport in the US in the 1950s and 1960s. He won the Masters 1958, 1960, 1962, and 1964; the US Open 1960; and the British Open 1961 and 1962.

Born in Pennsylvania, he won the US amateur title 1954, and went on to win all the world major professional trophies except the US PGA championship. In the 1980s he enjoyed a successful career on the US Seniors Tour.

CAREER HIGHLIGHTS

US Open: 1960
British Open: 1961–62
Masters: 1958, 1960, 1962, 1964
World Match-Play: 1964, 1967
US Ryder Cup: 1961, 1963*, 1965, 1967, 1971, 1973, 1975**

* playing captain;
** nonplaying captain

Palomar, Mount The 200-in/508-cm Hale telescope, shown pointing north, at Palomar Observatory, one of the Hale Observatories.

Palmer Geoffrey Winston Russell 1942– . New Zealand Labour politician, prime minister 1989–90, deputy prime minister and attorney-general 1984–89.

A graduate of Victoria University, Wellington, Palmer was a law lecturer in the US and New Zealand before entering politics, becoming Labor member for Christchurch in the House of Representatives 1979. He succeeded David ◊Lange on Lange's resignation as prime minister but resigned himself the following year.

Palmer Samuel 1805–1881. English landscape painter and etcher. He lived 1826–35 in Shoreham, Kent, with a group of artists who were all followers of William Blake and called themselves "the Ancients." Palmer's expressive landscape style during that period reflected a strongly spiritual inspiration.

Palmerston Henry John Temple, 3rd Viscount 1784–1865. British politician. Initially a Tory, in Parliament from 1807, he was secretary-at-war 1809–28. He broke with the Tories 1830 and sat in the Whig cabinets of 1830–34, 1835–41, and 1846–51 as foreign secretary. He was prime minister 1855–58 (when he rectified Aberdeen's mismanagement of the Crimean War, suppressed the Indian (Sepoy) Mutiny, and carried through the Second Opium War) and 1859–65 (when he almost involved Britain in the American Civil War on the side of the South).

He was responsible for the warship ◊*Alabama* going to the Confederate side in the American Civil War.

Palmerston North town on the SW coast of North Island, New Zealand; industries include textiles, dairy produce, and electrical goods; population (1986) 67,400.

Palm Springs resort and spa in S California, about 100 mi/160 km E of Los Angeles; population (1990) 40,181.

Palm Sunday in the Christian calendar, the Sunday before Easter and first day of Holy Week, commemorating Jesus' entry into Jerusalem, when the crowd strewed palm leaves in his path.

Palmyra ancient city and oasis in the desert of Syria, about 150 mi/240 km NE of Damascus. Palmyra, the biblical Tadmor, was flourishing by about 300 BC. It was destroyed AD 272 after Queen Zenobia had led a revolt against the Romans. Extensive temple ruins exist, and on the site is a village called Tadmor.

Palmyra coral atoll 1,000 mi/1,600 km SW of Hawaii, in the Line Islands, S Pacific, purchased by the US from a Hawaiian family 1979 for the storage of highly radioactive nuclear waste from 1986.

Palo Alto city in California, situated SE of San Francisco at the center of the high-tech region known as "Silicon Valley"; site of Stanford University; population (1990) 55,900.

Palomar, Mount the location, since 1948, of an observatory, 50 mi/80 km NE of San Diego, California. It has a 200-in/5-m reflector called the Hale.

Pamirs central Asian plateau mainly in the USSR, but extending into China and Afghanistan, traversed by mountain ranges. Its highest peak is Mount Communism (Kommunizma Pik, 24,600 ft/7,495 m) in the Akademiya Nauk range, the highest mountain in the USSR.

Pampas flat, treeless, Argentine plains, lying between the Andes and the Atlantic and rising gradually from the coast to the lower slopes of the mountains. The E Pampas contain large cattle ranches and the flax- and grain-growing area of Argentina; the W Pampas are arid and unproductive.

pampas grass any grass of the genus *Cortaderia*, native to South America, especially *C. argentea*, which is grown in gardens and has tall leaves and large panicles of white flowers.

Pamplona industrial city (wine, leather, shoes, textiles) in Navarre, N Spain, on the Arga river; population (1986) 184,000. A pre-Roman town, it was rebuilt by Pompey 68 BC, captured by the Visigoths 476, sacked by Charlemagne 778, became the capital of Navarre, and was taken by the Duke of Wellington in the Peninsular War 1813. An annual running of bulls takes place in the streets every July.

Pamyat (Russian "memory") nationalist Russian popular movement. Founded 1979 as a cultural and historical group attached to the Soviet Ministry of Aviation Industry, it grew from the mid-1980s, propounding a violently conservative and anti-Semitic Russian nationalist message.

Pan in Greek mythology, god (Roman Sylvanus) of flocks and herds, shown as a man with the horns, ears, and hoofed legs of a goat, and playing a shepherd's panpipe (syrinx).

panacea any supposed remedy for all known disease; a cure-all.

Pan-Africanist Congress (PAC) militant black South African nationalist group, which broke away from the African National Congress (ANC) 1959. More radical than the ANC, the Pan-Africanist Congress has a black-only policy for Africa. Since the 1970s, it has been weakened by internal dissent.

Panama country in Central America, on a narrow isthmus between the Caribbean and the Pacific Ocean, bounded W by Costa Rica and E by Colombia.

government The constitution was revised 1983, when a new, single-chamber legislative assembly of 67 members, elected by universal suffrage for a five-year term, was created. The president, elected in the same way for a similar period of office, is assisted by two elected vice-presidents and an appointed cabinet. There are a large number of political organizations, the most significant being represented in the assembly by two coalitions, the center-right National Democratic Union (Unade) and the center-left Democratic Opposition Alliance (ADO). Panama is divided into nine provinces, each with its own governor, appointed by the president. There are also three Indian reservations, which enjoy a high degree of self-government.

history For early history, see ◊American Indian. Panama was visited by Christopher ◊Columbus 1502. Vasco Núñez de ◊Balboa "discovered" the Pacific from the Darien isthmus 1513. Spanish settlements were sacked by Francis ◊Drake 1572–95 and Henry ◊Morgan 1668–71; Morgan destroyed the old city of Panama, which dated from 1519. Remains of Fort St Andrews, built by Scottish settlers 1698–1701, were discovered 1976. Panama remained part of the viceroyalties of Peru and New Granada until 1821, when it gained independence from Spain and joined Gran Colombia.

Panama achieved full independence 1903 with US support. At the same time the US bought the rights to build the Panama Canal and was given control of a ten-mile-wide strip of territory, known as the Canal Zone, in perpetuity. Panama was guaranteed US protection and an annuity. In

Panama
Republic of
(República de Panamá)

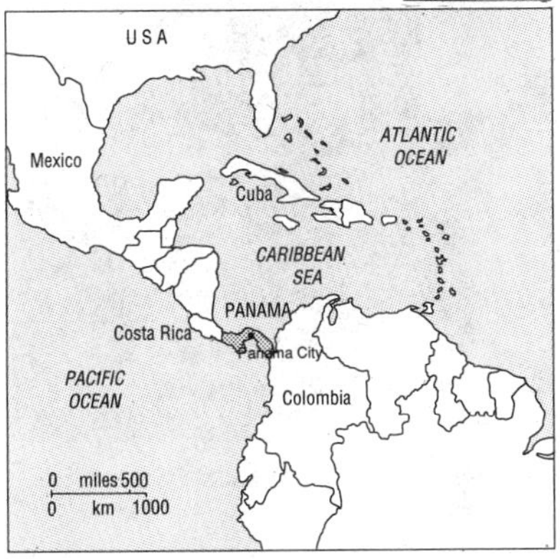
USA
Mexico
ATLANTIC OCEAN
Cuba
CARIBBEAN SEA
PANAMA
Costa Rica
Panama City
PACIFIC OCEAN
Colombia
0 miles 500
0 km 1000

area 29,768 sq mi/77,100 sq km
capital Panama City
cities Cristóbal, Balboa, Colón, David
physical coastal plains and mountainous interior; tropical rainforest in E and NW; Pearl Islands in Gulf of Panama
features Panama Canal; Barro Colorado Island in Gatun Lake (reservoir suppling the canal), a tropical forest reserve since 1923; Smithsonian Tropical Research Institute
head of state and government Guillermo Endara from 1989
political system emergent democratic republic
political parties Democratic Revolutionary Party (PRD), right-wing; Labor Party (PALA), right-of-center; Republican Party (PR), right-wing; National Liberal Republican Movement (MOLIRENA), left-of-center; Authentic Panama Party (PPA), centrist; Christian Democratic Party (PDC), center-left
exports bananas, petroleum products, copper, shrimp, sugar
currency balboa
population (1990 est) 2,423,000 (70% Mestizo, 14% W Indian, 10% European descent, 6% Indian (Cuna, Choco, Guayami)); growth rate 2.2% p.a.
life expectancy men 71, women 75 (1989)
language Spanish (official), English
religion Roman Catholic 93%, Protestant 6%
literacy 87% (1989)
GNP $4.2 bn (1988); $1,970 per head (1984)
chronology
1821 Achieved independence from Spain; joined Columbia.
1903 Full independence achieved on separation from Colombia.
1974 Agreement to negotiate full transfer of the Panama Canal from the US to Panama.
1977 US–Panama treaties transferred the canal to Panama, effective 1999, with the US guaranteeing its protection and an annual payment.
1984 Nicolas Ardito Barletta elected president.
1985 Barletta resigned; replaced by Eric Arturo del Valle.
1987 Gen Noriega resisted calls for his removal, despite suspension of US military and economic aid.
1988 Del Valle replaced by Manuel Solis Palma. Noriega, charged with drug smuggling by the US, declared a state of emergency.
1989 Opposition won election; Noriega declared results invalid; coup attempt failed; Noriega declared "maximum leader" by assembly; "state of war" with US announced; US invasion deposed Noriega, installed Guillermo Endara, winner of earlier elections; Noriega sought asylum in Vatican embassy, surrendered to US forces; taken to US for trial.

1939 Panama's protectorate status was ended by mutual agreement, and in 1977 two treaties were signed by Panama's president (1968–78), General Omar Torrijos Herara, and US President Carter. One transferred ownership of the canal to Panama effective 1999 and the other guaranteed its subsequent neutrality, with the conditions that only Panamanian forces would be stationed in the zone, and that the US would have the right to use force to keep the canal open if it became obstructed.

The 1980s saw a deterioration in the state of Panama's economy, with opposition to the austerity measures that the government introduced to try to halt the decline. Unade won 40 seats in the 1984 general election; ADO won 27 seats. After a very close result, Dr Nicolas Ardito Barletta, the Democratic Revolutionary Party (PRD) candidate, was declared president, but in 1985 he resigned, amid speculation that he had been forced to do so by the commander of the National Guard. Relations between Panama and the US deteriorated with the departure of President Barletta, and the Reagan administration cut and later suspended its financial aid.

Barletta was succeeded by Eric Arturo del Valle, but the country was, from 1983, effectively ruled by the army Commander in Chief, General Manuel Noriega. Although the 1977 Torrijos-Carter Canal Treaties specified that US forces in Panama were present purely to defend the canal, Noriega cooperated in allowing the US to use Panama as an intelligence, training, resupply, and weapons base for the Reagan administration's campaigns in Nicaragua and El Salvador.

In 1987 Noriega was accused of corruption, election rigging, involvement in the cocaine trade, and the murder of a political opponent. Noriega's forces were allegedly responsible for up to a dozen political killings between 1983 and 1989. Political parties, labor and student unions, and business groups united as the National Civic Crusade to campaign for his removal; demonstrations were suppressed by riot police. In July 1987 Noriega successfully resisted calls for his removal, despite the suspension of US military and economic aid. He declared the May 1989 assembly elections invalid and in Sept Francisco Rodriguez, with army backing, was made president. In the following month an attempted coup against Noriega was put down. In Dec 1989, after mounting harassment of Americans in the Canal Zone, US president Bush ordered troops to invade the country with the declared object of arresting Noriega and bringing him to trial. An estimated 7,000 people were killed and more than 15,000 made homeless in the US invasion. Noriega sought refuge in the Vatican embassy but eventually surrendered and was taken to the US to answer charges relating to drug trafficking. Guillermo Endara became president and worked to balance Panama's aims against pressures from the US, its most important foreign partner, in such areas as banking.

Panama Canal canal across the Panama isthmus in Central America, connecting the Pacific and Atlantic oceans; length 50 mi/80 km, with 12 locks. Built by the US 1904–14 after an unsuccessful attempt by the French, it was formally opened 1920. The Panama Canal Zone was acquired "in perpetuity" by the US 1903, comprising land extending about 3 mi/5 km on either side of the canal. The zone passed to Panama 1979, and control of the canal itself was ceded to Panama by the US in Jan 1990 under the terms of the Panama Canal Treaty 1977.

Panama City capital of the Republic of Panama, near the Pacific end of the Panama Canal; population (1980) 386,000. Products include chemicals, plastics, and clothing. An earlier Panama, to the NE, founded 1519, was destroyed 1671, and the city was founded on the present site 1673.

Pan-American Highway road linking the US with Central and South America; length 15,700 mi/25,300 km. Starting from the US-Canadian frontier (where it links with the Alaska Highway), it runs through San Francisco, Los Angeles, and Mexico City to Panama City, then down the W side of South America to Valparaiso, Chile, where it crosses the Andes and goes to Buenos Aires, Argentina. The road was first planned 1923.

Pan-American Union former name 1910–48 of the ◊Organization of American States.

Panay one of the Philippine islands, lying between Mindoro and Negros
area 4,446 sq mi/11,515 sq km
capital Iloilo
features mountainous, 7,265 ft/2,215 m in Madiaás
products rice, sugar, pineapples, bananas, copra, copper
history seized by Spain 1569; occupied by Japan 1942– 45.

Panchen Lama 10th incarnation 1935–1989. Tibetan spiritual leader, second in importance to the ◊Dalai Lama. A protégé of the Chinese since childhood, he is not indisputably recognized. When the Dalai Lama left Tibet 1959, the Panchen Lama was deputed by the Chinese to take over, but was stripped of power in 1964 for refusing to denounce the Dalai Lama. He did not appear again in public until 1978.

panchromatic in photography, a highly sensitive black-and-white film made to render all visible spectral colors in correct gray tones. It is always developed in total darkness.

pancreas in vertebrates, an accessory gland of the digestive system located close to the duodenum. When stimulated by ◊secretin, it secretes enzymes into the duodenum that digest starches, proteins, and fats. In humans, it is about 7 in/18 cm long, and lies behind and below the stomach. It contains groups of cells called the islets of Langerhans, which secrete the hormones insulin and glucagon that regulate the blood sugar level.

panda one of two carnivores of different families, native to NW China and Tibet. The giant panda *Ailuropoda melanoleuca* has black and white fur with black eye patches, and feeds mainly on bamboo shoots. It can grow up to 4.5 ft/1.5 m long, and weigh up to 300 lb/140 kg. The lesser panda *Ailurus fulgens*, of the raccoon family, is about 1.5 ft/50 cm long, and is black and chestnut, with a long tail. Destruction of pandas' natural habitats have made their extinction possible in the wild. There is dispute as to whether they should be included in the bear family or raccoon family, or classified as a family of their own.

The giant panda is the symbol of the Worldwide Fund for Nature (formerly the World Wildlife Fund), and the focus of conservation efforts.

Pandora in Greek mythology, the first mortal woman. Zeus sent her to Earth with a box of evils (to counteract the blessings brought to mortals

panda

lesser panda

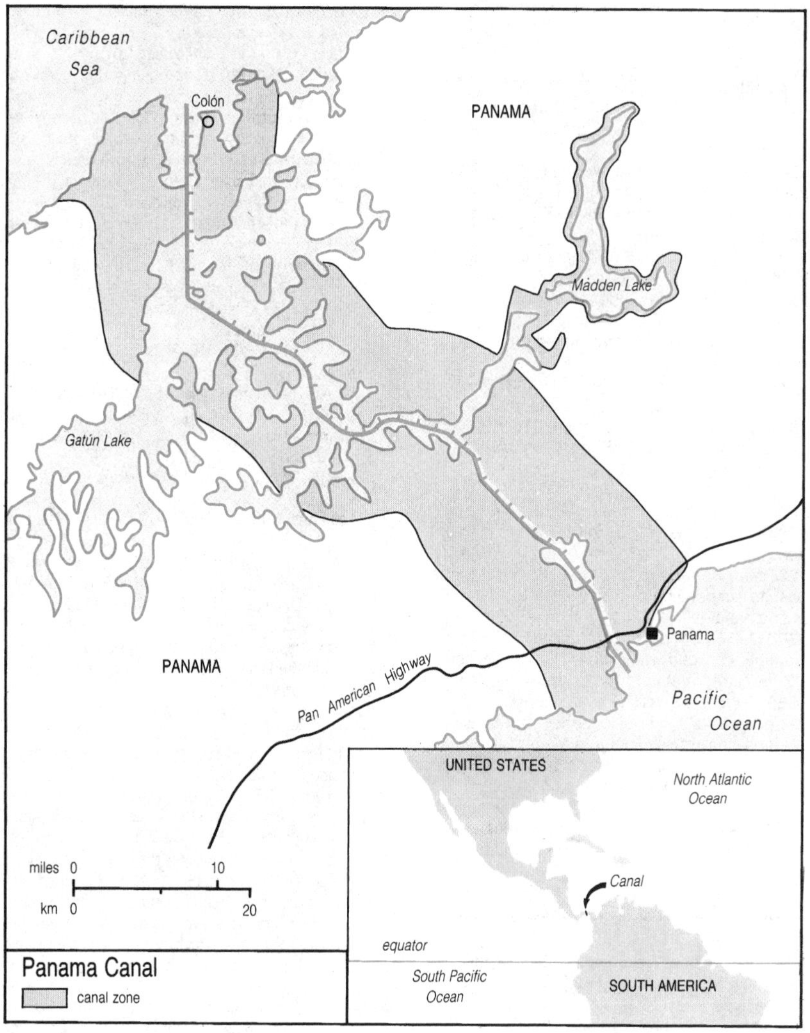
Caribbean Sea
Colón
PANAMA
Madden Lake
Gatún Lake
Panama
PANAMA
Pan American Highway
Pacific Ocean
miles 0 10
km 0 20
UNITED STATES
North Atlantic Ocean
Canal
equator
South Pacific Ocean
SOUTH AMERICA
canal zone
Panama Canal

by ◊Prometheus's gift of fire); she opened it, and they all flew out. Only hope was left inside as a consolation.

Pangaea or ***Pangea*** world continent, named by Alfred ◊Wegener, that may have existed between 250 and 200 million years ago, made up of all the continental masses. It may be regarded as a combination of ◊Laurasia in the north and ◊Gondwanaland in the south, the rest of Earth being covered by the ◊Panthalassa ocean.

Pan-Germanism movement that developed during the 19th century to encourage unity between German-speaking peoples in Austria, the Netherlands, Flanders, Luxembourg, and Switzerland. Encouraged by the unification of Germany after 1871, the movement had an increasingly high profile in the period up to 1914.

Pan-Germanism also had an impact in Belgium (Flemish separatism) and in Poland during World War I. Despite the defeat of Germany in 1919, its ideas were revived under Hitler's plans to expand through Europe.

pangolin or ***scaly anteater*** any toothless mammal of the orderr Pholidota. There is only one genus (*Manis*), with seven species found in tropical Africa and SE Asia. They are long-tailed and covered with large, overlapping scales. The elongated skull contains a long, extensible tongue. Pangolins measure up to 3 ft/1 m in length; some are arboreal and others are terrestrial. All live on ants and termites.

Panipat town in Punjab, India; scene of three decisive battles: 1526, when Babur (1483–1530), great-grandson of Tamerlane, defeated the emperor of Delhi and founded the Mogul empire; 1556, won by his descendant ◊Akbar; 1761, when the Mahrattas were defeated by ◊Ahmad Shah of Afghanistan.

Panjshir Valley the valley of the river Panjshir, which rises in the Panjshir range to the N of Kabul, E Afghanistan. It was the chief center of Mujaheddin rebel resistance against the Soviet-backed Najibullah government in the 1980s.

Pankhurst Emmeline (born Goulden) 1858–1928. English suffragist. Founder of the Women's Social and Political Union 1903, she launched the militant suffragist campaign 1905. In 1926 she joined the Conservative Party and was a prospective Parliamentary candidate.

pansy cultivated violet derived from the European wild pansy *Viola tricolor*, and including many different varieties and strains. The flowers are usually purple, yellow, cream, or a mixture, and there are many highly developed varieties bred for size, color, or special markings.

Pantanal a large area of swamp land in the Mato Grosso of SW Brazil, occupying 84,975 sq mi/220,000 sq km in the upper reaches of the Paraguay river; one of the world's great wildlife refuges; 530 sq mi/1,370 sq km were designated as a national park in 1981.

pansy

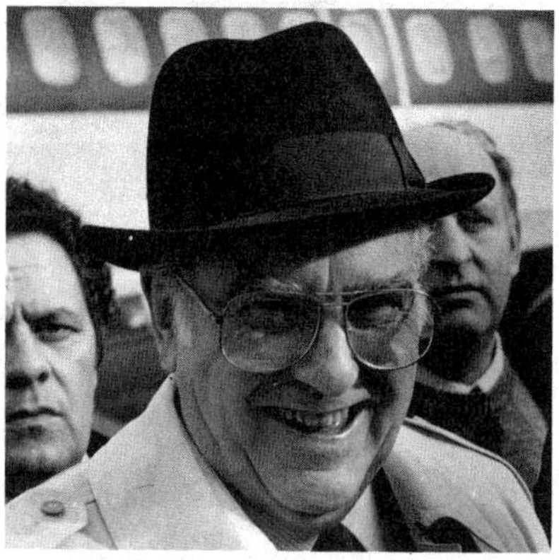

***Papandreou** Greece's first socialist prime minister, Andreas Papandreou.*

Pantelleria volcanic island in the Mediterranean, 62 mi/100 km SW of Sicily and part of that region of Italy

area 45 sq mi/115 sq km
town Pantelleria
products sheep, fruit, olives, capers
population (1981) 7,800
history Pantelleria has drystone dwellings dating from prehistoric times. The Romans called it *Cossyra* and sent people into exile there. Strategically placed, the island has been the site of many battles. It was strongly fortified by Mussolini in World War II but surrendered to the Allies June 11, 1943.

Panthalassa ocean that may have covered the surface of the Earth not occupied by the world continent ◊Pangaea between 250 and 200 million years ago.

pantheism (Greek *pan* "all"; *theos* "God") the doctrine that regards all of reality as divine, and God as present in all of nature and the universe. It is expressed in Egyptian religion and Brahmanism; stoicism, Neo-Platonism, Judaism, Christianity, and Islam can be interpreted in pantheistic terms. Pantheistic philosophers include Bruno, Spinoza, Fichte, Schelling, and Hegel.

pantheon originally a temple for worshiping all the gods, such as that in ancient Rome, rebuilt by ◊Hadrian and still used as a church. In more recent times, it is a building where famous people are buried (as in the Panthéon, Paris).

panther another name for ◊leopard.

pantothenic acid chemical formula $C_9H_{17}NO_5$) one of the water-soluble "B" ◊vitamins, occurring widely throughout a normal diet. There is no specific deficiency disease associated with pantothenic acid but it is known to be involved in the breakdown of fats and carbohydrates.

panzer German mechanized divisions and regiments in World War II, used in connection with armored vehicles, mainly tanks.

Paolozzi Eduardo 1924– . British sculptor, a major force in the Pop art movement in London in the mid-1950s. He typically uses bronze casts of pieces of machinery to create robotlike structures.

papacy the office of the ◊pope or bishop of Rome, as head of the Roman Catholic Church.

papal infallibility doctrine formulated by the Roman Catholic Vatican Council 1870, which stated that the pope, when speaking officially on certain doctrinal or moral matters, was protected from error by God, and therefore such rulings could not be challenged.

Papal States area of central Italy in which the pope was temporal ruler from 756 to the time of the country's unification in 1870.

Papandreou Andreas 1919– . Greek Socialist poli-

paper making

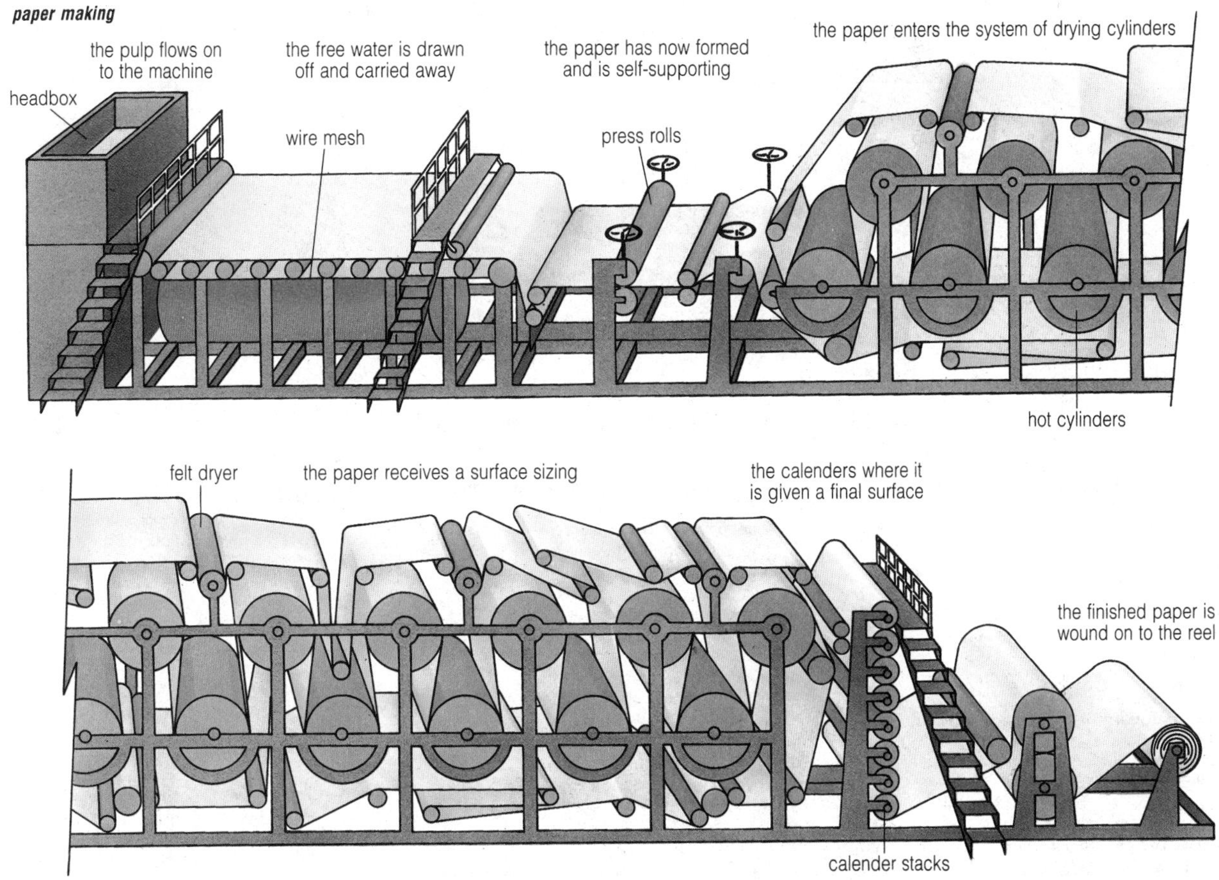
the pulp flows on to the machine
the free water is drawn off and carried away
the paper has now formed and is self-supporting
the paper enters the system of drying cylinders
headbox
wire mesh
press rolls
hot cylinders
felt dryer
the paper receives a surface sizing
the calenders where it is given a final surface
the finished paper is wound on to the reel
calender stacks

tician, founder of the Pan-Hellenic Socialist Movement (PASOK), and prime minister 1981–89, when he became implicated in the alleged embezzlement and diversion of funds to the Greek government of $200 million from the Bank of Crete, headed by George Koskotas, and lost the election.

Son of a former prime minister, he studied law in Athens and at Harvard. He was director of the Center for Economic Research in Athens 1961–64, and economic adviser to the Bank of Greece. He was imprisoned Apr–Dec 1967 for his political activities, after which he founded PASOK. After another spell in overseas universities, he returned to Greece 1974. He was leader of the opposition 1977–81, and became Greece's first Socialist prime minister. He was re-elected 1985, but was defeated 1989 after damage to his party and himself from the Koskotas affair. In Sep 1989 calls were made for criminal investigation of his wiretapping activities.

papaya tropical tree *Carica papaya* of the family Caricaceae, native from Florida to South America. Varieties are grown throughout the tropics. The edible fruits resemble a melon, with orange-colored flesh and numerous blackish seeds in the central cavity; they may weigh up to 20 lb/9 kg.

The fruit juice and the tree sap contain papain, an enzyme used to tenderize meat and aid digestion.

Papeete capital and port of French Polynesia on the NW coast of Tahiti; population (1983) 79,000. Products include vanilla, copra, and mother-of-pearl.

Papen Franz von 1879–1969. German right-wing politician. As chancellor 1932, he negotiated the Nazi-Conservative alliance that made Hitler chancellor 1933. He was envoy to Austria 1934–38 and ambassador to Turkey 1939–44. Although acquitted at the ◊Nuremberg trials, he was imprisoned by a German denazification court for three years.

paper thin, flexible material made in sheets from vegetable fibers (such as wood pulp) or rags and used for writing, drawing, printing, packaging, and various household needs. The name comes from ◊papyrus, a form of writing material made from water reed, used in ancient Egypt. The invention of true paper, originally made of pulped fishing nets and rags, is credited to Tsai Lun, Chinese minister of agriculture, AD 105.

Paper came to the West with Arabs who had learned the secret from Chinese prisoners of war in Samarkand in 768. It spread to Moorish Spain and to Byzantium in the 11th century, then to the rest of Europe. All early paper was handmade within frames.

With the spread of literacy there was a great increase in the demand for paper. Production by hand of single sheets could not keep pace with this demand and led to the invention, by Louis Robert in 1799, of a machine to produce a continuous reel of paper. Today most paper is made from ◊wood pulp on a Foudrinier machine, then cut to size. Recycling avoids some of the enormous waste of trees, and most papermakers plant and replant their own forests of fast-growing stock.

Paphos resort town on the SW coast of Cyprus; population (1985) 23,200; capital of Cyprus in Roman times and the legendary birthplace of Aphrodite who rose out of the sea. Archeological remains include the 2,300-year-old underground "Tombs of the Kings," the Roman villa of Dionysus, and the 7th-century Byzantine castle.

papier mâché a craft technique that involves building up layer upon layer of pasted paper, which is then baked or left to harden. Used for trays, decorative objects, and even furniture, it is often painted, lacquered, or decorated with mother of pearl.

Papineau Louis Joseph 1786–1871. Canadian politician. He led a mission to England to protest against the planned union of Lower Canada (Québec) and Upper Canada (Ontario), and demanded economic reform and an elected provincial legislature. In 1835 he gained the cooperation of William Lyon ◊Mackenzie in Upper Canada, and in 1837 organized an unsuccessful rebellion of the French against British rule in Lower Canada. He fled the country, but returned 1847 to sit in the United Canadian legislature until 1854.

Papp Joseph 1921–1991. US theater director and founder of the New York Shakespeare Festival 1954, free to the public and held in an open-air theater in Central Park. He also founded the New York Public Theatre 1967, an off-Broadway forum for new talent.

Productions directed by Papp include *The Merchant of Venice* and a musical version of *The Two Gentlemen of Verona* (Tony award 1972). The New York Public Theatre staged the first productions of the musicals *Hair* 1967 and *A Chorus Line* 1975. Many of Papp's productions achieved great success when transferred to Broadway.

pappus (plural pappi) in botany, a modified ◊calyx comprising a ring of fine, silky hairs, or sometimes scales or small teeth, that persists after fertilization. Pappi are found in members of the daisy family (Compositae) such as the dandelions *Taraxacum*, where they form a parachutelike structure that aids dispersal of the fruit.

Pap test or Pap smear common name for ◊cervical smear.

Papua original name of the island of New Guinea, but latterly its SE section, now part of ◊Papua New Guinea.

Papuan native to or inhabitant of Papua New Guinea; a speaker of a Papuan language, used mainly on the island of New Guinea, although some 500 are used in New Britain, the Solomon Islands, and the islands of the SW Pacific.

Papua New Guinea country in the SW Pacific, comprising the eastern part of the island of New Guinea, the New Guinea islands, the Admiralty islands, and part of the Solomon islands.

government The British monarch is the formal

Papua New Guinea

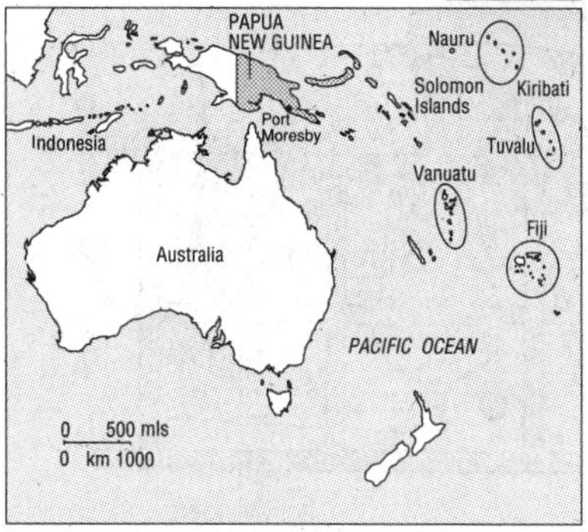
PAPUA
NEW GUINEA
Nauru
Solomon Islands
Kiribati
Port Moresby
Indonesia
Tuvalu
Vanuatu
Fiji
Australia
PACIFIC OCEAN
0 500 mls
0 km 1000

area 178,656 sq mi/462,840 sq km
capital Port Moresby (on E New Guinea)
cities Lae, Rabaul, Madang
physical mountainous; includes tropical islands of New Ireland, New Britain, and Bougainville; Admiralty Islands, D'Entrecasteaux Islands, and Louisiade Archipelago
features one of world's largest swamps on SW coast; world's largest butterfly, orchids; Sepik River
head of state Elizabeth II, represented by governor-general
head of government Rabbie Namaliu from 1988
political system constitutional monarchy
political parties Papua New Guinea Party (Pangu Pati: PP), urban-and coastal-oriented nationalist; People's Democratic Movement (PDM), 1985 breakaway from the PP; National Party (NP), highlands-based; Melanesian Alliance (MA), Bougainville-based autonomy; People's Progress Party (PPP), conservative
exports copra, coconut oil, palm oil, tea, copper, gold, coffee
currency kina
population (1989 est) 3,613,000 (Papuans, Melanesians, Pygmies, various minorities); growth rate 2.6% p.a.
life expectancy men 53, women 54 (1987)
language English (official); pidgin English, 715 local languages
religion Protestant 63%, Roman Catholic 31%, local faiths
literacy men 55%/women 36% (1985 est)
GNP $2.5 bn; $730 per head (1987)
chronology
1883 Annexed by Queensland: became the Australian Territory of Papua.
1884 NE New Guinea annexed by Germany; SE claimed by Britain.
1914 NE New Guinea occupied by Australia.
1921–42 Held as a League of Nations mandate.
1942–45 Occupied by Japan.
1975 Independence achieved from Australia, within the Commonwealth, with Michael Somare as prime minister.
1980 Julius Chan became prime minister.
1982 Somare returned to power.
1985 Somare challenged by deputy prime minister, Paias Wingti, who later formed a five-party coalition government.
1988 Wingti defeated on no-confidence vote and replaced by Rabbie Namaliu, who established a six-party coalition government.
1989 State of emergency imposed in Bougainville in response to separatist violence.
1991 Peace accord signed with Bougainville secessionists.

head of state, represented by a resident governor-general. The governor-general appoints the prime minister and cabinet, who are drawn from and responsible to the parliament.

The constitution from 1975 provides for a single-chamber legislature, the National Parliament, consisting of 109 members elected by universal suffrage for a five-year term, 89 representing local single-member constituencies and 20 provincial constituencies. Although Papua New Guinea is not a federal state, it has 20 provincial governments with a fair degree of autonomy. The 12 political parties include the Papua New Guinea Party (Pangu Pati: PP), People's Democratic Movement (PDM), National Party (NP), Melanesian Alliance (MA), and People's Progress Party (PPP).

history New Guinea has been inhabited for at least 10,000 years, probably by Asians arriving by way of Indonesia. It was visited by the Portuguese explorer Jorge de Menezes about 1526 and by Dutch traders in the 17th century. The Dutch East India Company took control of the western half of the island, and in 1828 it became part of the Netherlands East Indies. In 1884 the southeast was claimed by Britain, the north by Germany; the British part, Papua, was transferred to Australia 1905 and the German part after World War I, when Australia was granted a League of Nations mandate and then a trusteeship over the area.

Freed from Japanese occupation in 1945, the two territories were jointly administered by Australia and, after achieving internal self-government as Papua New Guinea, became fully independent within the ◊Commonwealth in 1975. The first prime minister after independence was Michael Somare, leader of the Pangu Pati (PP). Despite allegations of incompetence, he held office until 1980, when Julius Chan, leader of the PPP, succeeded him. Somare returned to power in 1982, but in 1985 he lost a no-confidence motion in parliament and was replaced by Paias Wingti, leader of the breakaway PDM, with former prime minister Chan as his deputy. In Aug 1987 Prime Minister Wingti returned to power with a slender majority of three votes. He announced a more independent foreign policy of good relations with the USSR, Japan, and China. In July 1988, following shifts in coalition alliances, Wingti lost a no-confidence vote and was replaced as prime minister by the former foreign minister and PP's new leader, Rabbie Namaliu. Somare became foreign minister in the new six-party coalition government. Faced with a deteriorating internal law and order situation—soldiers rioting in Port Moresby in Feb 1989 over inadequate pay increases—the government imposed a state of emergency on ◊Bougainville island from June 1989 because of the growing strength there of the guerrilla separatist movement, which had forced the closure of the island's Panguna copper mine a month earlier. An Interim peace accord—the "Endeavor Accord"—was signed on Aug 5, 1990 by the government and representatives of the secessionist Bougainville Revolutionary Army (BRA). The government had withdrawn its troops from the island March 1990. In May 1990 the BRA issued a unilateral declaration of independence, to which the government responded by imposing a blockade. This was to be lifted under the terms of the accord and new peace talks to commence.

papyrus type of paper made by the ancient Egyptians from the stem of the papyrus or paper reed *Cyperus papyrus*, family Cyperaceae.

Pará alternate name of the Brazilian port ◊Belém.

parabola in mathematics, a curve formed by cutting a right circular cone with a plane parallel to the sloping side of the cone; one of the family of curves known as ◊conic sections.

It can also be defined as a path traced out by

parabola

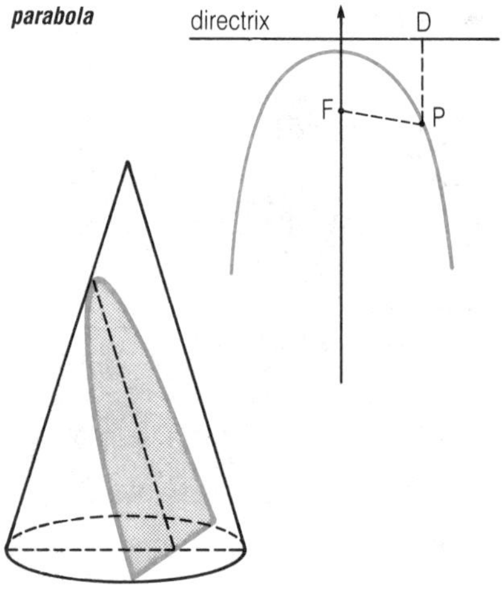
directrix
D
F
P

a point that moves in such a way that the distance from a fixed point (focus) is equal to its distance from a fixed straight line (directrix); it thus has an ◊eccentricity of 1.

The trajectories of missiles within the Earth's gravitational field approximate closely to parabolas (ignoring the effect of air resistance). The corresponding solid figure, the paraboloid, is formed by rotating a parabola about its axis. It is a common shape for headlight reflectors, dish-shaped microwave and radar aerials, and radiotelescopes, since a source of radiation placed at the focus of a paraboloidal reflector is propagated as a parallel beam.

Paracels (Chinese *Xisha*; Vietnamese *Hoang Sa*) group of about 130 small islands in the S China Sea. Situated in an oil-bearing area, they were occupied by China following a skirmish with Vietnam 1974.

Paracelsus Adopted name of Theophrastus Bombastus von Hohenheim 1493–1541. Swiss physician, alchemist, and scientist. He developed the idea that minerals and chemicals might have medical uses (iatrochemistry). He introduced the use of ◊laudanum (which he named) for pain-killing purposes. Although Paracelsus was something of a charlatan, and his books contain much mystical nonsense, his rejection of the ancients and insistence on the value of experimentation make him a leading figure in early science.

He lectured in Basel on the need for observational experience rather than traditional lore in medicine: he made a public bonfire of the works of his predecessors Avicenna and Galen. He was the disseminator in Europe of the medieval Islamic alchemists' theory that matter is composed of only three elements: salt, sulfur, and mercury.

paracentesis evacuation of unwanted fluid from a body tissue or cavity by means of a drainage tube.

paracetamol analgesic, particularly effective for musculoskeletal pain. It is as effective as aspirin in reducing fever, and less irritating to the stomach, but has little anti-inflammatory action (as for joint pain). An overdose can cause severe, often irreversible, liver and kidney damage.

Technically, it is acetaminophenol, a white crystalline powder $CH_3CONHC_6H_4OH$. It is sold under numerous trademarks (for example, Tylenol).

parachute any variously shaped, fabric, canopied device strapped to a person or a package, used to slow down their descent from a high altitude, or returning spent missiles or parts to a safe speed for landing, or sometimes to aid (through braking) the landing of a plane. It originally consisted of some two dozen panels of silk (later nylon) in a circular canopy with shroud lines to a harness. Modern designs enable the parachutist to exercise considerable control of direction and landing, as in ◊skydiving.

Leonardo da Vinci sketched a parachute design,

Paraguay
Republic of
(República del Paraguay)

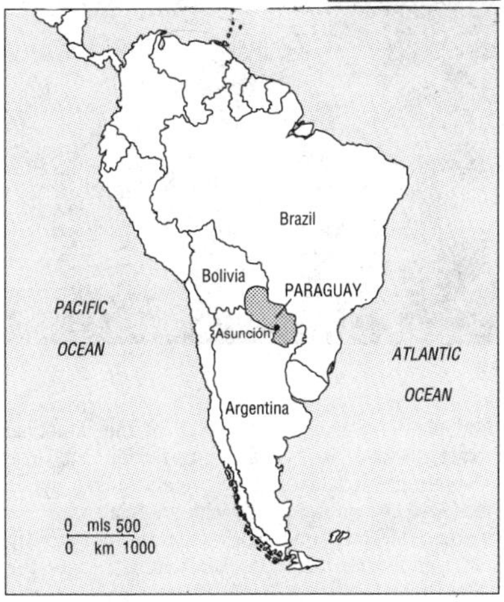
Brazil
Bolivia
PARAGUAY
PACIFIC
OCEAN
Asunción
ATLANTIC
OCEAN
Argentina
0 mls 500
0 km 1000

area 157,006 sq mi/406,752 sq km
capital Asunción
cities Presidente Stroessner, Pedro Juan Caballero; port Concepción
physical low marshy plain and marshlands; divided by Paraguay River; Paraná River in S
features Itaipú dam on border with Brazil; Gran Chaco plain with huge swamps
head of state and government Andrés Rodriguez from 1989
political system emergent democracy
political parties National Republican Association (Colorado Party), right-of-center; Liberal Party (PL), right-of-center; Radical Liberal Party (PLR), centrist
exports cotton, soy beans, timber, vegetable oil, maté
currency guaraní
population (1990 est) 4,660,000 (95% mixed Guaraní Indian-Spanish descent); growth rate 3.0% p.a.
life expectancy men 67, women 72 (1989)
language Spanish 6% (official); Guaraní 90%
religion Roman Catholic 97%
literacy men 91%/women 85% (1985 est)
GNP $7.4 bn; $1,000 per head (1987)
chronology
1811 Independence achieved from Spain.
1865–70 War with Argentina, Brazil, and Uruguay; much territory lost.
1932–35 Territory won from Bolivia during the Chaco War.
1940–48 Gen Higino Morinigo elected president.
1948–54 Political instability; six different presidents.
1954 Gen Alfredo Stroessner seized power.
1989 Stroessner ousted in coup led by Gen Andrés Rodriguez. Rodriguez elected president; Colorado Party won the congressional elections.

but the first descent, from a balloon, was not made until 1797 by Garnerin, and the first from an aircraft by Berry 1912. A parachute is typically folded into a pack from which it is released by a rip cord or other device. Modern parachutes are often small and rectangular. In parascending the parachuting procedure is reversed, the canopy (parafoil) to which the person is attached being towed behind a vehicle to achieve an ascent.

paradigm all those factors, both scientific and sociological, that influence the research of the scientist. The term, first used by the US historian of science T S ◊Kuhn, has subsequently spread to social studies and politics.

paradise (Persian "pleasure garden") in various religions, a place or state of happiness. Examples are the Garden of Eden and the Messianic kingdom; the Islamic paradise of the Koran is a place of sensual pleasure.

Paradise Lost an epic poem by John Milton, first published 1667. The poem describes the Fall of Man and the battle between God and Satan, as enacted through the story of Adam and Eve in the Garden of Eden. A sequel, *Paradise Regained*, was published 1671.

paraffin common name for ◊alkane, any member of the series of hydrocarbons with the general formula $C_nH_{2n}+_2$. The lower members are gases, such as methane (marsh or natural gas). The middle ones (mainly liquid) form the basis of gasoline, kerosene, and lubricating oils, while the higher ones (paraffin waxes) are used in ointment and cosmetic bases.

Paraguay landlocked country in South America, bounded NE by Brazil, S by Argentina, and NW by Bolivia.

government The 1967 constitution provides for a president and a two-chamber legislature, the National Congress, consisting of the Senate and Chamber of Deputies, all elected by universal suffrage for a five-year term. The president appoints and leads the cabinet, which is called the Council of Ministers.

The Senate has 30 members and the Chamber 60, and the party winning the largest number of votes in the congressional elections is allocated two-thirds of the seats in each chamber. A law passed in 1981 prescribes that a political party must have a minimum of 10,000 members and must contest at least a third of the constituencies before it can operate.

history For early history, see ◊American Indian. The Guaraní Indians had a settled agricultural civilization before the arrival of Europeans: Sebastian ◊Cabot 1526–30, followed by Spanish colonists, who founded the city of Asunción 1537. From about 1600–1767, when they were expelled, Jesuit missionaries administered much of the country. It became a province subordinate to the Spanish viceroyalty of Peru, then from 1776 part of the viceroyalty of Buenos Aires, and in 1811 Paraguay declared its independence.

The first president was J G R Francia (ruled 1816–40), a despot; he was followed by his nephew C A López and in 1862 by his son F S López, who involved Paraguay in a war with Brazil, Argentina, and Uruguay. Paraguay was invaded and López killed at Aquidaban 1870. When the war was finally over the population consisted mainly of women and children. Recovery was slow, with many revolutions. Continuing disputes with Bolivia over the frontier in the torrid Chaco zone of the north flared up into war 1932–35; arbitration by the US and five South American republics reached a peace settlement 1938.

Since 1940 Paraguay has been mostly under the control of military governments led by strong, autocratic leaders. General Morinigo was president 1940–47 and General Alfredo Stroessner 1954–89. During the US presidency of Jimmy ◊Carter the Stroessner regime came under strong criticism for its violation of human rights, and this resulted in a tempering of the general's iron rule. Criticism by the Reagan administration was less noticeable. Stroessner maintained his supremacy by ensuring that the armed forces and business community shared in the spoils of office and by preventing opposition groups from coalescing into a credible challenge. In the 1983 Congress elections the National Republican Party, led by the president, with the largest number of votes, automatically secured 20 Senate and 40 Chamber seats. The Radical Liberal Party placed second, with six Senate and 13 Chamber seats.

parallax

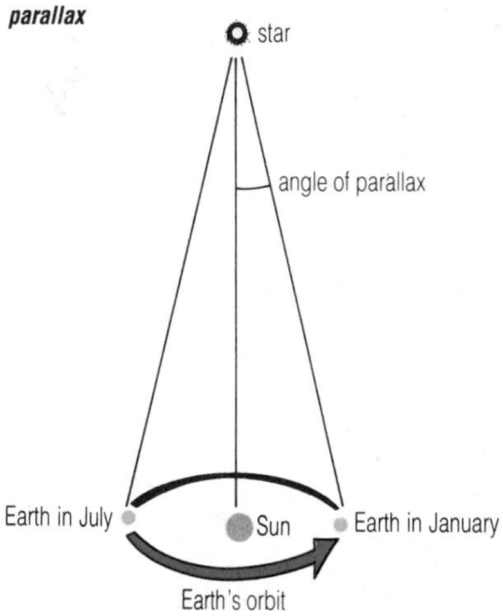
star
angle of parallax
Earth in July
Sun
Earth in January
Earth's orbit

Stroessner sought and won an eighth consecutive term only to be ousted, in Feb 1989, by General Andrés Rodriguez who, in May 1989, was elected president. The Colorado party was also successful in the congressional elections. During 1990–91, Rodriguez made progress on economic growth and on political democracy.

parakeet any of various small ◊parrots.

paraldehyde common name for ◊ethanal trimer.

parallax the change in the apparent position of an object against its background when viewed from two different positions. In astronomy, nearby stars show a shift caused by parallax when viewed from different positions on the Earth's orbit around the Sun. A star's parallax is used to deduce its distance.

Nearer bodies such as the Moon, Sun, and planets also show a parallax caused by the motion of the Earth. Diurnal parallax is caused by the Earth's rotation.

parallel circuit an electrical circuit in which the components are connected side by side. The current flowing in the circuit is shared by the components.

parallel computing or ***parallel processing*** an emerging computer technology that allows more than one computation at the same time. Currently, this means having a few computer processors working in parallel, but in future the number could run to thousands or millions.

The technique, which involves breaking down computations into small parts and performing thousands of them simultaneously, rather than in a linear sequence, offers the prospect of a vast improvement in working speed.

parallel lines and parallel planes in mathematics, straight lines or planes that always remain the same perpendicular distance from one another no matter how far they are extended. This is a principle of Euclidean geometry. Some non-Euclidean geometries, such as elliptical and hyperbolic geometry, however, reject Euclid's parallel axiom.

parallelogram in mathematics, a quadrilateral (four-sided plane figure) with opposite pairs of sides equal in length and parallel, and opposite angles equal. In the special case when all four sides are equal in length, the parallelogram is known as a rhombus, and when the internal angles are right angles, it is a rectangle or square.

The diagonals of a parallelogram bisect each other. Its area is the product of the length of one side and the perpendicular distance between that side and its parallel.

parallelogram of forces in physics and applied mathematics, a method of calculating the resultant (combined effect) of two different forces acting together on a object. Because a force has both magnitude and direction it is a ◊vector quantity

parallelogram

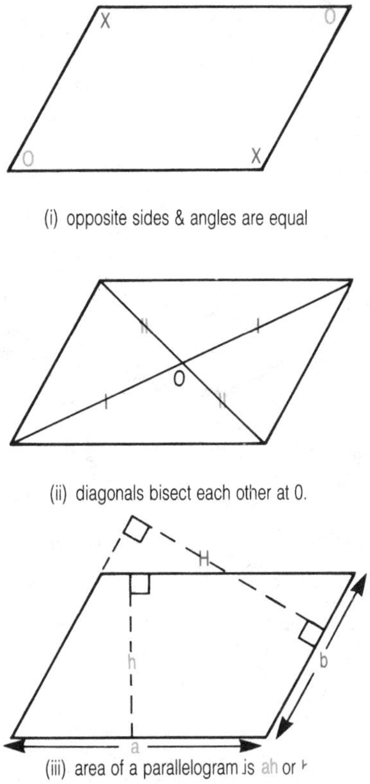
X
O
O
X
(i) opposite sides & angles are equal
O
(ii) diagonals bisect each other at O.
H
h
b
a
(iii) area of a parallelogram is ah or

and can be represented by a straight line. A second force acting at the same point in a different direction can be represented by another line drawn at an angle to the first. By completing the parallelogram (of which the two lines are sides) a diagonal may be drawn from the original angle to the opposite corner to represent the resultant force vector.

paralysis loss of voluntary movement due to failure of nerve impulses to reach the muscles involved. It may result from almost any disorder of the nervous system, including brain or spinal-cord injury, poliomyelitis, stroke, and progressive conditions such as a tumor or multiple sclerosis. Paralysis may also involve loss of sensation due to sensory-nerve disturbance.

Paramaribo port and capital of Surinam, South America, 15 mi/24 km from the sea on the river Surinam; population (1980) 193,000. Products include coffee, fruit, timber, and bauxite. It was founded by the French on an Indian village 1540, made capital of British Surinam 1650, and placed under Dutch rule from 1816 to 1975.

Paraná river in South America, formed by the confluence of the Río Grande and Paranaiba; the Paraguay joins it at Corrientes, and it flows into the Río de la Plata with the Uruguay; length 2,800 mi/4,500 km. It is used for hydroelectric power by Argentina, Brazil, and Paraguay.

Paraná industrial port (flour mills, meat canneries) and capital of Entre Rios province in E Argentina, on the Paraná river, 350 mi/560 km NW of Buenos Aires; population (1980) 160,000.

paranoia mental disorder marked by a single-channelled delusion, for example, that the patient is someone of great importance or the subject of a conspiracy.

paraplegia paralysis of the lower limbs, involving loss of both movement and sensation, usually due to spinal injury.

parapsychology (Greek *para* "beyond") study of phenomena that are not within range explicable by established science, for example, extra-sensory

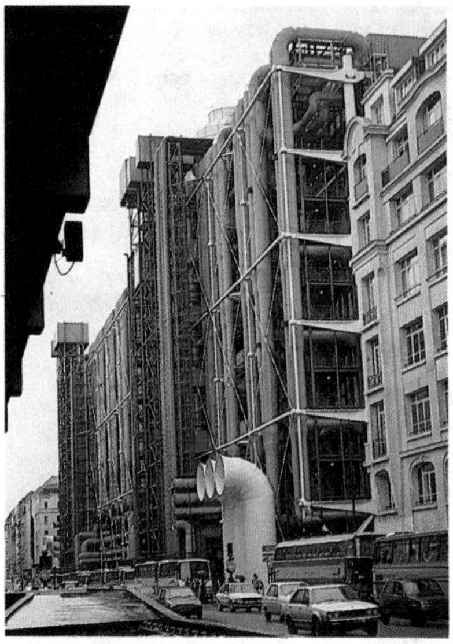

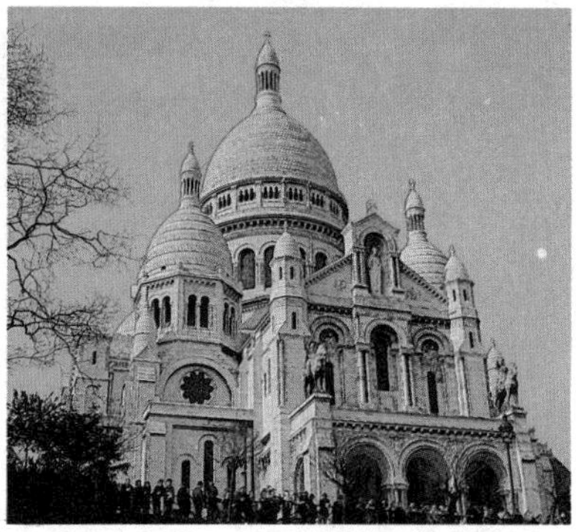

Paris *(top left) The Pompidou Center of art and culture (1977). (top right) The Basilica of Sacré Coeur (1919).*

perception. The faculty allegedly responsible for them, and common to humans and other animals, is known as *psi*.

Parapsychological phenomena include: mediumship, supposed contact with the spirits of the dead, usually via an intermediate "guide" in the other world; precognition, foreknowledge of events, as in "second sight"; telekinesis, movement of objects from one position to another by human mental concentration; and telepathy, a term coined by British essayist Myers (1843–1901) for "communication of impressions of any kind from one mind to another, independently of the recognized channels of sense." Most scientists are skeptical, but a chair of parapsychology was established 1984 at Edinburgh University, endowed by Arthur ◊Koestler.

paraquat $CH_3(C_5H_4N)_2CH_3{\cdot}2CH_3SO_4$ (technical name 1,1-dimethyl-4,4-dipyridylium) nonselective herbicide. Although quickly degraded by soil microorganisms, it is deadly to human beings if ingested.

parasite an organism that lives on or in another organism (called the "host"), and depends on it for nutrition, often at the expense of the host's welfare. Parasites that live inside the host, such as liver flukes and tapeworms, are called endoparasites; those that live on the outside, such as fleas and lice, are called ectoparasites.

parathyroid one of a pair of small ◊endocrine glands. Most tetrapod vertebrates, including humans, possess two such pairs, located behind the ◊thyroid gland. They secrete parathyroid hormone, which regulates the amount of calcium in the blood.

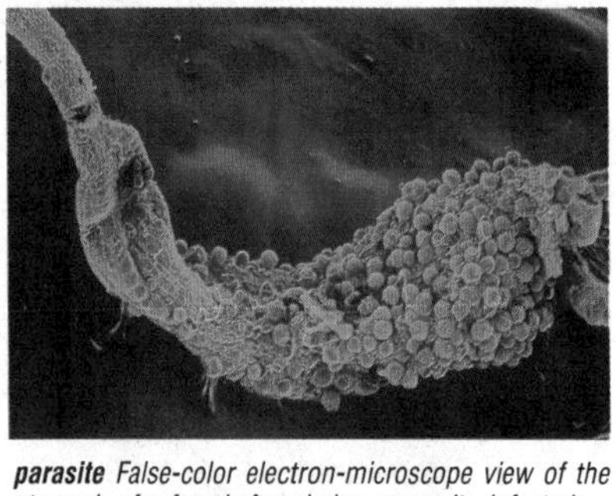

parasite *False-color electron-microscope view of the stomach of a female* Anopheles *mosquito infested with the malaria parasite* Plasmodium.

paratyphoid fever infective fever of the intestinal tract, similar to typhoid but milder and less dangerous. It is caused by bacteria of the genus *Salmonella* and is treated with antibiotics.

Parcae in Roman mythology, the three Fates of ancient Rome; their Greek counterparts are the Moirai.

Paré Ambroise 1509–1590. French surgeon who introduced modern principles to the treatment of wounds. As a military surgeon, Paré developed new ways of treating wounds and amputations, which greatly reduced the death rate among the wounded. He abandoned the practice of cauterization (sealing with heat), using balms and soothing lotions instead, and used ligatures to tie off blood vessels.

parenchyma a plant tissue composed of loosely packed, more or less spherical cells, with thin cellulose walls. Although parenchyma often has no specialized function, it is usually present in large amounts, forming a packing or ground tissue. It usually has many intercellular spaces.

parental care in biology, the time and energy spent by a parent in order to rear its offspring to maturity. Among animals, it ranges from the simple provision of a food supply for the hatching young at the time the eggs are laid (for example, many wasps) to feeding and protection of the young after hatching or birth, as in birds and mammals. In the more social species, parental care may include the teaching of skills—for example, female cats teach their kittens to hunt.

parent–teacher association (PTA) group attached to a school consisting of parents and teachers who support the school by fund raising and other activities.

Throughout the US, PTAs are active as political pressure groups and as a way to involve parents in the public education process.

Pareto Vilfredo 1848–1923. Italian economist and political philosopher, born in Paris. He produced the first account of society as a self-regulating and interdependent system that operates independently of human attempts at voluntary control. A vigorous opponent of socialism and liberalism, Pareto justified inequality of income on the grounds of his empirical observation (Pareto's law) that income distribution remained constant whatever efforts were made to change it.

A founder of welfare economics, he put forward a concept of "optimality," which contends that optimum conditions exist in an economic system if no one can be made better off without at least one other person becoming worse off.

Paris port and capital of France, on the River Seine; *département* in the Île de France region; area 40.5 sq mi/105 sq km; population (1982, metropolitan area) 8,707,000. Products include metal, leather, and luxury goods and chemicals, glass, and tobacco.

features the river Seine is spanned by 32 bridges; the oldest is the Pont Neuf 1578. Churches include Notre Dame cathedral built in the period 1163 to 1250; the Invalides, housing the tomb of Napoleon; the Gothic Sainte-Chapelle; and the 19th-century basilica of Sacré-Coeur, 410 ft/125 m high. Notable buildings include the Palais de Justice, the Hôtel de Ville, the Luxembourg Palace and Gardens. The former palace of the Louvre is a foremost art gallery; the Orsay Museum 1986 has Impressionist and other 19th-century paintings; the Pompidou Center (Beaubourg) 1977 exhibits modern art. Other landmarks are the Tuileries gardens, the Place de la Concorde, the Eiffel Tower, and the Champs-Elysées avenue leading to the Arc de Triomphe. Central Paris was replanned in the 19th century by Baron Haussmann. To the west is the Bois de Boulogne; Montmartre is in the north of the city; the university, founded about 1150, is on the Left Bank.

history Paris, the Roman Lutetia, capital of the Parisii, a Gaulish people, was occupied by Julius Caesar 53 BC. The Merovingian king Clovis made Paris the capital in about AD 508, and the city became important under the Capetian kings in the period 987 to 1328. Paris was occupied by the English between 1420 and 1436, and was beseiged by Henry IV between 1590 and 1594. The Bourbon kings did much to beautify the city. Napoleon I added new boulevards, bridges, and triumphal arches, as did Napoleon III. Paris was the center of the revolutions of 1789 to 1794, 1830, and 1848. It was beseiged by Prussia between 1870 and 1871, and by government troops during the Commune period (local Socialist government) from March to May 1871. During World War I it suffered from air raids and bombardment, and in World War II it was occupied by German troops between June 1940 and Aug 1944.

Paris in Greek legend, a prince of Troy whose abduction of Helen, wife of King Menelaus of Sparta, caused the Trojan war.

Paris Matthew c. 1200–1259. English chronicler. He entered St Albans Abbey 1217, and wrote a valuable history of England up to 1259.

Paris Club an international forum dating from the 1950s for the rescheduling of debts granted or guaranteed by official bilateral creditors; it has no fixed membership nor an institutional structure. In the 1980s it was closely involved in seeking solutions to the serious debt crises affecting many developing countries.

Paris Commune two periods of government in France:

The Paris municipal government 1789–94 was established after the storming of the ◊Bastille and remained powerful in the French Revolution until the fall of Robespierre 1794.

The ***provisional national government*** March 18–May 1871 was formed while Paris was besieged by the Germans during the Franco-Prussian War. It consisted of Socialists and left-wing republicans, and is often considered the first Socialist government in history. Elected after the right-wing National Assembly at Versailles tried to disarm the National Guard, it fell when the Versailles troops captured Paris and massacred 20,000–30,000 people May 21–28.

parish in the US, the ecclesiastical unit committed to one minister or priest. In Britain, a subdivision of a county often coinciding with an original territorial subdivision in Christian church administration, served by a parish church.

The origins of the parish lay in early medieval Italian cities, and by the 12th century, most of Christian Europe was divided into parishes. The parish has frequently been the center of community life, especially in rural areas.

Paris, Treaty of any of various peace treaties signed in Paris; they include:

1763 ending the ◊Seven Years' War
1783 recognizing American independence
1814 and 1815 following the abdication and final defeat of ◊Napoleon I
1856 ending the ◊Crimean War
1898 ending the ◊Spanish-American War
1919–20 the conference preparing the Treaty of ◊Versailles at the end of World War I was held in Paris
1946 after World War II the peace treaties between the ◊Allies and Italy, Romania, Hungary, Bulgaria, and Finland
1951 treaty signed by France, West Germany, Italy, Belgium, Netherlands and Luxemburg, embodying the Schuman Plan to set up a single coal and steel authority
1973 ending US participation in the ◊Vietnam war

parity in economics, equality of price, rate of exchange, wages, and buying power. Parity ratios may be used in the setting of wages to establish similar status to different work groups. Parity in international exchange rates means that those on a par with each other share similar buying power.

In the US, agricultural output prices are regulated by a parity system.

parity the state of a number, being either even or odd. In computing, a parity ◊bit is sometimes added to numbers to help ensure accuracy. The bit is chosen so that the total number of 1s, including the extra bit, is always of the same parity.

Park Merle 1937– . British ballerina, born in Rhodesia. She joined Sadler's Wells 1954, and by 1959 was a principal soloist with the Royal Ballet. She combined elegance with sympathetic appeal in such roles as Cinderella.

Parker *A virtuoso on the alto saxophone, jazz great Charlie Parker was able to improvise on any theme, from traditional ballads to rhythmic blues numbers.*

Paris Commune *Scenes of destruction under the provisional Socialist government. This statue of Napoleon had been on top of the Column Vendôme.*

Park Mungo 1771–1806. Scottish surgeon and explorer. He traced the course of the Niger river 1795–97 and probably drowned during a second expedition in 1805–06. He published *Travels in the Interior of Africa* 1799.

Park Chung Hee 1917–1979. President of South Korea 1963–79. Under his rule South Korea had one of the world's fastest-growing economies, but recession and his increasing authoritarianism led to his assassination 1979.

Parker Bonnie 1911–1943. US criminal; see ◊Bonnie and Clyde.

Parker Charlie (Charles Christopher). Nicknamed "Bird," "Yardbird." 1920–1955. US alto saxophonist and jazz composer, associated with the trumpeter Dizzy Gillespie in developing the ◊bebop style. His mastery of improvisation inspired performers on all jazz instruments.

Parker Dorothy (born Rothschild) 1893–1967. US writer and wit, a leading member of the Algonquin Round Table. She reviewed for the magazines *Vanity Fair* and *The New Yorker*, and wrote wittily ironic verses, collected in several volumes including *Not So Deep As a Well* 1940, and short stories.

She also wrote screenplays in Hollywood, having moved there from New York City along with other members of her circle.

Parkersburg city in NW West Virginia, where the Little Kanawha river flows into the Ohio river, N of Charleston. Industries include chemicals, glassware, paper, and plastics; population (1990) 33,862.

Parkes the site in New South Wales of the Australian National Radio Astronomy Observatory, featuring a radio telescope of 210-ft/64-m aperture. It is run by the Commonwealth Scientific and Industrial Research Organization.

Parkes Henry 1815–1896. Australian politician, born in the UK. He promoted education and the cause of federation, and suggested the official name "Commonwealth of Australia." He was five times premier of New South Wales 1872–91.

Parkinson Cyril Northcote 1909– . British historian, celebrated for his study of public and business administration, *Parkinson's Law* 1958, which included the dictum: "Work expands to fill the time available for its completion."

Parkinson James 1755–1824. British neurologist who first described Parkinson's disease.

Parkinson's disease or ***parkinsonism*** or ***paral-***

ysis agitans degenerative disease of the brain characterized by a progressive loss of mobility, muscular rigidity, tremor, and speech difficulties. The condition is mainly seen in people over the age of 50.

Parkinson's disease destroys a group of cells called the *substantia nigra* ("black substance") in the upper part of the ◊brainstem. These cells are concerned with the production of a neurotransmitter known as dopamine, which is essential to the control of voluntary movement. The almost total loss of these cells, and of their chemical product, produces the disabling effects.

The introduction of ◊L-dopa in the 1960s seemed at first the answer to Parkinson's disease. However, it became evident that long-term use of the drug brings considerable problems. At best, it postpones the terminal phase of the disease. Brain grafts with dopamine-producing cells were pioneered in the early 1980s, and attempts to graft Parkinson's patients with fetal brain tissue have been made. In 1989 a large US study showed that the drug deprenyl may slow the rate at which disability progresses in patients with early Parkinson's disease.

Parkman Francis 1823–1893. US historian and traveler who chronicled the European exploration and conquest of North America in such books as *The California and Oregon Trail* 1849 and *La Salle and the Discovery of the Great West* 1879.

Parkman viewed the defeat by England of the French at Québec 1759 (described in his *Montcalm and Wolfe* 1884) as the turning point of North American history, insofar as it swung the balance of power in North America toward the British colonies, which would form the United States of America.

parliament (French "speaking") the legislative body of a country. The world's oldest parliament is the Icelandic Althing from about AD 930. The UK parliament is usually dated from 1265. The Supreme Soviet of the USSR, with 1,500 members, may be the world's largest ◊legislature. The legislature of the US is called ◊Congress and comprises the ◊House of Representatives and the ◊Senate.

In the UK, Parliament is the supreme legislature, comprising the ◊House of Commons and the ◊House of Lords. The origins of Parliament are in the 13th century, but its powers were not established until the late 17th century. The powers of the Lords were curtailed 1911, and the duration of parliaments was fixed at five years, but any parliament may extend its own life, as happened during both world wars. It meets in the Palace of Westminster, London.

Parliament, Houses of the building where the UK legislative assembly meets. The present Houses of Parliament in London, designed in Gothic Revival style by the architects Charles Barry and A W Pugin, were built 1840–60, the previous building having burned down 1834. It incorporates portions of the medieval Palace of Westminster.

The Commons debating chamber was destroyed by incendiary bombs 1941: the rebuilt chamber (opened 1950) is the work of G G Scott and preserves its former character.

Parma city in Emilia-Romagna, N Italy; industries include food processing, textiles, and engineering; population (1988) 175,000. Founded by the Etruscans, it was the capital of the duchy of Parma 1545–1860. It has given its name to Parmesan cheese.

Parmenides c. 510–450 BC. Greek pre-Socratic philosopher, head of the Eleatic school (so called after Elea in S Italy). Against Heraclitus's doctrine of Becoming, Parmenides advanced the view that nonexistence was impossible, that everything was permanently in a state of being. Despite evidence of the senses to the contrary, motion and change are illusory—in fact, logically impossible—because their existence would imply a contradiction. Parmenides saw speculation and reason as more important than the evidence of the senses.

parrot

grey parrot of Africa

Parmigianino Francesco 1503–1540. Italian painter and etcher, active in Parma and elsewhere. He painted religious subjects and portraits in a Mannerist style, with elongated figures, for example *Madonna of the Long Neck* c. 1535 (Uffizi, Florence).

Parnassiens, Les school of French poets including Leconte de Lisle, Mallarmé, and Verlaine, which flourished 1866–76. Named after the review *Parnasse Contemporain*, it advocated "art for art's sake" in opposition to the ideas of the Romantics.

Parnassus mountain in central Greece, height 8,064 ft/2,457 m, revered as the abode of Apollo and the Muses. Delphi lies on its southern flank.

Parnell Charles Stewart 1846–1891. Irish nationalist politician. He supported a policy of obstruction and violence to attain ◊Home Rule, and became the president of the Nationalist Party 1877. In 1879 he approved the ◊Land League, and his attitude led to his imprisonment 1881. His career was ruined 1890 when he was cited as corespondent in a divorce case.

Parnell, born in County Wicklow, was elected member of Parliament for Meath 1875. He welcomed Gladstone's Home Rule Bill, and continued his agitation after its defeat 1886. In 1887 his reputation suffered from an unfounded accusation by *The Times* of complicity in the murder of Lord Frederick ◊Cavendish. Three years later came the adultery scandal, and for fear of losing the support of Gladstone, Parnell's party deposed him.

parody in literature and the other arts, a work that imitates the style of another work, usually with mocking or comic intent; it is related to ◊satire.

Parr Catherine 1512–1548. Sixth wife of Henry VIII of England. She had already lost two husbands when in 1543 she married Henry VIII. She survived him, and in 1547 married Lord Seymour of Sudeley (1508–1549).

Parramatta river inlet, W arm of Sydney Harbor, New South Wales, Australia. It is 15 mi/24 km long and is lined with industrial suburbs of Sydney: Balmain, Drummoyne, Concord, Parramatta, Ermington and Rydalmere, Ryde, and Hunter's Hill.

parrot any bird of the order Psittaciformes, abundant in the tropics, especially in Australia and South America. They all have hooked bills and feet adapted for tree climbing. The smaller species are commonly referred to as parakeets. They are mainly vegetarian, and range in size from the 3.5 in/8.5 cm pygmy parrot to the 40 in/100 cm Amazon parrot. The plumage is very colorful, and the call is commonly a harsh screech. The talent for imitating human speech is marked in the gray parrot *Psittacus erithacus* of Africa.

Several species are endangered. One of the rarest is the imperial parrot, found only in Dominica in the Caribbean, which is threatened by deforestation. In 1986, 600,000 parrots were caught and sold.

parsley

flower
seed heads

Parry William Edward 1790–1855. English admiral and Arctic explorer. He made detailed charts during explorations of the Northwest Passage 1819–20, 1821–23, and 1824–25.

He made an attempt to reach the North Pole 1827. The Parry Islands, Northwest Territories, Canada, are named after him.

parsec in astronomy, a unit (abbreviation pc) used for distances to stars and galaxies. One parsec is equal to 3.2617 ◊light-years, 2.063×10^5 ◊astronomical units, and 3.086×10^{13} km.

It is the distance at which a star would have a ◊parallax (apparent shift in position) of one second of arc when viewed from two points the same distance apart as the Earth's distance from the Sun; or the distance at which one astronomical unit subtends an angle of one second of arc.

Parsee or ***Parsi*** a follower of the religion ◊Zoroastrianism. The Parsees fled from Persia after its conquest by the Arabs, and settled in India in the 8th century AD. About 100,000 Parsees now live mainly in Bombay State.

Parsifal in Germanic legend, the father of ◊Lohengrin and one of the knights who sought the Holy Grail.

parsley biennial herb *Petroselinum crispum* of the carrot family Umbelliferae, cultivated for flavoring and its nutrient properties, being rich in Vitamin C and minerals. Up to 1.5 ft/45 cm high, it has pinnate, aromatic leaves and yellow umbelliferous flowers.

parsnip temperate Eurasian biennial *Pastinaca sativa* of the carrot family Umbelliferae, with a fleshy edible root.

Parsons Louella 1893–1972. US newspaper columnist. Born in Freeport, Illinois, Parsons began her newspaper career in Dixon, Illinois, soon after high school. Parsons was hired by the *New York Morning Telegraph* 1918 and later joined the ◊Hearst syndicate. She was moved to Hollywood by Hearst 1925 and began a Hollywood gossip column and a popular radio program "Hollywood Hotel" 1934. For over 40 years she exerted great influence over the lives of stars and studios.

Parsons Talcott 1902–1979. US sociologist, who attempted to integrate all the social sciences into a science of human action. He was professor of sociology at Harvard University from 1931 until his death, and author of over 150 books and articles. His theory of structural functionalism dominated US sociology from the 1940s to the 1960s, and as an attempt to explain social order and individual behavior, it was a major step in establishing sociology as an academic and scientific discipline.

part. abbreviation for participle.

parthenocarpy in botany, the formation of fruits without seeds. This phenomenon, of no obvious benefit to the plant, occurs naturally in some plants, such as bananas. It can also be induced in some fruit crops, either by breeding or by applying certain plant hormones.

Parthenon *The west front of the Parthenon, on the Acropolis in Athens, Greece.*

parthenogenesis the development of an ovum (egg) without any genetic contribution from a male. Parthenogenesis is the normal means of reproduction in a few plants (for example, dandelions) and animals (for example, certain fish). Some sexually reproducing species, such as aphids, show parthenogenesis at some stage in their life cycle.

In most cases, there is no sperm contribution of any kind, but in some the stimulus of being penetrated by a sperm is needed by the egg to start dividing, although the male's chromosomes are not combined with those of the female. Parthenogenesis can be artificially induced in many animals (such as sea urchins and rabbits) by cooling, pricking, or applying acid to an egg.

Parthenon temple of Athena Parthenos ("the Virgin") on the Acropolis at Athens; built 447–438 BC under the supervision of Phidias, and a perfect example of Doric architecture (designed by Callicrates and Ictinus). In turn a Christian church and Turkish mosque, it was then used as a gunpowder store and reduced to ruins when the Venetians bombarded the Acropolis 1687. Many Greek sculptures were removed from the Parthenon by the British diplomat Lord Elgin in the early 19th century to be studied and displayed in the British Musuem as the ◊Elgin marbles.

Parthia ancient country in W Asia in what is now NE Iran, capital Ctesiphon. Originating about 248 BC, it reached the peak of its power under Mithridates I in the 2nd century BC, and was annexed to Persia under the Sassanids AD 226. Parthian horsemen feigned retreat and shot their arrows unexpectedly backwards, hence "Parthian shot," a remark delivered in parting.

participle in grammar, a form of the verb, in English either a present participle ending in *-ing* (for example, "work*ing*" in "They were *working,*" "*working* men," and "a hard-*working* team") or a past participle ending in *-ed* in regular verbs (for example, "train*ed*" in "They have been *trained* well," "*trained* soldiers," and "a well-*trained* team").

particle physics the study of the properties of ◊elementary particles and of fundamental interactions (see ◊fundamental forces).

Pioneering research took place at the Cavendish laboratory, Cambridge, England. In 1895 Joseph Thomson discovered that all atoms contain identical, negatively charged particles called electrons that could easily be freed. By 1913 Ernest Rutherford had shown that electrons surround a very small, positively charged nucleus (which in the case of a hydrogen atom consists of a single positively charged particle, a proton, identified by James Chadwick in 1932). The nuclei of all the other elements are made up of protons and uncharged particles called neutrons.

1932 also saw the discovery of a particle (predicted in 1928 by Paul Dirac), with the mass of an electron, but an equal and opposite charge, called the positron. This was the first example of an antiparticle; it is now known that almost all particles have corresponding antiparticles. In 1933 Wolfgang ◊Pauli argued that a hitherto unsuspected particle must accompany electrons in beta-ray emission—the so-called electron-neutrino.

particle physics *The drift chamber of the Mark II particle detector at the Stanford Linear Accelerator center in California, which allows physicists to study the tracks of subatomic particles.*

particles and fundamental forces by the mid-1930s, four ◊fundamental forces had been identified: (1) The electromagnetic force acts between all particles with electric charge, and was thought to be related to the exchange between the particles of photons, packets of electromagnetic radiation. (2) In 1935 the Japanese physicist Hideki Yukawa suggested that the strong force (holding protons and neutrons together in the nucleus) was caused by the exchange of particles with a mass of about a tenth that of a proton; these particles, called pions (originally pi-mesons), were found by British physicist Cecil Powell in 1946. (3) Theoretical work on the weak force began with Enrico ◊Fermi in the 1930s. The existence of the particles that carry the weak force, the W and Z particles (weakons), was confirmed in 1983 at ◊CERN. (4) The fourth fundamental force, gravitation, is experienced by all matter, the postulated carrier of this force being the graviton.

leptons, hadrons, and quarks the electron, three types of neutrinos, and the muon are the leptons—particles with half-integral spin that "feel" the weak, but not the strong, force. The muon (found by US physicist Carl Anderson in cosmic radiation in 1937) produces the muon neutrino when it decays. The tauon, a surprise discovery of the 1970s, produces the tauon neutrino when it decays.

Hadrons (particles that "feel" the strong force) started to turn up in bewildering profusion in experiments in the 1950s and 1960s. They are classified into ◊mesons, with whole-number or zero spins, and baryons (which include protons and neutrons), with half-integral spins. It was shown in the early 1960s that if hadrons of the same spin are represented as points on suitable charts, simple patterns are formed. This symmetry enabled a hitherto unknown particle, the omega-minus, to be predicted from a gap in one of the patterns; it then turned up in experiments. In 1964, Murray Gell-Mann suggested that all hadrons were composed of just three types or "flavors" of a new particle with half-integral spin and a charge of magnitude either ⅓ or ⅔ that of an electron; Gell-Mann christened the particle ◊quark. Mesons are quark–antiquark pairs (spins either add to one or cancel to zero), and baryons are quark triplets. To account for new mesons, such as the psi, the number of quark flavors was discovered to be six by 1985 (up, down, top, bottom, strange, and charm).

particle, subatomic see ◊subatomic particle.

partisan member of an armed group that operates behind enemy lines or in occupied territories during wars. The name "partisans" was first given to armed bands of Russians who operated against Napoleon's army in Russia during 1812, but has since been used to describe Russian, Yugoslav, Italian, Greek, and Polish ◊Resistance groups against the Germans during World War II.

Partisan Review US intellectual and literary magazine, founded 1934 to express Marxist principles. In the later 1930s it departed from the orthodox line, and committed itself to Modernist literature.

During the 1950s the magazine published many of the major writers and critics of the time, including Saul Bellow, Mary McCarthy, and Lionel Trilling.

partnership two or more persons carrying on a common business for shared profit. The business can be of any kind—for instance, lawyers, shop owners, or window cleaners. A partnership differs from a corporation in that the individuals remain separate in identity and are not protected by limited liability, so that each partner is personally responsible for any debts of the partnership.

In a limited partnership, a general partner or partners with a limited liability manage the enterprise, while limited partners have no management rights and their liability is limited to their investment.

part of speech the grammatical function of a word, as categorized in the grammar of Western languages. The four major parts of speech are the noun, verb, adjective, and adverb; the minor parts of speech vary according to schools of grammatical theory, but include the article, conjunction, preposition, and pronoun.

In languages like Greek and Latin, the part of speech of a word tends to be invariable (usually marked by an ending, or ◊inflection); in English, it is much harder to recognize the function of a word simply by its form. Some English words may have only one function (for example, *and* as a conjunction). Others may have several functions (for example, *fancy,* which is a noun in the phrase "flights of *fancy,*" a verb in "*Fancy* that!," and an adjective in "a *fancy* hat").

partridge any of various medium-sized ground-dwelling fowl of the family Phasianidae, which also includes pheasants, quail, and chickens.

Partridges are Old World birds, some of which have become naturalized in North America, especially the European gray partridge *Perdix perdix,* with mottled brown back, gray speckled breast, and patches of chestnut on the sides.

Partridge Eric 1894–1979. New Zealand lexicographer. He studied at Oxford University and settled in England to write a number of dictionaries, including *A Dictionary of Slang and Unconventional English* 1934 and 1970, and *Dictionary of the Underworld, British and American* 1950.

Parvati in Hindu mythology, the consort of Siva in one of her gentler manifestations, and the mother of Ganesa, the god of prophecy; she is said to be the daughter of the Himalayas.

Pasadena city in SW California, part of Greater Los Angeles; population (1990) 131,591. Manufactures include electronic equipment and precision instruments. The California Institute of Technology and the Jet Propulsion Laboratory (administered jointly by the institute and the federal government) are here. Each New Year's Day, Pasadena is host to the Tournament of Roses parade and a major college football game at the Rose Bowl. Farmers from Indiana founded a settlement here 1874.

Pascagoula city in SE Mississippi at the mouth of the Pascagoula river, E of Biloxi. Industries include fishing, shipbuilding, paper, petroleum, and chemicals; population (1990) 25,899. A French fort 1718, it was at other times owned by Britain, Spain, and the free state of West Florida.

PASCAL high-level computer-programming language. Designed by Niklaus Wirth (1934–) in the 1960s as an aid to teaching programming, it is still widely used as such in universities, but is also recognized as a good general-purpose programming language.

Pascal's triangle

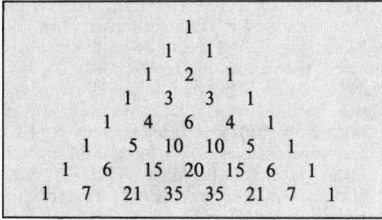

							1							
						1		1						
					1		2		1					
				1		3		3		1				
			1		4		6		4		1			
		1		5		10		10		5		1		
	1		6		15		20		15		6		1	
1		7		21		35		35		21		7		1

pascal SI unit (abbreviation Pa) of pressure, equal to one newton per square meter. It replaces ◊bars and millibars (10^5 Pa equals one bar). It is named after the French scientist Blaise Pascal.

Pascal Blaise 1623–1662. French philosopher and mathematician. He contributed to the development of hydraulics, the ◊calculus, and the mathematical theory of ◊probability.

In mathematics, Pascal is known for his work on conic sections and, with Pierre de Fermat, the probability theory. In physics, Pascal's chief work concerned fluid pressure and hydraulics. Pascal's principle states that the pressure everywhere in a fluid is the same, so that pressure applied at one point is transmitted equally to all parts of the container. This is the principle of the hydraulic press and jack.

Pascal's triangle is a triangular array of numbers in which each number is the sum of the pair of numbers above it. Plotted at equal distances along a horizontal axis, the numbers in the rows give the binomial probability distribution with equal probability of success and failure, such as when tossing fair coins.

In 1654 he went into the ◊Jansenist monastery of Port Royal and defended a prominent Jansenist, Antoine Arnauld (1612–1694), against the ◊Jesuits in his *Lettres Provinciales* 1656. His *Pensées* 1670 was part of an unfinished defense of the Christian religion.

Pasco city in SE Washington, on the Columbia river, seat of Franklin county; population (1990) 20,337.

Pas-de-Calais French name for the Strait of Dover and of the French *département* bordering it, of which Arras is the capital and Calais the chief port. See also ◊Nord-Pas-de-Calais.

pas de deux a dance for two performers. A *grand pas de deux* is danced by the prima ballerina and the premier danseur.

Pashto language or ***Pushtu*** Indo-European language, officially that of Afghanistan, also spoken in another dialect in N Pakistan.

Pasiphae in Greek mythology, wife of ◊Minos and mother of ◊Phaedra and of the ◊Minotaur, the offspring of her sexual union with a bull sent from the sea by the god ◊Poseidon.

Pasolini Pier Paolo 1922–1975. Italian poet, novelist, and film director, an influential figure of the postwar years. His writings (making much use of first Friulan and later Roman dialect) include the novels *Ragazzi di vita/The Ragazzi* 1955 and *Una vita violenta/A Violent Life* 1959. Among his films are *Il vangelo secondo Mateo/The Gospel According to St Matthew* 1964 and *I racconti de Canterbury/The Canterbury Tales* 1972.

Much of his work is colored by his experience of life in the poor districts of Rome, where he lived from 1950, and illustrates the decadence and inequality of society from his Marxist viewpoint.

pasqueflower plant *Anemone patens* of the buttercup family. It has a hairy stalk and hairy leaves near the base. The showy lavender-blue flowers are 2 in/5 cm across; native to the central US.

Passaic city in NW New Jersey, on the Passaic river, N of Jersey City. Manufactures include television cables, chemicals, plastics, pharmaceuticals, and clothing; population (1990) 58,041.

Passau town in SE Bavaria, Federal Republic of Germany, at the junction of the rivers Inn and Ilz with the Danube. The Treaty of Passau 1552 between Maurice, elector of Saxony, and the future emperor Ferdinand I allowed the Lutherans full religious liberty and prepared the way for the Peace of Augsburg: see ◊Reformation.

Pasteur *French chemist and scientist Louis Pasteur.*

Passchendaele village in W Flanders, Belgium, near Ypres. The Passchendaele ridge before Ypres was the object of a costly and unsuccessful British offensive in World War I, between July and Nov 1917; British casualties numbered nearly 400,000.

passion flower climbing plant of the tropical American genus *Passiflora*, family Passifloraceae. It bears distinctive flower heads comprising a saucer-shaped petal base, a fringelike corona, and a central stalk bearing the stamens and ovary. Some species produce edible fruit.

passion play play representing the death and resurrection of a god, such as Osiris, Dionysus, or Jesus; it has its origins in medieval ◊mystery plays. Traditionally, a passion play takes place every ten years at ◊Oberammergau, Germany.

pass laws South African laws that required the black population to carry passbooks (identity documents) at all times and severely restricted freedom of movement. The laws, a major cause of discontent, formed a central part of the policies of ◊apartheid. They were repealed 1986

Passover also called *Pesach* in Judaism, an eight-day spring festival which commemorates the exodus of the Israelites from Egypt and the passing over by the Angel of Death of the Jewish houses, so that only the Egyptian firstborn sons were killed.

The Last Supper was a Passover seder.

passport document issued by a national government authorizing the bearer to leave the country and guaranteeing the bearer the state's protection. Some countries require an intending visitor to obtain a special endorsement or visa.

Passy Frédéric 1822–1912. French economist, who shared the first Nobel Peace Prize 1901 with Jean-Henri Dunant. He founded the International League for Permanent Peace 1867, and was cofounder, with the English politician William Cremer (1828–1908), of the Inter-Parliamentary Conferences on Peace and on Arbitration 1889.

Pasternak Boris Leonidovich 1890–1960. Russian poet and novelist. His volumes of lyric poems include *A Twin Cloud* 1914 and *On Early Trains* 1943, and he translated Shakespeare's tragedies. His novel ◊*Dr Zhivago* 1957 was banned in the USSR as a "hostile act," and followed by a Nobel Prize (which he declined). *Dr Zhivago* has since been unbanned and Pasternak posthumously rehabilitated.

Pasteur Louis 1822–1895. French chemist and microbiologist who discovered that fermentation is caused by microorganisms. He also developed a vaccine for ◊rabies, which led to the foundation of the Institut Pasteur in Paris 1888.

Pasteur saved the French silkworm industry by identifying two microbial diseases that were decimating the worms. He discovered the pathogens responsible for ◊anthrax and chicken cholera, and developed vaccines for these diseases. He inspired his pupil ◊Lister's work in antiseptic surgery. Pasteurization to make dairy products free from the tuberculosis bacteria is based on his discoveries; see also ◊food technology.

pasteurization treatment of food to reduce the number of microorganisms it contains and so protect consumers from disease. Harmful bacteria are killed and the development of others is delayed. For milk, the method involves heating it to 161°F/72°C for 15 seconds followed by rapid cooling to 50°F/10°C or lower.

The experiments of Louis Pasteur on wine and beer in the 1850s and 1860s showed how heat treatment slowed the multiplication of bacteria and thereby the process of souring. Pasteurization of milk made headway in the dairy industries of Scandinavia and the US before 1900 because of the realization that it also killed off bacteria associated with the diseases of tuberculosis, typhoid, diphtheria, and dysentery.

Patagonia geographic area of South America, S of latitude 40° S, with sheep farming, and coal and oil resources. Sighted by Magellan 1520, it was claimed by both Argentina and Chile until divided between them 1881.

patchouli soft-wooded Indian shrub *Pogostemon heyneanus* of the mint family Labiateae, source of the perfume patchouli.

Patel Vallabhbhai Jhaverbhai 1875–1950. Indian political leader. A fervent follower of Mohandas Gandhi and a leader of the Indian National Congress, he held a number of positions in Nehru's first government after independence.

patella or ***knee cap*** a flat bone embedded in the knee tendon of birds and mammals, which protects the joint from injury.

paten flat dish of gold or silver used in the Christian church for holding the consecrated bread at the Eucharist.

patent or ***letters patent*** documents conferring the exclusive right to make, use, and sell an invention for a limited period. Ideas are not eligible; neither is anything not new.

In the US, the period of patent is 17 years. In 1987 the US began issuing patents for new animal forms (new types of livestock and assorted organisms) being created by DNA research, recombinant DNA, and other forms of genetic tampering.

Pater Walter Horatio 1839–1894. English critic. A stylist and supporter of "art for art's sake," he published *Studies in the History of the Renaissance* 1873, *Marius the Epicurean* 1885, *Imaginary Portraits* 1887, and other works.

Paternoster (Latin "our father") in the Roman Catholic Church, the Lord's Prayer. The opening words of the Latin version are *Pater noster*.

Paterson William 1745–1806. Irish-born US Supreme Court justice and political leader. Paterson immigrated to America with his family 1747 and graduated from Princeton 1763. Admitted to the bar 1769, he served as a member of the provincial congress 1775–76 and as New Jersey attorney general 1776–83. He was a member of the Constitutional Convention 1787 and was elected one of New Jersey's first US senators 1789. After serving as New Jersey governor 1790–93, Paterson was appointed to the US Supreme Court by President Washington, where he served as associate justice 1793–1806. He was noted for his vigorous prosecution of cases under the Sedition Act of 1798.

Pathan Muslim people of NW Pakistan and Afghanistan. Formerly a constant threat to the British Raj, the Pakistani Pathans are now claiming independence, with the Afghani Pathans, in their own state of Pakhtoonistan, although this has not yet been recognized.

Pathé Charles 1863–1957. French film pioneer who began his career selling projectors in 1896 and with the profits formed Pathé Frères with his brothers. In 1901 he embarked on film production and by 1908 had becomed the world's biggest

pasteurization

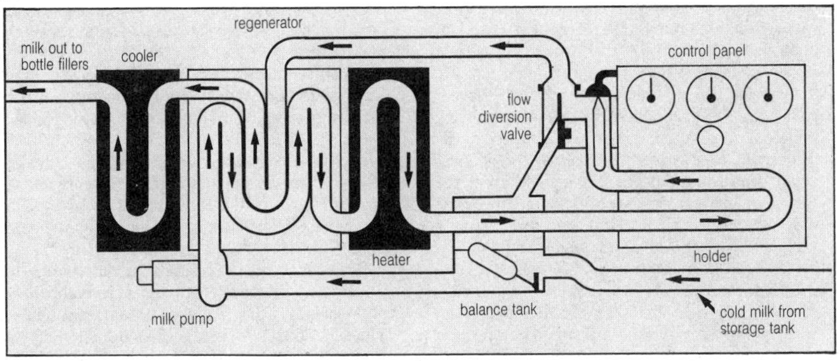
regenerator
milk out to bottle fillers
cooler
control panel
flow diversion valve
heater
holder
milk pump
balance tank
cold milk from storage tank

producer, with branches worldwide. He also developed an early color process and established a weekly newsreel, *Pathé Gazette*. World War I disrupted his enterprises and by 1918 he was gradually forced out of business by foreign competition.

pathogen (Greek "disease producing") in medicine, a bacterium or virus or other microorganism that causes disease. Most pathogens are ◊parasites, and the diseases they cause are incidental to their search for food or shelter inside the host. Nonparasitic organisms, such as soil bacteria or those living in our alimentary canal and feeding on waste foodstuffs, can also become pathogenic to a person whose immune system or liver is damaged. The larger parasites that can cause disease, such as nematode worms, are not usually described as pathogens.

pathology medical specialty concerned with the study of disease processes and how these provoke structural and functional chnges in the body and its tissues.

Patiala city in E Punjab, India; industries (textile and metalwork); population (1981) 206,254.

Patinir (also ***Patenier*** or ***Patinier***) Joachim c. 1485–1524. Flemish painter, active in Antwerp, whose inspired landscape backgrounds dominated his religious subjects. He is known to have worked with Matsys and to have painted landscape backgrounds for other artists' works.

Patmos Greek island in the Aegean, one of the Dodecanese; the chief town is Hora. St John is said to have written the New Testament Book of Revelation while in exile here.

Patna capital of Bihar state, India, on the river Ganges; population (1981) 916,000. It has remains of a hall built by the emperor Asoka in the 3rd century BC.

Paton Alan 1903–1988. South African writer. His novel *Cry, the Beloved Country* 1948 focused on racial inequality in South Africa. Later books include the study *Land and People of South Africa* 1956, *The Long View* 1968, and his autobiography *Toward the Mountain* 1980.

Born in Pietermaritzburg, he became a schoolmaster and in 1935 the principal of a reformatory near Johannesburg, which he ran along enlightened lines.

Patou Jean 1880–1936. French designer of sporting clothes (as worn by tennis player Suzanne ◊Lenglen) from 1922 and bias-cut white satin evening dresses 1929.

He created the perfume Joy 1926.

Patras (Greek *Patrai*) industrial city (hydroelectric installations, textiles, paper) in the NW Peloponnese, Greece, on the Gulf of Patras; population (1981) 141,500. The ancient Patrae is the only one of the 12 cities of ◊Achaea to survive.

patriarch (Greek "ruler of a family") in the Old Testament, one of the ancestors of the human race, and especially those of the ancient Hebrews, from Adam to Abraham, Isaac, Jacob, and his sons (who became patriarchs of the Hebrew tribes). In the Eastern Orthodox Church, the term refers to the leader of a national church.

patrician a member of the privileged class in ancient Rome, descended from the original citizens. After the 4th century BC the rights formerly exercised by the patricians alone were made available to the ◊plebeians, and patrician descent became only a matter of prestige.

Patrick, St 389–c. 461. Patron saint of Ireland. Born in Britain, probably in S Wales, he was carried off by pirates to six years' slavery in Antrim, Ireland before escaping either to Britain or Gaul—his poor Latin suggests the former—to train as a missionary. He is variously said to have landed again in Ireland 432 or 456, and his work was a vital factor in the spread of Christian influence there. His symbols are snakes and shamrocks; feast day Mar 17.

Patriot missile ground-to-air medium-range missile system used in an air defense role. It has high-altitude coverage, electronic jamming capability, and excellent mobility. It was tested in battle against ◊SCUD missiles fired by the Iraqis in the 1991 Gulf War.

patronage the power to give a favored appointment to an office or position in politics, business, or the church; or sponsorship of the arts. Patronage was for centuries bestowed mainly by individuals (often royal or noble) or by the church. In this century, patrons have tended to be political parties, the state, and—in the arts—private industry and foundations.

Patterson Harry 1929– . English novelist, born in Newcastle. He has written many thrillers under his own name, including *Dillinger* 1983, as well as under the pseudonym Jack Higgins, including *The Eagle Has Landed* 1975.

Patti Adelina 1843–1919. Anglo-Italian soprano renowned for her performances of Lucia in *Lucia di Lammermoor* and Amina in *La sonnambula*. At the age of 62 she was persuaded out of retirement to make a number of phonograph recordings, thus becoming one of the first opera singers to be recorded.

Patton George (Smith) 1885–1945. US general in World War II, known as "Blood and Guts." He commanded the 2nd Armored Division 1940, and in 1942 led the Western Task Force that landed at Casablanca, Morocco. After commanding the 7th Army, he led the 3rd Army across France and into Germany, and in 1945 took over the 15th Army.

Patton was an outspoken advocate of mobility and armor. He played a central role in stopping the German counteroffensive at the Battle of the ◊Bulge Dec 1944–Jan 1945.

Pau industrial city (electrochemical and metallurgical products) and resort, capital of Pyrénées-Atlantiques *département* in Aquitaine, SW France, near the Spanish border; population (1982) 131,500. It is the center of the ◊Basque area of France, and the site of fierce guerrilla activity.

Paul Elliot Harold 1891–1958. US author. His works include the novel *Indelible* 1922, about two young musicians, and the travel book *The Narrow Street/The Last Time I Saw Paris* 1942.

Paul Les. Adopted name of Lester Polfuss 1915– US inventor of the solid-body electric guitar in the early 1940s, and a pioneer of recording techniques including overdubbing and electronic echo. The Gibson Les Paul guitar was first marketed 1952 (the first commercial solid-body guitar was made by Leo ◊Fender). As a guitarist in the late 1940s and 1950s he recorded with the singer Mary Ford (1928–1977).

***Patton** An accomplished fencer, sailor, airplane pilot, and athlete, US General Patton demanded rigorous standards of individual fitness and unit training of his troops during World War II.*

Paul 1901–1964. King of the Hellenes from 1947, when he succeeded his brother George II. He was the son of Constantine I. In 1938 he married Princess Frederika (1917–), daughter of the Duke of Brunswick. Her involvement in politics brought her under attack.

Paul six popes, including:

Paul VI Giovanni Battista Montini 1897–1978. Pope from 1963. His encyclical *Humanae Vitae/Of Human Life* 1968 reaffirmed the church's traditional teaching on birth control, thus following the minority report of the commission originally appointed by Pope John, rather than the majority view.

He was born near Brescia, Italy. He spent more than 25 years in the Secretariat of State under Pius XI and Pius XII before becoming archbishop of Milan in 1954. In 1958 he was created a cardinal by Pope John, and in 1963 he succeeded him as pope, taking the name of Paul as a symbol of ecumenical unity.

Paul I 1754–1801. Tsar of Russia from 1796, in succession to his mother Catherine II. Mentally unstable, he pursued an erratic foreign policy and was assassinated.

Paul, St c. AD 3–c. 68. Christian missionary and martyr; in the New Testament, one of the apostles and author of 13 epistles. He is said to have been converted by a vision on the road to Damascus. His emblems are a sword and a book; feast day June 29.

The Hebrew form of his name is Saul. He was born in Tarsus (now in Turkey), son of well-to-do Pharisees, and had Roman citizenship. Originally opposed to Christianity, he took part in the stoning of St Stephen. After his conversion he made great missionary journeys, for example to ◊Philippi and ◊Ephesus, becoming known as the Apostle of the Gentiles (non-Jews). On his return to Jerusalem, he was arrested, appealed to Caesar, and (as a citizen) was sent to Rome for trial about 57 or 59. After two years in prison, he may have been released before his final arrest and execution under the emperor Nero.

St Paul's theology was rigorous on such questions as sin and atonement, and his views on the role of women were adopted by the Christian church generally.

Pauli Wolfgang 1900–1958. Austrian physicist, who originated Pauli's exclusion principle: in a given system no two electrons, protons, neutrons, or other elementary particles of half-integral spin can be characterized by the same set of ◊quantum numbers. He also predicted the existence of neutrinos. He won a Nobel Prize 1945 for his work on atomic structure.

Pauling Linus Carl 1901– . US chemist, author of fundamental work on the nature of the chemical bond and on the discovery of the helical structure of many proteins.

He has investigated the properties and uses of vitamin C as related to human health. He was awarded the Nobel Prize for Chemistry 1954. An outspoken opponent of nuclear testing, he also received the Nobel Peace Prize in 1962.

Paulus Friedrich von 1890–1957. German field marshal in World War II, commander of the forces that besieged Stalingrad (now Volgograd) in the USSR 1942–43; he was captured and gave evidence at the Nuremberg trials before settling in East Germany.

Pausanias 2nd century AD. Greek geographer, author of a valuably accurate description of Greece compiled from his own travels, *Description of Greece*, also translated as *Itinerary of Greece*.

Pavarotti Luciano 1935– . Italian tenor, whose operatic roles have included Rodolfo in *La Bohème*, Cavaradossi in *Tosca*, the Duke of Mantua in *Rigoletto*, and Nemorino in *L'Elisir d'amore*.

Pavia, Battle of battle 1525 between France and the Holy Roman Empire. The Hapsburg emperor Charles V defeated and captured Francis I; it signified the onset of Hapsburg dominance in Italy.

Pavlov Ivan Petrovich 1849–1936. Russian physiologist who studied conditioned reflexes in animals. His work had a great impact on behavioral theory (see ◊behaviorism) and ◊learning theory. See also ◊conditioning.

Pavlova Anna 1881–1931. Russian dancer. Prima ballerina of the Imperial Ballet from 1906, she left Russia 1913, and went on to become the world's most celebrated exponent of Classical ballet. With London as her home, she toured extensively with her own company, influencing dancers worldwide with roles such as Mikhail ◊Fokine's *The Dying Swan* solo 1905.

pawnbroker one who lends money on the security of goods held. The traditional sign of the premises is three gold balls, the symbol used in front of the houses of the medieval Lombard merchants of Italy.

pawpaw or ***papaw*** small tree *Asimina triloba* of the custard-apple family Annonaceae, native to the eastern US. It bears oblong fruits 5 in/13 cm long with yellowish, edible flesh.

Pawtucket city in NE Rhode Island, on the Blackstone river, NE of Providence. Industries include textiles, thread, machinery, and metal and glass products; population (1990) 72,644. It was the home of the first US water-powered cotton mill 1790.

Pax Roman goddess of peace; Greek counterpart ◊Irene.

Paxton Joseph 1801–1865. English architect, garden superintendent to the Duke of Devonshire from 1826 and designer of the Great Exhibition building 1851 (◊Crystal Palace), revolutionary in its structural use of glass and iron.

Paysandú city in Uruguay, capital of Paysandú department, on the river Uruguay; population (1985) 74,000. Canned meat is the main product. The city dates from 1772 and is linked by bridge 1976 with Puerto Colón in Argentina.

Pays de la Loire agricultural region of W France, comprising the *départements* of Loire-Atlantique, Maine-et-Loire, Mayenne, Sarthe, and Vendée; capital Nantes; area 12,391 sq mi/32,100 sq km; population (1986) 3,018,000. ndustries include shipbuilding and wine.

Paz Octavio 1914– . Mexican poet and essayist. His works reflect many influences, including Marxism, surrealism, and Aztec mythology. His celebrated poem *Piedra del sol/Sun Stone* 1957 uses contrasting images, centering upon the Aztec Calendar Stone (representing the Aztec universe), to symbolize the loneliness of individuals and their search for union with others. Nobel Prize for Literature 1990.

Paz Estenssoro Victor 1907– . President of Bolivia 1952–56, 1960–64, and 1985–89. He founded and led the Movimiento Nacionalista Revolucionario (Nationalist Revolutionary Movement; MNR), which seized power 1952. His regime extended the vote to Indians, nationalized the country's largest tin mines, embarked on a major program of agrarian reform, and brought inflation under control.

After holding a number of financial posts he entered politics in the 1930s and in 1942 founded the (MNR).

In exile in Argentina, during one of Bolivia's many periods of military rule, he returned in 1951 and became president in 1952. He immediately embarked on a program of political reform, retaining the presidency until 1956 and being re-elected 1960–64 and again in 1985, returning from near-retirement at the age of 77. During his long career he was Bolivian ambassador in London (1956–59) and a professor at London University (1966).

PCB abbreviation for ◊polychlorinated biphenyl; ◊printed circuit board.

PCP abbreviation for phencyclidine hydrochloride, a drug popularly known as ◊angel dust.

pea climbing plant *Pisum sativum*, family Leguminosae, with pods of edible seeds. The sweet pea *Lathyrus odoratus* of the same family is grown for its scented, butterfly-shaped flowers.

Peace river formed in British Columbia, Canada, by the union at Finlay Forks of the Finlay and Parsnip rivers and flowing through the Rocky Mountains and across Alberta to join the river Slave just N of Lake Athabasca; length 1,000 mi/1,600 km.

Peace Corps an organization of trained men and women, established in the US by President Kennedy 1961, providing skilled volunteer workers for the developing countries, especially in the fields of teaching, agriculture, and health. Living among the country's inhabitants, workers are paid only a small allowance to cover their basic needs and maintain health. The Peace Corps was inspired by the British program Voluntary Service Overseas.

peace movement the collective opposition to war. The Western peace movements of the late 20th century can trace their origins to the ◊pacifists of the 19th century and conscientious objectors during World War I. The campaigns after World War II have tended to concentrate on nuclear weapons, but there are numerous organizations devoted to peace, some wholly pacifist, some merely opposed to escalation.

Other organizations are concerned with the future of life on planet Earth and the environment. In the US, opposition to the Vietnam War, which grew from the late 1960s, was the primary post–World War II peace movement. It greatly influenced US politics and society, although Ban the Bomb opposition was older, a post–World War II posture against nuclear weapons.

peach tree *Prunus persica*, family Rosaceae. It has ovate leaves and small, usually pink flowers. The yellowish edible fruits have thick velvety skins; the ◊nectarine is a smooth-skinned variety.

peacock technically, the name for the male of any of various large pheasants. The name is most often used for the common peacock *Pavo cristatus*, a bird of the pheasant family, native to S Asia. It is rather larger than a pheasant. The male has a large fan-shaped tail, brightly colored with blue, green, and purple "eyes" on a chestnut background. The female (peahen) is brown with a small tail.

Peak District tableland of the S Pennines in NW Derbyshire, England. It is a tourist region and a national park (1951). The highest point is Kinder Scout, 2,088 ft/636 m.

Peale Charles Willson 1741–1827. American artist, head of a large family of painters. His portraits of leading figures in the Revolutionary War include the earliest known portrait of George Washington 1772.

Peale was also a naturalist, interested in paleontology and taxidermy, and an inventor. Five of Peale's 17 children also became painters—Titian Peale (1799–1885), animal painter; Rubens Peale (1784–1865), still-life painter; Raphaelle Peale (1774–1825), still-life and portrait painter; Rembrandt Peale (1778–1860), portrait and historical painter; and Franklin Peale (1795–1890), natural history painter. His brother James Peale (1749–1831) and James's daughters were portrait painters and miniaturists.

Peale Norman Vincent 1898– . US religious leader. After serving congregations in Brooklyn 1924–27 and Syracuse 1927–32, he became pastor of the Marble Collegiate Church in New York City. Through his radio program and book *The Art of Living* 1948, Peale became one of the best-known religious figures in the country. His *The Power of Positive Thinking* 1952 became a national bestseller. Peale was elected president of the Reformed Church in America in 1969.

Born in Bowersville, Ohio, Peale was educated at Ohio Wesleyan University and was ordained in the Methodist Episcopal Church in 1922.

peanut or ***groundnut*** or ***monkey nut*** South American vinelike annual plant *Arachis hypogaea*, family Leguminosae. After flowering, the flower stalks bend and force the pods into the earth to ripen underground. The nuts are a staple food in many tropical countries and widely grown in the southern US. They yield a valuable edible oil and are the basis for numerous processed foods.

pear tree *Pyrus communis*, family Rosaceae, native to temperate regions of Eurasia. It has a succulent edible fruit, less hardy than the apple.

pearl a shiny, hard, rounded abnormal growth composed of nacre (or ◊mother-of pearl), a chalky substance. It is secreted by many mollusks, and deposited in thin layers on the inside of the shell around a parasite, a grain of sand, or some other irritant body. After several years of the mantle (the layer of tissue between the shell and the body mass) secreting this nacre, a pearl is formed.

Although commercially valuable pearls are obtained from freshwater mussels and oysters, precious pearls come from the various species of the family Pteriidae (the pearl oysters) found in tropical waters off N and W Australia, off the California coast, in the Persian Gulf, and in the Indian Ocean.

Artificial pearls were first cultivated in Japan in 1893. A tiny bead of shell from a clam, plus a small piece of membrane from another pearl oyster's mantle (to stimulate the secretion of nacre) is inserted in oysters kept in cages in the sea for three years, and then the pearls are harvested. Because of their rarity, a large mussel pearl of perfect shape is worth more than that from an oyster.

Pearl Harbor an inlet of the Pacific Ocean where the US naval base is situated in Hawaii on Oahu Island. It was the scene of a Japanese surprise air attack on Dec 7, 1941, that brought the US into World War II. It took place while Japanese envoys were holding so-called peace talks in Washington. The local commanders Admiral Kummel and Lieutenant General Short were relieved of their posts and held responsible for the fact that the base, despite warnings, was totally unprepared at the time of the attack. About 3,300 US military personnel were killed, 4 battleships were lost, and a large part of the US Pacific fleet was destroyed or damaged. The Japanese, angered by US embargoes of oil and other war materiel and convinced that US entry into the war was inevitable, opted to strike a major blow in hopes of forcing US concessions. Instead, it galvanized public opinion and raised anti-Japanese sentiment to a fever pitch, with war declared thereafter.

Today it is a submarine base, supply center, and naval shipyard.

Pears Peter 1910–1986. English tenor. A cofounder with Benjamin ◊Britten of the Aldeburgh Festival, he was closely associated with the composer's work and sang the title role in *Peter Grimes.*

Pearse Patrick Henry 1879–1916. Irish poet prominent in the Gaelic revival, a leader of the ◊Easter Rising 1916. Proclaimed president of the provisional government, he was court-martialed and shot after its suppression.

Pearson Drew 1897–1969. US newspaper columnist. Born in Evanston, Illinois, and educated at Swarthmore College, Pearson worked as a foreign correspondent and joined the Washington bureau of the *Baltimore Sun* 1929. Although his frank, anonymously published exposé *Washington Merry-Go-Round* 1931 became a bestseller, he was fired from the *Sun* when his authorship became known. In 1932, however, he began openly publishing a syndicated column of the same name, working in conjunction with Robert Allen until 1942. Pearson continued the column alone until his death, after which it was taken over by Jack Anderson.

Pearson Karl 1857–1936. British statistician who followed Francis ◊Galton in introducing statistics and probability into genetics and who developed the concept of eugenics (improving the human race by selective breeding). He introduced the term ◊standard deviation into statistics.

Pearson Lester Bowles 1897–1972. Canadian politician, leader of the Liberal Party from 1958, prime minister 1963–68. As foreign minister 1948–57, he represented Canada at the United Nations, playing a key role in settling the ◊Suez Crisis 1956. Nobel Peace Prize 1957.

He served as president of the General Assembly 1952–53 and helped to create the UN Emergency Force (UNEF) that policed Sinai following the Egypt–Israel war of 1956. As prime minister, Pearson led the way to formulating a national medicare law.

Peary Robert Edwin 1856–1920. US polar explorer who, after several unsuccessful attempts, became the first person to reach the North Pole on Apr 6, 1909. In 1988 an astronomer claimed Peary's measurements were incorrect.

He sailed to Cape Sheridan in the *Roosevelt* with his aide Matthew Henson, and they then made a sled journey to the Pole.

One of his companions on an 1891 voyage was Frederick A. Cook who, in 1909, claimed he had reached the North Pole before Peary. Although Cook's claim is generally discredited, it continues to cast a shadow over Peary's achievment.

peasant a country-dweller engaged in small-scale farming. A peasant normally owns or rents a small amount of land, aiming to be self-sufficient and to sell surplus supplies locally.

In the UK, the move toward larger farms in the 18th century resulted in the disappearance of the independent peasantry, although the custom survives in smallholdings and Scottish crofts. Landowners in countries such as France, Spain, and Italy showed less direct interest in agriculture, so the tradition of small independent landholding remains a distinctive way of life today. See also ◊commune.

Peasants' Revolt the rising of the English peasantry June 1381.

Following the Black Death, there was a shortage of agricultural workers, which led to higher wages. The Statute of Labourers, enacted 1351, attempted to return wages to preplague levels. When a poll tax was enforced 1379, riots broke out all over England, especially in Essex and Kent. Led by Wat ◊Tyler and John ◊Ball, the rebels sacked Canterbury, and marched to London, where they continued plundering, burning John of Gaunt's palace at the Savoy, and taking the prisons at Newgate and Fleet. The young king Richard II attempted to appease the mob, who demanded an end to serfdom and feudalism. The rebels then took the Tower of London and murdered Archbishop Sudbury and Robert Hales. Again the king attempted to make peace at Smithfield, but Tyler was stabbed to death by William Walworth, the Lord Mayor of London. The king made concessions to the rebels, and they dispersed, but the concessions were revoked immediately.

peat fibrous organic substance found in ◊bogs and formed by the incomplete decomposition of plants such as sphagnum moss. The USSR, Canada, Finland, Ireland, and other places have large deposits, which have been dried and used as fuel from ancient times. Peat can also be used as a soil additive.

They began to be formed when glaciers retreated, about 9,000 years ago. Peat bogs grow at the rate of a millimeter a year, so that large-scale digging can result in destruction both of the bog and of specialized plants growing there.

Peat bogs allow for excellent preservation of organic materials (wood, leather, plant matter, animals), which usually decompose in archeological sites. Several in Scandinavia have been excavated and have provided data on prehistoric settlements. A number of ancient corpses, some the result of ritual murders, have also been found preserved in peat bogs.

pecan nut-producing ◊hickory tree *Carya illinoensis* or *C. pecan*, native to central US and N Mexico and now widely cultivated. The tree grows to over 150 ft/45 m, and the edible nuts are smooth-shelled, the kernel resembling a smoothly ovate walnut.

peccary one of two species of the New World genus *Tayassu* of piglike hoofed mammals. A peccary has a gland in the middle of the back which secretes a strong-smelling substance. Peccaries are blackish in color, covered with bristles, and have tusks that point downward. Adults reach a height of 16 in/40 cm, and a weight of 60 lb/25 kg.

Pechenga (Finnish *Petsamo*) ice-free fishing port in Murmansk, USSR, on the Barents Sea. Russia ceded Pechenga to Finland 1920 but recovered it under the 1947 peace treaty.

Pechora river in the USSR, rising in the N Urals. It transports coal, timber, and furs (June–Sept) to the Barents Sea, 1,125 mi/1,800 km to the N.

Peck (Eldred) Gregory 1916– . US film actor. One of Hollywood's most enduring stars, he was often cast as a decent man of great moral and physical strength, as in *The Old Gringo* 1989. His other films include *Spellbound* 1945, *Gentleman's Agreement* 1947, and *To Kill a Mockingbird* 1962, for which he won an Academy Award.

Peckinpah Sam 1925–1985. US film director, often of Westerns, usually associated with slow-motion, blood-spurting violence. His best films, such as *The Wild Bunch* 1969, exhibit a thoughtful, if depressing, view of the world and human nature.

Pécs city in SW Hungary, the center of a coal-mining area on the Yugoslavia frontier; population (1988) 182,000. Industries include metal, leather, and wine. The town dates from Roman times and was under Turkish rule 1543–1686.

pectoral in vertebrates, the upper area of the thorax associated with the muscles and bones used in moving the arms or forelimbs. In birds, the *pectoralis major* is the very large muscle used to produce a powerful downbeat of the wing during flight.

pediatrics medical specialty concerned with the care of children.

pedicel the stalk of an individual flower, which attaches it to the main floral axis, often developing in the axil of a bract.

pediment in architecture, the triangular part crowning the fronts of buildings in Classic styles. The pediment was a distinctive feature of Greek temples.

pedometer small portable instrument for counting the number of steps taken, and measuring the approximate distance covered by a person walking. Each step taken by the walker sets in motion a swinging weight within the instrument, causing the mechanism to rotate, and the number of rotations are registered on the instrument face.

pedomorphosis in biology, an alternative term for ◊neoteny.

Pedro two emperors of Brazil:

Pedro I 1798–1834. Emperor of Brazil 1822–31. The son of John VI of Portugal, he escaped to Brazil on Napoleon's invasion, and was appointed regent 1821. He proclaimed Brazil independent 1822 and was crowned emperor, but abdicated 1831 and returned to Portugal.

Pedro II 1825–1891. Emperor of Brazil 1831–89. He proved an enlightened ruler, but his antislavery measures alienated the landowners, who compelled him to abdicate.

Peel Robert 1788–1850. British Conservative politician. As home secretary 1822–27 and 1828–30, he founded the modern police force and in 1829 introduced Roman Catholic emancipation. He was prime minister 1834–35 and 1841–46, when his repeal of the ◊Corn Laws caused him and his followers to break with the party.

Peenemünde fishing village in Germany, used from 1937 by the Germans to develop the V2 rockets used in World War II.

peepul another name for ◊bo tree.

peerage in the UK, holders, in descending order, of the titles of duke, marquess, earl, viscount, and baron. Some of these titles may be held by a woman in default of a male heir. In the late 19th century they were augmented by the nonhereditary life peers and, from 1958, by a number of specially created life peers of either sex (usually long-standing members of the House of Commons). Since 1963 peers have been able to disclaim their titles, usually to take a seat in the Commons (where peers are disqualified from membership).

peer group in the social sciences, people who have a common identity based on such characteristics as similar social status, interests, age, or ethnic group. The concept has proved useful in analyzing the power and influence of coworkers, school friends, and ethnic and religious groups in socialization and social behavior.

Pegasus in astronomy, a constellation of the northern hemisphere, near Cygnus, and represented as the winged horse of Greek mythology.

It is the seventh-largest constellation in the sky and its main feature is a square outlined by four stars, one of which (Alpharata) is actually part of the adjoining constellation Andromeda. Diagonally across is Markab (or Alpha Pegasus), about 100 light-years distant.

Pegasus in Greek mythology, the winged horse that sprang from the blood of Medusa.

Hippocrene, the spring of the Muses on Mount Helicon, is said to have sprung from a blow of his hoof. He was transformed into a constellation.

pegmatite an extremely coarse-grained ◊igneous rock of any composition found in veins usually associated with large granite masses.

Pegu city in S Myanmar on the river Pegu, NE of Yangon; population (1983) 254,762. It was founded 573 and is home of the celebrated Shwemawdaw pagoda.

Péguy Charles 1873–1914. French Catholic Socialist, who established a Socialist publishing house in Paris. From 1900 he published on political topics *Les Cahiers de la Quinzaine/Fortnightly Notebooks* and on poetry, including *Le Mystère de* *la charité de Jeanne d'Arc/The Mystery of the Charity of Joan of Arc* 1897.

Pei I(eoh) M(ing) 1917– . Chinese-born American architect, noted for innovative modern design and high-technology structures, particularly the use of glass walls. His buildings include the Mile High Center in Denver, the National Airlines terminal (now owned by TWA) at Kennedy Airport in New York City, the John Hancock tower in Boston, and the National Gallery extension in Washington, DC. Pei's work in the 1980s included renovations to the Louvre Museum, Paris.

Peiping name, meaning "northern peace," 1928–49 of ◊Beijing in China.

Peipus, Lake (Estonian *Peipsi*, Russian *Chudskoye*) lake on the Estonian border in the USSR. Alexander Nevski defeated the Teutonic Knights on its frozen surface 1242.

Peirce Charles Sanders 1839–1914. US philosopher and logician, founder of ◊pragmatism (which he later called pragmaticism), who argued that genuine conceptual distinctions must be correlated with some differences of practical effect. He wrote extensively on the logic of scientific inquiry, suggesting that truth could be conceived of as the object of an ultimate consensus.

Born in Cambridge, Massachusetts, Peirce graduated from Harvard 1863, spent much of his life in government service, and was an astronomer and physicist before becoming a lecturer 1879–84 at Johns Hopkins University. His works include *How to Make Our Ideas Clear* 1878; his *Collected Papers* were published posthumously 1931–58.

Peking alternate name of ◊Beijing, capital of China.

pekingese breed of long-haired toy dog with a flat skull and flat face, typically less than 10 in/25 cm tall and weighing less than 11 lb/5 kg.

It was first bred at the Chinese court as the "imperial lion dog." The first specimens brought to the West were those taken during the Opium Wars when the Summer Palace in Beijing was looted 1860.

Peking man Chinese representative of an early species of human, found as fossils, 500,000–750,000 years old, in the cave of Choukoutien 1927 near Beijing (Peking). They used chipped stone tools, hunted game, and used fire. Similar varieties have been found in Java and E Africa. Their classification is disputed: some anthropologists classify them as *Homo erectus*, others as *Homo sapiens pithecanthropus*.

A skull found near Beijing 1927 was sent to the US 1941 but disappeared in transit; others have since been found.

Pelagius 360–420. British theologian. He taught that each person possesses free will (and hence the possibility of salvation), denying Augustine's doctrines of predestination and original sin. Cleared of heresy by a synod in Jerusalem 415, he was later condemned by the pope and the emperor.

pelargonium flowering plant of the genus *Pelargonium* of the ◊geranium family Geraniaceae, grown extensively in gardens, where it is familiarly known as geranium. Ancestors of the garden hybrids came from S Africa.

Pelé Adopted name of Edson Arantes do Nascimento 1940– . Brazilian soccer player. A prolific goal scorer, he appeared in four World Cup competitions 1958–70 and led Brazil to three championships (1958, 1962, 1970).

He spent most of his playing career with the Brazilian team, Santos, before ending it with the New York Cosmos in the US.

Pelée, Mont volcano on the island of Martinique; height 4,428 ft/1,350 m. It destroyed the town of St Pierre during its eruption 1902.

pelican any of a family (Pelecanidae) of large, heavy water birds remarkable for the pouch beneath the bill used as a fishing net and temporary store for catches of fish. Some species grow up to 6 ft/1.8 m, and have wingspans of 10 ft/3 m.

They include the American brown pelican *Pelicanus occidentalis*, which is marine, and dives for its food; the pinkish common pelican *P. onocrotalus* of Europe, Asia, and Africa; and the Australian black-backed pelican *P. conspicillatus*. The last two do not dive for food but dip their bills into the water while swimming.

Pelion mountain in Thessaly, Greece, near Mount ◊Ossa; height 5,079 ft/1,548 m. In Greek mythology it was the home of the ◊centaurs.

pellagra chronic disease of subtropical countries in which the staple food is corn, caused by deficiency of nicotinic acid (one of the B vitamins), which is contained in protein foods, beans and peas, and yeast. Symptoms include digestive disorders, skin eruptions, and mental disturbances.

pellitory-of-the-wall plant *Parietaria judaica* of the nettle family, found growing in cracks in walls and rocks and also on banks, in W and S Europe; widely cultivated in gardens. The stems are up to 3 ft/1 m and reddish, the leaves lance-shaped, and the greenish male and female flowers are separate but on the same plant.

Peloponnese (Greek *Peloponnesos*) peninsula forming the S part of Greece; area 8,318 sq mi/21,549 sq km; population (1981) 1,012,500. It is joined to the mainland by the narrow isthmus of Corinth and is divided into the nomes (administrative areas) of Argolis, Arcadia, Achaea, Elis, Corinth, Lakonia, and Messenia, representing its seven ancient states.

Peloponnesian War conflict between Athens and Sparta and their allies, 431–404 BC, originating in suspicions about the "empire-building" ambitions of Pericles. It was ended by ◊Lysander's destruction of the political power of Athens.

Pelops in Greek mythology, the son of ◊Tantalus, brother of ◊Niobe, and father of ◊Atreus. He gave his name to the southern part of mainland Greece, the Peloponnese.

pelota see ◊jai alai.

Peltier effect in physics, a change in temperature at the junction of two different metals produced when an electric current flows through them. The extent of the change depends on what the conducting metals are, and the nature of change (rise or fall in temperature) depends on the direction of current flow. It is the reverse of the ◊Seebeck effect. It is named after the French physicist Jean Charles Peltier (1785–1845), who discovered it 1834.

pelvis in vertebrates, the lower area of the abdomen featuring the bones and muscles used to move the legs or hindlimbs. The pelvic girdle is a set of bones that allows movement of the legs in relation to the rest of the body and provides sites for the attachment of relevant muscles.

Pemba coral island in the Indian Ocean, 30 mi/48 km NE of Zanzibar, and forming with it part of Tanzania

area 380 sq mi/984 sq km

capital Chake Chake

products cloves, copra

population (1985) 257,000.

pemmican preparation of dried lean bison or venison pounded into a paste with fat and dried berries and preserved as pressed cakes, once used as a food by Plains Indians. Similar preparations made from beef were used for high-energy rations by early Arctic explorers, and by mountaineers.

PEN abbreviation for Poets, Playwrights, Editors, Essayists, Novelists, literary association established 1921 by C A ("Sappho") Dawson Scott, to promote international understanding among writers.

penance a Roman Catholic sacrament, involving ◊confession of sins and receiving absolution, and works performed (or punishment self-inflicted) in atonement for sin. Penance is worked out now in terms of good deeds rather than routine repetition of prayers.

Penang (Malay *Pulau Pinang*) state in W Peninsular Malaysia, formed of Penang Island, Province Wellesley, and the Dindings on the mainland; area 398 sq mi/1,030 sq km; capital Penang (George

penguin

Town); population (1980) 955,000. Penang Island was bought by Britain from the ruler of Kedah 1785; Province Wellesley was acquired 1800.

penates the household gods of a Roman family. See ◊lares and penates.

Penda c. 577–654. King of Mercia from about 632. He raised Mercia to a powerful kingdom, and defeated and killed two Northumbrian kings, Edwin 632 and ◊Oswald 641. He was killed in battle by Oswy, king of Northumbria.

Penderecki Krzystof 1933– . Polish composer. His Expressionist works, such as the *Threnody for the Victims of Hiroshima* 1961 for strings, employ cluster and percussion effects. He later turned to religious subjects and a more orthodox style, as in the *Magnificat* 1974 and the *Polish Requiem* 1980–83.

Pendleton Act in US history, a civil service reform bill 1883 sponsored by senator George Pendleton (1825–1889) of Ohio that was designed to curb the power of patronage exercised by new administrations over a swelling federal bureaucracy. Initially about 10% of civil service appointments were made subject to competitive examinations administered by an independent Civil Service Commission.

pendulum a weight (called a "bob") swinging at the end of a rod or cord.

The regularity of a pendulum's swing was used in making the first really accurate clocks in the 17th century. Pendulums can be used for measuring the acceleration due to gravity (an important constant in physics), and in prospecting for oils and minerals. Specialized pendulums are used to measure velocities (ballistic pendulum) and to demonstrate the Earth's rotation (Foucault's pendulum).

Penelope in Greek legend, wife of ◊Odysseus. During his absence after the siege of Troy she kept her many suitors at bay by asking them to wait until she had woven a shroud for her father-in-law, but unraveled her work each night. When Odysseus returned, after 20 years, he killed her suitors.

penguin any of an order (Sphenisciformes) of marine flightless birds, mostly black and white, found in the S hemisphere. They range in size from 1.6 ft/40 cm to 4 ft/1.2 m tall, and have thick feathers to protect them from the intense cold. They are awkward on land, but their wings have evolved into flippers, making them excellent swimmers. Penguins congregate to breed in "rookeries," and often spend many months incubating their eggs while their mates are out at sea feeding.

Largest is the emperor penguin *Aptenodytes forsteri* 4 ft/1.2 m tall, whose single annual egg is brooded by the male in the warmth of a flap of his body skin, so that it rests on his feet. Among the small species is the jackass penguin *Sphenis-*

penicillin *Penicillium notatum is a species of fungus that was used as the original source of the antibiotic penicillin.*

cus demerss, which lays two eggs in a scraped hollow in the ground. Jackass penguins have declined in numbers, at first because of egg-collecting by humans, but more recently caused by overfishing, which deprives them of food, and to oil spills near their breeding colonies.

penicillin any of a group of ◊antibiotic compounds obtained from filtrates of molds of the genus *Penicillium* (especially *P. notatum*) or produced synthetically. Penicillin was the first antibiotic to be discovered (by Alexander ◊Fleming), and kills a broad spectrum of bacteria, many of which cause disease in humans.

The use of the original type of penicillin is limited by the increasing resistance of ◊pathogens and by allergic reactions in patients. Since 1941, numerous other antibiotics of the penicillin family have been discovered, which are more selective against, or resistant to, specific microorganisms.

peninsula tongue of land surrounded on three sides by water but still attached to a larger landmass. Florida is an example.

Peninsular War war 1808–14 caused by the French emperor Napoleon's invasion of Portugal and Spain. British expeditionary forces, combined with Spanish and Portuguese resistance, succeeded in defeating the French at Vimeiro 1808, Talavera 1809, ◊Salamanca 1812, and Vittoria 1813. The results were inconclusive, and the war was ended by Napoleon's abdication.

penis male reproductive organ, used for internal fertilization; it transfers sperm to the female reproductive tract. In mammals, the penis is made erect by vessels that fill with blood, and in most mammals (but not humans) is stiffened by a bone. It also contains the urethra, through which urine is passed. Snakes and lizards have a paired structure that serves as a penis, other reptiles a single organ. A few birds, mainly ducks and geese, also have a type of penis, as do snails, barnacles, and some other invertebrates. Many insects have a rigid, nonerectile male organ, usually referred to as an intromittent organ.

Penn Irving 1917– . US fashion, advertising, portrait, editorial, and fine art photographer. In 1948 he took the first of many journeys to Africa and the Far East, resulting in a series of portrait photographs of local people, avoiding sophisticated technique. He was associated for many years with *Vogue* magazine in the US.

Penn William 1644–1718. English Quaker and founder of Pennsylvania, born in London. He joined the Quakers 1667 and was imprisoned several times for his beliefs. In 1681 he obtained a grant of land in America, in settlement of a debt owed by Charles II to his father, on which he established the colony of Pennsylvania as a refuge for the persecuted Quakers. Penn made religious tolerance a cornerstone of his administration of the colony. He maintained good relations with neighboring colonies and with the Indians in the area, but his uptopian ideals were not successful for the most part.

In 1697 he presented a plan, never acted upon, for a union among the colonies. In 1701 he established, with his Charter of Privileges, a bicameral legislature as the government for Pennsylvania.

Pennsylvania

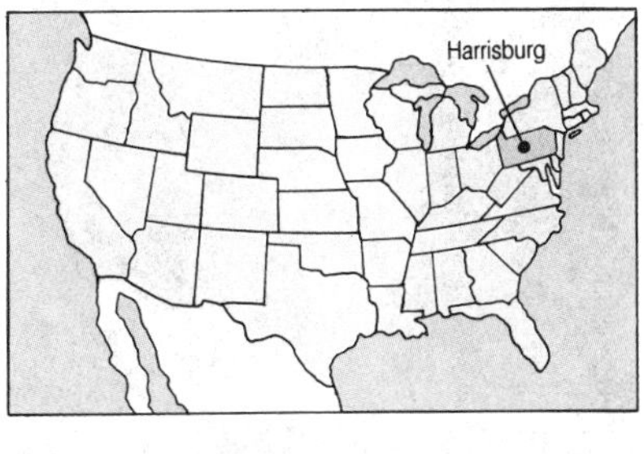
Harrisburg

Pennines mountain system, "the backbone of England," broken by a gap through which the river Aire flows to the E and the Ribble to the W; length (Scottish border to the Peaks in Derbyshire) 250 mi/400 km.

Pennsylvania state in NE US: nickname Keystone State

area 45,316, sq mi/117,400 sq km

capital Harrisburg

cities Philadelphia, Pittsburgh, Erie, Allentown, Scranton

population (1990) 11,881,643

features Allegheny mountains; rivers: Ohio, Susquehanna, Delaware; Independence National Historic Park, Philadelphia; Valley Forge National Historic Park; Gettysburg Civil War battlefield; Pennsylvania Dutch country; Poconos resort region

products hay, corn, mushrooms, cattle, poultry, dairy products, cement, coal, steel, petroleum products, pharmaceuticals, motor vehicles and equipment, electronic components, textiles

famous people Marian Anderson, Andrew Carnegie, Stephen Foster, Benjamin Franklin, Robert Fulton, Martha Graham, George C Marshall, Robert E Peary, Benjamin Rush, Gertrude Stein, John Updike

history disputed by Sweden, the Netherlands, and England early 17th century; granted to Quaker William ◊Penn 1682 by English King Charles II, after the 1664 capture of New Netherlands. The Declaration of Independence was proclaimed in Philadelphia, and many important Revolutionary War battles were fought here 1777–78. One of the original thirteen states, Pennsylvania was a leader in both agriculture and industry. The Battle of Gettysburg 1863 was a turning point in the Civil War for the Union cause. Until 1920, Pennsylvania was dominant in oil, coal, iron, steel, and textile production, but it already was losing its industrial lead when the Great Depression struck; by 1933, 37% of the work force was unemployed. Some areas never fully recovered, and the state now looks to agriculture, service-related industries, trade, and tourism for economic growth.

Pennsylvanian US term for the upper ◊Carboniferous period of geologic time, named after the US state.

pennyroyal European perennial plant *Mentha pulegium* of the mint family, with oblong leaves and whorls of purplish flowers. It is found growing in wet places on sandy soil.

A similar North American mint *Hedeoma pulegioides* that yields an aromatic oil is also called pennyroyal.

Pensacola port in NW Florida, on the Gulf of Mexico, with a large naval air-training station; industries include chemicals, synthetic fibers, and paper; population (1990) 58,165. The University of West Florida is here. Pensacola was founded by the Spanish 1696, passed to the British 1763, and returned to the Spanish again in the early 1780s. It was seized by US forces in 1814 and 1818 and was formally ceded with the rest of Florida in 1821. Union forces gained control of the city in 1862, during the Civil War.

pension a payment, not wages, made to a person (or his/her family) after fulfillment of certain conditions of service; an organized retirement plan. Pension plans vary widely, with some pensions calculated at a specified percentage of a worker's income, payable annually after retirement. Others provide lump-sum savings available for withdrawal at age 65. Employers sometimes match employee contributions; some plans are strictly employee contributions plus interest. Some plans are mandatory, others voluntary.

The most significant provider of retirement income in the US the is Social Security Administration, funded through nonvoluntary contributions assessed on both employers and employees. Unions make employer contributions to pension plans an important element of their contract negotiations, and accumulated pension funds have become important sources of investment capital. Under federal tax regulations, individuals can deposit specified maximum amounts into personal retirement funds, have their income tax liability reduced by that amount as a deduction, and have taxes on the fund's interest deferred until they withdraw the money at or after retirement.

pentadactyl limb the typical limb of the mammals, birds, reptiles and amphibians. These ◊vertebrates are all descended from primitive amphibians whose immediate ancestors were fleshy-finned fish.

The limb which evolved in those amphibians had three parts: a "hand/foot" with five digits (fingers/toes), a lower limb containing two bones, and an upper limb containing one bone. This basic pattern has persisted in all the terrestrial vertebrates, and those aquatic vertebrates (such as seals) which are descended from them. Natural selection has modified the pattern to fit different ways of life. In flying animals (birds and bats) it is greatly altered and in some vertebrates, such as whales and snakes, the limbs are greatly reduced or lost. Pentadactyl limbs of different species are an example of ◊homologous organs.

Pentagon the headquarters of the US Department of Defense, Arlington, Virginia. One of the world's largest office buildings (five-sided with a pentagonal central court), it houses the administrative and command headquarters for the US armed forces and has become synonymous with the defense-establishment bureaucracy.

Pentagon Papers Case a US Supreme Court decision (*New York Times* v *US*; *US* v *Washington Post*) 1971 dealing with the right of the federal government to enjoin the publication of sensitive or classified material. The federal government filed the suit against the *Times* and the *Post* to discontinue publication of portions of "The Pentagon Papers," a set of classified documents about US involvement in Vietnam. The government argued that the threat to national security warranted the infringement on First-Amendment rights. The Court ruled 6 to 3 to dismiss the government's suit, judging any suppression of the press, without proof of actual damage to national security, to be a violation of the First Amendment.

pentanol $C_5H_{11}OH$ (common name amyl alcohol) clear, colorless, oily liquid, usually having a characteristic choking odor. It is obtained by the fermentation of starches and from the distillation of petroleum.

Pentateuch Greek translation from the Hebrew of the first five books of the Bible, ascribed to Moses, and called the Torah by Jews.

pentathlon a five-sport competition. Modern pentathlon consists of former military training pursuits: swimming, fencing, running, horsemanship, and shooting. Formerly a five-event track and field competition for women, it was superseded by the ◊heptathlon 1981.

Pentecost in Judaism, the festival of *Shavuot*, celebrated on the 50th day after ◊Passover in commemoration of the giving of the Ten Commandments to Moses on Mt Sinai, and the end of the grain harvest; in the Christian church, the day on which the apostles experienced inspiration of the Holy Spirit, commemorated on Whit Sunday.

Pentecostal movement a Christian revivalist movement originating in the US 1906. Spiritual renewal is sought through baptism by the Holy Spirit, as experienced by the apostles on the first Pentecost. It represented a reaction against the rigid theology and formal worship of the traditional churches. Glossolalia, or speaking in tongues, often occurs. Pentecostalists believe in the literal word of the Bible and faith healing. They disapprove of alcohol, tobacco, dancing, the theater, gambling, and so on. It is an intensely missionary faith, and recruitment in person and on television has been very rapid since the 1960s: worldwide membership is more than 20 million, and it is the world's fastest growing sector of Christianity.

The Pentecostal movement dates from April 4, 1906, when members of the congregation of the Azusa Street Mission in Los Angeles experienced "baptism in the Spirit." Its appeal was to the poor and those alienated by the formalism and modernist theology of established denominations. It combined a highly emotional, informal approach to worship with an ethical emphasis on sobriety and hard work, and it became a way for poor and marginal groups to improve their economic and social status while retaining their religious faith.

The movement grew rapidly in the South and in impoverished urban areas, meanwhile dividing into dozens of small, contentious sects separated by doctrine and by such practices as faith healing. In the 1950s, faith healing, represented most prominently by Oral Roberts, was at its peak among Pentecostalists. After the 1960s, prosperity through faith became a dominant theme, taken up by Roberts and other television evangelists. But all the Pentecostal sects—ranging from the largest, the Assemblies of God, to small storefront churches—shared a rapturous, ecstatic tone that continued to have a powerful appeal in the US, Latin America, and Africa. The movement in Europe, after rapid growth in the early 20th century, had stabilized by midcentury. A similar movement within the Roman Catholic Church, the charismatic movement, won large numbers of followers from the 1960s.

Pentheus in Greek mythology, king of Thebes and grandson of ◊Cadmus. Opposed the worship of ◊Dionysus, he was destroyed by the god and his followers. His story is the subject of ◊Euripides' tragedy *The Bacchae*.

Penza industrial city (lumber mills, bicycles, watches, calculating machines, textiles) in the USSR, capital of Penza region, 350 mi/560 km SE of Moscow, at the junction of the Penza and Sura rivers; population (1987) 540,000. It was founded as a fort 1663.

peony any perennial plant of the genus *Paeonia*, family Paeoniaceae, remarkable for their brilliant flowers. Most popular are the common peony *P. officinalis*, the white peony *P. lactiflora*, and the taller tree peony *P. suffruticosa*.

Peoria city in central Illinois, on the Illinois river; a transport, mining, and agricultural center; population (1990) 113,504. Fort Crève Coeur was built here by the French explorer La Salle 1680 and became a trading center. The first US settlers arrived 1818, and the town was known as Fort Clark until 1825.

Pepin the Short c. 714–c. 768. King of the Franks from 751. The son of Charles Martel, he acted as ◊Mayor of the Palace to the last Merovingian king, Childeric III, deposed him and assumed the royal title himself, founding the ◊Carolingian dynasty. He was ◊Charlemagne's father.

pepper climbing plant *Piper nigrum* native to the E Indies, of the Old World pepper family Piperaceae. When gathered green, the berries are crushed to produce the seeds for the spice called black pepper. When the berries are ripe, the

Pepys *Diarist Samuel Pepys in a 1666 portrait by John Hayls.*

seeds are removed and the outer skin discarded, to produce white pepper. Sweet pepper comes from ◊capsicums native to the New World.

peppermint perennial herb *Mentha piperita* of the mint family, native to Europe, with ovate, aromatic leaves and purple flowers. Oil of peppermint is used in medicine and confectionery.

pepsin enzyme that breaks down proteins during digestion. It requires a strongly acidic environment and is found in the stomach.

peptide molecule comprising two or more ◊amino acid molecules (not necessarily different) joined by peptide bonds, whereby the acid group of one acid is linked to the amino group of the other (–CO·NH). The number of amino acid molecules in the peptide is indicated by referring to it as a di-, tri-, or polypeptide (two, three, or many amino acids).

Proteins are built up of interacting polypeptide chains with various types of bonds occurring between the chains. Incomplete hydrolysis (splitting up) of a protein yields a mixture of peptides, examination of which helps to determine the sequence in which the amino acids occur within the protein.

Pepusch Johann Christoph 1667–1752. German composer who settled in England about 1700. He contributed to John Gay's ballad operas *The Beggar's Opera* and *Polly*.

Pepys Samuel 1633–1703. English diarist. His diary, written 1659–69 (when his sight failed) in shorthand, was a unique record of both the daily life of the period and the intimate feelings of the man. It was not deciphered until 1825.

He was born in London, entered the navy office 1660, and was secretary to the Admiralty 1672–79, when he was imprisoned in the Tower of London on suspicion of being connected with the Popish Plot (see Titus ◊Oates).

Perak state of W Peninsular Malaysia; capital Ipoh; area 8,106 sq mi/21,000 sq km; population (1980) 1,805,000. It produces tin and rubber. The government is a sultanate. The other principal town is Taiping.

perborate any salt formed by the action of hydrogen peroxide on borates. Perborates contain the radical BO_3.

percentage a way of representing a number as a ◊fraction of 100. Thus 45 percent (45%) equals $^{45}/_{100}$, and 45% of 20 is $^{45}/_{100} \times 20 = 9$.

In general, if a quantity x changes to y, the percentage change is $100(x - y)/x$. Thus, if the number of people in a room changes from 40 to 50, the percentage increase is $(100 \times 10)/40 = 25\%$. To express a fraction as a percentage, its denominator must first be converted to 100, for example, $1/8 = 12.5/100 = 12.5\%$. The use of percentages often makes it easier to compare fractions that do not have a common denominator.

The percentage sign is thought to have been derived as an economy measure when recording in the old counting houses; writing in the numeric symbol for $^{25}/_{100}$ of a cargo would take two lines of parchment, and hence the "100" denominator was put alongside the 25 and rearranged to "%."

Perceval Spencer 1762–1812. British Tory politician. He became chancellor of the Exchequer 1807 and prime minister 1809. He was shot in the lobby of the House of Commons 1812 by a merchant who blamed government measures for his bankruptcy.

perch any of the largest order of spiny-finned bony fishes, the Perciformes, with some 8,000 species. This order includes the sea basses, cichlids, damselfishes, mullets, barracudas, wrasses, and gobies. Perches of the freshwater genus *Perca* are found in Europe, Asia, and North America. They have varied shapes and are usually a greenish color. They are very prolific, spawning when about three years old, and have voracious appetites.

The American yellow perch *P. flavescens*, which grows to 12 in/30 cm, is abundant in lakes and streams, feeding on insects and other fishes.

percussion instrument musical instrument played by being struck with the hand or a beater. Percussion instruments can be divided into those that can be tuned to produce a sound of definite pitch, and those without pitch.

Examples of tuned percussion instruments include:

kettledrum a hemispherical bowl of metal with a membrane stretched across the top, tuned by screwtaps around the rim

tubular bells suspended on a frame

glockenspiel (German *"bell play"*) a small keyboard of steel bars

xylophone similar to a glockenspiel, but with wooden rather than metal bars.

Instruments without definite pitch include:

snare drum with a membrane across both ends, and a "snare" that rattles against the underside when the drum is beaten

bass drum, which produces the lowest sound in the orchestra

tamborine a wooden hoop with a membrane stretched across it, and with metal jingles inserted in the sides

triangle a suspended triangular-shaped steel bar, played by striking it with a separate bar of steel. The sound produced can by clearly perceived even when played against a full orchestra

cymbals two brass dishes struck together

castanets two hollow shells of wood struck together

gong a suspended disk of metal struck with a soft hammer.

Percy Henry "Hotspur" 1364–1403. English soldier, son of the 1st Earl of Northumberland. In repelling a border raid, he defeated the Scots at Homildon Hill in Durham 1402. He was killed at the battle of Shrewsbury while in revolt against Henry IV.

Pereira capital of Risaralda department, central Colombia, situated at an altitude of 4,800 ft/1,463 m, overlooking the fertile Cauca valley, W of Bogota; population (1985) 390,000. Founded 1863, the city has developed into a chief center of the country's coffee and cattle industries.

Perelman S(idney) J(oseph) 1904–1979. US humorist, born in New York. He was often published in *The New Yorker* magazine, and wrote film scripts for the Marx Brothers. He shared the Academy Award for the film script of *Around the World in 80 Days* 1956.

perennating organ in plants, that part of a ◊biennial plant or herbaceous ◊perennial that allows it to survive the winter; usually a root, tuber, rhizome, bulb, or corm.

perennial plant a plant that lives for more than two years. Herbaceous perennials have aerial stems and leaves that die each autumn. They survive the winter by means of an underground storage (perennating) organ, such as a bulb or rhizome. Trees and shrubs or woody perennials have stems that persist above ground throughout the year,

percussion instrument

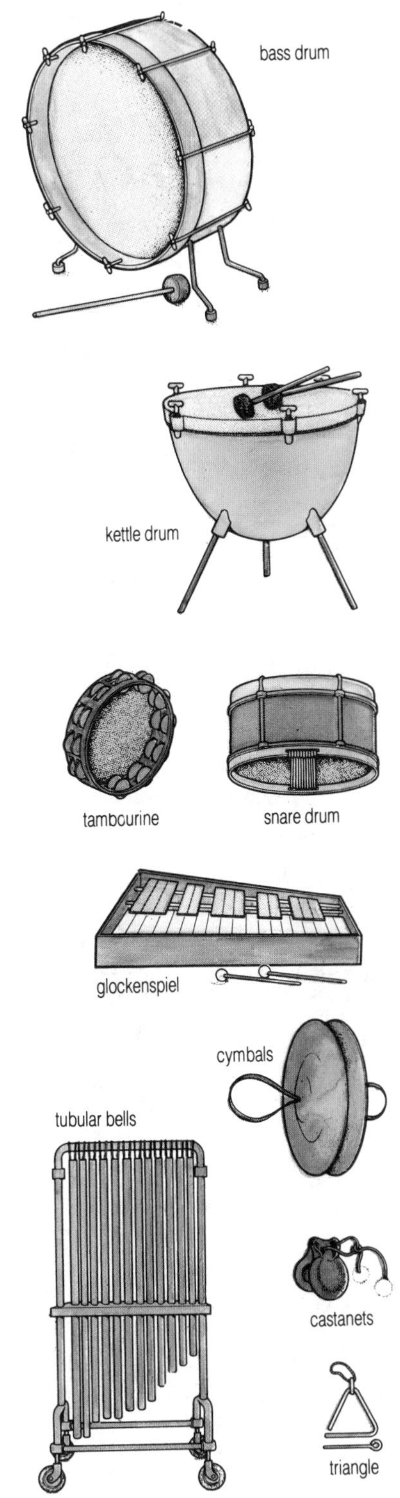
bass drum
kettle drum
tambourine
snare drum
glockenspiel
cymbals
tubular bells
castanets
triangle

and may be either ◊deciduous or ◊evergreen. See also ◊annual plant, ◊biennial plant.

Peres Shimon 1923– . Israeli Socialist politician, prime minister 1984–86. Peres emigrated from Poland to Palestine 1934, but was educated in the US. In 1959 he was elected to the Knesset (Israeli parliament). He became leader of the Labor Party 1977. Peres was prime minister, then foreign minister, under a power-sharing agreement with the leader of the Consolidation Party (Likud), Yitzhak ◊Shamir. From 1989 he was finance minister in a new Labor–Likud coalition.

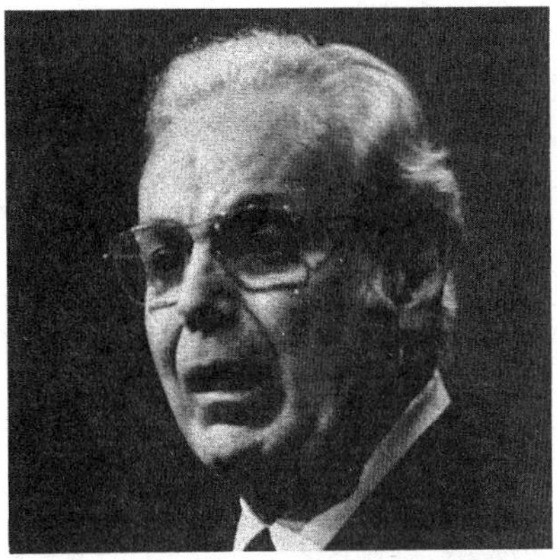

***Pérez de Cuéllar** Peruvian diplomat and secretary-general of the United Nations (1982–91) Javier Pérez de Cuéllar, Mexico City, 1984.*

perestroika (Russian "restructuring") in Soviet politics, the wide-ranging economic and political reforms initiated during Mikhail Gorbachev's leadership of the Soviet state.

It is also the title of a book by Gorbachev 1987.

The term was first proposed at the 26th Party Congress in 1979 and actively promoted by Gorbachev from 1985. Originally, in the economic sphere, perestroika was conceived as involving the "switching on to a track of intensive development" by automation and improved labor efficiency. It has evolved to attend increasingly to market indicators and incentives ("market socialism") and a gradual dismantlement of the Stalinist central-planning system, with decision-taking authority being devolved to self-financing enterprises.

Pérez de Cuéllar Javier 1920– . Peruvian diplomat, secretary-general of the United Nations from 1982–91. A delegate to the first UN General Assembly 1946–47, he subsequently held several ambassadorial posts. He raised the standing of the UN by his successful diplomacy in ending the Iran-Iraq war in 1988 and securing the independence of Namibia 1989. He was, however, unable to resolve the Gulf conflict resulting from Iraq's annexation of Kuwait 1990 before combat against Iraq by the UN coalition began in Jan 1991.

Pérez Galdós Benito 1843–1920. Spanish novelist, born in the Canary Islands. His works include the 46 historical novels in the cycle *Episodios nacionales* and the 21-novel cycle *Novelas españolas contemporáneos*, which includes *Doña Perfecta* 1876 and the epic *Fortunata y Jacinta* 1886–87, his masterpiece. In scale he has been compared to Balzac and Dickens.

perfect competition see ◊competition, perfect.

performance art staged artistic events, sometimes including music, painting, and sculpture. The events, which originated in the 1950s, are akin to happenings but less spontaneous.

perfume fragrant essence used to scent the body, cosmetics, and candles. More than 100 natural aromatic chemicals may be blended from a range of 60,000 flowers, leaves, fruits, seeds, woods, barks, resins, and roots,. combined by natural animal fixatives and various synthetics, the latter increasingly used even in expensive products.

Favored ingredients include ◊balsam, ◊civet, hyacinth, ◊jasmine, lily of the valley, musk (from the ◊musk deer), orange blossom, rose, and tuberose. Culture of the cells of such plants, on membranes that are constantly bathed in a solution to carry the essential oils away for separation, is now being adopted to reduce costs.

Perga ruined city of Pamphylia, 10 mi/16 km NE of Adalia, Turkey, noted for its local cult of Artemis. It was visited by the apostle Paul.

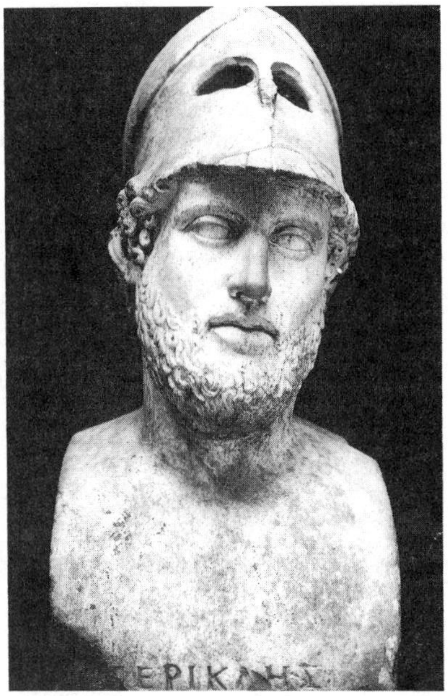

***Pericles** Bust of Pericles found near Tivoli, Italy, 1781. Under his rule, Greek culture reached its finest expression.*

Pergamum ancient Greek city in W Asia Minor, which became the capital of an independent kingdom 283 BC. As the ally of Rome it achieved great political importance in the 2nd century BC, and became a center of art and culture. Close to its site is the modern Turkish town of Bergama.

peri in Persian myth, a beautiful, harmless being, ranking between angels and evil spirits. Peris were ruled by Eblis, greatest of evil spirits.

Peri Jacopo 1561–1633. Italian composer, who served the ◊Medici family. His experimental melodic opera *Euridice* 1600 established the opera form and influenced Monteverdi. His first opera, *Dafne* 1597, with librettist Jacopo Corsi, is now lost.

perianth in botany, a collective term for the outer whorls of the ◊flower, which protect the reproductive parts during development. In most ◊dicotyledons the perianth is composed of two distinct whorls, the calyx of ◊sepals and the corolla of ◊petals, whereas in many ◊monocotyledons they are indistinguishable and the segments of the perianth are then known individually as tepals.

periastron in astronomy, the point at which an object traveling in an elliptical orbit around a star is at its closest to the star; compare ◊apastron.

pericarp the wall of a ◊fruit. It encloses the seeds and is derived from the ◊ovary wall. In fruits such as the acorn, the pericarp becomes dry and hard, forming a shell around the seed. In fleshy fruits the pericarp is typically made up of three distinct layers. The epicarp, or exocarp, forms the tough outer skin of the fruits, while the mesocarp is often fleshy and forms the middle layers. The innermost layer or endocarp, which surrounds the seeds, may be membranous or thick and hard, as in the ◊drupe (stone) of cherries, plums, and apricots.

Pericles c. 490–429 BC. Athenian politician, who dominated the city's affairs from 461 BC (as leader of the democratic party), and under whom Greek culture reached its height. He created a confederation of cities under the leadership of Athens, but the disasters of the ◊Peloponnesian War led to his overthrow 430 BC. Although quickly reinstated, he died soon after.

peridot a gem variety of the mineral ◊olivine. Peridotite is an ultrabasic (silica-poor) ◊igneous rock that consists almost entirely of olivine.

peridotite a rock consisting largely of the mineral

olivine; pyroxene and other minerals may also be present. Peridotite is an ultrabasic rock containing less than 45% silica by weight. It is believed to be one of the rock types making up the Earth's upper mantle, and is sometimes brought from the depths to the surface by major movements, or as inclusions in lavas.

perigee the point at which an object, traveling in an elliptical orbit around the Earth, is at its closest to the Earth.

Périgueux capital of Dordogne *département*, Aquitaine, France, on the river Isle, 79 mi/127 km ENE of Bordeaux; trading center for wine and truffles; population (1982) 35,392. The Byzantine cathedral dates from 984.

perihelion the point at which an object, traveling in an elliptical orbit around the Sun, is at its closest to the Sun.

Perim island in the strait of Bab-el-Mandeb, the S entrance to the Red Sea; part of South Yemen; area 5 sq mi/13 sq km.

period a punctuation mark (.). The term "period" is universally understood in English and is the preferred usage in North America; full stop is the preferred term in the UK. The period has two functions: to mark the end of a sentence and to indicate that a word has been abbreviated. It is also used in mathematics to indicate decimals and is then called a point.

period another name for menstruation; see ◊menstrual cycle.

period in physics, the time taken for one complete cycle of a repeated sequence of events. For example, the time taken for a pendulum to swing from side to side and back again is the period of the pendulum.

periodic table of the elements classification of the elements to reflect the periodic law, namely that the properties of the chemical elements recur periodically when the elements are arranged in increasing order of their ◊atomic number and are shown in related groups. Today's arrangement is by atomic numbers as devised by Moseley in 1913–14; the original tables were set up by atomic weights (masses), first proposed by Newlands in 1863 and expanded on by Mendeleyev and Meyer in 1869. There are similarities in the chemical properties of the elements in each of the main vertical groups and a gradation of properties along the horizontal periods. The periods correspond to the filling of successive electron shells, and the groups correspond to the number of valence electrons.

The continuous sequence of elements divides into seven periods and nine groups. The members of a group, and the subgroups (a) and (b) into which each group is divided, show similar chemical properties. The Roman numeral at the top of each group is equal to a valence (the minimum, as in group I, or the maximum, as in group VII) of the elements it contains.

periodontal disease formerly known as ***pyorrhea*** disease of the gums and bone supporting the teeth, caused by the accumulation of plaque and microorganisms; the gums recede, and the teeth eventually become loose and may drop out unless treatment is sought.

peripheral device in computing, any item of equipment attached to and controlled by a computer. Peripherals are typically for input from and output to the user (for example, a keyboard or printer), storing data (for example, a disk drive), communications (such as a modem), or for performing physical tasks (such as a ◊robot).

periscope optical instrument designed for observation from a concealed position such as from a submerged submarine. In its basic form it consists of a tube with parallel mirrors at each end, inclined at 45° to its axis.

The periscope attained prominence in naval and military operations of World War I.

peristalsis wavelike contractions, produced by the contraction of smooth ◊muscle, that pass along tubular organs, such as the intestines. The same term describes the wavelike motion of earthworms and other invertebrates, in which part of the body contracts as another part elongates.

periodic table of the elements

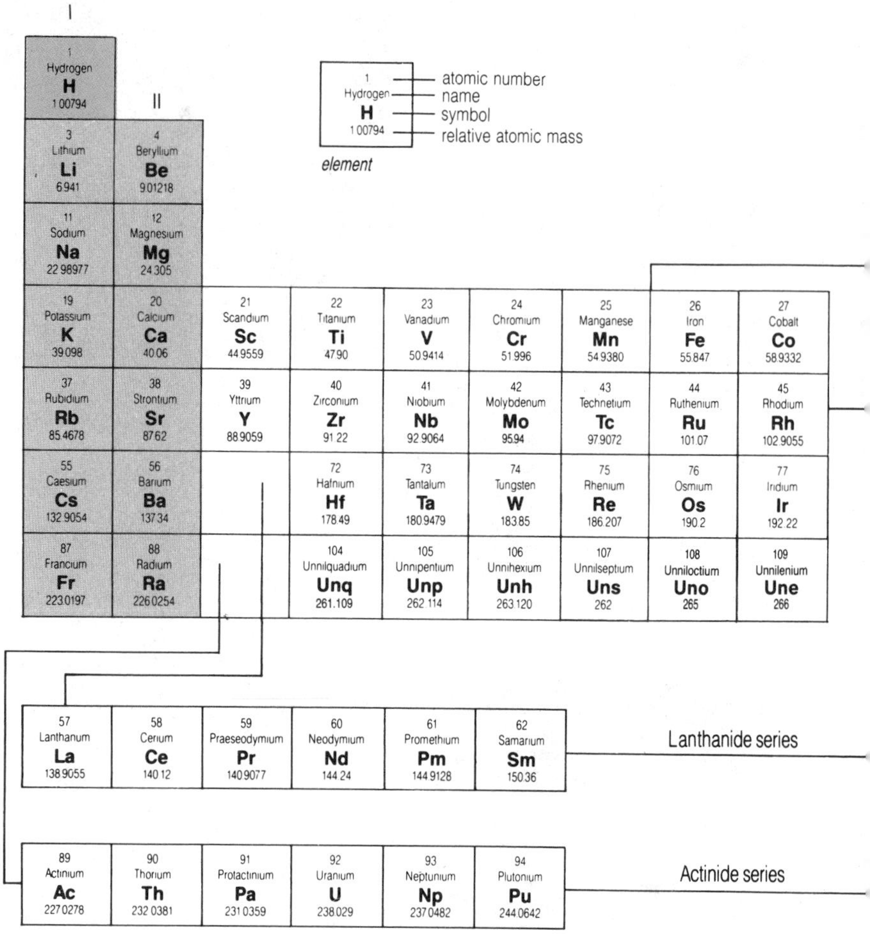
I
II
1 Hydrogen H 1.00794
atomic number
name
symbol
relative atomic mass
element
3 Lithium Li 6.941
4 Beryllium Be 9.01218
11 Sodium Na 22.98977
12 Magnesium Mg 24.305
19 Potassium K 39.098
20 Calcium Ca 40.06
21 Scandium Sc 44.9559
22 Titanium Ti 47.90
23 Vanadium V 50.9414
24 Chromium Cr 51.996
25 Manganese Mn 54.9380
26 Iron Fe 55.847
27 Cobalt Co 58.9332
37 Rubidium Rb 85.4678
38 Strontium Sr 87.62
39 Yttrium Y 88.9059
40 Zirconium Zr 91.22
41 Niobium Nb 92.9064
42 Molybdenum Mo 95.94
43 Technetium Tc 97.9072
44 Ruthenium Ru 101.07
45 Rhodium Rh 102.9055
55 Caesium Cs 132.9054
56 Barium Ba 137.34
72 Hafnium Hf 178.49
73 Tantalum Ta 180.9479
74 Tungsten W 183.85
75 Rhenium Re 186.207
76 Osmium Os 190.2
77 Iridium Ir 192.22
87 Francium Fr 223.0197
88 Radium Ra 226.0254
104 Unnilquadium Unq 261.109
105 Unnipentium Unp 262.114
106 Unnihexium Unh 263.120
107 Unnilseptium Uns 262
108 Unniloctium Uno 265
109 Unnilenium Une 266
57 Lanthanum La 138.9055
58 Cerium Ce 140.12
59 Praeseodymium Pr 140.9077
60 Neodymium Nd 144.24
61 Promethium Pm 144.9128
62 Samarium Sm 150.36
Lanthanide series
89 Actinium Ac 227.0278
90 Thorium Th 232.0381
91 Protactinium Pa 231.0359
92 Uranium U 238.029
93 Neptunium Np 237.0482
94 Plutonium Pu 244.0642
Actinide series

peritoneum the transparent tissue lining the abdominal cavity and curving around all the visceral organs of vertebrates.

peritonitis inflammation within the peritoneum, due to infection or other irritation. It is sometimes seen following a burst appendix. Peritonitis quickly proves fatal without treatment.

periwinkle in botany, trailing blue-flowered evergreen plants of the genus *Vinca* of the dogbane family Apocynaceae.

The related Madagascar periwinkle *Catharanthus roseus* produces chemicals that inhibit the division of cells and are used to treat leukemia.

periwinkle in zoology, any marine snail of the family Littorinidae, found on the shores of Europe and E North America. It has a conical spiral shell, and feeds on algae. Periwinkles range from 8 in/20 cm to 3 ft/1 m in length.

perjury the offense of deliberately making a false statement on ◊oath (or ◊affirmation) when appearing as a witness in legal proceedings, on a point material to the question at issue. In Britain and the US it is punishable by a fine, imprisonment, or both.

Perkins Anthony 1932– . US actor who played the mother-fixated psychopath Norman Bates in Hitchcock's *Psycho* 1960 and *Psycho II* 1982. He played shy but subtle roles in *Friendly Persuasion* 1956, *The Trial* 1962, and *The Champagne Murders* 1967. He also appears on the stage in London and New York.

Perkins Frances 1882–1965. US public official. Holding a succession of posts in state regulatory agencies, Perkins became a reformer of labor standards and served on the State Industrial Board 1923–29. Perkins was appointed New York State's industrial commissioner 1929 and became the first female cabinet officer when she served as secretary of labor under F D Roosevelt 1933–45. Under Truman she was a member of the federal civil service commission 1946–53.

Born in Boston and educated at Mount Holyoke, Perkins worked at Hull House in Chicago before receiving a master's degree in economics from Columbia University 1910.

Perlis border state of Peninsular Malaysia, NW Malaysia; capital Kangar; area 309 sq mi/800 sq km; population (1980) 148,000. It produces rubber, rice, coconuts, and tin. Perlis is ruled by a raja. It was transferred by Siam to Britain 1909.

Perm industrial city (shipbuilding, oil refining, aircraft, chemicals, lumber mills), and capital of Perm region, USSR, on the Kama near the Ural mountains; population (1987) 1,075,000. It was called Molotov 1940–57.

permafrost condition in which a deep layer of soil does not thaw out during the summer but remains at below 32°F/0°C for at least two years, despite thawing of the soil above. It is claimed that 26% of the world's land surface is permafrost.

Permafrost gives rise to a poorly drained form of grassland typical of N Canada, Siberia, and Alaska known as ◊tundra.

Permian period of geologic time 286–248 million years ago, the last period of the Paleozoic era. Its end was marked by a significant change in marine life, including the extinction of many corals and trilobites. Deserts were widespread, and

			III	IV	V	VI	VII	0
								2 Helium **He** 4.00260
			5 Boron **B** 10.81	6 Carbon **C** 12.011	7 Nitrogen **N** 14.0067	8 Oxygen **O** 15.9994	9 Fluorine **F** 18.99840	10 Neon **Ne** 20.179
			13 Aluminium **Al** 26.98154	14 Silicon **Si** 28.086	15 Phosphorus **P** 30.97376P	16 Sulphur **S** 32.06	17 Chlorine **Cl** 35.453	18 Argon **Ar** 39.948
28 Nickel **Ni** 58.70	29 Copper **Cu** 63.546	30 Zinc **Zn** 65.38	31 Gallium **Ga** 69.72	32 Germanium **Ge** 72.59	33 Arsenic **As** 74.9216	34 Selenium **Se** 78.96	35 Bromine **Br** 79.904	36 Krypton **Kr** 83.80
46 Palladium **Pd** 106.4	47 Silver **Ag** 107.868	48 Cadmium **Cd** 112.40	49 Indium **In** 114.82	50 Tin **Sn** 118.69	51 Antimony **Sb** 121.75	52 Tellurium **Te** 127.75	53 Iodine **I** 126.9045	54 Xenon **Xe** 131.30
78 Platinum **Pt** 195.09	79 Gold **Au** 196.9665	80 Mercury **Hg** 200.59	81 Thallium **Tl** 204.37	82 Lead **Pb** 207.37	83 Bismuth **Bi** 207.2	84 Polonium **Po** 210	85 Astatine **At** 211	86 Radon **Rn** 222.0176

63 Europium **Eu** 151.96	64 Gadolinium **Gd** 157.25	65 Terbium **Tb** 158.9254	66 Dysprosium **Dy** 162.50	67 Holmium **Ho** 164.9304	68 Erbium **Er** 167.26	69 Thulium **Tm** 168.9342	70 Ytterbium **Yb** 173.04	71 Lutetium **Lu** 174.97
95 Americium **Am** 243.0614	96 Curium **Cm** 247.0703	97 Berkelium **Bk** 247.0703	98 Californium **Cf** 251.0786	99 Einsteinium **Es** 252.0828	100 Fermium **Fm** 257.0951	101 Mendelevium **Me** 258.0986	102 Nobelium **No** 259.1009	103 Lawrencium **Lr** 260.1054

terrestrial amphibians and mammallike reptiles flourished. Cone-bearing plants (gymnosperms) came to prominence.

permutation in mathematics, a specified arrangement of a group of objects. It is the arrangement of a distinct objects taken b at a time in all possible orders. It is given by $a!/(a-b)!$, where "!" stands for ◊factorial. For example, the number of permutations of four letters taken from any group of six different letters is $6!/2! = (1 \times 2 \times 3 \times 4 \times 5 \times 6)/(1 \times 2) = 360$.

The theoretical number of four-letter "words" that can be made from an alphabet of 26 letters is $26!/22! = 358,800$.

Pernambuco state of NE Brazil, on the Atlantic
area 37,946 sq mi/98,281 sq km
capital Recife (former name Pernambuco)
features highlands; the coast is low and humid
population (1985) 6,776,000.

Peron Juan Domingo 1895–1974. President of Argentina 1946–55 and 1973–74. A professional army officer, Perón took part in the right-wing military coup that toppled Argentina's government in 1943.

As secretary of labor and social welfare in the new government, he developed a pro-labor program that won him the loyalty of the *descamisados* "shirtless ones." With their support, and the aid of his actress wife Eva ◊Perón, he was elected president in 1946. With Argentinian beef and wheat in high demand in the years following World War II, Perón was able to improve the country's economy substantially, but his increasingly dictatorial methods caused him to lose the support of the Roman Catholic Church. The death of his popular wife 1952 diminished his support among the workers, and in 1955 he was ousted by the military. Perón returned to Argentina 1973 and was elected president again; his third wife, Isabel Martínez de Perón became vice-president. Upon his death in 1974, she assumed the presidency but was soon ousted by the military.

Perón (María Estela) Isabel (born Martínez) 1931– . President of Argentina 1974–76, and third wife of Juan Perón. She succeeded him after he died in office, but labor unrest, inflation, and political violence pushed the country to the brink of chaos. Accused of corruption, she was held under house arrest for five years. She went into exile in Spain.

Perón María Eva (Evita) Duarte de 1919–1952. Argentinian populist leader, born in Buenos Aires. A successful film actress, she married Juan ◊Perón in 1945. When he became president the following year, she became his chief adviser and the unofficial minister of health and labor, devoting herself to helping the poor, improving education, and achieving women's suffrage. She was politically astute and sought the vice-presidency in 1951 but was opposed by the army and withdrew. After her death from cancer in 1952, Juan's political strength began to decline.

perpetual motion the idea that a machine can be designed and constructed in such a way that, once started, it will continue in motion indefinitely without requiring any further input of energy (motive power). Such a device contradicts the two laws of thermodynamics that state that (1) energy can neither be created nor destroyed (the law of conservation of energy) and (2) heat cannot by itself flow from a cooler to a hotter object. As a result, all practical (real) machines require a continuous supply of energy, and no heat engine is able to convert all the heat into useful work.

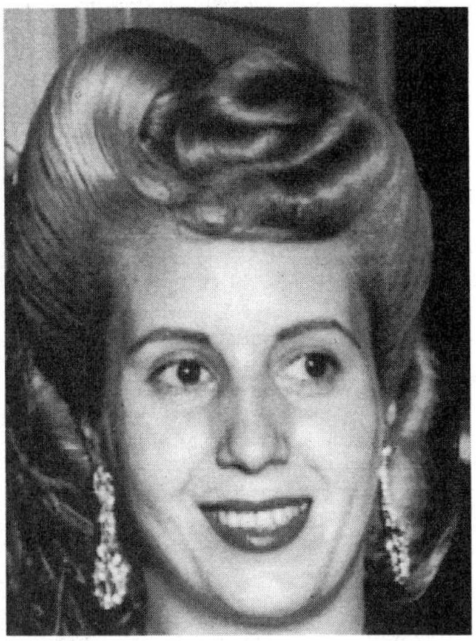

***Perón** Eva (Evita) Perón used her talents as a broadcaster and speaker to gain support for her husband Juan Perón, the Argentinian leader.*

Perpignan market town (olives, fruit, wine), resort, and capital of the Pyrénées-Orientales *département* of France, just off the Mediterranean coast, near the Spanish border; population (1982) 138,000. Overlooking Perpignan is the castle of the counts of Roussillon.

Perrault Charles 1628–1703. French author of the fairy tales *Contes de ma mère l'oye/Mother Goose's Fairy Tales* 1697, which include "Sleeping Beauty," "Little Red Riding Hood," "Blue Beard," "Puss in Boots," and "Cinderella."

Perrin Jean 1870–1942. French physicist who produced the crucial evidence that finally established the atomic nature of matter. Assuming the atomic hypothesis, Perrin demonstrated how the phenomenon of ◊Brownian movement could be used to derive precise values for ◊Avogadro's number. He was awarded the 1926 Nobel Prize for Physics.

perry fermented alcoholic beverage similar to hard cider, but made from pears, produced mainly in Normandy and the English West Country.

Perry Matthew Calbraith 1794–1858. US naval officer, commander of the expedition of 1853 that reopened communication between Japan and the outside world after 250 years' isolation. A show of evident military superiority, the use of steamships (thought by the Japanese to be floating volcanoes), and an exhibition of US technical superi-

***Perry** Commodore Matthew Perry, whose 1853 expedition to Japan led to the Treaty of Kanigawa, giving the US trading rights with Japan.*

ority enabled him to negotiate the Treaty of Kanagawa 1854, granting the US trading rights with Japan.

Born in Newport, Rhode Island, he fought in the War of 1812 and the Mexican War 1847. In the early 1800s he helped to found the African state of Liberia for free US blacks, and in the 1830s and 1840s he developed an engineering corps for the US navy. He was the younger brother of Oliver Hazard ◊Perry.

Perry Oliver Hazard 1785–1819. US naval officer. Born in South Kingston, Rhode Island, Perry began his naval career 1799 as a midshipman and saw action in the Tripolitan War. During the War of 1812 he played a decisive role in securing American control of Lake Erie. Ordered there in 1813, he supervised the construction of a small battle fleet and was responsible for the decisive victory over the British at the Battle of Put-in-Bay and participated in the Battle of the Thames.

Perry was sent to the Mediterranean after the war. He died of fever while on a cruise to South America.

Perse Saint-John. Adopted name of Alexis Saint-Léger 1887–1975. French poet and diplomat, a US citizen from 1940. His first book of verse, *Eloges* 1911, reflects the ambience of the West Indies, where he was born and raised. His later works include *Anabase* 1924, an epic poem translated by T S Eliot in 1930. Nobel Prize 1960.

Entering the foreign service in 1914, he was secretary-general 1933–40. He then emigrated permanently to the US, and was deprived of French citizenship by the Vichy government.

Persephone Greek goddess (Roman Proserpina), the daughter of Zeus and Demeter. She was carried off to the underworld as the bride of Pluto, who later agreed that she should spend six months of the year with her mother. The myth symbolizes the growth and decay of vegetation and the changing seasons.

Persepolis ancient capital of the Persian Empire, 40 mi/65 km NE of Shiraz. It was burned down after its capture in 331 BC by Alexander the Great.

Perseus in Greek mythology, son of Zeus and Danaë. He slew ◊Medusa, the Gorgon, rescued ◊Andromeda, and became king of Tiryns.

Perseus in astronomy, a constellation of the northern hemisphere, near Cassiopeia, and represented as the mythological hero. The eye of the decapitated Gorgon is represented by the variable star Algol. Perseus lies in the Milky Way and contains the Double Cluster, a twin cluster of stars. Every August the Perseid meteor shower radiates from its northern part.

Pershing John Joseph 1860–1948. US general who commanded the American Expeditionary Force sent to France 1917–18 during World War I. He was responsible for more than 2 million men and fought successfully to keep them a separate unit.

Born in Laclede, Missouri, Pershing graduated from West Point 1886 and served in the Spanish-American War 1898, the Philippines 1899–1903, and Mexico 1916–17. His distinguished service as commander of the American Expeditionary Forces in France earned him a newly created rank, general of the armies. His memoirs *My Experiences in the World War* 1931 earned him a Pulitzer prize in history 1932.

Persia, ancient kingdom in SW Asia. The early Persians were a nomadic Aryan people who migrated through the Caucasus to the Iranian plateau.

7th century BC The Persians were established in the present region of Fars, which then belonged to the Assyrians.

550 BC Cyrus the Great overthrew the empire of the Medes, to whom the Persians had been subject, and founded the Persian Empire.

539 BC Having conquered all Anatolia, Cyrus added Babylonia (including Syria and Palestine) to his empire.

529–485 BC Darius I organized an efficient centralized system of administration and extended Persian rule east into Afghanistan and NW India and as far north as the Danube, but the empire was weakened by internal dynastic struggles.

499–449 BC The Persian Wars with Greece ended Persian domination of the ancient world.

331 BC Alexander the Great drove the Persians under Darius III (died 330 BC) into retreat at Arbela on the Tigris, marking the end of the Persian Empire and the beginning of the Hellenistic period under the Seleucids.

AD 226 The Sassanian Empire was established in Persia and annexed Parthia.

637 Arabs took the capital, Ctesiphon, and introduced Islam in place of Zoroastrianism.

For modern history see ◊Iran.

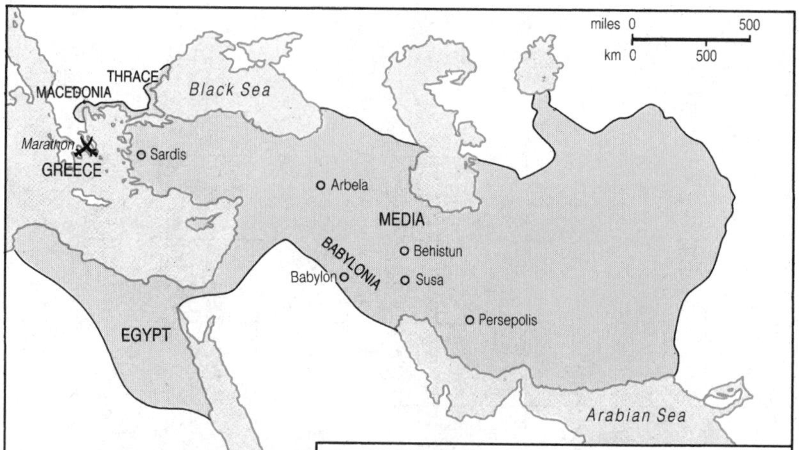
miles 0 500
km 0 500
THRACE
MACEDONIA
Black Sea
Marathon
GREECE
o Sardis
o Arbela
MEDIA
BABYLONIA
o Behistun
Babylon
o Susa
o Persepolis
EGYPT
Arabian Sea
Ancient Persia under Darius I c. 490 BC

Persian inhabitant of or native to Persia, now Iran, and referring to the culture and the language. Persian is the official language of Iran and is written in a modified Arabic script; it belongs to the Indo-Iranian branch of Indo-European. The Persians are descended from central Asians of S Russia (◊Aryans), who migrated S into the region about 2000 BC.

Persian art see ◊ancient art: art of early civilizations.

Persian Gulf or *Arabian Gulf* a large shallow inlet of the Arabian Sea; area 90,000 sq mi/ 233,000 sq km. It divides the Arabian peninsula from Iran and is linked by the Strait of Hormuz and the Gulf of Oman to the Arabian Sea. Oilfields surround it in the Gulf States of Bahrain, Iran, Iraq, Kuwait, Oman, Qatar, Saudi Arabia, and the United Arab Emirates.

Persian language member of the Indo-Iranian branch of the Indo-European language family and the official language of the state once known as Persia but now called Iran. Persian is known to its own speakers as Farsi, the language of the province of Fars (Persia proper). It is written in the Arabic script, from right to left, and has a large mixture of Arabic religious, philosophical, and technical vocabulary.

Persian literature before the Arab conquest it is represented by the sacred books of ◊Zoroastrianism known as the *Avesta* and later translated into Pahlavi, in which language there also appeared various secular writings. After the conquest the use of Arabic became widespread. The Persian language was revived during the 9th century, and the following centuries saw a succession of brilliant poets, including the epic writer Firdawsi, the didactic S'adi (1184–1291), the mystic Rumi (1207–73), the lyrical Hafiz, and Jami, who combined the gifts of his predecessors and is considered the last of the Classical poets. Omar Khayyam, who is well known outside Persia, is considered less important there. In the 16th and 17th centuries many writers worked in India, still using Classical forms and themes, and it was not until the revolutionary movements and contact with the West during the 20th century that Persian literature developed further.

Persian Wars a series of conflicts between Greece and Persia 499–449 BC. The eventual victory of Greece marked the end of Persian domination of the ancient world and the beginning of Greek supremacy.

499 BC Revolt of the Ionian Greeks against Persian rule.

490 BC Darius I of Persia defeated at Marathon.

480 BC Xerxes I victorious at Thermopylae (narrow pass from Thessaly to Locris, which Leonidas, king of Sparta, and 1,000 men defended to the death against the Persians); Athens was captured, but the Greek navy was victorious at ◊Salamis.

479 BC Greeks under Spartan general Pausanias (died c. 470) victorious at Plataea, driving the Persians from the country.

persimmon any tree of the genus *Diospyros* of the ebony family Ebenaceae, especially the common persimmon *D. virginiana* of the SE US. Up to 60 ft/19 m high, the persimmon has alternate oval leaves and yellow-green unisexual flowers. The small, sweet, orange fruits are edible.

The Japanese persimmon *D. kaki* has larger fruits and is widely cultivated.

personal computer (PC) another name for ◊microcomputer. The term is also used, more specifically, to mean the IBM Personal Computer and computers based on it.

The first IBM PC was introduced in 1981; it had 64 kilobytes of random access memory (RAM) and one floppy disk drive. It was followed in 1983 by the XT (with a hard-disk drive) and in 1984 by the AT (based on a more powerful ◊microprocessor). Many manufacturers have copied the basic design, which is now regarded as a standard for business microcomputers.

personality an individual's characteristic way of behaving across a wide range of situations.

Two broad dimensions of personality are ◊extroversion and ◊neuroticism. A number of more specific personal traits have also been described, including ◊psychopathy (antisocial behavior).

personification a figure of speech in which animals, plants, objects, and ideas are treated as if they were human or alive ("Clouds chased each other across the face of the moon"; "Nature smiled on their work and gave it her blessing"; "The future beckoned eagerly to them").

personnel management that part of management concerned with people at work and their relations within a firm. The main functions of the personnel manager usually include staff recruitment, training and welfare.

The term personnel management is somewhat misleading in that it is usually line managers who manage the work force, while personnel man-

Peru
Republic of
(República del Perú)

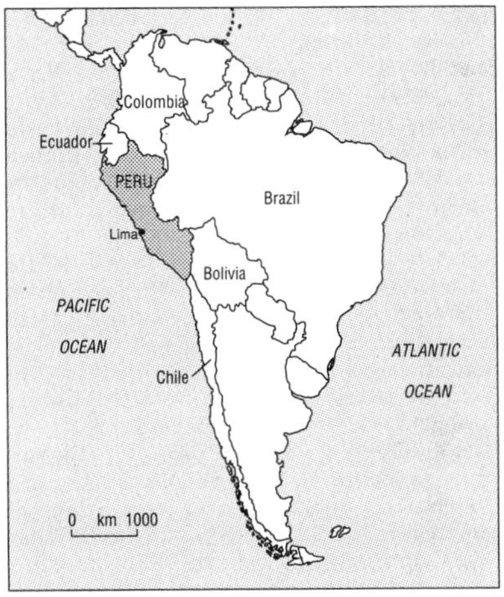
Colombia
Ecuador
PERU
Brazil
Lima
Bolivia
PACIFIC
OCEAN
ATLANTIC
OCEAN
Chile
0 km 1000

area 496,216 sq mi/1,285,200 sq km
capital Lima, including port of Callao
cities Arequipa, Iquitos, Chiclayo, Trujillo
physical Andes mountains N–S cover 27% separating Amazon river-basin jungle in NE from coastal plain in W; desert along coast N–S
features Lake Titicaca; Atacama Desert; Nazca lines, monuments of Machu Picchu, Chanchan, Charín de Huantar
head of state and government Alberto Fujimoro from 1990
political system democratic republic
political parties American Popular Revolutionary Alliance (APRA), moderate, left-wing; United Left (IU), left-wing
exports coca, coffee, alpaca, llama and vicuna wool, fish meal, lead (largest producer in South America), copper, iron, oil
currency new sol
population (1990 est) 21,904,000 (46% Indian, mainly Quechua and Aymara; 43% mixed Spanish-Indian descent); growth rate 2.6% p.a.
life expectancy men 61, women 66
language Spanish 68%, Quechua 27% (both official), Aymará 3%
religion Roman Catholic 90%
literacy men 91%/women 78% (1985 est)
GNP $19.6 bn (1988); $940 per head (1984)
chronology
1824 Independence achieved from Spain.
1849–74 Some 80,000–100,000 Chinese laborers arrived in Peru to fill menial jobs such as collecting guano.
1902 Boundary dispute with Bolivia settled.
1927 Boundary dispute with Colombia settled.
1942 Boundary dispute with Ecuador settled.
1948 Army coup, led by Gen Manuel Odria, installed a military government.
1963 Return to civilian rule, with Fernando Belaúnde Terry as president.
1968 Return of military government in a bloodless coup by Gen Juan Velasco Alvarado.
1975 Velasco replaced, in a bloodless coup, by Gen Morales Bermudez.
1980 Return to civilian rule, with Fernando Belaúnde as president.
1981 Boundary dispute with Ecuador renewed.
1985 Belaúnde succeeded by Social Democrat Alan García Perez.
1987 President García delayed the nationalization of Peru's banks after a vigorous campaign against the proposal.
1988 García pressured to seek help from the International Monetary Fund.
1989 The International Development Bank suspended credit to Peru because it was six months behind in debt payments. The annual inflation rate to April was 4,329.4%. Mario Vargas Llosa entered presidential race; his Democratic Front scored major victories in municipal elections Nov.
1990 In upset, political novice Alberto Fujimoro, the son of Japanese immigrants, forced a runoff in presidential election and defeated Vargas Llosa.

agers provide a mainly supportive and advisory service.

perspiration the excretion of water and dissolved substances from the ◊sweat glands of the skin of mammals. Perspiration has two main functions: body cooling by the evaporation of water from the skin surface, and excretion of waste products such as salts.

Perth industrial town in Tayside, E Scotland, on the river Tay; population (1981) 42,000. It was the capital of Scotland from the 12th century until James I of Scotland was assassinated here 1437.

Perth capital of Western Australia, with its port at nearby Fremantle on the Swan river; population (1986) 1,025,300. Products include textiles, cement, furniture, and vehicles. It was founded 1829 and is the commercial and cultural center of the state.

Peru country in South America, on the Pacific, bounded N by Ecuador and Colombia, E by Brazil and Bolivia, and S by Chile.

government The 1980 constitution provides for a president who is head of both state and government, elected by universal suffrage for a five-year term, and governing with an appointed council of ministers.

The two-chamber legislature, the National Congress, comprises a 60-member Senate and a 180-member Chamber of Deputies, also popularly elected for five years. Senators are elected on a national basis, but members of the Chamber are elected, through a system of proportional representation, from local constituencies. The two main political parties are the democratic left-wing American Popular Revolutionary Alliance (APRA) and the alliance of six left-wing parties, the Unified Left (IU).

history For early history, see ◊American Indian. The ◊Chimu culture flourished from about 1200 and was gradually superseded by the ◊Incan empire, building on 800 years of Andean civilization and covering a large part of South America. Civil war had weakened the Incas when the conquistador ◊Pizarro arrived from Spain 1532 and began raiding, looting, and enslaving the people. He executed the last of the Inca emperors, Atahualpa, 1533. Before Pizarro's assassination 1541, Spanish rule was firmly established.

A native revolt by ◊Túpac Amarú 1780 failed, and during the successful rebellions by the European settlers in other Spanish possessions in South America 1810–22, Peru remained the Spanish government's headquarters; it was the last to achieve independence 1824. It attempted union with Bolivia 1836–39. It fought a naval war against Spain 1864–66, and in the ◊Pacific War against Chile 1879–83 over the nitrate fields of the Atacama Desert, Peru was defeated and lost three provinces (one, Tacna, was returned 1929). Other boundary disputes were settled by arbitration 1902 with Bolivia, 1927 with Colombia, and 1942 with Ecuador. Peru declared war on Germany and Japan Feb 1945.

Peru was ruled by right-wing dictatorships from the mid-1920s until 1945, when free elections returned. Although Peru's oldest political organization, APRA, was the largest party in Congress, it was constantly thwarted by smaller conservative groups, anxious to protect their business interests. APRA was founded in the 1920s to fight imperialism throughout South America, but Peru was the only country where it became established.

In 1948 a group of army officers led by General Manuel Odría ousted the elected government, temporarily banned APRA, and installed a military junta. Odría became president 1950 and remained in power until 1956. In 1963 military rule ended, and Fernando Belaúnde Terry, the joint candidate of the Popular Action (AP) and Christian Democrats (PDC) parties, won the presidency, while APRA took the largest share of the Chamber of Deputies seats.

After economic problems and industrial unrest, Belaúnde was deposed in a bloodless coup 1968, and the army returned to government led by General Velasco Alvarado. Velasco introduced land reform, with private estates being turned into cooperative farms, but he failed to return any land to Indian peasant communities, and the Maoist guerrillas of *Sendero Luminoso* ("Shining Path") became increasingly active in the Indian region of S Peru.

Another bloodless coup, 1975, brought in General Morales Bermúdez. He called elections for the presidency and both chambers of Congress May 1980, and Belaúnde was re-elected. Belaúnde embarked on a program of agrarian and industrial reform, but at the end of his presidency, in 1985, the country was again in a state of economic and social crisis. His constitutionally elected successor was the young Social Democrat Alan García Pérez, who embarked on a program to cleanse the army and police of the old guard. By Feb 1986 about 1,400 had elected to retire. After trying to expand the economy with price and exchange controls, in July 1987 he announced his intention to nationalize the banks and insurance companies but delayed the move in Aug, after a vigorous campaign against the proposal.

In 1989 the International Development Bank suspended credit to Peru because it was six months behind in debt payments. The annual inflation rate to April was 4,329.4%. García Pérez declared his support for the Sandinista government in Nicaragua and criticized US policy throughout Latin America. The party of García Pérez, constitutionally barred from seeking re-election, saw its popularity slip in the Nov 1989 municipal elections. Novelist Mário Vargas Llosa, the candidate of the center-right Democratic Front coalition, was long considered the favorite to succeed García Pérez. However, Alberto Fujimoro, the son of Japanese immigrants and leader of a new party, Change 90, forced a run-off in April elections. A political novice, Fujimoro won a substantial victory in June. Soon after taking office he instituted a drastic economic adjustment program in an attempt to halt Peru's inflation and to pay foreign debt.

Peru Current formerly known as Humboldt Current cold ocean ◊current flowing north from the Antarctic along the W coast of South America to S Ecuador, then west. It reduces the coastal temperature, making the W slopes of the Andes arid because winds are already chilled and dry when they meet the coast.

Perugia capital of Umbria, Italy, 1,700 ft/520 m above the river Tiber, about 85 mi/137 km N of Rome; population (1988) 148,000. Its industries include textiles, liqueurs, and chocolate. One of the 12 cities of Etruria, it surrendered to Rome 309 BC. There is a university 1276, municipal palace 1281, and a 15th-century cathedral.

Perugino Pietro. Original name of Pietro Vannucci 1446–1523. Italian painter, active chiefly in Perugia. He taught Raphael who absorbed his soft and graceful figure style. Perugino produced paintings for the lower walls of the Sistine Chapel 1481 (Vatican) and in 1500 decorated the Sala del Cambio in Perugia.

Perutz Max 1914– . British biochemist who shared the 1962 Nobel Prize for Chemistry with John

Kendrew for work on the structure of the hemoglobin molecule.

Born in Austria, Perutz moved to Britain in 1936 to work with John Bernal (1901–1971) at Cambridge University. After internment in Canada as an alien during World War II he returned to Cambridge and completed his research in 1959.

Pesach the Hebrew name for the ◊Passover festival.

Pescadores (Chinese *Penghu*) group of about 60 islands off Taiwan, of which they form a dependency; area 50 sq mi/130 sq km.

Pescara town in Abruzzi, E Italy, at the mouth of the Pescara river, on the Adriatic; population (1988) 131,000. Hydroelectric installations supply Rome with electricity. It is linked to Yugoslavia by ferry.

Peshawar capital of North-West Frontier Province, Pakistan, 11 mi/18 km E of the Khyber Pass; population (1981) 555,000. Products include textiles, leather, and copper.

pessary medical device designed to be inserted into the vagina. Usually they are for administering drugs locally, made from glycerine or oil of theobromine, which melts within the vagina to release the contained substance; for example, a contraceptive, antibiotic, or antifungal agent. Others are used permanently to support a displaced womb.

Pessoa Fernando 1888–1935. Portuguese poet. Born in Lisbon, he was brought up in South Africa and was bilingual in English and Portuguese. His verse is considered to be the finest written in Portuguese this century. He wrote under three assumed names, which he called "heteronyms"—Alvaro de Campos, Ricardo Reis, and Alberto Caeiro—for each of which he invented a biography.

pest in biology, any insect, fungus, rodent, or other living organism that has a harmful effect on human beings, other than those that directly cause human diseases. Most pests damage crops or livestock, but the term also covers those that damage buildings, destroy food stores, and spread disease.

Pestalozzi Johann Heinrich 1746–1827. Swiss educator who advocated Rousseau's "natural" principles (of natural development and the power of example), and described his own theories in *Wie Gertrude ihre Kinder lehrt/How Gertrude Teaches her Children* 1801. He stressed the importance of mother and home in a child's education.

pesticide any chemical used in farming, gardening, and indoors to combat pests and the diseases they carry. Pesticides are of three main types: insecticides (to kill insects), fungicides (to kill fungal diseases), and herbicides (to kill plants, mainly those considered weeds). The safest pesticides are those made from plants, such as the insecticides pyrethrum and derris. More potent are synthetic products, such as chlorinated hydrocarbons. These products, including DDT and dieldrin, are highly toxic to wildlife and human beings, so their use is now restricted by law in some areas and is declining. Safer pesticides such as malathion are based on organic phosphorus compounds, but they still present hazards to health.

Pesticides were used to deforest SE Asia during the Vietnam war, causing death and destruction to the area's ecology and lasting health and agricultural problems.

pet animal kept for companionship and occasionally for status. Research suggests that interaction with a pet induces relaxation (slower heart rate and lower blood pressure). In 16th–17th century Europe, keeping animals in this way was thought suggestive of witchcraft.

Pétain Henri Philippe 1856–1951. French general and right-wing politician. His defense of Verdun 1916 during World War I made him a national hero. In World War II he became prime minister June 1940 and signed an armistice with Germany. Removing the seat of government to ◊Vichy, he established an authoritarian regime. He was imprisoned after the war.

Peter I As tsar of Russia, Peter I initiated a modernization and Westernization movement.

With the Allied invasion he was taken to Germany, but returned 1945 and was sentenced to death for treason, the sentence being commuted to life imprisonment.

petal part of a flower whose function is to attract pollinators such as insects or birds. Petals are frequently large and brightly colored and may also be scented. Some have a nectary at the base and markings on the petal surface, known as ◊honey guides, to direct pollinators to the source of the nectar. In wind-pollinated plants, however, the petals are usually small and insignificant, and sometimes absent altogether. Petals are derived from modified leaves, and are known collectively as a ◊corolla.

Some insect-pollinated plants also have inconspicuous petals, with large colorful ◊bracts or ◊sepals taking over their role, or strong scents that attract pollinators such as flies unaided.

Petaluma city in NW California, N of San Francisco, on the Petaluma river. It is an agricultural center for poultry and dairy products; population (1990) 43,184.

Peter Laurence J 1910–1990. Canadian writer and teacher, author (with Raymond Hull) of *The Peter Principle* 1969, in which he outlined the theory of how people tend to be promoted into positions for which they are incompetent.

Peter three tsars of Russia:

Peter I the Great 1672–1725. Tsar of Russia from 1682 on the death of his brother Tsar Feodor; he assumed control of the government 1689. He attempted to reorganize the country on Western lines; the army was modernized, a fleet was built, the administrative and legal systems were remodeled, education was encouraged, and the church was brought under state control. On the Baltic coast, where he had conquered territory from Sweden, Peter built his new capital, St Petersburg.

After a successful campaign against the Ottoman Empire 1696, he visited Holland and Britain to study Western techniques, and worked in Dutch and English shipyards. In order to secure an outlet to the Baltic, Peter undertook a war with Sweden 1700–21, which resulted in the acquisition of Estonia and parts of Latvia and Finland. A war with Persia 1722–23 added Baku to Russia.

Peter II 1715–1730. Tsar of Russia from 1727. Son of Peter the Great, he had been passed over in favor of Catherine I 1725 but succeeded her 1727. He died of smallpox.

Peter III 1728–1762. Tsar of Russia 1762. Weak-minded son of Peter I's eldest daughter, Anne, he was adopted 1741 by his aunt ◊Elizabeth, Empress of Russia, and at her command married the future Catherine II 1745. He was deposed in favor of his wife and probably murdered by her lover Alexius Orlov.

Peter I 1844–1921. King of Serbia from 1903. He was the son of Prince Alexander Karageorgevich and was elected king when the last Obrenovich king was murdered 1903. He took part in the retreat of the Serbian army 1915, and in 1918 was proclaimed first king of the Serbs, Croats, and Slovenes (renamed Yugoslavia in 1921).

Peter II 1923–1970. King of Yugoslavia 1934–45. He succeeded his father, Alexander I, and assumed the royal power after the overthrow of the regency 1941. He escaped to the UK after the German invasion, and married Princess Alexandra of Greece 1944. He was dethroned 1945 when Marshal Tito came to power and the Soviet-backed federal republic was formed.

Peter, St Christian martyr, the author of two epistles in the New Testament and leader of the apostles. He is regarded as the first bishop of Rome, whose mantle the pope inherits. His emblem is two keys; feast day June 29.

Originally a fisherman of Capernaum, on the Sea of Galilee, Peter may have been a follower of John the Baptist, and was the first to acknowledge Jesus as the Messiah. His real name was Simon, but he was nicknamed Kephas ("Peter," from the Greek for "rock") by Jesus, as being the rock upon which he would build his church. Tradition has it that he later settled in Rome; he was martyred during the reign of the emperor Nero, perhaps by crucifixion. Bones excavated from under the Basilica of St Peter's in the Vatican 1968 were accepted as his by Pope Paul VI.

Peterborough city in Cambridgeshire, England, noted for its 12th-century cathedral; population (1981) 115,400. It was designated a new town 1967. Nearby Flag Fen disclosed 1985 a well-preserved Bronze Age settlement of 660 BC.

Peter Damian, St real name Pietro Damianai 1007–1072. Italian monk who was associated with the initiation of clerical reform by Pope Gregory VII.

Peter I Island uninhabited island in the Bellingshausen Sea, Antarctica, belonging to Norway since 1931; area 69 sq mi/180 sq km.

Peter Lombard 1100–1160. Italian Christian theologian whose *Sententiarum libri quatuor* considerably influenced Catholic doctrine.

Peterloo massacre the events in St Peter's Fields, Manchester, England, Aug 16, 1819, when an open-air meeting in support of parliamentary reform was charged by yeomanry and hussars. Eleven people were killed and 500 wounded. The name was given in analogy with the Battle of Waterloo.

Peter Pan or ***The Boy Who Wouldn't Grow Up*** a play for children by James ◊Barrie, first performed in 1904. Peter Pan, an orphan with magical powers, arrives in the night nursery of the Darling children, Wendy, John, and Michael. He teaches them to fly and introduces them to the Never Never Land inhabited by fantastic characters, including the fairy Tinkerbell, the Lost Boys, and the pirate Captain Hook. The play was followed by a story, *Peter Pan in Kensington Gardens* 1906, and a book of the play 1911.

Peter Rabbit full title ***The Tale of Peter Rabbit*** first of the children's stories written and illustrated by English author Beatrix ◊Potter, published in 1900. The series, which included *The Tailor of Gloucester* 1902; *The Tale of Mrs Tiggy Winkle* 1904; *The Tale of Jeremy Fisher* 1906; and

petrel

Madeiran fork-tailed petrel

a sequel to Peter Rabbit, *The Tale of the Flopsy Bunnies* 1909, were based on her observation of family pets and wildlife around her home in the English Lake District.

Petersburg city in SE Virginia, on the Appomattox river, S of Richmond. Industries include tobacco products, textiles, leather products, boat building, and chemicals; population (1990) 38,386. It was the site of Fort Henry 1646, as well as of Revolutionary War and Civil War battles.

Peter's pence in the Roman Catholic Church, voluntary annual contribution to papal administrative costs; during the 10th–16th centuries it was a compulsory levy of one penny per household.

Peter the Hermit 1050–1115. French priest whose eloquent preaching of the First ◊Crusade sent thousands of peasants marching against the Turks, who massacred them in Asia Minor. Peter escaped and accompanied the main body of crusaders to Jerusalem.

petiole in botany, the stalk attaching the leaf blade, or ◊lamina, to the stem. Typically it is continuous with the midrib of the leaf and attached to the base of the lamina, but occasionally it is attached to the lower surface of the lamina (a peltate leaf), as in the nasturtium. Petioles that are flattened and leaflike are termed phyllodes. Leaves that lack a petiole are said to be ◊sessile.

Petipa Marius 1818–1910. French choreographer. For the Imperial Ballet in Russia he created masterpieces such as *La Bayadère* 1877, *The Sleeping Beauty* 1890, *Swan Lake* 1895 (with Ivanov), and *Raymonda* 1898, which are still performed.

petit point or ***tent stitch*** a short, slanting embroidery stitch used on open-net canvas for upholstery and cushions to form a solid background. It was common in the 18th century.

Petöfi Sándor 1823–1849. Hungarian nationalist poet. He published his first volume of poems 1844. He expressed his revolutionary ideas in the semiautobiographical poem "The Apostle," and died fighting the Austrians in the battle of Segesvár.

Petra (Arabic *Wadi Musa*) ancient city carved out of the red rock at a site in Jordan, on the eastern slopes of the Wadi el Araba, 56 mi/90 km S of the Dead Sea. An Edomite stronghold and capital of the Nabataeans in the 2nd century, it was captured by the Roman emperor Trajan 106 and destroyed by the Arabs in the 7th century. It was forgotten in Europe until 1812 when the Swiss traveler Jacob Burckhardt (1818–1897) came across it.

Petrarch (Italian ***Petrarca***) Francesco 1304–1374. Italian poet, born in Arezzo, a devotee of the Classical tradition. His *Il Canzoniere* is composed of sonnets in praise of his idealized love "Laura," whom he first saw 1327 (she was a married woman and refused to become his mistress).

From 1337 he often stayed in secluded study at his home at Vaucluse, near Avignon, and, eager to restore the glories of Rome, wanted to return the papacy there from Avignon. He was a friend of ◊Boccaccio, and supported ◊Rienzi's republic 1347.

petrel any of various families of seabirds, including (1)the worldwide storm petrels (family Procellariidae), which include the smallest seabirds (some only 5 in/13 cm long) and (2) the diving petrels (family Pelecanoididae) of the S hemisphere, which feed by diving underwater and are characterized by having nostril tubes. They include ◊fulmars and ◊shearwaters.

Most familiar is Wilson's storm petrel *Oceanites oceanicus*, which breeds in the S hemisphere and migrates to the N Atlantic in winter. Seldom coming to land except to breed, they lay a single egg in holes among the rocks. They are 7 in/18 cm long and sooty black with a white rump band.

Like other ground-nesting or burrow-nesting seabirds, petrels are vulnerable to predators such as rats that take eggs and nestlings. Several island species are in danger of extinction, including the Bermuda petrel *Pterodroma cahow* and the Freira petrel of Madeira *P. madeira*.

Petrie (William Matthew) Flinders 1853–1942. English archeologist who excavated sites in Egypt (the pyramids at Gîza, the temple at Tanis, the Greek city of Naucratis in the Nile delta, Tell el Amarna, Naquada, Abydos, and Memphis) and Palestine from 1880.

Petrie's work was exacting and systematic, and he developed dating sequences of pottery styles that correlated with dynastic and predynastic events.

petrochemical chemical derived from the processing of ◊petroleum. The petrochemical industry is a term embracing those industrial manufacturing processes that obtain their raw materials from the processing of petroleum.

petrodollars in economics, dollar earnings of nations that make up the ◊Organization of Petroleum Exporting Countries (OPEC).

Petrograd name 1914–24 of ◊Saint Petersburg, city in the USSR.

petroleum or ***crude oil*** natural mineral oil, a thick greenish-brown flammable liquid found underground in permeable rocks. Petroleum consists of hydrocarbons mixed with oxygen, sulfur, nitrogen, and other elements in varying proportions. It is thought to be derived from ancient organic material that has been converted by, first, bacterial action, then heat and pressure (but its origin may be chemical also). From crude petroleum, various products are made by distillation and other processes; for example, fuel oil, gasoline, kerosene, diesel oil, lubricating oil, paraffin wax, and petroleum jelly.

The organic material in petroleum was laid down millions of years ago (hence, fossil fuel). Petroleum is often found below ground level as large lakes floating on water but under a layer of ◊natural gas (mainly methane), in anticlines and other traps below impervious rock layers. Oil may flow naturally from wells under gas pressure from above or water pressure from below, causing it to rise up the borehole, but many oil wells require pumping to bring the oil to the surface.

The occurrence of petroleum was known in ancient times, and used medicinally by American Indians, but the exploitation of oil-fields began with the first commercial well in Pennsylvania 1859.

The US led in production until the 1960s, when the Middle East outproduced other areas, their immense reserves leading to a worldwide dependence on cheap oil for transport and industry. In 1961 the Organization of the Petroleum Exporting Countries (OPEC) was established to avoid exploitation of member countries; after OPEC's price rises in 1973, the International Energy Agency (IEA) was established 1974 to protect the interests of oil-consuming countries. New technologies were introduced to pump oil from offshore and from the Arctic (the Alaska pipeline) in an effort to avoid a monopoly by OPEC.

Petroleum products and chemicals are used in large quantities in the manufacture of detergents, artificial fibers, plastics, insecticides, fertilizers, pharmaceuticals, toiletries, and synthetic rubber. Aviation fuel is a volatile form of gasoline.

The burning of petroleum fuels is one cause of air pollution. The transport of oil can lead to major catastrophes—for example, the *Torrey Canyon* tanker lost off SW England, 1967, which led to an agreement by the international oil companies 1968 to pay compensation for massive shore pollution. The 1989 ◊oil spill in Alaska from the *Exxon Valdez* damaged the Prince William Sound's fragile environment, despite clean-up efforts. Drilling for oil involves the risks of accidental spillage and drilling-rig accidents. The problems associated with oil have led to the various ◊alternative energy technologies.

A new kind of bacterium was developed during the 1970s in the US, capable of "eating" oil as a means of countering oil spills. Its creation gave rise to the so-called Frankenstein law.

petroleum: chronology

1859	Edwin Drake drilled the world's first successful oil well in Titusville, Pennsylvania, to a depth of 70 ft/18 m.
1865	First oil pipeline, 32,000 ft/9,750 m long, constructed at Oil Creek, Pennsylvania, to carry oil from well to nearby coalfield.
1896	First offshore wells drilled from piers off the California coast.
1899	The first gravity meter produced.
1914	Reginald Fessenden patented the seismograph.
1939	The aircraft-borne magnetometer developed to measure magnetism of rocks.
1966	Oil discovered beneath the North Sea.
1967	The worst oil spill in British waters from the *Torrey Canyon*, which struck rocks at Lands End. Over 108,000 tons of oil was spilled.
1974	World's deepest oil well, 31,441 ft/10,941 m, drilled in Oklahoma.
1979	The oil rig *Ixtoc I* in the Gulf of Mexico accidentally released 545,000 tons of oil into the sea. The slick spread for 400 miles. Later the same year, the worst tanker spillage occurred. Two tankers, the *Atlantic Empress* and the *Aegean Captain*, collided off the island of Tobago, in the Caribbean Sea. Over 230,000 tons of oil was spilled.
1984	Exploratory well drilled off the coast of New England, in water of depth 6,942 ft/2,116 m—a world record.
1988	The Piper Alpha drilling rig in the North Sea caught fire in July, killing 167 people.
1989	The worst spill in American waters occurred when 55,000 tons of oil escaped from the *Exxon Valdez* off the Alaskan coast, near Prince William Sound.
1991	The worst spill to date was a consequence of the Gulf War when Iraqi forces opened the pipeline into the Persian Gulf and Coalition forces damaged it during Operation Desert Storm.

petrology branch of ◊geology that deals with the study of rocks, their mineral compositions, and their origins.

Petronius Gaius, died c. AD 66, known as Petronius Arbiter. Roman author of the licentious romance *Satyricon*. He was a companion of the emperor Nero and supervisor of his pleasures.

Petropavlovsk industrial city (flour, agricultural machinery, leather) in the Kazakh Republic, USSR, on the Ishim river, the Trans-Siberian railroad, and the Transkazakh line, opened 1953; population (1987) 233,000. A former caravan station, it was founded as a Russian fortress 1782.

Petropavlovsk-Kamchatskiy Pacific seaport and

Soviet naval base on the E coast of the Kamchatka peninsula, USSR; population (1987) 252,000.

Petrópolis hill resort in SE Brazil, founded by Pedro II; population (1980) 149,427.

Petrovsk former name (until 1921) of the Soviet port ◊Makhachkala.

Petrozavodsk industrial city (metal goods, cement, prefabricated houses, lumber mills), and capital of Karelia Republic, USSR, on the W shore of Lake Onega; population (1987) 264,000. Peter the Great established the township 1703 as an iron-working center; it was named Petrozavodsk 1777.

Petsamo Finnish name of the Murmansk port ◊Pechenga.

Pevsner Nikolaus 1902–1983. Anglo-German art historian. Born in Leipzig, he fled from the Nazis to England. He became an authority on architecture, especially English. His *Outline of European Architecture* was published 1942 and he wrote the series *The Buildings of England* (46 vols) 1951–74, in which he commented on every notable building in the country.

pewter any of various alloys of mostly tin with varying amounts of lead, copper, or antimony. Pewter has been known for centuries and was once widely used for domestic utensils but is now used mainly for ornamental ware.

peyote spineless cactus *Lophopora williamsii* of N Mexico and SW US. It has white or pink flowers. Its buttonlike tops contain the hallucinogen mescaline, which is used by American Indians in religious ceremonies.

Pfalz German name of the historic division of Germany, the ◊Palatinate.

Pforzheim city in Baden-Württemberg, Federal Republic of Germany, 16 mi/26 km SE of Karlsruhe; goldsmith industries; population (1988) 105,000. It was a Roman settlement, and the residence of the ◊margraves of Baden 1300–1565.

pH scale for measuring acidity or alkalinity. A pH of 7.0 (distilled water) indicates neutrality, below 7 is acid, while above 7 is alkaline.

The scale runs from 0 to 14. Strong acids, as used in car batteries, have a pH of about 2; acidic fruits such as citrus fruits are about pH 4. Fertile soils have a pH of about 6.5 to 7.0, while weak alkalis such as soap are 9 to 10. Corrosive alkalis such as lye are pH 13. The pH value of a solution equals the negative logarithm of the concentration of hydrogen ions.

Phaedra in Greek mythology, a Cretan, daughter of Minos and Pasiphae, married to ◊Theseus of Athens. Her adulterous passion for her stepson ◊Hippolytus led to her death in plays by Euripides, Seneca, and Racine.

Phaedrus c. 15 BC–c. AD 50. Roman fable writer, born in Macedonia. He was born a slave and freed by Emperor Augustus. The allusions in his fables (modeled on those of Aesop) caused him to be brought to trial by a minister of Emperor Tiberius. His work was popular in medieval times.

Phaethon in Greek mythology, the son of ◊Helios who was allowed for one day to drive the chariot of the Sun. Losing control of the horses, he almost set the Earth on fire and was killed by Zeus with a thunderbolt.

phage another name for a ◊bacteriophage, a virus that attacks bacteria.

phagocyte a type of ◊white blood cell, or leukocyte, that can engulf a bacterium or other invading microorganism. Phagocytes are found in blood, lymph, and other body tissues, where they also ingest foreign matter and dead tissue. A ◊macrophage differs in size and life span.

Phalangist member of a Lebanese military organization (Phalanges Libanaises), since 1958 the political and military force of the ◊Maronite Church in Lebanon. Its unbending right-wing policies and resistance to the introduction of democratic institutions helped contribute to the civil war in Lebanon.

The Phalanges Libanaises was founded 1936 by Pierre Gemayel after seeing the discipline and authoritarianism of Nazi Germany. Its initial aim was to protect the Maronite position in Lebanon; in 1958 it entered the political arena to oppose growing Arab nationalism.

Phalaris 570–554 BC. Tyrant of the Greek colony of Acragas (Agrigento) in Sicily. He is said to have built a hollow bronze bull in which his victims were roasted alive. He was killed in a people's revolt.

The *Letters of Phalaris* attributed to him were proved by the scholar Richard ◊Bentley to be a forgery of the 2nd century AD.

phalarope any of a genus *Phalaropus* of small, elegant shorebirds in the sandpiper family (Scolopacidae). They have the habit of spinning in the water to stir up insect larvae. They are native to North America, Britain, and polar regions of Europe.

The male phalarope is courted by the female and hatches the eggs. The female is always larger and more colorful.

The red-necked phalarope *P. lobatus*, gray *P. fulicarius*, and Wilson's phalarope *P. tricolor* can be found in North America.

phallus a model of the male sexual organ, used as a fertility symbol in ancient Greece, Rome, Anatolia, India, and many other parts of the world. In Hinduism ◊lingam, it is used as the chief symbolical representation of the deity Shiva.

phanerogam obsolete term for a plant that bears flowers or cones and reproduces by means of seeds, that is an ◊angiosperm and ◊gymnosperm, or a ◊seed plant. Plants such as mosses, fungi, and ferns were known as cryptogams.

Phanerozoic (Greek *phanero* "visible") eon in Earth history, consisting of the most recent 590 million years. It comprises the Paleozoic, Mesozoic, and Cenozoic eras. The vast majority of fossils come from this eon, owing to the evolution of hard shells and internal skeletons. The name means "interval of well-displayed life."

Pharaoh Hebrew form of the Egyptian royal title Per-'o. This term, meaning "great house," was originally applied to the royal household, and after about 950 BC to the king.

Pharisee (Hebrew "separatist") member of a ancient Hebrew political party and sect of Judiasm that formed in Roman-occupied Palestine in the 2nd century BC in protest against all movements favoring Hellenization. They were the party of the common man, standing for rabbi, prayer, and synagogue. They were opposed by the aristocratic Sadducees.

The Pharisees rejected political action, and in the 1st century AD the left wing of their followers, the Zealots, broke away to pursue a revolutionary nationalist policy. After the fall of Jerusalem and the destruction of the Temple AD 70, Pharisee ideas became the basis of orthodox Judaism as the people were dispersed throughout the W Roman empire.

pharmacology study of the origins, applications, and effects of chemical substances on living organisms. Products of the pharmaceutical industry range from aspirin to anticancer agents.

A wide range of resources have been investigated in the search for new and better drugs (human and plant molecular biology, newly discovered soil-grown molds, genetically engineered compounds, and monoclonal antibiotics).

pharynx the interior of the throat, the cavity at the back of the mouth. Its walls are made of muscle strengthened with a fibrous layer and lined with mucous membrane. The internal nostrils lead backwards into the pharynx, which continues downward into the esophagus and (through the epiglottis) into the windpipe. On each side, a Eustachian tube enters the pharynx from the middle ear cavity.

The upper part (nasopharynx) is an airway, but the remainder is a passage for food. Inflammation of the pharynx is named pharyngitis.

phase in physics, a stage in an oscillatory motion, such as a wave motion: two waves are in phase when their peaks and their troughs coincide. Otherwise, there is a phase difference, which has consequences in ◊interference phenomena and ◊alternating current electricity.

phenol

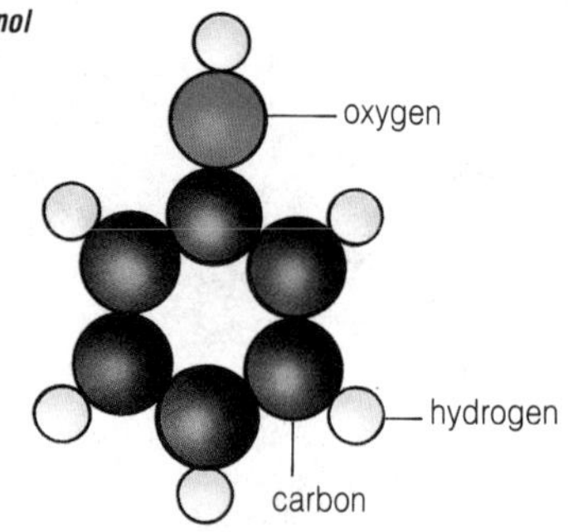
oxygen
hydrogen
carbon

phase see ◊Moon.

PhD abbreviation for Doctor of Philosophy degree.

pheasant any of various large, colorful Asiatic fowls of the family Phasianidae, which also includes grouse, quail and turkey. The plumage of the male Eurasian ring-necked or common pheasant *Phasianus colchicus* is richly tinted with brownish-green, yellow, and red markings, but the female is a camouflaged brownish color. The nest is made in the ground. The male is polygamous.

According to legend, this pheasant was introduced from Asia to Europe by the Argonauts, who brought them from the banks of the river Phasis. They have also been introduced to North America.

Among the more exotically beautiful pheasants of other genera, often kept as ornamental birds, are the golden pheasant *Chrysolophus pictus* from China and the argus pheasant *Argusianus argus* of Malaysia, which has metallic spots or "eyes" on the wings.

phencyclidine hydrochloride (PCP) technical name for ◊angel dust.

phenol member of a group of aromatic chemical compounds with weakly acidic properties, which are characterized by a hydroxyl (-OH) group attached directly to an aromatic ring. The simplest of the phenols, derived from benzene, is also known as phenol and has the formula C_6H_5OH. It is sometimes called carbolic acid and can be extracted from coal tar. Pure phenol consists of colorless, needle-shaped crystals which take up moisture from the atmosphere. It has a strong and characteristic smell and was once used as an antiseptic. It is, however, toxic by absorption through the skin.

phenomena in philosophy, a technical term used in ◊Kant's philosophy, describing things as they appear to us, rather than as they are in themselves.

phenomenalism a philosophical position that argues that statements about objects can be reduced to statements about what is perceived or perceivable. Thus J S Mill defined material objects as "permanent possibilities of sensation." Phenomenalism is closely connected with certain forms of ◊empiricism.

phenomenology the philosophical perspective, founded by the German philosopher ◊Husserl, that in the social sciences concentrates on phenomena as objects of perception (rather than as facts or occurrences that exist independently) in attempting to examine the ways people think about and interpret the world around them. It has been practiced by the philosophers Heidegger, Sartre, and Merleau-Ponty.

In contrast to positivism or "scientific" philosophy, phenomenology sees reality as essentially relative and subjective, and uses such tools as ethnomethodology and symbolic interactionism to focus on the structure of everyday life.

phenotype in genetics, the visible traits, those actually displayed by an organism. The phenotype is not a direct reflection of the ◊genotype because some alleles are masked by the presence of other, dominant alleles (see ◊dominance). The phenotype is further modified by the effects of the environment (for example, poor nutrition stunting growth).

phenylketonuria genetic condition in which the liver of a child cannot control the level of phenylalanine (an ◊amino acid derived from protein food) in the bloodstream in the normal way by excretion in the urine. It is controlled by special diet. Untreated, it causes severe mental handicap.

pheromone chemical signal (such as an odor) that is emitted by one animal and affects the behavior of others. Pheromones are used by many animal species to attract mates.

Phidias mid-5th century BC. Greek Classical sculptor. He supervised the sculptural program for the Parthenon (most of it preserved in the British Museum, London, and known as the Elgin marbles). He also executed the colossal statue of Zeus at Olympia, one of the Seven Wonders of the World.

He was a friend of the political leader Pericles, who made him superintendent of public works in Athens.

Phil. abbreviation for ◊Philadelphia.

Philadelphia industrial city and the world's largest freshwater port, on the Delaware River at the junction of the Schuylkill river, in Pennsylvania; population (1990) 1,585,577, metropolitan area (1990) 5,899,345. Products include refined oil, chemicals, textiles, processed food, printing and publishing, and transportation equipment. It is also a major port of entry and a financial, corporate, and research center. The University of Pennsylvania, the Franklin Institute, and Temple University are here, and the Philadelphia Orchestra and Museum of Art are among the nation's finest. Independence National Historic Park contains Independence Hall (1732–59), where the Declaration of Independence was adopted 1776, and the Liberty Bell.

Founded 1682 by William Penn as the "city of brotherly love," its religious tolerance caused it to become the most populous city in the Thirteen Colonies; it was the first capital of the US (before New York and Washington, DC). The Constitution was drafted here 1787. Benjamin Franklin lived and published here. By 1850 Philadelphia had more than 500,000 inhabitants. The Centennial Exposition, the first US international trade fair (world's fair), was held here 1876. Philadelphia reached a peak population of 2.1 million in 1950. Despite urban decay and substantial outmigration of people and industry since, it is the center of a large metropolitan area that extends into New Jersey and Delaware.

Philae island in the Nile, Egypt, above the first rapids, famed for the beauty of its temple of Isis (founded about 350 BC and in use until the 6th century AD). In 1977 the temple was re-erected on the nearby island of Agilkia above the flooding caused by the Aswan Dam.

philately the collection and study of postage stamps. It originated as a hobby in France about 1860.

Many countries earn extra revenue and cater to the philatelist by issuing sets of stamps to commemorate special events, anniversaries, and so on. There are many specialized fields of collection, from particular countries to specimens that have some defect; for example, contemporary issues that accidentally remain unperforated.

Philby Harry St John Bridger 1885–1960. British explorer. As chief of the British political mission to central Arabia 1917–18, he was the first European to visit the southern provinces of Najd. He wrote *The Empty Quarter* 1933, and *Forty Years in the Wilderness* 1957.

Philby "Kim" (Harold) 1912–1988. British intelligence officer from 1940 and Soviet agent from 1933. He was liaison officer in Washington 1949–51, when he was confirmed to be a double agent and asked to resign. Named in 1963 as having warned Guy Burgess and Donald Maclean

Philip II Philip II, King of Spain 1556–98.

(similarly double agents) that their activities were known, he fled to the USSR and became a Soviet citizen and general in the KGB. A fourth member of the ring was Anthony ◊Blunt.

Philip "King." Name given to Metacomet. c. 1639–1676. Wampanoag leader. Born in Rhode Island, he was the son of Wampanoag chieftain Massasoit. In 1662, after the death of his father and elder brother, Metacomet assumed power and was called "King Philip" by the English colonists. Growing tension over Indian vs. settlers' land rights led to Philip's arrest and the disarming of his people in 1671. The full-scale hostilities that broke out in 1675, known as King Philip's War, culminated with Philip's defeat and murder 1676. Although costly to the English, it ended Indian resistance in New England.

Philip Duke of Edinburgh 1921– . Prince of the UK, husband of Elizabeth II, and a grandson of George I of Greece and a great-great-grandson of Queen Victoria. He was born in Corfu, Greece but brought up in England.

A naturalized British subject, taking the surname Mountbatten, he married Princess Elizabeth (from 1952 Elizabeth II) in 1947, having the previous day received the title Duke of Edinburgh.

Philip six kings of France, including:

Philip II (Philip Augustus) 1165–1223. King of France from 1180. As part of his efforts to establish a strong monarchy and evict the English from their French possessions, he waged war in turn against the English kings Henry II, Richard I (with whom he also went on the Third Crusade), and John (against whom he won the decisive battle of Bouvines in Flanders 1214).

Philip IV the Fair 1268–1314. King of France from 1285. He engaged in a feud with Pope Boniface VIII and made him a prisoner 1303. Clement V (1264–1314), elected pope through Philip's influence 1305, moved the papal seat to Avignon 1309 and collaborated with Philip to suppress the ◊Templars, a powerful order of knights. Philip allied with the Scots against England and invaded Flanders.

Philip VI 1293–1350. King of France from 1328, first of the house of Valois, elected by the barons on the death of his cousin, Charles IV. His claim was challenged by Edward III of England, who defeated him at Crécy 1346.

Philip II of Macedon 382–336 BC. King of ◊Macedonia from 359 BC. He seized the throne from his nephew, for whom he was regent, conquered the Greek city states, and formed them into a league whose forces could be united against Persia. He was assassinated while he was planning this expedition, and was succeeded by his son ◊Alexander the Great. His tomb was discovered at Vergina, N Greece, in 1978.

Philip five kings of Spain, including:

Philip I the Handsome 1478–1506. King of Castile from 1504, through his marriage 1496 to Joanna the Mad (1479–1555). He was the son of the Holy Roman emperor Maximilian I.

Philip II 1527–1598. King of Spain from 1556. He was born at Valladolid, the son of the Hapsburg emperor Charles V, and in 1554 married Queen Mary of England. On his father's abdication 1556 he inherited Spain, the Netherlands, and the Spanish possessions in Italy and the Americas, and in 1580 annexed Portugal. His intolerance and lack of understanding of the Netherlanders drove them into revolt. Political and religious differences combined to involve him in war with England and, after 1589, with France. The defeat of the ◊Spanish Armada marked the beginning of the decline of Spanish power.

Philip V 1683–1746. King of Spain from 1700. A grandson of Louis XIV of France, he was the first Bourbon king of Spain. He was not recognized by the major European powers until 1713. See ◊Spanish Succession, War of the.

Philip, St 1st century AD. In the New Testament, one of the 12 apostles. He was an inhabitant of Bethsaida (N Israel), and is said to have worked as a missionary in Anatolia. Feast day May 3.

Philip Neri, St 1515–1595. Italian Roman Catholic priest who organized the Congregation of the Oratory (see ◊Oratorian). He built the oratory over the church of St Jerome, Rome, where prayer meetings were held and scenes from the Bible performed with music, originating the musical form ◊oratorio. Feast day May 26.

Philippeville former name (until 1962) of Algerian port of ◊Skikda.

Philippi ancient city of Macedonia founded by Philip of Macedon 358 BC. Near Philippi, Mark Antony and Augustus defeated Brutus and Cassius 42 BC. It was the first European town where St Paul preached the Epistle to the Philippians (about AD 53).

Philippines country on an archipelago of more than 7,000 islands W of the Pacific Ocean and S of the SE Asian mainland.

government The constitution was approved by plebiscite in Feb 1987. It provides for a US-style executive president who is elected for a nonrenewable six-year term and a two-chamber legislature or congress: a 24-member Senate and 250-member House of Representatives, with similar respective powers to their counterparts in the US. Senators are elected in national-level contests for six-year terms (a maximum of two consecutive terms). Representatives serve three-year terms (up to a maximum of three consecutive), with 200 being directly elected at the district level and up to a further 50 being appointed by the president from lists of "minority groups." The president appoints an executive cabinet, but, as in the US, while being unable to directly introduce legislation may impose vetoes on congressional bills that can only be overridden by two-thirds majorities in each chamber. There is also a "Bill of Rights" and 15-member Supreme Court.

history The people of the Philippine islands probably came from the ◊Malay Peninsula. They were seminomadic hunters and fishermen when the first Europeans, ◊Magellan's crew, arrived 1521, followed by conquering Spanish forces in 1565. Roman Catholicism was introduced during the reign of ◊Philip II (after whom the islands were named), replacing Islam, which had been spread by Arab traders and missionaries.

In 1898, the US sank the Spanish Armada in Manila Bay. Philippine nationalists proclaimed their independence, but were put down by US forces who killed 200,000 Filipinos, most of them civilians; 4,000 US soldiers died.

During the 19th century there were a series of armed nationalist revolts. These continued after the islands were ceded by Spain to the US in 1898, and increasing self-government was granted in 1916 and 1935. The Philippines were occupied by Japan 1942–45, before becoming a fully independent republic in 1946. A succession of presidents drawn from the islands' wealthy estate-owning elite followed, doing little to improve the lot of the peasant.

In 1965 President Diosdado Macapagal was defeated by Ferdinand ◊Marcos, the leader of the

Philippines
Republic of the
(Republika ng Pilipinas)

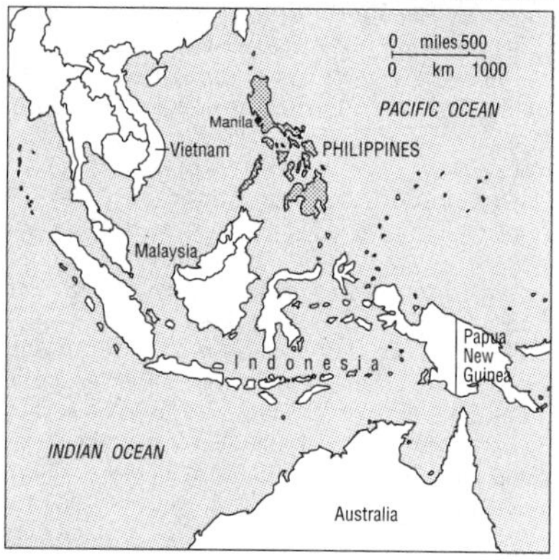

0 miles 500
0 km 1000
PACIFIC OCEAN
Manila
Vietnam
PHILIPPINES
Malaysia
Papua New Guinea
Indonesia
INDIAN OCEAN
Australia

area 115,800 sq mi/300,000 sq km
capital Manila (on Luzon)
cities Quezon City (Luzon), Zamboanga (Mindanao); ports Cebu, Davao (on Mindanao), and Iloilu
physical comprises over 7,000 islands; volcanic mountain ranges traverse main chain N–S; 50% still forested. The largest islands are Luzon 41,754 sq mi/108,172 sq km and Mindanao 36,372 sq mi/94,227 sq km; others include Samar, Negros, Palawan, Panay, Mindoro, Leyte, Cebu, and the Sulu group
features Luzon, site of Clark Field, US air base used as a logistical base in Vietnam War; Subic Bay, US naval base; Mindanao has active volcanoes Apo (9,370 ft/2,855 m) and Pinatubo (5,770 ft/1,759 m), and mountainous rainforest
head of state and government Corazón Aquino from 1986
political system emergent democracy
political parties People's Power, includings the PDP–Laban Party and the Liberal Party, centrist pro-Aquino; Nationalist Party, Union for National Action (UNA), and Grand Alliance for Democracy (GAD), conservative opposition groupings; Mindanao Alliance, Island-based decentralist body
exports sugar, copra (world's largest producer), and coconut oil, timber, copper concentrates, electronics, clothing
currency peso
population (1990 est) 66,647,000 (93% Malaysian); growth rate 2.4% p.a.
life expectancy men 63, women 69 (1989)
language Filipino; English and Spanish
religion Roman Catholic 84%, Protestant 9%, Muslim 5%
literacy 88% (1989)
GNP $38.2 bn; $667 per head (1988)
chronology
1565 Conquered by Spain.
1898 Ceded to the US after Spanish-American War.
1935 Granted internal self-government.
1942–45 Occupied by Japan.
1946 Independence achieved from US.
1965 Ferdinand Marcos elected president.
1983 Opposition leader Benigno Aquino murdered by military guard.
1986 Marcos overthrown by Corazón Aquino's People's Power movement.
1987 "Freedom constitution" adopted; People's Power won majority in congressional elections. Attempted right-wing coup suppressed. Communist guerrillas active. Government in rightward swing.
1988 Land Reform Act gave favorable compensation to large estateholders.
1989 Referendum on southern autonomy failed; Marcos died in exile; Aquino refused to permit burial in Philippines. Sixth and most serious coup attempt suppressed with US aid; Aquino declared state of emergency.
1990 Seventh coup attempt survived by President Aquino.
1991 June: eruption of Mount Pinatubo claimed at least 350 lives. US agreed to give up Clark Field airbase but keep Subic Bay naval base for ten more years. Sept: Philippines senate voted to urge withdrawal of all US forces.

Nationalist Party. Marcos initiated rapid economic development and some land reform. He was re-elected in 1969, but encountered growing opposition from Communist insurgents and Muslim separatists in the south. A high rate of population growth aggravated poverty and unemployment. Some months before his second term had been completed, Marcos declared martial law, suspended the constitution, and began to rule by decree. Intermittent referenda allowed him to retain power. Marcos's authoritarian leadership was criticized for corruption, and in 1977 the opposition leader, Benigno Aquino, was jailed under sentence of death for alleged subversion. In 1978 martial law was relaxed, the 1972 ban on political parties was lifted, and elections for an interim National Assembly were held, resulting in an overwhelming victory for Marcos.

In Jan 1981 martial law was lifted completely, and hundreds of political prisoners released. Marcos then won approval, by referendum, for a partial return to democratic government with himself as president, working with a prime minister and executive council. Political and economic conditions deteriorated, Communist guerrilla insurgency escalated, unemployment climbed to over 30% and the national debt increased. In 1983 Benigno Aquino, returning from self-imposed exile in the US, was shot dead on his arrival at Manila airport. A commission of inquiry reported that Aquino had been killed by the military guard escorting him as part of a broader conspiracy, although Marcos was widely suspected of involvement.

National Assembly elections were held in May 1984, amid violence and widespread claims of corruption, and although the government party stayed in power, the opposition registered significant gains. Then early in 1986 the main anti-Marcos movement, United Nationalist Democratic Organization (UNIDO), chose Corazón ◊Aquino, Benigno's widow, despite her political inexperience, to contest new elections for the presidency that Marcos had been persuaded to hold as a means of maintaining vital US economic and diplomatic support.

The campaign resulted in over 100 deaths, and large-scale electoral fraud was witnessed by international observers. On Feb 16, 1986 the National Assembly declared Marcos the winner, a result disputed by an independent electoral watchdog, the National Citizens' Movement for Free Elections (Namfrel). Corazón Aquino began a nonviolent protest, termed "people's power," which gathered massive popular support, backed by the Roman Catholic church; President Marcos came under strong international pressure, particularly from the US, to step down. On Feb 22, 1986 the army, led by Chief of Staff Lt-Gen Fidel Ramos and defense minister Juan Enrile, declared its support for Aquino, and on Feb 25 Marcos left for exile in Hawaii.

On assuming the presidency, Corazón Aquino dissolved the pro-Marcos National Assembly. She proceeded to govern in a conciliatory fashion, working with a coalition cabinet team comprising opposition politicians and senior military figures. She freed 500 political prisoners and granted an amnesty to the New People's Army (NPA) Communist guerrillas in an effort to end the 17-year-old insurgency and introduced a major rural-employment economic program, with land reforms opposed by property owners.

The new administration endured a series of attempted coups by pro-Marcos supporters and faced serious opposition from Juan Enrile, dismissed in Nov 1986. In Feb 1987 a new "freedom constitution" was overwhelmingly approved in a national plebiscite. This gave Aquino a mandate to rule as president until June 30, 1992. In the subsequent congressional elections, held in May 1987, Aquino's People's Power coalition won over 90% of the elected seats. However, in Aug 1987 the government was rocked by a coup attempt led by Colonel Gregorio "Gringo" Honasan, an army officer closely linked with Enrile, which claimed 53 lives. In response, Aquino effected a major cabinet reshuffle in Sept 1987 that signaled a shift to the right in the government's policy, with tougher measures being instituted toward the NPA and the Land Reform Act 1988 being diluted. Vice President Salvador Laurel, the former leader of UNIDO, was replaced as foreign minister. In Aug 1988 Laurel formed a new right-of-center opposition force, the Union for National Action (UNA) and become president of the revived Nationalist Party in May 1989. Aquino endured a further reverse in Nov 1989 when a regional referendum proposing the merging of the 13 southern provinces, including ◊Mindanao, into an "autonomous region" was rejected. This initiative had been made in an attempt to end the two decades long Muslim separatist struggle led by Moro National Liberation Front (MNLF).

After becoming president, Corazón Aquino enjoyed firm backing from the US. US economic and military aid to the Philippines between 1985 and 1989 was approximately $1.5 billion. In Dec 1989 US air support was provided to help foil a further Honasan-planned coup attempt. Aquino declared a state of emergency, giving her broad powers to impose order. The death of Marcos in exile Sept 28, 1989 provoked rallies of supporters demanding that his body be returned from Hawaii to the Philippines, a demand that Aquino refused. President Aquino survived another coup attempt in Oct 1990. A massive volcanic eruption in June 1991 led to the closure of Clark Air Force Base by the US and, in Oct, was a major factor in the US decision to withdraw from Subic Bay Naval Station. Imelda Marcos returned to the Philippines in Nov.

Philip the Good 1396–1467. Duke of Burgundy from 1419. He engaged in the Hundred Years' War as an ally of England until he made peace with the French at the Council of Arras 1435. He made the Netherlands a center of art and learning.

Philistine member of a seafaring, warlike people of non-Semitic origin who founded city-states on the Palestinian coastal plain in the 12th century BC, adopting a Semitic language and religion. They were at war with the Israelites in the 11th–10th centuries BC (hence the pejorative use of their name in Hebrew records for anyone uncivilized in intellectual and artistic terms). They were largely absorbed into the kingdom of Israel under King David, about 1000 BC.

Philips Anton 1874–1951. Dutch industrialist and founder of an electronics firm. The Philips Bulb and Radio Works 1891 was founded with his brother Gerard, at Eindhoven. Anton served as chair of the company 1921–51, during which time the firm became the largest producer of electrical goods outside the US.

Phillips Wendell 1811–1884. US reformer. Born in Boston and educated at Harvard, Phillips was admitted to the bar 1834. After attending the World Anti-Slavery Convention in London 1840, he became an outspoken abolitionist. A widely traveled lecturer, Phillips espoused a variety of social causes in addition to abolitionism, including feminism, prohibition, labor unionization, and improved treatment of American Indians.

Critical of the Mexican War and the conduct of

the American Civil War by Lincoln, Phillips was a reform candidate for governor of Massachusetts 1870.

Phillips curve a graph showing the relationship between percentage changes in wages and unemployment, and indicating that wages rise faster during periods of low unemployment as employers compete for labor. The implication is that the dual objectives of low unemployment and low inflation are inconsistent. The concept has been widely questioned since the early 1960s because of the apparent instability of the wages/unemployment relationship. It was developed by the British economist A(lban) W(illiam) Phillips (1914–1975), who plotted graphically wage and unemployment changes between 1861 and 1957.

Philoctetes in Greek mythology, a hero in the Trojan War who killed Paris.

On his way to the war, Philoctetes was bitten by a serpent and abandoned by his companions on the island of Lemnos. His friends came back to fetch him ten years later when they learned that the war could only be won with the poisoned arrows of Heracles, kept by Philoctetes. He used one of them to kill Paris, and soon afterward the Greeks captured Troy.

Philo Judaeus lived 1st century AD. Jewish philosopher of Alexandria, who in AD 40 undertook a mission to Caligula to protest against the emperor's claim to divine honors. In his writings Philo Judaeus attempts to reconcile Judaism with Platonic and Stoic ideas.

philology (Greek "love of language") in historical ◊linguistics, the study of the development of languages. It is also an obsolete term for the study of literature.

In this sense the scholars of Alexandria, who edited the Greek epics of Homer, were philologists. The Renaissance gave great impetus to this kind of study. Dutch scholars took the lead in the 17th century while Richard Bentley (1662–1742) made significant contributions in England. Comparative philology arose at the beginning of the 19th century from the study of Sanskrit, under Franz Bopp's (1791–1867) leadership. It was originally mainly concerned with the ◊Indo-European family of languages, while the Romantic movement greatly inspired the establishment of national philology throughout Europe and Asia.

philosophy (Greek "love of wisdom") branch of learning that includes metaphysics (the nature of Being), epistemology (theory of knowledge), logic (study of valid inference), ethics, and esthetics. Originally, philosophy included all intellectual endeavor, but over time traditional branches of philosophy have acquired their own status as separate areas of study. Philosophy is concerned with fundamental problems—including the nature of mind and matter, perception, self, free will, causation, time and space, and the existence of moral judgments—which cannot be resolved by a specific method. Contemporary philosophers are inclined to think of philosophy as an investigation of the fundamental assumptions that govern our ways of understanding and acting in the world.

Oldest of all philosophical systems is the Vedic system c. 2500 BC, but, like many other Eastern systems, it rests on a primarily mystic basis. The first scientific system originated in Greece in the 6th century BC with the Milesian school (Thales, Anaximander, Anaximenes). Both they and later pre-Socratics (Pythagoras, Xenophon, Parmenides, Zeno of Elea, Empedocles, Anaxagoras, Heraclitus, Democritus) were lively theorists, and ideas such as atomism, developed by Democritus, occur in later schemes of thought. In the 5th century Socrates, foremost among the teachers known as the Sophists, laid the foundation of ethics; Plato evolved a system of universal ideas; Aristotle developed logic. Later schools include Epicureanism (Epicurus), Stoicism (Zeno) and Skepticism (Pyrrho); the eclectics—not a school, they selected what appealed to them from various systems (Cicero and Seneca); and the Neoplatonists, infusing a mystic element into the system of Plato (Philo, Plotinus and, as disciple, Julian the Apostate).

The close of the Athenian schools of philosophy by Justinian AD 529 marks the end of ancient philosophy, though many of its teachers moved eastward; Greek thought emerges in Muslim philosophers such as Avicenna and Averroes, and the Jewish Maimonides. For the West the work of Aristotle was transmitted through Boethius. Study by medieval scholastic philosophers, mainly concerned with the reconciliation of ancient philosophy with Christian belief, began in the 9th century with John Scotus Erigena and includes Anselm, Abelard, Albertus Magnus, Thomas Aquinas, his opponent Duns Scotus, and William of Occam.

In the 17th century Descartes, with his rationalist determination to doubt and faith in mathematical proof, marks the beginning of contemporary philosophy, and was followed by Spinoza, Leibniz, and Hobbes. The empiricists, principally an 18th-century English school (Locke, Berkeley, Hume), turned instead to physics as indicating what can be known and how, and led up to the transcendental criticism of Kant. In the early 19th century Classical German idealism (Fichte, Schelling, Hegel) repudiated Kant's limitation of human knowledge; in France Comte developed the positivist thought that attracted Mill and Spencer. Notable also in the 19th century are the pessimistic atheism of Schopenhauer; the dialectical materialism of Marx and Engels; the work of Nietzsche and Kierkegaard, which led toward 20th-century existentialism; the pragmatism of William James and Dewey; and the absolute idealism at the turn of the century of the neo-Hegelians (Bradley, Royce).

Among 20th-century movements are the logical positivism of the Vienna Circle (Carnap, Popper, Ayer); the creative evolution of Bergson; Neo-Thomism, the revival of the medieval philosophy of Aquinas (Maritain); existentialism (Heidegger, Jaspers, Sartre); the phenomenology of Husserl, who influenced Ryle; and realism (Russell, Moore, Broad, Wittgenstein). Twentieth-century philosophers have paid great attention to the nature and limits of language, in particular in relation to the language used to formulate philosophical problems.

phlebitis inflammation of a vein. It is sometimes associated with blockage by a blood clot (◊thrombosis), in which case it is more accurately described as thrombophlebitis.

Phlebitis may occur as a result of the hormonal changes associated with pregnancy, or due to

philosophy: the great philosophers

name	*dates*	*nationality*	*representative work*
Heraclitus	*c.*544–483 BC	Greek	*On Nature*
Parmenides	*c.*510–*c.*450 BC	Greek	fragments
Socrates	469–399 BC	Greek	—
Plato	428–347 BC	Greek	*Republic*; *Phaedo*
Aristotle	384–322 BC	Greek	*Nichomachaen Ethics*; *Metaphysics*
Epicurus	341–270 BC	Greek	fragments
Lucretius	*c.*99–55 BC	Roman	*On the Nature of Things*
Plotinus	AD 205–270	Greek	*Enneads*
Augustine	354–430	N African	*Confessions*; *City of God*
Aquinas	*c.*1225–1274	Italian	*Summa Theologica*
Duns Scotus	*c.*1266–1308	Scottish	*Opus Oxoniense*
William of Occam	*c.*1285–1349	English	*Commentary of the Sentences*
Nicholas of Cusa	1401–1464	German	*De Docta Ignorantia*
Giordano Bruno	1548–1600	Italian	*De la Causa, Principio e Uno*
Bacon	1561–1626	English	*Novum Organum*; *The Advancement of Learning*
Hobbes	1588–1679	English	*Leviathan*
Descartes	1596–1650	French	*Discourse on Method; Meditations on the First Philosophy*
Pascal	1623–1662	French	*Pensées*
Spinoza	1632–1677	Dutch	*Ethics*
Locke	1632–1704	English	*Essay Concerning Human Understanding*
Leibniz	1646–1716	German	*The Monadology*
Vico	1668–1744	Italian	*The New Science*
Berkeley	1685–1753	Irish	*A Treatise Concerning the Principles of Human Knowledge*
Hume	1711–1776	Scottish	*A Treatise of Human Nature*
Rousseau	1712–1778	French	*The Social Contract*
Diderot	1713–1784	French	*D'Alembert's Dream*
Kant	1724–1804	German	*The Critique of Pure Reason*
Fichte	1762–1814	German	*The Science of Knowledge*
Hegel	1770–1831	German	*The Phenomenology of Spirit*
Schelling	1775–1854	German	*System of Transcendental Idealism*
Schopenhauer	1788–1860	German	*The World as Will and Idea*
Comte	1798–1857	French	*Cours de philosophie positive*
Mill	1806–1873	English	*Utilitarianism*
Kierkegaard	1813–1855	Danish	*Concept of Dread*
Marx	1818–1883	German	*Economic and Philosophical Manuscripts*
Dilthey	1833–1911	German	*The Rise of Hermeneutics*
Peirce	1839–1914	US	*How to Make our Ideas Clear*
Nietzsche	1844–1900	German	*Thus Spake Zarathustra*
Bergson	1859–1941	French	*Creative Evolution*
Husserl	1859–1938	German	*Logical Investigations*
Russell	1872–1970	English	*Principia Mathematica*
Lukács	1885–1971	Hungarian	*History and Class Consciousness*
Wittgenstein	1889–1951	Austrian	*Tractatus Logico-Philosophicus; Philosophical Investigations*
Heidegger	1889–1976	German	*Being and Time*
Gadamer	1900–	German	*Truth and Method*
Sartre	1905–1980	French	*Being and Nothingness*
Merleau Ponty	1908–1961	French	*The Phenomenology of Perception*
Quine	1908–	US	*Word and Object*
Foucault	1926–1984	French	*The Order of Things*

long-term use of contraceptive pills, or following prolonged immobility (which is why patients are mobilized as soon as possible after surgery). If a major vein is involved, nearly always in a leg, the part beyond the blockage swells and may remain engorged for weeks. It is very painful. Treatment is with ◊anticoagulant drugs and sometimes surgery.

phlebotomy the practice of blood-letting—withdrawing blood from a vein as a therapeutic measure.

phloem a tissue found in vascular plants whose main function is to conduct sugars and other food materials from the leaves, where they are produced, to all other parts of the plant.

Phloem is composed of sieve elements and their associated companion cells, together with some ◊sclerenchyma and ◊parenchyma cell types. Sieve elements are long, thin-walled cells joined end to end, forming sieve tubes; large pores in the end walls allow the continuous passage of nutrients. Phloem is usually found in association with ◊xylem, the water-conducting tissue, but unlike the latter it is a living tissue.

phlogiston a hypothetical substance formerly believed to have been produced during combustion. The term was invented by G Stahl (1660–1734). The phlogiston theory was replaced by the theory of oxygen gain/loss.

phlox any plant of the genus *Phlox*, native to North America and Siberia. They are small with alternate leaves and showy white, pink, red, or purple flowers.

Woodland phlox *P. divaricata* is native to central US.

Phnom Penh capital of Cambodia, on the Mekong River, 130 mi/210 km NW of Saigon; population (1989) 800,000. Industries include textiles and food-processing.

On Apr 17, 1975 the entire population (about 3 million) was forcibly evacuated by the Khmer Rouge; survivors later returned.

phobia an excessive irrational fear of an object or situation, for example, agoraphobia (fear of open spaces and crowded places), acrophobia (fear of heights), claustrophobia (fear of enclosed places). Behavior therapy is one form of treatment.

Phobos one of the two moons of Mars, discovered 1877 by the US astronomer Asaph Hall (1829–1907). It is an irregularly shaped lump of rock, cratered by ◊meteorite impacts. Phobos is 17 × 13 × 12 mi/27 × 22 × 19 km across and orbits Mars every 0.32 days at a distance of 5,840 mi/9,400 km from the planet's center. It is thought to be an asteroid captured by Mars' gravity.

Phoenicia ancient Greek name for N ◊Canaan on the E coast of the Mediterranean. The Phoenicians lived about 1200–332 BC. Seafaring traders and artisans, they are said to have circumnavigated Africa and established colonies in Cyprus, N Africa (for example Carthage), Malta, Sicily, and Spain. Their cities (Tyre, Sidon, and Byblos were the main ones) were independent states ruled by hereditary kings but dominated by merchant ruling classes. The fall of Tyre to Alexander the Great ended the separate history of Phoenicia.

The Phoenicians occupied the seaboard of Lebanon and Syria, N of Mount Carmel. Their exports included Tyrian purple dye and cloth, furniture (from the timber of Lebanon), and jewelry. Documents found 1929 at Ugarit on the Syrian coast give much information on their civilization; their deities included ◊Baal, Astarte or ◊Ishtar, and ◊Moloch. Competition from the colonies combined with attacks by the Sea Peoples, the Assyrians, and the Greeks on the cities in Phoenicia led to their ultimate decline.

phoenix mythical Egyptian bird that burned itself to death on a pyre every 500 years and rose rejuvenated from the ashes.

Phoenix capital of Arizona; industrial city (steel, aluminum, electrical goods, food processing) and tourist center on the Salt River; population (1990) 983,403. Settled 1868, Phoenix became the territorial capital 1889. The completion of a dam 1912 provided the water and power needed for economic development. Tremendous growth, beginning in the 1940s, has transformed Phoenix from what was largely a health resort and retirement community into a major economic center.

phosphorescence *Organic chemist working with phosphorescing solutions.*

Phoenix Islands group of eight islands in the South Pacific, included in Kiribati; total land area 11 sq mi/18 sq km. Drought has rendered them all uninhabitable.

phon unit of loudness, equal to the value in decibels of an equally loud tone with frequency 1,000 Hz. The higher the frequency, the louder a noise sounds for the same decibel value; thus an 80-decibel tone with a frequency of 20 Hz sounds as loud as 20 decibels at 1,000 Hz, and the phon value of both tones is 20. An aircraft engine has a loudness of around 140 phons.

phonetics identification, description, and classification of sounds used in articulate speech. These sounds are codified in the International Phonetic Alphabet (a highly modified version of the English/Roman alphabet).

A phoneme is the range of sound that can be substituted without change of meaning in the words of a particular language, for example; *r* and *l* form a single phoneme in Japanese but are two distinct phonemes in English. The study of phonemes is called phonemics, a branch of linguistics.

phonograph alternate name for ◊record player.

phony war the period in World War II between Oct 1939, when the Germans had occupied Poland, and Apr 1940, when the invasions of Denmark and Norway took place. During this time there were few signs of hostilities in Western Europe; indeed, Hitler made some attempts to arrange a peace settlement with Britain and France.

phosphate salt or ester of ◊phosphoric acid. Incomplete neutralization of phosphoric acid gives rise to acid phosphates (see acid salts and ◊buffer).

Phosphates are used as fertilizers, and lead to the development of healthy root systems. They are involved in many biochemical processes, often as part of complex molecules (see ◊ATP).

phosphor any substance that gives out visible light when it is illuminated by a beam of electrons or ultraviolet light. The television screen is coated on the inside with phosphors that glow when beams of electrons strike them. Fluorescent lamp tubes are also phosphor-coated.

phosphorescence in physics, the emission of light by certain substances after they have absorbed energy, whether from visible light, other electromagnetic radiation such as ultraviolet rays or X-rays, or cathode rays (a beam of electrons). When the stimulating energy is removed phosphorescence ceases, although it may persist for a short time after (unlike ◊fluorescence, which stops immediately).

The most common uses of phosphorescent substances (called phosphors) are as light-emitting coatings on the inside of television screens, in so-called fluorescent lamps and tubes, in Day-Glo paints, and as optical brighteners in detergents.

phosphoric acid acid derived from phosphorus and oxygen. Its commonest form (H_3PO_4) is also known as orthophosphoric acid, and is produced by the action of phosphorus pentoxide (P_2O_5) on water. It is used in rust removers and for rust-proofing iron and steel.

phosphorus (Greek *phosphoros* "bearer of light") highly reactive, nonmetallic element, symbol P, atomic number 15, atomic weight 30.9738. It occurs in nature as phosphates in the soil, in particular the mineral ◊apatite, and is essential to both plant and animal life. The element has three allotropic forms: a black powder; a white-yellow, waxy solid that ignites spontaneously in air to form the poisonous gas phosphorous pentoxide; and a red-brown powder that neither ignites spontaneously nor is poisonous. Compounds of phosphorus are used in fertilizers, various organic chemicals, for matches and fireworks, and in glass and steel.

Phosphorus was first identified in 1674 by German alchemist Hennig Brand (c. 1630–?), who prepared it from urine.

photocell or ***photoelectric cell*** a device for measuring or detecting light (or other electromagnetic radiation), since its electrical state is altered by the effect of light.

In a photoemissive cell, the radiation causes electrons to be emitted and a current to flow (◊photoelectric effect); a photovoltaic cell causes an ◊electromotive force to be generated in the presence of light across the boundary of two substances. A photoconductive cell, which contains a semiconductor, increases its conductivity when exposed to electromagnetic radiation. Photocells are used for photographers' exposure meters, burglar and fire alarms, automatic doors, and in solar energy arrays.

photochemical reaction any chemical reaction in which light is produced or light initiates the reaction. Light can initiate reactions by exciting atoms or molecules and making them more reactive: the light energy becomes converted to chemical energy. Many photochemical reactions set up a ◊chain reaction and produce ◊free radicals.

This type of reaction is seen in the bleaching of dyes or the yellowing of paper by sunlight. It is harnessed by plants in ◊photosynthesis and by humans in ◊photography. Chemical reactions that produce light are most commonly seen when materials are burned. Light-emitting reactions are used by living organisms in ◊bioluminescence. One photochemical reaction is the action of sunlight on car exhaust fumes, which results in the production of ◊ozone. Some large cities, such as Los Angeles, and Santiago, Chile, now suffer serious pollution due to photochemical smog.

photocopier machine that uses some form of photographic process to reproduce copies of documents or illustrations. Most modern photocopiers, as pioneered by the Xerox Corporation, use electrostatic photocopying, or xerography ("dry writing"). This employs a drum coated with a light-sensitive material such as selenium, which holds a pattern of static electricity charges corresponding to the dark areas of an image projected on to the drum by a lens. Finely divided pigment (toner) of opposite electric charge sticks to the charged areas of the drum and is transferred to a sheet of paper, which is heated briefly to melt the toner and stick it to the paper.

Additional functions include enlargement and reduction, copying on both sides of the sheet of paper, copying in color, collating, and stapling.

photoelectric effect in physics, the emission of ◊electrons from a substance (usually a metallic surface) when it is struck by ◊photons (quanta of electromagnetic radiation), usually those of visible light or ultraviolet radiation.

photofit system aiding the identification of wanted persons. Witnesses select photographs of a single feature (hair, eyes, nose, mouth), their choices

photography: chronology

1515	Leonardo da Vinci described the camera obscura.
1750	The painter Canaletto used a camera obscura as an aid to his painting in Venice.
1790	Thomas Wedgewood in England made photograms—placing objects on leather, sensitized using silver nitrate.
1826	Nicephore Niépce 1765–1833, a French doctor, produced the world's first photograph from nature on pewter plates with a camera obscura and an eight-hour exposure.
1835	Niépce, and L J M Daguerre produced the first *Daguerreotype camera photograph.*
1839	Daguerre was awarded an annuity by the French government and his process given to the world.
1841	Fox Talbot's Calotype process was patented—the first multicopy method of photography using a negative/positive process, sensitized with silver iodide.
1844	Fox Talbot published the first photographic book, *The Pencil of Nature.*
1845	Hill and Adamson began to use Calotypes for portraits in Edinburgh.
1851	Fox Talbot used a one-thousandth of a second exposure to demonstrate high-speed photography.
1855	Roger Fenton made documentary photographs of the Crimean war from a specially constructed wagon with portable darkroom.
1859	Nadar in Paris made photographs underground using battery powered arc lights.
1860	Queen Victoria was photographed by Mayall. Abraham Lincoln was photographed by Matthew Brady for political campaigning.
1861	Single lens reflex plate camera patented by Thomas Sutton.
1862	Nadar took aerial photographs over Paris.
1870	Julia Margaret Cameron used long lenses for her distinctive portraits.
1878	In the US Eadweard Muybridge analyzed the movements of animals through sequential photographs, using a series of cameras.
1880	A silver bromide emulsion was fixed with hypo. Photographs were first reproduced in newspapers in New York using the half-tone engraving process. The first twin-lens reflex camera was produced in London.
1889	Eastman Company in the US produced the Kodak No.1 camera and roll film, facilitating universal, hand-held snapshots.
1902	In Germany Deckel invented a prototype leaf shutter and Zeiss introduced the Tessar lens.
1904	The Autochrome color process was patented by the Lumière brothers.
1905	Alfred Steiglitz opened the gallery "291" in New York promoting photography. Lewis Hine used photography to expose the exploitation of children in American factories, causing protective laws to be passed.
1907	The autochrome process began to be factory-produced.
1914	Oskar Barnack designed a prototype Leica camera for Leitz in Germany.
1924	Leitz launched the first 35mm camera, the Leica, delayed because of World War I. It became very popular with photojournalists because it was quiet, small, dependable and had a range of lenses and accessories.
1929	Rolleiflex produced a twin-lens reflex camera in Germany.
1935	In the US, Mannes and Godowsky invented Kodachrome transparency film, which produced sharp images and rich color quality. Electronic flash was invented in the US. Social documentary photography received wide attention through the photographs of Dorothea Lange, Margaret Bourke-White, Arthur Rothstein, Walker Evans and others taken for the Farm Security Administration of the plight of the poor tenant farmers in the Midwest.
1936	*Life* magazine, significant for its photojournalism, was first published in the US.
1938	*Picture Post* magazine was introduced in the UK.
1940	Multigrade enlarging paper by Ilford was made available in the UK.
1945	The Zone system of exposure estimation published in the book *Exposure Record* by Ansel Adams.
1947	Polaroid black and white instant process film invented by Dr Edwin Land, who set up the Polaroid corporation in Boston, Massachusetts. Principles of holography demonstrated in England by Dennis Gabor.
1955	Kodak introduced Tri-X, a black and white 200 ASA film.
1959	The zoom lens invented in Germany by Voigtlander.
1960	Laser invented in the US, making holography possible. Polacolor, a self-processing color film, introduced by Polaroid, using a 60-second color film and dye diffusion technique.
1963	Cibachrome, paper and chemicals for printing directly from transparencies, was made available by Ciba-Geigy of Switzerland. One of the most permanent processes, it is marketed throughout the world.
1969	Photographs taken on the Moon by US astronauts.
1972	SX70 system, a single lens reflex camera with instant prints, produced by Polaroid.
1980	Ansel Adams sold an original print *Moonrise: Hernandez* for $45,000, a record price, in the US. Voyager 1 sent photographs of Saturn back to Earth across space.
1985	Minolta Corporation in Japan introduced the Minolta 7000—the world's first body-integral autofocus single lens reflex camera.

resulting in a composite likeness that is then rephotographed and circulated. It is a sophisticated development by Jacques Penry 1970 for the police of Scotland Yard, London, of the ◊identikit system.

photogram a picture produced on photographic material by exposing it to light, but without using a camera.

photography a process for producing images on sensitized materials by various forms of radiant energy, including visible light, ultraviolet, infrared, X-rays; radioactive radiation and electron beam.

photogravure ◊printing process that uses a plate prepared photographically, covered with a pattern of recessed cells in which the ink is held. See ◊gravure.

photometer instrument that measures luminous intensity, especially relative intensities from different sources. Bunsen's grease-spot photometer 1844 compares the intensity of a light source with a known source by each illuminating one half of a translucent area. Modern photometers use ◊photocells, as in a photographer's exposure meter. A ◊photomultiplier can also be used as a photometer.

photomultiplier instrument that detects low levels of electromagnetic radiation (usually visible light or ◊infrared radiation) and amplifies it to produce a detectable signal.

One type resembles a ◊photocell with an additional series of coated ◊electrodes (dynodes) between the ◊cathode and ◊anode. Radiation striking the cathode releases electrons (primary emission) which hit the first dynode, producing yet more electrons (◊secondary emission), which strike the second dynode. Eventually this produces a measurable signal up to 100 million times larger than the original signal by the time it leaves the anode. Similar devices, called image intensifiers, are used in television camera tubes that "see" in the dark.

photon the ◊elementary particle or quantum of energy in which light or other forms of electromagnetic radiation is emitted. It has both particle and wave properties; it has no charge, is considered massless but possesses momentum and energy. It is one of the ◊gauge bosons, a particle that cannot be subdivided, and is the carrier of the ◊electromagnetic force.

photoperiodism a biological mechanism that determines the timing of certain activities by responding to changes in day length. The flowering of many plants is initiated in this way. Photoperiodism in plants is regulated by a light-sensitive pigment, phytochrome. The breeding seasons of many temperate-zone animals are also triggered by increasing or declining day length, as part of their ◊biorhythms.

Autumn-flowering plants (for example, chrysanthemum and soybean) and autumn-breeding mammals (such as goats and deer) require days that are shorter than a critical length; spring-flowering and spring-breeding ones (such as radish and lettuce; birds) are triggered by longer days.

photosphere the visible surface of the Sun, which emits light and heat. About 200 mi/300 km deep, it consists of incandescent gas at a temperature of 5,800K (9,980°F/5,530°C).

Rising cells of hot gas produce a mottling of the photosphere known as granulation, each granule being about 620 mi/1,000 km in diameter. The photosphere is often marked by large, dark patches called ◊sunspots.

photosynthesis the process by which green plants, photosynthetic bacteria, and cyanobacteria utilize light energy from the Sun to produce food molecules (◊carbohydrates) from carbon dioxide and water. There are two stages. During the light reaction sunlight is used to split water (H_2O) into oxygen (O_2), protons (hydrogen ions, H^+), and electrons, and oxygen is given off as a byproduct. In the second-stage dark reaction, where sunlight is not required, the protons and electrons are used to convert carbon dioxide (CO_2) into carbohydrates (CH_2O). Photosynthesis depends on the ability of ◊chlorophyll to capture the energy of sunlight and to use it to split water molecules.

Other pigments, such as ◊carotenoids, are also involved in capturing light energy and passing it on to chlorophyll. Photosynthesis by cyanobacteria was responsible for the appearance of oxygen in the Earth's atmosphere 2 billion years ago, and photosynthesis by plants maintains the oxygen level today.

phototropism movement of part of a plant toward or away from a source of light. Leaves are positively phototropic, detecting the source of light and orientating themselves to receive the maximum amount.

phrase-structure grammar theory of language structure that proposes that a given language has several different potential sentence patterns, consisting of various sorts of phrases, which can be expanded in various ways.

For example, the sentence "The girl opened the door" contains a noun phrase, *the girl*, and a verb phrase, *opened the door*; the verb phrase can be further analyzed into a verb, *opened*, and a noun phrase, *the door*; and so on.

phrenology study of the shape and protuberances of

photosynthesis

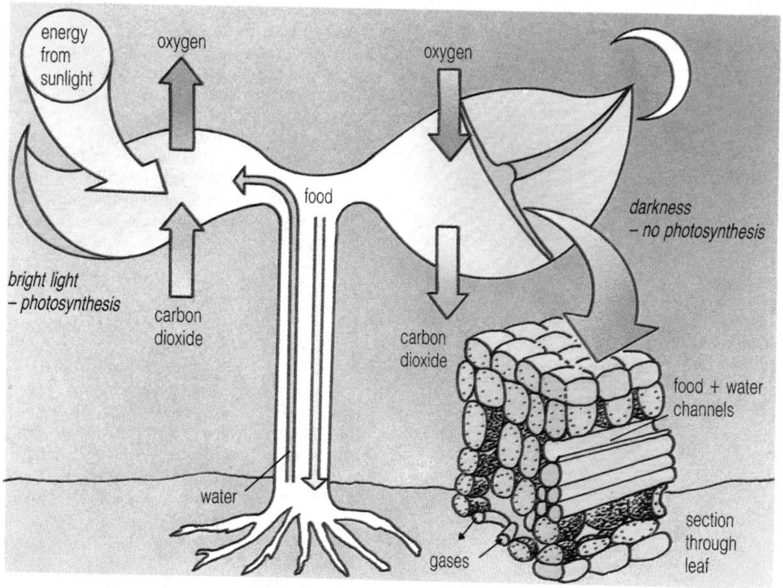
energy
from
sunlight
oxygen
oxygen
food
darkness
– no photosynthesis
bright light
– photosynthesis
carbon
dioxide
carbon
dioxide
food + water
channels
water
section
through
leaf
gases

the skull, based on the (now discredited) theory of the Viennese physician Dr Franz Josef ◊Gall that such features revealed measurable psychological and intellectual traits.

Phrygia former kingdom of W Asia covering the Anatolian plateau. It was inhabited in ancient times by an Indo-European people and achieved great prosperity in the 8th century BC under a line of kings bearing in turn the names Gordius and Midas, but then fell under Lydian rule. From Phrygia the cult of ◊Cybele was introduced into Greece and Rome.

Phryne Greek courtesan of the 4th century BC, famed for her beauty. She is said to have been the model for the Aphrodite of Cnidos by the Athenian sculptor Praxiteles.

Phyfe Duncan c. 1768–1854. Scottish-born US furniture maker. Phyfe immigrated with his family to America 1784. Settling in Albany, New York, and learning the cabinetmaker's trade, he established his own workshop in New York City 1792. There Phyfe gained a national reputation for his expensive and finely-worked furniture. Although derived from earlier English and Greco-Roman designs, the Phyfe style was distinctive in its simplicity of line with elaborate ornamentation and carving. In 1837 Phyfe brought his sons into the business, reorganizing his firm as Duncan Phyfe and Sons. He remained active until his retirement in 1847.

phylacteries in Judaism, another name for ◊tefillin.

phyllite a ◊metamorphic rock produced under increasing temperature and pressure, in which mica crystals are aligned so that the rock splits along their plane of orientation, the resulting break being shiny and smooth. It is intermediate between slate and schist.

phyllotaxis the arrangement of leaves on a plant stem. Leaves are nearly always arranged in a regular pattern and in the majority of plants they are inserted singly, either in a spiral arrangement up the stem, or on alternate sides. Other principal forms are opposite leaves, where two arise from the same node, and whorled, where three or more arise from the same node.

phylloxera any of a family (Phylloxeridae) of small plant-sucking insects (order Homoptera) that attack the leaves and roots of some plants.

The species *Phylloxera vitifolia*, a native of North America, attacks grapevines, laying its eggs under the bark. European vines are markedly susceptible and many French vineyards suffered by the arrival of the pest in Europe in the 19th century; most European vines are now grafted on to rootstock of the American vine, which is not as susceptible to the disease. Phylloxera insects (hemipteran) may be destroyed by spraying with carbon disulfide or petroleum.

phylogeny the historical sequence of changes that occurs in a given species during the course of its evolution. It was once erroneously associated with ontogeny (the process of development of a living organism).

phylum (plural phyla) a major grouping in biological classification. Mammals, birds, reptiles, amphibians, fishes, and tunicates belong to the phylum Chordata; the phylum Molluska consists of snails, slugs, mussels, clams, squid, and octopuses; the phylum Porifera contains sponges; and the phylum Echinodermata includes sea stars, sea urchins, and sea cucumbers. Among plants there are between four and nine phyla (or divisions) depending on the classification used. Related phyla are grouped together in a ◊kingdom; phyla are subdivided into ◊classes.

physical change in chemistry, a type of change that does not produce a new chemical substance, does not involve large energy changes, and that can be easily reversed (the opposite of a chemical change). Boiling and melting are examples of physical change.

physics the branch of science concerned with the ultimate laws that govern the structure of the universe, and the forms of matter and energy and their interactions. For convenience, physics is often divided into branches such as nuclear physics, particle physics, solid- and liquid-state physics, electricity, electronics, magnetism, optics, acoustics, heat, and thermodynamics. Before this century, physics was known as natural philosophy.

physiological psychology an aspect of ◊experimental psychology.

physiology the branch of biology that deals with the functioning of living animals, as opposed to anatomy, which studies their structures.

physiotherapy treatment of injury and disease by physical means such as exercise, heat, manipulation, massage, and electrical stimulation.

Piacenza industrial city (agricultural machinery, textiles, pottery) in Emilia-Romagna, N Italy, on the river Po, 40 mi/65 km SE of Milan; population (1988) 105,000. The Roman *Placentia*, Piacenza dates from 218 BC and has a 12th-century cathedral.

Piaf Edith. Adopted name of Edith Gassion 1915–1963. Parisian singer and songwriter, celebrated for her defiant song "Je ne regrette rien/I Regret Nothing."

Piaget Jean 1896–1980. Swiss psychologist distinguished by his studies of child development in relation to thought processes, and concepts of space, time, causality, and objectivity.

Piaget believed this was a vital framework for studying human intelligence and he stressed the interaction of biological and environmental factors.

piano or ***pianoforte*** a stringed musical instrument, played by felt-covered hammers activated from a keyboard, and capable of soft (piano) or loud (forte) tones, hence its name.

The first piano was constructed in 1704 and introduced in 1709 by Bartolommeo Christofori, a harpsichord-maker of Padua. It uses a clever mechanism to make the keyboard touch-sensitive. Extensively developed during the 18th century, the piano attracted admiration among many composers, although it was not until 1768 that Johann Christian Bach gave one of the first public recitals on the instrument. Further improvements in the keyboard action and tone by makers such as Broadwood, Erard, and Graf, together with a rapid expansion of published music by Haydn, Beethoven, Schubert and others, led to the development of the powerfully resonant concert grand and the mass production of smaller upright pianos for the home.

The player piano is designed to reproduce key-actions recorded on a perforated paper roll. The concert Duo-Art reproducing piano encoded more detailed information, such that audiences were unable to distinguish a live performance from a reproduced performance.

Piano Renzo 1937– Italian architect who designed (with Richard Rogers) the Pompidou Center, Paris, completed 1977. Among his other buildings are the Kansai Airport, Osaka, Japan and a sports stadium in Bari, Italy, both using new materials and making imaginative use of civil-engineering techniques.

Piazzi Giuseppe 1746–1826. Italian astronomer, director of Palermo Observatory. In 1801 he identified the first asteroid, which he named ◊Ceres.

Picabia Francis 1879–1953. French painter, a

physics: chronology

c. 400 BC	**The first "atomic" theory was put forward by Democritus.**
c. 250	Archimedes' principle of buoyancy was established.
45	The Julian calendar as used in most Western countries was introduced.
AD 1600	Magnetism was described by English physicist and physician William Gilbert.
c. 1610	The principle of falling bodies descending to earth at the same speed was established by Italian astronomer Galileo.
1642	The principles of hydraulics were put forward by French mathematician, physicist, and philosopher Blaise Pascal.
1643	The mercury barometer was invented by Italian physicist Evangelista Torricelli.
1656	The pendulum clock was invented by Dutch physicist and astronomer Christiaan Huygens.
1662	*Boyle's law* concerning gas was established by Irish physicist and chemist Robert Boyle.
c. 1665	English physicist Isaac Newton put forward the law of gravity, stating that the Earth exerts a constant force on falling bodies.
1677	The simple microscope was invented by Dutch microscopist Anton van Leeuwenhoek.
1690	The wave theory of light was propounded by Dutch physicist Christiaan Huygens.
1704	The corpuscular theory of light was put forward by Isaac Newton.
1714	The mercury thermometer was invented by German physicist (Gabriel) Daniel Fahrenheit.
1764	Specific and latent heats were described by Scottish chemist Joseph Black.

1771	The link between nerve action and electricity was discovered by Italian anatomist and physiologist Luigi Galvani.
c. 1787	*Charles's law* relating the pressure, volume, and temperature of a gas was established by French physicist and physical chemist Jacques Alexandre César Charles.
1795	The metric system was adopted in France.
1798	The link between heat and friction was discovered by Anglo-American physicist Benjamin Thomson Rumford (1753–1814).
1800	Italian physicist Alessandro Volta invented the Voltaic cell.
1801	Interference of light was discovered by British physicist Thomas Young.
1808	The "modern" atomic theory was propounded by British physicist and chemist John Dalton.
1811	Avogadro's hypothesis relating volumes and numbers of molecules of gases was proposed by Italian physicist and chemist Amedeo Avogadro.
1814	Fraunhofer lines in the solar spectrum were mapped by German physicist Joseph von Fraunhofer.
1815	Refraction of light was explained by French physicist Augustin Fresnel.
1819	The discovery of electromagnetism was made by Danish physicist Hans Oersted.
1821	The dynamo principle was described by British physicist and chemist Michael Faraday; the thermocouple was discovered by German physicist Thomas Seebeck.
1822	The laws of electrodynamics were established by French physicist and mathematician André Ampère.
1824	Thermodynamics as a branch of physics was proposed by French physicist Sadi Carnot.
1827	Ohm's law of electrical resistance was established by German physicist Georg Ohm; Brownian motion resulting from molecular vibrations was observed by British botanist Robert Brown.
1829	The law of gaseous diffusion was established by Scottish chemist Thomas Graham.
1831	Electromagnetic induction was discovered by Faraday.
1834	Faraday discovered self-induction.
1842	The principle of conservation of energy was observed by German physician and physicist Julius von Mayer.
c. 1847	The mechanical equivalent of heat was described by English physicist James Joule.
1849	A measurement of speed of light was put forward by French physicist Armand Fizeau (1819–1896).
1851	The rotation of the Earth was demonstrated by French physicist Jean Foucault.
1858	The mirror galvanometer, an instrument for measuring small electric currents, was invented by Scottish mathematician and physicist William Kelvin.
1859	Spectrographic analysis was made by German chemist Robert Bunsen (1811–1899) and German physicist Gustav Kirchhoff.
1861	Osmosis was discovered.
1873	Light was conceived as electromagnetic radiation by Scottish physicist James Maxwell.
1877	A theory of sound as vibrations in an elastic medium was propounded by British physicist John Rayleigh.
1880	Piezoelectricity was discovered by Polish scientist Pierre Curie.
1887	The existence of radio waves was predicted by German physicist Heinrich Hertz.
1895	X-rays were discovered by German physicist Wilhelm Röntgen; J J Thomson discovered the electron.
1896	The discovery of radioactivity was made by French physicist Antoine Becquerel.
1899	New Zealand physicist Ernest Rutherford discovered alpha and beta rays.
1900	Quantum theory was propounded by German physicist Max Planck; the discovery of gamma rays was made by French physicist Paul-Ulrich Villard (1860–1934).
1902	British physicist Oliver Heaviside discovered the ionosphere.
1904	The theory of radioactivity was put forward by Rutherford and British chemist Frederick Soddy.
1905	German-Swiss physicist Albert Einstein propounded his special theory of relativity.
1911	The discovery of the atomic nucleus was made by Rutherford.
1913	The Geiger counter was invented by German physicist Hans Geiger and Walther Müller.
1915	X-ray crystallography was discovered by William and Lawrence Bragg.
1916	Einstein put forward his general theory of relativity; mass spectrography was discovered by British physicist William Aston.
1922	The orbiting electron atomic theory was propounded by Danish physicist Niels Bohr.
1924	English physicist Edward Appleton made his study of the Heaviside layer.
1927	The uncertainty principle of atomic physics was established by German physicist Werner Heisenberg.
1928	Wave mechanics was introduced by Austrian physicist Erwin Schrödinger.
1931	The cyclotron was developed by US physicist Ernest Lawrence.
1932	The discovery of the neutron was made by Chadwick; the electron microscope was developed by Soviet-American physicist Vladimir Zworykin; the positron, the antiparticle of the electron, was discovered by US physicist Robert Millikan.
1934	Radioactivity was synthesized by Frédéric and Irène Joliot-Curie.
1939	Nuclear fission was discovered by Otto Hahn, Lise Meitner, and German chemist Fritz Strassman (1902–).
1942	The first controlled nuclear chain reaction was achieved by Italian physicist Enrico Fermi.
1956	The neutrino, an elementary particle, was discovered.
1960	The Mössbauer effect of atom emissions was discovered by German physicist Rudolf Mössbauer (1929–); the first maser was developed by American physicist Theodore Maiman (1927–).
1963	Maiman developed the first laser or light amplification by stimulated emission of radiation.
1964	Gell-Mann discovered the quark.
1971	The theory of superconductivity was announced, where electrical resistance in some metals vanishes above absolute zero.
1973	The discovery of pulsars was made by British scientist Antony Hewish.
1979	The discovery of the asymmetry of elementary particles was made by US physicists James W Cronin and Val L Fitch.
1982	The discovery of processes involved in the evolution of stars was made by US researchers S Chandrasekhar and William A Fowler.
1986	The discovery was made of high-temperature superconductors.
1988	The atomic clock was developed by US physicist Hans G Dehmelt.

Cubist from 1909. On his second visit to New York, 1915–16, he joined with Marcel Duchamp in the Dadaist revolt and later took the movement to Barcelona. He associated with the Surrealists for a time. His work was generally provocative and experimental.

Picardy (French *Picardie*) region of N France, including Aisne, Oise, and Somme *départements*
area 7,488 sq mi/19,400 sq km
population (1986) 1,774,000
products chemicals and metals
history in the 13th century the name Picardy was used to describe the feudal smallholdings N of Paris added to the French crown by Philip II. During the Hundred Years' War the area was hotly contested by France and England, but it was eventually occupied by Louis XI in 1477. Picardy once more became a major battlefield in World War I.

picaresque (Spanish *pícaro* "rogue") in literature, a genre of novels that takes for its heroes rogues and villains, telling their story in a series of loosely linked episodes. Examples include Daniel Defoe's *Moll Flanders*, Henry Fielding's *Tom Jones*, and Mark Twain's *Huckleberry Finn*.

Picasso Pablo 1881–1973. Spanish artist, active chiefly in France, one of the most inventive and prolific talents in 20th-century art. His Blue Period 1901–04 and Rose Period 1905–06 preceded the revolutionary *Les Demoiselles d'Avignon* 1907 (Metropolitan Museum of Art, New York), which paved the way for Cubism. In the early 1920s he was considered a leader of the Surrealist movement. In the 1930s his work included metal sculpture, book illustration, and the mural *Guernica* 1937 (Casón del Buen Retiro, Madrid), a comment on the bombing of civilians in the Spanish Civil War. He continued to paint into his 80s.

Born in Málaga, son of an art teacher, José Ruiz Blasco, and an Andalusian mother, Maria Picasso López; he discontinued use of the name Ruiz in 1898. He was a mature artist at ten, and at 16 was holding his first exhibition. In 1900 he made an initial visit to Paris, where he was to settle. From 1946 he lived mainly in the south of France where, in addition to painting, he experimented with ceramics, sculpture, sets for ballet (for example *Parade* in 1917 for Diaghilev), book illustrations (such as Ovid's *Metamorphoses*), and portraits (Stravinsky, Valéry, and others).

Piccard Auguste 1884–1962. Swiss scientist. In 1931–32, he and his twin brother, Jean Félix (1884–1963), made ascents to 55,000 ft/17,000 m in a balloon of his own design, resulting in useful discoveries concerning stratospheric phenomena such as ◊cosmic rays. He also built and used, with his son Jacques Ernest (1922–), bathyscaphs for research under the sea.

piccolo a woodwind instrument, the smallest member of the ◊flute family.

picketing a gathering of workers and their trade-union representatives, usually at the entrance to their place of work, to try to persuade others to support them in an industrial dispute. They often carry signs attached to pickets, hence the term.

Pickett George Edward 1825–1875. US military leader. At the outbreak of the American Civil War, he joined the Confederate army, rising to the rank of brigadier general 1862. Although he saw action in many battles, he is best remembered for leading the bloody, doomed "Pickett's Charge" at Gettysburg 1863. After the war Pickett declined further military appointments and retired to private life.

Born in Richmond, Virginia, Pickett graduated from West Point 1846 and was commended for bravery during the Mexican War. After service in Texas 1849–55, he was transferred to the Pacific Northwest.

Pickford Mary. Adopted name of Gladys Mary Smith 1893–1979. Canadian-born US actress. The first star of the silent screen, she was known as "America's Sweetheart," and played innocent ingenue roles into her thirties. She and her second husband (from 1920), Douglas ◊Fairbanks, Sr, were known as "the world's sweethearts." With her husband and Charlie ◊Chaplin, she founded United Artists studio 1919. For many years she was the wealthiest and most influential woman in Hollywood.

Her films include *Rebecca of Sunnybrook Farm* 1917, *Pollyanna* 1920, *Little Lord Fauntleroy* 1921, and *Coquette* 1929, her first talkie (Academy Award). She was presented a special Academy Award 1976.

Pico della Mirandola Count Giovanni 1463–1494. Italian mystic philosopher. Born at Mirandola, of which his father was prince, he studied Hebrew, Chaldean, and Arabic, showing particular interest in the Jewish and theosophical system, the ◊Kabbala. His attempt to reconcile the religious base of Christianity, Islam, and the ancient world earned Pope Alexander VI's disapproval.

Pict Roman term for a member of the peoples of N Scotland, possibly meaning "painted" (tattooed). Of pre-Celtic origin, and speaking a non-Celtic language, the Picts are thought to have inhabited much of England before the arrival of the Celtic Britons. They were united with the Celtic Scots under the rule of Kenneth MacAlpin 844.

PID (abbreviation for ***pelvic inflammatory disease***) serious gynecological condition characterized by lower abdominal pain, malaise, and fever; menstruation may be disrupted; infertility may result. Treatment is with antibiotics. The incidence of the disease is twice as high in women using intrauterine contraceptive devices (IUDs).

PID is potentially life-threatening, and, while mild episodes usually respond to antibiotics, surgery may be necessary in cases of severe or recurrent pelvic infection. The bacterium *Chlamydia trachomatis* (see ◊chlamydia) has been implicated in a high proportion of cases. The condition is increasingly common.

pidgin English originally a trade jargon or contact language between the British and the Chinese in the 19th century, but now commonly and loosely used to mean any kind of "broken" or "native" version of the English language.

Pidgin is believed to have been a Chinese pronunciation of the English word *business* (hence the expression, "This isn't my pigeon"). There have been many forms of pidgin English, often with common elements because of the wide range of contacts made by commercial shipping (see ◊pidgin languages). The original pidgin English of the Chinese ports combined words of English with a rough-and-ready Chinese grammatical structure. Melanesian pidgin English (also known as Tok Pisin) combines English and the syntax of local Melanesian languages. For example, the English pronoun "we" becomes both *yumi* (you and me) and *mifela* (me and fellow, excluding you). See also ◊Creole languages.

pidgin languages trade jargons, contact languages, or ◊lingua francas arising in ports and markets where people of different linguistic backgrounds meet for commercial and other purposes.

Generally, a pidgin comes into existence to answer short-term needs, for example Korean Bamboo English as used during the Korean war. Unless there is a reason for extending the life of such a hybrid form (in the case of Korean Bamboo English combining elements of English, Korean, and Japanese), it will fade away when the need passes. Usually a pidgin is a rough blend of the vocabulary of one (often dominant) language with the syntax or grammar of one or more other (often dependent) groups. Pidgin English in various parts of the world, *français petit negre*, and Bazaar Hindi or Hindustani are examples of pidgins that have served long-term purposes to the extent of being acquired by children as one of their everyday languages. At this point they become ◊creole languages.

Pieck Wilhelm 1876–1960. German communist politician. He was a leader of the 1919 ◊Spartacist revolt and a founder of the Socialist Unity Party 1946. He opposed both the Weimar Republic and Nazism. From 1949 he was president of East Germany; the office was abolished on his death.

Pierce *The 14th president of the United States of America, Franklin Pierce, a Democrat. 1853–1857.*

Piedmont (Italian *Piemonte*) region of N Italy, bordering Switzerland on the N and France on the W, and surrounded, except on the E, by the Alps and the Apennines; area 9,804 sq mi/ 25,400 sq km; population (1988) 4,377,000. Its capital is Turin, and towns include Alessandria, Asti, Vercelli, and Novara. It also includes the fertile Po river valley. Products include fruit, grain, cattle, automobiles, and textiles. The movement for the unification of Italy started in the 19th century in Piedmont, under the house of Savoy.

pier a structure built out into the sea from the coastline for use as a landing place or promenade.

Pierce Franklin 1804–1869. 14th president of the US. Born in Hillsboro, New Hampshire, Pierce was admitted to the bar 1827. He served in the New Hampshire state legislature 1829–33, the US House of Representatives 1833–37, and the US Senate 1837–42. Pierce subsequently returned to New Hampshire, serving briefly as US attorney and seeing action in the Mexican War. Chosen as a compromise candidate of the Democratic party, he was elected president 1852. Despite his expansionist foreign policy, North-South tensions grew more intense, and Pierce was denied renomination 1856.

Piercy Marge 1937– . US poet and novelist. Her fiction looks at the fringes of American social life and the world of the liberated woman. Her novels include the utopian *Woman on the Edge of Time* 1979, *Fly Away Home* 1984, and *Summer People* 1989.

Piero della Francesca c. 1420–1492. Italian painter, active in Arezzo and Urbino; one of the major artists of the 15th century. His work has a solemn stillness and unusually solid figures, luminous color, and compositional harmony. It includes a fresco series, *The Legend of the True Cross* (S Francesco, Arezzo), begun about 1452. Piero wrote two treatises, one on mathematics, one on the laws of perspective in painting.

Piero di Cosimo c. 1462–1521. Italian painter, known for his inventive pictures of mythological subjects, often featuring fauns and centaurs. He also painted religious subjects and portraits.

Pierre capital of South Dakota, located in the central part of the state, on the Missouri river, near the geographical center of North America. Industries include tourism and grain and dairy products; population (1990) 12,906. As Fort Pierre in the early 1800s, it served as a fur-trading post; in the late 1800s it was a supply center for gold miners.

Pietermaritzburg industrial city (footwear, furniture, aluminum, rubber, brewing), and capital, from 1842, of Natal, South Africa; population (1980) 179,000. Founded 1838 by Boer trekkers from

Piero della Francesca *Italian painter Piero della Francesca's* Baptism of Christ *c. 1439, now in the National Gallery, London.*

the Cape, it was named after their leaders, Piet Retief and Gert Maritz, killed by the Zulus.

Pietism religious movement within Lutheranism in the 17th century which emphasized spiritual and devotional faith rather than theology and dogma.

It was founded by Philipp Jakob Spener (1635–1705), a minister in Frankfurt, Germany, who emphasized devotional meetings for "groups of the Elect" rather than biblical learning; he wrote the *Pia Desideria* 1675. The movement was for many years associated with the University of Halle (founded 1694), Germany.

pietra dura (Italian "hard stone") an Italian technique of inlaying furniture with semiprecious stones, such as agate or quartz, in a variety of colors, to create pictures or patterns.

Pietro Berrettini da Cortona 1596–1669. Italian painter and architect, a major influence in the development of Roman High Baroque. His enormous fresco *Allegory of Divine Providence* 1633–39 (Barberini Palace, Rome) glorifies his patron the pope and the Barberini family, and gives a convincing illusion of reality.

piezoelectric effect property of some crystals (for example, ◊quartz) to develop an electromotive force or voltage across opposite faces when subjected to a mechanical strain, and, conversely, to expand or contract in size when subjected to an electromotive force. Piezoelectric crystal ◊oscillators are used as frequency standards (for example, replacing balance wheels in watches), and for producing ◊ultrasound.

The crystals are also used in phonograph pickups, transducers in ultrasonics, and certain gas lighters.

pig any even-toed hoofed mammal of family Suidae. The Near Eastern wild boar *Sus scrofa* is the ancestor of domesticated breeds; it is 4.5 ft/1.5 m long and 3 ft/1 m high, with formidable tusks, but not naturally aggressive. Pigs are omnivorous and have simple, nonruminating stomachs and thick hides.

Wild pigs include the ◊babirusa and the ◊wart hog. The farming of domesticated pigs was practiced during the Neolithic in the Near East and China at least 9,000 years ago, and pigs were a common farm animal in ancient Greece and Rome. Over 400 breeds evolved over the centuries, many of which have all but disappeared in more recent times with the development of intensive rearing systems; however, different environments and requirements have ensured the continuation of a variety of types. The Berkshire, Chester White, Poland, China, Saddleback, Yorkshire, Duroc, and Razorback are important surviving breeds. Modern indoor rearing methods favor the large white breeds, such as the Chester White and the originally Swedish Landrace, over colored varieties, which tend to be hardier and can survive better outdoors. Since 1960, hybrid pigs, produced by crossing two or more breeds, have become popular for their heavy but lean carcasses.

Pigalle Jean Baptiste 1714–1785. French sculptor. In 1744 he made the marble *Mercury* (Louvre, Paris), a lively, naturalistic work. His subjects ranged from the intimate to the formal, and included portraits.

Pigalle studied in Rome 1736–39. In Paris he gained the patronage of Madame de Pompadour, the mistress of Louis XV. His works include *Venus, Love and Friendship* 1758 (Louvre, Paris), a nude statue of *Voltaire* 1776 (Institut de France, Paris), and the grandiose *Tomb of Marechal de Saxe* 1753 (Strasbourg).

pigeon any bird of the family Columbidae, sometimes also called doves, distinguished by their large crops, which, becoming glandular in the breeding season, secrete a milky fluid ("pigeon's milk") that aids digestion of food for the young. They are found worldwide.

There are many species: domesticated varieties (including the city pigeon) derive from the Eurasian rock dove Columba livia. New World species include the mourning-doves, which live much of the time on the ground. The fruit pigeons of Australasia and the Malay regions are beautifully colored. In the US, there were once millions of passenger pigeons Ectopistes migratorius, but they have been extinct since 1914.

pigeon hawk another name for ◊merlin.

pig iron or ***cast iron*** the quality of iron produced in a ◊blast furnace. It contains about 4% carbon plus some other impurities.

Pigou Arthur Cecil 1877–1959. British economist, whose notion of the "real balance effect" (the "Pigou effect") contended that employment was stimulated by a fall in prices, because the latter increased liquid wealth and thus demand for goods and services.

pika or ***mouse-hare*** any small mammal of the family Ochotonidae, belonging to the order Lagomorpha (rabbits and hares). The single genus *Ochotona* contains about 15 species, most of which live in mountainous regions of Asia, although two species are native to North America. Pikas have short rounded ears, and most species are about 8 in/20 cm long, with greyish-brown fur and no visible tail. The warning call is a sharp whistle. They are vegetarian and in late summer cut grasses and other plants and place them in piles to dry as hay, which is then stored for the winter.

pike any of a family (Esocidae) in the order Salmoniformes, of slender, freshwater bony fishes with narrow pointed heads and sharp, pointed teeth. The northern pike *Esox lucius*, of North America and Eurasia, may reach 7 ft/2.2 m, and 20 lb/9 kg. Other kinds of pike include muskellunges, up to 7 ft/2.2 m long, and the smaller pickerels, both in the genus *Esox*.

Pike Zebulon Montgomery 1779–1813. US explorer and military leader. Born in Lamberton, New Jersey, Pike joined the army at age 15 and served in the Department of the West. In 1805 he was sent by the governor of the Louisiana Territory to explore the source of the Mississippi River. In 1806 he was sent to explore the Arkansas River and to contest Spanish presence in the area. After crossing Colorado and failing to reach the summit of the peak later named after him, he was captured by the Spanish, who released him 1807. Pike was later promoted to brigadier general and was killed in action in the War of 1812.

pikeperch any of various freshwater members of the perch family, resembling pikes, especially the walleye *Stizostedion vitreum*, common in Europe, W Asia, and North America. It reaches over 3 ft/1 m.

Pikes Peak mountain in the Rampart of the Rocky Mountains, Colorado; height 14,110 ft/4,300 m. It has commanding views, reachable by cog railroad and road. Pikes Peak was discovered 1806 by Zebulon Pike and first scaled 1820.

Pilate Pontius early 1st century AD. Roman procurator of Judea AD 26–36. Unsympathetic to the Jews, his actions several times provoked riots, and in AD 36 he was recalled to Rome to account for the brutal suppression of a Samaritan revolt. The New Testament Gospels describe his reluctant ordering of Jesus' crucifixion, but there has been considerable debate about his actual role in it; many believe that pressure was put on him by Jewish conservative priests. The Greek historian Eusebius says he committed suicide, but another tradition says he became a Christian, and he is regarded as a saint and martyr in the Ethiopian Coptic and Greek Orthodox churches.

pilchard any of various small, oily members of the herring family (Clupeidae), especially the commercial sardine of Europe *Sardina pilchardus*, and the California sardine *Sardinops sagax*.

piles popular name for ◊hemorrhoids.

pilgrimage journey to sacred places inspired by religious devotion. For Hindus, the holy places include Varanasi and the purifying river Ganges; for Buddhists, the places connected with the crises of Buddha's career; for the ancient Greeks, the shrines at Delphi and Ephesus among others; for Jews, the sanctuary at Jerusalem; and for Muslims, Mecca. The great centers of Christian pilgrimages have been, or still are, Jerusalem, Rome, the tomb of St James of Compostela in Spain, the shrine of Becket in Canterbury, England, and the holy places at La Salette and Lourdes in France.

Among Christians, pilgrimages were common by the 2nd century, and as a direct result of the growing frequency and numbers of pilgrimages there arose numerous hospices catering for pilgrims, the religious orders of knighthood, and the Crusades.

Pilgrimage of Grace rebellion against Henry VIII of England 1536–37, originating in Yorkshire and Lincolnshire. The uprising was directed against the policies of the monarch (such as the dissolution of the monasteries and the effects of ◊enclosure).

Pilgrims the emigrants who sailed from Plymouth, England, in the *Mayflower* on Sept 16, 1620, to found the first colony in New England at New Plymouth, Massachusetts. Of the 102 passengers, about a third were English Puritan refugees escaping religious persecution from Anglican England.

First known as Separatists, they were led by William Brewster, a wealthy layman, and William Bradford and had lived in Holland for 10 years. The voyagers had called themselves "Saints," the term "Pilgrim" not being applied to them until the 19th century. The Pilgrims originally set sail for Virginia in the *Mayflower* and *Speedwell* from Southampton on Aug 5, 1620, but had to put into Dartmouth when the latter needed repair. Bad weather then drove them into Plymouth Sound where the *Speedwell* was abandoned. After 2 months of sailing, they landed at Cape Cod in December and decided to stay, moving on to find Plymouth harbor and founding the Massachusetts colony. Considerable religious conflict had erupted between the 35 Puritans and the other, largely Anglican, passengers. Open mutiny was averted by the Mayflower Compact, which established the rights of the non-Puritans. About half their number died over the winter before they received help from the Indians; the survivors celebrated ◊Thanksgiving in the autumn of 1621.

The voyage was duplicated in 1957 with *Mayflower II*, a reproduction presented by Britain and now at Plymouth, Massachusetts.

Pilgrim's Progress an allegory by John Bunyan, published 1678–84, that describes the journey through life to the Celestial City of a man called Christian. On his way through the Slough of Despond, the House Beautiful, Vanity Fair, Doubting Castle, and other landmarks, he meets a number of allegorical figures.

This work was often the only other book an American pioneer family owned and read, besides the Bible.

Pilgrims' Way track running from Winchester to Canterbury, England, which was the route taken by medieval pilgrims visiting the shrine of Thomas à Becket. Some 120 mi/195 km long, the Pilgrims' Way can still be traced for most of its of its length.

pillory European instrument of punishment consisting of a wooden frame set on a post, with holes in which the prisoner's head and hands were secured. Bystanders threw whatever was available at the miscreant.

The pillory was similar to the ◊stocks. Its use for punishing petty offenders came to the Americas in colonial days and ended in the US in Delaware 1905.

the pill commonly used term for the contraceptive pill, based on female hormones. The combined pill, which contains estrogen and progesterone, stops the production of eggs, and makes the mucus produced by the cervix hostile to sperm. It is the most effective form of contraception apart from sterilization, being more than 99% effective.

The minipill or progesterone-only pill prevents implantation of a fertilized egg into the wall of the uterus. The minipill has a slightly higher failure rate, especially if not taken at the same time each day, but has fewer side effects and is considered safer for long-term use. Possible side effects of the pill include migraine or headache and high blood pressure. More seriously, estrogen-containing pills can slightly increase the risk of a blood clot forming in the blood vessels. This risk is increased in women over 35 if they smoke. Controversy surrounds other possible health effects of taking the pill. The evidence for a link with cancer is controversial (the pill may protect women from some forms of cancer). Once a woman ceases to take it, there is an increase in the chance of conceiving identical twins.

Pilobolous Dance Theater US troupe whimsically named after a light-sensitive fungus. Its members collectively choreograph surreal body-sculptures with a mixture of dance, gymnastics, and mime.

pilotfish small marine fish *Naucrates ductor* of the family Carangidae, which also includes pompanos. It hides below sharks, turtles, or boats, using the shade as a base from which to prey on smaller fish. It is found in all warm oceans and grows to about 1.2 ft/36 cm.

Pilsen German form of Czech town of ◊Plzeň.

Piłsudski Józef (Klemens) 1867–1935. Polish nationalist politician, dictator from 1926. Born in Russian Poland, he founded the Polish Socialist Party 1892 and was twice imprisoned for anti-Russian activities. During World War I he commanded a Polish force to fight for Germany but fell under suspicion of intriguing with the Allies and in 1917–18 was imprisoned by the Germans. When Poland became independent 1919, he was elected chief of state, and led an unsuccessful Polish attack on the USSR 1920. He retired 1923, but in 1926 led a military coup that established his dictatorship until his death.

Piltdown man a hoax; fossil skull fragments "discovered" by Charles Dawson at Piltdown, E Sussex, England, in 1913, and believed to be the earliest European human remains until proved a hoax in 1953 (the jaw was that of an orangutan).

pimento or ***allspice*** tree found in tropical parts of the New World. The dried fruits of the species *Pimenta dioica* are used as a spice. Also, a sweet variety of ◊capsicum pepper (more correctly spelled pimiento).

pimpernel any plant of the genus *Anagallis* of the primrose family Primulaceae. The European scarlet pimpernel *A. arvensis* grows in cornfields, the flowers opening only in full sunshine. It is naturalized in North America.

Pincus Gregory Goodwin 1903–1967. US biologist who, together with Min Chueh Chang and John Rock, developed the contraceptive pill in the 1950s.

As a result of studying the physiology of reproduction, Pincus conceived the idea of using synthetic ◊hormones to mimic the condition of pregnancy in women. This effectively prevents impregnation.

Pindar c. 552–442 BC. Greek poet, born near Thebes. He is renowned for his choral lyrics, the "Pindaric odes," written in honor of the victors of athletic games.

Pindling Lynden (Oscar) 1930– . Bahamian prime minister from 1967. After studying law in London, he returned to the island to join the newly formed Progressive Liberal Party and then became the first black prime minister of the Bahamas.

Pindus Mountains (Greek *Pindhos Oros*) range in NW Greece and Albania, between Epirus and Thessaly; highest point Smolikas, 8,638 ft/2,633 m.

pine any coniferous tree of the genus *Pinus*, family Pinaceae. There are 70–100 species, of which about 35 are native to North America. These are generally divided into two groupings: the soft pines and the hard pines. The former have needles in bundles of five and stalked cones without prickles; for example, eastern white pine *P. strobus*. Hard pines usually have needles in bundles of two or three and prickly cones; for example, jack pine *P. banksiana*. The oldest living species is probably the bristlecone pine *P. aristata*, native to California, of which some specimens are said to be 4,600 years old.

pineal body or ***pineal gland*** cone-shaped outgrowth of the vertebrate brain. In some lower vertebrates, this develops a rudimentary lens and retina, which show it to be derived from an eye, or pair of eyes, situated on the top of the head in ancestral vertebrates. The pineal still detects light (through the skull) in some fishes, lizards, and birds. Some lizards and the ◊tuatara have an opening in the skull for their pineal or "third eye." In fishes that can change color to match the background, the pineal perceives the light level and controls the color change. In birds, the pineal detects changes in daylight and stimulates breeding behavior as spring approaches.

Mammals also have a pineal gland, but it is located deeper within the brain. It secretes a hormonelike substance, melatonin, thought to influence rhythms of activity. In humans, it is a small piece of tissue attached to the posterior wall of the third ventricle of the brain.

pineapple plant *Ananas comosus* of the bromeliad family, native to South and Central America, but now cultivated in many other tropical areas, such as Hawaii and Queensland, Australia. The mauvish flowers are produced in the second year, and subsequently consolidate with their bracts into a fleshy fruit.

For export to world markets the fruits are cut unripe and lack the sweet juiciness typical of the canned pineapple (usually the smoother-skinned Cayenne variety), which is allowed to mature fully.

Pine Bluff city in SE Arkansas, on the Arkansas river, SE of Little Rock, seat of Jefferson county. Industries include paper, cotton, grain, and furniture; population (1990) 57,140.

Pinero Arthur Wing 1855–1934. British dramatist. A leading exponent of the "well-made" play, he enjoyed great contemporary success with his farces, beginning with *The Magistrate* 1885. More substantial social drama followed with *The Second Mrs Tanqueray* 1893, and comedies including *Trelawny of the "Wells"* 1898.

pine siskin streaked, tan, black, and yellow ◊finch *Carduelis pinus* of North America, about 5 in/12 cm long.

pink any annual or perennial plant of the genus *Dianthus* of the family Carophyllaceae. The stems have characteristically swollen nodes, and the flowers range in color from white through pink to purple. Deptford pink *D. armeria*, with deep pink flowers with pale dots, is native to Europe and naturalized in the US. Other members of the pink family include carnations, sweet williams, and baby's breath *Gypsophila paniculata*.

Pinkerton Allan 1819–1884. US detective, born in Glasgow, Scotland. He founded Pinkerton's National Detective Agency 1852 and built up the federal secret service from the espionage system he developed during the American Civil War. He thwarted an early assassination plot against Abraham ◊Lincoln and compiled the nation's most complete files on criminal activity. His agency became increasingly involved in the suppression of labor unrest. His men fought brutal battles against striking steelworkers 1892 and the ◊Molly Maguires.

Pink Floyd British psychedelic rock group, formed 1965. The original members were Syd Barrett (1946–), Roger Waters (1944–), Richard Wright (1945–), and Nick Mason (1945–). Their albums include *The Dark Side of the Moon* 1973 and *The Wall* 1979, with its spin-off film starring Bob Geldof.

Pinkham Lydia E 1819–1893. US entrepreneur and patent medicine proprietor, who claimed she could cure any "female complaint."

Pinkham began her manufacturing business in a cellar kitchen where she developed and mixed her own formulae. Although her claims of cures were never substantiated, her mixtures became increasingly popular, as was the Department of Advice she set up with an all-female staff to deal with the huge volume of inquiries the Lydia E. Pinkham Medicine Co. attracted.

pinna in botany, the primary division of a ◊pinnate leaf.

pinnate leaf a leaf that is divided up into many small leaflets, arranged in rows along either side of a midrib, as in ash trees (*Fraxinus*). It is a type of compound ◊leaf. Each leaflet is known as a pinna, and where the pinnae are themselves divided, the secondary divisions are known as pinnules.

Pinocchio a fantasy for children by Carlo ◊Collodi, published in Italy 1883 and in an English translation 1892. It tells the story of a wooden puppet that comes to life and assumes the characteristics of a human boy. His nose grows longer every time he tells a lie. A Walt Disney cartoon film, based on Collodi's story, was released in 1940 and brought the character to a wider audience.

Pinochet Ugarte Augusto 1915– . Military ruler of Chile from 1973, when a coup backed by the US Central Intelligence Agency ousted and killed President Salvador Allende. Pinochet took over the presidency and governed ruthlessly, crushing all opposition. He was voted out of power when general elections were held in Dec 1989 but remains head of the armed forces until 1997. In 1990 his attempt to reassert political influence was firmly censured by President Patricio Aylwin.

pint liquid or dry measure of volume or capacity. A liquid pint is equal to 16 fluid ounces or half a liquid quart (0.473 liter), while a dry pint is equal to half a dry quart (0.551 liter).

The British and Canadian imperial pint equals 0.568 liter.

Pinter Harold 1930– . English dramatist, originally an actor. He specializes in the tragicomedy of the breakdown of communication, broadly in the tradition of the Theater of the ◊Absurd, for example *The Birthday Party* 1958 and *The Caretaker* 1960. Later plays include *The Homecoming* 1965, *Old Times* 1971, *Betrayal* 1978, and *Mountain Language* 1988.

Pinturicchio (or Pintoricchio) pseudonym of Bernardino di Betto c. 1454–1513. Italian painter, active in Rome, Perugia, and Siena. His chief works are the frescoes in the Borgia Apartments in the Vatican, 1490s, and in the Piccolomini Library of Siena Cathedral, 1503–08. He is thought to have assisted ◊Perugino in decorating the Sistine Chapel, Rome.

pinworm ◊nematode worm *Enterobius vermicularis*, an intestinal parasite of humans.

Pinyin Chinese phonetic alphabet approved 1956 by the People's Republic of China, and used since 1979 in transcribing all names of people and places from Chinese ideograms into other languages using the English/Roman alphabet. For example, the former transcription Chou En-lai becomes Zhou Enlai, Hua Kuo-feng became Hua Guofeng, Teng Hsiao-ping became Deng Xiaoping, Peking became Beijing.

pion any of three ◊mesons (positive, negative, neutral) that play an important role in binding together the neutrons and protons in the nucleus of an atom. They belong to the ◊hadron class of ◊elementary particles.

Pioneer probes series of US solar-system space probes 1958–78. The probes *Pioneer 4–9* went into solar orbit to monitor the Sun's activity during the 1960s and early 1970s. *Pioneer 5*, launched 1960, was the first of a series to study the solar wind between the planets. *Pioneer 10*, launched March 1972, was the first probe to reach Jupiter (Dec 1973) and to leave the Solar System 1983. *Pioneer 11*, launched Apr 1973, passed Jupiter Dec 1974 and was the first probe to reach Saturn (Sept 1979), before also leaving the Solar System. *Pioneer 10* and *11* carry plaques containing messages from Earth in case they are found by other civilizations among the stars. Pioneer Venus probes were launched May and Aug 1978. One orbited Venus, and the other dropped three probes onto the surface. In early 1990 *Pioneer 10* was 4.4 billion mi/7.1 billion km from the Sun. Both it and *Pioneer 11* were still returning data-measurements of starlight intensity to Earth.

Pioneer 1, *2*, and *3*, launched 1958, were intended Moon probes, but *Pioneer 2*'s launch failed, and *1* and *3* failed to reach their target, although they did measure the ◊Van Allen radiation belts. *Pioneer 4* began to orbit the Sun after passing the Moon. *Pioneer 6* (1965), *7* (1966), *8* (1967), and *9* (1968) monitored solar activity.

pioneer species in ecology, those species that are the first to colonize and thrive in new areas. Coal heaps, recently cleared woodland, and new roadsides are areas where pioneer species will quickly appear. As the habitat matures other species take over, a process known as succession.

pipefish any of various long-snouted, thin, pipelike marine fishes in the same family (Syngnathidae) as ◊seahorses. The great pipefish *S. acus* grows up to 1.6 ft/50 cm, and the male has a brood pouch for eggs and developing young.

pipit any of various sparrow-sized ground-dwelling songbirds fo the genus *Anthus* of the family Motacillidae, which also includes wagtails.

The North American water pipit *A. spinoletta* lives near water in fields and on beaches. It is brown and tan with a slender bill.

piracy the taking of a ship, aircraft, or any of its contents, from lawful ownership, punishable under international law by the court of any country where the pirate may be found or taken. The contemporary equivalent is ◊hijacking. Piracy is also used to describe infringement of ◊copyright.

Algiers (see ◊corsairs), the West Indies (see ◊buccaneers), the coast of Trucial Oman (the Pirate Coast), Chinese and Malay waters, and such hideouts as Lundy Island, SW England, were long pirate haunts. Modern communications and the complexities of supplying and servicing modern vessels tend to eliminate piracy. However, it is still common in South America and SE Asian waters. Between the 16th and 19th centuries, the Barbary states of N Africa (Morocco, Algiers, Tunis, and Tripoli) were called the Pirate States.

The US sent a fleet to fight the Barbary pirates 1800–15, its first overseas naval and marine war, which was successfully concluded when Capt S ◊Decatur forced the dey of Algiers to cease the practice of holding US sailors hostage until tribute was paid.

***Piranesi** The 18th-century Italian architect Giambattista Piranesi worked in Rome on a series of etchings of the city in his day and in ancient times. This etching is called* Carceri d'Invenzione.

Piraeus port of both ancient and modern ◊Athens and main port of Greece, on the Gulf of Aegina; population (1981) 196,400. Constructed as the port of Athens about 493 BC, it was linked with that city by the Long Walls about 460 BC. After the destruction of Athens by Sulla 86 BC, Piraeus declined. Modern Piraeus is an industrial suburb of Athens.

Pirandello Luigi 1867–1936. Italian writer. His novel *Il fu Mattia Pascal/The Late Mattia Pascal* 1904 was highly acclaimed, along with many short stories. His plays include *La Morsa/The Vice* 1912, *Sei personaggi in cerca d'autore/Six Characters in Search of an Author* 1921, and *Enrico IV/Henry IV* 1922. The themes and treatment of his plays anticipated the work of Brecht, O'Neill, Anouilh, and Genet. Nobel Prize for Literature 1934.

Piranesi Giambattista 1720–1778. Italian architect who made powerful etchings of Roman antiquities and was a theorist of architecture, advocating imaginative use of Roman models. Only one of his designs was built, Sta Maria del Priorato, Rome.

piranha any South American freshwater fish of the genus *Serrusalmus*, in the same order as ◊cichlids. They can grow to 2 ft/60 cm long, and have razor-sharp teeth; some species may rapidly devour animals, especially if attracted by blood.

pirouette in dance, a movement comprising a complete turn of the body on one leg with the other raised.

Pirquet Clemens von 1874–1929. Austrian pediatrician and pioneer in the study of allergy.

Pisa city in Tuscany, Italy; population (1988) 104,000. It has a 11th–12th-century cathedral. Its famous campanile, the Leaning Tower of Pisa (repaired in 1990) is 180 ft/55 m high and about 16.5 ft/5 m out of perpendicular. The Leaning Tower has foundations only about 10 ft/3 m deep.

Pisa was a maritime republic in the 11th–12th

piranha

red
piranha

Pisa *The Leaning Tower of Pisa in Italy is 180 ft/ 55 m high and about 16.5 ft/5 m out of perpendicular.*

centuries. The university dates from 1338. The scientist Galileo was born here.

Pisanello nickname of Antonio Pisano c. 1395–1455. Italian artist active in Verona, Venice, Naples, Rome, and elsewhere. His panel paintings reveal a rich International Gothic style; his frescoes are largely lost. He was also an outstanding portrait medalist.

Pisano Andrea c. 1290–1348. Italian sculptor who made the earliest bronze doors for the Baptistery of Florence Cathedral, completed 1336.

Pisano Nicola (died c. 1284) and his son Giovanni (died after 1314). Italian sculptors and architects. They made decorated marble pulpits in churches in Pisa, Siena, and Pistoia. Giovanni also created figures for Pisa's baptistery and designed the façade of Siena Cathedral.

Pisces zodiac constellation, mainly in the northern hemisphere between Aries and Aquarius, near Pegasus. It is represented by two fish tied together by their tails. The Circlet, a delicate ring of stars, marks the head of the W fish in Pisces. The constellation contains the vernal ◊equinox, the point at which the Sun's path around the sky (the ◊ecliptic) crosses the celestial equator. The Sun reaches this point around March 21 each year as it passes through Pisces from mid-Mar to late Apr. In astrology, the dates for Pisces are between about Feb 19 and March 20 (see ◊precession).

Piscis Austrinus or ***Southern Fish*** constellation of the southern hemisphere near Capricornus. Its brightest star is ◊Fomalhaut.

Pisistratus c. 605–527 BC. Athenian politician. Although of noble family, he assumed the leadership of the peasant party and seized power 561 BC. He was twice expelled, but recovered power from 541 BC until his death. Ruling as a dictator under constitutional forms, he was the first to have the Homeric poems written down and founded Greek drama by introducing the Dionysiac peasant festivals into Athens.

Pissarro Camille 1831–1903. French painter, born in the West Indies. He went to Paris in 1855, met Corot, then Monet, and became a leading member of the Impressionists. He experimented with various styles, including ◊Pointillism, in the 1880s.

His son Lucien Pissarro (1863–1944) worked in the same style for a time.

pistachio deciduous Eurasian tree *Pistacia vera* of the cashew family Anacardiaceae, with green nuts, which are eaten salted or used to enhance and flavor foods.

pistil a general term for the female part of a flower, either referring to one single ◊carpel or a group of several fused carpels.

pistol any small ◊firearm designed to be fired with one hand. Pistols were in use from the early 15th century.

The problem of firing more than once without reloading was tackled by using many combinations of multiple barrels, both stationary and revolving. A breech-loading, multichambered revolver of as early as 1650 still survives; the first practical solution, however, was Samuel Colt's six-gun 1847. Behind a single barrel, a short six-chambered cylinder was rotated by cocking the hammer and a fresh round of ammunition brought into firing position. The automatic pistol, operated by gas or recoil, was introduced in Germany in the 1890s. Both revolvers and automatics remain in widespread military use.

Pistoia city in Tuscany, Italy, 10 mi/16 km NW of Florence; industries include steel, small arms, paper, pasta, and olive oil; population (1982) 92,500. Pistoia was the site of the Roman rebel Catiline's defeat 62 BC. It is surrounded by walls (1302) and has a 12th-century cathedral.

piston barrel-shaped device used in reciprocating engines (◊steam, ◊gasoline, ◊diesel) to harness power. Pistons are driven up and down in cylinders by expanding steam or hot gases. They pass on their motion via a connecting rod and crank to a ◊crankshaft, which turns the driving wheels. In a pump or compressor, the role of the piston is reversed, being used to move gases and liquids. See also ◊internal-combustion engine.

Piston Walter (Hamor) 1894–1976. US composer and teacher. He wrote a number of textbooks, including *Harmony* 1941 and *Orchestration* 1955. His Neo-Classical works include eight symphonies, a number of concertos, chamber music, the orchestral suite *Three New England Sketches* 1959, and the ballet *The Incredible Flautist* 1938.

He was well regarded as a teacher; his pupils included Leonard ◊Bernstein. He taught at Harvard University 1944–60.

Pitcairn Islands British colony in Polynesia, 3,300 mi/5,300 km NE of New Zealand

area 10 sq mi/27 sq km

capital Adamstown

features includes the uninhabited Henderson Islands, an unspoiled coral atoll with a rare ecology, and tiny Ducie and Oeno, annexed by Britain in 1902

products fruit and souvenirs to passing ships

population (1982) 54

language English

government the governor is the British high commissioner in New Zealand

history first settled 1790 by nine mutineers from the *Bounty* together with some Tahitians, their occupation remaining unknown until 1808.

pitch in chemistry, a black, sticky substance, hard when cold, but liquid when hot, used for waterproofing, roofing, and paving. It is made by the destructive distillation of wood or coal tar, and has been used since antiquity for caulking wooden ships.

pitch in music, the position of a note in the scale, dependent on the frequency of the predominant sound wave. In standard pitch, A above middle C has a frequency of 440 cycles per second (Hz). Perfect pitch is an ability to name or reproduce any note heard or asked for; it does not necessarily imply high musical ability.

pitchblende or ***uraninite*** brownish-black mineral, the major constituent of uranium ore, consisting mainly of uranium oxide (UO_2). It also contains some lead (the final, stable product of uranium decay) and variable amounts of most of the naturally occurring radioactive elements, which are products of either the decay or the fissioning of uranium isotopes. The uranium yield is 50–80%; it is also a source of radium, polonium, and actinium. Pitchblende was first studied by Pierre and Marie ◊Curie, who found radium and polonium in its residues in 1898.

Pitcher Molly. Nickname of Mary ◊McCauley

pitcher plant any of various insectivorous plants of the family Sarraceniaceae, especially the genera *Nepenthes* and *Sarracenia*, the leaves of which are shaped like a pitcher and filled with a fluid that traps and digests insects.

Pitman Isaac 1813–1897. English teacher and inventor of Pitman's shorthand. He studied Samuel Taylor's scheme for shorthand writing, and in 1837 published his own system, *Stenographic Soundhand*, fast, accurate, and adapted for use in many languages.

Pitot tube instrument that measures fluid (gas and liquid) flow. It is used to measure the speed of aircraft, and works by sensing pressure differences in different directions in the airstream. It was invented in the 1730s by the French scientist Henri Pitot (1695–1771).

It is a small, L-shaped tube that is inserted vertically into a flowing fluid with its open end facing upstream, thus measuring the total pressure of the fluid and indirectly the velocity of its flow.

Pitt William, the Elder, 1st Earl of Chatham 1708–1778. British Whig politician, "the Great Commoner." As paymaster of the forces 1746–55, he broke with tradition by refusing to enrich himself; he was dismissed for attacking Newcastle, the prime minister. He served effectively as prime minister in coalition governments 1756–61 (successfully conducting the Seven Years' War) and 1766–68.

Entering Parliament 1735, Pitt led the Patriot faction opposed to the Whig prime minister Walpole and attacked Walpole's successor, Carteret, for his conduct of the War of the Austrian Succession. He championed the Americans against the king, though rejecting independence, and collapsed during his last speech in the House of Lords—opposing the withdrawal of British troops—and died a month later.

Pitt William, the Younger 1759–1806. British Tory prime minister 1783–1801 and 1804–06. He raised the importance of the House of Commons, clamped down on corruption, carried out fiscal reforms and effected the union with Ireland. He attempted to keep Britain at peace but underestimated the importance of the French Revolution and became embroiled in wars with France from 1793; he died on hearing of Napoleon's victory at Austerlitz.

Son of William Pitt the Elder, he entered Cambridge University at 14 and Parliament at 22. He was the Whig Shelburne's chancellor of the Exchequer 1782–83, and with the support of the Tories and king's friends became Britain's youngest prime minister 1783.

pitta genus of tropical songless bird of order Passeriformes, genus *Pitta*, forming the family Pillidae. Some 20 species are native to SE Asia, W Africa, and Australia. They have round bodies, big heads, and are often brightly colored. They live on the ground and in low undergrowth, and can run from danger.

Pittsburgh industrial city (machinery, chemicals) and the nation's largest inland port, where the Allegheny and Monongahela rivers join to form the Ohio River in Pennsylvania; population (1990) 369,879, metropolitan area (1990) 2,242,798. Educational institutions include the University of Pittsburgh and Carnegie-Mellon University. Once a smoky, smoggy, steelmaking city, Pittsburgh was transformed by urban redevelopment from the 1960s and the demise of heavy industry into chiefly a corporate service center.

Established by the French as Fort Duquesne 1750, the site was taken by the British 1758 and renamed Fort Pitt. The main growth of the city's great iron and steel industry came after 1850.

Pittsfield city in W central Massachusetts on the

Housatonic River, just E of the New York border. Industries include electronics and tourism; population (1990) 48,622. Herman Melville wrote *Moby Dick* at his home here.

pituitary gland major ◊endocrine gland of vertebrates, situated in the center of the brain. The anterior lobe secretes hormones, some of which control the activities of other glands (thyroid, gonads, and adrenal cortex); others are direct-acting hormones affecting milk secretion, and controlling growth. Secretions of the posterior lobe control body water balance, and contraction of the uterus. The posterior lobe is regulated by nerves from the ◊hypothalamus, and thus forms a link between the nervous and hormonal systems.

Piura capital of the department of the same name in the arid NW of Peru, situated on the Piura river, 100 mi/160 km SW of Punta Pariñas; population (1981) 186,000. It is the westernmost point in South America and was founded 1532 by the conquistadors left behind by Pizarro. Cotton is grown in the surrounding area.

Pius 12 popes, including:

Pius IV 1499–1565. Pope from 1559, of the ◊Medici family. He reassembled the Council of Trent (see Counter-Reformation under ◊Reformation) and completed its work 1563.

Pius V 1504–1572. Pope from 1566. He excommunicated Elizabeth I of England, and organized the expedition against the Turks that won the victory of ◊Lepanto.

Pius VI (Giovanni Angelo Braschi) 1717–1799. Pope from 1775. He strongly opposed the French Revolution, and died a prisoner in French hands.

Pius VII 1742–1823. Pope from 1800. He concluded a ◊concordat with France 1801 and took part in Napoleon's coronation, but relations became strained. Napoleon annexed the papal states, and Pius was imprisoned 1809–14. After his return to Rome 1814, he revived the Jesuit order.

Pius IX 1792–1878. Pope from 1846. He never accepted the incorporation of the Papal States and of Rome in the kingdom of Italy, and proclaimed the dogmas of the Immaculate Conception of the Virgin 1854 and papal infallibility 1870; his pontificate was the longest in history.

Pius X (Giuseppe Melchiore Sarto) 1835–1914. Pope from 1903, canonized 1954. He condemned ◊Modernism in a manifesto 1907.

Pius XI (Achille Ratti) 1857–1939. Pope from 1922. He signed the ◊concordat with Mussolini 1929.

Pius XII (Eugenio Pacelli) 1876–1958. Pope from 1939. He was conservative in doctrine and politics, and condemned ◊Modernism. He proclaimed the dogma of the bodily assumption of the Virgin Mary 1950 and in 1951 restated the doctrine (strongly criticized by many) that the life of an infant must not be sacrificed to save a mother in labor. He was widely criticized for failing to speak out against atrocities committed by the Germans during World War II and has been accused of collusion with the Nazis.

pixel (contraction of "picture element") in computing, a single dot on a computer screen. All screen images are made up of a collection of pixels, with each pixel being either off (dark) or on (illuminated, possibly in color). The number of pixels available determines the screen's resolution. Typical resolutions of microcomputer screens vary from 320 × 200 pixels to 640 × 480 pixels, but screens with more than 1,000 × 1,000 pixels are now common for graphic (pictorial) displays.

Pizarro Francisco c. 1475–1541. Spanish conqueror of the Inca empire of Peru. Born in Spain, Pizarro traveled to the West Indies, where he met ◊Balboa and served as his lieutenant on the expedition that crossed Panama and resulted in their sighting of the Pacific Ocean 1513. While living in Panama, Pizarro heard of a wealthy Indian empire to the south, and beginning 1524 he explored the NW coast of South America, searching for gold and other riches. In 1531, with the permission of the king of Spain, he and 180 followers armed with cannon defeated the Inca king Atahualpa, later murdering him even though he gave them the large quantities of gold and silver they demanded. Pizarro founded Lima as the capital of Peru 1535. A feud then began among the Spanish leaders, and Pizarro was assassinated.

pizzicato (Italian "pinched") in music, an instruction to pluck a bowed stringed instrument (such as the violin) with the fingers of either the right or (infrequently) the left hand.

Plaatje Solomon Tshekiso 1876–1932. Pioneer South African black community leader who was the first secretary-general and founder of the ◊African National Congress 1912.

Place Francis 1771–1854. English Radical. He

plain

Animals of the plains depend on grasses and occasional trees for sustenance. Plant-eaters graze (feed on growing grass), browse (eat leaves, twigs and sparse vegetation), or forage (rummage for bulbs, roots and fruits). They are preyed upon by the meat-eaters.

African plain (savannah) wildlife and plants. 1. Baboon 2. Acacia tree 3. Eland 4. Low-growing shrubs 5. Giraffe 6. Elephant 7. Steenbok 8. Topi 9. Warthog 10. Weaver bird nests 11. Termite mound 12. Baobab tree 13. Lions 14. Rhinoceros

In temperate grasslands, where winter temperatures can fall far below freezing and summer temperatures rise to 104°F/40°C, many of the animals survive by living underground in burrows. In tropical grasslands, the climate is less extreme. Here a great variety of plants grow, and provide food for many more types of animals. The African grasslands support the world's largest wildlife populations.

Russian plain (steppe) wildlife and plants. 1. Shrubs and small trees 2. Grass snake 3. Lemmings 4. Field voles 5. Saiga antelope 6. Suslik 7. Marbled polecat 8. Black-bellied hamster

placenta

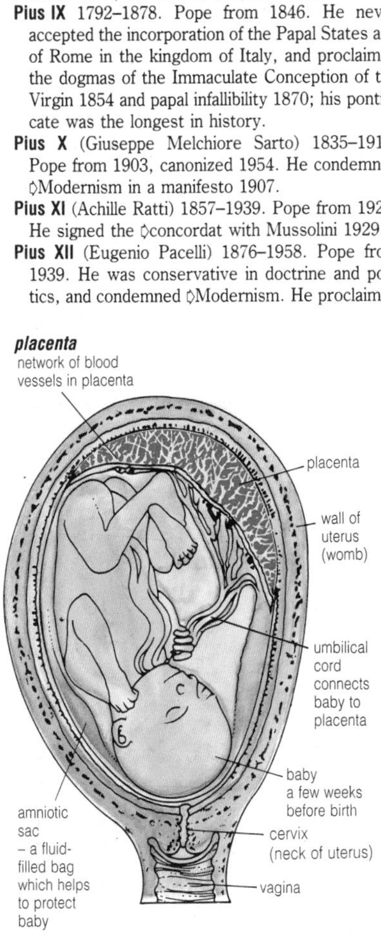
network of blood vessels in placenta
placenta
wall of uterus (womb)
umbilical cord connects baby to placenta
baby a few weeks before birth
amniotic sac – a fluid-filled bag which helps to protect baby
cervix (neck of uterus)
vagina

showed great powers as a political organizer, and made Westminster a center of pro-labor union Radicalism. He secured the repeal of the antiunion Combination Acts 1824.

placebo (Latin "I will please") any harmless substance, often called a "sugar pill," that has no chemotherapeutic value and yet produces physiological changes.

Its use in medicine is limited to drug trials, where it is given alongside the substance being tested, to compare effects. The "placebo effect," first named in 1945, demonstrates the control "mind" exerts over "matter," including causing changes in blood pressure, perceived pain, and rates of healing. Recent research finds the release of certain neurotransmitting substances in the production of the placebo effect.

placenta the vascular organ composed of maternal and embryonic tissue that attaches the developing ◊embryo or ◊fetus of placental mammals to the ◊uterus. Oxygen, nutrients, and waste products are exchanged between maternal and fetal blood across the placental membrane, but the two blood systems are not in direct contact. The placenta also produces hormones that regulate the progress of pregnancy. It is shed as part of the afterbirth.

It is now understood that a variety of materials, including drugs and viruses, can pass across the placental membrane. ◊HIV can be transmitted in this way.

The tissue in plants that joins the ovary to the ovules is also called a placenta.

placer deposit a detrital concentration of an economically important mineral, such as gold, but also other minerals such as cassiterite, chromite, and platinum metals. The mineral grains become concentrated during transport by water or wind because they are more dense than other detrital minerals such as quartz, and (like quartz) they are relatively resistant to chemical breakdown. Examples are the Witwatersrand gold deposits of South Africa, which are gold- and uranium-bearing conglomerates laid down by ancient rivers, and the placer tin deposits of the Malay Peninsula.

plague disease transmitted by fleas (carried by the black ◊rat) which infect the sufferer with the bacillus *Pasteurella pestis*. An early symptom is swelling of lymph nodes, usually in the armpit and groin; such swellings are called "buboes," hence bubonic plague. It causes virulent blood poisoning and the death rate is high.

Other and more virulent forms of plague are septicemic and pneumonic; the latter was fatal before the introduction of sulfa drugs and antibiotics. Outbreaks of plague still occur, mostly in poor countries, but never to the extent seen in the late Middle Ages. After the ◊Black Death, plague remained endemic for the next three centuries, the most notorious outbreak being the Great Plague of London in 1665, when about 100,000 of the 400,000 inhabitants died.

plaice any of various flatfishes of the flounder group, especially the genera *Pleuronectes* and *Hippoglossoides*. The American plaice *H. platessoides* grows to 2.5 ft/80 cm, and is valuable commercially.

plain or ***grassland*** land, usually flat, upon which grass predominates. The plains cover large areas of the Earth's surface, especially between the deserts of the tropics and the rainforests of the equator, and have rain in one season only. In such regions the climate belts move north and south during the year, bringing rainforest conditions at one time and desert conditions at another. Examples include the North European Plain, the High Plains of the US and Canada, and the Russian Plain also known as the ◊steppe.

Plains Indian member of any of the North American Indian peoples of the Great Plains, which extend over 2,000 mi/3,000 km from Alberta, Canada, to Texas. The Plains Indians were drawn from diverse linguistic stocks fringing the Plains but shared many cultural traits, especially the nomadic hunting of bison herds once horses

***Planck** One of the founders of 20th-century physics and formulator of the quantum theory, Max Planck was professor of theoretical physics at Berlin University.*

became available in the 18th century. The various groups include Blackfoot, Cheyenne, Comanche, Pawnee, and the Dakota or Sioux.

plainsong ancient chant of the Christian church first codified by Ambrose, bishop of Milan, and then by Pope Gregory in the 6th century. See ◊Gregorian chant.

Planck Max 1858–1947. German physicist who framed the quantum theory 1900.

He was appointed to the chair of physics at Kiel 1885 and Berlin 1889. Much of his early work was in thermodynamics. From 1930 to 1937, he was president of the Kaiser Wilhelm Institute. He was awarded the Nobel Prize for Physics 1918.

Planck's constant in physics, a fundamental constant (abbreviation h) that is the energy of one quantum of electromagnetic radiation (the smallest possible "packet" of energy; see ◊quantum theory) divided by the frequency of its radiation. Its value is 6.626196×10^{-34} joule seconds.

planet large celestial body in orbit around a star, composed of rock, metal, or gas. There are nine planets in the ◊Solar System.

The inner four, called the terrestrial planets, are small and rocky, and include the planet Earth. The outer planets (with the exception of Pluto) are called the giant planets and are large balls of rock, liquid, and gas; the largest is Jupiter, which contains more than twice as much mass as all the other planets combined. Planets do not produce light, but reflect the light of their parent star.

planetarium complex optical projection device by means of which the motions of stars and planets are reproduced on a domed ceiling representing the sky. Also, a building housing such a device, usually with auditoriums and scheduled lectures. About 60 such planetariums exist in the US.

planetary nebula shell of gas thrown off by a star at the end of its life. Planetary nebulae have nothing to do with planets. They were named by William Herschel, who thought their rounded shape resembled the disk of a planet. After a star has expanded to become a ◊red giant, its outer layers are ejected into space to form a planetary nebula, leaving the core as a ◊white dwarf at the center.

planetesimal body of rock in space, smaller than a planet, attracted to other such bodies during planet formation. According to modern solar nebula theory, the Sun and the planets are thought to have formed from a rotating dust cloud generated by a supernova explosion. On condensation, this cloud formed a central sun and a rotating disk, the material of which separated into rings of dust grains that began to stick together. Larger and larger clumps formed in each ring and eventually collected into bodies the size of present-day asteroids, called planetesimals. After numerous collisions, these bodies eventually formed the nucleus of the various planets of our Solar System.

A once-popular theory, called the planetesimal theory, held that planetesimals were formed from giant tongues of solar material torn from a preexisting sun by the gravitational attraction of a passing star. These planetesimals then ended up in orbits around the leftover sun in the plane of the passing star. As in the modern theory, the planetesimals then collided and coalesced into the present planets.

planimeter simple integrating instrument for measuring the area of a regular or irregular plane surface. It consists of two hinged arms: one is kept fixed and the other is traced around the boundary of the area. This actuates a small graduated wheel; the area is calculated from the wheel's change in position.

plankton small, often microscopic, forms of plant and animal life that drift in fresh or salt water, and are a source of food for larger animals.

plant an organism that carries out ◊photosynthesis, has cellulose cell walls and complex ◊eukaryotic cells, and is immobile. A few parasitic plants have lost the ability to photosynthesize but are still considered to be plants.

Plants are autotrophs, that is, they make carbohydrates from water and carbon dioxide, and are the primary producers in all food chains, so that all animal life is dependent on them. They play a vital part in the carbon cycle, removing carbon dioxide from the atmosphere and generating oxygen. The study of plants is known as botany.

Many of the lower plants (the algae and bryophytes) consist of a simple body, or thallus, on which the organs of reproduction are borne. Simplest of all are the threadlike algae, for example *Spirogyra*, which consist of a chain of cells. The seaweeds (algae) and mosses and liverworts (bryophytes) represent a further development, with simple, multicellular bodies that have specially modified areas in which the reproductive organs

planet

Planet	Main constituents	Atmosphere	Average distance from Sun in millions of mi	Time for one orbit in Earth-years	Diameter in thousands of mi	Average density if density of water is 1 unit
Mercury	rocky, ferrous	–	36	0.24	3.0	5.4
Venus	rocky, ferrous	carbon dioxide	67	0.61	7.5	5.2
Earth	rocky, ferrous	nitrogen, oxygen	93	1.00	7.9	5.5
Mars	rocky	carbon dioxide	142	1.88	4.2	3.9
Jupiter	liquid hydrogen, helium	–	484	11.86	88.7	1.3
Saturn	hydrogen, helium	–	887	29.50	75.0	0.7
Uranus	icy, hydrogen, helium	hydrogen, helium	1,783	84.00	31.6	1.2
Neptune	icy, hydrogen, helium	hydrogen, helium	2,794	164.80	30.2	1.7
Pluto	icy, rocky	methane	3,600	248.50	2.0	about 1

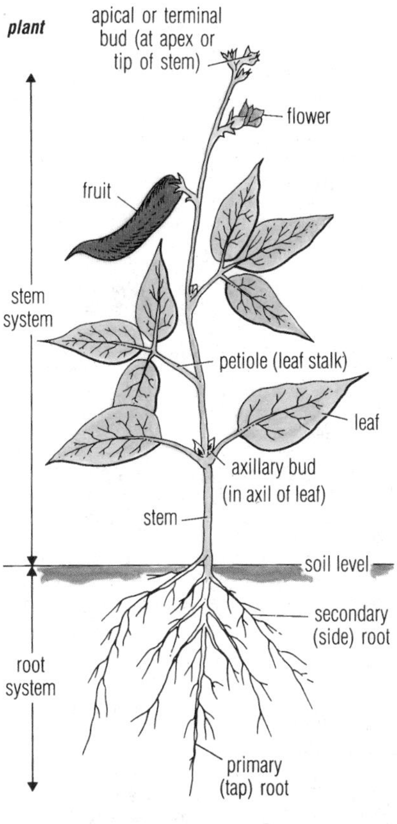
plant
apical or terminal bud (at apex or tip of stem)
flower
fruit
stem system
petiole (leaf stalk)
leaf
axillary bud (in axil of leaf)
stem
soil level
secondary (side) root
root system
primary (tap) root

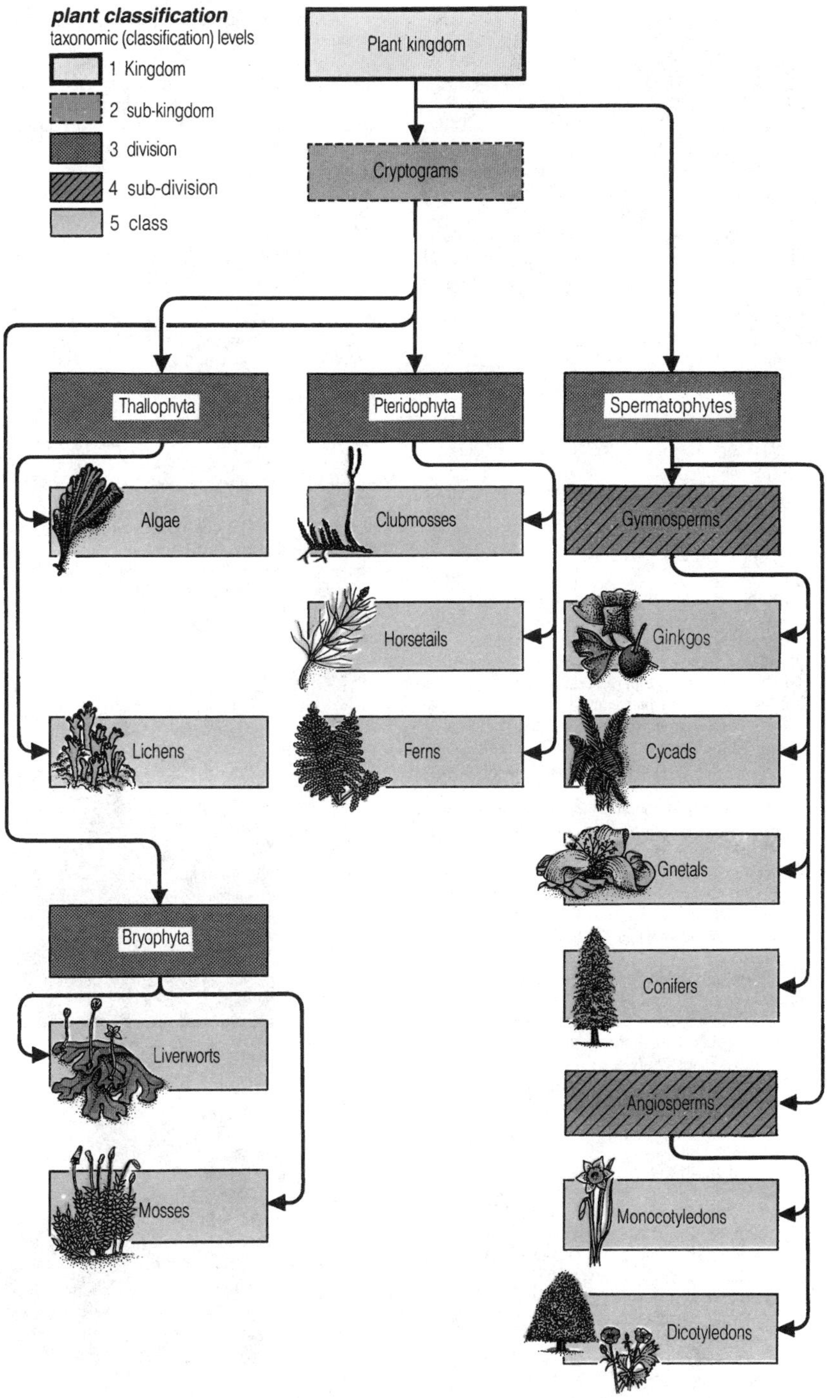
plant classification
taxonomic (classification) levels
1 Kingdom
2 sub-kingdom
3 division
4 sub-division
5 class
Plant kingdom
Cryptograms
Thallophyta
Pteridophyta
Spermatophytes
Algae
Clubmosses
Gymnosperms
Horsetails
Ginkgos
Lichens
Ferns
Cycads
Gnetals
Bryophyta
Conifers
Liverworts
Angiosperms
Mosses
Monocotyledons
Dicotyledons

are carried. Higher in the morphological scale are the ferns, club mosses, and horsetails (pteridophytes). Ferns produce leaflike fronds bearing sporangia on their undersurface in which the spores are carried. The spores are freed and germinate to produce small independent bodies carrying the sexual organs; thus the fern, like other pteridophytes and some seaweeds, has two quite separate generations in its life cycle (see ◊alternation of generations).

The pteridophytes have special supportive water-conducting tissues, which identify them as ◊vascular plants. This group includes all seed plants, that is the gymnosperms (conifers, yews, cycads, and ginkgo) and the angiosperms (flowering plants).

The seed plants are the largest group, and structurally the most complex. They are usually divided into three parts: root, stem, and leaves. Stems grow above or below ground. Their cellular structure is designed to carry water and salts from the roots to the leaves in the ◊xylem, and sugars from the leaves to the roots in the ◊phloem. The leaves manufacture the food of the plant by means of photosynthesis, which occurs in the ◊chloroplasts they contain. Flowers and cones are modified leaves arranged in groups, enclosing the reproductive organs from which the fruits and seeds result.

Plantagenet English royal house, reigning 1154–1399, whose name comes from the nickname of Geoffrey, Count of Anjou (1113–51), father of Henry II, who often wore in his hat a sprig of broom, *planta genista*. In the 1450s, Richard, duke of York, took it as a surname to emphasize his superior claim to the throne over Henry VI's.

plantain any plant of the genus *Plantago*, family Plantaginaceae. The great plantain *P. major* has oval leaves, grooved stalks, and spikes of green flowers with purple anthers followed by seeds, which are used in bird food. Many species are troublesome weeds. A type of ◊banana is also known as plantain.

plant classification the taxonomy or classification of plants. Originally the plant kingdom included bacteria, diatoms, dinoflagellates, fungi, and slime molds, but these are not now thought of as plants. The groups that are always classified as plants are the bryophytes (mosses and liverworts), pteridophytes (ferns, horsetails, and club mosses), gymnosperms (conifers, yews, cycads, and ginkgos), and angiosperms (flowering plants).

The basis of plant classification was established by ◊Linnaeus. Among the angiosperms, it is largely based on the number and arrangement of the flower parts.

The unicellular algae, such as *Chlamydomonas*, are often now put with the protists (single-celled organisms) instead of the plants. Some classification schemes even classify the multicellular algae (seaweeds and freshwater weeds) in a new kingdom, the Protoctista, along with the protists.

The angiosperms are split into monocotyledons (for example, orchids, grasses, lilies) and dicotyledons (for example, oak, cranberry, buttercup, and daisy).

plant hormone a substance produced by a plant that has a marked effect on its growth, flowering, leaf fall, fruit ripening, or some other process. Examples include ◊auxin, ◊gibberellin, ◊ethylene, and ◊cytokinin.

Unlike animal hormones, these substances are not produced by a particular area of the plant body, and they may be less specific in their effects. It has therefore been suggested that they should not be described as hormones at all.

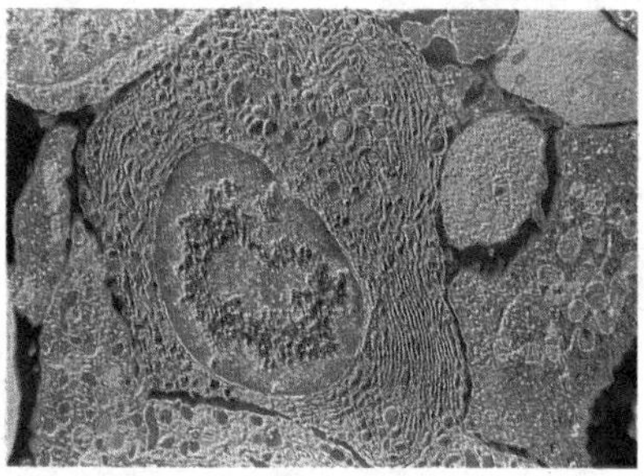

plasma *False-color electron-microscope view of a human plasmocyte (plasma cell). Plasmocytes are mature lymphocytes, or white blood cells, that synthesize and secrete the antibodies of the immune system.*

plaque any abnormal deposit on a body surface, especially the thin, transparent film of sticky protein (called mucin) and bacteria on tooth surfaces. If not removed, this film forms tartar (calculus), promotes tooth decay, and leads to gum disease. Another form of plaque is a deposit of fatty or fibrous material in the walls of blood vessels that can block blood flow or break free to form blood clots.

plasma in biology, the liquid part of the blood.

plasma in physics, an ionized gas produced at extremely high temperatures, as in the Sun and other stars, and which contains positive and negative charges in approximately equal numbers. It is a good electrical conductor. In thermonuclear reactions the plasma produced is confined through the use of magnetic fields.

plasmapheresis removal from the body of large quantities of blood, which is then divided into its components (plasma and blood cells) by centrifugal force in a continuous-flow cell separator. Once separated, the elements of the blood are isolated and available for specific treatment. Restored blood is then returned to the venous system of the patient.

Sometimes, donated blood is used.

plasmid a small, mobile piece of ◊DNA found in bacteria and used in ◊genetic engineering.

Plassey, Battle of a victory in India June 23, 1757, for the British under Robert ◊Clive, which brought Bengal under British rule.

plaster of Paris form of calcium sulfate, obtained from gypsum, mixed with water for making casts and molds.

plastic any of the stable synthetic materials that are fluid at some stage in their manufacture, when they can be shaped, and that later set to rigid or semirigid solids. Plastics today are chiefly derived from petroleum. Most are polymers, made up of long chains of identical molecules.

Processed by extrusion, injection-molding, vacuum-forming and compression, they emerge in consistencies ranging from hard and inflexible to soft and rubbery. They replace an increasing number of natural substances, being lightweight, easy to clean, durable, and capable of being rendered very strong, for example by the addition of carbon fibers, for building aircraft and other engineering projects.

Thermoplastics soften when warmed, then reharden as they cool. Examples of thermoplastics include polystyrene, a clear plastic used in kitchen utensils or (when expanded into a "foam" by gas injection) in insulation and ceiling tiles; polyethylene or polythene, used for containers and wrapping; and polyvinyl chloride (PVC), used for drainpipes, floor tiles, audio disks, shoes, and handbags.

Thermosets remain rigid once set, and do not soften when warmed. They include bakelite, used in electrical insulation and telephone receivers; epoxy resins, used in paints and varnishes, to laminate wood, and as adhesives; polyesters, used in synthetic textile fibers and, with fiberglass reinforcement, in car bodies and boat hulls; and polyurethane, prepared in liquid form as a paint or varnish, and in foam form for upholstery and in lining materials (where it may be a fire hazard). One group of plastics, the silicones, are chemically inert, have good electrical properties, and repel water. Silicones find use in silicone rubber, paints, electrical insulation materials, laminates, waterproofing for walls, stain-resistant textiles, and cosmetics.

Shape-memory polymers are plastics that can be crumpled or flattened and will resume their original shape when heated. They include trans-polyisoprene and polynorbornene. The initial shape is determined by heating the polymer to over 95°/35°C and pouring it into a metal mold. The shape can be altered with boiling water and the substance solidifies again when its temperature falls below 95°F.

Biodegradable plastics are increasingly in demand: Biopol was developed in 1990. The soil microbes involved build the plastic in their bodies from carbon dioxide and water (it constitutes 80% of their body). The unused parts of the microbe are dissolved away by heating in water. The discarded plastic can be placed in landfill sites where it breaks back down into carbon dioxide and water. It costs three to five times as much as ordinary plastics to produce.

Plasticine trademark for an oil-based modeling paste, used as a substitute for clay or wax. It was invented 1897 for children, but is also used by architects and engineers; the earliest space suits were modeled in Plasticine.

plastic surgery branch of surgery concerned with the repair of congenital disfigurement and the reconstruction of tissues damaged by disease or injury; and cosmetic surgery undergone for reasons of vanity to conform to some esthetic norm or counter the effects of aging; for example, the removal of bags under the eyes or a double chin.

plastid general name for a cell ◊organelle of plants that is enclosed by a double membrane and contains a series of internal membranes and vesicles. Plastids contain DNA and are produced by division of existing plastids. They can be classified into two main groups: the chromoplasts, which contain pigments such as ◊carotenes and ◊chlorophyll, and the leucoplasts, which are colorless; however, the distinction between the two is not always clear-cut.

◊Chloroplasts are the major type of chromoplast. They contain chlorophyll, are responsible for the green coloration of most plants, and perform

plate tectonics

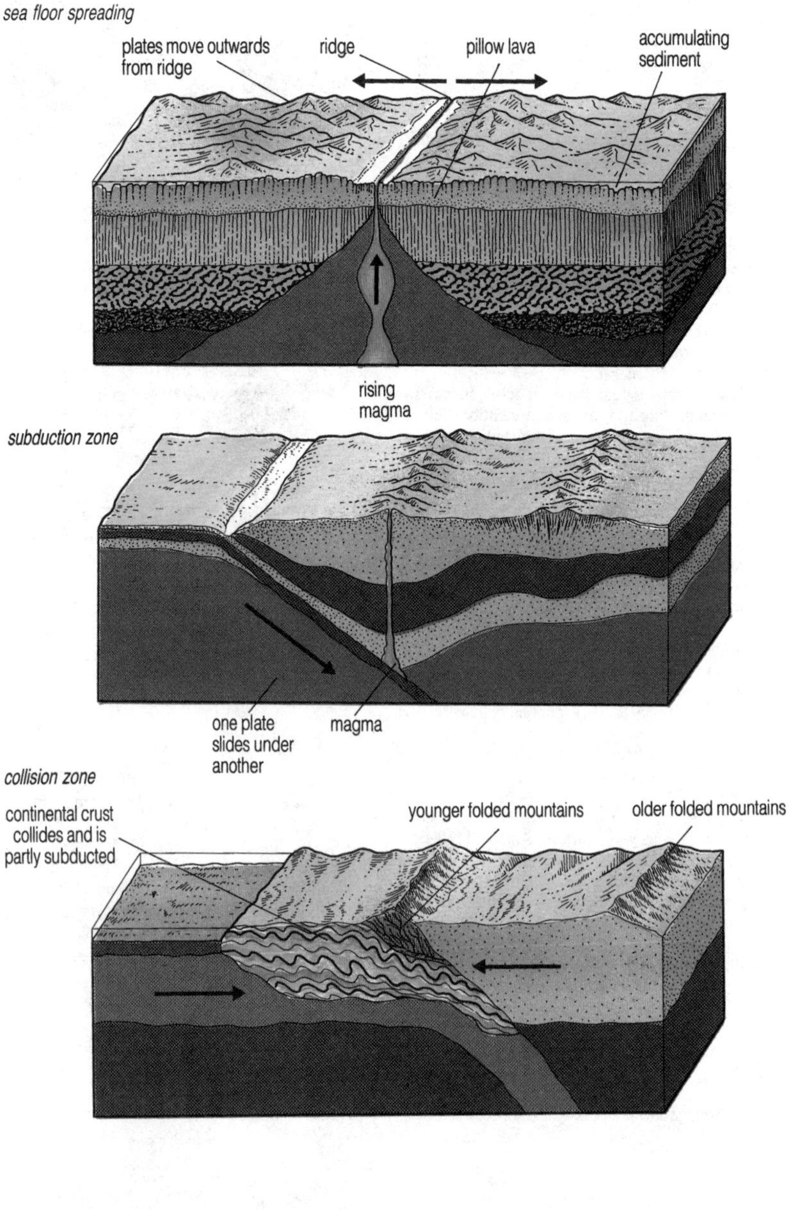
sea floor spreading
plates move outwards from ridge
ridge
pillow lava
accumulating sediment
rising magma
subduction zone
one plate slides under another
magma
collision zone
continental crust collides and is partly subducted
younger folded mountains
older folded mountains

◊photosynthesis. Other chromoplasts give the flower petals or the fruits their distinctive color. Leucoplasts are food-storage bodies and include amyloplasts, found in the roots of many plants, which store large amounts of starch.

Plataea, Battle of battle 479 BC, in which the Greeks defeated the Persians during the ◊Persian Wars.

plateau an elevated area of fairly flat land, or a mountainous region in which the peaks are at the same height. An intermontane plateau is one surrounded by mountains. A piedmont plateau is one that lies between the mountains and low-lying land. A continental plateau rises abruptly from low-lying lands or the sea.

platelet a tiny "cell" found in the blood, which helps it to clot. Platelets are not true cells, but membrane-bound cell fragments that bud off from large cells in the bone marrow.

plate tectonics concept that attributes ◊continental drift and ◊seafloor spreading to the continual formation and destruction of the outermost layer of the Earth. This layer is seen as consisting of major and minor plates, curved to the planet's spherical shape and with a jigsaw fit to one another. Convection currents within the Earth's mantle produce upwellings of new material along joint lines at the surface, forming ridges (for example the ◊Mid-Atlantic Ridge). The new material extends the plates, and these move away from the ridges. Where two plates collide, one overrides the other and the lower is absorbed back into the mantle. These "subduction zones" occur in the ocean trenches.

The moving plates consist of the Earth's ◊crust and the topmost solid layer of mantle, together called the ◊lithosphere. The plates move on a mobile layer of the mantle called the ◊asthenosphere. Some plates carry only ocean crust, others also carry continental crust. Only ocean crust is formed at mid-ocean ridges. The continents take little part in the generation and destruction of the plate material and are carried along passively on the moving plates.

The concept of continental drift was first put forward in 1915 by the German geophysicist Alfred Wegener; plate tectonics was formulated in the mid-1960s and has gained widespread acceptance among earth scientists.

Plath Sylvia 1932–1963. US poet and novelist. Plath's powerful, highly personal poems, often expressing a sense of desolation, are distinguished by their intensity and sharp imagery. Collections include *The Colossus* 1960; *Ariel* 1965, published after her death; and *Collected Poems* 1981, which was awarded a Pulitzer Prize. Her autobiographical novel, *The Bell Jar* 1961, deals with the events surrounding a young woman's emotional breakdown.

Born in Boston, Massachusetts, she attended Smith College and was awarded a Fulbright scholarship to study at Cambridge University, England, where she met the poet Ted Hughes, whom she married 1956; they separated in 1962. She committed suicide while living in London.

platinum heavy, soft, silver-white, malleable and ductile, metallic element, symbol Pt, atomic number 78, atomic weight 195.09. It is the namesake of and first of a group of six metallic elements (platinum, osmium, iridium, rhodium, ruthenium, and palladium) that possess similar traits, such as resistance to tarnish, corrosion, and attack by acid, and that often occur as free metals (◊native metals). They often occur in natural alloys with each other, the commonest of which is osmiridium. Both pure and as an alloy, platinum is used in dentistry, jewelry, and as a catalyst. The name derives from Spanish *platina*, the diminutive for *plata*, "silver."

Plato c. 428–347 BC. Greek philosopher, pupil of Socrates, teacher of Aristotle, and founder of the Academy. He was the author of philosophical dialogues on such topics as metaphysics, ethics, and politics. Central to his teachings is the notion of Forms, which are located outside the everyday world—timeless, motionless, and absolutely real.

platypus

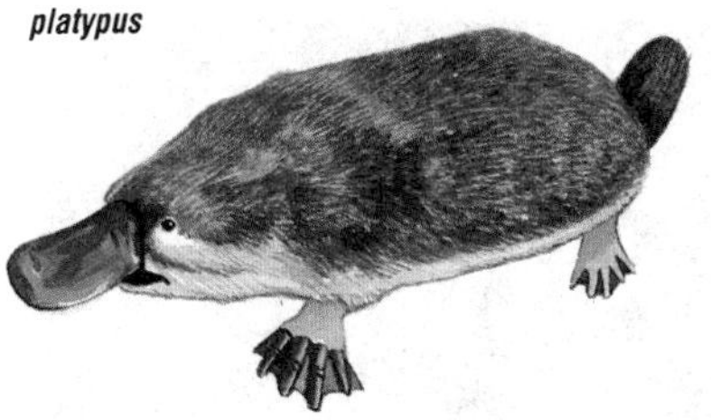

His philosophy has influenced Christianity and European culture, directly and through Augustine, the Florentine Platonists during the Renaissance, and countless others.

Born of a noble family, he entered politics on the aristocratic side, and in philosophy became a follower of Socrates. He traveled widely after Socrates's death, and founded the educational establishment the Academy in order to train a new ruling class.

Of his work, some 30 dialogues survive, intended for performance either to his pupils or to the public. The principal figure in these ethical and philosophical debates is Socrates and the early ones employ the Socratic method, in which he asks questions and traps the students into contradicting themselves; for example, *Iron*, on poetry. Other dialogues include the *Symposium*, on love, *Phaedo*, on immortality, and *Apology and Crito*, on Socrates' trial and death. It is impossible to say whether Plato's Socrates is a faithful representative of the real man or an articulation of Plato's own thought. Plato's philosophy rejects scientific rationalism (establishing facts through experiment) in favor of arguments, because mind, not matter, is fundamental, and material objects are merely imperfect copies of abstract and eternal "ideas." His political philosophy is expounded in two treatises, *The Republic* and *The Laws*, both of which describe ideal states (see ◊Utopia). Platonic love is inspired by a person's best qualities and seeks their development.

platypus monotreme, or egg-laying, mammal *Ornithorhynchus anatinus*, found in Tasmania and E Australia. Semiaquatic, it has small eyes, and no external ears, and jaws resembling a duck's beak. It lives in long burrows along river banks, where it lays two eggs in a rough nest. It feeds on water worms and insects, and when full-grown is 2 ft/60 cm long.

Plautus c. 254–184 BC. Roman dramatist, born in Umbria, who settled in Rome and worked in a bakery before achieving success as a dramatist. He wrote at least 56 comedies, freely adapted from Greek originals, of which 20 survive. Shakespeare based *The Comedy of Errors* on his *Menechmi*.

playa a temporary lake in a region of interior drainage. Such lakes are common features in arid desert basins fed by intermittent streams. The streams bring dissolved salts to the lakes, and when the lakes shrink during dry spells, the salts precipitate as evaporite deposits.

Player Gary 1935– . South African golfer, who won major championships in three decades and the first British Open 1959. A match-play specialist, he won the world title five times.

His total of nine "majors" is the fourth best of all time. He is renowned for wearing all-black outfits. In the 1980s he was a successful Seniors player.

CAREER HIGHLIGHTS

British Open: 1959, 1968, 1974
US Open: 1965
US Masters: 1961, 1974, 1978
US PGA: 1962, 1972
World Match-play: 1965–66, 1968, 1971, 1973

playing cards a set of small pieces of card with different markings, used in playing games. A standard set consists of a "deck" of 52 cards divided into four suits: hearts, clubs, diamonds, and spades. Within each suit there are 13 cards: nine are numbered (two through to ten), three are called face, picture (or court) cards (jack, queen, and king) and one is called the ace.

Playing cards probably originated in China or India, and first appeared in Europe in 14th-century Italy as the 78 cards (22 emblematic, including "the hanged man," and 56 numerals) of the ◊tarot cards, used both for gaming and in fortune-telling. However, in the 15th century they were reduced to the standard pack of 52 for most games, which include bridge, whist, poker, rummy, and cribbage.

pleadings in law, documents exchanged between the parties to court actions, which set out the facts that form the basis of the case they intend to present in court, and (where relevant) stating what damages or other remedy they are claiming.

plebeian a member of the unprivileged class in ancient Rome, composed of aliens, freed slaves, and their descendants. During the 5th–4th centuries BC plebeians waged a long struggle to win political and social equality with the patricians, eventually securing admission to the offices formerly reserved for patricians.

plebiscite referendum or direct vote by all the electors of a country or district on a specific question. Since the 18th century it has been employed on many occasions to decide to what country a particular area should belong; for example, in Upper Silesia and elsewhere after World War I; in the Saar 1935.

Pléiade, La group of seven poets in 16th-century France led by Pierre Ronsard who were inspired by Classical models to improve French verse. Their name is derived from the seven stars of the Pleiades group.

Pleiades in astronomy, a star cluster about 400 light-years away in the constellation Taurus, representing the Seven Sisters of Greek mythology. Its brightest stars (highly luminous, very young blue-white giants only a few million years old) are visible to the naked eye, but there are many fainter ones.

The stars of the Pleiades are still surrounded by traces of the reflection ◊nebula from which they formed, visible on long-exposure photographs.

Pleiades in Greek mythology, seven daughters of ◊Atlas, who asked to be changed into a cluster of stars to escape the pursuit of ◊Orion.

pleiotropy a process whereby a given gene influences several different observed characteristics of an organism.

Pleistocene first epoch of the Quaternary period of geologic time, beginning 1.8 million years ago and ending 10,000 years ago. Glaciers were abundant during the ◊Ice Age, and humans evolved into modern *Homo sapiens sapiens* by about 100,000 years ago.

Plekhanov Georgi Valentinovich 1857–1918. Russian Marxist revolutionary and theorist, founder of the ◊Menshevik party. He led the first populist demonstration in St Petersburg, became a Marxist and, with Lenin, edited the newspaper *Iskra* (spark). In 1903 his opposition to Lenin led to the Bolshevik-Menshevik split.

After the Bolshevik victory he lived in Finland.

Plenty, Bay of broad inlet on the NE coast of North Island, New Zealand, with the port of Tauranga. One of the first canoes bringing Maori immigrants landed here about 1350.

Plesetsk rocket-launching site, 105 mi/170 km south of Archangel, USSR. From here the USSR has launched satellites, mostly military, since 1966.

plesiosaur prehistoric carnivorous marine reptile of the Jurassic and Cretaceous periods, which reached a length of 36 ft/12 m, and had a long neck and paddlelike limbs. The pliosaurs evolved from the plesiosaurs.

Plessy v Ferguson a US Supreme Court decision

Plimsoll line

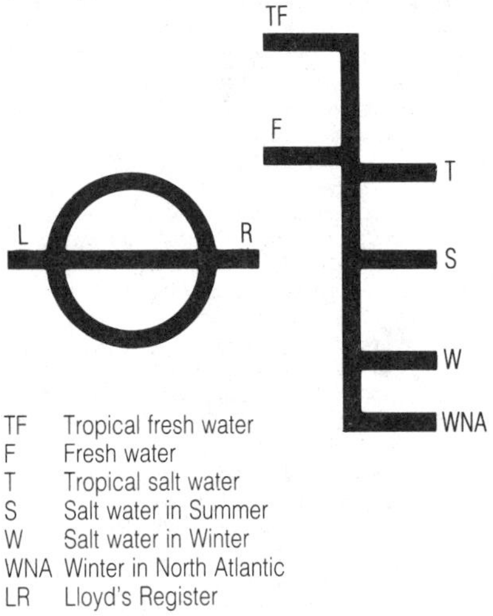
TF
F
T
L
R
S
W
WNA
TF Tropical fresh water
F Fresh water
T Tropical salt water
S Salt water in Summer
W Salt water in Winter
WNA Winter in North Atlantic
LR Lloyd's Register

1896 dealing with state-imposed segregation laws. Homer Plessy brought this case to the Supreme Court to test Louisiana segregation laws after he was arrested for refusing to leave a whites-only train car. He argued that such discrimination was prohibited by the 13th and 14th Amendments, which granted equal protection under the law. The Court ruled 8–1 against Plessy, holding that the 13th Amendment only prohibited slavery and that the 14th Amendment guaranteed only political but not social rights. The Court accepted a doctrine of separate but equal accommodations, a standard for segregation maintained until 1954 (see ◊*Brown* v *Board of Education*).

Plethon George Gemisthos 1353–1452. Byzantine philosopher who taught for many years at Mistra in Asia Minor. A Platonist, he maintained a resolutely anti-Christian stance and was the inspiration for many of the ideas of the 15th-century Florentine Platonic Academy.

pleural membrane one of a pair of membranes surrounding the lungs, protecting and lubricating them during breathing movements.

pleurisy inflammation of the pleura, the thin, secretory membrane that covers the lungs and lines the space in which they rest. Pleurisy is nearly always due to bacterial or viral infection, which can be treated with antibiotics. It renders breathing painful.

Normally the two lung surfaces move easily on one another, lubricated by small quantities of fluid. When the pleura is inflamed, the surfaces may dry up or stick together, making breathing difficult and painful. Alternatively, a large volume of fluid may collect in the pleural cavity, the space between the two surfaces, and pus (here called empyema) may accumulate. Pleurisy occurs in pneumonia and tuberculosis, but may also be a consequence of scarlet fever or rheumatism.

Pleven industrial town (textiles, machinery, ceramics) in N Bulgaria; population (1987) 134,000. In the Russo-Turkish War 1877, Pleven surrendered to the Russians after a siege of five months.

Plexiglas trademark for a clear, lightweight, tough plastic first produced 1930. It is widely used for watch glasses, advertising signs, domestic baths, motorboat windshields, aircraft canopies, and protective shields. Its chemical name is polymethylmethacrylate (PMMA).

Plimsoll line loading marking painted on the hull of merchant ships, first suggested by Samuel Plimsoll. It shows the depth to which a vessel may be safely (and legally) loaded.

Pliny the Elder (Gaius Plinius Secundus) c. AD 23–79. Roman scientist and historian; only his works on astronomy, geography, and natural history survive. He was killed in an eruption of Vesuvius.

plow Camel pulling a plow on Lanzarote, one of the Canary Islands.

Pliny the Younger (Gaius Plinius Caecilius Secundus) c. AD 61–113. Roman administrator, nephew of Pliny the Elder, whose correspondence is of great interest. Among his surviving letters are those describing the eruption of Vesuvius, his uncle's death, and his correspondence with the emperor ◊Trajan.

Pliocene ("almost recent") fifth and last epoch of the Tertiary period of geologic time, 5–1.8 million years ago. The earliest hominid (australopithecines) evolved in Africa; see also ◊human species.

pliosaur prehistoric carnivorous marine reptile, descended from the plesiosaurs, but with a shorter neck, and longer head and jaws. It was approximately 15 ft/5 m long. In 1989 the skeleton of one of a previously unknown species was discovered in northern Queensland, Australia. A hundred million years old, it lived in the sea that once covered the Great Artesian Basin.

Plisetskaya Maya 1925– . Soviet ballerina and actress. She attended the Moscow Bolshoi Ballet School and succeeded Ulanova as prima ballerina of the Bolshoi Ballet.

PLO abbreviation for ◊Palestine Liberation Organization.

Ploeşti industrial city (textiles, paper, petrochemicals; oil center) in SE Romania; population (1985) 234,000.

Plomer William 1903–1973. South African novelist, author of *Turbot Wolfe* 1925, an early criticism of South African attitudes to race. He settled in London in 1929 and wrote two autobiographical volumes.

plotter an ◊output device that draws pictures or diagrams under computer control. They are often used for producing business charts, architectural plans and engineering drawings. Flatbed plotters move a pen up and down across a flat drawing surface, while roller plotters roll the drawing paper past the pen as it moves from side to side.

Plovdiv industrial city (textiles, chemicals, leather, tobacco) in Bulgaria, on the river Maritsa; population (1987) 357,000. Conquered by Philip of Macedon in the 4th century BC, it was known as Philippopolis ("Philip's city").

plover any shore bird of the family Charadriidae, found worldwide. They are usually black or brown above, and white below, and have short bills. The largest of the ringed plovers is the killdeer *Charadrius vociferus*, called because of its cry.

The semipalmated plover *Charadrius semipalmatus* reaches 7 in/18 cm, has a black neck ring, and is common on beaches and lakeshores.

plow the most important agricultural implement, used for tilling the soil. The plow dates from about 3500 BC, when oxen were used to pull a simple wooden blade, or ard. In about 500 BC the iron share came into use.

By about AD 1000 horses as well as oxen were being used to pull wheeled plows, equipped with a plowshare for cutting a furrow, a blade for forming the walls of the furrow (called a colter), and a moldboard to turn a furrow. In the 18th century an innovation introduced by Robert Ransome (1753–1830), led to a reduction in the number of animals used to draw a plow: from an 8–12 oxer, or 6 horses, to a 2- or 4-horse plow. Steam plows came into use in some areas in the 1860s, superseded half a century later by tractor-drawn plows. The present plow consists of many "bottoms," each comprising a curved plowshare and angled moldboard. The bottom is designed so that it slices into the ground and turns the soil over.

plum tree *Prunus domestica*, bearing edible fruits that are smooth-skinned with a flat kernel. There are many varieties, including the Victoria, czar, egg-plum, greengage, and damson; the sloe *P. spinosa* is closely related. Dried plums are known as prunes.

plumbago alternate name for the mineral ◊graphite.

plumule the part of a seed embryo that develops into the shoot, bearing the first true leaves of the plant.

plur. abbreviation for plural.

pluralism in political science, the view that decision-making in contemporary liberal democracies is the outcome of competition among several interest groups in a political system characterized by free elections, representative institutions, and open access to the organs of power. This concept is opposed by corporatism and other approaches that perceive power to be centralized in the state and its principal elites (the Establishment).

pluralism in philosophy, the belief that reality consists of several different elements, not just two—matter and mind—as in ◊dualism.

Plutarch c. AD 46–120. Greek biographer whose *Parallel Lives* has the life stories of pairs of Greek and Roman soldiers and politicians, followed by comparisons between the two. Thomas North's 1579 translation inspired Shakespeare's Roman plays.

Plutarch was born in Chaeronea. He lectured on philosophy in Rome and was appointed procurator of Greece by Emperor Hadrian.

Pluto in astronomy, the smallest and, usually, outermost planet of the Solar System. Its highly elliptical orbit occasionally takes it within the orbit of Neptune, such as 1979–99. The existence of Pluto was predicted by calculation by Percival Lowell and the planet was located by Clyde ◊Tombaugh 1930. It orbits the Sun every 248.5 years at an average distance of 3.6 billion mi/5.8 billion km. Pluto has a diameter of about 2,000 mi/3,000 km and a mass about 0.005 that of Earth. It is of low density, composed of rock and ice, with frozen methane on its surface and a thin atmosphere.

Charon, Pluto's moon, was discovered 1978, revolving around Pluto with the same period as Pluto's rotation, remaining over the same point on Pluto's surface and showing the same face. The pair may be a double planet system.

Pluto in Greek mythology (Roman Dis), the lord of Hades, the underworld. He was the brother of Zeus and Poseidon.

plutonic rock an ◊igneous rock derived from magma that has cooled and solidified deep in the crust of the Earth; granites and gabbros are examples of plutonic rocks.

plutonium silvery-white, radioactive, metallic element of the ◊actinide series, symbol Pu, atomic number 94, atomic weight 239.13. It occurs in nature in minute quantities in ◊pitchblende and other ores, but is produced in quantity only synthetically. It has six allotropic forms (see ◊allotropy) and is one of three fissile elements (elements capable of splitting into other elements—the others are thorium and uranium). The element has awkward physical properties and is the most toxic substance known.

Its fissile isotope Pu-239 is usually made in ◊breeder reactors by bombarding uranium-238 with neutrons. Because Pu-239 is so easily synthesized from abundant uranium, it has been produced in large quantities (hundreds of thousands of pounds) by the weapons industry. It has a long half-life (24,000 years) during which time it remains highly toxic. It is dangerous to handle, difficult to store, and impossible to dispose of—it has become a human-made menace of global proportions. It was first produced in 1940 by Glenn Seaborg and his team at the University of California at Berkeley, by bombarding uranium with deuterons; this was the second transuranic element synthesized (after neptunium). It was named by them for the planet Pluto, since it comes after neptunium as the planet Pluto comes after Neptune.

Plymouth city and seaport in Devon, England, at the mouth of the river Plym, with dockyard, barracks, and naval base at Devonport; population (1981) 244,000.

The city rises N from the Hoe headland where tradition has it that ◊Drake played bowls before leaving to fight the Spanish Armada. John ◊Hawkins, Drake, and the *Mayflower* ◊Pilgrims sailed from Plymouth Sound. The city center was reconstructed after heavy bombing in World War II.

Plymouth Brethren a fundamentalist Christian Protestant sect characterized by extreme simplicity of belief, founded in Dublin about 1827 by the Reverend John Nelson Darby (1800–82). They have no ordained priesthood, affirming the ministry of all believers, and maintain no church buildings. They hold prayer meetings and Bible study in members' houses. An assembly of Brethren was held in Plymouth 1831 to celebrate the sect's arrival in England, but by 1848 the movement had split into "Open" and "Close" Brethren. The latter refuse communion with all those not of their persuasion.

There are some 65,000 in the US, divided into eight separate groups.

plywood manufactured panel of wood widely used in building. It consists of several thin sheets, or plies, of wood, glued together with the grain (direction of the wood fibers) of one sheet at right angles to the grain of the adjacent plies. This construction gives plywood equal strength in every direction.

Plzeň (German *Pilsen*) industrial city (heavy machinery, automobiles, beer) in W Czechoslovakia, capital of Západočeský region; 52 mi/84 km SW of Prague; population (1984) 174,000.

p.m. or P.M. abbreviation for post meridiem (Latin "after noon").

PM abbreviation for prime minister.

pneumatic drill drill operated by compressed air, used in mining and tunneling, for drilling shot holes (for explosives), and in road repairs for breaking up pavements. It contains an air-operated piston that delivers hammer blows to the drill ◊bit many times a second. The French engineer Germain Sommeiller (1815–71) developed the pneumatic drill 1861 for tunneling in the Alps.

pneumatophore an erect root that rises up above the soil or water and promotes ◊gas exchange. Pneumatophores, or breathing roots, are formed by certain swamp-dwelling trees, such as mangroves, since there is little oxygen available to the roots in waterlogged conditions. They have numerous pores or ◊lenticels over their surface, allowing gas exchange.

pneumectomy surgical removal of all or part of a lung.

pneumoconiosis disease of the lungs caused by dust, especially from coal, asbestos, or silica. Inhaled particles make the lungs gradually fibrous and the victim has difficulty breathing.

pneumonia inflammation of the lungs, generally due to bacterial or viral infection but also to particulate matter or gases. It is characterized by a buildup of fluid in the alveoli, the clustered air sacs (at the end of the air passages) where oxygen exchange takes place.

Symptoms include fever and pain in the chest. With widespread availability of antibiotics, infectious pneumonia is much less common than it was. However, it remains a dire threat to patients whose immune systems are suppressed (including transplant recipients and AIDS and cancer victims) and to those who are critically ill or injured. Pneumocystis pneumonia is a leading cause of death from AIDS.

pneumothorax the presence of air in the pleural cavity, between a lung and the chest wall. It may be due to a penetrating injury of the lung or to lung disease, or it may arise without apparent cause. Prevented from expanding normally, the lung is liable to collapse.

Pnom Penh alternate form of ◊Phnom Penh, capital of Cambodia.

Po longest river in Italy, flowing from the Cottian Alps to the Adriatic; length 415 mi/668 km. Its valley is fertile and contains natural gas. The river is heavily polluted with nitrates, phosphates, and arsenic.

PO abbreviation for Post Office.

Pobeda, Pik highest peak in the ◊Tian Shan mountain range on the Soviet-Chinese border; at 24,406 ft/7,439 m, it is the second highest mountain in the USSR.

Pocahontas c. 1595–1617. American Indian woman alleged to have saved the life of English colonist John Smith when he was captured by her father, Powhatan. Pocahontas was kidnapped 1613 by an Englishman, Samuel Argall, and she later married colonist John Rolfe (1585–1622) and was entertained as a princess at the English Court. Her marriage and conversion to Christianity brought about a period of peaceful relations between Indians and settlers, but she died of smallpox after her return to Virginia.

pochard any of various diving ducks found in Europe and North America especially the genus *Aythya*.

In North America, the canvasback *A. valisineria*, the redhead *A. americana*, the ring-necked *A. collaris*, and two species of scaup *A. marila* and *A. affinis* are pochards.

Po Chu-i alternative transliteration of ◊Bo Zhu Yi, Chinese poet.

pod in botany, a type of ◊fruit that is characteristic of legumes (plants belonging to the Leguminosae family), such as peas and beans. It develops from a single ◊carpel and splits down both sides when ripe to release the seeds.

In certain species the seeds may be ejected explosively due to uneven drying of the fruit wall, which sets up tensions within the fruit. In agriculture, "legume" is used to name the crops of the pea and bean family. "Grain legume" refers to those that are grown mainly for their dried seeds, such as lentils, chick peas, and soybeans.

podesta in the Italian ◊communes, the highest civic official, appointed by the leading citizens, and often holding great power.

Podgorica former name (until 1946) of ◊Titograd, city in Yugoslavia.

podiatry the medical profession that deals with the specialized care of feet. Some podiatric treatments involve the use of orthopedic devices to correct fallen arches or improve improper positioning of feet during walking.

Podolsk industrial city (oil refining, machinery, cables, cement, ceramics) in the USSR, 25 mi/40 km SW of Moscow; population (1987) 209,000.

podzol or ***podsol*** type of light-colored soil found predominantly under coniferous forests and moorlands in cool regions where rainfall exceeds evaporation. The constant downward movement of water leaches nutrients from the upper layers, making podzols poor agricultural soils.

The leaching of minerals such as iron, lime and alumina leads to the formation of a bleached zone, often also depleted of clay. These minerals can accumulate lower down the soil profile to form a hard, impermeable layer which restricts the drainage of water through the soil.

Poe *Daguerrotype of US author Edgar Allan Poe, particularly noted for his short stories and poetry.*

Poe Edgar Allan 1809–1849. US writer and poet. His short stories are renowned for their horrific atmosphere, as in "The Fall of the House of Usher" 1839 and "The Masque of the Red Death" 1842, and for their acute reasoning (ratiocination), as in "The Gold Bug" 1843 and "The Murders in the Rue Morgue" 1841 (in which the investigators Legrand and Dupin anticipate Arthur Conan Doyle's Sherlock Holmes). His most famous poem is "The Raven" 1845.

Born in Boston, he was orphaned 1811 and taken in by the wealthy Allan family of Richmond, Virginia. He was, however, disowned by the Allans when he was expelled from both the University of Virginia and West Point. Poe joined the army but was court-martialed for neglect of duty. Although he already had published *Tamerlane and Other Poems* 1827, *Al Aaraaf* 1829, and *Poems* 1831, he failed to earn a living by writing. He became editor of the *Southern Literary Messenger* in Richmond. In 1847 his wife died, an event he commemorated in his poem "Annabel Lee." He became an alcoholic and exhausted himself, dying at age 40. Poe was the first US poet to become internationally known and admired. His verse, of haunting lyric beauty, in, for example, "Ulalume" 1847 and "The Bells" 1849, influenced the French Symbolists.

poet laureate poet of the British royal household, so called because of the laurel wreath awarded to eminent poets in the Greco-Roman world. Early poets with unofficial status were Chaucer, Skelton, Spenser, Daniel, and Jonson.

Among later poets laureate have been Wordsworth, Tennyson, Cecil Day Lewis, John Betjeman, and Ted Hughes.

poetry the imaginative expression of emotion, thought, or narrative, frequently in metrical form and often using figurative language. Poetry has traditionally been distinguished from prose (ordinary written language) by rhyme or the rhythmical arrangement of words (meter), although the distinction is not always clear-cut.

A distinction is made between lyrical, or songlike, poetry (sonnet, ode, elegy, pastoral), and narrative, or story-telling, poetry (ballad, lay, epic). Poetic form has also been used as a vehicle for satire, parody, and expositions of philosophical, religious, and practical subjects.

Poetry: A Magazine of Verse US literary magazine, founded in Chicago 1912 by Harriet Monroe, with Ezra Pound as foreign editor. One of the "Little Magazines" of the early 20th century, and still published today, it introduced many major modern poets, including T S Eliot, Wallace Stevens, William Carlos Williams, Marianne Moore, and Carl Sandburg, and it printed the manifesto of Imagism.

pogrom (Russian "destruction") unprovoked violent attack on an ethnic group, particularly Jews, carried out with official sanction. The Russian pogroms against Jews began 1881, after the assassination of Tsar Alexander II, and again in 1903–06; persecution of the Jews remained constant until the Russian Revolution. Later there were pogroms in E Europe, especially in Poland after 1918, and in Germany under Hitler (see ◊Holocaust).

poikilothermy the condition in which an animal's body temperature is largely dependent on the temperature of the air or water in which it lives. It is characteristic of all animals except birds and mammals, which maintain their body temperatures by ◊homeothermy. Poikilotherms have behavioral means of temperature control, such as basking in the sun and then maintaining adequate temperatures by getting out of the Sun's direct rays. See ◊homeotherms ("warm-blooded animals"). Poikilotherms are often referred to as "coldblooded animals," but this is not really correct: their internal temperatures, regulated by behavioral means, are often as high as those of birds and mammals during the times they need to be active for feeding and reproductive purposes. The main difference is that their body temperatures fluctuate more than those of homeotherms.

Poincaré Jules Henri 1854–1912. French mathematician who developed the theory of differential equations and was a pioneer in ◊relativity theory. He suggested that Isaac Newton's laws for the behavior of the universe could be the exception rather than the rule. However, the calculation was so complex and time-consuming that he never managed to realize its full implication. He also published the first paper devoted entirely to ◊topology.

Poincaré Raymond Nicolas Landry 1860–1934. French politician, prime minister 1912–13, president 1913–20, and again prime minister 1922–24 (when he ordered the occupation of the Ruhr, Germany) and 1926–29.

Poindexter John Marlan 1936– . US rear admiral and Republican government official. In 1981 he joined the Reagan administration's National Security Council (NSC) and became national security adviser 1985. As a result of the ◊Irangate scandal, Poindexter was forced to resign 1986, along with his assistant, Oliver North.

A doctor in nuclear physics, Poindexter served in the US Navy, rising to become deputy head of naval educational training 1978–81. From 1983 he worked closely with the NSC head, Robert McFarlane, and took over when McFarlane left Dec 1985. Poindexter retired from the navy Dec 1987 and was found guilty on all counts April 1990, but his convictions were overturned on appeal Nov 1991.

poinsettia or ***Christmas flower*** winter-flowering shrub *Euphorbia pulcherrima*, with large red leaves encircling small greenish-yellow flowers. It is native to Mexico and tropical America and is a popular houseplant in North America and Europe.

pointe (French "toe of shoe") in dance, the tip of the toe. A dancer *sur les pointes* is dancing on her toes in blocked shoes, as popularized by Marie ◊Taglioni 1832.

Pointe-Noire chief port of the Congo, formerly (1950–58) the capital; population (1984) 297,000. Industries include oil refining and shipbuilding.

pointer breed of dog, often white mixed with black, tan, or dark brown, about 2 ft/60 cm tall, and weighing 62 lb/28 kgs.

They were bred to scent the position of game and indicate it by standing, nose pointed toward it, often with one forefoot raised, in silence.

Pointillism technique in oil painting developed in the 1880s by the Neo-Impressionist Seurat. He used small dabs of pure color laid side by side to create an impression of shimmering light when forms are viewed from a distance.

pointillism in music, a form of 1950s ◊serialism in which melody and harmony are replaced by complexes of isolated tones.

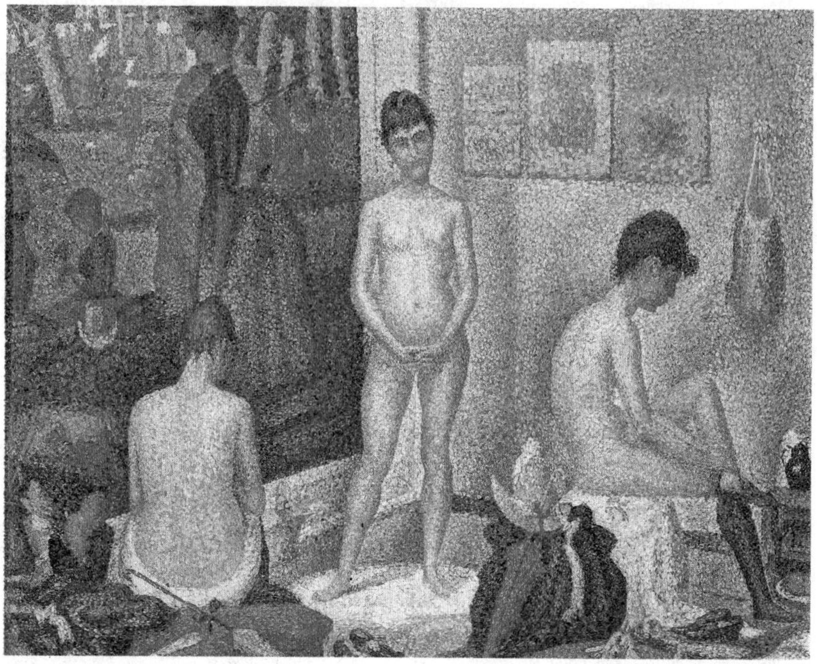

***Pointillism** French artist Georges Seurat developed the technique of pointillism (seen here in* Poseuses*). This painstakingly minute style evolved from Impressionist brushwork but was also based on scientific knowledge of the effects of color.*

point of sale in business premises, the point where a sale is transacted, for example, a supermarket checkout. In conjunction with electronic funds transfer, point of sale is part of the terminology of "cashless shopping," enabling buyers to transfer funds directly from their bank accounts to the shop's (see ◊EFTPOS).

poise unit (abbreviation P) of dynamic ◊viscosity (the property of liquids that determines how readily they flow). It is equal to one dyne-second per square centimeter. For most liquids the centipoise (one hundredth of a poise) is used. Water at 68°F/20°C has a viscosity of 1.002 centipoise.

Poiseuille's formula in physics, a relationship describing the rate of flow of a fluid through a narrow tube. For a capillary (very narrow) tube of length l and radius r with a pressure difference p between its ends, and a liquid of ◊viscosity η, the velocity of flow expressed as the volume per second is $\pi pr^4/8l\eta$. The formula was devised 1843 by the French physicist Jean Louis Poiseuille (1799–1869).

poison or ***toxin*** any chemical substance that, when introduced into or applied to the body, is capable of injuring health or destroying life. The liver is the organ that removes some poisons from the blood.

The majority of poisons may be divided into (1) corrosives, such as sulfuric, nitric, and hydrochloric acids; caustic soda; and mercuric chloride—all of which burn and destroy the parts with which they come into contact; (2) irritants, such as arsenic, copper sulfate, zinc chloride, silver nitrate, and green vitriol (iron sulfate)—all of which have an irritating effect on the stomach and bowels; (3) narcotics, such as opium, hydrocyanic acid, potassium cyanide, chloroform, and carbon monoxide—all of which affect the brainstem and spinal cord, inducing a stupor; and (4) narcoticoirritants, which can cause intense irritations and finally act as narcotics—for example, carbolic acid, foxglove, henbane, deadly nightshade (belladonna), tobacco, and many other substances of plant origin.

In noncorrosive poisoning every effort is made to remove the poison from the system as soon as possible—usually by vomiting induced by an emetic. For some corrosive and irritant poisons there are chemical antidotes, but for recently developed poisons (for example, the herbicide ◊paraquat) that produce proliferative changes in the system, there is no antidote. Drugs (legal and illegal), including nicotine and alcohol, are toxins to the human body.

In most countries the sale of poison, as such, is carefully controlled by law and, in general, only qualified and registered pharmacists and medical practitioners may dispense them, however, industrial and agricultural poisons are dumped into our waters and onto our lands, entering the food chain, and poisoning us and our planet.

poison ivy a North American plant *Rhus radicans* of the cashew family, having leaves composed of three leaflets, yellowish flowers, and ivory-colored, berrylike fruit. The leaves are variable and may be dull or shiny, leathery or thin, toothed or smooth-edged. It can grow as an erect shrub, trailing vine, or climber. All parts of the plant contain a heavy, nonvolatile oil that causes inflammation of the skin with itching rash, blisters, and/or swelling in susceptible persons. Numerous birds feed on the berries.

poison oak any of several North American subspecies of poison ivy *Rhus radicans*. Poison oak always grows as an erect shrub (to 10 in/25 cm tall) with three-parted leaves that are usually blunt-tipped and hairy on both sides. The irritating effects to humans are similar to those of poison ivy.

poison pill in business, a tactic to avoid hostile takeover by making the target unattractive. For example, a company may give a certain class of stockholders the right to have their shares redeemed at a very good price in the event of the company being taken over, thus involving the potential predator in considerable extra cost.

poison sumac a shrub or small tree *Rhus vernix* of the cashew family that thrives in a swampy habitat. Its large leaves are composed of 7–13 pointed leaflets, and it bears clusters of white globular fruit. All its parts contain a dangerous skin irritant more virulent than that of poison ivy or poison oak.

Poisson Siméon Denis 1781–1840. French applied mathematician. In probability theory he formulated the Poisson distribution, which is widely used in probability calculations. He published four treatises and several papers on aspects of physics, including mechanics, heat, electricity and magnetism, elasticity, and astronomy.

Poitevin in English history, relating to the reigns of King John and King Henry III. Poitevin derived from the region of France south of the Loire (Poitou), which was controlled by the English for most of this period.

Poitier Sidney 1924– . US actor and film director, the first black actor to become a star in Hollywood. He starred in *Something of Value* 1957, *Lilies of the Field* 1963, and *In the Heat of the Night* 1967; he directed *Stir Crazy* 1980.

Poitiers capital of Poitou-Charentes, W France; population (1982) 103,200; products include chemicals and clothing. The Merovingian king Clovis defeated the Visigoths under Alaric here 507; ◊Charles Martel stemmed the Saracen advance 732, and ◊Edward the Black Prince defeated the French 1356.

Poitou-Charentes region of W central France, comprising the *départements* of Charente, Charente-Maritime, Deux-Sèvres, and Vienne

capital Poitiers

area 9,959 sq mi/25,800 sq km

population (1986) 1,584,000

products dairy products, wheat, chemicals, metal goods; brandy is made at Cognac

history once part of the Roman province of Aquitaine, this region was captured by the Visigoths in the 5th century and taken by the Franks AD 507. The area was contested by the English and French until the end of the Hundred Years' War, when it was incorporated into France by Charles II.

poker card game of US origin, in which two to eight people play (usually for stakes) and try to obtain a "hand" of five cards ranking higher than those of their opponents. The best scoring hand wins the "pot."

Standard kinds of poker are five-card draw and stud. In draw poker, players receive five cards face down and then, after a round of betting, may "discard" up to three cards and "draw" replacement cards from the cards not dealt, in an attempt to improve their hands. A final round of betting follows. In stud, players receive one card (five-card stud) or two cards (seven-card stud) face down. Betting is done round by round as the remaining cards are dealt face up; players surmise the odds by viewing the exposed cards. The value of hands, in ascending order, is as follows: high card, one pair, two pairs, three-of-a-kind, straight (five cards in consecutive numerical order), flush (five cards of the same suit), full-house (three-of-a-kind plus 1 pair), four-of-a-kind, straight flush (5 cards of the same suit in consecutive order). Many variations exist; sometimes "wild cards" (such as deuces or one-eyed jacks) are designated.

pokeweed a tall North American herbaceous plant *Phytolacca americana* of the family Phytolaccaceae. It has pale greenish flowers and purple berries, the seeds of which are poisonous. North American Indians used the juice of the berries for staining.

Poland country in E Europe, bounded E by the USSR, S by Czechoslovakia, and W by the Federal Republic of Germany.

government Poland has a two-chamber legislature, comprising a 460-member lower assembly, the *Sejm* (parliament), and a 100-member upper chamber, the Senate. A two-ballot majority "run off" voting system is employed and terms are for four years. The Senate's members are elected in free, multiparty contests. The *Sejm* passes bills, adopts the state budget and economic plan, and appoints a 24-member executive council of ministers, headed by a chair, or prime minister. The Senate has the power of veto in specified areas, which can be overriden by a two-thirds *Sejm* vote. Both chambers jointly elect, for a six-year term, a French-style executive state president who is responsible for military and foreign affairs and has the authority to dissolve parliament, call referenda, veto bills, and impose martial law. It has been promised that when the current assembly-elected president has served his full term, the next chief executive will be directly elected by the public and the *Sejm* will be fully opened to multiparty competition for its seats. At the local level, there are elected people's councils in each of the country's 49 provinces (*voivodships*).

history In the 10th century the Polish tribes were first united under one Christian ruler, Mieczyslaw. Mongols devastated the country 1241, and thereafter German and Jewish refugees were encouraged to settle among the ◊Slav population. The first parliament met 1331, and Casimir the Great (1333–1370) raised the country to a high level of prosperity. Under the Jagellion dynasty (1386–1572) Poland became a great power, the largest country in Europe when it was united with Lithuania (1569–1776). Elected kings followed the death of the last Jagellion, a reactionary nobility wielded much power, and Poland's strength declined. But Stephen Bathory defeated Ivan the Terrible of Russia 1581, and in 1683 John III Sobieski forced the Turks to raise their siege of Vienna. In the mid-17th century a war against Russia, Sweden, and Brandenburg ended in the complete defeat of Poland, from which it was never allowed to recover.

Wars with the ◊Ottoman Empire, dissension among the nobles, quarrels at the election of every king, the continuance of serfdom, and the persecution of Protestants and Greek Orthodox Catholics laid the country open to interference by Austria, Russia, and Prussia, ending with partition 1772, and again 1793, when Prussia and Russia seized further areas. A patriotic uprising led by Tadeusz Kosciuszko was defeated, and Russia and Prussia occupied the rest of the country 1795. The Congress of ◊Vienna rearranged the division 1815 and reconstituted the Russian portion as a kingdom under the tsar. Uprisings 1830 and 1863 led to intensified repression and an increased attempt to Russianize the population.

Poland was revived as an independent republic 1918 under the leadership of Jósef Pilsudski, the founder of the PPS, taking advantage of the USSR's internal upheaval to advance into Lithuania and Ukraine before the Polish troops were driven back by the Red Army. Poland and the USSR then agreed on a frontier E of the ◊Curzon Line. Politically, the initial post-independence years were characterized by instability, 14 multiparty coalition governments holding power 1918–26. Pilsudski seized complete power in a coup and proceeded to govern in an increasingly authoritarian manner until his death in 1935. He was succeeded by a military regime headed by Smigly-Rydz. In April 1939 the UK and France concluded a pact with Poland to render military aid if it was attacked, and at the beginning of Sept Germany invaded (see ◊World War II). During the war, Western Poland was incorporated into the Nazi Reich, while the remainder, after a brief Soviet occupation of the east (1940–41), was

Poland
Republic of Poland
(Polska Rzeczpospolita)

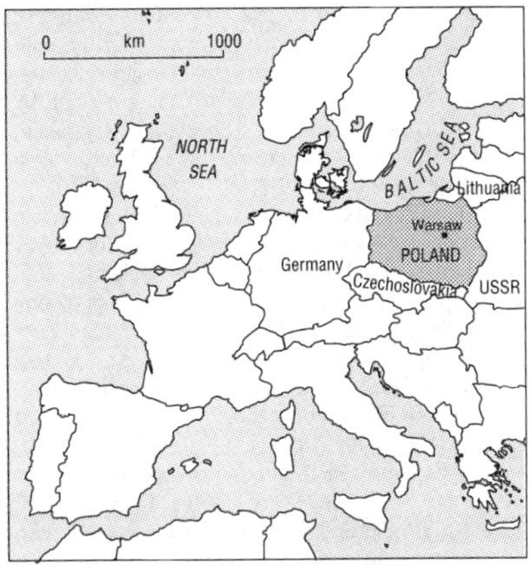
0 km 1000
NORTH SEA
BALTIC SEA
Warsaw
POLAND
Germany
Czechoslovakia
USSR

area 120,733 sq mi/312,700 sq km
capital Warsaw
cities Lódź, Kraków, Wroclaw, Poznań, Katowice, Bydgoszcz, Lublin; ports Gdánsk, Szczecin, Gdynia
physical part of the great plain of Europe; Vistula, Oder, and Neisse rivers; Sudeten, Tatra, and Carpathian mountains on S frontier
features last wild European bison (only in protected herds)
head of state Lech Wałesa from 1990
head of government Jan Krzysztof Bielecki from 1991
political system emergent democracy
political parties Social Democratic Party of the Polish Republic, 1990 successor to Polish United Worker's Party (PUWP), social democratic; Union of Social Democrats, radical breakaway from PUWP formed 1990; Solidarność (Solidarity) Parliamentary Club (OKP), anticommunist coalition; Center Alliance, right-of-center, christian democratic (modeled on Germany's CDU); Democratic-Social Movement
exports coal, softwood timber, chemicals, machinery, ships, vehicles, meat, copper (Europe's largest producer)
currency zloty
population (1990 est) 38,363,000; growth rate 0.6% p.a.
life expectancy men 66, women 74 (1989)
language Polish
religion Roman Catholic 95%
literacy 98% (1989)
GNP $276 bn (1988); $2,000 per head (1986)
chronology
1918 Poland revived as independent republic.
1939 German invasion and occupation.
1944 Germans driven out by Soviet forces.
1945 Polish boundaries redrawn at Potsdam Conference.
1947 Communist people's republic proclaimed.
1956 Poznań riots. Gomulka installed as Polish United Workers' Party (PUWP) leader.
1970 Gomulka replaced by Gierek after Gdańsk riots.
1980 Solidarity emerged as a free labor union following Gdańsk disturbances.
1981 Martial law imposed by Gen Jaruzelski.
1983 Martial law ended.
1984 Amnesty for political prisoners.
1985 Zbigniew Messner became prime minister.
1987 Referendum on economic reform rejected.
1988 Solidarity strikes and demonstrations called off after pay increases. Messner resigned; replaced by the reformist Mieczyslaw Rakowski.
1989 Solidarity relegalized; new "Socialist pluralist" constitution reached in church-state-union negotiations April. Widespread success for Solidarity in assembly elections, the first open elections in 40 years. First non-Communist government since World War II formed under Tadeusz Mazowiecki; economic restructuring undertaken on free market lines; W Europe and US create $1 bn aid package.
1990 PUWP dissolved; replaced by Social Democratic Party and breakaway Union of Social Democrats Jan. Lech Wałesa elected head of state; Prime Minister Mazowiecki resigned Dec.

treated as a colony. The country endured the full brunt of Nazi barbarism: a third of the educated elite were "liquidated" and, in all, six million Poles lost their lives, half of them Jews slaughtered in concentration camps.

A treaty between Poland and the USSR Aug 1945 (ratified 1946) established Poland's eastern frontier at the Curzon Line. Poland lost 70,000 sq mi/181,350 sq km in the east to the USSR but gained 39,000 sq mi/101,000 sq km in the west from Germany. After elections, a "people's republic" was established Feb 1947, and Poland joined ◊Comecon 1949 and the ◊Warsaw Pact 1955, remaining under close Soviet supervision, with the Soviet marshal Rokossovsky serving as minister for war 1949–56. A harsh Stalinist form of rule was instituted under the leadership of Boleslaw Bierut (1892–1956), involving rural collectivization, the persecution of Catholic church opposition, and the arrest of Cardinal Stefan Wyszynski 1953. In June 1956, serious strikes and riots, leading to 53 deaths, broke out in Poznan in opposition to Soviet "exploitation" and food shortages. The more pragmatic Wladyslaw ◊Gomulka took over as PUWP leader, reintroduced private farming, and released Cardinal Wyszynski.

A further outbreak of strikes and rioting in Gdańsk, Gdynia, and Szczecin Dec 1970 followed sudden food-price rises. This led to Gomulka's replacement as PUWP leader by the Silesia party boss Edward ◊Gierek, whose program aimed at raising living standards and consumer-goods production. The country's foreign debt grew, and food prices again triggered strikes and demonstrations June 1976. Opposition to the Gierek regime, which was accused of corruption, mounted 1979 after a visit to his homeland by the recently elected Pope ◊John Paul II. Strikes in Warsaw 1980, following a poor harvest and meat price increases, rapidly spread across the country. The government attempted to appease workers by entering into pay negotiations with unofficial strike committees, but at the Gdańsk shipyards demands emerged for permission to form free, independent labor unions. The government conceded the right to strike, and in Gdańsk 1980 the ◊Solidarity (Solidarność) union was formed under the leadership of Lech ◊Wałęsa.

In Sept 1980, the ailing Gierek was replaced as PUWP leader by Stanisław Kania, but unrest continued as the 10-million member Solidarity campaigned for a five-day working week and established a rural section. With food shortages mounting and PUWP control slipping, Kania was replaced as PUWP leader Oct 1981 by the prime minister, General Wojciech ◊Jaruzelski; the Soviet army was active on Poland's borders; and martial law was imposed Dec 13, 1981. Trade-union activity was banned, the leaders of Solidarity arrested, a night curfew imposed, and the Military Council of National Salvation established, headed by Jaruzelski. Five months of severe repression ensued, resulting in 15 deaths and 10,000 arrests. The US imposed economic sanctions.

In June 1982, curfew restrictions were eased, prompting further serious rioting in Aug. In Nov Wałęsa was released, and in Dec 1982 martial law was suspended (lifted 1983). The pope visited Poland 1983 and called for conciliation. The authorities responded by dissolving the Military Council and granting an amnesty to political prisoners and activists. In 1984, 35,000 prisoners and detainees were released on the 40th anniversary of the People's Republic, and the US relaxed its economic sanctions.

The Jaruzelski administration pursued pragmatic reform, including liberalization of the electoral system. Conditions remained tense, however, strained by the continued ban on Solidarity and by a threat (withdrawn 1986) to try Wałęsa for slandering state electoral officials. Economic conditions and farm output slowly improved, but Poland's foreign debt remained huge. During 1988 the nation's shipyards, coalmines, ports, and steelworks were paralyzed by a wave of Solidarity-led strikes for higher wages to offset the effect of recent price rises. With its economic strategy in tatters, the government of prime minister Zbigniew Messner resigned, being replaced, in Dec 1988, by a new administration headed by the reformist communist Mieczyslaw Rakowski, and the PUWP's politburo was infused with a new clutch of technocrats.

Following six weeks of PUWP-Solidarity-Church negotiations, an historic accord was reached in April 1989 under whose terms Solidarity was relegalized, the formation of opposition political associations tolerated, legal rights conferred upon the Catholic Church, the state's media monopoly lifted, and a new "Socialist pluralist" constitution adopted. In the subsequent national assembly elections, held in June 1989, Solidarity captured all but one of *Sejm* and Senate seats for which they were entitled to contest. In Sept 1989 a grand "coalition" was formed with Tadeusz ◊Mazowiecki, editor of Solidarity's newspaper, who became prime minister. Jaruzelski continued as president, and was reelected in July. The new government, which attracted generous financial aid from Western powers, proceeded to dismantle the command economy and encourage the private sector. A tough ◊IMF-approved austerity program was also instituted to solve the problem of hyperinflation, running up to 550% in 1989.

In April 1990 the Sejm (parliament) voted to restore May 3 (the anniversary of the creation of the 1791 constitution) and to cancel July 22 (anniversary of the 1944 Lublin Manifesto establishing communist rule) as a national holiday. Censorship was abolished in April. In 1990 living standards in Poland fell by 40%. Unemployment rose to over 1 million.

In July 1990 40 members of the 259-strong Solidarity caucus, under the leadership of Zbigniew Bujak and Wladyslaw Frasyniuk, established the Citizens" Movement of Democratic Action Party (ROAD) to provide a credible alternative to the Wałęsa-orientated Solidarity Center Alliance (SCA) established in May.

Wałęsa accused the government of delaying political and economic reform and forcing workers to bear the brunt of the austerity program. In July 100 SCA deputies and senators petitioned Jaruzelski to stand down to make way for Wałęsa. In Sept the Sejm passed a bill establishing a presidential term of five years.

In the first round of presidential elections, held on Nov 25, 1990, the rupture within Solidarity was exposed by both Prime Minister Mazowiecki and Lech Wałęsa contesting for the position. Having run a populist campaign, Wałęsa topped the poll with a 40% vote share, and Mazowiecki, defending an unpopular government, finished in third position, with 18% of the vote, behind Stanislav Tyminski, a previously obscure right-wing, returned-emigre Canadian businessman, who captured 23% of the vote. (In Dec Mazowiecki resigned as prime minister.) In the second round, held on Dec 9, Wałęsa defeated Tyminski.

In Oct 1991, Poland held its first parliamentary elections without guaranteed representation for the Communist Party. No dominant party emerged from the voting, and Wałęsa attempted to consolidate power in a coalition led by himself.

Polanski Roman 1933– . Polish film director and actor, born in Paris. He suffered a traumatic childhood in Nazi-occupied Poland, and later his wife, actress Sharon Tate, was the victim of murder in Hollywood by the Charles Manson "family." He left the US for Europe and his tragic personal life is reflected in a fascination with horror and violence in his work. His films include *Repulsion* 1965, *Cul de Sac* 1966, *Rosemary's Baby* 1968, *Tess* 1979, and *Frantic* 1988.

polar coordinates in mathematics, a way of defining the position of a point in terms of its distance r from a fixed point (the origin) and its angle θ to a fixed line or axis. The coordinates of the point are (r, θ).

Often the angle is measured in ◊radians, rather than degrees. The system is useful for defining positions on a plane in programming the operations of, for example, computer-controlled cloth- and metal-cutting machines.

Polaris or ***Pole Star*** or ***North Star*** the bright star closest to the north celestial pole, and the brightest star in the constellation Ursa Minor. Its position is indicated by the "pointers" in Ursa Major. Polaris is a yellow ◊supergiant about 700 light-years away.

It currently lies within 1° of the north celestial pole; ◊precession (Earth's axial wobble) will bring Polaris closest to the celestial pole (less than 0.5° away) about AD 2100. It is also known as Alpha Ursae Minoris.

polarized light ordinary light that can be regarded as electromagnetic vibrations at right angles to the line of propagation but in different planes. Light is said to be polarized when the vibrations take place in one particular plane. Polarized light is used to test the strength of sugar solutions, to measure stresses in transparent materials, and to prevent glare.

Ordinary light may be plane-polarized by reflection from a polished surface or by passing it through a Nicol prism or a synthetic polarizing film such as Polaroid.

Polaroid camera instant-picture camera, invented by Edwin Land in the US 1947. The original camera produced black-and-white prints in about one minute. Modern cameras can produce black-and-white prints in a few seconds, and color prints in less than a minute. An advanced model has automatic focusing and exposure. It ejects a piece of film on paper immediately after the picture has been taken. The film consists of layers of emulsion and color dyes together with a pod of chemical developer. When the film is ejected the pod bursts and processing occurs in the light, producing a paper-backed print.

polar reversal changeover in polarity of the Earth's magnetic poles. Studies of the magnetism retained in rocks at the time of their formation have shown that in the past the Earth's north magnetic pole repeatedly became the south magnetic pole, and vice versa.

Polar reversal seems to be relatively frequent, taking place three or four times every million years. The last occasion was 700,000 years ago. Distinctive sequences of magnetic reversals are used in dating rock formations. Movements of the Earth's molten core are thought to be responsible for both the Earth's magnetic field and its reversal.

Pole Reginald 1500–1558. English cardinal from 1536, who returned from Rome as papal legate on the accession of Mary I in order to readmit England to the Catholic church. He succeeded Cranmer as archbishop of Canterbury 1556.

polecat Old World weasel *Mustela putorius* with a brown back and dark belly and two yellow face patches. The body is about 20 in/50 cm long and it has a strong smell from anal gland secretions. It is native to Asia, Europe, and N Africa. In North America, ◊skunks are sometimes called polecats. A ferret is a domesticated polecat.

poles geographic north and south points of the axis about which the Earth rotates. The magnetic poles are the points toward which a freely suspended magnetic needle will point; however, they vary continually.

In 1985 the magnetic north pole was some 218 mi/350 km NW of Resolute Bay, Northwest Territories, Canada. It moves northward about 6 mi/10 km each year, although it can vary in a day about 50 mi/80 km from its average position. It is relocated every decade in order to update navigational charts. It is thought that periodic changes in the Earth's core cause a reversal of the magnetic poles (see ◊polar reversal). Many animals, including migrating birds and fish, are believed to orientate themselves partly using the Earth's magnetic field. A permanent scientific base collects data at the South Pole.

Pole Star ◊Polaris, the northern pole star. There is no bright star near the southern celestial pole.

police civil law-and-order force. In the US, law enforcement is the responsibility of municipal and state government except for violations of specific federal laws or cases in which state borders have been crossed. Unlike many countries, there is no national police force. The ◊Federal Bureau of Investigation assists state and local law-enforcement authorities.

The exercise of police power in the US is restricted and controlled in order to protect civil rights. Recent US Supreme Court decisions have relaxed some guidelines for searches.

poliomyelitis or ***polio*** an acute viral infection of the central nervous system affecting nerves that activate muscles. The disease used to be known as infantile paralysis. The polio virus is a common one, and mostly, its effects are confined to the throat and intestine, as in flu or a mild digestive upset. There may also be muscle stiffness in the neck and back. Paralysis is seen in about 1% of cases, and the disease is life-threatening only if the muscles of the throat and chest are affected. Cases of this kind, one entombed in an "iron lung," are today maintained on a respirator. Two kinds of vaccine are available, one injected (see ◊Salk) and one given by mouth.

Polish Corridor strip of land designated under the Treaty of ◊Versailles 1919 to give Poland access to the Baltic. It cut off East Prussia from the rest of Germany. When Poland took over the southern part of East Prussia 1945, it was absorbed.

Polish language member of the Slavonic branch of the Indo-European language family, spoken mainly in Poland. Polish is written in the Roman and not the Cyrillic alphabet and its standard form is based on the dialect of Poznań in W Poland.

Politburo contraction of "political bureau," a subcommittee (known as the Praesidium 1952–66) of the Central Committee of the Communist Party in the USSR and some other communist states, which lays down party policy. It consists of about 12 voting and 6 candidate (nonvoting) members.

Politian (Angelo Poliziano) pen name of Angelo Ambrogini 1454–1494. Italian poet, playwright, and exponent of humanist ideals. He was tutor to Lorenzo de ◊Medici's children, and professor at the University of Florence; he wrote commentaries and essays on Classical authors.

political action committee (PAC) in the US, any organization that raises funds for political candidates and in return seeks to commit them to a particular policy. It also spends money on changing public opinion. There were about 3,500 PACs in 1990, and they controlled some 25% of all funds spent in elections for ◊Congress.

Polk James Knox 1795–1849. the 11th president of the US 1845–49, a Democrat, born in North Carolina. He allowed Texas admission to the Union, and forced the war on Mexico that resulted in the annexation of California and New Mexico.

Polk was an associate of Andrew ◊Jackson, who influenced his strongly expansionist policies. A believer in ◊Manifest Destiny, Polk pursued war with Mexico but avoided armed conflict with Britain over the Oregon-Canada boundary.

polka folk dance in lively two-four time. The basic step is a hop followed by three short steps. It originated in Bohemia.

pollack marine fish *Pollachius virens* of the cod family, growing to 2.5 ft/75 cm, and found close to the shore on both sides of the N Atlantic.

Pollaiuolo Antonio c. 1432–1498 and Piero c. 1441–1496. Italian artists, active in Florence.

Polk *The 11th president of the United States of America, James K. Polk, a Democrat. 1845–1849.*

Both brothers were painters, sculptors, goldsmiths, engravers, and designers. Antonio is said to have been the first Renaissance artist to make a serious study of anatomy. The *Martyrdom of St Sebastian* 1475 (National Gallery, London) is considered a joint work.

The brothers also executed two papal monuments in St Peter's basilica, Rome. The major individual works are Piero's set of *Virtues* in Florence and Antonio's engraving *The Battle of the Nude Gods* about 1465. Antonio's work places a strong emphasis on the musculature of the human figure in various activities.

pollarding type of pruning whereby the young branches of a tree are severely cut back, about 6–12 ft/2–4 m above the ground, to produce a stumplike trunk with a rounded, bushy head of thin new branches. It is often practiced on willows, where the new branches or "poles" are cut at intervals of a year or more, and used for fencing and firewood. Pollarding is also used to restrict the height of many street trees. See also ◊coppicing.

pollen the grains of ◊seed plants that contain the male gametes. In ◊angiosperms pollen is produced within ◊anthers; in most ◊gymnosperms it is produced in male ◊cones. A pollen grain is typically yellow and, when mature, has a hard outer wall. Pollen of insect-pollinated plants (see ◊pollination) is often sticky and spiny and larger than the smooth, light grains produced by wind-pollinated species.

The outer wall of pollen grains from both insect-pollinated and wind-pollinated plants is often elaborately sculptured with ridges or spines so distinctive that individual species or genera of plants can be recognized from their pollen. Since pollen is extremely resistant to decay, useful information

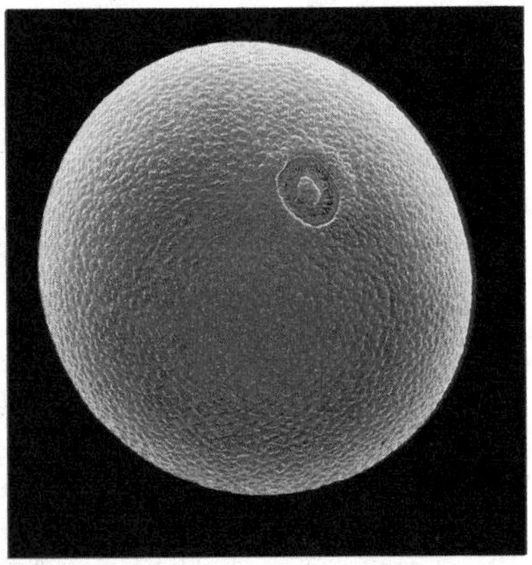

pollen *Electron-microscope picture of a pollen grain from cocksfoot grass, which is wind-pollinated.*

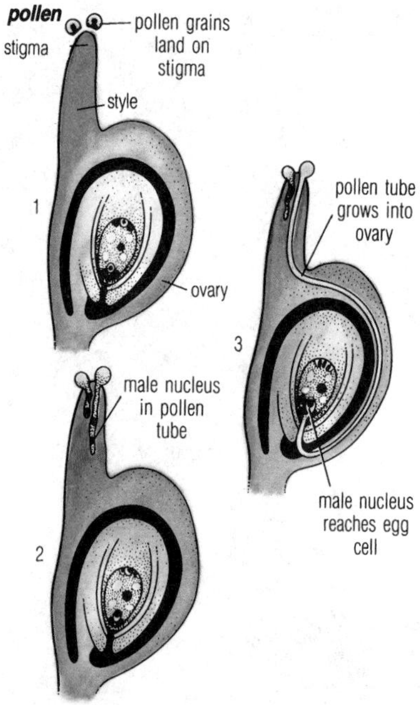
pollen
pollen grains land on stigma
stigma
style
1
ovary
pollen tube grows into ovary
3
male nucleus in pollen tube
2
male nucleus reaches egg cell

on the vegetation of earlier times can be gained from the study of fossil pollen. The study of pollen grains is known as palynology.

pollen tube an outgrowth from a pollen grain that grows toward the ◊ovule, following germination of the grain on the ◊stigma. In ◊angiosperms (flowering plants) the pollen tube reaches the ovule by growing down through the ◊style, carrying the male gametes inside. The gametes are discharged into the ovule and one fertilizes the egg cell.

pollination the process by which fertilization occurs in the sexual reproduction of higher plants. The male ◊gametes are contained in ◊pollen grains, which must be transferred from the ◊anther to the ◊stigma in ◊angiosperms, and from the male cone to the female cone in ◊gymnosperms. Self-pollination occurs when pollen is transferred to a stigma of the same flower, or to another flower on the same plant; cross-pollination occurs when pollen is transferred to another plant. This involves external pollen-carrying agents, such as wind (see ◊anemophily), water, insects, birds (see ◊ornithophily), bats, and other small mammals.

Animal pollinators carry the pollen on their bodies and are attracted to the flower by scent, or by the sight of the petals. Most flowers are adapted for pollination by one particular agent only. Those that rely on animals generally produce nectar, a sugary liquid, or surplus pollen, or both, on which the pollinator feeds. Thus the relationship between pollinator and plant is an example of mutualism, in which both benefit. However, in some plants, the pollinator receives no benefit (as in ◊pseudocopulation), while in others, nectar may be removed by animals that do not effect pollination.

Pollination of flowering plants also leads to the formation of the ◊endosperm, for which a second male gamete is needed; the pollination is therefore sometimes known as double fertilization.

pollinium a group of pollen grains that is transported as a single unit during pollination. Pollinia are common in orchids.

Pollock Jackson 1912–1956. US painter, a pioneer of Abstract Expressionism and the foremost exponent of the technique ◊action painting, a style he developed around 1946.

In the early 1940s Pollock moved from a vivid Expressionist style, influenced by Mexican muralists such as Siqueiros and by Surrealism, toward a semiabstract style. The paintings of this period are colorful and vigorous, using jumbled signs or symbols like enigmatic graffiti. He moved on to a more violently expressive abstract style, placing large canvases on the studio floor and dripping or hurling his paint on them. He continued to develop his style, producing even larger canvases in the 1950s.

Pollock v Farmer's Loan and Trust Co a US Supreme Court decision 1895 dealing with the right of Congress to levy a federal income tax. The Gorman Tariff Act 1894 imposed a 2% tax on all annual incomes over $4,000. The ensuing protests, including the test case, focused on three aspects of the tax: (1) it taxed income on state and municipal bonds, an infringement on states' rights; (2) it taxed income on land and private property, making it a direct tax not apportioned among the states according to population; and (3) it exempted certain people on the basis of personal income. The Court found 5–4 that these constitutional violations made the tax impermissible. This decision was rendered irrelevant in 1913 by the 16th Amendment, which empowered Congress to enact income taxes.

poll tax tax levied on every individual, without reference to his or her income or property. Being simple to administer, it was among the earliest sorts of tax (introduced in England 1377), but because of its indiscriminate nature (it is a regressive tax, in that it falls proportionately more heavily on poorer people) it has often proved unpopular.

In the US, the tax was widely used as a means of disenfranchising poor blacks in S states. It was made unconstitutional under the 24th Amendment 1964 for federal elections and 1966 for state races.

pollution the harmful effect on the environment of byproducts of human activity, principally industrial and agricultural processes—for example noise, smoke, auto emissions, chemical and ◊radioactive effluents in the air, seas and rivers, pesticides, radiation, sewage (see ◊sewage disposal), and household waste. Pollution contributes to the ◊greenhouse effect.

Pollution control involves higher production costs for the industries concerned, but failure to implement adequate controls may result in irreversible environmental damage and an increase in the incidence of diseases such as cancer. See also ◊nuclear safety.

Natural disasters may also cause pollution; volcanic eruptions, for example, cause ash to be ejected into the atmosphere and deposited on land surfaces.

Pollux in Greek mythology, the twin brother of ◊Castor.

Pollux brightest star in the constellation Gemini and the 17th brightest star in the sky. Pollux is a yellowish star with a true luminosity 35 times that of the Sun. It is 35 light-years away.

polo game played between two teams of four on horseback. It originated in Iran, spread to India and was first played in England 1869.

A typical game lasts about an hour, divided into 7.5 minute periods known as chukkers. A small ball is struck with the side of a mallet through goals at each end of the field.

Polo Marco 1254–1324. Venetian traveler and writer. He traveled overland to China 1271–75, and served the emperor Kublai Khan until he returned to Europe by sea 1292–95. He was captured while fighting for Venice against Genoa, and, while in prison 1296–98, dictated an account of his travels.

After his father (Niccolo) and uncle (Maffeo) returned from a trading journey to China 1260–69, Marco himself began his trip overland to China. Once there, he learned Mongolian and served the emperor Kublai Khan, returning nearly twenty years later by sea to his native country. His accounts of his travels remained the primary source of information about the Far East until the 19th century.

polonaise a Polish dance in stately three-four time, that was common in 18th century Europe. Chopin developed the polonaise as a pianistic form.

polonium radioactive, metallic element, symbol Po, atomic number 84, atomic weight 210. Polonium occurs in nature in small amounts and was isolated from ◊pitchblende. It is the element having the largest number of isotopes (27) and is 5,000 times as radioactive as radium, liberating considerable amounts of heat. It was the first element to have its radioactive properties recognized and investigated.

It was isolated in 1898 from the pitchblende residues analyzed by Pierre and Marie ◊Curie, and named for Marie Curie's native Poland.

Pol Pot (also known as Saloth Sar, Tol Saut, and Pol Porth) 1925– . Cambodian politician and Communist party leader; a member of the anti-French resistance under Ho Chi Minh in the 1940s. As leader of the Khmer Rouge, he overthrew the government 1975 and proclaimed Democratic Kampuchea with himself as premier. His policies were to evacuate cities and put people to work in the countryside. The Khmer Rouge also carried out a systematic large-scale extermination of the Western-influenced educated and middle classes (3–4 million) before the regime was overthrown by a Vietnamese invasion 1979. Pol Pot continued to help lead the Khmer Rouge until their withdrawal in 1989; in that year too he resigned from his last position within the Khmer Rouge, but he remained influential even though

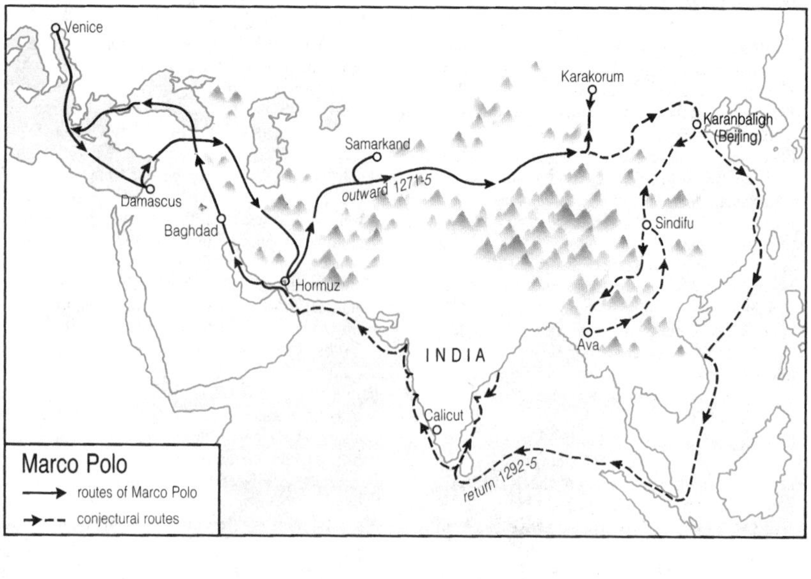
Venice
Karakorum
Karanbaligh (Beijing)
Samarkand
outward 1271–5
Damascus
Baghdad
Sindifu
Hormuz
INDIA
Ava
Calicut
return 1292–5
Marco Polo
routes of Marco Polo
conjectural routes

his role was undefined after the Cambodian peace agreement of Nov 1991.

Poltava industrial city (machinery, foodstuffs, clothing) in Ukraine, USSR, capital of Poltava region, on the river Vorskla; population (1987) 309,000. Peter the Great defeated ◊Charles XII of Sweden here 1709.

poltergeist (German "noisy ghost") unexplained phenomenon that invisibly moves objects or hurls them about, starts fires, or causes other mischief.

polyandry system whereby a woman is expected to have more than one husband at the same time. It is found in Tibet and certain parts of India, where polyandry takes the form of the marriage of one woman to several brothers, as a means of keeping intact a family's heritage and property. Although it is found in other areas, in practice, it is neither expected nor normative behavior (see ◊norm).

polyanthus cultivated variety of ◊primrose, with multiple flowers on one stalk, bred in a variety of colors.

Polybius c. 201–120 BC. Greek politician and historian. He was involved with the ◊Achaean League against the Romans and, following the defeat of the Macedonians at Pydna in 168 BC, he was taken as a political hostage to Rome. He returned to Greece in 151 and was present at the capture of Carthage by his friend Scipio in 146. His history of Rome in 40 books, covering the years 220–146, has largely disappeared.

Polycarp, St c. 69–c. 155. Christian martyr allegedly converted by St John the Evangelist. As bishop of Smyrna (modern Izmir, Turkey), on a vigorous struggle against various heresies for over 40 years. He was burned alive at a public festival; feast day Jan 26.

polychlorinated biphenyl (PCB) any of a group of chlorinated isomers of biphenal $(C_6H_5)_2$. They are dangerous industrial chemicals, valuable for their fire-resisting qualities. They constitute an environmental hazard because of their persistent toxicity. Since 1973 their use has been limited by international agreement.

polyester synthetic resin formed by the ◊condensation of polyhydric alcohols (alcohols containing more than one hydroxyl group) with dibasic acids (acids containing two replaceable hydrogen atoms). Polyesters are thermosetting ◊plastics, used in making synthetic fibers, such as Dacron, and constructional plastics. With fiberglass added as reinforcement, polyesters are used in car bodies and boat hulls.

polyethylene polymer of the gas ethylene (technically called ethene, C_2H_4). It is a tough, white translucent waxy thermoplastic (which means it can be repeatedly softened by heating). It is used for packaging, bottles, toys, electric cable, pipes and tubing.

Polyethylene is produced in two forms: low-density polyethylene, made by high-pressure polymerization of ethylene gas, and high-density polyethylene, which is made at lower pressure by using catalysts. This form, first made by German chemist Karl Ziegler, is more rigid at low temperatures and softer at higher temperatures than the low-density type.

polygamy the practice of having more than one spouse at the same time. It is found among many peoples and was common in most of the world. Normally it has been confined to the wealthy and to chiefs and nobles who can support several women and their offspring. Islam limits the number of legal wives a man may have to four. Certain Christian sects (for example, the Anabaptists of Munster, Germany, and the Mormons) have practiced polygamy, because it was the norm in the Old Testament. When the norm is for one husband and several wives, it is called polygyny; for one wife and several husbands, ◊polyandry. The most common expectation (although not necessarily the reality) was for polygyny. Polyandry was a very rare form of marriage, expected only where maintaining spare property or family heritage was important to the survival of the culture.

polygon

	number of sides	sum of interior angles (degrees)
triangle	3	180
quadrilateral	4	360
pentagon	5	540
hexagon	6	720
heptagon	7	900
octagon	8	1,080
decagon	10	1,440
duodecagon	12	1,800
icosagon	20	3,240

polygon in geometry, a plane (two-dimensional) figure with three or more straight-line sides. Common polygons have their own names, which define the number of sides (for example, triangle, quadrilateral, pentagon).

These are all convex polygons, having no interior angle greater than 180°. In general, the more sides a polygon has, the larger the sum of its internal angles and, in the case of a convex polygon, the more closely it approximates to a circle.

polygraph or ***lie detector*** an instrument that records graphically certain body activities, such as thoracic and abdominal respiration, blood pressure, pulse rate, and galvanic skin response (changes in electrical resistance of the skin). Marked changes in these activities when a person answers a question may indicate that the person is lying.

polyhedron in geometry, a solid figure with four or more plane faces. The more faces there are on a polyhedron, the more closely it approximates to a sphere. Knowledge of the properties of polyhedra is needed in crystallography and stereochemistry to determine the shapes of crystals and molecules.

There are only five types of regular polyhedra (with all faces the same size and shape), as was deduced by early Greek mathematicians; they are the tetrahedron (four equilateral triangular faces), cube (six square faces), octahedron (eight equilateral triangles), dodecahedron (12 regular pentagons) and icosahedron (20 equilateral triangles).

Polyhymnia in Greek mythology, the ◊Muse of singing, mime, and sacred dance.

Polykleitos 5th century BC. Greek sculptor whose *Spear Carrier* 450–440 BC (Roman copies survive) exemplifies the naturalism and harmonious proportions of his work. He created the legendary colossal statue of *Hera* in Argos, in ivory and gold.

polymer a compound made up of large, long-chain molecules composed of many repeated simple units (monomers). There are many polymers, both natural (cellulose, chitin, lignin) and synthetic (polyethylene and nylon, types of plastic). Synthetic polymers belong to two groups: thermosoftening and thermosetting (see ◊plastic).

polymerization the chemical union of two or more (usually small) molecules of the same kind to form a new compound.

Addition polymerization produces simple multiples of the same compound. Condensation polymerization joins molecules together with the elimination of water or another small molecule. Addition polymerization uses only a single monomer (basic molecule); condensation polymerization may involve two or more different monomers (copolymerization).

polymorphism in genetics, the coexistence of several distinctly different types in a ◊population. Examples include the different blood groups in humans and different color forms in some butterflies.

polymorphism in minerology, the ability of a substance to adopt different internal structures and external forms, in response to different conditions of temperature and/or pressure. For example, diamond and graphite are both forms of the element carbon, but they have very different properties and appearance.

Silica (SiO_2) also has several polymorphs, including quartz, tridymite, cristobalite, and stisthovite (the latter a very high pressure form found in meteoritic impact craters).

Polynesia

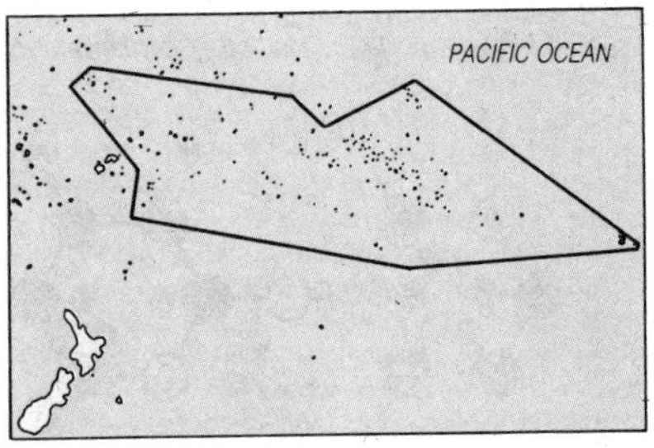
PACIFIC OCEAN

Polynesia islands of Oceania E of 170° E latitude, including Hawaii, Kiribati, Tuvalu, Fiji, Tonga, Tokelau, Samoa, Cook Islands, and French Polynesia.

Polynesian a member of any of the seafaring peoples of Polynesia. They migrated by canoe from S Asia in about 2000 BC, peopling the islands of the S Pacific for about 2,000 years, and settling Hawaii last, from Tahiti. The Polynesian languages belong to the Oceanic branch of the Austronesian family.

Polynesian languages see ◊Malayo-Polynesian languages.

Polynices in Greek mythology, son of ◊Oedipus and ◊Jocasta, and brother of ◊Eteocles. Denied his share in the kingship of Thebes by his brother, he induced his father-in-law, Adrastus of Argos, to lead the expedition of the ◊Seven against Thebes in which he and his brother died by each other's hands.

polynomial in mathematics, algebraic expression that has only one ◊variable (denoted by a letter). A polynomial of degree one, that is, whose highest ◊power of x is 1, as in $2x + 1$, is called a linear polynomial; $3x^2 + 2x + 1$ is quadratic; $4x^3 + 3x^2 + 2x + 1$ is cubic.

polyp or ***polypus*** small "stalked" benign tumor, most usually found on mucous membrane of the nose or bowels. Intestinal polyps are usually removed, since some have been found to be precursors of cancer.

polypeptide a long-chain ◊peptide.

Polyphemus in Greek mythology, a ◊Cyclops who imprisons ◊Odysseus and his companions in his cave on their homeward journey, and is finally blinded by them before they escape. His story forms the subject of Book Eleven of ◊Homer's *Odyssey*.

polyphony music combining two or more "voices" or parts, each with an individual melody.

polyploid in genetics, possessing three or more sets of chromosomes in cases where the normal complement is two sets (◊diploid). Polyploidy arises spontaneously and is common in plants (mainly among angiosperms), but rare in animals. Many crop plants are natural polyploids, including wheat, which has four sets of chromosomes per cell (durum wheat) or six sets (common wheat). Plant breeders can induce the formation of polyploids by treatment with a chemical, colchicine.

Matings between polyploid individuals and normal diploid ones are invariably sterile. Hence, an individual that develops polyploidy through a genetic aberration can initially only reproduce vegetatively, by parthenogenesis, or by self-fertilization (modes of reproduction that are common only among plants). Once a polyploid population is established, however, they can reproduce sexually.

polysaccharide

glucose molecules linked to form polysaccharide glycogen (animal starch)

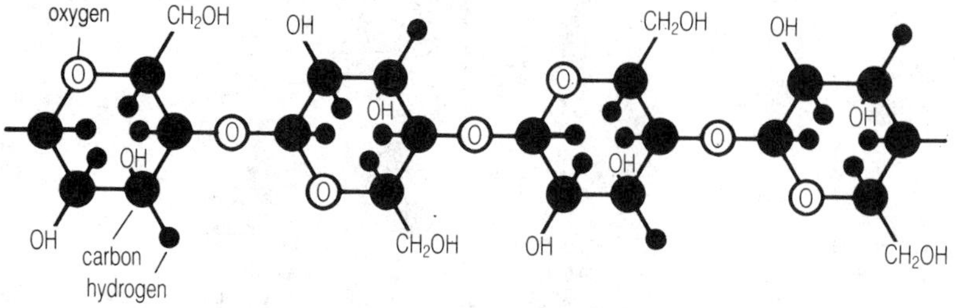
oxygen
CH_2OH
OH
O
OH
carbon
hydrogen
CH_2OH

polysaccharide a long-chain ◊carbohydrate made up of hundreds or thousands of linked simple sugars (monosaccharides) such as glucose and closely related molecules.

The polysaccharides are natural polymers. They either act as energy-rich food stores in plants (starch) and animals (glycogen), or have structural roles in the plant cell wall (cellulose, pectin) or the tough outer skeleton of insects and similar creatures (chitin). See also ◊carbohydrate.

polystyrene a type of ◊plastic.

polytheism the worship of many gods, as opposed to monotheism (belief in one god). Examples are the religions of ancient Egypt, Babylon, Greece, Rome, Mexico, and modern Hinduism.

polytonality in music, the simultaneous use of more than one ◊key. A combination of two keys is bitonality.

polyunsaturate a type of triglyceride (◊fat or oil) in which the long carbon chains of the ◊fatty acids contain several double bonds. By contrast, the carbon chains of saturated fats (such as lard) contain only single bonds.

The more double bonds the chains contain, the lower the melting point of the triglyceride. Unsaturated chains with several double bonds produce oils, such as vegetable and fish oils, which are liquids at room temperature. Saturated fats, with no double bonds, are solids at room temperature. The polyunsaturated fats used for margarines are produced by taking a vegetable or fish oil and turning some of the double bonds to single bonds, so that the product is semisolid at room temperature. This is done by bubbling hydrogen through the oil in the presence of a catalyst, such as platinum. The catalyst is later removed. Medical evidence suggests that polyunsaturated fats are less likely to contribute to cardiovascular disease than saturated fats, but there is also some evidence that they may have adverse effects on health. Monounsaturated oils, such as olive oil, with a single double bond, are probably healthier than either saturated or polyunsaturated fats. Butter contains both saturated and unsaturated fats, together with ◊cholesterol, which also plays a role in heart disease.

polyurethane polymer made from the monomer urethane; see ◊plastic.

polyvinyl chloride (PVC) a type of ◊plastic.

pome a type of ◊pseudocarp, or false fruit, typical of certain plants belonging to the Rosaceae family. The outer skin and fleshy tissues are developed from the ◊receptacle after fertilization, and the five ◊carpels (the true fruit) form the pome's core, which surrounds the seeds. Examples of pomes are apples, pears, and quinces.

pomegranate deciduous shrub or small tree *Punica granatum*, family Punicaceae, native to SW Asia but cultivated widely in tropical and subtropical areas. The round, leathery, reddish-yellow fruit contains numerous seeds that can be eaten fresh or made into wine.

Pomerania (Polish *Pomorze*, German *Pommern*) region along the S shore of the Baltic Sea, including the island of Rügen, forming part of Poland and (W of the Oder-Neisse line) East Germany 1945–1990, and the Federal Republic of Germany after unification in 1990. The chief port is Gdańsk. It was formerly a province of Germany.

pomeranian small breed of dog, about 6 in/15 cm, and 6.5 lb/3 kg. It has long straight hair with a neck frill, and the tail is carried over the back.

Pommern German form of ◊Pomerania, former province of Germany, now largely in Poland.

Pomona in Roman mythology, goddess of fruit trees.

Pomorze Polish form of ◊Pomerania, region of N Europe, now largely in Poland.

Pompadour Jeanne Antoinette Poisson, Marquise de 1721–1764. Mistress of ◊Louis XV of France from 1744, born in Paris. She largely dictated the government's ill-fated policy of reversing France's anti-Austrian policy for an anti-Prussian one. She acted as the patron of the Enlightenment philosophers Voltaire and Diderot.

Pompano Beach city in SE Florida, N of Fort Lauderdale, on the Atlantic Ocean. Tourism and fruit processing are important to the economy; population (1990) 72,411.

Pompeii ancient city in Italy, near ◊Vesuvius, 13 mi/21 km SE of Naples. In AD 63 an earthquake destroyed much of the city, which had been a Roman port and pleasure resort; it was completely buried beneath volcanic ash when Vesuvius erupted AD 79. Over 2,000 people were killed. Pompeii was rediscovered 1748 and the systematic excavation begun 1763 still continues.

Pompey the Great (Gnaeus Pompeius Magnus) 106–48 BC. Roman soldier and politician. Originally a supporter of ◊Sulla and the aristocratic party, he joined the democrats when he became consul with ◊Crassus 70 BC. He defeated ◊Mithridates VI of Pontus, and annexed Syria and Palestine. In 60 BC he formed the First Triumvirate with Julius ◊Caesar (whose daughter Julia he married) and Crassus, and when it broke down after 53 BC he returned to the aristocratic party. On the outbreak of civil war 49 BC he withdrew to Greece, was defeated by Caesar at Pharsalus 48 BC, and was murdered in Egypt.

Pompidou Georges 1911–1974. French conservative politician, president 1969–74. An adviser on General de Gaulle's staff 1944–46, he held administrative posts until he became director-general of the French House of Rothschild 1954, and even then continued in close association with de Gaulle, helping to draft the constitution of the Fifth Republic 1958–59. He negotiated a settlement with the Algerians 1961 and, as prime minister 1962–68, with the students in the revolt of May 1968, and was elected to the presidency on de Gaulle's resignation.

Ponce a major city and industrial port (iron, textiles, sugar, rum) in S Puerto Rico, population (1980) 161,739. The Catholic University of Puerto Rico is here. The settlement, established in the late 17th century, was named for the Spanish explorer Juan Ponce de León.

Ponce de León Juan 1460–1521. Spanish explorer who discovered Florida. He sailed on Columbus's second voyage to the Americas 1493 and settled in the colony on Hispaniola, later conquering Puerto Rico 1508–09 and becoming its governor. In 1513, while searching for the legendary "fountain of youth," he discovered Florida, exploring much of its E coast and part of the W coast. Ponce de León returned to Florida in 1521 and was wounded in a battle with Indians. He died soon after in Cuba.

Poncelet Jean 1788–1867. French mathematician, who worked on projective geometry. His book, started in 1814 and completed 1822, deals with the properties of plane figures unchanged when projected.

Pondicherry Union Territory of SE India; area 185 sq mi/480 sq km; population (1981) 604,000. Its capital is Pondicherry, and products include rice, peanuts, cotton, and sugar. Pondicherry was founded by France 1674 and changed hands several times among French, Dutch, and British before being returned to France 1814 at the close of the Napoleonic wars. Together with Karaikal, Yanam, and Mahé (on the Malabar Coast) it formed a French colony until 1954 when all were transferred to the government of India; since 1962 they have formed the Union Territory of Pondicherry. Languages spoken include French, English, Tamil, Telegu, and Malayalam.

pondweed any aquatic plant of the genus *Potamogeton* that either floats on the water or is sub-

Pompeii *The streets of the Roman resort of Pompeii were filled with volcanic ash, stones, and poisonous gases when nearby Vesuvius erupted* AD *79. The town was lost under the ash for nearly 1,700 years.*

merged. The leaves of floating pondweeds are broad and leathery, whereas leaves of the submerged forms are narrower and translucent; the flowers grow in green spikes.

Ponta Delgada port, resort, and chief commercial center of the Portuguese ◊Azores, on São Miguel; population (1981) 22,200.

Pontiac a motor-manufacturing city in Michigan, 24 mi/38 km NW of Detroit; population (1990) 71,166.

Pontiac c. 1720–1769. North American Indian, chief of the Ottawa from 1755. Allied with the French during the ◊French and Indian War, Pontiac was hunted by the British after the French withdrawal. He led the "Conspiracy of Pontiac" 1763–64 in an attempt to resist British persecution. He achieved remarkable success against overwhelming odds but eventually signed a peace treaty 1766.

Born near Detroit, Pontiac was murdered by a Peoria Indian in Illinois at the instigation of a British trader.

Pontine Marshes formerly malarial marshes in the Lazio region of Italy, near the coast 25 mi/40 km SE of Rome. They defied the attempts of the Romans to drain them, and it was not until 1926, under Mussolini's administration, that they were brought into cultivation. Products include cereals, fruit and vines, and sugar beet.

Pontormo Jacopo Carucci 1494–1557. Italian painter, active in Florence. He developed a dramatic Mannerist style, with lurid colors.

Pontormo worked in ◊Andrea del Sarto's workshop from 1512. An early work, *Joseph in Egypt* about 1515 (National Gallery, London), is already Mannerist. His mature style is demonstrated in *The Deposition* about 1525 (Sta Felicità, Florence), an extraordinary composition of interlocked figures, with rosy pinks, lime yellows, and pale apple greens illuminating the scene. The same distinctive colors occur in the series of frescoes 1522–25 for the Certosa monastery outside Florence.

Pontus kingdom of NE Asia Minor on the Black Sea from about 300 to 65 BC when its greatest ruler, ◊Mithridates VI, was defeated by ◊Pompey.

pony small horse under 4.5 ft/1.47 m (14.2 hands shoulder height).

Although of Celtic origin, all the pony breeds have been crossed with thoroughbred and Arab stock, except for the smallest—the hardy Shetland—less than 42 in/105 cm.

Pony Express, the a system of mail-carrying by relays of horse-riders that operated in the years 1860–61 between St Joseph, Missouri, and Sacremento, California, a distance of about 1,800 mi.

The Pony Express was a private venture by a company called Russell, Majors and Waddell. 157 stations were set up along the route and the riders, who included William Cody (Buffalo Bill), needed several changes of horses between each station.

poodle breed of dog, including standard (above 15 in/38 cm at shoulder), miniature (below 15 in/38 cm), and toy (below 11 in/28 cm) varieties. The long, curly coat, usually cut into an elaborate style, is usually either black or white, although grays and browns are also bred. The poodle probably originated in Russia, was naturalized in Germany, where it was used for retrieving ducks, and gained its name (from the German *pudeln*, "to splash"), and became a luxury dog in France.

pool or ***pocket billiards*** game derived from ◊billiards and played in many different forms. Originally popular in the US, it is now also played in Europe.

It is played with balls of different colors, each of which is numbered. The neutral ball (black) is the number eight ball. The most popular form of pool is eight-ball pool in which players have to sink all their own balls before the opponent, and then must sink the eight-ball to win the game. Other forms include sinking balls in numerical order (rotation), or sinking a designated ball into a designated pocket (straight pool).

Poole industrial town (chemicals, engineering, boat building, confectionery, pottery from local clay) and yachting center on Poole Harbor, Dorset, S England, 5 mi/8 km W of Bournemouth; population (1984) 123,000.

Pool Malebo lake on the border between the Congo Republic and Zaïre, formed by a widening of the Zaïre river, 350 mi/560 km from its mouth.

Poona former English spelling of ◊Pune, city in India; after independence in 1947 the form Poona was gradually superseded by Pune.

Pop Iggy. Adopted name of James Jewel Osterberg 1947– . US rock singer and songwriter, initially known as Iggy Stooge, lead singer with a seminal garage band called the Stooges (1967–74), famed for his self-destructive proto-punk performances. Later on in Pop's solo career his friend, David Bowie, contributed to *The Idiot* 1977, *Lust for Life* 1977, and *Blah, Blah, Blah* 1986.

Pop art movement of young artists in the mid-1950s and 1960s, reacting against the elitism of abstract art. Pop art used popular imagery drawn from advertising, comic strips, film, and television. It originated in Britain 1956 with Richard Hamilton, Peter Blake (1932–), and others, and broke through in the US with the paintings of flags and numbers by Jasper Johns 1958 and Andy Warhol's first series of soup cans 1962.

Pop art was so named by the British critic Lawrence Alloway (1926–). Richard Hamilton described it in 1957 as "popular, transient, expendable, low-cost, mass-produced, young, witty, sexy, gimmicky, glamorous, and big business." The artists often used repeating images and quoted from others' work. Among them were Roy Lichtenstein and Claes Oldenburg.

pope the bishop of Rome, head of the Roman Catholic Church, which claims he is the spiritual descendant of St Peter. Elected by the Sacred College of Cardinals, a pope dates his pontificate from his coronation with the tiara, or triple crown, at St Peter's Basilica, Rome. The pope had great political power in Europe from the early Middle Ages until the Reformation.

history

11th–13th centuries The papacy enjoyed its greatest temporal power under Gregory VII and Innocent III.

1309–78 The papacy came under French control (headquarters Avignon rather than Rome), "the Babylonian Captivity."

1378–1417 The "Great Schism" followed, with rival popes in Avignon and Rome.

16th century Papal political power further declined with the withdrawal of allegiance by the Protestant states at the Reformation.

1870 The Papal States in central Italy, which had been under the pope's direct rule from 756, merged with the newly united Italian state. At the Vatican Council the doctrine of papal infallibility was proclaimed.

1929 The Lateran Treaty recognized papal territorial sovereignty even in Italy only within the Vatican City.

1978 John Paul II became the first non-Italian pope since 1542.

Popé Pueblo leader. Born in the Tewa Pueblo, Popé was a leader of native resistance to Spanish political control and missionary activity in the New Mexico-Arizona area. Establishing his residence in Taos (in present-day New Mexico) in the 1670s, he began to plot a general uprising against the Spanish authorities. In August 1680 the Pueblo rose simultaneously throughout the area, forcing the Spanish to abandon Santa Fe and flee to El Paso. Pope held control of the area until his death, restoring the traditional ways of life. However, raids by Ute and Apache and severe drought led to the Spanish reconquest of the area 1692.

Pope Alexander 1688–1744. English poet and satirist. He established his reputation with the precocious *Pastorals* 1709 and *Essay on Criticism* 1711, which were followed by a parody of the heroic epic *The Rape of the Lock* 1712–14 and "Eloisa to Abelard" 1717. Other works include a highly Neo-Classical translation of Homer's *Iliad* and *Odyssey* 1715–26.

***Pope** English poet and satirist Alexander Pope, in a painting by William Hoare, c. 1739.*

Pope had a biting wit, which he expressed in the form of heroic couplets. As a Catholic, he was subject to discrimination, and he was embittered by a deformity of the spine. His edition of Shakespeare attracted scholarly ridicule, for which he revenged himself by a satire on scholarly dullness, the *Dunciad* 1728. His philosophy, including *An Essay on Man* 1733–34 and *Moral Essays* 1731–35, was influenced by ◊Bolingbroke. His finest mature productions are his *Imitations of the Satires of Horace* 1733–38 and his personal letters. Among his friends were the writers Swift, Arbuthnot, and Gay. His line "A little learning is a dangerous thing" is often misquoted.

poplar deciduous tree of the genus *Populus*, or cottonwood trees of the willow family Salicaceae. When ripe, the feathery seeds borne on elongate clusters are blown far and wide by the wind. Balsam poplar *P. balsamifera* and eastern cottonwood *P. deltoides* are native to North America. Eurasian white poplar *P. alba* and Lombardy poplar *P. nigra* are grown widely as ornamentals. Aspens belong to the same genus.

poplin a strong fabric, originally with a warp of silk and a weft of worsted, but now usually made from cotton, in a plain weave with a finely ribbed surface.

pop music short for popular music, umbrella term for contemporary music not classifiable as jazz or Classical. Pop became distinct from folk music with the advent of sound-recording techniques, but it incorporates blues, country and western, and music hall sounds; electronic amplification and other technological innovations have played a large part in the creation of new styles. The traditional format is a song of roughly three minutes with verse, chorus, and middle eight bars.

1910s The singer Al Jolson was one of the first recording stars. Ragtime was still popular.

1920s In the US Paul Whiteman and his orchestra, the country singer Jimmie Rodgers (1897–1933), the blues; in the UK the singer Al Bowlly (1899–1941, born in Mozambique).

1930s Crooner Bing Crosby and vocal groups such as the Andrews Sisters, front swing bands.

1940s Rhythm and blues evolved in the US while Frank Sinatra was a teen idol and Glenn Miller played dance music; the UK preferred singers such as Vera Lynn.

1950s In the US doo-wop (a vocal group style based on *a cappella* street-corner singing), rockabilly , and the rise of rock and roll (Elvis Presley, Chuck Berry). British pop records were often cover versions of US originals.

1960s The Beatles and the Mersey beat transcended UK borders, followed by the Rolling Stones. Hard rock (the Who, Led Zeppelin). Art rock (Genesis, Yes). In the US surf music (group harmony vocals or fast, loud, guitar-based instrumentals), Motown, folk rock (the Byrds, Bob Dylan), blues rock (Jimi Hendrix, Janis Joplin). Psychedelic rock evolved from 1966 on both sides of the Atlantic (The Doors, Pink Floyd, Jefferson Airplane).

1970s First half of the decade produced glitter rock (David Bowie), heavy metal, and disco (dance music with a very emphatic, mechanical beat); in the UK also pub rock (a return to basics, focusing on live performance). From 1976 punk; the US term New Wave encompassed bands not entirely within the punk idiom (Talking Heads, Elvis Costello).

1980s Punk continued as hardcore or mutated into gothic; dance music developed regional US variants: hip-hop (New York), go-go (Washington, DC), and house (Chicago). Live audiences grew, leading to anthemic stadium rock (U2, Bruce Springsteen) and increasingly elaborate stage performances (Michael Jackson, Prince). An interest in worldwide roots music sparked new fusions.

These songs are usually performed live and recorded for broadcast or home play as singles, albums, or music videos. An enormous industry has grown around the pop music field, worldwide, which dominates radio and has great influences on the young and contemporary life.

Popocatépetl (Aztec "smoking mountain") volcano in central Mexico, 30 mi/50 km SE of Mexico City; 17,526 ft/5,340 m. It last erupted 1920.

Popov Alexander 1859–1905. Russian physicist who devised the first ◊aerial, in advance of ◊Marconi (although he did not use it for radio communication). He also invented a detector for radio waves.

Popper Karl (Raimund) 1902– . Austrian philosopher of science. His theory of falsificationism says that although scientific generalizations cannot be conclusively verified, they can be conclusively falsified by a counterinstance; therefore, science is not certain knowledge but a series of "conjectures and refutations," approaching, though never reaching, a definitive truth. For Popper, psychoanalysis and Marxism are unfalsifiable and therefore unscientific.

His major work on the philosophy of science is *The Logic of Scientific Discovery* 1935. Other works include *The Poverty of Historicism* 1957 (about the philosophy of social science), *Conjectures and Refutations* 1963, and *Objective Knowledge* 1972.

Born and educated in Vienna, Popper became a naturalized British subject 1945 and was professor of logic and scientific method at the London School of Economics 1949–69. He opposes Wittgenstein's view that philosophical problems are merely pseudoproblems. Popper's view of scientific practice has been criticized by T S ◊Kuhn and other writers.

poppy any plant of the genus *Papaver*, family Papaveraceae, that bears brightly colored, often dark-centered, flowers and yields a milky sap. Species include the crimson European field poppy *P. rhoeas* and the Asian ◊opium poppies. Closely related are the California poppy *Eschscholtzia californica* and the yellow-horned or sea poppy *Glaucium flavum*.

popular front political alliance of liberals, Socialists, communists, and other center and left-wing parties against fascism. This policy was proposed by the Communist International 1935 and was adopted in France and Spain, where popular-front governments were elected 1936; that in France was overthrown 1938 and in Spain 1939. In Britain a popular-front policy was advocated by Sir Stafford Cripps and others, but rejected by the

population

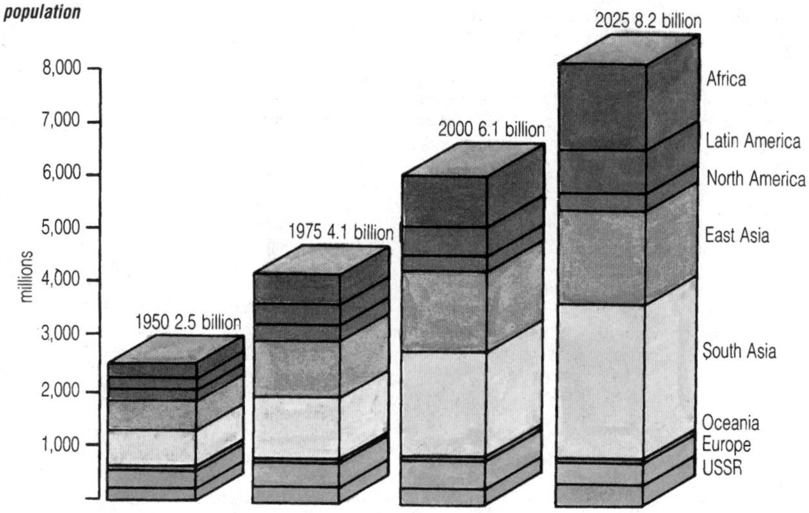
2025 8.2 billion
2000 6.1 billion
1975 4.1 billion
1950 2.5 billion
8,000
7,000
6,000
5,000
4,000
3,000
2,000
1,000
millions
Africa
Latin America
North America
East Asia
South Asia
Oceania
Europe
USSR

Labour Party. The resistance movements in the occupied countries during World War II represented a revival of the popular-front idea, and in postwar politics the term tends to recur whenever a strong right-wing party can be counterbalanced only by an alliance of those on the left.

population in biology and ecology, a group of animals of one species, living in a certain area and able to interbreed; the members of a given species in a ◊community of living things.

population cycle in biology, regular fluctuations in the size of a population, as seen in lemmings, for example. Such cycles are often caused by density-dependent mortality: high mortality due to overcrowding causes a sudden decline in the population, which then gradually builds up again. Population cycles may also result from an interaction between a predator and its prey.

population genetics the branch of genetics that studies the way in which the frequencies of different ◊alleles in populations of organisms change, as a result of natural selection and other processes.

Populism in US history, a late 19th-century political movement that developed out of farmers' protests against economic hardship. The Populist, or People's party was founded 1892 and ran several presidential candidates. It failed, however, to reverse increasing industrialization and the relative decline of agriculture in the US.

porcupine any ◊rodent with quills on its body, belonging to either of two families: (1) Old World porcupines (family Hystricidae) are terrestrial in habit and have long quills. The coloring is brown with black and white quills, or (2) New World porcupines (family Erethizontidae), tree-dwelling, with prehensile tails and much shorter quills.

porcupine fish another name for ◊globefish.

Porgy and Bess classic US folk opera 1935 by George and Ira Gershwin, based on the novel *Porgy* 1925 by DuBose Heyward, a story of the black residents of Catfish Row in Charleston, South Carolina.

Pori (Swedish *Björneborg*) ice-free industrial port (nickel and copper refining, lumber mills, paper, textiles) on the Gulf of Bothnia, SW Finland; population (1985) 79,000. A deepwater harbor was opened in 1985.

pornography obscene literature, pictures, photos, or films of no artistic merit, intended only to arouse sexual desire. See ◊obscenity law.

porphyria group of genetic disorders caused by an enzyme defect. It affects the digestive tract, causing abdominal distress; the nervous system, causing psychotic disorder, epilepsy, and weakness; the circulatory system, causing high blood pressure; and the skin, causing extreme sensitivity to light. No specific treatments exist.

In porphyria the body accumulates and excretes (rather than utilizes) one or more porphyrins, the pigments that combine with iron to form part of the oxygen-carrying proteins hemoglobin and myoglobin. It is known as the "royal disease" because sufferers included Mary Queen of Scots, James I, and (disputedly) George III.

porphyry any ◊igneous rock containing large crystals in a finer matrix.

porpoise any small whale of the faily Delphinidae that, unlike dolphins, have blunt snouts without

population

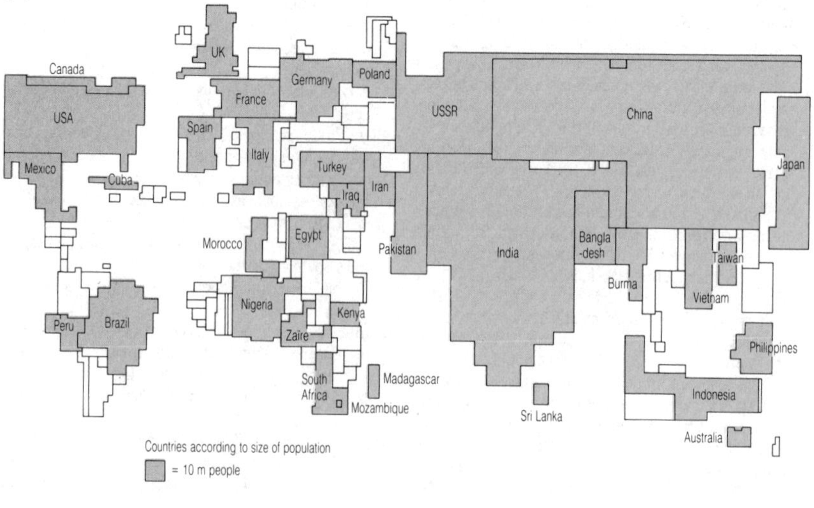
UK
Canada
Germany
Poland
France
USA
USSR
China
Spain
Italy
Turkey
Mexico
Cuba
Iraq
Iran
Japan
Morocco
Egypt
Pakistan
India
Bangla
-desh
Taiwan
Burma
Vietnam
Nigeria
Kenya
Peru
Brazil
Zaire
Philippines
South
Africa
Madagascar
Mozambique
Sri Lanka
Indonesia
Australia
Countries according to size of population
= 10 m people

porcupine

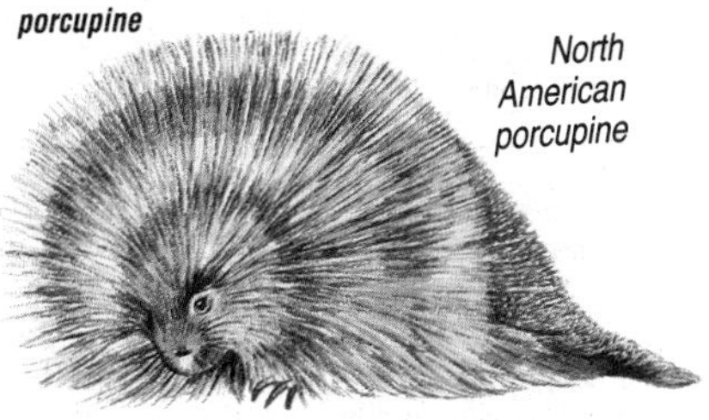
North
American
porcupine

"beaks." Common porpoises of the genus *Phocaena* can grow to 6 ft/1.8 m long, and feed on fish and crustaceans.

Porritt Jonathon 1950– . British environmental campaigner, director of ◊Friends of the Earth from 1984 to 1990. He has stood for election in both British and European elections as an Ecology (Green) Party candidate.

Porsche Ferdinand 1875–1951. German automotive engineer. The Volkswagen (German "people's car") was a product of the 1930s that became an international success (as the Beetle) in the 1950s–1970s. He also designed the original Porsche sports automobiles.

port sweet red, tawny or white dessert wine, fortified with brandy, made from grapes grown in the Douro basin of Portugal and exported from Oporto, hence the name.

Port Arthur industrial deepwater port (oil refining, shipbuilding, brass, chemicals) in Texas, 15 mi/24 km SE of Beaumont; population (1990) 58,724. Founded 1895, it gained importance with the discovery of petroleum near Beaumont in 1901.

Port Arthur former name (until 1905) of the port and naval base of Lüshun in NE China, now part of Lüdz.

Port-au-Prince capital and industrial port (sugar, rum, textiles, plastics) of Haiti; population (1982) 763,000.

Port Elizabeth industrial port (engineering, steel, food processing) in Cape province, South Africa, about 440 mi/710 km E of Cape Town on Algoa Bay; population (1980) 492,140.

Porter Cole (Albert) 1891–1964. US composer and lyricist of witty musical comedies. His shows include *The Gay Divorcee* 1932, *Anything Goes* 1934, *Kiss Me, Kate* 1948, and *Silk Stockings* 1955. He also wrote movie musicals, such as *Born to Dance* 1936 and *High Society* 1956.

Born in Indiana of an affluent family, Porter attended Yale and Harvard universities, then did military service during World War I. He became a member of the fashionable set in Europe during the 1920s and established himself with the revue *Paris* 1928. His clever, sophisticated lyrics and appealing melodies have made many of his songs standards, including "Night and Day," "I Get a Kick Out of You," "Begin the Beguine," "My Heart Belongs to Daddy," and "You're the Top."

Porter Edwin Stanton 1869–1941. US director of silent films, a pioneer of his time. His 1903 film *The Great Train Robbery* lasted 12 minutes which, for the period, was unusually long, and contained an early use of the close-up. More concerned with the technical than the artistic side of his films, which include *The Teddy Bears* 1907 and *The Final Pardon* 1912, Porter abandoned filmmaking 1916.

Porter Katherine Anne 1890–1980. US writer. She published three volumes of short stories (*Flowing Judas* 1930, *Pale Horse, Pale Rider* 1939, and *The Leaning Tower* 1944); a collection of essays, *The Days Before* 1952; and the allegorical novel *Ship of Fools* 1962 (made into a film 1965). Her *Collected Short Stories* 1965 won a Pulitzer prize.

Born in Indian Creek, Texas, Porter began her writing career after high school, working on newspapers and as a freelance, and lived in Mexico and then in Europe. Her short stories are notable for a depth and complexity usually found only in novels. Her correspondence is collected in *Letters of Katherine Anne Porter* 1990.

Porter Rodney Robert 1917–1985. British biochemist. In 1962 Porter proposed a structure for the antibody gamma globulin (IgG) in which the molecule was seen as consisiting of four chains. Porter was awarded, with Gerald ◊Edelman, the 1972 Nobel Prize for Medicine.

Porter William Sydney. Adopted name "O Henry." 1862–1910. US author. Born in Greensboro, North Carolina, Porter left home at an early age. Settling in Texas, he was convicted of embezzlement 1899 and served several years in prison. It was then that he began to write short stories under the distinctive pen name "O Henry." After his release 1902, he moved to New York City, where he contributed stories, many with surprise endings, to the *New York World*. Among the published collections of O Henry's most famous stories are *The Four Million* (including "The Gift of the Magi") 1906, *The Voice of the City* 1908, and *Rolling Stones* 1913.

Porterville city in S central California, N of Bakersfield. Industries include citrus fruits and olive oil; population (1990) 29,563.

Port Harcourt port (trading in coal, palm oil, and peanuts) and capital of Rivers state in SE Nigeria, on the river Bonny in the Niger delta; population (1983) 296,200. It is also an industrial center producing refined mineral oil, sheet aluminum, tires, and paints.

Port Kelang (Port Swettenham until 1971) Malaysian rubber port on the Strait of Malacca, 25 mi/40 km SW of Kuala Lumpur; population (1980) 192,080.

Portland industrial port (aluminum, paper, timber, lumber machinery, electronics) and capital of Multnomah County, NW Oregon; on the Columbia river, 108 mi/173 km from the sea, at its confluence with the Willamette river; population (1990) 437,319.

Portland industrial port and largest city of Maine, on Casco Bay, SE of Sebago Lake; population (1990) 64,358. The University of Southern Maine is here. Portland was first settled in 1632. The home of the poet Henry Wadsworth Longfellow, who was born here, is now a museum.

Portland William Henry Cavendish Bentinck, 3rd Duke of 1738–1809. British politician, originally a Whig, who in 1783 became nominal prime minister in the Fox–North coalition government. During the French Revolution he joined the Tories, and was prime minister 1807–09.

Port Louis capital of Mauritius, on the island's NW coast; population (1987) 139,000. Exports include sugar, textiles, watches, and electronic goods.

Port Moresby capital and port of Papua New Guinea on the S coast of New Guinea; population (1987) 152,000.

Porto (English *Oporto*) industrial city (textiles, leather, pottery) in Portugal, on the river Douro, 3 mi/5 km from its mouth; population (1984) 327,000. It exports port.

It is the second-largest city in Portugal and has a 12th-century cathedral.

Pôrto Alegre port and capital of Rio Grande do Sul state, S Brazil; population (1986) 2,705,000. It is a freshwater port for ocean-going vessels, and is Brazil's major commercial center.

Port-of-Spain port and capital of Trinidad and Tobago, on Trinidad; population (1988) 58,000.

Porto Novo capital of Benin, W Africa; population (1982) 208,258. It was a former Portuguese center for the slave and tobacco trade with Brazil and became a French protectorate 1863.

Porto Rico name until 1932 of ◊Puerto Rico, US island in the Caribbean.

Port Phillip Bay inlet off Bass Strait, Victoria, Australia, on which Melbourne stands.

Port Rashid port serving ◊Dubai in the United Arab Emirates.

Port Royal former capital of ◊Jamaica, at the entrance to Kingston harbor.

Port Said port in Egypt, on reclaimed land at the N end of the ◊Suez Canal; population (1983) 364,000. During the 1967 Arab-Israeli war the city was damaged and the canal blocked; Port Said was evacuated by 1969 but by 1975 had been largely reconstructed.

Portsmouth city and naval port in Hampshire, Eng-

Portugal

Republic of

(República Portuguesa)

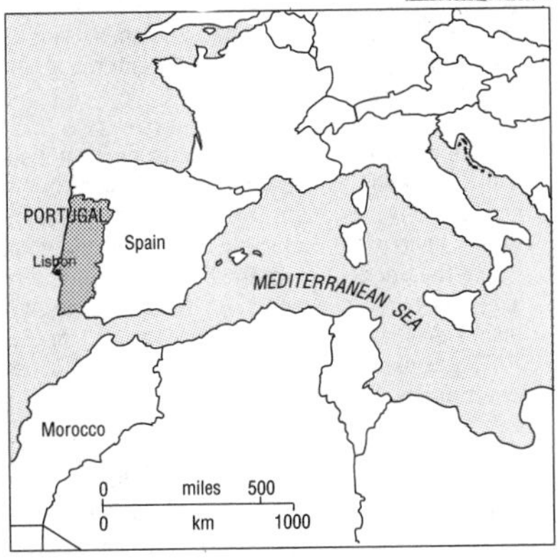
PORTUGAL
Lisbon
Spain
MEDITERRANEAN SEA
Morocco
0 miles 500
0 km 1000

area 35,521 sq mi/92,000 sq km (including Azores and Madeira)
capital Lisbon
cities Coimbra, ports Porto, Setúbal
physical mountainous in N, plains in S
features rivers Minho, Douro, Tagus, Guadiana; Serra da Estrélla mountains
head of state Mario Alberto Nobre Lopes Soares from 1986
head of government Cavaco Silva from 1985
political system democratic republic
political parties Social Democratic Party (PSD), moderate, left-of-center; Socialist Party (PS), progressive Socialist; Democratic Renewal Party (PRD), center-left; Democratic Social Center Party (CDS), moderate, left-of-center
exports wine, olive oil, resin, cork, sardines, textiles, clothing, pottery, pulpwood
currency escudo
population (1990 est) 10,528,000; growth rate 0.5% p.a.
life expectancy men 71, women 78 (1989)
language Portuguese
religion Roman Catholic 97%
literacy men 89%/women 80% (1985)
GNP $33.5 bn (1987); $2,970 per head (1986)
chronology
1928–68 Military dictatorship under Antonio de Oliveira Salazar.
1968 Salazar succeeded by Marcello Caetano.
1974 Caetano removed in military coup led by Gen Antonio Ribeiro de Spinola. Spinola replaced by Gen Francisco da Costa Gomes.
1975 African colonies became independent.
1976 New constitution, providing for return to civilian rule, adopted. Minority government appointed, led by Socialist party leader Mario Soares.
1978 Soares resigned.
1980 Francisco Balsemão formed center-party coalition after two years of political instability.
1982 Draft of new constitution approved, reducing powers of presidency.
1983 Center-left coalition government formed.
1985 Cavaco Silva became prime minister.
1986 Mario Soares elected first civilian president in 60 years. Portugal joined European Community.
1988 Portugal joined Western European Union.
1989 Constitution amended to allow state enterprises to be denationalized.
1991 Mario Soares reelected president.

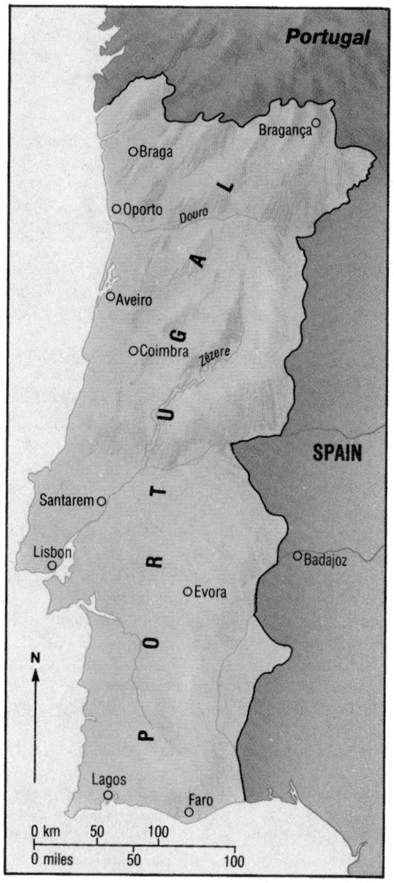
Portugal
Bragança
Braga
Oporto
Douro
PORTUGAL
Aveiro
Coimbra
Zêzere
SPAIN
Santarem
Lisbon
Badajoz
Evora
N
Lagos
Faro
0 km 50 100
0 miles 50 100

land, opposite the Isle of Wight; population (1981) 179,500.

Portsmouth port in Rockingham county, SE New Hampshire, on the estuary of the Piscataqua River; the state's only seaport; population (1990) 25,925. The nearby US Navy Yard (on Seavy's Island) dates from the 1790s and specializes in submarine construction and maintenance. Founded in 1623, Portsmouth was the state capital 1679–1775. The John Paul Jones House is here. The treaty ending the Russo-Japanese War was signed here 1905.

Portsmouth port and independent city in SE Virginia, on the Elizabeth River, seat of a US navy yard and training center; population (1990) 103,907. Manufactured goods include electronic equipment, chemicals, clothing, and processed food. Portsmouth was a British naval base during the American Revolution. During the Civil War the Confederacy briefly held the naval shipyard here and converted the scuttled steamship USS *Merrimack* into the ironclad warship *Virginia*. It engaged the Union's *Monitor* March 9, 1862, in Hampton Roads in the first naval battle between ironclad vessels.

Portugal country in SW Europe, on the Atlantic Ocean, bounded N and E by Spain.

government The 1976 constitution, revised 1982, provides for a president, elected by universal suffrage for a five-year term, and a single-chamber, 250-member assembly, similarly elected and serving a four-year term. The president, an active politician rather than a figurehead, appoints a prime minister who chooses the council of ministers, responsible to the assembly. A council of state, chaired by the president, acts as a supreme national advisory body.

history Portugal originated in the 11th century as a country subject to ◊León, while the south was ruled by the ◊Moors. It became an independent monarchy in the reign of Alfonso I (1128–85), who captured Lisbon 1147. Alfonso III (1248–79) expelled the Moors. During the 13th century the *Cortes*, an assembly representing nobles, clergy, and cities, began to meet and secured control of taxation. A commercial treaty with England was signed 1294, and an alliance established 1373. During the 15th century Portuguese mariners explored the African coast, opened the sea route to India, and reached Brazil, and colonists followed in the 16th century.

In 1580 Philip II of Spain seized the crown. The Portuguese rebelled against Spanish rule 1640, placed the house of Braganza on the throne, and after a long war forced Spain to recognize their independence 1668. Portugal fought as the ally of Britain in the War of the ◊Spanish Succession. France invaded Portugal 1807–11 (see ◊Peninsular War). A strong democratic movement developed, and after a civil war 1828–34, constitutional government was established. Carlos I was assassinated 1908; his son Manuel II was driven from the country by a revolution 1910, and a republic was proclaimed.

Portugal remained economically weak and corrupt until the start of the dictatorship of Dr Antonio de Oliveira ◊Salazar, prime minister from 1928. Social conditions were improved at the cost of personal liberties.

Salazar was succeeded as prime minister 1968 by Dr Marcello Caetano, who proved unable to liberalize the political system or deal with the costly wars in Portugal's colonies of Angola and Mozambique. Criticisms of his administration led to a military coup April 1974 to "save the nation from government." The Junta of National Salvation was set up, headed by General Antonio Ribeiro de Spinola. He became president a month later, with a military colleague replacing the civilian prime minister.

The new president promised liberal reforms, but after disagreements within the Junta, Spinola resigned Sept 1974 and was replaced by General Francisco da Costa Gomes. In 1975 there was a swing to the left among the military and President Gomes narrowly avoided a Communist coup by collaborating with the leader of the moderate Socialist Party (PS), Mario ◊Soares. In 1976 Portugal's first free assembly elections in 50 years were held. The PS won 36% of the vote, and Soares formed a minority government. The army chief, General Antonio Ramalho ◊Eanes, won the presidency, with the support of center and left-of-center parties.

After surviving precariously for over two years, Soares resigned 1978. A period of political instability followed, with five prime ministers in two and a half years, until, in Dec 1980, President Eanes invited Dr Francisco Balsemão, a cofounder of the Social Democratic Party (PSD), to form a center-party coalition. Dr Balsemão survived many challenges to his leadership, and in Aug 1982 the assembly approved his draft of a new constitution, which would reduce the powers of the president and move the country to a fully civilian government. In 1983 Soares entered a coalition with the PSD, whose leader was now the former finance minister, Professor Aníbal Cavaco Silva. In June 1985 the PS-PSD coalition broke up, and a premature general election was called. Cavaco Silva formed a minority government and was able to form a majority government after a landslide victory for the PSD July 1987. He has increased economic growth and raised living standards, and favors a free market and privatization.

In the 1986 presidential election Soares became Portugal's first civilian president for 60 years. He promised an open and cooperative presidency. Portugal entered the European Community 1986 and is a member of NATO. In July 1987 the Social Democrats won an absolute majority in parliament, with the PRD and Communists both losing seats. In June 1989 the parliament approved a series of measures that denationalized major industries and renounced the "Socialist economy." In Jan 1991, Soares was reelected to a 5-year term, while in Oct elections the PSD maintained its majority.

Portugal: former colonies

Name	*Colonized*	*Independent*
Brazil	1532	1822
Uruguay	1533	1828
Mozambique	1505	1975
Angola	1941	1975

Portuguese East Africa former name of ◊Mozambique.

Portuguese Guinea former name of ◊Guinea-Bissau.

Portuguese language member of the Romance branch of the Indo-European language family, the national language of Portugal, closely related to Spanish and strongly influenced by Arabic. It is also spoken in Brazil, Angola, Mozambique, and other former Portuguese colonies.

Portuguese literature under Provençal influence, medieval Portuguese literature produced popular ballads and troubadour songs. The Renaissance provided a stimulus for the outstanding work of the dramatist Gil Vicente and of the lyric and epic poet Camöens. In the 17th and 18th centuries there was a decline toward mere formality, but the *Letters of a Portuguese Nun*, attributed to Marianna Alcoforado, were a poignant exception and found echoes in the modern revolutionary period. No single figure has achieved international acclaim among the varied writers of the 19th and 20th centuries, although there is a lively tradition of writing in Brazil, and Angola developed its own school of Portuguese-African poetry.

Portuguese man-of-war any of a genus *Physalia* of phylum *Coelenterata* (see ◊coelenterate). They live in colonies, and have a large air-filled bladder (or "float") on top and numerous hanging tentacles made up of feeding, stinging, and reproductive individuals. The float can be 1 ft/30 cm long.

Portuguese West Africa former name of ◊Angola.

Poseidon Greek god (Roman Neptune), the brother of Zeus and Pluto. The brothers dethroned their father, Cronus, and divided his realm, Poseidon taking the sea; he was also worshiped as god of earthquakes. His son was ◊Triton.

Posen German ◊Poznań, city in Poland.

positivism a theory associated with the French philosopher Comte (1798–1857), and ◊empiricism, which confines genuine knowledge within the bounds of science and observation. The theory is hostile to theology and to metaphysics that overstep this boundary. Logical positivism developed in the 1920s. It rejected any metaphysical world beyond everyday science and common sense, and confined statements to those of formal logic or mathematics. It influenced, and became more widely known through the work of A J Ayer and the Vienna Circle.

On the basis of positivism, Comte constructed his "Religion of Humanity," in which the object of adoration was the Great Being, that is, the personification of humanity as a whole.

positron an ◊elementary particle that cannot be subdivided, one of the ◊leptons, having the same magnitude of mass and charge as an electron but, since it is the electron's antiparticle, exhibits a positive charge. The beta particle emitted from radioactive atoms during beta-plus decay is a positron.

possum another name for ◊opossum.

postcard a card with space for a written message that can be sent through the mail without an envelope. The postcard's inventor was Emmanual Hermann, of Vienna, who in 1869 proposed a "postal telegram," sent at a lower fee than a normal letter with an envelope. The first picture postcard was produced 1894.

poster advertising announcement for public display, often illustrated, first produced in France during the mid-19th century, when color ◊lithography came into its own.

Poster artists include Jules Chéret, Millais, Toulouse-Lautrec, and Charles Dana Gibson. Poster art flourished again in the 1960s, with an

Poseidon The Temple of Poseidon (northeast corner), Cape Sounion, Greece.

emphasis on psychedelic art and artists such as Rick Griffin, Peter Max, and Stanley Mouse in the US and Michael English and Martin Sharp in Britain.

Post-Impressionism the various styles of painting that followed Impressionism in the 1880s and 1890s. The term was first used by the British critic Roger Fry in 1911 to describe the works of Cézanne, van Gogh, and Gauguin. These painters moved away from the spontaneity of Impressionism, attempting to give their work more serious meaning and permanence.

Postmodernism a late 20th-century movement in the arts and architecture that rejects the preoccupation of ◊Modernism and ◊Functionalism with pure form and technique rather than content. Postmodern designers use an amalgam of style elements from the past, such as the Classical and the baroque, and apply them to spare modern forms. Their slightly off-key familiarity creates a more immediate appeal than the austerities of Modernism.

Post-Impressionism Paul Gauguin's Ea Haere la Oe Go! *(1893), Hermitage, St Petersburg.*

post-mortem (Latin "after death") alternate name for ◊autopsy.

potash general name for any potassium-containing mineral, most often applied to potassium carbonate (K_2CO_3) or potassium hydroxide (KOH). Potassium carbonate, originally made by roasting plants to ashes in earthenware pots, is commercially produced from the mineral sylvite (potassium chloride, KCl) and is used mainly in making artificial fertilizers, glass, and soap.

The potassium content of soils and fertilizers is commonly expressed as potash, although in this case it usually refers to potassium oxide (K_2O).

potassium soft, waxlike, silver-white, metallic element, symbol K (Latin *kalium*), atomic number 19, atomic weight 39.0983. It is one of the ◊alkali metals and has a very low density—it floats on water and is the second lightest metal (after lithium). It oxidizes rapidly when exposed to air and reacts violently with water. Of great abundance in the Earth's crust, it is widely distributed with other elements and found in salt and mineral deposits in the form of potassium aluminum silicates.

The element functions with sodium on the cellular level to make possible neuronal transmission and, so, is essential for animals; it is also essential for the growth of plants. It was discovered and named in 1807 by English chemist Humphry Davy, who isolated it from potash in the first instance of a metal being isolated by electric current. It was named for Dutch *potassa*, "potash."

potato perennial plant *Solanum tuberosum*, family Solanaceae, with edible tuberous roots that are rich in starch. Used by the Andean Indians for at least 2,000 years before the Spanish Conquest, the potato was introduced to Europe by the mid-16th century, and reputedly to England by Walter Raleigh. In Ireland, the potato famine in 1845, caused by a parasitic fungus, resulted in many thousands of deaths from starvation, and led to large-scale emigration to the US. See also ***sweet potato*** under ◊yam.

poteen Irish alcoholic liquor traditionally distilled from potatoes or barley and yeast, in home stills.

Potemkin Grigory Aleksandrovich, Prince Potemkin 1739–1791. Russian politician. He entered the army and attracted the notice of Catherine II, whose friendship he kept throughout his life. He was an active administrator who reformed the army, built the Black Sea Fleet, conquered the Crimea, developed S Russia, and founded the Kherson arsenal 1788 (the first Russian naval base on the Black Sea).

potential difference see ◊potential, electric

potential, electric the relative electrical state of an object. A charged ◊conductor, for example, has a higher potential than the earth, whose potential is taken by convention to be zero. An electric ◊cell (battery) has a potential in relation to emf (◊electromotive force), which can make current flow in an external circuit. The difference in potential between two points—the potential difference—is expressed in ◊volts; that is, a 12V battery has a potential difference of 12 volts between its negative and positive terminals.

potential energy ◊energy possessed by an object by virtue of its relative position or state (for example, as in a compressed spring). It is contrasted with ◊kinetic energy.

potentiometer in physics, an electrical ◊resistor that can be divided so as to compare, measure, or control voltages. A simple type consists of a length of uniform resistance wire (about 3 ft/1 m long) carrying a constant current provided by a battery connected across the ends of the wire. The source of potential difference (voltage) to be measured is connected (to oppose the cell) between one end of the wire, through a ◊galvanometer (instrument for measuring small currents), to a contact free to slide along the wire. The sliding contact is moved until the galvanometer shows no deflection. The ratio of the length of potentiometer wire in the galvanometer circuit to the total length of wire is then equal to the ratio of the unknown potential difference to that of the battery. In radio circuits, any rotary variable resistance (such as volume control) is referred to as a potentiometer.

Potomac river in W Virginia, Virginia, and Maryland, rising in the Allegheny mountains and flowing SE through Washington, DC into Chesapeake Bay. It is formed by the junction of the N Potomac, about 95 mi/150 km long, and the S Potomac, about 130 mi/210 km long, and is itself about 285 mi/460 km long. Large ships can sail upstream as far as Washington. The Potomac is of little economic importance, but historic sites such as Mount Vernon, the home of George Washington, are on its banks.

Potosí town in SW Bolivia; on the Cerro de Potosí slopes at 13,189 ft/4,020 m; it is one of the highest towns in the world; population (1982) 103,000. Silver, tin, lead, and copper are mined here. It was founded by Spaniards 1545; during the 17th and 18th centuries it was the chief silver-mining town and foremost city in South America.

potpourri mixture of dried flowers and leaves, for example, rose petals, lavender, and verbena, used to scent the air.

Potsdam capital of the state of Brandenburg, Federal Republic of Germany, on the river Havel SW of Berlin

population (1986) 140,000

products textiles, pharmaceuticals, and electrical goods

history a leading garrison town and Prussian military center, Potsdam was restored to its position

pottery and porcelain: chronology

BC 10000	Earliest known pottery in Japan; Near East.
c. 5000	Potter's wheel developed by the Egyptians.
c. 600–450	Black- and red-figured vases from Greece.
AD 6th century	Fine quality stoneware developed in China, as the forerunner of porcelain.
7–10th century	Tang porcelain in China.
10–13th century	Song porcelain in China.
14–17th century	Ming porcelain in China; Hispano-Moresque ware.
16th century	Majolica, an Italian tin-glazed earthenware with painted decoration, often large dishes with figures; faience (from Faenza, Italy) glazed earthenware and delftware.
17th century	Chinese porcelain first exported to the West; it was soon brought in large quantities (for example, the Nanking Cargo) as a ballast in tea clippers; delftware tin-glazed earthenware with white with blue decoration brought to perfection in Delft, Netherlands. In North America, colonists made bricks and tiles by 1612.
18th century	In 1710 the first European hardpaste porcelain was made in Dresden, Germany, by Böttger 1682–1719; the factory later transferred to Meissen. From 1769 hardpaste porcelain as well as softpaste made in ◊Sèvres, France, remarkable for its ground colors; c. 1760 cream-colored earthenware perfected (superseding delftware) by Josiah Wedgwood; he also devised stoneware, typically with white decoration in Neo-Classical designs on a blue ground, still among the wares made in Barlaston, Staffordshire; English softpaste made c. 1745–1810, first in Chelsea, later in Bow, Derby, and Worcester; English hardpaste first made in Plymouth 1768–70, and Bristol 1770–81, when the stock was removed to New Hall in Staffordshire; bone china c. 1789 first produced by Josiah Spode (1754–1827), Coalport, near Shrewsbury, and Thomas ◊Minton followed as did all English tableware of this type from 1815.
19th century	Large-scale production of fine wares, in Britain notably ◊Royal Worcester from 1862, and Royal (Crown) Derby from 1876. In the US, potteries established in New Jersey, Pennsylvannia, Ohio, New England, and the South made earthenware and stoneware utility items and earthware, stoneware, and bone china for tableware and fine ornaments.
20th century	A revival in the craft of the individual potter, for example, Bernard Leach, Lucie Rie, Maria Martinez. California potteries entered the world market.

Pound *US poet Ezra Pound founded the Imagist movement and influenced W B Yeats and James Joyce, but his mental instability led to 13 years in a psychiatric hospital.*

of capital of Brandenburg with the reunification of Germany 1990. The New Palace 1763–70 and Sans Souci were both built by Frederick the Great, and Hitler's Third Reich was proclaimed in the garrison church March 21, 1933. The Potsdam Conference took place here.

Potsdam Conference conference held at Potsdam (in what is now Germany) July 1945 between representatives of the US, the UK, and the USSR. They established the political and economic principles governing the treatment of Germany in the initial period of Allied control at the end of World War II, and sent an ultimatum to Japan demanding unconditional surrender on pain of utter destruction.

Potter Stephen 1900–1969. British author of humorous studies in how to outwit and outshine others, including *Gamesmanship* 1947, *Lifemanship* 1950, and *One Upmanship* 1952.

Potteries, the the home of the china and earthenware industries, in central England. Wedgwood and Minton are factory names associated with the Potteries.

pottery and porcelain ◊ceramics in domestic and ornamental use including:

earthenware made of porous clay and fired, whether unglazed (when it remains porous, for example, flowerpots, winecoolers) or glazed (rustic tableware);

stoneware made of nonporous clay with a high silica content, fired at high temperature, which is very hard;

bone china (softpaste) semiporcelain made of 5% bone ash and ◊kaolinite; first made in the West in imitation of Chinese porcelain;

porcelain (hardpaste) characterized by its hardness, ringing sound when struck, translucence, and shining finish, like that of a cowrie shell (Italian *porcellana*); made of kaolin and petuntse (fusible ◊feldspar consisting chiefly of silicates reduced to a fine, white powder); first developed in China. Porcelain is high-fired at 2,552°F/1,400°C.

potto arboreal, nocturnal, African prosimian primate *Perodicticus potto* belonging to the ◊loris family. It has a thick body, strong limbs, and grasping feet and hands, and grows to 16 in/40 cm long. It has horny spines along its backbone, which it uses in self-defense. It climbs slowly, and eats insects, snails, fruit, and leaves.

Poughkeepsie city in SE New York, on the Hudson River, N of New York City. Industries include chemicals, ball bearings, and cough drops. Vassar College is here; population (1990) 28,884. Settled by the Dutch 1687, it served as the temporary capital of New York 1717.

Poulenc Francis (Jean Marcel) 1899–1963. French composer and pianist. A self-taught composer of witty and irreverent music, he was a member of the group of French composers known as ◊Les Six. Among his many works are the operas *Les Mamelles de Tirésias* 1947, and *Dialogues des Carmélites* 1957, and the ballet *Les Biches* 1923.

Poulsen Valdemar 1869–1942. Danish engineer who in 1900 was the first to demonstrate that sound could be recorded magnetically—originally on a moving steel wire or tape; this was the forerunner of the tape recorder.

His discovery also led to motion picture sound recording systems (sound tape along the edge of the film).

poultry domesticated birds such as chickens, turkeys, ducks, and geese. They were domesticated for meat and eggs by early farmers in China, Europe, Egypt, and the Americas. Chickens were domesticated from the SE Asian jungle fowl *Gallus gallus* and then raised in the East as well as the West. Turkeys are New World birds, domesticated in ancient Mexico. Geese and ducks were domesticated in Egypt, China, and Europe.

Good egg-laying breeds of chicken are Leghorns, Minorcas, and Anconas; varieties most suitable for eating are Dorkings, Australorps, Brahmas, and Cornish; those useful for both purposes are Orpingtons, Rhode Island Reds, Wyandottes, Plymouth Rocks, and Jersey White Giants. Most farm poultry are hybrids, selectively crossbred for certain characteristics, including feathers and down. Since World War II, the development of battery-produced eggs and the intensive breeding of broiler fowls and turkeys has roused a public outcry against "factory" methods of farming. The birds are often kept constantly in small cages, have their beaks and claws removed to prevent them from pecking their neighbors, and given feed containing growth hormones and antibacterial drugs, which eventually make their way up the food chain to humans. Factory farming has led to a growing interest in deep-litter and free-range systems, although these account for only a small percentage of total production.

POUM acronym from Partido Obrero de Unificación Marxista ("Workers' Marxist Union Party") a small Spanish anti-Stalinist communist party led by Andrés Nin and Joaquín Maurín, prominent during the Spanish Civil War. Since Republican Spain received most of its external help from the USSR, the Spanish communist party used this to force the suppression of the POUM in 1937. POUM supporters included George Orwell, who chronicled events in his book *Homage to Catalonia*.

pound British standard monetary unit, issued as a gold sovereign before 1914, as a note 1914–83, and as a circular yellow metal alloy coin from 1983.

The pound is also the name given to the unit of currency in Egypt, Lebanon, Malta, Sudan, and Syria.

pound imperial unit (abbreviation lb) of mass equal to 16 ounces (7,000 grains) avoirdupois, or 12 ounces (5,760 grains) troy; the metric equivalents are 0.45 kg and 0.37 kg respectively. It derives from the Roman *libra*, which weighed 0.327 kg.

Pound Ezra 1885–1972. US poet who lived in London from 1908. His *Personae* and *Exultations* 1909 established the principles of the ◊Imagist movement. His largest work was the series of *Cantos* 1925–1969 (intended to number 100), which attempted a massive reappraisal of history.

In Paris 1921–25, he was a friend of the writers Gertrude Stein and Ernest Hemingway. He then settled in Rapallo, Italy. His anti-Semitism and sympathy with the fascist dictator Mussolini led him to broadcast from Italy in World War II, and he was arrested by US troops 1945. Found unfit to stand trial, he was confined in a mental hospital until 1958.

His first completely modern poem was *Hugh Selwyn Mauberley* 1920. He also wrote versions of Old English, Provençal, Chinese, ancient Egyptian, and other verse.

poundal imperial unit (abbreviation pdl) of force, now replaced in the SI system by the ◊newton. One poundal equals 0.1383 newtons.

It is defined as the force necessary to accelerate a mass of one pound by one foot per second per second.

Poussin Nicolas 1594–1665. French painter, active chiefly in Rome; court painter to Louis XIII 1640–43. He was one of France's foremost landscape painters in the 17th century. He painted mythological and literary scenes in a strongly Classical style: for example, *Rape of the Sabine Women* about 1636–37 (Metropolitan Museum of Art, New York).

Poussin went to Rome 1624 and studied Roman sculpture in the studio of ◊Domenichino. His style reflects painstaking preparation: he made small wax models of the figures in his paintings, experimenting with different compositions and lighting. Color was subordinate to line.

poverty the condition that exists when the basic needs of human beings (shelter, food, and clothing) are not being met.

In many countries, poverty is common and persistent, being reflected in poor nutrition, low life expectancy, and high levels of infant mortality. It may result from a country's complete lack of resources and an inability to achieve economic development.

Many different definitions of poverty exist, since there is little agreement on the standard of living (known as the poverty level) considered to be the minimum adequate level by the majority of people.

powder metallurgy method of shaping heat-resistant metals such as tungsten. Metal is pressed into a mold in powdered form and then sintered (heated to very high temperatures).

Powell Adam Clayton, Jr 1908–1972. US political leader. As pastor of the Abyssinian Baptist Church in Harlem, New York City, he became a leader of New York's black community and was elected to the US Congress 1944 and later became chairman of the House Education and Labor Committee. Due to charges of corruption, Powell was not allowed to take his seat in Congress 1967. Reelected 1968, he won back his seniority by a 1969 decision of the US Supreme Court.

Powell Anthony (Dymoke) 1905– . English novelist who wrote the series of 12 volumes *A Dance to the Music of Time* 1951–75 that begins shortly after World War I and chronicles a period of 50 years in the lives of Nicholas Jenkins and his circle of upper-class friends.

Powell Cecil Frank 1903–1969. English physicist, awarded a Nobel Prize 1950 for his use of photographic emulsion as a method of tracking charged nuclear particles.

Powell Colin (Luther) 1937– . US military leader, Army general who became chairman of the Joint Chiefs of Staff 1989, the first black to hold the post. He enhanced his reputation substantially by his efficient and calm leadership during the 1990–91 ◊Gulf War.

Born in New York City, Powell entered the army after college via the Reserve Officers' Training Corps (ROTC). He served two tours in Vietnam and held several key field command and staff posts, including National Security Advisor to President Reagan, before being named to the Joint Chiefs.

Powell Lewis Stanley 1907– . US jurist and associate justice of the US Supreme Court 1971–87. A conservative, Powell voted to restrict Fifth-Amendment guarantees against self-incrimination and for capital punishment. In *United States* v *Nixon* 1974, he sided with the majority in limiting executive privilege. In *Regents of the University of California* v *Bakke* 1978, he joined the majority in rejecting racial quotas as a basis for admission to an educational program.

Born in Suffolk, Virginia, Powell received his undergraduate and law degrees from Washington and Lee University and an MA in law from Harvard. Powell practiced in Virginia, becoming president of the American Bar Association 1964–65 and president of the American College of Trial Lawyers 1968–69. President Nixon appointed Powell to the Supreme Court 1971. He retired 1987 for health reasons.

Powell William 1892–1984. US film actor who costarred with Myrna Loy in the *Thin Man* series of films 1934–1947. He also played leading roles in *My Man Godfrey* 1936, *Life with Father* 1947, and *Mister Roberts* 1955. He retired 1955.

power in mathematics, that which is represented by an ◊exponent or index, denoted by a superior small numeral. A number or symbol raised to the power of two, that is, multiplied by itself, is said to be squared (for example, 3^2, x^2), and something raised to the power of three is said to be cubed (for example, 2^3, y^3).

power in physics, the rate of doing work or consuming energy. It is measured in watts (joules per second) or other units of work per unit time.

power of attorney in law, legal authority to act on behalf of another, for a specific transaction, or for a particular period.

Powys county in central Wales

area 1,961 sq mi/5,080 sq km

towns Llandrindod Wells (administrative headquarters)

features Brecon Beacons National Park; Black mountains; rivers: Wye, Severn, which both rise on Plynlimon; Lake Vyrnwy, artificial reservoir supplying Liverpool and Birmingham; alternative technology center near Machynlleth

products agriculture, dairy cattle, sheep

population (1987) 113,000

language 20% Welsh, English.

Poznań (German *Posen*) industrial city (machinery, aircraft, beer) in W Poland; population (1985) 553,000. Settled by German immigrants 1253, it passed to Prussia 1793 but was restored to Poland 1919.

pp abbreviation for perprocurationem; pianissimo.

PR abbreviation for Puerto Rico; public relations; proportional representation.

Prado Spanish art gallery (*Réal Museo de Pintura del Prado*/Royal Picture Gallery of the Prado), containing the national collection of pictures, founded by Charles III in 1785.

praemunire three English acts of Parliament passed 1353, 1365, and 1393, aimed to prevent appeal to the pope against the power of the king, and therefore an early demonstration of independence from Rome. The statutes were opposed by English bishops.

praetor in ancient Rome, a magistrate, elected annually, who assisted the ◊consuls and presided over the civil courts. After a year in office, a praetor would act as a provincial governor for a further year. The number of praetors was finally increased to eight.

pragmatism a philosophical tradition that interprets truth in terms of the practical effects of what is believed and, in particular, the usefulness of these effects.

The US philosopher ◊Peirce is often accounted the founder of pragmatism; it was further advanced by William James.

Prague (Czech *Praha*) city and capital of Czechoslovakia on the river Vltava; population (1985) 1,190,000. Industries include automobiles, aircraft, chemicals, paper and printing, clothing, brewing, and food processing. It became capital 1918.

Prague Spring the reform program introduced in Jan 1968 by Alexander Dubček was halted in Aug by a Soviet army invasion (see ◊Czechoslovakia). It was known as the Prague Spring from an annual music festival.

Praha Czech name for ◊Prague.

Praia port and capital of the Republic of Cape Verde, on the island of São Tiago (Santiago); population (1980) 37,500. Industries include fishing and shipping.

prairie dog any of the North American genus *Cynomys* of burrowing rodents in the squirrel family (Sciuridae). They grow to 12 in/30 cm, plus a short 3 in/8 cm tail. Their "towns" can contain up to several thousand individuals. Their barking cry has given them their name. Persecution by ranchers has brought most of the five species close to extinction.

Prakrit general name for the ancient Indo-European dialects of N India, contrasted with the sacred Classical language Sanskrit. The word is itself Sanskrit, meaning "natural," as opposed to *Sanskrit*, which means "perfected." The Prakrits are considered to be the ancestors of such modern N Indian languages as Hindi, Punjabi, and Bengali.

Prasad Rajendra 1884–1963. Indian politician. He was national president of the Indian National Congress and India's first president after independence.

praseodymium silver-white, malleable, metallic element of the ◊lanthanide series, symbol Pr, atomic number 59, atomic weight 140.907. It occurs in nature in the minerals monzanite and bastnasite, and its green salts are used to color glass and ceramics. It was named in 1885 by Australian chemist Carl von Welsbach (1858–1929).

He fractionated it from didymium (originally thought to be an element but actually a mixture of rare-earth metals consisting largely of neodymium, praseodymium, and cerium), and named it for its green salts and spectroscopic line from Greek *prasios*, "leek-green" and the suffix of di*dymium*.

Prato industrial town (woolens) in Tuscany, central Italy; population (1988) 165,000. The 12th-century cathedral has works of art by Donatello, Filippo Lippi, and Andrea della Robbia.

prawn any of various ◊shrimps of the suborder Natantia ("swimming"), of the crustacean order Decapoda, as contrasted with lobsters and crayfishes, which are able to "walk." Species called prawns are generally larger than species called shrimps.

Praxiteles mid-4th century BC. Greek sculptor, active in Athens. His *Aphrodite of Knidos* about 350 BC (known through Roman copies) is thought to have initiated the tradition of life-size freestanding female nudes in Greek sculpture.

prayer address to divine power, ranging from a magical formula to attain a desired end, to selfless communication in meditation. Within Christianity the Catholic and Orthodox churches sanction prayer to the Virgin Mary, angels, and saints as intercessors, whereas Protestantism limits prayer to God alone.

preadaptation in biology, the fortuitous possession of a character that allows an organism to exploit a new situation. In many cases, the character evolves to solve a particular problem that a species encounters in its preferred habitat, but once evolved may allow the organism to exploit an entirely different situation. Thus some early fishes, by maintaining a dual system of respiration in their possession of lungs for gulping air alongside gills for extracting oxygen from water, were able to give rise to exclusively air-breathing descendants living on land (the amphibians).

Precambrian in geology, the time from the formation of Earth (4.6 billion years ago) up to 590 million years ago. Its boundary with the succeeding Cambrian period marks the time when animals first developed hard outer parts (exoskeletons) and so left abundant fossil remains. It comprises about 85% of geologic time and is divided into two periods: the Archaean and the Proterozoic.

precedent the ◊common law principle that, in deciding a particular case, judges are bound to follow any applicable principles of law laid down by superior courts in earlier reported cases.

precession slow wobble of the Earth on its axis, like that of a spinning top. The gravitational pulls of the Sun and Moon on the Earth's equatorial bulge cause the Earth's axis to trace out a circle on the sky every 25,800 years. The position of the celestial poles (see ◊celestial sphere) is constantly changing caused by precession, as are the positions of the equinoxes (the points at which the celestial equator intersects the Sun's path around the sky). The precession of the equinoxes means that there is a gradual westward drift in the ecliptic—the path that the Sun appears to follow—and in the coordinates of objects on the celestial sphere; this is why the dates of the astrological signs of the zodiac no longer correspond to the times of year when the Sun actually passes through the constellations. For example, the Sun passes through Leo from mid-Aug to mid-Sept, but the astrological dates for Leo are between about July 23 and Aug 22.

precipitation meteorological term for water that falls to the Earth from the atmosphere. It includes ◊rain, ◊snow, sleet, ◊hail, ◊dew, and ◊frost.

predator an animal that must hunt and kill other animals for its food.

predestination the doctrine asserting that God has determined all events beforehand, including the ultimate salvation or damnation of the individual human soul; see ◊free will.

pref. in grammar, the abbreviation for prefix.

prefect French government official who, under the centralized Napoleonic system 1800–1984, was responsible for enforcing government policy in each *département* and *région*. In 1984 prefects were replaced by presidents of elected councils (see ◊France, government).

prefix letter or group of letters that can be added to the beginning of a word to make a new word. For example, *over*time, *out*rage, *non*sense.

pregnancy in humans, the period during which an embryo grows within the womb. It begins at conception and ends at birth, and the normal length is 40 weeks. Menstruation usually stops on conception. About one in five pregnancies fails, but most of these failures occur very early on, so the woman may notice only that her period is late. After the second month, the breasts become tense and tender, and the areas around the nipples become darker. Enlargement of the uterus can be felt at about the end of the third month, and thereafter the abdomen enlarges progressively. Pregnancy in animals is called ◊gestation.

Occasionally the fertilized egg implants not in the womb but in the ◊Fallopian tube, leading to an ectopic ("out of place") pregnancy. This will cause the woman severe abdominal pain and vaginal bleeding. If the growing fetus ruptures the tube, life-threatening shock may ensue.

pregnancy

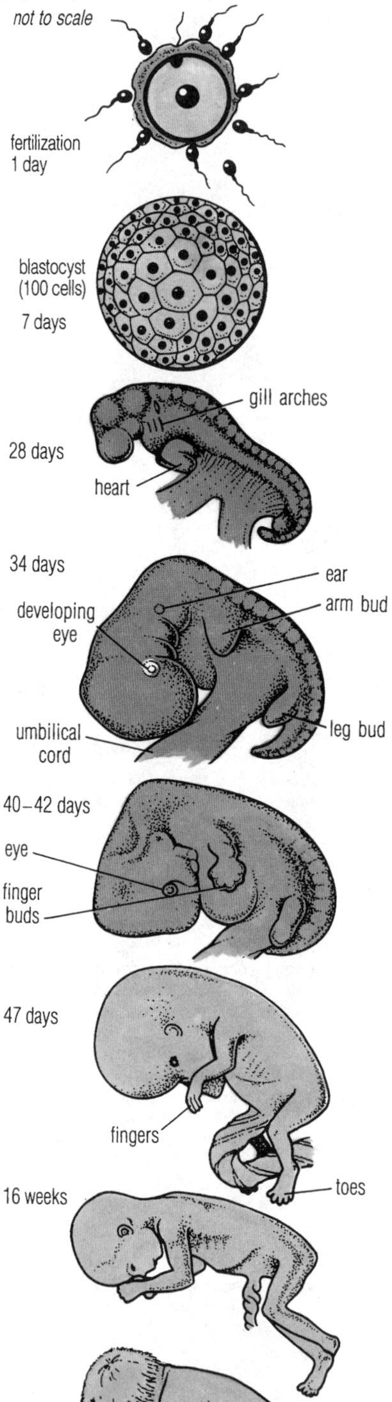
not to scale
fertilization
1 day
blastocyst
(100 cells)
7 days
gill arches
28 days
heart
34 days
ear
arm bud
developing
eye
umbilical
cord
leg bud
40–42 days
eye
finger
buds
47 days
fingers
toes
16 weeks
40 weeks

prehistoric art art of prehistoric cultures; see ◊ancient art.

prehistoric life the diverse organisms that inhabited Earth from the origin of life about 3.5 billion years ago to the time when humans began to keep written records about 3500 BC. During the course of evolution, new forms of life developed and many other forms, such as the dinosaurs, became extinct. Prehistoric life evolved over this vast timespan from simple bacterialike cells in the oceans to algae and protozoans and complex multicellar forms such as worms, mollusks, crustaceans, fishes, insects, land plants, amphibians, reptiles, birds, and mammals. On a geologic timescale, the ◊human species evolved relatively recently, about 4 million years ago, although the exact dating is a matter of some debate. See also ◊geologic time.

prehistory human cultures before the use of writing. A classification system was devised 1816 by the Danish archeologist Christian Thomsen, based on the predominant materials used by early humans for tools and weapons.

Stone Age Stone, mainly flint, was predominant. The Stone Age is divided into:

Old Stone Age (Paleolithic) 3,500,000–5000 BC. Tools were chipped into shape by early humans, or hominids, from Africa, Asia, the Middle East, and Europe as well as later Neanderthal and Cro-Magnon people; the only domesticated animals were dogs. Some Asians crossed the Bering land bridge to inhabit the Americas. Cave paintings were produced 20,000–8,000 years ago in many parts of the world, for example, Altamira, Spain; Lascaux, France; central Sahara; India; and Australia

***Middle Stone Age* (Mesolithic)** and ***New Stone Age* (Neolithic)** Stone and bone tools were ground and polished as well as chipped. In Neolithic times, agriculture and the domestication of goats, sheep, and cattle began. Stone Age cultures survived in the Americas, Asia, Africa, Oceania, and Australia until the 19th and 20th centuries.

Bronze Age Bronze tools and weapons began approximately 6000 BC in the Far East, and continued in the Middle East until about 1200 BC; in Britain it lasted from about 2000 to 500 BC. The heroes of the Greek poet Homer lived in the Bronze Age.

Iron Age Iron was hardened (alloyed) by the addition of carbon, so that it superseded bronze for tools and weapons; in the Old World generally from about 1000 BC.

prelude in music, a composition intended as the preface to further music, to set a mood for a stage work, as in Wagner's *Lohengrin*; as used by Chopin, a short piano work.

Premadasa Ranasinghe 1924– . Sri Lankan politician, a United National Party member of Parliament from 1960, prime minister from 1978, and president from 1988, having gained popularity through overseeing a major house-building and poverty-alleviation program. He has sought peace talks with the Tamil Tigers.

premenstrual syndrome (PMS) a hormonal condition comprising a number of physical and emotional features that occur cyclically before menstruation, and which disappear with its onset. Symptoms include mood changes, breast tenderness, a feeling of bloatedness, and headache.

Preminger Otto (Ludwig) 1906–1986. US film producer, director, and actor. Born in Vienna, he went to the US 1935. He directed *Margin for Error* 1942, *Laura* 1944, *The Moon is Blue* 1953, *The Man With the Golden Arm* 1955, *Anatomy of a Murder* 1959, *Skidoo!* 1968, and *Rosebud* 1974. His films are characterized by an intricate technique of story-telling, and a masterly use of the wide screen and the traveling camera.

premolar in mammals, one of the large teeth toward the back of the mouth. In herbivores they are adapted for grinding. In carnivores they may be carnassials. Premolars are present in milk ◊dentition as well as permanent dentition.

Premonstratensian a Roman Catholic monastic order founded 1120 by St Norbert (c. 1080–1134), a German bishop, at Prémontré, N France. Members were known as White Canons. The rule was a stricter version of that of the Augustinian Canons.

Prempeh I chief of the Ashanti people in W Africa. He became king 1888, and later opposed British attempts to take over the region. He was deported and in 1900 the Ashanti were defeated. He returned to Kumasi (capital of the Ashanti region) 1924 as chief of the people.

Prendergast Maurice 1859–1924. US painter who created a decorative watercolor style, using small translucent pools of color, inspired by the Impressionists.

He studied in Paris in the 1890s and was influenced by the ◊Nabis painters Bonnard and Vuillard. In 1898 he visited Italy. His *Umbrellas in the Rain, Venice* 1899 (Museum of Fine Arts, Boston) is typical.

preparatory school a private high school that prepares students for entrance to a college or university.

preposition in grammar, a ◊part of speech coming before a noun or a pronoun to show a location (*in*, *on*), time (*during*), or some other relationship (for example, figurative relationships in phrases like "*by* heart" or "*on* time").

In the sentence "Put the book *on* the table," *on* is a preposition governing the noun "table" and relates the verb "put" to the phrase "the table," indicating where the book should go. Some words of English that are often prepositional in function may, however, be used adverbially, as in the sentences, "He picked the book *up*" and "He picked *up* the book," in which the ordering is different but the meaning the same. In such cases *up* is called an adverbial particle and the form *pick up* is a phrasal verb.

Pre-Raphaelite Brotherhood (PRB) group of British painters 1848–53; Dante Gabriel Rossetti, John Everett Millais, and Holman Hunt were founding members. They aimed to paint serious subjects, to study nature closely, and to shun the influence of painterly styles post-Raphael. Their subjects were mainly biblical and literary, painted with

Pre-Raphaelite Brotherhood *Dante Gabriel Rossetti's* La Ghirlandata *1873. Minute detail and a vivid use of color mark this portrait as a work of the Pre-Raphaelite Brotherhood.*

obsessive naturalism. Artists associated with the group include Burne-Jones and William Morris.

Presbyterianism system of Christian Protestant church government, expounded during the Reformation by John Calvin in Geneva, which gives its name to the established church of Scotland and is also practiced in the US, England, the Netherlands, Switzerland, and elsewhere. There is no compulsory form of worship, and each congregation is governed by presbyters or elders (clerical or lay), who are of equal rank. Congregations are grouped in presbyteries, synods, and general assemblies.

Presbyterianism came to the American colonies in the 17th century with Scottish and northern Irish immigrants. The main body is the Presbyterian Church in the US, with more than 3 million members. Other groups include the Orthodox Presbyterian Church, the Bible Presbyterian Church, and the Associate Reformed Presbyterian Church. In Canada, most Presbyterians united with Congregationalists and Methodists in 1925 to form the United Church of Canada.

Prescott William Hickling 1796–1859. US historian, author of *History of the Reign of Ferdinand and Isabella, the Catholic* 1838, *History of the Conquest of Mexico* 1843, and *History of the Conquest of Peru* 1847.

prescription in medicine, an order written in a recognized form by a practitioner of medicine, dentistry, or veterinary surgery to a pharmacist for a preparation of medications to be used in treatment.

By tradition it is written in Latin, except for the directions addressed to the patient. It consists of (1) the superscription *recipe* ("take"), contracted to Rx; (2) the inscription or body, containing the names and quantities of the drugs to be dispensed; (3) the subscription, or directions to the pharmacist; (4) the signature, consisting of the contraction *Signa*, followed by directions to the patient; and (5) the patient's name, the date, and the practitioner's name.

preservative food ◊additive used to inhibit the growth of bacteria, yeasts, mold, and other microorganisms to extend the shelf-life of foods. The term sometimes refers to ◊antioxidants as well. All preservatives are potentially damaging to health if eaten in sufficient quantity. Both the amount used, and the foods in which they can be used, are restricted by law.

Alternatives to preservatives include faster turnover of food stocks, refrigeration, better hygiene in preparation, sterilization and pasteurization (see ◊food technology).

president in government, the usual title of the head of state in a republic; the power of the office may range from diplomatic figurehead to the actual head of the government. For presidents of the US, who head the executive branch and its agencies, see ◊United States and entries by name.

presidium the executive committee of the Supreme Soviet in the USSR; the ◊Politburo was known as the presidium 1952–66.

Presley Elvis (Aaron) 1935–1977. US singer, guitarist, and film star. He was born in Tupelo, Mississippi, and became the most influential performer of the rock-and-roll era. With his recordings for Sun Records in Memphis, Tennessee, 1954–55 and early hits such as "Heartbreak Hotel," "Hound Dog," and "Love Me Tender," all 1956, he created an individual performance style and vocal style, influenced by Southern blues, gospel music, country music, and rhythm and blues.

Presley's aggressive, sexual style of performance (he was called "Elvis the Pelvis") inspired controversy and earned him the adoration of millions of fans. In the mid-1950s Presley met Colonel Tom Parker, who would manage his career for his entire life. In addition to selling millions of records, Presley acted in 33 motion pictures and made numerous television appearances. From the late 1960s, he took a Las Vegas-based touring act on the road. He died at Graceland, his mansion in Memphis, in 1977, the victim of drug dependence.

Pressburg German name of ◊Bratislava, city in Czechoslovakia.

Pressburger Emeric 1902–1988. Hungarian director, producer, and screenwriter, known for his partnership with Michael ◊Powell.

press gang method used to recruit soldiers and sailors into the British armed forces in the 18th and early 19th centuries. In effect it was a form of kidnapping carried out by the services or their agents, often with the aid of armed men. This was similar to shanghaiing sailors for duty in the merchant marine, especially in the Far East.

pressure in physics, force per unit area. In a fluid (liquid or gas), pressure increases with depth. At the edge of Earth's atmosphere, pressure is zero, whereas at ground level it is about 1013.25 millibars (or 1 atmosphere). Pressure at a depth h in a fluid of density d is equal to hdg, where g is the acceleration due to gravity. The SI unit of pressure is the ◊pascal (newton per square meter), equal to 0.01 millibars. Pressure has also been measured using a mercury column (see ◊Torricelli); with 1 atmosphere equaling 760 mm of mercury.

Presley *Elvis Presley, originally a rock-and-roll singer, became a successful movie star and for many years was the most popular singer in the world.*

pressure cooker closed pot in which food is cooked in water under pressure, where water boils at a higher temperature than normal boiling point (212°F/100°C) and therefore cooks food quickly. The modern pressure cooker has a quick-sealing lid and a safety valve that can be adjusted to vary the steam pressure inside.

The French scientist Denis Papin invented the pressure cooker in England in 1679.

pressure group an interest group or lobby group that puts pressure on governments or parties to ensure laws and treatment favorable to its own interest. Pressure groups have played an increasingly prominent role in contemporary Western democracies. In general they fall into two types: groups concerned with a single issue, such as nuclear disarmament, and groups attempting to promote their own interest, such as oil producers.

Prester John legendary Christian prince. During the 12th and 13th centuries, Prester John was believed to be the ruler of a powerful empire in Asia. From the 14th to the 16th century, he was generally believed to be the king of Abyssinia (now Ethiopia) in N E Africa.

Preston industrial seaport (textiles, chemicals, electrical goods, aircraft, and shipbuilding), and administrative headquarters of Lancashire, NW England, on the river Ribble, 21 mi/34 km S of Lancaster; population (1983) 125,000. Cromwell defeated the Royalists at Preston in 1648. It is the birthplace of Richard Arkwright, inventor of cotton-spinning machinery.

pretender claimant to a throne. In British history, the term is widely used to describe the Old Pretender (◊James Francis Edward Stuart) and the Young Pretender (◊Charles Edward Stuart).

Pretoria administrative capital of the Republic of South Africa from 1910 and capital of Transvaal province from 1860; population (1985) 741,300. Industries include engineering, chemicals, iron, and steel. Founded 1855, it was named after Boer leader Andries Pretorius (1799–1853).

Previn André (George) 1929– . US conductor and composer, born in Berlin. After a period working as a composer and arranger in the US film industry, he concentrated on conducting. He was principal conductor of the London Symphony Orchestra 1968–79. He was appointed music director of Britain's Royal Philharmonic Orchestra 1985 (a post he relinquished the following year, staying on as principal conductor), and of the Los Angeles Philharmonic in 1986.

He has done much on television and on stage to popularize Classical music.

Prévost d'Exiles Antoine François 1697–1763. French novelist, known as Abbé Prévost, who combined a military career with his life as a monk. His *Manon Lescaut* 1731 inspired operas by Massenet and Puccini.

Priam in Greek mythology, the last king of Troy. He was killed by Pyrrhus, son of Achilles, when the Greeks entered the city of Troy concealed in a giant gift—a wooden horse.

Priapus Greek god of fertility, son of Dionysus and Aphrodite, represented as grotesquely ugly, with an exaggerated phallus. He was also a god of gardens, where his image was frequently used as a scarecrow.

Pribilof Islands group of four islands in the Bering Sea, of volcanic origin, 200 mi/320 km SW of Bristol Bay, Alaska. Named after Gerasim Pribilof, who reached them in 1786, they were sold by Russia to the US in 1867 with Alaska, of which they form part. They were made a fur-seal reservation in 1868.

Price Leontyne 1927– . US opera singer. She made her professional debut on Broadway 1952 and was cast by Ira Gershwin to sing one of the lead roles in his revival of *Porgy and Bess* 1952–54. Through concert and television performances, Price gained a national reputation and made her operatic debut in San Francisco 1957. She appeared at La Scala in Milan 1959 and became a regular member of the Metropolitan Opera in New York 1961.

Born in Laurel, Mississippi, and educated at Central State College in Ohio, Price was trained as a soprano at the Juilliard School of Music in New York.

Price Vincent 1911– . US actor who made his film debut in 1938 after a stage career. He is remembered for *Laura* 1944 and *Leave Her To Heaven* 1945 before becoming a star of horror films, including *Dragonwick* 1946, *House of Wax* 1953, the cult favorite *The Tingler* 1959, *The Fall of the House of Usher* 1960, and five more Roger Corman campy horrors through 1964. He is beloved for hosting TV's *Mystery* series.

prickly heat acute skin condition characterized by small white or red itchy blisters (miliaria), resulting from inflammation of the sweat glands in conditions of heat and humidity.

prickly pear cactus of the genus *Opuntia*, native to Central and South America, mainly Mexico and Chile, but naturalized in S Europe, N Africa, and Australia, where it is a pest. The common prickly pear *Opuntia vulgaris* is low-growing, with flat, oval-stem joints, bright yellow flowers, and prickly, oval fruit; the flesh and seeds of the peeled fruit have a pleasant taste.

Pride and Prejudice a novel by Jane Austen, published in 1813. Mr and Mrs Bennet, whose property is due to pass to a male cousin, William Collins, are anxious to secure good marriage settlements for their five daughters. Central to the story is the romance between the witty Elizabeth Bennet and the proud Mr Darcy.

Pride's purge the removal of about 100 Royalists and Presbyterians of the English House of Commons from Parliament by a detachment of soldiers led by Col Thomas Pride (died 1658) in 1648. They were accused of negotiating with Charles I and were seen as unreliable by the army. The remaining members were termed the ◊Rump and voted in favor of the king's trial.

Pride acted as one of the judges at the trial and also signed the king's death warrant. He opposed the plan to make Cromwell king.

Priestley J(ohn) B(oynton) 1894–1984. English novelist and playwright. His first success was a novel about traveling theater, *The Good Companions* 1929. He followed it with a realist novel about London life *Angel Pavement* 1930; later books include *Lost Empires* 1965 and *The Image Men* 1968. As a playwright he was often preoccupied with theories of time, as in *An Inspector Calls* 1945, but had also a gift for family comedy, for example, *When We Are Married* 1938.

He was also known for his wartime broadcasts and literary criticism, such as *Literature and Western Man* 1960.

Priestley Joseph 1733–1804. English chemist who identified oxygen 1774.

Prigg v Pennsylvania a US Supreme Court decision 1842 dealing with state and federal legislation about the removal of escaped slaves from "free" states. When Prigg, sent to recapture an escaped Maryland slave, was arrested for kidnapping under a Pennsylvania "personal liberty" law that prevented forcible seizure and removal of former slaves, he sued Pennsylvania in the US Supreme Court. The Court ruled the Pennsylvania law unconstitutional, upholding the federal Fugitive Slave Act and granting Congress absolute power over legislation about fugitive slaves. Many Northern states responded by passing laws that prohibited state officials from cooperating with the federal removal of runaways.

Prigogine Ilya 1917– . Russian-born Belgian chemist who, as a highly original theoretician, has made major contributions to the field of ◊thermodynamics for which work he was awarded the 1977 Nobel Prize for Physics. Earlier theories had considered systems at or about equilibrium.

***Priestly** English chemist Joseph Priestley, who discovered oxygen in 1774.*

Prigogine began to study "dissipative" or nonequilibrium structures frequently found in biological and chemical reactions.

primary in presidential election campaigns in the US, statewide elections to decide the candidates for the major parties. Held in 35 states, primaries begin with New Hampshire in Feb and continue until June; they operate under varying complex rules. Generally speaking, the number of votes received by a candidate governs the number of delegates who will vote for that person at the first ballot of the national conventions in July/Aug, when the final choice of candidate for both Democratic and Republican parties is made. Some delegates remain loyal to the last ballot, others make deals to benefit the state or local situation as the field of candidates narrows.

primary sexual characteristic the endocrine gland producing maleness and femaleness. In males it is the testis and in females the ovary.

primate in zoology, any member of the order of mammals that includes monkeys, apes, and humans (together called ◊anthropoids), as well as lemurs, bushbabies, lorises, and tarsiers (together called prosimians). Generally, they have forward-directed eyes, gripping hands and feet, opposable thumbs, and big toes. They tend to have nails rather than claws, with gripping pads on the ends of the digits, all adaptations to the arboreal, climbing mode of life.

primate in the Christian church, the official title of archbishops.

prime minister or ***premier*** head of a parliamentary government, usually the leader of the largest party. The first in Britain is usually considered to have been Robert ◊Walpole, but the office was not officially recognized until 1905. In some countries, such as Australia, a distinction is drawn between the prime minister of the whole country, and the premier of an individual state. In countries with an executive president, such as France, the prime minister is of lesser standing.

prime number a number that can be divided only by 1 or itself, that is, having no other factors. There is an infinite number of primes, the first ten of which are 2, 3, 5, 7, 11, 13, 17, 19, 23, and 29 (by definition, the number 1 is excluded from the set of prime numbers). The number 2 is the only even prime because all other even numbers have 2 as a factor.

Over the centuries mathematicians have sought general methods (algorithms) for calculating primes, from Eratosthenes' sieve to programs on powerful computers. Eratosthenes' method (dating from about 200 BC) is to write in sequence all numbers from 2, then, starting with 2, cross out every second number, thus eliminating numbers that can be divided by 2. Next, starting with 3, cross out every third number (whether or not it has already been crossed out), thus eliminating numbers divisible by 3. Continue the process for 5, 7, 11, 13, and so on. Numbers that remain are primes.

In 1989 researchers at Amdahl Corporation, Sunnyvale, California, calculated the largest

prime ministers of Britain

Sir Robert Walpole	(Whig)	1721
Earl of Wilmington	(Whig)	1742
Henry Pelham	(Whig)	1743
Duke of Newcastle	(Whig)	1754
Duke of Devonshire	(Whig)	1756
Duke of Newcastle	(Whig)	1757
Earl of Bute	(Tory)	1762
George Grenville	(Whig)	1763
Marquess of Rockingham	(Whig)	1765
Duke of Grafton	(Whig)	1766
Lord North	(Tory)	1770
Marquess of Rockingham	(Whig)	1782
Earl of Shelbourne	(Whig)	1782
Duke of Portland	(Coalition)	1783
William Pitt	(Tory)	1783
Henry Addington	(Tory)	1801
William Pitt	(Tory)	1804
Lord Grenville	(Whig)	1806
Duke of Portland	(Tory)	1807
Spencer Perceval	(Tory)	1809
Earl of Liverpool	(Tory)	1812
George Canning	(Tory)	1827
Viscount Goderich	(Tory)	1827
Duke of Wellington	(Tory)	1828
Earl Grey	(Whig)	1830
Viscount Melbourne	(Whig)	1834
Sir Robert Peel	(Conservative)	1834
Viscount Melbourne	(Whig)	1835
Sir Robert Peel	(Conservative)	1841
Lord J Russell	(Liberal)	1846
Earl of Derby	(Conservative)	1852
Lord Aberdeen	(Peelite)	1852
Viscount Palmerston	(Liberal)	1855
Earl of Derby	(Conservative)	1858
Viscount Palmerston	(Liberal)	1859
Lord J Russell	(Liberal)	1865
Earl of Derby	(Conservative)	1866
Benjamin Disraeli	(Conservative)	1868
W E Gladstone	(Liberal)	1868
Benjamin Disraeli	(Conservative)	1874
W E Gladstone	(Liberal)	1880
Marquess of Salisbury	(Conservative)	1885
W E Gladstone	(Liberal)	1886
Marquess of Salisbury	(Conservative)	1886
W E Gladstone	(Liberal)	1892
Earl of Rosebery	(Liberal)	1894
Marquess of Salisbury	(Conservative)	1895
Sir H Campbell-Bannerman	(Liberal)	1905
H H Asquith	(Liberal)	1908
H H Asquith	(Coalition)	1915
D Lloyd George	(Coalition)	1916
A Bonar Law	(Conservative)	1922
Stanley Baldwin	(Conservative)	1923
Ramsay MacDonald	(Labour)	1924
Stanley Baldwin	(Conservative)	1924
Ramsay MacDonald	(Labour)	1929
Ramsay MacDonald	(National)	1931
Stanley Baldwin	(National)	1935
N Chamberlain	(National)	1937
Sir Winston Churchill	(Coalition)	1940
Clement Attlee	(Labour)	1945
Sir Winston Churchill	(Conservative)	1951
Sir Anthony Eden	(Conservative)	1955
Harold Macmillan	(Conservative)	1957
Sir Alec Douglas-Home	(Conservative)	1963
Harold Wilson	(Labour)	1964
Edward Heath	(Conservative)	1970
Harold Wilson	(Labour)	1974
James Callaghan	(Labour)	1976
Margaret Thatcher	(Conservative)	1979
John Major	(Conservative)	1990

known prime number. It has 65,087 digits, and is more than a trillion trillion trillion times as large as the previous record holder. It took over a year of computation to locate the number and prove it was a prime.

prime rate the interest rate charged by commercial banks to their best customers. It is the lowest interest or base rate on which other rates are calculated according to the risk involved. Only borrowers who have the highest credit rating qualify for the prime rate.

Primitivism the influence on modern art (Kirchner, Modigliani, Picasso, and others) of aboriginal and folk cultures.

Primo de Rivera Miguel 1870–1930. Spanish soldier and politician, dictator from 1923 as well as premier from 1925. He was captain-general of Catalonia when he led a coup against the ineffective monarchy and became virtual dictator of Spain with the support of Alfonso XIII. He resigned 1930.

Primorye territory of the USSR in SE Siberia on the Sea of Japan; area 64,079 sq mi/165,900 sq km; population (1985) 2,136,000; capital is Vladivostok. Timber and coal are produced.

primrose any plant of the genus *Primula*, family Primulaceae, with showy five-lobed, tube-shaped flowers. The common primrose *P. vulgaris* is a woodland plant, native to Europe, bearing pale yellow flowers in spring. Related to it is the ◊cowslip.

prince a royal or noble title. In Rome and medieval Italy it was used as the title of certain officials, for example, *princeps senatus* (Latin "leader of the Senate"). The title was granted to the king's sons in 15th century France, and in England from Henry VII's time.

Prince Hal (Harold) 1928– . US director of musicals such as *Cabaret* 1968 and *Follies* 1971 on Broadway in New York, and *Evita* 1978 and *Sweeney Todd* 1980 in London's West End.

Prince Adopted name of Prince Rogers Nelson 1960– . US pop musician who composes, arranges, and produces his own records and often plays all the instruments. His albums, including *1999* 1982 and *Purple Rain* 1984, contain elements of rock, funk, and jazz.

His band, the Revolution, broke up after four years in 1986. His hits include "Little Red Corvette" from *1999*, "Kiss" from *Parade* 1986, and "Sign O' The Times" from the album of the same name 1987.

Prince Edward Island province of E Canada

area 2,200 sq mi/5,700 sq km

capital Charlottetown

features named after Prince Edward of Kent, father of Queen Victoria; Prince Edward Island National Park; Summerside Lobster Carnival

products potatoes, dairy products, lobsters, oysters, farm vehicles

population (1986) 127,000

history first recorded visit by Cartier 1534, who called it Isle St-Jean; settled by French; taken by British 1758; annexed to Nova Scotia 1763; separate colony 1769; settled by Scottish 1803; joined Confederation 1873.

In the late 1980s, there was controversy about whether to build a bridge to the mainland.

Princeton borough in Mercer County, W central New Jersey, 50 mi/80 km SW of New York; population (1990) 13,198. The seat of Princeton University, founded 1746 at Elizabethtown and moved to Princeton 1756.

Site of important Revolutionary War battle 1777.

Prince *US pop star Prince in concert, 1986.*

Prince Edward Island

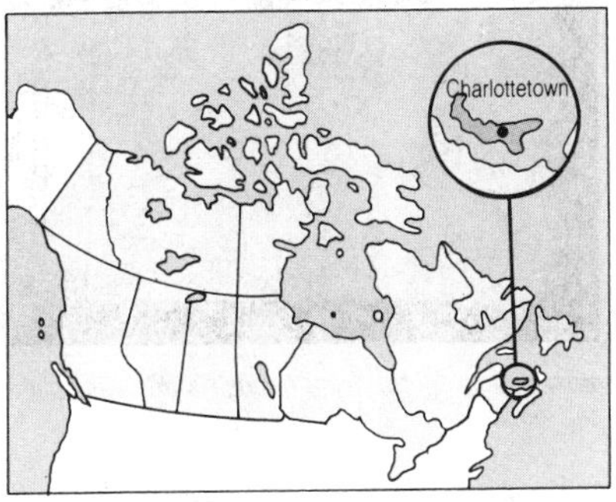
Charlottetown

Prince William Sound a channel in the Gulf of Alaska, extending 125 mi/200 km NW from Kayak Island. In March 1989 the oil tanker *Exxon Valdez* ran aground here, spilling 12 million gallons of crude oil in what was reckoned to be the world's greatest oil-pollution disaster.

printed circuit board (PCB) electrical circuit created by laying (printing) "tracks" of a conductor such as copper on to one or both sides of an insulating board. The PCB was invented 1936 by the Austrian scientist Paul Eisler, and was first used on a large scale in 1948.

Components such as integrated circuits (chips), resistors and capacitors can be soldered to the surface of the board (surface-mounted) or, more commonly, attached by inserting their connecting pins or wires into holes drilled in the board.

printed circuit board

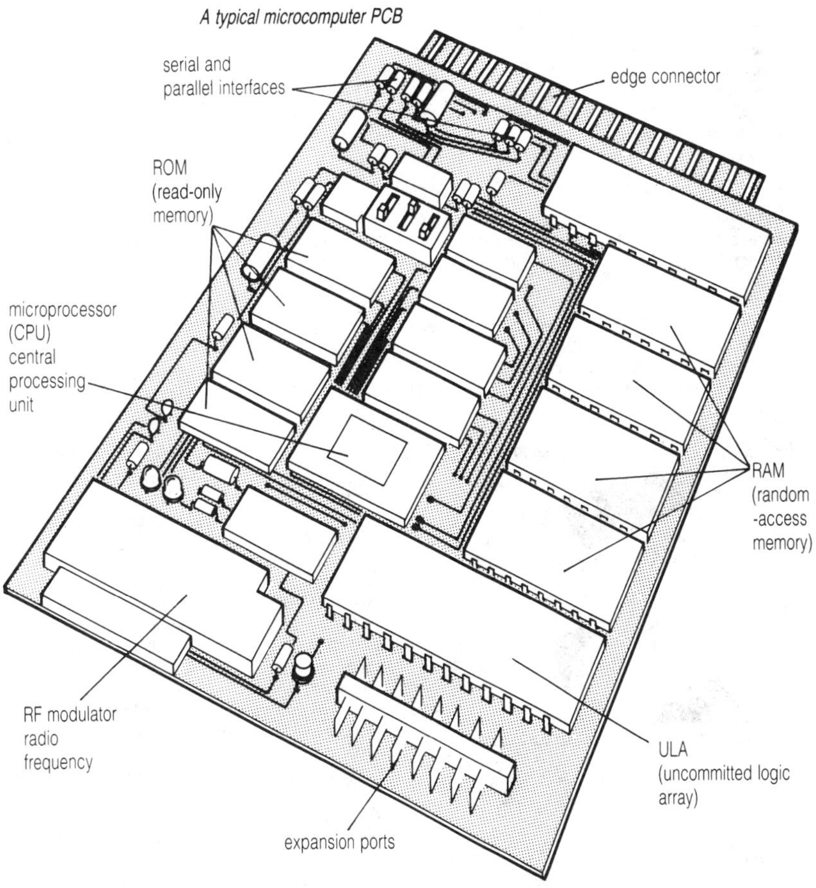
A typical microcomputer PCB
serial and
parallel interfaces
edge connector
ROM
(read-only
memory)
microprocessor
(CPU)
central
processing
unit
RAM
(random
-access
memory)
RF modulator
radio
frequency
ULA
(uncommitted logic
array)
expansion ports

printer in computing, an output device for producing printed copies of text or graphics. Types include the daisywheel, which produces good quality text, but no graphics; the dot matrix, which creates character patterns from a matrix of small dots, producing text and graphics; and the ◊laser printer, which produces high-quality text and graphics.

printing the reproduction of text or illustrative material on paper, as in books or newspapers, or on an increasing variety of materials; for example, on plastic containers. The first printing used woodblocks, followed by carved wood type or molded metal type and hand-operated presses. Modern printing is effected by electronically controlled machinery. Current printing processes include electronic phototypesetting with ◊offset printing, and ◊gravure print.

In China the art of printing from a single wooden block was known by the 6th century AD, and moveable type was being used by the 11th century. In Europe printing was unknown for another three centuries, and it was only in the 15th century that moveable type was reinvented, traditionally by Johannes ◊Gutenberg in Germany. William ◊Caxton introduced printing to England. There was no further substantial advance until, in the 19th century, steam power replaced hand-operation of printing presses, making possible long "runs"; hand-composition of type (each tiny metal letter was taken from the case and placed individually in the narrow stick that carried one line of text) was replaced by machines operated by a keyboard.

Linotype, a hot-metal process (it produced a line of type in a solid slug) used in newspapers, magazines, and books, was invented by Ottmar Mergenthaler 1886 and commonly used until the 1980s. The Monotype, used in bookwork (it produced a series of individual characters, which could be hand-corrected), was invented by Tolbert Lanston (1844–1913) in the US 1889. Important as these developments were, they represented no fundamental change but simply a faster method of carrying out the same basic typesetting operations. The actual printing process still involved pressing the inked type on to paper, a method called ◊letterpress.

In the 1960s this form of printing began to face increasing competition from ◊offset printing, a method that prints from an inked flat surface, and from the ◊gravure method (used for high-circulation magazines), which uses recessed plates.

The introduction of electronic phototypesetting machines, also in the 1960s, allowed the entire process of setting and correction to be done in the same way that a typist operates, thus eliminating the hot-metal composing room (with its hazardous fumes, lead scraps, and noise) and leaving only the making of plates and the running of the presses to be done traditionally. By the 1970s some final steps were taken to plateless printing, using various processes, such as a computer-controlled laser beam, or continuous jets of ink acoustically broken up into tiny equal-sized drops, which are electrostatically charged under computer control.

printmaking creating a picture or design by ◊printing from a plate (block, stone, or sheet) that holds ink or color. The oldest form of print is the woodcut, common in medieval Europe, followed by line ◊engraving from the 15th century, and ◊etching from the 17th century; colored woodblock prints flourished in Japan from the 18th century. ◊Lithography was invented 1796.

The German artist Dürer created outstanding woodcuts and line engravings and the Dutch painter Rembrandt was one of the first major artists to produce etchings.

prion an exceptionally small microorganism, a hundred times smaller than a virus. Composed of protein, and without any detectable amount of nucleic acid (genetic material), it is thought to cause diseases such as scrapie in sheep, and certain degenerative diseases of the nervous system in humans. How it can operate without nucleic acid is not yet known.

Researchers at the University of California 1982 first identified prions in living tissue.

prior, prioress in a Christian religious community, the deputy of either an abbot or abbess, responsible for discipline. In certain Roman Catholic orders, it is the principal of a monastery or convent.

Pripet (Russian *Pripyat*) river in W USSR, a tributary of the river Dnieper, which it joins 50 mi/80 km above Kiev, Ukraine, after a course of about 500 mi/800 km. The Pripet marshes near Pinsk were of strategic importance in both world wars.

printing

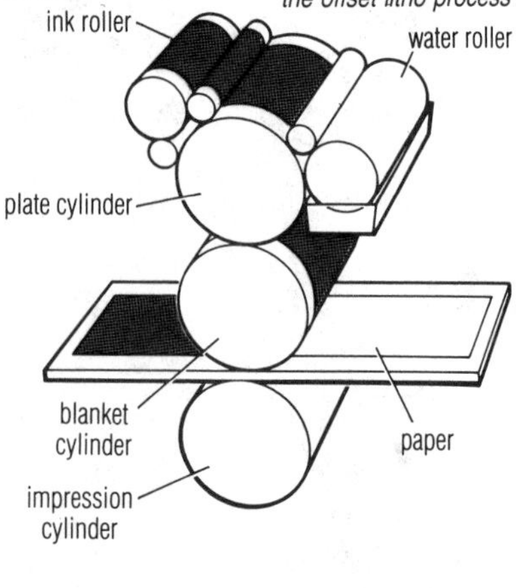
the offset litho process
ink roller
water roller
plate cylinder
blanket cylinder
paper
impression cylinder

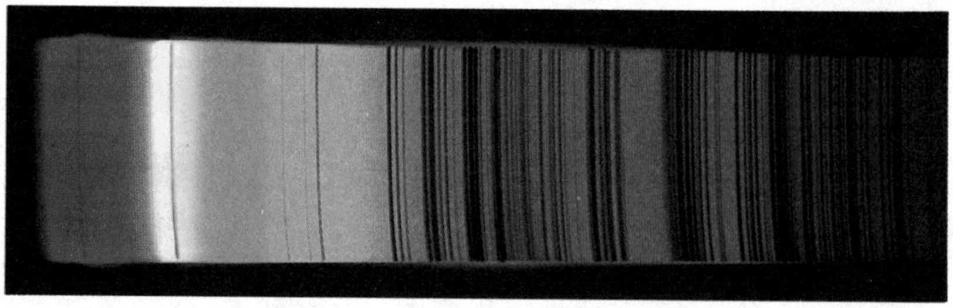

prism *White light passing through a prism is split into its constituent wavelengths, forming the colors of the rainbow.*

prism in mathematics, a solid figure whose cross section is constant in planes drawn perpendicular to its axis. A cube, for example, is a rectangular prism with all faces (bases and sides) the same shape and size.

prism in optics, a triangular block of transparent material (plastic, glass, silica) commonly used to "bend" a ray of light or split a beam into its spectral colors. Prisms are used as mirrors to define the optical path in binoculars, camera viewfinders, and periscopes. The dispersive property of prisms is used in the ◊spectroscope.

prison place of confinement for those accused of and/or convicted of contravening the law; after conviction most jurisdictions claim to aim at rehabilitation and deterrence as well as punishment. For major crimes, life imprisonment or death may be the sentence. Parole and probation programs exist, and "work-release" furlough programs allow convicts to work outside the prison or make family visits during their sentences.

The prison population in the US rose dramatically in the 1980s as stronger drug laws were passed and longer sentences imposed in that area. One result has been massive overcrowding, and several states are under court order not to exceed a specified number of prisoners. In some cases this means that a current prisoner must be released, often after serving only a fraction of the sentence, to make room for a new arrival. The US prison population is about 800,000.

Development of US prisons Loss of liberty was seen from the beginning as a punishment in the US. Prior to the late 18th century, prisons were viewed as a temporary restriction before exile, execution, or flogging was imposed as punishment. The US Constitution prohibited "cruel or unusual punishment," ending many of these methods of punishment; the isolated prison then came to be viewed as an institution in which discipline might be instilled and temptation removed. The system developed 1817 in Auburn, New York (to confine prisoners at night but require them to work during the day), was widely emulated because the use of prisoner labor reduced the costs and, it was hoped, inculcated respect for authority.

The modern system pursues rehabilitation as its goal by providing work (for pay), training, education, counseling, and the prospect of early release through the parole and probation systems. However, the high recidivism rates suggest that these programs do little to counter the background causes of criminal behavior.

Priština capital of Kosovo autonomous province, S Serbia, Yugoslavia; population (1981) 216,000.

Pritchett V(ictor) S(awdon) 1900– . English short-story writer, novelist, and critic, with an often witty and satirical style.

His short stories were gathered in *Collected Stories* 1982 and *More Collected Stories* 1983. His critical works include *The Living Novel* 1946 and biographies of the Russian writers Turgenev 1977 and Chekhov 1988.

privacy the right of the individual to be free from secret surveillance (by scientific devices or other means) and from the disclosure to unauthorized persons of personal data, as accumulated in computer databanks. Always an issue complicated by considerations of state security, public welfare (in the case of criminal activity), and other factors, it has been rendered more complex by present-day technology.

computer data All Western countries now have computerized-data protection. In the US the Privacy Act 1974 requires that there should be no secret databanks and that agencies handling data must ensure their reliability and prevent misuse (information gained for one purpose must not be used for another). The public must be able to find out what is recorded and how it is used, and be able to correct it. Under the Freedom of Information Act 1967, citizens and organizations have the right to examine unclassified files.

private enterprise sector of the economy in which economic activity is initiated through private capital and pursued for private profit. It is distinguished from ◊public spending, although public funds are often funneled into private enterprises, as with defense contractors or infrastructure development (public works contractors).

privateer a privately owned and armed ship commissioned by a state to attack enemy vessels. The crews of such ships were, in effect, legalized pirates; they were not paid but received a share of the spoils. Privateering existed from ancient times until the 19th century, when it was declared illegal by the Declaration of Paris 1856.

private school alternate name in England for a fee-paying independent school.

privatization the selling or transfer into private hands of state-owned, or public, assets and services (notably nationalized industries). Privatization of services involves the government contracting private firms to supply services previously supplied by public authorities. The proponents of privatization argue that the public benefits from theoretically greater efficiency from firms already in the competitive market; this also releases resources more appropriate for government use. Those against privatization believe that it transfers a country's assets from all the people to a controlling minority, that public utilities such as gas and water become private monopolies, and that a profit-making state-owned company raises prices.

The trend has grown worldwide, since inefficient state-run enterprises with little accountability required ever-larger subsidies. Governments in the US, the UK, France, Japan, and Italy have pursued the policy, as have a number of developing states that seek to stimulate economic activity. Poland and other East European states are moving away from the Communist system of state-run enterprises toward a free-market economy, in hopes of producing more and higher quality goods and services. See also ◊deregulation, ◊monetarism.

privet evergreen shrubs of the genus *Ligustrum* of the olive family Oleaceae, with dark green leaves, including the European common privet *L. vulgare*, with white flowers and black berries, naturalized in North America, and the native North American California privet *L. ovalifolium*, also known as hedge privet.

Privy Council originally the chief royal officials of the

Norman kings in Britain which, under the Tudors and early Stuarts, became the chief governing body. It was replaced from 1688 by the ◊cabinet, originally a committee of the council, and the council itself now retains only formal powers in issuing royal proclamations and orders-in-council. Cabinet ministers are automatically members, and it is presided over by the Lord President of the Council.

Prix Goncourt French literary prize for fiction, given by the Académie ◊Goncourt from 1903.

probability the likelihood or chance an event will occur, often expressed as odds, or in mathematics, numerically as a fraction or decimal. In general, the probability that *n* particular events will happen out of a total of *m* possible events is *n*/*m*. A certainty has a probability of 1; an impossibility has a probability of 0. Empirical probability is defined as the number of successful events divided by the total possible number of events.

In tossing a fair coin, the chance that it will land "heads" is the same as the chance that it will land "tails," that is, 1 to 1 or even; mathematically, this probability is expressed as ½ or 0.5. The odds against any chosen number coming up on the roll of a fair die are 6 to 1; the probability is ⅙ or 0.1666... . If two dice are rolled there are $6 \times 6 = 36$ different possible combinations. The probability of a double (two numbers the same) is 6/36 or ⅙ since there are six doubles in the 36 events: (1,1), (2,2), (3,3), (4,4), (5,5), and (6,6).

Probability theory was developed by the French mathematicians Blaise Pascal and Pierre de Fermat in the 17th century, initially in response to a request to calculate the odds of being dealt various hands at cards. Today probability plays a major part in the mathematics of atomic theory and finds application in insurance and statistical studies.

probate system for the administration of inheritance. Generally the function of probate (sometimes surrogate's) courts, probate determines the validity of wills and the satisfaction of requirements of inheritance law. In the cases of persons dying without wills (intestacy), probate courts appoint administrators of estates.

probation in law, the placing of offenders under the supervision of probation officers in the community, as an alternative to prison.

procedure in computing, a small part of a computer program, which performs a specific task, such as clearing the screen or sorting a file. In some programming languages there is an overlap between procedures, ◊functions, and subroutines. Careful use of procedures is an element of ◊structured programming. A procedural language, such as BASIC, is one in which the programmer describes a task in terms of how it is to be done, as opposed to a declarative language, such as PROLOG, in which it is described in terms of the required result.

processing cycle in computing, the sequence of steps performed repeatedly by a computer in the execution of a program. The computer's CPU (central processing unit) continuously works through a loop, involving fetching a program instruction from memory, fetching any data it needs, operating on the data, and storing the result in the memory, before fetching another program instruction.

processor in computing, another name for the central processing unit (◊CPU) or ◊microprocessor of a computer.

proconsul Roman ◊consul who went on to govern a province when his term ended.

Proconsul prehistoric ape skull found on Rusinga Island in Lake Victoria (Nyanza), E Africa, by Mary ◊Leakey. It is believed to be 20 million years old.

Procrustes (Greek "the stretcher") in Greek mythology, a robber who tied his victims to a bed; if they were too tall for it, he cut off the ends of their legs, and if they were too short, he stretched them.

Procyon or ***Alpha Canis Minoris*** brightest star in the constellation Canis Minor and the eighth brightest star in the sky. Procyon is a white star 11.5 light-years from Earth, with a mass of 1.7 Suns. It has a ◊white dwarf companion that orbits it every 40 years.

producer price index (PPI) measure of price changes. In 1978 the US government revised its reporting of wholesale price indexes to reflect separate price changes at three stages of the production process. Crude materials, intermediate goods, and finished goods were indexed separately, and each of these is a PPI. The finished goods index, the most cited PPI, and the ◊consumer price index are the two most common measures of inflation and cost of living.

productivity, biological in an ecosystem, the amount of material in the food chain produced by the primary producers (plants) that is available for consumption by animals. Plants turn carbon dioxide and water into sugars and other complex carbon compounds by means of photosynthesis. Their net productivity is defined as the quantity of carbon compounds formed, less the quantity used up by the respiration of the plant itself.

profit-sharing a system whereby an employer pays workers a share of the company's profits, which is often a percentage based on annual salary and invested by the employer in a retirement plan operated or overseen by the employer. It may be paid as cash or shares of stock in the firm. It originated in France in the early 19th century and was widely practiced for a time within the cooperative movement.

progesterone ◊steroid hormone that occurs in vertebrates. In mammals, it regulates the menstrual cycle and pregnancy. Progesterone is secreted by the corpus luteum (the ruptured Graafian follicle of a discharged ovum).

program music music that tells a story, depicts a scene or painting, or illustrates a literary or philosophical idea, such as Richard Strauss' *Don Juan*.

programming in computing, the activity of writing instructions in a programming language for the control of a computer. Applications programming is for end-user programs, such as accounts programs or word-processing packages. Systems programming is for operating systems and the like, which are concerned more with the internal workings of the computer.

There are several programming styles:

Procedural programming, in which programs are written as lists of instructions the computer obeys in sequence, is by far the most popular. It is the "natural" style, closely matching the computer's own sequential operation.

Declarative programming, such as in the programming language PROLOG, does not describe how to solve a problem, but rather describes the logical structure of the problem. Running such a program is more like proving an assertion than following a procedure.

Functional programming is a style based largely on the definition of functions. There are very few functional programming languages, HOPE and ML being the most widely used, though many more conventional languages (for example C) make extensive use of functions.

Object-oriented programming, the most recently developed style, involves viewing a program as a collection of objects that behave in certain ways when they are passed certain "messages." For example, an object might be defined to represent a table of figures, which will be displayed on screen when a "display" message is received.

programming language in computing, a special notation in which instructions for controlling a computer are written. Programming languages are designed to be easy for people to write and read, but must be capable of being mechanically translated (by a ◊compiler or an ◊interpreter) into the ◊machine code that the computer can execute.

program trading in finance, buying and selling a group of shares using a computer program to generate orders automatically whenever there is an appreciable movement in prices.

One form in use in the US in 1989 was index arbitrage, in which a program traded automatically whenever there was a difference between New York and Chicago prices of an equivalent number of shares. Program trading comprised some 14% of daily trading on the New York Stock Exchange by volume in Sept 1989, but was widely criticized for lessening market stability. It has been blamed, among other factors, for the Stock Market crashes of 1987 and 1989.

progression sequence of numbers each formed by a specific relationship to its predecessor. An arithmetical progression has numbers that increase or decrease by a common sum or difference (for example, 2, 4, 6, 8); a geometric progression has numbers each bearing a fixed ratio to its predecessor (for example, 3, 6, 12, 24); and a harmonic progression is a sequence with numbers whose ◊reciprocals are in arithmetical progression, for example 1, ½, ⅓, ¼.

progressive education teaching methods that take as their starting point children's own aptitudes and interests, and encourage them to follow their own investigations and lines of inquiry.

Progressivism in US history, the name of both a reform movement and a political party, active in the two decades before World War I. Mainly middle-class and urban-based, Progressives secured legislation at national, state, and local levels to improve the democratic system, working conditions, and welfare provision.

Prohibition in US history, the period 1920–33 when the 18th Amendment to the US Constitution was in force, and the manufacture, transportation, and sale of intoxicating liquors were illegal. It represented the culmination of a long campaign by Populists, Progressives, temperance societies, and the Anti-Saloon League. This led to ◊bootlegging (the illegal distribution of liquor, often illicitly distilled), widespread disdain for the law, speakeasies, and greatly increased organized crime activity, especially in Chicago and towns near the Canadian border. Public opinion insisted on repeal 1933.

The 18th Amendment was enforced by the Volstead Act 1919. Prohibition was repealed by the the 21st Amendment 1933.

projection see ◊map projection.

projector any apparatus that projects a picture on to a screen. In a slide projector, a lamp shines a light through the photographic slide or transparency, and a projection ◊lens throws an enlarged image of the slide onto the screen. A film projector has similar optics, but incorporates a mechanism that holds the film still while light is transmitted through each frame (picture). A shutter covers the film when it moves between frames.

prokaryote in biology, an organism whose cells lack organelles (specialized segregated structures such as nuclei, mitochondria, and chloroplasts). Prokaryote DNA is not arranged in chromosomes but forms a coiled structure called a nucleoid. The prokaryotes comprise only the bacteria and cyanobacteria; all other organisms are eukaryotes.

Prokhorov Aleksandr 1916– . Russian physicist whose fundamental work on microwaves in 1955 led to the construction of the first practical ◊maser (the microwave equivalent of the laser) by Charles ◊Townes, for which they shared the 1964 Nobel Prize for Physics.

Prokofiev Sergey (Sergeyevich) 1891–1953. Soviet composer. His music includes operas such as *The Love for Three Oranges* 1921; ballets for ◊Diaghilev, including *Romeo and Juliet* 1935; seven symphonies including the *Classical Symphony* 1916–17; music for films; piano and violin concertos; songs and cantatas (for example, that composed for the 30th anniversary of the October Revolution); and *Peter and the Wolf* 1936.

Prokopyevsk chief coal-mining city of the Kuzbas, Siberia, USSR, on the river Aba; population (1987) 278,000.

prolapse displacement of an organ due to the effects of strain in weakening the supporting tissues. The term is most often used with regard to the rectum (due to chronic bowel problems) or the uterus (following several pregnancies).

proletariat in Marxist theory, those classes in society that possess no property, and therefore depend on the sale of their labor or expertise (as opposed to the capitalists or bourgeoisie, who own the means of production, and the petty bourgeoisie, or working small-property owners). They are usually divided into the industrial, agricultural, and intellectual proletariat.

The term is derived from Latin *proletarii*, "the class possessing no property," whose contribution to the state was considered to be their offspring, *proles*.

PROLOG (acronym from programming in logic) computer-programming language based on logic. Invented in 1971 at the University of Marseilles, France, it did not achieve widespread use until more than ten years later. It is used mainly for ◊artificial intelligence programming.

PROM (acronym from programmable read-only memory) in computing, a memory device in the form of a silicon chip that can be programmed to hold information permanently. PROM chips are empty of information when manufactured, unlike ROM chips, which have memories built into them. Other memory devices are ◊EPROM and ◊RAM.

Prometheus in Greek mythology, a ◊Titan who stole fire from heaven for the human race. In revenge, Zeus had him chained to a rock where an eagle came each day to feast on his liver, which grew back each night, until he was rescued by ◊Hercules.

promethium radioactive, metallic element of the ◊lanthanide series, symbol Pm, atomic number 61, atomic weight 145. It occurs in nature only in extremely minute amounts, produced as a fission product/byproduct of uranium in ◊pitchblende and other uranium ores; for a long time it was considered not to occur in nature. The longest-lived isotope has a half-life of slightly more than 20 years.

Promethium is synthesized by neutron bombardment of neodymium and is a product of the fission of uranium, thorium, or plutonium; it can be isolated in large amounts from the fission-product debris of uranium fuel in nuclear reactors. It is used in phosphorescent paints and as an X-ray source.

It was named in 1949 for Prometheus, the Greek Titan, by G M Coryell for the element isolated by US physicists J A Marinsky and L E Glendenin.

prominence bright cloud of gas projecting from the Sun into space 60,000 mi/100,000 km or more. Quiescent prominences last for months and are held in place by magnetic fields in the Sun's corona. Surge prominences shoot gas into space at speeds of 600 mps/1,000 kps. Loop prominences are gases falling back to the Sun's surface after a solar ◊flare.

promissory note a written promise to pay on demand, or at a fixed future time, a specific sum of money to a named person or bearer. Like a check, it is negotiable if endorsed by the payee. A commercial paper is a form of promissory note that can be bought and sold. These forms of payment are usually issued by large corporations at times when credit is otherwise difficult to obtain. It is often those who are inferior credit risks who are asked to sign promissory notes.

pronghorn ruminant mammal *Antilocapra americana* constituting the family Antilocapridae, native to the W US. It is not a true antelope. It is light brown and about 3 ft/1 m high. It sheds its horns annually and can reach speeds of 60 mph/100 kph. The loss of prairies to agriculture, combined with excessive hunting, has brought this unique animal close to extinction.

pronghorn

pronoun in grammar, a ◊part of speech that is used in place of a noun, usually to save repetition of the noun (for example "The people arrived around nine o'clock. *They* behaved as though we were expecting *them*").

They, them, he, and *she* are personal pronouns (representing people); *this/these,* and *that/those* are demonstrative pronouns (demonstrating or pointing to something: "*this* book and not *that* book." Words like *that* and *who* can be relative pronouns in sentences like "She said *that* she was coming" and "Tell me *who* did it" relating one clause to another), and *myself* and *himself* are reflexive pronouns (reflecting back to a person, as in "He did it *himself*").

pronunciation the way in which words are rendered into human speech sounds; either a language as a whole ("French pronunciation") or a particular word or name ("what is the pronunciation of *allophony*?"). The pronunciation of languages forms the academic subject of ◊phonetics.

propaganda the systematic spreading (propagation) of information or disinformation, usually to promote a religious or political doctrine with the intention of instilling particular attitudes or responses.

Examples of the use of propaganda are the racial doctrines put forth by Nazism before and during World War II and some of the ideas and strategies propagated by the US and the Soviet Union during the ◊Cold War (1945–90). There are various forms of propaganda: black (a pack of lies), gray (half-truths and distortions), and white (the truth).

propane C_3H_8 gaseous hydrocarbon of the ◊alkane series, found in petroleum and used as fuel.

propanol or ***propyl alcohol*** third member of the homologous series of ◊alcohols. Propanol is usually a mixture of two isomeric compounds (see ◊isomer): propan-1-ol ($CH_3CH_2CH_2OH$) and propan-2-ol ($CH_3CHOHCH_3$). Both are colorless liquids that can be mixed with water and are used in perfumery.

propanone CH_3COCH_3 (common name acetone) colorless inflammable liquid used extensively as a solvent, as in nail-polish remover. It boils at 133.7°F/56.5°C, mixes with water in all proportions, and has a characteristic odor.

propellant the substance burned in a rocket for propulsion. Two propellants are used; oxidizer and fuel are stored in separate tanks and pumped independently into the combustion chamber. Liquid oxygen (oxidizer) and liquid hydrogen (fuel) are common propellants, used, for example, in the space shuttle main engines. The explosive charge that propels a projectile from a gun is also called a propellant.

propeller screwlike device used to propel some ships and airplanes. A propeller has a number of curved blades that describe a helical path as they rotate with the hub, and accelerates fluid (liquid or gas) backwards during rotation. Reaction to this backward movement of fluid sets up a propulsive thrust forwards. The marine screw propeller was developed by Francis Pettit Smith in Britain and Swedish-born John Ericson in the US and was first used 1839.

The airscrew is used to propel piston or turboprop ◊airplanes.

propene $CH_3CH{:}CH_2$ (common name propylene) second member of the alkene series of hydrocarbons. A colorless, flammable gas, it is widely used by industry to make organic chemicals, including polypropylene plastics.

propenoic acid $H_2C{:}CHCOOH$ (common name acrylic acid) acid obtained from the aldehyde propenal (acrolein) derived from glycerol or fats. Glasslike thermoplastic resins are made by polymerizing ◊esters of propenoic acid or methyl propenoic acid and used for transparent components, lenses, and dentures. Other acrylic compounds are used for adhesives, artificial fibers, and artists' acrylic paint.

proper motion the gradual change in the position of a star that results from its motion in orbit around our Galaxy, the Milky Way. Proper motions are slight and undetectable to the naked eye, but can be accurately measured on telescopic photographs taken many years apart. Barnard's Star is the star with the largest proper motion, 10.3 arc seconds per year.

Propertius Sextus c. 47–15 BC. Roman elegiac poet, a member of ◊Maecenas' circle, who wrote of his love for his mistress "Cynthia."

property the right to title and to control the use of a thing (such as land, a building, a work of art, or a computer program). In US law, a distinction is made between real property, which involves a degree of geographical fixity, and personal property, which does not. Property is never absolute, since any society places limits on an individual's property (such as the right to transfer that property to another). Different societies have held widely varying interpretations of the nature of property and the extent of the rights of the owner to that property.

prophet a person thought to speak from divine inspiration or who foretells the future.

In the Bible, one of the succession of saints and seers who preached and prophesied in the Hebrew kingdoms in Palestine from the 8th century BC until the suppression of Jewish independence in 586 BC, and possibly later. The chief prophets were Elijah, Amos, Hosea, and Isaiah. The prophetic books of the Old Testament constitute a division of the Hebrew Bible. In Islam, ◊Mohammed is believed to be the last and greatest of a long line of prophets beginning with Adam and including Moses and Jesus.

prophylaxis any measure taken to prevent disease, including exercise and ◊vaccination. Prophylactic (preventive) medicine is an aspect of public-health provision that is receiving increasing attention.

proportion two variable quantities x and y are proportional if, for all values of x, $y = kx$, where k is a constant. This means that if x increases, y increases in a linear fashion. A graph of x against y would be a straight line passing through the origin (the point $x = 0$, $y = 0$). y is inversely proportional to x if the graph of y against $1/x$ is a straight line through the origin. The corresponding equation is $y = k/x$. Many laws of science relate quantities that are proportional (for example ◊Boyle's Law).

prop root or ***stilt root*** a modified root that grows from the lower part of a stem or trunk down to the ground, providing a plant with extra support. Prop roots are common on some woody plants, such as mangroves, and also occur on a few herbaceous plants, such as corn. Buttress roots are a type of prop root found at the base of tree trunks, extended and flattened along the upper

prosthesis

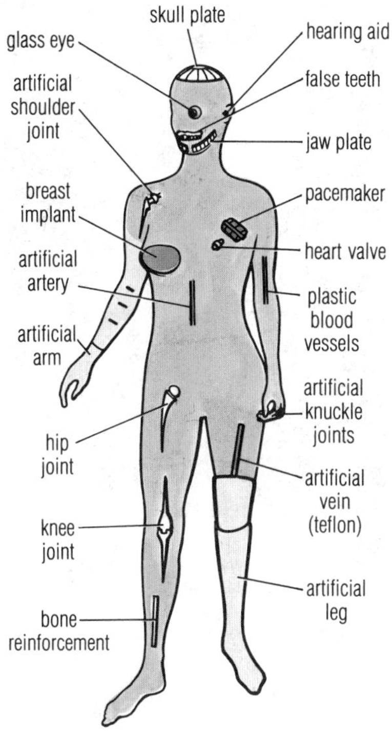
skull plate
glass eye
hearing aid
artificial shoulder joint
false teeth
jaw plate
breast implant
pacemaker
heart valve
artificial artery
plastic blood vessels
artificial arm
artificial knuckle joints
hip joint
artificial vein (teflon)
knee joint
artificial leg
bone reinforcement

edge to form massive triangular buttresses; they are common on tropical trees.

propyl alcohol common name for ◊propanol.

propylene common name for ◊propene.

prose spoken or written language without metrical regularity; in literature, prose corresponds more closely to the patterns of everyday speech than ◊poetry. In modern literature, however, the distinction between verse and prose is not always clear cut.

In Western literature prose was traditionally used for what is today called nonfiction—that is, history, biography, essays, and so on—while verse was used for imaginative literature. Prose came into its own as a vehicle for fiction with the rise of the ◊novel in the 18th century.

Proserpina Roman equivalent of ◊Persephone, goddess of the underworld.

Prost Alain 1955–. French racing-car driver. He won 44 races from 168 starts, and was world champion 1985, 1986, and 1989.

He raced in Formula One events from 1980 and he had his first Grand Prix win 1981 (French GP) driving a Renault. In 1984 he began driving for the McLaren team.

prostaglandin any of a group of complex fatty acids that act as messenger substances between cells. Effects include stimulating the contraction of smooth muscle (for example, of the womb during birth), regulating the production of stomach acid, and modifying hormonal activity. In excess, prostaglandins may produce inflammatory disorders such as arthritis. Synthetic prostaglandins are used to induce labor in humans and domestic animals.

The analgesic actions of substances such as aspirin are due to inhibition of prostaglandin synthesis.

prostate gland gland surrounding, and opening into, the urethra at the base of the bladder in male mammals. The prostate gland produces an alkaline fluid that is released during ejaculation; this fluid activates sperm, and prevents their clumping together.

prosthesis the replacement of a body part with an artificial substitute. Prostheses in the form of artificial limbs, such as wooden legs and metal hooks for hands, have been used for centuries, although artificial limbs are now more natural-looking and comfortable to wear. The comparatively new field of ◊bionics has developed myoelectric, or bionic, arms, which are electronically operated and worked by minute electrical impulses from body muscles. Other prostheses include hearing aids, false teeth and eyes, and for the heart, a ◊pacemaker and plastic heart valves and blood vessels.

prostitution receipt of money for sexual acts. Society's attitude toward it varies according to place and period. In some countries, tolerance is combined with licensing of brothels and health checks on the prostitutes (both male and female).

In the US, laws vary from state to state, with Nevada having some legalized prostitution. Where it remains illegal, it is often associated with drug abuse, street crime, and exploitation of children, and many communities expend large resources in an effort to control it.

protactinium (Latin *proto* "before" + actinium) a silver-gray, radioactive, metallic element of the ◊actinide series, symbol Pa, atomic number 91, atomic weight 231.036. It occurs in nature in very small quantities, in ◊pitchblende and other uranium ores. It has 14 known isotopes; the longest-lived, Pa-231, has a half-life of 32,480 years. The name comes from the Latin *proto* (before) and actinium, since it decays into the element actinium.

The element was discovered in 1913 (Pa-234, with a half-life of only 1.2 minutes) as a product of uranium decay by Kasimir Fajans and O Göhring; other isotopes were found in later years and the name was officially adopted in 1949, although it had been in use since 1918.

protandry in a flower, the state where the male reproductive organs reach maturity before those of the female. This is a common method of avoiding self-fertilization. See also ◊protogyny.

protease general term for an enzyme capable of splitting proteins. Examples include pepsin, found in the stomach, and trypsin, found in the small intestine.

protectionism in economics, the imposition of heavy duties or import quotas by a government as a means of discouraging the import of foreign goods likely to compete with domestic products. Price controls, quota systems and the reduction of surpluses are among the measures taken for agricultural products in the EC (see ◊agriculture). The opposite practice is ◊free trade.

protectorate formerly in international law, a small state under the direct or indirect control of a larger one. The 20th-century equivalent was a ◊trust territory. In English history the rule of Oliver and Richard ◊Cromwell 1653–59 is referred to as the Protectorate.

protein long-chain molecule composed of amino acids joined by ◊peptide bonds. Proteins are essential to all living organisms. As enzymes they regulate all aspects of metabolism. Structural proteins such as keratin and collagen make up the skin, claws, bones, tendons, and ligaments; muscle proteins produce movement; hemoglobin transports oxygen; and membrane proteins regulate the movement of substances into and out of cells.

For humans, protein is an essential part of the diet; it is found in meat, eggs, and cheese, as well as in beans and other legumes, whole grains, and other plant foods.

pro tem abbreviation for pro tempore (Latin "for the time being").

Proterozoic period of geologic time, 2.5 billion to 590 million years ago, the second division of the Precambrian era. It is defined as the time of simple life, since many rocks dating from this eon show traces of biological activity, and some contain the fossils of bacteria and algae.

Protestantism one of the main divisions of Christianity, which emerged from Roman Catholicism at the ◊Reformation. The chief Protestant denominations are the Episcopalian (Anglican Communion in the UK), Baptists, Christian Scientists, Congregationalists (United Church of Christ), Lutherans, Methodists, Pentecostals, and Presbyterians, with a total membership of about 300 million.

Protestantism takes its name from the protest of Luther and his supporters at the Diet of Spires 1529 against the decision to reaffirm the edict of the Diet of Worms against the Reformation. The ecumenical movement of the 20th century has attempted to reunite various Protestant denominations and, to some extent, the Protestant churches and the Catholic church.

Proteus in Greek mythology, an old man, the warden of the sea beasts of Poseidon, who possessed the gift of prophecy and could transform himself into any form he chose to evade questioning.

prothallus the short-lived gametophyte of many ferns and other ◊pteridophytes. It bears either the male or female sex organs, or both. Typically it is a small, green, flattened structure that is anchored in the soil by several ◊rhizoids and needs damp conditions to survive. The reproductive organs are borne on the lower surface close to the soil. See also ◊alternation of generations.

protist in biology, a single-celled organism which has a ◊eukaryotic cell, but which is not member of the plant, fungal, or animal kingdoms. The main protists are ◊protozoa.

Single-celled photosynthetic organisms, such as diatoms and dinoflagellates, are classified as protists or algae. Recently the term has also been used for members of the kingdom Protoctista, which features in certain five-kingdom classifications of the living world. This kingdom may include slime molds, all algae (seaweeds as well as unicellular forms), and protozoa.

protein

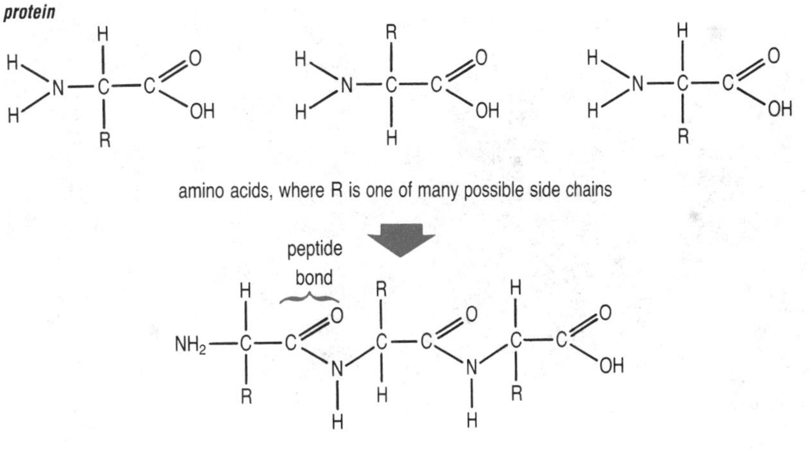
amino acids, where R is one of many possible side chains
peptide bond

protocol in computing, an agreed set of standards for the transfer of data between different devices. They cover transmission speed, format of data, and the signals required to synchronize the transfer. See also ◊interface.

Protocols of Zion forged document containing supposed plans for Jewish world conquest, alleged to have been submitted by ◊Herzl to the first Zionist Congress at Basel 1897, and published in Russia 1905. Although proved to be a forgery 1921, the document was used by Hitler in his anti-Semitic campaign 1933–45.

protogyny in a flower, the state where the female reproductive organs reach maturity before those of the male. Like ◊protandry, this is a method of avoiding self-fertilization, but it is much less common.

proton positively charged ◊elementary particle, a constituent of the nucleus of all atoms. It belongs to the ◊baryon group of ◊hadrons and is composed of two up quarks and one down quark. A proton is extremely long-lived, at least 10^{32} years. It carries a unit positive charge equal to the negative charge of an ◊electron. Its mass is almost 1,836 times that of an electron, or 1.673×10^{-24} g. The number of protons in the atom of an ◊element is equal to the atomic number of that element.

protonema the young ◊gametophyte of a moss, which develops from a germinating spore (see ◊alternation of generations). Typically it is a green, branched, threadlike structure that grows over the soil surface bearing several buds that develop into the characteristic adult moss plants.

proton number alternate name for ◊atomic number.

Proton rocket Soviet space rocket introduced 1965, used to launch heavy satellites, space probes, and the Salyut and *Mir* space stations.

Proton consists of up to four stages as necessary. It has never been used to launch humans into space.

protoplasm the contents of a living cell. Strictly speaking it includes all the discrete structures (organelles) in a cell, but it is often used simply to mean the jellylike material in which these float. The contents of a cell outside the nucleus are called ◊cytoplasm.

protozoan any of a group of single-celled, mainly heterotrophic organisms without rigid cell walls. Some, such as amoebas, ingest other cells, but most are ◊saprotrophs or parasites. They all require a fluid environment, and include ciliates, flagellates, rhizopods, and sporozoans.

protractor instrument used to measure a flat ◊angle.

Proudhon Pierre Joseph 1809–1865. French anarchist, born in Besançon. He sat in the Constituent Assembly of 1848, was imprisoned for three years, and had to go into exile in Brussels. He published *Qu'est-ce que la propriété/What is Property?* 1840 and *Philosophie de la misère/Philosophy of Poverty* 1846; the former contains the dictum "property is theft."

Proust Joseph Louis 1754–1826. French chemist. He was the first to state the principle of constant composition of compounds—that compounds consist of the same proportions of elements wherever found.

Proust Marcel 1871–1922. French novelist and critic. His immense autobiographical work *À la recherche du temps perdu/Remembrance of Things Past* 1913–27, consisting of a series of novels, is the expression of his childhood memories coaxed from his subconscious; it is also a precise reflection of life in provincial France at the end of the 19th century.

Born at Auteuil, Proust was a delicate, asthmatic child; until he was 35 he moved in the fashionable circles of Parisian society, but after the death of his parents 1904–05 he went into seclusion in a cork-lined room in his Paris apartment, and devoted the rest of his life to writing his masterpiece.

Prout William 1785–1850. British physician and chemist. In 1815 Prout published his hypothesis that the atomic weight of every atom is an exact and integral multiple of the hydrogen atom. The discovery of isotopes (atoms of the same element that have different masses) in the 20th century bore out his idea.

Provençal language member of the Romance branch of the Indo-European language family, spoken in and around Provence in SE France. It is now regarded as a dialect or patois.

During the Middle Ages it was in competition with French and was the language of the troubadours. It had a strong literary influence on such neighboring languages as Italian, Spanish, and Portuguese. Since the 19th century, attempts have been made to revive it as a literary language.

***Proust** During the 1890s, around the time this photograph was taken, Marcel Proust moved in fashionable Parisian circles, but shortly afterwards he became a virtual recluse, dedicating his time to his autobiographical work,* A la recherche du temps perdu.

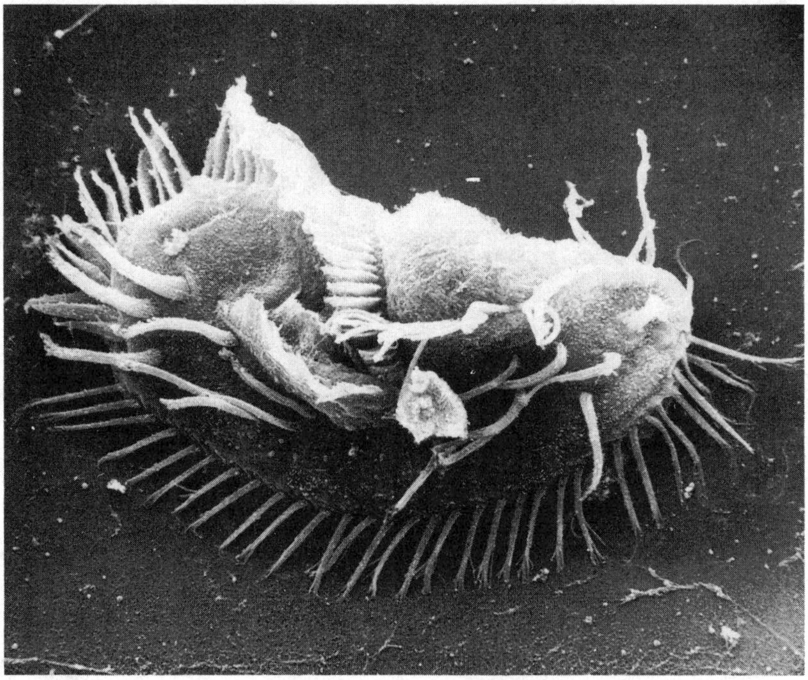

***protozoan** Scanning electron micrograph (SEM) of the ciliate protozoa Oxtricha. They are microscopic, unicellular and free-living, as well as being highly evolved and containing two kinds of nucleus. The cilia help in locomotion and feeding.*

Provençal literature Provençal literature originated in the 10th century and flowered in the 12th century with the work of the ◊troubadours. After the decline of the troubadours in the 13th century, Provençal disappeared as a literary medium from the 14th until the 19th centuries, when Jacques Jasmin (1798–1864) and others paved the way for the Félibrige group of poets, of whom the greatest are Joseph Roumanille (1818–1891), Frédéric Mistral (1830–1914), and Félix Gras (1844–1901).

Provence-Alpes-Côte d'Azur region of SE France, comprising the *départements* of Alpes-de-Haute-Provence, Hautes-Alpes, Alpes-Maritimes, Bouches-du Rhône, Var, and Vaucluse; area 12,120 sq mi/31,400 sq km; capital Marseilles; population (1986) 4,059,000. The Côte d'Azur, on the Mediterranean, is a tourist center. Provence was an independent kingdom in the 10th century, and the area still has its own language, Provençal.

Proverbs a book of the Old Testament traditionally ascribed to ◊Solomon. The Proverbs form a series of maxims on moral and ethical matters.

Providence industrial seaport (jewelry, silverware, textiles and textile machinery, watches, chemicals, meatpacking) and capital of Rhode Island, on Narragansett Bay and the Providence River, 27 mi/43 km from the Atlantic; population (1990) 160,728. Educational institutions include Brown University and the Rhode Island School of Design. Providence was founded 1636 by Roger Williams, who had been banished from Plymouth colony for his religious beliefs. By the early 18th century the community was thriving as a port for West Indian trade. It was an important base for American and French troops in the American Revolution.

Provincetown Players group of US actors, producers, and playwrights formed 1915 in Provincetown, Cape Cod, Massachusetts; they later moved to New York. Mounting new plays by Eugene O'Neill, Theodore Dreiser, e e cummings, and others, they opened the door to US experimental theater.

Provisions of Oxford provisions issued by Henry III of England 1258 under pressure from Simon de Montfort (1208–65) and the baronial opposition.

Prussia

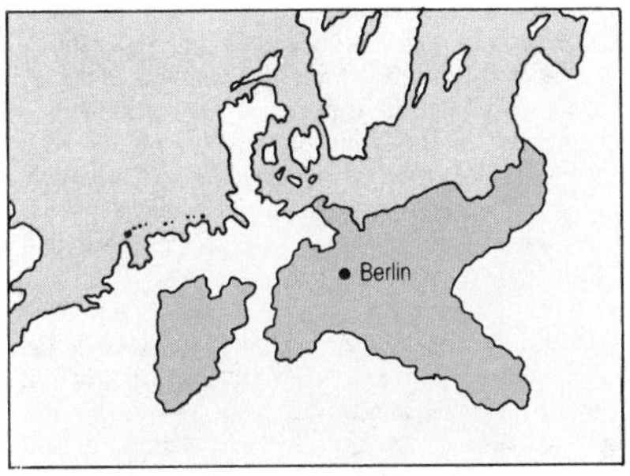
Berlin

They provided for the establishment of a baronial council to run the government, carry out reforms, and keep a check on royal power.

provitamin any precursor substance of a vitamin. Provitamins are ingested substances that become converted to active vitamins within the organism. One example is ergosterol (provitamin D_2), which through the action of sunlight is converted to calciferol (vitamin D_2); another example is B-carotene, which is hydrolyzed in the liver to vitamin A.

Provo city in N central Utah, on the Provo river, SE of Salt Lake City; seat of Utah county. Industries include iron and steel, food processing, and electronics. Brigham Young University is here; population (1990) 86,835.

Proxima Centauri the closest star to the Sun, 4.3 light-years away. It is a faint ◊red dwarf visible only with a telescope and is a member of the Alpha Centauri triple-star system.

It is called Proxima because it is about 0.1 light-years closer to us than its two partners.

proxy in law, a person authorized to stand in another's place; also the document conferring this right. The term usually refers to voting at meetings, but there may be marriages by proxy.

Prudhoe Bay a bay of the Arctic Ocean on the N coast (North Slope) of Alaska. An immense oil strike in the area in 1968 led to the construction of the 789-mi/1,270-km Trans-Alaska Pipeline, completed 1977, that carries oil from Prudhoe Bay to Valdez, on the S coast of Alaska. Almost 20% of US oil comes from the North Slope fields, although production has slowed.

Prud'hon Pierre 1758–1823. French Romantic painter. He became drawing instructor and court painter to the Emperor Napoleon's wives.

After winning the Prix de Rome 1784, Prud'hon visited Italy but, unlike his contemporary David, he was unaffected by the Neo-Classical vogue; his style is indebted to ◊Correggio.

Prunus genus of trees of the northern hemisphere, family Rosaceae, producing fruit with a fleshy, edible pericarp. The genus includes plums, cherries, peaches, apricots, and almonds.

Prussia N German state 1618–1945 on the Baltic coast. It was an independent kingdom until 1867, when it became, under ◊Bismarck, the military power of the North German Confederation and part of the German Empire 1871 under the Prussian king Wilhelm I. West Prussia became part of Poland under the ◊Versailles Treaty, and East Prussia was largely incorporated into the USSR after 1945.

1618 Formed by the union of ◊Brandenburg and the duchy of Prussia (established 1525).

1640–88 The country's military power was founded by ◊Frederick William, the "Great Elector."

1701 Prussia became a kingdom under Frederick I.

1713–40 Frederick William I expanded the army.

1740–86 Silesia, East Frisia, and West Prussia were annexed by ◊Frederick II the Great.

1806 ◊Frederick William III was defeated at Jena by Napoleon.

1815 After the Congress of Vienna Prussia regained its lost territories and also acquired lands in the Rhineland and Saxony.

1848 Bismarck suppressed the ◊revolution of 1848.

1864 War with Denmark resulted in the acquisition of Schleswig and Holstein.

1866 After the defeat of Austria, Prussia formed the North German Confederation with the territories of Hanover, Nassau, Frankfurt-am-Main, and Hesse-Cassel.

1871 After Prussia's victory in the Franco-Prussian War, the German Empire was proclaimed, under Bismarck's chancellorship, for Wilhelm I.

1918 Prussia became a republic after World War I.

1932 Prussia lost its local independence in Hitler's Germany and came under the control of the Reich.

1946 After World War II the Allies abolished Prussia altogether, dividing its territories among East and West Germany, Poland, and the USSR.

prussic acid former name for ◊hydrocyanic acid.

Prut a river that rises in the Carpathian Mountains of SW Ukraine, USSR and flows 565 mi/900 km to meet the Danube at Reni, USSR. For part of its course it follows the E frontier of Romania.

Przemyśl industrial city (timber, ceramics, flour milling, tanning, distilling, food processing, gas, engineering) in SE Poland; population (1981) 62,000.

Founded in the 8th century, it belonged alternately to Poland and Kiev in the 10th–14th centuries. An Austrian territory 1722–1919, it was a frontier fortress besieged by Soviet troops Sept 1914– March 1915 and was occupied by the Germans June 1941–July 1944.

Przhevalsky Nikolai Mikhailovitch 1839–1888. Russian explorer and soldier. In 1870 he crossed the Gobi Desert to Beijing and then went on to the upper reaches of the Chang Jiang River. His attempts to penetrate Tibet as far as Lhasa failed on three occasions, but he continued to explore the mountain regions between Tibet and Mongolia, where he made collections of plants and animals, including a wild camel and a wild horse (the species is now known as Przhevalsky's horse).

The Kirghiz town of Karakol on the eastern shores of Lake Issyk Kul where he died was renamed Przhevalsky in 1889.

PS abbreviation for post scriptum (Latin "after writing").

psalm a sacred poem or song of praise. The Book of Psalms in the Old Testament is divided into five books containing 150 psalms. They are traditionally ascribed to David, the second king of Israel.

pseudocarp a fruitlike structure that incorporates tissue that is not derived from the ovary wall. The additional tissues may be derived from floral parts such as the ◊receptacle and ◊calyx. For example, the colored, fleshy part of a strawberry develops from the receptacle and the true fruits are small ◊achenes—the "pips" embedded in its outer surface. Rose hips are a type of pseudocarp that consists of a hollow, fleshy receptacle containing a number of achenes within. Different types of pseudocarp include pineapples, figs, apples, and pears.

A coenocarpium is a fleshy, multiple pseudocarp derived from an ◊inflorescence rather than a single flower. The pineapple has a thickened central axis surrounded by fleshy tissues derived from the receptacles and floral parts of many flowers. A fig is a type of pseudocarp called a syconium, formed from a hollow receptacle with small flowers attached to the inner wall. After fertilization the ovaries of the female flowers develop into one-seeded achenes. Apples and pears are ◊pomes, another type of pseudocarp.

pseudocopulation the attempted copulation by a male insect with a flower. It results in ◊pollination of the flower and is common in the orchid family, where the flowers of many species resemble a

pseudocopulation

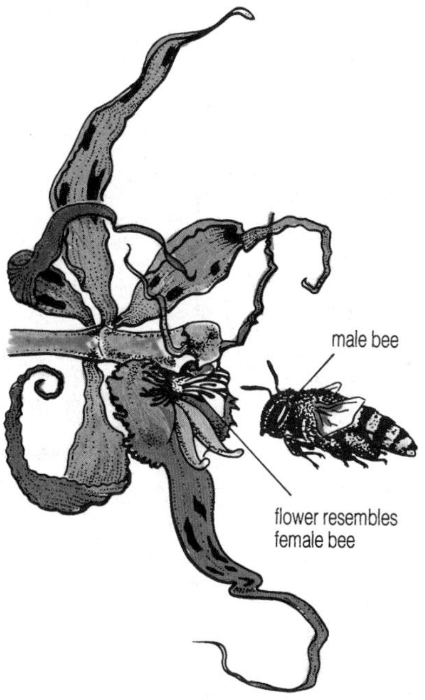
male bee
flower resembles female bee

particular species of female bee. When a male bee attempts to mate with a flower, the pollinia (groups of pollen grains) stick to its body. They are transferred to the stigma of another flower when the insect attempts copulation again.

pseudomorph a mineral that has replaced another *in situ* and has retained the external crystal shape of the original mineral.

psi in parapsychology, a hypothetical faculty common to humans and other animals said to be responsible for extra-sensory perception (ESP) and telekinesis.

Psilocybe genus of mushroom with hallucinogenic properties, including the Mexican sacred mushroom *P. mexicana*, which contains compounds with effects similar to LSD. A related species *P. semilanceata* is found in N Europe.

psittacosis infectious acute or chronic disease, contracted by humans from birds (especially parrots), which may result in pneumonia. It is caused by a bacterium (*Chlamydia psittaci*, see ◊chlamydia) and treated with antibiotics.

Pskov industrial city (food processing, leather) in USSR, on the Velikaya river, SW of St Petersburg; population (1987) 202,000. Dating from 965, it was independent 1348–1510.

psoriasis chronic, recurring skin disease characterized by raised, red, scaly patches, usually on the scalp, back, arms, and/or legs. Tar preparations, steroid creams, and ultraviolet light are used to treat it, and sometimes it disappears spontaneously. Psoriasis may be accompanied by a form of arthritis.

Psyche late Greek personification of the soul as a winged girl or young woman. The goddess Aphrodite was so jealous of Psyche's beauty that she ordered her son Eros, the god of love, to make Psyche fall in love with the worst of men. Instead, he fell in love with her himself.

psychedelic drug any drug that produces hallucinations or altered states of consciousness. Such sensory experiences may be in the auditory, visual, tactile, olfactory, or gustatory fields or in any combination. Among drugs known to have psychedelic effects are LSD (lysergic acid diethylamine), mescaline, and, to a mild degree, marijuana, along with a number of other plant-derived or synthetically prepared substances. Most of these drugs are known to cause temporary or recurring psychotic episodes.

psychology: chronology

1897	Wilhelm Wundt founded the first psychological laboratory in Leipzig.
1890	William James published the first comprehensive psychology text, *Principles of Psychology.*
1895	Freud's first book on psychoanalysis was published.
1896	The first clinical psychology clinic was founded by Witner at the University of Pennsylvania.
1903	Pavlov reported his early study on conditioned reflexes in animals.
1905	Binet and Simon developed the first effective intelligence test.
1908	A first textbook of social psychology was published by William McDougall.
1913	J B Watson published *Behaviorism*, which laid the basis for the school and doctrine of that name.
1926	Jean Piaget presented his first book on child development.
1947	Eysenck published *Dimensions of Personality*: a large scale study of neuroticism and extroversion.
1953	Skinner's *Science of Human Behavior*, a text of operant conditioning, was published.
1957	Chomsky's *Syntactic Structures*, which stimulated the development of psycholinguistics, the study of language processes, was published.
1963	Milgram's studies of compliance with authority indicated conditions under which individuals behave cruelly to others when instructed to do so.
1967	Neisser's *Cognitive Psychology* marked renewed interest in the study of cognition after years in which behaviorism had been dominant.
1972	Newell and Simon simulated human problem solving abilities by computer; an example of artificial intelligence.
1989	Jeffrey Masson attacked the fundamental principles of Freudian analytic psychotherapy in his book *Against Therapy.*

psychedelic rock or ***acid rock*** a type of pop music, involving advanced electronic equipment for both light and sound that appeared about 1966. The free-form improvisations and light shows of the hippie years by the 1980s had evolved into stadium performances with lasers and other special effects.

psychiatry the branch of medicine dealing with the diagnosis and treatment of mental disorder.

In practice there is considerable overlap between psychiatry and ◊clinical psychology, the fundamental difference being that psychiatrists are trained medical doctors (holding an MD degree) and may therefore prescribe drugs, whereas psychologists may hold a PhD but do not need a medical qualification to practice. See also ◊psychology and ◊psychoanalysis.

psychic a person allegedly possessed of parapsychological, or paranormal, powers.

psychoanalysis a theory and treatment method for neuroses, developed by ◊Freud. The main treatment method involves the free association of ideas, and their interpretation by patient and analyst. It is typically prolonged and expensive and its effectiveness has been disputed.

It emphasizes that the impact of early childhood sexuality and experiences, stored in the unconscious can lead to the development of adult emotional problems. Treatment involves recognizing these long-buried events in order to relieve actual pressure. Modern approaches, drawing from Freud's ideas, tend to be briefer and more problem-focused.

psychology the systematic study of human and animal behavior. The first psychology laboratory was founded 1879 by Wilhelm ◊Wundt at Leipzig, Germany. The subject includes diverse areas of study and application, among them the roles of instinct, heredity, environment, and culture; the processes of sensation, perception, learning, and memory; the bases of motivation and emotion; and the functioning of thought, intelligence, and language.

Experimental psychology emphasizes the application of rigorous and objective scientific methods to the study of a wide range of mental processes and behavior, whereas social psychology concerns the study of individuals within their social environment; for example, within groups and organizations. This has led to the development of related fields such as ◊occupational psychology, which studies human behavior at work, and ◊educational psychology. Clinical psychology concerns the understanding and treatment of mental health disorders, such as anxiety, phobias, or depression; treatment may include ◊behavior therapy, ◊cognitive therapy, ◊counseling, ◊psychoanalysis, or some combination of these.

Significant psychologists have included Gustav Fechner (1801–1887), founder of psychophysics; Wolfgang Köhler (1887–1967), one of the ◊gestalt or "whole" psychologists; Sigmund Freud and his associates Jung, Adler, and Rorschach; William James, Jean Piaget; Carl Rogers; Hans Eysenck; J B Watson, and B F Skinner. Modern studies have been diverse, for example the psychological causes of obesity; the nature of religious experience; and the underachievement of women seen as resulting from social pressures. Other related subjects are the nature of sleep and dreams, and the possible extensions of the senses, which leads to the more contentious ground of ◊parapsychology.

psychometrics the measurement of mental processes. This includes intelligence and aptitude testing to help in job selection and in the clinical assessment of cognitive deficiencies resulting from brain damage.

psychopathy a personality disorder characterized by chronic antisocial behavior (violating the rights of others, often violently) and an absence of feelings of guilt about the behavior.

Because the term has been misused to refer to any severe mental disorder, many psychologists now prefer the term "antisocial personality disorder."

psychosis or ***psychotic disorder*** a general term for a serious mental disorder where the individual commonly loses contact with reality and may experience hallucinations (seeing or hearing things that do not exist) or delusions (fixed false beliefs). For example, in a paranoid psychosis, an individual may believe that others are plotting against him or her. A major type of psychosis is ◊schizophrenia (which may be biochemically induced).

psychosomatic descriptive term for any physical symptom or disease thought to arise from emotional or mental factors.

The term "psychosomatic" has been applied to many conditions, including asthma, migraine, ◊hypertension, and peptic ulcers. Whereas it is unlikely that these and other conditions are wholly due to psychological factors, emotional states such as anxiety or depression do have a distinct influence on the frequency and severity of illness.

psychosurgery operation to achieve some mental effect. For example, lobotomy is the separation of the white fibers in the prefrontal lobe of the brain, as a means of relieving a deep state of anxiety.

It is irreversible and the degree of personality change is not predictable. Some states strictly regulate its use.

psychotherapy treatment approaches for psychological problems involving talking rather than surgery or drugs. Examples include ◊cognitive therapy and ◊psychoanalysis.

psychotic disorder another name for ◊psychosis.

pt abbreviation for pint.

Ptah Egyptian god, the divine potter, a personification of the creative force. He was worshiped at ◊Memphis, and often portrayed as a mummified man. He was the father of ◊Imhotep.

ptarmigan any of a genus (Lagopus) of hardy N ground-dwelling birds (family Phasianidae, which also includes ◊grouse), with feathered legs and feet.

The willow ptarmigan *L. lagopus*, found in bushes and heather in northern parts of North America, Europe, and Asia, grows to 15 in/38 cm and turns white in the winter.

pteridophyte a simple type of ◊vascular plant. The pteridophytes comprise four classes: the Psilosida, including the most primitive vascular plants, found mainly in the tropics; the Lycopsida, including the club mosses; the Sphenopsida, including the horsetails; and the Pteropsida, including the ferns. They are mainly terrestrial, non-flowering plants characterized by the presence of a vascular system; the possession of true stems, roots, and leaves; and by a marked ◊alternation of generations, with the sporophyte forming the dominant generation in the life cycle. They do not produce seeds.

The pteridophytes formed a large and dominant flora during the Carboniferous period, but many are now known only from fossils.

pterodactyl see ◊pterosaur.

pterosaur extinct flying reptile of the order Pterosauria, existing in the Mesozoic age. Pterosaurs were formerly assumed to be smooth-skinned gliders, but recent discoveries show that at least some were furry, probably warm-blooded, and may have had muscle fibers and blood vessels on their wings, stiffened by moving the hind legs, thus allowing controlled and strong flapping flight. They ranged from starling size to the largest with 40 ft/12 m wingspan. Some had horns on their heads that, when in flight, made a whistling to roaring sound.

PTO abbreviation for please turn over.

Ptolemy (Claudius Ptolemaeus) c. 100–AD 170. Egyptian astronomer and geographer, who worked in Alexandria. The *Almagest* developed the theory that Earth is the center of the universe, with the Sun, Moon, and stars revolving around it. In 1543 the Polish astronomer ◊Copernicus disproved the Ptolemaic system. Ptolemy's *Geography* was a standard source of information until the 16th century.

Ptolemy dynasty of kings of Macedonian origin who ruled Egypt over a period of 300 years; they included:

Ptolemy I c. 367–283 BC. Ruler of Egypt from 323 BC, king from 304. He was one of ◊Alexander the Great's generals, and possibly his half brother (and married his lover, ◊Thaïs). He established the library in Alexandria.

Ptolemy XIII 63–47 BC. Joint ruler of Egypt with his sister-wife Cleopatra; she put him to death.

ptomaine any of a group of toxic chemical substances (alkaloids) produced as a result of decomposition by bacterial action on proteins.

It is not the relevant factor in "food poisoning," which is usually caused by bacteria of the genus *Salmonella*.

puberty stage in human development when the individual becomes sexually mature. It may occur from the age of ten upward. The sexual organs take on their adult form and pubic hair grows. In girls, menstruation begins, and the breasts develop; in boys, the voice breaks and becomes deeper, and facial hair develops.

pubes the lowest part of the front of the human trunk, the region where the external generative organs are situated. The underlying bony structure, the pubic arch, is formed by the union in the midline of the two pubic bones, which are the front portions of the hip bones. In women it is more prominent than in men, to allow more room

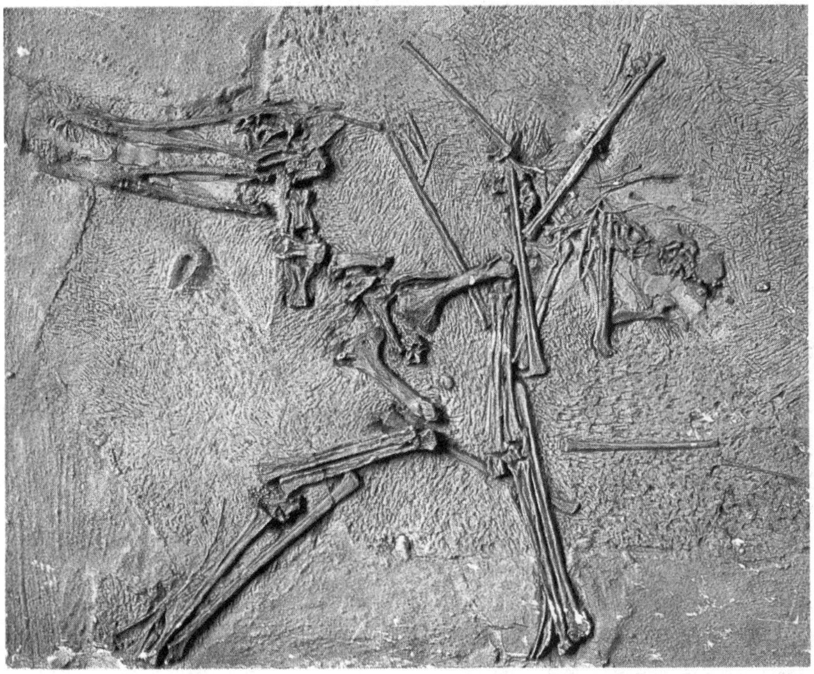

pterodactyl *Fossil remains of a pterodactyl, a flying reptile of the Mesozoic age, discovered in Wærttemberg, Germany.*

for the passage of the child's head at birth, and carries a pad of fat and connective tissue, the *mons veneris* (mountain of Venus), for its protection.

Public Against Violence (Slovak Verejnosť Proti Násil'u) the Slovak half of the Czechoslovak democratic movement, counterpart of the Czech organization ◊Civic Forum.

public corporation a management and administrative structure, similar to a private ◊corporation, established to run state-owned or nationalized enterprises. They are governed by a board of directors, although some level of government is either the sole or controlling stockholder.

Distinct from a publicly held corporation in the US, where shares are sold to the public, then traded in one of the stock markets, public corporations decline in number as the trend toward ◊privatization grows.

public school in the US and many English-speaking countries, "public" schools are maintained by the state, and "private" schools are independent institutions, supported by fees. In England, public schools are fee-paying independent schools.

Since the nation's founding, universal public education has become an important tradition in the US, and school attendance is compulsory to age 16. Public schools serve as the major method of socialization for immigrants. Since the 1960s, increasing numbers of middle-class whites have withdrawn their children from urban public school systems, choosing private or parochial (church-run) alternatives, thus compromising public education in the process.

public spending expenditure by government, covering the military, health, education, infrastructure, development projects, and the cost of servicing overseas borrowing.

A principal source of revenue to cover public expenditure is taxation. Most countries present their plans for spending in their annual budgets.

publishing the production of books for sale. The publisher arranges for the commissioning, editing, printing, binding, warehousing, and distribution to booksellers or book clubs. Although all rights in a book may be purchased by the publisher for a single outright fee, it is more usual that a fixed royalty is paid to the author on every copy sold, in return for the exclusive right to publish in an agreed territory.

Puccini Giacomo (Antonio Domenico Michele Secondo Maria) 1858–1924. Italian opera composer whose music shows a strong gift for melody and dramatic effect. His realist works include *Manon Lescaut* 1893, *La Bohème* 1896, *Tosca* 1900, *Madame Butterfly* 1904, and the unfinished *Turandot* 1926.

Pudovkin Vsevolod Illationovich 1893–1953. Russian film director whose films include the silent *Mother* 1926, *The End of St Petersburg* 1927, and *Storm over Asia* 1928; and the sound films *Deserter* 1933 and *Suvorov* 1941.

Giacomo Puccini

Puccini *Striving for perfection in the drama of his operas as much as in the scores, Italian composer Giacomo Puccini drove his libbretists Giacosa and Illica to produce "a libretto that would move the world."*

Puebla (de Zaragoza) industrial city (textiles, sugar refining, metallurgy, hand-crafted pottery and tiles) and capital of Puebla state, S central Mexico; population (1986) 1,218,000. Founded 1535 as Pueblo de los Angeles, it was later renamed after General de Zaragoza, who defeated the French here 1862.

Pueblo US intelligence vessel captured by the North Koreans Jan 1968, allegedly within their territorial waters. The crew, but not the ship, were released Dec 1968. A naval court recommended no disciplinary action.

Pueblo city in S central Colorado, on the Arkansas river, SE of Colorado Springs. Industries include steel, coal, lumber, and livestock and other agricultural products; population (1990) 98,640.

Pueblo Indian (Spanish pueblos, villages) generic name for a member of any of the farming groups of the SW US and N Mexico, living in communal villages of flat-topped adobe or stone structures arranged in terraces. Surviving groups include the Hopi and the Zuni.

puerperal fever infection of the genital tract of the mother after childbirth, due to lack of aseptic conditions. Formerly often fatal, it is now rare and treated with antibiotics.

Puerto Rico the Commonwealth of island of the West Indies (from 1898–1932, Porto Rico)
area 3,475 sq mi/9,000 sq km
capital San Juan
cities ports: Mayagüez, Ponce
population (1990) 3,522,037
features Old San Juan; nightclubs and casinos; rain forest of El Yunque; colonial-style San German; Arecibo Observatory
products apparel, textiles, pharmaceuticals, petroleum products, rum, refined sugar, coffee, computers, instruments, office machines, cattle, hogs, milk, cement
language Spanish and English (official)
religion Roman Catholic
government under the constitution of 1952, similar to that of the US, with a governor elected for four years and a legislative assembly with a senate and house of representatives
famous people Roberto Clemente, José Ferrer, Eugenio María de Hostos, Raul Julia, Rita Moreno, Luís Muñoz Marín
history visited 1493 by Columbus; annexed by Spain 1509; ceded to the US after the ◊Spanish-American War 1898; achieved commonwealth status with local self-government 1952.

This was confirmed in preference to independence by a referendum 1967, but there is both an independence movement and one preferring incorporation as a state of the US.

Puerto Sandino a major port on the Pacific W coast of Nicaragua, known as Puerto Somoza until 1979.

puff adder a variety of ◊adder.

puffball globulous fruiting body of certain ◊fungi that cracks with maturity, releasing the enclosed spores in the form of a brown powder; for example, the common puffball *Lycoperdon perlatum*.

puffer fish fish of the family Tetraodontidae. As a means of defense it inflates its body with air or water until it becomes spherical and the skin spines become erect. Puffer fishes are mainly found in warm waters, where they feed on mollusks, crustaceans, and coral. They vary in size, up to 20 in/50 cm long. The skin of some puffer fish is poisonous (25 times more toxic than cyanide), but they are prized as a delicacy (fugu) in Japan after the poison has been removed. Nevertheless about a hundred dead diners are recorded each year.

puffin any of various sea birds of the genus *Fratercula* of the ◊auk family, found in the N Atlantic and Pacific. It is about 14 in/35 cm long, with a white face and front, red legs, and a large deep

puffin

bill, very brightly colored in summer. It has short wings and webbed feet. Puffins are poor fliers, but excellent swimmers. They nest in rock crevices, or make burrows, and lay a single egg.

pug breed of small dog with short wrinkled face, chunky body, and tail curled over the hip. It weighs 13–18 lb/6–8 kg.

Puget Pierre 1620–1694. French Baroque sculptor who developed a powerful and expressive style. He created a muscular statue of the tyrant *Milo of Croton* 1672–82 (Louvre, Paris) for the garden of the palace of Versailles.

Puget worked in Italy 1640–43 and was influenced by ◊Michelangelo and ◊Pietro da Cortona. After 1682 he failed to gain further court patronage because of his stubborn temperament and his severe style.

Puget Sound an inlet of the Pacific Ocean on the W coast of Washington state.

Puglia (English *Apulia*) region of Italy, the southeastern "heel"; area 7,450 sq mi/19,300 sq km; capital Bari; population (1988) 4,043,000. Products include wheat, grapes, almonds, olives, and vegetables. The main industrial center is Taranto.

P'u-i (or ***Pu-Yi***) Henry 1906–1967. Last emperor of China (as Hsuan Tung) from 1908 until his deposition 1912; he was restored for a week 1917. After his deposition he chose to be called Henry. He was president 1932–34 and emperor 1934–45 of the Japanese puppet state of Manchukuo (see ◊Manchuria). Captured by Soviet troops, he was returned to China 1949 and put on trial in the new People's Republic of China 1950. Pardoned by Mao Zedong 1959, he became a worker in a botanical garden in Beijing.

pūjā worship, in Hinduism, Buddhism, and Jainism.

Pula commercial and naval port in W Croatia, Yugoslavia, on the Adriatic coast; population (1981) 77,278. A Roman naval base, *Colonia Pietas Julia*, it was seized by Venice in 1148, passed to Austria 1815, to Italy 1919, and to Yugoslavia 1947.

It has a Roman theater, and a castle and cathedral constructed under Venetian rule. There is an annual film festival.

Pulaski Casimir 1747–1779. Polish patriot and military leader in the American Revolution. Born in Padolia, Poland, Pulaski embarked on a military career early in life. After participating in the unsuccessful Polish defense against the Russian invasion 1770–72, he went into exile and was hired by Silas Deane and Benjamin Franklin to aid the American Revolutionary War effort. Arriving in America 1777, Pulaski was placed in command of the Continental cavalry. He spent the winter of 1777–78 at Valley Forge and after a personal dispute with General Anthony Wayne, was given an independent cavalry command. Pulaski died in action in the siege of Savannah.

Pulitzer Joseph 1847–1911. Hungarian-born US newspaper publisher. He acquired *The World* 1883 in New York City and, as a publisher, his format set the style for the modern newspaper. After his death, funds provided in his will established 1912 the school of journalism at Columbia University and the annual Pulitzer prizes in journalism, literature, and music.

Pulitzer came to the US 1864 and became a citizen 1867. A Democrat, he merged two St Louis newspapers and published 1878 the successful St Louis *Post-Dispatch*. He made *The World* into a voice of the Democratic Party. During a circulation battle with rival publisher William Randolph ◊Hearst's papers, he and Hearst were accused of resorting to "yellow journalism," or sensationalism. Pulitzer prizes have been awarded since 1917.

Pulitzer Prize for fiction (US)

1970	Jean Stafford *Collected Stories*
1972	Wallace Stegner *Angle of Repose*
1973	Eudora Welty *The Optimist's Daughter*
1975	Michael Shaara *The Killer Angels*
1976	Saul Bellow *Humboldt's Gift*
1978	James Alan McPherson *Elbow Room*
1979	John Cheever *The Stories of John Cheever*
1980	Norman Mailer *The Executioner's Song*
1981	John Kennedy Toole *A Confederacy of Dunces*
1982	John Updike *Rabbit is Rich*
1983	Alice Walker *The Color Purple*
1984	William Kennedy *Ironweed*
1985	Alison Lurie *Foreign Affairs*
1986	Larry McMurtry *Lonesome Dove*
1987	Peter Taylor *A Summons to Memphis*
1988	Toni Morrison *Beloved*
1989	Anne Tyler *Breathing Lessons*
1990	Oscar Hijuelos *The Mambo Kings Play Songs of Love*
1991	John Updike *Rabbit at Rest*

pulley simple machine consisting of a fixed, grooved wheel, sometimes in a block, around which rope or chain can be run. A simple pulley serves only to change the direction of the applied effort (as in a simple hoist for raising loads). The use of more than one pulley results in a mechanical advantage, so that a given effort can raise a heavier load.

The mechanical advantage depends on the arrangement of the pulleys. For instance, a block and tackle arrangement with three ropes supporting the load will lift it with one-third of the effort needed to lift it directly (if friction is ignored), giving a mechanical advantage of 3.

Pullman George 1831–1901. US engineer who developed the Pullman railroad car. In an attempt to improve the standard of comfort of rail travel, he built his first Pioneer Sleeping Car 1863. He formed the Pullman Palace Car Company 1867 and in 1881 the town of Pullman, Illinois, was built for his workers.

pulsar celestial source that emits pulses of energy at regular intervals, ranging from a few seconds to a few thousandths of a second. They were discovered 1967 and are thought to be rapidly rotating ◊neutron stars, which flash at radio and other wavelengths as they spin.

Over 400 radio pulsars are now known in our Galaxy, although a million or so may exist.

Two pulsars, one in the ◊Crab nebula and one in the constellation ◊Vela, give out flashes of visible light. Pulsars gradually slow down as they get older, and eventually the flashes fade. X-ray pulsars are caused by hot gas falling onto a spinning neutron star in a binary star system. Pulsars were discovered at the Mullard Radio Astronomy Observatory, Cambridge, England, by Jocelyn Bell (now ◊Burnell), a member of a team under Antony ◊Hewish.

pulse crop such as peas and beans. They are grown primarily for their seeds, which provide a concentrated source of vegetable protein, and make a vital contribution to human diets in poor countries where meat is scarce. Soybeans are the major temperate protein crop in the West; most are used for oil production or for animal feed. In Asia, most are processed into soy milk and beancurd. Peanuts dominate pulse production in the tropical world and are generally consumed as human food.

Pulses play a useful role in ◊crop rotations as they help to raise soil nitrogen levels as well as acting as break crops. In the mid-1980s, world production was about 50 million tons a year.

pulley

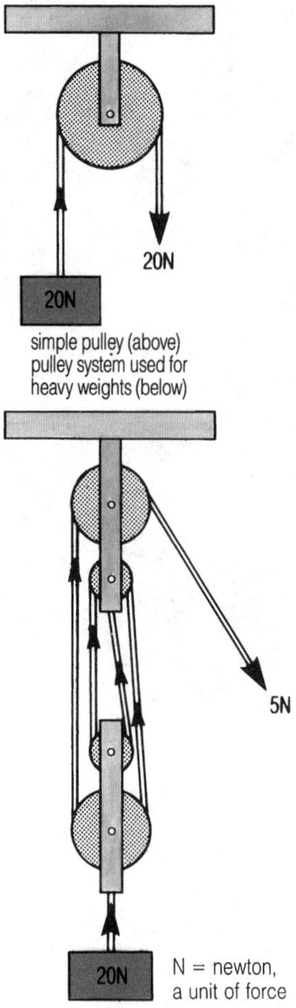
20N
20N
simple pulley (above)
pulley system used for
heavy weights (below)
5N
20N
N = newton,
a unit of force

pulse impulse transmitted by the heartbeat throughout the arterial systems of vertebrates. When the heart muscle contracts, it forces blood into the ◊aorta. Because the arteries are elastic, the sudden rise of pressure causes a throb or sudden swelling through them. The actual flow of the blood is about 2 ft/60 cm a second in humans. The pulse rate is generally about 70 per minute. The pulse can be felt where an artery is near the surface, such as in the wrist or the neck.

pulse-code modulation method of converting a continuous electrical signal (such as that produced by a microphone) into a series of pulses (a digital signal) for transmission along a telephone line.

In a process called ◊digital sampling, the continuous signal is sampled thousands of times a second and each part of the signal given a number related to its strength when sampled. The numbers are then converted into ◊binary code and transmitted as a series of pulses. At the receiving end the process is reversed. The advantages of the system arise because noise (static) on the line can easily be distinguished from the signal and removed; hence it is possible to send error-free messages. This has led to increasing use of the system in telephone, telegraph, and computer systems since its adoption in the 1960s. It is well suited to transmission along ◊optical fibers.

puma also called ***cougar*** or ***mountain lion*** large wild cat *Felis concolor* found in North and South America. Tawny-coated, it is 4.5 ft/1.5 m long with a 3 ft/1 m tail. It lives alone, with each male occupying a distinct territory; it eats deer, rodents, and cattle. It has been hunted nearly to extinction.

pumice a light volcanic rock produced by the frothing action of expanding gases during the solidification of lava. It has the texture of a hard sponge and is used as an abrasive.

pump any device for moving liquids and gases, or compressing gases. Some pumps, such as the traditional lift pump used to raise water from wells, work by a reciprocating (up-and-down) action. Movement of a piston in a cylinder with a one-way valve creates a partial vacuum in the cylinder, thereby sucking water into it. Gear pumps, used to pump oil in a car's lubrication system, have two meshing gears that rotate inside a housing, and the teeth move the oil. Rotary pumps contain a rotor with vanes projecting from it inside a casing, sweeping the oil around as they move.

pumped storage hydroelectric plant that uses surplus electricity to pump water back into a high-level reservoir. In normal working the water flows from this reservoir through the ◊turbines to generate power for feeding into the grid. At times of low power demand, electricity is taken from the grid to turn the turbines into pumps that then pump the water back again. This ensures that there is always a maximum "head" of water in the reservoir to give the maximum output when required.

pumpkin type of gourd *Cucurbita pepo* of the family Cucurbitaceae. The large, spherical fruit has a thick, orange rind, pulpy flesh, and many seeds.

pun a figure of speech, a play on words, or double meaning that is technically known as paronomasia (Greek "adapted meaning"). Double meaning can be accidental, often resulting from homonymy, or the multiple meaning of words; puns, however, are deliberate, intended as jokes or as clever and compact remarks.

Punch (Italian *Pulcinella*) the male character in the traditional ◊puppet play *Punch and Judy*, a hump-backed, hooknosed figure who fights with his wife, Judy.

punched card in computing, an early form of data storage and input, now almost obsolete. The 80-column card was widely used in the 1960s and 1970s. This was a thin card, measuring 7½ in/190 mm × 3⅓ in/84 mm, holding up to 80 characters of data encoded as small rectangular holes.

The punched card was invented by Joseph-Marie Jacquard (1752–1834) in about 1801 to control weaving looms. The first data processing machine using punched cards was developed by Herman ◊Hollerith in the 1880s for the US census.

punctuated equilibrium model an evolutionary theory developed by Niles Eldridge and Stephen Jay Gould 1972 to explain discontinuities in the fossil record. It claims that periods of rapid change alternate with periods of relative stability (stasis), and that the appearance of new lineages is a separate process from the gradual evolution of adaptive changes within a species.

The pattern of stasis and more rapid change is now widely accepted, but the second part of the theory remains unsubstantiated.

punctuation the system of conventional signs (punctuation marks) and spaces by means of which written and printed language is organized in order to be as readable, clear, and logical as possible.

It contributes to the effective layout of visual language; if a work is not adequately punctuated, there may be problems of ambiguity and unclear association among words. Conventions of punctuation differ from language to language, and there are preferred styles in the punctuation of a language like English. Some people prefer a fuller use of punctuation, while others punctuate lightly; comparably, the use of punctuation will vary according to the kind of passage being produced: a personal letter, a newspaper article, and a technical report are all laid out and punctuated in distinctive ways.

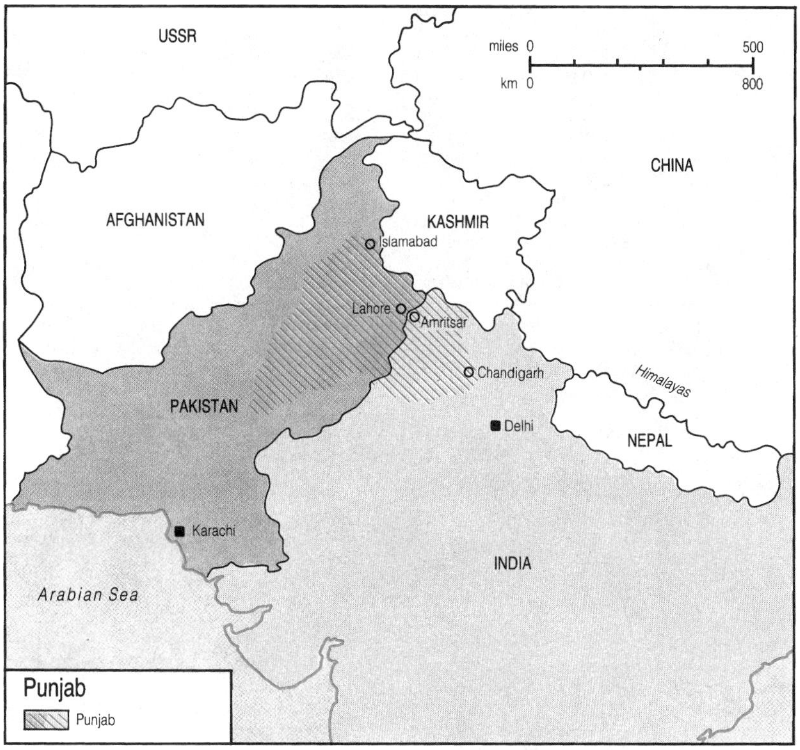
USSR
miles 0
500
km 0
800
CHINA
AFGHANISTAN
KASHMIR
Islamabad
Lahore
Amritsar
Chandigarh
Himalayas
PAKISTAN
Delhi
NEPAL
Karachi
INDIA
Arabian Sea
Punjab
Punjab

The standard punctuation marks and conventions are the ◊period, ◊comma, ◊colon, ◊semicolon, exclamation point, ◊question mark, ◊apostrophe, ◊asterisk, ◊hyphen, and ◊parenthesis (including dashes, brackets, and the use of parenthetical commas).

Pune or ***Poona*** city in Maharashtra, India; population (1985) 1,685,000. Products include chemicals, rice, sugar, cotton, paper, and jewelry.

Punic (Latin *Punicus* "a Phoenician") relating to ◊Carthage, ancient city in N Africa founded by the Phoenicians.

Punic Wars three wars between ◊Rome and ◊Carthage:

First 264–241 BC, resulted in the defeat of the Carthaginians under ◊Hamilcar Barca and the cession of Sicily to Rome

Second 218–201 BC, Hannibal invaded Italy, defeated the Romans under ◊Fabius Maximus at Cannae, but was finally defeated by ◊Scipio at Zama (now in Algeria)

Third 149–146 BC, ended in the destruction of Carthage and its possessions becoming the Roman province of Africa.

Punjab (Sanskrit "five rivers": the Indus tributaries Jhelum, Chnab, Ravi, Beas, and Sutlej). Former state of British India, now divided between India and Pakistan. Punjab was annexed by Britain 1849, after the Sikh Wars 1845–46 and 1848–49, and formed into a province with its capital at Lahore. Under the British, W Punjab was extensively irrigated, and land was granted to Indians who had served in the British army.

Punjab state of NW India

area 19,454 sq mi/50,400 sq km

capital Chandigarh

cities Amritsar

features mainly agricultural, crops chiefly under irrigation; longest life expectancy rates in India (59 for women, 64 for men); Harappa has ruins from the ◊Indus Valley civilization 2500 to 1600 BC

population (1981) 16,670,000

language Punjabi

religion 60% Sikh, 30% Hindu; there is friction between the two groups.

Punjab state of NE Pakistan

area 79,263 sq mi/205,344 sq km

capital Lahore

features wheat cultivation (by irrigation)

population (1981) 47,292,000

language Punjabi, Urdu

religion Muslim.

Punjabi inhabitant of or native to Punjab. The Punjabi language belongs to the Indo-Iranian branch of the Indo-European family.

Punjabi language member of the Indo-Iranian branch of the Indo-European language family, spoken in the Punjab provinces of India and Pakistan. It is considered by some to be a variety of Hindi, by others to be a distinct language.

Punjab massacres in the violence occurring after the partition of India 1947, more than a million people died while relocating in the Punjab. The eastern section became an Indian state, while the western area, dominated by the Muslims, went to Pakistan. Violence occurred as Muslims fled from eastern Punjab, and Hindus and Sikhs moved from Pakistan to ◊India.

punk a movement of disaffected youth of the late 1970s, manifesting itself in fashions and music designed to shock or intimidate. Punk rock stressed aggressive performance within a three-chord, three-minute format, as exemplified by such groups as the Sex Pistols 1975–78, the Slits 1977–82, and Johnny Thunders (with the Heartbreakers from 1975).

Punta Arenas (Spanish "sandy point") former name ***Magallanes*** seaport (trading in meat, wool, and oil), in Chile, capital of Magallanes province, on Magellan Strait, southernmost town on the American mainland; population (1982) 99,000.

pupa the nonfeeding, largely immobile stage of some insect life cycles, in which larval tissues are broken down, and adult tissues and structures are formed.

In many insects, it is exarate, with the appendages (legs, antennae, wings) visible outside the pupal case; in butterflies and moths, the pupa is called a chrysalis, and is obtect, with the appendages developing inside the case.

puppet figure manipulated on a small stage, usually by an unseen operator. The earliest known puppets are from 10th-century BC China. The types include finger or glove puppets (such as ◊Punch);

string marionettes (which reached a high artistic level in ancient Burma and Sri Lanka and in Italian princely courts from the 16th to 18th centuries, and for which the composer Haydn wrote his operetta *Dido* 1778); shadow silhouettes (operated by rods and seen on a lit screen, as in Java); and bunraku (devised in Osaka, Japan), in which three or four black-clad operators on stage may combine to work each puppet about 3 ft/1 m high.

During the 16th and 17th centuries puppet shows became popular with European aristocracy and puppets were extensively used as vehicles for caricature and satire until the 19th century, when they were offered as amusements for children in parks. In the 1920s Obraztsov founded the Puppet Theater in Moscow. Later in the 20th century interest was revived by television; for example, *The Muppet Show* in the 1970s.

In the US, Bil Baird (1904–) has created more than 2,000 puppets, many for film and television. He worked with Orson Welles, Ziegfeld, at the 1939 and 1965 New York world's fairs, for Radio City Music Hall, and for US State Department tours of India and the USSR. He opened a puppet theater in New York's Greenwich Village 1967.

Purana one of a number of sacred Hindu writings dealing with ancient times and events, and dating from the 4th century AD onward. The 18 main texts include the *Vishnu Purāna* and *Bhāgavata*, which encourage devotion to Vishnu, above all in his incarnation as Krishna.

Purcell Henry 1659–1695. English Baroque composer. His work can be highly expressive, for example, the opera *Dido and Aeneas* 1689 and music for Dryden's *King Arthur* 1691 and for *The Fairy Queen* 1692. He wrote more than 500 works, ranging from secular operas and incidental music for plays to cantatas and church music.

purchasing-power parity a system for comparing standards of living between different countries. Comparing the gross domestic product of different countries involves first converting them to a common currency (usually US dollars or pounds sterling), a conversion which is subject to large fluctuations with variations in exchange rates. Purchasing power parity aims to overcome this by measuring how much money in the currency of those countries is required to buy a comparable range of goods and services.

purdah (Persian and Hindu "curtain") the seclusion of women practiced by some Islamic and Hindu peoples. It had begun to disappear with the adoption of Western culture, but the fundamentalism of the 1980s revived it, for example, the wearing of the ◊*chador* (an all-enveloping black mantle), in Iran. The Koran actually requests only "modesty" in dress.

Purcell *Henry Purcell, whose work marks the high point of Baroque music in England.*

pure breeding line in genetics, a strain of individuals that when interbred produce genetically identical progeny. A pure breeding tall pea plant is ◊homozygous for the allele controlling height.

Pure Land Buddhism the dominant form of Buddhism in China and Japan. It emphasizes faith in and love of Buddha, in particular Amitābha (Amida in Japan, Amituofo in China), the ideal "Buddha of boundless light," who has vowed that all believers who call on his name will be reborn in his Pure Land, or Western Paradise. This also applies to women, who had been debarred from attaining salvation through monastic life. There are over 16 million Pure Land Buddhists in Japan.

Amidism developed in China in the 3rd century, where the Pure Land school was, according to tradition, founded by the monk Hui Yuan (334–417); it spread in Japan from the 10th century. The basic teachings are found in the *Sukhāvati vyū ha/Pure Land Sūtra*. The prayer *Namu Amida Butsu* or *Nembutsu* was in some sects repeated for several hours a day. The True Pure Land school (Jōdo Shinshū), founded by the Japanese monk Shinran (1173–1262), held that a single, sincere invocation was enough and rejected monastic discipline and the worship of all other Buddhas; this has become the largest school.

purgative or ***laxative*** in medicine, any preparation to ease or accelerate the emptying of the bowels, such as Epsom salts, senna, or castor oil. With a diet containing enough fiber, such aids should not normally be necessary.

purgatory in Roman Catholic belief, a purificatory state or place where the souls of those who have died in a state of grace can expiate their venial sins, with a limited amount of suffering.

purge the removal (for example from a political party) of suspected opponents or persons regarded as undesirable (often violently). In 1934 the Nazis carried out a purge of their party and a number of party leaders were executed for an alleged plot against Hitler. During the 1930s purges were conducted in the USSR under Joseph Stalin, carried out by the secret police against political opponents, Communist Party members, minorities, civil servants, and large sections of the armed forces' officer corps. Some 10 million people were executed or deported to labor camps from 1934 to 1938. Later purges include Communist purges in Hungary (1949), Czechoslovakia (1951), and China (1955).

Purim Jewish festival celebrated in Feb or March (the 14th of Adar in the Jewish calendar), commemorating ◊Esther, who saved the Jews from destruction in 473 BC during the Persian occupation.

The festival includes a complete reading of the Book of Esther (*Megilla*) in the synagogue, during which the listeners respond with stamping, whistling, and hissing to the names of the evil characters.

Puritan from 1564, a member of the Church of England who wished to eliminate Roman Catholic survivals in ritual, or substitute a presbyterian for an episcopal form of church government. The term also covers the separatists who withdrew from the church altogether.

The Puritans were characterized by a strong conviction of human sinfulness and the wrath of God and by a devotion to plain living and hard work. The Puritan immigrants who settled in New England in the 17th century, most of them Congregationalists and Presbyterians, had a profound, formative influence on American culture, political institutions, and education. See also ◊Congregationalism.

Purple Heart, Order of the the earliest US military award for distinguished service beyond the call of duty, established by George Washington 1782, when it was the equivalent of the modern Congressional Medal of Honor. Made of purple cloth bound at the edges, it was worn on the facings over the left breast. After the American Revolution, it lapsed until revived by Congress in 1932, when it was established as an award for those wounded in combat. The present Purple Heart is of bronze and enamel.

Pushkin *Russian author Aleksandr Pushkin, in an 1827 portrait by Vasily Tropinin.*

purpura condition marked by purplish patches on the skin or mucous membranes due to localized spontaneous bleeding. It may be harmless, as sometimes with the elderly, or linked with disease, allergy, or drug reactions.

pus yellowish liquid that forms in the body as a result of bacterial attack; it includes white blood cells (leukocytes) "killed in battle" with the bacteria, plasma, and broken-down tissue cells. An enclosed collection of pus is an abscess.

Pusan or ***Busan*** chief industrial port (textiles, rubber, salt, fishing) of South Korea; population (1985) 3,517,000. It was invaded by the Japanese 1592 and opened to foreign trade 1883.

Pushkin town NW of Leningrad, USSR; population 80,000. Founded by Peter the Great as Tsarskoe Selo ("tsar's village") 1708, it has a number of imperial summer palaces, restored after German troops devastated the town 1941–44. In the 1920s it was renamed Detskoe Selo ("children's village"), but since 1937 it has been known as Pushkin, after the poet, who was educated at the school that is now a museum commemorating him.

Pushkin Aleksandr 1799–1837. Russian poet and writer. He was exiled 1820 for his political verse and in 1824 was in trouble for his atheistic opinions. He wrote ballads such as *The Gypsies* 1827, and the novel in verse ◊*Eugene Onegin* 1823–31. Other works include the tragic drama *Boris Godunov* 1825, and the prose pieces *The Captain's Daughter* 1836 and *The Queen of Spades* 1834. Pushkin's range was wide, and his willingness to experiment freed later Russian writers from many of the archaic conventions of the literature of his time.

Pushtu another name for the ◊Pashto language.

Puss in Boots fairy tale, included in Charles ◊Perrault's collection. The youngest son of a poor miller inherits nothing from his father but a talking cat. By ingenuity and occasional magic, the cat enables the hero to become rich, noble, and the husband of a princess.

putrefaction decomposition of organic matter by microorganisms.

putsch Swiss German term for a violent seizure of political power, such as Hitler and Ludendorff's abortive beer-hall putsch Nov 1923, which attempted to overthrow the Bavarian government.

Puttnam David Terence 1941– English film producer who played a major role in reviving the

pyramid

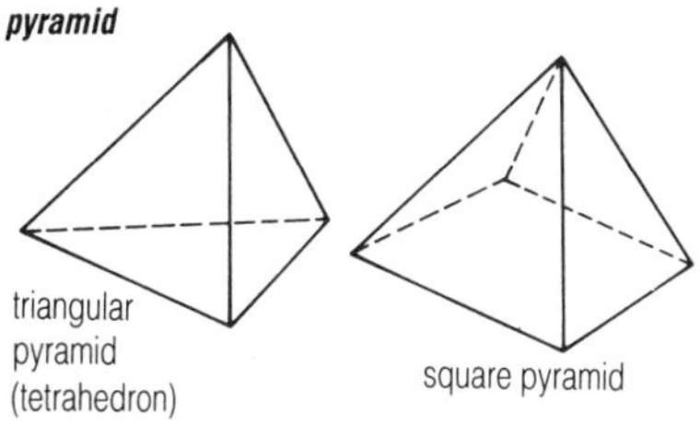
triangular
pyramid
(tetrahedron)
square pyramid

British film industry internationally. His films include *Chariots of Fire* 1981 and *The Killing Fields* 1984, both of which won several Academy Awards.

Puvis de Chavannes Pierre Cécile 1824–1898. French Symbolist painter. His major works are vast decorative schemes, mainly on mythological and allegorical subjects, for public buildings such as the Panthéon and Hôtel de Ville in Paris. His work influenced Gauguin.

The Boston Public Library, Massachusetts, also has his murals. His *Poor Fisherman* 1881 (Louvre, Paris) was a much admired smaller Symbolist work.

Puy, Le see ◊Le Puy, town in France.

Pu-Yi another transliteration of the name of the last Chinese emperor, Henry ◊P'u-i.

PVC abbreviation for polyvinylchloride, a type of ◊plastic derived from vinyl chloride (CH_2:CHCl).

pyelitis inflammation of the renal pelvis, the central part of the kidney where urine accumulates before discharge. It is caused by bacterial infection and is more common in women than in men.

Pygmalion in Greek legend, a king of Cyprus who fell in love with an ivory statue he had carved, and when Aphrodite brought it to life as Galatea, he married her.

Pygmy a member of any of the several small-statured, dark-skinned peoples of the rainforests of equatorial Africa (Negrillos) and Asia (the Negritos of parts of SE Asia and some Pacific islands).

Pylos port in SW Greece where the battle of ◊Navarino was fought 1827.

Pym Barbara 1913–1980. English novelist, born in Shropshire whose novels include *Some Tame Gazelle* 1950, *The Sweet Dove Died* 1978, and *A Few Green Leaves* 1980.

Pym John 1584–1643. English Parliamentarian, largely responsible for the ◊Petition of Right 1628. As leader of the Puritan opposition in the ◊Long Parliament from 1640, he moved the impeachment of Charles I's advisers Strafford and Laud, drew up the ◊Grand Remonstrance, and was the chief of five members of Parliament Charles I wanted arrested 1642. The five hid and then emerged triumphant when the king left London.

Pynchon Thomas 1937– . US novelist who created a bizarre, labyrinthine world in his books, the first of which was *V* 1963. *Gravity's Rainbow* 1973 represents a major achievement in 20th-century literature, with its fantastic imagery and esoteric language, drawn from mathematics and science.

Born in Glen Cove, New York, Pynchon graduated from Cornell University. His other works include *The Crying of Lot 49* 1966 and *Vineland* 1990. He also published short stories in *Slow Learner* 1984.

Pyongyang capital and industrial city (coal, iron, steel, textiles, chemicals) of North Korea; population (1984) 2,640,000.

pyorrhea former name for gum disease, now known as ◊periodontal disease.

pyramid in geometry, a solid figure with triangular side-faces meeting at a common vertex (point) and with a ◊polygon as its base. The volume *V* of a pyramid is given by $V = \frac{1}{3}Bh$, where *B* is the area of the base and *h* is the perpendicular height.

pyramid four-sided building with triangular sides used in ancient Egypt to enclose a royal tomb; for example, the Great Pyramid of Khufu/Cheops at Giza, near Cairo; 755 ft/230 m square and 481 ft/147 m high. In Babylon and Assyria broadly stepped pyramids (ziggurats) were used as the base for a shrine to a god: the Tower of Babel (see also ◊Babylon) was probably one of these.

Truncated pyramidal temple mounds were also built by the ancient Mexican and Peruvian civilizations, for example, at Teotihuacan and Cholula, near Mexico City; the latter is the world's largest in ground area (990 ft/300 m base, 195 ft/60 m high). Some New World pyramids were also used as royal tombs, for example, at the Mayan ceremonial center of Palenque.

pyramid of numbers in ecology, a diagram that shows how many plants and animals there are at different levels in a ◊food chain.

There are always far fewer individuals at the bottom of the chain than at the top because only about 10% of the food an animal eats is turned into flesh, so the amount of food flowing through the chain drops at each step. In a pyramid of numbers, the primary producers (usually plants) are represented at the bottom by a broad band, the plant-eaters are shown above by a narrower band, and the animals that prey on them by a narrower band still. At the top of the pyramid are the "top carnivores" such as lions and sharks, which are present in the smallest number.

Pyramus and Thisbe legendary Babylonian lovers whose story was retold by ◊Ovid. Pursued by a lioness, Thisbe lost her veil, and when Pyramus arrived at their meeting-place, he found it blood-stained. Assuming Thisbe was dead, he stabbed himself, and she, on finding his body, killed herself. In Shakespeare's *A Midsummer Night's Dream*, the "rude mechanicals" perform the story as a farce for the nobles.

Pyrenees (French *Pyrénées*; Spanish *Pirineos*) mountain range in SW Europe between France and Spain; length about 270 mi/435 km; highest peak Aneto (French Néthon) 11,172 ft/3,404 m. ◊Andorra is entirely within the range. Hydroelectric power has encouraged industrial development in the foothills.

pyrethrum popular name for some flowers of the genus *Chrysanthemum*, family Compositae. The ornamental species *C. coccineum*, and hybrids derived from it, are commonly grown in gardens. Pyrethrum powder, made from the dried flower heads of some species, is a powerful contact pesticide for aphids and mosquitoes.

pyridine C_5H_5N a heterocyclic compound (see ◊cyclic compounds). It is a liquid with a sickly smell that occurs in coal tar. It is soluble in water, acts as a strong ◊base, and is used as a solvent, mainly in the manufacture of plastics.

pyridoxine or ***vitamin B6*** $C_8H_{11}NO_3$ member of the ◊vitamin B complex. There is no clearly identifiable disease associated with deficiency but its absence from the diet can give rise to malfunction of the central nervous system and general skin disorders. Good sources are liver, meat, milk, and cereal grains. Related compounds may also show vitamin B6 activity.

pyrite a common iron ore, iron sulfide FeS_2; also called fool's gold because of its yellow metallic luster. Pyrite has a hardness of 6–6.5 on the Mohs' scale. It is used in the production of sulfuric acid.

pyroclastic in geology, pertaining to fragments of solidified volcanic magma, ranging in size from fine ash to large boulders, that are extruded during an explosive volcanic eruption; also the rocks that are formed by consolidation of such material. Pyroclastic rocks include tuff (ash deposit) and agglomerate (volcanic breccia).

pyrogallol $C_6H_3OH_3$ (techical name trihydroxybenzene) derivative of benzene, prepared from gallic acid. It is used in gas analysis for the measurement of oxygen because its alkaline solution turns black as it rapidly absorbs oxygen. It is also used as a developer in photography.

Pythagoras' theorem

for right-angled triangles

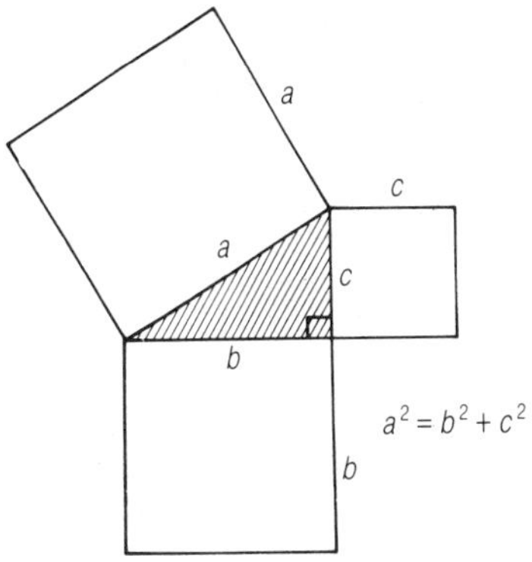
a
c
a
c
b
$a^2 = b^2 + c^2$
b

pyrometer ◊thermometer used for measuring high temperatures.

pyroxene any one of a group of minerals, silicates of calcium, iron, and magnesium with a general formula $XYSi_2O_6$, found in igneous and metamorphic rocks. The internal structure is based on single chains of silicon and oxygen. Diopside (X=Ca,Y=Mg) and augite (X=Ca,Y=Mg,Fe,Al) are common pyroxenes.

Jadeite ($NaAlSi_2O_6$), which is considered the more valuable form of jade, is also a pyroxene.

Pyrrho c. 360–c. 270 BC. Greek philosopher, founder of ◊Skepticism, who maintained that since certainty was impossible, peace of mind lay in renouncing all claims to knowledge.

Pyrrhus c. 318–272 BC. King of ◊Epirus from 307, who invaded Italy 280, as an ally of the Tarentines against Rome. He twice defeated the Romans but with such heavy losses that a "Pyrrhic victory" has come to mean a victory not worth winning. He returned to Greece 275 after his defeat at Beneventum, and was killed in a riot in Argos.

Pythagoras c. 580–500 BC. Greek mathematician and philosopher who formulated the Pythagorean theorem.

Much of his work concerned numbers, to which he assigned mystical properties. For example, he classified numbers into triangular ones (1, 3, 6, 10,...), which can be represented as a triangular array, and square ones (1, 4, 9, 16,...), which form squares. He also observed that any two adjacent triangular numbers add to a square number (for example, 1 + 3 = 4; 3 + 6 = 9; 6 + 10 = 16;...).

Pythagoras was the founder of a politically influential religious brotherhood in Croton, S Italy (suppressed in the 5th century). Its tenets included immortality of the soul and ◊transmigration.

Pythagorean theorem in geometry, theorem stating that in a right triangle, the square of the hypotenuse (the longest side) is equal to the sum of the squares of the other two sides (legs). If the hypotenuse is *c* units long and the lengths of the legs are *a* and *b*, then $c^2 = a^2 + b^2$.

The theorem provides a way of calculating the length of any side of a right triangle if the lengths of the other two sides are known. It is also used to determine certain trigonometrical relationships such as $\sin^2 \theta + \cos^2 \theta = 1$.

Pythagorus of Rhegium 5th century BC. Greek sculptor. He was born on Samos and settled in Rhegium (Reggio di Calabria), Italy. He made statues of athletes and is said to have surpassed his contemporary Myron in this field.

Pytheas 4th century BC. Greek navigator from Marseilles who explored the coast of W Europe at least as far N as Denmark, sailed around Britain, and reached ◊Thule (possibly the Shetlands).

Pythian Games ancient Greek festival in honor of ◊Apollo, celebrated near Delphi every four years.

python any constricting snake of the Old World subfamily Pythoninae of the family Boidae, which also includes ◊boas and the ◊anaconda. Pythons are found in the tropics of Africa, Asia, and Australia. Unlike boas, they lay eggs rather than producing living young. Some species are small, but the reticulated python *Python reticulatus* of SE Asia can grow to 33 ft/10 m.

pyx (Latin *pyxis* "small pox") in the Roman Catholic Church, the container used for the wafers of the sacrament.

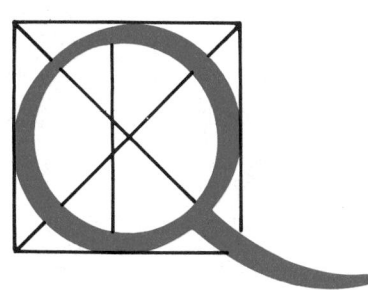

Qaboos bin Saidq 1940– . Sultan of Oman, the 14th descendant of the Albusaid family. Opposed to the conservative views of his father, he overthrew him in 1970 in a bloodless coup and assumed the sultanship. Since then he has followed more liberal and expansionist policies, while maintaining his country's position of international nonalignment.

Qaddafi alternate form of ◊Khaddhafi, Libyan leader.

Qadisiya, Battle of battle fought in S Iraq 637. A Muslim Arab force defeated a larger Zoroastrian Persian army and ended the ◊Sassanian Empire. The defeat is still resented in Iran, where Muslim Arab nationalism threatens to break up the Iranian state.

qat shrub *Catha edulis* of the staff-tree family Celastraceae. The leaves are chewed as a mild narcotic in some Arab countries. Its use was banned in ◊Somalia 1983.

Qatar country in the Middle East, occupying Qatar peninsula in the Arabian Gulf, bounded SW by Saudi Arabia and S by United Arab Emirates.

government A provisional constitution adopted 1970 confirmed Qatar as an absolute monarchy, with the emir holding all executive and legislative powers. The emir appoints and heads a council of ministers. An advisory council of 30 was established 1972, with limited powers to question ministers. There are no political parties.

history For early history, see ◊Arabia. Qatar, which used to be under ◊Bahrain's control, has had a treaty with Britain since 1868. It was part of the ◊Ottoman Empire from 1872 until World War I. The British government gave formal recognition 1916 to Sheik Abdullah al-Thani as Qatar's ruler, guaranteeing protection in return for an influence over the country's external affairs.

In 1968 Britain announced its intention of withdrawing its forces from the Persian Gulf area by 1981, and Qatar, having failed in an attempt to form an association with other Gulf states, became fully independent Sept 1, 1971. A new treaty of friendship with Britain replaced the former protectorate.

In 1972, while the emir, Sheik Ahmad, was out of the country, his cousin, the crown prince, Sheik Khalifa, led a bloodless coup; already prime minister, he declared himself also emir. He embarked on an ambitious program of social and economic reform, curbing the extravagances of the royal family. Qatar has good relations with most of its neighbors and is regarded as one of the more stable and moderate Arab states, although it devotes more than 43% of GNP to defense. Development programs are hampered by a lack of skilled workers. In the 1991 ◊Gulf War, Qatar's forces fought with the UN coalition against the Iraqi occupiers of Kuwait.

Qattara Depression tract of the Western Desert, Egypt, up to 400 ft/125 m below sea level. Its very soft sand makes it virtually impassable to vehicles, and it protected the left flank of the Allied armies before and during the battle of ◊Alamein 1942. Area 7,500 sq mi/20,000 sq km.

QED abbreviation for quod erat demonstrandum (Latin "which was to be proved").

qiblah the direction in which Muslims face to pray: the direction of Mecca. In every mosque this is marked by a niche (*mihrab*) in the wall.

Qin dynasty Chinese imperial dynasty 221–206 BC. ◊Shi Huangdi was its most renowned emperor.

Qingdao or ***Tsingtao*** industrial port (brewing) and summer resort in Shandong province, E China; population (1984) 1,229,500.

Qinghai or ***Tsinghai*** province of NW China

area 278,306 sq mi/721,000 sq km
capital Xining
features mainly desert, with nomadic herders
products oil, livestock, medical products
population (1986) 4,120,000; including many Tibetans and other minorities.

Qisarya Mediterranean port N of Tel Aviv–Jaffa, Israel; there are underwater remains of Herod the Great's port of Caesarea.

Qom or ***Qum*** holy city of Shiite Muslims, in central Iran, 90 mi/145 km S of Tehran; population (1986) 551,000.

The Islamic academy of Madresseh Faizieh 1920 became the headquarters of Ayatollah ◊Khomeini.

quadrathon a sports event in which the competitors must swim two miles, walk 30 miles, cycle 100 miles, and run 26.2 miles (a marathon) within 22 hours.

quadratic equation in mathematics, a polynomial equation of second degree (that is, an equation containing as its highest power the square of a single unknown variable, such as x^2). The general formula of such equations is $ax^2 + bx + c = 0$, in which a, b, and c are real numbers, and only the coefficient a cannot equal 0. In ◊coordinate geometry, a quadratic function represents a ◊parabola.

Depending on the value of the discriminant $b^2 - 4ac$, a quadratic equation has two real, two equal or two complex roots (solutions). When $b^2 - 4ac > 0$, there are two distinct real roots. When $b^2 - 4ac = 0$, there are two equal real roots. When $b^2 - 4ac < 0$, there are two distinct complex roots. Some quadratic equations can be solved by factorization, or the values of x can be found by using the formula for the general solution $x = [-b \pm \sqrt{(b^2 - 4ac)}]/2a$.

quadrille a square dance for four or more couples, or the music for the dance, which alternates between two and four beats in a bar.

quadrivium in medieval education, the four advanced liberal arts (arithmetic, geometry, astronomy, and music) which were studied after mastery of the trivium (grammar, rhetoric, and logic).

Quadruple Alliance in European history, three military alliances of four nations:

The Quadruple Alliance 1718 Austria, Britain, France, and the United Provinces (Netherlands) joined forces to prevent Spain from annexing Sardinia and Sicily

the Quadruple Alliance 1813 Austria, Britain, Prussia, and Russia allied to defeat the French emperor Napoleon; renewed 1815 and 1818. See Congress of ◊Vienna

the Quadruple Alliance 1834 Britain, France, Portugal, and Spain guaranteed the constitutional monarchies of Spain and Portugal against rebels in the Carlist War.

quaestor a Roman magistrate whose duties were mainly concerned with public finances. The quaestors originated as assistants to the consuls. Both urban and military quaestors existed, the latter being attached to the commanding generals in the provinces.

quagga South African zebra that became extinct in the 1880s. It was brown, with a white tail and legs, and unlike surviving zebra species, had stripes only on its head, neck, and forequarters.

Quai d'Orsay part of the left bank of the river Seine in Paris, where the French Foreign Office and

Qatar
State of
(Dawlat Qatar)

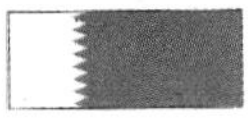

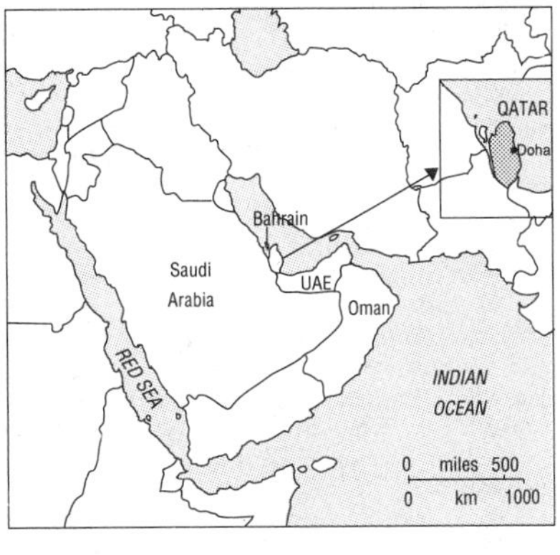
QATAR
Doha
Bahrain
Saudi
Arabia
UAE
Oman
RED SEA
INDIAN
OCEAN
0 miles 500
0 km 1000

area 4,402 sq mi/11,400 sq km
capital (and chief port) Doha
cities Dukhan, center of oil production
physical mostly flat desert with salt flats in S
features negligible rain and surface water, only 3% is fertile, but irrigation allows self-sufficiency in fruit and vegetables; extensive oil discoveries since World War II
head of state and government Sheik Khalifa bin Hamad al-Thani from 1972
political system absolute monarchy
political parties none
exports oil, natural gas, petrochemicals, fertilizers, iron, steel
currency riyal
population (1990 est) 498,000 (half in Doha; Arab 40%, Indian 18%, Pakistani 18%); growth rate 3.7% p.a.
life expectancy men 68, women 72 (1989)
language Arabic (official), English
religion Sunni Muslim 95%
literacy 60% (1987)
GNP $5.9 bn (1983); $35,000 per head
chronology
1916 Quatar became a British protectorate.
1970 Constitution adopted, confirming the emirate as an absolute monarchy.
1971 Independence achieved from Britain.
1972 Emir Sheik Ahmad replaced in bloodless coup by his cousin, Crown Prince Sheik Khalifa.

other government buildings are situated. The name has become synonymous with the Foreign Office itself.

quail any of several genera of small ground-dwelling birds of the family Phasianidae, which also includes grouse, pheasants, bobwhites, and prairie chickens.

The California quail *Callipepla californiensis* is one of five species of quail native to North America.

Quaker popular name, originally derogatory, for a member of the Society of ◊Friends.

qualitative analysis procedure for determining the identity of the component(s) of a single substance or mixture. A series of simple reactions and tests can be carried out on a compound to determine the elements present.

Quant Mary 1934– . British fashion designer. Her Chelsea boutique, Bazaar, revolutionized women's clothing and make-up and epitomized the "swinging London" of the 1960s.

quantitative analysis procedure for determining the precise amount of a known component present in a single substance or mixture. A known amount of the substance is subjected to particular procedures. Gravimetric analysis determines the mass of each constituent present; volumetric analysis determines the concentration of a solution by titration against a solution of known concentration.

quantity theory of money economic theory claiming that an increase in the amount of money in circulation causes a proportionate increase in prices.

The theory dates from the 17th century and was elaborated by the US economist Irving Fisher (1867–1947). Supported and developed by Milton Friedman, it forms the theoretical basis of ◊monetarism.

Quantrill William Clarke 1837–1865. US proslavery outlaw who became leader of a guerrilla unit on the Confederate side in the Civil War. Frank and Jesse ◊James were members of his gang (called Quantrill's Raiders).

quantum mechanics branch of physics dealing with the interaction of ◊matter and ◊radiation, the structure of the ◊atom, the motion of atomic particles, and with related phenomena (see ◊elementary particle and ◊quantum theory).

quantum number in physics, one of a set of four numbers that uniquely characterize an ◊electron and its state in an ◊atom. The principal quantum number n (= 1, 2, 3, and so on) defines the electron's main energy level. The orbital quantum number l ($= n - 1, n - 2$, and so on to l = 0) relates to angular momentum. The magnetic quantum number m ($= l, l - 1, l - 2$, and so on to 0 and then on to $\ldots -(l - 2), -(l - 1)$ and $-l$) describes the energies of electrons in a magnetic field. The spin quantum number m_s (= + ½ or −½) gives the spin direction of the electron.

The principal quantum number, defining the electron's energy level, corresponds to shells (energy levels) also known by their spectroscopic designations K, L, M, and so on. The orbital quantum number gives rise to a series of subshells designated s, p, d, f, and so on, of slightly different energy levels. The magnetic quantum number allows further subdivision of the subshells (making three subdivisions p_x, p_y, and p_z in the p subshell, for example, of the same energy level). No two electrons in an atom can have the same set of quantum numbers (the ◊Pauli exclusion principle).

quantum theory in physics, the theory that ◊energy does not have a continuous range of values, but is, instead, absorbed or radiated discontinuously, in multiples of definite, indivisible units called quanta. Just as earlier theory showed how light, generally seen as a wave motion, could also in some ways be seen as composed of discrete particles (◊photons), quantum mechanics shows how atomic particles such as electrons may also be seen as having wavelike properties. Quantum mechanics is the basis of particle physics, modern theoretical chemistry, and the solid-state physics that describes the behavior of the silicon chips used in computers.

quartz *Well-formed crystals of quartz, which are pyramidal in shape. These crystals are a pure form of quartz, so they are colorless.*

The theory began with the work of Max ◊Planck 1900 on radiated energy, and was extended by ◊Einstein to electromagnetic radiation generally, including ◊light. Niels ◊Bohr used it to explain the ◊spectrum of light emitted by excited hydrogen atoms. Later work by ◊Schrödinger, ◊Heisenberg, ◊Dirac, and others elaborated the theory to what is called quantum mechanics (or wave mechanics).

quarantine (from French *quarantaine* "40 days") any period for which people, animals, plants, or vessels may be detained in isolation when suspected of carrying contagious disease.

quark any of a group of basic ◊elementary particles that cannot be subdivided, of which all varieties plus their antiparticles total 36. They are the constituents of all ◊hadrons. There are six kinds, called "flavors' (up, down, top, bottom, strange, and charm), each having three varieties, called "colors" (red, green, and blue—but visual color is not meant, although the analogy is useful to ◊particle physics).

quart a unit of liquid or dry measure of volume or capacity. One liquid quart is equal to one-fourth of a gallon, or two pints, or 32 fluid ounces (0.946 liter), while a dry quart is equal to one-eighth of a peck, or two dry pints (1.101 liter).

The British and Canadian imperial quart equals two imperial pints or 1.136 liter.

quartz crystalline form of ◊silica SiO_2, one of the most abundant minerals of the Earth's crust (12% by volume). Quartz occurs in many different kinds of rock, including sandstone and granite. It ranks 7 on the Mohs' scale of hardness and is resistant to chemical or mechanical breakdown. Quartzes vary according to the size and purity of their crystals. Crystals of pure quartz are coarse, colorless, and transparent, and this form is usually called rock crystal. Impure colored varieties, often used as gemstones, include ◊agate, citrine quartz and ◊amethyst. Quartz is used in ornamental work and industry, where its reaction to electricity makes it valuable in electronic instruments (see ◊piezoelectric effect). Quartz can also be made synthetically.

Natural crystals that would take million of years to form can now be "grown" in pressure vessels to a standard that allows them to be used in optical and scientific instruments and in electronics, such as quartz wristwatches.

quartzite a ◊metamorphic rock consisting of pure quartz sandstone that has recrystallized under increasing heat and pressure.

quasar (from quasi-stellar object or QSO) in astronomy, a class of celestial objects far beyond our Galaxy, discovered 1964–65. Quasars appear starlike, but each emits more energy than 100 giant galaxies. They are thought to be at the center of distant galaxies, their brilliance emanating from the stars and gas falling toward an immense ◊black hole at their nucleus. Quasar light shows a large ◊red shift, indicating that they are very young and the most distant extragalactic objects known, the furthest lying over 10 billion light-years away. Some quasars emit radio waves (see ◊radio astronomy), which is how they were first identified 1963, but most are radio-quiet. About 3,000 are now known in a compact region of space, hence the suggestion that they spiral toward a massive black hole.

quasi-atom particle assemblage resembling an atom, in which particles not normally found in atoms become bound together for a brief period. Quasi-atoms are generally unstable structures, either because they are subject to matter–antimatter annihilation (positronium), or because one or more of their constituents is unstable (muonium).

Quasimodo Salvatore 1901–1968. Italian poet. His first book *Acque e terre/Waters and Land* appeared 1930. Later books, including *Nuove poesie/New Poetry* 1942, and *Il falso e vero verde/The False and True Green* 1956, reflect a growing preoccupation with the political and social problems of his time. Nobel Prize 1959.

quassia any tropical American tree of the genus *Quassia*, family Simaroubaceae, with a bitter bark and wood. The heartwood of *Q. amara* is a source of quassiin, an infusion of which was formerly used as a tonic; it is now used in insecticides.

The quassia family includes the Asian ailanthus *Ailanthus altissima*, also called the tree of heaven.

Quaternary period of geologic time that began 1.8 million years ago and is still in process. It is divided into the ◊Pleistocene and ◊Holocene epochs.

Quatre Bras, Battle of battle fought June 16, 1815 during the Napoleonic Wars, in which the British commander Wellington defeated French forces under Marshal Ney. It is named after a hamlet in Brabant, Belgium, 20 mi/32 km SE of Brussels.

Quayle (J) Dan(forth) 1947– . US Republican politician, an Indiana congressman from 1977, senator from 1981, vice president from 1989.

Born into a rich and powerful Indianapolis newspaper-owning family, Quayle was admitted to the Indiana bar 1974, and was elected to the House of Representatives 1976 and to the Senate 1980. When George Bush ran for president 1988, he selected Quayle as his running mate, admiring his conservative views and believing that Quayle could deliver the youth vote. This choice encountered heavy criticism because of Quayle's limited political experience. As vice president he was used frequently by the Bush administration to support conservative positions.

Que. abbreviation for ◊Québec.

Québec capital and industrial port (textiles, leather, timber, paper, printing and publishing) of Québec province, on the St Lawrence river, Canada; population (1986) 165,000, metropolitan area 603,000.

It was founded by the French explorer Samuel de ◊Champlain in 1608, and was a French colony 1608–1763. The British, under General ◊Wolfe, captured Québec 1759 after a battle on the nearby Plains of Abraham; both Wolfe and the French commander ◊Montcalm were killed. Québec is a center of French culture, and there are two universities, Laval 1663 (oldest in North America) and Québec 1969. Its picturesque old town survives below the citadel about 360 ft/110 m above the St Lawrence river.

Québec province of E Canada

area 594,710 sq mi/1,540,700 sq km

capital Québec

towns Montreal, Laval, Sherbrooke, Verdun, Hull, Trois-Rivières

features immense water-power resources (for example, the James Bay project)

products iron, copper, gold, zinc, cereals, potatoes, paper, textiles, fish, maple syrup (70% of world's output)

population (1986) 6,540,000

Quayle *US vice president Dan Quayle, who was elected as George Bush's Republican running mate in 1988.*

language French (the only official language since 1974, although 17% speak English). Language laws 1989 prohibit the use of English on street signs

history known as New France 1534–1763; captured by the British and became province of Québec 1763–90, Lower Canada 1791–1846, Canada East 1846–67; one of the original provinces 1867. Nationalist feelings 1960s (despite existing safeguards for Québec's French-derived civil law, customs, religion, and language) led to the foundation of the Parti Québecois by René Lévesque 1968. There was an uprising by Québec Liberation Front (FLQ) separatists 1970; a referendum on "sovereignty-association" (separation) was defeated 1980. Robert Bourassa and Liberals returned to power 1985 and enacted restrictive English-language legislation.

Québec Conference two conferences of Allied leaders in the city of Québec during World War II. The first conference 1943 approved the British admiral Mountbatten as supreme Allied commander in SE Asia and made plans for the invasion of France, for which the US general Eisenhower was to be supreme commander. The second conference Sept 1944 adopted plans for intensified air attacks on Germany, created a unified strategy against Japan, and established a postwar policy for a defeated Germany.

Quebec

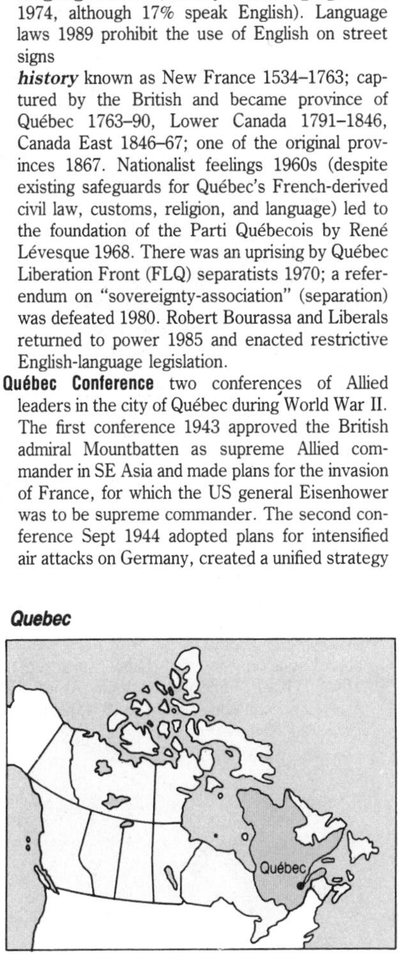
Québec

quebracho any of several South American trees of the cashew family Anacardiaceae, with very hard wood, chiefly the red quebracho *Schinopsis lorentzii*, used in tanning.

Quechua also ***Quichua*** or ***Kechua*** a member of a group of South American Indians of the Andean region, whose ancestors include the ◊Inca. The Quechua language is the second official language of Peru and is still spoken in Ecuador, Bolivia, Colombia, Argentina, and Chile.

QED abbreviation for *quod est demonstrandum*.

Queen Anne style style of decorative art in England 1700–20, characterized by plain, simple, curved or bowed lines, mainly in silver and furniture.

Queen Charlotte Islands archipelago about 100 mi/160 km off the coast of ◊British Columbia, W Canada, of which it forms part; area 3,780 sq mi/9,790 sq km; population 2,500. Graham and Moresby are the largest of about 150 islands. There are timber and fishing industries.

Queen Maud Land a region of Antarctica W of Enderby Land, claimed by Norway since 1939.

Queens a mainly residential borough and county at the NW end of Long Island, New York City. It has sports arenas (Shea Stadium, Forest Hills Tennis Club, and the National Tennis Center at Flushing Meadows), a botanical garden, a museum, and several branches of the City University of New York. Both La Guardia and Kennedy airports are here.

Queensberry John Sholto Douglas, 8th Marquess of Queensberry 1844–1900. British patron of boxing. In 1867 he formulated the Queensberry Rules, which form the basis of today's boxing rules.

Queensland state in NE Australia

area 666,699 sq mi/1,727,200 sq km

capital Brisbane

towns Gold Coast–Tweed, Townsville, Sunshine Coast, Toowoomba, Cairns

features Great Dividing Range, including Mount Bartle Frere 5,438 ft/1,657 m; Great Barrier Reef (collection of coral reefs and islands about 1,250 mi/2,000 km long off the E coast); City of Gold Coast vacation area in the S; Mount Isa mining area

Queensland

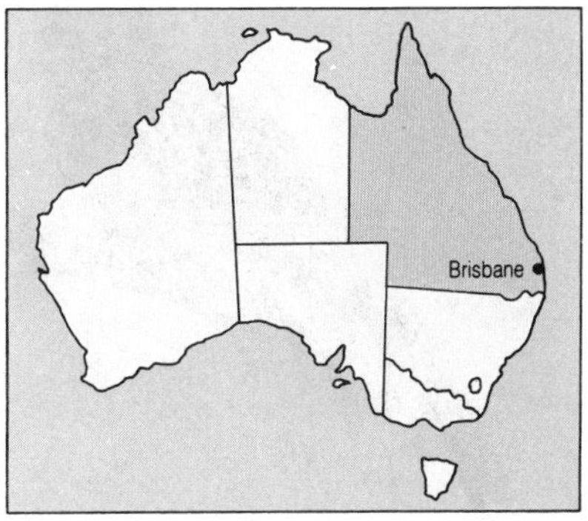
Brisbane

products sugar, pineapples, beef, cotton, wool, tobacco, copper, gold, silver, lead, zinc, coal, nickel, bauxite, uranium, natural gas

population (1987) 2,650,000

history part of New South Wales until 1859, when it became self-governing. In 1989 the ruling National Party was defeated after 32 years in power and replaced by the Labour Party.

Quemoy island off the SE coast of China, and administered, along with the island of Matsu, by Taiwan. Quemoy: area 50 sq mi/130 sq km; population (1982) 57,847. Matsu: 17 sq mi/44 sq km; population (1982) 11,000. When the islands were shelled from the mainland in 1960, the US declared they would be defended if attacked.

Queneau Raymond 1903–1976. French Surrealist poet and humorous novelist, author of *Zazie dans le Métro/Zazie in the Metro* 1959, portraying a precocious young Parisian woman.

question mark a punctuation mark (?), used to indicate inquiry or doubt. When indicating inquiry, it is placed at the end of a *direct question* ("Who is coming?") but never at the end of an *indirect question* ("He asked us who was coming"). When indicating doubt, it usually appears between brackets, to show that a writer or editor is puzzled or uncertain about quoted text.

Quetelet Lambert Adolphe Jacques 1796–1874. Belgian statistician. He developed tests for the validity of statistical information, and gathered and analyzed statistical data of many kinds. From his work on sociological data came the concept of the "average person."

Quetta summer resort and capital of Baluchistan, W Pakistan; population (1981) 281,000. Linked to Shikarpur by a gas pipeline in 1982.

quetzal long-tailed Central American bird (*Pharomachus mocinno) of the* ◊trogon family. The male is brightly colored, with green, red, blue, and white feathers, and is about 4.3 ft/1.3 m long including tail. The female is smaller and lacks the tail and plumage.

The quetzal eats fruit, insects, and small frogs and lizards. It is the national emblem of Guatemala, and was considered sacred by the Mayans and the Aztecs. The quetzal's forest habitat is rapidly being destroyed, and hunting of birds for trophies or souvenirs also threatens its survival.

Quetzalcoatl in pre-Columbian Mesoamerican cultures of Central America, a feathered serpent god of air and water. In his human form, he was said to have been fair-skinned and bearded and to have reigned on Earth during a golden age. He disappeared across the eastern sea, with a promise to return; ◊Cortés exploited the coincidence of description when he invaded. Ruins of Quetzalcoatl's temples survive in various ancient Mesoamerican ceremonial centers, including the one at Teotihuacán in Mexico. (See also ◊Aztec, ◊Mayan, and ◊Toltec civilizations).

Quevedo y Villegas Francisco Gómez de

quetzal

quince

1580–1645. Spanish novelist and satirist. His picaresque novel *La Vida del Buscón/The Life of a Scoundrel* 1626 follows the tradition of the roguish hero who has a series of adventures. *Sueños/Visions* 1627 is a brilliant series of satirical portraits of contemporary society.

Quezon City former capital of the Philippines 1948–76, NE part of metropolitan ◊Manila, on Luzon Island; population (1980) 1,166,000. It was named after the Philippines' first president, Manuel Luis Quezon (1878–1944).

Qufu or ***Chufu*** town in Shandong province, China; population 27,000. It is the birthplace of Kong Zi (◊Confucius) and the site of the Great Temple of Confucius.

Quiberon peninsula and coastal town in Brittany, NW France; in 1759 the British admiral ◊Hawke defeated a French fleet (under Conflans) in Quiberon Bay.

quietism a religious attitude, displayed periodically in the history of Christianity, consisting of passive contemplation and meditation to achieve union with God. The founder of modern quietism was the Spanish priest ◊Molinos who published a *Guida Spirituale/Spiritual Guide* 1675.

quilt a padded bed-cover or the method, as used to make padded covers or clothing. The padding is made by sewing in patterns—often diamond shapes or floral motifs—a layer of down, cotton, wool or other stuffing between two outer pieces of material.

Quilts have been made in the home for centuries throughout Europe, the East, and more recently the US. They are sometimes decorated with patchwork or embroidery.

In the US, group or family efforts resulted in quilting bees, where several people sewed and visited on certain days to finish the project (wedding, baby) and to have company in a vast, relatively unpopulated colonial farming region.

Quimby Fred(erick) 1886–1965. US film producer, head of MGM's short films department from 1926 to 1956. Among the cartoons produced by this department were the *Tom and Jerry* series and those directed by Tex ◊Avery.

quince small tree *Cydonia oblonga*, family Rosaceae, native to W Asia. The bitter, yellow, pear-shaped fruit is used in preserves.

Quincy Josiah 1772–1864. US public official. Born in Braintree, Massachusetts, Quincy was educated at Harvard and admitted to the bar 1793. Embarking on a political career as a staunch Federalist, he served in the US House of Representatives 1805–13, opposing the trade policies of the Jefferson administration and its acquisition of the Louisiana Territory. As an opponent of US involvement in the War of 1812, he resigned from Congress and returned to Boston, where he was mayor 1823–28.

Quincy also served as president of Harvard 1829–45 and wrote a number of historical works.

Quine Willard Van Orman 1908– . US philosopher and logician. In *Two Dogmas of Empiricism* 1951, he argued against the ◊analytic/◊synthetic distinction. In *Word and Object* 1960, he put forward the thesis of radical untranslatability, the view that a sentence can always be regarded as referring to many different things.

Born in Akron, Ohio, he graduated from Oberlin College and Harvard University. He was professor of philosophy at Harvard from 1936. He also wrote *Word and Object* 1960 and *Philosophy of Logic* 1970.

quinine antimalarial drug extracted from the bark of the cinchona tree. Peruvian Indians taught French missionaries how to use the bark 1630, but quinine was not isolated for another two centuries. It is a bitter alkaloid $C_{20}H_{24}N_2O_2$.

Other drugs against malaria have since been developed with fewer side effects, but quinine derivatives are still valuable in the treatment of unusually resistant strains.

Quinn Anthony 1915– . Mexican-born US actor, in films from 1935. He won an Academy Award for his role in *Viva Zapata!* 1952, another for his Gaugin in *Lust For Life* 1956, but became famous for the title role in *Zorba the Greek* 1964. He later often played variations on this larger-than-life character.

Quinquagesima (Latin "fiftieth") in the Christian church calendar, the Sunday before Lent and 50 days before Easter.

Quintana Roo state in SE Mexico, on the east of the ◊Yucatán peninsula, population (1980) 226,000. There are ◊Maya remains at Tulum; Cancun is a major resort and free port.

Quintero Serafín Alvarez and Joaquín Alvarez. Spanish dramatists; see ◊Alvarez Quintero.

Quintilian (Marcus Fabius Quintilianus) c. AD 35–95. Roman rhetorician. He was born at Calgurris, Spain, taught rhetoric in Rome from AD 68, and composed the *Institutio oratorio/The Education of an Orator*, in which he advocated a simple and sincere style of public speaking.

quipu (Quechua "knot") device used by the ◊Incas of ancient Peru to record numerical information, consisting of a set of knotted cords of one or several colors. Among its applications was the recording of granary and warehouse stores.

Quirinal one of the seven hills on which ancient Rome was built. Its summit is occupied by a palace built 1574 as a summer residence for the pope and occupied 1870–1946 by the kings of Italy. The name Quirinal is derived from that of Quirinus, local god of the ◊Sabines.

Quisling Vidkun 1887–1945. Norwegian politician. Leader from 1933 of the Norwegian Fascist Party, he aided the Nazi invasion of Norway 1940 by delaying mobilization and urging nonresistance. He was made premier by Hitler 1942, and was arrested and shot as a traitor by the Norwegians 1945. His name became a generic term for a traitor who aids an occupying force.

Quito capital and industrial city (textiles, chemicals, leather, gold, silver) of Ecuador, about 9,850 ft/3,000 m above sea level; population (1982) 1,110,250. It was an ancient settlement, taken by the Incas about 1470 and by the Spanish 1534. It has a temperate climate year round.

Quixote, Don novel by the Spanish writer ◊Cervantes, with a hero of the same name.

Qum alternate spelling of ◊Qom, city of Iran.

Qumran or ***Khirbet Qumran*** archeological site in Jordan, excavated from 1951, in the foothills NW of the Dead Sea. Originally an Iron Age fort (6th century BC), it was occupied in the late 2nd century BC by a monastic community, the ◊Essenes, until the buildings were burned by Romans AD 68. The monastery library had contained the ◊Dead Sea Scrolls, which had been hidden in caves for safekeeping and were discovered 1947.

quoits game in which a rubber, rope, or metal ring (quoit) is thrown at a peg (hob) from a point 54 ft/16.5 m away. The player whose quoit lands nearest the hob, within a circle 3 ft/1 m in diameter, gains one point. A quoit that encircles the hob is called a ringer and is worth two points.

quorum a minimum number of members required to be present for the proceedings of an assembly to be valid. The number of people required for a quorum may vary.

quota in international trade, a limitation on the quantities exported or imported. Restrictions may be imposed forcibly or voluntarily. The justifications of quotas include protection of a home industry from an influx of cheap goods, prevention of a heavy outflow of goods (usually raw materials) because there are insufficient numbers to meet domestic demand, allowance for a new industry to develop before it is exposed to competition, or prevention of a decline in the world price of a particular commodity.

qv abbreviation for quod vide (Latin "which see").

QwaQwa a black homeland of South Africa that achieved self-governing status in 1974; population (1985) 181,600.

Rabat capital of Morocco, industrial port (cotton textiles, carpets, leather goods) on the Atlantic coast, 110 mi/177 km W of Fez; population (1982) 519,000, Rabat-Salé 842,000. It is named after its original *ribat* or fortified monastery.

Rabaul largest port (trading in copra and cocoa) of Papua New Guinea, on the volcanic island of New Britain, SW Pacific; population (1980) 14,954. It was destroyed by British bombing after its occupation by the Japanese in 1942 but was rebuilt.

rabbi in Judaism, the chief religious leader of a synagogue or the spiritual leader (not a hereditory high priest) of a Jewish congregation; also, a scholar of Judaic law and ritual from the 1st century AD.

rabbit any of several genera of hopping mammals of the order Lagomorpha, which together with ◊hares constitute the family Leporidae. Rabbits differ from hares in bearing naked, helpless young and in occupying burrows.

The Old World rabbit (*Oryctolagus cuniculus*), originally from S Europe and N Africa, has now been introduced worldwide. It is bred for meat and for its fur, which is usually treated to resemble more expensive furs. It lives in interconnected burrows called "warrens," unlike cottontails (genus *Sylvilagus*), of which 13 species are native to North and South America.

Rabelais François 1495–1553. French satirist, monk, and physician, whose name has become synonymous with bawdy humor. He was educated in the Renaissance humanist tradition and was the author of satirical allegories, including *La Vie inestimable de Gargantua/The Inestimable Life of Gargantua* 1535 and *Faits et dits héroïques du grand Pantagruel/Deeds and Sayings of the Great Pantagruel* 1533, about two giants (father and son) Gargantua and Pantagruel.

Rabi Isidor Isaac 1898–1988. Russian-born US physicist who developed techniques to measure accurately the strength of the weak magnetic fields generated when charged elementary particles, such as the electron, spin about their axes. The work won for him the 1944 Nobel Prize for Physics.

rabies or ***hydrophobia*** disease of the central nervous system that can afflict all warm-blooded creatures. It is almost invariably fatal once symptoms have developed. Its transmission to humans is generally by a bite from a rabid dog.

After an incubation period, which may vary from ten days to more than a year, symptoms of fever, muscle spasm, and delirium develop. As the disease progresses, the mere sight of water is enough to provoke convulsions and paralysis. Death is usual within four or five days from the onset of symptoms. Injections of rabies vaccine and antiserum may save those bitten by a rabid animal from developing the disease. Louis ◊Pasteur was the first to produce a preventive vaccine, and the Pasteur Institute was founded to treat the disease. As a control measure for foxes and other wild animals, vaccination (by bait) is recommended. In France, foxes are now vaccinated against rabies with capsules distributed by helicopter.

Rabin Itzhak 1922– . Israeli prime minister 1974–77, who succeeded Golda Meir.

Rabuka Sitiveni 1948– . Fijian soldier and politician. When the 1987 elections in Fiji produced an Indian-dominated government he staged a bloodless coup, kidnapping the prime minister and his cabinet and heading an interim government. He soon stepped down, but remained influential behind the scenes.

raccoon any of several New World species of carnivorous mammals of the genus *Procyon*, in the family Procyonidae. The common raccoon *P. lotor* is about 2 ft/60 cm long, with a gray-brown body, a black and white ringed tail, and a black "mask" around its eyes. The crab-eating raccoon *P. cancrivorus* of South America is slightly smaller, and has shorter fur.

race in anthropology, the term applied to the varieties of modern humans, *Homo sapiens sapiens*, having clusters of distinctive physical traits in common. The three major varieties are ◊Caucasoid, ◊Mongoloid, and ◊Negroid. During the last 60,000 years, migrations and interbreeding have caused a range of variations to exist today, not distinct or "pure" races (which can exist only under conditions of isolation).

Rachel in the Old Testament, the favorite wife of ◊Jacob, and mother of ◊Joseph and Benjamin.

Rachel stage name of Elizabeth Félix 1821–1858. French tragic actress who excelled in fierce, passionate roles, notably Racine's *Phèdre*, which she took on tour to Europe, the US, and Russia.

Rachmaninov Sergei (Vasilevich) 1873–1943. Russian composer, conductor, and pianist. After the 1917 Revolution he went to the US. His dramatically emotional Romantic music has a strong melodic basis and includes operas, such as *Francesca da Rimini* 1906, three symphonies, four piano concertos, piano pieces, and songs. Among his other works are the *Prelude in C-sharp Minor* 1892 and *Rhapsody on a Theme of Paganini* 1934 for piano and orchestra.

Racine city and port of entry in SW Wisconsin on the Root river where it flows into Lake Michigan. Industries include automotive parts, farm machinery, and wax products; population (1990) 84,298.

raccoon

***Racine** The tragedies of Racine were part of the great flowering of dramatic and poetic writing in 17th-century France.*

Racine Jean 1639–1699. French dramatist and exponent of the Classical tragedy in French drama. His subjects came from Greek mythology and he observed the rules of Classical Greek drama. Most of his tragedies have women in the title role, for example *Andromaque* 1667, *Iphigénie* 1674, and *Phèdre* 1677. After the contemporary failure of *Phèdre* he no longer wrote for the secular stage, but influenced by Madame de ◊Maintenon wrote two religious dramas, *Esther* 1689 and *Athalie* 1691, which achieved posthumous success.

racism belief in, or set of implicit assumptions about, the superiority of one's own ◊race or ethnic group, often accompanied by prejudice against members of a race or ethnic group different from one's own. Racism may be used to justify ◊discrimination, verbal or physical abuse, or even genocide, as in Nazi Germany, or as practiced by European settlers against American Indians in both North and South America.

Many social scientists believe that even where there is no overt discrimination, racism exists as an unconscious attitude in many individuals and societies, based on a ◊stereotype or preconceived idea about different groups, which is damaging to individuals (both perpetrators and victims) and to society as a whole. See also ◊ethnicity.

rackets or ***racquets*** indoor game played on an enclosed court. It is regarded as the forerunner of many racket and ball games.

Although first played in the Middle Ages, rackets developed in the 18th century and was played against the walls of London buildings. See ◊squash.

rad (abbreviation of *r*adiation *a*bsorbed *d*ose) SI unit of absorbed dose of radiation. It is the dose when one kilogram of matter absorbs 0.01 joule of energy (formerly, the dose when one gram absorbs 100 ergs). Different types of radiation cause different amounts of damage for the same absorbed dose; the dose equivalent is measured in ◊rems.

radar (acronym for radio direction and ranging) device for locating objects in space, direction finding, and navigation by means of transmitted and reflected high-frequency radio waves.

The direction of an object is ascertained by transmitting a beam of shortwavelength (½–40 in/1–100 cm), shortpulse radio waves, and picking up the reflected beam. Distance is determined by timing the journey of the radio waves (traveling at the speed of light) to the object and back again. Radar is also used to detect objects underground, for example service pipes and in archeology. Contours of remains of ancient buildings can be detected down to 66 ft/20 m below ground.

Radar is essential to navigation in darkness, cloud, and fog, and is widely used in warfare to detect enemy aircraft and missiles. To avoid detection, various devices, such as modified shapes (to reduce their radar cross-section), radar-absorbent paints and electronic jamming are used. To pinpoint small targets ◊laser "radar," instead of ◊microwaves, has been developed. Chains of ground radar stations are used to warn of enemy attack—for example, North Warning System 1985, consisting of 52 stations across the Canadian Arctic and N Alaska. Radar is also used in ◊meteorology and ◊astronomy.

radar astronomy the bouncing of radio waves off objects in the Solar System, with reception and analysis of the "echoes." Radar contact with the Moon was first made 1945 and with Venus 1961. The travel time for radio reflections allows the distances of objects to be determined accurately. Analysis of the reflected beam reveals the rotation period and allows the object's surface to be mapped. The rotation periods of Venus and Mercury were first determined by radar. Radar maps of Venus were obtained first by Earth-based radar and subsequently by orbiting space probes.

Radcliffe Ann (born Ward) 1764–1823. English novelist, an exponent of the ◊Gothic novel or "romance of terror" who wrote, for example, *The Mysteries of Udolpho* 1794.

Radha in the Hindu epic ◊*Mahābhārata*, the wife of a cowherd who leaves her husband for love of Krishna (an incarnation of the god Vishnu). Her devotion to Krishna is seen by the mystical *bhakti* movement as the ideal of the love between humans and God.

radial circuit circuit used in household electric wiring in which all electrical appliances are connected to cables that radiate out from the main supply point or fuse box. In more modern systems, the appliances are connected in a ring, or ring circuit, with each end of the ring connected to the fusebox.

radian in mathematics, alternative unit to the ◊degree for measuring angles. It is the angle at the center of a circle when the center is joined to the two ends of an arc (part of the circumference) equal in length to the radius of the circle. There are 2π (approximately 6.284) radians in a full circle (360°).

One radian is approximately 57°, and 1° is π/180 or approximately 0.0175 radians. Radians are commonly used to specify angles in ◊polar coordinates.

radiation in physics, emission of radiant ◊energy as particles or waves—for example, heat, light, alpha particles, and beta particles (see ◊electromagnetic waves and ◊radioactivity). See also ◊atomic radiation.

radiation biology study of how living things are affected by radioactive (ionizing) emissions (see ◊radioactivity) and by electromagnetic (nonionizing) radiation (◊electromagnetic waves). Both are potentially harmful and can cause mutations as well as leukemia and other cancers; even low levels of radioactivity are very dangerous. Both are, however, used therapeutically, for example to treat cancer, when the radiation dose is very carefully controlled (radio therapy or X-ray therapy).

Radioactive emissions are harmful. Exposure to high levels produces radiation burns and radiation sickness, plus genetic damage (resulting in birth defects) and cancers in the longer term. Exposure to low-level ionizing radiation can also cause genetic damage and cancers, particularly leukemia.

Electromagnetic radiation is usually harmful only if exposure is to high-energy emissions, for example close to powerful radio transmitters or near radar-wave sources. Such exposure can cause organ damage, cataracts, loss of hearing, leukemia and other cancers, or premature aging. It may also affect the nervous system and brain, distorting their electrical nerve signals and leading to depression, disorientiation, headaches, and other symptoms. Individual sensitivity varies, but some people are affected by living under or near electric lines or by electrical equipment such as televisions, computers, and refrigerators.

radio

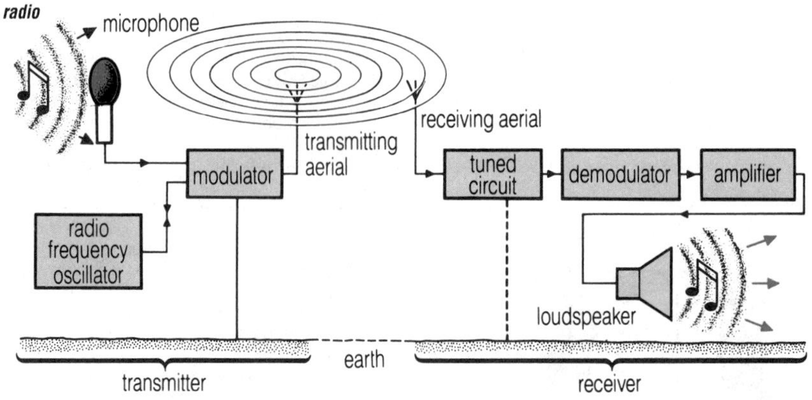
microphone
transmitting aerial
modulator
radio frequency oscillator
receiving aerial
tuned circuit
demodulator
amplifier
loudspeaker
earth
transmitter
receiver

radiation sickness sickness resulting from exposure to radiation, including X-rays, gamma rays, neutrons, and other nuclear radiation, as from weapons and fallout. Such radiation ionizes atoms in the body and causes nausea, vomiting, diarrhea, and other symptoms. The body cells themselves may be damaged even by very small doses, causing ◊leukemia; genetic changes may be induced in the germ plasm, causing infants to be born damaged or mutated.

radiation units units of measurement for radioactivity and radiation doses. Continued use of the units introduced earlier this century (the curie, rad, rem, and roentgen) has been approved while the derived SI units (becquerel, gray, sievert, coulomb) become familiar. One curie equals 3.7 $\times$ 10^{-10} becquerels (activity); one rad equals 10^{-2} gray (absorbed dose); one rem equals 10^{-2} sievert (dose equivalent); one roentgen equals 2.58 $\times$ 10^{-4} coulomb/kg (exposure to ionizing radiation).

The average radiation exposure per person per year in the US is 0.1 rem, of which 50% is derived from naturally occurring radon.

Radić Stjepan 1871–1928. Yugoslav nationalist politician, founder of the Croatian Peasant Party 1904. He led the Croat national movement within the Austro-Hungarian Empire and advocated a federal state with Croatian autonomy. His opposition to Serbian supremacy within Yugoslavia led to his assassination in parliament.

radical in chemistry, a group of atoms forming part of a molecule, which acts as a unit and takes part in chemical reactions without disintegration, yet often cannot exist alone; for example, the methyl radical $-CH_3$, or the carboxylic acid radical $-COOH$.

radical in politics, anyone with opinions more extreme than the main current of a country's major political party or parties. It is more often applied to those with left-wing opinions, although the radical right also exists.

Radical in Britain, supporter of parliamentary reform before the Reform Bill 1832. As a group the Radicals later became the progressive wing of the Liberal Party. During the 1860s (led by Cobden, Bright, and J S Mill) they campaigned for extension of the franchise, free trade, and ◊laissez-faire, but after 1870, under the leadership of Joseph Chamberlain and Dilke, they adopted a republican and semi-Socialist program. With the growth of ◊socialism in the later 19th century, Radicalism ceased to exist as an organized movement.

radicle the part of a plant embryo that develops into the primary root. Usually it emerges from the seed before the embryonic shoot, or ◊plumule, its tip protected by a root cap, or calyptra, as it pushes through the soil. The radicle may form the basis of the entire root system, or it may be replaced by adventitious (positioned on the stem) roots.

radio transmission and reception of radio waves. In radio transmission a microphone converts ◊sound waves (pressure variations in the air) into ◊electromagnetic waves that are then picked up by a receiving aerial and fed to a loudspeaker, which converts them back into sound waves.

The theory of electromagnetic waves was first developed by James Clerk ◊Maxwell 1864, given practical confirmation in the laboratory 1888 by Heinrich ◊Hertz, and put to practical use by ◊Marconi, who in 1901 achieved reception of a signal in Newfoundland transmitted from Cornwall, England. To carry the transmitted electrical signal, an ◊oscillator produces a carrier wave of high frequency; different stations are allocated different transmitting carrier frequencies. A modulator superimposes the audiofrequency signal on the carrier. There are two main ways of doing this: amplitude modulation (AM), used for long- and medium-wave broadcasts, in which the strength of the carrier is made to fluctuate in time with the audio signal; and frequency modulation (FM), as used for VHF broadcasts, in which the frequency of the carrier is made to fluctuate. The transmitting aerial emits the modulated electromagnetic waves, which travel outward from it.

In radio reception a receiving aerial picks up minute voltages in response to the waves sent out by a transmitter. A tuned circuit selects a particular frequency, usually by means of variable ◊capacitor connected across a coil of wire. A demodulator disentangles the audio signal from the carrier, which is now discarded, having served its purpose. An amplifier boosts the audio signal for feeding to the loudspeaker.

radioactive decay the spontaneous alteration of the nucleus of a radioactive ◊atom, which transmutes the atom from one atomic number to another, thereby producing another ◊element. This is accompanied by the emission of radiation, of which ◊alpha decay and ◊beta decay (beta-minus and beta-plus) are the most common forms. Less commonly occurring decay forms include heavy-ion emission, electron capture (k-capture and L-capture), fission (spontaneous and induced), neutron–proton exchange (neutron absorbed, proton ejected), spallation, and proton decay (rare). In all forms of decay except beta-minus, the atomic number decreases (in beta-minus it increases).

Radioactive Incident Monitoring Network (RIMNET) monitoring network at 46 (to be raised to about 90) Meteorological Office sites throughout the UK. It feeds into a central computer, and was installed in 1989 to record contamination levels from nuclear incidents such as the ◊Chernobyl disaster.

radioactive tracer any of various radioactive ◊isotopes used in labeled compounds; see ◊tracer.

radioactive waste any waste that emits radiation in excess of the background level. See ◊nuclear waste.

radioactivity spontaneous alteration of the nuclei of radioactive atoms, accompanied by the emission of radiation. It is the property exhibited by the radioactive ◊isotopes of stable elements and all isotopes of radioactive elements, and can be either natural or induced. See ◊radioactive decay.

Radioactivity establishes an equilibrium in parts of the nucleus of unstable radioactive substances, ultimately to form a stable arrangement of nucleons (protons and neutrons); that is, a non-radioactive (stable) element. This is most frequently accomplished by the emission of alpha particles (helium nuclei); beta particles (electrons and positrons); or gamma rays (electromagnetic waves of very high frequency). It takes place either directly, through a one-step decay, or indirectly, through a number of decays that transmute one element into another. This is called a decay series or chain, and sometimes produces an element more radioactive than its predecessor.

The instability of the particle arrangements in the nucleus of a radioactive atom (the ratio of neutrons to protons and/or the total number of both) determines the lengths of the ◊half-lives of the isotopes of that atom, which can range from fractions of a second to billions of years. All isotopes of atomic weights 210 and greater are radioactive. Beta and gamma radiation are both ionizing and are therefore dangerous to body tissues, especially if a radioactive substance is ingested or inhaled.

radio astronomy study of radio waves emitted naturally by objects in space, by means of a ◊radio telescope. Radio emission comes from hot gases (thermal radiation); electrons spiraling in magnetic fields (synchrotron radiation); and specific wavelengths (lines) emitted by atoms and molecules in space, such as the 8-in/21-cm line emitted by hydrogen gas. Radio astronomy began 1932 when Karl ◊Jansky detected radio waves from the center of our Galaxy, but the subject did not develop until after World War II. Radio astronomy has greatly improved our understanding of the evolution of stars, the structure of galaxies, and the origin of the universe.

Astronomers have mapped the spiral structure of the Milky Way from the radio waves given out by interstellar gas, and they have detected many individual radio sources within our Galaxy and beyond.

Among radio sources in our Galaxy are the remains of ◊supernova explosions, such as the ◊Crab nebula and ◊pulsars. Short-wavelength radio waves have been detected from complex molecules in dense clouds of gas where stars are forming. Searches have been undertaken for signals from other civilizations in the Galaxy, so far without success.

Strong sources of radio waves beyond our Galaxy include ◊radio galaxies and ◊quasars. Their existence far off in the universe demonstrates how the universe has evolved with time. Radio astronomers have also detected weak background radiation thought to be from the ◊Big Bang explosion that marked the birth of the universe.

radiocarbon dating or ***carbon dating*** method of dating organic materials (for example, bone or wood), used in archeology. Plants take up carbon dioxide gas from the atmosphere and incorporate it into their tissues, and some of that carbon dioxide contains the radioactive isotope of carbon, carbon-14. On death, the plant ceases to take up carbon-14 and that already taken up decays at a known rate, the half-life of 5,730 years, so that the time elapsed since the plant died can be measured in a laboratory. Animals take carbon-14 into their bodies from eating plant tissues, thus their remains can be similarly dated. After 120,000 years so little carbon-14 is left that no measure is possible (see ◊half-life).

radio, cellular portable telephone system; see ◊cellular phone.

radiochemistry chemical study of radioactive isotopes and their compounds (whether produced from naturally occurring radioactive or irradiated materials) and their use in the study of other chemical processes.

When such isotopes are used in labeled compounds, they enable the biochemical and physiological functioning of parts of the living body to be observed. They can help in the testing of new drugs, showing where the drug goes in the body and how long it stays there. They are also useful in diagnosis—for example, cancer, fetal abnormalities, and heart disease.

radio frequencies classification of, see ◊electromagnetic waves.

radio galaxy galaxy that is a strong source of electromagnetic waves of radio wavelengths. All galaxies, including our own, emit some radio waves, but radio galaxies are up to a million times more powerful.

In many cases the strongest radio emission comes not from the visible galaxy but from two clouds, invisible in an optical telescope, that can extend for millions of light-years either side of the galaxy. This double structure at radio wavelengths is also shown by some ◊quasars, suggesting a close relationship between the two types of object. In both cases, the source of energy is thought to be a massive black hole at the center. Some radio galaxies are thought to result from two galaxies in collision or recently merged.

radiography branch of science concerned with the use of radiation (particularly ◊X-rays) to produce images on photographic film or fluorescent screens. X-rays penetrate matter according to its nature, density, and thickness. In doing so they can cast shadows on photographic film, producing a radiograph. Radiography is widely used in medicine for examining bones and tissues and in industry for examining solid materials; for example, to check welded seams in pipelines.

radioisotope contraction of radioactive ◊isotope in physics, a naturally occurring or synthesized radioactive form of an element. Most radioisotopes are made by bombarding a stable element with neutrons in the core of a nuclear reactor. The radiations given off by radioisotopes are easy to detect (hence their use as ◊tracers), can in some instances penetrate substantial thicknesses of materials, and have profound effects (such as genetic ◊mutation) on living matter. Although dangerous, radioisotopes are used in the fields of medicine, industry, agriculture, and research.

Most natural isotopes of atomic mass 209 and under are not radioactive. Those from 210 and up are all radioactive.

radioisotope scanning the use of radioactive materials (radioisotopes or radionuclides) to pinpoint disease. It reveals the size and shape of the target organ and whether any part of it is failing to take up radioactive material, usually an indication of disease.

The speciality known as nuclear medicine makes use of the affinity of different chemical elements for certain parts of the body. Iodine, for instance, always makes its way to the thyroid gland. After being made radioactive, these materials can be given by mouth or injected, and then traced on scanners working on the Geiger-counter principle. The diagnostic record gained from radioisotope scanning is known as a scintigram.

radiometric dating method of dating rock by assessing the amount of ◊radioactive decay of naturally occurring ◊isotopes. The dating of rocks may be based on the gradual decay of uranium into lead. The ratio of the amounts of "parent" to "daughter" isotopes in a sample gives a measure of the time it has been decaying, that is, of its age. Different elements and isotopes are used depending on the isotopes present and the age of the rocks to be dated. Once-living matter can often be dated by ◊radiocarbon dating, employing the half-life of the isotope carbon-14, which is naturally present in organic tissue.

radiosonde balloon carrying a compact package of meteorological instruments and a radio transmitter, used to "sound," or measure, conditions in the atmosphere. The instruments measure temperature, pressure, and humidity, and the information gathered is transmitted back to observers on the ground. A radar target is often attached, allowing it to be tracked.

radio telescope instrument for detecting radio waves from the universe. Radio telescopes usually consist of a metal bowl that collects and focuses radio waves the way a concave mirror collects and focuses light waves. Other radio telescopes are shaped like long troughs, and some consist of simple rod-shaped aerials. Radio telescopes are much larger than optical telescopes because the wavelengths they are detecting are much longer than the wavelength of light. A large dish such as that at ◊Jodrell Bank, England, can see the radio sky less clearly than a small optical telescope sees the visible sky. The largest single dish is 1,000 ft/305 m across, at Arecibo, Puerto Rico.

Interferometry is a technique in which the output from two dishes is combined to give better resolution of detail than with a single dish. Very long baseline interferometry (VBLI) uses radio telescopes spread across the world to resolve minute details of radio sources. In aperture synthesis, several dishes are linked together to simulate the performance of a very large single dish. This technique was pioneered by Martin ◊Ryle at Cambridge, England, site of a radio telescope consisting of eight dishes in a line 3 mi/5 km long. The Very Large Array in New Mexico consists of 27 dishes arranged in a Y-shape, which simulates the performance of a single dish 17 mi/27 km in diameter.

radiotherapy treatment of disease by ◊radiation from X-ray machines or radioactive sources.

Radiation, which reduces the activity of dividing cells, is of special value for its effect on malignant tissues, certain nonmalignant tumors, and some diseases of the skin. Generally speaking, the rays of the diagnostic X-ray machine are not penetrating enough to be efficient in treatment, so for this purpose more powerful machines are required, operating from 10,000 to over 30 million volts. The lower-voltage machines are similar to conventional X-ray machines; the higher-voltage ones may be of special design; for example, linear accelerators and betatrons. Much radiation now given uses synthesized ◊radio isotopes. Radioactive cobalt is the most useful, since it produces gamma rays (highly penetrating), and it is used instead of very-high-energy X rays.

radish annual herb *Raphanus sativus*, family Cruciferae, grown for its fleshy, pungent, edible root, which is usually reddish but sometimes white or black.

radium white, radioactive, metallic element, symbol Ra, atomic number 88, atomic weight 226.02. It is one of the ◊alkaline-earth metals, found in nature in ◊pitchblende and other uranium ores. Radium decays in successive steps producing radon (a gas), polonium, and finally a stable isotope of lead. The isotope Ra-223 decays through the uncommon mode of heavy-ion emission, giving off carbon-14 and transmuting directly to lead. Since radium luminesces, it was used commercially in paints that glowed in the dark; when the hazards of ◊radioactivity became known its use was abandoned, but old factory sites and dump sites remain contaminated and many workers and neighbors contracted fatal cancers.

Of the 16 isotopes, the most common, Ra-226, has a half-life of 1,622 years. Because it emits rays (Latin *radius*), the element was named radium by its discoverers, Pierre and Marie ◊Curie, who in 1898 were investigating the nature of pitchblende.

rafflesia

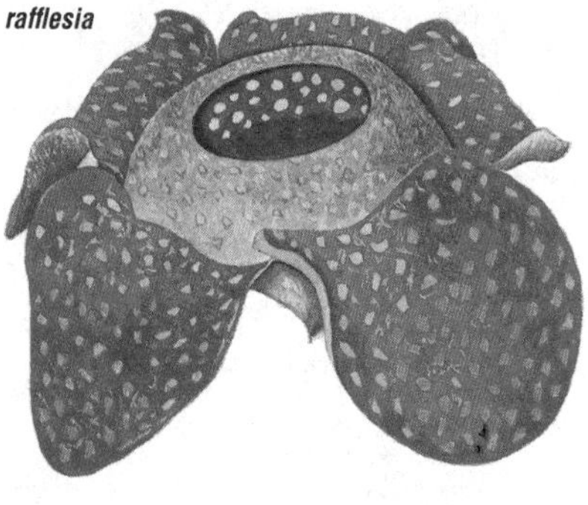

radius one of the two bones in the lower forearm of tetrapod (four-limbed) vertebrates.

Radom industrial city (flour-milling, brewing, tobacco, leather, bicycles, machinery; iron works) in Poland, 60 mi/96 km S of Warsaw; population (1985) 214,000. Radom became Austrian 1795 and Russian 1825 and was returned to Poland 1919.

radon colorless, odorless, gaseous, radioactive, nonmetallic element, symbol Rn, atomic number 86, atomic weight 222. It is grouped with the ◊inert gases and was formerly considered nonreactive but is now known to form some compounds with fluorine. Of the 20 known isotopes, only three occur in nature; the longest half-life is 3.82 days.

Radon is the densest gas known and occurs in small amounts in spring water, streams, and the air, being formed from the natural radioactive decay of radium. Ernest Rutherford discovered radon as the isotope Rn-220 in 1899, and Friedrich Dorn (1848–1916) in 1900; after several other chemists discovered additional isotopes, William Ramsay and R W Whytlaw-Gray isolated the element, which they named niton in 1908. The name radon (based on radium) was adopted in the 1920s.

Raeder Erich 1876–1960. German admiral. Chief of Staff in World War I, he became head of the navy in 1928, but was dismissed by Hitler in 1943 because of his failure to prevent Allied Arctic convoys from reaching the USSR. Sentenced to life imprisonment at the Nuremberg Trials of war criminals, he was released on grounds of ill health in 1955.

RAF abbreviation for Royal Air Force.

Rafelson Bob (Robert) 1934– . US film director who gained critical acclaim for his second film, *Five Easy Pieces* 1971. His other films include *Head* 1968, *The Postman Always Rings Twice* 1981, and *Black Widow* 1987.

Raffles Thomas Stamford 1781–1826. British colonial administrator, born in Jamaica. He served in the British East India Company, took part in the capture of Java from the Dutch 1811, and while governor of Sumatra 1818–23 was responsible for the acquisition and founding of Singapore 1819.

rafflesia or ***stinking corpse lily*** any parasitic plant without stems of the genus *Rafflesia*, family Rafflesiaceae, native to Malaysia, Indonesia, and Thailand. There are 14 species, several of which are endangered by logging of the forests where they grow; the fruit is used locally for medicine. The largest flowers in the world are produced by *R. arnoldiana*. About 3 ft/1 m across, they exude a smell of rotting flesh, which attracts flies to pollinate them.

Rafsanjani Hojatoleslam Ali Akbar Hashemi 1934– . Iranian politician and cleric, president from 1989. After training as a mullah (Islamic teacher) under Ayatollah ◊Khomeini in Qom, he acquired considerable wealth through his construction business but kept in touch with his exiled mentor. When the Ayatollah returned after the revolution of 1979–80, Rafsanjani became the speaker of the Iranian parliament and, after Khomeini's death, state president and effective political leader.

Raft George. Adopted name of George Ranft 1895–1980. US film actor, usually cast as a gangster (as in *Scarface* 1932). His later work included the comedy *Some Like it Hot* 1959.

raga (Sanskrit *rāga* "tone" or "color") in Indian music, a scale of notes and style of ornament for music associated with a particular mood or time of day; the equivalent term in rhythm is tala. A choice of raga and tala forms the basis of improvised music; however, a written composition may also be based on (and called) a raga.

Raglan FitzRoy James Henry Somerset, 1st Baron 1788–1855. English general. He took part in the Peninsular War under Wellington, and lost his right arm at Waterloo. He commanded the British forces in the Crimean War from 1854. The ***raglan sleeve***, cut right up to the neckline with no shoulder seam, is named after him.

Ragnarök or (German) ***Götterdämmerung*** in Norse mythology, the ultimate cataclysmic battle between gods and forces of evil, from which a new order will come.

ragtime syncopated music ("ragged time") in 2/4 rhythm, usually played on piano. It developed in the US among black musicians in the late 19th century; it was influenced by folk tradition, minstrel shows, and marching bands, and later was incorporated into jazz. Scott ◊Joplin was a leading writer of ragtime pieces, called "rags."

Ragusa town in Sicily, Italy, 34 mi/54 km SW of Syracuse; textile industries; population (1981) 64,492. It stands over 1,500 ft/450 m above the river Ragusa, and there are ancient tombs in caves nearby.

Ragusa Italian name (until 1918) for the Yugoslavian town of ◊Dubrovnik. Its English name was Arrogosa, from which the word "argosy" is derived, because of the town's fame for its trading fleets while under Turkish rule in the 16th century.

ragwort any of several perennial plants of the genus *Senecio*, family Compositae, usually with yellow-rayed flower heads; some are poisonous.

Golden ragwort or groundsel *S. aureus* is native to S US.

Rahman Sheik Mujibur 1921–1975. Bangladeshi Nationalist politician, president 1975. He was arrested several times for campaigning for the autonomy of East Pakistan. He won the elections 1970 as leader of the Awami League but was again arrested when negotiations with the Pakistan government broke down. After the civil war 1971, he became prime minister of the newly independent Bangladesh. He was presidential dictator Jan–Aug 1975, when he was assassinated.

Rafsanjani *The president of Iran, Ali Akbar Rafsanjani. He is viewed as the most pragmatic and influential member of Iran's post-Khomeini collective leadership.*

railroad *A replica of English inventor Robert Stephenson's* Rocket *(above); the original was built in 1829. The French TGV (overleaf) is one of the fastest passenger trains, traveling at speeds of 165 mph/260 kph. A locomotive on the Guayaquil-Quito line in Ecuador (below), the last steam-worked crossing in the Andes.*

Rahman Tunku Abdul 1903–1990. Malaysian politician, first prime minister of independent Malaya 1957–63 and of Malaysia 1963–70.

Born at Kuala Keda, the son of the sultan and his sixth wife, a Thai princess, the Tunku studied law in England. After returning to Malaysia he founded the Alliance Party 1952. The party was successful in the 1955 elections, and the Tunku became prime minister of Malaya on gaining independence 1957, continuing when Malaya became part of Malaysia 1963. His achievement was to bring together the Malay, Chinese, and Indian peoples within the Alliance Party, but in the 1960s he was accused of showing bias toward Malays. Ethnic riots followed in Kuala Lumpur 1969 and, after many attempts to restore better relations, the Tunku retired 1970. He has voiced criticism of the authoritarian leadership of Mahathir bin Mohamad.

raï type of Algerian pop music developed in the 1970s from the Bedouin song form *melhoun*, using synthesizers and electronic drums.

rail any wading bird of the family Rallidae, including the rails proper (genus *Rallus*), coots, moorhens, and gallinules.

Many oceanic islands have their own species of rail, often flightless, such as the Guam rail *R. owstoni* and Auckland Island rail *R. muelleri*. Several of these species have declined sharply, usually because of introduced predators such as rats and cats.

railroad method of transport in which trains convey passengers and goods along a twin rail track (at first made of wood but later of iron or steel with ties wedging them apart and relatively parallel). Following the work of English steam pioneers such as James ◊Watt, George ◊Stephenson built the first public steam railroad, from Stockton to Darlington, 1825. This heralded extensive railroad building in Britain, continental Europe, and

North America, providing a fast and economical means of transport and communication. After World War II, steam was replaced by electric and diesel engines. At the same time, the growth of road building, air services, and the trucking and automobile industries destroyed the supremacy of the railroads.

In North America the growth of railroads, such as the Union Pacific, during the 19th century made shipping from the midwest and western territories economical and helped the North to win the American Civil War. Railways were extended into Asia, the Middle East, Africa, and Latin America in the late 19th century. They were later important for troop and supply transport in both world wars.

With the increasing use of automobiles, inexpensive long-distance buslines, and truck freight lines after World War II, rising costs on the railroads meant higher fares, fewer passengers, and declining freight traffic. By 1970 many train services in the US had been discontinued or were under threat of extinction. Short-run commuter service survived, government-sponsored rail service was financed for some areas, and economical train trips are being reestablished to help counter automotive pollution. High-speed trains, developed in the 1970s, continue to serve passenger needs between large urban centers. Elsewhere in the world super-fast trains running on specially built tracks, such as the ◊Shinkansen (Japan) and ◊TGV (France) networks, are important to public transportation.

rain technically termed ***precipitation*** separate drops of water that fall to the Earth's surface from clouds. The drops are formed by the accumulation of droplets that condense from water vapor in the air.

The condensation is usually brought about by cooling, either when the air rises over a mountain range or when it rises above a cooler air mass.

rainbow arch in the sky displaying the seven colors of the ◊spectrum in bands. It is formed by the refraction, reflection, and dispersion of the Sun's rays through rain or mist. Its cause was discovered by ◊Theodoric of Freiburg in the 14th century.

rainbow coalition or ***rainbow alliance*** in politics, from the mid-1980s, a loose, left-of-center grouping of disparate elements, encompassing sections of society that are traditionally politically underrepresented, such as nonwhite ethnic groups. Its aims include promoting minority rights and equal opportunities.

"Rainbow" is a translation of French *Arc-en-Ciel*, a name brought into prominence by the Rev Jesse Jackson's campaign seeking to represent an alliance of nonwhite political groupings.

rainforest dense forest found on or near the ◊equator where the climate is hot and wet. Over half the tropical rainforests are in Central and South America, the rest in SE Asia and Africa. Although covering approximately 8% of the Earth's land surface, they comprise about 50% of all growing wood on the planet and harbor at least 40% of the Earth's species (plants and animals). Rainforests are being destroyed at an increasing rate as their valuable timber is harvested and land cleared for agriculture, causing problems of ◊deforestation, soil ◊erosion, and flooding. They also provide the bulk of the oxygen needed for plant and animal respiration. By 1990, 50% of the world's rainforest had been removed.

Rainforests can be divided into the following kinds: tropical, montane, upper montane or cloud, mangrove, and subtropical. They are characterized by a great diversity of species, usually of tall broad-leafed evergreen trees, with many climbing vines and ferns, some of which are a main source of raw materials for medicines. Rainforests comprise some of the most complex and diverse ecosystems on the planet and help to regulate global weather patterns. When deforestation occurs, the microclimate of the mature forest disappears; soil erosion and flooding become major problems since rainforests protect the shallow tropical soils.

Clearing of the rainforests may lead to a global warming of the atmosphere, and contribute to the ◊greenhouse effect. Deforestation also causes the salt level in the ground to rise to the surface, making the land unsuitable for farming or ranching.

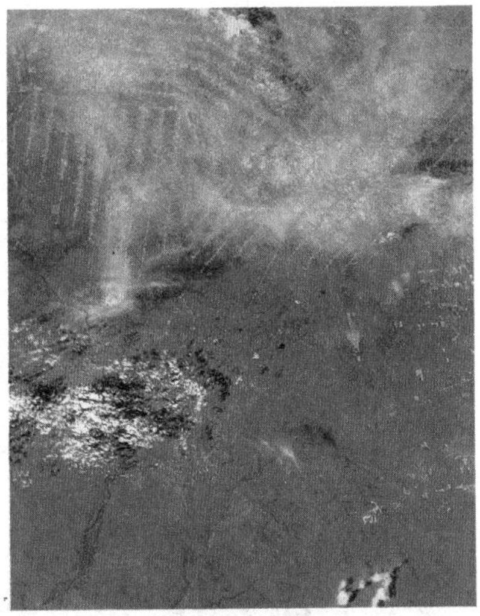

rainforest *Satellite image of the rainforest surrounding the Rondonia Development Project in western Brazil. The image shows the extensive deforestation associated with farm settlement spreading from a central road (running left to right). Deforested areas appear blue or white; dense vegetation is red.*

railroad: history

1500s	Tramways—wooden tracks along which trolleys ran—were in use in mines.
1789	Flanged wheels running on cast-iron rails first introduced; automobiles still horse-drawn.
1804	Richard Trevithick in England built the first steam locomotive, and ran it on the track at the Pen-y-darren ironworks in S Wales.
1825	George Stephenson in England built the first public railroad to carry steam trains—the Stockton and Darlington line—using his engine *Locomotion*.
1829	Stephenson designed his locomotive *Rocket*.
1830	Stephenson completed the Liverpool and Manchester Railway, the first steam passenger line. The first US-built locomotive, *Best Friend of Charleston*, went into service on the South Carolina Railroad.
1835	Germany pioneered steam railroads in Europe, using *Der Adler*, a locomotive built by Stephenson.
1863	Robert Fairlie, a Scot, patented a locomotive with pivoting driving bogies, allowing tight curves in the track (this was later applied in the Garratt locomotives). London opened the world's first underground railroad, powered by steam.
1869	The first US transcontinental railroad was completed at Promontory, Utah, when the Union Pacific and the Central Pacific railroads met. George Westinghouse of the US invented the compressed-air brake.
1879	Werner von Siemens demonstrated an electric train in Germany. Volk's Electric Railway along the Brighton seafront in England was the world's first public electric railroad.
1883	Charles Lartique built the first monorail, in Ireland.
1885	The trans-Canada continental railroad was completed, from Montreal in the east to Port Moody, British Columbia, in the west.
1890	The first electric underground railroad opened in London.
1901	The world's most successful monorail, the Wuppertal Schwebebahn, went into service in Germany.
1912	The first diesel locomotive took to the rails in Germany.
1938	The British steam locomotive *Mallard* set a steam-rail speed record of 125 mph/201 kph.
1941	Swiss Federal Railways introduced a gas-turbine locomotive.
1964	Japan National Railways inaugurated the 320 mi/515 km New Tokaido line between Osaka and Tokyo, on which run the 130 mph/210 kph "bullet" trains.
1973	British Rail's High Speed Train (HST) set a diesel rail speed record of 142 mph/229 kph.
1979	Japan National Railways' maglev test vehicle ML-500 attained a speed of 321 mph/517 kph.
1981	France's TGV superfast trains began operation between Paris and Lyons, regularly attaining a peak speed of 168 mph/270 kph.
1987	France and the UK began work on the Channel Tunnel, a railroad link connecting the two countries, running beneath the English Channel.
1989	A new world rail-speed record of 298 mph/482.4 kph was established by a French TGV train in Dec 1989.

Rainier III 1923– . Prince of Monaco from 1949. He was married to the US film actress Grace Kelly.

Rainier, Mount mountain in the ◊Cascade Range, Washington State; 14,415 ft/4,392 m, crowned by 14 glaciers and carrying dense forests on its slopes. It is a quiescent volcano. Mount Rainier national park was dedicated 1899.

Rais Gilles de 1404–1440. French marshal who fought alongside Joan of Arc. In 1440 he was hanged for the torture and murder of 140 children, but the court proceedings were irregular. He is the historical basis of the ◊Bluebeard character.

raisin dried grape, used for eating, baking, and the confection trade. The chief kinds are the common raisin, the sultana or seedless raisin, and the currant. They are produced in the Mediterranean area, California, and Australia.

Rajasthan state of NW India

area 132,089 sq mi/342,200 sq km

capital Jaipur

features includes the larger part of the Thar Desert, where India's first nuclear test was carried out

products oilseed, cotton, sugar, asbestos, copper, textiles, cement, glass

population (1981) 34,103,000

language Rajasthani, Hindi

religion 90% Hindu, 3% Muslim

history formed 1948; enlarged 1956.

Rajneesh meditation meditation based on the teachings of the Indian Shree Rajneesh (born Chaadra Mohan Jain), established in the early 1970s. Until 1989 he called himself Bhagwan (Hindi "God"). His followers, who number about half a million

rainforest

tropical rainforest habitat

Along the equator rising hot air draws winds in from the north and south. These winds, known as trade winds, are wet and their moisture falls as torrential rain as the air rises. The ensuing hot wet conditions encourage the prolific growth of thousands of plant species, giving rise to the tropical rainforest. The varied and abundant species of plant support many different species of animal. The rain runs off into huge rivers, such as the Amazon, the Zaïre and the Mekong.

The tropical rainforest runs in a belt along the equator, broken only by mountain ranges.

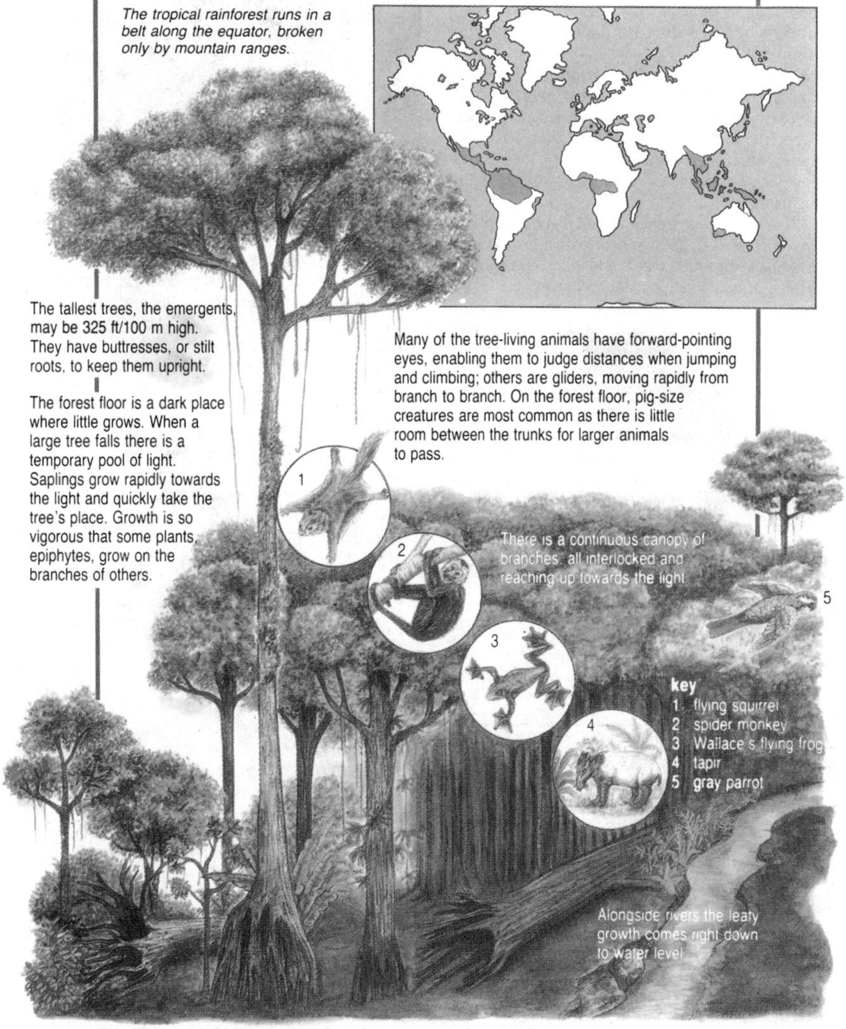
The tallest trees, the emergents, may be 325 ft/100 m high. They have buttresses, or stilt roots, to keep them upright.
The forest floor is a dark place where little grows. When a large tree falls there is a temporary pool of light. Saplings grow rapidly towards the light and quickly take the tree's place. Growth is so vigorous that some plants, epiphytes, grow on the branches of others.
Many of the tree-living animals have forward-pointing eyes, enabling them to judge distances when jumping and climbing; others are gliders, moving rapidly from branch to branch. On the forest floor, pig-size creatures are most common as there is little room between the trunks for larger animals to pass.
There is a continuous canopy of branches, all interlocked and reaching up towards the light
1
2
3
4
5
key
1 flying squirrel
2 spider monkey
3 Wallace's flying frog
4 tapir
5 gray parrot
Alongside rivers the leafy growth comes right down to water level

worldwide, regard themselves as Sannyas, or Hindu ascetics; they wear orange robes and carry a string of prayer beads. They are not expected to observe any specific prohibitions but to be guided by their instincts.

Rajneesh initially set up an ashram, or religious community, in Poona, NW India. He gained many followers, both Indian and Western, but his teachings also created considerable opposition, and in 1981 the Bhagwan moved his ashram to Oregon, calling himself "guru of the rich." He was deported in 1985 after pleading guilty to immigration fraud, and died 1990.

He taught that there is a basic energy in the world, bio-energy, and that individuals can release this by dynamic meditation, which involves breathing exercises and explosive physical activity. His followers are encouraged to live in large groups, so that children may grow up in contact with a variety of people.

Rajput a member of a Hindu people, predominantly soldiers and landowners, widespread over N India. The Rajput states of NW India are now merged in Rajasthan. The Rana family (ruling aristocracy of Nepal until 1951) was also Rajput.

Rajshahi capital of Rajshahi region, W Bangladesh; population (1981) 254,000. It trades in timber and vegetable oil.

Raleigh industrial city (food processing, electrical machinery, textiles) and capital of North Carolina; population (1990) 207,951. It benefits from the nearby presence of the Research Triangle Park, a regional research and manufacturing center for high-technology products. Educational institutions include North Carolina State University. The present site was named for Sir Walter Raleigh, selected to be the state capital 1788, and laid out 1792.

Raleigh or ***Ralegh*** Walter c. 1552–1618. English adventurer. He made colonizing and exploring voyages to North America 1584–87 and South America 1595, and naval attacks on Spanish ports. His aggressive actions against Spanish interests brought him into conflict with the pacific James I.

***Raleigh** English adventurer Sir Walter Raleigh, in a portrait by Nicholas Hilliard c. 1585.*

He was imprisoned for treason 1603–16 and executed on his return from an unsuccessful expedition to South America.

Raleigh was knighted 1584, and made several attempts 1584–87 to establish a colony in "Virginia" (now ◊North Carolina). In 1595 he led an expedition to South America (described in his *Discoverie of Guiana* 1596) and distinguished himself in expeditions against Spain in Cádiz 1596 and the Azores 1597. After James I's accession 1603 he was condemned to death on a charge of conspiracy, but was reprieved and imprisoned in the Tower of London, where he wrote his unfinished *History of the World*. Released 1616 to lead a gold-seeking expedition to the Orinoco River in South America, which failed disastrously, he was beheaded on his return under his former sentence.

Raleigh, Fort site of the first English settlement in America, at the N end of Roanoke Island, North Carolina, to which in 1585 Walter Raleigh sent 108 colonists from Plymouth, England, under his cousin Richard Grenville. In 1586 Francis Drake took the dissatisfied survivors back to England. The outline fortifications are preserved.

RAM (acronym from random access memory) in computing, a form of storage frequently used for the internal ◊memory of microcomputers. It is made up of a collection of ◊integrated circuits (chips). Unlike ◊ROM, RAM can be both read from and written to by the computer, but its contents are lost when the power is switched off. Today's microcomputers have up to 8 ◊megabytes of RAM.

Rama incarnation of ◊Vishnu, the supreme spirit of Hinduism. He is the hero of the epic poem the *Rāmāyana*, and he is regarded as an example of morality and virtue.

Ramadan in the Muslim ◊calendar, the ninth month of the year. Throughout Ramadan a strict fast is observed during the hours of daylight; Muslims are encouraged to read the whole Koran in commemoration of the Night of Power (which falls during the month) when, it is believed, Mohammed first received his revelations from the angel Gabriel.

Ramakrishna 1834–1886. Hindu sage, teacher, and mystic (one dedicated to achieving oneness with or a direct experience of God or some force beyond the normal world). Ramakrishna claimed that mystical experience was the ultimate aim of religions, and that all religions which led to this goal were equally valid.

Ramakrishna's most important follower, Swami Vivekananda (1863–1902), set up the Ramakrishna Society 1887, which now has centers for education, welfare, and religious teaching throughout India and beyond.

Raman Venkata 1888–1970. Indian physicist who in

1928 discovered what became known as the Raman effect: the scattering of monochromatic (single-wavelength) light when passed through a transparent substance. Awarded a Nobel prize in 1930, in 1948 he became director of the Raman Research Institute and national research professor of physics.

Ramat Gan industrial city (textiles, food processing) in W Israel, NE of Tel Aviv; population (1987) 116,000. It was established 1921.

Rāmāyana Sanskrit epic of c. 300 BC, in which Rama (an incarnation of the god Vishnu) and his friend Hanuman (the monkey chieftain) strive to recover Rama's wife, Sita, abducted by demon king Ravana.

Rambert Marie. Adopted name of Cyvia Rambam 1888–1982. British ballet dancer and teacher born in Warsaw, Poland, who became a British citizen 1918. One of the major innovative and influential figures in modern ballet, she was with the Diaghilev ballet 1912–13, opened the Rambert School 1920, and in 1926 founded the Ballet Rambert which she directed (renamed Rambert Dance Company 1987).

Rambouillet town in the south of the forest of Rambouillet, SW of Paris, France; population (1985) 22,500. The former royal château is now the presidential summer residence. A breed of sheep yielding fine woolen yarns is named after the town.

Rambouillet Catherine de Vivonne, Marquise de Rambouillet 1588–1665. French society hostess, whose salon at the Hôtel de Rambouillet in Paris included the writers Descartes, La Rochefoucauld, and Madame de Sévigné. The salon was ridiculed by the dramatist Molière in his *Les Précieuses ridicules* 1659.

Ram Das 1534–1581. Indian religious leader, fourth guru (teacher) of Sikhism 1574–81, who founded the Sikh holy city of Amritsar.

Rameau Jean-Philippe 1683–1764. French organist and composer. He wrote *Treatise on Harmony* 1722 and his varied works include keyboard and vocal music and many operas, such as *Castor and Pollux* 1737.

Ramillies, Battle of battle in which the British commander Marlborough defeated the French May 23, 1706, during the War of the ◊Spanish Succession, at a village in Brabant, Belgium, 13 mi/21 km N of Namur.

ramjet simple ◊jet engine used in some guided missiles. It only comes into operation at high speeds. Air is then "rammed" into the combustion chamber, into which fuel is sprayed and ignited.

Ram Mohun Roy 1770–1833. Indian religious reformer, founder 1830 of Brahma Samaj, a mystic cult.

Ramphal Shridath Surendranath ("Sonny") 1928– . Guyanese politician. He was minister of foreign affairs and justice 1972–75 and secretary-general of the British Commonwealth 1975–90.

Rampling Charlotte 1945– . British actress whose sometimes controversial films include *Georgy Girl* 1966, *The Night Porter/Il Portiere di Notti* 1974, and *Farewell My Lovely* 1975.

Ramsay Allan 1713–1784. Scottish portrait painter. After studying in Edinburgh and Italy, he established himself as a portraitist in London and became painter to George III in 1760. His Portraits include *The Artist's Wife* c. 1755 (National Gallery, Edinburgh).

Ramsay William 1852–1916. Scottish chemist who, with Lord Rayleigh, discovered argon 1894. In 1895 Ramsay produced helium and in 1898, in cooperation with Morris Travers, identified neon, krypton, and xenon. In 1903, with Frederick Soddy, he noted the production of helium from the transmutation of radium, which led to the discovery of the density and atomic weight of radium. Nobel Prize 1904. He continued his research on radioactive isotopes, isolating radon in 1908.

Ramses or ***Rameses*** 11 kings of ancient Egypt, including:

Ramses II *The temple of Ramses II at Abu Simbel, showing the head of a huge statue, carved in the rock.*

Ramses II or ***Rameses II*** king of Egypt about 1304–1236 BC, the son of Seti I. He campaigned successfully against the Hittites, and built two rock temples at ◊Abu Simbel in Upper Egypt.

Ramses III or ***Rameses III*** king of Egypt about 1200–1168 BC. He won a naval victory over the Philistines and other Middle Eastern peoples, and asserted his control over Palestine.

Rance river in Brittany, NW France, flowing into the English Channel between Dinard and St Malo, where a dam built 1960–67 (with a lock for ships) uses the 44-ft/13-m tides to feed the world's first successful tidal power station.

Rand shortened form of ◊Witwatersrand, a mountain ridge in Transvaal, South Africa.

Rand Ayn. Adopted name of Alice Rosenbaum 1905–1982. Russian-born US novelist. Her novel *The Fountainhead* 1943 (made into a film 1949), describing an idealistic architect who destroys his project rather than see it altered, displays her persuasive blend of virulent anticommunism and her fervent philosophy for individual enterprise. Her allegorical novel *Atlas Shrugged* 1957 was also a bestseller. Her beliefs won her a cult following.

Born and educated in St Petersburg, she came to the US 1926 and settled in Chicago. She became a US citizen 1931. Rand worked as a script writer in Hollywood and edited *The Objectivist*, a magazine that promoted Objectivism, her theory of self-interest and laissez-faire capitalism that is presented in her novels. Her other works include *We, the Living* 1936, *The Virtue of Selfishness* 1965, *Capitalism* 1966, *The New Left* 1971, and *Philosophy: Who Needs It?* 1982.

Rand Sally (Helen Gould Beck) 1904–1979. US exotic dancer. Born in Hickory County, Missouri, Rand joined the circus in her teenage years as an acrobat, later moving to Hollywood where she played supporting roles in a number of silent films. During the 1930s she worked as an exotic dancer in Chicago, developing her trademark nude dance routine to Chopin and Debussy, featuring the coy use of huge ostrich fans. Her appearances at the 1933 Chicago Exposition and at later fairs and expositions across the country made her a popular favorite. Rand played a featured role in a 1965 burlesque revival on Broadway and continued to dance until 1978.

Randolph Asa Philip 1889–1979. US labor and civil rights leader. Devoting himself to the cause of unionization, especially among black Americans, he founded the periodical *Messenger* 1917. After successfully organizing railroad workers, he served as the president of the Brotherhood of Sleeping Car Porters 1925–68. Named a vice-president of the American Federation of Labor and Congress of Industrial Organizations (AFL-CIO) 1957, Randolph was one of the organizers of the 1963 civil rights march on Washington.

Born in Crescent City, Florida, Randolph was educated at the City College of New York and became involved in labor-organizing activities while still in college.

random number one of a series of numbers that has no detectable pattern. Random numbers are used in ◊computer simulation and ◊computer games. It is impossible for an ordinary computer to generate true random numbers, but various techniques are available for obtaining pseudo-random numbers, these being close enough to true randomness for most purposes.

rangefinder instrument for determining the range or distance of an object from the observer; used to focus a camera or to sight a gun accurately.

Rangoon former name (until 1989) of ◊Yangon, capital of Myanmar.

Ranjit Singh 1780–1839. Indian maharajah. He succeeded his father as a minor Sikh leader 1792, and created a Sikh army that conquered Kashmir and the Punjab. In alliance with the British, he established himself as "Lion of the Punjab," ruler of the strongest of the independent Indian states.

Rank Joseph Arthur 1888–1972. British film magnate. Having entered films in 1933 to promote the Methodist cause, he proceeded to gain control of much of the industry through takeovers and forming new businesses. The Rank Organization still owns the Odeon chain of theaters and Pinewood Studios, although film is now a minor part of its activities.

Ranke Leopold von 1795–1886. German historian whose quest for objectivity in history had great impact on the discipline. His attempts to explain "how it really was" dominated both German and outside historical thought until 1914 and beyond.

Ransom John Crowe 1888–1974. US poet and critic, born in Tennessee. He was a leader of the Southern literary movement that followed World War I. He published his romantic but antirhetorical verse in, for example, *Poems About God* 1919, *Chills and Fever* 1924, and *Selected Verse* 1947. As a critic and teacher he was a powerful figure in the New Criticism movement, which shaped much literary theory from the 1940s to the 1960s.

At Kenyon College where he taught from 1937 to 1958, he founded the respected literary magazine *The Kenyon Review*.

Ransome Robert 1753–1830. English ironfounder and agricultural engineer, whose business earned a worldwide reputation in the 19th and 20th centuries. He introduced factory methods for the production of an improved range of plows from 1789. The firm remained at the forefront of advances in agricultural mechanization in connection with steam engines, threshing machines, and lawnmowers.

Rantoul city in E Illinois, S of Chicago. It is a trading center for agricultural products. Manufactures include electronic equipment and motorcycle parts; population (1990) 17,212.

Rao Raja 1909– . Indian writer, born at Hassan, Karnataka. He studied at Montpellier and the Sorbonne in France. He wrote about Indian independence from the perspective of a village in S India in *Kanthapura* 1938 and later, in *The Serpent and the Rope* 1960, about a young cosmopolitan intellectual seeking enlightenment. Collections of stories include *The Cow of the Barricades* 1947 and *The Policeman and the Rose* 1978.

Raoult Francois 1830–1901. French chemist. In 1882, while working at the University of Grenoble, Raoult formulated one of the basic laws of chemistry. Raoult's law enables the molecular

***Raphael** One of the great artists of the Italian High Renaissance, Raphael painted the allegorical* Vision of a Knight *about 1504, early in his career.*

weight of a substance to be determined by noting how much of it is required to depress the freezing point of a solvent by a certain amount.

Rapallo port and winter resort in Liguria, NW Italy, 15 mi/24 km SE of Genoa on the Gulf of Rapallo; population (1981) 29,300. Treaties were signed here 1920 (settling the common frontiers of Italy and Yugoslavia) and 1922 (canceling German and Russian counter-claims for indemnities for World War I).

Rapa Nui another name for ◊Easter Island, an island in the Pacific.

rape in botany, two plant species of the mustard family (Cruciferae), *Brassica rapa* and *B. napus*, grown for their seeds, which yield a pungent edible oil. The common turnip is a variety of the former, and the rutabaga of the latter.

rape in law, sexual intercourse without the consent of the subject. Most cases of rape are of women by men.

Some jurisdictions allow charges of rape to be brought against husbands replacing older legal doctrine asserting a wife's duty to submit to sex with her spouse. Sexual intercourse with a minor, not necessarily involving consent or penetration is defined as statutory rape (see ◊child abuse).

Raphael (Raffaello Sanzio) 1483–1520. Italian painter, one of the greatest of the High Renaissance, active in Perugia, Florence, and Rome (from 1508), where he painted frescoes in the Vatican and for secular patrons. His religious and mythological scenes are harmoniously composed; his portraits enhance the character of his sitters and express dignity. Many of his designs were engraved and much of his later work was the product of his studio.

Raphael was born in Urbino, the son of Giovanni Santi (died 1494), a court painter. In 1499 he went to Perugia, where he worked with ◊Perugino, whose graceful style is reflected in Raphael's *Marriage of the Virgin* 1504 (Brera, Milan). This work also shows his early concern for harmonious disposition of figures in the pictorial space. In Florence 1504–08 he studied the works of Leonardo da Vinci, Michelangelo, Masaccio, and Fra Bartolommeo. His paintings of this period include the *Ansidei Madonna* (National Gallery, London).

Pope Julius II commissioned him to decorate the papal apartments (the Stanze) in the Vatican. In Raphael's first fresco series there, *The School of Athens* 1509 is a complex but Classically composed grouping of Greek philosophers and mathematicians, centered on the figures of Plato and Aristotle. A second series of frescoes, 1511–14, includes the dramatic and richly colored *Mass of Bolsena*.

Raphael was increasingly flooded with commissions. Within the next few years he produced mythological frescoes in the Villa Farnesina in Rome 1511–12, cartoons for tapestries for the Sistine Chapel, Vatican (Victoria and Albert Museum, London), and the *Sistine Madonna* c. 1512 (Gemäldegalerie, Dresden, Germany). One of his pupils was ◊Giulio Romano.

Rapid Deployment Force former name (until 1983) of US ◊Central Command, a military strike force.

rap music rapid, rhythmic chant over a prerecorded repetitive backing track. Rap emerged in New York 1979 as part of the ◊hip-hop culture, although the usually macho, swaggering lyrics have roots in ritual boasts and insults.

rare-earth element alternate name for ◊lanthanide.

Ras el Khaimah or ***Ra's al Khaymah*** emirate on the Persian Gulf; area 652 sq mi/1,690 sq km; population (1980) 73,700. Products include oil, pharmaceuticals, and cement. It is one of the seven members of the ◊United Arab Emirates.

Rashdun the "rightly guided ones," the first four caliphs (heads) of Islam: Abu Bakr, Umar, Uthman, and Ali.

raspberry prickly cane plant *Rubus idaeus* of the Rosaceae family, with white flowers followed by red fruits. These are eaten fresh and used for jam and wine.

Rasputin (Russian "dissolute") Grigory Efimovich 1871–1916. Siberian Eastern Orthodox mystic and wandering "holy man," the illiterate son of a peasant. He acquired influence over the tsarina ◊Alexandra, wife of ◊Nicholas II, because of her faith in his power to ease her son's suffering from hemophilia, and he was able to make political and ecclesiastical appointments. His abuse of power and his notorious debauchery (reputedly including the tsarina) led to his being murdered by a group of nobles, who, when poison had no effect, dumped him in the river Neva after shooting him.

Rastafarianism religion originating in the West Indies, based on the ideas of Marcus ◊Garvey, who called on black people to return to Africa and set up a black-governed country there. When Haile Selassie (Ras Tafari, "Lion of Judah") was crowned emperor of Ethiopia 1930, this was seen as a fulfillment of prophecy and Rastafarians acknowledged him as the Messiah, the incarnation of God (Jah). The use of ganja (marijuana) is a sacrament. There are no churches. There were about one million Rastafarians by 1990.

Rastafarians identify themselves with the Chosen People, the Israelites, of the Bible. Ethiopia is seen as the promised land, while all countries outside Africa are Babylon, the place of exile. Many Rastafarians do not cut their hair, because of Biblical injunctions against this, but wear it instead in long dreadlocks, often covered in woolen hats in the Rastafarian colors of red, green, and gold. Food laws are very strict: for example, no pork, shellfish, salt, milk, or coffee.

Rastatt, Treaty of in 1714, agreement signed by Austria and France that supplemented the Treaty of ◊Utrecht and helped to end the War of the ◊Spanish Succession.

rat any of numerous long-tailed ◊rodents (especially of the families Muridae and Cricetidae) larger than mice and usually with scaly, naked tails. The genus *Rattus* in the family Muridae includes the rats found in human housing.

The brown rat *R. norvegicus* is about 8 in/20 cm with a tail of almost equal length. It is believed to have originated in central Asia, and is now found worldwide after being transported from Europe by ships. The black rat *R. rattus*, reponsible for the ◊plague, is smaller than the brown rat, but has larger ears, and a longer, more pointed snout. It does not interbreed with the brown rat.

Rathbone (Philip St John) Basil 1892–1967. South African-born British character actor, one of the film's great villains; he also played Sherlock Holmes (the fictional detective created by Arthur Conan Doyle) in several films. He worked mainly in Hollywood, in films such as *The Adventures of Robin Hood* 1938 and *The Hound of the Baskervilles* 1939.

rattlesnake

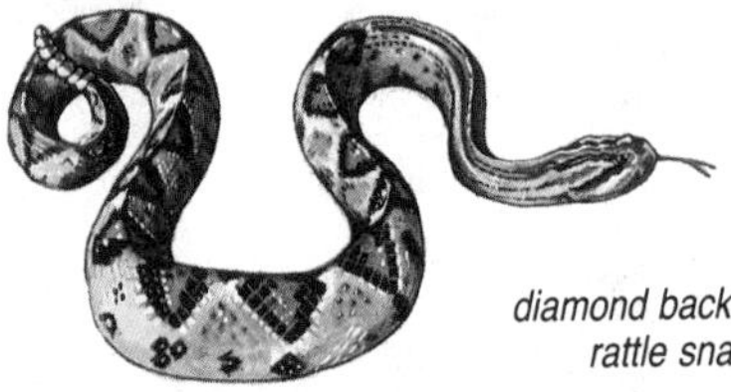

diamond backed rattle snake

Rathenau Walther 1867–1922. German politician. He was a leading industrialist and was appointed economic director during World War I, developing a system of economic planning in combination with capitalism. After the war he founded the Democratic Party, and became foreign minister 1922. The same year he signed the Rapallo Treaty of Friendship with the USSR, canceling German and Soviet counterclaims for indemnities for World War I, and soon after was assassinated by right-wing fanatics.

Rathlin island off the N Irish coast, in Antrim; St Columba founded a church here in the 6th century, and in 1306 Robert Bruce hid there after his defeat by the English at Methven.

rationalism in theology, the belief that human reason rather than divine revelation is the correct means of ascertaining truth and regulating behavior. In philosophy, rationalism takes the view that self-evident propositions deduced by reason are the sole basis of all knowledge (disregarding experience of the senses). It is usually contrasted with ◊empiricism, which argues that all knowledge must ultimately be derived from the senses.

Following the work of the philosophers Descartes and Spinoza, rationalism was developed by Leibnitz and Kant, through whom it influenced 19th-century idealism and 20th-century analytic philosophy.

rationalized units units for which the defining equations conform to the geometry of the system. Equations involving circular symmetry contain the factor 2π; those involving spherical symmetry 4π. ◊SI units are rationalized, ◊c.g.s. units are not.

rational number in mathematics, any number that can be expressed as an exact fraction (with a denominator not equal to 0), that is, as $a \div b$ where a and b are integers. For example, 2, $\frac{1}{4}$, $\frac{15}{4}$, $-\frac{3}{5}$ are all rational numbers, whereas π (which represents the constant 3.141592...) is not. Numbers such as π are called ◊irrational numbers.

Ratisbon English name for the German city of ◊Regensburg.

ratite flightless bird with a breastbone without the keel to which flight muscles are attached. Examples are ostrich, rhea, emu, cassowary, and kiwi.

rat-tail or ***grenadier*** any fish of the family Macrouridae of deep-sea bony fishes. They have stout heads and bodies, and long tapering tails. They are common in deep waters on the continental slopes. Some species have a light-emitting organ in front of the anus.

Also known as rat-tails are some of the ◊chimaeras.

Rattigan Terence 1911–1977. English playwright. His play *Ross* 1960 was based on T E Lawrence (Lawrence of Arabia).

Rattle Simon 1955–. English conductor. Principal conductor of the Birmingham Symphony Orchestra from 1980, he is renowned for his eclectic range and for interpretations of Mahler and Sibelius.

rattlesnake any of various New World pit ◊vipers of the genera *Crotalus* and *Sistrurus* (the massasaugas and pygmy rattlers), distinguished by horny flat segments of the tail, which rattle when vibrated as a warning to attackers. They can grow to 8 ft/2.5 m long. The venom injected by some rattlesnakes can be fatal.

There are 31 species distributed from S Canada to central South America. The eastern diamond back (*C. adamanteus*), from 2.8–8 ft/0.9–2.5 m, is at home in the flat pinelands of the S US.

Ratushinskaya Irina 1954– . Soviet dissident poet. Sentenced 1983 to seven years in a labor camp plus five years in internal exile for criticism of the Soviet regime, she was released 1986. Her strongly Christian work includes *Grey is the Colour of Hope* 1988.

Raunkiaer system method of classification devised by the Danish ecologist Christen Raunkiaer (1860–1938) whereby plants are divided into groups according to the position of their ◊perennating (overwintering) buds in relation to the soil surface. For example, plants in cold areas, such as the tundra, generally have their buds protected below ground, whereas in hot, tropical areas they are above ground and freely exposed. This scheme is useful for comparing vegetation types in different parts of the world.

The main divisions are phanerophytes with buds situated well above the ground; chamaephytes with buds borne within 10 in/25 cm of the soil surface; hemicryptophytes with buds at or immediately below the soil surface; and cryptophytes with their buds either beneath the soil (geophyte) or below water (hydrophyte).

Rauschenberg Robert 1925– . US Pop artist, a creator of happenings (art in live performance) and incongruous multimedia works such as *Monogram* 1959 (Moderna Museet, Stockholm), a car tire around the body of a stuffed goat daubed with paint. In the 1960s he returned to painting and used the silk-screen printing process to transfer images to canvas. He also made collages.

His works are spontaneous and use images and objects from everyday life.

Ravana in the Hindu epic *Rāmāyana*, demon king of Lankā (Sri Lanka) who abducted Sita, the wife of Rama.

Ravel Maurice Joseph 1875–1937. French composer. His work is characterized by its sensuousness, unresolved dissonances, and "tone color." Examples are the piano pieces *Pavane pour une infante défunte* 1899 and *Jeux d'eau* 1901, and the ballets *Daphnis et Chloë* 1912 and *Boléro* 1928.

raven any of several large ◊crows (genus *Corvus*). The common raven *C. corax* is about 2 ft/60 cm long, and has black, lustrous plumage. It is a scavenger, found only in the N hemisphere.

Raven, The US poem, written 1845 by Edgar Allan Poe, about a bereaved poet haunted by a raven that sonorously warns "Nevermore."

Ravenna historical city and industrial port (petrochemical works) in Emilia-Romagna, Italy; population (1988) 136,000. It lies in a marshy plain and is known for its Byzantine churches with superb mosaics.

Ravenna was a Roman port and naval station. It was capital of the W Roman emperors 404–93, of ◊Theodoric the Great 493–526, and later of the Byzantine exarchs (bishops) 539–750. The British poet Byron lived for some months in Ravenna, home of Countess Guiccioli, during the years 1819–21.

Ravi river in the Indian subcontinent, a tributary of the ◊Indus. It rises in India, forms the boundary between India and Pakistan for some 70 mi/110 km, and enters Pakistan above Lahore, the chief town on its 450-mi/725-km course. It is an important source of water for the Punjab irrigation canal system.

Rawalpindi city in Punjab province, Pakistan, in the foothills of the Himalayas; population (1981) 928,400. Industries include oil refining, iron, chemicals, and furniture.

Rawlinson Henry Creswicke 1810–1895. English orientalist and political agent in Baghdad in the Ottoman Empire from 1844. He deciphered the Babylonian cuneiform and Old Persian scripts of ◊Darius I's trilingual inscription at Behistun, Persia, continued the excavation work of A H Layard, and published a *History of Assyria* 1852.

Rawls John 1921– . US philosopher. In *A Theory of Justice* 1971, he revived the concept of the ◊"social contract" and its enforcement by civil disobedience.

Born in Baltimore, Maryland, Rawls taught at Princeton, Cornell, Massachusetts Institute of Technology, and Harvard.

ray any of several orders (especially Ragiformes) of cartilaginous fishes with a flattened body, winglike pectoral fins, and a whiplike tail. Species include the stingray, for example the Southern stingray *Dasyatis americana*, which has a serrated, poisonous spine on the tail, and the ◊torpedo fish.

Ray John 1627–1705. English naturalist who devised a classification system accounting for nearly 18,000 plant species. It was the first system to divide flowering plants into ◊monocotyledons and ◊dicotyledons, with additional divisions made on the basis of leaf and flower characters and fruit types.

Ray Man. US photographer and artist, see ◊Man Ray.

Ray Nicholas. Adopted name of Raymond Nicholas Kienzle 1911–1979. US film director, critically acclaimed for his socially aware dramas such as *Rebel Without a Cause* 1955. His later epics, such as *King of Kings* 1961, were less successful.

Ray Satyajit 1921– . Indian film director, renowned for his trilogy of life in his native Bengal: *Pather Panchali*, *Unvanquished*, and *The World of Apu* 1955–59. Later films include *The Chess Players* 1977 and *The Home and the World* 1984.

Rayburn Samuel Taliaferro 1882–1961. US political leader. After serving in the Texas state legislature 1907–12, he was elected to the US Congress as a Democrat 1912. Rayburn's tenure in the House 1912–61 was the longest on record. A supporter of the New Deal, he was elected majority leader 1937 and speaker 1940. With the exception of two terms, he served as speaker until his death. A leader of the Democratic party, Rayburn chaired the national conventions in 1948, 1952, and 1956.

Born in Roane County, Tennessee, and raised in Texas, Rayburn received a law degree from the University of Texas 1908.

Rayleigh John W Strutt, 3rd Baron 1842–1919. British physicist who wrote the standard *Treatise on Sound*, experimented in optics and microscopy, and, with William Ramsay, discovered argon. Nobel Prize 1904.

Raynaud's disease chronic condition in which the blood supply to the extremities is reduced by periodic spasm of the blood vessels on exposure to cold. It is most often seen in young women.

Attacks are usually brought on by cold or by emotional factors. Typically, the hands and/or feet take on a corpselike pallor, changing to blue as the circulation begins to return; initial numbness is replaced by a tingling or burning sensation. Drugs may be necessary to control the condition, particularly in severe cases where there is risk of gangrene.

Reagan *The 40th president of the United States of America, Ronald Reagan, a Republican. 1981–1989.*

Realism *Gustave Courbet's* The Stonebreakers *1849 (formerly Dresden State Museum, destroyed in World War II).*

rayon any of various shiny textile fibers and fabrics made from ◊cellulose. It is produced by pressing whatever cellulose solution is used through very small holes and solidifying the resulting filaments. A common type is ◊viscose, which consists of regenerated filaments of pure cellulose. Acetate and triacetate are kinds of rayon consisting of filaments of cellulose acetate and triacetate.

Rayon was originally made in the 1930s from the Douglas fir tree.

rays original name for ◊radiation of all types, such as X rays and gamma rays. See also ◊radioactivity and ◊radioactive decay.

razor sharpened metallic blade used to remove facial or body hair. Razors were known in the Bronze Age. The safety razor was patented by William Henson in 1847; a disposable version was produced by King Gillette at the start of the 20th century. The earliest electric razors date from the 1920s.

razorbill North Atlantic sea bird *Alca torda*, of the auk family, which breeds on cliffs, and migrates S in winter. It has a curved beak, and is black above and white below. It uses its wings as paddles when diving. Razorbills are common off Newfoundland.

re abbreviation for Latin "with regard to."

reaction in chemistry, the coming together of two or more atoms, ions, or molecules resulting in a chemical change. The nature of the reaction is portrayed by a chemical equation.

reaction principle principle stated by ◊Newton as his third law of motion: to every action, there is an equal and opposite reaction.

In other words, a force acting in one direction is always accompanied by an equal force acting in the opposite direction. This explains how ◊jet and rocket propulsion works and why a gun recoils after firing.

Reader's Digest magazine founded 1922 in the US to publish condensed articles and books, usually of an uplifting and conservative kind, along with in-house features. It has editions in many different languages and had the world's largest circulation until the mid-1980s.

Reading industrial town (cookies, electronics) on the river Thames; administrative headquarters of Berkshire, England; university 1892; population (1985) 138,000. It is an agricultural and horticultural center, and was extensively rebuilt after World War II. The writer Oscar Wilde spent two years in Reading jail.

Reading industrial city (textiles, special steels) in E Pennsylvania; population (1990) 78,380. Reading was laid out in 1748 and was an early iron- and steelmaking center, connected by canal and rail to nearby anthracite mines.

Reagan Ronald Wilson 1911– . US Republican politician, governor of California 1966–74, president 1981–89. A former Hollywood actor, Reagan was a hawkish and popular president. He adopted an aggressive policy in Central America, attempting to overthrow the leftist government of Nicaragua, and sending troops to ◊Grenada 1983. In 1987, ◊Irangate was investigated by the Tower Commission; Reagan admitted that US–Iran negotiations had become an "arms for hostages deal," but denied knowledge of resultant funds being illegally sent to the Contras in Nicaragua. He increased military spending (sending the national budget deficit to record levels), cut social programs, introduced deregulation of domestic markets, and cut taxes. His ◊Strategic Defense Initiative, announced 1983, proved controversial due to the cost and unfeasibility. He was succeeded by George ◊Bush.

Reagan was born in Tampico, Illinois, the son of a shoe salesman who was bankrupted during the Depression. He became a Hollywood actor 1937 and appeared in 50 films, including *Knute Rockne—All American* 1940 and *King's Row* 1942. As president of the Screen Actors' Guild 1947–52, he became a conservative, critical of the bureaucratic stifling of free enterprise, and named names before the House Un-American Activities Committee. He joined the Republican Party 1962, and his term as governor of California was marked by battles against students. Having lost the Republican presidential nomination 1968 and 1976 to Nixon and Ford respectively, Reagan won it 1980 and defeated President Carter. He was wounded in an assassination attempt 1981. The invasion of Grenada, following a coup there, generated a revival of national patriotism, and Reagan was re-elected by a landslide 1984. His insistence on militarizing space through the Strategic Defense Initiative, popularly called Star Wars, prevented a disarmament agreement when he met the Soviet leader ◊Gorbachev 1985 and 1986, but a 4% reduction in nuclear weapons was agreed 1987. In 1986, he ordered the bombing of Tripoli, Libya, in retaliation for the killing of a US soldier in Berlin by a guerrilla group.

realism in medieval philosophy, the theory that "universals" have existence, not simply as names for entities but as entities in their own right.

It is thus opposed to ◊nominalism. In contemporary philosophy, the term stands for the doctrine that there is an intuitively appreciated reality apart from what is presented to the consciousness. It is opposed to ◊idealism.

Realist philosophers include C D Broad and (although their views were later modified) Bertrand Russell and G E Moore; Wittgenstein was a significant later influence.

Realism in the arts and literature, an unadorned, naturalistic approach to the subject matter. The term realism may also refer to a socially conscious movement in mid-19th-century European art, a reaction against Romantic and Classical idealization and a rejection of conventional academic subjects, such as mythology, history, and sublime landscapes.

The painters Courbet and Daumier represent 19th-century Realism in France; both chose to paint scenes from contemporary life, sometimes using their art to expose injustice in society. Courbet shocked the public by exhibiting large canvases that depicted ordinary people.

real number in mathematics, any ◊rational (which include the integers) or ◊irrational number. Real numbers exclude ◊imaginary numbers, found in ◊complex numbers of the general form $a + bi$ where $i = \sqrt{-1}$, although these do include a real component a.

Realpolitik (German "politics of realism") the pragmatic pursuit of self-interest and power, backed up by force when convenient. The term was coined 1853 to describe ◊Bismarck's policies in Prussia during the 1848 revolutions.

real presence or transubstantiation in Christianity, the belief that there are present in the properly consecrated Eucharist the body and blood of Jesus. It is held by Roman Catholics, and in some sense by Anglo-Catholics.

real-time system in computing, a program that responds to events in the world as they happen, as, for example, an automatic pilot program in an aircraft must respond instantly to correct course deviations. Process control, robotics, games, and many military applications are examples of real-time systems.

Réaumur Réné Antoine Ferchault de 1683–1757. French metallurgist and entomologist. His definitive work on the early steel industry, published in 1722, described how to convert iron into steel and laid the foundations of the modern steel industry. He produced a six-volume work between 1734 and 1742 on the natural history of insects, the first books on entomology.

recall see ◊initiative, referendum, and recall.

Récamier Jeanne Françoise (born Bernard) 1777–1849. French society hostess, born in Lyon. At the age of 15 she married Jacques Récamier (died 1830), an elderly banker, and held a salon of literary and political celebrities.

received pronunciation (RP) see ◊English language.

receiver in law, person appointed by a court to collect and manage the assets of an individual, company, or partnership in serious financial difficulties. In the case of bankruptcy, the assets may be sold and distributed by a receiver to creditors.

In France, a receiver is known as a syndic, and in Germany as an administrator.

receptacle the enlarged end of a flower stalk to which the floral parts are attached. Normally the receptacle is rounded, but in some plants it is flattened or cup-shaped. The term is also used for the region on that part of some seaweeds which becomes swollen at certain times of the year and bears the reproductive organs.

receptor in biology, any cell capable of detecting stimuli. Receptors form part of the nervous system and are used by the body to gather information about the internal or external environment. There are several types, classified according to function. Some respond to light, some to mechanical force, and some to heat. They are essential for ◊homeostasis.

recession in economics, a fall in business activity lasting more than a fourth of a year, causing stagnation in a country's output.

The average decline has been about 10% although some recessions, such as 1981–82, can be longer and more severe.

recessive in genetics, an ◊allele that will show in

the ◊phenotype only if its partner allele on the paired chromosome is similarly recessive. Such an allele will not show if its partner is dominant, that is if the organism is ◊heterozygous for a particular characteristic. Alleles for blue eyes in humans, and for shortness in pea plants are recessive. Most mutant alleles are recessive and therefore are only rarely expressed (see ◊hemophilia and ◊sickle cell disease).

Recife industrial seaport (cotton textiles, sugar refining, fruit canning, flour milling) and naval base in Brazil; capital of Pernambuco state, at the mouth of the river Capibaribe; population (1980) 1,184,215. It was founded 1504.

reciprocal in mathematics, of a quantity, that quantity divided into 1. Thus the reciprocal of 2 is ½; of ⅔ is 3/2; of x^2 is $1/x^2$ or x^{-2}.

recitative in opera, on-pitch speechlike declamation of narrative episodes.

Recklinghausen industrial town (coal, iron, chemicals, textiles, engineering) in North Rhine–Westphalia, Federal Republic of Germany, 15 mi/24 km NW of Dortmund; population (1988) 118,000. It is said to have been founded by Charlemagne.

recombination in genetics, any process that recombines, or "shuffles," the genetic material, thus increasing genetic variation in the offspring. The two main processes of recombination both occur during meiosis (reduction division). One is ◊crossing over, in which chromosome pairs exchange segments; the other is the random reassortment of chromosomes that occurs when each gamete (sperm or egg) receives only one of each chromosome pair.

Reconquista (Spanish "reconquest") the Christian defeat of the ◊Moors 9th–15th centuries, and their expulsion from Spain.

Spain was conquered by the Muslims between 711 and 728, and its reconquest began with Galicia, Leon, and Castile. By the 13th century, only Granada was left in Muslim hands, but disunity within the Christian kingdoms left it unconquered until 1492, when it fell to ◊Ferdinand and Isabella.

Reconstruction in US history, the period 1865–77 after the ◊Civil War during which the nation was reunited under the federal government after the defeat of the ◊Confederacy.

Amendments to the US constitution, and to Southern state constitutions, conferred equal civil and political rights on blacks, although many Southern states, still opposed to these radical Republican measures, still practiced discrimination and segregation. During Reconstruction, industrial and commercial projects restored the economy of the South but failed to ensure racial equality, and the former slaves remained, in most cases, landless laborers, although emancipated slaves were assisted in finding work, shelter, and lost relatives through federal agencies. Reconstruction also resulted in an influx of Northern profiteers known as ◊carpetbaggers. Both the imposition of outside authority and the equal status conferred on former slaves combined to make Southerners bitterly resentful. Although Radical Republicans sought punitive measures against the South, they were restrained by President Abraham ◊Lincoln. When President Andrew ◊Johnson refused to agree to their program, the Radicals contrived to bring about his impeachment, failing by one vote to convict him.

recorder in music, an instrument of the ◊woodwind family, blown through one end, in which different notes are obtained by covering the holes in the instrument. Recorders are played in a consort (ensemble) of matching tone and comprise sopranino, descant, treble, and bass.

The descant, adopted into the orchestra, was gradually superseded by the flute, but was revived as a school music instrument. The full consort has since been reestablished for performing early music.

recording the process of storing information, or the information store itself. Sounds and pictures can be stored on disks or tape. The phonograph record or ◊compact disc stores music or speech as a spiral groove on a plastic disc and the sounds are reproduced by a record player. In ◊tape recording, sounds are stored as a magnetic pattern on plastic tape. The best-quality reproduction is achieved using ◊digital audio tape.

In digital recording the signals picked up by the microphone are converted into precise numerical values by computer. These values, which represent the original sound wave form, are recorded on tape or compact disc. When it is played back by ◊laser, the exact values are retrieved. When the signal is fed via an amplifier to a loudspeaker, sound waves exactly like the original ones are recreated. Pictures can be recorded on magnetic tape in a similar way by using a ◊videotape recorder. The video equivalent of a compact disc is the video disc.

record player device for reproducing sound recorded, usually in a spiral groove on a vinyl disk. A motor-driven turntable rotates the record at a constant speed, and a stylus or needle on the head of a pick-up is made to vibrate by the undulations in the record groove. These vibrations are then converted to electrical signals by a ◊transducer in the head (often a ◊piezoelectric crystal). After amplification, the signals pass to one or more loudspeakers, which convert them into sound.

The pioneers of the record player were ◊Edison, with his ◊phonograph, and Emile Berliner (1851–1929), who invented the predecessor of the vinyl record 1896. More recent developments are stereophonic sound and digital recording on compact disk.

Recruit scandal in Japanese politics, the revelation 1988 that a number of politicians and business leaders had profited from insider trading. It led to the resignation of several cabinet ministers, including Prime Minister Takeshita, whose closest aide committed suicide, and to the arrest of 20 people.

rectangle quadrilateral (four-sided figure) with opposite sides equal and parallel and with each interior angle a right angle (90°). Its area A is the product of the length l and width w; that is, $A = l \times w$. A rectangle with all four sides equal is a ◊square.

A rectangle is a special case of a ◊parallelogram. The diagonals of a rectangle bisect each other.

rectifier device used for obtaining one-directional current (DC) from an alternating source of supply (AC). Types include plate rectifiers, thermionic ◊diodes, and ◊semiconductor diodes.

rectum lowest part of the small intestine of mammals, which stores feces prior to elimination (defecation).

recursion in computing, a technique whereby a ◊function or ◊procedure calls itself into use to enable a complex problem to be broken down into simpler steps. For example, a function which returns the ◊factorial of a number, n, would obtain its result by multiplying n by the ◊factorial of $n - 1$.

recycling processing of industrial and household waste (such as paper, glass, and some metals) so that it can be reused, thus saving expenditure on scarce raw materials, slowing down the depletion of nonrenewable resources, and helping to reduce pollution.

red informal term for a leftist, revolutionary, or communist, which originated in the 19th century in the form "red republican," meaning a republican who favored a social as well as a political revolution, generally by armed violence. Red is the color adopted by Socialist and communist parties. To be soft on these political philosophies, one is thereby tainted "pink."

Red (1) River, W tributary of the ◊Mississippi River 1,018 mi/1,638 km long; so called because of the reddish soil sediment it carries. The stretch that forms the Texas-Oklahoma border is called Tornado Alley because of the storms caused by the collision in spring of warm air from the Gulf of Mexico with cold fronts from the N. The largest city on the river is Shreveport, Louisiana. (2) River, the Red River of the North, about 545 mi/877 km long, runs from North Dakota into Manitoba, Canada, and through Winnipeg, emptying into Lake Winnipeg. The fertile soil of the river valley produces large yields of wheat and other crops. (3) River in N Vietnam, 310 mi/500 km long, that flows into the Gulf of Tonkin. Its extensive delta is a main center of population.

Red and the Black, The French *Le Rouge et le noir* novel by Stendhal, published 1830. Julien Sorel, a carpenter's son, pursues social advancement by dishonorable means. Marriage to a marquis's daughter, a title, and an army commission are within his grasp when revelation of his murky past by a former lover destroys him.

Red Army former name of the army of the USSR. It developed from the Red Guards, volunteers who carried out the Bolshevik revolution, and received its name because it fought under the red flag. It was officially renamed the ***Soviet Army*** 1946. The Chinese revolutionary army was also called the Red Army.

Red Badge of Courage, The classic US novel of the American Civil War published 1895 by Stephen Crane, the story of the youth Henry Fleming, his cowardice, courage, and final sense of personal victory.

red blood cell or ***erythrocyte*** the most common type of blood cell, responsible for transporting oxygen around the body. It contains hemoglobin,

recycling *Crushed car bodies ready for recycling of the metal.*

which combines with oxygen from the lungs to form oxyhemoglobin. When transported to the tissues, these cells are able to release the oxygen because the oxyhemoglobin splits into its original constituents. Mammalian erythrocytes are disc-like with a depression in the center and no nucleus; they are manufactured in the bone marrow and, in humans, last for only four months before being destroyed in the liver and spleen. Those of other vertebrates are oval and nucleated.

Red Brigades (Italian *Brigate rosse*) extreme left-wing guerrilla groups active in Italy during the 1970s and early 1980s. They were implicated in many kidnappings and killings, including that of Christian Democrat leader Aldo Moro 1978.

Red Cloud (Sioux name ***Mahpiua Luta***) 1822–1909. Sioux leader. Born in the area of modern Nebraska, he became paramount chief of the Oglala Sioux in 1860. Thereafter Red Cloud led the armed resistance to the advance of white settlers along the Bozeman Trail. In 1869 Red Cloud signed the Fort Laramie Treaty and led his followers to the Red Cloud Agency in Nebraska. They moved to the Pine Ridge Agency in South Dakota 1878. Taking no part in the 1876 war that culminated in the Battle of the Little Bighorn, Red Cloud remained an advocate of accommodation with the US government.

Red Cross, the international relief agency founded by the Geneva Convention 1864 at the instigation of the Swiss doctor Henri ◊Dunant to assist the wounded and prisoners in war. Its symbol is a symmetrical red cross on a white ground. In addition to dealing with associated problems of war, such as refugees and the care of the disabled, the Red Cross is increasingly concerned with victims of natural disasters—floods, earthquakes, epidemics, and accidents.

Prompted by war horrors described by Dunant, the Geneva Convention laid down principles to ensure the safety of ambulances, hospitals, stores, and personnel distinguished by the Red Cross emblem. The Muslim equivalent is the Red Crescent.

The US National Red Cross was founded 1881.

redcurrant in botany, type of ◊currant.

Redding Otis 1941–1967. US soul singer and songwriter. He had a number of hits in the mid-1960s such as "My Girl" 1965, "Respect" 1967, and "(Sittin' on the) Dock of the Bay" 1968, released after his death in a plane crash.

red dwarf any star that is cool, faint, and small (about one-tenth the mass and diameter of the Sun). They burn slowly and have estimated lifetimes of 100 billion years. Red dwarfs may be the most abundant type of star but are difficult to see because they are so faint. Two of the closest stars to the Sun, ◊Proxima Centauri and ◊Barnard's Star, are red dwarfs.

Redford (Charles) Robert 1937– . US actor and film director. He became a star with *Barefoot In the Park* 1967 and a superstar appearing with Paul Newman in both *Butch Cassidy and the Sundance Kid* 1969 and *The Sting* 1973. His other films as an actor include *The Way We Were* 1973, *All the President's Men* 1976, *Out of Africa* 1985, and *Havana* 1991. He directed *Ordinary People* 1980 (Academy Award) and *The Milagro Beanfield War* 1988 and established the Sundance Institute in Utah for the development of theatrical talent.

red giant any large bright star with a cool surface. It is thought to represent a late stage in the evolution of a star like the Sun, as it runs out of hydrogen fuel at its center. Red giants have diameters between 10 and 100 times that of the Sun. They are very bright because they are so large, although their surface temperature is lower than that of the Sun, about 2,000–3,000K (3,000°–5,000°F/1,700°–2,700°C).

Redgrave Michael 1908–1985. British actor. His stage roles included Hamlet and Lear (Shakespeare), Uncle Vanya (Chekhov), and the schoolmaster in Rattigan's *The Browning Version*. He also appeared in films. He was the father of Vanessa and Lynn Redgrave, both actresses.

red-hot poker

Redgrave Vanessa 1937– . British actress. She has played Shakespeare's Lady Macbeth and Cleopatra on the stage, and the title role in the film *Julia* 1976 (Academy Award). She is active in left-wing politics. Daughter of Michael Redgrave.

Red Guards armed workers who took part in the ◊Russian Revolution of 1917.

The name was also given to the school and college students, wearing red armbands, active in the ◊Cultural Revolution in China 1966–68.

red-hot poker another name for tritoma.

Redmond John Edward 1856–1918. Irish politician, Parnell's successor as leader of the Nationalist Party 1890–1916. The 1910 elections saw him holding the balance of power in the House of Commons, and he secured the introduction of a ◊Home Rule bill, which was opposed by Protestant Ulster.

Redon Odilon 1840–1916. French Symbolist painter and graphic artist. He used fantastic symbols and images, sometimes mythological. From the 1890s he painted still lifes and landscapes. His work was much admired by the Surrealists.

Redon initially worked mostly in black and white, producing charcoal drawings and lithographs, but from 1890, in oils and pastels, he used color in a way that recalled the Impressionists. The head of Orpheus is a recurring motif in his work.

Redon made his reputation as a Symbolist in Paris around 1880.

Redoubt, Mount active volcanic peak rising to 10,197 ft/3,140 m W of Cook inlet in S Alaska. There have been recent eruptions in 1966 and 1989.

Redouté Pierre Joseph 1759–1840. French flower painter patronized by Empress Josephine and the Bourbon court. He taught flower drawing at the Museum of Natural History in Paris and produced volumes of delicate, highly detailed flowers, notably *Les Roses* 1817–24.

red pepper red fruit of various ◊capsicums.

Red Riding Hood traditional European fairy story. Little Red Riding Hood is on her way to visit her sick grandmother when she meets a wolf. After discovering where she is going he gets there before her, and eats and impersonates the grandmother. In Charles Perrault's version (1697) Red Riding Hood is eaten too, but later writers introduced a woodcutter to rescue her.

Red Scare, the in US history, campaign against radicals and dissenters which took place in the aftermath of World War I and the Russian Revolution, during a period of labor disorders and violence in the US.

Red Sea submerged section of the ◊Great Rift Valley (1,200 mi/2,000 km long and up to 200 mi/320 km wide). Egypt, Sudan, and Ethiopia (in Africa) and Saudi Arabia (Asia) are on its shores.

red shift in astronomy, the lengthening of the wavelengths of light from an object as a result of the object's motion away from us. It is an example of the ◊Doppler effect. The red shift in light from galaxies is evidence that the universe is expanding.

The lengthening of wavelengths causes the light to move or shift toward the red end of the ◊spectrum, hence the name. The amount of red shift can be measured by the displacement of lines in an object's spectrum. By measuring the amount of red shift in light from stars and galaxies, astronomers can tell how quickly these objects are moving away from us. A strong gravitational field can also produce a red shift in light; this is termed gravitational red shift.

redstart any of several New World wood warblers (family Parulidae), especially the American redstart (*Setophaga ruticulla*). The male is black and orange with white underparts. Old World redstarts are small ◊thrushes with reddish tails, belonging to the genus *Phoenicurus*.

Redstone rocket short-range US military missile, modified for use as a space launcher. Redstone rockets launched the first two ◊Mercury flights. A modified Redstone, *Juno 1*, launched the first US satellite, *Explorer 1*, in 1958.

red tape derogatory term for bureaucratic methods, derived from the fastening for departmental bundles of documents in Britain.

Red Terror term used by opponents to describe the Bolshevik seizure and retention of power in Russia after Oct 1917.

redwood giant coniferous tree. See ◊sequoia.

reed any of various perennial tall, slender grasses of wet or marshy environments; in particular, species of the genus *Phragmites*; also the stalk of any of these plants. The common reed *P. australis* attains a height of 10 ft/3 m, having stiff, erect leaves and straight stems bearing a plume of purplish flowers.

Reed Carol 1906–1976. British film producer and director, an influential figure in the British film industry of the 1940s. His films include *Odd Man Out* 1947, *The Fallen Idol* and *The Third Man* both 1950, and *Our Man in Havana* 1959.

Reed Ishmael 1938– . US novelist. His experimental, parodic, satirical novels exploit traditions taken from jazz and voodoo, and include *The Free-Lance Pallbearers* 1967, *Mumbo Jumbo* 1972, and *Reckless Eyeballing* 1986.

Reed John 1887–1920. US journalist and author. Born in Portland, Oregon, and educated at Harvard, Reed began his journalism career on the staff of the *American Magazine* 1911. Becoming involved in radical politics, he joined the staff of *Masses* 1913. He later published his accounts of overseas conflicts in *Insurgent Mexico* 1914 and *The War in Eastern Europe* 1916. As a supporter of the Bolsheviks, Reed published his account of the Russian Revolution in *Ten Days that Shook the World* 1919. Later indicted in the US for sedition, Reed fled to the Soviet Union, where he died in exile.

Reed Lou 1942– . US rock singer, songwriter, and former member (1965–70) of the seminal New York garage/avant-garde band the Velvet Underground. His solo work deals largely with urban alienation and angst, and includes the albums *Berlin* 1973, *Street Hassle* 1978, and *New York* 1989.

Reed Oliver 1938– . British actor, nephew of the director Carol Reed. He became a star through such films as *Women in Love* 1969, *The Devils* 1971, and *Castaway* 1987.

Reed Walter 1851–1902. US physician and medical researcher. His 1898 research into the causes and transmission of typhoid fever brought about significant control of the disease in army camps. Reed's greatest work was carried out 1900–01 in Cuba, where a yellow-fever epidemic was ravaging US troops. His breakthrough isolation of the aedes mosquito as the sole carrier of yellow fever led to the eradication of the deadly disease.

red shift

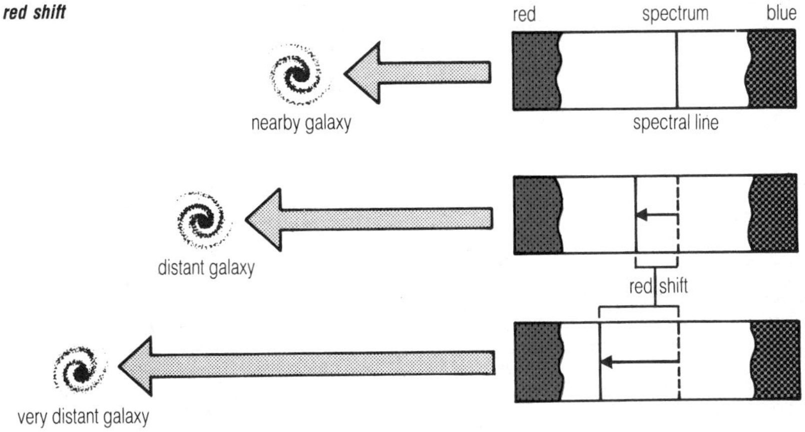
red
spectrum
blue
nearby galaxy
spectral line
distant galaxy
red shift
very distant galaxy

Born in Belroi, Virginia, Reed received an MD degree from the University of Virginia 1869. He joined the Army Medical Corps 1875, served as an army surgeon in Arizona 1876–89 and Baltimore 1890–93, and was professor at the Army Medical College 1893–1902.

reel in cinema, plastic or metal spool used for winding and storing film. As the size of reels became standardized it came to refer to the running time of the film: a standard 35-mm reel holds 900 ft/313 m of film, which runs for ten minutes when projected at 24 frames per second; hence a "two-reeler" was a film lasting 20 minutes. Today's projectors, however, hold bigger reels.

reeve in Anglo-Saxon England, an official charged with the administration of a shire or burgh, fulfilling functions similar to those of the later sheriff. After the Norman Conquest, the term tended to be restricted to the person elected by the villeins to oversee the work of the manor and to communicate with the manorial lord.

Reeves William Pember 1857–1932. New Zealand politician and writer. He was New Zealand minister of education 1891–96, and director of the London School of Economics 1908–19. He wrote poetry and the classic description of New Zealand, *Long White Cloud* 1898.

referee in sport, the official in charge of a game.

referee in science, one who reads and comments on a scientific paper before its publication, normally a scientist of at least equal standing to the author(s).

referee a quasi-judicial officer appointed by a court to take testimony or hear specified types of cases. These officials are sometimes called masters.

referendum procedure whereby a decision on proposed legislation is referred to the electorate for settlement by direct vote of all the people. It is most frequently employed in Switzerland, the first country to use it, but has also been used in Australia, New Zealand, Québec, and certain states of the US (see ◊initiative, referendum, and recall). It was used in the UK for the first time 1975 on the issue of membership of the European Community. Critics argue that referenda undermine parliamentary authority, but they do allow the elector to participate directly in decision-making. A similar device is the recall, whereby voters are given the opportunity of demanding the dismissal from office of officials. See also ◊initiative.

refining any process that purifies or converts something into a more useful form. Metals usually need refining after they have been extracted from their ores by such processes as smelting. Petroleum, or crude oil, needs refining before it can be used; the process involves ◊fractionation, the separation of the substance into separate components or "fractions."

Electrolytic metal-refining methods use the principle of ◊electrolysis to obtain pure metals. When refining petroleum, or crude oil, subsequent refinery processes to fractionation serve to convert the heavier fractions into more useful lighter products. The most important of these is ◊cracking. Other processes include ◊polymerization, hydrogenation, and reforming.

reflection the throwing back or deflection of waves, such as ◊light or ◊sound waves, when they hit a surface. The law of reflection states that the angle of incidence (the angle between the ray and a perpendicular line drawn to the surface) is equal to the angle of reflection (the angle between the reflected ray and a perpendicular to the surface).

reflex automatic response to a particular stimulus, controlled by the ◊nervous system. The receptor (for example, a sense organ) and the effector (such as a muscle) are linked directly (via the spinal ganglia or the lower brain, in vertebrates), making responses to stimuli very rapid. Reflex actions are most common in simple animals.

In animals with well-developed ◊central nervous systems, reflex actions can often be modified by other nerves that are under voluntary control. For example, most mammals learn to control the reflex that leads the bladder to be emptied as soon as it becomes full.

reflex anal dilatation controversial method of diagnosing anal abuse in children, which was at the center of speculation in Cleveland, NE England, in 1987 (see ◊child abuse). Repeated anal abuse stretches and damages the anal sphincter, with the result that when the anus is gently stretched apart during the test, it continues to dilate as a reflex action. The normal anal sphincter remains tightly closed.

reflex camera camera that uses a mirror and prisms to reflect light passing through the lens into the viewfinder, showing the photographer the exact scene that is being shot. When the shutter button is released the mirror springs out of the way, allowing light to reach the film. The most common type is the single-lens reflex (◊SLR) camera. The twin-lens reflex (◊TLR) camera has two lenses: one has a mirror for viewing, the other is used for exposing the film.

reflection

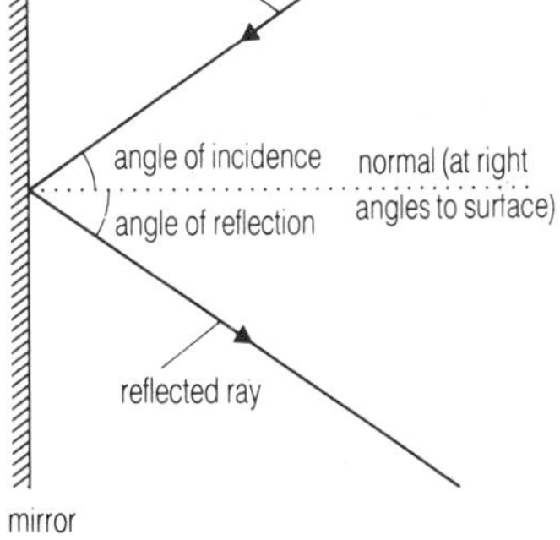
approaching or incident ray
angle of incidence
normal (at right angles to surface)
angle of reflection
reflected ray
mirror

refraction

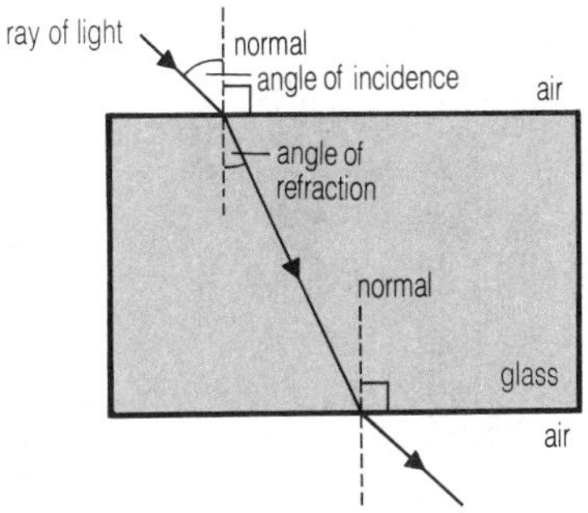
ray of light
normal
angle of incidence
air
angle of refraction
normal
glass
air

Reformation religious and political movement in 16th-century Europe to reform the Roman Catholic Church, and leading to the establishment of Protestant Churches. Anticipated from the 12th century by the Waldenses, Lollards, and Hussites, it became effective in the 16th century when the absolute monarchies gave it support by challenging the political power of the papacy and confiscating church wealth.

1517 The German priest Luther protested against the sale of ◊indulgences began the Reformation in Europe.

1519 Zwingli led the Reformation in Switzerland.

1529 The term "Protestant" was first used.

1533 Henry VIII renounced papal supremacy and proclaimed himself head of the Church of England.

1541 The French theologian Calvin established Presbyterianism in Geneva, Switzerland.

1559 The Protestant John Knox returned from exile to found the Church of Scotland.

1545–63 The Counter-Reformation was initiated by the Roman Catholic Church at the Council of Trent. It aimed at reforming abuses and regaining the lost ground by using moral persuasion and extending the Spanish Inquisition to other countries.

By 1648, at the end of the Thirty Years' War, the present European alignment had been reached, with the separation of Catholic and Protestant churches.

refraction the bending of a wave of light, heat, or sound when it passes from one medium to another. Refraction occurs because waves travel at different velocities in diferent media.

refractive index a measure of the refraction of a ray of light as it passes from one transparent medium to another. If the angle of incidence is i and the angle of refraction is r, the refractive index $n = \sin i / \sin r$. It is also equal to the speed of light in the first medium divided by the speed of light in the second, and it varies with the wavelength of the light.

refractory (of a material) able to resist high temperature, for example ◊ceramics made from clay, minerals, or other earthy materials. Furnaces are lined with silica and dolomite. Alumina (aluminum oxide) is an excellent refractory, often used for the bodies of spark plugs. Titanium and tungsten are often called refractory metals because they are temperature resistant. ◊Cermets are refractory materials made up of ceramics and metals.

refrigeration use of technology to transfer heat from cold to warm, against the normal temperature gradient, so that a body can remain substantially colder than its surroundings. Refrigeration equipment is used for the chiling and deep freezing of food (see ◊food technology), and in air conditioners and industrial processes.

Refrigeration is commonly achieved by a vapor-compression cycle, in which a suitable chemical (the refrigerant) travels through a long circuit of tubing, during which it changes from a vapor to a liquid and back again. A compression chamber makes it condense, and thus give out heat. In another part of the circuit, called the evaporator coils, the pressure is much lower, so the refrigerant evaporates, absorbing heat as it does so. The evaporation process takes place near the central

refrigeration

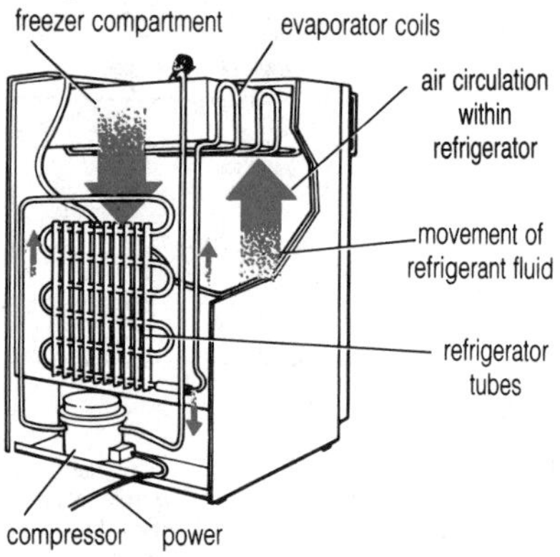
freezer compartment
evaporator coils
air circulation within refrigerator
movement of refrigerant fluid
refrigerator tubes
compressor
power

part of the refrigerator, which therefore becomes colder, while the compression process takes place near a ventilation grille, transferring the heat to the air outside. The most commonly used refrigerants in modern systems were ◊chlorofluorocarbons, but these are now being replaced by coolants that do not damage the ozone layer.

refugee a person fleeing from oppressive or dangerous conditions (such as political, religious, or military persecution) and seeking refuge in a foreign country. In 1990 there were an estimated 15 million refugees worldwide, whose resettlement and welfare were the responsibility of the United Nations High Commission for Refugees (UNCHR).

The term was originally applied to the French Huguenots who came to England after the revocation of the Edict of Nantes in 1685. Major refugee movements in 20th-century Europe include: Jews from the ◊pogroms of Russia 1881–1914 and again after the Revolution; White Russians from the USSR after 1917; Jews from Germany and other Nazi-dominated countries 1933–45; and the displaced people of World War II.

Elsewhere, the Palestinians represent the longest-running refugee problem. Many Chinese fled the mainland after the communist revolution of 1949, especially to Taiwan and Hong Kong; many Latin Americans fled from Cuba, Colombia, Brazil, Chile, Argentina, and Central America when new governments took power; and many people left Vietnam (the boat people) after the victory of the North over the South. Refugee movements created by natural disasters and famine have been widespread, most notably in Ethiopia and Sudan.

In 1990 the largest single refugee groupings were: Afghans (about 6 million, temporarily settled in Iran and Pakistan); Palestinians (2.3 million); Ethiopians (1.3 million, mostly Eritreans who have moved to Sudan); Mozambicans (1.2 million, displaced mostly to Malawi); Iraqis (600,000, predominantly Kurds who have settled in Iran); Somalis (400,000); Sudanese (400,000); Sri Lankan Tamils (300,000, who have fled to India); and Cambodians (300,000, who live in refugee camps in Thailand). A distinction is usually made by Western nations between "political" and so-called "economic" refugees, particularly when the refugees come from low-income countries (see ◊boat people).

Regan Donald 1918– . US Republican political adviser to Ronald ◊Reagan. He was secretary of the Treasury 1981–85, and chief of White House staff from 1985 until 1987, when he was forced to resign because of widespread belief of his complicity in the ◊Irangate scandal.

regelation phenomenon in which water refreezes to ice after it has been melted by pressure at a temperature below the freezing point of water. Pressure makes an ice skate, for example, form a film of water that freezes once again after the skater has passed.

Regency in Britain, the years 1811–20 during which ◊George IV (then Prince of Wales) acted as regent for his father ◊George III.

Regency style style of architecture and interior furnishings popular in England during the late 18th and early 19th centuries. The style is characterized by its restrained simplicity and its use of ancient Classical elements, often Greek.

regeneration in biology, regrowth of a new organ or tissue after the loss or removal of the original. It is common in plants, where a new individual can often be produced from a "cutting" of the original. In animals, regeneration of major structures is limited to lower organisms; certain lizards can regrow their tails if these are lost, and new flatworms can grow from a tiny fragment of an old one. In mammals, regeneration is limited to the repair of tissue in wound healing and the regrowth of peripheral nerves following damage.

Regensburg (English *Ratisbon*) city in Bavaria, Federal Republic of Germany, on the river Danube at its confluence with the Regen, 63 mi/100 km NE of Munich; population (1988) 124,000. It has many medieval buildings, including a Gothic cathedral 1275–1530. Regensburg stands on the site of a Celtic settlement dating from 500 BC. It became the Roman Castra Regina AD 179, the capital of the Eastern Frankish Empire, a free city 1245, and seat of the German *Diet* (parliament) 16th century–1806. It was included in Bavaria 1810.

regent person discharging the royal functions during a sovereign's minority or incapacity, or during a lengthy absence from the country. In England since the time of Henry VIII, Parliament has always appointed a regent or council of regency when necessary.

Regents of the University of California v Bakke a US Supreme Court decision 1978 dealing with "benign discrimination" in publicly funded schools. The case was a challenge to an affirmative-action program designed to remedy racial inequality in the University of California Medical School. Bakke, a white applicant denied admission to the school, sued the university on grounds of racial discrimination. He argued that his rejection was the result of a policy that accepted minority applicants at lower standards than those set for nonminorities. The Court sustained Bakke's complaint, ruling that any institution, regardless of motive, that discriminated solely because of race was in violation of the Civil Rights Act of 1964.

Reger (Johann Baptist Joseph) Max(imilian) 1873–1916. German composer and pianist. He taught at Munich 1905–07, was professor at the Leipzig Conservatoire from 1907, and was conductor of the Meiningen ducal orchestra 1911–14. His works include organ and piano music, chamber music, and songs.

reggae predominant form of West Indian popular music of the 1970s and 1980s, characterized by a heavily accented onbeat. The lyrics often refer to Rastafarianism. Musicians include Bob Marley (1945–81), Lee "Scratch" Perry (1940– , performer and producer), and the group Black Uhuru (1974–).

Reggio di Calabria industrial center (farm machinery, olive oil, perfume) of Calabria, S Italy; population (1988) 179,000. It was founded by Greeks about 720 BC.

Reggio nell'Emilia chief town of the province of the same name in Emilia-Romagna region, N Italy; population (1987) 130,000. It was here in 1797 that the Congress of the cities of Emilia adopted the tricolor flag that was later to become the national flag of Italy.

Regina industrial city (oil refining, cement, steel, farm machinery, fertilizers), and capital of Saskatchewan, Canada; population (1986) 175,000. It was founded 1882 as Pile O'Bones, and renamed in honor of Queen Victoria of England.

register in computing, a fast type of memory, often built into the computer's central processing unit (CPU). Some registers are reserved for special tasks, such as keeping track of the next command to be executed; others are used for holding frequently used data and for storing intermediate results.

Regulus brightest star in the constellation Leo and the 21st brightest star in the sky. Regulus has a true luminosity 160 times that of the Sun and is 85 light-years from Earth.

Rehnquist William Hubbs 1924– . US jurist; associate justice 1971–86 and chief justice 1986– of the US Supreme Court. As chief justice, he wrote the majority opinion for such cases as *Morrison* v *Olson* 1988, in which the court ruled that a special court can appoint special prosecutors to investigate crimes by high-ranking government officials, and *Hustler* v *Falwell* 1988, in which the Court ruled that public figures cannot be compensated for stress caused by parody that cannot possibly be taken seriously. Rehnquist dissented in *Texas* v *Johnson* 1989, in which the Court ruled that the burning of the US flag in protest is protected by individual rights set forth in the First Amendment. In 1990 Rehnquist dissented on the Court's ruling that it is unconstitutional for states to have the right to require a teenager to notify her parents before having an abortion.

Born in Milwaukee, Wisconsin, he graduated from Stanford University and the Stanford Law School. Rehnquist served as clerk to US Supreme Court Justice Robert Jackson before entering private practice in Phoenix, Arizona. He became active in Republican politics. In 1968 Rehnquist was appointed by President Nixon as an assistant US attorney general and in 1971 to the Supreme Court. As an associate justice, Rehnquist argued in dissent for the death penalty in *Furman* v *Georgia* 1972, and again in dissent, against the right to abortion in *Roe* v *Wade* 1973. Writing for the majority, Rehnquist held in *Rostken* v *Goldberg* 1981 that it is constitutional to exclude women for registering for the draft. He was appointed chief justice by President Reagan.

Rehoboam king of Judah about 932–915 BC, son of Solomon. Under his rule the Jewish nation split into the two kingdoms of Israel and Judah. Ten of the tribes revolted against him and took Jeroboam as their ruler, leaving Rehoboam only the tribes of Judah and Benjamin.

Rehoboth Gebeit district of Namibia to the south of Windhoek; area 12,420 sq mi/32,168 sq km; chief town Rehoboth. The area is occupied by the Basters, a mixed race of European-Nama descent.

Reich (German "empire") three periods in European history. The First Reich was the Holy Roman Empire 962–1806, the Second Reich the German Empire 1871–1918, and the ◊Third Reich Nazi Germany 1933–45.

Reich Wilhelm 1897–1957. Austrian doctor, who emigrated to the US 1939. He combined ◊Marxism and ◊psychoanalysis to advocate the positive effects of directed sexual energies and sexual freedom.

He held the view that neuroses were the result of repressed sexual energy that could be released only through orgasm. He extended Freud's hypothesis that sexuality determines personality, and concluded that orgastically potent individuals will spontaneously seek to do what is good and right.

His works include *Die Sexuelle Revolution/The Sexual Revolution* 1936–45 and *Die Funktion des Orgasmus/The Function of the Orgasm* 1948.

Reichstag German parliament building and lower legislative house during the German Empire 1871–1918 and Weimar Republic 1919–33.

Reichstag Fire burning of the German parliament building in Berlin Feb 27, 1933, less than a month after the Nazi leader Hitler became chancellor. The fire was used as a justification for the suspension of many constitutional guarantees and also as an excuse to attack the communists. There is still debate over Nazi involvement in the crime, not least because they were the main beneficiaries.

reindeer

Although three Bulgarians—◊Dimitrov, Popov, and Tanev—and a German, Torgler, were all indicted and tried in Leipzig, only a Dutch communist, Marinus van der Lubbe, was convicted, after being found at the scene of the crime and confessing.

Reichstein Tadeus 1897– . Swiss biochemist who investigated the chemical activity of the adrenal glands. By 1946 Reichstein had identified a large number of steroids secreted by the adrenal cortex, some of which would later be used in the treatment of Addison's disease. Reichstein shared the 1950 Nobel physiology or medicine prize with Edward ◊Kendall and Philip Hench (1896–1965).

reification alleged social process whereby relations between human beings are transformed into impersonal relations between things. Georg Lukács, in *History and Class Consciousness* 1923, analyzes this process as characteristic of capitalist society. Later Marxists have developed this analysis, thus extending Marx's early critique of alienation in the *Paris Manuscripts* 1844.

Reims (English *Rheims*) capital of Champagne-Ardenne region, France; population (1982) 199,000. It is the center of the champagne industry and has textile industries as well. It was known in Roman times as ***Durocorturum***. From 987 all but six French kings were crowned here. Ceded to England 1420 under the Treaty of Troyes, it was retaken by Joan of Arc, who had Charles VII consecrated in the 13th-century cathedral. In World War II, the German High Command formally surrendered here to US general Eisenhower May 7, 1945.

reincarnation belief that after death the human soul or the spirit of a plant or animal may live again in another human or animal. It is part of the teachings of many religions and philosophies, for example ancient Egyptian and Greek (the philosophies of Pythagoras and Plato), Buddhism, Hinduism, Jainism, certain Christian heresies (such as the Cathars), and theosophy. It is also referred to as transmigration or metempsychosis.

reindeer or ***caribou*** deer *Rangifer tarandus* of Arctic and subarctic regions, common to North America and Eurasia. About 4 ft/120 cm at the shoulder, it has a thick, brownish coat and broad hoofs well adapted to travel over snow. It is the only deer in which both sexes have antlers; up to 5 ft/150 cm long, they are shed in winter.

The Old World reindeer have been domesticated by the Lapps of Scandinavia for centuries. There are two types of North American caribou: the large woodland caribou of the more S regions, and the barren-ground caribou of the far N. Reindeer migrate S in winter, moving in large herds. They eat grass, small plants, and lichens.

Reinhardt Max 1873–1943. Austrian producer and director whose Expressionist style was predominant in German theater and film during the 1920s and 1930s. Directors such as Murnau and Lubitsch and actors such as Dietrich worked with him. He codirected the US film *A Midsummer Night's Dream* 1935.

In 1920 Reinhardt founded the Salzburg Festival. When the Nazis came to power, he lost his theaters and, after touring Europe as a guest director, went to the US, where he produced and directed. He founded an acting school and theater workshop in Hollywood.

Reisz Karel 1926– . Czech film director, originally a writer and film critic, who lived in Britain from 1938. His first feature film, *Saturday Night and Sunday Morning* 1960, was a critical and commercial success. His other movies include *Morgan* 1966, *The French Lieutenant's Woman* 1981, and *Sweet Dreams* 1986.

relational database ◊database in which data are viewed as a collection of linked tables. It is the most popular of the three basic database models, the others being network and hierarchical.

Its theoretical concepts were developed by E. F. Codd in the early 1970s.

relative atomic mass alternate name for ◊atomic weight.

relative density or ***specific gravity*** the density (at 68°F/20°C) of a solid or liquid relative to (divided by) the maximum density of water (at 39.2°F/4°C). The relative density of a gas is its density divided by the density of hydrogen (or sometimes dry air) at the same temperature and pressure.

relative humidity the concentration of water vapor in the air. It is expressed as a percentage of its moisture content to maximum amount that the air could contain at the same temperature and pressure. The higher the temperature the more water vapor the air can hold.

relativism philosophical position that denies the possibility of objective truth independent of some specific social or historical context or conceptual framework.

relativity the theory of the relative rather than absolute character of motion and mass and the interdependence of matter, time, and space, as developed by Albert ◊Einstein in two phases:

special theory (1905) Starting with the premises that (1) the laws of nature are the same for all observers in unaccelerated motion, and (2) the speed of light is independent of the motion of its source, Einstein postulated that the time interval between two events was longer for an observer in whose frame of reference the events occur in different places than for the observer for whom they occur at the same place.

general theory of relativity (1915) The geometrical properties of space-time were to be conceived as modified locally by the presence of a body with mass. A planet's orbit around the Sun (as observed in three-dimensional space) arises from its natural trajectory in modified space-time; there is no need to invoke, as Isaac Newton did, a force of ◊gravity coming from the Sun and acting on the planet. Einstein's theory predicted slight differences in the orbits of the planets from Newton's theory, which were observable in the case of Mercury. The new theory also said light rays should bend when they pass by a massive object, caused by the object's effect on local space-time. The predicted bending of starlight was observed during the eclipse of the Sun 1919, when light from distant stars passing close to the Sun was not masked by sunlight.

Einstein showed that for consistency with premises (1) and (2), the principles of dynamics as established by Newton needed modification; the most celebrated new result was the equation $E = mc^2$, which expresses an equivalence between mass (m) and ◊energy (E), c being the speed of light in a vacuum. Although since modified in detail, general relativity remains central to modern ◊astrophysics and ◊cosmology; it predicts, for example, the possibility of ◊black holes. General relativity theory was inspired by the simple idea that it is impossible in a small region to distinguish between acceleration and gravitation effects (as in an elevator one feels heavier when the elevator accelerates upward), but the mathematical development of the idea is formidable. Such is not the case for the special theory, which a nonexpert can follow up to $E = mc^2$ and beyond.

relay in electrical engineering, an electromagnetic switch. A small current passing through a coil of wire wound around an iron core attracts an ◊armature whose movement closes a pair of sprung contacts to complete a secondary circuit, which may carry a large current or activate other devices. The solid-state equivalent is a thyristor switching device.

relay neuron a nerve cell in the spinal cord, connecting motor neurons to sensory neurons. Relay neurons allow information to pass straight through the spinal cord, bypassing the brain. In humans such reflex actions, which are extremely rapid, cause the sudden removal of a limb from a painful stimulus.

relic part of some divine or saintly person, or something closely associated with them. Christian examples include the arm of St Teresa of Avila, the blood of St Januarius, and the ◊True Cross. Buddhist relics include the funeral ashes of the historic Buddha, placed in a number of stupas or burial mounds.

In medieval times relics were fiercely fought for, and there were a vast number of fakes. The cult was condemned by Protestant reformers but upheld by the Roman Catholic Church at the Council of Trent in the mid-16th century. Parallel nonreligious examples of the phenomenon include the display of the preserved body of Lenin in Moscow, USSR.

relief in architecture, carved figures and other forms that project from the background. The Italian terms *basso-rilievo* (low relief), *mezzo-rilievo* (middle relief), and *alto-rilievo* (high relief) are used according to the extent to which the sculpture projects. The French term *bas-relief* means low relief.

religion (Latin *religare* "to bind"; perhaps humans to God) code of belief or philosophy, which often involves the worship of a ◊God or gods. Belief in a supernatural power is not essential (absent in, for example, Buddhism and Confucianism), but faithful adherence is usually considered to be rewarded, for example by escape from human existence (Buddhism), by a future existence (Christianity, Islam), or by worldly benefit (Sōka Gakkai Buddhism).

Comparative religion studies the various faiths impartially, but often with the hope of finding common ground, to solve the practical problems of competing claims of unique truth or inspiration. The earliest known attempt at a philosophy of religious beliefs is contained in fragments written by Xenophones in Greece 6th century BC, and later Herodotus and Aristotle contributed to the study. In 17th-century China, Jesuit theologians conducted comparative studies. Toward the end of the 18th century English missionary schools in Calcutta compared the Bible with sacred Indian texts. The work of Charles Darwin in natural history and the growth of anthropology stimulated fresh investigation of religious beliefs; work by the Sanskrit scholar Max Müller (1823–1900), the Scottish anthropologist James Frazer, the German sociologist Max Weber, and the Romanian scholar Mircea Eliade has formed the basis for modern comparative religion.

Among the chief religions are:

ancient and pantheist religions of Babylonia, Assyria, Egypt, Greece, and Rome

oriental Hinduism, Buddhism, Jainism, Parseeism, Confucianism, Taoism, and Shinto

"religions of a book" Judaism, Christianity (the principal divisions are Roman Catholic, Eastern Orthodox, and Protestant), and Islam (the principal divisions are Sunni and Shiite)

combined derivation such as the Baha'is, the Unification Church, and Mormonism.

religious education the formal teaching of religion in schools.

In the US, religious education is prohibited in public (state-maintained) schools because of the

Religious festivals

Date	*Festival*	*Religion*	*Event Commemorated*
Jan 6	Epiphany	Western Christian	coming of the Magi
Jan 6–7	Christmas	Orthodox Christian	birth of Jesus
Jan 18–19	Epiphany	Orthodox Christian	coming of the Magi
Jan–Feb	New Year	Chinese	Return of Kitchen god to heaven
Feb–Mar	Shrove Tuesday	Christian	day before Lent
	Ash Wednesday	Christian	first day of Lent
	Purim	Jewish	story of Esther
	Mahashivaratri	Hindu	Siva
Mar–Apr	Palm Sunday	Western Christian	Jesus's entry into Jerusalem
	Good Friday	Western Christian	crucifixion of Jesus
	Easter Sunday	Western Christian	resurrection of Jesus
	Passover	Jewish	escape from slavery in Egypt
	Holi	Hindu	Krishna
	Holi Mohalla	Sikh	(coincides with Holi)
	Rama Naumi	Hindu	birth of Rama
	Ching Ming	Chinese	remembrance of the dead
Apr 13	Baisakhi	Sikh	founding of the Kalsa
Apr–May	Easter	Orthodox Christian	death and resurrection of Jesus
May–Jun	Shavuot	Jewish	giving of ten Comandments to Moses
	Pentecost (Whitsun)	Western Christian	Jesus's followers receiving the Holy Spirit
	Wesak	Buddhist	day of Buddha's birth, enlightenment and death
	Martyrdom of Guru Arjan	Sikh	death of fifth guru of Sikhism
June	Dragon Boat Festival	Chinese	Chinese martyr
	Pentecost	Orthodox Christian	Jesus's followers receiving the Holy Spirit
July	Dhammacakka	Buddhist	preaching of Buddha's first sermon
Aug	Raksha Bandhan	Hindu	family
Aug–Sept	Janmashtami	Hindu	birthday of Khrishna
Sept	Moon Festival	Chinese	Chinese hero
Sept–Oct	Rosh Hashana	Jewish	start of Jewish New Year
	Yom Kippur	Jewish	day of atonement
	Succot	Jewish	Israelites' time in the wilderness
Oct	Dusshera	Hindu	goddess Devi
Oct–Nov	Divali	Hindu	goddess Lakshmi
	Divali	Sikh	release of Guru Hargobind from prison
Nov	Guru Nanak's Birthday	Sikh	founder of Sikhism
Nov–Dec	Bodhi Day	Buddhist (Mahayana)	Buddha's enlightenment
Dec	Hanukkah	Jewish	recapture of Temple of Jerusalem
	Winter Festival	Chinese	time of feasting
Dec 25	Christmas	Western Christian	birth of Christ
Dec–Jan	Birthday of Guru Gobind Sind	Sikh	last (tenth) human guru of Sikhism
	Martyrdom of Guru Tegh Bahadur	Sikh	ninth guru of Sikhism

separation of church and state guaranteed under the First Amendment to the Constitution; however, the study of comparative religion is permitted, since it is theoretical and secular information, not sacred matter. Private parochial schools offer both state-approved courses and religious instruction.

REM US four-piece rock group formed 1980 in Georgia. Their songs are characterized by melodic bass lines, driving guitar, and evocative lyrics partly buried in the mix. Albums include *Reckoning* 1984 and *Green* 1988.

rem (acronym from roentgen equivalent man) SI unit of radiation dose equivalent. Some types of radiation do more damage than others for the same absorbed dose; the equivalent dose in rems is equal to the dose in rads multiplied by the relative biological effectiveness. One rem is approximately equivalent to the biological effect produced by one roentgen of X-ray or gamma-ray radiation. Humans can absorb up to 25 rems without immediate ill effects; 100 rems may produce radiation sickness; and more than 800 rems causes death.

Remarque Erich Maria 1898–1970. German novelist, a soldier in World War I, whose *All Quiet on the Western Front* 1929, one of the first antiwar novels, led to his being deprived of German nationality. He lived in Switzerland 1929–39, and then in the US.

Rembrandt Harmensz van Rijn 1606–1669. Dutch painter and etcher, one of the most prolific and significant artists in Europe of the 17th century. Between 1629 and 1669 he painted some 60 penetrating self-portraits. He also painted religious subjects and produced about 300 etchings and over 1,000 drawings. His group portraits include *The Anatomy Lesson of Dr Tulp* 1632 (Mauritshuis, The Hague) and *The Night Watch* 1642 (Rijksmuseum, Amsterdam).

After studying in Leiden and for a few months in Amsterdam (with a history painter), Rembrandt began his career 1625 in Leiden, where his work reflected knowledge of ◊Elsheimer and ◊Caravaggio, among others. He settled permanently in Amsterdam 1631 and obtained many commissions for portraits from wealthy merchants. The *Self-Portrait with Saskia* (his wife, Saskia van Uylenburgh) about 1634 (Gemäldegalerie, Dresden, Germany) displays their prosperity in warm tones and rich, glittering textiles.

Saskia died 1642, and that year Rembrandt's fortunes began to decline (he eventually became bankrupt 1656). His work became more somber and had deeper emotional content, and his portraits were increasingly melancholy: for example, *Jan Six* 1654 (Six Collection, Amsterdam). From 1660 onward he lived with Hendrickje Stoffels, but he outlived her, and in 1668 his only surviving child, Titus, died too.

Rembrandt had many pupils, including Gerard Dou and Carel Fabritius.

Remington Eliphalet 1793–1861. US inventor, gunsmith, and arms manufacturer (with his father) of the firm that bears his name. He supplied the US army with rifles in the Mexican War, then in 1856 the firm expanded into the manufacture of agricultural implements. His son Philo continued the expansion.

Remington Frederic 1861–1909. US artist and illustrator best known for his paintings, bronzes, and sketches of horses, characters, and scenes of the American West, which he recorded during several trips to the region. Born in Canton, New York, he trained at the Yale School of Fine Arts and at the Art Students League in New York City. He illustrated for Harper publications and other periodicals and for Theodore Roosevelt's *Ranch Life and the Hunting Trail* 1888. Remington wrote and illustrated *Pony Tracks* 1895, *Crooked Trails* 1898, and *John Ermine of Yellowstone* 1902. A correspondent for the Hearst syndicate during the Spanish American War, he came home to paint and sculpt. The Remington Museum was established in Ogdensburg, New York, near his family's home.

Remington Philo 1816–1889. US inventor and businessman, son of Eliphalet. He ran the arms business during the Civil War, when the firm had government contracts, and later supplied several European armies with his new breech-loading rifles. In 1873 he became interested in the manufacture of typewriters, the first being demonstrated at the Centennial Exhibition in Philadelphia. By 1878, he produced the first typewriter with a shift key, which provided lower case as well as upper case letters. In 1879 his firm began making sewing machines.

remora any of a family of warm-water fishes that have an adhesive disk on the head, by which they attach themselves to whales, sharks, and turtles. These provide the remora with shelter and transport, as well as food in the form of parasites on the host's skin.

remote sensing gathering and recording information from a distance, developed as a result of space technology. Space probes have sent back photographs and data about planets as distant as Neptune. Satellites such as *Landsat* have surveyed all the Earth's surface from orbit. Computer processing of data obtained by their scanning instruments, and the application of so-called false colors (generated by the computer), have made it possible to reveal surface features invisible in ordinary light. This has proved valuable in agriculture, forestry, and urban planning, and has led to the discovery of new deposits of minerals.

Remscheid industrial city in North Rhine–Westphalia, Federal Republic of Germany, where stainless-steel implements are manufactured; population (1988) 121,000.

REM sleep acronym for ***rapid-eye-movement sleep*** a phase of sleep that recurs several times nightly in humans and is associated with dreaming. The eyes flicker quickly beneath closed lids.

Remus in Roman mythology, the brother of ◊Romulus.

Renaissance period and intellectual movement in European cultural history that is traditionally seen as ending the Middle Ages and beginning modern times. The Renaissance started in Italy in the 14th century and flourished in W Europe until about the 17th century.

The aim of Renaissance education was to produce the "complete human being" (Renaissance man), conversant in the humanities, mathematics and science (including their application in war), the arts and crafts, and athletics and sport; to enlarge the bounds of learning and geographical knowledge; to encourage the growth of skepticism and free thought, and the study and imitation of Greek and Latin literature and art. The revival of interest in Classical Greek and Roman culture inspired artists such as Leonardo da Vinci, Michelangelo, and Dürer, architects such as Brunelleschi and Alberti, and writers such as Petrarch and Boccaccio. Scientists and explorers proliferated as well.

The beginning of the Italian Renaissance is usually dated in the 14th century with Petrarch and Boccaccio. The invention of printing (mid-15th century) and geographical discoveries helped spread the new spirit. Exploration by Europeans opened Africa, Asia, and the New World to trade, colonization, and imperialism. Biblical criticism by the Dutch humanist Erasmus and others contributed to the Reformation, but the Counter-Reformation almost extinguished the movement in

Rembrandt *One of Europe's most influential painters in the 17th century, the Dutch artist Rembrandt painted* Girl Leaning on a Windowsill *in 1645.*

16th-century Italy. In the visual arts Renaissance painting and sculpture later moved toward ◊Mannerism.

Figures of the Renaissance include the politician Machiavelli, the poets Ariosto and Tasso, the philosopher Bruno, the physicist Galileo, and the artists, Cellini and Raphael in Italy; the writers Rabelais and Montaigne in France, Cervantes in Spain, and Camoëns in Portugal; the astronomer Copernicus in Poland; and the politicians More and Bacon, and the writers Sidney, Marlowe, and Shakespeare in England.

The term "Renaissance," to describe the period of time, was first used in the 18th century.

Renaissance art movement in European art of the 15th and 16th centuries. It began in Florence, Italy, with the rise of a spirit of humanism and a new appreciation of the Classical past. In painting and sculpture this led to greater naturalism and interest in anatomy and perspective. Renaissance art peaked around 1500 with the careers of Leonardo da Vinci, Raphael, Michelangelo, and Titian in Italy and Dürer in Germany.

The Renaissance was heralded by the work of the early 14th-century painter Giotto in Florence, and in the early 15th century a handful of outstanding innovative artists emerged there: Masaccio in painting, Donatello in sculpture, and Brunelleschi in architecture. At the same time the humanist philosopher, artist, and writer Alberti recorded many of the new ideas in his treatises on painting, sculpture, and architecture. These ideas soon became widespread in Italy and many new centers of patronage formed. In the 16th century Rome superseded Florence as the center of activity and innovation, becoming the capital of the High Renaissance.

In northern Europe the Renaissance spirit is apparent in the painting of the van Eyck brothers in the early 15th century. Later, Dürer demonstrated a scientific and inquiring mind and, after his travels in Italy, brought many Renaissance ideas back to Germany. Hans Holbein the Younger brought some of the concerns of Renaissance art to England in the 16th century, but it was not until the 17th century that English taste was significantly affected.

Renault Mary. Adopted name of Mary Challans 1905–1983. English novelist who recreated the world of ancient Greece, with a trilogy on ◊Theseus and two novels on ◊Alexander: *Fire from Heaven* 1970 and *The Persian Boy* 1972.

René France-Albert 1935– . Seychelles left-wing politician, president from 1977 following a coup.

In 1964 René founded the left-wing Seychelles People's United Party, pressing for complete independence. When this was achieved, in 1976, he became prime minister and James Mancham, leader of the Seychelles Democratic Party, became president. René seized the presidency in 1977 and set up a one-party state. He has since followed a nonnuclear policy of nonalignment and has survived several attempts to remove him.

renewable resource natural resource that is replaced by natural processes in a reasonable amount of time. Soil, water, forests, plants, and animals are all renewable resources as long as they are properly conserved. Solar, wind, wave, and geothermal energies are based on renewable resources.

Reni Guido 1575–1642. Italian painter, active in Bologna and Rome (c. 1600–14), who is considered one of the greatest Italian artists of the 17th century. His work includes the fresco *Phoebus and the Hours Preceded by Aurora* 1613 (Casino Rospigliosi, Rome). His workshop in Bologna produced numerous religious images, including Madonnas.

Rennes industrial city (oil refining, chemicals, electronics, cars) and capital of Ille-et-Vilaine *département*, W France, at the confluence of the Ille and Vilaine, 35 mi/56 km SE of St Malo; population (1982) 234,000. It was the old capital of Brittany.

Its university specializes in Breton culture. The second ◊Dreyfus trial was held here 1899.

rennet extract, traditionally obtained from a calf's stomach, that contains the enzyme rennin, used to coagulate milk in the cheesemaking process. The enzyme can now be chemically produced.

rennin or ***chymase*** enzyme found in the gastric juice of young mammals, used in the digestion of milk.

Reno city in Nevada, known for gambling and easy divorces; population (1990) 133,850. Products include building materials and electronic equipment. The University of Nevada-Reno is here. Reno was settled 1858 and grew quickly with the discovery nearby of the Comstock Lode, a large gold and silver deposit. The transcontinental railroad reached Reno 1868.

Renoir Jean 1894–1979. French film director, son of the painter Auguste Renoir, whose films include *La Grande Illusion* 1937, and *La Règle du Jeu/The Rules of the Game* 1939. In 1975 he received an honorary Academy Award for his life's work.

Renoir Pierre-Auguste 1841–1919. French Impressionist painter. He met Monet and Sisley in the early 1860s and together they formed the nucleus of the Impressionist movement. He developed a lively, colorful painting style with feathery brushwork and painted many voluptuous female nudes, such as *The Bathers* c. 1884–87 (Philadelphia Museum of Art). In his later years he turned to sculpture.

Born in Limoges, Renoir trained as a porcelain painter. He joined an academic studio 1861 and the first strong influences on his style were the Rococo artists Boucher and Watteau and the Realist Courbet. In the late 1860s Renoir began to work outdoors. Painting with Monet, he produced many pictures of people at leisure by the river Seine. From 1879 he made several journeys abroad, to North Africa, the Channel Islands, Italy, and later to Britain, the Netherlands, Spain, and Germany. After his Italian visit of 1881 he moved toward a more Classical structure in his work, notably in *Les Parapluies/Umbrellas* c. 1881–84 (National Gallery, London). In 1906 he settled in the south of France. Many of his sculptures are monumental female nudes not unlike those of ◊Maillol.

reparation compensation paid by countries that start wars in which they are defeated, as by Germany in both world wars.

Repin Ilya Yefimovich 1844–1930. Russian painter. His work includes dramatic studies, such as *Barge Haulers on the Volga* 1873, and portraits, including those of Tolstoy and Mussorgsky.

replication in biology, production of copies of the genetic material, DNA; it occurs during cell division (◊mitosis and ◊meiosis). Most mutations are caused by mistakes during replication.

repression in psychology, unconscious process said

***Renoir** The French Impressionist Pierre-Auguste Renoir showed a more Classical approach in* Les Parapluies/The Umbrellas *c. 1881–84, painted after his visit to Italy in 1881.*

to protect a person from ideas, impulses, or memories that would threaten emotional stability were they to become conscious. See also ◊censor.

reprieve legal temporary suspension of the execution of a sentence of a criminal court. It is usually associated with the death penalty (◊capital punishment). It is distinct from a pardon (extinguishing the sentence) and commutation (alteration) of a sentence (for example, from death to life imprisonment).

reproduction process by which a living organism produces other organisms similar to itself. There are two kinds: ◊asexual reproduction and ◊sexual reproduction.

reproduction rate or ***fecundity*** in ecology, the rate at which a population or species reproduces itself.

reptile class (Reptilia) of vertebrates. Unlike amphibians, reptiles have hard-shelled, yolk-filled eggs that are laid on land and from which fully-formed young are born. Some snakes and lizards retain their eggs and give birth to live young. Reptiles are coldblooded and produced from eggs, and the skin is usually covered with scales. The metabolism is slow, and in some cases (some large snakes) intervals between meals may be months. Reptiles date back over 300 million years.

Many extinct forms are known, including the orders Pterosauria, Plesiosauria, Ichthyosauria, and Dinosauria. The chief living orders are the Chelonia (tortoises and turtles), Crocodilia (alligators and crocodiles), and Squamata, divided into three suborders: Lacertilia (lizards), Ophidia or Serpentes (snakes), and Amphisbaenia (worm lizards). The order Rhynchocephalia has one surviving species, the lizardlike tuatara of New Zealand.

Repton Humphrey 1752–1818. English garden designer, who coined the term "landscape gardening." He worked for some years in partnership with John ◊Nash. Repton preferred more formal landscaping than Capability ◊Brown, and was responsible for the landscaping of some 200 gardens and parks.

republic country where the head of state is not a monarch, either hereditary or elected, but usually a president whose role may or may not include political functions.

Republic, The treatise by the Greek philosopher Plato in which the voice of ◊Socrates is used to describe the ideal state, where the cultivation of truth, beauty, and goodness achieves perfection.

Republican Party one of the US's two main political parties, formed 1854 by a coalition of ◊slavery opponents, who elected their first president, Abraham ◊Lincoln, in 1860. The early Republican Party supported protective tariffs and favored genuine settlers (homesteaders) over land speculators. Toward the end of the century the Republican Party was identified with US imperialism and industrial expansion. With few intermissions, the Republican Party controlled Congress from the 1860s until defeated by the New Deal Democrats 1932. After an isolationist period before World War II, the Republican Party adopted an active foreign policy under ◊Nixon and ◊Ford, but the latter was defeated by Carter in the presidential election 1976. However, the party enjoyed landslide presidential victories for ◊Reagan and also carried the Senate 1980–86. ◊Bush won the 1988 presidential election but faced a Democratic Senate and House of Representatives.

Conservative tendencies and an antagonism of the legislature to the executive came to the fore after Lincoln's assassination, when Andrew Johnson, his Democratic and Southern successor, was impeached (although not convicted), and General ◊Grant was elected to the presidency 1868 and 1872. In the bitter period following the Civil War the party was divided into those who considered the South a beaten nation and those who wished to reintegrate the South into the country as a whole, but Grant carried through a liberal Reconstruction policy in the South.

It became divided during Theodore ◊Roosevelt's attempts at regulation and control of big business, and in forming the shortlived Progressive Party 1912, Roosevelt effectively removed the liberal influence from the Republican Party.

The Republican Party remained in eclipse until the election of ◊Eisenhower 1952, more a personal triumph than that of the party, whose control of Congress was soon lost and not regained by the next Republican president, ◊Nixon, 1968.

requiem in the Roman Catholic church, a mass for the dead. Musical settings include those by Palestrina, Mozart, Berlioz, and Verdi.

research the primary activity in science, a combination of theory and experimentation directed toward finding scientific explanations of phenomena. It is commonly classified into two types: pure research, involving theories with little apparent relevance to human concerns; and applied research, concerned with finding solutions to problems of social importance—for instance in medicine and engineering. The two types are linked in that theories developed from pure research may eventually be found to be of great value to society.

Scientific research is most often funded by government and industry, and so a nation's wealth and priorities are likely to have a strong influence on the kind of work undertaken.

reserpine psychoactive drug extracted from the root of SE Asian plants of the genus *Rauwolfia*, especially *R. serpentina* or serpent wood. It was once used as a tranquilizer for some mental illnesses and to treat hypertension. Suicidal depression is a possible side effect.

reserve currency in economics, a country's holding of internationally acceptable means of payment (major foreign currencies or gold); central banks also hold the ultimate reserve of money for their domestic banking sector. On the asset side of company balance sheets, undistributed profits are listed as reserves.

residue in chemistry, a substance or mixture of substances remaining in the original container after the removal of one or more components by a separation process.

The nonvolatile substance left in a container after ◊evaporation of liquid, the solid left behind after removal of liquid by filtration, and the substances left in a distillation flask after removal of components by distillation, are all residues.

resin substance exuded from pines, firs, and other trees in gummy drops that harden in air. Varnishes are common products of the hard resins, and ointments come from the soft resins.

Rosin is the solid residue of distilled turpentine, a soft resin. The name "resin" is also given to many synthetic products manufactured by polymerization; they are used in adhesives, plastics, and varnishes.

resistance in physics, that property of a substance that restricts the flow of electricity through it, associated with the conversion of electrical energy to heat; also the magnitude of this property. Resistance depends on many factors, such as the nature of the material, its temperature, dimensions, and thermal properties; degree of impurity; the nature and state of illumination of the surface; and the frequency and magnitude of the current. The SI unit of resistance is the ohm.

resistance movement opposition movement in a country occupied by an enemy or colonial power, especially in the 20th century. During World War II, resistance in E Europe took the form of ◊guerrilla warfare, for example in Yugoslavia, Greece, Poland, and by ◊partisan bands behind the German lines in the USSR. In more industrialized countries, such as France (where the underground movement was called the maquis), Belgium, and Czechoslovakia, sabotage in factories and on the railroads, propaganda, and the assassination of Germans and collaborators were priorities.

After World War II resistance movements grew in Palestine, South America, and European colonial possessions in Africa and Asia, aimed at unsettling established regimes.

resistor in physics, any component in an electrical circuit used to introduce ◊resistance to a current. Resistors are often made from wire-wound coils or pieces of carbon. ◊Rheostats and ◊potentiometers are variable resistors.

Resnais Alain 1922– . French film director whose work is characterized by the themes of memory and unconventional concepts of time. His films include *Hiroshima mon amour* 1959, *L'Année dernière à Marienbad/Last Year at Marienbad* 1961, and *Providence* 1977.

resonance rapid and uncontrolled increase in the size of a vibration when the vibrating object is subject to a force varying at its ◊natural frequency. In a trombone, for example, the length of the air column in the instrument is adjusted until it resonates with the note being sounded. Resonance effects are also produced by many electrical circuits. Tuning a radio, for example, is done by adjusting the natural frequency of the receiver circuit until it coincides with the frequency of the radio waves falling on the aerial.

Resonance has many physical applications. Children use it to increase the size of the movement on a swing, by giving a push at the same point during each swing. Soldiers marching across a bridge in step could cause the bridge to vibrate violently if the frequency of their steps coincided with its natural frequency. Resonance was the cause of the collapse of the Tacoma Narrows bridge, in 1940 when the frequency of the wind coincided with the natural frequency of the bridge.

resources materials that can be used to satisfy human needs. Because human needs are diverse and extend from basic physical requirements, such as food and shelter, to ill-defined esthetic needs, resources encompass a vast range of items. The intellectual resources of a society—its ideas and technologies—determine which aspects of the environment meet that society's needs, and therefore become resources. For example, in the 19th century, uranium was used only in the manufacture of colored glass. Today, with the advent of nuclear technology, it is a military and energy resource. Resources are often categorized into human resources, such as

respiration

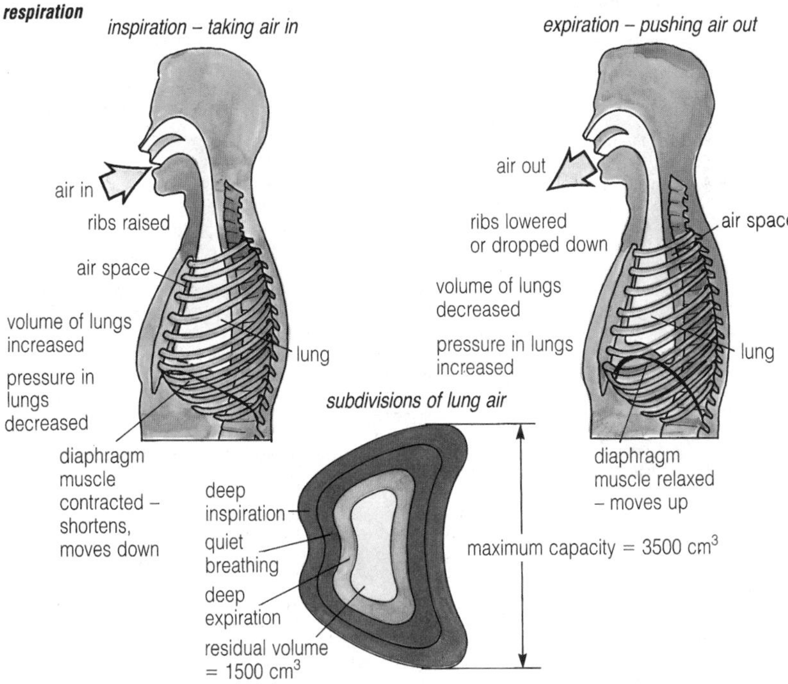
inspiration – taking air in
expiration – pushing air out
air in
ribs raised
air space
volume of lungs increased
pressure in lungs decreased
lung
diaphragm muscle contracted – shortens, moves down
air out
ribs lowered or dropped down
air space
volume of lungs decreased
pressure in lungs increased
lung
diaphragm muscle relaxed – moves up
subdivisions of lung air
deep inspiration
quiet breathing
deep expiration
residual volume = 1500 cm3
maximum capacity = 3500 cm3

labor, supplies, and skills, and natural resources, such as climate, fossil fuels, and water. Natural resources are divided into ◊nonrenewable resources and ◊renewable resources.

Nonrenewable resources include minerals such as coal, copper ores, and diamonds, which exist in strictly limited quantities. Once consumed they will not be replenished within the time span of human history. In contrast, water supplies, timber, food crops, and similar resources can, if managed properly, provide a steady yield virtually forever; they are therefore replenishable or renewable resources. Inappropriate use of renewable resources can lead to their destruction, as for example the cutting down of rainforests, with secondary effects, such as the decrease in oxygen and the increase in carbon dioxide and the ensuing ◊greenhouse effect. Some renewable resources, such as wind or solar energy, are continuous; supply is largely independent of people's actions.

Demands for resources made by rich nations are causing concern among many people who feel that the present and future demands of industrial societies cannot be sustained for more than a century or two, and that at the expense of the Third World and the global environment. Other authorities believe that new technologies will emerge, enabling resources currently of little importance to replace those being exhausted.

Respighi Ottorino 1879–1936. Italian composer, a student of ◊Rimsky-Korsakov, whose works include the symphonic poems *The Fountains of Rome* 1917 and *The Pines of Rome* 1924 (incorporating the recorded song of a nightingale), operas, and chamber music.

respiration biochemical process whereby food molecules are progressively broken down (oxidized) to release energy in the form of ◊ATP. In most organisms this requires oxygen, but in some bacteria the oxidant is the nitrate or sulfate ion instead. In all higher organisms, respiration occurs in the ◊mitochondria. Respiration is also used to mean breathing, although this is more accurately described as a form of ◊gas exchange.

respiratory distress syndrome (RDS) formerly hyaline membrane disease condition in which a newborn baby's lungs are insufficiently expanded to permit adequate oxygenation. Premature babies are most at risk. Such babies survive with the aid of intravenous fluids and oxygen, sometimes with assisted ventilation.

Normal inflation of the lungs requires the presence of a substance called surfactant to reduce the surface tension of the alveoli (air sacs) in the lungs. In premature babies, surfactant is deficient and the lungs become hard and glassy. As a result, the breathing is rapid, labored, and shallow, and there is the likelihood of ◊asphyxia. A synthetic replacement for surfactant has now been developed.

rest mass in physics, the mass of a body when its velocity is zero. For subatomic particles, it is their mass at rest or at velocities considerably below that of light. According to the theory of ◊relativity, at very high velocities, there is a relativistic effect that increases the mass of the particle.

Restoration in English history, period when the monarchy, in the person of Charles II, was reestablished after the English Civil War and the fall of the ◊Protectorate 1660.

Restoration comedy style of English theater, dating from the Restoration. It witnessed the first appearance of women on the English stage, most notably in the "breeches part," specially created in order to costume the actress in male attire, thus revealing her figure to its best advantage. The genre placed much emphasis on sexual antics. Examples include Wycherley's *The Country Wife* 1675, Congreve's *The Way of the World* 1700, and Farquhar's *The Beaux' Strategem* 1707.

resurrection in Christian, Jewish, and Muslim belief, the rising from the dead that all souls will experience at the Last Judgment. The Resurrection also refers to Jesus rising from the dead on the third day after his crucifixion, a belief central to Christianity and celebrated at Easter.

resuscitation steps taken to revive anyone on the brink of death. The most successful technique for life-threatening emergencies, such as electrocution, near-drowning, or heart attack, is mouth-to-mouth resuscitation. Medical and paramedical staff are trained in cardiopulmonary resuscitation: the use of specialized equipment and techniques to attempt to restart the breathing and/or heartbeat and stabilize the patient long enough for more definitive treatment.

retail sale of goods and services to a consumer. The retailer is the last link in the distribution chain. A retailer's purchases are usually made from a wholesaler.

The large range of retail outlets include vending machines, street peddlers, specialized shops, department stores, supermarkets, and cooperative stores. These are supplemented by auctions, door-to-door selling, telephone selling, and mail order.

retail price index (RPI) indicator of variations in the ◊cost of living, superseded in the US by the ◊consumer price index.

retina light-sensitive area at the back of the ◊eye connected to the brain by the optic nerve. It has several layers and in humans contains over a million rods and cones, sensory cells capable of converting light into nervous messages that pass down the optic nerve to the brain.

The image actually falling on the retina is highly distorted; research into the eye and the optic centers within the brain has shown that this poor quality image is processed to improve its quality.

retriever any of several breeds of hunting dogs developed for retrieving birds and other small game. The commonest breeds are the Labrador retriever, large, smooth-coated, and usually black or yellow; and the golden retriever, with either flat or wavy coat. They can grow to 2 ft/60 cm high and weigh 90 lb/40 kgs.

retrovirus any of a family (*Retroviridae*) of ◊viruses containing the genetic material ◊RNA rather than the more usual ◊DNA.

For the virus to express itself and multiply within an infected cell, its RNA must be converted to DNA. It does this by using a built-in enzyme known as reverse transcriptase (since the transfer of genetic information from DNA to RNA is known as ◊transcription, and retroviruses do the reverse of this). Retroviruses include those causing ◊AIDS and some forms of leukemia. See ◊immunity.

Réunion French island of the Mascarenes group, in the Indian Ocean, 400 mi/650 km E of Madagascar and 110 mi/180 km SW of Mauritius

area 970 sq mi/2,512 sq km

capital St Denis

physical forested, rising in Piton de Neiges to 10,072 ft/3,069 m

features administers five uninhabited islands, also claimed by Madagascar

products sugar, corn, vanilla, tobacco, rum

population (1987) 565,000

history explored by Portuguese (the first European visitors) 1513; annexed by Louis XIII of France 1642; overseas *département* of France 1946; overseas region 1972.

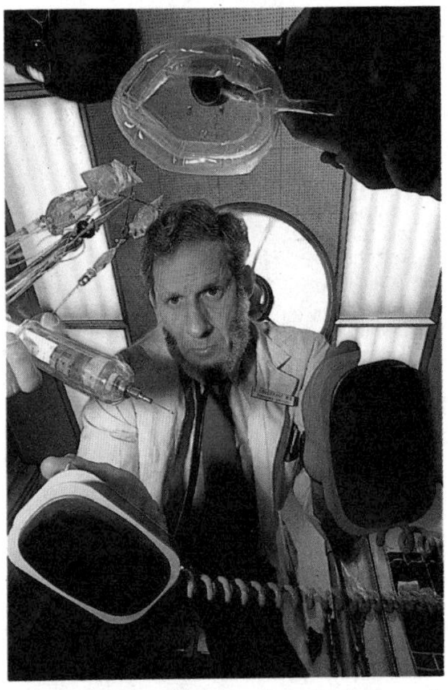

***resuscitation** A patient's-eye view of a doctor ready to resuscitate the patient after a severe heart attack.*

Réunion

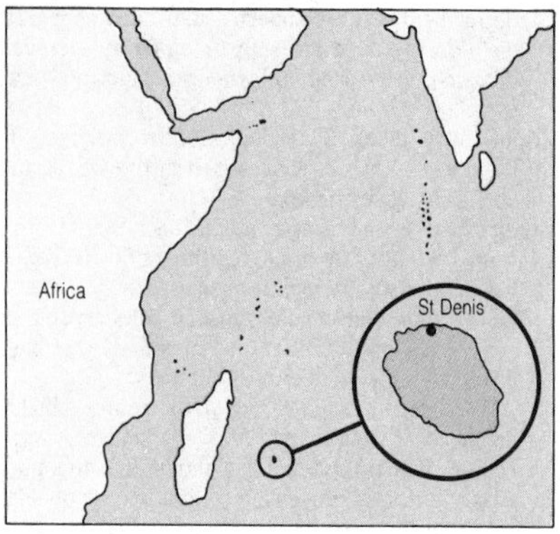
Africa
St Denis

Reus industrial city with an international airport in Catalonia, E Spain, 6 mi/10 km NW of Tarragona.

Reuter Paul Julius, Baron de 1816–1899. German founder of the international news agency Reuters. He began a continental pigeon post 1849, and in 1851 he set up a news agency in London. In 1858 he persuaded the press to use his news telegrams, and the service became worldwide.

The agency became a private trust 1916 and was taken over by the Newspaper Proprietors' Association 1926–41. It became a public company 1984.

Reval former name of the Soviet port of ◊Tallinn.

Revelation last book of the New Testament, traditionally attributed to the author of the Gospel of St John but now generally held to be the work of another writer. It describes a vision of the end of the world, of the Last Judgment, and of a new heaven and earth ruled by God from Jerusalem.

revenue sharing in the US, federal aid to state and local governments allocated under the State and Local Fiscal Assistance Act 1972.

Revere Paul 1735–1818. American revolutionary, a Boston silversmith, who carried the news of the approach of British troops to Lexington and Concord (see ◊American Revolution) on the night of April 18, 1775. On the next morning the first shots of the Revolution were fired at Lexington. Longfellow's poem *The Midnight Ride of Paul Revere* commemorates the event.

Revere, who took part in the ◊Boston Tea Party, was a courier for the Continental Congress, often riding from Boston to Philadelphia. In early 1775 he alerted rebels in New Hampshire that the British, under General Thomas ◊Gage were transporting supplies from Fort William and Mary. The New Hampshire militiamen captured quantities of munitions that proved decisive at the Battle of Bunker Hill. Revere was active throughout the Revolution and printed the first continental money.

reverse takeover in business, a ◊takeover where a company sells itself to another to avoid being itself the target of a purchase by an unwelcome predator. See ◊white knight.

revisionism political theory derived from Marxism that moderates one or more of the basic tenets of Marx, and is hence condemned by orthodox Marxists. The first noted Marxist revisionist was Eduard Bernstein, who in Germany in the 1890s questioned the inevitability of a breakdown in capitalism. After World War II the term became widely used by established Communist parties, both in E Europe and Asia, to condemn movements (whether more or less radical) that threatened the official party policy.

revolution any rapid, theoretical, violent change in the political, social, or economic structure of society. It is usually applied to political change: examples include the American Revolution, where the colonists broke free from their colonial ties and established a sovereign, independent nation; the French Revolution, where an absolute monarchy was overthrown by opposition from inside the country and a popular uprising; and the Russian Revolution, where a repressive monarchy was overthrown by those seeking to institute widespread social and economic changes based on a Socialist model. While political revolutions are often associated with violence, other types of change have just as much impact on society. Most notable is the Industrial Revolution of the mid-18th century. In the 1970s and 1980s a high-tech revolution could be identified, based on the increasing use of computers. In 1989–90 the ◊Eastern Bloc nations demonstrated against and voted out the ◊Communist Party, and in many cases created a pro-democracy revolution.

Revolutionary Wars: chronology

1791	Emperor ◊Leopold II and Frederick William II of Prussia issued the Declaration of Pillnitz inviting the European powers to restore the French king Louis XVI to power.
1792	France declared war on Austria, which formed a coalition with Prussia, Sardinia, and (from 1793), Britain, Spain, and the Netherlands; victories for France at ◊Valmy and Jemappes.
1793	French reverses until the reorganization by Lazare ◊Carnot.
1795	Prussia, the Netherlands, and Spain made peace with France.
1796	Sardinia forced to make peace by the Italian campaign of ◊Napoleon I, then a commander.
1797	Austria compelled to peace with France under the Treaty of ◊Campo-Formio.
1798	Napoleon's fleet, after its capture of Malta, was defeated by the British admiral ◊Nelson in Egypt at the Battle of the Nile (Aboukir Bay), and Napoleon had to return to France without his army; William Pitt the Younger, Britain's prime minister, organized a new coalition with Russia, Austria, Naples, Portugal, and Turkey.
1798–99	The coalition mounted its major campaign in Italy (under the Russian field marshal ◊Suvorov), but dissension led to the withdrawal of Russia.
1799	Napoleon, on his return from Egypt, reorganized the French army.
1800	June 14 Austrian army defeated by Napoleon at Marengo in NW Italy and again on Dec 3 (by Gen ◊Moreau) at Hohenlinden near Munich; the coalition collapsed.
1802	Treaty of Amiens truce between France and Britain, followed by the ◊Napoleonic Wars.

Revolutionary Wars series of wars 1791–1802 between France and the combined armies of England, Austria, Prussia, and others during the period of the French Revolution, and on ◊Napoleon's ambition to conquer Europe.

revolutions of 1848 series of revolts in various parts of Europe against monarchical rule. While some of the revolutionaries had republican ideas, many more were motivated by economic grievances. The revolution began in France with the overthrow of Louis Philippe and then spread to Italy, the Austrian Empire, and Germany, where the shortlived ◊Frankfurt Parliament put forward ideas about political unity in Germany. None of the revolutions enjoyed any lasting success, and most were violently suppressed within a few months.

Some concessions were made to both liberal and nationalist movements, and 1848 is regarded as ending the conservative domination of ◊Metternich.

revolver small handgun with a revolving chamber that holds the bullets.

revue stage presentation involving short satirical and topical items in the form of songs, sketches, and monologues; it originated in the late 19th century.

Turn-of-the-century revues were spectacular entertainments, notably those of Florenz Ziegfeld, but the "intimate revue" became increasingly popular, employing writers such as Noël Coward.

Reykjavik capital (from 1918) and chief port of Iceland, on the SW coast; population (1988) 93,000. Fish processing is the main industry. Reykjavik is heated by underground mains fed by volcanic springs. It was a seat of Danish administration from 1801 to 1918.

Reynaud Paul 1878–1966. French prime minister in World War II, who succeeded Edouard Daladier March 1940 but resigned June after the German breakthrough. He was imprisoned by the Germans until 1945, and again held government offices after the war.

Reynolds Burt 1936– . US film actor and director who excels in adventure films and comedies. He is known for doing his own stunts, since he started as a stuntman. His films include *Deliverance* 1972, the cult film *White Lightning* 1973, *Hustle* 1975, and *City Heat* 1984. He also appeared in 1991 as the lead in the television comedy series *Evening Shade*.

Reynolds Joshua 1723–1792. English portrait painter, active in London from 1752. He became the first president of the Royal Academy 1768. His portraits display a facility for striking and characterful compositions in a consciously grand manner. He often borrowed Classical poses, for example *Mrs Siddons as the Tragic Muse* 1784 (San Marino, California).

Reynolds was apprenticed to the portrait painter Thomas Hudson (1701–1779). From 1743 he practiced in Plymouth and London and 1749–52 completed his studies in Rome and Venice, concentrating on the antique and the High Renaissance masters.

After his return to London he became the leading portraitist of his day with pictures such as *Admiral Keppel* 1753–54 (National Maritime Museum, London).

Reynolds Osborne 1842–1912. British physicist and engineer who studied ◊fluid flow and devised the Reynolds number, which relates to turbulence in flowing fluids.

RGB (abbreviation of red-green-blue) method of connecting a color screen to a computer, involving three separate signals: red, green, and blue. All the colors displayed by the screen can be made up from these three component colors.

Rhadamanthys in Greek mythology, son of ◊Zeus and ◊Europa, ruler of ◊Elysium, and with ◊Minos and Aeacus judge of the dead.

rhapsody in music, instrumental ◊fantasia, often based on folk melodies, such as Lizst's *Hungarian Rhapsodies* 1853–54.

In ancient Greece, ***rhapsodes*** (Greek "stitchers of songs") were a class of reciters of epic poems, especially those of ◊Homer, who performed at festivals.

rhe unit of fluidity equal to the reciprocal of the ◊poise.

rhea one of two flightless birds of the family Rheidae. The common rhea *Rhea americana* is 5 ft/1.5 m high and is distributed widely in South America. The smaller Darwin's rhea *Pterocnemia pennata* occurs only in S South America. They differ from the ostrich in their smaller size and in having a feathered neck and head, three-toed feet, and no plumelike tail feathers.

Rhea in Greek mythology, a fertility goddess, one of the Titans, wife of Cronus and mother of several gods, including Zeus.

Rhee Syngman 1875–1965. Korean right-wing politician. A rebel under Chinese and Japanese rule, he became president of South Korea from 1948 until riots forced him to resign and leave the country 1960.

Rheims English version of ◊Reims.

Rheinland-Pfalz city in France. German name for the ◊Rhineland-Palatinate region, Federal Republic of Germany.

rhenium heavy, silver-white, metallic element, symbol Re, atomic number 75, atomic weight

rheostat

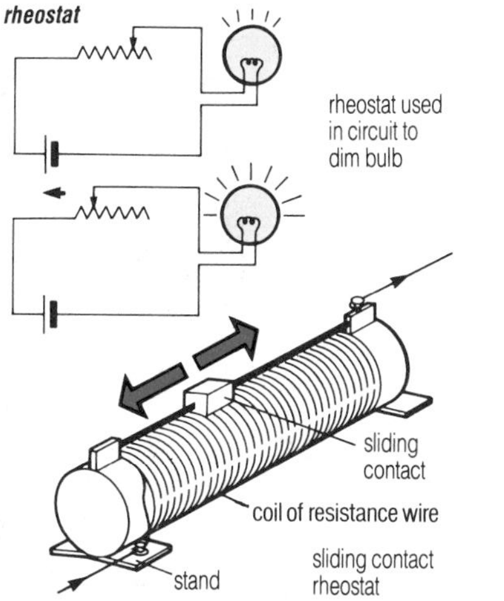
rheostat used
in circuit to
dim bulb
sliding
contact
coil of resistance wire
stand
sliding contact
rheostat

186.2. It has chemical properties similar to those of manganese and a very high melting point (5,756°F/3,180°C) that makes it valuable as an ingredient in alloys.

It was identified and named in 1925 by German chemists W Noddack (1893–1960), I Tacke, and O Berg from the Latin name *Rhenus* for the Rhine river.

rheostat in physics, a variable ◊resistor, usually consisting of a high-resistance wire-wound coil with a sliding contact. It is used to vary electrical resistance without interrupting the current (for example, when dimming lights). The circular type in electronics (which can be used, for example, as the volume control of an amplifier) is also known as a ◊potentiometer.

rhesus macaque monkey *Macaca mulatta*, found in N India and SE Asia. It has a pinkish face, red buttocks, and long, straight, brown-gray hair. It can grow up to 2 ft/60 cm long, with a 8 in/20 cm tail.

rhesus factor ◊protein on the surface of red blood cells of humans, which is involved in the rhesus blood group system. Most individuals possess the main rhesus factor (Rh+), but those without this factor (Rh–) produce ◊antibodies if they come into contact with it. The name comes from rhesus monkeys, in whose blood rhesus factors were first found.

If an Rh– mother carries an Rh+ fetus, she may produce antibodies if fetal blood crosses the ◊placenta. This is not normally a problem with the first infant because antibodies are only produced slowly. However, the antibodies continue to build up after birth, and a second Rh+ child may be attacked by antibodies passing from mother to fetus, causing the child to contract anemia, heart failure, or brain damage. In such cases, the blood of the infant has to be changed for Rh– blood. Alternatively, the problem can be alleviated by giving the mother anti-Rh globulin just after the first pregnancy, preventing the formation of antibodies.

rhetoric (Greek *rhetor* "orator") traditionally, the art of public speaking and debate. Rhetorical skills are valued in such occupations as politics, teaching, the law, religion, and broadcasting.

Accomplished rhetoricians need not be sincere in what they say; they should, however, be effective, or at least entertaining. Nowadays, "rhetoric" is often a pejorative term (for example, "Cut the rhetoric and tell us what you really think").

rhetorical question question, often used by public speakers and debaters, that either does not require an answer or for which the speaker intends to provide his or her own answer ("Where else in the world can we find such brave young men as these?").

rheumatic fever or ***acute rheumatism*** acute or

Rhine River

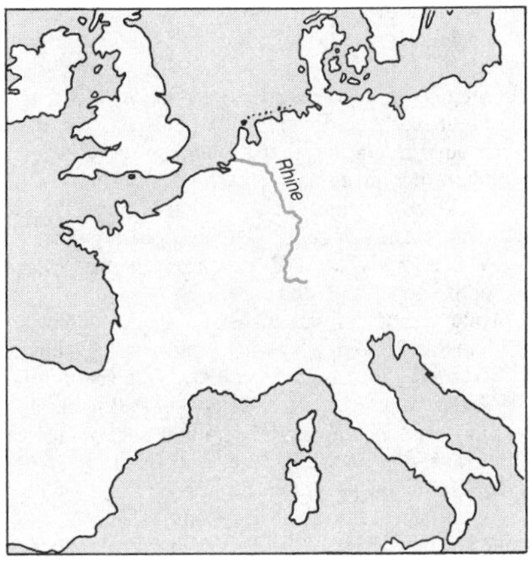
Rhine

chronic illness characterized by fever and painful swelling of joints. Some victims also experience involuntary movements of the limbs and head, a form of ◊chorea.

Rheumatic fever, which strikes mainly children and young adults, is always preceded by a streptococcal infection such as ◊scarlet fever or a severe sore throat, usually occurring a couple of weeks beforehand. It is treated with bed rest, antibiotics, and painkillers. The condition may give rise to malfunction of a heart valve.

rheumatism nontechnical term for a variety of ailments associated with inflammation and stiffness of the joints and muscles.

Rhine (German *Rhein*, French *Rhin*) European river rising in Switzerland and reaching the North Sea via Germany and the Netherlands; length 820 mi/1,320 km. Tributaries include the Moselle and the Ruhr. The Rhine is linked with the Mediterranean by the Rhine-Rhône Waterway, and with the Black Sea by the Rhine-Main-Danube Waterway.

The Lorelei is a rock in the river in Rhineland-Palatinate, Germany, with a remarkable echo; the German poet Brentano gave currency to the legend of a siren who lured sailors to death with her song, also subject of a poem by Heine.

Rhine Joseph Banks 1895–1980. US parapsychologist. His work at Duke University, North Carolina, involving controlled laboratory experiments in telepathy, clairvoyance, precognition, and psychokinesis, described in *Extra-Sensory Perception* 1934, made ESP a common term. See also ◊parapsychology.

Rhineland-Palatinate (German *Rheinland-Pfalz*) administrative region (German *Land*) of the Federal Republic of Germany

area 7,643 sq mi/19,800 sq km

capital Mainz

towns Ludwigshafen, Koblenz, Trier, Worms

physical wooded mountain country, river valleys of Rhine and Moselle

products wine (75% of German output), tobacco, chemicals, machinery, leather goods, pottery

population (1988) 3,611,000

history formed 1946 of the Rhenish ◊Palatinate and parts of Hessen, Rhine province, and Hessen-Nassau.

rhinoceros any odd-toed hoofed mammal of the

rhinoceros

Sumatran rhinoceros

family Rhinocerotidae. The one-horned Indian rhinoceros *Rhinoceros unicornis* is up to 6 ft/2 m at the shoulder, with a tubercled skin, folded into shield-like pieces; the African black rhinoceros *Diceros bicornis* is 5 ft/1.5 m high, with a prehensile upper lip for feeding on shrubs; the broad-lipped or "white" rhinoceros *Ceratotherium simum* is actually slaty-gray, with a squarish mouth for browsing grass. The latter two are smooth-skinned and two-horned. They are solitary and vegetarian, with poor eyesight but excellent hearing and smell. Needless slaughter has led to the near extinction of all species of rhinoceros, particularly the Sumatran rhinoceros and Javan rhinoceros.

An extinct hornless species, the baluchithere (genus *Baluchitherium*), reached 15 ft/4.5 m.

rhizoid hairlike outgrowth found on the ◊gametophyte generation of ferns, mosses and liverworts. Rhizoids anchor the plant to the substrate and can absorb water and nutrients. They may be composed of many cells, as in mosses, where they are usually brownish, or unicellular, as in liverworts, where they are usually colorless. Rhizoids fulfill the same functions as the ◊roots of higher plants but are simpler in construction.

rhizome horizontal underground plant stem. It is a ◊perennating organ in some species, where it is generally thick and fleshy, while in other species it is mainly a means of ◊vegetative reproduction, and is therefore long and slender, with buds all along it that send up new plants. The potato is a rhizome that has two distinct parts, the tuber being the swollen end of a long, cordlike rhizome.

rhm (abbreviation of roentgen–hour–meter) the unit of effective strength of a radioactive source that produces gamma rays. It is used for substances for which it is difficult to establish radioactive disintegration rates.

Rhode Island (officially Rhode Island and Providence Plantations) state in NE US; the smallest state of the US; nickname Ocean State

area 1,197 sq mi/3,100 sq km

capital Providence

cities Cranston, Woonsocket

population (1990) 1,003,464

features Narragansett Bay, with America's Cup yacht races; mansions of Newport; Block Island; Brown University; Rhode Island School of Design; University of Rhode Island

products poultry (Rhode Island Reds), jewelry, silverware, textiles, machinery, primary metals, rubber products, submarine assembly

famous people George M Cohan, Anne Hutchinson, Matthew C Perry, Oliver Hazard Perry, Gilbert Stuart, Roger Williams

history founded 1636 by Roger Williams, exiled from Massachusetts Bay colony for religious dissent; one of the original thirteen states. The principal trends in the 19th century were industrialization, immigration, and urbanization. Rhode Island is the most industrialized state, and it suf-

Rhode Island

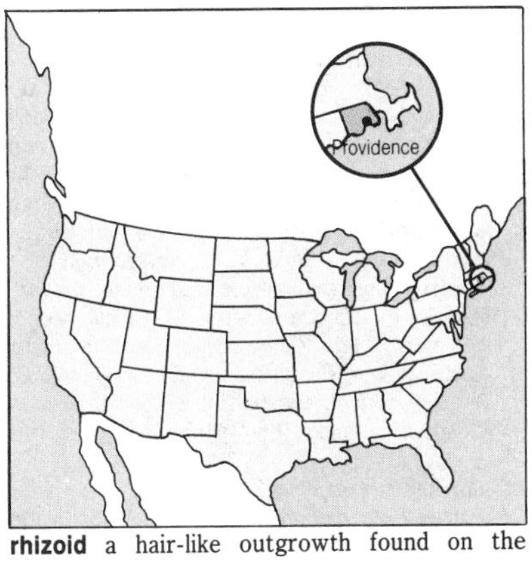
Providence

rhizoid a hair-like outgrowth found on the

fers from high unemployment, low-wage manufacturing industries, and susceptibility to recessions.

Rhodes (Greek *Rodhos*) Greek island, largest of the Dodecanese, in the E Aegean Sea
area 545 sq mi/1,412 sq km
capital Rhodes
products grapes, olives
population (1981) 88,000
history settled by Greeks about 1000 BC; the ◊Colossus of Rhodes (fell 224 BC), one of the ◊Seven Wonders of the World; held by the Knights Hospitallers of St John 1306–1522; taken from Turkish rule by the Italian occupation 1912; ceded to Greece 1947.

Rhodes Cecil (John) 1853–1902. South African politician, born in the UK, prime minister of Cape Colony 1890–96. Aiming at the formation of a South African federation and of a block of British territory from the Cape to Cairo, he was responsible for the annexation of Bechuanaland (now Botswana) in 1885. He formed the British South Africa Company in 1889, which occupied Mashonaland and Matabeleland, thus forming Rhodesia (now Zambia and Zimbabwe).

The ***Rhodes scholarships*** were founded at Oxford University, UK, under his will, for students from the Commonwealth, the US, and Germany.

Rhodes Zandra 1940– . English fashion designer known for the extravagant fantasy and luxury of her dress creations.

Rhodesia former name of ◊Zambia (Northern Rhodesia) and ◊Zimbabwe (Southern Rhodesia).

rhodium hard, silver-white, metallic element, symbol Rh, atomic number 45, atomic weight 102.905. It is one of the so-called platinum group of metals and is resistant to tarnish, corrosion, and acid. It occurs as a free metal (◊native metal) in the natural alloy osmiridium (osmium, iridium, platinum, and ruthenium) and is used in jewelry, electroplating, and thermocouples.

Rhodium was discovered in 1803 by English chemist William Wollaston (1766–1828) and named in 1804 from Greek *rhodon*, "rose," for the red color of its salts in solution.

rhododendron any of numerous shrubs of the genus *Rhododendron* of the heath family Ericaceae. Most species are evergreen. The leaves are usually dark and leathery, and the large racemes of flowers occur in all colors except blue. They thrive on acid soils. ◊Azaleas belong to the same genus.

Rhodope Mountains range of mountains on the frontier between Greece and Bulgaria, rising to 9,497 ft/2,925 m at Musala.

rhombus in geometry, an equilateral (all sides equal) ◊parallelogram. Its diagonals bisect each other at right angles, and its area is half the product of the lengths of the two diagonals. A rhombus whose internal angles are 90° is called a square.

A square, therefore, is the only rhombus that is also a rectangle.

Rhondda industrial town in Mid Glamorgan, Wales; population (1981) 81,725. Light industries have replaced coal-mining, formerly the main source of employment.

Rhône river of S Europe; length 500 mi/810 km. It rises in Switzerland and flows through Lake Geneva to Lyon in France, where at its confluence with the Saône the upper limit of navigation is reached. The river turns due S, passes Vienne and Avignon, and takes in the Isère and other tributaries. Near Arles it divides into the Grand and Petit Rhône, flowing respectively SE and SW into the Mediterranean W of Marseille.

Here it forms a two-armed delta; the area between the tributaries is the ◊Camargue, a desolate marsh. The Rhône is harnessed for hydroelectric power, the chief dam being at Genissiat in Ain *département*, constructed 1938–48. Between Vienne and Avignon it flows through a major wine-producing area.

Rhône-Alpes region of E France in the upper reaches of the Rhône; area 16,868 sq mi/43,700 sq km; population (1986) 5,154,000. It consists of the *départements* of Ain, Ardèche, Drôme, Isère, Loire, Rhône, Savoie, and Haute-Savoie. The chief town is Lyon. There are several notable wine-producing areas, including Chenas, Fleurie, and Beaujolais. Industrial products include chemicals, textiles, and motor vehicles.

rhubarb perennial plant *Rheum rhaponticum* of the buckwheat family Polygonaceae, grown for its pink, edible leaf stalks. The leaves are poisonous. There are also wild rhubarbs (genus *Rheum* native to Europe and Asia.

rhyme identity of sound, usually in the endings of lines of verse, such as *wing* and *sing*. Avoided in Japanese, it is a common literary device in other Asian and European languages. Rhyme first appeared in Europe in late Latin poetry but was not used in Classical Greek and Latin.

rhyolite ◊igneous rock, the fine-grained volcanic (extrusive) equivalent of granite.

Rhys Jean 1894–1979. British novelist, born in Dominica. Her works include *Wide Sargasso Sea* 1966, a recreation, set in a Caribbean island, of the life of Rochester's mad wife in *Jane Eyre* by Charlotte Brontë.

rhythm and blues (R & B) US popular music of the 1940s–60s, which drew on swing and jump-jazz rhythms and blues vocals and was a progenitor of rock and roll. It diversified into soul, funk, and other styles. R & B artists include Bo Diddley (1928–), Jackie Wilson (1934–84), and Etta James (c. 1938–).

rhythm method method of natural contraception that works by avoiding intercourse when the woman is producing egg cells (ovulating). The time of ovulation can be worked out by the calendar (counting days from the last period), by temperature changes, or by inspection of the cervical mucus. All these methods are unreliable because it is possible for ovulation to occur at any stage of the menstrual cycle.

RI abbreviation for ◊Rhode Island.

ria long narrow sea inlet, usually branching and surrounded by hills. A ria is deeper and wider toward its mouth, unlike a ◊fjord. It is formed by the flooding of a river valley due to either a rise in sea level or a lowering of a landmass.

rib long, usually curved bone that extends laterally from the ◊spine in vertebrates. Most fishes and many reptiles have ribs along most of the spine, but in mammals they are found only in the chest area. In humans, there are 12 pairs of ribs. The ribs protect the lungs and heart, and allow the chest to expand and contract easily.

At the rear, each pair is joined to one of the vertebrae of the spine. The upper seven are joined by ◊cartilage directly to the breast bone (sternum). The next three are joined by cartilage to the end of the rib above. The last two ("floating ribs") are not attached at the front.

Ribalta Francisco 1565–1628. Spanish painter, active in Valencia from 1599. Around 1615 he developed a dramatic Baroque style using extreme effects of light and shade (recalling Caravaggio), as in *St Bernard Embracing Christ* c. 1620–28 (Prado, Madrid).

Ribbentrop Joachim von 1893–1946. German Nazi politician and diplomat, born in the Rhineland. He joined the Nazi party 1932 and acted as Hitler's adviser on foreign affairs; he was German ambassador to Britain 1936–38 and foreign minister 1938–45, during which time he negotiated the Non-Aggression Pact between Germany and the Soviet Union. He was tried at Nuremberg as a war criminal 1946 and hanged.

Ribbentrop–Molotov pact see ◊Nazi-Soviet pact.

Ribera José (Jusepe) de 1591–1652. Spanish painter, active in Italy from 1616 under the patronage of the viceroys of Naples. His early work shows the impact of Caravaggio, but his colors gradually lightened. He painted many full-length saints and mythological figures and genre scenes, which he produced without preliminary drawing.

rice

grain
cross section of a grain

riboflavin or ***vitamin B_2*** ◊vitamin of the B complex whose absence in the diet causes stunted growth.

ribonucleic acid full name of ◊RNA.

ribosome in biology, the protein-making machinery of the cell. Ribosomes are located on the endoplasmic reticulum (ER) of eukaryotic cells, and are made of proteins and a special type of ◊RNA, ribosomal RNA. They receive messenger RNA (copied from the ◊DNA) and ◊amino acids, and "translate" the messenger RNA by using its chemically coded instructions to link amino acids in a specific order, to make a strand of a particular protein.

Ricardo David 1772–1823. English economist, author of *Principles of Political Economy* 1817. Among his discoveries were the principle of comparative advantage (that countries can benefit by specializing in goods they produce efficiently and trading internationally to buy others), and the law of diminishing returns (that continued increments of capital and labor applied to a given quantity of land will eventually show a declining rate of increase in output).

rice principal cereal of the wet regions of the tropics; derived from grass of the species *Oryza sativa*, probably native to India and SE Asia. The yield is very large, and rice is said to be the staple food of two-thirds of the world population.
cultivation Rice takes 150–200 days to mature in warm, wet conditions. During its growing period, it needs to be flooded either by the heavy monsoon rains or by adequate irrigation. This restricts the cultivation of swamp rice, the usual kind, to level land and terraces. A poorer variety, known as hill rice, is grown on hillsides. Outside Asia, there is some rice production in the Po valley of Italy, and in the US in Louisiana, the Carolinas, and California.
nutrition Rice contains 8–9% protein. Brown, or unhusked, rice has valuable B-vitamins that are lost in husking or polishing. Most of the the rice eaten in the world is, however, sold in polished form.
history Rice has been cultivated since prehistoric days in the East. New varieties with greatly increased protein content have been developed by gamma radiation for commercial cultivation, and yields are higher than ever before (see ◊green revolution).
byproducts Rice husks when burned provide a ◊silica ash that, mixed with lime, produces an excellent cement.

Rice Elmer 1892–1967. US playwright. His works include *The Adding Machine* 1923 and *Street Scene* 1929, which won a Pulitzer Prize and was made into an opera by Kurt Weill. Many of his plays deal with such economic and political issues as

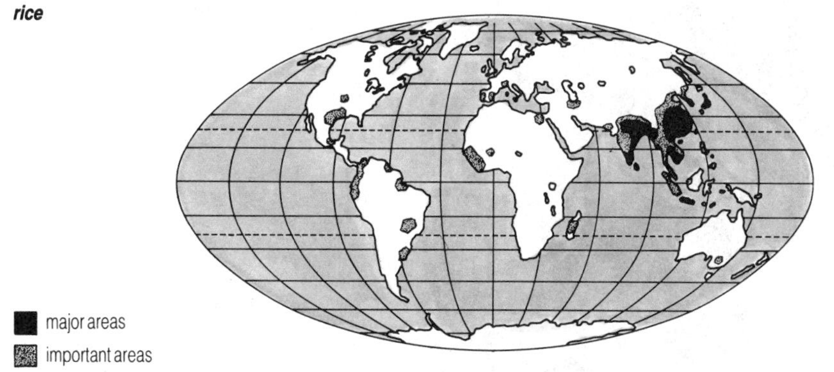
rice
major areas
important areas

the Depression (*We, the People* 1933) and racism (*American Landscape* 1939).

Rice Grantland 1880–1954. US sports journalist. Born in Murfreesboro, Tennessee, and educated at Vanderbilt University, Rice joined the staff of the *Nashville News* 1901. Gaining a reputation for vivid sports writing, he was hired by the *New York Mail* 1911 and worked for the *New York Herald Tribune* 1914–30. Rice succeeded Walter Camp in selecting the annual All-America football team.

After 1930 he wrote the column "The Sportlight," which set the standard for modern sports journalism. His autobiography, *The Tumult and the Shouting* was published 1954.

Rich Adrienne 1929– . US radical feminist poet, writer, and critic. Her poetry is both subjective and political, concerned with female consciousness, peace, and gay rights. Her works include *On Lies, Secrets and Silence* 1979 and *The Fact of a Doorframe: Poems, 1950–84* 1984.

In the 1960s her poetry was closely involved with the student and antiwar movements in the US but since then she has concentrated on women's issues. In 1974, when given the National Book Award, she declined to accept it as an individual, but with Alice Walker and Audrey Rich accepted it on behalf of all women.

Richard three kings of England:

Richard I the Lion-Hearted (French *Coeur-de-Lion*) 1157–1199. King of England from 1189, who spent all but six months of his reign abroad. He was the third son of Henry II, against whom he twice rebelled. In the third ◊Crusade 1191–92 he won victories at Cyprus, Acre, and Arsuf (against ◊Saladin), but failed to recover Jerusalem. While returning overland he was captured by the Duke of Austria, who handed him over to the emperor Henry VI, and he was held prisoner until a large ransom was raised. He then returned briefly to England, where his brother John I had been ruling in his stead. His later years were spent in warfare in France, where he was killed.

Richard II 1367–1400. King of England from 1377, effectively from 1389, son of Edward the Black Prince. He reigned in conflict with Parliament; they executed some of his associates 1388 and he some of the opposing barons 1397, whereupon he made himself absolute.

In 1399 his cousin Henry Bolingbroke, Duke of Hereford (later ◊Henry IV), returned from exile to lead a revolt; Richard II was deposed by Parliament and imprisoned in Pontefract Castle, where he died mysteriously.

Richard III 1452–1485. King of England from 1483. The son of Richard, Duke of York, he was created duke of Gloucester by his brother Edward IV, and distinguished himself in the Wars of the ◊Roses. On Edward's death 1483 he became protector to his nephew Edward V, and soon secured the crown for himself on the plea that Edward IV's sons were illegitimate. He proved a capable ruler, but the suspicion that he had murdered Edward V and his brother undermined his popularity. In 1485 Henry, Earl of Richmond (later ◊Henry VII), raised a rebellion, and Richard III was defeated and killed at ◊Bosworth.

Richards Theodore 1868–1928. US chemist. Working at Harvard University, Boston, for much of his career, Richards concentrated on determining as accurately as possible the atomic weights of a large number of elements. Nobel Prize 1914.

Richardson Dorothy 1873–1957. English novelist whose works were collected under the title *Pilgrimage* 1938. She pioneered the "stream of consciousness" technique used by Virginia ◊Woolf, who credited her with having invented "the psychological sentence of the feminine gender."

Richardson Henry Hobson 1838–1886. American architect, distinguished for his revival of ◊Romanesque style. He designed churches, university buildings, homes, railroad stations, and town libraries; Sever Hall and Austin Hall at Harvard University; and the monumental Marshall Field Wholesale Building, Chicago. His best-known work is Trinity Church in Copley Square, Boston.

Richardson Owen Williams 1879–1959. British physicist. He studied the emission of electricity from hot bodies, giving the name ◊thermionics to the subject. At Cambridge University, he worked under J J ◊Thomson in the Cavendish Laboratory. Nobel Prize 1928.

Richardson Ralph (David) 1902–1983. English actor. He played many stage parts, including Falstaff (Shakespeare), Peer Gynt (Ibsen), and Cyrano de Bergerac (Rostand). He shared the management of the Old Vic theater with Laurence Olivier 1944–50.

Richardson Samuel 1689–1761. English novelist,

Richard III *Portrait by an unknown artist of England's King Richard III, who was killed in battle by the forces of the future Henry VII.*

Richelieu *French churchman and politician Cardinal Richelieu, in a triple portrait by Philippe de Champaigne.*

one of the founders of the modern novel. *Pamela* 1740–41, written in the form of a series of letters and containing much dramatic conversation, was sensationally popular all across Europe, and was followed by *Clarissa* 1747–48 and *Sir Charles Grandison* 1753–54.

Richardson Tony 1928–1991. English director and producer. With George Devine he established the English Stage Company 1955 at the Royal Court Theatre, with productions such as *Look Back in Anger* 1956. His films include *Saturday Night and Sunday Morning* 1960, *A Taste of Honey* 1961, *Tom Jones* 1963, *Dead Cert* 1974, and *Joseph Andrews* 1977. He is the father of the actress Natasha Richardson.

Richelieu Armand Jean du Plessis de 1585–1642. French cardinal and politician, chief minister from 1624. He aimed to make the monarchy absolute; he ruthlessly crushed opposition by the nobility and destroyed the political power of the ◊Huguenots, while leaving them religious freedom. Abroad, he sought to establish French supremacy by breaking the power of the Hapsburgs; he therefore supported the Swedish king Gustavus Adolphus and the German Protestant princes against Austria and in 1635 brought France into the Thirty Years' War.

Born in Paris of a noble family, he entered the church and was created bishop of Luçon 1606 and a cardinal 1622. Through the influence of ◊Marie de' Medici he became ◊Louis XIII's chief minister 1624, a position he retained until his death. His secretary Père ◊Joseph was the original Grey Eminence.

Richland city in SE Washington, on the Columbia river, NW of Walla Walla. It is a center for research for the US Department of Energy and a major producer of plutonium for nuclear weapons; population (1990) 32,315. It grew as a residential community for employees of the Hanford Engineer Works that helped to develop the atomic bomb from 1943.

Richler Mordecai 1931– . Canadian novelist, born in Montreal. His novels, written in a witty, acerbic style, include *The Apprenticeship of Duddy Kravitz* 1959 and *St Urbain's Horseman* 1971. Later works include *Joshua Then and Now* 1980 and *Home Sweet Home* 1984.

Richmond industrial city and port on the James River and capital of Virginia; population (1990) 203,056. It is a major tobacco market and distribution, commercial, and financial center of the surrounding region. Its diversified manufactures include tobacco products, chemicals, paper and printing, and textiles. Educational institutions include the University of Richmond and Virginia Commonwealth University. The Museum of the Confederacy and Edgar Allan Poe Museum are here, as are the former homes of John Marshall and Robert E Lee and the graves of James Madison and Jefferson Davis. The first permanent colonial American settlement was established 1637. Richmond was the capital of the Confederacy 1861–65, and several Civil War battles were fought nearby.

Richter Burton 1931– . US high-energy physicist who, in the 1960s, designed the Stanford Positron Accelerating Ring (SPEAR). In 1974 Richter used SPEAR to produce a new particle, a hadeon, composed of a charmed quark and a charmed antiquark. The charmed quark had been first postulated by Sheldon ◊Glashow in 1964. Richter shared the 1976 Nobel Physics Prize with Samuel ◊Ting.

Richter Charles Francis 1900–1985. US seismologist, deviser of the ◊Richter scale used to measure the strength of the waves from earthquakes.

Richter Johann Paul Friedrich 1763–1825. German author, known as Jean Paul. He created a series of comic eccentrics in works such as the romance *Titan* 1800–03 and *Die Flegeljahre/The Awkward Age* 1804–05.

Richter Sviatoslav (Teofilovich) 1915– . Russian pianist, an outstanding interpreter of Schubert, Schumann, Rachmaninov, and Prokofiev.

Richter scale scale based on measurement of seismic waves, used to determine the magnitude of an ◊earthquake at the epicenter. The magnitude of an earthquake differs from the intensity, measured by the ◊Mercalli scale, which is subjective and varies from place to place for the same earthquake.

The magnitude is a function of the total amount of energy released, and each point on the Richter scale represents a tenfold increase in energy over the previous point. It is named after US seismologist Charles Richter.

Richter scale

Magnitude value	Relative amount of energy releases	Examples
1		
2		
3		
4	1	Carlisle, England 1979
5	30	San Francisco and New England 1979 Wrexham, Wales 1990
6	100	San Fernando 1971
7	30,000	Chimbote, Peru 1970 San Francisco 1989
8	1,000,000	Tangshan, China 1976 San Francisco 1906 Lisbon, Portugal 1755 Alaska 1964

Richthofen Ferdinand Baron von 1833–1905. German geographer and traveler who carried out extensive studies in China 1867–70 and subsequently explored Java, Thailand, Myanmar (Burma), Japan, and California.

Richthofen Manfred, Freiherr von (the "Red Baron") 1892–1918. German aviator. In World War I he commanded the 11th Chasing Squadron, known as Richthofen's Flying Circus, and shot down 80 aircraft before being killed in action.

ricin extremely toxic extract from the seeds of the ◊castor-oil plant. When combined with ◊monoclonal antibodies, ricin can attack cancer cells, particularly in the treatment of lymphoma and leukemia.

Ricin was used to assassinate the Bulgarian dissident Georgi Markov in London 1978.

Rickenbacker Edward Vernon 1890–1973. US racecar driver, aviator, and airline executive. Born in Columbus, Ohio, Rickenbacker became a racecar driver in his teenage years. By 1917 he had established a land speed record of 134 mph/216 kph. At the outbreak of World War I, he joined the army and was chosen for pilot's training in France. As a member of the 94th Aero Pursuit

Richthofen *German air ace Baron von Richthofen (center) during World War I with his 11th Chasing Squadron, "Richthofen's Flying Circus."*

Squadron, Rickenbacker gained fame as an air ace, downing 26 German aircraft in 4 months. Returning to private business after the war, he founded the Rickenbacker Motor Co 1921, but dissolved it and purchased Eastern Airlines 1938 (which he ran as president to 1959; chairman of the board to 1963). He left briefly to serve as an adviser to the War Department during World War II; he took on special missions and ditched his plane in the Pacific, drifting for 23 days before rescue.

rickets defective growth of bone in children due to an insufficiency of calcium deposits. The bones, which do not harden adequately, are bent out of shape. It is usually caused by a lack of vitamin D and insufficient exposure to sunlight. Renal rickets, also a condition of malformed bone, is associated with kidney disease.

Rickey Branch Wesley 1881–1965. US baseball executive. Born in Stockdale, Ohio, Rickey received a law degree from the University of Michigan 1911. Always active in athletics, he signed as a catcher with the St Louis Browns 1905–06. After playing with the New York Yankees 1907, he retired as a player. In 1913 he accepted a managerial job with the Browns and four years later became president of the St Louis Cardinals, the team he managed 1919–25. With the Cardinals, Rickey pioneered the minor-league system of developing talent. As president of the Brooklyn Dodgers 1942–50, he made baseball history by signing Jackie Robinson, the first black American to play in the major leagues.

Rickover Hyman George 1900–1986. Russian-born US naval officer. During World War II, Rickover worked on the atomic bomb project, headed the navy's nuclear reactor division, and served on the Atomic Energy Commission. He was responsible for the development of the first nuclear submarine, the *Nautilus,* 1954. He was promoted to the rank of admiral 1973. After retiring 1982, he became an outspoken critic of the dangers of nuclear research and development and the waste in military contracts.

Rickover immigrated to the US with his family 1906 and graduated from the US Naval Academy 1922. After further studies in engineering, he became a specialist in the electrical division of the Bureau of Ships.

Riefenstahl Leni 1902– . German filmmaker. Her film of the Nazi rallies at Nuremberg, *Triumph des Willens/Triumph of the Will* 1934, vividly illustrated Hitler's charismatic appeal but tainted her career. After World War II her work was blacklisted by the Allies until 1952.

She trained as a dancer, appearing in films in the 1920s, but in the early 1930s formed her own production company and directed and starred in *Das blaue Licht/The Blue Light* 1932. She also made a two-part documentary of the 1936 Berlin Olympics.

Unable to pursue her film career after being blacklisted, she turned to photography and is known for the volumes of photographs that have resulted from her visits to Africa, such as *The Last of the Nuba* 1973 and *Mein Afrika/My Africa* 1982.

Riel Louis 1844–1885. French-Canadian rebel, a champion of the Métis (an Indian-French people); he established a provisional government in Winnipeg in an unsuccessful revolt 1869–70 and was hanged for treason after leading a second revolt in Saskatchewan 1885.

Riemann Georg Friedrich Bernhard 1826–1866. German mathematician whose system of non-Euclidean geometry, thought at the time to be a mere mathematical curiosity, was used by Einstein to develop his general theory of ◊relativity.

Rienzi Cola di c. 1313–1354. Italian political reformer. In 1347, he tried to reestablish the forms of an ancient Roman republic. His second attempt seven years later ended with his assassination.

Riesman David 1909– . US sociologist, author of *The Lonely Crowd: A Study of the Changing American Character* 1950.

He made a distinction among "inner-directed," "tradition-directed," and "other-directed" societies; the first using individual internal values, the second using established tradition, and the third, other people's expectations, to develop cohesiveness and conformity within a society

Rietvelt Gerrit Thomas 1888–1964. Dutch architect, an exponent of De ◊Stijl. He designed the Schreder House at Utrecht 1924; he also designed colorful, minimalist chairs.

Rif, Er mountain range about 180 mi/290 km long on the Mediterranean seaboard of Morocco.

Riff member of a ◊Berber people of N Morocco, who under ◊Abd el-Krim long resisted the Spanish and French.

rifle ◊firearm that has spiral grooves (rifling) in its barrel. When a bullet is fired, the rifling makes it spin, thereby improving accuracy. Rifled guns came into use in the 16th century.

rift valley valley formed by the subsidence of a block of the Earth's ◊crust between two or more parallel ◊faults. Rift valleys are steep-sided and form where the crust is being pulled apart, as at ◊ocean ridges, or in the ◊Great Rift Valley of E Africa.

Rift Valley, Great volcanic valley formed 10–20 million years ago by a crack in the Earth's crust and running about 4,000 mi/6,400 km from the Jordan valley in Syria through the Red Sea to Mozambique in SE Africa. At some points its traces have been lost by erosion, but elsewhere, as in S Kenya, cliffs rise thousands of feet. It is marked by a series of lakes, including Lake Turkana (formerly Lake Rudolph), and volcanoes, such as Mount Kilimanjaro.

Rift Valley fever virus disease originating south of the Sahara. Hosted by sheep and cattle, it is spread by mosquitoes to humans, and a virulent strain reached Egypt 1977.

Riga capital and port of Latvia; population (1987) 900,000. A member of the ◊Hanseatic League from 1282, Riga has belonged in turn to Poland 1582, Sweden 1621, and Russia 1710. It was the capital of independent Latvia 1918–40 and was occupied by Germany 1941–44, before being annexed by the USSR. It again became independent Latvia's capital 1991.

Rigaud Hyacinthe 1659–1743. French portraitist, court painter to Louis XIV from 1688. His portrait of *Louis XIV* 1701 (Louvre, Paris) is characteristically majestic, with the elegant figure of the king enveloped in ermine and drapery.

Rigel brightest star in the constellation Orion. It is a blue-white supergiant with an estimated diameter 50 times that of the Sun. It is 900 light-years from Earth and is 50,000 times more luminous than our Sun. It is the seventh brightest star in the sky.

Rigg Diana 1938– . English actress. Her stage roles include Héloïse in *Abelard and Héloïse* 1970, and television roles include Emma Peel in *The Avengers* 1965–67 and Lady Deadlock in *Bleak House* 1985. She became the hostess for *Mystery Theater* on US public television 1989.

right ascension in astronomy, the coordinate on the ◊celestial sphere that corresponds to longitude on the surface of the Earth. It is measured in hours, minutes, and seconds eastward from the point where the Sun's path, the ecliptic, intersects the celestial equator; this point is called the vernal equinox.

right of way the right to pass over land belonging to another, such as a public right of way which can be a footpath; bridlepath, with horses permitted; or road, where vehicles are permitted. Other rights of way are ◊licenses (where personal permission is given) and ◊easements.

Rights of Man and the Citizen, Declaration of historic French document. According to the statement of the French National Assembly 1789, these rights include representation in the legislature; equality before the law; equality of opportunity; freedom from arbitrary imprisonment; freedom of speech and religion; taxation in proportion to ability to pay; and security of property. In 1946 were added equal rights for women; right to work, join a union, and strike; leisure, social security, and support in old age; and free education.

right triangle triangle in which one of the angles is a right angle (90°). It is the basic form of triangle for defining trigonometrical ratios (for example, sine, cosine, and tangent) and for which the ◊Pythagorean theorem holds true. The longest side of a right triangle is called the hypotenuse.

Its area is equal to half the product of the lengths of the two shorter sides. A triangle constructed with its longest side as the diameter of a circle with its opposite ◊vertex on the circumference is a right triangle. This is a fundamental theorem in geometry, first credited to the Greek mathematician Thales about 580 BC.

right wing the more conservative or reactionary section of a political party or spectrum. It originated in the French national assembly 1789, where the nobles sat in the place of honor on the president's right, whereas the commons were on his left (hence ◊left wing).

rigor medical term for shivering. Rigor mortis is the stiffness that ensues in a corpse soon after death, caused by the coagulation of muscle proteins.

Rigveda oldest of the ◊*Vedas*, the chief sacred writings of Hinduism. It consists of hymns to the Aryan gods, such as Indra, and to nature gods.

Riis Jacob August 1849–1914. Danish-born US journalist, photographer, and reformer. Riis immigrated to the US 1870. After working at a succession of jobs, he was hired as a reporter for the *New York Tribune* 1877. As police reporter for the *New York Evening Sun* 1888–99 he was exposed to the grim realities of urban life, and his photographic exposé of conditions in the New York slums, *How the Other Half Lives* 1890, made the American public aware of the poverty in its own midst.

As a social crusader, Riis later established a settlement house, named for him, in New York City. His autobiography, *The Making of an American*, appeared 1901.

Rijeka (Italian *Fiume*) industrial port (oil refining, distilling, paper, tobacco, chemicals) in NW Yugoslavia; population (1983) 193,044. It has changed hands many times and, after being seized by the Italian nationalist Gabriele ◊d'Annunzio 1919, was annexed by Italy 1924. It was ceded back to Yugoslavia 1949.

Riley James Whitcomb 1849–1916. US poet. Born in Greenfield, Indiana, Riley had little formal education and worked at a series of odd jobs before becoming the editor of a local newspaper. In 1877 he began to contribute light verse to the *Indianapolis Journal*. His use of the Midwestern vernacular and familiar themes earned him the unofficial title "The Hoosier Poet." His first collection of poems, *The Old Swimmin" Hole*, was published 1883. His later collections include *Rhymes of Childhood* 1890, *Poems Here at Home* 1893, and *Home Folks* 1900.

Rilke Rainer Maria 1875–1926. Austrian writer, born in Prague. His prose works include the semiautobiographical *Die Aufzeichnungen des Malte Laurids Brigge/Notebook of Malte Laurids Brigge* 1910, and his poetical works include *Die Sonnette an Orpheus/Sonnets to Orpheus* 1923 and *Duisener Elegien/Duino Elegies* 1923. His verse is characterized by a form of mystic pantheism that seeks to achieve a state of ecstasy in which existence can be apprehended as a whole.

Rimbaud (Jean Nicolas) Arthur 1854–1891. French Symbolist poet. His verse was chiefly written before the age of 20, notably *Les Illuminations* published 1886. From 1871 he lived with ◊Verlaine.

Although the association ended after Verlaine attempted to shoot him, it was Verlaine's analysis of Rimbaud's work 1884 that first brought him recognition. Rimbaud then traveled widely, working as a trader in North Africa 1880–91.

Rimini industrial port (pasta, footwear, textiles, furniture) and vacation resort in Emilia-Romagna, Italy; population (1988) 131,000. Its name in Roman times was Ariminum, and it was the terminus of the Flaminian Way from Rome. In World War II it formed the eastern strongpoint of the German "Gothic" defense line and was badly damaged in the severe fighting Sept 1944, when it was taken by the Allies.

Rimsky-Korsakov Nikolay Andreyevich 1844–1908. Russian composer. He used Russian folk idiom and rhythms in his Romantic compositions and published a text on orchestration. His operas include *The Maid of Pskov* 1873, *The Snow Maiden* 1882, *Mozart and Salieri* 1898, and *The Golden Cockerel* 1907, a satirical attack on despotism that was banned until 1909.

Other works include the symphonic poem *Sadko* 1867, the program symphony *Antar* 1869, and the symphonic suite *Scheherazade* 1888. He also completed works by other composers, for example, ◊Mussorgsky's *Boris Godunov*.

rinderpest acute viral disease of cattle (sometimes also sheep and goats) characterized by fever and bloody diarrhea, due to inflammation of the intestines. It can be fatal. Almost eliminated in the 1960s, it revived in Africa in the 1980s.

ring a circlet, usually of precious metal, sometimes set with gems, worn on a finger as a decoration or token. The origin of the wedding ring is uncertain, but betrothal rings were bestowed in Roman times. Rings were used for money in ancient Egypt and elsewhere. Their connection with the church still survives in instances such as the English coronation.

Ringling Charles 1863–1926. US circus promoter. Born in McGregor, Iowa, Ringling started a vaudeville act in 1882 with his brothers, John, Albert, Otto, and Alfred. The touring act eventually became a small circus and grew more popular after the purchase of an elephant in 1888. With Charles as business manager, the Ringling Brothers Circus toured widely. In 1907 they acquired the largest of their competitors, the Barnum and Bailey Circus, and established winter quarters in Sarasota, Florida.

With its three rings and large cast, the Ringlings' circus was touted as the "Greatest Show on Earth," the byword still most associated with the modern Ringling Brothers and Barnum and Bailey Circus.

ringworm any of various contagious skin infections due to related kinds of fungus, usually resulting in circular, itchy, discolored patches covered with scales or blisters. The scalp and feet (athlete's foot) are generally involved. Treatment is with ◊antifungal preparations.

***Río de Janeiro** The Sugar Loaf peak in Río de Janeiro.*

Rinzai (Chinese Lin-ch'i) school of Zen Buddhism introduced to Japan from China in the 12th century by the monk Eisai and others. It emphasizes rigorous monastic discipline and sudden enlightenment by meditation on a *kōan* (paradoxical question).

Río de Janeiro port and resort in Brazil; population (1980) 5,091,000, metropolitan area 10,217,000. The name (Portuguese "river of January") commemorates the arrival of Portuguese explorers Jan 1, 1502, but there is in fact no river. Sugar Loaf Mountain stands at the entrance to the harbor. It was the capital of Brazil 1822–1960.

Some colonial churches and other buildings survive; there are modern boulevards, including the Avenida Río Branco, and Copacabana is a luxurious beachside suburb.

Rio de Oro former district in the S of the province of Spanish Sahara. See ◊Western Sahara.

Río Grande river rising in the Rocky Mountains in S Colorado, and flowing S to the Gulf of Mexico, where it is reduced to a trickle by irrigation demands on its upper reaches; length 1,900 mi/3,050 km. Its last 1,500 mi/2,400 km form the US-Mexican border.

Río Grande do Norte state of NE Brazil; capital Natal; area 20,460 sq mi/53,000 sq km; population (1980) 1,900,750.

Riom town on the river Ambène, in the Puy-de-Dôme *département* of central France. In World War II, it was the scene Feb–Apr 1942 of the "war guilt" trials of several prominent Frenchmen by the ◊Vichy government. The accused included the former prime ministers ◊Blum and ◊Daladier, and Gen ◊Gamelin. The occasion turned into a wrangle over the reasons for French unpreparedness for war, and at the German dictator Hitler's instigation, the court was dissolved. The defendants remained in prison until released by the Allies 1945.

Río Muni the mainland portion of ◊Equatorial Guinea.

Río Negro river in South America, rising in E Colombia and joining the Amazon at Manáus, Brazil; length 1,400 mi/2,250 km.

Riopelle Jean Paul 1923– . Canadian artist, active in Paris from 1946. In the 1950s he developed an Abstract Expressionist style and produced colorful impasto (with paint applied in a thick mass) paintings and sculptures. His *Encounter* 1956 (Wallraf-Richartz Museum, Cologne, Germany) is a typically rough-textured canvas.

Río Tinto town in Andalusia, Spain; population (1983) 8,400. Its copper mines, first exploited by the Phoenicians, are now almost worked out.

RIP abbreviation for requiescat in pace (Latin "may he/she rest in peace").

Ripley Robert LeRoy 1893–1949. US cartoonist. Born in Santa Rosa, California, Ripley began cartooning as a teenager and was hired by the sports department of the *San Francisco Bulletin* 1910. In 1913 he became a sports cartoonist for the *New York Globe* and later began to present sports records in a series called "Believe It or Not!" Moving from sports to all kinds of oddities and obscure facts, Ripley took his column to the *New York Evening Post* in 1923 and later to national syndication. Through radio and film appearances and continued syndication, Ripley became a national celebrity and master of the bizarre.

ripple tank in physics, shallow water-filled tray used to demonstrate various properties of waves, such as reflection, refraction, diffraction, and interference, by programming and manipulating their movement.

Rip Van Winkle legendary character created by Washington Irving in his 1819 tale of a man who falls into a magical 20-year sleep, and wakes to find he has slumbered through the Revolutionary War.

RISC (acronym from reduced instruction-set computer) in computing, a processor on a single silicon chip that is faster and more powerful than others in common use today. By reducing the range of operations the processor can carry out, the chips are able to optimize those operations to execute more quickly. Computers based on RISC chips became commercially available in the late 1980s, but are less widespread than traditional processors.

Risorgimento movement for Italian national unity and independence from 1815. Leading figures in the movement included ◊Cavour, ◊Mazzini, and ◊Garibaldi. Uprisings in 1848–49 failed, but with help from France in a war against Austria—to oust it from Italian provinces in the north—an Italian kingdom was founded 1861. Unification was finally completed with the addition of Venetia 1866 and the Papal States 1870.

Ritter Tex (Woodward Maurice) 1905–1974. US singer and actor who was popular as a singing cowboy in B-films in the 1930s and 1940s. He sang the title song to *High Noon* 1952. His films include *Sing Cowboy Sing* 1937 and *Arizona Trail* 1943.

ritualization in ethology, a stereotype that occurs in certain behavior patterns when these are incorporated into displays. For example, the exaggerated and stylized head toss of the goldeneye drake during courtship is a ritualization of the bathing movement used to wet the feathers; its duration and form have become fixed. Ritualization may make displays clearly recognizable, so ensuring that individuals mate only with members of their own species.

river long water course or stream that flows down a slope along a bed between banks. It originates at a point called its source, and enters a sea or lake at its mouth, the ◊estuary. Along its length it may be joined by smaller rivers called tributaries. A river and its tributaries form a river system.

river

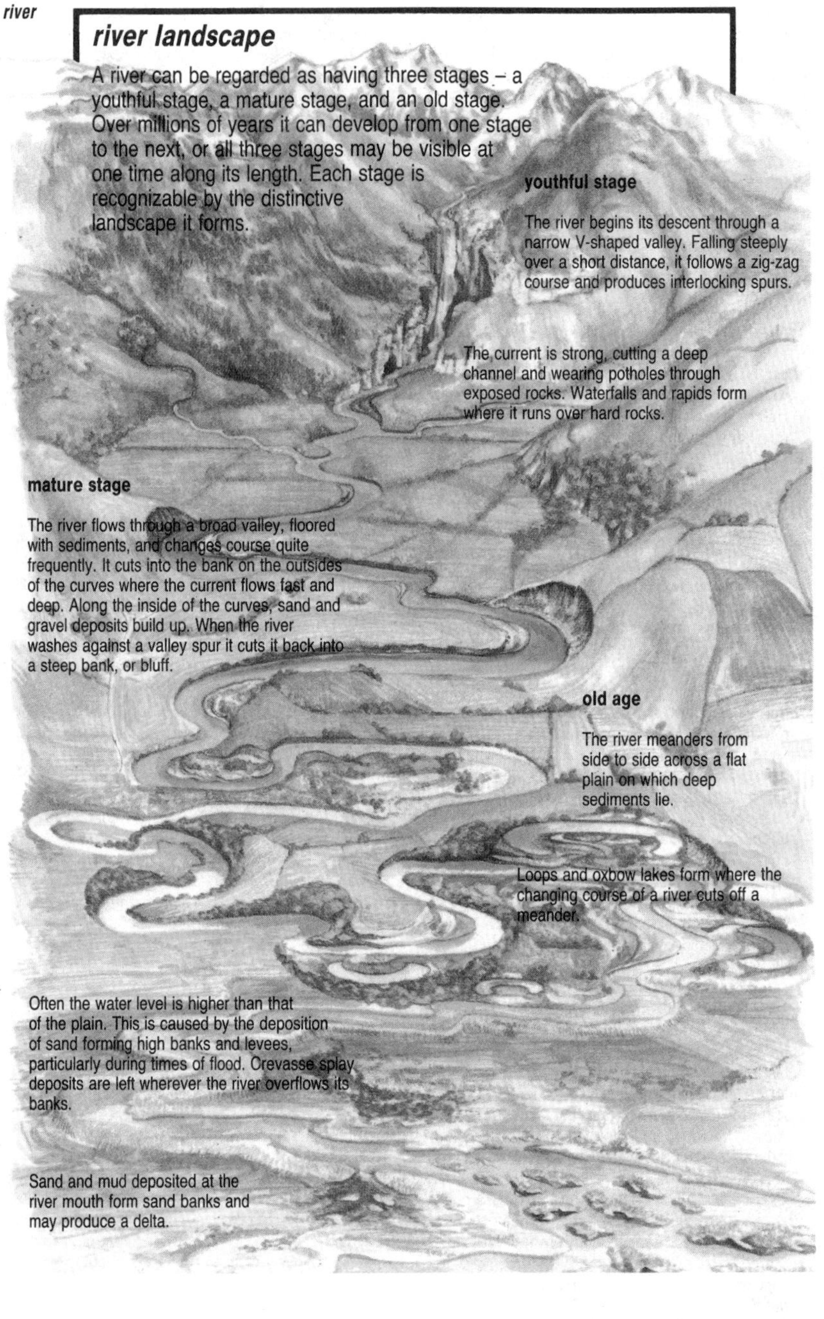
river landscape
A river can be regarded as having three stages – a youthful stage, a mature stage, and an old stage. Over millions of years it can develop from one stage to the next, or all three stages may be visible at one time along its length. Each stage is recognizable by the distinctive landscape it forms.
youthful stage
The river begins its descent through a narrow V-shaped valley. Falling steeply over a short distance, it follows a zig-zag course and produces interlocking spurs.
The current is strong, cutting a deep channel and wearing potholes through exposed rocks. Waterfalls and rapids form where it runs over hard rocks.
mature stage
The river flows through a broad valley, floored with sediments, and changes course quite frequently. It cuts into the bank on the outsides of the curves where the current flows fast and deep. Along the inside of the curves, sand and gravel deposits build up. When the river washes against a valley spur it cuts it back into a steep bank, or bluff.
old age
The river meanders from side to side across a flat plain on which deep sediments lie.
Loops and oxbow lakes form where the changing course of a river cuts off a meander.
Often the water level is higher than that of the plain. This is caused by the deposition of sand forming high banks and levees, particularly during times of flood. Crevasse splay deposits are left wherever the river overflows its banks.
Sand and mud deposited at the river mouth form sand banks and may produce a delta.

major rivers

Name and location	*km*	*mi*
Nile (NE Africa)	6,695	4,160
Amazon (South America)	6,570	4,080
Chiang Jiang (China)	6,300	3,900
Mississipi-Missouri (US)	6,020	3,740
Ob-Irtysh (USSR)	5,600	3,480
Huang He (China)	5,464	3,395
Zaïre (Africa)	4,500	2,800
Mekong (Asia)	4,425	2,750
Amur (Asia)	4,416	2,744
Lena (USSR)	4,400	2,730
Mackenzie (Canada)	4,241	2,635
Niger (Africa)	4,185	2,600
Yenisei (USSR)	4,100	2,550
Mississippi (US)	3,779	2,348
Madeira (Brazil)	3,240	2,013
Sao Francisco (Brazil)	3,199	1,988
Yukon (US)	3,185	1,979
Indus (Tibet/Pakistan)	3,180	1,975
Rio Grande (USA/Mexico)	3,050	1,900
Purus (Brazil)	2,993	1,860
Parana (Brazil)	2,940	1,827
Danube (Europe)	2,858	1,776
Brahmaputra (Asia)	2,850	1,770
Japura (Brazil)	2,816	1,750
Salween (Myanmar/China)	2,816	1,750
Euphrates (Iraq)	2,735	1,700
Tocantins (Brazil)	2,699	1,677
Zambezi (Africa)	2,650	1,650
Paraguay (Paraguay)	2,591	1,610
Orinoco (Venezuela)	2,600	1,600
Amu-Dar'ya (USSR)	2,540	1,578
Murray (SE Australia)	2,520	1,566
Ganges (India/Bangladesh)	2,510	1,560

Rivera Diego 1886–1957. Mexican painter, active in Europe until 1921. He received many public commissions for murals exalting the Mexican revolution. A vast cycle on historical themes (National Palace, Mexico City) was begun 1929. n the 1930s he visited the US and with Ben Shan produced murals for Rockefeller Center, New York City (later overpainted because he included a portrait of Lenin).

Rivera Primo de Spanish politician; see ◊Primo de Rivera.

river blindness another name for ◊onchocerciasis, a disease prevalent in Third World countries.

Riverside city in California, on the Santa Ana River E of Los Angeles; population (1990) 226,505. Founded 1870. It is the center of a citrus-growing district and has a citrus research station; the seedless orange was developed at Riverside 1873, and the research station, now part of the University of California-Riverside, saved the state's orange trees from obliteration by a virus in the 1940s. Manufactured products include irrigation and electronic equipment, aircraft engines, paper products, and plastics. A land-development company purchased the site and laid out the community 1870.

riveting method of joining metal plates. A hot metal pin called a rivet, which has a head at one end, is inserted into matching holes in two overlapping plates, then the other end is struck and formed into another head, holding the plates tight. Riveting is used in building construction, boilermaking, and shipbuilding.

Riviera the Mediterranean coast of France and Italy from Marseille to La Spezia.

The most exclusive section, with the finest climate, is the ◊Côte d'Azur, Menton–St Tropez, which includes Monaco. It has the highest property prices in the world.

Riyadh (Arabic *Ar Riyad*) capital of Saudi Arabia and of the Central Province, formerly the sultanate of Nejd, in an oasis, connected by rail with Damman on the Arabian Gulf; population (1986) 1,500,000.

Outside the city are date gardens irrigated from deep wells. There is a large royal palace and an Islamic university 1950.

Rizzio David 1533–1566. Italian adventurer at the court of Mary Queen of Scots. After her marriage to ◊Darnley, Rizzio's influence over her incited her husband's jealousy, and he was murdered by Darnley and his friends.

RNA ***ribonucleic acid*** nucleic acid involved in the process of translating ◊DNA, the genetic material, into proteins. It is usually single-stranded, unlike the double-stranded DNA, and consists of a large number of nucleotides strung together, each of which comprises the sugar ribose, a phosphate group, and one of four bases (uracil, cytosine, adenine, or guanine). RNA is copied from DNA by the assemblage of free nucleotides against an unwound portion (a single strand) of the DNA, with DNA serving as the template. In this process, uracil (instead of the thymine in DNA) is paired with adenine, and guanine with cytosine, forming ◊base pairs that then separate. The RNA then travels to the ribosomes where it serves to assemble proteins from free amino acids. In a few viruses, such as retroviruses, RNA is the only hereditary material.

RNA occurs in three major forms, each with a different function in the synthesis of protein molecules. ***Messenger RNA*** (mRNA) acts as the template for protein synthesis. Each ◊codon (a set of three bases) on the RNA molecule is matched up with the corresponding amino acid, in accordance with the ◊genetic code. This process (translation) takes place in the ribosomes, which are made up of proteins and ***ribosomal RNA*** (rRNA). ***Transfer RNA*** (tRNA) is responsible for combining with specific amino acids, and then matching up a special "anticodon" sequence of its own with a codon on the mRNA. This is how the genetic code is translated into proteins.

roach any freshwater fish of the Eurasian genus *Rutilus*, of the carp family, especially *R. rutilus* of N Europe. It is dark green above, whitish below, with reddish lower fins. It grows to 1.2 ft/ 35 cm.

Roach Hal 1892– . US film producer, usually of comedies, who was active from the 1910s to the 1940s. He worked with ◊Laurel and Hardy, and also produced films for Harold Lloyd and Charley Chase. His work includes *The Music Box* 1932, *Way Out West* 1936, and *Of Mice and Men* 1939.

road a specially constructed route for wheeled vehicles to travel on. Reinforced tracks became neccessary with the invention of wheeled vehicles in about 3000 BC and most ancient civilizations had some form of road network. The Romans developed engineering techniques that were not equaled for another 1,400 years.

Until the late 18th century most European roads were haphazardly maintained, making winter travel difficult. In the UK the turnpike system of collecting tolls created some improvement. The Scottish engineers Thomas Telford and John ◊McAdam introduced sophisticated construction methods in the early 19th century. Recent developments have included durable surface compounds, drainage, and machinery for rapid ground preparation.

In the US, the first roads were paved in colonial times, first with logs (corduroy roads), later with cobblestones and Belgian building blocks or brick, depending on the region. With the advent of motor vehicles, roads were constructed to reduce time spent draining, fixing flat tires, and seeking services; highways, parkways, freeways, and interstates now offer multilane, landscaped roads, with service areas at roadside, including motels, restaurants, and service stations.

roadrunner

greater roadrunner

roadrunner crested North American ground-dwelling bird *Geococcyx californianus* of the ◊cuckoo family, found in the SW US and Mexico. It can run at a speed of 15 mph/25 kph.

Roanoke (American Indian "shell money") industrial city (railroad repairs, chemicals, steel goods, furniture, textiles) in Virginia, on the Roanoke River; population (1980) 100,500. Founded in 1834 as Big Lick, it was a small village until 1881 when the repair shops of the Virginia Railway were set up here, after which it developed rapidly.

Robbe-Grillet Alain 1922– . French writer, the leading theorist of *le nouveau roman* ("the new novel"), for example his own *Les Gommes/The Erasers* 1953, *La Jalousie/Jealousy* 1957, and *Dans le labyrinthe/In the Labyrinth* 1959, which concentrates on the detailed description of physical objects. He also wrote the script for the film *L'Année dernière à Marienbad/Last Year in Marienbad* 1961.

Robben Island prison island in Table Bay, Cape Town, South Africa.

robbery in law, a variety of ◊theft: stealing from a person, using force, or the threat of force, to intimidate the victim.

Robbia, della Italian family of sculptors and architects, active in Florence. Luca della Robbia (1400–1482) created a number of major works in Florence, notably the marble *cantoria* (singing gallery) in the cathedral 1431–38 (Museo del Duomo), with lively groups of choristers. Luca also developed a characteristic style of glazed terracotta work.

Andrea della Robbia (1435–1525), Luca's nephew and pupil, and Andrea's sons continued the family business, inheriting the formula for the vitreous terracotta glaze. The blue and white medallions of foundling children 1463–66 on the Ospedale degli Innocenti, Florence, are typical. Many later works are more elaborate and highly colored, such as the frieze 1522 on the façade of the Ospedale del Ceppo, Pistoia.

Robbins Jerome 1918– . US dancer and choreographer. He choreographed the musicals *The King and I* 1951, *West Side Story* 1957, and *Fiddler on the Roof* 1964. First a chorus boy on Broadway, then a soloist with the newly formed American Ballet Theater 1941–46, Robbins was associate director of the New York City Ballet 1949–59. Robbins was ballet master of the New York City Ballet 1969–83, when he became joint ballet master-in-chief.

Among his ballets are *Fancy Free* 1940 (adapted with Leonard Bernstein into the musical *On the Town* 1944). He also choreographed *Facsimile* 1946 and *The Age of Anxiety* 1950 (again with Bernstein).

***Robeson** US singer and actor Paul Robeson, first acclaimed for his role as the lead in* The Emperor Jones, *was also an ardent supporter of black rights.*

Robert two dukes of Normandy, including:

Robert II c. 1054–1134. Eldest son of ◊William I (the Conqueror), succeeding him as duke of Normandy (but not on the English throne) 1087. His brother ◊William II ascended the English throne, and they warred until 1096, after which Robert took part in the First Crusade. When his other brother ◊Henry I claimed the English throne 1100, Robert contested the claim and invaded England unsuccessfully 1101. Henry invaded Normandy 1106 and captured Robert, who remained a prisoner in England until his death.

Robert three kings of Scotland:

Robert I Robert the Bruce 1274–1329. King of Scotland from 1306, and grandson of Robert de ◊Bruce. He shared in the national uprising led by William ◊Wallace, and, after Wallace's execution 1305, rose once more against Edward I of England, and was crowned at Scone 1306. He defeated Edward II at ◊Bannockburn 1314. In 1328 the treaty of Northampton recognized Scotland's independence and Robert as king.

Robert II 1316–1390. King of Scotland from 1371. He was the son of Walter (1293–1326), steward of Scotland, who married Marjory, daughter of Robert I. He was the first king of the house of Stuart.

Robert III c. 1340–1406. King of Scotland from 1390, son of Robert II. He was unable to control the nobles, and the government fell largely into the hands of his brother, Robert, duke of Albany (c. 1340–1420).

Roberts Frederick Sleigh ("Bobs"), 1st Earl 1832–1914. British field marshal. During the Afghan War of 1878–80 he occupied Kabul, and during the Boer War 1899–1902 he made possible the annexation of the Transvaal and Orange Free State.

Robeson Paul 1898–1976. US bass singer and actor. He graduated from Columbia University as a lawyer, but limited opportunities for blacks led him instead to the stage. He appeared in *The Emperor Jones* 1924 and *Showboat* 1928, in which he sang "Ol" Man River." He played *Othello* in 1930, and his films include *Sanders of the River* 1935 and *King Solomon's Mines* 1937. An ardent advocate of black rights, he had his passport withdrawn 1950–58 because of his association with left-wing movements. He then left the US to live in England.

Robespierre Maximilien François Marie Isidore de 1758–1794. French politician in the ◊French Revolution. As leader of the ◊Jacobins in the National Convention, he supported the execution of Louis XVI and the overthrow of the right-wing republican Girondins, and in July 1793 was elected to the Committee of Public Safety. A year later he was guillotined; many believe that he was a scapegoat for the Reign of ◊Terror since he ordered only 72 executions personally.

Robespierre, a lawyer, was elected to the National Assembly of 1789–91. His defense of democratic principles made him popular in Paris, while his disinterestedness won him the nickname of "the Incorruptible." His zeal for social reform and his attacks on the excesses of the extremists made him enemies on both right and left; a conspiracy was formed against him, and in July 1794 he was overthrown and executed by those who actually perpetrated the Reign of Terror.

robin one of two songbirds of the thrush family.

(1) North American thrush, the robin *Turdus migratorius*, 10 in/25 cm long, gray-brown with brick-red underparts. (2) Eurasian and African thrush *Erithracus rubecula*, 5 in/13 cm long, olive brown above with a red breast. Some Australian songbirds of several unrelated genera are also popularly called robins.

Robin Hood legendary English outlaw and champion of the poor against the rich. He is said to have lived in Sherwood Forest, Nottinghamshire, during the reign of Richard I (1189–99). He feuded with the sheriff of Nottingham, accompanied by Maid Marian and a band of followers known as his "merry men." He appears in ballads from the 13th century, but his first datable appearance is in Langland's *Piers Plowman* about 1377.

Robinson Edward G. Adopted name of Emanuel Goldberg 1893–1973. Romanian-born US film actor who emigrated with his family to the US in 1903. He was associated with gangster roles, such as *Little Caesar* 1930. He also performed in dramatic and comedy roles in film and on the stage and was a great art collector. He wrote two autobiographical volumes, *My Father, My Son* 1958 and *All My Yesterdays* 1973.

His other films include *The Ten Commandments* 1940, *Dr Ehrlich's Magic Bullet* 1944, *Double Indemnity* 1956, and *Soylent Green* 1973.

Robinson Edwin Arlington 1869–1935. US poet. His verse, dealing mainly with psychological themes in a narrative style, is collected in volumes such as *The Children of the Night* 1897, which established his reputation. He was awarded three Pulitzer Prizes in poetry: *Collected Poems* 1922, *The Man Who Died Twice* 1925, and *Tristram* 1928.

Well-known poems include "Richard Cory" and "Miniver Cheevy." He also published a series of long narrative poems based on Arthurian legends.

Robinson Jackie (Jack Roosevelt) 1919–1972. US baseball player, the first black to play in the major leagues. Born in Cairo, Georgia, Robinson attended the University of California at Los Angeles (UCLA) and joined the Kansas City Monarchs of the Negro National League 1945. He came to the attention of Branch ◊Rickey and was signed by a Brooklyn Dodgers minor league team. Robinson became the first black American in the major leagues 1947, playing second base for the Brooklyn Dodgers and winning rookie of the year honors. In 1949 he was the National League's batting champion and was voted the league's most valuable player. He had a career batting average of .311. After retirement as a player 1956, Robinson served as the New York governor's special assistant for community affairs 1966–68. He was elected to the Baseball Hall of Fame 1962.

Robinson Joan (Violet) 1903–1983. British economist who introduced Marxism to Keynesian economic theory. She expanded her analysis in *Economics of Perfect Competition* 1933.

Robinson John Arthur Thomas 1919–1983. British Anglican cleric, bishop of Woolwich 1959–69. A left-wing Modernist, he wrote *Honest to God* 1963, which was interpreted as denying a personal God.

Robinson Mary 1944– . Irish politician and president. Born in county Mayo, after convent school, Trinity College, Dublin and Harvard, she became a professor of law at 25. As a member of the

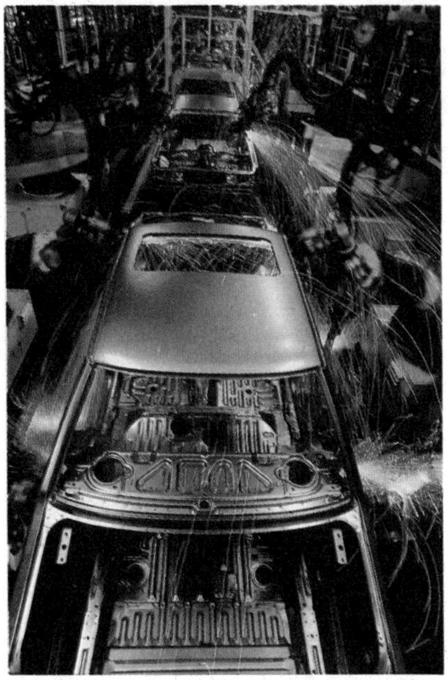

robot *Robots welding car bodies on the assembly lines of the Mazda car plant, Hiroshima, Japan.*

Labor Party, she began campaigning for women's rights in Ireland. After trying unsuccessfully to enter the Dáil (parliament) in 1990, she surprisingly won the presidency of her country, defeating the Fianna Fàil front-runner, Brian Lenihan.

Robinson Robert 1886–1975. English chemist, Nobel Prizewinner 1947 for his research in organic chemistry on the structure of many natural products, including flower pigments and alkaloids. He formulated the electronic theory now used in organic chemistry.

Robinson Sugar Ray. Adopted name of Walker Smith 1920–1989. US boxer, world welterweight champion 1945–51, defending his title five times. He defeated Jake LaMotta 1951 to take the middleweight title. He lost the title six times and won it seven times. He retired at the age of 45.

He was involved in the "Fight of the Century" with Randolph Turpin of the US 1951, and was narrowly beaten for the light-heavyweight title by Joey Maxim of the US 1952.

Robinson Crusoe *The Life and strange and surprising Adventures of Robinson Crusoe* novel by Daniel Defoe, published 1719, in which the hero is shipwrecked on an island and survives for years by his own ingenuity until rescued; based on the adventures of Alexander ◊Selkirk. The book had many imitators and is the first major English novel.

robot any machine controlled by electronic chip or computer that can be programmed to do work (robotics, as opposed to mechanical work, called automation). The most common types are robotic "arms"; when fixed to the floor or a workbench, they perform functions such as paint spraying or assembling parts in factories. Others include radio-directed or computer-controlled vehicles for carrying materials, and a miscellany of devices from cruise missiles and deep-sea and space-exploration craft to robotic toys.

Records of mechanical people and animals of all sizes that have been built go back more than 2,000 years. They are automatons, and it is only with the incorporation of the computer that the true robot could be built. A robot that plays guitar, and a cello, violin, and recorder robot ensemble, were marketed by a Japanese company 1989.

Rob Roy nickname of Robert MacGregor 1671–1734. Scottish Highland ◊Jacobite outlaw. After losing his estates, he lived by cattle theft and extortion. Captured, he was sentenced to banishment but pardoned 1727. He is a central

robot

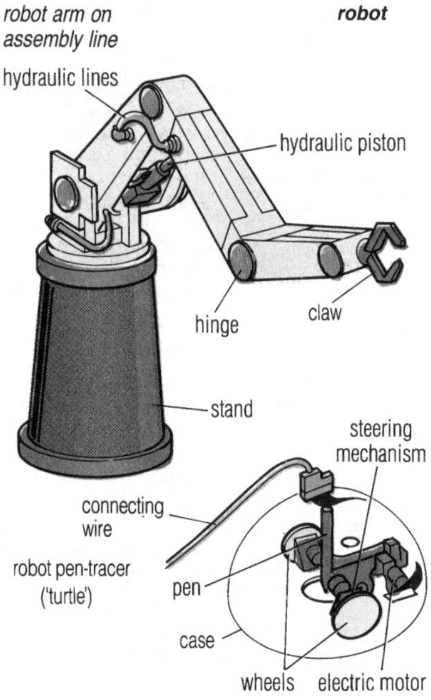
robot arm on assembly line
hydraulic lines
hydraulic piston
hinge
claw
stand
steering mechanism
connecting wire
robot pen-tracer ('turtle')
pen
case
wheels
electric motor

character in Walter Scott's historical novel *Rob Roy* 1817.

Robson Flora 1902–1984. English actress. Her successes include her role as Queen Elizabeth in the film *Fire Over England* 1931 and Mrs Alving in Ibsen's *Ghosts* 1959.

Rocard Michel 1930– . French Socialist politician, prime minister from 1988. A former radical, he joined the Socialist Party (PS) 1973, emerging as leader of its moderate social-democratic wing. He held ministerial office under Mitterrand 1981–85.

Rochefort industrial port (metal goods, machinery) in W France, SE of La Rochelle and 9 mi/15 km from the mouth of the Charente; population (1982) 27,716. The port dates from 1666 and it was from here that Napoleon embarked for Plymouth on the *Bellerophon* on his way to final exile in 1815.

Rochelle, La see ◊La Rochelle, port in W France.

Rochester industrial city (flour, Kodak films and cameras) in New York, on the Genesee River S of Lake Ontario; population (1990) 231,636. Its manufactured products include photographic equipment and optical and other precision instruments. It was the birthplace of the Xerox copier, and the world headquarters of the Eastman Kodak Company are here. The University of Rochester campus is in the suburbs, but Rochester is the home of the famed Eastman School of Music. The International Museum of Photography is at the George Eastman House. Permanent settlement began 1812, and growth was spurred by the completion of the Erie Canal 1825. During the mid-19th century, Rochester was a focus for abolitionism and women's rights; Susan B Anthony and Frederick Douglass lived here.

Rochester commercial center with dairy and food-processing industries in Minnesota; population (1990) 70,745. Rochester is the home of the noted Mayo Clinic, part of a medical center established 1889. The University of Minnesota medical school and the Mayo medical school are also here. The community was settled 1854 and named for Rochester, New York.

rochet in the Christian church, vestment worn mainly by Catholic and Anglican bishops and abbots. The Catholic rochet reaches to the knee, while the Anglican rochet is ankle length.

rock constitutent of the Earth's crust, composed of mineral particles and/or materials of organic origin consolidated into a hard mass as ◊igneous, ◊sedimentary, or ◊metamorphic rocks.

rock climbing *Rock climbing.*

rock and roll pop music born of a fusion of rhythm and blues and country and western and based on electric guitar and drums. In the mid-1950s, with the advent of Elvis Presley, it became the heartbeat of teenage rebellion in the West but was soon adopted by Eastern bloc countries and Third World nations. It found perhaps its purest form in late-1950s rockabilly; the blanket term "rock" later came to comprise a multitude of styles.

The term rock and roll was popularized by US disk jockey Alan Freed (1922–1965) beginning in 1951 on radio and in stage shows hosted by him.

rock climbing sport originally an integral part of mountaineering. It began as a form of training for Alpine expeditions and is now divided into three categories: the outcrop climb for climbs of up to 100 ft/30 m; the crag climb on cliffs of 100–1,000 ft/30–300 m, and the big wall climb, which is the nearest thing to Alpine climbing, but without the hazards of snow and ice.

Rockefeller John D(avison) 1839–1937. US industrialist, founder of the Standard Oil Company of Ohio 1870 (which achieved monopolistic control of 90% of US refineries). He also founded the philanthropic Rockefeller Foundation 1913, to which his son John D Rockefeller, Jr (1874–1960) devoted his life.

Born in Richford, New York, Rockefeller was brought up in Cleveland, Ohio, and after high school worked as a bookkeeper. By 1867, after oil was discovered in the US (in Pennsylvania), he and his produce-market partners went into the business of refining kerosene. From this company grew Standard Oil, which by 1911 had ruthlessly created a monopoly on US oil refining and distribution. It was broken up by a US Supreme Court ruling into smaller companies. Rockefeller then formed the General Education Board and the Rockefeller Foundation, philanthropic organizations that fostered educational programs in the South and at the University of Chicago and that funded medical research at the Rockefeller Institute in New York City.

rocket projectile driven by the reaction of gases produced by a fast-burning fuel. Unlike jet engines, which are also reaction engines, modern rockets carry their own oxygen supply to burn their fuel and are totally independent of any surrounding atmosphere. As rockets are the only form of propulsion available that can function in a vacuum, they are essential to exploration in outer space. ◊Multistage rockets have to be used, consisting of a number of rockets joined together. For warfare, rocket heads carry an explosive device.

Rockets have been valued as fireworks over the last seven centuries, but their intensive development as a means of propulsion to high altitudes, carrying payloads, started only in the interwar years with the state-supported work in Germany (primarily by Werner ◊von Braun) and of R H Goddard (1882–1945) in the US.

Two main kinds of rockets are used: one burns liquid propellants, the other solid propellants. The fireworks rocket uses gunpowder as a solid propellant. The ◊space shuttle's solid rocket boosters use a mixture of powdered aluminum in a synthetic rubber binder. Most rockets, however, have liquid propellants, which are more powerful and easier to control. Liquid hydrogen and kerosene are common fuels, while liquid oxygen is the most common oxygen provider, or oxidizer. One of the biggest rockets ever built, the *Saturn V* moon rocket, was a three-stage design, standing 365 ft/111 m high, weighed more than 3,000 tons on the launch pad, developed a takeoff thrust of some 7.5 million lb/3.4 million kg, and could place almost 150 tons into low Earth orbit. In the 1990s, the most powerful rocket system is the USSR Energia, which can place 110 tons into low Earth orbit. The US space shuttle can put only 26 tons into orbit. See ◊nuclear warfare and ◊missile.

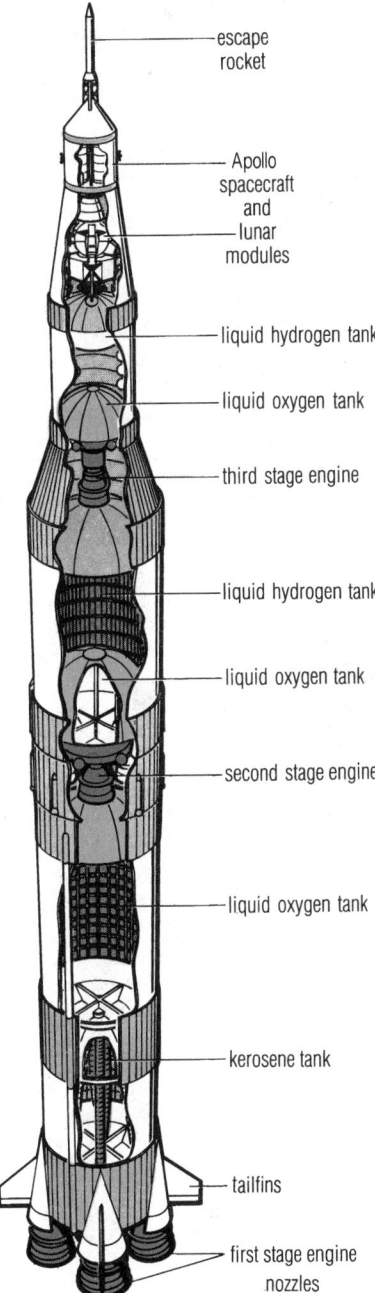

rocket
the Saturn V moon rocket

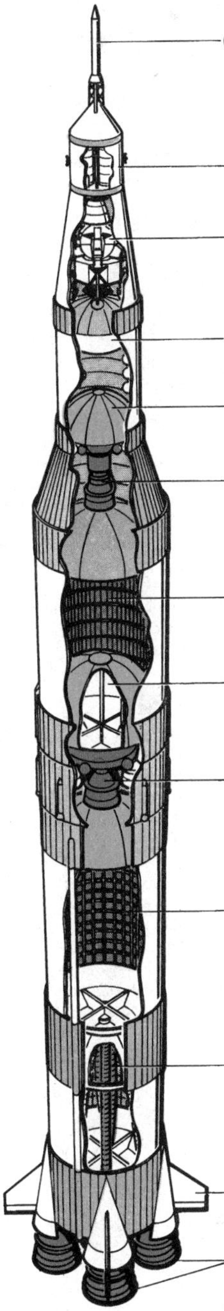
escape rocket
Apollo spacecraft and lunar modules
liquid hydrogen tank
liquid oxygen tank
third stage engine
liquid hydrogen tank
liquid oxygen tank
second stage engines
liquid oxygen tank
kerosene tank
tailfins
first stage engine nozzles

Rockford city in N Illinois, on the Rock river, NW of Chicago. Industries include automotive parts, furniture, machine tools, and food products; population (1990) 139,426.

Rock Hill city in N central South Carolina, S of Charlotte, North Carolina. Industries include chemicals, textiles, and paper products; population (1990) 41,643.

Rockingham Charles Watson Wentworth, 2nd Marquess of 1730–1782. British Whig politician, prime minister 1765–66 and 1782 (when he died in office); he supported the American claim to independence.

Rock Island city in NW Illinois, on the Mississippi river, W of Chicago. Industries include rubber and electronics. A US government arsenal is located here; population (1990) 40,552.

Rockne Knute Kenneth 1888–1931. Norwegian-born US football coach. Rockne immigrated with his family to the US 1893. As a student at Notre Dame University 1910–14, he was a star soccer player and became the school's head football coach 1918. Serving in that position until his death, Rockne established an unparalleled lifetime record of 105 wins, 12 losses, and 5 ties—with 5 undefeated, untied seasons. His greatest contribution to football was the extensive use of sophisticated formations and the forward pass. His book *Coaching, the Way of the Winner* was published 1925. His memoirs, *Autobiography*, appeared 1931.

rock opera musical using pop elements, such as Andrew ◊Lloyd Webber's *Jesus Christ Superstar* 1970.

Rockwell Norman 1894–1978. US painter and illustrator who is renowned for his magazine covers, mainly for *The Saturday Evening Post*, and cartoons portraying colorful, folksy American daily life.

His whimsical view of the ordinary activities of the nation at work and at play earned him huge popularity.

Rocky Mountains or ***Rockies*** largest North American mountain system. They extend from the junction with the Mexican plateau, N through the W central states of the US, through Canada to the Alaskan border, and then form part of the Continental Divide, which separates rivers draining into the Atlantic or Arctic oceans from those flowing toward the Pacific Ocean. Mount Elbert is the highest peak, 14,433 ft/4,400 m. Some geographers consider the Yukon and Alaska ranges as part of the system, making the highest point Mount Mckinley (Denali) 20,320 ft/6,194 m.)

Many large rivers rise in the Rocky Mountains, including the Missouri. Rocky Mountain National Park 1915 in Colorado has more than 107 named peaks over 10,000 ft/3,350 m. Because of the rugged terrain, the Rocky Mountains are sparsely populated. The chief economic asset is its minerals, including coal, petroleum, natural gas, copper, and gold. Lumbering is found in the N Rockies, and cattle and sheep are raised. The Rockies have US and Canadian national parks that attract many tourists.

rococo movement in the arts and architecture in 18th-century Europe, originating in France; a trend toward lightness, elegance, delicacy, and decorative charm. The term "rococo" refers to *rocaille* (rock- or shell-work), a style of interior decoration based on S-curves and scroll-like forms. Watteau's paintings and Sèvres porcelain belong to the French rococo vogue. The painters Boucher and Fragonard both painted typically decorative rococo panels for Parisian *hôtels* (town houses). In the 1730s the movement became widespread in Europe, notably in the churches and palaces of S Germany and Austria.

Other rococo features include the use of fantastic ornament, such as Grotesque and chinoiserie, and pretty, naturalistic details. Architectural and decorative ensembles, such as the Amalienburg pavilion at Nymphenburg near Munich, Germany, and the Hôtel de Soubise pavilion in Paris, exemplify the movement.

rodent any mammal of the worldwide order Roden-

Rodin *Bronze statue* Le Penseur/The Thinker *1904, the best-known work of French sculptor Auguste Rodin.*

tia, making up nearly half of all mammal species. Besides ordinary "cheek teeth," they have a single front pair of incisor teeth in both upper and lower jaw, which continue to grow as they are worn down.

They are often subdivided into three suborders: Sciuromorpha, including primitive rodents, with the squirrel as modern representatives; Caviomorpha, including all the South American rodents, of which the guinea pig is representative; and Myomorpha, rats and mice and their relatives.

rodeo originally a practical means of rounding up cattle in North America. It is now a professional sport in the US and Canada. Ranching skills such as bronco busting, bull riding, steer wrestling, and calf roping are all rodeo events. Because rodeo livestock is valuable, rules for its handling are laid out by the American Humane Association, yet criticism has been leveled at rodeos for cruel treatment of their animals.

Leading professionals earn in excess of $200,000 a season, and a world championship exists. One of the most widely known rodeo shows is the Calgary Stampede in Alberta.

Rodgers Richard (Charles) 1902–1979. US composer. He collaborated with librettist Lorenz Hart (1895–1943) on songs such as "Blue Moon" 1934 and musicals such as *On Your Toes* 1936, and with Oscar Hammerstein II (1895–1960) wrote musicals such as *Oklahoma!* 1943, *South Pacific* 1949, *The King and I* 1951, and *The Sound of Music* 1959.

Rodhos Greek name for the island of ◊Rhodes.

Rodin Auguste 1840–1917. French sculptor, often considered the greatest of his day. Through his work he freed sculpture from the idealizing conventions of the time by his realistic treatment of the human figure, introducing a new boldness of style and expression. Examples are *Le Penseur/The Thinker* 1880, *Le Baiser/The Kiss* 1886 (marble version in the Louvre, Paris), and *Les Bourgeois de Calais/The Burghers of Calais* 1885–95 (copy in Embankment Gardens, Westminster, London).

Rodin started his career as a mason, began to study in museums, and in 1875 visited Italy, where he was inspired by the work of Michelangelo. His statue *Bronze Age* 1877 was criticized for its total naturalism and accuracy. In 1880 he began the monumental bronze *Gates of Hell* for the Ecole des Arts Décoratifs in Paris (inspired by Ghiberti's bronze gates in Florence), a project that occupied him for many years and was unfinished at his death. Many of the figures designed for the gate became independent sculptures. During the 1890s he received two notable commissions, for statues of the writers *Balzac* 1897 (Musée Rodin, Paris) and *Hugo*. He also produced many drawings.

Rodney George Brydges Rodney, Baron 1718–1792. British admiral. In 1762 he captured Martinique, St Lucia, and Grenada from the French. In 1780 he relieved Gibraltar by defeating a Spanish squadron off Cape St Vincent. In 1782 he crushed the French fleet under Count de Grasse off Dominica, for which he was raised to the peerage.

Rodnina Irina 1949– . Soviet ice skater. Between 1969 and 1980 she won 23 world, Olympic, and European gold medals in pairs competitions. Her partners were Alexei Ulanov and then Alexsandr Zaitsev.

CAREER HIGHLIGHTS

Olympic champion: 1972, 1976, 1980
World champion: 1969–78
European champion: 1969–78

roebuck male of the Eurasian roe ◊deer.

roentgen or ***röntgen*** SI unit (abbreviation r) of radiation exposure, used for X and gamma rays. It is defined in terms of the number of ions produced in one cubic centimeter of air by the radiation.

Exposure to 1,000 roentgens gives rise to an absorbed dose of about 870 rads (8.7 grays), which is a dose equivalent of 870 rems (8.7 sieverts).

Roeselare (French *Roulers*) textile town in West Flanders province, NW Belgium; population (1985) 52,000. It was a major German base in World War I.

Roethke Theodore 1908–1963. US poet. His father owned a large nursery business, and the greenhouses and plants of his childhood provide the detail and imagery for much of his lyrical, personal, and visionary poetry. Collections include *Open House* 1941, *The Lost Son* 1948, *The Waking* 1953 (Pulitzer Prize), and the posthumous *Collected Poems* 1968.

Roe v Wade a US Supreme Court decision 1973 dealing with the constitutionality of state antiabortion laws. The case challenged a Texas statute prohibiting the abortion of a pregnancy that does not threaten the mother's life. The Court struck down the Texas law, ruling that state prohibition of abortion is unconstitutional on two grounds: (1) women are guaranteed the right to privacy by the 14th Amendment, and (2) unborn fetuses are not persons with the right to equal protection of the law. The highly controversial ruling limited state regulation to the prohibition of third-trimester abortions.

Rogers Carl 1902–1987. US psychologist who developed the client-centered approach to counseling and psychotherapy. This stressed the importance of clients making their own decisions and developing their own potential (self-actualization).

He emphasized the value of genuine interest on the part of a therapist who is also accepting and empathetic. Rogers's views became widely employed.

Rogers Ginger. Adopted name of Virginia Katherine McMath 1911– . US actress, dancer, and singer. She worked from the 1930s to the 1950s, often starring with Fred Astaire (in nine films 1933–39), including *Flying Down to Rio* 1933, *Top Hat* 1935, and *Swing Time* 1936. Her later work includes *Bachelor Mother* 1939, *Kitty Foyle* 1940, and *The Major and The Minor* 1942. She played on stage in the Broadway musicals *Hello, Dolly!*, and *Mame*.

Rogers Roy. Adopted name of Leonard Slye 1912– . US actor who moved to Hollywood from radio. He was a singing cowboy of the 1930s and 1940s, one of the Sons of the Pioneers. His first Roy Rogers film was *Under Westerm Stars* 1938, and he became "King of the Cowboys." He married his costar Dale Evans (who played in 20 of his films) in 1947. He played outside his own films in *Lake Placid Serenade* 1944, *Son of Paleface* 1952, *Alias Jesse James* 1959, and *Mackintosh and TJ* 1975.

Rogers Will (William Penn Adair) 1879–1935. US humorist. Born in Oologah Indian Territory (now Oklahoma), Rogers ended his formal education 1898 to work as a cowboy in Texas. He later traveled widely, performing in Wild West shows from 1902. In 1905 Rogers started his own vaudeville act of rope twirling and humorous banter. After beginning a Broadway career in 1915, which included Ziegfeld's Follies (1916–18, 1922, 1924–25), he moved to California to appear in motion pictures. From 1922 he wrote a humor column for *The New York Times*, and his wry comments on current affairs won him national popularity. Rogers was killed in a plane crash in Alaska with famed pilot Wiley Post.

Among his numerous books are *The Cowboy Philosopher on Prohibition* 1919 and *Ether and Me* 1929. *A Connecticut Yankee* 1931 and *State Fair* 1933 were two of his most popular films.

Roget Peter Mark 1779–1869. English physician, one of the founders of the University of London, and author of a *Thesaurus of English Words and Phrases* 1852, a text constantly revised and still in print, offering synonyms.

Röhm Ernst 1887–1934. German leader of the Nazi Brownshirts, the SA (◊Sturmabteilung). On the pretext of an intended SA *putsch* (uprising) by the Brownshirts, the Nazis had some hundred of them, including Röhm, killed June 29–30, 1934. It is sometimes called "the Night of the Long Knives" and has become a day of mourning for Jews and other politically aware groups.

Rohmer Eric. Adopted name of Jean-Marie Maurice Schérer 1920– . French film director and writer who was formerly a critic and television director. Part of the French new wave, his films are often concerned with the psychology of self-deception. They include *My Night at Maud's/Ma Nuit chez Maud* 1969, *Claire's Knee/Le Genou de Claire* 1970, and *The Marquise of O/La Marquise d'O/Die Marquise von O* 1976.

Rohmer Sax. Adopted name of Arthur Sarsfield Ward 1886–1959. English crime writer who created the sinister Chinese character Fu Manchu.

Roh Tae Woo 1932– . South Korean right-wing politician and general. He held ministerial office from 1981 under President Chun, and became chair of the ruling Democratic Justice Party 1985. He was elected president 1987, amid allegations of fraud and despite being connected with the massacre of about 2,000 antigovernment demonstrators 1980.

A Korean Military Academy classmate of Chun Doo Hwan, Roh fought in the Korean war and later, during the 1970s, became commander of the 9th Special Forces Brigade and Capital Security Command. Roh retired as a four-star general July 1981 and served as minister for national security, foreign affairs, and, later, home affairs.

Roland French hero whose real and legendary deeds of valor and chivalry inspired many medieval and later romances, including the 11th-century *Chanson de Roland* and Ariosto's *Orlando Furioso*. A knight of ◊Charlemagne, Roland was killed in 778 with his friend Oliver and the 12 peers of France at Roncesvalles (in the Pyrenees) by Basques. He headed the rearguard during Charlemagne's retreat from his invasion of Spain.

Roland de la Platière Jeanne Manon (born Philipon) 1754–1793. French intellectual politician, whose salon from 1789 was a focus of democratic discussion. Her ideas were influential after her husband Jean Marie Roland de la Platière (1734–1793) became minister of the interior 1792. As a supporter of the ◊Girondin party, opposed to Robespierre and Danton, she was condemned

Rolling Stones, The *English rock band The Rolling Stones, photographed shortly after their formation in 1962.*

to the guillotine 1793 without being allowed to speak in her own defense. Her last words were "O liberty! What crimes are committed in thy name!" While in prison she wrote *Mémoires*.

role in the social sciences, the part(s) a person plays in society, either in helping the social system to work or in fulfilling social responsibilities toward others. Role play refers to the way children learn adult roles by acting them out in play (mothers and fathers, cops and robbers). Everyone has a number of roles to play in a society: for example, a woman may be an employee, mother, and wife at the same time.

Role conflict arises where two or more of a person's roles are seen as incompatible, for example, a woman who is a daughter to a sick mother and a mother to a sick husband and child.

Sociologists distinguish between formal roles, such as those of a doctor or politician, and informal roles, such as those of mother or husband, which are based on personal relationships. Social roles involve mutual expectations: a doctor can fulfill that role only if the patients play their part; a father requires the support of his children. They also distinguish between ascribed roles (those we are born with) and achieved roles (those we attain).

roller any brightly colored bird of the Old World family Coraciidae, resembling crows but in the same order as kingfishers and hornbills. They grow up to 13 in/32 cm long. The name is derived from the habit of some species of rolling over in flight.

Rolling Stones, The British band formed 1962, once notorious as the "bad boys" of rock. Original members were Mick Jagger (1943–), Keith Richards (1943–), Brian Jones (1942–69), Bill Wyman (1936–), Charlie Watts (1941–), and Ian Stewart (1938–85). A rock-and-roll institution, the Rolling Stones were still performing and recording in the 1990s.

The Stones's earthy sound was based on rhythm and blues, and their rebel image was contrasted with the supposed wholesomeness of the early Beatles. Classic early hits include "Satisfaction" 1965 and "Jumpin' Jack Flash" 1968.

Rollins Sonny (Theodore Walter) 1930– . US tenor saxophonist and jazz composer. A leader of the "hard bop" school, he is known for the intensity and bravado of his music and for his skillful improvisation.

Rollo First duke of Normandy c. 860–932. Viking leader. He left Norway about 875 and marauded, sailing up the Seine to Rouen. He besieged Paris 886, and in 912 was baptized and granted the province of Normandy by Charles III of France. He was its duke until his retirement to a monastery 927. He was an ancestor of William the Conqueror.

Rolls Charles Stewart 1877–1910. British engineer who joined with Henry ◊Royce in 1905 to design and produce automobiles.

Rolls had trained as a mechanical engineer and worked in railroad production and as a car dealer before joining up with Royce. Before the business could flourish he died in a flying accident.

Rolls-Royce industrial company manufacturing automobiles and airplane engines, founded 1906 by Henry ◊Royce and Charles Rolls. The Silver Ghost car model was designed 1906, and produced until 1925, when the Phantom was introduced. In 1914, Royce designed the Eagle aircraft engine, used extensively in World War I. Royce also designed the Merlin engine, used in Spitfires and Hurricanes in World War II. Jet engines followed, and became an important part of the company.

ROM (acronym from read only memory) in computing, an electronic memory device; a computer's permanent store of vital information or programs. ROM holds data or programs that will rarely or never need to be changed but must always be readily available, for example, a computer's ◊operating system. It is an ◊integrated circuit (chip) and its capacity is measured in ◊kilobytes (thousands of characters).

ROM chips are loaded during manufacture with the relevant data and programs, which are not lost when the computer is switched off, as happens in ◊RAM.

Romagna area of Italy on the Adriatic coast, under papal rule 1278–1860 and now part of the region of ◊Emilia-Romagna.

Romains Jules. Adopted name of Louis Farigoule 1885–1972. French novelist, playwright and poet. His plays include the farce *Knock, ou le triomphe de la médecine/Dr Knock* 1923 and *Donogoo* 1930, and his novels include *Mort de quelqu'un/Death of a Nobody* 1911, *Les Copains/The Boys in the Back Room* 1913, and *Les Hommes de bonne volonté/Men of Good Will* (27 volumes) 1932–47.

Romains developed the theory of Unanimism, which states that every group has a communal existence greater than that of the individual, which intensifies the individual's perceptions and emotions.

Roman art sculpture and painting of ancient Rome, from the 4th century BC onward to the fall of the empire. Much Roman art was intended for public education, notably the sculpted triumphal arches and giant columns, such as *Trajan's Column* AD 106–113 and portrait sculptures of soldiers, politicians, and emperors. Surviving mural paintings (in Pompeii, Rome, and Ostia) and mosaic decorations show Greek influence. Roman art was to prove a lasting inspiration in the West.

Realistic portrait sculpture was an original development by the Romans. A cult of heroes began and in public places official statues were erected of generals, rulers, and philosophers. The portrait bust developed as a new art form from about 75 BC; these were serious, factual portraits of men to whose wisdom and authority, the busts implied, their subject nations should reasonably submit. Strict realism in portraiture gave way to a certain amount of Greek-style idealization in the propaganda statues of the emperors, befitting their semidivine status.

Narrative relief sculpture also flourished in Rome, linked to the need to commemorate publicly the military victories of their heroes. These appeared on monumental altars, triumphal arches, and giant columns such as *Trajan's Column*, on which Trajan's battles are recorded in relief like a cartoon strip winding its way around the column for about 655 ft/200 m. Gods and allegorical figures were featured with Rome's heroes on narrative relief sculptures, such as those on Augustus's giant altar to peace, the *Ara Pacis* 13–9 BC.

Very little Roman painting has survived, and much of what has is due to the volcanic eruption of Mount Vesuvius in AD 79 that buried the S Italian towns of Pompeii and Herculaneum under ash, thus preserving the lively and impressionistic wall paintings that decorated the villas of an art-loving elite. Common motifs were illusion and still life. A type of interior decoration known as Grotesque, rediscovered in Rome during the Renaissance, combined swirling plant motifs, strange animals, and tiny fanciful scenes. Grotesque was much used in later decorative schemes to quote the Classical period.

The art of mosaic was found throughout the Roman Empire. It was introduced from Greece and used for floors as well as walls and vaults, in *trompe l'oeil* (illusionary) effects, geometric patterns, and scenes from daily life and mythology.

Roman Britain period in British history from the mid-1st century BC to the mid-4th century AD. Roman relations with Britain began with Caesar's invasions of 55 and 54 BC, but the actual conquest was not begun until AD 43. England was rapidly Romanized, but north of York few remains of Roman civilization have been found. After several unsuccessful attempts to conquer Scotland the northern frontier was fixed at ◊Hadrian's Wall. During the 4th century Britain was raided by the Saxons, Picts, and Scots. The Roman armies were withdrawn 407 but there were partial reoccupations 417–c. 427 and c. 450. Roman towns include London, York, Chester, St Albans, Colchester, Lincoln, Gloucester, and Bath. The most permanent remains of the occupation were the system of military roads radiating from London.

Roman Catholicism one of the main divisions of the Christian religion, separate from the Eastern Orthodox Church from 1054, and headed by the pope. For history and beliefs, see ◊Christianity. Membership is about 585 million worldwide, with greatest concentrations in S Europe, Latin America, and the Philippines.

The Protestant churches separated from the Catholic with the Reformation in the 16th century, to which the Counter-Reformation was the Catholic response. An attempt to update Catholic doctrines in the late 19th century was condemned by Pope Pius X in 1907, and more recent moves have been rejected by John Paul II.

doctrine The Roman Catholic differs from the other Christian churches in that it acknowledges the supreme jurisdiction of the pope, infallible when he speaks *ex cathedra* ("from the throne"); in the doctrine of the Immaculate Conception (which states that the Virgin Mary, the mother of Jesus, was conceived without the original sin with which all other human beings are born); and in according a special place to the Virgin Mary.

organization The pope has (since the Second Vatican Council 1962–66) an episcopal synod of 200 bishops elected by local hierarchies to collaborate in the government of the church.

romance in literature, tales of love and adventure, in verse or prose, that became popular in France about 1200 and spread throughout Europe. There were Arthurian romances about the legendary King Arthur and his knights, and romances based on the adventures of Charlemagne and on Classical themes. In the 20th century the term "romantic novel" is often used disparagingly, to imply a contrast with a realist novel.

The term gradually came to mean any fiction remote from the conditions and concerns of everyday life. In this sense, romance is a broad term which can include or overlap with such genres as the ◊historical novel or ◊fantasy.

Romance languages branch of Indo-European languages descended from the Latin of the Roman Empire ("popular" or "vulgar" as opposed to "Classical" Latin). The present-day Romance languages with national status are French, Italian, Portuguese, Romanian, and Spanish.

Romansch (or Rhaeto-Romanic) is a minority language of Switzerland and one of the four official languages of the country, while Catalan and Gallego (or Galician) in Spain, Provençal in France, and Friulian and Sardinian in Italy are recognized as distinct languages with strong regional and/or literary traditions of their own.

Romanesque style of W European ◊architecture of the 8th to 12th centuries, marked by rounded arches, solid volumes, and emphasis on perpendicular elements.

Romanesque art a style of ◊medieval art.

Romania country in SE Europe, on the Black Sea,

Romania

USSR
Hungary
ROMANIA
Bucharest
Yugoslavia
BLACK SEA
Bulgaria
MEDITERRANEAN SEA
miles 500
0 km 1000

area 91,699 sq mi/237,500 sq km
capital Bucharest
cities Brasov, Timişoara, Cluj, Iasi; ports Galati, Constanta, Brăila
physical mountains surrounding a plateau, with river plains S and E
features Carpathian Mountains, Transylvanian Alps; river Danube; Black Sea coast; mineral springs
head of state Ion Iliescu from 1989
head of government Petre Roman from 1989
political system emergency provisional government from Dec 1989
exports petroleum products and oil-field equipment, electrical goods, automobiles, cereals
currency leu
population (1990 est) 23,269,000 (Romanians 89% Hungarians 7.9%, Germans 1.6%); growth rate 0.5% p.a.
life expectancy men 67, women 73 (1989)
language Romanian (official); Hungarian, German
religion Romanian Orthodox 80%, Roman Catholic 6%
literacy 98% (1988)
GNP $151 bn (1988); $6,400 per head
chronology
1944 Pro-Nazi Antonescu government overthrown.
1945 Communist-dominated government appointed.
1947 Boundaries redrawn. King Michael abdicated and People's Republic proclaimed.
1949 New constitution adopted. Joined Comecon.
1952 New Soviet-style constitution.
1955 Romania joined Warsaw Pact.
1958 Soviet occupation forces removed.
1965 New constitution adopted.
1974 Ceauşescu created president.
1985–86 Winters of austerity and power cuts.
1987 Workers demonstrated against austerity program.
1988–89 Relations with Hungary deteriorated over "systematization program."
1989 Announcement that all foreign debt paid off. Razing of villages and building of monuments to Ceauşescu; Communist orthodoxy reaffirmed; demonstrations violently suppressed; massacre in Timisoara; army joins uprising; heavy fighting; Ceauşescu and wife tried and executed; estimated 10,000 dead in civil warfare; power assumed by new military-dissident-reform Communist National Salvation Front, headed by Ion Iliescu.
1990 Securitate replaced by new Romanian Intelligence Service (RIS); religious practices resumed; mounting strikes and protests against effects of market economy.
1991 April: treaty on cooperation and good-neighborliness signed with USSR.

bounded N and E by the USSR, S by Bulgaria, SW by Yugoslavia, and NW by Hungary.
government Following the overthrow of the Ceauşescu regime in Dec 1989, an emergency interim administration, the council of the National Salvation Front, was established to hold power pending the framing of a new constitution and the holding of free multiparty elections during 1990. This council comprised 145 members, embracing military leaders, former anti-Ceauşescu communists, and dissident intellectuals, and included within it an 11-member executive bureau headed by the interim-president, Ion Iliescu.
history The earliest known inhabitants merged with invaders from ◊Thrace. Ancient Rome made it the province of Dacia; the poet Ovid was one of the settlers, and the people and language were Romanized. After the withdrawal of the Romans AD 275, Romania was occupied by ◊Goths, and during the 6th–12th centuries was overrun by ◊Huns, Bulgars, ◊Slavs, and other invaders. The principalities of Wallachia in the south, and Moldavia in the east, dating from the 14th century, fell to the ◊Ottoman Empire in the 15th and 16th centuries.

Turkish rule was exchanged for Russian protection 1829–56. In 1859 Moldavia and Wallachia elected Prince Alexander Cuza, under whom they were united as Romania from 1861. He was deposed 1866 and Prince Charles of ◊Hohenzollern-Sigmaringen elected. After the Russo-Turkish war 1877–78, in which Romania sided with Russia, the great powers recognized Romania's independence, and in 1881 Prince Charles became King Carol I.

Romania fought against Bulgaria in the Second ◊Balkan War 1913 and annexed S ◊Dobruja. It entered World War I on the Allied side 1916, was occupied by the Germans 1917–18, but received Bessarabia from Russia and ◊Bukovina and ◊Transylvania from the dismembered Hapsburg empire under the 1918 peace settlement, thus emerging as the largest state in the Balkans. During the late 1930s, to counter the growing popularity of the fascist ◊Iron Guard movement, ◊Carol II abolished the democratic constitution of 1923 and established his own dictatorship. In 1940 he was forced to surrender Bessarabia, N Transylvania, and S Dobruja to the USSR, Hungary, and Bulgaria, respectively, and abdicated when Romania was occupied by Germany in Aug. Power was assumed by Ion Antonescu (1882–1946, ruling in the name of Carol's son King ◊Michael), who signed the ◊Axis Pact Nov 1940 and declared war on the USSR June 1941. In Aug 1944, with the Red Army on Romania's borders, King Michael supported the ousting of the Antonescu government by a coalition of left and center parties, including the communists. Romania subsequently joined the war against Germany and in the Paris peace treaties 1947 recovered Transylvania but lost Bessarabia and N Bukovina to the USSR (they were included in ◊Moldavia and the ◊Ukraine) and S Dobruja to Bulgaria.

In the 1946 elections a Communist-led coalition achieved a majority and proceeded to force King Michael to abdicate. The new Romanian People's Republic was proclaimed Dec 1947 and dominated by the Romanian Communist Party, then termed the Romanian Workers' Party (RWP). Soviet-style constitutions were adopted in 1948 and 1952; Romania joined ◊Comecon 1949 and cosigned the ◊Warsaw Pact 1955; and a program of nationalization and agricultural collectivization was launched. After a rapid purge of opposition leaders, the RWP became firmly established in power, enabling Soviet occupation forces to leave the country 1958.

The dominant political personality 1945–65 was RWP leader and state president Gheorghe Gheorghiu-Dej. He was succeeded by Nicolae ◊Ceauşescu, who placed greater emphasis on national autonomy and proclaimed Romania a Socialist republic. Under Ceauşescu, Romania adopted a foreign-policy line independent of the USSR, condemned the 1968 invasion of Czechoslovakia, and refused to participate directly in Warsaw Pact maneuvers or allow Russian troops to enter the country. Ceauşescu called for multilateral nuclear disarmament and the creation of a Balkan nuclear-weapons-free zone and maintained warm relations with China.

At home, the secret police (Securitate) maintained a tight Stalinist rein on dissident activities, while a Ceauşescu personality cult was propagated, with almost 40 members of the president's extended family, including his wife Elena and son Nicu, occupying senior party and state positions. Economic difficulties mounted as Ceauşescu, pledging himself to repay the country's accumulated foreign debt (achieved 1989), embarked on an austerity program. This led to food shortages and widespread power cuts in the winters from 1985 onward; the army occupied power plants and brutally crushed workers' demonstrations in ◊Brasov in Nov 1987. After a referendum in 1986, military spending was cut by 5%. Ceauşescu was reelected general secretary of the RCP and state president in 1984–85 and again in 1989. From 1985 he refused to follow the ◊Gorbachev path of political and economic reform, even calling in the spring of 1989 for Warsaw Pact nations to intervene to prevent the opposition Solidarity movement from assuming power in Poland. The country's relations with neighboring Hungary also reached crisis point 1988–89 as a result of a Ceauşescu "systematization plan" to demolish 7,000 villages and replace them with 500 agro-industrial complexes, in the process forcibly resettling and "Romanizing" Transylvania-based ethnic Hungarians.

The unexpected overthrow of the Ceauşescu regime occurred in Dec 1989 when, in the city of Timisoara, ethnic Hungarians and Romanians joined forces to form an anti-Ceauşescu protest movement. Hundreds of demonstrators were killed in the state's subsequent crackdown on Dec 17. Four days later, an officially sponsored rally in Bucharest backfired when the crowd chanted anti-Ceauşescu slogans. Divisions between the military and Securitate rapidly emerged and on Dec 22 the army Chief of Staff, General Stefan Gusa, turned against the president. Ceauşescu attempted to flee, but was caught and summarily tried and executed on Christmas Day. Battles between Ceauşescu-loyal Securitate members and the army ensued in Bucharest, with several thousand being killed, but the army seizing the upper hand.

A National Salvation Front was established, embracing former dissident intellectuals, reform communists, and military leaders. At its head was Ion Iliescu (1930–), a Moscow-trained communist, while Petre Roman (1947–), an engineer without political experience, was appointed prime minister. The Front's council proceeded to relegalize the formation of alternative political parties and draft a new constitution. Faced with grave economic problems, it initiated a ban on the export of foodstuffs, the abandonment of Ceauşescu's "systematization program," the dissolution of the Securitate, the abolition of the RCP's leading role, and the relegalization of abortion and small-plot farming.

In April 1990 the government legalized the Eastern Rite Catholic Church and the Vatican re-established diplomatic relations. In July bills to create a legal market economy were presented to parliament by Roman. In Nov the leu was devalued, subsidies cut, and prices allowed to float. Industrial exports slumped and strikes increased. Economic chaos continued through 1991.

Romanian language member of the Romance branch of the Indo-European language family, spoken in Romania, Macedonia, Albania, and parts of N Greece. It has been strongly influenced by the Slavonic languages and by Greek. The Cyrillic alphabet was used until the 19th century, when a variant of the Roman alphabet was adopted.

Roman law legal system of ancient Rome that is now the basis of ◊civil law, one of the main European legal systems.

It originated under the republic, was developed under the empire, and continued in use in the Byzantine Empire until 1453. The first codification was that of the 12 Tables (450 BC), of which only fragments survive. Roman law assumed its final form in the codification of Justinian AD 528–34. An outstanding feature of Roman law was its system of international law (*jus gentium*), applied in disputes between Romans and foreigners or provincials, or between provincials of different states.

Roman numerals an ancient European number system using symbols different from Arabic numerals (the ordinary numbers 1, 2, 3, 4, 5, and so on). The seven key symbols in Roman numerals, as represented today, are I (1), V (5), X (10), L (50), C (100), D (500) and M (1,000). There is no zero, and therefore no place-value as is fundamental to the Arabic system. The first ten Roman numerals are I, II, III, IV (or IIII), V, VI, VII, VIII, IX, and X. When a Roman symbol is preceded by a symbol of equal or greater value, the values of the symbols are added (XVI = 16). When a symbol is preceded by a symbol of less value, the values are subtracted (XL = 40). A horizontal bar over a symbol indicates a factor of 1,000 ($\bar{X}$ = 10,000). Although addition and subtraction are fairly straightforward using Roman numerals, the absence of a zero makes other arithmetic calculations (such as multiplication) clumsy and difficult.

Although their role in mathematics is long obsolete, Roman numerals continue to enjoy a limited use as inscribed figures (for example, on timepiece faces, in the pagination of written material, or as dates on buildings or motion pictures).

Romano Giulio. See ◊Giulio Romano, Italian painter and architect.

Romanov dynasty rulers of Russia from 1613 to the ◊Russian Revolution 1917. Under the Romanovs, Russia developed into an absolutist empire. The first tsar was Michael; his most famous successors were ◊Peter the Great, ◊Catherine the Great, ◊Alexander I, ◊Nicholas I, and Alexander II. See also ◊Russian history.

Roman religion religious system that retained early elements of animism (with reverence for stones and trees) and totemism (see ◊Romulus and Remus), and had a strong domestic base in the ◊lares and penates, the cult of Janus and Vesta. It also had a main pantheon of gods derived from the Greek, which included Jupiter and Juno, Mars and Venus, Minerva, Diana, Ceres, and many lesser deities.

By the time of the empire, the educated classes tended toward Stoicism or Skepticism, but the following of mystery cults, especially within the army (see ◊Isis and ◊Mithraism), proved a strong rival to early Christianity. The deification of dead emperors served a political purpose and also retained the idea of family—that is, that those who had served the national family in life continued to care, as did one's ancestors, after their death.

Romansch member of the Romance branch of the Indo-European language family, spoken by some 50,000 people in the eastern cantons of Switzerland. It was accorded official status 1937 alongside French, German, and Italian. It is also known among scholars as Rhaeto-Romanic.

Romanticism *A blending of French and English romantic feeling in Gustav Doré's interpretation of the Arthurian legend in his illustrations of Tennyson's* Idylls – "The Ride to Camelot."

Romanticism in literature, music, and art, a style that emphasizes the imagination, emotions, and creativity of the individual artist. The term is often used to characterize the culture of 19th-century Europe, as contrasted with 18th-century ◊Classicism.

Inspired by social change and revolution (US, French) and reacting against the Classical restraint of the Augustan age and the ◊Enlightenment, the Romantics asserted the importance of how the individual feels about the world, natural and supernatural. The French painter Delacroix is often cited as the quintessential Romantic artist. Many of the later Romantics were strong nationalists, for example, Pushkin, Wagner, Verdi, Chopin.

In art, nostalgia for an imagined idyllic past and reverence for natural beauty were constant themes, inspiring paintings of grandiose landscapes, atmospheric ruins, historical scenes, portraits of legendary heroes, and so forth. Caspar David Friedrich in Germany, Frederick Church (1826–1900) and Frederic Remington in the US, and J M W Turner in England were outstanding landscape painters, while Henry Fuseli and William Blake represent a mystical and fantastic trend. The Romantic mood ranged from profound despair to dashing bravado.

Romanticism in music, term that generally refers to a preoccupation with the expression of emotion and with nature and folk history as a source of inspiration. Often linked with nationalistic feelings, the Romantic movement reached its height in the late 19th century, as in the works of Schumann and Wagner.

Romany a nomadic Caucasoid people, also called ◊Gypsy (a corruption of "Egyptian," since they were erroneously thought to come from Egypt). They are now believed to have originated in NW India, and live throughout the world. The Romany language (spoken in different dialects in every country where Gypsies live) is a member of the Indo-European family.

Rome *The center of activity in ancient Rome, the Roman Forum, here showing the Temple of Castor and Pollux, is now a major tourist attraction.*

In the 14th century they settled in the Balkan peninsula, spread over Germany, Italy, and France, and arrived in England about 1500. During World War II, Nazi Germany tried to exterminate them, along with Jews, Slavs, and political prisoners (see ◊concentration camp).

Rome city in central New York, on the Mohawk river, NW of Albany. Industries include copper and brass products, paint, and household appliances; population (1990) 44,350. Construction of the Erie Canal began here 1817.

Rome (Italian *Roma*) capital of Italy and of Lazio region, on the river Tiber, 17 mi/27 km from the Tyrrhenian Sea; population (1988) 2,817,000. Rome has few industries but is an important cultural, road, and rail center. A large section of the population finds employment in government offices. Remains of the ancient city include the Forum, Colosseum, and Pantheon.

history After the deposition of the last emperor, Romulus Augustus, 476, the papacy became the real ruler of Rome and from the 8th century was recognized as such. As a result of the French Revolution, Rome temporarily became a republic 1798–99, and was annexed to the French Empire 1808–14, until the pope returned on Napoleon's fall. During the 1848–49 revolution, a republic was established under Mazzini's leadership, but, in spite of Garibaldi's defense, was overthrown by French troops. In 1870 Rome became the capital of Italy, the pope retiring into the Vatican until 1929 when the Vatican City was recognized as a sovereign state. The occupation of Rome by the Fascists 1922 marked the beginning of Mussolini's rule, but in 1943 Rome was occupied by Germany and then captured by the Allies 1944. (For early history see ◊Rome, ancient.)

features E of the river are the seven hills on which it was originally built (Quirinal, Aventine, Caelian, Esquiline, Viminal, Palatine, and Capitol); to the W are the popular quarter of Trastevere, the more modern residential quarters of the Prati, and the Vatican. Among Rome's buildings are Castel Sant' Angelo (the mausoleum of the emperor Hadrian) and baths of Caracalla. Among the Renaissance palaces are the Lateran, Quirinal (with the Trevi fountain nearby), Colonna, Borghese, Barberini, and Farnese. There are a number of churches of different periods; San Paolo was founded by the emperor Constantine on St Paul's grave. The house where the English poet Keats died is near the Piazza di Spagna, known for the Spanish Steps.

Rome, ancient civilization based in Rome, which occupied first the Italian peninsula, then most of Europe, the Near East, and N Africa. It lasted for about 800 years. Traditionally founded 753 BC, Rome became a kingdom, then a self-ruling republic (and free of ◊Etruscan rule) 510 BC. From then, the history of Rome is one of continual expansion, interrupted only by civil wars in the period 133–27 BC, until the murder of Julius ◊Caesar and foundation of the empire under ◊Augustus and his successors. At its peak under ◊Trajan, the Roman Empire stretched from Britain to Mesopotamia and the Caspian Sea. A long

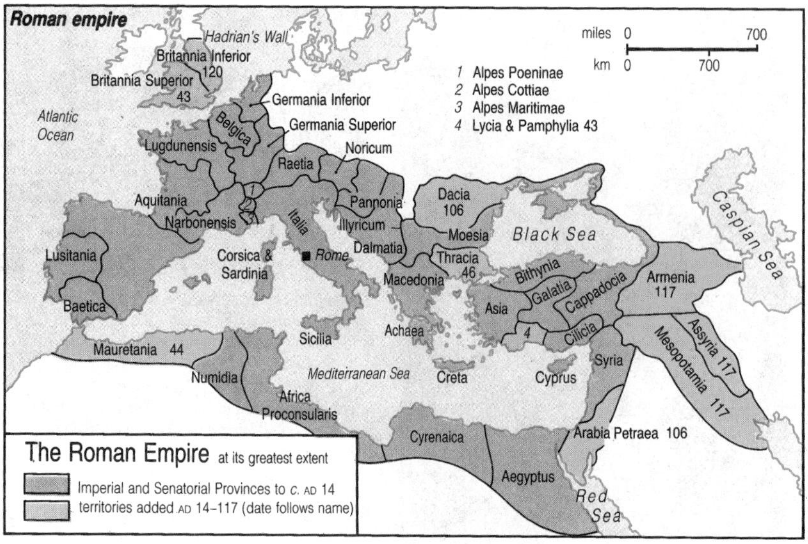
Roman empire
Hadrian's Wall
Britannia Inferior
120
Britannia Superior
43
Germania Inferior
Germania Superior
Atlantic Ocean
Belgica
Lugdunensis
Noricum
Raetia
Aquitania
Narbonensis
Pannonia
Dacia
106
Italia
Illyricum
Moesia
Black Sea
Caspian Sea
Lusitania
Corsica & Sardinia
Rome
Dalmatia
Thracia
46
Bithynia
Galatia
Cappadocia
Armenia
117
Macedonia
Baetica
Asia
Assyria 117
Mesopotamia 117
Cilicia
Achaea
Sicilia
Mauretania 44
Syria
Numidia
Mediterranean Sea
Creta
Cyprus
Africa Proconsularis
Cyrenaica
Arabia Petraea 106
Aegyptus
Red Sea
miles 0 700
km 0 700
1 Alpes Poeninae
2 Alpes Cottiae
3 Alpes Maritimae
4 Lycia & Pamphylia 43
The Roman Empire at its greatest extent
Imperial and Senatorial Provinces to c. AD 14
territories added AD 14–117 (date follows name)

train of emperors ruling by virtue of military, rather than civil, power marked the beginning of Rome's long decline; under ◊Diocletian, the empire was divided into two parts—East and West—although temporarily reunited under ◊Constantine, the first emperor formally to adopt Christianity. The end of the Roman Empire is generally dated by the sack of Rome by the Goths AD 410, or by the deposition of the last emperor in the west AD 476. The Eastern Empire continued until 1453 at ◊Constantinople.

The civilization of ancient Rome influenced the whole of W Europe throughout the Middle Ages, the Renaissance, and beyond, in the fields of art and architecture, literature, law, and engineering. See also ◊Latin.

735 BC According to tradition Rome was founded
510 The Etruscan dynasty of the Tarquins was expelled, and a republic was established, governed by two consuls, elected annually by the popular assembly, and a council of elders or Senate. The concentration of power in the hands of the aristocracy aroused the opposition of the plebeian masses
390 Rome sacked by Gauls
367 The plebeians secured the right to elect tribunes, the codification of the laws, and the right to marry patricians; it was enacted that one consul must be a plebeian
338 The cities of Latium formed into a league under Roman control
343–290 The Etruscans to the N and the Samnites to the SE were subdued during the 5th–4th centuries
280–272 The Greek cities of the south were conquered
264–241 First Punic War, ending in a Roman victory and the annexation of Sicily
238 Sardinia seized from Carthage and became a Roman province
226–222 Roman conquest of Cisalpine Gaul (Lombardy); conflict with Carthage, which was attempting to conquer Sicily
218 Hannibal invaded Italy and won a brilliant series of victories
202 Victory over Hannibal at Zama, followed by surrender of Carthage and relinquishing of its Spanish colonies
148 Three wars with Macedon were followed by its conversion into a province
146 After a revolt Greece became in effect a Roman province. In the same year Carthage was annexed. On the death of the king of Pergamum, Rome succeeded to his kingdom in Asia Minor
133 Tiberius Gracchus put forward proposals for agrarian reforms and was murdered by the senatorial party
123 Tiberius" policy was taken up by his brother Gaius Gracchus, who was likewise murdered
109–106 The leadership of the democrats passed to Marius
91–88 Social War: a revolt of the Italian cities compelled Rome to grant citizenship to all Italians
87–84 While Sulla was repelling an invasion of Greece by Mithridates, Marius seized power
82 On his return Sulla established a dictatorship and ruled by terror
70 His changes were reversed by Pompey and Crassus
66–62 Defeat of Mithradates and annexation of Syria and the rest of Asia Minor
60 Pompey formed an alliance with the democratic leaders Crassus and Caesar
51 Gaul conquered by Caesar as far as the Rhine
49 Caesar's return to Italy (crossing the ◊Rubicon) led to civil war between Caesar and Pompey
48 Defeat of Pompey at Pharsalus
44 Caesar's dictatorship ended by his assassination
32 The empire divided between Caesar's nephew Octavian in the W and Antony in the E; war between them
31 Defeat of Antony at ◊Actium
30 With the deaths of Antony and Cleopatra Egypt was annexed
27 Octavian took the name Augustus; he was by now absolute ruler, although in title only *princeps* (first citizen)
43 AD Augustus made the Rhine and the Danube its frontiers; Claudius added Britain
96–180 Under the Flavian emperors Nerva, Trajan, Hadrian, Antoninus Pius, and Marcus Aurelius Antoninus the empire enjoyed a golden age
115 Trajan conquered Macedonia; peak of Roman territorial expansion.
180 Marcus Aurelius Antoninus" death was followed by a century of war and disorder; a succession of generals were placed on the throne by their armies
284–305 Diocletian reorganized the empire as a centralized autocracy
324–37 Constantine I realized the political value of Christianity and became a convert
364 Constantine removed the capital to Constantinople, and the empire was divided
410 The Goths overran Greece and Italy, sacked Rome, and finally settled in Spain. The Vandals conquered Italy
451–52 The Huns raided Gaul and Italy
476 The last Western emperor was deposed.

Rome-Berlin Axis another name for the ◊Axis.

Romeo and Juliet romantic tragedy by William Shakespeare, first performed 1594–95. The play is concerned with the doomed love of Romeo and Juliet, victims of the bitter enmity between their respective families in Verona.

Rome, Sack of AD 410. The invasion and capture of the city of Rome by the Goths, generally accepted as marking the effective end of the Roman Empire.

Rome, Treaties of international agreements signed in March 1957 by Belgium, France, Germany, Italy, Luxemburg, and the Netherlands, which formally set up the ◊European Economic Community (EEC) for present member nations. Its terms proposed the abolition of internal tariffs between the six member countries, uniform external tariffs, the free movement of goods, capital, and people. A second Treaty set up the European Atomic Energy Commission (EURATOM) to develop nuclear energy for peaceful uses.

Rommel Erwin 1891–1944. German field marshal. He served in World War I, and in World War II he played an important part in the invasions of central Europe and France. He was commander of the N African offensive from 1941 (when he was nicknamed "Desert Fox") until defeated in the Battles of El ◊Alamein. He was commander in chief for a short time against the Allies in Europe 1944 but (as a sympathizer with the ◊Stauffenberg plot against Hitler) was forced to commit suicide. His son Manfred Rommel (1928–) became mayor of Stuttgart 1975.

Romney George 1734–1802. English portrait painter, active in London from 1762. He painted several portraits of Lady Hamilton, Admiral Nelson's mistress.

Romney was virtually self-taught. He set up as a portraitist in 1757, and in 1762 he went to London. There he became, with Gainsborough and Reynolds, one of the most successful portrait painters of the late 18th century.

Romulus in Roman mythology, legendary founder and first king of Rome, the son of Mars and Rhea Silvia, daughter of Numitor, king of Alba Longa. Romulus and his twin brother Remus were thrown into the Tiber by their great-uncle Amulius, who had deposed Numitor, but were suckled by a she-wolf and rescued by a shepherd. On reaching adulthood they killed Amulius and founded Rome.

Having murdered Remus, Romulus reigned alone until he disappeared in a storm; he was thereafter worshiped as a god under the name of Quirinus.

Romulus Augustulus born c. AD 461. Last Roman emperor in the West. He was made emperor by his father Orestes, a soldier, about 475 but was compelled to abdicate 476 by Odoacer, leader of the barbarian mercenaries, who nicknamed him Augustulus. Orestes was executed and Romulus Augustulus confined to a Neapolitan villa.

Roncesvalles village of N Spain, in the Pyrenees 5 mi/8 km S of the French border, the scene of the defeat of the rearguard of Charlemagne's army under ◊Roland, who with the 12 peers of France was killed 778.

rondo or ***rondeau*** form of instrumental music in which the principal section returns like a refrain. Rondo form is often used for the last movement of a sonata or concerto.

Rondônia state in NW Brazil; the center of Amazonian tin and gold mining and of experiments in agricultural colonization; area 93,876 sq mi/ 243,044 sq km; population (1986) 776,000. Known as the Federal Territory of ***Guaporé*** until 1956; it became a state in 1981.

Ronsard Pierre de 1524–1585. French poet, leader of the ◊Pléiade group of poets. Under the patronage of Charles IX, he published original verse in a lightly sensitive style, including odes and love sonnets, such as *Odes* 1550, *Les Amours/Lovers* 1552–53, and the "Marie" cycle, *Continuation des amours/Lovers Continued* 1555–56.

röntgen alternate spelling for ◊roentgen, unit of X-ray and gamma-ray exposure.

Röntgen (or ***Roentgen***) Wilhelm Konrad

1845–1923. German physicist who discovered X rays 1895. While investigating the passage of electricity through gases, he noticed the ◊fluorescence of a barium platinocyanide screen. This radiation passed through some substances opaque to light, and affected photographic plates. Developments from this discovery have revolutionized medical diagnosis.

He received a Nobel Prize 1901. The unit of electromagnetic radiation (X ray) is named roentgen or röntgen (r) after him.

rood alternate name for the cross of Christ, often applied to the large crucifix placed on a beam or screen at the entrance to the chancel of a church.

Roodepoort-Maraisburg gold-mining town in Transvaal, South Africa, 9 mi/15 km W of Johannesburg, at an altitude of 5,725 ft/1,745 m; population (1980) 165,315. Leander Starr ◊Jameson and his followers surrendered here in 1896 after an attempt to overthrow the government.

rook gregarious European ◊crow *Corvus frugilegus*. The plumage is black and lustrous and the face bare; it can grow to 18 in/45 cm long. Rooks nest in colonies at the tops of trees.

Roon Albrecht Theodor Emil, Graf von 1803–1879. Prussian field marshal. As war minister from 1859, he reorganized the army and made possible the victories over Austria 1866 (see ◊Prussia) and those in the ◊Franco-Prussian War 1870–71.

Rooney Mickey. Adopted name of Joe Yule Jr 1920– . US musician and actor who began his career in his parents' stage act when he was not yet two years old. He began in short films as a child called Mickey McGuire and became Rooney at age 12 when he started to appear in features such as *Manhattan Melodrama* 1954 and *A Midsummer Night's Dream* 1935. He played Andy Hardy opposite Judy Garland in the Hardy family series of B-films (1936–46) and starred with her in several musicals, including *Babes in Arms* 1939. He also starred in *Boys' Town* 1938, *Young Tom Edison* 1940, and *The Human Comedy* 1943. In later years he made character and cameo appearances and played on Broadway.

Roosevelt (Anna) Eleanor 1884–1962. US social worker, lecturer and First Lady; her newspaper column "My Day" was widely syndicated. She was a delegate to the UN general assembly and later chair of the UN commission on human rights 1946–51. She helped to draw up the Declaration of Human Rights at the UN 1945. Within the Democratic Party she formed the left-wing Americans for Democratic Action group 1947. She was married to President Franklin Roosevelt.

The niece of Theodore ◊Roosevelt, she was educated in Europe. Following her husband's death 1945, she continued to work on civil rights for US blacks and for human rights worldwide.

Roosevelt Franklin Delano 1882–1945. The 32nd president of the US 1933–45, a Democrat. He served as governor of New York 1929–33. Becoming president amid the ◊Depression, he launched the ◊New Deal economic and social reform program, which made him popular with the people. After the outbreak of World War II he introduced ◊Lend-Lease for the supply of war materials and services to the Allies and drew up the ◊Atlantic Charter of solidarity. Once the US had entered the war 1941 he spent much time in meetings with Allied leaders (see ◊Québec, ◊Tehran, and ◊Yalta conferences).

Born in Hyde Park, New York, of a wealthy family, Roosevelt was educated in Europe and at Harvard and Columbia universities, and became a lawyer. In 1910 he was elected to the New York state senate. He held the assistant secretaryship of the navy in Wilson's administrations 1913–21, and did much to increase the efficiency of the navy during World War I. He suffered from polio from 1921 but returned to politics, winning the governorship of New York State in 1929. When he first became president 1933, Roosevelt inculcated a new spirit of hope by his skillful "fireside chats" on the radio and his inaugural-address statement: "The only thing we have to fear is fear itself." Surrounding himself by a "◊Brain Trust" of experts, he immediately launched his reform program. Banks were reopened, federal credit was restored, the gold standard was abandoned, and the dollar devalued. During the first hundred days of his administration, major legislation to facilitate industrial and agricultural recovery was enacted. In 1935 he introduced the Utilities Act, directed against abuses in the large holding companies, and the ◊Social Security Act, providing for disability and retirement insurance. The presidential election 1936 was won entirely on the record of the New Deal. During 1935–36 Roosevelt was involved in a long conflict over the composition of the Supreme Court, following its nullification of major New Deal measures as unconstitutional. In 1938 he introduced measures for farm relief and the improvement of working conditions.

In his foreign policy, Roosevelt endeavored to use his influence to restrain Axis aggression, and to establish "good neighbor" relations with other countries in the Americas. Soon after the outbreak of war, he launched a vast rearmament program, introduced conscription, and provided for the supply of armaments to the Allies on a "cash-and-carry" basis. In spite of strong isolationist opposition, he broke a long-standing precedent in running for a third term, he was reelected 1940. He announced that the US would become the "arsenal of democracy." Roosevelt was eager for US entry into the war on behalf of the Allies. In addition to his revulsion for Hitler, he wanted to establish the US as a world power, filling the vacuum he expected to be left by the breakup of the British Empire. He was restrained by isolationist forces in Congress, and some argued that he welcomed the Japanese attack on Pearl Harbor.

The slaughter at Pearl Harbor Dec 7, 1941 incited public opinion, and the US entered the war. From this point on, Roosevelt concerned himself solely with the conduct of the war. He participated in the Washington 1942 and ◊Casablanca 1943 conferences to plan the Mediterranean assault, and the conferences in Québec, Cairo, and Tehran 1943, and Yalta 1945, at which the final preparations were made for the Allied victory. He was reelected for a fourth term 1944, but died 1945.

BLUE
CBS

Roosevelt *The 32nd president of the United States of America, Franklin Delano Roosevelt, a Democrat. 1933–1945.*

Roosevelt Theodore 1858–1919. the 26th president of the US 1901–09, a Republican. After serving as governor of New York 1898–1900 he became vice-president to ◊McKinley whom he succeeded as president on McKinley's assassination 1901. He campaigned against the great trusts (combines that reduce competition), while carrying on a jingoist foreign policy designed to enforce US supremacy over Latin America.

Roosevelt, born in New York, was elected to the state legislature 1881. He was assistant secretary of the Navy 1897–98, and during the Spanish-American War 1898 commanded a volunteer force of "rough riders." At age 42, Roosevelt was the youngest man to become president of the US. In office he became more liberal. He tackled business monopolies, initiated measures for the conservation of national resources, and introduced the Pure Food and Drug Act. He won the Nobel Peace Prize 1906 for his part in ending the Russo-Japanese war. Alienated after his retirement by the conservatism of his successor Taft, Roosevelt formed the Progressive or "Bull Moose" Party. As their candidate he unsuccessfully ran for the presidency 1912. During World War I he strongly advocated US intervention.

root the part of a plant that is usually underground, and whose primary functions are anchorage and the absorption of water and dissolved mineral

Roosevelt *The 26th president of the United States of America, Theodore Roosevelt, a Republican. 1901–1909.*

salts. Roots usually grow downward and toward water (that is, they are positively geotropic and hydrotropic; see ◊tropism). Plants, such as epiphytic orchids that grow above ground, produce aerial roots that absorb moisture from the atmosphere. Others, such as ivy, have climbing roots arising from the stems that serve to attach the plant to trees and walls.

The absorptive area of roots is greatly increased by the numerous, slender root hairs formed near the tips. A calyptra, or root cap, protects the tip of the root from abrasion as it grows through the soil.

Symbiotic associations occur between the roots of certain plants, such as clover, and various bacteria that fix nitrogen from the air (see ◊nitrogen fixation). Other modifications of roots include ◊contractile roots, ◊pneumatophores, ◊taproots, and ◊prop roots.

root in mathematics, another name for ◊square root; also any solution to a mathematical equation.

root crop ambiguous term for several different types of crop; in agriculture, it refers to turnips, rutabagas, and beets, which are actually enlarged hypocotyls and contain little root, whereas in trade statistics it refers to the tubers of potatoes, cassava, and yams. Roots have a high carbohydrate content, but their protein content rarely exceeds 2%. Consequently, communities relying almost exclusively upon roots may suffer from protein deficiency. Potatoes, cassava, and yams are second in importance only to cereals as human food. Food production for a given area from roots is greater than from cereals.

In the mid-1980s, world production of potatoes, cassava, and yams was just under 600 million tons. Potatoes are the major temperate root crop; the major tropical root crops are cassava (a shrub that produces starchy tubers), yams, and sweet potatoes. Root crops are also used as animal feed, and may be processed to produce starch, glue, and alcohol.

root hair tubular outgrowth from a cell on the surface of a plant root. It is a delicate structure, which survives for a few days only and does not develop into a root. New root hairs are continually being formed near the root tip to replace the ones that are lost. The majority of land plants possess root hairs, which greatly increase the surface area available for the absorption of water and mineral salts from the soil. The layer of the root's epidermis that produces root hairs is known as the piliferous layer.

root-mean-square (RMS) value obtained by taking the square root of the mean (average) of the squares of a set of values; for example the RMS value of four quantities a, b, c, and d is

$$\sqrt{[(a^2 + b^2 + c^2 + d^2)/4]}.$$

For an alternating current (AC), the RMS value is equal to the peak value divided by the square root of 2.

roots music or ***world music*** term originally denoting ◊reggae, later encompassing any music indigenous to a particular culture. Examples are W African *mbalax*, E African *soukous*, S African *mbaqanga*, French Antillean *zouk*, Javanese gamelan, Latin American salsa, Cajun music, and European folk music.

root

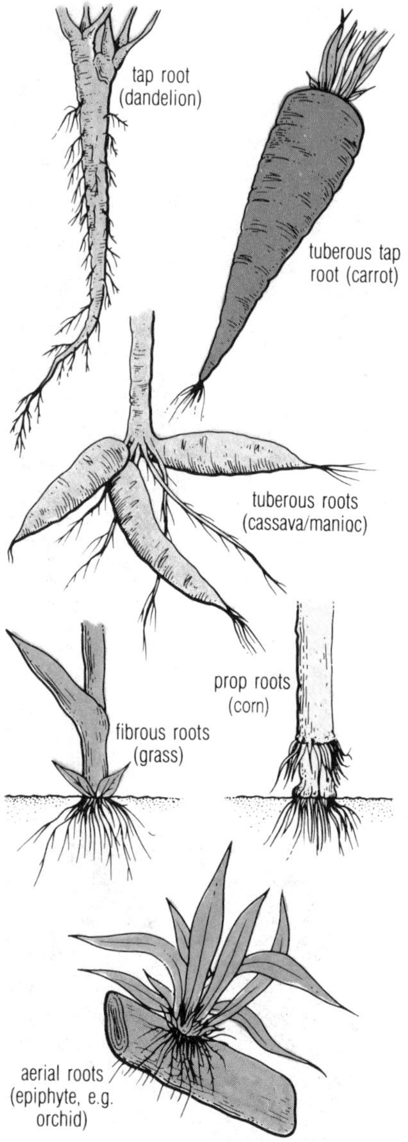

tap root (dandelion)
tuberous tap root (carrot)
tuberous roots (cassava/manioc)
prop roots (corn)
fibrous roots (grass)
aerial roots (epiphyte, e.g. orchid)

rope stout cordage with circumference over 1 in/2.5 cm. Rope is made similarly to thread or twine, by twisting yarns together to form strands, which are then in turn twisted around one another in the direction opposite to that of the yarns. Although ◊hemp is still used to make rope, nylon is increasingly used.

Roquefort a strong cheese made of sheep's and goats' milk and matured in caves, named after the village of Roquefort-sur-Soulzon in Aveyron *département*, France (population about 880).

Roraima, Mount plateau in the ◊Pacaraima range in South America, rising to 9,432 ft/2,875 m on the Brazil–Guyana–Venezuela frontier.

rorqual any of a family (Balenopteridae) of baleen whales, especially the genus *Balenoptera*, which includes the blue whale *B. musculus*, the largest of all animals, measuring 100 ft/30 m and more. The common rorqual or fin whale *B. physalus* is slate-colored and not quite so long.

The sei whale *B. borealis*, the minke whale *B. acutorostrata*, Bryde's whale *B. edeni*, and the humpbacked whale *Megaptera novaeangliae* also belong here. All are long-bodied whales with pleated throats.

Rorschach test in psychology, method of diagnosis involving the use of inkblot patterns that subjects are asked to interpret, to help indicate personality type, degree of intelligence, and emotional stability. It was invented by the Swiss psychiatrist Hermann Rorschach (1884–1922).

Rosa Salvator 1615–1673. Italian painter, etcher, poet, and musician, active in Florence 1640–49 and subsequently in Rome. He created wild, romantic, and sometimes macabre landscapes, seascapes, and battle scenes. He also wrote verse satires.

Born near Naples, Rosa spent much of his youth traveling in S Italy. He first settled in Rome in 1639 and established himself as a landscape painter. In Florence he worked for the ruling Medici family.

Rosario industrial river port (sugar refining, meat packing, maté processing) in Argentina, 175 mi/ 280 km NW of Buenos Aires, on the river Paraná; population (1980) 955,000. It was founded 1725.

rosary string of beads used in a number of religions, including Buddhism, Christianity, and Islam. The term also refers to a form of prayer used by Catholics, consisting of 150 ◊Ave Marias and 15 ◊Paternosters and Glorias, or to a string of 165 beads for keeping count of these prayers; it is linked with the adoration of the Virgin Mary.

Roscellinus Johannes c. 1050–c. 1122. Philosopher regarded as the founder of ◊scholasticism because of his defense of ◊nominalism (the idea that classes of things are simply names and have no objective reality) against ◊Anselm.

Roscius Gallus Quintus c. 126–62 BC. Roman actor, originally a slave, so gifted that his name became a byword for a great actor.

Roscoff port on the Brittany coast of France with a ferry link to Plymouth in England; population (1982) 4,000.

Roscommon (originally Ros-Comain, "wood around a monastery") county of the Republic of Ireland in the province of Connacht.

area 950 sq mi/2,460 sq km

towns county town Roscommon

physical bounded on the E by the river Shannon; lakes: Gara, Key, Allen; rich pastures

features remains of a castle put up in the 13th century by English settlers

population (1986) 55,000

rose any shrub or climber of the genus *Rosa*, family Rosaceae, with prickly stems and five-parted, fragrant flowers in many different colors. Numerous cultivated forms have been derived from the Eurasian sweetbrier or eglantine *R. rubiginosa* and dogrose *R. canina*. There are many climbing varieties, but the forms more commonly cultivated are bush roses and standards (cultivated roses grafted on to a brier stem).

Roseau formerly ***Charlotte Town*** capital of ◊Dominica, West Indies; population (1981) 20,000.

Rosebery Archibald Philip Primrose, 5th Earl of 1847–1929. British Liberal politician. He was

rose

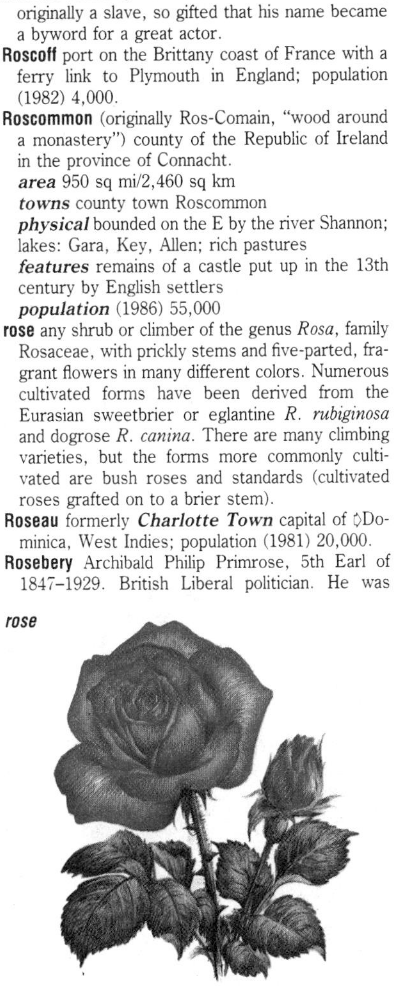

rosemary

foreign secretary 1886 and 1892–94, when he succeeded Gladstone as prime minister, but his government survived less than a year. After 1896 his imperialist views gradually placed him further from the mainstream of the Liberal Party.

Roseirs port at the head of navigation of the Blue Nile in Sudan. A hydroelectric scheme here provides the country with 70% of its electrical power.

rosemary evergreen shrub *Rosemarinus officinalis* of the mint family Labiatae, native to the Mediterranean and W Asia, with small, scented leaves. It is widely cultivated as a culinary herb and for the aromatic oil extracted from the clusters of pale purple flowers.

Rosenberg Alfred 1893–1946. German politician, born in Tallinn, Estonia. He became the chief Nazi ideologist and was minister for eastern occupied territories 1941–44. He was tried at ◊Nuremberg 1946 as a war criminal and hanged.

Rosenberg Julius 1918–53 and Ethel Greenglass 1915–53 US married couple, convicted of being leaders of a nuclear-espionage ring passing information from Ethel's brother via courier to the USSR. The Rosenbergs were executed after much public controversy and demonstration. They were the only Americans executed for espionage during peacetime.

Both were born in New York City; Julius owned a radio repair shop and was a member of the Communist Party. Despite an offer of clemency from the government, they both maintained their innocence right up to their executions. Other implicated Party members received long prison terms. The ◊Cold War atmosphere was one of widespread fear of the Soviet Union, and several major spy scandals had occurred at this time. The death penalty was ruled as justified because of the danger to the US from their actions. Recently published journals kept by ◊Khruschev further implicate the Rosenbergs.

Roses, Wars of the name given in the 19th century by novelist Walter Scott to civil wars in England 1455–85 between the houses of ◊Lancaster (badge, red rose) and ◊York (badge, white rose), both of whom claimed the throne through descent from the sons of Edward III. As a result of ◊Henry VI's lapse into insanity, Richard, Duke of York, was installed as protector of the realm. Upon his recovery, Henry forced York to take up arms in self-defense.

1455 Opened with battle of St Albans on May 22, a Yorkist victory (Henry VI taken prisoner). Four-year truce followed.

1459–61 War renewed until ◊Edward IV, son of York, having become king, confirmed his position by a victory at Towton on March 29, 1461. Henry, Margaret (his queen), and his son Edward fled.

1470 Civil war erupted within Yorkist ranks. ◊Warwick (who had helped Edward to the throne) allied with Henry's widow, Margaret, and deposed Edward, restoring Henry VI to the throne.

1471 Edward returned, defeated Warwick, April 14, and regained crown. May 4, Margaret was captured, her son killed, and her forces destroyed. Henry VI was murdered in the Tower of London.

1485 Yorkist rule ended with the defeat of ◊Richard III by the future ◊Henry VII at ◊Bosworth 22 Aug.

Rose Theatre former London theater near Southwark Bridge where many of Shakespeare's plays were performed. The excavation and preservation of the remains of the theater, discovered in 1989, caused controversy between government bodies and archeologists.

It was built in 1587 by the impresario Philip Henslowe (c. 1550–1616), who managed it to 1603; the theater was the site of the first performances of Shakespeare's plays *Henry VI* and *Titus Andronicus*.

Rosetta Stone slab of basalt with inscriptions from 197 BC, found near the town of Rosetta, Egypt, 1799. Giving the same text in three versions—Greek, hieroglyphic, and demotic script—it became the key to deciphering other Egyptian inscriptions.

Discovered during the French Revolutionary Wars by one of Napoleon's officers in the town now called Rashid, in the Nile delta, the Rosetta Stone was captured by the British 1801, and placed in the British Museum 1802. Demotic is a cursive script (for quick writing) derived from Egyptian hieratic, which in turn is a more easily written form of ◊hieroglyphic.

Rosh Hashanah two-day vacation that marks the start of the Jewish New Year (first new moon after the autumn equinox), traditionally announced by blowing a ram's horn (◊shofar).

Rosicrucians group of early 17th-century philosophers who claimed occult powers and employed the terminology of ◊alchemy to expound their mystical doctrines (said to derive from ◊Paracelsus). The name comes from books published in 1614 and 1615, attributed to Christian Rosenkreutz ("rosy cross"), most probably a pen name but allegedly a writer living around 1460. Several societies have been founded in Britain and the US that claim to be their successors, such as the Rosicrucian Fraternity (1614 in Germany, 1861 in the US).

Ross Betsy 1752–1836. American seamstress remembered as the maker of the first US flag. Born Elizabeth Griscom in Philadelphia to a devout Quaker family, she married upholsterer John Ross 1773. Upon his death 1776, she took over his business. According to popular legend, Ross was approached in June 1776 by family acquaintance George Washington to create an official flag for the new nation. Despite little historical substantiation, it is believed by many that the familiar red and white stripes with white stars on a field of blue was Ross's original concept. Becoming famous after the war, she continued in the upholstery business until her retirement 1827.

Ross James Clark 1800–1862. English explorer who discovered the magnetic North Pole 1831. He also went to the Antarctic 1839; Ross Island, Ross Sea, and Ross Dependency are named after him.

He is associated with ◊Parry and his uncle John Ross in Arctic exploration.

Ross John 1777–1856. Scottish rear admiral and explorer. He served in wars with France and made voyages of Arctic exploration in 1818, 1829–33, and 1850.

Ross Ronald 1857–1932. British physician and bacteriologist, born in India. From 1881 to 1899 he served in the Indian medical service, and during 1895–98 identified mosquitoes of the genus *Anopheles* as being responsible for the spread of malaria. Nobel Prize 1902.

Ross Dependency all the Antarctic islands and territories between 160° E and 150° W longitude and S of 60° S latitude; it includes Edward VII Land, Ross Sea and its islands, and parts of Victoria Land

Rosetta Stone *The Rosetta Stone, discovered in 1799 with inscriptions dating from 197 BC, provided the key to understanding Egyptian hieroglyphics.*

area 173,700 sq mi/450,000 sq km

features the Ross Ice Shelf (or Ross Barrier), a permanent layer of ice across the Ross Sea about 1,400 ft/425 m thick

population a few scientific bases with about 250 staff members, 12 of whom are present during winter

history given to New Zealand 1923. It is probable that marine organisms beneath the ice shelf had been undisturbed from the Pleistocene period until drillings were made 1976.

Rossellini Roberto 1906–1977. Italian film director. His World War II trilogy of films, *Roma città aperta/Rome, Open City* 1945, *Paisà/Paisan* 1946, and *Germania anno zero/Germany Year Zero* 1947, are considered landmarks in postwar European cinema.

In 1949 he made *Stromboli*, followed by other films in which his wife Ingrid Bergman appeared. After their divorce he made *General della Rovere* 1959 and embarked on television work including a feature-length film for French TV *La Prise de Pouvoir par Louis XIV/The Rise of Louis XIV* 1966.

Rossetti Christina (Georgina) 1830–1894. English poet, sister of Dante Rossetti and a devout High Anglican (see ◊Oxford movement). Her verse includes *Goblin Market and Other Poems* 1862 and expresses unfulfilled spiritual yearning and frustrated love. She was a skillful technician and made use of irregular rhyme and line length.

Rossetti Dante Gabriel 1828–1882. British painter and poet, a founding member of the ◊Pre-Raphaelite Brotherhood (PRB) in 1848. As well as romantic medieval scenes, he produced many idealized portraits of women. His verse includes "The Blessed Damozel" 1850. His sister was the poet Christina Rossetti.

Rosetti was a friend of the critic Ruskin, who helped establish his reputation as a painter, and of William Morris and his wife Jane, who became Rosetti's lover and the subject of much of his work.

Rossini Gioachino (Antonio) 1792–1868. Italian composer. His first success was the opera *Tancredi* 1813. In 1816 his "opera buffa" *Il barbiere di Siviglia/The Barber of Seville* was produced in Rome. During his fertile composition period 1815–23 he produced 20 operas, and created (with ◊Donizetti and ◊Bellini) the 19th-century Italian operatic style. After *Guillaume Tell/William Tell* 1829 he gave up writing opera and his later years were spent in Bologna and Paris.

Rossetti *Poet and painter Dante Gabriel Rossetti was a central figure in the Pre-Raphaelite movement.*

Among the works of this period are the *Stabat Mater* 1842 and the piano music arranged for ballet by ◊Respighi as *La Boutique fantasque/The Fantastic Toyshop* 1919.

Ross Island two islands in Antarctica:

Ross Island in Weddell Sea, discovered 1903 by the Swedish explorer Nordenskjöld, area about 1,500 sq mi/3,885 sq km;

Ross Island in Ross Sea, discovered 1841 by the British explorer James Ross, area about 2,500 sq mi/6,475 sq km, with the research stations Roos (New Zealand) and McMurdo (US). Mount Erebus (12,520 ft/3,794 m) is the world's southernmost active volcano; its lake of molten lava may provide a window on the ◊magma beneath the Earth's crust that fuels volcanoes.

Ross Sea Antarctic inlet of the S Pacific. See also ◊Ross Dependency and ◊Ross Island.

Rostand Edmond 1869–1918. French dramatist, who wrote *Cyrano de Bergerac* 1897 and *L'Aiglon* 1900 (based on the life of Napoleon III), in which Sarah Bernhardt played a leading role.

Rostock industrial port (electronics, fish processing, ship repair) in the state of Mecklenberg–West Pomerania, Federal Republic of Germany, on the river Warnow 8 mi/13 km S of the Baltic; population (1990) 250,000.

Founded 1189. In the 14th century Rostock became a powerful member of the ◊Hanseatic League. It was rebuilt in the 1950s and was capital of an East German district of the same name 1952–90.

Rostov-on-Don industrial port (shipbuilding, tobacco, automobiles, locomotives, textiles) in SW USSR, capital of Rostov region, on the river Don, 14 mi/23 km E of the Sea of Azov; population (1987) 1,004,000. Rostov dates from 1761 and is linked by river and canal with Volgograd on the Volga.

Rostropovich Mstislav 1927– . Russian cellist and conductor, deprived of Soviet citizenship in 1978 because of his sympathies with political dissidents. Prokofiev, Shostakovich, Khachaturian, and Britten wrote pieces for him. Since 1977 he has directed the National Symphony Orchestra, Washington, DC.

Rotary Club philanthropic society of business and professional people; founded by US lawyer Paul Harris (1878–1947) in Chicago 1905. It is now international, with some 750,000 members.

Roth Philip 1933– . US novelist whose portrayals of 20th-century Jewish-American life include *Goodbye Columbus* 1959 and *Portnoy's Complaint* 1969. His series of semiautobiographical novels about a writer, Nathan Zuckerman, includes *The Ghost Writer* 1979, *Zuckerman Unbound* 1981, *The Anatomy Lesson* 1984, and *The Counterlife* 1987. Psychosexual themes are prominent in his work. His *Patrimony* 1991 concerned his father's death.

Rothamsted agricultural research center in Hertfordshire, England, NW of St Albans.

Rothko Mark 1903–1970. Russian-born US painter, an Abstract Expressionist and a pioneer of Colour Field painting (abstract, dominated by areas of unmodulated, strong color). Rothko produced several series of paintings in the 1950s and 1960s, including one at Harvard University; one in the Tate Gallery, London; and one for a chapel in Houston, Texas, 1967–69.

He received his only training at New York City's Art Students League. During the 1930s he painted for the Federal Arts Project and, with Adolph Gottlieb, founded the expressionist group The Ten.

After his suicide 1970, his estate, consisting

primarily of a huge number of his paintings, became the subject of a long legal battle.

Rothschild German merchant banking family that began with Mayer Amschel (1744–1812) in Frankfurt-am-Main. His moneylending business expanded during the Napoleonic Wars at a time when loans were made to the various combatants and trade was established in goods in high demand, such as arms, cotton, and wheat. He was succeeded by his son Amschel Mayer (1773–1885) in Frankfurt. Four other sons went to the major European capitals to set up branches: Vienna, Salomon Mayer (1774–1855); London, Nathan Mayer (1777–1836); Paris, James Jakob (1792–1868); and Naples, Karl Mayer (1788–1855).

rotifer any of the tiny invertebrates, also called "wheel animalcules," of the phylum Rotifera. Mainly freshwater, some marine, rotifers have a ring of cilia that carries food to the mouth and also provides propulsion. Smallest of multicellular animals, few reach 0.02 in/0.05 cm.

Rotterdam industrial port (brewing, distilling, shipbuilding, sugar and petroleum refining, margarine, tobacco) in the Netherlands and one of the foremost ocean cargo ports in the world, in the Rhine-Maas delta, linked by canal 1866–90 with the North Sea; population (1988) 1,036,000.

Rotterdam dates from the 12th century or earlier, but the center was destroyed by German air attack 1940, and rebuilt; its notable art collections were saved. The philosopher Erasmus was born here.

Rottweiler breed of guard dog originating from Rottweil in S Germany. Large and powerful, up to 28 in/70 cm tall, it needs regular exercise, and has not proved successful as a pet. In Britain during the 1980s there were several cases of Rottweilers savaging young children.

Rouault Georges 1871–1958. French painter, etcher, illustrator, and designer. Early in his career he was associated with the ◊Fauves but created his own style using heavy, dark colors and bold brushwork. His subjects included sad clowns, prostitutes, and evil lawyers; from about 1940 he painted mainly religious works.

Rouault was born in Paris, the son of a cabinetmaker. He was apprenticed to a stained-glassmaker; later he studied under the Symbolist painter Gustave Moreau and became curator of Moreau's studio. *The Prostitute* 1906 (Musée Nationale d'Art Moderne, Paris) and *The Face of Christ* 1933 (Musée des Beaux-Arts, Ghent, Belgium) represent extremes of Rouault's painting style. He also produced illustrations and designed tapestries, stained glass, and sets for Diaghilev's Ballets Russes, and in 1948 he published a series of etchings entitled *Miserere*.

Roubaix town in Nord-Pay-de-Calais, N France, adjacent to Lille; population (1982) 102,000; major center of French woolen textile production.

Roubiliac or ***Roubillac*** Louis François c. 1705–1762. French sculptor, a Huguenot who fled religious persecution to settle in England 1732. He became a leading sculptor of the day, creating a statue of Handel for Vauxhall Gardens 1737 (Victoria and Albert Museum, London).

He also produced lively statues of historic figures, such as Newton, and an outstanding funerary monument, the *Tomb of Lady Elizabeth Nightingale* 1761 (Westminster Abbey, London).

Rouen industrial port (cotton textiles, electronics, distilling, oil refining) on the river Seine, capital of Haute-Normandie, NW France; population (1982) 380,000. Rouen was capital of ◊Normandy from 912. Lost by King ◊John 1204, it returned briefly to English possession 1419–49; Joan of Arc was burned in the square 1431. The novelist Flaubert was born here, and the hospital where his father was chief surgeon is now a Flaubert museum.

Rouget de Lisle Claude-Joseph 1760–1836. French army officer who composed, while in Strasbourg 1792, the "Marseillaise," the French national anthem.

roughage or ***dietary fiber*** part of the diet that is indigestible, consisting mostly of cellulose from plant cell walls. Roughage adds bulk to the intestinal contents, assisting the process of peristalsis, the muscular contractions forcing the food along the intestine. A high roughage content is believed to have several beneficial effects, including reduced cancer risks, since it helps more waste along quickly so that toxins and carcinogens have a reduced chance of initiating abnormal cell division.

roulette game of chance in which the players bet on a ball landing in the correct segment (numbered 0–36 and alternately colored red and black) on a rotating wheel.

Bets can be made on a single number, double numbers, 3, 4, 6, 8, 12, or 24 numbers. Naturally the odds are reduced the more numbers are selected. Bets can also be made on the number being odd or even, between 1 and 18 or 19 and 36, or being red or black. The odds are even in each of those cases, however, the advantage is with the banker, because the (zero) 0 gives all stakes to the bank unless a player bets on 0. The play is under the control of a croupier.

Roundhead member of the Parliamentary party during the English Civil War 1640–60, opposing the royalist Cavaliers. The term referred to the short hair then worn only by men of the lower classes.

roup contagious respiratory disease of poultry and game birds. It is characterized by swelling of the head and purulent catarrh.

Rousseau Henri "Le Douanier" 1844–1910. French painter, a self-taught naive artist. His subjects included scenes of the Parisian suburbs and exotic junglescapes, painted with painstaking detail, for example *Surprised! Tropical Storm with a Tiger* 1891 (National Gallery, London).

Rousseau served in the army for some years, then became a toll collector (hence *Le Douanier*, "the customs official"), and took up full-time painting in 1885. He exhibited at the Salon des Indépendants from 1886 to 1910 and was associated with the group led by Picasso and the poet Apollinaire, but his position was unique. As a naive and pompous person, he was considered ridiculous, yet admired for his inimitable style.

Rousseau Jean-Jacques 1712–1778. French social philosopher and writer, born in Geneva, Switzerland. *Discourses on the Origins of Inequality* 1754 made his name: he denounced civilized society and postulated the paradox of the superiority of the "noble savage." *Social Contract* 1762 emphasized the rights of the people over those of the government, and stated that a government could be legitimately overthrown if it failed to express the general will of the people. It was a significant influence on the French Revolution. In the novel *Emile* 1762 he outlined a new theory of education, based on natural development and the power of example, to elicit the unspoiled nature and abilities of children. *Confessions*, published posthumously 1782, was a frank account of his occasionally immoral life and was a founding work of autobiography.

Rousseau *French author Jean-Jacques Rousseau, whose writings struck fear into despotic governments throughout 18th-century Europe.*

rowan

Rousseau (Etienne-Pierre) Théodore 1812–1867. French landscape painter of the ◊Barbizon School. Born in Paris, he came under the influence of the British landscape painters Constable and Bonington, sketched from nature in many parts of France, and settled in Barbizon in 1848.

Rovaniemi capital of Lappi province, N Finland, and chief town of Finnish Lapland, situated just south of the Arctic Circle; population (1986) 32,769. After World War II the town was rebuilt by the architect Alvar Aalto, who laid out the main streets in the form of a reindeer's antlers.

rowan another name for the European ◊mountain ash tree.

Rowbotham Sheila 1943– . British Socialist, feminist, historian, lecturer, and writer. Her pamphlet *Women's Liberation and the New Politics* 1970 laid down fundamental approaches and demands of the emerging women's movement.

rowing propulsion of a boat by oars, either by one rower with two oars (sculling) or by crews (two, four, or eight persons) with one oar each, often with a coxswain.

Doggett's Coat and Badge 1715, begun for Thames watermen and also the first English race, still survives. Rowing as a sport began with the English Leander Club 1817, followed by the Castle Garden boat club, 1834. Major events include the world championship, first held in 1962 for men and 1974 for women, and the Boat Race, first held in 1829.

In the US the Harvard–Yale boat race is held on the Thames at New London, Connecticut, and national championships are held annually.

Rowling Wallace "Bill" 1927– . New Zealand Labour politician, party leader 1969–75, prime minister 1974–75.

Rowse A(lfred) L(eslie) 1903– . English popular historian. He published a biography of Shakespeare 1963, and in 1973 controversially identified the "Dark Lady" of Shakespeare's sonnets as Emilia Lanier, half-Italian daughter of a court musician, with whom the Bard is alleged to have had an affair 1593–95.

Royal Ballet title under which the British Sadler's Wells Ballet (at Covent Garden), Sadler's Wells Theatre Ballet, and the Sadler's Wells Ballet School were incorporated 1956.

Royal Botanic Gardens, Kew botanic gardens in Richmond, Surrey, England, popularly known as ◊Kew Gardens.

Royal Canadian Mounted Police (RCMP) Canadian national police force, known as the ◊Mounties.

Royal Greenwich Observatory the national astronomical observatory of the UK, founded 1675 at Greenwich, E London, England, to provide navigational information for sailors. After World

War II it was moved to Herstmonceux Castle, Sussex; in 1990 it was transferred to Cambridge. It also operates telescopes on La Palma in the Canary Islands, including the 165-in/4.2-m William Herschel Telescope, commissioned 1987.

The observatory was founded by King Charles II. The eminence of its work resulted in Greenwich Time's and the Greenwich Meridian's being adopted as international standards of reference 1884.

Royal Shakespeare Company (RSC) British professional theater company that performs Shakespearean and other plays. It was founded 1961 from the company at the Shakespeare Memorial Theatre 1932 (now the Royal Shakespeare Theatre) in Stratford-upon-Avon, Warwickshire, England.

Royal Society oldest and premier scientific society in Britain, originating 1645 and chartered 1660; Christopher ◊Wren and Isaac ◊Newton were prominent early members. Its Scottish equivalent is the Royal Society of Edinburgh 1783.

royalty in law, payment to the owner for rights to use or exploit literary or artistic copyrights and patent rights in new inventions of all kinds.

Oil, gas, and other mineral deposits are also subject to royalty payments.

Royce (Frederick) Henry 1863–1933. British engineer, who so impressed Charles ◊Rolls by the car he built for his own personal use 1904 that ◊Rolls-Royce Ltd was formed 1906 to produce automobiles and engines.

Royce Josiah 1855–1916. US idealist philosopher who in *The Conception of God* 1895 and *The Conception of Immortality* 1900 interpreted Christianity in philosophical terms.

Born in Grass Valley, California, Royce taught at the University of California and Harvard University. His philosophy saw God as cosmic purpose, which man embraces.

RPI abbreviation for retail price index; see ◊cost of living.

rpm abbreviation for revolutions per minute.

RSFSR abbreviation for ◊Russian Soviet Federal Socialist Republic, the largest constituent republic of the USSR.

RSVP abbreviation for *répondez s'il vous plaît* (French "please reply").

Ruanda alternate spelling of ◊Rwanda, country in central Africa.

Ruapehu volcano in New Zealand, SW of Lake Taupo; the highest peak in North Island, 9,175 ft/ 2,797 m.

Rub' al Khali (Arabic "empty quarter") vast sandy desert in S Saudi Arabia; area 250,000 sq mi/ 650,000 sq km. The British explorer Bertram Thomas (1892–1950) was the first European to cross it 1930–31.

rubber coagulated latex of a variety of plants, mainly from the New World. Most important is Para rubber, which derives from the tree *Hevea brasiliensis* of the spurge family. It was introduced from Brazil to SE Asia, where most of the world supply is now produced, the chief exporters being Malaysia, Indonesia, Sri Lanka, Cambodia, Thailand, Sarawak, and Brunei. At about seven years the tree, which may grow to 60 ft/20 m, is ready for "tapping." Small incisions are made in the trunk and the latex drips into collecting cups. In pure form, rubber is white and has the formula $(C_5H_8)_n$.

Other sources of rubber are the Russian dandelion *Taraxacum koksagyz*, which grows in temperate climates and can yield about 90 lb/40 kg of rubber per ton of roots, and guayule *Parthenium argentatum*, a small shrub of the compositae family, which grows in SW US and Mexico.

In the 20th century, world production of rubber has increased a hundredfold, and World War II stimulated the production of synthetic rubber to replace the supplies from Malaysian sources overrun by the Japanese. There are an infinite variety of synthetic rubbers adapted to special purposes, but economically foremost is SBR (styrene-butadene rubber). Cheaper than natural rubber, it is

***Rubens** Peter Paul Rubens was court painter in Antwerp, when he painted* Descent from the Cross *1611–14 for the Antwerp Cathedral.*

preferable for some purposes; for example, on car tires, where its higher abrasion-resistance is useful, and it is either blended with natural rubber or used alone for industrial molding and extrusions, shoe soles, hoses, and latex foam.

A synthetic "antirubber" was discovered in the US 1988. It expands when stretched and thins when squeezed, because of its microscopic structure, and can be used to repair cracks.

rubber another name for a ◊condom.

rubber plant Asiatic tree *Ficus elastica* of the mulberry family Moraceae, producing latex in its stem. With shiny, leathery, oval leaves, young plants are grown as house plants.

rubella technical term for ◊German measles.

Rubens Peter Paul 1577–1640. Flemish painter who brought the exuberance of Italian Baroque to N Europe, creating, with an army of assistants, innumerable religious and allegorical paintings for churches and palaces. These show mastery of drama in large compositions, and love of rich color. He also painted portraits and, in his last years, landscapes.

Rubens entered the Antwerp painters' guild 1598 and went to Italy in 1600, studying artists of the High Renaissance. In 1603 he visited Spain and in Madrid painted many portraits of the Spanish nobility. From 1604 to 1608 he was in Italy again, and in 1609 he settled in Antwerp and was appointed court painter to the archduke Albert and his wife Isabella. His *Raising of the Cross* 1610 and *Descent from the Cross* 1611–14, both in Antwerp Cathedral, show his brilliant painterly style. He went to France 1620, commissioned by the regent Marie de Médici to produce a cycle of 21 enormous canvases allegorizing her life (Louvre, Paris). In 1628 he again went to Madrid, where he met the painter Velázquez. In 1629–30 when he was diplomatic envoy to Charles I in London, he painted the ceiling of the Banqueting House in Whitehall.

Rubens's portraits range from intimate pictures of his second wife, such as *Hélène Fourment in a Fur Wrap* about 1638 (Kunsthistorisches Museum, Vienna), to dozens of portraits of royalty.

Rubicon ancient name of the small river flowing into the Adriatic that, under the Roman Republic, marked the boundary between Italy proper and Cisalpine Gaul. When ◊Caesar led his army across it 49 BC he therefore declared war on the Roman Republic (as Pompey had formed an army against him, thus beginning the civil war); hence to "cross the Rubicon" means to take an irrevocable step. It is believed to be the present-day Fiumicino, which rises in the Etruscan Apennines 10 mi/ 16 km WNW of San Marino and enters the Adriatic 10 mi/16 km NW of Rimini.

rubidium soft, silver-white, metallic element, symbol Rb, atomic number 37, atomic weight 85.47. It is one of the ◊alkali metals, ignites spontaneously in air, and reacts violently with water. It is used in photoelectric cells and vacuum-tube filaments.

Rubidium was discovered spectroscopically by Robert Bunsen and Gustav Kirchhoff in 1861, and named after Latin *rubidus*, "red," for the red lines in its spectrum.

Rubik Erno 1944– . Hungarian architect who invented the Rubik cube, a multicolored puzzle that can be manipulated and rearranged in only one correct way, but about 43 trillion wrong ones. Intended to help his students understand three-dimensional design, it became a fad that swept around the world.

Rubinstein Artur 1887–1982. Polish-born US pianist. He studied in Warsaw and Berlin and for 85 of his 95 years appeared with the world's major symphony orchestras, specializing in the music of Mozart, Chopin, Debussy, and the Spanish composers. He appeared in the US in 1906 and 1919, but it was not until a concert at Carnegie Hall 1937 that he was hailed as a genius in the US. He and his family emigrated to the US in the 1940s, and he became a citizen in 1946. Considered by many to be the greatest 20th-century piano virtuoso, he played with an intellectual and commanding tone, appeared in films, and made many distinctive recordings.

Rubinstein Helena 1882–1965. Polish-born cosmetics tycoon, who emigrated to Australia 1902, where she started a cosmetics business. She moved to Europe 1904 and later to the US, opening salons in London, Paris, and New York.

Rublev or ***Rublyov*** c. 1360–1430. Russian icon painter. Only one documented work of his survives, the *Holy Trinity* about 1411 (Tretyakov Gallery, Moscow). This shows a basically Byzantine style, but with a gentler expression.

He is known to have worked with ◊Theophanes the Greek in the Cathedral of the Annunciation in Moscow. In later life Rublev became a monk. The director Tarkovsky made a film of his life 1966.

ruby the red transparent gem variety of the mineral ◊corundum Al_2O_3, aluminum oxide. Small amounts of chromium oxide, Cr_2O_3, substituting for aluminum oxide, give ruby its color. Natural rubies are found mainly in Myanmar (Burma), but rubies can also be produced artificially and such synthetic stones are used in ◊lasers.

Ruda Śląska town in Silesia, Poland, with metallurgical industries, created 1959 by a merger of Ruda and Nowy Butom; population (1984) 163,000. Silesia's oldest mine is nearby.

rudd freshwater fish *Scardinius erythrophthalmus*, a type of minnow, belonging to the carp family (Cypridae), common in lakes and slow rivers of Europe; now introduced in the US. Brownish green above and silvery below, with red fins and golden eyes, it can reach a length of 1.5 ft/45 cm, and a weight of 2.2 lb/1 kgs.

Rude François 1784–1855. French Romantic sculptor. He produced the low-relief scene on the Arc de Triomphe, Paris, showing the capped figure of Liberty leading the revolutionaries (1833, known as *The Volunteers of 1792* or *The Marseillaise*).

Rude was a supporter of Napoleon, along with the painter David, and in 1814 both artists went into exile in Brussels for some years. Rude's other works include a bust of *David* 1831 and the monument *Napoleon Awakening to Immortality* 1854 (both in the Louvre, Paris).

Rudolf former name of Lake ◊Turkana in E Africa.

Rudolph 1858–1889. Crown prince of Austria, the

only son of Emperor Franz Joseph. From an early age he showed progressive views that brought him into conflict with his father. He conceived and helped to write a history of the Austro-Hungarian empire. In 1881, he married Princess Stephanie of Belgium, and they had one daughter, Elizabeth. In 1889 he and his mistress, Baroness Marie Vetsera, were found shot in his hunting lodge at Mayerling, near Vienna. The official verdict was suicide, although there were rumors that it was perpetrated by Jesuits, Hungarian nobles, or the baroness's husband.

Rudolph two Holy Roman emperors:

Rudolph I 1218–1291. Holy Roman emperor from 1273. Originally count of Hapsburg, he was the first Hapsburg emperor and expanded his dynasty by investing his sons with the duchies of Austria and Styria.

Rudolph II 1552–1612. Holy Roman emperor from 1576, when he succeeded his father Maximilian II. His policies led to unrest in Hungary and Bohemia, which led to the surrender of Hungary to his brother Matthias 1608 and religious freedom for Bohemia.

Rudra early Hindu storm god, most of whose attributes were later taken over by ◊Siva.

rue shrubby perennial herb *Ruta graveolens*, family Rutaceae, native to S Europe and temperate Asia. It bears clusters of yellow flowers. An oil extracted from the strongly scented, blue-green leaves is used in perfumery.

ruff bird *Philomachus pugnax* of the sandpiper family (Scolopacidae). The name is taken from the frill of erectile feathers developed in the breeding season around the neck of the male. The ruff is found across N Europe and Asia, and migrates S in winter. It is a casual migrant throughout North America.

Rugby market town and railroad junction in Warwickshire, England; population (1981) 59,500. Rugby School 1567 established its reputation under Thomas ◊Arnold. Rugby football originated here.

rugby contact sport that originated at the Rugby boys' school, England, 1823, when a boy picked up the ball and ran with it while playing soccer. Rugby is played with an oval ball. It is now played in two forms: Rugby League (for professionals) and Rugby Union (for amateurs).

Rügen a Baltic island in the state of Mecklenberg–West Pomerania, Federal Republic of Germany; area 358 sq mi/927 sq km. It is a vacation center, linked by causeway to the mainland; chief town Bergen, main port Sassnitz. As well as tourism there is agriculture and fishing, and chalk is mined. Rügen was annexed by Denmark 1168, Pomerania 1325, Sweden 1648, and Prussia 1815.

Ruhr river in the Federal Republic of Germany; it rises in the Rothaargebirge and flows W to join the Rhine at Duisburg. The Ruhr valley (142 mi/228 km), a metropolitan industrial area (petrochemicals, automobiles; iron and steel at Duisburg and Dortmund) was formerly a coal-mining center.

The area was occupied by French and Belgian troops 1923–25 in an unsuccessful attempt to force Germany to pay reparations laid down in the Treaty of Versailles. During World War II the Ruhr district was severely bombed. Allied control of the area from 1945 came to an end with the setting-up of the European Coal and Steel Community 1952.

Ruisdael or ***Ruysdael*** Jacob van c. 1628–1682. Dutch landscape painter, active in Amsterdam from about 1655. He painted rural scenes near his native town of Haarlem and in Germany, and exceled in depicting gnarled and weatherbeaten trees. The few figures in his pictures were painted by other artists.

Ruisdael was born in Haarlem, where he probably worked with his uncle, the landscape painter Salomon van Ruysdael (c. 1600–70). Jacob is considered the greatest realist landscape painter in Dutch art. ◊Hobbema was one of his pupils.

rule of law doctrine that no individual, however powerful, is above the law. The principle had a significant influence on attempts to restrain the arbitrary use of power by rulers and on the growth of legally enforceable human rights in many Western countries. It is often used as a justification for separating legislative from judicial power.

rum liquor fermented and distilled from sugar cane. Scummings from the sugarpans produce the best rum, molasses the lowest grade.

Rum or ***Rhum*** island of the Inner Hebrides, Highland region, Scotland, area 42 sq mi/110 sq km, a nature preserve from 1957. Haskeval is 2,432 ft/741 m high.

Rumania alternate spelling of ◊Romania.

ruminant any even-toed hoofed mammal with a rumen, the "first stomach" of its complex digestive system. Plant food is stored and fermented before being brought back to the mouth for chewing (chewing the cud) and then is swallowed to the next stomach. Ruminants include cattle, antelopes, goats, deer, and giraffes, all with a four-chambered stomach. Camels are also ruminants, but they have a three-chambered stomach.

rummy card game in which the players score by obtaining cards either of the same denomination or in sequence in the same suit. It probably derives from mah-jongg.

Rump, the English parliament formed between Dec 1648 and Nov 1653 after ◊Pride's Purge of the ◊Long Parliament to ensure a majority in favor of trying Charles I. It was dismissed 1653 by Cromwell, who replaced it with the Barebones Parliament. Reinstated after the Protectorate ended 1659 and the full membership of the Long Parliament restored by ◊Monk 1660, it dissolved itself shortly afterwards and was replaced by the Convention Parliament which brought about the restoration of the monarchy.

Rundstedt Karl Rudolf Gerd von 1875–1953. German field marshal in World War II. Largely responsible for the German breakthrough in France 1940, he was defeated on the Ukrainian front 1941. As commander in chief in France from 1942, he resisted the Allied invasion 1944 and in Dec launched the temporarily successful Ardennes offensive.

rune character in the oldest Germanic script, chiefly adapted from the Latin alphabet, the earliest examples being from the 3rd century, and found in Denmark. Runes were scratched on wood, metal, stone, or bone.

Runge Philipp Otto 1770–1810. German Romantic painter whose portraits, often of children, have a remarkable clarity and openness. He also illustrated fairy tales by the brothers Grimm.

runner in botany, aerial stem that produces new plants; a type of ◊stolon.

Runnymede meadow on the south bank of the river Thames near Egham, Surrey, England, where on June 15, 1215 King John put his seal to the ◊Magna Carta.

runner

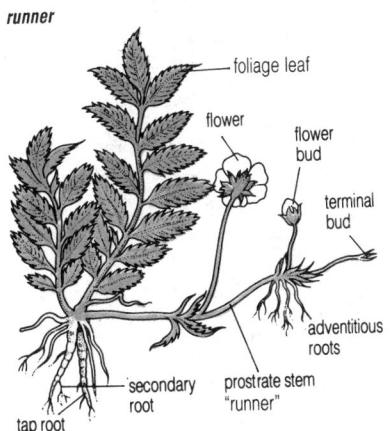

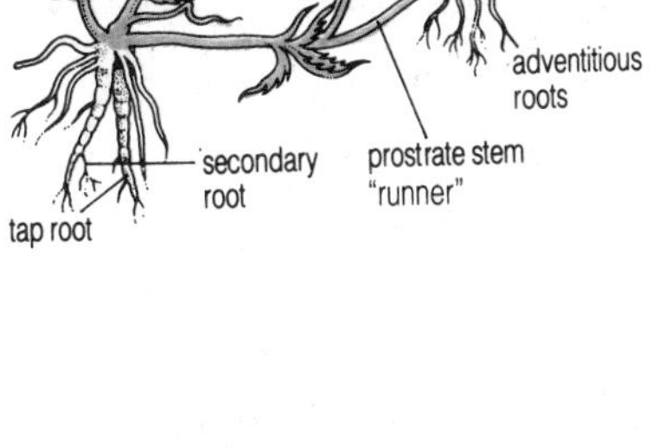
foliage leaf
flower
flower bud
terminal bud
adventitious roots
secondary root
prostrate stem "runner"
tap root

Runyon Damon 1884–1946. US journalist, primarily a sports reporter, whose short stories in *Guys and Dolls* 1932 deal wryly with the seamier side of New York City-life in his own invented jargon. He reached the height of his popularity in the 1930s, writing a syndicated newspaper feature "As I See It."

Rupert Prince 1619–1682. English Royalist general and admiral, born in Prague, son of the Elector Palatine Frederick V (1596–1632) and James I's daughter Elizabeth. Defeated by Cromwell at ◊Marston Moor and ◊Naseby in the Civil War, he commanded a privateering fleet 1649–52, until routed by Admiral Robert Blake, and, returning after the Restoration, was a distinguished admiral in the Dutch Wars. He founded the ◊Hudson's Bay Company.

Rupert's Land area of N Canada, of which Prince ◊Rupert was the first governor. Granted to the ◊Hudson's Bay Company 1670, it was later split among Québec, Ontario, Manitoba, and the Northwest Territories.

rupture in medicine, another name for ◊hernia.

Ruse (Anglicized name Rustchuk) Danube port in Bulgaria, linked by rail and road bridge with Giurgiu in Romania; population (1987) 191,000.

rush any grasslike plant of the genus *Juncus*, family Juncaceae, found in wet places in cold and temperate regions. The round stems and flexible leaves of some species have been used for making mats and baskets since ancient times.

Rush Benjamin 1745–1813. American physician and public official. Born in Bayberry, Pennsylvania, Rush was educated at the College of New Jersey and received his MD degree from the University of Edinburgh 1768. Committed to the cause of the American Revolution, he was a signer of the Declaration of Independence and was named surgeon general of the Continental army 1777. His involvement in agitation against Washington's leadership led to his resignation. After the war, Rush served on the medical faculty of the University of Pennsylvania 1780–97 and was active in public-health programs. From 1797 to his death he was treasurer of the US Mint.

Rushdie (Ahmed) Salman 1947– . British writer, born in India of a Muslim family. His novel *The Satanic Verses* 1988 (the title refers to verses deleted from the Koran) offended many Muslims with alleged blasphemy. In 1989 the Ayatollah Khomeini of Iran called for Rushdie and his publishers to be killed.

Rushdie was born in Bombay and later lived in Pakistan before moving to the UK. His earlier novels in the magic-realist style include *Midnight's Children* 1981, which deals with India from the date of independence and won the Booker Prize, and *Shame* 1983, set in an imaginary parallel of Pakistan. The furor caused by the publication of *The Satanic Verses* led to the withdrawal of British diplomats from Iran. In India and elsewhere, people were killed in demonstrations against the book and Rushdie was forced to go into hiding. *Haroun and the Sea of Stories*, a children's book, was published 1990.

Rushmore, Mount mountain in the Black Hills, South Dakota; height 6,203 ft/1,890 m. On its granite face are carved giant portrait heads of presidents Washington, Jefferson, Lincoln, and Theodore Roosevelt. The sculptor was Gutzon ◊Borglum.

Rusk Dean 1909– . US Democratic politician. He was secretary of state to presidents Kennedy and L B Johnson 1961–69, and became unpopular through his involvement with the ◊Vietnam war.

During World War II he fought in Burma (now Myanmar) and China and became deputy Chief of Staff of US forces. After the war he served in the Department of State, and as assistant secretary of state for Far Eastern affairs was prominent in ◊Korean War negotiations.

Ruskin John 1819–1900. English art critic and social critic. He published five volumes of *Modern Pain-*

ters 1843–60; *The Seven Lamps of Architecture* 1849, in which he stated his philosophy of art; and *The Stones of Venice* 1851–53, in which he drew moral lessons from architectural history. His writings hastened the appreciation of painters considered unorthodox at the time, such as ◊Turner and the ◊Pre-Raphaelite Brotherhood. His later writings were concerned with social and economic problems.

Born in London, the only child of a prosperous wine-merchant, Ruskin was able to travel widely and was educated at Oxford. In 1848 he married Euphemia "Effie" Chalmers Gray, but six years later the marriage was anulled.

From 1860 he devoted himself to social and economic problems, in which he adopted an individual and radical outlook exalting the "craftsman." He became increasingly isolated in his views. To this period belong a series of lectures and pamphlets (*Unto this Last* 1860, *Sesame and Lilies* 1865 on the duties of men and women, and *The Crown of Wild Olive* 1866).

Russell Bertrand (Arthur William), 3rd Earl Russell 1872–1970. English philosopher and mathematician, who contributed to the development of modern mathematical logic and wrote about social issues. His works include *Principia Mathematica* 1910–13 (with A N ◊Whitehead), in which he attempted to show that mathematics could be reduced to a branch of logic; *The Problems of Philosophy* 1912; and *A History of Western Philosophy* 1946. He was an outspoken liberal pacifist.

The grandson of Prime Minister John Russell, he was educated at Trinity College, Cambridge, where he specialized in mathematics and became a lecturer 1895. Russell's pacifist attitude in World War I lost him the lectureship, and he was imprisoned for six months for an article he wrote in a pacifist journal. His *Introduction to Mathematical Philosophy* 1919 was written in prison. He and his wife ran a progressive school 1927–32. After visits to the USSR and China, he went to the US 1938 and taught at many universities. In 1940, a US court disqualified him from teaching at City College of New York because of his liberal moral views. He later returned to England and was a fellow of Trinity College. He was a life-long pacifist except during World War II. From 1949 he advocated nuclear disarmament and until 1963 was on the Committee of 100, an offshoot of the Campaign for Nuclear Disarmament.

Among his other works are *Principles of Mathematics* 1903, *Principles of Social Reconstruction* 1917, *Marriage and Morals* 1929, *An Enquiry into Meaning and Truth* 1940, *New Hopes for a Changing World* 1951, and *Autobiography* 1967–69.

Russell Charles Taze 1852–1916. US founder of the ◊Jehovah's Witness sect 1872. Born in Pittsburgh, Russell, a successful businessman, began studying the Bible after encountering some Adventists and becoming convinced that Christ's return was imminent. On the basis of his studies he came to believe that Christ's "invisible return" had taken place in 1874 and that in 1914 a series of apocalyptic events would culminate in Christ's thousand-year reign on Earth. In 1879 he founded the journal that became *The Watchtower*, which spread his ideas. The movement under his leadership survived the failure of his prophecies in 1914, and it continued to grow rapidly after his death.

Russell Jane 1921– . US actress who was discovered by producer Howard Hughes. Her first film, *The Outlaw* (made 1940–43), was not released until 1950 owing to censorship problems. Her other films include *The Paleface* 1948, *Gentlemen Prefer Blondes* 1953, and *The Revolt of Mamie Stover* 1956. She retired in 1970.

Russell John, 1st Earl 1792–1878. British Liberal politician, son of the 6th Duke of Bedford. He entered the House of Commons 1813 and supported Catholic emancipation and the Reform Bill. He held cabinet posts 1830–41, became prime minister 1846–52, and was again a cabinet minister until becoming prime minister again 1865–66. He retired after the defeat of his Reform Bill 1866.

Russell Ken 1927– . English film director whose work includes *Women in Love* 1969, *Altered States* 1979, and *Salome's Last Dance* 1988.

He is often criticized for self-indulgence; some consider his work to contain gratuitous sex and violence, but others have high regard for its vitality and imagination. Other films include *The Music Lovers* 1971, *The Devils* 1971, *Tommy* 1975, *Lisztomania* 1975, and *Gothic* 1986.

Russia originally the name of the prerevolutionary Russian Empire (until 1917), and now accurately restricted to the ◊Russian Soviet Federal Socialist Republic only (RSFSR). It is incorrectly used to refer to the whole of the ◊Union of Soviet Socialist Republics (USSR).

Russian rulers 1547–1917

House of Rurik	
Ivan "the Terrible"	1547–84
Theodore I	1548–98
Irina	1598
House of Gudonov	
Boris Gudonov	1598–1605
Theodore II	1605
Usurpers	
Dimitri III	1605–06
Basil IV	1606–10
Interregnum	1610–1613
House of Romanov	
Michael Romanov	1613–45
Alexis	1645–76
Theodore III	1676–82
Peter I "Peter the Great" and Ivan V (brothers)	1682–96
Peter I, as Tsar	1689–1721
Peter I, as Emperor	1721–25
Catherine I	1725–27
Peter II	1727–30
Anna Ivanovna	1730–40
Ivan VI	1740–41
Elizabeth	1741–62
Peter III	1762
Catherine II "Catherine the Great"	1762–96
Paul I	1796–1801
Alexander I	1801–25
Nicholas I	1825–55
Alexander II	1855–81
Alexander III	1881–94
Nicholas II	1894–1917

Russian art painting and other products of the visual arts made in Russia and later in the USSR. From the 10th to the 17th century Russian art was dominated by the Eastern Orthodox Church and was influenced by various styles of Byzantine art. Painters such as Andrei Rublev produced icons, images of holy figures that were often considered precious. By the 17th century European influence had grown strong and in the 18th century the tsars imported European sculptors and painters. Early Russian Modernism 1910–30 anticipated Western trends but was then suppressed in favor of art geared to the sentimental glorification of workers.

Russian emigré artists carried their new vision to France, England, and the US after the Revolution. A new generation of post-Stalinist emigrés are to be found in the US and Israel.

Russian history the southern steppes of Russia were originally inhabited by nomadic peoples, and the northern forests by Slavonic peoples who slowly spread southward.

9th–10th centuries Viking chieftains established their own rule in Novgorod, Kiev, and other cities.

10th–12th centuries Kiev temporarily united the Russian peoples into an empire. Christianity was introduced from Constantinople 988.

13th century The Mongols (the Golden Horde) overran the southern steppes 1223, compelling the Russian princes to pay tribute.

14th century Byelorussia and Ukraine came under Polish rule.

1462–1505 Ivan III (the Great), prince of Moscow, threw off the Mongol yoke and united the northwest.

1547–84 Ivan IV (the Terrible) assumed the title of tsar and conquered Kazan and Astrakhan. During his reign the colonization of Siberia began.

1613 The first Romanov tsar, Michael, was elected after a period of chaos.

1667 Following a Cossack revolt, E Ukraine was reunited with Russia.

1682–1725 Peter I (the Great) modernized the bureaucracy and army. He founded a navy and a new capital, St Petersburg (now Leningrad); introduced Western education; and wrested the Baltic seaboard from Sweden. By 1700 the colonization of Siberia had reached the Pacific.

1762–96 Catherine II (the Great) annexed the Crimea and part of Poland and recovered W Ukraine and White Russia.

1798–1814 Russia intervened in the Revolutionary and Napoleonic Wars (1798–1801, 1805–07) and after repelling Napoleon's invasion, took part in his overthrow (1812–14).

1827–29 War with Turkey resulted from Russian attempts to dominate the Balkans.

1853–56 The ◊Crimean War.

1858–60 The treaties of Aigun 1858 and Peking 1860 were imposed on China, annexing territories north of the Amur and east of the Ussuri rivers.

1861 Serfdom was abolished (on terms unfavorable to the peasants). A rapid growth of industry followed, a working-class movement developed, and revolutionary ideas spread, culminating in the assassination of Alexander II in 1881.

1877–78 Balkan war with Turkey.

1898 The Social Democratic Party was founded.

1904–05 The occupation of Manchuria resulted in war with Japan (see ◊Russo-Japanese War).

1905 A revolution, although suppressed, compelled the tsar to accept a parliament (the Duma) with limited powers.

1914 Russo-German rivalries in the Balkans, which had brought Russia into an alliance with France 1895 and Britain 1907, were one of the causes of the outbreak of World War I.

1917 During World I, the ◊Russian Revolution began.

For subsequent history, see ◊Union of Soviet Socialist Republics.

Russian language member of the Slavonic branch of the Indo-European language family. The people of Russia proper refer to it as Great Russian, in contrast with Ukrainian (which they call Little Russian) and the language of Byelorussia (White Russian). It is written in the Cyrillic alphabet and is the standard means of communication throughout the USSR.

Russian literature literary works produced in Russia and later in the USSR. The earliest known works are sermons and chronicles and the unique prose poem "Tale of the Armament of Igor," belonging to the period in the 11th and 12th centuries when the center of literary culture was Kiev. By the close of the 14th century leadership had passed to Moscow, which was isolated from developments in the West until the 18th century; in this period are the political letters of Ivan the Terrible; the religious writings of the priest Avvakum (1620–81), who was the first to use vernacular Slavonic (rather than the elaborate Church Slavonic language) in literature; and traditional oral folk poems dealing with legendary and historical heroes, which were collected in the 18th and 19th centuries.

Modern Russian literature begins with Mikhail Lomonosov (1711–65) who fused elements of Church Slavonic with colloquial Russian to create an effective written medium. Among the earlier writers, working directly under French influence, were the fabulist Ivan Krylov (1768–1844) and the historian Nikolai Karamzin (1765–1826). In the 19th century poetry reached its greatest heights with Alexander Pushkin and the tempestuously Byronic Mikhail Lermontov, while prose was dominated by Nikolai Gogol. Typifying the intellectual unrest of the mid-19th century are the works of the prose writer Alexander Herzen, known for his memoirs.

The golden age of the 19th-century Russian novel produced works by literary giants such as Ivan Turgenev, Ivan Goncharov, Fyodor Dostoievsky, and Leo Tolstoy. In their wake came the humorous Nikolai Leskov (1831–95), the morbid Vsevolod Garshin (1855–88), and Vladimir Korolenko (1853–1921), and in drama the innovative genius of Anton Chekhov. Maxim Gorky rose above the pervasive pessimism of the 1880s and found followers in Alexander Kuprin (1870–1938) and Ivan Bunin; in contrast are the depressingly negative Leonid Andreyev and Mikhail Artsybashev. To the more mystic school of thought belong the novelist Dmitri Merezhkovsky (1865–1941) and the poet and philosopher Vladimir Soloviev (1853–1900), who molded the thought of the Symbolist poet Alexander Blok.

Many writers left the country at the time of the Revolution, but in the 1920s two groups emerged: the militantly Socialist LEF (Left Front of the Arts) led by the Futurist Mayakovsky, and the fellow-travelers of NEP (New Economic Policy) including Boris Pilnyak (1894–1938), Pasternak, Alexei Tolstoy, and Ehrenburg. Literary standards reached a low ebb during the first five-year plan (1928–32), when facts were compulsorily falsified in the effort to fortify socialism, but the novelist Sholokhov and poets Mandelshtam, Akhmatova, and Nikolai Tikhonov were notable in this period. More freedom was allowed by the subsequent Realism movement, seen for example in the works of Simonov and the poet Alexander Tvardovsky (1910–71).

During World War II censorship was again severe until the thaw after Stalin's death—when Vladimir Dudintsev published his *Not by Bread Alone* 1956—but was then soon renewed. Landmark events were the controversy over the award of a Nobel prize to Pasternak, the public statements by the poet Yevtushenko, and the imprisonment in 1966 of the novelists Andrei Sinyavsky (1926–) and Yuli Daniel (1926–) for smuggling their works abroad for publication. Other writers fled the country, such as Anatoly Kuznetsov (1929–), whose novel *The Fire* 1969 obliquely criticized the regime, and Solzhenitsyn, who found a different kind of disillusionment in the West. To evade censorship writers have also resorted to allegory, as in for example Vasili Aksyonov's *The Steel Bird* 1979, which grotesquely satirizes dictatorship. Among those apart from all politics was the nonsense-verse writer Kornei Chukovsky. The intellectual and cultural thaw under President Gorbachev heralded an era of literary revaluation as well as fresh discoveries of writers from the 1930s onward.

Russian orthodox church another name for the ◊Orthodox chruch.

Russian Revolution two revolutions of Feb and Oct 1917 (Julian calendar) that began with the overthrow of the Romanov dynasty and ended with the establishment of a communist soviet (council) state, the Union of Socialist Soviet Republics (USSR). The ***February Revolution*** (March, Western calendar) arose because of food and fuel shortages, the ongoing repressiveness of the tsarist government, and military incompetence in World War I. Riots in Petrograd led to the abdication of Tsar Nicholas II and the formation of a provisional government under Prince Lvov. They had little support as troops, communications, and transport were controlled by the Petrograd workers' and soldiers' council. ◊Lenin returned to Russia in April as head of the ◊Bolsheviks. Kerensky replaced Lvov as head of government in July. During this period, the Bolsheviks gained control of the soviets and advocated land reform (under the slogan "All power to the Soviets") and an end to their involvement in World War I.

The ***October Revolution*** was a coup on the night of Oct 25–26 (Nov 6–7, Western calendar). Bolshevik workers and sailors seized the government buildings and the Winter Palace, Petrograd. The second All-Russian Congress of Soviets, which met the following day, proclaimed itself the new government of Russia, and Lenin became leader. Bolsheviks soon took control of the cities, established worker control in factories, and nationalized the banks. The ◊Cheka (secret police) was set up to silence the opposition. The government concluded peace with Germany early in 1918 through the Treaty of ◊Brest-Litovsk, but civil war broke out in that year when anti-Bolshevik elements within the army attempted to seize power. The war lasted until 1922, when the Red Army, organized by ◊Trotsky, finally overcame "White" (Tsarist) opposition, but with huge losses, after which communist control was complete.

Some 2 million refugees fled during these years.

Russian Revolution: chronology

1894	Reign of Tsar Nicholas II begins.
1898	Formation of the Social Democratic Party among industrial workers under the influence of Plekhanov and Lenin.
1901	Formation of the Socialist Revolutionary Party.
1903	Split in Social Democratic Party at party's second congress (London Conference) into Bolsheviks and Menshiviks.
1905	Jan: "Bloody Sunday," where repression of workers in St Petersburg leads to widespread strikes and "1905 Revolution." Oct: strikes and the first "soviet" (local revolutionary council) in St Petersburg. October constitution provides for new parliament (Duma). Dec: insurrection of workers in Moscow. Punitive repression by the "Black Hundreds."
1914	July: outbreak of war between Russia and the Central Powers.
1917	March: outbreak of riots in St Petersburg. Tsar Nicholas abdicates. Provisional government established under Prince Lvov. Power struggles between government and Petrograd (St Petersburg) soviet. April: Lenin arrives in Petrograd. Demands transfer of power to soviets; an end to the war; the seizure of land by the peasants; control of industry by the workers. July: Bolsheviks attempt to seize power in Petrograd. Trotsky arrested and Lenin in hiding. Kerensky becomes head of provisional government. Sept: Kornilov coup,fails due to strike by workers. Kerensky's government weakened. Nov: Bolshevik Revolution. Military revolutionary committee and Red Guards seize government offices and the Winter Palace, arresting all the members of the provisional government. Second All-Russian Congress of Soviets creates the Council of Peoples Commissars as new governmental authority. Led by Lenin, with Trotsky as Commissar for War and Stalin as Commissar for National Minorities. Land Decree orders immediate distribution of land to the peasants. Banks are nationalized and national debt repudiated. Elections to the Constituent Assembly give large majority to the Socialist Revolutionary Party. Bolsheviks a minority.
1918	Jan: Constituent Assembly meets in Petrograd but almost immediately broken up by Red Guards. March: Treaty of Brest-Litovsk marks end of war with Central Powers but with massive losses of territory. July: murder of tsar and his family.
1918–22	Civil War in Russia between Red Army led by Trotsky and White Russian forces. Red Army ultimately victorious.
1923	July 6: constitution of USSR adopted.

Russian Soviet Federal Socialist Republic (abbreviated RSFSR; Russian *Rossiyskaya*) republic, constituent republic of the USSR 1922–91

area 6,592,658 sq mi/17,075,000 sq km

capital Moscow

cities Leningrad, Gorky, Rostov-on-Don, Volgograd

physical largest of the Soviet republics (occupies about three-quarters of the USSR); includes the fertile Black Earth district; extensive forests; the Ural Mountains with large mineral resources

features the heavily industrialized area around Moscow; Siberia; includes 16 autonomous republics

products three-quarters of the agricultural and industrial output of the USSR

population (1987) 145,311,000; 83% Russian

language Great Russian

religion traditionally Russian Orthodox

recent history (see also ◊Union of Soviet Socialist Republics) In the spring of 1991 the president of the Federation, Boris Yeltsin, who saw off a motion of no-confidence in the Federation's Congress of People's Deputies in April 1991 and secured its support for the direct election of an executive president, set about establishing new sovereign state structures (police, KGB, etc) within the republic. These included, in May 1991, its own KGB and independent television service. In the same month the RFSFR took charge, from the Union (federal) government of all coal mines within the Republic. In June 1991 Yeltsin, running under a Liberal-Radical banner, was popularly elected president, securing 57% of the first-round vote and trouncing former USSR premier Nikolai Ryzhkov, who, backed by the Russian Communist Party, captured 17% of the vote. In July 1991 President Yeltsin issued a sweeping decree to remove communist party cells from factories, farms, and government offices. The RFSFR also recognized the sovereignty of the Baltic republics, signing a state treaty with Lithuania in July 1991.

In the wake of the failed August 1991 anti-Gorbachev coup in the Soviet Union, the radical-democrat leaders of the Russian Republic became increasingly influential. They secured key posts in what remained of the reconstituted central union government, with Yeltsin emerging as the key power-broker within the USSR. In late 1991, Yeltsin led the republic to declare its independence and then made it the centerpiece in a new, looser union, the Commonwealth of Independent States (CIS), that superseded the USSR.

Autonomous Soviet Socialist Republics (capitals in parentheses): Bashkir (Ufa); Buryat (Ulan-Udé); Checheno-Ingush (Grozny); Chuvash (Cheboksary); Dagestan (Makhachkala); Kabardino-Balkar (Nalchik); Kalmyk (Elista); Karelia (Petrozavodsk); Komi (Syktyvkar); Mari (Yoshkar-Ola); Mordovia (Saransk); North Ossetia

Russian Soviet Federal Socialist Republic

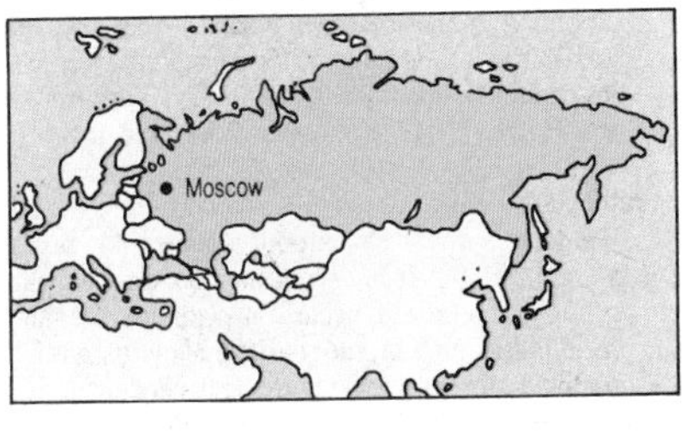
Moscow

(Ordzhonikidze); Tatar (Kazan); Tuva (Kizyl); Udmurt (Izhevsk); Yakut (Yakutsk).

Russo-Japanese War war between Russia and Japan 1904–05, which arose from conflicting ambitions in Korea and ◊Manchuria, specifically, the Russian occupation of Port Arthur (modern Lüda) 1896 and of the Amur province 1900. Japan successfully besieged Port Arthur May 1904–Jan 1905, took Mukden Feb 29–March 10, and on May 27 defeated the Russian Baltic fleet, which had sailed halfway around the world to Tsushima Strait. A peace was signed in Portsmouth, New Hampshire, US, Aug 23, 1905. Russia surrendered its lease on Port Arthur, ceded S Sakhalin to Japan, evacuated Manchuria, and recognized Japan's interests in Korea.

russula any fungus of the genus *Russula*, comprising many species. They are medium to large mushrooms with flattened caps, and many are brightly colored.

R. emetica is a common species found in damp places under conifers. Up to 3.5 in/9 cm across, the cap is scarlet, fading to cherry, and the gills are white. This toadstool tastes acrid and causes vomiting eaten raw, but some russulas are edible.

rust in botany, common name for the minute parasitic fungi of the order Uredinales, which appear on the leaves of their hosts as orange-red spots, later becoming darker. The commonest is the wheat rust *Puccinia graminis*.

rust reddish-brown oxide of iron or steel formed by the action of moisture and oxygen on the metal. It consists mainly of ferric oxide, Fe_2O_3, or ferric hydroxide, $Fe(OH)_3$.

rutabaga or ***swede*** annual or biennial plant *Brassica napus*, widely cultivated for its edible root, which is yellow, purple, or white. It is similar in taste to the turnip *Brassica rapa* but has more carbohydrates and sugars, is firmer fleshed, and longer keeping.

Ruth in the Old Testament, Moabite (see ◊Moab) ancestress of David (king of Israel) by her second marriage to Boaz. When her first husband died, she preferred to stay with her mother-in-law, Naomi, rather than return to her own people.

Ruth Babe (George Herman) 1895–1948. US baseball player, regarded by many as the greatest of all time. He played in ten ◊World Series and hit 714 home runs, a record that stood from 1935 to 1974 and led to the nickname "Sultan of Swat."

Ruth started playing 1914 as a pitcher-outfielder for the Boston Braves before moving to the Boston Red Sox later that year. He joined the New York Yankees 1920 and became one of the best hitters in the game. He hit 60 home runs in the 1927 season (a record beaten 1961 by Roger Maris). He is still the holder of the record for most bases in a season: 457 in 1921. Yankee Stadium is known as "the house that Ruth built" because of the money he brought into the club.

CAREER HIGHLIGHTS

games: 2,503
runs: 2,174
home runs: 714
average: 342
world series wins: 1915–16, 1918, 1923, 1927–28, 1932

Ruthenia or ***Carpathian Ukraine*** region of central Europe, on the S slopes of the Carpathian mountains, home of the Ruthenes or Russniaks. Dominated by Hungary from 10th century, it was part of Austria-Hungary until World War I. Divided among Czechoslovakia, Poland, and Romania 1918, it was independent for a single day in 1938, immediately occupied by Hungary, captured by the USSR 1944, and 1945–47 became incorporated into Ukraine Republic, USSR.

ruthenium hard, brittle, silver-white, metallic element, symbol Ru, atomic number 44, atomic weight 101.07. It is one of the so-called platinum group of metals; it occurs in platinum ores as a free metal and in the natural alloy osmiridium (osmium, iridium, platinum, and rhodium). It is used as a hardener in alloys and as a catalyst; its compounds are used as coloring agents in glass and ceramics.

***Rutherford** New Zealand physicist Ernest Rutherford (right), who was a pioneer researcher in radioactivity in a laboratory of England's Cambridge University.*

It was discovered in 1827 by Estonian chemist G W Osann, who produced it in impure form from residues of platinum ores, and named in 1828 for its place of discovery, the Ural mountains in Ruthenia (now part of the Ukraine, USSR). Pure ruthenium was isolated in 1845 by K K Klaus.

Rutherford Ernest 1871–1937. New Zealand-born British physicist, a pioneer of modern atomic science. His main research was in the field of radioactivity, and he discovered alpha, beta, and gamma rays. He named the nucleus, and was the first to recognize the ionizing nature of the atom. Nobel Prize 1908.

Rutherford Margaret 1892–1972. English film and theater actress who specialized in playing formidable yet jovially eccentric roles, one of the great character actresses. She became mildly successful in the mid 1930s but went on to her greatest success when she played Agatha Christie's Miss Marple, with her actor-husband Stringer Davis, in four films in the early 1960s and won an Academy Award for her role in *The VIPs* 1963.

She can also be seen in *Blithe Spirit* 1945, *Passport to Pimlico* 1949, *Mouse on The Moon* 1943, and Orson Welles's *Chimes at Midnight* 1966.

rutherfordium name proposed by US scientists for the element currently known as ◊unnilquadium (atomic number 104), to honor New Zealand physicist Ernest Rutherford. The symbol is Rf.

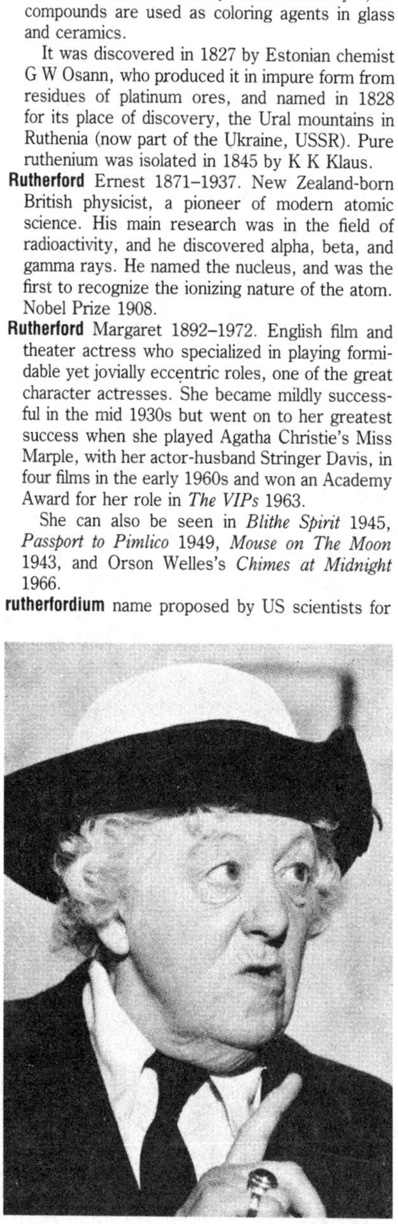

***Rutherford** British actress Margaret Rutherford, who is best known for portraying Miss Marple, an Agatha Christie character.*

rutile TiO_2, titanium oxide, a naturally occurring ore mineral of titanium. It is usually reddish brown to black, with a very bright (adamantine) surface luster. It crystallizes in the tetragonal system. Rutile is common in a wide range of igneous and metamorphic rocks and also occurs concentrated in sands; the coastal sands of E and W Australia are a major source. Rutile is also used as a pigment that gives a brilliant white to paint, paper, and plastics.

Rutledge Wiley Blount, Jr 1894–1949. US jurist and associate justice of the US Supreme Court 1943–49. He was known as a liberal, often dissenting from conservative Court decisions, such as in *Wolf* v *Colorado* 1949, which allowed illegally obtained evidence to be used against a defendant in state courts.

Born in Cloverport, Kentucky, Rutledge studied law at the University of Colorado and was admitted to the bar 1922. He became a teacher of law at the University of Colorado 1924–26, Washington University 1926–35, and the State University of Iowa 1935–39. In 1939 he was appointed judge of the US Court of Appeals for the District of Columbia. President F D Roosevelt appointed him to the Court 1943.

Ruwenzori mountain range on the frontier between Zaïre and Uganda, rising to 16,794 ft/5,119 m at Mount Stanley.

Ruysdael Jacob van. See ◊Ruisdael, Dutch painter.

Ruyter Michael Adrianszoon de 1607–1676. Dutch admiral who led his country's fleet in the wars against England. On June 1–4, 1666 he forced the British fleet under Rupert and Albemarle to retire into the Thames, but on July 25 was heavily defeated off the North Foreland, Kent. In 1667 he sailed up the Medway to burn three men-of-war at Chatham, and captured others.

Ruyter was mortally wounded in an action against the French fleet off Messina and died at Syracuse, Sicily.

Ruzicka Leopold Stephen 1887–1976. Swiss chemist. Born in Yugoslavia, Ruzicka settled in Switzerland in 1929. He began research on natural compounds such as musk and civet secretions. In the 1930s he investigated sex hormones, and in 1934 succeeded in extracting the male hormone androsterone from 7,000 gal/31,815 l of urine and synthesizing it. Ruzicka shared the 1939 Nobel Chemistry Prize with Butenandt.

Rwanda landlocked country in central Africa, bounded N by Uganda, E by Tanzania, S by Burundi, and W by Zaïre

government The 1978 constitution provides for a president and a single-chamber legislature, the National Development Council, all elected by universal adult suffrage for a five-year term. The president appoints and leads a council of ministers.

Rwanda is a one-party state, the sole legal party being the National Revolutionary Development Movement (MRND), whose leader is the president.

history For early history, see ◊Africa. The population comprises two ethnic groups: the agrarian Hutu, over 80%, were dominated by the pastoral Tutsi; there are also Pygmies.

Rwanda was linked to the neighboring state of Burundi, 1891–1919, within the empire of German East Africa, then under Belgian administration as a League of Nations mandate, and then as a United Nations trust territory.

In 1961 the monarchy was abolished, and Ruanda, as it was then called, became a republic. It achieved full independence 1962 as Rwanda, with Gregoire Kayibanda as its first president. Fighting broke out 1959 between the Hutu and the Tutsi, resulting in the loss of some 20,000 lives before an uneasy peace was agreed 1965.

Kayibanda was reelected president 1969, but by the end of 1972 the civil warfare had resumed,

Rwanda
Republic of
(Republika y'u Rwanda)

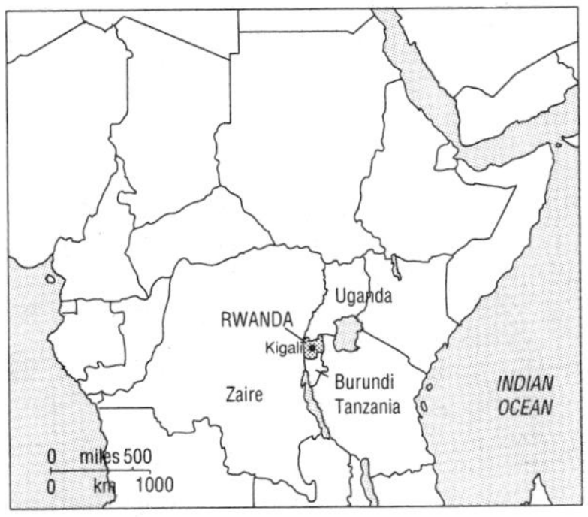
Uganda
RWANDA
Kigali
Burundi
Tanzania
Zaire
INDIAN OCEAN
0 miles 500
0 km 1000

area 10,173 sq mi/26,338 sq km
capital Kigali
cities Butare, Ruhengeri
physical high savanna and hills, with volcanic mountains in NW
features part of lake Kivu; highest peak Mount Karisimbi 14,792 ft/4,507 m; Kagera River (whose headwaters are the source of the Nile) and National Park
head of state and government Juvenal Habyarimana from 1973
political system one-party military republic
political parties National Revolutionary Movement for Development (MRND), nationalistic, Socialist
exports coffee, tea, pyrethrum
currency franc
population (1990 est) 7,603,000 (Hutu 90%, Tutsi 9%); growth rate 3.3% p.a.
life expectancy men 49, women 53 (1989)
language Kinyarwanda, French (official); Kiswahili religion Roman Catholic 54%, animist 23%, Protestant 12%, Muslim 9%
literacy men 50% (1989)
GNP $2.3 bn (1987); $323 per head (1986)
chronology
1916 Belgian troops occupied Rwanda; League of Nations mandated Rwanda and Burundi to Belgium as Territory of Ruanda-Urundi.
1959 Tribal warfare between Hutu and Tutsi.
1962 Independence from Belgium achieved, with Gregoire Kayibanda as president.
1972 Renewal of tribal fighting.
1973 Kayibanda ousted in a military coup led by Maj-Gen Juvenal Habyarimana.
1978 New constitution approved; Rwanda remained a military-controlled state.
1980 Civilian rule adopted.
1988 Refugees from Burundi massacres streamed into Rwanda.
1990 Rwandan Patriotic Army attacked government. Constitutional reforms promised.

and in 1973 the head of the National Guard, Maj Gen Juvenal Habyarimana, led a bloodless coup, ousting Kayibanda and establishing a military government. Meetings of the legislature were suspended, and the MRND was formed as the only legally permitted political organization. A referendum held at the end of 1978 approved a new constitution, but military rule continued. In Oct 1990 the government promised to reform the constitution.

Rwanda's population density has led to the cultivation of all arable land, soil erosion, and dependence on foreign aid.

Ryan Robert 1909–1973. US theater and film actor who was equally impressive in leading and character roles. His films include *Woman on the Beach* 1947, *The Set-Up* and *Caught* both 1949, *Billy Budd* 1962, and *The Wild Bunch* 1969.

He was cofounder of the UCLA Theater Group.

Ryazan industrial city (agricultural machinery, leather, shoes) dating from the 13th century, capital of Ryazan region, USSR, on the river Oka near Moscow; population (1987) 508,000.

Rybinsk port and industrial city (engineering) on the Volga, NE of Moscow in the Russian Soviet Federal Socialist Republic; population (1987) 254,000. Between 1984 and 1988 it was named Andropov after a president of the USSR.

Ryder Albert Pinkham 1847–1917. US painter who developed one of the most original styles of his time. He painted with broad strokes that tended to simplify form and used yellowish colors that gave his works an eerie, haunted quality. His works are poetic, romantic, and filled with unreality; *Death on a Pale Horse* 1910 (Cleveland Museum of Art) is typical.

Born in New Bedford, Massachusetts, he was self-taught and, as time passed, became more and more a recluse.

Ryder Cup golf tournament for professional men's teams from the US and Europe. It is played every two years, and the match is made up of a series of singles, foursomes, and fourballs played over three days.

Named after entrepreneur Samuel Ryder, who donated the trophy 1927, the tournament is played alternately in the US and Great Britain. The match was between the US and Great Britain 1927–71; US v. Great Britain and Ireland 1973–77, and US v. Europe from 1979.

Ryder Cup: winners

US: 1927, 1931, 1935, 1937, 1947, 1949, 1951, 1953, 1955, 1959, 1961, 1963, 1965, 1967, 1971, 1973, 1975, 1977, 1979, 1981, 1983, 1991
Great Britain: 1929, 1933, 1957
Europe: 1985, 1987
drawn: 1969, 1989

Rye town in East Sussex, England, notable for its literary associations; population (1985) 4,490. It was formerly a flourishing port (and one of the ◊Cinque Ports), but silt washed down by the river Rother has left it 2 mi/3 km inland.

rye cereal *Secale cereale* grown extensively in N Europe and other temperate regions. It was domesticated as a weed growing among the wheat. The flour is used to make dark-colored ("black") breads. Rye is grown mainly as a forage crop, but the grain is also used to make whiskey and breakfast cereals.

rye-grass any perennial, wiry grass of the genus *Lolium*, especially *L. perenne*, common in pastures and waste places. It grows up to 24 in/60 cm high, flowers in midsummer, and sends up abundant nutritious leaves, good for cattle. It is a Eurasian species but has been introduced to Australia and North America.

Rye House Plot conspiracy 1683 by English Whig extremists against Charles II for his Roman Catholic leanings. They intended to murder Charles and his brother James, Duke of York, at Rye House, Hoddesdon, Hertfordshire, but the plot was betrayed. The Duke of ◊Monmouth was involved, and alleged coconspirators, including Lord William ◊Russell and Algernon Sidney (1622–83) were executed for complicity.

Ryle Gilbert 1900–1976. British philosopher. His *The Concept of Mind* 1949 set out to show that

rye

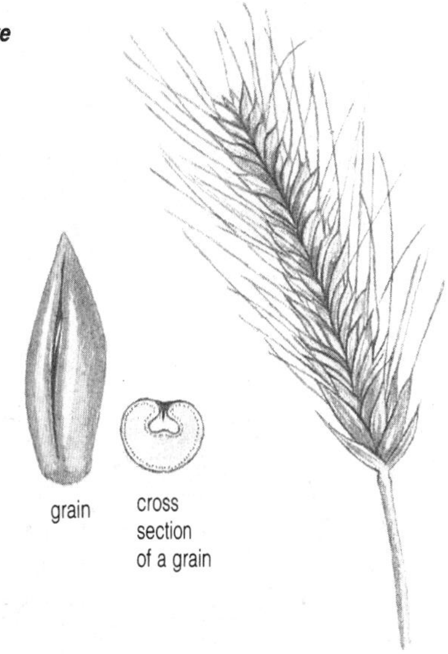
grain
cross section of a grain

the distinction between an inner and an outer world in philosophy and psychology cannot be sustained. He ridiculed the mind-body dualism of ◊Descartes as the doctrine of "the Ghost in the Machine."

Ryle Martin 1918–1984. English radioastronomer. At the Mullard Radio Astronomy Observatory, Cambridge, he developed the technique of sky-mapping using "aperture synthesis," combining smaller dish aerials to give the characteristics of one large one. His work on the distribution of radio sources in the universe brought confirmation of the ◊Big Bang theory. He won, with Antony ◊Hewish, the Nobel Prize for Physics 1974.

Ryukyu Islands southernmost island group of Japan, stretching toward Taiwan and including Okinawa, Miyako, and Ishigaki

area 870 sq mi/2,254 sq km
capital Naha, on Okinawa
features 73 islands, some uninhabited; subject to typhoons
products sugar, pineapples, fish
population (1985) 1,179,000
history originally an independent kingdom; ruled by China from the late 14th century until seized by Japan 1609 and controlled by the Satsuma feudal lords until 1868, when the Japanese government took over. Chinese claims to the islands were relinquished 1895. In World War II the islands were taken by US 1945 (see under ◊Okinawa); northernmost group, Oshima, restored to Japan 1953, the rest 1972.

Ryzhkov Nikolai Ivanovich 1929– . Soviet communist politician. He held governmental and party posts from 1975 before being brought into the Politburo and made prime minister 1985 by Gorbachev. A low-profile technocrat, Ryzhkov is viewed as a more cautious and centralist reformer than Gorbachev. As the author of unpopular economic reforms, he was nearly forced to resign, surviving with the support of Mikhail Gorbachev, only to suffer a heart attack in Dec 1990.

An engineering graduate from the Urals Polytechnic in Sverdlovsk, Ryzhkov rose to become head of the giant Uralmash engineering conglomerate. A member of the Communist Party from 1959, he became deputy minister for heavy engineering 1975. He then served as first deputy chair of Gosplan 1979–82 and Central Committee secretary for economics 1982–85 before becoming prime minister.

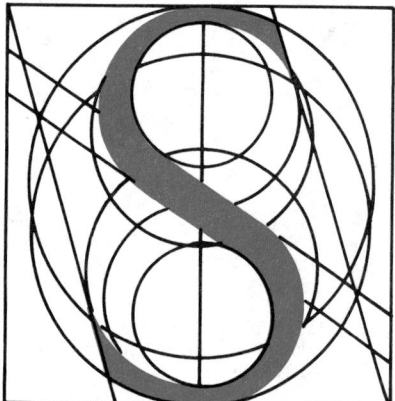

S abbreviation for south.

Saar (French *Sarre*) river in W Europe; it rises in the Vosges mountains, in France, and flows 149 mi/240 km N to join the river Moselle in Germany. Its valley has many vineyards.

Saarbrücken city on the river Saar, Federal Republic of Germany; population (1988) 184,000. It is situated on a large coalfield, and is an industrial center (engineering, optical equipment). It has been the capital of Saarland since 1919.

Saarinen Eero 1910–1961. Finnish-born US architect. Son of Eliel ◊Saarinen. He is known for a wide range of innovative modern designs using a variety of creative shapes for buildings. His works include the TWA terminal at Kennedy Airport in New York City; Dulles Airport outside Washington, DC; the General Motors Technical Center in Warren, Michigan; the Thomas J Watson Research Center in Yorktown, New York; Ezra Stiles and Morse colleges and the ice-hockey rink at Yale University; Kresge Auditorium at the Massachusetts Institute of technology; and US embassies in London and Oslo.

Saarinen Eliel 1873–1950. Finnish-born US architect and founder of the Finnish Romantic school. His most famous European work is the Helsinki railroad station. In the US he is particularly remembered for his designs for Cranbrook School in Bloomfield Hills, Michigan, and Christ Church in Minneapolis.

Saarland (French *Sarre*) *Land* (state) of the Federal Republic of Germany, crossed NW–S by the river Saar. Saarland is one-third forest.

area 992 sq mi/2,570 sq km

capital Saarbrücken

products cereals and other crops; cattle, pigs, poultry. Former flourishing coal and steel industries survive only by government subsidy

population (1988) 1,034,000

history in 1919, the Saar district was administered by France under the auspices of the League of Nations; a plebiscite returned it to Germany 1935; Hitler gave it the name Saarbrücken. Part of the French zone of occupation 1945, it was part of the economic union with France 1947. It was returned to Germany 1957; it is the smallest and poorest of the German *Länder* that were formerly part of West Germany.

Sabah self-governing state of the federation of Malaysia, occupying NE Borneo, forming (with Sarawak) East Malaysia; area 28,415 sq mi/73,613 sq km; population (1984) 1,177,000, of which the Kadazans form the largest ethnic group at 30%; also included are 250,000 immigrants from Indonesia and the Philippines. Its capital is Kota Kinabalu (formerly Jesselton), and its exports include hardwoods (25% of the world's supplies), rubber, fish, cocoa, palm oil, copper, copra, and hemp. It is chiefly mountainous (highest peak Mount Kinabalu 13,450 ft/4,098 m) and forested. The languages are Malay (official) and English, the religions Sunni Muslim and Christian (the Kadazans, among whom there is unrest about increasing Muslim dominance). Its government consists of a constitutional head of state with a chief minister, cabinet, and legislative assembly. In 1877–78 the Sultan of Sulu made concessions to the North Borneo Company, which was eventually consolidated with Labuan as a British colony 1946, and became the state of Sabah within Malaysia 1963. The Philippines advanced territorial claims on Sabah 1962 and 1968 on the grounds that the original cession by the Sultan was illegal, Spain having then been sovereign in the area.

Sabatier Paul 1854–1951. French chemist. He found in 1897 that if a mixture of ethene and hydrogen was passed over a column of heated nickel, the ethene changed into ethane. Further work revealed that nickel could be used to catalyze numerous chemical reactions. Sabatier shared the 1912 Nobel Prize for Chemistry with François ◊Grignard.

Sabbatarianism belief held by some Protestant Christians in the strict observance of the Sabbath, Sunday, following the fourth commandment of the ◊Bible. It began in the 17th century.

Sabbatarianism has taken various forms, including an insistence on the Sabbath lasting a full 24 hours; prohibiting sports and games and the buying and selling of goods on the Sabbath; and ignoring public vacations when they fall on a Sunday.

Sabbath (Hebrew *shābath*, "to rest") the seventh day of the week, commanded by God in the Old Testament as a sacred day of rest; in Judaism, from sunset Friday to sunset Saturday; in Christianity, Sunday (or, in some sects, Saturday).

sabin unit of sound absorption, used in acoustical engineering. One sabin is the absorption of one square foot (0.093 square meter) of a perfectly absorbing surface (such as an open window).

Sabin Albert 1906– . Polish-born US microbiologist whose involvement in the antipolio campaigns led to the development of a new, highly effective, live vaccine. The earlier vaccine, developed by the physicist Jonas ◊Salk, was based on heat-killed viruses. Sabin was convinced that a live form would be longer-lasting and more effective, and he succeeded in weakening the virus so that it lost its virulence. The vaccine can be orally administered.

Sabine a member of an ancient people of central Italy, conquered by the Romans and amalgamated with them in the 3rd century BC. The so-called rape of the Sabine women—a mythical attempt by ◊Romulus in the early days of Rome to carry off the Sabine women to colonize the new city—is frequently depicted in art.

sabka a flat shoreline zone in arid regions above the high-water mark in which the sediments are heavily laden with evaporites. These occur in the form of nodules, crusts, and crystalline deposits of halite, anhydrite, and gypsum, as well as mineral grains of various sorts. Some of the evaporites form from rapid evaporation of marine waters soaking through from the bordering tidal flats, but some can be derived also from sediment-laden continental waters coming down from adjoining highlands.

Sabkas are common features along the Persian Gulf. Former sabka environments can be deduced from the sedimentary record of much of the oil-rich Permian Basin of Texas, as an ancient sea moved back and forth across the continent.

sable marten *Martes zibellina*, about 20 in/50 cm long, and usually brown. It is native to N Eurasian forests, but now found mainly in E Siberia. The sable has diminished in numbers because of its valuable fur, which has long attracted hunters. Conservation measures and sable farming have been introduced to save it from extinction.

Sabu Adopted name of Sabu Dastagir 1924–1963. Indian child actor who was memorable as the hero of *The Thief of Baghdad* 1940. He acted in Britain and the US until the 1950s. His other films include *Elephant Boy* 1937 and *Black Narcissus* 1947.

saccharide the scientific term for a ◊sugar molecule. Saccharides can be joined together in long chains to form ◊polysaccharides.

saccharin $C_7H_5NO_3S$ (technical name ortho-sulfo benzimide) sweet, white, crystalline solid derived from coal tar and substituted for sugar. Since 1977 it has been regarded as potentially carcinogenic.

Sacco-Vanzetti Case murder trial of two anarchists in Massachusetts 1920–21. Italian immigrants Nicola Sacco (1891–1927) and Bartolomeo Vanzetti (1888–1927) were convicted of murder during an alleged robbery. The conviction was upheld on appeal, with application for retrial denied. Prolonged controversy delayed execution until 1927.

The two accused men were philosophical anarchists who had evaded the draft in World War I. Protests were made from many quarters arguing that the two were victims of the ◊Red Scare. Modern ballistics evidence suggests that one of the fatal shots was fired from Sacco's gun, but the judge's prejudice against the defendants' political views raised questions about the fairness of the trial. The case was extremely divisive at the time.

Sacher Paul 1906– . Swiss conductor. In 1926 he founded the Basle Chamber Orchestra, for which he has commissioned a succession of works from contemporary composers including Bartók, Stravinsky, and Britten.

Sacher-Masoch Leopold von 1836–1895. Austrian novelist. His books dealt with the sexual pleasure of having pain inflicted on oneself, hence ◊masochism.

Sachsen German form of ◊Saxony, former kingdom and state of Germany.

sackbut musical instrument of the ◊brass family, the forerunner of the trombone, common from the 14th century.

Sackville-West Vita (Victoria) 1892–1962. British poet and novelist, wife of Harold ◊Nicolson from 1913; *Portrait of a Marriage* 1973 by their son Nigel Nicolson described their married life. Her novels include *The Edwardians* 1930 and *All Passion Spent* 1931; she also wrote the pastoral poem *The Land* 1926. The fine gardens around her home at Sissinghurst, Kent, were created by her.

sacrament in Christian usage, observances forming the visible sign of inward grace. In the Roman Catholic Church there are seven sacraments: baptism, Holy Communion (Eucharist or mass), confirmation, rite of reconciliation (confession and penance), holy orders, matrimony, and the anointing of the sick.

Sacramento industrial port and capital (since 1854) of California, 80 mi/130 km NE of San Francisco; population (1990) 369,365, metropolitan area

Sacco-Venzetti *The Italian-American anarchists, Sacco and Venzetti, entering a Massachusetts courthouse during their trial for murder, 1920–21.*

1,481,102. It stands on the Sacramento River, which flows 382 mi/615 km through Sacramento Valley to San Francisco Bay. Industries include the manufacture of detergents and jet aircraft and food processing, including almonds, peaches, and pears. It was founded as Fort Sutter 1848 on land bought by John Sutter 1839. Its old town has been restored. A deepwater port channel to San Francisco Bay was completed 1963.

sacred cow any person, institution, or custom that is considered above criticism. The term comes from the Hindu belief that cows are sacred and must not be killed.

Sacred Thread ceremony Hindu initiation ceremony that marks the passage to maturity for boys of the upper three castes; it usually takes place between the ages of five and twelve. It is regarded as a second birth and the castes whose males are entitled to undergo the ceremony are called "twice born."

Sadat Anwar 1918–1981. Egyptian politician. Succeeding ◊Nasser as president 1970, he restored morale by his handling of the Egyptian campaign in the 1973 war against Israel. In 1974 his plan for economic, social, and political reform to transform Egypt was unanimously adopted in a referendum. In 1977 he visited Israel to reconcile the two countries, and shared the Nobel Peace Prize with Israeli prime minister Menachem Begin 1978. He was assassinated by Islamic fundamentalists.

Sadducee (Hebrew "righteous") member of the ancient Hebrew political party and sect of Judaism that formed in Roman-occupied Palestine in the 2nd century BC. They were the aristocratic group centered on the priesthood in Jerusalem until the final destruction of the Temple 70 AD. They opposed the Pharisees and were for Hellenization. They were the party of the priestly aristocrats, standing for the hereditary high priests, the Temple, and sacrifice. They denied the immortality of the soul and the existence of angels and maintained the religious law in all its strictness. Many of their ideas and rituals resurfaced in medieval Jewish sects after Pharisee ideas dominated the dispersed Jews of the W Roman empire.

Sacramento *The state capitol, where the legislature meets, in California's capital city. It was built 1860–69 in Classical style.*

Sade Donatien Alphonse François, Comte de, known as the *Marquis de Sade* 1740–1814. French soldier and author. He was imprisoned for sexual offenses and finally committed to an asylum. He wrote plays and novels dealing explicitly with a variety of sexual practices, including ◊sadism.

sadhu in Hinduism, a wandering holy man who devotes himself to the goal of *moksha*, or liberation from the cycle of reincarnation.

S'adi or ***Saadi***. Adopted name of Sheikh Moslih Addin c. 1184–c. 1291. Persian poet, author of *Bustan/Tree-garden* and *Gulistan/Flower-garden*.

sadism a tendency to derive pleasure (usually sexual) from inflicting physical or mental pain on others. The term is derived from the Marquis de ◊Sade.

Sadowa, Battle of (also known as the ***Battle of Königgrätz***) Prussian victory over the Austrian army 8 mi/13 km NW of Hradec Kralove (German *Königgrätz*) July 3, 1866, ending the ◊Seven Weeks' War. It confirmed Prussian hegemony over the German states and led to the formation of the North German Confederation 1867. It is named after the nearby village of Sadowa (Czech *Sadová*) in Czechoslovakia.

Sadat *President Anwar Sadat of Egypt, the first Arab leader to reconcile with Israel.*

sage

safety lamp portable lamp designed for use in places where flammable gases such as methane may be encountered, for example in coal mines. The electric head lamp used as a miner's working light has the bulb and contacts in protected enclosures. The flame safety lamp, now used primarily for gas detection, has the wick enclosed within a strong glass cylinder surmounted by wire gauzes. Humphrey ◊Davy 1815 and George ◊Stephenson each invented flame safety lamps.

safflower Asian plant *Carthamus tinctorius*, family Compositae. It is thistlelike, and widely grown for the oil from its seeds, which is used in cooking, margarine, and paints and varnishes; the seed residue is used as cattle feed.

saffron plant *Crocus sativus* of the iris family, probably native to SW Asia, and formerly widely cultivated in Europe; also the dried orange-yellow ◊stigmas of its purple flowers, used for coloring and flavoring.

Safi Atlantic port in Tensift province, NW Morocco; population (1981) 256,000. It exports phosphates and has fertilizer plants, sardine factories, and boat-building yards.

saga prose narrative written down in the 11th–13th centuries in Norway and Iceland. The sagas range from family chronicles, such as the *Landnamabok* of Ari (1067–1148), to legendary and anonymous works such as the *Njala* saga. Other sagas include the *Heimskringla* of Snorri Sturluson celebrating Norwegian kings (1178–1241), the *Sturlunga* of Sturla Thordsson (1214–84), and the legendary and anonymous *Laxdaela* and *Grettla* sagas.

Sagamihara city on the island of Honshu, Japan, with a large silkworm industry; population (1987) 489,000.

Sagan Carl 1934– . US physicist and astronomer, who became known for his popularization of science. A teacher at Cornell University from 1968, he also headed the Laboratory for Planetary Studies there. He has studied the possibility of life on other planets and the climatic effects of a nuclear war, and he has provided valuable data for several NASA space-probe missions. His works include *Intelligent Life in the Universe* 1966, with I S Shlovskii; *UFO's: A Scientific Debate* 1973, with Page Thornton; *Cosmic Connection: An Extraterrestrial Perspective* 1973; *Communication with Extraterrestrial Intelligence* 1973; *The Dragons of Eden* 1977; *Broca's Brain: Reflections on the Romance of Science* 1979; *Cosmos* 1980, based on his television series of that name; and *Contact* 1985.

Sagan Françoise 1935– . French novelist. Her studies of love relationships include *Bonjour Tristesse/Hello Sadness* 1954, *Un Certain Sourire/A Certain Smile* 1956, and *Aimez-vous Brahms?/Do You Like Brahms?* 1959.

Sagarmatha Nepalese name for Mount Everest, "the Goddess of the Universe," and the official name of the 476-sq mi/1,240-sq km Himalayan national park established 1976.

sage perennial herb *Salvia officinalis* with gray-green aromatic leaves used for flavoring. It grows up to 1.6 ft/50 cm high and has bluish-lilac or pink flowers.

Saginaw city and port in E Michigan on the Saginaw river, near Lake Huron, NW of Flint. Industries include automotive parts, metal products, salt, coal, and sugar beets; population (1990) 69,512. Saginaw was a lumber center until the late 19th century.

Sagittarius zodiac constellation in the southern hemisphere, represented as a centaur aiming a bow and arrow at neighboring Scorpius. The Sun passes through Sagittarius from mid-Dec to mid-Jan, including the winter solstice, when it is farthest south of the equator. The constellation contains many nebulae and ◊globular clusters, and open ◊star clusters. Kaus Australis and Nunki are its brightest stars. The center of our Galaxy, the Milky Way, is marked by the radio source Sagittarius A. In astrology, the dates for Sagittarius are between about Nov 22 and Dec 21 (see ◊precession).

sago the starchy material obtained from the pith of the sago palm *Metroxylon sagu*. It forms a nutritious food, and is used for manufacturing glucose and for sizing textiles.

Saguenay river in Québec, Canada, used for hydroelectric power as it flows from Lac St Jean SE to the St Lawrence estuary; length 475 mi/765 km.

Sahara the largest desert in the world, occupying 2,123,000 sq mi/5,500,000 sq km of N Africa from the Atlantic to the Nile, covering: W Egypt; part of W Sudan; large parts of Mauritania, Mali, Niger, and Chad; and southern parts of Morocco, Algeria, Tunisia, and Libya. Small areas in Algeria and Tunisia are below sea level, but it is mainly a plateau with a central mountain system, including the Ahaggar Mountains in Algeria, the Aïr Massif in Niger, and the Tibesti Massif in Chad, of which the highest peak is Emi Koussi 11,208 ft/3,415 m. The area of the Sahara has expanded by 251,000 sq mi/650,000 sq km in the last half century, but reforestation is being attempted in certain areas.

Oases punctuate the caravan routes, now modern roads. Resources include oil and gas in the N. Satellite observations have established a pattern below the surface of dried-up rivers that existed 2,000,000 years ago. Cave paintings confirm that 4,000 years ago running rivers and animal life existed.

Sahel (Arabic *sahil* "coast") marginal area to the S of the Sahara, from Senegal to Somalia, where the desert has extended because of a population explosion, poor agricultural practice, destruction of scrub, and climatic change.

Saida ancient Sidon port in Lebanon; population (1980) 24,740. It stands at the end of the Trans-Arabian oil pipeline from Saudi Arabia. Sidon was the chief city of ◊Phoenicia, a bitter rival of Tyre about 1400–701 BC, when it was conquered by ◊Sennacherib. Later a Roman city, it was taken by the Arabs AD 637 and fought over during the Crusades.

saiga antelope *Saiga tartarica* of E European and W Asian steppes and deserts. Buff-colored, whitish in winter, it stands 2.5 ft/75 cm at the shoulder, with a body about 5 ft/1.5 m long. Its nose is unusually large and swollen, an adaptation which may help warm and moisten the air inhaled, and keep out the desert dust. The saiga can run at 50 mph/80 kph.

Only the male has horns, which are straight and up to 1 ft/30 cm long. Once a vanishing species but now protected, the saiga has returned to some areas, and herds of thousands migrate with the changing seasons.

Saigon former name (until 1976) of ◊Ho Chi Minh City, Vietnam.

sailing pleasure cruising or racing a small and light vessel, whether sailing or power-driven. At the Olympic Games, seven categories exist: Soling, Flying Dutchman, Star, Finn, Tornado, 470, and Windglider or ◊windsurfing (boardsailing), which was introduced at the 1984 Los Angeles games. All these Olympic categories are sail-driven. The Finn and Windglider are solo events; the Soling class is for three-person crews; all other classes are for crews of two.

saint person eminently pious, especially one certified so in the Roman Catholic or Eastern Orthodox Church by ◊canonization. The term is also used in Buddhism for individuals who have led a virtuous and holy life, such as Kukai (775–835), founder of the Japanese Shingon sect of Buddhism. For individual saints, see under forename, for example ◊Paul, St.

The lives of thousands of Catholic saints have been collected by the Bollandists, a group of Belgian Jesuits. In 1970 Pope Paul VI revised the calendar of saints' days: excluded were Barbara, Catherine, Christopher, and Ursula (as probably nonexistent); optional veneration might be given to George, Januarius, Nicholas (Santa Claus), and Vitus; insertions for obligatory veneration include St Thomas More and the Uganda martyrs.

St Andrews a town at the E tip of Fife, Scotland, 12 mi/19 km SE of Dundee; population (1981) 11,400. Its university (1411) is the oldest in Scotland, and the Royal and Ancient Club (1754) is the ruling body in the sporting world of golf.

St Augustine port and vacation resort in Florida; population (1990) 11,692. Founded by the Spanish 1565, and the oldest permanent settlement in the US, it was burned by the English sea captain ◊Drake 1586 and ceded to the US 1821. It includes the oldest house (late 16th century) and oldest masonry fort (Castillo de San Marcos 1672) in the continental US.

St Bartholomew, Massacre of the slaughter of ◊Huguenots in Paris, Aug 24–Sept 17, 1572, and until Oct 3 in the provinces. About 25,000 people were believed to have been killed. When ◊Catherine de' Medici's plot to have ◊Coligny assassinated failed, she resolved to have all the Huguenot leaders killed, persuading her son Charles IX it was in the interests of public safety. Catherine received congratulations from all the Catholic powers, and the pope ordered a medal to be struck.

St Bernard breed of large, heavily built dog 2.5 ft/

sailing

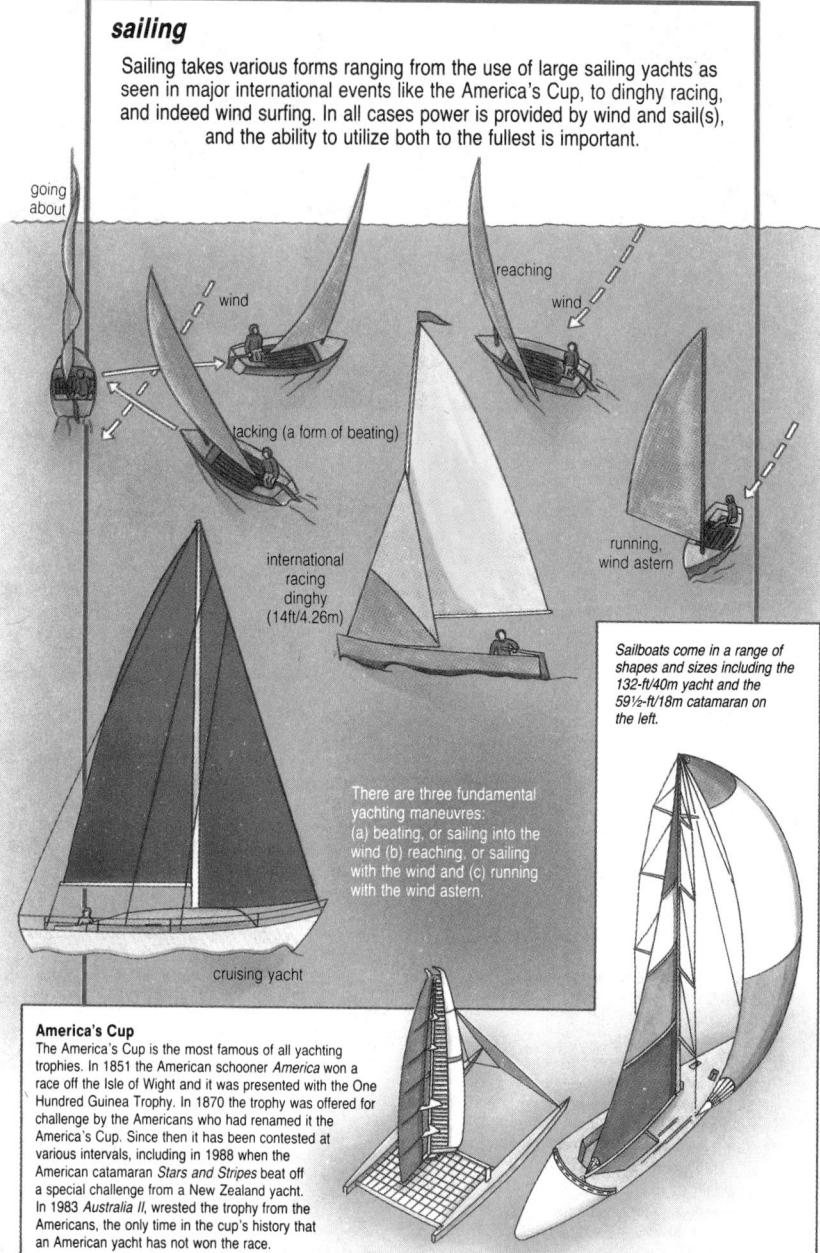

Sailing takes various forms ranging from the use of large sailing yachts as seen in major international events like the America's Cup, to dinghy racing, and indeed wind surfing. In all cases power is provided by wind and sail(s), and the ability to utilize both to the fullest is important.

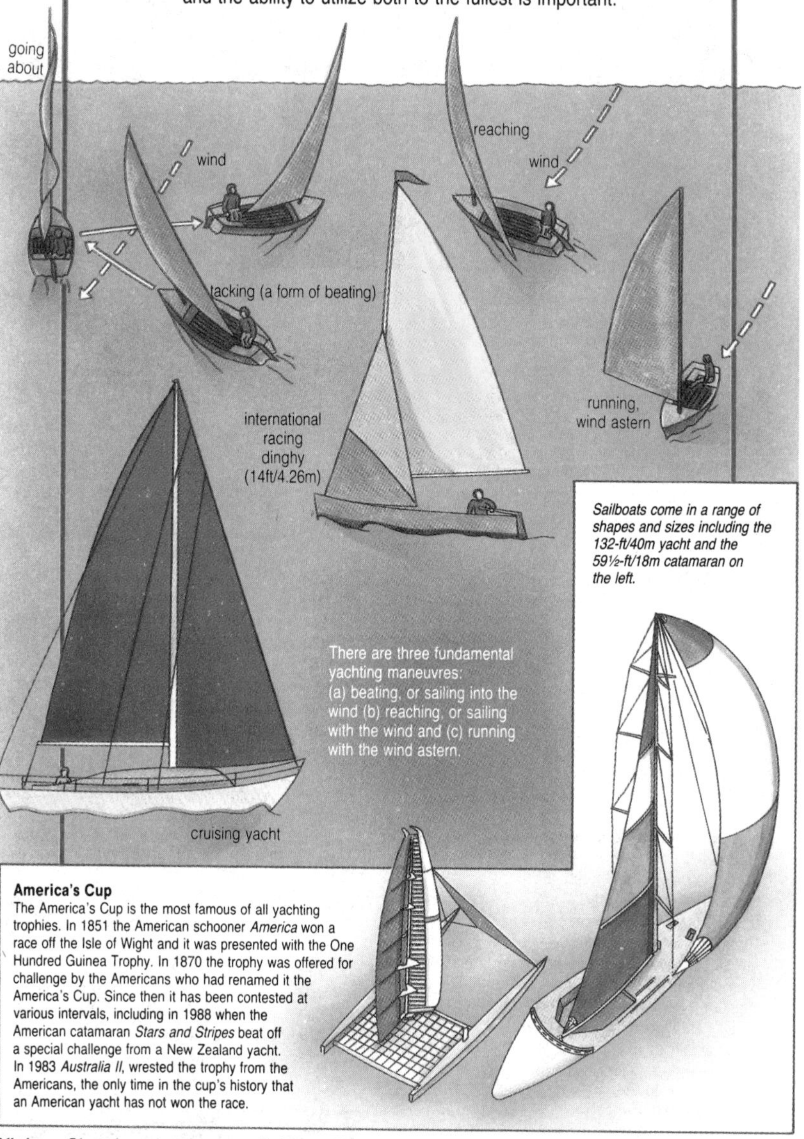
going about
wind
reaching
wind
tacking (a form of beating)
international racing dinghy (14ft/4.26m)
running, wind astern
cruising yacht
There are three fundamental yachting maneuvres: (a) beating, or sailing into the wind (b) reaching, or sailing with the wind and (c) running with the wind astern.

Sailboats come in a range of shapes and sizes including the 132-ft/40m yacht and the 59½-ft/18m catamaran on the left.

America's Cup
The America's Cup is the most famous of all yachting trophies. In 1851 the American schooner *America* won a race off the Isle of Wight and it was presented with the One Hundred Guinea Trophy. In 1870 the trophy was offered for challenge by the Americans who had renamed it the America's Cup. Since then it has been contested at various intervals, including in 1988 when the American catamaran *Stars and Stripes* beat off a special challenge from a New Zealand yacht. In 1983 *Australia II*, wrested the trophy from the Americans, the only time in the cup's history that an American yacht has not won the race.

St Christopher (St Kitts)–Nevis
Federation of

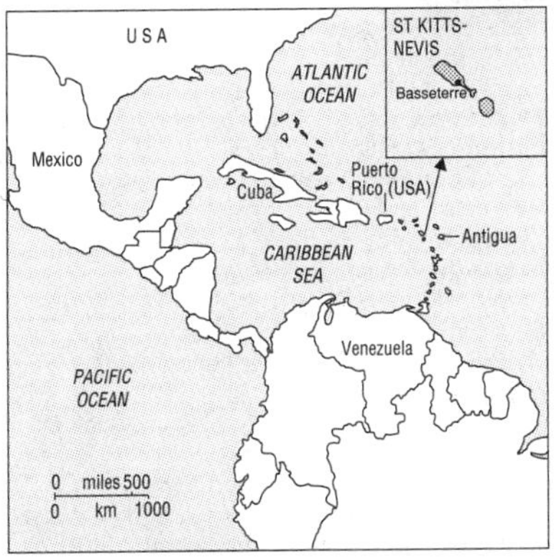
USA
ATLANTIC OCEAN
ST KITTS-NEVIS
Basseterre
Mexico
Cuba
Puerto Rico (USA)
Antigua
CARIBBEAN SEA
Venezuela
PACIFIC OCEAN
0 miles 500
0 km 1000

area 104 sq mi/269 sq km (St Kitts 68 sq mi, Nevis 36 sq mi)
capital Basseterre (on St Kitts)
cities Charlestown (largest on Nevis)
physical two volcanic islands in the Lesser Antilles
features first British West Indian island to be colonized
head of state Elizabeth II from 1983 represented by governor-general
head of government Kennedy Alphonse Simmonds from 1980
political system federal constitutional monarchy
political parties People's Action Movement (PAM), center-right; Nevis Reformation Party (NRP), Nevis-separatist; Labor Party, moderate, left-of-center
exports sugar, molasses, electronics, clothing
currency Caribbean dollar
population (1990 est) 45,800; growth rate 0.2% p.a.
life expectancy men 69/women 72
language English
religion Anglican 36%, Methodist 32%, other Protestant 8%, Roman Catholic 10% (1985 est)
literacy 90% (1987)
GNP $40 mn (1983); $870 per head
chronology
1871–56 Part of the Leeward Islands Federation.
1958–62 Part of the Federation of the West Indies.
1967 St Christopher, Nevis, and Anguilla granted internal self-government, within the British Commonwealth, with Robert Bradshaw, Labor Party leader, as prime minister.
1971 Anguilla left the federation.
1978 Bradshaw died; succeeded by Paul Southwell.
1979 Southwell died; succeeded by Lee L Moore.
1980 Coalition government led by Kennedy Simmonds. 1983 Full independence achieved within the Commonwealth.
1984 Coalition government reelected.
1989 Prime minister Simmonds won a third successive term.

St Helena

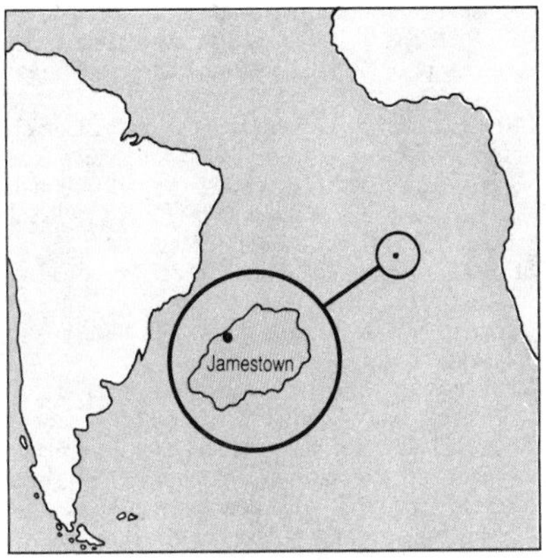
Jamestown

70 cm high at the shoulder, weight about 150 lb/70 kg. They have pendulous ears and lips, large feet, and drooping lower eyelids. They are usually orange and white.

They are named after the Augustinian monks of Grand St Bernard Hospice, Switzerland, who kept them for finding lost travelers in the Alps and to act as guides.

St Bernard Passes (Great St Bernard Pass and Little St Bernard Pass) passes through the ◊Alps.

St Christopher (St Kitts)-Nevis country in the West Indies, in the Leeward Islands.

government The islands of St Christopher and Nevis form a federal state within the ◊Commonwealth. The constitution dates from independence in 1983. The governor-general is the formal head of state, representing the British monarch, and appoints the prime minister and cabinet, who are drawn from and responsible to the assembly.

There is a single-chamber national assembly of 14 members, 11 elected by universal suffrage and 3 appointed by the governor-general, 2 on the advice of the prime minister and 1 on the advice of the leader of the opposition. There are three main political parties, the People's Action Movement (PAM), the Nevis Reformation Party (NRP), and the Labor Party.

Nevis Island has its own assembly of five elected and three nominated members, a prime minister and cabinet, and a deputy governor-general. It has the option to secede in certain conditions.

history The original ◊American Indian inhabitants were Caribs. St Christopher (then called Liamuiga) and Nevis were named by Christopher ◊Columbus in 1493. St Christopher became Britain's first West Indian colony 1623, and Nevis was settled soon afterwards. France also claimed ownership until 1713. Sugar plantations were worked by slaves.

The islands were part of the Leeward Islands Federation 1871–1956 and a single colony with the British Virgin Islands until 1960. In 1967 St Christopher (often called St Kitts), Nevis, and Anguilla attained internal self-government within the Commonwealth as associated states, and Robert Bradshaw, leader of the Labor Party, became the first prime minister. In 1970 the NRP was formed, calling for separation for Nevis, and the following year Anguilla, disagreeing with the government in St Christopher, chose to return to being a British dependency.

Bradshaw died in 1978 and was succeeded by his deputy, Paul Southwell. He died the following year, to be replaced by Lee L Moore. The 1980 general election produced a hung assembly, and, although Labor won more than 50% of the popular vote, a PAM-NRP coalition government was formed, with the PAM leader, Dr Kennedy Simmonds, as prime minister.

On Sept 1, 1983 St Christopher and Nevis became independent. In the 1984 general election the PAM-NRP coalition was decisively returned to office. In the 1989 general election, PAM won six of the eleven elective seats in the National asssembly and Dr Kennedy Simmonds continued in office.

St-Cloud town in the Île de France region, France; population about 29,000. The château, linked with Marie Antoinette and Napoleon, was demolished 1781, but the park remains. It is the site of the ◊Sèvres porcelain factory.

St-Denis industrial town, a northern suburb of Paris, France; population (1983) 96,000. ◊Abelard was a monk at the 12th-century Gothic abbey, which contains many tombs of French kings.

Sainte-Beuve Charles Augustin 1804–1869. French critic. He contributed to the *Revue des deux mondes/Review of the Two Worlds* from 1831. His articles on French literature appeared as *Causeries du lundi/Monday Chats* 1851–62, and his *Port Royal* 1840–59 is a study of Jansenism, a creed based on the teachings of St ◊Augustine.

St Elias Mountains mountain range on the Alaska–Canada border. Its highest peak, Mount Logan 19,850 ft/6,050 m, is Canada's highest mountain.

St Elmo's fire bluish, flamelike electrical discharge that sometimes occurs above ships' masts and other pointed objects or about aircraft in stormy weather. Although high voltage, it is low current and therefore harmless. St Elmo (or St Erasmus) is the patron saint of sailors.

Saint-Étienne city in S central France, capital of Loire *département*, Rhônes-Alpes region; population (1982) 317,000. Industries include the manufacture of aircraft engines, electronics, and chemicals, and it is the site of a school of mining, established 1816.

Saint-Exupéry Antoine de 1900–1944. French author who wrote the autobiographical *Vol de nuit/Night Flight* 1931 and *Terre des hommes/Wind, Sand, and Stars* 1939. His children's book *Le petit prince/The Little Prince* 1943 is also an adult allegory.

St Gallen (German *Sankt Gallen*) town in NE Switzerland; population (1987) 126,000. Industries include natural and synthetic textiles. It was founded in the 7th century by the Irish missionary St Gall, and the Benedictine abbey library has many medieval manuscripts.

Saint-Gaudens Augustus 1848–1907. Irish-born US sculptor; one of the leading Neo-Classical sculptors of his time. His monuments include the *Admiral Farragut* 1877 in Madison Square Park and the giant nude *Diana* that topped Stanford ◊White's Madison Square Garden, both in New York City, and the *Adams Memorial* 1891 in Rock Creek Cemetery, Washington, DC.

He was brought to the US as an infant, trained as a cameo cutter, studied at the National Academy of Design, and from 1867 traveled widely in Europe. After studying at the Ecole des Beaux-Arts in Paris, he returned to the US; established studios in New York City 1876 and Cornish, New Hampshire, 1885; and worked with the nation's major architects to produce public monuments. He also designed bronze medals, plaques, portrait tablets, and low reliefs. He was commissioned 1905 by President T Roosevelt to redesign US gold coinage; the 1907 double eagle ($20) was the only design approved before his death.

St George's port and capital of ◊Grenada; population (1986) 7,500, urban area 29,000.

St George's Channel stretch of water between SW Wales and SE Ireland, linking the Irish Sea with the Atlantic. It is 100 mi/160 km long and 50–90 mi/80–150 km wide. It is also the name of a channel between New Britain and New Ireland, Papua New Guinea.

St Germain-en-Laye, Treaty of 1919 treaty condemning the war between Austria and the Allies, signed at St Germain-en-Laye, a town 13 mi/21 km W of Paris. Representatives of the US signed it, but because the US Senate failed to ratify the Treaty of ◊Versailles, the Treaty of St Germain was not submitted to it. The US made a separate peace with Austria in 1921.

St Gotthard Pass a pass through the Swiss ◊Alps, at an altitude of 6,500 ft/2,000 m.

St Helena British island in the S Atlantic, 1,200 mi/1,900 km W of Africa, area 47 sq mi/122 sq km; population (1985) 5,900. Its capital is Jamestown, and it exports fish and timber. Ascension and Tristan da Cunha are dependencies.

St Helena became a British possession 1673, and a colony 1834. Napoleon died in exile here 1821.

St Helens, Mount volcanic mountain in Washington state. When it erupted in 1980 after being quiescent since 1857, it devastated an area of 230 sq mi/ 600 sq km and its height was reduced from 9,682 ft/2,950 m to 8,402 ft/2,560 m.

St Helier resort and capital of Jersey, Channel Islands; population (1981) 25,700. The "States of Jersey," the island legislature, sits here in the *salle des états*.

Saint John largest city of New Brunswick, Canada, on the Saint John River; population (1986) 121,000. It is a fishing port and has shipbuilding, timber, fish-processing, petroleum, refining, and textile industries. Founded by the French as Saint-Jean 1635, it was taken by the British 1758. After the American Revolution, several thousand Loyalists from the US settled here 1783, and it was the first Canadian city to be incorporated 1785.

St John, Order of (full title Knights Hospitallers of St John of Jerusalem) oldest order of Christian chivalry, named after the hospital at Jerusalem founded about 1048 by merchants of Amalfi for pilgrims, whose travel routes the knights defended from the Muslims. Today there are about 8,000 knights (male and female), and the Grand Master is the world's highest ranking Roman Catholic lay person.

On being forced to leave Palestine, the knights went to Cyprus 1291, to Rhodes 1309, and to Malta (granted to them by Emperor Charles V) 1530. Expelled by Napoleon (on his way to Egypt) 1798, they established their headquarters in Rome (Palazzo di Malta).

St John's capital and port of Antigua and Barbuda, on Antigua; population (1982) 30,000.

St John's capital and chief port of Newfoundland, Canada; population (1986) 96,000, urban area 162,000. The main industry is codfish processing; other products include textiles, fishing equipment, furniture, and machinery.

It was founded about 1528 and claimed for England by Humphrey ◊Gilbert 1582. Marconi's first transatlantic radio message was received on Signal Hill 1901. Memorial University was founded 1925.

St Joseph city in NW Missouri, on the Missouri river, NW of Kansas City. Industries include food processing, dairy products, metal products, concrete, and steel; population (1990) 71,852. In the mid-1800s, it served as the E terminus for the Pony Express.

Saint-Just Louis Antoine Léon Florelle de 1767–1794. French revolutionary. A close associate of ◊Robespierre, he became a member of the Committee of Public Safety 1793, and was guillotined with Robespierre.

St Kitts-Nevis contracted form of ◊St Christopher-Nevis.

Saint-Laurent Yves (Henri Donat Mathieu) 1936– . French couturier, partner to ◊Dior from 1954 and his successor 1957. He opened his own fashion house 1962.

St Lawrence river in E North America. From ports on the ◊Great Lakes it forms, with linking canals (which also give great hydroelectric capacity to the river), the St Lawrence Seaway for oceangoing ships, ending in the Gulf of St Lawrence. It is 745 mi/1,200 km long and is icebound annually for four months. The river's source is Lake Ontario. In its upper course the St Lawrence includes the scenic Thousand Islands and forms the border between the Canadian province of Ontario and the US state of New York. It then enters the province of Québec and flows past Montréal and the city of Québec. Below the latter, it broadens to a maximum width of 90 mi/145 km when it empties into the Gulf of St Lawrence, an arm of the Atlantic Ocean. French explorer Jacques Cartier discovered the river 1535, and the first permanent colonial settlement (city of Québec) was established 1608 by Samuel de Champlain.

St-Lô market town in Normandy, France, on the river Vire; population (1982) 24,800. In World War II it was almost entirely destroyed July 10–18, 1944, when US forces captured it from the Germans.

St Louis city in Missouri, on the Mississippi River; population (1990) 396,685, metropolitan area 2,444,099. Its industries include aerospace equipment, aircraft, vehicles, chemicals, electrical goods, steel, food processing, and beer. Its central US location makes it a warehousing and distribution center and a hub of rail, truck, and airline transportation. St Louis and Washington universities are here, and the University of Missouri has a campus in the city.

Founded as a French trading post 1764, it passed to the US 1803 under the ◊Louisiana Purchase. The Gateway Arch 1965 is a memorial by Eliel Saarinen to the pioneers of the West. A world's fair and the Olympic Games were held in the city 1904. After 1950, St Louis lost much of its population to the suburbs, and large areas fell into decay; redevelopment revived the center city in the late 1970s.

Saint Lucia country in the West Indies, one of the Windward Islands.

government The constitution dates from independence in 1979. The governor-general is the formal head of state, representing the British monarch. The governor-general appoints a prime minister and cabinet, drawn from and responsible to the House of Assembly.

There is a two-chamber parliament comprising the Senate, of 11 appointed members, and the House of Assembly, of 17 members, elected from single-member constituencies by universal suffrage. Six senators are appointed by the governor-general on the advice of the prime minister, three on the advice of the leader of the opposition, and two after wider consultation. Parliament has a life of five years.

There are three active political parties, the United Workers' Party (UWP), the St Lucia Labor Party (SLP) and the Progressive Labor Party (PLP).

history The early inhabitants were Carib Indians. ◊Columbus arrived 1502. The island was settled by the French 1635, who introduced ◊slavery, and ceded to Britain 1803.

Saint Lucia was a colony within the Windward Islands federal system until 1960, and acquired internal self-government 1967 as a West Indies associated state. The leader of the UWP, John Compton, became prime minister. In 1975 the associated states agreed to seek independence separately, and in Feb 1979, after prolonged negotiations, St Lucia achieved full independence within the ◊Commonwealth, with Compton as prime minister.

The SLP came to power in 1979 led by Allan Louisy, but a split developed within the party, and in 1981 Louisy was forced to resign, being replaced by the attorney general, Winston Cenac. Soon afterwards George Odlum, who had been Louisy's deputy, left with two other SLP members to form a new party, the PLP. For the next year the Cenac government had to fight off calls for a change of government that culminated in a general strike. Cenac eventually resigned, and in the general election 1982 the UWP won a decisive victory, enabling John Compton to return as prime minister. In new elections in April 1987, Compton's UWP was only narrowly returned by a 9:8 majority over the SLP.

St Lucia

USA
ATLANTIC
OCEAN
Mexico
ST LUCIA
Castries
Cuba
CARIBBEAN
SEA
Martinique
St Vincent
Venezuela
PACIFIC
OCEAN
0 miles 500
0 km 1000

area 238 sq mi/617 sq km
capital Castries
cities Vieux-Fort, Soufrière
physical mountainous with fertile valleys; mainly tropical forest
features volcanic peaks; Gros and Petit Pitons
head of state Elizabeth II from 1979 represented by governor-general
head of government John G M Compton from 1982
political system constitutional monarchy
political parties United Worker's Party (UWP), moderate, left-of-center; St Lucia Labor Party (SLP), moderate, left-of-center; Progressive Labor Party (PLP), moderate, left-of-center
exports coconut oil, bananas, cocoa, copra
currency Caribbean dollar
population (1990 est) 153,000; growth rate 2.8% p.a.
life expectancy 68 men, 73 women (1989)
language English; French patois
religion Roman Catholic 90%
literacy 78% (1989)
GNP $166 mn; $1,370 per head (1987)
chronology
1967 Granted internal self-government as a West Indies associated state.
1979 Independence achieved from Britain within the Commonwealth, with John Compton, leader of the United Workers' party (UWP), as prime minister. Allan Louisy, leader of the Saint Lucia Labor party (SLP), replaced Compton as prime minister.
1981 Louisy resigned; replaced by Winston Cenac.
1982 Compton returned to power at the head of a UWP government.
1987 Compton reelected with reduced majority.

St-Malo seaport and resort in the Ille-et-Vilaine *département*, W France, on the Rance estuary; population (1985) 47,500. It took its name from the Welshman Maclou, who was bishop here in about 640.

St Moritz winter sports center in SE Switzerland; it contains the Cresta Run (built 1885) for toboggans, bobsleds, and luges. It was the site of the Winter Olympics 1928 and 1948.

St-Nazaire industrial seaport in Pays de la Loire region, France; population (1982) 130,000. It stands at the mouth of the river Loire and in World War II was used as a German submarine base. Industries include shipbuilding, engineering, and food canning.

St-Omer town in Pas-de-Calais *département*, France, 26 mi/42 km SE of Calais; population (1985) 15,500. In World War I it was the site of British general headquarters from 1914 to 1916.

St Paul capital and industrial city of Minnesota, adjacent to ◊Minneapolis; population (1990) 272,235. Industries include electronics, publishing and printing, chemicals, refined petroleum, machin-

St Petersburg St Isaac's cathedral, St Petersburg (formerly Leningrad), USSR.

ery, and processed food. Educational institutions include Hamline University and Macalester College. The city is noted for its annual Winter Carnival and the St Paul Chamber Orchestra. French explorer Father Louis Hennepin visited the area 1680, but the first settlers did not arrive until 1838. St Paul became the territorial capital 1849. The first railroad reached here 1862.

St Petersburg seaside resort on the Gulf of Mexico and industrial city (space technology), W Florida; population (1990) 238,629. It is across Tampa Bay from Tampa. Besides aerospace and electronic equipment, the city produces boats and processed seafood. It is also a major tourist and retirement center. St Petersburg was platted 1884 and grew as a resort with the arrival of the railroad in the late 1880s.

St Petersburg formerly ***Leningrad*** capital of the Leningrad region, at the head of the Gulf of Finland; population (1987) 4,948,000. Industries include shipbuilding, machinery, chemicals, and textiles. It was renamed Petrograd 1914 and Leningrad 1924. In June 1991 the city's electors voted, by 55% to 43%, to restore the name it held under the tsars from 1703 to 1914. This vote secured parliamentary sanction in Sept 1991.

history capital of the Russian Empire 1709–1918, it was founded as an outlet to the Baltic 1703 by Peter the Great, who took up residence there 1712. St Petersburg was the center of all the main revolutionary movements from the Decembrist revolt 1825 up to the 1917 revolution. During the German invasion in World War II the city withstood siege and bombardment Sept 1941–Jan 1944.

In Aug 1991 the city's mayor, Anatoly Sobchak, and citizens, stood out against the attempted anti-Gorbachev coup.

St Petersburg is notable for its wide boulevards and the scale of its architecture. Most of its fine baroque and Neo-Classical buildings of the 18th and early 19th centuries survived World War II. Museums include the Winter Palace, occupied by the tsars until 1917, the Hermitage, the Russian Museum (formerly Michael Palace), and St Isaac's Cathedral. The oldest building is the fortress of St Peter and St Paul, on an island in the Neva, now a political prison. The university was established 1819.

St Petersburg became a seaport when it was linked with the Baltic by a ship canal built 1875–93. It is also linked by canal and river with the Caspian and Black seas, and in 1975 a seaway connection was completed via lakes Onega and Ladoga with the White Sea near Belomorsk, so that naval forces can reach the Barents Sea free of NATO surveillance.

St Petersburg is split up by the mouths of the Neva, which connects it with Lake Lagoda. The site is low and swampy, and the climate severe.

Saint-Pierre Jacques Henri Bernadin de 1737–1814. French author of the sentimental romance *Paul et Virginie* 1789.

St Pierre and Miquelon territorial collectivity of France, eight small islands off the S coast of Newfoundland

Saint-Simon Ahead of his time, French Socialist Comte de Saint-Simon advocated a "meritocracy" and the equality of women and men.

area St Pierre group 10 sq mi/26 sq km; Miquelon-Langlade group 83 sq mi/216 sq km
capital St Pierre
features the last surviving remnant of France's North American empire
products fish
population (1987) 6,300
language French
religion Roman Catholic
government French-appointed commissioner and elected local council; one representative in the National Assembly in France
history settled 17th century by Breton and Basque fishermen; French territory 1816–1976; overseas *département* until 1985; violent protests 1989 when France tried to impose its claim to a 200-mi/320-km fishing zone around the islands; Canada maintains that there is only a 12-mi/19-km zone.

St-Quentin town on the river Somme, Picardie, N France; population (1985) 69,000. It was the site of a Prussian defeat of the French 1871 and was almost obliterated in World War I. It is linked by canal to the industrial centers of Belgium and Germany. Its traditional textile production has been replaced by chemicals and metalworks.

Saint-Saëns (Charles) Camille 1835–1921. French composer, pianist, and organist. Among his many lyrical Romantic pieces are symphonies, concertos, the symphonic poem *Danse macabre* 1875, the opera *Samson et Dalila* 1877, and the orchestral *Carnaval des animaux/Carnival of the Animals* 1886.

Saint-Simon Claude Henri, Comte de 1760–1825. French Socialist who fought in the American Revolution and was imprisoned during the French Revolution. He advocated an atheist society ruled by technicians and industrialists in *Du Système industrielle/The Industrial System* 1821.

Saint-Simon Louis de Rouvroy, Duc de 1675–1755. French soldier, courtier, and politician whose *Mémoires* 1691–1723 are unrivaled as a description of the French court.

St-Tropez fishing port on the French Côte d'Azur; population (1985) 6,250. It became popular as a resort in the 1960s.

St Valentine's Day Massacre the murder in Chicago of seven unarmed members of the "Bugs" Moran gang on Feb 14, 1929 by members of Al Capone's gang disguised as policemen. The killings testified to the intensity of gangland warfare for the control of the trade in illicit liquor during ◊prohibition.

St Vincent and the Grenadines country in the Windward Islands, West Indies.

government The constitution dates from independence in 1979. The head of state is a resident governor-general representing the British monarch. The governor-general appoints a prime minister and cabinet, drawn from and responsible to the Assembly.

There is a single-chamber legislature, the House of Assembly, with 19 members, of which 13 are elected by universal suffrage, 4 appointed by the governor-general on the advice of the prime minister and 2 on the advice of the leader of the opposition. The Assembly has a life of five years.

There are a number of political parties, the most significant being the moderately left-of-center New Democratic Party (NDP) and the St Vincent Labor Party (SVLP).

history The original inhabitants were Carib Indians. ◊Columbus landed on St Vincent 1498. Claimed and settled by Britain and France, with African labor (see ◊slavery), the islands were ceded to Britain in 1783.

Collectively known as St Vincent, the islands were part of the West Indies Federation until 1962 and acquired internal self-government in 1969 as an associated state. They achieved full independence, within the ◊Commonwealth, as St Vincent and the Grenadines, in Oct 1979.

Until the 1980s two parties dominated politics in the islands, the SVLP and the People's Political Party (PPP). Milton Cato, SVLP leader, was prime minister at independence but his leadership was challenged in 1981 when a decline in the economy and his attempts to introduce new industrial-relations legislation resulted in a general strike. Cato survived mainly because of divisions in the opposition parties, and in 1984 the centrist NDP, led by an SVLP defector and former prime minister, James Mitchell, won a surprising victory. He was reelected 1989, his party winning all the assembly seats.

St Vitus's dance former name for ◊chorea, a nervous disorder. St Vitus, martyred under the Roman emperor Diocletian, was the patron saint of dancers.

Sakai city on the island of Honshu, Japan; population (1987) 808,000. Industries include engineering, aluminum, and chemicals.

Sakhalin (Japanese *Karafuto*) island in the Pacific, N of Japan which since 1947 forms with the ◊Kurils a region of the USSR; capital Yuzhno-Sakhalinsk (Japanese Toyohara); area 28,564 sq mi/74,000 sq km; population (1981) 650,000, including aboriginal ◊Ainu and Gilyaks. There are two parallel mountain ranges, rising to over 5,000 ft/1,525 m, which extend throughout its length, 600 mi/965 km. The economy is based on dairy farming, leguminous crops, oats, barley, and sugar beet. In the milder S, there is also timber, rice, wheat, fish, some oil and coal. The island was settled by both Russians and Japanese from the 17th century. In 1875 the S was ceded by Japan to Russia, but Japan regained it 1905, only to cede it again 1945. It has a missile base.

Sakharov Andrei Dmitrievich 1921–1989. Soviet physicist, known both as the "father of the Soviet H-bomb" and as an outspoken human-rights campaigner. Nobel Peace Prize 1975. He was elected to the Congress of the USSR People's Deputies (CUPD) 1989, where he emerged as leader of its radical reform grouping.

Sakharov was exempted from military service because of his skill at physics. In 1948 he joined Igor Tamm in developing the hydrogen bomb; he later protested against Soviet nuclear tests and was a founder of the Soviet Human Rights Committee. In 1980 he was arrested and sent to

St Vincent and the Grenadines

USA
ATLANTIC OCEAN
ST VINCENT and the GRENADINES
Kingstown
Mexico
Cuba
CARIBBEAN SEA
Martinique
St Lucia
Venezuela
PACIFIC OCEAN
0 miles 500
0 km 1000

area 150 sq mi/388 sq km, including Northern Grenadines 17 sq mi/43 sq km
capital Kingstown
cities Georgetown, Chateaubelair
physical volcanic mountains, thickly forested
features Mustique, one of the Grenadines, a vacation resort; Soufrière volcano
head of state Elizabeth II from 1979 represented by governor-general
head of government James Mitchell from 1984
political system constitutional monarchy
political parties New Democratic Party (NDP), moderate, left-of-center; St Vincent Labor Party (SVLP), moderate; left-of-center
exports bananas, tarros, sweet potatoes, arrowroot, copra
currency E Caribbean dollar
population (1990 est) 106,000; growth rate 4% p.a.
life expectancy men 69, women 74 (1989)
language English; French patois
religion 47% Anglican, 28% Methodist, 13% Roman Catholic
literacy 85% (1989)
GNP $188 mn; $1,070 per head (1987)
chronology
1783 Became a British Crown Colony.
1958–62 Part of the West Indies Federation.
1969 Granted internal self-government.
1979 Achieved full independence from Britain within the Commonwealth, with Milton Cato as prime minister.
1984 James Mitchell replaced Cato as prime minister.
1989 Mitchell decisively reelected.

internal exile in Gorky, following his criticism of Soviet action in Afghanistan. At the end of 1986 he was freed from exile and allowed to return to Moscow and resume his place in the Soviet Academy of Sciences.

Saki pen name of H(ugh) H(ector) Munro 1870–1916. Burmese-born British writer of ingeniously witty and bizarre short stories, often with surprise endings. He also wrote two novels *The Unbearable Bassington* 1912 and *When William Came* 1913.

Sakkara or ***Saqqara*** a village in Egypt, 10 mi/16 km S of Cairo, with 20 pyramids, of which the oldest (third dynasty) is the "Step Pyramid" designed by ◊Imhotep, whose own tomb here was the nucleus of the Aesklepieion, a center of healing in the ancient world.

Sakti the female principle in ◊Hinduism.

Śākyamuni the historical ◊Buddha, called Shaka in Japan (because Gautama was of the Śakya clan).

Saladin or ***Sala-ud-din*** 1138–1193. Born a Kurd, sultan of Egypt from 1175, in succession to the Atabeg of Mosul, on whose behalf he conquered Egypt 1164–74. He subsequently conquered Syria 1174–87 and precipitated the third ◊Crusade by his recovery of Jerusalem from the Christians 1187. Renowned for knightly courtesy, Saladin made peace with Richard I of England 1192.

Salado two rivers of Argentina, both rising in the Andes, and about 1,000 mi/1,600 km long. Salado del Norte, or ***Juramento***, flows from the Andes to join the Paraná; the Salado del Sud, or ***Desaguadero***, joins the Colorado and flows into the Atlantic S of Bahía Blanca.

Salam Abdus 1926– . Pakistani physicist. In 1967 he proposed a theory linking the electromagnetic and weak forces, also arrived at independently by Steven Weinberg. In 1979 he was the first person from his country to receive a Nobel Prize, which he shared with Weinberg and Sheldon Glashow.

Abdus Salam became a scientist by accident, when he won a scholarship to Cambridge in 1945 from the Punjab Small Peasants' welfare fund; he had intended to join the Indian civil service. He subsequently worked on the structure of matter at the Cavendish Laboratory.

Salamanca city in Castilla-León, W Spain, on the river Tormes, 162 mi/260 km NW of Madrid; population (1986) 167,000. It produces pharmaceuticals and wool. Its university was founded about 1230. It has a superbly designed square, the Plaza Mayor.

Salamanca, Battle of victory of the British commander Wellington over the French army in the ◊Peninsular War, July 22, 1812.

salamander any tailed amphibian of the order *Urodela*. They are sometimes confused with lizards, but unlike lizards they have no scales or claws. Salamanders have smooth or warty moist skin. The order includes some 300 species, arranged in nine families. Salamanders include hellbenders, mudpuppies, waterdogs, sirens, mole salamanders, newts, and lungless salamanders (dusky, woodland, and spring salamanders).

Salamis island off Piraeus, the port of ◊Athens, Greece; area 39 sq mi/101 sq km; population (1981) 19,000. The town of Salamis, on the west coast, is a naval station.

Salamis ancient city on the east coast of Cyprus, the capital under the early Ptolemies until its harbor silted up about 200 BC, when it was succeeded by Paphos in the southwest.

Salamis, Battle of naval battle off the coast of the island of Salamis in which the Greeks defeated the Persians 480 BC.

sal ammoniac former name for ◊ammonium chloride.

Salang Highway the main N–S route between Kabul, capital of Afghanistan, and the Soviet frontier; length 264 mi/422 km. The high-altitude Salang Pass and Salang Tunnel cross a natural break in the Hindu Kush mountains about 60 mi/100 km N of Kabul. This supply route was a major target of the Mujaheddin resistance fighters during the Soviet occupation of Aghanistan.

salat the daily prayers that are one of the Five Pillars of ◊Islam.

Muslims are required to pray five times a day, the first prayer being before dawn and the last after dusk. Prayer must be preceded by ritual washing and may be said in any clean place, facing the direction of Mecca. The prayers, which are recited in Arabic, follow a fixed series of words and movements.

salamander

***Salamis** The early Byzantine gymnasium at Salamis. Once the chief cities of ancient Cyprus, Salamis had a Christian community founded by Paul and Barnabas.*

Salazar Antonio de Oliveira 1889–1970. Portuguese prime minister 1932–68 who exercised a virtual dictatorship. A corporative constitution on the Italian model was introduced 1933, and until 1945 Salazar's National Union, founded 1930, remained the only legal party. Salazar was also foreign minister 1936–47 and during World War II he maintained Portuguese neutrality. But he fought long colonial wars in Africa (Angola and Mozambique) that impeded his country's economic development.

Salem industrial city (iron mining, textiles) in Tamil Nadu, India; population (1981) 515,000.

Salem city and manufacturing center in Massachusetts, 15 mi/24 km NE of Boston; population (1990) 38,091. Leather goods, electrical equipment, and machinery are manufactured here. Points of interest include Salem Maritime National Historic Site, the birthplace of Nathaniel Hawthorne, and the House of the Seven Gables 1668 that gave rise to his novel of the same name. Salem was settled 1626 and was the site of witchcraft trials 1692 that resulted in the execution of about 20 people.

Salem city in NW Oregon, settled about 1840 and made state capital 1859; population (1990) 107,786. It processes timber into wood products and has a prosperous fruit- and vegetable-canning industry. Williamette University is here. Salem was established by Methodist missionaries 1840–41 and became the territorial capital 1851.

Salerno port in Campania, SW Italy, 30 mi/48 km SE of Naples; population (1988) 154,000. It was founded by the Romans about 194 BC, destroyed by Charlemagne, and sacked by Holy Roman Emperor Henry VI 1194. The temple ruins of the ancient Greek city of ◊Paestum, with some of the earliest Greek paintings known, are nearby. Salerno has had a university (1150–1817, revived 1944) and medical school since medieval times.

Salic law a law adopted in the Middle Ages by several European royal houses, excluding women from succession to the throne. The name derives mistakenly from the Salian or northern division of the Franks, who supposedly practiced it.

salicylic acid HOC_6H_4COOH the active chemical constituent of aspirin, an analgesic drug. The acid and its salts (salicylates) occur naturally in many plants; concentrated sources include willow bark and oil of wintergreen.

When purified, salicylic acid is a white solid that crystallizes into prismatic needles at 318°F/159°C. It is used as an antiseptic, in food preparation and dyestuffs, and in the preparation of aspirin.

Salieri Antonio 1750–1825. Italian composer. He taught Beethoven, Schubert, and Liszt. He was the musical rival of Mozart (whom it has been suggested, without proof, that he poisoned) at the Emperor's court in Vienna, where he held the position of court composer.

Salinas city in W central California, S of San Jose. Fruits and vegetables, such as lettuce, are the economy's mainstay; population (1990) 108,777.

Salinas de Gortiari Carlos 1948– . Mexican politician, president from 1988, a member of the dominant Institutional Revolutionary Party (PRI).

Educated in Mexico and the US, he taught at Harvard and in Mexico before joining the government in 1971 and thereafter held a number of posts, mostly in the economic sphere, including finance minister. He narrowly won the 1988 presidential election, despite allegations of fraud.

Salinger J(erome) D(avid) 1919– . US writer, author of the classic novel of mid-20th-century adolescence *The Catcher in the Rye* 1951. He also wrote short stories about a Jewish family named Glass, including *Franny and Zooey* 1961.

Born in New York City, Salinger studied writing at Columbia University. In the late 1940s, he established an association with *The New Yorker*, which published most of his short stories. After *The Catcher in the Rye* became a classic, particularly among college students, he moved to New Hampshire, became increasingly reclusive, and published nothing after the mid-1960s. He also wrote *Nine Stories* 1953 and *Raise High the Roof Beam, Carpenters and Seymour: An Introduction* 1963.

Salisbury city in Wiltshire, England, 84 mi/135 km SW of London; population (1981) 35,355. The cathedral of St Mary, built 1220–66, is an example of Early English architecture; its decorated spire 404 ft/123 m is the highest in England. The cathedral library contains one of only four copies of the *Magna Carta*. Salisbury is an agricultural center, and industries include brewing and carpet manufacture. Another name for it is New Sarum, Sarum being a medieval Latin corruption of the ancient Romano-British name Sorbiodonum. Old Sarum, on a 300-ft/90-m hill to the N, was deserted when New Sarum was founded 1220 but was later again inhabited; it was brought within the town boundary 1953.

Salisbury former name (until 1980) of ◊Harare, capital of Zimbabwe.

Sailsbury Robert Arthur James Gascoyne-Cecil, 5th Marquess of 1893–1972. British Conservative politician. He was Dominions secretary 1940–42 and 1943–45, Colonial secretary 1942, Lord Privy Seal 1942–43 and 1951–52, and Lord President of the Council 1952–57.

saliva in vertebrates, a secretion from the salivary glands that aids the swallowing and digestion of food in the mouth. In mammals, it contains the enzyme amylase, which converts starch to sugar. The salivary glands of mosquitoes and other blood-sucking insects produce ◊anticoagulants.

Salk Jonas Edward 1914– . US physician and microbiologist. In 1954 he developed the original vaccine that led to virtual eradication of paralytic ◊polio in industrialized countries. He was director of the Salk Institute for Biological Studies, University of California, San Diego, 1963–75.

Sallinen Tyko 1879–1955. Finnish Expressionist painter. Inspired by ◊Fauvism on visits to France 1909 and 1914, he created visionary works relating partly to his childhood experiences of religion. He also painted Finnish landscape and peasant life, such as *Washerwoman* 1911 (Ateneum, Helsinki).

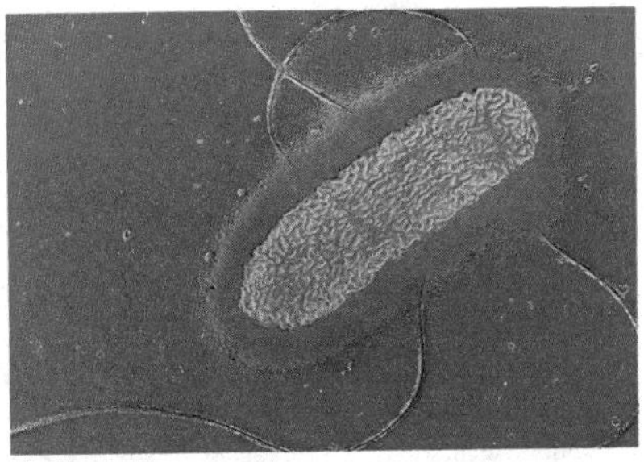

Salmonella *False-color electron-microscope view of the bacterium* Salmonella enteriditis, *a cause of food poisoning (× 8700).*

Sallust Gaius Sallustius Crispus 86–c. 34 BC. Roman historian, a supporter of Julius Caesar. He wrote accounts of Catiline's conspiracy and the Jugurthine War in an epigrammatic style.

salmon any of the various bony fishes of the family Salmonidae. More specifically the name is applied to several speciees of game fishes of the genera Salmo and Oncorhynchus of North America and Eurasia that mature in the ocean but, to spawn, return to the freshwater streams where they were born. Their normal color is silvery with a few dark spots, but the color changes at the spawning season. Salmon live in the sea, but return to spawn in the place they were spawned, often overcoming great obstacles to get there.

The spawning season is between Sept and Jan, although they occasionally spawn at other times. The orange eggs, about 0.25 in/6 mm in diameter, are laid on the river bed, fertilized by the male, and then covered with gravel by the female. The incubation period is from five weeks to five months. The young hatched fish are known as alevins, and when they begin feeding, they are called parr. At about two years old, the coat becomes silvery, and they are then smolts. Depending on the species, they may spend up to four years at sea before returning to their home streams to spawn (at this stage called grilse) and die.

Salmon are increasingly "farmed" in cages, and "ranched" (selectively bred, hatched, and fed before release to the sea). Stocking rivers indiscriminately with hatchery fish may destroy the precision of their homing instinct by interbreeding between those originating in different rivers.

Salmonella a very varied group of bacteria. They can be divided into three broad groups. One of these causes typhoid and paratyphoid fevers, while a second group causes Salmonella ◊food poisoning, which is characterized by stomach pains, vomiting, diarrhea, and headache. It can be fatal in infants and elderly people, but others usually recover in a few days without antibiotics. Most cases are caused by contaminated animal products, especially poultry meat and eggs.

Human carriers of the disease may seem well themselves but pass the bacteria on to others through unhygienic preparation of food. Domestic pets can also carry the bacteria while appearing healthy.

Salome 1st century AD. In the New Testament, granddaughter of the king of Judea, Herod the Great. Rewarded for her skill in dancing, she requested the head of John the Baptist from her stepfather ◊Herod Antipas.

Salomon Haym c. 1740–1785. Polish-born American financier. Salomon traveled extensively throughout Europe before settling permanently in New York 1772. As a successful merchant and supporter of American independence, he undertook the provisioning of Continental troops at the outbreak of the Revolutionary War. He was arrested briefly by the British as a spy 1776, and in 1778 he was captured and sentenced to death. After escaping, Salomon offered his financial services to the Continental Congress. From 1778 to 1782 he raised large public subscriptions for the continuance of the war.

salon (French "drawing room") a meeting place provided by a wealthy hostess for writers, artists, and musicians. The term was first used in 17th-century Paris to describe the gatherings of artists and intellectuals in the houses of rich and cultured ladies. The tradition of the "literary hostess" has continued in Europe and the US.

Salonika English name for ◊Thessaloniki, port and country in Greece.

salsa a Latin big-band dance music popularized by Puerto Ricans in New York City in the 1980s and by, among others, the Panamanian singer Rubén Blades (1948–).

salsify or ***vegetable oyster*** hardy biennial *Tragopogon porrifolius*, family Compositae. Its white fleshy roots and spring shoots are cooked and eaten.

SALT abbreviation for ◊Strategic Arms Limitation Talks, a series of US-Soviet negotiations 1969–79.

salt in chemistry, any compound formed from an acid and a base through the replacement of all or part of the hydrogen in the acid by a metal or electropositive radical. Common or table salt is sodium chloride (see ◊salt, common).

A salt may be produced by chemical reaction between an acid and a base, or by the displacement of hydrogen from an acid by a metal (see ◊displement activity). As a solid, the ions normally adopt a regular arrangement to form crystals. Some salts only form stable crystals as hydrates (when combined with water). A salt readily dissolves in water to give an electrolye (a solution that conducts electricity).

saltation (Latin *saltare* "to leap") in biology, the idea that an abrupt genetic change can occur in an individual, which then gives rise to a new species. The idea has now been largely discredited, although the appearance of ◊polyploid individuals can be considered an example.

salt, common sodium chloride (NaCl), found dissolved in sea water and as rock salt (halite) in large deposits and salt domes. Common salt is used extensively in the food industry as a preservative and for flavoring, and in the chemical industry to make chlorine and sodium. While common salt is an essential part of our diet, some medical experts believe that excess salt, largely from processed food, can lead to high blood pressure and increased risk of heart attacks.

Salt has historically been considered a sustaining substance, often taking on religious significance in ancient cultures. Roman soldiers were paid part of their wages as salt allowance (Latin *salerium argentinium*), hence the term "salary."

Salt Lake City capital of Utah, on the river Jordan, 11 mi/18 km SE of the Great Salt Lake; population (1990) 159,936. Founded 1847, it is the headquarters of the Church of Jesus Christ of Latter-Day Saints (Mormon Church). The Mormon Tabernacle, Mormon Temple, and University of Utah are here. Products include refined petroleum, metal goods, processed food, and textiles, and nearby mining adds to the city's economy. Salt Lake City became the territorial capital 1856.

Salton Sea brine lake in SE California, area 250 sq mi/650 sq km, accidentally created in the early 20th century during irrigation works from the Colorado River. It is used to generate electricity; see ◊solar ponds.

saltpeter former name for potassium nitrate (KNO_3), the compound used in making gunpowder (from about 1500). It occurs naturally, being deposited during dry periods in places with warm climates such as India.

saluki breed of dog resembling the greyhound. It is about 26 in/65 cm high, and has a silky coat, which is usually fawn, cream, or white.

Salt Lake City The Mormon Tabernacle in Salt Lake City, Utah, was dedicated in 1893 and took 40 years to build.

It is descended from the hound of the African desert Bedouins.

Salvador port and naval base in Bahia state, NE Brazil, on the inner side of a peninsula separating Todos Santos Bay from the Atlantic; population (1985) 2,126,000. Products include cocoa, tobacco, and sugar. Founded 1510, it was the capital of Brazil 1549–1763.

Salvador, El republic in Central America; see ◊El Salvador.

salvage saving or rescue, either as a whole or in part, of any property threatened with destruction, especially at sea. The term is used more specifically for compensation payable to those who, by voluntary effort, have saved a ship and/or its cargo and passengers from complete loss through shipwreck, fire, or enemy action.

Salvarsan historical proprietary name for arsphenamine (technical name 3,3-diamino-4,4-dihydroxyarsenobenzene dichloride), the first specific antibacterial agent, discovered by Paul Ehrlich in 1909. Because of its destructive effect on *Spirochaeta pallida*, it was used in the treatment of syphilis before the development of antibiotics.

Salvation Army Christian evangelical, social-service, and social-reform organization, originating 1865 in London, with the work of William ◊Booth. It has military titles for its officials, is renowned for its brass bands, and it publishes the weekly journal *War Cry*. Originally called the Christian Revival Association, it has been known since 1878 as the Salvation Army. It provides food-and-shelter missions for social derelicts and runs "thrift shops," selling second-hand merchandise to raise funds.

It was established in the US 1880 and in Canada 1881 and has conducted missionary work throughout the world. The American Rescue Workers split off from the organization in 1884, and the Volunteers of America withdrew in 1894 after disputes over organizational structure and autonomy. Doctrine and ritual have never been primary concerns of the Salvation Army, which devotes itself to preaching redemption from a sinful life. It currently has about 300,000 US members.

sal volatile another name for ◊smelling salts.

Salween river rising in E Tibet and flowing 1,740 mi/2,800 km through Myanmar (Burma) to the Andaman Sea; it has many rapids.

Salyut (Russian "salute") a series of seven space stations launched by the USSR 1971–82. Salyut was cylindrical in shape, 50 ft/15 m long, and weighed 21 tons. It housed two or three cosmonauts at a time, for missions lasting up to eight months.

Salyut 1 was launched Apr 19, 1971. It was occupied for 23 days in June 1971 by a crew of three, who died during their return to Earth when their ◊Soyuz ferry craft depressurized. *Salyut 2*, in 1973, broke up in orbit before occupation. The first fully successful Salyut mission was a 14-day visit to *Salyut 3* in July 1974. In 1984–85 a *Salyut 7* three-man cosmonaut team endured a record 237-day flight in an orbiting space station. In 1986, the Salyut series was superseded by ◊*Mir*, an improved design capable of being enlarged by additional modules sent up from Earth.

Crews observed Earth and the sky, and carried out processing of materials in weightlessness.

Salzburg capital of the state of Salzburg, W Austria, on the river Salzach, in W Austria; population (1981) 139,400. The city is dominated by the Hohensalzburg fortress. It is the seat of an archbishopric founded by St Boniface about 700 and has a 17th-century cathedral. Industries include stock rearing, dairy farming, forestry, and tourism.

It is the birthplace of the composer Wolfgang Amadeus Mozart and an annual music festival has been held here since 1920.

Salzburg federal province of Austria; area 2,779 sq mi/7,200 sq km; population (1987) 462,000. Its capital is Salzburg.

Salzedo Carlos 1885–1961. French-born harpist and composer. He studied in Paris and moved to New York, where he cofounded the International Composers' Guild. He did much to promote the harp as a concert instrument, and invented many unusual sounds.

Salzgitter city in Lower Saxony, Federal Republic of Germany; population (1988) 105,000.

samara in botany, a winged fruit, a type of ◊achene.

Samara name until 1935 of ◊Kuibyshev, a port in the USSR.

Samaria region of ancient Israel. The town of Samaria (now Sebastiyeh) on the west bank of the river Jordan was the capital of Israel in the 10th–8th centuries BC. It was renamed Sebarte in the 1st century BC by the Roman administrator Herod the Great. Extensive remains have been excavated.

Samaritan a member or descendant of the colonists forced to settle in Samaria (now N Israel) by the Assyrians after their occupation of the ancient kingdom of Israel 722 BC. Samaritans adopted a form of Judaism, but adopted only the *Pentateuch*, the five books of Moses of the Old Testament, and regarded their temple on Mount Gerizim as the true sanctuary. They remained a conservative, separate people and declined under Muslim rule, with only a few hundred, in a small community at Nablus, surviving today.

samarium hard, brittle, gray-white, metallic element of the ◊lanthanide series, symbol Sm, atomic number 62, atomic weight 150.4. It is widely distributed in nature and is obtained commercially from the minerals monzanite and bastnaesite. It is used only occasionally in industry, mainly as a catalyst in organic reactions. Samarium was discovered by spectroscopic analysis of the mineral samarskite and named in 1879 by French chemist Paul Lecoq de Boisbaudran (1838–1912) for its source.

Samarkand city in Uzbek Republic, USSR; capital of Samarkand region, near the river Zerafshan, 135 mi/217 km E of Bukhara; population (1987) 388,000. Industries include cotton-ginning, silk manufacture, and engineering.

Samarkand was the capital of the empire of ◊Tamerlane the 14th-century Mongol ruler who is buried here, and was once an major city on the ◊Silk Road. It was occupied by the Russians in 1868 but remained a center of Muslim culture until the Russian Revolution.

Samarra ancient town in Iraq, on the river Tigris, 65 mi/105 km NW of Baghdad; population (1970) 62,000. Founded 836 by the Abbasid Caliph Motassim, it was the Abbasid capital until 876 and is a place of pilgrimage for ◊Shi'ite Muslims.

samizdat (Russian "self-published") in the USSR, and eastern Europe before the 1989 uprisings, written material circulated underground to evade state censorship, for example reviews of Solzhenitsyn's banned novel *August 1914* 1972.

Samoa volcanic island chain in the SW Pacific. It is divided into Western Samoa and American Samoa.

Samoa, American group of islands 2,610 mi/4,200 km S of Hawaii, administered by the US

area 77 sq mi/200 sq km

capital Fagatogo on Tutuila

features five volcanic islands, including Tutuila, Tau, and Swain's Island, and two coral atolls. National park (1988) includes prehistoric village of Saua, virgin rainforest, flying foxes

exports canned tuna, handicrafts

currency US dollar

population (1990) 46,773

language Samoan and English

religion Christian

government as a non-self-governing territory of the US, under Governor A P Lutali, it is constitutionally an unincorporated territory of the US, administered by the Department of the Interior

history the islands were acquired by the US in Dec 1899 by agreement with Britain and Germany under the Treaty of Berlin. A constitution was adopted 1960 and revised 1967.

Samoa, Western country in the SW Pacific, in ◊Polynesia, NE of Fiji.

government Western Samoa is an independent state within the ◊Commonwealth. The 1962 constitution provides for a parliamentary system of government, with a constitutional head of state, a single-chamber legislative assembly, and a prime minister and cabinet drawn from and responsible to the assembly. The head of state is normally elected by the assembly for a five-year term, but the present holder of the office has been elected for life. The head of state appoints the prime minister and cabinet on the basis of assembly support.

The assembly (*Fono*) has 47 members, including 45 Samoans, who are elected by clan chiefs (holders of Matai titles) in 41 territorial constituencies, and 2, usually European, members who are elected from individual voter's roles. The assembly has a life of three years.

history The original inhabitants were Polynesians, and the first Europeans to reach the island group of Samoa, 1722, were Dutch. In the 19th century Germany, the UK, and the US had conflicting interests in the islands, sometimes called the Navigators' Islands, and administered them jointly from 1889 until 1899, when they were divided into American ◊Samoa and Western Samoa. Western Samoa was a German colony until World War I and from 1920 was administered by New Zealand, first as a League of Nations mandate and from 1946 as a United Nations trust territory.

Western Samoa was granted internal self-government gradually until it achieved full independence, within the Commonwealth, on Jan 1, 1962. The office of head of state was held jointly by two traditional rulers, but on the death of one of them, the other, Malietoa Tanumafili II, became the sole head of state for life. The prime minister at the time of independence was Fiame Mata Afa Mulinu'u. He lost power 1970 but regained it 1973 until his death 1975. In 1976 the first prime minister who was not of royal blood was elected, Tupuola Taisi Efi.

In 1979 the previously unorganized opposition politicians came together to form the Human Rights Protection Party (HRPP), and it won the 1982 election, Va'ai Kolone becoming prime minister. Later that year he was removed because of alleged voting malpractices and replaced by Tupuola Efi. Efi resigned a few months later when his budget was not approved; he was replaced by the new HRPP leader, Tofilau Eti Alesana. The HRPP won a decisive victory in the Feb 1985 general election, securing 31 *Fono* seats, and Tofilau Eti Alesana continued as prime minister. At the end of the year he resigned because of opposition to his budget proposals, which resulted in large scale defections from the HRPP. The head of state refused to call another election and

Samoa, Western
Independent State of
(Samoa i Sisifo)

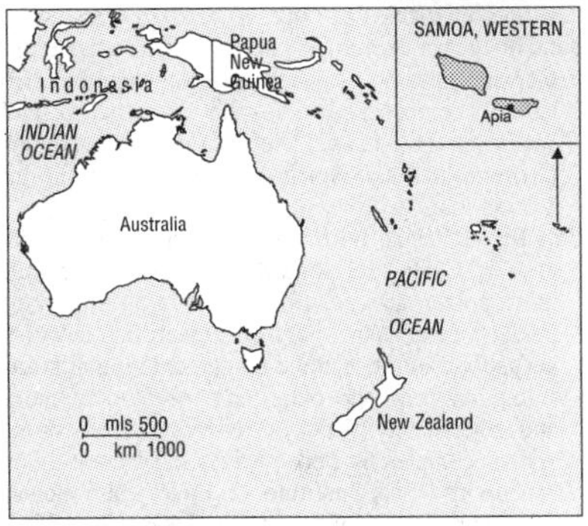
SAMOA, WESTERN
Apia
Papua
New Guinea
Indonesia
INDIAN OCEAN
Australia
PACIFIC
OCEAN
New Zealand
0 mls 500
0 km 1000

area 1,093 sq mi/2,830 sq km
capital Apia (on Upolu island)
physical comprises South Pacific islands of Savai'i and Upolu, with two smaller tropical islands and islets; mountain ranges on main islands
features lava flows on Savai'i
head of state King Malietoa Tanumafili II from 1962
head of government Tofilau Eti Alesana from 1988
political system constitutional monarchy
political parties Human Rights Protection Party (HRPP), led by Tofilau Eti Alesana; the Va'ai Kolone Group (VKG); Christian Democratic Party (CDP), led by Tupuola Taisi Efi. All "parties" are personality-based groupings
exports coconut oil, copra, cocoa, fruit juice, cigarettes, timber
currency talà
population (1989) 169,000; growth rate 1.1% p.a.
life expectancy men 64, women 69 (1989)
language English, Samoan (official)
religion Protestant 70%, Roman Catholic 20%
literacy 90% (1989)
GNP $110 mn (1987); $520 per head
chronology
1899–1914 German protectorate.
1920–61 Administered by New Zealand.
1959 Local government elected.
1961 Referendum favored independence.
1962 Independence achieved, with Fiame Mata'afa Mulinu'u as prime minister.
1975 Mata'afa died; succeeded by Tupuola Taisi Efi, first nonroyal prime minister.
1982 Va'ai Kolone became prime minister; replaced by Tupuola Efi. Assembly failed to approve budget; Tupuola Efi resigned; replaced by Tofilau Eti Alesana.
1985 Tofilau Eti resigned; head of state invited Va'ai Kolombe to lead the government.
1988 Elections produced a hung parliament, with first Tupuola Efi as prime minister and then Tofilau Eti Alesana.

Va'ai Kolone returned to lead a government that comprised independents as well as members of Tupuola Taisi Efi's (*Tupua Tamasese*) newly formed Christian Democratic Party (CDP). The general election of Feb 1988 produced a hung parliament with Tofilau Eti Alesana as the new premier.

Samos Greek island in the Aegean Sea, off the W coast of Turkey; area 184 sq mi/476 sq km; capital Limén Vathéos; population (1981) 31,600. Mountainous but fertile, it produces wine and olive oil. The mathematician Pythagoras was born here. The town of Teganion is on the site of the ancient city of Samos, which was destroyed by Darius I of Persia.

samovar (Russian "self-boiling") a metal urn with a fauceted spout, heated by charcoal, used for making tea.

samoyed breed of dog, originating in Siberia. It is about 60 lb/25 kg, and 23 in/58 cm tall. It resembles a ◊chow-chow, but has a more pointed face and a white or cream coat.

samphire or ***glasswort*** or ***sea asparagus*** perennial plant *Crithmum maritimum* found on sea cliffs in Europe. The aromatic leaves are fleshy and sharply pointed; the flowers grow in yellow-green umbels. It is used in salads, or pickled.

Samson 11th century BC. In the Old Testament, a hero of Israel. He was renowned for exploits of strength against the Philistines, which ended when his mistress Delilah cut off his hair, the source of his strength, as told in the Book of Judges.

Samsun Black Sea port and capital of a province of the same name in N Turkey; situated at the mouth of the Murat river in a tobacco-growing area; site of the ancient city of Amisus; population (1985) 280,000.

Samuel 11th–10th centuries BC. In the Old Testament, the last of the judges who ruled the ancient Hebrews before their adoption of a monarchy, and the first of the prophets; the two books bearing his name cover the story of Samuel and the reigns of kings Saul and David.

Samuelson Paul 1915– . US economist. He became professor at the Massachusetts Institute of Technology 1940 and was awarded a Nobel Prize 1970 for his application of scientific analysis to economic theory. His books include *Economics* 1948, a classic textbook, and *Linear Programming and Economic Analysis* 1958.

samurai feudal military caste in Japan from the mid-12th century until 1869, when the feudal system was abolished and all samurai pensioned off by the government. Many became leaders in various spheres of modern life. A samurai was an armed retainer of a *daimyō* (large landowner) with specific duties and privileges and a strict code of honor. A *rōnin* was a samurai without feudal allegiance.

From the 16th century, commoners were not allowed to carry swords, whereas samurai had two swords, and the higher class of samurai were permitted to fight on horseback. It is estimated that 8% of the population belonged to samurai families. A financial depression from about 1700 caused serious hardship to the samurai, beginning a gradual disintegration of their traditions and prestige, accelerated by the fall of the Tokugawa shogunate 1868, in which they had assisted. Under the new Meiji emperor they were stripped of their role, and many rebelled. Their last uprising was the Satsuma Rebellion 1877–78, in which 40,000 samurai took part.

San'a capital of Yemen, SW Arabia, 200 mi/320 km N of Aden; population (1986) 427,000. A walled city, with fine mosques and traditional architecture, it is rapidly being modernized.

San Andreas fault a geologic fault line stretching for 700 mi/1,125 km in a NW– SE direction through the state of California.

Two sections of the Earth's crust meet at the San Andreas fault, and friction is created as the coastal Pacific plate moves NW, rubbing against the American continental plate, which is moving slowly SE. The relative movement is only about 2 in/5 cm a year, which means that Los Angeles will reach San Francisco's latitude in 10 million years. The friction caused by this tectonic movement gives rise to periodic ◊earthquakes.

San Angelo city in W central Texas, where the North and Middle Concho rivers meet, SW of Abilene. Industries include wool, food processing, oil, livestock, and clay products; population (1990) 84,474.

***San'a** A view of the old city. A majority of the inhabitants still live within the city walls.*

San Antonio city in S Texas; population (1990) 935,933. A commercial and financial center, its industries include aircraft maintenance, oil refining, and meatpacking. Of great economic importance are Fort Sam Houston, four Air Force bases, South Texas Medical Center, and the Southwest Research Center, all within city limits. Educational institutions include Trinity University and the University of Texas at San Antonio. Points of interest include 18th-century Spanish missions and the Alamo, the Texan-occupied mission-fortress stormed in 1836 by Mexican troops who massacred the entire garrison. A Spanish mission and fort were established here on an Indian site 1718, and a community was laid out 1731. It passed from Spanish to Mexican rule 1821, to the Texas republic 1836, and to the US 1845.

San Bernardino city in California, 50 mi/80 km E of Los Angeles; population (1990) 164,164, metropolitan area 703,000. Manufactured products include processed food, steel, and aerospace and electronic equipment. Norton Air Force Base is just outside the city. San Bernardino was named by Spanish missionaries who arrived 1810. A group of Mormons platted the community in the 1850s.

San Cristóbal capital of Tachira state, W Venezuela, near the Colombian border; population (1981) 199,000. It was founded by the Spanish 1561 and stands on the ◊Pan-American Highway.

sanction economic or military measure taken by a state or number of states to enforce international law. Examples of the use of sanctions are the attempted economic boycott of Italy (1935–36) during the Abyssinian War, by the League of Nations; of Rhodesia, after its unilateral declaration of independence 1965, by the United Nations; the call for measures against South Africa on human-rights grounds, by the United Nations and other organizations from 1985; the

Sand *French novelist George Sand. Her affairs with a succession of artists and poets provided the inspiration for much of her work.*

economic boycott of Iraq (1990) in protest over its invasion of Kuwait, following resolutions passed by the United Nations.

Sanctorius Sanctorius 1561–1636. Italian physiologist who pioneered the study of ◊metabolism and invented the clinical thermometer and a device for measuring pulse rate.

Sanctorius introduced quantitative methods into medicine. For 30 years he weighed both himself and his food, drink, and waste products. He determined that over half of normal weight loss is due to "insensible perspiration."

sanctuary (Latin *sanctuarium* "sacred place") the holiest area of a place of worship; also, a place of refuge from persecution or prosecution, usually in or near a place of worship. The custom of offering sanctuary in specific places goes back to ancient times and was widespread in Europe in the Middle Ages.

The ancient Hebrews established six separate towns of refuge, and the Greek temple of Diana at Ephesus provided sanctuary within a radius of two stadia (about 475 yd/434 m). In Roman temples the sanctuary was the *cella* (inner room), in which stood the statue of the god worshiped there.

In the Middle Ages criminals or the hunted could take refuge for 40 days, then opt for safe passage out of the country.

sand loose grains of rock, sized 0.0008–0.0800 in/ 0.02–2.00 mm in diameter, consisting chiefly of ◊quartz, but owing their varying color to mixtures of other minerals. It is used in cement-making, as an abrasive, in glass-making, and for other purposes.

Sands are classified into marine, freshwater, glacial, and terrestrial. Some "light" soils contain up to 50% sand. Sands may eventually consolidate into ◊sandstone.

Sand George. Adopted name of Amandine Aurore Lucie Dupin 1804–1876. French author whose prolific literary output was often autobiographical. In 1831 she left her husband after nine years of marriage and, while living in Paris as a writer, had love affairs with Alfred de ◊Musset, ◊Chopin, and others. Her first novel, *Indiana* 1832, was a plea for women's right to independence.

Her other novels include *La mare au diable/ The Devil's Pool* 1846 and *La petite Fadette/The Little Fairy* 1848. In 1848 she retired to the château of Nohant, in central France.

sandbar ridge of sand built up by the currents across the mouth of a river or bay. A sandbar may be entirely underwater or it may form an elongated island that breaks the surface. A sandbar stretching out from a headland is a ***sand spit***.

Sandburg Carl August 1878–1967. US poet. He worked as a farm laborer and a bricklayer, and his poetry celebrates ordinary life in the US, as in *Chicago Poems* 1916, *The People, Yes* 1936, and *Complete Poems* 1951 (Pulitzer prize). In free verse, it is reminiscent of Walt Whitman's poetry. Sandburg also wrote a monumental biography of Abraham Lincoln, *Abraham Lincoln: The Prairie Years* 1926 (two volumes) and *Abraham Lincoln: The War Years* 1939 (four volumes; Pulitzer prize). *Always the Young Strangers* 1953 is his autobiography.

Born in Galesburg, Illinois, where a Lincoln-Douglas debate had taken place 1858, Sandburg left school after the eighth grade to work. After serving in the Spanish-American War, he briefly attended college but never graduated. *The American Songbag* 1927 is his collection of folk ballads and songs assembled during his travels around the US 1902-04. He also wrote *Smoke and Steel* 1920, *Slabs of the Sunburnt West* 1922, *Mary Lincoln, Wife and Widow* 1932, and *Storm Over the Land* 1942. Sandburg's children's books include *Rootabaga Stories* 1922.

Sanders George 1906–1972. Russian-born British actor, usually cast as a smooth-talking cad. Most of his film career was spent in the US where he starred in such films as *Rebecca* 1940, *The Moon and Sixpence* 1942, and *The Picture of Dorian Gray* 1944. From 1939 to 1942 he played The Saint and The Falcon in two films each.

sandgrouse any bird of the family Pteroclidae. They look like long-tailed grouse, but are closely related to pigeons instead. They live in warm, dry areas of Europe, Asia, and Africa and have long wings, short legs, and thick skin.

Sandgrouse may travel long distances to water to drink, and some carry water back to their young by soaking the breast feathers.

sand hopper or ***beachflea*** any of various small crustaceans belonging to the order Amphipeda, with laterally compressed bodies that live in beach sand and jump like fleas. The eastern sand hopper *Orchestia agilis* of North America is about 0.5 in/ 1.3 cm long.

San Diego Pacific port city and military and naval base in California; population (1990) 1,110,549, metropolitan area, 2,498,016. It is an important Pacific Ocean fishing port. Manufacturing includes aerospace and electronic equipment, metal fabricating, printing and publishing, seafood canning, and shipbuilding. The US Navy's largest operational complex is here. Educational institutions include the Salk Institute of Biological Studies, San Diego State University, the University of San Diego, and the University of California at San Diego, which includes the Scripps Institute of Oceanography in neighboring La Jolla. Attractions include the San Diego Zoo and Sea World. A 16-mi/26-km transit line opened 1981 connects to Tijuana, Mexico. San Diego's excellent deepwater harbor was discovered by Portuguese explorer João Rodriguez Cabrilho 1542. A Spanish mission and fort were established 1769. It passed to the US 1846 in the Mexican War. The coming of the railroad in 1884 began a period of rapid growth, particularly after 1940, with the establishment of military installations and defense-related industries.

Sandinista see ◊Nicaraguan revolution.

sandpiper any of various shorebirds belonging to the family Scolopacidae, which includes godwits, ◊curlews, and ◊snipes.

Other members of the family include yellow-

sandstone *Torridonian sandstone rock, shaped by the action of the waves at Loch Broom, Scotland. The layers in the rock are clearly visible.*

legs, tattlers, and dowitchers. The purple sandpiper *Calidris maritima* of E North America 9 in/23 cm long, has buff and brown plumage, orange-yellow legs, and a long, slender bill.

sandstone ◊sedimentary rocks formed from the consolidation of sand, with sand-sized grains (0.0025–0.08 in/0.0625–2.00 mm) in a matrix or cement. The principal component is quartz. Sandstones are classified according to the matrix or cement material (whether derived from clay or silt—for example, as calcareous sandstone, ferruginous sandstone, siliceous sandstone).

Sandwich resort and market town in Kent, England; population (1981) 4,184. It has many medieval buildings and was one of the ◊Cinque Ports, but recession of the sea has left the harbor useless since the 16th century.

Sandwich John Montagu, 4th Earl of 1718–1792. British politician. An inept First Lord of the Admiralty 1771–82 during the American Revolution; his corrupt practices were blamed for the British navy's inadequacies.

The Sandwich Islands (Hawaii) were named after him, as are sandwiches, which he invented so that he could eat without leaving the gaming table.

Sandwich Islands former name of ◊Hawaii, a group of islands in the Pacific.

San Francisco Pacific port city in California; population (1990) 723,959, metropolitan area of San Francisco-Oakland 3,686,602. The city stands on a peninsula, S of the Golden Gate 1937, the world's second-longest single-span bridge, 4,200 ft/1,280 m. The strait gives access to San Francisco Bay. Manufactured goods include textiles, fabricated metal products, electrical equipment, petroleum products, chemicals, and pharmaceuticals. San Francisco is also a financial, trade, corporate, and diversified service center, and tourism is important to its economy as well. Points of interest include Chinatown, Fisherman's Wharf, Nob and Telegraph hills, and Golden Gate Park. Educational institutions include San Francisco State University, the University of San Francisco, and the University of California at San Francisco. It is also connected by bridge to Berkeley, with the University of California at Berkeley campus.

In 1578 Sir Francis Drake's flagship, the *Golden Hind*, stopped near San Francisco on its voyage around the world. A Spanish fort and mission were established 1776. San Francisco was occupied 1846 during the war with Mexico and in 1906 was almost destroyed by an earthquake and subsequent fire that killed 452 people. It was the site of the drawing up of the United Nations Charter 1945 and of the signing of the peace treaty between the Allied nations and Japan 1951. Another destructive earthquake rocked the city 1989.

Sanger Frederick 1918– . English biochemist, the winner of two Nobel Prizes for Chemistry: one for his clarifying the structure of insulin, and the other, with two US scientists, for his work on the chemical structure of genes.

Sanger Margaret Higgins 1883–1966. US health reformer and crusader for birth control. Born in Corning, New York, Sanger received nursing degrees from White Plains Hospital and the Manhattan Eye and Ear Clinic. As a nurse, she saw the deaths and deformity caused by self-induced abortions and became committed to providing health and birth control education to the poor. In 1914 she founded the National Birth Control League and in 1917 was sent briefly to prison for opening in 1916 a public birth-control clinic in Brooklyn. She then founded and presided over the American Birth Control League 1921–28, the organization that later became the Planned Parenthood Federation of America, and the International Planned Parenthood Federation 1952. Sanger's *Autobiography* appeared 1938.

Sangha in Buddhism, the monastic orders, one of the Three Treasures of Buddhism (the other two are Buddha and the law, or dharma). The term Sangha is sometimes used more generally by Mahāyāna Buddhists to include all believers.

MODERATE
RATES

***San Francisco** A historic cable car ascends Powell Street in San Francisco, California. The city has recovered from disastrous earthquakes in 1906 and 1989.*

Sanhedrin (2nd century BC–1st century AD) ancient supreme court at Jerusalem headed by the Jewish high priest. Its functions were judicial, administrative, and religious.

The Great Sanhedrin was purely religious and continued on in Europe until c. 450 as the rabbinic patriarchate.

San José capital of Costa Rica; population (1984) 245,370. Products include coffee, cocoa, and sugar cane. Founded in 1737; capital since 1823.

San Jose city in Santa Clara Valley, California; population (1990) 782,248. It is the center of "Silicon Valley," the site of many high-technology electronic firms turning out semiconductors and other computer components. There are also electrical, aerospace, missile, rubber, metal, and machine industries, and it is a commercial and transportation center for orchard crops and wines produced in the area. San Jose State University is here, and the Lick Observatory is on nearby Mount Hamilton. San Jose was founded as California's first nonmilitary settlement in 1777 and served as the state capital 1849–51. The population increased more than sixfold between 1950 and 1980 as it was transformed from an agricultural to an industrial center.

San Juan capital of Puerto Rico; population (1990) 437,745. It is a port and industrial city. Products include chemicals, pharmaceuticals, machine tools, electronic equipment, textiles, plastics, and rum. The main campus of the University of Puerto Rico is here. San Juan was settled 1521 and remained under Spanish rule until 1898, when the island was ceded to the US.

San Luis Potosí silver-mining city and capital of San Luis Potosí state, central Mexico; population (1986) 602,000. Founded 1586 as a Franciscan mission, it became the colonial administrative headquarters and has fine buildings of the period.

San Marino small landlocked country within N central Italy.

San Marino
Republic of
(Repubblica di San Marino)

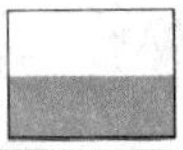

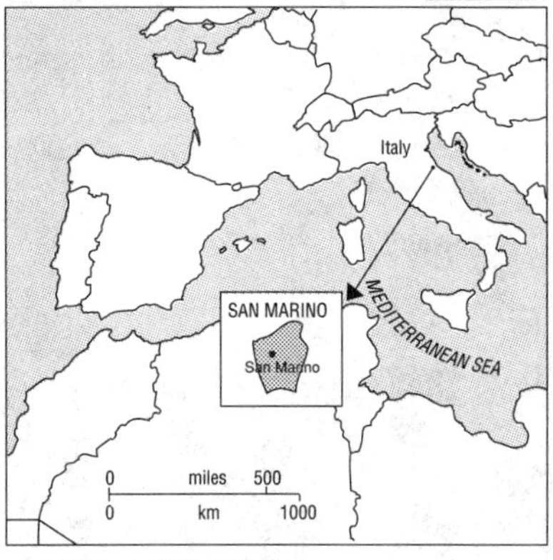
Italy
SAN MARINO
San Marino
MEDITERRANEAN SEA
0 miles 500
0 km 1000

area 24 sq mi/61 sq km
capital San Marino
cities Serravalle (industrial center)
physical on the slope of Mount Titano
features surrounded by Italian territory; one of the world's smallest states
head of state and government two captains-regent, elected for a six-month period
political system direct democracy
political parties San Marino Christian Democrat Party (PDCS), right-of-center; San Marino Communist Party (PCS), moderate Euro-communist; Socialist Unity Party (PSU) and Socialist Party (PSS), both left-of-center
exports wine, ceramics, paint, chemicals, building stone
currency Italian lira
population (1990 est) 23,000; growth rate 0.1% p.a.
life expectancy men 70, women 77
language Italian
religion Roman Catholic 95%
literacy 97% (1987)
chronology
1862 Treaty with Italy signed; independence recognized under Italy's protection.
1947–86 Governed by a series of left-wing and center-left coalitions.
1986 Formation of Communist and Christian Democrat "grand coalition."

government San Marino has no formal constitution. The single-chamber Great and General Council has 60 members, elected by universal suffrage for a five-year term. The council elects two of its members, one representing the capital and one the country, to serve a six-month period as captain's regent. Together they share the duties of head of state and head of government. They preside over a cabinet of ten, elected by the Council for a five-year term, called the Congress of State.

The country is divided into nine "castles," which correspond to the original nine parishes of the republic. Each castle is governed by a castle captain and an auxiliary council, both serving a one-year term.

history San Marino claims to be the world's oldest republic, founded by St Marinus in the 4th century; it is the only city-state to remain after the unification of Italy in the 19th century. It has had a treaty of friendship with Italy since 1862. Women had no vote until 1960.

San Marino's multiparty system mirrors that of the larger country that surrounds it. For the past 40 years it has been governed by a series of left-wing coalitions; the current one, the "grand coalition," which comprises the Communists (PCS), and Christian Democrats (PDCS), dates from July 1986. At the May 1988 council election the PDCS secured 27 seats and the PCS 18, while the opposition Socialist Unionist Party (PSU) captured 8 and the Socialist Party (PPS) 7 seats.

San Martín José de 1778–1850. South American revolutionary leader. Born in Argentina, he was educated in Spain and served in the Spanish army for more than 20 years. In 1812 he returned to Argentina to devote himself to the South American struggle for independence from Spain. In 1817 he and Bernardo O'Higgins led an army across the snow-covered Andes and attacked Spanish forces in Chile, liberating that country the following year. He helped liberate Peru 1821 and assumed the title "Protector of Peru" but resigned the following year and returned to Argentina. He went into exile in Europe 1824.

sannyasin in Hinduism, a person who has renounced worldly goods to live a life of asceticism and seek *moksha*, or liberation from reincarnation, through meditation and prayer.

San Pedro Sula main industrial and commercial city in NW Honduras, the second-largest city in the country; population (1986) 400,000. It trades in bananas, coffee, sugar, and timber and manufactures textiles, plastics, furniture, and cement.

San Salvador capital of El Salvador 30 mi/48 km from the Pacific, at the foot of San Salvador volcano (8,360 ft/2,548 m); population (1984) 453,000. Industries include food processing and textiles. Since its foundation 1525, it has suffered from several earthquakes.

sans-culotte (French "without knee breeches") in the French Revolution a member of the working classes, who wore trousers, as opposed to the aristocracy and bourgeoisie, who wore knee breeches.

San Sebastián port and resort in the Basque Country, Spain; population (1986) 180,000. It was formerly the summer residence of the Spanish court.

Sanskrit the dominant Classical language of the Indian subcontinent, a member of the Indo-Iranian group of the Indo-European language family, and the sacred language of Hinduism. The oldest form of Sanskrit is Vedic, the variety used in the *Vedas* and *Upanishads* (about 1500–700 BC).

Classical Sanskrit was systematized by Panini and other grammarians in the latter part of the 1st millennium BC and became fixed as the spoken and written language of culture, philosophy, mathematics, law, and medicine. It is written in Devanagari script and is the language of the two great Hindu epics, the *Mahābhārata* and the *Rāmāyana*, as well as many other Classical and later works. Sanskrit vocabulary has not only influenced the languages of India, Thailand, and Indonesia, but has also enriched several European languages, including English, with borrowed words as well as etymological bases.

Santa Ana commercial city in NW El Salvador, the second-largest city in the country; population (1980) 205,000. It trades in coffee and sugar.

Santa Ana periodic warm Californian ◊wind.

Santa Anna Antonio López 1794–1876. Mexican revolutionary who became general and dictator of Mexico for most of the years between 1824 and 1855.

A leader in achieving Mexican independence from Spain 1821, he led revolts against Emperor Agustín and two presidents, becoming president himself in 1833 and later assuming dictatorial powers. When the people of Texas, then part of Mexico, revolted against the Santa Anna government, he led the forces that captured the ◊Alamo in San Antonio 1836 but was wounded and captured later that year. Released after agreeing to independence for Texas, he returned to Mexico, where he regained political power. Defeated by US forces during the Mexican War 1846–48, Santa Anna was forced into exile, but he seized power again 1853, ruling as a dictator until he was forced from power for the last time 1855. For most of the next 20 years he lived in exile but returned to Mexico shortly before his death.

Santa Barbara oceanside city in S California; population (1990) 85,571. It is the site of a campus of the University of California. The Santa Ynez mountains are to the N. Manufactures include aircraft and aerospace equipment, precision instruments, and electronic components, but the city is better known for its wealthy residents and as a resort. A Spanish presidio and a mission (still in use) were built here in the 1780s, and the first American settler arrived 1816.

Santa Claus the American name, derived from the Dutch, for ◊St Nicholas. He is depicted as a fat, jolly old man with a long white beard, dressed in boots and a red hat and suit trimmed with white fur. He lives with Mrs Claus and his toy-making elves at the North Pole, and on Christmas Eve he travels in an airborne sleigh, drawn by eight reindeer, to deliver presents to good children, who are fast asleep when Santa arrives. The most popular legends claim that Santa lands his sleigh on rooftops, secretly entering homes through the chimney.

Santa Cruz city in W central California at the N end of Monterey Bay, SW of San Jose. A division of the University of California is here. Industries include tourism, food processing, fishing, and electronics; population (1990) 49,040.

Santa Cruz de la Sierra capital of Santa Cruz department in E Bolivia, the second-largest city in the country; population (1982) 377,000. Sugar cane and cattle were the base of local industry until newly discovered oil and natural gas led to phenomenal growth.

Santa Cruz de Tenerife capital of Tenerife and of the Canary Islands; population (1986) 211,000. It is a fuelling port and cable center. Industry also includes oil refining, pharmaceuticals, and trade in fruit. Santa Cruz was bombarded by the British admirals Blake 1657 and Nelson 1797 (the action in which he lost his arm).

Santa Fé capital of Santa Fé province, Argentina, on the Salado River 95 mi/153 km N of Rosario; population (1980) 287,000. It has shipyards and exports timber, cattle, and wool. It was founded 1573, and the 1853 constitution was adopted here.

Santa Fe capital of New Mexico, on the Santa Fe River, 40 mi/65 km W of Las Vegas; population (1990) 55,859, many Spanish-speaking. A number of buildings date from the Spanish period, including a palace 1609–10; the cathedral 1869 is on the site of a monastery built 1622. Santa Fe is known for American Indian jewelry and textiles; its chief industry is tourism. It is home to many artists and is noted for theater and opera. Santa Fe was founded 1610; it passed to Mexico 1821 and to the US 1846, during the Mexican War. It became the territorial capital 1851.

Santa Fé Trail US southern overland trade route 1821–80 from Independence, Missouri, to Santa Fé, New Mexico, established by trader William Becknell.

It passed through Raton Pass and between tributaries of the Kansas and Arkansas rivers. Later, to allow the passage of wheeled wagons, Becknell turned south and headed across the Cimarron Desert. This reduced the journey by 100 miles but increased the hardship and danger of Indian attack. The trade along the trail expanded to nearly 5,000 wagons carrying millions of dollars of goods each year. It was rendered obsolete in 1880 when railroad lines were extended to Santa Fé.

Santa Maria city in SW California, NW of Santa Barbara. Industries include oil, food processing, and dairy products; population (1990) 61,284.

Santander port on the Bay of Biscay, Cantabria, N Spain; population (1986) 189,000. Industries include chemicals, textiles, vehicles, and shipyards. It was sacked by the French marshal ◊Soult 1808 and was largely rebuilt after a fire

***Santiago** The Opera House in Santiago, Chile.*

1941. Paleolithic cave wall paintings of bison, wild boar, and deer were discovered at the nearby Altamira site 1879.

Santa Rosa city in NW California, N of San Francisco. Industries include wine, fruit, chemicals, and clothing; population (1990) 113,313.

Santayana George 1863–1952. Spanish-born US philosopher and critic. He developed his philosophy based on naturalism and taught that everything has a natural basis.

Born in Madrid, Santayana grew up in Spain and the US and graduated from Harvard University. He taught at Harvard 1889–1912. His books include *The Life of Reason* 1905–06, *Skepticism and Animal Faith* 1923, *The Realm of Truth* 1937, *Background of My Life* 1945; volumes of poetry; and the best-selling novel *The Last Puritan* 1935.

Sant'Elia Antonio 1888–1916. Italian architect. His drawings convey a ◊Futurist vision of a metropolis with skyscrapers, traffic lanes, and streamlined factories.

Santiago capital of Chile; population (1987) 4,858,000. Industries include textiles, chemicals, and food processing. It was founded 1541 and is famous for its broad avenues.

Santiago de Compostela city in Galicia, Spain; population (1986) 104,000. The 11th-century cathedral was reputedly built over the grave of Sant Iago el Mayor (St ◊James the Great), patron saint of Spain, and was one of the most popular places for medieval pilgrimage.

Santiago de Cuba port on the south coast of Cuba; population (1986) 359,000. Products include sugar, rum, and cigars.

Santiago de los Caballeros second-largest city in the Dominican Republic; population (1982) 395,000. It is a trading and processing center.

Santo Domingo capital and chief sea port of the Dominican Republic; population (1982) 1,600,000. Founded in 1496 by Bartolomeo, brother of Christopher Columbus, it is the oldest colonial city in the Americas. Its cathedral was built 1515–40.

Santos coffee-exporting port in SE Brazil, 45 mi/72 km SE of São Paulo; population (1980) 411,000. The soccer star Pélé played here for many years.

Sānusī Sidi Mohammed ibn Ali as c. 1787–1859. Algerian-born Muslim religious reformer. He preached a return to the puritanism of early Islam and met with much success in Libya, where he founded the sect named after him.

San Yu 1919– . Myanmar (Burmese) politician. A member of the Revolutionary Council that came to power 1962, he became president 1981 and was reelected 1985. He was forced to resign July 1988, along with Ne Win, after riots in Yangon (formerly Rangoon).

Saône river in E France, rising in the Vosges mountains and flowing 300 mi/480 km to join the Rhône at Lyon.

São Tomé e Príncipe
Democratic Republic of

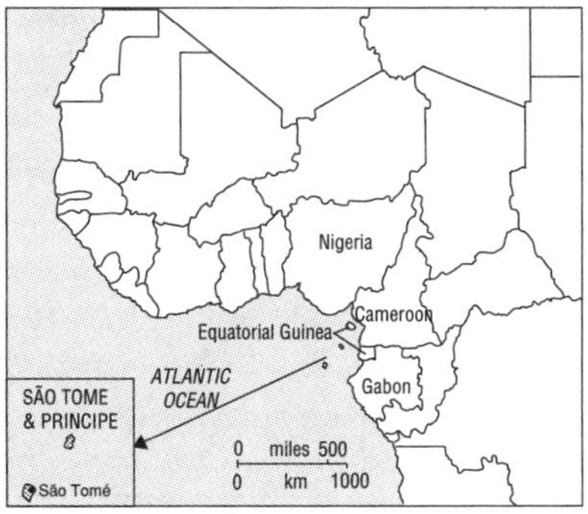
Nigeria
Equatorial Guinea
Cameroon
ATLANTIC
OCEAN
Gabon
SÃO TOME
& PRINCIPE
0 miles 500
0 km 1000
São Tomé

area 386 sq mi/1,000 sq km
capital São Tomé
cities Santo Antonio, Santa Cruz
physical comprises two main islands and several smaller ones, all volcanic; thickly forested and fertile
head of state and government Miguel Trovoada from 1991
political system emergent democracy
political parties Movement for the Liberation of São Tomé and Príncipe (MLSTP), nationalist Socialist
exports cocoa, copra, coffee, palm oil, kernels
currency dobra
population (1990 est) 125,000; growth rate 2.5% p.a.
life expectancy men 62, women 62
language Portuguese (official), Fang (Bantu)
religion Roman Catholic 80%, animist
literacy men 73%/women 42% (1981)
GNP $32 mn (1987); $384 per head (1986)
chronology
1471 Discovered by Portuguese.
1522–1973 A province of Portugal.
1973 Granted internal self-government.
1975 Independence achieved from Portugal, with Manuel Pinto da Costa as president.
1984 Formally declared itself a nonaligned state.
1987 President now popularly elected.
1988 Unsuccessful coup attempt against Pinto da Costa.
1990 New constitution approved.
1991 First multiparty elections held, Miguel Trovoada replaces Pinto da Costa.

São Paulo city in Brazil, 45 mi/72 km NW of its port Santos; population (1986) 8,490,700, metropolitan area 15,280,000. It is 3,000 ft/900 m above sea level, and 2° S of the Tropic of Capricorn. It is South America's leading industrial city, producing electronics, steel, and chemicals; it has meatpacking plants and is the center of Brazil's coffee trade. It originated as a Jesuit mission in 1554.

São Tomé port and capital of São Tomé e Principe, on São Tomé island, Gulf of Guinea; population (1984) 35,000.

São Tomé e Príncipe country in the Gulf of Guinea, off the coast of W Africa.

government The 1982 constitution describes the Movement for the Liberation of São Tomé e Príncipe (MLSTP) as the leading political force in the nation and the National People's Assembly as the supreme organ of the state. It has 40 members, all MLSTP nominees, elected by people's district assemblies for a five-year term. The president is also nominated by the MLSTP and elected for a five-year term by popular vote.

history The islands were uninhabited until the arrival of the Portuguese 1471, who brought convicts and exiled Jews to work on sugar plantations. Later ◊slavery became the main trade, and in the 19th century forced labor was used on coffee and cocoa plantations.

As a Portuguese colony, São Tomé e Príncipe was given internal self-government 1973. After the military coup in Portugal 1974, the new government in Lisbon formally recognized the liberation movement, MLSTP, led by Dr Manuel Pinto da Costa, as the sole representative of the people of the islands and granted full independence July 1975. Dr da Costa became the first president, and in Dec a National People's Assembly was elected. During the first few years of his presidency there were several unsuccessful attempts to depose him, and small opposition groups still operate from outside the country, mainly from Lisbon.

With a worsening economy, da Costa began to reassess his country's international links, which had made it too dependent on the Eastern bloc and, in consequence, isolated from the West. In 1984 he proclaimed that in future São Tomé e Príncipe would be a ◊nonaligned state, and the number of Angolan, Cuban, and Soviet advisers in the country was sharply reduced. Gradually São Tomé e Príncipe has turned toward nearby African states such as Gabon, Cameroon, and Equatorial Guinea, as well as maintaining its links with Lisbon. In 1987 the constitution was amended, making the president subject to election by popular vote, and in March 1988 an attempted coup against him was foiled. In Sept 1990 a new constitution, introducing multiparty politics was approved by referendum. In Jan 1991 multiparty elections were held for the assembly resulting in the ruling party losing its majority. In Mar the country's first free election led to the election of Miguel Trovoada after President Manuel Pinto da Costa withdrew.

sap the fluids that circulate through ◊vascular plants, especially woody ones. Sap carries water and food to plant tissues. Sap can be milky (as in rubber trees), resinous (as in pines), or syrupy (as in maples).

saponification in chemistry, the ◊hydrolysis (splitting) of an ◊ester by treatment with a strong alkali, resulting in the liberation of the alcohol from which the ester had been derived and a salt of the constituent fatty acid. The process is used in the manufacture of soap.

sapphire the deep blue, transparent gem variety of the mineral ◊corundum Al_2O_3, aluminum oxide.

***sapphire** Macrophotograph of sapphire, a gem variety of corundum.*

Small amounts of iron and titanium give it its color. A corundum gem of any color except red (which is a ruby) can be called a sapphire—for example, yellow sapphire.

Sappho c. 612–580 BC. Greek lyric poet, friend of the poet ◊Alcaeus and leader of a female literary coterie at Mytilene (now Lesvos, hence ◊lesbianism). Legend says she committed suicide when her love for the boatman Phaon was unrequited. Only fragments of her poems have survived.

Sapporo capital of ◊Hokkaido, Japan; population (1987) 1,555,000. Industries include rubber and food processing. It is a winter sports center and was the site of the 1972 Winter Olympics. The university was founded 1918. Giant figures are sculpted in ice at the annual snow festival.

saprophyte in botany, an obsolete term for a ◊saprotroph, an organism that lives in dead or decaying matter.

saprotroph (formerly ***saprophyte***) an organism that feeds on the excrement, or the dead bodies or tissues of others. They include most fungi (the rest being parasites), many bacteria and protozoa, animals such as dung beetles and vultures, and a few unusual plants, including several orchids. Saprotrophs cannot make food for themselves, so they are a type of ◊heterotroph. They are useful scavengers, and in sewage farms and refuse dumps break down organic matter into nutrients easily assimilable by green plants.

Saracen ancient Greek and Roman term for an Arab, used in the Middle Ages by Europeans for all Muslims. The equivalent term used in Spain was ◊Moor.

Saragossa English spelling of ◊Zaragoza, city in Aragon, Spain.

Sarajevo capital of Bosnia and Herzegovina, Yugoslavia; population (1982) 449,000. Industries include engineering, brewing, chemicals, carpets, and ceramics. It was the site of the 1984 Winter Olympics.

A Bosnian, Gavrilo Princip, assassinated Archduke ◊Francis Ferdinand here 1914, thereby precipitating World War I.

Sarasota city in SW Florida, on the Gulf of Mexico, S of Tampa. It is a resort town specializing in food processing and electronics research. It is the winter home of Ringling Brothers and Barnum and Bailey Circus; population (1990) 50,961.

Saratoga Springs city and spa in New York State; population (1990) 25,001. In 1777 the British general John ◊Burgoyne was defeated in two engagements nearby during the American Revolution.

Horse racing is popular during the summer.

Saratov industrial port (chemicals, oil refining) on the river Volga in the USSR; population (1987) 918,000. It was established in the 1590s as a fortress to protect the Volga trade route.

Sarawak state of Malaysia, on the NW corner of the island of Borneo; capital Kuching; area 48,018 sq mi/124,400 sq km; population (1986) 1,550,000. It has a tropical climate and produces timber, oil, rice, pepper, rubber, and coconuts. Sarawak was granted by the Sultan of Brunei to James Brooke 1841, who became "Rajah of Sarawak." It was a British protectorate from 1888 until captured by the Japanese in World War II. It was a Crown Colony from 1946 until 1963, when it became part of Malaysia.

sarcoma a type of malignant ◊tumor arising from the fat, muscles, bones, cartilage, or blood and lymph vessels and connective tissues. Sarcomas are much less common than ◊carcinomas.

sard or ***sardonyx*** a yellow or red-brown variety of ◊onyx.

sardine common name for various small fishes in the herring family (see ◊pilchard).

Sardinia (Italian *Sardegna*) mountainous island, special autonomous region of Italy; area 9,303 sq mi/24,100 sq km; population (1988) 1,651,000. Its capital is Cagliari, and it exports cork and petrochemicals. It is the second largest Mediterranean island and includes Costa Smeralda (Emerald Coast) tourist area in the NE and *nuraghi* (fortified Bronze Age dwellings). After centuries of foreign rule, it became linked 1720 with Piedmont, and this dual kingdom became the basis of a united Italy 1861.

Sardinia

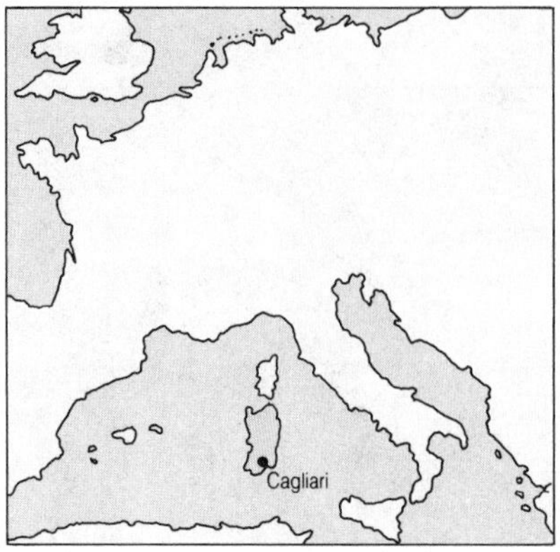
Cagliari

Sardou Victorien 1831–1908. French dramatist. He wrote plays with roles for Sarah Bernhardt and Henry Irving, for example *Fédora* 1882, *La Tosca* 1887 (the basis for the opera by Puccini), and *Madame Sans-Gêne* 1893. George Bernard ◊Shaw coined the expression "Sardoodledom" to express his disgust with the contrivances of the "well-made" play—a genre of which Sardou was the leading exponent.

Sargasso Sea part of the N Atlantic (between 40° and 80°W and 25° and 30°N) left static by circling ocean currents, and covered with floating weed *Sargassum natans*.

Sargent John Singer 1856–1925. US portrait painter. Born in Florence of American parents, he studied there and in Paris, then settled in London around 1885. He was a fashionable and prolific painter.

Sargent left Paris after a scandal concerning his décolleté portrait *Madame Gautreau* 1884. Later subjects included the actress Ellen Terry, President Theodore Roosevelt, and the writer Robert Louis Stevenson. He also painted watercolor landscapes and murals.

Sargon two Mesopotamian kings:

Sargon I king of Akkad c. 2370–2230 BC, and founder of the first Babylonian empire. Like Moses, he was said to have been found floating in a cradle on the local river, in his case the Euphrates.

Sargon II died 705 BC. King of Assyria from 722 BC. To keep conquered peoples from rising against him, he had whole populations moved from their homelands, including the Israelites from Samaria.

Sark one of the ◊Channel Islands, 6 mi/10 km E of Guernsey; area 2 sq mi/5 sq km; there is no town or village. It is divided into Great and Little Sark, linked by an isthmus, and is of great natural beauty. The Seigneurie of Sark was established by Elizabeth I, the ruler being known as Seigneur/Dame, and has its own parliament, the Chief Pleas. There is no income tax, and automobiles are forbidden; immigration is controlled.

Sarmatian a member of an Indo-European nomadic people who, from the 3rd century BC, slowly ousted the ◊Scythians from what is now southwest USSR. They had given way to the ◊Goths by the 3rd century AD.

Sarney Costa José 1930– . Brazilian politician, member of the Democratic Movement (PMDB), president 1985–90.

Sarney was elected vice-president in 1985 and within months, on the death of President Neves, became head of state. Despite earlier involvement with the repressive military regime, he and his party won a convincing victory in the 1986 general election. In Dec 1989, Ferdinando Collor de Mello of the Party for National Reconstruction was elected to succeed Sarney in March 1990.

Sarnoff David 1891–1971. Russian-born US broadcasting pioneer. Sarnoff immigrated with his family to New York 1900. After studying electrical engineering at the Pratt Institute, he was hired by the Marconi Wireless Co 1906. At first a telegraph operator, Sarnoff rose to become commercial manager of the company when it was taken over by the Radio Corporation of America (RCA) 1919. He was named general manager of RCA 1921 and founded the first radio network, the National Broadcasting Co (NBC), as a broadcast subsidiary 1926. Named RCA president 1930 and board chairman 1947, Sarnoff was an early promoter of television broadcasting during the 1940s and the first to manufacture color sets and to transmit color programs in the 1950s.

Saroyan William 1908–1981. US author. He wrote short stories, such as *The Daring Young Man on the Flying Trapeze* 1934, idealizing the hopes and sentiments of the "little man." His plays include *The Time of Your Life* (Pulitzer prize; refused) 1939, about eccentricity; *My Heart's in the Highlands* 1939; and *Talking to You* 1962.

Born in Fresno, California, Saroyan also wrote *The Human Comedy* 1942 and *One Day in the Afternoon of the World* 1964, both novels, and the novella *Boys and Girls Together* 1963. Other plays include *Love's Old Sweet Song* 1941 and *The Beautiful People* 1941. He also wrote autobiographical works, including *The Bicycle Rider in Beverly Hills* 1952 and *Here Comes, There Goes, You Know Who* 1961.

Sarraute Nathalie 1920– Russian-born French novelist whose books include *Portrait d'un inconnu/Portrait of a Man Unknown* 1948, *Les Fruits d'or/The Golden Fruits* 1964, and *Vous les entendez?/Do You Hear Them?* 1972. An exponent of the *nouveau roman*, Sarraute bypasses plot, character, and style for the half-conscious interaction of minds.

sarsaparilla drink prepared from the long twisted roots of several plants in the genus *Smilax* (family Liliaceae), native to Central and South America.

Sartre Jean-Paul 1905–1980. French author and philosopher, a leading proponent of ◊existentialism in postwar philosophy. He published his first novel, *La Nausée/Nausea*, 1937, followed by the trilogy *Les Chemins de la Liberté/Roads to Freedom* 1944–45 and many plays, including *Huis Clos/In Camera* 1944. *L'Etre et le néant/Being and Nothingness* 1943, his first major philosophical work, sets out a radical doctrine of human freedom. In the later work *Critique de la raison dialectique/Critique of Dialectical Reason* 1960 he tried to produce a fusion of existentialism and Marxism.

Sartre was born in Paris, and was the longtime companion of the feminist writer Simone de Beauvoir. During World War II he was a prisoner for nine months, and on his return from Germany joined the Resistance. As a founder of existentialism, he edited its journal *Les Temps modernes/Modern Times*, and expressed its tenets in his novels and plays. According to Sartre, people's awareness of their own freedom takes the form of anxiety, and they therefore attempt to flee from this awareness into what he terms *mauvaise foi* ("bad faith"); this is the theory he put forward in *L'Etre et le néant/Being and Nothingness*. In *Crime passionel/Crime of Passion* 1948 he attacked aspects of communism while remaining generally sympathetic. In his later work Sartre became more sensitive to the social constraints on people's actions. He refused the Nobel Prize for Literature 1964 for "personal reasons," but allegedly changed his mind later, saying he wanted it for the money.

Sary-Shagan weapons-testing area in Kazakhstan, USSR, near the Chinese border. In 1980 testing of beam weapons was detected there.

Sasebo seaport and naval base on the W coast of Kyushu, Japan; population (1985) 251,000.

Sask. abbreviation for ◊Saskatchewan.

Saskatchewan

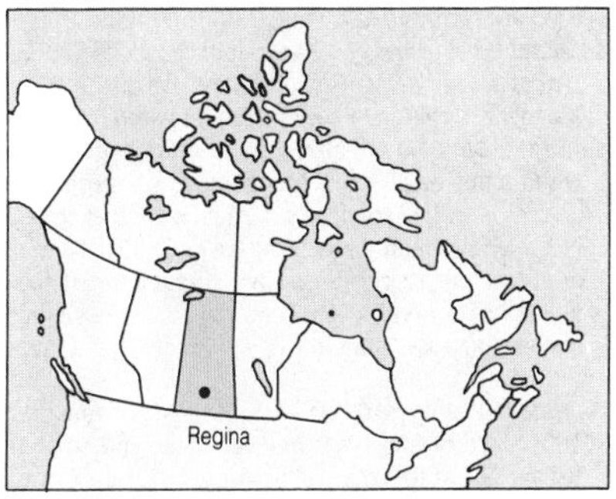
Regina

Saskatchewan (Cree *Kis-is-ska-tche-wan* "swift flowing") province of W Canada
area 251,788 sq mi/652,300 sq km
capital Regina
cities Saskatoon, Moose Jaw, Prince Albert
physical prairies in the S; to the N, forests, lakes, and subarctic tundra; Prince Albert National Park
products more than 60% of Canada's wheat; oil, natural gas, uranium, zinc, potash (world's largest reserves), copper, helium (the only western reserves outside the US)
population (1986) 1,010,000
history French trading posts established about 1750; owned by Hudson's Bay Company, first permanent settlement 1774; ceded to Canadian government 1870 as part of Northwest Territories; became a province 1905.

Saskatoon largest city in Saskatchewan, Canada; population (1986) 177,641. Industries include cement, oil refining, chemicals, metal goods, and processed foods. The University of Saskatchewan is here. Saskatoon was settled 1882.

Sassanian Empire Persian empire founded AD 224 by Ardashir, a chieftain in the area of what is now Fars, in Iran, who had taken over ◊Parthia; it was named for his grandfather, Sasan. The capital was Ctesiphon, near modern ◊Baghdad, Iraq. After a rapid period of expansion, when it contested supremacy with Rome, it was destroyed in 637 by Muslim Arabs at the Battle of ◊Qadisiya.

Sassari capital of the province of the same name, in the NW corner of Sardinia, Italy; population (1987) 121,000. Every May the town is the scene of the Sardinian Cavalcade, the greatest festival on the island.

Sassau-Nguesso Denis 1943– . Congolese Socialist politician, president from 1979. He progressively consolidated his position within the ruling left-wing Congolese Labor Party (PCT), at the same time as improving relations with France and the US.

Sassoon Siegfried 1886–1967. English writer, author of the autobiography *Memoirs of a Foxhunting Man* 1928. His *War Poems* 1919 express the disillusionment of his generation.

Educated at Cambridge, Sassoon enlisted in the army 1915, serving in France and Palestine. He published many volumes of poetry and three volumes of childhood autobiography, *The Old Century and Seven More Years* 1938, *The Weald of Youth* 1942, and *Siegfried's Journey* 1945. He wrote a biography of the novelist George Meredith 1948 and published *Collected Poems* in 1961.

sat in Hinduism, true existence or reality: the converse of illusion (*maya*).

Satan a name for the ◊devil.

satellite any small body that orbits a larger one; it may be natural or artificial. Natural satellites that orbit planets are called moons.

The first artificial satellite, *Sputnik 1*, was launched into orbit around the Earth by the USSR 1957. Artificial satellites are used for scientific purposes, communications, weather forecasting, and military purposes. The largest artificial satellites can be seen by the naked eye.

At any time, there are several thousand artificial satellites orbiting the Earth, including active satellites, satellites that have ended their working lives, and discarded sections of rockets. Artificial satellites eventually re-enter the Earth's atmosphere. Usually they burn up by friction, but sometimes debris falls to the Earth's surface, as with ◊Skylab and *Salyut 7*.

The US launched 23 nuclear-powered satellites 1961–77, of which four malfunctioned. The ◊Strategic Defense Initiative (Star Wars) program proposes sending as many as 100 nuclear reactors into space. The USSR has launched 39 nuclear reactors on orbiting satellites since 1965, of which six have malfunctioned.

More than 70,000 pieces of space junk, ranging from disabled satellites to tiny metal fragments, are careering around the Earth. The amount of waste is likely to increase, as the waste particles

satellite *Satellite image of North America showing cloud-free skies over much of the continent.*

largest planetary satellites

Planet	*Satellite*	*Diameter in mi*	*Mean distance from center of Primary in mi*	*Orbital period in days*	*Reciprocal mass (planet = 1)*
Jupiter	Ganymede	3,300	700,000	7.16	12,800
Saturn	Titan	3,200	759,000	15.95	4,200
Jupiter	Callisto	3,000	1,200,000	16.69	17,700
Jupiter	Io	2,240	257,000	1.77	21,400
Earth	Moon	2,160	238,857	27.32	81.3
Jupiter	Europa	1,900	417,000	3.55	39,000
Neptune	Triton	1,690	220,000	5.88	750

in orbit are continually colliding and fragmenting further.

satellite, applications the uses to which artificial satellites are put. These include:

scientific experiments and observation Many astronomical observations are best taken above the disturbing effect of the atmosphere. Satellite observations have been carried out by *IRAS* (*Infrared Astronomical Satellite*, 1983) which made a complete infrared survey of the skies, and *Solar Max* 1980, which observed solar flares. The *Hipparchos* satellite, launched 1989, is expected to measure the positions of the stars with unprecedented accuracy. Medical experiments are carried out aboard crewed satellites, such as the Soviet *Mir* and the US *Skylab*.

reconnaisance and mapping applications Apart from military use and routine mapmaking, the US *Landsat*, the French *SPOT*, and the equivalent USSR satellites have provided much useful information about water sources and drainage, vegetation, land use, geologic structures, oil and mineral locations, and snow and ice.

weather monitoring The US NOAA series of satellites, and others launched by the European space agency, Japan, and India, provide continuous worldwide observation of the atmosphere.

navigation The US Global Positioning System, when complete in 1993, will feature 18 Navstar satellites that will enable users (including walkers and motorists) to find their position to within 4.5 ft/1.5 m. The Transit system, launched in the 1960s, with 12 satellites in orbit, locates users to within 328 ft/100 m.

communications A complete worldwide communications network is now provided by satellites such as the US-run ◊Intelsat system.

satellite television transmission of broadcast signals through artificial communications satellites. Mainly positioned in ◊geostationary orbit, satellites have been used since the 1960s to relay television pictures around the world. Higher-power satellites have more recently been developed to broadcast signals to cable systems or directly to people's homes.

Satie Erik (Alfred Leslie) 1866–1925. French composer. His piano pieces, such as *Gymnopédies* 1888, often combine wit and melancholy. His orchestral works include *Parade* 1917, among whose sound effects is a typewriter. He was the mentor of the group of composers known as ◊*Les Six*.

satire a poem or piece of prose that uses wit, humor, or irony, often through ◊allegory or extended metaphor, to ridicule human pretensions or expose social evils. Satire is related to parody in its intention to mock, but satire tends to be more subtle and to mock an attitude or a belief, whereas parody tends to mock a particular work (such as a poem) by imitating its style, often with purely comic intent.

The Roman poets Juvenal and Horace wrote *Satires*, and the form became popular in Europe in the 17th and 18th centuries, used by Voltaire in France and by Pope and Swift in England. Both satire and parody are designed to appeal to the intellect rather than the emotions and both, to be effective, require a knowledge of the original attitude, person, or work that is being mocked (although much satire, such as *Gulliver's Travels* by Swift, can also be enjoyed simply on a literal level).

Satō Eisaku 1901–1975. Japanese conservative politician, prime minister 1964–72. He ran against Hayato Ikeda (1899–1965) for the Liberal Democratic Party leadership and succeeded him as prime minister, pledged to a more independent foreign policy. He shared a Nobel Peace Prize in 1974 for his rejection of nuclear weapons. His brother Nobosuke Kishi (1896–1987) was prime minister of Japan 1957–60.

satori in Zen Buddhism, awakening, the experience of sudden ◊enlightenment.

satrap title of a provincial governor in ancient Persia. Under Darius I, the Persian Empire was divided between some 20 satraps, each owing allegiance only to the king.

satsuma small, hardy, loose-skinned orange *Citrus reticulata* of the tangerine family, originally from Japan. It withstands cold conditions well.

saturated solution in physics, a solution obtained when a solvent (liquid) can dissolve no more of a solute (usually a solid) at a particular temperature. Normally, a slight fall in temperature causes some of the solute to crystallize out of solution. If this does not happen the phenomenon is called supercooling, and the solution is said to be supersaturated.

Saturday Evening Post popular US magazine founded 1821, specializing in family reading and known for its folksy Norman Rockwell covers. It was transformed into a modern magazine by G H Lorimer and remodeled again in the 1960s.

Saturn in astronomy, the second-largest planet in the Solar System, sixth from the Sun, and encircled by bright and easily visible equatorial rings. Viewed through a telescope it is white, but appears lemon-colored when seen at closer range (by the two ◊Voyager probes, for example). Saturn orbits the Sun every 29.46 years at an average distance of 886.7 million mi/1,427 million km. Its equatorial diameter is 75,000 mi/120,000 km, but its polar diameter is 7,450 mi/12,000 km smaller, a result of its fast rotation and low density, the lowest of any planet. Saturn spins on its axis every 10 hours 14 minutes at its equator, slowing to 10 hours 40 minutes at high latitudes. Its mass is 95 times that of Earth, and its magnetic field is 1,000 times stronger. Saturn is believed to have a small core of rock and iron, encased in ice and topped by a deep layer of liquid hydrogen. There are over 20 known moons, its largest being ◊Titan. The rings visible from Earth begin about 7,000 mi/11,000 km from the planet's surface and extend out to about 35,000 mi/56,000 km. Made of small chunks of ice and rock (averaging 3 ft/1 m across), they are 170,000 mi/275,000 km rim to rim but only 300 ft/100 m thick. The Voyager probes showed that the rings actually consist of thousands of closely spaced ringlets, looking like the grooves in a phonograph record.

Like Jupiter, Saturn's visible surface consists of swirling clouds, probably made of frozen ammonia at a temperature of –274°F/–170°C, although the markings in the clouds are not as prominent as Jupiter's. The space probes *Voyager 1* and *2* found winds reaching 1,100 mph/1,800 kph.

From Earth, Saturn's rings appear to be divided

satellite *Satellite receiving disk at the Pleumeur-Bodon receiving station in Brittany, France. The dish is 105 ft/32 m across and weighs 285 tons.*

Saturn *A color-enhanced image of Saturn and its rings, taken by the space probe* Voyager 1 *in 1980, at a range of 21 million mi/34 million km.*

into three main sections. Ring A, the outermost, is separated from ring B, the brightest, by the Cassini division (named after its discoverer ◊Cassini), 2,000 mi/3,000 km wide; the inner, transparent ring C is also called the Crepe Ring. Each ringlet of the rings is made of a swarm of particles of ice and rock, a few fractions of an inch to a few yards in diameter. Outside the A ring is the narrow and faint F ring, which the Voyagers showed to be twisted or braided. The rings of Saturn could be the remains of a shattered moon, or they may always have existed in their present form.

The Voyagers photographed numerous small moons orbiting Saturn, taking the total to 21–23, more than for any other planet. The largest moon, Titan, has a dense atmosphere. Saturn's major satellites, in order of mean distance from the planet, are:

Mimas mean distance 116,000 mi/186,000 km, diameter 245 mi/390 km;
Enceladus mean distance 147,900 mi/238,000 km, diameter 310 mi/500 km;
Tethys mean distance 183,300 mi/295,000 km, diameter 650 mi/1,050 km;
Dione mean distance 230,000 mi/370,000 km, diameter 700 mi/1,120 km;
Rhea mean distance 327,000 mi/527,000 km, diameter 950 mi/1,530 km;
Titan mean distance 759,000 mi/1,222,000 km, diameter 3,200 mi/5,150 km;
Hyperion mean distance 922,000 mi/1,483,000 km, shape irregular 230 × 175 × 140 mi/370 × 280 × 225 km;
Iapetus mean distance 2,200,000 mi/3,500,000 km, diameter 895 mi/1,440 km;
Phoebe mean distance 8,047,000 mi/12,950,000 km, diameter 100 mi/160 km.

Saturn in Roman mythology, the god of agriculture (Greek Cronus), whose period of rule was the ancient Golden Age. He was dethroned by his sons Jupiter, Neptune, and Pluto. At his festival, the Saturnalia in December, gifts were exchanged, and slaves were briefly treated as their masters' equals.

Saturn rocket family of large US rockets, developed by Wernher von Braun for the ◊Apollo project. The two-stage Saturn IB was used for launching Apollo spacecraft into orbit around the Earth. The three-stage Saturn V sent Apollo spacecraft to the Moon, and launched the ◊*Skylab* space station. The lift-off thrust of a Saturn V was 3,850 tons. After Apollo and *Skylab*, the Saturn rockets were retired in favor of the ◊Space Shuttle.

satyagraha (Sanskrit "insistence on truth") nonviolent resistance to British rule in India, as employed by Mahatma ◊Gandhi from 1918 to press for political reform; the idea owes much to the Russian writer ◊Tolstoy.

satyr in Greek mythology, a lustful, drunken woodland creature characterized by pointed ears, two horns on the forehead, and a tail. Satyrs attended the god of wine, ◊Dionysus. Roman writers confused satyrs with goat-footed fauns.

Saudi Arabia country on the Arabian peninsula, stretching from the Red Sea to the Arabian Gulf, bounded N by Jordan, Iraq, and Kuwait; E by Qatar and United Arab Emirates; SE by Oman; and S by Yemen.

government Saudi Arabia is an absolute monarchy with no written constitution, no legislature, and no political parties. The king rules, in accordance with Islamic law, by decree. He appoints and heads a council of ministers, whose decisions are the result of a majority vote but always subject to the ultimate sanction of the king.

history For early history, see ◊Arabia. The sultanate of Nejd in the interior came under Turkish rule in the 18th century. Present-day Saudi Arabia is almost entirely the creation of King Ibn Saud who, after the dissolution of the ◊Ottoman Empire in 1918, fought rival Arab rulers until, in 1926, he had established himself as the undisputed king of the Hejaz and sultan of Nejd. In 1932 Nejd and Hejaz became the United Kingdom of Saudi Arabia.

Oil was discovered in the 1930s, commercially exploited from the 1940s, and became the basis of the country's prosperity. Ibn Saud died 1953 and was succeeded by his eldest son, Saud. During King Saud's reign relations between Saudi Arabia and Egypt became strained, and criticisms of the king within the royal family grew, until in 1964 he abdicated in favor of his brother Faisal. Under King Faisal, Saudi Arabia became a leader among Arab oil producers.

In 1975 Faisal was assassinated by one of his nephews, and his half brother Khalid succeeded him. Khalid was in failing health and increasingly relied on his brother Fahd to perform the duties of government. King Khalid died of a heart attack in 1982 and was succeeded by Fahd.

Saudi Arabia has drawn up proposals for a permanent settlement of the Arab-Israeli dispute. It gave financial support to Iraq in its war with Iran. The ◊Iran-Iraq War also prompted Saudi Arabia to buy advanced missiles from the US. Islamic fundamentalists staged demonstrations in ◊Mecca in 1979 and 1987, leading to violence and worsening relations with Iran. In 1989 Saudi Arabia assumed a leading role in the search for a settlement of the Lebanese civil war, hosting a constitutional convention of Lebanese legislators in Taif.

On Aug 2, 1990 Iraq invaded and occupied neighboring Kuwait, threatening the security of Saudi Arabia. King Fahd turned to the US and UK for protection and a massive buildup of ground and air strength began, alongside Saudi Arabia's own forces. In return, King Fahd agreed to increase his oil output to offset the loss of Kuwaiti and Iraqi production, and to pay a substantial part of the cost of maintaining US and British forces. During the ensuing ◊Gulf War, Saudi Arabia served as the staging ground for the air and ground assaults on Iraqi forces. The country was hit by Iraqi missile strikes but suffered no serious damage. In Nov 1991, Saudi Arabia was one of the main participants in the historic Middle East peace conference in Spain.

Saul in the Old Testament, the first king of Israel. He was anointed by Samuel and warred successfully against the neighboring Ammonites and Philistines, but fell from God's favor in his battle against the Amalekites. He became jealous and suspicious of David and turned against him and Samuel. After being wounded in battle with the Philistines, in which his three sons died, he committed suicide.

Sault Ste Marie twin industrial ports on the Canadian/US border, one in Ontario and one in Michigan; population (1981) 82,902 and (1990) 14,689, respectively. They stand at the falls (French *sault*) in St Mary's River, which links Lakes Superior and Huron. The falls are bypassed by canals. Industries include steel, pulp, and agricultural trade.

Saumur town in Maine-et-Loire *département*, France, on the river Loire; population (1985) 34,000. The area is famous for its sparkling wines. The cavalry school, founded 1768, has since 1942 also been a training school for the French armed forces.

sauna a type of bath causing perspiration by means of dry heat. It consists of a small room in which the temperature is raised to about 200°F/90°C. The bather typically stays in it for only a few minutes and then follows it with a cold shower or swim. Saunas are popular in health clubs and sports centers.

The sauna derives from a Finnish dry-heat bath in which small quantities of steam could be produced by throwing cold water over hot stones; this was traditionally followed by a beating of the skin with birch twigs to stimulate the circulation, and a plunge into the lake or snow outdoors.

Saunders Cicely 1918– . English philanthropist, founder of the hospice movement, which aims to provide a caring and comfortable environment in which people with terminal illnesses can die.

Saunders Clarence 1881–1953. US retailer, who opened the first self-service supermarket, Piggly-Wiggly, in Memphis, Tennessee, 1919.

Saussure Horace de 1740–1799. Swiss geologist who made the earliest detailed and first-hand study of the Alps. He was a physicist at the University of Geneva. The results of his Alpine survey appeared in his classic work *Voyages des Alpes/Travels in the Alps* 1779–86.

Sauternes a sweet white table wine produced in the Gironde *département*, SW France. It takes its name from the village of Sauternes.

Savage Michael Joseph 1872–1940. New Zealand

Saudi Arabia

Kingdom of
(*al-Mamlaka al-'Arabiya as-Sa'udiya*)

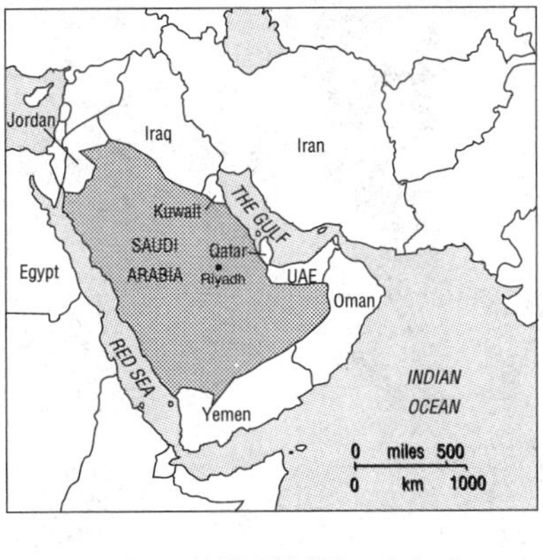
Jordan
Iraq
Iran
Kuwait
THE GULF
SAUDI ARABIA
Qatar
Riyadh
Egypt
UAE
Oman
RED SEA
INDIAN OCEAN
Yemen
0 miles 500
0 km 1000

area 849,400 sq mi/2,200,518 sq km
capital Riyadh
cities Mecca, Medina, Taif; ports Jidda, Dammam
physical desert, sloping to the Persian Gulf from a height of 9,000 ft/2,750 m in the W
features Nafud desert in N and the Rub'al Khali (Empty Quarter) in S, area 250,000 sq mi/650,000 sq km; there is a ban on women drivers so there are an estimated 300,000 chauffeurs
head of state and government King Fahd Ibn Abdul Aziz from 1982
political system absolute monarchy
political parties none
exports oil, petroleum products
currency rial
population (1990 est) 16,758,000 (16% nomadic); growth rate 3.1% p.a.
life expectancy men 64, women 67 (1989)
language Arabic
religion Sunni Muslim; Shiite minority
literacy men 34%/women 12% (1980 est)
GNP $70 bn (1988); $6,170 per head (1988)
chronology
1926–32 Territories united, and kingdom established.
1953 King ibn-Saud died and was succeeded by his eldest son, Saud.
1964 King Saud forced to abdicate; succeeded by his brother, Faisal.
1975 King Faisal assassinated; succeeded by his half-brother, Khalid.
1982 King Khalid died of a heart attack; succeeded by his brother, Crown Prince Fahd.
1987 Rioting by Iranian pilgrims caused 400 deaths in Mecca; diplomatic relations with Iran severed.
1990 Iraqi troops invaded and annexed Kuwait and massed on Saudi Arabian border. King Fahd called for help from US and UK forces.
1991 Saudi Arabia fights with UN coalition against Iraq; attends Middle East peace conference.

Savimbi Angolan guerrilla leader Jonas Savimbi, whose UNITA rebels fought against Angola's left-wing regime from 1975 until peace was signed in 1991.

Labour politician. As prime minister 1935–40, he introduced much social-security legislation.

savanna or ***savannah*** extensive open tropical grasslands, with scattered trees and shrubs. Savannas cover large areas of Africa, North and South America, and N Australia.

The name was originally given by Spaniards to the treeless plains of the tropical South American prairies. Most of North America's savannas have been built over.

Savannah city and port of Georgia, 18 mi/29 km W of the mouth of the Savannah River; population (1990) 137,560. Founded 1733, Savannah was the first city in the US to be laid out in geometrically regular blocks. Manufactures include paper products, aircraft, transportation equipment, chemicals, and food products. The *Savannah*, the first steam-powered ship to cross the Atlantic, was built here; most of the 25-day journey, in 1819, was made under sail. The first nuclear-powered merchant ship, launched by the US 1959, was given the same name. Founded by James Oglethorpe in 1733, Savannah is the oldest settlement in Georgia and was its capital 1754–86. World cotton prices were set by the exchange here from the late 18th century until 1895.

Savery Thomas c. 1650–1715. British engineer who invented the steam-driven water pump, precursor of the steam engine, in 1696.

The pump used a boiler to raise steam, which was condensed (in a separate condenser) by an external spray of cold water. The partial vacuum created sucked water up a pipe from the mine shaft; steam pressure was then used to force the water away, after which the cycle was repeated. Savery patented his invention in 1698.

Savimbi Jonas 1934– . Angolan soldier and right-wing revolutionary, founder of the National Union for the Total Independence of Angola (UNITA).

The struggle for independence from Portugal escalated in 1961 into a civil war. In 1966 Savimbi founded the right-wing UNITA, which he led against the left-wing People's Movement for the Liberation of Angola (MPLA), led by Agostinho Neto. Neto, with Soviet and Cuban support, became president when independence was achieved in 1975, while UNITA, assisted by South Africa, continued its fight. A ceasefire was agreed in June 1989, but the truce was abandoned after two months. A truce was finally signed in May 1991.

savings the amount of current income that is not spent on consumption. Distinct from ◊investments, which are considered expenditures for the production of goods for future consumption, savings usually takes the form of bank time deposits. The savings rate depends on many factors, such as interest rates, inflation rates, unemployment rates, and expectations for future earnings.

savings and loan association (S&L) a cooperative, mutual, savings organization that sells stock to its members. Created primarily to finance home mortgages, S&Ls at one time provided 40% of the funds for home purchases. From 1986, an industry-wide crisis developed when, in some parts of the US, declining real estate values and rising unemployment reduced the value of investments and the ability of borrowers to repay loans. For the first time, mergers were permitted across state lines in hopes that the healthier institutions could assume the debt of the weaker, but losses mounted. The Federal Home Loan Board (FHLBB) and the Federal Savings and Loan Insurance Corporation (FSLIC) were unable to reverse the tide or cover the losses. By 1989 the losses were enormous, and a federal bailout pledging more than $100 billion in taxpayer funds was negotiated.

Savonarola Girolamo 1452–1498. Italian reformer, a Dominican friar and an eloquent preacher. His crusade against political and religious corruption won him popular support, and in 1494 he led a revolt in Florence that expelled the ruling Medici family and established a democratic republic. His denunciations of Pope ◊Alexander VI led to his excommunication in 1497, and in 1498 he was arrested, tortured, hanged, and burned for heresy.

Savoy area of France between the Alps, Lake Geneva, and the river Rhône. A medieval duchy, it was made into the *départements* of Savoie and Haute-Savoie, in the Rhône-Alpes region.

Savoy was a duchy from the 14th century, with the capital Chambéry. In 1720 it became a province of the kingdom of Sardinia which, with Nice, was ceded to France in 1860 by Victor Emmanuel II (king of Italy from 1861) in return for French assistance in driving the Austrians from Italy.

sawfish any fish of an order *Prisitformes* of large, sharklike ◊rays, characterized by having a head with a flat, sawlike snout edged with teeth. The common sawfish *P. pectinatus*, also called the smalltooth, is more than 19 ft/6 m long. It has some 24 teeth along an elongated snout (6 ft/2 m) that can be used as a weapon.

Savonarola Italian Dominican monk Savonarola whose crusade against political and religious corruption led to the establishment of a democratic republic in Florence. His portrait is by Fra Bartolomeo.

sawfly any of several families of insects of the order Hymenoptera, related to bees, wasps, and ants, but lacking a "waist" on the body. The egg-laying tube (ovipositor) of the female is surrounded by a pair of sawlike organs, which she uses to make a slit in a plant stem to lay her eggs. Horntails are closely related.

Saw Maung 1929– . Myanmar (Burmese) soldier and politician. Appointed head of the armed forces in 1985 by ◊Ne Win, he led a coup to remove Ne Win's successor, Maung Maung, in 1988 and became leader of an emergency government, which, despite being defeated in the May 1990 election, remained in office.

Saxe French form of ◊Saxony, former kingdom of Germany.

Saxe-Coburg-Gotha Saxon duchy. Albert, the Prince Consort of Britain's Queen Victoria, was a son of the 1st Duke, Ernest I (1784–1844), who was succeeded by Albert's elder brother, Ernest II (1818–93). It remained the name of the British royal house until 1917, when it was changed to Windsor.

saxhorn a family of brass musical instruments played with valves, invented by the Belgian Adolphe Sax (1814–94) in 1845.

saxifrage any plant of the genus *Saxifraga*, family Saxifragaceae, occuring in rocky, mountainous, and alpine situations in the northern hemisphere. They are low plants with groups of small white, pink, or yellow flowers.

Early saxifrage *S. virginiensis* is native to North America.

Saxon member of a Teutonic people who invaded Britain in the early Middle Ages; see under ◊Anglo-Saxon.

Saxony (German *Sachsen*) administrative *Land* (state) of the Federal Republic of Germany

area 6,580 sq mi/17,036 sq km

capital Dresden

towns Leipzig, Chemnitz, Zwickau

products electronics, textiles, vehicles, machinery, chemicals, coal

population (1990) 5,000,000

history situated on the plain of the river Elbe N of the Erzebirge mountain range, Saxony takes its name from the early Saxon inhabitants whose territories originally reached as far west as the Rhine. Conquered by Charlemagne 792, Saxony became a powerful medieval German duchy. It was divided 1260 but reconstituted in 1424 when a new electorate embracing Thuringia, Meissen, and Wittenberg was formed. The electors of Saxony were also kings of Poland 1697–1763. The northern part of Saxony became a province of Prussia 1815, its king having sided with Napoleon. In 1946 Saxony became a region of East Germany and in 1952 it was split into the districts of Leipzig, Dresden, and Chemnitz (later named Karl-Marx-Stadt). The state of Saxony was restored 1990 following German reunification and the abolition of the former East German districts.

Saxony-Anhalt administrative *Land* (state) of the Federal Republic of Germany

area 10,000 sq mi/25,000 sq km

capital Magdeburg

cities Halle, Dessau

products chemicals, electronics, rolling stock, footwear, cereals, vegetables

population (1990) 3,000,000

history named after the medieval castle of Anhalt, the territory of Anhalt was divided and reunited many times before becoming a duchy 1863 and a member of the North German Confederation 1866. In 1946 it was joined to the former Prussian province of Saxony as a region of East Germany and in 1952 it was divided into the districts of Halle and Magdeburg. Following the reunification of Germany in 1990, Saxony-Anhalt was reconstituted as one of the five new *Landër* of the Federal Republic.

saxophone a large family of wind instruments com-

Saxony: chronology

792	Saxony was conquered by Charlemagne.
814	When Charlemagne's empire broke up after his death, Saxony became a dukedom.
13th century	It became an electorate (that is, ruled by an elector).
1483	Martin Luther was born in Saxony, and the ◊Reformation originated here.
1618–48	Saxony suffered much in the ◊Thirty Years' War.
18th century	Saxony became a kingdom.
1815	Because Saxony had supported Napoleon I, half the kingdom was given to Prussia by the Congress of Vienna, becoming the Prussian province of Saxony.
1866	The remaining kingdom joined the North German Confederation.
1871	Incorporated in the German Empire.
1918	At the end of World War I, the king abdicated and Saxony became one of the federal states of the German Republic.
1946	After World War II, Saxony was made a new administrative *Land* of East Germany as ◊Saxony-Anhalt.
1952	Saxony-Anhalt was merged with Leipzig region.
1990	Saxony was restored as a state of the Federal Republic of Germany.

bining woodwind and brass features, the single reed of the clarinet and the wide bore of the bugle. Invented in 1840 and patented in 1946 by Adolphe Sax (1814–94), a Belgian instrument maker, the saxophone is a lively and versatile instrument that has played a prominent part in the history of jazz. Four of the original eight sizes remain in common use: soprano, alto, tenor, and baritone. The soprano is usually straight, the others curved back at the mouthpiece end, and with an upturned bell.

Sayan Mountains range in the SE USSR, on the Mongolian border; the highest peak is Munku Sardik 11,451 ft/3,489 m. The mountains have coal, gold, silver, graphite, and lead resources.

Sayers Dorothy L(eigh) 1893–1957. English writer of crime novels featuring detective Lord Peter Wimsey and heroine Harriet Vane, including *Strong Poison* 1930, *The Nine Tailors* 1934, and *Gaudy Night* 1935. She also wrote religious plays for radio, and translations of Dante.

Say's law in economics, the "law of markets" formulated by Jean-Baptiste Say (1767–1832) to the effect that supply creates its own demand and that resources can never be under-used.

Widely accepted by Classical economists, the "law" was regarded as erroneous by J M Keynes in his analysis of the depression in Britain during the 1920s and 1930s.

sc. abbreviation for scilicet (Latin "let it be understood").

SC abbreviation for ◊South Carolina.

scabies contagious infection of the skin caused by the parasitic itch mite *Sarcoptes scaboi*, which burrows under the skin to deposit eggs. Treatment is by antiparasitic creams and lotions.

scabious any plant of the Eurasian genus *Scabiosa* of the teasel family Dipsacaceae, with many small, usually blue, flowers borne in a single head on a tall stalk. The small scabious *S. columbaria* and the Mediterranean sweet scabious *S. atropurpurea* are often cultivated.

Scafell Pike highest mountain in England, 3,210 ft/978 m. It is in Cumbria in the Lake District and is separated from Scafell (3,164 ft/964 m) by a ridge called Mickledore.

scalar quantity in mathematics and science, a quantity that has magnitude but no direction, as distinct from a ◊vector quantity, which has a direction as well as a magnitude. Temperature, mass, and volume are scalar quantities.

scalawag or ***scallywag*** in US history, a derogatory term for white Southerners who, during and after the Civil War of 1861–65, supported the Republican Party, emancipation, and enfranchisement.

The reforms instituted by the scalawags were widely resented in the South, and their influence diminished with the rise of the Democratic party in the South.

scale in music, a sequence of pitches that establishes a key, and in some respects the character of a composition. A scale is defined by its starting note and may be major or minor depending on the order of intervals. A chromatic scale is the full range of 12 notes: it has no key because there is no fixed starting point. A whole-tone scale is a six-note scale and is also indeterminate in key: only two are possible. A diatonic scale has seven notes, a pentatonic scale has five.

scale insect any small plant-sucking insect (order *Homoptera*) of the superfamily Cocceidea. Some species are major pests—for example the citrus mealy bug (genus *Pseudococcus*), which attacks citrus fruits in North America. The female is often wingless and legless, attached to a plant by the head and with the body covered with a waxy scale. The rare males are winged.

Scalia Antonin 1936– . US jurist and associate justice of the US Supreme Court 1986– . He concurred with the majority opinion of the court in *Texas* v *Johnson* 1989, that ruled constitutional the burning of the US flag in protest. He dissented in *Edwards* v *Aguillard* 1987 when the Court ruled that states may not mandate the teaching of the theory of creationism to counteract the teaching of the theory of evolution.

Born in Trenton, New Jersey, he graduated from Georgetown University and the Harvard University Law School. After practicing law in Cleveland, Scalia accepted a teaching position at the University of Virginia Law School in 1967. From 1971 he worked as a lawyer in the executive branch of the federal government, ultimately becoming assistant attorney general 1974, where he advised the Gerald Ford White House in the Watergate scandal. He later became professor of law at the University of Chicago, where he was known for his support of economic deregulation and judicial restraint. In 1982 President Reagan appointed Scalia to the US Court of Appeals for the District of Columbia. On the court, Scalia favored judicial restraint, circumscription of freedom of the press, and strong federal executive powers, especially in foreign policy areas. President Reagan appointed Scalia to the Supreme Court 1986.

scallop any marine bivalve ◊mollusk of the family Pectinidae, with a fan-shaped shell. There are two "ears" extending from the socketlike hinge. Scallops use "jet propulsion" to move through the water to escape predators such as starfish. The giant Pacific scallop found from Alaska to California can reach 8 in/20 cm width.

scaly anteater another name for the ◊pangolin.

Scandinavia peninsula in NW Europe, comprising Norway and Sweden; politically and culturally it also includes Denmark and Finland.

Scandinavian inhabitant of or native to Scandinavia (Denmark, Norway, Sweden, Iceland, and, often, Finland); also referring to the languages and cultures. The Scandinavian languages, including Faroese, belong to the Indo-European family.

scandium silver-white, metallic element of the ◊lanthanide series, symbol Sc, atomic number 21, atomic weight 44.956. Its compounds are found widely distributed in nature but only in minute amounts. The metal has little industrial importance.

Scandium is relatively more abundant in the Sun and other stars than on Earth. Scandium oxide (scandia) is used as a catalyst, in making crucibles and other ceramic parts, and scandium sulfate (in very dilute aqueous solution) is used in agriculture to improve seed germination.

The element was discovered and named in 1879 by Swedish chemist Lars Nilson (1840–1899), for Latin *Scandia*, because it occurs in the Scandinavian mineral euxenite, on which he worked.

scanner device, usually electronic, used to sense and reproduce an image. In medicine, scanners are used in diagnosis to provide images of internal organs. Magnetic resonance imaging was being used in 1990 to tell stale food from fresh: the image of a fresh vegetable is different from that of one frozen and thawed.

scanning in medicine, the noninvasive examination of body organs to detect abnormalities of structure or function. Detectable waves—for example ◊ultrasound, magnetic, or ◊X rays—are passed through the part to be scanned. Their absorption pattern is recorded, analyzed by computer, and displayed pictorially on a screen.

scanning tunneling microscope (STM) a microscope that produces a magnified image using a tiny tungsten probe, with a tip so fine that it may consist of a single atom, which moves across a specimen. The probe tip moves so close to the specimen surface that electrons jump (or tunnel) across the gap between the tip and the surface.

The magnitude of the electron flow (current) depends on the distance from the tip to the surface, and so by measuring the current, the contours of the surface can be determined. These can be used to form an image on a computer screen of the surface, with individual atoms resolved.

Scapa Flow expanse of sea in the Orkney Islands, Scotland, until 1957 a base of the Royal Navy. It was the main base of the Grand Fleet during World War I and in 1919 was the scene of the scuttling of 71 surrendered German warships.

scapolite a group of white or grayish minerals, silicates of sodium, aluminum, and calcium, common in metamorphosed limestones and forming at high temperatures and pressures.

scapula or ***shoulder blade*** large bone forming part of the pectoral girdle, assisting in the articulation of the arm with the chest region. Its flattened shape allows a large region for the attachment of muscles.

scarab any of a family Scarabaeidae of beetles, often brilliantly colored, and including ◊cockchafers, June beetles, and ◊dung beetles. The *Scarabeus sacer* was revered by the ancient Egyptians as the symbol of resurrection.

Scarlatti (Giuseppe) Domenico 1685–1757. Italian composer, eldest son of Alessandro ◊Scarlatti, who lived most of his life in Portugal and Spain in the service of the Queen of Spain. He wrote highly original harpsichord sonatas.

Scarlatti (Pietro) Alessandro (Gaspare) 1660–1725. Italian Baroque composer, Master of the Chapel at the court of Naples, who developed the opera form. He composed more than 100 operas, including *Tigrane* 1715, as well as church music and oratorios.

scarlet fever or ***scarlatina*** acute infectious disease, especially of children, caused by the bacterium *Streptococcus pyogenes*. It is marked by a sore throat and a bright red rash spreading from the upper to the lower part of the body. The rash is followed by the skin peeling in flakes. It is treated with antibiotics.

Scarlet Pimpernel, The a historical adventure novel by Baroness Orczy published in the UK 1905. Set in Paris during the Reign of Terror (1793–94), it describes the exploits of a group of Britons, called the League of the Scarlet Pimpernel, and their leader, Sir Percy Blakeney, who saved aristocrats from the Revolution.

scarp and dip in geology, the two slopes formed when a sedimentary bed outcrops as a landscape feature. The scarp is the slope that cuts across the bedding plane; the dip is the opposite slope which follows the bedding plane. The scarp is usually steep, while the dip is a gentle slope.

scent gland gland that opens onto the outer surface of animals, producing odorous compounds that are used for communicating between members of the same species (◊pheromones), or for discouraging predators.

Schechter v US a US Supreme Court decision 1935 dealing with the constitutionality of New Deal legislation over labor standards and trade practices. Found guilty under the National Industrial Recovery Act 1933 of violating minimum-wage and maximum-hours regulations, Schechter, a New York poultry dealer, appealed his case to the US Supreme Court. He argued that since he was a local dealer operating an exclusively intrastate trade, the case was outside federal jurisdiction. The Court found that Schechter's trade had no direct effect on interstate commerce and was therefore not subject to Congressional regulation. This was a serious blow to New Deal recovery policies.

Scheele Karl Wilhelm 1742–1786. Swedish chemist and pharmacist. In the book *Experiments on Air and Fire* 1777, he argued that the atmosphere was composed of two gases. One, which supported combustion (oxygen), he called "fire air," and the other, which inhibited combustion (nitrogen), he called "vitiated air." He thus anticipated Joseph ◊Priestley's discovery of oxygen by two years.

Scheer Reinhard 1863–1928. German admiral in World War I, commander of the High Sea Fleet in 1916 at the Battle of ◊Jutland.

Scheherazade the storyteller in the ◊*Arabian Nights*.

Scheldt (Dutch *Schelde*; French *Escaut*) river rising in Aisne *département*, N France, and flowing 250 mi/400 km to join the North Sea S of Walcheren, in the Netherlands. Antwerp is the chief town on the Scheldt.

Schelling Friedrich Wilhelm Joseph 1775–1854. German philosopher who began as a follower of Johann Fichte, but moved away from subjective ◊idealism, which treats the external world as essentially immaterial, toward a "philosophy of identity" (*Identitätsphilosophie*), in which subject and object are seen as united in the absolute. His early philosophy influenced ◊Hegel, but his later work criticizes Hegel, arguing that being necessarily precedes thought.

Schenck v US a US Supreme Court decision 1919 dealing with Congress's power to revoke First-Amendment rights. Schenck, an outspoken anti-draft activist, was convicted of providing aid and comfort to the enemy, in violation of the Espionage Act 1917. The Court unanimously upheld his conviction, ruling that Congress was obligated to interfere with the freedom of speech when it presented a "clear and present danger" to the well-being of the society.

Schenectady industrial city on the Mohawk river, New York State; population (1990) 65,566. It dates from 1662 was long noted as a producer of electrical goods.

Scherchen Hermann 1891–1966. German conductor. He collaborated with ◊Schoenberg, and in 1919 founded the journal *Melos* to promote contemporary music. He moved to Switzerland in 1933, and was active as a conductor and teacher. He wrote two texts, *Handbook of Conducting* and *The Nature of Music*. During the 1950s he founded a music publishing house, Ars Viva Verlag, and an electronic studio at Gravesano.

scherzo (Italian "joke") in music, a lively piece, usually in rapid triple (3/4) time; often used for the third movement of a symphony, sonata, or quartet.

Scheveningen seaside resort and northern suburbs of The ◊Hague, Netherlands. There is a ferry link with Great Yarmouth, England.

Schiaparelli Elsa 1896–1973. Italian couturier and knitwear designer. Her innovative fashion ideas included padded shoulders, sophisticated colors ("shocking pink"), and the pioneering use of zippers and synthetic fabrics.

Schiaparelli Giovanni (Virginio) 1835–1910. Italian astronomer who discovered the so-called "Martian canals." He studied ancient and medieval astronomy, discovered the asteroid 69 (Hesperia) April 1861, observed double stars, and revealed the connection between comets and meteors. In 1877 he was the first to draw attention to the linear markings on Mars, which gave rise to the "Martian canal" controversy. These markings are now known to be optical effects and not real lines.

Schick test injection of a small quantity of diphtheria toxin to ascertain whether or not a person is immune to the disease. If there is no immunity, a local inflammation develops.

Schiedam port in Zuid-Holland province, SW Netherlands, on the river Meuse, 3 mi/5 km W of Rotterdam; population (1987) 69,350. It is famous for its gin.

Schiele Egon 1890–1918. Austrian Expressionist artist. Originally a landscape painter, he was strongly influenced by Art Nouveau and developed a contorted linear style. His subject matter included portraits and nudes. In 1911 he was arrested for alleged obscenity.

Schiller Johann Christoph Friedrich von 1759–1805. German dramatist, poet, and historian. He wrote *Sturm und Drang* ("storm and stress") verse and plays, including the dramatic trilogy *Wallenstein* 1798–99. Much of his work concerns the aspirations for political freedom and the avoidance of mediocrity.

He was a qualified surgeon, but after the success of the play *Die Räuber/The Robbers* 1781, he devoted himself to literature and completed his tragedies *Fiesko/Fiasco* and *Kabale und Liebe/Love and Intrigue* 1783. Moving to Weimar in 1787, he wrote his more mature blank-verse drama *Don Carlos* and the hymn "An die Freude/Ode to Joy," later used by ◊Beethoven in his ninth symphony. As professor of history at Jena from 1789 he completed a history of the Thirty Years' War and developed a close friendship with ◊Goethe after early antagonism. His essays on esthetics include the piece of literary criticism *Über naive und sentimentalische Dichtung/Naive and Sentimental Poetry*. Schiller became the foremost German dramatist with his classic dramas *Wallenstein*, *Maria Stuart* 1800, *Die Jungfrau von Orleans/The Maid of Orleans* 1801, and *Wilhelm Tell/William Tell* 1804.

Schinkel Karl Friedrich 1781–1841. Prussian Neo-Classical architect. His major works include the Old Museum, Berlin, 1823–30, the Nikolaikirche in Potsdam 1830–37, and the Roman Bath 1833 in the park of Potsdam.

schipperke (Dutch "little boatman" from its use on canal barges) breed of tailless watchdog, bred in Belgium. It has black fur and erect ears, is about 1 ft/30 cm high, and weighs about 16 lb/7 kg.

schism a formal split over a doctrinal difference between religious believers, as in the ◊Great Schism in the Roman Catholic Church; over the doctrine of papal infallibility, as with the Old Catholics in 1879; and over the use of the Latin Tridentine mass 1988.

schist a foliated (laminated) ◊metamorphic rock arranged in parallel layers of ◊minerals — for example, mica, which easily splits off into thin plates.

schistosomiasis another name for ◊bilharzia.

schizocarp a type of dry ◊fruit that develops from two or more carpels and splits, when mature, to form separate one-seeded units known as mericarps.

The mericarps may be dehiscent, splitting open to release the seed when ripe, as in *Geranium*, or indehiscent, remaining closed once mature, as in mallow *Malva* and plants of the Umbelliferae family, such as the carrot *Daucus carota* and parsnip *Pastinaca sativa*.

schizophrenia a mental disorder, a psychosis of unknown origin (but evidence exists for a biochemical basis), which can lead to profound changes in personality and behavior including paranoia and hallucinations. Modern treatment approaches include drugs, family therapy, stress reduction, and rehabilitation, but they are not always successful.

Schlegel August Wilhelm von 1767–1845. German Romantic author, translator of Shakespeare, whose *Über dramatische Kunst und Literatur/Lectures on Dramatic Art and Literature* 1809–11 broke down the formalism of the old Classical criteria of literary composition. Friedrich von Schlegel was his brother.

Schlegel Friedrich von 1772–1829. German critic who (with his brother August) was a founder of the Romantic movement, and a pioneer in the comparative study of languages.

Schlesinger Arthur Meier, Jr 1917– . US historian. His first book, *The Age of Jackson*, won a Pulitzer prize 1945. After being named to the Harvard faculty 1946, he became active in Democratic politics, serving as a speechwriter in the presidential campaigns of Adlai Stevenson 1956 and John Kennedy 1960. Schlesinger was presidential assistant for Latin American Affairs 1961–64 and in 1967 became a professor at the City College of New York.

Born in Columbus, Ohio, the son of a prominent historian, Schlesinger was educated at Harvard and served as an intelligence officer during World War II.

Schlesinger John 1926– . English film and television director who was responsible for such British films as *Billy Liar* 1963 and *Darling* 1965. His first US film, *Midnight Cowboy* 1969, was a big commercial success and was followed by *Sunday, Bloody Sunday* 1971, *Marathon Man* 1976, and *Yanks* 1979.

Schleswig-Holstein *Land* (state) of Germany
area 6,060 sq mi/15,700 sq km
capital Kiel
towns Lübeck, Flensburg, Schleswig
features river Elbe, Kiel Canal, Heligoland
products shipbuilding, mechanical and electrical engineering, food processing
population (1988) 2,613,000
religion 87% Protestant; 6% Catholic
history Schleswig (Danish *Slesvig*) and Holstein were two duchies held by the kings of Denmark from 1460, but were not part of the kingdom; a number of the inhabitants were German, and Holstein was a member of the Confederation of the Rhine formed 1815. Possession of the duchies had long been disputed by Prussia, and when Frederick VII of Denmark died without an heir 1863, Prussia, supported by Austria, fought and defeated the Danes 1864, and in 1866 annexed the two duchies. A plebiscite held 1920 gave the northern part of Schleswig to Denmark, which made it the province of Haderslev and Aabenraa; the rest, with Holstein, remained part of Germany.

Schlieffen Plan military plan produced by German chief of general staff, General Count Alfred von Schlieffen (1833–1913) Dec 1905, that formed the basis of German military planning before World War I, and which inspired Hitler's plans for the conquest of Europe in World War II. It involved a simultaneous attack on Russia and France, the object being to defeat France quickly and then deploy all available resources against the Russians.

Schliemann Heinrich 1822–1890. German archeologist. He earned a fortune as a businessman, retiring in 1863 to pursue his life-long ambition to discover a historical basis for Homer's Iliad. In 1871 he began excavating at Hissarlik, Turkey, a site which yielded the ruins of nine consecutive cities and was indeed the site of Troy. His later excavations were at Mycenae 1874–76, where he discovered the ruins of the ◊Mycenean civilization.

Schluter Poul Holmskov 1929– . Danish right-wing politician, leader of the Conservative People's

Schnabel *Austrian pianist Artur Schnabel, who in 1938 emigrated to the US, where he became known for his interpretation of the German classics.*

Party (KF) from 1974 and prime minister from 1982. Having joined the KF in his youth, he trained as a lawyer and then entered the Danish parliament (Folketing) in 1964. His center-right coalition survived the 1987 election and was reconstituted, with Liberal support, in 1988.

Schmidt Helmut 1918– . German Socialist politician, member of the Social Democratic Party (SPD), chancellor of West Germany 1974–83. As chancellor, Schmidt introduced social reforms and continued Brandt's policy of ◊Ostpolitik. With the French president Giscard d'Estaing, he instigated annual world and European economic summits. He was a firm supporter of ◊NATO and of the deployment of US nuclear missiles in West Germany during the early 1980s.

Schmidt was elected to the Bundestag (federal parliament) in 1953. He was interior minister 1961–65, defense minister 1969–72, and finance minister 1972–74. He became federal chancellor (prime minister) on Willy ◊Brandt's resignation in 1974. Reelected 1980, he was defeated in the *Bundestag* in 1982 following the switch of allegiance by the SPD's coalition allies, the Free Democratic Party. Schmidt retired from federal politics at the general election of 1983, having encountered growing opposition from the SPD's left wing, who opposed his stance on military and economic issues.

Schmidt-Rottluff Karl 1884–1974. German Expressionist painter and printmaker, a founding member of the movement *Die* ◊Brücke in Dresden 1905, active in Berlin from 1911. Inspired by Vincent van Gogh and ◊Fauvism, he developed a vigorous style of brushwork and a bold palette. He painted portraits and landscapes and produced numerous woodcuts and lithographs.

Schnabel Artur 1882–1951. Austrian-born US pianist, teacher, and composer. He taught music at the Berlin State Academy 1925–30, but settled in the US in 1939, where he composed symphonies and piano works. He excelled at playing Beethoven and trained many of today's concert pianists.

Schneider Romy. Adopted name of Rosemarie Albach-Retty 1938–1982. Austrian film actress who starred in *Boccaccio '70* 1962, *Le Procès/Der Prozess* 1962, and *Ludwig* 1972.

Schoenberg Arnold (Franz Walter) 1874–1951. Austro-Hungarian composer, a US citizen from 1941. After Romantic early work such as *Verklärte Nacht* 1899 and the *Gurrelieder/Songs of Gurra* 1900–11, he experimented with ◊atonality (absence of key), producing works such as *Pierrot Lunaire* 1912 for chamber ensemble and voice, before developing the 12-tone system of musical composition. This was further developed by his pupils ◊Berg and ◊Webern.

After World War I he wrote several Neo-Classical works for chamber ensembles. He taught at the Berlin State Academy 1925–33. Driven from Germany by the Nazis, he settled in the US 1933, where he influenced music scoring for films. Later works include the opera *Moses and Aaron* 1932–51.

scholasticism the theological and philosophical systems that were studied in both Christian and Judaic schools in Europe in the medieval period. Scholasticism sought to integrate biblical teaching with Platonic and Aristotelian philosophy.

John Scotus (Erigena) is regarded as the founder, but the succession of "schoolmen," as scholastic philosophers were called, opened with Roscellinus at the end of the 11th century, when as a supporter of nominalism he was countered by Anselm, the champion of realism. The controversy over ◊universals thus begun continued for several centuries. William of Champeaux, Abelard, the English monk Alexander of Hales (died 1222), Albertus Magnus, and Peter Lombard played prominent parts, but more significant were Thomas Aquinas, whose writings became the Classical textbooks of Catholic doctrine, and the Franciscan Duns Scotus. In the late 12th century the Spanish philosopher Moses Maimonides published a work that helped to introduce Europe to an integrated approach to Aristotle. The last major scholastic philosopher was William of Occam, who, in the first half of the 14th century, restated ◊nominalism.

In the 20th century there has been a revival of interest in scholasticism, in the writings of Jacques Maritian (1882–1973) and other Catholic scholars.

school in education, an institution where instruction takes place. Some are accredited.

School District of Abington Township v Schempp a US Supreme Court decision 1963 dealing with mandatory religious worship in public schools. The case challenged the constitutionality of an Abington, Pennsylvania, statute that forced students to recite Bible verses and the Lord's Prayer in school. The Court ruled that such practice violated First-Amendment measures against establishing an official religion. Since the statute had no secular legislative purpose, it was declared invalid.

Schopenhauer Arthur 1788–1860. German philosopher whose *The World as Will and Idea* 1818 expounded an atheistic and pessimistic world view: an irrational will is considered as the inner principle of the world, producing an ever-frustrated cycle of desire, of which the only escape is esthetic contemplation or absorption into nothingness.

This theory struck a responsive chord in the philosopher Nietzsche, the composer Wagner, the German novelist Thomas Mann, and the English writer Thomas Hardy.

Schoenberg *Austro-Hungarian composer Arnold Schoenberg, who settled in the US in 1933, teaching at the University of California.*

Schubert *Austrian composer Franz Schubert, who created symphonies, chamber and piano music, and lieder (songs).*

Schreiner Olive 1862–1920. South African novelist and supporter of women's rights. Her autobiographical *The Story of an African Farm* 1883 describes life on the South African veld.

Schrödinger Erwin 1887–1961. Austrian physicist who advanced the study of wave mechanics (see ◊quantum theory). Born in Vienna, he became senior professor at the Dublin Institute for Advanced Studies 1940. He shared (with Paul ◊Dirac) a Nobel Prize 1933.

Schubert Franz (Peter) 1797–1828. Austrian composer. He was only 31 when he died, but his musical output was prodigious. His 13 symphonic efforts produced 7 complete and 6 incomplete works, most notable being (the "Unfinished") *Symphony No. 8* in B minor and (the "Great") *Symphony No. 9* in C major. He wrote chamber and piano music, including the "Trout Quintet," and over 600 *Leider* (songs) combining the Romantic expression of emotion with pure melody. They include the cycles *Die schöne Müllerin/The Beautiful Maid of the Mill* 1823 and *Die Winterreise/The Winter Journey* 1827.

Schulz Charles Monroe 1922– . US cartoonist. His idea for the "Peanuts" cartoon strip was accepted by United Features Syndicate 1950. As the characters Snoopy, Charlie Brown, Lucy, and Linus became famous throughout the country, Schulz further promoted them through merchandise lines and television specials. In 1967 a musical based on the "Peanuts" characters, *You're a Good Man, Charlie Brown*, played on Broadway.

Born in Minneapolis, Minnesota, Schulz gained his only formal training through a correspondence course with the Minneapolis Art Institute. He joined the staff of the *St Paul Pioneer Press* 1948.

Schumacher Fritz (Ernst Friedrich) 1911–1977. German writer and economist, whose *Small is Beautiful: Economics as if People Mattered* 1973 makes a case for small-scale economic growth without great capital expenditure.

Schuman Robert 1886–1963. French politician. He was prime minister 1947–48, and as foreign minister 1948–53 he proposed in May 1950 a common market for coal and steel (the Schuman Plan), which was established as the European Coal and Steel Community 1952, the basis of the European Community.

Schumann Clara (Josephine) (born Wieck) 1819–1896. German pianist. Born in Leipzig, she married Robert ◊Schumann in 1840 (her father had been his piano teacher). During his life and after his death she was devoted to popularizing his work, appearing frequently in European concert halls.

Schumann Robert Alexander 1810–1856. German Romantic composer. His songs and short piano pieces show simplicity combined with an ability to portray mood and emotion. Among his compositions are seven symphonies (three incomplete), a violin concerto, a piano concerto, sonatas, and song cycles, such as *Dichterliebe/Poet's Love* 1840. Mendelssohn championed many of his works.

Schumpeter Joseph A(lois) 1883–1950. US economist and sociologist, born in Moravia, now Czechoslovakia. In *Capitalism, Socialism and Democracy* 1942 he contended that Western capitalism, impelled by its very success, was evolving into a form of socialism because firms would become increasingly large and their managements increasingly divorced from ownership, while social trends were undermining the traditional motives for entrepreneurial accumulation of wealth.

He was deeply interested in mathematics, and he took part in the founding of the Econometric Society 1930. His writings established him as an authority on economic theory as well as the history of economic thought. Among other standard reference works, he wrote the *History of Economic Analysis* 1954, published posthumously.

Schurz Carl 1829–1906. German-born US editor and political leader. Named US minister to Spain 1861–62, he returned to see action as a staff officer in the American Civil War. After working briefly as editor of the *Detroit Post* 1866, he moved to St Louis and was elected to the US Senate, where he sat 1869–75. After serving as secretary of the interior under President Hayes 1877–81, Schurz became editor of the *New York Evening Post* 1881–83. A harsh critic of government corruption, he was president of the National Civil Service Reform League 1892–1901.

Schurz came to the US 1852, studied law, and was admitted to the Wisconsin bar 1859.

Schuschnigg Kurt von 1897–1977. Austrian chancellor 1934–38, in succession to ◊Dollfuss. He tried in vain to prevent Nazi annexation (*Anschluss*) but in Feb 1938 he was forced to accept a Nazi minister of the interior, and a month later Austria was occupied and annexed by Germany. He was imprisoned in Germany until 1945, when he went to the US; he returned to Austria 1967.

Schütz Heinrich 1585–1672. German composer, musical director to the Elector of Saxony from 1614. His works include *The Seven Last Words* c. 1645, *Musicalische Exequien* 1636, and the *Deutsche Magnificat/German Magnificat* 1671.

Schuyler Philip John 1733–1804. American public official. Born in Albany, New York, Schuyler inherited extensive real estate holdings in the Mohawk Valley. After service in the French and Indian War, he was elected to the provincial assembly 1768 and was a member of the Continental Congress 1775–77. At the outbreak of the American Revolution, he was named general in command of the Department of New York. Replaced in 1777, he returned to the Continental Congress 1778–81. A supporter of the US Constitution, Schuyler became one of New York's first US senators 1789–91 and later served 1797–98.

Schwarzkopf Elisabeth 1915– . German soprano, known for her dramatic interpretation of operatic roles, such as Elvira in *Don Giovanni* and the Marschallin in *Der Rosenkavalier*, as well as songs.

Schwarzkopf (H) Norman. Nicknamed "Stormin' Norman" 1934– . US general who was supreme commander of the Allied forces in the ◊Gulf War 1991. He planned and executed a blitzkrieg campaign, "Desert Storm," sustaining remarkably few casualties in the liberation of Kuwait. He was a battalion commander in the Vietnam War and deputy commander of the 1983 US invasion of Grenada.

A graduate from the military academy at West Point, Schwarzkopf obtained a master's degree in guided-missile engineering. He became an infantryman and later a paratrooper, and did two tours of service in Vietnam. Maintaining the 28-member Arab–Western military coalition against Iraq 1991 extended his diplomatic skills, and his success in

***Schwitters** German artist Kurt Schwitters, a Dadaist, painted* Opened by Customs *in 1937–38.*

the Gulf War made him a popular hero in the US, after which he retired.

Schwarzwald German name for the ◊Black Forest, coniferous forest in the Federal Republic of Germany.

Schweitzer Albert 1875–1965. French Protestant theologian, organist, and missionary surgeon. He founded the hospital at Lambaréné in Gabon in 1913, giving organ recitals to support his work there. He wrote a life of Bach and *Von reimarus zu Wrede/The Quest for the Historical Jesus* 1906 and was awarded the Nobel Peace Prize in 1952 for his teaching of "reverence for life."

Schwerin capital of the state of Mecklenberg–West Pomerania. Federal Republic of Germany, on the W shore of the lake of Schwerin; population (1990) 130,000; products include machinery and chemicals. Formerly the capital of ◊Mecklenburg and earlier of the old republic of Mecklenburg-Schwerin, Schwerin became capital of Mecklenberg–West Pomerania with the reunification of Germany 1990.

Schwinger Julian 1918– . US quantum physicist. His research concerned the behavior of charged particles in electrical fields. This work, expressed entirely through mathematics, combines elements from quantum theory and relativity theory.

Described as the "physicist in knee pants," he entered college in New York at the age of 15, transferred to Columbia University and graduated at 17. At the age of 29 he became Harvard University's youngest full professor.

Schwitters Kurt 1887–1948. German artist, a member of the ◊Dada movement. He moved to Norway in 1937 and to England in 1940. From 1918 he developed a variation on collage, using discarded rubbish such as buttons and bus tickets to create pictures and structures.

He called these art works *Merz* and produced a magazine of the same name from 1923. Later he created *Merzbau*, extensive constructions of wood and scrap, most of which were destroyed.

Schwyz capital of Schwyz canton, Switzerland; population (1980) 12,100. Schwyz was one of the three original cantons of the Swiss Confederation 1291, which gave its name to the whole country about 1450.

Sciascia Leonardo 1921–1989. Sicilian novelist who used the detective novel to explore the hidden workings of Sicilian life, as in *Il giorno della civetta/Mafia Vendetta* 1961.

sciatica persistent pain in the leg, along the sciatic nerve and its branches. Causes of sciatica include inflammation of the nerve or pressure on, or inflammation of, a nerve root leading out of the lower spine.

science (Latin *scientia* "knowledge") any systematic field of study or body of knowledge that aims, through experiment, observation, and deduction, to produce reliable explanation of phenomena, with reference to the material and physical world.

Activities such as healing, star-watching, and engineering have been practiced in many societies since ancient times. Pure science, especially physics (formerly called natural philosophy), had traditionally been the main area of study for philosophers. The European scientific revolution between about 1650 and 1800 replaced speculative philosophy with a new combination of observation, experimentation, and rationality.

Today, scientific research involves an interaction among tradition, experiment and observation, and deduction. The subject area called philosophy of science investigates the nature of this complex interaction, and the extent of its ability to gain access to the truth about the material world. It has long been recognized that induction from observation cannot give explanations based on logic. In the 20th century Karl ◊Popper has described ◊scientific method as a rigorous experimental testing of a scientist's ideas or hypotheses (see ◊hypothesis). The origin and role of these ideas, and their interdependence with observation, have been examined, for example, by the US thinker Thomas S ◊Kuhn, who places them in a historical and sociological setting. The sociology of science investigates how scientific theories and laws are produced, and questions the possibility of objectivity in any scientific endeavor. One controversial point of view is the replacement of scientific realism with scientific relativism, as proposed by Paul K ◊Feyerabend. Questions concerning the proper use of science and the role of science education are also restructuring this field of study.

Science is divided into separate areas of study, such as astronomy, biology, geology, chemistry, physics, and mathematics, although more recently attempts have been made to combine traditionally separate disciplines under such headings as ◊life sciences and ◊earth sciences. These areas are usually jointly referred to as the natural sciences. Physics and chemistry are usually separated out and called the physical or hard sciences, with mathematics left in a category of its own. The application of science for practical purposes is called technology. Social science is the systematic study of human behavior, and includes such areas as anthropology, economics, psychology, and sociology. One area of contemporary debate is whether the social-science disciplines are actually sciences; that is, whether the study of human beings is capable of scientific precision or prediction in the same way as natural science is seen to be.

science fiction or ***speculative fiction*** (also known as ***SF*** or ***sci-fi***) genre of fiction and film with an imaginary scientific, technological, or futuristic basis. It is sometimes held to have its roots in the works of Mary Shelley, notably *Frankenstein* 1818. Often taking its ideas and concerns from current ideas in science and the social sciences, science fiction aims to shake up standard perceptions of reality.

SF works often deal with alternative realities, future histories, robots, aliens, utopias and dystopias (often satiric), space and time travel, natural or human-made disasters, and psychic powers. Early practitioners were Jules Verne and H G Wells. In the 20th century the US pulp-magazine tradition of SF produced writers such as Arthur C Clarke, Isaac Asimov, Robert Heinlein, and Frank Herbert; a consensus of "pure storytelling" and traditional values was disrupted by writers associated with the British magazine *New Worlds* (Brian Aldiss, Michael Moorcock, J G Ballard) and by younger US writers (Joanna Russ, Ursula Le Guin, Thomas Disch, Gene Wolfe) who used the form for serious literary purposes and for political and sexual radicalism. Thriving SF traditions, only partly influenced by the Anglo-American one, exist in France, Germany, and Eastern Europe, especially the USSR. In the 1980s the cyberpunk school spread from the US, spearheaded by William Gibson and Bruce Sterling (1954–).

Science fiction writers include James Tiptree Jr (Alice Sheldon 1915–1987, US), Philip K Dick, John Brunner (1934– , UK), Samuel Delany (1942– , US), Stanislaw Lem (1921– , Poland), Boris and Arkady Strugatsky (1931– and 1925– , USSR), Harlan Ellison (1934–), Damon Knight (1922–), John Campbell (1910–1971), and Frederik Pohl (1919–)—the last four all US editors and anthologists.

Many mainstream writers have written SF, including Aldous Huxley (*Brave New World* 1932), George Orwell (*Nineteen Eighty-Four* 1949), and Doris Lessing (series of five books *Canopus in Argos: Archives* 1979–83).

science park site on which high-technology industrial businesses are housed near a university, so that they can benefit from the research expertise of the university's scientists. Science parks originated in the US in the 1950s.

scientific law in science, principles that are taken to be universally applicable.

Laws (for instance, ◊Boyle's law and ◊Newton's laws of motion) form the basic theoretical structure of the physical sciences, so that the rejection of a law by the scientific community is an almost inconceivable event. On occasion a law may be modified, as was the case when Einstein showed that Newton's laws of motion do not apply to objects traveling at speeds close to that of light.

scientific method in science, the belief that experimentation and observation, properly understood and applied, can avoid the influence of cultural and social values and so build up a picture of a reality independent of the observer.

Improved techniques and mechanical devices, which improve the reliability of measurements, may seem to support this theory; but the realization that observations of subatomic particles influence their behavior has undermined the view that objectivity is possible in science (see ◊uncertainty principle).

Scientology (Latin *scire* "to know" and Greek *logos* "branch of learning") an "applied religious philosophy" based on ◊dianetics, founded in California in 1954 by L Ron ◊Hubbard as the Church of Scientology. It claims to "increase man's spiritual awareness," but its methods of recruiting and retaining converts have been criticized. Its headquarters from 1959 have been in Sussex, England.

scilla any bulbous plant of the genus *Scilla*, family Liliaceae, bearing blue, pink, or white flowers, and including the spring squill *S. verna*.

Scilly Islands group of 140 islands and islets lying 25 mi/40 km SW of Land's End, England; administered by the Duchy of Cornwall; area 6.3 sq mi/16 sq km; population (1981) 1,850. The five inhabited islands are St Mary's, the largest, on which is Hugh Town, capital of the Scillies; Tresco, the second largest, with subtropical gardens; St Martin's, noted for beautiful shells; St Agnes; and Bryher.

Products include vegetables and flowers, and tourism is important. The islands have remains of Bronze Age settlements.

scintillation counter instrument for measuring very low levels of radiation. The radiation strikes a scintillator (a device that emits a unit of light when a charged elementary particle collides with it), whose light output is "amplified" by a ◊photomultiplier; the current pulses of its output are in turn counted or added by a scaler to give a numerical reading.

Scipio Africanus Major 237–c. 183 BC. Roman general. He defeated the Carthaginians in Spain 210–206, invaded Africa 204, and defeated Hannibal at Zama 202.

Scipio Africanus Minor c. 185–129 BC. Roman general, the adopted grandson of Scipio Africanus

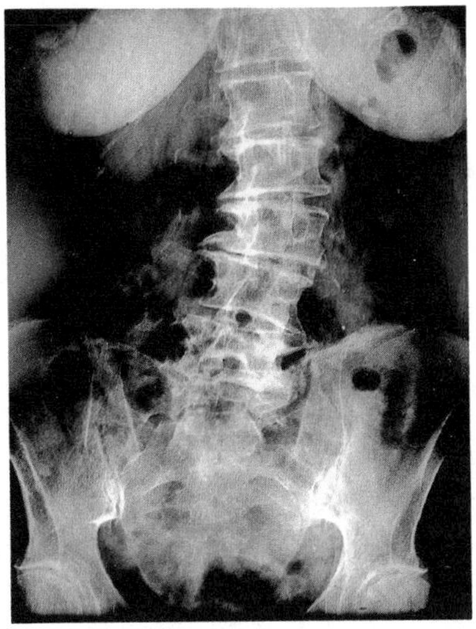

scoliosis X ray of the lumbar spine of a woman, aged 80, showing a prominent scoliosis (lateral curve).

Major, also known as Scipio Aemilianus. He destroyed Carthage 146, and subdued Spain 134. He was opposed to his brothers-in-law, the Gracchi (see under ◊Gracchus), and his wife is thought to have participated in his murder.

Scipio Publius Cornelius died 211 BC. Roman general, father of Scipio Africanus Major. Elected consul 218, during the 2nd Punic War, he was defeated by Hannibal at Ticinus and killed by the Carthaginians in Spain.

SCLC abbreviation for US civil-rights organization ◊Southern Christian Leadership Conference.

sclerenchyma a plant tissue whose function is to strengthen and support, composed of thick-walled cells that are heavily lignified (toughened). On maturity the cell inside dies, and only the cell walls remain.

Sclerenchyma may be made up of one or two types of cells: sclereids, occurring singly or in small clusters, are often found in the hard shells of fruits and in seed coats, bark, and the stem cortex; fibers, frequently grouped in bundles, are elongated cells, often with pointed ends, associated with the vascular tissue (◊xylem and ◊phloem) of the plant.

Some fibers provide useful materials, such as flax from *Linum usitatissimum* and hemp from *Cannabis sativa*.

sclerosis any abnormal hardening of body tissues or parts, especially the nervous system or walls of the arteries. See ◊multiple sclerosis, ◊arteriosclerosis, and ◊atherosclerosis.

Scofield Paul 1922– . English actor. His wide-ranging roles include the drunken priest in Greene's *The Power and the Glory*, Harry in Pinter's *The Homecoming*, and Salieri in Shaffer's *Amadeus*. He appeared as Sir Thomas More in both stage and film versions of Bott's *A Man for All Seasons*.

scoliosis lateral curvature of the spine. Correction by operations to insert bone grafts (thus creating a straight but rigid spine) has been replaced by insertion of an electronic stimulative device in the lower back to contract the muscles adequately.

Scopes monkey trial trial held in Dayton, Tennessee, 1925. John T Scopes, a science teacher at the high (secondary) school, was accused of teaching, contrary to a law of the state, Darwin's theory of evolution. He was fined $100, but this was waived on a technical point. The defense counsel was Clarence Darrow and the prosecutor William Jennings Bryan.

scopolamine another name for ◊hyoscine, a sedative drug.

scorched earth in warfare, the policy of burning and

scorpion

destroying everything that might be of use to an invading army, especially the crops in the fields. It was used to great effect in Russia in 1812 against the invasion of the French emperor Napoleon and again during World War II to hinder the advance of German forces in 1941.

Scorpio alternative term for ◊Scorpius.

scorpion any arachnid of the order Scorpiones. Common in the tropics and subtropics, scorpions have large pincers and long tails ending in upcurved poisonous stings, though the venom is not usually fatal to a healthy adult human. Some species reach 10 in/25 cm. They produce live young rather than eggs, and hunt chiefly by night.

scorpion fly any insect of the order Mecoptera. They have a characteristic downturned beak with jaws at the tip, and many males have a scorpion-like turned-up tail, giving them their common name. Most feed on insects or carrion. They are an ancient group with relatively few living representatives.

Scorpius or ***Scorpio*** zodiac constellation in the southern hemisphere between Libra and Sagittarius, represented as a scorpion. The Sun passes briefly through Scorpius in the last week of Nov. The heart of the scorpion is marked by the red supergiant star Antares. Scorpius contains rich Milky Way star fields, plus the strongest ◊X-ray source in the sky, Scorpius X-1. In astrology, the dates for Scorpius are between about Oct 24 and Nov 21 (see ◊precession).

Scorsese Martin 1942– . US director whose powerful films concentrate on complex characterization and the themes of alienation and guilt. His work includes *Mean Streets* 1973, *Taxi Driver* 1976, *Raging Bull* 1979, *After Hours* 1987, *The Last Temptation of Christ* 1988, and *The Grifters* 1991.

Scot inhabitant of Scotland, part of Britain; or person of Scottish descent. Originally the Scots were a Celtic (Gaelic) people of N Ireland who migrated to Scotland in the 5th century. Although English is today the main language, a distinct dialect called Lallans is spoken in the Scottish Lowlands. Scottish Gaelic is spoken by 1.3%, mainly in the Highlands. Norse elements are found in the dialect of Shetland.

Scotland the northernmost part of Britain, formerly an independent country, now part of the UK
area 30,297 sq mi/78,470 sq km
capital Edinburgh
cities Glasgow, Dundee, Aberdeen
features the Highlands in the N (see ◊Grampian Mountains); central Lowlands, including valleys of the Clyde and Forth, with most of the country's population and industries; Southern Uplands; and islands of the Orkneys, Shetlands, and Western Isles
industry electronics, aircraft and marine engines, oil, natural gas, chemicals, textiles, tourism
population (1987) 5,113,000
language English; Gaelic 1.3%, mainly in the Highlands
religion Presbyterian (Church of Scotland), Roman Catholic
famous people Robert Bruce, Walter Scott, Robert Burns, Robert Louis Stevenson, Adam Smith
government Scotland sends members to the UK Parliament at Westminster. Local government is on similar lines to that of England, but there is a

differing legal system (see ◊Scots Law). There is a movement for an independent or devolved Scottish assembly.

Scotland, history for early history, see also ◊Britain, ancient; ◊Celt; ◊Pict.

4th century BC Celts reached British Isles.
1st century AD Romans prevented by Picts from penetrating far into Scotland.
5th–6th centuries Christianity introduced from Ireland.
9th century Kenneth MacAlpin united kingdoms of Scotland.
946 Malcolm I conquered Strathclyde.
1015 Malcolm II conquered Lothian.
1263 Defeat of Haakon, king of Norway, at Battle of Largs.
1266 Scotland gained Hebrides from Norway at Treaty of Perth.
1292 Scottish throne granted by Edward I (attempting to annex Scotland) to John Baliol.
1297 Defeat of England at Stirling Bridge by Wallace.
1314 Robert Bruce defeated English at Bannockburn.
1328 Scottish independence recognized by England.
1371 First Stuart king, Robert II.
1513 James IV killed at Battle of Flodden.
1540s–1550s Knox introduced Calvinism to Scotland.
1565 Mary Queen of Scots married Darnley.
1566 Rizzio murdered.
1567 Darnley murdered.
1568 Mary fled to England.
1578 James VI took over government.
1587 Mary beheaded.
1592 Presbyterianism established.
1603 James VI became James I of England.
1638 Scottish rebellion against England.
1643 Solemn League and Covenant.
1651–1660 Cromwell conquered Scotland.
1679 Covenanters defeated at Bothwell Brig.
1689 Jacobites defeated at Killiecrankie.
1692 Massacre of Glencoe.
1707 Act of Union with England.
1715, 1745 Failed Jacobite risings against England.
18th and 19th centuries Highland clearances: tenant farmers evicted to make way for sheep.
1945 First Scottish member of Parliament elected.
1979 Referendum on Scottish directly elected assembly failed.
1989 Local real estate taxes replaced by "poll tax" despite wide opposition.
1990 350,000 warrants issued by March for nonpayment of poll tax.

Scotland Yard, New headquarters of the Criminal Investigation Department (CID) of Britain's London Metropolitan Police, established in 1878. It is named after its original location in Scotland Yard, off Whitehall.

Scots language the form of the English language as traditionally spoken and written in Scotland, regarded by some scholars as a distinct language.

It is also known as Inglis (now archaic, and a variant of "English"), Lallans ("Lowlands"), Lowland Scots (in contrast with the Gaelic of the Highlands and Islands), and "the Doric" (as a rustic language in contrast with the "Attic" or "Athenian" language of Edinburgh's literati, especially in the 18th century). It is also often referred to as Broad Scots in contrast to the anglicized language of the middle classes.

Scots derives from the Northumbrian dialect of Anglo-Saxon or Old English, and has been spoken in SE Scotland since the 7th century. During the Middle Ages it spread to the far north, blending with the Norn dialects of Orkney and Shetland (once distinct varieties of Norse). Scots has been a literary language since the 14th century, with a wide range of poetry, ballads, and prose records, including two national epic poems: Barbor's *Bruce* and Blind Harry's *Wallace*. With the transfer of the court to England upon the Union of the Crowns in 1603 and the dissemination of the King James Bible, Scots ceased to be a national and court language, but has retained its vitality among the general population and in various literary and ylinguistic revivals.

Scott George C(ampbell) 1927– . US actor of great range who played tough, authoritarian stage and film roles. His work includes *Dr Strangelove* 1964, *Patton* 1970 (Academy Award, which was declined), *The Hospital* 1971, and *Firestarter* 1984.

Scott (George) Gilbert 1811–1878. English architect. As the leading practical architect in the mid-19th-century Gothic revival in England, Scott was responsible for the building or restoration of many public buildings, including the Albert Memorial, the Foreign Office, and St Pancras Station, all in London.

Scott Giles Gilbert 1880–1960. English architect, grandson of George Gilbert Scott. He designed Liverpool Anglican Cathedral, Cambridge University Library, and Waterloo Bridge, London 1945. He supervised the rebuilding of the House of Commons after World War II.

Scott Paul (Mark) 1920–1978. English novelist, author of *The Raj Quartet* consisting of *The Jewel in the Crown* 1966, *The Day of the Scorpion* 1968, *The Towers of Silence* 1972, and *A Division of the Spoils* 1975, dealing with the British Raj in India.

Scott Peter (Markham) 1909–1989. British naturalist, artist, and explorer, founder of the Wildfowl Trust at Slimbridge in England, and a founder of the World Wildlife Fund (now World Wide Fund for Nature).

Scott's paintings were usually either portraits or bird studies. He published many books on birds and an autobiography *The Eye of the Wind* 1961. He was the son of the Antarctic explorer R F Scott.

Scott Randolph. Adopted name of Randolph Crane 1903–1987. US actor. He began his career in romantic films before becoming one of Hollywood's Western stars in the 1930s. His films include *Roberta* 1934, *Jesse James* 1939, and *Ride the High Country* 1962.

Scott Robert Falcon 1868–1912. known as Scott of the Antarctic. English explorer, who commanded two Antarctic expeditions, 1901–04 and 1910–12. On Jan 18, 1912 he reached the South Pole, shortly after ◊Amundsen, but on the return journey he and his companions died in a blizzard only a few miles from their base camp. His journal was recovered and published in 1913.

Scott Walter 1771–1832. Scottish novelist and poet. His first works were translations of German ballads, followed by poems such as "The Lady of the Lake" 1810 and "Lord of the Isles" 1815. He gained a European reputation for his historical novels such as *Heart of Midlothian* 1818, *Ivanhoe* 1819, and *The Fair Maid of Perth* 1828. His last years were marked by frantic writing to pay off his debts, after the bankruptcy of his publishing company in 1826.

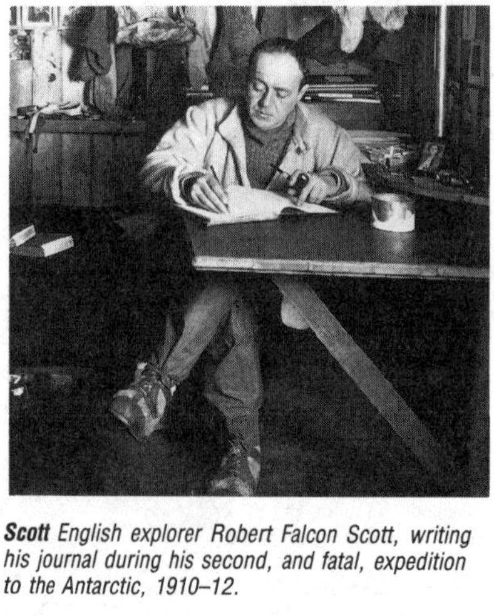

***Scott** English explorer Robert Falcon Scott, writing his journal during his second, and fatal, expedition to the Antarctic, 1910–12.*

***Scott** Despite the success of his Waverly novels, the last years of English author Sir Walter Scott were marred by frantic literary efforts to pay his creditors.*

Scott Winfield 1786–1866. US military leader. As a colonel in the War of 1812, he won distinction at the battles of Chippewa and Lundy's Lane. Promoted to brigadier general, he saw action in the Black Hawk 1832 and Seminole 1835–37 wars. In 1841 he became general in chief of the army. During the Mexican War he led the capture of Veracruz and Mexico City. An unsuccessful Whig candidate for president 1852, Scott was still head of the army at the outbreak of the Civil War but retired from active service 1861.

Born in Petersburg, Virginia, Scott attended the College of William and Mary and began his military career 1807.

Scottish Gaelic literature the earliest examples of Scottish Gaelic prose belong to the period 1000–1150, but the most significant early original composition is the history of the MacDonalds in the Red and Black Books at Clanranald. The first printed book in Scottish Gaelic was a translation of Knox's Prayer Book in 1567. Prose Gaelic is at its best in the folk tales, proverbs, and essays by writers such as Norman MacLeod in the 19th century and Donald Lamont in the 20th century. Scottish Gaelic poetry falls into two main categories. The older, syllabic verse was composed by professional bards. The chief sources of our knowledge of this are the Book of the Dean of Lismore (16th century), which is also the main early source for the Ossianic ballads; the panegyrics in the Books of Clanranald; and the Fernaig manuscript. Modern Scottish Gaelic poetry began in the 17th century but reached its zenith during the Jacobite period with Alexander MacDonald, Duncan Macintire, Rob Donn, and Dugald Buchanan. Only William Livingstone (1808–70) kept alive the old nationalistic spirit in the 19th century. During and after World War II a new school emerged, including Somhairle MacGilleathain, George Campbell-Hay, and Ruaraidh MacThómais.

Scout member of a worldwide youth organization that emphasizes character, citizenship, and outdoor life. It was founded (as the Boy Scouts) in England 1908 by Robert ◊Baden-Powell. His book *Scouting for Boys* 1908 led to the incorporation in the UK of the Boy Scout Association by royal charter in 1912.

The Boy Scouts of America was founded on the Baden-Powell model in 1910. There are about 3.5 million Boy Scouts in the US. Girl Scouts of the US was founded in 1912, following the same model. There are about 2 million Girl Scouts, including Brownies (aged 6–8), Juniors (9–11), Cadettes (12–14), and Seniors (14–17).

Scrabble trademark of a board game for two to four players, based on the crossword puzzle, in which lettered tiles of varying point values are used to form words on squares of varying point values. International competitions are now held.

Scranton industrial city on the Lackawanna River, Pennsylvania; population (1990) 81,805. Anthracite coal is mined nearby, but production has declined sharply, and the city now manufactures such products as electronic equipment, fabricated metal, clothing, plastic goods, and printed materials. The University of Scranton is here. Scranton was settled 1771 but developed chiefly with the erection of anthracite-fired iron furnaces 1840.

scrapie fatal disease of sheep and goats that attacks the central nervous system, causing deterioration of the brain cells. It is believed to be caused by a submicroscopic organism known as a prion and may be related to ◊bovine spongiform encephalopathy, the disease of cattle known as "mad cow disease."

screamer any South American marsh-dwelling bird of the family Anhimidae; there are only three species, all in the genus *Anhima*. They are about 2.6 ft/80 cm long, with short curved beaks, long toes, dark plumage, spurs on the fronts of the wings, and a crest or horn on the head.

It wades in wet forests and marshes, although the feet are scarcely webbed. Screamers are related to ducks and are placed in the same order, the Anseriformes.

screening form of preventive medicine that involves testing large numbers of apparently healthy people to detect early signs of disease.

screw in construction, cylindrical or tapering piece of metal or plastic (or formerly wood) with a helical groove cut into it. Each turn of a screw moves it forward or backwards by a distance equal to the pitch (the spacing between neighboring threads).

Its mechanical advantage equals $2r/P$, where P is the pitch and r is the radius of the thread. Thus the mechanical advantage of a tapering wood screw, for example, increases as it is rotated into the wood.

The thread is comparable to an inclined plane (wedge) wrapped around a cylinder or cone.

Scriabin Alexander (Nikolayevich) 1872–1915. Russian composer and pianist born in Moscow, whose powerfully emotional piano works—tone poems, such as *Prometheus* 1911, and symphonies, such as *Divine Poem* 1903—employed unusual harmonies to express his musical feelings.

Scribe member of an ancient Jewish group of Biblical scholars, both priests and laypersons, who studied the books of Moses and sat in the ◊Sanhedrin (supreme court). In the New Testament they are associated with the ◊Pharisees. Later, they are the copyists of Hebrew scripture.

Scribe Augustin Eugène 1791–1861. French dramatist. He achieved recognition with *Une Nuit de la garde nationale/Night of the National Guard* 1815, and with numerous assistants produced many plays of technical merit but little profundity, including *Bertrand et Raton/The School for Politicians* 1833.

scrip issue or ***subscription certificate*** in finance, a free issue of new shares to existing stockholders based on their holdings. It does not involve the raising of new capital as in a rights issue.

Scripps James Edmund 1835–1906. US publisher. Born in London, Scripps began his newspaper career in Chicago 1857. He later moved to Michigan and became part owner of the *Detroit Daily Advertiser* in the early 1860s. Scripps established the *Detroit Evening News* 1873 and with his younger brother Edward founded the *Cleveland Press* 1878. Two years later the Scripps brothers purchased the *St Louis Evening Chronicle* and the *Cincinnati Post* to create the first national newspaper chain. Scripps was also active in Republican politics.

scrofula tuberculosis of the lymph glands, especially of the neck, marked by enlargement, oozing, and scar formation. Treatment is with antibiotics and surgery. Scrofula is uncommon outside the Third World.

scrub bird one of two Australian birds of the genus *Atrichornis*, order Passeriformes. Both are about 7 in/18 cm long, rather wrenlike but long-tailed. Scrub birds are good mimics.

The noisy scrub bird *Atrichornis clamosus* was feared to be extinct, but has been rediscovered, although numbers are still low. The other species is called the rufous scrub bird *A. rufescens*.

Scud surface-to-surface ◊missile designed and produced in the USSR, which can be armed with a nuclear, chemical, or conventional warhead. The Scud-B, deployed on a mobile launcher, was the version most commonly used by the Iraqi army in the ◊Gulf War 1991. It is a relatively inaccurate weapon.

The Scud-B has a range of 180 mi/300 km; modified by the Iraqi army into the al-Hussayn, it was capable of projecting a smaller payload (about 1,100 lb/500 kg) for a distance of up to 650 km/400 mi, and was used during the Gulf War to hit Israel and Saudi Arabia.

Scullin James Henry 1876–1953. Australian Labor politician. He was leader of the Federal Parliamentary Labor Party 1928–35, and prime minister and minister of industry 1929–31.

sculpture the artistic shaping in relief or in the round of materials such as wood, stone, metal, and, more recently, plastic and other synthetics. The earliest sculptures are Paleolithic stone, bone, and ivory carvings. All ancient civilizations, including the Sumerian, Egyptian, Indian, Chinese, and New World, have left examples of sculpture. Traditional European sculpture descends from that of Greece, Rome, and Renaissance Italy. The indigenous tradition of sculpture in Africa (see ◊African art), South America, and the Caribbean has inspired much contemporary sculpture.

In the 20th century Alexander ◊Calder invented the mobile, in which the suspended components move spontaneously with the currents of air. An extension is the *structure vivante*, in which a mechanism produces a prearranged pattern produced by magnets, lenses, bubbles, and so on, accompanied by sound; leading exponents are Bury, Soto, and Takis. Another development has been the sculpture garden; for example, Hakore open-air museum in Japan and the Grizedale Forest sculpture project in the Lake District, England.

Major sculptors include:

Ancient Greek Phidias, Praxiteles

Renaissance Donatello, Verrochio, della Robbia, Michelangelo

Baroque Bernini, Falconet, Houdon, Grinling Gibbons

Neo-Classical Canova, Flaxman

20th-century American Remington, Saint-Gaudens, Lipchitz, Calder, David Smith

20th-century British Epstein, Henry Moore, Hepworth, Reg Butler, Caro

20th-century European Arp, Gaudier-Brzeska, Rodin, Maillol, Picasso, Mestrovic, Brancusi, Marini, Giacometti, Gabo, and Neizvestny.

scurvy disease caused by deficiency of vitamin C (ascorbic acid), which is contained in fresh vegetables and fruit. The signs are weakness and aching joints and muscles, progressing to bleeding of the gums and then other organs, and drying-up of the skin and hair. Treatment is by giving the vitamin.

scurvy grass plant *Cochlearia officinalis* of the crucifer family, growing on salt marshes and banks by the sea in the northern hemisphere. Shoots may grow low, or more erect up to 20 in/50 cm, with rather fleshy heart-shaped leaves; flowers are white or mauve and four-petaled. The edible, sharp-tasting leaves are a good source of vitamin C and were formerly eaten by sailors as a cure for scurvy.

scutage in medieval Europe, a feudal tax imposed on knights as a substitute for military service. It developed from fines for nonattendance at musters under the Carolingians, but in England by the 12th century it had become a purely fiscal measure designed to raise money to finance mercenary armies, reflecting the decline in the military significance of feudalism.

Scylla and Charybdis in Classical mythology, a sea-monster and a whirlpool, between which Odysseus had to sail. Later writers located them in the Straits of Messina, between Sicily and Italy.

scythe harvesting tool with long wooden handle and sharp, curving blade. It is similar to a ◊sickle. The scythe was in common use in the Middle East and Europe from the dawn of agriculture until the early 20th century, by which time it had generally been replaced by machinery.

Until the beginning of the 19th century, the scythe was used in the hayfield for cutting grass, but thereafter was applied to cereal crops as well, because it was capable of a faster work rate than the sickle. One man could mow 1 acre/0.4 hectares of wheat in a day with a scythe. Behind him came a team of workers to gather and bind the crop into sheaves and stand them in groups, or stooks, across the field.

Scythia region north of the Black Sea between the Carpathian mountains and the river Don, inhabited by the Scythians 7th–1st centuries BC. From the middle of the 4th century, they were slowly superseded by the Sarmatians. The Scythians produced ornaments and vases in gold and electrum with animal decoration.

SD abbreviation for ◊South Dakota.

SDI abbreviation for ◊Strategic Defense Initiative.

sea anemone invertebrate marine animal of the phylum Cnidaria with a tubelike body attached by the base to a rock or shell. The other end has an open "mouth" surrounded by stinging tentacles, which capture crustaceans and other small organisms. Many sea anemones are beautifully colored, especially those in tropical waters.

sea bass any marine fish of the family Serranidae, of perchlike appearance. Striped bass *Roccus saxatilis* of the E North American coast, is the best known.

Seaborg Glenn Theodore 1912– . US nuclear chemist associated with the preparation and synthesis of all the ◊transuranic elements with atomic numbers 94–105 at the Lawrence Radiation Laboratory, University of California at Berkeley. With Edwin M McMillan he produced plutonium in 1940, for which both shared the 1951 Nobel Prize for Chemistry.

During World War II he worked on the development of the first nuclear weapon, then served as chair of the US Atomic Energy Commission 1961–71. For his leadership in the development of nuclear chemistry and atomic energy, he received the 1959 Enrico Fermi award.

sea cucumber any echinoderm of the class Holothuroidea with a cylindrical body that is tough-skinned, knobbed, or spiny. The body may be several feet in length. Sea cucumbers are sometimes called "cotton-spinners" from the sticky filaments they eject from the anus in self-defense.

seafloor spreading growth of the ocean ◊crust outward (sideways) from midocean ridges. The concept of seafloor spreading has been combined with that of continental drift and incorporated into ◊plate tectonics.

Seafloor spreading was proposed by US geologist Harry Hess in 1962, based on his observations of midocean ridges and the relative youth of all ocean beds. In 1963, British geophysicists F Vine and D Matthews observed that the floor of the Atlantic Ocean was made up of rocks that could be arranged in strips, each strip being magnetized either normally or reversely (due to changes in the Earth's polarity when the North

sea horse

Pole becomes the South Pole and vice versa, termed ◊polar reversal). These strips were parallel and formed identical patterns on both sides of the midocean ridge. The inference was that each strip was formed at some stage in geologic time when the magnetic field was polarized in a certain way. The seafloor magnetic-reversal patterns could be matched to dated magnetic reversals found in terrestrial rock. It could then be shown that new rock forms continuously and spreads away from the midocean ridges, with the oldest rock located farthest away from the midline.

sea gull see ◊gull.

Seagull, The a play by Anton Chekhov, first produced in Russia 1896. It studies the jealousy between a mother and son, the son's vain search for identity, and his ultimate suicide.

sea horse any marine fish of several related genera, especially *Hippocqmpus*, of the family Syngnathidae, which includes the ◊pipefishes. The body is small and compressed and covered with bony plates raised into tubercles or spines. The tail is prehensile, and the tubular mouth sucks in small shellfish and larvae as food. The head and foreparts, usually carried upright, resemble those of a horse.

seakale perennial plant *Crambe maritima* of the family Cruciferae. In Europe the young shoots are cultivated as a vegetable.

seal any of two families (Otqriidae and Phocidae) of aquatic carnivorous mammals (sometimes placed in a separate order, the Pinnipedia). The eared seals or sea lions (Otariidae) have small external ears, unlike the true seals (Phocidae).

Seals have a streamlined body with thick blubber for insulation, and front and hind flippers. In true seals, the hind flippers provide the thrust for swimming, but they cannot be brought under the body for walking on land. Among eared seals (and walruses), the front flippers are the most important for swimming and the hind flippers can be brought forward under the body for walking. They feed on fish, squid, or crustaceans, and are commonly found in Arctic and Antarctic seas, but also in Mediterranean, Caribbean, and Hawaiian waters. For seal hunting, see ◊sealing.

True seals include the common or harbor seal *Phoca ritulina,* found in coastal regions over much of the northern hemisphere. The largest seal is the Southern elephant seal *Mirounga leonina,* which can be 20 ft/6 m long and weigh 4.5 tons; the smallest is the Baikal seql *Pusa sibirica,* only 4 ft/1.2 m long and the only seal to live entirely in fresh water. Eared seals include ◊sea lions and

seal

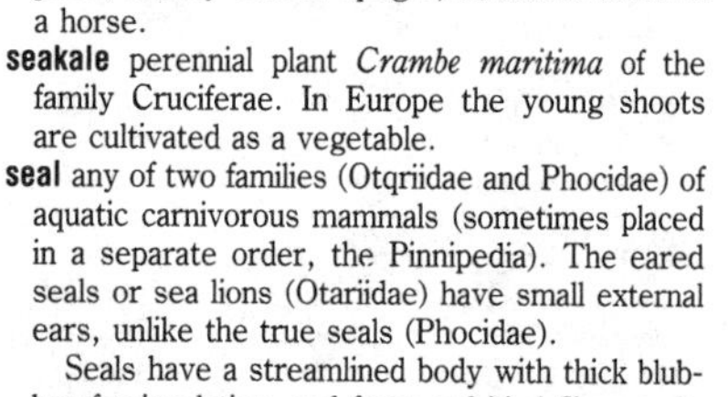

Mediterranean monk seal

fur seals. The rarest seals are the monk seals, the only species to live in warmer waters. The Caribbean monk seal *Monachus tropicalis* may already be extinct, and the Mediterranean *M. monachus* and Hawaiian *M. schauinslandi* species are both endangered, mainly caused by disturbance by humans.

seal mark or impression made in a block of wax to authenticate letters and documents. Seals were used in ancient China and are still used in China, Korea, and Japan.

sea law a set of laws dealing with fishing areas, ships, and navigation; see ◊maritime law.

sea lily any ◊echinoderm of the class Crinoidea. In most, the rayed, cuplike body is borne on a sessile stalk (permanently attached to a rock), and has feathery arms in multiples of five encircling the mouth. However, some sea lilies are free-swimming and unattached.

sealing the hunting of seals. Seals are killed for their meat, blubber and for their skins, which are sold as fine furs. Conservationists have campaigned to stop the killing of seals for fur, with some success.

sea lion any of several genera of ◊seals, of the family Otariidae (eared seals), which also includes the fur seals. These streamlined animals have large fore flippers which they use to row themselves through the water. The hind flippers can be turned beneath the body to walk on land.

There are two species of sea lion in the Northern hemisphere, three in the South. They feed on fish, squid, and crustaceans. Steller's sea lion *Eumetopias jubatus* lives in the N Pacific, large numbers breeding on the Aleutian Islands. Males may be up to 11 ft/3.4 m long, with a thick neck with the characteristic mane, and weigh up to a ton. Females are one-third the weight. The Californian sea lion *Zalophus californianus* only reaches 7 ft/2.3 m, and is the species most often seen in zoos and as a "performing seal."

Sealyham breed of terrier dog, named after the place in Pembrokeshire, Wales, where it originated in the 19th century as a cross of the Welsh and Jack Russell terriers. It reaches a height of 12 in/30 cm.

sea mouse any of a genus *Aphrodite* of large marine ◊annelid worms (polychaetes), with oval bodies covered in bristles and usually found on muddy sea floors.

seaplane airplane capable of taking off from, and landing on, water. There are two major types, floatplanes and flying boats. The floatplane is similar to an ordinary airplane but has floats in place of wheels; the flying boat has a broad hull shaped like a boat and may also have floats attached to the wing tips.

Seaplanes depend on smooth water for a good landing, and since World War II few have been built, although the first successful international airlines, such as Pan Am, relied on a fleet of flying boats in the 1920s and 1930s.

The seaplane was invented by Glenn ◊Curtiss.

sea robin any of a family (Triglidae) of spine-finned coastal fishes, especially the slender sea robin *Prionotus scitulus* of the Gulf and SE North American coast. They have large heads and creep along the sea bottom by means of three fingerlike appendages detached from the pectoral fins.

Sears Tower skyscraper in Chicago, rising 110 stories to a height of 1,454 ft/443 m. "Topped out" in 1973, it was then the world's tallest building. It was built as the headquarters of Sears, Roebuck & Co, to provide office accommodation for more than 16,000 people.

Seaside city in W central California, on the S shore of Monterey Bay, S of San Francisco. Industries include fruit processing; population (1990) 38,901.

sea slug any of an order (Nudibranchia) of marine gastropod mollusks in which the shell is reduced or absent. The order includes some very colorful forms, especially in the tropics. Tentacles on the back help take in oxygen. They are largely carnivorous, feeding on hydroids and ◊sponges. Most are under 1 in/2.5 cm long, and live on the sea bottom or on vegetation, although some live in open waters.

season climatic type, at any place, associated with a particular time of the year. The change in seasons is mainly due to the change in attitude of the Earth's axis in relation to the Sun, and hence the position of the Sun in the sky at a particular place. In temperate latitudes four seasons are recognized: spring, summer, autumn (fall), and winter. Tropical regions have two seasons—the wet and the dry. Monsoon areas around the Indian Ocean have three seasons: the cold, the hot, and the rainy.

The northern temperate latitudes have summer when the southern temperate latitudes have winter, and vice versa. During winter, the Sun is low in the sky and has less heating effect because of the oblique angle of incidence and because the sunlight has further to travel through the atmosphere. The differences between the seasons are more marked inland than near the coast, where the sea has a moderating effect on temperatures. In polar regions the change between summer and winter is abrupt; spring and autumn are hardly perceivable. In tropical regions, the belt of rain associated with the trade winds moves north and south with the Sun, as do the dry conditions associated with the belts of high pressure near the tropics. The monsoon's three seasons result from the influence of the Indian Ocean on the surrounding land mass of Asia in that area.

seasonal adjustment in statistics, an adjustment of figures designed to take into account influences that are purely seasonal, and relevant only for a short time. The resulting figures are then thought to reflect long-term trends more accurately.

seasonal affective disorder (SAD) recurrent depression characterized by an increased incidence at a particular time of year. One type of seasonal affective disorder increases in incidence in autumn and winter, and is associated with increased sleeping and appetite.

It has been suggested that seasonal affective disorder may be caused by a change in the release of melatonin, a hormone secreted in response to the diurnal variation in light and dark.

seasonal unemployment unemployment arising from the seasonal nature of some economic activities. An example is agriculture, which uses a smaller labor force in winter.

Seasonal employment can be created, however, as in the example of the retail sector in Western countries over the Christmas period.

sea squirt or ***tunicate*** any solitary or colonial-dwelling saclike ◊chordate of the class Ascidiacea. A pouch-shaped animal attached to a rock or other base, it draws in food-carrying water through one siphon and expels it through another after straining it through numerous gill slits. The young are free-swimming tadpole-shaped organisms, that, unlike the adults, have a ◊notochord.

Sea squirts have transparent or translucent tunics made of cellulose. They vary in size from a few millimeters to 12 in/30 cm in length and are cylindrical, circular, or irregular in shape.

SEATO abbreviation for ◊Southeast Asia Treaty Organization.

Seattle port (grain, timber, fruit, fish) of the state of Washington, situated between Puget Sound and Lake Washington; population (1990) 516,259, metropolitan area (with Everett) 2,559,164. It is a center for the manufacture of jet aircraft (Boeing) and also has shipbuilding, food processing, and paper industries.

There are two universities, Washington (1861) and Seattle (1891). First settled 1852, as the nearest port for Alaska, Seattle grew in the late 19th century with the arrival of a transcontinental railroad 1884 and the Klondike gold rush of the 1890s. Since World War II the economy has been dominated by the aerospace industry. The 607-ft-/185-m-high Space Needle was erected for the 1962 world's fair.

season

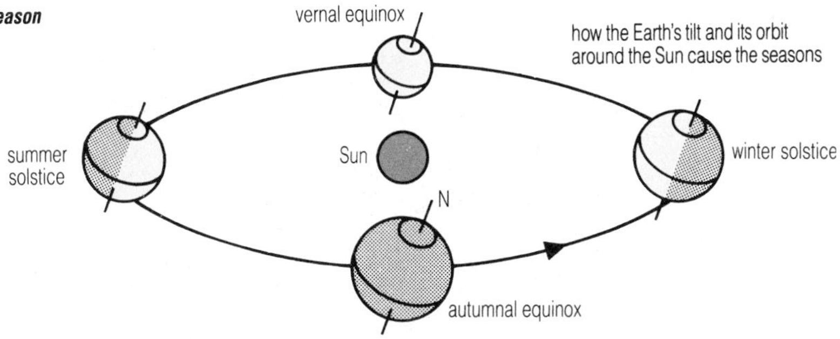
vernal equinox
how the Earth's tilt and its orbit around the Sun cause the seasons
summer solstice
Sun
winter solstice
N
autumnal equinox

sea turtle any of various marine species of ◊turtles, some of which grow up to a length of up to 8 ft/2.5 m. They are excellent swimmers, having legs that are modified to oarlike flippers but make them awkward on land. The shell is more streamlined and lighter than that of other turtles. They often travel long distances to lay their eggs on the beaches where they were born.

Species include the green turtle *Chelonia mydas*; the loggerhead *Caretta caretta*; the giant leatherback *Dermochelys coriacea* which can weigh half a ton; and the hawksbill *Eretmochelys imbricata*. Like many species of turtle, the hawksbill is now endangered, mainly through being hunted for its shell, which provides "tortoiseshell." Other turtles have suffered through destruction of their breeding sites (often for tourist developments) and egg-collecting.

sea urchin any of various orders of the class Echinoidea among the ◊echinoderms. They all have a globular body enclosed with plates of lime and covered with spines. Sometimes the spines are anchoring organs, and they also assist in locomotion. Sea urchins feed on seaweed and the animals frequenting them, and some are edible.

seaweed any of a vast collection of marine and freshwater, simple, multicellular plant forms belonging to the ◊algae and found growing from about high-water mark to depths of 100–200 m/300– 600 ft. Some have holdfasts, stalks, and fronds, sometimes with air bladders to keep them afloat, and are green, blue-green, red, or brown.

Many have traditionally been gathered for food, such as purple laver *Porphyra umbilicalis*, green laver *Ulva lactuca*, and carragheen moss *Chondrus crispus*. From the 1960s, seaweeds have been farmed, and the alginates extracted are used in convenience foods, ice cream, and animal feed, as well as in toothpaste, soap, and the manufacture of iodine and glass.

Sebastiano del Piombo c. 1485–1547. Italian painter, born in Venice, one of the great painters of the High Renaissance. Sebastiano was a pupil of ◊Giorgione and developed a similar style of painting. In 1511 he moved to Rome, where his friendship with Michelangelo (and rivalry with Raphael) inspired him to his greatest works, such as *The Raising of Lazarus* 1517–19 (National Gallery, London). He also painted powerful portraits.

Sebastian, St Roman soldier, traditionally a member of Emperor Diocletian's bodyguard until his Christian faith was discovered. He was martyred by being shot with arrows. Feast day Jan 20.

seaweed

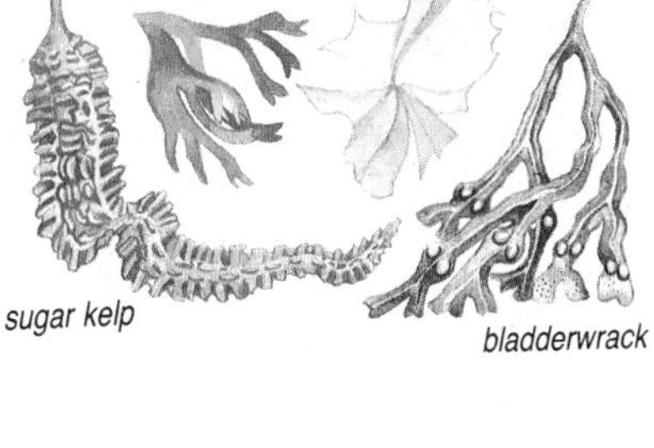
sea lettuce
dulse
sugar kelp
bladderwrack

Sebastopol alternate spelling of ◊Sevastopol, port in the USSR.

sec or ***s*** abbreviation for second, a unit of time.

secant in trigonometry, the function of an angle in a right triangle obtained by dividing the length of the hypotenuse (the longest side) by the length of the side adjacent to the angle. It is the ◊reciprocal of the cosine (sec = 1/cos).

Secchi Pietro Angelo 1818–1878. Italian astronomer and astrophysicist, who classified stellar spectra into four classes based on their color and spectral characteristics. He was the first to classify solar ◊prominences, huge jets of gas projecting from the Sun's surface.

secession (Latin *secessio* "apart") in politics, the withdrawal from a federation of states by one or more of its members, as in the secession of the Confederate states from the Union in the US 1860.

second basic ◊SI unit (abbreviation sec or s) of time, one-sixtieth of a minute. It is defined as the duration of 9,192,631,770 cycles of regulation (periods of the radiation corresponding to the transition between two hyperfine levels of the ground state) of the cesium-133 isotope. In mathematics, the second is a unit (symbol ″) of angular measurement, equaling one-sixtieth of a minute, which in turn is one-sixtieth of a degree.

secondary emission in physics, an emission of electrons from the surface of certain substances when they are struck by high-speed electrons or other particles from an external source. See also ◊photomultiplier.

secondary growth or ***secondary thickening*** the increase in diameter of the roots and stems of certain plants (notably shrubs and trees) that results from the production of new cells by the ◊cambium. It provides the plant with additional mechanical support and new conducting cells, the secondary ◊xylem and ◊phloem. Secondary growth is generally confined to ◊gymnosperms and, among the ◊angiosperms, to the dicotyledons. With just a few exceptions, the monocotyledons (grasses, lilies) exhibit only primary growth, resulting from cell division at the apical ◊meristems.

secondary market market for resale of purchase or shares, bonds, and commodities outside of organized stock exchanges and primary markets.

secondary sexual characteristic in biology, an external feature of an organism that is characteristic of its gender (male or female), but not the reproductive organs themselves. They include deepened voices and facial hair in men and breasts in women, combs in roosters, brightly colored plumage in many male birds, and manes in male lions. In many cases, they are involved in displays and contests for mates and have evolved by ◊sexual selection. Their development is stimulated by sex hormones.

secant

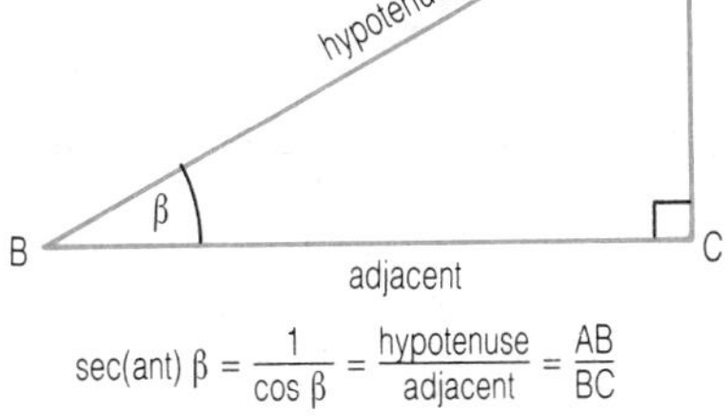
A
hypotenuse
β
B
adjacent
C

$$\sec(\text{ant})\,\beta = \frac{1}{\cos\beta} = \frac{\text{hypotenuse}}{\text{adjacent}} = \frac{AB}{BC}$$

Second World War alternate name for ◊World War II, 1939–45.

secretary bird ground-hunting, long-legged, mainly gray-plumaged bird of prey *Sagittarius serpentarius*, about 4 ft/1.2 m tall, with an erectile head crest. It is protected in southern Africa because it eats poisonous snakes.

It gets its name from the fact that its head crest supposedly looks like a pen behind a clerk's ear. It is the only member of its family Sagittaridae, in the same order (Falconiformes) as vultures, eagles, and hawks.

secretary of state the title of the cabinet official with responsibility for conducting the foreign affairs of the US. It is the senior cabinet post and is fourth in line of succession to the presidency in the event of death or incapacitation.

Secret Garden, The a novel for children by Frances Hodgson ◊Burnett published in the US 1911. Mary, a spoiled, sickly orphan, is sent from India to England to live at the house of her uncle, a crippled recluse. Her cultivation of the secret garden from a forgotten wilderness helps to transform her health and outlook and leads her to effect a similar change in her cousin Colin, who believed himself to be an invalid.

secretin hormone produced by the small intestine of vertebrates that stimulates the production of digestive secretions by the pancreas and liver.

secretion in biology, any substance (normally a fluid) produced by a cell or specialized gland, for example, sweat, saliva, enzymes, and hormones. The process whereby the substance is discharged from the cell is also known as secretion.

secret police government-run intelligence organizations such as the UK's Secret Service, the Soviet ◊KGB, or the US ◊Central Intelligence Agency.

secret service any government ◊intelligence organization.

The US Secret Service is a law-enforcement unit of the Treasury Department. It is charged with combating counterfeiters and has responsibility for protecting the president and other senior members of the government.

secret society society with membership by invitation only, often involving initiation rites, secret rituals, and dire punishments for those who break the code. Often founded for religious reasons or mutual benefit, some have become the province of corrupt politicians or gangsters, such as the ◊Mafia and the ◊Triad.

sect a small ideological group, usually religious in nature, that may have moved away from a main group, often claiming a monopoly of access to truth or salvation. Sects are usually highly exclusive. They demand strict conformity, total commitment to their code of behavior, and complete personal involvement, sometimes to the point of rejecting mainstream society altogether in terms of attachments, names, possessions, and family.

Most sects are shortlived, either because their appeal dies out and their members return to mainstream society, or because their appeal spreads and they become part of mainstream society (for example, early Christianity began as a small sect in Roman-ruled Palestine).

secularization the process through which religious thinking, practice, and institutions lose their religious and/or social significance. The concept is based on the theory, held by some sociologists, that as societies become industrialized their religious morals, values, and institutions give way to secular ones and some religious traits become common secular practices.

secular variable in astronomy, a star that, according to comparisons with ancient observations, has either increased or decreased substantially (and permanently) in brightness over the intervening centuries.

An example is Megrez (Delta Ursae Majoris), the faintest star in Ursa Major. According to 16th-century Danish astronomer Tycho Brahe, Megrez was of second magnitude, although the 2nd-century astronomer Ptolemy ranked it as somewhat fainter. Its current magnitude is 3.3.

It is unlikely that Megrez or any of the other secular variables has actually changed in brightness, and it seems either that the older values were subject to observational error, or that astronomers have misinterpreted those observations.

Securities and Exchange Commission (SEC) official US agency created in 1934, under Joseph P ◊Kennedy, to ensure full disclosure to the investing public and protection against malpractice in the securities (stocks and bonds) and financial markets (such as ◊insider trading).

The SEC, created in the wake of the 1929 stock market crash, operates under several major statutes. The Securities Act of 1933 is concerned with the accuracy of registration statements, made when a firm goes public and stock is offered for sale. The Securities Exchange Act of 1934 regulates trading in securities after they have been issued. The Investment Company Act 1940 regulates mutual funds, and the Investment Advisors Act of 1940 registers investment advisers. The SEC is also an impartial adviser to federal courts in bankruptcy cases involving publicly held corporations. Since 1988, the SEC has been authorized to pay bounties for information leading to conviction of inside traders.

Sedan town on the river Meuse, in Ardennes *département*, NE France; population (1982) 24,535. Industries include textiles and dyestuffs; the town's prosperity dates from the 16th–17th centuries, when it was a ◊Huguenot center. In 1870 Sedan was the scene of Napoleon III's surrender to Germany during the ◊Franco-Prussian War. It was the focal point of the German advance into France 1940.

sedan chair an enclosed chair for one passenger carried on poles by two bearers. Introduced into England by Sir Sanders Dunscombe in 1634, by the 18th century it was the equivalent of a one-person taxi. The name derives from S Italy rather than from the French town of Sedan.

sedative any medication with the effect of lessening nervousness, excitement, or irritation. Sedatives will induce sleep in larger doses. Examples are ◊barbiturates, ◊narcotics, and ◊benzodiazepines.

Seddon Richard John 1845–1906. New Zealand Liberal politician, prime minister 1893–1906.

seder meal that forms part of the Jewish festival of Passover, which celebrates the ◊Exodus.

sedge any perennial grasslike plants of the family Cyperaceae, especially the genus *Carex*, usually with three-cornered solid stems, common in low water or on wet and marshy ground.

Sedgemoor, Battle of in English history, a battle July 6, 1685 in which ◊Monmouth's rebellion was crushed by the forces of James II, on a tract of marshy land 3 mi/5 km SE of Bridgwater, Somerset.

sediment any loose material that has "settled"—deposited from suspension in water, ice, or air, generally as the water current or wind speed decreases. Typical sediments are, in order of increasing coarseness, clay, mud, silt, sand, gravel, pebbles, cobbles, and boulders.

Sediments differ from sedimentary rocks in which deposits are fused together in a solid mass of rock by a process called ◊diagenesis. Gravels are cemented into ◊conglomerates, rock screes into ◊breccias; sands become sandstones; muds become mudstones or shales; peat is transformed into coal.

sedimentary rock a rock formed by the accumulation and cementation of deposits that have been laid down by water, wind, ice, or gravity. Sedimentary rocks cover more than two-thirds of the Earth's surface and comprise three major categories: clastic, chemically precipitated, and organic. Clastic sediments are the largest group and are composed of fragments of pre-existing rocks; they include clays, sands, and gravels. Chemical precipitates include limestones such as chalk, and evaporated deposits such as gypsum and halite (rock-salt). Coal, oil shale, and limestone made of fossil material are examples of organic sedimentary rocks.

Most sedimentary rocks show distinct layering (stratification), caused by alterations in composition or by changes in rock type. These strata may become folded or fractured by the movement of the Earth's crust, a process known as deformation.

sedition the stirring up of discontent, resistance, or rebellion against the government in power.

Seebeck effect in physics, the generation of a voltage in a circuit containing two different metals, or semiconductors, by keeping the junctions between them at different temperatures. Discovered by the German physicist Thomas Seebeck (1770–1831), it is also called the thermoelectric effect, and is the basis of the ◊thermocouple. It is the opposite of the ◊Peltier effect (in which current flow causes a temperature difference between the junctions of different metals).

seed

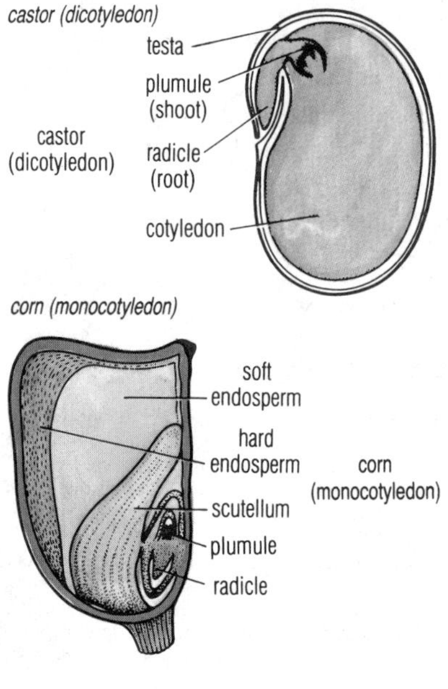
castor (dicotyledon)
testa
plumule (shoot)
castor (dicotyledon)
radicle (root)
cotyledon
corn (monocotyledon)
soft endosperm
hard endosperm
corn (monocotyledon)
scutellum
plumule
radicle

seed the reproductive structure of higher plants (◊angiosperms and ◊gymnosperms). It develops from a fertilized ovule and consists of an embryo and a food store, surrounded and protected by an outer seed coat, called the testa. The food store is contained either in a specialized nutritive tissue, the ◊endosperm, or in the ◊cotyledons of the embryo itself. In angiosperms the seed is enclosed within a ◊fruit, whereas in gymnosperms it is usually naked and unprotected, once shed from the female cone. Following ◊germination the seed develops into a new plant.

Seeds may be dispersed from the parent plant in a number of different ways. Agents of dispersal include animals, as with ◊burrs and fleshy edible fruits, and wind, where the seed or fruit may be winged or plumed. Water can disperse seeds or fruits that float, and various mechanical devices may eject seeds from the fruit, as in some pods or leguminous plants (see ◊legume).

There may be a delay in the germination of some seeds to ensure that growth occurs under favorable conditions (see ◊after-ripening, ◊dormancy). Most seeds remain viable for at least 15 years if dried to about 5% water and kept at −4°F/−20°C, although 20% of them will not survive this process.

seed drill machine for sowing cereals and other seeds, developed by Jethro ◊Tull in England 1701, although simple seeding devices were known in Babylon 2000 BC.

The seed is stored in a hopper and delivered by tubes into furrows in the ground. The furrows are made by a set of blades, or colters, attached to the front of the drill. A ◊harrow is drawn behind the drill to cover up the seeds.

seed plant or ***spermatophyte*** any seed-bearing plant. The seed plants are subdivided into two classes, the ◊angiosperms, or flowering plants, and the ◊gymnosperms, principally the cycads and conifers. Together they comprise the major types of vegetation found on land.

Angiosperms are the largest, most advanced, and most successful group of plants at the present time, occupying a highly diverse range of habitats. There are estimated to be about 250,000 different species. Gymnosperms differ from angiosperms in their ovules which are borne unprotected (not within an ◊ovary) on the scales of their cones. The arrangement of the reproductive organs, and their more simplified internal tissue structure, also distinguishes them from the flowering plants. In contrast to the gymnosperms, the ovules of angiosperms are enclosed within an ovary and many species have developed highly specialized reproductive structures associated with ◊pollination by insects, birds, or bats.

Seeger Pete 1919– . US folk singer and songwriter of antiwar protest songs, such as "Where Have All The Flowers Gone?" 1956 and "If I Had A Hammer" 1949.

Seeger was active in left-wing politics from the late 1930s and was a victim of the "witch-hunt" of Senator Joe ◊McCarthy in the 1950s. As a member of the vocal group *The Weavers* 1948–58, he popularized songs of diverse ethnic origin and had several hits.

Seeland German form of ◊Sjælland, the main island of Denmark.

Seferis George. Assumed name of Greek poet and diplomat Georgios Seferiades 1900–1971. Ambassador to Lebanon 1953–57 and to the UK 1957–62, he helped to resolve the Cyprus crisis. He published his first volume of lyrics 1931 and his *Collected Poems* 1950. Nobel Prize 1963.

Segar Elzie Crisler 1894–1938. US cartoonist. In 1919 he moved to New York, where he published "Thimble Theater," a comic strip featuring the various members of the Oyl family, including Olive and Castor. In 1929 Segar unveiled his most popular character: Popeye, the feisty, squint-eyed sailor. He also created the hamburger-loving Wimpy and the adventurous baby Swee'pea. These characters appeared in numerous animated films.

Born in Chester, Illinois, Segar worked at odd jobs before being hired as a cartoonist for the *Chicago Herald* and working briefly as a reporter for the *Chicago Evening American*.

Segovia town in Castilla-León, central Spain; population (1981) 50,760. Thread, fertilizer, and chemicals are produced. It has a Roman aqueduct with 118 arches in current use, and the Moorish ◊alcázar (fortress) was the palace of the monarchs of Castile. Isabella of Castile was crowned here 1474.

Segovia Andrés 1893–1987. Spanish virtuoso guitarist, for whom works were composed by De ◊Falla, ◊Villa-Lobos, and others.

Segrè Emilio 1905–1989. Italian physicist settled in the US, who in 1955 discovered the antiproton, a new form of ◊antimatter. He shared the 1959 Nobel Prize for Physics with Owen Chamberlain. Segrè had earlier discovered the first synthetic element, technetium (atomic number 43), in 1937.

Seifert Jaroslav 1901–1986. Czech poet who won state prizes, but became an original member of the Charter 77 human-rights movement. His works include *Mozart in Prague* 1970 and *Umbrella from Piccadilly* 1978. Nobel Prize 1984.

Seikan Tunnel the world's largest underwater tunnel, opened 1988, linking the Japanese islands of Hokkaido and Honshu, which are separated by the Tsungaru Strait; length 32.3 mi/51.7 km.

Seine French river rising on the Langres plateau NW of Dijon, and flowing 472 mi/774 km in a NW direction to join the English Channel near Le Havre, passing through Paris and Rouen.

seismology study of earthquakes and how their shock waves travel through the Earth. By examining the global pattern of waves produced by an earthquake, seismologists can deduce the nature of the materials through which they have passed. This leads to an understanding of the Earth's internal structure.

On a smaller scale artificial earthquake waves, generated by explosions or mechanical vibrators, can be used to search for subsurface features in, for example, oil or mineral exploration.

Sekhmet ancient Egyptian goddess of heat and fire. She was represented with the head of a lioness, and worshiped at Memphis as the wife of ◊Ptah.

Sekondi-Takoradi seaport of Ghana; population (1982) 123,700. The old port was founded by the Dutch. Takoradi has an artificial harbor, opened 1928, and railway engineering, boat building, and cigarette manufacturing industries.

Selangor state of the Federation of Malaysia; area 3,071 sq mi/7,956 sq km; population (1980) 1,516,000. It was under British protection from 1874 and was a Federated State 1895–1946. The capital was transferred to Shah Alam from Kuala Lumpur 1973. Klang is the seat of the Sultan and a center for rubber-growing and tin-mining; Port Klang (formerly Port Keland and, in 1971, Port Swettenham) exports tin.

Selective Draft Cases several US Supreme Court cases (including *Arver* v *US* 1918) dealing with the right of Congress to enact a mandatory military service law during wartime. The Court voted unanimously to uphold the Selective Draft Law, the World War I conscription act. The decision was based on a judgment that the right to establish a draft is implied in the Constitution in Congress's authority to declare war and maintain an army.

Selene in Greek mythology, the goddess of the Moon. She was the daughter of Titan, and the sister of Helios and Eos. In later times she was identified with ◊Artemis.

selenium gray, nonmetallic element, symbol Se, atomic number 34, atomic weight 78.96. It belongs to the sulfur group and occurs in several allotropic forms that differ in their physical and chemical properties. It is an essential trace element in human nutrition. Obtained from many sulfide ores and selenides, it is used as a red coloring for glass and enamel.

Because its electrical conductivity varies with the intensity of light, selenium is used extensively in photoelectric devices. It was discovered in 1817 by Swedish chemist Jöns Berzelius and named after Greek *Selene*, "Moon," because its properties follow those of tellurium, whose name derives from Latin *Tellus*, "Earth."

Seleucus I Nicator c. 358–280 BC. Macedonian general under Alexander the Great and founder of the Seleucid Empire. After Alexander's death 323 BC, Seleucus became governor and then (312 BC) ruler of Babylonia, founding the city of Seleucia on the river Tigris. He conquered Syria and had himself crowned king 306 BC, but his expansionist policies brought him into conflict with the Ptolemies of Egypt, and he was assassinated by Ptolemy Ceraunus. He was succeeded by his son Antiochus I.

self-induction or ***self-inductance*** in physics, the creation of a counter emf (◊electromotive force) in a coil because of variations in the current flowing through it.

Seljuk Empire empire of the Turkish people (converted to Islam during the 7th century) under the leadership of the invading Tatars or Seljuk Turks. The Seljuk Empire 1055–1243 included all Anatolia and most of Syria. It was succeeded by the ◊Ottoman Empire.

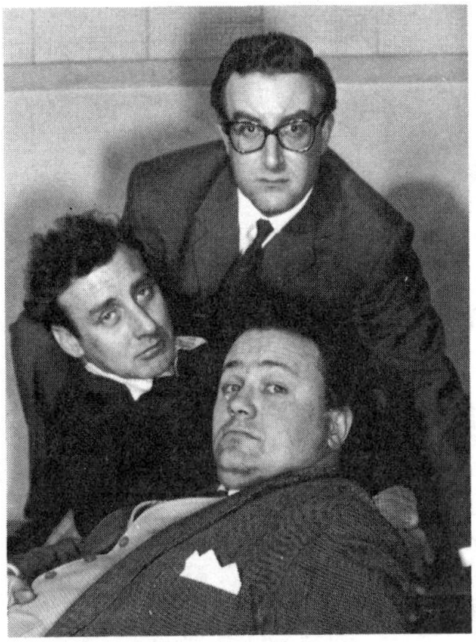

***Sellers** Comedian Peter Sellers (top center), who first won fame on British radio's* The Goon Show *1949–60, with radio cohorts Spike Milligan (left) and Harry Secombe (bottom).*

Selkirk Alexander 1676–1721. Scottish sailor marooned 1704–09 in the Juan Fernández Islands in the S Pacific. His story inspired Daniel Defoe to write *Robinson Crusoe*.

Sellers Peter 1925–1980. English comedian and film actor of great range and characterization. He made his name in the British radio comedy series *The Goon Show* 1949–60, and his films include *The Ladykillers* 1955, *I'm All Right Jack* 1959, *Lolita* 1962, *Dr Strangelove* 1964, five *Pink Panther* films 1964–78 (as the bumbling Inspector Clouseau), and *Being There* 1979.

seller's market a market in which sellers prosper because there is a strong demand for their goods or services, thus pushing up the price.

selva equatorial rainforest, such as that in the Amazon basin in South America.

Selznick David O(liver) 1902–1965. US film producer whose early work includes *King Kong*, *Dinner at Eight*, and *Little Women* all 1933. His independent company, Selznick International (1935–40), made such lavish films as *Gone With the Wind* 1939, *Rebecca* 1940, and *Duel in the Sun* 1946.

He had under contract Alfred Hitchcock and Ingrid Bergman who together made several films. He launched the careers of director George Cukor and actors Katharine Hepburn, Fred Astaire, Gregory Peck, and Joan Fontaine.

semantics branch of ◊linguistics dealing with the meaning of words.

semaphore a visual signaling code in which the relative positions of two movable pointers or hand-held flags stand for different letters or numbers. The system is used by ships at sea and for railroad signals.

Semarang port in N Java, Indonesia; population (1980) 1,027,000. There is a shipbuilding industry, and exports include coffee, teak, sugar, tobacco, kapok, and petroleum from nearby oilfields.

Semele in Greek mythology, mother of Dionysus by Zeus. At Hera's suggestion she demanded that Zeus should appear to her in all his glory, but when he did so she was consumed by lightning.

semelparity in biology, the occurrence of a single act of reproduction during an organism's lifetime. Most semelparous species produce very large numbers of offspring when they do reproduce, and normally die soon afterwards. Examples include the Pacific salmon and the pine looper moth. Many plants are semelparous, or ◊monocarpic. Repeated reproduction is called ◊iteroparity.

semen see ◊sperm.

Semenov Nikoly 1896– . Russian physical chemist who made significant contributions to the study of chemical chain reactions. Working mainly in Leningrad at the Institute for Chemical Physics, in 1956 he became the first Russian to gain the Nobel Prize for Chemistry, which he shared with Cyril ◊Hinshelwood.

semicircular canal one of three looped tubes that form part of the labyrinth in the inner ◊ear. They are filled with fluid and detect changes in the position of the head, contributing to the sense of balance.

semicolon punctuation mark (;) with a function halfway between the separation of sentence from sentence by means of a period, or full stop, and the gentler separation provided by a comma. It also helps separate items in a complex list: "pens, pencils, and paper; staples, such as rice and beans; tools, various; and rope."

Rather than the abrupt "We saw Mark last night. It was good to see him again," and the casual (and often condemned) "We saw Mark last night, it was good to see him again," the semicolon reflects a link in a two-part statement and is considered good style: "We saw Mark last night; it was good to see him again." In such cases an alternative is to use a comma followed by "and" or "but."

semiconductor crystalline material with an electrical conductivity between that of metals (good) and insulators (poor).

The conductivity of semiconductors can usually be improved by minute additions of different substances or by other factors. Silicon, for example, has poor conductivity at low temperatures, but this is improved by the application of light, heat, or voltage; hence silicon is used in transistors, rectifiers, and integrated circuits (silicon or computer chips).

semiology or ***semiotics*** the study of the function of signs and symbols in human communication, both in language and by various nonlinguistic means. Beginning with the notion of the Swiss linguist Ferdinand de Saussure (1857–1913) that no word or other sign (signifier) is intrinsically linked with its meaning (signified), it was developed as a scientific discipline, especially by ◊Lévi-Strauss and ◊Barthes.

Semiotics has combined with structuralism in order to explore the "production" of meaning in language and other sign systems and has emphasized the conventional nature of this production.

Semipalatinsk town in Kazakh Republic, USSR, on the river Irtysh; population (1987) 330,000. It was founded 1718 as a Russian frontier post and moved to its present site 1776. Industries include meatpacking, tanning, and flour-milling, and the region produces nickel and chromium. The Kyzyl Kum atomic-weapon-testing ground is nearby.

Semiramis lived c. 800 BC. Assyrian queen, later identified with the chief Assyrian goddess ◊Ishtar.

Semite a member of any of the peoples of the Near and Middle East originally speaking a Semitic language, and traditionally said to be descended from Shem, a son of Noah in the Bible. Ancient Semitic peoples include the Hebrews, Ammonites, Moabites, Edomites, Babylonians, Assyrians, Chaldaeans, Phoenicians, and Canaanites. The Semitic peoples founded the monotheistic religions of Judaism, Christianity, and Islam. They speak languages of the Hamito-Semitic branch of the Afro-Asiatic family.

Semitic languages branch of the ◊Hamito-Semitic family of languages.

Semmelweis Ignaz Philipp 1818–1865. Hungarian obstetrician who unsuccessfully pioneered ◊asepsis (better medical hygiene), later popularized by the British surgeon Joseph ◊Lister.

semaphore

flags are red and yellow
A
B
C
D
E
F
G
H
I
J
K
L
M
N
O
P
Q
R
S
T
U
V
W
X
Y
Z
attention
numerals follow
error
front

Semmelweis was an obstetric assistant at the General Hospital in Vienna at a time when 10% of women were dying of puerperal (childbed) fever. He realized that the cause was infectious matter carried on the hands of doctors treating the women after handling corpses in the postmortem room. He introduced aseptic methods (handwashing in chlorinated lime), and mortality fell to almost zero. Semmelweis was dismissed for his efforts, which were not widely adopted at the time.

Semmes Raphael 1809–1877. American naval officer. Born in Charles County, Maryland, Semmes joined the US Navy 1826 and rose to the rank of lieutenant 1836. After seeing action in the Mexican War, he was promoted to commander 1851. At the outbreak of the Civil War, he joined the Confederate navy and attacked Union shipping in the Atlantic. He was placed in command of the Confederate cruiser *Alabama* 1862, losing the ship in a battle with the USS *Kearsarge* in the English Channel 1864.

After the war Semmes was imprisoned briefly and thereafter practiced law. He also edited the *Memphis Daily Bulletin*.

Semtex a plastic explosive, manufactured in Czechoslovakia. It is safe to handle (it can only be ignited by a detonator), and difficult to trace, since it has no smell. It has been used by extremist groups in the Middle East and by the IRA in Northern Ireland.

Semtex is thought to have been the cause of an explosion that destroyed a Pan-American Boeing 747 in flight over Lockerbie, Scotland, in Dec 1988, killing 270 people.

Senanayake Don Stephen 1884–1952. First prime minister of independent Sri Lanka (formerly Ceylon) 1947–52.

Senanayake Dudley 1911–1973. Prime minister of Sri Lanka 1952–53, 1960, and 1965–70; son of Don Senanayake.

senate the Roman "council of elders." Originally consisting of the heads of patrician families, it was recruited from ex-magistrates and persons who had rendered notable public service, but was periodically purged by the censors. Although nominally advisory, it controlled finance and foreign policy.

The US Senate consists of 100 members, 2 from each state, elected for a six-year term. The term also refers to the upper house of the Canadian parliament and to the upper chambers of Italy and France. It is also given to the governing bodies in some universities, for example, the Faculty Senate.

Sendai city in Tojoku region, NE Honshu, Japan; population (1987) 686,000. Industries include metal goods (a metal museum was established 1975), textiles, pottery, and food processing.

Sendak Maurice 1928– . US writer and book illustrator, whose children's books with their deliberately arch illustrations include *Where the Wild Things Are* 1963, *In the Night Kitchen* 1970, and *Outside Over There* 1981.

Born in Brooklyn, New York, he attended the Art Students League and illustrated books for other authors. *Kenny's Window* 1956 was the first book that he both wrote and illustrated. *Very Far Away* 1957 and *The Sign on Rosie's Door* 1960 soon followed. He also designed several works for the stage, including an operatic version of *Where the Wild Things Are* and a production of Mozart's *Magic Flute*.

Sendero Luminoso (Shining Path) Maoist guerrilla group active in Peru, formed 1980 to overthrow the government. Until 1988 its activity was confined to rural areas. By June 1988 an estimated 9,000 people had been killed in the insurgency, about half of them guerrillas.

Seneca Lucius Annaeus c. 4 BC–AD 65. Roman Stoic playwright, author of essays and nine tragedies. He was tutor to the future emperor Nero but lost favor after the latter's accession to the throne and was ordered to commit suicide. His tragedies were accepted as Classical models by 16th-century dramatists.

Seneca Falls Convention, the in US history, a meeting in New York State July 1848 of women campaigning for greater rights. A Declaration of Sentiments, paraphrasing the US Declaration of Independence, called for female suffrage, equal educational and employment opportunities, and more legal rights.

Senefelder Alois 1771–1834. German engraver, born in Prague. He is thought to have invented ◊lithography.

Senegal river in W Africa, formed by the confluence of the Bafing and Bakhoy rivers and flowing 700 mi/1,125 km NW and W to join the Atlantic near St Louis, Senegal. In 1968 the Organization of Riparian States of the River Senegal (Guinea, Mali, Mauritania, and Senegal) was formed to develop the river valley, including a dam for hydroelectric power and irrigation at Joina Falls in Mali; its headquarters is in Dakar. The river gives its name to the Republic of Senegal.

Senegal country in W Africa, on the Atlantic, bounded N by Mauritania, E by Mali, S by Guinea and Guinea-Bissau, and enclosing Gambia on three sides.

government The constitution of 1963, amended, provides for a single-chamber legislature, the 120-member National Assembly, and a president who is head of state and head of government. The assembly and president are elected at the same time by universal suffrage to serve a five-year term. The president appoints and leads a council of ministers. The Senegalese Socialist Party (PS) is dominant.

Senegal's ten regions enjoy a high degree of autonomy, each having its own appointed governor and elected assembly and controlling a separate budget.

history For early history, see ◊Africa. Portuguese explorers arrived in the 15th century, and French settlers in the 17th. Senegal had a French governor from 1854, became part of ◊French West Africa 1895, and a territory 1946.

Senegal became an independent republic in Sept 1960, with ◊Leopold Sedar Senghor, leader of the Senegalese Progresssive Union (UPS), as its first president. Senghor was also prime minister 1962–70. UPS was the only legal party from 1966 until in Dec 1976 it was reconstituted as PS and two opposition parties were legally registered. In 1978 Senghor was decisively reelected.

Senghor retired at the end of 1980 and was succeeded by Abdou Diouf, who declared an amnesty for political offenders and permitted more parties to register. In the 1983 elections PS won 111 of the assembly seats and the main

Sendak *Condemned as disturbing by some parents and teachers, the creatures portrayed in* Where the Wild Things Are *by Maurice Sendak nonetheless convey extremely well the dreams and imaginings of childhood.*

opposition, the Senegalese Democratic Party (PDS), 8 seats. Later that year Diouf tightened control of his party and the government, abolishing the post of prime minister. This met open, sometimes violent, opposition, but he and the PS remained firmly in power.

In 1980 Senegal sent troops to Gambia to protect it against a suspected Libyan invasion, and it intervened again in 1981 to thwart an attempted coup. As the two countries came closer together, they agreed on an eventual merger, and the confederation of Senegambia came into being in Feb 1982. Senegal has always maintained close links with France, allowing it to retain military bases. In the Feb 1988 elections Diouf was reelected president with 73% of the vote, but his ruling party had a slightly reduced majority in the National Assembly. In April 1989 border disputes led to a severance of diplomatic relations with neighboring Mauritania, with more than 450 people killed during violent clashes between Senegalese and Mauretanians. Over 50,000 people were repatriated from both countries May 1989. In Aug formal recognition was given at the ending of the unsuccessful federation with Gambia, Senegambia.

senescence in biology, the deterioration in physical and reproductive capacities associated with old age. See ◊aging.

Senghor 1906– . First president of independent Senegal 1960–80. He was also a well-known poet and a founder of Negritude, a black literary and philosophical movement.

Educated at the Sorbonne in Paris, Senghor was a strong advocate of pride in his native Africa. He served in the French army during World War II, an experience that aided him in leading his country, French West Africa, to independence 1956 as Senegal. His works, written in French, include *Songs of the Shade* 1945, *Éthiopiques* 1956, and *On African Socialism* 1961. He was a founder of the journal *Présence Africaine*.

senile dementia a general term associated with old age; see ◊dementia and ◊Alzheimer's Disease.

Sennacherib died 681 BC. King of Assyria from 705 BC. Son of ◊Sargon II, he rebuilt the city of Nineveh on a grand scale, sacked Babylon 689, and defeated ◊Hezekiah, king of Judah, but failed to take Jerusalem. He was assassinated by his sons, and one of them, Esarhaddon, succeeded him.

Sennett Mack. Adopted name of Michael Sinnott 1880–1960. Canadian-born US film director. Born in Richmond, Québec, Sennett moved to New York 1904, where he began to perform in vaudeville. After working as an actor in Biograph Studio films under D W Griffith 1908–11, he founded his own film production company, the Keystone Company 1911. As director, Sennett made hundreds of short slapstick comedies, cast Charles ◊Chaplin in his first feature film (*Tillie's Punctured Romance* 1914), and started the career of Gloria Swanson. In the following years, Sennett developed the slapstick style of comedy, featuring the first flying custard pie and his Keystone Kops. Before his career ended, with the advent of sound films, he had directed most of Hollywood's major silent film stars. His studio closed 1933.

sense organ any organ that an animal uses to gain information about its surroundings. All sense organs have specialized receptors (such as light receptors in an eye) and some means of translating their response into a nerve impulse that travels to the brain. The main human sense organs are the eye, which detects light and color (different wavelengths of light); the ear, which detects sound (vibrations of the air) and gravity; the nose, which detects some of the chemical molecules in the air; and the tongue, which detects some of the chemicals in food, giving a sense of taste. There are also many small sense organs in the skin, including pain sensors, temperature sensors, and pressure sensors, contributing to our sense of touch.

Research suggests that our noses may also be sensitive to magnetic forces, giving us an innate "sense of direction." This sense is well developed in other animals, as are a variety of senses that we do not share. Some animals can detect small electric discharges, underwater vibrations, minute vibrations of the ground, or sounds that are below (infrasound) or above (ultrasound) our range of hearing. Sensitivity to light varies greatly. Most mammals cannot distinguish different colors, whereas some birds can detect the polarization of light. Many insects can see light in the ultraviolet range, which is beyond our spectrum, while snakes can form images of infrared radiation (radiant heat). In many animals, light is also detected by another organ, the pineal gland, which "sees" light filtering through the skull, and measures the length of the day to keep track of the seasons.

Seoul or ***Sŏul*** capital of the Republic of Korea (South Korea), near the Han River, with its chief port at Inchon; population (1985) 9,646,000. Industries include engineering, textiles, food processing, electrical and electronic equipment, chemicals, and machinery. It was the capital of Korea 1392–1910 and has a 14th-century palace and six universities. It was the site of the 1988 Summer Olympics.

sepal part of a flower, usually green, that surrounds

Senegal
Republic of
(*République du Sénégal*)

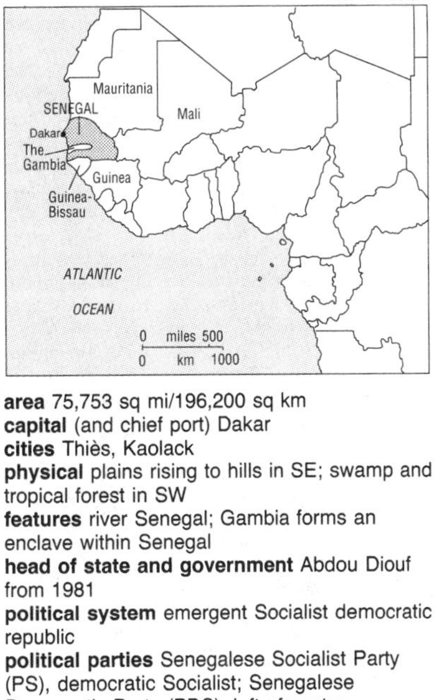
Mauritania
SENEGAL
Mali
Dakar
The Gambia
Guinea
Guinea-Bissau
ATLANTIC
OCEAN
0 miles 500
0 km 1000

area 75,753 sq mi/196,200 sq km
capital (and chief port) Dakar
cities Thiès, Kaolack
physical plains rising to hills in SE; swamp and tropical forest in SW
features river Senegal; Gambia forms an enclave within Senegal
head of state and government Abdou Diouf from 1981
political system emergent Socialist democratic republic
political parties Senegalese Socialist Party (PS), democratic Socialist; Senegalese Democratic Party (PDS), left-of-center
exports peanuts, cotton, fish, phosphates
currency franc CFA
population (1990 est) 7,740,000; growth rate 3.1% p.a.
life expectancy men 51, women 54 (1989)
language French (official); African dialects
religion Muslim 80%, Roman Catholic 10%, animist
literacy men 37%/women 19% (1985 est)
GNP $2 bn (1987); $380 per head (1984)
chronology
1659 Became a French colony.
1854–65 Interior occupied.
1902 Became a territory of French West Africa.
1959 Formed the Federation of Mali with French Sudan.
1960 Independence achieved from France but withdrew from the federation. Léopold Sedar Senghor, leader of the Senegalese Progressive Union (UPS), became president.
1966 UPS declared the only legal party.
1974 Pluralist system reestablished.
1976 UPS reconstituted as Senegalese Socialist Party (PS). Prime Minister Abdou Diouf nominated as Senghor's successor.
1980 Senghor resigned; succeeded by Diouf. Troops sent to defend Gambia.
1981 Military help again sent to Gambia.
1982 Confederation of Senegambia came into effect.
1983 Diouf reelected. Post of prime minister abolished.
1988 Diouf decisively reelected.
1989 Violent clashes between Senegalese and Mauritanians in Dakar and Nouakchott killed more than 450 people; over 50,000 people repatriated from both countries. Senegambia federation abandoned.

and protects the flower in bud. The sepals are derived from modified leaves, and collectively known as the ◊calyx.

In some plants, such as the marsh marigold *Caltha palustris*, where true ◊petals are absent, the sepals are brightly colored and petal-like, taking over the role of attracting insect pollinators to the flower.

separation of powers an approach to limiting the powers of government by separating governmental functions into the executive, legislative, and judiciary. The concept has its fullest practical expression in the the US constitution (see ◊federalism.

Sephardi (plural Sephardim) a Jew descended from those expelled from Spain and Portugal in the 15th century, or from those forcibly converted during the Inquisition to Christianity (Marranos). Many settled in North Africa and in the Mediterranean countries, as well as in Holland, England, and Dutch colonies in the New World. Sephardim speak Ladino, a 15th-century Romance dialect, as well as the language of their nation.

sepoy an Indian soldier in the service of the British or Indian army in the days of British rule in India. The Indian Mutiny 1857–58 was thus known as the ◊Sepoy Rebellion or Mutiny.

Sepoy Rebellion the revolt 1857–58 of the Indian soldiers (sepoys) against the British in India; also known as the Sepoy, or Indian, Mutiny. The uprising was confined to the north, from Bengal to the Punjab, and central India. The majority of support came from the army and recently dethroned princes, but in some areas it developed into a peasant uprising and general revolt. It included the seizure of Delhi by the rebels, its siege and recapture by the British, and the defense of Lucknow by a British garrison. The mutiny led to the end of rule by the ◊British East India Company and its replacement by direct British crown administration.

sepsis general term for infection; any poisoned state due to the introduction of disease-causing organisms from outside into the bloodstream.

septicemia technical term for ◊blood poisoning.

Septuagesima in the Christian church calendar, the 3rd Sunday before Lent; the 70th day before Easter.

Septuagint (Latin *septuagint*, seventy) the oldest Greek version of the Old Testament or Hebrew Bible, traditionally made by 70 scholars.

seq. abbreviation for sequentes (Latin "the following").

sequoia two species of conifer in the redwood family Taxodiaceae, native to western US. The redwood *Sequoia sempervirens* is a long-lived timber tree, and one specimen, the Howard Libbey Redwood, is the world's tallest tree at 361 ft/110 m, with a circumference of 44 ft/13.4 m. The giant sequoia *Sequoiadendron giganteum* reaches up to 100 ft/30 m in circumference at the base, and grows almost as tall as the redwood. It is also (except for the bristlecone pine) the oldest living tree, some specimens being estimated at over 3,500 years of age.

Sequoya George Guess 1770–1843. American Indian scholar and leader. After serving with the US army in the Creek War 1813–14, he made a study of his own Cherokee language and created a syllabary which was approved by the Cherokee council 1821. This helped thousands of Indians toward literacy and resulted in the publication of books and newspapers in their own language.

Sequoya went on to write down ancient tribal history. In later life he became political representative of the Western tribes in Washington, negotiating for the Indians when the US government forced resettlement in Indian territory in the 1830s. A type of giant redwood tree, the ◊sequoia, is named after him, as is a national park in California.

Serang alternate form of ◊Ceram, an Indonesian island.

seraph (plural ***seraphim***) in Christian and Judaic belief, an ◊angel of the highest order. They are mentioned in the book of Isaiah in the Old Testament.

sequoia

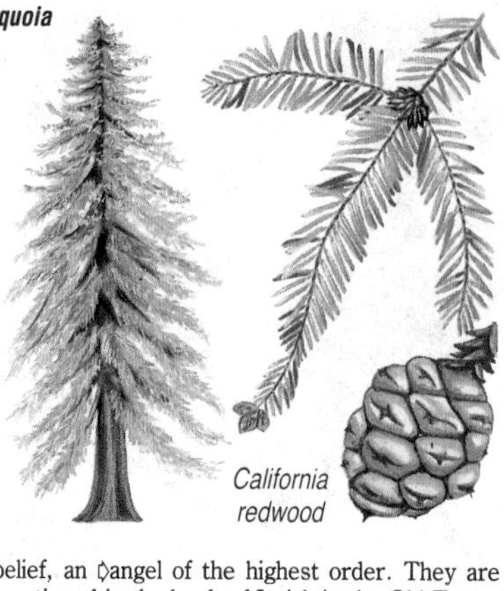
California redwood

Serapis ancient Greco-Egyptian god, a combination of Hades and Osiris, invented by the Ptolemies; his finest temple was the Serapeum in Alexandria.

Serbia (Serbo-Croat *Srbija*) constituent republic of Yugoslavia, which includes Kosovo and Vojvodina
area 34,122 sq mi/88,400 sq km
capital Belgrade
physical fertile Danube plains in the N, mountainous in the S; features includes the autonomous provinces of ◊Kosovo, capital Priština, of which the predominantly Albanian population demands unification with Albania, and ◊Vojvodina, capital Novi Sad, largest town Subotica, with a predominantly Serbian population
population (1986) 9,660,000
language the Serbian variant of Serbo-Croat, sometimes written in Cyrillic script
religion Serbian Orthodox
history the Serbs settled in the Balkans 7th century and became Christians 9th century. They were united as one kingdom about 1169 and under Stephen Dushan (1331–55) founded an empire covering most of the Balkans. After their defeat at Kosovo 1389 they came under the domination of the Turks, who annexed Serbia 1459. Uprisings 1804–16, led by Kara George and Milosh Obrenovich, forced the Turks to recognize Serbia as an autonomous principality under Milosh. The assassination of Kara George on Obrenovich's orders gave rise to a long feud between the two houses. After a war with Turkey 1876–78, Serbia became an independent kingdom. On the assassination of the last Obrenovich 1903 the Karageorgevich dynasty came to the throne. The two Balkan Wars 1912–13 greatly enlarged Serbia's territory at the expense of Turkey and Bulgaria. Serbia's designs on Bosnia and Herzegovina, backed by Russia, led to friction with Austria, culminating in the outbreak of war 1914. Serbia was completely overrun 1915–16 and was occupied until 1918, when it became the nucleus of the new kingdom of the Serbs, Croats, and Slovenes, later ◊Yugoslavia.

After unrest in Kosovo in the 1980s a campaign by the hard-line Serbian party chief, Milosevic, culminated in the adoption of a new multiparty constitution in 1990, stripping the republics of Kosovo and Vojvodina of their autonomy. The election of Milosevic as president in Dec 1990 sparked more uprisings. In 1991 Serbia called for secession and Serb-Croatian clashes broke out in Croatia. The federal army intervened, but fighting continued through the year. In Sept 1991 President Bush accused the Serb-dominated federal army of aggression toward Croatia and the EC, and then the UN intervened, imposing economic sanctions. After several attempts, a ceasefire with Croatia was agreed upon in Jan 1992.

sere a type of plant ◊succession developing in a particular habitat. A ***lithosere*** is a succession starting on the surface of bare rock. A ***hydrosere*** is a succession in shallow fresh water, beginning with planktonic vegetation and the growth of pondweeds and other aquatic plants, and ending with the development of swamp. A ***plagiosere*** is the sequence of communities that develops following the clearing of the existing vegetation.

serenade a musical piece for chamber orchestra or wind instruments in several movements, originally intended for evening entertainment, such as Mozart's *Eine kleine Nachtmusik/A Little Night Music*.

serfdom the legal and economic status of peasants under ◊feudalism. Serfs could not be sold like slaves, but they were not free to leave their master's estate without his permission. They had to work the lord's land without pay for a number of days every week and pay a percentage of their produce to the lord every year. They also served as soldiers in the event of conflict. Serfs also had to perform extra labor at harvest time and other busy seasons; in return they were allowed to cultivate a portion of the estate for their own benefit.

In England serfdom died out between the 14th and 17th centuries, but it lasted in France until 1789, in Russia until 1861, and in most other European countries until the early 19th century.

Sergel Johan Tobias 1740–1814. German-born Swedish Neo-Classical sculptor, active mainly in Stockholm. His portraits include *Gustaf III* (Royal Palace, Stockholm) and he made terracotta figures such as *Mars and Venus* (National Museum, Stockholm).

Sergius, St of Radonezh 1314–1392. Patron saint of Russia, who founded the Eastern Orthodox monastery of the Blessed Trinity near Moscow 1334. Mediator among Russian feudal princes, he inspired the victory of Dmitri, Grand Duke of Moscow, over the Tatar khan Mamai at Kulikovo, on the upper Don, 1380.

serialism in music, an alternate name for the ◊twelve-tone system of composition.

It usually refers to post-1950 compositions in which further aspects such as dynamics, durations, and attacks are brought under serial control. These other series may consist of fewer than 12 degrees while some pitch series can go higher.

series circuit an electric circuit in which the components are connected end to end, so that the current flows through them all one after the other.

Serlio Sebastiano 1475–1554. Italian architect and painter, author of *L'Architettura* 1537–51, which set down practical rules for the use of the Classical orders, and was used by architects of the Neo-Classical style throughout Europe.

Serpens constellation of the equatorial region of the sky, representing a serpent coiled around the body of Ophiuchus. It is the only constellation divided into two halves: Serpens Caput, the head (on one side of Ophiuchus), and Serpens Cauda, the tail (on the other side). Its main feature is the Eagle nebula.

serpentine a group of minerals, hydrous magnesium silicate, $Mg_3Si_2O_5(OH)_4$, occurring in soft ◊metamorphic rocks and usually dark green. The fibrous form chrysotile is a source of ◊asbestos; other forms are antigorite, talc, and meerschaum. Serpentine minerals are formed by hydration of ultrabasic rocks during metamorphism. Rare snake-patterned forms are used in ornamental carving.

Serpent Mound earthwork built by Hopewell Indians 2nd–1st centuries BC in Ohio. It is 1,330 ft/405 m long, 4 ft/1.3 m high, and about 19 ft/6 m across and may have been constructed in the shape of a snake for religious purposes.

Serpent Mound is in a state park in Adams County, Ohio.

Serra Junipero 1713–1784. Spanish missionary and explorer of California. Born in Majorca, Spain, Serra joined the Franciscan order 1730. After receiving a doctorate in theology, he served on the faculty of the University of Palma 1743–49. Pursuing a missionary career, he arrived in Mexico City 1750. Having served in Querétaro 1750–58, he was transferred to Baja California with the expulsion of the Jesuits from Mexico 1767. Two years later he led a missionary expedition to Alta California and spent the remainder of his life establishing missions throughout the region.

serum clear fluid that remains after blood clots. It is blood plasma with the anticoagulant proteins removed, and contains ◊antibodies and other proteins, as well as the fats and sugars of the blood. It can be produced synthetically, and is used to protect against disease.

serval African wild cat *Felis serval*. It is a slender, long-limbed cat, about 3 ft/1 m long, with a yellowish-brown, black-spotted coat. It has large, sensitive ears, with which it locates its prey, mainly birds and rodents.

Servan-Schreiber Jean Jacques 1924– . French Radical politician, and founder of the magazine *L'Express* 1953. His *Le Défi americain* 1967 maintained that US economic and technological dominance would be challenged only by a united left-wing Europe. He was president of the Radical Party 1971–75 and 1977–79.

Servetus Michael (Miguel Serveto) 1511–1553. Spanish Christian Anabaptist theologian and physician. He was a pioneer in the study of the circulation of the blood and found that it circulates to the lungs from the right chamber of the heart. He was burned alive by the church reformer Calvin in Geneva, Switzerland, for publishing attacks on the doctrine of the Trinity.

service industry commercial activity that provides and charges for various services to customers (as opposed to manufacturing or supplying goods), such as restaurants, the tourist industry, cleaning, hotels, and the retail trade (shops and supermarkets).

With the decline in the manufacturing sector in many Western countries, service industries have become major employers of labor.

services, armed the air, sea, and land forces of a country; see ◊army, ◊navy, ◊air force; also called the armed forces.

service tree deciduous Eurasian tree *Sorbus domestica* of the rose family Rosaceae, with alternate pinnate leaves, white flowers, and small, edible, oval fruit. The wild service tree *Sorbus torminalis* has oblong rather than pointed leaflets. It is related to the ◊mountain ash.

servomechanism automatic control system used in aircraft, motor automobiles, and other complex machines. A specific input, such as moving a lever or joystick, causes a specific output, such as feeding current to an electric motor that moves, for example, the rudder of the aircraft. At the same time, the position of the rudder is detected and fed back to the central control, so that small adjustments can continually be made to maintain the desired course.

sesame annual plant *Sesamum indicum* of the family Pedaliaceae, probably native to SE Asia. It produces oily seeds used for food and soap making.

sessile in botany, a leaf, flower, or fruit that lacks a stalk and sits directly on the stem, as with the sessile acorns of certain ◊oaks. In zoology, it is an animal that normally stays in the same place, such as a barnacle or mussel. The term is also applied to the eyes of ◊crustaceans when these lack stalks and sit directly on the head.

sessile in botany, a leaf, flower, or fruit that lacks a stalk and sits directly on the stem, as with the acorns of the California white oak *Querais lobata*. In zoology, it is an animal that normally stays in the same place, such as a barnacle or mussel. The term is also applied to the eyes of crustaceans when these lack stalks and sit directly on the head.

Sessions Roger (Huntington) 1896–1985. US composer whose Modernist, dissonant works include *The Black Maskers* incidental music 1923, eight symphonies, and *Concerto for Orchestra* 1971. He was instrumental in increasing the understanding and appreciation of modern music.

Born in Brooklyn, New York, he attended Harvard and Yale, then studied under Ernest Bloch. He became a leading teacher of composition, serving on the faculties of Boston University, Princeton University, the University of California at Berkeley, and the Juilliard School of Music.

set

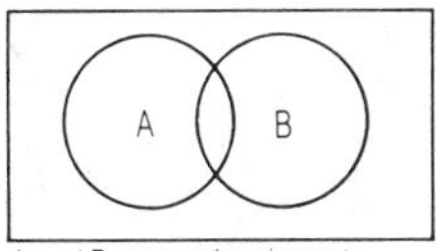
A
B
A and B are overlapping sets

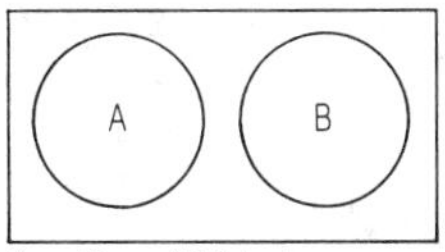
A
B
A and B are disjoint sets

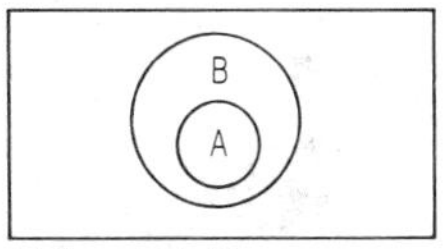
B
A
A is the subset of B

Set in Egyptian mythology, the god of night, the desert, and all evils. He was the murderer of ◊Osiris, portrayed as a grotesque animal.

set in mathematics, any collection of defined things (elements), provided the elements are distinct and that there is a rule to decide whether an element is a member of a set. It is usually denoted by a capital letter and indicated by curly brackets { }.

For example, let L represent the set that consists of all the letters of the alphabet. The symbol $\in$ stands for "is a member of"; thus p $\in L$ means that p belongs to the set consisting of all letters, and 4 $\notin L$ means that 4 does not belong to the set consisting of all letters.

There are various types of sets. A finite set has a limited number of members, such as {letters of the alphabet}; an infinite set has an unlimited number of members, such as {all whole numbers}; an empty or null set has no members, such as the number of people who have swum across the Atlantic Ocean, written as {} or ø; a single-element set has only one member, such as days of the week beginning with M, written as {Monday}. Equal sets have the same members; for example, if W = {days of the week} and S = {Sunday, Monday, Tuesday, Wednesday, Thursday, Friday, Saturday}, it can be said that $W = S$. Sets with the same number of members are equivalent sets. Sets with some members in common are intersecting sets; for example, if R = {red playing cards} and F = {face cards}, then R and F share the members that are red face cards. Sets with no members in common are disjoint sets, such as {minerals} and {vegetables}. Sets contained within others are subsets; for example, {vowels} is a subset of {letters of the alphabet}. Sets and their interrelationships are often illustrated by a ◊Venn diagram.

Sète town on the Mediterranean coast of France, in Hérault *département*, SW of Montpellier; population (1982) 40,466. It is a seaport and handles fish, wine, brandy, and chemicals. It was founded 1666 as an outlet to the Canal du Midi.

Seton Ernest Thompson, born Ernest Seton Thompson. 1860–1946. Canadian author and naturalist, born in England. He illustrated his own books with drawings of animals. He was the founder of the Woodcraft Folk youth movement, a nonreligious alternative to the scouting movement.

Seton St Elizabeth Ann Bayley 1774–1821. US religious leader. Born in New York, Seton was devoted to the service of the poor and established the Society for the Relief of Poor Widows with Small Children 1797. After a trip to Italy and the death of her first husband, she joined the Roman Catholic Church 1805. In 1809, with her own funds, she established a Catholic elementary school in Baltimore. Soon afterward becoming a nun, she formed the Sisters of St Joseph and founded St Joseph's College for Women 1809. Known as "Mother Seton," she was proclaimed the first American saint 1975.

setter any of various breeds of sporting dog, about 2.2 ft/66 cm high, and weighing about 55 lb/25 kg. They have long, smooth coats, feathered tails, and spaniellike faces. They are called "setters" because they were trained in crouching or "setting" on the sight of game to be pursued.

The Irish setter is a rich red; the English setter is usually white with black, tan, or liver markings; and the Gordon setter is black and brown.

Settlement, Act of in Britain, a law passed 1701 during the reign of King William III, designed to ensure a Protestant succession to the throne by excluding the Roman Catholic descendants of James II in favor of the Protestant House of Hanover. Elizabeth II still reigns under this Act.

settlement out of court a compromise reached between the parties to a legal dispute. Most civil legal actions are settled out of court, reducing legal costs, and avoiding the uncertainty of the outcome of a trial.

Seurat Georges 1859–1891. French artist. He originated, with Paul Signac, the Neo-Impressionist technique of ◊Pointillism (painting with small dabs rather than long brushstrokes). Examples of his work are *The Bathers, Asnières* 1884 (National Gallery, London) and *Sunday on the Island of La Grande Jatte* 1886 (Art Institute of Chicago).

Seurat also departed from Impressionism by evolving a more formal type of composition based on the Classical proportions of the ◊golden section, rather than aiming to capture fleeting moments of light and movement.

Seuss, Dr see ◊Geisel, Theodore Seuss.

Sevastopol or ***Sebastopol*** port, resort, and fortress in the Crimea, Ukraine Republic, USSR; population (1987) 350,000. It is the base of the Soviet Black Sea fleet and also has shipyards and a wine-making industry. Founded by Catherine II 1784, it was successfully besieged by the English and French in the Crimean War (Oct 1854–Sept 1855), and in World War II by the Germans (Nov 1941–July 1942), but was retaken by the Soviets 1944.

Seven against Thebes in Greek mythology, the attack of seven captains led by Adrastus king of Argos on the seven gates of ancient Thebes, prompted by the rivalry between the two sons of Oedipus, ◊Polynices and ◊Eteocles, for the kingship of Thebes. The subject of tragedies by ◊Aeschylus and ◊Euripides (*The Phoenician Women*), and of the epic *Thebaid* by the Roman poet Statius, it forms the background to other Greek tragedies by ◊Sophocles (Antigone, Oedipus at Colonus) and Euripides (Suppliant Women).

seven deadly sins in Christian theology, anger, avarice, envy, gluttony, lust, pride, and sloth.

Seventh Day Adventist often called an ◊Adventist. A member of the Protestant religious sect of the same name. It originated in the US in the fervent expectation of Christ's Second Coming, or advent, that swept across New York State following William Miller's prophecy that Christ would return on Oct 22, 1844. When this failed to come to pass, a number of Millerites, as his followers were called, reinterpreted his prophetic speculations and continued to maintain that the millennium was imminent. Adventists observe Saturday as the Sabbath and emphasize healing and diet; many are vegetarians. The sect has about 500,000 members in the US.

The chief author of what became Seventh Day Adventist doctrine was Ellen G White, and the sect considers her works canonical. She held that Christ's judgment of humanity had begun in 1844

Seurat *French artist Georges Seurat painted* The Bathers, Asnières *in his pointillist technique in 1883–84.*

Seville *Seville cathedral (1401–1520), the largest medieval cathedral in Europe, occupies the site of a Moorish mosque. The Giralda, or bell tower, was probably built as a symbol of Moorish power.*

and would continue in preparation for his return and thousand-year reign on Earth.

Seven Weeks' War war 1866 between Austria and Prussia, engineered by the German chancellor ◊Bismarck. It was nominally over the possession of ◊Schleswig-Holstein, but it was actually to confirm Prussia's superseding Austria as the leading German state. The Battle of ◊Sadowa was the culmination of von ◊Moltke's victories.

Seven Wonders of the World in antiquity, the pyramids of Egypt, the hanging gardens of Babylon, the temple of Artemis at Ephesus, the statue of Zeus at Olympia, the mausoleum at Halicarnassus, the Colossus of Rhodes, and the Pharos (lighthouse) at Alexandria.

Seven Years' War (French and Indian War) war 1756–63 arising from the conflict between Austria and Prussia, and between France and Britain over colonial supremacy. Britain and Prussia defeated France, Austria, Spain, and Russia; Britain gained control of India and many of France's colonies, including Canada. Spain ceded Florida to Britain in exchange for Cuba. Fighting against great odds, Prussia was eventually successful in becoming established as one of the great European powers. The war ended with the Treaty of Paris 1763, signed by Britain, France, and Spain.

severe combined immune deficiency (SCID) rare condition in which a baby is born without the body's normal defenses against infection. The child must be kept within a transparent plastic tent until a matched donor can provide a bone-marrow transplant (bone marrow is the source of disease-fighting cells in the body).

Severin Tim 1940– . Writer, historian, and traveler who has re-enacted several "classic" voyages. In 1961 he retraced the Marco Polo route in Asia and four years later canoed the length of the Mississippi. His Brendan Voyage 1977 followed the supposed transatlantic route taken by St Brendan in the 7th century; the Ulysses Voyage took him from Troy to Ithaca 1985; and a journey on horseback retraced the route to the Middle East taken by the Crusaders 1987–88.

Severn river of Wales and England, rising on the NE side of Plynlimmon, N Wales, and flowing 210 mi/338 km through Shrewsbury, Worcester, and Gloucester to the Bristol Channel. The Severn bore is a tidal wave up to 6 ft/2 m high.

S England and S Wales are linked near Chepstow by a rail tunnel 1873–85 over the Severn, and a road bridge 1966.

Severus Lucius Septimus 146–211. Roman emperor. Born in N Africa, he held a command on the Danube when in 193 the emperor Pertinax was murdered. Proclaimed emperor by his troops, Severus proved an able administrator; he was the only African to become emperor. He died at York while campaigning in Britain against the Caledonians.

Severus of Antioch 467–538. Christian bishop, one of the originators of the Monophysite heresy. As patriarch of Antioch (from 512), Severus was the leader of opposition to the Council of Chalcedon 451, an attempt to unite factions of the early church, by insisting that Christ existed in one nature only. He was condemned by the emperor Justin I in 518, and left Antioch for Alexandria, never to return.

Sévigné Marie de Rabutin-Chantal, Marquise de 1626–1696. French writer. In her letters to her daughter, the Comtesse de Grignan, she paints a vivid picture of contemporary customs and events.

Seville (Spanish *Sevilla*) city in Andalucia, Spain, on the Guadalquivir River, 60 mi/96 km N of Cadiz; population (1986) 668,000. Products include machinery, spirits, porcelain, pharmaceuticals, silk, and tobacco.

Formerly the center of a Moorish kingdom, it has a 12th-century Alcázar palace, and a 15th–16th-century Gothic cathedral. Seville was the birthplace of the artists Murillo and Velázquez.

Sèvre two French rivers from which the *département* of Deux Sèvres takes its name. The ***Sèvre Nantaise*** joins the Loire at Nantes; the ***Sèvre Niortaise*** flows into the Bay of Biscay.

Sèvres town in the Île de France region of France, now a Paris suburb; population about 21,000. The state porcelain factory was established in the park of ◊St-Cloud 1756, and it is also the site of a national museum of ceramics.

Sèvres fine porcelain produced at a factory in Sèvres, France, since the early 18th century. It is characterized by the use of intensely colored backgrounds (such as pink and royal blue), against which flowers are painted in elaborately embellished frames, often in gold.

It became popular after the firm's patronage by Louis XV's mistress, Madame de ◊Pompador.

Sèvres, Treaty of the last of the treaties that ended World War I. Negotiated between the Allied powers and the Ottoman Empire, it was finalized in Aug 1920 but never ratified by the Turkish government.

The treaty reduced the size of Turkey by making concessions to the Greeks, Kurds, and Armenians, as well as ending Turkish control of Arab lands. Its terms were rejected by the newly created nationalist government and the treaty was never ratified. It was superseded by the Treaty of Lausanne in 1923.

sewage disposal the disposal of human excreta and other waterborne waste products from houses, streets, and factories. Conveyed through sewers to sewage plants, sewage has to undergo a series of treatments to be acceptable for discharge into rivers or the sea, according to various local laws and ordinances.

In the industrialized countries of the West, most industries are responsible for disposing of their own wastes. Government agencies establish industrial waste-disposal standards. In most countries, sewage plants for residential areas are the responsibility of local authorities. The solid waste (sludge) may be spread over fields as a fertilizer or, in a few countries, dumped at sea.

Sèvres *A characteristic piece of Sèvres porcelain.*

sewing machine

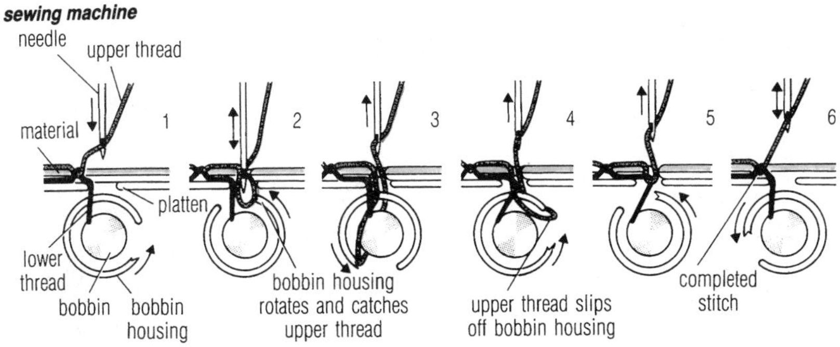
needle
upper thread
material
1
2
3
4
5
6
platten
lower thread
bobbin
bobbin housing
bobbin housing rotates and catches upper thread
upper thread slips off bobbin housing
completed stitch

sextant

simplified diagram of a sextant

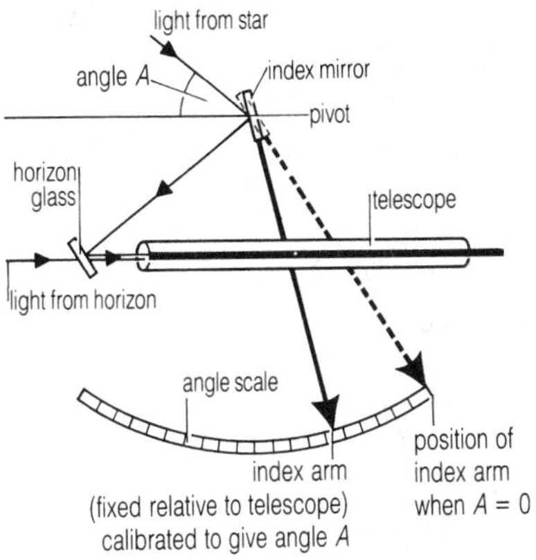
light from star
angle A
index mirror
pivot
horizon glass
telescope
light from horizon
angle scale
index arm (fixed relative to telescope) calibrated to give angle A
position of index arm when A = 0

Raw sewage, or sewage that has not been treated properly, is one serious source of water pollution. A significant proportion of bathing beaches in densely populated regions have unacceptably high bacterial content, largely as a result of untreated sewage being discharged into rivers and the sea.

The use of raw sewage as a fertilizer (long practiced in China) has the drawback that disease-causing microorganisms can survive in the soil and be transferred to people or animals by consumption of subsequent crops.

Seward William Henry 1801–1872. US public official. A lawyer, he was elected to the New York state senate 1830 and served as governor 1838–42 and US senator 1849–61. An active abolitionist, Seward became a leader of the Republican Party and was appointed secretary of state by Lincoln. Although seriously wounded in the 1865 assassination plot against Lincoln, Seward continued to serve as secretary of state under Andrew Johnson, purchasing Alaska from Russia 1867 for $7.2 million.

Born in Florida, New York, Seward was educated at Union College and was admitted to the bar 1822.

Sewell Anna 1820–1878. English author whose only published work, *Black Beauty* 1877, tells the life story of a horse. Although now read as a children's book, it was written to encourage sympathetic treatment of horses by adults.

sewing machine apparatus for the mechanical sewing of cloth, leather, and other materials by a needle, powered by hand, treadle, or belted electric motor. The popular lockstitch machine, using a double thread, was invented independently in the US by both Walter Hunt 1834 and Elias ◊Howe 1846. Howe's machine was the basis of the machine patented 1851 by Isaac ◊Singer. In the latest microprocessor-controlled sewing machines, as many as 25 different stitching patterns can be selected by push button.

sex determination the process by which the sex of an organism is determined. In many species, the sex of an individual is dictated by the two sex chromosomes (X and Y) it receives from its parents. In mammals, some plants, and a few insects, males are XY, and females XX; in birds, reptiles, some amphibians, and butterflies the reverse is the case. In bees and wasps, males are produced from unfertilized eggs, females from fertilized eggs. Environmental factors can affect some fish and reptiles, such as turtles, where sex is influenced by the temperature at which the eggs develop.

Many fish have a very flexible system of sex determination, which can be affected by external factors. For example, most members of the sea-bass family start as females and later reverse their sex, depending on the particular local sex ratio, to become males.

sexism belief in (or set of implicit assumptions about) the superiority of one's own sex, often accompanied by a ◊stereotype or preconceived idea about the opposite sex. Sexism may also be accompanied by ◊discrimination on the basis of sex, generally as practiced by men against women. See also ◊chauvinism.

The term sexism, coined by analogy with racism, was first used in the 1960s by feminist writers to describe language or behavior that implied women's inferiority. Examples include the contentious use of male pronouns to describe both men and women, and the assumption that some jobs are typically performed only by one sex.

sex linkage in genetics, the tendency for certain characteristics to occur exclusively, or predominantly, in one sex only. Human examples include red-green color blindness and hemophilia, both found predominantly in males. In both cases, these characteristics are ◊recessive and are determined by genes on the ◊X chromosome.

Since females possess two X chromosomes, any such recessive ◊allele on one of them is likely to be masked by the corresponding allele on the other. In males (who have only one X chromosome paired with a largely inert Y chromosome) any gene on the X chromosome will automatically be expressed. Color blindness and hemophilia can appear in females, but only if they are ◊homozygous for these traits, due to inbreeding, for example.

Sex Pistols, The UK punk rock group (1975–78) that became notorious under the guidance of their manager, Malcolm McLaren. They released one album, *Never Mind the Bollocks, Here's the Sex Pistols* 1977. Members included Johnny Rotten (John Lydon, 1956–) and Sid Vicious (John Ritchie, 1957–79).

sextant navigational instrument for determining latitude by measuring the angle between some heavenly body and the horizon. It was invented by John Hadley (1682–1744) in 1730 and can be used only in clear weather.

When the horizon is viewed through the right-hand side horizon glass, which is partly clear and partly mirrored, the light from a star can be seen at the same time in the mirrored left-hand side by adjusting an index mirror. The angle of the star to the horizon can then be read on a calibrated scale.

Sexton Anne 1928–1974. US poet. She studied with Robert Lowell and wrote similarly confessional poetry, as in *To Bedlam and Part Way Back* 1960 and *All My Pretty Ones* 1962. She committed suicide, and her *Complete Poems* appeared posthumously 1981.

sexual reproduction a reproductive process in organisms that requires the union, or ◊fertilization, of gametes (such as eggs and sperm). These are usually produced by two different individuals, although self-fertilization occurs in a few ◊hermaphrodites such as tapeworms. Most organisms other than bacteria and cyanobacteria show some sort of sexual process. Except in some lower organisms, the gametes are of two distinct types called eggs and sperm. The organisms producing the eggs are called females, and those producing the sperm, males. The fusion of a male and female gamete produces a zygote, from which a new individual develops. The alternatives to sexual reproduction are binary fission, budding, vegetative reproduction, parthenogenesis, and spore formation.

sexual selection a process similar to ◊natural selection but relating exclusively to success in finding a mate for the purpose of sexual reproduction and producing offspring. Sexual selection occurs when one sex (usually but not always the female) invests more effort in producing young than the other. Members of the other sex compete for access to this limited resource (usually males competing for the chance to mate with females). Sexual selection often favors features that increase a male's attractiveness to females (such as the pheasant's "tail") or enable males to fight with one another (such as a deer's antlers). More subtly, it can produce hormonal effects by which the male makes the female unreceptive to other males, causes the abortion of fetuses already conceived, or removes the sperm of males who have already mated with a female.

Seychelles country in the Indian Ocean, off E Africa, N of Madagascar.

government Seychelles is a republic within the ◊Commonwealth. The constitution of 1979 makes Seychelles a one-party state, the party being the

sexual reproduction

female reproductive system

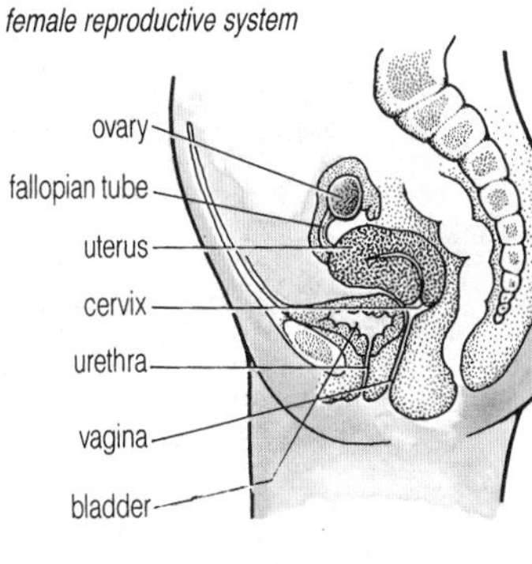
ovary
fallopian tube
uterus
cervix
urethra
vagina
bladder

male reproductive system

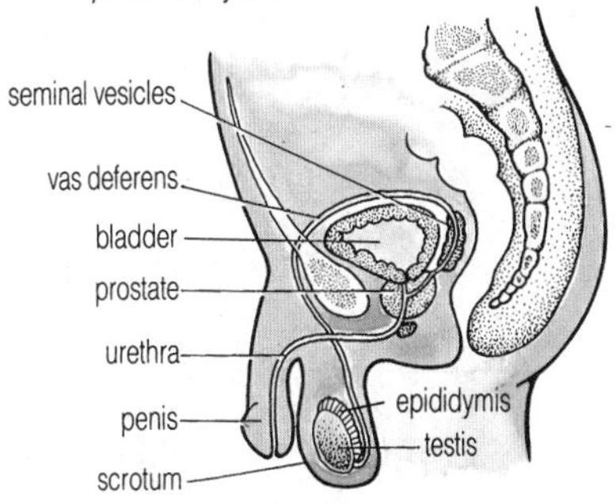
seminal vesicles
vas deferens
bladder
prostate
urethra
penis
scrotum
epididymis
testis

Seychelles
Republic of

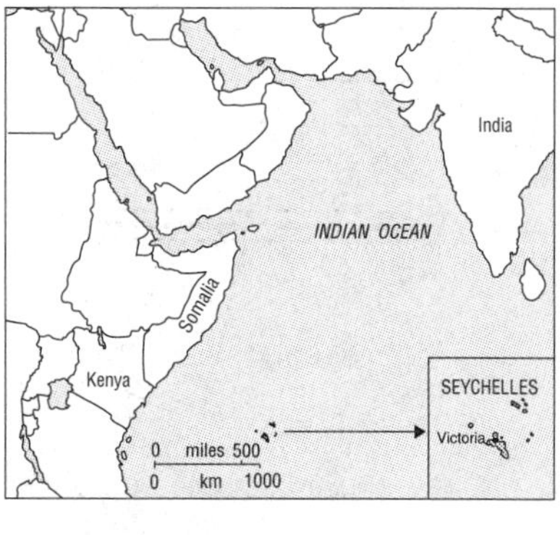
India
INDIAN OCEAN
Somalia
Kenya
SEYCHELLES
Victoria
0 miles 500
0 km 1000

area 175 sq mi/453 sq km
capital Victoria (on Mahé island)
cities Cascade, Port Glaud, Misere
physical comprises two distinct island groups, one concentrated, the other widely scattered, totaling over 100 islands and islets
features Aldabra atoll, containing world's largest tropical lagoon; the unique "double coconut" (cocode-mer); tourism is important
head of state and government France-Albert René from 1977
political system one-party Socialist republic
political parties Seychelles People's Progressive Front (SPPF), nationalistic Socialist
exports copra, cinnamon
currency Seychelles rupee
population (1990) 71,000; growth rate 2.2% p.a.
life expectancy 66 years (1988)
language Creole (Asian, African, European mixture) 95%, English, French (all official)
religion Roman Catholic 90%
literacy 80% (1989)
GNP $175 mn; $2,600 per head (1987)
chronology
1814 Incorporated as dependency of Mauritius.
1903 Became a separate colony.
1975 Internal self-government granted.
1976 Independence achieved from Britain as a republic within the Commonwealth, with Mancham as president.
1977 René ousted Mancham in an armed coup and took over presidency.
1979 New constitution adopted; Seychelles People's Progressive Front (SPPF) sole legal party.
1981 Attempted coup by South African mercenaries thwarted.
1984 René reelected.
1987 Coup attempt foiled.
1989 René reelected.

Seychelles People's Progresssive Front (SPPF). The president, who is both head of state and head of government, and the single-chamber legislature, the National Assembly, both serve a five-year term. The president and 23 of the 25 assembly members are elected by universal suffrage, and 2 are appointed by the president.

history For early history, see ◊Africa. The islands were probably visited by the Portuguese about 1500 and became a French colony 1744. Seychelles was ceded to Britain by France in 1814 and was ruled as part of ◊Mauritius until it became a Crown Colony in 1903.

In the 1960s several political parties were formed, campaigning for independence, the most significant being the Seychelles Democratic Party (SDP), led by James Mancham, and the Seychelles People's United Party (SPUP), led by Albert René. René demanded complete independence, while Mancham favored integration with Britain. In 1975 internal self-government was agreed. The two parties then formed a coalition government with Mancham as prime minister. In June 1976 Seychelles became an independent republic within the Commonwealth, with Mancham as president and René as prime minister.

The following year René staged an armed coup while Mancham was attending a Commonwealth conference in London and declared himself president. After a brief suspension of the constitution, a new one was adopted, creating a one-party state, with the SPUP being renamed the Seychelles People's Progressive Front. René, as the only candidate, was formally elected president in 1979 and then reelected in 1984 and 1989. There have been several unsuccessful attempts to overthrow him, the last reported in 1987.

René has followed a policy of ◊nonalignment and has forbidden the use of port facilities to vessels carrying nuclear weapons. He has maintained close links with Tanzania, which has provided military support.

Seyfert galaxy type of galaxy whose small, bright center is caused by hot gas moving at high speed around a massive central object, possibly a ◊black hole. Almost all Seyferts are spiral galaxies. They seem to be closely related to ◊quasars but are about 100 times fainter. They are named after their discoverer Carl Seyfert (1911–1960).

Seymour Jane c. 1509–1537. Third wife of Henry VIII, whom she married in 1536. She died soon after the birth of her son Edward VI.

Seymour Lynn 1939– . Canadian ballerina of rare dramatic talent. She was principal dancer of the Royal Ballet from 1959 and artistic director of the Munich State Opera Ballet 1978–80.

Sezession (German "secession") various groups of German and Austrian artists in the 1890s who "seceded" from official academic art institutions in order to found new schools of painting. The first was in Munich, 1892; the next, linked with the paintings of Gustav ◊Klimt, was the Vienna Sezession 1897; the Berlin Sezession followed in 1899.

In 1910 the members of the group *Die* ◊Brücke formed the Neue Sezession when they were rejected by Berlin's first Sezession.

Sfax (Arabic *Safaqis*) port and second-largest city in Tunisia; population (1984) 232,000. It is the capital of Sfax district, on the Gulf of Gabès and lies about 150 mi/240 km SE of Tunis. Products include leather, soap, and carpets; there are also salt works and phosphate workings nearby. Exports include phosphates, olive oil, dates, almonds, esparto grass, and sponges.

Sforza Italian family that ruled the duchy of Milan 1450–99, 1512–15, and 1522–35. Its court was a center of Renaissance culture and its rulers prominent patrons of the arts.

The family's original name was Attendoli but it took the name Sforza (Italian "force") in the early 13th century. Francesco Sforza (1401–1466) obtained Milan by marriage to a Visconti in 1441; then his son Galeazzo (1444–1476) ruled and became a patron of the arts. After his assassination, his brother Ludovico (1451–1508) seized power, made Milan one of the most powerful Italian states, and became a great patron of artists, especially ◊Leonardo da Vinci. He was ousted by Louis XII of France 1499, restored 1512–15, then ousted again. His son Francesco (1495–1535) was reestablished 1522 by Emperor Charles V, but with no male heirs, Milan passed to Charles 1535.

SFSR abbreviation for Soviet Federal Socialist Republic.

's-Gravenhage Dutch name for The ◊Hague.

Shaanxi or ***Shensi*** province of NW China
area 75,579 sq mi/195,800 sq km
capital Xian
physical mountains; Huang He valley, one of the earliest settled areas of China
products iron, steel, mining, textiles, fruit, tea, rice, wheat
population (1986) 30,430,000.

Shaba formerly (until 1972) Katanga region of ◊Zaïre; area 191,828 sq mi/496,965 sq km; population (1984) 3,874,000. Its main town is ◊Lubumbashi, formerly Elisabethville.

Shache alternate name for ◊Yarkand, a city in China.

shackle obsolete unit of length, used at sea for measuring cable or chain. One shackle is 15 fathoms (90 ft/27 m).

Shackleton Ernest 1874–1922. Irish Antarctic explorer. In 1907–09, he commanded an expedition that reached 88° 23′ S latitude, located the magnetic South Pole, and climbed Mount ◊Erebus.

He was a member of Scott's Antarctic expedition 1901–04, and also commanded the expedition 1914–16 to cross the Antarctic, when he had to abandon his ship, the *Endurance*, crushed in the ice of the Weddell Sea. He died on board the *Quest* on his fourth expedition 1921–22 to the Antarctic.

shad any of several marine fishes, especially the genus *Alosa*, the largest (2 ft/60 cm long and 6 lb/2.7 kg in weight) of the herring family (Clupeidae). They migrate in shoals to breed in rivers.

The American shad *A. sapidissima*, once common along the Atlantic coast, was badly affected by stream pollution but is now making a comeback. It was successfully introduced along the Pacific in 1870. The gizzard shad *Dorosoma cepedianum* has been widely introduced into fresh waters of the US as food for other fishes.

shadoof or ***shaduf*** machine for lifting water, consisting typically of a long, pivoted wooden pole acting as a lever, with a weight at one end. The other end is positioned over a well, for example. The shadoof was in use in ancient Egypt and is still used in Arab countries today.

SHAEF abbreviation for Supreme Headquarters Allied Expeditionary Force. World War II military center established Feb 15, 1944 in London, where final plans were made for the Allied invasion of Europe (under US general Eisenhower).

Shaffer Peter 1926– English playwright. His plays include *Five Finger Exercise* 1958, the historical epic *The Royal Hunt of the Sun* 1964, *Equus* 1973, and *Amadeus* 1979 about the composer Mozart.

Shaftesbury Anthony Ashley Cooper, 1st Earl of 1621–1683. English politician, a supporter of the Restoration of the monarchy. He became Lord Chancellor in 1672, but went into opposition in 1673 and began to organize the ◊Whig Party. He headed the Whigs' demand for the exclusion of the future James II from the succession, secured the passing of the ◊Habeas Corpus Act in 1679, then, when accused of treason in 1681, fled to Holland.

Shaftesbury Anthony Ashley Cooper, 7th Earl of 1801–1885. British Tory politician. He strongly supported the Ten Hours Act of 1847 and other factory legislation, including the 1842 act forbidding the employment of women and children underground in mines. He was also associated with the movement to provide free education for the poor.

shag common name for the double-crested ◊cormorant *Phalacrocorax auritis*.

shah (more formally, Shahanshah "king of kings") traditional title of ancient Persian rulers, and also of those of the recent ◊Pahlavi dynasty in Iran.

Shah Jahan 1592–1666. Mogul emperor of India 1628–58. During his reign the ◊Taj Mahal and the Pearl Mosque at Agra were built. From 1658 he was a prisoner of his son Aurangzeb.

Shahn Ben 1898–1969. US artist, born in Lithuania, a Social Realist painter. His work included draw-

Shah Jahan *Mogul portrait c. 1632–33 of Shah Jahan, who built the Taj Mahal.*

ings and paintings on the ◊Dreyfus case and the ◊Sacco and Vanzetti case in which two Italian anarchists were accused of murders. He painted murals for Rockefeller Center, New York City (with the Mexican artist Diego Rivera), and the Federal Security Building, Washington, DC, 1940–42.

Shaka or ***Chaka*** c. 1787–1828. Zulu chief who formed a Zulu empire in SE Africa. He seized power from his half brother 1816 and then embarked on a bloody military campaign to unite the Zulu clans. He was assassinated in 1828 by two half brothers.

Shaker popular name for a member of the Christian sect of the United Society of Believers in Christ's Second Appearing (and an offshoot of the ◊Quakers). This was founded by James and Jane Wardley in England about 1747 and taken to North America 1774 by Ann Lee (1736–84), the wife of a Manchester blacksmith, known as Mother Ann. She founded a colony in New York, and eventually 18 colonies existed in several states. Separation from the world in self-regulating farm communities, prescribed modes of simple dress and living conditions, celibacy, and faith healing characterized their way of life. The name was applied because of their ecstatic trembling and shaking during worship.

Mrs Lee held that God had appeared in his masculine aspect as Jesus and would appear a second time in a female aspect, which her followers identified with her. She held that sex is inherently sinful, and Shakers were forbidden to marry. New members were supplied to the colonies through conversion and adopting orphans, but by the 20th century their numbers steadily declined, and today there are only a few Shakers left. Shaker design became renowned for pleasing but austere simplicity.

Shakespeare William 1564–1616. English dramatist and poet. Established in London by 1589 as an actor and a playwright, he was England's unrivaled dramatist until his death, and is considered the greatest English playwright. His plays, written in blank verse, can be broadly divided into

Shakespeare *Portrait c. 1610, attributed to John Taylor, of William Shakespeare, England's greatest playwright.*

lyric plays, including ◊*Romeo and Juliet* and ◊*A Midsummer Night's Dream*; comedies, including *The Comedy of Errors, As You Like It, Much Ado About Nothing,* and *Measure For Measure*; historical plays, such as *Henry VI* (in three parts), *Richard III,* and *Henry IV* (in two parts), which often showed cynical political wisdom; and tragedies, such as ◊*Hamlet*, ◊*Macbeth*, and ◊*King Lear*. He also wrote numerous sonnets.

Born in Stratford-on-Avon, the son of a wool dealer, he was educated at the grammar school, and in 1582 married Anne Hathaway. They had a daughter, Susanna, in 1583, and twins Hamnet (died 1596) and Judith in 1595. Early plays, written around 1589–93, were the tragedy *Titus Andronicus*; the comedies *The Comedy of Errors, The Taming of the Shrew,* and *The Two Gentlemen of Verona*; the three parts of *Henry VI*; and *Richard III*. About 1593 he came under the patronage of the Earl of ◊Southampton, to whom he dedicated his long poems *Venus and Adonis* 1593 and *The Rape of Lucrece* 1594; he also wrote for him the comedy *Love's Labour's Lost*, satirizing ◊Raleigh's circle, and seems to have dedicated to him his sonnets written around 1593–96, in which the mysterious "Dark Lady" appears.

From 1594 Shakespeare was a member of the Chamberlain's (later the King's) company of players, and had no rival as a dramatist, writing, for example, the lyric plays *Romeo and Juliet, A Midsummer Night's Dream,* and *Richard II* 1594–95, followed by *King John* and *The Merchant of Venice* in 1596. The Falstaff plays of 1597–99—*Henry IV* (parts I and II), *Henry V*, and *The Merry Wives of Windsor* (said to have been written at the request of Elizabeth I)—brought his fame to its height. He wrote *Julius Caesar* 1599. The period ended with the lyrically witty *Much Ado about Nothing, As You Like It,* and *Twelfth Night* about 1598–1601.

With *Hamlet* begins the period of the great tragedies, 1601–08: *Othello, Macbeth, King Lear, Timon of Athens, Antony and Cleopatra,* and *Coriolanus*. This "darker" period is also reflected in the comedies *Troilus and Cressida, All's Well that Ends Well,* and *Measure for Measure* around 1601–04.

It is thought that Shakespeare was only part author of *Pericles*, which is grouped with the other plays of around 1608–11—*Cymbeline, The Winter's Tale,* and *The Tempest*—as the mature romance or "reconciliation" plays of the end of his career. During 1613 it is thought that Shakespeare collaborated with John Fletcher on *Henry VIII* and *Two Noble Kinsmen*. He had already retired to Stratford in about 1610, where he died on April 23, 1616.

Shakespeare: the plays

Title	*First Performed*
Early Plays	
Henry VI Part I	1589–92
Henry VI Part II	1589–92
Henry VI Part III	1589–92
The Comedy of Errors	1592–93
The Taming of the Shrew	1593–94
Titus Andronicus	1593–94
The Two Gentlemen of Verona	1594–95
Love's Labors Lost	1594–95
Romeo and Juliet	1594–95
Histories	
Richard III	1592–93
Richard II	1593–96
King John	1596–97
Henry IV Part I	1597–98
Henry IV Part II	1597–98
Henry V	1599
Roman Plays	
Julius Ceasar	1599–1600
Antony and Cleopatra	1607–08
Coriolanus	1607–08
The "Great" or "Middle" Comedies	
Midsummer Night's Dream	1595–96
The Merchant of Venice	1596–97
Much Ado About Nothing	1598–99
As You Like It	1599–1600
The Merry Wives of Windsor	1600–01
Twelfth Night	1601–02
The Great Tragedies	
Hamlet	1600–01
Othello	1604–05
King Lear	1605–06
Macbeth	1605–06
Timon of Athens	1607–08
The "Dark" Comedies	
Troilus and Cressida	1601–02
All's Well That Ends Well	1602–03
Measure for Measure	1604–05
Late Plays	
Pericles	1608–09
Cymbeline	1609–10
The Winter's Tale	1610–11
The Tempest	1611–12
Henry VIII	1612–13

Shakhty town in the Donbas region of the Russian Soviet Federal Socialist Republic, 50 mi/80 km NE of Rostov; population (1987) 225,000. Industries include anthracite mining, stone quarrying, textiles, leather, and metal goods. It was known as Aleksandrovsk Grushevskii until 1921.

shale a fine-grained and finely laminated ◊sedimentary rock composed of silt and clay that parts easily along bedding planes. It differs from mudstone in that the latter splits into flakes. Oil shale contains kerogen, a solid bituminous material that yields ◊petroleum when heated.

shallot small onion *Allium ascalonicum* in which bulbs are clustered like garlic; used for cooking and in pickles.

Shalmaneser five Assyrian kings including:

Shalmaneser III king of Assyria 859–824 BC who pursued an aggressive policy and brought Babylon and Israel under the domination of Assyria.

shaman a ritual leader, one who acts as intermediary between society and the supernatural world in many indigenous cultures of Asia, Africa, and the Americas. Also known as a medicine man, seer, or sorcerer, the shaman is expected to use white magic powers to cure illness and control good and evil spirits. The term is used for any tribal sorcerer or medicine man regardless of geography.

Shamir Yitzhak 1915– . Israeli politician, born in Poland; foreign minister under Menachem Begin 1980–83, prime minister 1983–84, and again foreign minister in the ◊Peres unity government

Shanghai *The commercial center of Shanghai, the largest city in China.*

from 1984. In Oct 1986, he and Peres exchanged positions, Shamir becoming prime minister and Peres taking over as foreign minister. He was reelected 1989 and formed a new coalition government with Peres 1990. Shamir was a leader of the ◊Stern Gang of guerrillas (1940–48) during the British mandate rule of Palestine.

shamrock any of several trifoliate ◊clovers and cloverlike plants of the family Leguminosae. One is said to have been used by St Patrick to illustrate the doctrine of the Holy Trinity, and it was made the national badge of Ireland.

Shan a member of a people of the mountainous borderlands separating Thailand, Myanmar (Burma), and China. They are related to the Laos and Thais, and their language belongs to the Sino-Tibetan family.

Shandong or ***Shantung*** province of NE China
area 59,174 sq mi/153,300 sq km
capital Jinan
cities ports: Yantai, Weihai, Qingdao, Shigiusuo
features crossed by the Huang He River and the ◊Grand Canal; Shandong Peninsula
products cereals, cotton, wild silk, varied minerals
population (1986) 77,760,000

Shanghai port on the Huang-pu and Wusong rivers, Jiangsu province, China, 15 mi/24 km from the Chang Jiang estuary; population (1986) 6,980,000, the largest city in China. The municipality of Shanghai has an area of 2,239 sq mi/5,800 sq km and a population of 12,320,000. Industries include textiles, paper, chemicals, steel, agricultural machinery, precision instruments, shipbuilding, flour and vegetable-oil milling, and oil refining. It handles about 50% of China's imports and exports.

Shanghai is reckoned to be the most heavily populated area in the world with an average of 65 sq ft/6 sq m of living space and 2.6 sq yd/2.2 sq m of road per person.

features Notable buildings include the Jade Buddha Temple 1882, the former home of the revolutionary ◊Sun Yat-sen, the house where the First National Congress of the Communist Party of China met secretly in 1921, and the house, museum, and tomb of the writer Lu Xun.

history Shanghai was a city from 1360 but became significant only after 1842, when the treaty of Nanking opened it to foreign trade. The international settlement then developed, which remained the commercial center of the city after the departure of European interests 1943–46.

Shankar Ravi 1920– . Indian composer and musician. A virtuoso of the ◊sitar, he has composed film music and founded music schools in Bombay and Los Angeles.

Shankara 799–833. Hindu philosopher who wrote commentaries on some of the major Hindu scriptures, as well as hymns and essays on religious ideas. Shankara was responsible for the final form of the Advaita Vedanta school of Hindu philosophy, which teaches that Brahman, the supreme being, is all that exists in the universe, everything else is illusion. Shankara was fiercely opposed to Buddhism and may have influenced its decline in India.

Shannon longest river in Ireland, rising in County Cavan and flowing 240 mi/386 km through Loughs Allen and Ree and past Athlone, to reach the Atlantic through a wide estuary below Limerick. It is also the major source of electric power in the republic, with hydroelectric installations at and above Ardnacrusha, 3 mi/5 km N of Limerick.

Shannon Claude Elwood 1916– . US mathematician whose paper *The Mathematical Theory of Communication* 1948 marks the beginning of the science of information theory. He argued that information data and ◊entropy are analogous, and obtained a quantitive measure of the amount of information in a given message.

Shansi alternative transliteration of the Chinese province of ◊Shanxi.

Shantou or ***Swatow*** port and industrial city in SE China; population (1970) 400,000. It was opened as a special foreign trade area 1979.

Shantung alternative transliteration of the Chinese province of ◊Shandong.

Shanxi or ***Shansi*** province of NE China
area 60,641 sq mi/157,100 sq km
capital Taiyuan
features a drought-ridden plateau, partly surrounded by the ◊Great Wall
products coal, iron, fruit
population (1986) 26,550,000
history saw the outbreak of the Boxer Rebellion 1900.

Shaoshan the birthplace in the Chinese province of Hunan of the Communist leader ◊Mao Zedong.

SHAPE abbreviation for Supreme Headquarters Allied Powers Europe, situated near Mons, Belgium, and the headquarters of NATO's Supreme Allied Commander Europe (SACEUR).

Shapiro Karl 1913– . US poet. He was born in Baltimore, and his work includes the striking *V Letter* 1945, written after service in World War II. Later volumes of poetry include *Poems of a Jew* 1958. He has also written numerous critical works.

Shapley Harlow 1885–1972. US astronomer, whose study of ◊globular clusters showed that they were arranged in a halo around the Galaxy and that the Galaxy was much larger than previously thought. He realized that the Sun was not at the center of the Galaxy as then assumed, but two-thirds of the way out to the rim. Shapley joined the Mount Wilson Observatory, California, 1914.

Shari'a the law of ◊Islam believed by Muslims to be based on divine revelation, and drawn from a number of sources, including the Koran, the Hadith, and the consensus of the Muslim community. From the latter part of the 19th century, the role of the Shari'a courts in the majority of Muslim countries began to be taken over by secular courts, and the Shari'a to be largely restricted to family law.

Sharif Omar. Adopted name of Michael Shalhoub 1932– . Egyptian-born actor (of Lebanese parents) who was Egypt's top male star before breaking into international films after his successful appearance in *Lawrence of Arabia* 1962. His other films include *Dr Zhivago* 1965, *Funny Girl* 1968, and *Funny Lady* 1975.

Sharjah or ***Shariqah*** third largest of the seven member states of the ◊United Arab Emirates, situated on the Arabian Gulf NE of Dubai; area 1,004 sq mi/2,600 sq km; population (1985) 269,000. Since 1952 it has included the small state of Kalba. In 1974 oil was discovered offshore. Industries include ship repair, cement, paint, and metal products.

shark any of various orders of cartilaginous fishes (class Chondrichthyes), found thoughout the oceans of the world. They have tough, usually gray, skin covered in denticles (small toothlike scales). A shark's streamlined body has side pectoral fins, a high dorsal fin, and a forked tail with a large upper lobe. Five open gill slits are visible on each side of the generally pointed head. Most sharks are fish-eaters, and a few will attack humans. They range from several feet in length to the great white shark *Carcharodon carcharias*, 30 ft/9 m long, and the harmless plankton-feeding whale shark *Rhincodon typus*, over 50 ft/15 m in length.

shark

great white shark

Relatively few attacks on humans lead to fatalities, and research suggests that the attacking sharks are not searching for food, but attempting to repel "rivals" from their territory. Game fishing for "sport," the eradication of sharks in swimming and recreation areas, and their industrial exploitation as a source of leather, oil, and protein have reduced their numbers.

Sharon coastal plain in Israel between Haifa and Tel Aviv, and a subdistrict of Central district; area 134 sq mi/348 sq km; population (1983) 190,400. It has been noted since ancient times for its fertility.

Sharon city in W Pennsylvania on the Shenango river, N of Pittsburgh, near the Ohio border. Industries include steel products and electronics; population (1990) 17,493.

Sharpeville black township in South Africa, 40 mi/65 km S of Johannesburg and N of Vereeniging; 69 people were killed here when police fired on a crowd of antiapartheid demonstrators on March 21, 1960.

The massacre took place during a campaign launched by the Pan-Africanist Congress against the pass laws (laws requiring nonwhite South Africans to carry identity papers). On the anniversary of the massacre in 1985, during funerals of people who had been killed protesting against unemployment, 19 people were shot by the police at Langa near Port Elizabeth.

Sharpey-Schäfer Edward Albert 1850–1935. English physiologist and one of the founders of endocrinology. He made important discoveries relating to the hormone ◊adrenaline, and to the ◊pituitary and other ◊endocrine, or ductless, glands.

Shasta, Mount dormant volcano rising to a height of 14,162 ft/4,317 m in the Cascade Range, N California.

Shastri Lal Bahadur 1904–1966. Indian politician, prime minister 1964–66. He campaigned for national integration, and secured a declaration of peace with Pakistan at the Tashkent peace conference 1966.

Before independence, he was imprisoned several times for civil disobedience. Because of his small stature, he was known as "the Sparrow."

Shatt-al-Arab (Persian *Arvand*) the waterway formed by the confluence of the rivers ◊Euphrates and ◊Tigris; length 120 mi/190 km to the Persian Gulf. Basra, Khorramshahr, and Abadan stand on it.

Its lower reaches form a border of disputed demarcation between Iran and Iraq. In 1975 the two countries agreed on the deepest water line as the frontier, but Iraq repudiated this 1980; the dispute was a factor in the Iran–Iraq war 1980–88.

Shaw George Bernard 1856–1950. Irish dramatist. He was also a critic and novelist, and an early member of the Socialist ◊Fabian Society. His plays combine comedy with political, philosophical, and polemic aspects, aiming to make an impact on his audience's social conscience as well as their emotions. They include *Arms and the Man* 1894, *Devil's Disciple* 1897, *Man and Superman* 1905, *Pygmalion* 1913, and *St Joan* 1924. Nobel prize 1925.

Born in Dublin, the son of a civil servant, Shaw

came to London in 1876, where he became a brilliant debater and supporter of the Fabians, and worked as a music and drama critic. He wrote five unsuccessful novels before his first play, *Widowers' Houses*, was produced in 1892. Attacking slum landlords, it allied him with the realistic, political, and polemical movement in the theater, pointing to people's responsibility to improve themselves and their social environment.

The volume *Plays: Pleasant and Unpleasant* 1898 also included *The Philanderer*; *Mrs Warren's Profession*, dealing with prostitution and banned until 1902, and *Arms and the Man* about war. *Three Plays for Puritans* 1901 contained *The Devil's Disciple*, *Caesar and Cleopatra* (a companion piece to the play by Shakespeare), and *Captain Brassbound's Conversion*, written for the actress Ellen ◊Terry. *Man and Superman* 1903 expounds his ideas of evolution by following the character of Don Juan into hell for a debate with the devil.

The "antiromantic" comedy *Pygmalion*, first performed 1913, was written for the actress Mrs Patrick ◊Campbell (and later converted to a musical as *My Fair Lady*). Later plays included *Heartbreak House* 1917, *Back to Methuselah* 1921, and the historical *St Joan* 1924.

Altogether Shaw wrote more than 50 plays and became a byword for wit. His theories were further explained in the voluminous prefaces to the plays, and in books such as *The Intelligent Woman's Guide to Socialism and Capitalism* 1928. He was also an unsuccessful advocate of spelling reform and a prolific letter-writer.

shawm in music, an early form of oboe.

Shays Daniel c. 1747–1825. American political agitator. Born in W Massachusetts, Shays served in the 5th Massachusetts Regiment during the American Revolution, seeing action at the battles of Bunker Hill, Ticonderoga, and Saratoga. Returning to civilian life 1780, Shays led an armed uprising of hard-pressed farmers 1786 against the refusal of the state government to offer economic relief. Shays' Rebellion was suppressed 1787 by a Massachusetts militia force, but its effect within the state was to turn public attention to the plight of the western farmers, and on a national level it underlined the need for a stronger central government.

Shchedrin N. Adopted name of Mikhail Evgrafovich Saltykov 1826–1889. Russian writer whose works include *Fables* 1884–85, in which he depicts misplaced "good intentions," and the novel *The Golovlevs* 1880. He was a satirist of pessimistic outlook.

He was exiled for seven years for an early story that proved too liberal for the authorities, but later held official posts.

Shearer (Edith) Norma 1900–1983. Canadian-born US actress who starred in silent films and in talkies such as *Private Lives* 1931, *Romeo and Juliet* 1936, *Marie Antoinette* 1938, and *The Women* 1939. She was married to MGM executive Irving Thalberg and retired after *Her Cardboard Lover* 1942.

shearwater any sea bird of the genus *Puffinus*, in the same family (Procellariidae) as the diving ◊petrels.

The sooty shearwater *P. griseus* is common on both North Atlantic coasts.

sheath another name for a ◊condom.

Sheba ancient name for south ◊Yemen (Sha'abijah). It was once renowned for gold and spices. According to the Old Testament, its queen visited Solomon; until 1975 the Ethiopian royal house traced its descent from their union.

Sheboygan city in E Wisconsin, on Lake Michigan, N of Milwaukee. Industries include wood, food, plastic, and enamel products; population (1990) 49,676.

Shechem ancient town in Palestine, capital of Samaria. In the Old Testament, it is the traditional burial place of Joseph; nearby is Jacob's well. Shechem was destroyed about AD 67 by the Roman emperor Vespasian; on its site stands Nablus (a corruption of Neapolis) built by the Roman emperor ◊Hadrian.

Sheeler Charles 1883–1965. US painter. Born in Philadelphia, he was associated with precisionism, a movement that used sharply defined shapes to represent objects. He is best known for his paintings of factories and urban landscapes (for example, *American Landscape* 1930). His style was to photograph his subjects before painting them.

sheep any of various ruminant, even-toed, hoofed mammals of the family Bovidae. Wild species survive in the uplands of central and eastern Asia, North Africa, southern Europe, and North America. The domesticated breeds are all classified as *Ovis aries* and are descended from wild sheep of the Neolithic Near East. The original species may be extinct but was probably closely related to the surviving mouflon *O. musimom* of Sardinia and Corsica. Various breeds of sheep are reared worldwide for meat, wool, milk, and cheese, and for rotation on arable land to maintain its fertility.

Only a small proportion of European and North American breeds are still in full commercial use. Among those, the Rambouillet breed is used extensively in the US for its fine wool, and the Columbia is a popular meat-producing breed.

sheepdog any of several breeds of dog, bred originally for herding sheep. The Old English sheepdog is gray or blue-gray, with white markings, and is about 22 in/56 cm tall at the shoulder. The Shetland sheepdog is much smaller, 36 cm/14 in tall, and shaped more like a long-coated collie. Sheepdogs were fomerly used by shepherds and farmers to tend sheep. Border collies are now used for this job.

Sheffield industrial city on the river Don, South Yorkshire, England; population (1986) 538,700. From the 12th century, iron smelting was the chief industry, and by the 14th century, Sheffield cutlery, silverware, and plate were made. During the Industrial Revolution the iron and steel industries developed rapidly. It now produces alloys and special steels, cutlery of all kinds, permanent magnets, drills, and precision tools. Other industries include electroplating, type-founding, and the manufacture of optical glass.

sheik the leader or chief of an Arab family or village.

Shelburne William Petty FitzMaurice, 2nd Earl of 1737–1805. British Whig politician. He was an opponent of George III's American policy, and as prime minister in 1783, he concluded peace with the United States of America.

shelduck duck *Tadorna tadorna* with a dark green head and red bill, with the rest of the plumage strikingly marked in black, white, and chestnut. Widely distributed in Europe and Asia, it lays 10–12 white eggs in rabbit burrows on sandy coasts, and is usually seen on estuary mudflats.

shelf sea relatively shallow sea, usually no deeper than 650 ft/200 m, overlying the continental shelf around the coastlines. Most fishing and marine mineral exploitations are carried out in shelf seas.

shellac a resin derived from secretions of the ◊lac insect.

Shelley Mary Wollstonecraft 1797–1851. English writer, the daughter of Mary Wollstonecraft and William Godwin. In 1814 she eloped with the poet Percy Bysshe Shelley, whom she married in 1816. Her novels include ◊*Frankenstein* 1818, *The Last Man* 1826, and *Valperga* 1823.

Shelley Percy Bysshe 1792–1822. English lyric poet, a leading figure in the Romantic movement. Expelled from Oxford university for atheism, he fought all his life against religion and for political freedom. This is reflected in his early poems such as *Queen Mab* 1813. He later wrote tragedies including *The Cenci* 1818, lyric dramas such as *Prometheus Unbound* 1820, and lyrical poems such as "Ode to the West Wind."

Born near Horsham, Sussex, he was educated at Eton school and University College, Oxford, where his collaboration in a pamphlet *The Necessity of Atheism* 1811 caused his expulsion. While

***Shelley** English poet Percy Bysshe Shelley, who eloped to Switzerland with Mary Wollstonecraft, died by drowning in a sailing accident.*

living in London he fell in love with 16-year-old Harriet Westbrook, whom he married 1811. He visited Ireland and Wales, writing pamphlets defending vegetarianism and political freedom, and in 1813 published privately *Queen Mab*, a poem with political freedom as its theme. Meanwhile he had become estranged from his wife and in 1814 left England with Mary Wollstonecraft Godwin, whom he married after Harriet drowned herself 1816. *Alastor*, written 1815, was followed by the epic *The Revolt of Islam*, and by 1818 Shelley was living in Italy. Here he produced the tragedy *The Cenci*; the satire on Wordsworth, *Peter Bell the Third* 1819; and the lyric drama *Prometheus Unbound* 1820. Other works of the period are "Ode to the West Wind" 1819; "The Cloud" and "The Skylark," both 1820; "The Sensitive Plant" and "The Witch of Atlas"; "Epipsychidion" and, on the death of the poet Keats, "Adonais" 1821; the lyric drama *Hellas* 1822; and the prose *Defence of Poetry* 1821. In July 1822 Shelley was drowned while sailing near La Spezia, and his ashes were buried in Rome.

shellfish popular name for mollusks, crustaceans, including the whelk, periwinkle, mussel, oyster, lobster, crab, and shrimp.

shell shock or ***combat neurosis*** or ***battle fatigue*** any of the various forms of mental disorder that affect soldiers exposed to heavy explosions or extreme ◊stress. Shell shock was first diagnosed during World War I.

Following the Vietnam War, many veterans were found to be suffering from post-traumatic shock-syndrome, in which recurring "flashbacks" to combat experiences torment the sufferer.

Shema in Judaism, prayer from the Torah, recited by orthodox men every morning and evening, which affirms the special relationship of the Jews with God.

It begins with the Hebrew for "Hear, O Israel, the Lord our God, the Lord is One."

Shenandoah river in Virginia 55 mi/89 km long, a tributary of the Potomac, which it joins at Harper's Ferry, West Virginia. The river is not navigable but has several hydroelectric facilities, and the Shenandoah valley is one of the nation's main apple-growing regions. In the Civil War, Union general Philip Sheridan laid waste to the valley 1864–65.

Shensi former name for the Chinese province of ◊Shanxi.

Shenyang industrial city and capital of Liaoning province, China; population (1986) 4,200,000. It was the capital of the Manchu emperors 1644–1912.

Their tombs are nearby. Historically known as Mukden, it was taken from Russian occupation by the Japanese in the Battle of Mukden Feb 20–March 10, 1905, and was again taken by the Japanese 1931.

Shenzen a Special Economic Zone established in 1980 opposite Hong Kong on the coast of Guangdong province, S China. Its status provided much of the driving force of its spectacular development in the 1980s when its population rose from 20,000 in 1980 to 600,000 in 1989. Part of the population is "rotated" newcomers from other provinces who return to their homes after a few years spent learning foreign business techniques.

Shepard Alan Bartlett, Jr 1923– . US astronaut. He undertook the first crewed US space flight, the suborbital *Mercury-Redstone 3* mission on board the *Freedom 7* capsule May 1961, and commanded the *Apollo 14* lunar landing mission 1971. Born in East Derry, New Hampshire, he graduated 1944 from the US Naval Academy at Annapolis and served as a fighter pilot, test pilot, and aircraft-readiness officer for the Atlantic fleet before becoming an astronaut.

Shepard Sam 1943– . US dramatist and actor. His work combines colloquial American dialogue with striking visual imagery, and includes *The Tooth of Crime* 1972 and *Buried Child* 1978, for which he won the Pulitzer Prize. *Seduced* 1979 is based on the life of the recluse Howard Hughes. He has acted in a number of films, including *The Right Stuff* 1983, *Fool for Love* 1986, based on his play of the same name, and *Steel Magnolias* 1989.

shepherd's purse annual plant *Capsella bursa-pastoris* of the Cruciferae family, distributed worldwide in temperate zones. It is a persistent weed with white flowers followed by heart-shaped, seed-containing pouches from which its name derives.

Sheraton Thomas c. 1751–1806. English designer of elegant inlaid furniture. He was influenced by his predecessors ◊Hepplewhite and ◊Chippendale.

Sheridan Philip Henry 1831–1888. Union general in the American ◊Civil War. Recognizing Sheridan's aggressive spirit, General Ulysses S ◊Grant gave him command of his cavalry in 1864, and soon after of the Army of the Shenandoah Valley, Virgina. Sheridan laid waste to the valley, cutting off grain supplies to the Confederate armies. In the final stage of the war, Sheridan forced General Robert E ◊Lee to retreat to Appomattox and surrender.

Born in Albany, New York, Sheridan graduated from West Point 1853. Following the war, Sheridan led troops at the Mexican border and hastened the collapse of the regime of Emperor Maximilian. Sheridan served as military governor of Texas and Louisiana during ◊Reconstruction; his policies were so harsh that he was removed by President Andrew ◊Johnson. He was made general in chief of the US army 1883–88.

Sheridan Richard Brinsley 1751–1816. Irish dramatist and politician, born in Dublin. His social comedies include *The Rivals* 1775, celebrated for the character of Mrs Malaprop, *The School for Scandal* 1777, and *The Critic* 1779. In 1776 he became lessee of the Drury Lane Theatre. He became a member of Parliament in 1780.

sheriff (Old English *scīr* "shire," *gerēfa* "reeve") in the US, in all states but Rhode Island, the chief elected officer of a county law-enforcement agency, usually responsible for enforcement in unincorporated areas of the county and for the operation of the jail. The sheriff is also the officer of the local court who serves papers and enforces court orders.

Sherman city in NE Texas, N of Dallas. It is a processing and shipping center for agricultural products; textiles, electronics, and machinery are manufactured; population (1990) 31,601.

Sherman Roger 1721–1793. American public official; signer of the Declaration of Independence, Articles of Confederation, and US Constitution. After service in Connecticut's provincial legislature, he became superior court judge 1766–85. A supporter of American independence, he was a member of the Continental Congress 1774–81 and 1783–84. As a delegate to the Constitutional Convention 1787, he introduced the "Connecticut Compromise" that provided for a bicameral federal legislature. Sherman served in the US House of Representatives 1789–91 and Senate 1791–93.

Born in Newton, Massachusetts, Sherman moved to Connecticut 1743. He later studied law and was admitted to the bar 1754.

Sherman William Tecumseh 1820–1891. Union general in the American ◊Civil War. In 1864 he captured and burned Atlanta; continued his march eastward, to the sea, laying Georgia waste; and then drove the Confederates northward. He was US Army chief of staff 1869–83.

Born in Lancaster, Ohio, Sherman graduated from West Point 1840. He served in the Mexican War and then became a banker. Early in the Civil War he served at the First Battle of Bull Run 1861 and Shiloh 1862. He replaced General U S ◊Grant as commander of the West 1864 and launched his Georgia campaign. Despite the ruthlessness of his campaign to capture Atlanta and the widespread destruction he inflicted as he marched to the sea, he was conciliatory in victory, offering terms that had to be repudiated by President A Johnson. Following the war, there was a move to nominate Sherman for president, but he announced that he would not run if nominated and would not serve if elected. He succeeded Grant as commander of the army 1869.

Sherman Anti-Trust Act in US history, an act of Congress 1890, named after senator John Sherman (1823–1900) of Ohio, designed to prevent powerful corporations from monopolizing industries and restraining trade for their own benefit. Relatively few prosecutions of such trusts were successful under the act.

Sherpa member of a people in NE Nepal related to the Tibetans and renowned for their mountaineering skill. They frequently work as support staff and guides for climbing expeditions. A Sherpa, Tensing Norgay, was one of the first two men to climb to the summit of Everest.

Sherrington Charles Scott 1857–1952. English neurophysiologist, who studied the structure and function of the nervous system. *The Integrative Action of the Nervous System* 1906 formulated the principles of reflex action. Nobel Prize for Medicine (with E D ◊Adrian) 1932.

's-Hertogenbosch (French *Bois-le-Duc*) capital of North Brabant, the Netherlands, on the river Meuse, 28 mi/45 km SE of Utrecht; population (1988) 193,000. It has a Gothic cathedral and was the birthplace of the painter Hieronymus Bosch.

Sherwood Robert 1896–1955. US dramatist. His plays include *The Petrified Forest* 1934, *Idiot's Delight* 1936, *Abe Lincoln in Illinois* 1938, and *There Shall Be No Night* 1940. For each of the last three he received a Pulitzer prize.

A member of the ◊Algonquin Round Table, Sherwood worked as a magazine editor during the 1920s. Later he became Franklin Roosevelt's speechwriter and adviser and held various political offices. After World War II he produced little important theatrical material except for the Academy Award-winning film *The Best Years of Our Lives* 1946.

Sherwood Forest a hilly stretch of woodland in W Nottinghamshire, England, area about 200 sq mi/520 sq km. Formerly a royal forest, it is associated with the legendary outlaw ◊Robin Hood.

Shetland Islands islands off N coast of Scotland
area 541 sq mi/1,400 sq km
towns Lerwick (administrative headquarters), on Mainland, largest of 19 inhabited islands
physical over 100 islands including Muckle Flugga (latitude 60° 51′ N) the northernmost of the British Isles
products processed fish, handknits from Fair Isle and Unst, miniature ponies. Europe's largest oil port is Sullom Voe, Mainland
population (1987) 22,000
language dialect derived from Norse, the islands having been a Norse dependency from the 8th century until 1472.

Shevardnadze Edvard 1928– . Soviet politician, foreign minister from 1985. A supporter of ◊Gorbachev, he was first secretary of the Georgian Communist Party from 1972 and an advocate of economic reform. In 1985 he became foreign minister and a member of the Politburo and worked for détente and disarmament. In late 1990 he announced his intention to resign in an unexpected and unusually outspoken attack on the Soviet leadership, and he left office in Jan 1991, only to return to office later in the year.

SHF in physics, the abbreviation for superhigh ◊frequency.

Shiah or ***Shiite*** member of one of the two main sects of ◊Islam.

Shidehara Kijuro 1872–1951. Japanese politician and diplomat, prime minister 1945–46. As foreign minister 1924–27 and 1929–31, he promoted conciliation with China, and economic rather than military expansion. After a brief period as prime minister 1945–46, he became speaker of the Japanese Diet (parliament) 1946–51.

shield in geology, alternate name for ◊craton.

shield in technology, any material used to reduce the amount of radiation (electrostatic, electromagnetic, heat, nuclear) reaching from one region of space to another, or any material used as a protection against falling debris, as in tunneling. Electrical conductors are used for electrostatic shields, soft iron for electromagnetic shields, and poor conductors of heat for heat shields. Heavy materials such as lead and concrete are used for protection against X rays and nuclear radiation. See also ◊biological shield, and ◊heat shield.

Shihchiachuang alternative transliteration of the city of ◊Shijiazhuang in China.

Shi Huangdi or ***Shih Huang Ti*** 259–210 BC. Emperor of China. He succeeded to the throne of the state of Qin in 246 BC and reunited the country as an empire by 228 BC. He burned almost all existing books in 213 BC to destroy ties with the past; rebuilt the ◊Great Wall; and was buried at Xian in a tomb complex guarded by 10,000 life-size terracotta warriors (excavated by archeologists in the 1980s).

He had so overextended his power that the dynasty and the empire collapsed with the death of his weak successor in 207 BC.

Shiite or ***Shiah*** member of a sect of ◊Islam who believe that ◊Ali was ◊Mohammed's first true successor. They are doctrinally opposed to the ◊Sunni Muslims. Holy men have greater authority in the Shiite sect than in the Sunni sect. They are prominent in Iran and Lebanon and are also found in Iraq and Bahrain. Breakaway subsects include the Alawite sect, to which the ruling party in Syria belongs; and the Ismaili sect, with the ◊Aga Khan IV (1936–) as its spiritual head.

Shijiazhuang or ***Shihchiachuang*** city and major railroad junction in Hebei province, China; population (1986) 1,160,000. Industries include textiles, chemicals, printing, and light engineering.

Shikoku smallest of the four main islands of Japan, S of Honshu, E of Kyushu; area 7,257 sq mi/18,800 sq km; population (1986) 4,226,000; chief town Matsuyama. Products include rice, wheat, soybeans, sugar cane, orchard fruits, salt, and copper.

It has a mild climate, and annual rainfall in the S can reach 105 in/266 cm. The highest point is Mount Ishizuchi (6,498 ft/1,980 m). A suspension bridge links Shikoku to Awajishima Island over the Naruto whirlpool in the Seto Naikai (Inland Sea).

Shillong capital of Meghalaya state, NE India; population (1981) 109,244. It was the former capital of Assam.

Shimonoseki seaport in the extreme SW of Honshu, Japan; population (1985) 269,000. It was opened to foreign trade 1890. The first of the ◊Sino-Japanese Wars ended with a treaty signed at Shimonoseki 1895. Industries include fishing, shipbuilding, engineering, textiles, and chemicals.

shingles common name for ◊herpes zoster, a disease characterized by infection of sensory nerves, with pain and eruption of blisters along the course of the affected nerves.

Shinkansen (Japanese "new trunk line") the fast railroad network operated by Japanese Railways, on which the bullet trains run. The network, opened 1964, uses specially built straight and level track, on which average speeds of 100 mph/160 kph are attained.

The Shinkansen between Tokyo and Osaka carried 270,000 passengers a day by 1990.

Shinto the indigenous religion of Japan. It combines an empathetic oneness with natural forces and loyalty to the reigning dynasty as descendants of the Sun goddess, Amaterasu-Omikami. Traditional Shinto followers stressed obedience and devotion to the emperor, and an aggressive nationalistic aspect was developed by the Meiji rulers. Today Shinto has discarded these aspects.

Shinto is the Chinese transliteration of the Japanese Kami-no-Michi, the Way or Doctrine of the Gods. Its holiest shrine is at Ise, near Kyoto, where in the temple of the Sun Goddess is preserved the mirror that she is supposed to have given to Jimmu, the first emperor, in the 7th century BC. Sectarian Shinto consists of 130 sects; the sects are officially recognized but not state-supported (as was state Shinto until its disestablishment after World War II and Emperor Hirohito's disavowal of his divinity 1946).

ship large seagoing vessel. The ancient Chinese, Japanese, Greeks, Phoenicians, Romans, and Vikings used ships extensively for trade, exploration, and warfare. The 14th century was the era of European seafaring exploration by sailing ship, largely aided by the invention of the compass. In the 15th century Britain's Royal Navy was first formed, but in the 16th–19th centuries the Spanish and Dutch fleets dominated the shipping lanes of both the Atlantic and Pacific. The ultimate sailing ships, the fast US and British tea clippers, were built in the 19th century. Also in the 19th century, iron was first used for some shipbuilding instead of wood. Steam-propelled ships of the late 19th century were followed by compound engine and turbine-propelled vessels from the early 20th century.

The Chinese, Japanese, Greeks and Phoenicians built wooden ships, propelled by oar or sail. The Romans and Carthaginians built war galleys equipped with rams and several tiers of rowers. The oak ships of the Vikings were built for rough seas and propelled by oars and sail. The Crusader fleet of Richard the Lion-Hearted was largely of sail. The invention of the compass in the 14th century led to exploration by sailing ship, especially by the Portuguese, resulting in the discovery of "new worlds." In the 15th Henry VIII built the *Great Harry*, the first double-decked English warship. In the 16th century ships were short and high-sterned. In the 1840s iron began replacing wood in shipbuilding, pioneered by ◊Brunel's *Great Britain* 1845.

The US and Britain experimented with steam propulsion as the 19th century opened. The paddle-wheel-propelled *Comet* appeared 1812, the Canadian *Royal William* crossed the Atlantic 1833, and the English *Great Western* steamed from Bristol to New York 1838. Pettit Smith first used the screw propeller in the *Archimedes* 1839, and after 1850 the paddle wheel was used mainly on inland waterways, especially the great rivers of the Americas. The introduction of the compound engine and turbine (the latter 1902) completed the revolution in propulsion until the advent of nuclear-powered vessels after World War II, chiefly submarines (which are considered boats, not ships). More recently ◊hovercraft and ◊hydrofoil boats have been developed for specialized purposes, such as short-distance ferries. Sailing ships in automated form for cargo purposes, and ◊maglev ships, are also planned.

Shiraz ancient walled city of S Iran, the capital of Fars province; population (1986) 848,000. It is known for its wines, carpets, and silverwork and for its many mosques.

shire an administrative area formed in Britain for the purpose of raising taxes in Anglo-Saxon times. By AD 1000 most of southern England had been divided in Shires with fortified strongholds at their centers. The Midland counties of England are still known as The Shires; for example Derbyshire, Nottinghamshire, and Staffordshire.

Shiré Highlands an upland area of S Malawi, E of the Shiré River; height up to 5,800 ft/1,750 m. Tea and tobacco are grown there.

Shirer William L(awrence) 1904– . US journalist and historian. From 1937 to 1941, Shirer worked with E R ◊Murrow covering the events leading up to the outbreak of World War II for the Columbia Broadcasting System (CBS). He remained a columnist and commentator for CBS until 1947 and for the Mutual Broadcasting System 1947–49. His best-known book is *The Rise and Fall of the Third Reich* 1960. Other works include *The Nightmare Years: 1930–1940* 1984.

Born in Chicago, Shirer was educated at Coe College and joined the Paris bureau of the *Chicago Tribune* 1926. Traveling widely throughout Europe, he joined the Paris staff of the *New York Herald Tribune* 1934.

Shizuoka city in Chubo region, Honshu, Japan; population (1985) 468,000. Industries include metal and food processing and especially tea.

Shkodër (Italian *Scutari*) town on the river Bojana, NW Albania, SE of Lake Shkodër, 12 mi/19 km from the Adriatic; population (1983) 71,000. Products include woolens and cement. During World War I it was occupied by Austria 1916–18, and during World War II by Italy.

shock in medicine, circulatory failure marked by a sudden fall of blood pressure and resulting in pallor, sweating, fast (but weak) pulse, and sometimes complete collapse. Causes include disease, injury, and psychological trauma.

In shock, the blood vessels dilate and the pressure falls below that necessary to supply the tissues of the body, especially the brain. Treatment depends on the cause. Rest is needed, and, in the case of severe blood loss, restoration of the normal circulating volume.

shock absorber in technology, any device for absorbing the shock of sudden jarring actions or movements. Shock absorbers are used in conjunction with coil springs in most motor-vehicle suspension systems and are usually of the telescopic type, consisting of a piston in an oil-filled cylinder. The resistance to movement of the piston through the oil creates the absorbing effect.

Shockley William 1910–1989. US physicist and amateur geneticist, who worked with John ◊Bardeen and Walter ◊Brattain on the invention of the ◊transistor. They were jointly awarded a Nobel Prize 1956. During the 1970s Shockley was severely criticized for his claim that blacks were genetically inferior to whites in terms of intelligence.

He donated his sperm to the bank in S California established by the plastic-lens millionaire Robert Graham for the passing on of the genetic code of geniuses.

shoebill or ***whale-headed stork*** large, gray, long-legged, swamp-dwelling African bird *Balaeniceps rex*. Up to 5 ft/1.5 m tall, it has a large wide beak 8 in/20 cm long, with which it scoops fish, mollusks, reptiles, and carrion out of the mud.

Shoemaker Willie (William Lee) 1931– . US jockey, whose career 1949–90 was outstandingly successful. He rode 8,833 winners from 40,351 mounts and his earnings exceeded $123 million. He retired Feb 3, 1990 after finishing 4th on Patchy Groundfog at Santa Anita, California.

He was the leading US jockey 10 times. After his retirement he became a successful trainer before an automobile accident 1991 left him paralyzed.

CAREER HIGHLIGHTS

US Triple Crown wins:
Kentucky Derby: 1955, 1959, 1965, 1986
Preakness Stakes: 1963, 1967
Belmont Stakes: 1957, 1959, 1962, 1967, 1975
Leading US money winner: 1951, 1953–54, 1958–64

shofar in Judaism, a ram's horn blown in the synagogue as a call to repentance at the new-year festivals of Rosh Hashanah and Yom Kippur.

shogi Japanese board game. It probably derives from the same Indian sources as chess, but is more complex.

shogun in Japanese history, the hereditary commander in chief of the army. Though nominally subject to the emperor (Mikado) and acting in his name, the shoguns–by successive usurpations of power–became the real rulers of Japan from 1192 to 1868, when the emperor resumed power, feudalism was abolished, and the ◊samurai pensioned off.

Shogun is an abbreviation of the official title *Seii-Tai-Shōgun* ("barbarian-subduing commander"), first given to an imperial guard for his subugation of the Ainu people 794. Yoritomo Minamoto (died 1199) seized power 1185 and was granted the title 1192. From then on shoguns were military dictators of the Minamoto or Fujiwara clan; the Tokugawa shogunate took over 1603–1867.

Sholapur town in Maharashtra state, India; population (1981) 514,860. Industries include textiles, leather goods, and chemicals.

Sholokhov Mikhail Aleksandrovich 1905–1984. Soviet novelist. His *And Quiet Flows the Don* 1926–40 depicts the Don Cossacks through World War I and the Russian Revolution. Nobel Prize 1965.

Shona member of a S African Bantu-speaking people, comprising approximately 80% of the population of Zimbabwe. They also occupy the land between the Save and Pungure rivers in Mozambique, and smaller groups are found in South Africa, Botswana, and Zambia. The Shona language belongs to the Niger-Congo family.

shoot in botany, a general term for parts of a ◊vascular plant growing above ground, comprising a stem bearing leaves, buds, and flowers. The shoot develops from the ◊plumule of the embryo.

short circuit direct connection between two points in an electrical circuit. Its relatively low resistance means that a large current flows through it, bypassing the rest of the circuit, and this may cause the circuit to overheat dangerously.

shorthand any system of rapid writing, such as the abbreviations practiced by the Greeks and Romans. The first perfecter of an entirely phonetic system was Isaac ◊Pitman, by which system speeds of about 300 words a minute are said to be attainable.

The earliest shorthand system to be based on the alphabet was that of John Willis published 1603. Later alphabetic systems in England were devised by Thomas Shelton 1630 (used by the diarist Pepys) and Thomas Burney 1750, used by novelist Charles Dickens as a reporter. In the US, the most popular system is that of Irish-born John Robert Gregg (1867–1948) 1888.

Stenotype machines, using selective keyboards enabling several word contractions to be printed at a time, are equally speedy and accurate. Abbreviations used can be transferred by the operator to a television screen, enabling the deaf to follow the spoken word.

Short Parliament the English Parliament that was summoned by Charles I on April 13, 1640 to raise funds for his war against the Scots. It was succeeded later in the year by the ◊Long Parliament.

When it became clear that the parliament opposed the war and would not grant him any money, he dissolved it May 5 and arrested some of its leaders.

short story a short work of prose fiction, which typically either sets up and resolves a single narrative point or depicts a mood or an atmosphere. Celebrated short-story writers include Chekhov, Kipling, Maupassant, Saki, Borges, Poe, and Hemingway.

Shostakovich Dmitry (Dmitriyevich) 1906–1975. Soviet composer. His music is tonal, expressive, and sometimes highly dramatic; it has not always been to official Soviet taste. He wrote 15 symphonies, chamber music, ballets, and operas, the latter including *Lady Macbeth of Mtsensk* 1934, which was suppressed as "too divorced from the proletariat," but revived as *Katerina Izmaylova* 1963.

shot put in athletics, the sport of putting overhand from the shoulder, from within the confines of a circle, a metal ball (or shot). Standard shot weights are 16 lb/7.26 kg for men and 8.8 lb/4 kg for women.

shoveler fresh-water duck *Anas clypeata*, so named after its long and broad flattened beak. Spending the summer in N Europe or North America, it winters further south.

The male has a green head, white and brown body plumage, and can grow up to 1.7 ft/50 cm long. The female is speckled brown.

show trial public and well-reported trials of people accused of crimes against the state. In the USSR in the 1930s and 1940s, Stalin carried out show trials against economic saboteurs, Communist Party members, army officers, and even members of the Bolshevik leadership.

Shrapnel Henry 1761–1842. British army officer who invented shells containing bullets, to increase the spread of casualties, first used 1804; hence the word shrapnel to describe shell fragments.

Shreveport port on the Red River, Louisiana; population (1990) 198,525. Industries include oil, natural gas, steel, telephone equipment, glass, and timber. It was founded 1836 and named after Henry Shreeve, a riverboat captain who cleared a giant logjam.

The discovery of oil nearby 1906 stimulated economic growth.

shrew insectivorous mammal of the family Soricidae, found in Eurasia and the Americas. It is mouse-like, but with a long nose and pointed teeth. Its high metabolic rate means that it must eat almost constantly.

The common shrew *Sorex araneus* is about 3 in/ 7.5 cm long. The pigmy shrew *Sorex minutus* is only about 2 in/50 cm long.

Shrewsbury market town on the river Severn, Shropshire, England; population (1985) 87,300. It is the administrative headquarters of the county. To the E is the site of the Roman city of Viroconium (larger than Pompeii). In the 5th century, as Pengwern, Shrewsbury was capital of the kingdom of Powys, which later became part of Mercia. In the battle of Shrewsbury 1403, Henry IV defeated the rebels led by Hotspur (Sir Henry ◊Percy).

shrike "butcher-bird" of the family Laniidae, of which there are over 70 species, living mostly in Africa, but also in Eurasia and North America. They often impale insects and small vertebrates on thorns. They can grow to 14 in/35 cm long, and have gray, black, or brown plumage.

shrimp a crustacean related to the ◊prawn. It has a cylindrical, semitransparent body, with ten jointed legs. Some shrimps grow as large as 10 in/25 cm long.

Shropshire county in W England. Sometimes abbreviated to Salop, it was officially so known from 1974 until local protest reversed the decision 1980.

area 1,347 sq mi/3,490 sq km

towns Shrewsbury (administrative headquarters), Telford, Oswestry, Ludlow

physical bissected, on the Welsh border, NW to SE by the river Severn; Ellesmere, the largest of several lakes; the Clee Hills rise to about 1,800 ft/ 610 m in the SW

features Ironbridge Gorge open-air museum of industrial archeology, with the Iron Bridge 1779

products chiefly agricultural: sheep and cattle

population (1987) 397,000

shroud of Turin Christian relic; see ◊Turin shroud.

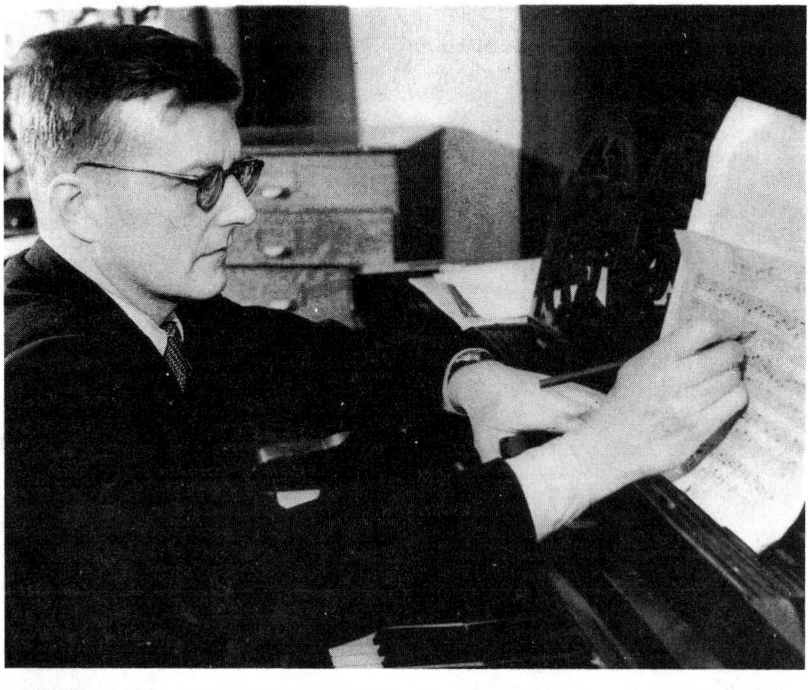

Shostakovich *Soviet composer Dmitry Shostakovich's works were sometimes suppressed by Soviet authorities.*

Shrove Tuesday in the Christian calendar, the day before the beginning of Lent. It is also known as Mardi Gras.

shrub a perennial woody plant that typically produces several separate stems, at or near ground level, rather than the single trunk of most trees. A shrub is usually smaller than a tree, but there is no clear distinction between large shrubs and small trees.

Shultz George P 1920– . US Republican politician, economics adviser to President ◊Reagan 1980–82, and secretary of state 1982–89.

Shultz taught as a labor economist at the University of Chicago before serving in the 1968–74 ◊Nixon administration, including secretary of labor 1969–70 and secretary of the treasury 1972–74. As secretary of state he was in charge of the formulation of US foreign policy. He was pragmatic and moderate, against the opposition of Defense Secretary Caspar ◊Weinberger.

Shute Nevil. Adopted name of English novelist Nevil Shute Norway 1899–1960. Among his books are *A Town Like Alice* 1949 and *On the Beach* 1957.

shuttle diplomacy form of international diplomacy prominent in the 1970s in which an independent mediator would travel between belligerent parties, in the attempt to achieve a compromise solution.

SI abbreviation for Système International [d'Unités] (French "International System [of Metric Units]").

Siachen Glacier Himalayan glacier at an altitude of 17,000 ft/5,236 m in the Karakoram mountains of N Kashmir. Occupied by Indian forces 1984, the glacier has been the focal point of a territorial dispute between India and Pakistan since independence 1947. Three wars in 1947, 1965, and 1971 resulted in the establishment of a temporary boundary between the two countries through the province of Jammu and Kashmir, but the accords failed to define a frontier in the farthest reaches of N Kashmir. Pakistan responded to the 1984 Indian action by sending troops to the heights of the nearby Baltoro Glacier.

sial in geochemistry and geophysics, term denoting the substance of the Earth's continental ◊crust, as distinct from the ◊sima of the ocean crust. The name is derived from silica and alumina, its two main chemical constituents.

Sialkot city in Punjab province, E Pakistan; population (1981) 302,000. Industries include the manufacture of surgical and sports goods, metalware, carpets, textiles, and leather goods.

siamang the largest ◊gibbon *Symphalangus syndactylus*, native to Malaysia and Sumatra. Siamangs have a large throat pouch to amplify the voice, making the territorial "song" extremely loud. They are black-haired, up to 3 ft/90 cm tall, with very long arms (a span of 5 ft/150 cm).

Sian former name of ◊Xian, China.

Sibelius Jean (Christian) 1865–1957. Finnish composer. His works include nationalistic symphonic poems such as *En Saga* 1893 and *Finlandia* 1900, a violin concerto 1904, and seven symphonies.

He studied the violin and composition at Helsinki and went on to Berlin and Vienna. In 1940 he abruptly ceased composing and spent the rest of his life as a recluse.

Siberia Asian region of the USSR extending from the Urals to the Pacific

area 4,650,000 sq mi/12,050,000 sq km

towns Novosibirsk, Omsk, Krasnoyarsk, Irkutsk

features long and extremely cold winters

products hydroelectric power from rivers Lena, Ob, and Yenisei; forestry; mineral resources, including gold, diamonds, oil, natural gas, iron, copper, nickel, cobalt

history overrun by Russia in the 17th century, it was used from the 18th century to exile political and criminal prisoners. The first Trans-Siberian Railway 1892–1905 from Leningrad (via Omsk, Novosibirsk, Irkutsk, and Khabarovsk) to Vladivostok, approximately 5,400 mi/8,700 km, began to open it up. A popular front was formed 1988, campaigning for ecological and political reform.

Sibyl in Roman mythology, priestess of Apollo. She offered to sell ◊Tarquinius nine collections of prophecies, the Sibylline Books, but the price was too high. When she had destroyed all but three, he bought those for the identical price, and these were kept for consultation in emergency at Rome.

sic (Latin "thus," "so") sometimes found in brackets within a printed quotation to show that an apparent error is in the original.

Sichuan or ***Szechwan*** province of central China
area 219,634 sq mi/569,000 sq km
capital Chengdu
towns Chongqing
features surrounded by mountains, it was the headquarters of the Nationalist government 1937–45, and China's nuclear research centers are here. It is China's most populous administrative area
products rice, coal, oil, natural gas
population (1986) 103,200,000

Sicily (Italian *Sicilia*) largest Mediterranean island, an autonomous region of Italy; area 9,920 sq mi/25,700 sq km; population (1988) 5,141,000. Its capital is Palermo, and towns include the ports of Catania, Messina, Syracuse, and Marsala. It exports Marsala wine, olives, citrus, refined oil and petrochemicals, pharmaceuticals, potash, asphalt, and marble. The autonomous region of Sicily also includes the islands of ◊Lipari, Egadi, Ustica, and ◊Pantelleria. Etna, 10,906 ft/3,323 m high, is the highest volcano in Europe; its last major eruption was in 1971.

Conquered by most of the major powers of the ancient world, it flourished under the Greeks who colonized Sicily during the 8th–5th centuries BC. It was invaded by Carthage and became part of the Roman empire 241 BC–AD 476. In the Middle Ages it was ruled successively by the Arabs; the Normans 1059–1194, who established the Kingdom of the Two Sicilies (that is, Sicily and the southern part of Italy); the German emperors; and then the Angevins, until the popular revolt known as the ***Sicilian Vespers*** 1282. Spanish rule was invited and continued in varying forms, with a temporary displacement of the Spanish Bourbons by Napoleon, until ◊Garibaldi's invasion 1860 resulted in the two Sicilies being united with Italy 1861.

sick building syndrome malaise diagnosed in the early 1980s among office workers and thought to be caused by such pollutants as formaldehyde (from furniture and insulating materials), benzene (from paint), and the solvent trichloroethylene, concentrated in air-conditioned buildings. Symptoms include headache, sore throat, tiredness, colds, and flu. Studies have found that it can cause a 40% drop in productivity and a 30% rise in absenteeism.

Work on improving living conditions of astronauts showed that the causes were easily and inexpensively removed by potted plants in which interaction is thought to take place between the plant and microorganisms in its roots. Among the most useful (along with their target pollutants) are chrysanthemums (benzene), English ivy and the peace lily (trichloroethylene), and the spider plant (formaldehyde).

sickle harvesting tool of ancient origin characterized by a curving blade with serrated cutting edge and short wooden handle. It was widely used in the Middle East and Europe for cutting wheat, barley, and oats from about 10,000 BC to the 19th century.

sickle-cell disease hereditary chronic blood disorder common among people of black African descent. It is characterized by distortion and fragility of the red blood cells, which are lost too rapidly from the circulation. This often results in ◊anemia.

People with this disease have abnormal red blood cells (sickle cells), containing a defective ◊hemoglobin. The presence of sickle cells in the

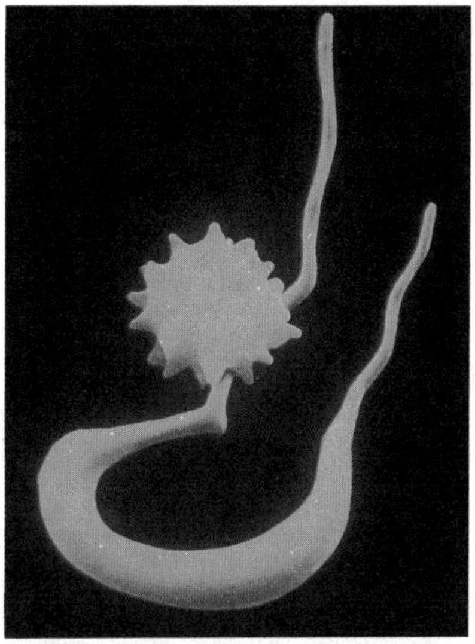

sickle-cell disease *Scanning electron micrograph of the abnormal type of red blood cell that causes sickle-cell anemia.*

blood, with or without accompanying anemia, is called sicklemia. It confers a degree of protection against ◊malaria because fewer normal red blood cells are available to the parasites for infection.

Siddons Sarah 1755–1831. Welsh actress. Her majestic presence made her suited to tragic and heroic roles such as Lady Macbeth, Zara in Congreve's *The Mourning Bride*, and Constance in *King John*.

She toured the provinces with Roger Kemble, her father, until she appeared in London to immediate acclaim in in Otway's *Venice Preserv'd* 1774. This led to her appearing with ◊Garrick at Drury Lane. She retired in 1812.

sidereal period the orbital period of a planet around the Sun, or of a moon around a planet, with reference to a background star. The sidereal period of a planet is in effect its "year."

sidewinder type of rattlesnake *Crotalus cerastes* that lives in the deserts of the SW US and Mexico, and moves by throwing its coils into a sideways "jump" across the sand. It can grow up to 2.5 ft/75 cm long.

Sidi Barrâni coastal settlement in Egypt, about 230 mi/370 km W of Alexandria, the scene of heavy fighting 1940–42 during World War II.

Sidi-Bel-Abbès trading city in Algeria; population (1983) 187,000. Because of its strategic position, it was the headquarters of the French Foreign Legion until 1962.

Siding Spring Mountain peak 250 mi/400 km NW of Sydney, site of the 154-in/3.9-m Anglo-Australian Telescope, opened 1974, which was the first big telescope to be fully computer controlled. It is one of the most powerful telescopes in the southern hemisphere.

Sidney Philip 1554–1586. English poet and soldier, author of the sonnet sequence *Astrophel and Stella* 1591; *Arcadia* 1590, a prose romance; and *Apologie for Poetrie* 1595, the earliest work of English literary criticism.

Sidon alternate name for ◊Saida, Lebanon.

SIDS acronym for sudden infant death syndrome, the technical name for ◊crib death.

Siegel Don(ald) 1912– . US film director who made thrillers, Westerns, and police dramas. He also directed *Invasion of the Body Snatchers* 1956. His other films include *Madigan* 1968, *Dirty Harry* 1971, and *The Shootist* 1976.

Siegen city in North Rhine–Westphalia, Federal Republic of Germany; population (1988) 107,000.

Siegfried legendary Germanic hero. It is uncertain whether his story has a historical basis, but it was

Sidney *English poet and soldier Philip Sidney, who died fighting the Spanish in the Netherlands.*

current about AD 700. In the poems of the Norse Elder ◊Edda and in the prose Völsunga Saga, Siegfried appears under the name of ◊Sigurd. A version of the story is in the German *Nibelungenlied/Song of the Nibelung*.

Siegfried Line in World War I the defensive line established 1918 by the Germans in France; in World War II the Allies' name for the West Wall, the German defensive line established along its western frontier, from the Netherlands to Switzerland.

Siemens German family of four brothers, creators of a vast industrial empire. The eldest, Ernst Werner von Siemens (1812–92), founded the original electrical firm of Siemens und Halske 1847 and made many advances in telegraphy. William (Karl Wilhelm) (1823–83) moved to England in 1884 and perfected the open-hearth production of steel, pioneered the development of the electric locomotive and the laying of transoceanic cables, and improved the electric generator.

siemens SI unit (abbreviation S) of electrical conductance, the reciprocal of the ◊impedance of an electrical circuit. One siemens equals one ampere per volt. It was formerly called the mho or reciprocal ohm.

Siena city in Tuscany, Italy; population (1985) 60,670. Founded by the Etruscans, it has medieval architecture by ◊Pisano and Donatello, including a 13th-century Gothic cathedral, and many examples of the Sienese school of painting that flourished from the 13th to the 16th centuries. The *Palio* ("banner," in reference to the prize) is a horse race in the main square, held annually since the Middle Ages.

Sienkiewicz Henryk 1846–1916. Polish author. His books include *Quo Vadis?* 1895, set in Rome at the time of Nero, and the 17th-century historical trilogy *With Fire and Sword*, *The Deluge*, and *Pan Michael* 1890–93.

Sierra Leone country in W Africa, on the Atlantic, bounded N and E by Guinea and SE by Liberia.
government The 1978 constitution makes Sierra Leone a one-party state, the party being the All People's Congress (APC). The constitution also provides for a president, who is both head of state and head of government, and a single-chamber legislature, the House of Representatives. The House has 127 members, 105 elected for five years by universal suffrage, 12 paramount chiefs, one for each district, and 10 additional members appointed by the president. The president, who is also leader and secretary general of the APC, is endorsed by the party as the sole candidate and then popularly elected for a seven-year term. The president appoints a cabinet and two vice-presidents.
history For early history, see ◊Africa. Freetown, the capital, was founded by Britain 1787 for homeless Africans rescued from ◊slavery. Sierra Leone became a British colony 1808.

Sierra Leone achieved full independence, as a constitutional monarchy within the ◊Common-

Sierra Leone
Republic of

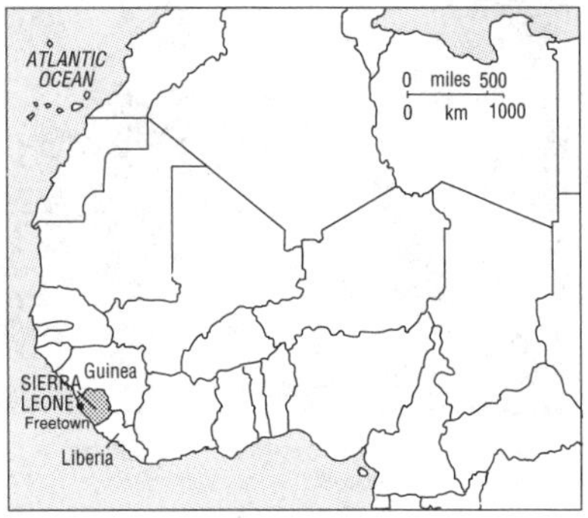
ATLANTIC
OCEAN
0 miles 500
0 km 1000
SIERRA
LEONE
Guinea
Freetown
Liberia

area 27,710 sq mi/71,740 sq km
capital Freetown
cities Bo, Kenema, Makeni
physical mountains in E; hills and forest; coastal mangrove swamps
features hot and humid climate (138 in/3,500 mm rainfall p.a.
head of state and government Joseph Saidu Momoh from 1985
political system one-party republic
political parties All People's Congress (APC), moderate Socialist
exports palm kernels, cocoa, coffee, ginger, diamonds, bauxite, rutile
currency leone
population (1990 est) 4,168,000; growth rate 2.5% p.a.
life expectancy men 41, women 47 (1989)
language English (official); local languages
religion Muslim 39%, animist 52%, Protestant 6%, Roman Catholic 2% (1980 est)
literacy men 38%/women 21% (1985 est)
GNP $965 mn (1987); $320 per head (1984)
chronology
1896 Hinterland declared a British protectorate.
1961 Independence achieved from Britain within the Commonwealth, with Milton Margai, leader of Sierra Leone People's Party (SLPP), as prime minister.
1964 Milton succeeded by his half brother, Albert Margai.
1967 Election results disputed by army, who set up a National Reformation Council and forced the governor general to leave.
1968 Army revolt made Siaka Stevens, leader of the All-People's Congress (APC), prime minister.
1971 New constitution adopted, making Sierra Leone a republic, with Stevens as president.
1978 APC declared only legal party. Stevens sworn in for another seven-year term.
1985 Stevens retired; succeeded by Maj Gen Joseph Momoh.
1989 Attempted coup against president Momoh foiled.
1991 Momoh "welcomes" multiparty democracy.

wealth, in 1962, with Sir Milton Margai, leader of the Sierra Leone People's Party (SLPP), as prime minister. He died in 1964 and was succeeded by his half brother, Dr Albert Margai. The 1967 general election was won by the APC, led by Dr Siaka Stevens, but the result was disputed by the army, which assumed control and temporarily forced the governor-general to leave the country. In 1968 another army revolt brought back Stevens as prime minister, and in 1971, after the constitution had been changed to make Sierra Leone a republic, he became president. He was reelected in 1976, and the APC, having won the 1977 general election by a big margin, began to demand the creation of a one-party state. To this end, a new constitution was approved by referendum in 1978, and Stevens was sworn in as president.

Stevens, who was now 80, did not run in 1985, and the APC endorsed the commander of the army, Maj Gen Joseph Momoh, as the sole candidate for the party leadership and presidency. Momoh appointed a civilian cabinet and dissociated himself from the policies of his predecessor, who had been criticized for failing to prevent corruption within his administration. The last elections for the House of Representatives were held in May 1982 but annulled because of alleged irregularities. It was reported in Oct 1989 that an attempted coup against the government had been put down.

Sierra Madre chief mountain system of Mexico, consisting of three ranges, enclosing the central plateau of the country; highest point Pico de Orizaba 18,700 ft/5,700 m. The Sierra Madre del Sur ("of the south") runs along the SW Pacific coast.

Sierra Nevada mountain range of S Spain; highest point Mulhacén 11,425 ft/3,481 m.

Sierra Nevada mountain range in E California; highest point Mount Whitney 14,500 ft/4,418 m. It includes the King's Canyon, Sequoia, and Yosemite Valley national parks. About 400 mi/640 km in length, the Sierra Nevada separates California from the rest of the continent. In 1848 settlers found gold in its W foothills, touching off the great 1849 gold rush. Silver mines have been opened on its E side.

sievert SI unit (abbreviation Sv) of radiation dose equivalent. It is defined as the absorbed dose of ionizing radiation (modified to account for different types of radiation causing different effects in biological tissue) of one joule per kilogram. One sievert equals 100 ◊rem.

Sieyes Emmanuel-Joseph 1748–1836. French cleric and constitutional theorist who led the bourgeois attack on royal and aristocratic privilege in the ◊States General (parliament) 1788–89. Active in the early years of the French Revolution, he later retired from politics, but reemerged as an organizer of the coup that brought Napoleon I to power in 1799.

Siger of Brabant 1240–1282. Medieval philosopher, a follower of ◊Averroës, who taught at the University of Paris, and whose distinguishing between reason and Christian faith led to his works being condemned as heretical 1270. He refused to recant and was imprisoned. He was murdered while in prison.

sight the detection of light by an ◊eye, which can form images of the outside world.

Sigismund 1368–1437. Holy Roman emperor from 1411. He convened and presided over the council of Constance 1414–18, where he promised protection to the religious reformer ◊Huss, but imprisoned him after his condemnation for heresy and acquiesced in his burning. King of Bohemia from 1419, he led the military campaign against the ◊Hussites.

Sigma Octantis the star closest to the south celestial pole (see ◊celestial sphere), in effect the southern equivalent of ◊Polaris, although far less conspicuous. Situated just less than 1° from the south celestial pole in the constellation Octans, Sigma Octantis is 120 light-years away.

Signac Paul 1863–1935. French artist. In 1884 he joined with Georges Seurat in founding the Société des Artistes Indépendants and developing the technique of ◊Pointillism.

Signac, born in Paris, was inspired by the Impressionist painter Monet. He laid down the theory of Neo-Impressionism in his book *De Delacroix au Néo-Impressionisme* 1899. From the 1890s he developed a stronger and brighter palette. He and Matisse painted together in the south of France 1904–05.

signal any sign, gesture, sound, or action that conveys information. Examples include the use of flags (◊semaphore), light (traffic and railroad signals), radio telephony, radio telegraphy (◊Morse code), and electricity (telecommunications and computer networks).

The International Code of Signals used by shipping was drawn up by an international committee and published 1931. The codes and abbreviations used by aircraft are dealt with by the International Civil Aviation Organization, established 1944.

Signorelli Luca c. 1450–1523. Italian painter, active in central Italy. About 1483 he was called to the Vatican to complete frescoes on the walls of the Sistine Chapel.

He produced large frescoes in Orvieto Cathedral, where he devoted a number of scenes to *The Last Judgment* 1499–1504. The style is sculptural and dramatic, reflecting late 15th-century Florentine trends, but Signorelli's work is more imaginative. He settled in Cortona and ran a workshop producing altarpieces.

Sigurd in Norse mythology, a hero who appears in both the ◊*Nibelungenlied/Song of the Nibelung* (under his German name of ◊Siegfried) and the ◊*Edda*.

Sihanouk Norodom 1922– . Cambodian politician, king 1941–55, prime minister 1955–70. His government was overthrown 1970 by a military coup led by Lon Nol. With Pol Pot's resistance front, he overthrew Lon Nol 1975 and again became prime minister 1975–76, when he was forced to resign by the ◊Khmer Rouge.

Educated in Vietnam and Paris, he was elected king of Cambodia 1941. He abdicated 1955 in favor of his father, founded the Popular Socialist Community, and governed as prime minister 1955–70.

After he was deposed in 1970, Sihanouk established a government in exile in Beijing and formed a joint resistance front with Pol Pot. This movement succeeded in overthrowing Lon Nol April 1975 and Sihanouk was reappointed head of state, but in April 1976 he was forced to resign by the communist Khmer Rouge leadership. Based in North Korea, he became the recognized head of the Democratic Kampuchea government in exile 1982, leading a coalition of three groups opposing the Vietnamese-installed government. International peace conferences aimed at negotiating a settlement repeatedly broke down, fighting intensified, and the Khmer Rouge succeeded in taking some important provincial capitals. In 1990 Sihanouk returned to live in the "liberated zone" of W Cambodia, and in Nov 1991, after the Cambodian peace treaty was signed, returned to Phnom Penh.

Sikhism religion professed by 16 million Indians, living mainly in the Punjab. Sikhism was founded by Nanak (1469–c. 1539). Sikhs believe in a single God who is the immortal creator of the universe and who has never been incarnate in any form, and in the equality of all human beings; Sikhism is strongly opposed to caste divisions. Their holy book is the ◊*Adi Granth*. Guru Gobind Singh (1666–1708) instituted the Khanda-di-Pahul, the Baptism of the Sword, and established the *Khalsa* ("pure"), the company of the faithful. The Khalsa wear the five Ks: *kes*, long hair; *kangha*, a comb; *kirpan*, a sword; *kachh*, short trousers; and *kara*, a steel bracelet. Sikh men take the last name "Singh" ("lion") and women "Kaur" ("princess").
beliefs Human beings can make themselves ready to find God by prayer and meditation but can achieve closeness to God only as a result of God's *nadar* (grace). Sikhs believe in ◊reincarnation and that the ten human gurus were teachers through whom the spirit of Guru Nanak was passed on to live today in the *Guru Granth Sahib* and the Khalsa.
practice Sikhs do not have a specific holy day, but hold their main services on the day of rest of the country in which they are living. Daily prayer is important in Sikhism, and the gurdwara func-

tions as a social as well as religious center; it contains a kitchen, the *langar*, where all, male and female, Sikh and non-Sikh, may eat together as equals. Sikh women take the same role as men in religious observances, for example, in reading from the *Guru Granth Sahib* at the gurdwara. Festivals in honor of the ten human gurus include a complete reading of the *Guru Granth Sahib*; Sikhs also celebrate at the time of some of the major Hindu festivals, but their emphasis is on aspects of Sikh belief and the example of the gurus. Sikhs avoid the use of all nonmedicinal drugs and, in particular, tobacco.

history On Nanak's death he was followed as guru by a succession of leaders who converted the Sikhs (the word means "disciple") into a military confraternity which established itself as a political power. The last of the gurus, Guru Gobind Singh, was assassinated by a Muslim 1708, and since then the *Guru Granth Sahib* has taken the place of a leader.

Upon the partition of India many Sikhs migrated from W to E Punjab, and in 1966 the efforts of Sant Fateh Singh (c. 1911–72) led to the creation of a Sikh state within India by partition of the Punjab. However, the Akali separatist movement agitates for a completely independent Sikh state, Khalistan, and a revival of fundamentalist belief and was headed from 1978 by Sant Jarnail Singh Bhindranwale (1947–84), killed in the siege of the Golden Temple, ◊Amritsar. In retaliation for this, the Indian prime minister Indira Gandhi was assassinated in Oct of the same year by her Sikh bodyguards. Heavy rioting followed, in which 1,000 Sikhs were killed. Mrs Gandhi's successor, Rajiv Gandhi, reached an agreement for the election of a popular government in the Punjab and for state representatives to the Indian parliament with the moderate Sikh leader Sant Harchand Singh Longowal, who was himself killed 1985 by Sikh extremists.

Sikh Wars two wars in India between the Sikhs and the British:

The ***First Sikh War*** 1845–46 followed an invasion of British India by Punjabi Sikhs. The Sikhs were defeated and part of their territory annexed.

The ***Second Sikh War*** 1848–49 arose from a Sikh revolt in Multan. The Sikhs were defeated, and the British annexed the Punjab.

Si-Kiang alternative transliteration of ◊Xi Jiang, Chinese river.

Sikkim or ***Denjong*** state of NE India; formerly a protected state, it was absorbed by India 1975, the monarchy being abolished. China does not recognize India's sovereignty.

area 7,300 sq2,818 mi/ km

capital Gangtok

features Mount Kangchenjunga; wildlife including birds, butterflies, and orchids

products rice, grain, tea, fruit, soybeans, carpets, cigarettes, lead, zinc, copper

population (1981) 316,000

language Bhutia, Lepecha, Khaskura (Nepali) — all official

religion Mahayana Buddhism, Hinduism

Sikorski Władysław 1881–1943. Polish general and statesman; prime minister 1922–23, and 1939–45 of the Polish government-in-exile in London during World War II. He was killed in an airplane crash near Gibraltar under controversial circumstances.

Sikorsky Igor 1889–1972. Ukrainian-born US engineer who built the first practical helicopter. He emigrated to the US 1918, where he first constructed multiengined flying boats. His first helicopter (the VS300) flew 1939 and a commercial version (the R3) went into production 1943.

silage fodder preserved through controlled fermentation in a silo, an airtight structure that presses green crops. The term also refers to stacked crops that may be preserved indefinitely.

Silenus in Greek mythology, the son of Hermes, or Pan, and companion of ◊Dionysus. He is portrayed as a jovial old man, usually drunk.

Silesia long-disputed region of Europe because of its geographical position, mineral resources, and industrial potential; now in Poland and Czechoslovakia. Dispute began in the 17th century with claims on the area by both Austria and Prussia. It was seized by Prussia's Frederick the Great, which started the War of the ◊Austrian Succession; this was finally recognized by Austria 1763, after the Seven Years' War. After World War I, it was divided in 1919 among newly formed Czechoslovakia, revived Poland, and Germany, which retained the major part. In 1945, after World War II, all German Silesia east of the Oder-Neisse line was transferred to Polish administration; about 10 million inhabitants of German origin, both there and in Czechoslovak Silesia, were expelled.

The chief towns (with their German names) are: Wroclaw (Breslau), Katowice (Kattowitz), Zabrze (Hindenburg), Chorzow (Königshütte), Gliwice (Gleiwitz), and Bytom (Beuthen) in Poland, and Opava (Troppau) in Czechoslovakia.

silhouette a profile or shadow portrait filled in with black or a dark color. A common pictorial technique in the late 18th and early 19th centuries, it was named after Etienne de Silhouette (1709–67), a French finance minister who made paper cutouts as a hobby.

silica silicon dioxide, SiO_2, the composition of the most common mineral group, of which the most familiar form is quartz. Other silica forms are ◊chalcedony, chert, opal, tridymite, and cristobalite. Chalcedony includes some semiprecious forms: gem varieties include agate, onyx, sardonyx, carnelian, and tiger's eye.

silicate compound containing silicon and oxygen combined together as a negative ion (◊anion), together with one or more metal ◊cations.

Common natural silicates are sands (common sand is the oxide of silicon known as silica). Glass is a manufactured complex polysilicate material in which other elements (boron in borosilicate glass) have been incorporated.

silicate one of a group of minerals containing silicon and oxygen in tetrahedral units of SiO_4, bound together in various ways to form specific structural types. Silicates are the chief rock-forming minerals. Most rocks are composed, wholly or in part, of silicates (the main exception being limestones).

Generally, additional cations are present in the structure, especially Al^{3+}, Fe^{2+}, Mg^{2+}, Ca^{2+}, Na^+, K^+, but quartz and other polymorphs of SiO_2 are also considered to be silicates; stishorite (a high pressure form of SiO_2) is a rare exception to the usual tetrahedral coordination of silica and oxygen.

In orthosilicates, the oxygens are all ionically bonded to cations such as Mg^{2+} or Fe^{2+} (as olivines), and are not shared between tetrahedra. All other silicate structures involve some degree of oxygen sharing between adjacent tetrahedra. For example, beryl is a ring silicate based on tetrahedra linked by sharing oxygens to form a circle. Pyroxenes are single chain silicates, with chains of linked tetrahedra extending in one direction through the structure; amphiboles are similar but have double chains if tetrahedra. In micas, which are sheet silicates, the tetrahedra are joined to form continuous sheets that are stacked upon one another. Framework silicates, such as feldspars and quartz, are based on three-dimensional frameworks of tetrahedra in which all oxygens are shared.

silicon brittle, nonmetallic element, symbol Si, atomic number 14, atomic weight 28.086. It is the second most abundant element (after oxygen) in the Earth's crust and occurs in amorphous and crystalline forms. In nature it is found only in combination with other elements, chiefly with oxygen in silica (silicon dioxide, SiO_2) and silicates. These form the mineral ◊quartz, which makes up most sands, gravels, and beaches.

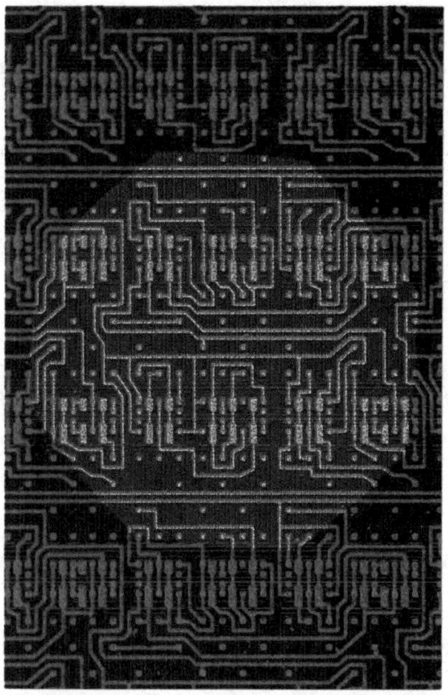

silicon chip *False-color microscope image of a computer memory chip. The tiny circuit components and interconnections are etched onto the chip during manufacturing.*

Pottery glazes and glassmaking are based on the use of silica sands and date back into prehistory. Today the crystalline form of silicon is used as a deoxidizing and hardening agent in steel; it has become the basis of the electronics industry because of its ◊semiconductor properties, being used to make silicon chips for microprocessors.

The element was isolated by Swedish chemist Jöns Berzelius in 1823, having been named in 1817 by Scottish chemist Thomas Thomson for Latin *silicium*, "silica," and by analogy with bor*on* and carb*on* because of its chemical resemblance to these elements.

silicon chip ◊integrated circuit with microscopically small electrical components on a piece of silicon crystal only a few millimeters square.

One may contain more than a million components. A chip is mounted in a rectangular plastic package and linked via gold wires to metal pins, so that it can be connected to a printed circuit board for use in electronic devices, such as computers, calculators, televisions, car dashboards, and domestic appliances.

Silicon Valley nickname given to Santa Clara county, California, since the 1950s the site of many high-technology electronic firms, whose prosperity is based on the silicon chip.

silicosis chronic disease of miners and stone cutters who inhale ◊silica dust, which makes the lung tissues fibrous and less capable of aerating the blood. It is a form of ◊pneumoconiosis.

silk fine soft thread produced by the larva of the ◊silkworm moth when making its cocoon. It is soaked, carefully unwrapped, and used in the manufacture of textiles. The introduction of synthetics originally harmed the silk industry, but rising standards of living have produced an increased demand for real silk. It is manufactured in China, India, Japan, and Thailand.

Silk Road ancient medieval overland route of about 4,000 mi/6,400 km by which silk was brought from China to Europe in return for trade goods; it ran west via the Gobi Desert, Samarkand, and Antioch to Mediterranean ports in Greece, Italy, the Near East, and Egypt.

silk-screen printing or ***serigraphy*** method of ◊printing based on stencils. It can be used to print on most surfaces, including paper, plastic, cloth, and wood. An impermeable stencil (either paper or photographic) is attached to a finely meshed silk screen that has been stretched on a wooden frame, so that the ink passes through to the area beneath only where the image is required. The design can also be painted directly on to the screen with varnish. A series of screens can be used to add successive layers of color to the design.

The process was developed in the early 20th century for commercial use and adopted by many artists from the 1930s onward.

silkworm usually the larva of the common silkworm moth *Bombyx mori*. After hatching from the egg and maturing on the leaves of white mulberry trees (or a synthetic substitute), it "spins" a protective cocoon of fine silk thread 900 ft/275 m long. It is killed before emerging as a moth to keep the thread intact, and several threads are combined to form the commercial silk thread woven into textiles.

Other moths produce different fibers, such as tussah from *Antheraea mylitta*. The raising of silkworms is called sericulture and began in China about 2000 BC. Chromosome engineering and artificial selection practiced in Japan have led to the development of different types of silkworm for different fibers.

sillimanite aluminum silicate, Al_2SiO_5, a mineral that occurs either as white to brownish prismatic crystals or as minute white fibers. It is an indicator of high temperature conditions in metamorphic rocks formed from clay sediments. Andalusite, kyanite, and sillimanite are all polymorphs of Al_2SiO_5.

Sillitoe Alan 1928– . English novelist, who wrote *Saturday Night and Sunday Morning* 1958, about a working-class man in Nottingham, Sillitoe's hometown. He also wrote *The Loneliness of the Long Distance Runner* 1959, *Life Goes On* 1985, many other novels, and poems, plays, and children's books.

Sills Beverly. Adopted name of Belle Silverman 1929– . US coloratura soprano. She was a child radio star who became one of the world's most dramatically gifted opera singers, making her debut at 17 in Philadelphia. She joined the New York City Opera 1955. She appeared at such European opera houses as La Scala, Milan 1969, and Covent Garden, London 1970. Her Metropolitan Opera debut was in 1975; in 1979 she became director of the New York City Opera, announcing her retirement in 1988. She wrote an autobiography, *Bubbles* 1976 followed by a second, *Beverly* 1988.

silo in farming, an airtight tower in which ◊silage is made by the fermentation of freshly cut grass and other forage crops. In military technology, a silo is an underground chamber for housing and launching a ballistic missile.

Silone Ignazio. Adopted name of Secondo Tranquilli 1900–1978. Italian novelist. His novel *Fontamara* 1933 deals with the hopes and disillusionment of a peasant village from a Socialist viewpoint. His other works include *Una manciata di more/A Handful of Blackberries* 1952.

Silurian period of geologic time 438–408 million years ago, the third period of the Paleozoic era. Silurian sediments are mostly marine and consist of shales and limestone. Luxuriant reefs were built by corallike organisms. The first land plants began to evolve during this period, and there were many ostracoderms (armored jawless fishes). The first jawed fishes (called acanthodians) also appeared.

Silvanus a Roman woodland deity identified in later times with ◊Pan.

silver white, lustrous, extremely malleable and ductile, metallic element, symbol Ag (from Latin *argentum*), atomic number 47, atomic weight 107.868. It occurs in nature in ores and as a free metal (◊native metal); the chief ores are sulfides, from which the metal is extracted by smelting with lead. It is the best metallic conductor of both heat and electricity; its most useful compounds are the chloride and bromide, which darken on exposure to light and are the basis of photographic emulsions.

Silver is used ornamentally, for jewelry and tableware; for coinage; in eletroplating, electrical contacts, and dentistry; and as a solder. It has been mined since prehistory and was originally worked from the free-metal sources. Its name is an ancient non-Indo-European one, *silubr*, borrowed by the Germanic branch as *silber*.

silver age period of Latin literature after the death of ◊Augustus, with a florid and rhetorical writing style; authors included Seneca, Juvenal, and Suetonius.

silverberry a North American shrub *Eleagnus commutata* of the oleaster family, having twigs marked with brown and silver scales and bearing silvery yellow, fragrant flowers. The silvery berrylike fruits are edible.

silverfish wingless insect, a type of ◊bristletail.

Sim Alistair 1900–1976. Scottish comedy actor. Possessed of a marvelously expressive face, he was ideally cast in eccentric roles, as in the title role in *Scrooge* 1951. His other films include *Inspector Hornleigh* 1939, *Green for Danger* 1945, and *The Belles of St Trinians* 1954.

sima in geochemistry and geophysics, term denoting the substance of the Earth's oceanic ◊crust, as distinct from the ◊sial of the continental crust. The name is derived from silica and magnesia, its two main chemical constituents.

Simenon Georges 1903–1989. Belgian crime writer. Initially a pulp fiction writer, in 1931 he created Inspector Maigret of the Paris Sûreté, who appeared in a series of detective novels.

Simeon Stylites, St c. 390–459. Syrian Christian ascetic, who practiced his ideal of self-denial by living for 37 years on a platform on top of a high pillar. Feast day Jan 5.

Simferopol city in the Crimea, Ukraine, USSR; population (1987) 338,000. Industries include the manufacture of soap and tobacco. It is on the site of the Tatar town of Ak-Mechet, conquered by the Russians 1783 and renamed.

Simenon *Georges Simenon, Belgian novelist of the world of crime.*

simile (Latin "likeness") a figure of speech that in English uses the conjunctions *like* and *as* to express comparisons ("run like the devil"; "as deaf as a post"). It is sometimes confused with ◊metaphor.

Simla capital of Himachal Pradesh state, India, 7,500 ft/2,300 m above sea level, population (1980) 70,604. It was the summer administrative capital of British India 1864–1947.

Simmons Jean 1929– . English actress of stage and screen who worked in Hollywood from the 1950s onward. She starred in the films *Black Narcissus* 1947, *Guys and Dolls* 1955, and *Spartacus* 1960. She retired in the early 1970s.

Simon Claude 1913– . French novelist. Originally an artist, he abandoned "time structure" in such novels as *La Route de Flandres/The Flanders Road* 1960, *Le Palace* 1962, and *Histoire* 1967. His later novels include *Les Géorgiques* 1981 and *L'Acacia* 1989. Nobel Prize 1985.

Simon Herbert 1916– . US social scientist. He researched decision making in business corporations and argued that maximum profit was seldom the chief motive. He attempted to examine the psychological factors involved in decision making and created the concept of "satisfying behavior" as motivation for some decisions. He also was deeply involved in the effort to create artificial intelligence technology capable of analyzing the factors that influence human problem-solving processes. He was awarded the Nobel Prize for Economics 1978.

Simon (Marvin) Neil 1927– . US playwright. His stage plays (which were made into films) include the wryly comic *Barefoot in the Park* 1963, *The Odd Couple* 1965, and *The Sunshine Boys* 1972, and the more serious, autobiographical, trilogy *Brighton Beach Memoirs* 1983, *Biloxi Blues* 1985, and *Broadway Bound* 1986. He has also written screenplays and cowritten musicals, including *Sweet Charity* 1966, *Promises, Promises* 1968, and *They're Playing Our Song* 1978.

Simon Paul 1942– . US pop singer and songwriter. In a folk-rock duo with Art Garfunkel (1942–), he had such hits as "Mrs Robinson" 1968 and "Bridge Over Troubled Water" 1970. Simon's solo work includes the critically acclaimed album *Graceland* 1986, for which he drew on Cajun and African music.

Simone Martini. Sienese painter; see ◊Martini, Simone.

simony in the Christian church, the buying and selling of church preferments, now usually regarded as a sin.

The term is derived from Simon Magus (Acts 8) who offered money to the Apostles for the power of the Holy Ghost.

simple harmonic motion (SHM) oscillatory or vibrational motion in which an object (or point) moves so that its acceleration toward a central point is proportional to its distance from it. A simple example is a pendulum, which also demonstrates another feature of SHM, that the maximum deflection is the same on each side of the central point.

A graph of the varying distance with respect to time is a sine curve, a characteristic of the oscillating current or voltage of an alternating current (AC), which is another example of SHM.

Simplon (Italian *Sempione*) Alpine pass Switzerland-Italy. The road was built by Napoleon 1800–05, and the Simplon Tunnel 1906, 12.3 mi/19.8 km, is one of Europe's longest.

Simpson Wallis Warfield, Duchess of Windsor 1896–1986. US socialite, twice divorced, who married ◊Edward VIII 1937, who abdicated to marry "the woman he loved." He was given the title Duke of Windsor by his brother, George IV, who succeeded him.

Simpson Desert desert area in Australia, chiefly in Northern Territory; area 56,000 sq mi/145,000 sq km. It was named after a president of the South

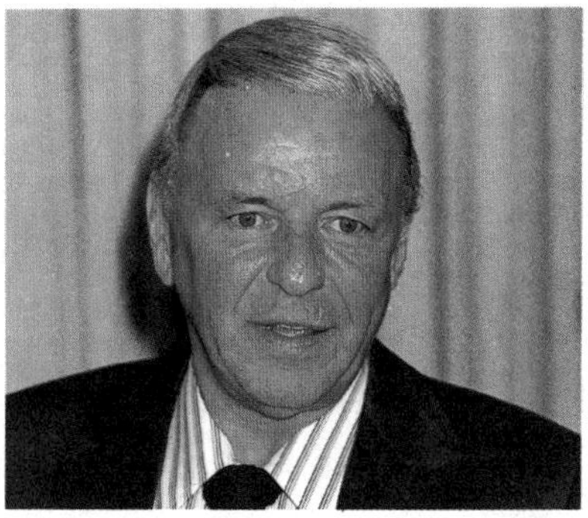

Sinatra *US singer and film actor Frank Sinatra.*

Australian Geographical Society who financed its exploration.

simultaneous equations in mathematics, two or more algebraic equations that each contain two or more unknown quantities that may have a unique solution. For example, in the case of two linear equations with two unknown variables, such as (i) $x + 3y = 6$ and (ii) $3y - 2x = 4$, the solution will be those unique values of x and y that are valid for both equations. Linear simultaneous equations can be solved by using algebraic manipulation to eliminate one of the variables, ◊coordinate geometry, or matrices (see ◊matrix).

For example, by using algebra, both sides of equation (i) could be multiplied by 2, which gives $2x + 6y = 12$. This can be added to equation (ii) to get $9y = 16$, which is easily solved: $y = {}^{16}\!/_{9}$. The variable x can now be found by inserting the known y value into either original equation and solving for x. Another method is by plotting the equations on a graph, because the two equations represent straight lines in coordinate geometry and the coordinates of their point of intersection are the values of x and y that are true for both of them. A third method of solving linear simultaneous equations involves manipulating matrices. If the equations represent either two parallel lines or the same line, then there will be no solutions or an infinity of solutions respectively.

sin transgression of the will of God or the gods, as revealed in the moral code laid down by a particular religion. In Roman Catholic theology, a distinction is made between mortal sins, which, if unforgiven, result in damnation, and venial sins, which are less serious. In Islam, the one unforgivable sin is shirk, denial that Allah is the only god.

In Christian belief, humanity is in a state of original sin and therefore in need of redemption through the crucifixion of Jesus. The sacrament of ◊penance is seen as an earthly means of atonement for sin.

Sinai Egyptian peninsula, at the head of the Red Sea; area 25,000 sq mi/65,000 sq km. Resources include oil, natural gas, manganese, and coal; irrigation water from the river Nile is carried under the Suez Canal.

Sinai was occupied by Israel 1967–82. After the Battle of Sinai 1973, Israel began a gradual withdrawal from the area, under the disengagement agreement 1975, and the Camp David peace treaty 1979 and restored the whole of Sinai to Egyptian control by Apr 1982.

Sinai, Battle of battle Oct 6–24, 1973 which took place during the Yom Kippur War between Egypt and Israel. In one of the longest tank battles ever, the Israelis crossed the Suez canal Oct 16 cutting off the Egyptian 3rd Army.

Sinai, Mount (Arabic *Gebel Mûsa*) mountain near the tip of the Sinai Peninsula; height 7,500 ft/ 2,285 m. According to the Old Testament this is where ◊Moses received the Ten Commandments from God.

Egypt established a religious complex (Jewish-Muslim-Christian) at Mount Sinai 1979.

Sinan 1489–1588. Ottoman architect, chief architect from 1538 to ◊Suleiman the Magnificent. Among the hundreds of buildings he designed are the Suleimaniye in Istanbul, a mosque complex, and the Topkapi Saray, palace of the Sultan (now a museum).

Sinatra Frank (Francis Albert) 1915– . US singer and film actor. In the 1930s and 1940s he sang songs such as "Night and Day" and "You'd Be So Nice To Come Home To" with the Harry James and Tommy Dorsey bands. He was celebrated for his love ballads, which were unmatched in phrasing and emotion, and gives concerts into the 1990s. From 1943 to 1945, he was soloist on "Your Hit Parade" earning even wider popularity.

After a slump in his career, he established himself as an actor. *From Here to Eternity* 1953 won him an Academy Award. His later career includes films, television and club appearances, forming a record company (Reprise), and his idiosyncratic rendering of the song "My Way."

Sinclair Upton 1878–1968. US novelist. His concern for social reforms is reflected in *The Jungle* 1906, an important example of naturalistic writing, which exposed the horrors of the Chicago meat-packing industry and led to a change in food-processing laws; *Boston* 1928; and his Lanny Budd series 1940–53, including *Dragon's Teeth* 1942, which won the Pulitzer Prize.

He was a committed Socialist who was actively involved in politics.

Sind province of SE Pakistan, mainly in the Indus delta

area 54,393 sq mi/140,914 sq km

capital and chief seaport Karachi

population (1981) 19,029,000

language 60% Sindi; others include Urdu, Punjabi, Baluchi, Puhsto

features Sukkur Barrage, which enables water from the Indus River to be used for irrigation

history annexed 1843, it became a province of British India, and part of Pakistan on independence. There is agitation for its creation as a separate state, Sindhudesh.

Sinding Christian (August) 1856–1941. Norwegian composer. His works include four symphonies, piano pieces (including *Rustle of Spring*), and songs. His brothers Otto (1842–1909) and Stephan (1846–1922), were painter and sculptor, respectively.

sine in trigonometry, a function of an angle in a right triangle defined as the ratio of the length of the side opposite the angle to the length of the hypotenuse (the longest side).

Various properties in physics vary sinusoidally; that is, they can be represented diagramatically by a sine wave (a graph obtained by plotting values of angles against the values of their sines). Examples include ◊simple harmonic motion, such as the way alternating current (AC) electricity varies with time.

sinfonietta an orchestral work that is of a shorter, lighter nature than a ◊symphony.

sine of an angle

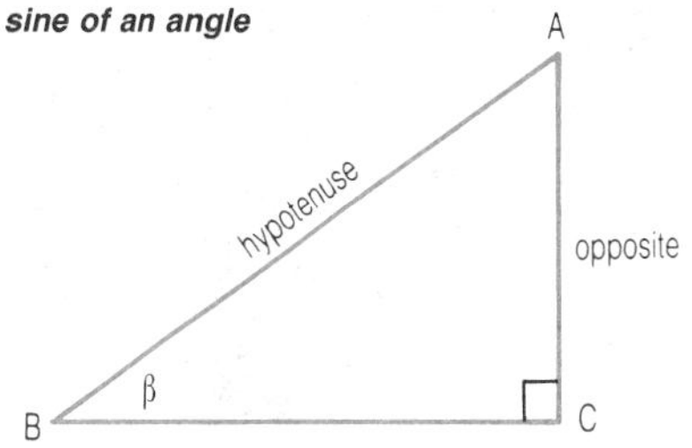
A
hypotenuse
opposite
B
β
C

$$\sin(e)\,\beta = \frac{\text{opposite}}{\text{hypotenuse}} = \frac{AC}{AB}$$

Singapore (Sanskrit *Singa pura*, "city of the lion") country in SE Asia, off the tip of the Malay Peninsula.

government Singapore has a single-tier system of government. The constitution of 1965 provided for a one-chamber parliament, whose 81 members are elected for five-year terms by universal suffrage from single-member constituencies on a winner-take-all basis. Parliament debates and votes on legislation and elects, for a four-year term, a ceremonial head of state (president). Executive power is held by a prime minister and cabinet drawn from the majority party within parliament. The dominant party in Singapore since independence has been the conservative People's Action Party (PAP).

history For early history, see ◊Malay Peninsula. Singapore was leased as a trading post in 1819 from the sultan of Johore by the British East India Company, on the advice of Stamford ◊Raffles, at a time when it was a swampy jungle. It passed to the crown in 1858 and formed part of the ◊Straits Settlements 1867–1942.

During World War II, Singapore functioned as a vital British military base in the Far East. Designed to be invulnerable to naval attack, it was invaded by land and occupied by Japan Feb 1942–Sept 1945. Singapore became a separate British crown colony in 1946 and fully self-governing, with ◊Lee Kuan Yew as prime minister, from 1959. It joined the Federation of ◊Malaysia in 1963 but seceded in 1965, alleging discrimination against the federation's Chinese members. A new independent republic of Singapore was thus formed in Sept 1965, which remained within the ◊Commonwealth.

The new republic's internal political affairs were dominated by Prime Minister Lee Kuan Yew's PAP, which gained a monopoly of all parliamentary seats in the elections between 1968 and 1980. Under Lee's stewardship, Singapore has developed rapidly as a commercial and financial entrepot and as a center for new export industries. Today its inhabitants enjoy the highest standard of living in Asia outside Japan and Brunei.

During the early 1980s, as the pace of economic

sine wave

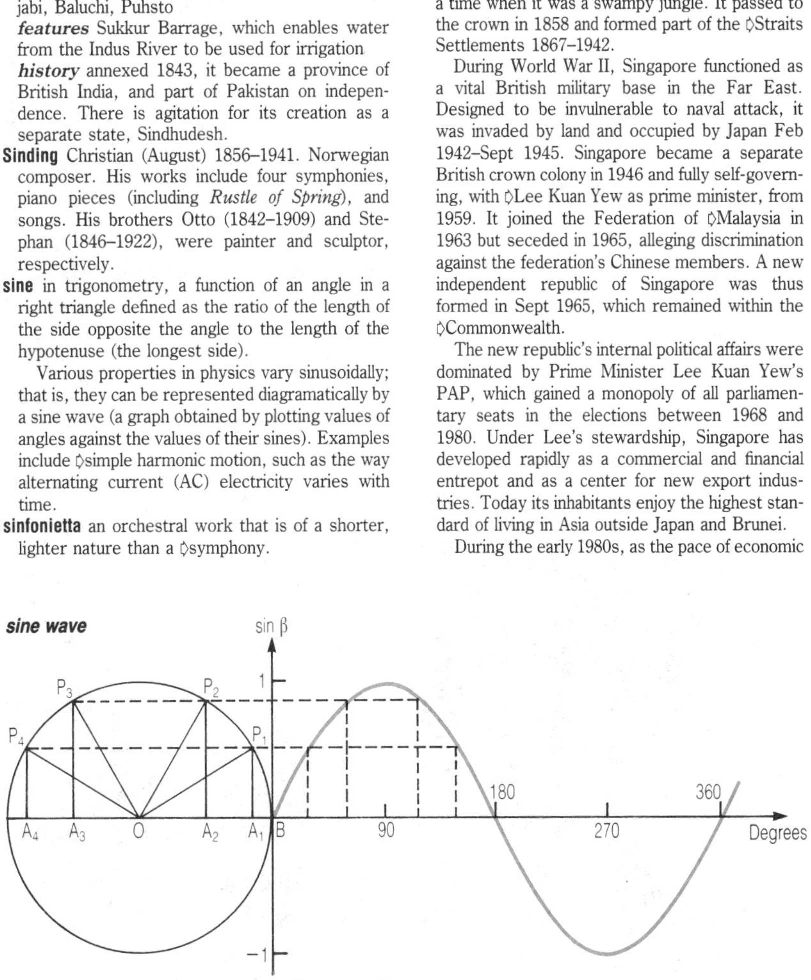
sin β
1
-1
P3
P2
P4
P1
180
360
A4
A3
O
A2
A1
B
90
270
Degrees

Note: $B\hat{O}P_4 = 180° - B\hat{O}P_1$ $\Rightarrow \sin B\hat{O}P_4 = \sin B\hat{O}P_1$

$B\hat{O}P_3 = 180° - B\hat{O}P_2$ & $\sin B\hat{O}P_3 = \sin B\hat{O}P_2$

Singapore
Republic of

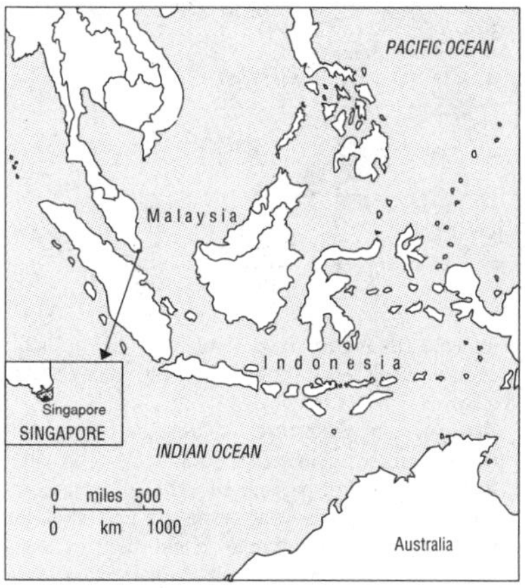
PACIFIC OCEAN
Malaysia
Indonesia
Singapore
SINGAPORE
INDIAN OCEAN
0 miles 500
0 km 1000
Australia

area 240 sq mi/622 sq km
capital Singapore City
cities Jurong, Changi
physical comprises Singapore Island, low and flat, and 57 small islands
features Singapore Island is joined to mainland by causeway across Strait of Johore; temperature range 69°–93°F/21°–34°C
head of state Wee Kim Wee from 1985
head of government Goh Chok Tong from 1990
political system liberal democracy with strict limits on dissent
political parties People's Action Party (PAP) conservative; Worker's Party (WP), Socialist; Singapore Democratic Party (SDP), liberal pluralist
exports electronics, petroleum products, rubber, machinery, vehicles
currency Singapore dollar (S$2.86 = £July 1, 1991)
population (1990 est) 2,703,000 (Chinese 75%, Malay 14%, Tamil 7%); growth rate 1.2% p.a.
life expectancy men 71, women 77 (1989)
language Malay (national tongue), Chinese, Tamil, English (all official)
religion Buddhist, Taoist, Muslim, Hindu, Christian
literacy men 93%/women 79% (1985 est)
GDP $19.9 bn (1987); $7,616 per head
chronology
1819 Singapore leased to British East India Company.
1858 Placed under crown rule.
1942 Invaded and occupied by Japan.
1945 Japanese removed by British forces.
1959 Independence achieved from Britain; Lee Kuan Yew became prime minister.
1963 Joined new Federation of Malaysia.
1965 Left federation to become independent republic.
1984 Opposition made advances in parliamentary elections.
1986 Opposition leader convicted of perjury, prohibited from standing for election.
1988 Ruling conservative party elected to all but one of available assembly seats; increasingly authoritarian rule.
1990 Lee Kuan Yew resigned as prime minister; replaced by Goh Chok Tong.

growth briefly slowed, opposition to the Lee regime began to surface, with support for the PAP falling from 76% to 63% in the Dec 1984 election and two opposition deputies winning parliamentary seats for the first time. Lee responded by taking a firmer line against dissent, with J B Jeyaretnam, the Workers' Party leader, being conveniently found guilty of perjury in Nov 1986 and deprived of his parliamentary seat. Support for the PAP held steady, at 62%, in the Sept 1988 election and the opposition won only one seat. Plans were unveiled to create a new position of elected executive president. In Nov 1990 Lee resigned, handing over to his deputy, Goh Chok Tong, but remaining a senior member of the cabinet.

Singapore allied itself closely with the US 1965–74. Since the mid-1970s, however, it has pursued a neutralist foreign policy and improved its relations with China. It is a member of ◊ASEAN.

Singapore *Singapore's city skyline.*

Singapore City capital of Singapore, on the SE coast of the island of Singapore; population (1980) 2,413,945. It is an oil refining center and port.

Singer Isaac Bashevis 1904–1991. Polish-born US novelist and short-story writer. His works, written in Yiddish, then translated into English, often portray traditional Jewish life in Poland and the US, and the loneliness of old age. They include *Gimpel the Fool* 1957, *The Slave* 1960, *Shosha* 1978, *Old Love* 1979, *Lost in America* 1981, *The Image and Other Stories* 1985, and *The Death of Methuselah* 1988. He has also written plays and books for children. In 1978 he was awarded the Nobel Prize for Literature.

He fled Nazi-dominated Europe and became a US citizen 1942.

Singer Isaac Merit 1811–1875. US inventor of domestic and industrial sewing machines. Within a few years of opening his first factory 1851, he became the world's largest manufacturer (despite charges of patent infringement by Elias ◊Howe), and by the late 1860s more than 100,000 Singer sewing machines were in use in the US alone. To make his machines available to the widest market, Singer became the first manufacturer to offer attractive installment credit terms.

Singer *US novelist Isaac Bashevis Singer, born in Poland, received the Nobel Prize for Literature in 1978.*

Singh Vishwanath Pratap 1931– Indian politician, prime minister 1989–90. As a member of the Congress (I) Party, he held ministerial posts under Indira Gandhi and Rajiv Gandhi, and from 1984, led an anticorruption drive. When he unearthed an arms-sales scandal in 1988, he was ousted from the government and party and formed a broad-based opposition alliance, the ◊Janata Dal, which won the Nov 1989 election. Mounting caste and communal conflict split the Janata Dal and forced him out of office in Nov 1990.

Singh was born in Allahabad, the son of a local raja. He was minister of commerce 1976–77 and 1983, Uttar Pradesh chief minister 1980–82, minister of finance 1984–86, and of defense 1986–87, when he discovered the embarrassing Bofors scandal. Respected for his probity and sense of principle, Singh emerged as one of the most popular politicians in India.

Singh, Gobind see ◊Gobind Singh, Sikh guru.

single party state another name for ◊one party state.

single-sideband transmission radio-wave transmission using either the frequency band above the carrier wave frequency, or below, instead of both (as now).

Sing Sing name until 1901 of the village of Ossining, New York, with a state prison of that name from 1825 to 1969, when it was renamed the Ossining State Correctional Facility.

singularity in astrophysics, the point at the center of a ◊black hole at which it is predicted that the infinite gravitational forces will compress the infalling mass of the collapsing star to infinite density. It is a point in space-time at which the known laws of physics break down. Singularity is thought, in the ◊Big Bang theory of the origin of the universe, to be the point from which the expansion of the universe began.

Sinhalese member of the majority population of Sri Lanka; also their language and culture. The Sinhalese language belongs to the Indo-Iranian branch of the Indo-European family.

Sining alternative transliteration of the city of ◊Xining, Tsinghai province, W central China.

Sinkiang-Uighur former name of ◊Xinjian Uygur, autonomous region of NW China.

Sinn Féin (Gaelic "We ourselves") Irish nationalist party founded by Arthur Griffith (1872–1922) in

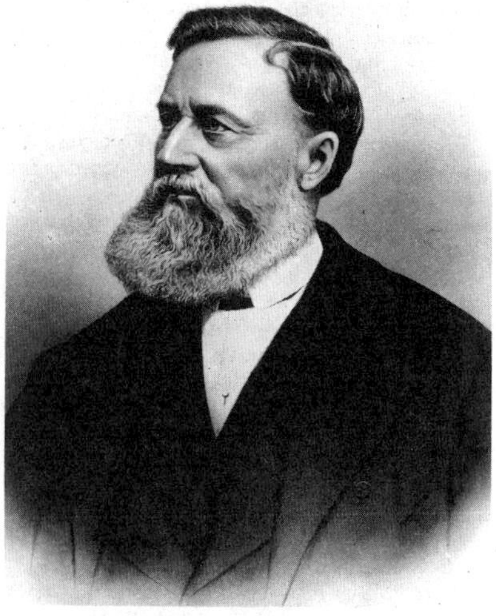

Singer *US inventor of the sewing machine, Isaac Merit Singer succeeded in mass-producing and selling them around the world.*

1905; in 1917 ◊de Valera became its president. It is the political wing of the Irish Republican Army and is similarly split between comparative moderates and extremists. In 1985 it gained representation in 17 of 26 district councils in Northern Ireland.

Sino-Japanese Wars wars waged by Japan against China to expand to the mainland.

First Sino-Japanese War 1894–95. Under the treaty of Shimonoseki, Japan secured the "independence" of Korea, cession of Taiwan and the nearby Pescadores Islands, and the Liaodong peninsula (for a naval base). France, Germany, and Russia pressured Japan into returning the last-named, which Russia occupied 1896 to establish Port Arthur (now Lüda); this led to the Russo-Japanese War 1904–05.

Second Sino-Japanese War 1931–45.

1931–32 The Japanese occupied Manchuria, which they formed into the puppet state of Manchukuo. They also attacked Shanghai, and moved into NE China.

1937 Chinese leaders Chiang Kai-shek and Mao Zedong allied to fight the Japanese; war was renewed as the Japanese overran NE China and seized Shanghai and Nanjing.

1938 Japanese capture of Wuhan and Guangzhou was followed by the transfer of the Chinese capital to Chongqing; a period of stalemate followed.

1941 Japanese attack on the US (see ◊Pearl Harbor) led to the extension of lend-lease aid to China and US entry into war against Japan and its allies.

1944 A Japanese offensive threatened Chongqing.

1945 The Chinese received the Japanese surrender at Nanjing in Sept, after the Allies had concluded World War II.

Sino-Soviet split period of strained relations between the two major communist powers, China and the USSR, during the early 1960s, thus dividing the communist world. The tension was based partly on differences in ideology but also involved rivalry for leadership and old territorial border claims. The Chinese Communists also criticized the USSR for supplying aircraft to India and for withdrawing technical and military aid to China in 1960. The USSR supported India in its border warfare with China between 1961 and 1962.

Sinuiju capital of North Pyongan province, near the mouth of the Yalu River, North Korea; population (1984) 754,000. It was founded 1910.

sinusitis painful inflammation of one of the sinuses, or air spaces, that surround the nasal passages. Most cases clear with antibiotics and nasal decongestants, but some require surgical drainage.

Sinusitis most frequently involves the maxillary sinuses, within the cheek bones, producing pain around the eyes, toothache, and a nasal discharge.

Sioux member of a group of North American ◊Plains Indians (also called the Dakota), now living on reservations in South Dakota and Nebraska, and among the general public. When gold was discovered in their treaty territory, the US sent in troops to remove them 1876. Under chiefs Crazy Horse and Sitting Bull they defeated Lt Col George Custer at Little Bighorn, Montana; as a result, Congress abrogated the Fort Laramie Treaty of 1868 (which had given the Sioux a large area in the Black Hills of Dakota). Gold, uranium, coal, oil, and natural gas have been found there since, and the Sioux pressed for and were awarded $160 million compensation 1980.

Sioux City city in NW Iowa, on the Missouri river, near Iowa's border with Nebraska and South Dakota. Industries include food processing, fabricated metals, fertilizer, and meatpacking. It is the head of navigation for the Missouri river; population (1990) 80,505.

Sioux Falls largest city in South Dakota; population (1990) 100,814. Its industry (electrical goods and agricultural machinery) is powered by the Big Sioux River over the Sioux Falls 100 ft/30 m. Large stockyards, slaughterhouses, and meatpacking plants are also here. Sioux Falls was founded 1856 but was abandoned during the Sioux Indian uprising of 1862. It was resettled with the establishment of Fort Dakota here 1865.

siphon tube in the form of an inverted U with unequal arms. When it is filled with liquid and the shorter arm is placed in a tank or reservoir, liquid flows out of the longer arm provided that its exit is below the level of the surface of the liquid in the tank.

It works on the principle that the pressure at the liquid surface is atmospheric pressure, whereas at the lower end of the longer arm it is less than atmospheric pressure, causing flow to occur.

siren in Greek mythology, a sea nymph who lured sailors to their deaths along rocky coasts by her singing. ◊Odysseus, in order to hear the sirens safely, tied himself to the mast of his ship and stuffed his crew's ears with wax.

Sirius or ***Dog Star*** or ***Alpha Canis Majoris*** the brightest star in the sky, 8.7 light-years from Earth in the constellation Canis Major. Sirius is a white star with a mass 2.35 times that of the Sun, a diameter 1.8 times that of the Sun, and a luminosity of 23 Suns. It is orbited every 50 years by a white dwarf, Sirius B.

Sirk Douglas. Adopted name of Claus Detlef Sierck 1900–1987. German film director of Danish descent, who studied in Germany but left 1937 because of the Nazi regime, and eventually went to Hollywood. During the 1950s he made a series of lurid American melodramas slick with color and lush decor. Commercially successful at the time for these qualities, the films were also subsequently praised by critics for their implicit critiques of American postwar capitalist society, including *All that Heaven Allows* 1956 and *Written on the Wind* 1957. He retired 1959 and returned to Germany.

sirocco a hot, normally dry and dust-laden wind that blows from the deserts of N Africa, across the Mediterranean into S Europe. It occurs mainly in the spring. The name "sirocco" is also applied to any hot oppressive wind.

Sirte, Gulf of gulf off the coast of Libya, on which Benghazi stands. Access to the gulf waters has been a cause of dispute between Libya and the US.

sisal strong fiber made from various species of ◊agave, such as *Agave sisalina.*

Sisley Alfred 1839–1899. French Impressionist painter whose landscapes include views of Port-Marly and the river Seine, painted during floods in 1876.

Sisley studied in an academic studio in Paris, where he met Monet and Renoir. They took part in the First Impressionist Exhibition 1874. Unlike most other Impressionists, Sisley's style developed slowly and surely, without obvious changes.

Sistine Chapel a chapel in the Vatican, Rome, begun under Pope Sixtus IV in 1473 by Giovanni del Dolci, and decorated by (among others) ◊Michelangelo. It houses the conclave that meets to select a new pope.

Built to the proportions of Solomon's temple in the Old Testament (its height one-half and its width one-third of its length), it has frescoes on the walls (emphasizing the authority and legality of the papacy) by ◊Botticelli, ◊Ghirlandaio, and on the altar wall and ceiling by Michelangelo.

Sisulu Walter 1912– . South African civil-rights activist, one of the first full-time secretary generals of the African National Congress (ANC), in 1964, with Nelson Mandela. He was imprisoned following the 1964 ◊Rivonia Trial for opposition to the apartheid system and released, at the age of 77, as a gesture of reform by President F W ◊De Klerk 1989.

Sisyphus in Greek mythology, king of Corinth who, after his evil life, was condemned in the underworld to roll a huge stone uphill, which always fell back before he could reach the top.

Sita in Hinduism, the wife of Rama, an avatar (manifestation) of the god Vishnu; a character in the ◊*Rāmāyana* epic, characterized by chastity and kindness.

sitar Indian stringed instrument. It has a pear-shaped body, long neck, and an additional gourd resonator at the opposite end. A principal solo instrument, it has seven metal strings extending over movable frets and two concealed strings that provide a continuous singing drone.

sitatunga herbivorous antelope *Tragelaphus spekei* found in several swamp regions in Central Africa. The hooves are long and splayed to help progress on soft surfaces. They are up to about 4 ft/1.2 m high at the shoulder; the males have thick horns up to 3 ft/90 cm long. Males are dark grayish brown, females and young are chestnut, all with whitish markings on the rather shaggy fur.

Sitting Bull c. 1834–1893. North American Indian chief who agreed to ◊Sioux resettlement 1868. When the treaty was broken by the US, he led the Sioux against Lieutenant Colonel ◊Custer at the Battle of the ◊Little Bighorn 1876. He was pursued by the US Army and forced to flee to Canada. He was allowed to return 1881, and he toured in the Wild West show of "Buffalo Bill" ◊Cody. He settled on a Dakota reservation and was killed during his arrest on suspicion of involvement in Indian agitations.

Sitwell Edith 1887–1964. English poet whose series of poems *Façade* was performed as recitations to the specially written music of William ◊Walton from 1923.

Sitwell Sacheverell 1897–1988. English poet and art critic. His work includes *Southern Baroque Art* 1924 and *British Architects and Craftsmen* 1945; poetry; and prose miscellanies such as *Of Sacred and Profane Love* 1940 and *Splendor and Miseries* 1943.

SI units (French Système International d'Unités) standard system of scientific units used by scientists worldwide. Originally proposed in 1960, it replaces the m.k.s., ◊c.g.s., and ◊f.p.s. systems. It is based on seven basic units: the meter (m)

Sitting Bull *Sioux leader Sitting Bull, whose forces annihilated George Armstrong Custer's troops at the Battle of the Little Big Horn in 1876.*

Siva Nataraja: *Siva as Lord of the Dance. A bronze statue from Madras State, probably Tanjore-Pudukottai region. It is of the Chola dynasty, which ruled in the 10th century* AD.

for length, kilogram (kg) for weight, second (s) for time, ampere (A) for electrical current, kelvin (K) for temperature, mole (mol) for amount of substance, and candela (cd) for luminosity.

Siva or ***Shiva*** in Hinduism, the third chief god (with Brahma and Vishnu). As Mahadeva (great lord), he is the creator, symbolized by the phallic *lingam*, who restores what as Mahakala he destroys. He is often sculpted as Nataraja, performing his fruitful cosmic dance. His consort or female principle (*sakti*) is Parvati, otherwise known as Durga or Kali.

Six Articles act introduced by Henry VIII in England in 1539 to settle disputes over dogma in the English Church. The articles affirmed belief in transubstantiation, communion in one kind only, auricular confession, monastic vows, celibacy of the clergy, and private masses. The act was repealed in 1547.

Six Counties the six counties that form northern Ireland: Antrim, Armagh, Down, Fermanagh, Londonderry, and Tyrone.

Six-Day War common name for one of the ◊Arab-Israeli Wars.

Six, Les a group of French 20th-century composers; see ◊Les Six.

Sixtus five popes, including:

Sixtus IV 1414–1484. pope from 1471. He built the Sistine Chapel in the Vatican, which is named after him.

Sixtus V 1521–1590. pope from 1585. He supported the Spanish Armada against Britain and the Catholic League against Henry IV of France.

SJ abbreviation for Society of Jesus (see ◊Jesuits).

Sjælland or ***Zealand*** the main island of ◊Denmark, on which Copenhagen is situated; area 2,700 sq mi/7,000 sq km; population (1970) 2,130,000. It is low-lying with an irregular coastline. The chief industry is dairy farming.

Skagerrak arm of the North Sea between the S coast of Norway and the N coast of Denmark. In May 1916 it was the scene of the Battle of ◊Jutland.

Skåne or ***Scania*** area of S Sweden. It is a densely populated and fertile agricultural region, comprising the counties of Malmöhus and Kristianstad. Malmö and Hälsingborg are leading centers. It was under Danish rule until ceded to Sweden 1658.

skate several species of flatfish of the ray group. The common skate *Raja batis* is up to 6 ft/1.8 m long and grayish, with black specks. The egg-cases ("mermaids' purses") are often washed ashore by the tide.

skateboard single flexible board mounted on wheels, and steerable by weight positioning. As a land alternative to surfing, skateboards developed in California in the 1960s and became a worldwide craze in the 1970s. Skateboarding is practiced in urban environments and has enjoyed a revival since the late 1980s.

skating self-propulsion on ice by means of bladed skates, or on other surfaces by skates with small rollers (wheels of wood, metal, or plastic). The chief competitive ice-skating events are figure skating, for singles or pairs, ice-dancing, and simple speed skating.

The roller skate was the invention of James L Plympton, who opened the first rink at Newport, Rhode Island, 1866; events are as for ice-skating with European and world championships.

Ice-skating became possible as a world sport from the opening of the first artificial ice rink in London, England, 1876. The first world ice-skating championships were held in 1896.

skeleton the rigid or semirigid framework that supports an animal's body, protects its internal organs, and provides anchorage points for its muscles. The skeleton may be composed of bone and cartilage (vertebrates), chitin (arthropods), calcium carbonate (mollusks and other invertebrates, or silica (many protists).

It may be internal, forming an ◊endoskeleton, or external, forming an ◊exoskeleton. Another type of skeleton, found in invertebrates such as earthworms, is the hydrostatic skeleton. This gains partial rigidity from fluid enclosed within a body cavity. Because the fluid cannot be compressed, contraction of one part of the body results in extension of another part, giving peristaltic motion.

Skepticism ancient philosophical view that absolute knowledge of things is ultimately unobtainable, hence the only proper attitude is to suspend judgment. Its origins lay in the teachings of the Greek philosopher Pyrrho, who maintained that peace of mind lay in renouncing all claims to knowledge.

It was taken up in a less extreme form by the Greek ◊Academy in the 3rd and 2nd centuries BC. Academic skeptics claimed that although truth is finally unknowable, a balance of probabilities can be used for coming to decisions. The most radical form of skepticism is known as ◊solipsism, which maintains that the self is the only thing that can be known to exist.

skiffle a style of British popular music, introduced by singer and banjo player Lonnie Donegan (1931–) in 1956, using improvised percussion instruments such as tea chests and washboards.

skiing self-propulsion on snow by means of elongated runners (skis) for the feet, slightly bent upward at the tip. It is a popular recreational sport, as cross-country ski touring or as downhill runs on mountain trails; events include downhill; slalom, in which a series of turns between flags have to be negotiated; cross-country racing; and ski jumping, when jumps of over 490 ft/150 m are achieved from ramps up to 295 ft/90 m high. Speed-skiing uses skis approximately one-third longer and wider than normal, with which speeds of up to 125 mph/200 kmph have been recorded. Recently, monoboarding or the use of a single, very broad ski, similar to a surf board, used with the feet facing the front and placed together, has become increasingly popular. See ◊surfing.

Skiing was known as a means of transportation over snow in N Europe and Asia from about 3000 BC. It developed into a sport when innovations in ski design made it possible to maneuver more accurately, around 1896. Ski resorts then began as a winter-vacation business in Europe and the US, but not until the 1970s did skiing become a recreation for any but the wealthy or for those who lived in ski conditions. Today it is one of the most popular winter sport activities in the US, with ski schools and camps, as well as overcrowded resorts in New England and the Rocky Mountain states. The Alpine World Cup was first held in 1967.

Skikda trading port in Algeria; population (1983) 141,000. Products include wine, citrus, and vegetables. It was founded by the French 1838 as Philippeville and renamed after independence 1962.

skeleton

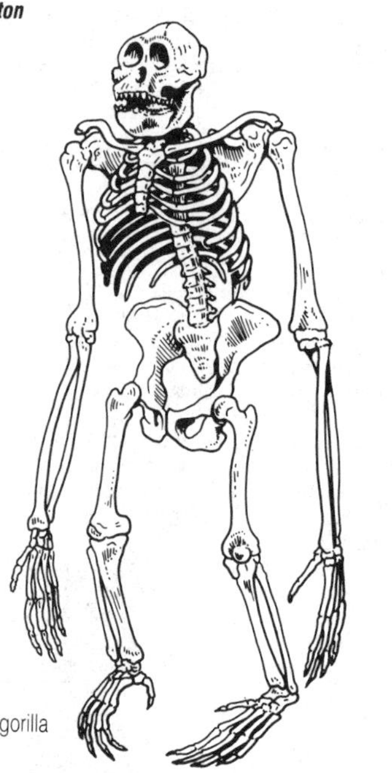

gorilla

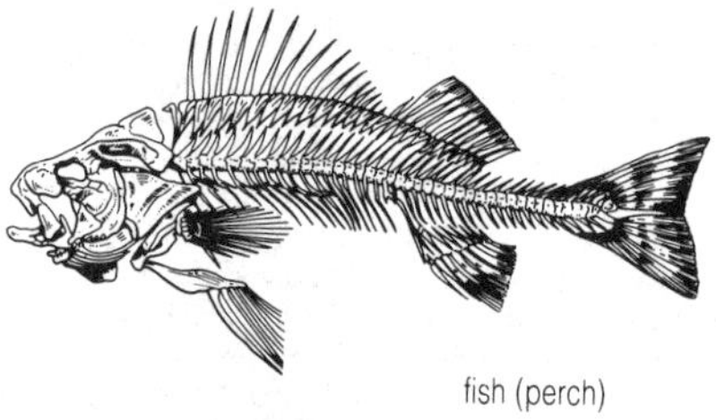

fish (perch)

crab
(carapace and exoskeleton)

stag beetle (exoskeleton)

skiing *Swiss skier Pirmin Zurbriggen at the World Championships 1989.*

skin the covering of the body of a vertebrate. In mammals, the outer layer (epidermis) is dead and protective, and its cells are constantly being rubbed away and replaced from below. The lower layer (dermis) contains blood vessels, nerves, hair roots, and sweat and sebaceous glands, and is supported by a network of fibrous and elastic cells.

Skin grafting is the repair of injured skin by placing pieces of skin, taken from elsewhere on the body, over the injured area. The field of medicine dealing with skin is called dermatology.

skink lizard of the family Scincidae, a large family of about 700 species found throughout the tropics and subtropics. The body is usually long, and the legs reduced. Some are actually legless and rather snakelike. Many are good burrowers, or can "swim" through sand, like the sandfish genus *Scincus* of N Africa. Some skinks lay eggs, others bear live young.

Skinks include the three-toed skink *Chalcides chalcides* of S Europe and NW Africa, up to 1.3 ft/40 cm long, of which half is tail, and the stump-tailed skink *Tiligua rugosus* of Australia, which stores fat in its triangular tail, looks the same at either end, and feeds on fruit as well as small animals.

Skinner B(urrhus) F(rederic) 1903–1990. US psychologist, a radical behaviorist who rejected mental concepts, having seen the organism as a "black box" where internal processes are not significant in predicting behavior. He studied operant conditioning and maintained that behavior is shaped and maintained by its consequences.

His text *The Behavior of Organisms* 1938 set forth his argument that a certain behavior may be obtained by positive reinforcement or eliminated by withholding reinforcement. He applied his conditioning technique to education—pioneering programmed learning—and to clinical work with psychotic patients. He devised a teaching machine to reinforce learning by reward.

Skolimowski Jerzy 1938– . Polish film director, formerly a writer, active both in his own country and other parts of Europe. His films include *Deep End* 1970, *The Shout* 1978, and *Moonlighting* 1982.

skin

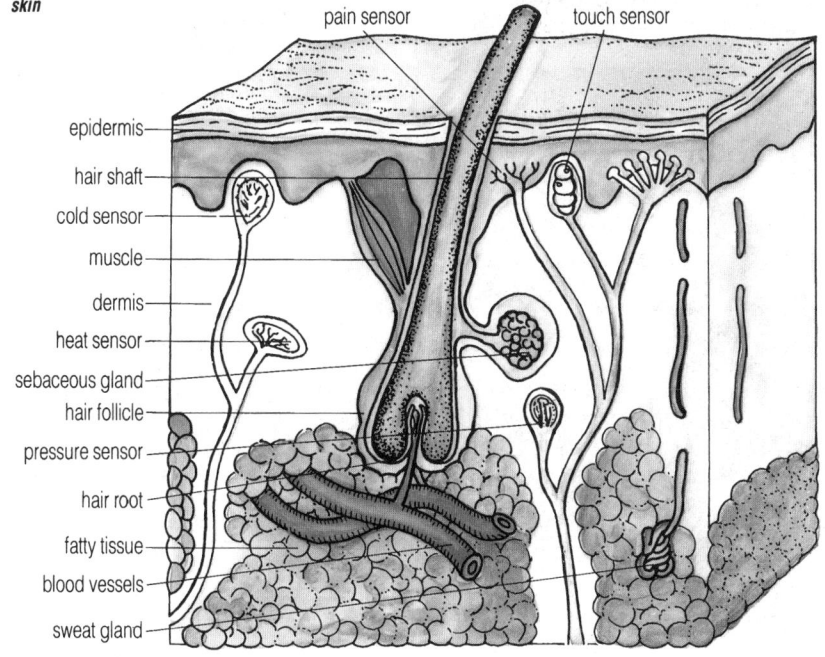

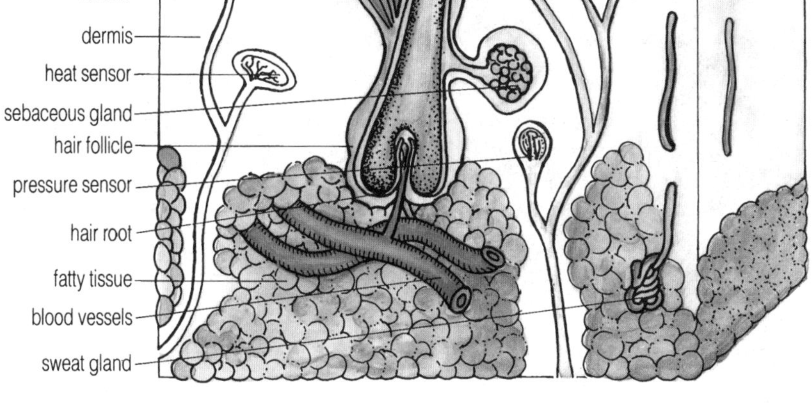
pain sensor
touch sensor
epidermis
hair shaft
cold sensor
muscle
dermis
heat sensor
sebaceous gland
hair follicle
pressure sensor
hair root
fatty tissue
blood vessels
sweat gland

Skopje capital and industrial city of Macedonia, Yugoslavia; population (1981) 506,547. Industries include iron, steel, chromium mining, and food processing.

It stands on the site of an ancient town destroyed by an earthquake in the 5th century and was taken in the 13th century by the Serbian king Milutin, who made it his capital. Again destroyed by an earthquake 1963, Skopje was rebuilt on a safer site nearby. It is an Islamic center.

skua dark-colored gull-like seabird living in arctic and antarctic waters. Skuas can grow up to 2 ft/60 cm long, and are good fliers. They are aggressive scavengers, and will seldom fish for themselves but force gulls to disgorge their catch, and will also eat chicks of other birds.

The largest species is the great skua *Stercorarius skua* of the N Atlantic, 2 ft/60 cm long and dark brown on the upper parts.

skull in vertebrates, the collection of flat and irregularly shaped bones (or cartilage) that enclose the brain and the organs of sight, hearing, and smell, and provide support for the jaws. In mammals, the skull consists of 22 bones joined by sutures. The floor of the skull is pierced by a large hole for the spinal cord and a number of smaller apertures through which other nerves and blood vessels pass.

The bones of the face include the upper jaw, enclose the sinuses, and form the framework for the nose, eyes, and roof of the mouth cavity. The lower jaw is hinged to the middle of the skull at its lower edge. The opening to the middle ear is located near the jaw hinge. The plate at the back of the head is jointed at its lower edge with the upper section of the spine. Inside, the skull has various shallow cavities into which fit different parts of the brain.

The human skull has evolved from robust to gracile in the past 5.5 million years; it exhibits ◊neoteny (infantilism), whereby the youthful features of ancient ◊human species are retained in the adult skulls of modern humans—probably to make room for the evolving and enlarging brain.

skunk North American mammal of the weasel family. The common skunk *Mephitis mephitis* has a long, arched body, short legs, a bushy tail, and black fur with white streaks on the back. In self-defense, it discharges a foul-smelling fluid.

skunk cabbage either of two disagreeably smelling North American plants of the arum family Araceae: *Symplocarpus foetidus*, of the E, growing in wet soils and having large, cabbagelike leaves and a fleshy blunt spike of tiny flowers in a purple, hooded sheath; or *Lysichiton americanum* of the W, having similar appearance except that the sheath enclosing a more elongated flower spike is yellow.

skydiving the sport of freefalling from an aircraft at a height of up to 12,000 ft/3,650 m ft, performing aerobatics, and opening a parachute when 2,000 ft/600 m from the ground.

Skye largest island of the Inner Hebrides, Scotland; area 672 sq mi/1,740 sq km; population (1987) 8,100. It is separated from the mainland by the Sound of Sleat. The chief port is Portree. The economy is based on crofting, tourism, and livestock.

Skylab US space station, launched May 14, 1973, made from the adapted upper stage of a Saturn V rocket. At 82.5 tons, it was the heaviest object ever put into space, and was 84 ft/25.6 m long. *Skylab* contained a workshop for carrying out experiments in weightlessness, an observatory for monitoring the Sun, and cameras for photographing the Earth's surface.

Damaged during launch, it had to be repaired by the first crew of astronauts. Three crews, each of three astronauts, occupied *Skylab* for periods of up to 84 days, at that time a record duration for

skull

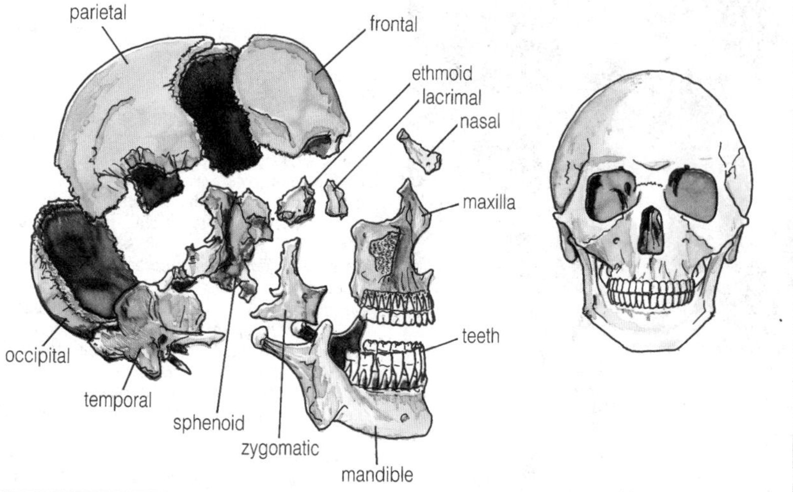
parietal
frontal
ethmoid
lacrimal
nasal
maxilla
teeth
occipital
temporal
sphenoid
zygomatic
mandible

human spaceflight. *Skylab* entered Earth's atmosphere and fell on July 11, 1979, dropping debris on W Australia.

skylark a type of ◊lark.

Skyros or ***Skiros*** Greek island, the largest of the northern ◊Sporades; area 81 sq mi/210 sq km; population (1981) 2,750. It is known for its furniture and weaving. The English poet Rupert Brooke is buried here.

skyscraper a building so tall that it appears to "scrape the sky," popularized in New York, where land prices were high and the geology permitted such methods of construction.

The world's tallest free-standing structure is the CN (Canadian National) Tower, Toronto, 1,821 ft/555 m. In Manhattan, New York City, are the Empire State Building (1930–32), 102 stories and 1,250 ft/381 m high, and the 1970s twin towers of the World Trade Center 1,361 ft/415 m, but these were surpassed by the Sears Tower (1973–74) 1,454 ft/443 m in Chicago. Chicago was the home of the first skyscraper, the Home Insurance Building (1885), which was built ten stories high with an iron and steel frame. A rigid steel frame is the key to skyscraper construction, taking all the building loads. The walls simply "hang" from the frame (curtain walling), and they can thus be made from relatively light materials such as glass and aluminum.

Skyscrapers were made possible by the 1850s elevators, but the introduction of the 1880s metal-frame construction in Chicago allowed for advances and are now found in cities throughout the world.

slag in chemistry, the molten mass of impurities that is produced in the smelting or refining of metals.

The slag produced in the manufacture of iron in a ◊blast furnace floats on the surface above the molten iron. It contains mostly silicates, phosphates, and sulfates of calcium. When cooled, the solid is broken up and used as a core material in the foundations of roads and buildings.

slaked lime $Ca(OH)_2$ (technical name calcium hydroxide) substance produced by adding water to quicklime (calcium oxide, CaO). Much heat is given out, and the solid crumbles as it absorbs water. A solution of slaked lime is called ◊limewater.

slang extremely informal language usage. It is not usually accepted in formal speech or writing and includes expressions that may be impolite or taboo in conventional terms.

Forms of slang develop among particular groups, for example soldiers, teenagers, and criminals, and are often extended into more general use because social conditions make them fashionable or people have grown accustomed to using them. Some types of slang are highly transient; others may last across generations and gain currency in the standard language. Because slang is often vivid, suggestive, and linked with subjects such as defecation, urination, sex, blasphemy, drink, and drugs, many people find it offensive. It is, however, pervasive in its influence.

slate a fine-grained, usually gray metamorphic rock that splits readily into thin slabs along its ◊cleavage plane. It is the metamorphic equivalent of ◊shale.

Slate is highly resistant to atmospheric conditions and can be used for writing on with chalk (actually gypsum). Quarrying slate takes such skill and time that it is now seldom used for roof and sill material except in restoring historic buildings.

Slater Samuel 1768–1835. British-born US industrialist. Slater was trained in machinery manufacture and worked as a mechanical supervisor in a textile mill. Immigrating to the US 1789 with detailed knowledge of British industrial technology, he was quickly hired by several American machine manufacturing firms. In 1791 he supervised the construction of a mill, based on the design of the English model, in Providence, Rhode Island, and eventually established his own manufacturing company 1798. His business acumen as mill owner and banker made him a central figure in the New England textile industry.

Slaughterhouse Cases two related US Supreme Court cases (*The Butchers' Benevolent Association of New Orleans* v *The Crescent City Livestock Landing and Slaughter Co*; *Esteban* v *Louisiana*) 1873 brought against the Louisiana legislature for its law granting one slaughterhouse exclusive rights to operate in New Orleans. The suits claimed that this monopoly was in violation of the privileges and immunities clause of the 14th Amendment because it prevented citizens from pursuing the professions of their choice. The Court upheld the Louisiana monopoly statute by 5 to 4, implementing a narrow interpretation of the 14th Amendment that left the protection of most civil rights to state governments.

Slav member of an Indo-European people, speaking closely related Slavonic languages. Their ancestors are believed to have included the ◊Sarmatians and ◊Scythians. Moving west from Central Asia, they settled E and SE Europe during the 2nd and 3rd millennia BC. There are now three groups: Eastern (Russians, Byelorussians, and Ukrainians); Western (Poles, Czechs, Slovaks, and Sorbs or Wends); and Southern (Serbs, Croats, Slovenes, Macedonians, and Bulgars).

The present Slavic nations emerged around the 5th and 6th centuries AD. By the 7th century they were the predominant population of E and SE Europe. During the 9th century they adopted Christianity.

slavery the enforced servitude of one person to another or one group to another. Slavery goes back to prehistoric times, but declined in Europe after the fall of the Roman Empire. During the imperialism of Spain, Portugal, and Britain in the 16th–18th centuries and in the American South in the 17th–19th centuries, slavery became a mainstay of an agricultural factory economy, with millions of Africans abducted to work on plantations in North and South America. Millions more died in the process, but the profits from this trade were enormous. Slavery was abolished in the British Empire 1833 and in the US at the end of

Skylab *A close-up view of the* Skylab *space station cluster, taken from the command module during the "fly-around" inspection. Launched in 1973,* Skylab *completed numerous important experiments before reentering the Earth's atmosphere and disintegrating in 1979.*

skyscraper

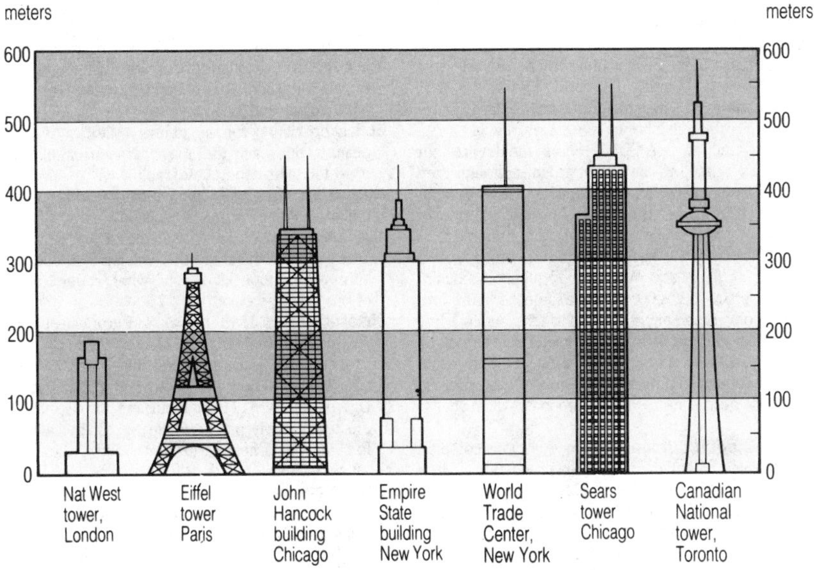
meters
meters
600
500
400
300
200
100
0
Nat West tower, London
Eiffel tower Paris
John Hancock building Chicago
Empire State building New York
World Trade Center, New York
Sears tower Chicago
Canadian National tower, Toronto

the Civil War 1863–65, but continues illegally in some countries.

Chattel slavery involves outright ownership of the slave by a master, but there are forms of partial slavery where an individual is tied to the land, or to another person, by legal obligations, as in ◊serfdom.

As a social and economic institution, slavery originated in the times when humans adopted sedentary farming methods of subsistence rather than more mobile forms of hunting and gathering. Slave labor became commonplace in ancient Greece and Rome, when it was used to cultivate large estates and to meet the demand for personal servants in the towns. Slaves were created through the capture of enemies, through birth to slave parents, through sale into slavery by free parents, and as a means of punishment.

After the fall of the Roman Empire in the 5th century, slavery persisted in Arab lands and in central Europe, where many Slavs were captured and taken as slaves to Germany (hence the derivation of the word). In Spain and Portugal, where the reconquest of the peninsula from the Moors in the 15th century created an acute shortage of labor, captured Muslims were enslaved. They were soon followed by slaves from Africa, imported by the Portuguese prince Henry the Navigator after 1444. Slaves were used for a wide range of tasks, and a regular trade in slaves was established between the Guinea Coast and the slave markets of the Iberian peninsula.

Slavery became of major economic importance after the 16th century with the European conquest of South and Central America. Needing a labor force but finding the indigenous inhabitants unwilling or unable to cooperate, the Spanish and Portuguese conquerors used ever-increasing numbers of slaves drawn from Africa. These slaves had a great impact on the sugar and coffee plantations. A lucrative triangular trade was established with alcohol, firearms, and textiles being shipped from Europe to be traded for slaves in Africa. The slaves would then be shipped to South or Central America where they would be traded for staples such as molasses and later raw cotton. In 1619 the first black slaves landed in an English colony in North America (Virginia).

The vast profits became a major element in the British economy and the West Indian trade in general. It has been estimated that the British slave trade alone shipped 2 million slaves from Africa to the West Indies between 1680 and 1786. The total slave trade to the Americas in the single year of 1790 may have exceeded 70,000. According to another estimate, during the nearly 400 years of the slave trade, a total of 15 million slaves were delivered to buyers and some 40 million Africans lost their lives in the notorious "middle crossing." Anti-slavery movements and changes in the political and economic structure of Europe helped to bring about the abolition of slavery in most of Europe during the later 18th and early 19th century, followed by abolition in overseas territories somewhat later.

Only in the Southern states of the US did slavery persist as a major, if not essential, component of the economy—providing the labor force for the cotton and other plantations. While the Northern states abolished slavery in the 1787–1804 period, the Southern states insisted on protecting the institution. Slavery became an issue in the economic struggles between Southern plantation owners and Northern industrialists in the first half of the 19th century, a struggle that culminated in the American Civil War.

Despite the common perception to the contrary, the war was not fought primarily on the slavery issue. Abraham Lincoln, however, saw the political advantages of promising freedom for Southern slaves, and the Emancipation Proclamation was enacted in 1863. This was reinforced after the war by the 13th, 14th, and 15th amendments to the US Constitution (1865, 1868, and 1870), which abolished slavery altogether and guaranteed citizenship and civil rights to former slaves. Apart from the moral issues, there has also been a good deal of debate on the economic efficiency of slavery as a system of production in the US. It has been argued that plantation owners might have been better off employing labor, although the effect of emancipating vast numbers of slaves could, and did, have enormous political and social repercussions in the Reconstruction period following the Civil War.

Although outlawed in most countries of the world, various forms of slavery continue to exist—as evidenced by the steps taken by international organizations such as the League of Nations between the World Wars and the United Nations since 1945 to curb such practices.

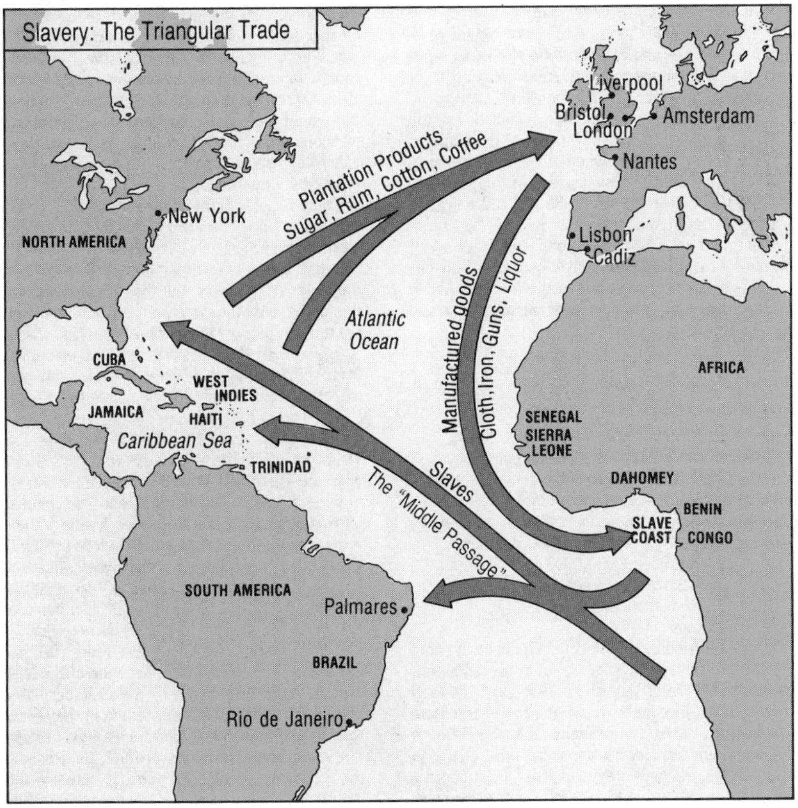
Slavery: The Triangular Trade
Liverpool
Bristol
London
Amsterdam
Nantes
Lisbon
Cadiz
New York
NORTH AMERICA
Plantation Products
Sugar, Rum, Cotton, Coffee
Manufactured goods
Cloth, Iron, Guns, Liquor
Atlantic Ocean
AFRICA
CUBA
WEST INDIES
JAMAICA
HAITI
Caribbean Sea
TRINIDAD
SENEGAL
SIERRA LEONE
DAHOMEY
BENIN
SLAVE COAST
CONGO
Slaves
The "Middle Passage"
SOUTH AMERICA
Palmares
BRAZIL
Rio de Janeiro

Slavic languages or ***Slavonic languages*** branch of the Indo-European language family spoken in central and E Europe, the Balkans, and parts of N Asia. The family comprises the southern group (Serbo-Croatian, Slovenian, and Macedonian in Yugoslavia, and Bulgarian in Bulgaria); the western group (Czech and Slovak in Czechoslovakia, Sorbian in Germany, and Polish and its related dialects); and the eastern group (Russian, Ukrainian, and Byelorussian in the USSR).

There is such a high degree of uniformity among the Slavic languages that scholars speak of a "dialect continuum" in which the users of one variety understand fairly well much of what is said in other varieties. Some Slavic languages, like

Polish, are written in the Roman alphabet while others, like Russian, use the Cyrillic alphabet.

Slavkov Czech name of ◊Austerlitz.

Slavophile intellectual and political group in 19th-century Russia that promoted the idea of an Eastern European orientation for the empire in opposition to those who wanted the country to adopt Western methods and ideas of development.

SLBM abbreviation for submarine-launched ballistic missile; see ◊nuclear warfare.

sleep a state of reduced awareness and activity that occurs at regular intervals in most mammals and birds, though there is considerable variation in the amount of time spent sleeping. Sleep differs from hibernation in that it occurs daily rather than seasonally, and involves less drastic reductions in metabolism. The function of sleep is unclear. People deprived of sleep become irritable, uncoordinated, forgetful, hallucinatory, and even psychotic.

In humans, sleep is linked with hormone levels and specific brain electrical activity, including delta waves, quite different from the brain's waking activity. REM (rapid eye movement) phases, associated with dreams, occur at regular intervals during sleep, when the eyes move rapidly below closed lids.

Species that do not have distinct periods of sleep (most invertebrates and fishes, for example) have short intervals of reduced activity throughout a given 24-hour period.

Extensive periods of sleep may have developed to make animals inconspicuous at times when they would be vulnerable to predators.

sleeping pill any pill or capsule that contains a drug (especially one of the ◊barbiturates) that induces sleep; in small doses, such drugs may relieve anxiety.

sleeping sickness or ***trypanosomiasis*** infectious disease of tropical Africa. Early symptoms include fever, headache, and chills, followed by ◊anemia and joint pains. Later, the disease attacks the central nervous system, causing drowsiness, lethargy, and, if left untreated, death. Sleeping sickness is caused by either of two ◊trypanosomes, *Trypanosoma gambiense* or *T. rhodesiense*. Control is by eradication of the tsetse fly, which transmits the disease to humans.

A viral infection of the brain, ◊encephalitis, is also sometimes called sleeping sickness; sleeping sickness in cattle is called nagana; see also ◊trypanosomiasis.

sleet precipitation consisting of a mixture of water and ice. Technically, it refers to precipitation in the form of ice pellets smaller than 0.2 in/5 mm. The icy coating when rain freezes on trees and streets is also called sleet.

Slidell John 1793–1871. American public official. Born in New York and educated at Columbia University, Slidell moved to New Orleans 1819 and was admitted to the bar. He served as district attorney 1829–33 and US congressman 1843–45. He was named minister to Mexico by President Polk 1845–48 and later served in the US Senate 1853–61. Resigning at the outbreak of the Civil War, he was named Confederate representative to France and was taken prisoner on the high seas by the US Navy. Released in 1862, Slidell remained in exile in France after the war but died on the British Isle of Wight.

slide rule mathematical instrument with pairs of logarithmic sliding scales, used for rapid calculations, including multiplication, division, and the extraction of square roots. It has been generally superseded by the electronic calculator.

It was invented 1622 by the English mathematician William Oughtred. A later version was devised by the French army officer Amédée Mannheim (1831–1906).

Sligo county in the province of Connacht, Republic of Ireland, situated on the Atlantic coast of NW Ireland; area 695 sq mi/1,800 sq km; population (1986) 56,000. The county town is Sligo; there is livestock and dairy farming.

Slim William Joseph, 1st Viscount 1891–1970. British field marshal in World War II. He commanded the 1st Burma Corps 1942–45, stemming the Japanese invasion of India, and then forcing the Japanese out of Burma (now Myanmar). He was governor-general of Australia 1953–60.

slime mold or ***myxomycete*** an extraordinary organism which shows some features of ◊fungi and some of ◊protozoa. Slime molds are not closely related to any other group, although they are often classed, for convenience, with the fungi. ***Cellular slime molds*** go through a phase of living as single cells, looking like amebas, and feed by engulfing the bacteria found in rotting wood, dung, or damp soil. When a food supply is exhausted, up to 100,000 of these amebas form into a colony resembling a single sluglike animal and migrate to a fresh source of bacteria. The colony then takes on the aspect of a fungus, and forms long-stalked fruiting bodies which release spores. These germinate to release amebas, which repeat the life cycle.

Plasmodial slime molds have a more complex life cycle involving sexual reproduction. They form a slimy mass of protoplasm with no internal cell walls, which slowly spreads over the bark or branches of trees.

Sloan John 1871–1951. US painter. He was encouraged to paint by Robert ◊Henri, with whom he later organized "The Eight," a group of realists who were against academic standards. He moved to New York 1904 and helped to organize the avant-garde Armory Show 1913. He was president of the Society of Independent Artists 1918–44 and taught at the Art Students League 1916–37. His paintings of working-class urban life pioneered the field of American realism.

Born in Lock Haven, Pennsylvania, he started as a newspaper illustrator for several Philadelphia newspapers.

sloe fruit of the ◊blackthorn.

sloth South American mammal, about 2.3 ft/70 cm long, of the order Edentata. Sloths are grayish brown and have small rounded heads, rudimentary tails, and prolonged forelimbs. Each foot has long curved claws adapted to clinging upside down from trees. They are vegetarian.

Species include the three-toed sloth or ai *Bradypus tridactylus*, and the two-toed sloth *Choloepus didactylus* of northern South America.

Slovakia region of E ◊Czechoslovakia settled in the 5th–6th centuries by Slavs; occupied by the Magyars in the 10th century; part of the kingdom of Hungary until 1918, when it became a province of Czechoslovakia. Slovakia was a puppet state under German domination 1939–45, and was abolished as an administrative division in 1949. Its capital and chief town was Bratislava.

Slovene a member of the Slavic people of Slovenia (NW Yugoslavia), and parts of the Austrian Alpine provinces of Styria and Carinthia; their language resembles Serbo-Croat.

Slovenia or ***Slovenija*** republic; formerly constituent republic of NW Yugoslavia

area 7,836 sq mi/20,300 sq km

capital Ljubljana

physical mountainous; rivers: Sava, Drava

features the wealthiest republic: contains 7% of the population of Yugoslavia but produces 15% of Yugoslavia's gross national product

products grain, sugarbeet, livestock, timber, cotton and woolen textiles, steel, vehicles

population (1986) 1,930,000; 89% Slovenes

language Slovene, resembling Serbo-Croat, written in Roman characters

religion Roman Catholic

history settled by the Slovenes 6th century; until 1918 the Austrian province of Carniola; an autonomous republic of Yugoslavia 1946. In Sept 1989 it voted to give itself the right to secede from Yugoslavia and to prevent the Yugoslavian government from interfering in Slovene affairs. In June 1991 Slovenia declared itself independent. European nations gradually recognized its independence, including the European Community Jan 1992.

slow-worm harmless species of lizard *Anguis fragilis*, common in Europe. Superficially resembling a snake, it is distinguished by its small mouth and movable eyelids. It is about 1 ft/30 cm long, and eats worms and slugs.

SLR abbreviation for single-lens reflex, a type of ◊camera in which the image is seen in the lens used for taking the photograph.

slug air-breathing gastropod related to the snails, but with absent or much reduced shell.

slug obsolete unit of mass, equal to 32.17 lb/14.6 kg. It is the mass that will have an acceleration of one foot per second when under a force of one pound weight.

Sluter Claus c. 1380–1406. N European Gothic sculptor, probably of Dutch origin, active in Dijon, France. His work includes the *Well of Moses* c. 1395–1403 (now in the grounds of a hospital in Dijon); and the kneeling mourners, or *gisants*, for the tomb of his patron Philip the Bold, Duke of Burgundy (Dijon Museum and Cleveland Museum, Ohio).

small arms one of the two main divisions of firearms, guns that can be carried by hand. The first small arms were portable handguns in use in the late 14th century, supported on the ground and ignited by hand. Today's small arms range from breech-loading single shot rifles and shotguns to sophisticated automatic and semiautomatic weapons.

The matchlock, which evolved during the 15th century, used a match of tow and saltpeter gripped by an S-shaped lever, which was rocked toward the touch hole with one finger, enabling the gun to be held, aimed, and fired in much the same way as today. Front and back sights, followed by a curved stock that could be held against the shoulder (in the hackbut or Hookgun), gave increased precision. The difficulty of keeping a match alight in wet weather was overcome by the introduction of the wheel lock, in about 1515, in which a shower of sparks was produced by a spring-drawn steel wheel struck by iron pyrites. This cumbrous and expensive mechanism evolved into the simpler flintlock in about 1625, operated by flint striking steel and in general use for 200 years until a dramatic advance, the "percussion cap," invented in 1810 by a sport-loving Scottish cleric Alexander Forsyth (1769–1843), removed the need for external igniters. Henceforth, weapons were fired by a small explosive detonator placed behind or within the base of the bullet, struck by a built-in hammer.

The principles of rifling, breech-loading, and the repeater, although known since the 16th century, were not successfully exploited until the 19th century. It was known that imparting a spin made the bullet's flight truer, but the difficulty of making the bullet bite the grooves had until then prevented the use of rifling. The Baker rifle, issued to the British Rifle Brigade in 1800, was loaded from the front of the barrel (muzzle) and had a mallet for hammering the bullets into the grooves.

The first breechloader was von Dreyse's "needle gun," issued to the Prussian army in 1842, in which the detonator was incorporated with the cartridge. By 1870 breech-loading was in general use, being quicker, and sweeping the barrel out after each firing. An early rifle with bolt action was the Lee-Metford 1888, followed by the Lee-Enfield, both having a magazine beneath the breech, containing a number of cartridges. A modified model is still used by the British army. US developments favored the repeater (such as the Winchester) in which the fired case was extracted and ejected, the hammer cocked, and a new charge inserted into the chamber, all by one reciprocation of a finger lever. In the semiautomatic, part of the explosion energy performs the same operations: the Garand, long used by the US army, is of this type. Completely automatic weapons were adopted during World

War II. Improvements since then have concentrated on making weapons lighter and faster-firing, as with the M-16, extensively used by US troops in the Vietnam war.

small claims court in the US, a court that deals with small civil monetary claims, using a simple procedure, often without attorney intervention.

small intestine the length of alimentary canal between the stomach and the large intestine, consisting of the duodenum and the ileum. It is responsible for digesting and absorbing food.

The wall is glandular, producing mucus and enzymes to aid digestion, and muscular so that food can be moved down the gut. Absorption, the passage of small molecules across the wall, is made more efficient by the presence of numerous villi, small fingerlike projections that increase the surface area.

smallpox acute, highly contagious viral disease, marked by aches, fever, vomiting, and skin eruptions leaving pitted scars. Widespread vaccination programs have almost eradicated this often fatal disease.

It was endemic in Europe until the development of vaccination by Edward ◊Jenner about 1800, and remained so in Asia, where a virulent form of the disease (variola major) entailed a fatality rate of 30% until the World Health Organization campaign from 1967, which resulted in its virtual eradication by 1980. The virus now survives chiefly in storage in various research institutes.

smell a sense that responds to chemical molecules in the air. It works by having receptors for particular chemical groups, into which the airborne chemicals must fit to trigger a message to the brain.

A sense of smell is used to detect food and to communicate with other animals (see ◊pheromone and ◊scent gland). Aquatic animals can sense chemicals in water, but whether this sense should be described as "smell" or "taste" is debatable.

smelling salts or ***sal volatile*** a mixture of ammonium carbonate, bicarbonate, and carbamate together with other strong-smelling substances, formerly used as a restorative for dizziness or fainting.

smelt small fish, usually marine, although some species are freshwater, and some live in lakes. They occur in Europe and North America. The most common European smelt is the sparling *Osmerus eperlanus*.

Smersh formerly the main administration of counterintelligence in the USSR, established 1942. It was a subsection of the ◊KGB.

Smetana Bedřich 1824–1884. Czech composer, whose music has a distinct national character, as in for example the operas *The Bartered Bride* 1866 and *Dalibor* 1868, and the symphonic suite *My Country* 1875–80. He conducted the National Theatre of Prague 1866–74.

Smith Adam 1723–1790. Scottish economist, often regarded as the founder of political economy. His *The Wealth of Nations* 1776 defined national wealth in terms of labor. The cause of wealth is explained by the division of labor—dividing a production process into several repetitive operations, each carried out by different workers. Smith advocated the free working of individual enterprise, and the necessity of "free trade."

He was born in Kirkcaldy, and was professor of moral philosophy at Glasgow 1752–63. He published *Theory of Moral Sentiments* 1759.

Smith Al (Alfred Emanuel) 1873–1944. US political leader. Born in New York, Smith left school in his teens and became involved in local Democratic politics. After serving in the New York state assembly 1905–15 he became New York County sheriff 1915–17. In 1918 he was elected governor of New York. He was defeated for reelection 1920 but was victorious in 1922, 1924, and 1926. In 1928 he became the first Roman Catholic to receive a presidential nomination. In his lively, yet unsuccessful, campaign against Herbert Hoover he was called "The Happy Warrior."

Smith Bessie 1894–1937. US jazz and blues singer, born in Chattanooga, Tennessee. Known as the "Empress of the Blues," she established herself in the 1920s after she was discovered by Columbia Records. She made over 150 recordings accompanied by such greats as Louis Armstrong and Benny Goodman.

Her popularity waned in the Depression and she died after an auto accident.

Smith David 1906–1965. US sculptor and painter whose work made a lasting impact on sculpture after World War II. He trained as a steel welder in a car factory. His pieces are large openwork metal abstracts.

Smith turned first to painting and then, about 1930, to sculpture. Using welded steel, he created abstract structures influenced by the metal sculptures of Picasso. In the 1940s and 1950s he developed a more linear style. The *Cubi* series of totemlike abstracts, some of them painted, was designed to be placed in the open air.

Smith Ian Douglas 1919– . Rhodesian politician. He was a founder of the Rhodesian Front 1962 and prime minister 1964–79. In 1965 he made a unilateral declaration of Rhodesia's independence and, despite United Nations sanctions, maintained his regime with tenacity. In 1979 he was succeeded as prime minister by Bishop Abel Muzorewa, when the country was renamed Zimbabwe. He was suspended from the Zimbabwe parliament in April 1987 and resigned in May as head of the white opposition party.

Smith John 1580–1631. English colonist. After an adventurous early life he took part in the colonization of Virginia, acting as president of the North American colony 1608–09. He explored New England in 1614, which he named, and published pamphlets on America and an autobiography. He traded with the Indians, which may have kept the colonists alive in the early years.

During an expedition among the American Indians he was captured, and his life is said to have been saved by the intervention of the chief's daughter, ◊Pocahontas.

Smith John Maynard. British biologist, see ◊Maynard Smith.

Smith Joseph 1805–1844. US founder of the ◊Mormon religious sect.

Born in Vermont, he received his first religious call in 1820, and in 1827 claimed to have been granted the revelation of the *Book of Mormon* (an ancient American prophet), inscribed on gold plates and concealed a thousand years before in a hill near Palmyra, New York. He founded the Church of Jesus Christ of Latter-day Saints in Fayette, New York, 1830. The headquarters of the church was moved to Kirkland, Ohio, 1831; to Missouri 1838; and to Nauvoo, Illinois, 1840. Smith began the construction of a Mormon temple at Nauvoo, organized a private army to defend the sect from its enemies, and declared his candidacy for president. Hostility to Smith intensified when rumors that he had taken several wives began to circulate; Smith publicly opposed polygamy and acknowledged only one wife. He was jailed after some of his followers destroyed the printing press of a newspaper that had attacked him, and a mob stormed the jail and killed him. Historians still differ on whether Smith practiced polygamy; some have concluded that he secretly married more than 20 women. Some of his followers who accompanied Brigham ◊Young to Salt Lake City openly espoused polygamy; those who organized a separate branch in Missouri, headed by Smith's son, strongly opposed it. Smith's chief works are *Doctrines and Covenants* and *Pearl of Great Price*.

Smith Kate 1909–1986. US singer. Born in Greenville, Virginia, Smith made her Broadway debut 1926. After a succession of singing roles, she gained national fame as a radio personality. Beginning in 1936, she starred in a weekly program and adopted the popular tune "When the Moon Comes over the Mountain" as her theme song. Smith became one of the most beloved entertainers in the US, especially noted for her rousing renditions of "God Bless America." She was featured in a popular television show, "The Kate Smith Hour," 1950–56.

Smith Maggie (Margaret Natalie) 1934– . English actress of stage and screen who is also a highly talented comedienne. Her films include *The Prime of Miss Jean Brodie* 1969 (for which she won an Academy Award), *California Suite* 1978, *A Private Function* 1984, and *A Room with a View* 1986. She also appears in television drama and in the London and Broadway stage, most recently in *Leave It to Lettice*.

Smith William 1769–1839. British geologist, the founder of stratigraphy, or the science of identifying rock strata by their contained fossils. He also produced the first geologic maps of England and Wales.

Smithson James 1765–1829. British chemist and mineralogist. The Smithsonian Institution in Washington, DC, was established in 1846, as "an establishment for the increase and diffusion of knowledge," following his bequest of $100,000 for this purpose.

Branches of the institution include research laboratories, collections, and exhibits in a wide range of fields in the arts and sciences. It sponsors scientific expeditions and publishes their results.

smoker vent on the ocean floor, associated with an ◊ocean ridge, through which hot, mineral-rich ground water erupts into the sea, forming thick clouds of suspended material. The clouds may be dark or light, depending on the mineral content, thus producing "white smokers" or "black smokers."

Sea water percolating through the sediments and crust is heated in the active area beneath and dissolves minerals from the hot rocks. As the charged water is returned to the ocean, the sudden cooling causes these minerals to precipitate from solution, so forming the suspension.

smoking inhaling the fumes from burning substances, generally ◊tobacco in the form of ◊cigarettes. The practice can be habit-forming and is dangerous to health, since carbon monoxide and other toxic materials result from the combustion process. A direct link between lung cancer and tobacco smoking was established in 1950; the habit is also linked to respiratory and coronary heart diseases. In the West, smoking is now forbidden in many public places because even passive smoking—breathing in fumes from other people's cigarettes—can be harmful.

Some illegal drugs, such as ◊crack and ◊opium, are also smoked.

Smolensk city on the river Dnieper, W USSR; population (1987) 338,000. Industries include textiles, distilling, and flour milling. It was founded 882 as the chief town of a Slavic tribe and was captured by Napoleon 1812. The Germans took the city 1941, and it was liberated by the Soviets 1943. Nearby is ◊Katyn Forest.

smooth muscle a muscle capable of slow contraction over a period of time. Its presence in the wall of the alimentary canal allows slow rhythmic movements known as ◊peristalsis, which cause food to be mixed and forced along the gut. Smooth muscle has a microscopic structure distinct from other forms, and is not under conscious control.

smuggling the illegal import or export of prohibited goods or the evasion of customs duties on dutiable goods. Smuggling has a long tradition in most border and coastal regions; goods smuggled include tobacco, spirits, diamonds, gold, and illegal drugs.

Restrictions on imports, originally a means of preventing debasement of coinage (for example, in 14th-century England), were later used for raising revenue, mainly on luxury goods, and led to a flourishing period of smuggling during the 18th century in goods such as wine, brandy, tea, tobacco, and lace.

The smuggling of illegal substances such as cocaine and marijuana into the US from Mexico and various South American contries is a serious problem today.

smut in botany, any parasitic ◊fungus of the order Ustilaginales, which infects flowering plants, particularly cereal grasses.

Smuts Jan Christian 1870–1950. South African politician and soldier; prime minister 1919–24 and 1939–48. He supported the Allies in both world wars and was a member of the British imperial war cabinet 1917–18.

During the Second ◊South African War (1899–1902) Smuts commanded the Boer forces in his native Cape Colony. He subsequently worked for reconciliation between the Boers and the British, and on the establishment of the Union of South Africa, he became minister of the interior 1910–12 and defense minister 1910–20. During World War I he commanded the South African forces in E Africa 1916–17. He was prime minister 1919–24 and minister of justice 1933–39; on the outbreak of World War II he succeeded General Hertzog as premier. He was made a field marshal in 1941.

Smyrna former name of the Turkish port of ◊Izmir.

snail air-breathing gastropod mollusk, with a spiral shell. There are thousands of species, on land and in water.

The typical snails of the genus *Helix* have two species in Europe. The common garden snail *Helix aspersa* is very destructive to plants. The Roman snail *Helix pomatia* is "corralled" for the gourmet food market. Overcollection has depleted the population. The French eat as much as 11 lb/5 kg of snails per capita each year.

Snake tributary of the Columbia River, in NW US; length 1,038 mi/1,670 km. It flows 40 mi/65 km through Hell's Canyon, one of the deepest gorges in the world.

Extensive irrigation in S Idaho makes possible the farmland that grows Idaho potatoes and other crops.

snake reptile of the suborder Serpentes of the order Squamata, which also includes lizards. Snakes are characterized by an elongated limbless body, possibly evolved because of subterranean ancestors. One of the striking internal modifications is the absence or greatly reduced size of the left lung. The skin is covered in scales, which are markedly wider underneath where they form. There are 3,000 species found in the tropic and temperate zones, but none in New Zealand, Ireland, Iceland, and near the poles. Only three species are found in Britain: the adder, smooth snake, and grass snake.

In all except a few species, scales are an essential aid to locomotion. A snake is helpless on glass where scales can effect no "grip" on the surface; progression may be undulant, "concertina," or creeping, or a combination of these. Detailed vision is limited at a distance, though movement is immediately seen; hearing is restricted to ground vibrations (sound waves are not perceived); the sense of touch is acute; besides the sense of smell through the nasal passages, the flickering tongue picks up airborne particles which are then passed to special organs in the mouth for investigation; and some (rattlesnakes) have a cavity between eye and nostril which is sensitive to infrared rays (useful in locating warm-blooded prey in the dark). All snakes are carnivorous, and often camouflaged for better concealment in hunting as well as for their own protection. Some are oviparous and others ovoviviparous, that is, the eggs are retained in the oviducts until development is complete; in both cases the young are immediately self-sufficient.

The majority of snakes belong to the Colubridae, chiefly harmless, such as the common grass snake of Europe, but including the deadly African boomslang *Dispholidus typus*. The venomous families include the Elapidae comprising the true ◊cobras, the New World coral snakes, and the

snow *Snow crystal showing characteristic hexagonal symmetry.*

Australian taipan, copperhead, and death adder; the Viperidae (see ◊viper), and the Hydrophiidae, aquatic sea-snakes. Antisera against snakebite (made from the venom) are expensive to prepare and store, and specific to one snake species, so that experiments have been made with more widely valid treatment; for example, trypsin, a powerful protein-degrading enzyme, has proven effective against the cobra/mamba group. Among the more primitive snakes are the Boidae, which still show links with the lizards and include the boa constrictor, anaconda, and python. These kill by constriction but their victims are usually comparatively small animals.

snapdragon perennial herbaceous plant of the genus *Antirrhinum*, family Scrophulariaceae, with spikes of brightly colored two-lipped flowers.

Snell Willebrord 1581–1626. Dutch mathematician and physicist who devised the basic law of refraction, known as Snell's law, in 1621. This states that the ratio between the sine of the angle of incidence and the sine of the angle of refraction is constant. The laws describing the reflection of light were well known in antiquity, but the principles governing the refraction of light were little understood. Snell's law was published by ◊Descartes in 1637.

snipe European marsh bird of the family Scolopacidae, order Charadriiformes; species include common snipe *Gallinago gallinago*, and the rare great snipe *Gallinago media*, of which the males hold spring gatherings to show their prowess. It is closely related to the ◊woodcock.

snooker indoor game derived from ◊billiards (via ◊pool). It is played with 22 balls: 15 red, 1 each of yellow, green, brown, blue, pink, and black, and 1 white cueball. Red balls are worth one point when sunk, while the colored balls have ascending values from two points for the yellow to seven points for the black. The world professional championship was first held in 1927. The world amateur championship was first held in 1963.

The game, invented in 1875 by British officers serving in India, did not gain popularity among the British until the 1920s. Since then it has grown to become one of the biggest television sports in the UK, and it is gaining in popularity across Europe, the Far East, and the US.

snoring loud noise during sleep made by vibration of the soft palate (the rear part of the roof of the mouth) caused by streams of air entering the nose and mouth at the same time. It is most common when the nose is partially blocked.

It is common in men, but women and children also snore.

snow precipitation in the form of soft, white, crystalline flakes caused by the condensation in air of excess water vapor below freezing point. Light reflecting in the crystals, which have a basic hexagonal (six-sided) geometry, gives snow its white appearance.

Snow C(harles) P(ercy), Baron Snow 1905–1980. English novelist and physicist. He held government scientific posts in World War II and 1964–66. His sequence of novels *Strangers and Brothers* 1940–64 portrayed English life from 1920 onward. His *Two Cultures* (Cambridge Rede lecture 1959) discussed the absence of communication between literary and scientific intellectuals in the West, and added the phrase "the two cultures" to the language.

snowdrop

Snowdon (Welsh *Y Wyddfa*) highest mountain in Wales, 3,560 ft/1,085 m above sea level. It consists of a cluster of five peaks. At the foot of Snowdon are the Llanberis, Aberglaslyn, and Rhyd-ddu passes. A rack railroad ascends to the summit from Llanberis. Snowdonia, the surrounding mountain range, was made a national park 1951. It covers 845 sq mi/2,188 sq km of mountain, lakes, and forest land.

Snowdon Anthony Armstrong-Jones, Earl of Snowdon 1930– . English portrait photographer. In 1960 he married Princess Margaret; they were divorced in 1978.

snowdrop bulbous plant *Galanthus nivalis*, family Amaryllidaceae, native to Europe, with white, bell-shaped flowers, tinged with green, in early spring.

snow leopard a type of ◊leopard.

Snow White traditional European fairy tale. Snow White is a princess persecuted by her jealous stepmother. Taking refuge in a remote cottage inhabited by seven dwarfs, she is tricked by the disguised queen into eating a poisoned apple. She is woken from apparent death by a prince.

Snowy Mountains range in the Australian Alps, chiefly in New South Wales, near which Snowy River rises; both river and mountains are known for a hydroelectric and irrigation system.

snuff finely powdered ◊tobacco for sniffing up the nostrils (or sometimes chewed or rubbed on the gums) as a stimulant or sedative. Snuff taking was common in 17th-century England and the Netherlands. It spread in the 18th century to other parts of Europe, but was largely superseded by cigarette smoking.

Snyders Frans 1579–1657. Flemish painter of hunting scenes and still lifes. Based in Antwerp, he was a pupil of ◊Brueghel the Younger and later assisted ◊Rubens and worked with ◊Jordaens. In 1608–09 he traveled in Italy. He exceled at painting fur, feathers, and animals fighting.

soap a mixture of the sodium salts of various ◊fatty acids: palmitic, stearic, and oleic acid. It is made by the action of caustic soda or caustic potash on fats of animal or vegetable origin. Soap makes grease and dirt disperse in water in a similar manner to a ◊detergent.

Soap was mentioned by Galen in the 2nd century for washing the body, although the Romans seem to have washed with a mixture of sand and oil. Soap was manufactured in Britain from the 14th century, but better-quality soap was imported from Castile or Venice.

soap opera a television or radio melodrama. It originated in the US as a series of daytime programs sponsored by soap powder and detergent manufacturers. The popularity of the genre has led to soap operas being shown at peak viewing times in many languages and countries.

soapstone or ***steatite*** compact, massive form of impure ◊talc.

Soares Mario 1924– . Portuguese Socialist politician, president from 1986. Exiled in 1970, he returned to Portugal in 1974, and, as leader of the

Portuguese Socialist Party, was prime minister 1976–78. He resigned as party leader in 1980, but in 1986 he was elected Portugal's first Socialist president.

Sobieski John, alternate name for ◊John III, king of Poland.

soca Latin Caribbean music, a mixture of soul and calypso.

socage Anglo-Saxon term for the free tenure of land by the peasantry. Sokemen, holders of land by this tenure, formed the upper stratum of peasant society at the time of the ◊Domesday Book.

soccer ball game originating in the UK, popular in Europe, the Middle East, and Latin America. It is played between two teams each of 11 players, on a field 100–130 yd/90–120 m long and 50–100 yd/45–90 m wide, with a spherical, inflated (traditionally leather) ball, circumference 27 in/ 0.69 m. The object of the game is to send the ball with the feet or head into the opponents' goal, an area 8 yd/7.31 m wide and 8 ft/2.44 m high.

A team is broadly divided into defense (the goalkeeper and defenders), midfield (whose players collect the ball from the defense and distribute it to the attackers), and attack (forwards or strikers). The number of players assigned to each role varies according to the tactics adopted, but a typical formation is 4–4–2 (four defenders, excluding goalkeeper, four midfield, and two forwards).

The field has a halfway line marked with a center circle, two penalty areas, and two goal areas. Corner kicks are taken from a 1 yd/1 m segment, when the ball goes behind the goal-line off a defender; a ball kicked over the sidelines is thrown in by one of the opposing side. Only the goalkeeper is allowed to touch the ball with the hands and only then in an assigned penalty area. For major offenses committed within the defenders' penalty area, a penalty kick may be awarded by the referee to the attacking team. This is taken 12 yd/11 m from the goal center, with only the goalkeeper inside the area and standing still on the goal-line.

The game is started from the center spot. It is played for two periods of 45 minutes each, the teams changing ends at half-time. The game is controlled by a referee; two linesmen bring rule infringements to the referee's attention.

Played in England from the 14th century, soccer developed in the 19th century and the first set of rules were drawn up at Cambridge University 1848. The modern game is played in the UK according to the rules laid down by the Football Association, founded 1863. Slight amendments to the rules take effect in certain competitions and overseas matches as laid down by the sport's world governing body, Fédération Internationale de Football Association (FIFA, 1904). FIFA organizes the competitions for the World Cup, held every four years from 1930.

world cup

recent winners
1950 Uruguay
1954 West Germany
1958 Brazil
1962 Brazil
1966 England
1970 Brazil
1974 West Germany
1978 Argentina
1982 Italy
1986 Argentina
1990 West Germany

Sochi seaside resort in the USSR, on the Black Sea; population (1987) 317,000. In 1976 it became the world's first "no smoking" city.

Social and Liberal Democrats official name for the British political party formed 1988 from the former Liberal Party and most of the Social Democratic Party. The common name for the party is the Liberal Democrats.

social behavior in zoology, behavior concerned with altering the behavior of other individuals of the same species. Social behavior allows animals to live harmoniously in groups by establishing hierarchies of dominance to discourage disabling fighting. It may be aggressive or submissive (for example, cowering and other signals of appeasement), or designed to establish bonds (such as social grooming or preening).

The social behavior of mammals and birds is generally more complex than that of lower organisms, and involves relationships with individually recognized animals. Thus, courtship displays allow individuals to choose appropriate mates and form the bonds necessary for successful reproduction. In the social systems of bees, wasps, ants, and termites, an individual's status and relationships with others is largely determined by its biological form, as a member of a caste of workers, soldiers, or reproductives; see ◊eusociality.

social contract the idea that government authority derives originally from an agreement between ruler and ruled in which the former agrees to provide order in return for obedience from the latter. It has been used to support both absolutism (◊Hobbes) and democracy (◊Locke, ◊Rousseau).

social credit theory, put forward by C H Douglas (1879–1952), that economic crises are caused by bank control of money, which leads to shortage of purchasing power. His remedy was payment of a "social dividend." There have been provincial social-credit governments in Canada, but the central government has always vetoed the plan.

social democracy political ideology or belief in the gradual evolution of a democratic ◊socialism within existing political structures. The earliest was the German *Sozialdemokratische Partei* (SPD), today one of the two major German parties, created in 1875 from August Bebel's earlier German Social Democratic Workers' Party, itself founded 1869. Parties along the lines of the German model were founded in the last two decades of the 19th century in a number of countries including Austria, Belgium, Holland, Hungary, Poland, and Russia. The British Labor Party is in the social democratic tradition.

Social Democratic Party (SDP) British centrist political party formed 1981 by members of Parliament who resigned from the Labour Party. The 1983 and 1987 general elections were fought in alliance with the Liberal Party as the ***Liberal/ SDP Alliance***. A merger of the two parties was voted for by the SDP 1987, and the new party became the ◊Social and Liberal Democrats, leaving a weak SDP that folded 1990.

social history the branch of history that documents the living and working conditions of people rather than affairs of state.

History became a serious branch of study in the 18th century, but was confined to ancient civilizations and to recent political and religious history. Only in the early 20th century did historians begin to study how people lived and worked in the past. In recent years television programs, books, and museums have helped to give social history a wide appeal.

socialism movement aiming to establish a classless society by substituting public for private ownership of the means of production, distribution, and exchange. The term has been used to describe positions as widely apart as anarchism and social democracy. Socialist ideas appeared in Classical times; in early Christianity; among later Christian sects such as the ◊Anabaptists and ◊Diggers; and, in the 18th and early 19th centuries, were put forward as systematic political aims by Jean-Jacques ◊Rousseau, Claude ◊Saint-Simon François ◊Fourier, and Robert ◊Owen, among others. See also Karl ◊Marx and Friedrich ◊Engels, who developed the theme in *The Communist Manifesto* 1848 and *Das Kapital/Capital* 1867–94.

The late 19th and early 20th centuries saw a division between those who reacted against Marxism leading to social-democratic parties and those who emphasized the original revolutionary significance of Marx's teachings. Weakened by these divisions, the Second ◊International (founded in 1889) collapsed in 1914, right-wing Socialists in all countries supporting participation in World War I while the left opposed it. The Russian Revolution removed socialism from the sphere of theory to that of practice and was followed in 1919 by the foundation of the Third International, which completed the division between right and left. This lack of unity, in spite of the temporary successes of the popular fronts in France and Spain in 1936–38, facilitated the rise of fascism and National Socialism (◊Nazism).

After World War II, Socialist and communist parties tended to formal union in Eastern Europe, although the rigid communist control that ensued was later modified in some respects in, for example, Poland, Romania, and Yugoslavia. Subsequent tendencies to broaden communism were suppressed in Hungary (1956) and Czechoslovakia (1968). In 1989, however, revolutionary change throughout Eastern Europe ended this rigid control. In Western Europe a communist takeover of the Portuguese revolution failed 1975–76, and elsewhere, as in France under ◊Mitterrand, attempts at Socialist-communist cooperation petered out. Most countries in Western Europe have a strong Socialist party, for example, in Germany the Social Democratic Party and in Britain the ◊Labour Party.

Socialist realism artistic censorship doctrine set up by the USSR during the 1930s setting out the optimistic, Socialist terms in which society should be portrayed in works of art—in music and the visual arts as well as writing. Artists whose work was censured in this way include the composer Shostakovich, and the writers Solzhenitsyn and Sholokhov.

The policy was used as a form of censorship of artists whose work, it was felt, did not follow the approved Stalinist party line, or was too "Modern." The policy was relaxed after Stalin's death, but remains somewhat in force despite the changes engendered by the Soviet era of *glasnost* at the end of the 1980s.

socialization the process, beginning in childhood, by which a person learns how to become a member of a society, learning its norms, customs, laws, and ways of living. The main agents of socialization are the family, school, peer groups, work, religion, and the mass media. The main methods of socialization are direct instruction, rewards and punishment, imitation, experimentation, role play, and interaction.

Some agents of socialization, such as the family and the peer group, may conflict with each other, offering alternative goals, values, and styles of behavior. Socialization is of particular interest to psychologists, anthropologists, and sociologists, but there are diverse opinions about its methods and effects.

social mobility the movement of groups and individuals up and down the social scale in a classed society. The extent or range of social mobility varies in different societies. Individual social mobility may occur through education, marriage, talent, and so on; group mobility usually occurs through change in the occupational structure caused by new technological or economic developments.

The caste system of India and the feudalism of medieval Europe are cited as examples of closed societies, where little social mobility was possible; the class system of Western industrial societies is considered relatively open and flexible.

Social Realism in painting, art that realistically depicts subjects of social concern, such as poverty and deprivation. The French artist Courbet provides a 19th-century example of the genre. Subsequently, in the US, the Ashcan School and Ben Shahn are among those described as Social Realists.

social science the group of academic disciplines that

investigate how and why people behave the way they do, as individuals and in groups. The term originated with the 19th-century French thinker Auguste ◊Comte. The academic social sciences are generally listed as sociology, economics, anthropology, political science, and psychology.

Western thought about society has been influenced by the ideas and insights of such great theorists as Plato, Aristotle, Machiavelli, Rousseau, Hobbes, and Locke. The study of society, however, can be traced to the great intellectual period of the 18th century called the Enlightenment, and to the industrial and political revolutions of the 18th and 19th centuries, to the moral philosophy of ◊positivism. Comte attempted to establish the study of society as a scientific discipline, capable of precision and prediction in the same way as natural science, but it overlaps extensively with such subject areas as history, geography, law, philosophy, and even biology. Although some thinkers—such as Marx—have attempted to synthesize the study of society within one theory, none has yet achieved what Einstein has done for physics or Charles Darwin for biology. A current debate is whether the study of people can or should be a science.

social security state provision of financial aid to alleviate poverty and to provide income to retired persons and disabled workers. The term "social security" was first applied officially in the US, in the Social Security Act 1935. The term usually refers specifically to old-age pensions, which have a contributory element, unlike "welfare." The federal government is responsible for social security (medicare, retirement, survivors', and disability insurance); unemployment insurance is covered by a joint federal-state system for industrial workers, but few in agriculture are covered; and welfare benefits are the responsibility of individual states, with some federal assistance. The program is an important source of income for the growing population of retired Americans. Politically sacrosanct, the benefits pose a growing burden for the working-age population.

The concept of such payments developed in the late 19th century in Europe—for example, compulsory social insurance in Germany from 1883. In the US the program was developed as part of the effort to cope with the effects of the ◊Depression from 1929, when large numbers of Americans were without income.

society the organization of people into communities or groups. Social science, in particular sociology, is the study of human behavior in a social context. Various aspects of society are discussed under ◊class, ◊community, ◊culture, ◊kinship, ◊norms, ◊role, ◊socialization, and ◊status.

Society Islands (French *Archipel de la Société*) an archipelago in ◊French Polynesia, divided into Windward Islands and Leeward Islands; area 650 sq mi/1,685 sq km; population (1983) 142,000. The administrative headquarters is Papeete on ◊Tahiti. The Windward Islands (French *Îles du Vent*) have an area of 460 sq mi/1,200 sq km and a population (1983) of 123,000. They comprise Tahiti, Moorea (area 51 sq mi/132 sq km; population 7,000), Maio (or Tubuai Manu; 3.5 sq mi/9 sq km; population 200), and the smaller Tetiaroa and Mehetia. The Leeward Islands (French *Îles sous le Vent*) have an area of 156 sq mi/404 sq km and a population of 19,000. They comprise the volcanic islands of Raiatea (including the main town of Uturoa), Huahine, Bora-Bora, Maupiti, Tahaa, and four small atolls. Claimed by France 1768, the group became a French protectorate 1843 and a colony 1880.

Socinianism form of 17th-century Christian belief which rejects such traditional doctrines as the Trinity and original sin, named after Socinus, the Latinized name of Lelio Francesco Maria Sozzini (1525–62), Italian Protestant theologian. It is an early form of ◊Unitarianism.

His views on the nature of Christ were developed by his nephew, Fausto Paolo Sozzini (1539–1604), who also taught pacifist and anarchist doctrines akin to Tolstoy's. Socinianism denies the divinity of Jesus but emphasizes his virtues.

sociology the systematic study of society, in particular of social order and social change, social conflict and social problems. It studies institutions such as the family, law, and the church, as well as concepts such as norm, role, and culture. Sociology attempts to study people in their social environment according to certain underlying moral, philosophical, and political codes of behavior.

Sociology today reflects a variety of perspectives and traditions. Its focus tends to be on contemporary industrial society, sometimes comparing it with preindustrial society, and occasionally drawing on such related disciplines as history, geography, politics, economics, psychology, and anthropology. Its concerns range from theories of social order and change to detailed analyses of small groups, individuals, and the routines of daily life. The relation between theory and method is one part of the current debate about whether sociology is or should be a science, and whether it can or should be free of ideology.

Socotra Yemeni island in the Indian Ocean; capital Tamridah; area 1,351 sq mi/3,500 sq km. Under British protection from 1886, it became part of South Yemen 1967 and is used as a military base by the USSR.

Socrates c. 469–399 BC. Athenian philosopher. He wrote nothing but was immortalized in the dialogues of his pupil Plato. In his desire to combat the skepticism of the ◊sophists, Socrates asserted the possibility of genuine knowledge. In ethics, he put forward the view that the good person never knowingly does wrong. True knowledge emerges through dialogue and systematic questioning and an abandoning of uncritical claims to knowledge.

The effect of Socrates's teaching was disruptive since he opposed tyranny. Accused in 399 on charges of impiety and corruption of youth, he was condemned by the Athenian authorities to die by drinking hemlock.

Socratic method method of teaching used by Socrates, in which he aimed to guide pupils to clear thinking on ethics and politics by asking questions and then exposing their inconsistencies in cross-examination. This method was effective against the ◊sophists.

soda ash former name for sodium carbonate (Na_2CO_3).

soda lime powdery mixture of calcium hydroxide and sodium hydroxide or potassium hydroxide, used in medicine and as a drying agent.

Soddy Frederick 1877–1956. English physical chemist, who pioneered research into atomic disintegration and coined the term ◊isotope. He was awarded a Nobel Prize in 1921 for investigating the origin and nature of isotopes.

Söderberg Hjalmar (Eric Fredrik) 1869–1941. Swedish writer. His work includes the short, melancholy novels *Förvillelser*/*Aberrations* 1895, *Martin Bircks ungdom*/*The Youth of Martin Birck* 1901, *Doktor Glass*/*Dr Glass* 1906, and the play *Gertrud* 1906.

sodium soft, waxlike, silver-white, metallic element, symbol Na (from Latin *natrium*), atomic number 11, atomic weight 22.898. It is one of the ◊alkali metals and has a very low density, being light enough to float on water. It is the sixth most abundant element (the fourth most abundant metal) in the Earth's crust. Sodium is highly reactive, oxidizing rapidly when exposed to air and reacting violently with water. Its most familiar compound is sodium chloride (common salt), which occurs naturally in the oceans and in salt deposits left by dried-up ancient seas.

Other sodium compounds are of great industrial importance and thousands of tons are manufactured annually. Sodium functions with potassium on the cellular level to make possible neuronal transmission, and so it is an essential nutrient for animals. It was named in 1807 by Humphry Davy, because he isolated it from caustic *soda* (sodium hydroxide).

sodium chloride or ***common salt*** or ***table salt*** NaCl white, crystalline compound found widely in nature. It is a typical ionic solid with a high melting point (1,473.8°F/801°C); it is soluble in water, insoluble in organic solvents; and is a strong electrolyte when molten or in aqueous solution. Found in concentrated deposits, it is widely used in the food industry as a flavoring and preservative, and in the chemical industry in the manufacture of sodium, chlorine, and sodium carbonate.

Sodom and Gomorrah two ancient cities in the Dead Sea area of the Middle East, recorded in the Old Testament (Genesis) as being destroyed by fire and brimstone for their wickedness.

Sofia or ***Sofiya*** capital of Bulgaria since 1878; population (1987) 1,129,000. Industries include textiles, rubber, machinery, and electrical equipment. It lies at the foot of the Vitosha Mountains.

softball bat-and-ball game similar to ◊baseball. Among the differences between the two sports are playing-field dimensions and equipment specifications. Softball diamonds are smaller overall. The distance between bases is 60 ft/18.3 m; pitchers stand 46 ft/14 m from home plate; and the softball itself (which is about as hard as a baseball) is approximately 12 in/30.5 cm in circumference (a baseball is about 9 in/23 cm). In proportional terms of weight to size, a softball is lighter than a baseball and therefore, when pitched or batted, generally will not attain the speed and distance of a well-hit baseball. Softball bats can be no longer than 34 in/86.4 cm.

A regulation softball game is seven innings (for baseball it is nine), but actual play (rules, actions, and objectives) is so alike in both games that the technical differences cannot disguise the fact that softball is the legitimate offspring of baseball. The one element of play that is significantly distinct, however, is the execution of the pitch; a legally delivered softball must be thrown underhand. Pitching defines the two styles of softball play: fast pitch and slow pitch. Of the nearly 175,000 teams registered with the US Amateur Softball Association, more than 80% play slow-pitch softball.

The slow-pitch game customarily is played with 10-player teams, the tenth being a fourth outfielder or a "short fielder" (covering the area between infield and outfield). The arc of a slow-pitched ball must not be less than 3 ft/0.9 m, and the ball must cross home plate in a downward motion. Both bunting and base stealing are illegal in slow-pitch games. Some slow-pitch teams use a ball that is as large as 16 in/40.6 cm in circumference. Bunting and stealing are allowed in fast-pitch games, but it is never legal in softball for a runner to get a "jump" on a steal by leaving the base before the ball is pitched.

soft currency a vulnerable currency that tends to fall in value on foreign-exchange markets because of political or economic uncertainty. Governments are unwilling to hold soft currencies in their foreign-exchange reserves, preferring strong or hard currencies, which are easily convertible.

software in computing, a collection of programs and procedures for making a computer perform a specific task, as opposed to ◊hardware, the term used to describe the machine. Software is created by programmers and either distributed on a suitable medium, such as the ◊floppy disk, or built into the computer in the form of ◊firmware. Examples of software include ◊operating systems, ◊compilers, and application programs, such as payrolls. No computer can function without some form of software.

software project lifecycle in computing, the various stages of development in the writing of a major program (software), from the identification of a requirement to the installation, maintenance, and support of the finished program. The process includes ◊systems analysis and ◊systems design.

softwood any coniferous tree, or the wood from it. In general this type of wood is softer and easier to work, but in some cases less durable, than wood from flowering (or angiosperm) trees.

Sogne Fjord longest and deepest fjord in ◊Norway, 115 mi/185 km long and 4,080 ft/1,245 m deep.

soil loose covering of broken rocky material and decaying organic matter overlying the bedrock of the Earth's surface. Various types of soil develop under different conditions: deep soils form in warm wet climates and in valleys; shallow soils form in cool dry areas and on slopes. Pedology, the study of soil, is significant because of the relative importance of different soil types to agriculture. The organic content of soil is widely variable, ranging from zero in some desert soils to almost 100% in peats.

soil creep gradual movement of soil down a slope. As each soil particle is dislodged by a raindrop it moves slightly further downhill. This eventually results in a mass downward movement of soil on the slope.

Manifestations of soil creep are the formation of terracettes (steplike ridges along the hillside), leaning walls and telegraph poles, and trees that grow in a curve to counteract progressive leaning.

soil erosion the wearing away and redistribution of the Earth's soil layer. It is caused by the action of water, wind, and ice, and also by improper methods of ◊agriculture. If unchecked, soil erosion results in the formation of ◊deserts.

If the rate of erosion exceeds the rate of soil formation (from rock) then the land will decline and eventually become fertile. The removal of forests or other vegetation often leads to serious soil erosion, because plant roots bind soil, and without them the soil is free to wash or blow away, as in the American ◊dust bowl. The effect is worse on hillsides, and there has been devasting loss of soil where forests have been cleared from mountainsides, as in Madagscar. Improved agricultural practices are needed to combat soil erosion. Windbreaks, such as hedges or strips planted with coarse grass, are valuable. Organic farming can reduce soil erosion by as much as 75%.

soil mechanics a branch of engineering that studies the nature and properties of the soil. Soil is investigated during construction work to ensure that it has the mechanical properties necessary to support the foundations of dams, bridges, and roads.

Soissons market town in Picardie region, N France; population (1982) 32,000. The chief industry is metallurgy. In 486 ◊Clovis defeated the Gallo-Romans here, ending their rule in France.

Sokol Czechoslovak educational and athletic organization founded in 1862, which plays an important part in public life. The movement also flourishes in Poland, Bulgaria, Yugoslavia, and other Slavonic countries. Until 1948 it was nonpolitical.

Sokoto trading center and capital of Sokoto state, NW Nigeria; population (1983) 148,000.

Sokoto state in Nigeria, established 1976; capital Sokoto; area 39,565 sq mi/102,500 sq km; population (1984) 7,609,000. It was a ◊Fula sultanate from the 16th century until occupied by the British 1903.

solar energy *Solar dishes at the Themis experimental solar-power station at Targassone in the French Pyrénées.*

solar system

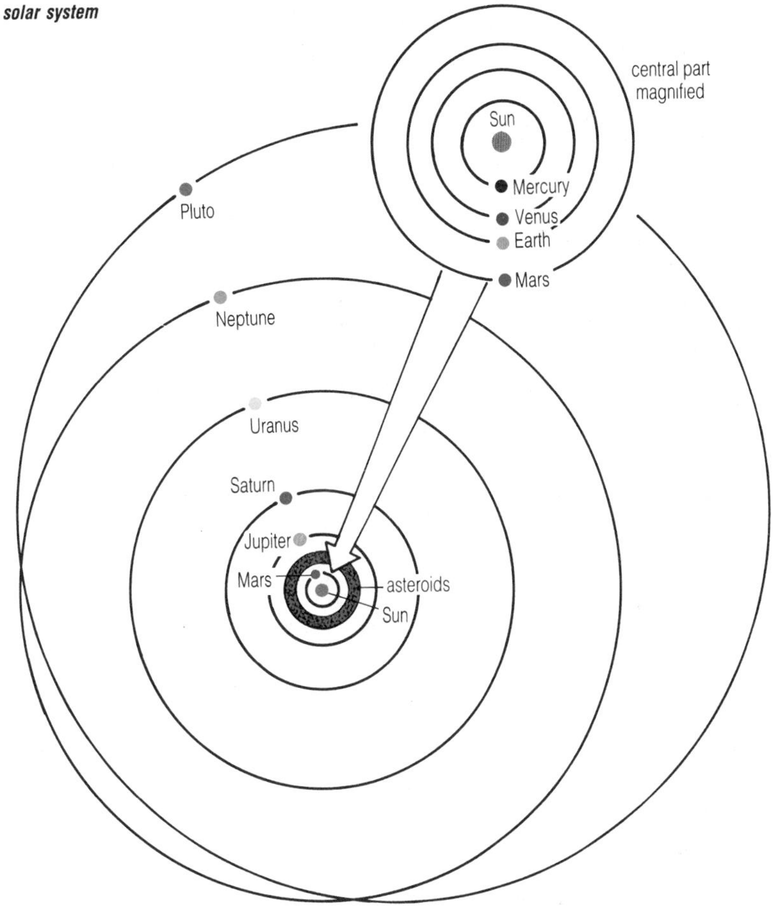
central part magnified
Sun
Mercury
Venus
Earth
Mars
Pluto
Neptune
Uranus
Saturn
Jupiter
Mars
asteroids
Sun

solan goose another name for the ◊gannet.

solar energy energy derived from the Sun's radiation. The amount of energy falling on just 0.3861 sq mi/1 sq km is about 4,000 megawatts, enough to heat and light a small town. In one second the Sun gives off 13 million times more energy than all the electricity used in the US in one year. Solar heaters have industrial or domestic uses. They usually consist of a black (heat-absorbing) panel containing pipes through which air or water, heated by the Sun, is circulated, either by thermal ◊convection or by a pump.

Solar energy may also be harnessed indirectly using solar cells (photovoltaic cells) made of panels of ◊semiconductor material (usually silicon), which generate electricity when illuminated by sunlight. Although it is difficult to generate a high output from solar energy compared to sources such as nuclear or fossil-fuel energy, it is a major nonpolluting and renewable energy source used as far north as Scandinavia as well as in the SW US and in Mediterranean countries.

A solar furnace, such as that built in 1970 at Odeillo in the French Pyrénées, has thousands of mirrors to focus the Sun's rays; it produces uncontaminated intensive heat for industrial and scientific or experimental purposes. Advanced schemes have been proposed that will use giant solar reflectors in space that would harness ◊solar energy and beam it down to earth in the form of ◊microwaves. Despite their low running costs, their high installation cost and low power output have meant that solar cells have found few applications outside space probes and artificial satellites. Solar heating is, however, widely used for domestic purposes in many parts of the world.

solar pond natural or artificial "pond," for example the Dead Sea, in which salt becomes more soluble in the Sun's heat. Water at the bottom becomes saltier and hotter, and is insulated by the less salty water layer at the top. Temperatures at the bottom reach about 212°F/100°C and can be used to generate electricity.

solar radiation radiation given off by the Sun, consisting mainly of visible light, ◊ultraviolet radiation, and ◊infrared radiation, although the whole spectrum of ◊electromagnetic waves is present, from radio waves to X-rays. High-energy charged particles such as electrons are also emitted, especially from solar ◊flares. When these reach the Earth, they cause magnetic storms (disruptions of the Earth's magnetic field), which interfere with radio communications.

Solar System the Sun (a star) and all the bodies orbiting it: the nine planets (Mercury, Venus, Earth, Mars, Jupiter, Saturn, Uranus, Neptune, and Pluto), their moons, the asteroids, and the comets. Thought to have formed from a cloud of gas and dust in space about 4.6 billion years ago, the Sun contains 99% of the mass of the Solar System. The outer edge of the Solar System is not clearly defined, marked only by the limit of the Sun's gravitational influence, which extends about 1.5 light-years, almost halfway to the nearest star, Proxima Centauri, 4.3 light-years away.

solar wind stream of atomic particles, mostly protons and electrons, from the Sun's corona, flowing outward at speeds of between 200 mps/300 kps and 600 mps/1,000 kps.

The fastest streams come from "holes" in the Sun's corona that lie over areas where no surface activity occurs. The solar wind pushes the gas of comets' tails away from the Sun, and "gusts" in the solar wind cause geomagnetic disturbances and aurorae on Earth.

solder any of various alloys used when melted for

joining metals such as copper, its common alloys (brass and bronze), and tin-plated steel, as used for making food cans. Soft solders (usually alloys of tin and lead, sometimes with added antimony) melt at low temperatures (about 392°F/200°C), and are widely used in the electrical industry for joining copper wires. Hard (or brazing) solders, such as silver solder (an alloy of copper, silver, and zinc), melt at much higher temperatures and form a much stronger joint.

A necessary preliminary to making any solder joint is thorough cleaning of the surfaces of the metal to be joined (to remove oxide) and the use of a flux (to prevent the heat applied to melt the solder from reoxidizing the metal).

sole flatfish found in temperate and tropical waters. The common sole *Solea solea*, also called Dover sole, is found in the southern seas of NW Europe. Up to 1.6 ft/50 cm long, it is a prized food fish, as is the sand or French sole *Pegusa lascaris* further south.

solenodon rare insectivorous shrewlike mammal, genus *Solenodon*. There are two species, one each on Cuba and Hispaniola, and they are threatened with extinction caused by introduced predators. They are about 1 ft/30 cm long with a 10 in/25 cm tail, slow-moving, and produce venomous saliva.

solenoid a coil of wire, usually cylindrical, in which a magnetic field is created by passing an electric current through it (see ◊electromagnet). This field can be used to move an iron rod placed on its axis. Mechanical valves attached to the rod can be operated by switching the current on or off, so converting electrical energy into mechanical energy. Solenoids are used to relay energy from the battery of a car to the starter motor by means of the ignition switch.

sole proprietorship or ***sole trader*** one person who runs a business, receiving all profits and responsible for all liabilities. Most small businesses are headed by sole proprietors.

Solferino, Battle of Napoleon III's victory over the Austrians 1859 at a village near Verona, N Italy, 5 mi/8 km S of Lake Garda.

solicitor general the second-ranking member of the US Department of Justice, charged with representing the federal government before the US Supreme Court, and any other courts, and who must approve any appeal the federal government might take to an apellate court.

solid in physics, a state of matter that holds its own shape (as opposed to a liquid, which takes up the shape of its container, or a gas, which totally fills its container). According to ◊kinetic theory, the atoms or molecules in a solid are not free to move but merely vibrate about fixed positions, such as those in crystal lattices.

Solidarity (Polish *Solidarność*) the national confederation of independent labor unions in Poland, formed under the leadership of Lech ◊Wałęsa Sept 1980. An illegal organization from 1981 to 1989, it now heads the Polish government and divisions have emerged in the leadership.

Solidarity emerged from a summer of industrial disputes caused by the Polish government's attempts to raise food prices. The strikers created a trade-union movement independent of the Communist Party, and protracted negotiations with the government led to recognition of Solidarity in exchange for an acceptance of the leading role of the Communist Party in Poland. Continuing unrest and divisions in Solidarity's leadership led to the declaration of martial law in Dec 1981; the union was banned and its leaders were arrested. Wałęsa was released Dec 1982, and Solidarity continued to function as an underground organization. It was legalized again April 1989 following a further wave of strikes under its direction and round-table talks with the government. In the elections of June 1989 it won almost every seat open to it, and formed the senior partner in a "grand coalition" government formed Sept 1989 with Tadeusz ◊Mazowiecki as prime minister. After Wałęsa was elected president of Poland 1990, he left the confederation, and by mid-1991 Solidarity found itself opposing some of its former leader's economic policies and with diminished national influence.

Solidarity's achievements inspired the successful "people power" movements in other E European countries during 1989, as well as the formation of more independent labor unions in the USSR.

solid-state circuit a circuit where all the components (resistors, capacitors, transistors, and diodes) and interconnections are made at the same time, and by the same processes, in or on one piece of single-crystal silicon. The small size of this construction accounts for its use in electronics for space vehicles and aircraft.

Solingen city in North Rhine–Westphalia, Federal Republic of Germany; population (1988) 158,000. It was once a major producer of swords and today makes high-quality steel for razor blades and cutlery.

solipsism in philosophy, a view that maintains that the self is the only thing that can be known to exist. It is an extreme form of ◊skepticism. The solipsist sees himself or herself as the only individual in existence, assuming other people to be a reflection of his or her own consciousness.

soliton nonlinear solitary wave that maintains its shape and velocity, and does not widen and disperse in the normal way. Such behavior is characteristic of the waves of ◊energy that constitute the particles of atomic physics, and the mathematical equations that sum up the behavior of solitons are being used to further research nuclear fusion and superconductivity.

It is so named after a solitary wave seen on a canal by Scottish engineer John Scott Russell (1808–82), who raced after it on his horse.

Solomon c. 974–c. 937 BC. in the Old Testament, third king of Israel, son of David by Bathsheba. During a peaceful reign, he was famed for his wisdom and his alliances with Egypt and Phoenicia. The much later biblical Proverbs, Ecclesiastes, and Song of Songs are attributed to him. He built the temple in Jerusalem with the aid of heavy taxation and forced labor, resulting in the revolt of N Israel.

Solomon Islands country in the W Pacific, E of New Guinea, comprising many hundreds of islands, the largest of which is Guadalcanal.

government The constitution dates from 1978 and creates a constitutional monarchy within the ◊Commonwealth, with a resident governor-general representing the UK monarch as head of state. There is a single-chamber legislature, the National Parliament, with 38 members elected by universal suffrage for a four-year term. The governor-general appoints a prime minister and cabinet drawn from and collectively responsible to the parliament.

The two main political parties are the Solomon Islands United Party (SIUPA) and the People's Alliance Party (PAP).

history The islands were inhabited by Melanesians, and were sighted by a 1568 expedition from Peru led by the Spanish navigator Álvaro de Mendaña. They became a British protectorate in the 1890s.

The Solomon Islands were given internal self-government 1976, with Peter Kenilorea, leader of the SIUP, as chief minister. He became prime minister when they achieved full independence, within the Commonwealth, in 1978. In 1981 he was replaced by Solomon Mamaloni of the People's Progressive Party. Kenilorea had been unable to devolve power to the regions while preserving the unity of the state, but Mamaloni created five ministerial posts specifically for provincial affairs.

In the 1984 general election SIUPA won 13 seats and the opposition, now PAP, 12. Sir Peter Kenilorea, as he had become, was put back into office at the head of a coalition government. He immediately abolished the five provincial ministries. Kenilorea, after narrowly surviving a series of no confidence motions resigned again as prime minister in Dec 1986, following allegations that he had accepted US $47,00 of French aid to repair cyclone damage to his home village in Malaita province. Kenilorea remained in the cabinet of his successor, Ezekiel Alebua, a fellow SIUPA member and became deputy prime minister from Feb 1988. In the general election of Feb 1989 support for the SIUPA halved to 6 seats and the PAP, led by Mamaloni, reemerged, with 14 seats, as the dominant party. Mamaloni formed a coalition government that promised to reform the constitution so as to establish a republic and also to reduce the influence of "foreign aid personnel."

In its external relations, the Solomon Islands, under the SIUPA administrations, has pursued a moderate pro-Western course. However, during the 1981–84 Mamaloni administrations relations with the US were strained by the government's refusal to allow nuclear-powered warships within the Island's territorial waters. In pursuit of a new, broader "Pacific strategy," the Solomon Islands joined Papua New Guinea and Vanuatu in forming the Spearhead Group March 1988, with the aim of preserving ◊Melanesian cultural traditions and securing independence for the French dependency of ◊New Caledonia.

Solomon's seal any perennial plant of the genus *Polygonatum* of the lily family Liliaceae, found growing in moist, shady woodland areas. They have bell-like white or greenish-white flowers drooping from the leaf axils of arching stems, followed by blue or black berries.

Great Solomon's seal *P. commutatum* is native to E North America.

Solon c. 638–558 BC. Athenian statesman. As one of the chief magistrates about 594 BC, he carried out the revision of the constitution that laid the foundations of Athenian democracy.

Soloviev Vladimir Sergeyevich 1853–1900. Russian philosopher and poet whose blending of neo-Platonism and Christian mysticism attempted to link all aspects of human experience in a doctrine of divine wisdom. His theories, expressed in poems and essays, influenced Symbolist writers such as ◊Blok.

Solti Georg 1912– . Hungarian-born British conductor. He was music director at Covent Garden 1961–71, and became director of the Chicago Symphony Orchestra 1969. He was also principal conductor of the London Philharmonic Orchestra 1979–83.

solubility in physics, a measure of the amount of solute (usually a solid or gas) that will dissolve in a given amount of solvent (usually a liquid) at a particular temperature. Solubility may be expressed as grams of solute per 100 grams of solvent or, for a gas, in parts per million (ppm) of solvent.

solution two or more substances mixed to form a single, homogenous phase. One of the substances is the solvent and the others (solutes) are said to be dissolved in it.

The constituents of a solution may be solid, liquid, or gaseous. The solvent is normally the substance that is present in greatest quantity, although when one of them is a liquid this is considered to be the solvent even if it is not the major substance.

Solvay process industrial process for the manufacture of sodium carbonate.

It is a multistage process in which carbon dioxide is generated from limestone and passed through ◊brine saturated with ammonia. Sodium hydrogen carbonate is isolated and heated to yield sodium carbonate. All intermediate byproducts are recycled so that the only ultimate byproduct is calcium chloride.

solvent substance, usually a liquid, that will dissolve

Solomon Islands

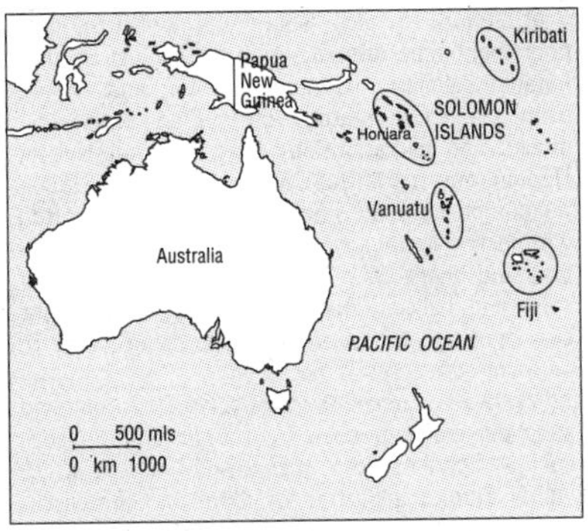
Kiribati
Papua New Guinea
SOLOMON ISLANDS
Honiara
Vanuatu
Australia
Fiji
PACIFIC OCEAN
0 500 mls
0 km 1000

area 10,656 sq mi/27,600 sq km
capital Honiara (on Guadalcanal)
cities Gizo, Yandina
physical comprises all but the northernmost islands (which belong to Papua New Guinea) of a Melanesian archipelago stretching nearly 900 mi/1,500 km. The largest is Guadalcanal (area 2,510 sq mi/6,500 sq km); others are Malaita, San Cristobal, New Georgia, Santa Isabel, Choiseul; mainly mountainous and forested
features rivers ideal for hydroelectric power
head of state Elizabeth II represented by governor-general
head of government Solomon Mamaloni from 1989
political system constitutional monarchy
political parties People's Alliance Party (PAP), center-left; Solomon Islands United Party (SIUPA), right-of-center
exports fish products, palm oil, copra, cocoa, timber
currency Solomon Island dollar
population (1990 est) 314,000 (Melanesian 95%, Polynesian 4%); growth rate 3.9% p.a.
life expectancy men 66, women 71
language English (official); 120 Melanesian dialects
religion Anglican 34%, South Sea Evangelical 17%, Roman Catholic 19%
literacy 60% (1989)
GNP $141 mn; $420 per head (1987)
chronology
1978 Independence achieved from Britain within the Commonwealth, with Peter Kenilorea as prime minister.
1981 Solomon Mamaloni replaced Kenilorea as prime minister.
1984 Kenilorea returned to power, heading a coalition government.
1986 Kenilorea resigned after allegations of corruption; replaced by his deputy, Ezekiel Alebua.
1988 Kenilorea elected deputy prime minister. Joined Vanuatu and Papua New Guinea to form the Spearhead Group, aiming to preserve Melanesian cultural traditions and secure independence for the French territory of New Caledonia.
1989 Solomon Mamaloni (People's Action Party) elected prime minister; formed PAP-dominated coalition.

another substance (see ◊solution). Although the commonest solvent is water, in popular use the term refers to low-boiling-point organic liquids that are harmful if used in a confined space. They can give rise to respiratory problems, liver damage, and neurological complaints.

Typical organic solvents are petroleum distillates (in glues), xylol (in paints), alcohols (for synthetic and natural resins such as shellac), esters (in lacquers, including nail varnish), ketones (in cellulose lacquers and resins), and chlorinated hydrocarbons (as paint stripper and dry-cleaning fluids). Some solvents have a pleasant odor which has given rise to the dangerous practice of solvent abuse or ◊glue-sniffing.

Solway Firth inlet of the Irish Sea, formed by the estuaries of the rivers Eden and Esk, at the western end of the border between England and Scotland.

Solzhenitsyn Alexander (Isayevich) 1918– . Soviet novelist, a US citizen from 1974. After military service, he was in prison and exile 1945–57 for anti-Stalinist comments. Much of his writing is semiautobiographical and highly critical of the system, including *One Day in the Life of Ivan Denisovich* 1962 which deals with the labor camps under Stalin, and *The Gulag Archipelago* 1973, an exposé of the whole Soviet labor camp network. This led to his expulsion from the USSR 1974.

He was awarded a Nobel Prize in 1970. Other works include *The First Circle* and *Cancer Ward* both 1968. His autobiography, *The Oak and the Calf*, appeared 1980. He has adopted a Christian position, and his criticism of Western materialism is also stringent.

soma intoxicating drink made from the fermented sap of the *Asclepias acida* plant, used in Indian religious ritual as a sacrifice to the gods. As *haoma*, its consumption also constituted the central rite in Zoroastrian ritual. Some have argued that the plant was in fact a hallucogenic mushroom.

Somali member of a group of E African peoples from the Horn of Africa. Although the majority of Somalis live in the Somali Republic, there are minorities in Ethiopia and Kenya. Their Cushitic language belongs to the Hamitic branch of the Afro-Asiatic family.

Somalia country in the Horn of Africa, on the Indian Ocean.

government The 1979 constitution defines Somalia as a Socialist state with power in the hands of the Somali Revolutionary Socialist Party (SRSP). As in most Socialist states, the party and the state system operate alongside each other, with the president bestriding both. The president is chosen by the party as head of state and head of government and is secretary general of the party and president of its politburo. Party policy is formulated by the 51-member central committee, operating through 13 bureaus and sanctioned by the Politburo. A council of ministers, appointed by the president, implements these policies. In the 177-member People's Assembly, 6 are presidential nominees and 171 elected by secret ballot for a five-year term from a single list of candidates approved by the party.

history For early history, see ◊Africa. Somalia developed around Arab trading posts that grew into sultanates. A British protectorate of Somaliland was established 1884–87, and Somalia, an Italian protectorate, 1889. The latter was a colony from 1927 and incorporated into Italian East Africa 1936; it came under British military rule 1941–50, when as a United Nations trusteeship it was again administered by Italy.

Somalia became a fully independent republic in 1960 through a merger of the two former colonial territories. Since then, Somalia has been involved in disputes with its neighbors because of its insistence on the right of all Somalis to self-determination, wherever they have settled. This has frequently applied to those living in the Ogaden district of Ethiopia and in NE Kenya. A dispute over the border with Kenya resulted in a break in diplomatic relations with Britain 1963–68. The dispute with Ethiopia led to an eight-month war in 1978, in which Somalia was defeated by Ethiopian troops assisted by Soviet and Cuban weapons and advisers. Some 1.5 million refugees entered Somalia, and guerrilla fighting continues in Ogaden. There was a rapprochement with Kenya in 1984 and, in 1986, the first meeting for ten years between the Somalian and Ethiopian leaders.

The first president of Somalia was Aden Abdullah Osman, who was succeeded in 1967 by Dr

Somalia

Somali Democratic Republic
(Jamhuriyadda Dimugradiga Somaliya)

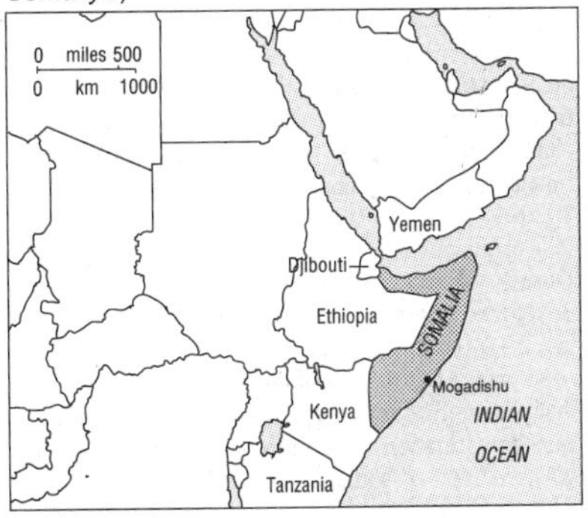
0 miles 500
0 km 1000
Yemen
Djibouti
Ethiopia
SOMALIA
Mogadishu
Kenya
INDIAN OCEAN
Tanzania

area 246,220 sq mi/637,700 sq km
capital Mogadishu
cities Hargeisa, Kismayu, port Berbera
physical mainly flat, with hills in N
features occupies a strategic location on the Horn of Africa
head of state Ali Mahdi Mohammed from 1991
head of government Mohammed Ali Samantar from 1987
political system one-party Socialist republic
Somali Revolutionary Socialist Party (SRSP), nationalist, Socialist
exports livestock, skins, hides, bananas, fruit
currency Somali shilling
population (1990 est) 8,415,000 (including 350,000 refugees from Ethopia and 50,000 in Djibouti); growth rate 3.1% p.a.
life expectancy men 53, women 53 (1989)
language Somali, Arabic (both official), Italian, English
religion Sunni Muslim 99%
literacy 40% (1986)
GNP $1.5 bn; $290 per head (1987)
chronology
1960 Independence achieved from Italy and Britain.
1963 Border dispute with Kenya; diplomatic relations with the UK broken.
1968 Diplomatic relations with the UK restored.
1969 Army coup led by Maj Gen Mohammad Siyad Barre; constitution suspended, Supreme Revolutionary Council set up; name changed to Somali Democratic Republic.
1978 Defeated in eight-month war with Ethiopia. Armed insurrection began in north.
1979 New constitution for Socialist one-party state adopted.
1982 Somali National Movement, antigovernment formed. Oppressive countermeasures by government.
1987 Barre reelected president.
1989 Dissatisfaction with government and increased guerrilla activity in north.
1990 Civil war intensified. Constitutional reforms promised.
1991 Mogadishu captured by rebels. Ali Mahdi Mohammed named president; free elections promised. Secession of NE Somalia, as the Somaliland Republic, announced. Peace talks commenced. Ceasefire agreed.

Abdirashid Ali Shermarke of the Somali Youth League (SYL), which had become the dominant political party. In Oct 1969, President Shermarke was assassinated, and the army seized power under the Commander in Chief, Maj Gen Mohamed Siad Barre. He suspended the 1960 constitution, dissolved the national assembly, banned all political parties, and formed a military government. In 1970 he declared Somalia a Socialist state.

In 1976, the junta transferred power to the newly created SRSP (Somali Revolutionary Socialist Party) and three years later the constitution for a one-party state was adopted. Some unofficial opposition groups operate outside the country, from Ethiopia and London. Over the next few years Barre consolidated his position by increasing the influence of his own clan and reducing that of his northern rival, despite often violent opposition. In 1982 the antigovernment Somali National Movement (SNM) was formed. Oppressive countermeasures by the government led to an estimated 50,000–60,000 civilian deaths by 1990 and 400,000 refugees fleeing to Ethiopia. All post was censored in the north, identity cards were necessary for travel within the country, and contact with foreigners was discouraged.

Barre was reelected in Jan 1987, although the Somali National Movement had taken control of large parts of the north and east of the country. Foreign workers were evacuated from Hargeisa, the capital of N Somalia, June 1988. In riots June 1989 an estimated 400 people were killed by government troops; the government claimed only 24 people died. Government soldiers, pursuing refugees believed to be SNM rebels, crossed into Kenya Sept 1989 and killed four Kenyan policemen. Kenya threatened reprisals even as Prime Minister Samantar announced the release of all political prisoners. He ruled out talks with the SNM. In Oct 1990 the government announced that it would hold a referendum, within 12 months, for greater liberalization, including electoral reform. In 1991 Barre lost power to Ali Mahdi Mohammed.

Somaliland region of Somali-speaking peoples in E Africa including the former British Somaliland Protectorate (established 1887) and Italian Somaliland (made a colony 1927, conquered by Britain 1941 and administered by Britain until 1950)—which both became independent 1960 as the Somali Democratic Republic, the official name for ◊Somalia—and former French Somaliland, which was established 1892, became known as the Territory of the Afars and Issas 1967, and became independent as ◊Djibouti 1977.

Somerset county in SW England

area 1,336 sq mi/3,460 sq km

towns administrative headquarters Taunton; Wells, Bridgwater, Glastonbury, Yeovil

physical rivers Avon, Parret, and Exe; marshy coastline on the Bristol Channel; Mendip Hills (including Cheddar Gorge and Wookey Hole, a series of limestone caves where Old Stone Age flint implements and bones of extinct animals have been found); the Quantock Hills; Exmoor

products engineering, dairy products, cider, Exmoor ponies

population (1987) 452,000

famous people Henry Fielding.

Somerset Edward Seymour, 1st Duke of c. 1506–1552. English politician. Created Earl of Hertford after Henry VIII's marriage to his sister Jane, he became Duke of Somerset and Protector (regent) for Edward VI in 1547. His attempt to check enclosure (the transfer of land from common to private ownership) offended landowners and his moderation in religion upset the Protestants, and he was beheaded on a fake treason charge in 1552.

Somerville Mary (born Fairfax) 1780–1872. Scottish scientific writer, who produced several widely used textbooks, despite having just one year of formal education. Somerville College, Oxford, is named after her.

Her main works were *Mechanism of the Heavens* 1831 (a translation of ◊Laplace's treatise on celestial mechanics), *On the Connexion of Physical Sciences* 1834, *Physical Geography* 1848, and *On Molecular and Microscopic Science* 1869.

Somme river in N France, on which Amiens and Abbeville stand; length 150 mi/240 km. It rises in Aisne *département* and flows W through Somme *département* to the English Channel.

Somme, Battle of the Allied offensive in World War I July–Nov 1916 at Beaumont-Hamel-Chaulnes, on the river Somme in N France, during which severe losses were suffered by both sides. It was the first battle in which tanks were used. The German offensive around St Quentin March–April 1918 is sometimes called the Second Battle of the Somme.

Sommeiler Germain 1815–1871. French engineer who built the Mont Cenis Tunnel, 7 mi/12 km long, between Switzerland and France. The tunnel was drilled with his invention the ◊pneumatic drill.

Sommerfeld Arnold 1868–1951. German physicist, who demonstrated that difficulties with Niels ◊Bohr's model of the atom, in which electrons move around a central nucleus in circular orbits, could be overcome by supposing that electrons adopt elliptical orbits.

Somoza Anastasio 1896–1956. Nicaraguan soldier and politician. As head of the Nicaraguan army, he deposed President Juan Bautista Sacasa, his uncle, 1936 and assumed the presidency the following year, ruling as a dictator until his assassination 1956. During his rule, Somoza exiled most of his political foes and amassed a fortune. He was succeeded by his sons Luis Somoza Debayle (1922–1967; president 1956–63) and Anastasio ◊Somoza Debayle (1925–1980; president 1967–72, 1974–79).

Somoza Debayle Anastasio 1925–1980. Nicaraguan soldier and politician, president 1967–72 and 1974–79. The second son of Anastasio Somoza García, he succeeded his brother Luis Somoza Debayle (1922–1967; president 1956–63) as president of Nicaragua in 1967, to head an even more oppressive regime. He was removed by Sandinista guerrillas in 1979, and assassinated in Paraguay 1980.

sonar (acronym for sound navigation and ranging) a method of locating underwater objects by the reflection of ultrasonic waves. The time taken for an acoustic beam to travel to the object and back to the source enables the distance to be found since the velocity of sound in water is known. Sonar devices, or echo sounders were developed 1920.

The process is similar to that used in ◊radar. During World War I and after, the Allies developed and perfected an apparatus for detecting the presence of enemy U-boats beneath the sea surface by the use of ultrasonic echoes. Originally named ASDIC (from antisubmarine detection investigation committee), in 1963 the name was changed to sonar.

sonata (Italian "sounded") a piece of instrumental music written for a soloist or a small ensemble and consisting of a series of related movements.

sonata form in music, the structure of a movement, typically involving division into exposition, development, and recapitulation sections. It is the framework for much Classical music, including sonatas, ◊symphonies, and ◊concertos.

Sondheim Stephen (Joshua) 1930– . US composer and lyricist. He wrote the witty and sophisticated lyrics of Leonard Bernstein's *West Side Story* 1957 and composed musicals, including *A Little Night Music* 1973, *Pacific Overtures* 1976, *Sweeney Todd* 1979, *Into the Woods* 1987, and *Sunday in the Park with George* 1989.

sone unit of subjective loudness. A tone of 40 decibels above the threshold of hearing with a frequency of 1000 hertz is defined as one sone; any sound that seems twice as loud as this has a value of two sones, and so on. A loudness of one sone corresponds to 40 ◊phons.

son et lumière (French "sound and light") the outdoor night-time dramatization of the history of a notable building, monument, town, and so on, using theatrical lighting effects, sound effects, music, and narration; invented by Paul Robert Houdin, curator of the Château de Chambord.

song composition for one or more singers, often with instrumental accompaniment, such as madrigals and chansons. Common forms include folk song and ballad. The term "song" is used for secular music, whereas motet and cantata tend to be forms of sacred music.

song cycle a sequence of songs related in mood and sung as a group, used by romantic composers such as Schubert, Schumann, and Hugo Wolf.

Songhai Empire a former kingdom of NW Africa, founded in the 8th century, which developed into a powerful Muslim empire under the rule of Sonni Ali (reigned 1464–92). It superseded ◊Mali and extended its territory, occupying an area that included parts of present-day Guinea, Burkina Faso, Senegal, Gambia, Mali, Mauritania, Niger, and Nigeria. In 1591 it was invaded and overthrown by Morocco.

Song of Myself the longest poem in Walt Whitman's ◊*Leaves of Grass*, relating the poet, the "single separate person," to the democratic "en masse." It was regularly revised from its original form of 1855 to incorporate new experiences and "cosmic sensations."

sonic boom noise like a thunderclap that occurs when an aircraft passes through the ◊sound barrier, or begins to travel faster than the speed of sound. It happens when the cone-shaped shock wave caused by the plane touches the ground.

sonnet fourteen-line poem of Italian origin introduced to England by Thomas ◊Wyatt in the form used by Petrarch (rhyming *abba abba cdcdcd* or *cdecde*) and followed by Milton and Wordsworth; Shakespeare used the form *abab cdcd efef gg*.

sonoluminescence emission of light by a liquid that is subjected to high-frequency sound waves. The rapid changes of pressure induced by the sound cause minute bubbles to form in the liquid, which then collapse. Light is emitted at the final stage of the collapse, probably because it squeezes and heats gas inside the bubbles.

Sons of Liberty in American colonial history, the name adopted by those colonists opposing the ◊Stamp Act of 1765. Merchants, lawyers, farmers, artisans, and laborers joined what was an early instance of concerted resistance to British rule, causing the repeal of the Act March 1766.

Sontag Susan 1933– . US critic, novelist, and screenwriter. Her novel *The Benefactor* appeared in 1963, and she established herself as a critic with the influential cultural essays of *Against Interpretation* 1966 and *Styles of Radical Will* 1969. More recent studies, showing the influence of French structuralism, are *On Photography* 1976 and the powerful *Illness as Metaphor* 1978 and *Aids and its Metaphors* 1989.

Soochow alternative transliteration of the Chinese city of ◊Suzhou.

Soong Ching-ling 1890–1981. Chinese politician, wife of the ◊Guomindang Nationalist leader founder ◊Sun Yat-sen; she remained a prominent figure in Chinese politics after his death, being a vice chair of the People's Republic of China from 1959.

Sophia Electress of Hanover 1630–1714. Twelfth child of Frederick V, elector palatine of the Rhine and king of Bohemia, and Elizabeth, daughter of James I of England. She married the elector of Hanover in 1658. Widowed in 1698, she was recognized in the succession to the English throne in 1701, and when Queen Anne died without issue in 1714, her son George I founded the Hanoverian dynasty.

sophist (Greek "wise man") one of a group of 5th-century BC lecturers on culture, rhetoric, and politics. Skeptical about the possibility of achieving genuine knowledge, they applied bogus reasoning and were concerned with winning arguments rather than establishing the truth. ◊Plato regarded them as dishonest and sophistry came to mean fallacious reasoning.

Sophocles 495–406 BC. Greek dramatist who, with Aeschylus and Euripides, is one of the three great tragedians. He modified the form of tragedy by introducing a third actor and developing stage scenery. He wrote some 120 plays, of which seven tragedies survive. These are *Antigone* 441 BC, *Oedipus Tyrannus, Electra, Ajax, Trachiniae, Philoctetes* 409 BC, and *Oedipus at Colonus* 401 BC.

Sophocles lived in Athens when the city was ruled by Pericles, a period of great prosperity. His many friends included the historian Herodotus. In his tragedies, human will plays a greater part than that of the gods, as in the plays of Aeschylus, and his characters are generally heroic. This is perhaps what he meant when he said of Euripides "He paints men as they are" and of himself "I paint men as they ought to be." A large fragment of his satyr play (a tragedy treated in a grotesquely comic fashion) *Ichneutae* also survives.

Sopwith Thomas Octave Murdoch 1888–1989. English designer of the Sopwith Camel biplane, used in World War I, and joint developer of the Hawker Hurricane fighter plane used in World War II.

sorbic acid $CH_3CH{:}CHCH{:}CHCOOH$ tasteless acid found in the fruit of the mountain ash (genus *Sorbus*) and prepared synthetically. It is widely used in the preservation of food—for example, cider, wine, soft drinks, animal feeds, bread, and cheese.

Sorbonne common name for the University of Paris, originally a theological institute founded 1253 by Robert de Sorbon, chaplain to Louis IX.

Richelieu ordered the reconstruction of the buildings in 1626, which were again rebuilt in 1885. In 1808, the Sorbonne became the seat of the Académie of Paris and of the University of Paris. It is the most prestigious French university.

Sorbus genus of deciduous trees and shrubs of the northern hemisphere, family Rosaceae, including American and Eurasian ◊mountain ashes; the latter include ◊whitebeam and ◊service tree.

Sorel Georges 1847–1922. French philosopher who believed that socialism could only come about through a general strike; his theory of the need for a "myth" to sway the body of the people was used by fascists.

Sørensen Søren 1868–1939. Danish chemist who in 1909 introduced the concept of using the ◊pH scale as a measure of the acidity of a solution. On Sørensen's scale, still used today, a pH of 7 is neutral; higher numbers represent alkalinity, and lower numbers acidity.

sorghum also called ***great millet*** or ***Guinea corn*** any cereal grass of the genus *Sorghum*, native to Africa but cultivated widely in India, China, the US, and S Europe. The seeds are used for making bread. Durra is a member of the genus.

sorrel (Old French *sur* "sour") any of several plants of the genus *Rumex* of the buckwheat family Polygonaceae. *R. acetosa* is grown for its bitter salad leaves. ◊Dock plants are of the same genus.

Sorrento town on the Gulf of Naples, SW Italy; population (1981) 17,301. It has been a vacation resort since Roman times.

sorus in ferns, a group of sporangia, the reproductive structures that produce ◊spores. They occur on the lower surface of fern fronds.

SOS internationally recognized distress signal, using letters of the ◊Morse code.

Sosnowiec chief city of the Darowa coal region in the Upper Silesian province of Katowice, S Poland; population (1985) 255,000.

soul according to many religions, the intangible and immortal part of a human being that survives the death of the physical body.

Judaism, Christianity, and Islam all teach that at the end of the world each soul will be judged and assigned to heaven or hell on its merits. According to orthodox Jewish doctrine, most souls first spend time in purgatory to be purged of their sins, and are then removed to paradise. In Christianity the soul is that part of the person that can be redeemed from sin through divine grace. In other religions, such as Hinduism, the soul is thought to undergo ◊reincarnation until the individual reaches enlightenment and is freed from the cycle of rebirth. According to the teachings of Buddhism, no permanent self or soul exists.

soul music style of ◊rhythm and blues sung by, among others, Sam Cooke (1931–64), Aretha Franklin (1942–), and Al Green (1946–). A synthesis of blues, gospel music, and jazz, it emerged in the 1950s. Its lyrics are emotionally intense and earthy.

Soult Nicolas Jean de Dieu 1769–1851. Marshal of France. He held commands in Spain in the Peninsular War, where he sacked the port of Santander 1808, and was Chief of Staff at the Battle of ◊Waterloo. He was war minister 1830–40.

sound physiological sensation received by the ear, originating in a vibration (pressure variation in the air) that communicates itself to the air, and travels in every direction, spreading out as an expanding sphere. All sound waves in air travel with a speed dependent on the temperature; under ordinary conditions, this is about 1,070 ft/330 m per second. The pitch of the sound depends on the number of vibrations imposed on the air per second, but the speed is unaffected. The loudness of a sound is dependent primarily on the amplitude of the vibration of the air.

The lowest note audible to a human being has a frequency of about 20 ◊hertz (vibrations per second), and the highest one of about 15,000 Hz; the lower limit of this range varies little with the person's age, but the upper range falls steadily from adolescence onward.

Sound, the strait dividing SW Sweden from Denmark and linking the ◊Kattegat and the Baltic; length 70 mi/113 km; width 3–37 mi/5–60 km.

sound barrier the concept that the speed of sound, or sonic speed (about 760 mph/1,220 kph at sea level), constitutes a speed limit to flight through the atmosphere, since a badly designed aircraft suffers severe buffeting at near sonic speed caused by the formation of shock waves. US test pilot Chuck Yeager first flew through the "barrier" in 1947 in a Bell X-1 rocket plane. Now, by careful design, aircraft such as Concorde can fly at supersonic speed with ease, though they create in their wake a ◊sonic boom.

sound synthesis the generation of sound (usually music) by electronic ◊synthesizer.

soundtrack band at one side of a movie film on which the accompanying sound is recorded. Usually it takes the form of an optical track (a pattern of light and shade). The pattern is produced on the film when signals from the recording microphone are made to vary the intensity of a light beam. During playback, a light is shone through the track on to a photocell, which converts the pattern of light falling on it into appropriate electrical signals. These signals are then fed to loudspeakers to recreate the original sounds.

Souphanouvong Prince 1912– . Laotian politician, president 1975–86. After an abortive revolt against French rule in 1945, he led the guerrilla organization Pathet Lao, and in 1975 became the first president of the Republic of Laos. He resigned after suffering a stroke.

source language in computing, the language in which programs are originally written, as opposed to ◊machine code, which is the form in which they are carried out by the computer. The translation from source language to machine code is done by a ◊compiler or ◊interpreter program within the computer.

Sousa John Philip 1854–1932. US bandmaster and composer of marches, such as "The Stars and Stripes Forever!" 1897. He became known as a brilliant bandmaster during his tenure as leader of the Marine Band 1880–92. He went on to form the Sousa Band 1892 and toured internationally with this group until his death. In addition to about 140 stirring marches, he composed operettas, symphonic poems, suites, waltzes, and songs.

sousaphone a form of large bass ◊tuba, suggested by US bandmaster John Sousa, designed to wrap round the player in a circle and having a forward-facing bell.

Souter David Hackett 1939– . US jurist and associate justice of the US Supreme Court 1990– . Born in Melrose, Massachusetts, he graduated from Harvard College, received a Rhodes scholarship to Oxford University, and graduated from the Harvard Law School. After private practice in New Hampshire, Souter served as state assistant and deputy attorney general before being appointed state attorney general 1976. He became a judge on the state trial court 1978 and was named to the state supreme court 1983. He was appointed by President Bush to the US Court of Appeals for the First Circuit 1990 and to the Supreme Court later in 1990.

South Africa country on the southern tip of Africa, bounded N by Namibia, Botswana, and Zimbabwe and NE by Swaziland and Mozambique.

government The 1984 constitution is based on racial discrimination. The legislature and government are dominated by the descendants of Europeans, termed Whites in the context of ◊apartheid. There is only conditional participation in government for non-Whites, in the form of Coloureds, or persons of mixed European and African descent, and Asians. Black Africans are completely unrepresented at national level.

The three-chamber parliament consists of the House of Assembly, for Whites; the House of Representatives, for Coloureds; and the House of Delegates, for Indians. The House of Assembly has 178 members, 166 elected by universal White suffrage, 4 nominated by the president on the basis of one for each province, and 8 elected by the 166. The House of Representatives has 85 members, 80 elected by universal Coloured suffrage, 2 nominated by the president and 3 elected by the 80. The House of Delegates has 45 members, 40 elected by universal Indian suffrage, two nominated by the president, and three elected by the 40 directly elected members. Each house is responsible for its "own affairs," meaning matters affecting only Whites, Coloureds, or Indians, as the case may be. General legislation applying to all races, including Black Africans, has to be approved by all three houses and the president. Members of all three houses serve a five-year term.

The state president, who combines the roles of head of state and head of government, is elected for the duration of Parliament by an 88-member electoral college: 50 from the House of Assembly, 25 from the House of Representatives and 13 from the House of Delegates. The president appoints and presides over a cabinet dominated by Whites and is advised by an appointed council of 60 members: 20 from the House of Assembly, 10 from the House of Representatives, 5 from the House of Delegates, and 25 chosen by the president. There are also 3 advisory ministers' councils: one for the whole country, one for the Coloured community, and one for the Indians. Each of South Africa's four provinces has an adminstrator, appointed by the president, and an elected provincial council.

history For early history, see ◊Africa. The area was originally inhabited by Bushmen and Hottentots. Bantus, including Sotho, Swazi, Xhosa, and Zulu, settled there before the 17th century. The

South Africa
Republic of
(Republiek van Suid-Afrika)

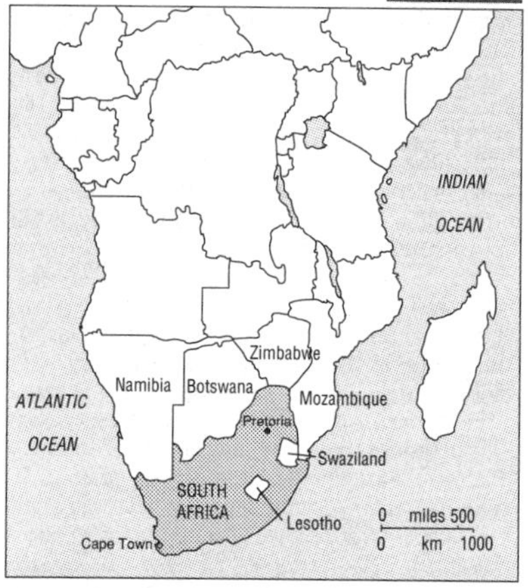
INDIAN
OCEAN
ATLANTIC
OCEAN
Zimbabwe
Namibia
Botswana
Mozambique
Pretoria
Swaziland
SOUTH AFRICA
Lesotho
Cape Town
0 miles 500
0 km 1000

area 472,148 sq mi/1,223,181 sq km (includes Walvis Bay and independent black homelands)
capital Cape Town (legislative), Pretoria (administrative), Bloemfontein (judicial)
cities Johannesburg; ports Cape Town, Durban, Port Elizabeth, East London
physical southern end of large plateau, fringed by mountains and lowland coastal margin
territories Marion Island and Prince Edward Island in the Antarctic
features Drakensberg Mountains. Table Mountain; Limpopo and Orange rivers; the Veld and the Karoo; part of Kalahari Desert; Kruger National Park
head of state and government F W de Klerk from 1989
political system restricted democracy
political parties White: National Party (NP), right-of-center, racist; Conservative Party of South Africa (CPSA), extreme right, racist; Democratic Party (DP), left-of-center, multiracial.
Coloureds: Labor Party of South Africa, left-of-center; People's Congress Party, right-of-center. Indian: National People's Party, right-of-center; Solidarity Party, left-of-center
exports corn, sugar, fruit; wool; gold (world's largest producer), platinum, diamonds, uranium, iron and steel, copper
currency rand
population (1990 est) 39,550,000 (73% Black: Zulu, Xhosa, Sotho, Tswana; 18% White: 3% mixed, 3% Asiatic); growth rate 2.5% p.a.
life expectancy whites 71, Asians 67, blacks 58
language Afrikaans and English (both official); Bantu
religion Dutch Reformed Church 40%, Anglican 11%, Roman Catholic 8%, other Christian 25%; Hindu, Muslim
literacy whites 99%, Asians 69%, blacks 50% (1989)
GNP $81 bn; $1,890 per head (1987)
chronology
1910 Union of South Africa formed from two British colonies and two Boer republics.
1912 African National Congress (ANC) formed.
1948 Apartheid system of racial discrimination initiated by Daniel Malan, leader of National Party (NP).
1955 Freedom Charter adopted by African National Congress (ANC).
1958 Malan succeeded as prime minister by Hendrik Verwoerd.
1960 ANC banned.
1961 South Africa withdrew from Commonwealth and became a republic.
1962 ANC leader Nelson Mandela jailed.
1964 Mandela, Walter Sisulu, Govan Mbeki, and five other ANC leaders sentenced to life imprisonment.
1966 Verwoerd assassinated and succeeded by B J Vorster.
1976 Soweto uprising.
1977 Death in custody of Pan African Congress activist Steve Biko.
1978 Vorster resigned and was replaced by Pieter W Botha.
1984 New constitution adopted, giving segregated representation to Coloureds and Asians and making Botha president. Nonaggression pact with Mozambique signed but not observed.
1985 Growth of violence in black townships.
1986 Commonwealth agreed on limited sanctions. US Congress voted to impose sanctions. Some major multinational companies closed down their South African operations.
1987 Government formally acknowledged the presence of its military forces in Angola.
1988 Botha announced "limited constitutional reforms." South Africa agreed to withdraw from Angola and recognize Namibia's independence as part of regional peace accord.
1989 Botha gave up NP leadership and state presidency. Democratic Party (DP) launched. F W de Klerk became president. Walter Sisulu and other ANC activists released; De Klerk allowed ANC rallies; beaches and public facilities desegregated. Elections held in Namibia to create independence government.
1990 ANC ban lifted; Nelson Mandela released from prison. National Party membership opened to all races. Oliver Tambo returned. Daily average of 35 murders and homicides recorded.
1991 Meeting between Mandela and Zulu leader Buthelezi resulted in agreement to end fighting between ANC and Inkatha. Mandela elected ANC president. Revelations of government financial support for Inkatha threatened ANC cooperation. De Klerk announced repeal of remaining apartheid laws and introduced legislation to abolish racial controls on land ownership. South Africa readmitted to Olympic sports community.

◊Cape of Good Hope was rounded by Bartolomeu ◊Diaz 1488; the coast of ◊Natal was sighted by Vasco da ◊Gama 1497. The Dutch ◊East India Company founded Cape Town 1652 as a port of call on the way to the Indies.

Occupied by Britain 1795 and 1806, Cape Town and the hinterland were purchased by Britain 1814 for £6 million. Britons also settled in Natal, on the coast near ◊Durban, 1824. In 1836 some 10,000 Dutch, wishing to escape from British rule, set out north on the Great Trek and founded the republic of ◊Transvaal and the ◊Orange Free State; they also settled in N Natal, which became part of Cape Colony 1844 and a separate colony 1856. The Orange Free State was annexed by Britain 1848 but became independent 1854.

The discovery of diamonds at Kimberley, Cape Colony, 1867, and of gold in Transvaal 1886, attracted prospectors, who came in conflict with the Dutch farmers, the ◊Boers. Britain attempted to occupy Transvaal 1877–81 but withdrew after a severe defeat at Majuba (see ◊South African Wars). Denial of citizenship rights to the migrant miners (*uitlanders*) in Transvaal, and the imperialist ambitions of Cecil ◊Rhodes and others, led to the Jameson Raid (see L S ◊Jameson) and the Boer War 1899–1902 (see ◊South African Wars), won by Britain.

In 1910 the Union of South Africa was formed, comprising the provinces of Cape of Good Hope, Natal, Orange Free State, and Transvaal. A Boer rebellion on the outbreak of ◊World War I was speedily crushed by Jan ◊Smuts. South Africa occupied German SW Africa (see ◊Namibia). Between the wars the union was alternately governed by the republican nationalists under ◊Hertzog and the South African Party under Smuts, who supported the ◊Commonwealth connection. Hertzog wanted South Africa to be neutral in ◊World War II, but Smuts took over as premier, and South African troops fought with the Allies.

The National Party (NP) came to power 1948 and has ruled South Africa ever since. Its leader, Daniel Malan, initiated the policy of apartheid, attempting to justify it as "separate but equal" development. In fact, all but the White minority are denied a voice in the nation's affairs. In the 1950s the ◊African National Congress (ANC) led a campaign of civil disobedience until it and other similar movements were, in 1960, declared illegal, and in 1964 the ANC leader Nelson Mandela was sentenced to life imprisonment for alleged sabotage. He became a central symbol of Black opposition to the apartheid regime remaining in prison until 1990.

Malan was succeeded 1958 by Hendrik ◊Verwoerd, who withdrew from the Commonwealth rather than abandon apartheid, and the Union became the Republic of South Africa 1961. Verwoerd was assassinated 1966, but his successor, B J ◊Vorster, pursued the same policy. Pass laws restricting the movement of Blacks within the country had been introduced, causing international outrage, and ten "homelands" (Bantustans; see ◊Black National State) were established to contain particular ethnic groups. By the 1980s thousands of the apartheid regime's opponents had been imprisoned without trial and more than 3,000,000 people had been forcibly resettled in Black townships. International condemnation of police brutality followed the news of the death in detention of the Black community leader Steve Biko 1977. Despite all this, the NP continued to increase its majority at each election, with the White opposition parties failing to unseat the NP. Both the Conservative Party (CP) and the Democratic Party (DP) made gains in Sept 1989 elections, with the ruling NP losing one fourth of its seats. Its new total was only nine seats more than was required for a majority, its worst electorial showing since coming to power 1948.

In 1978 Vorster resigned and was succeeded by Pieter W ◊Botha. He embarked on constitutional reform to involve Coloureds and Asians, but not Blacks, in the governmental process. This led to a clash within the NP, and in March 1982 Dr Adries Treurnicht, leader of the hardline (*verkrampte*) wing, and 15 other extremists were expelled. They later formed a new party, the Conservative Party of South Africa (CPSA). Although there were considerable doubts about Botha's proposals in the Coloured and Indian communities as well as among the Whites, they were approved by 66% of the voters in an all-White referendum and came into effect Sept 1984. In 1985 a number of apartheid laws were amended or repealed, including the ban on sexual relations or marriage between people of different races and the ban on mixed racial membership of political parties, but the underlying inequalities in the system remained and dissatisfaction of the Black community grew. In the 1986 cabinet of 21, including Botha, there were 19 Whites, 1 Coloured, and 1 Indian. The main Coloured parties are the Labor Party of South Africa, led by the Rev Allan Hendrickse, and the People's Congress Party. The main Indian parties are the National People's Party, led by Amichand Rajbani, and the Solidarity Party, led by Dr J N Reddy.

In May 1986 South Africa attacked what it claimed to be guerrilla strongholds in Botswana, Zambia, and Zimbabwe. The exiled ANC leader Oliver ◊Tambo was receiving increasing moral

South America

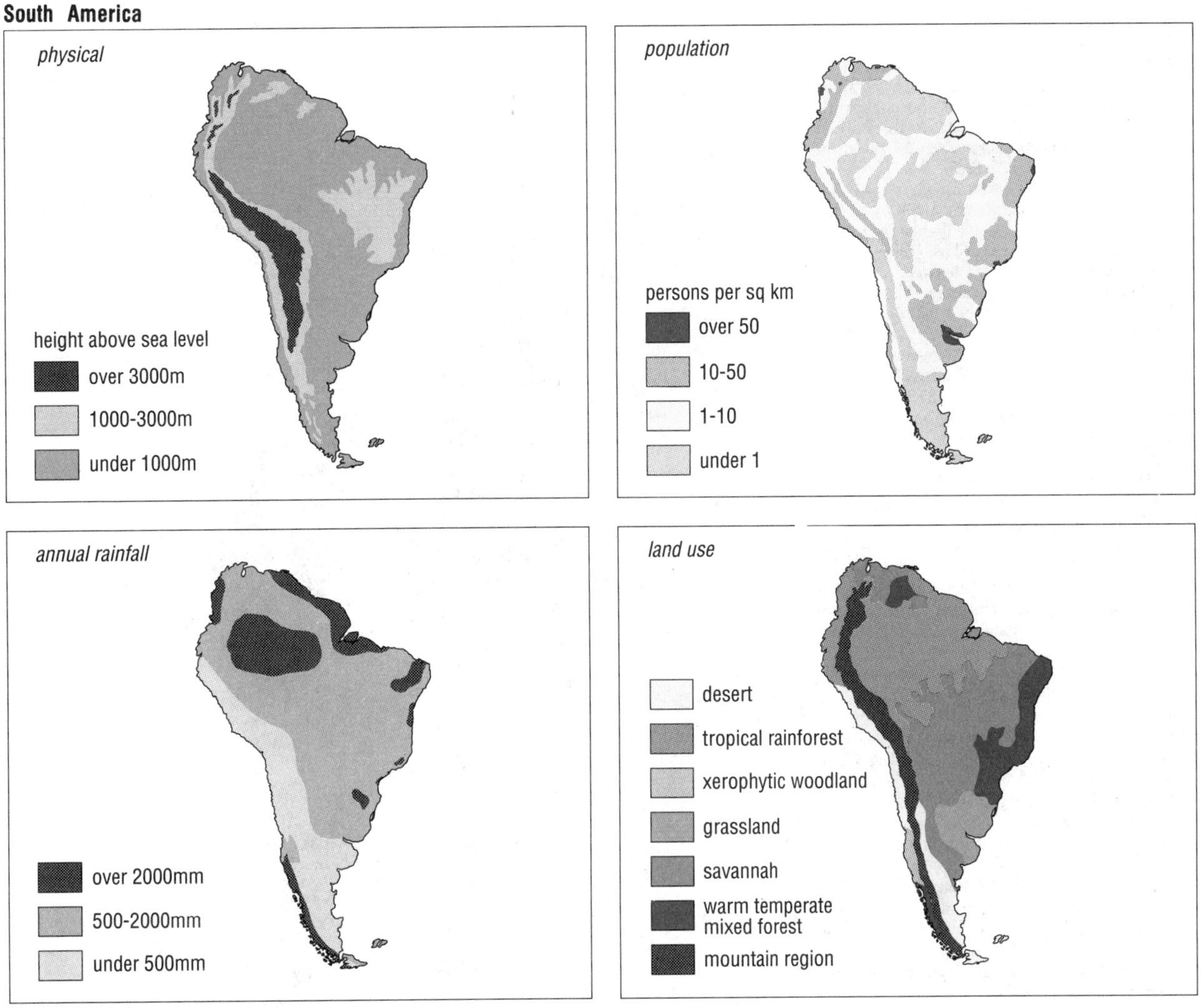
physical
height above sea level
over 3000m
1000-3000m
under 1000m
population
persons per sq km
over 50
10-50
1-10
under 1
annual rainfall
over 2000mm
500-2000mm
under 500mm
land use
desert
tropical rainforest
xerophytic woodland
grassland
savannah
warm temperate mixed forest
mountain region

support in meetings with politicians throughout the world, and Winnie ◊Mandela, during her husband's continuing imprisonment, was "banned" repeatedly for condemning the system publicly. Non-violent resistance was advocated by Bishop ◊Tutu, the ◊Inkatha movement, and others. A state of emergency was declared June 1986, a few days before the tenth anniversary of the first ◊Soweto uprising, marked by a strike in which millions of Blacks participated. Serious rioting broke out in the townships and was met with police violence, causing hundreds of deaths. Between 1980 and 1990 1,070 people were judicially executed.

Abroad, calls for economic ◊sanctions against South Africa grew during 1985 and 1986. At the Heads of Commonwealth conference 1985 the Eminent Persons' Group (EPG) of Commonwealth politicians was conceived to investigate the likelihood of change in South Africa without sanctions. In July 1986 the EPG reported that there were no signs of genuine liberalization. Reluctantly, Britain's prime minister, Margaret Thatcher, agreed to limited measures. Some Commonwealth countries, notably Australia and Canada, took additional independent action. The US Congress eventually forced President Reagan to move in the same direction. Between 1988 and 1990 economic sanctions cost the South African treasury more than $4 billion in lost revenue. The decisions by individual multinational companies to close down their South African operations (see ◊disinvestment) may, in the long term, have the greatest effect.

At the end of 1988 South Africa signed a peace agreement with Angola and Cuba, which included the acceptance of Namibia's independence, and in 1989, under UN supervision, free elections took place there. In Feb 1989 state president Botha suffered a stroke that forced him to give up the NP leadership and later the presidency. He was succeeded in both roles by F W de Klerk, who promised major constitutional reforms. Meanwhile the nonracialist Democratic Party was launched, advocating universal adult suffrage, and made significant progress in the Sept 1989 Whites-only assembly elections. Despite de Klerk's release of the veteran ANC activist, Walter Sisulu, and some of his colleagues, in Oct 1989, Nelson Mandela remained a prisoner and the new president's promises of political reform were treated with skepticism by the opposition, until he announced the lifting of the ban on the ANC, followed, on Feb 11, 1990, by the release of Mandela. In Sept President de Klerk declared membership of the National Party open to all races. In Dec ANC president Oliver Tambo returned triumphantly and in Jan 1991 a meeting between Nelson Mandela and Zulu leader Chief Buthelezi was arranged.

In Feb 1991 President de Klerk announced the intended repeal of all remaining apartheid laws, and the most oppressive laws were repealed in June. In July 1991, South Africa was readmitted to the Olympic community. With growing opposition from the extreme right-wing activists, the abandonment of apartheid and the establishment of a fully democratic political system will require considerable skill from both de Klerk and Mandela.

South Africa: territorial divisions

Provinces	*Capital*	*Area in sq km*
Cape of Good Hope	Cape Town	721,000
Natal	Pietermaritzburg	86,965
Transvaal	Pretoria	286,064
Orange Free State	Bloemfontein	129,152
		1,223,181
Administered territory		
SW Africa (Namibia)	Windhoek	823,167
Walvis Bay		1,124
		2,047,472

South African literature the founder of South African literature in English was Thomas Pringle (1789–1834), who published lyric poetry and the prose *Narrative of a Residence in South Africa*. More recent poets are Roy Campbell and Francis C Slater (1876–1959). The first work of South African fiction to receive attention outside the country was Olive Schreiner's *Story of an African Farm* 1833; later writers include Sarah Gertrude Millin, Pauline Smith (1882–1959), William Plomer (1903–73), Laurens van der Post, Alan Paton, Nadine Gordimer, and playwright Athol Fugard (1932–).

Original writing in ◊Afrikaans developed rapidly after the South African War, and includes works by the lyricists C Louis Leipoldt (1880–1947), Jan Celliers (1865–1940), and Eugène Marais (1871–1936); the satirical sketch and story writer C J Langenhoven; and the student of wildlife "Sangiro" (A A Peinhar), author of *The Adventures of a Lion Family*, which became popular in English translation. In more recent years the intellectual barriers imposed by South Africa's isolation have prevented its writers from becoming more widely known, but there has been much spirited work, including that of the novelists André P Brink (1935–) and Etienne Leroux (1922–), and the poet Ingrid Jonker (1933–1965).

Notable works by blacks include the autobiographical *Down Second Avenue* 1959, by Ezekiel Mphahlele (1919–); and the drama *The Rhythm of Violence* 1964, by Lewis Nkosi (1936–).

South African Wars two wars between the Boers (settlers of Dutch origin) and the British; essentially fought for the gold and diamonds of the Transvaal.

The War of 1881 was triggered by the attempt of the Boers of the ◊Transvaal to reassert the independence surrendered 1877 in return for British aid against African peoples. The British were defeated at Majuba, and the Transvaal again became independent.

The War of 1899–1902, also known as the Boer War, was preceded by the armed Jameson Raid into the Boer Transvaal; a failed attempt, inspired by the Cape Colony prime minister Rhodes, to precipitate a revolt against Kruger, the Transvaal president. The *uitlanders* (non-Boer immigrants) were still not given the vote by the Boers, negotiations failed, and the Boers invaded British territory, besieging Ladysmith, Mafeking (now Mafikeng), and Kimberley. The war ended with the Peace of Vereeniging following the Boer defeat.

South America fourth largest of the continents, nearly twice as large as Europe, extending S from ◊Central America

area 6,893,429 sq mi/17,854,000 sq km

largest cities (over 3.5 million inhabitants) Buenos Aires, São Paulo, Rio de Janeiro, Bogotá, Santiago, Lima, Caracas

features Andes in the W; Brazilian and Guiana highlands; central plains from the Orinoco basin to Patagonia; Parana-Paraguay-Uruguay system flowing to form the La Plata estuary; Amazon river basin, with its remaining great forests and their rich fauna and flora

products coffee; cocoa; sugar; bananas; oranges; wine; meat and fish products; cotton; wool; handicrafts; minerals including oil, silver, iron ore, copper

population (1985) 263,300,000: originally ◊American Indians, who survive chiefly in Bolivia, Peru, and Ecuador and are increasing in number. In addition there are many mestizo (people of mixed Spanish or Portuguese and Indian ancestry) elsewhere; many people originally from Europe, largely Spanish, Italian, and Portuguese; and many of African descent, originally imported as slaves

language Spanish, Portuguese (chief language in Brazil), many Indian languages

religion Roman Catholic, Indian beliefs

history (for the archaic and later American Indian cultures, see ◊American Indian):

16th century arrival of Europeans, with the Spanish (◊Pizarro) and Portuguese conquest; the American Indians were mainly killed, assimilated, or, where considered unsuitable for slave labor, replaced by imported slaves from Africa.

18th century revolt of ◊Túpac Amaru.

19th century Napoleon's toppling of the Spanish throne opened the way for the liberation of its colonies (led by ◊Bolívar and ◊San Martín). Brazil became independent peacefully. Large-scale European immigration took place (Hispanic, Italian, and German). Interstate wars took a heavy toll — for example, the Paraguay War (see under ◊Paraguay) and ◊Pacific War.

20th century rapid industrialization and high population growth. In the 1980s heavy indebtedness incurred to fund economic expansion led to

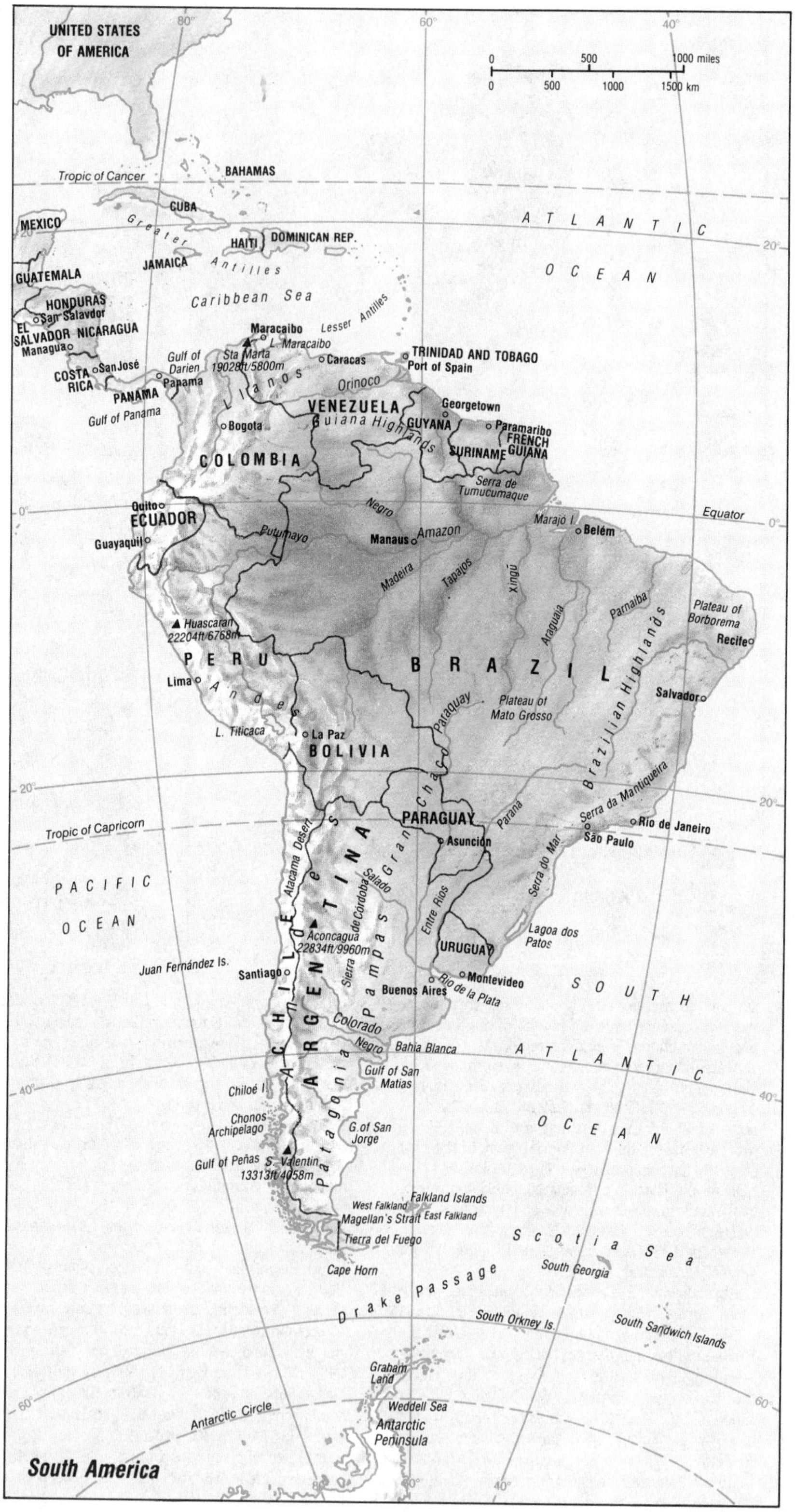
UNITED STATES OF AMERICA
0 500 1000 miles
0 500 1000 1500 km
Tropic of Cancer
BAHAMAS
CUBA
MEXICO
HAITI
DOMINICAN REP.
JAMAICA
Greater Antilles
GUATEMALA
HONDURAS
Caribbean Sea
EL SALVADOR
San Salvador
NICARAGUA
Managua
Lesser Antilles
Maracaibo
L. Maracaibo
COSTA RICA
San José
Gulf of Darien
Sta Marta 19028ft/5800m
Caracas
TRINIDAD AND TOBAGO
Port of Spain
Panama
PANAMA
Gulf of Panama
Llanos
Orinoco
VENEZUELA
Georgetown
Bogota
Guiana Highlands
GUYANA
Paramaribo
FRENCH GUIANA
SURINAME
COLOMBIA
Serra de Tumucumaque
Quito
ECUADOR
Guayaquil
Putumayo
Negro
Manaus
Amazon
Marajo I.
Belém
Equator
Madeira
Tapajós
Xingu
Parnaiba
Plateau of Borborema
Recife
Huascaran 22204ft/6768m
Araguaia
PERU
BRAZIL
Lima
Andes
Paraguay
Plateau of Mato Grosso
Brazilian Highlands
Salvador
L. Titicaca
La Paz
BOLIVIA
Serra da Mantiqueira
Gran Chaco
PARAGUAY
Tropic of Capricorn
Parana
Rio de Janeiro
São Paulo
Atacama Desert
Asunción
Serra do Mar
PACIFIC OCEAN
ARGENTINA
Salado
Sierra de Córdoba
Entre Rios
Aconcagua 22834ft/9960m
Lagoa dos Patos
URUGUAY
Juan Fernández Is.
Santiago
Montevideo
Buenos Aires
Rio de la Plata
Pampas
CHILE
Colorado
Negro
Bahia Blanca
SOUTH ATLANTIC OCEAN
Gulf of San Matias
Chiloé I.
Chonos Archipelago
G. of San Jorge
Patagonia
Gulf of Peñas
S. Valentin 13313ft/4058m
Falkland Islands
West Falkland
East Falkland
Magellan's Strait
Tierra del Fuego
Scotia Sea
Cape Horn
South Georgia
Drake Passage
South Orkney Is.
South Sandwich Islands
Graham Land
Weddell Sea
Antarctic Circle
Antarctic Peninsula
ATLANTIC OCEAN
South America

an inability to meet interest payments in the world slump.

1946–55 Perón president in Argentina.

1952 revolution in Bolivia limits large landowners, nationalizes tin mines.

1970–73 elected Socialist regime under Salvador Allende in Chile ended in military coup.

1982 Falklands War between the UK and Argentina.

1985 Brazil inaugurates first civilian president since 1964.

1989 democratic transition of power in Argentina. Initial steps taken toward reestablishment of relations with Britain.

Southampton port in Hampshire, S England; population (1981) 204,604. Industries include engineering, chemicals, plastics, flour-milling, and tobacco; it is also a passenger and container port.

South Australia

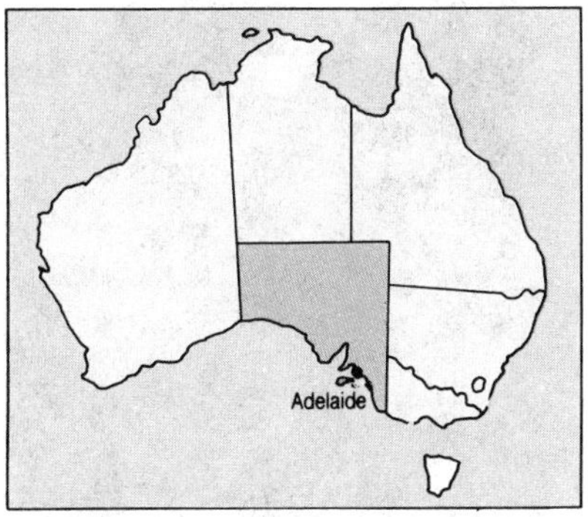
Adelaide

The *Mayflower* set sail from here en route to North America in 1620, as did the *Titanic* on its fateful maiden voyage in 1912. There is a university, established in 1952.

South Arabia, Federation of former grouping (1959–67) of Arab emirates and sheikdoms, joined by ◊Aden 1963. The western part of the area was claimed by ◊Yemen, and sporadic fighting and terrorism from 1964 led to British withdrawal 1967 and the proclamation of the Republic of South Yemen.

South Asia Regional Cooperation Committee (SARCC) organization established 1983 by India, Pakistan, Bangladesh, Nepal, Sri Lanka, Bhutan, and the Maldives to cover agriculture, telecommunications, health, population, sports, art, and culture.

South Australia state of the Commonwealth of Australia
area 379,824 sq mi/984,000 sq km
capital Adelaide (chief port)
towns Whyalla, Mount Gambier
features Murray Valley irrigated area, including wine-growing Barossa Valley; lakes: ◊Eyre, ◊Torrens; mountains: Mount Lofty, Musgrave, Flinders; parts of the ◊Nullarbor Plain, and Great Victoria and Simpson deserts; experimental rocket range in the arid N at Woomera. At Maralinga, British nuclear tests were made 1963 in which Aborigines were said to have died
products meat and wool (80% of area cattle and sheep grazing), wines and spirits, dried and canned fruit, iron (Middleback Range), coal (Leigh Creek), copper, uranium (Roxby Downs), oil and natural gas in the NE, lead, zinc, iron, opals, household and electrical goods, vehicles
population (1987) 1,388,000; 1% Aborigines
history possibly known to the Dutch in the 16th century; surveyed by ◊Tasman 1644; first European settlement 1834; province 1836; state 1901.

South Bend city on the St Joseph River, N Indiana; population (1990) 105,511. Industries include the manufacture of agricultural machinery, trucks, and aircraft equipment. The University of Notre Dame is on the outskirts. The community developed around a fur-trading post established 1823.

South Carolina state in SE US; nickname Palmetto State
area 31,112 sq mi/80,600 sq km
capital Columbia

South Carolina

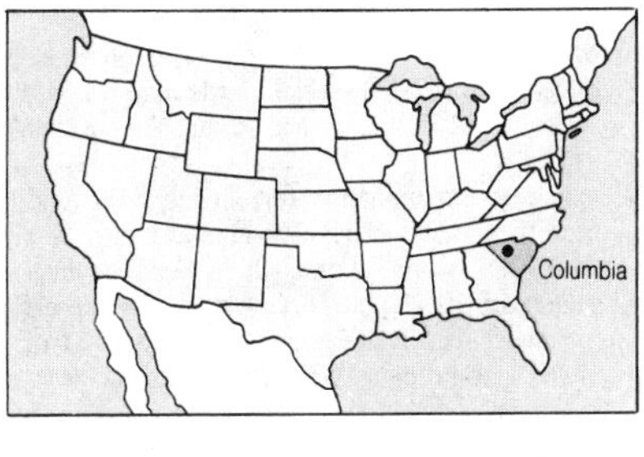
Columbia

South Dakota

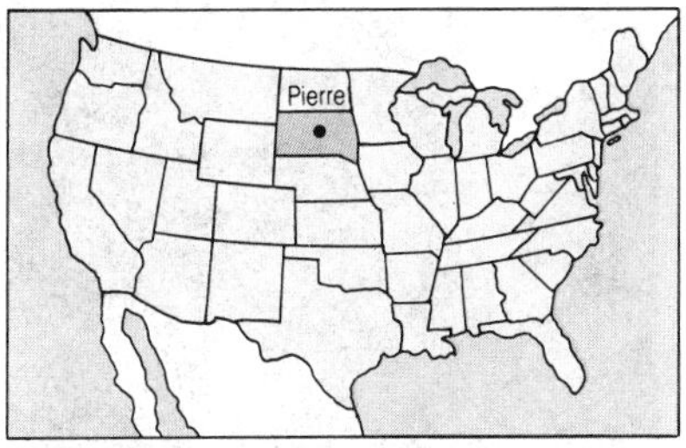
Pierre

cities Charleston, Greenville-Spartanburg
population (1990) 3,486,703
features large areas of woodland; subtropical climate in coastal areas; antebellum Charleston; Myrtle Beach and Hilton Head Island ocean resorts
products tobacco, soybeans, lumber, textiles, clothing, paper, wood pulp, chemicals, nonelectrical machinery, primary and fabricated metals
famous people John C Calhoun, "Dizzy" Gillespie, DuBose Heyward, Francis Marion, John B Watson
history explored first by De Gordillo for Spain 1521; Charles I gave the area (known as Carolina) to Robert Heath (1575-1649) in 1629, and the first English settlement was in 1670 at Albemarle Point, but poor conditions drove the settlers to Charles Town (now Charleston). South Carolina, one of the original thirteen states, was the first state to secede from the Union 1860, and the first battle of the Civil War took place at Fort Sumter in Charleston Harbor, April 12, 1861. Union troops caused widespread destruction in the closing months of the war 1865, including the burning of Columbia. Under Reconstruction, the state was readmitted to the Union 1868, and federal troops left 1877. Tenant farming, or sharecropping, replaced plantation slave labor and, beginning around 1890, tobacco and soybeans replaced rice and cotton as the main crops. Textiles became the state's leading industry after 1900. After 1954, desegregation proceeded very slowly but peaceably. In 1989 Hurricane Hugo devastated coastal areas in the state.

South Dakota state in NW US; nickname Coyote State/Sunshine State
area 77,123 sq mi/199,800 sq km
capital Pierre
cities Sioux Falls, Rapid City, Aberdeen
population (1990) 696,004
physical Great Plains; Black Hills (which include Mount Rushmore, on whose granite face giant relief portrait heads of US presidents Washington, Jefferson, Lincoln, and T Roosevelt are carved); Badlands
products cereals, hay, livestock, gold (second-largest US producer), meat products
famous people Crazy Horse, Ernest O Lawrence, George McGovern, Sitting Bull
history first explored 1743 by Verendrye for France; claimed by France 18th century; passed to the US as part of the Louisiana Purchase 1803; explored by Lewis and Clark 1804–06; first permanent settlement, Fort Pierre 1817, reached by first Missouri River steamboat 1831. A gold rush brought thousands of prospectors and settlers to the Black Hills by railroad 1873–74, and South Dakota became a state 1889. In the 20th century, dam construction along the Missouri river, rural electrification, and reclamation of arid land helped raise the standard of living, but economic opportunities remain limited.

Southeast Asia Treaty Organization (SEATO) former collective defense system (analogous to NATO in Europe) established 1954 by Australia, France, New Zealand, Pakistan, the Philippines, Thailand, the UK, and the US, with Vietnam, Cambodia, and Laos as protocol states. After the Vietnam war, SEATO was phased out by 1977.

South East Cape southernmost point of Australia, in Tasmania.

Southend-on-Sea resort in Essex, England; population (1981) 157,100. Industries include light engineering and boat-building. The shallow water of the Thames estuary enabled the building of a pier 1.25 mi/2 km long.

Southern and Antarctic Territories French overseas territory created 1955. It comprises the islands of St Paul and Amsterdam (26 sq mi/67 sq km); the Kerguelen and Crozet Islands (7,515 sq km/ 2,901 sq mi); and Adélie Land on Antarctica itself (165,500 sq mi/432,000 sq km). All are uninhabited, except for research stations.

Southern Christian Leadership Conference (SCLC) US civil rights organization founded 1957 by Martin Luther ◊King, Jr, and led by him until his assassination 1968. It advocated nonviolence and passive resistance, and it sponsored the 1963 march on Washington, DC that focused national attention on the civil rights movement. Its nonviolent philosophy was increasingly challenged by militants in the civil rights movement, and it lost its central position in the movement. The Rev Jesse ◊Jackson began his association with the civil rights movement with King at the SCLC.

Southern Cross popular name for the constellation ◊Crux.

southern lights common name for the ◊aurora australis, colored light in the southern skies.

Southern US fiction part of a long tradition of fiction and *belles lettres* in the US South since Edgar Allan Poe, often distinctively different from other US fiction. In the 20th century, a remarkable literary revival began, exemplified by the work of Ellen Glasgow and William Faulkner, dealing with the experience of a defeated agrarian region with proud traditions. Among 20th-century writers are Thomas Wolfe, Robert Penn Warren, Katherine Anne Porter, Eudora Welty, William Styron, and Margaret Mitchell, author of *Gone With the Wind* 1936. The Southern Gothic school includes Flannery O'Connor and Carson McCullers.

Writers of the 19th century include William Gilmore Simms, Joel Chandler Harris, and George Washington Cable.

Southey Robert 1774–1843. English poet and author, friend of Coleridge and Wordsworth. In 1813 he became poet laureate but is better known for his *Life of Nelson* 1813, and for his letters.

South Georgia island in the S Atlantic, a British crown colony administered with the South Sandwich Islands; area 1,450 sq mi/3,757 sq km. South Georgia lies 800 mi/1,300 km SE of the Falkland Islands, of which it was a dependency until 1985. The British Antarctic Survey has a station on nearby Bird Island.

South Georgia was visited by Cap James Cook 1775. The explorer Edward Shackleton is buried there. The chief settlement, Grytviken, was established as a whaling station 1904 and abandoned 1966; it was reoccupied by a small military garrison after the Falklands War 1982.

South Glamorgan county in S Wales
area 162 sq mi/420 sq km
towns Cardiff (administrative headquarters), Barry, Penarth
features fertile Vale of Glamorgan; Welsh Folk Museum at St Fagans, near Cardiff
products dairy farming, industry (steel, plastics, engineering) in the Cardiff area
population (1987) 400,000
language 6% Welsh; English.

South Holland (Dutch *Zuid-Holland*) low-lying coastal province of the Netherlands
area 1,123 sq mi/2,910 sq km
population (1988) 3,208,000
capital The Hague
cities Rotterdam, Dordrecht, Leiden, Delft, Gouda
products bulbs, horticulture, livestock, dairy products, chemicals, textiles

history once part of the former county of Holland that was divided into two provinces in 1840.

South Korea see ◊Korea, South.

Southland Plain plain on S South Island, New Zealand, on which Invercargill stands. It is an agricultural area with sheep and dairy farming.

South Orkney Islands group of barren, uninhabited islands in ◊British Antarctic Territory, SE of Cape Horn; area 240 sq mi/622 sq km. They were discovered by the naval explorer Capt George Powell 1821. Argentina, which lays claim to the islands, maintained a scientific station there 1976–82.

South Sandwich Islands actively volcanic uninhabited British Dependent Territory; area 130 sq mi/337 sq km. Along with ◊South Georgia, 470 mi/750 km to the NW, it is administered from the Falkland Islands. They were claimed by Capt Cook 1775 and annexed by the UK 1908 and 1917. They were first formally claimed by Argentina 1948. In Dec 1976, 50 Argentine "scientists" landed on Southern Thule and were removed June 1982. There is an ice-free port off Cumberland Bay. Over 21 million penguins breed on Zavadovski Island.

South Sea Bubble financial crisis in Britain in 1720. The South Sea Company, founded 1711, which had a monopoly of trade with South America, offered in 1719 to take over more than half the national debt in return for further concessions. Its £100 shares rapidly rose to £1,000, and an orgy of speculation followed. When the "bubble" burst, thousands were ruined. The discovery that cabinet ministers had been guilty of corruption led to a political crisis.

South Shetland Islands archipelago of 12 uninhabited islands in the South Atlantic, forming part of ◊British Antarctic Territory; area 1,785 sq mi/4,622 sq km.

South, the historically, the states of the US bounded on the N by the ◊Mason-Dixon Line, the Ohio River, and the E and N borders of Missouri, with an agrarian economy based on plantations worked by slaves, and which seceded from the Union 1861, beginning the American Civil War, as the ◊Confederacy. The term is now loosely applied in a geographic and cultural sense, with Texas often regarded as part of the Southwest rather than the South. By its broadest definition, the South consists of 16 states (including Texas and Oklahoma) and the District of Columbia, with an area of 898,575 sq mi/2,327,309 sq km and a population (1983) of 79.5 million. Houston is the largest city.

South West Africa former name (until 1968) of ◊Namibia.

South Yorkshire metropolitan county of England, created 1976, originally administered by an elected council; its powers reverted to district councils from 1986.

area 602 sq mi/1,560 sq km

towns Barnsley (administrative headquarters), Sheffield, Doncaster

features river Don; part of Peak District National Park

products metal work, coal, dairy, sheep, arable farming

population (1987) 1,296,000.

Soutine Chaim 1894–1943. Lithuanian-born French Expressionist artist. He painted landscapes and portraits, including many of painters active in Paris in the 1920s and 1930s. He had a distorted style, using thick application of paint (impasto) and brilliant colors.

sovereignty absolute authority within a given territory. The possession of sovereignty is taken to be the distinguishing feature of the state, as against other forms of community. The term has an internal aspect, in that it refers to the ultimate source of authority within a state, such as a parliament or monarch, and an external aspect, where it denotes the independence of the state from any outside authority.

Sovetsk town in Kaliningrad region, USSR. In 1807 Napoleon signed peace treaties with Prussia and Russia here. Until 1945 it was known as Tilsit and was part of East Prussia.

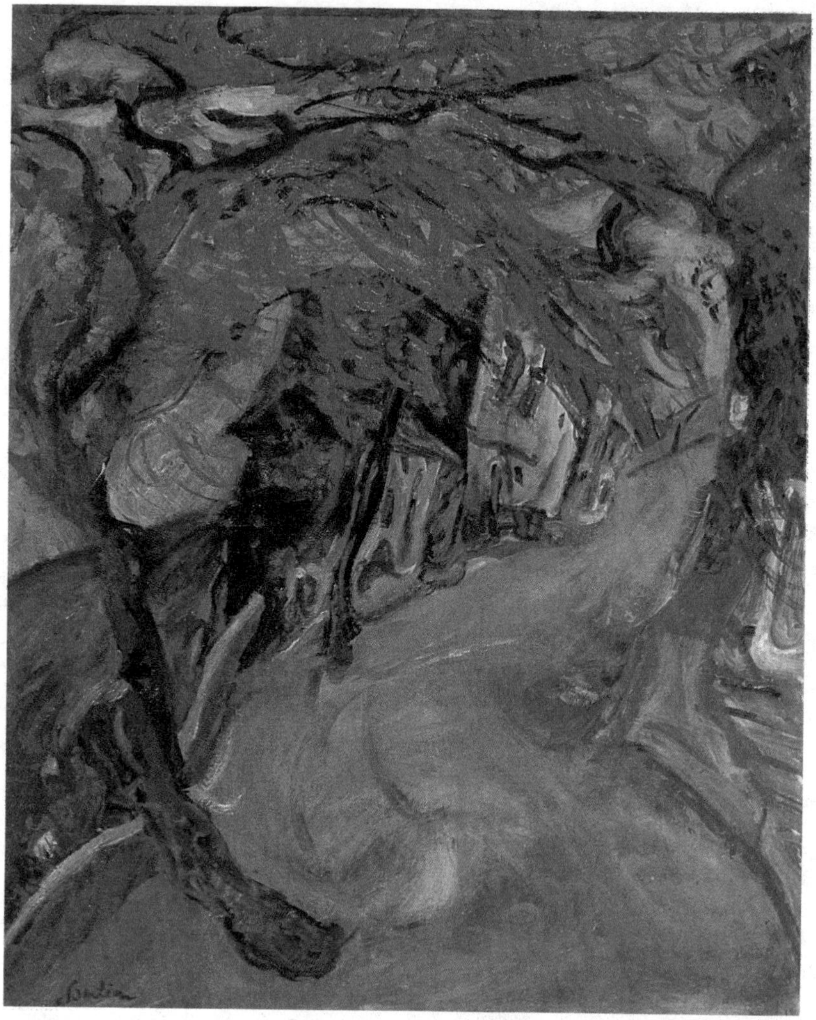

Soutine *Born in Lithuania, French Expressionist artist Chaim Soutine was particularly active during the 1920s and 1930s when he painted* The Road up the Hill *c. 1924.*

soviet (Russian "council") originally a strike committee elected by Russian workers in the 1905 revolution; in 1917 these were set up by peasants, soldiers, and factory workers. The soviets sent delegates to the All-Russian Congress of Soviets to represent their opinions to a future government. They were later taken over by the ◊Bolsheviks.

Soviet Central Asia formerly ***Turkestan*** an area of the USSR comprising the republics of ◊Kazakhstan, ◊Uzbekistan, ◊Tadzhikistan, ◊Turkmenistan, and ◊Kirghizia.

These were conquered by Russia as recently as 1866–73 and until 1917 were divided into the Khanate of Khiva, the Emirate of Bokhara, and the Governor-Generalship of Turkestan. The Soviet government became firmly established 1919, and in 1920 the Khan of Khiva and the Emir of Bokhara were overthrown and People's Republics set up. Turkestan became an Autonomous Soviet Socialist Republic 1921. Boundaries were redistributed 1925 along nationalist lines, and Uzbekistan, Tadzhikistan, and Turkmenistan became republics of the USSR, along with Bokhara and Khiva. The area populated by Kazakhs was united with Kazakhstan, which became a Union Republic 1936, the same year as Kirghizia. Shortfalls in agricultural production led to the establishment in 1962 of a Central Asian Bureau to strengthen centralized control by the Party Praesidium in Moscow. These republics are the home of most Soviet Muslims, and strong nationalist sentiment persists. Major civil disturbances erupted in 1990–91, and the republics demonstrated their resolve to leave the Soviet Union.

Soviet Far East geographical, not administrative, division of Asiatic USSR, on the Pacific coast. It includes the Amur, Lower Amur, Kamchatka, and Sakhalin regions and Khabarovsk and Maritime territories.

Soviet Jew a member of an ethnic minority in the USSR for whom the ◊Jewish Autonomous Region was created.

Soviet Union alternate name for the ◊Union of Soviet Socialist Republics (USSR).

sovkhoz state-owned farm in the USSR where the workers are state employees. The sovkhoz differs from the kolkhoz where the farm is run by a ◊collective.

Soweto (acronym from South West Township) racially segregated urban settlement in South Africa, SW of Johannesburg; population (1983) 915,872.

It began as a shanty town in the 1930s and is now the largest black city in South Africa, but until 1976 its population could have status only as temporary residents, serving as a workforce for Johannesburg. There were serious riots in June 1976, sparked by a ruling that Afrikaans be used in African schools there. Reforms followed, but

***Soyuz** The crew of the Soviet spacecraft* Soyuz 37 *before launch on July 23, 1980. Soviet cosmonaut Vikto Gorbatko (left) teamed with Pham Tuan, the first Vietnamese in space.*

riots flared up again in 1985 and have continued into the 1990s.

soybean plant *Glycine max* of the pea family (Leguminosae) native to E Asia, in particular Japan and China. Originally grown as a forage crop, it is increasingly used for human consumption in cooking oils and margarine, as a flour, or processed and extruded as textured vegetable protein (TVP).

Soyinka Wole 1934– . Nigerian author who was a political prisoner in Nigeria 1967–69. His works include the play *The Lion and the Jewel* 1963; his prison memoirs *The Man Died* 1972; *Aké, The Years of Childhood* 1982, an autobiography, and *Isara*, a fictionalized memoir 1989. He was the first African to receive the Nobel Prize for Literature, in 1986.

Soyuz (Russian "union") series of Soviet spacecraft, capable of carrying up to three cosmonauts. Soyuz spacecraft consist of three parts: a rear section containing engines; the central crew compartment; and a forward compartment that gives additional room for working and living space. They are used for ferrying crews up to space stations. *Soyuz 1* crashed on its first flight April 1967, killing the lone pilot, Vladimir Komarov. Yet in 1968 *Soyuz 3* had the first manned rendezvous and possible docking by a cosmonaut; in 1969 *Soyuz 6* had three spacecraft and seven men put into Earth orbit simultaneously for the first time; and in 1971 *Soyuz 11* linked up with the first space station, *Salyut 1*, although three cosmonauts died on reentry due to loss of pressure in the spacecraft.

Spa town in Liège province, Belgium; population (1982) 9,600. Celebrated since the 14th century for its mineral springs, it has given its name to similar centers elsewhere.

Spaak Paul-Henri 1899–1972. Belgian Socialist politician. From 1936 to 1966 he held office almost continuously as foreign minister or prime minister. He was an ardent advocate of international peace.

space the void that exists beyond Earth's atmosphere. Above 75 mi/120 km, very little atmosphere remains, so objects can continue to move quickly without extra energy. The space between the planets is not entirely empty, but filled with the tenuous gas of the ◊solar wind as well as dust specks.

The space between stars is also filled with thin gas and dust. Evidence also exists for highly rarefied gas in the space between clusters of galaxies, and for that between individual galaxies.

Spacek Sissy (Mary Elizabeth) 1949– . US film actress who starred in *Badlands* 1973 and *Carrie* 1976, in which she played a repressed telekinetic teenager. Her other films include *Coal Miner's Daughter* 1979 and *Missing* 1982.

Spacelab small space station built by the European Space Agency, carried in the cargo bay of the Space Shuttle, in which it remains throughout each flight, returning to Earth with the Shuttle. Spacelab consists of a pressurized module in which astronauts can work, and a series of pallets,

***Space Shuttle** The Space Shuttle* Columbia, *which can carry up a cargo of about 30 tons into space and return with one of about 15 tons.*

open to the vacuum of space, on which equipment is mounted.

Spacelab is used for astronomy, Earth observation, and experiments utilizing the conditions of weightlessness and vacuum in orbit. The pressurized module can be flown with or without pallets, or the pallets can be flown on their own, in which case the astronauts remain in the Shuttle's own crew compartment. All the sections of Spacelab can be reused many times. The first Spacelab mission lasted ten days in Nov–Dec 1983.

space probe any instrumented object sent beyond Earth to collect data from other parts of the Solar System and from deep space. The first probe was the Soviet *Lunik 1*, which flew past the Moon 1959. Other probes include *Giotto*, the Moon probes, and the Mariner, Pioneer, Viking, and Voyager series.

space program a space exploration program dominated by the USSR and the US. See ◊space probe and ◊Space Shuttle.

Space Shuttle reusable US crewed spacecraft, first launched April 12, 1981. It was developed by NASA to reduce the cost of using space for commercial, scientific, and defense purposes. After leaving its payload in space, the Space Shuttle orbiter can be flown back to Earth like any conventional airplane and is then available for reuse.

Four orbiters were built: *Columbia, Challenger, Discovery,* and *Atlantis. Challenger* was destroyed in a midair explosion just over a minute into its tenth launch Jan 28, 1986, killing all seven crew members. The inquiry showed that the cold weather had made the rocket unsafe and that it was launched because of the pressure put on the ground crew by the companies who were using the Shuttle. Flights were postponed until *Discovery* was launched again Sept 29, 1988. At the end of the 1980s, an average of $375 million dollars had been spent on each Space Shuttle mission.

The Space Shuttle orbiter is 122 ft/37.2 m long and weighs 75 tons. Although most of its cargoes will be unmanned, two to eight crew members may occupy the orbiter's nose section for up to 30 days. In its cargo bay the orbiter can carry up to 32 tons of satellites, scientific equipment, ◊Spacelab, or military payloads. At launch, the Shuttle's three main engines are fed with liquid fuel from a cylindrical tank attached to the orbiter; this tank is discarded shortly before the Shuttle

***Space Shuttle** Liftoff of the Space Shuttle* Atlantis *on Oct 18, 1989, carrying a crew of five and the spacecraft* Galileo, *sent toward Jupiter.*

reaches orbit. Two additional solid-fuel boosters provide the main thrust for launch but are jettisoned after two minutes.

space sickness or ***space adaptation syndrome*** feeling of nausea, sometimes accompanied by vomiting, experienced by about 40% of all astronauts during their first few days in space. It is akin to travel sickness and is thought to be caused by confusion of the body's balancing mechanism, located in the inner ear, by weightlessness. The sensation passes after a week or so as the body adapts.

space station any large structure designed for human occupation in space for extended periods of time. Space stations are used for carrying out astronomical observations and surveys of Earth, as well as for biological studies and the processing of materials in weightlessness. The first space station was ◊*Salyut 1*, and the US has launched ◊*Skylab*.

space suit protective suit worn by astronauts and cosmonauts in space. It provides an insulated, air-conditioned cocoon in which people can live and work for hours at a time while outside the spacecraft. Inside the suit is a cooling garment that keeps the body at a comfortable temperature even during vigorous work. The suit provides air to breathe and removes exhaled carbon dioxide and moisture. The suit's outer layers insulate the occupant from the extremes of hot and cold in space (–240°F/–150°C in the shade to +350°F/180°C in sunlight), and from the impact of small meteorites. Some space suits have a jet-propelled backpack, which the wearer can use to move about.

space-time in physics, combination of space and time used in the theory of ◊relativity. When developing relativity, Einstein showed that time was in many respects like an extra dimension (or direction) to space. Space and time can thus be considered as entwined into a single entity, rather than two separate things.

Space-time is considered to have four dimensions: three of space and one of time. In relativity theory, events are described as occurring at points in space-time. The general theory of relativity describes how space-time is distorted by the presence of material bodies, an effect that we observe as gravity.

spadix a type of ◊inflorescence consisting of a long, fleshy axis bearing many small, stalkless flowers. It is partially enclosed by a large bract or ◊spathe. A spadix is characteristic of plants belonging to

Spain
(España)

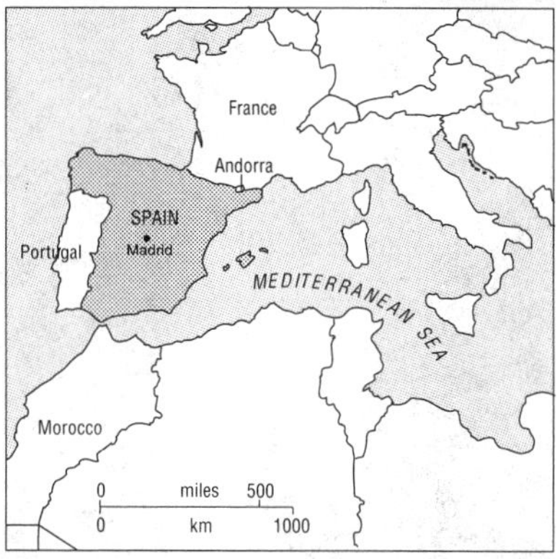
France
Andorra
SPAIN
Madrid
Portugal
MEDITERRANEAN SEA
Morocco
0 miles 500
0 km 1000

area 194,960 sq mi/504,750 sq km
capital Madrid
cities Zaragoza, Seville, Murcia, Córdoba; ports Barcelona, Valencia, Cartegena, Málaga, Cádiz, Vigo, Santander, Bilbao
physical central plateau with mountain ranges; lowlands in S
territories Balearic and Canary Islands; in N Africa: Ceuta, Melilla, Alhucemas, Chafarinas Is, Peñón de Vélez
features rivers Ebro, Douro, Tagus, Guadiana, Guadalquivir; Iberian Plateau (Meseta); Pyrenees, Cantabrian Mountains, Andalusian Mountains, Sierra Nevada
head of state Juan Carlos I from 1975
head of government Felipe González Marquez from 1982
political system constitutional monarchy
political parties Socialist Workers' Party (PSOE), democratic Socialist; Popular Alliance (AP), center-right; Christian Democrats (DC), centrist; Liberal Party (PL), left-of-center
exports citrus fruits, grapes, pomegranates, vegetables, wine, sherry, olive oil, canned fruit and fish, iron ore, cork, vehicles, textiles, petroleum products, leather goods, ceramics
currency peseta
population (1990 est) 39,623,000; growth rate 0.2% p.a.
life expectancy men 74, women 80 (1989)
language Spanish (Castilian, official), Basque, Catalan, Galician, Valencian, and Majorcan
religion Roman Catholic 99%
literacy 97% (1989)
GNP $288 bn (1987); $4,490 per head (1984)
chronology
1936–39 Civil war; Gen Francisco Franco became head of state and government; facist party Falange declared only legal political organization.
1947 Gen Franco announced return to the monarchy after his death, with Prince Juan Carlos as his successor.
1975 Franco died; succeeded as head of state by King Juan Carlos I.
1978 New constitution adopted with Adolfo Suárez, leader of the Democratic Centre Party, prime minister.
1981 Suárez resigned; succeeded by his deputy, Calvo-Sotelo. Attempted military coup thwarted.
1982 Socialist Workers' Party (PSOE), led by Felipe González, won a sweeping electoral victory. Basque separatist organization (ETA) stepped up its guerrilla campaign.
1985 ETA's campaign spread to vacation resorts.
1986 Referendum confirmed NATO membership. Spain joined the European Community.
1988 Spain joined the Western European Union. PSOE lost seats to hold only parity after general election.
1989 Talks between government and ETA collapsed and truce ended.

the family Araceae, including the arum lily *Zantedeschia aethiopica*.

Spain country in SW Europe, on the Iberian Peninsula between the Atlantic and the Mediterranean, bounded N by France and W by Portugal.

government The 1978 constitution puts a hereditary monarch as formal head of state. The monarch appoints a prime minister, called president of government, and a council of ministers, all responsible to the national assembly, *las Cortes Generales*. The *Cortes* consists of two chambers, the Chamber of Deputies, with 350 members, and the Senate, with 208. Deputies are elected by universal suffrage through a system of proportional representation, and 208 of the senators are directly elected to represent the whole country and 49 to represent the regions. All serve a four-year term.

Spain has developed a regional self-government whereby each of the 50 provinces has its own council (*Diputación Provincial*) and civil governor. The devolution process was extended 1979 when 17 autonomous communities were approved, each with a parliament elected for a four-year term.

history Pre-Roman Spain was inhabited by Iberians, ◊Basques, ◊Celts, and Celtiberians. ◊Greece and ◊Phoenicia established colonies on the coast from the 7th century BC; ◊Carthage dominated from the 5th century, trying to found an empire in the southeast. This was conquered by Ancient ◊Rome about 200 BC, and after a long struggle all Spain was absorbed into the Roman Empire. At the invitation of Rome the Visigoths (see ◊Goths) set up a kingdom in Spain from the beginning of the 5th century AD until the invasion by the ◊Moors 711. Christian resistance held out in the north, and by 1250 they had reconquered all Spain except ◊Granada. During this struggle a number of small kingdoms were formed, all of which by the 13th century had been absorbed by ◊Castile and ◊Aragon. The marriage of ◊Ferdinand of Aragon to Isabella of Castile 1469 united their domains on their accession 1479. The conquest of Granada 1492 completed the unification of Spain.

Under Ferdinand and Isabella, Charles I (see ◊Charles V of the ◊Holy Roman Empire), and ◊Philip II, Spain became one of the greatest

Spain: territorial divisions

Regions and provinces	*Area sq km*
Andalucía	
Almería, Cádiz, Córodoba, Granada, Huelva, Jaén, Málaga, Sevilla	87,300
Aragón	
Huesca, Teruel, Zaragoza	47,700
Asturias	10,600
Basque Country	
Álava, Guipúzcoa, Vizcaya	7,300
Canary Islands	
Las Palmas, Santa Cruz de Tenerife	7,300
Cantabria	5,300
Castilla-La Mancha	
Albacete, Ciudad Real, Cuenca, Guadalajara, Toledo	79,200
Castilla-León	
Ávila, Burgos, León, Palencia, Salamanca, Segovia, Soria, Valladolid, Zamora	94,100
Catalonia	
Barcelona, Gerona, Lérida, Tarragona	31,900
Extremadura	
Badajoz, Cáceres	41,600
Galicia	
La Coruña, Lugo, Orense, Pontevedra	29,400
Madrid	8,000
Murcia	11,300
Navarra	10,400
La Rioja	5,000
Valencian Community	
Alicante, Castellón, Valencia	23,300
Ceuta	18
Melilla	14
	499,732

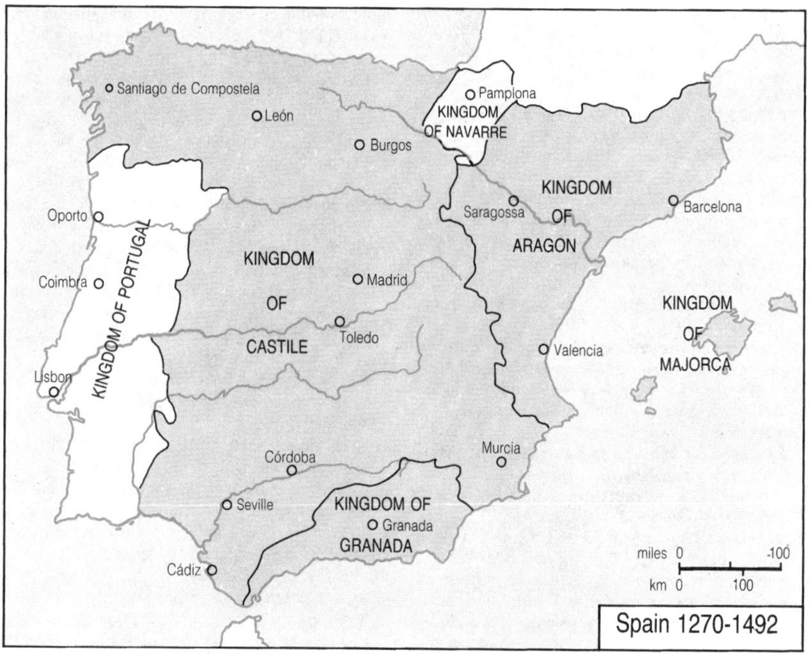
Santiago de Compostela
León
Pamplona
KINGDOM OF NAVARRE
Burgos
KINGDOM OF ARAGON
Saragossa
Barcelona
Oporto
KINGDOM OF PORTUGAL
Coimbra
KINGDOM OF CASTILE
Madrid
Toledo
Valencia
KINGDOM OF MAJORCA
Lisbon
Córdoba
Murcia
Seville
KINGDOM OF GRANADA
Granada
Cádiz
miles 0 100
km 0 100

Spain 1270-1492

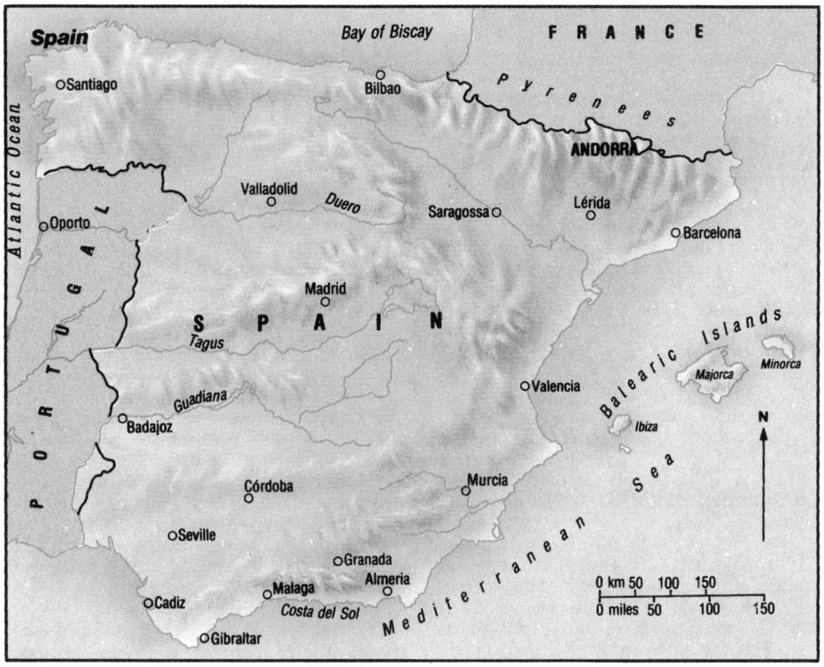
Spain
Bay of Biscay
FRANCE
Pyrenees
ANDORRA
Atlantic Ocean
Santiago
Bilbao
Valladolid
Duero
Saragossa
Lérida
Oporto
Barcelona
PORTUGAL
Madrid
SPAIN
Tagus
Balearic Islands
Majorca
Minorca
Valencia
Ibiza
Guadiana
Badajoz
N
Córdoba
Murcia
Sea
Seville
Granada
Almeria
Malaga
Cadiz
Costa del Sol
Mediterranean
Gibraltar
0 km 50 100 150
0 miles 50 100 150

powers in the world. The discoveries of ◊Columbus, made on behalf of Spain, were followed by the conquest of most of Central and South America. Naples and Sicily were annexed 1503, Milan 1535, Portugal 1580, and Charles I inherited the Netherlands, but with the revolt in the Netherlands and the defeat of the Armada 1588, Spain's power began to decline. The loss of civil and religious freedom, constant wars, inflation, a corrupt bureaucracy, and the expulsion of the Jews and Moors undermined the economy. By the peace of Utrecht that concluded the War of the ◊Spanish Succession 1713, Spain lost Naples, Sicily, Milan, Gibraltar, and its last possessions in the Netherlands.

The 18th century saw reforms and economic progress, but Spain became involved in the ◊Revolutionary and ◊Napoleonic wars, first as the ally, then as the opponent of France. France occupied Spain 1808 and was expelled with British assistance 1814. Throughout the 19th century conflict raged between monarchists and liberals; revolutions and civil wars took place 1820–23, 1833–39, and 1868, besides many minor revolts, and a republic was temporarily established 1873–74.

Spain lost its American colonies between 1810 and 1830 and after the ◊Spanish-American War 1898 ceded Cuba and the Philippines to the US.

Republicanism, socialism, and anarchism grew after 1900; ◊Primo de Rivera's dictatorship 1923–30 failed to preserve the monarchy under ◊Alfonso XIII, and in 1931 a republic was established. In 1936 the Popular Front, a center-left alliance, took office and introduced agrarian and other reforms that aroused the opposition of the landlords and the Catholic church. A military rebellion led by General Francisco ◊Franco resulted in the Spanish ◊Civil War 1936–39. Franco, who was supported by the German Nazis and Italian Fascists, won the war, establishing a military dictatorship.

In 1947 Franco allowed the revival of a legislature with limited powers and announced that after his death the monarchy would be restored, naming the grandson of the last monarch, Prince Juan Carlos de Bourbon, as his successor. Franco died 1975, and King Juan Carlos became head of state. There followed a slow but steady progress to democratic government, with the new constitution endorsed by referendum 1978.

Spain faced two main internal problems, the demands for independence by regional extremists and the possibility of a right-wing military coup. The aims of the ruling Democratic Centre Party (UCD), led by Adolfo Suárez, included a devolution of power to the regions (Basque, Catalonia, and eventually Andalucia), entry into NATO, and membership of the European Community. In 1981 Suárez suddenly resigned and was succeeded by his deputy, Calvo Sotelo. He was immediately confronted with an attempted army coup in Madrid, while at the same time the military commander of Valencia declared a state of emergency there and sent tanks out on the streets. Both uprisings failed, and the two leaders were tried and imprisoned. Sotelo's decision to take Spain into NATO was widely criticized, and, after defections from the party, he was forced to call a general election Oct 1982. The result was a sweeping victory for the Socialist Workers Party (PSOE), led by Felipe Gonzalez.

The Basque separatist organization, ETA, had stepped up its campaign for independence with widespread terrorist activity, spreading in 1985 to the Mediterranean vacation resorts and threatening Spain's lucrative tourist industry. In 1985 unemployment reached 22%.

The PSOE had fought the election on a policy of taking Spain out of NATO and carrying out extensive nationalization. Once in office, however, Gonzalez showed himself to be a pragmatist. His nationalization program was highly selective, and he left the decision on NATO to a referendum. In Jan 1986 Spain became a full member of the European Community, and in March the referendum showed popular support for remaining in NATO. In the July 1986 election the PSOE won 184 seats in the Chamber of Deputies, and Gonzalez returned for another term as prime minister. In Nov 1988 Spain, with Portugal, became a member of the ◊Western European Union (WEU). In the Nov 1989 general election PSOE won only 175 seats in the 350-member National Assembly but retained power under prime minister Gonzales. Major tax reforms were passed in 1991 in an effort to help the nation's struggling economy.

Spalato Italian name for ◊Split, a port in Yugoslavia.

Spallanzani Lazzaro 1729–1799. Italian priest and biologist. He disproved the theory that microbes spontaneously generate out of rotten food by showing that they would not grow in flasks of broth that had been boiled for 30 minutes and then sealed.

Spandau suburb of Berlin, Germany. The chief war criminals condemned at the Nuremberg Trials in 1946 were imprisoned in the fortress there. The last of them was the Nazi leader Rudolf Hess, and the prison was demolished following his death in 1987.

spaniel any of several breeds of dog, characterized by large, drooping ears and a wavy, long, silky coat.

The ***springer*** (English and Welsh), about 45 lb/20 kg and 20 in/50 cm tall, is so called because of its use for "springing" game. The ***cocker*** (English and American) is smaller (25 lb/12 kg, 15 in/40 cm tall), and of various colors. The ***Sussex spaniel*** is believed to be the oldest variety, weighs 45 lb/20 kg, is 15 in/40 cm tall, and is a golden liver color.

Spanish an inhabitant of Spain or a person of Spanish descent, as well as the culture and Romance language of such persons. The standard Spanish language, Castilian, originated in the kingdoms of Castile and Aragon (Catalan and Basque languages are also spoken in Spain).

Spanish-American War brief war 1898 between Spain and the US over Spanish rule in Cuba and in the Philippines; the complete defeat of Spain made the US a colonial power. The war began in Cuba when the US battleship *Maine* was blown up in Havana harbor, allegedly by the Spanish. Other engagements included the Battle of Manila Bay, in which Commander George Dewey's navy destroyed the Spanish fleet in the Philippines, and the taking of the Cuban port cities of El Caney and San Juan Heights (in which Theodore Roosevelt's regiment, the Rough Riders, was involved), thus destroying the Spanish fleet there. The Treaty of Paris ceded the Philippines, Guam, and Puerto Rico to the US; Cuba became independent. The US paid $20 million to Spain. Thus ended Spain's colonial presence in the Americas.

Spanish architecture the architecture of Spain has been influenced by both Classical and Islamic traditions. Styles include Roman (3rd–5th centuries); Asturian (9th century), taking its name from the district in NW Spain that was unconquered by the Moors; Mozarabic (9th–11th centuries), a style of Spanish Christian architecture, showing the influence of Islamic architecture; Romanesque (11th–12th centuries); Gothic (13th–16th centuries); Renaissance (15th–17th centuries), which is based on Italian models; Baroque (17th–18th centuries), a style that reached its peak in the fantastic designs of Churriguera and his followers; Neo-Classical (18th–19th centuries); Modern, including the works of Oscar Niemeyer and Antonio ◊Gaudí.

Spanish Armada the fleet sent by Philip II of Spain against England in 1588. Consisting of 130 ships, it sailed from Lisbon and carried on a running fight up the Channel with the English fleet of 197 small ships under Howard of Effingham and Francis ◊Drake. The Armada anchored off Calais but was forced to put to sea by fireships, and a general action followed off Gravelines. What remained of the Armada escaped around the N of Scotland and W of Ireland, suffering many losses by storm and shipwreck on the way. Only about half the original fleet returned to Spain.

Spanish art painting and sculpture of Spain.

painting

late 15th–16th centuries Italian and Flemish influences contributed to Spanish Renaissance painting. The painters of this period include Bartolomé Bermejo (1440–95), Alonzo Sánchez Coello (1515–90), Luis de Vargas (1502–68), Francisco de Herrera the Elder, Juan de Juanes (1523–79), Juan Navarrette (1526–79), Luis de Morales (1509–86), and El Greco.

17th century The leading Spanish artist was Velázquez.

18th century Goya was to exert a great influence on European art of the following century.

20th century Painters include the Cubist Juan Gris, the Surrealists Joan Miró and Salvador Dali, and Pablo Picasso, widely regarded as the most innovative painter of the century.

sculpture Spanish sculptors include Berruguete (c. 1488–1561), El Greco, Montañes (1568–1649), Alonso Cano (1601–67), Julio González (1876–1942), and Pablo Picasso.

Spanish Civil War 1936–39. See ◊Civil War, Spanish.

Spanish fly alternate name for a European blister ◊beetle. *Lytta vesicatoria*, once used in powdered form as a dangerous diuretic and supposed aphrodisiac.

Spanish Guinea former name of the Republic of ◊Equatorial Guinea.

Spanish language member of the Romance branch of the Indo-European language family, traditionally known as Castilian and originally spoken only in NE Spain. As the language of the court, it has been the standard and literary language of the Spanish state since the 13th century. It is now a world language, spoken in Mexico and all South and Central American countries (except Brazil, Guyana, Suriname, and French Guiana) as well as in the Philippines, Cuba, Puerto Rico, and much of the US that borders on Spanish-speaking countries or has large Latin American immigrant communities.

Castilian Spanish has never succeeded in supplanting such regional languages as Basque, Gallego or Galician, and Catalan. Because of the long Muslim dominance of the S Iberian peninsula, Spanish has been influenced by Arabic. Words in English of Spanish origin include *bronco, cargo, galleon, mosquito, ranch*, and *sherry*.

Spanish literature of the Classical Spanish epics, the 12th-century *El cantar de Mio Cid* is the only complete example. The founder of Castilian prose was King Alfonso X, El Sabio (the Wise), who also wrote lyric poetry in the Galician dialect. The first true poet was the 14th-century satirist Juan Ruiz (c. 1283–1350), archpriest of Hita. To the 15th century belong the Marquis of Santillana (Iñigo López de Mendoza), poet, critic, and collector of proverbs; chivalric romances, such as the *Amadis de Gaula*; ballads dealing with the struggle against the Moors; and the *Celestina*, a novel in dramatic form. The flowering of verse drama began with Lope de Rueda (died 1565) and reached its height with Lope de Vega and Calderón de la Barca. In poetry the golden age of the 15th–16th centuries produced the lyrical Garcilaso de la Vega; the patriotic Fernando de Herrera (1534–97); the mystics Santa Teresa and Luis de León; the elaborate style of Luis de Góngora (1561–1627), who popularized the decadent "gongorism"; and the biting satire of Francisco de Quevedo. In fiction there developed the pastoral romance, for example Jorge de Montemayor's *Diana*; the picaresque novel, established by the anonymous *Lazarillo del Tormes*; and the work of Cervantes. In the 18th century the Benedictine Benito J Feijoo introduced scientific thought to Spain, and French influence emerged in the comedies of Leandro F de Moratín (1760–1828) and others. Typical of the romantic era were the poets and dramatists Angel de Saavedra (Duque de Rivas) (1791–1865) and José Zorilla (1817–93), and the lyricist José de Espronceda (1810–42). Among 19th-century novelists were Pedro de Alarcón (1833–91), Emilia, condesa de Pardo Bazán (1852–1921), and Vicente Blasco Ibáñez (1867–1928); a 19th-century dramatist is José Echegaray (1832–1916).

The "Generation of 1898" included the philosophers Miguel de Unamuno (1864–1936) and José Ortega y Gasset (1883–1955); the novelist Pío Baroja (1872–1956); the prose writer Azorín (José Martínez Ruiz, 1874–1967); and the Nobel prizewinning poet Juan Ramón Jiménez (1881–1958). The next generation included novelist Camilo José Cela (1916–); the poets Antonio Machado (1875–1939), Rafael Alberti (1902–), Luis Cernuda (1902–63), and the Nobel Prizewinner Vincente Aleixandre (1898–); and the dramatists Jacinto Benavente (1866–1954), the brothers Quintero, and Federico García Lorca. The Civil War and the strict censorship of the Franco government disrupted mid-20th century literary life, but later names include the novelists Rafael Sánchez Ferlosio (1927–) and Juan Goytisolo (1931–); and the poets Blas de Otero (1916–) and José Hierro (1922–).

Spanish Main term often used to describe the Caribbean in the 16th–17th centuries, but more properly the South American mainland between the river Orinoco and Panama.

Spanish Sahara former name for the ◊Western Sahara.

Spanish Succession, War of the war 1701–14 of Britain, Austria, the Netherlands, Portugal, and Denmark (the Allies) against France, Spain, and Bavaria. It was caused by Louis XIV's acceptance of the Spanish throne on behalf of his grandson, Philip V of Spain, in defiance of the Partition Treaty of 1700, under which it would have passed to Archduke Charles of Austria (later Holy Roman Emperor Charles VI).

Peace was made by the Treaties of Utrecht 1713 and Rastatt 1714. Philip V was recognized as king of Spain, thus founding the Spanish branch of the Bourbon dynasty. Britain received Gibraltar, Minorca, and Nova Scotia; and Austria received Belgium, Milan, and Naples.

Spanish Town town in Middlesex county, Jamaica; population (1982) 89,000. Founded by Diego Columbus about 1525, it was the capital of Jamaica 1535–1871.

Spark Muriel 1918– . Scottish novelist. She is a Catholic convert, and her works are enigmatic satires: *The Ballad of Peckham Rye* 1960, *The Prime of Miss Jean Brodie* 1961, *The Only Problem* 1984, and *Symposium* 1990.

spark chamber electronic device for recording tracks of charged subatomic ◊particles, decay products, and rays. In combination with a stack of photographic plates, a spark chamber enables the point where an interaction has taken place to be located, to within a cubic centimeter. At its simplest, it consists of two smooth threadlike ◊electrodes that are positioned 1–2 cm apart, the space between being filled by an inert gas such as neon. Sparks jump through the gas along the ionized path created by the radiation.

spark plug a plug that produces an electric spark in the cylinder of a gasoline engine to ignite the fuel mixture. It consists essentially of two electrodes insulated from one another. High-voltage (18,000 V) electricity is fed to a central electrode via the distributor. At the base of the electrode, inside the cylinder, the electricity jumps to another electrode earthed to the engine body, creating a spark. See also ◊ignition coil.

sparrow any of a family (Passeridae) of small Old World birds of the order Passeriformes with short, thick bills, including the now worldwide house or English sparrow *Passer domesticus*. Many numbers of the New World family Emberizidae, which includes ◊warblers, orioles, and buntings are also called sparrows, for example the North American song sparrow *Melospize melodia*.

sparrow hawk alternate (but no longer correct) name for the American ◊kestrel. The name now only refers to a small woodland ◊hawk *Accipiter nisus* found in Eurasia and N Africa. It has a long tail and short wings. The male grows to 11 in/28 cm long, and the female 15 in/38 cm. It hunts small birds.

Sparta ancient Greek city-state in the S Peloponnese (near Sparte), developed from Dorian settlements in the 10th century BC. The Spartans, known for their military discipline and austerity, took part in the Persian and Peloponnesian wars.

The Dorians formed the ruling race in Sparta, the original inhabitants being divided into *perioeci* (tributaries without political rights) and helots or serfs. The state was ruled by two hereditary kings, and under the constitution attributed to Lycurgus all citizens were trained for war from childhood hence the Spartans became proverbial for their indifference to pain or death, their contempt for luxury and the arts, and their harsh treatment of the helots. They distinguished themselves in the ◊Persian and ◊Peloponnesian wars, but defeat by the Thebans in 371 BC marked the start of their decline. The ancient city was destroyed by the Visigoths in AD 396.

Spartacist member of a group of left-wing radicals in Germany at the end of World War I, founders of the Spartacus League, which became the German Communist party in 1919. The league participated in the Berlin workers' revolt of Jan 1919, which was suppressed by the Freikorps on the orders of the Socialist government. The agitation ended with the murder of Spartacist leaders Karl ◊Liebknecht and Rosa ◊Luxemburg.

Spartacus died 71 BC. Thracian gladiator who in 73 BC led a revolt of gladiators and slaves at Capua. He was eventually caught by ◊Crassus and crucified.

Spartakiad sports games held every four years in the USSR (so named after ancient Sparta's stress on physical fitness for state service), in which about 10,000 Soviet athletes compete (foreigners were admitted from 1979).

Spartanburg city in NW South Carolina, NW of Columbia. In the foothills of the Blue Ridge Mountains, it is an agricultural center. Its industries include food products, furniture, textiles, paper, and plumbing supplies; population (1990) 43,467.

spastic person with ◊cerebral palsy. The term is also applied generally to limbs with impaired movement, stiffness, and resistance to passive movement, and to any body part (such as the colon) affected with spasm.

spathe in flowers, the single large bract surrounding the type of inflorescence known as a ◊spadix. It is sometimes brightly colored and petal-like, as in the brilliant scarlet spathe of the flamingo plant *Anthurium andreanum* from South America; this serves to attract insects.

spa town a town with a spring, the water of which, it is claimed, has the power to cure illness and restore health. Spa treatment involves drinking and bathing in the naturally mineralized spring water.

The name derives from the Belgian town of Spa, whose mineral springs have attracted patients since the 14th century. The earliest spas date from Roman times.

speakeasy a bar that illegally sold alcoholic beverages during the ◊Prohibition period (1920–33) in the US. The term is probably derived from the need to speak quickly or quietly to the doorkeeper in order to gain admission.

speaker the presiding officer in the US House of Representatives. The speaker is second in line of succession to the presidency in the event of death or incapacitation.

spearmint perennial herb *Mentha spicata* of the mint family Labiatae, with aromatic leaves and spikes of purple flowers, used for flavoring dishes.

special drawing right (SDR) the right of a member state of the ◊International Monetary Fund to apply for money to finance its balance of payments deficit. Originally, the SDR was linked to gold and the US dollar. After 1974 SDRs were defined in terms of a "basket" of the 16 currencies of countries doing 1% or more of the world's trade. In 1981 the SDR was simplified to a weighted average of US dollars, French francs, German marks, Japanese yen and UK sterling.

special education education, often in separate "special schools," for children with specific physical or mental problems or disabilities.

In the US, the federal department of education has been leading the recent movement toward "mainstreaming," which calls for the integration of students with special needs into the normal school system whenever practical.

speciation the emergence of a new species during

evolutionary history. One cause of speciation is the geographical separation of populations of the parent species, followed by reproductive isolation and selection for different environments so that they no longer produce viable offspring when they interbreed. Other causes are ◊assortative mating and the establishment of a ◊polyploid population.

species in biology, a distinguishable group of organisms that resemble each other or consist of a few distinctive types (as in ◊polymorphism), and that can all interbreed to produce fertile offspring. Species are the lowest level in the system of biological classification.

Related species are grouped together in a genus. Within a species there are usually two or more separate ◊populations, which may in time become distinctive enough to be designated subspecies or varieties, and could eventually give rise to new species through ◊speciation. Around 1.4 million species have been identified so far, of which 750,000 are insects, 250,000 are plants, and 41,000 are vertebrates. In tropical regions there are roughly two species for each temperate-zone species. It is estimated that one species becomes extinct every day through habitat destruction.

specific gravity alternative term for ◊relative density.

specific heat capacity in physics, quantity of heat required to raise unit mass (1 kg) of a substance by one ◊kelvin (1°C). The unit of specific heat capacity in the SI system is the ◊joule per kilogram kelvin (J kg^{-1} K^{-1}).

speckle interferometry technique whereby large telescopes can achieve high resolution of astronomical objects despite the adverse effects of the atmosphere through which light from the object under study must pass. A long-exposure photograph is formed from many individual images, or "speckles," which together form the final picture. The technique was introduced by the French astronomer Antoine Labeyrie 1970.

spectroscopy the study of spectra (obtained by the use of an optical instrument called a spectroscope) associated with atoms or molecules in solid, liquid, or gaseous phase. Spectroscopy can be used to identify unknown compounds and is an invaluable tool to scientists, industry (for example, pharmaceuticals for purity checks), and medical workers.

Emission spectroscopy is the study of the characteristic series of sharp lines in the spectrum produced when an ◊element is heated. Thus an unknown mixture can be analyzed for its component elements. Related is absorption spectroscopy, dealing with atoms and molecules as they absorb energy in a characteristic way. Again, dark lines can be used for analysis. More detailed structural information can be obtained using infrared spectroscopy (concerned with molecular vibrations) or nuclear magnetic resonance (NMR) spectroscopy (concerned with interactions between adjacent atomic nuclei).

spectrum (plural ***spectra***) in physics, an arrangement of frequencies or wavelengths when electromagnetic radiations are separated into their constituent parts. Visible light is part of the ◊electromagnetic spectrum and most sources emit waves over a range of wavelengths that can be broken up or "dispersed"; white light can be separated into red, orange, yellow, green, blue, indigo, and violet.

The visible spectrum was first studied by ◊Newton, who showed in 1672 how white light could be broken up into different colors.

There are many types of spectra, both emission and absorption, for radiation and particles, used in ◊spectroscopy. An incandescent body gives rise to a continuous spectrum where the dispersed radiation is distributed uninterruptedly over a range of wavelengths. An element gives a line spectrum—one or more bright discrete lines at characteristic wavelengths. Molecular gases give band spectra in which there are groups of close-packed lines shaded in one direction of wavelength. In an absorption spectrum dark lines or spaces replace the characteristic bright lines of the absorbing medium. The mass spectrum of an element is obtained from a mass spectrograph and shows the relative proportions of its constituent ◊isotopes.

speculum (plural ***specula***) medical instrument to aid examination of an opening into the body; for example, the nose or vagina. The speculum allows the opening to be widened, permitting the passage of instruments. Many specula also have built-in lights to illuminate the cavity being examined.

Spee Maximilian, Count von Spee 1861–1914. German admiral, born in Copenhagen. He went down with his flagship in the 1914 battle of the Falkland Islands, and the *Graf Spee* battleship was named after him.

speech recognition in computing, techniques whereby a computer can understand ordinary speech. Spoken words are divided into "frames," each lasting about one-thirtieth of a second, which are converted to a wave form. These are then compared with a series of stored frames to determine the most likely word. Research into speech recognition started in 1938, but the technology became sufficiently developed for commercial applications only in the late 1980s.

There are three types: separate word recognition for distinguishing up to several hundred separately spoken words; connected speech recognition for speech in which there is a short pause between words; and continuous speech recognition for normal but carefully articulated speech.

speech synthesis computer-based technology for the generation of speech. A speech synthesizer is controlled by a computer, which supplies strings of codes representing basic speech sounds (phonemes); these together make up words. Speech synthesis applications include children's toys, car and aircraft warning systems, and talking books for the blind.

speed the rate at which an object moves. Speed in miles per hour is calculated by dividing the distance traveled in miles by the time taken in hours. Speed is a ◊scalar quantity, as the direction of motion is not involved. This makes it different from velocity, which is a ◊vector quantity.

speed of light the speed at which light and other ◊electromagnetic waves travel through empty space. Its value is 186,281 mi per second/299,792 km per second. The speed of light is the highest speed possible, according to the theory of ◊relativity, and its value is independent of the motion of its source and of the observer. It is impossible to accelerate any material body to this speed because it would require an infinite amount of energy.

speed of sound the speed at which sound travels through a medium, such as air or water. In air at a temperature of 32°F/0°C, the speed of sound is 1,087 ft/331 m per second. At higher temperatures, the speed of sound is greater; at 64°F/18°C it is 1,123 ft/342 m per second. It is greater in liquids and solids; for example, in water it is around 4,724 ft/1,440 m per second, depending on the temperature.

speedometer instrument attached to the transmission of a vehicle by a flexible drive shaft, which indicates the speed of the vehicle in miles and/or kilometers per hour on a dial easily visible to the driver.

speedwell any flowering plant of the genus *Veronica* of the snapdragon family Scrophulariaceae. Of the many wild species, most are low-growing with small, bluish flowers.

Brookline speedwell *V. americana* grows in marshes all across North America.

Speke John Hanning 1827–1864. British explorer. He joined British traveler Richard ◊Burton on an African expedition in which they reached Lake Tanganyika 1858; Speke became the first European to see Lake ◊Victoria.

His claim that it was the source of the Nile was disputed by Burton, even after Speke and James ◊Grant made a second confirming expedition 1860–63. Speke accidentally shot himself, in England, the day before he was due to debate the matter publicly with Burton.

sperm

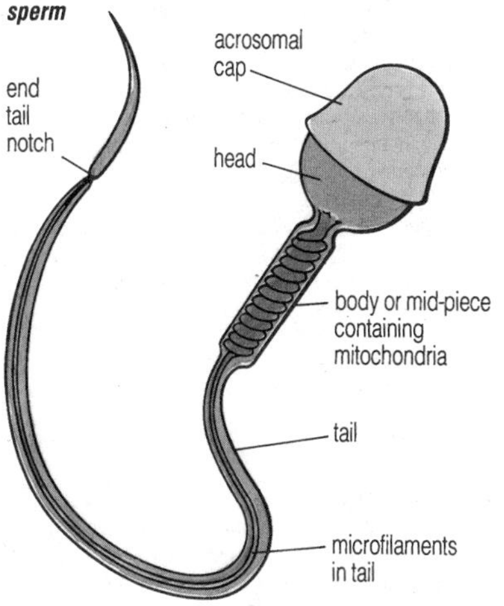
acrosomal cap
end tail notch
head
body or mid-piece containing mitochondria
tail
microfilaments in tail

speleology scientific study of caves, their origin, development, physical structure, flora, fauna, folklore, exploration, mapping, photography, cave-diving, and rescue work. Potholing, which involves following the course of underground rivers or streams, has become a popular sport.

Speleology first developed in France in the late 19th century, where the Société de Spéléologie was founded in 1895.

Spencer Herbert 1820–1903. British philosopher. He wrote *Social Statics* 1851, expounding his *laissez-faire* views on social and political problems, *Principles of Psychology* 1855, and *Education* 1861. In 1862 he began his ten-volume *System of Synthetic Philosophy*, in which he extended Charles ◊Darwin's theory of evolution to the entire field of human knowledge. The chief of the ten volumes are *First Principles* 1862 and *Principles* of biology, psychology, sociology, and ethics. Other works are *The Study of Sociology, Man v. the State, Essays*, and an autobiography.

Spender Stephen (Harold) 1909– . English poet and critic. His earlier poetry has a left-wing political content, as in *Twenty Poems* 1930, *Vienna* 1934, *The Still Centre* 1939, and *Poems of Dedication* 1946. Other works include the verse drama *Trial of a Judge* 1938, the autobiography *World within World* 1951, and translations. His *Journals 1939–83* were published 1985.

Spengler Oswald 1880–1936. German philosopher whose *Decline of the West* 1918 argued that civilizations go through natural cycles of growth and decay. He was admired by the Nazis.

Spenser Edmund c. 1552–1599. English poet, who has been called the "poet's poet" because of his rich imagery and command of versification. He is known for his moral allegory *The Faerie Queene*, of which six books survive (three published 1590 and three 1596). Other books include *The Shepheard's Calendar* 1579, *Astrophel* 1586, the love sonnets *Amoretti* and the *Epithalamion* 1595.

Born in London and educated at Cambridge university, in 1580 he became secretary to the Lord Deputy in Ireland and at Kilcolman Castle completed the first three books of *The Faerie Queene*. In 1598 Kilcolman Castle was burned down by rebels, and Spenser with his family narrowly escaped. He died in London, and was buried in Westminster Abbey.

sperm or ***semen*** the fluid containing the male ◊gametes (sperm cells) of animals. Usually, each sperm cell has a head capsule containing a nucleus, a middle portion containing ◊mitochondria (which provide energy), and a long tail (flagellum).

In most animals, sperm cells (sometimes called "sperm" for short) are motile, and are propelled by a long flagellum, but in some (such as crabs and lobsters) they are nonmotile. The term is sometimes used for the motile male gametes (◊antherozoids) of lower plants.

spermaceti glistening waxlike substance, not a true oil, contained in the cells of the huge, almost rectangular "case" in the head of the sperm whale, amounting to about 3 tons. It rapidly changes in density with variations in temperature. It was formerly used in lubricants and cosmetics, but in 1980 a blend of fatty acids and esters from tallow and coconut oil was developed as a substitute.

spermatophore small, nutrient-rich packet of ◊sperm produced in invertebrates, newts, and cephalopods.

spermatophyte in botany, another name for a ◊seed plant.

spermicide any cream, jelly, pessary, or other preparation that kills the sperm cells in semen. Spermicides are used for contraceptive purposes, usually in combination with a ◊condom or ◊diaphragm. Sponges impregnated with spermicide have also been developed. Spermicide used alone is only 75% effective in preventing pregnancy.

Sperry Elmer Ambrose 1860–1930. US engineer who developed various devices using ◊gyroscopes, such as gyrostabilizers (for ships and torpedoes) and gyro-controlled autopilots.

The first gyrostabilizers dated from 1912, and during World War I Sperry designed a pilotless aircraft that could carry up to 990 lb/450 kg of explosives a distance of 100 mi/160 km (the first flying bomb) under gyroscopic control. By the mid-1930s ***Sperry autopilots*** were standard equipment on most large ships.

Spey river in Highland and Grampian regions, Scotland, rising SE of Fort Augustus, and flowing 107 mi/172 km to the Moray Firth between Lossiemouth and Buckie. It has salmon fisheries at its mouth.

Speyer (English *Spires*) ancient city on the Rhine, in Rhineland-Palatinate, Federal Republic of Germany, 16 mi/26 km S of Mannheim; population (1983) 43,000. It was at the Diet of Spires 1529 that Protestantism received its name.

sphalerite the chief ore of zinc, composed of zinc sulfide with a small proportion of iron, formula (Zn,Fe)S. It is brown with a non-metallic luster unless an appreciable amount of iron is present (up to 26% by weight). Sphalerite usually occurs in ore veins in limestones, where it is often associated with galena. It crystallizes in the cubic system but does not normally form perfect cubes.

sphere in mathematics, a circular solid figure with all points on its surface the same distance from the center. For a sphere of radius r, the volume $V = \frac{4}{3}\pi r^3$ and the surface area $A = 4\pi r^2$.

sphincter ring of muscle found at various points in the alimentary canal, which contracts and relaxes to control the movement of food. The ***pyloric sphincter***, at the base of the stomach, controls the release of the gastric contents into the duodenum. After release the sphincter contracts, closing off the stomach.

Sphinx a mythological creature, represented in Egyptian, Assyrian, and Greek art as a lion with a human head. In Greek myth the Sphinx was female and killed travelers who failed to answer a riddle; she killed herself when ◊Oedipus gave the right answer.

sphygmomanometer instrument for measuring blood pressure. Consisting of an inflatable arm cuff joined by a rubber tube to a pressure-recording device (often a column-of-mercury scale), it is used, together with a stethoscope, to measure arterial blood pressure.

Spica or ***Alpha Virginis*** brightest star in the constellation Virgo and the 16th brightest star in the sky. Spica has a true luminosity over 2,000 times that of the Sun and is 275 light-years from Earth. It is also a spectroscopic ◊binary star, the components of which orbit each other every four days.

spice any aromatic vegetable substance used as a condiment and for flavoring food. Spices are mostly obtained from tropical plants, and include pepper, nutmeg, ginger, and cinnamon. They have little food value but increase the appetite and may facilitate digestion.

Sphinx *The avenue of ram sphinxes at the temple of Karnak in Luxor, Egypt.*

spicebush an aromatic E North American shrub *Lindera benzoin* of the laurel family Lauraceae, with leathery, elliptical leaves. Its red, aromatic berries can be dried and crushed for use as a spice and its leaves for tea.

Spice Islands former name of the ◊Moluccas, a group of islands in the Malay Archipelago.

spicules, solar in astronomy, short-lived jets of hot gas in the upper ◊chromosphere of the Sun. Spiky in appearance, they move at high velocities along lines of magnetic force to which they owe their shapes, and last for a few minutes each. Spicules are usually seen to form at about 45° to the vertical, and appear to disperse material into the ◊corona.

spider any arachnid (eight-legged animal) of the order Araneae. There are about 30,000 known species. Unlike insects, the head and breast are merged to form the cephalothorax, connected to the abdomen by a characteristic narrow waist. There are eight legs, and usually eight simple eyes. On the under-surface of the abdomen are spinnerets, usually six, which exude a viscid fluid. This hardens on exposure to the air to form silky threads, used to make silken egg cases, silk-lined tunnels, or various kinds of webs and snares for catching prey that is then wrapped. The fangs of spiders inject substances to subdue and digest prey, the juices of which are then sucked in to the stomach by the spider. The cross spider *Araneus diadematus* spins webs of remarkable beauty.

Spiders are found everyhwere in the world except Antarctica. Species of interest include the zebra spider *Salticus scenicus*, a longer-sighted species which stalks its prey and has pads on its feet which enable it to walk even on glass; the poisonous ◊tarantula and ◊black widow; the only aquatic species of spider, the water spider *Argyroneta aquatica*, which fills a "diving bell" home with air trapped on the hairs of the body; and the largest members of the group, the bird-eating spider genus *Mygale* of South America, with a body about 2.4–3.5 in/6–9 cm long and a leg-span of 1 ft/30 cm. Spider venom is a powerful toxin that paralyzes its prey.

Spielberg Steven 1947– . US film director, writer, and producer. His highly successful films, including *Jaws* 1975, *Close Encounters of the Third Kind* 1977, *Raiders of the Lost Ark* 1981, and *ET* 1982, have given popular cinema a new "respectable" appeal. He also directed *Indiana Jones and the Temple of Doom* 1984, *The Color Purple* 1985, *Empire of the Sun* 1987, *Indiana Jones and the Last Crusade* 1989, and *Hook* 1991.

spikelet in botany, one of the units of a grass ◊inflorescence. It comprises a slender axis on which one or more flowers are borne.

Each individual flower or floret has a pair of scalelike bracts, the glumes, and is enclosed by a membranous lemma and a thin, narrow palea, which may be extended into a long, slender bristle, or awn.

spikenard Himalayan plant *Nardostachys jatamansi* of the valerian family Valerianaceae; its underground stems give a perfume used in Eastern aromatic oils. Also, a North American plant *Aralia racemosa* of the ginseng family, with fragrant roots.

Spillane Mickey (Frank Morrison) 1918– . US crime novelist, born in Brooklyn, New York. He began by writing for pulp magazines and became known for violent and sexually explicit crime novels featuring his "one-man police force" hero Mike Hammer; for example, *Vengeance is Mine* 1950 and *The Long Wait* 1951.

His other works include *I, The Jury* 1947, *Day of the Guns* 1964, and *The Delta Factor* 1968. Some were made into films during the era of ◊film noir, and a TV series was based on Mike Hammer. He also wrote *Kiss Me, Deadly* 1952, *The Death Dealers* 1965, *Survival . . . Zero* 1970, *The Last Cop Out* 1973, and *The Day the Sea Rolled Back* 1979.

spina bifida congenital defect in which part of the spinal cord and its membranes are exposed, due to incomplete development of the spine (vertebral column).

Spina bifida, usually present in the lower back, varies in severity. The most seriously affected

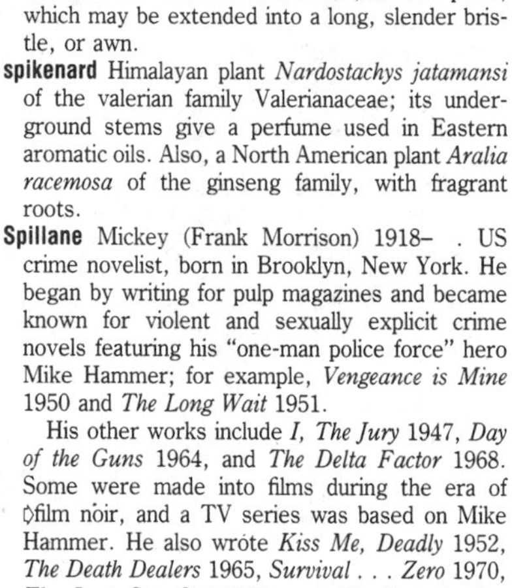

Spielberg *US film director Steven Spielberg, holding the Fellowship Award received at the British Academy of Film and Television Arts Awards, 1986.*

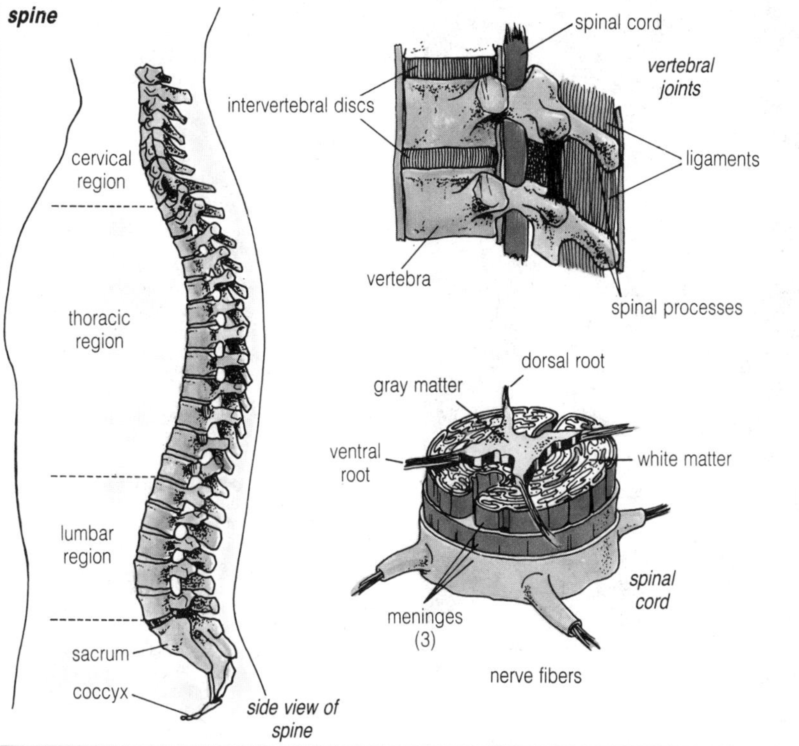
cervical
region
thoracic
region
lumbar
region
sacrum
coccyx
side view of
spine
intervertebral discs
spinal cord
vertebral
joints
ligaments
vertebra
spinal processes
dorsal root
gray matter
ventral
root
white matter
spinal
cord
meninges
(3)
nerve fibers

spine

babies may be paralyzed below the waist. There is also a risk of mental retardation and death from hydrocephalus, which is often associated. Surgery is performed to close the spinal lesion shortly after birth, but this does not usually cure the disabilities caused by the condition.

spinach annual plant *Spinacia oleracea* of the goosefoot family Chenopodiaceae. It is native to Asia and widely cultivated for its leaves, which are eaten as a vegetable.

spinal cord major component of the ◊central nervous system in vertebrates. It is a thick cord of nerve tissue enclosed by dorsal extensions from each vertebra along the spinal column. It runs from the medulla oblongata of the brain all the way down the back.

spinal tap another term for ◊lumbar puncture, a medical test.

spine the backbone of vertebrates. It consists of separate disk-shaped bony units (vertebrae), processes that enclose and protect the spinal cord. The spine connects with the skull, ribs, back muscles, and pelvis.

In humans, there are 7 cervical vertebrae in the neck; 12 thoracic in the upper trunk; 5 lumbar in the lower back; the sacrum (consisting of 5 vertebrae fused together, joined to the hipbones); and the coccyx (4 vertebrae, fused into a tailbone). The human spine has four curves (front to rear), which allow for the increased size of the chest and pelvic cavities, and for a degree of spring so as to minimize jolting of the internal organs.

spinel a group of "mixed oxide" minerals consisting mainly of the oxides of magnesium and aluminum, $MgAl_2O_4$ and $FeAl_2O_4$. Spinels crystallize in the cubic system, forming octahedral crystals. They are found in high-temperature igneous and metamorphic rocks. The aluminum oxide spinel contains gem varieties, such as the ruby spinels of Sri Lanka and Myanmar (Burma).

spinet a keyboard instrument, similar to a ◊harpsichord but smaller, which has only one string for each note.

spinning the art of drawing out and twisting fibers (originally wool or flax) into threads, by hand or machine. Synthetic fibers are extruded as a liquid through the holes of a spinneret.

spinning machine machine for drawing out fibers and twisting them into a long thread, or yarn. Spinning was originally done by hand, then with the spinning wheel, and in about 1767 in England James ◊Hargreaves built the spinning jenny, a machine that could spin 8, then 16, bobbins at once. Later, Samuel ◊Crompton's spinning mule 1779 had a moving carriage carrying the spindles and is still in use today.

Also used is the ring-spinning frame introduced in the US in 1828 where sets of rollers moving at various speeds draw out finer and finer thread, which is twisted and wound onto rotating bobbins. Originally, some 9,000 years ago, spinning was done by hand using a distaff (a cleft stick holding a bundle of fibers) and a weighted spindle, which was spun to twist the thread. In the 1300s the spinning wheel came to in Europe, though it had been in use earlier in the East. It provided a way of turning the spindle mechanically.

By the next century, the wheel was both spinning and winding the yarn onto a bobbin, but further mechanical development did not occur until the 18th century.

Spinoza Benedict or Baruch 1632–1677. Dutch philosopher who believed in a rationalistic pantheism that owed much to Descartes's mathematical appreciation of the universe. Mind and matter are two modes of an infinite substance that he called God or Nature, good and evil being relative. He was a determinist, believing that human action was motivated by self-preservation.

Ethics 1677 is his main work. *A Treatise on Religious and Political Philosophy* 1670 was the only one of his works published during his life, and was attacked by Christians. He was excommunicated by the Jewish community in Amsterdam on charges of heretical thought and practice 1656. He was a lens-grinder by trade.

spiny anteater alternate name for ◊echidna.

spiracle in insects, the opening of a ◊trachea, through which oxygen enters the body and carbon dioxide is expelled. In cartilaginous fishes (sharks and rays), the same name is given to a circular

***Spinoza** The Dutch philosopher Benedict Spinoza is known for his philosophy of rational pantheism.*

opening that marks the remains of the first gill slit.

In tetrapod vertebrates, the spiracle of early fishes has evolved into the Eustachian tube, which connects the middle ear cavity with the pharynx.

spiral a common curve such as that traced by a flat coil of rope. Various kinds of spirals can be generated mathematically—for example, an equiangular or logarithmic spiral (in which a tangent at any point on the curve always makes the same angle with it) and an ◊involute. It also occurs in nature as a normal consequence of accelerating growth, such as the spiral shape of the shells of snails and some other mollusks.

spirea herbaceous plant or shrub of the genus *Spiraea*, family Rosaceae, including many cultivated species with ornamental panicles of flowers.

spiritualism a belief in the survival of the human personality and in communication between the living and those who have "passed on." The spiritualist movement originated in the US in 1848. Adherents to this religious denomination practice mediumship, which claims to allow clairvoyant knowledge of distant events and spirit healing. The writer Arthur Conan Doyle and the Victorian prime minister Gladstone were converts.

spit ◊sandbar (sand ridge) projecting into a body of water and growing out from land, deposited by a current carrying material from one direction to another across the mouth of an inlet.

Spitsbergen the main island in the Norwegian archipelago of ◊Svalbard.

spittle alternate name for ◊cuckoo spit.

spittlebug alternate name for ◊froghopper.

Spitz Mark Andrew 1950– . US swimmer. He won a record seven gold medals at the 1972 Olympic Games, all in world record times.

He won 11 Olympic medals in total (4 in 1968) and set 26 world records between 1967 and 1972.

CAREER HIGHLIGHTS

Olympic medals
gold
4 × 100 meters freestyle relay 1968, 1972
4 × 200 meters freestyle relay 1968, 1972
4 × 100 meters medley relay 1972
100 meters freestyle 1972
200 meters freestyle 1972
100 meters butterfly 1972
200 meters butterfly 1972
silver
100 meters butterfly 1968
bronze
100 meters freestyle 1968

spleen organ in vertebrates, part of the lymphatic system, which helps to process ◊lymphocytes. It also regulates the number of red blood cells in circulation by destroying old cells, and stores iron. It is situated behind the stomach.

splenectomy surgical removal of the ◊spleen.

Split (Italian *Spalato*) port in Yugoslavia, on the Adriatic; population (1981) 236,000. Industries include engineering, cement, and textiles, and it is also a tourist resort.

The Roman emperor Diocletian retired here in 305.

Spock Benjamin McLane 1903– . US pediatrician and writer on child care. His *Common Sense Book of Baby and Child Care* 1946 urged less rigidity in bringing up children than had been advised by previous generations of writers on the subject, but this was misunderstood as advocating permissiveness. He was also active in the peace movement, especially during the Vietnam war.

In his later work he stressed that his common-sense approach had not implied rejecting all discipline, but that his main aim was to give parents the confidence to trust their own judgment rather than rely on books by experts who did not know a particular child.

Spode Josiah 1754–1827. English potter. He developed bone porcelain (made from bone ash, china stone, and kaolinite) around 1800, which was produced at all English factories in the 19th century. Spode became potter to King George III in 1806.

spoils system in the US, the granting of offices and favors among the supporters of a party in office. The spoils system, a type of ◊patronage, was used by President Jefferson and was enlarged in scope by the 1820 Tenure of Office Act, which gave the president and Senate the power to reappoint posts that were the gift of the government after each four-year election.

The system reached a peak under the presidency of Ulysses S Grant (1869–77). In the 20th century, civil-service posts in large cities were often filled on the recommendation of newly elected political leaders. The system was epitomized by the Democratic Party "machine" of Richard Daley (1902–76), mayor of Chicago 1955–76.

The term is derived from a speech after an election victory by Secretary of State William Marcy: "To the victor belong the spoils of the enemy."

Spokane city on the Spokane River, E Washington State; population (1990) 177,196. It is situated in a mining, timber, and rich agricultural area and is the seat of Gonzaga University. Spokane was incorporated 1881 and was the site of Expo '74 (International Exposition of Environment).

Spoleto town in Umbria, central Italy; population (1985) 37,000. There is an annual opera and drama festival established by Gian Carlo ◊Menotti. It was a papal possession 1220–1860 and has Roman remains and medieval churches.

sponge any saclike simple invertebrate of the phylum Porifera, usually marine. A sponge has a hollow body, its cavity lined by cells bearing flagellae, whose whiplike movements keep water circulating, bringing a stream of food particles. The body walls are strengthened with protein (as in the bath sponge) or small spikes of silica, or a framework of calcium carbonate.

sponsorship a form of advertising in sports, music, broadcasting, and the arts. Sponsorship became a major source of finance for sport in the 1970s and takes several forms. Many companies sponsor sporting events, while others give money to individuals who wear the company's logo or motifs while performing. Rock tours are also commonly sponsored by advertisers, although some performers refuse in principle to endorse a product in this way. Art exhibitions are often sponsored by large companies, a form of corporate funding for tax deductions.

In the US radio broadcasts were sponsored by consumer goods and services companies; this continued as television programs became the prime mode of home entertainment. The object for sponsors, often, is a "name" association with a particular show, event, or personality, thus enhancing product image.

spore *The earthstar* Geastrum triplex *is so called because its outer covering splits into a star shape. A water droplet has just landed on top of the fungus, inducing it to expel a spore cloud.*

spontaneous generation or ***abiogenesis*** the erroneous belief that living organisms can arise spontaneously from nonliving matter. This survived until the mid-19th century, when the French chemist Louis Pasteur demonstrated that a nutrient broth would not generate microorganisms if it was adequately sterilized. The theory of ◊biogenesis holds that spontaneous generation cannot now occur; it is thought, however, to have played an essential role in the origin of ◊life on this planet 4 billion years ago.

spooling in computing, a process in which information to be printed is stored temporarily in a file, the printing being carried out later. It is used to prevent a relatively slow printer from holding up the system at critical times, and to enable several computers or programs to share one printer.

spoonbill any of several large wading birds of the ibis family (Threskiornithidae), characterized by a long, flat bill, dilated at the tip in the shape of a spoon. Spoonbills are white or pink, and up to 3 ft/90 cm tall.

The roseate spoonbill *Ajaia ajaja* of North and South America is found in shallow open water, which it sifts for food.

spoonerism the exchange of elements in a flow of words. Usually a slip of the tongue, a spoonerism can also be contrived for comic effect (for example "a troop of Boy Scouts" becoming "a scoop of Boy Trouts"). William Spooner (1844–1930) gave his name to the phenomenon.

Sporades Greek island group in the Aegean Sea. The chief island of the Northern Sporades is ◊Skyros. The Southern Sporades are more usually referred to as the ◊Dodecanese.

sporangium a structure in which ◊spores are produced.

spore a small reproductive or resting body, usually consisting of just one cell. Unlike a ◊gamete, it does not need to fuse with another cell in order to develop into a new organism. Spores are produced by the lower plants, most fungi, some bacteria, and certain protozoa. They are generally light and easily dispersed by wind movements.

Plant spores are haploid and are produced by the sporophyte, following ◊meiosis; see ◊alternation of generations.

sporophyte the diploid spore-producing generation in the life cycle of a plant that undergoes ◊alternation of generations.

sport an activity pursued for exercise or pleasure, performed individually or in a group, usually involving the testing of physical capabilities and often taking the form of a competitive game.

Many sports can be traced to the ancient civilizations. Wrestling took place in what is now Iraq more than 4,000 years ago; a form of hockey was played in Egypt about 2050 BC; and falconry, boxing, track and field athletics, and fencing were all played more than 4,000 years ago. They were organized into the Olympic games in ancient Greece 776 BC.

The real development of the majority of sports as competitions, rather than pastimes, was in the 18th and 19th centuries, when sports such as baseball, soccer, cricket, rugby, golf, tennis, and many more became increasingly popular. The traditional sports have changed very little over the years but televised events have led to more and more competitions within each sport.

SPQR abbreviation for *Senatus Populusque Romanus* (Latin "the Senate and the Roman People").

Spratly Islands (Chinese *Nanshan Islands*) a group of small islands, coral reefs, and sandbars dispersed over a distance of 600 mi/965 km in the South China Sea. Used as a submarine base by the Japanese during World War II, the islands are claimed in whole or part by the People's Republic of China, Taiwan, Malaysia, Vietnam (which calls the islands Truong Sa), and the Philippines (which calls them Kalayaan). The islands are of strategic importance, commanding the sea passage from Japan to Singapore, and in 1976 oil was discovered.

spreadsheet in computing, a program that mimics a sheet of ruled paper, divided into columns and rows. The user enters values in the sheet, then instructs the program to perform some operation on them, such as totaling a column or finding the average of a series of numbers. Highly complex numerical analyses may be built up from these simple steps.

Spreadsheets are widely used in business for forecasting and financial control. The first spreadsheet program, VisiCalc, appeared in 1979.

spring device, usually a metal coil, that returns to its original shape after being stretched or compressed. Springs are used in some machines (such as clocks) to store energy, which can be released at a controlled rate. In other machines (such as engines) they are used to close valves.

In vehicle-suspension systems, springs are used to cushion passengers from road shocks. These springs are used in conjunction with ◊shock absorbers to limit their amount of travel. In bedding and upholstered furniture springs add comfort.

spring in geology, a natural flow of water from the ground, formed at the point of intersection of the water table and the ground's surface. The source of water is rain that has percolated through the overlying rocks. During its underground passage, the water may have dissolved mineral substances that may then be precipitated at the spring (hence, a mineral spring).

A spring may be continuous or intermittent and depends on the position of the water table and the topography.

springbok South African antelope *Antidorcas marsupialis* about 2.6 ft/0.8 m at the shoulder, with head and body 4 ft/1.3 m long. It may leap 10 ft/3 m or more in the air when startled or playing,

spring

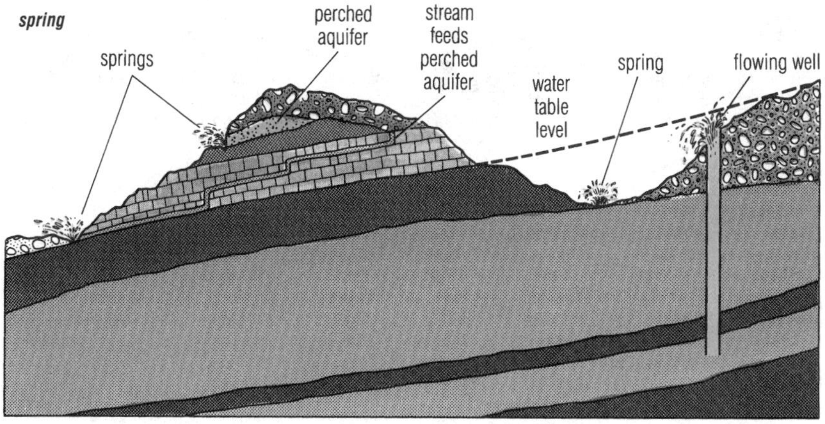
springs
perched aquifer
stream feeds perched aquifer
water table level
spring
flowing well

and has a fold of skin along the middle of the back which is raised to a crest in alarm. Springboks once migrated in herds of over a million, but are now found only in small numbers where protected.

Springdale city in NW Arkansas, NW of Little Rock. Industries include food and livestock processing; population (1990) 29,941.

Springfield city in W Oregon on the Willamette river, E of Eugene. Industries include lumber, animal feeds, and agricultural products; population (1990) 44,683.

Springfield capital and agricultural and mining center of Illinois; population (1990) 105,227. Abraham Lincoln lived and practiced law in Springfield from 1837 until he became president 1861. His home and tomb are historic sites. Sangamon State University is here. Springfield was settled 1818 and became the state capital 1837.

Springfield city in S central Massachusetts; population (1990) 156,983. It was the site (1794–1968) of the US arsenal and armory, known for the Springfield rifle. Basketball originated here 1891, and points of interest include the National Basketball Hall of Fame. The community dates from 1636.

Springfield city and agricultural center in Missouri; population (1990) 140,494. Industries include electronic equipment and processed food. The city is also a tourist center for the Ozark Mountains and the home of Southwest Missouri State University. Springfield was settled 1829.

springhare alternate name for ◊jumping hare.

Springs city in Transvaal, South Africa, 25 mi/40 km E of Johannesburg; population (1980) 154,000. It is a mining center, producing gold, coal, and uranium.

Springsteen Bruce 1949– US rock singer, songwriter, and guitarist, born in New Jersey. Springsteen began his early career in the late 1960s playing small East Coast clubs, where he earned a cult following. His music combines melodies in traditional rock idiom and reflective lyrics about working-class life on albums such as *Born to Run* 1975 and *Born in the USA* 1984.

In concerts with the E Street Band, playing long ambitious sets, his performance is electrifying. "The Boss" won many new fans in the mid-1980s performing in a series of sold-out stadium concerts across the US stadium events.

springbok

spruce coniferous tree of the genus *Picea* of the pine family, found over much of the northern hemisphere. Pyramidal in shape, spruces have rigid, prickly needles and drooping, leathery cones. Some are important forestry trees, such as sitka spruce *P. sitchensis*, native to W North America, and the Norway spruce *P. abies*, now planted widely in North America.

Spurs, Battle of the victory 1513 over the French at Guinegate, NW France, by Henry VII of England; the name emphasizes the speed of the French retreat.

Sputnik (Russian "fellow traveler") series of ten Soviet Earth-orbiting satellites. *Sputnik 1* was the first artificial satellite, launched Oct 4, 1957. It weighed 185 lb/84 kg, with a 23-in/58-cm diameter, and carried only a simple radio transmitter, which allowed scientists to track it as it orbited Earth. It burned up in the atmosphere 92 days later. *Sputnik 2*, launched Nov 3, 1957, weighed about 1,100 lb/500 kg, and carried the dog Laika, the first living creature in space. Unfortunately, there was no way to return the dog to Earth, and it died in space.

sq abbreviation for square (measure).

SQL (abbreviation of structured query language) a computer language designed for use with ◊relational databases. Although it can be used by programmers in the same way as other languages, it is often used as a means for programs to communicate with each other. Typically, one program (called the "client") uses SQL to request data from a database "server."

Squanto c. 1580–1622. Pawtuxet ally of the Plymouth colonists. Also known as Tisquantum, he was born in SE New England and kidnapped to England 1605 by the English explorer George Weymouth. After residing in England and providing Fernando Gorges with information on the native peoples of New England, he returned there 1619 as a guide for Capt John Slaine. With his own tribe wiped out by an epidemic, Squanto settled among the Wampanoag. After serving as interpreter for Wampanoag chief Massasoit in his dealings with the Pilgrims, Squanto eventually settled in Plymouth, living there until his death.

***Springsteen** US rock singer, songwriter, and guitarist Bruce Springsteen.*

spruce

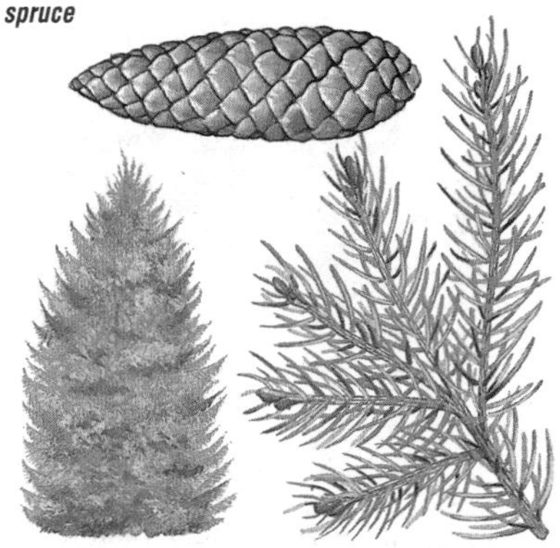

square in geometry, a quadrilateral (four-sided) plane figure with all sides equal and each angle a right angle. Its diagonals bisect each other at right angles. The area A of a square is the length l of one side multiplied by itself ($A = l \times l$). Similarly, any quantity multiplied by itself is also a square, represented by an exponent (power) of 2; for example, $4 \times 4 = 4^2 = 16$ and $6.8 \times 6.8 = 6.8^2 = 46.24$.

An algebraic term is squared by doubling its exponent and squaring its coefficient if it has one; for example, $(x^2)^2 = x^4$ and $(6y^3)^2 = 36y^6$. A number that has a whole number as its ◊square root is known as a perfect square; for example, 25, 144 and 54,756 are perfect squares (with roots of 5, 12 and 234, respectively).

square root in mathematics, a number that when squared (multiplied by itself) equals a given number. For example, the square root of 25 (written $\sqrt{25}$) is ±15, because $5 \times 5 = 25$, and $(-5) \times (-5) = 25$. As an ◊exponent, a square root is represented by ½, for example, $16^{1/2} = 4$.

Negative numbers (less than 0) do not have square roots that are ◊real numbers. Their roots are represented by ◊complex numbers, in which the square root of −1 is given the symbol i (that is, $i^2 = -1$). Thus the square root of −4 is

$$\sqrt{[(-1) \times 4]} = \sqrt{-1} \times \sqrt{4} = 2i.$$

squash game usually played by two people on an enclosed court, derived from ◊rackets. It became a popular sport in the 1970s and then a fitness craze as well as a competitive sport. There are two forms of squash: the American form which is played in North and some South American countries and the English which is played mainly in Europe, Pakistan, and Commonwealth countries such as Australia and New Zealand. Two players use rackets and a small rubber ball which, in the English form, is softer than that used in the American sport. The ball is hit against a wall (the front wall) and when serving, must be above a line about 6 ft/1.83 m high. Thereafter the ball must be hit alternately by both players against the front wall, within certain limitations, but rebounds off the other three walls are permitted. The object is to win points by playing shots the opponent cannot return to the wall.

squill bulb-forming perennial plant of the genus *Scilla*, family Liliaceae, found growing in dry places near the sea in W Europe. Cultivated species usually bear blue flowers either singly or in clusters at the top of the stem.

squint or ***strabismus*** common condition in which one eye deviates in any direction. A squint may

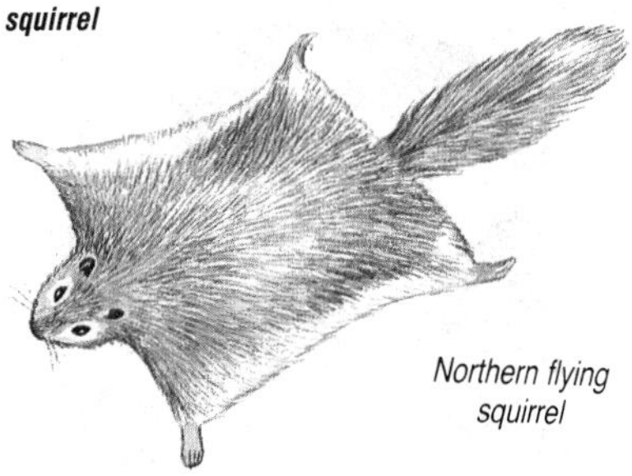
squirrel

Northern flying squirrel

be convergent (with the bad eye turned inward), divergent (outward), or, in rare cases, vertical. A convergent squint is also called cross-eye.

There are two types of squint: paralytic, arising from disease or damage involving the extraocular muscles or their nerve supply; and nonparalytic, which may be inherited or due to some refractive error within the eye. Nonparalytic (or concomitant) squint is the typical condition seen in small children. It is treated by corrective glasses, exercises for the eye muscles, or surgery.

squirrel rodent of the family Sciuridae. Squirrels are found worldwide except for Australia, Madagascar, and polar regions. Some are tree dwellers; these generally have bushy tails, and some, with membranes between their legs, are called ◊flying squirrels. Others are terrestrial, generally burrowing forms called ground squirrels; these includes chipmunks, gophers, marmots, and prairie dogs.

The small red squirrel *Tamia sciurus* to 14 in/35 cm including the tail, of Alaska, Canada, the Rocky Mountains, and NE US, builds large tree nests and accomulates the cones of spruce and other conifers for winter use. The larger eastern gray squirrel *Sciurus carlinensis* of E North America grows to 20 in/50 cm including tail, stores nuts and acorns, and is a common sight in city parks and suburbs.

Sri Lanka island in the Indian Ocean, off the southeast coast of India.

government Under the 1978 constitution, the head of state and chief executive is the president, directly elected by universal suffrage for six-year terms. A two-term limit applies and voting is by the single transferable vote system. The president appoints and dismisses cabinet ministers, including the prime minister, and may hold selected portfolios and dissolve parliament. Parliament, which is known as the National State Assembly, is a single-chamber body with supreme legislative authority. There are 225 members, directly elected by a complex system of proportional representation for six-year terms. A two-thirds parliamentary majority is required to alter the constitution.

history The aboriginal people, the Veddas (of whom a few may remain in jungle areas), were conquered about 550 BC by the Sinhalese from N India under their first king, Vijaya. In the 3rd century BC the island became a world center of Buddhism. The spice trade brought Arabs, who called the island Serendip, and Europeans, who called it Ceylon. Portugal established settlements 1505, taken over by the Netherlands 1658 and by Britain 1796. Ceylon was ceded to Britain 1802 and became a crown colony.

Under British rule Tamils from S India (Hindus who had been settled in the north and east for centuries) took up English education and progressed rapidly in administrative careers. Many more Tamils immigrated to work on the tea and rubber plantations developed in central Sri Lanka near Kandy. Conflicts between the Sinhalese majority and the Tamils surfaced during the 1920s as Nationalist politics developed. In 1931, universal suffrage was introduced for an elected legislature and executive council in which power

Sri Lanka

Democratic Socialist Republic of (until 1972 **Ceylon**)
Prajathanrika Samajawadi Janarajaya Sri Lanka

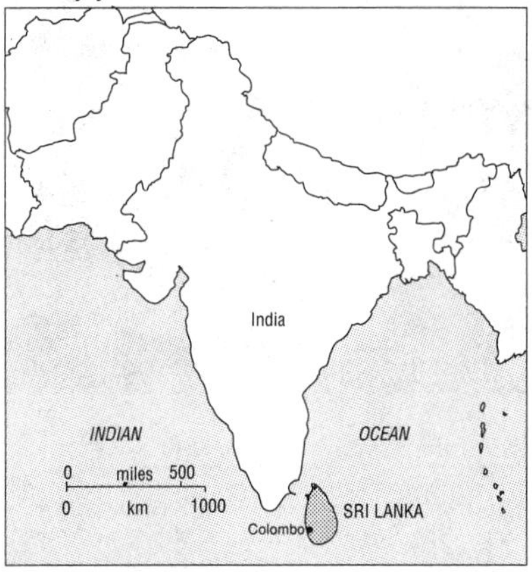
India
INDIAN
OCEAN
0 miles 500
0 km 1000
SRI LANKA
Colombo

area 25,328 sq mi/65,600 sq km
capital (and chief port) Colombo
cities Kandy; ports Jaffna, Galle, Negombo, Trincomalee
physical flat in N and around the coast; hills and mountains in S and central interior
features Adam's Peak (7,538 ft/2,243 m); ruined cities of Anuradhapura, Polonnaruwa
head of state Ranasinghe Premadasa from 1989
head of government Dingiri Banda Wijetunge from 1989
political system liberal democratic republic
political parties United National Party (UNP), right-of-center; Sri Lanka Freedom Party (SLFP), left-of-center; Tamil United Liberation Front (TULF), Tamil autonomy; Eelam People's Revolutionary Liberation Front (EPLRF), Indian-backed Tamil-secessionist "Tamil Tigers"
exports tea, rubber, coconut products, graphite, sapphires, rubies, other gemstones
currency Sri Lanka rupee
population (1990 est) 17,135,000 (Sinhalese 74%, Tamils 17%, Moors 7%); growth rate 1.8% p.a.
life expectancy men 67, women 72 (1989)
language Sinhala, Tamil (both official); English
religion Buddhist 69%, Hindu 15%, Muslim 8%, Christian 7%
literacy 87% (1988)
GNP $7.2 bn; $400 per head (1988)
chronology
1802 Ceylon became a British colony.
1948 Ceylon achieved independence from Britain within the Commonwealth.
1956 Sinhalese established as official language.
1959 Prime Minister Solomon Bandaranaike assassinated.
1972 Socialist Republic of Sri Lanka proclaimed.
1978 Presidential constitution adopted by new Jayawardene government.
1983 Tamil guerrilla violence escalated; state of emergency imposed.
1987 Violence continued despite cease-fire policed by Indian troops.
1988 Left-wing guerrillas campaigned against Indo-Sri Lankan peace pact. Prime Minister Premadasa elected president.
1989 Premadasa became president; Wijetunge, prime minister. Leaders of the TULF and JVP assassinated.
1990 IPKF withdrawn by March. Violence continued.

was shared with the British, and in Feb 1948 independence was achieved.

Between 1948 and 1972, Sri Lanka remained a dominion within the British Commonwealth with a titular governor-general. The United National Party (UNP), led consecutively by Don and Dudley ◊Senanayake, held power until 1956, when the radical Socialist and more narrowly Sinhalese Sri Lanka Freedom Party (SLFP), led by Solomon ◊Bandaranaike, gained electoral victory and established Sinhalese rather than English as

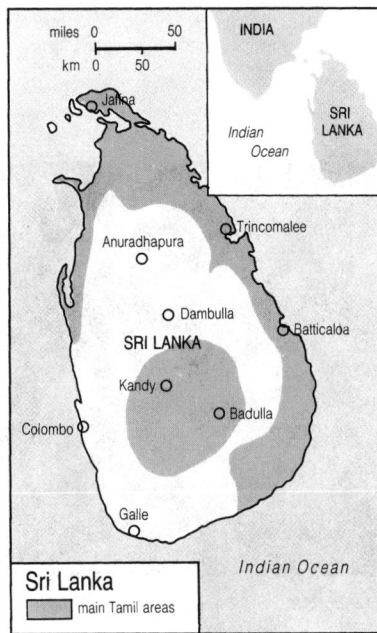

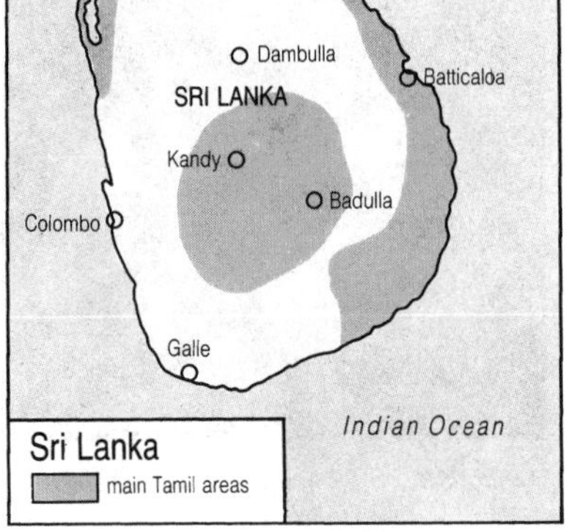
miles 0 50
km 0 50
INDIA
Indian Ocean
SRI LANKA
Jaffna
Trincomalee
Anuradhapura
Dambulla
Batticaloa
SRI LANKA
Kandy
Badulla
Colombo
Galle
Indian Ocean
Sri Lanka
main Tamil areas

the official language to be used for entrance to universities and the civil service. This precipitated Tamil riots, culminating in the prime minister's assassination by a Buddhist monk Sept 1959. Bandaranaike's widow, Sirimavo, became prime minister and held office until 1977, except for UNP interludes 1960 and 1965–70. She implemented a radical economic program of nationalization and land reform, a pro-Sinhalese educational and employment policy, and an independent ◊nonaligned defense policy.

In 1972 the Senate upper chamber was abolished, and the new national name Sri Lanka "Resplendent Island" adopted. Economic conditions deteriorated, spawning a serious wave of strikes 1976, while Tamil complaints of discrimination bred a separatist movement calling for the creation of an independent Tamil state (Eelam) in the north and east. The Tamil United Liberation Front (TULF) coalition was formed 1976 to campaign for this goal and emerged as the second-largest party in parliament from the elections July 1977, easily won by the UNP led by Junius Jayawardene. The new government remodeled the 1972 constitution and introduced a new freer-market economic program, which recorded initial success. In Oct 1980 Sirimavo Bandaranaike was deprived of her civil rights for six years for alleged abuses of power. The guerrilla activities of the Liberation Tigers of Tamil Eelam (LTTE) in the north and east provoked the frequent imposition of a state of emergency. In 1982 Jayawardene was re-elected president, and the life of parliament was prolonged by referendum.

The violence escalated 1983, causing the deaths of over 400 people, mainly Tamils in the Jaffna area. This prompted legislation outlawing separatist organizations, including the TULF. The near civil war has cost thousands of lives and blighted the country's economy; the tourist industry has collapsed, foreign investment dried up, and aid donors have become reluctant to prop up a government seemingly bent on imposing a military solution. All-party talks with Indian mediation repeatedly failed to solve the Tamil dispute, but in July 1987, amid protest riots, with several demonstrators killed by police, President Jayawardene and the Indian prime minister Rajiv ◊Gandhi signed a peace pact. It proposed to make Tamil and English official languages, create a semiautonomous homeland for the Tamils in the north and east, recognize the Tigers (once disarmed) as their representatives, and hold a referendum 1988 in the eastern province, which has pockets of Sinhalese and 32% Muslims. To police this agreement, a 7,000-strong Indian Peace Keeping Force (IPKF) was despatched to the Tiger-controlled Jaffna area. The Tamil Tigers put down their weapons and agreed to talks with the Sri Lankan government April 1989.

This employment of Indian troops served to fan unrest among the Sinhala community who viewed the July 1987 Colombo Accord as a "sell-out" to Tamil interests. Protest riots erupted in the south around Colombo and senior UNP politicians, including President Jayawardene were targeted for assassination by the resurfaced Sinhala-Marxist terrorist organization, the People's Liberation Front (JVP). In the north, despite an additional 50,000 reinforcements being sent, the IPKF failed to capture the Tiger's leader Velupillai Prabhakaran, who continued to wage a guerrilla war from fresh bases in the rural east.

Jayawardene being unable, under the terms of the constitution, to seek a second term, prime minister Ranasinghe ◊Premadasa stood for the governing party in the presidential election of Dec 1989 and defeated the SLFP's Sirimavo Bandaranaike, who called for the immediate withdrawal of the IPKF in a campaign that was marred by JVP-induced violence. A member of the lowly *dhobi* (washerman) caste, Premadasa was the country's first national leader not to be drawn from the privileged *Goyigama* elite. The state of emergency, which had been imposed in May 1983, was temporarily lifted for the National Assembly elections that followed in Feb 1989 and in which the UNP secured a narrow overall majority. After the election, finance minister Dingri Banda Wijetunge was appointed prime minister and proceeded, with President Premadasa, to work for national reconciliation. Round-table negotiations were held with Tiger leaders in June 1989 and in Sept 1989 agreement was reached with India that the IPKF would be withdrawn by April 1990. Despite these moves the civil war, with its two fronts in the north and south, continued, with the death toll exeeding 1,000 a month. Among those assassinated during 1989 was Appapillai Amirthalingam, the leader of the TULF, and Rohana Wijeweera, who had led the JVP since its formation in 1967.

Sri Lanka remains a member of the Commonwealth and ◊nonaligned movement and joined the ◊South Asian Association for Regional Cooperation 1985. India withdrew its troops from Sri Lanka in March 1990. Tamil separatists were accused in the 1991 assassination of India's Rajiv Gandhi.

Srinagar summer capital of the state of ◊Jammu and Kashmir, India; population (1981) 520,000. It is a beautiful resort, intersected by waterways, and has carpet, papier mâché, and leather industries. The university of Jammu and Kashmir was established 1948.

SS Nazi elite corps (German *Schutz-Staffel* "protective squadron") established 1925. Under ◊Himmler its 500,000 membership included the full-time Waffen-SS (armed SS), which fought in World War II, and spare-time members. The SS performed state police duties and was brutal in its treatment of the Jews and others in the concentration camps and occupied territories. It was condemned at the Nuremberg Trials of war criminals.

SSR abbreviation for Soviet Socialist Republic.

stability in physics, how difficult it is to move an object from a position of ◊equilibrium. A stable object returns to its rest position after being shifted slightly. An unstable object topples or falls when shifted slightly.

stabilizer one of a pair of fins fitted to the sides of a ship, especially one governed automatically by a ◊gyroscope mechanism, designed to reduce side-to-side rolling of the ship in rough weather.

stadholder or ***stadtholder*** the leader of the United Provinces of the Netherlands from the 15th to the 18th century.

Originally provincial leaders appointed by the central government, stadholders were subsequently elected in the newly independent Dutch republic. For much of their existence they competed with the States General (parliament) for control of the country. The stadholders later became dominated by the house of ◊Orange-Nassau. In 1747 the office became hereditary, but was abolished in 1795.

Staël Anne Louise Germaine Necker, Madame de 1766–1817. French author, daughter of the financier ◊Necker. She wrote semiautobiographical novels such as *Delphine* 1802 and *Corinne* 1807, and the critical work *De l'Allemagne* 1810, on German literature. She was banished from Paris by Napoleon in 1803 because of her advocacy of political freedom.

Staffordshire county in W central England
area 1,050 sq mi/2,720 sq km
towns Stafford (administrative headquarters), Stoke-on-Trent
features largely flat, comprising the Vale of Trent and its tributaries; Cannock Chase; Keele University 1962; Staffordshire bull terriers
products coal in N; china and earthenware in the Potteries and the upper Trent basin
population (1987) 1,028,000
famous people Peter de Wint

Staffordshire porcelain pottery from Staffordshire, England, one of the largest pottery-producing regions in the world, built up around an area rich in clay. Different companies, the first of which was Longton, have produced stoneware and earthenware from the 17th century onward. See also the ◊Potteries, and ◊pottery and porcelain.

stagflation economic condition (experienced in the US in the 1970s) in which rapid inflation is accompanied by stagnating, even declining, output and by increasing unemployment. It is a recently coined term to explain a condition that violates many of the suppositions of Classical economics. Under the Carter administration, interest rates skyrocketed, prices rose dramatically, and a deep recession occurred. The 1973 increase in ◊OPEC petroleum prices was a major contributing factor.

Stahl Georg Ernst 1660–1734. German chemist who produced a fallacious theory of combustion. He was professor of medicine at Halle, and physician to the king of Prussia. He argued that objects burn because they contain a combustible substance, phlogiston. Substances rich in phlogiston, such as wood, burn almost completely away. Metals, which are low in phlogiston, burn less well. Chemists spent much of the 18th century evaluating Stahl's theories before they were finally proved false by ◊Lavoisier.

stained glass colored pieces of glass that are joined by lead strips to form a pictorial window design.

The art is said to have originated in the Middle East. At first only one monumental figure was represented on each window, but by the middle of the 12th century, incidents in the life of Jesus or of one of the saints were commonly depicted. Fine examples of medieval stained glass are to be found in the cathedrals of Canterbury, Lincoln, Chartres, Cologne, and Rouen. More recent designers include William ◊Morris, Edward ◊Burne-Jones, and Marc ◊Chagall. Since World War II the use of thick, faceted glass joined by cement (common in the 6th century) has been revived.

stalactite and stalagmite *Large stalagmites with stalactites above in Cave of the Black Spring (Ogof Ffynnon Dhu) in South Wales, Great Britain.*

stainless steel widely used ◊alloy of iron, chromium, and nickel that resists rusting. Its chromium content also gives it a high tensile strength.

It is used for cutlery and kitchen fittings. Stainless steel was first produced in the UK 1913 and in Germany 1914.

stalactite and stalagmite cave structures formed by the deposition of calcite dissolved in ground water. Stalactites grow downward from the roofs or walls and can be icicle-shaped, straw-shaped, curtain-shaped, or formed as terraces. Stalagmites grow upward from the cave floor and can be conical, fir-cone-shaped, or resemble a stack of saucers. Growing stalactites and stalagmites may meet to form a continuous column from floor to ceiling.

Stalactites are formed when ground water, hanging as a drip, loses a proportion of its carbon dioxide into the air of the cave. This reduces the amount of calcite that can be held in solution, and a small trace of calcite is deposited. Successive drips build up the stalactite over many years. In stalagmite formation the calcite comes out of the solution because of agitation—the shock of a drop of water hitting the floor is sufficient to remove some calcite from the drop. The different shapes result from the splashing of the falling water.

Stalin Joseph. Adopted name (Russian "steel") of Joseph Vissarionovich Djugashvili 1879–1953. Soviet politician. A member of the October Revolution Committee 1917, Stalin became general secretary of the Communist Party 1922. After ◊Lenin's death 1924, Stalin sought to create "socialism in one country" and clashed with ◊Trotsky, who denied the possibility of socialism inside Russia until revolution had occurred in W Europe.

Stalin *Soviet leader Stalin taking the salute during a march past of workers in Red Square, Moscow, in May 1932.*

EVERLAST

Stallone *US actor Sylvester Stallone specializes in portraying virile and violent men, such as the title character in* Rambo *1985.*

Stalin won this ideological struggle by 1927, and a series of five-year plans was launched to collectivize industry and agriculture from 1928. All opposition was eliminated in the Great Purge 1936–38. During World War II, Stalin intervened in the military direction of the campaigns against Nazi Germany. His role was denounced after his death by Khrushchev and other members of the Soviet regime.

Born in Georgia, the son of a shoemaker, he was educated for the priesthood but was expelled from his seminary for Marxist propaganda. He became a member of the Social Democratic Party 1898, and joined Lenin and the Bolsheviks 1903. He was repeatedly exiled to Siberia 1903–13. He then became a member of the Communist Party's ◊Politburo, and sat on the October Revolution Committee. Stalin rapidly consolidated a powerful following (including ◊Molotov); in 1921 he became commissar for nationalities in the Soviet government, responsible for the decree granting equal rights to all peoples of the Russian Empire, and was appointed general secretary of the Communist Party 1922. As dictator in the 1930s, he disposed of all real and imagined enemies.

Stalingrad former name (1925–61) of the Soviet city of ◊Volgograd.

Stalinsk former name (1932–61) of ◊Novokuznetsk, city in USSR.

Stallone Sylvester 1946– . US film actor. He played bit parts and occasional leads in exploitation films before starring in *Rocky* 1976 and its sequels, which he also wrote. His later films have mostly been based around violence, and include *F.I.S.T.* 1978, *First Blood* 1982, and the *Rambo* series from 1985.

Stamboul the old part of the Turkish city of ◊Istanbul, the area formerly occupied by ◊Byzantium.

stamen the male reproductive organ of a flower. The stamens are collectively referred to as the ◊androecium. A typical stamen consists of a stalk, or filament, with an anther, the pollen-bearing organ, at its apex, but in some primitive plants, such as *Magnolia*, the stamen may not be markedly differentiated.

The number and position of the stamens are significant in the classification of flowering plants. Generally the more advanced plant families have fewer stamens, but they are often positioned more effectively so that the likelihood of successful pollination is not reduced.

Stamford city in SW Connecticut, on Long Island Sound, NE of New York City. Industries include computers, hardware, rubber, plastics, and pharmaceuticals; population (1990) 108,056.

Stamp Act UK act of Parliament in 1765 that sought to raise enough money from the American colonies to cover the cost of their defense. Refusal to use the required tax stamps and a blockade of British merchant shipping in the colonies forced repeal of the act the following year. It was a precursor of the ◊American Revolution.

The act provoked vandalism and looting in America, and the Stamp Act Congress in Oct of that year (the first intercolonial congress) declared the act unconstitutional, with the slogan "No taxation without representation," because the colonies were not represented in the British Parliament.

standard atmosphere alternate term for ◊atmosphere, an unit of pressure.

standard deviation in statistics, a measure of the spread of data. The deviation (difference) of each of the data items from the mean is found, and their values squared. The mean value of these squares is then calculated. The standard deviation is the square root of this mean.

To simplify the calculations, the formula used for a sample standard deviation s is $s = \sqrt{[\Sigma(x_i - \bar{x})^2 \div (n - 1)]}$, where x_i is a particular value of the n pieces of data, and $\bar{x}$ is the sample mean. For example, to find the standard deviation of the ages of a group of eight people in a room, the mean is first found (in this case by adding all the ages together and dividing the total by 8), and the deviations between all the individual ages and the mean calculated. Thus, if the ages of the eight people are 14, 14½, 15, 15½, 16, 17, 19, and 21, the mean age is 132 ÷ 8 = 16.5. The deviations between the individual ages and this mean age are –2.5, –2.0, –1.5, –1.0, –0.5, +0.5, +2.5 and +4.5. These values are then squared to give 6.25, 4.00, 2.25, 1.00, 0.25, 0.25, 6.25, and 20.25, with a mean value of 40.5 ÷ 8 = 5.0625. The square root of this figure is 2.25, which is the standard deviation in years.

standard form a method of writing numbers often used by scientists, particularly for very large or very small numbers. The numbers are written with one digit before the decimal point and multiplied by a power of 10. The number of digits given after the decimal point depends on the accuracy required. For example, the ◊speed of light is 1.8628×10^5 mi per second.

standard gravity the acceleration due to gravity, generally taken as 32.38204 ft per second/ 9.81274 m per second. See ◊*g* scale.

stamen

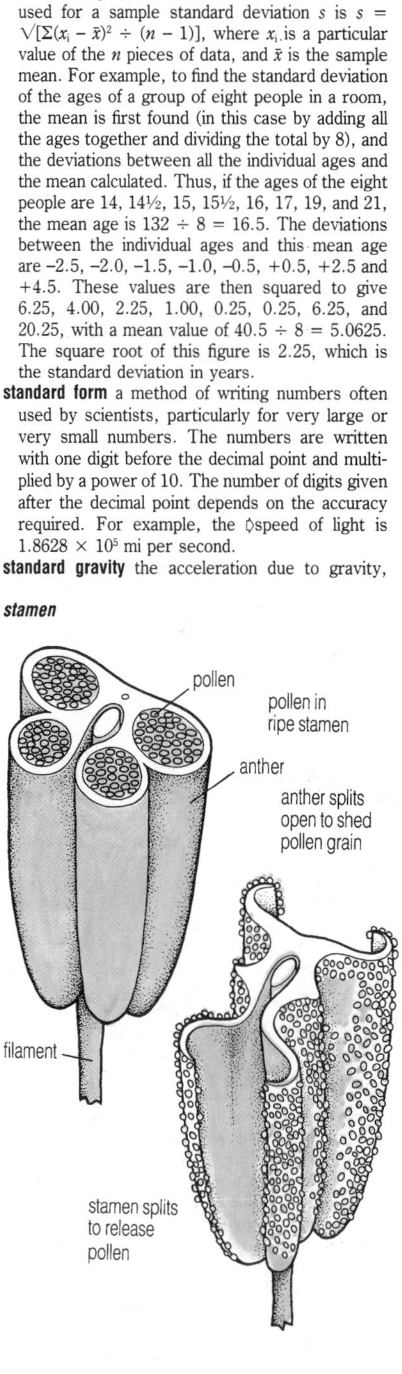

pollen
pollen in ripe stamen
anther
anther splits open to shed pollen grain
filament
stamen splits to release pollen

standard illuminants three standard light intensities, A, B, and C, used for illumination when phenomena involving color are measured. A is the light from a filament at 2,848 K (4667°F/2,575°C), B is noon sunlight, and C is normal daylight. B and C are defined with respect to A. Standardization is necessary because colors appear different when viewed in different lights.

standard of living in economics, the measure of consumption and welfare of a country, community, class, or person. Individual standard-of-living expectations are heavily influenced by the income and consumption of other people in similar jobs and social circumstances, as well as the size of the family in relation to the income.

Universal measures of standards of living cannot be applied to individuals. National income and gross national product, which measure a country's wealth, do not take into account unpaid work (housework and family labor) or quality of life and do not show the distribution of wealth or reflect the particular national or individual aspirations, duties, or responsibilities, which differ widely from person to person, class to class, and country to country.

Standard Oil Co of New Jersey et al v US a US Supreme Court decision 1911 dealing with the dissolution of unreasonable corporate monopolies. The Standard Oil Co, ordered to dissolve after being convicted of an attempt to eliminate free competition in the industry, appealed to the Supreme Court. The Court upheld the conviction formulating a new subjective definition of an illegal trust as "an unreasonable attempt" to restrain competition in trade.

standard temperature and pressure (STP) in chemistry, a standard set of conditions for experimental measurements, to enable comparisons to be made between sets of results. Standard temperature is 0°C and standard pressure 1 atmosphere (101,325 Pa).

standard time alternate name for ◊zone standard time.

standard volume in physics, the volume occupied by one kilogram molecule (the molecular mass in kilograms) of any gas at standard temperature and pressure. Its value is approx 22.414 cubic meters.

standing crop in ecology, the total number of individuals of a given species alive in a particular area at any moment. It is sometimes measured as the weight (or ◊biomass) of a given species in a sample section.

standing order in banking, an instruction (banker's order) by a depositor with the bank to pay a certain sum of money at regular intervals. In some cases, the bank may be billed by a third party such as a supplier of gas or electricity, who is authorized by the depositor to invoice the bank directly, which in turn will pay out the sum demanded (known as direct debit).

standing wave a wave in which the positions of ◊nodes (positions of zero vibration) and antinodes (positions of maximum vibration) do not move. Standing waves result when two similar waves travel in opposite directions through the same space.

For example, when a sound wave is reflected back along its own path, as when a stretched string is plucked, a standing wave is formed. In this case the antinode remains fixed at the center and the nodes are at the two ends. Water and ◊electromagnetic waves can form standing waves in the same way.

Standish Miles c. 1584–1656. Colonial American military leader. Meeting the Puritan Separatists who were about to embark for America, he agreed to serve as their military adviser. Arriving in New England, Standish led negotiations with the Wampanoag and supervised the Plymouth colonists' military training. After returning to England in 1625 to obtain a charter for Plymouth Colony, he became one of its chief investors 1627.

He later established the nearby town of Duxbury and settled there 1637.

Born in Lancashire, England, Standish began his military career as a mercenary in the Dutch rebellion against the Spanish. Although one of the most influential figures in colonial New England, Standish is best remembered through Longfellow's *The Courtship of Miles Standish*, a narrative poem presumably more fictitious than historical.

Stanford Charles Villiers 1852–1924. British composer and teacher, born in Ireland. A leading figure in the 19th-century renaissance of British music, his many works include operas such as *Shamus O'Brien* 1896, seven symphonies, chamber music, and church music. Among his pupils were Vaughan Williams, Holst, and Bridge.

Stanford Leland 1824–1893. US public official and railroad developer. Settling in California 1856, he became a successful merchant in Sacramento and was elected governor 1861. In the same year, he became president of the Central Pacific Railroad and exerted his political influence to gain government concessions for its transcontinental route. Stanford was one of the founders of the Southern Pacific Railroad 1870. He later served in the US Senate 1885–93 and endowed Stanford University.

Born in Watervliet, New York, Stanford was educated at Cazenovia Seminary and was admitted to the bar 1848.

Stanislavsky Konstantin Sergeivich 1863–1938. Russian actor, director, and teacher. He founded the Moscow Art Theatre 1898 and directed productions of Chekhov and Gorky. He was the originator of ◊Method acting, described in *My Life in Art* 1924 and other works.

The Method had considerable influence on acting techniques in Europe and the US (resulting in the founding of the ◊Actors Studio). He rejected the declamatory style of acting in favor of a more realistic approach, concentrating on the psychological basis for the development of character.

Stanley town on E Falkland, capital of the ◊Falkland Islands; population (1986) 1,200. After changing its name only once between 1843 and 1982, it was renamed five times in the space of six weeks during the Falklands War in April–June 1982.

Stanley Henry Morton 1841–1904. Welsh-born US explorer and journalist who made four expeditions to Africa. He and David ◊Livingstone met at Ujiji 1871 and explored Lake Tanganyika. He traced the course of the river Zaïre (Congo) to the sea 1874–77, established the Congo Free State (Zaïre) 1879–84, and charted much of the interior 1887–89.

Stanley fought in the Confederate army in the US Civil War. He worked for the *New York Herald* from 1867, and in 1871 he was sent by the editor James Gordon Bennett (1795–1872) to find the ailing Livingstone, which he did on Nov 10. From Africa he returned to the UK and was elected to Parliament 1895.

Stanley Wendell 1904–1971. US biochemist who succeeded, in 1935, in crystallizing the tobacco mosaic virus (TMV). He demonstrated that, despite its crystalline state, TMV remained infectious. Together with John Northrop and James Sumner, Stanley received the 1946 Nobel Prize for Chemistry.

Stanley Cup North American ◊ice-hockey playoffs held at the end of the regular season in the National Hockey League (NHL). It was inaugurated in 1917 and named after Lord Stanley of Preston, former governor-general of Canada.

Stanley Falls former name (until 1972) of ◊Boyoma Falls, on the Zaïre River.

Stanley Pool former name (until 1972) of ◊Pool Malebo, on the Zaïre River.

Stanleyville former name (until 1966) of the Zaïrean port of ◊Kisangani.

Stanton Edwin McMasters 1814–1869. US public official. Born in Steubenville, Ohio, Stanton attended Kenyon College and was admitted to the bar 1836. Having gained a reputation as a skilled lawyer, he was appointed US attorney general by President Buchanan 1860. Although a Democrat, Stanton was named secretary of war by Republican president Lincoln 1862. In that position he was an effective, if autocratic administrator.

Although retained in office by Andrew Johnson, Stanton eventually broke with him over Reconstruction policies and was forced to resign 1868. He was named to the US Supreme Court 1869 by Grant but died before taking office.

Stanton Elizabeth Cady 1815–1902. US feminist who, with Susan B ◊Anthony, founded the National Woman Suffrage Association 1869, the first women's movement in the US and was its first president. She and Anthony wrote and compiled the *History of Women's Suffrage* 1881–86. Stanton also worked for the abolition of slavery.

She organized the International Council of Women in Washington, DC. Her publications include *Degradation of Disenfranchisement* and *Solitude of Self* 1892, and in 1885 and 1898 she published a two-part feminist critique of the Bible: *The Woman's Bible*.

Stanwyck Barbara. Adopted name of Ruby Stevens 1907–1990. US film actress. Often cast as an independently minded woman of the world, she also excelled in villainous roles, as in *Double Indemnity* 1944. Her other films include *Stella Dallas* 1937, *Ball of Fire* 1942, and *Executive Suite* 1954. In later years she was especially known for her TV Western series "The Big Valley." She was presented with a special Academy Award in 1981 for her life's work.

stanza (Italian "resting or stopping place") a group of lines in a poem. Each stanza has a set, repeatable pattern of meter and rhyme and is usually divided from the following stanza by a line of space.

staple in medieval Europe, a riverside town where merchants had to offer their wares for sale before proceeding to their destination, a practice that constituted a form of toll; such towns were particularly common on the Rhine.

In English usage, it referred to a town appointed as the exclusive market for a particular commodity, especially wool. The wool staple was established by the English crown in Calais 1353. This form of monopoly trading was abandoned 1617.

star luminous globe of gas, producing its own heat and light by nuclear reactions. Stars are born from ◊nebulae and consist mostly of hydrogen and helium gases. Surface temperatures range from 3,600°F/2,000°C to above 54,000°F/30,000°C, and the corresponding colors range from red to blue-white. The brightest stars have masses 100 times that of the Sun and emit as much light as millions of suns; they live for less than a million years before exploding as ◊supernovae. The faintest stars are the ◊red dwarfs, less than one-thousandth the brightness of the Sun.

The smallest mass possible for a star is about 8% that of the Sun (80 times the mass of the planet Jupiter), otherwise nuclear reactions do not occur. Objects with less than this critical mass shine only dimly and are termed brown dwarfs. There is no firm distinction between a small brown dwarf and a large planet, like Jupiter. Toward the end of its life, a star like the Sun swells up into a ◊red giant, before losing its outer layers as a ◊planetary nebula, and finally shrinking to become a ◊white dwarf. See also ◊binary star, ◊Hertzsprung–Russell diagram, ◊supergiant, and ◊variable star.

starch widely distributed, high-molecular-mass ◊carbohydrate, produced by plants as a food store; main dietary sources are cereals, legumes, and tubers, including potatoes. It consists of varying proportions of two ◊glucose polymers (◊polysaccharides): straight-chain (amylose) and branched (amylopectin) molecules.

Purified starch is a white powder used to stiffen textiles and paper and as a raw material for making various chemicals. It is used in the food industry as a thickening agent. Chemical treatment of starch gives rise to a range of "modified starches" with varying properties. Hydrolysis (splitting) of starch by acid or enzymes generates a variety of "glucose syrups" or "liquid glucose" for use in the food industry. Complete hydrolysis of starch with acid generates the ◊monosaccharide glucose only. Incomplete hydrolysis or enzymic hydrolysis yields a mixture of glucose, maltose and nonhydrolyzed fractions called "dextrins."

starfish

crown of thorns starfish

Star Chamber in English history, a civil and criminal court, named after the star-shaped ceiling decoration of the room in the Palace of Westminster, London, where its first meetings were held. Created in 1487 by Henry VII, the Star Chamber comprised some 20 or 30 judges. It was abolished 1641 by the ◊Long Parliament.

star cluster group of related stars, usually held together by gravity. Members of a star cluster are thought to form together from one large cloud of gas in space. Open clusters such as the Pleiades contain from a dozen to many hundreds of young stars, loosely scattered over several light-years. ◊Globular clusters are larger and much more densely packed, containing perhaps 100,000 old stars.

starfish or ***seastar*** any ◊echinoderm of the subclass Asteroidea with arms radiating from a central body. Usually there are five arms, but some species have more. They are covered with spines and small pincerlike organs. There are also a number of small tubular processes on the skin surface that assist in locomotion and respiration. Starfish are predators, and vary in size from 0.5 in/1.2 cm to 3 ft/90 cm.

Some species use their suckered tube feet to pull open the shells of bivalve mollusks, then evert the stomach to surround and digest the animal inside. The poisonous and predatory crown-of-thorns of the Pacific is very destructive to coral and severely damaged Australia's Great Barrier Reef when it multiplied prolifically in the 1960–70s, but by 1990 it had itself practically disappeared, perhaps because of attack by parasites.

starling any member of a large widespread Old World family (Sturnidae) of chunky, dark, generally gregarious birds of the order Passeriformes. The European starling *Sturnus vulgaris*, common in N Eurasia, has been naturalized in North America from the late 19th century. The black, speckled plumage is glossed with green and purple. Its own call is a bright whistle, but it is a mimic of the songs of other birds. It is about 8 in/20 cm long.

Strikingly gregarious in feeding, flight, and roosting, it often becomes a pest in large cities, where it becomes attached to certain buildings as "dormitories," returning each night from omnivorous foraging in the countryside. If disturbed, starlings have been known to lay eggs in the nests of other birds before starting a new nest with their mate elsewhere.

Starling Ernest Henry 1866–1927. English physiologist who discovered ◊secretin and coined the word "hormone." He formulated Starling's law, which states that the force of the heart's contraction is a function of the length of the muscle fibers. He is considered one of the founders of endocrinology.

Star of David or ***Magen David*** six-pointed star (made with two equilateral triangles), a symbol of Judaism since the 17th century. It is the central motif on the flag of Israel, and, since 1897, the emblem of Zionism.

START abbreviation for ◊Strategic Arms Reduction Talks.

Star Wars popular term for the ◊Strategic Defense Initiative announced by US president Reagan in 1983.

state or ***nation-state*** territory that forms its own domestic and foreign policy, acting through laws that are typically decided by a government and carried out, by force if necessary, by agents of that government.

Although most nation-states are members of the United Nations, this is not a completely reliable criterion: some are not members by choice, like Switzerland; some have been deliberately excluded, like Taiwan; and some are members but do not enjoy complete national sovereignty, like Byelorussia and Ukraine, which both form part of the USSR.

The classic definition of a state is given by R M MacIver (*The Modern State* 1926): "An association which, acting through law as promulgated by a government endowed to this end with coercive power, maintains within a community territorially demarcated the universal external conditions of social order." There are four essential elements in this definition: that people have formed an association to create and preserve social order; that the community comprising the state is clearly defined in territorial terms; that the government representing the people acts according to promulgated laws; and that it has power to enforce these laws.

Today, the state is seen as the nation-state so that any community that has absolute sovereignty over a specific area is a state. Thus the so-called states of the US, which are to some degree subject to the will of the federal government, are not states in international terms, nor are colonial or similar possessions, which, too, are subject to an overriding authority.

In a ◊federation, the units are also often called states, such as the United States of Mexico, the United States of Brazil, and the United States of America, but they are units of a nation-state.

state change in science, a change in the physical state (solid, liquid, or gas) of a material. For instance, melting, boiling, evaporation, and their opposites (solidification and condensation) are state changes.

These changes require energy in the form of heat, called ◊latent heat, even though the temperature of the material does not change during the transition between states.

State Department (Department of State) US government department responsible for ◊foreign relations, headed by the ◊secretary of state, the senior cabinet officer of the executive branch.

Staten Island island in New York harbor, part of New York City, comprising the county of Richmond and, since 1975, the borough of Staten Island; area 60 sq mi/155 sq km. Staten Island is the city borough with the smallest population. Although mainly residential, it has oil refineries, docks, diversified manufactures, city garbage dumps, and the new nuclear home port of the US Navy. It is linked to Manhattan by ferry, to Brooklyn by the Verrazano-Narrows Bridge, and to New Jersey by the Outerbridge Crossing. Colonial settlement began 1661 by the Dutch; it passed to the English 1664 and became part of the city 1898. Residents petitioned 1989 and voted 1990 to take a step toward separation from New York City, since they feel they are exploited by but inadequately serviced by the city.

States General former French parliament that consisted of three estates—nobility, clergy, and commons. First summoned in 1302, it declined in importance as the power of the crown grew. It was not called at all between 1614 and 1789 when the crown needed to institute fiscal reforms to avoid financial collapse. Once called, the demands made by the States General formed the first phase in the ◊French Revolution.

States General is also the name of the Dutch parliament.

states of matter the forms (solid, liquid, or gas) in which material can exist. Whether a material is solid, liquid, or gas depends on its temperature and the pressure on it. The transition between states takes place at definite temperatures, called melting point and boiling point.

◊Kinetic theory describes how the state of a material depends on the movement and arrangement of its atoms or molecules. A hot ionized gas or ◊plasma is often called the fourth state of matter, but ◊liquid crystals, ◊colloids, and glass also have a claim to this title.

static electricity ◊electric charge that is stationary, usually acquired by a body by means of electrostatic induction or friction. Rubbing different materials can produce static electricity, as seen in the sparks produced on combing one's hair or removing a nylon shirt. In some processes static electricity is useful, as in paint spraying where the parts to be sprayed are charged with electricity of opposite polarity to that on the paint droplets, and in ◊xerography.

statics branch of mechanics concerned with the behavior of bodies at rest and forces in equilibrium, and distinguished from ◊dynamics.

stations of the Cross in the Christian church, a series of 14 crosses, usually each with a picture or image, depicting the 14 stages in Jesus's journey to the Crucifixion.

statistical mechanics branch of physics in which the properties of large collections of ◊particles are predicted by considering the motions of the constituent particles.

statistics the branch of mathematics concerned with the collection and interpretation of data. For example, to determine the ◊mean age of the children in a school, a statistically acceptable answer might be obtained by calculating an average based on the ages of a representative sample, consisting, for example, of a random tenth of the pupils from each class. ◊Probability is the branch of statistics dealing with predictions of events.

status in the social sciences, an individual's social position, or the esteem in which he or she is held by others in society. Both within and among most occupations or social positions there is a status hierarchy. Status symbols, such as insignia of office or an expensive car, often accompany high status.

The two forms of social prestige may be separate or interlinked. Formal social status is attached to a certain social position, occupation, role, or office. Informal social status is based on an individual's own personal talents, skills, or personality. Sociologists distinguish between ascribed status, which is bestowed by birth, and achieved status, the result of one's own efforts.

The German sociologist Max Weber analyzed social stratification in terms of three separate but interlinked dimensions: class, status, and power. Status is seen as a key influence on human behavior, on the way people evaluate themselves and others.

Staudinger Hermann 1881–1965. German organic chemist, founder of macromolecular chemistry, who carried out pioneering research into the structure of albumen and cellulose. Nobel Prize 1953.

Stauffenberg Claus von 1907–1944. German colonel in World War II who, in a conspiracy to assassinate Hitler, planted a bomb in the dictator's headquarters conference room in the Wolf's Lair at Rastenburg, East Prussia, July 20, 1944. Hitler was merely injured, and Stauffenberg and 200 others were later executed by the Nazi regime.

staurolite a silicate mineral, $FeAl_4Si_2O_{10}(OH)_2$. It forms brown crystals that may be twinned in the form of a cross. It is a useful indicator of medium grade (moderate temperature and pressure) in metamorphic rocks formed from clay sediments.

Stavanger seaport and capital of Rogaland county, SW Norway, population (1988) 96,000. It has fish-canning, oil, and shipbuilding industries.

Stavropol a territory of the Russian Soviet Federal Socialist Republic, lying N of the Caucasus mountains; area 31,128 sq mi/80,600 sq km; population (1985) 2,715,000. The capital is Stavropol. Irrigated land produces grain and sheep are also reared. There are natural gas deposits.

Stavropol formerly (1935–43) ***Voroshilovsk*** town SE of Rostov, in the N Caucasus, USSR; population (1987) 306,000. Founded 1777 as a fortress town, it is now a market center for an agricultural area and makes agricultural machinery, textiles, and food products.

STD abbreviation for sexually transmitted disease, a term encompassing not only traditional ◊venereal disease, but also a growing list of conditions, such as ◊AIDS and scabies, which are known to be spread primarily by sexual contact. Other diseases that are sexual in origin include viral ◊hepatitis and cancer of the cervix.

steady-state theory theory that the universe is in a steady state: it appears the same wherever (and whenever) viewed. This seems to be refuted by the existence of cosmic background radiation, however. The theory was proposed 1948 by Hermann Bondi, Thomas Gold (1920–), and Fred Hoyle.

stealth technology the development of aircraft and missiles that have low radar, infrared, and optical signatures and thus can penetrate an enemy's defenses with minimum detection. This is accomplished by using nonconventional airframe shapes, engine placements, construction materials, and coatings. In 1980 the US announced that it had developed such piloted aircraft, in both fighter and bomber types. The F-117 fighter was used by the US in the Persian Gulf war 1991.

steam in chemistry, a dry, invisible gas formed by vaporizing water. The visible cloud that normally forms in the air when water is vaporized is due to minute suspended water particles. Steam is widely used in chemical and other industrial processes and for the generation of power.

steam engine engine that uses the power of steam to produce useful work. It was the principal power source during the British Industrial Revolution in the 18th century. The first successful steam engine was built 1712 by Thomas Newcomen: steam was admitted to a cylinder as a piston moved up, and was then condensed by a spray of water, allowing air pressure to force the piston downward. James Watt improved Newcomen's engine in 1769 by condensing the steam outside the cylinder (thus saving energy formerly used to reheat the cylinder) and by using steam to force the piston upward. Watt also introduced the double-acting engine, in which steam is alternately sent to each end of the cylinder. The compound engine (1781) uses the exhaust from one cylinder to drive the piston of another. The high-pressure steam engine was developed 1802 by Richard Trevithick, and led to the development of the steam locomotive. A later development was the steam ◊turbine, still used today to power ships and generators in power stations. See ◊internal combustion engine.

stearic acid $CH_3(CH_2)_{16}COOH$ saturated long-chain ◊fatty acid, soluble in alcohol and ether but not in water. It is found in many fats and oils, and is used to make soap and candles and as a lubricant. The salts of stearic acid are called stearates.

stearin a mixture of stearic and palmitic acids, used to make soap.

Stębark Polish name (since 1945) for the village of ◊Tannenberg, formerly in East Prussia, now part of Poland.

steel alloy or mixture of iron and up to 1.7% carbon, sometimes with other elements, such as manga-

***Steen** Dutch genre painter Jan Steen's* The Harpsichord Lesson, *now in the Wallace Collection, London.*

nese, phosphorus, sulfur, and silicon. The US, the USSR, and Japan are the main steel producers. Steel has innumerable uses, including ship and automobile manufacture, skyscraper frames, and machinery of all kinds.

Steels with only small amounts of other metals are called carbon steels. These steels are far stronger than pure iron, with properties varying with the composition. Alloy steels contain greater amounts of other metals. Low-alloy steels have less than 5% of the alloying material; high-alloy steels have more. Low-alloy steels containing up to 5% silicon with relatively little carbon have a high electrical resistance and are used in power transformers and motor or generator cores, for example. Stainless steel is a high-alloy steel containing at least 11% chromium. Steels with up to 20% tungsten are very hard and are used in high-speed cutting tools. About 50% of the world's steel is now made from scrap.

Steel is produced by removing impurities, such as carbon, from raw or pig iron, produced by a ◊blast furnace. The main industrial process is the ◊basic-oxygen process, in which molten pig iron and scrap steel is placed in a container lined with heat-resistant, alkaline (basic) bricks. A pipe or lance is lowered near to the surface of the molten metal and pure oxygen blown through it at high pressure. The surface of the metal is disturbed by the blast and the impurities are oxidized (burned out). The open-hearth process is an older steelmaking method in which molten iron and limestone are placed in a shallow bowl or hearth (see ◊open-hearth furnace). Burning oil or gas is blown over the surface of the metal, and the impurities are oxidized. High-quality steel is made in an electric furnace. A large electric current flows through electrodes in the furnace, melting a charge of scrap steel and iron. The quality of the steel produced can be controlled precisely because the temperature of the furnace can be maintained exactly and there are no combustion by-products to contaminate the steel. Electric furnaces are also used to refine steel, producing the extra-pure steels used, for example, in the petrochemical industry.

The steel produced is cast into ingots, which can be worked when hot by hammering (forging) or pressing between rollers to produce sheet steel. Alternatively, the continuous-cast process, in which the molten metal is fed into an open-ended mold cooled by water, produces an unbroken slab of steel.

steel band type of musical ensemble common in the West Indies, consisting mostly of percussion instruments made from oil drums that give a sweet, metallic ringing tone.

Steele Richard 1672–1729. Irish essayist who founded the journal *The Tatler* 1709–11, in which Joseph ◊Addison collaborated. They continued their joint work in *The Spectator*, also founded by Steele, 1711–12, and *The Guardian* 1713. He also wrote plays, such as *The Conscious Lovers* 1722.

Steen Jan 1626–1679. Dutch painter. Born in Leiden, he was also active in The Hague, Delft, and Haarlem. He painted humorous everyday scenes, mainly set in taverns or bourgeois households, as well as portraits and landscapes.

Steep Point the westernmost extremity of Australia, in Western Australia, NW of the Murchison River.

Stefan Joseph 1835–1893. Austrian physicist who established one of the basic laws of heat radiation in 1874, since known as the ◊Stefan–Boltzmann law. This states that the heat radiated by a hot body is proportional to the fourth power of its absolute temperature.

Stefan–Boltzmann constant in physics, a constant relating the energy emitted by a black body (a hypothetical body that absorbs or emits all the energy falling on it) to its temperature. Its value is 5.6697×10^{-8} W m^{-2} K^{-4}.

Stefan–Boltzmann law in physics, a law that relates the energy, E, radiated away from a perfect emitter (a ◊black body), to the temperature, T, of that body. It has the form $M = \sigma T^4$, where M is the energy radiated per unit area per second, T is the temperature, and σ is the Stefan–Boltzmann constant.

Steffens Lincoln 1866–1936. US journalist. Born in San Francisco and educated at Berkeley, Steffens joined the staff of the *New York Evening Post* 1892. An expert in financial affairs, Steffens served as editor of the *New York Commercial Advertiser* 1897–1901 and later joined the staff of *McClure's Magazine*. Intent on exposing corruption and fraud in high places, he joined forces with writers Ida Tarbell and Ray Stannard Baker and initiated the style of investigative journalism since known as "muckraking." Steffens later covered the Mexican Revolution and befriended Lenin. His *Autobiography* appeared 1931.

Steichen Edward 1897–1973. Luxembourg-born US photographer, who with Alfred ◊Stieglitz helped to establish photography as an art form. His style evolved during his career from painterly impressionism to realism.

During World War I he helped to develop aerial photography, and in World War II he directed US naval-combat photography. He turned to fashion and advertising 1923–38, working mainly for *Vogue* and *Vanity Fair* magazines. He was in charge of the Museum of Modern Art's photography collection 1947–62, where in 1955 he organized the renowned "Family of Man" exhibition.

Steiermark German name for ◊Styria, province of Austria.

Steiger Rod(ney Stephen) 1925– . US character actor who often played leading film roles. His work includes *On the Waterfront* 1954, *In the Heat of the Night* 1967 (Academy Award), and the title role in *W C Fields and Me* 1976.

Stein Aurel 1862–1943. Hungarian archeologist and explorer who carried out projects for the Indian government in Chinese Turkestan and Tibet 1900–15.

Stein Gertrude 1874–1946. US writer who influenced authors Ernest ◊Hemingway, Sherwood ◊Anderson, and F Scott ◊Fitzgerald with her conversational tone, cinematic technique, use of repetition, and absence of punctuation: devices intended to convey immediacy and realism. Her work includes the self-portrait *The Autobiography of Alice B Toklas* 1933.

Born in Allegheny, Pennsylvania, Stein went to Paris 1903 after medical school at Johns Hopkins University and lived there, writing and collecting art, for the rest of her life. She settled in with her brother, also a patron of the arts, and a companion/secretary, Alice B Toklas (1877–1967). In her home she held court to a "lost generation" of expatriate US writers and modern artists (Picasso, Matisse, Braque, Gris). She also wrote *The Making of Americans* 1906–11, *Composition as Explanation* 1926, *Tender Buttons* 1941, *Mrs. Reynolds* 1952, and the operas (with composer Virgil Thomson) *Four Saints in Three Acts* 1929 and *The Mother of Us All* 1947. A tour of the US 1934 resulted in *Everybody's Autobiography* 1937.

Steinbeck John (Ernst) 1902–1968. US novelist. His realist novels, such as *In Dubious Battle* 1936, *Of Mice and Men* 1937, and *The Grapes of Wrath* 1939 (Pulitzer prize 1940), portray agricultural life in his native California, where migrant farm laborers from the Oklahoma dust bowl struggled to survive. He received the Nobel Prize for Literature in 1962.

Born in Salinas, California, Steinbeck worked as a laborer to support his writing career, and his experiences supplied him with authentic material for his books. He first achieved success with *Tortilla Flat* 1935, a humorous study of the lives of Monterey *paisanos* (farmers). His early naturalist works are his most critically acclaimed. Later books include *Cannery Row* 1944, *The Wayward Bus* 1947, *East of Eden* 1952, *Once There Was a War* 1958, *The Winter of Our Discontent* 1961, and *Travels with Charley* 1962. He also wrote screenplays for films, notably *Viva Zapata!* 1952. His best-known short story is the fable "The Pearl."

Steinberg Saul 1914– . Romanian-born US artist. He was educated at the University of Bucharest and received his doctorate in architecture from the Reggio Politecnico in Milan 1940. Embarking on a career as a painter and cartoonist, he immigrated to the US 1942. After service as an American intelligence officer in Italy during World War II, Steinberg became a regular cover illustrator for the *New Yorker*. Collections of his paintings, cartoons, and murals were exhibited at galleries throughout the country. He was inducted into the National Institute of Arts and Letters 1968.

Steinem Gloria 1934– . US journalist and liberal feminist who emerged as a leading figure in the US women's movement in the late 1960s. She was also involved in radical protest campaigns against racism and the Vietnam War. She co-founded the Women's Action Alliance 1970 and *Ms* magazine. In 1983 a collection of her articles was published as *Outrageous Acts and Everyday Rebellions*.

Steiner Max(imilian Raoul) 1888–1971. Austrian composer of film music who lived in the US from 1914. He composed his first film score in 1929 and produced some of motion pictures' finest music, including the scores to *King Kong* 1933, *Gone with the Wind* 1939, and *Casablanca* 1942.

Steiner Rudolf 1861–1925 Austrian philosopher, originally a theosophist (see ◊Blavatsky), who developed his own mystic and spiritual teaching, anthroposophy, designed to develop the whole human being. His method of teaching is followed by a number of schools named after him, although the schools also include the possibilities for pupils to take state exams.

Steinmetz Charles 1865–1923. US engineer who formulated the Steinmetz hysteresis law in 1891, which describes the dissipation of energy that occurs when a system is subject to an alternating magnetic force.

He worked on the design of alternating current transmission and from 1894 to his death served as consulting engineer to General Electric.

Stella Frank 1936– . US painter, a pioneer of the hard-edged geometric trend in abstract art that followed Abstract Expressionism. From around 1960 he also experimented with the shape of his canvases.

Stella Joseph 1877–1946. Italian-born US painter. He painted cubistic and futuristic views of New York City, such as his *Brooklyn Bridge* 1919–20 and *New York Interpreted* 1920–22. Stella's works are mostly mechanical and urban scenes, although his later paintings include tropical landscapes.

stem the main supporting axis of a plant that bears the leaves, buds, and reproductive structures; it may be simple or branched. The plant stem usually grows above ground, although some grow underground, including ◊rhizomes, ◊corms, and ◊tubers. Stems contain a continuous vascular system that conducts water and food to and from all parts of the plant.

The point on a stem from which a leaf or leaves arise is called a node, and the space between two successive nodes is the internode. In some plants, the stem is highly modified; for example, it may form a leaflike ◊cladode or it may be twining (as in many climbing plants), or fleshy and swollen to store water (as in cacti and other succulents). In plants exhibiting ◊secondary growth, the stem may become woody, forming a main trunk, as in trees, or a number of branches from ground level, as in shrubs.

Stendhal pen name of Marie Henri Beyle 1783–1842. French novelist. His novels ◊*Le Rouge et le noir/The Red and the Black* 1830 and *La Chartreuse de Parme/The Charterhouse of Parme* 1839 were pioneering works in their treatment of disguise and hypocrisy; a review of the latter by ◊Balzac in 1840 furthered Stendhal's reputation.

Born in Grenoble, Stendhal served in Napoleon's armies and took part in the ill-fated Russian campaign. Failing in his hopes of becoming a prefect, he lived in Italy from 1814 until suspicion of espionage drove him back to Paris in 1821, where he lived by literary hackwork. From 1830 he was a member of the consular service, spending his leaves in Paris.

Stephen c. 1097–1154. King of England from 1135. A grandson of William I, he was elected king 1135, although he had previously recognized Henry I's daughter ◊Matilda as heiress to the throne. Matilda landed in England 1139, and civil war disrupted the country until 1153, when Stephen acknowledged Matilda's son, Henry II, as his own heir.

Stephen I, St 975–1038. King of Hungary from 997, when he succeeded his father. He completed the conversion of Hungary to Christianity and was canonized in 1803.

Stephen, St died c. AD 35. The first Christian martyr; he was stoned to death. Feast day Dec 26.

Stephens Alexander Hamilton 1812–1883. American public official. As one of the leaders of the Whig Party in the US House of Representatives 1843–59, Stephens, from Georgia, opposed the Mexican War and remained a strong defender of slavery. In 1861 he was chosen vice-president of the Confederacy. Arrested and briefly imprisoned at the end of the Civil War, he served again as US congressman 1872–82 and as Georgia governor 1882–83.

Born in Taliaferro County, Georgia, Stephens was educated at the University of Georgia and was admitted to the bar 1834. He served in the Georgia state legislature 1836–41.

Stephens John Lloyd 1805–1852. US explorer in Central America, with Frederick ◊Catherwood. He recorded his findings of ruined Mayan cities in his two-volume *Incidents of Travel in Central America, Chiapas and Yucatan* 1841–43.

Stephenson George 1781–1848. English engineer who built the first successful steam locomotive, and who also invented a safety lamp in 1815. He was appointed engineer of the Stockton and Darlington Railway, the world's first public railroad, in 1821, and of the Liverpool and Manchester Railway in 1826. In 1829 he won a £500 prize with his locomotive *Rocket*.

Stephenson Robert 1803–1859. English civil engineer who constructed railroad bridges such as the high-level bridge at Newcastle upon Tyne, England, and the Menai and Conway tubular bridges in Wales. He was the son of George Stephenson.

steppe the temperate grasslands of Europe and Asia. Sometimes the term refers to other temperate grasslands and semiarid desert edges.

Steppenwolf a novel by Hermann Hesse, published 1927. Henry Haller ("Steppenwolf") is contemplating suicide, but comes to terms with the world around him following a visit to the surreal Magic Theatre.

Steptoe Patrick Christopher 1913–1988. English obstetrician who pioneered ◊in vitro fertilization. Steptoe, together with biologist Robert Edwards, was the first to succeed in implanting in the womb an egg fertilized outside the body. The first "test-tube baby" was Louise Brown, born by Caesarean section in 1978.

steradian SI unit (abbreviation sr) of measure of solid (three-dimensional) angles, the three-dimensional equivalent of the ◊radian. One steradian is the angle at the center of a sphere when an area on the surface of the sphere equal to the square of the sphere's radius is joined to the center.

Sterea Ellas-Evvoia the region of central Greece and Eubea, occupying the southern part of the Greek mainland between the Ionian and Aegean seas and including the island of Euboea; population (1981) 1,099,800; area 9,421 sq mi/24,391 sq km. The chief city is Athens.

stereophonic sound system of sound reproduction using two complementary channels leading to two loudspeakers, which gives a more natural depth to the sound. Stereo recording began with the introduction of two-track magnetic tape in the 1950s. See ◊hi-fi.

stereotype (Greek "fixed impression") a fixed, exaggerated, and preconceived description about a certain type of person, group, or society. It is based on prejudice rather than fact, but by repetition and with time, stereotypes become fixed in people's minds, resistant to change or factual evidence to the contrary.

The term, originally used for a method of duplicate printing, was adopted in a social sense by the US journalist Walter Lippman in 1922. Stereotypes can prove dangerous when used to justify persecution and discrimination. Some sociologists believe that stereotyping reflects a power structure in which one group in society uses labelling to keep another group "in its place."

sterilization any surgical operation to terminate the possibility of reproduction. In women, this is normally achieved by sealing or tying off the ◊Fallopian tubes (tubal ligation) so that fertilization can no longer take place. In men, the transmission of sperm is blocked by ◊vasectomy.

Sterilization is a safe alternative to ◊contraception and may be encouraged by governments to limit population growth or as part of a selective-breeding policy (see ◊eugenics).

sterilization the killing or removal of living organisms such as bacteria and fungi. A sterile environment is necessary in medicine, food processing, and some scientific experiments. Methods include heat treatment (such as boiling), the use of chemicals (such as disinfectants), irradiation with gamma rays, and filtration. See also ◊asepsis.

sterling silver ◊alloy containing 925 parts of silver and 75 parts of copper. The copper hardens the silver, making it more useful.

Stern Otto 1888–1969. German physicist. Stern studied with Einstein in Prague and Zürich, where he became a lecturer in 1914. After World War I he demonstrated by means of the Stern–Gerlach apparatus that elementary particles have wavelike properties as well as the properties of matter that had been demonstrated. He left Germany for the US in 1933. Nobel Prize 1943.

Sternberg Josef von 1894–1969. Austrian film director who lived in the US from childhood. He worked with Marlene Dietrich on *The Blue Angel/Der blaue Engel* 1930 and other films. He favored striking imagery over narrative in his work, which includes *Underworld* 1927 and *Blonde Venus* 1932.

Sterne Laurence 1713–1768. Irish writer, creator of the comic antihero Tristram Shandy. *The Life and Opinions of Tristram Shandy, Gent* 1760–67, an eccentrically whimsical and bawdy novel, foreshadowed many of the techniques and devices of 20th-century novelists, including James Joyce. His other works include *A Sentimental Journey through France and Italy* 1768.

Sterne, born in Clonmel, Ireland, took orders in 1737 and became vicar of Sutton-in-the-Forest, Yorkshire, in the next year. In 1741 he married Elizabeth Lumley, producing an unhappy union largely because of his infidelity. He had a sentimental love affair with Eliza Draper, of which the *Letters of Yorick to Eliza* 1775 is a record.

Stern Gang formal name ***Fighters for the Freedom of Israel*** a Zionist guerrilla group founded 1940 by Abraham Stern (1907–42). The group carried out anti-British attacks during the UK mandate rule in Palestine, both on individuals and on strategic targets. Stern was killed by British forces in 1942, but the group survived until 1948, when it was outlawed with the creation of the independent state of Israel.

sternum large flat bone at the front of the chest, joined to the ribs. It gives protection to the heart and lungs. During open heart surgery the sternum must be cut to give access to the thorax.

steroid in biology, any of a group of cyclic, unsaturated alcohols (lipids without fatty acid components), which, like sterols, have a complex molecular structure consisting of four carbon rings. Steroids include the sex hormones, such as ◊testosterone, the corticosteroid hormones produced by the ◊adrenal gland, bile acids, and ◊cholesterol. The term is commonly used to refer to ◊anabolic steroid.

sterol any of a group of solid, cyclic, unsaturated alcohols, with a complex structure that includes four carbon rings; cholesterol is an example. Steroids are derived from sterols.

stethoscope instrument used to ascertain the condition of the heart and lungs by listening to their action. It consists of two earpieces connected by flexible tubes to a small plate that is placed against the body. It was invented in 1819 in France by René Théophile Hyacinthe ◊Laënnec.

Stettin German name for the Polish city of ◊Szczecin.

Steuben Friedrich Wilhelm von, Baron 1730–1794. Prussian military leader in the American Revolution. Born in Prussia, Steuben began his military career in the Seven Years' War. After leaving active duty 1763, he was a functionary in the court of Hohenzollern-Hechingen 1764–75 and was made a baron. Seeking employment as an officer in the American Revolution, Steuben left Europe and joined Washington at Valley Forge 1778. Named inspector general of the Continental army, he was placed in charge of training and compiled a manual of military regulations. He later saw action in the South and was present at Yorktown.

Steubenville city in E Ohio, on the Ohio river, S of Youngstown, near the West Virginia border. Industries include steel, coal, paper, and chemicals; population (1990) 22,125. Originally Fort Steuben, it was built 1786 to protect government land agents from the Indians.

Stevens George 1904–1975. US film director who began as a director of photography. He made films such as *Swing Time* 1936 and *Gunga Din* 1939, and his reputation grew steadily, as did the length of his films. His later work included *A Place in the Sun* 1951, *Shane* 1953, and *Giant* 1956.

Stevens John Paul 1920– . US jurist and associate justice of the US Supreme Court 1975– . He was a moderate whose opinions and dissents were wide ranging. He argued for Congressional authority to regulate wages in *National League of Cities* v *Usery* 1976, that the death penalty is not by definition cruel and unusual punishment in *Jurek* v *Texas* 1976, and held, in a dissent, that minority contracting guarantees are unconstitutional in *Fullilove* v *Klutznick* 1980. He also argued that a state cannot require the teaching of creationism to counteract the teaching of evolution in *Edwards* v *Aguillard* 1987 and that the burning of the US flag in protest is unconstitutional in *Texas* v *Johnson*.

Born in Chicago, Illinois, he graduated from the University of Chicago and Northwestern University Law School and served as clerk to US

Supreme Court Justice Wiley Rutledge. After entering private practice, Stevens also taught at Chicago and Northwestern before being appointed judge of the US Court of Appeals for the Seventh Circuit. President Ford appointed him to the Supreme Court in 1975.

Stevens Siaka Probin 1905–1988. Sierra Leone politician, president 1971–85. He was the leader of the moderate left-wing All People's Congress (APC), from 1978 the country's only legal political party.

Stevens was a policeman, industrial worker, and labor unionist before founding the APC. He became prime minister in 1968 and in 1971, under a revised constitution, became Sierra Leone's first president. He created a one-party state based on the APC, and remained in power until his retirement at the age of 80.

Stevens Wallace 1879–1955. US poet. An insurance company executive, he was not recognized as a major poet until late in life. His volumes of poems include *Harmonium* 1923, *The Man with the Blue Guitar* 1937, and *Transport to Summer* 1947. *The Necessary Angel* 1951 is a collection of essays. An elegant and philosophical poet, he won the Pulitzer Prize 1954 for his *Collected Poems*.

Stevenson Adlai 1900–1965. US Democratic politician. He is best known as the losing Democratic nominee in two presidential elections against Dwight ◊Eisenhower 1952 and 1956. He served in the F D ◊Roosevelt administration in the 1930s and 1940s and became a successful reform-minded governor of Illinois 1949–52. He was named ambassador to the UN by John ◊Kennedy 1961.

Born in Los Angeles, California, Stevenson graduated from Princeton University and Northwestern Law School 1926. He practiced law in Chicago, where he became active on the Council on Foreign Relations and the Committee to Defend America by Aiding the Allies.

Stevenson Robert Louis 1850–1894. Scottish novelist and poet, author of the adventure novel *Treasure Island* 1883. Later works included the novels *Kidnapped* 1886, *The Master of Ballantrae* 1889, *Dr Jekyll and Mr Hyde* 1886, and the anthology *A Child's Garden of Verses* 1885.

Stevenson was born in Edinburgh. He studied at the university there and qualified as a lawyer, but never practiced. Early works include *An Island Voyage* 1878 and *Travels with a Donkey* 1879. In 1879 he went to the US, married Fanny Osbourne, and, returning to Britain in 1880, published a volume of stories, *The New Arabian Nights* 1882, and essays, for example *Virginibus Puerisque* 1881, and *Familiar Studies of Men and Books* 1882. The humorous *The Wrong Box* 1889 and the novels *The Wrecker* 1892 and *The Ebb-tide* 1894 were written in collaboration with his stepson, Lloyd Osbourne (1868–1920). In 1890 he settled at Vailima, in Samoa, where he sought a cure for the tuberculosis of which he died.

Stewart James 1908– . US actor. He made his Broadway debut in 1932 and soon after worked in Hollywood. Speaking with a soft drawl, he specialized in the role of the stubbornly honest, ordinary American in such films as *Mr Smith Goes to Washington* 1939, *The Philadelphia Story* 1940 (Academy Award), *It's a Wonderful Life* 1946, *Harvey* 1950, *The Man from Laramie* 1955, and *The FBI Story* 1959. His films with director Alfred ◊Hitchcock include *Rope* 1948, *Rear Window* 1954, *The Man Who Knew Too Much* 1956, and *Vertigo* 1958.

Born in Indiana, Pennsylvania, he was an air force pilot in World War II.

Stewart Potter 1915–1985. US jurist and associate justice of the US Supreme Court 1958–81. Seen as a moderate, he is known for opinions upholding civil rights for minorities and for opinions on criminal procedure. In writing the majority opinion in *Elkins* v *United States* 1960 he stated the Court's prohibition of the use of evidence illegally obtained by state officials in federal criminal trials. He dissented in both *Escabedo* v *Illinois* 1964 and *Miranda* v *Arizona*, which gave defendants expanded procedural rights, and in *In re Gault* 1967, which gave juveniles due process rights. In other cases he ruled for defendants' rights.

***Stewart** Actor James Stewart portraying a dedicated FBI investigator in the film* The FBI Story *1959.*

Born in Chicago, Illinois, Stevens graduated from Yale and Yale Law School and entered private practice in New York City and Cincinnati, Ohio. He was appointed judge of the US Court of Appeals for the Sixth Circuit 1954. In 1958 President Eisenhower appointed him to the Supreme Court.

Stewart Island volcanic island divided from South Island, New Zealand, by the Foveaux Strait; area 676 sq mi/1,750 sq km; population (1981) 600. Industries include farming, fishing, and granite quarrying. Oban is the main settlement.

stickleback any fish of the family Gasterosteidae, found in marine and fresh waters of the N hemisphere. It has a long body that can grow to 7 in/18 cm. The spines along a stickleback's back take the place of the first dorsal fin, and can be raised to make the fish difficult to eat for predators. The male builds a nest for the female's eggs, which he then guards.

The common three-spined stickleback, *Gasterosteus aculeatus*, up to 4 in/10 cm, is found in freshwater habitats and also in brackish estuaries.

Stieglitz Alfred 1864–1946. US photographer, who was mainly responsible for the recognition of photography as an art form. After forming the multimedia Photo-Secession Group at 291 Fifth Avenue, New York, with Edward ◊Steichen, he began the magazine *Camera Work* 1902–17. Through exhibitions, competitions, and publication at his galleries, he helped establish a photographic esthetic.

He was also instrumental in promoting modern art, both by European and American artists. He was the first exhibitor to show such painters and sculptors as Picasso, Cézanne, Rodin, Matisse, Brancusi, and Georgia O'Keeffe, who became his wife 1924. His cloud series, the portraits of O'Keeffe, and his studies of New York City, are his most famous works.

stigma in a flower, the surface at the tip of a ◊carpel that receives the ◊pollen. It often has short outgrowths, flaps, or hairs to trap pollen and may produce a sticky secretion to which the grains adhere.

stigmata impressions or marks corresponding to the five wounds Jesus received at his crucifixion, which are said to have appeared spontaneously on St Francis and other saints.

Stijl, de (Dutch "the style") a group of 20th-century Dutch artists and architects led by ◊Mondrian from 1917. The name came from a magazine, *De Stijl*, founded 1917 by Mondrian and Theo van Doesburg (1883–1931). They believed in the concept of the "designer"; that all life, work, and leisure should be surrounded by art; and that everything functional should also be esthetic. The group had a strong influence on the ◊Bauhaus school.

Stilicho Flavius AD 359–408. Roman general, of ◊Vandal origin, who campaigned successfully against the Visigoths and Ostrogoths. He virtually ruled the western empire as guardian of Honorius (son of ◊Theodosius I) but was executed on the orders of Honorius when he was suspected of wanting to make his own son successor to another son of Theodosius in the eastern empire.

Stilwell Joseph Warren 1883–1946. US general, nicknamed "Vinegar Joe." In 1942 he became US military representative in China, when he commanded the Chinese forces cooperating with the British (with whom he quarreled) in Burma; he later commanded all US forces in the Chinese, Burmese, and Indian theaters until recalled to the US 1944 after differences over nationalist policy with ◊Chiang Kai-shek. Stilwell sought engagement of 30 divisions of Chinese nationalist troops in battle against the Japanese. Chiang Kai-shek refused, preferring to reserve his forces for use against the Chinese Communists in the anticipated Chinese civil war. At Chiang's insistence, President F D ◊Roosevelt recalled Stilwell, giving him command of the US 10th Army on the Japanese island of Okinawa.

Born in Palatka, Florida, Stilwell graduated from West Point 1904.

Stimson Henry Lewis 1867–1950. US politician. He was war secretary in Taft's cabinet 1911–13, Hoover's secretary of state 1929–33, and F D Roosevelt's war secretary 1940–45.

stimulant any drug that acts on the brain to increase alertness and activity; for example, ◊amphetamine. When given to children, stimulants may have a paradoxical, calming effect. Stimulants cause liver damage, are habit-forming, have limited therapeutic value, and are now prescribed only to treat ◊narcolepsy and to reduce the appetite in dieting.

stimulus any change in environmental factors, such as light, heat, or pressure, which can be detected by an organism's receptors.

stinkhorn any foul-smelling fungus of the genus *Phallus*, especially *P. impudicus*; they first appear on the surface as white balls.

stinkwood various trees with unpleasant-smelling wood. The S African tree *Ocotea bullata*, family Lauraceae, has offensive-smelling wood when newly felled, but fine, durable timber used for furniture. Another stinkwood is *Gustavia augusta* from tropical America.

stipule an outgrowth arising from the base of a leaf or leaf stalk in certain plants. Stipules usually occur in pairs or fused into a single semicircular structure.

They may have a leaflike appearance, as in rose plants *Rosa*; be spiny, as in black locust *Robinia pseudoacacia*; or look like small scales. In some species they are large and contribute significantly to the photosynthetic area, as in the garden pea *Pisum sativum*.

Stirling administrative headquarters of Central region, Scotland, on the river Forth; population (1981) 39,000. Industries include the manufacture of agricultural machinery, textiles, and carpets. The castle, which guarded a key crossing of the river, predates the 12th century and was long a Scottish royal residence. Wallace won a victory at Stirling bridge 1297. Edward II of England (in raising a Scottish siege of the town) went into battle at Bannockburn 1314 and was defeated by Robert I (the Bruce).

stoat alternate name for the ◊ermine or short-tailed weasel *Mustela erminea* used for Old World members of this N hemisphere species.

stock in the US, each share of stock represents proportional ownership in a corporation. Once offered by a corporation going public, stock can be bought and sold on a ◊stock exchange, but the corporation has no obligation to buy it back. Sold to raise capital, stock gives the holder specified rights, including the right to examine the books and the right to vote for the directors. Dividends can be paid, in cash or in stock, if or when the corporation declares a profit.

stock in botany, any of several herbaceous plants of the genus *Matthiola* of the crucifer family, commonly grown as garden ornamentals. Many cultivated varieties, including simple-stemmed, queen's, and ten-week, have been derived from the wild stock *M. incana*; *M. bicornis* becomes aromatic at night and is known as night-scented (or evening) stock.

stock-car racing sport popular in the UK and the US, but in two different forms. In the UK, the automobiles are "old bangers," which attempt to force the other automobiles off the track or to come to a standstill. This format is popular in the US as "demolition derbies."

In the US, the automobiles are high-powered automobiles that race on specially-built tracks, at distances of over 400–500 mi/640–800 km; the sport is governed by the National Association for Stock Car Auto Racing (NASCAR) founded 1947.

stock exchange institution for the buying and selling of stock in publicly held corporations. An exchange trades in stocks that are already issued. Trading is done only by members who have purchased or inherited a "seat" on the exchange. They can act as brokers for nonmembers, on a commission basis, or as floor brokers, acting for other members. Registered traders have no contact with the public but trade only their private accounts. The world's largest exchanges are in New York, London, and Tokyo, and stock prices are watched carefully as indicators of confidence in the economy.

Stockhausen Karlheinz 1928– . German composer of avant-garde music, who has continued to explore new musical sounds and compositional techniques since the 1950s. His major works include *Gesang der Jünglinge* 1956 and *Kontakte* 1960 (electronic music); *Klavierstücke* 1952–85; *Momente* 1961–64, revised 1972; *Mikrophonie I* 1964; and *Sirius* 1977. Since 1977 all his works have been part of *Licht*, a cycle of seven musical ceremonies, intended for performance on the evenings of a week. He has completed *Donnerstag* 1980, *Samstag* 1984, and *Montag* 1988.

Stockholm capital and industrial port of Sweden; population (1988) 667,000. It is built on a number of islands. Industries include engineering, brewing, electrical goods, paper, textiles, and pottery.

A network of bridges links the islands and the mainland; an underground railroad was completed 1957. The 18th-century royal palace stands on the site of the 13th-century fortress that defended the trading settlements of Lake Mälar, around which the town first developed. The old town is well preserved and has a church 1264. The town hall was designed by Ragnar Östberg 1923. Most of Sweden's educational institutions are in Stockholm (including the ◊Nobel Institute). The warship *Wasa* (built for King Gustavus Adolphus) sank in the harbor 1628 was raised in 1961 and is preserved in a museum.

Stock Market crash, 1929 Wall Street crash, 1929 a panic in the US following an artificial stock market boom 1927–29 fed by speculation of shares bought on 10% margin. On Oct 24, 1929, 13 million shares changed hands, with further heavy selling on Oct 28, and the disposal of 16 million shares on Oct 29. Many stockholders were ruined, banks and businesses failed, and unemployment rose to approximately 17 million during the Great Depression 1929–40 that ensued.

The repercussions of the Depression as experienced throughout the US were also felt in Europe, worsened by the reduction of US loans. A world economic crisis followed the crash, which was countered by the New Deal program of President F D Roosevelt and eventually by rearming for World War II.

stock rights issue in finance, new shares offered to existing stockholders to raise new capital. Shareholders receive a discount on the market price while the company benefits from not having the costs of a relaunch of the new issue.

The amount of shares offered depends on the capital the company needs. In a "one for one rights issue," a stockholder is offered one share for each that he or she already holds. For companies this is the least expensive way of raising more capital.

stocks European punishment device, a wooden frame with holes used until the 19th century to confine the legs and sometimes the arms of minor offenders, exposing them to public humiliation. The ◊pillory had a similar purpose.

Stockton industrial river port (agricultural machinery, food processing) on the San Joaquin River in California; population (1990) 210,943. The University of the Pacific is here. Stockton was founded in the late 1840s as a supply center for the California gold rush. The deepwater channel to San Francisco Bay was completed 1933.

Stockton-on-Tees port city on the river Tees, Cleveland, NE England; population (1981) 155,000. There are shipbuilding, steel, and chemical industries, and it was the starting point for the world's first passenger railroad 1825.

stoicism (Greek *stoa* "porch") a Greek school of philosophy, founded about 300 BC by Zeno of Citium. The stoics were pantheistic materialists who believed that happiness lay in accepting the law of the universe. They emphasized human brotherhood, denounced slavery, and were internationalist. The name is derived from the porch on which Zeno taught.

In the 3rd and 2nd centuries BC, stoics took a prominent part in Greek and Roman revolutionary movements. After the 1st century BC stoicism became the philosophy of the Roman ruling class and lost its revolutionary significance; outstanding stoics of this period were Seneca, Epictetus, and Marcus Aurelius Antoninus.

Stoke-on-Trent city in Staffordshire, England, on the river Trent; population (1981) 253,000. It is the heart of the ◊Potteries and a major ceramic center. Other industries include steel, chemicals, engineering machinery, paper, rubber, and coal.

Stoke was formed 1910 from Burslem, Hanley, Longton, Stoke-upon-Trent, Fenton, and Tunstall. The ceramics factories of ◊Minton and ◊Wedgwood are here.

Stoker Bram (Abraham) 1847–1912. Irish novelist, actor, theater manager, and author. His novel ◊*Dracula* 1897 crystallized most aspects of the traditional vampire legend and became the source for all subsequent fiction and films on the subject.

Stoker wrote a number of other stories and novels of fantasy and horror, such as *The Lady of the Shroud* 1909.

stokes unit (abbreviation St) of kinematic viscosity (rate of flow of a liquid).

Liquids with higher kinematic viscosity have higher turbulence than those with low kinematic viscosity. It is found by dividing the dynamic viscosity in ◊poise by the density of the liquid.

Stokes George Gabriel 1819–1903. Irish physicist. During the late 1840s, he studied the ◊viscosity (resistance to relative motion) of fluids. This culminated in Stokes' law, $F = 6\pi\epsilon r v$, which applies to a force acting on a sphere falling through a liquid, where ϵ is the liquid's viscosity and r and v are the radius and velocity of the sphere.

Stokowski Leopold 1882–1977. US conductor, born in London. An outstanding experimentalist, he introduced modern music (for example, Mahler's Eighth Symphony) to the US; appeared in several films; and conducted the music for Walt Disney's animated film *Fantasia* 1940.

He led the Philadelphia Orchestra 1912–38, established the All-American Youth Orchestra, and gave low-priced concerts at the New York City Centre.

STOL (acronym for short takeoff and landing) aircraft fitted with special devices on the wings (such as sucking flaps), that increase aerodynamic lift at low speeds. Small passenger and freight STOL craft may become common with the demand for small airports, especially in difficult terrain.

stolon a type of ◊runner.

stoma (plural ***stomata***) in botany, a pore in the epidermis of a plant. Each stoma is surrounded by a pair of guard cells that are crescent shaped when the stoma is open but can collapse to an oval shape, thus closing off the opening between them. Stomata allow the exchange of carbon dioxide and oxygen (needed for ◊photosynthesis and ◊respiration) between the internal tissues of the plant and the outside atmosphere. They are also the main route by which water is lost from the plant, and they can be closed to conserve water, the movements being controlled by changes in turgidity of the guard cells.

Stomata occur in large numbers on the aerial parts of a plant, and on the undersurface of leaves, where there may be as many as 300,000 per square inch.

stomach the first cavity in the digestive system of animals. In mammals it is a bag of muscle situated just below the diaphragm. Food enters it from the esophagus, is digested by the acid and ◊enzymes secreted by the stomach lining, and then passes into the duodenum. Some plant-eating mammals have multichambered stomachs that harbor bacteria in one of the chambers to assist in the digestion of ◊cellulose. The gizzard is part of the stomach in birds.

stone (plural ***stone***) British unit (abbreviation st) of mass (chiefly used to express body mass) equal to 14 pounds avoirdupois (6.35 kg).

Stone Harlan Fiske 1872–1946. US jurist; associate justice 1925–41 and chief justice 1941–46 of the US Supreme Court. During World War II he authored opinions favoring federal war powers and regulation of aliens.

Born in Chesterfield, New Hampshire, Stone graduated from Amherst College and Columbia University School of Law. He practiced in New York City and taught at Columbia, serving as dean of the law school 1910–23. President Coolidge appointed Stone US attorney general 1924 and to the US Supreme Court 1925. As an associate justice, Stone favored judicial restraint, the

stoma

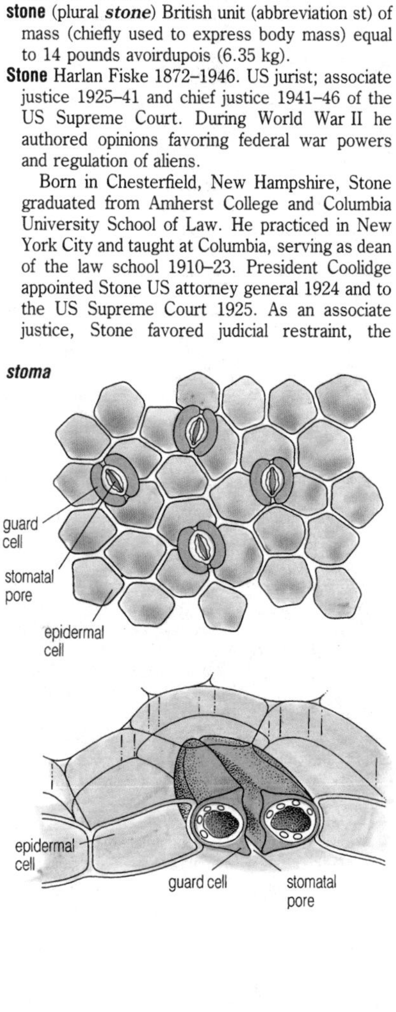
guard cell
stomatal pore
epidermal cell
epidermal cell
guard cell
stomatal pore

stomach

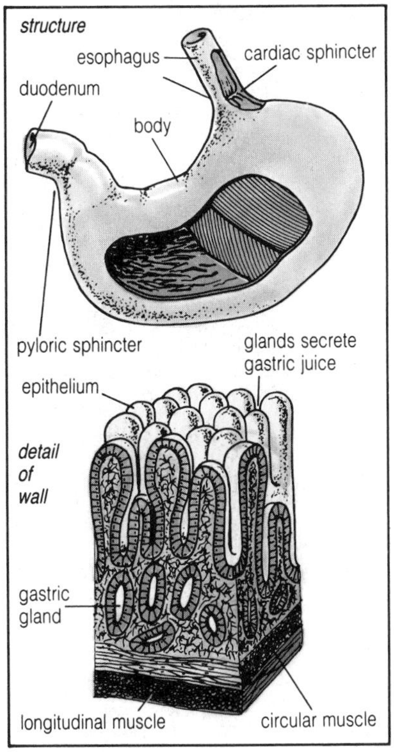
structure
esophagus
cardiac sphincter
duodenum
body
pyloric sphincter
glands secrete gastric juice
epithelium
detail of wall
gastric gland
longitudinal muscle
circular muscle

making of decisions on constitutional rather than personal grounds. He dissented from numerous conservative decisions opposing President F D Roosevelt's New Deal legislation. He supported voting rights and use of the Constitution's commerce clause to justify federal legislation regulating interstate commerce. In 1941 Roosevelt appointed Stone chief justice.

Stone Lucy 1818–1893. US feminist orator and editor. Married to the radical Henry Blackwell in 1855, she gained wide publicity when, after a mutual declaration rejecting the legal superiority of the man in marriage, she chose to retain her own surname despite her marriage. The epithet "Lucy Stoner" was coined to mean a woman who advocated doing the same.

In the 1860s she helped to establish the American Woman Suffrage Association and founded and edited the Boston *Woman's Journal*, a suffragist paper that was later edited by her daughter Alice Stone Blackwell (1857–1950).

***Stone** The phrase "Lucy Stoner" was coined for women who followed Lucy Stone's example and kept their maiden name after marriage; she even refused to open letters addressed to her under her husband's surname.*

***Stonehenge** The standing stones of Stonehenge are one of Europe's most importanı neolithic temples. Constructed in three main stages, it served not only as a burial complex but also as a permanent stone calendar.*

Stone Robert 1937– . US novelist and journalist. His *Dog Soldiers* 1974 is a classic novel about the moral destructiveness of the Vietnam war. *A Flag for Sunrise* 1982 similarly explores the political and moral consequences of US intervention in a corrupt South American republic. Among his other works is *Children of Light* 1986.

Stone Age the developmental stage of humans in ◊prehistory before the use of metals, when tools and weapons were made chiefly of stone, especially flint. The Stone Age is subdivided into the Old or Paleolithic, the Middle or Mesolithic, and the New or Neolithic. The people of the Old Stone Age were hunters, whereas the Neolithic people took the first steps in agriculture, the domestication of animals, weaving, and pottery.

stonechat small insectivorous ◊thrush *Saxicola torquata* frequently found in Eurasia and Africa on open land with bushes. The male has a black head and throat, tawny breast, and dark back; the female is browner.

stonecrop any of several plants of the genus *Sedum* of the orpine family Crassulaceae, a succulent herb with fleshy leaves and clusters of starlike flowers. They are characteristic of dry, rocky places and some grow on walls.

stonefish any of a family (Synanceiidae) of tropical marine bony fishes with venomous spines and bodies resembling encrusted rocks.

stonefly any insect of the order Plecoptera, with a long tail and antennae and two pairs of membranous wings. They live near fresh water. There are over 1,300 species.

The aquatic larvae live mainly in streams with stony bottoms.

Stonehenge megalithic monument dating from about 2000 BC on Salisbury Plain, Wiltshire, England. It consisted originally of a circle of 30 upright stones, their tops linked by lintel stones to form a continuous circle about 100 ft/30 m across. Within the circle was a horseshoe arrangement of five trilithons (two uprights plus a lintel, set as five separate entities), and a so-called "altar stone"—an upright pillar—on the axis of the horseshoe at the open, NE end, which faces in the direction of the rising sun. It has been suggested that it served as an observatory.

The local sandstone, or sarsen, was used for the uprights, which measure 18 ft/5.5 m by 7 ft/2 m and weigh some 26 tons each. To give true perspective, they were made slightly convex. A secondary circle and horseshoe were built of bluestones, originally brought from Pembrokeshire, Wales.

Stonehenge is one of a number of prehistoric structures on Salisbury Plain, including about 400 round ◊barrows.

stoneware a very hard opaque pottery made of nonporous clay with feldspar and a high silica content, fired at high temperature.

Stoppard Tom 1937– . Czechoslovak-born British playwright, whose works use wit and wordplay to explore logical and philosophical ideas. He wrote *Rosencrantz and Guildenstern are Dead* 1967. This was followed by comedies including *The Real Inspector Hound* 1968, *Jumpers* 1972, *Travesties* 1974, *Dirty Linen* 1976, *The Real Thing* 1982, and *Hapgood* 1988. He has also written for radio, television, and the cinema.

store or ***shop***, a building or part of a building used for the retail sale of goods. Roman *stoae* were market stalls enclosed by an arcaded walkway; stores changed little from ancient times until the latter part of the 19th century, when concentration of population and greater availability of manufactured goods gave rise to the department store, in effect a number of small specialty shops under one roof, and to the chain store and the supermarket.

With the spread of chain stores to several cities, all having the same ownership, the relationship between retailers and manufacturers changed. Direct links with factories bypassed middlemen (wholesalers) and lowered costs, in some cases forcing small independent stores to focus on narrow specialties not otherwise available. In the 1970s in the US, to coincide with the population shift out of urban centers, enclosed shopping malls of up to 250 specialty stores, anchored by at least one large department store, were constructed in many suburban areas. These "controlled shopping environments" have music, free parking, movie theaters, restaurants, and, in some instances, even child-care facilities. The idea has been adopted in the UK and elsewhere, although resistance is rising from those who wish to preserve the viability of downtown (urban center) areas.

stork any of a family (Ciconiidea) of long-legged, long-necked wading birds with long, powerful wings, and long bills used for spearing prey. Some species grow up to 5 ft/1.5 m tall.

Species include the Eurasian white stork *Ciconia ciconia*, which is encouraged to build on rooftops as a luck and fertility symbol; and the jabiru *Jabiru mycteria* of the Americas. Up to 5 ft/ 1.5 m high, it is white plumaged, with a black and red head.

Storting the Norwegian parliament, which consists of 150 representatives, elected every four years.

Story Joseph 1779–1845. US jurist and associate justice of the US Supreme Court 1811–45. On the Court he wrote several decisions defining the role of federal courts in admiralty law. The most notable was *United States* v *Schooner Amistad* 1841, in which the Court ordered black slaves who had seized a slaving ship repatriated to Africa. He also wrote the Court's decision in *Martin* v *Hunter's Lessee* 1816, which established the Court as final arbiter of constitutional issues. He was also a member of the Court when it decided *Dartmouth College* v *Woodward* 1819 and *McCulloch* v *Maryland* 1819, enhancing Congressional authority over states' rights. Story became professor of law at Harvard 1829–45 in addition to his court duties.

Born in Marblehead, Massachusetts, Story was a graduate of Harvard College and practiced law in Massachusetts. He served in the Massachusetts legislature 1805–08 and the US House of Representatives 1808–09, before returning to the Massachusetts legislature, of which he became speaker 1811. President Madison appointed Story to the Supreme Court 1811.

Stoss Veit. Also known as ***Wit Stwosz*** c. 1450–1533. German sculptor and painter, active in Nuremberg and Poland. He carved a wooden altarpiece with high relief panels in St Mary's, Krakow, a complicated design with numerous figures that centers on the *Death of the Virgin*.

Stoss was born in Nuremberg and returned there from Poland. The figure of St Roch in Sta Annunziata, Florence, shows his characteristic figure style and sculpted drapery.

Stowe Harriet Beecher 1811–1896. US suffragist, abolitionist, and author of the antislavery novel *Uncle Tom's Cabin*, first published serially 1851–52. The inspiration came to her in a vision in 1848, and the book brought immediate success.

Stowe was a daughter of Congregationalist minister Lyman ◊Beecher and in 1836 married C E Stowe, a professor of theology. Her book was radical in its time and did much to spread antislavery sentiment, but in the 20th century was criticized for sentimentality and racism.

***Stowe** US novelist Harriet Beecher Stowe, who stirred abolitionist sentiment with her novel* Uncle Tom's Cabin.

She also published other works from 1856, including the New England novels *The Minister's Wooing* 1859 and *Old-Town Folks* 1869, as well as essays and religious poems.

strabismus technical term for a ◊squint.

Strabo c. 63 BC–AD 24. Greek geographer and historian, who traveled widely to collect first-hand material for his *Geography*.

Strachey (Giles) Lytton 1880–1932. English critic and biographer, a member of the ◊Bloomsbury Group of writers and artists. He wrote *Landmarks in French Literature* 1912. The mocking and witty treatment of Cardinal Manning, Florence Nightingale, Thomas Arnold, and General Gordon in *Eminent Victorians* 1918 won him recognition. His biography of *Queen Victoria* 1921 was more affectionate.

Stradivari Antonio. (Latin form ***Stradivarius***) 1644–1737. Italian stringed instrument maker, generally considered the greatest of all violin makers. He was born in Cremona and studied there with Nicolo ◊Amati. He produced more than 1,100 instruments from his family workshops, including violins, violas, cellos, guitars, and several lesser types.

Straits Settlements former province of the ◊East India Company 1826–58, and British crown colony 1867–1946; it comprised Singapore, Malacca, Penang, Cocos Islands, Christmas Island, and Labuan.

Stralsund, Peace of in 1369, the peace between Waldemar IV of Denmark and the Hanseatic League (association of N German trading towns) that concluded the Hanse war 1362–69.

Denmark had unsuccessfully attempted to reduce the power of the Hanseatic League in Scandinavia, and by this peace, Waldemar had to recognize the League's trading rights in his territories and assent to an enlargement of its privileges.

Strand Paul 1890–1976. US photographer who used large-format cameras for his strong, clear, close-up photographs of natural objects.

Strasberg Lee 1902–1982. US actor and artistic director of the ◊Actors Studio from 1948, who developed Method acting from ◊Stanislavsky's system; pupils have included Marlon Brando, Paul Newman, Julie Harris, Kim Hunter, Geraldine Page, Al Pacino, and Robert DeNiro.

In 1931 Strasberg was one of the founders of the Group Theatre, with Harold Clurman and Cheryl Crawford. It became known for its experimental plays, such as *Men in White* 1934 (Pulitzer Prize). He founded the Lee Strasberg Institute of Theater 1969. Strasberg made his film acting debut in *The Godfather II* 1974. He is the father of the actress Susan Strasberg.

Strasbourg city on the river Ill, in Bas-Rhin *département*, capital of Alsace, France; population (1982) 373,000. Industries include car manufacture, tobacco, printing and publishing, and preserves. The ◊Council of Europe meets here, and sessions of the European Parliament alternate between Strasbourg and Luxembourg.

Seized by France 1681, it was surrendered to Germany 1870–1919 and 1940–44. It has a 13th-century cathedral.

Strassburg Gottfried von lived c. 1210. German poet, author of the unfinished epic *Tristan und Isolde*, which inspired the German composer ◊Wagner.

strata (singular stratum) layers or ◊beds of ◊sedimentary rock.

Strategic Arms Limitation Talks (SALT) a series of US-Soviet discussions aimed at reducing the rate of nuclear-arms buildup. The talks, delayed by the Soviet invasion of Czechoslovakia 1968, began in 1969 between US President Lyndon Johnson and Soviet leader Brezhnev. Neither the SALT I accord (effective 1972–77) nor SALT II called for reductions in nuclear weaponry, merely a limit on the expansion of these forces. SALT II was mainly negotiated by US President Ford before 1976 and signed by Soviet leader Brezhnev and President Carter in Vienna in 1979. It was never fully ratified because of the Soviet occupation of Afghanistan, although the terms of the accord were respected by both sides until President ◊Reagan exceeded its limitations during his second term 1985–89. SALT talks were superseded by START (Strategic Arms Reduction Talks) negotiations under Reagan, and the first significant reductions began under Soviet President Gorbachev.

Strategic Arms Reduction Talks (START) a phase in US-Soviet peace discussions. START began with talks in Geneva 1983, leading to the signing of the ◊Intermediate Nuclear Forces (INF) treaty 1987. In 1989 proposals for reductions in conventional weapons were added to the agenda. As the Cold War drew to a close from 1989, the two nations moved rapidly toward total agreement, and in July 1991 the START treaty was signed in Moscow.

Strategic Defense Initiative (SDI) also called ***Star Wars*** an attempt by the US to develop a defense system against incoming nuclear missiles, based in part outside the Earth's atmosphere. It was announced by President Reagan March 1983, and the research had by 1990 cost over $16.5 billion. In 1988, the joint Chiefs of Staff announced that they expected to be able to intercept no more than 30% of incoming missiles. Scientists maintain that the system is basically unworkable.

The essence of the SDI is to attack enemy missiles at several different stages of their trajectory, using advanced laser and particle-beam technology, thus increasing the chances of disabling them. Israel, Japan, and the UK are among the nations assisting in SDI research and development. In 1987 Gorbachev acknowledged that the USSR was developing a similar defense system.

Stratford port and industrial town in SW Ontario, Canada; population (1981) 26,000. It is the site of a Shakespeare festival.

Stratford-upon-Avon market town on the river Avon, in Warwickshire, England; population (1981) 21,000. It is the birthplace of William ◊Shakespeare.

The Royal Shakespeare Theatre 1932 replaced an earlier building 1877–79 that burned down in 1926. Shakespeare's birthplace contains relics of his life and times. His grave is in the parish church; his wife Anne Hathaway's cottage is nearby.

Strathclyde region of Scotland
area 5,367 sq mi/13,900 sq km
towns Glasgow (administrative headquarters), Paisley, Greenock, Kilmarnock, Clydebank, Hamilton, Coatbridge, Prestwick
features includes some of Inner ◊Hebrides; river Clyde; part of Loch Lomond; Glencoe, site of the massacre of the Macdonald clan; Breadalbane; islands: Arran, Bute, Mull
products dairy, pig, and poultry products; shipbuilding; engineering; coal from Ayr and Lanark; oil-related services
population (1987) 2,333,000, half the population of Scotland
famous people David Livingstone, William Burrell.

stratigraphy branch of geology that deals with the sequence of formation of ◊sedimentary rock layers and the conditions under which they were formed. Its basis was developed by William ◊Smith, a British canal engineer. In archeology, stratigraphic layers are excavated and the remains in each studied to identify and date prehistoric sites.

Stratigraphy involves both the investigation of sedimentary structures to determine ancient geographies and environments, and the study of fossils for identifying and dating purposes.

stratosphere that part of the atmosphere 6–25 mi/ 10–40 km from Earth, where the temperature slowly rises from a low of –67°F/–55°C to around

32°F/0°C. The air is rarefied and at around 15 mi/ 25 km much ◊ozone is concentrated.

Straus Oscar 1870–1954. Austrian composer, born in Vienna. He is remembered for the operetta *The Chocolate Soldier* 1909.

Strauss Franz-Josef 1915–1988. German conservative politician, leader of the West German Bavarian Christian Social Union (CSU) party 1961–88, premier of Bavaria 1978–88.

Strauss Johann (Baptist) 1825–1899. Austrian conductor and composer, the son of Johann Strauss (1804–49). In 1872 he gave up conducting and wrote operettas, such as *Die Fledermaus* 1874, and numerous waltzes, such as *The Blue Danube* and *Tales from the Vienna Woods*, which gained him the title "The Waltz King."

Strauss Richard (Georg) 1864–1949. German composer and conductor. He followed the German Romantic tradition but had a strongly personal style, characterized by his bold, colorful orchestration. He first wrote tone poems such as *Don Juan* 1889, *Till Eulenspiegel's Merry Pranks* 1895, and *Also sprach Zarathustra* 1896. He then moved on to opera with *Salome* 1905, and *Elektra* 1909, both of which have elements of polytonality. He reverted to a more traditional style with *Der Rosenkavalier* 1911.

He spent his final years in the US, teaching and composing at the Eastman School of Music in New York.

Stravinsky Igor 1882–1971. Russian composer, later of French (1934) and US (1945) nationality. He studied under ◊Rimsky-Korsakov and wrote the music for the Diaghilev ballets *The Firebird* 1910, *Petrushka* 1911, and *The Rite of Spring* 1913 (controversial at the time for their unorthodox rhythms and harmonies). His versatile work ranges from his Neo-Classical ballet *Pulcinella* 1920, to the choral-orchestral *Symphony of Psalms* 1930. He later made use of serial techniques in works such as the *Canticum Sacrum* 1955 and the ballet *Agon* 1953–57.

strawberry low-growing perennial plant of the genus *Fragaria*, family Rosaceae, widely cultivated for its red, fleshy fruits, which are rich in vitamin C. Wild strawberry (*F. virginiana*) has small aromatic fruits and grows over much of the E half of North America. Cultivated strawberries are hybrids between North American wild species and European species.

streamlining shaping a body so that it offers the least resistance when traveling through a medium such as air or water. Aircraft, for example, must be carefully streamlined to reduce air resistance, or ◊drag.

High-speed aircraft must have swept-back wings, supersonic craft a sharp nose and narrow body.

stream of consciousness narrative technique in which a writer presents directly the uninterrupted flow of a character's thoughts, impressions, and feelings, without the conventional devices of dialogue and description. It first came to be widely used in the early 20th century. Leading exponents have included the novelists Virginia Woolf, James Joyce, and William Faulkner.

Molly Bloom's soliloquy in Joyce's *Ulysses* is a good example of the technique. The English writer Dorothy Richardson (1873–1957) is said to have originated the technique in her novel sequence *Pilgrimage*, the first volume of which was published 1915 and the last posthumously. The term "stream of consciousness" was introduced by the philosopher William James in 1890.

Streep Meryl (Mary Louise) 1949– . US actress known for her strong character roles. She became a leading star of the 1980s, winning numerous awards. Her films include *The Deer Hunter* 1978, *Kramer vs Kramer* 1979 (Academy Award), *The French Lieutenant's Woman* 1980, *Sophie's Choice* 1982 (Academy Award), *Out of Africa* 1985, *Ironweed* 1988, and *A Cry in the Dark* 1989.

Street J(abez) C(urry) 1906–1989. US physicist

Streep *US actress Meryl Streep is known for her portrayal of strong, independent women, such as Karen Blixen in* Out of Africa *1985.*

who, with Edward C Stevenson, discovered the muon (an ◊elementary particle) in 1937.

streetcar or ***trolley*** transport system, widespread in the US and Europe from the late 19th to the mid-20th century, where wheeled vehicle ran on parallel rails. It originated in British collieries in the 18th century, and the earliest passenger system was in New York City, 1832. They are powered either by electric conductor rails below ground or conductor arms connected to electrified overhead wires. They were designed for urban and interurban service and vast networks ran from the city to city, especially in the NE US, where they ran more often to small towns than did the railroads. Greater flexibility was achieved with trolley buses, similarly powered by conductor arms overhead but without tracks. From the 1930s–1960s most were retired. In the 1980s both trams and trolley buses were in some areas being revived. Both vehicles have the advantage of being nonpolluting to the local environment, since they produce no exhaust gases. However, electricity *is* polluting at the source.

Streisand Barbra (Barbara Joan) 1942– . US singer and actress who became a film star in *Funny Girl* 1968. Her subsequent films include *What's Up Doc?* 1972, *The Way We Were* 1973, and *A Star is Born* 1979. *Yentl* 1983 was her masterwork, which she directed, scripted, composed, and starred in.

streptomycin antibiotic drug discovered in 1944, used to treat tuberculosis, influenzal meningitis, and other infections, some of which are unaffected by ◊penicillin.

Streptomycin is derived from a soil bacterium (*Streptomyces griseus*) or synthesized.

stress in psychology, any event or situation that makes demands on a person's mental or emotional resources. Stress can be caused by overwork,

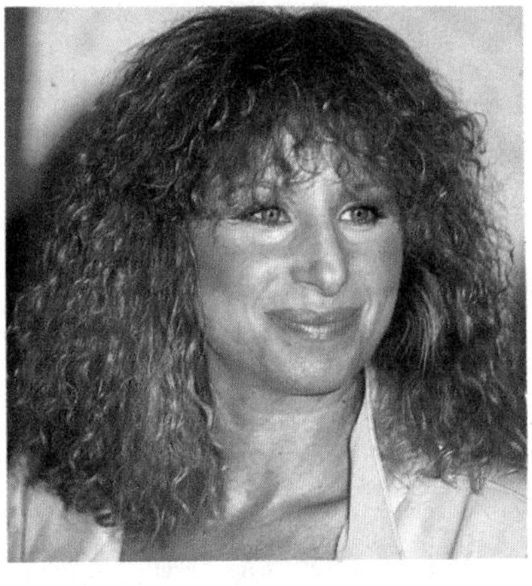

Streisand *US singer, actress, and entertainer Barbra Streisand. Her comic appeal ensured her success in films such as* Funny Girl *1968.*

AVG·STRINDBERG
FVRVSVND·JVLI·1899·

Strindberg *Drawing of Swedish dramatist August Strindberg by his friend Carl Larsson.*

anxiety about exams, money, or job security, unemployment, bereavement, poor relationships, marriage breakdown, sexual difficulties, poor living or working conditions, and constant exposure to loud noise.

Many changes that are apparently "for the better," such as being promoted at work, going to a new school, moving house, and getting married, are also a source of stress. Stress can cause, or aggravate, physical illnesses, among them psoriasis, eczema, asthma, and stomach and mouth ulcers. Apart from removing the source of stress, acquiring some control over it and learning to relax when possible are the best treatments.

stress and strain in the science of materials, measures of the deforming force applied to a body (stress) and of the resulting change in its shape (strain). For a perfectly elastic material, stress is proportional to strain (◊Hooke's law).

stridulatory organs in insects, organs that produce sound when rubbed together. Crickets rub their wings together, but grasshoppers rub a hind leg against a wing. Stridulation is thought to be used for attracting mates, but may also serve to mark territory.

Temperatures can be determined from the stridulations of crickets: adding 40 to the number of chirps counted in 15 seconds gives the approximate temperature in Fahrenheit.

strike stoppage of work by employees (with picketing), often as members of a labor union, to obtain or resist change in wages, hours, or conditions. A "lockout" is a weapon of an employer to thwart or enforce such change by preventing employees from working. Another measure is "work to rule," when production is virtually brought to a halt by strict observance of union rules.

Strikes may be "official" (union-authorized) or "wildcat" (undertaken spontaneously) and may be accompanied by a sit-in or work-in, the one being worker occupation of a factory and the other continuation of work in a plant the employer wishes to close. In a "sympathetic" strike, action is in support of other workers on strike elsewhere, possibly in a different industry. See also ◊industrial relations.

Strindberg August 1849–1912. Swedish playwright and novelist. His plays, influential in the development of dramatic technique, are in a variety of styles including historical plays, symbolic dramas (the two-part *Dödsdansen/The Dance of Death* 1901) and "chamber plays" such as *Spöksonaten/The Ghost [Spook] Sonata* 1907. *Fadren/The*

Father 1887 and *Fröken Julie/Miss Julie* 1888 are among his works.

Born in Stockholm, he lived mainly abroad after 1883, having been unsuccessfully prosecuted for blasphemy in 1884 following publication of his short stories *Giftas/Marrying*. His life was stormy and his work has been criticized for its hostile attitude to women, but he is regarded as one of Sweden's greatest writers.

stringed instrument musical instrument that produces a sound by making a stretched string vibrate. Today the strings are made of gut, metal, and Pearlon (a plastic). Types of stringed instruments include:
bowed violin family, viol family;
plucked guitar, ukelele, lute, sitar, harp, banjo, lyre;
plucked mechanically harpsichord;
struck mechanically piano, clavichord;
hammered dulcimer.

strip mining or ***open-pit mining*** mining from the surface rather than by tunneling underground. Coal, iron ore, and phosphates are often extracted by strip mining. Often the mineral deposit is covered by soil, which must first be stripped off, usually by large machines such as walking draglines and bucket-wheel excavators. The ore deposit is then broken up by explosives and collected from the surface.

One of the largest excavations in the world has been made by open-pit mining at the Bingham Canyon copper mine in Utah, measuring 2,590 ft/790 m deep and 2.3 mi/3.7 km across.

strobilus in botany, a reproductive structure found in most ◊gymnosperms and some ◊pteridophytes, notably the club mosses. In conifers the strobilus is commonly known as a ◊cone.

stroboscope instrument for studying continuous periodic motion by using light flashing at the same frequency as that of the motion; for example, rotating machinery can be optically "stopped" by illuminating it with a stroboscope flashing at the exact rate of rotation.

Stroessner Alfredo 1912– . Military leader and president of Paraguay 1954–89. As head of the armed forces from 1951, he seized power in a coup in 1954 sponsored by the right-wing ruling Colorado Party. Accused by his opponents of harsh repression, his regime spent heavily on the military to preserve his authority. Despite criticisms of his government's civil rights record, he was reelected seven times and remained in office until ousted in an army-led coup in 1989.

Stroheim Erich von. (Erich Oswald) 1885–1957. Austrian actor and director who worked in Hollywood from 1914. Successful as an actor in villainous roles, his career as a director was wrecked by his extravagance, so he returned to acting in international films such as *La Grande Illusion* 1937 and *Sunset Boulevard* 1950. He directed *Greed* 1923 and *Queen Kelly* 1928 (unfinished).

stroke in medicine, a sudden interruption of the blood supply to the brain. It is also termed a cerebrovascular accident or apoplexy. Strokes are caused by a sudden bleed in the brain (cerebral hemhorrhage) or interruption of the blood supply to part of the brain due to ◊embolism or ◊thrombosis. They vary in severity from producing almost no symptoms to proving rapidly fatal. In between are those (often recurring) that leave a wide range of impaired function, depending on the size and location of the event.

Transient ischemic attacks, or "mini-strokes," with effects lasting only briefly (minutes to weeks), require investigation to try to forestall the possibility of a subsequent full-blown stroke.

The disease of the arteries that predisposes to stroke is ◊atherosclerosis. High blood pressure (◊hypertension) is also a precipitating factor. Strokes can sometimes be prevented by surgery (as in the case of some ◊aneurysms), or by use of ◊anticoagulant drugs or vitamin E or daily aspirin to minimize the risk of stroke due to blood clots.

Stromboli Italian island in the Tyrrhenian Sea, one of the ◊Lipari Islands; area 5 sq mi/12 sq km. It has an active volcano, 3,039 ft/926 m high. The island produces Malmsey wine and capers.

strong force one of the four ◊fundamental forces of nature, the other three being the electromagnetic force, the gravitational force, and the weak force. It is the strongest of all the forces, acts only over very small distances within the nucleus of the atom (10^{-13} cm), and is responsible for binding together ◊quarks to form ◊hadrons. The particle that is the carrier of the strong force is the ◊gluon, of which there are eight kinds, each with zero mass and zero charge.

strontium soft, ductile, pale-yellow, metallic element, symbol Sr, atomic number 38, atomic weight 87.62. It is one of the ◊alkaline-earth metals, widely distributed in small quantities only as a sulfate or carbonate. Strontium salts burn with a red flame and are used in fireworks and signal flares.

The radioactive isotopes Sr-89 and Sr-90 (half-life 25 years) are some of the most dangerous products of the nuclear industry; they are fission products in nuclear explosions and in the reactors of nuclear power plants. Strontium is chemically similar to calcium and deposits in bones and other tissues, where the radioactivity is damaging. The element was named in 1808 by English chemist Humphry Davy, who isolated it by electrolysis, for Strontian, a mining location in Scotland where it was first found.

strophanthus any tropical plant of the genus *Strophanthus* of the dogbane family Apocynaceae, native to Africa and Asia. Seeds of the handsome climber *S. gratus* yield a poison, strophantin, used on arrows in hunting, and in medicine as a heart stimulant.

structuralism 20th-century philosophical movement that has influenced such areas as linguistics, anthropology, and literary criticism. Inspired by the work of the Swiss linguist Ferdinand de Saussure (1857–1913), structuralists believe that objects should be analyzed as systems of relations, rather than as positive entities.

Saussure proposed that language is a system of arbitrary signs, meaning that there is no intrinsic link between the "signifier" (the sound or mark) and the "signified" (the concept it represents). Hence any linguistic term can only be defined by its differences from other terms. His ideas were taken further by Roman Jakobson (1896–) and the Prague school of linguistics, and were extended into a general method for the social sciences by the French anthropologist Claude Lévi-Strauss. The French writer Roland Barthes took the lead in applying the ideas of structuralism to literary criticism, arguing that the critic should identify the structures within a text that determine its possible meanings, independently of any reference to the real. This approach is radicalized in Barthes' later work and in the practice of "deconstruction," pioneered by the French philosopher Jacques Derrida (1930–). Here the text comes to be viewed as a "decentered" play of structures, lacking any ultimately determinable meaning.

structured programming in computing, the process of writing a program in small, independent parts. This allows a more easily controlled program development and the individual design and testing of the component parts. Structured programs are built up from units called modules, which normally correspond to single procedures or functions. Some programming languages, such as PASCAL and Modula-2, are more suited to structured programming than others.

strychnine $C_{21}H_{22}O_2N_2$ bitter-tasting, poisonous alkaloid. It is a poison that causes violent muscular spasms, and is usually obtained by powdering the seeds of plants of the genus *Strychnos* (for example *Strychnos nux vomica*). Curare is a related drug.

Stuart or ***Stewart*** royal family who inherited the Scottish throne in 1371 and the English throne in 1603.

Stuart Gilbert Charles 1755–1828. American artist. Born in North Kingstown, Rhode Island, and trained by the Scottish painter Cosmo Alexander, Stuart later became a protégé of Benjamin ◊West 1776–82. Gaining fame as one of the foremost portraitists in England, he worked in Ireland 1787–93 and eventually returned to the US, setting up a studio in Philadelphia 1794. Stuart, best known for his portraits of George Washington, lived in Washington, DC 1803–05, producing portraits of various prominent public figures. He resided in Boston from 1805 until his death.

Stuart John McDougall 1815–1866. Scottish-born Australian explorer. He went with Charles ◊Sturt on his 1844 expedition, and in 1860, after two unsuccessful attempts, crossed the center of Australia from Adelaide in the southeast to the coast of Arnhem Land. He almost lost his life on the return journey.

Stubbs George 1724–1806. English artist, known for paintings of horses. After the publication of his book of engravings *The Anatomy of the Horse* 1766, he was widely commissioned as an animal painter.

Stubbs began his career as a portrait painter and medical illustrator in Liverpool. In 1754 he went to Rome, continuing to study nature and anatomy. Before settling in London in the 1760s he rented a farm and carried out a series of dissections of horses, which resulted in his book of engravings. The dramatic *Lion Attacking a Horse* 1770 (Yale University Art Gallery, New Haven, Connecticut) and the peaceful *Reapers* 1786 (Tate Gallery, London) show the variety of mood in his painting.

Students for a Democratic Society (SDS) US student movement, founded 1962, which steered a middle line between Marxism and orthodox left-wing politics; its members opposed racism and imperialism. At its peak it had some 100,000 members. In 1968 they were split by the hardline Weatherman faction, which aimed for violent revolution and control from above.

Stukeley William 1687–1765. English antiquarian and pioneer archeologist, who made some of the earliest accurate observations about Stonehenge 1740 and Avebury 1743. He originated the popular (but erroneous) idea that both were built by Druids.

sturgeon any of a family (Acipenseridae) of large, primitive, bony fishes with five rows of bony plates, small sucking mouths, and chin barbels used for exploring the bottom of the water for prey.

The beluga sturgeon *Huso huso* of the Caspian sea can reach a length of 25 ft/8 m and weigh 3,300 lb/1,500 kg.

North American species include the Atlantic sturgeon *Acipenser oxyrhynchus*, over 10 ft/3 m long.

Sturges Preston. Adopted name of Edmond Biden 1898–1959. US film director and writer who enjoyed great success with a series of comedies in the early 1940s, including *Sullivan's Travels* 1941, *The Palm Beach Story* 1942, and *The Miracle of Morgan's Creek* 1943.

Sturluson Snorri 1179–1241. Icelandic author of the Old Norse poems called ◊Eddas and the *Heimskringla*, a saga chronicle of Norwegian kings until 1177.

Sturm Abteilung (SA) German terrorist militia, also known as Brownshirts, of the ◊Nazi Party, established 1921 under the leadership of ◊Röhm, in charge of physical training and political indoctrination.

Sturm und Drang (German "storm and stress") German early Romantic movement in literature and music, from about 1775, concerned with the

Stuttgart *Staatsgalerie in Stuttgart, the capital of the German state of Baden-Wærttemberg.*

depiction of extravagant passions. Writers associated with the movement include Herder, Goethe, and Schiller. The name is taken from a play by Friedrich von Klinger 1776.

Sturt Charles 1795–1869. British explorer and soldier. In 1828 he sailed down the Murrumbidgee River in SE Australia to the estuary of the Murray in circumstances of great hardship, charting the entire river system of the region.

Born in India, he served in the army, and in 1827 discovered with the Australian explorer Hamilton Hume the river ◊Darling. Drawn by his concept of a great inland sea, he set out for the interior in 1844, crossing what is now known as the Sturt Desert, but failing to penetrate the Simpson Desert.

Stuttgart capital of Baden-Württemberg, Federal Republic of Germany; population (1988) 565,000. Industries include publishing and the manufacture of vehicles and electrical goods.

It is the headquarters of US European Command (Eucom). The philosopher ◊Hegel was born here.

Stuyvesant Peter 1610–1672. Dutch colonial leader. Born in Holland, Stuyvesant worked as an official of the Dutch West India Company. Named governor of Curacao 1643, he lost his right leg in a battle on nearby St Maarten. He was appointed director general of New Netherland 1646 and arrived there the following year. He reorganized the administration of the colony and established a permanent boundary with Connecticut by the Treaty of Hartford 1650. Forced to surrender the colony to the British 1664, Stuyvesant remained there for the rest of his life.

style in flowers, the part of the ◊carpel bearing the ◊stigma at its tip. In some flowers it is very short or completely lacking, while in others it may be long and slender, positioning the stigma in the most effective place to receive the pollen.

Usually the style withers after fertilization but in certain species, such as rock clematis *Clematis verticillaris*, it develops into a long feathery plume that aids dispersal of the fruit.

Styria (German *Steiermark*) alpine province of SE Austria; area 6,330 sq mi/16,400 sq km; population (1987) 1,181,000. Its capital is Graz, and its industries include iron, steel, lignite, vehicles, electrical goods, and engineering. An independent state from 1056 until it passed to the ◊Hapsburgs in the 13th century, it was annexed by Germany in 1938.

Styx in Greek mythology, the river surrounding the underworld.

Suárez González Adolfo 1933– . Spanish politician, prime minister 1976–81. A friend of King Juan Carlos, he was appointed by the king to guide Spain into democracy after the death of the fascist dictator Franco.

subatomic particle any of the subdivisions of the atom, including those ◊elementary particles that combine to form all ◊matter. See also ◊particle physics.

subduction zone the region where two plates of the Earth's rigid lithosphere collide, and one plate descends below the other into the semiliquid asthenosphere. Subduction occurs along deep-sea trenches, most of which encircle the Pacific Ocean; portions of the ocean plate slide beneath other plates carrying continents.

Deep-sea trenches are usually associated with volcanic ◊island arcs and deep-focus earthquakes (more than 185 mi/300 km below the surface), both the result of disturbances caused by the plate subduction. The Aleutian Trench bordering Alaska is an example of an active subduction zone, which has produced the Aleutian Island arc.

sublimation in chemistry, the conversion of a solid to vapor without passing through the liquid phase.

Some substances that do not sublime at atmospheric pressure can be made to do so at low pressures. This is the principle of freeze-drying, during which ice sublimes at low pressure.

subliminal message a message delivered beneath the human conscious threshold of perception. It may be visual (words or images flashed between the frames of a cinema or TV film), or aural (a radio message broadcast constantly at very low volume).

Attempts to use subliminal perception in advertising have raised public fears of manipulation; there is little evidence to show that such messages are effective.

submarine vessel capable of traveling and functioning under water, used in research and military operations. The first underwater boat was constructed for James I of England by the Dutch scientist Cornelius van Drebbel (1572–1633) in 1620. In the 1760s, the American David Bushnell (1742–1824) designed a submarine called *Turtle* for attacking British ships, and in 1800, Robert Fulton designed a submarine called *Nautilus* for Napoleon for the same purpose. John P Holland, an Irish emigrant to the US, designed a submarine about 1875, which was used by both the US and the British navies at the turn of the century. A naval submarine, or submersible torpedo boat, the *Gymnote*, was launched by France 1888. The conventional submarine of World War I was driven by diesel engine on the surface and by battery-powered electric motors underwater. The diesel engine also drove a generator that produced electricity to charge the batteries. In both world wars submarines, from the oceangoing to the midget type, played a vital role. The first nuclear-powered submarine, the *Nautilus*, was launched by the US 1954. In oceanography, salvage, and pipe-laying, smaller submarines called ◊submersibles are used.

submersible vessel designed to operate under water, especially a small submarine used by engineers and research scientists as a ferry craft to support diving operations. The most advanced submersibles are the so-called lock-out type, which have two compartments: one for the pilot, the other to carry divers. The diving compartment is pressurized and provides access to the sea.

Subotica largest town in Vojvodina, NW Serbia, Yugoslavia; population (1981) 155,000. Industries include chemicals and electrical machinery.

subpoena (Latin "under penalty") in law, a writ requiring someone who might not otherwise come forward of his or her own volition to give evidence before a court or judicial official at a specific time and place.

subsidiary a company that is legally controlled by another company having 50% or more of its shares.

subsidy government payment or concession granted to a state or private company, or an individual. A subsidy may be provided to keep prices down, to stimulate the market for a particular product, or because it is perceived to be in the public interest.

The payment of subsidies may distort the market, create shortages, reduce efficiency, or waste resources that could be used more beneficially elsewhere. Export subsidies are usually condemned because they represent unfair competition.

Many countries provide subsidies for transport systems and public utilities such as water, gas, and electricity supplies. Subsidies are also given for art, science, and religion when they cannot be self-supporting to the standards perceived desirable.

subsistence farming term used for farming when the produce is enough to feed only the farmer and family and there is no surplus to sell.

substrate in biochemistry, a compound or mixture of compounds acted on by an enzyme. The term also refers to a substance such as ◊agar that provides the nutrients for the metabolism of microorganisms. Since the enzyme systems of microorganisms regulate their metabolism, the essential meaning is the same.

subway or ***underground*** rail service that runs underground. The first underground line in the world was in London. Opened 1863, it was essentially a roofed-in trench. The London Underground is still the longest, with over 250 mi/400 km of routes. Many major cities throughout the world have extensive systems; New York's subway system and Moscow's, each handles millions of passengers a day.

succession in ecology, series of changes that occur in the structure and composition of the vegetation in a given area from the time it is first colonized by plants (primary succession), or after it has

submersibles

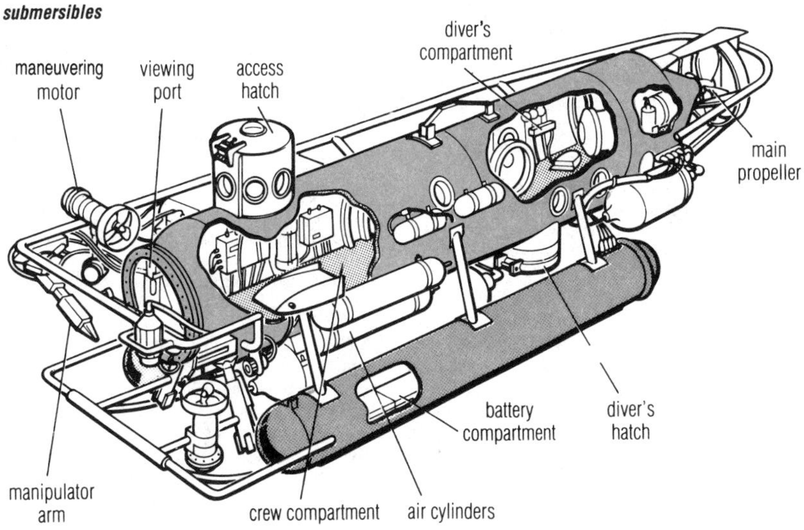
diver's compartment
maneuvering motor
viewing port
access hatch
main propeller
battery compartment
diver's hatch
manipulator arm
crew compartment
air cylinders

succession

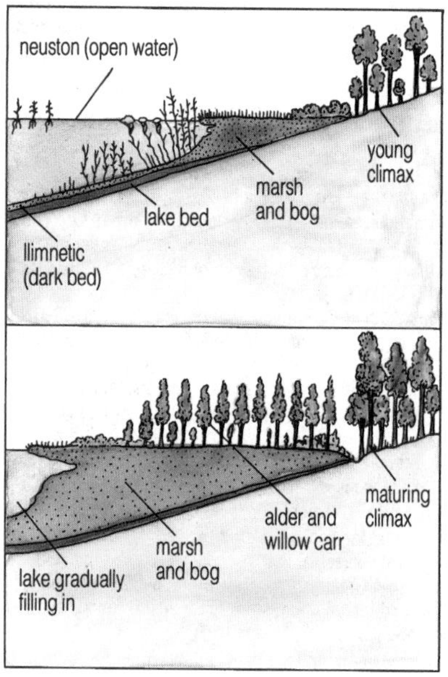
neuston (open water)
young climax
marsh and bog
lake bed
limnetic (dark bed)
maturing climax
alder and willow carr
marsh and bog
lake gradually filling in

been disturbed by fire, flood, or clearing (secondary succession).

If allowed to proceed undisturbed, succession leads naturally to a stable ◊climax community (for example, oak and hickory forest or savannah grassland) that is determined by the climate and soil characteristics of the area.

Succot or ***Sukkoth*** in Judaism, a harvest festival celebrated in Oct, also known as the Feast of Booths, which commemorates the time when the Israelites lived in the wilderness during the ◊Exodus from Egypt. As a reminder of the shelters used in the wilderness, huts are built and used for eating and sleeping during the seven days of the festival.

succubus a female spirit; see ◊incubus.

succulent plant a thick, fleshy plant that stores water in its tissues, for example, cacti and stonecrops *Sedum*. Succulents live either in areas where water is very scarce, such as deserts, or in places where it is not easily obtainable because of the high concentrations of salts in the soil, as in salt marshes. See also ◊xerophyte.

Suceava capital of Suceava county, N Romania; population (1985) 93,000. Industries include textiles and lumber. It was a former center of pilgrimage and capital of Moldavia 1388–1564.

sucker fish another name for ◊remora.

suckering in plants, reproduction by new shoots (suckers) arising from an existing root system rather than from seed. Plants that produce suckers include elm, dandelion, and members of the rose family.

sucrase enzyme capable of digesting sucrose into its constituent molecules of glucose and fructose.

In mammals this action takes place within the wall of the intestine, the products of the reaction being liberated into the lumen. This is an example of intracellular digestion.

Sucre legal capital and judicial seat of Bolivia; population (1985) 87,000. It stands on the central plateau at an altitude of 9,320 ft/2,840 m. The city was founded in 1538, its cathedral dates from 1553, and the University of San Francisco Xavier 1624 is probably the oldest in South America. The first revolt against Spanish rule in South America began here May 25, 1809.

Sucre Antonio José de 1795–1830. South American revolutionary leader. As chief lieutenant of Simón ◊Bolívar, he won several battles in freeing the colonies of Ecuador and Bolivia from Spanish rule, and in 1826 became president of Bolivia. After a mutiny by the army and invasion by Peru, he resigned in 1828 and was assassinated in 1830 on his way to join Bolívar.

Sudan

Democratic Republic of
(Jamhuryat es-Sudan)

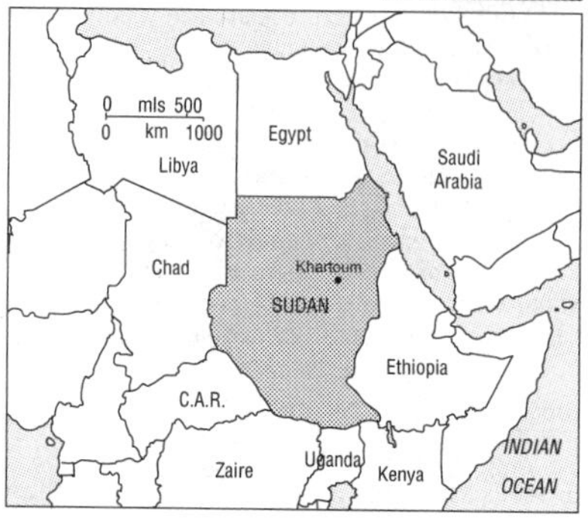
0 mls 500
0 km 1000
Egypt
Libya
Saudi Arabia
Chad
Khartoum
SUDAN
Ethiopia
C.A.R.
Zaire
Uganda
Kenya
INDIAN OCEAN

area 967,489 sq mi/2,505,800 sq km
capital Khartoum
cities Omdurman, Juba, Wadi Medani, al-Obeid, Kassala, Atbara, al-Qadarif, Kosti; chief port Port Sudan
physical fertile valley of Nile River separates Libyan Desert in W from high rocky Nubian Desert in E
features Sudd swamp; largest country in Africa
head of state and government Gen Omar Hasan Ahmed el-Bashir from 1989
political system military republic
political parties New National Umma Party (NNUP), Islamic, nationalist; Democratic Unionist Party (DUP), moderate, nationalist; National Islamic Front, Islamic nationalist
exports cotton, gum arabic, sesame seed, peanuts, sorghum
currency Sudanese pound
population (1990 est) 25,164,000; growth rate 2.9% p.a.
life expectancy men 51, women 55 (1989)
language Arabic 51% (official); tribal languages
religion Sunni Muslim 73%, animist 18%, Christian 9% (in south)
literacy 30% (1986)
GNP $8.5 bn (1988); $330 per head (1988)
chronology
1820 Sudan ruled by Egypt.
1885 Revolt led to capture of Khartoum.
1896–98 Anglo-Egyptian offensive led by Lord Kitchener subdued revolt.
1899 Sudan administered as an Anglo-Egyptian condominium.
1955 Civil war between Muslim north and non-Muslim south broke out.
1956 Sudan achieved independence from Britain and Egypt as a republic.
1958 Military coup replaced civilian government with Supreme Council of the Armed Forces.
1964 Civilian rule reinstated.
1969 Coup led by Col Gaafar Mohammed Nimeri established Revolutionary Command Council (RCC); name changed to Democratic Republic of Sudan.
1970 Union with Egypt agreed in principle.
1971 New constitution adopted; Nimeri confirmed as president; Sudanese Socialist Union (SSU) declared only legal party.
1972 Proposed Federation of Arab Republics, comprising Sudan, Egypt, and Syria, abandoned. Addis Ababa conference proposed autonomy for southern provinces.
1974 National assembly established.
1983 Nimeri reelected. *Sharia* (Islamic law) introduced.
1985 Nimeri deposed in a bloodless coup led by Gen Swar al-Dahab; transitional military council set up. State of emergency declared.
1986 More than 40 political parties fought general election; coalition government formed.
1987 Virtual civil war with Sudan People's Liberation Movement (SPLM).
1988 Al-Mahdi formed a new coalition. Another flare-up of civil war between north and south created tens of thousands of refugees. Floods made 1.5 million people homeless. Peace pact signed with Sudan People's Liberation Movement.
1989 Sadiq Al-Mahdi overthrown in coup led by Gen Omar Hasan Ahmed el-Bashir.
1990 Civil war continued with new SPLM offensive.

sucrose $C_{12}H_{22}O_{10}$ ◊disaccharide known commonly as ◊sugar, cane sugar, or beet sugar.

A single molecule of sucrose consists of a ◊glucose molecule and a ◊fructose molecule bonded together. Sucrose does not have the reducing properties associated with most simple carbohydrates.

Sudan country in NE Africa, S of Egypt, with a Red Sea coast; it is the largest country in Africa.

government After a military coup April 1985 a transitional constitution was introduced, providing for a 264-member legislative assembly, a supreme council under a president, and a council of ministers led by a prime minister. The assembly is charged with the task of producing a new constitution and, after a further transitional period, of declaring itself a parliament, subject to election every four years.

history In ancient times, the region was known as ◊Nubia and was taken over by the kingdoms of Upper and Lower Egypt. The Nubians were later converted to Coptic Christianity in the 6th century and to Islam in the 15th century when Arabs invaded. Sudan was again ruled by Egypt from 1820. A revolt began 1881, led by a sheik who took the title of ◊Mahdi and captured ◊Khartoum 1885. It was subdued by an Anglo-Egyptian army under ◊Kitchener 1896–98 and administered as an Anglo-Egyptian condominium from 1899.

The Sudan, as it was called, achieved independence as a republic 1956. Two years later a coup ousted the civil administration, and a military government was set up, which in 1964 was itself overthrown and civilian rule was reinstated. Five years later the army returned in a coup led by Colonel Gaafar Mohammed Nimeri. All political bodies were abolished, the Revolutionary Command Council (RCC) set up, and the country's name changed to the Democratic Republic of Sudan. Close links were soon established with Egypt, and in 1970 an agreement in principle was reached for eventual union. In 1972 this should have become, with the addition of Syria, the Federation of Arab Republics, but internal opposition blocked both developments. In 1971 a new constitution was adopted, Nimeri confirmed as president, and the Sudanese Socialist Union (SSU) declared to be the only party.

The most serious problem confronting Nimeri was open aggression between the Muslim north and the chiefly Christian south, which had started as long ago as 1955. At a conference in Addis Ababa 1972 he granted the three southern provinces a considerable degree of autonomy, but fighting continued. Nimeri had come to power in a left-wing revolution but soon turned to the West, and the US, for support. By 1974 he had established a national assembly, but his position still relied on army backing. In 1983 he was reelected for a third term, but his regional problems persisted. By sending more troops south against the Sudan People's Liberation Army he alienated the north and then caused considerable resentment in the south by replacing the penal code with strict Islamic law. His economic policies contributed to the widespread unrest.

In March 1985 a general strike was provoked by a sharp devaluation of the Sudanese pound and an increase in bread prices. Nimeri was in the US when army mutiny threatened. One of his supporters, General Swar al-Dahab, took over in a bloodless coup. He set up a transitional military council and held elections for a legislative assembly April 1986, contested by more than 40 parties, the three most significant being the New National Umma Party (NNUP), which won 99 seats; the Democratic Unionist Party (DUP), 63 seats; and the National Islamic Front, 51 seats. A coalition government was formed, with Ahmed Ali El-Mirghani (DUP) as president of the Supreme Council and Oxford-educated Sadiq al-Mahdi (NNUP) as prime minister. Strikes and shortages persisted, with inflation running at about 100% and the highest national debt in Africa, and in July 1987 a state of emergency was declared. In Oct 1987 the prime minister announced the breakup of the government of national unity and the formation of a new coalition. In Dec 1988 the signing of a peace agreement with the Sudan People's Liberation Movement (SPLM), led by John Garang, threatened to split the coalition government and eventually led to a military takeover, by General Ahmed el-Bashir, in July 1989. El-Bashir established a 15-man revolutionary council with himself as head of state and government. Just weeks before the successful coup, the military foiled the second attempt in six months to restore Nimeri to power. Bashir's government arrested Al-Mahdi and announced that its first priority was to bring an end to the six-year war between the Muslim north and the Christian and animist south. The civil war and famine remained a problem in 1991, when the government announced the division of the country into nine provinces, to be governed under federal system.

sudden infant death syndrome (SIDS) in medicine, the technical name for ◊crib death.

Sudbury city in Ontario, Canada; population (1986) 149,000. A buried meteorite there yields 90% of the world's nickel.

Sudetenland mountainous region of N Czechoslovakia, annexed by Germany under the ◊Munich Agreement 1938; returned to Czechoslovakia 1945.

Suetonius (Gaius Suetonius Tranquillius) c. AD 69–140. Roman historian, author of *Lives of the Caesars* (Julius Caesar to Domitian).

Suez (Arabic *El Suweis*) port at the Red Sea terminus of the ◊Suez Canal; population (1985) 254,000. Industries include oil refining and the manufacture of fertilizers. It was reconstructed after the ◊Arab-Israeli Wars in 1979.

Suez Canal artificial waterway, 100 mi/160 km long, from Port Said to Suez, linking the Mediterranean and Red seas, separating Africa from Asia, and providing the shortest eastward sea route from Europe. It was opened 1869, nationalized 1956, blocked by Egypt during the Arab-Israeli war 1967, and not reopened until 1975.

The French Suez Canal Company was formed 1858 to execute the scheme of Ferdinand de Lesseps. The canal was opened 1869, and in 1875 British prime minister ◊Disraeli acquired a major stockholding for Britain from the khedive of Egypt. The 1888 Convention of Constantinople opened it to all nations. The Suez Canal was administered by a company with offices in Paris controlled by a council of 33 (10 of them British) until 1956 when it was forcibly nationalized by President ◊Nasser of Egypt. The new Damietta port complex on the Mediterranean at the mouth of the canal was inaugurated July 1986. The port is designed to handle 16 million tons of cargo.

Suez Crisis military confrontation Oct–Dec 1956 following the nationalization of the ◊Suez Canal by President Nasser of Egypt. In an attempt to reassert international control of the canal, Israel

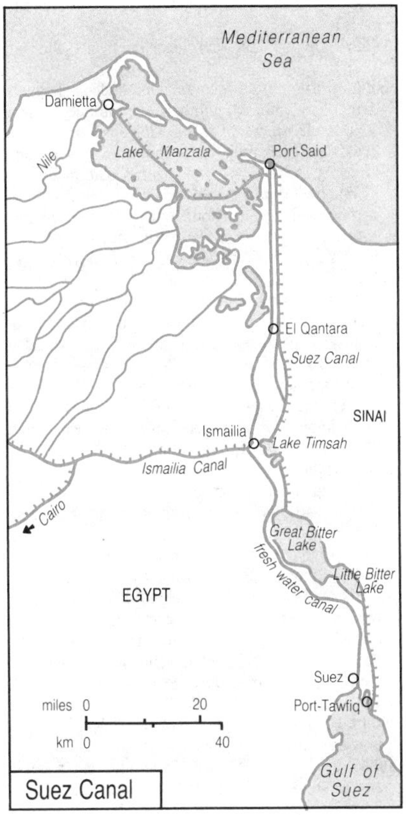
Mediterranean Sea
Damietta
Nile
Lake Manzala
Port-Said
El Qantara
Suez Canal
SINAI
Ismailia
Lake Timsah
Ismailia Canal
Cairo
Great Bitter Lake
fresh water canal
Little Bitter Lake
EGYPT
Suez
Port-Tawfiq
miles 0 20
km 0 40
Gulf of Suez
Suez Canal

launched an attack, after which British and French troops landed. Widespread international censure (Soviet protest, US nonsupport, and considerable domestic opposition) forced the withdrawal of British and French troops. The crisis resulted in the resignation of British prime minister Eden.

suffix letter or group of letters added to the end of a word in order to form a new word. For example, the suffix *-ist* can be added to *sex* to form the word *sexist*.

Suffolk county of E England

area 1,467 sq mi/3,800 sq km

towns Ipswich (administrative headquarters), Bury St Edmunds, Lowestoft, Felixstowe

physical low undulating surface and flat coastline; rivers: Waveney, Alde, Deben, Orwell, Stour; part of the Norfolk Broads

features Minsmere marshland bird reserve, near Aldeburgh; site of ◊Sutton Hoo (7th-century ship-burial); site of "Sizewell B," planned as the first of Britain's pressurized-water nuclear reactor (PWR) plants (approved 1987)

products cereals, sugar beet, working horses (Suffolk punches), fertilizers, agricultural machinery

population (1987) 635,000

famous people John Constable, Thomas Gainsborough, Elizabeth Garrett Anderson, Benjamin Britten, George Crabbe.

suffragan (Latin *suffragor* "vote for, support") in the Christian church, an assistant bishop, appointed to work in a part of the diocese.

suffragist a woman fighting for the right to vote. In the US, the suffragist movement officially began at the ◊Seneca Falls Convention 1848. Elizabeth Cady ◊Stanton and Susan B ◊Anthony founded the National Woman Suffrage Association 1869. At about the same time, Lucy ◊Stone formed the American Woman Suffrage Association. The two groups merged 1890 as the National American Woman Suffrage Association. The perseverance of this group and others led to the ratification of the 19th Amendment 1920, which gave US women the right to vote.

Sufism a mystical movement of ◊Islam which originated in the 8th century. Sufis believe that deep intuition is the only real guide to knowledge. The movement has a strong strain of asceticism. The name derives from the *suf*, a rough woolen robe worn as an indication of disregard for material things. There are a number of groups or brotherhoods within Sufism, each with its own method of meditative practice, one of which is the whirling dance of the ◊dervishes.

sugar any sweet, soluble crystalline carbohydrate, either a monosaccharide or disaccharide. The major sources are tropical sugar cane *Saccharum officinarum*, which accounts for about two-thirds of production, and temperate sugar beet *Beta vulgaris*. ◊Honey also contains sugars.

Cane, which is a grass, usually yields over 9 tons of sugar per acre per year; sugar beet rarely exceeds 3 tons per acre per year. Beet sugar is more expensive to produce, but is often subsidized by European governments wishing to support the agricultural sector and to avoid overdependence on the volatile world sugar market. Minor quantities of sugar are produced from the sap of maple trees, and from sorghum and date palms. Sugar is a major source of energy, but also contributes to tooth decay.

Monosaccharides are the simplest sugars; examples include fructose and glucose, both obtained from fruit and honey. Disaccharides are sugars which, when hydrolyzed by dilute acids, give two of either the same or different simple sugars (monosaccharides). Examples are sucrose from sugar cane and sugar beet, which breaks down to glucose and fructose. Polysaccharides, such as starch and cellulose, hydrolyze to many simple sugars. Sucrose is produced commercially from sugar cane by crushing the stem. Molasses is the uncrystallized syrup drained from the crystallized sugar, then refined by stages to "pure" whiteness. Fermented unrefined molasses produces rum. Highly refined forms of sugar include cube, granulated, confectioner's, and icing.

Sugar is also produced from sugar beet; the pulp remaining from the process is used as cattle feed. The fibrous residue of sugar cane, called bagasse, is used in the manufacture of paper, cattle feed, and fuel; and new types of cane are being bred for low sugar and high fuel production.

history

c. 700 BC sugar first refined in India

c. 650 BC first bee husbandry in the Mediterranean and Mexico, for honey

c. 1300 sugar industry spread from Arab countries to Spain (Italy main trader) and to Latin America by the Spanish (16th–17th centuries)

1319 first record of sugar in England

18th century rise in European consumption

late 18th century Margraf isolated sugar in beet

1885 beet and cane sugar trade

sugar maple E North American ◊maple tree *Acer saccharum*.

Suger c. 1081–1151. French historian and politician, regent of France during the Second Crusade. In 1122 he was elected abbot of St Denis, Paris, and was counselor to, and biographer of, Louis VI and Louis VII. He began the reconstruction of St Denis as the first large-scale Gothic building.

Suharto Raden 1921– . Indonesian politician and general. He ousted Sukarno to become president in 1967. He ended confrontation with Malaysia, invaded East Timor in 1975, and reached a cooperation agreement with Papua New Guinea 1979. His authoritarian rule has met domestic opposition from the left. He was reelected in 1973, 1978, 1983, and 1988.

suicide (Latin "to kill oneself") self-murder; the victim is also termed a suicide.

It is often considered a crime in law, with consequences for a suicide's estate, or criminal prosecution for unsuccessful attempt. It is also a crime in terms of some religious law. Aiding and abetting another's suicide is often considered illegal. Survivors of joint suicides may be charged

Suharto *General Suharto, president of Indonesia.*

with manslaughter. In some cultures, suicide is considered honorable behavior, such as suicide in ancient Rome, historic ◊hara-kiri in Japan, or historic suttee in India.

suite in music, formerly a grouping of old dance forms; later the term came to be used to describe a set of instrumental pieces, sometimes assembled from a stage work, such as Tchaikovsky's *Nutcracker Suite* 1891–92.

Sukarno Achmed 1901–1970. Indonesian nationalist, president 1945–67. During World War II he cooperated in the local administration set up by the Japanese, replacing Dutch rule. After the war he became the first president of the new Indonesian republic, becoming president-for-life in 1966; he was ousted by ◊Suharto.

Sukkur or ***Sakhar*** port in Sind province, Pakistan, on the river Indus; population (1981) 191,000. The Sukkur river–Lloyd Barrage 1928–32 lies to the W.

Sulawesi formerly ***Celebes*** island in E Indonesia, one of the Sunda Islands; area (with dependent islands) 73,000 sq mi/190,000 sq km; population (1980) 10,410,000. It is mountainous and forested and produces copra and nickel.

Suleiman or ***Solyman*** 1494–1566. Ottoman sultan from 1520, known as the Magnificent and the Lawgiver. Under his rule, the Ottoman Empire flourished and reached its largest extent. He made conquests in the Balkans, the Mediterranean, Persia, and N Africa, but was defeated at Vienna in 1529 and Valletta (on Malta) in 1565. He was a patron of the arts, a poet, and an administrator.

Suleiman captured Belgrade (now in Yugoslavia) in 1521, the Mediterranean island of Rhodes in 1522, defeated the Hungarians at Mohács in 1526, and was halted in his advance into Europe only by his failure to take Vienna, capital of the Austro-Hungarian Empire, after a siege Sept–Oct 1529. In 1534 he turned more successfully against Persia, and then in campaigns against the Arab world took almost all of N Africa and the Red Sea port of Aden. Only the ◊Knights of Malta inflicted severe defeat on both his army and fleet when he tried to take Valletta in 1565.

sulfate SO_4^{2-} salt or ester derived from sulfuric acid. Most sulfates are water soluble (the exceptions are lead, calcium, strontium, and barium sulfates), and require a very high temperature to decompose them.

The commonest sulfates seen in the laboratory are coppper(II) sulfate ($CuSO_4$), iron(II) sulfate ($FeSO_4$), and aluminum sulfate ($Al_2(SO_4)_3$). The ion is detected in solution by using barium chloride or barium nitrate to precipitate the insoluble sulfate.

sulfide compound of sulfur and another element in which sulfur is the more ◊electronegative element. Sulfides occur in a number of minerals. Some of the more volatile sulfides have extremely unpleasant odors (hydrogen sulfide smells of bad eggs).

sulfite SO_3^{2-} salt or ester derived from sulfurous acid.

sulfur brittle, pale-yellow, nonmetallic element, symbol S, atomic number 16, atomic weight 32.064. It occurs in three allotropic forms: two crystalline (rhombic and monoclinic) and one amorphous. It burns in air with a blue flame and a stifling odor; it is insoluble in water but soluble in carbon disulfide. It is found abundantly in volcanic regions and occurs in nature in combination with metals and other substances, as well as a free, brittle, crystalline solid.

Sulfur is a constituent of proteins. Its greatest industrial use is in the commercial preparation of sulfuric acid to treat phosphate rock in producing fertilizers. It is also used in making paper, matches, gunpowder, and fireworks; in vulcanizing rubber; and in medicines and insecticides. It has been known since ancient times and was called *sulphur*, later *sulfur*, in Latin.

sulfur dioxide SO_2 a pungent gas, produced by burning sulfur in air or oxygen.

It is used widely for disinfecting food vessels and equipment, and as a preservative in some food products. It occurs in industrial flue gases and is a major cause of ◊acid rain.

sulfuric acid H_2SO_4 (also called oil of vitriol) dense, oily, colorless liquid that gives out heat when added to water. It is used extensively in the chemical industry, gasoline refining, and in manufacturing fertilizers, detergents, explosives, and dyes.

sulfurous acid H_2SO_3 solution of sulfur dioxide (SO_2) in water. It is a weak acid.

Sulla Lucius Cornelius 138–78 BC. Roman general and politician, a leader of the senatorial party. Forcibly suppressing the democrats in 88 BC, he departed for a successful campaign against ◊Mithridates VI of Pontus. The democrats seized power in his absence, but on his return Sulla captured Rome and massacred all opponents. As dictator, his reforms, which strengthened the Senate, were backward-looking and shortlived. He retired 79 BC.

Sullivan Arthur (Seymour) 1842–1900. English composer who wrote operettas in collaboration with William Gilbert, including *HMS Pinafore* 1878, *The Pirates of Penzance* 1879, and *The Mikado* 1885. Their partnership broke down in 1896. Sullivan also composed serious instrumental, choral, and operatic works—for example, the opera *Ivanhoe* 1890—which he valued more highly than the operettas.

Sullivan John L(awrence) 1858–1918. US prize-fighter. Born in Boston, Sullivan briefly attended Boston College before beginning a professional boxing career. He won the heavyweight championship from Paddy Ryan 1882 and in the following years toured widely throughout the US and British Isles. In 1892 Sullivan lost his title to James "Gentleman Jim" Corbett in the first championship bout held according to the Marquis of Queensbury rules. After his retirement from the ring, Sullivan became a popular vaudevillian and was a saloonkeeper in New York.

Sullivan Louis Henry 1856–1924. US architect, a leader of the Chicago school of architects and an early developer of the ◊skyscraper. His skyscrapers include the Wainwright Building, St Louis 1890 and the Guaranty Building, Buffalo 1894. Other notable works include the Chicago Auditorium and the Carson Pirie and Scott department store, Chicago. He was the teacher of Frank Lloyd ◊Wright.

Sully Maximilien de Béthune, Duc de 1560–1641. French politician who served with the Protestant ◊Huguenots in the wars of religion, and, as Henry IV's superintendent of finances 1598–1611, aided French recovery.

Sully-Prudhomme Armand 1839–1907. French poet who wrote philosophical verse including *Les Solitudes/Solitude* 1869, *La Justice/Justice* 1878, and *Le Bonheur/Happiness* 1888. Nobel Prize 1901.

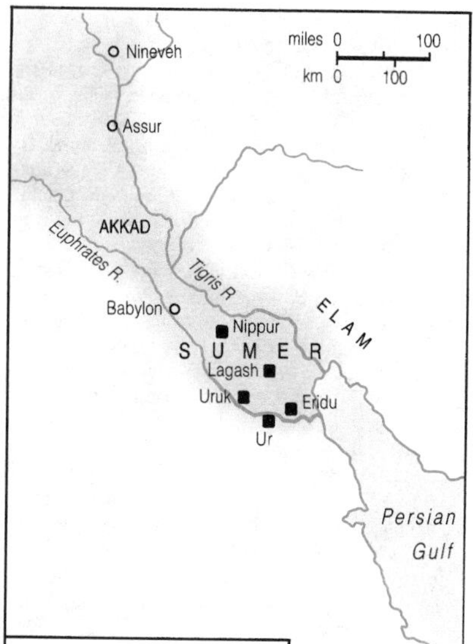
Nineveh
Assur
miles 0 100
km 0 100
AKKAD
Euphrates R.
Tigris R.
Babylon
ELAM
Nippur
SUMER
Lagash
Uruk
Eridu
Ur
Persian Gulf

Sumerian civilization
■ city states

Sulu Archipelago group of about 870 islands off SW Mindanao in the Philippines, between the Sulawesi and Sulu seas; area 1,042 sq mi/2,700 sq km; population (1980) 361,000. The capital is Jolo, on the island (the largest) of the same name. Until 1940 the islands were an autonomous sultanate.

sumac any bush or tree of the genus *Rhus* of the cashew family, having pinnate compound leaves and clusters of small reddish fruits. Staghorn sumac *Rhus typhina*, growing to 36 ft/11 m tall, is common in North America. Included too are several poisonous plants (sometimes referred to collectively as the genus *Toxicodendron*), such as ◊poison ivy, ◊poison sumac, and certain Japanese sumacs.

Sumatra or ***Sumatera*** second-largest island of Indonesia, one of the Sunda Islands; area 182,800 sq mi/473,600 sq km; population (1980) 28,016,000. E of a longitudinal volcanic mountain range is a wide plain; both are heavily forested. Products include rubber, rice, tobacco, tea, timber, tin, and petroleum.

Northern Sumatra is rapidly being industrialized, and the Asakan River (rising in Lake Toba) was dammed for power 1974. The main towns are Palembang, Padang, and Benkuelen.

A Hindu empire was founded in the 8th century, but Islam was introduced by Arab traders from the 13th century and by the 16th century was adopted throughout the island.

Sumer the earliest civilization in the world, located in the Tigris–Euphrates valleys of Mesopotamia, now in S Iraq, a part of the Near East's fertile crescent. It is dated to about 3500 BC, had writing, trade, irrigation systems, great planned city-states (such as Ur and Eridu) with public works and temple complexes, and was ruled by a theocracy—all supported by taxation of the surrounding agricultural villages. Centralized control over the region (an empire) was first asserted by neighboring Akkad, about 2300 BC, and after 2000 BC, Sumer was absorbed by the Babylonian empire.

Sumerian civilization the world's earliest ◊civilization, dated about 3500 BC, and located at the confluence of the Tigris and Euphrates rivers in lower Mesopotamia (present-day Iraq). It was a city-state with priests as secular rulers. Sumerian culture was based on the taxation of the surplus produced by agricultural villagers to support the urban ruling class and its public-works program, which included state-controlled irrigation. Cities

sumo wrestling *A sumo wrestling exhibition match in Paris, France, 1986.*

included ◊Lagash, ◊Eridu, and ◊Ur. Trade with Egypt and the Indus valley led to the formation of the ancient ◊Egyptian civilization and the ◊Indus Valley civilization.

summons in law, a court order officially delivered, requiring someone to appear in court on a certain date.

Sumner Charles 1811–1874. US political leader. Born in Boston and educated at Harvard, Sumner was admitted to the bar 1833. After a period of travel in Europe, he taught at Harvard, lectured on abolitionism and pacifism, and was elected to the US Senate as a FreeSoil Democrat 1852. For his fierce opposition to any compromise on the issue of slavery, Sumner was badly beaten by South Carolina congressman Preston Brooks 1856. Although long an invalid, he was a Republican leader in Congress during the Civil War. A supporter of Radical Reconstruction, he opposed Grant's renomination 1872.

Sumner James 1887–1955. US biochemist. In 1926 he succeeded in crystallizing the enzyme urease and demonstrating its protein nature. For this work Sumner shared the 1946 Nobel Prize for Chemistry with John Northrop and Wendell Stanley.

sumo wrestling national sport of Japan. Fighters of larger than average size (rarely less than 285 lb/130 kg) try to push, pull, or throw each other out of a circular ring.

Fighters follow a traditional diet and eat a great deal to build up body weight. In the ring, they try to get their center of gravity as low to the ground as possible. Championships, lasting up to 15 days each, are held six times a year in Japan; millions of fans watch the contests live and on television. Sumo wrestling originated as a religious ritual performed at Shinto shrines. In the 17th and 18th centuries it evolved into a popular spectator sport.

sumptuary law a law restraining excessive individual consumption, such as expenditure on food and dress, or attempting to control religious or moral conduct.

The Romans had several sumptuary laws; for example, the *lex Orchia* in 181 BC limited the number of dishes at a feast. In England sumptuary laws were introduced by Edward III and Henry VII.

Sun the ◊star at the center of the Solar System. Its diameter is 865,000 mi/1,392,000 km; its temperature at the surface is about 6,000K (10,000°F/5,800°C), and at the center 15,000,000K (15,000,000°C/27,000,000°F). It is composed of about 70% hydrogen and 30% helium, with other elements making up less than

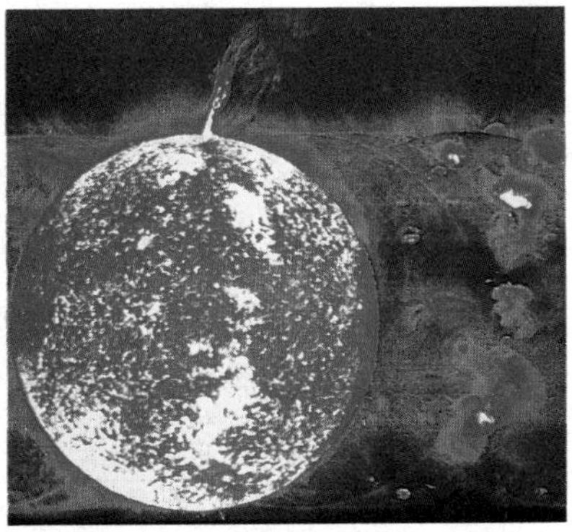

Sun *Ultraviolet image of the solar disk and solar prominence, recorded by the* Skylab *space station in 1973.*

1%. The Sun's energy is generated by nuclear fusion reactions that turn hydrogen into helium at its center. It is about 4.7 billion years old, with a predicted lifetime of 10 billion years.

At the end of its life, it will expand to become a ◊red giant the size of Mars' orbit, then shrink to become a ◊white dwarf. The Sun spins on its axis every 25 days near its equator but more slowly toward its poles. Its rotation can be followed by watching the passage of dark ◊sunspots across its disk. Sometimes bright eruptions called ◊flares occur near sunspots. Above the Sun's ◊photosphere lies a layer of thinner gas called the ◊chromosphere, visible only by means of special instruments or at eclipses. Tongues of gas called ◊prominences extend from the chromosphere into the corona, a halo of hot, tenuous gas surrounding the Sun. Gas boiling from the corona streams outward through the Solar System, forming the ◊solar wind. Activity on the Sun, including sunspots, flares, and prominences, waxes and wanes during the solar cycle, which peaks every 11 years or so. The unmanned space probe *Pioneer 9* achieved solar orbit in 1968 and reported data on solar radiation.

Sunbelt popular name for the S and SW continental US because of the warm climate. The Sunbelt is growing much faster in population than the N US, with a steady migration of retirees and high-tech and service industries. The 20 states that, roughly, comprise the Sunbelt have a population of more than 110 million. The largest city in the Sunbelt is Los Angeles.

Sun City alternate name for ◊Mmabatho, resort in Bophuthatswana, South Africa.

Sunda Islands islands W of the Moluccas, in the Malay Archipelago, the greater number belonging to Indonesia. They are so named because they lie largely on the Indonesian extension of the Sunda continental shelf. The Greater Sundas include Borneo, Java (including the small island of Madura), Sumatra, Sulawesi, and Belitung. The Lesser Sundas (Indonesian *Nusa Tenggara*) are all Indonesian and include Bali, Lombok, Flores, Sumba, Sumbawa, and Timor.

sun dance religious ceremony performed by certain ◊Plains Indians at the time of the summer solstice.

Sunday first day of the week; in Christianity, Sunday is set aside for worship in commemoration of Jesus' resurrection, and in predominantly Christian societies banks, offices, and many shops are generally closed. It replaced the Jewish ◊Sabbath, or day of rest, observed on Saturday.

"Blue laws," which restricted commercial activities, entertainment, and the purveying of alcoholic beverages on Sunday, have been repealed in many parts of the US since the 1950s.

Sunderland port in Tyne and Wear, NE England; population (1981) 196,150. Industries were formerly only coal-mining and shipbuilding but have now diversified to electronics, glass, and furniture. There is a polytechnic and a civic theater, the Sunderland Empire.

sundew any insectivorous plant of the genus

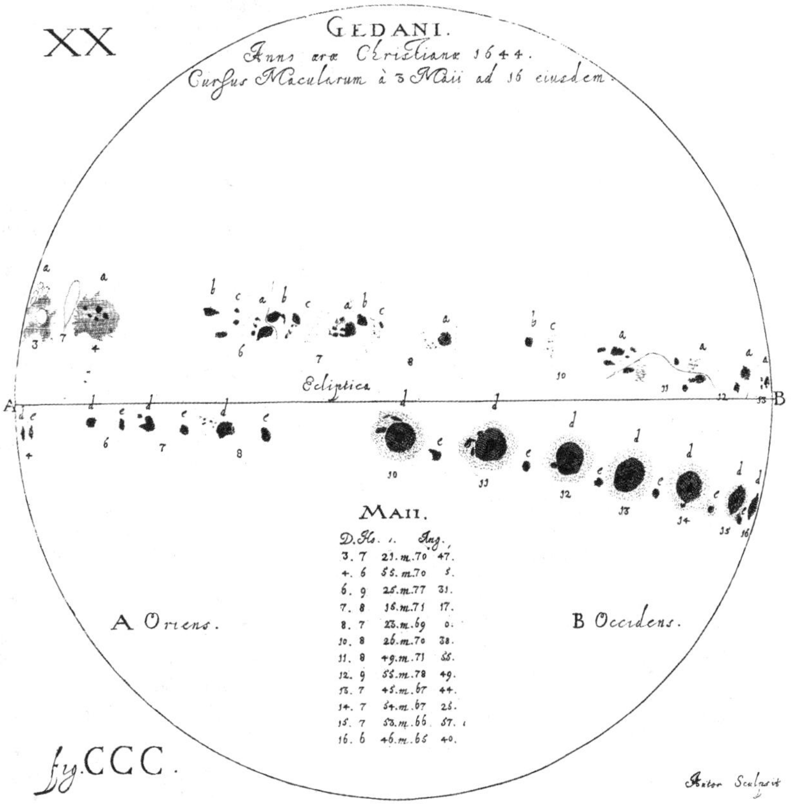
XX
GEDANI.
Ecliptica
A
B
MAII.
A Oriens.
B Occidens.
fig. CCC.

sunspot *A line drawing by Hevelius of sunspots observed as long ago as May 1644.*

Drosera, family Droseraceae, with viscid hairs on the leaves for catching prey.

sundial instrument measuring time by means of a shadow cast by the Sun. Almost completely superseded by the proliferation of clocks, it survives ornamentally in gardens. The dial is marked with the hours at graduated distances, and a style or gnomon (parallel to Earth's axis and pointing to the north) casts the shadow.

Sundsvall port in E Sweden; population (1986) 93,000. It has oil, timber, and wood-pulp industries.

sunfish any of various small members of the North American family (Centrarchidae) of freshwater bony fishes with compressed, almost circular bodies ranging from 6 in/15 cm to 12 in/30 cm and including bluegills, pumpkinseeds, rock bass, and crappies. The considerably larger basses also belong to this family. Ocean sunfishes of the family Molidae have disc-shaped, abruptly truncated bodies. The 10 ft/3 m species *Mola mola* is found worldwide.

sunflower tall plant of the genus *Helianthus*, family Compositae. The common sunflower *H. annuus*, probably native to Mexico, grows to 15 ft/4.5 m in favorable conditions. It is commercially cultivated in central Europe, the US, and the USSR for the oil-bearing seeds that follow the yellow-petaled flowers.

Sungari river in Manchuria, NE China, that joins the Amur on the Siberian frontier; length 800 mi/1,300 km.

Sunni member of the larger of the two main sects of ◊Islam, with about 680 million adherents. Sunni Muslims believe that the first four caliphs were all legitimate successors of the prophet Mohammed, and that guidance on belief and life should come from the Koran and the Hadith, and from the Shari'a, not from a human authority or spiritual leader. Imams in Sunni Islam are educated lay teachers of the faith and prayer leaders.

sunspot dark patch on the surface of the Sun, actually an area of cooler gas, thought to be caused by strong magnetic fields that block the outward flow of heat to the Sun's surface. Sunspots consist of a dark central umbra, about 4,000K (6,700°F/3,700°C), and a lighter surrounding penumbra, about 5,500K (9,400°F/5,200°C). They last from several days to over a month, ranging in size from 1,250 mi/2,000 km to groups stretching for over 62,000 mi/100,000 km. The number of sunspots visible at a given time varies from none to over 100 in a cycle averaging 11 years.

sunstroke a form of ◊heat stroke caused by excessive exposure to the Sun.

Sun Yat-sen or ***Sun Zhong Shan*** 1867–1925. Chinese revolutionary leader and statesman, founder of the ◊Guomindang (Nationalist party) 1894, and provisional president of the Republic of China 1912 after playing a vital part in deposing the emperor. He was president of a breakaway government from 1921.

Sun Yat-sen was the son of a Christian farmer. After many years in exile he returned to China during the 1911 revolution that overthrew the Manchu dynasty and was provisional president of the republic in 1912. In an effort to bring unity to China, he soon resigned in favor of the military leader Yuan Shih-k'ai. As a result of Yuan's increasingly dictatorial methods, Sun established an independent republic in S China based in Canton 1921. He was criticized for lack of organizational ability, but his "three people's principles" of nationalism, democracy, and social reform are accepted by both the Nationalists and the Chinese Communists.

Sun Yat-sen *Sun Yat-Sen, founder of the Nationalist Guomindang party and the guiding force behind the Chinese revolution in 1911.*

superactinide any of a theoretical series of superheavy, radioactive elements, starting with atomic number 113, that extend beyond the ◊transactinide series in the periodic table. They do not occur in nature and none have yet been synthesized.

It is postulated that this series has a group of elements that have half-lives longer than those of the transactinide series. This group, centered on element 114, is referred to as the "island of stability," based on the nucleon arrangement. The longer half-lives will, it is hoped, allow enough time for their chemical and physical properties to be studied when they have been synthesized.

Super Bowl US professional championship, inaugurated 1966. It is the annual end-of-season contest between the American Football Conference (AFC) and National Football Conference (NFC) champions. See ◊football.

supercomputer the fastest, most powerful type of computer, capable of performing its basic operations in picoseconds (trillionths of a second), rather than nanoseconds (billionths of a second), like most other computers.

To achieve these extraordinary speeds, supercomputers use several processors working together and techniques such as cooling processors down to nearly ◊absolute zero temperature, so that their components conduct electricity many times faster than normal.

superconductivity in physics, increase in electrical conductivity at low temperatures. The resistance of some metals and metallic compounds decreases uniformly with decreasing temperature until at a critical temperature (the superconducting point), within a few degrees of absolute zero (0K/−459.67°F/−273.16°C), the resistance suddenly falls to zero.

In this superconducting state, an electric current will continue indefinitely after the magnetic field has been removed, provided that the material remains below the superconducting point. In 1986 IBM researchers achieved superconductivity with some ceramics at −405°F/−243°C; Paul Chu at the University of Houston, Texas, achieved superconductivity at −290°F/−179°C, a temperature that can be sustained using liquid nitrogen.

Some metals, such as platinum and copper, do not become superconductive; as the temperature decreases, their resistance decreases to a certain point but then rises again. Superconductivity can be nullified by the application of a large magnetic field. Superconductivity has been produced in a synthetic organic conductor that would operate at much higher temperatures, thus cutting costs. The phenomenon was discovered by the Dutch scientist, Kamerlingh Onnes (1853–1926) in 1911.

supercooling in physics, the lowering in temperature of a ◊saturated solution without crystallization taking place, forming a supersaturated solution. Usually crystallization rapidly follows the introduction of a small (seed) crystal or agitation of the supercooled solution.

superego in Freudian psychology, the element of the human mind concerned with the ideal, responsible for ethics and self-imposed standards of behavior. It is characterized as a form of conscience, restraining the ◊ego, and responsible for feelings of guilt when the moral code is broken.

supergiant the largest and most luminous type of star known, with a diameter of up to 1,000 times that of the Sun and absolute magnitudes of between −5 and −9.

Superior, Lake largest and deepest of the Great Lakes and the largest freshwater lake in the world; area about 31,700 sq mi/82,100 sq km. It is bordered by the Canadian province of Ontario and the US states of Minnesota, Wisconsin, and Michigan. As the westernmost of the Great Lakes, Superior is at the W end of the St Lawrence Seaway. Duluth, Minnesota, is the largest US city on its shores, and with its sister city, Superior, Wisconsin, it is the busiest Great Lakes port, shipping grain and iron ore to the US and Europe. Also on Lake Superior is Canada's busiest Great Lakes port, Thunder Bay, Ontario, shipping coal and grain chiefly to points in E Canada.

superior planet planet that is farther away from the Sun than the Earth. Included are all the planets from Mars outward.

Superman the first comic-strip superhero, created 1938 in the US by writer Jerome Siegel and artist Joseph Shuster, later featured in films, television, and other media. In the German philosopher ◊Nietzsche's work, his ideal future human being was the ◊*Übermensch*, or Superman.

supermarket a large self-service shop selling food and household goods. The first, Piggly-Wiggly, was introduced by US retailer Clarence Saunders in Memphis, Tennessee, 1919.

supernova the explosive death of a star; it temporarily attains a brightness of 100 million Suns or more, so that it can shine as brilliantly as a small galaxy for a few days or weeks.

Type I supernovae are thought to occur in ◊binary star systems in which gas from one star falls on to a white dwarf, causing it to explode. Type II supernovae occur in stars ten or more times as massive as the Sun, which suffer runaway internal nuclear reactions at the ends of their lives, leading to explosions. These are thought to leave behind ◊neutron stars and ◊black holes. Gas ejected by such an explosion causes an expanding radio source, such as the ◊Crab nebula. Supernovae are thought to be the main source of elements heavier than hydrogen and helium.

The last supernova occurring in our Galaxy was in 1604, but supernovae have occurred since in other galaxies. In 1987 a supernova visible to the unaided eye occurred in the Large ◊Magellanic Cloud, a small neighboring galaxy. Eta Carinae, an unusual star in the constellation Carina in the southern hemisphere, may become a supernova in a few hundred years.

superpower term used to describe the US and the USSR from the end of World War II 1945, when they emerged as significantly stronger than any other country.

supersaturation in chemistry, the state of a solution that has a higher concentration of solute than would normally be obtained in a ◊saturated solution.

Many solutes have a higher ◊solubility at high temperatures. If a hot saturated solution is cooled slowly, sometimes the excess solute does not come out of solution. This is an unstable situation and the introduction of a small solid particle will encourage the release of excess solute.

supersonic speed speed greater than that at which sound travels, measured in ◊Mach numbers. In dry air at 32°F/0°C, sound travels at about 727 mph/1,170 kph, but decreases with altitude until, at 39,000 ft/12,000 m, it is only 658 mph/1,060 kph, remaining constant below that height.

When an aircraft passes the ◊sound barrier, shock waves are built up that give rise to ◊sonic boom, often heard at ground level.

Superstring Theory in physics and astronomy, the theory that attempts to link the four ◊fundamental forces. It postulates that each force emerged separately during the expansion of the very early universe from the ◊Big Bang. It also postulates viewing matter as tiny vibrating strings instead of particles within a universe of more than the currently known four dimensions. Continuing research pursues a model based on a ten-dimensional universe, present at ◊singularity. At the Big Bang, the ten dimensions split into two components, with four dimensions expanded into the current observable universe while the other six dimensions contracted to a point in space.

supply in economics, the production of goods or services for a market in anticipation of an expected ◊demand. There is no guarantee that supply will match actual demand.

supply and demand one of the fundamental approaches to economics, which examines and compares the supply of a good with its demand (usually in the form of a graph of supply and demand curves plotted against price). For a typical good, the supply curve is upward sloping (the higher the price, the more the manufacturer is willing to sell), while the demand curve is downward-sloping (the cheaper the good, the more demand there is for it). The point where the curves intersect is the equilibrium price at which supply equals demand.

support environment in computing, a collection of programs (◊software) used to help people design and write other programs. At its simplest, this includes a text editor (word-processing software) and a ◊compiler for translating programs into executable form; but it can also include interactive debuggers for helping to locate faults, data dictionaries for keeping track of the data used, and rapid prototyping tools for producing quick, experimental mock-ups of programs.

suprarenal gland alternate name for the ◊adrenal gland.

Supremacy, Acts of two UK acts of Parliament 1534 and 1559, which established Henry VIII and Elizabeth I respectively as head of the English church in place of the pope.

Suprematism Russian abstract-art movement developed about 1913 by ◊Malevich. The Suprematist paintings gradually became more severe, until in 1918 they reached a climax with the *White on White* series showing white geometrical shapes on a white ground.

Suprematism was inspired in part by Futurist and Cubist ideas. Early paintings such as *Black Square* 1915 (Russian Museum, Leningrad) used purely geometrical shapes in bold dynamic compositions. The aims of the movement were expressed by Malevich as "the supremacy of pure feeling or perception in the pictorial arts—the expression of nonobjectivity."

Supreme Court the highest US judicial tribunal, composed since 1869, of a chief justice (William Rehnquist from 1986) and eight associate justices. Appointments are made for life by the president, with the advice and consent of the Senate, and justices can be removed only by impeachment.

The US Supreme Court hears appeals from decisions of the US Court of Appeals and from the state supreme courts. It also adjudicates questions of constitutional propriety and conflicts between the executive and legislative branches of the federal government. See also individual biographies and court decisions.

Supremes, The US vocal group, pioneers of the Motown sound, formed 1959 in Detroit. Beginning in 1962, the group was a trio comprising, initially, Diana Ross (1944–), Mary Wilson (1944–), and Florence Ballard (1943–76). One of the most successful female groups of the 1960s, they had a string of pop hits beginning with "Where Did Our Love Go?" 1964 and "Baby Love" 1964. Diana Ross left to pursue a solo career 1969.

Sur or ***Soûr*** Arabic name for the Lebanese port of ◊Tyre.

Surabaya port on the island of Java, Indonesia; population (1980) 2,028,000. It has oil refineries and shipyards and is a naval base.

Surat city in Gujarat, W India, at the mouth of the Tapti; population (1981) 913,000. The chief industry is textiles. The first East India Company trading post in India was established here 1612.

surd term for the mathematical root of a quantity that can never be exactly expressed because it is an ◊irrational number—for example, $\sqrt{3} = 1.732050808...$.

surface-area-to-volume ratio the ratio of an animal's surface area (the area covered by its skin) to its total volume. This is high for small animals, but low for large animals such as elephants.

The ratio is important for endothermic (warm-blooded) animals because the amount of heat lost by the body is proportional to its surface area, whereas the amount generated is proportional to its volume. Very small birds and mammals, such as hummingbirds and shrews, lose a lot of heat and need a high intake of food to maintain their body temperature. Elephants, on the other hand, are in danger of overheating, which is why they have no fur.

surface tension in physics, the property that causes the surface of a liquid to behave as if it were covered with a weak elastic skin; this is why a needle can float on water. It is caused by the exposed surface's tendency to contract to the smallest possible area because of unequal cohesive forces between ◊molecules at the surface. Allied phenomena include the formation of droplets, the concave profile of a meniscus, and the ◊capillary action by which water soaks into a sponge.

surfing sport of riding on the crest of large waves while standing on a narrow, keeled surfboard, usually of light synthetic material such as fiberglass, about 6 ft/1.8 m long (or 8–9 ft/2.4–7 m known as the Malibu), as first developed in Hawaii and Australia. ◊Windsurfing is a recent development.

surgeon fish any fish of the tropical marine family Acanthuridae. It has a flat body up to 1.7 ft/50 cm long, is brightly colored, and has a movable spine on each side of the tail that can be used as a weapon.

surgery in medicine, originally the removal of diseased parts or foreign substances from the body through cutting and other manual operations. It now includes such techniques as beamed high-energy ultrasonic waves, binocular magnifiers for microsurgery, and lasers.

Circumstances permitting, surgery is carried out under sterile conditions using an ◊anesthetic. There are many specialized fields, including cardiac (heart), orthopedic (bones and joints), ophthalmic (eye), neuro (brain and nerves), thoracic (chest), renal (kidney), and fetal (the developing embryo) surgery; other specialities include ◊microsurgery, cosmetic and ◊plastic surgery, and ◊transplant surgery.

Historically, surgery for abscesses, amputation, dental problems, trepanning, and childbirth were practiced by the ancient civilizations of both the Old World and the New World. During the Middle Ages, Arabic surgeons passed their techniques on to Europe, where, during the Renaissance, anatomy and physiology were pursued. By the 19th century, anesthetics and Joseph ◊Lister's discovery of antiseptics became the basis for successful surgical practices. The 20th century's use of antibiotics and blood ◊transfusions has made surgery less dangerous.

Suriname country on the northern coast of South America, on the Atlantic, between Guyana and French Guiana.

government The constitution was suspended in 1980, and in 1982 an interim president took office as head of state, with ultimate power held by the army through its Commander in Chief who is also chair of the Supreme Council, the country's controlling group. A nominated 31-member national assembly was established in Jan 1985, consisting of 14 military, 11 labor union, and 6 business

Suriname
Republic of

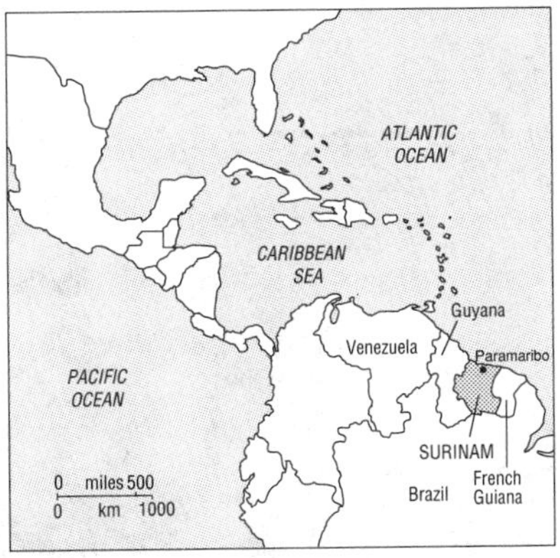
ATLANTIC OCEAN
CARIBBEAN SEA
Guyana
Venezuela
Paramaribo
PACIFIC OCEAN
SURINAM
French Guiana
Brazil
0 miles 500
0 km 1000

area 63,243 sq mi/163,820 sq km
capital Paramaribo
cities Nieuw Nickorie, Brokopondo, Nieuw Amsterdam
physical hilly and forested, with flat and narrow coastal plain
features Suriname River
head of state and government (interim) Johan Kraag from 1991
political system emergent democratic republic
political parties Party for National Unity and Solidarity (KTPI), Indonesian, left-of-center; Suriname National Party (NPS), Creole, left-of-center; Progressive Reform Party (VHP), Indian, left-of-center; members of Front for Democracy and Development (FDD)
exports alumina, alluminum, bauxite, rice, timber
currency Suriname guilder
population (1990 est) 408,000 (Hindustani 37%, Creole 31%, Javanese 15%) growth rate 1.1% p.a.
life expectancy men 66, women 71 (1989)
language Dutch (official); Sranan (Creole), English, others
religion Christian 30%, Hindu 27%, Muslim 20%
literacy 65% (1989)
GNP $1.1 bn (1987); $2,920 per head (1985)
chronology
1954 Achieved internal self-government as Dutch Guiana.
1975 Independence achieved from the Netherlands, with Dr Johan Ferrier as president and Henck Arron as prime minister; 40% of the population emigrated to the Netherlands.
1980 Arron's government overthrown in army coup; Ferrier refused to recognize military regime; appointed Dr Henk Chin A Sen to lead civilian administration. Army replaced Ferrier with Dr Chin A Sen.
1982 Army, led by Lt Col Desi Bouterse, seized power, setting up a Revolutionary People's Front.
1985 Ban on political activities lifted.
1986 Antigovernment rebels brought economic chaos to Suriname.
1987 New constitution approved.
1988 Ramsewak Shankar elected president.
1989 Bouterse rejected peace accord reached by President Shankar with guerrilla insurgents, vowed to continue fighting.
1990 Shankar deposed in army coup.
1991 Johan Kraag became interim president, serving until Ronald Venetiaan won the elections in Sept.

nominees. It was given 27 months in which to prepare a new constitution.

history For early history, see ◊American Indian, ◊South America. Founded as a colony by the English 1650, Suriname became Dutch in 1667. In 1954, as Dutch Guiana, it was made an equal member of the Kingdom of the Netherlands, with internal self-government. Full independence was achieved in 1975, with Dr Johan Ferrier as president and Henck Arron, leader of the Suriname National Party (NPS), as prime minister. In 1980 Arron's government was overthrown in an army coup, but President Ferrier refused to recognize the military regime and appointed Dr Henk Chin A Sen, of the Nationalist Republican Party, to head a civilian administration. Five months later the army staged another coup, and President Ferrier was replaced by Dr Chin A Sen. The new president announced details of a draft constitution that would reduce the army's role in government, whereupon the army, led by Lt Col Desi Bouterse, dismissed Dr Chin A Sen and set up the Revolutionary People's Front.

There followed months of confusion in which a state of siege and then martial law were imposed. From Feb 1980 to Jan 1983 there were six attempted coups by different army groups. Because of the chaos and killings of opposition leaders, Netherlands and US aid was stopped, and Bouterse turned to Libya and Cuba for assistance. The partnership among the army, the labor unions, and business, which had operated since 1981, broke up in 1985, and Bouterse turned to the traditional parties that had operated before the 1980 coup: the NPS, the left-wing Indian VHP, and the Indonesian KTPI. The ban on political activity was lifted, and leaders of the three main parties were invited to take seats on the Supreme Council, with Wym Udenhout as prime minister. The Nov 1987 election was won by the three-party FDD and Rameswak Shankar was elected president of the National Assembly. In March 1989 a new constitution was approved prior to an election in Nov. In Jan 1991 the assembly elected Johan Kraag as caretaker president, followed by Ronald Venetiaan, who won the Sept elections.

Surrealism movement in art, literature, and film that developed out of ◊Dada around 1922. Led by André ◊Breton, who produced the *Surrealist Manifesto* 1924, the Surrealists were inspired by the thoughts and visions of the subconscious mind. They explored varied styles and techniques, and the movement became the dominant force in Western art between World Wars I and II.

Surrealism followed the Freudian theory of the unconscious. In art it encompassed ◊Masson's automatic drawings, paintings based on emotive semiabstract forms (Ernst, Miró, Tanguy), and dreamlike images painted in a realistic style (Dali, Magritte). The poets Aragon and Eluard and the film-maker Buñuel were also part of the movement.

Surrey county in S England

area 641 sq mi/1,660 sq km

towns Kingston upon Thames (administrative headquarters), Guildford, Woking

features rivers: Thames, Mole, Wey; hills: Box and Leith; North Downs; Runnymede, Thameside site of the signing of ◊Magna Carta; Yehudi ◊Menuhin School; Kew Palace and Royal Botanic Gardens

products market garden vegetables, agricultural products, service industries

population (1987) 1,000,000

famous people John Galsworthy.

surrogacy the practice whereby a woman is sought, and usually paid, to bear a child for a couple or a single parent.

Surtsey a volcanic island 12 mi/20 km SW of Heimaey in the Westman Islands of Iceland. The island was created following an underwater volcanic eruption in Nov 1963.

surveying the accurate measurements of the Earth's crust, or of land features or buildings. It is used to establish boundaries, and to evaluate the topography for engineering work. The measurements used are both linear and angular, and geometry and trigonometry are applied in the calculations.

Sūrya in Hindu mythology, the Sun-god, son of the sky-god Indra. His daughter, also named Surya, is a female personification of the Sun.

Susa (French *Sousse*) port and commercial center in NE Tunisia; population (1984) 83,500. It was founded by the Phoenicians and has Roman ruins.

suslik small Eurasian ground ◊squirrel *Citellus citellus*.

suspensory ligament in the ◊eye, a ring of fiber supporting the lens.

The ligaments themselves attach to the ciliary muscles, the circle of muscle mainly responsible for changing the shape of the lens during ◊accommodation. If the ligaments are put under tension, the lens becomes flatter, and therefore able to focus on objects in the far distance.

Susquehanna river rising in central New York State, and flowing 444 mi/715 km to Chesapeake Bay. It is used for hydroelectric power. On the strength of its musical name, Samuel ◊Coleridge planned to establish a communal settlement here with his fellow poet Robert Southey.

Sussex former county of England, on the S coast, now divided into ◊East Sussex and ◊West Sussex.

According to tradition, the Saxon Ella landed here 477, defeated the inhabitants, and founded the kingdom of the South Saxons, which was absorbed by Wessex 825.

sustained-yield cropping in ecology, the removal of surplus individuals from a ◊population of organisms so that the population maintains a constant size. This usually requires selective removal of animals of all ages and both sexes to ensure a balanced population structure. Excessive cropping of young females, for example, may lead to fewer births in following years, and a fall in population size. Appropriate cropping frequencies can be determined from an analysis of a ◊life table.

Sutherland Donald 1934– . Canadian-born US film actor who usually appears in offbeat roles. He starred in *M*A*S*H* 1970, and his subsequent films include *Klute* 1971, *Don't Look Now* 1973, and *Revolution* 1986. He is the father of actor Kiefer Sutherland.

Sutherland Earl Wilbur Jr 1915–1974. US physiologist, discoverer of cyclic AMP, a chemical "messenger" made by a special enzyme in the wall of living cells. Many hormones operate by means of this messenger. Nobel Prize for Medicine 1971.

Sutherland Graham (Vivian) 1903–1980. English painter, graphic artist, and designer, active mainly in France from the late 1940s. He painted portraits, landscapes, and religious subjects.

In the late 1940s Sutherland turned increasingly to characterful portraiture. His portrait of *Winston Churchill* 1954 was disliked by its subject and eventually burned on the instructions of Lady Churchill (studies survive).

Sutherland Joan 1926– . Australian soprano. She went to England in 1951, where she made her debut the next year in *The Magic Flute*; later roles included *Lucia di Lammermoor*, Donna Anna in *Don Giovanni*, and Desdemona in *Otello*. She retired from the stage in 1990.

She usually performed under the baton of her husband, conductor Richard Bonynge.

Sutlej river in Pakistan, a tributary of the river ◊Indus; length 851 mi/1,370 km.

sūtra in Buddhism, discourse attributed to the historical Buddha. In Hinduism, the term generally describes any sayings that contain moral instruction.

suttee Hindu custom whereby a widow committed suicide by joining her husband's funeral pyre, often under public and family pressure. Banned in the 17th century by the Mogul Emperors, the custom continued even after it was made illegal under British rule 1829. There continue to be sporadic revivals.

Sutton Hoo archeological site in Suffolk, England, where in 1939 a Saxon ship burial was excavated. It is the funeral monument of Raedwald, king of the East Angles, who died about 624 or 625. The jewelry, armor, and weapons discovered were placed in the British Museum, London.

suture any thread or wire used in surgery to stitch

***Sutherland** British artist Graham Sutherland's* Study for Origins of the Land *1950 Courtauld Collection, London.*

***Suzhou** The Tiger Hill Pagoda near Suzhon, China. Built in 961, it is 5° out of perpendicular, making the top about 6 ft (2 m) out from the vertical.*

together the edges of a wound or incision. Also, the stitch itself.

Suva capital and industrial port of Fiji, on Viti Levu; population (1981) 68,000. It produces soap and coconut oil.

Suvorov Aleksandr Vasilyevich 1729–1800. Russian field marshal, victorious against the Turks 1787–91, the Poles 1794, and the French army in Italy 1798–99 in the Revolutionary Wars.

Suzhou or *Soochow*; formerly ***Wuhsien*** (1912–49) city S of the Yangtze River delta and E of the ◊Grand Canal, in Jiangsu province, China; population (1983) 670,000. It has embroidery and jade-carving traditions and Shizilin and Zhuozheng gardens. The city dates from about 1000 BC, and the name Suzhou from the 7th century AD; it was reputedly visited by the Venetian Marco ◊Polo.

Suzman Helen 1917– . South African politician and human-rights activist. A university lecturer concerned about the inhumanity of the apartheid system, she joined the white opposition to the ruling National Party and became a strong advocate of racial equality, respected by black communities inside and outside South Africa. In 1978 she received the United Nations Human Rights Award. She retired from active politics in 1989.

Suzuki Zenkō 1911– . Japanese politician. Originally a Socialist member of the Diet in 1947, he became a conservative (Liberal Democrat) in 1949, and was prime minister 1980–82.

Svalbard Norwegian archipelago in the Arctic Ocean. The main island is Spitsbergen; other islands include North East Land, Edge Island, Barents Island, and Prince Charles Foreland.
area 23,938 sq mi/62,000 sq km
towns Long Year City on Spitsbergen
features weather and research stations. Wildlife includes walrus and polar bear; fossil palms show that it was in the tropics 40 million years ago
products coal, phosphates, asbestos, iron ore, and galena—all mined by the USSR and Norway
population (1982) 4,000; 62% Russian, 36% Norwegian
history under the Svalbard Treaty 1925, Norway has sovereignty, but allows free scientific and economic access to others.

Svedberg Theodor 1884–1971. Swedish chemist. In 1924 he constructed the first ultracentrifuge, a machine that allowed the rapid separation of particles by mass. Nobel Prize for Chemistry 1926.

Svengali a person who molds another into a performer and masterminds his or her career. The original Svengali was a character in the novel *Trilby* 1894 by George ◊Du Maurier.

Sverdlovsk formerly ***Ekaterinburg*** (until 1924) industrial town in W USSR, in the E foothills of the Urals; population (1987) 1,331,000. Industries include copper, iron, platinum, engineering, and chemicals. Tsar ◊Nicholas II and his family were murdered here 1918.

Svetambara ("white-clad") a sect of Jain monks (see ◊Jainism) who wear white loincloths, as opposed to the *Digambaras* sect which believes that total nudity is correct for the Jain monk.

Svevo Italo. Adopted name of Ettore Schmitz 1861–1928. Italian novelist whose books include *As a Man Grows Older* 1898 and *Confessions of Zeno* 1923.

Swabia (German *Schwaben*) historic region of SW Germany, an independent duchy in the Middle Ages. It includes Augsburg and Ulm and forms part of the *Länder* (states) of Baden-Württemberg, Bavaria, and Hessen.

Swahili member of an African people inhabiting Zanzibar and adjoining coastal areas of Kenya and Tanzania. The Swahili are not an isolated group, but are part of a mixed coastal society engaged in fishing and trading.

The Swahili language belongs to the N Bantu group of the Niger-Congo family. It contains many Arabic roots and is used as a lingua franca in many parts of Africa.

Swahili language language of Bantu origin and strongly influenced by Arabic, a widespread ◊lingua franca of E Africa and the national language of Tanzania (1967) and Kenya (1973).

swallow any bird of the family Hirundinidae, of small, insect-eating birds in the order Passeriformes, with long, narrow wings and deeply forked tails. Swallows feed while flying.

Species include the barn swallow *Hirundo rustica* and the purple martin *Progne subis*.

swami title of respect for a Hindu teacher.

swamp permanently or periodically waterlogged tract of wet, spongy land, often overgrown with plant growth.

swan several large, long-necked, aquatic, web-footed birds of the family Anatidae, which also includes ducks and geese.

Species include the Old World mute swan *Cygnus olor*, with all-white plumage, now introduced in parks worldwide; the black swan of Australia, *Cygnus atratus*. The North American trumpeter swan *Cygnus buccinator* is the largest, with a wingspan of 8 ft/2.4 m. This species was nearly extinct by 1900, and although numbers have recovered, it is still endangered. Pairing is generally for life, and the young are called cygnets.

Swann v Charlotte-Mecklenburg Board of Education a US Supreme Court decision 1971 dealing with methods of court-ordered desegregation in public schools. The Court unanimously upheld a district court order implementing its own desegregation plan after the school board's proved unsatisfactory. Among the methods judged legitimate in the forced desegregation of delinquent school systems were busing, racial quotas, and the rearrangement of school districts.

Swansea (Welsh *Abertawe*) port and administrative headquarters of West Glamorgan, S Wales, at the mouth of the river Tawe where it meets the Bristol Channel; population (1981) 168,000. It has oil refineries and metallurgical industries.

Swanson Gloria. Adopted name of Gloria Josephine Mae Svenson 1897–1983. US actress, a star of silent films who influenced American tastes and fashion for more than 20 years. She was second only to Mary Pickford in fame and in 1926 she formed her own production company with Joseph Kennedy as her financial backer. She retired in 1932 but made several major comebacks. Her work includes *Sadie Thompson* 1928, *Queen Kelly* 1928 (unfinished), and *Sunset Boulevard* 1950, for which she received an Academy Award nomination.

SWAPO (South West Africa People's Organization) organization formed 1959 in South West Africa (now ◊Namibia) to oppose South African rule. SWAPO guerrillas, led by Sam Nujoma, began attacking with support from Angola. In 1966 SWAPO was recognized by the United Nations

Swaziland
Kingdom of

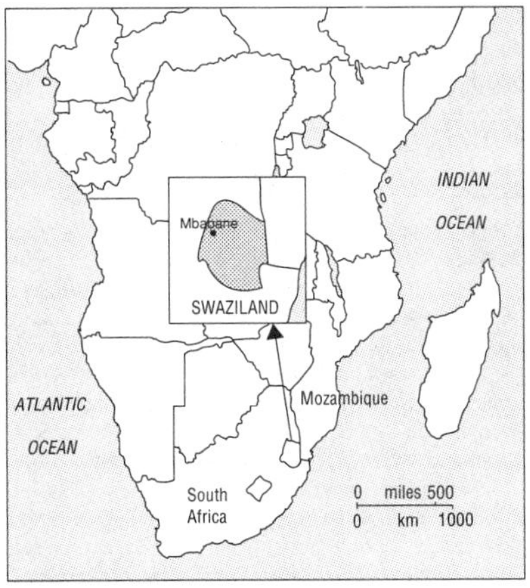
INDIAN
OCEAN
Mbabane
SWAZILAND
ATLANTIC
OCEAN
Mozambique
South
Africa
0 miles 500
0 km 1000

area 6,716 sq mi/17,400 sq km
capital Mbabane
cities Manzini, Big Bend
physical central valley; mountains in W (Highveld); plateau in E (Lowveld and Lubombo plateau)
features landlocked enclave between South Africa and Mozambique
head of state and government King Mswati III from 1986
political system near-absolute monarchy
political parties Imbokodvo National Movement (INM), nationalistic monarchist
exports sugar, canned fruit, woodpulp, asbestos
currency lilangeni
population (1990 est) 779,000; growth rate 3% p.a.
life expectancy men 47, women 54 (1989)
language Swazi 90%, English (both official)
religion Christian 57%; animist
literacy men 70%/women 66% (1985 est)
GNP $539 mn; $750 per head (1987)
chronology
1903 Swaziland became a special High Commission territory.
1967 Achieved internal self-government.
1968 Independence achieved from Britain, within the Commonwealth, as the Kingdom of Swaziland, with King Sobhuza II as head of state.
1973 The king suspended constitution and assumed absolute powers.
1978 New constitution adopted.
1982 King Sobhuza died, and his place was taken by one of his wives, Dzeliewe, until his son, Prince Makhosetive, reached the age of 21.
1983 Queen Dzeliewe ousted by another wife, Ntombi.
1984 After royal power struggle, it was announced that the crown prince would become king at 18.
1986 Crown prince formally invested as King Mswati III.
1987 Power struggle developed between advisory council Liqoqo and Queen Ntombi over accession of king. Mswati dissolved parliament; new government elected with Sotsha Dlamini as prime minister.

as the legitimate government of Namibia and won the first independent election 1989.

swastika (Sanskrit "svastika") cross in which the bars are extended at right angles in the same clockwise or counterclockwise direction. An ancient good-luck symbol in both the New and the Old Worlds and an Aryan and Buddhist mystic sign, it was adopted by Hitler as the emblem of the Nazi Party and incorporated into the German national flag 1935–45.

Swatow another name for the Chinese port of ◊Shantou.

Swazi member of the majority group of people in Swaziland. The Swazi are primarily engaged in cultivating and raising livestock, but many work in industries in South Africa. The Swazi language belongs to the Bantu branch of the Niger-Congo family.

Swazi kingdom Southern African kingdom, established by Sobhuza I (died 1839), and named after his successor Mswati (ruled 1840–75).

Swaziland country in SE Africa, bounded by Mozambique and the Transvaal province of South Africa.

government Swaziland is a monarchy within the ◊Commonwealth. Under the 1978 constitution the monarch is head of both state and of government, and chooses the prime minister and cabinet. There is a two-chamber legislature, the *Libandla*, consisting of a 20-member Senate and a 50-member House of Assembly. Ten senators are appointed by the sovereign and ten elected by and from an 80-member electoral college, made up of two representatives from each of the country's 40 chieftancies (*Tinkhundla*). Forty of the House of Assembly deputies are also elected by the electoral college, with the remaining ten appointed by the monarch.

The constitution makes the Imbokodvo National Movement (INM) the only legal political party, although there are at least three opposition groups based outside Swaziland.

history For early history, see ◊South Africa. Its original autonomy was guaranteed by Britain and the Transvaal, and Swaziland became a special High Commission territory in 1903. The South African government repeatedly asked for Swaziland to be placed under its jurisdiction, but this call was resisted by the British government as well as by the people of Swaziland. In 1967 the country was granted internal self-government and 1968 full independence within the Commonwealth, with King Sobhuza II as head of state. In 1973 the king suspended the constitution and assumed absolute powers. In 1978 the new constitution was announced.

King Sobhuza died in 1982, and the role of head of state passed to the queen mother, Dzeliwe, until the king's heir, Prince Makhosetive, should reach the age of 21 in 1989, but a power struggle developed within the royal family. Queen Dzeliwe was ousted by another of King Sobhuza's wives, Ntombi, who became queen regent in Oct 1983, and in April 1986 the crown prince was formally invested as King Mswati III. He has a supreme advisory body, the *Liqoqo*, all of whose 11 members are appointed by him. By June 1987 a power struggle had developed between the *Liqoqo* and Queen Ntombi over the accession of her son, Mswati III.

Swaziland needs to maintain good relations with South Africa as well as with other African states, and this has often been difficult, since the formerly banned African National Congress (ANC) has tried to use it as a base.

sweat gland gland within the skin of mammals that produces surface perspiration. In primates, sweat glands are distributed over the whole body, but in most other mammals they are more localized; for example, in cats and dogs, they are restricted to the feet and around the face.

sweatshop a workshop or factory where employees work long hours under substandard conditions for low wages. Exploitation of labor in this way is associated with unscrupulous employers, who often employ illegal immigrants in their labor force, or children. At the turn of the century, women were employed on a large scale, since they would work for less money than men. Such exploitation led to the rise of labor unions and the labor movement.

Sweatt v Painter a US Supreme Court decision 1950 dealing with racial discrimination in publicly funded schools. Herman Sweatt, a black prospective law student, filed the suit against administrators of the University of Texas after being denied admission because of his race. The defendants argued that a separate law school for blacks was soon to be opened. The Court maintained the separate but equal doctrine but ruled that the black law school was decidedly inferior to the white one. The university was found guilty of violating the equal protection clause of the 14th Amendment.

Sweden country in N Europe on the Baltic Sea, bounded W by Norway and NE by Finland.

government Sweden has a hereditary monarch as formal head of state and a popularly elected government. The constitution from 1809, several times amended, is based on four fundamental laws: the Instrument of Government Act, the Act of Succession, the Freedom of the Press Act, and the *Riksdag* Act. The *Riksdag* is a single-chamber parliament of 349 members, elected by universal suffrage, through a system of proportional representation, for a three-year term.

The prime minister is nominated by the Speaker of the *Riksdag* and confirmed by a vote of the whole house. The prime minister chooses a cabinet, and all are then responsible to the *Riksdag*. The king or queen now has a purely formal role; the normal duties of a constitutional monarch, such as dissolving parliament and deciding who should be asked to form an administration, are undertaken by the Speaker.

history S Sweden has been inhabited since about 6000 BC. The Swedish Vikings in AD 800–1060 sailed mainly to the E and founded the principality of ◊Novgorod. In the mid-12th century the Swedes in the N were united with the Goths in the S and accepted Christianity. A series of crusades from the 12th to the 14th centuries brought Finland under Swedish rule. Sweden, Norway, and Denmark were united under a Danish dynasty 1397–1520. ◊Gustavus Vasa was subsequently elected king of Sweden; he established Lutheranism as the state religion 1527. The Vasa line ruled until 1818, when the French marshal Bernadotte established the present dynasty.

Sweden's territorial ambitions led to warfare in Europe from the 16th to the 18th centuries (see ◊Gustavus Adolphus, ◊Thirty Years' War, ◊Charles X, ◊Charles XII) which left the country impoverished. Science and culture flourished under Gustavus III 1771–91. Sweden lost Finland to Russia 1809 but seized Norway 1814, a union dissolved 1905.

Sweden has a long tradition of neutrality and political stability and a highly developed social welfare system. The office of ombudsman is a Swedish invention, and Sweden was one of the first countries to adopt a system of open government.

The Social Democratic Labor Party (SAP) was continuously in power 1951–76, usually in coalition. In 1969 the leadership of the party changed hands, and Olof Palme became prime minister. He carried out two major reforms of the constitution, reducing the chambers in parliament from two to one 1971 and 1975 removing the last of the monarch's constitutional powers. In 1976 the general election was fought on the issue of the level of taxation needed to fund the welfare system, and Palme was defeated. Thorbjorn

Sweden

Kingdom of
(Konungariket Sverige)

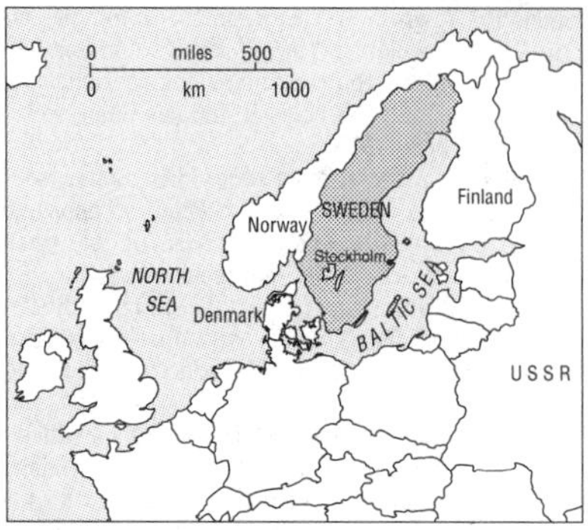
0 miles 500
0 km 1000
Finland
Norway
SWEDEN
Stockholm
NORTH SEA
Denmark
BALTIC SEA
USSR

area 173,745 sq mi/450,000 sq km
capital Stockholm
cities Göteborg, Malmö, Uppsala, Norrköping, Västerås
physical mountains in W; plains in S; thickly forested; more than 20,000 islands off the Stockholm coast
features lakes, including Vänern, Vättern, Mälaren, Hjälmaren; islands of Öland and Gotland; wild elk
head of state Carl XVI Gustaf from 1973
head of government Ingvar Carlsson from 1986
political system constitutional monarchy
political parties Social Democratic Labor party (SAP), moderate, left-of-center; Moderate Party, right-of-center; Liberal Party, center-left; Centre Party, centrist; Christian Democratic Party, Christian, centrist; Left (Communist) Party, European, Marxist; Green, ecological
exports aircraft, vehicles, ballbearings, drills, missiles, electronics, petrochemicals, textiles, furnishings, ornamental glass, paper, iron and steel
currency krona
population (1990 est) 8,407,000 (including 17,000 Lapps and 1.2 million postwar immigrants from Finland, Turkey, Yugoslavia, Greece, Iran, other Nordic countries); growth rate 0.1% p.a.
life expectancy men 74, women 81 (1989)
language Swedish; Finnish and Lapp-speaking minorities
religion Lutheran (official) 95%
literacy 99% (1989)
GNP $179 bn; $11,783 per head (1989)
chronology
12th century United as an independent nation.
1397–1520 Under Danish rule.
1914–45 Neutral in both world wars.
1951–76 Social Democratic Labor Party (SAP) in power.
1969 Olof Palme became SAP leader and prime minister.
1971 Constitution amended, creating a single-chamber *Riksdag*, the governing body.
1975 Monarch's constitutional powers reduced.
1976 Thorbjörn Fälldin, leader of the Centre Party, became prime minister, heading center-right coalition.
1982 SAP, led by Palme, returned to power.
1985 SAP formed minority government, with Communist support.
1986 Olof Palme murdered. Ingvar Carlsson became prime minister and SAP party leader.
1988 SAP re-elected with reduced majority; Green Party increased its vote dramatically.
1990 SAP government resigned. Sweden to apply for European Community membership.
1991 Formal application for EC membership submitted.

Fälldin, leader of the Centre Party, formed a center-right coalition government. The Fälldin administration fell 1978 over its wish to follow a nonnuclear energy policy, and it was replaced by a minority Liberal government led by Ola Ullsten. Fälldin returned 1979, heading another coalition, and in a referendum the following year there was a narrow majority in favor of continuing with a limited nuclear-energy program. Fälldin remained in power until 1982, when the Social Democrats, with Olof Palme, returned with a minority government. Palme was soon faced with deterioriating relations with the USSR, arising from suspected violation of Swedish territorial waters by Soviet submarines. The situation had improved substantially by 1985. After the general election in that year, Palme's party had 159 *Riksdag* seats, and he was able to continue with Communist support. The Moderate Party won. In Feb 1986, Olof Palme was murdered by an unknown assailant in the center of Stockholm. A suspect was arrested and convicted, but freed upon appeal. Palme's deputy, Ingvar Carlsson, took over as prime minister and leader of the SAP. In the Sept 1988 general election Carlsson and the SAP were reelected with a reduced majority. The Green Party won enough votes to gain representation in the *Riksdag*, the first new party to gain a seat in 70 years. In Feb 1990, with mounting opposition to its economic policies, the government resigned, leaving Carlsson as a caretaker prime minister. In Dec the *Riksdag* supported the government's decision to apply for EC membership. Elections in Sept 1991 led to the defeat of Carlsson's government. He was succeeded as prime minister by Carl Bildt.

Swedenborg Emanuel 1688–1772. Swedish theologian and philosopher. He trained as a scientist, but from 1747 concentrated on scriptural study, and in *Divine Love and Wisdom* 1763 concluded that the Last Judgment had taken place in 1757, and that the New Church, of which he was the prophet, had now been inaugurated. His writings are the scriptures of the sect popularly known as Swedenborgians, and his works are kept in circulation by the Swedenborg Society, London.

Swedish architecture the style of building in Sweden.

medieval The Romanesque cathedrals of Uppsala (brick) and Lund (stone) are from the 11th century. Gothic churches include Riddarholms church in Stockholm and the cathedral in Linköping. The former Hanseatic city of Visby, Gotland, has three Gothic churches and the ruins of 12 more; some medieval domestic buildings have also survived there within the old city wall.

Swedish art painting and sculpture of Sweden. A geometrically stylized dragon ornament characterized Swedish art and crafts before and during the Viking period. Bright and cheerful folk art flourished in church and secular decorations from the Middle Ages into the 19th century. Although the main movements in European art have successively taken hold in Sweden, artists have repeatedly returned to a national tradition.

5000–500 BC Animal pictures carved in or painted on rock can be found in central Sweden.

500 BC–11th century AD Bronze and gold jewelry; memorial stones carved with runes and ornaments.

12th–16th centuries Woven tapestries show the geometrically stylized animals that also occur in jewelry and carvings. Churches were decorated with lively, richly ornamented frescoes. Wooden sculptures were initially stiff and solemn, later more realistic and expressive.

17th century Sculptors and portrait painters who had studied Italian Baroque were patronized by Sweden's rulers.

18th century Swedish Rococo was more restrained than its French models; chinoiserie was popular because of Swedish trade with the orient. Alexander Roslin (1718–1793) was one of several portrait painters who continued their career in France. Rococo was supplanted toward the end of the century by a light Neo-Classical style known as Gustavian. The sculptor J T Sergel based his strong, sensual work on studies of ancient art in Rome.

19th century Academic history painting was superseded by the work of artists influenced by the French Impressionists and by the nationalist spirit current in many countries. The watercolor interiors by Carl Larsson (1853–1919) of his home were very popular. Anders Zorn (1860–1920) loved color and nudes. Bruno Liljefors (1860–1939) specialized in paintings of animals.

early 20th century The Romantic nationalist Jugend style can be seen in the monumental sculptures of Carl Milles (1875–1955) throughout Sweden and in the US. Albert Engström (1869–1940) was a prolific illustrator and cartoonist. Nils von Dardel (1888–1943) was an early Surrealist painter.

late 20th century Figurative art predominated, ranging from the dreamlike, symbolic paintings of Lena Cronqvist, Åosa Moberg, and others to the realistic still-life graphics of Philip von Schantz (1928–).

Swedish language member of the Germanic branch of the Indo-European language family, spoken in Sweden and Finland and closely related to Danish and Norwegian.

sweet cicely plant *Myrrhis odorata* of the carrot family Umbelliferae, native to S Europe; the root is eaten as a vegetable, and the aniseed-flavored leaves are used in salads.

Also, one of several North American plants (genus *Osmorhiza*) of the same family with clusters of small white flowers.

sweet pea plant of the ◊pea family.

sweet potato tropical American plant *Ipomea batatas* of the morning-glory family Convolvulaceae; the white-orange tuberous root is used as a source of starch and alcohol and eaten as a vegetable.

sweet william biennial to perennial plant *Dianthus barbatus* of the pink family Caryophyllaceae, native to S Europe. It is grown for its fragrant red, white, and pink flowers.

Sweyn I died 1014. King of Denmark from c. 986, and nicknamed "Forkbeard." He raided England, finally conquered it in 1013, and styled himself king, but his early death led to the return of ◊Ethelred II.

swift any fast-flying, short-legged bird of the family Apodidae, of which there are about 75 species, found largely in the tropics. They are 4–11 in/9–23 cm long, with brown or gray plumage, long, pointed wings, and usually a forked tail. They are capable of flying 70 mph/110 kph.

The chimney swift *Chaetura pelagica*, which breeds in North America, is 5.5 in/13 cm long, with a cigar-shaped body and a short, stubby, superficially unforked tail.

Swift Jonathan 1667–1745. Irish satirist and Anglican cleric, author of *Gulliver's Travels* 1726, an allegory describing travel to lands inhabited by giants, miniature people, and intelligent horses. Other works include *The Tale of a Tub* 1704, attacking corruption in religion and learning; contributions to the Tory paper *The Examiner*, of which he was editor 1710–11; the satirical *A Modest Proposal* 1729, which suggested that children of the poor should be eaten; and many essays and pamphlets.

Swift, born in Dublin, became secretary to the diplomat William Temple (1628–1699) at Moor Park, Surrey, where his friendship with the child "Stella" (Hester Johnson 1681–1728) began in 1689. Returning to Ireland, he was ordained in the Church of England 1694, and in 1699 was made a prebendary of St Patrick's, Dublin. In 1710 he became a Tory pamphleteer, and obtained the deanery of St Patrick in 1713. His *Journal to Stella* is a series of letters, 1710–13, in which he described his life in London. "Stella" remained the love of his life, but "Vanessa" (Esther Vanhomrigh 1690–1723), a Dublin woman who had fallen in love with him, jealously wrote to her rival in 1723 and so shattered his relationship with both women. From about 1738 his mind began to fail.

***Swift** Irish satirist Jonathan Swift published his work anonymously, except for* Gulliver's Travels, *the only work for which he received payment.*

Swift and Co v US a US Supreme Court decision 1905 dealing with federal regulation of local business transactions. When the meatpacking industry colluded to fix the price of fresh meat in Chicago, the federal government issued an injunction against price fixing. The beef trust appealed, arguing that local commerce was outside of federal jurisdiction. The Court upheld the injunction, ruling that, since the local transaction affected businesses that participated in interstate trade, the federal government had the power to regulate it.

swim bladder thin-walled, air-filled sac found between the gut and the spine in bony fishes. Air enters the bladder from the gut or from surrounding ◊capillaries, and changes of air pressure within the bladder maintain buoyancy whatever the water depth.

In evolutionary terms, the swim bladder of higher fishes is a derivative of the lungs present in all primitive fishes (not just lungfishes).

swimming self-propulsion of the body through water. As a competitive sport there are four strokes: crawl, breaststroke, backstroke, and butterfly. (In freestyle events, the crawl is usually used, since it is the "fastest" stroke for most swimmers; but any stroke may be used). Distances of races vary from 20 yds up to the mile or more. Swimming meets are held in pools and at beach clubs (for the events longer than the mile).

Swimming has been known since ancient times, and was part of the training of Greek and Roman warriors. Competitive swimming is known to have taken place in Japan 36 BC, and became compulsory in schools there in 1603. Fear of infection prevented Europeans from swimming during the Middle Ages, but during the late 19th century swimming pools with chlorine as a disinfectant began to be built at major schools and universities. By the early 20th century in the US, public pools were features of parks and clubs, and swimming, diving, and water polo were part of the sports revival that gave pleasure to the leisured classes. Swimming has become a popular pastime and competitive sport for age-grade, school, amateur, and senior contestants in all parts of the US.

swingwing

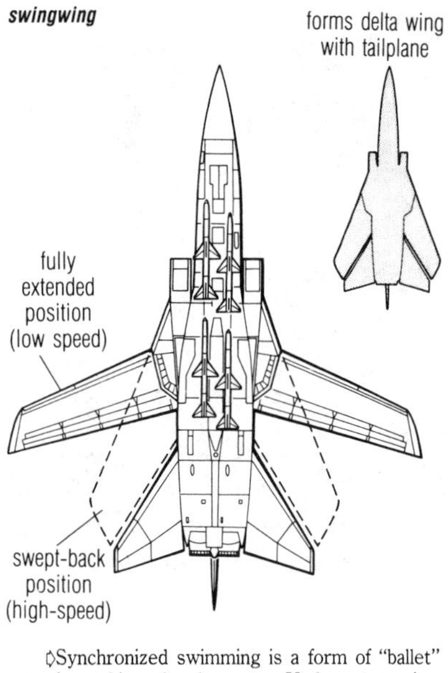
forms delta wing
with tailplane
fully
extended
position
(low speed)
swept-back
position
(high-speed)

◊Synchronized swimming is a form of "ballet" performed in and under water. Underwater swimming developed with the invention of such equipment as flippers, snorkel, and self-contained underwater breathing apparatus (scuba). See also ◊diving. Swimming has been included in the Olympic Games since 1896 for men and 1912 for women. The world championships were introduced in 1973, later held in 1975 and 1978 and every four years since.

Swinburne Algernon Charles 1837–1909. English poet. He attracted attention with the choruses of his Greek-style tragedy *Atalanta in Calydon* 1865, but he and ◊Rossetti were attacked in 1871 as leaders of "the fleshly school of poetry," and the revolutionary politics of *Songs before Sunrise* 1871 alienated others.

swine flu virulent, highly contagious form of influenza, infecting swine and communicable to people.

swine vesicular disease virus disease (porcine enterovirus) closely resembling foot and mouth disease, and communicable to humans. It may have originated in the infection of pigs by a virus that causes flulike symptoms in people.

swing music jazz style popular in the 1930s–40s. A big-band sound with a simple harmonic base of varying tempo from the rhythm section (percussion, guitar, piano), harmonic brass and woodwind sections (sometimes strings), and superimposed solo melodic line from, for example, trumpet, clarinet, or saxophone. Exponents included Benny Goodman, Duke Ellington, and Glenn Miller, who introduced jazz to a mass white audience.

swingwing correctly ***variable-geometry wing*** aircraft wing that can be moved during flight to provide a suitable configuration for either low-speed or high-speed flight. The British engineer Barnes ◊Wallis developed the idea of the swingwing, first used on the US-built Northrop X-4, and now used in several aircraft, including the US F-111, F-114, and the B-1, the European Tornado, and several Soviet-built aircraft. These craft have their wings projecting nearly at right angles for takeoff and landing and low-speed flight, and swung back for high-speed flight.

Swinton Ernest 1868–1951. British soldier and historian. He served in South Africa and in World War I, and was the inventor of the tank in 1916.

Swiss Family Robinson, The a children's adventure story by Swiss author Johann Wyss, first published in German 1812–13 and expanded by subsequent editors and translators. Modeled on Defoe's *Robinson Crusoe*, it tells of a Swiss family shipwrecked on a desert island and the lessons taught to the children by their adventures there.

Switzerland landlocked country in W Europe, bounded N by Germany, E by Austria, S by Italy, and W by France.

government Switzerland is a federation of 20 cantons and 6 half-cantons (canton is the name for a political division, derived from Old French). The constitution dates from 1874 and provides for a two-chamber federal assembly, consisting of the National Council and the Council of States. The National Council has 200 members, elected by universal suffrage, through a system of proportional representation, for a four-year term. The Council of States has 46 members, each canton electing two representatives and each half-canton one. Members of the Council of States are elected for three or four years, depending on the constitutions of the individual cantons.

The federal government is in the hands of the Federal Council, consisting of seven members elected for a four-year term by the assembly, each heading a specific federal department. The federal assembly also appoints one member to act as federal head of state and head of government for a year, the term of office beginning on Jan 1. The federal government is allocated specific powers by the constitution with the remaining powers left with the cantons, each having has its own constitution, assembly, and government. At a level below the cantons are more than 3,000 communes, whose populations range from fewer than 20 to 350,000. Direct democracy is encouraged through communal assemblies and referenda.

history The region was settled by peoples that the Romans called Helvetians or Transalpine Gauls, and it became a province of the Roman empire after Julius Caesar's conquest. In 1291 the cantons of Schwyz, Uri, and Lower Unterwalden formed the Everlasting League to defend their liberties against their ◊Hapsburg overlords. More towns and districts joined them, and there were 13 cantons by 1513. The Reformation was accepted during 1523–29 by Zürich, Berne, and Basel, but the rural cantons remained Catholic. Switzerland gradually won more freedom from Hapsburg control until its complete independence was recognized by the Treaty of ◊Westphalia 1648.

A peasant uprising 1653 was suppressed. A French invasion 1798 established the Helvetic Republic with a centralized government; this was modified by Napoleon's Act of Mediation 1803, which made Switzerland a democratic federation. The Congress of ◊Vienna 1815 guaranteed Swiss neutrality, and Switzerland received Geneva and other territories, increasing the number of cantons to 22. After a civil war between the *Sonderbund* (a union of the Catholic cantons Lucerne, Zug, Freiburg, and Valais) and the Liberals, a revised federal constitution, giving the central government wide powers, was introduced 1848; a further revision 1874 increased its powers and introduced the principle of the referendum.

Switzerland, for centuries a neutral country, has been the base for many international organizations and the host of many international peace conferences. A referendum 1986 rejected the advice of the government and came out overwhelmingly against membership of the United Nations. Its domestic politics have been characterized by coalition governments and a stability that has enabled it to become one of the world's richest countries (per person).

Of several political parties, the most significant are the Radical Democratic Party, the Social Democratic Party, the Christian Democratic Party, the People's Party, and the Liberal Party. Women were not allowed to vote in federal elections until 1971. The first female cabinet minister was appointed 1984. After the Oct 1987 election, the four-party coalition continued in power, although there was a significant increase in the number of seats held by the Green Party. In 1989, a referendum found widespread dissatisfaction with the citizen army and military service requirements. In Aug 1991 the country celebrated its 700th anniversary.

swordfish marine bony fish *Xiphias gladius*, the only member of its family (Xiphiidae), characterized by a long swordlike beak protruding from the upper jaw. It may reach 15 ft/4.5 m in length and weigh 1000 lb/450 kg.

Switzerland

Swiss Confederation
(German *Schweiz*, French *Suisse*, Romansch *Svizzera*)

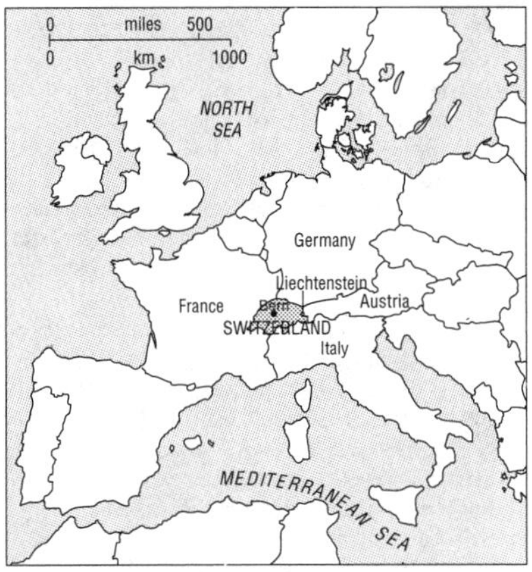
0 miles 500
0 km 1000
NORTH SEA
Germany
Liechtenstein
France
Bern
Austria
SWITZERLAND
Italy
MEDITERRANEAN SEA

area 15,946 sq mi/41,300 sq km
capital Bern
cities Zürich, Geneva, Lausanne; river port Basel (on the Rhine)
physical most mountainous country in Europe (Alps and Jura mountains); highest peak Dufourspitze 15,203 ft/4,634 m in Apennines
features winter sports area of the upper valley of the river Inn (Engadine); lakes Maggiore, Lucerne, Geneva. Constance
head of state and government Flavio Cotti from 1991
government federal democratic republic
political parties Radical Democratic Party (FDP), radical, center-left; Social Democratic party (SPS), moderate, left-of-center; Christian Democratic Party (PDC), Christian, moderate, centrist; People's Party (SVP), center-left; Liberal Party (PLS), federalist, center-left; Green Party, ecological
exports electrical goods, chemicals, pharmaceuticals, watches, precision instruments, confectionery
currency Swiss franc
population (1990 est) 6,628,000; growth rate 0.2% p.a.
life expectancy men 74, women 82 (1989)
language German 65%, French 18%, Italian 12%, Romansch 1% (all official)
religion Roman Catholic 50%, Protestant 48%
literacy 99% (1989)
GNP $111 bn (1988); $26,309 per head (1987)
chronology
1648 Became independent of the Holy Roman Empire.
1798–1815 Helvetic Republic established by French Revolutionary armies.
1847 Civil war resulted in greater centralization.
1971 Women given the vote in federal elections.
1984 First female cabinet minister appointed.
1986 Referendum rejected proposal for membership of United Nations.
1989 Referendum supported abolition of citizen army and military service requirements.

sycamore

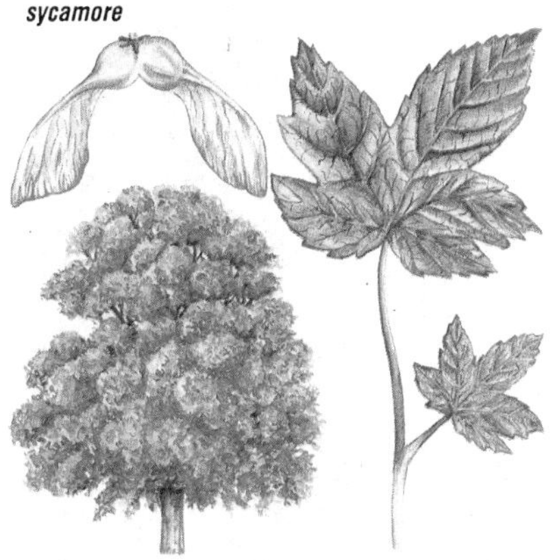

sycamore or ***plane tree*** Eurasian trees of the genus *Platanus* of the family Plantanaceae. Species include the oriental plant *P. orientalis*, a favorite tree of the Greeks and Romans; the American sycamore *P. occidentalis* of the E US; and the Arizona sycamore *P. Wrightii*. All species have pendulous burlike fruits and some grow to 100 ft/ 30 m high.

Sydenham Thomas 1624–1689. English physician, the first person to describe measles and to recommend the use of quinine for relieving symptoms of malaria. His original reputation as "the English Hippocrates" rested upon his belief that careful observation is more useful than speculation. His *Observationes medicae* was published in 1676.

Sydney capital and port of New South Wales, Australia; population (1986) 3,431,000. Industries include engineering, oil refining, electronics, scientific equipment, chemicals, clothing, and furniture. It is a financial center, and has three universities. The 19th-century Museum of Applied Arts and Sciences is the most popular museum in Australia.

Originally a British penal colony 1788, Sydney developed rapidly following the discovery of gold in the surrounding area. The main streets still follow the lines of the original wagon tracks, and the Regency Bligh House survives. Modern landmarks are the harbor bridge (single span 1,652 ft/ 503.5 m) 1923–32, Opera House 1959–73, Centre Point Tower 1980.

Sydow Max von (Carl Adolf) 1929– . Swedish actor associated with the director Ingmar Bergman. He made his US debut as Jesus in *The Greatest Story Ever Told* 1965. His other films include *The Seventh Seal* 1957, *The Exorcist* 1973, and *Hannah and her Sisters* 1985.

syenite a gray, crystalline, plutonic (intrusive) ◊igneous rock, consisting of feldspar and hornblende; other minerals may also be present, including small amounts of quartz.

Sykes Percy Molesworth 1867–1945. English explorer, soldier, and administrator who surveyed much of the territory in SW Asia between Baghdad, the Caspian Sea, and the Hindu Kush during World War I (1914–18).

In 1894 he was the first British consul to Kerman (now in Iran) and Persian Baluchistan. Later he raised and commanded the South Persian Rifles. His histories of Persia and Afghanistan were published in 1915 and 1940.

Syktyvkar capital of Komi Republic, USSR; population (1987) 224,000. Industries include timber, paper, and tanning. It was founded 1740 as a Russian colony.

Sylhet capital of Sylhet region, NE Bangladesh; population (1981) 168,000. It is a tea-growing center and also produces rice, jute, and sugar. There is natural gas nearby. It is the former capital of a Hindu kingdom and was conquered by Muslims in the 14th century. In the 1971 civil war, which led to the establishment of Bangladesh, it was the scene of heavy fighting.

Sydney *The Opera House in Sydney, Australia.*

syllogism a set of philosophical statements devised by Aristotle in his work on logic. It establishes the conditions under which a valid conclusion follows or does not follow by deduction from given premises. The following is an example of a valid syllogism: "All men are mortal, Socrates is a man, therefore Socrates is mortal."

Sylvanus in Roman mythology, another version of ◊Silvanus.

symbiosis any relationship between two organisms of different species, where both partners benefit from the association. A well-known example is the pollination relationship between insects and flowers, where the insects feed on nectar and carry pollen from one flower to another. This kind of relationship is better known as ◊mutualism. Strictly speaking, symbiosis refers to continuous, intimate contact between mutually benefiting species, such as the fungus and alga in ◊lichen.

symbol in general, something that stands for something else. A symbol may be an esthetic device or a sign used to convey information visually, thus saving time, eliminating language barriers, or overcoming illiteracy.

Symbols are used in art, mathematics, music, and literature; for practical use in science and medicine; for road signs; and as warnings—for example, a skull and crossbones to indicate dangerous contents.

symbolic interactionism sociological method, founded by the US pragmatist George Mead, that studies the behavior of individuals and small groups through observation and description, viewing people's appearance, gestures, and language as symbols they use to interact with others in social situations. In contrast to theories such as Marxism or functionalism that attempt to analyze society as a whole through economic or political systems, it takes a perspective of society from within, as created by people themselves.

symbolic processor computer purpose-built to run so-called symbol-manipulation programs rather than programs involving a great deal of numerical computation. They exist principally for the ◊artificial intelligence language ◊LISP, although some have also been built to run ◊PROLOG.

symbolism in the arts, the use of symbols as a device for concentrating or intensifying meaning. In particular, the term is used for a late 19th-century movement in French poetry, associated with Verlaine, Mallarmé, and Rimbaud, who used words for their symbolic rather than their concrete meaning.

Symbolism a movement in late 19th-century painting that emerged in France inspired by the trend in poetry. The subjects were often mythological, mystical, or fantastic. Gustave Moreau was a leading Symbolist painter.

Other Symbolist painters included Puvis de Chavannes and Odilon Redon in France, Böcklin in Switzerland, and Burne-Jones in the UK. Statuesque female figures were often used to embody qualities or emotions.

symmetry the property of having similar parts arranged around a line, point, or plane. A circle is symmetrical about its center, for example. In a wider sense, symmetry is present if a change in the system leaves the essential features of the system unchanged; for example, reversing the sign of electric charges does not change the electrical behavior of an arrangement of charges.

symphonic poem in music, a term originated by Liszt for his 13 one-movement orchestral works that interpret a story from literature or history, also used by many other composers. Richard Strauss preferred the title "tone poem."

symphony a musical composition for orchestra, traditionally in four separate but closely related movements. It developed from the smaller ◊sonata form, the Italian overture, and the dance suite of the 18th century.

Haydn established the mature form of the symphony, written in slow, minuet, and allegro movements. Mozart and Beethoven (who replaced the ◊minuet with the scherzo) expanded the form, which has been developed further by successive composers: Brahms, Tchaikovsky, Bruckner, Dvořák, Mahler, Sibelius, Vaughan Williams, Piston, Prokofiev, Nielsen, Shostakovich, and Stravinsky.

synagogue a Jewish place of worship, also called a temple by the non-Orthodox. As an institution it dates from the destruction of the Temple in Jerusalem AD 70, although it had been developing from the time of the Babylonian Exile as a substitute for the Temple. In antiquity it was a public meeting hall where the Torah was also read, but today it is used primarily for prayer and services. A service requires a quorum (*minyan*) of ten adult Jewish men.

In addition to the ark (the sacred ornamented enclosure that holds the Torah scrolls) the synagogue contains a raised platform (*bimah*) from which the service is conducted, with seats for the hereditary high priests. The rest of the congregation sits or stands facing it. Two tablets above the ark are inscribed with the Ten Commandments. In Orthodox synagogues women sit apart from the men.

synapse the junction between two ◊nerve cells, or between a nerve cell and a muscle (a neuromuscular junction), across which a nerve impulse is transmitted . The two cells involved are not in direct contact but separated by a narrow gap called the synaptic cleft. The threadlike extension, or ◊axon, of the transmitting nerve cell has a slightly swollen terminal point, the synaptic knob. This forms one half of the synaptic junction and houses membrane-bound vesicles, which contain a chemical ◊neurotransmitter. When nerve impulses reach the knob, the vesicles release the transmitter and this flows across the gap and binds itself to special receptors on the receiving cell's membrane. If the receiving cell is a nerve cell, the other half of the synaptic junction will be one or more extensions called ◊dendrites; these will be stimulated by the neurotransmitter to set up an impulse, which will then be conducted along the length of the nerve cell and on to its own axons. If the receiving cell is a muscle cell, it will be stimulated by the neurotransmitter to contract.

Synapsida group of mammallike reptiles living 315–195 million years ago, whose fossil record is largely complete, and who were for a while the dominant land animals, before being replaced by the dinosaurs. The true mammals are their descendants.

synchronized swimming a swimming discipline that demands artistry as opposed to speed. Competitors, either individual (solo) or in pairs, perform rhythmic routines to music, which include difficult but graceful movements called "stunts," similar to diving positions. Points are awarded for interpretation and style, and stunt performance (multiplied by a degree of difficulty scale as in ◊diving). It was introduced into the Olympic swimming program in 1984.

Water ballet is the theatrical form of the competitive event. Water ballets using dozens of swimmers are performed at outdoor theaters for entertainment, since Billy Rose invented the form for swimming champion Eleanor Holm in the 1920s. Esther Williams, another swimming champion, popularized water ballet in Hollywood films of the 1940s.

syncline geologic term for a fold in the rocks of the Earth's crust in which the layers or ◊beds dip inward, thus forming a troughlike structure with a sag in the middle. The opposite structure, with the beds arching upward, is an ◊anticline.

syncopation in music, the deliberate upsetting of rhythm by shifting the accent to a beat that is normally unaccented.

syncope medical term for any temporary loss of consciousness, as in ◊fainting.

syndicalism (French *syndicat* "labor union") political movement that rejected parliamentary activity in favor of direct action, culminating in a revolutionary general strike to secure worker ownership and control of industry. The idea originated under Robert ◊Owen's influence in the 1830s, acquired its name and its more violent aspects in France from the philosopher ◊Sorel, and also reached the US (see ◊Industrial Workers of the World). After 1918 syndicalism was absorbed in communism, although it continued to have an independent existence in Spain until the late 1930s.

syndrome in medicine, a set of signs and symptoms that always occur together, thus characterizing a particular condition or disorder.

synecdoche (Greek "accepted together") a figure of speech that either uses the part to represent the whole ("There were some *new faces* at the meeting," rather than *new people*), or the whole to stand for the part ("The West Indies beat England at cricket," rather than naming the national teams in question).

synergy (Greek "combined action") in architecture, the augmented strength of systems, where the strength of a wall is greater than the added total of its individual units.

synergy in medicine, the "cooperative" action of two or more drugs, muscles, or organs; applied especially to drugs whose combined action is more powerful than their simple effects added together.

Synge J(ohn) M(illington) 1871–1909. Irish playwright, a leading figure in the Irish dramatic revival of the early 20th century. His six plays reflect the speech patterns of the Aran Islands and W Ireland. They include *In the Shadow of the Glen* 1903, *Riders to the Sea* 1904, and *The Playboy of the Western World* 1907, which caused riots at the Abbey Theatre, Dublin, when first performed.

Synge Richard 1914– . British biochemist who investigated paper ◊chromatography (a means of separating mixtures). By 1940 techniques of chromatography for separating proteins had been devised. Still lacking were comparable techniques for distinguishing the amino acids that constituted the proteins. By 1944, Synge and his colleague Archer Martin had worked out a procedure, known as ascending chromatography, which filled this gap and won them the 1952 Nobel Prize for Chemistry.

synodic period the interval between successive ◊oppositions of a superior planet (those from Mars outward) or inferior ◊conjunctions of an inferior planet (Venus or Mercury).

synonymy near or identical meaning between or among words. There are very few strict synonyms in any language, although there may be many near-synonyms, depending upon the contexts in which the words are used. Thus *brotherly* and *fraternal* are synonyms in English, but a *brotherhood* is not at all the same as a *fraternity*.

synovial fluid viscous yellow fluid that bathes movable joints between the bones of vertebrates. It nourishes and lubricates the ◊cartilage at the end of each bone.

Synovial fluid is secreted by a membrane that links movably jointed bones. The same kind of fluid is found in bursae, the membranous sacs that buffer some joints, such as in the shoulder and hip region.

synovitis inflammation of the membranous lining of a joint, or of a tendon sheath, caused by injury or infection.

synthesis in chemistry, the formation of a substance or compound from more elementary compounds. The synthesis of a drug can involve several stages from the initial material to the final product; the complexity of these stages is a major factor in the cost of production.

synthesizer device that uses electrical components to produce sounds, such as conventional musical instruments, or in free creativity. In preset synthesizers, the sound of various instruments is produced by a built-in computer-type memory. In programmable synthesizers any number of new instrumental or other sounds may be produced at the will of the performer. Speech synthesizers can break down speech into 128 basic elements (allophones), which are then combined into words and sentences, as in the voices of electronic teaching aids.

In preset synthesizers the memory triggers all the control settings required to produce the sound of a trumpet or violin. For example, the "sawtooth" sound wave produced by a violin is artificially produced by an electrical tone generator, or oscillator, and then fed into an electrical filter set to have the resonances characteristic of a violin body.

synthetic any material made from chemicals. Since the 1900s, more and more of the materials used in everyday life are synthetics, including plastics (polythene, polystyrene), ◊synthetic fibers (nylon, acrylics, polyesters), synthetic resins, and synthetic rubber. Most naturally occurring organic substances are now made synthetically, especially pharmaceuticals.

synthetic

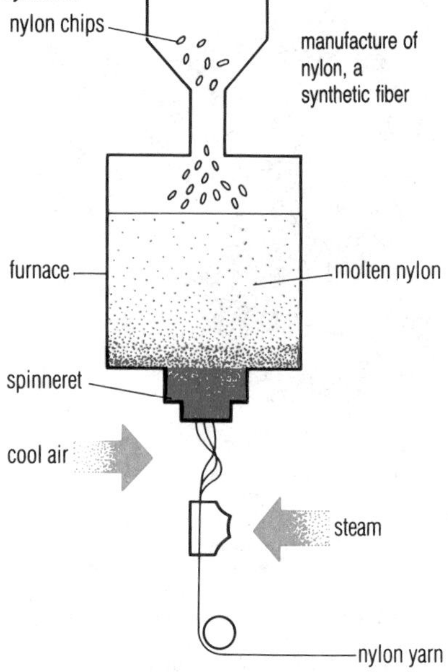
nylon chips
furnace
molten nylon
spinneret
cool air
steam
nylon yarn

manufacture of nylon, a synthetic fiber

synthetic in philosophy, a term employed by ◊Kant to describe a judgment in which the predicate is not contained within the subject; for example, "The flower is blue" is synthetic, since every flower is not blue. It is the converse of ◊analytic.

synthetic fiber fiber made by chemical processes, unknown in nature. There are two kinds. One is made from natural materials that have been chemically processed in some way; ◊rayon, for example, is made by processing the cellulose in wood pulp. The other type is the true synthetic fiber, made entirely from chemicals. ◊Nylon was the original synthetic fiber, made from chemicals obtained from petroleum (crude oil).

Fibers are drawn out into long threads or filaments, usually by so-called "spinning" methods, melting or dissolving the parent material and then forcing it through the holes of a perforated plate, or spinneret.

syphilis venereal disease caused by the spiral-shaped bacterium (spirochete) *Treponema pallidum*. Untreated, it runs its course in three stages over many years, often starting with a painless hard sore, or chancre, developing within a month on the area of infection (usually the genitals). The second stage, months later, is a rash with arthritis, hepatitis, and/or meningitis. The third stage, years later, leads eventually to paralysis, blindness, insanity, and death. The Wassermann test is a diagnostic blood test for syphilis.

With widespread availability of antibiotics, syphilis is now increasingly cured in the industrialized world, at least to the extent that the final stage of the disease is rare. The risk remains that the disease may go undiagnosed or that it may be transmitted by a pregnant woman to her fetus. It has been implicated in the onset of ◊AIDS symptoms.

Syracuse industrial city on Lake Onondaga, in New York State; population (1990) 163,860. Industries include the manufacture of electrical and other machinery, paper, and food processing. There are canal links with the ◊Great Lakes, and the Hudson and St Lawrence rivers. Syracuse University is here. Syracuse was settled in the 1780s on the site of a former Iroquois capital and developed as a salt-mining center.

Syria

Syrian Arab Republic
(al-Jamhuriya al-Arabya as-Suriya)

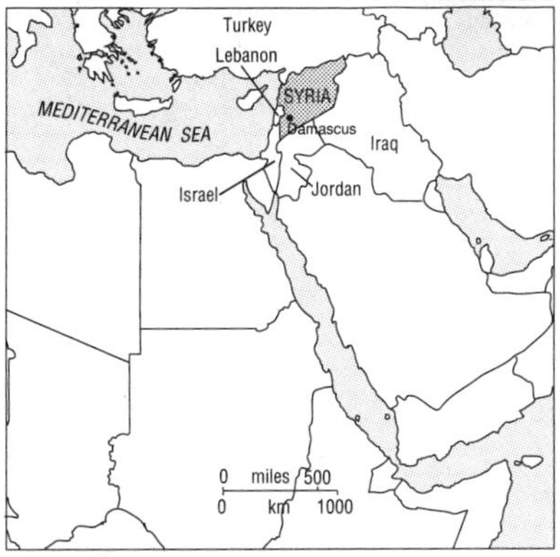
Turkey
Lebanon
SYRIA
MEDITERRANEAN SEA
Damascus
Iraq
Israel
Jordan
0 miles 500
0 km 1000

area 71,506 sq mi/185,200 sq km
capital Damascus
cities Aleppo, Homs, Hama; chief port Latakia
physical mountains alternate with fertile plains and desert areas; Euphrates River
features Mount Hermon, Golan Heights; crusader castles (Krak des Chevaliers); Phoenician city sites (Ugarit), ruins of ancient Palmyra
head of state and government Hafez al-Assad from 1971
political system Socialist republic
political parties National Progressive Front (NPF), pro-Arab, Socialist; Communist Action Party, Socialist
exports cotton, cereals, oil, phosphates, tobacco
currency Syrian pound
population (1990 est) 12,471,000; growth rate 3.5% p.a.
life expectancy men 67, women 69 (1989)
language Arabic 89% (official), Kurdish 6%, Armenian 3%
religion Sunni Muslim 74%; ruling minority Alawite, and other Islamic sects 16%; Christian 10%
literacy men 76%/women 43% (1985 est)
GNP $17 bn (1986); $702 per head
chronology
1946 Achieved full independence from France.
1958 Merged with Egypt to form the United Arab Republic (UAR).
1961 UAR disintegrated.
1967 Six-Day War resulted in the loss of territory to Israel.
1970–71 Syria supported Palestinian guerrillas against Jordanian troops.
1971 Following a bloodless coup, Hafez al-Assad became president.
1973 Israel consolidated its control of the Golan Heights after the Yom Kippur War.
1976 Substantial numbers of troops committed to the civil war in Lebanon.
1978 Assad reelected.
1981–82 Further military engagements in Lebanon.
1982 Islamic militant uprising suppressed; 5,000 dead.
1984 Presidents Assad and Gemayel approved a plan for government of national unity in Lebanon.
1985 Assad secured the release of US hostages held in an aircraft hijacked by extremist Shiite group. Assad reelected.
1987 Improved relations with US and attempts to secure the release of Western hostages in Lebanon.
1989 Diplomatic relations with Morocco restored. Continued fighting in Lebanon; Syrian forces reinforced in Lebanon; diplomatic relations with Egypt restored.
1990 Diplomatic relations with Britain restored.
1991 Syria fights against Iraq in Gulf War, attends Middle East peace conference.

Syracuse (Italian *Siracusa*) industrial port (chemicals, salt) in E Sicily; population (1988) 124,000. It has a cathedral and remains of temples, aqueducts, catacombs, and an amphitheater. Founded 734 BC by the Corinthians, it became a center of Greek culture under the elder and younger ◊Dionysius. After a three-year siege it was taken by Rome 212 BC. In AD 878 it was destroyed by the Arabs, and the rebuilt town came under Norman rule in the 11th century.

Syria country in W Asia, on the Mediterranean, bounded N by Turkey, E by Iraq, S by Jordan, and SW by Israel and Lebanon.

government The 1973 constitution provides for a president, elected by universal adult suffrage for a seven-year term, who appoints and governs with the help of a prime minister and a council of ministers. There is a single-chamber legislature, the 195-member *Majlis al-Sha'ab*, also elected by universal adult suffrage.

history Ancient Syria was inhabited by various small kingdoms that fought against Israel and were subdued by the Assyrians. It was subsequently occupied by Babylonia, Persia, and Macedonia but gained prominence under Seleucus Nicator, founder of ◊Antioch 300 BC, and ◊Antiochus the Great. After forming part of the Roman and Byzantine empires, it was conquered by the Saracens 636. During the Middle Ages, Syria was the scene of many of the Crusaders' exploits.

Syria was part of the ◊Ottoman Empire 1516–1918. It was occupied by British and French troops 1918–19 and in 1920 placed under French mandate. Syria became independent in 1946 and three years later came under military rule.

In 1958 Syria merged with Egypt to become the United Arab Republic (UAR), but after an army coup in 1961 Syria seceded, and the independent Syrian Arab Republic was established. In 1963 a government was formed, mainly from members of the Arab Socialist Renaissance (Ba'ath) Party, but three years later the army removed it. In 1970 the moderate wing of the Ba'ath Party, led by Lt Gen Hafez al-Assad, secured power in a bloodless coup, and in the following year Assad was elected president.

Since then President Assad has remained in office without any serious challenges to his leadership. He is head of state, head of government, secretary general of the Ba'ath Arab Socialist Party, and president of the National Progressive Front (NPF), an umbrella organization for the five main Socialist parties. Syria is therefore in reality, if not in a strictly legal sense, a one-party state. Since 1983 Assad's health has suffered but no obvious successor has emerged. In the 1986 elections the NPF won 151 of the 195 seats.

Externally Syria has played a leading role in Middle East affairs. In the Six-Day War 1967 it lost territory to Israel, and after the Yom Kippur War 1973 Israel formally annexed the Golan Heights, which had previously been part of Syria. During 1976 Assad increasingly intervened in the civil war in Lebanon, eventually committing some 50,000 troops to the operations. Relations between Syria and Egypt cooled after President Sadat's Israel peace initiative 1977 and the subsequent ◊Camp David agreements. Assad has consistently opposed US-sponsored peace moves in Lebanon, arguing that they infringed upon Lebanese sovereignty. He has also questioned Yasser Arafat's leadership of the Palestine Liberation Organization (PLO) and supported opposition to him.

In 1984 President Assad and the Lebanese president Amin Gemayel approved plans for a government of national unity in Lebanon, which would give equal representation to Muslims and Christians, and secured the reluctant agreement of Nabih Berri of the Shi'ite Amal Militia and Walid Joumblatt, leader of the ◊Druse. Fighting still continued, and Assad's credibility suffered, but in 1985 his authority proved sufficient to secure the release of 39 US hostages from an aircraft hijacked by the extremist Shi'ite group Hezbollah (Party of God). In Nov 1986 Britain broke off diplomatic relations after claiming to have proof of Syrian involvement in international terrorism, when a Syrian citizen attempted to blow up an Israeli plane at Heathrow, London. In July 1987 Syria instigated a crackdown on the pro-Iranian Hezbollah party. Syria has been leaning to the west, its policies in Lebanon in direct conflict with Iran's dream of an Islamic republic, and its crumbling economy has been promised Arab aid if Damascus switches allegiance. In June 1987, following a private visit by former US president Jimmy ◊Carter, Syria's relations with the US began to improve, and efforts were made to arrange the release of Western hostages in Lebanon, a process that continued through 1991.

After Iraq's invasion of Kuwait in Aug 1990, Syria sided with other Arab states and the UN coalition against Iraq, contributing troops for the ◊Gulf War. In Nov 1991 Syria attended the historic Middle East peace conference in Spain.

Syriac language ancient Semitic language, originally the Aramaic dialect spoken in and around Edessa (now in Turkey) and widely used in W Asia from about 700 BC to AD 700. From the 3rd to 7th centuries it was a Christian liturgical and literary language.

syringa common, but incorrect, name for the ◊mock orange *Philadelphus*. The genus *Syringa* includes ◊lilac *Syringa vulgaris*, and is not related to mock orange.

Système International d'Units see ◊SI units.

systemic in medicine, relating to or affecting the body as a whole. A systemic disease is one where the effects are present throughout the body, as opposed to local disease, such as ◊conjunctivitis, which is confined to one part.

systems analysis in computing, the investigation of a business activity or clerical procedure, with a view to deciding if and how it can be computerized. The analyst discusses the existing procedures with the people involved, observes the flow of data through the business, and draws up an outline specification of the required computer system (see also ◊systems design).

systems design in computing, the detailed design of an application. The designer breaks the system down into component programs and designs the required input forms, screen layouts, and printouts. Systems design forms a link between systems analysis and ◊programming.

Szczecin (German *Stettin*) industrial (shipbuilding, fish processing, synthetic fibers, tools, iron) port on the river Oder, in NW Poland; population (1989) 391,000.

A ◊Hanseatic port from 1278, it was Swedish from 1648 until 1720, when it was taken by Prussia. It was Germany's chief Baltic port until captured by the Russians in 1945, and came under Polish administration. ◊Catherine the Great of Russia was born here.

Szechwan alternate spelling for the central Chinese province of ◊Sichuan.

Szeged port on river Tisza and capital of Csongrad county, S Hungary; population (1988) 188,000. The chief industry is textiles, and the port trades in timber and salt.

Székesfehérvár industrial city (metal products) in W central Hungary; population (1988) 113,000. It is a market center for wine, tobacco, and fruit.

Szent-Gyorgi Albert 1893–1986. Hungarian-born US biochemist who isolated vitamin C and studied the chemistry of muscular activity. Nobel Prize for Medicine 1937.

In 1928 Szent-Gyorgi isolated a substance from

the adrenal glands that he named hexuronic acid; when he found the same substance in cabbages and oranges, he suspected that he had finally isolated vitamin C.

Szilard Leo 1898–1964. Hungarian-born US physicist who, in 1934, was one of the first scientists to realize that nuclear fission, or atom splitting, could lead to a chain reaction releasing enormous amounts of instantaneous energy. He emigrated to the US in 1938 and there influenced ◊Einstein to advise President Roosevelt to begin the nuclear arms program. In postwar years he turned his attention to the newly emerging field of molecular biology.

Szymanowski Karol (Maliej) 1882–1937. Polish composer of orchestral works, operas, piano music, and violin concertos. He was director of the Conservatoire in Warsaw from 1926.

T

Tabah or ***Taba*** small area of disputed territory, 0.6 mi/1 km long, between Eilat (Israel) to the east and the Sinai Desert (Egypt) to the west on the Red Sea. Under an Anglo-Egyptian-Turkish agreement 1906, the border ran through Tabah; under a British survey of 1915 headed by T E Lawrence (of Arabia, who made "adjustments" allegedly under British government orders) it runs to the E. Taken by Israel 1967, Tabah was returned to Egypt 1989.

Table Bay inlet on the SW coast of the Cape of Good Hope, South Africa, on which Cape Town stands. It is overlooked by Table Mountain (highest point Maclear's Beacon 3,568 ft/1,087 m), the cloud often above it being known as the "tablecloth."

table tennis or ***ping pong*** indoor game played on a rectangular table by two or four players. It was developed in Britain about 1880 and derived from lawn tennis. World championships were first held in 1926.

Play takes place on a table measuring 9 ft/2.74 m long by 5 ft/1.52 m wide. Across the middle is a 6 in/15.25 cm high net over which the ball must be hit. The players use small, wooden paddles covered in sponge or rubber. A feature of the game is the amount of spin put on the small plastic ball. Points are scored by forcing the opponent(s) into an error. The first to score 21 wins the game. Volleying is not allowed. A match may consist of three or five games. In doubles play, the players must hit the ball in strict rotation.

Tabligh (Arabic "revival") missionary movement in Islam, which developed after 1945 and feeds the militant organizations for the "true Islamic state"; there is an annual gathering at Tongi, near Dhaka.

Tadzhikistan

Dushanbe

taboo (Polynesian *tabu*, "forbidden") prohibition applied to magical and religious objects. In psychology and the social sciences the term refers to practices that are generally prohibited because of religious or social pressures; for example, incest is forbidden in most societies.

Tabora trading center in W Tanzania; population (1978) 67,400. It was founded about 1820 by Arab traders of slaves and ivory.

Tabriz city in NW Iran; population (1986) 972,000. Industries include metal casting, carpets, cotton, and silk textiles.

Tacitus Publius Cornelius c. AD 55–c. 120. Roman historian. A public orator in Rome, he was consul under Nerva 97–98 and proconsul of Asia 112–113. He wrote histories of the Roman Empire, *Annales* and *Historiae*, covering the years AD 14–68 and 69–97 respectively. He also wrote a *Life of Agricola* 97 (he married Agricola's daughter in 77) and a description of the German tribes, *Germania* 98.

Tacna city in S Peru; population (1988) 138,000. It is undergoing industrialization. In 1880 Chile defeated a combined Peruvian-Bolivian army nearby and occupied Tacna until 1929.

Tacoma port in Washington State, on Puget Sound, 25 mi/40 km S of Seattle; population (1990) 176,664. It is a lumber and shipping center, with fishing and boat-building industries. Manufactures include primary metals, wood and paper products, chemicals, and processed foods. Educational institutions include the University of Puget Sound and Pacific Lutheran University. Founded 1868, it developed after being chosen as the terminus of the Northern Pacific Railroad 1873.

Tadmur Arabic name for the ancient city of ◊Palmyra in Syria.

Tadzhikistan republic, formerly constituent republic of S central USSR 1929–91, part of Soviet Central Asia.

area 55,251 sq mi/143,100 sq km
capital Dushanbe
features few areas below 11,000 ft/3,500 m; includes ◊Communism Peak; health resorts and mineral springs
products fruit, cereals, cotton, cattle, sheep, silks, carpets, coal, lead, zinc, chemicals, oil, gas
population (1987) 4,807,000; 59% Tadzhik, 23% Uzbek, 11% Russian or Ukrainian
language Tadzhik, similar to Farsi (Persian)
religion Sunni Muslim
recent history formed 1924 from the Tadzhik areas of Bokhara and Turkestan. It experienced a devastating earthquake Jan 1989 (274 people died) and ethnic conflict 1989–90.In Dushanbe, 18 were killed in Feb 1990 in rioting against Communist Party Headquarters. In late 1991, Tadzhikistan proclaimed its independence, joining the new Commonwealth of Independent States (CIS) in Dec 1991.

Taegu largest inland city of South Korea after Seoul; population (1985) 2,031,000.

Taejon (Korean "large rice paddy") capital of South Chungchong province, central South Korea; population (1985) 866,000. Korea's tallest standing Buddha and oldest wooden building are found NE of the city at Popchusa in the Mount Songnisan National Park.

tae kwon do Korean ◊martial art similar to ◊karate, which includes punching and kicking. It was included in the 1988 Olympic Games as a demonstration sport.

Tafawa Balewa Alhaji Abubakar 1912–1966. Nigerian politician, prime minister from 1957 to 1966, when he was assassinated in a coup d'état.

taffeta (Persian "spun") originally light, plain-weave silk fabric with a high luster (today also manufactured from man-made fibers).

Taft Robert Alphonso 1889–1953. US Republican senator 1939–53; candidate for the presidential nomination 1940, 1944, 1948, 1952. He sponsored the Taft-Hartley Labor Act 1947, restricting union power.

Born in Cincinnati, Ohio, he was the son of President W H ◊Taft. Known as "Mr Republican," he was the standard-bearer of the conservative wing of the Republican Party, and he was lost in the liberal tide that swept the US during the 1930s. He was further isolated by his resistance to US involvement against Nazi Germany, a view he held as late as 1943.

Taft William Howard 1857–1930. 27th president of the US 1909–13, a Republican; chief justice of the US 1921–30. He was secretary of war 1904–08 in Theodore ◊Roosevelt's administration, but as president his conservatism provoked Roosevelt to run against him in the 1912 election.

Born in Cincinnati, Ohio, Taft graduated from Yale University and Cincinnati Law School. His first interest was always the judiciary, although he accepted a post as governor of the Philippines and took responsibility for the construction of the ◊Panama Canal. His single term as president was characterized by struggles against progressives, although he prosecuted more trusts than had his predecessor. As chief justice of the Supreme Court, he supported a minimum wage.

Taganrog port in the NE corner of the Sea of Azov, S USSR, W of Rostov; population (1987) 295,000. Industries include iron, steel, metal goods, aircraft, machinery, and shoes. A museum commemorates the playwright Chekhov, who was born here.

Tagliacozzi Gaspare 1546–1599. Italian surgeon who pioneered plastic surgery. He was the first to repair noses lost in duels or through ◊syphilis. He also carried out repair of ears. His method involved taking flaps of skin from the arm and grafting them into place.

Taglioni Marie 1804–1884. Italian dancer. A ballerina of ethereal style and exceptional lightness, she was the first to use ◊pointe work, or dancing on the toes, as an expressive part of ballet rather than as sheer technique. She created many roles, including the title role in *La Sylphide* 1832, first performed at the Paris Opéra, and choreographed by her father Filippo (1771–1871). Marie's brother Paolo (1808–1884) was a choreographer and ballet master at Berlin Court Opera 1856–83, and his daughter Marie (1833–1891) danced in Berlin and London, creating many roles in her father's ballets.

Tagore Rabindranath 1861–1941. Bengali Indian writer, born in Calcutta, who translated into English his own verse *Gitanjali* ("song offerings") 1912 and his verse play *Chitra* 1896. Nobel Prize 1913.

He was an ardent nationalist and urged social reform.

Tagus (Spanish *Tajo*, Portuguese *Tejo*) river rising in Aragon, Spain, and reaching the Atlantic at Lisbon, Portugal; length 626 mi/1,007 km. At Lisbon it is crossed by the April 25 (formerly Salazar) Bridge, so named in honor of the 1974 revolution. The Tagus-Segura irrigation scheme serves the rainless Murcia/Alicante region for early fruit and vegetable growing.

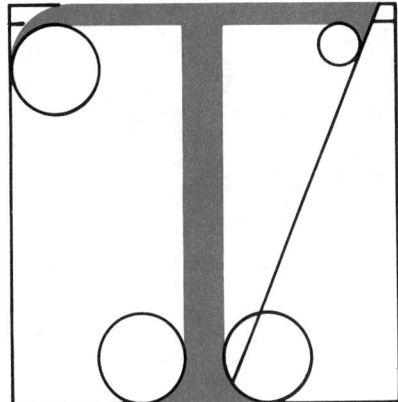

Taft *The 27th president of the United States of America, William H Taft, a Republican. 1909–1913.*

Tagore *Indian writer Rabindranath Tagore in 1920.*

Tahiti largest of the Society Islands, in ◊French Polynesia; area 402 sq mi/1,042 sq km; population (1983) 116,000. Its capital is Papeete. Tahiti was visited by Capt James ◊Cook 1769 and by ◊Bligh of the *Bounty* 1788. It came under French control 1843 and became a colony 1880.

Tai member of any of the groups of SE Asian peoples who speak Tai languages, all of which belong to the Sino-Tibetan language family. There are over 60 million speakers, the majority of whom live in Thailand. Tai peoples are also found in SW China, NW Myanmar (Burma), Laos, and N Vietnam.

T'ai Chi series of 108 complex, slow-motion movements, each named and designed (for example, The White Crane Spreads its Wings) to ensure effective circulation of the *chi*, or intrinsic energy of the universe, through the mind and body. It derives partly from the Shaolin ◊martial arts of China and partly from ◊Taoism.

taiga or ***boreal forest*** Russian name for the forest zone S of the ◊tundra, found across the N hemisphere. Here, dense forests of conifers (spruces and hemlocks), birches, and poplars occupy glaciated regions punctuated with cold lakes, streams, bogs, and marshes. Winters are prolonged and very cold, but the summer is warm enough to promote dense growth. The varied fauna and flora are in delicate balance because the conditions of life are so precarious. This ecology is threatened by mining, forestry, and pipeline construction.

Taine Hippolyte Adolphe 1828–1893. French critic and historian. He analyzed literary works as products of period and environment, as in *Histoire de la littérature anglaise/History of English Literature* 1863 and *Philosophie de l'art/Philosophy of Art* 1865–69.

taipan species of small-headed cobra *Oxyuranus scutellatus* found in NE Australia and New Guinea. It is about 10 ft/3 m long, and has a brown back and yellow belly. Its venom is fatal within minutes.

Taipei or ***Taibei*** capital and commercial center of Taiwan; population (1987) 2,640,000. Industries include electronics, plastics, textiles, and machinery.

The National Palace Museum 1965 houses the world's greatest collection of Chinese art, taken there from the mainland 1948.

Taiwan country in SE Asia, officially the Republic of China, occupying the island of Taiwan between the E China Sea and the S China Sea.

government The 900-member National Assembly (Kuo-Min Ta-Hui) elects the president and vice-president and has power to amend the constitution of 1947. Its members, originally elected from mainland China, have retained their seats since their constituencies fell under Communist Chinese control 1949, and are termed "life members." Fresh elections have only been held for seats vacated by deceased deputies.

Taiwan's president, elected for a six-year term, is head of state and Commander in Chief of the armed forces, and promulgates laws. The president works with a cabinet, the Executive *Yuan*, headed by a prime minister (Lee Huan from 1989), responsible to a single-chamber legislature, the Legislative *Yuan*. The Legislative *Yuan* comprises 260 members, some of them presidential appointees but the majority "life members" from former mainland seats. Since 1972, 70 vacated seats have, on average, been subject to fresh elections at three-yearly intervals. Three Control, Judicial, and Examination *Yuans* also exist, with the tasks of investigating the work of the executive, interpreting the constitution, and overseeing entrance examinations for public offices.

The dominant political force is the Nationalist Party of China (Kuomintang), which is still primarily staffed at its senior levels by pre-1949 mainlanders though their numbers are being rapidly reduced through "natural attrition." It is anticommunist and Chinese nationalist. The principal opposition party is the Democratic Progressive Party (DPP), which is heir to an earlier, informal, nonparty "tangwai" opposition grouping.

history Taiwan, then known as Formosa ("The Beautiful"), was settled by ◊China from the 15th century, briefly occupied by the Dutch during the mid-17th century, and annexed by the Manchu dynasty 1683. It was ceded to Japan under the terms of the Treaty of Shimonoseki after the 1895 Sino-Japanese war and not regained by China until the Japanese surrender Aug 1945.

In Dec 1949 Taiwan became the refuge for the Chinese Nationalist government forces of ◊Chiang Kai-shek, which were compelled to evacuate the mainland after their defeat by the Communist troops of ◊Mao Zedong. Chiang and his Nationalist followers, though only a 15% minority, dominated the island and maintained an army of 600,000 in the hope of reconquering the mainland, over which they still claimed sovereignty. They continued to be recognized by the US as the legitimate government of China, and occupied China's United Nations and Security Council seats until Oct 1971 when they were expelled and replaced by the People's Republic.

Taiwan was protected by US naval forces during the Korean war 1950–53 and signed a mutual defense treaty with the US 1954. Benefiting from such security, the country enjoyed a period of rapid economic growth during the 1950s and 1960s, emerging as an export-oriented, newly industrialized country. Political power during these years was concentrated in the hands of the Kuomintang and the armed forces led by Presi-

Taiwan
Republic of China
(Chung Hua Min Kuo)

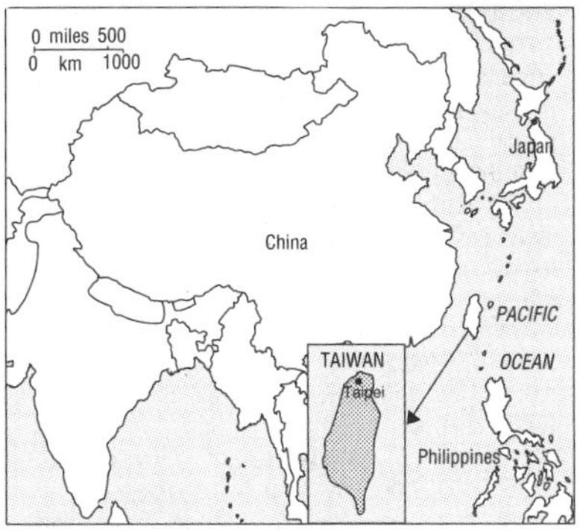
0 miles 500
0 km 1000
Japan
China
PACIFIC
OCEAN
TAIWAN
Taipei
Philippines

area 13,965 sq mi/36,179 sq km
capital Taipei
cities ports Keelung, Kaohsiung
physical island (formerly Formosa) off People's Republic of China; mountainous, with lowlands in W
features Penghu (Pescadores), Jinmen (Quemoy), Mazu (Matsu) islands
head of state Lee Teng-hui from 1988
head of government Lee Huan from 1989
political system emergent democracy
political parties Nationalist Party of China (Kuomintang: KMT), anticommunist, Chinese nationalist; Democratic Progressive Party (DPP), centrist-pluralist, pro-self-determination grouping; Workers' Party (Kungtang), left-of-center
exports textiles, steel, plastics, electronics, foodstuffs
currency New Taiwan dollar
population (1990) 20,454,000 (84% Taiwanese, 14% mainlanders); growth rate 1.4% p.a.
life expectancy 70 men, 75 women (1986)
language Mandarin Chinese (official); Taiwan, Hakka dialects
religion officially atheist; Taoist, Confucian, Buddhist, Christian
literacy 90% (1988)
GNP $119.1 bn; $6,200 per head (1988)
chronology
1683 Taiwan (Formosa) annexed by China.
1895 Ceded to Japan.
1945 Recovered by China.
1949 Flight of Nationalist government to Taiwan after Chinese communist revolution.
1954 US-Taiwanese mutual defense treaty.
1971 Expulsion from United Nations.
1972 Commencement of legislature elections.
1975 President Chiang Kai-shek died; replaced as Kuomintang leader by his son, Chiang Ching-kuo.
1979 US severed diplomatic relations and annulled security pact.
1986 Opposition party to the nationalist Kuomintang formed.
1987 Martial law lifted.
1988 President Chiang Ching-kuo died; replaced by Taiwanese-born Lee Teng-hui.
1989 Kuomintang won first free assembly elections.
1990 Formal move toward normalization of relations with China.
1991 State of emergency that had existed since 1948 declared over.

dent Chiang Kai-shek, with martial law imposed and opposition activity outlawed. During the 1970s the Taiwanese government was forced to adjust to rapid external changes as the US adopted a new policy of détente toward Communist China. In Jan 1979 this culminated in the full normalization of Sino-US relations, the severing of Taiwanese-US diplomatic contacts, and the annulment of the US's 1954 security pact. Other Western nations followed suit in ending diplomatic relations with Taiwan during the 1970s and early 1980s.

These developments, coupled with generational change within the Kuomintang, have prompted a slow review of Taiwanese policies, both domestic and external. Chiang Kai-shek died April 1975 and his son Chiang Ching-kuo (1910–88) became party chair and, from 1978, state president. Under his stewardship, a program of gradual democratization and "Taiwanization" was adopted, with elections being held for "vacated seats" within the National Assembly and Legislative Yuan and native Taiwanese being more rapidly inducted into the Kuomintang. In the Dec 1986 elections a formal opposition party, the Democratic Progressive Party (DPP), led by Chiang Peng-chien, was tolerated and captured 22% of the vote to the Kuomintang's 69%. In July 1987 martial law was lifted and replaced with a national-security law under which demonstrations and the formation of opposition parties were legalized, so long as they forswore communism and supported Taiwanese independence, and press restrictions were lifted.

President Chiang was succeeded on his death by ◊Lee Teng-hui, a Taiwan-born Christian who had been vice-president since 1984. The new president, who headed the party's modernizing technocrat wing, accelerated the pace of reform. Many "old guard" figures were retired during 1988–89 and a plan for phasing out by 1992, through voluntary retirement, up to 200 mainland constituencies and replacing them with Taiwanese deputies was approved. In the Dec 1989 Legislative Yuan elections, the first to be freely held on the island, the Kuomintang's vote share fell to 59% and the DPP increased its number of seats from 12 to 21. In Sept 1990, following the death of a 95-year-old legislator, the "ancient guard," Chinese-born Kuomintang members became a minority within Taiwan's parliament for the first time, and their influence rapidly declined. In 1991 the "state of emergency" that had existed since 1948 was declared over. The Apr 30 announcement paved the way for better relations with China and for domestic reforms.

Taiyuan capital of Shanxi province, NE China; population (1986) 1,880,000. Industries include iron, steel, agricultural machinery, and textiles. It is a walled city, founded in the 5th century AD, on the river Fen He, and is the seat of Shanxi University.

Ta'iz third-largest city of N Yemen; situated in the south of the country at the center of a coffee-growing region; population (1980) 119,500. Cotton, leather, and jewelry are also produced.

Taizé ecumenical Christian community based in the village of that name in SE France. Founded in 1940 by Swiss theologian Roger Schutz (1915–), it has been since the 1960s a communal center for young Christians.

Tajik or ***Tadzhik*** speaker of any of the Tajiki dialects that belong to the Iranian branch of the Indo-European family. The Tajiks have long been associated with neighboring Turkic peoples and their language contains Altaic loan words. The Tajiks inhabit Tadzhikistan and parts of Uzbekistan (USSR), and Afghanistan.

Taj Mahal white marble mausoleum built 1634–56 on the river Jumna near Agra, India. Erected by Shah Jehan to the memory of his favorite wife, Mumtaz Mahal, it is a celebrated example of Indo-Islamic architecture, the fusion of Muslim and Hindu styles.

It took some 20,000 workers to build the Taj Mahal, which has a central dome and minarets on each corner. Every facade is inlaid with semi-precious stones. Ransacked in the 18th century, it was restored in the early 20th century and is a symbol of India to the world.

Tajo Spanish name for the river ◊Tagus.

takahe flightless bird *Notornis mantelli* of the rail family: native to New Zealand. It is about 2 ft/60 cm tall, with blue and green plumage and a red beak. The takahe was thought to have become extinct at the end of the 19th century, but in 1948 small numbers were rediscovered in the tussock grass of a mountain valley on South Island.

Takao Japanese name for ◊Kaohsiung, a city on the W coast of Taiwan.

takeover in business, the acquisition by one company of a sufficient number of shares in another company to have effective control of that company—usually 51%, although a controlling stake may be as little as 30%. Takeovers may be agreed or contested; methods employed include the ◊dawn raid, and methods of avoiding an unwelcome takeover include ◊reverse takeover, ◊poison pills or inviting a ◊white knight to make a takeover bid.

Takeshita Noboru 1924– . Japanese right-wing politician. Elected to parliament as a Liberal Democratic Party (LDP) deputy 1958, he became president of the LDP and prime minister Oct 1987. He and members of his administration were shown in the ◊Recruit scandal to have been

Taj Mahal *More than 20,000 workers were employed in the construction of the Taj Mahal (1634–56) in Agra, N India, built by Shah Jehan as a mausoleum for his favorite wife.*

involved in insider-trading and in April 1989 he resigned.

Takoradi port in Ghana, administered with ◊Sekondi.

Talavera de la Reina town in Castilla-León, central Spain, on the river Tagus, 75 mi/120 km SW of Madrid; population (1981) 64,100. It produces soap, pharmaceuticals, and textiles. Spanish and British forces defeated the French here in the ◊Peninsular War 1809.

Talbot William Henry Fox 1800–1877. English pioneer of photography. He invented the paper-based ◊calotype process, the first ◊negative/positive method. Talbot made ◊photograms several years before Daguerre's invention was announced.

talc mineral, hydrous magnesium silicate, $Mg_3Si_4O_{10}(OH)_2$. It occurs in tabular crystals, but the massive impure form, known as soapstone or steatite, is more common. It is formed by the alteration of magnesium compounds, and usually found in metamorphic rocks. Talc is very soft, ranked 1 on the Mohs' scale of hardness. It is used in powdered form in cosmetics, lubricants, and as an additive in paper manufacture.

French chalk and potstone are varieties of talc. Soapstone has a greasy feel to it, and is used for carvings such as Eskimo sculptures.

Talcahuano port and chief naval base in Biobio region, Chile; population (1987) 231,000. Industries include oil refining and timber.

Talien part of the port of ◊Lüda, China.

Taliesin lived c. 550. Legendary Welsh poet, a bard at the court of the king of Rheged in Scotland. Taliesin allegedly died at Taliesin (named after him) in Dyfed.

Talking Heads US new-wave rock group formed 1975 in New York. Their nervy minimalist music is inspired by African rhythms; albums include *More Songs About Buildings and Food* 1978, *Little Creatures* 1985, and *Naked* 1988.

The vocalist, David Byrne (1952–), has also composed avant-garde and ballet music and made the film *True Stories* 1986.

tallage English tax paid by cities, boroughs, and royal ◊demesnes, first levied under Henry II as a replacement for ◊danegeld. It was abolished in 1340.

Tallahassee capital of Florida; population (1990) 124,773. It is an agricultural and lumbering center. Florida Agricultural and Mechanical University and Florida State University are here. The Spanish explorer Hernando de Soto found an Indian settlement here 1539. The site was chosen as the Florida territorial capital 1821. During the Civil War, it was the only Confederate capital E of the Mississippi River not captured by Union troops.

Talleyrand Charles Maurice de Talleyrand-Périgord 1754–1838. French politician and diplomat. As bishop of Autun 1789–91 he supported moderate reform during the ◊French Revolution, was excommunicated by the pope, and fled to the US during the Reign of Terror (persecution of antirevolutionaries). He returned and became foreign minister under the Directory 1797–99 and under Napoleon 1799–1807. He represented France at the Congress of ◊Vienna 1814–15.

Tallinn (German Reval) naval port and capital of Estonia; population (1987) 478,000. Industries include electrical and oil-drilling machinery, textiles, and paper. Founded 1219, it was a member of the ◊Hanseatic League; passed to Sweden 1561 and to Russia 1750. Vyshgorod castle (13th century) and other medieval buildings remain. It is a yachting center.

Tallis Thomas c. 1505–1585. English composer in the polyphonic style. He wrote masses, anthems, and other church music.

Talmud the two most important works of post-Biblical Jewish literature, the Babylonian and the Palestinian (or Jerusalem) Talmud provide a compilation of ancient Jewish law and tradition. The Babylonian Talmud was edited at the end of the 5th century AD and is the more authoritative version for later Judaism; both Talmuds are written in a mix of Hebrew and Aramaic. They contain the commentary (*gemara*) on the ◊*Mishna* (early rabbinical commentaries compiled c. AD 200), and the material can be generally divided into *halakhah*, consisting of legal and ritual matters, and *aggadah*, concerned with ethical, theological, and folklorist matters.

Talleyrand *The French politician Talleyrand, whose diplomatic skills kept him in office during and after the French Revolution.*

talus the pile of rubble and sediment that forms an ascending slope at the foot of a mountain range or cliff, also in front of a ◊cave.

The rock fragments that form a talus are usually slide rock or pieces broken off by frost action. As fragments are loosened they clatter downward in a series of free falls, bounces, and slides. With time, the rock waste builds in a heap or sheet of rubble that may eventually bury even the upper cliffs, and the growth of the talus then stops. Usually, however, erosional forces decompose the rock waste so that a talus stays restricted to lower slopes.

Tamale town in NE Ghana; population (1982) 227,000. It is a commercial center, dealing in rice, cotton, and peanuts.

tamandua tree-living toothless anteater *Tamandua tetradactyla* found in tropical forests and tree savannah from S Mexico to Brazil. About 1.8 ft/56 cm long with a prehensile tail of equal length, it has strong foreclaws with which it can break into nests of tree ants and termites, which it licks up with its narrow tongue.

Tamar in the Old Testament, the sister of ◊Absalom. She was raped by her half brother Amnon, who was then killed by Absalom.

tamarack coniferous tree *Larix laricina*; a type of ◊larch native to boggy soils in North America, where it is used for timber.

tamarind evergreen tropical tree *Tamarindus indica*, family Leguminosae, native to the Old World, with pinnate leaves and reddish-yellow flowers, followed by pods. The pulp surrounding the seeds is used medicinally and as a flavoring.

tamarisk any small tree or shrub of the genus *Tamarix*, flourishing in warm, salty, desert regions of Europe and Asia where no other vegetation is found. The common tamarisk *T. gallica* has scale-like leaves and spikes of very small, pink flowers.

Tambo Oliver 1917– . South African nationalist politician, in exile 1960–90, president of the African National Congress (ANC) 1977–91.

Tambo was expelled from teacher training for organizing a student protest and joined the ANC 1944. He set up a law practice with Nelson ◊Mandela in Johannesburg 1952. In 1956 Tambo, with other ANC members, was arrested on charges of treason; he was released the following year. When the ANC was banned in 1960, he left South Africa to set up an external wing. He became acting ANC president in 1967 and president in 1977, during Mandela's imprisonment. Because of poor health, he was given the honorary post of national chairman July 1991, and Mandela became president of the ANC.

tamborine musical percussion instrument of ancient origin, almost unchanged since Roman times, consisting of a shallow drum with a single skin and loosely set jingles in the rim that increase its effect.

Tambov city in W central USSR; population (1987) 305,000. Industries include engineering, flour milling, and the manufacture of rubber and synthetic chemicals.

Tamerlane or ***Tamburlaine*** or ***Timur i Leng*** 1336–1405. Mongol ruler of ◊Samarkand from 1369 who conquered Persia, Azerbaijan, Armenia, and Georgia. He defeated the ◊Golden Horde 1395, sacked Delhi 1398, invaded Syria and Anatolia, and captured the Ottoman sultan in Ankara 1402; he died invading China.

Tamil member of any of the groups of S Indian and Sri Lankan peoples speaking Tamil, a member of the Dravidian family of languages. The majority of Tamils live in the Indian state of Tamil Nadu (formerly Madras), although there are approximately 3 million Tamils in Sri Lanka.

Tamil language Dravidian language of SE India, spoken principally in the state of Tamil Nadu and also in N Sri Lanka. It is written in its own distinctive script.

Tamil Nadu formerly (until 1968) Madras State state of SE India

area 50,219 sq mi/130,100 sq km

capital Madras

products mainly industrial: cotton, textiles, silk, electrical machinery, tractors, rubber, sugar refining

population (1981) 48,297,000

language Tamil

history the present state was formed 1956. Tamil Nadu comprises part of the former British Madras presidency (later province) formed from areas taken from France and Tipu Sahib, the sultan of Mysore, in the 18th century, which became a state of the Republic of India 1950. The northeast was detached to form Andhra Pradesh 1953; other areas went to Kerala and Mysore (now Karnataka) 1956, and the Laccadive Islands (now Lakshadweep) became a separate Union Territory.

Taming of the Shrew, The comedy by William Shakespeare, first performed 1593–94. Bianca, who has many suitors, must not marry until her sister Katherina (the shrew) has done so. Petruchio agrees to woo Katherina so that his friend Hortensio may marry Bianca. Petruchio succeeds in "taming" Katherina but Bianca marries another.

Tammany Hall Democratic Party organization in New York City. It originated 1789 as the Society of St Tammany, named after an American Indian chief. It was dominant from 1800 until the 1970s and gained a reputation for bossism; its domination was broken by Mayor ◊La Guardia in the 1930s and by Mayor ◊Koch in the 1970s.

Tammuz in Sumerian legend, a vegetation god, who died at midsummer and was brought back from the underworld in spring by his lover Ishtar. His cult spread over Babylonia, Syria, Phoenicia and Palestine. In Greek mythology Tammuz appears as ◊Adonis.

Tampa port and resort on Tampa Bay in W Florida; population (1990) 280,015. Industries include fruit and vegetable canning, shipbuilding, and the manufacture of fertilizers, clothing, beer, and cigars. The University of South Florida and Busch Gardens are here. Tampa was settled 1823, and a fort was built the next year that was taken from Confederate forces by Union troops in the Civil War. Economic growth was spurred in the 1880s

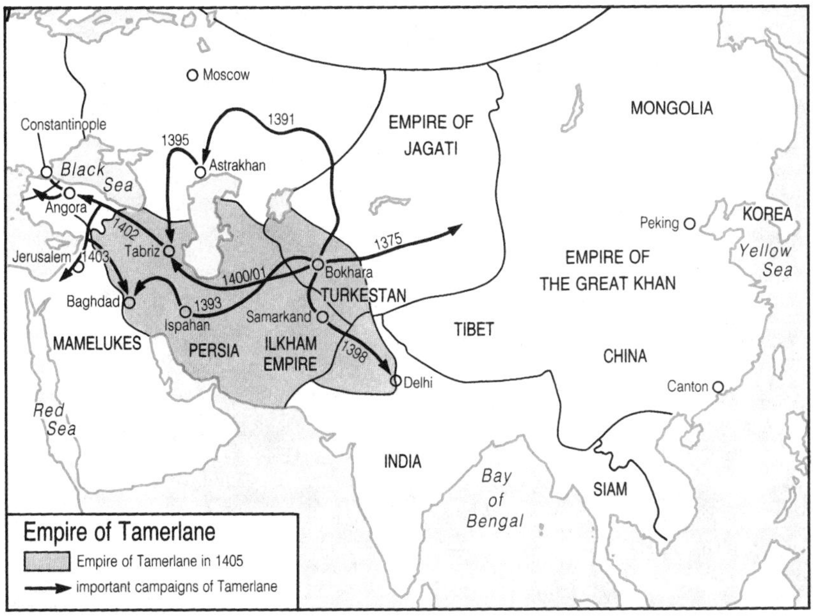
Moscow
Constantinople
1391
1395
Astrakhan
Black Sea
Angora
1402
Jerusalem
1403
Tabriz
1375
Bokhara
1400/01
Baghdad
1393
Ispahan
Samarkand
TURKESTAN
MAMELUKES
PERSIA
ILKHAM EMPIRE
1398
Delhi
Red Sea
EMPIRE OF JAGATI
MONGOLIA
Peking
KOREA
Yellow Sea
EMPIRE OF THE GREAT KHAN
TIBET
CHINA
Canton
INDIA
Bay of Bengal
SIAM
Empire of Tamerlane in 1405
important campaigns of Tamerlane
Empire of Tamerlane

by the discovery of phosphates in the area, the arrival of the railroad, and the establishment of a cigar-making industry.

Tampere (Swedish Tammerfors) city in SW Finland; population (1988) 171,000, metropolitan area 258,000. It is the second-largest city in Finland. Industries include textiles, paper, footwear, and turbines.

Tampico port on the Rio Pánuco, 6 mi/10 km from the Gulf of Mexico, in Tamaulipas state, Mexico; population (1980) 268,000. Industries include oil refining and fishing.

Tana lake in Ethiopia, 5,900 ft/1,800 m above sea level; area 1,390 sq mi/3,600 sq km. It is the source of the Blue Nile.

Tanabata Japanese "star festival" celebrated annually on July 7, introduced from China in the 8th century. It is dedicated to Altair and Vega, two stars in the constellation Aquila, which are united once yearly in the Milky Way. According to legend they represent two star-crossed lovers allowed by the gods to meet on that night.

tanager any of various New World passerine birds, of the family Emberizidae, which also includes ◊blackbirds, ◊orioles, and grackles. Tanagers that breed in N America all belong to the genus *Piranga* and include the scarlet tanager (P. olivacea), about 7 in/18 cm long. There are about 230 species in forests of Central and South America; all males are brilliantly colored.

Tanagra ancient city in ◊Boeotia, central Greece. Sparta defeated Athens there 457 BC. Terracotta statuettes called tanagra were excavated in 1874.

Tanaka Kakuei 1918– . Japanese right-wing politician, leader of the dominant Liberal Democratic Party (LDP) and prime minister 1972–74. In 1976 he was charged with corruption and resigned from the LDP but remained a powerful faction leader.

In the Diet from 1947, Tanaka was minister of finance 1962–65 and of international trade and industry 1971–72, before becoming LDP leader. In 1974 he had to resign the premiership because of allegations of corruption and 1976 he was arrested for accepting bribes from the Lockheed Corporation while premier. He was found guilty in 1983, but remained in the Diet as an independent deputy pending appeal. He was also implicated in the 1988–89 ◊Recruit scandal of insider trading.

Tananarive former name for ◊Antananarivo, the capital of Madagascar.

Taney Roger Brooke 1777–1864. US lawyer and chief justice of the United States. In 1835 he succeeded John Marshall as chief justice of the US Supreme Court. In 1857 he ruled in the Dred Scott case that Congress had no right to ban slavery in the territories, a decision that gravely aggravated sectional tensions.

Born in Calvert County, Maryland, Taney was educated at Dickinson College and was admitted to the bar 1799. He served as a Maryland state senator 1816–21, state attorney general 1827–31, President Jackson's attorney general 1831, and US secretary of the treasury 1833–35.

Tanga seaport and capital of Tanga region, NE Tanzania, on the Indian Ocean; population (1978) 103,000. The port trades in sisal, fruit, cocoa, tea, and fish.

Tanganyika former British colony in E Africa that now forms the mainland of ◊Tanzania.

Tanganyika, Lake lake 2,534 ft/772 m above sea level in the Great Rift Valley, E Africa, with Zaïre to the W, Zambia to the S, and Tanzania and Burundi to the E. It is about 400 mi/645 km long, with an area of about 31,000 sq km/12,000 sq mi, and is the deepest lake (1,435 m/4,710 ft) in Africa. The mountains around its shores rise to about 8,860 ft/2,700 m. The chief ports are Bujumbura (Burundi), Kigoma (Tanzania), and Kalémié (Zaïre).

Tange Kenzo 1913– . Japanese architect. His works include the National Gymnasium, Tokyo, for the 1964 Olympics, and the city of Abuja, planned to replace Lagos as the capital of Nigeria.

tangent in trigonometry, a function of an acute angle in a right triangle, defined as the ratio of the length of the side opposite the angle to the length of the side adjacent to it; a way of expressing the slope of a line. In geometry, a tangent is a straight line that touches a curve and has the same slope as the curve at the point of contact. At a ◊maximum or minimum, the tangent to a curve has zero slope.

tangent of an angle

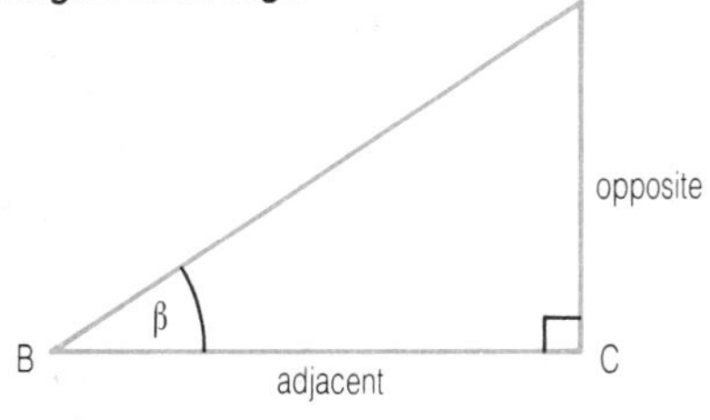
A
opposite
β
B
adjacent
C

$$\tan(\text{gent})\ \beta = \frac{\sin\beta}{\cos\beta} = \frac{\text{opposite}}{\text{adjacent}} = \frac{AC}{BC}$$

tangerine small ◊orange *Citrus reticulata*.

Tangier or ***Tangiers*** or ***Tanger*** port in N Morocco, on the Strait of Gibraltar; population (1982) 436,227. It was a Phoenician trading center in the 15th century BC.

Captured by the Portuguese in 1471, it passed to England 1662 as part of the dowry of Catherine of Braganza, but was abandoned 1684, and later became a lair of ◊Barbary pirates. From 1923 Tangier and a small surrounding enclave became an international zone, administered by Spain 1940–45. In 1956 it was transferred to independent Morocco and became a free port 1962.

tango a couples dance of Latin-American origin or the music for it. The dance consists of two long sliding steps followed by three short steps and stylized body positions.

Tangshan industrial city in Hebei province, China; population (1986) 1,390,000. Almost destroyed by an earthquake 1976, with 200,000 killed, it was rebuilt on a new site, coal seams being opened up under the old city.

Tanguy Yves 1900–1955. French Surrealist painter, who lived in the US from 1939. His inventive canvases feature semiabstract creatures in a barren landscape.

Tanguy was inspired to paint by de ◊Chirico's work and in 1925 he joined the Surrealist movement. He soon developed his characteristic style with bizarre, slender forms in a typically Surrealist wasteland.

Tanizaki Jun-ichirō 1886–1965. Japanese novelist. His works include a version of ◊Murasaki's *The Tale of Genji* 1939–41, *The Makioka Sisters* in three volumes 1943–48, and *The Key* 1956.

His work matured when he moved from Tokyo after the 1923 earthquake to the Kyoto-Osaka region, where ancient tradition is stronger.

tank armored fighting vehicle that runs on tracks and is fitted with weaponry capable of destroying life and property and defeating other tanks. The term was originally a code name for the first effective tracked and armored fighting vehicle, invented by the British soldier and scholar Ernest Swinton, and used in the battle of the Somme 1916.

A tank consists of a body or hull of thick steel, on which are mounted machine guns and a larger gun. The hull contains the crew (usually consisting of a commander, driver, and one or two soldiers), engine, radio, fuel tanks, and ammunition. The tank travels on caterpillar tracks that enable it to cross rough ground and debris.

tanker ship with tanks for carrying crude oil, liquefied gas, or molasses in bulk. Currently the biggest oil tanker is the Greek-owned *Hellas Fos*, of 555,051 tons deadweight.

Tannenberg, Battle of two battles, named after a village now in N Poland:

1410 the Poles and Lithuanians defeated the Teutonic Knights, establishing Poland as a major power;

1914 during World War I, when Tannenberg was part of East Prussia, ◊Hindenburg defeated the Russians.

tannic acid or ***tannin*** $C_{14}H_{10}O_9$ yellow astringent substance, composed of several ◊phenol rings, occurring in the bark, wood, roots, fruits, and galls (growths) of certain trees, such as the oak. It precipitates gelatin to give an insoluble compound, used in the manufacture of leather from hides (tanning).

tanning treating animal skins to preserve them and make them into leather. In vegetable tanning, the prepared skins are soaked in tannic acid. Chrome tanning, which is much quicker, uses solutions of chromium salts.

Tannu-Tuva former independent republic in NE Asia; see ◊Tuva.

tansy perennial herb *Tanacetum vulgare*, family Compositae, native to Europe. The yellow flower heads grow in clusters, and the aromatic leaves are used in cooking.

tantalum hard, ductile, lustrous, gray-white, met-

Tanzania

United Republic of
(Jamhuri ya Muungano wa Tanzania)

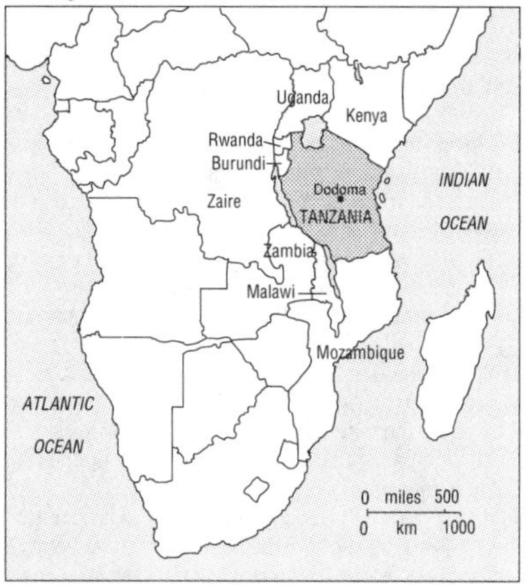
Uganda
Kenya
Rwanda
Burundi
Zaire
Dodoma
TANZANIA
INDIAN OCEAN
Zambia
Malawi
Mozambique
ATLANTIC OCEAN
0 miles 500
0 km 1000

area 364,865 sq mi/945,000 sq km
capital Dodoma
cities Zanzibar Town, Mwanza; chief port Dar es Salaam
physical central plateau; lakes in N and W; coastal plains; lakes Victoria, Tanganyika, and Niasa
features comprises islands of Zanzibar and Pemba; Mount Kilimanjaro, 19,340 ft/5,895 m, the highest peak in Africa; Serengeti National Park, Olduvai Gorge; Ngorongoro Crater 9 mi/14.5 km across, 2,500 ft/762 m deep
head of state and government Ndugu Ali Hassan Mwinyi from 1985
political system one-party Socialist republic
political parties Revolutionary Party of Tanzania (CCM), African, Socialist
exports coffee, cotton, sisal, cloves, tea, tobacco, cashew nuts, diamonds
currency Tanzanian shilling
population (1990 est) 26,070,000; growth rate 3.5% p.a.
life expectancy men 49, women 54 (1989)
language Kiswahili, English (both official)
religion Muslim 35%, Christian 35%, traditional 30%
literacy 85% (1987)
GNP $4.9 bn; $258 per head (1987)
chronology
1946–62 Came under United Nations (UN) trusteeship.
1961 Independence achieved from Britain, within the Commonwealth, with Julius Nyerere as prime minister.
1962 Tanganyika became a republic with Nyerere as president.
1964 Tanganyika and Zanzibar became the United Republic of Tanzania with Nyerere as president.
1967 East African Community (EAC) formed. Arusha Declaration.
1977 Revolutionary Party of Tanzania (CCM) proclaimed the only legal party. EAC dissolved.
1978 Ugandan forces repulsed after crossing into Tanzania.
1979 Tanzanian troops sent to Uganda to help overthrow the president, Idi Amin.
1984 Nyerere announced his retirement but stayed on as CCM leader. Prime Minister Edward Sokoine killed in a traffic accident.
1985 Ali Hassan Mwinyi elected president.
1990 Nyerere surrendered party leadership.

allic element, symbol Ta, atomic number 73, atomic weight 180.948. It occurs with niobium in tantalite and other minerals. It can be drawn into wire with a very high melting point and great tenacity, useful for lamp filaments subject to vibration. It is also used in alloys, for corrosion-resistant laboratory apparatus and chemical equipment, as a catalyst in manufacturing synthetic rubber, in tools and instruments, and in rectifiers and capacitors.

It was discovered and named in 1802 by Swedish chemist Anders Ekeberg (1767–1813) for the mythological Greek figure Tantalus.

Tantalus in Greek mythology, a king whose crimes were punished in ◊Tartarus by food and drink he could not reach.

Tantrism forms of Hinduism and Buddhism that emphasize the division of the universe into male and female forces that maintain its unity by their interaction; this gives women equal status with men. Tantric Hinduism is associated with magical and sexual yoga practices that imitate the union of Siva and Sakti, as described in religious books known as the *Tantras*. In Buddhism, the *Tantras* are texts attributed to the Buddha, describing methods of attaining enlightenment.

Tantric Buddhism, practiced in medieval India, depended on the tuition of teachers and the use of yoga, mantras, and meditation to enable its followers to master themselves and gain oneness with the universe.

Tanzania country in E Africa, on the Indian Ocean, bounded N by Uganda and Kenya; S by Mozambique, Malawi, and Zambia; and W by Zaïre, Burundi, and Rwanda.

government The 1977 constitution made Tanzania a one-party Socialist republic with the Revolutionary Party of Tanzania (CCM). The president is chosen by the party to serve a maximum of two five-year terms. The president appoints two vice presidents from members of the National Assembly, and if the president comes from the mainland, the first vice-president must come from Zanzibar. The second vice-president is termed prime minister. The president also appoints and presides over a cabinet.

The single-chamber National Assembly has 243 members: 118 directly elected by universal suffrage for the mainland, 50 for the islands of Zanzibar and Pemba, 25 regional commissioners, 15 nominated by the president and 35 indirectly elected, to represent specific sections, including women and party organizations.

history For early history, see ◊Africa. Zanzibar was under Portuguese control during the 16th–17th centuries. In 1822 it was united with the nearby island of Pemba. It was a British protectorate 1890–1963, when it became an independent sultanate; an uprising followed, and the sultan was overthrown 1964.

Tanganyika was a German colony 1884–1914, until conquered by Britain during World War I; it was a British League of Nations mandate 1920–46 and came under United Nations (UN) trusteeship 1946–62. It achieved full independence, within the ◊Commonwealth, in 1961, with Julius ◊Nyerere as prime minister. He gave up the post some six weeks after independence to devote himself to the development of the Tanganyika African National Union (TANU), but in Dec 1962, when Tanganyika became a republic, he returned to become the nation's first president.

Tanzania was founded by the union of Tanganyika and Zanzibar in April 1964. Nyerere became president of the new United Republic of Tanzania and dominated the nation's politics for the next 20 years, being reelected in 1965, 1970, 1975, and 1980. Known throughout Tanzania as Mwalimu ("teacher"), he established himself as a Christian Socialist who attempted to put into practice a philosophy that he believed would secure his country's future. He committed himself in the Arusha Declaration of 1967 (the name comes from the N Tanzanian town where he made his historic statement) to building a Socialist state for the millions of poor peasants through a series of village cooperatives (*ujamas*). Nyerere became one of Africa's most respected politicians. In the final years of his presidency economic pressures, domestic and international, forced him to compromise his ideals and accept a more capitalistic society than he would have wished, but his achievements have included the best public health service on the African continent, according to UN officials, and a universal primary school system.

Relations between Tanzania and its neighbors have been variable. The East African Community (EAC) of Tanzania, Kenya, and Uganda, formed in 1967, broke up in 1977, and relations between Tanzania and the more capitalistic Kenya became uneasy. In 1979 Nyerere sent troops to support the Uganda National Liberation Front in its bid to overthrow President Idi Amin. This enhanced Nyerere's reputation but damaged his country's economy. Tanzania also supported the liberation movements in Mozambique and Rhodesia.

In 1977 TANU and the Afro-Shirazi Party of Zanzibar merged to become the Revolutionary Party of Tanzania (CCM), and this was made the only legal political organization. Nyerere retired from the presidency at the end of 1985 but remained as CCM chair. The president of Zanzibar, Ali Hassan Mwinyi, was adopted as the sole presidential candidate by the CCM congress in Dec 1985.

In May 1990 Julius Nyerere announced his retirement as party chair and in Aug 1990 he was replaced by President Mwinji.

Taoism Chinese philosophical system, traditionally founded by the Chinese philosopher Lao Zi 6th century BC, though the scriptures, *Tao Te Ching*, were apparently compiled 3rd century BC. The "tao" or "way" denotes the hidden principle of the universe, and less stress is laid on good deeds than on harmonious interaction with the environment, which automatically ensures right behavior. The second major work is that of Zhuangzi (c. 389–286 BC), *The Way of Zhuangzi*. The magical side of Taoism is illustrated by the *I Ching* or *Book of Changes*, a book of divination.

This magical, ritualistic aspect of Taoism developed from the 2nd century AD and was largely responsible for its popular growth; it stresses physical immortality, and this was attempted by means ranging from dietary regulation and fasting to alchemy. By the 3rd century, worship of gods had begun to appear, including that of the stove god Tsao Chun. From the 4th century, rivalry between Taoists and Mahayana Buddhists was strong in China, leading to persecution of one religion by the other; this was resolved by mutual assimilation, and Taoism developed monastic communities similar to those of the Buddhists.

Taormina coastal resort in E Sicily, at the foot of Mount Etna; population (1985) 9,000. It has an ancient Greek theater.

tap dancing rapid step dance, derived from clog dancing. Its main characteristic is the tapping of toes and heels (a shuffle-slap) accentuated by steel taps affixed to the shoes. It was popularized in ◊vaudeville and in 1930s films by dancers such as Fred Astaire and Bill "Bojangles" Robinson (1878–1949).

tape recording, magnetic method of recording electric signals on a layer of iron oxide, or other magnetic material, coating a thin plastic tape. The electrical impulses are fed to the electromagnetic recording head, which magnetizes the tape in accordance with the frequency and amplitude of the original signal. The impulses may be audio (for sound recording), video (for television), or data (for computer). For playback, the tape is passed over the same, or another, head to convert magnetic into electrical signals, which are then amplified for reproduction. Tapes are easily demagnetized (erased) for reuse, and come in cassette, cartridge, or reel form.

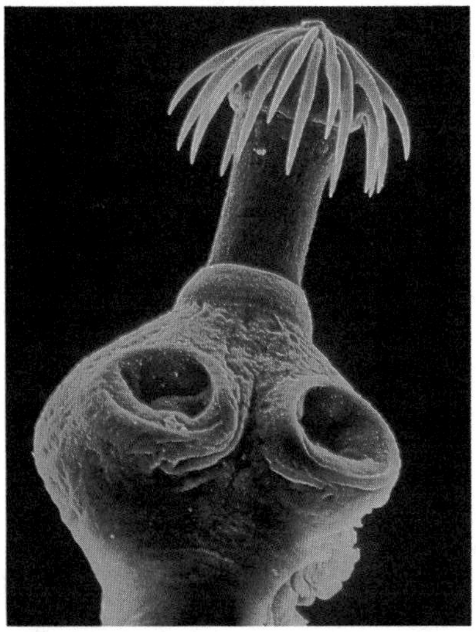

tapeworm Electron microscope picture of the head of a tapeworm showing the hooks used to cling on to the host's tissues (x 200).

tapestry ornamental woven textile used for wall hangings, furniture, and curtains. The tapestry design is threaded into the warp with various shades of yarn.

Tapestries have been woven for centuries in many countries, and during the Middle Ages the art was practiced in monasteries. European tapestries of the 13th century frequently featured oriental designs brought back by the Crusaders. The great European centers of tapestry weaving were in Belgium, France, and England. The ◊Gobelins tapestry factory of Paris was made a royal establishment in the 17th century. In England, William ◊Morris established the Merton Abbey looms in the late 19th century. Other designers have included ◊Raphael, ◊Rubens, and ◊Burne-Jones. The ◊Bayeux Tapestry is an embroidery rather than a true tapestry.

tapeworm any of various parasitic flatworms of the class Cestoda. They lack digestive and sense organs, can reach 50 ft/15 m in length, and attach themselves to the host's intestines by means of hooks and suckers. Tapeworms are made up of hundreds of individual segments, each of which develops into a functional hermaphroditic reproductive unit capable of producing numerous eggs. The larvae of tapeworms usually reach humans in imperfectly cooked meat or fish, causing anemia and intestinal disorders.

tapioca gelatinous, granular starch used in cooking, produced from the ◊cassava root, a New World plant.

tapir any of the odd-toed hoofed mammals (perissodactyls) of the single genus *Tapirus*, now constituting the family Tapiridae. There are four species living in the American and Malaysian tropics. Their general body form is rounded in back and tapering up front, with a short tail and a short trunk. They reach 3 ft/1 m at the shoulder and weigh up to 770 lb/350 kgs. Their survival is in danger because of destruction of the forests.

The Malaysian tapir *Tapirus indicus* is black with a large white patch on the back and hindquarters. The three South American species are dark to reddish brown.

taproot in botany, a single, robust, main ◊root that is derived from the embryonic root, or ◊radicle, and grows vertically downward, often to considerable depth. Taproots are often modified for food storage and are common in biennial plants such as the carrot *Daucus carota*, where they act as ◊perennating organs.

tar dark brown or black viscous liquid obtained by the destructive distillation of coal, shale, and wood. Tars consist of a mixture of hydrocarbons, acids, and bases. ◊Creosote and ◊paraffin are produced from wood tar. See also ◊coal tar.

Tara Hill ancient religious and political center in County Meath, S Ireland. The site of a palace and coronation place of many Irish kings, abandoned in the 6th century. St ◊Patrick preached here.

Taranaki peninsula in North Island, New Zealand, dominated by Mount ◊Egmont; volcanic soil makes it a rich dairy-farming area, and cheese is manufactured there.

tarantella peasant dance of southern Italy; also a piece of music composed for, or in the rhythm of, this dance in fast six-eight time.

Taranto naval base and port in Puglia region, SE Italy; population (1988) 245,000. It is an important commercial center, and its steelworks are part of the new industrial complex of S Italy. It was the site of the ancient Greek Tarentum, founded in the 8th century BC by ◊Sparta, and was captured by the Romans 272 BC.

tarantula wolf spider *Lycosa tarantula* with a 1 in/2.5 cm body. It spins no web, relying on its speed in hunting to catch its prey. The name "tarantula" is also used for any of the numerous large, hairy spiders of the family Theraphosidae with large poison fangs native to SW US and tropical America.

In the Middle Ages, its bite was thought to cause hysterical ailments for which dancing was the cure, hence the dance named "tarantella."

Tarawa port and capital of Kiribati; population (1985) 21,000.

Tarbell Ida Minerva 1857–1944. US journalist. After graduate studies at the Sorbonne, she was an editor and contributor to *McClure's Magazine* 1894–1906. Her exposés of corruption in high places made her one of the most prominent "muckrakers" in the US. Tarbell's book *The History of the Standard Oil Company* 1904 sparked antitrust reform. From 1906 to 1915 she joined Lincoln Steffens and Ray Stannard Baker on the staff of the *American Magazine*. Her autobiography, *All in a Day's Work*, appeared 1939.

Born in Erie County, Pennsylvania, Tarbell was educated at Allegheny College and became an editor of the *Chautauquan* 1883.

tare alternative common name for ◊vetch.

tariff tax on imports or exports from a country. Tariffs have generally been used by governments to protect home industries from lower-priced foreign goods, and have been opposed by supporters of free trade. For a tariff to be successful, it must not provoke retaliatory tariffs from other countries. Organizations such as the European Community, EFTA, and the General Agreement on Tariffs and Trade (GATT) 1948 have worked toward mutual lowering of tariffs between countries.

Tarim Basin (Chinese *Tarim Pendi*) internal drainage area in Xinjiang Uygur province, NW China, between the Tien Shan and Kunlun mountains; area about 350,000 sq mi/900,000 sq km. It is crossed by the Tarim He river and includes the lake of Lop Nur. The Taklimakan desert lies to the S of the Tarim He.

Tarkington Booth 1869–1946. US novelist, born in Indiana, author of *Monsieur Beaucaire* 1900 and novels of the Midwest, such as *The Magnificent Ambersons* 1918; filmed 1941 by Orson Welles. His novels for young people, which include *Penrod* 1914, are classics. He was among the best-selling authors of the early 20th century.

Tarkovsky Andrei 1932–1986. Soviet film director whose work is characterized by unorthodox cinematic techniques and visual beauty. His films include the science fiction *Solaris* 1972, *Mirror* 1975, and *The Sacrifice* 1986.

Tarn river in SW France, rising in the Cévennes and flowing 217 mi/350 km to the Garonne. It cuts the limestone plateaus in picturesque gorges.

taro or eddo plant *Colocasia esculenta* of the arum family Araceae, native to tropical Asia; the tubers are edible and are the source of Polynesian poi (a fermented food).

tarragon

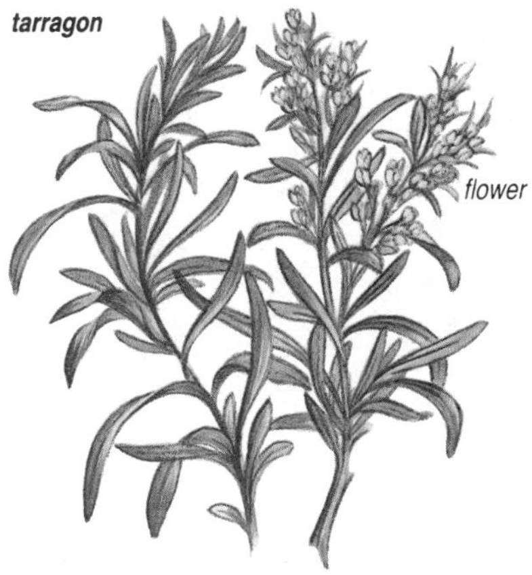
flower

tarot cards fortune-telling aid consisting of 78 cards: the minor arcana in four suits (resembling playing cards) and the major arcana, 22 cards with densely symbolic illustrations that have links with astrology and the ◊Kabbala.

history Of unknown (probably medieval) origin, the earliest known reference to tarot cards is from 1392. The pack may have been designed in Europe in the early 14th century as a repository of Gnostic ideas then being suppressed by the Christian church. Since the 18th century the tarot has interested occult scholars.

tarpon a large silver-sided fish *Tarpon atlanticus* of the family Megalopidae. It reaches 6 ft/2 m and may weigh 300 lb/135 kg. It lives in warm W Atlantic waters.

Tarquinius Superbus lived 5th century BC. Last king of Rome 534–510 BC. He abolished certain rights of Romans, and made the city powerful. He was deposed when his son Sextus raped ◊Lucretia.

tarragon perennial bushy herb *Artemisia dracunculus* of the daisy family Compositae, native to the Old World, growing to 5 ft/1.5 m, with narrow leaves and small green-white flower heads arranged in groups. Tarragon contains an aromatic oil; its leaves are used to flavor salads, pickles, and tartar sauce. It is closely related to wormwood.

Tarragona port in Catalonia, Spain; population (1986) 110,000. Industries include petrochemicals, pharmaceuticals, and electrical goods. It has a cathedral and Roman remains, including an aqueduct and amphitheater.

Tarrasa town in Catalonia, NE Spain; industries include textiles and fertilizers; population (1986) 160,000.

Tarshish city mentioned in the Old Testament, probably the Phoenician settlement of Tartessus in Spain.

tarsier any of three species of the prosimian primates, genus *Tarsius* of the East Indies and the Phillippines. These survivors of early primates are about the size of a rat with thick, light-brown fur, very large eyes, and long feet and hands. They are nocturnal, arboreal, and eat insects and lizards.

Tarsus city in Içel province, SE Turkey, on the river Pamuk; population (1980) 121,000. Formerly the capital of the Roman province of Cilicia, it was the birthplace of St ◊Paul.

tartan woolen cloth woven in specific plaid patterns individual to Scottish clans, with stripes of different widths and colors criss-crossing on a colored background; used in making skirts, kilts, trousers, and other articles.

Developed in the 17th century, tartan was banned after the 1745 ◊Jacobite rebellion, and not legalized again until 1782.

tartaric acid $HCOO(CHOH)_2COOH$ organic acid present in vegetable tissues and fruit juices in the form of salts of potassium, calcium, and magnesium. It is used in carbonated drinks and baking powders.

Tasmania

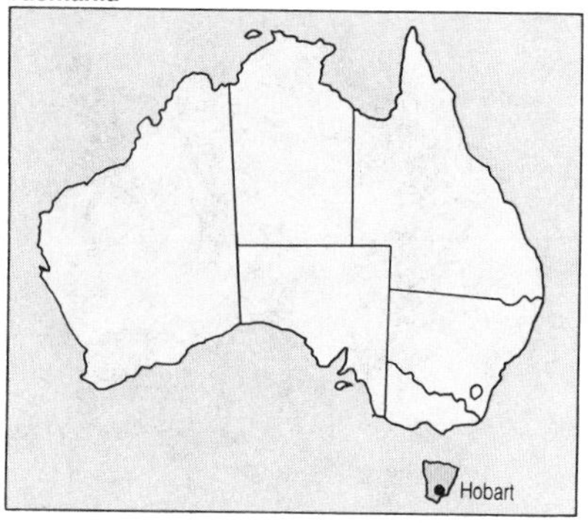
Hobart

Tartarus in Greek mythology, a part of ◊Hades, the underworld, where the wicked were punished.

Tartini Giuseppe 1692–1770. Italian composer and violinist. In 1728 he founded a school of violin playing in Padua. A leading exponent of violin technique, he composed the *Devil's Trill* sonata.

Tartu city in Estonia; industries include engineering and food processing; population (1981) 107,000. Once a stronghold of the ◊Teutonic Knights, it was taken by Russia 1558 and then held by Sweden and Poland but returned to Russian control 1704.

Tarzan fictitious hero inhabiting the African rainforest, created by US writer Edgar Rice ◊Burroughs in *Tarzan of the Apes* 1914, with numerous sequels. He and his partner Jane have featured in films, comic strips, and television serials.

Tarzan, raised by apes from infancy, is in fact a British peer, Lord Greystoke. He has enormous physical strength and the ability to communicate with animals. Jane Porter, an American, falls in love with him while on safari and elects to stay.

Tasaday member of an indigenous people of the rainforests of Mindanao in the ◊Philippines, discovered by anthropologists in the 1960s.

Tashkent capital of Uzbekistan, S central USSR; population (1987) 2,124,000. Industries include the manufacture of mining machinery, chemicals, textiles, and leather goods. Founded in the 7th century, it was taken by the Turks in the 12th century and captured by Tamerlane 1361. In 1865 it was taken by the Russians. It was severely damaged by an earthquake 1966.

A temporary truce between Pakistan and India over ◊Kashmir was established at the Declaration of Tashkent 1966.

Tasman Abel Janszoon 1603–1659. Dutch navigator. In 1642, he was the first European to see Tasmania. He also made the first European sightings of New Zealand, Tonga, and Fiji.

Tasmania former name (until 1856) Van Diemen's Land island off the S coast of Australia; a state of the Commonwealth of Australia
area 26,171 sq mi/67,800 sq km
capital Hobart
cities Launceston (chief port)
features an island state (including small islands in the Bass Strait, and Macquarie Island); Franklin River, a wilderness area saved from a hydroelectric scheme 1983, which also has a prehistoric site; unique fauna including Tasmanian devil, Tasmanian "tiger"
products wool, dairy products, apples and other fruit, timber, iron, tin, coal, copper, silver
population (1987) 448,000
history the first European to visit here was Abel Tasman 1642; the last of the Tasmanian Aboriginals died 1876. Tasmania joined the Australian Commonwealth as a state 1901.

Tasmanian devil carnivorous marsupial *Sarcophilus harrisii*, in the same family (Dasyuridae) as native "cats." It is about 2.1 ft/65 cm long with a 10 in/25 cm bushy tail. It has a large head, strong teeth, and is blackish with white patches on the chest and hind parts. It is nocturnal, carnivorous, and can be ferocious when cornered. It has recently

Tasmanian devil

become extinct in Australia and survives only in remote parts of Tasmania.

Tasmanian wolf or thylacine carnivorous marsupial *Thylacinus cynocephalus*, in the family Dasyuridae. It is doglike in appearance and can be nearly 6 ft/2 m from nose to tail tip. It was hunted to probable extinction in the 1930s, but there are still occasional unconfirmed reports of sightings.

The dingo exterminated the Tasmanian wolf on the Australian mainland. Also known as Tasmanian tiger.

Tasman Sea the part of the ◊Pacific Ocean between SE Australia and NW New Zealand. It is named after the Dutch explorer Abel Tasman.

Tass acronym for the Soviet news agency Telegrafnoye Agentstvo Sovyetskovo Soyuza.

Tasso Torquato 1544–1595. Italian poet, author of the romantic epic poem of the First Crusade *La Gerusalemme Liberata/Jerusalem Delivered* 1574, followed by the *Gerusalemme Conquistata/Jerusalem Conquered*, written during the period from 1576 when he was mentally unstable.

At first a law student at Padua, he overcame his father's opposition to a literary career by the success of his romantic poem *Rinaldo* 1562, dedicated to Cardinal Luigi d'Este, who took him to Paris. There he met the members of the ◊Pléiade group of poets. Under the patronage of Duke Alfonso d'Este of Ferrara, he wrote his pastoral play *Aminta* in 1573.

taste sense that detects some of the chemical constituents of food. The human ◊tongue can distinguish only four basic tastes (sweet, sour, bitter, and salty) but it is supplemented by the nose's sense of smell. What we refer to as taste is really a composite sense made up of both taste and smell.

Tatar or ***Tartar*** member of a Turkic-speaking, mainly Muslim people, the descendants of the mixed Mongol and Turkic followers of ◊Genghis Khan, called the Golden Horde because of the wealth they gained by plunder. They now live mainly in Tatar and Uzbekistan (where they were deported from the Crimea 1944) and SW Siberia, USSR. Their language belongs to the Altaic family.

Tatar Autonomous Republic administrative region of W central USSR
area 26,250 sq mi/68,000 sq km
capital Kazan
products oil, chemicals, textiles, timber
population (1986) 3,537,000
history territory of Volga-Kama Bulgar state from 10th to 13th centuries; conquered by Mongols until 15th century; conquered by Russia 1552; became an autonomous republic 1920.

Tate Jeffrey 1943– . English conductor. He was appointed principal conductor of the English Chamber Orchestra in 1985 and principal conductor of the Royal Opera House, Covent Garden, London, in 1986. He has conducted opera in Paris, in Geneva, and at the Metropolitan Opera, New York. He qualified as a doctor of medicine before turning to a career in music.

Tate Gallery art gallery (British art from the late 16th century, and international from 1810) in London. Endowed by the sugar merchant Henry Tate (1819–1899), it was opened 1897.

Tati Jacques. Adopted name of Jacques Tatischeff 1908–1982. French comic actor, director, and writer. He portrayed Monsieur Hulot, a character who embodies polite opposition to modern mechanization, in a series of films including *Les Vacances de M Hulot/Monsieur Hulot's Holiday* 1953.

Tatlin Vladimir 1885–1953. Russian artist, cofounder of ◊Constructivism. After encountering Cubism in Paris 1913 he evolved his first Constructivist works, using raw materials such as tin, glass, plaster, and wood to create abstract sculptures that he suspended in the air.

Tatra Mountains range in central Europe, extending for about 40 mi/65 km along the Polish-Czechoslovakian border; the highest part of the central ◊Carpathians.

tatting lacework in cotton, made since medieval times by knotting and looping a single thread with a small shuttle.

Tatum Art(hur) 1910–1956. US jazz pianist who, in the 1930s worked mainly as a soloist. Tatum is considered among the most technically brilliant of jazz pianists and his technique and chromatic harmonies influenced many musicians, such as Oscar Peterson (1925–). He improvised with the guitarist Tiny Grimes (1916–) in a trio from 1943.

Tatum Edward Lawrie 1909–1975. US microbiologist. For his work on biochemical genetics, he shared the 1958 Nobel Prize for Medicine with George Beadle and Joshua Lederberg.

Taube Henry 1915– . US chemist who established the basis of inorganic chemistry through his study of the loss or gain of electrons by atoms during chemical reactions.

He was awarded a Nobel Prize for Chemistry in 1983 for his work on electron transference between molecules in chemical reactions.

Tau Ceti one of the nearest stars visible to the naked eye, 11.9 light-years from Earth in the constellation Cetus. It has a diameter slightly less than that of the Sun and an actual luminosity about 45% that of the Sun. Its similarity to the Sun is sufficient to suggest that Tau Ceti may possess a planetary system, although observations have yet to reveal evidence of this.

Taunus Mountains mountain range in Hessen, Federal Republic of Germany, where there are several mineral spas.

Taupo largest lake in New Zealand, in a volcanic area of hot springs; area 239 sq mi/620 sq km. It is the source of the Waikato River.

Taurus zodiac constellation in the northern hemisphere near Orion, represented as a bull. The Sun passes through Taurus from mid-May to late June. Its brightest star is Aldebaran, seen as the bull's red eye. Taurus contains the Hyades and Pleiades open ◊star clusters, and the Crab nebula. In astrology, the dates for Taurus are between about 20 Apr and May 20 (see ◊precession).

Taurus Mountains (Turkish *Toros Dağlari*) mountain range in S Turkey, forming the southern edge of the Anatolian plateau and rising to over 12,000 ft/3,656 m.

Taussig Helen Brooke 1898–1986. US cardiologist who developed surgery for "blue" babies. Such babies never fully develop the shunting mechanism in the circulatory system that allows blood to be oxygenated in the lungs before passing to the rest of the body. The babies are born chronically short of oxygen and usually do not survive without surgery.

tautology repetition of the same thing in different words, or the ungrammatical use of unnecessary words: for example, it is tautologous to say that something is *most unique*, since something unique cannot, by definition, be comparative.

taxation the raising of money from individuals and organizations by state and local governments, to pay for the goods and services they provide. Taxation can be direct (a deduction from income) or indirect (added to the purchase price of goods or services—that is, a tax on consumption).

The most common form of indirect taxation in the US is the sales tax, applied to the purchase price of items. The most common form of direct taxation is the income tax, withheld from paychecks and imposed by most of the states as well as the federal government.

Taxation can be an important economic and social policy tool. By themselves, taxes would reduce economic activity by taking money out of circulation. The benefit of taxes, then, depends on the use to which the funds are put. A redistribution of resources takes place when funds collected from taxpayers are used to pay contractors to build housing or provide food or education for the poor. The tax structure helps determine the distribution of resources. For example, progressive taxes take an increasing percentage of income as it rises; proportional tax rates take the same percentage of income across all levels; and regressive rates take a higher percentage as income is reduced. Direct taxes tend to be proportional or progressive, whereas indirect taxes are generally regressive, since they take a higher percentage of income from the poor.

Taxes have important social as well as economic purposes. High excise taxes, applied to specific commodities, can be used either to raise tax revenues or to try to discourage consumption of those items, examples being cigarettes, liquor, gasoline, and luxury items. In some states following the Civil War, poll taxes were used to disenfranchise poor blacks who could not afford to pay them. Corporate taxes must find a delicate balance, since rates that are too high can drive businesses from one state to another or, in extreme instances, force them to relocate in another country, or cease operating entirely.

During the Reagan administrations, it was argued by supply-side economists that reductions in tax rates would actually produce increased revenues by stimulating a growth in overall economic activity. Conversely, it was held that increased tax rates would yield decreased revenue by discouraging growth. Federal taxation was simplified and rates reduced by Congress to some of the lowest rates among industrialized nations 1987.

tax avoidance the conducting of financial affairs in such a way as to keep tax liability to a minimum within the law.

tax deductible an item that may be offset against tax liability, such as the cost of a car where it is required as a business expense, is termed "tax deductible."

tax evasion failure to meet tax liabilities by illegal action, such as not declaring income. Tax evasion is a criminal offense.

tax haven country or state where taxes are much lower than elsewhere. It is often used by companies of another country that register in the tax haven to avoid tax. Any business transacted is treated as completely confidential. Tax havens include the Channel Islands, Switzerland, Bermuda, the Bahamas, and Liberia.

taxis (plural ***taxes***) or ***tactic*** movement in botany, the movement of a single cell, such as a bacterium, protozoan, single-celled alga, or gamete, in response to an external stimulus. A movement directed toward the stimulus is described as positive taxis, and away from it as negative taxis. The alga *Chlamydomonas*, for example, demonstrates positive phototaxis by swimming toward a light source to increase the rate of photosynthesis. Chemotaxis is a response to a chemical stimulus, as seen in many bacteria that move toward higher concentrations of nutrients.

tax loophole gap in the law that can be exploited to gain a tax advantage not intended by the government when the law was made.

Taxodium tree genus of the redwood family (Taxodiaceae). Also called ◊wormwood.

taxonomy another name for the ◊classification of living organisms.

tax shelter investment opportunity designed to reduce the tax burden on an individual or group of individuals but at the same time to stimulate finance in the direction of a particular location or activity. Such shelters might be tax-exempt or lightly taxed securities in government or a local authority, or in forestry or energy projects.

Taylor *English-born actress Elizabeth Taylor with costar Montgomery Clift in a scene from* Raintree County *1957.*

Tay longest river in Scotland; length 118 mi/189 km. Rising in NW Central region, it flows NE through Loch Tay, then E and SE past Perth to the Firth of Tay, crossed at Dundee by the Tay Bridge, before joining the North Sea. The Tay has salmon fisheries; its main tributaries are the Tummel, Isla, and Earn.

Taylor Elizabeth 1932– . English-born US actress. Noted for both her beauty and acting skill since childhood, her films include *Lassie Come Home* 1942, *National Velvet* 1944, *Father of the Bride* 1950, *Giant* 1956, *Raintree County* 1957, *Cat On a Hot Tin Roof* 1958, *Butterfield 8* 1960 (Academy Award), *Cleopatra* 1963, and *Who's Afraid of Virginia Woolf?* 1966 (Academy Award). She appeared on Broadway in *The Little Foxes* 1981 and has appeared in TV movies, including *Malice in Wonderland*, portraying Louella Parsons.

Her many husbands included the actors Michael Wilding, Eddie Fisher, and Richard ◊Burton (twice).

Taylor Frederick Winslow 1856–1915. US engineer and management consultant, the founder of scientific management. His ideas, published in *Principles of Scientific Management* 1911, were based on the breakdown of work to the simplest tasks, the separation of planning from execution of tasks, and the introduction of time-and-motion studies. His methods were clearly expressed in assembly-line factories, but have been criticized for degrading and alienating workers and producing managerial dictatorship.

Taylor Zachary (1784–1850) 12th president of the US 1849–50. A veteran of the War of 1812 and a hero of the Mexican War (1846–48), he then left the military for politics. Nominated by the Whigs in 1848, he defeated opponents Lewis Cass and Martin van Buren for the presidency but died less than one and a half years into his term. He was succeeded by Vice President Millard Fillmore.

Born in Virginia, Taylor grew up in frontier Kentucky. He began 40 years of army service in 1808 and played a key role in Ft Harrison's defense during the War of 1812. Most of his military career was spent on the frontier, and he distinguished himself in campaigns against the Indians. In the Seminole Wars in Florida his successes led to his promotion to brigadier general and command of the Florida department (1838–40). By now known by his nickname "Old Rough and Ready," Taylor won his greatest fame in the Mexican War. While commander of the US forces occupying the recently-annexed Texas, he opposed Mexican forces on President Polk's orders.

In spring 1846, Taylor advanced into Mexico and almost immediately won several battles and a promotion to major general. By fall he had taken Monterrey and in Feb 1847 defeated Santa Anna at Buena Vista.

His short presidency was dominated by controversies over the slavery issue, with Taylor supporting the anti-slavery elements that were pushing for the admission to the Union of more free states. Taylor died unexpectedly of cholera while the Compromise of 1850 was being shaped.

Tay-Sachs disease inherited disorder, due to a defective gene, causing an enzyme deficiency that leads to blindness, retardation, and death in childhood. Because of their enforced isolation and inbreeding during hundreds of years, it is most common in people of E European Jewish descent.

Tayside region of Scotland
area 2,973 sq mi/7,700 sq km
cities Dundee (administrative headquarters), Perth, Arbroath, Forfar
features river Tay; ◊Grampian Mountains; lochs: Tay and Rannoch; hills: Ochil and Sidlaw; vales of the North and South Esk
products beef and dairy products, soft fruit from the fertile Carse of Gowrie (SW of Dundee)
population (1987) 394,000
famous people James Barrie.

Taylor *The 12th president of the United States of America, Zachary Taylor, a Whig. 1848–1850.*

TB abbreviation for the infectious disease ◊tuberculosis.

Tbilisi formerly Tiflis capital of Georgia, SW USSR; population (1987) 1,194,000. Industries include textiles, machinery, ceramics, and tobacco. Dating from the 5th century, it is a center of Georgian culture, with fine medieval churches. Anti-Russian demonstrations were quashed here by troops 1981 and 1989, the latter following rejected demands for autonomy from the Abkhazia enclave, resulting in 19 or more deaths from poison gas (containing chloroacetophenone) and 100 injured.

T cell or ***T lymphocyte*** immune cell (see ◊immunity and ◊lymphocyte) that plays several roles in the blood stream to maintain the body's defenses. T cells are so called because they mature in the ◊thymus.

There are three main types of T cells: T helper cells (Th cells), which allow other immune cells to go into action; T suppressor cells (Ts cells), which stop specific immune reactions from occurring; and T cytotoxic cells (Tc cells), which kill cells that are cancerous or infected with viruses. Like ◊B cells, to which they are related, T cells have surface receptors that make them specific for particular antigens.

Tchaikovsky Pyotr Il'yich 1840–1893. Russian composer. His strong sense of melody, personal expression, and brilliant orchestration are clear throughout his many Romantic works, which include eight symphonies (one is incomplete and the *Manfred* is unnumbered), three piano concertos and a violin concerto, operas (for example, *Eugene Onegin* 1879), ballets (for example, *The Nutcracker* 1892), orchestral fantasies (for example, *Romeo and Juliet* 1870), and chamber and vocal music.

Professor of harmony at Moscow in 1865, he later met ◊Balakirev, becoming involved with the nationalist movement in music. He was the first Russian composer to establish a reputation with Western audiences.

He conducted the opening night program at Carnegie Hall, in New York City, 1891.

tea evergreen shrub *Camellia sinensis*, family Theaceae, of which the fermented, dried leaves are infused to make a beverage of the same name. Known in China as early as 2737 BC, tea was first brought to Europe AD 1610 and rapidly became a fashionable drink. In 1823 it was found growing wild in N India, and plantations were later established in Assam and Sri Lanka; producers today include Africa, South America, the USSR, Indonesia, and Iran.

Growing naturally to 40 ft/12 m, the tea plant is restricted in cultivation to bushes 4 ft/1.5 m high. The young shoots and leaves are picked every five years. After 24 hours spread on shelves in withering lofts, they are broken up by rolling machines to release the essential oils, and then left to ferment. This process is halted by passing the leaves through ovens where moisture is removed and the blackish-brown black tea emerges ready for sifting into various grades. Green tea is steamed and quickly dried before fermentation, remaining partly green in color.

Tea was not in use in England or the American colonies until 1657. It remained expensive as long as cargoes had to be brought from China in sailing ships, the fast tea clippers. Methods of consumption vary: in Japan special teahouses and an elaborate tea ceremony have evolved; in England afternoon tea has its own ritual; and in Tibet hard slabs of compressed tea are used as money before being finally brewed.

In the US, tea with lemon and honey is a cold remedy, but iced tea has become a year-round soft drink, sold in cans like colas. After the American Revolution, the new US citizens turned away from tea (as being British) and imported ◊coffee instead. Only after 200 years did tea revive its popularity in the US.

teak tropical Asian timber tree *Tectona grandis*, family Verbenaceae, with yellowish wood used in furniture and shipbuilding.

teal any of various small, shortnecked dabbling ducks of the genus *Anas*. The drakes generally have a bright head and wing markings. The green-winged teal *A. crecca* is about 14 in/35 cm long.

Teapot Dome Scandal US political scandal that revealed the corruption of President ◊Harding's administration. It centered on the leasing of naval oil reserves in 1921 at Teapot Dome, Wyoming, without competitive bidding, as a result of bribing Secretary of the Interior Albert B Fall (1861–1944). Fall was tried and imprisoned 1929. A Senate investigation revealed that Fall had accepted gifts and loans totaling $400,000. The US Supreme Court nullified the leases 1927. The two oil-company executives involved were acquitted on technicalities, but one of them, Harry Sinclair, was later imprisoned for jury tampering and contempt of the Senate.

tear gas any of various volatile gases that produce irritation and tearing of the eyes, used by police against crowds and used in chemical warfare. The gas is delivered in pressurized, liquid-filled canisters or grenades, thrown by hand or launched from a specially adapted rifle. Gases such as mace cause violent coughing and blinding tears, which pass when the victim breathes fresh air, and there are no lasting effects. Blister gases (such as mustard gas) and nerve gases are more harmful and may cause permanent injury or death.

teasel erect, prickly, biennial herb *Dipsacus fullonum*, family Dipsacaceae, native to Eurasia. The dry, spiny seed heads were once used industrially to tease, or raise the nap of, cloth.

Tebaldi Renata 1922– . Italian dramatic soprano, renowned for the controlled purity of her voice and for her roles in ◊Puccini operas.

technetium silver-gray, radioactive, metallic element, symbol Tc, atomic number 43, atomic weight 98.906. It occurs in nature only in extremely minute amounts, produced as a fission product from uranium in ◊pitchblende and other uranium ores. Technetium is a superconductor and is used as a hardener in steel alloys and as a medical tracer. Its longest-lived isotope, Tc-99, has a half-life of 216,000 years.

It was synthesized in 1937 (named in 1947) by Italian physicists Carlo Perrier and Emilio Segrè, who bombarded molybdenum with deuterons, looking to fill a missing spot in the ◊periodic table of the elements, since at that time it was considered not to occur in nature, thus it was named for *technetos*, Greek for "artificial" or "contrived." It was later isolated in large amounts from the fission-product debris of uranium fuel in nuclear reactors.

Technicolor trade name for a film color process using three separate negatives of blue, green, and red images. It was invented by Daniel F Comstock and Herbert T Kalmus in the US 1922. Originally, Technicolor was a two-color process in which superimposed red and green images were projected on to the screen by a special projector.

This initial version proved expensive and imperfect, but when the three-color process was introduced 1932, the system was widely adopted, culminating in its use in *The Wizard of Oz* and *Gone with the Wind* both 1939. Despite increasing competition, Technicolor remains the most commonly used color process for cinematography.

technocracy society controlled by technical experts such as scientists and engineers. The term was invented by US engineer W H Smyth 1919 to describe his proposed "rule by technicians," and was popularized by James Burham (1903–) in *Managerial Revolution* 1941.

technology the practical application of science in everyday life. The growth of technology began with the ◊Industrial Revolution in the second half of the 18th century with the invention of the steam engine. The introduction of electricity as a power source and of the internal combustion engine (leading to the motorcar and aircraft) in the early 20th century transformed everyday life in the industrialized countries. The pace of technological development escalated in the middle and late 20th century with the introduction of ◊electronics, ◊nuclear power, ◊computers, ◊robots, and space ◊satellites. Areas of current development include information technology (the use of computers to store, retrieve, and manipulate information by using systems such as ◊teletext and ◊videotext), medical technology (organ ◊transplants and ◊tomography), military technology (such as the US ◊Strategic Defense Initiative), energy (◊solar energy and tidal power stations, communications (the ◊cellular phone and ◊optical fibers), and entertainment (many developments in ◊television and ◊video). See also ◊engineering.

Humans are distinguished from other animals by their 5-million-year development of tools and technology. Almost every human process for getting food and shelter depends on complex technological systems, now elaborated by engineers, architects, and other specialists.

tectonics in geology, the study of the deformation of rocks on the Earth's surface. On a small scale tectonics involves the formation of ◊folds and ◊faults, but on a large scale ◊plate tectonics deals with the movement of the Earth's crust as a whole.

Tecumseh 1768–1813. North American Indian chief of the Shawnee. He attempted to unite the Indian peoples from Canada to Florida against the encroachment of white settlers, but the defeat of his brother Tenskwatawa, popularly known as "the Prophet," at the battle of Tippecanoe in Nov 1811 by then-governor of the Indiana Territory W H ◊Harrison, largely destroyed the confederacy built by Tecumseh. He allied himself with the British in the War of 1812, during which he helped take Detroit, fomented the Creek War 1813 in the South, and led an invasion of Ohio. He was killed in Canada at the Battle of the Thames 1813, a battle won by Harrison, who would campaign for the presidency 1840 largely on the strength of his military exploits against Tecumseh.

Tedder Arthur William, 1st Baron 1890–1967. UK marshal of the Royal Air Force in World War II. As deputy supreme commander under US general Eisenhower 1943–45, he was largely responsible for the initial success of the 1944 Normandy landings.

Tees river flowing from the Pennines in Cumbria, England, to the North Sea via Tees Bay in ◊Cleveland; length 80 mi/130 km.

Teesside industrial area at the mouth of the river Tees, Cleveland, NE England; population (1981) 382,700. Industries include high-technology, capital-intensive steelmaking; chemicals; an oil-fuel terminal; and the main North Sea natural-gas terminal. Middlesbrough is a major port.

tefillin or ***phylacteries*** in Judaism, two small leather boxes containing scrolls from the Torah, that are strapped to the left arm and the forehead by Jewish men for daily prayer.

telecommunications

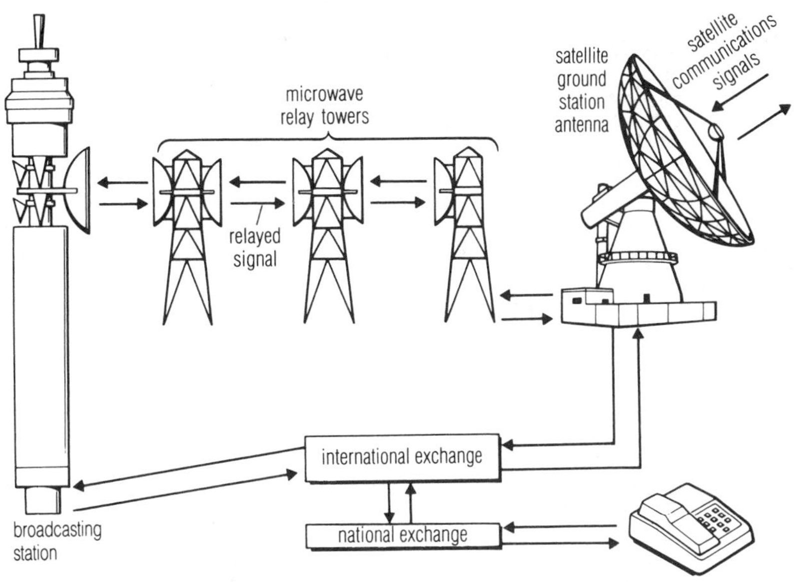

microwave relay towers
satellite ground station antenna
satellite communications signals
relayed signal
international exchange
broadcasting station
national exchange

Teflon trade name for polytetrafluoroethene (PTFE), a tough, waxlike, heat-resistant plastic used for coating nonsticking cookware and in gaskets and bearings.

Tegucigalpa capital of Honduras, population (1986) 605,000. It has textile and food-processing industries. It was founded 1524 as a gold and silver mining center.

Tehran capital of Iran; population (1986) 6,043,000. Industries include textiles, chemicals, engineering, and tobacco. It was founded in the 12th century and made the capital 1788 by Mohammed Shah. Much of the city was rebuilt in the 1920s and 1930s. Tehran is the site of the Gulistan Palace (the former royal residence).

Tehran Conference conference held 1943 in Tehran, Iran, the first meeting of World War II Allied leaders Churchill, Roosevelt, and Stalin. The chief subject discussed was coordination of Allied strategy in W and E Europe.

Teilhard de Chardin Pierre 1881–1955. French Jesuit theologian, paleontologist, and philosopher. He is best known for his creative synthesis of nature and religion, based on his fieldwork and fossil studies. Publication of his *Le Phénomène humain/The Phenomenon of Man*, written 1938–40, was delayed (due to his unorthodox views) until after his death by the embargo of his superiors. He saw humanity as being in a constant process of evolution, moving toward a perfect spiritual state.

Tej Bahadur 1621–1675. Indian religious leader, ninth guru (teacher) of Sikhism 1664–75, executed for refusing to renounce his faith.

Tejo Portuguese name for the river ◊Tagus.

Te Kanawa Kiri 1944– . New Zealand opera singer. Her first major role was the Countess in Mozart's *The Marriage of Figaro* at Covent Garden, London, 1971. She sang at the wedding of Prince Charles in 1980.

tektite (Greek *tektos* "molten") small, rounded glassy stone, found in certain regions of the Earth, such as Australasia. They are probably the scattered drops of molten rock thrown out by the impact of a large ◊meteorite.

Tel Aviv officially ***Tel Aviv–Jaffa*** city in Israel, on the Mediterranean Sea; population (1987) 320,000. Industries include textiles, chemicals, sugar, printing, and publishing. Tel Aviv was founded 1909 as a Jewish residential area in the Arab town of Jaffa, with which it was combined 1949; their ports were superseded 1965 by Ashdod to the S.

telecommunications communications over a distance, generally by electronic means. Long-distance voice communication was pioneered 1876 by Alexander Graham Bell, when he invented the telephone as a result of Faraday's discovery of electromagnetism. Today it is possible to communicate with most countries by telephone cable, or by satellite or microwave link, with over 100,000 simultaneous conversations and several television channels being carried by the latest satellites. Integrated-services digital network (ISDN) is a system that transmits voice and image data on a single transmission line by changing them into digital signals, making videophones and high-quality fax possible; the world's first large-scale center of ISDN began operating in Japan 1988. The chief method of relaying long-distance calls on land is microwave radio transmission.

The first mechanical telecommunications systems were the ◊semaphore and heliograph (using flashes of sunlight), invented in the mid-19th century, but the forerunner of the present telecommunications age was the electric telegraph. The earliest practicable telegraph instrument was invented by W F Cooke and Charles ◊Wheatstone in Britain 1837 and used by railroad companies. In the US, Samuel Morse invented a signaling code, ◊Morse code, which is still used, and a recording telegraph, first used commercially between England and France 1851. As a result of ◊Hertz's discoveries using electromagnetic waves, ◊Marconi pioneered a "wireless" telegraph, ancestor of the radio. He established wireless communication between England and France 1899 and across the Atlantic 1901. The modern telegraph uses teleprinters to send coded messages along telecommunications lines. Telegraphs are keyboard-operated machines that transmit a five-unit Baudot code (see ◊baud). The receiving teleprinter automatically prints the received message.

The drawback to long-distance voice communication via microwave radio transmission is that the transmissions follow a straight line from tower to tower, so that over the sea the system becomes impracticable. A solution was put forward 1945 by the science-fiction writer Arthur C Clarke, when he proposed a system of communications satellites in an orbit 22,300 mi/35,900 km above the equator, where they would circle the Earth in exactly 24 hours, and thus appear fixed in the sky. Such a system is now in operation internationally, by ◊Intelsat. The satellites are called geosynchronous or geostationary satellites (syncoms). The first to be successfully launched,

telecommunications chronology

1794	Claude Chappe in France built a long-distance signaling system using semaphore.
1839	Charles Wheatstone and William Cooke devised an electric telegraph in England.
1843	Samuel Morse transmitted the first message along a telegraph line in the US, using his Morse code of signals—short (dots) and long (dashes).
1858	The first transatlantic telegraph cable was laid.
1876	Alexander Graham Bell invented the telephone.
1877	Thomas Edison invented the carbon transmitter for the telephone.
1894	Marconi pioneered wireless telegraphy in Italy, later moving to England.
1900	Fessenden in the US first broadcast voice by radio.
1901	Marconi transmitted the first radio signals across the Atlantic.
1904	Fleming invented the thermionic valve.
1907	Charles Krumm introduced the forerunner of the teleprinter.
1920	Stations in Detroit and Pittsburgh began regular radio broadcasts.
1922	The BBC began its first radio transmissions, for the London station 2LO.
1932	The Post Office introduced the Telex in Britain.
1956	The first transatlantic telephone cable was laid.
1962	Telstar pioneers transatlantic satellite communications, transmitting live TV pictures.
1966	Charles Kao in England advanced the idea of using optical fibers for telecommunications transmissions.
1969	Live TV pictures were sent from astronauts on the Moon back to Earth.
1975	The Post Office announced Prestel, the world's first viewdata system, using the telephone lines to link a computer data bank with the TV screen.
1977	The first optical fiber cable was installed in California.
1986	*Voyager 2* transmitted images of the planet Uranus over a distance of 2 billion mi/3 billion km, the signals taking 2 hours 45 minutes to make the journey back to Earth.
1988	Videophones introduced in Japan.
1989	*Voyager 2* transmitted images of the planet Neptune; the first transoceanic optical fiber cable, capable of carrying 40,000 simultaneous telephone conversations, was laid between Europe and the US.

telescope

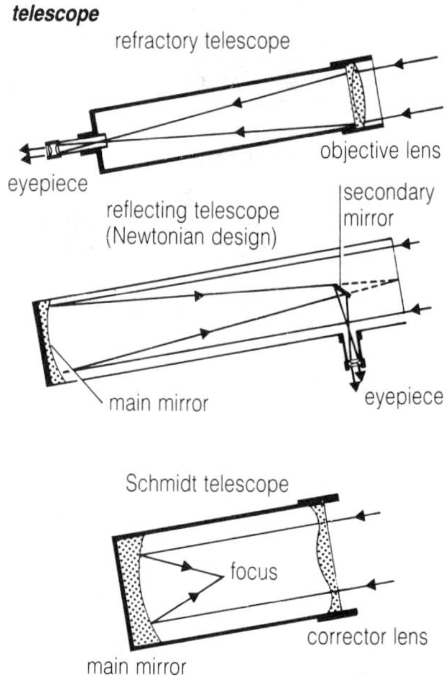
refractory telescope
objective lens
eyepiece
reflecting telescope
(Newtonian design)
secondary
mirror
main mirror
eyepiece
Schmidt telescope
focus
corrector lens
main mirror

by Delta rocket from Cape Canaveral, was *Syncom 2* in July 1963. Many such satellites are now in use, concentrated over heavy traffic areas such as the Atlantic, Indian, and Pacific oceans. Telegraphy, telephony, and television transmissions are carried simultaneously by high-frequency radio waves. They are beamed to the satellites from large dish antennae or Earth stations, which connect with international networks.

Recent advances include the use of fiber-optic cables consisting of fine fiberglass for telephone lines instead of the usual copper cables. The telecommunications signals are transmitted along the fibers on pulses of laser light.

telegraphy transmission of coded messages along wires by means of electrical signals. The first modern form of telecommunication, it now uses printers for the transmission and receipt of messages. Telex is an international telegraphy network.

Telemachus in Greek mythology, son of ◊Odysseus and ◊Penelope. He attempts to control the conduct of his mother's suitors in ◊Homer's *Odyssey* while his father is believed dead, but on Odysseus' return helps him to kill them, with the support of the goddess ◊Athene.

Telemann Georg Philipp 1681–1767. German Baroque composer, organist, and conductor at the Johanneum, Hamburg, from 1721. He was one of the most prolific composers ever, producing 25 operas, 1,800 church cantatas, hundreds of other vocal works, and 600 instrumental works.

telemetry measurement at a distance, in particular the systems by which information is obtained and sent back by instruments on board a spacecraft. See ◊remote sensing.

telepathy "the communication of impressions of any kind from one mind to another, independently of the recognized channels of sense," as defined by F W H Myers, a 19th-century investigator of psychic phenomena, who coined the term.

telephone instrument for communicating by voice over long distances, invented by Alexander Graham ◊Bell 1876. The transmitter (mouthpiece) consists of a carbon microphone, with a diaphragm that vibrates when a person speaks into it. The diaphragm vibrations compress grains of carbon to a greater or lesser extent, altering their resistance to an electric current passing through them. This sets up variable electrical signals, which travel along the telephone lines to the receiver of the person being called. There they cause the magnetism of an electromagnet to vary, making a diaphragm above the electromagnet vibrate and give out sound waves, which mirror those that entered the mouthpiece originally.

telephone tapping method of listening in on a telephone conversation; in the US and the UK a criminal offense if carried out without a warrant or the consent of the person concerned. See also ◊privacy.

Telephone tapping, or the use of "wire taps," has become an important although controversial tool in the efforts against organized crime, drug trafficking, and foreign intelligence information.

telephoto lens photographic lens of longer focal length than normal that takes a very narrow view and gives a large image through a combination of telescopic and ordinary photographic lenses.

teleprinter or ***teletypewriter*** transmitting and receiving device used in telecommunications to handle coded messages. Teleprinters are automatic typewriters keyed telegraphically to convert typed words into electrical signals (using a 5-unit Baudot code, see ◊baud) at the transmitting end, and signals into typed words at the receiving end.

telescope optical instrument that magnifies images of faint and distant objects. It is used to sight over land and sea and is a major research tool in astronomy. Some are attached to cameras. A telescope with a large aperture, or opening, can distinguish finer detail and fainter objects than can one with a small aperture. The refracting telescope uses lenses, and the reflecting telescope uses mirrors. A third type, the catadioptric telescope, with a combination of lenses and mirrors, is used increasingly. See also ◊radio telescope.

In a refractor, light is collected by a ◊lens called the object glass or objective, which focuses light down a tube, forming an image magnified by an eyepiece. Invention of the refractor is attributed to a Dutch optician, Hans ◊Lippershey, 1608. The largest refracting telescope in the world, at ◊Yerkes Observatory, Wisconsin, has an aperture of 40 in/102 cm.

In a reflector, light is collected and focused by a concave mirror. The first reflector was built about 1670 by Isaac ◊Newton. Large mirrors are cheaper to make and easier to mount than large lenses, so all the largest telescopes are reflectors. The largest reflector, with a 236-in/6-m mirror, is at Zelenchukskaya, USSR. Telescopes with larger apertures are planned, some of which will be composed of numerous smaller mirrors. The first such multiple-mirror telescope was installed on Mount Hopkins, Arizona 1979. It consists of six mirrors of 72-in/1.8-m aperture, which perform like a single 176-in/4.5-m mirror. Schmidt telescopes are used for taking wide-field photographs of the sky. They have a main mirror plus a thin lens at the front of the tube to increase the field of view.

Large telescopes can now be placed in orbit above the distorting effects of the Earth's atmosphere. Telescopes in space have been used to study ◊infrared, ◊ultraviolet and ◊X-rays that have not penetrated the atmosphere; they carry much information about the births, lives, and deaths of stars and galaxies. The 95-in/2.4-m Hubble Space Telescope was launched by the US in April 1990 in an attempt to see the sky more clearly than can any telescope on Earth.

televangelist in North America, a fundamentalist Christian minister, often of a Pentecostal church, who hosts a television show and solicits donations from viewers. Well-known televangelists include Jim Bakker, convicted in 1989 of fraudulent misuse of donations, and Jimmy Swaggart.

television (TV) reproduction at a distance by radio waves of visual images. For transmission, a television camera converts the pattern of light it takes in into a pattern of electrical charges. This is scanned line by line by a beam of electrons from an electron gun, resulting in variable electrical signals that represent the visual picture. These vision signals are combined with a radio carrier wave and broadcast. The TV aerial picks up the wave and feeds it to the receiver (TV set). This separates out the vision signals, which pass to a cathode-ray tube. The vision signals control the strength of a beam of electrons from an electron gun, aimed at the screen and making it glow more or less brightly. At the same time the beam is made to scan across the screen line by line, mirroring the action of the gun in the TV camera. The result is a recreation of the pattern of light that entered the camera. Thirty pictures are built up each second with interlaced scanning in North America (25 in Europe), with a total of 525 lines in North America and Japan (625 lines in Europe).

television channels In addition to transmissions received by all viewers, the 1970s and 1980s saw the growth of pay-television cable networks, which are received only by subscribers, and of devices, such as those used in the Qube system (USA), which allow the viewers' opinions to be transmitted instantaneously to the studio

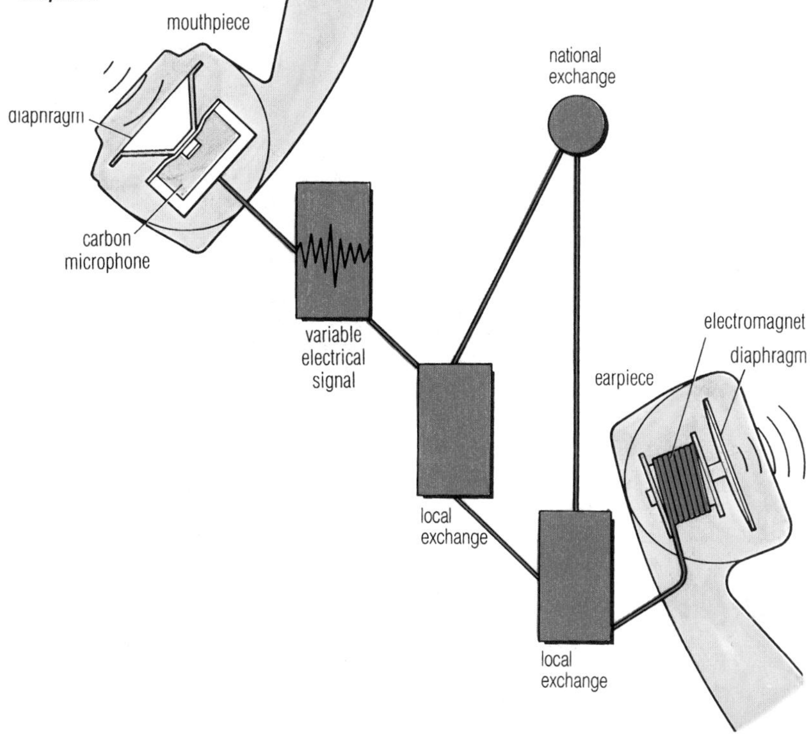
mouthpiece
diaphragm
carbon
microphone
variable
electrical
signal
national
exchange
local
exchange
earpiece
electromagnet
diaphragm
local
exchange
telephone

via a response button, so that, for example, a home viewing audience can vote in a talent competition. The number of program channels continues to increase, following the introduction of satellite-beamed TV signals.

Further use of TV sets has been brought about by ◊videotext and the use of video recorders to tape programs for playback later or to play prerecorded videocassettes, and by their use as computer screens and for security systems. Extended-definition television gives a clear enlargement from a microscopic camera and was first used in 1989 in neurosurgery to enable medical students to watch brain operations.

history In 1873 it was realized that, since the electrical properties of the nonmetallic chemical element selenium vary according to the amount of light to which it is exposed, light could be converted into electrical impulses, making it possible to transmit such impulses over a distance and then reconvert them into light. The chief difficulty was seen to be the "splitting of the picture" so that the infinite variety of light and shade values might be transmitted and reproduced.

In 1908 Campbell-Swinton pointed out that cathode-ray tubes would best effect transmission and reception. Mechanical devices were used at the first practical demonstration of television, given by J L Baird in London Jan 27, 1926, and cathode-ray tubes were used experimentally in the UK from 1934.

color television Baird gave a demonstration of color television in London 1928, but it was not until Dec 1953 that the first successful system was adopted for broadcasting, in the US. This is called the NTSC system, since it was developed by the National Television System Committee, and variations of it have been developed in Europe, for example SECAM (sequential and memory) in France and PAL (phase alternation by line) in West Germany. The three differ only in the way color signals are prepared for transmission. When there was no agreement on a universal European system 1964, in 1967 the UK, West Germany, the Netherlands, and Switzerland adopted PAL while France and the USSR adopted SECAM. In 1989 the European Community agreed to harmonize TV channels from 1991, allowing any station to show programs anywhere in the EC.

The method of color reproduction is related to that used in color photography and printing. It uses the principle that any colors can be made by mixing the primary colors red, green, and blue in appropriate proportions. In color television the receiver reproduces only three basic colors: red, green, and blue. The effect of yellow, for example, is reproduced by combining equal amounts of red and green light, while white is formed by a mixture of all three basic colors. Signals indicate the amounts of red, green, and blue light to be generated at the receiver.

To transmit each of these three signals in the same way as the single brightness signal in black and white television would need three times the normal band width and reduce the number of possible stations and programs to one-third of that possible with monochrome television. The three signals are therefore coded into one complex signal, which is transmitted as a more or less normal black and white signal and produces a satisfactory—or compatible—picture on black and white receivers. A fraction of each primary red, green, and blue signal is added together to produce the normal brightness, or luminance, signal. The minimum of extra coloring information is then sent by a special subcarrier signal, which is superimposed on the brightness signal. This extra coloring information corresponds to the hue and saturation of the transmitted color, but without any of the fine detail of the picture. The impression of sharpness is conveyed only by the brightness signal, the coloring being added as a broad color wash. The various color systems differ only in the way in which the coloring information is sent on the subcarrier signal.

The color receiver has to amplify the complex signal and decode it back to the basic red, green, and blue signals; these primary signals are then applied to a color cathode-ray tube. The color display tube is the heart of any color receiver. Many designs of color picture tube have been invented; the most successful of these is known as the "shadow mask tube." It operates on similar electronic principles to the black and white television picture tube, but the screen is composed of a fine mosaic of over one million dots arranged in an orderly fashion. One-third of the dots glow red when bombarded by electrons, one-third glow green, and one-third blue. There are three sources of electrons, respectively modulated by the red, green, and blue signals. The tube is arranged so that the shadow mask allows only the red signals to hit red dots, the green signals to hit green dots, and the blue signals to hit blue dots. The glowing dots are so small that from a normal viewing distance the colors merge into one another and a picture with a full range of colors is seen.

In the US, TV technology was pioneered by David ◊Sarnoff and Lee ◊De Forest and sets became available in the 1930s, but few performances were televised until the late 1940s, when local and network shows were scheduled in major cities and, by coaxial cable, across the nation. Live performances gave way to videotaped shows by the late 1950s, and color sets became popular from the 1960s. Cable networks began operating in the 1980s and satellite dishes were added to many homes and businesses to help receive the extensive cable networks.

Tell Wilhelm (William) legendary 14th-century Swiss archer, said to have refused to salute the Hapsburg badge at Altdorf on Lake Lucerne. Sentenced to shoot an apple from his son's head, he did so, then shot the tyrannical Austrian ruler Gessler, symbolizing his people's refusal to submit to external authority.

The first written account of the legend dates from 1474, the period of the wars of the Swiss against Charles the Bold of Burgundy; but the story of a man showing his skill with the crossbow in such a way is much earlier. The legend has been used for plays (by Schiller, 1804) and an opera (Rossini, 1829), as well as in filmed versions.

Tell el Amarna site of the ancient Egyptian capital ◊Akhetaton. The ◊Amarna tablets were found there.

Teller Edward 1908– . Hungarian-born US physicist. Born in Budapest, Teller received his PhD from the University of Leipzig 1930. After a period of research at Göttingen 1931–33 and with Niels Bohr in 1934, he immigrated to the US and became a faculty member of George Washington University 1935. Teller joined the staff of Columbia University 1941 and the University of Chicago 1942 to work with Enrico Fermi on atomic fission. From 1941 to 1945 he was also a member of the Manhattan Project, which developed the first atomic bombs. In 1946 Teller was appointed professor at the University of Chicago and played a central role in the development and testing of the first hydrogen bomb 1952.

From 1958 to 1975 he was associated with the Lawrence Livermore laboratories (for radiation and weapons research) at the University of California at Berkeley. One of the most controversial of nuclear scientists, he advocated the nuclear weapons buildup for supremacy over the USSR, including weapons in space (SDI or "Star Wars"), and opposed all test-ban treaties.

tellurium silver-white, semimetallic (◊metalloid) element, symbol Te, atomic number 52, atomic weight 127.60. Chemically it is similar to sulfur and selenium, and it is considered as one of the sulfur group. It occurs naturally in telluride minerals; it is used in coloring glass blue–brown, in the electrolytic refining of zinc, in electronics, and as a catalyst in refining petroleum.

It was discovered by Austrian mineralogist Franz Müller (1740–1825) in 1782, and named in 1798 by German chemist Martin Klaproth from Latin *Tellus*, the Roman goddess of the Earth.

Tellus the goddess of the Earth in Roman religion, identified with a number of other agricultural gods and celebrations.

Telstar US communications satellite, launched July

television transmitter

television transmitter (essentials)

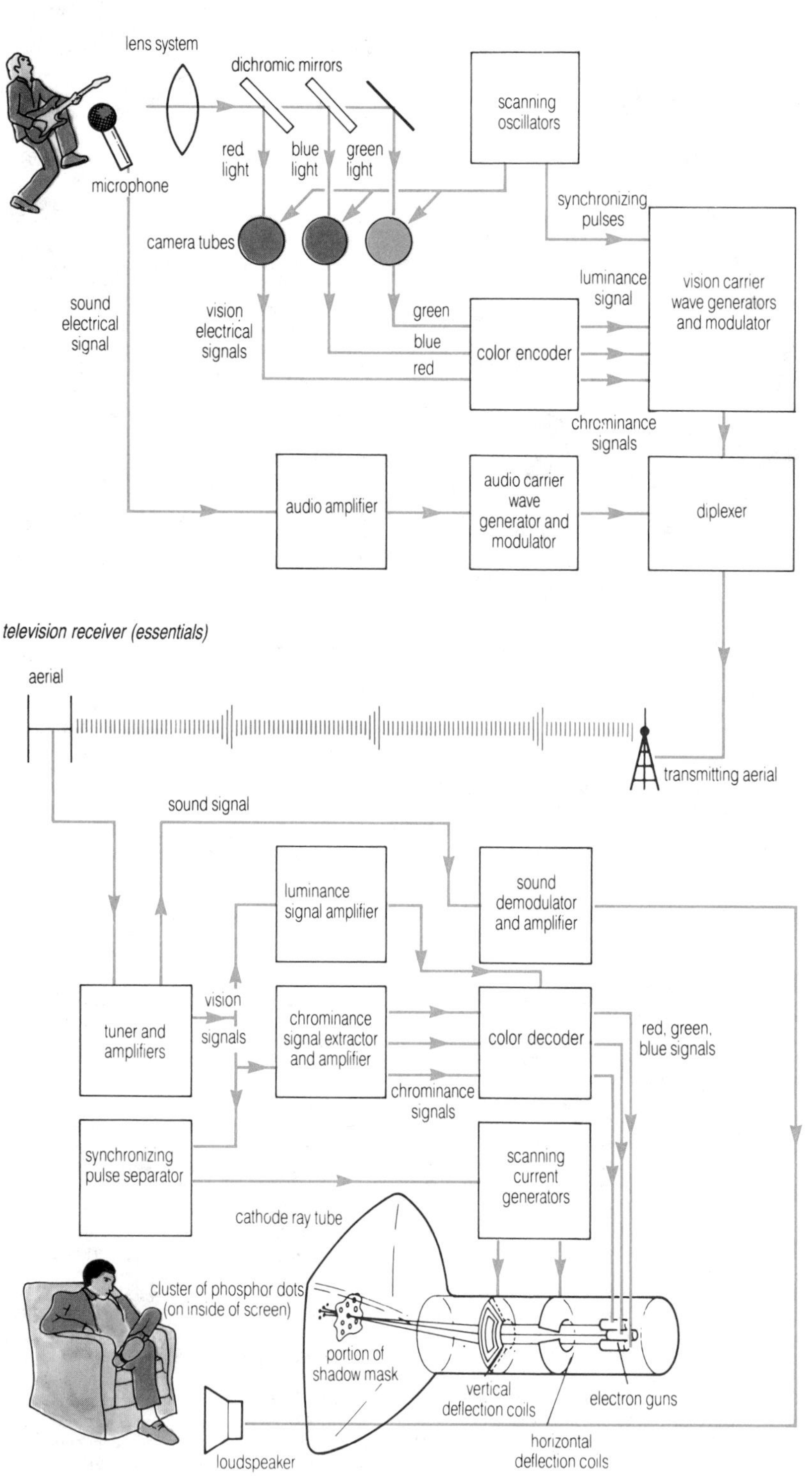
lens system
dichromic mirrors
scanning oscillators
microphone
red light
blue light
green light
synchronizing pulses
camera tubes
luminance signal
vision carrier wave generators and modulator
sound electrical signal
vision electrical signals
green
blue
red
color encoder
chrominance signals
audio amplifier
audio carrier wave generator and modulator
diplexer
television receiver (essentials)
aerial
transmitting aerial
sound signal
luminance signal amplifier
sound demodulator and amplifier
vision signals
tuner and amplifiers
chrominance signal extractor and amplifier
color decoder
red, green, blue signals
chrominance signals
synchronizing pulse separator
scanning current generators
cathode ray tube
cluster of phosphor dots (on inside of screen)
portion of shadow mask
vertical deflection coils
electron guns
horizontal deflection coils
loudspeaker

10, 1962, which relayed the first live television transmissions between the US and Europe. *Telstar* orbited the Earth in 158 minutes, and so had to be tracked by ground stations, unlike the geosynchronous satellites of today.

Tema port in Ghana; population (1982) 324,000. It has the largest artificial harbor in Africa, opened 1962, as well as oil refineries and a fishing industry.

temp. abbreviation for temperature; temporary.

tempera painting medium in which powdered pigments are bound together, usually with egg yolk and water. A form of tempera was used in ancient Egypt, and egg tempera was the foremost medium for panel painting in late medieval and early Renaissance Europe. It was gradually superseded by oils from the late 15th century onward.

temperament in music, a system of tuning the pitches of a mode or scale; in folk music to preserve its emotional or ritual meaning, in Western music to allow maximum flexibility for changing key. J S Bach wrote *The Well-Tempered Clavier* to demonstrate the superiority of this system of tuning.

temperance movement societies dedicated to curtailing the consumption of alcohol by total prohibition, local restriction, or encouragement of declarations of personal abstinence ("the pledge"). They were first set up in the US, Ireland, and Scotland, then in the N of England in the 1830s.

The proponents of temperance were drawn from evangelical or nonconformist Christians, labor unionists, Chartists, members of cooperatives, the self-help movement, and the Church of England. After 1871 the movement supported the ◊Liberal Party in its attempts to use the licensing laws to restrict the consumption of alcoholic beverages.

temperature the state of hotness or coldness of a body, and the condition that determines whether or not it will transfer heat to, or receive heat from, another body according to the laws of ◊thermodynamics. It is measured in degrees Celsius (before 1948 called centigrade), kelvin, or Fahrenheit.

The normal temperature of the human body is about 98.4°F/36.9°C. Variation by more than a degree or so indicates ill-health, a rise signifying excessive activity (usually due to infection), and a decrease signifying deficient heat production (usually due to lessened vitality).

temperature regulation the ability of an organism to control its internal body temperature.

Although some plants have evolved ways of resisting extremes of temperature, sophisticated mechanisms for maintaining the correct temperature are found in multicellular animals. Such mechanisms may be behavioral, as when a lizard moves into the shade in order to cool down. Mammals and birds have internal control (see ◊medulla) and are known as ◊homeotherms. These animals are insulated with fat, hair, or feathers to conserve heat produced by metabolic activities. Other adaptations allow heat to leave the body when the animal is in danger of overheating, for instance during intense activity. Such mechanisms include sweating, increased flow of blood through the skin, and panting.

tempering heat treatment for improving the properties of metals, often used for steel alloys. The metal is heated to a certain temperature and then cooled suddenly in a water or oil bath.

Tempest, The romantic drama by William Shakespeare, first performed 1611–12. Prospero, usurped as duke of Milan by his brother Antonio, lives on a remote island with his daughter Miranda and Caliban, a deformed creature. Prospero uses magic to shipwreck Antonio and his party on the island and, with the help of the spirit Ariel, regains his dukedom.

Templar member of a Christian military order, founded in Jerusalem 1119, the Knights of the Temple of Solomon. The knights took vows of poverty, chastity, and obedience and devoted themselves to the recovery of Palestine from the Muslims.

They played an important part in the Crusades of the 12th and 13th centuries. The enormous wealth of the order aroused the envy of Philip IV of France, who arranged for charges of heresy to be brought against its members 1307, and the order was suppressed 1308–12.

Temple city in central Texas, S of Waco. Industries include building materials, steel, furniture, and railroad supplies; population (1990) 46,109.

Temple Shirley 1928– . US actress who became the most successful child star of the 1930s. The charming, curly-haired, dimpled tot's films include *Bright Eyes* 1934, in which she sang "On the Good Ship Lollipop"; *Little Miss Marker* 1934; *The Little Colonel* 1935; *Captain January* 1936; *Heidi* 1937; and *The Little Princess* 1939.

As Shirley Temple Black, she was active in the Republican Party and diplomatic affairs. She was a delegate to the United Nations 1969–70, US

Temple *Shirley Temple, the most successful child star of the 1930s, salutes and wins the hearts of moviegoers in* Bright Eyes *1934, for which she received an Academy Award.*

chief of protocol 1976–77, and ambassador to Ghana and Czechoslovakia.

Temple of Jerusalem the center of Jewish national worship in both ancient and modern days. The Western or Wailing Wall is the surviving part of the western wall of the platform of the enclosure of the Temple. Solomon built the Temple c. 950 BC but it was destroyed by Nebuchadnezzer in 586 BC. It was rebuilt in the late 6th century BC, restored by the ◊Maccabees and later by Herod the Great, but destroyed by the Romans in AD 70. Since then, Jews have come here to pray, to mourn their dispersion and the loss of their homeland.

The Mosque of Omar now stands on the site. Under Jordanian rule Jews had no access, but they retook this part of the city during the 1967 war, and made it available to all.

Templer Gerald 1898–1979. British field marshal. He served in both world wars, but is especially remembered for his work as high commissioner in Malaysia 1952–54, during the period of fighting against communist insurgents.

tempo (Italian "time") in music, the speed at which a piece is played.

Temuco market town and capital of Araucanía region, Chile; population (1987) 218,000.

tenant farming system whereby farmers rent their holdings from a landowner in return for the use of agricultural land.

tench European freshwater bony fish *Tinca tinca*, a member of the carp family, now established in North America. It is about 18 in/45 cm long, weighing 4.5 lb/2 kgs, colored olive-green above and gray beneath. The scales are small and there is a barbel at each side of the mouth.

Ten Commandments in the Old Testament, the laws given by God to the Hebrew leader Moses on Mt Sinai, engraved on two tablets of stone. They are: to have no other gods besides Jehovah; to make no idols; not to misuse the name of God; to keep the sabbath holy; to honor one's parents; not to commit murder, adultery, or theft; not to give false evidence; not to be covetous. They form the basis of Jewish and Christian moral codes; the "tablets of the Law" given to Moses are also mentioned in the Koran. The giving of the Ten Commandments is celebrated in the Jewish festival of *Shavuot* (see ◊Pentecost).

tendon or sinew cord of tough, fibrous connective tissue that joins muscle to bone in vertebrates. Tendons are largely composed of the protein collagen, and because of their inelasticity are very

tendrils

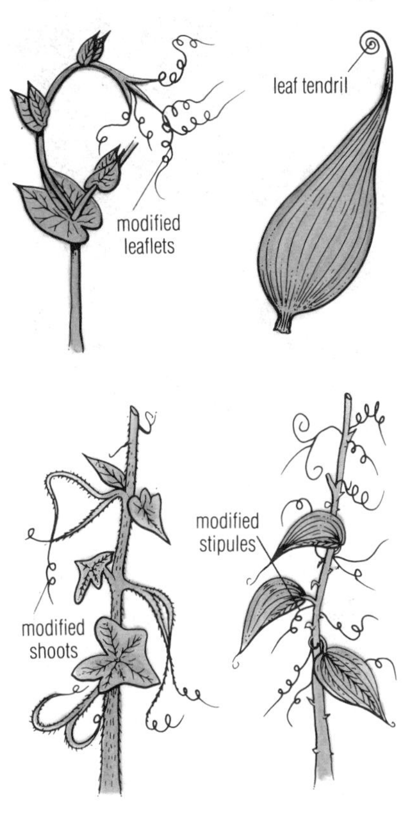
leaf tendril
modified leaflets
modified stipules
modified shoots

efficient at transforming muscle power into movement.

tendril in botany, a slender, threadlike structure that supports a climbing plant by coiling around suitable supports, such as the stems and branches of other plants. It may be a modified stem, leaf, leaflet, flower, leaf stalk, or stipule (a small appendage on either side of the leaf stalk), and may be simple or branched. The tendrils of Virginia creeper *Parthenocissus quinquefolia* are modified flower heads with suckerlike pads at the end that stick to walls, while those of the grapevine *Vitis* grow away from the light and thus enter dark crevices where they expand to anchor the plant firmly.

Tenerife largest of the ◊Canary Islands, Spain; area 795 sq mi/2,060 sq km; population (1981) 557,000. Santa Cruz is the main town, and Pico de Teide is an active volcano.

Teng Hsiao-ping alternate spelling of ◊Deng Xiaoping, Chinese politician.

Teniers family of Flemish painters, active in Antwerp. David Teniers the Younger (David II, 1610–1690) became court painter to Archduke Leopold William, governor of the Netherlands, in Brussels. He painted scenes of peasant life.

As curator of the archduke's art collection, David Teniers made many copies of the pictures and a collection of engravings, *Theatrum Pictorium* 1660. His peasant scenes are humorous and full of vitality, inspired by ◊Brouwer.

His father, David Teniers the Elder (David I, 1582–1649), painted religious pictures.

Tennessee state in E central US; nickname Volunteer State

area 42,151 sq mi/109,200 sq km

capital Nashville

cities Memphis, Knoxville, Chattanooga, Clarksville

features Tennessee Valley Authority (TVA); Great Smoky Mountains National Park; Grand Old Opry, Nashville; Beale Street Historic District and Graceland, estate of Elvis Presley, Memphis; research centers, including Oak Ridge National Laboratory

products cereals, cotton, tobacco, soybeans, livestock, timber, coal, zinc, copper, chemicals

population (1990) 4,877,185

famous people Davy Crockett, David Farragut, Aretha Franklin, W C Handy, Cordell Hull, Andrew Jackson, Andrew Johnson, Dolly Parton, John Crow Ransom, Bessie Smith

history explored by De Soto for Spain 1521, La Salle for France 1670s, and Needham and Arthur for England 1680s; first settled 1757. After England obtained the region as settlement of the French and Indian War 1763, it was occupied by settlers from Virginia and the Carolinas. It became a state 1796. Tennessee was deeply divided in the Civil War and was a major war theater, with the battles of Shiloh, Murfreesboro, Chattanooga, and Nashville among those fought

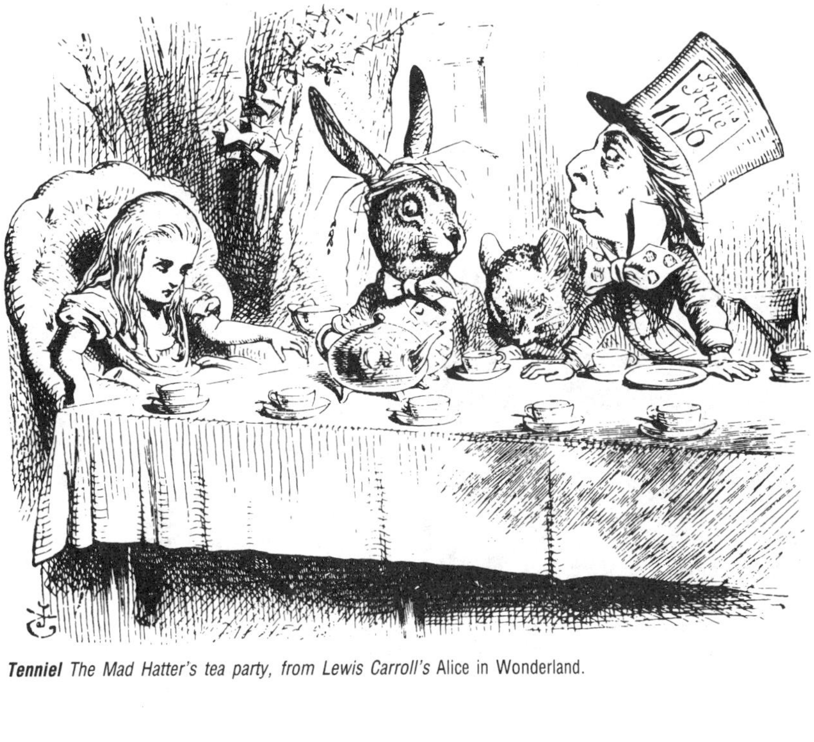

Tenniel *The Mad Hatter's tea party, from Lewis Carroll's* Alice in Wonderland.

Tennessee

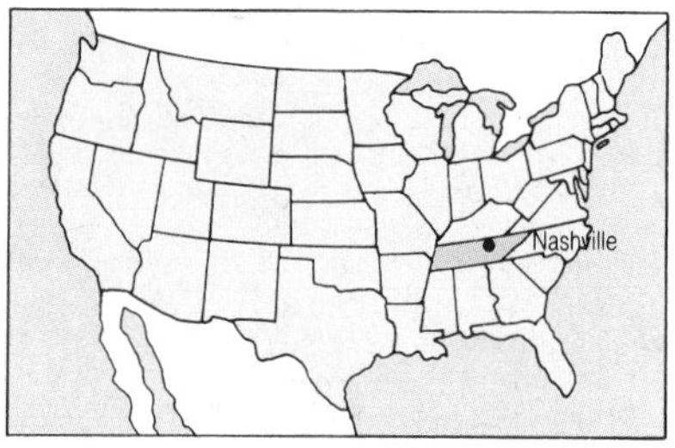
Nashville

in the state. With Tennessean Andrew Johnson in the White House, it was the only former Confederate state not to have a military government imposed during Reconstruction. Coal and iron deposits attracted Northern capital, and by the early 1880s, flour, wool, and paper mills were established in all the urban areas. Both prohibitionism and religious fundamentalism were strong; in 1925 the Scopes evolution trial was held in Dayton, and the law against the teaching of the theory of evolution in public schools was not repealed until 1967. The 1930s brought major development in the form of the federal Tennessee Valley Authority and prepared the state for the industrialization that followed World War II.

Tennessee Valley Authority (TVA) US government corporation founded 1933 to develop the Tennessee river basin (an area of some 40,000 sq mi/ 104,000 sq km) by building hydroelectric power stations, producing and distributing fertilizers, and similar activities. The TVA was one of President F D Roosevelt's ◊New Deal measures, promoting economic growth by government investment.

Its two major functions were to control the destructive flooding that had long plagued the valley and to provide employment in a 7-state area hard hit by the ◊Depression. There were 32 major dams incorporated into a massive river-control system that also provided electric power for a wide region. Today about half of TVA's electrical output is devoted to defense installations surrounding the generating plants. The TVA has undertaken reforestation projects and agricultural research.

Tenniel John 1820–1914. English cartoonist, illustrator of Lewis Carroll's *Alice's Adventures in Wonderland* 1865 and *Through the Looking-Glass* 1872.

tennis racket and ball game invented toward the end of the 19th century. It was introduced by Major Clopton Wingfield at a Christmas party at Nantclwyn, Wales in 1873. His game was then called "Sphairistike." It derived from ◊court tennis. Although played on different surfaces (grass, wood, shale, clay, concrete), it is sometimes still called "lawn tennis."

The aim of the two or four players is to strike the ball into the prescribed area of the court, with oval-headed rackets (strung with gut or nylon), in

tennis *Germany's Boris Becker (above) playing in England's Stella Artois tournament 1987.*
Argentina's Gabriela Sabatini (above right) playing in the US Open tournament 1988.

such a way that it cannot be returned. The game is won by those first winning four points (called 15, 30, 40, game), unless both sides reach 40 (deuce), when two consecutive points are needed to win. A set is won by winning six games with a margin of two over opponents, although a tie-break system operates, that is, at six games to each side (or in some cases eight), except in the final set. Major events include the ◊Davis Cup first contested in 1900 for international men's competition; the annual All England Tennis Club championships (originating 1877), an open event for players of both sexes at Wimbledon; and the US, French, and Australian Opens.

tennis: recent winners

Wimbledon championships
men's singles
1980 Björn Borg *(Sweden)*
1981 John McEnroe *(US)*
1982 Jimmy Connors *(US)*
1983 John McEnroe *(US)*
1984 John McEnroe *(US)*
1985 Boris Becker *(West Germany)*
1986 Boris Becker *(West Germany)*
1987 Pat Cash *(Australia)*
1988 Stefan Edberg *(Sweden)*
1989 Boris Becker *(West Germany)*
1990 Stefan Edberg *(Sweden)*
1991 Michael Stich *(Germany)*
women's singles
1980 Evonne Goolagong-Cawley *(Australia)*
1981 Chris Evert-Lloyd *(US)*
1982 Martina Navratilova *(US)*
1983 Martina Navratilova *(US)*
1984 Martina Navratilova *(US)*
1985 Martina Navratilova *(US)*
1986 Martina Navratilova *(US)*
1987 Martina Navratilova *(US)*
1988 Steffi Graf *(West Germany)*
1989 Steffi Graf *(West Germany)*
1990 Martina Navratilova *(US)*
1991 Steffi Graf *(Germany)*
United States Open
men's singles
1980 John McEnroe *(US)*
1981 John McEnroe *(US)*
1982 Jimmy Connors *(US)*
1983 Jimmy Connors *(US)*
1984 John McEnroe *(US)*
1985 Ivan Lendl *(Czechoslovakia)*
1986 Ivan Lendl *(Czechoslovakia)*
1987 Ivan Lendl *(Czechoslovakia)*
1988 Mats Wilander *(Sweden)*
1989 Boris Becker *(West Germany)*
1990 Pete Sampras *(US)*
1991 Stefan Edberg *(Sweden)*
women's singles
1979 Tracy Austin *(US)*
1980 Chris Evert-Lloyd *(US)*
1981 Tracy Austin *(US)*
1982 Chris Evert-Lloyd *(US)*
1983 Martina Navratilova *(US)*
1984 Martina Navratilova *(US)*
1985 Hana Mandlikova *(Czechoslovakia)*
1986 Martina Navratilova *(US)*
1987 Martina Navritilova *(US)*
1988 Steffi Graf *(West Germany)*
1989 Steffi Graf *(West Germany)*
1990 Gabriela Sabatini *(Argentina)*
1991 Monica Seles *(Yugoslavia)*

Tennstedt Klaus 1926– . East German conductor, musical director of the London Philharmonic Orchestra 1983–87. He is renowned for his interpretations of works by Mozart, Beethoven, Bruckner, and Mahler.

Tennyson Alfred, 1st Baron Tennyson 1809–1892. English poet, poet laureate 1850–96, whose verse has a majestic, musical quality. His works include "The Lady of Shalott," "The Lotus Eaters," "Ulysses," "Break, Break, Break," "The Charge of the Light Brigade"; the longer narratives *Locksley Hall* 1832 and *Maud* 1855; the elegy *In Memoriam* 1850; and a long series of poems on the Arthurian legends *The Idylls of the King* 1857–85.

Tennyson was born at Somersby, Lincolnshire. The death of A H Hallam (a close friend during his years at Trinity College, Cambridge) 1833 prompted the elegiac *In Memoriam*, unpublished until 1850, the year in which he succeeded Wordsworth as poet laureate and married Emily Sellwood.

tenure employment terms and conditions. Security of tenure is often granted to the judiciary, civil servants, educators, and others in public office, where impartiality and freedom from political control are considered necessary.

The length of tenure depends on the service involved, and termination of it would only occur in exceptional cases, such as serious misconduct.

Tenzing Norgay. Known as Sherpa Tenzing 1914–1986. Nepalese mountaineer. In 1953 he was the first, with Edmund Hillary, to reach the summit of Mount Everest.

He had previously made 19 Himalayan expeditions as a porter. He subsequently became a director of the Himalayan Mountaineering Institute, Darjeeling.

Teotihuacán huge ancient city in central Mexico, a religious center of Mesoamerican civilization that was inhabited by many cultures from 6000 BC on. It is one of the best excavated archeological sites in Mexico.

Teplice industrial (peat-and lignite-mining, glass, porcelain, cement, paper) city and spa in Czechoslovakia; population (1984) 54,000.

tequila Mexican alcoholic liquor made from a distilled mash obtained from the ◊agave plant. It is named after the place, near Guadalajara, where the Conquistadors first developed it from Aztec *pulque*, which would keep for only a day.

teratogen any nongenetic agent that can induce deformities in the fetus if absorbed by the mother during pregnancy. Teratogens include some drugs (notably alcohol and ◊thalidomide), other chemicals, certain disease organisms, and radioactivity.

terbium soft, silver-gray, metallic element of the ◊lanthanide series, symbol Tb, atomic number 81, atomic weight 158.925. It occurs in gadolinite and other ores, with yttrium and ytterbium, and is used in lasers, semiconductors, and television tubes. It was named in 1843 by Swedish chemist Karl Mosander (1797–1858) for the town of Ytterby, Sweden, where it was first found.

Terborch Gerard 1617–1681. Dutch painter of small-scale portraits and genre (everyday) scenes, mainly of soldiers at rest or wealthy families in their homes. He traveled widely in Europe. *The Peace of Münster* 1648 (National Gallery, London) is an official group portrait.

Terbrugghen Hendrik 1588–1629. Dutch painter, a leader of the Utrecht school with Honthorst. He

tennis

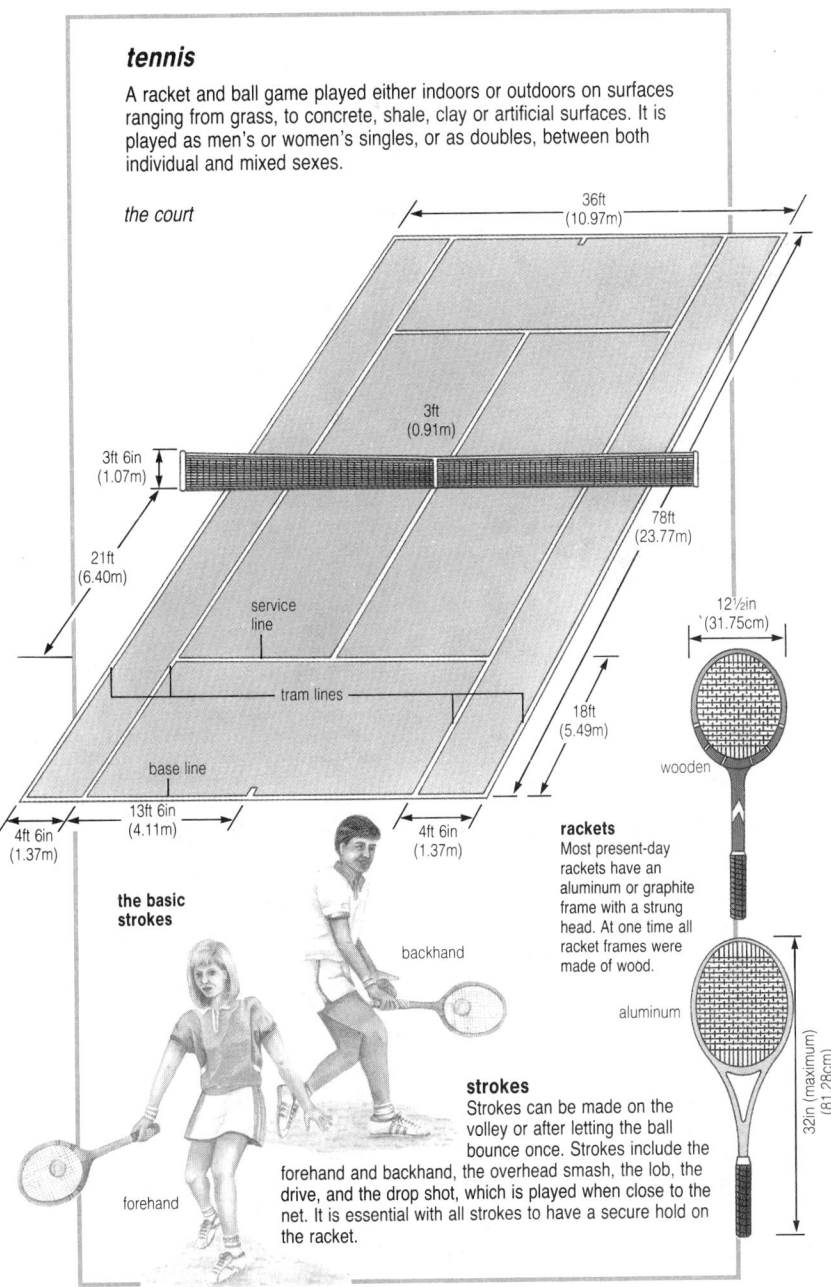

A racket and ball game played either indoors or outdoors on surfaces ranging from grass, to concrete, shale, clay or artificial surfaces. It is played as men's or women's singles, or as doubles, between both individual and mixed sexes.

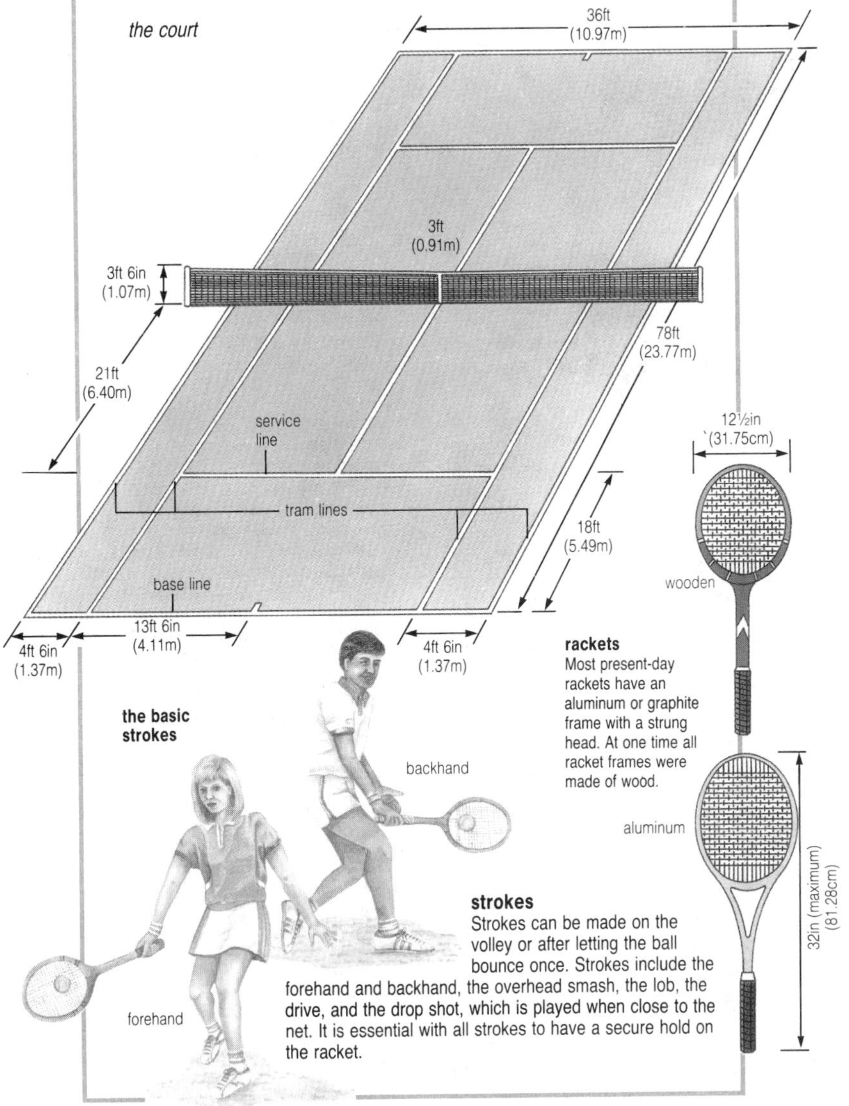
the court
36ft
(10.97m)
3ft
(0.91m)
3ft 6in
(1.07m)
21ft
(6.40m)
78ft
(23.77m)
service line
tram lines
18ft
(5.49m)
base line
13ft 6in
(4.11m)
4ft 6in
(1.37m)
4ft 6in
(1.37m)
12½in
(31.75cm)
wooden
aluminum
32in (maximum)
(81.28cm)
the basic strokes
backhand
forehand

rackets
Most present-day rackets have an aluminum or graphite frame with a strung head. At one time all racket frames were made of wood.

strokes
Strokes can be made on the volley or after letting the ball bounce once. Strokes include the forehand and backhand, the overhead smash, the lob, the drive, and the drop shot, which is played when close to the net. It is essential with all strokes to have a secure hold on the racket.

visited Rome around 1604 and was inspired by Caravaggio's work. He painted religious subjects and genre (everyday) scenes.

Terence (Publius Terentius Afer) 190–159 BC. Roman dramatist, born in Carthage and brought as a slave to Rome, where he was freed and came under ◊Scipio's patronage. His surviving six comedies (including *The Eunuch* 161 BC) are subtly characterized and based on Greek models.

Terengganu alternate spelling of ◊Trengganu, state in Peninsular Malaysia.

Teresa, St 1515–1582. Spanish mystic, born in Avila. She became a Carmelite nun, and in 1562 founded a new and stricter order. She was subject to fainting fits, during which she saw visions. She wrote *The Way to Perfection* 1583 and an autobiography, *Life of the Mother Theresa of Jesus*, 1611. In 1622 she was canonized, and in 1970 was made the first female Doctor of the Church.

Tereshkova Valentina Vladimirovna 1937– . Soviet cosmonaut, the first woman to fly in space. In June 1963 she made a three-day flight in *Vostok 6*, orbiting the Earth 48 times.

term in architecture, a pillar in the form of a pedestal supporting the bust of a human or animal figure. Such objects derive from Roman boundary marks sacred to Terminus, the god of boundaries, whose feast day was Feb 23.

terminal in computing, a device consisting of a keyboard and ◊VDT (or, in older systems, a teleprinter) to enable the operator to communicate with the computer. The terminal might be physically attached to the computer or linked to it over a telephone line.

termite any member of the insect order Isoptera. Termites are soft-bodied social insects living in large colonies which include one or more queens (of relatively enormous size and producing an egg every two seconds), much smaller kings, and still smaller soldiers, workers, and immature forms. Termites build galleried nests of soil particles that may be 20 ft/6 m high.

One group, the Macrotermitinae, constructs fungus gardens from its own feces by infecting them with a special fungus that digests the feces and renders them edible. Termites may dispose of a fourth of the vegetation litter of an area, and their fondness for wood (as in houses and other buildings) brings them into conflict with humans. The wood is broken down in their stomachs by numerous microorganisms living in ◊symbiosis with their hosts. Some species construct adjustable air vents in their nests, and one species moistens the inside of the nest with water to keep it cool.

tern any of various lightly-built seabirds placed in the same family (Laridae) as gulls and characterized by pointed wings and bill and usually a forked tail. Terns plunge-dive after aquatic prey. They are 8–20 in/20–50 cm long, and usually colored in combinations of white and black.

The common tern *Sterna hirundo* has white underparts, gray upper wings, and a black crown on its head. The Arctic tern *Sterna paradisea* migrates from N parts of Greenland, North America, and Europe to the Antarctic.

Terni industrial city in the valley of the Nera river, Umbria region, central Italy; population (1987) 111,000. The nearby Marmore Falls, the highest in Italy, were created by the Romans in order to drain the Rieti marshes.

Terpsichore in Greek mythology, the ◊Muse of dance and choral song.

terracotta (Italian "baked earth") brownish-red baked clay, usually unglazed, used in building, sculpture, and pottery. The term is specifically applied to small figures or figurines, such as those found at ◊Tanagra. Excavations at Xian, China, have revealed life-size terracotta figures of the army of the Emperor Shi Huangdi dating from the 3rd century BC.

terrapin general name for any turtle that frequents fresh or brackish water. The name is sometimes specifically used for the tidewater diamondback terrapins (genus *Malaclemys*) of E North America.

Terre Adélie French name for ◊Adélie Land, Antarctica.

Terre Haute city in W Indiana, on the Wabash River; industries include plastics, chemicals, and glass; population (1990) 57,483. Points of interest include the birthplace of author Theodore Dreiser and the home of labor leader Eugene V Debs. Indiana State University is here. Terre Haute was laid out 1816.

terrier any of various breeds of highly intelligent, active dogs. They are usually small. Types include the bull, cairn, fox, Irish, Scottish, Sealyham, Skye, and Yorkshire terriers. They were originally bred for hunting rabbits and following quarry such as foxes down into burrows.

The small Parson Jack Russell terrier was recognized by the Kennel Club 1990 as a variant of the fox terrier.

territorial behavior in biology, any behavior that serves to exclude other members of the same species from a fixed area or ◊territory. It may involve aggressively driving out intruders, marking the boundary (with dung piles or secretions from special scent glands), conspicuous visual displays, characteristic songs, or loud calls.

territorial waters area of sea over which the adjoining coastal state claims territorial rights. This is most commonly a distance of 12 nautical mi/22.2 km from the coast, but, increasingly, states claim fishing and other rights up to 200 mi/320 km.

territory in animal behavior, a fixed area from which an animal or group of animals excludes other members of the same species. Animals may hold territories for many different reasons; for example, to provide a constant food supply, to monopolize potential mates, or to ensure access to refuges or nest sites. The size of a territory depends in part on its function: some nesting and mating territories may be only a few square yards,

termite

termite – a typical termite mound

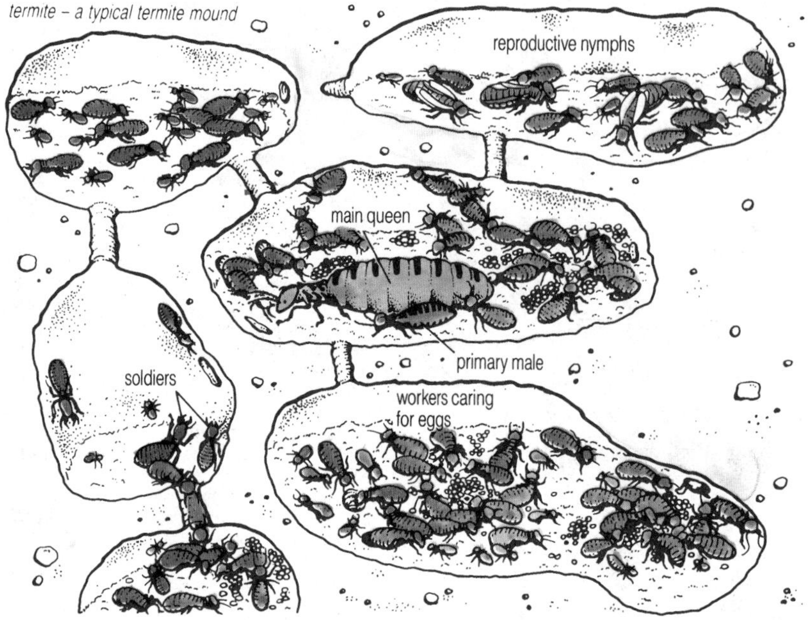
reproductive nymphs
main queen
soldiers
primary male
workers caring
for eggs

whereas feeding territories may be as large as hundreds of square miles.

terrorism systematic violence in the furtherance of political aims, often by small ◊guerrilla groups, such as the Fatah Revolutionary Council led by Abu Nidal, a splinter group that split from the Palestine Liberation Organization in 1973.

Terror, Reign of the period of the ◊French Revolution when the Jacobins were in power (Oct 1793–July 1794) under Maximilien ◊Robespierre and instituted mass persecution of their opponents. About 1,400 were executed, mainly by guillotine, until public indignation rose and Robespierre was overthrown in July 1794.

Terry Alfred Howe 1827–1890. US military leader. He served with distinction in the Civil War as colonel of the 2nd Connecticut militia and was promoted to brigadier general 1865. After the war he was placed in command of the Department of Dakota and also served in the Department of the South 1869–72. He was George ◊Custer's commander in the 1876 Sioux War, later negotiated with Sitting Bull, and supervised the opening of the Northern Plains.

Born in Hartford, Connecticut, Terry was educated at Yale University and was admitted to the bar 1849.

Terry Ellen 1847–1928. British actress, leading lady to Henry ◊Irving from 1878. She excelled in Shakespearean roles, such as Ophelia in *Hamlet*. She had a correspondence with the playwright G B Shaw.

Terry-Thomas Adopted name of Thomas Terry Hoar Stevens 1911–1990. British film comedy actor, who portrayed upper-class English fools in such films as *I'm All Right Jack* 1959, *It's a Mad, Mad, Mad, Mad World* 1963, and *How to Murder Your Wife* 1965.

tertiary in the Roman Catholic church, a member of a "third order" (see under ◊holy orders); a lay person who, while marrying and following a normal employment, attempts to live in accordance with a modified version of the rule of one of the religious orders. The first such order was founded by St ◊Francis 1221.

Tertiary period of geologic time 65–1.8 million years ago, divided into into five epochs: Paleocene, Eocene, Oligocene, Miocene, and Pliocene. During the Tertiary, mammals took over all the ecological niches left vacant by the extinction of the dinosaurs, and became the prevalent land animals. The continents took on their present positions, and climatic and vegetation zones as we know them became established. Within the geologic time column the Tertiary follows the Cretaceous period and is succeeded by the Quaternary period.

Tertullian Quintus Septimius Florens AD 155–222. Carthaginian Father of the Church, the first major Christian writer in Latin; he became a leading exponent of ◊Montanism.

terza rima poetical meter used in Dante's *Divine Comedy*, consisting of three-line stanzas in which the second line rhymes with the first and third of the following stanza. Shelley's "Ode to the West Wind" is another example.

tesla SI unit (abbreviation T) of ◊magnetic flux density. One tesla represents a flux density of one ◊weber per square meter, or 10^4 ◊gauss. It is named after the Croatian engineer Nikola Tesla.

Tesla Nikola 1856–1943. Croatian electrical engineer who emigrated to the US 1884. He invented fluorescent lighting, the Tesla induction motor, and the Tesla coil, and developed the ◊alternating current (AC) electrical supply system.

Test Act act of Parliament passed in England in 1673, more than 100 years after similar legislation in Scotland, requiring holders of public office to renounce the doctrine of ◊transubstantiation and take the sacrament in an Anglican church, thus excluding Catholics, Nonconformists, and non-Christians from office. Its clauses were repealed in 1828–29. Scottish tests were abolished in 1889. In Ireland the Test Act was introduced in 1704 and English legislation on oaths of allegiance and religious declarations were made valid there in 1782. All these provisions were abolished in 1871.

Test Ban Treaty agreement signed by the US, the USSR, and the UK Aug 5, 1963 contracting to test nuclear weapons only underground. In the following two years 90 other nations signed the treaty, the only major nonsignatories being France and China, which continued underwater and ground-level tests.

testis (plural ***testes***) the organ that produces ◊sperm in male (and hermaphrodite) animals. In vertebrates it is one of a pair of oval structures that are usually internal, but in mammals (other than elephants and marine mammals), the paired testes (or testicles) descend from the body cavity during development, to hang outside the abdomen in a scrotal sac.

testosterone in vertebrates, hormone secreted chiefly by the testes, but also by the ovaries and the cortex of the adrenal glands. It promotes the development of secondary sexual characteristics

tetra

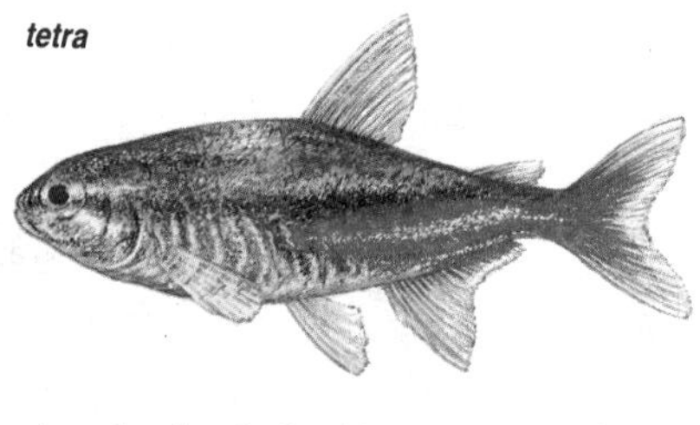

in males. In animals with a breeding season, the onset of breeding behavior is accompanied by a rise in the level of testosterone in the blood.

Synthetic or animal testosterone is used to treat inadequate development of male characteristics or (illegally) to aid athletes' muscular development. Like other sex hormones, testosterone is a ◊steroid.

tetanus or ***lockjaw*** acute disease caused by the toxin of the bacillus *Clostridium tetani*, which usually enters the body through a wound. The bacterium is chiefly found in richly manured soil. Untreated, in seven to ten days tetanus produces muscular spasm and rigidity of the jaw spreading to the other muscles, convulsions, and death. There is a preventive vaccine series, and the disease may be treatable with tetanus antitoxin and antibiotics.

Tethys in Greek mythology, one of the ◊Titans, the wife of the god ◊Oceanus.

Tethys Sea sea that once separated ◊Laurasia from ◊Gondwanaland; roughly corresponding to the present-day Mediterranean.

Tet Offensive in the Vietnam War, a prolonged attack mounted by the Vietcong against Saigon (now Ho Chi Minh City) and other South Vietnamese cities and hamlets beginning Jan 30, 1968. Although the Vietcong were finally forced to withdraw, the Tet Offensive brought into question the ability of the South Vietnamese and their US allies to win the war.

Some 84,000 Communist Vietcong took part in the offensive, with 32,000 being killed by mid-Feb. The fighting in Saigon was especially fierce, and in Hue, which the Vietcong controlled for almost a month, 3,000 civilians were executed. The US Marine base at Khe San was besieged for almost three months, and although the Vietcong were finally repulsed with heavy losses, the US later abandoned the base.

tetra any of various brightly colored tropical bony fishes of the family Characidae, formerly placed in the genus *Tetragonopterus*.

tetracycline one of a group of antibiotic substances having in common the four-ring structure of chlortetracycline, the first member of the group to be isolated. They are prepared synthetically or obtained from certain bacteria of the genus *Streptomyces*. They are broad-spectrum antibiotics, effective against a wide range of disease-causing bacteria. The most commonly used tetracycline has the chemical formula $C_{22}H_{24}N_2O_8$.

tetrahedron (plural tetrahedra) in geometry, a solid

tetrahedron

regular tetrahedron

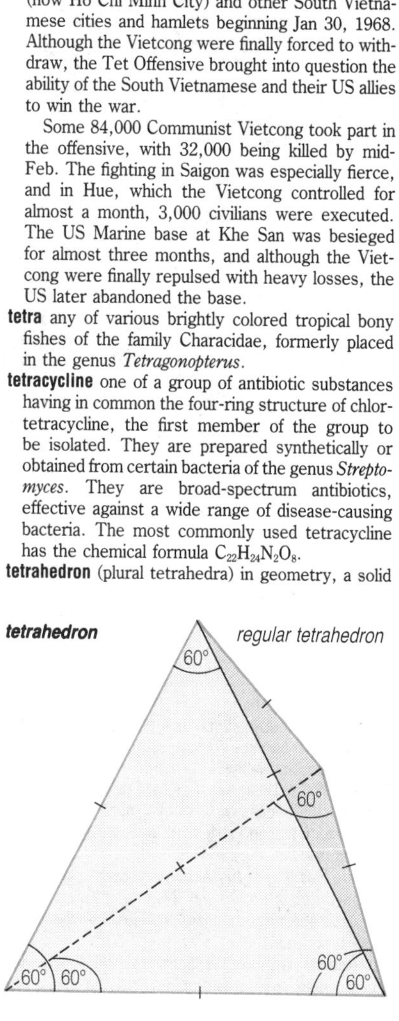
60°
60°
60°
60°
60°
60°

Texas

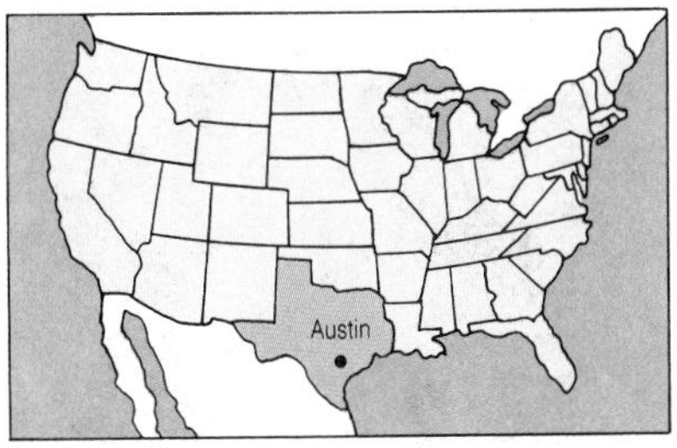
Austin

figure (◊polyhedron) with four triangular faces; that is, a ◊pyramid on a triangular base. A regular tetrahedron has equilateral triangles as its faces.

In chemistry and crystallography, tetrahedra describe the shapes of some molecules and crystals; for example, the carbon atoms in a crystal of diamond are arranged in space as a set of interconnected regular tetrahedra.

tetrapod (Latin "four-legged") type of ◊vertebrate. The group includes mammals, birds, reptiles, and amphibians. Birds are included because they evolved from four-legged ancestors, the forelimbs having become modified to form wings. Even snakes are tetrapods, since their lack of limbs is secondary.

Tetuán or ***Tétouan*** town in NE Morocco, near the Mediterranean coast, 40 mi/64 km SE of Tangier; population (1982) 372,000. Products include textiles, leather, and soap. It was settled by Moorish exiles from Spain in the 16th century.

Teutonic Knight member of a German Christian military order, the Knights of the Teutonic Order, founded 1190 by Hermann of Salza in Palestine. They crusaded against the pagan Prussians and Lithuanians from 1228 and controlled Prussia until the 16th century. Their capital was Marienburg (now Malbork, Poland).

The Teutonic Knights were originally members of the German aristocracy who founded an order of hospitallers in Acre 1190 and became a military order 1198. They wore white robes with black crosses. They were based in Palestine until 1268 when they were expelled by the Mamelukes (rulers of Egupt), after which they concentrated on taking Roman Catholicism into E Europe under the control of the pope. They were prevented from expanding into Russia by ◊Alexander Nevski at the battle of Lake Peipus 1243, but they ruthlessly colonized Prussia 1226–1283. By the 15th century, pressure from neighboring powers and the decline of the crusader ideal led to their containment within East Prussia. Their influence ended 1525 when their grand master Albert of Brandenburg was converted to Lutheranism and declared Prussia to be a secular duchy.

Texarkana twin cities that straddle the Texas-Arkansas border. Industries include furniture, lumber, cotton, and sand and gravel; population (1990) 22,631 (Texas), 31,656 (Arkansas).

Texas state in SW US; nickname Lone Star State.
area 266,803 sq mi/691,200 sq km
capital Austin
cities Houston, Dallas-Fort Worth, San Antonio, El Paso, Corpus Christi, Lubbock
features rivers: Rio Grande, Red; arid Staked Plains, reclaimed by irrigation; the Great Plains; Gulf Coast resorts; Lyndon B Johnson Space Center, Houston; Alamo, San Antonio; Big Bend and Guadalupe Mountains national parks
products rice, cotton, sorghum, wheat, hay, livestock, shrimp, meat products, lumber, wood and paper products, petroleum (nearly one-third of US production), natural gas, sulfur, salt, uranium, chemicals, petrochemicals, nonelectrical machinery, fabricated metal products, transportation equipment, electric and electronic equipment
population (1990) 16,986,510
famous people Stephen F Austin, James Bowie, George Bush, Buddy Holly, Sam Houston, Howard Hughes, Lyndon Johnson, Janis Joplin, Katherine Anne Porter, Sam Rayburn, Tina Turner, Willie Nelson, Babe Didrikson Zaharias
history explored by Cabeza de Vaca and Coronado in the 16th and 17th centuries; settled by the Spanish at Ysleta (near El Paso) 1682; part of Mexico 1821–36. Americans led by Stephen Austin settled along the Brazos River from 1821. Santa Anna massacred the Alamo garrison 1836 but was defeated by Sam Houston at San Jacinto the same year. Texas became an independent republic 1836–45, with Houston as president; in 1845 it became a state of the US. Texas joined the Confederacy in the Civil War but saw little fighting and rejoined the Union 1870. The economy flourished with the development of the cattle industry; in 1901 oil was struck, leading to the development of the petroleum and petrochemical industries. Aircraft and other high technology contributed to the industrialization of Texas during and after World War II. Texas is the only state in the US previously to have been an independent republic.

Texas City city in SE Texas on Galveston Bay, SE of Houston. Industries include tin, chemicals, oil, and grains; population (1990) 40,822.

Texas v White a US Supreme Court decision 1869 that dealt with the legal status of Confederate and Reconstruction governments. The provisional Reconstruction government of Texas sued for the return of property sold by the Confederate government during the Civil War. The case raised the question of which, if either, of the two governments was the valid, legal representative of Texas with the power to control state finances. The Court ruled that since secession was unconstitutional the Confederate state government had never existed as a legal body. It therefore had no right to dispose of state property. The Court also ruled that the provisional postwar government was a valid legal state government with the right to sue in the name of the people of Texas.

Texel or ***Tessel*** largest and most westerly of the ◊Frisian Islands, in North Holland province, the Netherlands; area 73 sq mi/190 sq km. Den Burg is the chief settlement.

textile (Latin *texere* "to weave") woven fabric; formerly a material woven from natural spun thread, now loosely extended to machine knits and spunbonded fabrics (in which a web of fiber is created and then fuse-bonded by passing it through controlled heat).
natural Textiles made from natural fibers include cotton, linen, silk, and wool (including angora, llama, and many others). For particular qualities, such as flame resistance or water and stain repellence, these may be combined with synthetic fibers or treated with various chemicals;
synthetic The first commercial synthetic thread was "artificial silk," or rayon (see ◊Chardonnet), with filaments made from modified cellulose (wood pulp) and known according to later methods of manufacture as viscose (using caustic soda and carbon disulfide) or acetate (using acetic acid). The first fully synthetic textile fiber was ◊nylon 1937; these two, along with acrylics (such as Orlon, used in knitwear), polyesters (such as Terylene), and spandex or elastomeric fibers (such as Lycra), form the basis of most of today's industry;
geotextiles These are made from plastic and synthetic fibers; either felted for use as filters or stabilizing grids, or woven for strength. They form part of drainage systems, road foundations, and barriers to sea and river defenses against erosion.

TGV abbreviation for *train à grande vitesse* (French "high-speed train") French electrically powered train that provides the world's fastest rail service. Introduced in 1981, it holds the world speed record for a train of 301.5 mph/482.4 kmh (about half the speed of a passenger jet aircraft), reached at a stretch near Tours in 1989. In its regular service, the TGV covers the 264 mi/425 km distance between Paris and Lyon in two hours.

Thackeray William Makepeace 1811–1863. English novelist and essayist, born in Calcutta, India. He was a regular contributor to *Fraser's Magazine* and *Punch*. *Vanity Fair* 1847–48 was his first novel, followed by *Pendennis* 1848, *Henry Esmond* 1852 (and its sequel *The Virginians* 1857–59), and *The Newcomes* 1853–55, in which Thackeray's tendency to sentimentality is most marked.

Son of an East India Company official, he was educated at Cambridge. He studied law, and then art in Paris, before ultimately settling to journalism in London. Other works include *The Book of Snobs* 1848 and the fairy tale *The Rose and the Ring* 1855.

Thailand country in SE Asia on the Gulf of Siam, bounded E by Laos and Cambodia, S by Malaysia, and W by Myanmar (Burma).
government Under the constitution of 1978, Thailand is ruled by a hereditary monarch working with a two-chamber legislature, the National Assembly. The monarch is head of state and head of the armed forces and appoints a prime minister on the advice of the National Assembly. The prime minister and a selected cabinet formulate policy and are in charge of day-to-day government administration. These ministers may speak but not vote at National Assembly meetings; they must not be serving military officers.

The upper house of the National Assembly, the Senate (Wuthisapha) comprises 268 members who are appointed for six-year terms by the monarch on the recommendation of the prime minister. Senators must not be members of any political party. The lower house, the House of Representatives (Saphaphutan) comprises 357 members who are elected from single-member constituencies by universal suffrage for four-year terms.

Far-left parties, such as the Communist Party, are outlawed, as are parties that field candidates in fewer than half the nation's constituencies. Effective political power in Thailand remains ultimately with the army leadership.
history Thailand has an ancient civilization, with Bronze Age artifacts from as early as 4000 BC. Siam, as it was called until 1939 (and from 1945 to 1949), has been united as a kingdom since 1350; the present dynasty dates from 1782. It was reached by Portuguese traders in 1511, followed by the British East India Company and the Dutch in the 17th century. Treaties of friendship and trade 1826 and 1855 established Britain as the paramount power in the region and opened Siam to foreign commerce. The US presence was especially welcomed, since Americans brought the printing press, smallpox vaccination, and other medical advances to a country that was fascinated by technology. Anglo-French diplomatic agreements of 1896 and 1904 established Siam as a neutral buffer kingdom between British Burma and French Indochina.

After World War I, a movement for national renaissance developed, which culminated in a coup against the absolute monarch King Prajadhipok and the establishment instead of a constitutional monarchy and an elected, representative system of government 1932. The name of Muang Thai ("Land of the Free") was adopted 1939. Thailand was occupied by Japan 1941–44. The government collaborated, but there was a guerrilla resistance movement. A period of instability followed the Japanese withdrawal, King Ananda Mahidol was assassinated 1946, and the army assumed power in a coup 1947 led by Field Marshal Pibul Songgram.

The army retained control during the next two decades, with the leader of the military junta periodically changed by a series of bloodless coups: Field Marshal Pibul Songgram 1947–57, Field Marshal Sarit Thanarat 1958–63, and General Thanom Kittikachorn 1964–73. The monarch,

Thailand
Kingdom of
(*Prathet Thai* or *Muang-Thai*, formerly **Siam**)

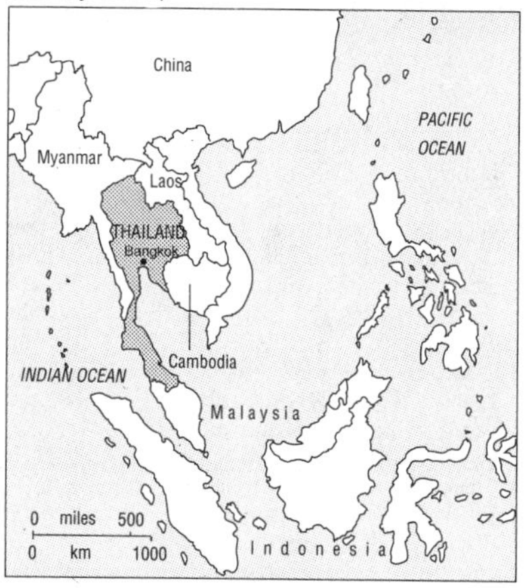
China
PACIFIC OCEAN
Myanmar
Laos
THAILAND
Bangkok
Cambodia
INDIAN OCEAN
Malaysia
Indonesia
0 miles 500
0 km 1000

area 198,108 sq mi/513,115 sq km
capital (and chief port) Bangkok
cities Chiangmai, Nakhon Sawan river port
physical mountainous, semiarid plateau in NE, fertile central region, tropical isthmus in S
features rivers Chao Phraya, Mekong, Salween; archaeological sites featuring tools and weapons from the Bronze Age
head of state King Bhumibol Adulyadej from 1946
head of government Anand Panyarachun from 1991
political system emergent democracy
political parties Thai Nation (Chart Thai), conservative, probusiness; Democratic Party (Prachipat), right-of-center, promonarchist; Social Action Party (Kij Sangkhom), right-of-center; Citizen's Party (Rassadorn), conservative
exports rice, textiles, rubber, tin (fifth largest producer), rubies, sapphires, corn, tapioca
currency baht
population (1990 est) 54,890,000 (Thai 75%, Chinese 14%); growth rate 2% p.a.
life expectancy men 62, women 68 (1989)
language Thai and Chinese (both official); regional dialects
religion Buddhist 95%, Muslim 4%
literacy 89% (1988)
GNP $52 bn (1988); $771 per head (1988)
chronology
1782 Siam absolutist dynasty commenced.
1896 Anglo-French agreement recognized Siam as independent buffer state.
1932 Constitutional monarchy established.
1939 Name of Thailand adopted.
1941–44 Japanese occupation.
1947 Military seized power in coup.
1972 Withdrawal of Thai troops from South Vietnam.
1973 Military government overthrown.
1976 Military reassumed control.
1980 Gen Prem Tinsulanonda assumed power.
1983 Civilian government formed; martial law maintained.
1988 Prime Minister Prem resigned; replaced by Chatichai Choonhavan.
1989 Thai pirates continued to murder, pillage, and kidnap Vietnamese "boat people" at sea.
1991 Military seized power in coup. Martial law ended.

King ◊Bhumibol Adulyadej, was only a figurehead, and experiments with elected assemblies were undertaken 1957–58 and 1968–71. During this era of junta rule, Thailand allied itself with the US and encountered serious Communist guerrilla insurgency along its borders with ◊Laos, ◊Cambodia, and ◊Malaysia. Despite achievements in the economic sphere, the junta was overthrown by violent student riots in Oct 1973. A democratic constitution was adopted a year later, and free elections were held in 1975 and 1976. A series of coalition governments lacked stability, and the military assumed power again 1976–77, annulling the 1974 constitution.

The army supreme commander, General Kriangsak Chomanan, held power 1977–80 and promulgated a new constitution in Dec 1978. This established a mixed civilian and military form of government under the monarch's direction. Having deposed Kriangsak in Oct 1980, General Prem Tinsulanonda (1920–) formally relinquished his army office and headed the civilian coalition governments that were formed after the parliamentary elections of April 1983 and July 1986.

Attempted coups in April 1983 and Sept 1985 (the latter involving General Kriangsak) were easily crushed by Prime Minister Prem, who ruled in a cautious apolitical manner and retained the confidence of the army leadership and the public. Under his stewardship, the country achieved a rapid rate of economic growth, 9–10% a year, emerging as an export-oriented newly industrializing country. However, during the spring of 1988 divisions began to emerge within the ruling coalition and parliament was dissolved in April 1988. Following the general election of July 1988, a six-party coalition, consisting of the Thai Nation, Democratic, Social Action, Rassadorn, United Democratic and Muan Chon parties, was formed, which asked Prem to come into parliament and assume its leadership. Prem declined this offer for "personal" reasons and the Thai Nation's leader took over as premier. He proceeded to pursue a growth-oriented policy course similar to his predecessor's.

The civil war in Cambodia and Laos, which resulted in the flight of more than 500,000 refugees to Thailand from 1975, provided justification for continued quasi-military rule and the maintenance of martial law. Thailand was drawn closer to its ◊ASEAN allies, and its relations with China have seen a thaw. Thailand was drawn more deeply into the Cambodian civil war, with the shelling in 1989 of a refugee camp in Thailand, but tensions eased after the Cambodian peace agreement 1991.

Thaïs 4th century BC. Greek courtesan, mistress of ◊Alexander the Great and later wife of ◊Ptolemy I, king of Egypt. She allegedly instigated the burning of ◊Persepolis.

thalassemia or ***Cooley's anemia*** chronic hereditary blood disorder that is widespread in the Mediterranean countries and found also in Africa and Asia. It is characterized by an abnormality of the red blood cells and bone marrow, with enlargement of the spleen.

Thalberg Irving Grant 1899–1936. US film executive. Born in Brooklyn, New York, Thalberg was hired 1918 as assistant to Carl Laemmle, president of Universal Pictures Corporation in New York. Having moved to Hollywood 1919, Thalberg, "the boy genius," was named head of the studio 1923, leaving to become vice-president in charge of production for Metro-Goldwyn-Mayer 1924. Throughout the rest of his brief career, he displayed an uncanny eye for talent and a consummate skill in business matters. Among his most memorable productions were *Grand Hotel* 1932, *Mutiny on the Bounty* 1935, and *A Night at the Opera* 1935.

Thales 640–546 BC. Greek philosopher and scientist. He made advances in geometry, predicted an eclipse of the Sun 585 BC, and, as a philosophical materialist, theorized that water was the first principle of all things, that the Earth floated on

Thatcher *Thatcher, the first prime minister to be reelected for a third term of office since Lord Liverpool.*

water, and so proposed an explanation for earthquakes. He lived in Miletus in Asia Minor.

Thalia in Greek mythology, the ◊Muse of comedy and pastoral poetry.

thalidomide ◊hypnotic drug developed in the 1950s for use as a sedative. When taken in early pregnancy, it caused malformation of the fetus (such as abnormalities in the limbs) in over 5,000 recognized cases, and the drug was withdrawn.

thallium soft, bluish-white, malleable, metallic element, symbol Tl, atomic number 81, atomic weight 204.37. It is a poor conductor of electricity. Its compounds are poisonous and are used as insecticides and rodent poisons; some are used in the optical-glass and infrared-glass industries and in photoelectric cells.

Discovered spectroscopically in 1861 by its green line, thallium was isolated and named by William Crookes for Greek *thallos*, "young green shoot."

thallus any plant body that is not divided into true leaves, stems, and roots. It is often thin and flattened, as in the body of a seaweed, lichen, or liverwort, and the gametophyte generation (◊prothallus) of a fern.

Some flowering plants (◊angiosperms) that are adapted to an aquatic way of life may have a very simple plant body that is described as a thallus (for example, duckweed *Lemna*).

Thames river in S England; length 210 mi/338 km. It rises in the Cotswolds above Cirencester and is tidal as far as Teddington. Below London there is protection from flooding by means of the Thames barrier. The headstreams unite at Lechlade.

thane or ***thegn*** Anglo-Saxon hereditary nobleman rewarded by the granting of land for service to the monarch or a lord.

Thanksgiving (Day) national holiday in the US (fourth Thursday in November) and Canada (second Monday in October), first celebrated by the Pilgrim settlers in Massachusetts after their first harvest 1621. It was proclaimed a national US vacation 1863.

Since 1942 the US vacation has been celebrated, by act of Congress, on the fourth Thursday in November. The original day of thanksgiving was proclaimed by Massachusetts governor William Bradford after the Pilgrims had survived their first winter, due largely to help from their Indian ally Massasoit.

Thant, U 1909–1974. Burmese diplomat, secretary general of the United Nations 1962–71. He helped to resolve the US-Soviet crisis over the Soviet installation of missiles in Cuba, and he made the controversial decision to withdraw the UN peacekeeping force from the Egypt– Israel border 1967 (see ◊Arab-Israeli Wars).

Thar Desert or ***Indian Desert*** desert on the borders of ◊Rajasthan and Pakistan; area about 96,500 sq mi/250,000 sq km.

Thatcher Margaret Hilda (born Roberts) 1925– British Conservative politician, prime minister

1979–1990. She was education minister 1970–74, and Conservative party leader from 1975. In 1982 she sent British troops to recapture the Falkland Islands from Argentina. She confronted trade-union power during the miners' strike 1984–85, sold off majority stakes in many public utilities to the private sector, and reduced the influence of local government through such measures as the abolition of metropolitan councils, the control of expenditure through "rate-capping," and the introduction of the community charge or ◊poll tax from 1989. In 1990 splits in the cabinet over the issues of Europe and consensus government forced her resignation. An astute Parliamentary tactician, she tolerated little disagreement, either from the opposition or from within her own party.

thaumatrope in photography, a disk with two different pictures at opposite ends of its surface. The images combine into one when rapidly rotated because of the persistence of visual impressions.

theater performance by actors for an audience; it may include ◊drama, dancing, music, ◊mime, and ◊puppets. The term is also used for the place or building in which dramatic performances take place. Theater history can be traced to Egyptian religious ritualistic drama as long ago as 3200 BC. The first known European theaters were in Greece from about 600 BC.

history The earliest Greek theaters were open spaces around the altar of Dionysus. The great stone theater at Athens was built about 500 BC, and its semicircular plan provided for an audience of 20,000–30,000 people sitting in tiers on the surrounding slopes; it served as a model for the theaters that were erected in all the main cities of the Graeco-Roman world. After the collapse of the Roman Empire the theaters were deserted. Examples of Roman theaters still exist at Orange, France, near St Albans, England, and elsewhere.

In medieval times, temporary stages of wood and canvas, one for every scene, were set up side by side in fairgrounds and market squares for the performance of mimes and ◊miracle plays.

Small enclosed theaters were built in the 16th century, for example in Vicenza, Italy (by the architect Palladio). The first London theater was built in Shoreditch 1576 by James ◊Burbage, who also opened the first covered theater in London, the Blackfriars 1596. His son was responsible for building the ◊Globe Theatre, the venue for Shakespeare's plays.

In the US, the center of commercial theater is New York City, with numerous theaters on or near ◊Broadway, although Williamsburg, Virginia (1716), and Philadelphia (1766) had the first known American theaters. The ◊Yiddish theater thrived on New York City's Lower East Side from the late 19th century into the mid-20th century, with many actors, singers, directors, and playwrights becoming stars on Broadway and in Hollywood. The "little theaters," off-Broadway, developed to present less commercial productions, often by new playwrights, and of these the first was the Theater Guild (1919); off-off-Broadway then developed as ◊fringe or alternative theater.

In Britain repertory theaters (theaters running a different play every few weeks) proliferated until World War II, for example, the ◊Old Vic; and in Ireland the ◊Abbey became the first state-subsidized theater 1924. Although the repertory movement declined from the 1950s with the spread of cinema and television, a number of regional community theaters developed. Recently established theaters are often associated with a university or are part of a larger cultural center.

The ◊Comédie Française in Paris (founded by Louis XIV 1690 and given a permanent home 1792) was the first national theater. In Britain the ◊National Theatre company was established 1963; other national theaters exist in Stockholm, Moscow, Athens, Copenhagen, Vienna, Warsaw, and elsewhere.

theater chronology

c. 3200 BC	Beginnings of Egyptian religious drama, essentially ritualistic.
c. 600 BC	Choral performances (dithyrambs) in honor of Dionysus formed beginnings of Greek tragedy, according to Aristotle.
500–300 BC	Great age of Greek drama that included tragedy, comedy, and satyr plays (grotesque farce).
468 BC	Sophocles' first victory at Athens festival. His use of a third actor altered the course of the tragic form.
458 BC	Aeschylus' *Oresteia* first performed.
c. 425–388 BC	Comedies of Aristophanes including *The Birds* 414, *Lysistrata* 411, and *The Frogs* 405. In tragedy the importance of the chorus diminished under Euripedes, author of *The Bacchae* 405.
c. 350 BC	Menander's "New Comedy" of social manners developed.
c. 240 BC–AD 500	Emergence of Roman drama, adapted from Greek originals. Plautus, Terence, and Seneca were the main playwrights.
c. AD 375	Kālidāsa's *Sakuntalā* marked the height of Sanskrit drama in India.
c. 1250–1500	European mystery (or miracle) plays flourished, first in the churches, later in marketplaces, and were performed in England by town guilds.
c. 1375	Nō (or Noh) drama developed in Japan.
c. 1495	*Everyman*, the best known of all the morality plays, first performed.
1500–1600	Italian *commedia dell'arte* troupes performed popular, improvised comedies; they were to have a large influence on Molière and on English harlequinade and pantomime.
c. 1551	Nicholas Udall wrote *Ralph Roister Doister*, the first English comedy.
c. 1576	First English playhouse, The Theatre, built by James Burbage in London.
1587	Marlowe's play *Tamburlaine the Great* marked the beginning of the great age of Elizabethan and Jacobean drama in England.
c. 1589	Kyd's play *Spanish Tragedy* was the first of the "revenge" tragedies.
c. 1590–1612	Shakespeare's greatest plays, including *Hamlet* and *King Lear*, were written.
1604	Inigo Jones designed *The Masque of Blackness* for James I, written by Ben Jonson.
1614	Lope de Vega's *Fuenteovejuna* marked Spanish renaissance in drama. Other writers include Calderón de la Barca.
1637	Corneille's *Le Cid* established Classical tragedy in France.
1642	Act of Parliament closed all English theaters.
1660	With the restoration of Charles II to the English throne, dramatic performances recommenced. The first professional actress appeared as Desdemona in Shakespeare's *Othello*.
1664	Molière's *Tartuffe* was banned for three years by religious factions.
1667	Racine's first success, *Andromaque*.
1680	Comédie Française formed by Louis XIV.
1700	Congreve, the greatest exponent of Restoration comedy, wrote *The Way of the World*.
1716	First known American theater built in Williamsburg, Virginia.
1728	Gay's *The Beggar's Opera* first performed.
1737	Stage Licensing Act in England required all plays to be approved by the Lord Chamberlain before performance.
1747	The actor Garrick became manager of the Drury Lane Theatre, London.
1773	In England, Goldsmith's *She Stoops to Conquer* and Sheridan's *The Rivals* 1775 established the "comedy of manners." Goethe's *Götz von Berlichingen* was the first *Sturm und Drang* play (literally, storm and stress).
1781	Schiller's *Die Räuber/The Robbers*.
1784	Beaumarchais' *Le Mariage de Figaro/The Marriage of Figaro* (written 1778).
1814	Edmund Kean's London debut as Shylock in Shakespeare's *The Merchant of Venice*.
1830	Hugo's *Hernani* caused riots in Paris. His work marked the beginning of a new Romantic drama, changing the course of French theater.
1878	Henry Irving became actor-manager of the Lyceum with Ellen Terry as leading lady.
1879	Ibsen's *A Doll's House*, an early example of realism in European theater.
1888	Strindberg wrote *Miss Julie*.
1893	Shaw wrote *Mrs Warren's Profession* (banned until 1902 because it deals with prostitution). Shaw's works brought the new realistic drama to Britain and introduced social and political issues as subjects for the theater.
1895	Wilde's comedy *The Importance of Being Earnest*. Alfred Jarry's *Ubu Roi*, a forerunner of Surrealism.
1896	The first performance of Chekhov's *The Seagull* failed.
1899	Abbey Theatre, Dublin, founded by W B Yeats and Lady Gregory, marked the beginning of an Irish dramatic revival.
1904	Chekhov's *The Cherry Orchard*.
1919	Theater Guild founded in the US to perform less commercial new plays.
1920	*Beyond the Horizon*, O'Neill's first play, marked the beginning of serious theater in the US.
1921	Pirandello's *Six Characters in Search of an Author* introduced themes of the individual and exploration of reality and appearance.
1928	Brecht's *Die Dreigroschenoper/The Threepenny Opera* with score by Kurt Weill; other political satires by Čapek and E Rice. In the US Jerome Kern's *Show Boat* with Paul Robeson, and other musical comedies by Cole Porter, Irving Berlin, and George Gershwin, became popular.
1930s	US social-protest plays of Odets, Hellman, Wilder, and Saroyan.
1935	T S Eliot's *Murder in the Cathedral*.
1935–39	WPA Federal Theater Project in the US.
1938	Publication of Artaud's *Theater and Its Double*.
1943	The first of the musicals, *Oklahoma!*, opened.
1944–45	Sartre's *Huis Clos/In Camera*; Anouilh's *Antigone*; Arthur Miller's *Death of a Salesman*.
post-1945	Resurgence of German-language theater, including Borchert, Frisch, Dürrenmatt, and Weiss.
1947	Tennessee Williams's *A Streetcar Named Desire*. First Edinburgh Festival, Scotland, with fringe theater events.
1953	Arthur Miller's *The Crucible* opened in the US; *En attendant Godot/Waiting for Godot* by Beckett exemplified the Theater of the Absurd.
1956	English Stage Company formed at the Royal Court Theatre to provide a platform for new dramatists. Osborne's *Look Back in Anger* included in its first season.
1957	Bernstein's *West Side Story* opened in New York.
1960	Pinter's *The Caretaker* produced in London.
1960s	Off-off-Broadway theater, a more daring and experimental type of drama, began to develop in New York.
1961	Royal Shakespeare Company formed in the UK under directorship of Peter Hall.
1963–64	UK National Theatre Company formed at the Old Vic under the directorship of Laurence Olivier.
1967	Success in US of *Hair*, first of the "rock" musicals.
1968	Abolition of theater censorship in the UK.
1975	*A Chorus Line*, to become the longest-running musical, opened in New York.
1980	Howard Brenton's *The Romans in Britain* led in the UK to a private prosecution of the director for obscenity.
1989	Discovery of the remains of the 16th-century Rose and Globe theaters, London.
1992	Agatha Christie's *The Mousetrap* entered its 40th year, the longest-running play in the world.

thebaine $C_{19}H_{21}NO_3$ highly poisonous extract of ◊opium.

Thebes capital of Boeotia in ancient Greece. In the Peloponnesian War it was allied with Sparta against Athens. For a short time after 371 BC when Thebes defeated Sparta at Leuctra, it was the most powerful state in Greece. Alexander the Great destroyed it 336 BC and although it was restored, it never regained its former power.

Thebes Greek name of an ancient city (Niut-Ammon) in Upper Egypt, on the Nile. Probably founded under the first dynasty, it was the center of the worship of Ammon, and the Egyptian capital under the New Kingdom about 1600 BC. Temple ruins survive near the villages of Karnak and Luxor, and in the nearby Valley of the Kings are buried the 18th–20th dynasty kings, including Tutankhamen and Amenhotep III.

theft dishonest appropriation of another's property with the intention of depriving him or her of it permanently.

In the US it is an informal name for the crime of ◊larceny.

thegn alternate spelling of ◊thane.

theism belief in the existence of gods, but more specifically in that of a single personal God, at once immanent (active) in the created world and transcendent (separate) from it.

Themis in Greek mythology, one of the ◊Titans, the daughter of Uranus and Gaia. She was the personification of law and order.

Themistocles c. 525–c. 460 BC. Athenian soldier and politician. Largely through his policies in Athens (creating its navy and strengthening its walls) Greece was saved from Persian conquest. He fought with distinction in the Battle of ◊Salamis 480 BC during the Persian War. About 470 he was accused of embezzlement and conspiracy against Athens, and banished by Spartan influence. He fled to Asia, where Artaxerxes, the Persian king, received him with favor.

Theocritus c. 310–c. 250 BC. Greek poet whose *Idylls* became models for later pastoral poetry. Probably born in Syracuse, he spent much of his life in Alexandria.

theodolite instrument for the measurement of horizontal and vertical angles, used in surveying. It consists of a small telescope mounted so as to move on two graduated circles, one horizontal and the other vertical, while its axes pass through the center of the circles. See also ◊triangulation.

Theodora 508–548. Byzantine empress from 527. She was originally the mistress of Emperor Justinian before marrying him in 525. She earned a reputation for charity, courage, and championing the rights of women.

The daughter of a bear keeper, Theodora became an actress and, as mistress and later wife of the Emperor, the most influential woman in Europe, since Justinian consulted her on all affairs of state.

Theodoric of Freiburg c. 1250–1310. German scientist and monk. He studied in Paris 1275–77. In his work *De Iride/On the Rainbow* he describes how he used a water-filled sphere to simulate a raindrop, and determined that colors are formed in the raindrops and that light is reflected within the drop and can be reflected again, which explains secondary rainbows.

Theodoric the Great c. 455–526. King of the Ostrogoths from 474 in succession to his father. He invaded Italy 488, overthrew King Odoacer (whom he murdered) and established his own Ostrogothic kingdom there, with its capital in Ravenna. He had no strong successor, and his kingdom eventually became part of the Byzantine Empire of Justinian.

Theodosius II 401–450. Byzantine emperor from 408, who defeated the Persians 421 and 441, and from 441 bought off ◊Attila's Huns with tribute.

theology the study of God or gods, either by reasoned deduction from the natural world or through revelation, as in the scriptures of Christianity, Islam, or other religions.

Theophanes the Greek 14th century. Byzantine painter active in Russia. He influenced painting in Novgorod, where his frescoes in Our Savior of the Transfiguration are dated to 1378. He also worked in Moscow with Andrei ◊Rublev.

theorbo a large 17th-century ◊lute with a double neck and two sets of strings.

theory in science, a set of ideas, concepts, principles, or methods used to explain a wide set of observed facts. Among the major theories of science are ◊relativity, ◊quantum theory, ◊evolution, and ◊plate tectonics.

theosophy any religious or philosophical system based on intuitive insight into the nature of the divine, but especially that of the Theosophical Society, founded in New York 1875 by Madame Helena Petrovna Blavatsky and H S Olcott. It was based on Hindu ideas of ◊karma and ◊reincarnation, with ◊nirvana as the eventual aim.

Theravāda one of the two major forms of ◊Buddhism, common in S Asia (Sri Lanka, Thailand, Cambodia, and Myanmar); the other is the later Mahāyāna.

Theresa Mother. Born Agnes Bojaxhiu 1910– . Roman Catholic nun. She was born in Skopje, Albania, and at 18 entered a Calcutta convent and became a teacher. In 1948 she became an Indian citizen and founded the Missionaries of Charity, an order for men and women based in Calcutta that helps abandoned children and the dying. Nobel Peace Prize 1979.

Thérèse of Lisieux, St 1873–1897. French saint. She was born in Alençon, and entered a Carmelite convent in Lisieux at 15, where her holy life induced her superior to ask her to write her spiritual autobiography. She advocated the "Little Way of Goodness" in small things in everyday life, and became known as the "Little Flower of Jesus." She died of tuberculosis and was canonized 1925.

therm unit of energy defined as 10^5 British thermal units; equivalent to 1.055×10^8 joules. It is no longer in scientific use.

thermal capacity the heat energy, C, required to increase the temperature of an object by one degree. It is measured in joules per degree, J/°C or J/K. If an object has mass m and is made of a substance with ◊specific heat capacity c, then $C = mc$.

thermal conductivity in physics, the ability of a substance to conduct heat. Good thermal conductors, like good electrical conductors, are generally materials with many free electrons (such as metals).

Thermal conductivity is expressed in units of joules per second per meter per Kelvin ($J\ s^{-1}\ m^{-1}\ K^{-1}$). For a block of material of cross-sectional area a and length l, with temperatures T_1 and T_2 at its end faces, the thermal conductivity £gL equals $Hl/at(T_2 - T_1)$, where H is the amount of heat transferred in time t.

thermal expansion in physics, expansion that is due to a rise in temperature. It can be expressed in terms of linear, area, or volume expansion.

The coefficient of linear expansion α is the increase in unit length per degree temperature rise; area, or superficial, expansion β is the increase in unit area per degree; and volume, or cubic, expansion γ is the increase in unit volume per degree. As a close approximation, $\beta = 2\alpha$ and $\gamma = 3\alpha$.

Thermidor 11th month of the French Revolutionary calendar, which gave its name to the period after the fall of the Jacobins and the proscription of Robespierre by the National Convention 9 Thermidor 1794.

thermionics branch of electronics dealing with the emission of electrons from matter under the influence of heat. Thermionics was named by O W ◊Richardson.

thermionic tube an electronic tube, used in telegraphy and telephony and in radio and radar, using space conduction by thermionically emitted electrons from an electrically heated cathode. Classification is into diode, triode, and multielectrode tubes, but in most applications they have been replaced by ◊transistors.

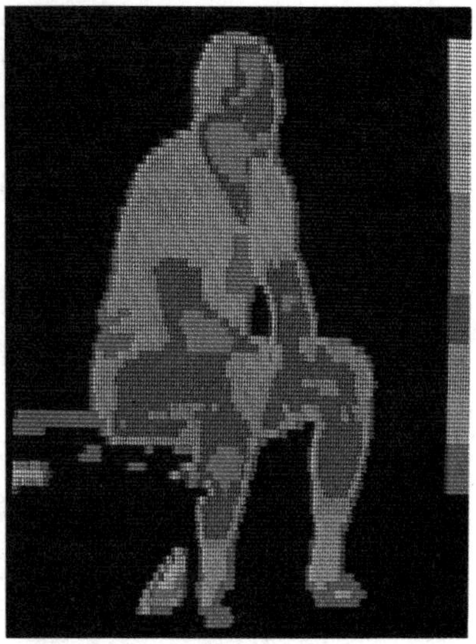

thermography Thermogram, or heat image, of a man. The warmest parts of his body show as spots of red; the cooler areas are blue, green, and purple.

thermistor device whose electrical ◊resistance falls as temperature rises. The current passing through a thermistor increases rapidly as its temperature rises, and so they are used in electrical thermometers.

thermite process method used in incendiary devices and welding operations. It uses a powdered mixture of aluminum and (usually) iron oxide, which, when ignited, gives out enormous heat. The oxide is reduced to iron, which is molten at the high temperatures produced. This can be used to make a weld. The process was discovered 1895 by German chemist Hans Goldschmidt (1861–1923).

thermocouple electric temperature-measuring device consisting of a circuit having two wires made of different metals welded together at their ends. A current flows in the circuit when the two junctions are maintained at different temperatures (◊Seebeck effect). The electromotive force generated—measured by a millivoltmeter—is proportional to the temperature difference.

thermodynamics branch of physics dealing with the transformation of heat into and from other forms of energy. It is the basis of the study of the efficient working of engines, such as the steam and internal combustion engines. The three laws of thermodynamics are (1) energy can be neither created nor destroyed, heat and mechanical work being mutually convertible; (2) it is impossible for an unaided self-acting machine to convey heat from one body to another at a higher temperature; and (3) it is impossible by any procedure, no matter how idealized, to reduce any system to the ◊absolute zero of temperature (0K/–273°C) in a finite number of operations. Put into mathematical form, these laws have widespread applications in physics and chemistry.

thermography photographic recording of heat patterns. It is used medically as an imaging technique to identify "hot spots" in the body—for example, tumors, where cells are more active than usual.

It was developed in the 1970s and 1980s by the military to assist night vision by detecting the body heat of an enemy or the hot engine of a tank. It uses a photographic method (using infrared light) called the Aga system.

thermoluminescence the release in the form of light of stored energy from a substance heated by ◊irradiation. It occurs with most crystalline substances to some extent. It is used in archeology to date pottery, and by geologists in studying terrestrial rocks and meteorites.

thermometer

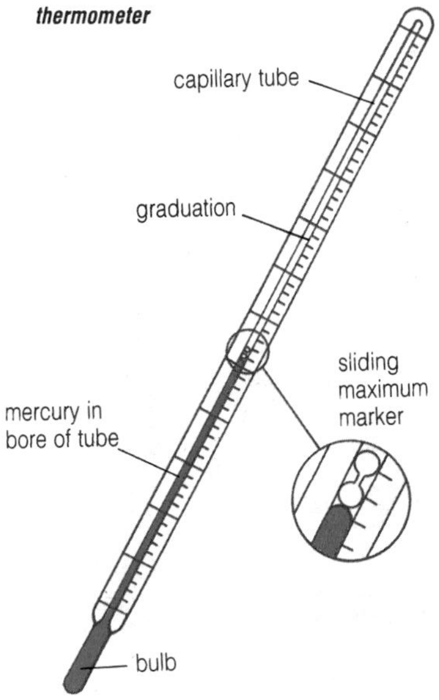
capillary tube
graduation
sliding maximum marker
mercury in bore of tube
bulb

thermometer instrument for measuring temperature. There are many types, designed to measure different temperature ranges to varying degrees of accuracy. Each makes use of a different physical effect of temperature.

Expansion of a liquid is employed in common liquid-in-glass thermometers, such as those containing mercury or alcohol. The more accurate gas thermometer uses the effect of temperature on the pressure of a gas held at constant volume. A resistance thermometer takes advantage of the change in resistance of a conductor (such as a platinum wire) with variation in temperature. Another electrical thermometer is the ◊thermocouple. Mechanically, temperature change can be indicated by the change in curvature of a bimetallic strip (as commonly used in a thermostat).

Thermopylae, Battle of battle during the ◊Persian wars 480 BC when Leonidas, king of Sparta, and 1,000 men defended the pass of Thermopylae to the death against a much greater force of Persians. The pass led from Thessaly to Locris in central Greece.

Thermos originally a trademarked name for a container for keeping things either hot or cold for several hours. It has two silvered glass walls enclosing a vacuum, filled into a metal or plastic outer case. This design reduces the three forms of heat transfer: radiation (prevented by the silvering) and conduction and convection (prevented by the vacuum). A vacuum flask is therefore equally efficient at keeping cold liquids hot, or hot liquids cold. It was invented by James Dewar (1842–1923) about 1872 to store liquefied gases.

thermosphere layer in the Earth's ◊atmosphere above the mesosphere and below the exosphere. Its lower level is about 50 mi/80 km above the ground, but its upper level is undefined. The ionosphere is located in the thermosphere. In the thermosphere the temperature rises with increasing height to several thousand degrees Celsius. However, because of the thinness of the air, very little heat is actually present.

Theroux Paul (Edward) 1941– . US novelist and travel writer whose works include the novels *Saint Jack* 1973, *The Mosquito Coast* 1981, *Doctor Slaughter* 1984, and *My Secret History* 1989, and accounts of his travels by train *The Great Railway Bazaar* 1975, *The Old Patagonian Express* 1979, *Kingdom by the Sea* 1983, and *Riding the Iron Rooster* 1988.

thesaurus (Greek "treasure") collection of synonyms or words with related meaning. Thesaurus compilers include ◊Pliny, Francis ◊Bacon, Comenius (1592–1670), and Peter Mark ◊Roget, whose work was published 1852.

Theseus legendary hero of ◊Attica, supposed to have united the states of the area under a constitutional government in Athens. Ariadne, whom he later abandoned on Naxos, helped him find his way through the Labyrinth to kill the ◊Minotaur. He also fought the Amazons and was one of the ◊Argonauts.

Thespis 6th century BC. Greek poet, born in Attica, said to have introduced the first actor into plays (previously presented by choruses only), hence the word thespian for an actor. He was also said to have invented tragedy and to have introduced the wearing of linen masks.

Thessaloniki (English *Salonika*) port in Macedonia, NE Greece, at the head of the Gulf of Thessaloniki, the second-largest city of Greece; population (1981)706,200. Industries include textiles, shipbuilding, chemicals, brewing, and tanning. It was founded from Corinth by the Romans 315 BC as Thessalonica (to whose inhabitants St Paul addressed two epistles), captured by the Saracens AD 904 and by the Turks 1430, and restored to Greece 1912.

Thessaly (Greek *Thessalia*) region of E central Greece, on the Aegean; area 5,367 sq mi/ 13,904 sq km; population (1981) 695,650. It is a major area of cereal production. It was an independent state in ancient Greece and later formed part of the Roman province of ◊Macedonia. It was Turkish from the 14th century until incorporated in Greece 1881.

The Three Musketeers romance by Dumas *père*, published 1844–45. D'Artagnan, a poor gentleman, joins forces with three of King Louis XIII's musketeers, Athos, Porthos, and Aramis, in a series of adventures.

Thetis in Greek mythology, daughter of Nereus, and mother of ◊Achilles, to whom she brings armor forged by ◊Hephaestus in ◊Homer's Iliad. Fated to have a son more powerful than his father, she was married by the gods to a mortal Peleus.

thiamine or vitamin B_1 ◊vitamin of the B complex. Its absence from the diet causes the disease beriberi.

Thibault Anatole-François. Real name of French writer Anatole ◊France.

Thibodaux city in SE Louisiana, SW of New Orleans. It is an agricultural center for sugar, dairy products, vegetables, and cotton; population (1980) 15,810.

Thiers Louis Adolphe 1797–1877. French politician and historian, first president of the Third Republic 1871–73. He held cabinet posts under Louis Philippe, led the parliamentary opposition to Napoleon III from 1863, and as head of the provisional government 1871 negotiated peace with Prussia and suppressed the briefly autonomous ◊Paris Commune.

His economic policies facilitated the nation's recovery after the Franco-Prussian War.

Thimbu or ***Thimphu*** capital since 1962 of the Himalayan state of Bhutan; population (1982) 15,000.

thing assembly of freemen in the Norse lands (Scandinavia) during the medieval period. It could encompass a meeting of the whole nation (*Althing*) or of a small town or community (*Husthing*).

thing-in-itself (German *Ding-an-sich*) technical term in the philosophy of ◊Kant, employed to denote the unknowable source of the sensory component of our experience. Later thinkers, including ◊Fichte and ◊Hegel, denied the coherence of this concept.

think tank popular name for research foundations, generally private, that gather experts to study policy questions and make recommendations. There are think tanks representing positions across the political spectrum, and they are sometimes funded according to the viewpoints they represent.

Thin Man, The 1934 novel by the US writer Dashiell Hammett, introducing the suave-tough-guy style of detective fiction. It was made into a light-hearted film series 1934–47, starring William Powell (1892–1984) and Myrna Loy (1905–).

Third Reich (Third Empire) term used by the Nazis to describe Germany during the years of Hitler's dictatorship after 1933.

The idea of the Third Reich was based on the existence of two previous German empires, the medieval Holy Roman Empire and the second empire 1871–1918. The term was coined by the German writer Moeller van den Bruck (1876–1925) in the 1920s.

Third World term originally applied collectively to those countries of Africa, Asia, and Latin America that were not aligned with either the Western bloc (First World) or Communist bloc (Second World). The term later took on economic connotations and was applied to those 120 countries that were underdeveloped, as compared to the industrialized free-market countries of the West and the industrialized Communist countries. Third World countries are the poorest, as measured by their income per capita, and are concentrated in Asia, Africa, and Latin America. They are divided into low-income countries, including China and India; middle-income countries, such as Nigeria, Indonesia, and Bolivia; and upper-middle-income countries, such as Brazil, Algeria, and Malaysia.

Problems associated with developing countries include high population growth and mortality rates; poor educational and health facilities; heavy dependence on agriculture and commodities for which prices and demand fluctuate; high levels of underemployment, and, in some cases, political instability. Third World countries, led by the Arab oil-exporting countries, account for over 75% of all arms imports. The economic performance of developing countries in recent years has been mixed, with sub-Saharan Africa remaining in serious difficulties and others, as in Asia, making significant progress. Failure by many developing countries to meet their enormous foreign debt obligations has led to stringent terms being imposed on loans by industrialized countries, as well as rescheduling of loans (deferring payment).

Thirteen Colonies the 13 American colonies that signed the ◊Declaration of Independence from Britain 1776. Led by George Washington, the Continental Army defeated the British army in the ◊American Revolution 1776–81 to become the original 13 United States of America: Connecticut, Delaware, Georgia, Maryland, Massachusetts, New Hampshire, New Jersey, New York, North Carolina, Pennsylvania, Rhode Island, South Carolina, and Virginia. They were united first under the ◊Articles of Confederation and from 1789, the US ◊constitution.

38th parallel the demarcation line between North (People's Democratic Republic of) and South (Republic of) Korea, agreed at the Yalta Conference 1945 and largely unaltered by the Korean War 1950–53.

35 mm width of photographic film, the most popular format for the camera today. The 35-mm camera falls into two categories, the ◊SLR and the ◊rangefinder.

Thirty-Nine Articles a set of articles of faith defining the doctrine of the Anglican Church; see under Anglican Communion.

Thirty Years' War major war 1618–48 in central Europe. Beginning as a German conflict between Protestants and Catholics, it gradually became transformed into a struggle to determine whether the ruling Austrian Hapsburg family would gain control of all Germany. The war caused serious economic and demographic problems in central Europe.

1618–20 A Bohemian revolt against Austrian rule was defeated. Some Protestant princes continued the struggle against Austria.

1625–27 Denmark entered the war on the Protestant side.

1630 Gustavus Adolphus of Sweden intervened on the Protestant side, overrunning N Germany.

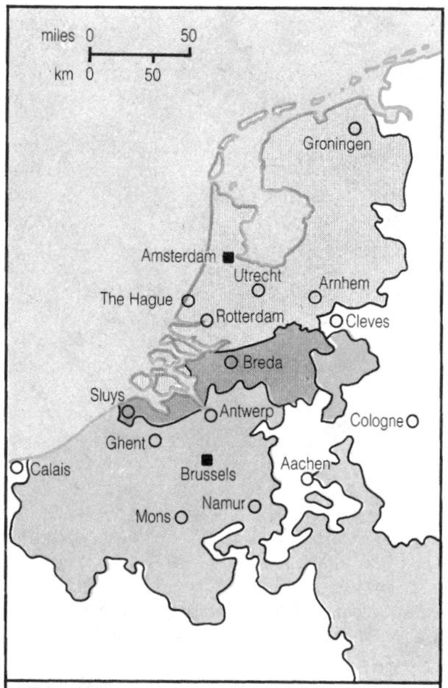
miles 0 50
km 0 50
Groningen
Amsterdam
Utrecht
Arnhem
The Hague
Rotterdam
Cleves
Breda
Sluys
Antwerp
Cologne
Ghent
Calais
Brussels
Aachen
Namur
Mons

Thirty Years' War
The Netherlands after the Peace of Westphalia 1648
United Provinces
The Generality, i.e. areas seized from the Spanish Netherlands by the United Provinces
Spanish Netherlands

1631 The Catholic commander Tilly stormed Magdeburg.

1632 Tilly was defeated at Breitenfeld and the Lech, and was killed. The German general Wallenstein was defeated at the Battle of Lützen; Gustavus Adolphus killed.

1634 When the Swedes were defeated at Nördlingen, ◊Richelieu brought France into the war to inflict several defeats on Austria's Spanish allies. Wallenstein was assassinated.

1648 The Treaty of Westphalia gave France S Alsace, and Sweden got certain Baltic provinces, the emperor's authority in Germany becoming only nominal. The mercenary armies of Wallenstein, Tilly, and Mansfeld devastated Germany.

thistle species of prickly plant of several genera, such as *Carduus* and *Cirsium*, in the family Compositae, found in the N hemisphere. The stems are spiny, the flower heads purple, white, or yellow and cottony, and the leaves deeply indented with prickly margins. The thistle is the Scottish national emblem.

Thomas Clarence 1948– . US Supreme Court justice (1991–). Born in Savannah, Georgia, he received a law degree from Yale University Law School (1974). President Reagan appointed him head of the civil rights division of the Department of Education 1981 and the head of the Equal Employment Opportunities Commission 1982. Thomas served there until 1990, when President Bush appointed him a justice on the US Court of Appeals. In 1991 he was nominated to the Supreme Court to succeed Thurgood Marshall, and after extremely bitter and sensational confirmation hearings, Thomas was confirmed by the Senate and took his seat on the Court.

thistle

Thomas Dylan (Marlais) 1914–1953. Welsh poet. His poems include the celebration of his 30th birthday "Poem in October" and the evocation of his youth "Fern Hill" 1946. His radio play *Under Milk Wood* 1954 and the short stories of *Portrait of the Artist as a Young Dog* 1940 are autobiographical.

Born in Swansea, son of the English teacher at the local grammar school where he was educated, he worked as a reporter on the *South Wales Evening Post*, then settled as a journalist in London and published his first volume *Eighteen Poems* in 1934.

Thomas Lowell (Jackson) 1892–1981. US journalist. Born in Woodington, Ohio, Thomas was educated at Northern Indiana University and the University of Denver and joined the staff of the *Chicago Journal* 1912. After receiving an MA from Princeton 1915, he served as a special observer for President Wilson during World War I. His first-person account of the Arab Revolt was published as *With Lawrence in Arabia* 1924. In 1930 Thomas became a radio commentator for the Columbia Broadcasting System and was on the air for 46 years. Traveling to all World War II theaters of combat and to remote areas of the world, he became one of America's best-known journalists.

Thomas Norman Mattoon 1884–1968. US political leader. As pastor of the East Harlem Church he first confronted the problem of urban poverty and joined the Socialist party 1918. Leaving the ministry for political activism, he was one of the founders of the American Civil Liberties Union 1920 and served as a director of the League for Industrial Democracy 1922–37. Six-time Socialist candidate for president 1928–48 and a brilliant speaker, he noted that by 1950 most of his so-called radical platform had been adopted by the US, such as Social Security and public-health programs. He published *A Socialist's Faith* 1951.

Born in Marion, Ohio, Thomas graduated from Princeton 1905 and after study at the Union Theological Seminary was ordained a Presbyterian minister 1911.

Thomas Seth 1785–1859. US clock manufacturer. Born in Wolcott, Connecticut, Thomas was trained as a carpenter and cabinetmaker. In 1807 he joined Silas Hoadley and Eli Terry in a partnership in Plymouth, Connecticut, for the production of clocks. Thomas established his own firm 1812 and became enormously successful in the manufacture of affordable shelf clocks. In 1853 the firm was reorganized as the Seth Thomas Clock Company and continued to prosper into the 20th century. Its base of operations, Plymouth Hollow, Connecticut, was renamed Thomaston.

Thomas, St in the New Testament, one of the 12 Apostles, said to have preached in S India, hence the ancient churches there were referred to as the "Christians of St Thomas." He is not the author of the Gospel of St Thomas, the Gnostic collection of Jesus' sayings.

Thomas à Kempis 1380–1471. German Augustinian monk who lived at the monastery of Zwolle. He took his name from his birthplace Kempen; his real surname was Hammerken. His *De Imitatio Christi/Imitation of Christ* is probably the most widely known devotional work ever written.

Thomas Aquinas, St see ◊Aquinas.

Thomism in philosophy, the method and approach of Thomas ◊Aquinas. Neo-Thomists apply this philosophical method to contemporary problems.

Thompson David 1770–1857. Canadian explorer and surveyor who mapped extensive areas of W Canada, including the Columbia River, for the Hudson's Bay Company 1789–1811.

Thompson John Taliaferro 1860–1940. US colonel, inventor of the Thompson submachine-gun (see ◊machine gun).

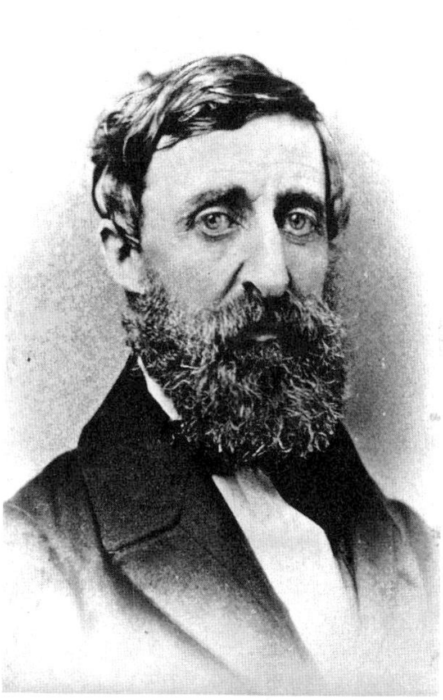

***Thoreau** Author and naturalist Henry David Thoreau, whose views on peaceful resistance to unjust laws were widely adopted in the US in the 20th century.*

Thomsen Christian (Jürgensen) 1788–1865. Danish archeologist. He devised the classification of prehistoric cultures into Stone Age, Bronze Age, and Iron Age.

Thomson Elihu 1853–1937. US inventor. He founded, with E J Houston, the Thomson–Houston Electric Company 1882, later merging with the Edison Company to form the General Electric Company. He made advances into the nature of the ◊electric arc and invented the first high-frequency ◊dynamo and ◊transformer.

Thomson George Paget 1892–1975. English physicist. His work on ◊interference phenomena in the scattering of electrons by crystals helped to confirm the wave-like nature of particles. He shared a Nobel Prize with C J ◊Davisson 1937.

Thomson J(oseph) J(ohn) 1856–1940. English physicist who discovered the ◊electron. He was responsible for organizing the Cavendish atomic research laboratory at Cambridge University. His work inaugurated the electrical theory of the atom and led to ◊Aston's discovery of ◊isotopes. Nobel Prize 1906.

Thomson Virgil 1896–1989. US composer and critic. His large body of work, characterized by a clarity and simplicity of style, includes operas such as *Four Saints in Three Acts* (libretto by Gertrude Stein) 1934; orchestral, choral, and chamber music; and film scores.

Thor in Norse mythology, god of thunder (his hammer), and represented as a man of enormous strength defending humanity against demons. He was the son of Odin and Freya, and Thursday is named after him.

thorax in tetrapod vertebrates, the part of the body containing the heart and lungs, and protected by the rib cage; in arthropods, the middle part of the body, between the head and abdomen.

In mammals the thorax is separated from the abdomen by the muscular diaphragm. In insects the thorax bears the legs and wings. The thorax of spiders and crustaceans is fused with the head, to form the cephalothorax.

Thoreau Henry David 1817–1862. US author and naturalist. His work *Walden, or Life in the Woods* 1854 stimulated the back-to-nature movement, and he completed some 30 volumes based on his daily nature walks. His essay "Civil Disobedience"

1849, prompted by his refusal to pay taxes, advocated peaceful resistance to unjust laws and had a wide impact, even in the 20th century.

Born in Concord, Massachusetts, Thoreau graduated from Harvard University. His friend, transcendentalist Ralph Waldo ◊Emerson, encouraged him to write and offered him land near Walden Pond on which to set up his experiment 1845–47 in living a life close to nature, requiring little manual labor and allowing him time to write. His other works include *A Week on the Concord and Merrimack Rivers* 1849 and, published posthumously, *Excursions* 1863, *The Maine Woods* 1864, *Cape Cod* 1865, and *A Yankee in Canada* 1866.

thorium dark-gray, radioactive, metallic element of the ◊actinide series, symbol Th, atomic number 90, atomic weight 232.038. It occurs throughout the world in small quantities in minerals such as thorite and is widely distributed in monzanite beach sands. It is one of three fissile elements (the others are uranium and plutonium), and its longest-lived isotope has a half-life of 1.39×10^{10} years. Thorium is used to strengthen alloys. It was discovered by Jöns Berzelius in 1828 and was named by him for the Norse god Thor.

thorn apple or jimson weed annual plant *Datura stramonium* of the nightshade family, growing to 6 ft/2 m in northern temperate and subtropical areas; native to America and naturalized worldwide. It bears white or violet trumpet-shaped flowers and capsulelike fruit that split to release black seeds. All parts of the plant are poisonous. The fruit of the ◊hawthorn is also called thorn apple.

thoroughbred horse bred for racing purposes. All racehorses are thoroughbreds, and all male thoroughbreds are direct descendants of one of three stallions imported into Britain during the 17th and 18th centuries: the Darley Arabian, Byerley Turk, and Godolphin Barb.

Thorpe Jim (James Francis) 1888–1953. US athlete. Born in Prague, Oklahoma, Thorpe attended the Carlisle Indian School in Pennsylvania. An outstanding soccer player, he was named All-American in 1911 and 1912. A member of the 1912 US Olympic Team in Stockholm, Thorpe won gold medals for the decathlon and pentathlon. However, when he admitted to having played semiprofessional baseball, he was forced to return his medals. Thorpe later played major-league baseball 1913–19 and professional football 1917–29. He was posthumously elected to the Football Hall of Fame 1963, and his Olympic medals were restored by the Amateur Athletic Union 1973.

Thorwaldsen Bertel 1770–1844. Danish Neo-Classical sculptor. He went to Italy on a scholarship in 1796 and stayed in Rome for most of his life, producing portraits, monuments, and religious and mythological works. Much of his work is housed in the Thorwaldsen Museum, Copenhagen.

Thoth in Egyptian mythology, god of wisdom and learning. He was represented as a scribe with the head of an ◊ibis, the bird sacred to him.

Thothmes four Egyptian kings of the 18th dynasty, including:

Thothmes I king of Egypt 1540–1501 BC. He founded the Egyptian empire in Syria.

Thothmes III king of Egypt about 1500–1446 BC. He extended the empire to the river Euphrates, and conquered Nubia. He was a grandson of Thothmes I.

Thousand and One Nights collection of Oriental tales, also known as the ◊Arabian Nights.

Thousand Islands group of about 1,700 islands in the upper St Lawrence River, on the border between Canada and the US. Most of them are in Ontario, Canada; the rest are in the US state of New York. Some are in Canada's St Lawrence Islands National Park; many of the others are privately owned. The largest is Wolfe Island in Ontario, 49 sq mi/127 sq km. The islands are popular summer resorts.

Thrace (Greek *Thráki*) ancient empire (6000 BC–AD 300) in the Balkans, SE Europe, formed by parts of modern Greece and Bulgaria. It was held successively by the Greeks, Persians, Macedonians, and Romans.

The area was divided 1923 into western Thrace (the Greek province of Thráki) and eastern Thrace (European Turkey). The heart of the ancient Thracian Empire was Bulgaria, where since 1945 there have been tomb finds of gold and silver dishes, drinking vessels, and jewelry with animal designs. The legend of ◊Orpheus and the cult of ◊Dionysus were both derived by the Greeks from Thrace. The area was conquered by Persia 6th–5th centuries BC and by Macedonia 4th–2nd centuries BC. From AD 46 it was a Roman province, then part of the Byzantine Empire, and Turkish from the 15th century until 1878; it was then subject to constant dispute until after World War I.

threadworm kind of ◊nematode.

Three Mile Island island in the Shenandoah River near Harrisburg, Pennsylvania, site of a nuclear power station that was put out of action following a major accident in March 1979. Opposition to nuclear power in the US was reinforced after this accident and safety standards reassessed.

Three Rivers English name for the Canadian port of ◊Trois-Rivières.

Three Sisters, The play by Anton Chekhov, first produced 1901. A family, bored and frustrated by life in the provinces, dream that if they move to Moscow their problems will disappear. However, apathy prevents the dream becoming reality.

threshing agricultural process of separating cereal grains from the plant. Traditionally, the work was carried out by hand in winter months using the flail, a jointed beating stick. Today, threshing is done automatically inside the combine harvester at the time of cutting.

From the late 18th century, through the work of Andrew ◊Meikle and others, machine threshing slowly overtook the flail and made rapid progress after 1850.

thrift or ***sea pink*** any plant of the genus *Armeria*, family Plumbaginaceae. *A. maritima* occurs on seashores and cliffs in Europe. The leaves are small and linear; the dense round heads of pink flowers rise on straight stems.

thrips any of an order (Thysanoptera) of tiny insects, usually with feathery wings.

Many of the 3,000 species live in flowers and suck their juices, causing damage and spreading disease. Others eat fungi, decaying matter, or smaller insects.

throat in human anatomy, the passage that leads from the back of the nose and mouth to the ◊trachea and ◊esophagus. It includes the ◊pharynx and the ◊larynx, the latter being at the top of the trachea. The word "throat" is also used to mean the front part of the neck, both in humans and other vertebrates; for example, in describing the plumage of birds. In engineering, it is any narrowing entry, such as the throat of a carburetor.

thrombosis condition in which a blood clot forms in a vein or artery, causing loss of circulation to the area served by the vessel. If it breaks away, it often travels to the lungs, causing pulmonary embolism.

Thrombosis in veins of the legs is often seen in association with ◊phlebitis, and in arteries with ◊atheroma. Thrombosis increases the risk of heart attack (myocardial ◊infarct) and stroke. It is treated by surgery and/or anticoagulant drugs.

throwing event field event. There are four at most major international track and field meets: ◊discus, ◊hammer, ◊javelin, and ◊shot put.

thrush any bird of the large worldwide family Turdidae (order Passeriformes), found worldwide, known for their song. Thrushes are usually brown with speckles of other colors. They are between 5–12 in/12–30 cm long.

North American species include the hermit thrush *Catharus guttatus*, a beautiful songster; the wood thrush *Hylocichla mustelina*; and the American robin *Turdus migratorius*. European species include the song thrush *Turdus philomelos* and the mistle thrush *T. viscivorus*.

thrush infection usually of the mouth (particularly in infants), but also sometimes of the vagina, caused by a yeastlike fungus (genus *Candida*). It is seen as white patches on the mucous membranes.

Thrush, also known as candidiasis, may be caused by antibiotics removing natural antifungal agents from the body. It is treated with a further antibiotic.

Thucydides 460–400 BC. Athenian historian, who exercised command in the ◊Peloponnesian War with Sparta 424 with so little success that he was banished until 404. In his *History of the Peloponnesian War*, he attempted a scientific impartiality.

thug originally a member of a Hindu sect who strangled travelers as sacrifices to ◊Kali, the goddess of destruction. The sect was suppressed about 1830.

Thule Greek and Roman name for the northernmost land known. It was applied to the Shetlands, the Orkneys, and Iceland, and by later writers to Scandinavia.

thulium soft, silver-white, malleable and ductile, metallic element, of the ◊lanthanide series, symbol Tm, atomic number 69, atomic weight 168.94. It is the least abundant of the rare-earth metals and was first found in gadolinite and various other minerals. It is used in arc lighting.

The X-ray-emitting isotope Tm-170 is used in portable X-ray units. Thulium was named in 1886 by French chemist Paul Lecoq de Boisbaudran for the northland, Thule, in Latin.

Thunder Bay city and port on Lake Superior, Ontario, Canada, formed by the union of Port Arthur and its twin city of Fort William to the S; industries include shipbuilding, timber, paper, wood pulp, and export of wheat; population (1986) 122,000.

Thunderbird legendary bird of the North American Indians, the creator of storms.

He produces thunder by flapping his wings; lightning by opening and closing his eyes.

Thünen Johann von 1785–1850. German economist and geographer who believed that the success of a state depends on the well-being of its farmers. His book *The Isolated State* 1820, a pioneering study of land use, includes the earliest example of ◊marginal productivity theory, a theory which he developed to calculate the natural wage for a farmworker. He has been described as the first modern economist.

Thurber James (Grover) 1894–1961. US humorist. His short stories, written mainly for the *New Yorker* magazine, include "The Secret Life of Walter Mitty" 1932, and his doodle drawings include fanciful impressions of dogs.

Born in Columbus, Ohio, Thurber was partially blind as a result of an accident in childhood; he became totally blind in the last ten years of his life but continued to work. His stories and sketches are collected in *Is Sex Necessary?* (with E B White) 1929, *The Middle-Aged Man on the Flying Trapeze* 1935, *The Last Flower* 1939, and *My World and Welcome to It* 1942. He also wrote adult fairy tales—*Many Moons* 1943, *The Great Quillow* 1944, *The White Deer* 1945, *The 13 Clocks* 1950, and *The Wonderful O* 1957—and a play, *The Male Animal* 1940.

Thuringia administrative *Land* (state) of the Federal Republic of Germany

area 5,980 sq mi/15,482 sq km;

capital Erfurt;

cities Weimar, Gera, Jena, Eisenach;

products machine tools, optical instruments, steel, vehicles, ceramics, electronics, glassware, timber;

population (1990) 2,500,000;

history historic, densely forested region of Germany that became a province 1918 and a region of East Germany 1946. It was split into the districts of Erfurt, Gera, and Suhl 1952 but reconstituted as a state following German reunification 1990.

Thursday Island island in Torres Strait, Queensland, Australia; area 1.5 sq mi/4 sq km; chief center Port Kennedy. It is a center of the pearl-fishing industry.

Thyestes in Classical mythology, son of ◊Pelops and brother of ◊Atreus. His rivalry with Atreus for the kingship of Mycenae was continued by their sons, Aegisthus and Agamemnon.

thylacine another name for the ◊Tasmanian wolf.

thyme herb, genus *Thymus*, of the mint family Labiatae. Garden thyme *T. vulgaris*, native to the Mediterranean, grows to 1 ft/30 cm high, and has pinkish flowers. Its aromatic leaves are used for seasoning.

thymus organ in vertebrates, situated in the upper chest cavity in humans. The thymus processes ◊lymphocyte cells to produce T-lymphocytes (T denotes "thymus-derived"), which are responsible for binding to specific invading organisms and killing them or rendering them harmless.

The thymus reaches full size at puberty, and shrinks thereafter; the stock of T-lymphocytes is built up early in life, so this function diminishes in adults, but the thymus continues to function as an ◊endocrine gland, producing the hormone thymosin, which stimulates the activity of the T-lymphocytes.

thyristor type of ◊rectifier, an electronic device that conducts electricity in one direction only. The thyristor is composed of layers of ◊semiconductor material sandwiched between two electrodes called the anode and cathode. The current can be switched on by using a third electrode called the gate.

Thyristors are used to control mains-driven motors and in lighting dimmer controls.

thyroid ◊endocrine gland of vertebrates, situated in the neck in front of the trachea. It secretes several hormones, among them thyroxin, a hormone containing iodine. This stimulates growth, metabolism, and other functions of the body. Excessive action produces Graves's disease, characterized by bulging eyeballs and an elevated metabolism, while deficient action produces ◊myxedema in adults and dwarfism in juveniles.

thyrotoxicosis synonym for ◊hyperthyroidism.

Tiahuanaco or ***Tihuanaco*** site of a Peruvian city, S of Lake Titicaca in the Andes, which gave its name to the 8th–14th-century civilization that preceded the Inca and built many of the roads the Inca are credited with building.

Tiananmen Square (Chinese "Square of Heavenly Peace") paved open space in central Beijing (Peking), China, the largest public square in the world (area 0.14 sq mi/0.4 sq km). On 3–June 4, 1989, more than 1,000 unarmed protesters were killed by government troops in a massacre that crushed China's emerging prodemocracy movement.

Hundreds of thousands of demonstrators had occupied the square from early May, calling for political reform and the resignation of the Communist leadership. They were led by students, 3,000 of whom staged a hunger strike in the square. The massacre that followed was sanctioned by the old guard of leaders, including Deng Xiaoping.

Tianjin or ***Tientsin*** port and industrial and commercial city in Hubei province, central China; population (1986) 5,380,000. The special municipality of Tianjin has an area of 1,544 sq mi/4,000 sq km and a population of 8,190,000. Its handmade silk and wool carpets are renowned. Dagan oil-field is nearby. Tianjin was opened to foreign trade 1860 and occupied by the Japanese 1937.

Tian Shan (Chinese *Tien Shan*) mountain system on the Soviet-Chinese border. Pik Pobedy on the Xinjiang–Kirghizia border is the highest peak at 24,415 ft/7,440 m.

tiara triple crown worn by the pope, or a semicircular headdress worn by women for formal occasions. The term was originally applied to a headdress worn by the ancient Persians.

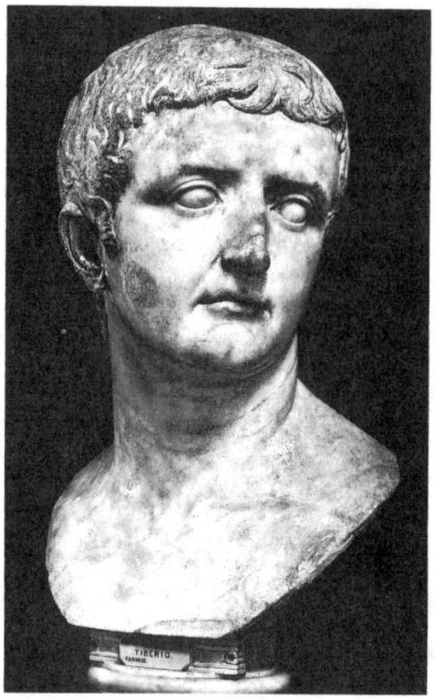

Tiberius *A bust of the Roman emperor Tiberius.*

Tiber (Italian *Tevere*) river in Italy on which Rome stands; length from the Apennines to the Tyrrhenian Sea 250 mi/400 km.

Tiberias, Lake or ***Sea of Galilee*** lake in N Israel, 689 ft/210 m below sea level, into which the ◊Jordan flows; area 66 sq mi/170 sq km. The first Israeli ◊kibbutz (cooperative settlement) was founded nearby 1909.

Tiberius Claudius Nero 42 BC–AD 37. Roman emperor, the stepson, adopted son, and successor of Augustus from AD 14. A distinguished soldier, he was a conscientious ruler under whom the empire prospered.

Tibesti Mountains range in the central Sahara, N Chad; highest peak Emi Koussi 11,208 ft/3,415 m.

Tibet autonomous region of SW China (Pinyin form ***Xizang***)

area 471,538 sq mi/1,221,600 sq km

capital Lhasa

features Tibet occupies a barren plateau bounded south and southwest by the Himalayas and north by the Kunlun Mountains, traversed west to east by the Bukamagna, Karakoram, and other mountain ranges, and having an average elevation of 13,000–15,000 ft/4,000–4,500 m. The Sutlej, Brahmaputra, and Indus rivers rise in Tibet, which has numerous lakes, many of which are salty. The ◊yak is the main domestic animal.

government Tibet is an autonomous region of China, with its own People's Government and People's Congress. The controlling force in Tibet is the Communist Party of China, represented locally by First Secretary Wu Jinghua from 1985

products wool, borax, salt, horn, musk, herbs, furs, gold, iron pyrites, lapis lazuli, mercury, textiles, chemicals, agricultural machinery

population (1986) 2,030,000; many Chinese have settled in Tibet

religion Traditionally Lamaist (a form of Mahāyāna Buddhism)

history Tibet was an independent kingdom from the 5th century AD. It came under nominal Chinese rule about 1700. Independence was regained after a revolt 1912. China regained control 1951 when the historic ruler and religious leader, the ◊Dalai Lama, was driven from the country and the monks (who formed 25% of the population) were forced out of the monasteries. Between 1951 and 1959 the Chinese People's Liberation Army (PLA) controlled Tibet, although the Dalai Lama returned as nominal spiritual and temporal head of state. In 1959 a Tibetan uprising spread from bordering regions to Lhasa and was supported by the Tibet local government. The rebellion was suppressed by the PLA, prompting the Dalai Lama and 9,000 Tibetans to flee to India. The Chinese proceeded to dissolve the Tibet local government, abolish serfdom, collectivize agriculture, and suppress ◊Lamaism. In 1965 Tibet became an autonomous region of China. Chinese rule continued to be resented, however, and the economy languished.

From 1979, the leadership in Beijing adopted a more liberal and pragmatic policy toward Tibet. Traditional agriculture, livestock, and trading practices were restored (under the 1980 slogan "relax, relax, and relax again"), a number of older political leaders and rebels were rehabilitated or pardoned, and the promotion of local Tibetan cadres was encouraged. In addition, a somewhat more tolerant attitude toward Lamaism has been adopted (temples damaged during the 1965–68 Cultural Revolution are being repaired) and attempts, thus far unsuccessful, have been made to persuade the Dalai Lama to return from exile.

Pro-independence demonstrations erupted in Lhasa in Sept–Oct 1987, repeatedly throughout 1988, and in March 1989 and were forcibly suppressed by Chinese troops. In May and Oct 1988 peacefully demonstrating monks and civilians were shot by police. In 1989 many anti-China demonstrators were shot and all foreigners were expelled. These clashes exhibit the continuing strength of nationalist feeling. The country is of immense strategic importance to China, being the site of 50,000–100,000 troops and a major nuclear missile base at Nagchuka.

Tibetan member of a Mongolian people inhabiting Tibet who practice Mahayana Buddhism, introduced in the 7th century. Since China's Cultural Revolution 1966–68, refugee communities formed in India and Nepal. The Tibetan language belongs to the Sino-Tibetan language family.

tibia the anterior of the pair of bones found between the ankle and the knee. In humans, the tibia is the shinbone.

tick any of an arachnid group (Ixodoidea) of large

tide

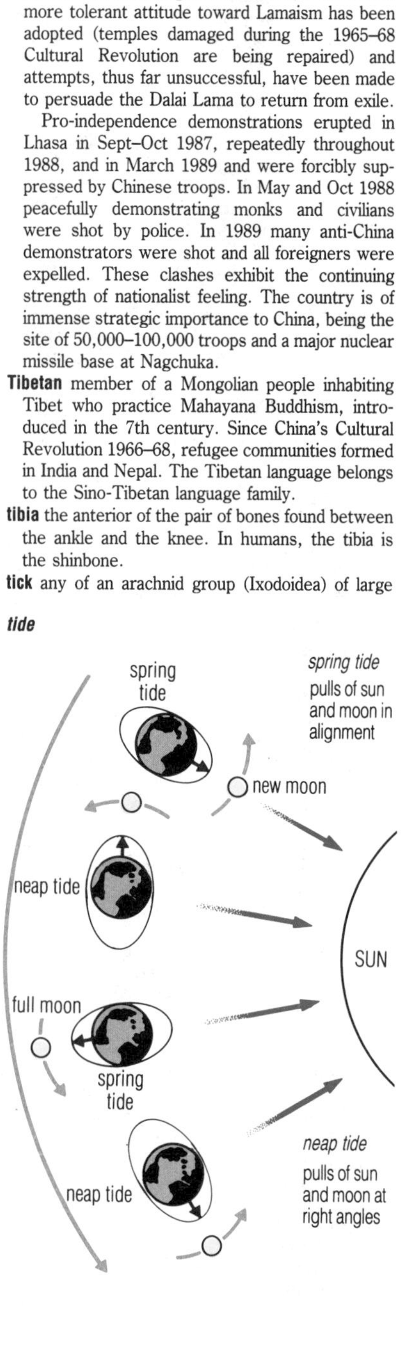
spring tide
spring tide
pulls of sun and moon in alignment
new moon
neap tide
SUN
full moon
spring tide
neap tide
pulls of sun and moon at right angles
neap tide

***Tiepolo** Italian Rococo painter Giovanni Tiepolo's* Immaculate Conception, *which was commissioned in 1767.*

bloodsucking mites. Many carry and transmit diseases to mammals (including humans) and birds.

tidal power a specialized form of ◊hydro-electric power, harnessing the twice daily surge of the tides to generate electricity. This has been done successfully at the Rance estuary in Brittany, France since 1966.

tidal wave misleading name for a ◊tsunami.

tide rise and fall of sea level due to the gravitational forces of the Moon and Sun. High water occurs at an average interval of 12 hr 24 min 30 sec. The highest or spring tides are at or near new and full Moon; the lowest or neap tides when the Moon is in its first or third quarter. Some seas, such as the Mediterranean, have very small tides.

Other factors affecting sea level are (1) a combination of naturally high tides with storm surge, as sometimes happens along the low-lying coasts of Germany and the Netherlands; (2) the water walls created by typhoons and hurricanes, such as often hit Bangladesh; (3) underwater upheavals in the Earth's crust that may cause a ◊tsunami; and (4) global temperature change melting the polar ice caps.

Tieck Johann Ludwig 1773–1853. German Romantic poet and collector of folk tales, some of which he dramatized, such as "Puss in Boots."

Tien Shan Chinese form of ◊Tian Shan, mountain system of central Asia.

Tientsin alternate form of ◊Tianjin, industrial city in NE China.

Tiepolo Giovanni Battista 1696–1770. Italian painter, born in Venice. He created monumental Rococo decorative schemes in palaces and churches in NE Italy, SW Germany, and Madrid 1762–70. The style is light-hearted, the palette light and warm, and he made great play with illusion.

Tiepolo painted religious and historical or allegorical pictures: for example, scenes from the life of Cleopatra 1745 (Palazzo Labia, Venice) and from the life of Frederick Barbarossa 1757 (Kaisersaal, Würzburg Palace). His sons were among his many assistants.

Tierra del Fuego island group divided between Chile and Argentina. It is separated from the mainland of South America by the Strait of Magellan, and Cape Horn is at the southernmost point. Chief town, Ushuaia, Argentina, is the world's southernmost town. Industries include oil and sheep farming.

To the S of the main island is Beagle Channel (named after the ship of the scientist Charles Darwin's voyage), with three islands at the E end, finally awarded 1985 to Chile rather than Argentina.

Tiffany Louis Comfort 1848–1933. US artist and glassmaker, son of Charles Louis Tiffany, who founded Tiffany and Company, the New York City jewelers. He produced stained-glass windows, iridescent Favrile (from Latin *faber* "craftsman") glass, and lampshades in the Art Nouveau style. He used glass that contained oxides of iron and other elements to produce rich colors.

In 1881 he founded his own decorating firm. By 1893, he began producing his glass art objects, which remained popular through the 1920s and enjoyed a resurgence of popularity from the 1950s on.

Tiflis former name (until 1936) of the city of ◊Tbilisi in the USSR.

tiger largest of the great cats *Panthera tigris*, formerly found in much of central and S Asia but nearing extinction because of hunting and the destruction of its natural habitat. The tiger can grow to 12 ft/3.6 m long and weigh 660 lb/300 kgs; it has a yellow-orange coat with black stripes. It is solitary, and feeds on large ruminants. It is a good swimmer.

Man-eating tigers are rare and are the result of weakened powers or shortage of game. The striped markings—black on reddish fawn—are present from birth, although rare cream or black specimens have been known.

In Sumatra there are about 800 tigers left, and many are killed each year by poachers. They are continually losing their jungle habitat: companies plunder the forest for timber and minerals, and then farmers move in and take over the land.

Tigré or ***Tigray*** region in the northern highlands of Ethiopia; area 25,444 sq mi/65,900 sq km. The chief town is Mekele. The region had an estimated population of 2.4 million in 1984, at a time when drought and famine were driving large numbers of people to fertile land in the south or into neighboring Sudan. From 1978 a guerrilla group known as the Tigré People's Liberation Front (TPLF) fought for regional autonomy. In 1989 government troops were forced from the province, and the TPLF advanced towards Addis Ababa, playing a key role in the fall of the Ethiopian government in May 1991.

Tigris (Arabic *Shatt Dijla*) river flowing through Turkey and Iraq (see also ◊Mesopotamia), joining the ◊Euphrates above Basra, where it forms the ◊Shatt-al-Arab; length 1,000 mi/1,600 km.

Tijuana city and resort in NW Mexico; population (1980) 461,257; known for horse races and casinos. ◊San Diego adjoins it across the US border.

Tikhonov Nikolai 1905– . Soviet politician. He was a close associate of President Brezhnev, joining the Politburo 1979, and was prime minister (chair of the Council of Ministers) 1980–85. In Apr 1989 he was removed from the central committee.

Tilden Samuel Jones 1814–1886. US political leader. As chairman of the New York state Democratic committee 1866–74, he campaigned against the Tammany Hall Organization and its leader, William "Boss" Tweed. Tilden was elected governor on a reform ticket 1874. He received the Democratic presidential nomination 1876, and although he received a plurality of popular votes, the 1877 electoral college awarded the majority of electoral votes to Rutherford B Hayes.

Born in New Lebanon, New York, Tilden was educated at Yale and New York universities and was admitted to the bar 1841.

till deposit of clay, mud, gravel, and boulders left by a glacier. Till is unsorted, all sizes of fragments mixed up together, and it shows no stratification; that is, it does not form clear layers or ◊beds.

Tillich Paul Johannes 1886–1965. Prussian-born US theologian. Tillich received his PhD from the University of Breslau 1911. Ordained a pastor in the Evangelical Lutheran Church 1912, he served as a chaplain during World War I. In 1929 he was appointed professor of philosophy at the University of Frankfurt, a post from which he was removed by the Nazis. Tillich came to the US 1933 and served as professor of theology at the Union Theological Seminary 1933–55, Harvard University 1955–62, and the University of Chicago 1962–65. He is best remembered for his *Systematic Theology* 1951–63.

Tilly Jan Tserkles, Count von 1559–1632. Flemish commander of the army of the Catholic League and imperial forces in the ◊Thirty Years' War. Notorious for his storming of Magdeburg, E Germany, 1631, he was defeated by the Swedish king Gustavus Adolphus at Breitenfeld and at the river Lech in SW Germany, where he was mortally wounded.

Tilsit former name (until 1945) of the Soviet town of ◊Sovetsk.

timber wood used in construction, furniture, and paper pulp. Hardwoods include tropical mahogany, teak, ebony, rosewood, temperate oak, elm, beech, and eucalyptus. All except eucalyptus are slow-growing, and world supplies are near exhaustion. Softwoods are comprised of the conifers (pine, fir, spruce, and larch), which are quick to grow and easy to work but inferior in quality of grain. White woods include ash, birch, and cottonwood; all have light-colored timber, are fast-growing, and can be used through modern methods as veneers on cheaper timber.

Timbuktu or ***Tombouctou*** town in Mali; population (1976) 20,500. A camel caravan center from the 11th century on the fringe of the Sahara, since 1960 it has been surrounded by the southward movement of the desert, and the former canal link with the river Niger is dry. Products include salt.

time the continuous passage of existence, recorded by division into hours, minutes, and seconds. Formerly the measurement of time was based on the Earth's rotation on its axis, but this was found to be irregular. Therefore the second, the standard ◊SI unit of time, was redefined 1956 in terms of the Earth's annual orbit of the Sun, and 1967 in terms of a radiation pattern of the element cesium.

Universal time (UT), based on the Earth's actual rotation, was replaced by coordinated universal time (UTC) 1972, the difference between the two involving the addition (or subtraction) of leap seconds on the last day of June or Dec. National observatories make standard time available in various countries. From 1986 the term Greenwich Mean Time was replaced by UTC. However, the Greenwich meridian, adopted 1884, remains that from which all longitudes are measured, and the world's standard time zones are calculated from it.

time and motion study process of analysis applied to a job or number of jobs to check the efficiency of the work method, equipment used, and the worker. Its findings are used to improve performance.

Time and motion studies were introduced in the US by Frederick Taylor (1856–1915) at the beginning of the 20th century. Since then, the practice has spread throughout the industrialized world.

time-sharing in computing, a way of enabling several users to access the same computer at the same time. The computer rapidly switches between programs, giving each user the impression that he or she has sole use of the system.

Timişoara capital of Timiş county, W Romania; population (1985) 319,000. The revolt against the

Ceauşescu regime began here in Dec 1989 when demonstrators prevented the arrest and deportation of a popular protestant minister who was promoting the rights of ethnic Hungarians. This soon led to large pro-democracy rallies.

Timon an Athenian of the age of ◊Pericles notorious for his misanthropy, which was reported and elaborated by Classical authors, and became the subject of the play by ◊Shakespeare.

Timor largest and most easterly of the Lesser Sunda Islands, part of Indonesia; area 12,973 sq mi/ 33,610 sq km. West Timor (capital Kupang) was formerly Dutch and was included in Indonesian independence. East Timor (capital Dili) was an overseas province of Portugal until it was annexed by Indonesia 1975. Guerrilla warfare by local people seeking independence continues. Since 1975 over 500,000 have been killed or have resettled in West Timor, according to Amnesty International. Products include coffee, corn, rice, and coconuts.

Timothy in the New Testament, companion to St ◊Paul, both on his missionary journeys and in prison. Two of the Pauline epistles are addressed to him.

tin soft, silver-white, malleable and somewhat ductile, metallic element, symbol Sn (from Latin *stannum*), atomic number 50, atomic weight 118.69. Tin exhibits ◊allotropy, having three forms: the familiar lustrous metallic form above 55.8°F/ 13.2°C; a brittle form above 321.8°F/161°C; and a gray powder form below 55.8°F/13.2°C (commonly called tin pest or tin disease). The metal is quite soft (slightly harder than lead) and can be rolled, pressed, or hammered into extremely thin sheets; it has a low melting point. Its chief source is the mineral cassiterite. In nature it occurs rarely as a free metal (◊native metal). It resists corrosion and is therefore used for coating and plating other metals.

Tin and copper smelted together form the oldest desired alloy, bronze; since the Bronze age (3,500 BC) that alloy has been the basis of both useful and decorative materials. The mines of Cornwall were the principal Western source from then until the 19th century, when rich deposits were found in South America, Africa, and Southeast Asia. Tin is also alloyed with metals other than copper to make solder and pewter. It was recognized as an element by Antoine Lavoisier, but the name is very old and comes from the Germanic form *zinn*.

tinamou any fowllike bird of the South American order Tinamiformes, of which there are some 45 species. They are up to 16 in/40 cm long, and their drab color provides good camouflage. They are excellent runners but poor flyers and are thought to be related to the ratites (flightless birds). Tinamous are mainly vegetarian, but sometimes eat insects. They escape predators by remaining still or by burrowing through dense cover.

Tinbergen Jan 1903–1988. Dutch economist. He shared a Nobel Prize 1969 with Ragnar Frisch for his work on ◊econometrics (the mathematical-statistical expression of economic theory).

Tinbergen Nikolaas 1907– . Dutch zoologist. He was one of the founders of ◊ethology, the scientific study of animal behavior in natural surroundings. Specializing in the study of instinctive behavior, he shared a Nobel prize with Konrad Lorenz and Karl von ◊Frisch 1973. He is the brother of Jan Tinbergen.

Tindouf Saharan oasis in the Aïn-Sefra region of Algeria, crossed by the Agadir–Dakar desert route. There are large iron deposits in the area; the oasis is a base for exiled Polisario guerrillas of the Western Sahara.

Ting Samuel 1936– . US high-energy physicist. In 1974 he detected a new subatomic particle, known as the J particle, similar to the ψ (psi) particle found by Burton ◊Richter, with whom he shared the 1976 Nobel Prize for Physics.

tinnitus in medicine, constant internal sounds, inaudible to others. The phenomenon may originate from noisy conditions (drilling, machinery, or loud music) or from infection of the middle or inner ear. The victim may become overwhelmed by the relentless noise in the head.

In some cases there is a hum at a frequency of about 40 Hz, which resembles that heard by people troubled by environmental ◊hum but may include whistles and other noises resembling a machine workshop. Being in a place where external noises drown the internal ones gives some relief, and devices may be worn that create pleasant, soothing sounds to override them.

Tipperary *Celtic crosses, with their characteristic intertwined ornamentation, are found in the Irish countryside. This is the E face of South Cross at Ahenny in Tipperary.*

tin ore mineral from which tin is extracted, principally cassiterite, SuO_2. The chief producers today are Malaysia, Thailand, and Bolivia.

tinplate milled steel coated with tin, the metal used for most "tin" cans. The steel provides the strength, and the tin provides the corrosion resistance, ensuring that the food inside is not contaminated. Tinplate may be made by ◊electroplating or by dipping in a bath of molten tin.

Tintoretto real name Jacopo Robusti 1518–1594. Italian painter, active in Venice. His dramatic religious paintings are spectacularly lit and full of movement, such as his canvases of the lives of Christ and the Virgin in the Scuola di San Rocco, Venice, 1564–88.

Tintoretto was so named because his father was a dyer (*tintore*). He was a student of ◊Titian and admirer of Michelangelo. *Miracle of St Mark Rescuing a Slave* 1548 (Accademia, Venice) marked the start of his successful career. In the Scuola di San Rocco he created a sequence of heroic scenes with bold gesture and foreshortening and effects of supernatural light. He also painted canvases for the Doge's Palace.

Tiomkin Dimitri 1899–1979. Russian composer who lived in the US from 1925. From 1930 he wrote Hollywood film scores, including music for *Duel in the Sun* 1946, *The Thing* 1951, and *Rio Bravo* 1959. His score for *High Noon* 1952 won him an Academy Award.

Tipperary county in the Republic of Ireland, province of Munster, divided into N and S regions. North Tipperary: administrative headquarters Nenagh; area 772 sq mi/2,000 sq km; population (1986) 59,000. South Tipperary: administrative headquarters Clonmel; area 872 sq mi/2,260 sq km; population (1986) 77,000. It includes part of the Golden Vale, a dairy-farming region.

Tippett Michael (Kemp) 1905– . English composer whose works include the operas *The Midsummer Marriage* 1952 and *The Knot Garden* 1970; four symphonies; *Songs for Ariel* 1962; and choral music including *The Mask of Time* 1982.

Tirana or ***Tiranë*** capital (since 1920) of Albania; population (1983) 206,000. Industries include metallurgy, cotton textiles, soap, and cigarettes. It was founded in the early 17th century by Turks when part of the Ottoman Empire. Although the city is now largely composed of recent buildings, some older districts and mosques have been preserved.

tire inflatable (pneumatic) rubber casing fitted to the wheel rims of bicycles and motor vehicles. The first pneumatic rubber tire was patented by R W Thompson 1845, but it was John Boyd Dunlop of Belfast who independently reinvented pneumatic tires for use with bicycles 1888–89. ◊Vulcanization, used in tire manufacture, was invented by Charles ◊Goodyear in 1844.

Tiresias or ***Teiresias*** in Greek mythology, a man blinded by the gods and given the ability to predict the future.

According to the poet Ovid, Tiresias once saw two snakes mating, struck at them, and was changed into a woman. Seven years later, in a repetition of the same scene, he reverted back to manhood. Later, he was called upon to settle a dispute between the two gods Zeus and Hera on whether men or women enjoy sex more. He declared for women, and as a result Hera blinded him, but Zeus gave him the gift of foresight.

Tîrgu Mureş city in Transylvania, Romania, on the river Mureş; population (1978) 137,000. With a population comprising approximately equal numbers of ethnic Hungarians and Romanians, the city was the scene of rioting between the two groups following Hungarian demands for greater autonomy in 1990; six people were killed.

Tirol federal province of Austria; area 4,864 sq mi/ 12,600 sq km; population (1987) 610,000. Its capital is Innsbruck, and it produces diesel engines, optical instruments, and hydroelectric power. Tirol was formerly a province (from 1363) of the Austrian Empire, divided 1919 between Austria and Italy (see ◊Trentino–Alto Adige).

Tirpitz Alfred von 1849–1930. German admiral. As secretary for the navy 1897–1916, he created the modern German navy and planned the World War I U-boat campaign.

Tirso de Molina pen name of Gabriel Telléz 1571–1648. Spanish dramatist and monk who wrote more than 400 plays, of which eight are extant, including comedies, historical and biblical dramas, and a series based on the legend of Don Juan.

Tiruchirapalli formerly Trichinopoly ("three-headed demon") city in Tamil Nadu, India; chief industries are cotton textiles, cigars, and gold and silver filigree; population (1981) 362,000. It is a place of pilgrimage and was the capital of Tamil kingdoms during the 10th to 17th centuries.

Tiryns ancient Greek city in the Peloponnese on the plain of Argos, with remains of the ◊Mycenean culture.

Tiselius Arne 1902–1971. Swedish chemist who developed a powerful method of chemical analysis known as ◊electrophoresis. He applied his new techniques to the analysis of animal proteins. Nobel Prize 1948.

Tissot James (Joseph Jacques) 1836–1902. French painter who produced detailed portraits of Victorian high society during a ten-year stay in England.

In the 1880s Tissot visited Palestine. His religious works were much admired.

tissue in biology, any kind of cellular fabric that

occurs in an organism's body. Several kinds of tissue can usually be distinguished, each consisting of cells of a particular kind bound together by cell walls (in plants) or extracellular matrix (in animals). Thus, nerve and muscle are different kinds of tissue in animals, as are ◊parenchyma and ◊sclerenchyma in plants.

tissue culture process by which cells from a plant or animal are removed from the organism and grown under controlled conditions in a sterile medium containing all the necessary nutrients. Tissue culture can provide information on cell growth and differentiation, and is also used in plant propagation and drug production. See also ◊meristem.

tissue plasminogen activator (TPA) naturally occurring substance in the body tissues that activates the enzyme plasmin, which is able to dissolve blood clots. Human TPA, produced in bacteria by genetic engineering, has been used to try to dissolve blood clots in the coronary arteries of heart-attack victims.

Tisza tributary of the river Danube, rising in the USSR and flowing through Hungary to Yugoslavia; length 601 mi/967 km.

Titan in astronomy, largest moon of the planet Saturn, with a diameter of 3,200 mi/5,150 km and a mean distance from Saturn of 759,000 mi/1,222,000 km. It was discovered 1655 by Christiaan Huygens and is the second-largest moon in the Solar System (only Ganymede, of Jupiter, is larger).

Titan is the only moon in the Solar System with a substantial atmosphere (mostly nitrogen), topped with smoggy orange clouds that obscure the surface, which may be covered with liquid ethane lakes. Its surface atmospheric pressure is greater than Earth's. Radar signals suggest that Titan has dry land as well as oceans (among the planets of the Solar System, only Earth has both).

Titan in Greek mythology, any of the giant children of Uranus and Gaia, who included Cronus, Rhea, Themis (mother of Prometheus and personification of law and order), and Oceanus. Cronus and Rhea were in turn the parents of Zeus, who ousted Cronus as the ruler of the world.

Titanic British passenger liner, supposedly unsinkable, that struck an iceberg and sank off the Grand Banks of Newfoundland on its first voyage April 14–15, 1912; 1,513 lives were lost. In 1985 it was located by robot submarine 2.5 mi/4 km down in an ocean canyon, preserved by the cold environment. In 1987 salvage operations began.

titanium strong, light-weight, silver-gray, metallic element, symbol Ti, atomic number 22, atomic weight 47.90. Its compounds occur in practically all igneous rocks and their sedimentary deposits. It is very strong and resistant to corrosion, so it is used in building high-speed aircraft and spacecraft; it is also widely used in making alloys, as it unites with almost every metal except copper and aluminum. Titanium oxide is used in high-grade white pigments.

The element was discovered in 1791 by English mineralogist William Gregor (1761–1817) and named in 1796 by German chemist Martin Klaproth for Titan, one of the Giants of Greek mythology. It was not obtained in pure form until 1925.

titanium ore one of the minerals from which titanium is extracted, principally ilmenite, $FeTiO_3$, and rutile, TiO_2. Both these ore minerals are found either in rock formations or concentrated in heavy mineral sands. Brazil, India, and Canada are major producers.

Titan rocket family of US space rockets, developed from the Titan intercontinental missile. Two-stage Titan rockets launched the ◊Gemini crewed missions. More powerful Titans, with additional stages and strap-on boosters, were used to launch spy satellites and space probes, including ◊Viking and ◊Voyager.

tithe formerly, payment exacted from the inhabitants of a parish for the maintenance of the church and its incumbent; some religious groups continue the practice by giving 10% of members' incomes to charity.

Titian *A portrait of the Holy Roman Emperor Charles V by Titian.*

It was originally the grant of a tenth of all agricultural produce made to priests in Hebrew society. In the Middle Ages the tithe was adopted as a tax in kind paid to the local parish church, usually for the support of the incumbent, and stored in a special tithe ◊barn; as such, it survived into contemporary times. In Protestant countries, these payments were often appropriated by lay landlords.

Titian anglicized form of the name of Tiziano Vecellio c. 1487–1576. Italian painter, active in Venice, one of the greatest artists of the High Renaissance. In 1533 he became court painter to Charles V, Holy Roman emperor, whose son Philip II of Spain later became his patron. Titian's work is richly colored, with inventive composition. He produced a vast number of portraits, religious paintings, and mythological scenes, including *Bacchus and Ariadne* 1520–23, *Venus and Adonis* 1554, and the *Entombment of Christ* 1559.

Titian probably studied with Giovanni ◊Bellini but also learned much from ◊Giorgione and seems to have completed some of Giorgione's unfinished works, such as *Noli Me Tangere* (National Gallery, London). His first great painting is the *Assumption of the Virgin* 1518 (Church of the Frari, Venice), typically sublime in mood, with upward-thrusting layers of figures. Three large mythologies painted in the next few years for the dukes of Ferrara show yet more brilliant use of color, and numerous statuesque figures suggest the influence of Classical art. By the 1530s Titian's reputation was widespread.

In the 1540s Titian visited Rome to paint the pope; in Augsburg, Germany, 1548–49 and 1550–51 he painted members of the imperial court. In his later years he produced a series of mythologies for Philip II, notably *The Rape of Europa* 1562 (Isabella Stewart Gardner Museum, Boston, Massachusetts). His handling became

Tito *Marshal Tito, who became president of Yugoslavia after World War II, led guerrilla resistance to the Germans during the war.*

increasingly free and his palette somber, but his work remained full of drama. He made an impact not just on Venetian painting but on art throughout Europe.

Titicaca lake in the Andes, 12,500 ft/3,810 m above sea level; area 3,200 sq mi/8,300 sq km, the largest lake in South America. It is divided between Bolivia (port at Guaqui) and Peru (ports at Puno and Huancane). It has enormous edible frogs.

titmouse any of a family (Paridae) of small birds of the order Passeriformes, found worldwide except in South America and Australia. There are 65 species, all agile and hardy, and often seen hanging upside down from twigs to feed. In North America many of the species are called chickadees.

North American species include the tufted titmouse *Parus bicolor*, with a gray crest, and the black-capped chickadee *P. atricapillus*.

Tito adopted name of Josip Broz 1892–1980. Yugoslav soldier and communist politician, in power from 1945. In World War II he organized the National Liberation Army to carry on guerrilla warfare against the German invasion 1941, and was created marshal 1943. As prime minister 1946–53 and president from 1953, he followed a foreign policy of "positive neutralism."

Born in Croatia, Tito served in the Austrian army during World War I, was captured by the Russians, and fought in the Red Army during the civil wars. Returning to Yugoslavia 1923, he became prominent as a communist and during World War II as ◊partisan leader against the Nazis. In 1943 he established a provisional government and gained Allied recognition (previously given to the ◊Chetniks), and with Soviet help proclaimed the federal republic 1945. As prime minister, he settled the Yugoslav minorities question on a federal basis, and in 1953 took the newly created post of president (for life from 1974). In 1948, he was criticized by the USSR and other communist countries, for his successful system of decentralized profit-sharing workers' councils, and became a leader of the ◊nonaligned movement.

Titograd formerly (until 1948) ***Podgorica*** capital of Montenegro, Yugoslavia; population (1981) 132,300. Industries include metal working, furniture making, and tobacco. It was damaged in World War II and after rebuilding was renamed in honor of Marshal Tito. It was the birthplace of the Roman emperor Diocletian.

Titus Flavius Sabinus Vespasianus AD 39–81. Roman emperor from AD 79. Eldest son of ◊Vespasian, he stormed Jerusalem 70 to end the Jewish revolt in Roman Palestine. He completed the Colosseum, and enjoyed a peaceful reign, except for ◊Agricola's campaigns in Britain.

Titusville city in E Florida, on the Indian River, E of Orlando. Industries include citrus fruits and

toad

western spadefoot toad

sport fishing. The Kennedy Space Center is nearby; population (1990) 39,394.

Tivoli town NE of Rome, Italy; population (1981) 52,000. It has remains of Hadrian's villa, with gardens; and the Villa d'Este with Renaissance gardens laid out 1549 for Cardinal Ippolito d'Este.

Tlatelolco, Treaty of international agreement signed 1967 in Tlatelolco, Mexico, prohibiting nuclear weapons in Latin America.

Tlemcen (Roman *Pomaria*) town in NW Algeria; population (1983) 146,000. Carpets and leather goods are made, and there is a 12th-century mosque.

Tlingit member of a North American Indian people of the NW coast, living in S Alaska and N British Columbia. They are especially known for carving wooden totem poles that include such animals as the raven, whale, octopus, beaver, bear, wolf, and the mythical "thunderbird." Their language is related to the Athabaskan languages.

TLR camera twin-lens reflex camera that has a viewing lens of the same angle of view and focal length mounted above and parallel to the taking lens.

TM abbreviation for ◊transcendental meditation.

TN abbreviation for ◊Tennessee.

TNT abbreviation for trinitrotoluene, $CH_3C_6H_2(NO_2)_3$, a powerful high explosive. It is a yellow solid, prepared in several isomeric forms from ◊toluene by using sulfuric and nitric acids.

toad general name for any of the more terrestrial warty-skinned members of the tailless amphibians (order Anura) especially the genus *Bufo*, family Bufonidae. Actually, there are no hard and fast rules for distinguishing betweeen frogs and toads. Members of the genus *Bufo* occur worldwide, except in the Australian and polar regions.

The American toad *B. americanus* reaches 3.5 in/9 cm and is found from suburban backyards to mountain wildernesses throughout the NE US.

toadflax any small plant of the genus *Linaria* of the snapdragon family Scrophulariaceae, with spurred, two-lipped flowers.

toadstool inedible or poisonous type of ◊fungus with a fleshy, gilled fruiting body on a stalk.

tobacco large-leaved plant of the genus *Nicotiana* of the family Solanaceae, native to tropical parts of the Americas. The species *N. tabacum* is widely cultivated as an annual in warm, dry climates for use in cigars and cigarettes, and in powdered form as snuff. The worldwide profits of the tobacco industry are estimated to be over £10 billion annually.

The leaves are cured, or dried, and matured in storage for two to three years before use. Introduced to Europe as a medicine in the 16th century, tobacco was recognized from the 1950s as a major health hazard; see ◊cancer. The leaves also yield the alkaloid nicotine, a colorless oil, one of the most powerful poisons known, and addictive in humans. It is used in insecticides.

Tobago island in the West Indies; part of the republic of ◊Trinidad and Tobago.

Tobin James 1918– . US Keynesian economist. He was awarded a Nobel Prize 1981 for his "general equilibrium" theory, which states that other criteria than monetary considerations are applied by households and firms when making decisions on consumption and investment. He is critical of monetarists for putting too much emphasis on a single asset—money—and he has analyzed the impact of changes in fiscal or monetary policy on the economy as a whole. He also has examined the process of portfolio selection, considering the trade-off between risk and yield across a broad range of assets.

Born in Champaign, Illinois, Tobin received his undergraduate and graduate degrees from Harvard. He taught at Yale, becoming the Sterling Professor of Economics from 1957. He served on the President's Council of Economic Advisers during President Kennedy's administration. Tobin's works include the three-volume *Essays in Economics* 1971–82 and *The New Economics, One Decade Older* 1974.

toboggan flat-bottomed sled, curved upward and backwards at the front, used on snow or ice slopes or banked artificial courses.

Tobolsk river port and lumber center at the confluence of the Tobol and Irtysh rivers in N Tyumen, W Siberia, USSR; population (1985) 75,000. It was founded by ◊Cossacks 1587; Tsar Nicholas II was exiled here 1917.

Tobruk Libyan port; population (1984) 94,000. Occupied by Italy 1911, it was taken by Britain 1941 during World War II, and unsuccessfully besieged by Axis forces Apr–Dec 1941. It was captured by Germany June 1942 after the retreat of the main British force to Egypt, and this precipitated the replacement of Auchinleck by Montgomery as British commander.

toccata in music, a display piece for keyboard instruments, such as the organ.

Tocqueville Alexis de 1805–1859. French politician and political scientist, author of the first analytical study of the US constitution, *De la Démocratie en Amérique/Democracy in America* 1835, and of a penetrating description of France before the Revolution, *L'Ancien Régime et la Révolution/The Old Regime and the Revolution* 1856.

Elected to the Chamber of Deputies 1839, Tocqueville became vice-president of the Constituent Assembly and minister of foreign affairs 1849. He retired after Napoleon III's coup 1851.

Todt Fritz 1891–1942. German engineer, who was responsible for building the first autobahns (German expressways) and, in World War II, the Siegfried Line and the Atlantic Wall.

tofu or ***dofu*** or ***dowfu*** bean curd derived from soy milk. It is a good source of protein and naturally low in fat.

Tofu comes in three varieties: smooth and firm, in small white blocks, used for stir-frying or steaming; as a junketlike solid used in making dips, salad dressings, or ice cream; and hard, fermented and/or seasoned cakes, which may be sliced and eaten or used in cooking. The flavor is bland, but it combines readily with other ingredients; the fermented and seasoned tofu has the taste and texture of various cheeses.

tog unit of measure of thermal insulation used in the textile trade; a light summer suit provides 1.0 tog.

The tog-value of an object is equal to ten times the temperature difference (in 8°C) between its two surfaces when the flow of heat is equal to one watt per square meter; one tog equals 0.645 ◊clo.

Togare stage name of Georg Kulovits 1900–1988. Austrian wild-animal tamer and circus performer. Togare invented the character of the exotic Oriental lion tamer after watching Douglas Fairbanks in the 1923 film *The Thief of Baghdad*. In his circus appearances he displayed a nonchalant disregard for danger.

Togliatti or ***Tolyatti***, formerly Stavropol, port on the river Volga, W central USSR; industries include engineering and food processing; population (1987) 627,000. The city was relocated in the 1950s after a flood and renamed after the Italian communist Palmiro Togliatti.

Togliatti Palmiro 1893–1964. Founding member of the Italian Communist Party in 1921 and effectively its leader for almost 40 years from 1926 until his death. In exile from 1926 until 1944, he returned after the fall of the Fascist dictator Mussolini to become a member of Badoglio's government and held office until 1946.

Togliatti trained as a lawyer, served in the army, and was wounded during World War I. He was associated with the revolutionary wing of the Italian Socialist party that left to form the Communist Party in 1921. From 1922 to 1924 he edited the newspaper *Il Comunista* and became a member of the party's central committee. He was in Moscow when Mussolini outlawed the party, and stayed there to become a leading member of the ◊Comintern, joining the Secretariat in 1935. Returning to Italy after Mussolini's downfall, he advocated coalition politics with other leftist and democratic parties, a policy which came to fruition in the elections of 1948 where the communists won 135 seats.

Togo country in W Africa, bounded W by Ghana, E by Benin, and N by Burkina Faso.

government The 1979 constitution created a one-party, Socialist republic based on the Assembly of the Togolese People (RPT). The president is elected by universal suffrage for a seven-year term and is eligible for re-election. The president is head of state and head of government, appointing and presiding over a council of ministers, and is also president of RPT.

There is a single-chamber legislature, the National Assembly, of 77 members, elected by universal suffrage from a list of RPT nominees and serving for five years. There is an illegal opposition party, the Togolese Movement for Democracy, which is based in Paris.

history For early history, see ◊Africa. Called Togoland, the country was a German protectorate 1885–1914, when it was captured by Anglo-French forces. It was divided between Britain and France in 1922 under a League of Nations mandate and continued under United Nations trusteeship from 1946. In 1956 British Togoland voted for integration with Ghana, where it became Volta region 1957.

French Togoland voted to become an autonomous republic within the French union. The new Togolese republic achieved internal self-government in 1956 and full independence in 1960. Sylvanus Olympio, leader of the United Togolese (UT) party, became president in an unopposed election in April 1961. In 1963 Olympio was killed in a military coup and his brother-in-law Nicolas Grunitzky, who had gone into exile, was recalled to become president.

In 1967 Grunitzky was, in turn, deposed in a bloodless military coup, led by Lt-Gen Etienne Gnassingbé Eyadéma. The new constitution was suspended; Eyadéma assumed the presidency and banned all political activity. Six years later he founded a new party, the Socialist, nationalist RPT, and declared it the only legal political organization. Between 1967 and 1977 there were several attempts to overthrow him but by 1979 Eyadéma felt sufficiently secure to propose a new coalition and embark on a policy of gradual democratization. An attempt to overthrow him in Oct 1986, by mercenaries from Burkina Faso and Ghana, was easily thwarted. In 1990 his government asserted that the Togolese people did not want a multi-party political system.

Tōgō Heihachirō 1846–1934. Japanese admiral who commanded the fleet at the battle of ◊Tsushima 1905, when Japan defeated the Russians and effectively ended the Russo-Japanese War of 1904–05.

Tohoku mountainous region of N Honshu island, Japan; population (1986) 9,737,000; area 25,867 sq mi/66,971 sq km. Timber, fruit, fish, and livestock are produced. The chief city is Sendai. Aomori in the NE is linked to Hakodate on the island of Hokkaido by the Seikan tunnel, the world's longest underwater tunnel.

Tōjō Hideki 1884–1948. Japanese general and premier 1941–44 during World War II. Promoted to chief of staff of Japan's Guangdong army in Manchuria 1937, he served as minister for war

Togo
Republic of
(République Togolaise)

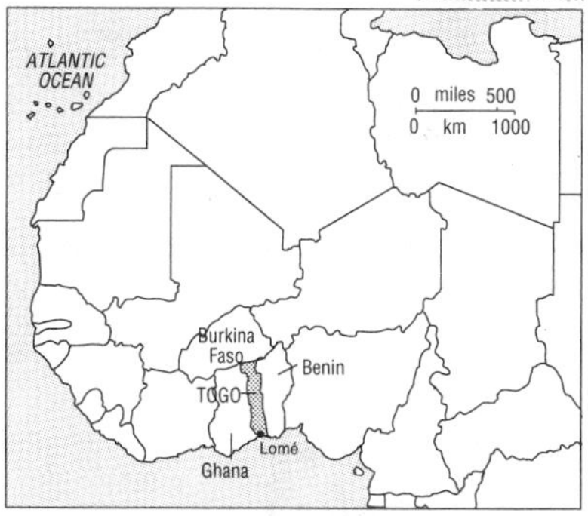
ATLANTIC OCEAN
0 miles 500
0 km 1000
Burkina Faso
Benin
TOGO
Lomé
Ghana

area 21,930 sq mi/56,800 sq km
capital Lomé
cities Sokodé, Kpalimé
physical two savanna plains, divided by range of hills NE--SW; coastal lagoons and marsh
features EEC Lomé conventions signed 1975 and 1979 in Lome1, establishing trade links with developing countries
head of state and government Etienne Gnassingbé Eyadéma from 1967
political system one-party Socialist republic
political parties Assembly of the Tongolese People (RPT), nationalist, Socialist
exports phosphates, cocoa, coffee, coconuts
currency franc CFA
population (1990 est) 3,566,000; growth rate 3% p.a.
life expectancy men 53, women 57 (1989)
language French (official), local languages
religion animist 46%, Catholic 28%, Muslim 17%, Protestant 9%
literacy men 53%/women 28% (1985 est)
GNP $1.3 bn (1987); $240 per head (1985)
chronology
1922 Divided between Britain and France under League of Nations mandate.
1946 Continued under United Nations trusteeship.
1960 Independence achieved from France as the Republic of Togo with Sylvanus Olympio as head of state.
1963 Olympio killed in a military coup. Nicolas Grunitzky became president.
1967 Grunitzky replaced by Lt Gen Etienne Gnassingbé Eyadéma in bloodless coup.
1973 Assembly of Togolese People (RPT) formed as sole legal political party.
1979 Eyadéma returned in election.
1986 Attempted coup failed.
1991 Constitutional talks promised, but progress restricted.

1940–41. He was held responsible for defeats in the Pacific 1944 and forced to resign. After Japan's defeat, he was hanged as a war criminal.

tokamak experimental machine designed by Soviet scientists to investigate controlled nuclear fusion. It consists of a doughnut-shaped chamber surrounded by electromagnets capable of exerting very powerful magnetic fields. The fields are generated to confine a very hot (millions of degrees) ◊plasma of ions and electrons, keeping it away from the chamber walls.

Tokay sweet white wine made near the Hungarian town of Tokaj; also the grape from which it is made.

Tokelau formerly Union Islands overseas territory of New Zealand, 300 mi/480 km N of Western Samoa, comprising three coral atolls: Atafu, Fakaofo, and Nukunonu; area 4 sq mi/10 sq km; population (1980) 1,700. The islands belong to the Polynesian group. Their resources are small, and until 1975 many of the inhabitants settled in New Zealand, which has administered them since 1926 when they were separated from the British Gilbert and Ellice islands colony.

Tokugawa military family that controlled Japan as ◊shoguns 1603–1867. Iyeyasu or Ieyasu Tokugawa (1542–1616) was the Japanese general and politician who established the Tokugawa shogunate. The Tokugawa were feudal lords who ruled about one-fourth of Japan.

Tokyo capital of Japan, on Honshu Island; population (1987) 8,209,000, metropolitan area over 12,000,000. The Sumida river delta separates the city from its suburb of Honjo. It is Japan's main cultural and industrial center (engineering, chemicals, textiles, electrical goods). Founded in the 16th century as Yedo (or Edo, it was renamed when the emperor moved his court there from Kyoto 1868. An earthquake 1923 killed 58,000 people. The city was severely damaged by Allied bombing in World War II. The subsequent rebuilding has made it into one of the world's most modern cities.

Features include the Imperial Palace, National Diet (parliament), Asakusa Kannon Temple (7th century, rebuilt after World War II), National Theatre, National Museum and other art collections, Tokyo University 1877, Tokyo Disneyland, and the National Athletic Stadium.

Toland Gregg 1904–1948. US director of film photography who used deep focus to good effect in such films as *Wuthering Heights* 1939, *Citizen Kane* 1941, *The Grapes of Wrath* 1940, and *The Best Years of our Lives* 1946.

Toledo city on the river Tagus, Castilla–La Mancha, central Spain; population (1982) 62,000. It was the capital of the Visigoth kingdom 534–711 (see ◊Goth), then became a Moorish city, and was the Castilian capital 1085–1560.

In the 12th century, Toledo had a flourishing steel industry and a school of translators, run by Archbishop Raymond (1125–1151), writing Latin versions of Arabic philosophical works. The painter El Greco worked here from about 1575 (his house and garden are preserved), and the local landscape is the setting of Cervantes" novel *Don Quixote*.

Toledo port on Lake Erie, Ohio, at the mouth of the Maumee River; industries include food processing and the manufacture of vehicles, electrical goods, and glass; population (1990) 332,943. The University of Toledo is here. A French fort was built 1700, but permanent settlement did not begin until after the War of 1812.

Tolkien J(ohn) R(onald) R(euel) 1892–1973. English writer who created the fictional world of Middle Earth in *The Hobbit* 1937 and the trilogy *The Lord of the Rings* 1954–55, fantasy novels peopled with hobbits, dwarves, and strange magical creatures. His work developed a cult following in the 1960s and had many imitators. At Oxford University he was professor of Anglo-Saxon 1925–45 and Merton professor of English 1945–59.

Tolstoy Leo Nikolaievich 1828–1910. Russian novelist who wrote *Tales from Sebastopol* 1856, ◊*War and Peace* 1863–69, and ◊*Anna Karenina* 1873–77. From 1880 Tolstoy underwent a profound spiritual crisis and took up various moral positions, including passive resistance to evil, rejection of authority (religious or civil) and private ownership, and a return to basic mystical Christianity. He was excommunicated by the Orthodox Church, and his later works were banned.

Tolstoy was born of noble family at Yasnaya Polyana, near Tula, and fought in the Crimean War. His first published work was *Childhood* 1852, the first part of the trilogy that was completed with *Boyhood* 1854 and *Youth* 1857; later books include *What I Believe* 1883 and *The Kreutzer Sonata* 1889, and the novel *Resurrection* 1900. His desire to give up his property and live as a peasant disrupted his family life, and he finally fled his home and died of pneumonia at the railroad station at Astapovo.

Toltec member of an ancient American Indian people who ruled much of Mexico in the 10th–12th centuries, with their capital at Tula, and built new ceremonial centers in the Mayan territories of Yucatán. After the Toltecs' fall in the 13th century, the Aztecs took over much of their former territory, except for the regions regained by the Maya.

toluene or ***methyl benzene*** $C_6H_5CH_3$ colorless, flammable liquid, insoluble in water, derived from petroleum. It is used as a solvent, in aircraft fuels, in preparing phenol (carbolic acid, used in making resins for adhesives, pharmaceuticals, and as a disinfectant), and the powerful high explosive ◊TNT.

Tomasi Giuseppe, Prince of Lampedusa. Italian writer; see ◊Lampedusa.

tomato annual plant *Lycopersicon esculentum* of the nightshade family Solanaceae, native to South America. It is widely cultivated for the many-seeded red fruit (technically a berry), used in salads and cooking.

Tombaugh Clyde (William) 1906– . US astronomer who discovered the planet ◊Pluto 1930.

Born in Streator, Illinois, Tombaugh became an assistant at the Lowell Observatory in Flagstaff, Arizona, in 1929 and photographed the sky in search of an undiscovered remote planet as predicted by the observatory's founder, Percival ◊Lowell. Tombaugh found Pluto on Feb 18, 1930, from plates taken three weeks earlier. He continued his search for new planets across the entire sky; his failure to find any placed strict limits on the possible existence of planets beyond Pluto, although calculations still lead astronomers to conclude that one more planet, or possibly a body such as a brown dwarf, may exist, thereby explaining the great eccentricity of Pluto's orbit.

Tombstone former silver-mining town in the desert of SE Arizona. The gunfight at the OK Corral, with deputy marshal Wyatt Earp, his brothers, and "Doc" Holliday against the Clanton gang, took place here Oct 26, 1881.

Tom Jones, The History of novel by Henry Fielding, published 1749. It describes the complicated, and not always reputable, early life of Tom Jones, an orphan, who is good-natured but hot-headed.

Tommy gun popular name for Thompson submachine-gun; see ◊machine gun.

tomography the obtaining of plane-section X-ray photographs, which show a "slice" through any object. Crystal detectors and amplifiers can be used that have a sensitivity 100 times greater than X-ray film, and, in conjunction with a computer system, can detect, for example, the difference between a brain tumor and healthy brain tissue.

Godfrey Hounsfield was a leading pioneer in the development of this technique. In modern medical imaging there are several types, such as the ◊CAT scan (computerized axial tomography).

Tom Sawyer, The Adventures of novel by US author Mark Twain, published 1876. It describes the childhood escapades of Tom Sawyer and his friends Huckleberry Finn and Joe Harper in a small Mississippi community before the Civil War. It and its sequel *The Adventures of Huckleberry Finn* 1885 are remarkable for their rejection of the high moral tone prevalent in 19th-century children's literature.

Tomsk city on the river Tom, W central Siberia; industries include synthetic fibers, timber, distilling, plastics, and electrical motors; population (1987) 489,000. It was formerly a gold-mining town and the administrative center of much of Siberia.

Tom Thumb Midget performer General Tom Thumb (Charles Stratton), who joined P T Barnum's circus at the age of five, with his wife Lavinia Warren. He stood 3 ft 4 in/1 m tall as an adult.

Tonga
Kingdom of
(*Pule'anga Fakatu'i 'o Tonga*)
or **Friendly Islands**

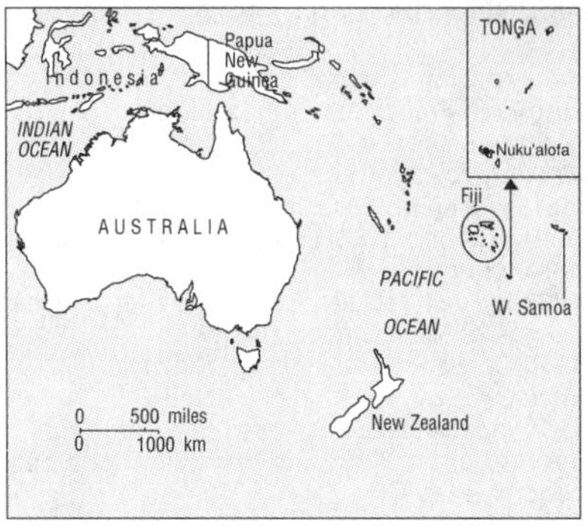
TONGA
Papua
New
Guinea
Indonesia
INDIAN
OCEAN
AUSTRALIA
Nuku'alofa
Fiji
PACIFIC
OCEAN
W. Samoa
New Zealand
0 500 miles
0 1000 km

area 290 sq mi/750 sq km
capital Nuku'alofa (on Tongatapu island)
cities Pangai, Neiafu
physical three groups of islands in SW Pacific, mostly coral formations, but actively volcanic in W
features of 170 islands in Tonga group, 36 are inhabited
head of state King Taufa'ahau Tupou IV from 1965
head of government Fatafehi Tu'ipelehake from 1965
political system absolute monarchy
political parties none
currency Tongan dollar or pa'anga
population (1988) 95,000; growth rate 2.4% p.a.
life expectancy men 69, women 74 (1989)
language Tongan (official), English
religion Wesleyan 47%, Roman Catholic 14%, Free Church of Tonga 14%, Mormon 9%, Church of Tonga 9%
literacy 93% (1988)
GNP $65 mn (1987); $430 per head
chronology
1831 Tongan dynasty founded by Prince Taufa'ahau Tupou.
1900 Became a British protectorate.
1965 Queen Salote died; succeeded by her son, King Taufa'ahau Tupou IV.
1970 Independence achieved from Britain within the Commonwealth.

Tom Thumb tiny hero of English folk tale, whose name has often been given to those of small stature, including Charles Sherwood Stratton 1838–1883, nicknamed General Tom Thumb by P T Barnum.

ton unit (abbreviation t) of mass. The short ton, used in the US and Canada, is 2,000 lb/907 kg. The long ton, used in the UK, is 2,240 lb/1,016 kg. The metric ton or tonne is 1,000 kg/2,205 lb.

In shipping, gross tonnage is calculated in units of volume (called register tons) equal to 100 cu ft/2.8 cu m; it measures the total internal volume of a ship. Net register tonnage is the amount of gross tonnage (in register tons) used for carrying cargo or passengers. Displacement tonnage is the weight of the vessel, in terms of the number of long tons of sea water displaced when the ship is loaded to its load line; it is used to describe warships, and one displacement ton equals 35 cubic feet. Deadweight tons are used for cargo haulage.

tonality in music, the observance of a key structure; that is, the recognition of the importance of a tonic or key note and of the diatonic scale built upon it. See also ◊atonality and ◊polytonality.

tone poem in music, another name for ◊symphonic poem, as used, for example, by Richard Strauss.

Tonga country in the SW Pacific, in ◊Polynesia.

government Tonga is an independent hereditary monarchy within the ◊Commonwealth. Its constitution dates from 1875 and provides for a monarch who is both head of state and head of government. The monarch chooses and presides over the Privy Council, a cabinet of nine ministers appointed for life.

There is a single-chamber legislature, the Legislative Assembly, of 29 members, which include the monarch, the Privy Council, nine hereditary nobles, and nine representatives of the people, elected by universal adult suffrage. The assembly has a life of three years. There are no political parties in Tonga.

history The original inhabitants were Polynesians, and the first European visitors to the islands were Dutch, 1616 and 1643 (Abel Tasman). Captain Cook dubbed them the Friendly Islands 1773. The contemporary Tongan dynasty was founded in 1831 by Prince Taufa'ahau Tupou, who assumed the designation King George Tupou I when he ascended the throne. He consolidated the kingdom by conquest, encouraged the spread of Christianity and granted a constitution. Tonga became a British protectorate from 1900, but under the terms of revised treaties of 1958 and 1967 recovered increased control over its internal affairs.

Queen Salote Tupou III died 1965 and was succeeded by her son, Prince Tupouto'a Tungi, who as King Tupou IV led his nation to full independence, within the Commonwealth, 1970. He is still the country's ruler.

Tongariro volcanic peak at the center of North Island, New Zealand. Sacred to the Maori, the mountain was presented to the government by chief Te Heuheu Tukino IV 1887. It was New Zealand's first national park and the fourth to be designated in the world.

tongue in tetrapod vertebrates, a muscular organ usually attached to the floor of the mouth. It has a thick root anchored at the base to a skeletal system (the hyoid apparatus), formed from what were gill supports in fishes. The tongue is covered with a ◊mucous membrane containing nerves and "taste buds" in mammals. It directs food to the teeth and into the throat for chewing and swallowing. In humans, it is crucial for speech; in other animals, for lapping up water and for grooming. In some animals, such as frogs, it can be flipped forward to catch insects; in others, such as anteaters, it serves to reach for food found in deep holes.

tonka South American tree *Dipteryx odorata*, family Leguminosae. The fruit, a dry fibrous pod, encloses a black aromatic bean used in flavoring, perfumery, and the manufacture of snuff and tobacco.

Tonkin or ***Tongking*** former region of Vietnam, on the China Sea; area 39,951 sq mi/103,500 sq km. Under Chinese rule from 111 BC, Tonkin became independent AD 939 and remained self-governing until the 19th century. A part of French Indochina 1885–1946, capital Hanoi, it was part of North Vietnam from 1954 and was merged into Vietnam after the Vietnam War.

Tonkin Gulf Incident clash that triggered US entry into the Vietnam War in Aug 1964. Two US destroyers (USS *C Turner Joy* and USS *Maddox*) reported that they were fired on by North Vietnamese torpedo boats. It is unclear whether hostile shots were actually fired, but the reported attack was taken as a pretext for retaliatory air raids against North Vietnam. On Aug 7 the US Congress passed the Tonkin Resolution, which allowed President Johnson "to take all necessary steps, including the use of armed forces" to help SEATO (South-East Asia Treaty Organization) members "defend their freedom." This resolution formed the basis for the considerable increase in US military involvement in the Vietnam War; it was repealed 1970.

Tonkin, Gulf of part of the South China Sea, with oil resources. China and Vietnam disagree over their respective territorial boundaries in the area.

Tonle Sap or ***Great Lake*** lake on a tributary of the ◊Mekong river, W Cambodia; area 1,000 sq mi/2,600 sq km to 2,500 sq mi/6,500 sq km at the height of the monsoon. During the June–Nov wet season it acts as a natural flood reservoir.

Tönnies Ferdinand 1855–1936. German social theorist and philosopher, one of the founders of the sociological tradition of community studies and urban sociology through his key work, ◊*Gemeinschaft–Gesellschaft* 1887.

Tönnies contrasted the nature of social relationships in traditional societies and small organizations (*Gemeinschaft*, "community") with those in industrial societies and large organizations (*Gesellschaft*, "association"). He was pessimistic about the effect of industrialization and urbanization on the social and moral order, seeing them as a threat to traditional society's sense of community.

tonsils in higher vertebrates, masses of lymphoid tissue situated at the back of the mouth and throat (palatine tonsils), and on the rear surface of the tongue (lingual tonsils). The tonsils contain many ◊lymphocytes and are part of the body's defense system against infection.

The adenoids are sometimes called pharyngeal tonsils.

tonsure the full or partial shaving of the head as a symbol of entering the clerical or monastic orders. Until 1973 in the Roman Catholic Church, the crown was shaved (leaving a surrounding fringe to resemble Jesus' crown of thorns); in the Eastern Orthodox Church the hair is merely shorn close. For Buddhist monks, the entire head is shaved except for a topknot.

Tonton Macoute member of a private army of death squads on Haiti. The Tontons Macoutes were initially organized by François ◊Duvalier, president of Haiti 1957–71, and continued to terrorize the population under his successor J C Duvalier. It is alleged that the organization continued to operate after Duvalier's exile to France.

Tony award annual award by the League of New York Theaters to playwrights, performers, and technicians in ◊Broadway plays. It is named after the US actress and producer Antoinette Perry (1888–1946).

tool any implement that gives the user a ◊mechan-

tooth

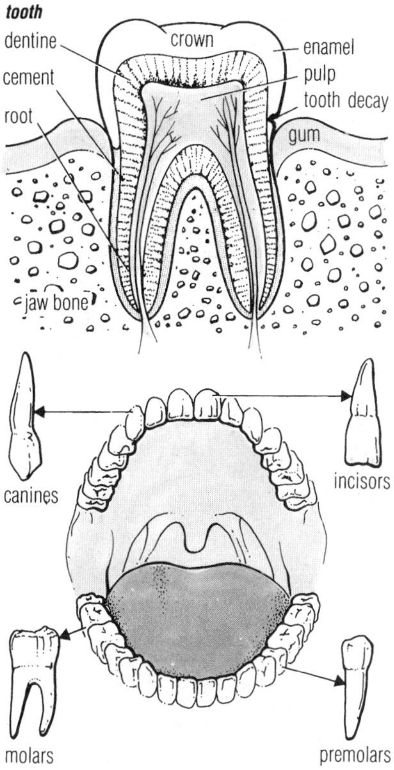
dentine
crown
enamel
cement
pulp
tooth decay
root
gum
jaw bone
canines
incisors
molars
premolars

topology

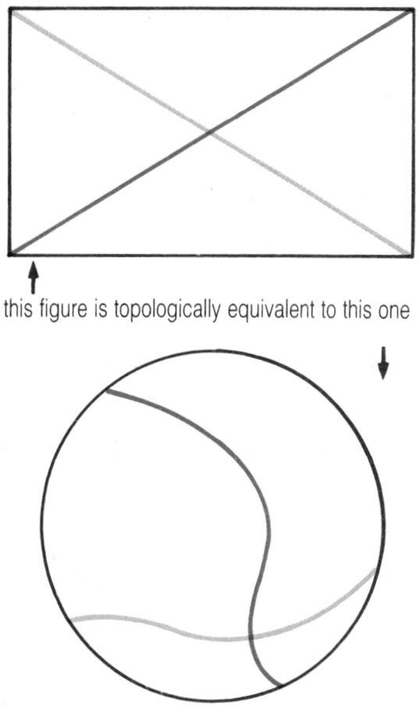
this figure is topologically equivalent to this one

ical advantage, such as a hammer or a saw; a machine tool is a tool operated by power. Tools are the basis of industrial production; the chief machine tool is the ◊lathe. The industrial potential of a country is often calculated by the number of machine tools available. Automatic control of machine tools, a milestone in industrial development, is known as ◊automation, and electronic control is called robotics (see ◊robot).

tooth in vertebrates, one of a set of hard, bonelike structures in the mouth, used for biting and chewing food, and in defense and aggression. In humans, the first set (20 milk teeth) appear from age six months to two and a half years. The permanent ◊dentition replaces these from the sixth year onward, the wisdom teeth (third molars) sometimes not appearing until the age of 25 or 30. Adults have 32 teeth: two incisors, one canine (eye tooth), two premolars, and three molars on each side of each jaw. Each tooth consists of an enamel coat (hardened calcium deposits), dentine (a thick, bonelike layer), and an inner pulp cavity, housing nerves and blood vessels. Mammalian teeth have roots surrounded by cementum, which fuses them into their sockets in the jawbones. The neck of the tooth is covered by the ◊gum, while the enamel-covered crown protrudes above the gum line.

The chief diseases of teeth are misplacements resulting from defect or disturbance of the toothgerms before birth, eruption out of their proper places, and caries (decay; see ◊cavity).

Toowoomba town and commercial and industrial (coal-mining, iron-working, engineering, clothing) center in the Darling Downs, SE Queensland, Australia; population (1987) 79,000.

topaz mineral, aluminum fluosilicate, $Al_2SiO_4(F,OH)_2$. It is usually yellow, but pink if it has been heated, and is used as a gemstone when transparent. It ranks 8 on the Mohs' scale of hardness.

tope slender shark *Galeorhinus galeus* ranging through temperate and tropical seas. Dark gray above and white beneath, it reaches 6 ft/2 m in length. The young are born well-formed, sometimes 40 at a time.

tope tumulus found in India and SE Asia; a Buddhist monument usually built over a relic of Buddha or his disciples. They date from 400–300 BC including ones at Sanchi, near Bhilsa, central India.

Topeka capital of Kansas; population (1990) 119,883. It is a commercial center for an agricultural area, and its manufactures include processed food, printed materials, and rubber and metal products. The Menninger Foundation, a noted psychiatric center, is here. The community was platted 1854 and developed as a railroad center. It was made the state capital 1861.

topi or ***korrigum antelope*** *Damaliscus korrigum* of equatorial Africa, head and body about 5.5 ft/1.7 m long, 3.5 ft/1.1 m high at the shoulder, with a chocolate-brown coat.

topiary clipping of trees and shrubs into ornamental shapes, originated by the Romans in the 1st century and revived in the 16th–17th centuries in formal European and American gardens.

topography the surface shape and aspect of the land, and its study. Topography deals with relief and contours, the distribution of mountains and valleys, the patterns of rivers, and all other features, natural and artificial, that produce the landscape.

topology branch of geometry that deals with those properties of a figure that remain unchanged even when the figure is transformed (bent or stretched)—for example, when a square painted on a rubber sheet is deformed by distorting the sheet. Topology has scientific applications, as in the study of turbulence in fluids. The map of the London Underground system is an example of the topological representation of the rail network.

Connectivity is preserved, but metric (distance, etc.) relations are not. A topological problem (studied extensively by the Norwegian mathematician Oystein Ore) is to provide a proof that only four colors are needed in producing a map to give all adjoining areas different colors.

topsoil the upper, cultivated layer of soil, which may vary in depth from 3 to 18 in/8 to 45 cm. It contains organic matter, the decayed remains of vegetation, which plants need for active growth.

Torah in ◊Judaism, the first five books of the Hebrew Bible (Christian Old Testament), which are called the Five Books of Moses. Handwritten in Hebrew on parchment scrolls by biblical scribes, the Torah contains a traditional history of the world from the Creation to the death of Moses; it also includes the Hebrew people's ◊covenant with the one God, rules for religious observance, and guidelines for social conduct, including the Ten Commandments.

In every synagogue Torah scrolls are housed in a sacred enclosure, the ark, and are treated with great respect. Jews believe that by observing the guidelines laid down in the Torah, they fulfill their part of their covenant with God.

Torbay district in S Devon, England; population (1981) 116,000. It was created 1968 by the union of the seaside resorts of Paignton, Torquay, and Brixham.

Torgau town in Leipzig county, Federal Republic of Germany; population 20,000. In 1760, during the Seven Years' War, Frederick II of Prussia defeated the Austrians nearby, and in World War II the US and Soviet forces first met here.

Torino Italian name for the city of ◊Turin.

tornado extremely violent revolving storm with swirling, funnel-shaped clouds, caused by a rising column of warm air propelled by strong wind. A tornado can rise to a great height, but with a diameter of only a few hundred yards or meters or less. Tornadoes move with wind speeds of 100–300 mph/160–480 kph, destroying everything in their path. They are common in the central US and Australia.

torong musical instrument of the native Tay people of central Vietnam (Nguyen) and now common throughout Vietnam. It consists of differing lengths of hanging bamboo that are struck with a stick.

Toronto (North American Indian "place of meeting") formerly (until 1834) York port on Lake Ontario, capital of Ontario, Canada; metropolitan population (1985) 3,427,000. It is Canada's main industrial and commercial center (banking, shipbuilding, automobiles, farm machinery, food processing, publishing) and also a cultural center, with theaters and a film industry. The Skydome 1989, a sports arena with a retractable roof dome, seats up to 53,000 and is bigger than the Roman Coliseum. A French fort was established 1749, and the site became the provincial capital 1793.

torpedo or ***electric ray*** any of an order (***Torpediniformes***) of mainly tropical rays (cartilaginous fishes), whose electric organs between the pectoral fin and the head can give a powerful shock. They can grow to 6 ft/180 cm in length.

The electric ray *Torpedo nobiliana* is found on both sides of the Atlantic.

torpedo self-propelled underwater missile, invented 1866 by British engineer Robert ◊Whitehead. Modern torpedoes are homing missiles; some resemble mines in that they lie on the seabed until activated by the acoustic signal of a passing ship. A television camera enables them to be remotely controlled, and in the final stage of attack they lock on to the radar or sonar signals of the target ship.

Torquay resort in S Devon, England, part of the district of ◊Torbay.

torque the turning effect of force on an object. A turbine produces a torque that turns an electricity generator in a power station. Torque is measured by multiplying the force by its perpendicular distance from the turning point.

torque converter device similar to a turbine, filled with oil, used in automatic transmission systems in motor vehicles and locomotives to transmit power (torque) from the engine to the gears.

Torquemada Tomás de 1420–1498. Spanish Dominican monk, confessor to Queen Isabella I. In 1483 he revived the ◊Inquisition on her behalf, and at least 2,000 "heretics" were burned; Torquemada also expelled the Jews from Spain 1492, with a resultant decline of the economy.

torr unit of pressure equal to 1/760 of an ◊atmosphere, used mainly in high-vacuum technology.

One torr is equivalent to 133.322 pascals, and for practical purposes is the same as the millimeter of mercury. It is named after Evangelista ◊Torricelli.

Torrens salt lake 25 ft/8 m below sea level in E South Australia; area 2,239 sq mi/5,800 sq km. It is reduced to a marsh in dry weather.

Torreón industrial and agricultural city in Coahuila

tortoise

state, N Mexico, on the river Nazas at an altitude of 3,700 ft/1,127 m; population (1986) 730,000. Before the arrival of the railroad 1907 Torreón was the largest of the three Laguna cotton-district cities (with Gómez Palacio and Ciudad Lerdo). Since then it has developed as a major thoroughfare and commercial center.

Torres-García Joaquim 1874–1949. Uruguayan artist, born in Montevideo. In Paris from 1926, he was influenced by ◊Mondrian and others and, after going to Madrid in 1932, by Inca, and Nazca pottery. His mature style is based on a grid pattern derived from the esthetic proportion of the ◊golden section.

Torres Strait channel separating New Guinea from Australia, with scattered reefs; width 80 mi/130 km. The first European to sail through it was the Spanish navigator Luis Vaez de Torres 1606.

Torricelli Evangelista 1608–1647. Italian physicist and pupil of ◊Galileo who devised the mercury ◊barometer.

torsion in physics, the state of strain set up in a twisted material; for example, when a thread, wire, or rod is twisted, the torsion set up in the material tends to return the material to its original state. The torsion balance, a sensitive device for measuring small gravitational or magnetic forces, or electric charges, balances these against the restoring force set up by them in a torsion suspension.

tort (Latin "to twist") in law, a wrongful act for which someone can be sued for damages in a civil court. It includes such acts as libel, trespass, injury done to someone (whether intentionally or by negligence), and inducement to break a contract (although breach of contract itself is not a tort).

In general a tort is distinguished from a crime in that it affects the interests of an individual rather than of society at large, but some crimes can also be torts (for example, assault).

tortoise any member of the family Testudinidae, the land-living members of the order Chelonia, which includes all ◊turtles, terrestrial or aquatic. The shell of tortoises is generally more domed than that of aquatic turtles; their hind legs are stumpy and columnar; the front legs are often shovel-shaped for digging. Tortoises are herbivorous and occur in the warmer regions of all continents except Australia. Tortoises range in size from 4 in/10 cm to 5 ft/150 cm, and some are known to live for 150 years.

Best-known in the pet trade is the small spur-thighed tortoise *Testudo graece* found in Asia Minor, the Balkans, and N Africa. The giant species of the Galapagos and Seychelles may reach a length of 5 ft/1.5 m and weigh over 500 lb/225 kg. They can yield about 200 lb/90 kg of meat, hence their almost complete extermination by sailors in passing ships. North American tortoises are reprsented by four species of gopher tortoises (genus *Gophenus*) living in the SW US and Mexico.

Tortoise shell is the semitransparent shell of the marine hawksbill turtle.

Tortuga (French La Tortue "turtle") island off the N coast of ◊Haiti; area 69 sq mi/180 sq km. It was a pirate lair during the 17th century.

Toruń (German *Thorn*) industrial (electronics, fertilizers, synthetic fibers) river port in N Poland, on the Vistula; population (1982) 183,000. It was founded by the ◊Teutonic Knights 1230 and is the birthplace of the astronomer Copernicus.

Tory Party the forerunner of the British ◊Conservative Party about 1680–1830. It was the party of the squire and parson, as opposed to the Whigs (supported by the trading classes and Nonconformists). The name is still applied colloquially to the Conservative Party. In the US a Tory was an opponent of the break with Britain in the Revolutionary War 1775–83.

Toscana Italian name for the region of ◊Tuscany.

Toscanini Arturo 1867–1957. Italian conductor. He made La Scala, Milan (where he conducted 1898–1903, 1906–08, and 1921–29), the world's leading opera house. Opposed to the Fascist regime, in 1936 he returned to the US, where he had conducted at the Metropolitan Opera 1908–15. The NBC Symphony Orchestra was formed for him in 1937. He retired in 1954.

total internal reflection the complete reflection of a beam of light that occurs from the surface of an optically "less dense" material. For example, a beam from an underwater light source can be reflected from the surface of the water, rather than escaping through the surface. Total internal reflection can only happen if a light beam hits a surface at an angle greater than the ◊critical angle for that particular pair of materials.

Total internal reflection is used as a means of reflecting light inside ◊prisms and ◊optical fibers. Light is contained inside an optical fiber not by the cladding around it, but by the ability of the internal surface of the glass-fiber core to reflect 100% of the light, thereby keeping it trapped inside the fiber.

totalitarianism government control of all activities within a country, overtly political or otherwise, as in fascist or communist dictatorships. Examples of totalitarian regimes are Italy under Benito ◊Mussolini 1922–45; Germany under Adolph ◊Hitler 1933–45; the USSR under Joseph ◊Stalin from 1930s until his death in 1953; more recently Romania under Nicolae ◊Ceauşescu 1974–89.

totemism (Algonquin Indian "mark of my family") the belief in individual or clan kinship with an animal, plant, or object. This totem becomes an emblem and is sacred to those concerned. They are forbidden to eat or desecrate it; marriage within the clan is usually forbidden. Totemism occurs among Pacific Islanders and Australian Aborigines, and was formerly prevalent throughout Europe, Africa, and Asia. Most North and South American Indian societies had totems as well.

Totem poles are carved by Native Americans of the NW coast of North America and incorporate totem objects (carved and painted) as a symbol of the people or to commemorate the dead.

Totila died 522. King of the Ostrogoths, who warred with the Byzantine emperor Justinian for Italy, and was killed by General Narses at the battle of Taginae 552 in the Apennines.

Totò Adopted name of Antonio de Curtis Gagliardi Ducas Comneno di Bisanzio 1898–1967. Italian comedian who moved to films from the music hall. His films, such as *Totò le Moko* 1949 and *L'Oro di Napoli/Gold of Naples* 1954, made him something of a national institution.

toucan any South and Central American forest-dwelling bird of the family Ramphastidae. Toucans have very large, brilliantly colored beaks and often handsome plumage. They live in small flocks, eat fruits, seeds, and insects; and lay their eggs in holes in trees. They grow to 2 ft/64 cm in length. There are 37 species.

touch sensation produced by specialized nerve endings in the skin. Some respond to light pressure, others to heavy pressure. Temperature detection may also contribute to the overall sensation of touch. Many animals, such as nocturnal ones, rely on touch more than humans do. Some have

toucan

specialized organs of touch that project from the body, such as whiskers or antennae.

touch screen in computing, an input device allowing the user to communicate with the computer by touching a display screen with a finger. In this way, the user can point to a required ◊menu option or item of data. Touch screens are used less widely than other pointing devices such as the ◊joystick or ◊mouse.

Typically, the screen detects the finger either through a sensitive membrane or when the finger interrupts a grid of light beams crossing the screen surface.

touch sensor in a computer-controlled ◊robot, a device used to give the robot a sense of touch, allowing it to manipulate delicate objects or move automatically about a room. Touch sensors provide the feedback necessary for the robot to adjust the force of its movements and the pressure of its grip. The main types include the strain gauge and the microswitch.

Toulon port and capital of Var *département*, SE France, on the Mediterranean Sea, 30 mi/48 km SE of Marseille; population (1983) 410,000. It is the chief Mediterranean naval station of France. Industries include oil refining, chemicals, furniture, and clothing. Toulon was the Roman Telo Martius and was made a port by Henry IV. It was occupied by the British 1793, and Napoleon first distinguished himself in driving them out. In World War II the French fleet was scuttled here to avoid its passing to German control.

Toulouse capital of Haute-Garonne *département*, S France, on the river Garonne SE of Bordeaux; population (1982) 541,000. The chief industries are textiles and aircraft construction (Concorde was built here). Toulouse was the capital of the Visigoths (see ◊Goth) and later of Aquitaine 781–843.

Toulouse has a 12th–13th-century cathedral. The Duke of Wellington repulsed the French marshal Soult at Toulouse 1814 in the ◊Peninsular War.

Toulouse-Lautrec Henri Marie Raymond de 1864–1901. French artist, associated with the Impressionists. He was active in Paris, where he painted entertainers and prostitutes. From 1891 his lithograph posters were a great success.

Toulouse-Lautrec showed an early gift for drawing, to which he turned increasingly after a riding accident at the age of 15 left him with crippled and stunted legs. In 1882 he began to study art in Paris. He admired Goya's etchings and Degas's work, and in the 1880s he met Gauguin and was inspired by Japanese prints. Lautrec became a familiar figure drawing and painting in the dance halls, theaters, cafés, circuses, and brothels. Many of his finished works have the spontaneous character of sketches. He often painted with thinned-out oils on cardboard.

touraco any fruit-eating African bird of the family Musophagidae. They have long tails, erectile

Toulouse-Lautrec *French artist Henri Toulouse-Lautrec's* The Two Friends *1894, Tate Gallery, London.*

Toussaint L'Ouverture *An 1805 print showing the Haitian revolutionary leader Pierre Toussaint L'Ouverture. Born a slave, he became governor of Haiti during the French Revolution.*

crests, and short, rounded wings. The largest are 28 in/70 cm long.

The white-cheeked touraco *Touraco leucotis* resembles a multicolored magpie.

Touraine former province of W central France, now part of the *départements* of Indre-et-Loire and Vienne; capital Tours.

Tourcoing town in Nord *département*, France, part of metropolitan Lille; population (1983) 102,000. It is situated near the Belgian border, and has been a textile center since the 12th century.

Tour de France French road race for professional cyclists held annually over approximately 3,000 mi/4,800 km of primarily French roads. The race takes about three weeks to complete and the route varies each year, often taking in adjoining countries, but always ending in Paris. A separate stage is held every day, and the overall leader at the end of each stage wears the coveted "yellow jersey" (French *maillot jaune*).

First held in 1903, it is now the most watched sporting event in the world, with more than 10 million spectators. Although it is a race for individuals, sponsored teams of 12 riders take part, each with its own "star" rider whom team members support.

Tour de France: recent winners

1981	Bernard Hinault *(France)*
1982	Bernard Hinault *(France)*
1983	Laurent Fignon *(France)*
1984	Laurent Fignon *(France)*
1985	Bernard Hinault *(France)*
1986	Greg LeMond *(US)*
1987	Stephen Roche *(Ireland)*
1988	Pedro Delgado *(Spain)*
1989	Greg LeMond *(US)*
1990	Greg LeMond *(US)*
1991	Miguel Indurain (Spain)

tourmaline hard, brittle mineral, a complex of various metal silicates, but mainly sodium aluminum borosilicate.

Small tourmalines are found in granites and gneisses. The common varieties range from black (schorl) to pink, and the transparent gemstones may be colorless (achroite), rose pink (rubellite), green (Brazilian emerald), blue (indicolite, verdelite, Brazilian sapphire), or brown (dravite).

Tournai (Flemish *Doornik*) town in Hainaut province, Belgium, on the river Scheldt; population (1983) 67,000. Industries include carpets, cement, and leather. It stands on the site of a Roman relay post and has an 11th-century Romanesque cathedral.

Tours industrial (chemicals, textiles, machinery) city and capital of the Indre-et-Loire *département*, W central France, on the river Loire; population (1982) 263,000. It has a 13th–15th-century cathedral. An ancient city and former capital of ◊Touraine, it was the site of the French defeat of the Arabs 732 under ◊Charles Martel. Tours became the French capital for four days during World War II.

Toussaint L'Ouverture Pierre Dominique c. 1743–1803. Haitian revolutionary leader, born a slave. He joined the insurrection of 1791 against the French colonizers and was made governor by the revolutionary French government. He expelled the Spanish and British, but when the French emperor Napoleon reimposed slavery he revolted, was captured, and died in prison in France. In 1983 his remains were returned to Haiti.

Tower John 1925– . US Republican politician, a senator from Texas 1961–83. Despite having been a paid arms-industry consultant, he was selected in 1989 by President Bush to serve as defense secretary, but the Senate refused to approve the appointment because of Tower's previous heavy drinking.

Tower, in 1961 the first Republican to be elected senator for Texas, emerged as a military expert in the Senate, becoming chair of the Armed Services Committee in 1981. After his retirement from the Senate in 1983, he acted as a consultant to arms manufacturers and chaired the 1986–87 Tower Commission, which investigated aspects of the ◊Irangate arms-for-hostages scandal.

Tower of London fortress on the Thames bank to the east of the City. The keep, or White Tower, was built about 1078 by Bishop Gundulf on the site of British and Roman fortifications. It is surrounded by two strong walls and a moat (now dry), and was for centuries a royal residence and the principal state prison. Today it is a barracks, an armory, and a museum.

Townes Charles 1915– . US physicist who in 1953 designed and constructed the first ◊maser. For this work, he shared the 1964 Nobel Prize with Soviet physicists Nikolai Basov (1922–) and Aleksandr ◊Prokhorov.

town planning the design of buildings or groups of buildings in a physical and social context, concentrating on the relationship between various buildings and their environment, as well as on their uses. See also ◊garden city; ◊Mumford.

Townshend Charles 1725–1767. British politician, chancellor of the Exchequer 1766–67. The Townshend Acts, designed to assert Britain's traditional authority over its colonies, resulted in widespread resistance. Among other things they levied taxes on imports (such as tea, glass, and paper) into the North American colonies. Opposition in the colonies to taxation without representation (see ◊Stamp Act) precipitated the American Revolution.

Townsville port on Cleveland Bay, N Queensland, Australia; population (1987) 108,000. It is the center of a mining and agricultural area and exports meat, wool, sugar, and minerals, including gold and silver.

toxemia condition in which poisons are spread throughout the body by the bloodstream, such as those produced by ◊pathogens or by localized cells in the body.

Toxemia of pregnancy is a potentially serious condition marked by high blood pressure, ◊edema, and sometimes convulsions. Arising from unknown causes, it disappears when pregnancy is over.

toxic poisonous or harmful. Radioactivity, air and water pollutants, and poisons ingested or inhaled—for example, lead from car exhausts, asbestos, and chlorinated solvents are some toxic substances that occur in the environment; generally the effects take some time to become apparent (anything from a few hours to many years). The cumulative effects of toxic waste pose a serious threat to the ecological stability of the planet.

toxicity tests tests carried out on new drugs, cosmetics, food additives, pesticides, and other synthetic chemicals to see whether they are safe for humans to use. They aim to identify potential toxins, carcinogens, teratogens, and mutagens.

Traditionally such tests use live animals such as rats, rabbits, and mice. Animal tests have become a target for criticism by ◊animal rights activists and ◊antivivisection groups, and alternatives have been sought. These include tests on human cells cultured in a test tube and on bacteria.

toxic shock syndrome rare blood poisoning triggered by use of tampons. Symptoms include fever, vomiting, diarrhea, rashes, and sometimes kidney and respiratory failure leading to death. The cause is a toxin produced by the bacterium *Staphylococcus aureus*, which is normally harmlessly present in the body.

toxin any chemical molecule that can damage the living body. In vertebrates, toxins are broken down by ◊enzyme action, mainly in the liver.

toxocariasis infection of humans by a canine intestinal worm, which results in a swollen liver and sometimes eye damage.

toxoplasmosis disease transmitted to humans by animals, often in pigeon or cat excrement. It causes flulike symptoms and damages the central nervous system, eyes, and visceral organs; it is caused by a protozoan, *Toxoplasma gondii*.

Toynbee Arnold Joseph 1889–1975. English historian whose *A Study of History* 1934–61 was an attempt to discover the laws governing the rise and fall of civilizations.

Trabzon formerly Trebizond port on the Black Sea, NE Turkey, 220 mi/355 km SW of Batum; population (1985) 156,000. Its exports include fruit, tobacco, and hides.

trace element chemical element necessary for the health of a plant or animal, but only in minute quantities. For example, iodine is needed by the thyroid gland of mammals for making hormones that control growth and body chemistry, and for all metabolic processes.

tracer in science, a small quantity of a radioactive ◊isotope (form of an element) used to follow the path of a chemical reaction or a physical or biological process. The location (and possibly concen-

trachea

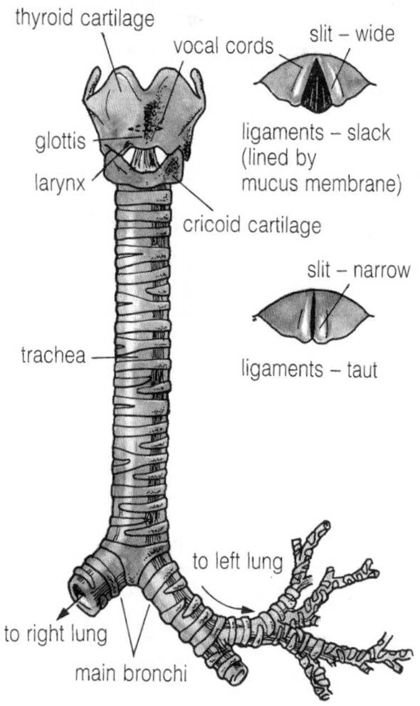
thyroid cartilage
vocal cords
slit – wide
glottis
larynx
ligaments – slack (lined by mucus membrane)
cricoid cartilage
slit – narrow
trachea
ligaments – taut
to left lung
to right lung
main bronchi

tration) of the tracer is usually detected by using a Geiger–Muller counter.

For example, the activity of the thyroid gland can be followed by giving the patient an injection containing a small dose of a radioactive isotope of iodine, which is selectively absorbed from the bloodstream by the gland.

trachea tube that forms an airway in air-breathing animals. In land-living ◊vertebrates, including humans, it is also known as the windpipe and runs from the larynx to the upper part of the chest. Its diameter is about 0.6 in/1.5 cm and its length 4 in/10 cm. It is strong and flexible, and reinforced by rings of ◊cartilage. In the upper chest, the trachea branches into two tubes: the left and right bronchi, which enter the lungs. Insects have a branching network of tubes called tracheae, which conduct air from holes (◊spiracles) in the body surface to all the body tissues. The finest branches of the tracheae are called tracheoles.

Some spiders also have tracheae but, unlike insects, they possess gilllike lungs (book lungs) and rely on their circulatory system to transport gases throughout the body.

tracheid cell found in the water-conducting tissue (◊xylem) of many plants, including gymnosperms (conifers) and pteridophytes (ferns). It is long and thin with pointed ends. The cell walls are thickened by ◊lignin, except for numerous small rounded areas, or pits, through which water and dissolved minerals pass from one cell to another. Once mature, the cell itself dies and only its walls remain.

tracheotomy surgical opening in the windpipe (trachea), usually created for the insertion of a tube to enable the patient to breathe. It is done either to bypass the airway impaired by disease or injury, or to safeguard it during surgery or a prolonged period of mechanical ventilation.

trachoma chronic eye infection, resembling severe ◊conjunctivitis. The conjunctiva becomes inflamed, with scarring and formation of pus, and there may be damage to the cornea. It is caused by a viruslike organism (◊chlamydia), and is a disease of dry tropical regions. Although it responds well to antibiotics, numerically it remains the biggest single cause of blindness worldwide.

Tractarianism another name for the ◊Oxford Movement, 19th-century movement for Catholic revival within the Church of England.

tractor in agriculture, a powerful motor vehicle, commonly having large rear wheels or caterpillar tracks, used for pulling farm machinery and loads.

Tracy Spencer 1900–1967. US actor distinguished for his understated, seemingly effortless natural performances. His films include *Captains Courageous* 1937 and *Boys' Town* 1938 (for both of which he won Academy Awards), and he starred in nine films with Katharine Hepburn, including *Adam's Rib* 1949 and *Guess Who's Coming to Dinner* 1967, his final performance.

His other films include *Bad Day at Black Rock* 1955, *The Last Hurrah* 1958, *The Old Man and the Sea* 1958, and *Inherit the Wind* 1960. He was one of Hollywood's most versatile performers.

trademark name or symbol that is distinctive of a marketed product. The owner may register the mark to prevent its unauthorized use.

Tradescant John 1570–1638. English gardener and botanist, who traveled widely in Europe and is thought to have introduced the cos lettuce (a kind of romaine lettuce) to England from the Greek island bearing the same name. His son, John Tradescant the Younger (1608–1662), undertook three plant-collecting trips to Virginia, and the Swedish botanist Carl Linnaeus named the genus *Tradescantia* (the spiderworts) in his honor.

tradescantia any plant of the genus *Tradescantia* of the family Commelinaceae, native to North and Central America. The spiderwort *T. virginiana* is a cultivated garden plant; the wandering jew *T. albiflora* is a common house plant, with green oval leaves tinged with pink or purple or silver-striped.

trade wind prevailing wind that blows toward the equator from the northeast and southeast. Trade winds are caused by hot air rising at the equator and the consequent movement of air from north and south to take its place. The winds are deflected toward the west because of the Earth's west-to-east rotation. The unpredictable calms known as the ◊doldrums lie at their convergence.

The trade-wind belts move north and south about 5° with the seasons. The name is derived from the obsolete expression "to blow *trade*" meaning consistently in a constant direction, which indicates the trade winds' importance to navigation in the days of cargo-carrying sailing ships.

Trafalgar, Battle of battle Oct 21, 1805 in the ◊Napoleonic Wars. The British fleet under Admiral Nelson defeated a Franco-Spanish fleet; Nelson was mortally wounded. It is named after Cape Trafalgar, a low headland in SW Spain, near the western entrance to the Straits of Gibraltar.

tragedy in the theater, a play dealing with a serious theme, traditionally one in which a character meets disaster either as a result of personal failings or circumstances beyond his or her control. Historically the Greek view of tragedy, as defined by Aristotle and expressed by the great tragedians Aeschylus, Euripides, and Sophocles, has been predominant in the western tradition. In the 20th century tragedies in the narrow Greek sense of dealing with exalted personages in an elevated manner have virtually died out. Tragedy has been replaced by dramas with "tragic" implications or overtones, as in the work of Ibsen, O'Neill, Tennessee Williams, Pinter, and Osborne, for example, or by the hybrid tragicomedy.

The Greek view of tragedy provided the subject matter for later tragic dramas, but it was the Roman Seneca (whose works were intended to be read rather than acted) that influenced the Elizabethan tragedies of Marlowe and Shakespeare. French Classical tragedy developed under the influence of both Seneca and an interpretation of Aristotle that gave rise to the theory of unities of time, place, and action, as observed by Racine, one of its greatest exponents. In Germany the tragedies of Goethe and Schiller led to the exaggerated ◊melodrama, which replaced pure tragedy. In the 18th century unsuccessful attempts were made to "domesticate" tragedy. In the 20th century "tragedy" has come to refer to dramas with "tragic" implications for individuals or society.

tragopan

western

tragicomedy drama that contains elements of tragedy and comedy; for example, Shakespeare's "reconciliation" plays, such as *The Winter's Tale*, which reach a tragic climax but then lighten to a happy conclusion. A tragicomedy is the usual form for plays in the tradition of the Theater of the ◊Absurd, such as Samuel ◊Beckett's *En attendant Godot/Waiting for Godot* 1953 and Tom ◊Stoppard's *Rosencrantz and Guildenstern are Dead* 1967.

tragopan any of several species of bird of the genus *Tragopan*, a short tailed pheasant living in wet forests along the S Himalayas. Tragopans are brilliantly colored with arrays of spots, long crown feathers and two blue erectile crests. All have been reduced in numbers by destruction of their habitat. The western tragopan is the rarest, as a result of extensive deforestation.

Males inflate colored wattles and throat pouches in their spring courtship displays.

train line of connected ◊***railroad*** cars pulled by a locomotive.

Trajan Marcus Ulpius (Trajanus) AD 52–117. Roman emperor and soldier, born in Seville. He was adopted as heir by ◊Nerva, whom he succeeded AD 98.

He was a just and conscientious ruler, corresponded with Pliny about the Christians, and conquered Dacia (Romania) 101–07 and much of ◊Parthia. Trajan's Column, Rome, commemorates his victories.

trance mental state in which the subject loses the ordinary perceptions of time and space, and even of his or her own body.

In this highly aroused state, often induced by rhythmic music, "speaking in tongues" (glossolalia) may occur (see ◊Pentecostal Movement); this usually consists of the rhythmic repetition of apparently meaningless syllables, with a euphoric return to consciousness. It is also practiced by native American and Australian Aboriginal healers, Afro-Brazilian spirit mediums, and Siberian shamans.

tranquilizer common name for any drug for reducing anxiety or tension (◊anxiolytic), such as ◊benzodiazepines. (Antipsychotic drugs are not tranquilizers.)

transactinide any of a series of nine radioactive, metallic elements with atomic numbers that extend beyond the ◊actinide series, those from 104 (rutherfordium) to 112 (unnamed). They are grouped because of their expected chemical similarities (they are all bivalent), the properties differing only slightly with atomic number. All have ◊half-lives that measure less than two minutes.

Trans-Alaskan Pipeline one of the world's greatest civil engineering projects, the construction of a pipeline to carry petroleum (crude oil) 800 mi/1,285 km from N Alaska to the ice-free port of Valdez. It was completed 1977 after three years' work and much criticism by ecologists.

The engineers had to elevate nearly half the pipeline on supports above ground level to avoid thawing the permafrost (permanently frozen ground), which would have caused much environmental damage. They also had to cross 600 rivers and streams, two mountain ranges, and allow for earthquakes.

Trans-Amazonian Highway or ***Transamazonica*** road in Brazil linking Recife in the E with the provinces of Rondonia, Amazonas, and Acre in the W. Begun as part of the Brazilian National Integration Program (PIN) in 1970, the Trans-Amazonian Highway was designed to enhance national security, aid the industrial development of the N of Brazil, and act as a safety valve for the overpopulated coastal regions.

Transcaucasia region of the USSR S of the Caucasus. It includes Armenia, Azerbaijan, and ◊Georgia, which formed the Transcaucasian Republic 1922, broken up 1936 when each became a separate republic of the USSR.

transcendentalism a form of philosophy inaugurated in the 18th century by Immanuel Kant and developed in the US in the mid-19th century into a mystical and social doctrine. As opposed to metaphysics in the traditional sense, transcendental philosophy is concerned with the conditions of possibility of experience, rather than the nature of being. It seeks to show the necessary structure of our "point of view" on the world.

Introduced to England, transcendentalism influenced the writers Samuel Coleridge and Thomas Carlyle. In the US it was taken up in New England about 1840–60, influenced by European Romanticism, by Henry Thoreau, Ralph Waldo Emerson, the feminist Margaret Fuller (1810–50), and Orestes Brownson, who saw God as immanent in nature and the human soul. Transcendentalism had religious, philosophical, and political implications, shaping American ideals of self-reliance, attitudes toward reform and slavery-abolition, feminism, and various forms of Utopian idealism displayed in the movement's experimental community at Brook Farm near Boston, Massachusetts. Emphasizing the role of the poet and the need for an original US literature, it also had literary consequences, and out of it came Emerson's essays and poems, Jones Very's poetry, Thoreau's *Walden* 1854, and, less directly, the novels and stories of Nathaniel Hawthorne, and Walt Whitman's *Leaves of Grass* 1855.

transcendental meditation (TM) technique of focusing the mind, based in part on Hindu meditation. Meditators are given a *mantra* (a special word or phrase) to repeat over and over to themselves; such meditation is believed to benefit the practitioner by relieving stress and inducing a feeling of well-being and relaxation. It was introduced to the West by Maharishi Mahesh Yogi and popularized by the Beatles in the late 1960s.

transcription in living cells, the process by which the information for the synthesis of a protein is transferred from the ◊DNA strand on which it is carried to the messenger ◊RNA strand involved in the actual synthesis.

It occurs by the formation of ◊base pairs when a single strand of unwound DNA serves as a template for assembling the complementary nucleotides that make up the new RNA strand.

transducer power-transforming device that enables ◊energy in any form (electrical, acoustical, mechanical) to flow from one transmission system to another.

The energy flowing to and from a transducer may be of the same or of different forms. For example, an electric motor receives electrical energy and delivers it to a mechanical system; a phonograph pickup crystal receives mechanical energy from the stylus and delivers it as electrical energy; and a loudspeaker receives an electrical input and delivers an acoustical output.

transfer orbit elliptical path followed by a spacecraft moving from one orbit to another, designed to save fuel by moving for most of the journey in free fall.

Space probes travel to the planets on transfer orbits. A probe aimed at Venus has to be "slowed

transfer orbit

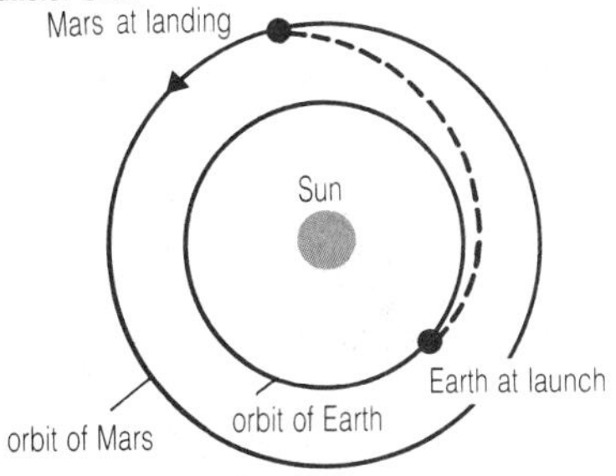
Mars at landing
Sun
Earth at launch
orbit of Earth
orbit of Mars

down" relative to the Earth, so that it enters an elliptical transfer orbit with its perigee (point of closest approach to the Sun) at the same distance as the orbit of Venus; toward Mars, the vehicle has to be "speeded up" relative to the Earth, so that it reaches its apogee (farthest point from the Sun) at the same distance as the orbit of Mars. Geosynchronous transfer orbit is the path followed by satellites to be placed in ◊geosynchronous orbit around the Earth (an orbit coincident with Earth's rotation). A small rocket is fired at the transfer orbit's apogee to place the satellite in geosynchronous orbit.

transformational grammar theory of language structure initiated by Noam ◊Chomsky, which proposes that below the actual phrases and sentences of a language (its surface structure) there lies a more basic layer (its deep structure), which is processed by various transformational rules when we speak and write.

Below the surface structure "the girl opened the door" would lie the deep structure "the girl open + (past tense) the door." Note that there is usually more than one way in which a deep structure can be realized; in this case, "the door was opened by the girl."

transformer device in which, by electromagnetic induction, an alternating current (AC) of one voltage is transformed to another voltage, without change of ◊frequency. Transformers are widely used in electrical apparatus of all kinds, and in particular in power transmission where high voltages and low currents are utilized.

A transformer has two coils, a primary for the input and a secondary for the output, wound on a common iron core. The ratio of the primary to the secondary voltages (and currents) is directly (and inversely) proportional to the number of turns in the primary and secondary coils.

transfusion intravenous delivery of blood or blood products (plasma, red cells) into a patient's circulation to make up for deficiencies due to disease, injury, or surgical intervention.

Blood transfusion, first successfully pioneered in humans 1818, remained highly risky until the discovery of blood groups, by Karl ◊Landsteiner 1900, indicated the need for compatibility of donated blood. Today, cross-matching is carried out to ensure the patient receives the right type of blood.

transgenic organism a plant, animal, bacterium, or other living organism which has had a foreign gene added to it by means of ◊genetic engineering.

transistor solid-state electronic component, made of ◊semiconductor material, with three or more ◊electrodes, that can regulate a current passing through it. A transistor can act as an amplifier, ◊oscillator, ◊photocell, or switch, and (unlike earlier electron tubes) usually operates on a very small amount of power. Transistors commonly consist of a tiny sandwich of ◊germanium or ◊silicon, alternate layers having different electrical properties. A crystal of pure germanium or silicon would act as an insulator (nonconductor).

By introducing impurities in the form of atoms of other materials (for example, boron, arsenic, or indium) in minute amounts, the layers may be made either n-type, having an excess of electrons, or p-type, having a deficiency of electrons. This enables electrons to flow from one layer to another in one direction only.

Transistors have had a great impact on the electronics industry, and are now made in thousands of millions each year. They perform many of the same functions as thermionic tubes but have the advantages of greater reliability, long life, compactness, and instantaneous action, no warming-up period being necessary. They are widely used in most electronic equipment, including portable radios and televisions, computers, satellites, and space research, and are the basis of the ◊integrated circuit (silicon chip). They were invented at Bell Telephone Laboratories in the US in 1948 by John ◊Bardeen and Walter ◊Brattain, developing the work of William ◊Shockley.

transit in astronomy, the passage of a smaller object across the visible disk of a larger one. Transits of the inferior planets (Venus and Mercury) occur when they pass directly between the Earth and Sun, and are seen as tiny dark spots against the Sun's disk.

Other forms of transit include the passage of a satellite or its shadow across the disk of Jupiter and the passage of planetary surface features across the central ◊meridian of that planet as seen from Earth. The passage of an object in the sky across the observer's meridian is also known as a transit.

transition metal any of a group of metallic elements that have incomplete inner electron shells and exhibit variable valency—for example, cobalt, copper, iron, and molybdenum. They are excellent conductors of electricity and generally form highly colored compounds.

Transjordan former name (1923–49) of the Hashemite kingdom of ◊Jordan.

Transkei largest of South Africa's Bantustans, or homelands, extending northeast from the Great Kei River, on the coast of Cape Province, to the border of Natal; area 16,910 sq mi/43,808 sq km; population (1985) 3,000,000, including small white and Asian minorities. It became self-governing 1963, and achieved full "independence" 1976. Its capital is Umtata, and it has a port at Mnganzana. It is one of the two homelands of the Xhosa people (the other is Ciskei), and products include livestock, coffee, tea, sugar, corn, and sorghum. Its government consists of a president (paramount chief Tutor Nyangelizwe Vulinolela Ndamase from 1986–) and single-chamber national assembly.

translation in literature, the rendering of words from one language to another. The first recorded named translator was Livius Andronicus, who translated Homer's *Odyssey* from Greek to Latin in 240 BC.

translation in living cells, the process by which proteins are synthesized. During translation, the information coded as a sequence of nucelotides in messenger ◊RNA is transformed into a sequence of amino acids in a peptide chain. The process involves the "translation" of the ◊genetic code. See also ◊transcription.

translocation the movement of soluble materials through ◊vascular plants.

Roots, stems and leaves all possess ◊vascular bundles, groups of hollow fibers that transport fluids and dissolved substances. Two types of tube exist within the bundles: ◊xylem for the upward transport of inorganic materials from root to leaf, and ◊phloem for the downward movement of organic substance formed during photosynthesis. Lower plants such as mosses lack these structures and are therefore less able to grow in dry areas.

transmigration of souls another name for ◊reincarnation.

transpiration the loss of water from a plant by evaporation. Most water is lost from the leaves through pores known as ◊stomata, whose primary function is to allow ◊gas exchange between the internal plant tissues and the atmosphere. Transpiration from the leaf surfaces causes a continu-

transpiration

transpiration

During photosynthesis, carbon dioxide enters the leaves of a plant through the stomata. A leaf that is permeable to carbon dioxide is also permeable to water vapor. Therefore, water is lost from the plant. The evaporation of water from the leaves is called transpiration. It produces a transpiration stream, which is a tension that draws water up the vessels of the stem. The tension can be sufficiently great to draw water up trees 328 ft/100 m tall.

Transpiration rates can be measured using a potometer.

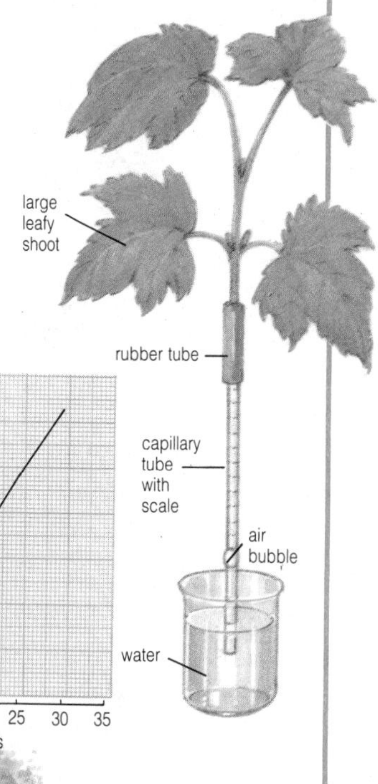
large leafy shoot
rubber tube
capillary tube with scale
air bubble
water

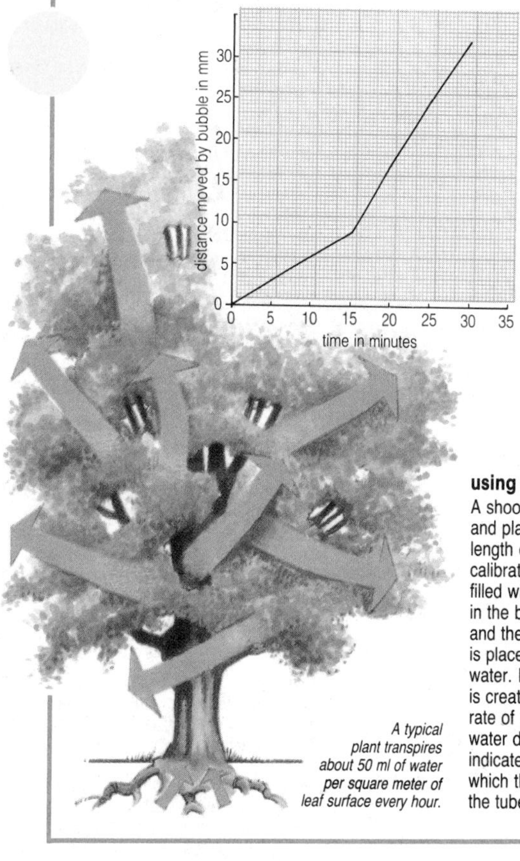
distance moved by bubble in mm
0
5
10
15
20
25
30
0
5
10
15
20
25
30
35
time in minutes

A typical plant transpires about 50 ml of water per square meter of leaf surface every hour.

using a potometer

A shoot is cut from a tree and placed in the top of a length of rubber tubing. A calibrated capillary tube, filled with water, is inserted in the bottom of the tubing and the whole arrangement is placed in a beaker of water. If a small air bubble is created in the tube, the rate of movement of the water due to transpiration is indicated by the speed with which the bubble moves up the tube.

ous upward flow of water from the roots via the ◊xylem, which is known as the transpiration stream.

A single corn plant has been estimated to transpire 64 gal/245 l of water in one growing season.

transplant in medicine, the transfer of a tissue or organ from one human being to another or from one part of the body to another (skin grafting). In most organ transplants, the operation is for life-saving purposes, though the immune system tends to reject foreign tissue. Careful matching and immunosuppressive drugs must be used, but these are not always successful.

Corneal grafting, which may restore sight to a diseased or damaged eye, was pioneered 1905, and is the oldest successful human transplant procedure. Of the internal organs, kidneys were first transplanted successfully in the early 1950s and are the most readily received by the body. Recent transplant also encompasses hearts, lungs, livers, pancreatic, bone, and bone-marrow tissue. Most transplant material is taken from cadaver donors, usually those suffering death of the ◊brainstem, or from frozen tissue banks. In rare cases, kidneys, corneas, and part of the liver may be obtained from living donors. Besides the shortage of donated material, the main problem facing transplant surgeons is rejection of the donated organ by the new body.

transputer electronic device introduced in computers to increase computing power. In the circuits of a standard computer the processing of data takes place in sequence. In a transputer's circuits processing takes place in parallel, greatly reducing computing time for programs written specifically for the transputer.

transsexual a person who identifies himself or herself completely with the opposite sex, believing that the wrong sex was assigned at birth. Unlike transvestism, which is the desire to dress in clothes traditionally worn by the opposite sex, transsexuals think and feel emotionally in a way typically considered appropriate to members of the opposite sex, and may undergo surgery to modify external sexual characteristics.

Trans-Siberian Railway railroad line connecting the cities of European Russia with Omsk, Novosibirsk, Irkutsk, and Khabarovsk, and terminating at Vladivostok on the Pacific. It was built 1891–1905; from Leningrad to Vladivostok is about 5,400 mi/8,700 km. A 1,928 mi/3,102 km northern line was completed 1984 after ten years' work.

transubstantiation in Christian theology, the doctrine that the whole substance of the bread and wine changes into the substance of the body and blood of Jesus when consecrated in the ◊Eucharist.

transuranic any chemical element with an atomic number greater than that of uranium (92). All are radioactive. Neptunium, plutonium, and perhaps americium occur in nature; the rest are synthesized elements only. The first were synthesized in 1940, neptunium and then plutonium.

Research in transuranics is pursued mainly at the Lawrence Radiation Laboratories of the University of California at Berkeley; the Joint Institute for Nuclear Research in Dubna, USSR; and the Institute for Heavy Ion Research in Darmstadt, Germany.

Transvaal province of NE South Africa, bordering Zimbabwe to the north; area 101,325 sq mi/262,499 sq km; population (1985) 7,532,000. Its capital is Pretoria, and towns include Johannesburg, Germiston, Brakpan, Springs, Benoni, Krugersdorp, and Roodepoort. Products include diamonds, coal, iron ore, copper, lead, tin, manganese, meat, corn, tobacco, and fruit. The main rivers are the Vaal and Limpopo with their tributaries. Swaziland forms an enclave on the Natal border. It was settled by *Voortrekkers*, Boers who left Cape Colony in the Great Trek from 1831. Independence was recognized by Britain 1852, until the settlers" difficulties with the conquered Zulus led to British annexation 1877. It was made a British colony after the South African War 1899–1902, and in 1910 became a province of the Union of South Africa.

Transylvania mountainous area of central and NW Romania, bounded to the south by the Transylvanian Alps (an extension of the ◊Carpathians), formerly a province, with its capital at Cluj. It was part of Hungary from about 1000 until its people voted to unite with Romania 1918. It is the home of the vampire legends.

Trapani port and naval base in NW Sicily, about 30 mi/48 km N of Marsala; population (1981) 72,000. It trades in wine, salt, and fish.

trapezium in geometry, a four-sided plane figure (quadrilateral) with no two sides parallel.

trapezoid in geometry, a four-sided plane figure (quadrilateral) with exactly two sides parallel. If the parallel sides have lengths a and b and the perpendicular distance between them is h (the height of the trapezoid), its area $A = \frac{1}{2}h(a + b)$.

An isosceles trapezoid has its sloping sides (legs) equal, is symmetrical about a line drawn through the midpoints of its parallel sides, and has equal base angles.

Trappist member of a Roman Catholic order of monks and nuns, renowned for the strictness of their rule, which includes the maintenance of silence, manual labor, and a vegetarian diet. It originated 1664 at La Trappe, in Normandy, as a reformed version of the ◊Cistercian order under which it is now once more governed.

trasformismo (Italian "transformation") government by coalition, using tactics of reforming new cabinets and political alliances, often between conflicting interest groups, in order to retain power. The term has been applied cynically to describe changing the appearance while the essence remains the same. It was first used to describe the way the Italian nationalist leader Cavour held on to power.

Traven B(en). Adopted name of Herman Feige 1882–1969. German-born US novelist whose true

transuranic

Atomic Number	Name	Symbol	Year discovered	Source of first preparation	Isotope identified	Half life of first isotope identified
Actinide series						
93	neptunium	Np	1940	Irradiation of uranium-238 with neutrons	Np^{239}	2.35 days
94	plutonium	Pu	1941	Bombardment of uranium-238 with deutrons	Pu^{238}	86.4 years
95	americium	Am	1944	Irradiation of plutonium-239 with neutrons	Am^{241}	458 years
96	curium	Cm	1944	Bombardment of plutonium-239 with helium ions	Cm^{242}	162.5 days
97	berkelium	Bk	1949	Bombardment of americium-241 with helium ions	Bk^{243}	4.5 hours
98	californium	Cf	1950	Bombardment of curium-242 with helium ions	Cf^{245}	44 minutes
99	einsteinium	Es	1952	Irradiation of uranium-238 with neutrons in first thermonuclear explosion	Es^{253}	20 days
100	fermium	Fm	1953	Irradiation of uranium-238 with neutrons in first thermonuclear explosion	Fm^{255}	16 hours
101	mendelevium	Md	1955	Bombardment of einsteinium-253 with helium ions	Md^{256}	1.5 hours
102	nobelium	No	1958	Bombardment of curium-246 with carbon ions	No^{255}	3 seconds
103	lawrencium	Lr	1961	Bombardment of californium-252 with boron ions	Lr^{257}	8 seconds
Super-heavy elements						
104	unnilquadium* (old name rutherfordium)	Rf	1969	Bombardment of californium-249 with ions of carbon-12	Ru^{257}	4 seconds
105	unnilpentium* (old name hahnium)	Ha	1970	Bombardment of californium-249 with nuclei of nitrogen-15 ions	Ha^{260}	1.6 seconds
106	unnilsexium*		1974	Bombardment of californium-249 with oxygen-18 ions	$U6^{263}$	0.9 seconds
107	unnilseptium*	Uns	1977	Bombardment of bismuth-209 with nuclei of chromium-54	U7	2 milliseconds
108	unniloctium*	Uno	1984	Bombardment of lead-208	$U8^{265}$	a few milliseconds
109	unnilnonium*		1982	Bombardment of bismuth-209	U9	5 milliseconds

*Names for elements 104–109 are as proposed by the International Union for Pure and Applied Chemistry in 1980.

identity was not revealed until 1979. His books include the bestseller *The Death Ship* 1926 and *The Treasure of the Sierra Madre* 1934, which was made into a film starring Humphrey Bogart in 1948.

Born in a part of Germany now in Poland, he was in turn known as the anarchist Maret Rut, Traven Torsvan, and Hollywood scriptwriter Hal Croves. Between the two world wars he lived in obscurity in Mexico and avoided recognition.

Travers Morris William 1872–1961. English chemist who, with William Ramsay, between 1894 and 1908 first identified what were called the ◊inert or noble gases: krypton, xenon, and radon.

treadmill wheel turned by foot power (often by a domesticated animal) and used, for instance, to raise water from a well or grind corn.

treason act of betrayal, in particular against the sovereign or the state to which the offender owes allegiance.

In the US, treason is defined in the Constitution as the crime of "levying war against [the United States], or adhering to their enemies, giving them aid and comfort." Congress has the power to declare the punishment for treason.

Treasure Island adventure story for children by R L ◊Stevenson, published in 1883. Jim Hawkins, the story's narrator, sets sail with Squire Trelawney in the *Hispaniola*, armed with a map showing the location of buried treasure. Attempts by the ship's crew of pirates, including Long John Silver, to seize the map are foiled after much fighting and the squire finds the treasure.

treaty written agreement between two or more states. Treaties take effect either immediately on signature or, more often, on ratification. Ratification involves a further exchange of documents and usually takes place after the internal governments have approved the terms of the treaty. Treaties are binding in international law, the rules being laid down in the Vienna Convention on the Law of Treaties 1969.

Trebizond former English name of ◊Trabzon, a city in Turkey.

miles 0 150
km 0 150
CZECHOSLOVAKIA
U.S.S.R.
Vienna
AUSTRIA
R. Danube
Budapest
R. Prut
HUNGARY
R. Tisza
TRANSYLVANIA
ROMANIA
Belgrade
Bucharest
YUGOSLAVIA
R. Danube
Black Sea
BULGARIA
Transylvania

tree perennial plant with a woody stem, usually a single stem or "trunk," made up of ◊wood, and protected by an outer layer of ◊bark. It absorbs water through a ◊root system. There is no clear dividing line between ◊shrubs and trees, but sometimes a minimum height of 20 ft/6 m is used to define a tree.

A treelike form has evolved independently many times in different groups of plants. Among the ◊angiosperms, or flowering plants, most trees are ◊dicotyledons. This group includes trees such as oak, beech, ash, chestnut, lime, and maple, and they are often referred to as ◊broad-leaved trees because their leaves are broader than those of conifers, such as pine and spruce. In temperate regions angiosperm trees are mostly ◊deciduous (that is, they lose their leaves in winter), but in the tropics most angiosperm trees are evergreen. There are fewer trees among the ◊monocotyledons, but the palms and bamboos (some of which are treelike) belong to this group. The ◊gymnosperms include many trees and they are classified into four orders: Cycadales (including cycads and sago palms), Coniferales (the conifers), Ginkgoales (including only one living species, the ginkgo, or maidenhair tree), and Taxales (including yews). Apart from the ginkgo and the larches (conifers), most gymnosperm trees are evergreen. There are also a few living trees in the ◊pteridophyte group, known as tree ferns. In the swamp forests of the Carboniferous era, 300 million years ago, there were giant treelike horsetails and club mosses in addition to the tree ferns. The world's oldest trees are found in the Pacific forest of North America, some more than 2,000 years old.

Tree Herbert Beerbohm 1853–1917. British actor and theater manager, half brother of Max ◊Beerbohm. Noted for his Shakespeare productions, he was founder of the ◊Royal Academy of Dramatic Art (RADA).

trefoil several ◊clover plants of the genus *Trifolium* of the pea family Leguminosae, the leaves of which are divided into three leaflets. The name is also used for other plants with leaves divided into three lobes.

Bird's-foot trefoil *Lotus corniculatus*, also of the pea family, is a low-growing perennial found in grassy places throughout Europe, N Asia, and parts of Africa. Its has five leaflets to each leaf, but the first two are bent back so it appears to have only three. The yellow flowers, often tinged orange or red, are borne in heads with only a few blooms.

trematode parasitic flatworm with an oval nonsegmented body, of the class Trematoda, including the ◊fluke.

tremor minor ◊earthquake.

Trengganu or ***Terengganu*** state of E Peninsular Malaysia; capital Kuala Trengganu; area 5,018 sq mi/13,000 sq km; population (1980) 541,000. Its exports include copra, black pepper, tin, and tungsten; there are also fishing and offshore oil industries.

Trent third longest river of England; length 170 mi/275 km. Rising in the S Pennines, it flows first S and then NE through the Midlands to the Humber. It is navigable by barge for nearly 100 mi/160 km.

Trent, Council of Conference held 1545–63 by the Roman Catholic Church at Trento, N Italy initiating the ◊Counter-Reformation; see also ◊Reformation.

Trentino–Alto Adige autonomous region of N Italy, comprising the provinces of Bolzano and Trento; capital Trento; chief towns Trento in the Italian-speaking southern area, and Bolzano-Bozen in the northern German-speaking area of South ◊Tirol (the region was Austrian until ceded to Italy 1919); area 5,250 sq mi/13,600 sq km; population (1988) 882,000.

Trento capital of Trentino–Alto Adige region, Italy, on the Adige River; population (1988) 101,000. Industries include the manufacture of electrical goods and chemicals. The Council of ◊Trent was held here 1545–63.

Trenton capital of New Jersey, on the Delaware River; population (1990) 88,675. It has metal-working and ceramics industries. It was first settled by Quakers 1679; George Washington defeated the British here 1776. It became state capital 1790.

trepang ◊sea cucumbers used as food.

trespass going on to the land of another without authority. In law, a landowner has the right to eject a trespasser by the use of reasonable force and can sue for any damage caused.

A trespasser injured on another's land cannot usually recover damages from the landowner unless the latter did him or her some positive injury.

Treurnicht Andries Petrus 1921– . South African Conservative Party politician. A former minister of the Dutch Reformed Church, he was elected to the South African parliament as a National Party member but left it to form a new right-wing Conservative Party, opposed to any dilution of the ◊apartheid system.

Trevelyan George Macaulay 1876–1962. British historian. Regius professor of history at Cambridge 1927–40, he pioneered the study of social history, as in his *English Social History* 1942.

Trèves French name for ◊Trier, a city in the Federal Republic of Germany.

Treviso city in Veneto, NE Italy; population (1981) 88,000. Its industries include the manufacture of machinery and ceramics. The 11th-century cathedral has an altarpiece by Titian.

Trevithick Richard 1771–1833. British engineer, constructor of a steam road locomotive 1801 and the first steam engine to run on rails 1804.

Triad secret society, founded in China as a Buddhist cult AD 36. It became known as the Triad because the triangle played a significant part in the initiation ceremony. Today it is reputed to be involved in organized crime (drugs, gambling, prostitution) among overseas Chinese. Its headquarters are alleged to be in Hong Kong.

In the 18th century it became political, aiming at the overthrow of the Manchu dynasty, and

triangle

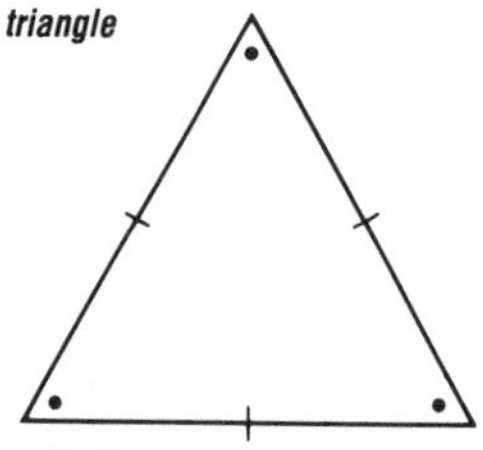

Equilateral triangle: all the sides are the same length; all the angles are equal to 60°

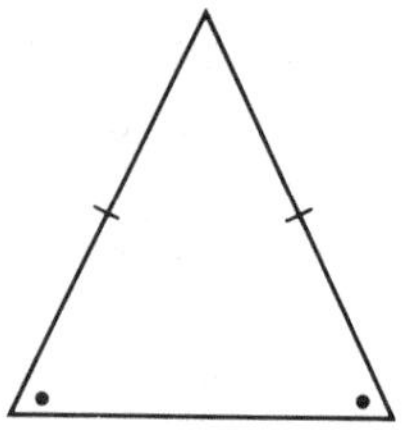

Isosceles triangle: two sides and two angles are the same

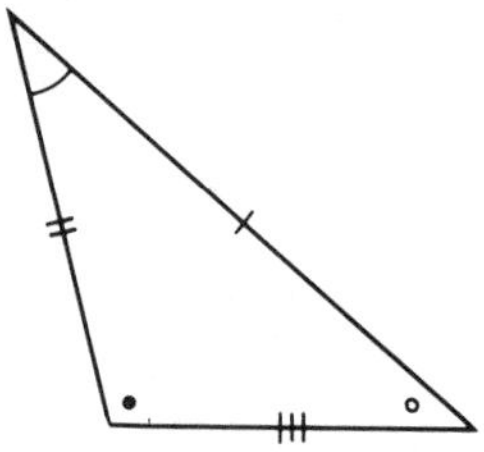

Scalene triangle: all the sides and angles are different

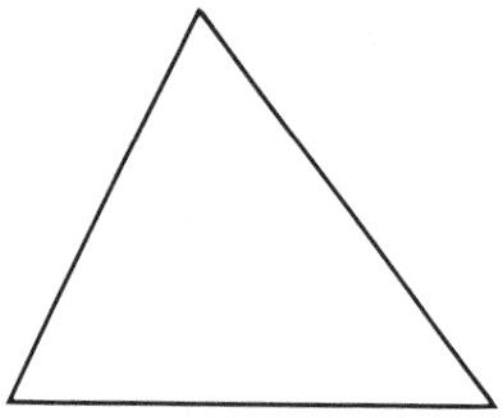

Acute-angle triangle: each angle is acute (less than 90°)

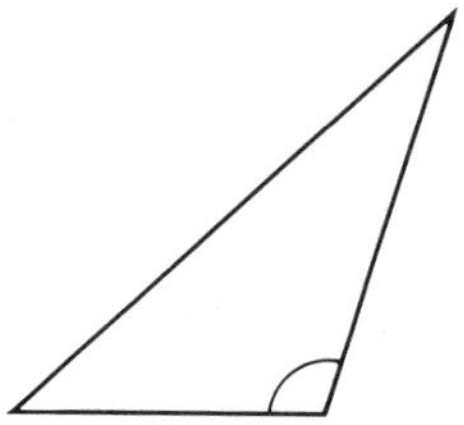

Obtuse-angle triangle: one angle is obtuse (more than 90°)

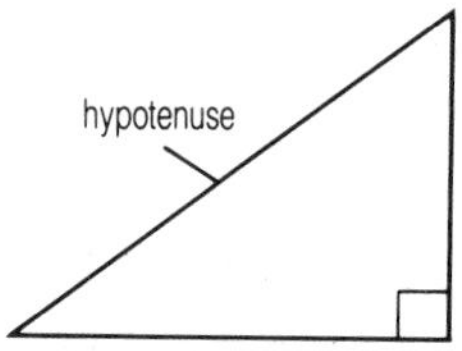
hypotenuse

A right-angle triangle has one angle of 90°, the *hypotenuse* is the side opposite the right angle

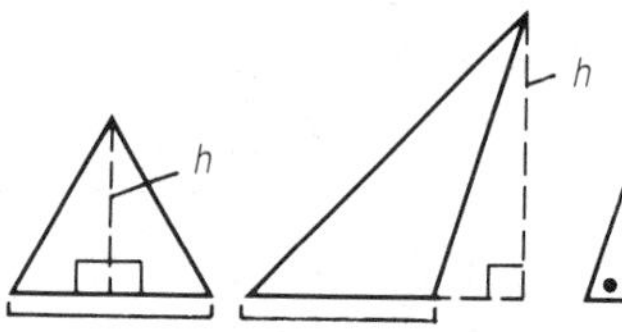
h
h
l
l

Area of triangle = ½*lh*

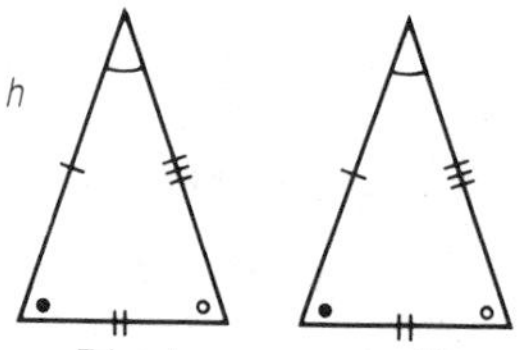

Triangles are *congruent* if corresponding sides and corresponding angles are equal

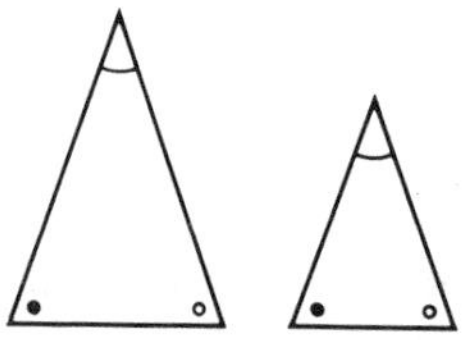

Similar triangles have corresponding angles that are equal; they therefore have the same shape

backed the Taiping Rebellion 1851 and Sun Yat-sen's establishment of a republic 1912.

trial by ordeal in the Middle Ages, a test of guilt or innocence by which God's judgment of the case was supposedly revealed through the accused's exposure to fire, water, or blessed bread. The practice originated with the Franks in the 8th century, and survived until the 13th century. In the ordeal by cold water, the accused would be bound and thrown into the water. If he or she sank, it would prove innocence, but if they remained alive, it would show guilt.

If the accused ate blessed bread, the theory was that the guilty would not be able to swallow it.

Trial, The (German *Der Prozess*) novel by Franz Kafka, published 1925. It deals with the sinister circumstances in which a man is arrested for no apparent reason, and with his consequent feelings of guilt and alienation, culminating in his "execution."

triangle in geometry, a three-sided plane figure, the sum of whose interior angles is 180°. Triangles can be classified by the relative lengths of their sides. A scalene triangle has no sides of equal length; an isosceles triangle has at least two equal sides; an equilateral triangle has three equal sides (and three equal angles of 60°).

Triangles can also be classified by their angle measures: a right triangle has one right (90°) angle; an acute triangle has three acute (less than 90°) angles; an obtuse triangle has one obtuse (greater than 90°) angle; an equiangular triangle has three equal angles. (All equilateral triangles are equiangular, and vice versa.) If the length of one side of a triangle is l and the perpendicular distance from that side to the opposite corner is h (the height or altitude of the triangle), its area $A = \frac{1}{2}(l \times h)$.

triangle of forces method of calculating the force produced by two other forces (the resultant). It is based on the fact that if three forces acting at a point can be represented by the sides of a triangle, the forces are in equilibrium. See ◊parallelogram of forces.

triangulation technique used in surveying and navigation to determine distances, using the properties of the triangle. To begin, surveyors measure a certain length exactly to provide a base line. From each end of this line they then measure the angle to a distant point, using a ◊theodolite. They now have a triangle in which they know the length of one side and the two adjacent angles. By simple trigonometry they can work out the lengths of the other two sides.

To make a complete survey of the region, they repeat the process, building on the first triangle.

Trianon two palaces in the park at ◊Versailles, France: Le Grand Trianon built for Louis XIV, and Le Petit Trianon for Louis XV.

Triassic period of geologic time 248–213 million years ago, the first period of the Mesozoic era. The continents were fused together to form the world continent ◊Pangaea. Triassic sediments contain remains of early dinosaurs and other reptiles now extinct. By late Triassic times, the first mammals had evolved.

triathlon test of stamina involving three sports: swimming 2.4 mi/3.8 km, cycling 112 mi/180 km, and running a marathon 26 mi/42.195 km 385 yd, each one immediately following the last.

It was first established as a sport in the US 1974. The most celebrated event is the Hawaii Ironman.

Tribal Areas, Federally Administered part of the

mountainous frontier of NW Pakistan with Afghanistan, comprising the districts of Malakand, Mohmand, Khyber, Kurram, and Waziristan, administered directly from Islamabad; area 27,219 sq km/10,507 sq mi; population (1985) 2,467,000; chief towns are Wana, Razmak, Miram Shah.

tribal society way of life in which people govern their own affairs as independent local communities without central government organizations or states. They may be found in parts of SE Asia, New Guinea, South America, and Africa.

As the world economy expands, natural resources belonging to tribal peoples are coveted and exploited for farming or industrial use and the people are frequently dispossessed. Pressure groups such as Survival International and Cultural Survival have been established in some Western countries to support the struggle of tribal peoples for property rights as well as civil rights within the borders of the countries of which they are technically a part.

tribune Roman magistrate of ◊plebeian family, elected annually to defend the interests of the common people; only two were originally chosen in 494 BC, but there were later ten. They could veto the decisions of any other magistrate.

triceratops any of a genus (*Triceratops*) of massive, horned ornithiscian dinosaurs. They had three horns and a neck frill. Up to 25 ft/8 m long, they lived in the Cretaceous period.

Trichinopoly former name for ◊Tiruchirapalli, a city in India.

trichloromethane technical name for ◊chloroform.

tricolor (French *tricouleur*) the French national flag of three vertical bands of red, white, and blue. The red and blue were the colors of Paris and the white represented the royal house of Bourbon. The flag was first adopted on July 17, 1789, three days after the storming of the Bastille during the French Revolution.

tricoteuse (French "knitter") in the French Revolution, one of the women who sat knitting in the National Convention and beneath the guillotine.

tricuspid valve a flap of tissue situated on the right side of the ◊heart between the atrium and the ventricle. It prevents blood flowing backwards when the ventricle contracts.

As with all the valves, its movements are caused by pressure changes during the beat rather than by any intrinsic muscular activity. As the valve snaps shut a vibration passes through the chest cavity and is detectable as the first sound of the heart beat.

Trier (French *Trèves*) city in Rhineland-Palatinate, Federal Republic of Germany; population (1984) 95,000. Once the capital of the Treveri, a Celto-Germanic tribe, it became known as Augusta Treverorum under the Roman emperor Augustus about 15 BC and was the capital of an ecclesiastical principality during the 14th–18th centuries. Karl Marx was born here.

Trieste port on the Adriatic, opposite Venice, in Friuli-Venezia-Giulia, Italy; population (1988) 237,000, including a large Slovene minority. It is the site of the International Centre for Theoretical Physics, established 1964.

Trieste was under Austrian rule from 1382 (apart from Napoleonic occupation 1809–14) until transferred to Italy 1918. It was claimed after World War II by Yugoslavia, and the city and surrounding territory were divided 1954 between Italy and Yugoslavia.

triggerfish any marine bony fish of the family Balistidae, with a laterally compressed body, up to 2 ft/60 cm long, and deep belly. They have small mouths but strong jaws and teeth. The first spine on the dorsal fin locks into an erect position, which allows them to fasten themselves securely in crevices for protection, and can only be moved by depressing the smaller third ("trigger") spine.

There are many species, found mainly in warm waters, and some are very colorful.

Triglav mountain in the Julian Alps, rising to 9,393 ft/2,863 m. It is the highest peak in Yugoslavia.

trigonometry branch of mathematics that solves problems relating to plane and spherical triangles. Its principles are based on the fixed proportions of sides for a particular angle in a right triangle, the simplest of which are known as the ◊sine, ◊cosine, and ◊tangent (so-called trigonometrical ratios). It is of practical importance in navigation, surveying, and simple harmonic motion in physics. Invented by ◊Hipparchus, trigonometry was developed by ◊Ptolemy of Alexandria and was known to early Hindu and Arab mathematicians.

triiodomethane technical name for ◊iodoform.

Trilling Lionel 1905–1975. US author and literary critic. His books of criticism include *The Liberal Imagination* 1950, *Beyond Culture* 1965, and *The Experience of Literature* 1967. Trilling also gained acclaim for his annotated editions of the works of Matthew Arnold and John Keats. He published frequent reviews and essays and was a visiting professor at Oxford 1964–65 and Harvard 1969–70.

Born in New York and educated at Columbia University, Trilling joined the Columbia English Department faculty 1932. He received his PhD 1938 and was appointed professor 1948.

trillium any of various perennial herbaceous woodland plants of the genus *Trillium* of the lily family. They have a whorl of three leaves around the erect stem. The single terminal flower has three green sepals and three usually maroon or white petals. The nodding trillium *Trillium cernuum* ranges across most of the eastern half of North America.

trilobite any of a large class (Trilobita) of extinct, marine, invertebrate arthropods of the Paleozoic era, with a flattened, oval body, 0.4–26 in/1–65 cm long. The hard-shelled body was divided by two deep furrows into three lobes.

Some were burrowers, others were swimming and floating forms. Their worldwide distribution, many species, and the immense quantities of their remains make them useful in geologic dating.

Trimurti the Hindu triad of gods, representing the Absolute Spirit in its three aspects: Brahma, personifying creation; Vishnu, preservation; and Siva, destruction.

Trinidad town in Beni region, N Bolivia, near the river Mamoré, 250 mi/400 km NE of La Paz; population (1980) 36,000. It is built on an artificial earth mound, above flood-level, the work of a little-known early American Indian people.

Trinidad and Tobago country in the West Indies, off the coast of Venezuela.

government Trinidad and Tobago is an independent republic within the ◊Commonwealth. The 1976 constitution provides for a president as head of state and a two-chamber parliament, consisting of a senate of 31 members and a house of representatives of 36. The president appoints the prime minister and cabinet, who are collectively responsible to parliament. The president also appoints the senators, 16 on the advice of the prime minister, 6 on the advice of the leader of the opposition, and 9 after wider consultation. The 36 members of the House of Representatives are elected by universal adult suffrage. Parliament has a life of five years.

Tobago was given its own House of Assembly 1980. It has 15 members, 12 popularly elected and 3 chosen by the majority party.

history For early history, see ◊American Indian. Trinidad and Tobago were visited by Columbus 1498. Trinidad was colonized by Spain from 1532 and ceded to Britain 1802, having been captured 1797. Tobago was settled by the Netherlands in the 1630s and subsequently occupied by various countries before being ceded to Britain by France 1814. Trinidad and Tobago were amalgamated 1888 as a British colony.

Trinidad and Tobago's first political party, the People's National Movement (PNM), was formed 1956 by Dr Eric Williams, and when the colony achieved internal self-government 1959 he became the first chief minister. Between 1958 and 1961 it was a member of the Federation of the West Indies but withdrew and achieved full independence, within the Commonwealth, 1967, Williams becoming the first prime minister.

A new constitution was adopted 1976 that made Trinidad and Tobago a republic. The former governor-general, Ellis Clarke, became the first president and Williams continued as prime minister. He died March 1981 without having nominated a successor, and the president appointed George Chambers; the PNM formally adopted him as leader May 1981. The opposition, a moderate left-wing party grouping led by the deputy prime minister, Arthur Robinson, was during the next few years reorganized as the National Alliance for Reconstruction (NAR), until in the 1986 general election it swept the PNM from power and Arthur Robinson became prime minister.

An attempted coup in July 1990 resulted in the capture of Prime Minister Robinson. In Aug 1990 the rebels surrendered and an injured Robinson was released. The PNM returned to power in Dec 1991 elections.

triggerfish

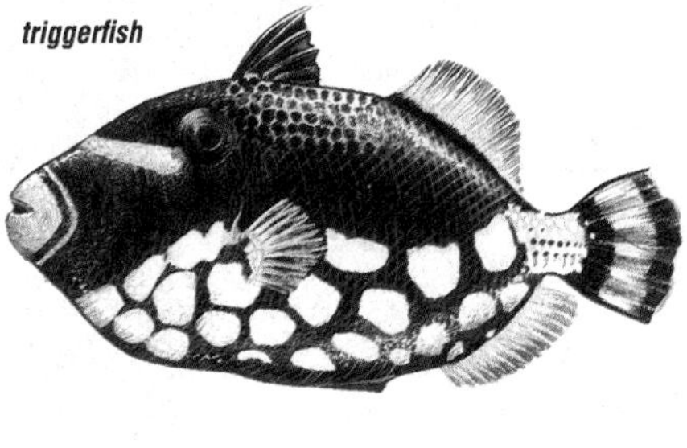

Trinitarianism belief in the Christian Trinity.

Trinity in Christianity, the union of three persons—Father, Son, and Holy Ghost/Spirit—in one godhead. The precise meaning of the doctrine has been the cause of unending dispute, and was the chief cause of the split between the Eastern Orthodox and Roman Catholic churches. Trinity Sunday occurs on the Sunday after Pentecost.

triode three-electrode thermionic tube containing an anode and a cathode (as does a ◊diode) with an additional negatively based control grid. Small variations in voltage on the grid bias result in large variations in the current. The triode was commonly used in amplifiers until largely superseded by the ◊transistor. The tube was invented by the US radio engineer Lee De Forest.

Tripitaka (Pāli "three baskets") the canonical texts of Theravāda Buddhism, divided into three parts.

Triple Alliance pact from 1882 between Germany, Austria-Hungary, and Italy to offset the power of Russia and France. It was last renewed 1912, but during World War I Italy's initial neutrality gradually changed and it denounced the alliance 1915. The term also refers to other alliances: 1668—England, Holland, and Sweden; 1717—Britain, Holland, and France (joined 1718 by Austria); 1788—Britain, Prussia, and Holland; 1795—Britain, Russia, and Austria.

Triple Entente alliance of Britain, France, and Russia 1907–17. In 1911 this became a military alliance and formed the basis of the Allied powers in World War I against the Central Powers, Germany and Austria-Hungary.

The failure of the alliance system to create a stable balance of power, coupled with widespread horror of the carnage created by World War I, led to attempts to create international cooperation with the League of Nations.

Tripoli (Arabic *Tarabolus esh-sham*) port in N Lebanon, 40 mi/65 km NE of Beirut; population (1980) 175,000. It stands on the site of the Phoenician city of Oea.

Tripoli (Arabic *Tarabolus al-Gharb*) capital and chief port of Libya, on the Mediterranean; population

Trinidad and Tobago
Republic of

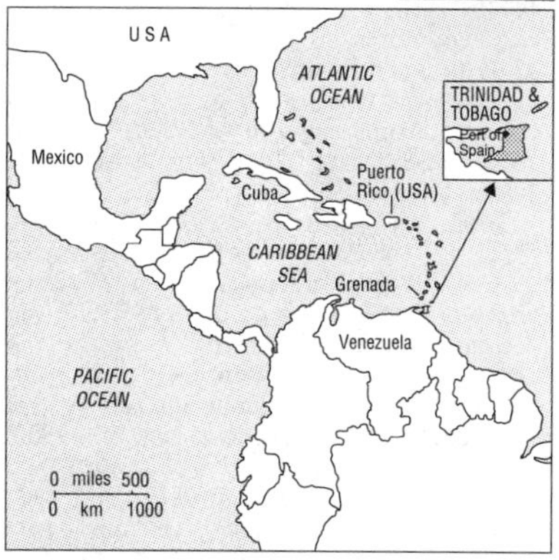
USA
ATLANTIC
OCEAN
TRINIDAD &
TOBAGO
Port of
Spain
Mexico
Puerto
Rico (USA)
Cuba
CARIBBEAN
SEA
Grenada
Venezuela
PACIFIC
OCEAN
0 miles 500
0 km 1000

area Trinidad 1,864 sq mi/4,828 sq km and Tobago 116 sq mi/300 sq km
capital Port-of-Spain
cities San Fernando, Arima, Scarborough (Tobago)
physical comprises two main islands and some smaller ones; coastal swamps and hills E–W
features Pitch Lake, a self-renewing source of asphalt used by 16th-century explorer Walter Raleigh to repair his ships
head of state Noor Hassanali from 1987
head of government Arthur Robinson from 1986
political system democratic republic
political parties National Alliance for Reconstruction (NAR), nationalistic, left-of-center; People's National Movement (PNM), nationalistic, moderate, centrist
exports oil, petroleum products, chemicals, sugar, cocoa
currency Trinidad and Tobago dollar
population (1990 est) 1,270,000 (40% African descent, 40% Indian, 16% European, Chinese and others 2%), 1.2 million on Trinidad; growth rate 1.6% p.a.
life expectancy men 68, women 72 (1989)
language English (official), Hindi, French, Spanish
religion Roman Catholic 32%, Protestant 29%, Hindu 25%, Muslim 6%
literacy 97% (1988)
GNP $4.5 bn; $3,731 per head (1987)
chronology
1888 Trinidad and Tobago united as a British colony.
1956 People's National Movement (PNM) founded.
1959 Granted internal self-government, with PNM leader Eric Williams as chief minister.
1962 Independence achieved from Britain, within the Commonwealth, with Williams as prime minister.
1976 Became a republic, with Ellis Clarke as president and Williams as prime minister.
1981 Williams died and was succeeded by George Chambers, with Arthur Robinson as opposition leader.
1986 Arthur Robinson became prime minister.
1990 Attempted antigovernment coup defeated.
1991 Dec elections return PNM to power.

(1980) 980,000. Products include olive oil, fruit, fish, and textiles. Tripoli was founded about the 7th century BC by Phoenicians from Oea (now Tripoli in Lebanon). It was a base for Axis powers during World War II. In 1986 it was bombed by the US Air Force in response to international guerrilla activity.

Tripolitania former province of Libya, stretching from Cyrenaica in the east to Tunisia in the west. Italy captured it from Turkey 1912, and the British captured it from Italy 1942 and controlled it until it was incorporated into the newly independent United Kingdom of Libya, established 1951. In 1963 Tripolitania was subdivided into administrative divisions.

Triptolemos in ancient Greek religion associated with ◊Demeter and ◊Persephone in the ◊Eleusinian Mysteries, and entrusted and sent out into the world by them with the task of teaching agriculture to humanity.

Tripura state of NE India since 1972, formerly a princely state; between Bangladesh and Assam
area 4,053 sq mi/10,500 sq km
capital Agartala
features agriculture on a rotation system in the jungle, now being superseded by modern methods
products rice, cotton, tea, sugar cane; steel, jute
population (1981) 2,060,000
language Bengali
religion Hindu.

trireme ancient Greek warship with three banks of oars as well as sails, 115 ft/38 m long. They were used at the battle of ◊Salamis and by the Romans until the 4th century AD.

Tristan hero of Celtic legend who fell in love with Iseult, the bride he was sent to win for his uncle King Mark of Cornwall; the story became part of the Arthurian cycle and is the subject of Wagner's opera *Tristan und Isolde*.

Tristan Flora 1803–1844. French Socialist writer and activist, author of *Promenades dans Londres/The London Journal* 1840, a vivid record of social conditions, and *L'Union ouvrière/Workers' Union* 1843, an outline of a workers's utopia.

Tristan da Cunha group of islands in the S Atlantic, part of the British dependency of St Helena
area 42 sq mi/110 sq km;
features comprises four islands: Tristan, Gough, Inaccessible, and Nightingale. Tristan consists of a single volcano 6,761 ft/2,060 m; it is an important meteorological and radio station;
government administrator, plus island council, as a dependency of ◊St Helena;
products crawfish;
population (1982) 325;
language English;
history the first European to visit the then uninhabited islands was the Portuguese admiral after whom they are named, in 1506; they were annexed by Britain 1816. Believed to be extinct, the Tristan volcano erupted 1961 and the population were evacuated, but in 1963 they chose to return.

Tristano Lennie (Lennard Joseph) 1919–1978. US jazz pianist and composer. An austere musician, he gave an academic foundation to the school of "cool jazz" in the 1940s and 1950s, which was at odds with the bebop tradition. He was also active as a teacher.

Tristram Shandy novel by Laurence Sterne, published 1759–67. The work, a forerunner of the 20th century stream-of-consciousness novel, has no coherent plot and uses typographical devices to emphasize the author's disdain for the structured novels of his contemporaries.

triticale cereal crop of recent origin that is a cross between wheat *Triticum* and rye *Secale*. It can produce heavy yields of high-protein grain, principally for use as animal feed.

tritium radioactive isotope of hydrogen, three times as heavy as ordinary hydrogen, consisting of one proton and two neutrons. It has a half-life of 12.5 years.

Triton in Greek mythology, a merman sea-god, the son of ◊Poseidon and the sea-goddess Amphitrite. He is shown blowing on a conch shell.

Triton in astronomy, the largest of Neptune's moons and one of the four largest in the Solar System. It has a diameter of 1,690 mi/2,720 km and orbits Neptune every 5.88 days in a retrograde (east-to-west) direction. Its surface has many fault lines and a bright polar region that reflects 90% of the sunlight it receives. Its atmosphere is composed of nitrogen and methane, and has a pressure only 0.00001 that of the Earth at sea level. Triton was discovered by Galle 1846, one month after the discovery of Neptune.

Other surface features include what appear to be frozen lakes, perhaps formed when material ejected from Triton's interior froze in low-lying areas of the surface. Chemical reaction between the material on Triton's surface and solar radiation are probably responsible for the pinkish coloring across the southern hemisphere. The low number of craters suggests that the surface may be fairly young on the geologic time scale, perhaps less than 500 million years. It is possible that Triton may still be volcanically active. Dark streaks near its south pole may be formed from liquid nitrogen thrown up into the atmosphere to heights of several tens of miles, becoming frozen and then being blown by gentle winds and deposited across the surface. The features resemble streaks seen elsewhere in the Solar System.

triumvir one of a group of three administrators sharing power in ancient Rome, as in the First Triumvirate 60 BC: Caesar, Pompey, Crassus; and Second Triumvirate 43 BC: Augustus, Antony, and Lepidus.

Trivandrum capital of Kerala, SW India; population (1981) 483,000. It has chemical, textile, and rubber industries. Formerly the capital of the princely state of Travancore, it has many palaces, an old fort, and a shrine.

trivium in medieval education, the three lower liberal arts (grammar, rhetoric, and logic) studied before the ◊quadrivium.

trogon any of an order (Trogoniformes) of tropical birds, up to 1.7 ft/50 cm long, with resplendent plumage, living in the Americas and Afro-Asia. Most striking is the ◊quetzal.

Trois-Rivières port on the St Lawrence River, Québec, Canada; population (1986) 129,000. The chief industry is the production of newsprint.

Trojan horse in computing, a program that appears to function normally but, undetected by the normal user, causes damage to other files or circumvents security procedures. The earliest appeared in the UK in about 1988.

Trojan horse seemingly innocuous but treacherous gift from an enemy. In Greek legend, during the siege of Troy, the Greek army left an enormous wooden horse outside the gate of the city and retreated. When the Trojans had brought it in, Greek soldiers emerged from within the hollow horse and opened the city gates to enable it to be captured.

Trollope Anthony 1815–1882. English novelist who delineated provincial English middle-class society in his Barchester series of novels. *The Warden* 1855 began the series, which includes *Barchester Towers* 1857, *Doctor Thorne* 1858, and *The Last Chronicle of Barset* 1867.

trombone ◊brass wind musical instrument developed from the sackbut. It consists of a tube bent double, varied notes being obtained by an inner sliding tube. Usual sizes of trombone are alto, tenor, bass, and contra-bass.

trompe l'oeil (French "deceives the eye") painting technique that gives a convincing illusion of three-dimensional reality. It has been common in most periods in the West, from Classical Greece through the Renaissance and later.

Tromsø fishing port and the largest town in NW Norway, on Tromsø island; population (1988) 49,000.

Trondheim fishing port in Norway; population (1988) 136,000. It has canning, textile, margarine, and soap industries. It was the medieval capital of Norway, and Norwegian kings are crowned in the cathedral.

trophic level in ecology, the position occupied by a species (or group of species) in a ◊food chain. The main levels are primary producers (photosynthetic plants), primary consumers (herbivores),

Trotsky *Leon Trotsky in 1917, the year of the Russian Revolution.*

secondary consumers (carnivores), and decomposers (bacteria and fungi).

tropics the area between the tropics of Cancer and Capricorn, defined by the parallels of latitude approximately 23°30′ N and S of the equator. They are the limits of the area of Earth's surface in which the Sun can be directly overhead.

tropine $C_8H_{15}NO$ poisonous crystalline solid formed by the hydrolysis of the ◊alkaloid atropine.

tropism or ***tropic movement*** the directional growth of a plant, or part of a plant, in response to an external stimulus. If the movement is directed toward the stimulus it is described as positive; if away from it, it is negative. Geotropism, the response of plants to gravity, causes the root (positively geotropic) to grow downward, and the stem (negatively geotropic) to grow upward. Phototropism occurs in response to light, hydrotropism to water, chemotropism to a chemical stimulus, and thigmotropism, or haptotropism, to physical contact, as in the tendrils of climbing plants when they touch a support and then grow around it.

Tropic movements are the result of greater rate of growth on one side of the plant organ than the other. Tropism differs from a ◊nastic movement in being influenced by the direction of the stimulus.

troposphere lower part of the Earth's ◊atmosphere extending about 6.5 mi/10.5 km from the Earth's surface, in which temperature decreases with height to about –76°F/–60°C except in local layers of temperature inversion. The ***tropopause*** is the upper boundary of the troposphere above which the temperature increases slowly with height within the ◊atmosphere.

Trotsky Leon. Adopted name of Lev Davidovitch Bronstein 1879–1940. Russian revolutionary. He joined the Bolshevik party and took a leading part in the seizure of power 1917 and raising the Red Army that fought the Civil War 1918–20. In the struggle for power that followed ◊Lenin's death 1924, ◊Stalin defeated Trotsky, and this and other differences with the Communist Party led to his exile 1929. He settled in Mexico, where he was assassinated with an ice pick at Stalin's instigation. Trotsky believed in world revolution and in permanent revolution, and was an uncompromising, if liberal, idealist.

Trotsky became a Marxist in the 1890s and was imprisoned and exiled for opposition to the tsarist regime. He lived in W Europe from 1902 until the 1905 revolution, when he was again imprisoned but escaped to live in exile until 1917. Although as a young man Trotsky admired Lenin, when he worked with him organizing the revolution of 1917, he objected to Lenin's dictatorial ways. He was second in command until Lenin's death. Trotsky's later works are critical of the Soviet regime; for example, *The Revolution Betrayed* 1937. His greatest work is his magisterial *History of the Russian Revolution* 1932–33. Official Soviet recognition of responsibility for his assassination through the secret service came in 1989.

Trotskyism form of Marxism advocated by Leon Trotsky. Its central concept is that of permanent revolution. In his view a proletarian revolution, leading to a Socialist society, could not be achieved in isolation, so it would be necessary to instigate further revolutions throughout Europe and ultimately worldwide. This was in direct opposition to the Stalinist view that socialism should be built and consolidated within individual countries.

Trotskyism developed in an attempt to reconcile Marxist theory with actual conditions in Russia in the early 20th century, but it was never officially accepted within the USSR. Instead it has found much support worldwide, primarily in Third World countries, and the Fourth ◊International, which Trotsky founded in 1937, has sections in over 60 countries.

troubador one of a group of poet musicians in Provence and S France in the 12th–13th centuries, which included both nobles and wandering minstrels. The troubadors originated a type of lyric poetry devoted to themes of courtly love and the idealization of women and to glorifying the deeds of their patrons, reflecting the chivalric ideals of the period. Little is known of the music, which was passed down orally.

Among the troubadors were Bertran de Born (1140–c. 1215), who was mentioned by Dante, Arnaut Daniel, and Bernard de Ventador. The troubador tradition spread to other parts of Europe, including northern France (the *trouvères*) and Germany (the *minnesingers*).

trout any of various bony fishes in the salmon family, popular for sport and food, usually speckled and found mainly in fresh water. They are native to the N hemisphere.

Common US species are the rainbow trout *Salmo gairdneri*, brook trout *Salvelinus fontinalis*, and lake trout *Salvelinus malma*. Some European trout have been introduced to the US and vice versa; some are raised in trout farms.

Troy city in E New York, E of Albany on the E bank of the Hudson river; seat of Rensselear county, incorporated 1816. Industries include apparel, abrasives, metals, paper, automobile and railroad parts, and processed foods. Rensselaer Polytechnic Institute 1824 and Russell Sage College 1916 are here; population (1990) 54,269. A Mohegan Indian fortress, it was explored by Henry Hudson 1609, granted by the Dutch East India Company as a patroonship to Kiliaen Van Rensselaer, and founded as a town 1786.

Troy (Latin *Ilium*) ancient city of Asia Minor, besieged in the ten-year Trojan War (mid-13th century BC), which the poet Homer described in the *Iliad*. The city fell to the Greeks who first used the stratagem of leaving behind, in a feigned retreat, a large wooden horse containing armed infiltrators to open the gates. Believing it to be a religious offering, the Trojans took it within the walls.

Nine cities found one beneath another at the site Hissarlik, near the Dardanelles, were originally excavated by Heinrich ◊Schliemann from 1874 to 1890. Recent research suggests that the seventh, sacked and burned about 1250 BC, is probably the Homeric Troy, which was succeeded by a shanty town sacked by the ◊Sea Peoples about 780 BC. It has been suggested that Homer's tale of war might have a basis in fact, for example, a conflict arising from trade rivalry (Troy was on a tin trade route), which might have been triggered by such an incident as Paris running off with ◊Helen. The wooden horse may have been a votive offering left behind by the Greeks after ◊Poseidon (whose emblem was a horse) had opened breaches in the city walls for them by an earthquake.

Troyes industrial (textiles and food processing) town in Champagne-Ardenne, NE France; population (1982) 65,000. The Treaty of Troyes 1420 made Henry V of England heir to the French crown.

troy system system of units used for precious metals and gems. The pound troy (0.37 kg) consists of 12 ounces (each of 120 carats) or 5,760 grains (each equal to 65 mg).

Trucial States former name (until 1971) of the ◊United Arab Emirates. It derives from the agreements made with Britain 1820 to ensure a truce in the area and to suppress piracy and slavery.

Trudeau Pierre (Elliott) 1919– . Canadian Liberal politician. He was prime minister 1968–79 and won again by a landslide Feb 1980. In 1980 his work helped to defeat the Québec independence movement in a referendum. He repatriated the constitution from Britain 1982, but by 1984 had so lost support that he resigned.

True Cross the instrument of Jesus' crucifixion, supposedly found by St Helena, the mother of the emperor Constantine, on the hill of the ◊Calvary 326.

She is reputed to have placed most of it in a church built on the site and to have taken the rest to Constantinople. During the Middle Ages, a large number of relics were claimed to be fragments of the True Cross and were preserved and exhibited in churches and cathedrals.

Truffaut François 1932–1984. French New Wave film director whose gently comic films include *Jules et Jim* 1961 and *La Nuit américaine/Day for Night* 1973 (Academy Award). His prize-winning (Cannes) *The 400 Blows* 1959 was the first in a series of semiautobiographical films. His later work includes *The Story of Adèle H* 1975 and *The Last Metro* 1980. He was influenced by Alfred Hitchcock and also drew on Surrealist and comic traditions. He played one of the leading roles in Steven Spielberg's *Close Encounters of a Third Kind* 1977.

His interest in film led to a job as film critic for *Cahiers du Cinema* during the 1950s before embarking on his career as director.

truffle subterranean fungus of the order Tuberales. Certain species are valued as edible delicacies; in particular, *Tuber melanosporum*, generally found growing under oak trees. It is native to the Périgord region of France but cultivated in other areas as well. It is rounded, blackish brown, covered with warts externally, and with blackish flesh.

Dogs and pigs are traditionally used to discover truffles, but in 1990 an artificial "nose" developed at the University of Manchester Institute of Science and Technology, England, proved more effective in tests in Bordeaux.

Trujillo city in NW Peru, with its port at Salaverry; population (1988) 491,000. Industries include engineering, copper, sugar milling, and vehicle assembly.

Trujillo Molina Rafael (Leónidas) 1891–1961. Dictator of the Dominican Republic from 1930. As commander of the Dominican Guard, he seized power and established a ruthless dictatorship. He was assassinated.

Truman Harry S 1884–1972. 33rd president of the US 1945–53, a Democrat. In Jan 1945 he became vice-president to F D Roosevelt, and president when Roosevelt died in April that year. He played an important role at the ◊Potsdam Conference, used ◊atomic bombs against Japan to end World War II, launched the ◊Marshall Plan to restore Western Europe's postwar economy, and nurtured the European Community and NATO (including the rearmament of West Germany). He believed in the ◊United Nations (UN) and when South Korea was invaded by North Korea 1950, had US forces join the UN forces, with General ◊MacArthur at their head. He fired MacArthur

Truman *The 33rd president of the United States of America, Harry S Truman, a Democrat. 1945–1953.*

1951 when the general's war policy conflicted with UN aims.

Born in Lamar, Missouri, he was an officer in World War I, was a partner in a clothing store that was bankrupted by the ◊Depression, and ran for various local political offices. He became a senator 1934, was selected as Roosevelt's fourth-term vice-president 1944, succeeded to the presidency 1945, and in 1948 was elected for a second term in an upset victory over Republican Thomas Dewey (1902–1971). At home, Truman had difficulty with Congress and with labor groups in converting the economy back to peacetime conditions; he also failed to prevent the Congressional witch hunts on suspected Communists (see ◊Hiss, ◊McCarthy). He enunciated the Truman Doctrine, which called for aid to nations threatened by Communist expansion. His policy of ◊containment initiated the long ◊cold war with the Soviet Union. Truman retired to Independence, Missouri.

Truman Doctrine President Harry Truman's 1947 dictum that the US would "support free peoples who are resisting attempted subjugation by armed minorities or by outside pressures." It was used to justify sending aid to Greece following World War II and sending US troops abroad; for example, to Korea.

Trumbull John 1756–1843. American artist. Born in Lebanon, Connecticut, the son of Governor Jonathan Trumbull, he was educated at Harvard and saw action during the Revolutionary War. In 1780 he traveled to England to study art with Benjamin ◊West and was briefly imprisoned for espionage. In 1789 Trumbull returned to the US to work on a series of historical paintings of Revolutionary War scenes; the most famous was his depiction of the signing of the Declaration of Independence. From 1793 to 1804 he undertook diplomatic assignments in England. He later served as president of the American Academy of Fine Arts 1817–36.

trumpet small high-register ◊brass wind instrument; a doubled tube with valves.

trumpeter any of a family (Psophiidae) of South American birds, up to 20 in/50 cm tall, genus *Psophia*, related to the cranes. They have long legs, a short bill, and dark plumage. The name is also applied to the trumpeter ◊swan.

Truong Sa one of the ◊Spratly Islands, in the South China Sea.

trust arrangement whereby a person or group of people holds property for the benefit of others entitled to the beneficial interest.

A trust can be a legal arrangement under which A is empowered to administer property belonging to B for the benefit of C. A and B may be the same person; B and C may not. A ◊unit trust holds and manages a number of marketable securities; by buying a "unit" in such a trust, the purchaser has a proportionate interest in each of the securities so that his or her risk is spread. Nowadays, an investment trust is not a trust, but a public company investing in marketable securities money subscribed by its stockholders who receive dividends from the income earned. A charitable trust, such as the Ford Foundation, administers funds for charitable purposes. A business trust is formed by linking several companies by transferring shares in them to trustees; or by the creation of a holding company, whose shares are exchanged for those of the separate companies. Competition is thus eliminated, and in the US both types were outlawed by the Sherman Antitrust Act 1890 (first fully enforced by "trust buster" Theodore ◊Roosevelt, as in the breakup of the Standard Oil Company of New Jersey by the Supreme Court 1911).

trust territory territory formerly held under the United Nations trusteeship system to be prepared for independence, either former ◊mandates, territories taken over by the Allies in World War II, or those voluntarily placed under the UN by the administering state.

Truth Sojourner. Adopted name of Isabella Baumfree, later Isabella Van Wagener 1797–1883. US antislavery and women's suffrage campaigner. Born a slave, she ran away and became involved with religious groups. In 1843 she was "commanded in a vision" to adopt the name Sojourner Truth. She published an autobiography, *The Narrative of Sojourner Truth*, in 1850.

truth table in computing, a diagram showing the effect of a particular ◊logic gate on every combination of inputs.

trypanosome any parasitic flagellate protozoan of the genus *Trypanosoma* that lives in the blood of vertebrates, including humans. They often cause serious diseases, called trypanosomiases, such as sleeping sickness or Chagas' disease, and are transmitted by the bite of such insects as tsetse flies or assassin bugs.

trypanosomiasis any of a set of debilitating long-term diseases caused by a trypanosome (protozoan of the genus *Trypanosoma*). They include sleeping sickness (nagana) in Africa, transmitted by the bites of ◊tsetse flies, and ◊Chagas' disease in the Americas, spread by assassin bugs.

Trypanosomes can live in the bloodstream of humans and other vertebrates. Millions of people are affected in warmer regions of the world; the diseases also affect cattle, horses, and wild animals, which form a reservoir of infection.

trypsin enzyme occurring in the small intestine that digests proteins into smaller molecules. Trypsin is secreted by the pancreas in the form of trypsinogen, which is converted into active trypsin by the intestinal enzyme enterokinase. It is also used by industry in the preparation of baby foods.

Ts'ao Chan alternate spelling of the Chinese novelist ◊Cao Chan.

tsar or ***czar*** the Russian imperial title, derived from Latin *caesar*.

Tsaritsyn former name (until 1925) of ◊Volgograd, a city in the USSR.

Tsavo national park in SE Kenya, established 1948. One of the world's largest, it occupies 8,036 sq mi/20,821 sq km.

Tschiffley Aimé Felix 1895–1954. Swiss writer and traveler whose 10,000 mi/16,000 km journey on horseback from Buenos Aires to New York was known as "Tschiffley's Ride," recounted in *Southern Cross to Pole Star* 1933.

tsetse any member of the genus *Glossina* of African flies, some of which transmits the disease nagana to cattle and sleeping sickness to human beings. They grow up to 0.6 in/1.5 cm long.

Tsinan another spelling of ◊Jinan, capital of Shandong province, E China.

Tsingtao another spelling of ◊Qingdao, port in E China.

Tsiolkovsky Konstantin 1857–1935. Russian scientist. He published the first practical paper on astronautics 1903, dealing with space travel by rockets using liquid propellants, such as liquid oxygen.

Tsumeb principal mining center (diamonds, copper, lead, zinc) of N Namibia, NW of Grootfontein; population 13,500.

tsunami (Japanese "harbor wave") giant wave generated by an undersea ◊earthquake or other disturbance. In the open ocean it may take the form of several successive waves, traveling at tens of miles per hour but with an amplitude (height) of approximately 3 feet. In the coastal shallows, tsunamis slow down and build up, producing towering waves that can sweep inland and cause great loss of life and property.

Before each wave there may be a sudden, unexpected withdrawal of water from the beach. Used synonymously with tsunami, the popular term "tidal wave" is misleading.

Tsung Dao Lee 1926– . US physicist whose research centered on the physics of weak interactions between particles. In 1956 Lee proposed that such interactions might disobey certain key assumptions, for instance the conservation of parity. He shared the 1957 Nobel Prize for Physics with his colleague Chen Ning Yang (1922–).

Lee originally trained in China; but a scholarship sent him to the US in 1946, working mostly on particle physics at the Princeton Institue of Advanced Study and at the University of California.

Tsushima Japanese island between Korea and Japan in Tsushima Strait; area 702 sq km/ 271 sq mi. The Russian fleet was destroyed by the Japanese here May 27, 1905 in the ◊Russo-Japanese War. The chief settlement is Izuhara.

Tsvetayeva Marina 1892–1941. Russian poet, born in Moscow. She wrote mythic, romantic, frenetic verse, including *The Demesne of the Swans*. *Selected Poems* was translated 1971.

Tuamotu Archipelago two parallel ranges of 78 atolls, part of ◊French Polynesia; area 266 sq mi/ 690 sq km; population (1983) 11,800, including the ◊Gambier Islands to the E. The atolls stretch 1,300 mi/2,100 km N and E of the Society Islands. The administrative headquarters is Apataki. The largest atoll is Rangiroa, the most significant is Hao; they produce pearl shell and copra. Mururoa and Fangataufa atolls to the SE have been a French nuclear test site since 1966. Spanish explorers landed 1606, and the islands were annexed by France 1881.

Tuareg a member of a nomadic Berber people of the west and central Sahara.

tuatara lizardlike reptile *Sphenodon punctatus*, found only on a few islands off New Zealand. It grows up to 2.3 ft/70 cm long, is greenish-black, and has a spiny crest down its back. On the top of its head is the ◊pineal organ, or so-called "third eye," linked to the brain, which probably acts as a kind of light meter.

It is the sole survivor of the reptilian order Rhynchocephalia. It lays eggs in burrows that it shares with seabirds, and has the longest incubation period of all reptiles (up to 15 months).

tuba large bass ◊brass wind musical instrument.

tube or ***electron tube*** in electronics, a glass tube containing gas at low pressure, which is used to control the flow of electricity in a circuit. Three or more metal electrodes are inset into the tube. By varying the voltage on one of them, called the grid electrode, the current through the tube can be controlled, and the tube can act as an amplifier. They have been replaced for most applications by ◊transistors. However, they are still used in high-power transmitters and amplifiers, and in some hi-fi systems.

tuber swollen region of an underground stem or root, usually modified for storing food. The potato is a stem tuber, as shown by the presence of terminal and lateral buds, the "eyes" of the potato. Root tubers, developed from adventitious roots, lack these. Both types of tuber can give rise to new individuals and so provide a means of ◊vegetative reproduction.

Unlike a bulb, a tuber persists for one season only; new tubers developing on a plant in the following year are formed in different places. See also ◊rhizome.

tuber

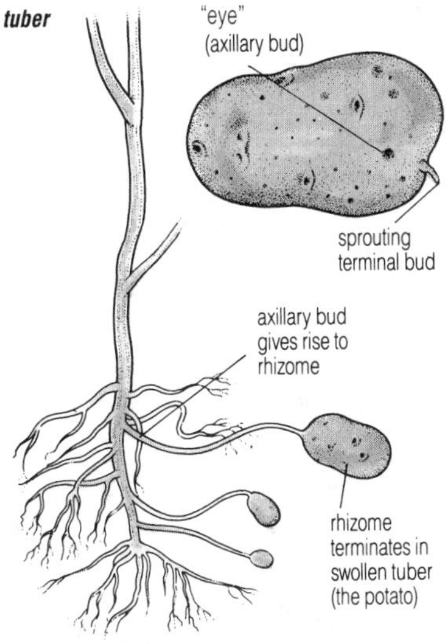
"eye"
(axillary bud)
sprouting
terminal bud
axillary bud
gives rise to
rhizome
rhizome
terminates in
swollen tuber
(the potato)

tuberculosis (TB) formerly known as consumption or phthisis infectious disease caused by the bacillus *Mycobacterium tuberculosis*. It takes several forms, of which pulmonary tuberculosis is by far the most common.

In pulmonary TB, a patch of inflammation develops in the lung, with formation of an abscess. Often, this heals spontaneously, leaving only scar tissue. The dangers are of rapid spread through both lungs (what used to be called "galloping consumption") or the development of miliary tuberculosis (spreading in the bloodstream to other sites) or tuberculous ◊meningitis. The first antituberculosis drug, streptomycin, was developed in 1944.

In practice, most people who are infected do not become ill, and, with public-health measures such as screening people for disease (patch tests) and pasteurization of milk, active tuberculosis is rare in the affluent part of the world. It still threatens, however, where there is malnutrition and overcrowding. Vulnerable populations may be protected by means of the ◊BCG vaccine.

tuberose Mexican flowering plant *Polianthes tuberosa* of the ◊agave family, grown as a sweet-smelling greenhouse plant.

Tübingen town in Baden-Württemberg, Federal Republic of Germany, on the river Neckar, 30 km/19 m S of Stuttgart; population (1985) 75,000. Industries include paper, textiles, and surgical instruments. It was capital of the French zone of occupation after World War II.

Tubman Harriet Ross 1821–1913. US abolitionist. Born a slave in Maryland, she escaped to Philadelphia (where slavery was outlawed) 1849. She set up the Underground Railroad, a secret network of sympathizers, to help slaves escape to the North and Canada. During the American ◊Civil War she served as a spy for the Union army. She spoke against slavery and for women's rights, and founded schools for emancipated slaves after the Civil War.

Tubman William V S 1895–1971. Liberian politician. The descendant of US slaves, he was a lawyer in the US. After his election to the presidency of Liberia 1944 he concentrated on uniting the various ethnic groups. Re-elected several times, he died naturally in office despite frequent assassination attempts.

Tubuai Islands or ***Austral Islands*** chain of volcanic islands and reefs 800 mi/1,300 km long in ◊French Polynesia, S of the Society Islands; area 57 sq mi/148 sq km; population (1983) 6,300. The main settlement is Mataura on Tubuai. They were visited by Captain Cook 1777 and annexed by France 1880.

Tucana constellation of the southern hemisphere, represented as a toucan. It contains the second most prominent ◊globular cluster in the sky, 47 Tucanae, and the Small ◊Magellanic Cloud. It is one of the 11 constellations named by Johann Bayer (1572–1625) early in the 17th century to complement the 65 constellations delineated by the ancients.

Tucson resort city in the Sonora Desert in SE Arizona; population (1990) 405,390. It stands 2,500 ft/760 m above sea level, and the Santa Catalina Mountains to the NE rise to about 9,000 ft/2,750 m. Industries include aircraft, electronics, and copper smelting. The University of Arizona is here, and Kitt Peak National Observatory is in the area. An Indian village was on the site when a Jesuit mission was founded about 1700. A Spanish fort, and eventually a settlement, grew around the mission. Tucson passed from Mexico to the US 1853 and was the territorial capital 1867–77. Growth has been rapid since World War II.

Tucumán or ***San Miguel de Tucumán*** capital of Tucumán province, NW Argentina, on the Rio Sali, in the foothills of the Andes; population (1980) 497,000. Industries include sugar mills and distilleries. Founded 1565, Tucumán was the site of the signing of the Argentine declaration of independence from Spain 1816.

tucu-tuco any member of the genus *Ctenomys*, a burrowing South American rodent about 8 in/ 20 cm long with a 3 in/7 cm tail. It has a large head, sensitive ears, and enormous incisor teeth.

Tuco-tucos spend most of their time below ground in a burrow system, generally one animal to a burrow. The name tucu-tuco is an attempt to imitate the bubbling call.

Tudor English dynasty descended from the Welsh Owen Tudor (c. 1400–1461), the second husband of Catherine of Valois (the widow of Henry V of England). Their son Edmund married Margaret Beaufort (1443–1509), the great-granddaughter of ◊John of Gaunt, and was the father of Henry VII, who ascended the throne 1485. The dynasty ended with the death of Elizabeth I 1603.

The dynasty was portrayed in a favorable light in Shakespeare's history plays.

tufa or ***travertine*** a soft, porous, ◊limestone rock, white in color, deposited from solution from carbonate-saturated ground water around hot springs and in caves.

Tu Fu or ***Du Fu*** 712–770. Chinese poet who wrote about the social injustices of his time, peasant suffering, and war, as in "The Army Carts."

Tukano member of an indigenous South American Indian people of the Vaupés region on the Colombian-Brazilian border, numbering approximately 2,000.

Tula city in W central USSR, on the river Upa, 121 mi/193 km S of Moscow; population (1987) 538,000. Industries include engineering and metallurgy. Site of the government ordnance factory, founded 1712 by Peter the Great.

Tula de Allende town in Mexico, near the site of the ancient Toltec Indian capital.

Tulare city in S central California, S of Fresno, in the San Joaquin Valley. Industries include food processing, wine, and dairy products; population (1990) 33,249. It was built 1871 as a division headquarters for the Southern Pacific Railroad.

tulip plant of the genus *Tulipa*, family Liliaceae, usually with single goblet-shaped flowers on the end of an upright stem and leaves of a narrow oval shape with pointed ends. It is widely cultivated as a garden flower.

Tulipa gesnerana, from which most of the garden cultivars have been derived, probably originated in the Middle East. Quickly adopted in Europe during the 16th century, it became a craze in 17th-century Holland when extravagant prices were paid for bulbs of rare colors. Today it is commercially cultivated on a large scale in the Netherlands and East Anglia, England.

The tulip tree *Liriodendron tulipifera* of the

tulip

eastern US is a member of the magnolia family, with large, tulip-shaped blooms.

Tull Jethro 1674–1741. English agriculturist who about 1701 developed a drill that enabled seeds to be sown mechanically and spaced so that cultivation between rows was possible in the growth period. His major work, *Horse-Hoeing Husbandry*, was published 1731.

Tulsa city in NE Oklahoma, on the Arkansas river, NE of Oklahoma City. It is an oil-producing and aerospace center; other industries include mining, machinery, metals, and cement; population (1990) 367,302.

tumor overproduction of cells in a specific area of the body, often leading to a swelling or lump. Tumors are classified as benign or malignant (see ◊cancer).

Benign tumors grow more slowly, do not invade surrounding tissues, do not spread to other parts of the body, and do not usually recur after removal. However, some benign tumors can be dangerous, such as in areas like the brain. The most familiar types of benign tumor are warts on the skin. In some cases, there is no sharp dividing line between benign and malignant tumors.

tuna any of various large marine bony fishes of the mackerel family, especially the genus *Thunnus*, popular as food and game. Albacore *T. alalunga*, bluefin tuna *T. thynnus*, and yellowfin tuna *T. albacores* are commercially important.

Tunbs, the two islands in the Strait of Hormuz, formerly held by Ras al Khaimah and annexed from other Gulf states by Iran 1971; their return to their former owners was an Iraqi aim in the Iran–Iraq War.

tundra region of high latitude almost devoid of trees, resulting from the presence of ◊permafrost. The vegetation consists mostly of grasses, sedges, heather, mosses, and lichens. Tundra stretches in a continous belt across N North America and Eurasia.

tung oil oil used in paints and varnishes, obtained from trees of the genus *Aleurites*, family Euphorbiaceae, native to China.

tungsten hard, heavy, gray-white, metallic element, symbol W (from German *Wolfram*), atomic number 74, atomic weight 183.85. It occurs in the minerals wolframite, scheelite, and hubertite. It has the highest melting point of any metal (6,170°F/3,410°C) and is added to steel to make it harder, stronger, and more elastic; its other uses include high-speed cutting tools, electrical elements, and thermionic couplings. Its salts are used in the paint and tanning industries.

Tungsten was first recognized in 1781 by Swedish chemist Karl Scheele in the ore scheelite (originally called *tung sten*, "heavy stone," in Swedish). It was isolated in 1783 by the Spanish chemists Fausto D'Elhuyar (1755–1833) and his brother Juan José (1754–1796).

tungsten ore one of the two main minerals, wolframite $(FeMn)WO_4$, and scheelite, $CaWO_4$, from which tungsten is extracted. Most of the world's tungsten reserves are in China, but the main suppliers are Bolivia, Australia, Canada, and the US.

Tunguska Event explosion at Tunguska, central Siberia, Russia, in June 1908 which devastated around 2,500 sq mi/6,500 sq km of forest. It is thought to have been caused by either a cometary nucleus or a fragment of ◊Encke's comet. The magnitude of the explosion was equivalent to an atomic bomb and produced a colossal shock wave; a bright falling object was seen 375 mi/600 km away and was heard up to 625 mi/1,000 km away.

An expedition to the site was made in 1927. The central area of devastation was occupied by trees that were erect but stripped of their branches. Farther out, to a radius of 12 mi/20 km, trees were flattened and laid out radially.

tundra

tundra habitat

The landscape around the ice caps at the North and South Poles consists of an open treeless plain called tundra, or muskeg in North America. Winters last for about eight or nine months and the temperature can fall to −85°F (−30°C). The ground is frozen for most of the year, and in the summer there is only time for the topmost layer of soil to thaw. The meltwater cannot drain away and this gives rise to a waterlogged landscape where only low stunted plants grow. Insects flourish during the short summer, and birds migrate into the area to feed on them. Other animals winter in the forests in warmer latitudes and migrate into the region in the summer.

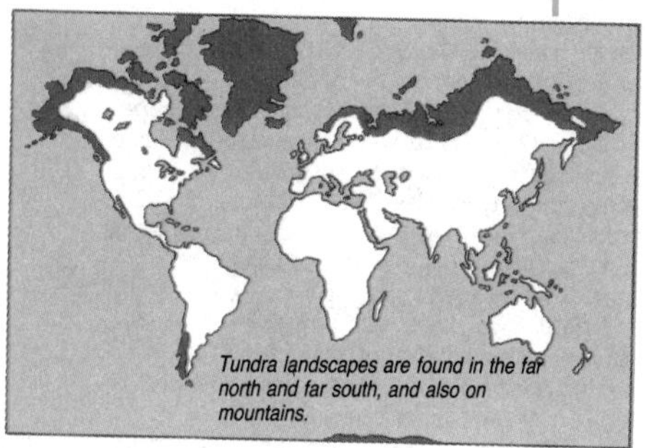
Tundra landscapes are found in the far north and far south, and also on mountains.

Herds of reindeer migrate into the area in the summer to feed on vegetation. Clouds of insects emerge from the ponds and lakes to take advantage of the brief period of sunlight.
reindeer
Water from a spring may freeze underground and eventually force up a dome-shaped hill of ice known as a a pingo.
insects
Arctic hare
Arctic foxes
Expansion and contraction of freezing soil produces wedges of ice that split the ground into polygonal shapes. The outlines of the polygons are marked by channels of rocks or by distinctive vegetation.
Some animals, such as Arctic foxes, develop a white coat in winter.
In the summer only the top several feet of soil can thaw. Below this the ground remains permanently frozen – a condition known as permafrost.
ducks
Canada geese
In winter, the low ground-hugging plants are blanketed and insulated by snow.

tunicate alternative name for ◊sea squirt.

tuning fork in music, a device for providing a reference pitch. It is made from hardened metal and consists of parallel bars about 4 in/10 cm long joined at one end and terminating in a blunt point. When the fork is struck and the point placed on a wooden surface, a pure tone is heard. There are tuning forks for each musical pitch; A is known as "concert pitch," since the instruments of the orchestra and the singers of the chorus are tuned to A above middle C.

Tunis capital and chief port of Tunisia; population (1984) 597,000. Industries include chemicals and textiles. Founded by the Arabs, it was occupied by the French 1881 and by the Axis powers 1942–43. The ruins of ancient ◊Carthage are to the NE.

Tunisia country in N Africa, on the Mediterranean, bounded SE by Libya and W by Algeria.

government The constitution was adopted 1959, providing for a president who is both head of state and head of government, elected by universal suffrage for a five-year term and eligible for reelection. The president governs through an appointed council of ministers. There is a single-chamber national assembly of 141 members, elected in the same way and for the same term as the president.

history Founded as ◊Carthage by the Phoenicians in the 8th century BC, Tunisia was under Arab rule from the 7th century AD until it became part of the ◊Ottoman Empire 1574. It harbored the ◊Barbary pirates until the 19th century. It became a French protectorate 1881.

Tunisia

Tunisian Republic
(al-Jumhuriya at-Tunisiya)

MEDITERRANEAN SEA
Tunis
TUNISIA
Algeria
Libya
0 miles 500
0 km 1000

area 63,378 sq mi/164,150 sq km
capital (and chief port) Tunis
cities ports Sfax, Sousse, Bizerta
physical arable and forested land in N graduates toward desert in S
features fertile island of Jerba, linked to mainland by causeway and identified with the island of lotus-eaters; Shott el Jerid salt lakes; holy city of Kairouan, ruins of Carthage
head of state and government Zine el Abdin Ben Ali from 1987
political system emergent democratic republic
political parties Constitutional Democratic Rally (RDC), nationalist, moderate, Socialist
exports oil, phosphates, chemicals, textiles, food, olive oil
currency dinar
population (1990 est) 8,094,000; growth rate 2% p.a.
life expectancy men 68, women 71 (1989)
language Arabic (official), French
religion Sunni Muslim 95%; Jewish, Christian
literacy men 68%/women 41% (1985 est)
GNP $9.6 bn (1987); $1,163 per head (1986)
chronology
1883 Became a French protectorate.
1955 Granted internal self-government.
1956 Independence achieved from France as a monarchy, with Habib Bourguiba as prime minister.
1957 Became a republic with Bourguiba as president.
1975 Bourguiba made president for life.
1985 Diplomatic relations with Libya severed.
1987 Bourguiba removed Prime Minister Rashed Sfar and appointed Zine el Abdin Ben Ali. Ben Ali declared Bourguiba incompetent and seized power.
1988 Constitutional changes toward democracy announced. Diplomatic relations with Libya restored.
1989 Government party, RDC, won all assembly seats in general election.
1991 Crackdown on religious fundamentalists.

The Socialist Destourien Party (PSD), founded 1934 by Habib Bourguiba, led Tunisia's campaign for independence from France. The country achieved internal self-government 1955 and full independence 1956, with Bourguiba as prime minister. A year later the monarchy was abolished, and Tunisia became a republic, with Bourguiba as president. A new constitution was adopted 1959, and the first national assembly elected. Between 1963 and 1981 PSD was the only legally recognized party, but since then others have been allowed. In Nov 1986 PSD won all the assembly seats, while other parties boycotted the elections.

President Bourguiba followed a distinctive foreign policy, establishing links with the Western powers, including the US, but joining other Arab states in condemning the US-inspired Egypt–Israel treaty. He allowed the Palestine Liberation Organization (PLO) to use Tunis as its headquarters, and this led to an Israeli attack 1985

Tunisia *The fortified mosque or* ribat *in Sousse.*

that strained relations with the US. Diplomatic links with Libya were severed 1985.

Bourguiba's firm and paternalistic rule, and his long period in Tunisian politics, made him a national legend, evidenced by the elaborate mausoleum that was built in anticipation of his death. However, in Nov 1987 he was deposed and replaced by Zine al-Abidine Ben Ali. In July 1988, a number of significant constitutional changes were announced, presaging a move to more pluralist politics, but in the April 1989 elections the RDC won all 141 assembly seats. In 1991, Tunisia opposed US actions in the Gulf War.

tunnel passageway through a mountain, under a body of water, or under ground. Tunneling is a significant branch of civil engineering in both mining and transport. In the 19th century there were two major advances: the use of compressed air within underwater tunnels to balance the external pressure of water, and the development of the tunnel shield to support the face and assist excavation. In recent years there have been notable developments in linings (for example, concrete segments and steel liner plates), and in the use of rotary diggers and cutters and explosives.

Major tunnels include:

Orange–Fish River (South Africa) 1975, longest irrigation tunnel, 51 mi/82 km;

Chesapeake Bay Bridge-Tunnel (USA) 1963, combined bridge, causeway, and tunnel structure, 17.5 mi/28 km;

St Gotthard (Switzerland–Italy) 1980, longest road tunnel, 10.1 mi/16.3 km;

Seikan (Japan) 1964–85, longest rail tunnel, Honshu–Hokkaido, under Tsugaru Strait, 33.5 mi/53.9 km, 14.5 mi/23.3 km under water (however, a bullet-train service is no longer economical);

Simplon (Switzerland–Italy) 1906, longest rail tunnel on land, 12.3 mi/19.8 km;

Rogers Pass (Canada) 1989, longest tunnel in the western hemisphere, 22 mi/35 km long, through the Selkirk Mountains, British Columbia.

A ◊Channel tunnel, or Chunnel, beneath the English Channel was first planned as a military measure by the French emperor Napoleon 1802. Later, in the 1880s, excavations were made from both shores but work was halted by Parliament for security reasons. In 1986 a plan for twin rail tunnels was approved by the French and British governments, and work is under way with a schedule for completion in the early 1990s.

Tunney Gene 1898–1978. US prizefighter. As a professional he won the US light-heavyweight title 1922. Tunney began to fight as a heavyweight in 1924 and was the upset winner over heavyweight champion Jack Dempsey 1926. Tunney retained the title against Dempsey in the famous "Long Count" bout 1927 and retired undefeated 1928. He later became a successful businessman and published *A Man Must Fight* 1932 and *Arms for Living* 1941.

Born in New York, Tunney attended LaSalle Academy and worked as a steamship clerk 1912–17. As an amateur boxer, he won the US armed forces championship in Paris 1919.

Túpac Amarú adopted name of José Gabriel Condorcanqui c. 1742–1781. Peruvian Indian revolutionary leader, executed for his revolt against Spanish rule 1780; he claimed to be descended from the last chieftain of the Incas.

Tupamaros urban guerrilla movement operating in Uruguay, largely active in the 1960s–70s, named after the 18th-century revolutionary Túpac Amarú.

turbine engine in which steam, water, gas, or air (see ◊windmill) is made to spin a rotating shaft by pushing on angled blades, like a fan. Turbines are among the most powerful machines. Steam turbines are used to drive generators in power stations and ships' propellers; water turbines spin the generators in hydroelectric power plants; and gas turbines (as jet engines) power most aircraft and drive machines in industry.

The high-temperature, high-pressure steam for steam turbines is raised in boilers heated by furnaces burning coal, oil, or gas, or by nuclear energy. A steam turbine consists of a shaft, or rotor, which rotates inside a fixed casing (stator). The rotor carries "wheels" consisting of blades, or vanes. The stator has vanes set between the vanes of the rotor, which direct the steam through the rotor vanes at the optimum angle. When steam expands through the turbine, it spins the rotor by ◊reaction. The steam engine of Hero of Alexandria (130 BC), called the *eolipile*, was the prototype of this type of turbine, called a reaction turbine. Modern development of the reaction turbine is largely due to Charles ◊Parsons. Less widely used is the impulse turbine, patented by Carl Gustaf Patrick de Laval (1845–1913) 1882. It works by directing a jet of steam at blades on a rotor. Similarly there are reaction and impulse water turbines: impulse turbines work on the same principle as the water wheel and consist of sets of buckets arranged around the edge of a wheel; reaction turbines look much like propellers and are fully immersed in the water. In a gas turbine a compressed mixture of air and gas, or vaporized fuel, is ignited, and the hot gases produced expand through the turbine blades, spinning the rotor. In the industrial gas turbine, the rotor shaft drives machines. In the jet engine, the turbine drives the compressor, which supplies the compressed air to the engine, but most of the power developed comes from the jet exhaust in the form of propulsive thrust.

turbocharger turbine-driven device fitted to engines to force more air into the cylinders, producing extra power. The turbocharger consists of a "blower," or compressor, driven by a turbine, which in most units is driven by the exhaust gases leaving the engine.

turbofan the type of jet engine used by most airliners, so called because added to the conventional ◊turbojet engine is a huge front fan. The fan sends air not only into the engine for combustion but also noncombusted air around the engine for additional thrust. This results in a faster and more fuel-efficient propulsive jet. See ◊jet propulsion.

turbojet jet engine that derives its thrust from a jet of hot exhaust gases.

turbocharger

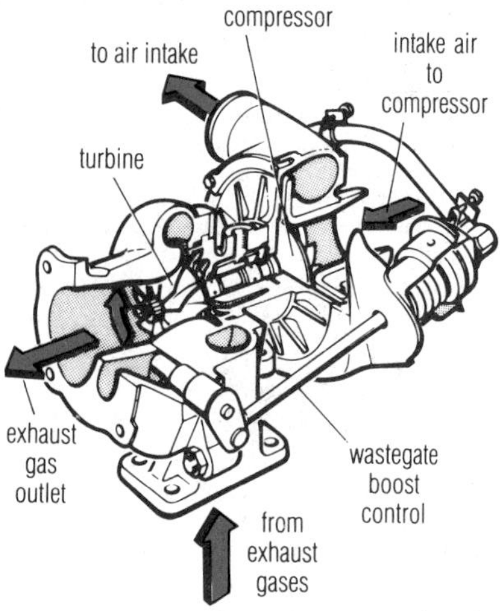
compressor
to air intake
intake air to compressor
turbine
exhaust gas outlet
wastegate boost control
from exhaust gases

A single-shaft turbojet consists of a shaft (rotor) rotating in a casing. At the front is a multiblade compressor, which takes in and compresses air and delivers it to one or more combustion chambers. Fuel (kerosene) is then sprayed in and ignited. The hot gases expand through a nozzle at the rear of the engine after spinning a ◊turbine. The turbine drives the compressor. Reaction to the backward stream of gases produces a forward propulsive thrust.

turboprop jet engine that derives its thrust partly from a jet of exhaust gases, but mainly from a propeller powered by a turbine in the jet exhaust. Turboprops are more economical than turbojets but can be used only at relatively low speeds.

A turboprop typically has a twin-shaft rotor. One shaft carries the compressor and is spun by one turbine, while the other shaft carries a propeller and is spun by a second turbine.

turbot any of various flatfishes of the flounder group prized as food, especially *Scophthalmus maximus* found in European waters. It grows up to 3 ft/1 m long and weighs up to 30 lb/14 kg. It is brownish above and whitish underneath.

Turenne Henry de la Tour d'Auvergne, Vicomte de 1611–1675. French marshal under Louis XIV, known for his siege technique.

Turgenev Ivan Sergeievich 1818–1883. Russian writer, notable for poetic realism, pessimism, and skill in characterization. His works include the play *A Month in the Country* 1849, and the novels *A Nest of Gentlefolk* 1858, *Fathers and Sons* 1862, and *Virgin Soil* 1877. His series *A Sportsman's Sketches* 1852 criticized serfdom.

turgor the rigid condition of a plant caused by the fluid contents of a plant cell exerting a mechanical pressure against the cell wall. Turgor supports plants that do not have woody stems.

Turgot Anne Robert Jacques 1727–1781. French finance minister 1774–76, whose reforming economies led to his dismissal.

Turin (Italian *Torino*) capital of Piedmont, NW Italy, on the river Po; population (1988) 1,025,000. Industries include iron, steel, automobiles, silk and other textiles, fashion goods, chocolate, and wine. It was the first capital of united Italy 1861–64.

Turing Alan Mathison 1912–1954. British mathematician and logician. In 1936 he described a "universal computing machine" that could theoretically be programmed to solve any problem capable of solution by a specially designed machine. This concept, now called the Turing machine, foreshadowed the digital computer.

Turing studied at King's College, Cambridge, and became a fellow there in 1935. He studied at Princeton, New Jersey, 1936–38. During World War II he worked on the Ultra project in the team that cracked the German Enigma code. He is

turkey

believed to have been the first to suggest the possibility of machine learning and artificial intelligence. His test for distinguishing between real (human) and simulated (computer) thought is known as the Turing test: with a person in one room and the machine in another, an interrogator in a third room asks questions of both to try to identify them. When the interrogator cannot distinguish between them by questioning, the machine will have reached a state of human-like intelligence.

Turin shroud ancient piece of linen bearing the image of a body, claimed to be that of Jesus. Independent tests carried out 1988 by scientists in Switzerland, the US, and the UK showed that the cloth of the shroud dated from between 1260 and 1390. The shroud, property of the pope, is kept in Turin Cathedral, Italy.

Turk member of any of the Turkic-speaking peoples of Asia and Europe, especially the principal ethnic group of Turkey. Turkic languages belong to the Altaic family and include Uzbek, Ottoman, Turkish, Azerbaijani, Turkoman, Tatar, Kirghiz, and Yakut.

Turkana, Lake formerly Lake Rudolf lake in the Great Rift Valley, 1,230 ft/375 m above sea level, with its northernmost end in Ethiopia and the rest in Kenya; area 3,475 sq mi/9,000 sq km. It is saline, and shrinking by evaporation. Its shores were an early human hunting ground, and valuable remains have been found that are accurately datable because of undisturbed stratification.

Turkestan area of central Asia divided among USSR (Kazakh, Kirghiz, Tadzhik, Turkmen, and Uzbek republics), Afghanistan, and China (part of Xinjiang Uygur).

turkey any of several large game birds of the pheasant family, native to the Americas. The wild turkey *Meleagris galloparvo* reaches a length of 4.3 ft/1.3 m, and is native to North and Central American woodlands. The domesticated turkey derives from the wild species. The ocellated turkey *Agriocharis ocellata* is found in Central America; it has eyespots on the tail.

The domesticated turkey was introduced to Europe in the 16th century. Since World War II, it has been intensively bred, in the same way as the chicken. It is gregarious, except at breeding time.

Turkey country between the Black Sea and the Mediterranean, bounded E by the USSR and Iran, S by Iraq and Syria.

government The constitution of 1982 provides for a single-chamber legislature of 450 members, the National Assembly, and a president who is both head of state and head of government. The president is elected by the assembly for a seven-year term. The assembly is elected by universal suffrage for a five-year term.

history The Turks originally came from Mongolia and spread into Turkestan in the 6th century AD. During the 7th century they adopted Islam. In 1055 the ◊Seljuk Turks secured political control of the caliphate and established an empire in Asia Minor. The ◊Ottoman Turks, driven from central Asia by the Mongols, entered the service of the Seljuks, and Osman I founded a kingdom of his own 1299. Having overrun Asia Minor, the Ottomans began their European conquests by seizing Gallipoli 1354, captured Constantinople 1453, and by 1480 were masters of the Balkans. By 1550 they had conquered Egypt, Syria, Arabia, Mesopotamia, Tripoli, and most of Hungary; thereafter the empire ceased to expand, although Cyprus was taken 1571 and Crete 1669.

The Christian counter-offensive opened 1683 with the defeat of the Turks before Vienna; in 1699 the Turks lost Hungary, and in 1774 Russia ousted them from Moldavia, Wallachia, and the Crimea. In the Balkans there was an unsuccessful revolt in Serbia 1804, but in 1821–29 Greece threw off Turkish rule. Russia's attempts to exploit this situation were resisted by Britain and France, which in the Crimean War (1854–56) fought on the Turkish side. The Bulgarian uprising of 1876 led to a new war between Turkey and Russia, and by the Treaty of Berlin 1878 Turkey lost Bulgaria, Bosnia, and Herzegovina. A militant nationalist group, the Young Turks, secured the grant of a constitution 1908; Italy took advantage of the ensuing crisis to seize Tripoli in 1911–12, while the Balkan states in 1912–13 expelled the Turks from Albania and Macedonia. Turkey entered World War I on the German side 1914, only to lose Syria, Arabia, Mesopotamia, and its nominal suzerainty in Egypt.

The Greek occupation of Izmir 1919 provoked the establishment of a nationalist congress with Mustafa Kemal (◊Atatürk) as president. Having defeated Italian and French forces, he expelled the Greeks 1922. Peace was concluded 1923 with the Treaty of ◊Lausanne and Turkey was proclaimed an independent republic with Kemal as its first president. He introduced a policy of westernization and a new legal code. He died 1938, but his People's Party remained in power.

Turkey's first free elections were held 1950 and won by the Democratic Party (DP), led by Celal Bayar and Adnan Menderes. Bayar became president and Menderes prime minister. In 1960, after a military coup, President Bayar was imprisoned and Menderes executed. A new constitution was adopted 1961 and civilian rule restored, but with the leader of the coup, General Cemal Gursel, as president. There followed a series of civilian governments, led mainly by the veteran politician Ismet Inonu until 1965, when the Justice Party (JP), led by Suleyman Demirel, came to power. Prompted by strikes and student unrest, the army forced Demirel to resign 1971, and for the next two years the country came under military rule again.

A civilian government was restored 1973, a coalition led by Bulent Ecevit. The following year Turkey sent troops to Cyprus to protect the Turkish-Cypriot community, resulting in the effective partition of the island. Ecevit's government fell when he refused to annex N Cyprus, and in 1975 Suleyman Demirel returned at the head of a right-wing coalition. Elections held 1977 were inconclusive, and Demirel precariously held on to power until 1978 when Ecevit returned, leading another coalition. He was faced with a deteriorating economy and outbreaks of sectional violence and by 1979 had lost his working majority and resigned.

Demirel returned in Nov, but the violence continued and in Sept 1980 the army stepped in and set up a national security council, with Bulent Ulusu as prime minister. Martial law was imposed, political activity suspended, and a harsh regime established. Strong international pressure was put on Turkey to return to a more democratic system of government, and in May 1983 political parties were allowed to operate again. The old parties reformed under new names and in Nov three of them contested the assembly elections: the conservative Motherland Party (ANAP), the

Turkey

Republic of
(Türkiye Cumhuriyeti)

USSR
BLACK SEA
Bulgaria
Greece
Ankara
TURKEY
Iran
Syria
Iraq
MEDITERRANEAN SEA
0 miles 500
0 km 1000

area 300,965 sq mi/779,500 sq km
capital Ankara
cities ports Istanbul and Izmir
physical central plateau surrounded by mountains
features Bosporus and Dardanelles; Mount Ararat; Taurus Mountains in SW (highest peak Kaldi Daĝ, 12,255 ft/3,734 m); sources of rivers Euphrates and Tigris in E; archeological sites include Catal Hüyük, Ephesus, and Troy; rock villages of Cappadocia; historic towns (Antioch, Iskenderun, Tarsus)
head of state Turgot Ozal from 1989
head of government Vildirim Akbulut from 1989
political system democratic republic
political parties Motherland Party (ANAP), Islamic, nationalist, right-of-center; Social Democratic Populist Party (SDPP), moderate, left-of-center; True Path Party (TPP), center-right
exports cotton, yarn, hazelnuts, citrus, tobacco, dried fruit, chromium ores
currency Turkish lira
population (1990 est) 56,549,000 (85% Turkish, 12% Kurdish); growth rate 2.1% p.a.
life expectancy men 63, women 66 (1989)
language Turkish (official); Kurdish, Arabic
religion Sunni Muslim 98%
literacy men 86%/women 62% (1985)
GNP $62 bn (1987); $1,160 per head (1986)
chronology
1919–22 Turkish War of Independence provoked by Greek occupation of Izmir. Mustafa Kemal (Atatürk), leader of nationalist congress, defeated Italian, French, and Greek forces.
1923 Treaty of Lausanne established Turkey as independent republic under Kemal. Westernization began.
1950 First free elections; Adnan Menderes became prime minister.
1960 Menderes executed after military coup by Gen Cemal Gürsel.
1965 Suleyman Demirel became prime minister.
1971 Army forced Demirel to resign.
1973 Civilian rule returned under Bulent Ecevit.
1974 Turkish troops sent to protect Turkish community in Cyprus.
1975 Demirel returned to head of a right-wing coalition.
1978 Ecevit returned, in the face of economic difficulties and factional violence.
1979 Demeril returned. Violence grew.
1980 Army took over, and Bulent Ulusu became prime minister. Harsh repression of political activists attracted international criticism.
1982 New constitution adopted.
1983 Ban on political activity lifted. Turgut Ozal became prime minister.
1987 Ozal maintained majority in general election.
1988 Improved relations and talks with Greece.
1989 Turgot Ozal elected president. Application for EC membership refused.
1991 Turkey sides with UN coalition against Iraq in Gulf War; Conflict with Kurdish minority continues.

Nationalist Democracy Party (MDP), and the Populist Party (SDHP). ANAP won 212 assembly seats, SDHP 117, and MDP 71, and ANAP's leader, Turgut Ozal, became prime minister. Since 1984 there has been guerrilla fighting in ◊Kurdistan, and a separatist Kurdish Workers' Party (PKK) is active.

After World War II Turkey felt itself threatened by the USSR and joined a number of military alliances, including NATO 1952 and the Baghdad Pact 1955, which became the Central Treaty Organization 1959 and was dissolved 1979. Turkey strengthened Western links and by 1987 was making overtures to the European Community. During the 1990–91 ◊Gulf War, Turkey supported the UN forces, allowing use of vital bases in the country.

turkish bath a type of bathing that involves exposure to warm air and steam, followed by massage and cold water immersion. Originating from Roman and East Indian traditions, the concept was introduced to Western Europe by the Crusaders but only became popular when hot water could be supplied in sufficient quantities.

Turkish language language of central and W Asia, the national language of Turkey. Originally written in Arabic script, the Turkish of Turkey has been written in a variant of the Roman alphabet since 1928. Varieties of Turkish are spoken in NW Iran and several of the Asian republics of the USSR, and all have been influenced by Arabic and Persian.

Turkish literature for centuries Turkish literature was based on Persian models, but under ◊Suleiman the Great (1494–1566) the Golden Age began, of which the poet Fuzuli (died 1563) is the great exemplar, and continued in the following century with the great poet satirist Nefi of Erzerum (died 1635) and others. During the 19th century westernization overtook Turkish literature, as in the use of French models by Ibrahim Shinasi Effendi (1826-1871), poet and prose writer. Effendi was cofounder of the New School with Mehmed Namik Kemal (1840–1880), poet and author of the revolutionary play *Vatan/The Fatherland*, which led to his exile by the sultan. Unlike these, the poet Tevfik Fikret (1867–1915) turned rather to Persian and Arabic than to native sources for his vocabulary. The poet Mehmed Akif (1873–1936) was the author of the words of the Turkish national anthem, and the work of the contemporary poet and novelist Yashar Kemal (1923–) describes the hard life of the peasant (*Memed, My Hawk* 1955 and *The Wind from the Plain* 1961).

Turkmenistan republic, formerly constituent republic of the USSR 1924–91, part of Soviet Central Asia
area 188,455 sq mi/488,100 sq km
capital Ashkhabad
features Kara Kum "Black Sands" desert, which occupies most of the republic, area about 120,000 sq mi/310,800 sq km (on its edge is Altyn Depe, "golden hill," site of a ruined city with a ziggurat); river Amu Darya
products silk, sheep, astrakhan fur, carpets, oil, chemicals
population (1987) 3,361,000; 69% Turkmenian, 13% Russian, 9% Uzbek, 3% Kazakh
language West Turkic, closely related to ◊Turkish
religion Sunni Muslim.

Turkmenistan

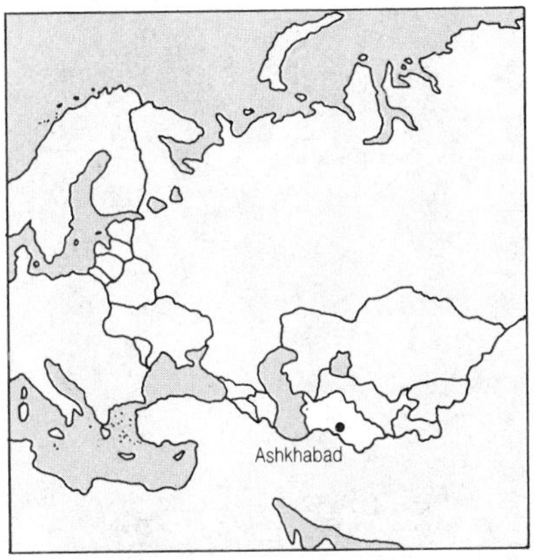
Ashkhabad

Turkoman or ***Turkmen*** member of a Turkic-speaking people living around the Kara-Kum desert, to the E of the Caspian Sea, along the borders of Afghanistan and Iran, and within several republics in the USSR. Their language belongs to the Turkic branch of the Altaic family.

Turks and Caicos Islands British crown colony in the West Indies, the SE archipelago of the Bahamas
area 166 sq mi/430 sq km
capital Cockburn Town on Grand Turk features a group of 30 islands, of which six are inhabited. The largest is the uninhabited Grand Caicos; others include Grand Turk (population 3,100), South Caicos (1,400), Middle Caicos (400), North Caicos (1,300), Providenciales (1,000), and Salt Cay (300); since 1982 the Turks and Caicos have developed as a tax haven
government governor, with executive and legislative councils (chief minister from 1985 Nathaniel Francis, Progressive National Party)
exports crayfish and conch (flesh and shell)
population (1980) 7,500, 90% of African descent
language English, French Creole
religion Christian
history secured by Britain 1766 against French and Spanish claims, the islands were a Jamaican dependency 1873–1962, and in 1976 attained internal self-government. The chief minister, Norman Saunders, resigned 1985 after his arrest in Miami on drug charges, of which he was convicted

Turku (Swedish *Åbo*) port in SW Finland, near the mouth of the river Aura, on the Gulf of Bothnia; population (1988) 262,000. Industries include shipbuilding, engineering, textiles, and food processing. It was the capital of Finland until 1812.

turmeric perennial plant *Curcuma longa* of the ginger family, native to India and the East Indies; also the ground powder from its tuberous rhizomes, used in curries to give a yellow color, and as a dyestuff.

Turner Frederick Jackson 1861–1932. US historian, professor at Harvard University 1910–24. He emphasized the significance of the frontier in US historical development, attributing the distinctive character of US society to the influence of changing frontiers over three centuries of westward expansion.

Turner John Napier 1929– . Canadian Liberal politician, prime minister 1984. He was elected to the House of Commons 1962 and served in the cabinet of Pierre Trudeau until resigning 1975. He succeeded Trudeau as party leader and prime minister 1984, but lost the 1984 and 1988 elections. Turner resigned as leader 1989, and returned to his law practice. He was replaced as Liberal Party chief by Herbert Gray in Feb 1990.

Turner Joseph Mallord William 1775–1851. English landscape painter. He traveled widely in Europe, and his landscapes became increasingly Romantic, with the subject often transformed in scale and

Turner The Fighting Téméraire *1838 by English landscape painter J M W Turner, who was noted for his interpretation of light.*

flooded with brilliant, hazy light. Many later works anticipate Impressionism, for example *Rain, Steam and Speed* 1844 (National Gallery, London).

A precocious talent, Turner went to the Royal Academy schools in 1789. In 1792 he made the first of several European tours, from which numerous watercolor sketches survive. His early oil paintings show Dutch influence, but by the 1800s he had begun to paint landscapes in the grand manner, reflecting the styles of ◊Claude Lorrain and Richard ◊Wilson.

Many of Turner's most dramatic works are set in Europe or at sea: for example, *Shipwreck* 1805, *Snowstorm: Hannibal Crossing the Alps* 1812 (both Tate Gallery, London), and *The Slave Ship* 1839 (Museum of Fine Arts, Boston, Massachusetts).

Turner Lana (Julia Jean Mildred Frances) 1920– US actress who appeared as a sultry blonde beauty in melodramatic films of the 1940s and 1950s such as *Peyton Place* 1958. Her other films include the classic version of *The Postman Always Rings Twice* 1946, *The Three Musketeers* 1948, and *Imitation of Life* 1959.

Her debut was in *They Won't Forget* 1937, after her legendary "discovery" at a Hollywood soda fountain at the age of 16. By the mid 1940s she was a star, and she proved her acting ability in *The Bad and the Beautiful* 1952. In the 1960s, she starred in glossy Douglas Sirk and Ross Hunter productions.

Turner Nat 1800–1831. US slave, who led 60 slaves in the most serious US slave revolt—the Southampton Insurrection of 1831—to capture an armory in Southampton County, Virginia. Before he and 16 of the others were hanged, at least 55 people throughout the region, 24 of them children, had been killed. He thought himself divinely appointed to lead the slaves to freedom. He eluded capture for 6 weeks following the uprising, which so alarmed slave owners that repressive measures forbidding the educating of any blacks were swiftly enacted. Widespread torture and execution followed as owners exacted retribution, and the abolition movement in the South was abandoned.

Turner Tina. Adopted name of Annie Mae Bullock 1938– . US rhythm-and-blues singer who recorded 1960–76 with her husband, Ike Turner (1931–), including *River Deep, Mountain High* 1966, produced by Phil Spector. She achieved success in the 1980s as a solo artist, recording albums such as *Private Dancer* 1984, and also becoming a successful live performer.

turnip biennial plant *Brassica rapa* cultivated in temperate regions for its edible white- or yellow-fleshed root and the young leaves, which are used as a green vegetable. Closely allied to it is the swede *Brassica napus*.

turnstone any of a genus (*Arenaria*) of small wading shorebirds, especially the ruddy turnstone *A. interpres*, which breeds in the Arctic and migrates to the southern hemisphere. It is seen on rocky beaches, turning over stones for small crustaceans and insects. It is about 9 in/23 cm long, has a summer plumage of black and chestnut above, white below, and is duller in winter.

turpentine solution of resins distilled from the sap of conifers, used in varnish and as a paint solvent but now largely replaced by ◊white spirit.

Turpin Ben 1874–1940. US comedian, a star of silent films. His hallmark was being cross-eyed, and he parodied screen stars and their films. His work includes *The Shriek of Araby* 1923, *A Harem Knight* 1926, and *Broke in China* 1927.

Turpin Dick 1706–1739. English highwayman. The son of an innkeeper, he turned to highway robbery, cattle-thieving, and smuggling, and was hanged.

Turner *US singer Tina Turner in London, 1986.*

turtle

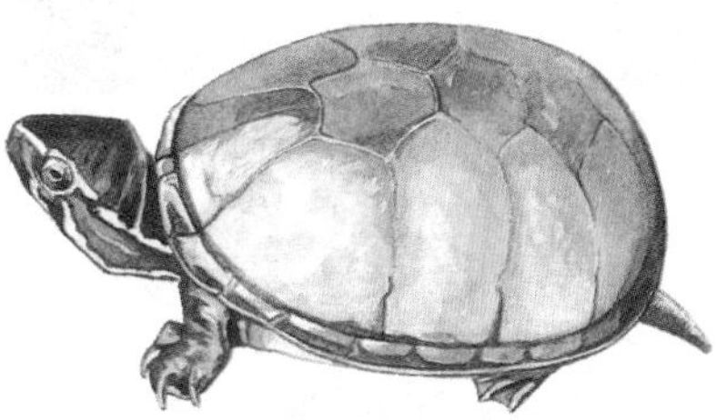

turquoise a mineral, hydrous basic copper aluminum phosphate. Blue-green, blue, or green, it is a gemstone. Turquoise is found in Iran, Turkestan, Mexico, and southwestern US.

turtle any member of the reptilian order Chelonia, characterized by a horn-covered bony shell consisting of an upper and lower portion joined along the sides. The main divisions are the hidden-necked turtles (Cryptodira) that withdraw their heads in an S-shaped vertical curve and the side-necked turtles (Pleurodira) that withdraw their heads in a horizontal, sideways curve. See also ◊terrapin, ◊tortoise, and ◊sea turtle.

Tuscaloosa city in W central Alabama, on the Black Warrior River, SW of Birmingham. Industries include chemicals, tires, paper, and lumber. The University of Alabama 1831 is here; population (1990) 77,759. It was originally founded by Creek Indians 1809.

Tuscan in Classical architecture, one of the five types of column; see ◊order.

Tuscany (Italian *Toscana*) region of central Italy; area 8,878 sq mi/23,000 sq km; population (1988) 3,568,000. Its capital is Florence, and towns include Pisa, Livorno, and Siena. The area is mainly agricultural, with many vineyards, such as in the Chianti hills; it also has lignite and iron mines and marble quarries. The Tuscan dialect has been adopted as the standard form of Italian. Tuscany was formerly the Roman Etruria, and inhabited by Etruscans around 500 BC. In medieval times the area was divided into small states, united under Florentine rule during the 15th–16th centuries. It became part of united Italy 1861.

Tussaud Madame (Anne Marie Grosholtz) 1761–1850. French wax-modeler. In 1802 she established an exhibition of wax models of celebrities in London. It was destroyed by fire 1925, but reopened 1928.

Born in Strasbourg, she went to Paris 1766 to live with her wax-modeler uncle, Philippe Curtius, whom she soon surpassed in technique. During the French Revolution they were forced to take death masks of many victims and leaders (some still exist in the Chamber of Horrors).

Tutankhamen king of Egypt of the 18th dynasty, about 1360–1350 BC. A son of Ikhnaton (also called Amenhotep III), he was about 11 at his accession. In 1922 his tomb was discovered by the British archeologists Lord Carnarvon and Howard Carter in the Valley of the Kings at Luxor, almost untouched by tomb robbers. The contents included many works of art and his solid-gold coffin, which are now displayed in a Cairo museum.

Tutu Desmond (Mpilo) 1931– . South African priest, Anglican archbishop of Cape Town and general secretary of the South African Council of Churches 1979–84. One of the leading figures in the struggle against apartheid in the Republic of South Africa, he received the 1984 Nobel Peace Prize.

Tuva (Russian *Tuvinskaya*) autonomous republic (administrative unit) of the USSR, NW of Mongolia

capital Kyzyl

area 65,813 sq mi/170,500 sq km

population (1986) 284,000

features good pasture; gold, asbestos, cobalt

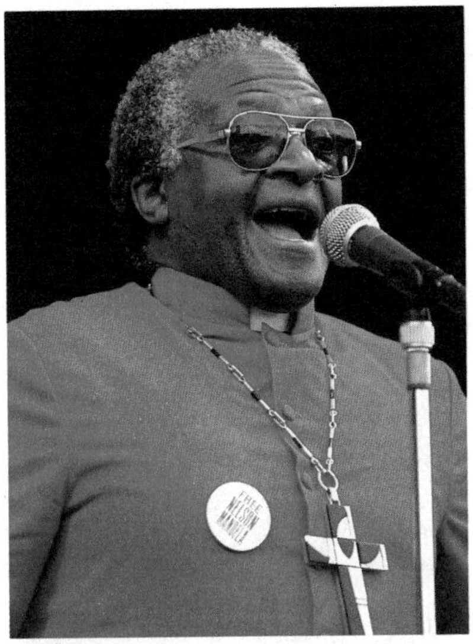

Tutu *South African Anglican archbishop Desmond Tutu. A prominent civil rights campaigner, he is pictured speaking at Nelson Mandela's 70th-birthday concert in 1988.*

history part of Mongolia until 1911 and declared a Russian protectorate 1914, after the 1917 revolution it became the independent Tannu-Tuva republic 1920, until incorporated in the USSR as an autonomous region 1944. It was made the Tuva Autonomous Republic 1961.

Tuvalu country in the SW Pacific, on the former Ellice Islands; part of ◊Polynesia.

government The constitution dates from 1978 when Tuvalu became an independent state within the ◊Commonwealth, accepting the British monarch as head of state, represented by a resident governor-general, who must be a Tuvaluan citizen and is appointed on the recommendation of the prime minister.

There is a single-chamber parliament of 12 members and a prime minister and cabinet elected by and responsible to it. Members of Parliament are elected by universal suffrage for a four-year term. There are no political parties. Each of the inhabited atolls of the Tuvalu group has its own elected island council, responsible for local affairs.

history The islands were inhabited by Melanesians, and were invaded and occupied by Samoans during the 16th century. They were first reached by Europeans in 1765. During the mid-19th century European slave traders captured indigenous Melanesians for forced labor on plantations in South America. As a result of this, and the importation of European diseases, the population declined from an estimated 20,000 to barely 3,000. Originally known as the Ellice Islands, they were a British protectorate 1892–1915 and part of the Gilbert and Ellice Islands colony 1915–75, when they became a separate British colony.

In 1978 the Ellice Islands became fully independent within the Commonwealth, reverting to their old name of Tuvalu, meaning "eight standing together." Because of its small size, Tuvalu is a "special member" of the Commonwealth and does not have direct representation at meetings of heads of government. Its first prime minister was Toaripi Lauti, replaced 1981 as a result of his alleged involvement in an investment scandal, by Dr Tomasi Puapua, who was re-elected 1985. In 1986 a poll was taken to decide whether Tuvalu should remain a constitutional monarchy or become a republic. Only one atoll favored republican status. Following new elections in Sept 1989, Puapua was replaced as prime minister by Bikenibeu Paeniu, whose new administration pledged to reduce the country's dependence on foreign aid, which contributes more than a fourth of gross domestic product.

Tver former name (until 1932) of ◊Kalinin, city in the USSR.

TVP (abbreviation of texturized vegetable protein) a meat substitute usually made from soybeans. In manufacture, the soya-bean solids (what remains after oil has been removed) are ground finely and mixed with a binder to form a sticky mixture. This is forced through a spinneret and extruded into fibers, which are treated with salts and flavorings, wound into hanks, and then chopped up to resemble meat chunks.

Twain Mark. Adopted name of Samuel Langhorne Clemens 1835–1910. US writer. He established his reputation with the comic masterpiece *The Innocents Abroad* 1869 and two classic American novels, in dialect, *The Adventures of Tom Sawyer* 1876 and *The Adventures of Huckleberry Finn* 1885. He also wrote satire, as in *A Connecticut Yankee at King Arthur's Court* 1889.

Born in Florida, Missouri, Twain grew up along

Twain *US novelist Mark Twain, best remembered for* The Adventures of Huckleberry Finn *1885, was also noted for his biting satire.*

the Mississippi River in Hannibal, Missouri, the setting for many of his major works, and was employed as a riverboat pilot before he moved west; taking a job as a journalist, he began to write. The famous tale "The Celebrated Jumping Frog of Calaveras County" was his first success. After a trip by boat to the Holy Land, he wrote *The Innocents Abroad*. As his writing career blossomed, he also became a lecturer very much in demand. By 1870 he married, and a few years later he and his wife settled in Hartford, Connecticut.

Huckleberry Finn is considered Twain's masterpiece, for its use of the vernacular, vivid characterization and descriptions, and its theme, underlying the humor, of man's inhumanity to man. He also wrote *Roughing It 1872, The Gilded Age* 1873, *Old Times on the Mississippi* 1875, *The Prince and the Pauper* 1882, *Life on the Mississippi* 1883, *Pudd'nhead Wilson* 1894, and *Personal Recollections of Joan of Arc* 1896. His later works, such as *The Mysterious Stranger*, unpublished until 1916, are less humorous and more pessimistic. He is recognized as one of America's finest and most characteristic writers.

Tweed river rising in SW Borders region, Scotland, and entering the North Sea at Berwick-upon-Tweed, Northumberland; length 97 mi/156 km.

tweed cloth made of woolen yarn, usually of several shades, but in its original form without a regular pattern and woven on a hand loom in the more remote parts of Ireland, Wales, and Scotland.

Harris Tweed is made on the island of Harris in the Outer Hebrides; it is highly durable and largely weatherproof. Today, it is often machine-woven, patterned, and processed.

Tweed William Marcy. Nicknamed "Boss." 1823–1878. US political leader, he emerged as the leader of Tammany Hall (a New York City Democratic club, founded 1789) and was elected to the city board of supervisors 1856. Serving in various municipal offices, and from 1867 in the state senate, Tweed, by then a master of graft, controlled government spending and accumulated a fortune estimated at somewhere between $45 million and $200 million. Arrested on charges of forgery and larceny, Tweed was convicted and sentenced to prison 1873–75. Shortly thereafter he was rearrested and jailed, and in December 1875 he escaped to Spain via Cuba. His anonymity in Spain was subverted by a Thomas ◊Nast cartoon, from which Tweed was recognized and sent back to New York, where he died in prison.

Born in New York City, Tweed worked briefly as a clerk in his father's brush factory. Becoming involved in municipal politics, he served as an alderman 1852–56 and in the US House of Representatives 1853–55.

Twelfth Day the 12th and final day of the Christmas celebrations, 6 Jan; the feast of the ◊Epiphany.

Tuvalu
South West Pacific State of
(formerly **Ellice Islands**)

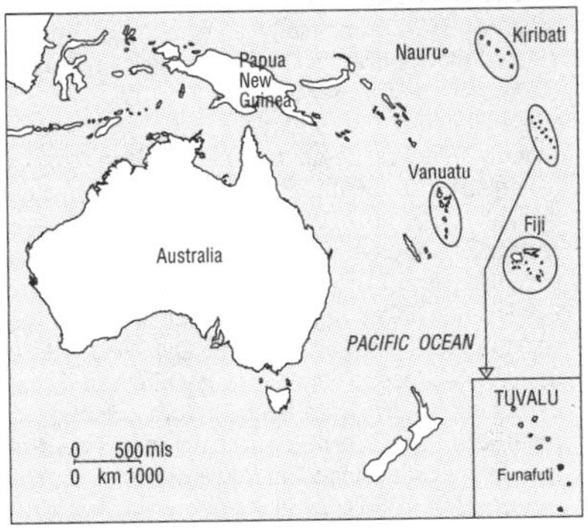
Papua New Guinea
Nauru
Kiribati
Vanuatu
Fiji
Australia
PACIFIC OCEAN
TUVALU
Funafuti
0 500 mls
0 km 1000

area 9.5 sq mi/25 sq km
capital Funafuti
physical nine low coral atolls forming a chain of 650 mi/579 km in the SW Pacific
features the name means "cluster of eight" islands (there are nine, but one is very small)
head of state Elizabeth II from 1978 represented by governor-general
head of government Bikenibeu Paeniu from 1989
political system liberal democracy
political parties none, members are elected to parliament as independents
exports copra, handicrafts, stamps
currency Australian dollar
population (1990 est) 9,000 (Polynesian 96%); growth rate 3.4% p.a.
life expectancy 60 men, 63 women (1989)
language Tuvaluan, English
religion Christian, (Protestant)
literacy 96% (1985)
GDP (1983) $711 per head
chronology
1892 Became a British protectorate forming part of the Gilbert and Ellice Islands group.
1916 The islands acquired colonial status.
1975 The Ellice Islands were separated from the Gilbert Islands.
1978 Independence achieved from Britain within the Commonwealth with Toaripi Lauti as prime minister.
1981 Dr Tomasi Puapua replaced Lauti as premier.
1986 Islanders rejected proposal for republican status.
1989 Bikenibeu Paeniu elected new prime minister.

Twelfth Night comedy by William Shakespeare, first performed 1601–02. The plot builds on misunderstandings and mistaken identities, leading to the successful romantic unions of Viola and her twin brother Sebastian with Duke Orsino and Olivia respectively, and the downfall of Olivia's steward Malvolio.

Twelver member of a Shiite Muslim sect who believes that the 12th imam (Islamic leader) did not die, but is waiting to return toward the end of the world as the Mahdi, the "rightly guided one," to establish a reign of peace and justice on Earth.

twelve-tone system or ***twelve-note system*** system of musical composition in which the 12 notes of the chromatic scale are arranged in a particular order, called a "series" or "tone-row." A work using the system consists of restatements of the series in any of its formations. ◊Schoenberg and ◊Webern were exponents of this technique.

twin one of two young produced from a single pregnancy. Human twins may be genetically identical, having been formed from a single fertilized egg that split into two cells, both of which became implanted. Nonidentical twins are formed when two eggs are fertilized at the same time.

two-stroke cycle operating cycle for internal combustion piston engines. The engine cycle is completed after just two strokes (movement up or down) of the piston, which distinguishes it from the more common ◊four-stroke cycle. Power mowers and lightweight motorcycles use two-stroke gasoline engines, which are cheaper and simpler than four-strokes.

Most marine diesel engines are also two-strokes. In a typical two-stroke motorcycle engine, fuel mixture is drawn into the crankcase as the piston moves up on its first stroke to compress the mixture above it. Then the compressed mixture is ignited, and hot gases are produced, which drive the piston down on its second stroke. As it moves down, it uncovers an opening (port) that allows the fresh fuel mixture in the crankcase to flow into the combustion space above the piston. At the same time, the exhaust gases leave through another port.

TX abbreviation for ◊Texas.

Tyche the personification of Chance in Classical Greek thought whose cult developed in the ◊Hellenistic and Roman periods, when it was identified with that of the Roman ◊Fortuna.

tycoon person who has acquired great wealth through business achievements. Examples include J Pierpont ◊Morgan (1837–1913) and John D ◊Rockefeller (1839–1937).

Tyler city in NE Texas, SE of Dallas. Industries include oil, roses, vegetables, furniture, and plastics; population (1990) 75,450.

Tyler John 1790–1862. 10th president of the US 1841–45, succeeding Benjamin ◊Harrison, who died after only one month in office. Tyler was the first US vice-president to succeed to the presidency. Because he was not in favor of many of the Whig Party's policies, he was constantly at odds with the cabinet and Congress, until elections forced the Whigs from power and enabled Tyler to reorganize his cabinet. His government negotiated the Webster–Ashburton Treaty, which settled the Maine-New Brunswick, Canada, boundary dispute 1842 and annexed Texas 1845.

Tyler, a lawyer, served in the US House of Representatives 1817–21 and in the Senate 1827–36, representing his home state of Virginia, of which he was governor 1825–27.

Tyler Wat died 1381. English leader of the ◊Peasants' Revolt of 1381. After taking Canterbury he led the peasant army to Blackheath and occupied London. King Richard II met the rebels and promised to redress their grievances, which included the imposition of a poll tax. At another conference at Smithfield, Tyler was murdered.

tympanum or ***ear drum*** membrane capable of vibrating in response to vibrations passing from the outer ◊ear.

***Tyler** The 10th president of the United States of America, John Tyler, a Whig. 1841–1845.*

It is composed of two layers of epidermis with connective tissue sandwiched between them. Vibrations set up by the sound waves are transferred to the tiny bones of the inner ear, which themselves pass vibrations through to the inner ear and ◊cochlea.

Tynan Kenneth 1927–1980. British author and theater critic, a leading cultural figure of the radical 1960s. He devised the nude revue *Oh Calcutta!* 1969, first staged in New York.

Tyndale William 1492–1536. English translator of the Bible. The printing of his New Testament (the basis of the King James Version) was begun in Cologne 1525 and, after he had been forced to flee, completed in Worms. He was strangled and burned as a heretic at Vilvorde in Belgium.

Tyndall John 1820–1893. Irish physicist who in 1869 studied the scattering of light by invisibly small suspended particles. Known as the Tyndall effect, it was first observed with ◊colloidal solutions, in which a beam of light is made visible when it is scattered by minute colloidal particles (whereas a pure solvent does not scatter light). Similar scattering of blue wavelengths of sunlight by particles in the atmosphere makes the sky look blue (beyond the atmosphere, the sky is black).

Tyne river of NE England formed by the union of the North Tyne (rising in the Cheviot Hills) and South Tyne (rising in Cumbria) near Hexham, Northumberland, and reaching the North Sea at Tynemouth; length 45 mi/72 km. Kielder Water (1980) in the N Tyne Valley is Europe's largest artificial lake, 7.5 mi/12 km long and 0.5 mi/0.8 km wide, and supplies the industries of Tyneside, Wearside, and Teesside.

Tyne and Wear metropolitan county in NE England, created 1974, originally administered by an elected metropolitan council; its powers reverted to district councils 1986

area 208 sq mi/540 sq km

towns Newcastle-upon-Tyne (administrative headquarters), South Shields, Gateshead, Sunderland

features bisected by the rivers Tyne and Wear; includes part of ◊Hadrian's Wall; Newcastle and Gateshead, linked with each other and with the coast on both sides by the Tyne and Wear Metro (a light railroad using existing suburban lines, extending 34 mi/54 km beneath both cities)

products once a center of heavy industry, it is now being redeveloped and diversified.

population (1987) 1,136,000

famous people Thomas Bewick, Robert Stephenson, Harry Patterson ("Jack Higgins").

typeface style of printed lettering. Books, newspapers, and other printed matter are set in various styles of lettering; each style was designed and is named; examples include Times and ◊Baskerville. Since printing was invented, each alphabet was designed to exhibit distinguishing characteristics for ease of reading or ornamental purposes. See also ◊typography.

typewriter *Today's streamlined electronic models are a far cry from this Waverley typewriter of 1895, but the principle of a hand-operated machine for producing printed characters on paper remains the same.*

type metal ◊alloy of tin, lead, and antimony, for making the metal type used by printers.

typesetting the means by which text, or copy, is prepared for ◊printing, now usually carried out by computer. Text is keyed on a typesetting machine in a similar way to typing. Laser or light impulses are projected onto light-sensitive film that, when developed, can be used to make plates for printing.

typewriter keyboard machine that produces characters on paper. The first practical typewriter was built 1867 in Milwaukee, Wisconsin, by C L Sholes, C Glidden, and S W Soulé. By 1874 ◊Remington and Sons, the gun makers, produced under contract the first machines for sale and in 1878 patented the first with lower-case as well as upper-case (capital) letters.

The QWERTY keyboard was designed 1873 by Sholes to slow down typists who were too fast for their mechanical keyboards. Later developments include tabulators from about 1898, portable machines about 1907, the gradual introduction of electrical operation (allowing increased speed, since the keys are touched, not depressed), proportional spacing 1940, and the rotating typehead with stationary plates 1962. More recent typewriters work electronically, are equipped with a memory, and can be given an interface that enables them to be connected to a computer.

typhoid fever acute infectious disease of the digestive tract, caused by the bacterium *Salmonella typhi*, and usually contracted through a contaminated water supply. It is characterized by bowel hemorrhage and damage to the spleen. Treatment is with antibiotics.

The symptoms begin 10–14 days after ingestion and include fever, headache, cough, constipation, and rash. Fluids and cold baths are helpful. The combined TAB vaccine protects both against typhoid and the milder, related condition known as ***paratyphoid fever***.

typhoon violently revolving storm, a type of ◊cyclone.

typhus acute infectious disease, often fatal, caused by bacteria transmitted by lice, fleas, mites, and ticks. Symptoms include fever, headache, and rash. Typhus is epidemic among people living in overcrowded conditions. Treatment is by antibiotics.

The microorganisms responsible are of the genus *Rickettsia*, especially *R. prouazekii*. A preventive vaccine exists.

typography design and layout of the printed word. Typography began with the invention of writing and developed as printing spread throughout Europe following the invention of metal moveable type by Johann ◊Gutenberg about 1440. Hundreds of variations have followed since, but the basic design of the Frenchman Nicholas Jensen (c. 1420–1480), with a few modifications, is still the ordinary ("roman") type used in printing.

Ease of reading is sought in text typefaces; ornament is sought in display typefaces. Type sizes are measured in points and picas: there are 6 picas to the inch and 12 points to the pica, or 72 points to the inch.

Tyr in Norse mythology, the god of battles, whom the Anglo-Saxons called Týw, hence "Tuesday."

tyrannosaurus any of a genus *Tyrannosaurus* of gigantic flesh-eating ◊dinosaurs, order Saurischia, which lived in North America and Asia about 70 million years ago. They had two feet, were up to 50 ft/15 m long, 20 ft/6.5 m tall, weighed 10 tons, and had teeth 6 in/15 cm long.

Only a few whole skeletons are known; the most complete was discovered 1989 in Hell Creek, Montana, and will be preserved in the Museum of the Rockies, Bozeman, Montana.

Tyson *US boxer and former heavyweight champion of the world, Mike Tyson.*

Tyre (Arabic *Sur* or *Soûr*) town in SW Lebanon, about 50 mi/80 km S of Beirut, formerly a port until its harbor silted up; population about 14,000. It stands on the site of the ancient city of the same name, a seaport of ◊Phoenicia.

history Built on the mainland and two small islands, the city was a commercial center, known for its purple dye. Besieged and captured by Alexander the Great 333–332 BC, it came under Roman rule 64 BC and was taken by the Arabs AD 638. The Crusaders captured it 1124, and it never recovered from the destruction it suffered when retaken by the Arabs 1291. In the 1970s it became a Palestinian guerrilla stronghold and was shelled by Israel 1979.

Tyrol variant spelling of ◊Tirol, state of Austria.

Tyrone county of Northern Ireland

area 1,220 sq mi/3,160 sq km

towns Omagh (county town), Dungannon, Strabane, Cookstown

features rivers: Derg, Blackwater, Foyle; Lough Neagh

products mainly agricultural

population (1981) 144,000.

Tyson Mike 1966– . US heavyweight boxer, undisputed world champion from Aug 1987 to Feb 1990. He won the WBC heavyweight title 1986 when he beat Trevor Berbick to become the youngest world heavyweight champion. He beat James "Bonecrusher" Smith for the WBA title 1987 and later that year became the first undisputed champion since 1978 when he beat Tony Tucker for the IBF title. He was undefeated until 1990 when he lost the championship in an upset to James "Buster" Douglas. A conviction for rape in February 1992 appeared to end his career.

He turned professional 1985. Of Tyson's first 25 opponents, 15 were knocked out in the first round.

Tyumen oldest town in Siberia, central USSR (founded 1586), on the river Nitsa; population (1987) 456,000. Industries include oil refining, machine tools, and chemicals.

Tzu-Hsi alternate transliteration of ◊Zi Xi dowager empress of China.

U2 Irish rock band U2 that became international stars in the 1980s.

uakari

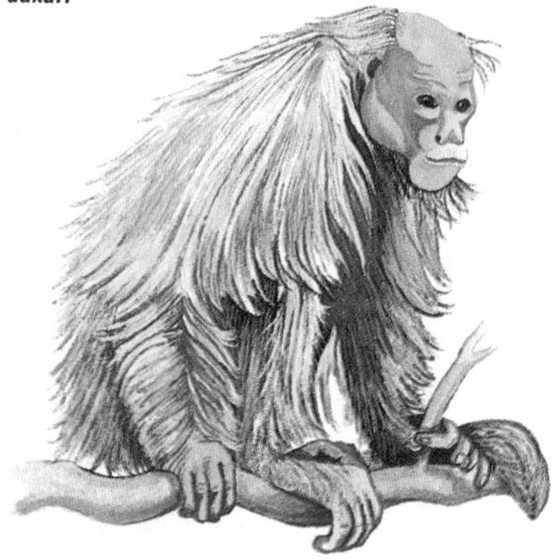

U-2 a US military reconnaissance airplane, used in secret flights over the USSR from 1956 to photograph military installations. In 1960 a U-2 was shot down over the USSR and the pilot, Gary Powers, was captured and imprisoned. He was exchanged for a US-held Soviet agent two years later.

The U-2 affair led to the cancellation of a proposed meeting in Moscow between President Eisenhower and Soviet leader Khrushchev, precipitating a greatly increased Soviet arms spending in the 1960s and 1970s. U-2 flights in 1962 revealed the construction of Soviet missile bases in Cuba. Designed by Richard Bissell, the U-2 flew higher (70,000 ft/21,000 m) and farther (2,200 mi/3,500 km) than any previous plane.

U2 Irish rock group formed 1977 by singer Bono Vox (born Paul Hewson, 1960–), guitarist Dave "The Edge" Evans (1961–), bassist Adam Clayton (1960–), and drummer Larry Mullen (1961–). Committed Christians, they play socially concerned stadium rock, and their albums include *The Unforgettable Fire* 1984, *The Joshua Tree* 1987, and the soundtrack from their documentary film *Rattle and Hum* 1988.

uakari any of several rare South American monkeys of the genus *Cacajao*. There are three species. They have bald faces and long fur. About 1.8 ft/55 cm long in head and body, and with a comparatively short 6 in/15 cm tail, they rarely leap, but are good climbers, remaining in the tops of the trees in swampy forests and feeding largely on fruit. The black uakari is in danger of extinction because it is found in such small numbers already, and the forests where it lives are fast being destroyed.

Ubangi-Shari former name for the ◊Central African Republic.

Übermensch (German "Superman") in the writings of Nietzsche, the ideal to which humans should aspire, set out in *Thus Spake Zarathustra* 1883–85. The term was popularized in George Bernard Shaw's play *Man and Superman* 1903.

U-boat (German *Unterseeboot* "undersea boat") German submarine. The title was used in both world wars.

Uccello Paolo. Adopted name of Paolo di Dono 1397–1475. Italian painter, active in Florence, celebrated for his early use of perspective. His surviving paintings date from the 1430s onward. Decorative color and detail dominate his later pictures. His works include *St George and the Dragon* c. 1460 (National Gallery, London).

Uccello is recorded as an apprentice in Lorenzo Ghiberti's workshop in 1407. His fresco *The Deluge* c. 1431 (Sta Maria Novella, Florence) shows his concern for pictorial perspective, but in later works this aspect becomes superficial. His three battle scenes painted in the 1450s for the Palazzo Medici, Florence, are now in the Ashmolean Museum, Oxford; National Gallery, London; and the Louvre, Paris.

Udaipur or ***Mecvar*** industrial city (cotton, grain) in Rajasthan, India, capital of the former princely state of Udaipur; population (1981) 232,588. It was founded 1568 and has several palaces (two on islands in a lake) and the Jagannath Hindu temple 1640.

Udall Nicholas 1504–1556. English schoolmaster and playwright. He was the author of *Ralph Roister Doister* about 1553, the first known English comedy.

UDI (acronym for unilateral declaration of independence) usually applied to the declaration of Ian Smith's Rhodesian Front government on Nov 11, 1965, announcing the independence of Rhodesia (now Zimbabwe) from Britain.

Udine industrial city (chemicals, textiles) NE of Venice, Italy; population (1984) 101,000. Udine was the capital of Friuli in the 13th century and passed to Venice 1420.

Uccello The 15th-century Italian painter Paolo Uccello, known for his early use of perspective, as in St George and the Dragon *c. 1460, National Gallery, London.*

Uganda
Republic of

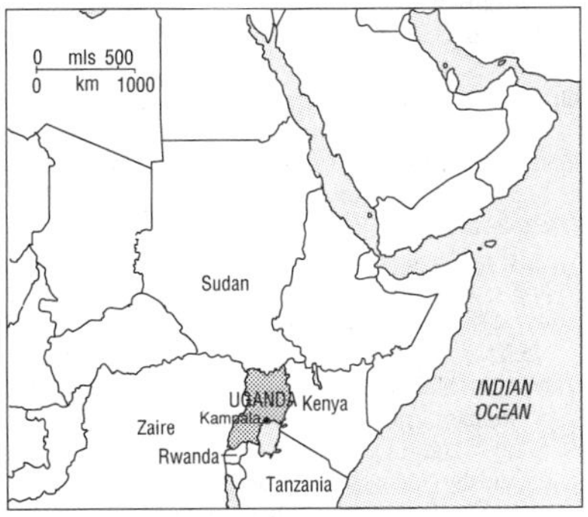
0 mls 500
0 km 1000
Sudan
UGANDA
Kenya
Zaire
Rwanda
Tanzania
INDIAN OCEAN

area 91,351 sq mi/236,600 sq km
capital Kampala
cities Jinja, M'Bale, Entebbe, Masaka
physical plateau with mountains in W; forest and grassland; arid in NE
features Ruwenzori Range (Mount Margherita 16,765 ft/5,110 m); national parks with wildlife (chimpanzees, crocodiles, Nile perch to 160 lb/70 kg); Owen Falls on White Nile where it leaves Lake Victoria; Lake Albert in W
head of state and government Yoweri Museveni from 1986
political system emergent democratic republic
political parties National Resistance Movement (NRM), left-of-center; Democratic Party (DP), center-left; Conservative Party (CP), center-right; Uganda People's Congress (UPC), left-of-center; Uganda Freedom Movement (UFM), left-of-center
exports coffee, cotton, tea, copper
currency Uganda new shilling
population (1990 est) 17,593,000 (largely the Baganda, from whom the country is named; also Langi and Acholi, some surviving Pygmies); growth rate 3.3% p.a.
life expectancy men 49, women 51 (1989)
language English (official); Kiswahili, Luganda, and other African languages
religion Roman Catholic 33%, Protestant 33%, Muslim 16%, animist
literacy men 70%/women 45% (1985 est)
GNP $3.6 bn (1987); $220 per head
chronology
1962 Independence achieved from Britain within the Commonwealth with Milton Obote as prime minister.
1963 Proclaimed a federal republic with King Mutesa II as president.
1966 King Mutesa ousted in coup led by Obote, who ended the federal status and became executive president.
1969 All opposition parties banned after assassination attempt on Obote.
1971 Obote overthrown in army coup led by Maj Gen Idi Amin; ruthlessly dictatorial regime established; nearly 49,000 Ugandan Asians expelled; over 300,000 opponents of regime killed.
1978 Amin forced to leave country by opponents backed by Tanzanian troops. Provisional government set up with Yusuf Lule as president. Lule replaced by Godfrey Binaisa.
1978–79 Fighting broke out against Tanzanian troops.
1980 Binaisa overthrown by army. Elections held and Milton Obote returned to power.
1985 After opposition by National Resistance Army (NRA), and indiscipline in army, Obote ousted by Brig Basilio Okello; power-sharing agreement entered into with NRA leader Yoweri Museveni.
1986 Agreement ended; Museveni became president, heading broad-based coalition government.

Udmurt (Russian *Udmurtskaya*) autonomous republic in the W Ural foothills, central USSR
area 16,200 sq mi/42,100 sq km
capital Izhevsk
products timber, flax, potatoes, peat, quartz
population (1985) 1,559,000; 58% Russian, 33% Udmurt, 7% Tatar
history conquered in the 15th–16th centuries; constituted the Votyak Autonomous Region 1920; name changed to Udmurt 1932; Autonomous Republic 1934.

Uelsmann Jerry 1934– . US photographer who produced dreamlike images, created by synthesizing many elements into one with great technical skill.

Ufa industrial city (engineering, oil refining, petrochemicals, distilling, timber) and capital of the Republic of Bashkir, central USSR, on the river Bielaia, in the W Urals; population (1987) 1,092,000. It was founded by Russia 1574 as a fortress.

Uffizi art gallery in Florence, Italy. Its collection is one of the finest in Europe, based on that of the Medici family.

Uganda landlocked country in E Africa, bounded N by Sudan, E by Kenya, S by Tanzania and Rwanda, and W by Zaïre.
government The 1969 constitution provides for a single-chamber national assembly of 126 elected members and a president who is both head of state and head of government. In 1985 a military coup suspended the constitution and dissolved the National Assembly. The National Resistance Council (NRC) is an interim legislative body.
history For early history, see ◊Africa. Uganda was a British protectorate 1894–1962. Uganda became an independent member of the ◊Commonwealth in 1962, with Dr Milton Obote, leader of the Uganda People's Congress (UPC), as prime minister. In 1963 it was proclaimed a federal republic; King Mutesa II became president, ruling through a cabinet. King Mutesa was deposed in a coup 1966, and Obote became executive president. One of his first acts was to end the federal status. After an attempt to assassinate him in 1969 Obote banned all opposition and established what was effectively a one-party state.

In 1971 Obote was overthrown in an army coup led by Maj-Gen Idi ◊Amin Dada, who suspended the constitution and all political activity and took legislative and executive powers into his own hands. Obote fled to Tanzania. Amin proceeded to wage what he called an "economic war" against foreign domination, resulting in the mass expulsion of Asians, many of whom settled in Britain. In 1976 Amin claimed that large tracts of Kenya historically belonged to Uganda and accused Kenya of cooperating with the Israeli government in a raid on Entebbe airport to free hostages held in a hijacked aircraft. Relations with Kenya became strained, and diplomatic links with Britain were severed. During the next two years the Amin regime carried out a widespread campaign against any likely opposition, resulting in thousands of deaths and imprisonments.

In 1978, when Amin annexed the Kagera area of Tanzania, near the Uganda border, the Tanzanian president, Julius Nyerere, sent troops to support the Uganda National Liberation Army (UNLA), which had been formed to fight Amin. Within five months Tanzanian troops had entered the Uganda capital, Kampala, forcing Amin to flee, first to Libya and then to Saudi Arabia. A provisional government, drawn from a cross-section of exiled groups, was set up, with Dr Yusuf Lule as president. Two months later Lule was replaced by Godfrey Binaisa who, in turn, was overthrown by the army. A military commission made arrangements for national elections, which were won by the UPC, and Milton Obote came back to power.

Obote's government was soon under pressure from a range of exiled groups operating outside the country and guerrilla forces inside, and he was only kept in office by the presence of Tanzanian troops. When they were withdrawn in June 1982 a major offensive was launched against the Obote government by the National Resistance Movement (NRM) and the National Resistance Army (NRA), led by Dr Lule and Yoweri Museveni. By 1985 Obote was unable to control the army, which had been involved in indiscriminate killings, and he was ousted in July in a coup led by Brig Tito Okello. Obote fled to Kenya and then Zambia, where he was given political asylum.

Okello had little more success in controlling the army and, after a brief period of power-sharing with the NRA, fled to Sudan in Jan 1986. Museveni was sworn in as president and announced a policy of national reconciliation, promising a return to normal parliamentary government within three to five years. He formed a cabinet in which most of Uganda's political parties were represented. Museveni worked at consolidating his hold domestically, reviving the economy, and improving African relations, as in the nonaggression treaty signed with Sudan in 1990.

Uganda Martyrs 22 Africans, of whom 12 were boy pages, put to death 1885–87 by King Mwanga of Uganda for refusing to renounce Christianity. They were canonized as the first African saints of the Roman Catholic Church in 1964.

Ugarit ancient trading-city kingdom (modern Ras Shamra) on the Syrian coast. It was excavated by the French archeologist Claude Schaeffer (1898–1982) from 1929, with finds dating from about 7000 to the 15th–13th centuries BC, including the earliest known alphabet.

ugli fruit trademark for a bumpy-skinned cultivated Jamaican citrus fruit, a three-way cross between a grapefruit, a tangerine, and an orange.

Sweeter than a grapefruit but sharper than a tangerine, with rough skin, it is eaten fresh or used in jams and preserves for a sweet-sour flavor. It is native to the East Indies and its name comes from its misshapen appearance.

UHF (abbreviation for ultra high frequency) referring to radio waves of very short wavelength, used, for example, for television broadcasting.

Uhland Johann Ludwig 1787–1862. German poet, author of ballads and lyrics in the Romantic tradition.

uitlander (Dutch "foreigner") in South African history, term applied by the Boer inhabitants of the Transvaal to immigrants of non-Dutch origin (mostly British) in the late 19th century. The uitlanders' inferior political position in the Transvaal led to the Second ◊South African War 1899–1902.

Ujiji port on Lake Tanganyika, Tanzania, where Henry ◊Stanley found David Livingstone 1871; population (1970) 17,000. It was originally an Arab trading post for slaves and ivory.

Ujung Pandang formerly (until 1973) Macassar or Makassar chief port (trading in coffee, rubber, copra, and spices) on Sulawesi, Indonesia, with fishing and food-processing industries; population (1980) 709,000. Established by the Dutch 1607.

UK abbreviation for the ◊United Kingdom.

Ukraine republic, formerly constituent republic of the SE USSR from 1923 to 1991
area 233,089 sq mi/603,700 sq km
capital Kiev
towns Kharkov, Donetsk, Odessa, Dnepropetrovsk, Lvov, Zaporozhe, Krivoi Rog
physical Russian plain: Carpathian and Crimean Mountains; rivers: Dnieper (with the Dnieper dam 1932), Donetz, Bug
products grain, 60% of Soviet coal reserves, oil, various minerals
population (1987) 51,201,000; 74% Ukrainian, 21% Russian, 2% Russian-speaking Jews. Some

Ukraine

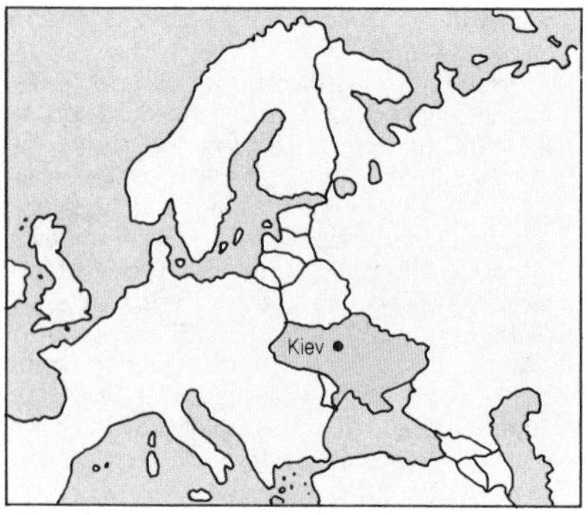
Kiev

1.5 million émigrés live in the US, 750,000 in Canada

language Ukrainian (Slavonic), with a literature that goes back to the Middle Ages

famous people Ivan Kotlyarevsky and Taras Shevchenko

religion traditionally Ukrainian Orthodox; also Ukrainian Catholic

recent history a state by the 9th century; under Polish rule from the 14th century; Russia absorbed E Ukraine 1667, the rest 1793, from Austrian rule; proclaimed itself a people's republic 1918; from 1920, one of the republics of the USSR; overrun by Germans in World War II. In the famine of 1932–33 more than 7.5 million people died. In Sept 1989 the RUK or Ukrainian Popular Movement for Perestroika was launched in Kiev, aiming at confederation of autonomous republics in the USSR. In addition, Ukrainian catholics called for a lift on the ban on the Ukrainian Uniate Church (banned since 1946). In July 1990 the Ukraine voted to proclaim sovereignty.

On Aug 24 1991, in the wake of the failed anti-Gorbachev coup in the USSR, the republic declared its independence and suspended the activities of its Communist Party. During the coup, the president, Leonid Kravchuk, had adopted an ambivalent stance. During the late fall, as the government structure of the Soviet Union collapsed, the Ukraine allied itself with the Russian Republic and Byelorussia to form a new governing arrangement, which evolved into the Commonwealth of Independent States (CIS) by the end of 1991.

Ukrainian language member of the Slavonic branch of the Indo-European language family, spoken in the Ukraine. It is closely related to Russian and is sometimes referred to by Russians as Little Russian, although this is a description that Ukrainians generally do not find appropriate. Ukrainian-speaking communities are also found in Canada and the US.

ukulele a type of small four-stringed ◊guitar.

Ulaanbaatar or ***Ulan Bator*** and (until 1924) ***Urga*** capital of the Mongolian Republic; a trading center producing carpets, textiles, vodka; population (1988) 500,000.

Ulanova Galina 1910– . Soviet dancer. Prima ballerina of the Bolshoi Theatre Ballet 1944–61, she exceled as Juliet and Giselle and created the principal role of Katerina in Prokofiev's *The Stone Flower*.

Ulan-Ude formerly (until 1934) Verkhne-Udinsk industrial city (lumber mills, automobiles, glass) and capital of the Republic of Buryat in SE USSR, on the river Ibla and the Trans-Siberian railroad; population (1987) 351,000. It was founded as a Cossack settlement in the 1660s.

Ulbricht Walter 1893–1973. East German communist politician, in power 1960–71. He lived in exile in the USSR during Hitler's rule 1933–45. A Stalinist, he became first secretary of the Socialist Unity Party in East Germany 1950 and (as chair of the Council of State from 1960) was instrumental in the building of the Berlin Wall 1961. He established East Germany's economy and recognition outside the Eastern European bloc.

ulcer any persistent breach in a body surface (skin or mucous membrane). It may be caused by infection, irritation, or tumor.

Common ulcers include stomach, peptic, mouth (aphthous), intestinal (see ◊colitis), and varicose. The disintegration of tissue is often accompanied by the discharge of pus and blood. Bleeding stomach ulcers can be repaired without an operation by the use of endoscopy. A flexible fiber-optic tube is passed into the stomach and under direct vision a remote-controlled stitching machine sews up the ulcer.

Uleåborg Swedish name for the Finnish port of ◊Oulu.

Ullman Liv 1939– . Norwegian actress who was critically acclaimed for her roles in first Swedish and then international films. Her work includes *Persona* 1966, the title role in *Pope Joan* 1972, and *Autumn Sonata* 1978.

Ulm industrial city (vehicles, agricultural machinery, precision instruments, textiles) in Baden-Württemberg, Federal Republic of Germany, on the river Danube; population (1988) 101,000. Its Gothic cathedral with the highest stone spire ever built (528 ft/161 m) escaped damage in World War II when two-thirds of Ulm was destroyed.

It was a free imperial city from the 14th century to 1802. Albert Einstein was born here.

ulna one of the two bones found in the lower limb of the tetrapod (four-limbed) vertebrate.

Ulsan industrial city (vehicles, shipbuilding, oil refining, petrochemicals) in South Kyongsang province, SE South Korea; population (1985) 551,000.

Ulster former kingdom in Northern Ireland, annexed by England 1461, from Jacobean times a center of English, and later Scottish, settlement on land confiscated from its owners; divided 1921 into Northern Ireland (counties Antrim, Armagh, Down, Fermanagh, Londonderry, and Tyrone) and the Republic of Ireland (counties Cavan, Donegal, and Monaghan).

Ultra abbreviation of Ultra Secret, term used by the British in World War II from spring 1940 to denote intelligence gained by deciphering German signals.

ultrabasic in geology, an igneous rock with a lower silica content than basic rocks (less than 45% silica).

Ultramontanism (Latin "beyond the mountains," that is, the Alps) in the Roman Catholic Church, the tenets of an Italian movement that stresses papal authority rather than nationalism in the church.

ultrasonics the study and application of the sound and vibrations produced by ultrasonic pressure waves (see ◊ultrasound).

ultrasound pressure waves similar in nature to sound waves but occurring at frequencies above 20,000 Hz (cycles per second), the approximate upper limit of human hearing (15–16 Hz is the lower limit). ◊Ultrasonics is concerned with the study and practical application of these phenomena.

The earliest practical application was to detect submarines during World War I, but recently the field of ultrasonics has greatly expanded. Frequencies above 80,000 Hz have been used to produce echoes as a means of measuring the depth of the sea or to detect flaws in metal, and in medicine, high-frequency pressure waves are used to investigate various body organs. Ultrasonic pressure waves transmitted through the body are absorbed and reflected to different degrees by different body tissues. By recording the "echoes," a picture (sonogram) of the different structures being scanned can be built up. Ultrasound scanning is valued as a safe, noninvasive technique which often eliminates the need for exploratory surgery. Free of the risks of ionizing radiation, unlike X-rays and computerized axial tomography (◊CAT scan), it is especially valuable in obstetrics, where it has revolutionized fetal evaluation and diagnosis. High-power ultrasound has been used with focusing arrangements to destroy deep-lying tissue in the body, and extremely high frequencies of 1,000 MHz (megahertz) or more are used in ultrasonic microscopes.

ultrasound scanning or ***ultrasonography*** in medicine, the use of ultrasonic pressure waves to create a diagnostic image. It is a safe, noninvasive technique that often eliminates the need for exploratory surgery.

The sound waves transmitted through the body are absorbed and reflected to different degrees by different body tissues. By recording the "echoes," a picture of the various structures being scanned can be built up. Free of the risks of ionizing radiation (see ◊radioactivity), unlike X-rays and ◊CAT scan, ultrasound scanning is especially valuable in obstetrics, where it has revolutionized fetal evaluation and diagnosis.

ultraviolet astronomy the study of cosmic ultraviolet emissions using artificial satellites. The US has launched a series of satellites for this purpose, receiving the first useful data in 1968. Only a tiny percentage of solar ultraviolet radiation penetrates the atmosphere, this being the less dangerous longer-wavelength ultraviolet. The dangerous shorter-wavelength radiation is absorbed by gases in the ozone layer high in the Earth's upper atmosphere.

The US Orbiting Astronomical Observatory (OAO) satellites provided scientists with a great deal of information regarding cosmic ultraviolet emissions. *OAO-1*, launched 1966, failed after only three days, although *OAO-2*, put into orbit 1968, operated for four years instead of the intended one year, and carried out the first ultraviolet observations of a supernova and also of Uranus. *OAO-3* (*Copernicus*), launched 1972, continued transmissions into the 1980s and discovered many new ultraviolet sources. The *International Ultraviolet Explorer* (*IUE*), launched Jan 1978 and still operating in the early 1990s, observed all the main objects in the Solar System (including Halley's comet), stars, galaxies, and the interstellar medium.

ultraviolet radiation light rays invisible to the human eye, of wavelengths from about 4×10^{-4} to 5×10^{-6} millimeters (where the ◊X-ray range begins). Physiologically, they are important but also dangerous, causing the formation of vitamin D in the skin and producing sunburn in excess. They are strongly germicidal and may be produced artificially by mercury vapor and arc lamps for therapeutic use.

Much of ultraviolet radiation may be detected with ordinary photographic plates or films. It can also be studied by its fluorescent effect on certain materials. The desert iguana, *Disposaurus dorsalis*, uses it to locate the boundaries of its territory and to find food.

Ulundi capital of the "homeland" KwaZulu in Natal, South Africa.

Ulysses a novel by James Joyce, published 1922. It employs stream of consciousness, linguistic experimentation, and parody to describe in enormous detail a single day (June 16, 1904) in the life of its characters in Dublin.

It was first published in Paris but, because of obscenity prosecutions, not until 1933 in the US.

Ulysses Roman name for ◊Odysseus, Greek mythological hero.

Umar 2nd caliph (head) of Islam, a strong disciplinarian. Under his rule Islam spread to Egypt and Persia. He was assassinated in Medina.

Umayyad alternate spelling of ◊Omayyad, Arab dynasty.

Umberto two kings of Italy:

Umberto I 1844–1900. King of Italy from 1878, who joined the Triple Alliance in 1882 with Germany and Austria-Hungary; his colonial ventures included the defeat at Aduwa, Abyssinia, 1896. He was assassinated by an anarchist.

Umberto II 1904–1983. Last king of Italy 1946. On the abdication of his father, Victor Emmanuel III, he ruled May 9–June 13, 1946, when he had to abdicate since a referendum established a republic. He retired to Portugal.

umbilical cord the connection between the ◊embryo and the ◊placenta of placental mammals. It has one vein and two arteries, transporting oxygen and nutrients to the developing young, and removing waste products. At birth, the connection between the young and the placenta is no longer necessary. The umbilical cord drops off or is severed, leaving a scar called the navel.

umbrella portable protection against the rain (when used in the sun it is usually called a parasol or sunshade). In use in China for more than a thousand years, umbrellas were also held over the rulers of ancient Egypt and Assyria as symbols of power and had a similar significance for Aztec and African rulers and dignitaries of the Roman Catholic Church.

Umbria mountainous region of Italy in the central Apennines; including the provinces of Perugia and Terni; area 3,281 sq mi/8,500 sq km; population (1988) 818,000. Its capital is Perugia, and it includes the river Tiber. Industry includes wine, grain, olives, tobacco, textiles, chemicals, and metalworking. This is the home of the Umbrian school of artists, including Raphael.

Umm al Qaiwain one of the ◊United Arab Emirates.

Umtali former name (until 1982) for the town of ◊Mutare in Zimbabwe.

Umtata capital of the South African Bantu homeland of Transkei; population (1976) 25,000.

UN abbreviation for the ◊United Nations.

Una in Classical Roman religion, goddess of the moon.

Unamuno Miguel de 1864–1936. Spanish writer of Basque origin, exiled 1924–30 for criticism of the military directorate of Primo de ◊Rivera. His works include mystic poems and the study *Del sentimiento trágico de la vida/The Tragic Sense of Life* 1913, about the conflict of reason and belief in religion.

uncertainty principle or ***indeterminacy principle*** in quantum mechanics, the principle that it is meaningless to speak of a particle's position, momentum, or other parameters, except as results of measurements; measuring, however, involves an interaction (such as a ◊photon of light bouncing off the particle under scrutiny), which must disturb the particle, though the disturbance is noticeable only at an atomic scale. The principle implies that one cannot, even in theory, predict the moment-to-moment behavior of such a system.

It was established by Werner ◊Heisenberg, and gave a theoretical limit to the precision with which a particle's momentum and position can be measured simultaneously: the more accurately the one is determined, the more uncertainty there is in the other.

Uncle Remus US folk tales by Joel Chandler Harris of Brer Rabbit, Brer Fox, and others, taken from black plantation legends in the 1870s and 1880s, and part of the tradition of US Southern humor.

Uncle Sam nickname for the US government. It was coined during the War of 1812, by opponents of US policy. It was probably derived from the initials US placed on government property.

Uncle Tom's Cabin best-selling US novel by Harriet Beecher Stowe, written 1851–52. A sentimental but powerful portrayal of the cruelties of slave life on Southern plantations, it promoted the call for abolition. The heroically loyal slave Uncle Tom has in the 20th century become a byword for black subservience.

Uncle Vanya a play by Anton Chekhov, first produced 1897. Serebryakov, a retired professor, realizes the futility of his intellectual ideals when faced with the practical demands of life.

unconformity *The Great Unconformity, in Colorado's Grand Canyon, dramatically illustrates—with the sharp division between the Hakatai shales and the overlying Tennessee sandstone—the break in sedimentary rocks that characterizes unconformity.*

unconformity in geology, a break in the sequence of ◊sedimentary rocks. It is usually seen as an eroded surface, with the ◊beds above and below lying at different angles. An unconformity represents an ancient land surface, where exposed rocks were worn down by erosion and later covered in a renewed cycle of deposition.

unconscious in psychoanalysis, part of the personality of which the individual is unaware, and which contains impulses or urges that are held back, or repressed, from conscious awareness.

UNCTAD acronym for United Nations Commission on Trade and Development.

underground economy unofficial economy of a country, which includes undeclared earnings from a second job ("moonlighting") and enjoyment of undervalued goods and services (such as company "perks"), designed for tax evasion purposes. In industrialized countries, it has been estimated to equal about 10% of ◊gross domestic product.

Underground Railroad in US history, a network established in the North before the American ◊Civil War to provide sanctuary and assistance for escaped black slaves. Safe houses, transport facilities, and "conductors" existed to lead the slaves to safety in the North and Canada, although the number of fugitives who secured their freedom by these means may have been exaggerated.

Undset Sigrid 1882–1949. Norwegian novelist, author of *Kristin Lavransdatter* 1920–22, a strongly Catholic novel set in the 14th century. Nobel Prize 1928.

unemployment lack of paid employment. Unemployment is generally subdivided into frictional unemployment, the inevitable temporary unemployment of those moving from one job to another; cyclical unemployment, caused by a downswing in the business cycle; seasonal unemployment, in an area where there is high demand only during vacation periods, for example; and structural unemployment, where changing technology or other long-term change in the economy results in large numbers without work. Periods of widespread unemployment in Europe and the US in the 20th century include 1929–1930s, and the years since the mid-1970s.

Many Third World countries suffer from severe unemployment and underemployment; the problem is exacerbated by rapid growth of population and lack of skills. In industrialized countries unemployment has been a phenomenon since the mid-1970s, when the rise in world oil prices caused a downturn in economic activity, and greater use of high technology has improved output without the need for more jobs. The average unemployment rate in industrialized countries (the members of the Organization for Economic Cooperation and Development) rose to 11% in 1987 compared with only 3% in 1970, with some countries, such as Spain and Ireland, suffering around 20%. There continues to be a great deal of youth unemployment despite government training and job creation schemes. In 1989 the US official unemployment rate was 5.3%, but it is estimated that 20% to 25% of those who want employment cannot find any (and have never had a job or are out of work longer than unemployment compensation pays benefits, so are not counted by labor statisticians). In China, nearly a fourth of the urban labor force is unemployed.

UNEP acronym for United Nations Environmental Program.

UNESCO acronym for United Nations Educational, Scientific, and Cultural Organization, an agency of the UN, established 1946, with its headquarters in Paris. The US, contributor of 25% of its budget, withdrew 1984 on grounds of its overpoliticization and mismanagement, and Britain followed 1985.

Ungaretti Giuseppe 1888–1970. Italian poet who lived in France and Brazil. His lyrics show a cosmopolitan independence from Italian poetic tradition. His poems, such as the *Allegria di naufragi/Joy of Shipwrecks* 1919, are of great simplicity.

Ungava district in N Québec and Labrador, Canada, E of Hudson Bay; area 351,780 sq mi/911,110 sq km. It has large deposits of iron ore.

ungulate general name for any hoofed mammal. Included are the odd-toed ungulates (perissodactyls) and the even-toed ungulates (artiodactyls), along with subungulates such as elephants.

UNHCR abbreviation for United Nations High Commission for Refugees.

Uniate Church any of the ◊Orthodox churches that accept the Catholic faith and the supremacy of the pope, and are in full communion with the Roman Catholic Church, but retain their own liturgy and separate organization.

In the Ukraine, USSR, despite being proscribed 1946–89, the Uniate Church claimed some 4.5 million adherents when it was once more officially recognized.

UNICEF acronym for United Nations International Children's Emergency Fund.

unicellular organism an animal or plant consisting of a single cell. Most are invisible without a microscope but a few, such as the giant ◊amoeba, may be just visible to the naked eye. The main groups of unicellular organisms are bacteria, protozoa, unicellular algae, and unicellular fungi or yeasts. Some become disease-causing agents, ◊pathogens.

unicorn mythical animal referred to by Classical writers, said to live in India and resembling a horse, but with one spiralled horn growing from the forehead.

It was especially important in medieval Christian symbolism and lore.

unidentified flying object or ***UFO*** any light or object seen in the sky whose immediate identity is not apparent. Despite unsubstantiated claims, there is no evidence that UFOs are alien spacecraft. On investigation, the vast majority of sightings turn out to have been of natural or identifiable objects, notably bright stars and planets, meteors, aircraft, and satellites, or to have been perpetrated by pranksters. The term flying saucer was coined in 1947 and has been in use since.

Unification Church or ***Moonies*** church founded in Korea 1954 by the Reverend Sun Myung ◊Moon. The number of members (often called "moonies") is about 200,000 worldwide. The theology unites Christian and Taoist ideas and is based on Moon's book *Divine Principle*, which teaches that the original purpose of creation was to set up a perfect family, in a perfect relationship with God.

This was thwarted by the Fall of Man, and history is seen as a continuous attempt to restore the original plan, now said to have found its fulfillment in Reverend and Mrs Moon. The Unification Church teaches that marriage is essential for spiritual fulfillment, and marriage partners are sometimes chosen for members by Reverend Moon, although individuals are free to reject a chosen partner. Marriage, which takes the form of mass blessings by Reverend and Mrs Moon, is the most important ritual of the church; it is preceded by the wine or engagement ceremony.

There are few other rituals, although there is a weekly pledge, which is a ceremony of rededication. Accusations that the church engages in a cultlike programming of members, and its business, political, and journalistic activities have given it a persistently controversial and derogatory reputation.

unified field theory in physics, the theory that attempts to explain the four ◊fundamental forces (strong, weak, electromagnetic, and gravitational) in terms of a single unified force (see ◊particle physics).

Research was begun by Albert Einstein and, by 1971, a theory developed by Steven Weinberg, Sheldon Glashow, Abdus Salam, and others, had demonstrated the link between the weak and electromagnetic forces. The next stage is to develop a theory (called the ◊Grand Unified Theory, or GUT) that combines the strong nuclear force with the electroweak force. The final stage will be to incorporate the gravitational force into the scheme. Work on the ◊Superstring Theory indicates that this may be the ultimate "theory of everything."

uniformitarianism in geology, the principle that processes that can be seen to occur on the Earth's surface today are the same as those that have occurred throughout geologic time. For example, desert sandstones containing sand-dune structures must have been formed under conditions similar to those present in deserts today. The principle was formulated by James ◊Hutton and expounded by Charles ◊Lyell.

unilateralism in politics, support for unilateral nuclear disarmament: scrapping a country's nuclear weapons without waiting for other countries to agree to do so at the same time.

Union, Act of 1707 act of Parliment that brought about the union of England and Scotland; that of 1801 united England and Ireland. The latter was revoked when the Irish Free State was constituted in 1922.

Soviet Union

The Soviet Republics
LATVIA
ESTONIA
Moscow
BYELORUSSIA
LITHUANIA
UKRAINE
RUSSIA
MOLDAVIA
GEORGIA
ARMENIA
AZERBAIJAN
UZBEKISTAN
TURKMENIA
KAZAKHSTAN
TADZHIKISTAN
KIRGHIZIA
Aral Sea
Black Sea
Caspian Sea
Turkey
NAGORNO-KARABAKH
Iran
Afghanistan
Pakistan

Union of Soviet Socialist Republics (USSR) country in N Asia and E Europe, stretching from the Baltic Sea and the Black Sea to the Arctic and Pacific oceans.

government Under the 1977 constitution, amended in 1989, the USSR is a federal state comprising 15 constituent union republics (see table), but the country's government moved toward a looser arrangement with the republics in 1990–91. Each union republic enjoys, in theory, the right of secession and has its own constitution, legislature, and government (Council of Ministers) that is responsible for local administration. A number of union republics in turn include autonomous republics and regions in which special regard is paid to local culture, customs, and languages. The central (federal) government is solely responsible for defense, foreign policy, foreign trade, communications, and heavy industries. By the end of 1991 the entire governing structure was undergoing change leading to stronger republics and a weak central authority.

The highest organ of the Moscow-based central government is the Congress of the USSR People's Deputies (CUPD), which comprises 2,250 members. Of these, 750 are elected every five years by universal suffrage, and in competitive contests, from demographically equal-sized single-member constituencies from across the USSR. A further 750 are elected to national-territorial constituencies on the basis of 32 deputies per union republic, 11 from each of the 20 autonomous republics, 5 from each of the 8 autonomous regions and 1 from each of the 10 national districts within the Russian Soviet Federal Socialist Republic (RSFSR). The remaining 750 seats in the CUPD are allocated among 32 officially recognized "social organizations," with the Communist Party and labor unions each being accorded 100 seats and the Communist Youth League (Komsomol) 75.

The CUPD, which was created in 1989 by adding the 750 "social organization" seats to the existing 1,500 members of the former Supreme Soviet (though the former "reserved seats" are set to be abolished when the CUPD is next elected). It functions as an "overarching" constitutional assembly rather than as a legislature. It convenes for several days each year to decide key constitutional, political and socioeconomic questions and elects, at its outset, a state president, vice-president, prime minister, who is chair of the 60–70-member council of ministers (the body that has charge of the USSR's day-to-day executive administration), and the chair of the Supreme Court. The state president has responsibility for directing defense and foreign policy and for guiding the drafting of legislation. From its ranks, the CUPD also elects, by secret ballot, 542 members to serve in a Supreme Soviet that, meeting in spring and summer sessions for eight months a year, functions as the country's effective legislature. Its members are elected in accordance with regional quotas, with a proportion being annually rotated. Like its predecessor, it is divided into two chambers, the 271-member Soviet of Nationalities, whose task it is to concentrate on legislation that specifically affects the territorial subdivisions of the USSR, and the 271-member Soviet of the Union, which concentrates on civil rights, socioeconomic, military, and international matters. The state president presides over the Supreme Soviet's presidium. Approval from the Supreme Soviet and its committees is required for the prime minister's nominated minis-

USSR: constituent republics: December 1991

Republic	*Capital*	*Area in sq km*	*Date of joining USSR*
Armenia	Yerevan	29,800	1936**
Azerbaijan	Baku	86,600	1936**
Byelorussia	Minsk	207,600	1922
Estonia	Tallinn	45,100	1940***
Georgia	Tbilisi	69,700	1936**
Kazakhstan	Alma-Ata	2,717,300	1936*
Kirghizia	Frunze	198,500	1936*
Latvia	Riga	63,700	1940***
Lithuania	Vilnius	65,200	1940***
Moldavia	Kishinev	33,700	1940
RSFSR	Moscow	17,075,000	1922
Tadzhikistan	Dushanbe	143,100	1929*
Turkmenistan	Ashkhabad	488,100	1924*
Ukraine	Kiev	603,700	1922
Uzbekistan	Tashkent	447,400	1924*
USSR	Moscow	22,274,500	1922

*Formerly Autonomous Republics with the USSR
**Formerly part of the Trans-Caucasian Soviet Socialist Republic, which joined the USSR 1922
***Became independent nations, Sept 1991

Union of Soviet Socialist Republics

(USSR);
(Soyuz Sovyetskikh Sotsialisticheskikh Respublik)

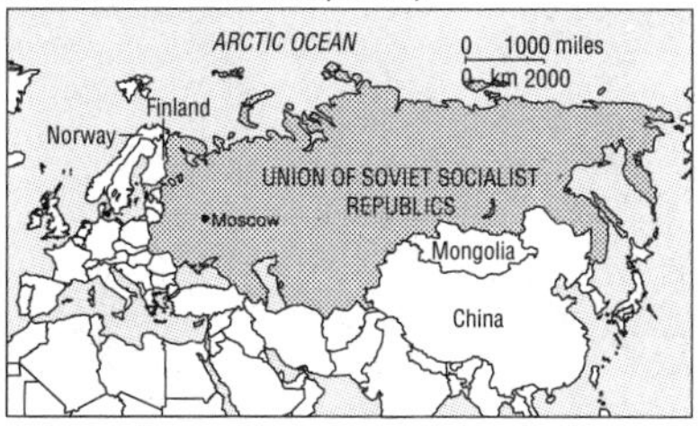
ARCTIC OCEAN
0 1000 miles
0 km 2000
Finland
Norway
UNION OF SOVIET SOCIALIST REPUBLICS
Moscow
Mongolia
China

area 8,590,274 sq mi/22,402,200 sq km
capital Moscow
cities Kiev, Tashkent, Kharkov, Gorky, Novosibirsk, Minsk, Sverdlovsk, Kuibyshev, Chelyabinsk, Dnepropetrovsk, Tbilisi; ports St Petersburg, Odessa, Baku, Archangel, Murmansk, Vladivostok, Vostochny, Rostov, Riga
physical Ural Mountains separate European and Asian plain; Caucasus Mountains in S between Black Sea and Caspian Sea, mountain ranges in SE; coniferous forests and tundra in Siberia; desert in Central Asia
features Pamirs and Altai mountains; Kara Kum Desert; Aral Sea; rivers (in Europe) Don, Dnieper, Volga, Dvina, Pechora, Dneister, Neva, Kuban, and (in Asia) Ob, Yenisei, Lena, Amur, Amu Darya and Syr Darya; lakes Ladoga, Onega, Baikal, and Balkhash; largest country in the world
head of state and government Mikhail Gorbachev 1988–91
political system communism
political parties Communist Party of the Soviet Union; Russian United Workers' Front, conservative; Democratic Union in Moscow, pluralist, intelligentsia-led
exports cotton, timber, iron and steel, nonferrous metals, electrical equipment, machinery, oil and natural gas, vehicles
currency ruble
population (1990 est) 290,939,000 (125 nationalities; 52% Russian, 17% Ukrainian); growth rate 1% p.a.
life expectancy men 64, women 74 (1989)
language Russian (official); Slavic 75% (Russian, Ukrainian, Byelorussian), Altaic 12% (Turkish, Mongolian, others), Uralian 3%, Caucasian 2%
religion atheist 60%; Russian Orthodox 22%, Sunni Muslim 11% Protestant 2%, Roman Catholic 1%, Jewish 1%
literacy 99% (1989)
GNP $734 bn (1984); $3,000 per head (1987)
chronology
1917 Revolution: provisional democratic government established by Mensheviks. Communist takeover by Bolsheviks under Lenin.
1922 Soviet Union established.
1924 Death of Lenin.
1928 Stalin emerged as absolute ruler after ousting Trotsky.
1930s Purges of Stalin's opponents took place.
1939 Nonaggression pact signed with Germany.
1941–45 Great Patriotic War against Germany.
1949 Comecon created.
1953 Stalin died. Beria removed. "Collective leadership" in power.
1955 Warsaw Pact created.
1956 Khrushchev made February "secret speech." Hungarian uprising.
1957–58 Ousting of "antiparty" group and Bulganin.
1960 Sino-Soviet rift.
1962 Cuban missile crisis.
1964 Khrushchev ousted by new "collective leadership."
1968 Czechoslovakia invaded.
1969 Sino-Soviet border war.
1972 SALT I arms-limitation agreed with US.
1977 Brezhnev elected president.
1979 SALT II. Soviet invasion of Afghanistan.
1980 Kosygin replaced as prime minister by Tikhonov.
1980–81 Polish crisis.
1982 Deaths of Suslov and Brezhnev. Andropov became Communist Party leader.
1984 Chernenko succeeded Andropov.
1985 Gorbachev succeeded Chernenko and introduced wide-ranging reforms. Gromyko appointed president.
1986 Gorbachev's power consolidated at 27th Party Congress. Chernobyl nuclear disaster.
1987 USSR and US agreed to scrap intermediate-range nuclear missiles. Boris Yeltsin, Moscow party chief, dismissed for criticizing the slow pace of reform.
1988 Nationalists challenged in Kazakhstan, Baltic republics, Armenia, and Azerbaijan. Earthquake killed 100,000 in Armenia. Constitution radically overhauled; private sector encouraged at Special All-Union Party Conference. Gorbachev replaced Gromyko as head of state.
1989 Troops withdrew from Afghanistan. General election held, with candidate choice for new congress of People's Deputies. 20 killed in nationalist riots in Georgia. 74 members of CPSU Central Committee removed, ¼ of the total. Gorbachev elected state president; conservative communist regimes in Eastern Europe overthrown. Relations with Chinese normalized. Lithuania allowed multiparty elections. Gorbachev and US president Bush declared end of Cold War; Gorbachev renounced "Brezhnev doctrine"; Soviet Union admitted invasion of Afghanistan and intervention in Czechoslovakia to have been mistakes; Gorbachev opposed calls to modify Soviet constitution; economic problems mounted; Lithuanian Communist Party declared independence from Moscow.
1990 Troops sent to Azerbaijan during civil war with Armenia. CPSU Central Committee agreed to end one-party rule. Gorbachev opposed independence of Baltic republics; sanctions imposed on Lithuania; elections showed strength of liberal Communists. Summit meeting with President Bush. Supreme Soviet passed law allowing freedom of religious expression, ending official atheism.
1991 Pact between Moscow and 9 of the 15 republics, aimed at achieving stable relations. Boris Yeltsin elected president of the Russian Federation. Gorbachev and Yeltsin agreed to cooperate. Leningrad changed its name back to St Petersburg. A coup by hard-line communists removed Gorbachev from power Aug but they were forced to step down by the resistance of the people and the strong opposition of Yeltsin. Gorbachev was restored, but his position was undermined by Yeltsin who led the way in a rapid dissolution of communist rule, the KGB, and all existing communist structures. Independence of the republics of Latvia, Lithuania, and Estonia was formally and internationally acknowledged. Gorbachev helped convene Middle East conference in Spain in Nov but his power continued to decline. In Nov and Dec the republics seceded from the union piecemeal and a new federated arrangement emerged, the Commonwealth of Independent States (CIS).

terial team, nine nominees actually being rejected in July 1989.

Lower-level elected soviets operate at the village, town, regional, and republic levels. However, the dominating force in the country is the Communist Party of the Soviet Union (CPSU). The CPSU, with 18 million members, is the only currently permitted political party in the USSR and forms a second and parallel form of government that dominates the state tier. It is set up like a pyramid with at its base over 400,000 primary party branches in factories and villages. The party, being organized on "democratic centralist" lines, is controlled from above. The CPSU's highest authority is its Party Congress, which meets every five years and includes 5,000 selected members. Congress ratifies party programs and elects a Central Committee of currently 251 full members to assume authority over the party between congresses.

The Central Committee meets twice a year and elects the Politburo of normally eleven full members and seven candidates and the specialist twelve-member administrative Secretariat. The Politburo is the most powerful political body in the USSR. It meets fortnightly as an executive cabinet, controls and determines the policy of the CPSU, and sets out the medium-and long-term goals for the nation. Its members select from their ranks the party leader, or general secretary (since March 1985 Mikhail Gorbachev), who presides over the Secretariat and serves in practice as the leader of the Soviet Union.

The CPSU dominates the state system of government through the control it exercises over appointments and candidatures in elections. More than 85% of CUPD delegates are members of the CPSU, while the state's policy-making and executive organs, the Presidium and Council of Ministers, are tightly controlled by leading members of the CPSU Central Committee and Politburo. This inner circle of CPSU leaders determines state and party policy. However, growing factional divisions within the party elite, combined with the administrative reforms of 1988–89, have meant that there is growing debate within the CUPD, Supreme Soviet, and the CPSU's Central Committee and Congress. A gradual power shift away from party toward state executive organs is becoming increasingly evident.

history For early history, see ◊Russian history; also Armenia, Azerbaijan, Byelorussia, Estonia, Georgia, Kirghizia, Latvia, Lithuania, Moldavia, Russia, Tadzhikistan, Turkmenistan, the Ukraine, and Uzbekistan.

The Union of Soviet Socialist Republics was formed 1922, and a constitution adopted 1923. Lenin, who had led the new regime, died 1924, and an internal party controversy broke out between Stalin and Trotsky over the future of socialism and the necessity of world revolution. Trotsky was expelled 1927, and Stalin's policy of socialism in one country adopted. During the first two five-year plans 1928–39, heavy and light industries were developed, and agriculture collectivized.

The country was transformed as industry grew at an annual (official) rate of 16% with, as a consequence, the size of the manual workforce quadrupling and the urban population doubling. However, the social cost was enormous, with millions dying in the Ukraine and Kazakhstan famine of 1932–34, as well as in the political purges and liquidations launched during the 1920s and 1930s. Leading party figures, including Bulkharin, Kamenev, and Zinoviev were victims of these "show trial" purges. In the process, the Soviet political system was deformed, as inner-party democracy gave way to autocracy based around a Stalinist personality cult.

From 1933 the USSR put forward a policy of collective resistance to aggression. In 1939 it concluded a nonaggression pact with Germany, and Poland was invaded and divided between them. The USSR invaded ◊Finland 1939 but signed a brief peace 1940. For events 1941–45, see ◊World War II. 25 million Russians perished during this "Great Patriotic War." During the immediate postwar years the USSR concentrated on consolidating its empire in Eastern Europe and on providing indirect support to anticolonial movements in the Far East. Relations with the West, particularly the US, sharply deteriorated. On the death of Stalin in March 1953 a collective leadership, including Nikita Khrushchev (CPSU first or general secretary 1953–64), Georgi Malenkov (prime minister 1953–55), Nikolai Bulganin (prime minister 1955–58), Vyacheslav Molotov (foreign minister 1953–56), and Lazar Kaganovich, assumed power. They combined to remove the secret-police chief Lavrenti Beria in Dec 1953 and introduced a new legal code that regularized the political system. Strong differences emerged within the collective leadership over future political and economic reform, and a fierce succession struggle developed.

Khrushchev emerged dominant from this contest, ousting Malenkov, Molotov, and Kaganovich (the "antiparty" group) June 1957 and Bulganin June 1958 to combine the posts of prime minister and party first secretary. At the 1961 Party Congress, Khrushchev introduced a new party program for rapid agricultural, industrial, and technological development to enable the USSR to move ahead of the US in economic terms by 1980 and attain full Communism. He launched a "virgin lands" cultivation campaign in Kazakhstan, increased rural incentives and decentralized industrial management through the creation of new regional economic councils (*sovnarkhozy*). In addition, Khrushchev introduced radical new party rule changes, sanctioned a cultural thaw, and enunciated the principle of "peaceful coexistence" with the West to divert resources from the defense sector. These reforms enjoyed initial success; having exploded its first hydrogen bomb 1953 and launched a space satellite (Sputnik I) 1957, the USSR emerged as a serious technological rival to the US. But Khrushchev's liberalization policy and his denunciation of the errors and crimes of the Stalin era at the Feb 1956 Party Congress had serious repercussions among the USSR's satellites—a nationalist revolt in Hungary and a breach in relations with Yugoslavia and China—while his administrative reforms were fiercely opposed by senior party and state officials. After a series of poor harvests in overcropped Kazakhstan and the ◊Cuban missile crisis 1962, these opponents succeeded in ousting Khrushchev at the Central Committee meeting Oct 1964.

A new and conservative collective leadership, based around the figures of Leonid Brezhnev (CPSU general secretary 1964–82), Alexei Kosygin (prime minister 1964–80), Nikolai Podgorny (state president 1965–77), and Mikhail Suslov (ideology secretary 1964–82), assumed power and immediately abandoned Khrushchev's *sovnarkhozy* and party reforms and reimposed strict censorship in the cultural sphere. Priority was now given to the expansion and modernization of the Soviet armed forces, including the creation of a naval force with global reach. This, coupled with the Warsaw Pact invasion of Czechoslovakia 1968, resulted in a renewal of the ◊cold war 1964–70. During the later 1960s, Leonid Brezhnev, through inducting his supporters into the CPSU Politburo and Secretariat, slowly emerged as the dominant figure. He governed in a cautious and consensual manner and brought into the Politburo leaders from all the significant centers of power, including the ◊KGB (Yuri Andropov), the army (Marshal Andrei Grechko), and the diplo-

Union of Soviet Socialist Republics
Arctic Circle
IRE.
UNITED KINGDOM
North Sea
NORWAY
SWEDEN
FINLAND
Svalbard
Franz Josef
Barents Sea
Novaya Zemlya
Kara Sea
NETH.
BELG.
GERMANY
FRANCE
Stockholm
Helsinki
Murmansk
Baltic Sea
Tallinn
St Petersburg
EST.
LAT.
Riga
LITH.
Vilnius
POLAND
Warsaw
North European Plain
Archangel
Pechora
AUSTRIA
CZECHOSLOVAKIA
HUNGARY
YUGOSLAVIA
Minsk
Dnieper
Moscow
Nizhniy Novgorod
Perm
Kazan
Ural Mountains
Kiev
ROMANIA
Kishinev
Odessa
Bucharest
BULGARIA
GR.
Steppes
Don
Volga
Kharkov
Saratov
Kuibyshev
Ekaterinburg
Chelyabinsk
Istanbul
Black Sea
Rostov-on-Don
Volgograd
Omsk
TURKEY
Ankara
Astrakhan
Caucasus
Caspian Sea
Irtysh
Tbilisi
Yerevan
Baku
Aral Sea
Syr Darya
L. Balkhash
LEB.
SYRIA
IS.
JOR.
Tigris
Euphrates
Turanian Plain
Amu Darya
Krasnovodsk
Ashkhabad
Tashkent
Alma Ata
Bishkek
Elburz Mts
Tehran
Baghdad
IRAQ
Zagros
IRAN
Bukhara
Samarkand
Dushanbe
Hindu Kush
KUWAIT
AFGHANISTAN
Kabul
Karakoram Range
Persian Gulf
Islamabad
Lahore
SAUDI ARABIA
Riyadh
PAKISTAN
Indus
U.A.E.
Muscat
OMAN
Karachi
Arabian Sea
INDIA
YEMEN

matic service (Andrei Gromyko). Working with Prime Minister Kosygin, Brezhnev introduced a series of minor economic reforms and gave new priority to agricultural and consumer-goods production. He oversaw the framing of a new constitution 1977 where the limits for internal dissent were clearly set out and the "Brezhnev doctrine" was also promulgated 1968, establishing the power of the Soviet Union to intervene to preserve Socialism in E Europe as it did in Czechoslovakia.

Brezhnev, who became the new state president May 1977, emerged as an international figure during the 1970s, frequently meeting Western leaders during a new era of détente. The landmarks of this period were the Salt-1 and Salt-2 Soviet-US arms-limitation agreements of 1972 and 1979 (see ◊strategic arms limitation) and the Helsinki Accord 1975, which brought Western recognition of the postwar division of Eastern Europe. Another cultural thaw resulted in the emergence of a vocal dissident movement. The political and military influence of the USSR was extended into Africa with the establishment of new Communist governments in Mozambique 1974, Angola and Ethiopia 1975, and South Yemen 1978. The détente era was brought to an end by the Soviet invasion of Afghanistan Dec 1979 and the ◊Polish crisis 1980–81. The final years of the Brezhnev administration were ones

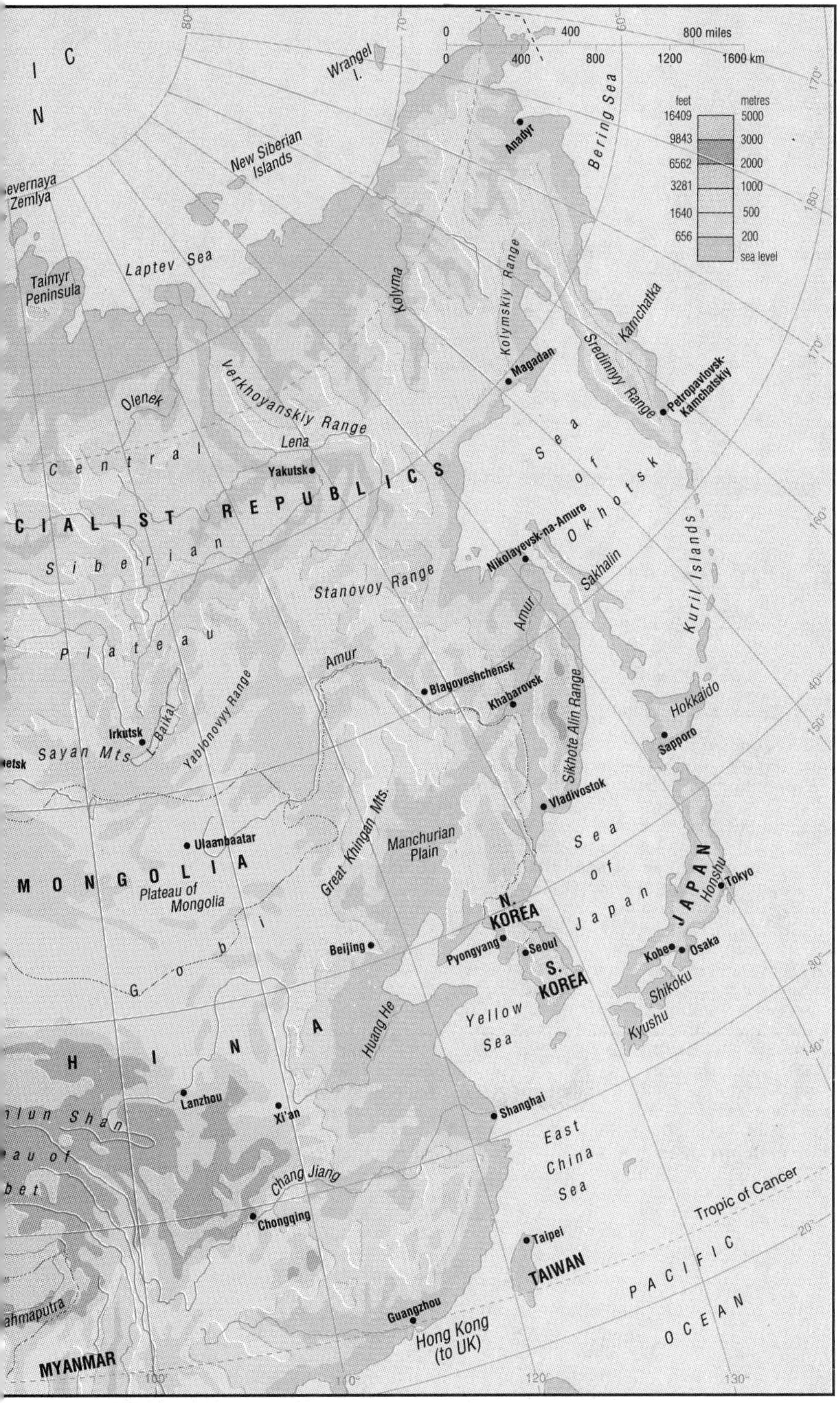
0 400 800 miles
0 400 800 1200 1600 km
feet metres
16409 5000
9843 3000
6562 2000
3281 1000
1640 500
656 200
sea level
Wrangel I.
New Siberian Islands
Severnaya Zemlya
Laptev Sea
Taimyr Peninsula
Bering Sea
Anadyr
Kolyma
Kolymskiy Range
Kamchatka
Sredinnyy Range
Petropavlovsk-Kamchatskiy
Magadan
Verkhoyanskiy Range
Olenek
Lena
Yakutsk
Central Siberian Plateau
CIALIST REPUBLICS
Sea of Okhotsk
Nikolayevsk-na-Amure
Sakhalin
Kuril Islands
Stanovoy Range
Amur
Blagoveshchensk
Khabarovsk
Sikhote Alin Range
Hokkaido
Sapporo
Irkutsk
Baikal
Yablonovyy Range
Sayan Mts
Vladivostok
Ulaanbaatar
MONGOLIA
Plateau of Mongolia
Great Khingan Mts.
Manchurian Plain
Sea of Japan
JAPAN
Honshu
Tokyo
N. KOREA
Pyongyang
Seoul
S. KOREA
Beijing
Gobi
Kobe
Osaka
Shikoku
Kyushu
Yellow Sea
Huang He
CHINA
Lanzhou
Xi'an
Shanghai
East China Sea
Chang Jiang
Chongqing
Tropic of Cancer
Taipei
TAIWAN
PACIFIC OCEAN
Guangzhou
Hong Kong (to UK)
MYANMAR

of hardening policy, mounting corruption, and economic stagnation.

Yuri Andropov, the former KGB chief, was elected CPSU leader on Brezhnev's death Nov 1982 and began energetically to introduce a series of radical economic reforms aimed at streamlining and decentralizing the planning system and inculcating greater labor discipline. Andropov also launched a major campaign directed against corrupt and complacent party and state bureaucrats. These measures had a perceptible impact on the Soviet economy during 1983, but when Andropov died Feb 1984 he was succeeded by the cautious and elderly Brezhnev supporter, Konstantin Chernenko. Chernenko held power as a stop-gap leader for 13 months, his sole initiative being a renewed search for détente with the US that was rejected by the hardline Reagan administration.

On Chernenko's death March 1985, power was transferred to a new generation led by Mikhail Gorbachev, the protégé of Andropov, at 54 the CPSU's youngest leader since Stalin. Gorbachev introduced a number of reforms. He began to free farmers and factory managers from bureaucratic interference and to increase material incentives in a "market Socialist" manner. Working with Ideology Secretary Yegor Ligachev and Prime Minister Nikolai Ryzhkov, he restructured the party and state bureaucracies and replaced cautious Brezhnevites with ambitious new technocrats. Ligachev soon became the leading voice for the conservative wing of the Politburo and was increasingly considered an obstacle to Gorbachev's policies of *glasnost* ("openness"). Ligachev was demoted to the agriculture portfolio, and he was openly ridiculed and accused of corruption. Gorbachev made explicit his renunciation of the "Brezhnev doctrine" 1989.

These changes were not lost on the opposition leaders in the Baltic republics or on Communist deputies in the newly assertive Soviet Parliament. Lithuania declared that it would permit free elections, then the Lithuanian Communist party declared its independence from Moscow. By Jan 1990, Gorbachev was faced with growing calls for secession from the Soviet Union, and he had been forced to reconsider his earlier opposition to a multiparty system in the Soviet Union itself. He also was forced to declare a state of emergency and dispatch thousands of troops to quell near civil warfare between Armenians and Azerbaijanis who were fighting each other for religious and territorial reasons, as well as the Soviet forces sent to suppress the violence.

Working with the foreign secretary, Edvard Shevardnadze, Gorbachev made skillful use of the foreign media to make a case against space weapons and nuclear testing. He met US President Reagan at Geneva and Reykjavik Nov 1985 and Oct 1986, and, at the Washington summit in Dec 1987, he concluded a treaty designed to eliminate medium-range Intermediate Nuclear Forces (INF) from European soil. This treaty was formally ratified at the Moscow summit of May–June 1988. As part of the new détente initiative, the USSR also effected a full withdrawal of its troops from Afghanistan in Feb 1989 and made broad cutbacks in the size of its conventional forces during 1989–90.

Gorbachev pressed for an acceleration (*uskoreniye*) of his domestic, economic, and political program of restructuring (*perestroika*) from 1987, but faced growing opposition both from conservatives grouped around Ligachev and radicals led by Boris Yeltsin. Gorbachev's *glasnost* policy helped fan growing nationalist demands for secession among the republics of the Baltic and Transcaucasia. To add momentum to the reform process, Gorbachev convened, in June 1988, a special 4,991 member All-Union Party Conference, the first since 1941. At this meeting a radical constitutional overhaul was approved. A new "super-legislature," the CUPD, was created, from which a full-time working parliament was subsequently to be elected, headed by a state president with increased powers. The members of this CUPD were to be chosen in competition with one another. The authority of the local soviets was enhanced and their structures made more democratic, while, in the economic sphere, it was agreed to reintroduce private leasehold farming, reform the price system and allow some private enterprise.

The June 1988 reforms constituted the most fundamental reordering of the Soviet policy since the "Stalinist departure" of 1928, entailing the creation of a new type of "Socialist democracy," as well as a new mixed, private–public economic system. In May 1989, the CUPD elected Gorbachev as its chair, and thus as state president. During 1989 this movement toward "Socialist pluralism" was furthered by Gorbachev's abandonment of the ◊Brezhnev doctrine and his sanctioning of the establishment of noncommunist and "reform communist" governments elsewhere in Eastern Europe. This led to the ruling regimes there being overthrown in a wave of "people's power." In Feb 1990, the CPSU Central Committee agreed to create a new directly elected state executive presidency on US and French models.

In March 1990 the Soviet parliament authorized private ownership of the means of production, forbidden since the NED during the 1920s. Further, constitutional amendments made in 1990 supported the right of self-determination, includ-

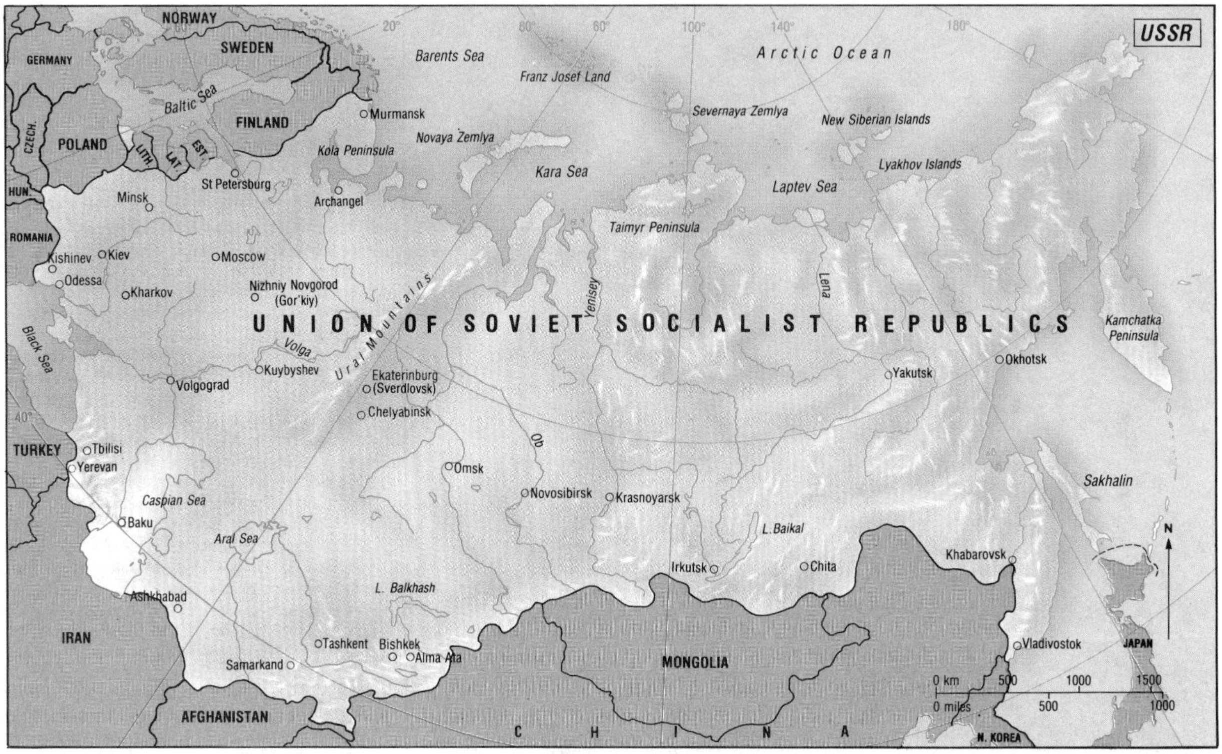
USSR
NORWAY
SWEDEN
GERMANY
FINLAND
POLAND
CZECH.
HUN.
ROMANIA
TURKEY
IRAN
AFGHANISTAN
MONGOLIA
C H I N A
JAPAN
N. KOREA
Barents Sea
Franz Josef Land
Arctic Ocean
Severnaya Zemlya
New Siberian Islands
Lyakhov Islands
Laptev Sea
Kara Sea
Novaya Zemlya
Kola Peninsula
Murmansk
Baltic Sea
St Petersburg
Archangel
Minsk
Taimyr Peninsula
Kishinev
Kiev
Moscow
Odessa
Kharkov
Nizhniy Novgorod (Gor'kiy)
Ural Mountains
Yenisey
Lena
UNION OF SOVIET SOCIALIST REPUBLICS
Kamchatka Peninsula
Black Sea
Volga
Kuybyshev
Volgograd
Ekaterinburg (Sverdlovsk)
Chelyabinsk
Yakutsk
Okhotsk
Tbilisi
Yerevan
Omsk
Ob
Novosibirsk
Krasnoyarsk
Sakhalin
Caspian Sea
Baku
Aral Sea
L. Baikal
Irkutsk
Chita
Khabarovsk
Ashkhabad
L. Balkhash
Tashkent
Bishkek
Alma Ata
Samarkand
Vladivostok
N
0 km 500 1000 1500
0 miles 500 1000

ing secession of republics, and ended the CPSU's monopoly of power. The Gorbachev reform program showed signs of running out of control during 1989–90 as a result both of growing nationalist tensions and mounting popular discontent over the failure of *perestroika* to improve living standards.

In their Dec 1989 summit meeting at Malta, Gorbachev and US president Bush were able to declare an end to the Cold War, which opened the possibility of most-favored-nation trading status with the US, membership in the ◊GATT, and an influx of Western investment. A Gorbachev trip to Canada and the US followed in May–June 1990.

During 1990–91, Gorbachev faced unprecedented domestic pressures and was nearly toppled from power by a 3-day coup in Aug 1991. Ultimately, he remained in office but with reduced influence, finding himself forced to rely on Boris ◊Yeltsin, president of the Russian Federation, for support. As the nation's economy disintegrated, Gorbachev had first to allow dissident republics greater autonomy and then in the cases of Estonia, Latvia, and Lithuania, independence (Sept 1991).

Later in the fall, the Russian Federation—followed by Byelorussia, the Ukraine, and other republics—seceded from the Soviet Union's central authority and formed their own loose federation of independent republics.

Political developments accelerated in the Soviet Union in Nov and Dec, pushed by the economic crisis with the country and the nationalist aspirations of the various constituent republics. Ultimately, a new form of government, an association called the Commonwealth of Independent States (CIS), emerged.

The growing power of the individual republics became apparent in late Nov when the Group of Seven industrial countries reached a Soviet debt deferral agreement with the USSR and included 8 of the republics as signatories. On Dec 8 the most powerful of the republics—Russia, Byelorussia, and Ukraine—agreed to form the CIS, a development denounced by Gorbachev. By mid-Dec, the 5 Central Asian republics (Kazakhstan, Kirghizia, Tadzhikistan, Turkemenistan, and Uzbekistan) had announced that they would join the CIS, and Gorbachev had agreed on a transfer of power from the centralized government to the CIS. The remaining republics (Armenia, Azerbaijan, and Moldavia) except Georgia, torn by civil war, joined the others in signing agreements on Dec 21 to establish the commonwealth, formally designated as an alliance of independent states. The formal dissolution of the USSR came on Dec 25 as Gorbachev resigned as president.

unit standard quantity in relation to which other quantities are measured. There have been many systems of units. Some ancient units, such as the day, the foot, and the pound, are still in use. ◊SI units, the latest version of the metric system, are widely used in science.

UNITA acronym for National Union for the Total Independence of Angola. Angolan nationalist movement backed by South Africa, which continued to wage guerrilla warfare against the ruling MPLA regime after the latter gained control of the country in 1976. The UNITA leader Jonas ◊Savimbi founded the movement 1966. A June 1989 ceasefire was abandoned after two months.

Unitarianism a Christian denomination that rejects the orthodox doctrine of the Trinity and gives a preeminent position to Jesus as a religious teacher, while denying his deity. Unitarians

United Arab Emirates

(UAE) (*Ittihad al-Imarat al-Arabiyah*) federation of the emirates of **Abu Dhabi, Ajman, Dubai, Fujairah, Sharjah, Umm al Qaiwain, Ras al Khaimah**

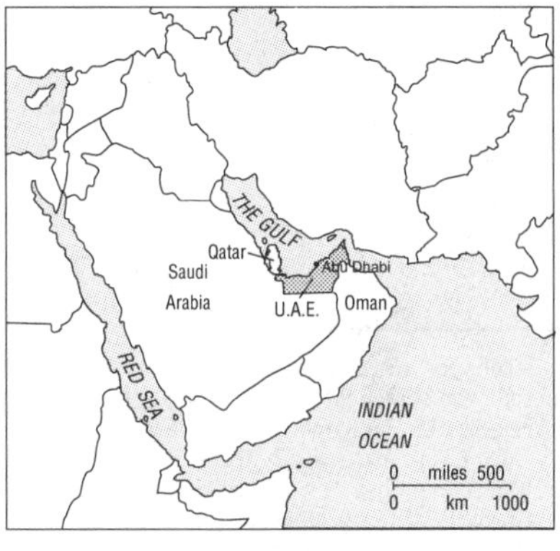
THE GULF
Qatar
Abu Dhabi
Saudi Arabia
U.A.E.
Oman
RED SEA
INDIAN OCEAN
0 miles 500
0 km 1000

total area 32,292 sq mi/83,657 sq km
capital Abu Dhabi
cities (chief port) Dubai
physical desert and flat coastal plain; mountains in E
features linked by their dependence on oil revenues
head of state and government Zayed Bin Sultan al-Nahayan of Abu Dhabi from 1971
political system absolutism
political parties none
exports oil, natural gas, fish, dates
currency UAE dirham
population (1990 est) 2,250,000 (10% nomadic); growth rate 6.1% p.a.
life expectancy men 68, women 72 (1989)
language Arabic (official); Farsi, Hindi, Urdu, English
religion Muslim 96%, Christian, Hindu
literacy 68% (1989)
GNP $22 bn (1987); $11,900 per head
chronology
1952 Trucial Council established.
1971 Federation of Arab Emirates formed; later dissolved. Six Trucial States formed United Arab Emirates, with ruler of Abu Dhabi, Sheik Zayed, as president.
1972 The seventh state joined.
1976 Sheik Zayed threatened to relinquish presidency unless progress toward centralization became more rapid.
1985 Diplomatic and economic links with USSR and China established.
1987 Diplomatic relations with Egypt restored.
1990–91 Iraqi invasion of Kuwait opposed; UAE fights with UN coalition.
1991 Bank of Commerce and Credit International controlled by Abu Dhabi's ruler collapses.

believe in individual conscience and reason as a guide to right action, rejecting the doctrines of original sin, the atonement, and eternal punishment. See also ◊Arianism and ◊Socinianism.

Unitarianism arose independently in the 16th century in Poland, where its chief exponent was Faustus Socinus (1539–1604), and in the Transylvanian region of Hungary and Romania. During the 17th century a number of English writers began to accept Jesus's humanity while denying the doctrine of the Trinity. The movement grew amid the ◊rationalism of the 18th century, and the first Unitarian chapel was established in London 1774. American Unitarianism emerged as a secession movement from the Congregational Church in New England. Its most eloquent spokesman was William Ellery Channing (1780–1842). The transcendentalism of ◊Emerson and ◊Thoreau was a major influence on American Unitarianism. In the 20th century, Unitarianism became identified closely with a liberal political stance and the cause of world peace, and its specific Christian affinities have been replaced gradually by a rational commitment to the moral and spiritual progress of humanity. The chief Unitarian body in the US is the Unitarian Universalist Association, formed 1961 by the merger of the American Unitarian Association and the Universalist Church.

Unitas John Constantine 1933– . US football player. Born in Pittsburgh, Unitas was a football star for the University of Louisville and was drafted by the Pittsburgh Steelers of the National Football League (NFL) 1955. Released after a single season, he was signed by the Baltimore Colts 1956. As Colt quarterback for 17 seasons, Unitas led the team to 5 NFL championship titles in the years 1958–71. Following his release from the Colts, Unitas played for the San Diego Chargers 1973. One of the greatest passers in the history of the game, he was elected to the Football Hall of Fame 1979.

United Arab Emirates federation in SW Asia, on the Arabian Gulf, bounded SW by Saudi Arabia and SE by Oman.

government A provisional constitution for the United Arab Emirates (UAE) has been in effect since Dec 1971 and provides a federal structure for a union of seven sheikdoms. The highest authority is the Supreme Council of Rulers, which includes all seven sheiks. Each is a hereditary emir and an absolute monarch in his own country. The council elects two of its members to be president and vice-president of the federal state for a five-year term. The president then appoints a prime minister and council of ministers.

There is a federal National Council of 40 members appointed by the emirates for a two-year term, and this operates as a consultative assembly. There are no political parties.

history For early history, see ◊Arabia. In 1952 the seven sheikdoms of Abu Dhabi, Ajman, Dubai, Fujairah, Ras al Khaimah, Sharjah, and Umm al Qaiwain set up, on British advice, the Trucial Council, consisting of all seven rulers, with a view to eventually establishing a federation. In the 1960s the Trucial States, as they were known, became very wealthy through the exploitation of oil deposits.

The whole area was under British protection, but in 1968 the British government announced that it was withdrawing its forces within three years. The seven Trucial States, with Bahrain and Qatar, formed the Federation of Arab Emirates, that was intended to become a federal state, but in 1971 Bahrain and Qatar seceded to become independent nations. Six of the Trucial States then combined to form the United Arab Emirates. The remaining sheikdom, Ras al Khaimah, joined Feb 1972. Sheik Zayed Bin al-Nahayan, the ruler of Abu Dhabi, became the first president.

In 1976 Sheik Zayed, disappointed with the slow progress toward centralization, was persuaded to accept another term as president only with assurances that the federal government would be given more control over such activities as defense and internal security. In recent years the United Arab Emirates has played an increasingly prominent role in Middle East affairs, and in 1985 it established diplomatic and economic links with the USSR and China.

In the 1990–91 ◊Gulf War, the UAE firmly opposed Iraq's invasion of Kuwait and contributed troops and economic support to the UN coalition that defeated Iraq. The international financial scandal surrounding the 1991 collapse of the Bank of Commerce and Credit International (BCCI) had serious implications for the UAE because Abu Dhabi's ruler held a controlling interest in the bank.

Supreme Council of Rulers:
Abu Dhabi Sheik Zayed Bin Sultan al-Nahayan, president (1966);
Dubai Sheik Maktoum bin Rashid al-Maktoum (1990);
Sharjah Sheik Sultan Bin Mohammed al-Quasimi (1972);
Ras al Khaimah Sheik Saqr Bin Mohammed al-Quasimi (1948);
Umm al Qaiwain Sheik Rashid Bin Ahmad al-Mu'alla (1981);
Ajman Sheik Humaid Bin Rashid al-Nuami (1981);
Fujairah Sheik Hamad Bin Mohammed al-Sharqi (1974).

United Arab Republic union formed 1958, broken 1961, between ◊Egypt and ◊Syria. Egypt continued to use the name after the breach until 1971.

United Artists (UA) Hollywood film studio formed 1919 by silent-screen stars Charles Chaplin, Mary Pickford, and Douglas Fairbanks, and director D W Griffith, in order to take control of their artistic and financial affairs. Smaller than the other major studios, UA concentrated on producing the works of independent filmmakers and adaptations of literary works in the 1930s and 1940s, including *Wuthering Heights* 1939, *Rebecca* 1940, and *Major Barbara* 1941. The company nearly collapsed after the box-office disaster of Michael Cimino's *Heaven's Gate* 1980, and UA was subsequently bought by MGM.

United Australia Party Australian political party formed by Joseph ◊Lyons 1931 from the right-wing Nationalist Party. It was led by Robert Menzies after the death of Lyons. Considered to have become too dominated by financial interests, it lost heavily to the Labor Party 1943, and was reorganized as the ◊Liberal Party 1944.

United Democratic Front moderate multiracial political organization in South Africa, founded 1983. It was an important focus of antiapartheid action in South Africa until 1989, when the African National Congress and Pan-Africanist Congress were unbanned.

United Irishmen society formed 1791 by Wolfe Tone to campaign for parliamentary reform in Ireland. It later became a secret revolutionary group.

Inspired by the republican ideals of the French Revolution, the United Irishmen was initially a debating society, calling for reforms such as the right of Catholics to vote in Irish elections, but after an attempt to suppress it in 1793, the organization became secret, looking to France for military aid. An attempted insurrection in 1798 was quickly defeated and the leaders captured.

United Kingdom (UK) country in NW Europe off the coast of France, consisting of England, Scotland, Wales, and Northern Ireland.

government The UK is a constitutional monarchy with parliamentary government. There is no written constitution. Cabinet government, which is at the heart of the system, is founded on rigid convention, and the relationship between the monarch as head of state and the prime minister as head of government is similarly based. Parliament is sovereign, in that it is free to make and unmake any laws that it chooses, and the government is subject to the laws that Parliament makes, as interpreted by the courts.

Parliament has two legislative and debating chambers, the House of Lords and the House of Commons. The House of Lords has three main kinds of members: those who are there by accident of birth, the hereditary peers; those who are there because of some office they hold; and those who are appointed to serve for life, the life peers. There are nearly 800 hereditary peers. Among those sitting by virtue of their position are 2 archbishops and 24 bishops of the Church of England and 9 senior judges, known as the law lords. The appointed life peers include about 65 women, or peeresses. The House of Commons has 650 members, elected by universal adult suffrage from single-member geographical constituencies, each constituency containing, on average, about 65,000 electors.

Although the House of Lords is termed the upper house, its powers, in relation to those of the Commons, have been steadily reduced so that now it has no control over financial legislation and merely a delaying power, of a year, over other bills. Before an act of Parliament becomes law it must pass through a five-stage process in each chamber—first reading, second reading, committee stage, report stage, and third reading—and then receive the formal royal assent. Bills, other than financial ones, can be introduced in either house, but most begin in the Commons.

The monarch appoints as prime minister the leader of the party with most support in the House of Commons, and he or she, in turn, chooses and presides over a cabinet. The voting system, which does not include any form of proportional representation, favors two-party politics, and both chambers of Parliament are physically designed to accommodate two parties, the ruling party sitting on one side of the presiding Speaker and the opposition on the other. The party with the second-largest number of seats in the Commons is recognized as the official opposition, and its leader is paid a salary out of public funds and provided with an office within the Palace of Westminster, as the Houses of Parliament are called.

history For early history, see ◊Britain, ancient; ◊England, history; ◊Scotland, history; ◊Wales, history; ◊Ireland, history. The term "United Kingdom" became official 1801, but was in use from 1707, when the Act of Union combined Scotland and England into the United Kingdom of Great Britain. Cabinet government developed under Robert Walpole, in practice the first prime minister (1721–42). Two ◊Jacobite rebellions sought to restore the Stuarts to the throne until the Battle of ◊Culloden 1746, after which the Scottish Highlanders were brutally suppressed. The American colonies that became the US were lost in the ◊American Revolution.

The Act of Ireland 1801 united Britain and Ireland. This was the time of the ◊Industrial Revolution, the mechanization of production that shifted the balance of political power from the landowner to the industrial capitalist and created an exploited urban working class. In protest, the ◊Luddites destroyed machinery. Agricultural ◊enclosures were driving the small farmers off the land. The alliance of the industrialists with the ◊Whigs produced a new party, the Liberals, with an ideology of ◊free trade and nonintervention in economic affairs. In 1832 they carried a Reform Bill transferring political power from the aristocracy to the middle classes and for the next 40 years the Liberal Party was a major force. The working classes, who had no vote, created their own organizations in the labor unions and ◊Chartism; their attempts to seek parliamentary reform were brutally suppressed (at the ◊Peterloo Massacre 1819). The Conservative minister Robert Peel introduced a number of domestic reforms, including the repeal of the Corn Laws 1846.

After 1875 the UK's industrial monopoly was

United Kingdom
of Great Britain and Northern Ireland (UK)

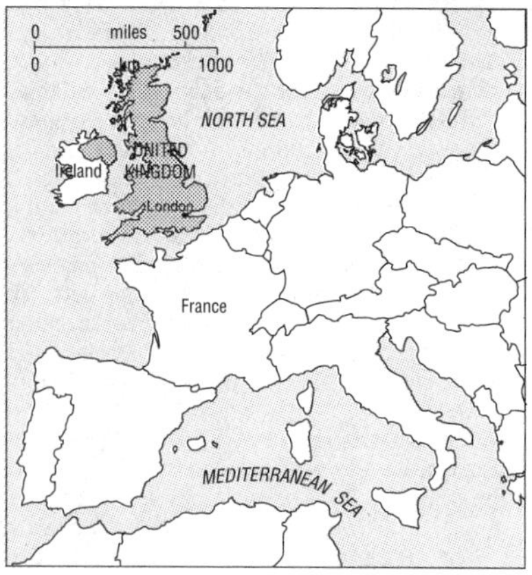
0 miles 500
0 km 1000
NORTH SEA
UNITED KINGDOM
Ireland
London
France
MEDITERRANEAN SEA

area 94,247 sq mi/244,100 sq km
capital London
cities Birmingham, Glasgow, Leeds, Sheffield, Liverpool, Manchester, Edinburgh, Bradford, Bristol, Belfast, Newcastle-upon-Tyne, Cardiff
physical became separated from European continent about 6000 BC; rolling landscape, increasingly mountainous toward the N, with Grampian Mountains in Scotland, Pennines in N England, Cambrian Mountains in Wales; rivers include Thames, Severn, and Spey
territories Anguilla, Bermuda, British Antarctic Territory, British Indian Ocean Territory, British Virgin Islands, Cayman Islands, Falkland Islands, Gibraltar, Hong Kong (until 1997), Montserrat, Pitcairn Islands, St Helena and Dependencies (Ascension, Tristan da Cunha), Turks and Caicos Islands
features milder climate than N Europe because of Gulf Stream; considerable rainfall. Nowhere further than 74.5 mi/120 km from sea; indented coastline, various small islands
head of state Elizabeth II from 1952
head of government John Major from 1990
political system liberal democracy
political parties Conservative and Unionist Party, right-of-center; Labour Party, moderate, left-of-center; Social and Liberal Democrats, center-left; Scottish National Party (SNP), Scottish nationalist; Plaid Cymru (Welsh Nationalist Party), Welsh nationalist; Official Ulster Unionist Party (OUP), Northern Ireland moderate right-of-center; Democratic Unionist Party (DUP), Northern Ireland, right-of-center; Social Democratic Labor Party (SDLP), Northern Ireland, moderate, left-of-center; Ulster People's Unionist Party (UPUP), Northern Ireland, militant right-of-center; Sinn Féin, Northern Ireland, pro-united Ireland; Green Party, ecological
exports cereals, rape, sugar beet, potatoes, meat and meat products, poultry, dairy products, electronic and telecommunications equipment, engineering equipment and scientific instruments, oil and gas, petrochemicals, pharmaceuticals, fertilizers, film and television programs, aircraft
currency pound sterling
population (1990 est) 57,121,000 (81.5% English, 9.6% Scottish, 1.9% Welsh, 2.4% Irish, 1.8% Ulster); growth rate 0.1% p.a.
religion Christian (55% Protestant, 10% Roman Catholic); Muslim, Jewish, Hindu, Sikh
life expectancy men 72, women 78 (1989)
language English, Welsh, Gaelic
literacy 99% (1989)
GNP $758 bn; $13,329 per head (1988)
chronology
1707 Act of Union between England and Scotland under Queen Anne.
1783 Loss of N American colonies that form US; Canada retained.
1801 Act of Ireland united Britain and Ireland.
1832 Great Reform Bill became law, shifting political power from upper to middle class.
1867 Second Reform Bill, extending the franchise, introduced by Disraeli and passed.
1911 Powers of House of Lords curbed.
1914 Irish Home Rule Bill introduced.
1914–18 World War I.
1920 Home Rule Act incorporated NE of Ireland (Ulster) into the United Kingdom of Great Britain and Northern Ireland.
1921 Ireland, except for Ulster, became a dominion (Irish Free State, later Eire, 1937).
1931 National government; unemployment reached 3 million.
1939 World War II began.
1940 Winston Churchill became head of coalition government.
1945 Labour government under Clement Attlee; welfare state established.
1956 Suez crisis.
1970 Conservatives under Edward Heath defeated Labour.
1972 Parliament prorogued in Northern Ireland; direct rule from Westminster began.
1973 UK joined European Community.
1974 Three-day week, coal strike; Wilson replaced Heath.
1976 James Callaghan replaced Wilson as prime minister.
1977 Liberal-Labour pact.
1979 Victory for Conservatives under Margaret Thatcher.
1981 Formation of Social Democratic Party (SDP). Riots occurred in inner cities.
1982 Unemployment over 3 million. Falklands War.
1983 Thatcher reelected.
1984–85 Coal strike, the longest in British history.
1987 Thatcher reelected for third term.
1988 Liberals and most of SDP merged into the Social and Liberal Democrats, leaving a splinter SDP. Inflation and interest rates rose.
1989 Labour Party launched new Policy Review. David Owen announced that the SDP would no longer be able to fight in all national constituencies and would operate as a "guerilla force."
1990 Riots as poll tax introduced in England. Troops sent to the Persian Gulf following Iraq's invasion of Kuwait. British hostages held in Iraq, later released. Britain joined European exchange-rate mechanism. Thatcher replaced by John Major as Conservative leader and prime minister.
1991 British troops took part in US-led war against Iraq under United Nations umbrella. Support was given to the USSR during the dissolution of communism and the restoration of independence to the republics. John Major visited Beijing to sign agreement with China on new Hong Kong airport. At home, Britain suffered severe economic recession.

challenged by Germany and the US. To seek new markets and sources of raw materials, the Conservatives under Disraeli launched the UK on a career of imperialist expansion in Egypt, South Africa, and elsewhere. Canada, Australia, and New Zealand became self-governing dominions.

The domestic issues after 1900 were social reform and home rule for Ireland; the Labour Party emerged from an alliance of labor unions and small Socialist bodies 1900; the ◊suffragists were active until ◊World War I. After the war a wave of strikes culminated in the general strike 1926; three years later a world economic crisis precipitated the Depression that marked the 1930s and brought to power a coalition government 1931.

The following years were dominated by unemployment, which reached almost 3 million in 1933, and the approach of ◊World War II. The death of George V Jan 1936 brought Edward VIII to the throne, closely followed by the ◊Abdication crisis precipitated by his desire to marry US divorcee Wallis Simpson. In Dec 1936, Edward VIII abdicated, and George VI came to the throne.

In 1939 the Germans invaded Poland, and Britain entered World War II by declaring war on Germany. In 1940 Winston Churchill became prime minister, leader of the Conservative Party, and head of a coalition government. The country sustained intensive bombardment in the "Battle of Britain" July—Oct 1940, and the "blitz" of night bombing which effected London and Coventry particularly. Following the defeat of Germany 1945, the Labour Party, led by Clement Attlee, gained power.

In 1945 the UK was still nominally at the head of an empire that covered a fourth of the world's surface and included a fourth of its population, and, although two world wars had gravely weakened it, many of its citizens and some of its politicians still saw it as a world power. The reality of its position soon became apparent when the newly elected Labour government confronted the problems of rebuilding the war-damaged economy. This renewal was greatly helped, as in other W European countries, by support from the US through the ◊Marshall Plan. Between 1945 and 1951 the Labour government carried out an ambitious program of public ownership and investment and laid the foundations of a national health service and welfare state. During the same period the dismemberment of the British Empire, restyled the British ◊Commonwealth, was begun, a process that was to continue into the 1980s.

When in 1951 the Conservative Party was returned to power, under Winston Churchill, the essential features of the welfare state and the public sector were retained. In 1955 Churchill, in his 81st year, handed over power to the foreign secretary, Anthony Eden. In 1956 Eden found himself confronted by the takeover of the Suez Canal by the president of Egypt, Gamal Nasser. Eden's perception of the threat posed by Nasser was not shared by everyone, even within the Conservative Party. The British invasion of Egypt, in conjunction with France and Israel, brought widespread criticism and was abandoned in the face of pressure from the US and the United Nations. Eden resigned, on the grounds of ill health, and the Conservatives chose Harold Macmillan as their new leader and prime minister.

By the early 1960s, the economy had improved, living standards had risen, and Prime Minister Harold Macmillan was known as "Supermac." Internationally, he established working relationships with the US presidents Eisenhower and Kennedy. He also did much for the Commonwealth, but he was sufficiently realistic to see that the UK's long-term economic and political future lay in Europe. By the mid-1950s the framework for the European Community (EC) had been created, with the UK an onlooker rather than a participant. The Conservatives won the 1959 general election with an increased majority, and in 1961 the first serious attempt was made to join the EC, only to have it blocked by the French president, Charles de Gaulle.

Despite rising living standards, the UK's economic performance was not as successful as that of many of its competitors, such as West Germany and Japan. There was a growing awareness that there was insufficient investment in industry, that young talent was going into the professions or financial institutions rather than manufacturing, and that training was poorly planned and inadequately funded. It was against this background that Macmillan unexpectedly resigned 1963, on the grounds of ill health, and was succeeded by

United Kingdom
United Kingdom
ATLANTIC
OCEAN
SHETLAND
ORKNEY
The districts of Northern Ireland
1 Londonerry
2 Limavady
3 Coleraine
4 Ballymoney
5 Moyle
6 Larne
7 Ballymena
8 Magherafelt
9 Cookstown
10 Strabane
11 Omagh
12 Fernanagh
13 Dungannon
14 Craigavon
15 Armagh
16 Newry and Mourne
17 Banbridge
18 Down
19 Lisburn
20 Antrim
21 Newtownabbey
22 Carrickfergus
23 North Down
24 Arda
25 Castlereagh
26 Belfast
WESTERN ISLES
HIGHLAND
GRAMPIAN
SCOTLAND
NORTH SEA
TAYSIDE
FIFE
CENTRAL
Edinburgh
LOTHIAN
STRATHCLYDE
BORDERS
DUMFRIES AND GALLOWAY
NORTHUMBERLAND
TYNE AND WEAR
DONEGAL
N. IRELAND
DURHAM
CLEVELAND
CUMBRIA
ISLE OF MAN
SLIGO
LEITRIM
MAYO
CAVAN
LONGFORD
LOUTH
ROSCOMMON
WEST MEATH
MEATH
NORTH YORKSHIRE
LANCASHIRE
W. YORKS
HUMBERSIDE
GALWAY
OFFALY
KILDARE
DUBLIN
Dublin
IRELAND
GREATER MANCHESTER
MERSEYSIDE
S. YORKS
LAOIS
WICKLOW
CLARE
CHESHIRE
DERBYSHIRE
NOTTINGHAMSHIRE
LINCOLNSHIRE
CARLOW
CLWYD
GWYNEDD
SHROPSHIRE
STAFFORDSHIRE
LIMERICK
TIPPERARY
KILKENNY
WEXFORD
LEICESTERSHIRE
NORFOLK
WALES
WEST MIDLANDS
WARWICKSHIRE
NORTHAMPTONSHIRE
CAMBRIDGESHIRE
KERRY
CORK
WATERFORD
POWYS
HEREFORD AND WORCESTER
BEDFORDSHIRE
SUFFOLK
St. George's Channel
DYFED
BUCKS
HERTFORD
ESSEX
GLOUCESTERSHIRE
GWENT
OXFORDSHIRE
WEST GLAMORGAN
MID GLAMORGAN
SOUTH GLAMORGAN
Cardiff
AVON
GREATER LONDON
London
ENGLAND
BERKSHIRE
WILTSHIRE
SURREY
KENT
SOMERSET
HAMPSHIRE
WEST SUSSEX
EAST SUSSEX
Str. of Dover
DEVON
DORSET
ISLE OF WIGHT
CORNWALL
ENGLISH CHANNEL
Isles of Scilly
Alderney
Guernsey
Channel Is. (Br.)
Jersey
ATLANTIC OCEAN
FRANCE
0 50 100 150 miles
0 100 200 km
58°
54°
50°
4°
2°
0°

the foreign secretary, Lord Home, who immediately renounced his title to become Alec Douglas-Home.

In the general election 1964 the Labour Party won a slender majority, and its leader, Harold Wilson, became prime minister. The election had been fought on the issue of the economy. Wilson created the Department of Economic Affairs (DEA) to challenge the short-term conservatism of the Treasury, and brought in a leading labor unionist to head a new Department of Technology. In an early general election 1966 Wilson increased his Commons majority, but his promises of fundamental changes in economic planning, industrial investment, and improved work practices were not fulfilled. The DEA was disbanded 1969 and an ambitious plan for the reform of industrial relations was dropped in the face of trade-union opposition.

In 1970 the Conservatives returned to power under Edward Heath. He, too, saw institutional change as one way of achieving industrial reform and created two new central departments (Trade and Industry, Environment) and a "think tank" to advise the government on long-term strategy, the Central Policy Review Staff (CPRS). He attempted to change the climate of industrial relations through a long and complicated Industrial Relations Bill. He saw entry into the EC as the "cold shower of competition' that industry needed, and membership was negotiated 1972.

Heath's "counter-revolution," as he saw it, was frustrated by the labor unions, and the sharp rise in oil prices 1973 forced a U-turn in economic policy. Instead of abandoning "lame ducks" to their fate, he found it necessary to take ailing industrial companies, such as Rolls-Royce, into public ownership. The introduction of a statutory incomes policy precipitated a national miners' strike in the winter of 1973–74, and Heath decided to challenge the unions by holding an early general election 1974. The result was a hung Parliament, with Labour winning the biggest number of seats but no single party having an overall majority. Heath tried briefly to form a coalition with the Liberals and, when this failed, resigned.

Harold Wilson returned to the premiership, heading a minority government, but in another general election later the same year won enough additional seats to give him a working majority. He had taken over a damaged economy and a nation puzzled and divided by the events of the previous years. He turned to Labour's natural ally and founder, the trade-union movement, for support and jointly they agreed on a "social contract": the government pledged itself to redress the imbalance between management and unions created by the Heath industrial-relations legislation, and the unions promised to cooperate in a voluntary industrial and incomes policy. Wilson met criticism from a growing left-wing movement within his party, impatient for radical change. In March 1976 Wilson, apparently tired and disillusioned, retired in midterm.

Wilson was succeeded by James Callaghan, his senior by some four years. In the other two parties, Heath had unexpectedly been ousted by Margaret Thatcher, and the Liberal Party leader, Jeremy Thorpe, had resigned after a personal scandal and been succeeded by the young Scottish MP David Steel. Callaghan was now leading a divided party and a government with a dwindling parliamentary majority. Later in 1976 an unexpected financial crisis arose from a drop in confidence in the overseas exchange markets, a rapidly falling pound, and a drain on the country's foreign reserves. After considerable debate within the cabinet, both before and afterwards, it was decided to seek help from the International Monetary Fund and submit to its stringent economic policies. Within weeks the crisis was over and within months the economy was showing clear signs of improvement.

In 1977, to shore up his slender parliamentary majority, Callaghan entered into an agreement with the new leader of the Liberal Party, David Steel. Under the "Lib-Lab Pact" Labour pursued moderate, nonconfrontational policies in consultation with the Liberals, who, in turn, voted with the government, and the economy improved dramatically. The Lib-Lab Pact had effectively finished by the autumn of 1978, and soon the social contract with the unions began to disintegrate. Widespread and damaging strikes in the public sector badly affected essential services during what became known as the "winter of discontent." At the end of March 1979 Callaghan lost a vote of confidence in the House of Commons and was forced into a general election.

The Conservatives returned to power under the UK's first female prime minister, Margaret Thatcher. She inherited a number of inflationary public-sector pay awards that, together with a

United Kingdom
Shetland Is
Orkney Is
Pentland Firth
North Minch
North West Highlands
Outer Hebrides
Inner Hebrides
Skye
Rhum
Coll
Tiree
Mull
Jura
Islay
Arran
L. Ness
Ben Nevis 4402ft/1342m
Grampian Mts
Dee
Tay
Forth
Clyde
Tweed
Southern Uplands
Cheviot Hills
ATLANTIC
OCEAN
NORTH
SEA
Mts of Antrim
North Channel
Sperrin Mts
L. Neagh
L. Erne
Tyne
Cumbrian Mts
Scafell Pike 3208ft/978m
Tees
North York Moors
Pennines
I. of Man
IRISH SEA
L. Mask
L. Corrib
Central Plain
Liverpool Bay
Ribble
Mersey
Wicklow Mts
Shannon
Barrow
Snowdon 3559ft/1085m
Cambrian Mts
Trent
The Wash
The Fens
Welland
Ouse
Cardigan Bay
Severn
Avon
Macgillycuddys Reeks 3415ft/1041m
Blackwater
Mts of Kerry
St. George's Channel
Cotswolds
Thames
London
North Downs
South Downs
Str. of Dover
Bristol Channel
Exmoor
Dartmoor
ENGLISH CHANNEL
Isles of Scilly
Alderney
Guernsey
Channel Is. (Br.)
Jersey
FRANCE
0 50 100 150 miles
0 100 200 km
58°
54°
50°
4°
2°
0°

budget that doubled the rate of value added tax, resulted in a sharp rise in prices and interest rates. The Conservatives were pledged to reduce inflation and did so by mainly monetarist policies, which caused the number of unemployed to rise from 1.3 million to 2 million in the first year. Thatcher had experience in only one government department, and it was nearly two years before she made any major changes to the cabinet she inherited from Heath. In foreign affairs Zimbabwe became independent 1980 after many years, and without the bloodshed many had feared.

Meanwhile, changes were taking place in the other parties. Callaghan resigned the leadership of the Labour Party 1980 and was replaced by the left-winger Michael Foot, and early in 1981 three Labour shadow cabinet members, David Owen, Shirley Williams, and William Rodgers, with the former deputy leader Roy Jenkins (collectively dubbed the "Gang of Four"), broke away to form a new centrist group, the ◊Social Democratic Party (SDP). The new party made an early impression, winning a series of by-elections within months of its creation. From 1983 to 1988 the Liberals and the SDP were linked in an electoral pact, the Alliance. They advocated the introduction of a system of ◊proportional representation, which would ensure a fairer parity between votes gained and seats won.

Unemployment continued to rise, passing the 3 million mark in Jan 1982, and the Conservatives and their leader were receiving low ratings in the public-opinion polls. An unforseen event rescued them, the invasion of the Falkland Islands by Argentina. Thatcher's decision to send a battle fleet to recover the islands paid off. The general election 1983 was fought with the euphoria of the Falklands victory still in the air and the Labor Party, under its new leader, divided and unconvincing. The Conservatives had a landslide victory, winning more Commons seats than any party since 1945, although with less than half the popular vote. Thatcher was able to establish her position firmly, replacing most of her original cabinet.

The next three years were marked by rising unemployment and growing dissent: a dispute at the government's main intelligence-gathering station, GCHQ; a bitter and protracted miners' strike; increasing violence in Northern Ireland; an attempted assassination of leading members of the Conservative Party during their annual conference; and riots in inner-city areas of London, Bristol, and Liverpool. The government was further embarrassed by its own prosecutions under the Official Secrets Act and the resignations of two prominent cabinet ministers. With the short-term profits from North Sea oil and an ambitious privatization program, the inflation rate continued to fall and by the winter of 1986–87 the economy was buoyant enough to allow the chancellor of the Exchequer to arrange a pre-election spending and credit boom.

Leadership changes took place by 1987 in two of the other parties. Michael Foot was replaced by his Welsh protégé, Neil Kinnock; Roy Jenkins was replaced by David Owen as SDP leader, to be succeeded in turn by Robert MacLennan Sept 1987, when the SDP and Liberal parties voted to initiate talks toward a merger. Despite high unemployment and Thatcher's increasingly authoritarian style of government, the Conservatives were reelected June 1987.

The merger of the Liberal and Social Democratic parties was an acrimonious affair, with the SDP, led by David Owen, refusing to join the merged party and operating as a rival group. Paddy Ashdown emerged as the leader of the new party.

In a cabinet reshuffle July 1989, Geoffrey Howe was replaced as foreign secretary by John Major. In Oct 1989 the chancellor of the Exchequer, Nigel Lawson, resigned because of disagreements with the prime minister, and Major replaced him. Douglas Hurd took over the foreign office. In Dec 1989 Mrs Thatcher won the party leadership election. The government was widely criticized for its decision forcibly to repatriate Vietnamese "boat people" and for the perceived over-liberality of its decision to give UK right of abode to the families of 50,000 "key" Hong Kong citizens, after the transfer of the colony to China in 1997. David Owen announced that the SDP would no longer be able to fight in all national constituencies and would only operate as a "guerrilla force." The Green Party polled 2 million votes in the European elections. The Labour Party launched a new Policy Review.

In Sept 1990 the House of Commons was recalled for an emergency debate that endorsed the government's military activities in the Gulf. In Oct, shortly before the Conservative annual conference, the government announced that it was joining the European Exchange Rate Mechan-

United Nations peacekeeping forces

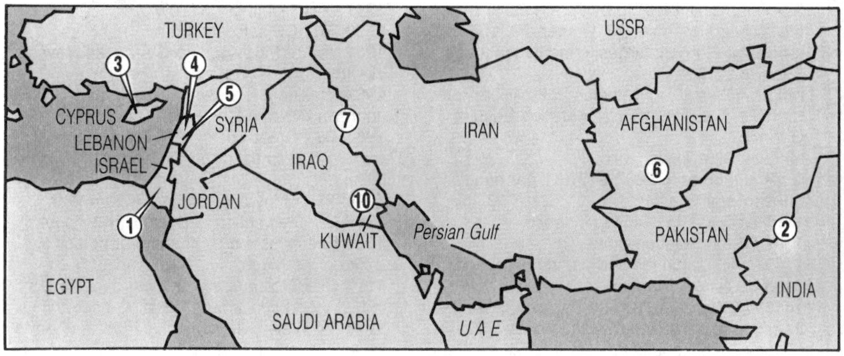
TURKEY
USSR
CYPRUS
LEBANON
ISRAEL
SYRIA
IRAQ
IRAN
AFGHANISTAN
JORDAN
KUWAIT
Persian Gulf
PAKISTAN
INDIA
EGYPT
SAUDI ARABIA
UAE
1
2
3
4
5
6
7
10

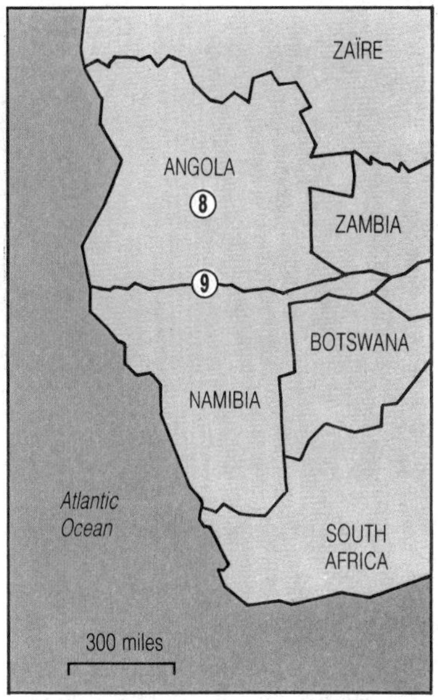
ZAÏRE
ANGOLA
ZAMBIA
BOTSWANA
NAMIBIA
Atlantic Ocean
SOUTH AFRICA
300 miles
8
9

Key No.	Began	Location	Key No.	Began	Location
①	June 1948	Sinai; Beirut*	⑥	Apr 1988	Afghanistan
②	Jan 1949	India–Pakistan border areas	⑦	Aug 1988	Iran–Iraq border
③	Mar 1964	Cyprus	⑧	Jan 1989	Cuba withdrawal from Angola
④	June 1974	Golan Heights	⑨	Apr 1989	Namibia
⑤	Mar 1978	Southern Lebanon	⑩	Feb 1991	Kuwait–Iraq border

ism (ERM). In Nov the deputy prime minister, Geoffrey Howe, resigned. After a dramatic resignation speech by Howe, strongly critical of Thatcher, Michael Heseltine announced his candidacy for the leadership of the Conservative Party. Having failed to gain a clear victory in the first ballot of the leadership election, Thatcher was eventually persuaded by her colleagues to withdraw from the contest. In the subsequent second ballot Michael Heseltine (131 votes) and Douglas Hurd (56) conceded that John Major (185) had won. He consequently became party leader and prime minister.

United Nations (UN) association of nation-states (successor to the ◊League of Nations) for international peace, security, and cooperation, with its headquarters in New York City. Its charter was drawn up at the San Francisco Conference 1945, based on proposals drafted at the Dumbarton Oaks conference. The original intention was that the UN's Security Council would preserve the wartime alliance of the US, USSR, and Britain (with France and China also permanent members) in order to maintain the peace. This never happened because of the outbreak of the Cold War, but the UN has played a positive role in many other areas such as refugees, development assistance, disaster relief, and cultural cooperation.

United Provinces of Central America political union 1823–38 between the the Central American states of Costa Rica, El Salvador, Guatemala, Honduras, and Nicaragua. The union followed the break-up of the Spanish empire and was initially dominated by Guatemala. Its unity was more apparent than real, and the federation fell apart in 1838. Subsequent attempts at reunification foundered.

United States (US), officially ***United States of America*** (USA), country in North America, extending from the Atlantic to the Pacific oceans, bounded N by Canada and S by Mexico, and including the outlying states of Alaska and Hawaii.

government The US is a federal republic comprising 50 states and the District of ◊Columbia. Under the 1787 constitution, which has had 26 amendments, the constituent states are reserved considerable powers of self-government. The federal government concentrated originally on military and foreign affairs and the coordination of interstate concerns, leaving legislation in other spheres to the states, each with its own constitution, elected legislature, governor, supreme court, and local taxation powers. Since the 1930s, however, the federal government has increasingly attempted to run the country and has therefore impinged upon state affairs. It has become the principal revenue-raising and spending agency.

The executive, legislative, and judicial branches of the federal government are deliberately separate from each other, working in a system of checks and balances. At the head of the executive branch is a president elected every four years in a national contest by universal adult suffrage but votes are counted at the state level on a winner-take-all basis, with each state (and the District of Columbia) being assigned votes (equivalent to the number of its congressional representatives) in a national electoral college that formally elects the president. The president serves as head of state, the armed forces, and the federal civil service. He or she is restricted to a maximum of two terms and, once elected, cannot be removed except through impeachment and subsequent conviction by Congress. The president works with a personally selected (appointed) cabinet team, subject to the Senate's approval, whose members are prohibited from serving in the legislature.

The second branch of government, Congress, the federal legislature, comprises two houses, the 100-member Senate and the 435-member House of Representatives. Senators serve six-year terms, and there are two from each state regardless of its size and population. Every two years a third of the seats come up for election. Representatives are elected from state congressional districts of roughly equal demographic sizes and serve two-year terms.

Congress operates through a system of specialized standing committees in both houses. The Senate is the more powerful chamber of Congress, since its approval is required for key federal appointments and for the ratification of foreign treaties. The president's policy program needs the approval of Congress, and the president addresses Congress in Jan for an annual "State of the Union" speech and sends periodic "messages" and "recommendations." The success of a president to carry out his platform depends on voting support in Congress, bargaining skills, and public support.

Proposed legislation, to become law (an Act of Congress), requires the approval of both houses of Congress as well as the signature of the president. If differences exist, "conference committees" are convened to effect compromise agreements. The president can impose a veto, which can be overridden only by two-thirds majorities in both houses. Constitutional amendments require two-thirds majorities from both houses and the support of three-quarters of the nation's 50 state legislatures.

The third branch of government, the judiciary, headed by the Supreme Court, interprets the written US Constitution to ensure that a correct balance is maintained between federal and state institutions and the executive and legislature and to uphold the Constitution, especially the civil rights described in the first ten (the ◊Bill of Rights) and later amendments. The Supreme Court comprises nine judges appointed by the president with the Senate's approval, who serve life terms and can only be removed by impeachment, trial, and conviction by Congress.

Two broad political parties, divided regionally and ideologically, dominate US politics: the Democrats and the Republicans. During the 1930s the Democrats became pre-eminent both at the local and congressional levels. The party is dominated by its northeast liberal wing, which, since the Depression, supports social reform through federal funds and government intervention, but the conservative southern wing is also powerful. The Republicans are more conservative than the Democrats and have been most successful during recent decades in presidential contests, often because of support by conservative Southern Democrats. Republicans are strongest in the central and western states and adhere, in general, to a big-business, "small government" philosophy. Both parties have a relatively weak national organization and seldom vote as a block in Congress. Party organization is centered instead at the state and local levels.

The US administers a number of territories, including American Samoa and the US Virgin Islands, which have local legislatures and a governor. These territories, as well as the "self-governing territories" of Puerto Rico and Guam, each send a nonvoting delegate to the US House of Representatives.

The District of Columbia, centered around the city of Washington, DC, is the site of the Federal legislature, judiciary, and executive. Since 1971 it has sent one nonvoting delegate to the House and since 1961 its citizens have been able to vote in presidential elections (the District having three votes in the national electoral college).

United States of America

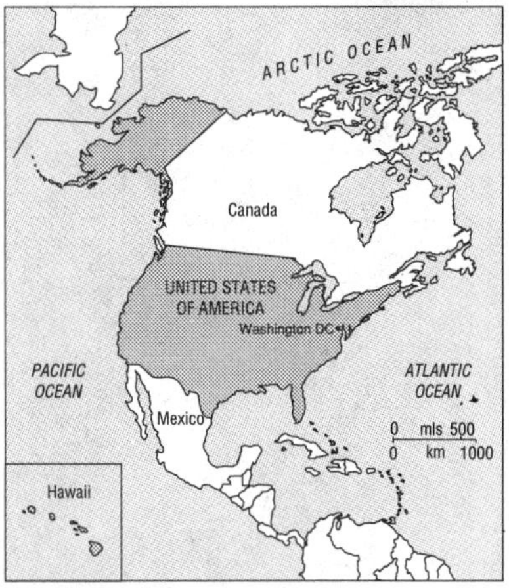
ARCTIC OCEAN
Canada
UNITED STATES OF AMERICA
Washington DC
PACIFIC OCEAN
ATLANTIC OCEAN
Mexico
0 mls 500
0 km 1000
Hawaii

area 3,618,770 sq mi/9,368,900 sq km
capital Washington DC
cities New York, Los Angeles, Chicago, Philadelphia, Detroit, San Francisco, Washington, Dallas, San Diego, San Antonio, Houston, Boston, Baltimore, Phoenix, Indianapolis, Memphis, Honolulu, San José
physical topography and vegetation from tropical (Hawaii) to arctic (Alaska) zones; mountain ranges parallel with the E and W coasts; the Rocky Mountains separate rivers emptying into the Pacific from those flowing into the Gulf of Mexico; Great Lakes; rivers include Hudson, Mississippi, Missouri, Colorado, Columbia, Snake, Rio Grande, Ohio
features see individual states
territories the commonwealths of Puerto Rico, and Northern Marianas; the federated states of Micronesia; Guam, the US Virgin Islands, American Samoa, Wake Island, Midway Islands, Marshall Islands, Belau, and Johnston and Sand Islands
head of state and government George Bush from 1989
political system liberal democracy
political parties Democratic Party liberal, center; Republican Party, center-right
exports
currency US dollar
population (1990 est) 250,372,000 (ethnic minorities include 26,500,000 black, about 20,000,000 Hispanic, and 1,000,000 American Indians, of whom 50% are concentrated in Arizona, California, New Mexico, North Carolina, Oklahoma); growth rate 0.9% p.a.
life expectancy men 72, women 79 (1989)
language English; largest minority language Spanish
religion 79 million Protestant, 52 million Roman Catholic, 6 million Jewish, 4 million Eastern Orthodox
literacy 99% (1989)
GNP $3,855 bn (1983); $13,451 per head
chronology
1776 Declaration of Independence.
1787 US constitution drawn up.
1789 Washington elected as first president.
1803 Louisiana Purchase.
1812–14 War of 1812 with England, arising from commercial disputes caused by Britain's struggle with Napoleon.
1819 Florida purchased from Spain.
1836 The battle of the Alamo, Texas, won by Mexico.
1841 First wagon train left Missouri for California.
1846–48 Mexican War resulted in cession to US of Arizona, California, Colorado (part), Nevada, New Mexico, Texas, and Utah.
1846 Mormons, under Brigham Young, founded Salt Lake City, Utah.
1848–49 California gold rush.
1860 Lincoln elected president.
1861–65 Civil War between North and South.
1865 Slavery abolished. Lincoln assassinated.
1867 Alaska bought from Russia.
1890 Battle of Wounded Knee, the last major battle between American Indians and US troops.
1898 War with Spain ended with the Spanish cession of Philippines, Puerto Rico, and Guam; it was agreed that Cuba be independent.
1898 Hawaii annexed.
1917–18 US entered World War I.
1919–1921 Wilson's 14 Points become base for League of Nations.
1920 Women achieved the vote.
1924 American Indians made citizens by Congress.
1929 Wall Street stock-market crash.
1933 F D Roosevelt's New Deal to alleviate the Depression put into force.
1941–45 The Japanese attack on Pearl Harbor Dec 1941 precipitated US entry into World War II.
1945 The US ended war in the Pacific by dropping A-bombs on Hiroshima and Nagasaki, Japan.
1950–53 US involvement in Korean War. McCarthy anti-Communist investigations (HUAC) began; became a "witch hunt."
1954 Civil Rights legislation began with the ending of segregation in public schools.
1957 Civil Rights bill on voting.
1958 First US satellite in orbit.
1961 Bay of Pigs abortive CIA-backed invasion of Cuba.
1963 President Kennedy assassinated; L B Johnson assumed the presidency.
1964–68 "Great Society" civil-rights and welfare measures in the Omnibus Civil Rights bill.
1964–75 US involvement in Vietnam War.
1965 US intervention in Dominican Republic.
1969 Neil Armstrong was the first person to walk on the Moon.
1973 OPEC oil embargo almost crippled US industry and consumers. Inflation began.
1973–74 Watergate scandal began in effort to reelect Nixon and ended just before impeachment; Nixon resigned as president; replaced by Gerald Ford, who "pardoned" Nixon.
1975 Final US withdrawal from Vietnam.
1979 US-Chinese diplomatic relations normalized.
1979–80 Iranian hostage crisis; relieved by Reagan concessions and hostages released on his inauguration day, Jan 1981.
1981 Space shuttle mission was successful.
1983 US invasion of Grenada.
1986 "Irangate" scandal over secret US government arms sales to Iran, with proceeds to anti-government Contra guerrillas in Nicaragua.
1987 Reagan and Gorbachev (for USSR) signed INF treaty. Wall Street stock-market crash caused by program trading.
1988 US became world's largest debtor nation, owing $532 billion, in Republican bid to control Congress under Reagan and Bush.
1989 Bush met Gorbachev at Malta, end to Cold War declared; high-level delegation sent to China amid severe criticism; large troop reductions and budget cuts announced for US military; US invaded Panama, Gen Noriega taken into custody.
1990 Bush and Gorbachev met. South Africa's Nelson Mandela, freed in South Africa, toured US. US troops sent to Middle East as part of UN multinational force following Iraq's invasion of Kuwait.
1991 In Jan–Feb US-led assault drove Iraq from Kuwait in Gulf War. In July a Strategic Arms Reduction Treaty (START), to reduce the number of long-range nuclear weapons held, was signed at the US-Soviet summit held in Moscow. In Nov, Bush co-hosted Middle East conference in Spain.

history For early history, see ◊American Indian. The Spanish first settled in Florida 1565. The first permanent English settlement was at Jamestown, Virginia, 1607. In 1620 English ◊Pilgrims landed at Plymouth and founded the colony of Massachusetts and, later, Connecticut. English Catholics founded Maryland 1634; English Quakers founded Pennsylvania 1682. A Dutch settlement 1611 on Manhattan Island, named New Amsterdam 1626, was renamed New York after it was taken by England 1664. In the 18th century the English colonies were threatened by French expansion from the Great Lakes to Louisiana until the English won the French and Indian War (in Europe called the Seven Years' War 1756–63).

In 1775, following years of increasing tension, the 13 colonies (New Hampshire, Massachusetts, Rhode Island, Connecticut, New York, New Jersey, Pennsylvania, Delaware, Virginia, North Carolina, South Carolina, Maryland, and Georgia) rose against the British government, assembled at the Continental Congress, and fought British troops in Massachusetts, at Lexington and Concord. Meeting in Philadelphia in 1776, they declared themselves to be "free and independent states." Led by Gen George Washington, they defeated George III's armies in the ◊American Revolution. By the Treaty of Paris 1783 Britain recognized the independence of the 13 colonies. The Constitution came into force 1789. Washington was unanimously elected as the first president.

The ◊Louisiana territory was bought from Napoleon 1803, and Florida from Spain 1819. Napoleon's trade blockade of British shipping led indirectly to the ◊War of 1812. Expansion to the west, called Manifest Destiny, reached the Pacific, and the Mexican War 1846–48 secured the areas of California, Utah, New Mexico, and Texas. ◊Alaska was purchased from Russia 1867. Hawaii ceded itself to the US 1898.

The ◊Civil War 1861–65 put an end to slavery but left ill feeling between north and south. It stimulated additional industrial development in the N, as well as the construction of roads and railroads, which continued until the end of that century.

Involvement in international affairs really began with the Spanish–American War 1898, which involved the US in Cuba, Puerto Rico, and the Philippines. The Panama Canal Zone rights were leased 1903. After trying to maintain an isolationist stance, under President Woodrow Wilson, the US entered ◊World War I in 1917; it was not a party to the Treaty of Versailles but made peace by separate treaties 1921. A period of isolationism followed. The country's economic, industrial, and agricultural expansion was brought to a halt by the stock-market crash 1929, which marked the start of the ◊Depression. President Franklin Roosevelt's ◊New Deal 1933 tackled but did not solve the problem, and only preparations for ◊World War II brought full employment. The US did not declare war until Japan attacked ◊Pearl Harbor on Honolulu Dec 1941.

The US, having emerged from the war as a superpower, remained internationalist during the prosperity of the postwar era. Under the presidency of Harry S Truman (Democrat) a doctrine of intervention in support of endangered "free peoples" and of containing the spread of communism was devised by secretaries of state George

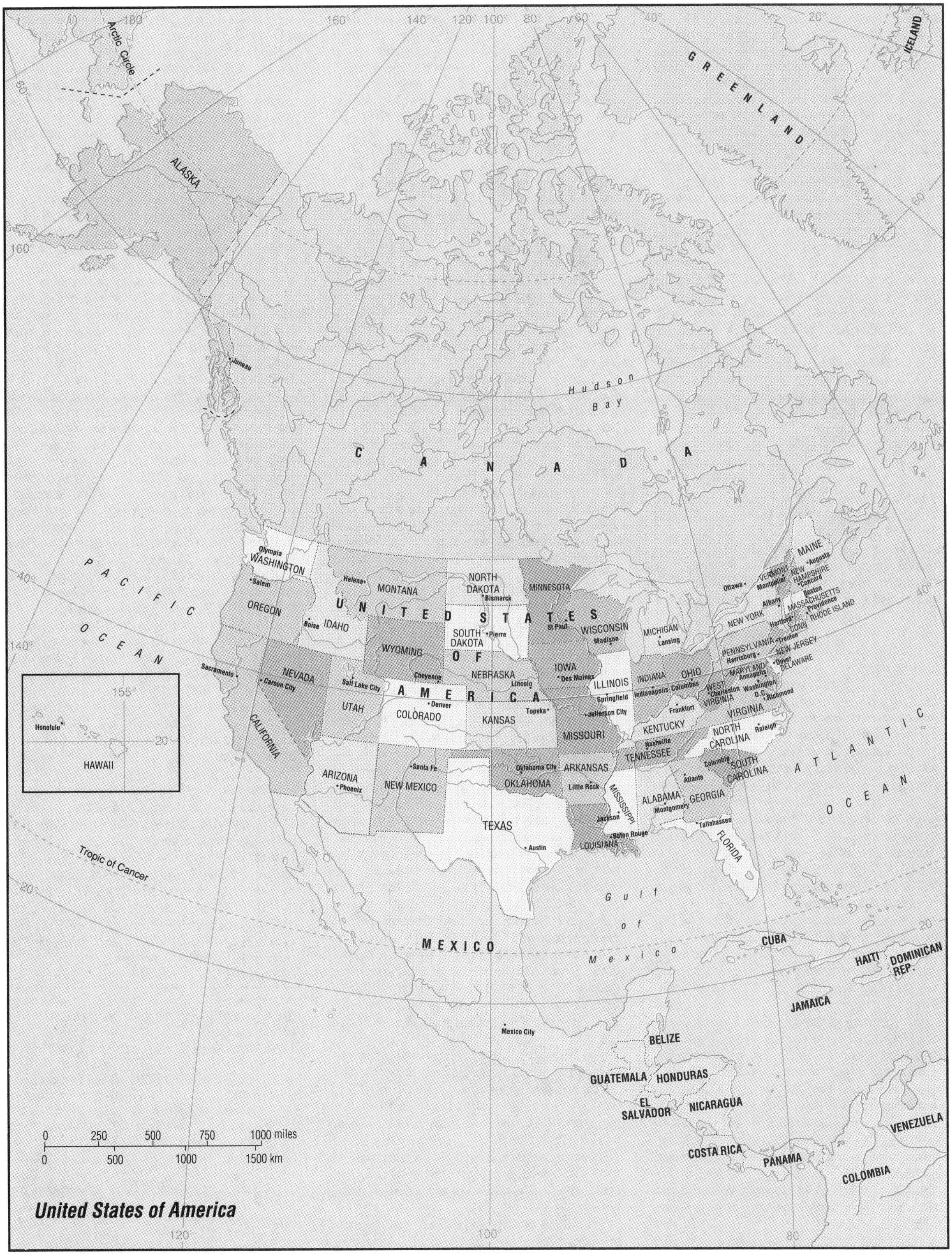
Arctic Circle
ALASKA
GREENLAND
ICELAND
Hudson Bay
CANADA
PACIFIC OCEAN
ATLANTIC OCEAN
UNITED STATES OF AMERICA
Juneau
Olympia
WASHINGTON
Salem
OREGON
Boise
IDAHO
Helena
MONTANA
NORTH DAKOTA
Bismarck
SOUTH DAKOTA
Pierre
MINNESOTA
St Paul
WISCONSIN
Madison
MICHIGAN
Lansing
WYOMING
Cheyenne
NEBRASKA
Lincoln
IOWA
Des Moines
ILLINOIS
Springfield
INDIANA
Indianapolis
OHIO
Columbus
Sacramento
Carson City
NEVADA
Salt Lake City
UTAH
Denver
COLORADO
KANSAS
Topeka
Jefferson City
MISSOURI
Frankfort
KENTUCKY
Nashville
TENNESSEE
CALIFORNIA
ARIZONA
Phoenix
Santa Fe
NEW MEXICO
Oklahoma City
OKLAHOMA
ARKANSAS
Little Rock
MISSISSIPPI
Jackson
ALABAMA
Montgomery
Atlanta
GEORGIA
Columbia
SOUTH CAROLINA
NORTH CAROLINA
Raleigh
VIRGINIA
Richmond
WEST VIRGINIA
Charleston
Washington D.C.
MARYLAND
Annapolis
DELAWARE
Dover
NEW JERSEY
Trenton
PENNSYLVANIA
Harrisburg
NEW YORK
Albany
Hartford
CONN
RHODE ISLAND
Providence
MASSACHUSETTS
Boston
NEW HAMPSHIRE
Concord
VERMONT
Montpelier
MAINE
Augusta
Ottawa
TEXAS
Austin
Baton Rouge
LOUISIANA
Tallahassee
FLORIDA
Honolulu
HAWAII
Tropic of Cancer
Gulf of Mexico
MEXICO
Mexico City
CUBA
HAITI
DOMINICAN REP.
JAMAICA
BELIZE
GUATEMALA
HONDURAS
EL SALVADOR
NICARAGUA
COSTA RICA
PANAMA
VENEZUELA
COLOMBIA
0 250 500 750 1000 miles
0 500 1000 1500 km

United States of America

◊Marshall and Dean ◊Acheson. This led to the US's safeguarding of Greece and Nationalist Taiwan 1949 and its participation in the ◊Korean War 1950–53. The US, in addition, helped to create new global and regional bodies designed to maintain the peace—the United Nations (UN, 1945), the Organization of American States (OAS, 1948), the North Atlantic Treaty Organization (NATO, 1949), the South-East Asia Treaty Organization (SEATO, 1954)—and launched the Marshall Plan 1947 to begin strengthening the capitalist economies of its allies while fending off similar strategies of the USSR-dominated Eastern Bloc. This began the ◊Cold War. Domestically, President Truman sought to introduce liberal reforms designed at extending civil and welfare rights under the slogan "a fair deal." These measures were blocked by a combination of Southern Democrats and Republicans in Congress. Truman's foreign policy was criticized as being "soft on communism" between 1950 and 1952, as a wave of anti-Soviet hysteria, spearheaded by Senator Joseph McCarthy, swept the nation.

This rightward shift in the public mood brought Republican victory in the congressional and presidential elections 1952, with popular military commander General Dwight D Eisenhower becoming president. He was re-elected by an increased margin Nov 1956. Working with Secretary of State John Foster Dulles, Eisenhower adhered to the Truman–Acheson doctrine of "containment," while at home he pursued a policy of "progressive conservatism" designed to encourage business enterprise. The Eisenhower era was one of growth, involving the migration of southern blacks to the northern industrial cities and rapid expansion in the educational sector. In the southern states, where racial segregation and discrimination was openly practiced, a new civil-rights movement developed under the leadership of Dr Martin Luther King, Jr. Promising a "New Frontier" program of social reform, John F Kennedy (Democrat) won the presidential election Nov 1960 and emerged as an active supporter of civil rights and space exploration and an opponent of communism abroad (see ◊Bay of Pigs). He was assassinated Nov 1963.

It was left to his vice-president and successor, Lyndon B Johnson, to oversee the passage of additional reforms, called the "Great Society" by Johnson. These measures, which included the Equal Opportunities, Voting Rights, Housing, and Medicare acts, guaranteed blacks their civil rights and extended the reach and responsibilities of the federal government. They were buttressed by the judicial rulings of the Supreme Court, led by Chief Justice Earl Warren. Abroad, President Johnson escalated US involvement in the ◊Vietnam War (1964–73), which polarized public opinion and deeply divided the Democratic Party into "hawks and doves."

Johnson declined to run for reelection Nov 1968, and his vice-president, Hubert Humphrey, was defeated by Republican Richard Nixon. Working with National Security Adviser Henry ◊Kissinger, Nixon escalated the Vietnam conflict by invading neighboring Cambodia (leading to the Kent State demonstration and shootings) before he began a gradual disengagement, launching a policy of ◊détente that brought an improvement in relations with the Soviet Union (see ◊Strategic Arms Limitation Talks) and a visit to Communist China 1973. Nixon, faced with a divided opposition led by the liberal George McGovern, had gained re-election by an overwhelming margin Nov 1972, but during the campaign, Nixon's staff had broken into the Democratic Party's ◊Watergate headquarters. When this and the attempts at cover-up came to light, the scandal forced the resignation of the president Aug 1974, just short of impeachment.

Watergate shook the US public's confidence in the Washington establishment. Gerald Ford, who had been appointed vice-president when Spiro Agnew was forced to step down Dec 1973, pardoned Nixon and kept the services of Kissinger and the policy of détente when he became president. He faced a hostile, Democrat-dominated Congress that introduced legislation curbing the unauthorized power of the presidency, attemping to mend fences both at home and abroad. He also had to deal with an economic recession and increased OPEC oil prices that began under Nixon 1973.

Ford ran in the presidential election Nov 1976 but was defeated by Washington outsider and Democrat Jimmy Carter, who promised open and honest government. Carter was a fiscal conservative but social liberal, who sought to extend welfare provision through greater administrative efficiency. He substantially ended the fuel crisis through enforced conservation in the energy bills 1978 and 1980. In foreign relations President Carter emphasized human rights. In the Middle East, he moved close to a peace settlement 1978–79 (see ◊Camp David Agreements) and in Jan 1979 the US's diplomatic relations with Communist China were fully normalized.

The Carter presidency was, however, brought down by two foreign-policy crises 1979–80: the fall of the shah of Iran and the Soviet invasion of Afghanistan. The president's leadership style, military economies, and moralistic foreign policy were blamed by the press for weakening US influence abroad. There was a swell of anti-communist feeling and mounting support for a new policy of rearmament and selective interventionism. President Carter responded to this new mood by enunciating the hawkish ◊Carter Doctrine 1980 and supporting a new arms-development program, but his popularity plunged during 1980 as economic recession gripped the country and US embassy staff members were held hostage by Shiite Muslim fundamentalists in Tehran.

The Republican Ronald Reagan benefited from Carter's difficulties and was elected Nov 1980, when the Democrats also lost control of the Senate. The new president had risen to prominence as an effective, television-skilled campaigner. He purported to believe in a return to traditional Christian and family values and promoted a domestic policy of supply-side economics, decentralization, and deregulation. The early years of the Reagan presidency witnessed substantial reductions in taxation, with cutbacks in federal welfare programs that created serious hardships in many sectors as economic recession gripped the nation.

Reagan rejected détente and spoke of the USSR as an "evil empire" that needed to be checked by a military buildup and a readiness to employ force. This led to a sharp deterioration in Soviet-US relations, ushering in a new Cold War during the Polish crisis 1981. He was reelected on a wave of optimistic patriotism Nov 1984, defeating the Democrat ticket of Walter ◊Mondale and Geraldine ◊Ferraro by a record margin. A radical tax-cutting bill passed in Congress, and in 1986 a large budget and trade deficit developed (as a spending economy was developed to control Congress). At home and overseas the president faced mounting public opposition to his interventions in Central America. The new Soviet leader Mikhail ◊Gorbachev pressed unsuccessfully for arms reduction during superpower summits at Geneva (Nov 1985) and Reykjavik (Oct 1986), but a further summit Dec 1987, with an agreement to scrap intermediate-range nuclear missiles, appeared to promise a new détente.

In Nov 1986 the Republican party lost control of the Senate in the midterm elections, just before the disclosure of a scandal concerning US arms sales to Iran in return for hostages held in Beirut, with the profits illegally diverted to help the Nicaraguan Contra (anticommunist) guerrillas.

The ◊Irangate scandal briefly dented public confidence in the administration and forced the dismissal and resignation of key cabinet members, including national security adviser John Poindexter, in Nov 1986, and chief of staff Donald Regan, in Feb 1987. During the last two years of his presidency, a more consensual Reagan was on view and, helped by his Dec 1987 arms reduction deal, he left office with much of his popular affection restored.

Reagan's popularity transferred itself to vice-president George Bush who, despite selecting the inexperienced Dan Quayle as his running-mate and despite opposition charges that he had been indirectly involved in the Irangate proceedings, defeated the Democrat's candidate Michael Dukakis in the presidential election of Nov 1988.

Bush came to power, after six years of economic growth, a time of uncertainty. Reagan's tax-cutting policy had led to mounting Federal trade and budget deficits, which had served to turn the US into a debtor nation for the first time in its history and had precipitated a stock market crash in Oct 1987. Retrenchment was thus needed and this became concentrated, during 1989–90, in the military sphere, being helped by continuing Soviet moves toward both conventional and nuclear forces reduction. Domestically, Bush set as the goal for his presidency to work to create a "kinder, gentler nation," and unveiled a number of initiatives in the areas of education, drug control and the environment designed to deal with problems that had surfaced during the Reagan years. (In 1990, almost 500,000 children were suffering from malnutrition and at least 100,000 people were homeless.) The start of his presidency was marred by the Senate's rejection of his nominee to be Defence Secretary, John Tower, as a result of criticisms of Tower's lifestyle and his links to defense contracting companies. With his overthrowing of the corrupt Panamanian leader, General Manuel Noriega in Dec 1989, Bush began to establish his presidency.

In Sept 1990 the Senate confirmed David Souter, a conservative jurist from New Hampshire who had been nominated by President Bush, as a new Supreme Court justice. He replaced justice William Brennan, a veteran liberal, who resigned in July following a stroke. Souter's appointment appeared likely to strengthen the conservative majority that had been established within the Court as did the confirmation in 1991 of Clarence Thomas after long and bitter Congressional hearings.

The US responded to Iraq's unprovoked invasion and annexation of Kuwait on Aug 2, 1990 by coordinating, in the United Nations, the passage of a series of resolutions damanding Iraq's unconditional withdrawal and imposing comprehensive economic sanctions. By late Nov the US had sent more than 230,000 troops and support personnel to Saudi Arabia to form the core of a 400,000-strong Western and Arab "desert shield" with the object of defending the Saudi frontier and, if necessary, dislodging Iraq from Kuwait. A further 150,000 US troops were sent in early Dec.

In Jan 1991 the ◊Gulf War heated up as US-led forces launched air attacks against Iraqi forces in Kuwait and Iraq. The bombing was followed in Feb by a ground offensive that drove Iraq from Kuwait. Bush followed US success in the war by pushing for and convening a Middle East peace conference in Spain in Nov 1991. Domestically, the US had less success as the economic recession continued. A Bush trip to Australia and East Asia to press for trade concessions ended in Japan in Jan 1992 with little progress.

US: presidents and elections

Year	*President*	*Losing candidate(s)*
1789	1. George Washington (F)	No opponent
1792	reelected	No opponent
1796	2. John Adams (F)	Thomas Jefferson (DR)
1800	3. Thomas Jefferson (DR)	Aaron Burr (DR)
1804	reelected	Charles Pinckney (F)
1808	4. James Madison (DR)	Charles Pinckney (F)
1812	reelected	DeWitt Clinton (F)
1816	5. James Monroe (DR)	Rufus King (F)
1820	reelected	John Quincy Adams (DR)
1824	6. John Quincy Adams (DR)	Andrew Jackson (DR)
	Henry Clay (DR)	William H Crawford (DR)
1828	7. Andrew Jackson (D)	John Quincy Adams (NR)
1832	reelected	Henry Clay (NR)
1836	8. Martin Van Buren (D)	William Henry Harrison (W)
1840	9. William Henry Harrison (W)	Martin Van Buren (D)
	10. John Tyler (W)[1]	
1844	11. James K Polk (D)	Henry Clay (W)

1848	12. Zachary Taylor (W)	Lewis Cass (D)
	13. Millard Fillmore (W)[2]	
1852	14. Franklin Pierce (D)	Winfield Scott (W)
1856	15. James Buchanan (D)	John C Fremont (R)
1860	16. Abraham Lincoln (R)	Stephen Douglas (D)
	John Breckinridge (D)	John Bell (Const. Union)
1864	reelected	George McClellan (D)
	17. Andrew Johnson (D)[3]	
1869	18. Ulysses S Grant (R)	Horatio Seymour (D)
1872	reelected	Horace Greeley (D-LR)
1876	19. Rutherford B Hayes (R)	Samuel Tilden (D)
1880	20. James A Garfield (R)	Winfield Hancock (D)
	21. Chester A Arthur (R)[4]	
1884	22. Grover Cleveland (D)	James Blaine (R)
1888	23. Benjamin Harrison (R)	Grover Cleveland (D)
1892	24. Grover Cleveland (D)	Benjamin Harrison (R)
		James Weaver (P)
1896	25. William McKinley (R)	William J Bryan (D-P)
1900	reelected	William J Bryan (D)
	26. Theodore Roosevelt (R)[5]	
1904	reelected	Alton B Parker (D)
1908	27. William H Taft (R)	William J Bryan (D)
1912	28. Woodrow Wilson (D)	Theodore Roosevelt (PR)
		William H Taft (R)
1916	reelected	Charles E Hughes (R)
1920	29. Warren G Harding (R)	James M Cox (D)
1924	30. Calvin Coolidge (R)	John W Davis (D)
		Robert M LaFollette (PR)
1928	31. Herbert Hoover (R)	Alfred E Smith (D)
1932	32. Franklin D Roosevelt (D)	Herbert Hoover (R)
		Norman Thomas (Socialist)
1936	reelected	Alfred Landon (R)
1940	reelected	Wendell Willkie (R)
1944	reelected	Thomas E Dewey (R)
	33. Harry S Truman (D)[6]	
1948	reelected	Thomas E Dewey (R)
		J Strom Thurmond (SR)
		Henry A Wallace (PR)
1952	34. Dwight D Eisenhower (R)	Adlai E Stevenson (D)
1956	reelected	Adlai E Stevenson (D)
1960	35. John F Kennedy (D)	Richard M Nixon (R)
	36. Lyndon B Johnson (D)[7]	
1964	reelected	Barry M Goldwater (R)
1968	37. Richard M Nixon (R)	Hubert H Humphrey (D)
		George C Wallace
1972	reelected	George S McGovern (D)
	38. Gerald R Ford (R)[8]	
1976	39. Jimmy Carter (D)	Gerald R Ford (R)
1980	40. Ronald Reagan (R)	Jimmy Carter (D)
		John B Anderson (Independent)
1984	reelected	Walter Mondale (D)
1988	41. George Bush (R)	Michael Dukakis (D)

(F) Federalist; (D) Democrat; (R) Republican; (DR) Democrat-Republican; (NR) National Republican; (W) Whig; (P) People's; (PR) Progressive; (S) States' Rights; (LR) Liberal Republican.

[1] Became president 1841 on death of Harrison.
[2] Became president 1850 on death of Taylor.
[3] Became president 1865 on assassination of Lincoln.
[4] Became president 1881 on assassination of Garfield.
[5] Became president 1901 on assassination of McKinley.
[6] Became president 1945 on death of F D Roosevelt.
[7] Became president 1963 on assassination of Kennedy.
[8] Became president 1974 on resignation of Nixon.

United States

State	*Capital*	*Area sq km*	*Date of joining the Union*
Alabama	Montgomery	134,700	1819
Alaska	Juneau	1,531,100	1959
Arizona	Phoenix	294,100	1912
Arkansas	Little Rock	137,800	1836
California	Sacramento	411,100	1850
Colorado	Denver	269,700	1876
Connecticut	Hartford	13,000	1788
Delaware	Dover	5,300	1787
Florida	Tallahassee	152,000	1845
Georgia	Atlanta	152,600	1788
Hawaii	Honolulu	16,800	1959
Idaho	Boise	216,500	1890
Illinois	Springfield	146,100	1818
Indiana	Indianapolis	93,700	1816
Iowa	Des Moines	145,800	1846
Kansas	Topeka	213,200	1861
Kentucky	Frankfort	104,700	1792
Louisiana	Baton Rouge	135,900	1812
Maine	Augusta	86,200	1820
Maryland	Annapolis	31,600	1788
Massachusetts	Boston	21,500	1788
Michigan	Lansing	151,600	1877
Minnesota	St Paul	218,700	1858
Mississippi	Jackson	123,600	1817
Missouri	Jefferson City	180,600	1821
Montana	Helena	381,200	1889
Nebraska	Lincoln	200,400	1867
Nevada	Carson City	286,400	1864
New Hampshire	Concord	24,000	1788
New Jersey	Trenton	20,200	1787
New Mexico	Santa Fé	315,000	1912
New York	Albany	127,200	1788
North Carolina	Raleigh	136,400	1789
North Dakota	Bismarck	183,100	1889
Ohio	Columbus	107,100	1803
Oklahoma	Oklahoma City	181,100	1907
Oregon	Salem	251,500	1859
Pennsylvania	Harrisburg	117,400	1787
Rhode Island	Providence	3,100	1790
South Carolina	Columbia	80,600	1788
South Dakota	Pierre	199,800	1889
Tennessee	Nashville	109,200	1796
Texas	Austin	691,200	1845
Utah	Salt Lake City	219,900	1896
Vermont	Montpelier	24,900	1791
Virginia	Richmond	105,600	1788
Washington	Olympia	176,700	1889
West Virginia	Charleston	62,900	1863
Wisconsin	Madison	145,500	1848
Wyoming	Cheyenne	253,400	1890
District of Columbia	Washington	180	
Total		9,391,880	

US v American Tobacco Co a US Supreme Court decision 1911 dealing with the distinction between reasonable and unreasonable formations of trusts. The American Tobacco Co appealed to the Supreme Court after being convicted of monopolistic practices by the federal government. The federal district court had ordered the dissolution of the company, but the Supreme Court revised this decision on the grounds that the attempts to restrain trade had not been unreasonable. The Court ordered that the company be reorganized but not dissolved.

US v Butler a US Supreme Court decision 1936 concerning a New Deal policy of using federal taxing powers to regulate the economy. The challenge was brought against the Agricultural Adjustment Act (AAA), which taxed food processing to pay for farm subsidies, thereby discouraging the planting of certain crops. The Court ruled the AAA invalid on the grounds that it taxed with the purpose of regulating agricultural production.

US v Classic a US Supreme Court decision 1941 dealing with Congress's right to interfere with the operation of state primaries. Convicted of fraud in a Louisiana state primary, Classic appealed on the grounds that primaries, as functions of state political parties, were not subject to government regulation. The Court upheld Classic's conviction, ruling 4 to 3 that the primary had clear impact on the selection of federal representatives. Since Congress had the responsibility to monitor and regulate federal elections, state primaries were judged to be under Congressional authority.

US v Darby Lumber Co a US Supreme Court decision 1941 that decided the issue of federal control of commerce, overturning ◊*Hammer* v *Dagenhart* 1918. The case dealt with the constitutionality of the Fair Labor Standards Act (FLSA) of 1938, which established maximum hours and minimum wages for workers. The interstate sale of any products manufactured in violation of the standards was strictly prohibited. The Court upheld the FLSA ruling that commerce is an integrated whole, not divisible into state and federal spheres. According to the unanimous decision, it was not the Court's role to judge the motives of Congressional legislation; Congress had the right to regulate national commerce without judicial interference.

US v E C Knight Co a US Supreme Court decision 1895 dealing with the right of the federal government to restrict the formation of corporate monopolies. The American Sugar Co established a 98% monopoly on sugar manufacturing in the US when it purchased the E C Knight Sugar Co, its leading competitor. The Justice Department filed suit against Knight for conspiracy to violate federal antitrust legislation. The Court ruled 8 to 1 that manufacturing was distinct from commerce and therefore outside of federal regulatory jurisdiction. The charges against Knight were dropped, virtually nullifying an important provision of the Sherman Antitrust Act 1890.

US v Gouveja a US Supreme Court decision 1984 dealing with the constitutional right of accused persons to an attorney. The case was brought to appeal the conviction of six prison inmates for a murder committed in the prison. The six argued that their right to counsel had been violated when they were detained without lawyers during the initial investigation. The Court ruled that the right to counsel applies only to "adversarial judicial proceedings," not to preliminary investigations.

US v Nixon a US Supreme Court decision 1974 dealing with the extent to which a US president may exercise executive privilege in a criminal investigation. During the ◊Watergate investigations, President Nixon cited this privilege in refusing to produce certain tape recordings that had been subpoened by Special Prosecutor Jaworski. The Court ruled unanimously that while the president had certain privileges, they were subject to definition by the judiciary, the final interpreters of the Constitution. According to the Court, given the circumstances of the criminal investigation, Jaworski had the power to overrule presidential autonomy, requiring Nixon to yield the tapes.

United States architecture little survives of the earliest native American architecture, although the early settlers in each region recorded the house and village styles of the local Indians. The most notable prehistoric remains are the cliff dwellings in the Southwest. Archeologists have also discovered traces of structures associated with the moundbuilding peoples in the Mississippi river valley. Subsequent architectural forms are those that came with colonizers from European cultures, those adapted to American conditions and social development, and, most recently, those that were developed and innovated by American architects.

16th and 17th centuries Earliest European architectural influences were those of the Spanish colonizers, coming N from their Mexican colony or from early settlements in Florida; most were small or transitory. Spanish influence in the Southwest and California grew through the 19th century and continued in the 20th. The dominant American colonial architecture came to the east coast from 17th-century English immigrants, but also from Dutch, Swedish, and German settlers. Generally, new arrivals attempted to reconstruct the architecture they had known in their home countries, making adaptations to available materials and craftsmanship. Wood tended to be the material of choice in the northern colonies; wood, brick, and stone in the middle colonies; and wood and brick in the southern colonies. The earliest styles were primarily for farm homes and some urban dwellings, churches, and a few public buildings. Houses most often were small, had massive chimney stacks, and were timber-framed with brick, clapboard, or wattle-and-daub walls. Early churches and civic buildings were like large houses rather than imposing edifices. By the end of the century, with more settlers, greater resources, and more skilled builders, more elegant and elaborate examples of Jacobean and Queen Anne style were built, and more imposing public architecture was constructed, such as William and Mary College in Williamsburg, Virginia.

18th century Neo-Classical style dominated and was referred to as Georgian architecture, although designs lagged behind English sources, and the scale of projects was generally modest. No architects set up offices, but itinerant master craftsmen with plan-and-model books, working for educated colonial sponsors, diffused European style developments along the eastern seaboard. Many fine homes were built, with distinct variations preferred in each of the colonial regions. Many churches and public buildings were influenced by British architect Christopher Wren. As settlement moved inland, the rough-hewn timber or log cabin became an American architectural mainstay. Other, finer, buildings from this period include numerous plantation houses, such as Westover or Carters Grove in Virginia; Dutch patroon mansions along the Hudson river in New York or in E Pennsylvania; the then Virginia capital of Williamsburg; churches with steeples, such as Old North Church in Boston, Christ Church in Philadelphia, Christ Church in Williamsburg; public buildings, such as the Old State House or Faneuil Hall in Boston, Independence Hall in Philadelphia, or Charles Bulfinch's new State House in Boston; and numerous urban structures.

19th century Early in the century, Neo-Classical patterns were used to design the new republic's buildings, such as the Capitol and the ◊White House in Washington, DC. The style was given strong inspiration by Thomas Jefferson, especially after his stay in Europe. He introduced and promoted a revival of Renaissance architecture based on Andrea Palladio and otherwise helped define what is now known as Federal-period architecture. His own work is best seen in his Virginia home, Monticello (which started as an 18th-century Georgian project and which he transformed throughout his life); in his design for the Virginia state capitol in Richmond, adapted from the Roman Maison Carré at Nimes, France; and in his harmonious plan for the campus of the University of Virginia at Charlottesville. Other structures from the first half of the century include the Greek-revival work of Charles Bulfinch and Benjamin Latrobe (notably in their work on the US Capitol). After the Civil War, Romanesque forms in stone and brick were promoted by Henry Hobson Richardson. An appreciation for and adaptation of French Renaissance design emerged, as well as a Romantic revival of Gothic architecture in both domestic and public buildings.

20th century Architecture in the early 20th century often combined the elements of earlier times and cultures; pseudo-English Tudor, French Provincial, and Spanish Mission models were built for residences, but Stanford White's Beaux Arts style dominated office buildings, clubs, mansions, and theaters, such as his Madison Square Garden in New York City. Most dramatically, this was the century of the modern architect, and Americans became internationally famous for innovative and creative design, since the ◊skyscraper became the fundamental US contribution to world architecture. Spare, functional Modernist form predominated by midcentury, but by the 1980s a return to softening elements was promoted by Post-Modernists. Notable 20th-century US architects include Frank Lloyd Wright, Louis Henry Sullivan, Walter Gropius, Ludwig Mies van der Rohe, Eliel and Eero Saarinen, I M Pei, Philip Johnson, Kevin Roche, Minoru Yamasaki, and Edward Durrell Stone.

United States art painting and sculpture in the US from colonial times to the present. The unspoiled American landscapes romantically depicted in the 18th and 19th centuries gave way to realistic and Modernistic city scenes in the 20th. Modern movements have flourished in the US, among them Abstract Expressionism and Pop art.

colonial the first American-born artist in the European tradition was the portraitist Robert Feke (1705–1750). The historical painter Benjamin West, working mainly in England, encouraged the portraitist John Singleton Copley. Charles Willson Peale and Gilbert Stuart, a student of West's, painted the founders of the new nation.

19th century the recording of the Indians' lifeways by George Catlin, the dramatic landscapes of Washington Allston, the nature pictures of Audubon, the seascapes of Winslow Homer, the art of the West of Frederic Remington, the realism of Thomas Eakins, and the Romantic landscapes of the Hudson River school found in the works of such artists as Thomas Cole, Asher B Durand, Martin Johnson Heade, and Frederick Edwin Church represent the vitality of US art in this century. The Impressionist-influenced James Whistler and Mary Cassatt and the society painter John Singer Sargent were active mainly in Europe.

early 20th century the members of the Ashcan school, led by Robert Henri, introduced social realism in art; they depicted slum squalor and city life. The group was actually known as The Eight and also included John Sloan, George Luks, William Glackens, Everett Shinn, Maurice Prendergast, Ernest Lawson, and Arthur B Davies. The infamous New York Armory Show 1913 introduced Europe's most avant-garde styles, Cubism and Futurism; Dada arrived soon after, and New York City vied with Paris as the world capital of art. In the 1930s and 1940s, several major European artists emigrated to the US, notably Max Ernst, Max Beckmann, Piet Mondrian, Hans Hoffmann, and Lyonel Feininger. The giant heads of presidents were carved out of Mount Rushmore by G Borglum.

mid-20th century Abstract Expressionism was practiced by the inventor of action painting, Jackson Pollock, his wife Lee Krasner, and the spiritual Mark Rothko. More politically concerned, Ben Shahn created influential graphics. The sculptor Alexander Calder invented mobiles.

late 20th century the Pop-art movement, begun in the 1950s with Robert Rauschenberg and Jasper Johns and led by such artists as Andy Warhol, was a reaction against abstract art. It used precise and distorted images from the media, such as advertising, film, television, and comic strips. Andy Warhol painted soup cans 1962; Jasper Johns painted flags and numbers; Roy Lichtenstein used comic-strip characters to depict romance and heroism; Claes Oldenburg made soft sculptures of everyday items, many times their normal size. It led to multimedia works and performance art in the following decades.

By the 1990s, extremely high prices were being paid at auction for works of art by well-known artists; museum facilities were expanded to house donated collections and traveling exhibitions; and the designs for art exhibitions, their catalogs, and posters had become, in some ways, art forms in themselves.

United States literature early US literature falls into two distinct periods: colonial writing 1620–1776, largely dominated by the Puritans, and post-Revolutionary literature after 1787, when the ideal of US literature developed, and poetry, fiction, and drama began to evolve on national principles.

colonial period 1607–1765 Literature of this period includes travel books and religious verse, but is mainly theological: Roger Williams, Cotton Mather, and Jonathan Edwards were typical Puritan writers. Benjamin Franklin's *Autobiography* is the first work of more than historical interest.

post-Revolutionary period 1785–1820 This period produced much political writing, by Thomas Paine, Thomas Jefferson, and Alexander Hamilton, and one noteworthy poet, Philip Freneau.

early 19th century The influence of English Romantics became evident, notably on the poems of William Cullen Bryant (1794–1878), Washington Irving's tales, Charles Brockden Brown's Gothic fiction, and James Fenimore Cooper's novels of frontier life. During 1830–60 intellectual life was centered in New England, which produced the essayists Ralph Waldo Emerson, Henry Thoreau, and Oliver Wendell Holmes; the poets Henry Wadsworth Longfellow, James Lowell, and John Whittier; and the novelists Nathaniel Hawthorne and Louisa May Alcott. Outside the New England circle were the novelists Edgar Allan Poe and Herman Melville.

post-Civil War period 1865–1900 The disillusionment of this period found expression in the realistic or psychological novel. Ambrose Bierce and Stephen Crane wrote realistic war stories; Mark Twain and Bret Harte dealt with western life; the growth of industrialism led to novels of social realism, notably the works of William Howells and Frank Norris; and Henry James and his disciple Edith Wharton developed the novel of psychological analysis among the well-to-do. The dominant poets were Walt Whitman and Emily Dickinson.

short story This form has attracted many of the major novelists from Hawthorne, Poe, and James onward, and was popularized as a form by O Henry; writers specializing in it have included Ring Lardner, Katharine Anne Porter, Flannery O'Connor, William Saroyan, Eudora Welty, Grace Paley, and Raymond Carver.

drama The US produced a powerful group of playwrights between the wars including Eugene O'Neill, Maxwell Anderson, Lillian Hellman, Elmer Rice, Thornton Wilder, and Clifford Odets. They were followed by Arthur Miller and Tennessee Williams. A later generation now includes Edward Albee, Neil Simon, David Mamet, John Guare, and Sam Shepard.

poetry Poets like Edwin Arlington Robinson, Carl Sandburg, Vachel Lindsay, Robert Frost, and Edna St Vincent Millay extended the poetic tradition of the 19th century, but after the ◊Imagist movement of 1912–14 an experimental modern tradition arose with Ezra Pound, T S Eliot, William Carlos Williams, Marianne Moore, "HD" (Hilda Doolittle), and Wallace Stevens. Attempts at writing the modern US epic include Pound's *Cantos*, Hart Crane's *The Bridge*, and William Carlos Williams's *Paterson*. Among the most striking post-World War II poets are Karl Shapiro, Theodore Roethke, Robert Lowell, Charles Olson, Sylvia Plath, Gwendolyn Brooks, Denize Levertov, John Ashbery, A R Ammons, and Allen Ginsberg.

literary criticism Irving Babbitt (1865–1933), George Santayana, H L Mencken, and Edmund Wilson (1895–1972) were dominant figures, followed by Lionel Trilling (1905–75), Van Wyck Brooks, Yvor Winters (1900–68), and John Crowe Ransom, author of *The New Criticism* 1941, which stressed structural and linguistic factors. More recently US criticism has been influenced by French literary theory and the journalistic criticism of Gore Vidal, Tom Wolfe, George Plimpton, and Susan Sontag.

Recent US literature increasingly expresses the cultural pluralism, regional variety, and the historical and ethnic range of US life. Feminism and minority consciousness have been brought to the fore by authors such as Alice Walker, Toni Morrison, and Maya Angelou.

fiction since 1900 The main trends have been realism, as exemplified in the work of Jack London, Upton Sinclair, and Theodore Dreiser, and modernist experimention. After World War I, Sherwood Anderson, Sinclair Lewis, Ernest Hemingway, William Faulkner, Thomas Wolfe, F Scott Fitzgerald, John Dos Passos, Henry Miller, and Richard Wright established the main literary directions. Among the internationally known novelists since World War II have been John O'Hara, James Michener, Eudora Welty, Truman Capote, J D Salinger, Saul Bellow, John Updike, Norman Mailer, Vladimir Nabokov, Bernard Malamud, Philip Roth, Ralph Ellison, and James Baldwin.

Bestselling authors of popular fiction include Harold Robbins, Jaqueline Suzanne, Judith Krav-itz, and Stephen King.

United World Colleges six colleges worldwide with admission by scholarship for students aged 16–18. Their curriculum demands both academic achievement and service to the community.

They were the inspiration of German educator Kurt ◊Hahn.

universal in philosophy, a property that is incorporated by all the individual things of a specific class: for example, all red things incorporate "redness." Many philosophical debates have centered on the status of universals, including the medieval debate between ◊nominalism and ◊realism.

universal indicator mixture of ◊pH ◊indicators, each of which changes color at a different pH value. The indicator is a different color at different values of pH, ranging from red (at pH1) to purple (at pH13).

The pH of a substance may be found by adding a few drops of universal indicator and noting the color, or by dipping in an absorbent paper strip that has been impregnated with the indicator.

universal joint flexible coupling used to join rotating shafts; for example, the drive shaft in a car. In a typical universal joint the ends of the shafts to be joined end in U-shaped yokes. They dovetail into each other and pivot flexibly about an X-shaped spider. This construction allows side-to-side and up-and-down movement, while still transmitting rotary motion.

Universal Postal Union an agency of the United Nations responsible for collaboration of postal services. It was first established in 1875, and became an agency of the UN in 1947, with headquarters in Berne, Switzerland.

universal time (UT) another name for ◊Greenwich Mean Time. It is based on the rotation of the Earth, which is not quite constant. Since 1972, UT has been replaced by universal time coordinated (UTC), which is based on uniform atomic time; see ◊time.

universe all of space and its contents, the study of which is called cosmology. The universe is thought to be between 10 billion and 20 billion years old and is mostly empty space, dotted with ◊galaxies for as far as telescopes can see. The most distant detected galaxies and ◊quasars lie 10 billion light-years or more from Earth and are moving farther apart as the universe expands. Several theories attempt to explain how the universe came into being and evolved—for example, the ◊Big Bang theory of an expanding universe originating in a single explosive event, and the contradictory ◊steady-state theory.

Apart from those galaxies within the ◊Local Group, all the galaxies we see display ◊red shifts in their spectra, indicating that they are moving away from us. The farther we look into space, the greater are the observed red shifts, which implies that the more distant galaxies are receding at ever greater speeds. This observation led to the theory of an expanding universe, first proposed by Edwin Hubble 1929, and to Hubble's law, which states that the speed with which one galaxy moves away from another is proportional to its distance from it. Current data suggest that the galaxies are moving apart at a rate of 30–60 mps/50–100 kps for every million ◊parsecs of distance.

university an institution of higher learning for those who have completed primary and secondary education.

In the US there are both state universities (funded by the individual states) and private universities. The oldest universities in the US are all private: Harvard 1636, William and Mary 1693, Yale 1701, Pennsylvania 1741, and Princeton 1746. Typically, a university offers advanced degrees in addition to the four-year bachelor's degree; is made up of colleges, such as liberal arts, sciences, law, medicine; and offers some special degrees such as divinity, technical, and vocational. Recent innovations include universities serving international areas, for example, the Middle East Technical University 1961 in Ankara, Turkey, supported by the United Nations; the United Nations University in Tokyo 1974; and the British Open University 1969, based on a mixed media curriculum.

The first European university was established in the 9th century at Salerno, Italy, and was followed in the 12th century by Bologna in Italy, Paris, Oxford, and Cambridge.

Unix ◊operating system designed for minicomputers but becoming increasingly popular on large microcomputers, workstations and supercomputers. It was developed by Bell Laboratories in the late 1960s, and is closely related to the programming language ◊C. Its wide range of functions and flexibility have made it widely used by universities and in commercial software.

unnilennium synthesized radioactive element of the ◊transactinide series, symbol Une, atomic number 109, atomic weight 266. It was first produced in 1982 at the Institute for Heavy Ion Research in Darmstadt, Germany, by fusing bismuth and iron nuclei; it took a week to obtain a single new, fused nucleus. The element is as yet unnamed; temporary identification was assigned until a name is approved by the International Union of Pure and Applied Chemistry.

unnilhexium synthesized radioactive element of the ◊transactinide series, symbol Unh, atomic number 106, atomic weight 263. It was first synthesized in 1974 by two institutions, each of which claims priority. The University of California at Berkeley bombarded californium with oxygen nuclei to get isotope 263; the Joint Institute for Nuclear Research in Dubna, USSR, bombarded lead with chromium nuclei to obtain isotopes 259 and 260. The element is as yet unnamed; temporary identification was assigned until a name is approved by the International Union of Pure and Applied Chemistry.

unniloctium synthesized radioactive element of the ◊transactinide series, symbol Uno, atomic number 108, atomic weight 265. It was first synthesized in 1984. The element is as yet unnamed; temporary identification was assigned until a name is approved by the International Union of Pure and Applied Chemistry.

unnilpentium synthesized radioactive, metallic element of the ◊transactinide series, symbol Unp, atomic number 105, atomic weight 262. Six isotopes have been synthesized, each with very short (fractions of a second) half-lives. Two institutions claim to have been the first to produce it: the Joint Institute for Nuclear Research in Dubna, USSR, in 1967 (proposed name nielsbohrium); and the University of California at Berkeley, who dispute the Soviet's claim, in 1970 (proposed name hahnium). Temporary identification was assigned until a name is approved by the International Union of Pure and Applied Chemistry (IUPAC).

unnilquadium synthesized radioactive, metallic element, the first of the ◊transactinide series, symbol Unq, atomic number 104, atomic weight 262. It is produced by bombarding californium with carbon nuclei and has ten isotopes, the longest-lived of which, Unq-262, has a half-life of 70 seconds. Two institutions claim to be the first to have synthesized it: the Joint Institute for Nuclear Research in Dubna, USSR, in 1964 (proposed name kurchatovium); and the the University of California at Berkeley, in 1969 (proposed name rutherfordium). Each disputes the other's claim. Temporary identification was assigned until a name is approved by the International Union of Pure and Applied Chemistry (IUPAC).

unnilseptium synthesized radioactive element of the ◊transactinide series, symbol Uns, atomic number 107, atomic weight 262. It was first synthesized by the Joint Institute for Nuclear Research in Dubna, USSR, in 1976; in 1981 the Institute for Heavy Ion Research in Darmstadt, Germany, confirmed its existence. The element is as yet unnamed; temporary identification was assigned until a name is approved by the International Union of Pure and Applied Chemistry.

Uno Sōsuke 1923– . Japanese conservative politician, member of the Liberal Democratic Party (LDP). Having held various cabinet posts since 1976, he was designated prime minister in June 1989 in an attempt to restore the image of the LDP after several scandals. He resigned after only a month in office when his affair with a prostitute became public knowledge.

untouchable or ***harijan*** a member of the lowest Indian ◊caste, formerly forbidden to be touched by members of the other castes.

Upanishad one of a collection of Hindu sacred treatises, written in Sanskrit, connected with the ◊Vedas but composed later, about 800–200 BC. Metaphysical and ethical, their doctrine equated the atman (self) with the Brahman (supreme spirit)—*"Tat tvam asi"* ("Thou art that")—and developed the theory of the transmigration of souls.

upas tree SE Asian tree *Antiaris toxicaria* of the mulberry family Moraceae, with a poisonous latex used for arrows, and traditionally reputed to kill all who fell asleep under it.

Updike John (Hoyer) 1932– . US writer. Associated with *The New Yorker* magazine from 1955, he soon established a reputation for polished prose, poetry, and criticism. His novels include *The Poorhouse Fair* 1959, *The Centaur* 1963, *Couples* 1968, *The Witches of Eastwick* 1984, *Roger's Version* 1986, and *S.* 1988 and deal with the tensions and frustrations of contemporary US middle-class life and their effects on love and marriage.

Born in Shillington, Pennsylvania, Updike graduated from Harvard University. Two characters recur in Updike's novels: the former basketball player "Rabbit" Angstrom, who matures in the series *Rabbit, Run* 1960, *Rabbit Redux* 1971, *Rabbit is Rich* 1981 (Pulitzer prize), and *Rabbit at Rest* 1990; and the novelist Henry Bech, who appears in *Bech: A Book* 1970 and *Bech is Back* 1982. Other novels by Updike include *Of the Farm* 1965, *A Month of Sundays* 1972, *Marry Me* 1976, and *The Coup* 1978. His short-story collections include *The Same Door* 1959, *Pigeon Feathers* 1962, *Museums and Women* 1972, and *Problems* 1979. His body of work includes essay collections, such as *Hugging the Shore* 1983, and the play *Buchanan Dying* 1974.

Upper Austria (German *Oberösterreich*) mountainous federal province of Austria, drained by the Danube; area 4,632 sq mi/12,000 sq km; population (1987) 1,294,000. Its capital is Linz. In addition to wine, sugar-beet and grain, there are reserves of oil. Manufactured products include textiles, chemicals, and metal goods.

Upper Volta former name (until 1984) of ◊Burkina Faso.

Uppsala city in Sweden, NW of Stockholm; population (1988) 160,000. Industries include engineering and pharmaceuticals. The botanist Linnaeus lived here. The university was founded 1477; there are a Gothic cathedral and Viking relics.

Ur ancient city of the ◊Sumerian civilization, now in S Iraq. Excavations by the British archeologist Leonard Woolley show that it was inhabited 3500 BC. He discovered evidence of a flood that may have inspired the *Epic of* ◊Gilgamesh as well as the biblical account, and remains of ziggurats, or step pyramids, as well as social and cultural materials.

uremia excess of urea (a nitrogenous waste product) in the blood, caused by kidney damage.

Ural Mountains (Russian *Ural'skiy Khrebet*) mountain system running from the Arctic to the Caspian Sea, traditionally separating Europe from Asia. The highest peak is Naradnaya 6,214 ft/1,894 m. It has vast mineral wealth.

The middle Urals is one of the most industrialized regions of the USSR. Perm, Chelyabinsk, Sverdlovsk, Magnitogorsk, and Zlatoust are major industrial centers.

Urania in Greek mythology, the ◊Muse of astronomy.

uraninite uranium oxide, UO_2, an ore mineral of uranium, also known as pitchblende when occurring in massive form. It is black or brownish-black, very dense, and radioactive. It occurs in veins and as massive crusts, usually associated with granite rocks.

uranium hard, lustrous, silver-white, malleable and ductile, radioactive, metallic element of the ◊actinide series, symbol U, atomic number 92, atomic weight 238.029. It is the most abundant radioactive element in the Earth's crust, its decay giving rise to essentially all radioactive elements in nature; its final decay product is the stable element lead. Uranium combines readily with most elements to form compounds that are extremely poisonous. Small amounts of some compounds have been used in the ceramics industry to make orange-yellow glazes and as mordants in dyeing; however, this was discontinued when the dangerous effects of radiation became known. The chief ore is ◊pitchblende, in which the element was discovered by German chemist Martin Klaproth in 1789; he named it after the planet Uranus, which had been discovered in 1781.

Uranium is one of three fissile elements (the others are thorium and plutonium). It was long considered (erroneously) to be the element with the highest atomic number to occur in nature. The isotopes U-238 and U-235 have been used to help determine the age of the Earth.

Uranium-238, which comprises about 99% of all naturally occuring uranium, has a half-life of 4.51×10^9 years. Because of its abundance, it is the isotope from which fissile plutonium is produced in nuclear ◊breeder reactors. The fissile isotope U-235 has a half-life of 7.13×10^8 years and comprises about 0.7% of naturally occuring uranium; it is used directly as a fuel for nuclear reactors and in the manufacture of nuclear weapons.

uranium ore material from which uranium is extracted, often a complex mixture of minerals. The main ore is uraninite (or pitchblende), Uo_2, which is commonly found with sulfide minerals. The US, Canada, and South Africa are the main producers in the West.

Uranus in Greek mythology, the primeval sky-god. He was responsible for both the sunshine and the rain, and was the son and husband of ◊Gaia, the goddess of the Earth. Uranus and Gaia were the parents of ◊Cronus and the ◊Titans.

Uranus the seventh planet from the Sun, discovered by William ◊Herschel 1781. It is twice as far out as the sixth planet, Saturn. Uranus has a diameter of 31,600 mi/50,800 km and a mass 14.5 times that of Earth. It orbits the Sun in 84 years at an average distance of 2,870 million1,783 mi/ kmllion

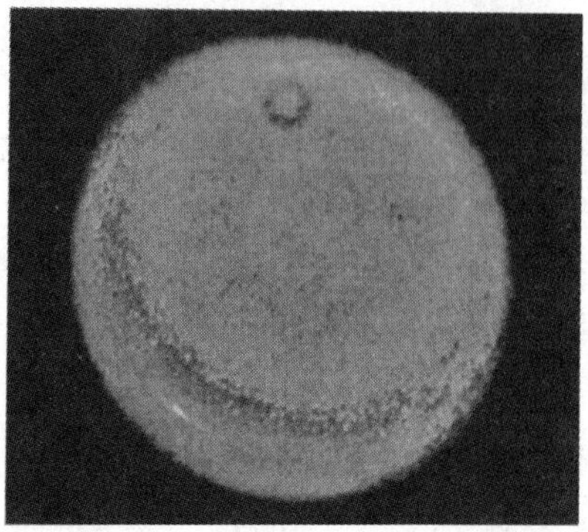

Uranus *False-color image of clouds in the upper atmosphere of Uranus, seen from* Voyager 2.

mi. The spin axis of Uranus is tilted at 98°, so that one pole points toward the Sun, giving extreme seasons. It has 15 moons and in 1977 was discovered to have thin rings around its equator.

Uranus has a peculiar magnetic field, whose axis is tilted at 60° to its axis of spin and is displaced about one-third of the way from the planet's center to its surface. Observations of the magnetic field show that the solid body of the planet rotates every 17.2 hours. Uranus spins from east to west, the opposite of the other planets, with the exception of Venus and possibly Pluto. The rotation rate of the atmosphere varies with latitude, from about 16 hours in midsouthern latitudes to longer than 17 hours at the equator.

Data derived from the space probe *Voyager 1* in 1986 revealed that Uranus is covered with a cloud layer under which a hot ocean of superheated water exists. The pressure caused by the thick atmosphere keeps the water from boiling away and the heat keeps the pressure from solidifying the water. This has led to suggestions that the planet may have formed from the coalescence of comets. Other discoveries were that the pole facing the Sun is no hotter than the pole facing away and that four known methane clouds in the atmosphere rotate with the planet, not in the expected opposite direction. *Voyager 2* detected ten rings, composed of chunky rock and large ice boulders, around the planet's equator, and found ten small moons in addition to the five visible from Earth. Titania, the largest moon, has a diameter of 1,000 mi/1,610 km. The rings are charcoal black and may be debris of former "moonlets" that have broken up.

Urban six popes, including:

Urban II c. 1042–1099. Pope 1088–99. He launched the First ◊Crusade at the Council of Clermont in France 1095.

Urbana city in E central Illinois, E of Springfield. Industries include food processing, electronics, and metal products. The University of Illinois 1867 is here; population (1990) 36,344.

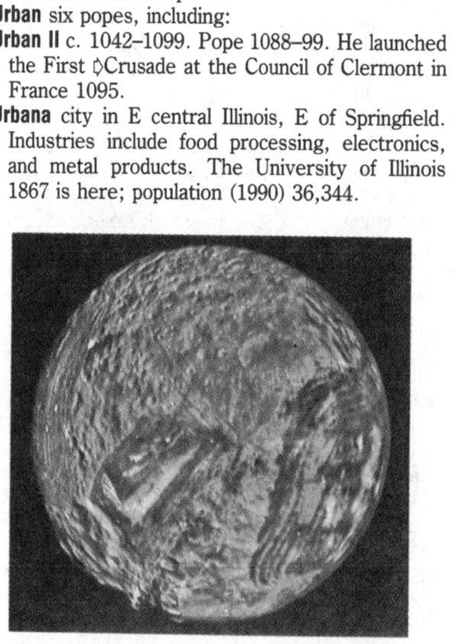

Uranus *A mosaic of photographs of the battered face of Miranda, the fourth largest moon of Uranus, seen from* Voyager 2.

urbanization the process by which the proportion of a population living in or around towns and cities increases through migration as the agricultural population decreases. The growth of urban concentrations in the US and Europe is a relatively recent phenomenon, dating back only about 150 years to the beginnings of the Industrial Revolution (although the world's first cities were built more than 5,000 years ago.)

Urbanization has had a major effect on the social structures of industrial societies, affecting not only where people live but how they live, and urban sociology has emerged as a distinct area of study.

urban legend any story that is part of a largely new mode of folklore thriving in big cities, mainly in the US, in the mid-20th century, and passed along, usually orally, and always at second or later hand. Some of the material – hitchhikers that turn out to be ghosts, spiders breeding in elaborate hairstyles—is preindustrial in origin, but transformed to fit new circumstances; others, notably about the pet or baby in the microwave oven or about people living in department stores, are of their essence entirely new.

urban renewal the adaptation of existing buildings and neighborhoods in towns and cities to meet changes in economic, social, and environmental requirements, rather than demolishing them.

Urban renewal has increased since the early 1970s, when it became less expensive to renew than to rebuild. A major objective is to preserve the historical and cultural character of a locality, at the same time improving the environment and meeting new demands, such as those imposed by automobile traffic.

Urdu language member of the Indo-Iranian branch of the Indo-European language family, related to Hindi and written not in Devanagari but in Arabic script. Urdu is strongly influenced by Persian and Arabic. It is the official language of Pakistan and a language used by Muslims in India.

urea $CO(NH_2)_2$ waste product formed in the mammalian liver when nitrogen compounds are broken down. It is excreted in urine. When purified, it is a white, crystalline solid. In industry it is used to make urea–formaldehyde plastics (or resins), pharmaceuticals, and fertilizers.

uremia excess of urea (a nitrogenous waste product) in the blood, caused by kidney damage.

ureter tube connecting the kidney to the bladder. Its wall contains fibers of ◊smooth muscle, whose contractions aid the movement of urine out of the kidney.

urethra in mammals a tube connecting the bladder to the exterior. It carries urine, and in males, semen.

Urey Harold Clayton 1893–1981. US chemist. In 1932 he isolated ◊heavy water and discovered ◊deuterium, for which he was awarded the 1934 Nobel Prize for Chemistry.

During World War II he as a member of the Manhattan Project that produced the atomic bomb, but after the war he advocated nuclear disarmament and world government.

Urga former name (until 1924) of ◊Ulaanbaatar, the capital of Mongolia.

uric acid $C_5H_4N_4O_3$ a nitrogen-containing waste substance, formed from the breakdown of food and body protein. It is the usual excretory material in insects, reptiles, and birds. (The white part of bird and reptile exrement is uric acid.)

Humans and other primates produce some uric acid as well as urea, the normal nitrogen-waste product of mammals, adult amphibians, and many marine fishes. If formed in excess and not excreted, uric acid may be deposited in sharp crystals in the joints and other tissues, causing gout; or it may form stones (calculi) in the kidneys or bladder.

urim and thummim two mysterious objects in the breastplate of the high priests of the ancient Hebrews, which were used for divination.

urinary system the system of organs that removes

urinary system

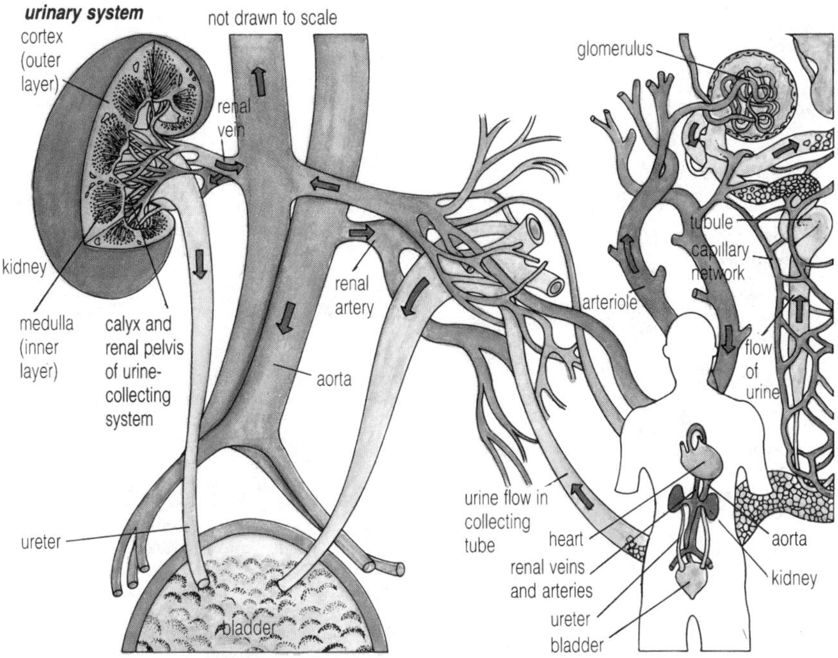
not drawn to scale
cortex (outer layer)
renal vein
kidney
medulla (inner layer)
calyx and renal pelvis of urine-collecting system
renal artery
aorta
ureter
bladder
glomerulus
tubule
capillary network
arteriole
flow of urine
urine flow in collecting tube
heart
renal veins and arteries
ureter
bladder
aorta
kidney

urine

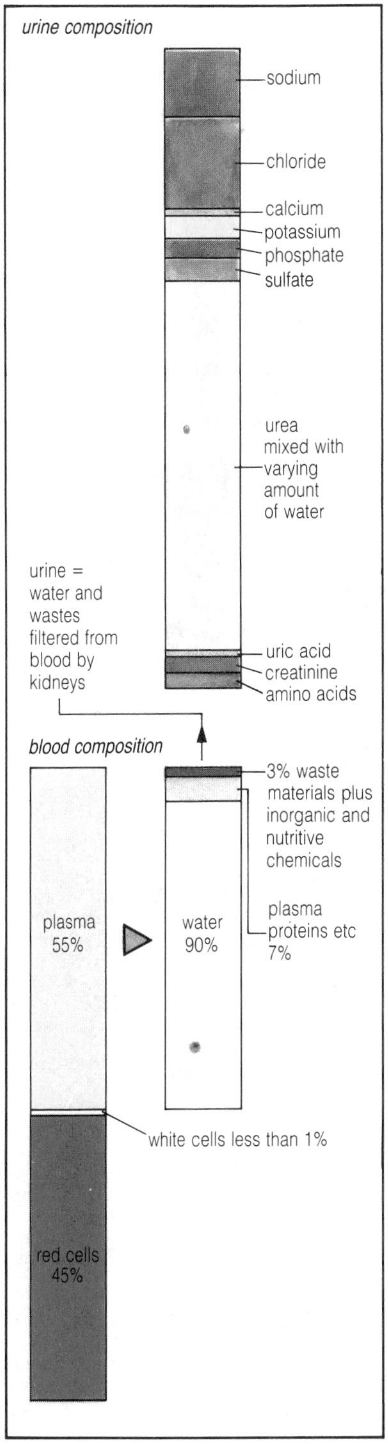
urine composition
sodium
chloride
calcium
potassium
phosphate
sulfate
urea mixed with varying amount of water
urine = water and wastes filtered from blood by kidneys
uric acid
creatinine
amino acids
blood composition
3% waste materials plus inorganic and nutritive chemicals
plasma proteins etc 7%
plasma 55%
water 90%
white cells less than 1%
red cells 45%

nitrogeneous waste products and excess water from the bodies of animals. In vertebrates, it consists of a pair of kidneys, which produce urine; ureters, which drain the kidneys; and (in bony fishes, amphibians, some reptiles, and mammals) a bladder, which stores the urine before its discharge. In mammals, the urine is expelled through the urethra; in other vertebrates, the urine drains into a common excretory chamber called a ◊cloaca, and the urine is not discharged separately.

urine amber-colored fluid made by the kidneys from the blood. It contains excess water, salts, proteins, waste products in the form of urea, a pigment, and some acid.

The kidneys pass it through two fine tubes (ureters) to the bladder, which may act as a reservoir for up to 1.5 pt/0.7 l at a time. In mammals, it then passes into the urethra, which opens to the outside by a sphincter (constricting muscle) under voluntary control. In reptiles and birds, nitrogenous wastes are discharged as an almost solid substance made mostly of ◊uric acid, rather than urea.

Ursa Major (Latin "Great Bear") the third-largest constellation in the sky, in the north polar region. Its seven brightest stars make up the familiar shape of the Big Dipper. The second star of the "handle" of the dipper, called Mizar, has a companion star, Alcor. Two stars forming the far side of the "bowl" (one of them, Dubhe, being the constellation's brightest star) act as pointers to the north pole star, Polaris.

Ursa Minor (Latin "Little Bear") constellation in the northern sky. It is shaped like a little dipper, with the north pole star, Polaris, at the end of the handle. It contains the orange subgiant Kochab, about 95 light-years from Earth.

Ursula, St 4th century AD. English legendary saint, supposed to have been martyred with 11 virgins (misread as 11,000 in the Middle Ages) by the Huns in the Rhineland.

Ursuline a Roman Catholic religious order, founded in Brescia, Italy, by St Angela Merici 1537; it carries out educational work among girls.

urticaria or ***nettle rash*** or ***hives*** irritant skin condition characterized by itching, burning, stinging, and the spontaneous appearance of raised patches of skin. Treatment is usually by antihistamines or steroids taken orally or applied as lotions. Its causes are varied and include allergy and stress.

Uruguay country in South America, on the Atlantic, bounded N by Brazil and W by Argentina.

government The 1966 constitution provides for a president who is head of state and head of government, elected by universal suffrage for a five-year term, and a two-chamber legislature, comprising a senate and a federal chamber of deputies. The president is assisted by a vice-president and presides over a council of ministers.

The Senate has up to 30 members and the Chamber of Deputies 99, all elected for a five-year term by universal suffrage through a system of proportional representation. The voting system ensures that there are at least two deputies representing each of the republic's 19 departments.

history For early history, see ◊American Indian. The area was settled by both Spain 1624 and Portugal 1680, but Spain secured the whole in the 18th century. In 1814 Spanish rule was overthrown under the leadership of José Artigas, dictator until driven out by Brazil 1820. Disputed between Argentina and Brazil 1825–28, Uruguay was declared independent 1828, although not recognized by its neighbors until 1853.

The names of Uruguay's two main political parties, the liberal Colorado (the Reds) and the conservative Blanco (the Whites), are derived from the colors of the flags carried in the civil war 1836. From 1951 to 1966 there was a collective leadership called "collegiate government," and then a new constitution was adopted and a single president elected, the Blanco candidate, Jorge Pacheco Areco. His presidency was marked by high inflation, labor unrest, and growing guerrilla activity by the ◊Tupamaros.

In 1972 Pacheco was replaced by the Colorado candidate, Juan Maria Bordaberry Arocena. Within a year the Tupamaros had been crushed, and all other left-wing groups banned. Bordaberry now headed a repressive regime, under which the normal democratic institutions had been dissolved. In 1976, he refused any movement toward constitutional government, was deposed by the army, and Dr Aparicio Méndez Manfredini was made president. Despite promises to return to democratic government, the severe repression continued, and political opponents were imprisoned.

In 1981 the deteriorating economy made the army anxious to return to constitutional government, and a retired general, Gregorio Alvarez Armellino, was appointed president for an interim period. Discussions between the army and the main political parties failed to agree on the form of constitution to be adopted, and civil unrest, in the shape of strikes and demonstrations, grew. By 1984 antigovernment activity had reached a crisis point, and eventually all the main political leaders signed an agreement for a "Program of National Accord." The 1966 constitution, with some modifications, was restored, and in 1985 a general election was held. The Colorado Party won a narrow majority, and its leader, Dr Julio Maria Sanguinetti, became president. The army stepped down, and by 1986 President Sanguinetti was presiding over a government of national

Uruguay
Oriental Republic of
(República Oriental del Uruguay)

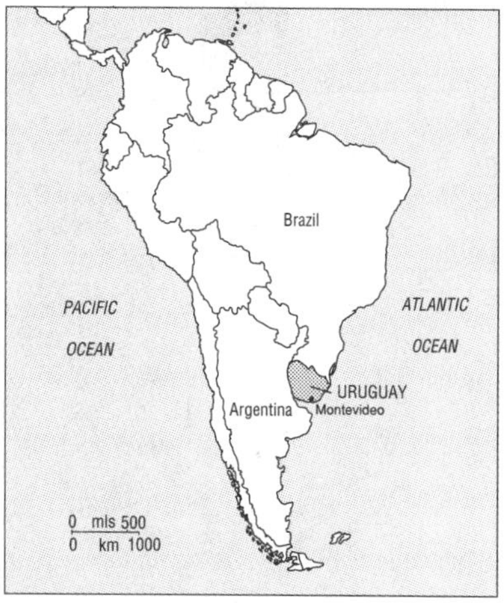
Brazil
PACIFIC OCEAN
ATLANTIC OCEAN
URUGUAY
Argentina
Montevideo
0 mls 500
0 km 1000

area 68,031 sq mi/176,200 sq km
capital Montevideo
cities Salto, Paysandú
physical grassy plains (pampas) and low hills
features rivers Negro, Uruguay, Río de la Plata
head of state and government Luis Lacalle Herrera from 1989
political system democratic republic
political parties Colorado Party (PC), progressive, center-left; National (Blanco) Party (PN), traditionalist, right-of-center; Amplio Front (FA), moderate, left-wing
exports meat and meat products, leather, wool, textiles
currency nuevo peso
population (1990 est) 3,002,000 (Spanish, Italian; mestizo, mulatto, black); growth rate 0.7% p.a.
life expectancy men 68, women 75 (1989)
language Spanish
religion Roman Catholic 66%
literacy 96% (1984)
GNP $7.5 bn; $2,470 per head (1988)
chronology
1825 Independence declared from Brazil.
1930 First constitution adopted.
1956 Blanco party in power, with Jorge Pacheco Areco as president.
1972 Colorado party returned, with Juan Maria Bordaberry Arocena as president.
1976 Bordaberry deposed by army; Dr Méndez Manfredini became president.
1984 Violent antigovernment protests after ten years of repressive rule.
1985 Agreement reached between the army and political leaders for return to constitutional government. Colorado party won general election; Dr Julio Maria Sanguinetti became president.
1986 Government of national accord established under President Sanguinetti's leadership.
1989 Luis Lacalle elected president.

accord in which all the main parties—Colorado, Blanco, and the left-wing Broad Front—were represented. In the Nov 1989 elections Luis Lacalle Herrera (PN) was narrowly elected president, with 37% of the vote compared with 30% for his PC opponent. After his inauguration in 1990, he concentrated his efforts on economic problems.

Urumchi alternate spelling of Urumqi, city in China.

Urumqi or ***Urumchi*** industrial city and capital of Xinjiang Uygur autonomous region, China, at the N foot of the Tian Shan mountains; population (1986) 1,147,000. It produces cotton textiles, cement, chemicals, iron, and steel.

US abbreviation for the United States of America.

USA abbreviation (official) for the ◊United States of America; US Army.

USDA abbreviation for the US Department of Agriculture.

user interface in computing, the procedures and methods through which the user operates a program. These might include ◊menus, input forms, error messages, and keyboard procedures. A graphical user interface is one that uses icons and allows the user to make menu selections with a mouse (see also ◊WIMP).

The study of human–computer interaction to achieve easier and more effective use of the device and greater human satisfaction is the subject of a subbranch of ◊ergonomics, which has become a focus for many national and international research programs.

USGS abbreviation for the US Geological Survey, part of the department of the interior.

Ushant (French *Ouessant*) French island 11 mi/18 km W of Brittany, area 9 sq mi/15 sq km, off which the British admiral Richard ◊Howe defeated the French navy 1794 on "the Glorious First of June." The chief town is Lampaul.

Ushuaia southernmost town in the world, at the tip of Tierra del Fuego, Argentina, less than 620 mi/1,000 km from Antarctica; population (1980) 11,000. It is a free port and naval base.

USIA abbreviation for US Information Agency.

Usküb Turkish name of ◊Skopje, a city in Yugoslavia.

Usküdar suburb of Istanbul, Turkey; formerly a separate town, which under the name Scutari was the site of the hospital set up by Florence Nightingale during the Crimean War.

USO abbreviation for United Service Organizations.

USP abbreviation for US Pharmacopoeia.

USS abbreviation for US Ship.

USSR abbreviation for the ◊Union of Soviet Socialist Republics.

Ussuri river in E Asia, tributary of the Amur. Rising N of Vladivostok and joining the Amur S of Khabarovsk, it forms part of the border between the Chinese province of Heilongjiang and the USSR. There were military clashes 1968–69 over the sovereignty of Damansky Island (Chenpao).

Ustinov Peter 1921– . English stage and film actor, writer, and director. He won an Academy Award for *Spartacus* 1960. Other film appearances include *Topkapi* 1964, *Death on the Nile* 1978, and *Evil under the Sun* 1981.

Ust-Kamenogorsk river port and chief center of the nuclear industry in the USSR, situated in the Altai mountains, on the river Irtysh; population (1987) 321,000.

usury former term for charging interest on a loan of money. In medieval times, usury was held to be a sin, and Christians were forbidden to lend (although not to borrow).

The practice of charging interest is still regarded as usury in some Muslim countries.

Utagawa Kuniyoshi. Japanese printmaker; see ◊Kuniyoshi Utagawa.

Utah state in W US; nickname Beehive State/Mormon State.

Utah

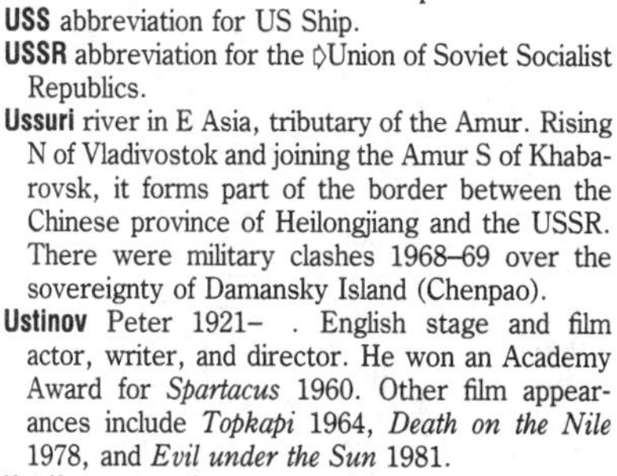
Salt Lake City

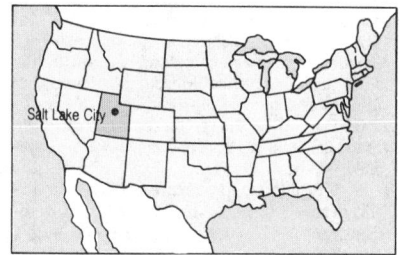

area 84,881 sq mi/219,900 sq km
capital Salt Lake City
cities Provo, Ogden
physical Colorado Plateau to the E, mountains in center, Great Basin to the W, Great Salt Lake
features Great American Desert; Colorado River system; Dinosaur and Rainbow Bridge national monuments; five national parks: the Arches, Bryce Canyon, Canyonlands, Capitol Reef, Zion; auto racing at Bonneville Salt Flats; Mormon temple and tabernacle, Salt Lake City
products wool, gold, silver, copper, coal, salt, steel
population (1990) 1,722,850
famous people Brigham Young
history explored first by Franciscan friars for Spain 1776; Great Salt Lake discovered by US frontiersman Jim Bridger 1824; part of the area ceded by Mexico 1848; developed by Mormons, still by far the largest religious group in the state; territory 1850, but not admitted to statehood until 1896 because of Mormon reluctance to relinquish plural marriage. The world's largest open-pit copper mine began 1906 at Bingham Canyon. Largely because of the high birth rate, the state's population has more than doubled since World War II.

Utamaro Kitagawa 1753–1806. Japanese artist of the *ukiyo-e* ("floating world") school who created muted color prints of beautiful women, including informal studies of prostitutes.

His style was distinctive: his subject is often seen close up, sometimes from unusual angles or viewpoints, and he made use of bold curvaceous lines and highly decorative textiles.

uterus hollow muscular organ of female mammals, located between the bladder and rectum, and connected to the Fallopian tubes above and the vagina below. The embryo develops within the uterus, and in placental mammals is attached to it after implantation via the ◊placenta and umbilical cord. The lining of the uterus changes during the ◊menstrual cycle. In humans and other higher primates, it is a single structure, but in other mammals it is paired.

The outer wall of the uterus is composed of smooth muscle, capable of powerful contractions (induced by hormones) during childbirth.

U Thant Burmese diplomat, see ◊Thant, U.

Uthman another spelling of ◊Othman, third caliph of Islam.

Utica industrial city (engine parts, clothing) in central New York State; population (1990) 68,637. The settlement 1773 was on the site of an Iroquois center and British fort. Utica was an important textile center from about 1850 to 1950. The first Woolworth store was opened here 1879.

utilitarianism a philosophical theory of ethics outlined by the philosopher Jeremy ◊Bentham and developed by John Stuart Mill. According to utilitarianism, an action is morally right if it has consequences that lead to happiness, and wrong if it brings about the reverse. Thus society should aim for the greatest happiness of the greatest number.

Utopia (Greek "no place") any ideal state in literature, named after philosopher Thomas More's ideal commonwealth in his book *Utopia* 1516.

Others versions include Plato's *Republic*, Bacon's *New Atlantis* 1626, and *City of the Sun* by the Italian Tommaso Campanella (1568–1639). Utopias are a common subject in ◊science fiction.

Utrecht a province of the Netherlands lying SE of Amsterdam, on the Kromme Rijn (crooked Rhine)
area 513 sq mi/1,330 sq km
population (1988) 965,000
capital Utrecht
cities Amersfoort, Zeist, Nieuwegeun, Veenendaal
products chemicals, livestock, textiles, electrical goods
history ruled by the bishops of Utrecht in the Middle Ages, the province was sold to the emperor Charles V of Spain 1527. It became a

Utrillo *French artist Maurice Utrillo, noted for his street scenes, as in* Street at Sannóis *1913.*

center of Protestant resistance to Spanish rule and, with the signing of the Treaty of Utrecht, became one of the seven United Provinces of the Netherlands 1579.

Utrecht, Treaty of treaty signed 1713 that ended the War of the ◊Spanish Succession. Philip V was recognized as the legitimate king of Spain, thus founding the Spanish branch of the Bourbon dynasty and ending the French king Louis XIV's attempts at expansion; the Netherlands, Milan, and Naples were ceded to Austria; Britain gained Gibraltar; the duchy of Savoy was granted Sicily.

Utrecht, Union of in 1579, the union of seven provinces of the N Netherlands—Holland, Zeeland, Friesland, Groningen, Utrecht, Gelderland, and Overijssel—that became the basis of opposition to the Spanish crown and the foundation of the present-day Dutch state.

Utrillo Maurice 1883–1955. French artist. He painted townscapes of his native Paris, many depicting Montmartre, often from postcard photographs.

Utrillo was the son of Suzanne Valadan, a trapeze-performer who was encouraged to become an artist herself after posing as a model for many painters of the day. His work from 1908 to 1914 is considered his best.

Uttar Pradesh state of India
area 113,638 sq mi/294,400 sq km
capital Lucknow
towns Kanpur, Varanasi, Agra, Allahabad, Meerut
features most populas state; Himalayan peak Nanda Devi 25,655 ft/7,817 m
population (1981) 110,858,000
famous people Indira Gandhi, Ravi Shankar
language Hindi
religion 80% Hindu, 15% Muslim
history formerly the heart of the Mogul Empire and generating point of the ◊Indian Mutiny 1857 and subsequent opposition to British rule; see also the ◊United Provinces of ◊Agra and ◊Oudh.

UV in physics, abbreviation for ultraviolet.

uvula fleshy flap that hangs at the back of the throat in humans.

Uzbek member of certain Turkic-speaking peoples of the Uzbek Soviet Republic (where they form 70% of the population) and neighboring regions.

Uzbekistan

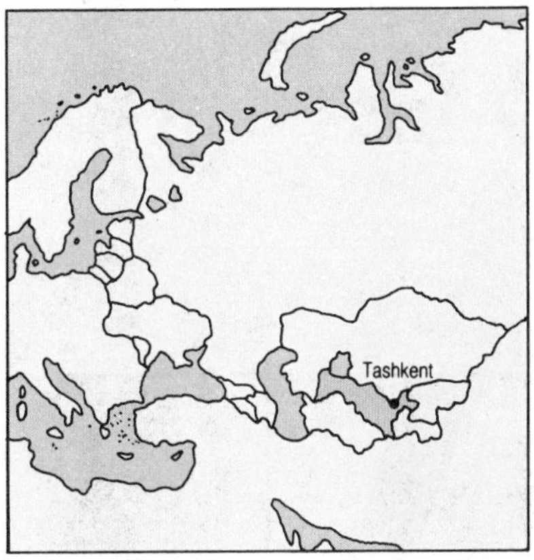
Tashkent

Uzbekistan republic, formerly constituent republic of the USSR, 1924–91, in Soviet Central Asia.
area 172,741 sq mi/447,400 sq km
capital Tashkent
cities Samarkand
physical oases in the deserts; rivers: Amu Darya, Syr Darya; Fergana Valley
products rice, dried fruit, vines (all grown by irrigation); cotton, silk
population (1987) 19,026,000; 69% Uzbek, 11% Russian, 4% Tadzhik, 4% Tatar
language Uzbek
religion Sunni Muslim
history part of Turkestan, it was conquered by Russia 1865–76. The Tashkent soviet gradually extended its power 1917–24, and Uzbekistan became a constituent republic of the USSR 1925.

Some 160,000 Mesketian Turks were forcibly transported from their native Georgia to Uzbekistan by Stalin 1944. In June 1989 Tashlak, Yaipan, and Fergana were the scenes of riots in which Mesketian Turks were attacked. In Sept 1989 an Uzbek nationalist organization, the *Birhik* ("Unity") Peoples' Movement, was formed.

In the wake of the failed Aug 1991 anti-Gorbachev coup in the USSR, the republic's parliament declared its independence. President Islam Karimov, who had initially supported the anti-Gorbachev junta, resigned from the Communist Party Politburo and Central Committee. In Dec 1991, Uzbekistan joined the new federation, the Commonwealth of Independent States (CIS).

V

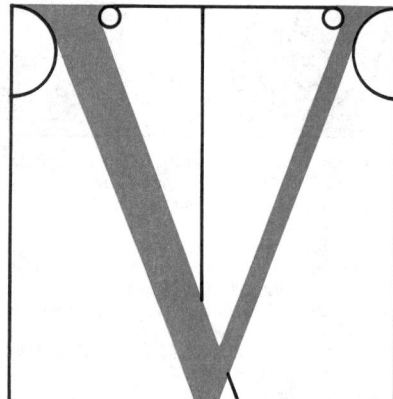

V in roman numerals, symbol for five; in physics, symbol for volt.

v in physics, abbreviation for velocity.

V1, V2 (German *Vergeltungswaffe* "revenge weapons") German flying bombs of World War II, launched against Britain in 1944 and 1945. The V1, also called the doodle-bug and buzz bomb, was an uncrewed monoplane carrying a bomb, powered by a simple kind of jet engine called a pulse jet. The V2, a rocket bomb with a preset guidance system, was the first long-range ballistic ◊missile. It was 47 ft/14 m long, carried a 1-ton warhead, and hit its target at a speed of 3,000 mph/5,000 kph.

The V2 was developed by the rocket engineer Wernher ◊von Braun. After the war captured V2 material became the basis of the space race in both the USSR and the US.

Vaal river in South Africa, the chief tributary of the Orange. It rises in the Drakensberg and for much of its course of 750 mi/1,200 km it separates Transvaal from Orange Free State.

vaccination the use of specially modified ◊pathogens (bacteria and viruses) to confer immunity to the diseases with which they are associated. When injected or taken by mouth, a vaccine stimulates the production of antibodies to protect against that particular disease. Vaccination is the oldest form of ◊immunization.

vaccine any preparation of modified viruses or bacteria that is introduced into the body, usually either orally or by a hypodermic syringe, to induce the specific ◊antibody reaction that produces ◊immunity against a particular disease.

In 1796, Edward ◊Jenner was the first to inoculate a child successfully with cowpox virus to produce immunity to smallpox. His method, the application of an infective agent to an abraded skin surface, is still used in smallpox inoculation.

vacuole in biology, a fluid-filled, membrane-bound cavity inside a cell. It may be a reservoir for fluids that the cell will secrete to the outside, or filled with other excretory products or essential nutrients that the cell needs to store. In amebas (single-cell animals), vacuoles are sites for digestion of engulfed food particles. A plant cell usually has a large central vacuole to increase its surface area for food absorption.

vacuum in general, a region completely empty of matter; in physics, any enclosure in which the gas pressure is considerably less than atmospheric pressure (101,325 pascals).

vacuum cleaner cleaning device invented 1901 by the Scot Hubert Cecil Booth 1871–1955. Having seen an ineffective dust-blowing machine, he reversed the process so that his machine (originally on wheels, and operated from the street by means of tubes running into the house) operated by suction.

Vadodara formerly (until 1976) Baroda industrial city (metal goods, chemicals, textiles) and rail junction in Gujarat, India; population (1981) 744,881.

Vaduz capital of the European principality of Liechtenstein; population (1984) 5,000. Industries include engineering and agricultural trade.

vagina the front passage in female mammals, linking the uterus to the exterior. It admits the penis during sexual intercourse, and is the birth canal down which the fetus passes during delivery.

vaginismus spasmodic contraction of the entrance to the vagina during attempted intercourse, thus preventing the entrance of the penis. It is usually of psychological origin, although it may be due to inflammation of the vagina, causing a reflex contraction.

Vail Alfred Lewis 1807–1859. US communications pioneer. Born in Morristown, New Jersey, Vail was educated at New York University and worked as a mechanic at his father's iron foundry. Having a close association with Samuel ◊Morse in 1837, he developed an improved design for the telegraph mechanism, beginning production of the new model 1838. With Congressional funding for a telegraph line between Washington and Baltimore, Vail renewed his working relationship with Morse 1844. Vail's book *The American Electro Magnetic Telegraph* was published 1845, and he retired from business 1849.

Vairochana the cosmic Buddha, Dainichi in Japan; central to esoteric Buddhism.

Valdai Hills small forested plateau between St Petersburg and Moscow, where the Volga and W Dvina rivers rise. The Viking founders of the Russian state used it as a river route center to reach the Baltic, Black, Caspian, and White seas. From the 15th century it was dominated by Moscow.

Valdemar alternate spelling of ◊Waldemar, name of four kings of Denmark.

Valdivia industrial port (shipbuilding, leather, beer, soap) and resort in Chile; population (1983) 115,500. It was founded 1552 by the Spanish conquistador Pedro de Valdivia (c. 1500–54), conqueror of Chile.

Valdívia Pedro de c. 1497–1554. Spanish explorer who traveled to Venezuela around 1530 and accompanied Francisco ◊Pizarro on his second expedition to Peru. He then went south into Chile, where he founded the cities of Santiago 1541 and Valdívia 1544. In 1552 he crossed the Andes to explore the Negro River. He was killed by Araucanian Indians.

Valence market town and capital of Drôme *département*; SE France, on the Rhône river; population (1982) 68,100. Industries include electrical goods and components for aerospace. It is of pre-Roman origin and has a Romanesque cathedral consecrated 1095.

valence the combining capacity of an ◊atom or ◊radical, determined by the number of electrons that an atom will add, lose, or share when it reacts with another atom. Elements that lose electrons (such as hydrogen and the ◊metals) have a positive valence; those that add electrons (such as oxygen and other nonmetals) have a negative valence.

valence electron electron in the outermost shell of an ◊atom. It is the valence electrons that are involved in the formation of ionic and covalent bonds (see ◊molecule). The number of electrons in this outermost shell represents the maximum possible ◊valency for many elements and matches the number of the group that the element occupies in the ◊periodic table of the elements.

Valencia industrial city (textiles, leather, sugar) and agricultural center in Carabobo state, N Venezuela, on the Cabriales River; population (1981) 624,000. It is 1,569 ft/478 m above sea level and was founded 1555.

Valencia industrial city (wine, fruit, chemicals, textiles, ship repair) in Valencia region, E Spain; population (1986) 739,000. The Valencian Community, consisting of Alicante, Castellón, and Valencia, has an area of 8,994 sq mi/23,300 sq km and a population of 3,772,000.

Valencia was ruled by El ◊Cid 1094–99, after he recaptured it from the Moors. There is a cathedral of the 13th–15th centuries and a university 1500.

Valenciennes industrial town in Nord *département*, NE France, near the Belgian border, once known for its lace; population (1982) 349,500. It became French in 1678.

valency shell the outermost shell of electrons in an ◊atom. It contains the ◊valence electrons. Elements with four or more electrons in their outermost shell can show variable ◊valency. Chlorine can show valencies of 1, 3, 5, and 7 in different compounds.

valency shell

group number	I	II	III	IV	V	VI	VII
element	Na	Mg	Al	Si	P	S	Cl
atomic number	11	12	13	14	15	16	17
electron arrangement	2.8.1	2.8.2	2.8.3	2.8.4	2.8.5	2.8.6	2.8.7
valencies	1	2	3	4(2)	5(3)	6(2)	7(1)

Valentine, St According to tradition a bishop of Terni martyred at Rome, now omitted from the calendar of saints' days as probably nonexistent. His festival was Feb 14, but the custom of sending "valentines" to a loved one on that day seems to have arisen because the day accidentally coincided with the Roman mid-February festival of ◊Lupercalia.

Valentino Rudolph. Adopted name of Rodolfo d'Antonguolla 1895–1926. Italian-born US film actor. He came to the US 1913 and worked as a gardener and a dancer in New York City before appearing as a dancer in a 1918 Hollywood film. He became the screen idol of his day, the archetypal romantic lover of the silent screen. His films include *The Four Horsemen of the Apocalypse* 1921, *The Sheik* 1922, *Blood and Sand* 1922, *Monsieur Beaucaire* 1924, *The Eagle* 1925, and *Son of the Sheik* 1926. His fans never forgot him after a premature death from peritonitis.

valerian perennial plant of either of two genera, *Valeriana* and *Centranthus*, family Valerianaceae, native to the northern hemisphere, with clustered heads of fragrant tubular flowers in red, white, or pink. The root of the common valerian or garden heliotrope *Valeriana officinalis* is used medicinally to relieve flatulence and as a sedative.

Valéry Paul 1871–1945. French poet and mathematician. His poetry includes *La Jeune Parque/The Young Fate* 1917 and *Charmes/Enchantments* 1922.

Valhalla in Norse mythology, the hall in ◊Odin's

palace where he feasts with the souls of heroes killed in battle.

Valkyrie in Norse mythology, any of the female attendants of ◊Odin. They select the most valiant warriors to die in battle and escort them to Valhalla.

Valladolid industrial town (food processing, vehicles, textiles, engineering), and capital of Valladolid province, Spain; population (1986) 341,000.

It was the capital of Castile and Leon in the 14th–15th centuries, then of Spain until 1560. The Catholic monarchs Ferdinand and Isabella were married at Valladolid 1469. The explorer Columbus died here, and the home of the writer Cervantes is preserved. It has a university founded in 1346 and a cathedral 1595.

Vallandigham Clement Laird 1820–1871. US political leader. He served in the Ohio legislature 1845–47 and the US House of Representatives 1858–63. A staunch Democrat, he supported Stephen Douglas for president 1860 and, as leader of the "Copperheads," opposed many of Lincoln's war policies. Defeated for reelection to the House and arrested for sedition 1862, Vallandigham was deported to the Confederacy. Returning to Ohio 1864, he remained a strong foe of the Radical Republicans until his death.

Born in New Lisbon, Ohio, and educated at Washington and Jefferson College, Vallandigham was admitted to the bar 1842.

Valle d'Aosta autonomous region of NW Italy; area 1,274 sq mi/3,300 sq km; population (1988) 114,000, many of whom are French-speaking. It produces wine and livestock. Its capital is Aosta.

Vallee Rudy 1901–1986. US singer. Establishing a clean-cut, college-boy image, Vallee became one of the most popular "crooners" of the 1920s with his trademark megaphone and theme song, "My Time Is Your Time." He formed his own band 1928 and hosted a radio program. After service in the Coast Guard in World War II, Vallee appeared in films and on Broadway.

Born Hubert Prior Vallee in Island Pond, Vermont, and raised in Maine, Vallee toured with local bands throughout his teenage years. After studying at the University of Maine and Yale, he traveled widely, making appearances in England and throughout the US.

Valle-Inclán Ramón Maria de 1866–1936. Spanish author of erotic and symbolist works including *Sonatas* 1902–05 and, set in South America, the novel *Tirano Banderas/The Tyrant* 1926.

Vallejo city in NW California, on San Pablo Bay, NE of Berkeley. Industries include fruits, flour processing, and petroleum refining; population (1990) 109,199. It served as California's capital 1852–53.

Vallejo Mariano Guadelupe 1808–1890. Military leader in colonial California. Born in Monterey, California, Vallejo chose a military career early in life. A supporter of Mexican independence, he was stationed in Alta California and helped put down an Indian uprising at San Jose 1829. Through the 1830s, Vallejo consistently opposed the rule of autocratic governors sent from Mexico City and in 1838 became the military commander of the province. He was briefly imprisoned during the Bear Flag revolt 1849 but later chose to become a citizen of the state of California, serving as a member of the state senate.

Valletta capital and port of Malta; population (1987) 9,000, but the urban harbor area is 101,000.

It was founded 1566 by the Knights of ◊St John of Jerusalem and named after their grand master Jean de la Valette (1494–1568), who fended off a Turkish siege May–Sept 1565. The 16th-century palace of the grand masters survives. Malta was formerly a British naval base and was under heavy attack in World War II.

Valley Forge site in Pennsylvania 20 mi/32 km NW of Philadelphia, where George ◊Washington's army spent the winter of 1777–78 in terrible hardship during the ◊American Revolution.

Of the 10,000 men who spent the winter there, 2,500 died of disease and the rest suffered from lack of rations and other supplies; many deserted. During that winter, Washington introduced Prussian officers who trained the irregulars. The Franco-American alliance 1778 boosted morale and brought new recruits to the army, which emerged from the ordeal to inflict heavy losses on the British.

Valley of Ten Thousand Smokes valley in SW Alaska, on the Alaska Peninsula, where in 1912 Mount Katmai erupted in one of the largest volcanic explosions ever known, though without loss of human life since the area was uninhabited. It was dedicated in 1918 as the Katmai National Monument. Thousands of fissures on the valley floor continue to emit steam and gases.

Valley of the Kings burial place of ancient kings opposite ◊Thebes, Egypt, on the left bank of the Nile.

Valois branch of the Capetian dynasty, originally counts of Valois, (see Hugh ◊Capet) in France, members of which occupied the French throne from Philip VI 1328 to Henry III 1589.

Valona Italian form of ◊Vlorë, port in Albania.

Valparaíso industrial port (sugar, refining, textiles, chemicals) in Chile; capital of Valparaíso province, on the Pacific; population (1987) 279,000. Founded 1536, it was occupied by the English naval adventurers ◊Drake 1578 and ◊Hawkins 1595, pillaged by the Dutch 1600, and bombarded by Spain 1866; it has also suffered from earthquakes.

value-added tax (VAT) a tax on goods and services. VAT is imposed by the European Community on member states. The tax varies from state to state. An agreed proportion of the tax money is used to fund the EC.

VAT is applied at each stage of the production of a commodity, and it is charged only on the value added at that stage. It is not levied, unlike sales tax, on the sale of the commodity, but at this stage the VAT paid at earlier stages of the commodity's manufacture cannot be reclaimed. In the UK food, newspapers, and books are exempt from VAT.

A form of VAT was introduced in Japan 1989, its unpopularity contributing to the downfall of Prime Minister Takeshita. Canada imposed a VAT (termed GST) from 1991.

valve in control engineering, a device that controls the flow of a fluid or along a pipeline. Inside a valve, a plug moves to widen or close the opening through which the fluid passes.

Common valves include the cone or needle valve, the globe valve, and butterfly valve, all named after the shape of the plug. Specialized valves include the one-way valve, which permits fluid flow in one direction only, and the safety valve, which cuts off flow under certain conditions.

valve a structure for controlling the direction of the blood flow. In humans and other vertebrates, the contractions of the beating heart cause the correct blood flow into the arteries because a series of valves prevent back flow. Diseased valves, detected as "heart murmurs," have decreased efficiency. The tendency for low pressure venous blood to collect at the base of limbs under the influence of gravity is counteracted by a series of small valves within the veins. It was the existence of these valves that prompted the 17th-century physician William Harvey to suggest that the blood circulated around the body.

Vámbéry Arminius 1832–1913. Hungarian traveler and writer who crossed the deserts of Central Asia to Khiva and Samarkand dressed as a ◊dervish, a classic journey described in his *Travels and Adventures in Central Asia* 1864.

vampire in Slavic folklore, an "undead" corpse that sleeps by day in its native earth, and by night, often in the form of a bat, sucks the blood of the living. ◊Dracula is a vampire in popular fiction.

vampire bat any South and Central American bat of the family Desmodontidae, of which there are three species. The common vampire *Desmodus rotundus* is found from N Mexico to central Argentina; its head and body grow to 3.5 in/9 cm. Vampires feed on the blood of mammals; they slice a piece of skin from a victim with their sharp incisor teeth and lap up the flowing blood.

vampire bat

Vampires feed on all kinds of mammals including horses, cattle, and occasionally humans. They fly low and settle on the ground before running to a victim. The bite is painless and the loss of blood is small; the victim seldom comes to any harm. Vampire bats are intelligent and among the few mammals to manifest altruistic behavior (they adopt orphans and help other bats in need).

Van city in Turkey on a site on Lake Van that has been inhabited for more than 3,000 years; population (1985) 121,000. It is a commercial center for a fruit- and grain-producing area.

vanadium silver-white, malleable and ductile, metallic element, symbol V, atomic number 23, atomic weight 50.942. It occurs in certain iron, lead, and uranium ores and is widely distributed in small quantities in igneous and sedimentary rocks. It is used to make steel alloys, to which it adds tensile strength.

Spanish mineralogist Andrés del Rio (1764–1849) and Swedish chemist Nils Sefströ m (1787–1845) discovered vanadium independently, the former in 1801 and the latter in 1831. Del Rio named it "erythronium," but was persuaded by other chemists that he had not in fact discovered a new element; Sefströ m gave it its present name, after the Norse goddess of love and beauty, Vanadis (or Freya).

Van Allen James Alfred 1914– . US physicist whose instruments aboard the first US satellite *Explorer 1* in 1958 led to the discovery of the ◊Van Allen radiation belts. He studied captured German V2 rockets after World War II and went on to pioneer high-altitude research with rockets. He became professor of physics at the University of Iowa 1951. Born in Mount Pleasant, Iowa, Van Allen received a PhD in physics from the University of Iowa 1939.

Van Allen radiation belts two zones of charged particles around the Earth's magnetosphere, discovered 1958 by US physicist James Van Allen. The atomic particles come from the Earth's upper atmosphere and the ◊solar wind, and are trapped by the Earth's magnetic field. The inner belt lies 620–3,100 mi/1,000–5,000 km above the equator, and contains ◊protons and ◊electrons. The outer belt lies 9,300–15,500 mi/15,000–25,000 km above the equator but is lower around the magnetic poles. It contains mostly electrons from the solar wind.

Van Buren Martin 1782–1862. Eighth president of the US 1837–41, a Democrat, who had helped establish the ◊Democratic Party. He was president during the Panic of 1837, the worst US economic crisis until that time, caused by land speculation in the West. Refusing to intervene, he advocated the establishment of an independent treasury, one not linked to the federal government. He attempted to hold the Southern states in the Union by advocating a strict states' rights position on slavery. He adhered to Jeffersonian principles of nonintervention in economic affairs,

Van Allen radiation belts

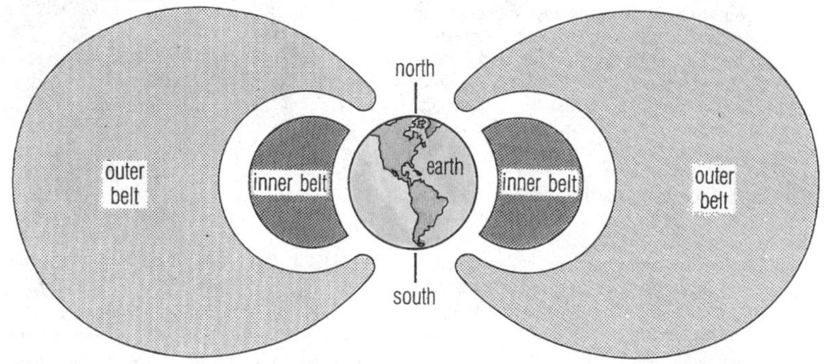
north
outer belt
inner belt
earth
inner belt
outer belt
south

van de Graaff generator

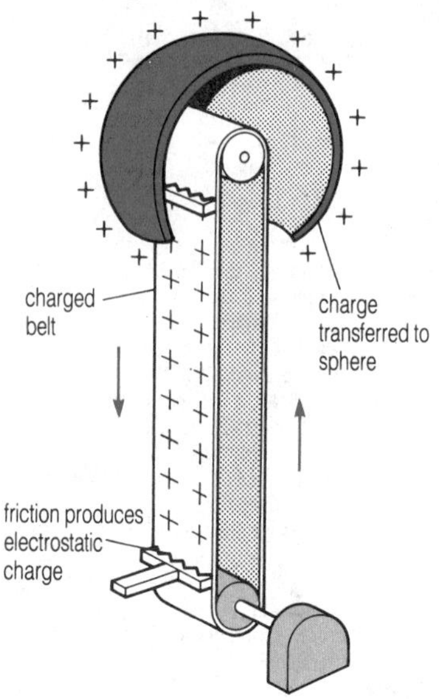
charged belt
charge transferred to sphere
friction produces electrostatic charge

worsening the depression and leading to his 1840 defeat.

Born of Dutch ancestry in Kinderhook, New York, he was a US senator from New York 1821–28, governor of New York 1829, US secretary of state 1829–31, and US vice-president 1833–37. As president, his refusal to annex Texas alienated many Southerners despite his reluctance to express his antislavery sentiment in public policy. He unsuccessfully campaigned for the presidency 1840, 1848.

Vance Cyrus 1917– . US Democratic politician, secretary of state 1977–80. He resigned because he did not support President Carter's abortive mission to rescue the US hostages in Iran. In 1991 he was named by the United Nations to help mediate the Yugoslav crisis.

Van Cortlandt Stephanus 1643–1700. Dutch-American colonial official. Born in New Amsterdam (now New York), the son of a prominent family of Dutch settlers, Van Cortlandt became a prosperous merchant and expanded his landholdings after the English conquest of the colony in 1664. A long-time colonel in the provincial militia, he served on the governor's council and in 1677 became the first native-born mayor of New York. He was a local judge 1677–91 and justice of the provincial supreme court 1691–1700.

Van Buren *The 8th president of the United States of America, Martin Van Buren, a Democrat. 1837–1841.*

Vancouver industrial city (oil refining, engineering, shipbuilding, aircraft, timber, pulp and paper, textiles, fisheries) in Canada, its chief Pacific seaport, on the mainland of British Columbia; population (1986) 1,381,000.

It is situated on Burrard Inlet, at the mouth of the Fraser River. The site was taken possession of by George Vancouver for Britain 1792. It was settled by 1875, under the name of Granville, and was renamed when it became a city 1886, having been reached by the Canadian Pacific Railroad.

Vancouver city in SW Washington, on the Columbia river, N of Portland, Oregon.

It is a manufacturing and shipping center for agriculture and lumber; population (1990) 46,380. It began as a trading post for the Hudson's Bay Co. 1825.

Vancouver George c. 1758–1798. British navigator who made extensive exploration of the W coast of North America.

He accompanied James ◊Cook on two voyages, and served in the West Indies. He also surveyed parts of Australia, New Zealand, Tahiti, and Hawaii.

Vancouver Island island off the W coast of Canada, part of British Columbia

area 12,404 sq mi/32,136 sq km

towns Victoria, Nanaimo, Esquimalt (naval base)

products coal, timber, fish

history visited by British explorer Cook 1778; surveyed 1792 by Capt George Vancouver.

Vandal member of a Germanic people related to the ◊Goths. In the 5th century AD the Vandals moved from N Germany to invade Roman ◊Gaul and Spain, many settling in Andalusia (formerly Vandalitia) and others reaching N Africa 429. They sacked Rome 455 but accepted Roman suzerainty in the 6th century.

van de Graaff Robert Jemison 1901–1967. US physicist who from 1929 developed a high-voltage generator, which in its modern form can produce more than a million volts. It consists of an endless vertical conveyor belt that carries electrostatic charges (resulting from friction) up to a large hollow sphere supported on an insulated stand. The lower end of the belt is earthed, so that charge accumulates on the sphere. The size of the voltage built up in air depends on the radius of the sphere, but can be increased by enclosing the generator in an inert atmosphere, such as nitrogen.

Vandenberg Arthur Hendrick 1884–1951. US public official. Active in Republican state politics, he was named to fill a vacant US Senate seat 1928 and

Vanderbilt *American tycoon Cornelius Vanderbilt, who made his fortune developing steamship and railroad lines.*

remained in that office for the next 23 years. Although initially an isolationist, Vandenberg supported F D Roosevelt's war policies and was a supporter of the United Nations 1945. He was chairman of the Senate Foreign Relations Committee 1946–48.

Born in Grand Rapids, Michigan, Vandenberg briefly attended the University of Michigan Law School, leaving to join the staff of the *Grand Rapids Herald*, of which he became editor 1906.

Vanderbilt Cornelius 1794–1877. US industrialist who made a fortune in steamships and (from the age of 70) by financing railroads. He defeated stock raids and takeover attempts by other financiers in the process of amassing a fortune of more than $100 million. Despite his wealth, he did not engage in any philanthropic activities until near his death, when he gave $1 million to what would become Vanderbilt University. See also Jay ◊Gould.

Born in Port Richmond, New York, Vanderbilt, at the age of 16, began a ferry operation between Staten Island and Manhattan. By 1829, he had established his own steamship line, at first to service local New York and New England ports, and from 1850 to reach California by a shorter route, through Nicaragua. In the 1860s he began to acquire and merge railroad lines in New York and Chicago.

Vanderbilt William Henry 1821–1885. US financier and railroad promoter. Born in New Brunswick, New Jersey, son of financier Cornelius Vanderbilt, he was given control of the Staten Island Railroad 1857. He was named vice-president of the New York and Harlem Railroad 1864, acquired other railroads, and became president of the New York Central Railroad 1877. As the head of a railroad trust, he was deeply involved in rate fixing and strongly opposed government regulation of the railroad industry. Vanderbilt, famous for his contemptuous phrase "The public be damned," retired in 1883.

Van der Post Laurens (Jan) 1906– . South African writer whose books, many of them autobiographical, reflect his openness to diverse cultures and his belief in the importance of intuition, individualism, and myth in human experience. A formative influence was his time spent with the San Bushmen of the Kalahari while growing up, and whose disappearing culture he recorded in *The Lost World of the Kalahari* 1958, *The Heart of the Hunter* 1961, and *Testament to the Bushmen* 1984.

His first novel *In a Province* 1934 was an indictment of racism in South Africa; later works include *Flamingo Feather* 1955, *The Hunter and the Whale* 1967, *A Story like the Wind* 1972, and *A Far-off Place* 1974. He wrote about Japanese prisoner-of-war camps in *The Seed and the Sower* 1963.

Van der Waals Johannes Diderik 1837–1923. Dutch physicist who was awarded a Nobel Prize in 1910 for his theoretical study of gases. He emphasized the forces of attraction and repulsion between atoms and molecules in describing the behavior of real gases, as opposed to the ideal gases dealt with in ◊Boyle's law and ◊Charles's law.

Van Devanter Willis 1859–1941. US Supreme Court justice. Born in Marion, Indiana, Van Devanter was educated at Asbury University and received a law degree from the University of Cincinnati 1881. Settling in Cheyenne, Wyoming, he served as city attorney 1887–88 and chief justice of the territorial supreme court 1888–90. He was active in Republican politics and served as assistant US attorney general 1897–1903 and federal circuit judge 1903–10. He was appointed to the US Supreme Court by President Taft 1910. A staunch conservative, Van Devanter was a bitter opponent of the New Deal until his retirement 1937.

van Diemen Anthony 1593–1645. Dutch admiral, see ◊Diemen, Anthony van.

Van Doren Mark 1894–1972. US poet and writer. He published his first collection, *Spring Thunder*, in 1924. His anthology *Collected Poems* 1939 won a Pulitzer prize. Van Doren was an editor of *The Nation* 1924–28 and published the novels *The Transients* 1935 and *Windless Cabins* 1940.

Born in Hope, Illinois, Van Doren was educated at the University of Illinois and received his PhD 1920 from Columbia University, where he taught English 1920–59. His autobiography appeared in 1958 and his last collection of poems, *Good Morning*, in 1973.

van Dyck Anthony. Flemish painter, see ◊Dyck, Anthony van.

Vane Henry 1613–1662. English politician. In 1640 elected a member of the ◊Long Parliament, he was prominent in the impeachment of Archbishop ◊Laud and in 1643–53 was in effect the civilian head of the Parliamentary government. At the Restoration of the monarchy he was executed.

Vane John 1923– . British pharmacologist who discovered the wide role of prostaglandins in the human body, produced in response to illness and stress. He shared the 1982 Nobel Prize for Physiology or Medicine with Sune Gergstrom and Bengt Samuelsson of Sweden.

Vänern, Lake largest lake in Sweden, area 2,140 sq mi/5,550 sq km.

van Eyck Jan. Flemish painter, see ◊Eyck, Jan van.

van Gogh Vincent. Dutch painter, see ◊Gogh, Vincent van.

Vanguard early series of US Earth-orbiting satellites and their associated rocket launcher. *Vanguard 1* was the second US satellite, launched March 17, 1958 by the three-stage Vanguard rocket. Tracking its orbit revealed that Earth is slightly pear-shaped. The series ended Sept 1959 with *Vanguard 3*.

vanilla any climbing orchid of the genus *Vanilla*, native to tropical America but cultivated elsewhere, with fragrant, large, white or yellow flowers. The dried and fermented fruit, or podlike capsules, of *Vanilla planifolia* are the source of the vanilla flavoring used in cooking and baking.

Annual world production of vanilla pods is estimated at 1,500 tons. Vanilla flavoring (vanillin) can now be produced artificially from waste sulfite liquor, a byproduct of paper pulp-making.

Vanity Fair a novel by William Makepeace Thackeray, published in the UK 1847–48. It deals with the contrasting fortunes of the tough orphan Becky Sharp and the soft-hearted, privileged Amelia Sedley, who first meet at Miss Pinkerton's Academy for young ladies.

van Leyden Lucas. Dutch painter, see ◊Lucas van Leyden.

van Meegeren Hans. Dutch forger, see ◊Meegeren, Han van.

Van Rensselaer Stephen 1764–1839. American public official. At the start of the War of 1812, he commanded American forces at New York State's northern border but suffered a serious defeat at Queenstown, Canada. Van Rensselaer was a US congressman 1822–29, and as president of the New York Canal Commission 1825–39 he oversaw the construction of the Erie Canal. He founded the Rensselaer Polytechnic Institute 1824.

Born in New York and educated at Harvard, Van Rensselaer inherited extensive real estate holdings and served in the New York state assembly 1789–91, in the state senate 1791–96, and as a major general in the militia.

van t'Hoff Jacobus Henricus 1852–1911. Dutch physical chemist. He explained the "asymmetric" carbon atom occurring in optically active compounds. His greatest work—the concept of chemical affinity as the maximum work obtainable from a reaction—was shown with measurements of osmotic and gas pressures, and reversible electric batteries. He was the first recipient of the Nobel Prize for Chemistry in 1901.

Vanuatu group of islands in the S Pacific, part of ◊Melanesia.

government Vanuatu is an independent republic within the ◊Commonwealth. The constitution dates from independence in 1980. It provides for a president, who is formal head of state, elected for a five-year term by an electoral college consisting of parliament and the presidents of the country's regional councils. Parliament consists of a single chamber of 46 members, elected by universal suffrage, through a system of proportional representation, for a four-year term. From among their members they elect a prime minister who then appoints and presides over a council of ministers.

history Originally settled by Melanesians, the islands were reached from Europe 1606 by the Portuguese navigator Pedro Fernandez de Queiras. Called the New Hebrides, they were jointly administered by France and Britain from 1906.

Vanuatu escaped Japanese occupation during World War II. In the 1970s two political parties were formed, the New Hebrides National Party, supported by British interests, and the Union of New Hebrides Communities, supported by France. Discussions began in London about eventual independence, and they resulted in the election of a representative assembly in Nov 1975. Independence was delayed because of objections by the National Party, which had changed its name to the Vanuaaku Party (VP). A government of national unity was formed in Dec 1978 with Father Gerard Leymang as chief minister and the VP leader, Father Walter Lini, as his deputy. In 1980 a revolt by French settlers and plantation workers in the island of Espiritu Santo was put down by British, French, and Papua New Guinean troops.

Later in 1980 the New Hebrides became independent, within the Commonwealth, as the Republic of Vanuatu. The first president was George Kalkoa, who adopted the name *Sokomanu* ("leader of thousands"), and the first prime minister was Father Lini. In the 1983 general election the VP won 24 seats, and Father Lini continued as prime minister. The Union of Moderate Parties won 12 seats.

Lini proceeded to pursue a left-of-center, nonaligned foreign policy, which included support for the Kanak separatist movement in New Caledonia. This soured relations with France and provoked mounting opposition within parliament. Despite the VP retaining its majority after the Nov 1987 general election, this opposition continued, prompting Lini, in July 1988, to expel from parliament his rival Barak Sope. Lini was then

Vanuatu
Republic of
(Ripablik Blong Vanuatu)

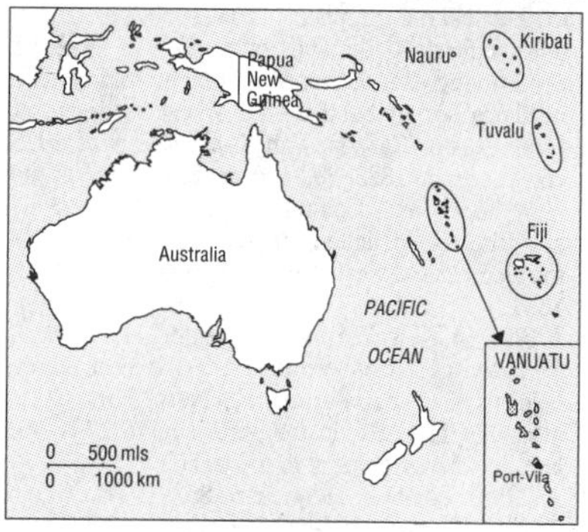
Papua New Guinea
Nauru
Kiribati
Tuvalu
Fiji
Australia
PACIFIC
OCEAN
VANUATU
Port-Vila
0 500 mls
0 1000 km

area 5,714 sq mi/14,800 sq km
capital Vila (on Efate island)
cities Luganville (on Espiritu Santo)
physical comprises 70 islands, including Espiritu Santo, Malekala, and Efate; densely forested, mountainous
features three active volcanoes
head of state Fred Timakata from 1989
head of government Walter Lini from 1980
political system democratic republic
political parties Vanuaaki Pati (VP: "Party of Our Land"), Melanesian Socialist; Union of Moderate Parties (UMP), Francophone opposition grouping
exports copra, fish, coffee, cocoa
currency vatu
population (1988) 149,400 (94% Melanesian); growth rate 3.3% p.a.
life expectancy men 67, women 71 (1989)
language Bislama 82%, English, French (all official)
literacy 20%
religion Presbyterian 40%, Roman Catholic 16%, Anglican 14%, animist 15%
GDP $125 million (1987); $927 per head
chronology
1906 Islands jointly administered by France and Britain.
1975 Representative assembly established.
1978 Government of national unity formed, with Father Gerard Leymang as chief minister.
1980 Revolt on the island of Espiritu Santo delayed independence but it was achieved within the Commonwealth with George Sokomanu as president and Father Walter Lini as prime minister.
1988 Attempt by Sokomanu to unseat Lini led to Sokomanu's arrest for treason.
1989 Sokomanu sentenced to six years' imprisonment and succeeded as president by Fred Timakata.

dismissed as prime minister and Parliament dissolved by president Sokomanu, who appointed his nephew Sope head of an interim government. However, the Supreme Court ruled these actions unconstitutional and security forces loyal to Lini arrested the president, Sope and opposition leader Maxime Carlot (who were each later sentenced to 5–6 years imprisonment) and reinstated the former prime minister. Fred Timakata, formerly the minister of health, was elected president by the state's electoral college in Jan 1989.

Externally, since independence, Vanuatu has sought to promote greater cooperation among the states of the Pacific region. As part of this strategy, along with Papua New Guinea and the Solomon Islands, it formed, in March 1988, the "Spearhead Group," whose aim is to preserve Melanesian cultural tradition and campaign for New Caledonia's independence.

Var river in S France, rising in the Maritime Alps and flowing generally SSE for 84 mi/134 km into the Mediterranean near Nice. It gives its name to a *département* in the Provence-Alpes-Côte d'Azur region.

Varanasi or ***Benares*** holy city of the Hindus in Uttar Pradesh, India, on the river Ganges; population (1981) 794,000. There are 1,500 golden shrines, and a 3-mi/5-km frontage to the Ganges with sacred stairways (ghats) for purification by bathing.

At the burning ghats, the ashes of the dead are scattered on the river to ensure a favorable reincarnation. There are two universities 1916 and 1957.

Varangian member of a widespread Swedish Viking people in E Europe and the Balkans; more particularly a member of the Byzantine imperial guard founded 988 by Vladimir of Kiev (955–1015), which lasted until the fall of Constantinople 1453.

From the late 11th century, the Byzantine guard included English and Norman mercenaries, as well as Scandinavians. It was feared and respected as an elite military force, and occasionally dabbled in politics.

Varèse Edgard 1885–1965. French composer, who settled in New York 1916 where he founded the New Symphony Orchestra 1919 to advance the cause of modern music. His work is experimental and often dissonant, combining electronic sounds with orchestral instruments, and includes *Hyperprism* 1923, *Intégrales* 1931, and *Poème Electronique* 1958.

Vargas Getúlio 1883–1954. President of Brazil 1930–45 and 1951–54. He overthrew the republic 1930 and in 1937 he set up a totalitarian, profascist state known as the Estado Novo. Ousted by a military coup 1945, he returned as president 1951 but, amid mounting opposition and political scandal, committed suicide 1954.

Vargas Llosa Mario 1937– . Peruvian novelist and politician, author of *La ciudad y los perros/The Time of the Hero* 1963 and *La guerra del fin del mundo/The War at the End of the World* 1982.

As a writer he belongs to the magic realist school. *La tía Julia y el escribidor/Aunt Julia and the Scriptwriter* 1977 is a humorously autobiographical novel.

Vargas Llosa began as a communist and turned to the political right. He ran unsuccessfully for the presidency in 1990. He has been criticized for being out of touch with Peru's large Quechua Indian community.

Varèse *An experimental composer, Edgard Varèse rejected the Classical tradition. He shocked audiences of his day by introducing dissonant brass and percussion effects into the orchestra; he was a pioneer of electronic music.*

variable in mathematics, a changing quantity (one that can take various values), as opposed to a ◊constant. For example, in the algebraic expression $y = 4x^3 + 2$, the variables are x and y, whereas 4 and 2 are constants.

A variable may be dependent or independent. Thus if y is a ◊function of x, written $y = f(x)$, such that $y = 4x^3 + 2$, the domain of the function includes all values of the independent variable x while the range (or codomain) of the function is defined by the values of the dependent variable y.

variable-geometry wing technical name for a ◊swingwing, a type of moveable aircraft wing.

variable star star whose brightness changes, either regularly or irregularly, over a period ranging from a few hours to months or even years. The ◊Cepheid variables regularly expand and contract in size every few days or weeks.

Stars that change in size and brightness at less precise intervals include long-period variables such as the red giant Mira in the constellation Cetus (period about 330 days), and irregular variables such as some red supergiants. Eruptive variables emit sudden outbursts of light. Some suffer flares on their surfaces, while others, such as a ◊nova, result from transfer of gas between a close pair of stars. A ◊supernova is the explosive death of a star. In an ◊eclipsing binary, the variation is due not to any change in the star itself but to the periodical eclipse of a star by a close companion; see ◊Epsilon Aurigae and ◊Algol.

variations in music, a form based on constant repetition of a simple theme, each new version being elaborated or treated in a different manner. The theme is easily recognizable, either as a popular tune or—as a gesture of respect—as the work of a fellow composer, for example, Brahms honors Bach in the *Variations on the St Antony Chorale*.

varicose veins or ***varicosis*** condition where the veins become swollen and twisted. The veins of the legs are most often affected, although other vulnerable sites include the rectum (◊hemorrhoids) and testes.

Some people have an inherited tendency to varicose veins, and the condition often appears in pregnant women, but obstructed blood flow is the direct cause. They may cause a dull ache or may be the site for ◊thrombosis, infection, or ulcers. The affected veins can be injected with a substance that causes them to shrink, or surgery may be needed.

variegation a description of plant leaves or stems that exhibit patches of different colors. The term is usually applied to plants that show white, cream, or yellow on their leaves, caused by areas of tissue that lack the green pigment ◊chlorophyll. Variegated plants are bred for their decorative value, but they are often considerably weaker than the normal, uniformly green plant. Many will not breed true and require ◊vegetative reproduction.

The term is sometimes applied to abnormal patchy coloring of petals, as in the variegated petals of certain tulips, caused by a virus infection. A mineral deficiency in the soil may also be the cause of variegation.

Varna port in Bulgaria, on an inlet of the Black Sea; population (1987) 306,000. Industries include shipbuilding and the manufacture of chemicals.

Varna was a Greek colony in the 6th century BC and part of the Ottoman Empire 1391–1878; it was renamed Stalin 1949–56.

varnish a solution of resins or resinous gums dissolved in linseed oil, turpentine, or other solvents; the synthetic equivalents. It is used to give a shiny, sealed surface to furniture and interior fittings.

Varuna in early Hindu mythology, the sky god and king of the universe.

varve a pair of thin sedimentary beds, one coarse

vascular bundle

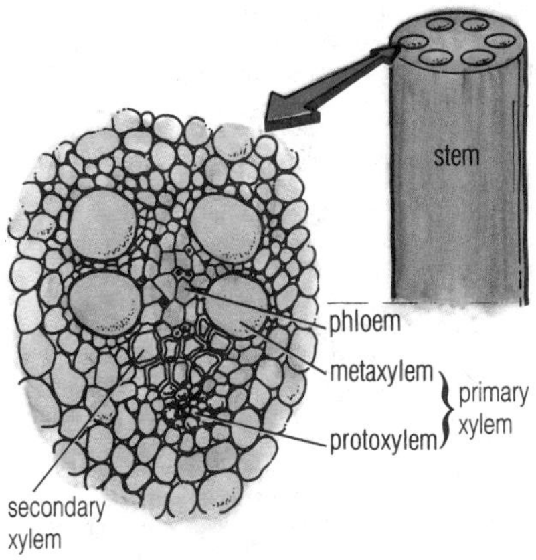
stem
phloem
metaxylem
protoxylem
primary xylem
secondary xylem

Vatican City State

(Stato della Città del Vaticano)

miles 500
km 1000
Italy
VATICAN CITY
Rome
MEDITERRANEAN SEA

area 109 acres/0.4 sq km

physical forms an enclave in the heart of Rome, Italy
features Vatican Palace, official residence of the pope; basilica and square of St Peter's; churches in and near Rome, the pope's summer villa at Castel Gandolfo; the world's smallest state
head of state and government John Paul II from 1978
political system absolute Catholic
currency Vatican City lira; Italian lira
population (1985) 1,000
language Latin (official), Italian
religion Roman Catholic
chronology
1929 Three treaties recognized sovereignty of the pope.
1947 New Italian constitution confirmed the sovereignty of the Vatican City State.
1978 John Paul II became the first non-Italian pope for more than 400 years.
1985 New concordat signed under which Roman Catholicism ceased to be Italy's state religion.

and one fine, representing a cycle of thaw followed by an interval of freezing, in lakes of glacial regions.

Each couplet thus constitutes the sedimentary record of a year, and by counting varves in glacial lakes a record of absolute time elapsed can be determined. Summer and winter layers often are distinguished also by color, with lighter layers representing summer deposition, and darker layers the result of dark clay settling from water while the lake was frozen.

Vasarély Victor 1908– . French artist, born in Hungary. In the 1940s he developed his precise geometric compositions, full of visual puzzles and effects of movement, which he created with complex arrangements of hard-edged geometric shapes and subtle variations in colors.

He was active in Paris from 1930 and in the south of France from 1960. He initially worked as a graphic artist, concentrating on black and white images.

Vasari Giorgio 1511–1574. Italian art historian, architect, and painter, author of *Lives of the Most Excellent Architects, Painters and Sculptors* 1550 (enlarged and revised 1568), in which he proposed the theory of a Renaissance of the arts beginning with Giotto and culminating with Michelangelo. He designed the Uffizi Palace, Florence.

Vasari was a prolific Mannerist painter. His basic view of art history has remained unchallenged, despite his prejudices and his delight in often ill-founded, libelous anecdotes.

Vasco da Gama Portuguese navigator; see ◊Gama.

vascular bundle a strand of primary conducting tissue (a "vein") in vascular plants, consisting mainly of water-conducting tissues, metaxylem and protoxylem, which together make up the primary ◊xylem, and nutrient-conducting tissue, ◊phloem. It extends from the roots to the stems and leaves. Typically the phloem is situated nearest to the epidermis and the xylem toward the center of the bundle. In plants exhibiting ◊secondary growth, the xylem and phloem are separated by a thin layer of vascular ◊cambium, which gives rise to new conducting tissues.

vascular plant a plant containing vascular bundles. ◊Pteridophytes (ferns, horsetails, and club mosses), ◊gymnosperms (conifers and cycads), and ◊angiosperms (flowering plants) are all vascular plants.

vas deferens in male vertebrates, a tube conducting sperm from the testis to the urethra. The sperms are carried in a fluid secreted by various glands, and can be transported very rapidly when the smooth muscle in the wall of the vas deferens undergoes rhythmic contractions, as in sexual intercourse.

vasectomy male sterilization; an operation to cut and tie the duct (vas deferens) that carries sperm from the testes to the penis. Vasectomy does not affect sexual performance, but the semen produced at ejaculation no longer contains sperm.

Some surgical attempts to reopen the duct have been successful, and some have opened spontaneously, thus making conception possible.

vassal in medieval Europe, a person who paid feudal homage to a superior lord (see ◊feudalism), and who promised military service and advice in return for a grant of land. The term was used from the 9th century.

The relationship of vassalage was the mainstay of the feudal system and declined along with it during the transition to ◊bastard feudalism.

Vassar Matthew 1792–1868. British-born US businessman and educational philanthropist. Vassar came to the US with his family 1796. He worked in his father's brewery in Poughkeepsie, New York, before establishing his own firm 1811. Vassar successfully expanded his business interests and real estate investments. A proponent of higher education for women, he endowed Vassar Female College in Poughkeepsie 1861. The school opened 1865 with a full college curriculum and became one of the finest women's educational institutions in the US. In 1969 it became coeducational.

Vassilou Georgios Vassos 1931– . Greek-Cypriot politician and entrepreneur, president from 1988. A self-made millionaire, he entered politics as an independent and in 1988 won the presidency, with Communist Party support. He has since, with United Nations help, tried unsuccessfully to heal the rift between the Greek and Turkish communities.

Vatican Bank bank of the Vatican City State, officially Institute of Religious Works (IOR).

Vatican City State sovereign area surrounded by the city of Rome, Italy.

government The pope, elected for life by the Sacred College of ◊Cardinals, is absolute head of state. He appoints a pontifical commission to administer the state's affairs on his behalf and under his direction.

history The pope has traditionally been based in Rome, where the Vatican has been a papal residence since 1377. The Vatican Palace is one of the largest in the world and contains a valuable collection of works of art.

The Vatican City State came into being through the Lateran Treaty of 1929, under which Italy recognized the sovereignty of the pope over the city of the Vatican. The 1947 Italian constitution reaffirmed the Lateran Treaty, and under its terms, Roman Catholicism became the state religion in Italy, enjoying special privileges. This remained so until under a new 1984 Concordat (ratified 1985) Catholicism ceased to be the state religion. Karol Wojtyla, formerly archbishop of Krakow in Poland, has been pope since 1978 under the title of ◊John Paul II. In 1982 Roberto Calvi, known as "God's banker" because of his ties with the Vatican, was found hanged under a London bridge shortly before the collapse of the Italian bank of which he was chair, Banco Ambrosiano, and warrants were issued in Italy against three Vatican Bank executives held responsible for the crash. The warrants were annulled 1987 because the affairs of the Vatican Bank, officially known as the Institute for Religious Works (IOR), are outside Italian jurisdiction.

Vatican Councils Roman Catholic ecumenical councils called by Pope Pius IX 1869 (which met 1870) and by Pope John XXIII 1959 (which met 1962). These councils deliberated over major elements of church policy.

Vauban Sébastien le Prestre de 1633–1707. French marshal and military engineer. In Louis XIV's wars he conducted many sieges and rebuilt many of the fortresses on France's east frontier.

Vaucluse mountain range in SE France, part of the Provence Alps, E of Avignon, rising to 4,075 ft/ 1,242 m. It gives its name to a *département*. The Italian poet Petrarch lived in the Vale of Vaucluse 1337–53.

vaudeville variety entertainment in theaters, popular in the US from the 1890s to the 1920s. Consisting of 10 to 15 acts, ranging from singers and dancers to magicians, jugglers, acrobats, and comedians, it was the equivalent of the English music hall.

The forerunners of vaudeville, variety shows held in cities and frontier settlements, were often coarse and lewd and intended largely for male audiences. By the 1890s these shows had become suitable family entertainment. Many performers who later became famous for their stage and

Vatican City State *St Peter's Square in the Vatican City State, central Rome, Italy.*

vector quantity

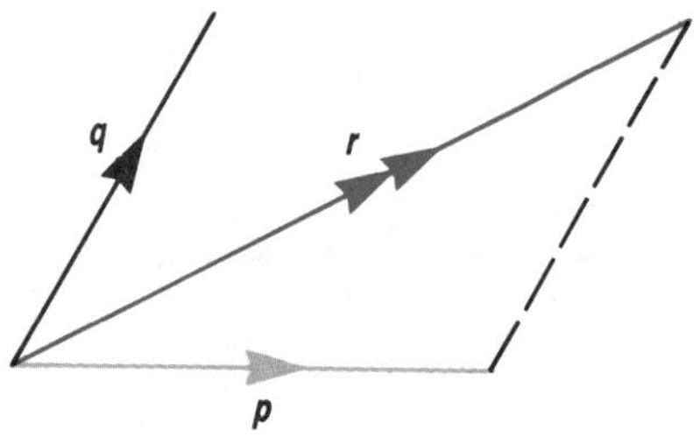
q
r
p

screen work—George Burns, W C Fields, and Will Rogers, for instance—began their careers as vaudeville artists. Vaudeville declined during the 1930s because of the economic hardships of the Depression and the growth of radio and motion pictures. It all but disappeared by the end of World War II, with the advent of television.

Vaughan Williams Ralph 1872–1958. English composer. His style was tonal and often evocative of the English countryside through the use of folk themes. Among his works are the orchestral *Fantasia on a Theme by Thomas Tallis* 1910; the opera *Sir John in Love* 1929, featuring the Elizabethan song "Greensleeves"; and nine symphonies 1909–57.

vb in grammar, abbreviation for ◊verb.

VDT (abbreviation of video display terminal) an electronic output device for displaying the data processed by a computer on a screen. The oldest and the most popular type is the ◊cathode ray tube (CRT), which uses essentially the same technology as a television screen. Other types use plasma display technology and ◊liquid crystal displays.

Veblen Thorstein Bunde 1857–1929. US social critic. Born in Cato, Wisconsin, and raised in Minnesota, Veblen was educated at Carleton College and received his PhD from Yale 1884. He taught at the University of Chicago 1892–1906 and edited the *Journal of Political Economy* 1892–1905. Veblen's insights on culture and economics were expressed in his books *The Theory of the Leisure Class* 1899 and *The Theory of Business Enterprise* 1904.

He also held teaching positions at Stanford University 1906–09 and the University of Missouri 1911–18 and was a founder of the New School for Social Research in New York 1919.

vector quantity any physical quantity that has both magnitude and direction, such as the velocity or acceleration of an object, as distinct from a scalar quantity, which has magnitude but no direction, such as speed, density, or mass. A vector is represented geometrically by an arrow whose length corresponds to its magnitude, and in an appropriate direction. Vectors can be added graphically by constructing a triangle of vectors (such as the triangle of forces commonly employed in physics and engineering).

If two forces p and q are acting on a body at A, then the parallelogram of forces is drawn to determine the resultant force and direction r. p, q, and r are vectors. In technical writing, it is denoted by bold (clarendon) type, or underlined or overlined.

Veda (Sanskrit "divine knowledge") the most sacred of the Hindu scriptures, hymns written in an old form of Sanskrit; the oldest may date from 1500 or 2000 BC. The four main collections are: the *Rigveda* (hymns and praises); *Yajurveda* (prayers and sacrificial formulae); *Sâmaveda* (tunes and chants); and *Atharvaveda*, or Veda of the Atharvans, the officiating priests at the sacrifices.

Vedānta school of Hindu philosophy that developed the teachings of the *Upanishads*. One of its teachers was Śamkara, who lived in S India in the 8th century AD and is generally regarded as a manifestation of Siva. He taught that there is only one reality, Brahman, and that knowledge of Brahman leads finally to *moksha*, or liberation from reincarnation.

Vedda member of the aboriginal peoples of Sri Lanka, who occupied the island before the arrival of the Aryans around 550 BC. They live mainly in the central highlands, and many practice shifting cultivation.

Veeck William Louis, Jr 1914–1986. US baseball executive. In 1941 he bought a minor league baseball team in Milwaukee and pioneered marketing promotions that would later become standard in professional sports. After service in the US Marines during World War II, he became part owner of the Cleveland Indians, helping to guide the team to a World Series victory 1948. As owner of the St Louis Browns 1951–53 and Chicago White Sox 1959–61, he introduced innovations in the sale of television rights and the drafting of amateurs.

Born in Chicago, son of the owner of major league baseball's Chicago Cubs, Veeck attended Kenyon College.

Vega or ***Alpha Lyrae*** the brightest star in the constellation Lyra and the fifth brightest star in the sky. It is a blue-white star, 27 light-years from Earth, with a luminosity 50 times that of the Sun.

In 1983 the *Infra-Red Astronomy Satellite* (*IRAS*) discovered a ring of dust around Vega, possibly a disk from which a planetary system is forming.

vegan a vegetarian who eats no foods of animal origin whatever, including fish, eggs, and milk.

Theoretically vegans are at risk of a deficiency of vitamin B_{12}, which is needed by the body for blood cell and nerve formation (see ◊vitamin); it can be obtained from fortified soy products and yeast extracts. Vegans ensure an adequate supply of calcium from greens, seeds, nuts and soy products, and vitamin D from sunshine.

vegetarian a person who eats only foods obtained without slaughter, for humanitarian, esthetic, or health reasons. Vegans abstain from all foods of animal origin.

vegetative reproduction a type of ◊asexual reproduction in plants that relies not on spores, but on multicellular structures formed by the parent plant. Some of the main types are ◊stolons and runners, ◊gemmae, ◊bulbils, sucker shoots produced from roots, (such as in the creeping thistle *Cirsium arvense*), ◊tubers, ◊bulbs, ◊corms, and ◊rhizomes. Vegetative reproduction has long been exploited in horticulture and agriculture, with various methods employed to multiply stocks of plants.

Veidt Conrad 1893–1943. German film actor, memorable as the sleepwalker in *Das Kabinett des Dr Caligari/The Cabinet of Dr Caligari* 1919 and as the evil caliph in *The Thief of Baghdad* 1940. An international film star from the 1920s, he moved to Hollywood in the 1940s, where he played the Gestapo officer in *Casablanca* 1942.

Veil Simone 1927– . French politician. A survivor of Hitler's concentration camps, she was minister of health 1974–79 and framed the French abortion bill. In 1979–81 she was president of the European Parliament.

vein in animals with a circulatory system, any vessel that carries blood from the body to the heart. Veins contain valves that prevent the blood from running back when moving against gravity. They always carry deoxygenated blood, with the exception of the veins leading from the lungs to the heart in birds and mammals, which carry newly oxygenated blood.

The term is also used more loosely for any system of channels that strengthens living tissues and supplies them with nutrients—for example, leaf veins (see ◊vascular bundle), and the veins in insects' wings.

Vela constellation of the southern hemisphere near Carina, or the Keel, represented as the sails of a ship. It contains large wisps of gas (called the Gum nebula after its discoverer), believed to be the remains of one or more ◊supernovae. Vela also contains the second optical ◊pulsar (pulsar that flashes at a visible wavelength) to be discovered.

Its four brightest stars are second-magnitude, one of them being Suhail, about 490 light-years from Earth.

Velázquez Diego Rodríguez de Silva y 1599–1660. Spanish painter, born in Seville, the outstanding Spanish artist of the 17th century. In 1623 he became court painter to Philip IV in Madrid, where he produced many portraits of the royal family as well as occasional religious paintings, genre scenes, and other subjects. *Las Meninas/The Ladies-in-Waiting* 1655 (Prado, Madrid) is a complex group portrait that includes a self-portrait, but nevertheless focuses clearly on the doll-like figure of the Infanta Margareta Teresa.

His early work in Seville shows exceptional realism and dignity, delight in capturing a variety of textures, rich use of color, and contrasts of light and shade. In Madrid he was inspired by works by Titian in the royal collection and by Rubens, whom he met in 1628. He was in Italy 1629–31 and 1648–51; on his second visit he painted *Pope Innocent X* (Doria Gallery, Rome).

Velázquez's work includes an outstanding formal history painting, *The Surrender of Breda* 1634–35 (Prado), studies of the male nude, and a reclining female nude, *The Rokeby Venus* about 1648 (National Gallery, London). Around half of the 100 or so paintings known to be by him are owned by the Prado, Madrid.

velcro (from "velvet" and "crochet") a system of hooks and eyes for fastening clothing, developed by Swiss inventor Georges de Mestral (1902–1990) after studying why burrs stuck to his trousers and noting that they were made of thousands of tiny hooks.

Velde, van de family of Dutch artists. Both Willem van de Velde the Elder (1611–1693) and his son Willem van de Velde the Younger (1633–1707) painted sea battles for Charles II and James II (having settled in London 1672). Another son, Adriaen van de Velde (1636–1672), painted landscapes.

Willem the Younger achieved an atmosphere of harmony and dignity in highly detailed views of fighting ships at sea. The National Maritime Museum in Greenwich, London, has a fine collection of his works.

veldt subtropical grassland in South Africa, equivalent to the ◊Pampas of South America.

vellum a type of parchment, often rolled in scrolls, made from the skin of a calf, kid, or lamb. It was used from the late Roman Empire and Middle Ages for exceptionally important documents and the finest manuscripts. For example, *Torahs* (the five books of Moses) are always written in Hebrew on parchment. The modern term now describes thick, high-quality paper that resembles fine parchment.

velocity the speed of an object in a given direction. Velocity is a ◊vector quantity, since its direction is important as well as its magnitude (or speed).

The velocity at any instant of a particle traveling in a curved path is in the direction of the tangent to the path at the instant considered.

velocity ratio (VR), or distance ratio in a machine, the ratio of the distance moved by an effort force to the distance moved by the machine's load in the same time. It follows that the velocities of the effort and the load are in the same ratio. Velocity ratio has no units.

velvet a fabric of silk, cotton, nylon, or other textile, with a short, thick pile. Utrecht, Netherlands, and Genoa, Italy, are traditional centers of manufacture. It is woven on a double loom, then cut between the center pile to form velvet nap.

vena cava one of the large, thin-walled veins found just above the ◊heart, formed from the junction of several smaller veins. The posterior vena cava receives oxygenated blood returning from the lungs, and empties into the left atrium. The anterior vena cava collects deoxygenated blood returning from the rest of the body and passes it into the right side of the heart, from where it will be pumped into the lungs.

Venda ◊Black National State from 1979, near the Zimbabwe border, in South Africa
area 2,510 sq mi/6,500 sq km
capital Thohoyandou
cities MaKearela
features homeland of the Vhavenda people
government executive president (paramount chief P R Mphephu in office from Sept 1979) and national assembly—not recognized outside South Africa
products coal, copper, graphite, construction stone
population (1980) 343,500
language Luvenda, English.

Vendée river in W France that rises near the village of La Châtaigneraie and flows 45 mi/72 km to join the Sèvre Niortaise 7 mi/11 km E of the Bay of Biscay.

Vendée, Wars of the in the French Revolution, a series of peasant uprisings against the revolutionary government that began in the Vendée *département*, W France 1793, and spread to other areas of France, lasting until 1795.

vendetta (Italian "vengeance") any prolonged feud, in particular one in which the relatives of a dishonored or murdered person seek revenge on the wrongdoer or members of the family. The tradition is Mediterranean, known in Europe and the US as a way of settling wrongs in Corsica, Sardinia, and Sicily, as practiced by the ◊Mafia.

Vendôme Louis Joseph, Duc de Vendôme 1654–1712. Marshal of France under Louis XIV, who lost his command after defeat by the British commander Marlborough at Oudenaarde, Belgium, 1708, but achieved successes in the 1710 Spanish campaign during the War of the ◊Spanish Succession.

venereal disease (VD) any disease mainly transmitted by sexual contact, although commonly the term is used specifically for gonorrhea and syphilis, both occurring worldwide, chlamydia, a problem in the US, and chancroid ("soft sore") and ◊lymphogranuloma venerum, seen mostly in the tropics. The term sexually transmitted diseases (◊STDs) is more often used to encompass a growing list of conditions passed on primarily, but not exclusively, in this way.

Venetia Roman name of that part of NE Italy which later became the republic of Venice, including the Veneto region.

Veneto region of NE Italy, comprising the provinces of Belluno, Padova (Padua), Treviso, Rovigo, Venezia (Venice), and Vicenza; area 7,102 sq mi/18,400 sq km; population (1988) 4,375,000. Its capital is Venice, and towns include Padua, Verona, and Vicenza. The Veneto forms part of the N Italian plain, with the delta of the river Po; it includes part of the Alps and Dolomites, and Lake Garda. Products include cereals, fruit, vegetables, wine, chemicals, shipbuilding, and textiles.

Venezia Italian form of ◊Venice, city, port, and naval base on the Adriatic.

Veneziano Domenico. Italian painter, see ◊Domenico Veneziano.

Venezuela country in northern South America, on the Caribbean Sea, bounded E by Guyana, S by Brazil, and W by Colombia.

government Venezuela is a federal republic of 20 states, 2 federal territories, and a federal district based on the capital, Caracas. The 1961 constitution provides for a president, who is head of state and head of government, and a two-chamber national congress, consisting of a senate and a chamber of deputies. The president is elected by universal suffrage for a five-year term and may not serve two consecutive terms. The president appoints and presides over a council of ministers.

The Senate has 44 members elected by universal suffrage, on the basis of two representatives for each state and two for the federal district, plus any living ex-presidents. The Chamber has 196 deputies, also elected by universal suffrage. Both chambers serve five-year terms.

history For early history, see ◊American Indian, ◊South America. Columbus visited Venezuela 1498, and there was a Spanish settlement from 1520. In 1811 a rebellion against Spain began, led by Simón Bolívar, and Venezuela became independent 1830.

After a long history of dictatorial rule, Venezuela adopted a new constitution 1961, and three years later Rómulo Betancourt became the first president to have served a full term of office. He was succeeded by Dr Raúl Leoni 1964 and by Dr Rafael Caldera Rodríguez 1969. The latter did much to bring economic and political stability, although underground abductions and assassinations still occurred. In 1974 Carlos Andrés Rodríguez, of the Democratic Action Party (AD), became president, and stability increased. In 1979 Dr Luis Herrera, leader of the Social Christian Party (COPEI), was elected.

Against a background of growing economic problems, the 1983 general election was contested by 20 parties and 13 presidential candidates. It was a bitterly fought campaign and resulted in the election of Dr Jaime Lusinchi as president and a win for the Democratic Action Party (AD) in Congress, with 109 Chamber and 27 Senate seats. COPEI won 60 Chamber and 16 Senate seats, and the Socialist Movement (MAS) 10 Chamber and 2 Senate seats. President Lusinchi's austere economic policies were unpopular, and he tried to conclude a social pact between the government, labor unions, and business. He reached an agreement with the government's creditor bankers for a rescheduling of Venezuela's large public debt.

In 1988 Venezuela suspended payment on its foreign debt, which had grown due to a drop in oil prices since the 1970s. In Feb 1989, newly elected president Carlos Andrés Pérez instituted price increases and other austerity measures designed to satisfy loan terms imposed by the International Monetary Fund. Riots followed in which at least 300 people were killed. In May a general strike was declared to protest the austerity program. Elections held in Dec were boycotted by the main opposition groups. At a meeting in Caracas in May 1991, the leaders of the Andean Common Market countries agreed to create a Latin American free trade zone.

Venezuela
Republic of
(República de Venezuela)

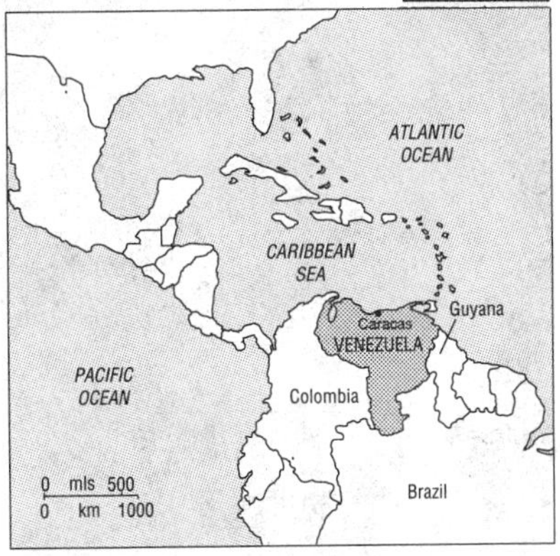
ATLANTIC OCEAN
CARIBBEAN SEA
PACIFIC OCEAN
Guyana
Caracas
VENEZUELA
Colombia
Brazil
0 mls 500
0 km 1000

area 352,162 sq mi/912,100 sq km
capital Caracas
cities Barquisimeto, Valencia; port Maracaibo
physical Andes Mountains and Lake Maracaibo in NW; central plains (llanos); delta of river Orinoco in E; Guiana Highlands in SE
features Angel Falls, world's highest waterfall
head of state and government Carlos Andrés Pérez from 1988
government federal democratic republic
political parties Democratic Action Party (AD), moderate, left-of-center; Christian Social Party (COPEI), Christian center-right; Movement toward Socialism (MAS), left-of-center
exports coffee, timber, oil, aluminum, iron ore, petrochemicals
currency bolívar
population (1990 est) 19,753,000 (mestizos 70%, white [Spanish, Portuguese, Italian] 20%, black 9%, amerindian 2%); growth rate 2.8% p.a.
life expectancy men 67, women 73 (1989)
religion Roman Catholic 96%, Protestant 2%
language Spanish (official), Indian languages 2%
literacy 88% (1989)
GNP $47.3 bn (1988); $2,629 per head (1985)
chronology
1961 New constitution adopted, with Rómulo Betancourt as president.
1964 Dr Raúl Leoni became president.
1969 Dr Rafael Caldera became president.
1974 Carlos Andrés Pérez Rodríguez became president.
1979 Dr Luis Herrera became president.
1984 Dr Jaime Lusinchi became president; social pact established between government, labor unions, and business; national debt rescheduled.
1987 Widespread social unrest triggered by inflation; student demonstrators shot by police.
1988 Andrés Pérez elected president. Payments suspended on foreign debts (increase due to drop in oil prices).
1989 Economic austerity program enforced by $4.3 billion loan from International Monetary Fund. Price increases triggered riots in which 300 people were killed; martial law declared Feb. General strike May; elections boycotted by opposition groups.

Venice (Italian *Venezia*) city, port, and naval base, capital of Veneto, Italy, on the Adriatic; population (1988) 328,000. The old city is built on piles on low-lying islands. Apart from tourism, industries include glass, jewelry, textiles, and lace. Venice was an independent trading republic from the 10th century, ruled by a doge, or chief magistrate, and was one of the centers of the Italian Renaissance.

It is now connected with the mainland and its industrial suburb, Mestre, by road and rail viaduct. The Grand Canal divides the city and is crossed by the Rialto bridge; transport is by traditional gondola or *vaporetto* (water bus).

St Mark's Square has the 11th-century Byzantine cathedral of San Marco, the 9th–16th-century campanile (rebuilt 1902), and the 14th–15th-century Gothic Doge's Palace (linked to the former state prison by the 17th-century Bridge of Sighs). The nearby Lido is a bathing resort. The Venetian School of artists includes the Bellinis, Carpaccio, Giorgione, Titian, Tintoretto, and Veronese.

Venice was founded in the 5th century by refugees from mainland cities sacked by the Huns, and became a wealthy independent trading republic in the 10th century, stretching by the mid-15th century to the Alps and including Crete. It was governed by an aristocratic oligarchy, the Council of Ten, and a senate, which appointed the doge 697–1797. Venice helped defeat the Ottoman Empire in the naval battle of Lepanto 1571 but the republic was overthrown by Napoleon 1797. It passed to Austria 1815 but finally became part of the kingdom of Italy 1866.

Venizelos Eleuthérios 1864–1936. Greek politician

born in Crete, leader of the Cretan movement against Turkish rule until the union of the island with Greece in 1905. He later became prime minister of the Greek state on five occasions, 1910–15, 1917–20, 1924, 1928–32, and 1933, before being exiled to France in 1935.

Having led the fight against Turkish rule in Crete, Venizelos became president of the Cretan assembly and declared the union of the island with Greece in 1905. As prime minister of Greece from 1910, he instituted financial, military, and constitutional reforms and took Greece into the Balkan Wars 1912–13. As a result, Greece annexed Macedonia, but attempts by Venizelos to join World War I on the Allied side led to his dismissal by King Constantine. Leading a rebel government in Crete and later in Salonika, he declared war on Bulgaria and Germany and secured the abdication of King Constantine.

As prime minister again from 1917 he attended the Paris Peace Conference in 1919. By provoking a war with Turkey over Anatolia in 1920 he suffered an electoral defeat. On his last return to office in 1933, he was implicated in an uprising by his supporters and fled to France, where he died.

Venn diagram in mathematics, a diagram representing a ◊set or sets and the logical relationships between them. Sets are drawn as circles. An area of overlap between two circles (sets) contains elements that are common to both sets, and thus represents a third set. Circles that do not overlap represent sets with no elements in common (disjoint sets). The method is named after the British logician John Venn (1834–1923).

Vent, Îles du French name for the Windward Islands, part of the ◊Society Islands in ◊French Polynesia. The Leeward Islands are known as the Îles sous le Vent.

Ventris Michael (George Francis) 1922–1956. English archeologist. Deciphering Minoan Linear B, the language of the tablets found at Knossos and Pylos, he showed that it was a very early form of Greek, thus revising existing views on early Greek history. *Documents in Mycenean Greek*, written with John Chadwick, was published shortly after he died in a road accident.

Ventura city in SW California, on the Pacific Ocean, NW of Los Angeles. Industries include oil and agricultural products, such as citrus fruits and lima beans; population (1980) 83,475.

venture capital or ***risk capital*** financing provided by venture capital companies, individuals, and merchant banks for medium-or long-term business ventures that are not their own and in which there is a strong element of risk.

In recent years, there has been a large growth in the number of companies specializing in providing venture capital.

Venturi Robert 1925– US architect. He pioneered Postmodernism through his books, *Complexity and Contradiction in Architecture* 1967 and *Learning from Las Vegas* 1972. In 1986 he was commissioned to design an extension to the National Gallery, London.

Venus the second planet from the Sun. It orbits the Sun every 225 days at an average distance of 67.2 million mi/108.2 million km and can approach the Earth to within 38 million 24 mi/kmllion mi, closer than any other planet. Its diameter is 7,500 mi/12,100 km and its mass is 0.82 that of Earth. Venus rotates on its axis more slowly than any other planet, once every 243 days and from east to west, the opposite direction to the other planets (except Uranus and possibly Pluto). Venus is shrouded by clouds of sulfuric acid droplets that sweep across the planet from east to west every four days. The atmosphere is almost entirely carbon dioxide, which traps the Sun's heat by the ◊greenhouse effect and raises the planet's surface temperature to 900°F/480°C, with an atmospheric pressure 90 times that at Earth's surface.

The surface of Venus consists mainly of plains dotted with eroded craters, presumably formed

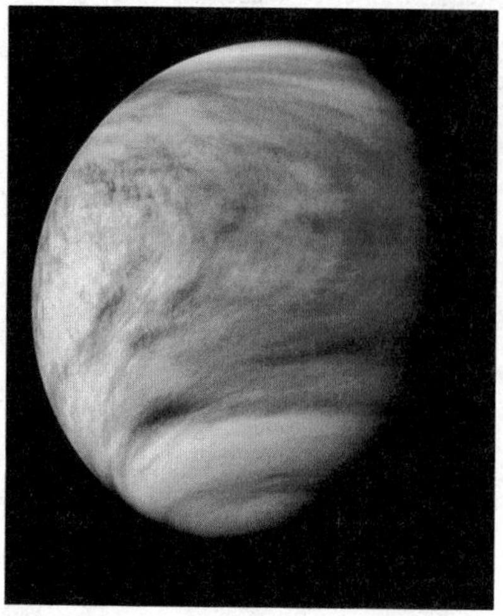

Venus *Venus photographed from a Pioneer probe. The planet has a cloud cover that permanently obscures its surface.*

by meteorite impacts. The largest highland area is Aphrodite Terra near the equator, half the size of Africa. The highest mountains are on the N highland region of Ishtar Terra, where the massif of Maxwell Montes rises to 35,000 ft/10,600 m above the average surface level. The highland areas on Venus were formed by volcanoes, which may still be active.

The first artificial object to hit another planet was the Soviet probe *Venera 3*, which crashed on Venus March 1, 1966. Later Venera probes parachuted down through the atmosphere and landed successfully on its surface, analyzing surface material and sending back information and pictures. In Dec 1978 a US Pioneer Venus probe (see ◊Pioneer) went into orbit around the planet and mapped most of its surface by radar, which penetrates clouds.

Venus in Roman mythology, the goddess of love (Greek Aphrodite).

Venus flytrap insectivorous plant *Dionea muscipula* of the sundew family, native to the SE US; its leaves have two hinged blades that close and entrap insects.

Veracruz port (trading in coffee, tobacco, and vanilla) in E Mexico, on the Gulf of Mexico; population (1980) 305,456. Products include chemicals, sisal, and textiles. It was founded by the Spanish conquistador Cortés as Villa Nueva de la Vera Cruz ("new town of the true cross") on a nearby site 1519 and transferred to its present site 1599.

verb the grammatical part of speech for what someone or something does (*to go*), experiences (*to live*), or is (*to be*). Verbs involve the grammatical categories known as number (singular or plural: "He *runs*; they *run*"), voice (active or passive: "She *writes* books; it *is written*"), mood (statements, questions, orders, emphasis, necessity, condition), aspect (completed or continuing action: "She *danced*; she *was dancing*"), and tense (variation according to time: simple present tense, present progressive tense, simple past tense, and so on).

Verbs are formed from nouns and adjectives by adding affixes (prison: *imprison*; light: *enlighten*; fresh: *freshen up*; pure: *purify*). Some words function as both nouns and verbs (*crack*, *run*), both adjectives and verbs (*clean*; *ready*), and as nouns, adjectives, and verbs (*fancy*).

types of verb A transitive verb takes a direct object ("He *saw* the house").

An intransitive verb has no object ("She *laughed*").

An auxiliary or helping verb is used to express

Venus *The* Venus de Milo *in the Louvre, Paris.*

tense and/or mood ("He *was* seen"; "They *may* come").

A modal verb or modal auxiliary generally shows only mood; common modals are *may/might, will/would, can/could, shall/should, must*.

The infinitive of the verb usually includes *to* (*to go, to run* and so on), but may be a bare infinitive (for example, after modals, as in "She may *go*").

A regular verb forms tenses in the normal way (*I walk: I walked: I have walked*); irregular verbs do not (*swim: swam: swum; put: put: put*; and so on). Because of their conventional nature, regular verbs are also known as weak verbs, while some irregular verbs are strong verbs with special vowel changes across tenses, as in *swim: swam: swum* and *ride: rode: ridden*.

A phrasal verb is a construction in which a particle attaches to a usually single-syllable verb (for example, *put* becoming *put up*, as in "He put up some money for the project," and *put up with*, as in "I can't put up with this nonsense any longer").

verbena any plant of the genus *Verbena*, family Verbenaceae, of about 100 species, mostly found in

Venus flytrap

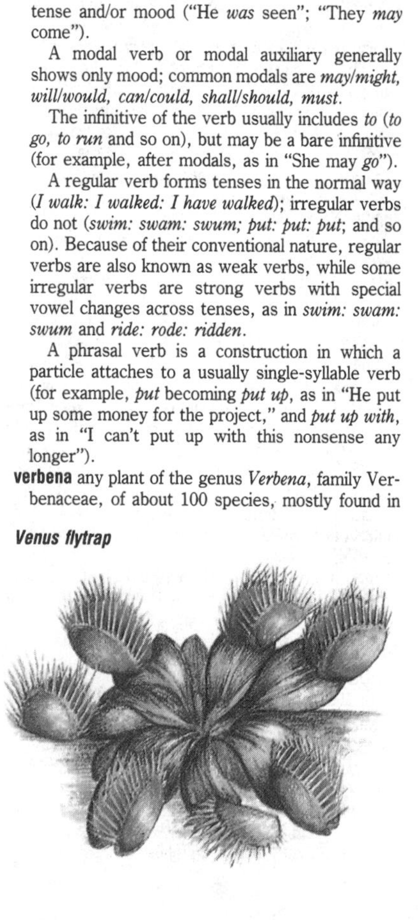

***Verdi** Giuseppe Verdi, whose operas inspired the heroes of the* Risorgimento.

the American tropics. The leaves are fragrant and the tubular flowers arranged in close spikes in colors ranging from white to rose, violet, and purple. The garden verbena is a hybrid annual.

Vercingetorix Gallic chieftain. Leader of a revolt of all the tribes of Gaul against the Romans 52 BC. He lost, was captured, displayed in Julius Caesar's triumph 46 BC, and later executed. This ended the Gallic resistance to Roman rule.

Verdi Giuseppe (Fortunino Francesco) 1813–1901. Italian opera composer of the Romantic period, who took his native operatic style to new heights of dramatic expression. In 1842 he wrote the opera *Nabucco*, followed by *Ernani* 1844 and *Rigoletto* 1851. Other works include *Il Trovatore* and *La Traviata* both 1853, *Aïda* 1871, and the masterpieces of his old age, *Otello* 1887 and *Falstaff* 1893. His *Requiem* 1874 commemorates Alessandro ◊Manzoni.

verdict in law, a jury's decision, usually a finding of "guilty" or "not guilty."

verdigris green-blue coating of copper ethanoate that forms naturally on copper, bronze, and brass. It is an irritating, greenish, poisonous compound made by treating copper with ethanoic acid, and was formerly used in wood preservatives, antifouling compositions, and green paints.

Verdun fortress town in NE France on the Meuse. During World War I it became the symbol of French resistance, withstanding a German onslaught in 1916.

Vergil alternate spelling for ◊Virgil, Roman poet.

vérité (French "realism"), as in *cinéma vérité*, used to describe a realistic or documentary style.

Verlaine Paul 1844–1896. French lyric poet who was influenced by the poets Baudelaire and ◊Rimbaud. His volumes of verse include *Poèmes saturniens/Saturnine Poems* 1866, *Fêtes galantes/Amorous Entertainments* 1869 and *Romances sans paroles/Songs without Words* 1874. In 1873 he was imprisoned for attempting to shoot Rimbaud. His later works reflect his attempts to lead a reformed life. He was acknowledged as leader of the ◊Symbolist poets.

Vermeer Jan 1632–1675. Dutch painter, active in Delft. Most of his pictures are ◊genre scenes, with a limpid clarity and distinct air of stillness, and a harmonious palette often focusing on yellow and blue. He frequently depicted solitary women in domestic settings, as in *The Lacemaker* (Louvre, Paris).

Vermeer is thought to have spent his whole life in Delft. There are only 35 paintings ascribed to him. His work fell into obscurity until the mid- to late 19th century, but he is now ranked as one of the greatest Dutch artists.

In addition to genre scenes, his work comprises one religious painting, a few portraits, and two townscapes, of which the fresh and naturalistic *View of Delft* c. 1660 (Mauritshuis, The Hague) triggered the revival of interest in Vermeer. *The*

***Vermeer** Dutch artist Jan Vermeer often painted women in domestic settings, as in* A Young Woman standing at a Virginal *c. 1670, National Gallery, London.*

Artist's Studio c. 1665–70 (Kunsthistorisches Museum, Vienna) is one of his most elaborate compositions; the subject appears to be allegorical, but the exact meaning remains a mystery.

Vermont state in NE US; nickname Green Mountain State

area 9,611 sq mi/24,900 sq km

capital Montpelier

cities Burlington, Rutland, Barre

population (1990) 562,758

features noted for brilliant autumn foliage and winter sports; Green Mountains; Lake Champlain

products apples, maple syrup, dairy products, kaolinite, granite, marble, slate, business machines, paper and allied products

famous people Ethan Allen, Ira Allen, Chester A Arthur, Calvin Coolidge, George Dewey, John Dewey, Stephen A Douglas, Dorothy Canfield Fisher, James Fisk

history explored by Champlain from 1609; first French settlement at Fort Ste Anne 1666; first English settlers 1724 at Fort Drummer (now Brattleboro). England controlled the area from 1763 after the French and Indian War. The Green Mountain Boys, organized 1764 to protect Vermont from New York's territorial claims, captured Ticonderoga and Crown Point from the British 1775. Statehood was achieved 1791. After the Civil War—in which half the men of military age joined the army, and one of seven lost his life—young people tended to move W, and the state economy stagnated. Tourism now accounts for more than 20% of the gross state product. The "back to the earth" movement has brought new farmers, businesses, and second-home owners to

Vermont

Montpelier

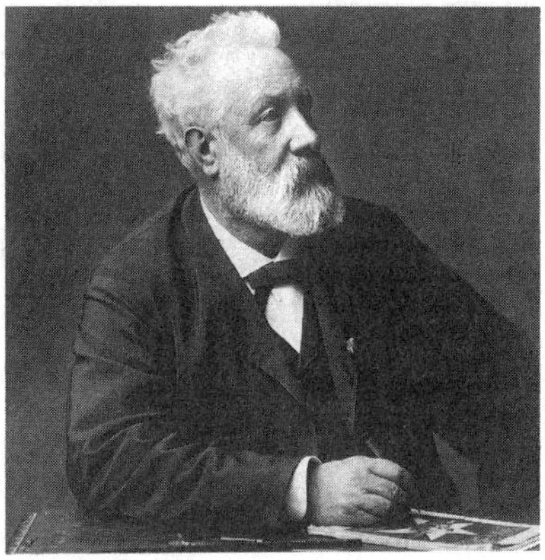

***Verne** French adventure and science-fiction novelist Jules Verne.*

Vermont, so the population and cultural activities continue to grow.

vermouth sweet or dry white wine flavored with bitter herbs and fortified with alcohol. It is made in France, Italy, and the US.

vernal equinox see ◊equinox.

vernalization the stimulation of flowering by exposure to cold. Certain plants will not flower unless subjected to low temperatures during their development. For example, winter wheat will flower in summer only if planted in the previous autumn. However, by placing partially germinated seeds in low temperatures for several days, the cold requirement can be supplied artificially, allowing the wheat to be sown in the spring.

Verne Jules 1828–1905. French author of tales of adventure that anticipated future scientific developments: *Five Weeks in a Balloon* 1862, *Journey to the Center of the Earth* 1864, *Twenty Thousand Leagues under the Sea* 1870, and *Around the World in Eighty Days* 1873.

vernier device for taking readings on a graduated scale to a fraction of a division. It consists of a short divided scale that carries an index or pointer and is slid along a main scale. It was invented by Pierre Vernier.

Vernier Pierre 1580–1637. French mathematician who invented a means of making very precise measurements with what is now called the vernier scale. He was a French government official and in 1631 published a book explaining his method called "a new mathematical quadrant."

Verona industrial city (printing, paper, plastics, furniture, pasta) in Veneto, Italy, on the Adige; population (1988) 259,000. It also trades in fruit and vegetables.

Its historical sights include one of the largest Roman amphitheaters in the world, Castelvecchio—the 14th-century residence of the Scaligers, the tomb of Juliet, and a 12th-century cathedral.

Veronese Paolo c. 1528–1588. Italian painter, born in Verona, active mainly in Venice (from about 1553). He specialized in grand decorative schemes, such as his ceilings in the Doge's Palace in Venice, with *trompe l'oeil* effects and inventive detail. The subjects are religious, mythological, historical, and allegorical.

Titian was a major influence, but Veronese also knew the work of Giulio Romano and Michelangelo. His decorations in the Villa Barbera at Maser near Vicenza show his skill at illusionism and a typically Venetian use of rich color; they are also characteristically full of inventive fantasy. He took the same approach to religious works, and as a result his *Last Supper* 1573 (Accademia, Venice, renamed *The Feast in the House of Levi*) was the subject of a trial by the Inquisition, since the holy event seems to be almost subordinated by profane details: figures of drunkards, soldiers conversing, dogs, and so on.

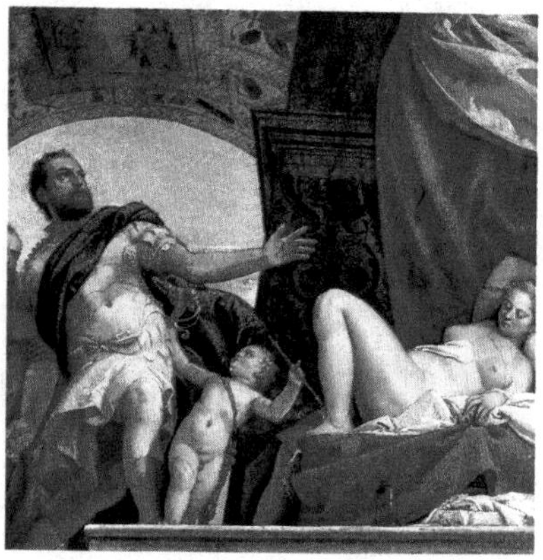

Veronese *Italian painter Paolo Veronese, who was noted for his allegorical subjects, as in* Allegory of Love, III *1570s, National Gallery, London.*

Veronica, St a woman of Jerusalem who, according to tradition, lent her veil to Jesus to wipe the sweat from his brow on the road to Calvary, whereupon the image of his face was printed upon it. A relic alleged to be the actual veil is preserved in St Peter's, Rome.

Verrocchio Andrea del 1435–1488. Italian painter, sculptor, and goldsmith, born in Florence, where he ran a large workshop and received commissions from the Medici family. The vigorous equestrian statue of *Bartolomeo Colleoni*, begun 1481 (Campo SS Giovanni e Paolo, Venice), was his last work.

Verrocchio was a pupil of ◊Donatello and himself the early teacher of Leonardo da Vinci. In his *Baptism* c. 1472 (Uffizi, Florence) Leonardo is said to have painted the kneeling angel shown in profile. Verrocchio's sculptures include a bronze *Christ and St Thomas* 1465 (Orsanmichele, Florence) and *David* 1476 (Bargello, Florence).

Versailles city in N France, capital of Les Yvelines *département*, on the outskirts of Paris; population (1982) 95,240. It grew up around the palace of Louis XV. Within the palace park are two small châteaux, Le Grand and Le Petit ◊Trianon, built for Louis XIV (by Jules-Hardouin ◊Mansart) and Louis XV (by Jacques Gabriel 1698–1782) respectively.

Versailles, Treaty of peace treaty after World War I between the Allies and Germany, signed June 28, 1919. It established the League of Nations. Germany surrendered Alsace-Lorraine to France, and large areas in the east to Poland, and made smaller cessions to Czechoslovakia, Lithuania, Belgium, and Denmark. The Rhineland was demilitarized, German rearmament was restricted, and Germany agreed to pay reparations for war damage. The treaty was never ratified by the US, which made a separate peace with Germany and Austria 1921.

verse arrangement of words in a rhythmic pattern, which may depend on the length of syllables (as in Greek or Latin verse), or on stress, as in English.

Classical Greek verse depended upon quantity, a long syllable being regarded as occupying twice the time taken up by a short syllable. Long and short syllables were combined in feet, examples of which are:

dactyl (long, short, short);
spondee (long, long);
anapaest (short, short, long);
iamb (short, long);
trochee (long, short).

Rhyme (repetition of sounds in the endings of words) was introduced to Western European verse in late Latin poetry, and alliteration (repetition of the same initial letter in successive words) was the dominant feature of Anglo-Saxon poetry. Both these elements helped to make verse easily remembered in the days when it was spoken rather than written.

Form The Spenserian stanza (in which ◊Spenser wrote *The Faerie Queene*) has nine iambic lines rhyming ababbcbcc. In English, the ◊sonnet has 14 lines, generally of ten syllables each; it has several rhyme schemes.

Blank verse, consisting of unrhymed five-stress lines, as used by Marlowe, Shakespeare, and Milton develops an inner cohesion that replaces the props provided by rhyme and stanza. It became the standard meter for English dramatic and epic poetry.

◊***Free verse***, or *vers libre*, avoids rhyme, stanza form, and any obvious rhythmical basis.

vertebrate any animal with a backbone. The 41,000 species of vertebrates include mammals, birds, reptiles, amphibians, and fishes. They include most of the larger animals, but in terms of numbers of species are only a tiny proportion of the world's animals. The zoological taxonomic group Vertebrata is a subgroup of the ◊phylum Chordata.

vertex (plural *vertices*) in geometry, a point shared by three or more sides of a solid figure; the point farthest from a figure's base; or the point of intersection of two sides of a plane figure or the two rays of an angle.

vertical takeoff and landing craft (VTOL) aircraft that can take off and land vertically. Helicopters, airships, and balloons can do this, as can a few fixed-wing airplanes. See ◊helicopter, ◊convertiplane.

vertigo dizziness; a whirling sensation accompanied by a loss of any feeling of contact with the ground. It may be due to temporary disturbance of the sense of balance (as in spinning for too long on one spot), psychological reasons, disease, or intoxication.

Verwoerd Hendrik (Frensch) 1901–1966. South African right-wing Nationalist Party politician, prime minister 1958–66. As minister of native affairs 1950–58, he was the chief promoter of apartheid legislation (segregation by race). He made the country a republic 1961. He was assassinated in 1966.

Very Large Array (VLA) the largest and most complex single-site radio telescope in the world. It is located on the Plains of San Augustine, 50 mi/80 km west of Socorro, New Mexico. It consists of 27 dish antennae, each 82 ft/25 m in diameter, arranged along three equally spaced arms forming a Y-shaped array. Two of the arms are 13 mi/21 km long, and the third, to the north, is 11.8 mi/19 km long. The dishes are mounted on railroad tracks enabling the configuration and size of the array to be altered as required.

There are four standard configurations of antennae ranging from A (the most extended) through B and C to D. In the A configuration the antennae are spread out along the full extent of the arms and the VLA can map small, intense radio sources with high resolution. The smallest configuration, D, uses arms that are just 0.4 mi/0.6 km long for mapping larger sources. Here the resolution is lower, although there is greater sensitivity to fainter, extended fields of radio emission. Pairs of dishes can also be used as separate interferometers (see ◊radio telescope), each dish having its own individual receivers that are remotely controlled, enabling many different frequencies to be studied.

Vesalius Andreas 1514–1564. Belgian physician who revolutionized anatomy. His great innovations were to perform postmortem dissections and to make use of illustrations in teaching anatomy.

The dissections (then illegal) enabled him to discover that ◊Galen's system of medicine was based on fundamental anatomical errors. Vesalius's book *De Humani Corporis Fabrica/On The Structure of the Human Body* 1543, together with the astronomer Copernicus's major work, published in the same year, marked the dawn of modern science.

Vesey Denmark c. 1767–1822. American resistance leader. Probably born on the Caribbean island of St Thomas, he was purchased 1781 by Capt John Vesey and taken to Charleston, South Carolina, 1783. In 1800 Vesey bought his own freedom for $600 and established himself as a carpenter. An outspoken and eloquent critic of the institution of slavery, he was arrested 1822 on suspicion of fomenting a rebellion among local slaves. Although only circumstantial evidence was brought against him in court, Vesey and five other black leaders were subsequently hanged.

Vespasian (Titus Flavius Vespasianus) 9–79 AD. Roman emperor from AD 69. He was the son of a moneylender, and had a distinguished military career. He was proclaimed emperor by his soldiers while he was campaigning in Palestine. He reorganized the eastern provinces, and was a capable administrator.

vespers the seventh of the eight canonical hours in the Catholic Church.

The phrase Sicilian Vespers refers to the massacre of the French rulers in Sicily in 1282, signaled by vesper bells on Easter Monday.

Vespucci Amerigo 1454–1512. Florentine merchant. The Americas were named after him as a result of the widespread circulation of his accounts of his explorations. His accounts of the voyage 1499–1501 indicate that he had been to places he could not possibly have reached (the Pacific Ocean, British Columbia, Antarctica).

Vesta in Roman mythology, the goddess of the hearth (Greek Hestia). In Rome, the sacred flame in her shrine in the Forum was kept constantly lit by the six Vestal Virgins.

vestigial organ in biology, an organ that remains in diminished form after it has ceased to have any significant function in the adult organism. In humans, the appendix is vestigial, having once had a digestive function in our ancestors.

Vesuvius (Italian *Vesuvio*) active volcano SE of Naples, Italy; height 4,190 ft/1,277 m. In 79 BC it destroyed the cities of Pompeii, Herculaneum, and Oplonti.

vetch trailing or climbing plants of several genera, family Leguminosae, with pinnate leaves (leaves on either side of the stem) and purple, yellow, or white flowers, including the fodder crop alfalfa *Medicago sativa*.

veterinary science the study, prevention, and cure of disease in animals. More generally, it covers animal anatomy, breeding, and relations to humans.

The American Veterinary Medical Association was formed 1883.

veto (Latin "I forbid") exercise by a sovereign, a branch of the legislature, or other political power, of the right to prevent the enactment or operation of a law, or the taking of some course of action.

Under the US Constitution, the president may veto legislation, although that veto may, in turn, be overruled by a two-thirds majority in Congress. At the United Nations, it takes only one veto for the Security Council to turn down a resolution.

Veuster Joseph de 1840–1889. Belgian missionary, known as Father Damien. He entered the order of the Fathers of the Sacred Heart at Louvain, went to Hawaii, and from 1873 was resident priest in the leper settlement at Molokai. He eventually became infected and died there.

VHF (abbreviation for very high frequency) referring to radio waves that have very short wavelengths. They are used for interference-free ◊FM (frequency-modulated) transmissions. VHF transmitters have a relatively short range because the waves cannot be reflected over the horizon like longer radio waves.

v.i. the abbreviation for verb intransitive.

Viborg industrial town (brewing, engineering, textiles, tobacco) in Jutland, Denmark; population

(1981) 28,700. It is also the Swedish name for ◊Vyborg, port and naval base in the USSR.

vibraphone an electrically amplified musical percussion instrument resembling a ◊xylophone but with metal keys. Spinning disks within the resonating tubes give the instrument a vibrato sound that can be controlled in speed and worked with a foot pedal.

viburnum any small tree or shrub of the genus *Viburnum* of the honeysuckle family Caprifoliaceae, found in temperate and subtropical regions, including the ◊wayfaring tree, the laurustinus, and the guelder rose of Europe and Asia, and the North American blackhaws and arrowwoods.

Vicenza city in Veneto region, NE Italy, capital of Veneto province, manufacturing textiles and musical instruments; population (1988) 110,000.

It has a 13th-century cathedral and many buildings by ◊Palladio, including the Teatro Olimpico 1583.

viceroy the chief officer of the crown in many Spanish and Portuguese American colonies who had ultimate responsibility for administration and military matters. The office of viceroy was also used by the British crown to rule India.

Vichy health resort with thermal springs, known to the Romans, on the river Allier in Allier *département*, central France. During World War II it was the seat of the French general ◊Pétain's government 1940–44 (known also as the Vichy government), which collaborated with the Nazis.

Vichy government in World War II, the right-wing government of unoccupied France after the country's defeat by the Germans in June 1940, named after the spa town of Vichy, France where the national assembly was based under Prime Minister Pétain until the liberation 1944. Vichy France was that part of France not occupied by German troops until Nov 1942. Authoritarian and collaborationist, the Vichy regime cooperated with the Germans even after they had moved to the unoccupied zone in Nov 1942.

Vico Giambattista 1668–1744. Italian philosopher, considered the founder of the modern philosophy of history. He rejected Descartes's emphasis on the mathematical and natural sciences, and argued that we can understand history more adequately than nature, since it is we who have made it. He believed that the study of language, ritual, and myth was a way of understanding earlier societies. His cyclical theory of history (the birth, development, and decline of human societies) was put forward in *New Science* 1725.

He postulated that society passes through a cycle of four phases: the divine, or theocratic, when people are governed by their awe of the supernatural; the aristocratic, or "heroic" (Homer, *Beowulf*); the democratic and individualistic; and chaos, a fall into confusion that startles people back into supernatural reverence. This is expressed in his dictum *verum et factum convertuntur* ("the true and the made are convertible"). His belief that the study of language and rituals was a better way of understanding early societies was a departure from the traditional ways of writing history either as biographies or as preordained God's will. He was born in Naples and was professor of rhetoric there 1698. He became historiographer to the king of Naples 1735.

Victor Emmanuel three kings of Italy, including:

Victor Emmanuel II 1820–1878. First king of united Italy from 1861. He became king of Sardinia on the abdication of his father Charles Albert 1849. In 1855 he allied Sardinia with France and the UK in the Crimean War. In 1859 in alliance with the French he defeated the Austrians and annexed Lombardy. By 1860 most of Italy had come under his rule, and in 1861 he was proclaimed king of Italy. In 1870 he made Rome his capital.

Victor Emmanuel III 1869–1947. King of Italy from the assassination of his father, Umberto I, 1900. He acquiesced in the Fascist regime of Mussolini from 1922 and, after the dictator's fall 1943, relinquished power to his son Umberto II, who cooperated with the Allies. Victor Emmanuel formally abdicated 1946.

Victoria *Queen Victoria reading official dispatches at Frogmore, England, with an Indian servant in attendance, 1893.*

Victoria 1819–1901. Queen of the UK from 1837, when she succeeded her uncle William IV, and empress of India from 1876. In 1840 she married Prince ◊Albert of Saxe-Coburg and Gotha. Her relations with her prime ministers ranged from the affectionate (Melbourne and Disraeli) to the stormy (Peel, Palmerston, and Gladstone). Her golden jubilee 1887 and diamond jubilee 1897 marked a waning of republican sentiment, which had developed with her withdrawal from public life on Albert's death.

Only child of Edward, duke of Kent, fourth son of George III, she was born in London. She and Albert had four sons and five daughters. After Albert's death 1861 she lived mainly in retirement. Nevertheless, she kept control of affairs, refusing the prince of Wales (Edward VII) any active role.

Victoria city in S Texas, on the Guadalupe river, near the Gulf of Mexico. It is a transportation center for oil, natural gas, chemicals, and dairy products; population (1990) 55,076.

Victoria industrial port (shipbuilding, chemicals, clothing, furniture) on Vancouver Island, capital of British Columbia, Canada; population (1986) 66,303.

It was founded as Fort Victoria 1843 by the Hudson's Bay Company. Its university was founded 1964.

Victoria port and capital of the Seychelles, on Mahé island; population (1985) 23,000.

Victoria district of ◊Hong Kong, rising to 1,800 ft/554 m at Victoria Park.

Victoria state of SE Australia
area 87,854 sq mi/227,600 sq km
capital Melbourne
towns Geelong, Ballarat, Bendigo
physical part of the Great Dividing Range, running E–W and including the larger part of the Australian Alps; Gippsland lakes; shallow lagoons on the coast; the ◊mallee shrub region
products sheep, beef cattle, dairy products, tobacco, wheat, vines for wine and dried fruit, orchard fruits, vegetables, gold, brown coal (Latrobe Valley), oil and natural gas (Bass Strait)
population (1987) 4,184,000; 70% in the Melbourne area
history annexed for Britain by Captain Cook 1770; settled in the 1830s; after being part of New South Wales became a separate colony 1851, named after the queen; became a state 1901

Victoria Cross British decoration for conspicuous bravery in wartime, instituted by Queen Victoria 1856.

Victoria Falls or ***Mosi-oa-tunya*** waterfall on the river Zambezi, on the Zambia–Zimbabwe border. The river is 5,580 ft/1,700 m wide and drops 400 ft/120 m to flow through a 30-m/100-ft wide gorge.

The falls were named after Queen Victoria by the Scottish explorer Livingstone in 1855.

Victoria, Lake or ***Victoria Nyanza*** largest lake in Africa; area over 26,800 sq mi/69,400 sq km; length 255 mi/410 km. It lies on the equator at an

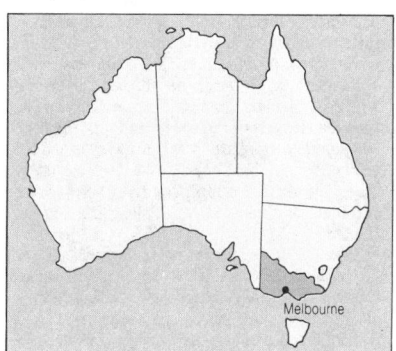

Victoria

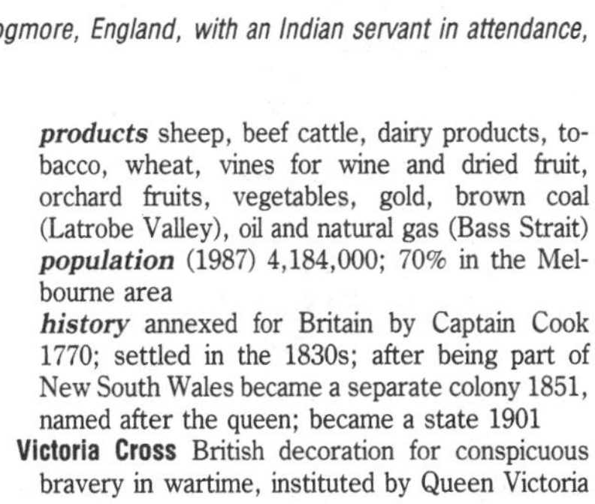
Melbourne

vicuña

video tape recorder

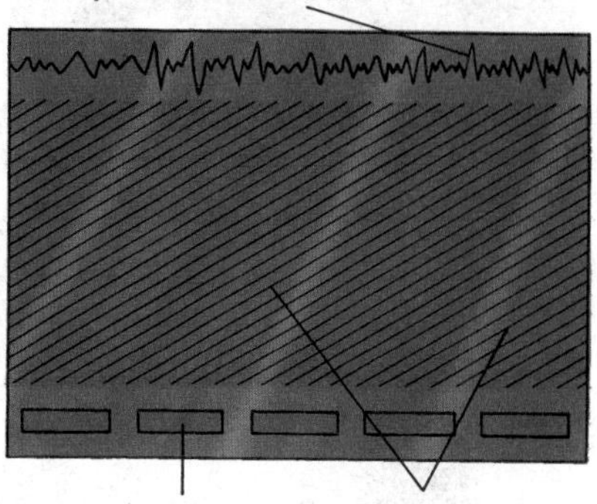
sound track
control track
video tracks

altitude of 3,728 ft/1,136 m, bounded by Uganda, Kenya, and Tanzania. It is a source of the Nile.

The British explorer Speke named it after Queen Victoria 1858.

Victorian a period of English architecture, furniture making, and decorative art between the mid- and late 19th century in England, covering the reign of Queen Victoria 1837–1901. Victorian style was often very ornate, markedly so in architecture, and Victorian Gothic drew upon the original Gothic architecture of medieval times. It was also an era when increasing mass-production by machines threatened the existence of crafts and craft skills.

vicuña ◊ruminant mammal *Lama vicugna* of the camel family that lives in herds on the Andean plateau. It can run at speeds of 30 mph/50 kph. It has good eyesight, fair hearing, and a poor sense of smell. It was hunted close to extinction for its meat and soft brown fur, which was used in textile manufacture, but the vicuña is now a protected species; populations are increasing thanks to strict conservation measures.

Vidal Gore 1925– . US writer and critic. Much of his fiction deals satirically with history and politics and includes the novels *Myra Breckinridge* 1968, *Burr* 1973, *Empire* 1987, and *Hollywood* 1990, plays and screenplays, including *Suddenly Last Summer* 1958, and essays, such as *Armageddon?* 1987.

video camera or ***camcorder*** portable television camera that takes moving pictures electronically on magnetic tape. It produces an electrical output signal corresponding to rapid line-by-line scanning of the field of view. The output is recorded on video cassette and is played back on a television screen via a video cassette recorder.

video cassette recorder (VCR) device for recording on and playing back video cassettes. In the home they are used mainly to record broadcast programs for future viewing and to view rented or owned video cassettes of commercial films.

Video recording works in the same way as audio ◊tape recording: the picture information is stored as a line of varying magnetism, or track, on a plastic tape covered with magnetic material. The main difficulty—the huge amount of information needed to reproduce a picture—is overcome by arranging the video track diagonally across the tape. During recording, the tape is wrapped around a drum in a spiral fashion. The recording head rotates inside the drum. The combination of the forward motion of the tape and the rotation of the head produces a diagonal track. The audio signal accompanying the video signal is recorded as a separate track along the edge of the tape.

Two VCR systems were introduced by Japanese firms in the 1970s. The Sony Betamax was considered technically superior, but Matsushita's VHS had larger marketing resources behind it and after some years became the sole system on the market.

video disc disk with pictures and sounds recorded on it, played back by laser. The video disc works in the same way as a ◊compact disc.

The video disc (originated by Baird 1928; commercially available from 1978) is chiefly used to provide commercial films for private viewing. Most systems use a 12 in/30 cm rotating vinyl disk coated with a reflective material. Laser scanning recovers picture and sound signals from the surface where they are recorded as a spiral of microscopic pits.

video game electronic game played on a visual-display screen or, by means of special additional or built-in components, on the screen of a television set. The first commercially sold was a simple bat-and-ball game developed in the USA in 1972, but complex variants are now available in color and with special sound effects.

video tape recorder (VTR) device for recording visuals and sound on spools of magnetic tape. It is used in television broadcasting.

videotex or ***videotext*** any of various systems in which information (text) is displayed on a television (video) screen. There are two basic systems. In one, information is broadcast using the standard television signals; in the other information is relayed to the screen from a central data bank via the telephone network. The use of telephone lines in the latter system allow for conveniences such as home banking and shopping and other applications involving a two-way information process. Both systems require the use of a television receiver with decoding device.

Vidor King 1894–1982. US film director who made epics such as *The Big Parade* 1925 and *Duel in the Sun* 1946. He has been praised as a cinematic innovator, and received an honorary Academy Award in 1979. His other films include *The Crowd* 1928 and *Guerra e Pace/War and Peace* 1956.

Vienna (German *Wien*) capital of Austria, on the Danube river at the foot of the Wiener Wald (Vienna Woods); population (1986) 1,481,000. Industries include engineering and the production of electrical goods and precision instruments.

The United Nations city 1979 houses the United Nations Industrial Development Organization (UNIDO) and the International Atomic Energy Agency (IAEA).

features Renaissance and baroque architecture; the Hofburg (former imperial palace); the 18th-century royal palaces of Schönbrunn and Belvedere, with formal gardens; the Steiner house 1910 by Adolf Loos; and several notable collections of paintings. Vienna is known for its theater and opera. Sigmund Freud's home is a museum, and there is a university 1365.

history Vienna was the capital of the Austro-Hungarian Empire 1278–1918 and the commercial center of E Europe. The old city walls were replaced by a wide street, the Ringstrasse, 1860. After much destruction in World War II the city was divided into US, British, French, and Soviet occupation zones 1945–55. Vienna is associated with J Strauss waltzes, as well as the music of Haydn, Mozart, Beethoven, and Schubert and the development of atonal music.

Also figuring in Vienna's cultural history were the Vienna Sezession group of painters, the philosophical Vienna Circle, and the origins of psychoanalysis originated here.

Vienna, Congress of international conference held 1814–15 that agreed the settlement of Europe after the Napoleonic Wars. National representatives included the Austrian foreign minister Metternich, Alexander I of Russia, the British foreign secretary Castlereagh and military commander Wellington, and the French politician Talleyrand.

Its final act created a kingdom of the Netherlands, a German confederation of 39 states, Lombardy-Venetia subject to Austria, and the kingdom of Poland. Monarchs were restored in Spain, Naples, Piedmont, Tuscany, and Modena; Louis XVIII was confirmed king of France.

Vientiane capital and chief port of Laos on the Mekong river; population (1985) 377,000.

Vietcong (Vietnamese "Vietnamese Communists") in the Vietnam war 1954–75, the members of the National Front for the Liberation of South Vietnam, founded 1960, who fought the South Vietnamese and US forces. The name was coined by the South Vietnamese government to differentiate these Communist guerrillas from the ◊Vietminh.

Viète François 1540–1603. French mathematician who developed algebra and its notation. He was the first mathematician to use letters of the alphabet to denote both known and unknown quantities.

Vietminh the Vietnam Independence League, founded 1941 to oppose the Japanese occupation of Indochina and later directed against the French colonial power. The Vietminh were instrumental in achieving Vietnamese independence through military victory at Dien Bien Phu 1954.

Vietnam country in SE Asia, on the South China Sea, bounded N by China and W by Cambodia and Laos.

government Under the constitution 1980, the highest state authority and sole legislative chamber in Vietnam is the National Assembly, composed of 496 members directly elected every five years by universal suffrage. The assembly meets twice a year and elects from its ranks a permanent, 15-member council of state, whose chair acts as state president, to function in its absence. The executive government is the council of ministers, headed by the prime minister, which is responsible to the National Assembly.

The dominating force in Vietnam is the Communist Party (Dang Cong san Viet-Nam), headed since 1986 by Nguyen Van Linh (1914–). It is controlled by a politburo, and is prescribed a "leading role" by the constitution.

history Originally settled by SE Asian hunters and agriculturalists, Vietnam was founded 208 BC in the Red River delta in the north, under Chinese overlordship. Under direct Chinese rule 111 BC–AD 939, it was thereafter at times nominally subject to China. It annexed land to the south and defeated the forces of Kublai Khan 1288. European traders arrived in the 16th century. The country was united under one dynasty 1802.

France conquered Vietnam between 1858–1884, and it joined Cambodia, Laos, and Annam as the French colonial possessions of Indochina. French Indochina was occupied by Japan 1940–45.

◊Ho Chi Minh, who had built up the Vietminh (Independence) League, overthrew the Japanese-supported regime of Bao Dai, the former emperor of Annam, Sept 1945. French attempts to regain control and restore Bao Dai led to bitter fighting 1946–54, and final defeat of the French at Dien Bien Phu. At the 1954 Geneva Conference the country was divided along the 17th parallel of latitude into Communist North Vietnam, led by Ho Chi Minh, with its capital at Hanoi, and pro-Western South Vietnam, led by Ngo Dinh Diem

Vietnam

Socialist Republic of
(Công Hòa Xã Hôi Chu Nghĩa Viêt Nam)

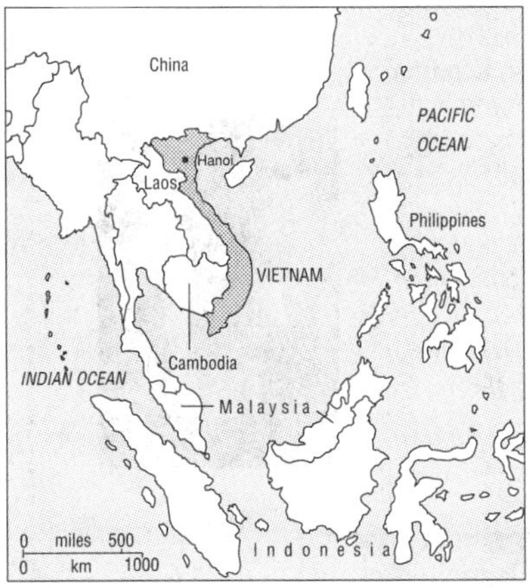
China
PACIFIC OCEAN
Hanoi
Laos
Philippines
VIETNAM
Cambodia
INDIAN OCEAN
Malaysia
Indonesia
0 miles 500
0 km 1000

area 127,259 sq mi/329,600 sq km
capital Hanoi
cities ports Ho Chi Minh City (formerly Saigon), Da Nang, and Haiphong
physical Red River and Mekong deltas, center of cultivation and population; tropical rainforest; mountainous in N and NW
features Karst hills of Halong Bay, Cham Towers
head of state Vo Chi Cong from 1987
head of government Do Muoi from 1988
political system communism
exports rice, rubber, coal, iron, apatite
currency dong
population (1990 est) 68,488,000 (750,000 refugees, majority ethnic Chinese left 1975–79, some settled in SW China, others fled by sea—the "boat people"—to Hong Kong and elsewhere); growth rate 2.4% p.a.
life expectancy men 62, women 66 (1989)
language Vietnamese (official), French, English, Khmer, Chinese, tribal
religion Buddhist, Taoist, Confucian, Christian
literacy 78% (1989)
GNP $12.6 bn; $180 per head (1987)
chronology
1945 Japanese removed from Vietnam.
1946 Commencement of Vietminh war against French.
1954 France defeated at Dien Bien Phu. Vietnam divided along 17th parallel.
1964 US troops entered Vietnam War.
1973 Paris ceasefire agreement.
1975 Saigon captured by North Vietnam.
1976 Socialist Republic of Vietnam proclaimed.
1978 Admission into Comecon. Invasion of Cambodia.
1979 Sino-Vietnamese border war.
1986 Retirement of old-guard leaders.
1987–88 Over 10,000 political prisoners released.
1988–89 Troop withdrawals from Cambodia continued.
1989 "Boat people" leaving Vietnam murdered and robbed at sea by Thai pirates; Hong Kong forcibly repatriated some Vietnamese refugees; troop withdrawal from Cambodia ostensibly completed.

(the former premier to Bao Dai), with its capital at Saigon.

Within South Vietnam, the Communist guerrilla National Liberation Front, or Vietcong, gained strength, being supplied with military aid by North Vietnam and China. The US gave strong backing to the incumbent government in South Vietnam and became, following the Aug 1964 ◊Tonkin Gulf incident, actively embroiled in the ◊Vietnam War. The years 1964–68 witnessed an escalation in US military involvement to 500,000 troops. From 1969, however, as a result of mounting casualties and domestic opposition, the US gradually began to withdraw its forces and sue for peace. A ceasefire agreement was negotiated Jan 1973 but was breached by the North Vietnamese, who proceeded to move south, surrounding and capturing Saigon (which was renamed Ho Chi Minh City) April 1975.

The Socialist Republic of Vietnam was proclaimed July 1976, and a program to integrate the south was launched. The new republic encountered considerable problems. The economy was in ruins, the two decades of civil war having claimed the lives of more than 2 million; it maimed 4 million, left more than half the population homeless, and resulted in the destruction of 70% of the country's industrial capacity. In addition, the new Communist administration faced opposition from the intelligentsia (many of whom were imprisoned) and from rural groups, who refused to cooperate in the drive to collectivize southern agriculture. In Dec 1978 Vietnam was at war again, toppling the pro-Chinese Khmer Rouge government in Kampuchea (now Cambodia) led by Pol Pot and installing a puppet administration led by Heng Samrin. A year later, in response to accusations of maltreatment of ethnic Chinese living in Vietnam, China mounted a brief, but largely unsuccessful, punitive invasion of North Vietnam Feb 17–March 16, 1979. These actions, coupled with the contemporary campaigns against private businesses in the south, induced the flight of about 700,000 Chinese and middle-class Vietnamese from the country 1978–79, often by sea (the "boat people"). Economic and diplomatic relations with China were severed as Vietnam became closer to the Soviet Union, being admitted into Comecon June 1978.

Despite considerable economic aid from the Eastern bloc, Vietnam did not reach its planned growth targets 1976–85. This forced policy adjustments, extending incentives and decentralizing decision-making, 1979 and 1985. Further economic liberalization followed the death of Le Duan (1907–1986), effective leader since 1969, and the retirement at the Dec 1986 Communist Party Congress of other prominent "old guard" leaders, including Prime Minister Pham Van Dong and President Truong Chinh. Under the pragmatic lead of Nguyen Van Linh, a "renovation" program was launched. The private marketing of agricultural produce and formation of private businesses were now permitted, agricultural cooperatives were partially dismantled (farmers were given 15-year land leases instead), foreign "joint venture" inward-investment was encouraged and more than 10,000 political prisoners were released. Economic reform proved most successful in the south. In general, however, the country faced a severe economic crisis from 1988, with inflation, famine conditions in rural areas, and rising urban unemployment inducing a further flight of "boat people" refugees during 1989–90, predominantly to Hong Kong. In Dec 1989, the British colony of ◊Hong Kong began the forced repatriation of some Vietnamese refugees. Earlier in the year, Vietnam announced the final withdrawal of its troops from Cambodia.

In May 1991, Van Linh resigned as party chief because of poor health and was succeeded by Do Muoi, a supporter of Van Linh's policies. Vo Van Kiet became premier in Aug.

Vietnamese member of the majority group (90%) of peoples inhabiting Vietnam and referring to their language and culture, which is also called Annamese. Although Annamese is an independent language, it has been influenced by Chinese and there are Khmer loan words.

Vietnam War *American troops of the 1st Cavalry Division (Airmobile), Vietnam 1967.*

Vietnam War 1954–1975 war to reunify the nation, between communist North Vietnam and US-backed South Vietnam, who were opposed to reunification. Following the division of French Indochina into North and South Vietnam and the Vietnamese defeat of the French 1954, US involvement in Southeast Asia grew through the ◊SEATO pact. Noncommunist South Vietnam was viewed, in the context of the 1950s and the ◊cold war, as a bulwark against the spread of communism throughout SE Asia. Advisers and military aid were dispatched to the region at increasing levels because of the so-called domino theory, which contended that the fall of South Vietnam would precipitate the collapse of neighboring states. Corruption and inefficiency within the South Vietnamese government led the US to assume ever greater responsibility for the war effort, until 1 million US combat troops were engaged.

In the US, the draft, the high war casualties, and the undeclared nature of the war resulted in growing domestic resistance, which caused social unrest and forced President Johnson to abandon reelection plans. President Nixon first expanded the war to Laos and Cambodia but finally phased out US involvement; his national security adviser Henry Kissinger negotiated a peace treaty 1973 with North Vietnam, which soon conquered the South and united the nation. Between 1961 and 1975, 56,555 US soldiers were killed; also some 200,000 South Vietnamese soldiers, plus 1 million North Vietnamese soldiers, and 500,000 civilians died.

Although US forces were never militarily defeated, Vietnam was considered a most humiliating political defeat for the US.

1954 Under the Geneva Convention the former French colony of Indochina was divided into the separate states of North and South Vietnam. Within South Vietnam the communist Vietcong, supported by North Vietnam and China, attempted to seize power and unify north and south. The US began to provide military advisers to support the South Vietnamese, who opposed unification.

1964 The Tonkin Gulf Incident, when North Vietnamese torpedo boats allegedly attacked two US destroyers, prompted the US to send troops.

1967 Several large-scale invasion attempts by North Vietnam were defeated by indigenous and US forces.

1968 Tet Offensive in South Vietnam; My Lai massacre by US troops.

1973 In the US, the unpopularity of sending troops to an undeclared war led to the start of US withdrawal. A peace treaty was signed between North and South Vietnam.

1975 South Vietnam was invaded by North Vietnam in March.

1976 South Vietnam was annexed by North Vietnam, and the two countries were renamed the Socialist Republic of Vietnam.

Vigée-Lebrun Elisabeth 1755–1842. French portrait painter, trained by her father (a painter in pastels) and ◊Greuze. She became painter to Queen Marie Antoinette in the 1780s (many royal portraits survive).

At the outbreak of the Revolution 1789 she left France and traveled in Europe, staying in St Petersburg, Russia, 1795–1802. She resettled in Paris 1809. She published an account of her travels, *Souvenirs* 1835–37, written in the form of letters.

Vigeland Gustav 1869–1943. Norwegian sculptor. He studied in Oslo and Copenhagen and with ◊Rodin in Paris 1892. His program of sculpture in Frogner Park, Oslo, conceived in 1900, was never finished. The style is heavy and monumental; the sculpted figures and animals enigmatic.

vigilante in US history, originally a member of a "vigilance committee," a self-appointed group to maintain public order in the absence of organized authority. The vigilante tradition continues with present-day urban groups patrolling streets and subways to deter muggers and rapists, for example, the Guardian Angels in New York, and the Community Volunteers in London.

Early vigilante groups included the "Regulators" in South Carolina in the 1760s, and in Pennsylvania 1794 during the Whiskey Rebellion. Many more appeared in the 19th century in frontier towns. Once authorized police forces existed, vigilante groups such as the post-Civil War ◊Ku Klux Klan operated outside the law, often as perpetrators of mob violence such as lynching.

Vigny Alfred, Comte de 1797–1863. French romantic writer whose works include the historical novel *Cinq-Mars* 1826, the play *Chatterton* 1835, and poetry, such as, for example, in *Les Destinées/Destinies* 1864.

Vigo industrial port (oil refining, leather, paper, distilling) and naval station on Vigo bay, Galicia, NW Spain; population (1986) 264,000.

Vigo Jean. Adopted name of Jean Almereyda 1905–1934. French director of intensely lyrical experimental films. He made only two short films: *A Propos de Nice* 1930, and *Taris Champion de Natation* 1934; and two feature films: *Zéro de conduite/Nothing for Conduct* 1933, and *L'Atalante* 1934.

Viipuri Finnish name of ◊Vyborg, port and naval base in the USSR.

Viking or ***Norseman*** Medieval Scandinavian sea warrior, who traded with and raided Europe in the 8th–11th centuries, and often settled there. In France they were given ◊Normandy. Under Sweyn I they conquered England 1013, and his son Canute was king of England as well as Denmark and Norway. In the east they established the first Russian state and founded ◊Novgorod. They reached the Byzantine Empire in the south, and in the west sailed the seas to Ireland, Iceland, Greenland, and North America; see ◊Eric the Red, Leif ◊Ericsson, ◊Vinland.

In their narrow, shallow-draft, highly maneuverable longships, the Vikings penetrated far inland along rivers. They plundered for gold and land, and the need for organized resistance accelerated the growth of the feudal system. In England and Ireland they were known as "Danes." They created settlements, for example in York, and greatly influenced the development of the English language. The Vikings had a sophisticated literary culture (◊sagas), and an organized system of government with an assembly (◊thing). As ◊"Normans" they achieved a second conquest of England 1066.

Viking

In their narrow, shallow-draughted and highly manoeuvreable longships, the Vikings spread from their Scandinavian homelands to fight, trade and settle through most of the coastal regions of 8th to 11th-century Europe. They established kingdoms in the British Isles, Normandy, and Russia. As Normans they founded a kingdom in Sicily and in 1066 achieved a second conquest of England. They are believed to have sailed to North America and as far south as the Byzantine Empire where Swedish Vikings (Varangians) formed the imperial guard.

A stone cross (below) from Yorkshire, England depicting a well-armed Viking warrior. His weapons include a spear, sword, axe and dagger.

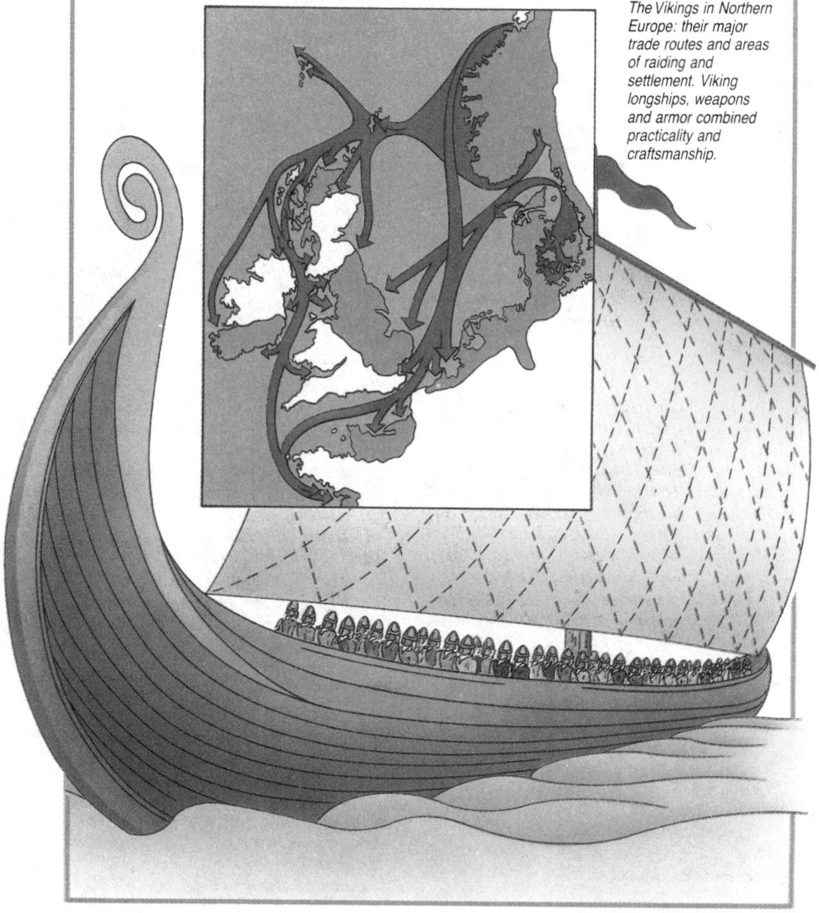

The Vikings in Northern Europe: their major trade routes and areas of raiding and settlement. Viking longships, weapons and armor combined practicality and craftsmanship.

The Swedish Varangians were invited to settle differences among the Slav chieftains in Russia 862. The Varangians also formed the imperial guard in Constantinople.

Viking art sculpture and design of the Vikings, including woodcarving and metalwork. Their intricate interlacing ornament is similar to that found in Celtic art. The dragon is a recurring motif.

After conversion to Christianity in the 10th century, the traditional Viking ornament continued: for example, carvings on the wooden stave churches of Norway, in Borgund and Urnes. Viking art was gradually absorbed into the Romanesque style.

Viking probes two US space probes to Mars, each one consisting of an orbiter and a lander. They were launched Aug 20 and Sept 9, 1975. The probes transmitted color pictures, and analyzed the soil; no definite signs of life were found.

Viking 1 carried life detection labs and landed on July 20, 1976 for detailed research and photos. Designed to work for 90 days, it operated for six and a half years, going silent in Nov 1982. *Viking 2* was similar in setup to *Viking 1*; it landed on Mars Sept 3, 1976 and functioned for three and a half years.

Vila or ***Port-Vila*** port and capital of Vanuatu, on the SW of Efate island; population (1988) 15,000.

Villa-Lobos Heitor 1887–1959. Brazilian composer. His style was based on folk tunes collected on travels in his country; for example, in the *Bachianas Brasileiras* 1930–44, he treats them in the manner of Bach. His works range from guitar

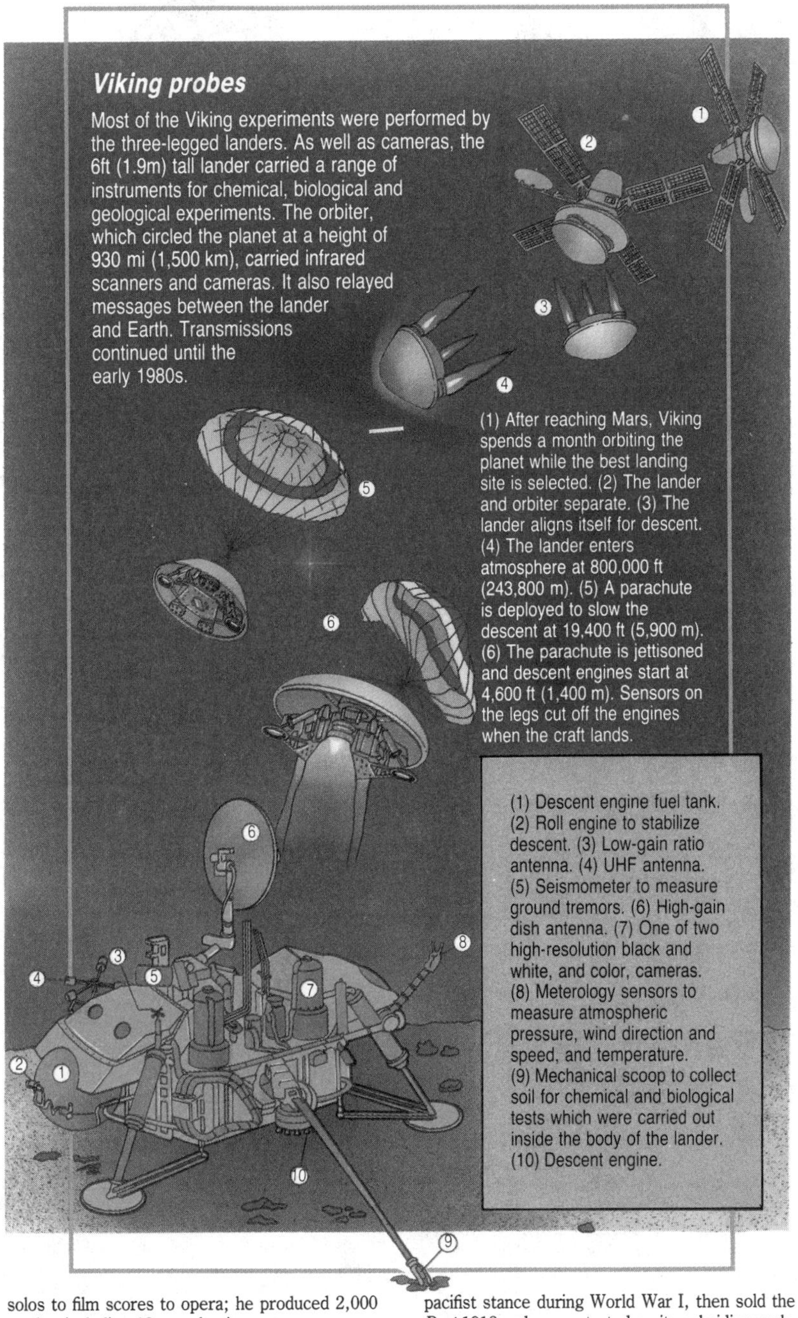
Viking probes
Most of the Viking experiments were performed by the three-legged landers. As well as cameras, the 6ft (1.9m) tall lander carried a range of instruments for chemical, biological and geological experiments. The orbiter, which circled the planet at a height of 930 mi (1,500 km), carried infrared scanners and cameras. It also relayed messages between the lander and Earth. Transmissions continued until the early 1980s.
(1) After reaching Mars, Viking spends a month orbiting the planet while the best landing site is selected. (2) The lander and orbiter separate. (3) The lander aligns itself for descent. (4) The lander enters atmosphere at 800,000 ft (243,800 m). (5) A parachute is deployed to slow the descent at 19,400 ft (5,900 m). (6) The parachute is jettisoned and descent engines start at 4,600 ft (1,400 m). Sensors on the legs cut off the engines when the craft lands.
(1) Descent engine fuel tank. (2) Roll engine to stabilize descent. (3) Low-gain ratio antenna. (4) UHF antenna. (5) Seismometer to measure ground tremors. (6) High-gain dish antenna. (7) One of two high-resolution black and white, and color, cameras. (8) Meterology sensors to measure atmospheric pressure, wind direction and speed, and temperature. (9) Mechanical scoop to collect soil for chemical and biological tests which were carried out inside the body of the lander. (10) Descent engine.

solos to film scores to opera; he produced 2,000 works, including 12 symphonies.

Villard Henry 1835–1900. German-born US journalist and financier. Villard immigrated to the US 1853 and settled in Illinois. As a journalist, he covered the American Civil War for the New York *Herald* and *Tribune*. After the war, he traveled in Europe and became interested in railroad development. He became president of the Oregon and California Railroad 1876, served as president of the Northern Pacific Railroad 1881–84, and was Northern Pacific's chairman of the board 1889–93. An astute investor, he was president of the Edison General Electric Co. 1890–92 and the *New York Evening Post* 1881–1900.

Villard Oswald Garrison 1872–1949. US editor. Born in Germany during the European travels of his father Henry ◊Villard, he was educated at Harvard and joined the staff of the *Philadelphia Press* 1893. Moving to the *New York Evening Post*, he became president and owner upon his father's death 1900. He became unpopular for his pacifist stance during World War I, then sold the *Post* 1918 and concentrated on its subsidiary publication, *The Nation*. As editor 1918–32, Villard became a leading spokesman for liberal causes. He was a founder of the National Association for the Advancement of Colored People (NAACP) and active in antiwar movements. His autobiography, *Fighting Years*, appeared in 1939.

Villehardouin Geoffroy de c. 1160–1213. French historian, the first to write in the French language. He was born near Troyes, and was a leader of the Fourth ◊Crusade, of which his *Conquest of Constantinople* (c. 1209) is an account.

villeinage the system of serfdom that prevailed in Europe in the Middle Ages. A villein was a peasant who gave dues and services to his lord in exchange for land. In France until the 13th century, "villeins" could refer to rural or urban nonnobles, but after this, it came to mean exclusively rural nonnoble freemen. In Norman England, it referred to free peasants of relatively high status.

Their social position declined until, by the early 14th century, their personal and juridicial status was close to that of serfs. After the mid-14th century, as the effects of the Black Death led to a severe labor shortage, their status improved. By the 15th century villeinage had been supplanted by a system of free tenure and labor in England, but it continued in France until 1789.

Villella Edward 1936– . US ballet dancer whose energetic, virile style popularized the male role in Balanchine's New York City Ballet, from his debut in 1957. He studied with Balanchine and performed until the 1970s in a large repertoire, including *The Prodigal Son*.

Villiers de l'Isle Adam Philippe Auguste Mathias, Comte de 1838–1889. French poet, the inaugurator of the Symbolist movement. He wrote the drama *Axel* 1890; *Isis* 1862, a romance of the supernatural; verse; and short stories.

Villon François 1431–c. 1465. French poet who used satiric humor, pathos, and lyric power in works written in *argot* (slang) of the time. Very little of his work survives, but it includes the *Ballade des dames du temps jadis/Ballad of the Ladies of Former Times*, *Petit Testament* 1456, and *Grand Testament* 1461.

Born in Paris, he dropped his surname (Montcorbier or de Logos) to assume that of a canon—a relative who sent him to study at the Sorbonne, where he graduated 1449 and took his MA 1452. In 1455 he stabbed a priest in a street fight and had to flee the city. Pardoned the next year, he returned to Paris but was soon in flight again after robbing the College of Navarre. He stayed briefly at the court of the duke of Orléans until sentenced to death for an unknown offense, from which he was saved by the amnesty of a public holiday. Theft and public brawling continued to occupy his time, in addition to the production of the *Grand Testament* 1461. A sentence of death in Paris, commuted to ten-year banishment in 1463, is the last that is known of his life.

villus plural ***villi*** small fingerlike projection extending into the interior of the small intestine and increasing the absorptive area of the intestinal wall. Digested food, including sugars and amino acids, pass into the villi and are carried away by the circulating blood.

Vilnius capital of Lithuania; population (1987) 566,000. Industries include engineering and the manufacture of textiles, chemicals, and foodstuffs. Its university was founded 1578.

From a 10th-century settlement, Vilnius became the Lithuanian capital 1323 and a center of Polish and Jewish culture. It was then Polish from 1386 until the Russian annexation 1795. Claimed by both Poland and Lithuania after World War I, it was given to Poland 1921, occupied by the USSR 1939, and immediately transferred to Lithuania. The city was the focal point of Lithuania's agitation for independence from the USSR, 1989–91, and became the country's capital when independence was realized in 1991.

Vimy Ridge hill in N France, taken in World War I by Canadian troops during the battle of Arras, Apr 1917, at the cost of 11,285 lives. It is a spur of the ridge of Nôtre Dame de Lorette, 5 mi/8 km NE of Arras.

Vincennes the University of Paris VIII, usually known as Vincennes after the suburb of E Paris where it was founded in 1970 (following the 1968 student rebellion) for blue-collar workers. By 1980, it had 32,000 students. In June 1980, it was moved to the industrial suburb of St-Denis.

Vincent de Paul, St c. 1580–1660. French Roman Catholic priest and founder of the two charitable orders of Dazarists 1625 and Sisters of Charity 1634. After being ordained 1600, he was captured by Barbary pirates and held as a slave in Tunis until he escaped 1607. He was canonized 1737; feast day July 19.

Vincent of Beauvais c. 1190–1264. French scholar, encyclopedist, and Dominican priest. A chaplain to the court of Louis IX, he is remembered for

violet

his *Speculum majus/Great Mirror* 1220–44, a reference work summarizing contemporary knowledge on virtually every subject, including science, natural history, literature, and law. It also contained a history of the world from the creation.

It is noteworthy for its positive attitude to Classical literature, which had undergone a period of eclipse in the preceding centuries.

vincristine an ◊alkaloid extracted from the blue periwinkle plant (*Vinca rosea*). Developed as an anticancer agent, it has revolutionized the treatment of childhood acute leukemias; it is also included in ◊chemotherapy regimens for some lymphomas (cancers arising in the lymph tissues) and lung and breast cancers. Side effects, such as nerve damage and loss of hair, are severe but usually reversible.

vine or ***grapevine*** any of various climbing woody plants of the genus *Vitis*, family Vitaceae, especially *V. vinifera*, native to Asia Minor and cultivated from antiquity. Its fruit is eaten or made into wine or other fermented drinks; dried fruits of certain varieties are known as raisins and currants. Many other species of climbing plant are also termed vines.

vinegar sour liquid consisting of a 4% solution of acetic acid produced by the oxidation of alcohol. It is used to flavor food, in salad dressing, and as a preservative in pickling. Malt vinegar is brown and made from malted cereals; white vinegar is distilled from it. Other sources of vinegar include cider, wine, and honey. Balsamic vinegar is wine vinegar aged in wooden barrels.

Vineland city in SW New Jersey, N of Millville. Industries include foundry products, glassware, chemicals, and vegetables; population (1990) 54,780.

Vinland Norse name for the area of North America, probably the coast of Nova Scotia or New England, which the Norse adventurer and explorer Leif ◊Ericsson visited c. 1000. It was named after the wild grapes that grew there and is celebrated in an important Norse saga.

Vinson Frederick Moore 1890–1953. US jurist and chief justice of the US Supreme Court 1946–53. Vinson was known for opinions defending the propriety of wide-ranging federal intervention in social and economic matters. He wrote the decision upholding the contempt convictions of union leader John L Lewis in *United States* v *United Mine Workers* 1947 and a dissent in *Youngstown Sheet and Tube Co* v *Sawyer* 1952, revoking presidential nationalization of the steel industry during the Korean war. He was conservative on issues of national security, most notably in *Rosenberg* v *United States* 1953, denying a stay of execution of convicted spies Ethel and Julius Rosenberg. He supported civil rights, writing the majority opinion in *Shelly* v *Kraemer* 1948, ruling that state courts may not enforce discrimination by private landlords, and *McLaurin* v *Oklahoma State Regents* 1950, attacking the "separate but equal" doctrine.

Born in Louisa, Kentucky, Vinson received his undergraduate and law degrees from Center College and became a lawyer active in Democratic politics, ultimately serving as a member of the US House of Representatives 1924–28 and 1930–38. He was appointed judge of the US Court of Appeals for the District of Columbia 1939. During

violin

bow
viola
violin
double bass
cello

World War II he was chief judge of the US Emergency Court of Appeals and director of the Office of Economic Stabilization. President Truman appointed Vinson secretary of the Treasury 1945 and chief justice 1946.

Vinson Massif highest point in ◊Antarctica, rising to 16,863 ft/5,140 m in the Ellsworth Mountains.

viola a bowed, stringed musical instrument of the ◊violin family.

violet plant of the genus *Viola*, family Violaceae, with toothed leaves and mauve, blue, or white flowers, such as the Canada violet *V. canadensis* and primrose violet *V. primulifolia* of North America and the sweet violet *V. odorata* of Europe. Pansies are also a kind of violet.

viol family a family of bowed 6-stringed fretted instruments prominent in the 16th–18th centuries, before their role was taken by the ◊violin family. Developed for close-harmony chamber music, they have a pure and restrained tone. Viols have six strings a flat back and narrow shoulders.

Members of the family include treble, alto, tenor, bass (or viola da gamba), and double bass (or violone). The smaller instruments are rested on the knee, not held under the chin. They are tuned in fourths, like a guitar. The only viol to survive in use in the symphony orchestra is the double bass, which was modified to have 4 strings and no frets.

violin a bowed, 4-stringed musical instrument, the smallest and highest pitched of the violin family. The strings are tuned in fifths (G, D, A, and E), with G as the lowest, tuned below middle C.

The violin had its origins in Italy in a variety of small-sized 3- and 4-stringed designs during the first third of the 16th century, with the classic form being finalized shortly after c. 1535 by the Cremonese master Andrea ◊Amati. Guarneri and Stradiveri apprenticed at the Amati workshop and soon constructed violins based on his pattern. Some of these very violins from the 16th century are still being played, studied, collected, and emulated by luthiers. Today's violin has not changed in form since that time, but in the late 18th century, aspects of the design were modified to produce a bigger sound and greater projection for the concert hall and to allow for evolving virtuoso expression. These include a lengthened finger-

viper

common viper

board, an angled neck, and larger sized basebar and soundpost.

violin family a family of bowed 4-stringed unfretted musical instruments developed in Italy during the 14th century, which eventually superseded the viol family and formed the basis of the modern orchestra. The ◊violin, viola, and cello are tuned in fifths; the double bass is descended from the double bass viol (or violone) and is tuned in fourths.

Viollet-le-Duc Eugène Emmanuel 1814–1849. French architect. Leader of the Gothic revival in France, he also restored medieval buildings.

violoncello or ***cello*** a bowed, stringed musical instrument of the ◊violin family.

VIP abbreviation for very important person.

viper any front-fanged venomous snake of the family Viperidae. Vipers range in size from 1 ft/30 cm to 10 ft/3 m, and often have diamond or jagged markings. Most give birth to live young.

There are 150 species of viper. The true vipers, sub family *Viperinae*, abundant in Africa and SW Asia, include the ◊adder *Vipera berus*, the African puff adder *Bitis arietans* and the horned viper of North Africa *Cerastes cornutus*. The second subfamily *Crotalinae* includes the mostly New World pit vipers (such as ◊rattlesnakes and ◊copperheads of the Americas), which have a heat-sensitive pit between each eye and nostril.

Virchow Rudolf Ludwig Carl 1821–1902. German pathologist, the founder of cellular pathology. Virchow was the first to describe leukemia (cancer of the blood). In his book *Die Cellulare Pathologie/Cellular Pathology* 1858, he proposed that disease is not due to sudden invasions or changes, but to slow processes in which normal cells give rise to abnormal ones.

Virgil (Publius Vergilius Maro) 70–19 BC. Roman poet who wrote the *Eclogues* 37 BC, a series of pastoral poems; the *Georgics* 30 BC, four books on the art of farming; and his epic masterpiece, the ◊*Aeneid*.

Virgil, born near Mantua, came of the small farmer class. He was educated in Cremona and Mediolanum (Milan) and studied philosophy and rhetoric in Rome before returning to his farm, where he began the *Eclogues* 43 BC. He wrote the *Georgics* at the suggestion of his patron, Maecenas, to whom he introduced Horace. Virgil devoted the last 11 years of his life to the composition of the *Aeneid*, considered the greatest epic poem in Latin literature and a major influence on later European literature.

virginal in music, a small type of ◊harpsichord.

Virginia state in E US; nickname Old Dominion
area 40,762 sq mi/105,600 sq km

Virginia

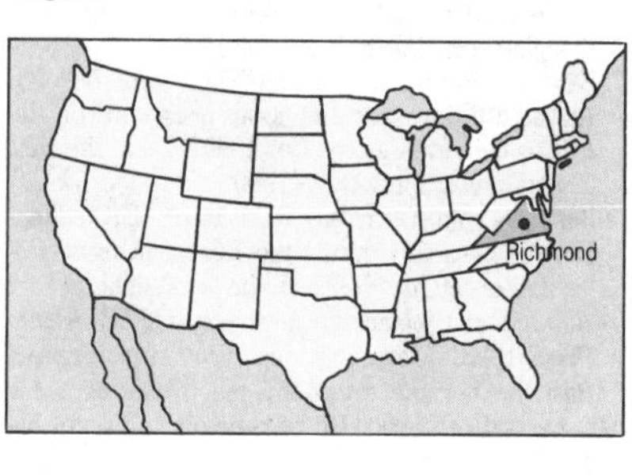
Richmond

Virgin Islands

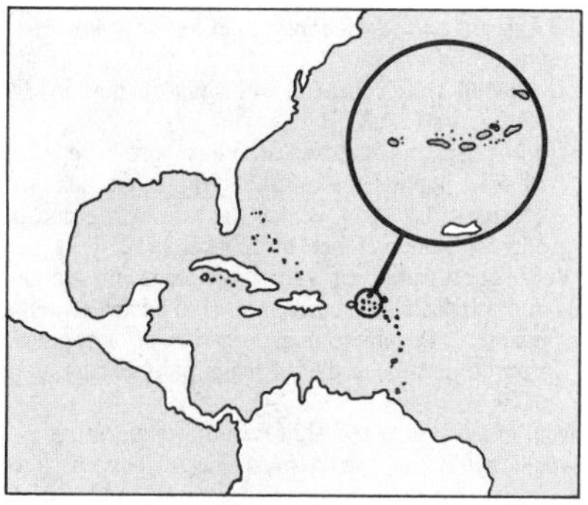

capital Richmond
cities Norfolk, Virginia Beach, Newport News, Hampton, Chesapeake, Portsmouth
population (1990) 6,187,358
features Blue Ridge mountains, which include the Shenandoah National Park; Arlington National Cemetery; Mount Vernon (home of George Washington 1752–99); Monticello (Thomas Jefferson's home near Charlottesville); Stratford Hall (Robert E Lee's birthplace at Lexington); Williamsburg restoration; Jamestown and Yorktown historic sites
products sweet potatoes, corn, tobacco, apples, peanuts, coal, ships, trucks, paper, chemicals, processed food, textiles
famous people Richard E Byrd, Ella Fitzgerald, Patrick Henry, Thomas Jefferson, Robert E Lee, James Madison, George C Marshall, John Marshall, James Monroe, Edgar Allan Poe, John Tyler, Booker T Washington, George Washington, Woodrow Wilson
history named in honor of Elizabeth I; Jamestown first permanent English settlement in the New World 1607, slavery was introduced there 1619; settled by planters of indigo and tobacco; took a leading part in the American Revolution; one of the original thirteen states. It joined the Confederacy in the Civil War, with Richmond the Confederate capital. Virginia was the principal theater of the war, and defeat left it devastated and bereft of its W section–the new state of West Virginia. The postwar period was marked by gradual economic recovery, and segregation was dismantled in the 1960s. Virginia has benefited from military industries and the growth of the federal government in neighboring Washington, DC.

Virginia Beach city in SE Virginia, on Chesapeake Bay, E of Norfolk. It is a resort center; population (1990) 393,069. The colonists who settled Jamestown first landed here 1607.

Virginia creeper or ***woodbine*** an E North American climbing vine *Parthenocissus quinquefolia* of the grape family, having tendrils, palmately compound leaves, green flower clusters, and blue berries consumed by numerous birds but inedible to humans.

Virgin Islands group of about 100 small islands, northernmost of the Leeward Islands in the Antilles, West Indies. Tourism is the main industry. They comprise the US Virgin Islands—St Thomas (with the capital, Charlotte Amalie), St Croix, St John, and about 50 small islets; area 135 sq mi/ 350 sq km; population (1990) 101,809—and the British Virgin Islands—Tortola (with the capital, Road Town), Virgin Gorda, Anegada, Jost van Dykes, and about 40 islets; area 58 sq mi/ 150 sq km; population (1987) 13,250.

Christopher Columbus reached these islands 1493. They were divided between Britain and Denmark 1666. Denmark sold its islands to the US 1917; they form an unincorporated territory, with residents electing a governor and legislature. The British Virgin Islands have partial internal self-government.

Virgo zodiac constellation, the second largest in the sky. It lies between Leo and Virgo and is represented as a maiden holding an ear of wheat. The Sun passes through Virgo from late Sept to the end of Oct. Virgo's brightest star is the first-magnitude Spica, a blue-white star about 250 light-years from Earth. Virgo contains the nearest large cluster of galaxies to us, 50 million light-years away, consisting of about 3,000 galaxies centered on the giant elliptical galaxy M87. Also in Virgo is the nearest ◊quasar, 3c273, an estimated 3 billion light-years distant. In astrology, the dates for Virgo are between about Aug 23 and Sept 22 (see ◊precession).

virion the smallest unit of a mature ◊virus.

Virtanen Artturi Ilmari 1895–1973. Finnish chemist who from 1920 made discoveries in agricultural chemistry. Because green fodder tends to ferment and produce a variety of harmful acids, it cannot be preserved for long. Virtanen prevented the process from starting by acidifying the fodder. In this form it lasted longer and remained nutritious. Nobel Prize 1945.

virtual memory in computing, a technique whereby a portion of external ◊memory is used as an extension of internal memory. The contents of an area of ◊RAM are stored on, say, a hard disk while they are not needed, and brought back into main memory when required. The process, which is called either paging or segmentation, is hidden from the programmer, to whom the computer's internal memory appears larger than it really is.

virus an infectious particle consisting of a core of nucleic acid (DNA or RNA) enclosed in a protein shell. Viruses are acellular and able to function and reproduce only if they can invade a living cell to use the cell's system to replicate themselves. In the process they may disrupt or alter the host cell's own DNA. The healthy human body reacts by producing an antiviral protein, ◊interferon, which prevents the infection spreading to adjacent cells.

Viruses have recently been found to be very abundant in seas and lakes with between 5 and 10 million per milliliter of water at most sites tested, but up to 250 million per milliliter in one polluted lake. These viruses infect bacteria and possibly, single-celled algae. They may play a crucial role in controlling the survival of bacteria and algae in the plankton.

Among diseases caused by viruses are canine distemper, chickenpox, common cold, herpes, influenza, rabies, smallpox, yellow fever, AIDS, and many plant diseases. Recent evidence implicates viruses in the development of some forms of cancer (see ◊oncogenes).

bacteriophage a virus that infects bacterial cells.
retrovirus a virus of special interest because it has an RNA genome, and can code for DNA from this RNA, in a unique process called reverse transcription.
viroid discovered in 1971. A viroid is even smaller than a virus; it consists of a single strand of nucleic acid with no protein coat. Viroids may cause stunting in plants and some rare diseases in animals, including humans. It is debatable whether viruses and viroids are truly living organisms, since they are incapable of an independent existence. Outside the cell of another organism they remain completely inert. The origin of viruses is also unclear, but it is believed that they are degenerate forms of life, derived from cellular organisms, or pieces of nucleic acid that have broken away from the genome of some higher organism and taken up a parasitic existence.
antiviral drug difficult drugs to develop because viruses replicate by using the genetic machinery of host cells, so that drugs tend to affect the host cell as well as the virus. Acyclovir (used against the herpes group of diseases) is one of the few drugs so far developed that is successfully selective in its action. It is converted to its active form by an enzyme that is specific to the virus, and it then specifically inhibits viral replication. Some viruses have shown developing resistance to the few antiviral drugs available.

virus in computing, a piece of ◊software that can replicate itself and transfer itself from one computer to another, without the user being aware of it. Some viruses are relatively harmless, but others can damage or destroy data. They are written by anonymous programmers, often maliciously, and are spread along telephone lines or on ◊floppy disks. Most are very difficult to eradicate.

Visalia city in central California, in the San Joaquin Valley, SE of Fresno.

It is an agricultural center for grapes, citrus fruits, and dairy products; population (1990) 75,636.

Visby historic town and bishopric on the Swedish island of Gotland in the Baltic that became the center of German ◊Hanseatic League.

It was founded as a Viking trading post on the route from Novgorod to the west. During the 12th and 13th centuries, the Scandinavian population became outnumbered by German colonists, and Visby became the nucleus of the Hanseatic League. In 1361, it was conquered by Waldemar IV. It possesses impressive fortifications, dated from the time of the Hanse, and many Gothic churches.

viscacha Argentinian pampas and scrubland-dwelling rodent *Lagostomus maximus* of the chinchilla family. It is up to 2.2 ft/70 cm long with a 8 in/ 20 cm tail, and weighs 15 lb/7 kgs. It is gray and black and has a large head and small ears. Viscachas live in warrens of up to 30 individuals. They are nocturnal, and feed on grasses, roots, and seeds.

Four species of Mountain viscachas genus *Lagidium*, also called Peruvian hares, are smaller and have long ears and tails and are found in rocky places feeding by day on sparse vegetation.

Visconti dukes and rulers of Milan 1277–1447. They originated as north Italian feudal lords under Matteo I Visconti (1250–1322), who attained dominance over the city as a result of alliance with the Holy Roman emperors. Despite papal opposition, by the mid-14th century they ruled 15 other major towns in northern Italy. The duchy was inherited by the ◊Sforzas 1447.

They had no formal title until Gian Galeazzo (1351–1402) bought the title of duke from Emperor Wenceslas IV (1361–1419). On the death of the last male Visconti, Filippo Maria, 1447, the duchy was inherited by his son-in-law, Francesco Sforza.

Visconti Luchino 1906–1976. Italian film, opera, and theater director. The film *Ossessione* 1942 pioneered Neo-Realist cinema despite being subject to censorship problems from the fascist government; later works include *Rocco and his Brothers* 1960, *The Leopard* 1963, *The Damned* 1969, and *Death in Venice* 1971. His powerful social commentary led to clashes with the Italian government and Roman Catholic Church.

His stage work introduced Tennessee Williams, Arthur Miller, Sartre, and Cocteau to Italy.

viscose yellowish, syrupy solution made by treating cellulose with sodium hydroxide and carbon disulfide. The solution is then regenerated as continuous filament for the making of ◊rayon and as cellophane.

viscosity in physics, the resistance of a fluid to flow, caused by its internal friction, which makes it resist flowing past a solid surface or other layers of the fluid. It applies to the motion of an object moving through a fluid as well as the motion of a fluid passing by an object.

Fluids such as pitch, treacle, and heavy oils are highly viscous; for the purposes of calculation, many fluids in physics are considered to be perfect, or nonviscous.

viscount in the UK peerage, the fourth degree of nobility, between earl and baron.

Vishnu in Hinduism, the second in the triad of gods (with Brahma and Siva) representing three aspects of the supreme spirit. He is the Preserver, and is believed to have assumed human appearance in nine *avatāras*, or incarnations, in such forms as Rama and Krishna. His worshipers are the Vaishnavas.

Visigoth member of the western branch of the ◊Goths, an E Germanic people.

vision defects abnormalities of the eye that cause less than perfect sight. In a nearsighted eye, the lens is fatter than normal, causing light from distant objects to be focused in front and not on the retina. A person with this complaint, called ◊myopia, cannot see clearly for distances over a few meters, and needs glasses with diverging lenses. Farsightedness, also called hypermetropia or presbyopia, is caused by an eye lens thinner than normal that focuses light from distant objects behind the retina. The sufferer cannot see close objects clearly, and needs converging-lens glasses. There are other vision defects, such as ◊color blindness.

vision system a computer-based device for interpreting visual signals from a video camera. Computer vision is important in robotics where sensory abilities would considerably increase the flexibility and usefulness of a robot.

Although some vision systems exist for recognizing simple shapes, the technology is still in its infancy.

Vistula (Polish *Wisła*) river in Poland, that rises in the Carpathians and runs SE to the Baltic at Gdańsk; length 677 mi/1,090 km. It is heavily polluted, carrying into the Baltic every year large quantities of industrial and agricultural waste, including phosphorus, oil, nitrogen, mercury, cadmium, and zinc.

vitalism the idea that living organisms derive their characteristic properties from a universal life force. In the present century, this view is associated with the philosopher Henri ◊Bergson.

vitamin any of various chemically unrelated organic compounds that are necessary in small quantities for the normal functioning of the body. Many act as coenzymes, small molecules that enable ◊enzymes to function effectively. They are normally present in adequate amounts in a balanced diet. Deficiency of a vitamin will normally lead to a metabolic disorder ("deficiency disease"), which can be remedied by sufficient intake of the vitamin. They are generally classified as water-soluble (B and C) or fat-soluble (A, D, E, and K).

Scurvy (the result of vitamin C deficiency) was observed at least 3,500 years ago, and sailors from the 1600s were given fresh sprouting cereals or citrus-fruit juice to prevent or cure it. The concept of scurvy as a deficiency disease, however, caused by the absence of a specific substance, emerged later. In the 1890s a Dutch doctor, Christiaan ◊Eijkman, discovered that he could cure hens suffering from a condition like beriberi by feeding them on whole-grain, rather than polished, rice. In 1912 Casimir Funk, a Polish-born biochemist, had proposed the existence of what he called "vitamines," but it was not fully established until about 1915 that several deficiency diseases were preventable and curable by extracts from certain foods. By then it was known that two groups of factors were involved, one being water-soluble and present, for example, in yeast, rice-polishings, and wheat germ, and the other being fat-soluble and present in egg yolk, butter, and fish-liver oils. The water-soluble substance, known to be effective against beriberi, was named vitamin B. The fat-soluble vitamin complex was at first called vitamin A. With improving analytical techniques these have been subsequently separated into their various components, and others have been discovered.

vitamin C alternate name for ◊ascorbic acid.

Vitebsk industrial city (glass, textiles, machine tools, shoes) in NE Byelorussia, USSR, on the Dvina River; population (1987) 347,000. Vitebsk dates from the 10th century and has been Lithuanian, Russian, and Polish.

Vitoria capital of Alava province, in the Basque country, N Spain; population (1986) 208,000. Products include motor vehicles, agricultural machinery, and furniture.

vitreous humor transparent jellylike substance behind the lens of the vertebrate ◊eye. It gives rigidity to the spherical form of the eye and allows light to pass through to the retina.

vitriol any of a number of sulfate salts. Blue, green, and white vitriols are copper, ferrous, and zinc sulfate, respectively. Oil of vitriol is sulfuric acid.

Vitruvius (Marcus Vitruvius Pollio) 1st century BC. Roman architect whose ten-volume interpretation of Roman architecture, *De architectura*, influenced the Renaissance architects Alberti and Palladio.

Vittorio Veneto industrial town (motorcycles, agricultural machinery, furniture, paper, textiles) in Veneto, NE Italy, site of the final victory of Italy and its allies over Austria Oct 1918; population (1981) 30,000.

Vitus, St Christian saint, perhaps Sicilian, who was martyred in Rome early in the 4th century. Feast day June 15.

Vivaldi Antonio (Lucio) 1678–1741. Italian Baroque composer, violinist, and conductor. He wrote 23 symphonies, 75 sonatas, over 400 concertos, including the *Four Seasons* (about 1725) for violin and orchestra, over 40 operas, and much sacred music. His work was largely neglected until the 1930s.

Known as the Red Priest, because of his flaming hair color, Vivaldi spent much of his church career teaching music at a girl's orphanage. He wrote many of his famous works for them and for himself.

vivipary in animals, a method of reproduction in which the embryo develops inside the body of the female from which it gains nourishment (in contrast to ◊ovipary and ◊ovovivipary). Vivipary is best developed in placental mammals, but also occurs in some arthropods, fishes, amphibians, and reptiles that have placentalike structures. In plants, it is the formation of young plantlets or bulbils instead of flowers. The term also describes seeds that germinate prematurely, before falling from the parent plant.

Premature germination is common in mangrove trees, where the seedlings develop sizable spearlike roots before dropping into the swamp below; this prevents their being washed away by the tide.

vivisection literally, cutting into a living animal. Used originally to mean experimental surgery or dissection practiced on a live subject, the term is often used by ◊antivivisection campaigners to include any experiment on animals, surgical or otherwise.

viz abbreviation for *videlicet* (Latin "that is to say," "namely").

Vizcaya Basque form of ◊Biscay, a bay in the Atlantic off France and Spain. It is also the name of one of the three Spanish Basque provinces.

Vladimir I St 956–1015. Russian saint, prince of Novgorod, and grand duke of Kiev. Converted to Christianity 988, he married Anna, Christian sister of the Byzantine emperor ◊Basil II, and established the Byzantine rite of Orthodox Christianity as the Russian national faith.

Vladivostok port (naval and commercial) in E USSR at the Amur Bay on the Pacific coast; population (1987) 615,000. It is kept open by icebreakers during winter. Industries include shipbuilding and the manufacture of precision instruments.

It was established 1860 as a military port. It is the administrative center of the Far East Science Centre 1969, with subsidiaries at Petropavlovsk, Khabarovsk, and Magadan.

Vlaminck Maurice de 1876–1958. French artist who painted brilliantly colored landscapes as an early member of the ◊Fauves. He later abandoned Fauve color. He also wrote poetry, novels, and essays.

Initially he was inspired by van ◊Gogh but by 1908 ◊Cézanne had become the chief influence. Vlaminck was a multitalented eccentric: his pastimes included cycling, playing the violin, and farming.

VLF in physics, the abbreviation for very low ◊frequency.

Vlissingen Dutch form of ◊Flushing, a port in SW Netherlands.

Vlorë port and capital of Vlorë province, SW Albania, population (1980) 58,000. A Turkish possession from 1464, it was the site of the declaration of independence by Albania 1912.

VLSI (abbreviation of very large-scale integration) in electronics, the current level of advanced technology in the microminiaturization of ◊integrated circuits, and an order of magnitude smaller than ◊LSI.

voc. in grammer, the abbreviation for vocative.

vocal cords the paired folds, ridges, or cords of tissue within a mammal's larynx, and a bird's syrinx. Air passing over the folds or membranes makes them vibrate, producing sounds. Muscles in the larynx change the pitch of the sounds produced, by adjusting the tension of the vocal cords.

vocational education education relevant to a specific job or career.

Community colleges provide two-year training in the trades as well as secretarial, business, accounting, and other business and job-related studies. Technical colleges may be two-year, four-year, or prestigious advanced degree institutions, such as the Massachusetts Institute of Technology or Rensselaer Polytechnical Institute.

vocative in the grammar of certain inflected languages, for example Latin, the form of a word, especially a name, that is used to indicate that a person or thing is being addressed.

vodka strong colorless alcoholic liquor distilled from rye, potatoes, or barley.

Vogel Hans-Jochen 1926– . German Socialist politician, chair of the Social Democratic Party (SPD) from 1987. A former leader of the SPD in Bavaria and mayor of Munich, he served in the Brandt and Schmidt West German governments in the 1970s as housing and then justice minister and then, briefly, as mayor of West Berlin.

A centrist, compromise figure, Vogel unsuccessfully contested the 1983 federal election as chancellor candidate for the SPD and in 1987 replaced Brandt as party chair.

voice sound produced through the mouth and by the passage of air between the ◊vocal cords. In humans the sound is much amplified by the hollow sinuses of the face, and is modified by the movements of the lips, tongue, and cheeks.

voiceprint a print produced by a sound spectograph showing frequency and intensity changes in the human voice when visually recorded. It enables individual speech characteristics to be determined. First used as evidence in criminal trials in the US in 1966, voiceprints were banned in 1974 by the US Court of Appeal as "not yet sufficiently accepted by scientists."

Voight Jon 1938– . US film actor who starred with Dustin Hoffman in *Midnight Cowboy* 1969. His subsequent films include *Deliverance* 1972, *Coming Home* 1978, and *Runaway Train* 1985.

Vojvodina autonomous area in N Serbia, Yugoslavia; area 8,299 sq mi/21,500 sq km; population (1986) 2,050,000, including 1,110,000 Serbs and 390,000 Hungarians. Its capital is Novi Sad.

vol abbreviation for volume.

volatile in chemistry, term describing a substance that readily passes from the liquid to the vapor phase. Volatile substances have a high vapor pressure.

volcanic rock ◊igneous rock formed at the surface of the Earth. It is usually fine-grained, unlike the more coarse-grained intrusive (under the surface) types of igneous rocks. Volcanic rock can be either lava (solidified magma) or a pyroclastic deposit (fragmentary lava or ash) such as tuff (volcanic ash that has fused to form rock).

Basalt and andesite are the main types of lava. Rhyolite often occurs as a pyroclastic deposit.

volcano

volcanoes

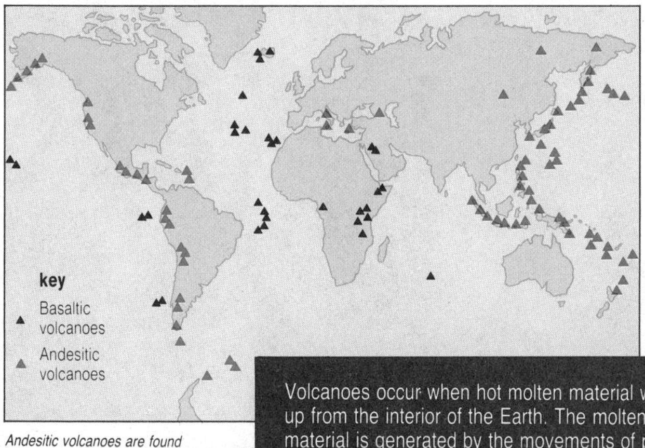
key
Basaltic volcanoes
Andesitic volcanoes

Andesitic volcanoes are found where areas of the Earth's surface are being pushed together. They take their name from the Andes mountains in South America. Basaltic volcanoes form where areas of the Earth's surface are pulling apart, and usually erupt from the ocean floor.

Volcanoes occur when hot molten material wells up from the interior of the Earth. The molten material is generated by the movements of plate tectonics and is known as lava when it appears at the surface. The volcanic mountain is formed by the build-up of solidified lava and ash around the vent or crack in the Earth's surface.

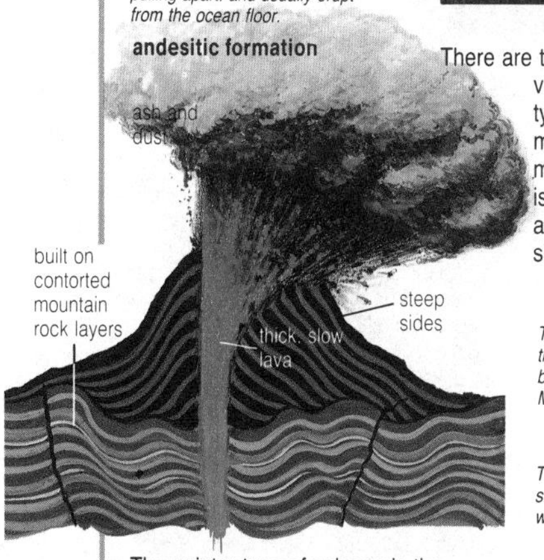
andesitic formation
ash and dust
built on contorted mountain rock layers
steep sides
thick, slow lava

There are two main types of volcano. The more violent is the andesitic volcano which is typical of island arcs and coastal mountain chains. The molten rock is mostly derived from plate material and is rich in silica. This makes it very stiff and it solidifies to form high, steep-sided volcanic mountains.

The stiff lava of an andesitic volcano often clogs the volcanic vent. Eruptions can be violent as the blockage is blasted free, as in the eruption of Mount Saint Helens in North America in 1980.

The black silica-poor lava from a basaltic volcano, such as those in Hawaii or Iceland, often forms wrinkled ropy surfaces before it sets.

The quieter type of volcano is the basaltic type which is found along rift valleys and ocean ridges, and also over 'hot spots' beneath the Earth's crust. The molten material is derived from the Earth's mantle and is quite runny. It flows for some distance over the surface before it sets and so forms broad low volcanoes.

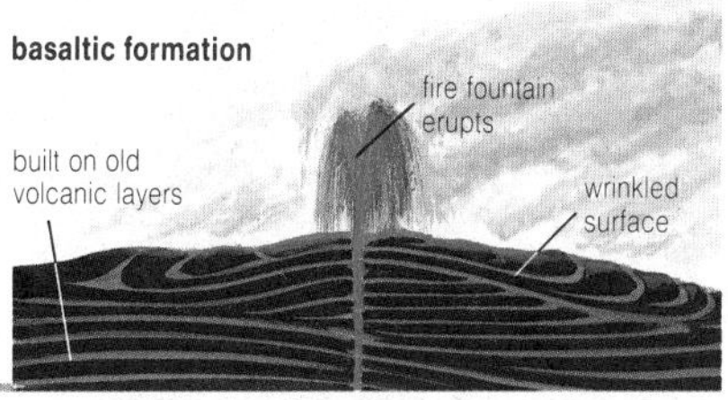
basaltic formation
fire fountain erupts
built on old volcanic layers
wrinkled surface

volcano vent in the Earth's ◊crust from which molten rock, lava, ashes, and gases are ejected. Usually it is cone-shaped with a pitlike opening at the top called the crater. Some volcanoes, for example Stromboli and Vesuvius in Italy, eject the material with explosive violence; others are quiet and the lava simply rises into the crater and flows over the rim.

Volcanoes are closely associated with the movements of lithospheric plates (the top layer of the Earth's structure), particularly around plate boundaries—due to the movements of ◊plate tectonics. Many volcanoes are submarine and occur along midocean ridges. The chief terrestrial volcanic regions are around the Pacific rim (Cape Horn to Alaska); the central Andes of Chile (with the world's highest volcano, Guallatiri, 19,900 ft/6,060 m); North Island, New Zealand; Hawaii; Japan; and Antarctica. There are about 600 active volcanoes on Earth. Volcanism has helped shape other members of the Solar System, including the Moon, Mars, Venus, and Jupiter's moon Io.

Some volcanoes may be inactive for long periods.

Volcker Paul 1927– . US economist. As chair of the board of governors of the Federal Reserve System 1979–87, he controlled the amount of money in circulation in the US. He was succeeded by Alan Greenspan.

vole any of various rodents of the family Cricetidae, subfamily Microtinae, distributed over Europe, Asia, and North America, and related to hamsters and lemmings. They are charcterized by stout bodies and short tails. They have brown or gray fur, and blunt noses, and some species reach a length of 12 in/30 cm. They feed on grasses, seeds, aquatic plants, and insects. Many show remarkable fluctuations in numbers over 3–4 year cycles.

The most common genus is *Microtus*, which includes some 45 species distributed across North America and Eurasia.

Volga longest river in Europe; 2,290 mi/3,685 km, 2,200 mi/3,540 km of which are navigable. It drains most of the central and eastern parts of European USSR, rises in the Valdai plateau, and flows into the Caspian Sea 55 mi/88 km below Astrakhan.

The Soviet Union is going ahead with plans for diverting water from N-flowing rivers, E and W of the Urals, to irrigate the croplands of central Asia. Diversion of water into the S-flowing Volga from the Sukhona River and surrounding lakes is due for completion 1990. A canal stretching 1,500 mi/2,415 km from the river Ob to Amu Darya is still in the planning stage.

Volgograd formerly (until 1925) Tsaritsyn, and (1925–61) Stalingrad industrial city (metal goods, machinery, lumber mills, oil refining) in SW USSR, on the river Volga; population (1987) 988,000.

Its successful defense 1942–43 against Germany was a turning point in World War II.

Völkerwanderung (German "nations wandering") the migration of peoples, usually with reference to the Slavic and Germanic movement in Europe 2nd–11th centuries AD.

Volkswagen (VW) German car manufacturer. The original VW, with its distinctive beetle shape, was first designed in 1933 and produced in Germany 1936, a design by Ferdinand Porsche. It was still in production in Latin America in the late 1980s, by which time it had exceeded 20 million sales worldwide.

volleyball an indoor and outdoor team game played on a court between two teams of six players each. A net is placed across the center of the court, and players hit the ball (only once each, not more than three times per side) with their hands, the aim being to ground it in the opponents' court.

Originally called Mintonette, the game was invented 1895 by William G Morgan in Massachusetts, as a rival to the newly developed basketball. The playing area measures 59 ft/18 m by 29 ft 6 in/9 m. The ball is slightly smaller and lighter than a basketball. The world championships were first held in 1949 for men, and 1952 for women.

volt SI unit (abbreviation V) of electromotive force or electric potential. A small battery usually has a potential of one or two volts; the domestic electricity supply in the US is 110 volts. A high-tension transmission line may carry up to 765,000 volts.

The absolute volt is defined as the potential difference necessary to produce a current of one ampere through an electric circuit with a resistance of one ohm. It can also be defined as the potential difference that requires one joule of work to move a positive charge of one coulomb from the lower to the higher potential. It is named after the Italian scientist Alessandro Volta.

Volta main river in Ghana, about 1,000 mi/1,600 km long, with two main upper branches, the Black and White Volta. It has been dammed to provide power.

Volta Alessandro 1745–1827. Italian physicist. He invented the voltaic pile (the first battery), the electrophorus (an early electrostatic generator), and an ◊electroscope.

Born in Como, he was a professor there and at Pavia. The ◊volt is named after him.

Voltaire Adopted name of François-Marie Arouet 1694–1778. French writer who believed in ◊deism, and devoted himself to tolerance, justice, and humanity. He was threatened with arrest for *Lettres philosophiques sur les anglais/Philosophical Letters on the English* 1733 (essays in favor of English ways, thought, and political practice) and had to take refuge. Other writings include *Le Siècle de Louis XIV/The Age of Louis XIV* 1751; *Candide* 1759, a parody on ◊Leibniz's "best of all possible worlds"; and *Dictionnaire philosophique* 1764.

Born in Paris, the son of a notary, he adopted his pen name 1718. He was twice imprisoned in the Bastille and exiled from Paris between 1716 and 1726 for libelous political verse. *Oedipe/Oedipus*, his first essay in tragedy, was staged 1718.

Voltaire *French writer and philosopher Voltaire.*

While in England 1726–29 he dedicated an epic poem on Henry IV, *La Henriade/The Henriade*, to Queen Caroline, and on returning to France published the successful *Histoire de Charles XII/History of Charles XII* 1731, and produced the play *Zaïre* 1732. He took refuge with his mistress, the Marquise de ◊Châtelet, at Cirey in Champagne, where he wrote the play *Mérope* 1743 and much of *Le Siècle de Louis XIV*. Among his other works are histories of Peter the Great, Louis XV, and India; *La Pucelle/The Maid*, on Joan of Arc; the satirical tale *Zadig* 1748; and the tragedy *Irène* 1778. From 1751 to 1753 he stayed at the court of Frederick II (the Great) of Prussia, who had long been an admirer, but the association ended in deep enmity. From 1754 he established himself near Geneva—after 1758 at Ferney, just across the French border. His remains were transferred in 1791 to the Panthéon in Paris.

voltmeter instrument for measuring potential difference (voltage). It has a high internal resistance (so that it passes only a small current), and is connected in parallel with the component across which potential difference is to be measured. A common type is constructed from a sensitive current-detecting moving-coil ◊galvanometer placed in series with a high-value resistor (multiplier). To measure an AC (◊alternating-current) voltage, the circuit must usually include a rectifier; however, a moving-iron instrument can be used to measure alternating voltages without the need for such a device.

volume in geometry, the space occupied by a three-dimensional solid object. A prism (such as a cube) or a cylinder has a volume equal to the area of the base multiplied by the height. For a pyramid or cone, the volume is equal to one-third of the area of the base multiplied by the perpendicular height. The volume of a sphere is equal to $\frac{4}{3}\pi r^3$, where r is the radius. Volumes of irregular solids may be calculated by the technique of ◊integration.

vomiting the expulsion of the contents of the stomach through the mouth. It may have numerous causes, including direct irritation of the stomach, severe pain, dizziness, and emotion. Sustained or repeated vomiting is always a serious symptom, because it may indicate serious disease, and because dangerous loss of water, salt, and acid may result (as in ◊bulimia).

von Braun Wernher 1912–1977. German rocket engineer who developed German military missiles (V1 and V2) during World War II and later worked for ◊NASA in the US.

During the 1940s his research team at Peenemünde on the Baltic coast produced the V1 unguided missile, called the "buzz bomb" and supersonic V2 rockets. In the 1950s von Braun was part of the team that produced rockets for US satellites (the first, *Explorer I*, was launched early 1958) and early space flights by astronauts.

von Gesner Konrad 1516–1565. Swiss naturalist who produced an encyclopedia of the animal world, the *Historia animalium* 1551–58.

Gesner was a victim of the Black Death and could not complete a similar project on plants. He is considered a founder of the science of zoology, but was also an expert in languages and an authority on the Classical writers.

Neumann *US mathematician John von Neumann, born in Hungary, known particularly for his pioneering work on computer design, also made important contributions to quantum physics and logic.*

von Karajan Herbert Austrian conductor. See ◊Karajan, Herbert von.

Vonnegut Kurt, Jr 1922– . US writer whose work generally has surrealistic elements, satire, and fantasy and depicts the flaws of contemporary society. His novel *Slaughterhouse Five* 1969 mixes his World War II experience of the firebombing of Dresden, Germany, with a fantasy world on the planet Tralfamadore with the science-fiction element dominated by absurdism and earthly black humor.

Born in Indianapolis, Indiana, Vonnegut graduated from Cornell University and the University of Chicago. In the 1960s and 1970s his work became very popular, particularly among college students. Other novels include *Player Piano* 1952, *The Sirens of Titan* 1958, *Cat's Cradle* 1963, *Breakfast of Champions* 1973, *Slapstick* 1976, *Jailbird* 1979, *Deadeye Dick* 1982, *Galapagos* 1985, and *Hocus Pocus* 1990. His short stories are collected in *Welcome to the Monkey House* 1968. His autobiography was published as *Palm Sunday* 1981.

Von Neumann John 1903–1957. Hungarian-born US scientist and mathematician, known for his pioneering work on computer design. He invented his celebrated "rings of operators" (called Von Neumann algebras) in the late 1930s, and also contributed to set theory, games theory, cybernetics (with his theory of self-reproducing automata, called Von Neumann machines), and the development of the atomic and hydrogen bombs.

He was born in Budapest and became an assistant professor of physical mathematics at Berlin University before moving to Princeton, in 1929, where he later became professor of mathematics. In the early 1940s he described a design for a stored-program computer.

voodoo a set of magical beliefs and practices, followed in some parts of Africa, South America, and the West Indies, especially Haiti. It arose in the 17th century on slave plantations as a combination of Roman Catholicism and W African religious traditions; believers retain membership in the Roman Catholic church. Beliefs include the existence of loa, spirits who closely involve themselves in human affairs, and some of whose identities mesh with those of Christian saints. The loa are invoked by the priest (*houngan*) or priestess (*manbo*) at ceremonies, during which members of the congregation become possessed by the spirits and go into trance.

A voodoo temple (*houmfort*) has a central post from which the loa supposedly descend to "mount" the worshiper. The loa can be identified by the characteristic behavior of the possessed person. Loa include Baron Samedi, who watches over the land of the dead; Erzulie, the black Virgin or Earth goddess; Ogu, a warrior, corresponding to St James the Great; and Legba, the lord of the road and interpreter between humans and spirits, who corresponds to St Anthony the hermit.

Vorarlberg ("in front of the Arlberg") alpine federal province of W Austria draining into the Rhine and Lake Constance; area 1,004 sq mi/2,600 sq km; population (1987) 314,000. Its capital is Bregenz. Industries include forestry and dairy farming.

Voronezh industrial city (chemicals, construction machinery, electrical equipment) and capital of the Voronezh region of the USSR, S of Moscow on the Voronezh river; population (1987) 872,000. There has been a town on the site since the 11th century.

Voroshilov Klement Efremovich 1881–1969. Marshal of the USSR. He joined the Bolsheviks 1903 and was arrested many times and exiled, but escaped. He became a Red Army commander in the civil war 1918–20, a member of the central committee 1921, commissar for war 1925, member of the Politburo 1926, marshal 1935. He was removed as war commissar 1940 after defeats on the Finland front and failing to raise the German siege of Leningrad. He was a member of the committee for defense 1941–44 and president of the Presidium of the USSR 1953–60.

Voroshilovgrad formerly (until 1935 and 1958–70) Lugansk industrial city (locomotives, textiles, mining machinery) in Ukraine Republic, USSR; population (1987) 509,000.

Vorster Balthazar Johannes 1915–1983. South African Nationalist politician, prime minister 1966–78, and president 1978–79. During his premiership some elements of apartheid were allowed to lapse, and attempts were made to improve relations with the outside world. He resigned the presidency because of a financial scandal.

Vosges mountain range in E France, rising in the Ballon de Guebwiller to 4,667 ft/1,422 m and forming the W edge of the Rhine rift valley.

Voskhod (Russian "ascent") Soviet spacecraft used

in the mid-1960s; it was modified from the single-seat Vostok and was the first spacecraft capable of carrying two or three cosmonauts. During *Voskhod 2*'s flight 1965, Alexei Leonov made the first space walk.

Vostok (Russian "east") the first Soviet spacecraft, used 1961–63. Vostok was a metal sphere 7.5 ft/2.3 m in diameter, capable of carrying one cosmonaut. It made flights lasting up to five days. *Vostok 1* carried the first person into space, Yuri ◊Gagarin.

vote expression of opinion by ballot, show of hands, or other means. For direct vote, see ◊plebiscite and ◊referendum. In parliamentary elections the results can be calculated in a number of ways.

In the US the voting age is 18. Conditions of residence vary from state to state and registration is required some weeks before election day. Until declared illegal 1965, literacy tests or a ◊poll tax were often used to prevent black people from voting in the South. Voter registration and turnout in the US remains the lowest in the industrialized world. In 1988, 37% of potential voters failed to register and barely 50% bothered to vote in the presidential election, so that George Bush became president with the support of only 27% of the people.

Voyager probes two US space probes, originally ◊Mariners. *Voyager 1*, launched Sept 5, 1977, passed Jupiter March 1979 and reached Saturn Nov 1980. *Voyager 2* was launched earlier, Aug 20, 1977, on a slower trajectory that took it past Jupiter July 1979, Saturn Aug 1981, Uranus Jan 1986, Neptune Aug 1989, and on to Pluto. Like the ◊Pioneer probes, the Voyagers are on their way out of the Solar System. Their tasks now include helping scientists to locate the position of the heliopause, the boundary at which the influence of the Sun gives way to the forces exerted by other stars. Both Voyagers carry specially coded long-playing records called "Sounds of Earth" for the enlightenment of any other civilizations that might find them.

Voyager 2 was not intended to visit Uranus and Neptune, but the project's scientists were able to reprogram its computer to take it past those planets after it was discovered that the systems were still functioning. It passed by Neptune at an altitude of 3,000 mi/4,800 km; its radio signals took 4 hours 6 minutes to reach Earth.

Vranitzky Franz 1937– . Austrian Socialist politician, federal chancellor from 1986. Vranitzky first went into banking and in 1970 became adviser on economic and financial policy to the minister of finance. After a return to the banking world he entered the political arena through the Socialist Party of Austria (SPÖ), and became minister of finance in 1984. He succeeded Fred Sinowatz as federal chancellor in 1986, heading an SPÖ-ÖVP (Austrian People's Party) coalition.

VT abbreviation for ◊Vermont.

v.t. in grammar, the abbreviation for verb transitive.

Vuillard (Jean) Edouard 1886–1940. French painter and printmaker, a founding member of les ◊Nabis. His work is mainly decorative, with an emphasis on surface pattern reflecting the influence of Japanese prints. With ◊Bonnard he produced numerous lithographs and paintings of simple domestic interiors, works that are generally categorized as *intimiste*.

Vulcan in Roman mythology, the god of fire and destruction, later identified with the Greek god ◊Hephaestus.

vulcanization technique for hardening rubber by heating it with, and chemically combining it with, sulfur. The process also makes the rubber stronger and more elastic. If the sulfur content is increased to as much as 30%, the product is the inelastic solid known as ebonite.

More expensive alternatives to sulfur, such as selenium and telurium, are used to vulcanize rubber for specialized products such as vehicle tires. The process was discovered accidentally by US inventor Charles ◊Goodyear 1839 and patented 1844.

Accelerators can be added to speed the vulcanization process, which takes from a few minutes for small objects to an hour or more for vehicle tires. Molded objects are often shaped and vulcanized simultaneously in heated molds; other objects may be vulcanized in hot water, hot air, or steam.

vulcanology study of ◊volcanoes and the geologic phenomena that cause them.

Vulgate (Latin "common") the Latin translation of the Bible produced by St Jerome in the 4th century.

It is the oldest surviving version of the entire Bible and differs from earlier Latin translations in working from the Hebrew rather than the Greek. In 1546 it was adopted by the Council of Trent as the official Roman Catholic Bible and was later used for official English versions like the Douai.

Vulpecula small constellation in the northern hemisphere of the sky just south of Cygnus, represented as a fox. It contains a major ◊planetary nebula, the Dumbbell, and the first ◊pulsar (pulsating radio source) to be discovered.

vulture

vulture any of various carrion-eating birds of prey with naked heads and necks and with keen senses of sight and smell. Vultures are up to 3.3 ft/1 m long, with wingspans of up to 11.5 ft/3.5 m. The plumage is usually dark, and the head brightly colored.

True vultures are placed in the family Accipitridae along with hawks and eagles and are found only in the Old World. American vultures are placed in a family of their own (Cathartidae) and include turkey vultures and ◊condors. The vulture has keen senses of sight and smell. Its eyes are adapted to give an overall view with a magnifying area in the center, enabling it to locate possible food sources and see the exact site in detail.

Vyborg (Finnish Viipuri) port (trading in timber and wood products) and naval base in E Karelia, USSR, on the Gulf of Finland, 70 mi/112 km NW of Leningrad; population (1973) 51,000. Products include electrical equipment and agricultural machinery. Founded by the Swedes 1293, it was Finnish 1918–40.

Vyshinsky Andrei 1883–1954. Soviet politician. As commissar for justice, he acted as prosecutor at Stalin's treason trials 1936–38. He was foreign minister 1949–53 and often represented the USSR at the United Nations.

W abbreviation for west; in physics, symbol for watt.

WA abbreviation for ◊Washington (state); ◊Western Australia.

Wace Robert c. 1100–1175. Anglo-Norman poet and chronicler of early chivalry. His major works, both written in Norman French, were *Roman de Brut* (also known as *Geste des Bretons*) 1155, containing material relating to the legends of King ◊Arthur, and *Roman de Rou* (or *Geste des Normanz*) 1160–62, covering the history of Normandy.

Waco city in E central Texas, on the Brazos river, S of Fort Worth. It is an agricultural shipping center for cotton, grain, and livestock; industries include airplane parts, glass, cement, tires, and textiles; population (1990) 103,590. Baylor University 1845 is here.

Waddenzee European estuarine area (tidal flats, salt marshes, islands, and inlets) N of the Netherlands and the Federal Republic of Germany, and W of Denmark; area 4,000 sq mi/10,000 sq km. It is the nursery for the North Sea fisheries, but the ecology is threatened by tourism and other development.

wadi in arid regions of the Middle East, a steep-sided valley containing an intermittent stream that flows in the wet season.

Wadi Halfa frontier town in Sudan, NE Africa, on Lake Nuba (the Sudanese section of Lake Nasser, formed by the Nile dam at Aswan, Egypt, which partly flooded the archeological sites here).

Wafd (Arabic "deputation") the main Egyptian nationalist party between World Wars I and II. Under Nahas Pasha it formed a number of governments in the 1920s and 1930s. Dismissed by King Farouk in 1938, it was reinstated by the British in 1941. The party's pro-British stance weakened its claim to lead the nationalist movement, and the party was again dismissed by Farouk in 1952, shortly before his own deposition. Wafd was banned in Jan 1953.

Wagner *German composer Richard Wagner.*

wafer in microelectronics, a "superchip" some 3–4 in/8–10 cm in diameter, for which wafer-scale integration (WSI) is used to link the equivalent of many individual ◊silicon chips, improving reliability, speed, and cooling.

wage and price controls government directives freezing or limiting wages and prices, usually in time of emergency, such as wars or in the event of severe ◊inflation.

The use of such controls in the US has been relatively rare, the strongest control occurring during World War II. Under President Nixon, wages and prices were frozen for 90 days in 1971. Since then, presidents have preferred to use persuasion rather than impose controls.

Wagner Honus (John Peter) 1874–1955. US baseball player. Born in Mansfield, Pennsylvania, Wagner began his professional baseball career 1895 and was signed as a shortstop by the Louisville club of the National League 1897. He was acquired by the Pittsburgh Pirates 1899 and remained there until his retirement 1917. He was a consistent hitter with an impressive lifetime batting average of .329. In addition to his fielding skills, he was a great runner; his career record of 722 stolen bases won him the nickname "The Flying Dutchman." Wagner was elected to the Baseball Hall of Fame 1936.

Wagner Richard 1813–1883. German opera composer. He revolutionized the 19th-century conception of opera, envisaging it as a wholly new art form in which musical, poetic, and scenic elements should be unified through such devices as the *leitmotif*. His operas include *Tannhäuser* 1845, *Lohengrin* 1850, and *Tristan und Isolde* 1865. In 1872 he founded the Festival Theatre in Bayreuth; his masterpiece *Der Ring des Nibelungen/The Ring of the Nibelung*, a sequence of four operas, was first performed there in 1876. His last work, *Parsifal*, was produced in 1882.

Wagner's early career was as director of the Magdeburg Theatre, where he unsuccessfully produced his first opera *Das Liebesverbot/Forbidden Love* in 1836. He lived in Paris 1839–42 and conducted the Dresden Opera House 1842–48. He fled Germany to escape arrest for his part in the 1848 revolution, but in 1861 he was allowed to return. He won the favor of Ludwig II of Bavaria in 1864 and was thus able to set up the Festival Theatre in Bayreuth. The Bayreuth tradition was continued by his wife Cosima (Liszt's daughter, whom he married after her divorce from Hans von ◊Bülow), by his son Siegfried Wagner (1869–1930), a composer of operas such as *Der Bärenhäuter*; and by later descendants.

Wagner Robert Ferdinand 1877–1953. German-born US public official. He came to the US 1885, was educated at the City College of New York, and was admitted to the bar 1900. He served as a Democrat in the state assembly 1905–09 and senate 1909–18 and as a justice of the state supreme court 1919–26. Wagner served in the US Senate 1927–49. Deeply concerned with labor and welfare issues, he was a strong supporter of the New Deal and helped draft the National Industrial Recovery Act of 1933 and the National Labor Relations Act of 1935.

Wagner-Jauregg Julius 1857–1940. Austrian neurologist. He received a Nobel Prize in 1927 for his work on the use of induced fevers in treating mental illness.

Wagram, Battle of battle in July 1809 when French troops under Emperor Napoleon won an important victory over the Austrian army under Archduke Charles near the village of Wagram, NE of Vienna, Austria. The outcome forced Austria to concede general defeat to the French.

wagtail any slim narrow-billed bird of the genus *Motacilla*, about 7 in/18 cm long, with a characteristic flicking movement of the tail. There are about 30 species, found mostly in Eurasia and Africa.

Wahabi a puritanical Saudi Islamic sect founded by Mohammed ibn-Abd-al-Wahab (1703–92), which regards all other sects as heretical. By the early 20th century it had spread throughout the Arabian peninsula; it still remains the official ideology of the Saudi Arabian kingdom.

Waikato river on North Island, New Zealand, 220 mi/355 km long; Waikato is also the name of the dairy area the river traverses; chief town Hamilton.

Wailing Wall or (in Judaism) ***Western Wall*** the remaining part of the ◊Temple in Jerusalem, a sacred site of pilgrimage and prayer for Jews. There they offer prayers either aloud ("wailing") or on pieces of paper placed between the stones of the wall.

Waitaki river in SE South Island, New Zealand, that flows 135 mi/215 km to the Pacific. The Benmore hydroelectric installation has created an artificial lake.

Waite Morrison Remick 1816–1888. US lawyer and chief justice of the US. He was appointed chief justice of the US by President Grant 1874. As chief justice, he presided over constitutional challenges to Reconstruction, but Waite is best remembered for his decisions upholding the right of states to regulate public utilities.

Born in Lyme, Connecticut, and educated at Yale, Waite settled in Ohio, where he was admitted to the bar 1839. After serving in the state legislature 1849–50, he returned to private practice. A staunch Republican, he was named US counsel in the 1871 *Alabama* claims case.

Waite Terry (Terence Hardy) 1939– . British religious adviser from 1980 to the archbishop of Canterbury, Dr Robert Runcie. Waite undertook many overseas assignments and disappeared in 1987 while making inquiries in Beirut, Lebanon, about European hostages. Worldwide efforts to secure his release long proved unsuccessful, but he was finally released in Nov 1991.

Waits Tom 1949– . US singer and songwriter, with a characteristic gravelly voice. His songs typically deal with urban street life, and have jazz-influenced arrangements. He has written music for and acted in several films, including Jim Jarmusch's *Down by Law* 1986.

Wajda Andrzej 1926– . Polish film director, one of the major figures in postwar European cinema. His films are concerned with the predicament and disillusion of individuals caught up in political events. His works include *Ashes and Diamonds* 1958, *Man of Marble* 1977, *Man of Iron* 1981, *Danton* 1982, and *Korczak* 1990.

He was also mentor to filmmaker Roman Polanski.

Wakefield industrial city (chemicals, machine tools), administrative headquarters of West Yorkshire,

Waite *British negotiator Terry Waite was taken hostage in Lebanon in 1987, while seeking the release of hostages, and was released 1991.*

Waldheim *Austrian president Kurt Waldheim, elected in 1986 despite his wartime service with the Nazis in Yugoslavia. He was secretary-general of the United Nations 1972–81.*

England, on the river Calder, south of Leeds; population (1981) 310,200. The Lancastrians defeated the Yorkists here 1460, during the Wars of the ◊Roses.

Wake Islands a small Pacific atoll comprising three islands 2,300 mi/3,700 km W of Hawaii, under US Air Force administration since 1972; area 3 sq mi/ 8 sq km; population (1980) 300. It was discovered by Captain William Wake 1841, annexed by the US 1898, and uninhabited until 1935 when it was made an air staging point, with a garrison. It was occupied by Japan 1941–45.

Wakhan Salient narrow strip of territory in Afghanistan bordered by the USSR, China, and Pakistan. It was effectively annexed by the USSR in 1980 to halt alleged arms supplies to Afghan guerrillas from China and Pakistan.

Waksman Selman Abraham 1888–1973. US biochemist, born in Ukraine. He coined the word "antibiotic" for bacteria-killing chemicals derived from microorganisms. Waksman was awarded a Nobel Prize in 1952 for the discovery of streptomycin, an antibiotic used against tuberculosis.

Walachia alternate spelling of ◊Wallachia, part of Romania.

Walcheren island in Zeeland province, Netherlands, in the estuary of the Scheldt
area 80 sq mi/200 sq km
capital Middelburg
cities Flushing (Vlissingen)
features flat and for the most part below sea level
products dairy, sugar-beet and other root vegetables
history a British force seized Walcheren in 1809; after 7,000 of the garrison of 15,000 had died of malaria, the remainder were withdrawn. It was flooded by deliberate breaching of the dykes to drive out the Germans 1944–45, and in 1953 by abnormally high tides.

Wald George 1906– . US biochemist who explored the chemistry of vision. He found that a crucial role was played by the retinal pigment rhodopsin, derived in part from vitamin A. For this he shared the 1967 Nobel Prize for Physiology or Medicine with Ragnar Granit (1900–) and Haldan Hartline (1903–).

Wald Lillian D 1867–1940. US public health administrator and founder of New York City's Henry Street Settlement House 1895. Born in Cincinnati, Ohio, Wald graduated from the New York Hospital Training School for Nurses 1891. She later worked as a nurse in some of New York's poorest neighborhoods, especially the Lower East Side, and began to provide medical, nutritional, educational, and social-welfare programs for children and adults. In 1912 she founded the National Organization for Public Health Nursing and was also active in union and antiwar activities. Her memoirs, *House on Henry Street*, appeared 1915.

Waldemar or ***Valdemar*** four kings of Denmark, including:

Waldemar I the Great 1131–1182. King of Denmark from 1157, who defeated rival claimants to the throne and overcame the ◊Wends on the Baltic island of Rügen in 1169.

Waldemar II the Conqueror 1170–1241. King of Denmark from 1202. He was the second son of Waldemar I and succeeded his brother Canute VI. He gained control of land N of the river Elbe (which he later lost), as well as much of Estonia, and he completed the codification of Danish law.

Waldemar IV 1320–1375. King of Denmark from 1340, responsible for reuniting his country by capturing Skåne (S Sweden) and the island of Gotland in 1361. However, the resulting conflict with the ◊Hanseatic League led to defeat by them, and in 1370 he was forced to submit to the Peace of Stralsund.

Walden or ***Life in the Woods*** 1854, classic literary work of US Transcendentalism, the record kept by Henry David Thoreau of his attempt to "front the essential facts of life" by building a simple cabin at Walden Pond, near Concord, Massachusetts, and observing nature there.

Waldenses also known as ***Waldensians*** or ***Vaudois*** Protestant religious sect, founded about 1170 by Peter Waldo, a merchant of Lyons. They were allied to the ◊Albigenses. They lived in voluntary poverty, refused to take oaths or take part in war, and later rejected the doctrines of transubstantiation, purgatory, and the invocation of saints. Although subjected to persecution until the 17th century, they spread in France, Germany, and Italy, and still survive in Piedmont.

Waldheim Kurt 1918– . Austrian politician and diplomat, president from 1986. He was secretary general of the United Nations 1972–81, having been Austria's representative there 1964–68 and 1970–71. He was elected president of Austria despite revelations that during World War II he had been an intelligence officer in an army unit responsible for transporting Jews to death camps. His election led to some diplomatic isolation of Austria, and in 1991 he announced that he would not run for reelection.

Wales (Welsh *Cymru*) Principality of; constituent part of the United Kingdom, in the west between the British Channel and the Irish Sea.
area 8,021 sq mi/20,780 sq km
capital Cardiff
cities Swansea
features Snowdonia mountains (Snowdon 3,561 ft/1,085 m, the highest point in England and Wales) in the NW and in the SE the Black Mountain, Brecon Beacons, and Black Forest ranges; rivers Severn, Wye, Usk, and Dee
exports traditional industries (coal and steel) have declined, but varied modern and high-technology ventures are being developed. Tourism is important
population (1987) 2,836,000
language Welsh 19% (1981), English
religion Nonconformist Protestant denominations; Roman Catholic minority
government returns 38 members to the UK Parliament.

Wales: Counties

County	*Administrative Headquarters*	*Area sq km*
Clwyd	Mold	2,420
Dyfed	Carmarthen	5,770
Gwent	Cwmbran	1,380
Gwynedd	Caernarvon	3,870
Mid Glamorgan	Cardiff	1,020
Powys	Llandrindod Wells	5,080
South Glamorgan	Cardiff	420
West Glamorgan	Swansea	820
		20,780

Wales: history for ancient history, see also ◊Britain, ancient.
c. 400 BC Wales occupied by Celts from central Europe.
AD 50–60 Wales became part of the Roman Empire.
c. 200 Christianity adopted.
c. 450–600 Wales became the chief Celtic stronghold in the west since the Saxons invaded and settled in S Britain. The Celtic tribes united against England.
8th century Frontier pushed back to ◊Offa's Dyke.
9th–11th centuries Vikings raided the coasts. At this time Wales was divided into small states organized on a clan basis, although princes such as Rhodri (844–878), Howel the Good (c. 904–949), and Griffith ap Llewelyn (1039–1063) temporarily united the country.
11th–12th centuries Continual pressure on Wales from the Normans across the English border was resisted, notably by ◊Llewelyn I and II.
1277 Edward I of England accepted as overlord by the Welsh.
1284 Edward I completed the conquest of Wales that had been begun by the Normans.
1294 Revolt against English rule put down by Edward I.
1350–1500 Welsh nationalist uprisings against the English; the most notable was that led by Owen Glendower.
1485 Henry Tudor, a Welshman, became Henry VII of England.
1536–43 Acts of Union united England and Wales after conquest under Henry VIII. Wales sent representatives to the English Parliament; English law was established in Wales; English became the official language.
18th century Evangelical revival made Nonconformism a powerful factor in Welsh life. A strong coal and iron industry developed in the south.
19th century The miners and ironworkers were militant supporters of Chartism, and Wales became a stronghold of labor unionism and socialism.
1893 University of Wales founded.

Wałesa Labor union leader Lech Wałesa, who founded Solidarity, was elected president of Poland in 1990.

1920s–30s Wales suffered from industrial depression; unemployment reached 21% 1937, and a considerable exodus of population took place.

post-1945 Growing nationalist movement and a revival of the language, earlier suppressed or discouraged (there is a Welsh television channel).

1966 Plaid Cymru, the Welsh National Party, returned its first member to Westminster.

1979 Referendum rejected a proposal for limited home rule.

1988 Bombing campaign against real-estate agents selling Welsh properties to English buyers.

For other history, see also ◊England, history; ◊United Kingdom.

Wałesa Lech 1947– . Polish trade-union leader and president of Poland from 1990, founder of ◊Solidarity (Solidarność) in 1980, an organization, independent of the Communist Party, which forced substantial political and economic concessions from the Polish government 1980–81 until being outlawed. Nobel Peace Prize 1983.

Wałesa, as an electrician at the Lenin shipyard at Gdańsk, became a trade-union organizer. A series of strikes led by Wałesa, a devout Catholic, drew wide public support. In Dec 1981 Solidarity was outlawed and Wałesa arrested, following the imposition of martial law by the Polish leader General Jaruzelski. Wałesa was released in 1982.

After leading a further series of strikes during 1988, he negotiated an agreement with the Jaruzelski government in Apr 1989 under the terms of which Solidarity once more became legal and a new, semipluralist "Socialist democracy" was established. The coalition government elected in Sept 1989 was dominated by Solidarity. In 1990 elections he overcame objections within the solidarity movement to win the presidency.

Wales, Church in the Welsh Anglican Church, independent from the ◊Church of England.

The Welsh church became strongly Protestant in the 16th century, but in the 17th and 18th centuries declined from being led by a succession of English-appointed bishops. Disestablished by an act of Parliament in 1920, with its endowments appropriated, the Church in Wales today comprises six dioceses (with bishops elected by an electoral college of clergy and lay people) with an archbishop elected from among the six bishops.

Wales, Prince of title conferred on the eldest son of the United Kingdom's sovereign. Prince ◊Charles was invested as 21st prince of Wales at Caernarvon in 1969 by his mother, Elizabeth II.

walkabout Australian Aboriginal term for a nomadic ritual return into the bush by an urbanized Aboriginal; also used more casually for any similar excursion.

Walker Alice 1944– . US poet, novelist, critic, and essay writer. She was active in the US civil-rights movement in the 1960s and, as a black woman, wrote about the double burden of racist and sexist oppression that such women bear. Her novel *The Color Purple* 1983 (film, 1985) won the Pulitzer Prize.

Born in Eatonton, Georgia, she also wrote the novels *The Third Life of Grange Copeland* 1970, *Meridian* 1976, and *The Temple of My Familiar* 1989. Walker's collections of poems include *Once* 1968 and *Revolutionary Petunias* 1973; her short stories and essays are collected in *Love and Trouble: Stories of Black Women* 1973 and *In Search of Our Mothers' Gardens: Womanist Prose* 1983.

Walker Jimmy (James John) 1881–1946. US public official. In 1925 Walker was elected mayor of New York City and in that position became a popular personality, familiarly known to his constituents as "Jimmy." Although Walker made great improvements to the city's infrastructure, he was charged with graft and forced to resign 1932.

Born in New York, Walker attended St Francis Xavier College and was admitted to the bar 1912. Becoming active in Democratic party politics, he served in the state assembly 1909–15 and the state senate 1915–25, where he became a protégé of Al Smith.

Walker William 1824–1860. US adventurer who for a short time established himself as president of a republic in NW Mexico, and was briefly president of Nicaragua 1856–57. He was eventually executed and is now regarded as a symbol of US imperialism in Central America.

wallaby any of various small and medium-sized members of the ◊kangaroo family.

Wallace Alfred Russel 1823–1913. English naturalist who collected animal and plant specimens in South America and SE Asia, and independently arrived at a theory of evolution by natural selection similar to that proposed by ◊Charles Darwin.

Wallace George Corley 1919– . US politician who was opposed to integration. He was governor of Alabama 1963–67, 1971–79, and 1983–87. He contested the presidency in 1968 on the American Independent Party ticket and in 1972 campaigned for the Democratic nomination but was shot at a rally and became partly paralyzed. Wallace moderated his staunchly anti-integration views and was elected for a fourth term as governor by a populist coalition of blacks and whites 1982. He retired 1987.

Wallace was born in Clio, Alabama, and held various state jobs before being elected to the governorship for the first time. During the 1963 integration of the University of Alabama, he defied a court order and stood on the steps to prevent access to black students; he later complied with the order. His wife served as governor 1967–71 when he was ineligible to run for a third consecutive term.

Wallace Henry Agard 1888–1965. US editor and public official. Although his father was a prominent Republican, the younger Wallace joined the Democratic party 1928. He was appointed secretary of the treasury by Franklin Roosevelt 1933 and served as vice-president during Roosevelt's third term 1941–45. Wallace later broke with Truman and, after serving as editor of the *New Republic* 1946–47, was the unsuccessful Progressive party candidate for president 1948.

Born in Adair County, Iowa, Wallace was educated at Iowa State College and in 1910 joined the staff of the family-owned periodical *Wallace's Farmer*.

Wallace Lewis "Lew" 1827–1905. US general and novelist. He served in the Mexican War and the American Civil War and subsequently became governor of New Mexico and minister to Turkey. He was credited with saving Washington, DC from capture by Confederate forces and served on the tribunal that tried those accused of conspiring to assassinate Abraham ◊Lincoln. He wrote several historical novels, including *The Fair God* 1873 and *Ben Hur* 1880.

Wallace divide or ***Wallace line*** an imaginary line running down the Lombok Strait in SE Asia, between the island of Bali and the islands of Lombok and Sulawesi. It was identified by the naturalist A R Wallace as separating the S Asian (Oriental) and Austronesian biogeographical regions, each of which has its own distinctive animals.

Subsequently, others have placed the boundary between these two regions at different points in the Malay archipelago, citing overlapping migration patterns.

Wallachia independent medieval principality, founded 1290, with allegiance to Hungary until 1330 and under Turkish rule 1387–1861, when it was united with Moldavia to form Romania.

Wallenberg Raoul 1912–1947. Swedish businessman who attempted to rescue several thousand Jews from German-occupied Budapest in 1944, during World War II.

There he tried to rescue and support Jews in safe houses, and provided them with false papers to save them from deportation to extermination camps. After the arrival of Soviet troops in Budapest, he reported to the Russian commander in Jan 1945 and then disappeared. The Soviet government later claimed that he died of a heart attack in July 1947. However, rumors persisted that he was alive and held in a Soviet prison camp.

Wallenstein Albrecht Eusebius Wenzel von 1583–1634. German general who, until his defeat at Lützen in 1632, led the Hapsburg armies in the Thirty Years' War. He was assassinated.

wallflower perennial garden plant *Cheiranthus cheiri*, family Cruciferae, with fragrant red or yellow flowers in spring.

Wallis Hal (Harold Brent) 1899–1986. US film producer. Born in Chicago, Wallis left school at an early age and worked briefly for the General Electric Co. After moving to Los Angeles 1922, he joined the staff of the Warner Brothers studios. He was named publicity director 1924 and was promoted to studio manager 1928. Wallis distinguished himself as a shrewd businessman with a keen eye for choosing potential box-office successes and was named chief executive in charge of production 1933. He left Warner Brothers 1944 to establish his own company, Hal Wallis Productions.

Wallis and Futuna two island groups in the SW Pacific, an overseas territory of France; area 143 sq mi/367 sq km; population (1983) 12,400. They produce copra, yams and bananas. Discovered by European sailors in the 18th century, the islands became a French protectorate 1842 and an overseas territory 1961.

Walloon member of a French-speaking, chiefly Celtic people of SE Belgium and adjacent areas of France.

Wall Street the financial center of the US on lower Manhattan Island in New York City. It is often synonymous with the New York Stock Exchange, which is housed there. The street was so named because of a stockade erected by the Dutch 1653.

walnut genus *Juglans* of trees of the family Juglandaceae, closely related to ◊hickories. Walnuts have pinnately compound leaves and nuts enclosed in a thick leathery husk. Six species, including the black walnut *J. nigra* and the butternut *J. cinerea* are native to the US. About 15 other species occur in South America and Eurasia. The English walnut *J. regia*, originally from SE Europe and Asia, is cultivated widely for its nut crop.

Walpole Horace, 4th Earl of Orford 1717–1797. English novelist and politician, the son of Robert Walpole. He was a Whig member of Parliament 1741–67. He converted his house at Strawberry Hill, Twickenham (then a separate town SW of London), into a Gothic castle; his *The Castle of*

walnut

Otranto 1764 established the genre of the Gothic, or "romance of terror," novel.

Walpole Robert, 1st Earl of Orford 1676–1745. British Whig politician, the first "prime minister" as First Lord of the Treasury and chancellor of the Exchequer 1715–17 and 1721–42. He encouraged trade and tried to avoid foreign disputes (until forced into the War of Jenkins's Ear with Spain in 1739).

Opponents thought his foreign policies worked to the advantage of France. He held favor with George I and George II, struggling against ◊Jacobite intrigues, and received an earldom when he eventually retired in 1742.

Walpurga, St English abbess who preached Christianity in Germany. Walpurgis Night, the night of May 1 (one of her feast days), became associated with witches' sabbaths and other superstitions. Her feast day is Feb 25.

Walras Léon 1834–1910. French economist. In his *Éléments d'économie politique pure* 1874–77 he attempted to develop a unified model for general equilibrium theory (a hypothetical situation in which demand equals supply in all markets). He also originated the theory of diminishing marginal utility of a good (the increased value to a person of consuming more of a product).

walrus Arctic marine carnivorous mammal *Odobenus rosmarus* of the same family (Otaridae) as the eared ◊seals. It can reach 13 ft/4 m in length, and weigh up to 3,000 lb/1,400 kg. It has webbed flippers, a bristly moustache, and large tusks. It is gregarious except at breeding time and feeds mainly on mollusks. It has been hunted close to extinction for its ivory tusks, hide, and blubber. The Alaskan walrus is rarer than the African elephant, and is close to extinction.

Walsall industrial town (castings, tubes, electrical equipment, leather goods) in the West Midlands, England, 8 mi/13 km NW of Birmingham; population (1981) 179,000.

Walsh Raoul 1887–1981. US film director who was originally an actor. He made a number of outstanding films, including *The Thief of Baghdad* 1924, *The Roaring Twenties* 1939, and *White Heat* 1949. He retired in 1964.

Walther von der Vogelweide c. 1170–1230. German poet, greatest of the ◊Minnesingers, whose songs dealt mainly with courtly love. Of noble birth, he lived in his youth at the Austrian ducal court in Vienna, adopting a wandering life after the death of his patron in 1198. His lyrics deal mostly with love, but also with religion and politics.

walrus

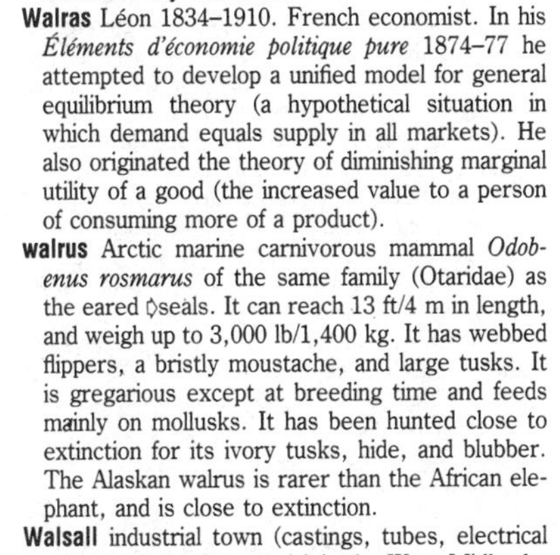

Walton Ernest 1903– . Irish physicist who, as a young doctoral student at the Cavendish laboratory in Cambridge, England, collaborated with John ◊Cockcroft on investigating the structure of the atom. In 1932 they succeeded in splitting the atom; for this experiment they shared the 1951 Nobel Prize for Physics.

Walton Izaak 1593–1683. English author of the classic fishing text *Compleat Angler* 1653. He was born in Stafford, and settled in London as an ironmonger. He also wrote short biographies of the poets George Herbert and John Donne and the theologian Richard Hooker.

Walton William (Turner) 1902–1983. English composer. Among his works are *Façade* 1923, a series of instrumental pieces designed to be played in conjunction with the recitation of poems by Edith Sitwell; the oratorio *Belshazzar's Feast* 1931; and *Variations on a Theme by Hindemith* 1963.

waltz a ballroom dance in three-four time evolved from the Austrian *Ländler* (traditional peasants' country dance) and later made popular by the ◊Strauss family in Vienna.

Walvis Bay chief port of Namibia, SW Africa; population (1980) 26,000. It was a fishing industry with allied trades. It was a detached part (area 425 sq mi/1,100 sq km) of Cape Province from 1884 but administered by South Africa from 1922 until Namibian independence in 1990.

wampum cylindrical beads ground from sea shells, of white and purple, for ceremony, currency, and in decoration by North American Indians of the NE woodlands.

Wanamaker John 1838–1922. US retailer. Born in Philadelphia, Wanamaker worked as a delivery boy and store clerk, founding the dry goods firm of Brown and Wanamaker with his brother-in-law 1861. He established his own firm, John Wanamaker and Company, 1869. Wanamaker's greatest innovation was the development of the modern department store. Renting an abandoned railroad depot 1876, he merchandised goods in distinct departments; he publicized his stores through extensive advertising.

A staunch Republican, Wanamaker served as postmaster general in the Benjamin Harrison administration 1889–93.

Wandering Jew in medieval legend, a Jew named Ahasuerus, said to have insulted Jesus on his way to Calvary and been condemned to wander the world until the Second Coming.

Wang An 1920–1990. Chinese-born engineer, who emigrated to the US in 1945 and founded Wang Laboratories 1951; it subsequently became one of the world's largest suppliers of word-processing equipment. In 1948 he invented core memory, the world's most common computer memory in the 1950s.

Wankel engine rotary gasoline engine developed by the German engineer Felix Wankel (1902–) in the 1950s. It operates according to the same stages as the ◊four-stroke gasoline engine cycle, but these stages take place in different sectors of a figure-eight chamber in the space between the chamber walls and a triangular rotor. Power is produced once on every turn on the rotor. The Wankel engine is simpler in construction than the four-stroke piston gasoline engine, and produces rotary power directly (instead of via a crankshaft). Problems with rotor seals have prevented its widespread use.

wapiti alternate name for ◊elk.

war an act of force, usually on behalf of the state, intended to compel a declared enemy to obey the will of the other. The aim is to render the opponent incapable of further resistance by destroying its capability and will to bear arms in pursuit of its own aims. War is therefore a continuation of politics carried on with violent and destructive means, as an instrument of policy.

War and Peace a novel by Leo Tolstoy, published 1863–69. It chronicles the lives of three noble families in Russia during the Napoleonic Wars and is notable for its complex characters and optimistic tone.

waratah Australian shrub or tree of the family Proteaceae, including the crimson-flowered *Telopea speciosissima*, emblem of New South Wales.

War between the States another (usually Southern) name for the American ◊Civil War.

warbler any of two families of songbirds, order Passeriformes.

American or wood warblers (family Parulidae) are small, insect-eating forms, often brightly colored, such as the yellow warbler, prothonotary warbler, and dozens of others. This group is sometimes placed in the same family (Emberizidae) with sparrows and ◊orioles. Old World warblers (family Sylviidae) are typically slim and dull-plumaged above, lighter below, insectivorous, and fruit-eating, overwhelmingly represented in Eurasia and Africa. These are sometimes considered a subgroup of the same family (Muscicapidae) that includes thrushes.

Warburg Otto 1878–1976. German biochemist who in 1923 devised a manometer (pressure gauge) sensitive enough to measure oxygen uptake of respiring tissue. By measuring the rate that cells absorb oxygen under differing conditions, he was able to show that enzymes called cytochromes enable cells to process oxygen. Nobel Prize for Medicine 1931. Warburg also demonstrated that cancerous cells absorb less oxygen than normal cells.

war crime offense (such as murder of a civilian or a prisoner of war) that contravenes the internationally accepted laws governing the conduct of wars, particularly The Hague Convention 1907 and the Geneva Convention 1949. A key principle of the law relating to such crimes is that obedience to the orders of a superior is no defense.

Ward Artemus. Adopted name of Charles Farrar Browne 1834–1867. US humorist who achieved great popularity with comic writings such as *Artemus Ward: His Book* 1862 and *Artemus Ward: His Travels* 1865, and with his deadpan lectures. He influenced Mark Twain.

Ward Montgomery 1843–1913. US retailer. He pioneered the mass marketing of clothing and personal items through the mails. Serving the needs of farm families in remote rural areas, Ward constantly expanded his catalog from its inception in 1872. Although Ward himself retired from the day-to-day operations of the firm in 1886, the business continued to expand, eventually moving its headquarters to the Ward Tower in Chicago 1900.

Born in Chatham, New Jersey, Ward left school in his teens to become a traveling representative for several Midwestern dry goods firms.

warfarin poison that induces fatal internal bleeding in rats; neutralized with sodium hydroxide, it is used in medicine as an anticoagulant: it prevents blood clotting by inhibiting the action of vitamin K. It can be taken orally and begins to act several days after the initial dose.

Warfarin is a crystalline powder, $C_{19}H_{16}O_4$. ◊Heparin may be given in treatment at the same time and discontinued when warfarin takes effect. It is often given as a preventive measure, to reduce the risk of ◊thrombosis or ◊embolism after major surgery.

Warhol Andy 1928–1987. US Pop artist and filmmaker. He made his name in 1962 with paintings of Campbell's soup cans, Coca-Cola bottles, and film stars. In his New York studio, the Factory, he produced series of garish silk-screen prints. His films include the semidocumentary *Chelsea Girls* 1966 and *Trash* 1970.

Warhol was born in Pittsburgh, where he studied art. In the 1950s he became a leading commercial artist in New York. With the breakthrough of

Pop art, his bizarre personality and flair for self-publicity made him a household name.

He was a pioneer of multimedia events with the Exploding Plastic Inevitable touring show in 1966 featuring the Velvet Underground (see Lou ◊Reed). In 1968 he was shot and nearly killed by a radical feminist, Valerie Solanas.

In the 1970s and 1980s Warhol was primarily a society portraitist, although his activities included a magazine (*Interview*) and a cable TV show.

His early silk-screen series dealt with car crashes and suicides, Marilyn Monroe, Elvis Presley, and flowers. His films, beginning with *Sleep* 1963 and ending with *Bad* 1977, have a strong documentary or improvisational element. His books include *The Philosophy of Andy Warhol (From A to B and Back Again)* 1975 and *Popism* 1980.

warlord in China, any of the provincial leaders who took advantage of central government weakness, after the death of the first president of Republican China 1912, to organize their own private armies and fiefdoms. They engaged in civil wars until Chiang Kai-shek's Northern Expedition against them 1926, but they exerted power until the Communists came to power under Mao Zedong 1949.

Warner Deborah 1959– . British theater director. Discarding period costume and furnished sets, she adopted an uncluttered approach to the classics, including productions of many Shakespeare plays and Sophocles's *Electra*.

Warner Robins city in central Georgia, S of Macon. Industries include nuts, fruits, and airplane parts; population (1990) 43,726.

warning coloration in biology, an alternative term for ◊aposematic coloration.

War of 1812 a war between the US and Britain caused by British interference with American trade (shipping) as part of Britain's economic warfare against Napoleonic France. US sailors were impressed from American ships, and a blockade was imposed on US shipping by Britain. Also, British assistance was extended to Indians harassing the NW settlements (see ◊Tecumseh). President Madison authorized the beginning of hostilities against the British on the high seas and in Canada. US forces failed twice in attempts to invade British-held Canada but achieved important naval victories, while in 1814 British forces occupied Washington, DC and burned the White House and the Capitol. A treaty signed at Ghent, Belgium, in Dec 1814 ended the conflict. Before news of the treaty reached the US, American troops under Andrew ◊Jackson defeated the British at New Orleans 1815.

War Powers Act US Congressional legislation passed 1973, over President Nixon's veto, aimed at restricting the president's introduction of US forces into potentially hostile situations without Congressional declaration of war. The measure calls for notification of Congress by the president of plans to dispatch military forces and sets a time limit by which either Congress must approve or the forces must be withdrawn. The act has been considered unconstitutional by each president since its passage, and its provisions generally have been ignored by both Congress and presidents.

warrant officer an officer in the US armed forces who holds office on a warrant rather than a commission. Such officers rank above noncommissioned officers but below commissioned officers.

Warren city in NE Ohio, on the Mahoning river, NW of Youngstown. Industries include steel and iron products, tools, and paint; population (1990) 50,793.

Warren Earl 1891–1974. US jurist and chief justice of the US Supreme Court 1953–69. He served as governor of California 1943–53. As chief justice, he presided over a moderately liberal court, taking a stand against racial discrimination and ruling that segregation in schools was unconstitutional. He headed the commission that investigated 1963–64 President Kennedy's assassination.

Born in Los Angeles, Warren graduated from the University of California at Berkeley 1914 and practiced law in the San Francisco area. He became active in the Republican party and in 1938 was appointed California's attorney general, which paved the way for the governorship. He was appointed to the Supreme Court by President Eisenhower. His most important ruling was in *Brown* v *Board of Education* 1954, in which the Court unanimously ruled against segregation in public schools and made it illegal to classify races for discrimination purposes. The Warren Court oversaw the reapportionment by population of many election districts in cases such as *Reynolds* v *Sims* 1964. Other rulings involved individual rights, especially in criminal procedures, as in *Miranda* v *Arizona* 1966, which ruled in favor of a defendant being informed of his or her rights at the time of arrest. The Warren Commission 1963–64, appointed by President Johnson, reached the controversial conclusion that no conspiracy was involved in the assassination of President Kennedy. Warren retired from the Court 1969 and was succeeded by Warren ◊Burger.

Warren Joseph 1741–1775. Colonial American physician and revolutionary leader. Born in Roxbury, Massachusetts, and educated at Harvard, Warren established a private medical practice in Boston. With the enactment of the Stamp Act 1765, he became a full-time political activist. As a leader of the Massachusetts opposition to British colonial rule, Warren served in the provincial congress and committee of safety. In April 1775 he sent Paul Revere and William Dawes to warn the countryside of the approach of the British. Appointed major general of the Massachusetts militia, he was killed at the Battle of Bunker Hill.

Warren Robert Penn 1905–1989. US author. Born in Guthrie, Kentucky, and educated at Vanderbilt University, Warren received an MA degree from Berkeley 1927 and became a leading figure in the Southern literary revival. A faculty member at Vanderbilt 1931–34; Louisiana State University 1934–42; the University of Minnesota 1942–50; and Yale University 1950–56, 1961–73, Warren was a respected critic, poet, and novelist. His novel *All the King's Men* won the Pulitzer Prize for Fiction 1947. Among his collections of poems are *Brother to Dragons* 1953 and *Promises*, which won the Pulitzer Prize for Poetry 1958. He won this prize a second time 1979 and was the first official US poet laureate 1986–88.

Warrington industrial town (metal goods, chemicals, brewing) in Cheshire, NW England, on the Mersey river; population (1985) 178,000. A trading center since Roman times, it was designated a "new town" 1968.

Warrumbungle Range mountain range of volcanic origin in New South Wales, Australia. ◊Siding Spring Mountain 2,819 ft/859 m is the site of an observatory; the Breadknife is a 90-m/300-ft high rock only 5 ft/1.5 m wide; the highest point is Mount Exmouth 4,030 ft/1,228 m. The name is Aboriginal and means "broken-up small mountains."

Warsaw (Polish *Warszawa*) capital of Poland, on the river Vistula; population (1985) 1,649,000. Industries include engineering, food processing, printing, clothing, and pharmaceuticals.

Founded in the 13th century, it replaced Kraków as capital in 1595. Its university was founded in 1818. It was taken by the Germans Sept 27, 1939, and 250,000 Poles were killed during two months of street fighting that started Aug 1, 1944. It was finally liberated Jan 17, 1945. The old city was virtually destroyed in World War II but has been reconstructed. Marie Curie was born here.

Warsaw Pact military alliance established 1955 between the USSR and E European communist states as a response to the admission of West Germany into NATO. The pact was formally dissolved on July 1, 1991, a recognition of the vastly changed political and military situation in Europe.

wart hog

warship a fighting ship armed and crewed for war. The supremacy of the battleship at the beginning of the 20th century was superseded during World War I by the development of ◊submarine attack, and was rendered obsolete in World War II with the growth of long-range air attack. Today the largest and most important surface warships are the ◊aircraft carriers.

wart protuberance composed of a local overgrowth of skin. The common wart (*verruca vulgaris*) is due to a virus infection. It usually disappears spontaneously within two years, but can be treated with peeling applications, burning away (cautery), or freezing (cryosurgery).

wart hog African wild ◊pig *Phacochoerus aethiopicus*, which has a large head with a bristly mane, fleshy pads beneath the eyes, and four large tusks. It has short legs and can grow to 2.5 ft/80 cm at the shoulder.

Warwick Richard Neville, Earl of 1428–1471. English politician, called the Kingmaker. During the Wars of the ◊Roses he fought at first on the Yorkist side against the Lancastrians, and was largely responsible for placing Edward IV on the throne. Having quarrelled with him, he restored Henry VI in 1470, but was defeated and killed by Edward at Barnet, Hertfordshire.

washing soda $Na_2CO_3.10H_2O$ (technical name sodium carbonate decahydrate) substance added to washing water to "soften" it (see ◊water softener).

Washington state in NW US; nickname Evergreen State/Chinook State

area 68,206 sq mi/176,700 sq km

capital Olympia

cities Seattle, Spokane, Tacoma

population (1990) 4,866,692

features Columbia River; national parks: Olympic (Olympic Mountains), Mount Rainier (Cascade Range), North Cascades; 90 dams

products apples and other fruits, potatoes, livestock, fish, timber, processed food, wood products, paper and allied products, aircraft and aerospace equipment, aluminum

famous people William E Boeing, Bing Crosby, William O Douglas, Jimi Hendrix, Mary McCarthy, Theodore Roethke

history explored by the Spanish, British, and Americans in the 18th century; settled from 1811;

Washington

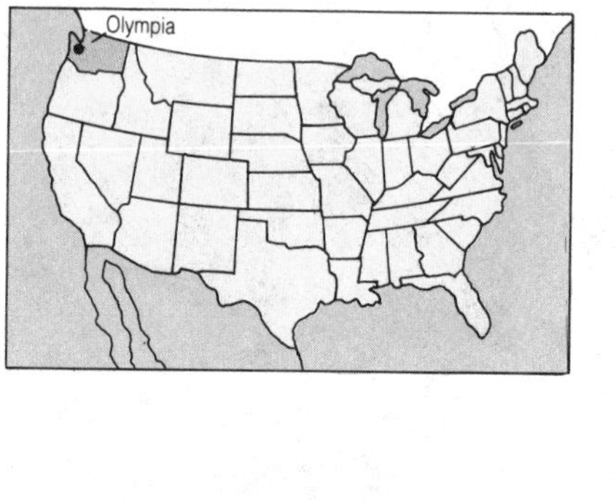
Olympia

***Washington** Teacher and reformer Booker T Washington, who founded Tuskegee Institute (1881) to improve higher education opportunities for blacks.*

***Washington** The 1st president of the United States of America, George Washington, a Federalist. 1789–1797.*

rival American and British territorial claims threatened war in the early 1840s that was settled by the Oregon Treaty 1846; became a territory 1853; arrival of transcontinental railroad 1883; statehood 1889; radical labor activity repressed 1919. The New Deal era brought many public-works projects, and Boeing became the largest employer in World War II. Mount St Helens erupted here 1980, and many in the state are now fighting to close the antiquated and dangerous nuclear plant at Hanford.

Washington Booker T(aliaferro) 1856–1915. US educationor, pioneer in higher education for black people in the South. He was the founder and first principal of Tuskegee Institute, Alabama, in 1881, originally a training college for blacks, which has become a respected academic institution. He maintained that economic independence was the way to achieve social equality.

Washington George 1732–1799. Commander of the American forces during the Revolutionary War and 1st president of the US 1789–97, known as "the father of his country." An experienced soldier, he had fought in campaigns against the French during the ◊French and Indian War. He was elected to the Virginia House of Burgesses 1759 and was a leader of the Virginia militia, gaining valuable exposure to wilderness fighting. As a strong opponent of the British government's policy, he sat in the Continental Congresses of 1774 and 1775, and on the outbreak of the ◊American Revolution was chosen commander in chief of the Continental army. After many setbacks, he accepted the surrender of British general Cornwallis at Yorktown 1781.

After the war Washington retired to his Virginia estate, Mount Vernon, but in 1787 he reentered politics as president of the Constitutional Convention in Philadelphia and was elected US president 1789. Although he attempted to draw his ministers from all factions, his aristocratic outlook alienated his secretary of state, Thomas Jefferson, with whose resignation in 1793 the two-party system originated. Washington accepted the fiscal policy championed by Alexander ◊Hamilton and oversaw the payment of the foreign and domestic debt incurred by the new nation. He also shaped the powers of the presidency, assuming some implied powers not specified in the Constitution—among them, the power to create a national bank.

Washington was reelected president 1793 but refused to serve a third term, setting a precedent that was followed until 1940. In his farewell address 1796, he maintained that the US should avoid European quarrels and entangling alliances. He died and was buried at Mount Vernon.

Washington Convention an alternate name for ◊CITES, the international agreement that regulates trade in endangered species.

Washington, DC (District of Columbia) national capital of the US, on the Potomac River

area 69 sq mi/180 sq km

population (1990) metro, 3,923,574; city, 606,900

features designed by French engineer Pierre L'Enfant (1754–1825) and completed by Andrew Ellicott and Benjamin Banneker. Among buildings of architectural note are the Capitol, the Pentagon, the White House, the Washington Monument, and the Jefferson and Lincoln memorials. The National Gallery has an outstanding collection of paintings; libraries include the Library of Congress, the National Archives, and the Folger Shakespeare Library. The Smithsonian Institution and its several museums are on the National Mall

history The District of Columbia, initially land ceded from Maryland 1788 and Virginia 1789, was established by an act of Congress 1790–91 and was first used as the seat of Congress Dec 1, 1800. The Virginia portion was returned 1846. The right to vote in national elections was not granted to residents until 1961. Local self-rule began 1975.

Wash, the bay of the North Sea between Norfolk and Lincolnshire, England.

wasp any of several families of winged stinging insects of the order Hymenoptera, characterized by a thin stalk between the thorax and the abdomen. Wasps can be social or solitary. Among social wasps, the queens devote themselves to egg laying, the fertilized eggs producing female workers; the males come from unfertilized eggs and have no sting. The larvae are fed on insects, but the mature wasps feed mainly on fruit and sugar. In winter, the fertilized queens hibernate, but the other wasps die.

Paper wasps, family Vespidae, include the common paper wasp *Polistes annularis*, hornets and yellow jackets (both genus *Vespula*). Potter wasps, mason wasps, and mud daubers all use mud with which to construct their nests.

Wassermann August von 1866–1925. German professor of medicine. In 1907 he discovered a diagnostic blood test for ◊syphilis, known as the Wassermann reaction.

waste materials that are no longer needed and are discarded. Examples are household waste, industrial waste (which usually contains toxic chemicals), medical waste (which may contain organisms that cause disease), and nuclear waste (which is ◊radioactive; see also ◊nuclear safety). Waste may be reused or not, safe or toxic; by

Washington DC *The Capitol building (1793) in Washington DC, chosen to be the capital of the US in 1790 by George Washington.*

◊recycling, some materials in waste can be reclaimed for further use. In the US, 40 tons of solid waste are generated annually per person.

waste disposal depositing waste. Methods of waste disposal vary according to the materials in the waste and include incineration, burial at designated sites, and dumping at sea. Organic waste can be treated and reused as fertilizer (see ◊sewage disposal). Nuclear and toxic waste is usually buried or dumped at sea, although this does not negate the danger of ◊radioactivity. See also ◊nuclear safety.

Waste disposal is an increasing problem in the late 20th century. Environmental groups, such as Greenpeace and Friends of the Earth, are campaigning for more recycling, a change in lifestyle so that less waste (from packaging and containers to nuclear materials) is produced, and safer methods of disposal.

Waste Land, The a poem by T S Eliot, first published 1922. It expressed the prevalent mood of depression after World War I and is a key work of Modernism in literature.

watch portable timepiece. In the early 20th century increasing miniaturization, mass production, and, in World War I, the advantages of the wristband led to the watch moving from the pocket to the wrist. Watches were also subsequently made waterproof, antimagnetic, self-winding, and shock-resistant. In 1957 the electric watch was developed, and in the 1970s came the digital watch, in which all moving parts are dispensed with.

history Traditional mechanical watches with analog dials (hands) are based on the invention by Peter Henlein (1480–1542) of the mainspring as the energy store. By 1675 the invention of the balance spring allowed watches to be made small enough to move from waist to pocket. By the 18th century pocketwatches were accurate, and by the 20th century wrist watches were introduced. In the 1950s battery-run electromagnetic watches were developed; in the 1960s electronic watches were marketed, which use the ◊piezoelectric oscillations of a quartz crystal to mark time and an electronic circuit to drive the hands. In the 1970s quartz watches without moving parts were developed—the solid-state watch with a display of digits. Some include a tiny calculator and functions such as date, alarm, stopwatch, and reminder beeps.

water H_2O liquid without color, taste, or odor. It is an oxide of hydrogen. Water begins to freeze solid at 32°F/0°C, and to boil at 212°F/100°C. When liquid, it is virtually incompressible; frozen, it expands by 1/11 of its volume. At 39.2°F/4°C, one cubic centimeter of water has a mass of one gram, its maximum density, forming the unit of specific gravity. It has the highest known specific heat and acts as an efficient solvent, particularly when hot. Most of the world's water is in the sea; less than 0.01% is fresh water.

It occurs as standing (oceans, lakes) and running (rivers, streams) water, rain, and vapor and supports all forms of Earth's life.

Water covers 70% of the Earth's surface. Water supply in sparsely populated regions usually comes from underground water rising to the surface in natural springs, supplemented by pumps and wells. Urban sources are deep artesian wells, rivers, and reservoirs, usually formed from enlarged lakes or dammed and flooded valleys,

wasp

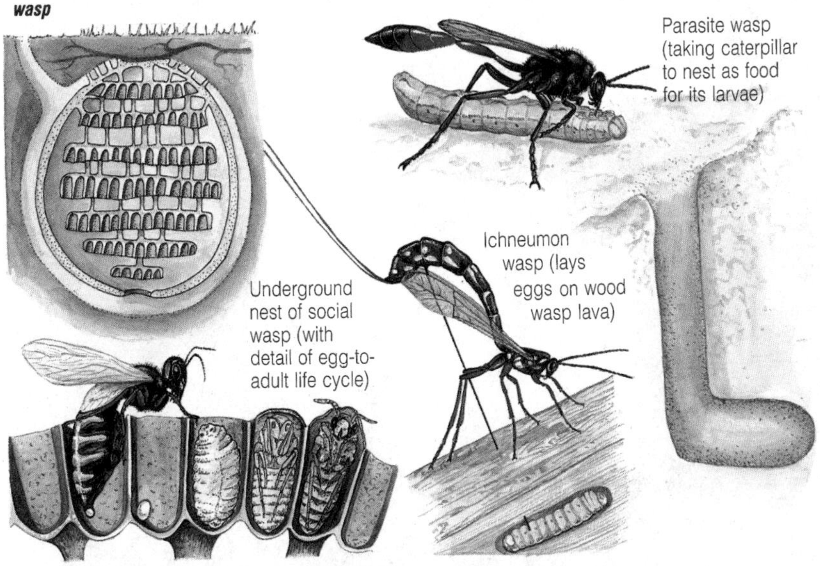
Parasite wasp (taking caterpillar to nest as food for its larvae)
Ichneumon wasp (lays eggs on wood wasp lava)
Underground nest of social wasp (with detail of egg-to-adult life cycle)

from which water is conveyed by pipes, conduits, and aqueducts to filter beds. As water seeps through layers of shingle, gravel, and sand, harmful organisms are removed and the water is then distributed by pumping or gravitation through mains and pipes. Often other substances are added to the water, such as chlorine and fluorine; ◊aluminum sulfate is the most widely used chemical in water treatment. In towns, besides industrial demands, domestic and municipal (road washing, sewage) needs account for about 30 gal/135 l per head each day. In coastal desert areas, such as the Arabian peninsula, desalination plants remove salt from sea water. The Earth's waters, both fresh and saline, have been polluted by industrial and domestic chemicals, some of which are toxic and others radioactive.

Water Babies, The a fantasy by British author Charles ◊Kingsley, published in England 1863. Tom, an orphan child, is employed to climb up chimneys and clear out the soot. While engaged in this task, he inadvertently frightens a girl, Ellie, and runs away. He drowns and is immortalized as an amphibious "water baby." After redeeming his moral character by the instruction of Mrs Bedonebyasyoudid and Mrs Doasyouwouldbedoneby, Tom is reunited with Ellie, who drowns while trying to reach him.

water boatman any water ◊bug of the family Corixidae that feeds on plant debris and algae. It has a flattened body 0.6 in/1.5 cm long, with oarlike legs.

The name is sometimes also used for the backswimmers, genus *Notonecta*, which are superficially similar, but which can fly and which belong to a different family (Notonectidae) of bugs.

water-borne disease disease associated with poor water supply. In the Third World four-fifths of all illness is caused by water-borne diseases, with ◊diarrhea being the leading cause of childhood death. Malaria, carried by mosquitoes dependent on stagnant water for breeding, affects 400 million people every year and kills five million. Polluted water is also a problem in industrialized nations, where industrial dumping of chemicals, hazardous, and ◊radioactive wastes cause a range of disease from ◊headache to ◊cancer. See also ◊radiation sickness.

waterbuck any of several African ◊antelopes of the genus *Kobus* which usually inhabit swampy tracts and reedbeds. They vary in size from 6–7.25 ft/1.4–2.1 m long and are up to 4.5 ft/1.4 m tall at the shoulder, and have long brown fur. The large curved horns, normally carried only by the males, have corrugated surfaces. Some species have white patches on the buttocks. Lechwe, kor, and defassa are alternative names for some of the species.

Waterbury city in W Connecticut, on the Naugatuck River; population (1990) 108,961. Products include clocks, watches, brass and copper ware, and plastics. It was founded 1674.

watercolor painting method of painting with pigments mixed with water, known in China as early as the 3rd century. The art as practiced today began in England in the 18th century with the work of Paul Sandby and was developed by Thomas Girtin and J M W Turner. Other watercolorists were Raoul Dufy, Paul Cézanne, and John Marin.

The technique of watercolor painting requires great skill since its transparency rules out overpainting, and many artists prefer acrylic paint which, as well as drying rapidly, is easier to handle.

watercress perennial aquatic plant *Nasturtium officinale* of the crucifer family, found in Europe and Asia, and cultivated as a salad crop.

water cycle in ecology, the natural circulation of water through the ◊biosphere. Water is lost from the Earth's surface to the atmosphere either by evaporation from the surface of lakes, rivers, and oceans or through the transpiration of plants. This atmospheric water forms clouds that condense to deposit moisture on the land and sea as rain or snow. The water that collects on land flows to the ocean in streams and rivers.

waterfall a cascade of water in a stream or river, which occurs when an area of underlying soft rock has been eroded to form a steep, vertical drop. As the river ages, continuing erosion causes the waterfall to move upstream and lose height until it becomes a series of rapids, and eventually disappears.

major waterfalls

Name and location	*Total drop m*	*ft*
Angel Falls (Venezuela)	979	3,212
Yosemite (US)	739	2,425
Mardalsfossen—South (Norway)	655	2,149
Tugela Falls (South Africa)	614	2,014
Cuquenan (Venezuela)	610	2,000
Sutherland (South Island, New Zealand)	580	1,903
Takkakaw Falls (Canada)	503	1,650
Ribbon Fall, Yosemite (US)	491	1,612
Great Karamang River Falls (Guyana)	488	1,600
Mardalsfossen—North (Norway)	468	1,535
Della Falls (Canada)	440	1,443
Gavarnie (France)	422	1,385
Skjeggedal (Norway)	420	1,378
Glass Falls (Brazil)	404	1,325
Krimml (Austria)	400	1,312
Trummelbach (Switzerland)	400	1,312
Silver Strand Falls, Yosemite (US)	357	1,170
Wallaman, Stony Creek (Australia)	346	1,137
Wollomombi (Australia)	335	1,100
Cusiana River Falls (Colombia)	300	984
Giessbach (Switzerland)	300	984
Skykkjedalsfossen (Norway)	300	984
Staubbach (Switzerland)	300	984

waterflea any aquatic crustacean in the order Cladocera, of which there are over 400 species. The commonest species is *Daphnia pulex*, used in the pet trade to feed tropical fish.

Waterford port and county town of County Waterford, SE Republic of Ireland, on the Suir; population (1986) 41,000. Handmade Waterford crystal glass (34% lead content instead of the normal 24%) was made here until 1851 and again from 1951.

waterfowl any water bird, but especially any member of the family Anatidae, which consists of ducks, geese, and swans.

Watergate US political scandal, named after the building in Washington, DC that housed the Democrats' campaign headquarters in the 1972 presidential election. Five men, hired by the Republican Committee to Re-elect the President (CREEP), were caught after breaking in to the Watergate with complex electronic surveillance equipment. Over the next two years, investigations by the media and a Senate committee revealed that the White House was implicated in the break-in, and that there was a "slush fund," used to finance unethical activities.

In Aug 1974, President ◊Nixon was forced by the Supreme Court to surrender to Congress tape recordings of conversations he had held with administration officials, and these indicated his complicity in a cover-up. Nixon resigned rather than face virtually certain impeachment for obstruction of justice and other crimes, the only US president to have left office through resignation.

water hyacinth tropical aquatic plant *Eichhornia crassipes* of the pickerelweed family Pontederiaceae. In one growing season 25 plants can produce 2 million new plants. It is liable to choke waterways, depleting the water of nutrients and blocking the sunlight, but can be used as a purifier of sewage-polluted water as well as in making methane gas, compost, concentrated protein, paper, and baskets. Originating in South America, it now grows in more than 50 countries.

water lily aquatic plant of the family Nymphaeaceae. The fleshy roots are embedded in mud and the large round leaves float on the water. The cup-shaped flowers may be white, pink, yellow, or blue.

The white water lily *Nymphaea odorata* is common in E North America as is the yellow-flowered spatterdock *Nuphar advena*. *Victoria regia*, with leaves about 6 ft/2 m in diameter, occurs in South America.

Waterloo, Battle of battle on June 18, 1815 in which British forces commanded by Wellington defeated the French army of Emperor Napoleon near the village of Waterloo, 8 mi/13 km S of Brussels, Belgium. Wellington had 68,000 soldiers (of whom 24,000 were British, the remainder being German, Dutch, and Belgian) and Napoleon had 72,000. Napoleon found Wellington's army isolated from his allies and began a direct offensive to smash them, but the British held on until joined by the Prussians under General Blücher. Four days later Napoleon abdicated for the second and final time.

The French casualties numbered about 37,000, the British 13,000, and the Prussians 7,000.

water meadow an irrigated meadow. By flooding the land for part of each year, increased yields of hay are obtained. Water meadows were common in Italy, Switzerland, and England (from 1523).

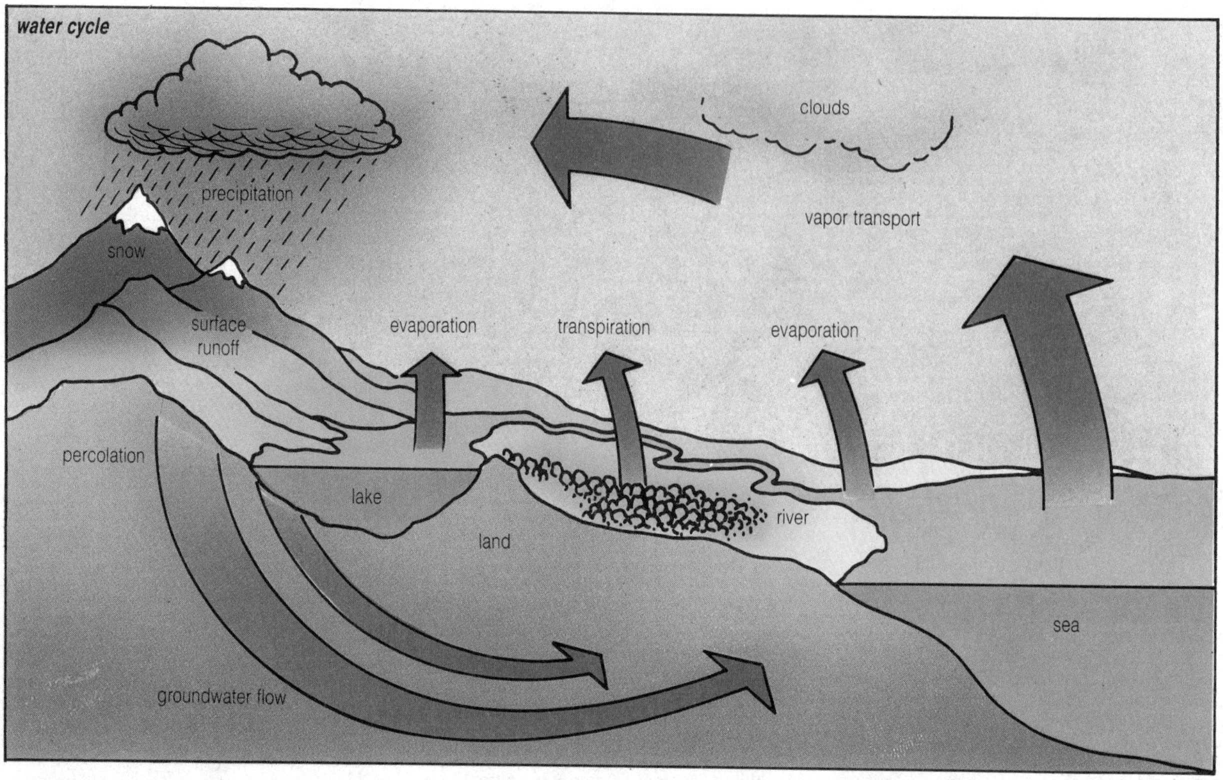
water cycle
clouds
precipitation
vapor transport
snow
surface runoff
evaporation
transpiration
evaporation
percolation
lake
land
river
sea
groundwater flow

watermelon large ◊melon *Citrullus vulgaris* of the gourd family, native to tropical Africa, with pink, white, or yellow flesh studded with black seeds and a green rind. It is widely cultivated in subtropical regions.

water mill machine that harnesses the energy in flowing water to produce mechanical power, typically for milling (grinding) grain. Water from a stream is directed against the paddles of a water wheel to make it turn. Simple gearing transfers this motion to the millstones. The modern equivalent of the water wheel is the water turbine, used in ◊hydroelectric power plants.

Although early step wheels were used in ancient China and Egypt, and parts of the Middle East, the familiar vertical water wheel came into widespread use in Roman times. There were two types: undershot, in which the wheel simply dipped into the stream, and the more powerful overshot, in which the water was directed at the top of the wheel. The Domesday Book records over 7,000 water mills in Britain. Water wheels remained a prime source of mechanical power until the development of a reliable steam engine in the 1700s, not only for milling, but also for metalworking, crushing and grinding operations, and driving machines in the early factories. The two were combined to form paddlewheel steamboats in the 18th century.

water pollution see ◊pollution, ◊water, ◊waste, ◊leaching, and ◊sewage disposal.

water polo a water sport developed in England 1869, originally called "soccer-in-water." The aim is to score goals, as in soccer, at each end of a swimming pool. It is played by two teams of seven (from squads of 13).

An inflated ball is passed among the players, who must swim around the pool without touching the bottom. A goal is scored when the ball is thrown past the goalkeeper and into a net.

water skiing a water sport in which a person is towed across water on a ski or skis, wider than those used for skiing on snow, by means of a rope (75 ft/23 m long) attached to a speedboat. Competitions are held for overall performances, slalom, tricks, and jumping.

The first person known to have "danced on water" on a wooden plank was Eliseo of Tarentum in the 14th century. In 1922, Ralph Samuelson (US) pioneered the sport as it is known today. Its governing body, the Union Internationale de Ski Nautique, was founded in 1946. World championships were first held 1949.

water softener any substance or unit that removes the hardness from water. Hardness is caused by the presence of calcium and magnesium ions, which combine with soap to form an insoluble scum, prevent lathering, and cause deposits to build up in pipes and cookware (kettle fur). A water softener replaces these ions with sodium ions, which are fully soluble and cause no scum.

water strider any of various insect-eating aquatic ◊bugs of the family Gerridae that use their long legs to skate along the water surface without breaking through.

water table level of ground below which the rocks are saturated with water. Thus above the water table water will drain downward, and where the water table cuts the surface of the ground, a spring results. The water table usually follows surface contours, and it varies with rainfall.

Regions with high water tables and dense industrialization have problems with the ◊pollution of the water table. In the US, New Jersey, Florida, and Louisiana have water tables contaminated by both industrial ◊wastes and saline seepage from the ocean.

water table

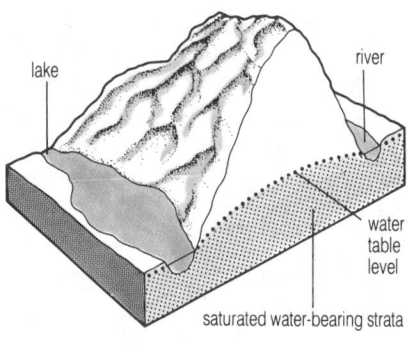

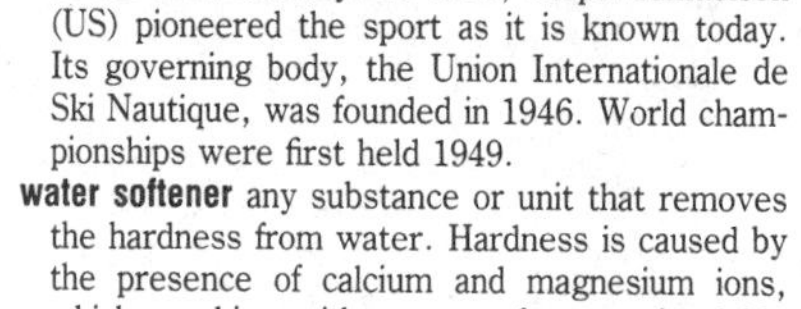
lake
river
water table level
saturated water-bearing strata

Waterton Charles 1783–1865. British naturalist who traveled extensively in South and North America 1804–24. In the UK, he was the first person to protest against pollution from industry, and created a nature preserve around his home in Yorkshire.

Watkins Gino (Henry George) 1907–1932. English polar explorer whose expeditions in Labrador and Greenland helped to open up an Arctic air route during the 1930s. He was drowned in a kayak accident while leading an expedition in Greenland.

Watson James Dewey 1928– . US biologist whose 1950s research on the molecular structure of DNA (the genetic code), in collaboration with Francis ◊Crick, earned him a shared Nobel Prize in 1962. Based on earlier works, they were able to show that DNA formed a double helix of two spiral strands held together by base pairs.

Watson John Broadus 1878–1958. US psychologist, founder of behaviorism. He rejected introspection (observation by an individual of his or her own mental processes) and regarded psychology as the study of observable behavior, within the scientific tradition.

Watson-Watt Robert Alexander 1892–1973. Scottish physicist who developed a forerunner of ◊radar. During a long career in government service (1915–1952) he proposed in 1935 a method of radiolocation of aircraft—a key factor in the Allied victory over German aircraft in World War II.

watt SI unit (abbreviation W) of power (the rate of expenditure or consumption of energy). A light bulb may use 40, 100, or 150 watts of power; an electric heater will use several kilowatts (thousands of watts).

The absolute watt is defined as the power used when one joule of work is done in one second. In electrical terms, the flow of one ampere of current through a conductor whose ends are at a potential difference of one volt uses one watt of power (watts = volts × amps). One watt equals 0.00134 horsepower. It is named after the Scottish engineer James Watt.

Watt James 1736–1819. Scottish engineer who developed the steam engine. He made ◊Newcomen's steam engine vastly more efficient by

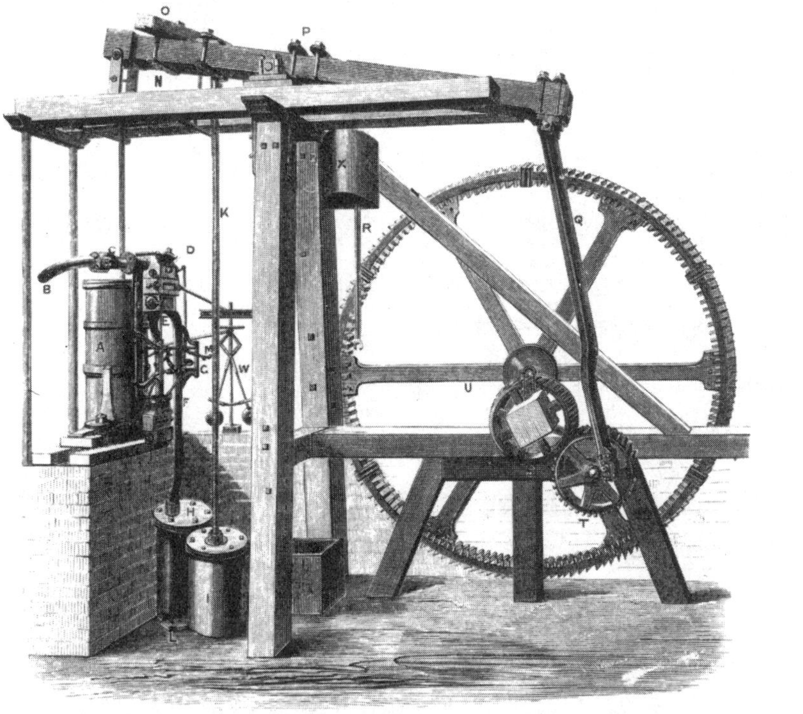

Watt *Drawing published 1865 of Scottish engineer James Watt's prototype steam engine,* Old Bess. *In this engine, reciprocating motion was turned into rotary motion by a sun-and-planet gear train.*

cooling the used steam in a condenser separate from the main cylinder.

Steam engines incorporating governors, sun-and-planet gears, and other devices of his invention were successfully built by him in partnership with Matthew Boulton and were vital to the ◊Industrial Revolution.

Watteau Jean-Antoine 1684–1721. French Rococo painter. He developed a new category of genre painting known as the *fête galante,* scenes of a kind of aristocratic pastoral fantasy world. One of these pictures, *The Embarkation for Cythera* 1717 (Louvre, Paris), won him membership in the French Academy.

Watteau was born in Valenciennes. At first inspired by Flemish genre painters, he produced tavern and military scenes. His early years in Paris, from 1702, introduced him to fashionable French paintings and in particular to decorative styles and theatrical design. He was also influenced by ◊Giorgione and ◊Rubens.

Watteau *French artist Jean-Antoine Watteau painted* Giles and his family *about 1717.*

wattle certain species of ◊acacia in Australia, where their fluffy golden flowers are the national emblem. The leathery leaves, adapted to drought conditions, further avoid loss of water through transpiration by turning their edges to the direct rays of the sun. Wattles are used for tanning and in fencing.

wattle and daub a method of constructing walls consisting of upright stakes bound together with withes (strong flexible shoots or twigs, usually of willow), and covered in mud or plaster. This was the usual way of building houses in medieval Europe; it was also the traditional method used in Australia, Africa, the Middle East, and the Far East.

Watts Alan (Witson) 1915–1973. British-born US philosopher. Educated in England, Watts was a longtime student of Eastern religions and published *The Spirit of Zen* 1936. He emigrated to the US 1939, graduated from the Seabury-Weston Theological Seminary, and was ordained in the Episcopal Church 1944. Briefly serving as chaplain at Northwestern University, he moved to California and taught philosophy at the College of the Pacific 1951–57. As a popular lecturer and author, he became a spiritual leader of the "beat generation" of the 1950s. His books include *The Way of Zen* 1957.

Waugh Evelyn (Arthur St John) 1903–1966. English novelist. His social satires include *Decline and Fall* 1928, *Vile Bodies* 1930, and *The Loved One* 1948. A Roman Catholic convert from 1930, he developed a serious concern with religious issues in *Brideshead Revisited* 1945. *The Ordeal of Gilbert Pinfold* 1957 is largely autobiographical.

Wausau city in central Wisconsin, on the Wisconsin river, NW of Green Bay. Industries include dairy products, paper products, insurance, chemicals, and plastics; population (1990) 37,060.

wave in the oceans, the formation of a ridge or swell by wind or other causes. Freak or "episodic" waves form under particular weather conditions at certain times of the year, traveling long distances in the Atlantic, Indian, and Pacific oceans. They are considered responsible for the sudden disappearance, without distress calls, of many ships. A ◊tsunami is a type of freak wave.

Freak waves become extremely dangerous when they reach the shallow waters of the continental shelves at 100 fathoms (600 ft/180 m), especially when they meet currents, for example, the Agulhas Current to the east of South Africa, and the Gulf Stream in the N Atlantic. A wave height of 112 ft/34 m has been recorded.

wave in physics, a disturbance consisting of a series of oscillations that propagate through a medium (or space). There are two types: in a longitudinal wave (such as a ◊sound wave) the disturbance is parallel to the wave's direction of travel; in a transverse wave (such as an ◊electromagnetic wave) it is perpendicular. The medium only vibrates as the wave passes; it does not travel outward from the source with the waves.

wavelength the distance between successive crests of a ◊wave. The wavelength of a light wave determines its color; red light has a wavelength of about 700 nanometers, for example. The complete range of wavelengths of electromagnetic waves is called the electromagnetic ◊spectrum.

Wavell Archibald, 1st Earl 1883–1950. British field marshal in World War II. As commander in chief Middle East, he successfully defended Egypt against Italy July 1939. He was transferred as Commander in Chief India in July 1941, and was viceroy 1943–47.

wax solid fatty substance of animal, vegetable, or mineral origin. Waxes are composed variously of ◊esters, ◊fatty acids, free ◊alcohols, and solid hydrocarbons.

Mineral waxes are obtained from petroleum and vary in hardness from the soft petroleum jelly (or petrolatum) used in ointments to the hard paraffin wax employed for making candles and waxed paper for drinks cartons.

Animal waxes include beeswax, the wool wax lanolin, and spermaceti from sperm whale oil; they are used mainly in cosmetics, ointments, and polishes. Another animal wax is tallow, a form of suet obtained from cattle and sheep's fat, once widely used to make candles and soap. Sealing wax is made from lac or shellac, a resinous substance obtained from secretions of ◊scale insects.

Vegetable waxes, which usually occur as a waterproof coating on plants that grow in hot, arid regions, include carnauba wax (from the leaves of the carnauba palm) and candelilla wax, both of which are components of hard polishes such as car waxes.

waxbill any of a group of small mainly African seed-eating birds in the family Estrildidae, order Passeriformes, which also includes the grass finches of Australia. Waxbills grow to 6 in/15 cm long, are brown and gray with yellow, red, or brown markings, and have waxy-looking red or pink beaks.

They sometimes raise the young of ◊whydahs, who lay their eggs in waxbill nests.

wax myrtle an evergreen bush or tree *Myrica cerifera* of the barberry family, native to SE North America. Its fruit consists of grayish nutlets coated with a wax that is collected for making scented candles; 1 lb/0.5 kg of nutlets immersed in hot water yields about 4 oz/115 g of wax. The fruit is eaten by ground-dwelling birds such as bobwhite and wild turkey.

waxwing any of several fruit-eating birds of order Passeriformes, family Bombycillidae. They are found in the N hemisphere. The Bohemian waxwing *B. garrulus* of North America and Eurasia is about 7 in/18 cm long, and is greyish brown above with a reddish-chestnut crest, black streak at the eye, and variegated wings. It undertakes mass migrations in some years.

wayfaring tree European shrub *Viburnum lantana* of the honeysuckle family, with clusters of fragrant white flowers, found on limy soils; naturalized in the NE US.

Wayne Anthony ("Mad Anthony") 1745–1796. American Revolutionary War officer and Indian

Wayne *Movie star John Wayne, famous for his cowboy and military films, in* The Man Who Shot Liberty Valance.

fighter. He secured a treaty 1795 that made possible the settlement of Ohio and Indiana. He built Fort Wayne, Indiana.

A surveyer and farmer, he was briefly active in politics before the Revolution. He assisted Benedict ◊Arnold in his retreat from Québec, held a variety of increasingly important commands, was with George Washington at Valley Forge 1777–78, took Stony Point, New York, and was then trapped by Cornwallis's superior force at Green Spring, Virginia, but escaped and served under General Greene in Georgia before retiring to farming and business interests. President Washington recalled him 1792 as a major general to command the Army of the West against the Indians.

Wayne John. Adopted name of Marion Morrison 1907–1979. US actor. Nicknamed "Duke" from the name of a dog he once owned, Wayne was the archetypal Western hero. His films include *Stagecoach* 1939, *Red River* 1948, *She Wore a Yellow Ribbon* 1949, *The Searchers* 1956, *Rio Bravo* 1959, *The Man Who Shot Liberty Valance* 1962, and *True Grit* 1969 (Academy Award).

Wayne also appeared in many war films, such as *The Sands of Iwo Jima* 1945, *In Harm's Way* 1965, and *The Green Berets* 1968. His other films include *The Quiet Man* 1952 and *The High and the Mighty* 1954. He was also active in conservative politics.

Waziristan mountainous territory in Pakistan, on the border with Afghanistan, inhabited by Waziris and Mahsuds.

Wazyk Adam 1905– . Polish writer who made his name with *Poem for Adults* 1955, a protest against the regime that preceded the fall of the Stalinists in 1956. In 1957 he resigned with others from the Communist Party, disappointed by First Secretary Gomulka's illiberalism. He also wrote novels and plays.

weak force one of the four ◊fundamental forces of nature, the other three being the gravitational force, the electromagnetic force, and the strong force. It causes radioactive decay and other subatomic reactions. The particle that is the carrier of the weak force is called either the ◊weakon or the intermediate vector boson (comprising the positively and negatively charged W particles and the neutral Z particle).

weakon one of the ◊gauge bosons, three particles that cannot be subdivided (the positive and negative W particle and the neutral Z particle) and are carriers of the weak force.

Weald, the (Old English "forest") area between the North and South Downs, England, once thickly wooded, and forming part of Kent, Sussex, Surrey, and Hampshire. Now an agricultural area, it produces fruit, hops, and vegetables. In the Middle Ages its timber and iron ore made it the industrial heart of England.

weapon any implement used for attack and defense, from simple clubs, spears, and bows and arrows in prehistoric times to machine guns and nuclear bombs in modern times. The first revolution in warfare came with the invention of ◊gunpowder and the development of cannons and shoulder-held guns. Many other weapons now exist, such as grenades, shells, torpedoes, rockets, and guided missiles. The ultimate in explosive weapons are the atomic (fission) and hydrogen (fusion) bombs. They release the enormous energy produced when atoms split or fuse together (see ◊nuclear warfare). There are also chemical and bacteriological weapons.

weapons, history:

13th century Gunpowder brought to the West from China (where it was long in use but only for fireworks).

about 1300 Guns invented by the Arabs, with bamboo muzzles reinforced with iron.

1346 Battle of Crécy in which gunpowder was probably used in battle for the first time.

1376 Explosive shells used in Venice.

17th century Widespread use of guns and cannon in the Thirty Years' War and English Civil War.

1800 Henry Shrapnel invented shrapnel for the British army.

1862 Machine gun invented by Richard Gatling in the Civil War and used against American Indians in the US.

1863 TNT discovered by German chemist J Wilbrand.

1867 Dynamite patented by Alfred Nobel.

1915 Poison gas (chlorine) used for the first time by the Germans in World War I.

1916 Tanks used for the first time by the British at Cambrai in World War I.

1945 First test explosion and military use of atom bomb by US against Japan in World War II.

1954–73 Vietnam War, use of chemical warfare (defoliants and other substances) by the US.

1983 Star Wars or Strategic Defense Initiative research announced by US to develop space laser and particle-beam weapons for use in space.

1991 SCUD missiles used by Iraq in ◊Gulf War.

Wear river in NE England; length 67 mi/107 km. From its source in the Pennines it flows east, past Durham to meet the North Sea at Sunderland.

weathering

Frost, wind, rain and sunshine all have a part to play in the gradual wearing away of the landscape. As soon as an area of rock is exposed on the surface of the Earth, it is attacked over time by the weather, which reduces it to sand and rubble. This material is carried downwards by gravity, rivers and glaciers and redeposited in low areas. Eventually it may be turned back into solid rock.

Frost shattering produces spiky peaks.
In mountainous areas the water that collects in rock cracks freezes regularly. As it does so, it expands, forcing the rocks apart.
ice
A combination of temperature, moisture and chemical effects can wear away the outer skin of a rock. As a result it may peel off, layer by layer. This process is known as onion-skin weathering.
The debris broken off the peaks by the frost piles up as slopes of scree.
Soft soil may be washed away by the rain. Where a boulder provides protection only the surrounding soil may be washed away, leaving the boulder on a soil pedestal.
The debris produced by weathering forms the basis of soil. It can work its way downhill in a process known as soil creep, causing trees to bend and posts to lean.
The carbon dioxide in rainwater produces weak carbonic acid. This reacts with some minerals, and causes spheroidal weathering of dolerite, the opening up of cracks called grykes in limestone, and the decay of granite into china clay.
Soil creep may give rise to a stepped appearance – terracettes – on a hillside.

weathering

Physical weathering	
temperature changes	weakening rocks by expansion and contraction
frost	wedging rocks apart by the expansion of water on freezing
rain	making loose slopes unstable
wind	wearing away rocks by sandblasting, and moving sand dunes along
unloading	the loosening of rock layers by release of pressure after the erosion and removal of those layers above
Chemical weathering	
carbonation	the breakdown of calcite by reaction with carbonic acid in rainwater
hydrolysis	the breakdown of feldspar into kaolinite by reaction with carbonic acid in rainwater
oxidation	the breakdown of iron-rich minerals due to rusting
hydration	the expansion of certain minerals due to the uptake of water
Gravity	
soil creep	the slow downslope movement of surface material
landslide	the rapid downward movement of solid material
avalanche	scouring by ice, snow, and accumulated debris
Rivers	
abrasion	wearing away stream beds and banks by trundling boulders along
corrasion	the wear on the boulders themselves as they are carried along
Glaciers	
deepening	of valleys by the weight of ice scouring of rock surfaces by embedded rocky debris
Sea	
hydraulic effect	expansion of air pockets in rocks and cliffs by constant hammering by waves
abrasion and corrasion	see *Rivers*

weasel any of various small shortlegged lithe carnivirous mammals with bushy tails, especially the genus *Mustela*, found worldwide except Australia. They feed mainly on small rodents, although some, like the mink *M. vison* hunt aquatic prey. Most are 5–10 in/12–25 cm long, excluding tail.

Included are the North American long-tailed weasel, the N hemisphere ermine or stoat, the Eurasian polecat, and the endangered North American black-footed ferret. In cold regions the coat color of several species changes to white during the winter.

weather the day-to-day variations of meteorological and climatic conditions at a particular place. See ◊meteorology and ◊climate.

weathering process by which exposed rocks are broken down by the action of rain, frost, wind, and other elements of the weather. Two types of weathering are recognized: physical and chemical. They usually occur together.

Physical weathering involves such effects as: frost wedging, in which water trapped in a crack in a rock expands on freezing and splits the rock; sand blasting, in which exposed rock faces are worn away by sand particles blown by the wind; and ◊soil creep, in which soil particles gradually move downhill under the influence of gravity.

Chemical weathering is a process by which carbon dioxide in the atmosphere combines with rainwater to produce weak carbonic acid, which may then react with certain minerals in the rocks and break them down. Examples are the solution of caverns in limestone terrains, and the breakdown of feldspars in granite to form kaolinite or kaolin, thus loosening the other minerals present—quartz and mica—which are washed away as sand.

Although physical and chemical weathering normally occur together, in some instances it is difficult to determine which type is involved. For example, onion-skin weathering, which produces rounded ◊inselbergs in arid regions, such as Ayers Rock in central Australia, may be caused by the daily physical expansion and contraction of the surface layers of the rock in the heat of the Sun, or by the chemical reaction of the minerals just beneath the surface during the infrequent rains of these areas.

weaver any small bird of the family Ploceidae, order Passeriformes, mostly about 6 in/15 cm long, which includes the house ◊sparrow. The majority of weavers are African, a few Asian. The males use grasses to weave elaborate globular nests in bushes and trees. Males are often more brightly colored than females.

Many kinds are polygamous, so build several nests, and some species build large communal nests with many chambers. One species, the red-billed African quelea *Quelea quelea,* lives and breeds in flocks numbering many thousands of individuals; the flocks migrate to follow food sources. Their destructive power can equal that of locusts.

weaving the production of ◊textile fabric by means of a loom. The basic process is the interlacing at right angles of longitudinal threads (the warp) and horizontal threads (the weft), the latter being carried across from one side of the loom to the other by a type of bobbin called a shuttle.

The technique of weaving has been in use worldwide since ancient times and has been mechanized only since the 19th century. Hand looms are still used, in many societies; for example, in the manufacture of tweeds in the British Isles. They may be horizontal or vertical; industrial looms are generally vertical. In the hand-loom era the ◊Jacquard machine, the last in a series of inventions for producing complicated designs, was perfected in the early 19th century.

Webb (Martha) Beatrice (born Potter) 1858–1943 and Sidney (James), Baron Passfield 1859–1947. English social reformers, writers, and founders of the London School of Economics 1895. They were early members of the Socialist ◊Fabian Society, and were married in 1892. They argued for social insurance in their minority report (1909) of the Poor Law Commission, and wrote many influential books, including *The History of Trade Unionism* 1894, *English Local Government* 1906, and *Soviet Communism* 1935.

Sidney Webb was a member of the Labour Party executive 1915–25, entered Parliament in 1922, and held several government posts.

weaver

Webber Andrew Lloyd English composer of musicals: see ◊Lloyd Webber.

weber SI unit (abbreviation Wb) of ◊magnetic flux (the magnetic field strength multiplied by the area through which the field passes). One weber equals 10^8 ◊maxwells.

A change of flux at a uniform rate of one weber per second in an electrical coil with one turn produces an electromotive force of one volt in the coil.

Weber Carl Maria Friedrich Ernst von 1786–1826. German composer who established the Romantic school of opera with *Der Freischütz* 1821 and *Euryanthe* 1823. He was *Kapellmeister* at Breslau 1804–06, Prague 1813–16, and Dresden 1816. He died during a visit to London where he produced his opera *Oberon* 1826, written for the Covent Garden theater.

Weber Ernst Heinrich 1795–1878. German anatomist and physiologist, brother of Wilhelm Weber. He applied hydrodynamics to study blood circulation, and formulated Weber's law, relating response to stimulus.

Weber Max 1864–1920. German sociologist, one of the founders of modern sociology. He emphasized cultural and political factors as key influences on economic development and individual behavior.

Weber argued for a scientific and value-free approach to research, yet highlighted the importance of meaning and consciousness in understanding social action. His ideas continue to stimulate thought on social stratification, power, organizations, law, and religion.

Key works include *The Protestant Ethic and the Spirit of Capitalism* 1902, *Economy and Society* 1922, *The Methodology of the Social Sciences* 1949, and *The Sociology of Religion* 1920.

Weber Max 1881–1961. Russian-born US painter and sculptor. He immigrated to New York 1891, where he studied painting. Traveling in Europe 1905–09, he was strongly influenced by Parisian avant-garde painters of the cubist and futurist schools. He was a prominent figure in importing these styles to the US and also became famous for his futuristic sculpture.

Weber Wilhelm Eduard 1804–1891. German physicist, who studied magnetism and electricity, brother of Ernst Weber. Working with Karl Gauss, he made sensitive magnetometers to measure magnetic fields, and instruments to measure direct and alternating currents. He also built an electric telegraph. The SI unit of magnetic flux, the weber, is named after him.

Webern Anton (Friedrich Wilhelm von) 1883–1945. Austrian composer. A pupil of ◊Schoenberg, whose 12-tone technique he adopted. He wrote works of extreme brevity; for example, the oratorio *Das Augenlicht* 1935, and songs to words by Stefan George and poems of Rilke.

Webster Daniel 1782–1852. US politician and orator, born in Salisbury, New Hampshire. He sat in the US House of Representatives 1813–27 and the Senate 1827–41, 1845–50, at first as a ◊Federalist and later as a ◊Whig. He was secretary of state 1841–43, 1850–52, and negotiated the Webster-Ashburton Treaty 1842, which fixed the Maine-Canada boundary. His celebrated "seventh of March" speech in the Senate 1850 helped secure a compromise on the slavery issue. He argued that the Congress was powerless under the Constitution to interfere with slavery, and he maintained that the breakup of the Union would produce an even greater evil.

Webster John c. 1580–1634. English dramatist, who ranks after Shakespeare as the greatest tragedian of his time and is the Jacobean whose plays are most frequently performed today. His two great plays *The White Devil* 1608 and *The Duchess of*

weaving loom

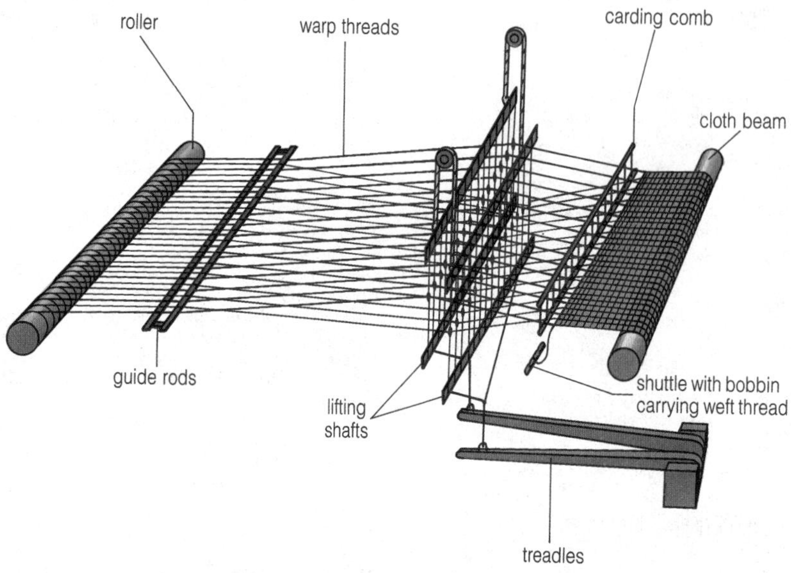
roller
warp threads
carding comb
cloth beam
guide rods
lifting shafts
shuttle with bobbin carrying weft thread
treadles

Malfi 1614 are dark, violent tragedies obsessed with death and decay and infused with poetic brilliance.

Webster Noah 1758–1843. US lexicographer, whose books on grammar and spelling and *American Dictionary of the English Language* 1828 standardized US English.

Webster learned 26 languages and began the scientific study of ◊etymology. Following the American Revolution, he was prompted by patriotic sentiment to create schoolbooks that would impart that sentiment to young students. His *Blue-Backed Speller* sold nearly 100 million copies in a century.

Weddell James 1787–1834. British Antarctic explorer. In 1823, he reached 75°S latitude and 35°W longitude, in the Weddell Sea, which is named after him. .

Weddell Sea an arm of the S Atlantic Ocean that cuts into the Antarctic continent SE of Cape Horn; area 3,000,000 sq mi/8,000,000 sq km. Much of it is covered with thick pack ice for most of the year.

Wedekind Frank 1864–1918. German dramatist. He was a forerunner of Expressionism with *Frühlings Erwachen/The Awakening of Spring* 1891, and *Der Erdgeist/The Earth Spirit* 1895 and its sequel *Der Marquis von Keith. Die Büchse der Pandora/Pandora's Box* 1904 was the source for Berg's opera *Lulu*.

wedge block of triangular cross-section that can be used as a simple machine. An ax is a wedge: it splits wood by redirecting the energy of the downward blow sideways, where it exerts the force needed to split the wood.

Wedgwood Josiah 1730–1795. English pottery manufacturer. He set up business in Staffordshire in the early 1760s to produce his agateware and his unglazed blue or green stoneware decorated with white Neo-Classical designs, using pigments of his own invention.

weedkiller or ***herbicide*** chemical that kills some or all plants. Selective herbicides are effective with cereal crops because they kill all broad-leaved plants without affecting grasslike leaves. Those that kill all plants include sodium chlorate and ◊paraquat; see also ◊Agent Orange. The widespread use of weedkillers in agriculture has led to a dramatic increase in crop yield but also to pollution of soil and ◊water supplies and killing birds and small animals, as well as creating a health hazard for humans.

Weems Mason Locke 1759–1825. American clergyman and author. Born in Anne Arundel County, Maryland, Weems studied for the ministry in England and was ordained in the Anglican church 1784. Returning to America, he served as a parish clergyman until 1792. Thereafter he still insisted on being addressed as "Parson Weems." After becoming the sales agent of a Philadelphia publisher, Weems settled in Virginia 1795 and became an author. He is best remembered for the many editions of his biography *The Life and Memorable Actions of George Washington*, which contained the first published version of the legendary cherry tree story.

weever fish any of a family (Trachinidae) of marine bony fishes of the perch family, especially the genus *Trachinus*, with poison glands on dorsal fin and gill cover that can give a painful sting. It grows up to 2 in/5 cm long, has eyes near the top of the head, and lives on sandy seabeds.

weevil any of a superfamily (Curculionoidea) of ◊beetles, usually less than 0.25 in/6 mm long, and with a head prolonged into a downward beak, which is used for boring into plant stems and trees for feeding.

The larvae are usually white and the adults green, black, or brown. The grain weevil *Sitophilus granarius* is a serious pest of stored grain and the boll weevil *Anthonomus grandis* damages cotton crops.

Wegener Alfred Lothar 1880–1930. German meteorologist and geophysicist, whose theory of ◊continental drift, expounded in *Origin of Continents and Oceans* 1915, was originally known as Wegener's hypothesis. His ideas can now be explained in terms of plate tectonics, the idea that the Earth's crust consists of a number of plates, all moving with respect to one another.

weight the force exerted on an object by ◊gravity. The weight of an object depends on its mass—the amount of material in it—and the strength of the Earth's gravitational pull, which decreases with height. Consequently, an object weighs less at the top of a mountain than at sea level. On the Moon, an object weighs only one-sixth of its weight on Earth, because the pull of the Moon's gravity is one-sixth that of the Earth.

weightlessness condition in which there is no gravitational force acting on a body, either because gravitational force is canceled out by equal and opposite acceleration, or because the body is so far outside a planet's gravitational field that no force is exerted upon it.

weight lifting the sport of lifting the heaviest possible weight above one's head to the satisfaction of judges. In international competitions there are two standard lifts: snatch and jerk.

In the snatch, the bar and weights are lifted from the floor to a position with the arms outstretched and above the head in one continuous movement. The arms must be locked for two seconds for the lift to be good. The jerk is a two-movement lift: from the floor to the chest, and from the chest to the outstretched position. The aggregate weight of the two lifts counts. The International Weightlifting Federation was formed 1920, although a world championship was first held 1891. The first women's world championship was held in 1987 in Florida.

Weil Simone 1909–1943. French writer who became a practicing Catholic after a mystical experience in 1938. Apart from essays, her works (advocating political passivity) were posthumously published, including *Waiting for God* 1951, *The Need for Roots* 1952, and *Notebooks* 1956.

Weill Kurt (Julian) 1900–1950. German composer, US citizen from 1943. He wrote chamber and orchestral music and collaborated with ◊Brecht on operas such as *Die Dreigroschenoper/The Threepenny Opera* 1928 and *Aufsteig und Fall der Stadt Mahagonny/The Rise and Fall of the City of Mahagonny* 1930, all attacking social corruption (*Mahagonny* caused a riot at its premiere in Leipzig). He tried to evolve a new form of ◊music theater, using subjects with a contemporary relevance and the simplest musical means. In 1935 he left Germany for the US where he wrote a number of successful scores for Broadway, among them the antiwar musical *Johnny Johnson* 1936 (including the often covered "September Song") and *Street Scene* 1947 based on an Elmer Rice play of the Depression.

Weil's disease infectious disease of animals (also known as leptospirosis), which is occasionally transmitted to human beings, usually by contact with water contaminated with rat urine. It is characterized by acute fever, and infection may spread to the liver, kidneys, and heart.

The usual form occurring in humans is caused by a spiral-shaped bacterium (spirochete) that is a common parasite of rats. The condition responds poorly to antibiotics, and death may result.

Weimar town the state of Thuringia, Federal Republic of Germany, on the river Elm; population (1990) 80,000. Products include farm machinery and textiles. It was the capital of the grand duchy of Saxe-Weimar 1815–1918; in 1919 the German National Assembly drew up the constitution of the new Weimar Republic here. The writers Goethe, Schiller, and Herder, and the composer Liszt lived in the town. The former concentration camp of Buchenwald is nearby.

Weimar Republic the constitutional republic in Germany 1919–33, which was crippled by the election of antidemocratic parties to the ◊Reichstag (parliament), and then subverted by the Nazi leader Hitler after his appointment as chancellor in 1933. It took its name from the city where in Feb 1919 a constituent assembly met to draw up a democratic constitution.

Weinberg Steven 1933– . US physicist, who in 1967 demonstrated, together with Abdus ◊Salam, that the weak nuclear force and the electromagnetic force are variations of a single underlying force, now called the electroweak force. Their theory involved the prediction of a new interaction, the neutral current (discovered in 1973), which required the presence of charm (see ◊quark). Weinberg and Salam shared a Nobel Prize with Sheldon ◊Glashow in 1979.

Weinberger Caspar (Willard) 1917– . US Republican politician. He served under presidents Nixon and Ford, and was Reagan's defense secretary 1981–87.

weir a low wall built across a river to raise the water level. The oldest surviving weir in England is at Chester, across the river Dee, dating from around 1100.

Weir Peter 1938– . Australian film director. His

Weizman *Chaim Weizman, Russian-born chemist and Zionist leader, who in 1948 became the first president of Israel.*

films have an atmospheric quality and often contain a strong spiritual element. They include *Picnic at Hanging Rock* 1975, *Witness* 1985, and *The Mosquito Coast* 1986.

Weirton city in West Virginia, on the Ohio River, W of Pittsburgh. Industries include coal, steel, chemicals, and cement; population (1990) 22,124.

Weiser Conrad 1696–1760. Colonial American public official, born in Germany. Weiser immigrated to America 1710, settling in New York's Hudson Valley. Moving to Berks County, Pennsylvania, 1729, Weiser became familiar with the language and customs of the local Iroquois and was frequently used as an official interpreter in government dealings with them. Due to his efforts, peace conferences were held in Philadelphia in 1731 and 1736.

He later negotiated treaties with the Iroquois to open up western lands to colonial settlement. Weiser later served as judge of Berks County 1752–60 and as colonel of the militia.

Weismann August 1834–1914. German biologist. His failing eyesight forced him to turn from microscopy to theoretical work. In 1892 he proposed that changes to the body do not in turn cause an alteration of the genetic material.

This "central dogma" of biology remains of vital importance to biologists supporting the Darwinian theory of evolution. If the genetic material can be altered only by chance mutation and recombination, then the Lamarckian view that acquired bodily changes can subsequently be inherited becomes obsolete.

Weismuller Johnny (Peter John) 1904–1984. US film actor, formerly an Olympic swimmer, who played Tarzan in a long-running series of films for MGM and RKO including *Tarzan the Ape Man* 1932, *Tarzan and His Mate* 1934, and *Tarzan and the Leopard Woman* 1946.

Weizmann Chaim 1874–1952. Zionist leader, the first president of Israel (1948–52), and chemist. Born in Russia, he became a naturalized British subject, and as director of the navy's laboratories 1916–19 discovered a process for manufacturing acetone, a solvent. He conducted the negotiations leading up to the Balfour Declaration, which favored a Jewish state. He became head of the Hebrew University in Jerusalem, then in 1948 became the first president of the new republic of Israel.

Weizsäcker Richard, Baron von 1920– . German Christian Democrat politician, president from 1984. He began his career as a lawyer and was also active in the German Protestant church and in Christian Democratic Union party politics. He was elected to the West German Bundestag (parliament) in 1969 and served as mayor of West Berlin from 1981, before being elected federal president in 1984.

Welch Raquel. Adopted name of Raquel Tejada 1940– . US actress, a sex symbol of the 1960s in such films as *One Million Years BC* 1966, *Myra Breckinridge* 1970, and *The Three Musketeers* 1973.

Welch Robert H W, Jr 1899–1985. US businessman and anticommunist crusader. Over the years, he supported conservative political causes and by the 1950s had become an outspoken anticommunist. He founded the magazine *American Opinion* 1956 and organized the John Birch Society 1958. A strong supporter of losing Republican presidential candidate Barry Goldwater in 1964, Welch later became increasingly venomous in his accusations against supposed communist agents and sympathizers.

Born in Chowan County, North Carolina, Welch was educated at the University of North Carolina and joined the family candy business in Boston 1922.

welding joining pieces of metal (or nonmetal) at faces rendered plastic or liquid by heat or pressure (or both). Forge (or hammer) welding, employed by blacksmiths since early times, was the only method available until the late 19th century. The principal processes, today, are gas and arc welding, in which the heat from a gas flame or an electric arc melts the faces to be joined. Additional "filler metal" is usually added to the joint.

Resistance welding is another electric method in which the weld is formed by a combination of pressure and resistance heating from an electric current. Recent developments include electric-slag, electron-beam, high-energy laser, and the still experimental radio-wave energy-beam welding processes.

Weldon Fay 1931– . British novelist and dramatist whose work deals with feminist themes, often in an ironic or comic manner. Novels include *The Fat Woman's Joke* 1967, *Female Friends* 1975, *Remember Me* 1976, *Puffball* 1980, *The Life and Loves of a She-Devil* 1984, and *The Hearts and Lives of Men* 1988. She has also written plays for the stage, radio, and television.

Welensky Roy 1907–1991. Rhodesian politician. He was instrumental in the creation of a federation of N Rhodesia (now Zambia), S Rhodesia (now Zimbabwe), and Nyasaland (now Malawi) in 1953 and was prime minister 1956–63, when the federation was disbanded. His S Rhodesian Federal Party was defeated by Ian Smith's Rhodesian Front in 1964. In 1965, following Smith's Rhodesian unilateral declaration of S Rhodesian independence from Britain, Welensky left politics.

Welhaven Johan Sebastian Cammermeyer 1807–1873. Norwegian poet, professor of philosophy at Christiania (now Oslo) 1839–68. A supporter of the Dano-Norwegian culture, he is considered one of the greatest Norwegian masters of poetic form. His works include the satiric *Norges Daemring* 1834.

Welland Ship Canal Canadian waterway, part of the ◊St Lawrence Seaway, linking Lake Erie to Lake Ontario.

Welles Gideon 1802–1878. US public official. Born in Glastonbury, Connecticut, and educated at Norwich University, Welles served as editor of the *Hartford Times* 1826–36. As an active Democrat he served in the state legislature 1827–35 and held other state and federal offices. In 1854 he became one of the founders of the Republican Party. Welles was appointed secretary of the navy by President Lincoln 1861 and in that position supervised the expansion of the Union naval forces and advocated the development of ironclads. An opponent of President Grant, he joined the Liberal Republicans 1872.

Welles *US actor and director Orson Welles, whose most notable movie was* Citizen Kane *1941.*

Welles (George) Orson 1915–1985. US actor and director. He produced a radio version of H G Wells's novel *The War of the Worlds* 1938. He then produced, directed, and starred in *Citizen Kane* 1941, in which he used innovative lighting techniques, camera angles and movements, creating a landmark in the history of cinema, yet he directed very few films subsequently in Hollywood. His numerous performances as an actor include the character of Harry Lime in *The Third Man* 1949.

A child prodigy, Welles made his acting debut at 16 in Dublin and toured with Katherine Cornell's company in the US. In 1937 he founded the Mercury Theater, New York, with John Houseman, where their repertory productions included a modern-dress version of *Julius Caesar*. The realistic radio broadcast of H G Wells's *The War of the Worlds* in 1938 caused panic and fear of Martian invasion in the US. He directed the films *The Magnificent Ambersons* 1942, *The Lady From Shanghai* 1948 with his wife Rita Hayworth, *Touch of Evil* 1958, and *Chimes at Midnight* 1967, a Shakespeare adaptation. As his career declined he became a familiar voice and face in US television commercials, and made guest appearances on television shows.

Wellesley Richard Colley, Marquess of 1760–1842. British administrator; brother of the Duke of Wellington. He was governor general of India 1798–1805, and by his victories over the Mahrattas of W India greatly extended the territory under British rule. He was foreign secretary 1809–12, and lord lieutenant of Ireland 1821–28 and 1833–34.

Wellington capital and industrial port (woolen textiles, chemicals, soap, footwear, bricks) of New Zealand in North Island on Cook Strait; population (1987) 351,000. The harbor was first sighted by Captain Cook in 1773.

Founded 1840 by Edward Gibbon Wakefield as the first settlement of the New Zealand Company, it has been the seat of government since 1865, when it replaced Auckland. Victoria University was founded 1897. A new assembly hall (designed by the British architect Basil Spence and popularly called "the beehive" because of its shape) was opened in 1977 alongside the original parliament building.

Wellington Arthur Wellesley, 1st Duke of 1769–1852. British soldier and Tory politician. As commander in the ◊Peninsular War, he expelled the French from Spain in 1814. He defeated Napoleon Bonaparte at Quatre-Bras and Waterloo in 1815, and was a member of the Congress of Vienna. As prime minister 1828–30, he was forced to concede Roman Catholic emancipation.

Wellington *Arthur Wellesley, 1st Duke of Wellington, known as the Iron Duke.*

Wells H(erbert) G(eorge) 1866–1946. English writer of "scientific romances" such as *The Time Machine* 1895 and *The War of the Worlds* 1898. His later novels had an antiestablishment, anticonventional humor remarkable in its day, for example *Kipps* 1905 and *Tono-Bungay* 1909. His many other books include *Outline of History* 1920 and *The Shape of Things to Come* 1933, a number of his prophecies from which have since been fulfilled. He also wrote many short stories.

Wells Ida Bell 1862–1931. US journalist and political activist. Born in Holly Springs, Mississippi, Wells was educated in a segregated school and became a teacher in Memphis, Tennessee. Losing her job in 1891 as the result of a suit she had filed against state segregation laws, she began a career of political activism. Moving to New York City, she joined the staff of *New York Age* and embarked on extensive lecture tours. Bell married and settled in Chicago 1895. She served as secretary of the National African-American Council 1898–1902 and as a Chicago probation officer 1913–16.

Welsh people of ◊Wales; see also ◊Celts. The term is thought to be derived from an old Germanic term for "foreigner," and so linked to Walloon (Belgium) and Wallachian (Romania). It may also derive from the Latin *Volcae*, the name of a Celtic people of France.

Welsh corgi breed of dog with a foxlike head and pricked ears. The coat is dense, with several varieties of coloring. Corgis are about 1 ft/30 cm at the shoulder, and weigh up to 27 lb/12 kgs.

There are two types, the Pembrokeshire and the heavier Cardiganshire. They were originally bred for cattle herding. Their size was an advantage because cattle were unable to bend low enough to gore them.

Welsh language or ***Cymraeg*** member of the Celtic branch of the Indo-European language family, spoken chiefly in the rural north and west of Wales; it is the strongest of the surviving Celtic languages, and in 1981 was spoken by 18.9% of the Welsh population.

Welsh has been in retreat in the face of English expansion since the accession of the Welsh Henry Tudor (as Henry VII) to the throne of England. Modern Welsh, like English, is not a highly inflected language, but British, the Celtic ancestor of Welsh, is. The continuous literature of Welsh, from the 6th century onward, contains the whole range of change from British to present-day Welsh. Nowadays, few Welsh people speak only Welsh; they are either bilingual or speak only English.

Wells *English journalist and novelist H G Wells.*

Welsh literature the chief remains of early Welsh literature are contained in the Four Ancient Books of Wales—the Black Book of Carmarthen, the Book of Taliesin, the Book of Aneirin, and the Red Book of Hergest—anthologies of prose and verse of the 6th–14th centuries. Characteristic of Welsh poetry is the bardic system, which ensured the continuance of traditional conventions; most celebrated of the 12th-century bards was Cynddelw.

The English conquest of 1282 involved the fall of the princes who supported these bards, but after a period of decline a new school arose in South Wales with a new freedom in form and sentiment, the most celebrated poet in the 14th-century being Dafydd ap Gwilym, and in the next century the Classical metrist Dafydd ap Edmwnd. With the Reformation biblical translations were undertaken, and Morgan Llwyd and Ellis Wynn o Lasynys wrote religious prose. Popular meters resembling those of England developed, for example the poems of Huw Morys.

In the 18th century the Classical poetic forms revived with Goronwy Owen, and the Eisteddfod (song festival) movement began: popular measures were used by the hymn-writer William Williams. The 19th century saw few notable figures save the novelist Daniel Owen, but the foundation of a Welsh university and the work there of Sir John Morris Jones (1864–1929) produced a 20th-century revival, including Thomas Gwynn Jones (1871–1949), W J Gruffydd (1881–1954), and Robert Williams Parry (1884–1956). Later poets included J Kitchener Davies (1902–52), Saunders Lewis (1893–), and in the period after World War II Waldo Williams (1904–71), Euros Bowen (1904–), and Bobi Jones (1929–). Outside Wales, those who have expressed the Welsh spirit in English include Henry Vaughan, Edward Thomas, Vernon Watkins (1906–67), Dylan Thomas, and Ronald Thomas.

Weltpolitik (German "world politics") term applied to German foreign policy after about 1890, which represented Emperor Wilhelm II's attempt to make Germany into a world power through an aggressive foreign policy on colonies and naval building combined with an increase in nationalism at home.

Welty Eudora 1909– . US novelist and short-story writer, born in Jackson, Mississippi. Her works reflect life in the American South and are notable for their creation of character and accurate rendition of local dialect. Her novels include *Delta Wedding* 1946, *Losing Battles* 1970, and *The Optimist's Daughter* 1972.

The Collected Stories of Eudora Welty appeared in 1980. The autobiographical work *One Writer's Beginnings* 1984 is a warm recounting of the people, places, and incidents that influenced Welty's work.

welwitschia woody plant *Welwitschia mirabilis* of the order Gnetales, found in the deserts of SW Africa. It has a long, water-absorbent taproot and may live a hundred years.

Wenceslas, St 907–929. Duke of Bohemia who attempted to Christianize his people and was murdered by his brother. He is patron saint of Czechoslovakia and the "good King Wenceslas" of a popular carol. Feast day Sept 28.

Wenchow former name of Chinese town ◊Wenzhou.

Wends the NW Slavonic peoples who settled E of the rivers Elbe and Saale in the 6th–8th centuries. By the 12th century most had been forcibly Christianized and absorbed by invading Germans; a few preserved their identity and survive as the Sorbs of Lusatia (Germany/Poland).

Wenzhou industrial port (textiles, medicine) in Zhejiang, SE China; population (1984) 519,000. It was opened to foreign trade 1877 and is now a special economic zone.

werewolf in folk belief, a human being either turned by spell into a wolf or having the ability to assume a wolf form. The symptoms of ◊porphyria may have fostered the legends.

Werfel Franz 1890–1945. Austrian poet, dramatist, and novelist, a leading Expressionist. His works include the poems "Der Weltfreund der Gerichtstag"/"The Day of Judgment" 1919; the plays *Juarez und Maximilian* 1924, and *Das Reich Gottes in Böhmen/The Kingdom of God in Bohemia* 1930; and the novels *Verdi* 1924 and *Das Lied von Bernadette/The Song of Bernadette* 1941.

Born in Prague, he lived in Germany, Austria, and France, and in 1940 escaped from a French concentration camp to the US, where he died. In 1929 he married Alma Mahler, daughter of the composer Gustav Mahler.

Wergeland Henrik 1808–1845. Norwegian lyric poet. He was a leader of the Norwegian revival and is known for his epic *Skabelsen, Mennesket, og Messias/Creation, Humanity, and Messiah* 1830.

wergild or ***wergeld*** in Anglo-Saxon and Germanic law during the Middle Ages, the compensation paid by a murderer to the relatives of the victim, its value dependent on the social rank of the deceased. It originated in European tribal society as a substitute for the blood feud (essentially a form of ◊vendetta), and was replaced by punishments imposed by courts of law during the 10th and 11th centuries.

Werner Abraham Gottlob 1750–1815. German geologist, one of the first to classify minerals systematically. He also developed the later discarded theory of neptunianism—that the Earth was initially covered by water, with every mineral in suspension: as the water receded, layers of rocks "crystallized."

Werner Alfred 1866–1919. Swiss chemist. He was awarded a Nobel Prize in 1913 for his work on valency theory, which gave rise to the concept of coordinate bonds and coordination compounds. He demonstrated that different three-dimensional arrangements of atoms in inorganic compounds gives rise to optical isomerism (the rotation of polarized light in opposite directions by molecules that contain the same atoms but are mirror images of each other).

Wesberry v Sanders a US Supreme Court decision 1964 dealing with apportionment of Congressional districts. After a suit against Georgia's apportionment statute was dismissed by the federal circuit court, the case was appealed to the Supreme Court. The Court ruled that all Congressional districts must be equal in size of voting population. The Georgia statute was declared invalid because its unequal apportionment gave greater voting power to residents of certain districts.

Wesermünde name until 1947 of ◊Bremerhaven, a port in the Federal Republic of Germany.

Wesley Charles 1707–1788. English Methodist, brother of John ◊Wesley and one of the original Methodists at Oxford. He became a principal preacher and theologian of the Wesleyan Methodists, and wrote some 6,500 hymns.

Wesley John 1703–1791. English founder of ◊Methodism. When the pulpits of the Church of England were closed to him and his followers, he took the gospel to the people. For 50 years he rode about the country on horseback, preaching daily, largely in the open air. His sermons became the doctrinal standard of the Wesleyan Methodist Church.

Wesley went to Oxford University together with his brother Charles, where their circle was nicknamed Methodists because of their religious

West *British journalist and novelist Rebecca West took her pen name from a character in Ibsen's play* Rosmersholm.

West, American: chronology

1550	Horses introduced by the Spanish. Francisco Coronado's expedition into the SW.
1775	Wilderness Road opened by Daniel Boone.
1804	Meriwether Lewis and William Clark explored the ◊Louisiana Purchase lands for President Jefferson.
1805	Zebulon Pike (see ◊Pikes Peak) explored the Mississippi.
1819	Major Stephen Long, a US government topographical engineer, explored the Great Plains.
1822	◊Santa Fé Trail established.
1824	Great Salt Lake discovered by Jim Bridger, "mountain man," trapper, and guide.
1836	Defeat of Davy Crockett and other Texans by Mexicans at the Battle of the ◊Alamo.
1840–60	◊Oregon Trail in use.
1846	Mormon trek to Utah under Brigham ◊Young.
1846–48	◊Mexican War.
1849–56	◊California gold rush.
1860	Pony Express (St Joseph, Missouri–San Francisco, California) April 3–Oct 22; superseded by the telegraph.
1863	On Jan 1 the first homestead was filed; followed by the settlement of the Western Prairies and Great Plains.
1865–90	Wars against the Indians, accompanied by rapid extermination of the buffalo, upon which much of Great Plains and Indian life depended.
1867–80s	Period of the "cattle kingdom," and cow trails such as the Chisholm Trail from Texas to the railheads at Abilene, Wichita, and Dodge City.
1869	First transcontinental railroad completed by Central Pacific company, building eastward from Sacramento, California, and Union Pacific company, building westward from Omaha, Nebraska.
1876	Battle of Little Bighorn; see George ◊Custer and ◊Plains Indians.
1890	Battle of ◊Wounded Knee; official census declaration that the West no longer had a frontier line.

observances. He was ordained in the Church of England in 1728 and in 1735 he went to the American colony of Georgia as a missionary. On his return he experienced "conversion" in 1738, and from being rigidly High Church developed into an ardent Evangelical.

Wessex the kingdom of the West Saxons in Britain, said to have been founded by Cerdic about AD 500, covering present-day Hampshire, Dorset, Wiltshire, Berkshire, Somerset, and Devon. In 829 Egbert established West Saxon supremacy over all England. Thomas ◊Hardy used the term Wessex in his novels for the SW counties of England.

West Benjamin 1738–1820. American Neo-Classical painter, active in London from 1763. He enjoyed the patronage of George III for many years and painted historical pictures.

West was born in Pennsylvania. His *Death of General Wolfe* 1770 (National Gallery, Ottawa) began a vogue for painting recent historical events in contemporary costume. Many early American artists studied with him, including Washington Allston, Gilbert Stuart, and J S Copely.

West Mae 1892–1980. US vaudeville, stage, and film actress. She wrote her own plays and film dialogue, setting herself up as a provocative sex symbol and the mistress of verbal innuendo. She appeared on Broadway in *Sex* 1926, *Drag* 1927, and *Diamond Lil* 1928, which was the basis of the film (with Cary Grant) *She Done Him Wrong* 1933. Her other films include *I'm No Angel* 1933, *Going to Town* 1934, *My Little Chickadee* 1944 (with W C Fields), *Myra Breckenridge* 1969, and *Sextette* 1977. Both her plays and her films led to legal battles over censorship.

Two of her often quoted lines are "Come up and see me," and "Beulah, peel me a grape." Her autobiography, *Goodness Had Nothing to Do with It*, was published 1959.

West Nathanel. Adopted name of Nathan Weinstein 1904–1940. US black-humor novelist. His surrealist-influenced novels capture the absurdity and extremity of American life and the dark side of the American dream. *The Day of the Locust* 1939 explores the violent fantasies induced by Hollywood, where West had been a screenwriter.

Miss Lonelyhearts 1933 is about a newspaper advice columnist who feels the misfortunes of his correspondents; *A Cool Million* 1934 satirizes the rags-to-riches dream of success.

West Rebecca. Adopted name of Cicily Isabel Fairfield 1892–1983. British journalist and novelist, an active feminist from 1911. *The Meaning of Treason* 1959 deals with the spies Burgess and Maclean. Her novels have political themes and include *The Fountain Overflows* 1956 and *The Birds Fall Down* 1966.

West African Economic Community international organization established 1975 to end barriers in trade and to achieve cooperation in development; members include Burkina Faso, Ivory Coast, Mali, Mauritania, Niger, and Senegal; Benin and Togo have observer status.

West, American the Great Plains region of the US to the east of the Rocky Mountains from Canada to Mexico.

West Bank area (2,270 sq mi/5,879 sq km) on the W bank of the river Jordan; population (1988) 866,000. The West Bank was taken by the Jordanian army 1948 at the end of the Arab-Israeli war that followed the creation of the state of Israel; and was captured by Israel during the Six-Day War June 5–10, 1967. The continuing Israeli occupation and settlement of the area has created tensions with the Arab population.

In 1988 King Hussein announced that Jordan was cutting "legal and administrative ties" with the West Bank, leaving responsibility for Arabs in the region to the ◊Palestine Liberation Organization (which was already the de facto position).

West Bengal state of NE India
capital Calcutta
towns Asansol, Durgarpur
physical occupies the west part of the vast alluvial plain created by the rivers Ganges and Brahmaputra, with the Hooghly river; annual rainfall in excess of 100 in/250 cm
products rice, jute, tea, coal, iron, steel, cars, locomotives, aluminium, fertilizers
population (1981) 54,486,000
history created 1947 from the former British province of Bengal, with later territories added: Cooch Behar 1950, Chandernagore 1954, and part of Bihar 1956.

West Bromwich industrial town (metalworking, springs, tubes) in West Midlands, England, NW of Birmingham; population (1981) 155,000.

Westerlies prevailing winds from the W that occur in both hemispheres between latitudes of about 35° and 60°. Unlike the ◊trade winds, they are very variable and produce stormy weather.

The Westerlies blow mainly from the SW in the northern hemisphere and the NW in the southern hemisphere, bringing moist weather to the W coast of the landmasses in these latitudes.

western genre of popular fiction and film based on the landscape and settlement of the American West, with emphasis on the conquest of Indian territory. It developed in American ◊dime novels and ◊frontier literature. The western became established in written form with such novels as Owen Wister's *The Virginian* 1902 and Zane Grey's *Riders of the Purple Sage* 1912. From the earliest silent films, movies extended the western mythology and, with Italian "spaghetti" westerns and Japanese westerns, established it as an international form.

The romance of the American frontiersman confronting his wilderness was first popularized in J F ◊Cooper's ◊Leatherstocking Tales 1823–41 and the American hunter stories of Karl May and soon evolved into a national fascination with the West specifically. From the mid-19th century, in stylized form, came frontier tales of cowboy rangers or lawmen portraying good, with Indians, cattle rustlers, or gunmen portraying evil. Most are set vaguely in the post-Civil War era. The characters are sometimes based on real persons, such as Kit Carson, Annie Oakley, Wyatt Earp, and Bat Masterson.

Most westerns are nostalgic, written after the frontier officially closed in 1890. *The Virginian* is the "serious" version of the form, but prolific writers such as Grey; Frederick Faust (Max Brand), who wrote *Destry Rides Again* 1930; and Louis L'Amour, who wrote *Hondo* 1953, developed its pulp possibilities and its place in universal fantasy.

Westerns have provided endless sources for motion pictures (◊Western film), among them *The Great Train Robbery* 1903, *The Covered Wagon* 1923, *Cimarron* 1931, *Stagecoach* 1939, *The Gunfighter* 1950, *High Noon* 1952, *Shane* 1953, *True Grit* 1969, and *Dances with Wolves* 1990. "The Lone Ranger" was a popular serialized western on radio and television. Other western series on television included "Gunsmoke," "Bonanza," "Bat Masterson," and "Wyatt Earp."

Western Australia state of Australia
area 974,843 sq mi/2,525,500 sq km
capital Perth
towns main port Fremantle, Bunbury, Geraldton, Kalgoorlie-Boulder, Albany
features largest state in Australia; Monte Bello Islands; rivers Fitzroy, Fortescue, Gascoyne, Murchison, Swan; NW coast subject to hurricanes ("willy-willies"); ◊Lasseter's Reef
products wheat, fresh and dried fruit, meat and dairy products, natural gas (NW shelf) and oil (Canning Basin), iron (the Pilbara), copper, nickel, uranium, gold, diamonds

Western Australia

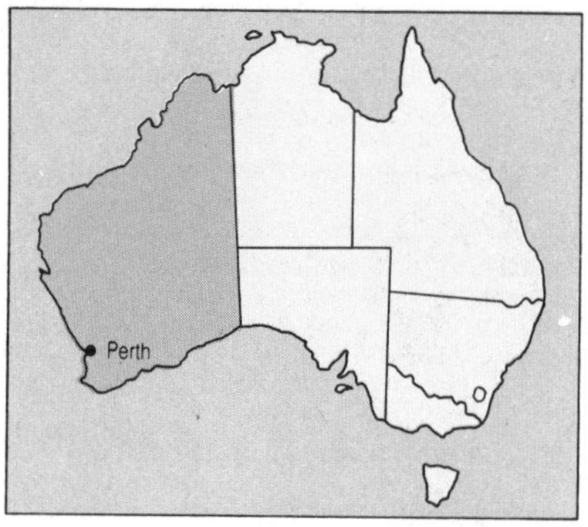
Perth

population (1987) 1,478,000
history a shortlived convict settlement at King George Sound 1826; the state founded at Perth 1829 by Captain James Stirling (1791–1865); self-government 1890; state 1901.

Western European Union (WEU) organization established 1955 as a consultative forum for military issues among the W European governments: Belgium, France, Holland, Italy, Luxembourg, the UK, West Germany, and (from 1988) Spain and Portugal.

Policy is agreed during meetings of the foreign ministers of the member nations, with administrative work carried out by a permanent secretariat and specialist committees. The WEU is charged under its charter with ensuring close cooperation with NATO. During its early years the WEU supervised the gradual rearmament of West Germany and the transfer of the Saarland back to West German rule 1957. Recently attempts have been made, particularly by France, to transform the WEU into a coordinating body for W European military policy and to frame a "charter of security principles."

Western film genre of films based loosely on the history of the American ◊West and evolved from the written Western. As a genre, the Western is virtually as old as the cinema. Postwar Italian "spaghetti Westerns" and Japanese Westerns established it as an international form. In the 1980s only *Pale Rider* 1985 and *Young Guns* 1988 were commercially successful.

A memorable early example is *The Great Train Robbery* 1903. The silent era produced such epics as *The Iron Horse* 1924, and the genre remained popular into the coming of sound. The 1930s saw the rise of singing cowboys (Gene Autry) and many epics, such as *Union Pacific* 1939, whereas the 1940s often saw star vehicles (Roy Rogers) or dwelt on specific historical events (including Custer's last stand in *They Died With Their Boots On* 1941). The 1950s brought more realism and serious issues, such as the treatment of the Indians. The Westerns of the 1960s contained an increased amount of violence, partly caused by the influence of the Italian "spaghetti Westerns" (often directed by Sergio ◊Leone), a development carried further into the 1970s with films such as *The Wild Bunch* 1969. The artistic and commercial disaster of *Heaven's Gate* 1980 suggested the virtual death of the genre, but the success of *Young Guns* spurred interest, especially in a 1990s TV series based on that theme, and *Dances with Wolves*, emphasizing the American Indian perspective, achieved critical and commercial success.

Western Isles island area of Scotland, comprising the Outer Hebrides (Lewis, Harris, North and South Uist, and Barra); unofficially the Inner and Outer Hebrides generally
area 1,120 sq mi/2,900 sq km
towns Stornoway on Lewis (administrative headquarters)
features divided from the mainland by the Minch channel; Callanish monolithic circles of the Stone Age on Lewis
products Harris tweed, sheep, fish, cattle
population (1987) 31,000.

Western Provinces in Canada, the provinces of ◊Alberta, ◊British Columbia, ◊Manitoba, and ◊Saskatchewan.

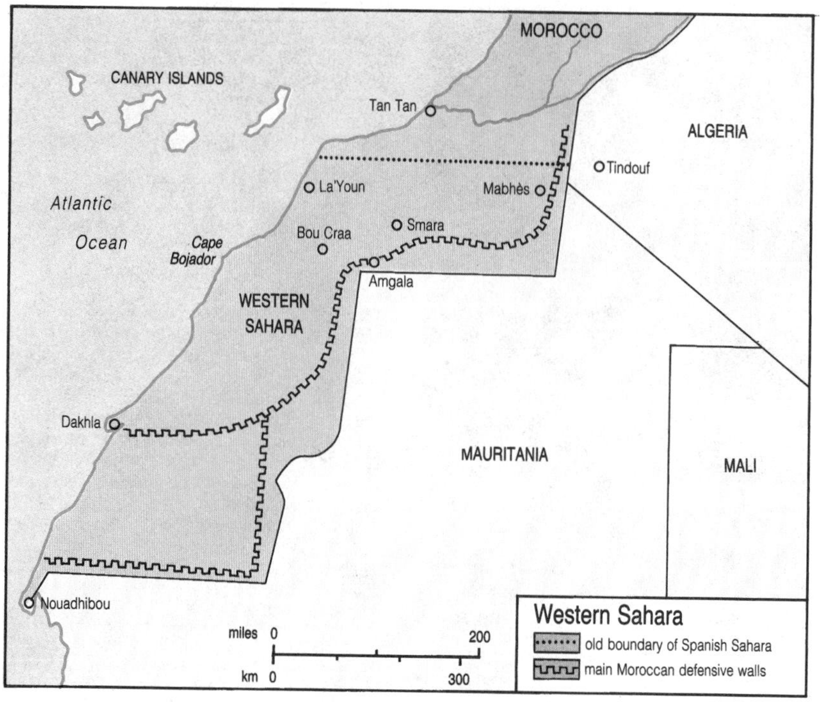
MOROCCO
CANARY ISLANDS
Tan Tan
ALGERIA
Tindouf
La'Youn
Mabhès
Atlantic
Ocean
Cape
Bojador
Bou Craa
Smara
Amgala
WESTERN
SAHARA
Dakhla
MAURITANIA
MALI
Nouadhibou
miles 0
200
km 0
300
old boundary of Spanish Sahara
main Moroccan defensive walls
Western Sahara

Western Sahara formerly Spanish Sahara disputed territory in NW Africa bounded to the N by Morocco, to the W and S by Mauritania, and to the E by the Atlantic Ocean. A peace plan, accepted in principle Aug 30, 1988, by Morocco and Polisario, calls for a cease-fire and a UN-supervised referendum on the future of the territory
area 103,011 sq mi/266,800 sq km
capital La'Youn (Arabic al-Aaiún)
cities phosphate mining town of Bou Craa
features electrically monitored fortified wall enclosing the phosphate area
exports phosphates
currency dirham
population (1988) 181,400; another estimated 165,000 live in refugee camps near Tindouf, SW Algeria. Ethnic composition: Sawrawis (traditionally nomadic herders)
language Arabic
religion Sunni Muslim
government administered by Morocco
history This 1,000-km-long Saharan coastal region, which during the 19th century separated French-dominated Morocco and Mauritania, was designated a Spanish "sphere of influence" in 1884 as it lies opposite the Spanish-ruled Canary Islands. On securing its independence in 1956, Morocco laid claim to and invaded this "Spanish Sahara" territory, but was repulsed. Moroccan interest was rekindled from 1965, following the discovery of rich phosphate resources at Bou-Craa, and within Spanish Sahara a pro-independence nationalist movement developed, spearheaded by the Popular Front for the Liberation of Saguia al Hamra and Rio de Oro (Polisario), which was established in 1973. After the death of the Spanish ruler General Franco, Spain withdrew and the territory was partitioned between Morocco and Mauritania. Polisario rejected this partition, declared their own independent Saharan Arab Democratic Republic (SADR), and proceeded to wage a guerrilla war, securing indirect support from Algeria and, later, Libya. By 1979 they had succeeded in their struggle against Mauritania—which withdrew from their southern sector and concluded a peace agreement with Polisario—and in 1982 the SADR was accepted as a full member of the ◊Organization of African Unity. By the end of 1990, 70 countries had granted diplomatic recognition to the SADR.

Morocco, which occupied the Mauritanian-evacuated zone, still retained control over the bulk of the territory, including the key towns and phosphate mines, which they protected with a 2,500-km-long "electronic defensive wall." From the mid-1980s this wall was gradually extended outward as Libya and Algeria reduced their support for Polisario and drew closer to Morocco. In 1988, Morocco and the Polisario Front agreed to United Nations-sponsored plans for a cease-fire and a referendum in Western Sahara, based on 1974 voting rolls, to decide the territory's future. However, divisions persisted during 1989 and 1990 over the terms of the referendum and sporadic fighting continued.

Western Samoa see ◊Samoa, Western.

West Germany see ◊Germany, West.

West Indian inhabitant of or native to the West Indies, or person of West Indian descent. The West Indies are culturally heterogenous; in addition to the indigenous Carib and Arawak Indians, there are peoples of African, European, and Asian descent, as well as peoples of mixed descent.

West Indies archipelago of about 1,200 islands, dividing the Atlantic from the Gulf of Mexico and the Caribbean. The islands are divided into:
Bahamas
Greater Antilles Cuba, Hispaniola (Haiti, Dominican Republic), Jamaica, and Puerto Rico
Lesser Antilles Aruba, Netherlands Antilles, Trinidad and Tobago, the Windward Islands (Grenada, Barbados, St Vincent, St Lucia, Martinique, Dominica, Guadeloupe), the Leeward Islands (Montserrat, Antigua, St Christopher (St Kitts)–Nevis, Barbuda, Anguilla, St Martin, British and US Virgin Islands, and many smaller islands.

West Indies, Federation of the federal union 1958–62 comprising Antigua, Barbados, Dominica, Grenada, Jamaica, Montserrat, St Christopher (St Kitts)-Nevis and Anguilla, St Lucia, St Vincent, and Trinidad and Tobago. This federation came to an end when first Jamaica and then Trinidad and Tobago withdrew.

Westinghouse George 1846–1914. US inventor and manufacturer. The most profitable of his designs was an air brake for railroad automobiles, perfected 1869. Westinghouse later devised a system of railroad signals and an efficient means of distributing natural gas. His greatest success came with the establishment of the Westinghouse Electric Co 1886, through which he adapted alternating current for domestic and industrial use.

Born in Central Bridge, New York, Westinghouse served in the American Civil War as a teenager. Later working in his father's tool shop, he became an inventor.

West Irian former name of ◊Irian Jaya.

Westman Islands small group of islands off the south coast of Iceland. In 1973 volcanic eruption caused the population of 5,200 to be temporarily evacuated, and added 1 sq mi/2.5 sq km to the islands' area. Heimaey is one of Iceland's chief fishing ports.

Westminster, City of borough of central Greater London, on the N bank of the Thames between Kensington and the City of London; population (1986) 176,000. It encompasses Bayswater, Belgravia, Mayfair, Paddington, Pimlico, Soho, St John's Wood, and Westminster.

Westminster Abbey Gothic church in central London, officially the Collegiate Church of St Peter. It was built 1050–1745 and consecrated under Edward the Confessor in 1065. The west towers are by Hawksmoor 1740. Since William I nearly all English monarchs have been crowned in the abbey, and several are buried there; many poets are buried or commemorated there, at Poets' Corner.

In the abbey, the Coronation Chair includes the Stone of Scone, on which Scottish kings were crowned, brought here by Edward I in 1296; Poets' Corner was begun with the burial of ◊Spenser 1599. Westminster School, a public school with ancient and modern buildings nearby, was once the Abbey School.

Westmoreland William Childs 1914– . US military leader. Born in Spartanburg County, South Carolina, Westmoreland was a 1936 graduate of West Point. After service as an artillery officer during World War II, he saw action in the Korean conflict and served in various administrative capacities at the Pentagon 1953–58. He was superintendent of West Point 1960–63 and served as commander of US forces in Vietnam 1964–68. An aggressive advocate of expanded US military involvement in Vietnam, he was replaced in 1968 and ended his active military career as army chief of staff 1968–72.

Weston Edward 1886–1958. US photographer. A founding member of the "f/64" group (after the smallest lens opening), a school of photography advocating sharp definition. He is noted for the technical mastery, composition, and clarity in his California landscapes, clouds, gourds, cacti, and nude studies.

In his photography, Weston aimed for realism. He never used artificial light and seldom enlarged, cropped, or retouched his negatives. His esthetic principle dominated American photography for many years.

Weston-super-Mare seaside resort and town in Avon, SW England, on the Bristol Channel; population (1984) 170,000. Industries include plastics and engineering.

West Pakistan a province of ◊Pakistan.

West Palm Beach city on the SE coast of Florida, on the lagoon Lake Worth, N of Miami. Industries include transistors, aircraft parts, building materials, and citrus fruits. It is a resort, and tourism is important to the economy; population (1990) 67,643.

Westphalia independent medieval duchy, incorporated in Prussia by the Congress of Vienna 1815, and made a province 1816 with Münster as its capital. From 1946 it has been part of the West German and then (from 1990) German *Land* (region) of ◊North Rhine–Westphalia.

West Virginia

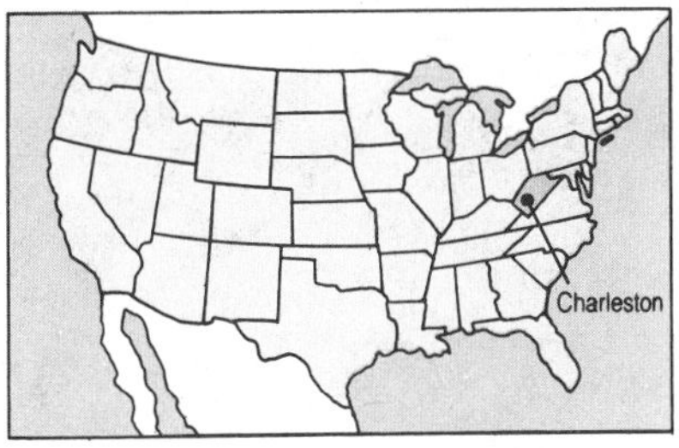
Charleston

Westphalia, Treaty of agreement 1648 ending the ◊Thirty Years' War. The peace marked the end of the supremacy of the Holy Roman Empire and the emergence of France as a dominant power. It recognized the sovereignty of the German states, Switzerland, and the Netherlands; Lutherans, Calvinists, and Roman Catholics were given equal rights.

West Point former fort in New York State, on the Hudson River, 50 mi/80 km N of New York City, site of the US Military Academy (commonly referred to as West Point), established in 1802. Women were admitted 1976. West Point has been a military post since 1778.

West Virginia state in E central US; nickname Mountain State

area 24,279 sq mi/62,900 sq km

capital Charleston

cities Huntington, Wheeling

physical Allegheny Mountains; Ohio River

features port of Harper's Ferry, restored as when John Brown seized the US armory 1859

products apples, corn, poultry, dairy and meat products, coal, natural gas, oil, chemicals, synthetic fibers, plastics, steel, glass, pottery

population (1990) 1,793,477

famous people Pearl Buck, Thomas "Stonewall" Jackson, Walter Reuther, Mary Lee Settle, Cyrus Vance

history explorers and fur traders 1670s; first settlement at Mill Creek 1731 by Morgan Morgan; German settlements 1730s; coal discovered on the Coal River 1742; industrial development early 19th century. On the secession of Virginia from the Union 1861, West Virginians dissented and formed a new state 1863. Industrial expansion was accompanied by labor strife in the early 20th century. Long one of the poorest parts of the country, West Virginia reached its peak population in 1950. The decline of employment in coal mining and heavy industry has hampered the state's economic life.

West Virginia State Board of Education v Barnette one of the "flag salute" Supreme Court cases 1943 dealing with mandatory recitation of the pledge of allegiance in public school. Barnette issued a legal challenge to a West Virginia statute requiring all public-school children to salute the flag. A Jehovah's Witness, he argued that his child's First-Amendment freedom of religion was being denied, since reciting the pledge was against his religious principles. The Court invalidated the law because it violated First-Amendment rights to freedom of religion, speech, and thought.

weta flightless insect *Deinacrida rugosa*, 3.5 in/8.5 cm long, resembling a large grasshopper, found on offshore islands of New Zealand.

Wexford seaport and county town of Wexford, Republic of Ireland; population (1981) 15,000. Products include textiles, cheese, and agricultural machinery. It was founded by the Danes in the 9th century and devastated by Cromwell 1649.

Weyden Rogier van der c. 1399–1464. Netherlandish painter, official painter to the city of Brussels from 1436. He painted portraits and religious subjects, such as *The Last Judgment* c. 1450 (Hôtel-Dieu, Beaune). His refined style had considerable impact on Netherlandish painting.

Little is known of his life, and none of his works have been dated, but he was widely admired in his day and his paintings were sent to Italy, Spain, France, and Germany. His *Deposition* before 1443 (Prado, Madrid) shows the influence of Robert ◊Campin.

Weymouth seaport and resort in Dorset, S England; population (1981) 46,000. It is linked by ferry to France and the Channel Islands. Weymouth, dating from the 10th century, was the first place in England to suffer from the Black Death 1348 and was popularized as a bathing resort by George III.

whale any marine mammal of the order Cetacea, with front limbs modified into flippers and with internal vestiges of hind limbs. When they surface

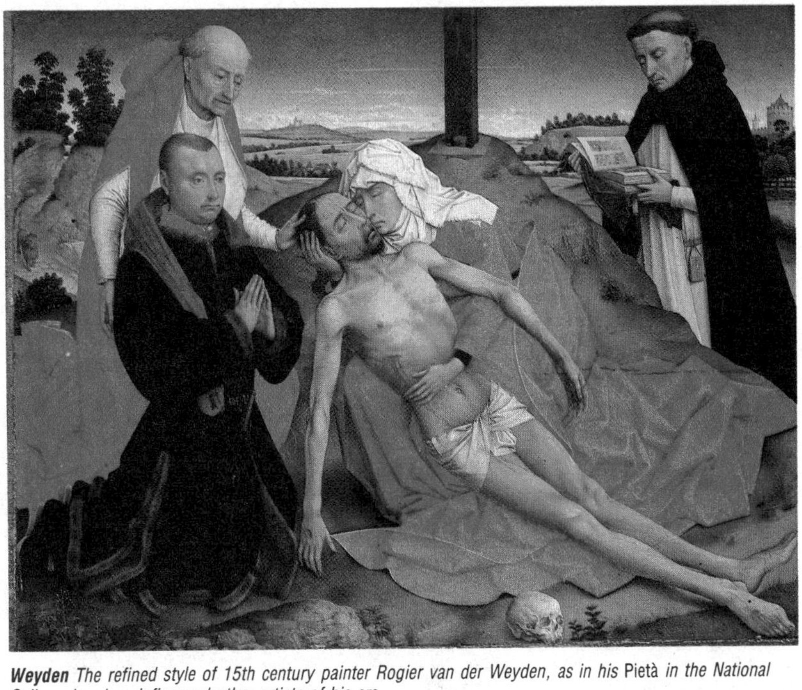

Weyden *The refined style of 15th century painter Rogier van der Weyden, as in his* Pietà *in the National Gallery, London, influenced other artists of his era.*

whale

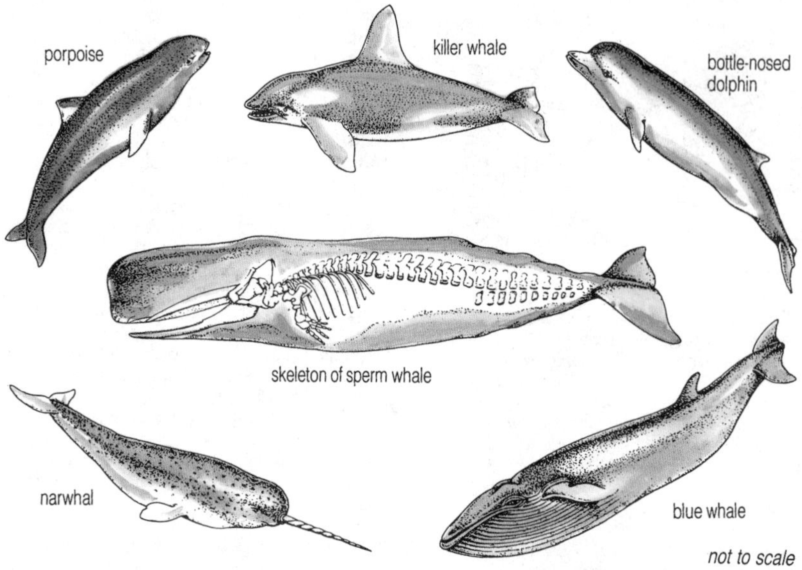
porpoise
killer whale
bottle-nosed dolphin
skeleton of sperm whale
narwhal
blue whale
not to scale

to breathe, they eject air in a "spout" through the blowhole (single or double nostrils) in the top of the head. There were hundreds of thousands of whales at the beginning of the 20th century, but they have been hunted close to extinction. The order is divided into the toothed whales (Odontoceti) and the baleen whales (Mysteciti). The toothed whales include ◊dolphins and ◊porpoises, along with large forms such as sperm whales. The baleen whales, with plates of modified mucous membrane called baleen in the mouth, are all large in size and include finback whales and right whales. See ◊whaling.

They are extremely intelligent and have a complex communication system, known as "songs." Mass strandings where whales swim onto a beach occur occasionally for unknown reasons; it may have something to do with pollution. Group loyalty is strong, and whales may follow a confused leader to disaster.

The blue whale *Sibaldus musculus*, one of the finback whales (or rorquals), is 100 ft/31 m long, and weighs over 100 tons. It is the largest animal ever to inhabit the planet. It feeds on plankton, strained through its whalebone "plates." The common rorqual *Balenoptera physalas* is slate-colored, and not quite so large. Largest of the toothed whales, which feed on fish and larger animals, is the sperm whale *Physeter catodon* (see ◊spermaceti). The killer whale is a large member of the dolphin family (Delphinidae), and is often exhibited in oceanaria. Killer whales in the wild have 8–15 special calls, and each family group, or "pod," has its own particular dialect: they are the first mammals known to have dialects in the same way as human language. See also ◊bowhead whale.

Whale James 1886–1957. English film director. He initially went to Hollywood to film his stage success *Journey's End* 1930 and went on to direct four horror films: *Frankenstein* 1931, *The Old Dark House* 1932, *The Invisible Man* 1933, and *Bride of Frankenstein* 1935. He also directed *Showboat* 1936.

whaling the hunting of whales for whale oil (made from the thick layer of fat under the skin called "blubber"), used for food and cosmetics; for the large reserve of oil in the head of the sperm whale, used in the leather industry; and for ambergris, a waxlike substance from the intestines, used in making perfumes. There are synthetic substitutes for all these products. Whales are also killed for their meat, which is eaten by the Japanese and used a pet food in the US and Europe. A protest movement has been moderately successful since the 1960s.

The International Whaling Commission, established in 1946, failed to enforce quotas on whale killing until world concern about the possible extinction of the whale mounted in the 1970s. By the end of the 1980s, 90% of blue, fin, humpback, and sperm whales had been wiped out. Low reproduction rates mean that protected species are slow to recover. After 1986 only Iceland, Japan, Norway, and the USSR have continued with limited whaling for "scientific purposes," but Japan has been repeatedly discovered in commercial whaling and pirates also operate. In 1991, Japan held a "final" whale feast before conforming to the regulations of the International Whaling Commission.

Wharton Edith (born Jones) 1862–1937. US novelist. Her work, known for its subtlety and form and influenced by her friend Henry James, was mostly set in New York society. It includes *The House of Mirth* 1905, which made her reputation; the grim, uncharacteristic novel of New England *Ethan Frome* 1911; *The Custom of the Country* 1913, and *The Age of Innocence* 1920.

wheat cereal plant derived from the wild *Triticum*, a grass native to the Middle East. It is one of the earliest of the domesticated grains (c. 10,000 BC), the chief cereal used in breadmaking, and it is widely cultivated in temperate climates suited to its growth. Wheat is killed by frost, and damp renders the grain soft, so warm, dry regions produce the most valuable grain.

The main wheat-producing areas of the world are Ukraine in the USSR, the prairie states of the US, the Punjab in India, the prairie provinces of Canada, parts of France, Poland, S Germany, Italy, Argentina, and SE Australia. Flour is milled from the ◊endosperm; the coatings of the grain produce bran. Semolina is also prepared from wheat; it is a meal byproduct from the manufacture of fine flour.

wheat

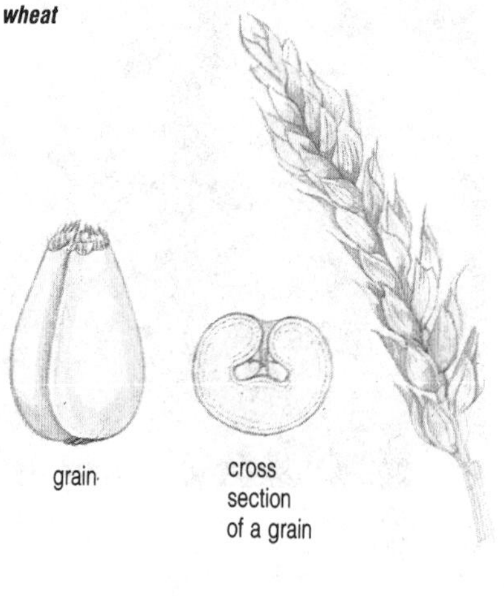
grain
cross section of a grain

wheatear small (6 in/15 cm long) migratory bird *Oenanthe oenanthe* of the family Muscicapidae, in the order Passeriformes. The family also includes the thrushes. Wheatears are found throughout the Old World and also breed in far N parts of North America. The plumage is light gray above and white below, with a white patch on the back, a black face-patch, and black and white wings and tail.

Wheatstone Charles 1802–1875. English physicist and inventor. He patented a railroad telegraph in 1837 and devised the Wheatstone bridge, an electrical network for measuring resistance. He also invented the harmonica and the concertina.

Wheeler Mortimer 1890–1976. English archeologist. As director-general of archeology in India 1944–48 he revealed the ◊Indus Valley civilization. He helped to popularize archeology by his television appearances.

Wheeling city in NW West Virginia on the Ohio river, SW of Pittsburgh, Pennsylvania. Industries include coal and natural-gas processing, iron and steel, textiles, glass, pottery, paper, and chemicals; population (1990) 34,882. Fort Henry, site of the last battle 1782 of the Revolutionary War, is here.

whelk any of various families of large marine snails with a thick spiral shell, especially the family Buccinidae. Whelks are scavengers, and also eat other shellfish. The largest grow to 16 in/40 cm long. Tropical species, such as the conches, can be very colorful.

The common northern whelk *Buccinum undatum* is widely distributed around the North Sea and Atlantic.

Whewell William 1794–1866. British physicist and philosopher who coined the term "scientist" along with such words as "Eocene" and "Miocene," "electrode," "cathode," and "anode." Most of his career was connected with Cambridge University, where he became the Master of Trinity College. His most enduring influence rests on two works of great scholarship, *The History of the Inductive Sciences* 1837 and *The Philosophy of the Inductive Sciences* 1840.

whey watery byproduct of the cheesemaking process, which is drained off after the milk has been heated and ◊rennet (a curdling agent) added to induce its coagulation.

Whig Party in the UK, predecessor of the Liberal Party. The name was first used of rebel ◊Covenanters and then of those who wished to exclude James II from the English succession (as a Roman Catholic). They were in power continuously 1714–60 and pressed for industrial and commercial development, a vigorous foreign policy, and religious toleration. During the French Revolution, the Whigs demanded parliamentary reform in Britain, and from the passing of the Reform Bill in 1832 became known as Liberals.

Whig Party in the US, political party opposed to the autocratic presidency of Andrew Jackson from 1834. The Whig presidents were W H Harrison, Taylor, and Fillmore. The party diverged over the issue of slavery 1852; the Northern Whigs joined the Republican party; the Southern or "Cotton" Whigs joined the Democrats. The title was taken from the British Whig Party which supported Parliament against the king. During the American Revolution, colonial patriots described themselves as Whigs, while those remaining loyal to Britain were known as Tories.

whimbrel a ◊curlew *Numenius phaeopus* with a medium-sized down-curved bill, streaked brown plumage, and striped head. About 1.3 ft/40 cm

wheat

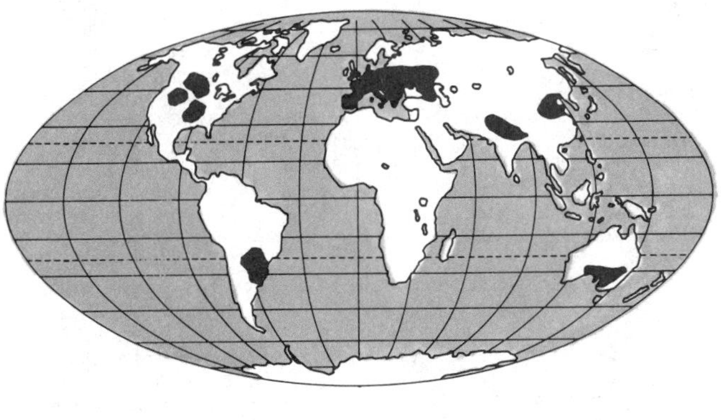

major areas

long, it breeds in the Arctic, and winters in Africa, S North America, South America, and S Asia.

whippet breed of dog resembling a small greyhound. It grows to 22 in/56 cm at the shoulder, and 20 lb/ 9 kg in weight.

The whippet was developed in England for racing. It was probably produced by crossing a terrier and a greyhound.

Whipple Fred Lawrence 1906– . US astronomer whose hypothesis in 1949 that the nucleus of a comet is like a dirty snowball was confirmed 1986 by space-probe studies of ◊Halley's comet. He was director of the Smithsonian Astrophysical Observatory 1955–73.

Whipple George 1878–1976. US physiologist whose research interest concerned the formation of hemoglobin in the blood. He showed that anemic dogs, kept under restricted diets, responded well to a liver regime, and that their hemoglobin quickly regenerated. This work led to a cure for pernicious anemia.

whippoorwill North American ◊nightjar *Caprimulgus vociferus*, so called from its cry.

whip snake any of the various species of nonpoisonous slender-bodied tree-dwelling snakes of the New World genus *Masticophis*, family Colubridae, also called coachwhips. They are closely allied to members of the genus *Coluber* of SW North America, Eurasia, Australasia, and N Africa, some of which are called whip snakes in the Old World, but racers in North America. They grow to about 5 ft/1.5 m in length, move very quickly, and are partially arboreal. They feed on rodents, small birds, lizards, sucker frogs, and insects. All lay eggs.

whiskey (Gaelic *uisge beatha*, water of life) a strong alcoholic liquor made from a fermented mash of various cereals: Scotch whiskey from malted barley; Irish whiskey usually from barley, and American whiskey and bourbon from rye and corn. Scotch and other whiskeys are usually blended; pure malt whiskeys are the most expensive. Whiskey is generally aged in wooden casks for 4–12 years.

The spelling "whisky" usually refers to Scotch or Canadian drink and "whiskey" to Irish or American. The earliest written record of whiskey comes from Scotland 1494 but the art of distillation is thought to have been known before this time.

whist a card game for four, predecessor of ◊bridge, in which the partners try to win a majority of the 13 tricks (the highest card played being the winner of the trick).

Whistler James Abbott McNeill 1834–1903. US painter and etcher, active in London from 1859. His riverscapes and portraits show subtle composition and color harmonies: for example, *Arrangement in Grey and Black: Portrait of the Painter's Mother* 1871 (Louvre, Paris).

He settled in Chelsea, London, and painted views of the Thames including *Old Battersea Bridge* (c. 1872–75) (Tate Gallery, London). In 1877 the art critic John ◊Ruskin published an article on his *Nocturne in Black and Gold: The Falling Rocket* (now in Detroit) that led to a libel trial in which Whistler was awarded symbolic damages of a farthing (a fourth of an old penny). Whistler described the trial in his book *The Gentle Art of Making Enemies* 1890.

Whistler was born in Lowell, Massachusetts. He originally attended West Point, left after failing a course, and worked as a draftsman. In 1855 he went to Paris where he was associated with the Impressionists.

Whitby port and resort in N Yorkshire, England, on the North Sea coast; population (1981) 14,000. Industries include boat building, fishing, and plastics. Remains of a Benedictine abbey built 1078 survive on the site of the original foundation by St Hilda 657, which was destroyed by the Danes 867. Captain Cook's ship *Resolution* was built in Whitby, where he had served his apprenticeship, and he sailed from here on his voyage to the Pacific in 1768.

Whitby, Synod of council summoned by King Oswy of Northumbria in 664, which decided to adopt the Roman rather than the Celtic form of Christianity for Britain.

Whistler *US artist James Whistler lived from 1859 in England, where he painted* Miss Cicely Alexander, harmony in grey and green *1872, Tate Gallery, London.*

White counter-revolutionary, especially during the Russian civil wars 1917–21. Originally the term described the party opposing the French Revolution, when the royalists used the white lily of the French monarchy as their badge.

White E(lwyn) B(rooks) 1899–1985. US writer, long associated with *The New Yorker* magazine and renowned for his satire, such as *Is Sex Necessary?* 1929 (with the humorist James Thurber).

With William Strunk Jr., he published *The Elements of Style* 1935, considered a definitive style manual for the English language. White also wrote children's classics: *Stuart Little* 1945, *Charlotte's Web* 1952, and *The Trumpet of the Swan* 1970.

White Edward Douglass, Jr 1845–1921. US jurist; associate justice 1894–1911 and chief justice 1911–21 of the US Supreme Court. During White's service the Court made important decisions on US economic policy. In *United States* v *E C Knight and Co* 1895 he joined the majority in weakening the Sherman Antitrust Act by removing manufacture of goods from its purview. In *Standard Oil Co.* v *United States* 1911 and *United States* v *American Tobacco Co* the Court created the still-current legal definition of trusts in restraint of trade (see ◊monopoly). In *McCray* v *United States* 1904 he wrote the Court's decision expanding federal taxing power. He also participated in several cases that refined US labor policy in civil rights cases and in the *Selective Draft Law Cases* 1918.

Born in Lafourche Parish, Louisiana, White attended Mount St Mary's College (Maryland), the Jesuit College (New Orleans), and Georgetown University, but left his college studies to serve in the Confederate Army. After the Civil War he studied law at the University of Louisiana Law School in New Orleans; he was admitted to the bar 1868. He entered private practice in his home state and became active in Democratic politics. He was elected to the state senate 1874 and was a justice of the Louisiana supreme court 1878–80. He was elected to the US Senate 1891. In 1893 President Cleveland nominated White to the Supreme Court. President Taft nominated White as chief justice.

White Patrick 1912–1990. Australian novelist. Born in London, he settled in Australia in the 1940s. His novels include *The Aunt's Story* 1948, *The Tree of Man* 1955, *Voss* 1957 (based on the 19th-century explorer Leichhardt), *The Vivisector* 1970, *The Eye of the Storm* 1973, *The Twyborn Affair* 1979, his autobiography *Flaws in the Glass* 1981, and his last work *Memoirs of Many in One* 1986. He won the Nobel Prize for Literature in 1973.

White Stanford 1853–1906. US architect. Born in New York City and trained in architecture during an apprenticeship with the firm of Gambril and Richardson, White became one of the most prominent US architects of the 19th century. After a year of study in Europe, he was one of the founders of the architectural firm of McKim, Mead and White 1879. Specializing in the Renaissance style, White designed, among many famous projects, the original Madison Square Garden and the Washington Square Arch, both in New York City. A flamboyant and arrogant personality, he was murdered in the rooftop restaurant of Madison Square Garden by the husband of a former lover.

White T(erence) H(anbury) 1906–1964. English writer who retold the Arthurian legend in four volumes of *The Once and Future King* 1938–58.

whitebait any of the fry (young) of various silvery fishes, especially ◊herring. It is also the name for a Pacific smelt *Osmerus mordax*.

whitebeam tree *Sorbus aria*, native to S Europe, usually found growing on chalk or limestone. It can reach 60 ft/20 m. It takes its name from the pinnately compound leaves, which have a dense coat of short white hairs on the underside.

It is a type of ◊mountain ash.

white blood cell or ***leukocyte*** one of a number of different cells that play a part in the body's defenses and give immunity against disease. Some (◊phagocytes and ◊macrophages) engulf invading microorganisms, others kill infected cells, while ◊lymphocytes produce more specific immune responses (see ◊B cell and ◊T cell). White blood cells are colorless, with clear or granulated cytoplasm, and are capable of independent amoeboid movement. Unlike mammalian red blood cells, they possess a nucleus. Human blood contains about 11,000 leukocytes to the cubic millimeter—about one to every 500 red cells. However, these cells are not confined to the blood; they also occur in the ◊lymph and elsewhere in the body's tissues.

White blood cell numbers may be reduced (leucopenia) by starvation, pernicious anemia, and certain infections, such as typhoid and malaria. An increase in their numbers (leukocytosis) is a reaction to normal events such as digestion, exertion, and pregnancy, and to abnormal ones such as loss of blood, cancer, and most infections.

white dwarf small, hot ◊star, the last stage in the life of a star such as the Sun. White dwarfs have a mass similar to that of the Sun, but are only 1% of the Sun's diameter, similar in size to the Earth. Most have surface temperatures of 14,400°F/8,000°C or more, hotter than the Sun. Yet, being so small, their overall luminosities may be less than 1% of that of the Sun.

White dwarfs consist of degenerate matter in which gravity has packed the protons and electrons together as tightly as is physically possible, so that a spoonful of it weighs several tons. White dwarfs are thought to be the shrunken remains of stars that have exhausted their internal energy supplies. They slowly cool and fade over billions of years.

Whitefield George 1714–1770. British Methodist evangelist. He was a student at Oxford University and took orders in 1738, but was suspended for his unorthodox doctrines and methods. For many years he traveled through Britain and America, and by his preaching contributed greatly to the Great Awakening. He died while visiting New England.

whitefish any of various freshwater fishes, genera *Coregonus* and *Prosopium* of the salmon family, found in lakes and rivers of North America and Eurasia. They include the whitefish *C. clupeaformis* and cisco *C. artedi*.

Whitehead Alfred North 1861–1947. English philosopher and mathematician. In his "theory of organism," he attempted a synthesis of metaphysics and science. His works include *Principia Mathematica* 1910–13 (with Bertrand ◊Russell), *The Concept of Nature* 1920, and *Adventures of Ideas* 1933.

He was professor of applied mathematics at London University 1914–24, and professor of philosophy at Harvard University, 1924–37. Other works include *Principles of Natural Knowledge* 1919, *Science and the Modern World* 1925, and *Process and Reality* 1929.

Whitehorse capital of Yukon Territory, Canada; population (1986) 15,199. Whitehorse is on the NW Highway. It replaced Dawson as capital in 1953.

White House official residence of the president of the US, in Washington, DC. It is a plain edifice of sandstone, built in the Italian Renaissance style 1792–99 to the designs of James Hoban, who also restored it after it was burned by the British 1814; it was then painted white to hide the scars.

The structure was completely restored 1948–52 by the Truman administration; the interior was redecorated 1960–63 by First Lady Jacqueline Kennedy. The offices of the president's staff in the White House and nearby buildings are often collectively referred to as "The White House." The president's study and ceremonial office is known from its shape as the Oval Office. The building includes living quarters for the president, the presidential family, and staff and public rooms for dinners, concerts, and receptions. The presidential apartment is separate from the rest of the mansion, which is open to visitors and public tours as a museum. The name White House, first recorded in 1811, is often adapted to refer to other residences of the president, for example Little White House, at Warm Springs, Georgia, where F D Roosevelt died; Western White House, at San Clemente, California, where Nixon had a home.

white knight in business, a company invited by the target of a takeover bid to make a rival bid. The company invited to bid is usually one that is already on good terms with the target company.

Whiteman Paul 1890–1967. US dance-band and swing orchestra leader specializing in "symphonic jazz." He commissioned George Gershwin's *Rhapsody in Blue*, conducting its premiere in 1924.

whiteout "fog" of grains of dry snow caused by strong winds in temperatures of between 0°F/–18°C and 30°F/–1°C. The uniform whiteness of

White House *The official residence of the US president, the White House was burned by the British in 1814 during the War of 1812.*

***Whitman** US poet Walt Whitman, whose breaking away from conventional form made him one of the most influential writers of his generation.*

the ground and air causes disorientation in humans.

White Russia English translation of ◊Byelorussia, republic of the USSR.

White Sea (Russian *Beloye More*) gulf of the Arctic Ocean, on which the port of Archangel stands. There is a Soviet warship construction base, including nuclear submarines, at Severodvinsk. The North Dvina and Onega rivers flow into it, and there are canal links with the Baltic, Black, and Caspian seas.

White Terror general term used by Socialists and Marxists to describe a right-wing counterrevolution, for example, the attempts by the Chinese Guomindang to massacre the communists 1927–31; see ◊White.

whitethroat any of several Old World warblers of the genus *Sylvia*, found in scrub, hedges, and wood clearings of Eurasia in summer, migrating to Africa in winter. They are about 5.5 in/14 cm long.

whiting any of various edible marine bony fishes, especially the silver hake and various kingfishes, genus *Menticirrhus*.

Whitlam Gough (Edward) 1916– . Australian politician, leader of the Labor Party 1967–78 and prime minister 1972–75.

Whitman Walt(er) 1819–1892. US poet who published *Leaves of Grass* 1855, which contains the symbolic "Song of Myself." It used unconventional free verse (with no rhyme or regular rhythm) and scandalized the public by its frank celebration of sexuality.

Born at West Hill (Huntington, Long Island), New York, as a young man Whitman worked as a printer, teacher, and journalist. In 1865 he published *Drum-Taps*, a volume inspired by his work as an army nurse during the Civil War. *Democratic Vistas* 1871 is a collection of his prose pieces. He also wrote an elegy for Abraham Lincoln, "When Lilacs Last in the Dooryard Bloom'd." He preached a particularly American vision of individual freedom and human brotherhood. Such poets as Ezra Pound, Wallace Stevens, and Allen Ginsberg show his influence in their work.

Whitney Eli 1765–1825. US inventor who in 1794 patented the ◊cotton gin, a device for separating cotton fiber from its seeds. Also a manufacturer of firearms, he created a standarization system that was the precursor of the assembly line.

Born in Westborough, Massachusetts, Whitney graduated from Yale 1792. His invention of the cotton gin revolutionized the cotton industry in the South. In a shop in New Haven, Connecticut, he manufacturered muskets under a contract from the US government, using power-driven tools to produce interchangeable parts.

Whitney v California a US Supreme Court decision 1927 dealing with state legislation restricting freedom of speech and assembly. Charlotte Whitney had been convicted, under a California law outlawing membership in organizations advocating political or industrial violence, for her activities in the Communist Labor Party. She appealed to the Supreme Court for protection under the First Amendment. The Court upheld the California law, ruling that states were obligated to thwart "all threats to the American form of government, no matter how remote."

Whitsunday Christian church festival held seven weeks after Easter, commemorating the descent of the Holy Spirit on the Apostles. The name is probably derived from the white garments worn by candidates for baptism at the festival.

Whittier John Greenleaf 1807–1892. US poet who was a powerful opponent of slavery, as shown in the verse *Voices of Freedom* 1846. Among his other works are *Legends of New England in Prose and Verse, Songs of Labor* 1850, and the New England nature poem *Snow-Bound* 1866.

He was also a journalist and humanitarian. Many of his poems have been set to music, and are sung as church hymns.

Whittington Dick (Richard) 13th–14th centuries. English cloth merchant who was mayor of London 1397–98, 1406–07, and 1419–20. According to legend, he came to London as a poor boy with his cat when he heard that the streets were paved with gold and silver. His cat first appears in a play from 1605.

Whittle Frank 1907– . British engineer who patented the basic design for the turbojet engine in 1930. In the Royal Air Force he worked on jet propulsion 1937–46. In May 1941 the Gloster E 28/39 aircraft first flew with the Whittle jet engine. Both the German (first operational jet planes) and the US jet aircraft were built using his principles.

WHO acronym for ◊World Health Organization.

Who, The English rock group, formed 1964, with a hard, aggressive sound, high harmonies, and a stage show that often included destroying their instruments. Their albums include *Tommy* 1969, *Who's Next* 1971, and *Quadrophenia* 1973. Originally a mod band, The Who comprised Pete Townshend (1945–), guitar and songwriter; Roger Daltrey (1944–), vocals; John Entwhistle (1944–), bass; Keith Moon (1947–1978), drums.

wholesale the business of selling merchandise to anyone other than the final customer. Most manufacturers or producers sell in bulk to a wholesale organization which distributes the smaller quantities required by retail outlets.

whooping cough or ***pertussis*** acute infectious disease, seen mainly in children, caused by colonization of the air passages by the bacterium *Bordetella pertussis*. There may be catarrh, mild fever, and loss of appetite, but the main symptom is violent coughing, associated with the sharp intake of breath that is the characteristic "whoop," and often followed by vomiting and severe nose bleeds. The cough may persist for weeks.

Although debilitating, the disease is seldom serious in older children, but infants are at risk both from the illness itself and from susceptibility to other conditions, such as ◊pneumonia. Immunization lessens the incidence and severity of whooping cough.

whortleberry a form of ◊bilberry.

whydah any of various African birds of genus *Vidua*, order Passeriformes, of the weaver family. They lay their eggs in the nest of waxbills, which rear the young. Young birds resemble young waxbills, but the adults do not resemble adult waxbills. Males have long tail feathers used in courtship displays.

Whymper Edward 1840–1911. English mountaineer. He made the first ascent of many Alpine peaks, including the Matterhorn 1865, and in the Andes scaled Chimborazo and other mountains.

WI abbreviation for ◊West Indies; ◊Wisconsin.

Wichita industrial city (oil refining, aircraft, motor vehicles) in S Kansas; population (1990) 304,011. Wichita State University is here. Wichita was founded about 1867 and became a stopover on the Chisholm cattle-driving trail; when the railroad arrived 1872, the city became a major cattle-shipping point. Petroleum was discovered nearby 1915, and aircraft manufacture began 1920.

Wichita Falls city in N Texas, on the Wichita river, S of the Oklahoma border. It is an important petroleum-processing center. Other industries include leather goods, textiles, foodstuffs, electronics, and pharmaceutical goods; population (1990) 96,259.

wide-angle lens a photographic lens of shorter focal length than normal, taking in a wider angle of view.

Widmark Richard 1914– . US actor who made his film debut in *Kiss of Death* 1947 as a psychopath. He subsequently appeared in a great variety of *film noir* roles as well as *The Alamo* 1960, *Madigan* 1968, and *Coma* 1978.

Wieland Christoph Martin 1733–1813. German poet and novelist. After attempts at religious poetry, he came under the influence of Voltaire and Rousseau, and wrote novels such as *Agathon* 1766–67 and the satirical *Abderiten* 1774, and tales in verse such as *Musarion* 1768, *Oberon* 1780, and others. He translated Shakespeare into German 1762–66.

Wien German name for ◊Vienna, capital of Austria.

Wien Wilhelm 1864–1928. German physicist who studied radiation and established the principle, since known as Wien's law, that the wavelength at which the radiation from an idealized radiating body is most intense is inversely proportional to the body's absolute temperature. (That is, the hotter the body, the shorter the wavelength.) For this, and other work on radiation, he was awarded the 1911 Nobel Prize for Physics.

Wiene Robert 1880–1938. German film director of the bizarre Expressionist film *Das Kabinett des Dr Caligari/The Cabinet of Dr Caligari* 1919. He also directed *Orlacs Hände/The Hands of Orlac* 1924, *Der Rosenkavalier* 1926, and *Ultimatum* 1938.

Wiener Norbert 1894–1964. US mathematician. Born in Columbia, Missouri, Wiener was a child prodigy, attending Tufts University at an early age and receiving his PhD from Harvard at age 19. Joining the mathematics faculty at the Massachusetts Institute of Technology 1919, he became one of the pioneers in the development of computer logic. During World War II, Wiener helped to perfect sophisticated weapons guidance systems. Best known for his book *Cybernetics* 1948, he laid the theoretical groundwork for information feedback systems. Two volumes of memoirs were published as *Ex-Prodigy* 1953 and *I Am a Mathematician* 1956.

Wiener Werkstätte (German "Vienna Workshops") a group of artisans and artists, founded in Vienna 1903 by Josef Hoffmann and Kolo Moser who were both members of the Vienna ◊Sezession. They designed objects, ranging from furniture and jewelry to metal and books, in a rectilinear Art Nouveau style influenced by Charles Rennie Mackintosh. The workshop, financed by Fritz Wärndorfer, closed in 1932.

Wien's law in physics, a law of radiation stating that the wavelength carrying the maximum energy is inversely proportional to the body's absolute temperature: the hotter a body is, the shorter the wavelength. It has the form $\lambda_{max}T$ = constant, where λ_{max} is the wavelength of maximum intensity and T is the temperature. The law is named after the German physicist Wilhelm Wien.

Wiesbaden spa town and capital of Hessen, Federal Republic of Germany, on the Rhine 12 mi/20 km W of Frankfurt; population (1988) 267,000. Products include cement, plastics, wines and spirits; most of the German sparkling wine cellars are in this area. Wiesbaden was the capital of the former duchy of Nassau from the 12th century until 1866.

Wiesel Elie 1928– . Romanian-born US academic and human-rights campaigner. He was held by the ◊Nazis in Buchenwald ◊concentration camp during World War II and assiduously documented wartime atrocities against the Jews in an effort to alert the world to the dangers of racism and violence. The recipient of the 1986 Nobel Peace Prize, he sought to remind new generations of the Nazi atrocities so that they might never be repeated. He is considered the most eloquent spokesman of the death-camp survivors.

wig artificial head of hair, either real or synthetic, worn as an adornment, disguise, or to conceal baldness. Wigs were known in the ancient world and have been found on Egyptian mummies. Today they remain part of the uniform of judges, lawyers, and some parliamentary officials in the UK and certain Commonwealth countries.

Wigan industrial town (food processing, engineering, paper) in Greater Manchester, NW England; population (1981) 80,000. The Wigan Alps are a recreation area with ski slopes and water sports created from industrial dereliction including colliery spoil heaps.

wigeon any of two species of dabbling duck of genus *Anas*. The American wigeon *A. americana*, about 19 in/48 cm long, is found along both coasts in winter and breeds inland. Males have a white-capped head and a green eye stripe.

The Eurasian wigeon *A. penelope* has a dark head without eye stripe. It is a regular winter visitor along both North American coasts.

Wiggin Kate Douglas 1856–1923. US writer, born in Philadelphia. She was a pioneer in the establishment of kindergartens in the US, and wrote the children's classic *Rebecca of Sunnybrook Farm* 1903 and its sequels.

Wight, Isle of island and county in S England.

area 147 sq mi/380 sq km

towns Newport (administrative headquarters), resorts: Ryde, Sandown, Shanklin, Ventnor

features the Needles, a group of pointed chalk rocks up to 100 ft/30 m high in the sea to the W; the Solent, the sea channel between Hampshire and the island (including the anchorage of Spithead opposite Portsmouth, used for naval reviews); Cowes, venue of Regatta Week and headquarters of the Royal Yacht Squadron; Osborne House, near Cowes, a home of Queen Victoria, for whom it was built 1845; Farringford, home of Tennyson, near Freshwater

products chiefly agricultural; tourism is important

population (1987) 127,000

history called Vectis ("separate division") by the Romans, who conquered it AD 43. Charles I was imprisoned 1647–48 in Carisbrooke Castle, now ruined.

Wightman Cup annual tennis competition between international women's teams from the US and the UK. The trophy, first contested in 1923, was donated by Hazel Hotchkiss Wightman (1886–1974), a former US tennis player who won singles, doubles, and mixed-doubles titles in the US Championships 1909–1911. Because of US domination of the contest it was abandoned in 1990, but it is to be reinstated in 1991 with the UK side assisted by European players.

Wigner Eugene Paul 1902– . Hungarian-born US physicist who introduced the notion of parity into nuclear physics with the consequence that all nuclear processes should be indistinguishable from their mirror images. For this, and other work on nuclear structure, he shared the 1963 Nobel Prize for Physics with Maria ◊Goeppert-Mayer and Hans Jensen (1906–1973).

Wilberforce William 1759–1833. English reformer who was instrumental in abolishing slavery in the British Empire. He entered Parliament in 1780; in 1807 his bill for the abolition of the slave trade was passed, and in 1833, largely through his efforts, slavery was abolished throughout the empire.

***Wilde** Irish writer and poet Oscar Wilde was a leading figure of the Aesthetic movement.*

Wilbur Richard 1921– . US poet, whose witty verse is found in several volumes including *Poems 1943–56* 1957 and *The Mind Reader* 1971.

Wilde Cornel(ius Louis) 1915–1989. US actor and film director. He starred in *A Song to Remember* 1945, *Leave Her To Heaven* 1945, and *Forever Amber* 1947. He produced, directed, and starred (with his wife Jean Wallace) in several films from 1955, including *Storm Fear* 1955, *Maracaibo* 1958, *The Naked Prey* 1966, *Beach Red* 1967, and *No Blade of Grass* 1970. His originality reveals him to be a primitive of the camera, at home in African adventure.

Wilde Oscar (Fingal O'Flahertie Wills) 1854–1900. Irish writer. With his flamboyant style and quotable conversation, he dazzled London society and, on his lecture tour in 1882, the US. He published his only novel, *The Picture of Dorian Gray* 1891, followed by witty plays including *A Woman of No Importance* 1893 and *The Importance of Being Earnest* 1895. In 1895 he was imprisoned for two years for homosexual offenses; he died in exile.

Wilde was born in Dublin and studied at Dublin and Oxford, where he became known as a supporter of the Aesthetic movement ("art for art's sake"). He published *Poems* 1881, and also wrote fairy tales and other stories, criticism, and a long, anarchic political essay, "The Soul of Man Under Socialism" 1891. His elegant social comedies include *Lady Windermere's Fan* 1892 and *An Ideal Husband* 1895. The drama *Salome* 1893, based on the biblical character, was written in French; considered scandalous by the British censor, it was first performed in Paris 1896 with the actress Sarah Bernhardt in the title role.

Among his lovers was Lord Alfred ◊Douglas, whose father provoked Wilde into a lawsuit that led to his social and financial ruin and imprisonment. The long poem *Ballad of Reading Gaol* 1898 and a letter published as *De Profundis* 1905 were written in jail to explain his side of the relationship. After his release from prison in 1897, he lived in France and is buried in Paris.

wildebeest another name for ◊gnu.

Wilder Billy 1906– . Austrian-born US screenwriter and film director who arrived in the US in 1934. He directed and coscripted *Double Indemnity* 1944, *The Lost Weekend* (Academy Award for best director) 1945, *Sunset Boulevard* 1950, *Some Like it Hot* 1959, and the Academy Award-winning *The Apartment* 1960.

He specialized in "smart" romances and worked with Charles Brackett on film scripts such as *Ninotchka* 1939 directed by Lubitsch and produced by Wilder. He won the Thalberg Award 1987.

Wilder Thornton (Niven) 1897–1975. US playwright and novelist. He won Pulitzer prizes for the novel *The Bridge of San Luis Rey* 1927 and for the plays *Our Town* 1938 and *The Skin of Our Teeth* 1942. His farce *The Matchmaker* 1954 was made into a film 1958. In 1964 it was adapted into the hit stage musical *Hello, Dolly!*, also made into a film. His plays are innovative in that they are overtly philosophical, they generally employ no props or scenery, and the characters often directly address the audience.

wilderness area of uncultivated and uninhabited land, which is usually located some distance from towns and cities. In the US wilderness areas are specially designated by Congress and protected by federal agencies; some are "forever wild."

wild type in genetics, the naturally occurring gene for a particular character that is typical of most individuals of a given species, as distinct from new genes that arise by mutation.

Wilhelm (English *William*) two emperors of Germany:

Wilhelm I 1797–1888. King of Prussia from 1861 and emperor of Germany from 1871; the son of Friedrich Wilhelm III. He served in the Napoleonic Wars 1814–15 and helped to crush the 1848 revolution. After he succeeded his brother Friedrich Wilhelm IV to the throne of Prussia, his policy was largely dictated by his chancellor ◊Bismarck, who secured his proclamation as emperor.

Wilhelm II 1859–1941. Emperor of Germany from 1888, the son of Frederick III and Victoria, daughter of Queen Victoria of Britain. In 1890 he forced Chancellor Bismarck to resign and began to direct foreign policy himself, which proved disastrous. He encouraged warlike policies and built up the German navy. In 1914 he first approved Austria's ultimatum to Serbia and then, when he realized war was inevitable, tried in vain to prevent it. In 1918 he fled to Holland, after Germany's defeat and his abdication.

Wilhelmshaven North Sea industrial port, resort, and naval base in Lower Saxony, Germany, on Jade Bay; population (1983) 99,000. Products include chemicals, textiles, and machinery.

Wilkes John 1727–1797. British Radical politician, imprisoned for his political views; member of Parliament 1757–64 and from 1774. He championed parliamentary reform, religious toleration, and US independence.

Wilkes, born in Clerkenwell, London, entered Parliament as a Whig in 1757. His attacks on the Tory prime minister Bute in his paper *The North Briton* led to his outlawry in 1764; he fled to France, and on his return in 1768 was imprisoned. He was four times elected MP for Middlesex, but the Commons refused to admit him and finally declared his opponent elected. This secured him strong working- and middle-class support, and in 1774 he was allowed to take his seat in Parliament.

Wilkes Barre city in NE Pennsylvania, on the Susquehanna river, SW of Scranton. Industries include furniture, textiles, wire and tobacco products, and heavy machinery; population (1990) 47,523.

Wilkins Maurice Hugh Frederick 1916– . New Zealand scientist. In 1962 he shared the Nobel Prize for Medicine with Francis ◊Crick and James ◊Watson for his work on the molecular structure of nucleic acids, particularly ◊DNA, using X-ray diffraction.

Wilkins began his career as a physicist working on luminescence and phosphorescence, radar, and the separation of uranium isotopes, and worked in the US during World War II on the development of the atomic bomb. After the war he turned his attention from nuclear physics to biophysics, and studied the genetic effects of ultrasonic waves, nucleic acids, and viruses by using ultraviolet light.

Wilkins William 1778–1839. English architect who pioneered the Greek revival in England with his design for Downing College, Cambridge. His other works include the main block of University College London 1827–28 and the National Gallery, London, 1834–38.

will in law, declaration of how a person wishes his

or her property to be disposed of after death. It also appoints administrators of the estate (◊executors) and may contain wishes on other matters, such as place of burial or use of organs for transplant. Wills must comply with formal legal requirements of the local jurisdiction.

Willard Frances Elizabeth Caroline 1839–1898. US educator. Born in Churchville, New York, and raised in Wisconsin, Willard was educated at the Northwestern Female College in Evanston, Illinois. After a career as a teacher, she was appointed dean of women at Northwestern University 1873. Becoming increasingly committed to the cause of the prohibition of alcohol, she served as president of the Women's Christian Temperance Union 1879–98. Willard was also elected President of the National Council of Women 1888.

Willem Dutch form of ◊William.

William four kings of England:

William I the Conqueror c. 1027–1087. King of England from 1066. He was the illegitimate son of Duke Robert the Devil and succeeded his father as duke of Normandy in 1035. Claiming that his relative King Edward the Confessor had bequeathed him the English throne, William invaded the country in 1066, defeating ◊Harold II at Hastings, Sussex, and was crowned king of England.

He was crowned in Westminster Abbey on Christmas Day 1066. He completed the establishment of feudalism in England, compiling detailed records of land and property in the Domesday Book, and kept the barons firmly under control. He died in Rouen after a fall from his horse and is buried in Caen, France. He was succeeded by his son William II.

William II Rufus, the Red c. 1056–1100. King of England from 1087, the third son of William I. He spent most of his reign attempting to capture Normandy from his brother ◊Robert II, duke of Normandy. His extortion of money led his barons to revolt and caused confrontation with Bishop Anselm. He was killed while hunting in the New Forest, and was succeeded by his brother Henry I.

William III of Orange 1650–1702. King of Great Britain and Ireland from 1688, the son of William II of Orange and Mary, daughter of Charles I. He was offered the English crown by the parliamentary opposition to James II. He invaded England in 1688 and in 1689 became joint sovereign with his wife, ◊Mary II. He spent much of his reign campaigning, first in Ireland, where he defeated James II at the battle of the Boyne 1690, and later against the French in Flanders. He was succeeded by Anne.

William IV 1765–1837. King of Great Britain and Ireland from 1830, when he succeeded his brother George IV; third son of George III. He was created duke of Clarence 1789, and married Adelaide of Saxe-Meiningen (1792–1849) in 1818. During the Reform Bill crisis he secured its passage by agreeing to create new peers to overcome the hostile majority in the House of Lords. He was succeeded by Victoria.

William three kings of the Netherlands:

William I 1772–1844. King of the Netherlands 1815–40. He lived in exile during the French occupation 1795–1813 and fought against the emperor Napoleon at Jena and Wagram. The Austrian Netherlands were added to his kingdom by the Allies in 1815, but secured independence (recognized by the major European states in 1839) by the revolution of 1830. William's unpopularity led to his abdication in 1840.

William II 1792–1849. King of the Netherlands 1840–49, son of William I. He served with the British army in the Peninsular War and at Waterloo. In 1848 he averted revolution by conceding a liberal constitution.

William III 1817–1890. King of the Netherlands 1849–90, the son of William II. In 1862 he abolished slavery in the Dutch East Indies.

William the Lion 1143–1214. King of Scotland from 1165. He was captured by Henry II while invading England in 1174, and forced to do homage, but Richard I abandoned the English claim to suzerainty for a money payment in 1189. In 1209 William was forced by King John to renounce his claim to Northumberland.

William the Silent 1533–1584. Prince of Orange from 1544. He was appointed governor of Holland by Philip II of Spain in 1559, but joined the revolt of 1572 against Spain's oppressive rule and, as a Protestant from 1573, became the national leader. He briefly succeeded in uniting the Catholic southern and Protestant northern provinces, but the former provinces submitted to Spain while the latter formed a federation in 1579 which repudiated Spanish suzerainty in 1581. He became known as "the Silent" because of his absolute discretion. He was assassinated by a Spanish agent.

William of Malmesbury c. 1080–c. 1143. English historian and monk. He compiled the *Gesta regum/ Deeds of the Kings* about 1120–40 and *Historia novella*, which together formed a history of England to 1142.

Williams (George) Emlyn 1905–1987. Welsh actor and playwright. His plays, in which he appeared, include *Night Must Fall* 1935 and *The Corn Is Green* 1938. He gave early encouragement to the actor Richard Burton.

Williams John (Christopher) 1942– . Australian guitarist, whose extensive repertoire includes contemporary music and jazz.

Williams Roger c. 1603–1683. American colonist, founder of the Rhode Island colony 1636, based on democracy and complete religious freedom.

He came to America as a Puritan minister in Massachusets 1631 but was banished from the colony 1635 for his "dangerous opinions"; he deplored theocracy and advocated separation of church and state. He then founded Providence 1636, disavowed Puritanism 1639, and returned to England to secure a patent with full religious freedom for his colony in the face of threats from the Puritans. He subsequently returned to Rhode Island and was the colony's president 1654–57; there he founded the first Baptist Church in America. Williams tried to maintain good relations with the Indians of the region, although he fought against them in the Pequot War and King Philip's War.

Williams Ted (Theodore Samuel) 1918– . US baseball player. Born in San Diego, California, Williams was signed by the Boston Red Sox and made his major league debut 1939. Named rookie of the year, Williams went on to a 19-season career with the Red Sox (interrupted by service in World War II and the Korean war), during which he established a lifetime batting average of .344. He was six times the American League batting champion and twice won the most valuable player award. In 1947 he became only the second player (Rogers ◊Hornsby was first) to twice win the Triple Crown (leading the league in batting, home runs, and runs batted in for a season). Williams retired as a player 1960 and served as manager of the Washington Senators 1969–71 and the Texas Rangers 1972. He was elected to the Baseball Hall of Fame 1966.

Williams Tennessee (Thomas Lanier) 1911–1983. US playwright, born in Mississippi. His work is characterized by fluent dialogue and searching analysis of the psychological deficiencies of his characters. His plays, usually set in the Deep South against a background of decadence and degradation, include, most notably, *The Glass Menagerie* 1945, *A Streetcar Named Desire* 1947, and *Cat on a Hot Tin Roof* 1955, the latter two of which earned Pulitzer Prizes. Many of his plays have been made into successful theatrical films, several of which were directed memorably by Elia Kazan. His other plays include *Suddenly Last Summer* 1958 and *Sweet Bird of Youth* 1959. After writing *The Night of the Iguana* 1961, also awarded the Pulitzer Prize, he entered a period of ill health, and none of his subsequent plays succeeded. However, his earlier work earned him a reputation as one of America's pre-eminent playwrights.

***Williams** US playwright Tennessee Williams. All his most influential works are set in the Deep South where he grew up.*

Williams William Carlos 1883–1963. US poet. His spare images and language reflect everyday speech. His epic poem *Paterson* 1946–58 celebrates his hometown in New Jersey. *Pictures from Brueghel* 1963 won him, posthumously, a Pulitzer prize. His vast body of prose work includes novels, short stories, and the play *A Dream of Love* 1948. His work had a great impact on younger US poets.

Williamsburg historic city in Virginia; population (1990) 11,530. Founded in 1632, capital of the colony of Virginia 1699–1779, much of it has been restored to its 18th-century appearance. The College of William and Mary 1693 is one of the oldest in the US.

Williamsport city in N central Pennsylvania, on the Susquehanna river, N of Harrisburg. Industries include electronics, plastics, metals, lumber, textiles, and aircraft parts; population (1990) 31,933. It is the birthplace 1939 of Little League baseball.

William the Marshall 1st Earl of Pembroke c. 1146–1219. English knight, regent of England from 1216. After supporting the dying Henry II against Richard (later Richard I), he went on a crusade to Palestine, was pardoned by Richard, and was granted an earldom in 1189. On King John's death he was appointed guardian of the future Henry III, and defeated the French under Louis VIII to enable Henry to gain the throne.

He grew up as a squire in Normandy and became tutor in 1170 to Henry, son of Henry II of England. William's life was a model of chivalric loyalty, serving four successive kings of England.

Willkie Wendell Lewis 1892–1944. US political leader. After service in World War I, he became corporate counsel for a private utility and an outspoken opponent of the economic policies of the New Deal, for which reason Willkie was nominated as the 1940 Republican presidential candidate. After losing to F D Roosevelt he continued as a leader of the liberal wing of the Republican party. Becoming committed to the cause of international cooperation, he published *One World* 1942.

Born in Elwood, Indiana, and educated at Indiana University, Willkie was admitted to the bar 1916.

willow

willow any tree or shrub of the genus *Salix*, family Salicaceae. There are over 350 species, mostly in the northern hemisphere, and they flourish in damp places. The leaves are often lance-shaped, and the male and female catkins are found on separate trees.

North American species include black willow *S. nigra* and Pacific willow *S. lasiandra*. The weeping willow *S. babylonica* is a native of China, cultivated worldwide.

willowherb plant of the genus *Epilobium*, a perennial weed. Fireweed *E. angustifolium* is common in woods and waste places, especially after forest fires in areas bordering the Arctic. It grows to 4 ft/1.2 m with long terminal racemes of red or purplish flowers.

Wills Helen Newington 1905– . US tennis player. Born in Centerville, California, Wills was educated at the University of California and won her first US women's title 1923 and her first Wimbledon championship 1927. In the course of an unparalleled amateur tennis career, Wills went on to win the US title six more times and Wimbledon seven more times. In addition to many other doubles and singles titles, Wills won two gold medals in the 1924 Paris Olympics. From 1929 to 1937 she played under her married name, Helen Wills Moody.

Wilmington industrial port and city (chemicals, textiles, shipbuilding, iron and steel goods; headquarters of Du Pont enterprises) in Delaware; population (1990) 71,529. Founded by Swedish settlers as Fort Christina 1638, it was taken from the Dutch and renamed by the British in the 1664.

Wilmington port city in SE North Carolina, on the Cape Fear river, near the Atlantic Ocean. Its manufactures include textiles, tobacco, lumber, and chemicals. Tourism is important to the economy; population (1990) 55,530.

Wilms' tumor or ***nephroblastoma*** one of the rare cancers of infancy, arising in the kidneys. Often the only symptom is abdominal swelling. Treatment is by removal of the affected kidney (nephrectomy), followed by radiotherapy and ◊cytotoxic drugs.

Wilson Angus (Frank Johnstone) 1913– . British novelist, short-story writer, and biographer whose acidly humorous books include *Anglo-Saxon Attitudes* 1956 and *The Old Men at the Zoo* 1961.

His nonfiction includes *Emile Zola* 1952, *The World of Charles Dickens* 1970, and *The Strange Ride of Rudyard Kipling* 1977.

Wilson Brian 1942– . US pop musician, founder member of the Beach Boys pop group.

Wilson Charles Thomson Rees 1869–1959. British physicist who in 1911 invented the Wilson ◊cloud chamber, an apparatus for studying subatomic particles. He shared a Nobel Prize in 1927.

Wilson Edmund 1895–1972. US critic and writer. Perhaps the foremost American social and literary critic of the 20th century, he was an editor of *Vanity Fair* 1920–21, the *New Republic* 1926–31, and *The New Yorker* 1944–48. Among his most influential works are *Axel's Castle* 1931, a survey of symbolism, and *The Wound and the Bow* 1941, a study of the relationship of neurosis to creativity.

Born in Red Bank, New Jersey, Wilson graduated from Princeton 1916. Other works include satirical sketches in *Memoirs of Hecate County* 1946, and two works of social history, *To the Finland Station* 1940, on revolutionary ideology, and *The American Earthquake* 1958, about the Great Depression. He edited his friend F Scott ◊Fitzgerald's posthumous *The Crack-Up* 1956. His *Patriotic Gore* 1962 surveys Civil War literature.

Wilson Edward O 1929– . US zoologist who has done important research in biogeography, the study of the distribution of species, and sociobiology, the evolution of behavior. His works include *Sociobiology: The New Synthesis* 1975 and *On Human Nature* 1978.

Wilson (James) Harold, Baron Wilson of Rievaulx 1916– . British Labor politician, party leader from 1963, prime minister 1964–70 and 1974–76. His premiership was dominated by the issue of UK admission to membership of the European Community, the social contract (unofficial agreement with the labor unions), and economic difficulties.

Wilson, born in Huddersfield, West Yorkshire, was president of the Board of Trade 1947–51 (when he resigned because of social service cuts). In 1963 he succeeded Gaitskell as Labor leader and became prime minister the following year, increasing his majority in 1966. He formed a minority government in Feb 1974 and achieved a majority of three in Oct 1974. He resigned in 1976 and was succeeded by James Callaghan. He was knighted in 1976 and became a peer in 1983.

Wilson (Thomas) Woodrow 1856–1924. Twenty-eighth president of the US 1913–21, a Democrat. He kept the US out of World War I until 1917 and in Jan 1918 issued his ◊Fourteen Points as a basis for a just peace settlement. At the peace conference in Paris he secured the inclusion of the ◊League of Nations covenant in individual peace treaties, but these were not ratified by Congress, so the US did not join the League. He was awarded the Nobel Peace Prize 1919.

Wilson, born in Staunton, Virginia, was educated at Princeton University, of which he became president 1902–10. In 1910 he became governor of New Jersey. Elected US president 1912 against Theodore Roosevelt and William Howard Taft, he initiated antitrust legislation and secured valuable economic and social reforms in his progressive "New Freedom" program. Wilson also instituted a federal income tax, the first since the Civil War. He strove to keep the US neutral during World War I, but the unrestricted German U-boat campaign, sensationalized by the sinking of the British liner *Lusitania* (with 128 Americans lost), forced him to declare war 1917. His refusal to compro-

Wilson *The 28th president of the United States of America, Woodrow Wilson, a Democrat. 1913–1921.*

mise on the text of the League of Nations' proposal contributed to its defeat in Congress. In 1919 Wilson suffered a stroke during a nationwide campaign to gain support for the League and retired from public life.

wilting the loss of rigidity (◊turgor) in plants, caused by a decreasing wall pressure within the cells making up the supportive tissues. Wilting is most obvious in plants which have little or no wood.

Wimbledon English tennis center used for international championship matches, situated in south London. There are currently 18 courts.

The first center was at Worple Road when it was the home of the All England Croquet Club. Tennis was first played there in 1875, and in 1877 the club was renamed the All England Lawn Tennis and Croquet Club. The first All England championship was held in the same year. The club and championship moved to their present home in Church Road in 1922.

Martina ◊Navratilova won six successive women's titles at Wimbledon 1982–87; of the men Björn ◊Borg won five successive titles 1976–80, and William Renshaw won six 1881–86. The youngest male winner was 17-year-old West German Boris ◊Becker 1985. The Wimbledon championship is one of the sport's four Grand Slam events; the others are the US Open, first held 1881 as US Championships, becoming US Open in 1968; French Championships, and Australian Championships.

Wimbledon: recent winners

men's singles
1980 Björn Borg *(Sweden)*
1981 John McEnroe *(US)*
1982 Jimmy Connors *(US)*
1983 John McEnroe *(US)*
1984 John McEnroe *(US)*
1985 Boris Becker *(West Germany)*
1986 Boris Becker *(West Germany)*
1987 Pat Cash *(Australia)*
1988 Stefan Edberg *(Sweden)*
1989 Boris Becker *(West Germany)*
1990 Stefan Edberg *(Sweden)*
1991 Michael Stich (Germany)
women's singles
1980 Evonne Goolagong-Cawley *(Australia)*
1981 Chris Evert-Lloyd *(US)*
1982 Martina Navratilova *(US)*
1983 Martina Navratilova *(US)*
1984 Martina Navratilova *(US)*
1985 Martina Navratilova *(US)*
1986 Martina Navratilova *(US)*
1987 Martina Navratilova *(US)*
1988 Steffi Graf *(West Germany)*
1989 Steffi Graf *(West Germany)*
1990 Martina Navratilova *(US)*
1991 Steffi Graf (Germany)

WIMP (acronym from *w*indows, *i*cons, *m*enus, *p*ointing device) in computing, a type of ◊user interface, in which programs and files appear as ◊icons, menus drop down from a bar along the top of the screen, and data are displayed in rectangular areas, called windows, which the operator can manipulate in various ways. The operator uses a pointing device, typically a ◊mouse, to make selections and initiate actions.

Winchell Walter 1897–1972. US journalist, born in New York. He was a columnist for the *New York Mirror* 1929–69, and his bitingly satiric writings were syndicated throughout the US.

Winchester cathedral city and administrative headquarters of Hampshire, on the river Itchen; population (1984) 93,000. Tourism is important, and there is also light industry. Originally a Roman town, Winchester was the capital of Wessex. Winchester Cathedral is the longest medieval church in Europe and was remodeled from Norman-Romanesque to Perpendicular Gothic under the patronage of William of Wykeham (founder of Winchester College 1382), who is buried there, as are Saxon kings, St Swithun, and the writers Izaac Walton and Jane Austen.

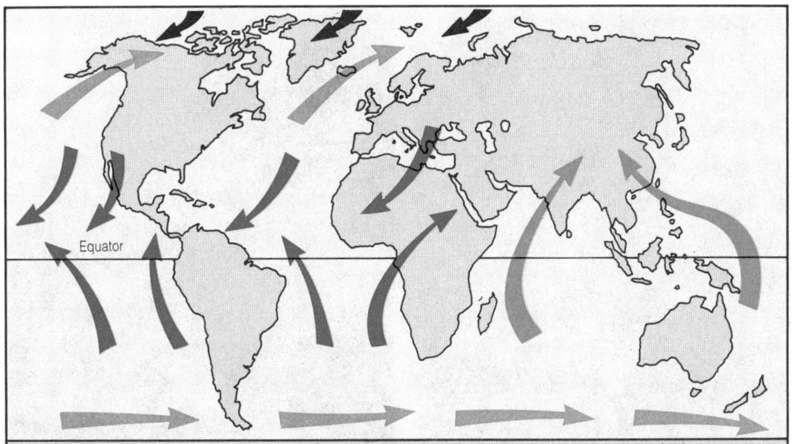
Equator
Trades
Westerlies
Monsoons
Polar Easterlies
World wind patterns in the Northern hemisphere's summer

Winchester disk alternate name for ◊hard disk.

wind lateral movement of the Earth's atmosphere from high- to low-pressure areas. Although modified by features such as land and water, there is a basic worldwide system of ◊trade winds, ◊Westerlies, ◊monsoons, and others.

A belt of low pressure (the ◊doldrums) lies along the equator. The trade winds blow toward this from the horse latitudes (areas of high pressure at about 30° N and 30° S of the equator), blowing from the NE in the northern hemisphere, and from the SE in the southern. The Westerlies (also from the horse latitudes) blow north of the equator from the SW and south of the equator from the NW.

Cold winds blow outward from high-pressure areas at the poles. More local effects result from landmasses heating and cooling faster than the adjacent sea, producing onshore winds in the daytime and offshore winds at night.

The ◊monsoon is a seasonal wind of S Asia, blowing from the SW in summer and bringing the rain on which crops depend. It blows from the NE in winter.

Famous or notorious warm winds include the chinook of the eastern Rocky Mountains, North America; the föhn of Europe's Alpine valleys; the sirocco (Italy)/khamsin (Egypt)/sharav (Israel), spring winds that bring warm air from the Sahara and Arabian deserts across the Mediterranean; and the Santa Ana, a periodic warm wind from the inland deserts that strikes the California coast.

The dry northerly bise (Switzerland) and the mistral, which strikes the Mediterranean area of France, are unpleasantly cold winds.

windchill factor or ***windchill index*** an estimate of how much colder it feels when a wind is blowing. It is the sum of the temperature (in °F below zero) and the wind speed (in miles per hour). So for a wind of 15 mph at an air temperature of –5°F, the windchill factor is 20.

Windermere largest lake in England, in Cumbria, 10.5 mi/17 km long and 1 mi/1.6 km wide.

wind farm array of windmills or ◊wind turbines used for generating electrical power. A wind farm at Altamont Pass, California, consists of 300 wind turbines, the smallest producing 60 kW and the largest 750 kW of electricity. To produce 1,200 megawatts of electricity (an output comparable with that of a nuclear power station), a wind farm would need to occupy around 140 sq mi/370 sq km.

Denmark has built the world's first offshore wind farm, off Vindeby on Lolland Island in the North Sea.

Windhoek capital of Namibia; population (1988) 115,000. It is just N of the Tropic of Capricorn, 180 mi/290 km from the west coast.

wind instrument a musical instrument that uses the performer's breath to make a column of air vibrate. The pitch of the note is controlled by the length of the column. The main types are ◊woodwind instruments and ◊brass instruments.

Wind in the Willows, The a fantasy for children by British author Kenneth ◊Grahame, published in the UK 1908. The story relates the adventures of a group of humanlike animals—Rat, Mole, Badger, and Toad. It was dramatized by A A ◊Milne as *Toad of Toad Hall* 1930.

windmill mill with sails or vanes that, by the action of wind upon them, drive machinery for grinding corn or pumping water, for example. Wind turbines, designed to use wind power on a large scale, usually have a propeller-type rotor mounted on a tall shell tower. The turbine drives a generator for producing electricity.

Windmills were used in the East in ancient times, and in Europe they were first used in Germany and the Netherlands in the 12th century. The main types of traditional windmill are the post mill, which is turned around a post when the direction of the wind changes, and the tower mill, which has a revolving turret on top. It usually has a device (fantail) that keeps the sails pointing into the wind. In the US windmills were used by the colonists and later a light type, with steel sails

windmill

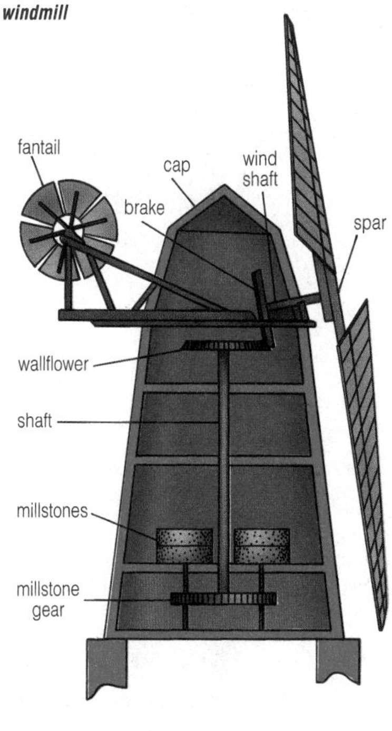
fantail
cap
wind shaft
brake
spar
wallflower
shaft
millstones
millstone gear

windsurfing *French windsurfing champion Pascal Maka.*

wine *The upper valley of the Douro river, the center of Portugal's port-wine region. Terraced vineyards, olive groves, and fields of corn surround a typical* quinta *(estate) near Peso de Regna.*

supported on a long steel girder shaft, was introduced for use on farms.

wind power the harnessing of wind energy to produce power. The wind has long been used as a source of energy: sailing ships and windmills are ancient inventions. After the energy crisis of the 1970s ◊wind turbines began to be used to produce electricity on a large scale. By the year 2000, 10% of Denmark's energy is expected to come from wind power.

Windscale former name of Sellafield, nuclear power station in Cumbria, England.

Windsor industrial lake port (car engines, pharmaceuticals, iron and steel goods, paint, bricks) in Ontario, SE Canada, opposite Detroit, Michigan; population (1986) 254,000. It was founded as a Hudson's Bay Company post 1853.

Windsor, House of official name of the British royal family since 1917, adopted in place of Saxe-Coburg-Gotha. Since 1960 those descendants of Elizabeth II not entitled to the prefix HRH (His/Her Royal Highness) have borne the surname Mountbatten-Windsor.

Windsor town in Berkshire, S England, on the river Thames; population (1981) 28,000. It is the site of Windsor Castle and Eton College (public school) 1540 and has a 17th-century guildhall designed by Christopher Wren.

Windsor Duchess of. Title of Wallis Warfield ◊Simpson.

Windsor Duke of. Title of ◊Edward VIII.

windsurfing or ***boardsailing*** or ***sailboarding*** water sport combining elements of surfing and sailing. The windsurfer stands on a board 8–13 ft/2.5–4 m long, which is propelled and steered by means of a sail attached to a mast that is articulated at the foot. The sport was first developed in the US in 1968. Since 1984 the sport has been included in the Olympic Games as part of the yachting events. Using the Lechner board, speeds in excess of 40 knots have been achieved. In 1992 men and women began competing in their individual categories. There are also annual boardsailing world championships.

wind tunnel test tunnel in which air is blown over, for example, a stationary model aircraft, motor vehicle, or locomotive to simulate the effects of movement. Lift, drag, and airflow patterns are observed by the use of special cameras and sensitive instruments. Wind-tunnel testing assesses aerodynamic design, preparatory to full-scale construction.

wind turbine windmill of advanced aerodynamic design connected to an electricity generator and used in ◊wind-power installations. Wind turbines can be either large propeller-type rotors mounted on a tall tower, or flexible metal strips fixed to a vertical axle at top and bottom. The world's largest wind turbine is on Hawaii, in the Pacific Ocean. It has two blades about 150 ft/50 m long on top of a tower 20 stories high.

An example of a propeller turbine is found at Tvind in Denmark and has an output of some 2 megawatts. Other machines use novel rotors, such as the "egg-beater" design developed at Sandia Laboratories in New Mexico.

Windward Islands islands in the path of the prevailing wind, notably: West Indies see under ◊Antilles; ◊Cape Verde Islands; ◊French Polynesia (Tahiti, Moorea, and Makatea).

wine alcoholic beverage, usually made from fermented grape pulp, although wines have also traditionally been made from many other fruits such as damsons and elderberries. Red wine is the product of the grape with the skin; white wine of the inner pulp of the grape; and rosé from the first pressing of red grapes. The sugar content is converted to ethyl alcohol by the yeast *Saccharomyces ellipsoideus*, which lives on the skin of the grape. For dry wine the fermentation is allowed to go on longer than for sweet or medium; ◊Champagne (sparkling wine from the Champagne region of France) is bottled while still fermenting, but other sparkling wines are artificially carbonated. Some wines are fortified with additional alcohol obtained from various sources, and with preservatives. Some of the latter may cause dangerous side effects (see ◊additive). For this reason, organic wines, containing no preservatives, have recently become popular. The largest wine-producing countries are Italy, France, the USSR, and Spain; others include almost all European countries, Australia, South Africa, the US, and Chile.

A vintage wine is produced during a good year (as regards quality of wine, produced by favorable weather conditions) in recognized vineyards of a particular area; France has a guarantee of origin (*appellation controlée*), as do Italy (*Denominazione di Origine Controllata*), Spain (*Denominacíon Controllata*), and Germany (a series of graded qualities running from *Qualitätswein* to *Beerenauslese*).

wine

wing in biology, the modified forelimb of birds and bats, or the membranous outgrowths of the ◊exoskeleton of insects, which give the power of flight. Birds and bats have two wings. Bird wings have feathers attached to the fused digits ("fingers") and forearm bones, while bat wings consist of skin stretched between the digits. Most insects have four wings, which are strengthened by wing veins. The wings of butterflies and moths are covered with scales. The hind pair of a fly's wings are modified to form two knoblike balancing organs (halteres).

wing *comparison of wing shapes*

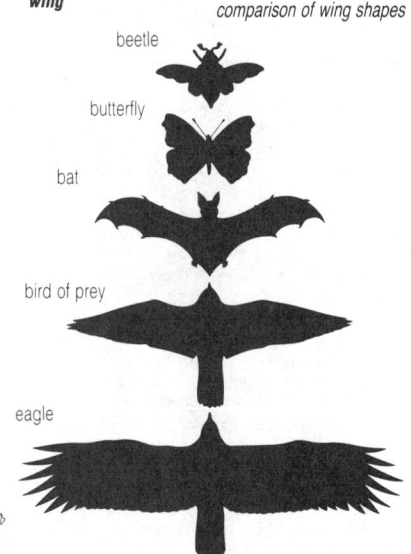

beetle
butterfly
bat
bird of prey
eagle

Winnie-the-Pooh collection of children's stories by British author A A ◊Milne, published in 1926, illustrated by E H Shepard. The stories featured the author's son Christopher Robin, his teddy bear Winnie-the-Pooh, and a group of toy animals, including Piglet, Eeyore, Rabbit, Owl, Kanga and Roo, and Tigger. Further stories appeared in *The House at Pooh Corner* 1928.

Winnipeg capital and industrial city in Manitoba, Canada, on the Red River of the North, S of Lake Winnipeg; population (1986) 594,551, the largest Canadian city W of Toronto. The chief manufactured products are processed foods and transportation equipment. The University of Manitoba and University of Winnipeg are here.

Established as Winnipeg 1870 on the site of earlier forts, the city expanded with the arrival of the Canadian Pacific Railroad 1881. The city annexed several adjacent communities 1972.

Winnipeg, Lake lake in S Manitoba, Canada, draining much of the Canadian prairies; area 9,460 sq mi/24,500 sq km.

Winston-Salem city in N central North Carolina, NE of Charlotte. Its industries include tobacco products, textiles, clothing, and furniture. Wake Forest University 1834 is here; population (1980) 131,885.

wintergreen any of several plants of the genus *Gaultheria* of the heath family Ericaceae, especially *G. procumbens* of NE North America, creeping underground and sending up tiny shoots. Oil of wintergreen, used in treating rheumatism, is extracted from its leaves. Wintergreen is also the name for various plants of the family Pyrolaceae, including the genus *Pyrola* and the green pipsissewa *Chimaphila maculata* of N North America and Eurasia.

Winterhalter Franz Xavier 1805–1873. German portraitist. He became court painter to Grand Duke Leopold at Karlsruhe, then, in 1834, moved to Paris and enjoyed the patronage of European royalty.

Winter Haven city in central Florida, E of Lakeland. It is a center for citrus-fruit processing and shipping. Other industries include tourism, cigars, and alcohol; population (1990) 24,725.

Winterthur Swiss town and spa NE of Zürich; population (1987) 108,000. Manufacturing includes engines and textiles.

Winter War the USSR's invasion of Finland Nov 30, 1939–March 12, 1940, also called the Russo-Finnish War.

The Soviets set up a Finnish puppet government in E Karelia, but their invasion forces were at first repulsed by the greatly outnumbered Finnish troops under Marshal Mannerheim. In Feb 1940 the Finnish lines were broken by a million-strong Soviet offensive. In the March armistice Finland ceded part of Karelia to the USSR.

Winthrop John 1588–1649. American colonist and first governor of the Massachusetts Bay Colony. Born in England and educated at Cambridge, Winthrop studied law at Gray's Inn and was admitted to the Inner Temple 1628. A devout Puritan and one of the founders of the Massachusetts Bay Company, he departed for New England with a large group of settlers 1630. A founder of the city of Boston, he served as Massachusetts governor or deputy governor until his death. Deeply conservative, he favored the prosecution and banishment of Anne ◊Hutchinson 1638. His *History of New England from 1630 to 1649* was published 1825.

wire thread of metal, made by drawing a rod through progressively smaller-diameter dies. Fine-gauge wire is used for jewelry, musical instrument strings, and electrical power transmission; heavier-gauge wire is used to make load-bearing cables.

Gold, silver, and bronze wire has been found in the ruins of Troy and in ancient Egyptian tombs. From early times to the 14th century, wire was made by hammering metal into sheets, cutting thin strips, and making the strips round by hammering them. The Romans made wire by hammering heated metal rods.

Wire drawing was introduced in Germany in the 14th century. In this process, a metal rod is pulled (drawn) through a small hole in a mold (die). Until the 19th century this was done by hand; now all wire is drawn by machine. Metal rods are pulled through a series of progressively smaller tungsten carbide dies to produce large-diameter wire, and through diamond dies for very fine wire. The die is funnel-shaped, with the smaller opening smaller than the diameter of the rod. The rod, which is pointed at one end, is coated with a lubricant to allow it to slip through the die. Pincers pull the rod through until it can be wound round a drum. The drum then rotates, drawing the wire through the die and winding it into a coil.

There are many kinds of wire for different uses: silver wire, used for musical instrument strings and jewelry; galvanized wire (coated with zinc), which does not rust; ◊barbed wire and wire mesh for fencing; and wire cable, made by weaving thin wires into ropes. Needles, pins, nails, and rivets are made from wire.

wireworm the larva of ◊click beetles.

Wisconsin

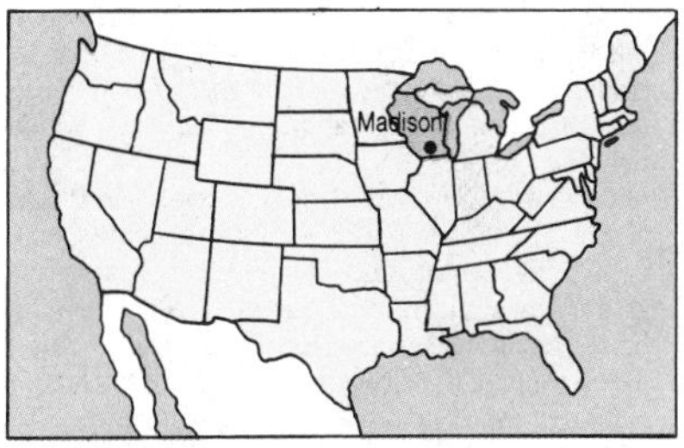
Madison

Wisconsin state in N central US; nickname Badger State

area 56,163 sq mi/145,500 sq km

capital Madison

cities Milwaukee, Green Bay, Racine

population (1990) 4,891,769

features lakes: Superior, Michigan; Mississippi River; Door peninsula

products leading US dairy state; corn, hay, industrial and agricultural machinery, engines and turbines, precision instruments, paper products, automobiles and trucks, plumbing equipment

famous people Edna Ferber, Harry Houdini, Robert La Follette, Joseph McCarthy, Spencer Tracy, Orson Welles, Thornton Wilder, Frank Lloyd Wright

history explored by Jean Nicolet for France 1634; originally settled near Ashland by the French; passed to Britain 1763; included in US 1783. Wisconsin became a territory 1836 and a state 1848. Lumbering emerged as a major industry in the late 19th century, and Milwaukee became an industrial center. Germans, Scandinavians, and Poles settled in large numbers. In the early 20th century, Wisconsin became noted for pioneering progressive legislation.

Wise Robert 1914– . US film director who began as a film editor. His debut was a horror film, *Curse of the Cat People* 1944; he progressed to such large-scale projects as *The Sound of Music* 1965 and *Star* 1968. His other films include *The Body Snatcher* 1945 and *Star Trek: The Motion Picture* 1979.

Wise Stephen Samuel 1874–1949. Hungarian-born US religious leader. He was ordained as a reform rabbi 1893 and served congregations in New York City 1893–1900 and Portland, Oregon, 1900–07. Returning to New York City 1907, he became rabbi of the Free Synagogue. An ardent Zionist, Wise attended the Versailles Peace Conference and served as president of the American Jewish Congress 1924–49. His autobiography, *Challenging Years*, appeared 1949.

Born in Budapest, Wise immigrated to the US with his family 1875. Educated at the City College of New York, he received a PhD from Columbia University 1901.

wisent another name for the European ◊bison.

Wister Owen 1860–1938. US novelist who created the genre of the ◊Western. He was born in Philadelphia, a grandson of the British actress Fanny Kemble, and became known for stories of cowboys, including *The Virginian* 1902. He also wrote *Roosevelt: The Story of a Friendship 1880–1919* 1930, about his relationship with US president Theodore Roosevelt.

wisteria any climbing shrub of the genus *Wisteria*, including *W. sinensis*, of the family Leguminosae, native to eastern USA and east Asia. Wisterias have racemes of bluish, white, or pale mauve flowers, and pinnate leaves (leaves on either side of the stem).

Witan or ***Witenagemot*** council of the Anglo-Saxon kings, the forerunner of Parliament, but including only royal household officials, great landowners, and top churchmen.

witchcraft the alleged possession and exercise of magical powers—black magic if used with evil intent, and white magic if benign. Its origins lie in traditional beliefs and religions. Practitioners of witchcraft (see ◊shaman) have often had considerable skill in, for example, herbal medicine and traditional remedies; this prompted the World Health Organization in 1976 to recommended the integration of traditional healers into the health teams of African states.

The Christian church persecuted witches in Europe between the 15th and 17th centuries and in North America (see ◊Salem). The last official execution of a witch in Europe was that of Anna Goddi, hanged in Switzerland in 1782. ◊Obi is the witchcraft of black Africa imported to the West Indies, and includes Christian elements; ◊voodoo is a similar cult.

witch hazel any flowering shrub or small tree of the genus *Hamamelis* of the witch-hazel family, native to North America and E Asia, especially *H. virginiana*. An astringent extract prepared from the bark or leaves is used in medicine as an eye lotion and a liniment.

witch-hunt persecution of minority political-opposition or socially nonconformist groups without any regard for their guilt or innocence. Witch-hunts are often accompanied by a degree of public hysteria; for example, the ◊McCarthy anti-communist hearings during the 1950s in the US.

withholding tax personal income tax on wages, salaries, dividends, or other income that is taxed at the source, to ensure that it reaches the tax authority. Those not liable to the tax have to reclaim it by filing a tax return.

witness in law, a person who was present at some event (such as an accident, a crime, or the signing of a document) or has relevant special knowledge (such as a medical expert) and can be called on to give evidence in a court of law.

Witt Johann de 1625–1672. Dutch politician, grand pensionary of Holland and virtual prime minister from 1653. His skillful diplomacy ended the Dutch Wars of 1652–54 and 1665–67, and in 1668 he formed a triple alliance with England and Sweden against Louis XIV of France. He was murdered by a rioting mob.

Wittelsbach Bavarian dynasty, who ruled Bavaria as dukes from 1180, electors from 1623, and kings 1806–1918.

Witten city in North Rhine–Westphalia, Federal Republic of Germany; population (1988) 102,000.

Wittenberg town in the state of Saxony-Anhalt, Federal Republic of Germany, on the river Elbe, SW of Berlin; population (1981) 54,000. Wittenberg university was founded 1502, but transferred to Halle 1815. Luther preached in the Stadtkirche (in which he is buried), nailed his 95 theses to the door of the Schlosskirche 1517, and taught philosophy at the university. The artists Lucas Cranach, father and son, lived here.

Wittgenstein Ludwig 1889–1951. Austrian philosopher. *Tractatus Logico-Philosophicus* 1922 postulated the "picture theory" of language: that words represent things according to social agreement. He subsequently rejected this idea, and developed the idea that usage was more important than convention.

The picture theory said that it must be possible to break down a sentence into "atomic propositions" whose elements stand for elements of the real world. After he rejected this idea, his later philosophy developed a quite different, anthropological view of language: words are used according to different rules in a variety of human activities—different "language games" are played with them. The traditional philosophical problems arise through the assumption that words (like "exist" in the sentence "Physical objects do not really exist") carry a fixed meaning with them, independent of context.

He taught at Cambridge University, England, in the 1930s and 1940s. *Philosophical Investigations* 1954 and *On Certainty* 1969 were published posthumously.

Witwatersrand or ***the Rand*** the economic heartland of S Transvaal, South Africa. Its reef, which stretches nearly 62 mi/100 km, produces over half the world's gold. Gold was first found there in 1854. The chief city of the region is Johannesburg. Forming a watershed between the Vaal and the Olifant rivers, the Rand comprises a series of parallel ranges which extend 60 mi/100 km E–W and rise to 1,525–1,830 m/5,000–6,000 ft above sea level. Gold occurs in reefs that are mined at depths of up to 10,000 ft/3,050 m.

Wizard of Oz, The Wonderful classic US children's tale of Dorothy's journey by the yellow brick road to an imaginary kingdom, written by L Frank Baum in 1900. It had many sequels and was made into a musical film 1939 with Judy Garland.

woad biennial plant *Isatis tinctoria*, family Cruciferae, native to Europe, with arrow-shaped leaves and clusters of yellow flowers. Ancient Britons used the blue dye from its leaves as a body paint in battle.

Wodehouse P(elham) G(renville) 1881–1975. English novelist, a US citizen from 1955, whose humorous novels portray the accident-prone world of such characters as the socialite Bertie Wooster and his invaluable and impeccable manservant Jeeves, and Lord Emsworth of Blandings Castle with his prize pig, the Empress of Blandings.

From 1906, Wodehouse also collaborated on the lyrics of Broadway musicals by Jerome Kern, Gershwin, and others. He spent most of his life in the US. Staying in France in 1941, during World War II, he was interned by the Germans; he made some humorous broadcasts from Berlin, which were taken amiss in Britain at the time, but he was later exonerated, and was knighted in 1975. His work is admired for its style and geniality, and includes *Indiscretions of Archie* 1921, *Uncle Fred in the Springtime* 1939, and *Aunts Aren't Gentlemen* 1974.

Woden or ***Wodan*** the foremost Anglo-Saxon god, whose Norse counterpart is ◊Odin.

Wöhler Friedrich 1800–1882. German chemist and student of ◊Berzelius who in 1828 synthesized the first organic compound (◊urea) from an inorganic compound (ammonium cyanate), opening a new era in organic chemistry. He also devised a new method 1827 that isolated the metals aluminum, beryllium, and yttrium from their ores.

wolf any of two species of large wild dogs of the genus *Canis*. The gray or timber wolf *C. lupus*, of North America and Eurasia, is highly social, measures up to 3 ft/90 cm at the shoulder, and weighs up to 100 lb/45 kg. It has been greatly reduced in numbers except for isolated wilderness regions.

The red wolf *C. niger*, generally more slender and smaller (average weight about 35 lb/15 kg) and tawnier in color, may be extinct in the wild. It used to be restricted to S central US.

Wolf Hugo (Filipp Jakob) 1860–1903. Austrian composer, whose songs are in the German *Lieder* tradition. He also composed the opera *Der Corregidor* 1895 and orchestral works, such as *Italian Serenade* 1892.

Wolfe James 1727–1759. British soldier. He fought at the battles of Dettingen, Falkirk, and ◊Culloden. With the outbreak of the Seven Years' War (the French and Indian War in North America), he served in Canada and played a conspicuous part in the siege of the French stronghold of Louisburg 1758. He was promoted to major-general 1759 and commanded a victorious expedition against Montcalm in Québec on the Plains of Abraham, during which both commanders were killed. The British victory established their supremacy over Canada.

Wolfe Thomas 1900–1938. US novelist. He wrote four long and hauntingly powerful autobiographical novels, mostly of the South: *Look Homeward, Angel* 1929, *Of Time and the River* 1935, and *The Web and the Rock* 1939, and *You Can't Go Home Again* 1940 (the last two published posthumously).

Born in Asheville, North Carolina, Wolfe studied playwriting at the University of North Carolina and Harvard University. He settled in New York City, with hopes of becoming a playwright. His first novel, *Look Homeward, Angel*, was a realistic, brutal view of the South and Southern family life, the result of six years of work with Scribner's editor Maxwell Perkins. He also wrote *The Story of a Novel* 1936 and the short-story collections *From Death to Morning* 1935 and *The Hills Beyond* 1941.

Wolfe Tom. Adopted name of Thomas Kennerly, Jr 1931– . US journalist and novelist. In the 1960s he was a founder of the "New Journalism," which brought fiction's methods to reportage. Wolfe recorded American mores and fashions in pop style essays in *The Kandy-Kolored Tangerine-Flake Streamline Baby* 1965. His sharp style is applied to the New York City of the 1980s in his best-selling novel *The Bonfire of the Vanities* 1988 (film 1990).

Born in Richmond, Virginia, Wolfe graduated from Yale University and worked at newspaper and magazine reporting. He also wrote *The Electric Kool-Aid Acid Test* 1968; *Radical Chic and Mau-Mauing the Flak Catchers* 1970; *The Painted Word* 1975, about art; *The Right Stuff* 1979, about the first US astronauts; and *From Bauhaus to Our House* 1981, about modern architecture.

Wolf-Ferrari Ermanno 1876–1948. Italian composer whose operas include *Il segreto di Susanna/Susanna's Secret* 1909 and the realistic tragedy *I gioielli di Madonna/The Jewels of the Madonna* 1911.

wolfram alternate name for ◊tungsten.

wolframite iron manganese tungstate. $(Fe,Mn)Wo_4$, an ore mineral of tungsten. It is dark gray with a submetallic surface luster, and often occurs in hydrothermal veins in association with ores of tin.

Wolfsburg town NE of Brunswick in Federal Republic of Germany, chosen 1938 as the Volkswagen ("people's car") factory site; population (1988) 122,000.

Wollaston William 1766–1828. British chemist and physicist. He amassed a large fortune through his discovery in 1804 of how to make malleable platinum. He went on to discover the new elements palladium in 1804 and rhodium in 1805. He also contributed to optics through the invention of a number of ingenious and still useful measuring instruments.

Wollongong industrial city (iron, steel) in New South Wales, Australia, 40 mi/65 km S of Sydney; population (1985, with Port Kembla) 238,000.

Wollstonecraft Mary 1759–1797. British feminist, member of a group of radical intellectuals called the English Jacobins, whose book *Vindication of the Rights of Women* 1792 demanded equal educational opportunities for women. She married William Godwin and died giving birth to a daughter, Mary (see Mary ◊Shelley).

wombat

Wolseley Garnet Joseph, 1st Viscount 1833–1913. British field marshal who, as Commander in Chief 1895–1900, began modernizing the army.

Wolsey Thomas c. 1475–1530. English cleric and politician. In Henry VIII's service from 1509, he became archbishop of York 1514, cardinal and Lord Chancellor in 1515, and began the dissolution of the monasteries. His reluctance to further Henry's divorce from Catherine of Aragon, partly because of his ambition to be pope, led to his downfall in 1529. He was charged with high treason in 1530 but died before being tried.

Wolverhampton industrial city (metalworking, chemicals, tires, aircraft, commercial vehicles) in West Midlands, England, 12 mi/20 km NW of Birmingham; population (1984) 254,000.

wolverine largest land member *Gulo gulo* of the weasel family (Mustelidae), found in Europe, Asia, and North America. It is stocky in build, about 3.3 ft/1 m long. Its long, thick fur is dark-brown on the back and belly and lighter on the sides. It covers food that it cannot eat with an unpleasant secretion. Destruction of habitat and trapping for its fur have greatly reduced its numbers.

wombat any of a family (Vombatidae) of burrowing, herbivorous marsupials, native to Tasmania and S Australia. They are about 3.3 ft/1 m long, heavy, with a big head, short legs and tail, and coarse fur.

The two living species include the common wombat *Vombatus ursinus* of Tasmania and SE Australia, and *Lasiorhirnus latifrons*, the plains wombat of S Australia.

women's movement the campaign for the rights of women, including social, political, and economic equality with men. Early European campaigners of the 17th–19th centuries fought for women's right to own property, to have access to higher education, and to vote (see ◊suffragist). Once women's suffrage was achieved in the 20th century, the emphasis of the movement shifted to the goals of equal social and economic opportunities for women, including employment. A continuing area of concern in industrialized countries is the contradiction between the now generally accepted principle of equality and the demonstrable inequalities that remain between the sexes in state policies and in everyday life.

Pioneer 19th-century feminists, considered radical for their belief in the equality of the sexes, include Mary Wollstonecraft and Emmeline Pankhurst in the UK, and Susan B Anthony and Elizabeth Cady Stanton in the US.

The women's movement gained worldwide impetus after World War II with such theorists as Simone de ◊Beauvoir, Betty ◊Friedan, Kate ◊Millett, Gloria ◊Steinem, and Germaine ◊Greer, and the founding of the National Organization of Women (NOW) in New York 1966. From the late 1960s the radical and militant wing of the movement argued that women were oppressed by the male-dominated social structure as a whole, which they saw as pervaded by ◊sexism, despite legal concessions toward equality of the sexes.

In the US the Equal Employment Opportunity Commission, a government agency, was formed in 1964 to end discrimination (including sex dis-

Wonder *US multiinstrumentalist and singer Stevie Wonder began his career with Motown Records at the age of ten.*

crimination) in hiring, but the Equal Rights Amendment (ERA), a proposed constitutional amendment prohibiting sex discrimination was passed by Congress in 1972 but failed to be ratified by the necessary majority of 38 states.

women's services the organized military use of women on a large scale, a 20th-century development. First, women replaced men in factories, on farms, and in noncombat tasks during wartime; they are now found in combat units in many countries, including the US, Cuba, the UK, the USSR, and Israel.

Wonder Stevie. Adopted name of Steveland Judkins Morris 1950– . US pop musician, singer, and songwriter, associated with Motown Records. Blind from birth, he had his first hit, "Fingertips," at the age of 12. Later hits, most of which he composed and sang, and on which he also played several instruments, include "My Cherie Amour" 1973, "Master Blaster (Jammin')" 1980, and the album *Innervisions* 1973.

wood the hard tissue beneath the bark of many perennial plants; it is composed of water-conducting cells, or secondary ◊xylem, and gains its hardness and strength from deposits of ◊lignin. Hardwoods, such as oak, and softwoods, such as pine, have commercial value as structural material and for furniture.

The central wood in a branch or stem is known as heartwood and is generally darker and harder than the outer wood; it consists only of dead cells. As well as providing structural support, it often contains gums, tannins, or pigments which may impart a characteristic color and increased durability. The surrounding sapwood is the functional part of the xylem that conducts water.

The secondary xylem is laid down by the vascular ◊cambium which forms a new layer of wood annually, on the outside of the existing wood and visible as an ◊annual ring when the tree is felled; see ◊dendrochronology.

Commercial wood can be divided into two main types: hardwood, containing xylem vessels and obtained from angiosperms (for example, oak) and softwood, containing only ◊tracheids, obtained from gymnosperms (for example, pine). Although in general softwoods are softer than hardwoods, this is not always the case: balsa, the softest wood known, is a hardwood, while pitch pine, very dense and hard, is a softwood. A superhard wood is produced in wood-plastic combinations (WPC), in which wood is impregnated with liquid plastic (monomer) and the whole is then bombarded with gamma rays to polymerize the plastic.

Wood Grant 1892–1942. US painter based mainly in his native Iowa. Although his work is highly stylized, he struck a note of hard realism in his studies of farmers, such as *American Gothic* 1930 (Art Institute, Chicago).

He also painted landscapes and somewhat humorous scenes, for example *Daughters of Revolution* 1932 (Cincinnati Art Museum), which satirized membership in patriotic societies.

Wood Natalie. Adopted name of Natasha Gurdin 1938–1981. US film actress who began as a child star. Her films include *Miracle on 34th Street* 1947, *Rebel Without A Cause* 1955, *The Searchers* 1956, *Splendor In the Grass* 1961, *Gypsy* 1962, and *Bob & Carol & Ted & Alice* 1969. She was married to actor Robert Wagner and died by drowning.

wood carving an art form practiced in many parts of the world since prehistoric times, for example, the NW Pacific coast of North America, in the form of totem poles, and W Africa where there is a long tradition of woodcarving, notably in Nigeria. Wood carvings survive less often than sculpture in stone or metal unless they are preserved in hot, dry, (Egypt, China) or cool, wet (Scandinavian bogs, estuarine) conditions.

woodcock two species of shore birds, genus *Scolopax*, of the family Scolopacidae, which also includes dowitchers and snipes.

The American woodcock *S. minor*, about 11 in/28 cm long, is shortlegged and shortnecked, with a long, straight bill. It nests in moist woodlands and thickets throughout E North America. The Eurasian woodcock *S. rusticola*, somewhat larger, is similar in appearance and habits.

woodcut print made by a woodblock in which a picture or design has been cut in relief. The woodcut is the oldest method of ◊printing, invented in China in the 5th century AD. In the Middle Ages woodcuts became popular in Europe, illustrating early printed books and broadsides.

woodland

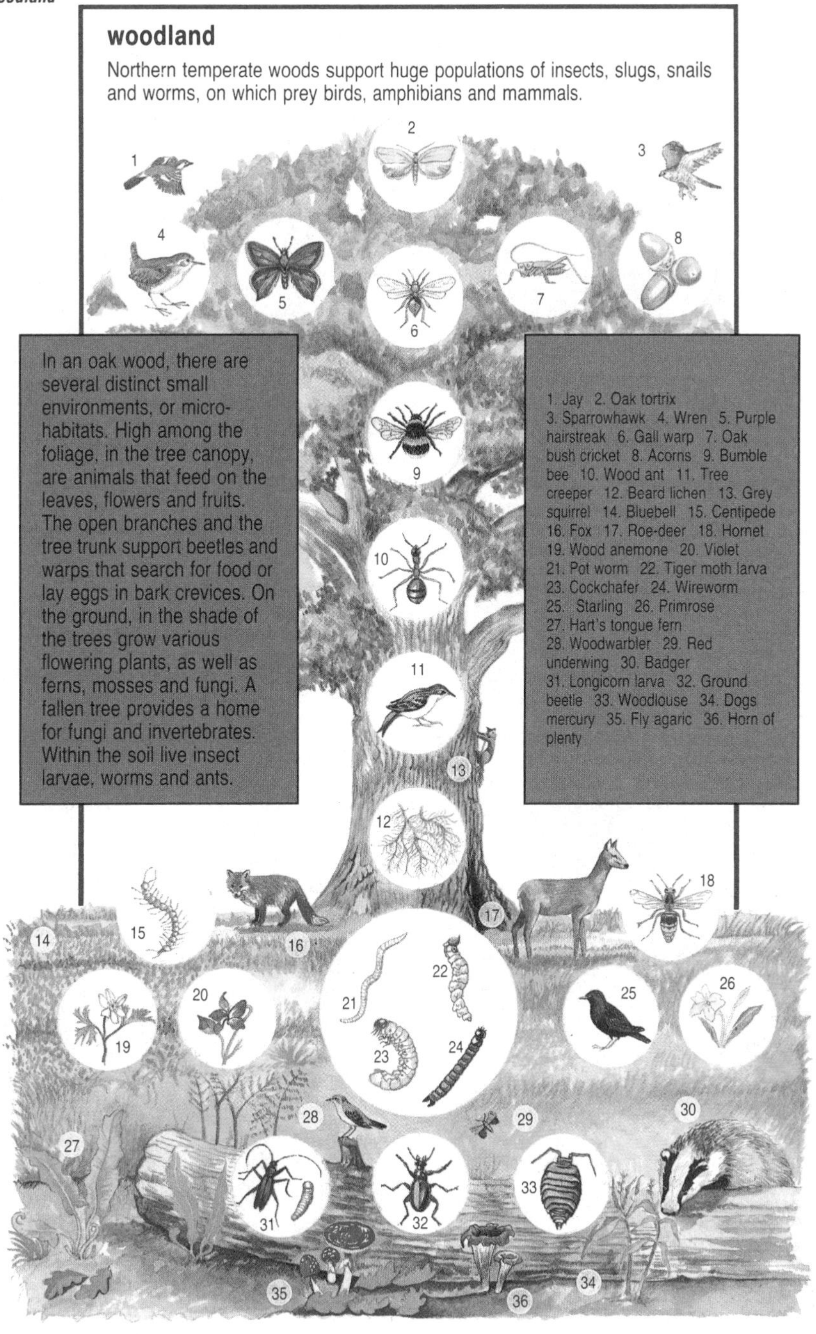
woodland
Northern temperate woods support huge populations of insects, slugs, snails and worms, on which prey birds, amphibians and mammals.
In an oak wood, there are several distinct small environments, or microhabitats. High among the foliage, in the tree canopy, are animals that feed on the leaves, flowers and fruits. The open branches and the tree trunk support beetles and warps that search for food or lay eggs in bark crevices. On the ground, in the shade of the trees grow various flowering plants, as well as ferns, mosses and fungi. A fallen tree provides a home for fungi and invertebrates. Within the soil live insect larvae, worms and ants.
1. Jay 2. Oak tortrix 3. Sparrowhawk 4. Wren 5. Purple hairstreak 6. Gall warp 7. Oak bush cricket 8. Acorns 9. Bumble bee 10. Wood ant 11. Tree creeper 12. Beard lichen 13. Grey squirrel 14. Bluebell 15. Centipede 16. Fox 17. Roe-deer 18. Hornet 19. Wood anemone 20. Violet 21. Pot worm 22. Tiger moth larva 23. Cockchafer 24. Wireworm 25. Starling 26. Primrose 27. Hart's tongue fern 28. Woodwarbler 29. Red underwing 30. Badger 31. Longicorn larva 32. Ground beetle 33. Woodlouse 34. Dogs mercury 35. Fly agaric 36. Horn of plenty

woodpecker

The German artist Dürer was an early exponent of the technique. Multicolored woodblock prints were developed in Japan in the mid-18th century.

woodland area in which trees grow more or less thickly; generally smaller than a forest. Temperate climates, with four distinct seasons per year, tend to support a mixed woodland habitat, with some conifers but mostly broad-leaved and deciduous trees, shedding their leaves in autumn and regrowing them in spring. In the Mediterranean region and parts of the southern hemisphere, the trees are mostly evergreen.

Temperate woodlands grow in the zone between the cold coniferous forest and the tropical forests of the hotter climates near the equator. They develop in areas where the closeness of the sea keeps the climate mild and moist.

woodlouse any of the several families of mostly terrestrial crustaceans of the order Isopoda (especially the sow bugs, genera *Onisais* and *Porcellio*) that live in damp places under rocks or fallen timber. They have rounded oval, evenly segmented bodies and flat undersides. Some species of sow bugs can roll up when threatened. The pill bugs (family Armadillidiidae) typically roll up. Rock slaters (family Ligiidae) are amphibious on ocean beaches.

woodpecker bird of the family Picidae, which drills holes in trees to obtain insects. There are about 200 species worldwide. The largest of these, the imperial woodpecker *Campephilus imperialis* of Mexico, is very rare and may already be extinct.

North American woodpeckers include four species of sapsuckers (genus *Sphyrapicus*), which drill and then tap holes in trees for sap and the attracted insects. The pileated woodpecker *Dryocopus pileatus* is the largest, about 17 in/43 cm long, with a red crest.

wood pulp wood that has been processed into a pulpy mass of fibers. Its main use is for making paper, but it is also used in making ◊rayon and other cellulose fibers and plastics.

There are two methods of making wood pulp: mechanical and chemical. In the former, debarked logs are ground with water (to prevent charring) by rotating grindstones; the wood fibers are physically torn apart. In the latter, log chips are digested with chemicals (such as sodium sulfite). The chemicals dissolve the material holding the fibers together.

Woodstock the first free rock festival, held near Bethel, New York State, over three days in Aug 1969. It was attended by 400,000 people, and performers included the Band, Country Joe and the Fish, the Grateful Dead, Jimi Hendrix, Jefferson Airplane, and The Who. The festival was a landmark in the youth culture of the 1960s (see ◊hippie) and was recorded in the film *Woodstock*.

Woodward Joanne 1930– . US actress, active in film, television, and theater. She was directed by her husband Paul Newman in the film *Rachel Rachel* 1968, and also starred in *The Three Faces of Eve* 1957, *They Might Be Giants* 1971, and *Harry and Son* 1984. She has appeared with Newman in several films including *Mr and Mrs Bridge* 1991.

Woodward Robert 1917–1979. US chemist who worked on synthesizing a large number of complex molecules. These included quinine 1944, cholesterol 1951, chlorophyll 1960, and vitamin

woodwind

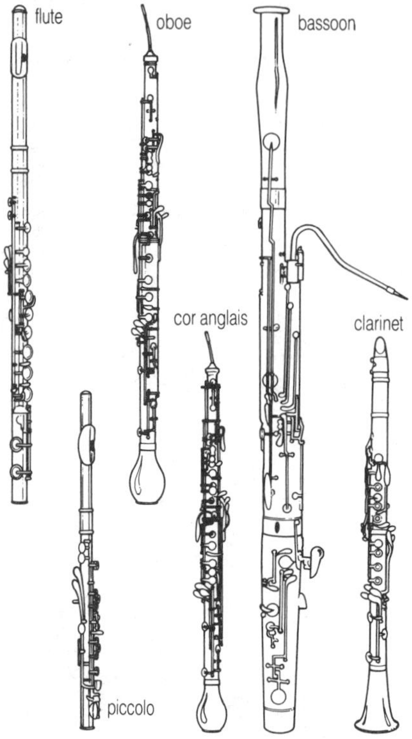
flute
oboe
bassoon
cor anglais
clarinet
piccolo

B_{12} 1971. Woodward worked throughout his career at Harvard University, Boston. Nobel Prize 1965.

woodwind musical instrument from which sound is produced by blowing into a tube, causing the air within to vibrate. Woodwind instruments include those, like the flute, originally made of wood but now more commonly of metal. The saxophone, made of metal, is an honorary woodwind because it is related to the clarinet. The oboe, bassoon, flute, and clarinet make up the normal woodwind section of an orchestra.

Woodwind instruments fall into two categories: reed instruments, in which air vibrates a reed (a thin piece of cane attached to the mouthpiece through which air is blown); and those without a reed, which sound when air is blown into or across a tube. In both cases, different notes are obtained by changing the length of the tube by covering holes along it. Reed instruments include clarinet, oboe (evolved from the medieval shawm and hautboy), cor anglais, saxophone, and bassoon. Woodwind instruments without a reed include recorder, flute, and piccolo.

There is an enormous variety of woodwind instruments throughout the world.

woodworm common name for the larval stage of certain wood-boring beetles. Dead or injured trees are their natural target, but they also attack structural timber and furniture.

Included are the furniture beetle *Anobium punctatum*, which attacks older timber; the powder-post beetle genus *Lyctus*, attacks newer timber; the ◊deathwatch beetle, whose presence always coincides with fungal decay, and wood-boring ◊weevils. Special wood preservatives have been developed to combat woodworm infestation, which has markedly increased since about 1950.

wool the natural hair covering of the sheep, and also of the llama, angora goat, and some other ◊mammals. The domestic sheep *Ovis aries* provides the great bulk of the fibers used in (textile) commerce. Lanolin is a byproduct.

Sheep have been bred for their wool since ancient times. Hundreds of breeds were developed in the Middle East, Europe, and Britain over the centuries, several dozen of which are still raised for their wool today. Most of the world's finest wool comes from the merino sheep, originally from Spain. In 1797 it was introduced into Australia, which has become the world's largest producer of merino wool; South Africa and South America are also large producers. Wools from crossbred sheep (usually a cross of one of the British breeds class with a merino) are produced in New Zealand. Since the 1940s, blendings of wool with synthetic fibers have been developed for textiles.

Woolf Virginia (née Virginia Stephen) 1882–1941. English novelist and critic. Her first novel, *The Voyage Out* 1915, explored the tensions experienced by women who want marriage and a career. In *Mrs Dalloway* 1925 she perfected her "stream of consciousness" technique. Among her later books are *To the Lighthouse* 1927, *Orlando* 1928, and *The Years* 1937, which considers the importance of economic independence for women.

Woollcott Alexander 1887–1943. US theater critic and literary figure. He served as *The New York Times*'s theater critic 1914-22, eventually working in the same capacity for the New York *Herald*, *Sun*, and *World*. Woollcott was also a regular contributor to the *New Yorker* and hosted the radio interview program "Town Crier" 1929–42. He appeared on stage in *The Man Who Came to Dinner* 1939 as a character based on himself. Woollcott became famous as a member of the Algonquin Hotel "Round Table" of wits in New York City and wrote several books, including *While Rome Burns* 1934.

Born in Phalanx, New Jersey, Woollcott was educated at Hamilton College and joined the staff of the *Times* 1909.

Woolley (Charles) Leonard 1880–1960. British archeologist. He excavated at Carchemish in Syria, Tell el Amarna in Egypt, Atchana (the ancient Alalakh) on the Turkish-Syrian border, and Ur in Iraq.

Woolman John 1720–1772. American Quaker, born in Ancocas (now Rancocas), New Jersey. He was one of the first antislavery agitators and left an important *Journal*. He supported those who refused to pay a tax levied by Pennsylvania, to conduct the French and Indian War, on the grounds that it was inconsistent with pacifist principles.

Woolsey Theodore Dwight 1801–1889. US educator. He served as president of Yale 1846–71 and oversaw its expansion into a modern university with specialized departments and graduate degrees. After his retirement as president, Woolsey remained a member of the Yale Corporation 1871–85. Later in life he became increasingly interested in questions of politics and law. He was the author of *Political Science* 1878 and *Communism and Socialism* 1880.

Born in New York and educated at Yale University, Woolsey studied classics in Europe and was appointed to the Yale faculty as a professor of Greek 1831.

Woolworth Frank Winfield 1852–1919. US entrepreneur. He opened his first successful "five and ten cent" store in Lancaster, Pennsylvania, in 1879, and, together with his brother C S Woolworth (1856–1947), built up a chain of similar stores throughout the US, Canada, the UK, and Europe.

Woonsocket city in N Rhode Island, on the Blackstone river, NW of Providence. Industries include rubber, chemicals, and woolen goods; population (1990) 43,877.

Worcester cathedral city with industries (gloves, shoes, Worcester sauce; Royal Worcester porcelain from 1751) in Hereford and Worcester, W central England, administrative headquarters of the county, on the river Severn; population (1985) 76,000. The cathedral dates from the 13th and 14th centuries. The birthplace of the composer Elgar at nearby Broadheath is a museum. At the Battle of Worcester 1651 Cromwell defeated Charles I.

Wordsworth *One of the greatest English poets, Wordsworth turned to nature for his inspiration, in particular to his native Lake District. This portrait is by Benjamin Haydon.*

World War I: chronology

outbreak	On June 28 the heir to the Austrian throne was assassinated in Sarajevo, Serbia; on July 28 Austria declared war on Serbia; as Russia mobilized, Germany declared war on Russia and France, taking a short cut in the west by invading Belgium; on Aug 4 Britain declared war on Germany.
1914 Western Front	The German advance reached within a few miles of Paris, but an Allied counter-attack at Marne drove them back to the Aisne River; the opposing lines then settled into trench warfare.
Eastern Front	The German commander Hindenburg halted the Russian advance through the Ukraine and across Austria-Hungary at the Battle of Tannenberg in E Prussia.
Africa	On Sept 16 all Germany's African colonies were in Allied hands.
Middle East	On Nov 1 Turkey entered the war on the side of the Central Powers and soon attacked Russia in the Caucasus Mountains.
1915 Western Front	Several offensives on both sides resulted in insignificant gains. At Ypres, Belgium, the Germans used poison gas for the first time.
Eastern Front	The German field marshals Mackensen and Hindenburg drove back the Russians and took Poland.
Middle East	British attacks against Turkey in Mesopotamia (Iraq), the Dardanelles, and at Gallipoli were all unsuccessful.
Italy	declared war on Austria; Bulgaria joined the Central Powers.
war at sea	Germany declared all-out U-boat war, but the sinking of the British ocean liner *Lusitania* (with Americans among the 1,198 lost) led to demands that the US enter the war.
1916 Western Front	German attack at Verdun was countered by the Allies on the Somme, where tanks were used for the first time.
Eastern Front	Romania joined the Allies but was soon overrun by Germany.
Middle East	Kut-al-Imara, Iraq, was taken from the British by the Turks.
war at sea	The Battle of Jutland between England and Germany which, although indecisive, put a stop to further German naval participation in the war.
1917	The US entered the war in April. The UK launched the third battle at Ypres and by Nov had taken Passchendaele.
1918 Eastern Front	On March 3 Soviet Russia signed the Treaty of Brest-Litovsk with Germany, ending Russian participation in the war (the Russian Revolution 1917 led into their civil war 1918–21).
Western Front	Germany began a final offensive. In April the Allies appointed the French marshal Foch supreme commander, but by June (when the first US troops went into battle) the Allies had lost all gains since 1915, and the Germans were on the Marne. The battle at Amiens marked the launch of the victorious Allied offensive.
Italy	At Vittorio Veneto the British and Italians finally defeated the Austrians.
German capitulation	began with naval mutinies at Kiel, followed by uprisings in the major cities. Kaiser Wilhelm II abdicated, and on Nov 11 the armistice was signed.
1919	June 18, peace treaty of Versailles. (The US signed a separate peace accord with Germany and Austria 1921.)

Worcester industrial port (textiles, engineering, printing) in central Massachusetts, on the Blackstone River; population (1990) 169,759. Educational institutions include Clark University and Worcester Polytechnic Institute. It was permanently settled 1713.

Worcester Porcelain Factory English porcelain factory, since 1862 the Royal Worcester Porcelain Factory. The factory was founded 1751 and produced a hard-wearing type of softpaste porcelain, mainly as tableware and decorative china.

word in computing, a unit of storage. The size of a word varies from one computer to another. In a popular microcomputer, it is 16 ◊bits or 2 ◊bytes; on many mainframes it is 32 bits.

word processor in computing, a program that allows the input, amendment, manipulation, storage, and retrieval of text; or a computer system that runs such software. Since word-processing programs became available to the method has been gradually replacing the typewriter for producing letters or other text.

Wordsworth William 1770–1850. English Romantic poet. In 1797 he moved with his sister Dorothy

World War I *Men of Britain's Middlesex Regiment wheeling wounded from the trenches of the Somme to medical facilities, Nov 1916.*

World War I *(left) Soldiers struggling to move a field gun in muddy conditions. (right) Prisoners from Guilemont pass by troops, Sept 1916.*

to Somerset to be near ◊Coleridge, collaborating with him on *Lyrical Ballads* 1798 (which included "Tintern Abbey"). From 1799 he lived in the Lake District, and later works include *Poems* 1807 (including "Intimations of Immortality") and *The Prelude* (written by 1805, published 1850). He was appointed poet laureate in 1843.

Born in Cockermouth, Cumbria, he was educated at Cambridge University. In 1791 he returned from a visit to France, having fallen in love with Marie-Anne Vallon, who bore him an illegitimate daughter. In 1802 he married Mary Hutchinson. *The Prelude* was written to form part of the autobiographical work *The Recluse*, never completed.

work in physics, a measure of the result of transferring energy from one system to another to cause an object to move. Work should not be confused with ◊energy (the capacity to do work, which is also measured in ◊joules) or with ◊power (the rate of doing work, measured in joules per second).

Work W is equal to the product of the force F used and the distance d moved by the object in the direction of that force ($W=F \times d$). For example, the work done when a force of 10 newtons moves an object 5 meters against some sort of resistance is 50 newton-meters (= 50 joules).

World Bank popular name for the International Bank for Reconstruction and Development, established 1945 under the 1944 Bretton Woods agreement, which also created the International Monetary Fund. The World Bank is a specialized agency of the United Nations that borrows in the commercial market and lends on commercial terms. The International Development Association is an arm of the World Bank.

The World Bank now earns almost as much money from interest and loan repayments as it hands out in new loans every year. Over 60% of the bank's loans goes to suppliers outside the borrower countries for such things as consultancy services, oil, and machinery. Control of the bank is vested in a board of executives representing national governments, whose votes are apportioned according to the amount they have funded the bank. The US, with the largest fund, has nearly 20% of the vote and always appoints the board's president.

World Cup the most prestigious competition in international soccer, but which also features in the calendars of rugby union, cricket, and other sports. Most World Cup events are held every four years but the skiing World Cup is an annual event.

World Health Organization (WHO) agency of the United Nations established 1946 to prevent the spread of diseases and to eradicate them. In 1990–91 it had staff of 4,500 operating throughout the world.

Its headquarters are in Geneva, Switzerland.

World Intellectual Property Organization (WIPO) specialist agency of the United Nations established 1974 to coordinate the international protection (initiated by the Paris convention 1883) of inventions, trademarks, and industrial designs, and also literary and artistic works (as initiated by the Berne convention 1886).

World Meteorological Organization agency, part of the United Nations since 1950, that promotes the international exchange of weather information through the establishment of a worldwide network of meteorological stations. It was founded as the International Meteorological Organization 1873, and its headquarters are now in Geneva, Switzerland.

World Series annual ◊baseball competition between the winning teams of the National League (NL) and American League (AL). It is a best-of-seven series played each October. The first modern World Series was played in 1903 (as a best-of-nine series): the AL's Boston Pilgrims defeated the NL's Pittsburgh Pirates in eight games.

World War I 1914–1918. War between the Central European Powers (Germany, Austria-Hungary, and allies) on one side and the Triple Entente (Britain and the British Empire, France, and Russia) and their allies, including the US (which entered 1917), on the other side. An estimated 10 million lives were lost and twice that number were wounded. It was fought on the Eastern and Western Fronts, in the Middle East, Africa, and at sea. Toward the end of the war Russia withdrew because of the ◊Russian Revolution 1917. The Peace Treaty of Versailles 1919 was the formal end to the war.

World War II 1939–1945. war between Germany, Italy, and Japan (the Axis powers) on one side, and Britain, the Commonwealth, France, the US, the USSR, and China (the Allied powers) on the other. An estimated 55 million lives were lost, 20 million of them citizens of the USSR. The war was fought in the Atlantic and Pacific Theaters. In 1945, Germany surrendered (May) but Japan fought on until the US dropped atomic bombs on Hiroshima and Nagasaki (July).

World Wide Fund for Nature (WWF, formerly the World Wildlife Fund) an international organization established 1961 to raise funds for conservation by public appeal. Its headquarters are in Gland, Switzerland. Projects include conservation of particular species, for example, the tiger and giant panda, and special areas, such as the Simen Mountains, Ethiopia.

World Wildlife Fund former and US name of the World Wide Fund for Nature.

worm any of various elongated limbless invertebrates belonging to several phyla. Worms include the ◊flatworms, such as ◊flukes and ◊tapeworms; the roundworms or ◊nematodes, such as the eelworm and the hookworm; the marine ribbon worms or nemerteans; and the segmented worms or ◊annelids.

In 1979, giant sea worms about 10 ft/3 m long, living within tubes created by their own excretions, were discovered in hydrothermal vents 8,000 ft/2,450 m beneath the Pacific NE of the Galápagos Islands.

WORM (acronym from *w*rite *o*nce *r*ead *m*any times) in computing, a storage device, similar to ◊CD-ROM. The computer can write to the disk directly, but cannot subsequently erase or overwrite the same area. WORMs are mainly used for archiving and backup copies.

Worms industrial town in Rhineland-Palatinate, Federal Republic of Germany, on the Rhine; population (1984) 73,000. Liebfraumilch wine is produced here. The Protestant reformer Luther appeared before the Diet (Assembly) of Worms 1521 and was declared an outlaw by the Roman Catholic Church.

World War I *American troops in Alsace during World War I.*

World War II *Lili Sédin, 1940. Pilots at a Royal Air Force Fighter aerodrome in France race to their Hurricane aircraft.*

wormwood any plant of the genus *Artemisia*, family Compositae, especially the aromatic herb *A. absinthium*, the leaves of which are used in ◊absinthe. ◊Tarragon is a member of this genus.

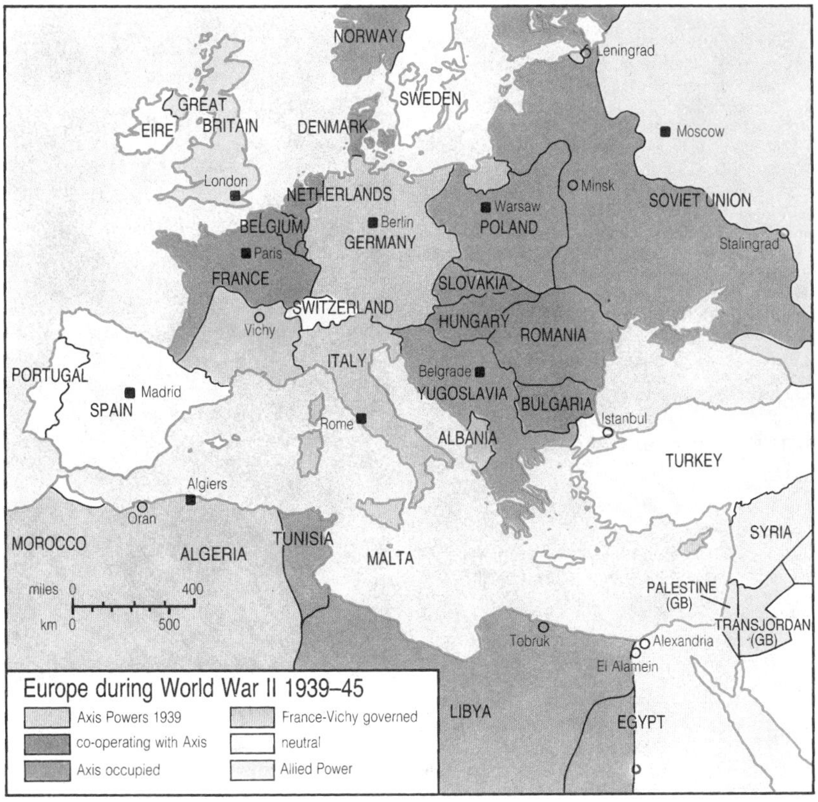
NORWAY
Leningrad
SWEDEN
GREAT BRITAIN
EIRE
DENMARK
Moscow
London
NETHERLANDS
Minsk
SOVIET UNION
Warsaw
POLAND
BELGIUM
Berlin
GERMANY
Paris
Stalingrad
FRANCE
SLOVAKIA
SWITZERLAND
HUNGARY
Vichy
ROMANIA
ITALY
PORTUGAL
Madrid
SPAIN
Belgrade
YUGOSLAVIA
BULGARIA
Rome
Istanbul
ALBANIA
TURKEY
Algiers
Oran
MOROCCO
ALGERIA
TUNISIA
MALTA
SYRIA
miles 0 400
km 0 500
PALESTINE (GB)
TRANSJORDAN (GB)
Tobruk
Alexandria
El Alamein
Europe during World War II 1939–45
Axis Powers 1939
co-operating with Axis
Axis occupied
France-Vichy governed
neutral
Allied Power
LIBYA
EGYPT

Wörner Manfred 1934– . German politician, NATO secretary-general from 1988. He was elected for the conservative Christian Democratic Union (CDU) to the West German Bundestag (parliament) in 1965 and, as a specialist in strategic affairs, served as defense minister under Chancellor Kohl 1982–88. A proponent of closer European military collaboration, he succeeded the British politician Peter Carrington as secretary general of NATO in July 1988.

Worrall Denis John 1935– . South African politician, member of the white opposition to apartheid. A coleader of the Democratic Party (DP), he was elected to parliament in 1989.

A former academic and journalist, Worrall joined the National Party and was made ambassador to London 1984–87. On his return to South Africa he resigned from the NP and in 1988 established the Independent Party (IP), which later merged with other white opposition parties to form the reformist DP, advocating dismantling of the apartheid system and universal adult suffrage.

Wounded Knee site on the Oglala Sioux Reservation, South Dakota, of a confrontation between the US Army and American Indians. Sitting Bull was killed, supposedly resisting arrest, on Dec 15, 1890, and on Dec 29 a group of Indians involved in the Ghost Dance Movement (aimed at resumption of Indian control of North America with the aid of the spirits of dead braves) were surrounded and 153 killed.

In 1973 the militant American Indian Movement, in the siege of Wounded Knee Feb 27–May 8, held hostages and demanded a government investigation of the Indian treaties.

Wouvermans family of Dutch painters, based in Haarlem. The brothers Philips Wouvermans (1619–1668), Pieter Wouvermans (1623–1682), and Jan Wouvermans (1629–1666) specialized in landscapes with horses and riders and in military scenes.

W particle type of ◊elementary particle.

wpm abbreviation for words per minute.

wrack any of the large brown ◊seaweeds characteristic of rocky shores. The bladder wrack *Fucus vesiculosus* has narrow, branched fronds up to

World War II *USS Bunker Hill takes two Kamikazes in 30 seconds on May 11, 1945, in the Leyte Gulf.*

Wren *The largest of London's churches and symbol of Christopher Wren's architectural achievement, St Paul's Cathedral, built 1675–1710.*

3.3 ft/1 m long, with oval air bladders, usually in pairs on either side of the midrib or central vein.

Wrangel Ferdinand Petrovich, Baron von 1794–1870. Russian vice admiral and Arctic explorer, after whom Wrangel Island (Ostrov Vrangelya) in the Soviet Arctic is named.

Wrangel Peter Nicolaievich, Baron von 1878–1928. Russian general, born in St Petersburg. He commanded a division of Cossacks in World War I, and in 1920, after succeeding Anton Denikin as commander in chief of the White army, lost to the Bolsheviks in the Crimea.

wrasse any bony fish of the family Labridae, found in temperate and tropical seas. They are slender and often brightly colored, with a single long dorsal fin. They have elaborate courtship rituals, and some species can change their coloring and sex. Species vary in size from 2 in/5 cm to 6.5 ft/2 m.

The hogfish *L. maximus*, found along S Atlantic shores of North America, is a fine food fish up to 2 ft/0.6 m long, with rapidly changing reddish colors.

Wray Fay 1907– . US film actress who starred in *King Kong* 1933 after playing the lead in Erich von Stroheim's *The Wedding March* 1928, and starring in *Doctor X* 1932 and *The Most Dangerous Game* 1932.

wren any of a family (Troglodytidae) of small birds of order Passeriformes, with slender, slightly curved bills, and uptilted tails.

The house wren of North America *Troglodytes aedon* is common in brush, farmyard, and park.

Wren Christopher 1632–1723. English architect, designer of St Paul's Cathedral, London, built 1675–1710; many London churches including St Bride's, Fleet Street, and St Mary-le-Bow, Cheapside; the Royal Exchange; Marlborough House; and the Sheldonian Theatre, Oxford.

Wren studied mathematics, and in 1660 became a professor of astronomy at Oxford University. His opportunity as an architect came after the Great Fire of London 1666. He prepared a plan for rebuilding the city, but it was not adopted. Instead, Wren was commissioned to rebuild 51 City churches and St Paul's Cathedral. The west towers of Westminster Abbey, often attributed to him, were the design of his pupil Hawksmoor.

Wren P(ercival) C(hristopher) 1885–1941. British novelist. Drawing on his experiences in the French and Indian armies, he wrote adventure novels including *Beau Geste* 1924, dealing with the Foreign Legion.

wrestling sport popular in ancient Egypt, Greece, and Rome, and included in the Olympics from 704 BC. The two main modern international styles are Greco-Roman, concentrating on above-waist holds, and freestyle, which allows the legs to be used to hold or trip; in both the aim is to throw the opponent to the ground.

Many countries have their own forms of wrestling. *Glima* is unique to Iceland; *Kushti* is the national style practiced in Iran; *Schwingen* has been practiced in Switzerland for hundreds of years; and ◊sumo is the national sport of Japan. World championships for freestyle wrestling have existed since 1951 and since 1921 for Greco-Roman style. Greco-Roman was included in the first Olympic program 1896; freestyle made its debut 1904. Competitors are categorized according to weight: there are ten weight divisions in each style of wrestling.

Wright Frank Lloyd 1869–1959. US architect, who, as a student of Louis ◊Sullivan 1888–93, rejected Neo-Classicist styles for "organic architecture," in which buildings reflected their natural surroundings. Among his buildings are the Robie house 1909 in Chicago; his Spring Green, Wisconsin, home Taliesin East 1925; Falling Water, near Pittsburgh, Pennsylvania, 1936, a house built straddling a waterfall; the Johnson Wax Company Administration building, Racine, Wisconsin, 1938, and the company's Laboratory Tower 1949; the high-rise Price Company Tower, Bartlesville, Oklahoma, 1953; and the Guggenheim Museum, New York, 1959.

Wright also designed buildings in Japan from 1915 to 1922, most notably the Imperial Hotel in Tokyo 1922. In 1938 he built his winter home in the Arizona desert, Taliesin West, and established an architectural community there. He

Wright *US architect Frank Lloyd Wright at 87. The originality of his work stands out in city buildings like the Guggenheim Museum in New York 1959. He condemned the growing congestion of cities and encouraged closeness to nature.*

World War II: chronology

Sept 1939	German invasion of Poland; Britain and France declared war on Germany; the USSR invaded Poland; fall of Warsaw (Poland divided between Germany and USSR).
Nov	The USSR invaded Finland.
March 1940	Soviet peace treaty with Finland.
April	Germany occupied Denmark, Norway, the Netherlands, Belgium, and Luxembourg. In Britain, a coalition government was formed under Churchill.
May	Germany outflanked the defensive French Maginot Line.
May–June	Evacuation of 337,131 Allied troops from Dunkirk, France, across the Channel to England.
June	Italy declared war on Britain and France; the Germans entered Paris; the French prime minister Pétain signed an armistice with Germany and moved the seat of government to Vichy.
July–Oct	Battle of Britain between British and German air forces.
Sept	Japanese invasion of French ◊Indochina.
Oct	Abortive Italian invasion of Greece.
April 1941	Germany occupied Greece and Yugoslavia.
June	Germany invaded the USSR; Finland declared war on the USSR.
July	The Germans entered Smolensk, USSR.
Dec	The Germans within 25 mi/40 km of Moscow, with Leningrad under siege. First Soviet counter-offensive. Japan bombed Pearl Harbor, Hawaii, and declared war on the US and Britain. Germany and Italy declared war on the US.
Jan 1942	Japanese conquest of the Philippines.
June	Naval battle of Midway, the turning point of the Pacific War.
Aug 2	German attack on Stalingrad (now Volgograd), USSR.
Oct–Nov	Battle of El Alamein in N Africa, turn of the tide for the Western Allies.
Nov	Soviet counter-offensive on Stalingrad.
Jan 1943	Casablanca Conference issued Allied demand of unconditional surrender; the Germans retreated from Stalingrad.
March	The USSR drove the Germans back to the river Donetz.
May	End of Axis resistance in N Africa.
July	A coup by King Victor Emmanuel and Marshal Badoglio forced Mussolini to resign.
Aug	Beginning of campaign against the Japanese in Burma (now Myanmar); US Marines landed on Guadalcanal, Solomon Islands.
Sept	Italy surrendered to Allies; Mussolini rescued by Germans who set up Republican Fascist government in northern Italy; Allied landings at Salerno; the USSR retook Smolensk.
Oct	Italy declared war on Germany.
Nov	US Navy defeated the Japanese in Battle of Guadalcanal.
Nov–Dec	Allied leaders met at Tehran Conference.
Jan 1944	Allied landing in Nazi-occupied Italy: Battle of Anzio.
March	End of German U-boat campaign in the Atlantic.
May	Fall of Monte Cassino, S Italy.
June	D-day: Allied landings in Nazi-occupied and heavily defended Normandy.
July	Bomb plot of German generals against Hitler failed.
Aug	Romania joined Allies.
Sept	Battle of Arnhem on the Rhine; Soviet armistice with Finland.
Oct	The Yugoslav guerrilla leader Tito and Soviets entered Belgrade.
Dec	German counter-offensive, Battle of the Bulge.
Feb 1945	The Soviets reached the German border; Yalta conference; Allied bombing campaign over Germany (Dresden destroyed); US reconquest of the Philippines completed; the Americans landed on Iwo Jima, S of Japan.
April	Hitler committed suicide; Mussolini captured by Italian partisans and shot.
May	German surrender to the Allies.
June	US troops completed the conquest of Okinawa (one of the Japanese Ryukyu Islands).
July	Potsdam Conference issued Allied ultimatum to Japan.
Aug	Atomic bombs dropped by the US on Hiroshima and Nagasaki; Japan surrendered.

always designed the interiors and the furnishing for his projects, to create a total environment for his patrons.

Wright Richard 1908–1960. US novelist. He was one of the first to depict the condition of black people in 20th-century US society with *Native Son* 1940 and the autobiography *Black Boy* 1945.

Between 1932 and 1944 he was active in the Communist party. Shortly thereafter he became a permanent expatriate in Paris. His other works include *White Man, Listen!* 1957, originally a series of lectures.

Wright Sewall 1889–1988. US geneticist and statistician. During the 1920s he helped modernize Charles ◊Darwin's theory of evolution, using statistics to model the behavior of populations of genes.

Wright's work on genetic drift centered on a phenomenon occurring in small isolated colonies where the chance disappearance of some types of gene leads to evolution without the influence of natural selection.

Wright Wilbur 1867–1912 and Orville 1871–1948. US inventors; brothers who pioneered piloted, powered ◊flight. Inspired by ◊Lilienthal's gliding, they perfected their piloted glider 1902. In 1903 they built their first powered machine, a 12-hp 750-lb/341-kg plane, and became the first to make a successful powered flight, near Kitty Hawk, North Carolina. Orville flew 120 ft/36.6 m in 12 sec; Wilbur, 852 ft/260 m in 59 sec.

Both brothers were born in Dayton, Ohio, and became interested in flight at early ages. They devised a wing-control system and added a rudder and a balancing tail to existing gliders. By 1903 they had built and flown a power-driven plane; they received a patent in 1906 and in 1909 set up the American Wright Corp to produce planes for the War Department. After Wilbur's death Orville did research and served on the National Advisory Committee for Aeronautics 1915–48.

writ in law, a document issued by a court requiring performance of certain actions.

Examples include a writ of ◊habeas corpus, a writ of certiorari by which the US Supreme Court calls up cases from inferior courts for review, or writ of attachment of property in civil litigation.

writing any written form of communication using a set of symbols: see ◊alphabet, ◊cuneiform, ◊hieroglyphic. The last two used ideographs (picture writing) and phonetic word symbols side by side, as does modern Chinese. Syllabic writing, as in Japanese, develops from the continued use of a symbol to represent the sound of a short word. Some 8,000-year-old inscriptions, thought to be pictographs, were found on animal bones and tortoise shells in Henan province, China, at a Neolithic site at Jiahu. They are thought to predate by 2,500 years the oldest known writing (Mesopotamian cuneiform of 3,500 BC).

Wroclaw industrial river port in Poland, on the river Oder; population (1985) 636,000. Under the German name of Breslau, it was the capital of former German Silesia. Industries include shipbuilding, engineering, textiles, and electronics.

wrought iron fairly pure iron containing some beads of slag, widely used for construction work before the days of cheap steel. It is strong, tough, and easy to machine. It is made in a puddling furnace, invented by Henry Colt in England 1784. Pig iron is remelted and heated strongly in air with iron ore, burning out the carbon in the metal, leaving relatively pure iron and a slag containing impurities. The resulting pasty metal is then hammered to remove as much of the remaining slag as possible. It is still used in fences and grating.

wt abbreviation for weight.

Wuchang former city in China; amalgamated with ◊Wuhan.

Wuhan river port and capital of Hubei province, China, at the confluence of the Han and Chang Jiang rivers, formed 1950 as one of China's greatest industrial areas by the amalgamation of Hankou, Hanyang, and Wuchang; population (1986) 3,400,000. It produces iron, steel, machine tools, textiles, and fertilizer.

A center of revolt in both the Taiping Rebellion 1851–65 and the 1911 revolution, it had an anti-Mao revolt 1967 during the Cultural Revolution.

Wuhsien another name for ◊Suzhou, a city in China.

Wundt Wilhelm Max 1832–1920. German physiologist, who regarded psychology as the study of internal experience or consciousness. His main psychological method was introspection; he also studied sensation, perception of space and time, and reaction times.

Wuppertal industrial town in North Rhine–Westphalia, Federal Republic of Germany, 20 mi/32 km E of Düsseldorf; population (1988) 374,000. Industries include textiles, plastics, brewing, and electronics. It was formed 1929 (named 1931) by uniting Elberfield (13th century) and Barmen (11th century).

Württemberg former kingdom (1805–1918) in SW Germany that joined the German Reich in 1870. Its capital was Stuttgart. In 1946 it was divided between the administrative West German *Länder* of Württemberg-Baden and Württemberg-Hohenzollern, from 1952 it was part of the *Land* of ◊Baden-Württemberg.

Würzburg industrial town (engineering, printing, wine, brewing) in NW Bavaria, Federal Republic of Germany; population (1988) 127,000. The bishop's palace was decorated by Tiepolo.

Wuthering Heights a novel by Emily Brontë, published in the UK 1847, that chronicles the tumultuous relationship of Heathcliff and Catherine.

Heathcliff is taken in as a child by the Earnshaw family and forms an intense relationship with Catherine Earnshaw but is cruelly treated by her brother Hindley. Heathcliff flees, believing Catherine has rejected him, but returns after a few years to wreak his revenge. He marries Isabella, sister of Catherine's husband, and when Catherine dies in childbirth, Heathcliff forces her daughter Cathy to marry his son Linton. When Linton dies, Cathy turns to Hindley's son Hareton.

WV abbreviation for ◊West Virginia.

WWF abbreviation for ◊World Wide Fund for Nature (formerly World Wildlife Fund).

WY abbreviation for ◊Wyoming.

Wyatt Thomas c. 1503–1542. English poet. He was

employed on diplomatic missions by Henry VIII, and in 1536 was imprisoned for a time in the Tower of London, suspected of having been the lover of Henry's second wife, Anne Boleyn. In 1541 Wyatt was again imprisoned on charges of treason. With the Earl of Surrey, he pioneered the sonnet in England.

Wycherley William 1640–1710. English Restoration playwright. His first comedy *Love in a Wood* won him court favor in 1671, and later bawdy works include *The Country Wife* 1675 and *The Plain Dealer* 1676.

Wycliffe John c. 1320–1384. English religious reformer. H attacked abuses in the church, maintaining that the Bible rather than the church was the supreme authority. He criticized such fundamental doctrines as priestly absolution, confession, and indulgences, and set disciples to work on translating the Bible into English. He sent out bands of traveling preachers, was denounced as a heretic, but died peacefully at Lutterworth.

Wye river in Wales and England; length 130 mi/208 km. It rises on Plynlimmon, NE Dyfed, flowing SE and E through Powys, and Hereford and Worcester, then follows the Gwent–Gloucestershire border before joining the river Severn south of Chepstow.

Wyeth Andrew (Newell) 1917– . US painter. His portraits and landscapes, usually in watercolor or tempera, are naturalistic, minutely detailed, and often have a strong sense of the isolation of the countryside: for example, *Christina's World* 1948 (Museum of Modern Art, New York).

Born in Chadds Ford, Pennsylvania, the son of artist-illustrator N C ◊Wyeth, he is among the most popular of contemporary US artists. His paintings depict people of the land, especially Wyeth's own surroundings in Chadds Ford and Maine, where his summer home is located. His son James Browning Wyeth (1946–) also is an artist.

Wyeth N(ewel) C(onvers) 1882–1944. US artist and illustrator. Born in Needham, Massachusetts, he was trained by illustrator Howard Pyle. Wyeth became the foremost US illustrator of his time as well as an accomplished muralist. He illustrated over 20 children's classics including *Treasure Island, The Adventures of Tom Sawyer, Robin Hood,* and *The Yearling.* Among his students were his daughter Henriette and his son Andrew ◊Wyeth.

Wyler William 1902–1981. German-born film director who lived in the US from 1922. He directed *Wuthering Heights* 1939, *Mrs Miniver* 1942, *Ben-Hur* 1959, and *Funny Girl* 1968, among others.

Wyndham John. Adopted name of John Wyndham Parkes Lucas Beynon Harris 1903–1969. English science-fiction writer who wrote *The Day of the Triffids* 1951, *The Chrysalids* 1955, and *The Midwich Cuckoos* 1957. A recurrent theme in his work is people's response to disaster, whether caused by nature, aliens, or human error.

Wynne-Edwards Vera 1906– . English zoologist who argued that animal behavior is often altruistic and that animals will behave for the good of the group, even if this entails individual sacrifice. Her study *Animal Dispersal in Relation to Social Behavior* was published in 1962.

The theory that animals are genetically programmed to behave for the good of the species has since fallen into disrepute. From this dispute grew a new interpretation of animal behavior, seen in the work of biologist E O Wilson.

Wyoming state in W US: nickname Equality State

area 97,812 sq mi/253,400 sq km

capital Cheyenne

cities Casper, Laramie

population (1990) 453,588

Wyoming

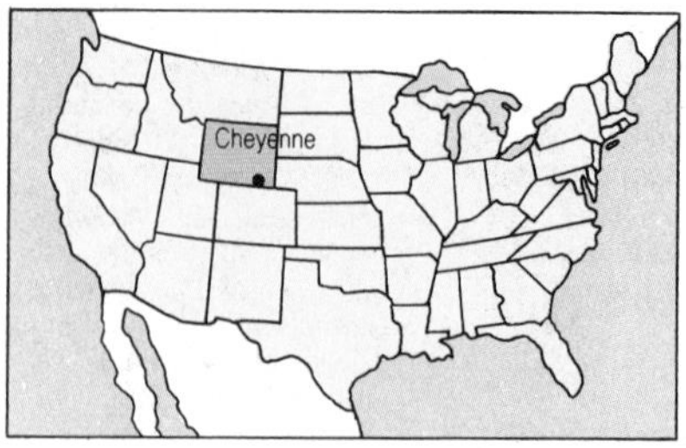
Cheyenne

features Rocky Mountains; national parks: Yellowstone (including the geyser Old Faithful), Grand Teton

products oil, natural gas, sodium salts, coal, uranium, sheep, beef

famous people Buffalo Bill Cody, J C Penney, Jackson Pollock

history acquired by US from France as part of the Louisiana Purchase 1803; first explored 1807 by trapper John Colter, who found the Yellowstone area and its geysers and hot springs; Fort Laramie, a trading post, settled 1834. The Union Pacific Railroad came through 1867–68; Wyoming then became a territory and passed a pioneering woman's suffrage act. Statehood came 1890. Despite the development of its energy resources, Wyoming remains sparsely settled, with large ranches dotting the arid landscape.

WYSIWYG (acronym from *w*hat *y*ou *s*ee *i*s *w*hat *y*ou *g*et) in computing, a program that attempts to display on the screen a faithful representation of the final printed output. For example, a WYSIWYG ◊word processor would show actual line widths, page breaks, and the sizes and styles of type.

xerophyte

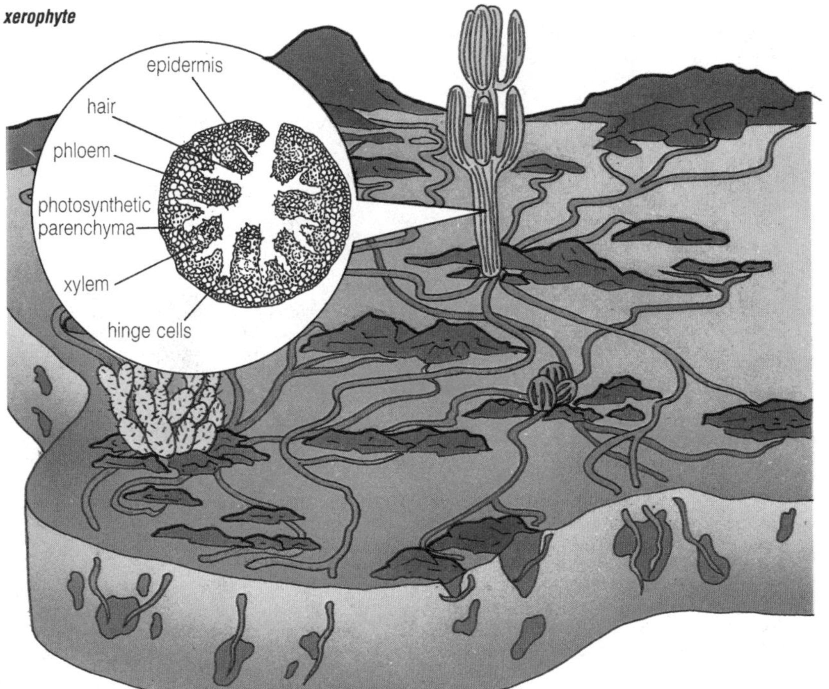
epidermis
hair
phloem
photosynthetic parenchyma
xylem
hinge cells

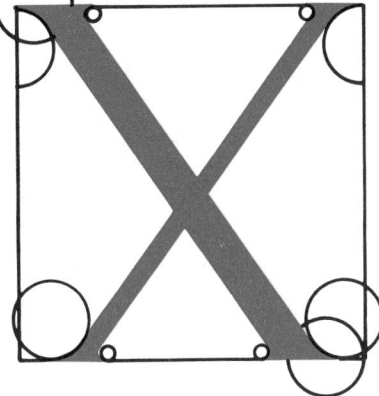

X Roman numeral ten; a person or thing unknown.

x in mathematics, an unknown quantity.

xanthophyll yellow pigment in plants that, like ◊chlorophyll, is responsible for the production of carbohydrates by photosynthesis.

Xavier, St Francis 1506–1552. Spanish Jesuit missionary. He went to the Portuguese colonies in the East Indies, arriving at Goa in 1542. He was in Japan 1549–51, establishing a Christian mission that lasted for 100 years. He returned to Goa in 1552, and sailed for China, but died of fever there. He was canonized in 1622.

X chromosome the larger of the two sex chromosomes, the smaller being the ◊Y chromosome. These two chromosomes are involved in sex determination. Genes carried on the X chromosome produce the phenomenon of ◊sex linkage.

xenon colorless, odorless, gaseous, nonmetallic element, symbol Xe, atomic number 54, atomic weight 131.30. It is grouped with the ◊inert gases and was long believed not to enter into reactions, but is now known to form some compounds, mostly with fluorine. It is a heavy gas present in very small quantities in the air (about one part in 20 million).

Xenon is used in bubble chambers, light bulbs, vacuum tubes, and lasers. It was discovered in 1898 in a residue from liquid air by William Ramsay and Morris Travers (1872–1961) and named by them for Greek *xenos*, "foreign" or "strange."

Xenophon c. 430–354 BC. Greek historian, philosopher, and soldier. He was a disciple of ◊Socrates (described in Xenophon's *Symposium*). In 401 he joined a Greek mercenary army aiding the Persian prince Cyrus, and on the latter's death took command. His *Anabasis* describes how he led 10,000 Greeks on a 1,000-mile march home across enemy territory. His other works include *Memorabilia* and *Apology*.

xerography dry, electrostatic method of producing images, without the use of negatives or sensitized paper, invented in the US by Chester Carlson in 1938 and applied in the Xerox ◊photocopier. Toner powder is sprayed on paper in highly charged areas and fixed with heat.

xerophyte a plant adapted to live in dry conditions. Common adaptations to reduce the rate of ◊transpiration include a reduction of leaf size, sometimes to spines or scales; a dense covering of hairs over the leaf to trap a layer of moist air (as in edelweiss); and permanently rolled leaves or leaves that roll up in dry weather (as in vinemesquite grass). Many desert cacti are xerophytes.

Xerxes c. 519–465 BC. King of Persia from 485 BC when he succeeded his father Darius and continued the Persian invasion of Greece. In 480, at the head of an army of some 400,000 men and supported by a fleet of 800 ships, he crossed the ◊Hellespont strait (now the Dardanelles) over a bridge of boats. He defeated the Greek fleet at Artemisium and captured and burned Athens, but Themistocles retaliated by annihilating the Persian fleet at Salamis and Xerxes was forced to retreat. He spent his later years working on a grandiose extension of the capital Persepolis and was eventually murdered in a court intrigue.

Xhosa member of a South African people, living mainly in the Black National State of ◊Transkei. Their Bantu language belongs to the Niger-Congo family.

Xiamen formerly (until 1979) Amoy port on Ku Lang island in Fujian province, SE China; population (1984) 533,000. Industries include textiles, food products, and electronics. It was one of the original five treaty ports used for trade under foreign control 1842–1943 and a special export-trade zone from 1979.

Xian industrial city and capital of Shaanxi province, China; population (1986) 2,330,000. It produces chemicals, electrical equipment, and fertilizers.

It was the capital of China under the Zhou dynasty (1126–255 BC); under the Han dynasty (206 BC–AD 220), when it was called Changan ("long peace"); and under the Tang dynasty 618–906, as Siking ("western capital"). The Manchus called it Sian ("western peace"), now spelled Xian. It reverted to Changan 1913–32, was Siking 1932–43, and again Sian from 1943. It was here that the imperial court retired after the Boxer Rebellion 1900.

Its treasures include the 600-year-old Ming wall; the pottery soldiers buried to protect the tomb of the first Qin emperor, Shi Huangdi; Big Wild Goose Pagoda, one of the oldest in China; and the Great Mosque 742.

Xian Incident kidnapping of the Chinese generalissimo and politician ◊Chiang Kai-shek Dec 12, 1936, by one of his own generals, to force his cooperation with the Communists against the Japanese invaders.

Xi Jiang or ***Si-Kiang*** river in China, that rises in Yunnan and flows into the South China Sea; length 1,200 mi/1,900 km. Guangzhou lies on the N arm of its delta, and Hong Kong island at its mouth. The name means "west river."

Xingú river (Amazon tributary) and region in Pará, Brazil. In 1989 Xingú Indians protested at the creation of a vast, intrusive lake for the Babaquara and Kararao dams of the Altamira complex.

Xinhua official Chinese news agency.

Xining or ***Sining*** industrial city and capital of Qinghai province, China; population (1982) 873,000.

Xinjiang Uygur or ***Sinkiang Uighur*** autonomous region of NW China

area 635,665 sq mi/1,646,800 sq km

capital Urumqi

features largest of Chinese administrative areas; Junggar Pendi (Dzungarian Basin) and Tarim Pendi (Tarim Basin, which includes ◊Lop Nor, China's nuclear testing ground, although the research centers were moved to the central province of Sichuan 1972) separated by the Tyan Shan mountains

products cereals, cotton, fruit in valleys and oases; uranium, coal, iron, copper, tin, oil

population (1986) 13,840,000

religion 50% Muslim

history under Manchu rule from the 18th century. Large sections were ceded to Russia 1864 and 1881; China has raised the question of their return and regards the 480-km/300-mi

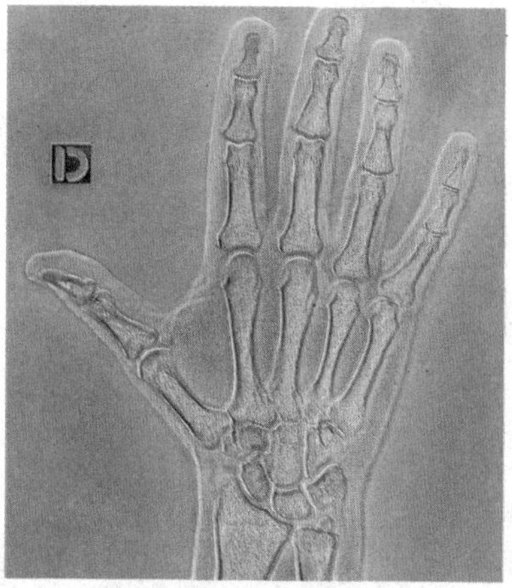

***X ray** X ray of a human hand and wrist, obtained using xerography.*

frontier between Xinjiang Uygur and Soviet Tadzikistan as undemarcated.

Xizang Chinese name for ◊Tibet, an autonomous region of SW China from 1965.

Xochimilco lake about 7 mi/11 km SE of Mexico City, Mexico, which features floating gardens, all that remains of an ancient water-based agricultural system.

X ray band of electromagnetic radiation in the wavelength range 10^{-11} to 10^{-9} m (between gamma rays and ultraviolet radiation; see ◊electromagnetic waves). Applications of X rays make use of their short wavelength (such as X-ray crystallography) or their penetrating power (as in medical X rays of internal body tissues). X rays are dangerous and can cause cancer.

X rays were discovered by Wilhelm Röntgen in 1895 and formerly called roentgen rays. They are produced when high-energy electrons from a

X-ray

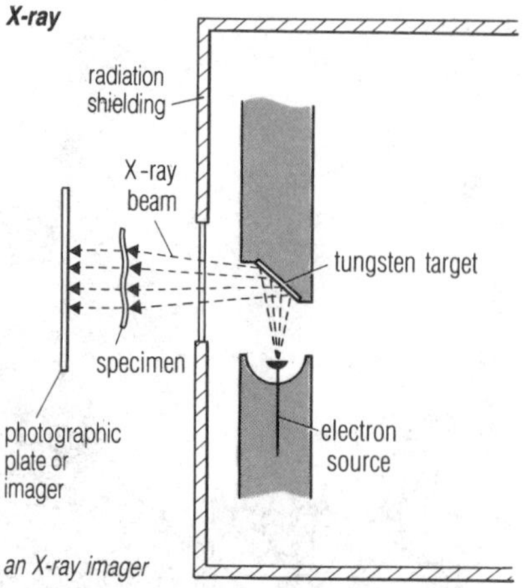
radiation shielding
X-ray beam
tungsten target
specimen
photographic plate or imager
electron source

an X-ray imager

heated filament cathode strike the surface of a target (usually made of tungsten) on the face of a massive heat-conducting anode, between which a high alternating voltage (about 100 kV) is applied.

X-ray astronomy detection of X rays from intensely hot gas in the universe. Such X rays are prevented from reaching the Earth's surface by the atmosphere, so detectors must be placed in rockets and satellites. The first celestial X-ray source, Scorpius X-1, was discovered by a rocket flight in 1962.

Since 1970, special satellites have been orbited to study X rays from the Sun, stars, and galaxies. Many X-ray sources are believed to be gas falling onto ◊neutron stars and ◊black holes.

X-ray diffraction method of studying the atomic and molecular structure of crystalline substances by using ◊X rays. X rays directed at such substances spread out as they pass through the crystals caused by ◊diffraction (the slight spreading of waves around the edge of an opaque object) of the rays around the atoms. By using measurements of the position and intensity of the diffracted waves, it is possible to calculate the shape and size of the atoms in the crystal. The method has been used to study substances such as ◊DNA that are found in living material.

xylem a tissue found in ◊vascular plants, whose main function is to conduct water and dissolved mineral nutrients from the roots to other parts of the plant. Xylem is composed of a number of different types of cell, and may include long, thin, usually dead cells known as ◊tracheids; fibers (schlerenchyma); thin-walled ◊parenchyma cells; and conducting vessels.

In most ◊angiosperms (flowering plants) water is moved through these vessels. Most ◊gymnosperms and ◊pteridophytes lack vessels and depend on tracheids for water conduction.

Non-woody plants contain only primary xylem, derived from the procambium, whereas in trees and shrubs this is replaced for the most part by secondary xylem, formed by ◊secondary growth from the actively dividing vascular ◊cambium. The cell walls of the secondary xylem are thickened by a deposit of ◊lignin, providing mechanical support to the plant; see ◊wood.

xylophone musical ◊percussion instrument in which wooden bars of varying lengths are arranged according to graded pitch, or as a piano keyboard, over resonators to produce sounds when struck with hammers.

XYZ Affair in American history, an incident 1797–98 in which the French were accused of demanding a $250,000 bribe to French foreign minister ◊Talleyrand before agreeing to negotiate with US envoys in Paris in an attempt to resolve a crisis in Franco-US relations caused by the war in Europe and by French raids on American shipping. Three French agents (referred to by President John Adams 1797 as X, Y, and Z) held secret talks with the envoys over the money. Publicity fueled anti-French feelings in the US and led to increased military spending.

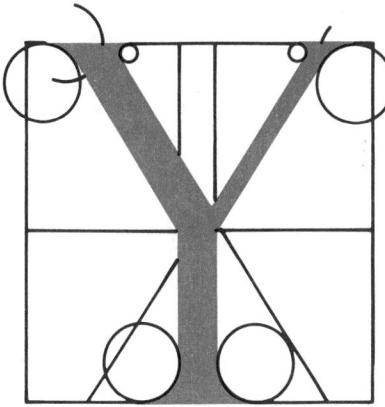

Yahweh see ◊Jahweh.

Yahya Khan Agha Mohammed 1917–1980. Pakistani president 1969–71. His mishandling of the Bangladesh separatist issue led to civil war, and he was forced to resign.

Yahya Khan fought with the British army in the Middle East during World War II, escaping German capture in Italy. Later, as Pakistan's chief of army general staff, he supported General Ayub Khan's 1958 coup and in 1969 became military ruler. Following defeat by India in 1971, he resigned and was under house arrest 1972–75.

yak species of cattle *Bos grunniens*, family Bovidae, which lives in wild herds at high altitudes in Tibet. It stands about 6 ft/2 m at the shoulder and has long shaggy hair on the underparts. It has large, upward-curving horns and humped shoulders. The yak has a thick coat as well as its own form of central heating through the fermentation in progress in its stomach. It is in danger of becoming extinct.

In the wild, yaks are brown or black, but the domesticated variety, which is half the size of the wild form, may be white. It is used for milk, meat, leather, and as a beast of burden.

yak

Yakima city in S central Washington, on the Yakima River, SE of Seattle. It is an agricultural processing center for sugar beets, apples, hops, and livestock, and produces cider and flour; population (1990) 54,827.

Yakut (Russian *Yakutskaya*) autonomous Soviet Socialist Republic in NE USSR
area 1,197,760 sq mi/3,103,000 sq km
capital Yakutsk
features one of world's coldest inhabited places; river Lena
products furs, gold, natural gas, some agriculture in the S
population (1986) 1,009,000; 50% Russians, 37% Yakuts
history the nomadic Yakuts were conquered by Russia 17th century; Yakut became a Soviet republic 1922.

Yakutsk capital of Yakut republic, USSR, on the Lena river; population (1987) 184,000. Industries include timber, tanning, and brick-making. It is the coldest point of the Arctic in NE Siberia and has an institute for studying the permanently frozen soil area (permafrost).

yakuza (Japanese "good for nothing") Japanese gangster. Organized crime in Japan is highly structured, and the various syndicates between them employed some 110,000 people in 1989, with a turnover of an estimated 1.5 trillion yen. The *yakuza* are unofficially tolerated and very powerful.

Their main areas of activity are prostitution, pornography, sports, entertainment, and moneylending; they have close links with the construction industry and with some politicians. There is considerable rivalry between gangs. Many *yakuza* have one or more missing fingertips, a self-inflicted ritual injury in atonement for an error.

Yale lock trademark for a key-operated pin-tumbler cylinder ◊lock invented by US locksmith Linus Yale Jr (1821–1868) in 1865 and still widely used.

Yale University US university, founded 1701, now located in New Haven, Connecticut. It was named after Elihu Yale (1648–1721), born in Boston, Massachusetts, one-time governor of Fort St George, Madras, India.

Yale is considered one of the preeminent US universities, attracting great numbers of foreign students as well as superior US high school graduates. Presidents George Bush and Gerald Ford, among many prominent Americans, attended Yale.

Yalow Rosalind 1921– . US physicist who developed radioimmunoassay (RIA), a technique for detecting minute quantities of hormones present in the blood. It can be used to discover a range of hormones produced in the hypothalamic region of the brain.

Yalta Conference in 1945, a meeting at which the Allied leaders Churchill (UK), Roosevelt (USA), and Stalin (USSR) completed plans for the defeat of Germany in World War II and the foundation of the United Nations. It took place in Yalta, a Soviet vacation resort in the Crimea.

Yalu river forming the N boundary between North Korea and Jilin and Liaoning provinces (Manchuria) in China; length 491 mi/790 km. It is only navigable near the mouth and is frozen from Nov to Mar.

yam any climbing plant of the genus *Dioscorea*, family Dioscoreaceae, cultivated in tropical regions; its starchy tubers are eaten as a vegetable. The Mexican yam *D. composita* contains a chemical used in the manufacture of contraceptive pills.

Yamagata Aritomo 1838–1922. Japanese soldier, politician, and prime minister 1889–93 and 1898. As war minister 1873 and chief of the imperial general staff 1878, he was largely responsible for the modernization of the military system. He returned as chief of staff during the Russo-Japanese War 1904–05 and remained an influential political figure until he was disgraced in 1921 for having meddled in the marriage arrangements of the crown prince.

Yamal Peninsula peninsula in NW Siberia, USSR, with gas reserves estimated at 212 trillion cu ft/6 trillion cu m; supplies are piped to W Europe.

Yamamoto Gombei 1852–1933. Japanese admiral and politician. As prime minister 1913–14, he began Japanese expansion into China and initiated political reforms. He again became premier 1923 but resigned the following year.

Yamoussoukro capital designate of ◊Ivory Coast; population (1986) 120,000. The economy is based on tourism and agricultural trade. A basilica, completed 1990, rivals St Peter's in Rome in scale.

Yamuna alternate name for the ◊Jumna river in India.

Yanamamo member of a South American Indian people, numbering approximately 15,000, who live in S Venezuela and N Brazil. The Yanamamo language is divided into several dialects, although there is a common ritual language.

Yan'an or ***Yenan*** industrial city in Shaanxi province, central China; population (1984) 254,000. The ◊Long March ended here Jan 1937, and it was the communist headquarters 1936–47 (the caves in which Mao lived are preserved).

Yangon since 1989 the name for Rangoon capital and chief port of Myanmar on the Yangon river, 20 mi/32 km from the Indian Ocean; population (1983) 2,459,000. Products include timber, oil, and rice. The city Dagon was founded on the site 746 AD; it was given the name Rangoon (meaning "end of conflict") by King Alaungpaya 1755.

Yang Shangkun 1907– . Chinese communist politician. He held a senior position in the party 1956–66 but was demoted during the Cultural Revolution. He was rehabilitated 1978, elected to the Politburo 1982, and to the position of state president 1988.

The son of a wealthy Sichuan landlord and a veteran of the ◊Long March 1934–35 and the war against Japan 1937–45, Yang rose in the ranks of the Chinese Communist Party (CCP) before being purged for alleged revisionism in the Cultural Revolution. He was a trusted supporter of Deng Xiaoping.

Yangtze-Kiang former name for ◊Chang Jiang, greatest Chinese river.

Yangzhou formerly ***Yangchow*** canal port in Jiangsu province, E China, on the Chang Jiang river; population (1984) 382,000. Among its features are gardens and pavilions. It is an artistic center for crafts, jade carving, and printing.

Yankee initially, a disparaging term for a Dutch freebooter, later applied to English settlers by colonial Dutch in New York. Now it may be a colloquial term for a New Englander, any US northerner (used in the South), or any American (used outside the US). A "real" Yankee refers to a member of a New England founding family.

Yantai formerly Chefoo ice-free port in Shandong province, E China; population (1984) 700,000. A special economic zone, its industries include tourism, wine, and fishing.

Yaoundé capital of Cameroon, 130 mi/210 km E of the port of Douala; population (1984) 552,000. Industry includes tourism, oil refining, and cigarette manufacturing.

Established by the Germans as a military port 1899, it became capital of French Cameroon 1921.

yapok nocturnal ◊opossum *Chironectes minimus* found in tropical South and Central America. It is about 1.1 ft/33 cm long, with a 1.3 ft/40 cm tail. It has webbed hind feet and thick fur, and is the only aquatic marsupial. The female has a watertight pouch.

yard imperial unit (abbreviation yd) of length, equivalent to 3 ft/0.9144 m; also sometimes used to denote a cubic yard (0.7646 cubic meters) as of topsoil.

yardang ridge formed by wind erosion from a dried-up riverbed or similar feature, as in Chad, China,

Yalta Conference The Allied leaders of World War II, Stalin of the USSR (left), Roosevelt of the US (center), and Churchill of the UK, met at the Yalta Conference in 1945 to plan the final defeat of Germany and the future of postwar Europe.

Peru, and North America. On the planet Mars, yardangs occur on a massive scale.

Yarkand or ***Shache*** walled city in Xinjiang Uygur region of China, in an oasis of the Tarim basin, on the caravan route to India and W USSR; a center of Islamic culture; population (1985) 100,000.

Yarmouth or ***Great Yarmouth*** vacation resort and port in Norfolk, England, at the mouth of the river Yare; population (1981) 55,000. Formerly a fishing town, it is now a leading base for North Sea oil and gas and is also a container port.

Yaroslavl industrial city (textiles, rubber, paints, commercial vehicles) in the USSR, capital of Yaroslavl region, on the river Volga 155 mi/ 250 km NE of Moscow; population (1987) 634,000.

yarrow or ***milfoil*** perennial herb *Achillea millefolium* of the family Compositae, with feathery, scented leaves and flat-topped clusters of white or pink flowers.

yashmak traditional Muslim face veil, worn by devout Muslim women in the presence of men.

yaws contagious tropical disease common in the West Indies, W Africa, and some Pacific islands, characterized by red, raspberrylike eruptions on the face, toes, and other parts of the body, sometimes followed by lesions of the skin and bones. It is caused by a spirochete (*Treponema pertenue*), a bacterium related to the one that causes ◊syphilis. Treatment is by antibiotics.

Yazd or ***Yezd*** silk-weaving town in central Iran, in an oasis on a trade route; population (1986) 231,000.

yd abbreviation for yard.

year a unit of time measurement, based on the orbital period of the Earth around the Sun.

The tropical year (also called equinoctal and solar year), from one spring ◊equinox to the next, lasts 365.2422 days. It governs the occurrence of the seasons, and is the period on which the calendar year is based. The sidereal year is the time taken for the Earth to complete one orbit relative to the fixed stars, and lasts 365.2564 days (about 20 minutes longer than a tropical year). The difference is due to the effect of ◊precession, which slowly moves the position of the equinoxes. The anomalistic year is the time taken by any planet in making one complete revolution from perihelion to perihelion; for the Earth this period is about 5 minutes longer than the sidereal year due to the gravitational pull of the other planets. The calendar year consists of 365 days, with an extra day added at the end of Feb each leap year. Leap years occur in every year that is divisible by four, except that a century year is not a leap year unless it is divisible by 400. Hence 1900 was not a leap year, but 2000 will be.

yeast one of various sincle-celled fungi (especially the genus *Saccharomyces*) that form masses of minute circular or oval cells by budding. When placed in a sugar solution the cells multiply and convert the sugar into alcohol and carbon dioxide. Yeasts are used as fermenting agents in baking, brewing, and the making of wine and spirits. Brewer's yeast *S. cerevisiae* is a rich source of vitamin B.

yeast

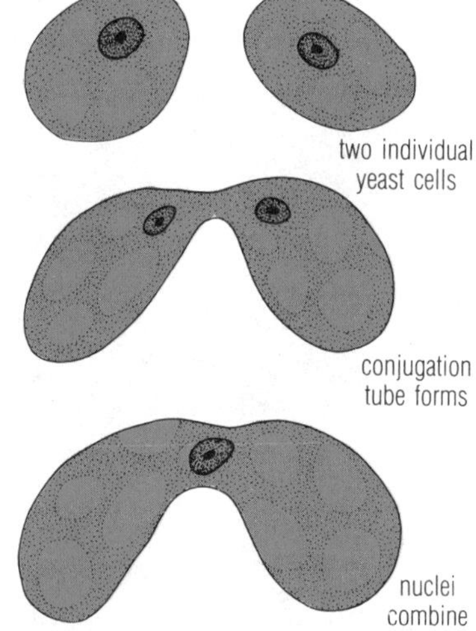
two individual yeast cells
conjugation tube forms
nuclei combine

Yeats Irish poet and dramatist W B Yeats.

Yeats Jack Butler 1871–1957. Irish painter and illustrator. His vivid scenes of Irish life, for example *Back from the Races* 1925 (Tate Gallery, London), and Celtic mythology reflected a new consciousness of Irish nationalism. He was the brother of the poet W B Yeats.

Yeats W(illiam) (B)utler 1865–1939. Irish poet. He was a leader of the Celtic revival and a founder of the Abbey Theatre in Dublin. His early work was romantic and lyrical, as in the poem "The Lake Isle of Innisfree" and plays *The Countess Cathleen* 1892 and *The Land of Heart's Desire* 1894. His later books of poetry include *The Wild Swans at Coole* 1917 and *The Winding Stair* 1929. He was a senator of the Irish Free State 1922–28. Nobel prize 1923.

Yeats was born in Dublin. His early poetry, such as *The Wind Among the Reeds* 1899, is romantically and exotically lyrical, and he drew on Irish legend for his poetic plays, including *Deirdre* 1907, but broke through to a new sharply resilient style with *Responsibilities* 1914. In his personal life there was also a break: the beautiful Maude Gonne, to whom many of his poems had been addressed, refused to marry him, and in 1917 he married Georgie Hyde-Lees, whose work as a medium reinforced his leanings toward mystic symbolism, as in the prose work *A Vision* 1925 and 1937. His later volumes of verse include *The Tower* 1928 and *Last Poems and Two Plays* 1939. His other prose works include *Autobiographies* 1926, *Dramatis Personae* 1936, *Letters* 1954, and *My Theologies* 1959.

yellow archangel flowering plant *Lamiastrum galeobdolon* of the mint family Labiatae, found over much of Europe. It grows up to 2 ft/60 cm tall and has nettlelike leaves and whorls of yellow flowers, the lower lips streaked with red in early summer.

yellow fever acute tropical viral disease, prevalent in the Caribbean area, Brazil, and on the west coast of Africa. Its symptoms are a high fever and yellowish skin (jaundice, possibly leading to liver failure); the heart and kidneys may also be affected.

Before the arrival of Europeans, yellow fever was not a problem because indigenous people had built up an immunity. The disease was brought under control after the discovery that it is carried by the mosquito *Aëdes aegypti*. The first effective vaccines were produced by Max Theiler of South Africa, for which he was awarded the 1951 Nobel Prize for Medicine.

yellowhammer Eurasian bird *Emberiza citrinella* of the bunting family Emberizidae. About 6.5 in/ 16.5 cm long, the male has a yellow head and underside, a chestnut rump, and a brown-streaked back. The female is duller.

The name is sometimes also used for a subspecies of the northern flicker *Colaptes auratus*, a North American woodpecker with a spotted belly and yellow underwings.

Yellowknife capital of Northwest Territories,

yellowhammer

Canada, on the N shore of Great Slave Lake; population (1986) 11,753. It was founded 1935 when gold was discovered in the area and became the capital 1967.

Yellow River English name for the ◊Huang He river, China.

Yellow Sea gulf of the Pacific Ocean between China and Korea; area 180,000 sq mi/466,200 sq km. It receives the Huang He (Yellow river) and Chang Jiang.

Yellowstone National Park largest US nature preserve; area explored 1807 by John Colter, a trapper; established 1872 on a broad plateau in the Rocky Mountains, chiefly in NW Wyoming, but also in SW Montana and E Idaho; area 3,469 sq mi/8,983 sq km. The park contains more than 3,000 geysers and hot springs, including periodically erupting Old Faithful. It is one of the world's great wildlife refuges. Much of the park was ravaged by forest fires 1988.

Yeltsin Boris Nikolayevich 1931– . Soviet "reform" politician, president of the Russian Republic from 1990. He was Moscow party chief 1985–87, when he was dismissed after criticizing the slow pace of political and economic reform. He was reelected March 1989 with an 89% share of the vote, defeating an "official Communist Party" candidate, and was elected to the Supreme Soviet in May 1989. He supported the Baltic states in their calls for greater independence and demanded increasingly more radical economic reform. In April 1991 the Russian Republic congress voted him emergency powers, enabling him to rule by decree, and two months later he was popularly elected president of the Republic. His enhanced position after the failure of the anti-Gorbachev coup, 1991, made him the key power-broker within the Soviet Union, and in Dec 1991 he surpassed Gorbachev's influence. He directed the Russian Federation's secession from the Soviet Union and the formation of a new, decentralized nation, the Commonwealth of Independent States (CIS), with himself as the most powerful leader.

Yemen country in SW Asia, bounded N by Saudi Arabia, E by Oman, S by the Gulf of Aden, and W by the Red Sea.

government The unification of North and South Yemen was proclaimed May 1990, followed by a 30-month period of implementation overseen by a presidential council. Many political parties were legalized or created and, following the approval of a new constitution in May 1991, a general election was scheduled for Nov 1992.

history North Yemen was a kingdom in the 2nd millennium BC before it came under, successively, Egyptian, Roman, and Ethiopian rule. It adopted Islam 628, formed part of the ◊Ottoman Empire 1538–1630, and was occupied by Turkey in the 19th century. For the early history of South Yemen, see ◊Arabia. The last king of North Yemen, Imam Muhammad, was killed in a military coup 1962. The declaration of the new Yemen Arab Republic (YAR) provoked a civil war between royalist forces, assisted by Saudi Arabia, and republicans, helped by Egypt. By 1967 the republicans, under Marshal Abdullah al-Sallal, had won. Later that year Sallal was deposed while on a foreign visit, and a Republican Council took over.

The People's Democratic Republic of Yemen (South Yemen) was founded 1967 by the union of ◊Aden and the Federation of South Arabia, both of which had been under British rule or protection. Before Britain withdrew, two rival factions fought for power, the Marxist National Liberation Front (NLF) and the Front for the Liberation of Occupied South Yemen (FLOSY). The NLF eventually won and assumed power as the National Front (NF). On the third anniversary of independence, Nov 1 1970, the country was renamed the People's Democratic Republic of Yemen.

The accession of the left-wing NF government caused hundreds of thousands of people to flee to more moderate North Yemen. This resulted in clashes between the South Yemen government and mercenaries operating from North Yemen, and war broke out 1971. The Arab League arranged a cease-fire 1972, and the two countries signed an agreement to merge, but the agreement was not honored.

In North Yemen the pro-Saudi Col Ibrahim al-Hamadi seized power 1974, but he was assassinated in 1977, and Col Ahmed ibn Hussein al-Ghashmi, another member of the Military Command Council that Hamadi had set up 1974, took over. In 1978 a gradual move towards a more constitutional form of government was started, with the appointment of the Constituent People's Assembly, the dissolution of the Military Command Council, and the installation of Ghashmi as president. In 1978 Ghashmi was killed, and Col Ali Abdullah Saleh took over as president.

In the aftermath of Ghashmi's death, the South Yemen president Rubayi Ali was deposed and executed. Two days later the three political parties of South Yemen agreed to merge to form a "Marxist–Leninist vanguard party," the Yemen Socialist Party (YSP), and Abdul Fattah Ismail became its secretary general. In Dec 1978 Ismail was appointed head of state but four months later resigned and went into exile in the USSR. He was succeeded by Ali Nasser Muhammad.

In 1979 South Yemen's neighbors became concerned when a 20-year Treaty of Friendship and Cooperation was signed, allowing the USSR to station troops in the country, and three years later an aid agreement between the two countries was concluded. A subsequent aid agreement with Kuwait helped to reduce anxieties.

War broke out again between the two Yemens after the assassination of President Ghashmi of North Yemen. The Arab League again intervened to arrange a cease-fire 1979, and for the second time the two countries agreed to unite. This time definite progress was made so that by 1983 a joint Yemen council was meeting at six-month intervals, and in March 1984 a joint committee on foreign policy sat for the first time in Aden.

In North Yemen President Saleh was reelected for a further five years 1983, and again 1988, while in South Yemen Ali Nasser Muhammad was reelected secretary general of the YSP and its political bureau for another five years 1985. He soon began taking steps to remove his opponents, his personal guard killing three bureau members. This led to a short civil war and the dismissal of Ali Nasser from all his posts in the party and the government. A new administration was formed, headed by Haydar Abu Bakr al-Attas, which immediately committed itself to eventual union with North Yemen.

A draft constitution of the unified state of Yemen was published Dec 1989 and in Jan 1990 the border between the two countries was opened to allow free movement for all citizens. Unification was proclaimed May 22, with Ali Abdullah Saleh as leader of the new Republic of Yemen with San'aa as its capital.

Yemen, North former country in SW Asia. It was

Yemen
Republic of Yemen
(al Jamhuriya al Yamaniya)

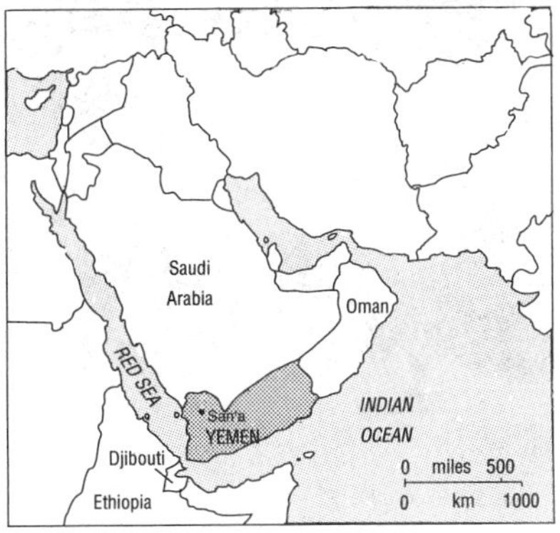
Saudi Arabia
Oman
RED SEA
San'a
YEMEN
INDIAN OCEAN
Djibouti
Ethiopia
0 miles 500
0 km 1000

area 205,367 sq mi/531,900 sq km
capital San'a
cities Ta'iz; and chief port Aden
physical hot, moist coastal plain, rising to plateau and desert
features once known as *Arabia felix* because of its fertility, includes islands of Perim (in strait of Bab-el-Mandeb, at S entrance to Red Sea), Socotra, and Kamaran
head of state and government Ali Abdullah Saleh from 1978
political system authoritarian republic
political parties none
exports cotton, coffee, grapes, vegetables
currency rial
population (1990 est) 11,000,000; growth rate 2.7% p.a.
life expectancy men 47, women 50
language Arabic
religion Sunni Muslim 63%, Shiite Muslim 37%
literacy men 20%/women 3% (1985 est)
GNP $4.9 bn (1983); $520 per head
chronology
1918 Yemen became independent.
1962 North Yemen declared the Arab Republic of Yemen (YAR), with Abdullah al-Sallal as president. Civil war broke out between royalists and republicans.
1967 Civil war ended with the republicans victorious. Sallal deposed and replaced by a Republican Council. The People's Republic of South Yemen was formed.
1971–72 War between South Yemen and YAR; union agreement not kept.
1974 Ibrahim al-Hamadi seized power in North Yemen, and a Military Command Council was set up.
1977 Hamadi assassinated and replaced by Ahmed ibn Hussein al-Ghashmi.
1978 Constituent People's Assembly appointed and Military Command Council dissolved. Ghashmi killed by envoy from South Yemen; succeeded by Ali Abdullah Saleh. War broke out again between the two Yemens.
1979 Cease-fire agreed with commitment to future union.
1983 Saleh elected president of North Yemen for a further five-year term.
1984 Joint committee on foreign policy for the two Yemens met in Aden.
1988 President Saleh reelected.
1989 Draft constitution created for unified Yemen.
1990 Two Yemens merge.
1991 New constitution approved.

***Yevtushenko** A master of the conversational, confessional style, the Soviet poet Yevtushenko has walked a thin line between Communist idealism and the raising of sensitive issues in works such as "Stalin's Heirs" 1956 and "Babi Yar" 1961.*

united with South Yemen 1990 as the Republic of Yemen.

Yemen, South former country in SW Asia. It was united with North Yemen 1990 as the Republic of Yemen.

yen the standard currency of Japan.

Yenan former name for city of ◊Yan'an in the Chinese province of Shaanxi.

Yenisei river in Asian USSR, rising in Tuva region and flowing across the Siberian plain into the Arctic Ocean; length 2,550 mi/4,100 km.

Yeomen of the Guard English military corps, popularly known as Beefeaters, the sovereign's bodyguard since the corps was founded by Henry VII in 1485. Its duties are now purely ceremonial.

There are Yeomen warders at the Tower of London, and the uniform and weapons are much as they were in Tudor times. The nickname "Beefeaters" is supposed to have originated in 1669 when the Grand Duke of Tuscany ascribed their fine appearance to beef.

Yerevan industrial city (tractor parts, machine tools, chemicals, bricks, bicycles, wine, fruit canning) and capital of Armenian Republic, USSR, a few miles N of the Turkish border; population (1987) 1,168,000. It was founded 7th century and was alternately Turkish and Persian from the 15th century until ceded to Russia 1828.

Its university was founded 1921. The city has seen mounting inter-ethnic violence and Armenian nationalist demonstrations since 1988, fanned by the ◊Nagorno-Karabakh dispute.

Yerkes Observatory astronomical center in Wisconsin, founded by George Hale in 1897. It houses the world's largest refracting optical ◊telescope, with a lens of diameter 40 in/102 cm.

Yersin Alexandre Emile Jean 1863–1943. Swiss bacteriologist who discovered the bubonic plague bacillus in Hong Kong in 1894 and prepared a serum against it.

Yesenin Sergei alternate form of ◊Esenin, Russian poet.

yeti Tibetan for the ◊abominable snowman.

Yevtushenko Yevgeny Aleksandrovich 1933– . Soviet poet, born in Siberia. He aroused controversy with his anti-Stalinist "Stalin's Heirs" 1956, published with Khrushchev's support, and "Babi Yar" 1961. His autobiography was published in 1963.

yew any evergreen coniferous tree of the genus *Taxus* of the family Taxaceae, native to the northern hemisphere. The leaves and bright red

yew

berrylike seeds are poisonous; the wood is hard and close-grained.

The western or Pacific yew *T. brevifolia* is native to North America. English yew *T. baccata* is widely cultivated as an ornamental.

Yezd alternate name for the Iranian town of ◊Yazd.

Yezidis Islamic sect originating as disciples of the Sufi saint Sheik Adi ibn Musafir (12th century). The beliefs of its adherents mingle folk traditions with Islam, also incorporating features of Judaism and Christianity (they practice circumcision and baptism), and include a cult of the Fallen Angel who has been reconciled with God.

Yezo another name for ◊Hokkaido, northernmost of the four main islands of Japan.

Yggdrasil in Scandinavian mythology, the world tree, a sacred ash that spans heaven and hell. It is is evergreen and tended by the Norns, goddesses of past, present, and future.

Yggdrasil has three roots with a spring under each one. One root covers Nifelheim, the realm of the dead; another runs under Jotunheim, where the giants live; the third under Asgard, home of the gods. By the Norns' well at the third root, the gods regularly gather to confer. Various animals inhabit and eat of the tree.

Yichang port at the head of navigation of the Chang Jiang, Hubei province, China; population (1982) 175,000.

Yiddish language member of the west Germanic branch of the Indo-European language family, deriving from 13th–14th-century Rhineland German and spoken by northern, central, and eastern European Jews, who have carried it to Israel, the USA, and many other parts of the world. It is written in the Hebrew alphabet and has many dialects reflecting European areas of residence, as well as many borrowed words (from Polish, Russian, Lithuanian, etc.).

In the US, Yiddish has had a powerful impact on English, best heard in the argot of New York City, in the film and stage communities, and in the national media. Such words as *bagel, chutzpah, kibbitz, mensh, nosh, schlemiel, schmaltz,* and *schmuck* have entered the American language, but are less used in Britain. The novelist and short-story writer Isaac Bashevis ◊Singer writes in Yiddish.

yin and yang Chinese for "dark" and "bright" respectively, referring to the passive (characterized as feminine, negative, intuitive) and active (characterized as masculine, positive, intellectual) principles of nature. Their interaction is believed to maintain equilibrium and harmony in the universe and to be present in all things. In Taoism and Confucianism they are represented by two interlocked curved shapes within a circle, one white, one black, with a spot of the contrasting color within the head of each.

Yinchuan capital of Ningxia autonomous region, NW China; population (1984) 383,000.

Yippie member of the Youth International Party (YIP), led by Abbie ◊Hoffmann and Jerry Rubin, known for their antics during the 1960s as they mocked the US political process.

Ymir in Scandinavian mythology, the first living being, a giant who grew from melting frost. Among his descendants, the god Odin and his two brothers killed Ymir and created heaven and earth from parts of his body.

yoga (Sanskrit "union") Hindu philosophical system attributed to Patanjali, who lived about 150 BC at Gonda, Uttar Pradesh, India. He preached mystical union with a personal deity through the practice of self-hypnosis and a rising above the senses by abstract meditation, adoption of special postures, and ascetic practices. As practiced in the West, yoga is more a system of mental and physical exercise, and of induced relaxation as a means of relieving stress.

yogurt also called ***yoghurt*** or ***yoghourt*** semisolid curdlike dairy product made from milk. Heat-treated, homogenized milk is inoculated with active cultures of bacteria. Yogurt was originally made by nomadic tribes of Central Asia, from mare's milk in leather pouches attached to their saddles. It spread to the Asian and Mediterranean regions, where it is drunk plain, but honey, sugar, and fruit were added in Europe and the US, and the product was made solid and creamy, to be eaten with a spoon.

Heat-treated, homogenized milk is inoculated with a culture of *Streptococcus lactis* and *Lactobacillus bulgaricus* in equal amounts, which change the lactose in the milk to lactic acid.

Yogyakarta city in Java, Indonesia, capital 1945–1949; population (1980) 399,000. The Buddhist pyramid shrine to the NW at Borobudur (400 ft/122 m square) was built AD 750–850.

Yokohama Japanese port on Tokyo Bay; population (1987) 3,072,000. Industries include shipbuilding, oil refining, engineering, textiles, glass, and clothing.

In 1859 it was the first Japanese port opened to foreign trade. From then it grew rapidly from a small fishing village to the chief center of trade with Europe and the US. Almost destroyed in an earthquake 1923, it was again rebuilt after World War II.

Yokosuka Japanese seaport and naval base (1884) on Tokyo Bay, S of Yokohama; population (1984) 428,000.

yolk a store of food, mostly in the form of fats and proteins, found in the ◊eggs of many animals. It provides nourishment for the growing embryo.

yolk sac the sac containing the yolk in the egg of most vertebrates. The term is also used for the membranous sac formed below the developing mammalian embryo and connected with the umbilical cord.

Yom Kippur the Jewish Day of ◊Atonement.

Yom Kippur War the surprise attack October 1973 War caused by the Arab advance on Israel; see ◊Arab-Israeli Wars. It is named after the Jewish vacation on which it began, the holiest day of the Jewish year.

yoni in Hinduism, an image of the female genitalia as an object of worship, a manifestation of ◊Sakti; the male equivalent is the lingam.

Yonkers city in Westchester county, New York, on the Hudson River, just N of the Bronx, New York City; population (1990) 188,082. Principal products include machinery, processed food, metal goods, chemicals, clothing, and electric and electronic equipment. Sarah Lawrence College is here. Yonkers was a Dutch settlement from about 1650.

Yonne French river, 180 mi/290 km long, rising in central France and flowing N into the Seine; it gives its name to a *département* in Burgundy region.

York cathedral and industrial city (railroad rolling stock, scientific instruments, sugar, chocolate, and glass) in North Yorkshire, N England

population (1985) 102,000

features The Gothic York Minster, containing medieval stained glass. Much of the 14th-century city wall survives. Jorvik Viking Centre opened 1984 after excavation of site at Coppergate, con-

yoga

lotus
headstand
triangle
backward bend

tains wooden remains of Viking houses. National Railway Museum and the 19th-century railroad station; and the university 1963.

history York was a British city, traditionally the capital of the N of England, before becoming from AD 71 the Roman fortress of Eboracum. Recent excavations of the Roman city have revealed the fortress, baths and temples to Serapis and Mithras. The first bishop of York (Paulinus) was consecrated 627 in the wooden church that first preceded York Minster. Paulinus baptized King Edwin there 627, and York was created an archbishopric 732. In the 10th century it was a Viking settlement. Its commercial prosperity depended on the wool trade in the Middle Ages.

York English dynasty founded by Richard, duke of York (1411–60). He claimed the throne through his descent from Lionel, duke of Clarence (1338–1368), third son of Edward III, whereas the reigning monarch, Henry VI of the rival house of Lancaster, was descended from the fourth son. The argument was fought out in the ◊Wars of the Roses. York was killed at the Battle of Wakefield 1460, but next year his son became King Edward IV, in turn succeeded by his son Edward V and then by his brother Richard III, with whose death at Bosworth the line ended. The Lancastrian victor in that battle was crowned Henry VII and consolidated his claim by marrying Edward IV's eldest daughter, Elizabeth.

York city in S Pennsylvania, SE of Harrisburg. It is an agricultural processing center for the area and manufactures paper products, building materials, and heavy machinery; population (1990) 42,192. The Articles of Confederation were adopted here during the Continental Congress 1777–78.

York Alvin Cullum, "Sergeant" 1887–1964. US war hero. Born in Pall Mall, Tennessee, York was trained as a blacksmith and, although a conscientious objector, was drafted as a private in the 82nd Infantry Division in World War I. On Oct 8, 1918, during the Battle of the Argonne Forest, York led a charge against a German position in which he and his comrades captured 132 prisoners and 35 machine guns. Promoted to the rank of sergeant and awarded the Congressional Medal of Honor and the French Croix de Guerre, York returned to private life after the war. A film biography, *Sergeant York*, appeared in 1940.

Yoruba member of a W African people from SW Nigeria and E Benin. They number approximately 12 million, and their language belongs to the Kwa branch of the Niger-Congo family.

Yosemite area in the Sierra Nevada, E California, a national park from 1890; area 1,189 sq mi/ 3,079 sq km. It includes Yosemite Gorge, Yosemite Falls (2,500 ft/762 m in three leaps) with many other lakes and waterfalls, and groves of giant sequoias.

Yoshida Shigeru 1878–1967. Japanese politician who served as prime minister of Occupied Japan for most of the postwar 1946–54 period.

Young Brigham 1801–1877. US ◊Mormon religious leader, born in Vermont. He joined the Mormons, or Church of Jesus Christ of Latter-day Saints, in 1832, and three years later was appointed an apostle. He led the first Mormon mission to England, in Liverpool 1840, and he was preaching in the E US in 1844 when the Mormon prophet and leader Joseph ◊Smith was murdered in Nauvoo, Illinois, at that time the headquarters of the church. Young returned to Illinois, assumed leadership of most of Smith's distraught followers, and led them away from persecution to a new home near the Great Salt Lake in Utah, establishing a theocratic colony there under his strict and efficient administration. He was appointed governor of Utah territory 1850 and defied federal pressure to repudiate the Utah Mormon practice of polygamy. Young himself had 27 wives and fathered 56 children.

Young Cy (Denton True) 1867–1955. US baseball player. Born in Gilmore, Ohio, Young played for the Cleveland Nationals 1890–98, St Louis Cardinals 1899–1900, Boston Red Sox 1901–08, Cleveland Indians 1909–11, and Boston Braves 1911. As a pitcher of unequaled skill and stamina, Young (nicknamed "Cy" for his "cyclone" pitch) established a lifetime record of 511 victories; 16 times he finished the season with 20 or more wins, 5 times exceeding 30. He was elected to the Baseball Hall of Fame 1937. The Cy Young Award, given annually to the outstanding pitcher in both the American and National leagues, is named for him.

Young John Watts 1930– . US astronaut, the first person to make six space flights. Born in San Francisco, he became a NASA astronaut in 1962 and chief of the Astronaut Office in 1975. His first flight was on *Gemini 3* in 1965, followed by *Gemini 10* in 1966. He flew on *Apollo 10* in 1969 and landed on the Moon with *Apollo 16* in 1972. He was commander of the first flight of the Space

***Yosemite** The entrance to the Yosemite Valley in Yosemite National Park, California. The park, established in 1890, is noted for its giant sequoias and the triple-cascade Yosemite Falls.*

Shuttle *Columbia* in 1981 and commanded the ninth Shuttle flight in 1983.

Young Lester (Willis) 1909–1959. US tenor saxophonist and jazz composer. He was a major figure in the development of his instrument for jazz music from the 1930s and was an accompanist for the singer Billie Holiday, who gave him the nickname "President," later shortened to "Pres."

Young Thomas 1773–1829. British physicist who revived the wave theory of light and in 1801 identified the phenomenon of ◊interference. A child prodigy, he had mastered most European languages and many of the Eastern tongues by the age of 20. He had also absorbed the physics of Newton and the chemistry of Lavoisier. He further displayed his versatility by publishing an account of the Rosetta stone that played a crucial role in the stone's eventual decipherment by Jean François ◊Champollion.

Young Ireland Irish nationalist organization, founded 1840 by William Smith O'Brien (1803–1864), who attempted an abortive insurrection of the peasants against the British in Tipperary in 1848. O'Brien was sentenced to death, but later pardoned.

Young Italy Italian nationalist organization founded 1831 by Giuseppe ◊Mazzini while in exile in Marseille. The movement, which was immediately popular, was followed the next year by Young Germany, Young Poland, and similar organizations. All the groups were linked by Mazzini in his Young Europe movement, but none achieved much practical success; attempted uprisings by Young Italy in 1834 and 1844 failed miserably. It was superseded in Italy by the ◊Risorgimento.

Young Men's Christian Association (YMCA) international organization founded 1844 by George Williams (1821–1905) in London and in the US 1851. It aims at self-improvement—spiritual, intellectual, and physical. There are about 12 million members in the US in 2,200 groups. YMCAs provide dormitories and rooms for both transients and residents; educational, sports, and civic programs; and recreation facilities for members and for military troops in wartime.

Young Plan scheme devised by US entrepreneur Owen D Young to reschedule German payments of war reparations in 1929.

Young Pretender nickname of ◊Charles Edward Stuart, claimant to the Scottish and English thrones.

***Young** Mormon leader Brigham Young in 1846. He led the church to its present home in Salt Lake City, Utah.*

Youngstown industrial city (fabricated metals) in E Ohio, on the Mahoning River; population (1990) 95,732. Youngstown was laid out 1797, and the city's first steel plant was established 1892, close to coal and iron deposits. Ten thousand workers lost their jobs when three steel plants shut down 1977.

Youngstown Sheet and Tube Co v Sawyer a US Supreme Court decision 1952 dealing with the right of the US president to nationalize private industry during wartime. The case arose over President Truman's seizure of steel mills during the Korean war. A crucial part of the war effort, the steel industry had been on the brink of a national strike. The Court ruled that the president's actions were illegal because neither Congressional legislation nor the Constitution had empowered him to intervene in labor disputes or to nationalize property.

Young Turk member of a reformist movement of young army officers in the Ottoman Empire founded 1889. The movement was instrumental in the constitutional changes of 1908 and the abdication of Sultan Abdul-Hamid II 1909. It gained prestige during the Balkan Wars 1912–13 and encouraged Turkish links with the German empire. Its influence diminished after 1918. The term is now used for a member of any radical or rebellious faction within a party or organization.

Young Women's Christian Association (YWCA) organization for the welfare of women and girls, founded London 1855. The first YWCA in the US was formally established 1858 in New York City; another followed in Boston, Massachusetts, 1866. Both were in response to the effects of the Industrial Revolution on women. Its facilities and activities are similar to those of the YMCA.

Yourcenar Marguerite. Adopted name of Marguerite de Crayencour 1903–1987. French writer, born in Belgium. She first gained recognition as a novelist in France in the 1930s with books such as *La Nouvelle Euridyce/The New Euridyce* 1931. In 1939 she settled in the US. Her evocation of past eras and characters, exemplified in *Les Mémoires d'Hadrien/The Memoirs of Hadrian* 1951, brought her acclaim as a historical novelist. In 1980 she became the first woman to be elected to the French Academy.

Youth Hostels Association (YHA) a registered charity founded in Britain 1930 to promote knowledge and care of the countryside by providing cheap overnight accommodation for young people on active vacations (such as walking or cycling). Types of accommodation range from castles to log cabins.

YHA is a member of the International Youth Hostel Federation, with over 3 million members and 5,000 youth hostels in 58 countries.

In the US, the American Youth Hostels provides information, equipment, trips, and accommodation for hiking, biking, skiing, canoeing, and horseback riding for people of all ages.

Ypres (Flemish *Ieper*) Belgian town in W Flanders, 25 mi/40 km S of Ostend, a site of fighting in World War I. The Menin Gate 1927 is a memorial to British soldiers lost in the three major battles fought around the town 1914–17.

Ysselmeer alternate spelling of ◊IJsselmeer, lake in the Netherlands.

ytterbium soft, lustrous, silvery, malleable and ductile element of the ◊lanthanide series, symbol Yb, atomic number 70, atomic weight 173.04. It occurs with (and resembles) yttrium in gadolinite and other minerals; it is used in making steel and other alloys.

In 1878 Swiss chemist Jean-Charles de Marignac gave the name ytterbium (after the Swedish town of Ytterby, near where it was found) to what he believed to be a new element. French chemist Georges Urbain (1872–1938) discovered in 1907 that this was in fact a mixture of two elements: ytterbium and lutetium.

yttrium silver-gray, metallic element, symbol Y, atomic number 39, atomic weight 88.905. It is associated with and resembles the rare-earth elements (◊lanthanides), occuring in gadolinite, xenotime, and other minerals. It is used in color-television tubes and to reduce steel corrosion.

The name derives from the Swedish town of Ytterby, near where it was found, and was proposed in 1822 by Swedish chemist Carl Mosander, who isolated the element in 1843.

Yuba City city in N central California, on the Feather river, N of San Francisco. It is an agricultural trading center for nuts, fruits, rice, and dairy products; population (1990) 27,437.

Yucatán peninsula in Central America, divided among Mexico, Belize, and Guatemala; area 70,000 sq mi/180,000 sq km. Tropical crops are grown. It is inhabited by ◊Maya Indians and contains the remains of their civilization.

There are ruins at Chichén Itzá and Uxmal. The Mexican state of Yucatán has an area of 14,823 sq mi/38,402 sq km, and a population (1980) of 1,035,000. Its capital is Mérida.

yucca plant of the genus *Yucca*, family Liliaceae, with over 40 species found in Latin America and southwest USA. The leaves are stiff and sword-shaped and the flowers white and bell-shaped.

Yugoslavia country in SE Europe, on the Adriatic Sea, bounded W by Italy, N by Austria and Hungary, E by Romania and Bulgaria, and S by Greece and Albania.

government Under the 1974 constitution, amended 1981, Yugoslavia is a federal republic consisting of six Socialist republics and two Socialist autonomous provinces (Kosovo and Vojvodina, which lie within Serbia), each with its own assembly. The federal republic itself has a two-chamber legislative assembly comprising the 220-member Federal Chamber and the 88-member Chamber of Republics and Provinces, whose members are indirectly elected every four years, with fixed quotas assigned to the constituent republics and autonomous provinces.

The legislature elects the executive branch of government which, since May 1980 consists of a nine-member collective presidency, comprising the head of the Communist Party together with a representative from each republic and province. The presidency's members are appointed for five-year terms, with titular leadership of the body rotating annually. Day-to-day government administration is carried out by the Federal Executive Council (headed by a president or prime minister), whose members are elected by the legislature for four-year terms.

The controlling political party is the Communist Party (League of Communists of Yugoslavia), which is controlled by a 23-member presidium (with a rotating presidency) and directs the broader Socialist Alliance of the Working People of Yugoslavia. The dominating practice is that of self-management, with elected workers' assemblies at all levels.

history Originally inhabited by nomadic peoples from the central Asian plateau, and later by Slavs, it came under the rule of the Greek and then the Roman empires. During the early medieval period the present-day republics of Yugoslavia existed as substantially independent bodies, the most important being the kingdom of Serbia. During the 14th and 15th centuries much of the country was conquered by the Turks and incorporated into the Ottoman Empire. The exceptions were mountainous Montenegro, which survived as a sovereign principality, and Croatia and Slovenia in the NW, which formed part of the Austro-Hungarian Hapsburg empire. Anti-Ottoman uprisings secured Serbia a measure of autonomy from the early 19th century and full independence from 1878, and the new kingdom proceeded to enlarge its territory, at Turkey and Bulgaria's expense, during the Balkan Wars of 1912–13. However, not until the collapse of the Austro-Hungarian empire at the end of World War I were Croatia and Slovenia liberated from foreign control. A new "Kingdom of the Serbs, Croats and Slovenes" was formed in Dec 1918, with the Serbian Peter Karageorgevic at its helm, to which Montenegro acceded following its people's deposition of its own ruler, King Nicholas.

Peter I died 1921 and was succeeded by his son Alexander, who renamed the country Yugoslavia ("nation of the South Slavs") and who, faced with opposition from the Croatians at home and from the Italians abroad, established a military dictatorship 1929. He was assassinated Oct 1934 in Marseille, France, by a Macedonian with Croatian dissident links. Alexander's young son ◊Peter II succeeded, and a regency under the latter's uncle Paul (1893–1976) was set up that came under increasing influence from Germany and Italy. The regency was briefly overthrown by pro-Allied groups March 1941, precipitating a successful invasion by German troops. Peter II fled, while two guerrilla groups—the pro-royalist, Serbian-based Chetniks, led by General Draza ◊Mihailovič, and the Communist partisans, led by Josip Broz (Marshal ◊Tito)—engaged in resistance activities.

Tito established a provisional government at liberated Jajce in Bosnia and Herzegovina Nov 1943 and proclaimed the Yugoslav Federal Republic Nov 1945 after the expulsion, with Soviet help, of the remaining German forces. Elections were held, a Communist constitution on the Soviet model was introduced, and remaining royalist opposition crushed. Tito broke with Stalin 1948 and, with the constitutional law of 1953, adopted a more liberal and decentralized form of communism centered around workers' self-management and the support of private farming. Tito became the dominating force in Yugoslavia and held the newly created post of president from 1953 until his death May 1980.

In foreign affairs, the country sought to maintain a balance between East and West and played

Yugoslavia

Socialist Federal Republic of
(Socijalistička Federativna Republika Jugoslavija)

0 miles 500
0 km 1000
Austria
Hungary
Romania
Belgrade
YUGOSLAVIA
ADRIATIC SEA
Italy
Bulgaria
Albania
Greece
MEDITERRANEAN SEA

area 98,739 sq mi/255,800 sq km
capital Belgrade
cities Zagreb, Skopje, Ljubljana; ports Split, Rijeka
physical mountainous, with river Danube plains in N and E; limestone (Karst) features in NW
features constituent republics of Bosnia and Herzegovina, Croatia, Macedonia, Montenegro, Serbia (including the autonomous provinces of Kosovo and Vojvodina), and Slovenia; scenic Dalmatian coast and Dinaric Alps; Lake Shkodër
head of state vacant from March 15, 1991
head of government Ante Marković from 1989
political system Socialist pluralist republic
political parties League of Communists of Yugoslavia (SKJ), Marxist-Leninist-Titoist; nationalist parties in the republics
exports machinery, electrical goods, chemicals, clothing, tobacco
currency dinar
population (1990 est) 24,107,000 (Serbs 36%, Croats 20%, Muslims 9%, Slovenes 8%, Albanians 8%, Macedonians 6%, Montenegrins 3%, Hungarians 2%, 5.5% declared "Yugoslavs"); growth rate 0.6% p.a.
life expectancy men 69, women 75 (1989)
language Serbo-Croat, Macedonian, Slovenian
religion Eastern Orthodox 41% (Serbs), Roman Catholic 12% (Croats), Muslim 3%
literacy 90% (1989)
GNP $154.1 bn; $6,540 per head (1988)
chronology
1917–18 Creation of Kingdom of the Serbs, Croats, and Slovenes.
1929 Name of Yugoslavia adopted.
1941 Invaded by Germany.
1945 Communist federal republic formed under leadership of Tito.
1948 Split with USSR.
1953 Self-management principle enshrined in constitution.
1961 Nonaligned movement formed under Yugoslavia's leadership.
1974 New constitution adopted.
1980 Tito died; collective leadership assumed power.
1987 Threatened use of army to curb unrest.
1988 Economic difficulties: 1,800 strikes, inflation 250%, 20% unemployment. Ethnic unrest in Montenegro and Vojvodina; party reshuffled and government resigned.
1989 Reformist Croatian Ante Markovic became prime minister. Twenty-nine died in ethnic riots in Kosovo province; state of emergency imposed. Inflation to May 490%; tensions with ethnic Albanians rose.
1990 Multiparty systems established in Slovenia and Croatia.
1991 Several republics called for secession. President resigned. Clashes between Serbs and Croats in Croatia. Slovenia and Croatia declared themselves independent; the federal army intervened. Slovenia accepted EC-sponsored peace pact. Fighting continued in Croatia.
1992 Serbia-Croatia ceasefire established; EC recognizes Slovenia's independence.

a leading role in the creation of the ◊nonaligned movement 1961. Domestically, the nation experienced continuing regional discontent, in particular in ◊Croatia where a violent separatist movement gained ground in the 1970s. To deal with these problems, Tito encouraged further decentralization and devolution of power to the constituent republics. A system of collective leadership and the regular rotation of office posts was introduced to prevent the creation of regional cliques. This collective leadership has held power since Tito's death. However, the problems of regionalist unrest have grown worse since 1980, notably in Kosovo (see ◊Serbia) and ◊Bosnia, where Albanian and Islamic nationalism respectively are strong.

This regionalist discontent has been fanned by a general decline in living standards since 1980, caused by a mounting level of foreign debt, the service of which absorbs more than 10% of GNP, and a spiralling inflation rate, which reached 200% in 1988 and 700% in 1989. From 1987 to 1988 the federal government under the leadership of prime minister Branko Mikulic, a Bosnian, instituted a "market Socialist" program of prices and wages decontrol and the greater encouragement of the private sector and foreign "inward investment." However, the short term consequence of this restructuring program was a period of increased economic austerity and a rise in the unemployment rate to 15%. Following a wave of strikes and mounting internal disorder, Mikulic was replaced as prime minister in Jan 1989 by Ante Marković, a reformist Croatian. The unity of the ruling Communist party began to crumble between 1988 and 1990 as both personal and ideologically based feuds developed between the leaders of its republican branches. Slobodan Milosević, the hardline Serbian party chief, began to wage a populist campaign designed to terminate Kosovo and Vojvodina's autonomous province status and secure their reintegration within Serbia. This led to a violent ethnic Albanian backlash in Kosovo during 1989–90 and to growing pressure in more liberal, pro-pluralist Croatia and Slovenia for their republics to break away from the federation. The schism within the Communist Party was confirmed Jan 1990 when its Congress had to be abandoned following a walk-out by the Slovene delegation.

In the republic of Serbia a new multiparty constitution was approved July 1990 and came into force Sept. It effectively stripped Kosovo and Vojvodina of their autonomy. The Albanians of Kosovo reacted defiantly by calling a general strike on Sept 3 and by convening an underground parliament that proclaimed a new, unrecognized, constitution for the autonomous province. In multi-party elections held in Serbia in Dec, Slobodan Milosević was elected president by a landslide margin and his Serbian Socialist Party achieved an assembly majority.

In July 1990 the Slovenian Assembly issued a proclamation of full republican sovereignty and in Sept moved toward confrontation with the federal army by proclaiming control of its own defense.

In Croatia, ethnic tension between the majority Croat and minority Serb populations increased following the election April–May 1990 of a right-wing Croat nationalist government led by Franje Tudman.

Attempts to stem the rising tide of ethnic conflict and political disintegration continued into 1991 but eventually failed. In May 1991 the bloodiest clashes between Croats and Serbs since World War II occurred in the self-proclaimed Serbian Autonomous Region of Krajina (within Croatia). In a referendum held throughout Croatia on May 19, 1991 93% voted for the republic to become a sovereign and independent country within a loose confederation of Yugoslav sovereign states. Slovenia, which had voted for independence in a December 1990 referendum, announced that it would secede from Yugoslavia by June 26, 1991. This caused conflict between the republic's territorial defense force and the Serbian-dominated Yugoslav National Army.

On June 25, 1991, both Slovenia and Croatia issued unilateral declarations of indepedence, or "dissociation," from the Yugoslav federation, though declaring their continued willingness to discuss the formation of a new, much looser Yugoslav confederation. Neither Slovenian nor Croatian independence was recognized by foreign countries. This precipitated military confrontations between the federal army and the republican forces from June 27, 1991, initially directed against newly established Slovene border posts. An initial ceasefire included a three-month suspension in the implementation of Slovenia's independence. Although this deal soon fell apart, it was agreed that the Yugoslav National Army, which had been surprisingly unsuccessful, would withdraw during July 1991 from Slovenia, which seemed set to secure its independence eventually. However, beginning in July the civil war intensified in ethnically mixed Croatia. Despite constant efforts by the EC and the UN, including economic sanctions, to halt civil war, strife continued. Croatia was devastated by the war. A Serbia-Croatia ceasefire was established in Jan 1992.

Yugoslavia: constituent republics

Republic	*Capital*	*Area sq km*
Bosnia and Herzegovina	Sarajevo	51,100
Croatia*	Zagreb	56,500
Macedonia	Skopje	25,700
Montenegro	Titograd	13,800
Serbia	Belgrade	88,400
Kosovo	Pristina	10,900
Vojvodina	Novi Sad	21,500
Slovenia*	Ljubljana	20,300
*proclaimed independence 1991		255,800

Yugoslav literature Yugoslavian literature begins in the 9th century with the translation into Slavonic of the church service books. Its chief glory is folk poetry, in particular the song cycles dealing with the battle of Kosovo and the hero Marko Kraljevíac. After centuries of national repression a revival occurred, notably under Dositej Obradović (1739–1811). Poets of the earlier 19th century include bishop Petar Njegoš (1813–1851), France Prešern (1800–1849), and Ivan Mažuranić (1814–1890). Later, Russian influence predominated. Twentieth-century writers include the novelists Ivan Cankar (1876–1918), Ivo Andrić (1892–1974), and Miroslav Krleža (1893–), whose collected works cover 36 volumes, and the poet Oton Župančič (1878–1949).

Yukon Territory

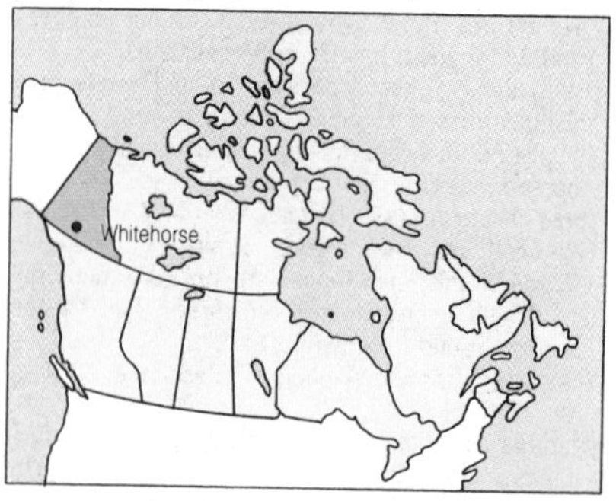
Whitehorse

Yukawa Hideki 1907–1981. Japanese physicist who predicted the existence of the subatomic particle called the ◊meson 1935. Nobel Prize 1949.

Yukon territory of NW Canada
area 186,631 sq mi/483,500 sq km
capital Whitehorse
cities Dawson, Mayo
features named after its chief river, the Yukon; includes the highest point in Canada, Mount Logan 19,850 ft/6,050 m; Klondike Gold Rush International Historical Park, which extends into Alaska
products gold, silver, lead, zinc
population (1986) 24,000
history settlement dates from the gold rush 1896–1910, when 30,000 people moved to the ◊Klondike River valley (silver is now worked there). It became separate from the Northwest Territories 1898, with Dawson as the capital 1898–1951. Construction of the Alcan Highway during World War II helped provide the basis for further development.

Yukon river in North America, 1,979 mi/3,185 km long, flowing from Yukon Territory from Lake Tagish into Alaska where it empties into the Bering Sea.

Yungning former name 1913–45 for Chinese port of ◊Nanning.

Yunnan province of SW China, adjoining Myanmar, Laos, and Vietnam
area 168,373 sq mi/436,200 sq km
capital Kunming
physical rivers: Chang Jiang, Salween, Mekong; crossed by the Burma Road; mountainous and well forested
products rice, tea, timber, wheat, cotton, rubber, tin, copper, lead, zinc, coal, salt
population (1986) 34,560,000.

Yuzovka former name (1872–1924) for the town of ◊Donetsk, Ukraine, USSR, named after the Welshman John Hughes who established a metallurgical factory there in the 1870s.

Zaïre

Republic of
(*République du Zaïre*) (formerly **Congo**)

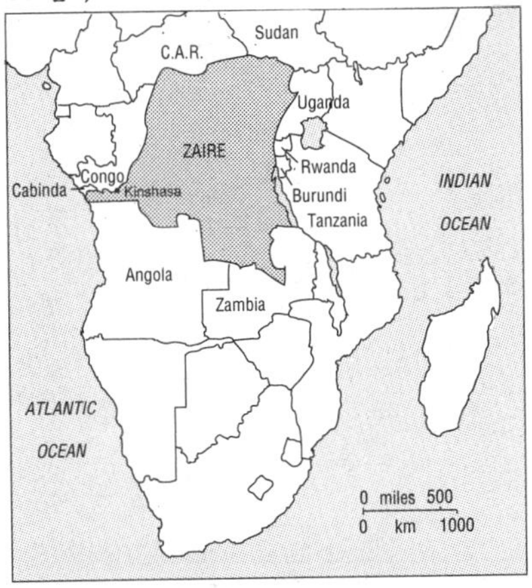

Sudan
C.A.R.
Uganda
ZAIRE
Congo
Kinshasa
Cabinda
Rwanda
Burundi
Tanzania
INDIAN
OCEAN
Angola
Zambia
ATLANTIC
OCEAN
0 miles 500
0 km 1000

area 905,366 sq mi/2,344,900 sq km
capital Kinshasa
cities Lubumbashi, Kananga, Kisangani; ports Matadi, Boma
physical Zaïre River basin has tropical rainforest and savanna; mountains in E and W
features lakes Tanganyika, Mobutu Sésé Séko, Edward; Ruwenzori Mountains
head of state and of government Mobuto Sésé Séko Kuku Ngbendu wa Zabanga from 1965
political system Socialist pluralist republic
political parties Popular Movement of the Revolution (MPR), African Socialist
exports coffee, copper, cobalt (80% of world output), industrial diamonds, palm oil
currency zaïre
population (1990 est) 35,330,000; growth rate 2.9% p.a.
life expectancy men 51, women 54 (1989)
language French (official), Swahili, Lingala, and other African languages
religion Christian 70%, Muslim 10%
literacy men 79%/women 45% (1985 est)
GNP $5 bn (1987); $127 per head
chronology
1907 Congo Free State annexed to Belgium.
1960 Independence achieved from Belgium as Republic of the Congo. Civil war broke out between central government and Katanga province.
1963 Katanga war ended.
1967 New constitution adopted.
1970 Col Mobutu elected president.
1971 Country became the Republic of Zaïre, with the Popular Movement of the Revolution (MPR) the only legal political party.
1974 Foreign-owned businesses and plantations seized by Mobutu and given in political patronage.
1977 Original owners of confiscated properties invited back. Mobutu reelected; Zaïrians invaded Katanga province from Angola, repulsed by Belgian paratroops.
1978 Second unsuccessful invasion from Angola.
1988 Potential rift with Belgium avoided.
1990 Mobutu announced end of ban on multiparty politics, following internal dissent.
1991 Military unrest, rioting and opposition demands force Moloutu to agree to share power.

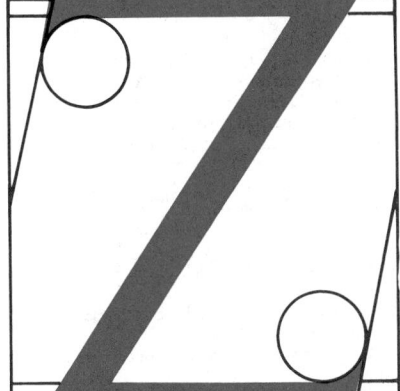

Z in physics, the symbol for impedance (electricity and magnetism).

Zaandam industrial port (timber, paper) in North Holland province, the Netherlands, on the Zaan river, NW of Amsterdam, since 1974 included in the municipality of ◊Zaanstad.

Zaanstad industrial town in W Netherlands which includes the port of ◊Zaandam; population (1988) 129,000.

Zabrze industrial city (coal-mining, iron, chemicals) in Silesia, S Poland; formerly the German town of Hindenburg; population (1985) 198,000.

Zadar (Italian *Zara*) port and resort in Croatia, W Yugoslavia; population (1981) 116,000. It was alternately held and lost by the Venetian republic from the 12th century until its seizure by Austria 1813. It was the capital of Dalmatia 1815–1918 and part of Italy from 1920 until 1947, when it became part of Yugoslavia. The city was sacked by the army of the Fourth Crusade 1202, which led to the Crusade being excommunicated by Pope Innocent III.

Zadkine Ossip 1890–1967. French Cubist sculptor, born in Russia, active in Paris from 1909. His art represented the human form in dramatic, semiabstract terms, as in the monument *To a Destroyed City* 1953 (Rotterdam).

Zagorsk town 45 mi/70 km NE of Moscow, USSR; population (1983) 111,000. The Trinity Monastery of St Sergius 1337, surrounded by a fortified wall, has a large collection of medieval Russian architecture and art.

Zagreb industrial city (leather, linen, carpets, paper, and electrical goods) and capital of Croatia, Yugoslavia, on the Sava river; population (1981) 1,174,512.

Zagreb was a Roman city (Aemona) and has a Gothic cathedral. Its university was founded 1874.

Zahir ud-din Mohammed 1483–1530. First Great Mogul of India from 1526, called Baber (Arabic "lion"). He was the great-grandson of the Mongol conqueror Tamerlane and, at the age of 12, succeeded his father, Omar Sheik Mirza, as ruler of Ferghana (Turkestan). In 1526 he defeated the emperor of Delhi at Panipat in the Punjab, captured Delhi and ◊Agra (the site of the Taj Mahal), and established a dynasty that lasted until 1858.

Zahir Shah Mohammed 1914– . King of Afghanistan 1933–73. Zahir, educated in Kabul and Paris, served in the government 1932–33 before being crowned king. He was overthrown in 1973 by a republican coup and went into exile. He has been a symbol of national unity for the ◊Mujaheddin Islamic fundamentalist resistance groups.

zaibatsu (Japanese "financial clique") Japanese industrial conglomerate (see ◊cartel).

The old, family-owned Japanese *zaibatsu* had been involved in the military buildup preceding World War II, and were in 1945, after the country's defeat, broken up by the authorities of the US occupation. Similar conglomerates soon formed in the course of Japan's industrial revival. By the late 1980s there were six *zaibatsu* with 650-member companies among them, employing 6% of the country's work force and controlling more than 2% of the world economy.

za'im in Lebanon, a political leader, originally the holder of a feudal office. The office is largely hereditary; an example is the Jumblatt family, traditional leaders of the Druse party. The pattern of Lebanese politics has been that individual *za'im*, rather than parties or even government ministers, wield effective power.

Zaïre country in central Africa, bounded to the N by the Central African Republic and Sudan, to the E by Uganda and Tanzania, to the W by Congo, to the SW by Angola, and to the SE by Zambia.

government Zaïre is a one-party state, based on the Popular Movement of the Revolution (MPR). Under the 1978 constitution, the leader of the MPR is automatically elected president for a nonrenewable seven-year term. The president, head of state and head of government, appoints and presides over the National Executive Council. There is a single-chamber legislature, the National Legislative Council, whose 210 members are elected by universal suffrage for a five-year term. Ultimate power lies with the MPR, whose highest policy-making body is the 80-member Central Committee, which elects the 14-member Political Bureau.

history The area was originally peopled by central African hunters and agriculturalists. The name Zaïre (from *Zadi*, "big water") was given by Portuguese explorers who arrived on the country's Atlantic coast in the 15th century. The great medieval kingdom of Kongo, centered on the banks of the Zaïre river, was then in decline, and the subsequent slave trade weakened it further. The interior was not explored by Europeans until the arrival of ◊Stanley and ◊Livingstone in the 1870s, partly financed by Leopold II of Belgium, who established the Congo Free State under his personal rule 1885. Local resistance was suppressed, and the inhabitants were exploited. When the atrocious treatment of local labor was made public, Belgium annexed the country as a colony, the Belgian Congo, 1908, and conditions were marginally improved.

Zaïre was given full independence in June 1960 as the Republic of the Congo. The new state was intended to be governed centrally from Leopoldville by President Joseph Kasavubu and Prime Minister Patrice Lumumba, but Moise Tshombe immediately declared the rich mining province of Katanga independent under his leadership. Fighting broke out, which was not quelled by Belgian troops, and the United Nations (UN) Security Council agreed to send a force to restore order and protect lives. Meanwhile, disagreements

Zaïre River

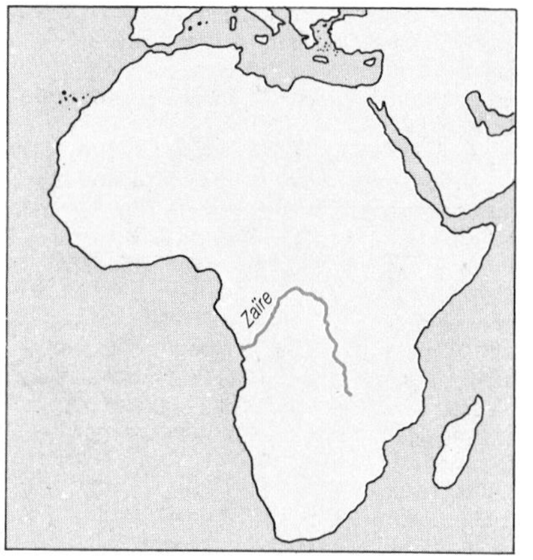
Zaïre

between Kasavubu and Lumumba on how the crisis should be tackled prompted the Congolese army commander, Col Joseph-Désiré ◊Mobutu, to step in and temporarily take over the government. Lumumba was imprisoned and later released, and five months later power was handed back to Kasavubu. Soon afterwards Lumumba was murdered and the white mercenaries employed by Tshombe were thought to be responsible. The outcry that followed resulted in a new government being formed, with Cyrille Adoula as prime minister.

During the fighting between Tshombe's mercenaries and UN forces the UN secretary general, Dag ◊Hammarskjöld, flew to Katanga province to mediate and was killed in an airplane crash on the border with Northern Rhodesia. The attempted secession of Katanga was finally stopped in 1963 when Tshombe went into exile, taking many of his followers with him to form the Congolese National Liberation Front (FNLC). In July 1964 Tshombe returned from exile, and President Kasavubu appointed him interim prime minister until elections for a new government could be held. In Aug the country was renamed the Democratic Republic of the Congo.

A power struggle soon developed between Kasavubu and Tshombe, and again the army, under Mobutu, intervened, establishing a "second republic" in Nov 1965. A new constitution was adopted 1967, Tshombe died in captivity 1969, and 1970 Mobutu was elected president for a seven-year term. The following year the country became the Republic of Zaïre, and 1972 the Popular Movement of the Revolution (MPR) was declared the only legal political party. In the same year the president became known as Mobutu Sese Seko.

Mobutu, reelected 1977, carried out a large number of political and constitutional reforms. He gradually improved the structure of public administration and brought stability to what had once seemed an ungovernable country, although he faced two revolts in Katanga province. The first in March 1977 was put down with the support of Moroccan forces airlifted to Zaïre by France. The second in May 1978 was repulsed by French and Belgian paratroopers. Both invasions were instigated by the Congolese National Liberation Front, operating from bases in Angola. However, the harshness of some of his policies brought international criticism and 1983 he offered amnesty to all political exiles.

Often criticized for his authoritarian rule, Mobutu approved in Jan 1991 the formation of opposition political parties. By the fall, opponents forced him to agree to share power as the country's economy disintegrated and rebellious soldiers and mobs ransacked Zaire's cities. Many observers felt that Mobutu's concessions to his political enemies were only temporary.

Zaïre River formerly (until 1971) Congo second longest river in Africa, rising near the Zambia-Zaïre border (and known as the Lualaba River in the upper reaches) and flowing 2,800 mi/4,500 km to the Atlantic, running in a great curve that crosses the equator twice, and discharging a volume of water second only to the Amazon. The chief tributaries are the Ubangi, Sangha, and Kasai.

Navigation is interrupted by dangerous rapids up to 100 mi/160 km long, notably from the Zambian border to Bukama; below Kongolo, where the gorge known as the Gates of Hell is located; above Kisangani, where the Stanley Falls are situated; and between Kinshasa and Matadi.

Boma is a large port on the estuary; Matadi is a port 50 mi/80 km from the Atlantic, for ocean-going ships; and at Pool Malebo (formerly Stanley Pool), a widening of the river 350 mi/560 km from its mouth, which encloses the marshy island of Bamu, are Brazzaville on the western shore and Kinshasa on the southwestern. The Inga dam supplies Matadi and Kinshasa with electricity.

history The mouth of the Zaïre was seen by the Portuguese navigator Diego Cão 1482, but the vast extent of its system became known to Europeans only with the explorations of Livingstone and Stanley. Its navigation from source to mouth was completed by the expedition 1974 led by the English explorer John Blashford-Snell (1936–), supported by President Mobutu.

Zákinthos or ***Zante*** southernmost of the ◊Ionian Islands, Greece; area 158 sq mi/410 sq km; population (1981) 30,000. Products include olives, currants, grapes, and carpets.

Zama, Battle of battle fought in 202 BC in Numidia (now Algeria), in which the Carthaginians under Hannibal were defeated by the Romans under Scipio, so ending the Second Punic War.

Zambezi river in central and SE Africa; length 1,650 mi/2,650 km from NW Zambia through Mozambique to the Indian Ocean, with a wide delta near Chinde. Major tributaries include the Kafue in Zambia.

It is interrupted by rapids, and includes on the Zimbabwe–Zambia border the Victoria Falls (*Mosi-oa-tunya*) and Kariba Dam, which forms the reservoir of Lake Kariba with large fisheries.

Zambia
Republic of

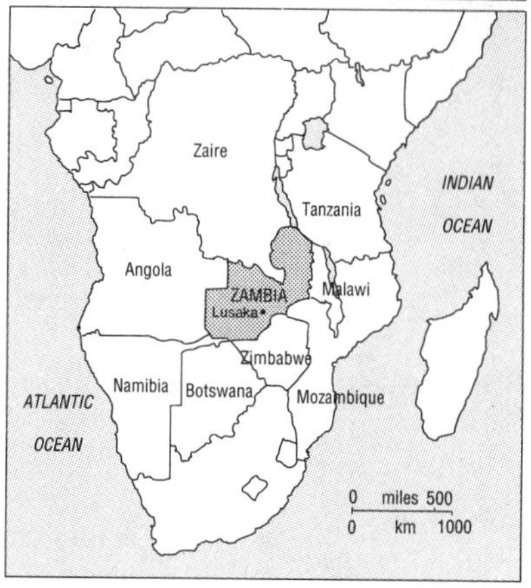
Zaire
INDIAN
OCEAN
Tanzania
Angola
ZAMBIA
Lusaka
Malawi
Zimbabwe
Namibia
Botswana
Mozambique
ATLANTIC
OCEAN
0 miles 500
0 km 1000

area 290,579 sq mi/752,600 sq km
capital Lusaka
cities Kitwe, Ndola, Kabwe, Chipata, Livingstone
physical forested plateau cut through by rivers
features Zambezi River, Victoria Falls, Kariba Dam
head of state and government Frederick Chiluba from 1991
political system Socialist pluralist republic
political parties United National Independence Party (UNIP), African Socialist; Movement for Multiparty Democracy (MMD); National Democratic Alliance (Nada)
exports copper, cobalt, zinc, emeralds, tobacco
currency kwacha
population (1990 est) 8,119,000; growth rate 3.3% p.a.
life expectancy men 54, women 57 (1989)
language English (official); Bantu dialects
religion Christian 66%, animist; Hindu, Muslim
literacy 54% (1988)
GNP $2.1 bn (1987); $304 per head (1986)
chronology
1899–1924 As Northern Rhodesia, under administration of the British South Africa company.
1924 Became a British protectorate.
1964 Independence achieved from Britain, within the Commonwealth, as the Republic of Zambia with Kenneth Kaunda as president.
1972 United Independence Party (UNIP) declared the only legal party.
1976 Support for the Patriotic Front in Rhodesia declared.
1980 Unsuccessful coup against President Kaunda.
1985 Kaunda elected chair of the Front Line States.
1987 Kaunda elected chair of the Organization of African Unity (OAU).
1988 Kaunda reelected unopposed for sixth term.
1990 Multiparty system announced for 1991.
1991 Kaunda ousted in country's first free elections. Frederick Chiluba succeeds.

Zambia landlocked country in central Africa, with Tanzania and Zaïre to the N, Angola to the W, Zimbabwe and Mozambique to the S, and Malawi to the E.

government Zambia is an independent republic within the ◊Commonwealth. It was proclaimed a one-party state in 1972, and the constitution was adopted 1973. The party is the United National Independence Party (UNIP), and its president is the state president, elected by universal suffrage for a five-year term, and who may be re-elected. The president governs with an appointed cabinet and is advised by the House of Chiefs, consisting of chiefs from the country's nine provinces. There is a single-chamber national assembly of 135 members, 125 elected by universal suffrage and 10 nominated by the president. The assembly has a life of five years. Ultimate power lies with UNIP, whose Central Committee is chaired by the president.

history For early history, see ◊Africa. The country was visited by Portuguese in the late 18th century and by ◊Livingstone 1851. As Northern Rhodesia it became a British protectorate 1924, together with the former kingdom of Barotseland (now Western province), taken under British protection at the request of its ruler 1890.

From 1953 the country, with Southern Rhodesia (now Zimbabwe) and Nyasaland (now Malawi), was part of the Federation of Rhodesia and Nyasaland, dissolved 1963. Northern Rhodesia became an independent republic 1964, within the Commonwealth, with Dr Kenneth ◊Kaunda, leader of the United Independence Party (UNIP), as its first president. Between 1964 and 1972, when it was declared a one-party state, Zambia was troubled with frequent outbreaks of violence because of disputes within the governing party and conflicts between the country's more than 70 tribes.

Zambia was economically dependent on neighboring white-ruled Rhodesia but tolerated liberation groups operating on the border, and relations between the two countries deteriorated.

The border was closed 1973, and 1976 Kaunda declared his support for the Patriotic Front, led by Robert Mugabe and Joshua Nkomo, which was fighting the white regime in Rhodesia. In 1980 there was an unsuccesful coup against the president, allegedly promoted by South Africa. Despite his imposition of strict economic policies, Kaunda was re-elected 1983. In 1985 he was appointed to succeed President Nyerere of Tanzania as chair of the black African ◊Front Line States. In Oct 1988 he was re-elected, unopposed, for a sixth consecutive term. In Sept 1990 President Kaunda announced that, without a referendum, a multiparty system would be introduced by October 1991. Free elections in Nov 1991 led unexpectedly to Kaunda's defeat by Frederick Chiluba.

Zamenhof Lazarus Ludovik 1859–1917. Polish inventor of the international language ◊Esperanto in 1887.

Zampieri Domenico. Italian Baroque painter, known as ◊Domenichino.

Zante Italian name for the Ionian island of ◊Zákinthos, Greece.

ZANU (acronym for Zimbabwe African National Union) political organization founded in 1963 by the Reverend Ndabaningi Sithole and later led by Robert Mugabe. It was banned 1964 by Ian Smith's Rhodesian Front government, against which it conducted a guerrilla war from Zambia until the free elections of 1980, when the ZANU Patriotic Front party, led by Mugabe, won 63% of the vote. In 1987 it merged with ◊ZAPU in preparation for making Zimbabwe a one-party state.

Zanzibar island region of Tanzania
area 640 sq mi/1,658 sq km (50 mi/80 km long)
towns Zanzibar
products cloves, copra
population (1985) 571,000
history settled by Arab traders in the 7th century; became a sultanate; under British protection 1890–1963. Together with the island of Pemba, some nearby islets, and a strip of mainland territory, it became a republic. It merged with Tanganyika as Tanzania 1964.

Zanzotto Andrea 1921– . Italian poet. A teacher from the Veneto, he has published much verse, including the collection *La beltà/Beauty* 1968, with a strong metaphysical element.

Zapata Emiliano 1879–1919. Mexican Indian revolutionary leader. He led a revolt against dictator Porfirio Díaz (1830–1915) from 1911 under the slogan "Land and Liberty," to repossess for the indigenous Mexicans the land taken by the Spanish. By 1915 he was driven into retreat, and was assassinated.

Zaporozhye formerly (until 1921) ***Aleksandrovsk*** industrial city (steel, chemicals, aluminum goods, pig iron, magnesium) in Ukraine, USSR, on the Dnieper river; capital of Zaporozhye region and site of the Dnieper Dam; population (1987) 875,000. It was occupied by Germany 1941–43.

Zapotec member of a North American Indian people of S Mexico, now numbering approximately 250,000, living mainly in Oaxaca. The Zapotec language, which belongs to the Oto-Mangean family, has nine dialects. The ancient Zapotec built the ceremonial center of Monte Albán 1000–500 BC, developing one of the classic Mesoamerican civilizations by AD 300, but declined under pressure from the Mixtecs from 900 until the Spanish Conquest 1530s.

ZAPU (acronym for Zimbabwe African People's Union) political organization founded by Joshua Nkomo in 1961 and banned 1962 by the Rhodesian government. It engaged in a guerrilla war in alliance with ◊ZANU against the Rhodesian regime until late 1979. In the 1980 elections ZAPU was defeated and was then persecuted by the ruling ZANU Patriotic Front party. In 1987 the two parties merged.

Zara Italian name for ◊Zadar, port on the Adriatic coast of Yugoslavia.

Zaragoza (English *Saragossa*) industrial city (iron,

zebra

steel, chemicals, plastics, canned food, electrical goods) in Aragon, Spain; population (1986) 596,000. The medieval city walls and bridges over the river Ebro survive, and there is a 15th-century university.
history Founded as Salduba in pre-Roman days, it took its present name from Roman conqueror Caesar Augustus; later it was captured by Visigoths and Moors and was taken in 1118 by Alfonso the Warrior, King of Navarre and Aragon, after a nine-month siege. It remained capital of Aragon until the end of the 15th century. From June 1808 to Feb 1809, in the Peninsular War, it resisted a French siege. Maria Augustin, known as the "Maid of Zaragoza," died 1859, became a national hero for her part in the defense; her story is told in Byron's *Childe Harold* 1812–18.

zarzuela Spanish musical theater form combining song, dance, and speech. It originated as an amusement for royalty in the 17th century. It found an early exponent in the playwright Calderón de la Barca. Often satirical, it gained renewed popularity in the 20th century with the works of Frederico Moreno Tórroba (1891–1982).

zazen formal seated meditation in Zen Buddhism. Correct posture and breathing are necessary.

Zealand another name for ◊Sjælland, main island of Denmark, and for ◊Zeeland, SW province of the Netherlands.

zebra black and white striped member of the horse genus *Equus* found in Africa; the stripes serve as camouflage or dazzle and confuse predators. It is about 5 ft/1.5 m high at the shoulder, with a stout body, and a short, thick mane. Zebras live in family groups and herds on mountains and plains, and can run at up to 40 mph/60 kph. Males are usually solitary.

The mountain zebra *E. zebra* was once common in Cape Colony and Natal and still survives in parts of South Africa and Angola. It has long ears and is silvery-white with black or dark brown markings. Grevy's zebra *E. grevyi* is much larger, with finer and clearer markings; it inhabits Ethiopia and Somalia; Burchell's or the common zebra *E. burchelli*, which is intermediate in size, has white ears, a long mane, and full tail; it roams the plains north of the Orange River in South Africa.

zebu any of a species of ◊cattle *Bos indicus* found domesticated in E Asia, India, and Africa. It is usually light-colored, with large horns and a large, fatty hump near the shoulders. It is used for pulling loads, and is held by some Hindus to be sacred. There are about 30 breeds.

Zebus have been crossbred with other species of cattle in hot countries to pass on their qualities of heat tolerance and insect resistance. In the US, they are called Brahman cattle.

Zedekiah last king of Judah 597–586 BC. Placed on the throne by Nebuchadnezzar, he rebelled, was forced to witness his sons' execution, then was blinded and sent to Babylon. The witness to these events was the prophet Jeremiah, who describes them in the Old Testament.

Zeeland province of the SW Netherlands
area 691 sq mi/1,790 sq km
capital Middelburg
cities Vlissingen, Terneuzen, Goes
population (1988) 356,000
products cereals, potatoes
features mostly below sea level, Zeeland is protected by a system of dykes
history Disputed by the counts of Flanders and Holland during the Middle Ages, Zeeland was annexed to Holland in 1323 by Count Willam III.

Zeeman Pieter 1865–1943. Dutch physicist who discovered in 1896 that when light from certain elements, such as sodium or lithium (when heated), is passed through a spectroscope in the presence of a strong magnetic field, the spectrum splits into a number of distinct lines. This is known as the Zeeman effect and won him a share of the 1902 Nobel Prize for Physics.

Zeffirelli Franco 1923– . Italian theater, opera and film director and stage designer, acclaimed for his stylish designs and lavish productions. His films include *La Traviata* 1983, and *Otello* 1986.

From the late 1960s he was known primarily as a film director. His credits include *The Taming of the Shrew* 1967, *Romeo and Juliet* 1968, *Endless Love* 1981, and *Hamlet* 1991.

Zeiss Carl 1816–1888. German optician. He opened his first workshop in Jena in 1846, and in 1866 joined forces with Ernst Abbe (1840–1905) producing cameras, microscopes, and binoculars.

Zelenka Jan Dismas 1679–1745. Bohemian composer who worked at the court of Dresden and became director of church music in 1729. His compositions were rediscovered in the 1970s.

zemstvo Russian provincial or district councils established by Tsar Alexander II in 1864. They were responsible for local administration until the revolution of 1917.

Zen abbreviation of Japanese *zenna*, "quiet mind concentration," a form of ◊Buddhism introduced from India to Japan via China in the 12th century. *Koan* (paradoxical questions), tea-drinking, and sudden enlightenment are elements of Zen practice. Soto Zen was spread by the priest Dogen (1200–1253), who emphasized work, practice, discipline, and philosophical questions to discover one's Buddha-nature in the "realization of self."

Zendavesta the sacred scriptures of ◊Zoroastrianism, today practiced by the Parsees. They comprise the *Avesta* (liturgical books for the priests); the *Gathas* (the discourses and revelations of Zoroaster); and the *Zend* (commentary upon them).

Zenger John Peter 1697–1746. Colonial American printer and newspaper editor, born in Germany. Zenger immigrated to New York 1710 and was apprenticed to a printer. Establishing his own press 1726, Zenger became active in local political affairs. As editor of the *New York Weekly Journal*, he publicized his opposition to New York governor William Cosby. In 1734 the *Journal*'s virulent anti-government stance led to Zenger's arrest for seditious libel. Acquitted by a jury in 1735, he published *A Brief Narrative of the Case and Trial of John Peter Zenger* and remained a spokesman for the principle of freedom of the press.

zenith the uppermost point of the celestial horizon, immediately above the observer; the ◊nadir is below, diametrically opposite. See ◊celestial sphere.

Zenobia queen of Palmyra AD 266–272. She assumed the crown as regent for her sons, after the death of her husband Odaenathus, and in 272 was defeated at Emesa (now Homs) by Aurelian and taken captive to Rome.

Zeno of Citium c. 335–262 BC. Greek founder of the stoic school of philosophy in Athens, about 300 BC.

Zeno of Elea c. 490–430 BC. Greek philosopher who pointed out several paradoxes that raised "modern" problems of space and time. For exam-

Zeppelin *The Hindenburg disaster, May 6, 1937, when all those on board were killed.*

ple, motion is an illusion, since an arrow in flight must occupy a determinate space at each instant, and therefore must be at rest.

zeolite any of the hydrous aluminum silicates, also containing sodium, calcium, barium, strontium, and potassium, chiefly found in igneous rocks and characterized by a ready loss or gain of water. Zeolites are used as "sieves" to separate mixtures because they are capable of selective absorption. They have a high ion-exchange capacity and can be used to make gasoline, benzene, and toluene from low-grade raw materials, such as coal and methanol.

zeppelin see ◊airship.

Zeppelin Ferdinand, Count von 1838–1917. German airship pioneer. On retiring from the army in 1891, he devoted himself to the study of aeronautics, and his first airship was built and tested in 1900. During World War I a number of Zeppelin airships bombed England. They were also used for luxury passenger transport but the construction of hydrogen-filled airships with rigid keels was abandoned after several disasters in the 1920s and 1930s. Zeppelin also helped to pioneer large multiengine bomber planes.

Zermatt tourist center in the Valais canton, Switzerland, at the foot of the Matterhorn; population (1985) 3,700.

Zernicke Frits 1888–1966. Dutch physicist who developed the phase-contrast microscope 1935. Earlier microscopes allowed many specimens to be examined only after they had been transformed by heavy staining and other treatment. The phase-contrast microscope allowed living cells to be directly observed by making use of the difference in refractive indices between specimens and medium. Nobel Prize for Physics 1953.

Zeus in Greek mythology, chief of the gods (Roman Jupiter). He was the son of Cronus, whom he overthrew; his brothers included Hades and Poseidon, his sisters Demeter and Hera. As the supreme god he dispensed good and evil and was the father and ruler of all humankind. His emblems are the thunderbolt and aegis (shield), representing the thundercloud.

He ate his pregnant first wife Metis (goddess of wisdom), fearing their child (Athena) would be greater than himself. His second wife was Hera, but he also fathered children by other women and goddesses. The offspring, either gods and goddesses or godlike humans, included Apollo, Artemis, Castor and Pollux/Polydeuces, Dionysus, Hebe, Hercules, Hermes, Minos, Perseus, and Persephone.

Zhangjiakou formerly Changchiakow historic town and trade center in Hebei province, China, 100 mi/160 km NW of Beijing, on the Great Wall; population (1980) 1,100,000. Zhangjiakou is on the border of Inner Mongolia (its Mongolian name is *Kalgan*, "gate") and on the road and railroad to Ulaanbaatar in Mongolia. It developed under the Manchu dynasty, and was the center of the tea trade from China to Russia.

Zhao Ziyang 1918– . Chinese politician, prime minister from 1980, and secretary of the Chinese Communist Party (CCP) 1987–89. His reforms included self-management and incentives for workers and factories. He lost his secretaryship and other posts after the Tiananmen Square massacre in Beijing June 1989.

Zhao, son of a wealthy landlord from Henan province, joined the Communist Youth League 1932 and worked underground as a CCP official during the liberation war 1937–49. He rose to prominence in the party in Guangdong from 1951. As a supporter of the reforms of Liu Shaoqi, he was dismissed during the 1966–69 Cultural Revolution, paraded through Canton in a dunce's cap, and sent to Inner Mongolia.

He was rehabilitated by Zhou Enlai 1973 and

Zhao Ziyang *An economic expert with a pragmatic outlook, Zhao Ziyang became China's prime minister in 1980.*

Zhou Enlai *Chinese politician and prime minister Zhou Enlai, 1971*

sent to China's largest province, Sichuan, as first party secretary 1975. Here he introduced radical and successful market-oriented rural reforms. Deng Xiaoping had him inducted into the Politburo 1977. After six months as vice premier, Zhao was appointed prime minister 1980 and assumed, in addition, the post of CCP general secretary Jan 1987. His economic reforms were criticized for causing inflation, and his liberal views of the pro-democracy demonstrations that culminated in the student occupation of Tiananmen Square led to his downfall.

Zhdanov former name (1948 to 1989) of ◊Mariupol, port in Ukraine, USSR.

Zhejiang or ***Chekiang*** province of SE China
area 39,295 sq mi/101,800 sq km
capital Hangzhou
features smallest of the Chinese provinces; the base of the Song dynasty 12th–13th centuries; densely populated
products rice, cotton, sugar, jute, corn; timber on the uplands
population (1986) 40,700,000.

Zhengzhou or ***Chengchow*** industrial city (light engineering, cotton textiles, foods) and capital (from 1954) of Henan province, China, on the Huang Ho; population (1986) 1,590,000.

In the 1970s the earliest city found in China, from 1500 BC, was excavated near the walls of Zhengzhou. The Shaolin temple, where the martial art of kung fu originated, is nearby.

Zhitomir capital of Zhitomir region in Ukraine, USSR, W of Kiev; population (1987) 287,000. It is a timber and grain center and has furniture factories. Zhitomir dates from the 13th century.

Zhivkov Todor 1911– . Bulgarian Communist Party (BCP) leader 1954–89, prime minister 1962–71, president 1971–89. His period in office was one of caution and conservatism.

Zhivkov, a printing worker, joined the BCP in 1932 and was active in the resistance 1941–44. After the war, he was elected to the National Assembly and soon promoted into the BCP secretariat and Politburo. As BCP first secretary, Zhivkov became the dominant political figure in Bulgaria after the death of Vulko Chervenkov in 1956. Zhivkov was elected to the new post of state president in 1971 and lasted until the Eastern bloc upheavals of 1989.

Zhonghua Renmin Gonghe Guo Chinese for People's Republic of ◊China.

Zhou Enlai or ***Chou En-lai*** 1898–1976. Chinese politician. Zhou, a member of the Chinese Communist Party (CCP) from the 1920s, was prime minister 1949–76 and foreign minister 1949–58. He was a moderate Maoist and weathered the Cultural Revolution. He played a key role in foreign affairs.

Born into a declining mandarin gentry family near Shanghai, Zhou studied in Japan and Paris, where he became a founding member of the overseas branch of the CCP. He adhered to the Moscow line of urban-based revolution in China, organizing communist cells in Shanghai and an abortive uprising in Nanchang 1927. In 1935 Zhou supported the election of Mao Zedong as CCP leader and remained a loyal ally during the next 40 years. He served as liaison officer 1937–46 between the CCP and Chiang Kai-shek's nationalist Guomindang government. In 1949 he became prime minister, an office he held until his death Jan 1976.

Zhou, a moderator between the opposing camps of Liu Shaoqi and Mao Zedong, restored orderly progress after the Great Leap Forward (1958–60) and the Cultural Revolution (1966–69), and was the architect of the Four Modernizations program in 1975. Abroad, Zhou sought to foster Third World unity at the Bandung Conference 1955, averted an outright border confrontation with the USSR by negotiation with Prime Minister Kosygin 1969, and was the principal advocate of détente with the US during the early 1970s.

Zhubov scale scale for measuring ice coverage, used in the USSR. The unit is the ball; one ball is 10% coverage, two balls 20%, and so on.

Zhu De or ***Chu Teh*** 1886–1976. Chinese Red Army leader from 1931. He devised the tactic of mobile guerrilla warfare and organized the ◊Long March to Shaanxi 1934–36. He was made a marshal 1955.

The son of a wealthy Sichuan landlord, Zhu served in the Chinese Imperial Army before supporting Sun Yat-sen in the 1911 revolution. He studied communism in Germany and Paris 1922–25 and joined the Chinese Communist Party (CCP) on his return, becoming commander in chief of the Red Army. Working closely with Mao Zedong, Zhu organized the Red Army's Jiangxi breakout 1931 and led the 18th Route Army during the liberation war 1937–49. He served as head of state (chair of the Standing Committee of the National People's Congress) 1975–76.

Zhukov Georgi Konstantinovich 1896–1974. Marshal of the USSR in World War II and minister of defense 1955–57. As chief of staff from 1941, he defended Moscow 1941, counterattacked at Stalingrad in 1942, organized the relief of Leningrad 1943, and led the offensive from the Ukraine March 1944 which ended in the fall of Berlin. He subsequently commanded the Soviet occupation forces in Germany.

Zhukov joined the Bolsheviks and the Red Army 1918 and led a cavalry regiment in the Civil War 1918–20. His army defeated the Japanese forces in Mongolia 1939. At the end of World War II, he headed the Allied delegation that received the German surrender. Under the Khruschev regime he was denounced 1957 for obstructing party work and encouraging a Zhukov cult, but was restored 1965.

Zia ul-Haq *Pakistani president General Mohammad Zia ul-Haq.*

Zia ul-Haq Mohammad 1924–1988. Pakistani general, in power from 1977 until his death, probably an assassination, in an aircraft explosion. He became army chief of staff 1976, led the military coup against Zulfiqar Ali ◊Bhutto 1977, and became president 1978. Zia introduced a fundamentalist Islamic regime and restricted political activity.

Zia was a career soldier from a middle-class Punjabi Muslim family. As army chief of staff, his opposition to the Soviet invasion of Afghanistan 1979 drew support from the US, but his refusal to commute the death sentence imposed on Zulfiqar Ali Bhutto was widely condemned. He lifted martial law 1985. The US Central Intelligence Agency is widely rumored to have engineered his death.

Ziegler Karl 1898–1973. German organic chemist. In 1963 he shared a Nobel Prize with Giulio Natta of Italy for his work on the chemistry and technology of large polymers. He combined simple molecules of the gas ethylene (now called ethene) into the long-chain plastic polyethylene (polythene).

ziggurat in ancient Babylonia and Assyria, a step pyramid of sun-baked brick faced with glazed bricks or tiles on which stood a shrine. The Tower of Babel as described in the Bible may have been a ziggurat.

Zimbabwe extensive stone architectural ruins near Victoria in Mashonaland, Zimbabwe. The structure was probably the work of a highly advanced Bantu-speaking people from Zaïre or Ethiopia, smelters of iron, who were in the area before AD 300. The new state of Zimbabwe took its name from these ruins.

Zimbabwe landlocked country in central Africa, with Mozambique to the E, Zambia to the N, and South Africa to the S.

government Zimbabwe is an independent republic within the ◊Commonwealth. Its constitution dates from 1980 and provides for a president who is formal head of state, a two-chamber parliament consisting of the Senate and the House of Assembly, and a prime minister and cabinet drawn from and responsible to Parliament.

In recognition of the rights of the white minority, there were two sets of constituencies for parlimentary elections, a "common roll" that included all voters, and a "white roll" for white voters. The white roll was abolished in 1987. The Senate has 40 members, 24 indirectly elected through an electoral college, 5 elected by Mashona chiefs, 5 chiefs sitting "ex officio," and 6 appointed by the president. The House of Assembly has 100 members elected by universal suffrage, through a party list system of proportional representation. Both chambers serve a five-year term and are subject to dissolution within that period. The president is elected by Parliament for a six-year term and in turn appoints the prime minister and cabinet on the basis of parliamentary support.

The main political party is the Zimbabwe African National Union–Patriotic Front (ZANU–PF), which merged with the Patriotic Front (PF, formerly the Zimbabwe African People's Union, ZAPU) in Dec 1989.

history For early history, see ◊Africa. There was a Bantu-speaking civilization in the area before AD 300. By 1200 ◊Mashonaland, now E Zimbabwe, was an major settlement of the Shona people, who had moved in from the N and erected stone buildings. The name Zimbabwe means "stone house" in Bantu. In the 15th century the Shona empire, under Mutota, expanded across Zimbabwe before it fell to the Rozwi, who ruled until the 19th century. Portuguese explorers reached the area in the early 16th century. In 1837 the Matabele, a Bantu people, in retreat after unsuccessful battles with the ◊Boers, settled in W Zimbabwe. Mashonaland and ◊Matabeleland together with what is now Zambia, were granted to the British South Africa Company 1889, and the whole was named ◊Rhodesia 1895 in honor of Cecil ◊Rhodes. King ◊Lobengula of Matabeleland accepted British protection 1888 but rebelled 1893; he was defeated, but 1896 after the ◊Jameson Raid the Matabele once more unsuccessfully tried to regain their independence. The portion of the area south of the Zambezi River, then known as Southern Rhodesia, became self-governing 1923 and a member of the Federation of Rhodesia and Nyasaland 1953.

African nationalists were campaigning for full democracy, and the African National Congress (ANC), which had been present since 1934, was reconvened 1957 under the leadership of Joshua Nkomo. It was banned 1959, and Nkomo went into exile to become leader of the National Democratic Party (NDP), which had been formed by some ANC members. When the NDP was banned 1961, Nkomo created the Zimbabwe African People's Union (ZAPU); this was banned 1962. In 1963 a splinter group developed from ZAPU, the Zimbabwe African National Union (ZANU), led by the Rev Ndabaningi Sithole, with Robert ◊Mugabe as its secretary general.

After the dissolution of the Federation of Rhodesia and Nyasaland 1963 the leader of the Rhodesian Front party (RF), Winston Field, became the first prime minister of Rhodesia. The RF was a group of white politicians committed to maintaining racial segregation. In Apr 1964 Field resigned and was replaced by Ian ◊Smith, who rejected terms for independence proposed by Britain that required clear progress toward majority rule. Four months later ZANU was banned, and Nkomo and Mugabe imprisoned. In Nov 1965, after further British attempts to negotiate a formula for independence, Smith annulled the 1961 constitution and unilaterally announced Rhodesia's independence. Britain broke off diplomatic and trading links and the United Nations initiated economic sanctions, but these were bypassed by many multinational companies. The British prime minister, Harold Wilson, had abortive talks with Smith 1966 and 1968.

In 1969 Rhodesia declared itself a republic and adopted a new constitution, with white majority representation in a two-chamber legislature. Armed South African police at times supported the Smith regime against ZAPU and ZANU guerrillas. In 1972 another draft agreement for independence was rejected by the British government as not acceptable to the Rhodesian people "as a whole." A conference in Geneva 1975 was attended by deputations from the British government, the Smith regime, and the African nationalists, represented by Bishop Abel ◊Muzorewa, president of the African National Council, which had been formed 1971 to oppose the earlier independence arrangements, and Robert Mugabe and Joshua Nkomo, who had been released from detention and had jointly formed the Patriotic Front.

At the beginning of 1979 Smith produced a new "majority rule" constitution, which contained an inbuilt protection for the white minority but which he had managed to get Muzorewa to accept. In June 1979 Bishop Muzorewa was pronounced prime minister of what was to be called Zimbabwe Rhodesia. The new constitution was denounced by Mugabe and Nkomo as another attempt by Smith to perpetuate the white domination, and they continued to lead the Zimbabwe African National Liberation Army from bases in neighboring Mozambique.

In Aug 1979 the new British prime minister, Margaret ◊Thatcher, under the influence of her foreign secretary, Lord Carrington, and President Kaunda of Zambia, agreed to the holding of a constitutional conference in London at which all shades of political opinion in Rhodesia would be represented. The conference, in Sept 1979, resulted in what became known as the ◊Lancaster House Agreement and paved the way for full independence. A member of the British cabinet, Lord

Zimbabwe
Republic of

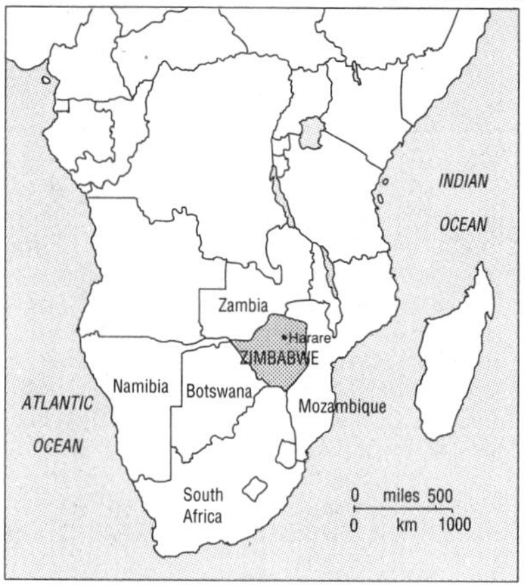
INDIAN
OCEAN
Zambia
•Harare
ZIMBABWE
Namibia
Botswana
Mozambique
ATLANTIC
OCEAN
South
Africa
0 miles 500
0 km 1000

area 150,695 sq mi/390,300 sq km
capital Harare
cities Bulawayo, Gweru, Kwekwe, Mutare, Hwange
physical high plateau with central high veld and mountains in E; rivers Zambezi, Limpopo
features Hwange National Park, part of Kalahari Desert; ruins of Great Zimbabwe
head of state and government Robert Mugabe from 1987
political system effectively one-party Socialist republic
political parties Zimbabwe African National Union–Patriotic Front (ZANU–PF), African Socialist.
exports tobacco, asbestos, cotton, coffee, gold, silver, copper
currency Zimbabwe dollar
population (1990 est) 10,205,000 (Shona 80%, Ndbele 19%; about 100,000 whites); growth rate 3.5% p.a.
life expectancy men 59, women 63 (1989)
language English (official); Shona, Sindebele
religion Christian; Muslim, Hindu, animist
literacy men 81%/women 67% (1985 est)
GNP $5.5 bn (1988); $275 per head (1986)

chronology
1880s–1923 As Southern Rhodesia, under administration of British South Africa Company.
1923 Became a self-governing British colony.
1961 Zimbabwe African People's Union (ZAPU) formed, with Joshua Nkomo as leader.
1962 ZAPU declared illegal.
1963 Zimbabawe African National Union (ZANU) formed, with Robert Mugabe as secretary general.
1964 Ian Smith became prime minister. Nkomo and Mugabe imprisoned.
1965 ZANU banned. Smith declared unilateral independence.
1966–68 Abortive talks between Smith and UK prime minister Harold Wilson.
1974 Nkomo and Mugabe released.
1975 Geneva conference set date for constitutional independence.
1979 Smith produced new constitution and established a government with Bishop Abel Muzorewa as prime minister. New government denounced by Nkomo and Mugabe. Conference in London agreed independence arrangements (Lancaster House Agreement).
1980 Independence achieved from Britain, with Robert Mugabe as prime minister.
1981 Rift between Mugabe and Nkomo.
1982 Nkomo dismissed from the cabinet, leaving the country temporarily.
1984 ZANU–People's Front (PF) Party Congress agreed to create a one-party state in future.
1985 Relations between Mugabe and Nkomo improved. Troops sent to Matabeleland to suppress rumored insurrection; 5,000 civilians killed.
1986 Joint ZANU–PF rally held amid plans for merger.
1987 White-roll seats in the assembly were abolished. President Banana retired; Mugabe combined posts of head of state and prime minister with the title executive president.
1988 Nkomo returned to the cabinet and appointed vice-president.
1989 Opposition party, the Zimbabwe Unity Movement, formed by Edgar Tekere; draft constitution renouncing Marxism-Leninism as state ideology created; ruling party merged with opposition groups to form one-party state.
1990 Opposition to creation of one-party state.
1991 State of emergency declared over.

Soames, was sent to Rhodesia as governor-general to arrange a timetable for independence. Economic and trade sanctions were lifted. A small Commonwealth Monitoring Force supervised the disarming of the thousands of guerrilla fighters who brought their weapons and ammunition from all parts of the country.

A new constitution was adopted, and elections were held, under independent supervision, in Feb 1980. They resulted in a decisive win for Robert Mugabe's ZANU–PF party. The new state of Zimbabwe became fully independent in April 1980, with the Rev Canaan Banana as president and Robert Mugabe as prime minister. During the next few years a rift developed between Mugabe and Nkomo and between ZANU–PF and ZAPU supporters. Nkomo was accused of trying to undermine Mugabe's administration and was dismissed from the cabinet. Fearing for his safety, he spent some months in the UK. ZAPU was opposed to the 1984 proposal by ZANU–PF for the eventual creation of a one-party Socialist state.

Mugabe's party increased its majority in the 1985 elections with 63 seats against 15 and early in 1986 he announced that the separate seats for the whites in the assembly would be abolished within a year. Relations between the two parties and the two leaders eventually improved and by 1986 discussions of a merger were under way. In Dec 1989 a draft constitution was created that renounced Marxism-Leninism as the state ideology and created a one-party state, fusing the governing party and opposition groups. A new opposition group headed by former Mugabe ally Edgar Tekere challenged the AZNU–PG but did not do well in the Jan 1990 voting. Subsequently, Mugabe announced that he would work to achieve a one-party state gradually, and in 1991 the country ended the state emergency that had existed for 25 years.

zinc hard, brittle, bluish-white, metallic element, symbol Zn, atomic number 30, atomic weight 65.37. The principal ore is spalerite or zinc blende (zinc sulfide, ZnS). Zinc is little affected by air or moisture at ordinary temperatures; its chief uses are in alloys such as brass and in coating metals (for example galvanized iron). Its compounds include zinc oxide, used in ointments (as an astringent) and cosmetics, paints, glass, and printing ink.

Zinc has been used as a component of brass since the Bronze Age, but it was not recognized as a separate metal until 1746, when it was described by German chemist Andreas Sigismund Marggraf (1709–1782). The name derives from the Germanic *zint*, "point," the shape of the crystals on smelting.

zinnia

zinc ore mineral from which zinc is extracted, principally sphalerite, (Zn,Fe)S, but also zincite, ZnO_2, and smithsonite, Zn,CO_3, all of which occur in mineralized veins. Ores of lead and zinc often occur together, and are common worldwide; Canada, the US, and Australia are major producers.

Zinneman Fred(erick) 1907– . Austrian film director who has lived in the US from 1921. His films include *High Noon* 1952, *The Nun's Story* 1959, *The Day of the Jackal* 1973, and *Five Days One Summer* 1982.

zinnia any annual plant of the genus *Zinnia*, family Compositae, native to Mexico and South America, notably the cultivated hybrids of *Z. elegans*, with brightly colored, daisylike flowers.

Zinoviev Alexander 1922– . Soviet philosopher whose satire on the USSR, *The Yawning Heights* 1976, led to his exile 1978. *The Reality of Communism* 1984 outlined the argument that communism is the natural consequence of masses of people living under deprived conditions, and thus bound to expand.

Zinoviev Grigory 1883–1936. Russian politician. A prominent Bolshevik, he returned to Russia in 1917 with Lenin and played a leading part in the Revolution. As head of the Communist ◊International 1919, his name was attached to a forgery, the Zinoviev letter, inciting Britain's communists to rise, which helped to topple the Labor government in 1924. As one of the "Old Bolsheviks," he was seen by Stalin as a threat. He was accused of complicity in the murder of the Bolshevik leader Sergei Kirov 1934, and shot.

Zion Jebusite (Amorites of Canaan) stronghold in Jerusalem captured by King David, and the hill on which he built the Temple, symbol of Jerusalem and of Jewish national life.

Zionism a political movement advocating the reestablishment of a Jewish homeland in Palestine, the "promised land" of the Bible, with its capital Jerusalem, the "city of Zion."

1896 As a response to European ◊anti-Semitism, Theodor Herzl published his *Jewish State*, outlining a scheme for setting up an autonomous Jewish commonwealth under Ottoman Turkish suzerainty.

1897 The World Zionist Congress was established in Basel, Switzerland, with Herzl as its first president. *Hatikva* (The Hope) was adopted as the Zionist anthem, which was the unofficial anthem of Palestine until 1948 when it was sung at the proclamation of the State of Israel on May 14.

1917 The ◊Balfour Declaration was secured from Britain by Chaim Weizmann. It promised the Jews a homeland in Palestine.

1940–48 Jewish settlement in the British mandate of Palestine led to armed conflict between militant Zionists (see ◊Irgun, ◊Stern Gang) and both Palestinian Arabs and the British.

1947 In Nov the United Nations (UN) divided Palestine into Jewish and Arab states, with Jerusalem as an international city.

1948 The Jews in Palestine proclaimed the State of Israel on May 14, but the Arab states rejected both the partition of Palestine and the existence of Israel. The armies of Iraq, Syria, Lebanon, Trans-Jordan, Saudi Arabia, Yemen, and Egypt crossed Israel's borders and attacked en masse but were defeated by the Israeli army (*Haganah*).

1948–73 In addition to constant border sniping and clashes, one or more Arab nations have attacked Israel in the on-going ◊Arab-Israeli wars of 1956, 1967, and 1973.

1975 The General Assembly of the UN condemned Zionism as "a form of racism and racial discrimination"; among those voting against the resolution were the US and the members of the European Community.

1991 Attacked during ◊Gulf War by Iraqi missiles and criticized for its adamant attitude against Palestinian aspirations, Israel meets with Arab nations for the first time in a historic Middle East peace conference held in Spain. UN General Assembly repeals its 1975 resolution condemning Zionism.

zipper fastening device used in clothing, invented in the US by Whitcomb Judson in 1891, originally for doing up shoes. It has two sets of interlocking teeth, meshed by means of a slide that moves up and down.

zircon zirconium silicate, $ZrSiO_4$, a mineral that occurs in small quantities in a wide range of igneous, sedimentary, and metamorphic rocks. It is very durable and is resistant to erosion and weathering. It is usually colored brown, but can be other colors, and when transparent may be used as a gemstone.

zirconium lustrous, grayish-white, strong, ductile, metallic element, symbol Zr, atomic number 40, atomic weight 91.22. It occurs in nature as the mineral zircon (zirconium silicate), from which it is obtained commercially. It is used in some ceramics, alloys for wire and filaments, steel manufacture, and nuclear reactors, where its low neutron absorption is advantageous.

It was isolated in 1824 by Swedish chemist Jöns Berzelius. The name was proposed by Humphry Davy in 1808, based on the Germanic *zirkon*, from the Persian *zargun*, "golden."

zither a member of a family of musical instruments that have strings attached across a flat soundboard and are plucked, bowed, or struck with a beater to play a note. Examples are the ◊dulcimer, the Japanese ◊koto, and a 45-stringed folk instrument from Austria and Germany.

Zi Xi or ***Tz'u-hsi*** 1836–1908. Dowager empress of China. She was presented as a concubine to the emperor Hsien-feng. On his death 1861 she became regent for her son T'ung Chih and, when he died in 1875, for her nephew Guang Xu (1871–1908).

Zlatoust industrial city (metallurgy) in Chelyabinsk region, USSR, in the S Urals; population (1987) 206,000. It was founded 1754 as an iron-and copper-working settlement, destroyed 1774 by a peasant uprising, but developed as an armaments center from the time of Napoleon's invasion of Russia.

zodiac the zone of the heavens containing the paths of the Sun, Moon, and planets. When this was devised by the ancient Greeks, only five planets were known, making the zodiac about 16° wide. The stars in it are grouped into 12 signs (constellations), each 30° in extent: Aries, Taurus, Gemini, Cancer, Leo, Virgo, Libra, Scorpius, Sagittarius, Capricornus, Aquarius, and Pisces. Because of the ◊precession of the equinoxes, the current constellations do not cover the same areas of sky as the zodiacal signs of the same name.

zodiacal light cone-shaped light sometimes seen extending from the Sun along the ◊ecliptic, visible after sunset or before sunrise. It is due to thinly spread dust particles in the central plane of the Solar System. It is very faint and requires a dark, clear sky to be seen.

Zoë c. 978–1050. Byzantine empress who ruled from 1028 until 1050. She gained the title by marriage to the heir apparent Romanus III Argyrus, but was reputed to have poisoned him (1034) in order to marry her lover Michael. He died 1041 and Zoë and her sister Theodora were proclaimed joint empresses. Rivalry led to Zoë marrying Constantine IX Monomachus with whom she reigned until her death.

zoetrope an optical toy with a series of pictures on the inner surface of a cylinder. When the pictures are rotated and viewed through a slit, it gives the impression of continuous motion.

Zola *French novelist and reformer Emile Zola.*

zodiac *A 15th-century rendering of the 12 signs of the zodiac, also now popularly known as astrological signs.*

Zog Ahmed Beg Zogu 1895–1961. King of Albania 1928–39. He became prime minister of Albania in 1922, president of the republic in 1925, and proclaimed himself king in 1928. He was driven out by the Italians in 1939 and settled in England.

Zola Émile Edouard Charles Antoine 1840–1902. French novelist and social reformer. With *La Fortune des Rougon/The Fortune of the Rougons* 1867 he began a series of some 20 naturalistic novels, portraying the fortunes of a French family under the Second Empire. They include *Le Ventre de Paris/The Underbelly of Paris* 1873, *Nana* 1880, and *La Débâcle/The Debacle* 1892. In 1898 he published *J'accuse/I Accuse*, a pamphlet indicting the persecutors of ◊Dreyfus, for which he was prosecuted for libel but later pardoned.

Born in Paris, Zola was a journalist and clerk until his *Contes à Ninon/Stories for Ninon* 1864 enabled him to devote himself to literature. Some of the titles in *La Fortune des Rougon/The Fortune of the Rougons* series are *La Faute de l'Abbé Mouret/The Simple Priest* 1875, *L'Assommoir/Drunkard* 1878, *Germinal* 1885 and *La Terre/Earth* 1888. Among later novels are the trilogy *Trois Villes/Three Cities* 1894–98, and *Fécondité/Fecundity* 1899.

Zollverein 19th-century German customs union, begun under Prussian auspices in 1828; the union included most German-speaking states except Austria by 1834.

Although designed to remove tariff barriers and facilitate trade within the German confederation, the Zollverein also had a political effect in isolating Austria. The Austrians were committed to trade tariffs to protect their agriculture and industry; thus their inability to join the Zollverein served to increase Prussian power in the confederation.

Zomba former capital of Malawi, 20 mi/32 km W of Lake Shirwa; population (1985) 53,000. It was replaced by Lilongwe as capital 1975 but remains the university town.

zombie a corpse believed to be reanimated by a spirit and enslaved. The idea, widespread in Haiti, possibly arose from voodoo priests using the nerve poison tetrodotoxin (from the puffer fish) to produce a semblance of death from which the victim afterwards physically recovers. Those eating incorrectly prepared puffer fish in Japan have been similarly affected.

zone standard time or ***standard time*** the time in any of the 24 time zones, each an hour apart, into which the Earth is divided. The respective times depend on their distances, east or west of Greenwich, England. In North America the eight zones (Atlantic, Eastern, Central, Mountain, Pacific, Alaska, Hawaii-Aleutian, and Samoa) use the mean solar times of meridians 15° apart, starting with 60° longitude. (See also ◊time.)

zone system in photography, a system of exposure

estimation invented by Ansel ◊Adams that groups infinite tonal gradations into ten zones, zone 0 being black and zone 10 white. An ◊f-stop change in exposure is required from zone to zone.

zoo abbreviation of zoological gardens, a place where animals are kept in captivity. Originally created purely for visitor entertainment and education, zoos have become major centers for the breeding of endangered species of animals.

Notable zoos exist in New York, San Diego, Toronto, Chicago, London, Paris, Berlin, Moscow, and Beijing (Peking).

zoology the branch of biology concerned with the study of animals. It includes description of present-day animals, the study of evolution of animal forms, anatomy, physiology, embryology, behavior, and geographical distribution.

zoom lens a photographic lens that, by variation of focal length, allows speedy transition from long shots to close-ups.

zoonosis any infectious disease that can be transmitted to humans by other vertebrate animals. Probably the most feared example is ◊rabies. The transmitted microorganism sometimes causes disease only in the human host, leaving the animal host unaffected.

Zorach v Clausen a US Supreme Court decision 1952 dealing with the inclusion of religious studies in public school education. A New York City program that exempted some public school students from the required curriculum to pursue religious studies elsewhere was challenged as an unconstitutional marriage of church and state. The Court upheld the "release program," ruling that the division between church and state was not meant to be absolute.

Zoroaster or ***Zarathustra*** c. 628–c. 551 BC. Persian prophet and religious teacher, founder of Zoroastrianism.

Zoroastrianism pre-Islamic Persian religion founded by Zoroaster, and still practiced by the ◊Parsees in India. The ◊*Zendavesta* are the sacred scriptures of the faith. The theology is dualistic, Ahura Mazda or Ormuzd (the good God) being in conflict with Ahriman (the evil God), but the former is assured of eventual victory.

The return of Zoroaster will presage the resurrection of the dead and the creation of a paradise on Earth by Ahura Mazda. The free choice of good or evil renders believers responsible for their fate after death in heaven or hell. Procreation and life are valued, but death defiles—hence the custom of exposing corpses to be devoured by vultures. Worship is at altars on which the sacred fire burns.

Zorrilla y Moral José 1817–1893. Spanish poet and playwright. Born in Valladolid, he based his plays chiefly on national legends, such as the *Don Juan Tenorio* 1844.

Zouave member of a corps of French infantry soldiers, first raised in 1831 from the Zouaoua tribe in Algeria. The term came to be used for soldiers in other cores modeled on the French Zouaves.

Z particle type of ◊elementary particle.

Zsigmondy Richard 1865–1929. Austrian chemist who devised and built an ultramicroscope in 1903. The microscope's illumination was placed at right angles to the axis. (In a conventional microscope the light source is placed parallel to the instrument's axis.) Zsigmondy's arrangement made it possible to observe gold particles with a diameter of 10-millionth of a millimeter. Nobel Prize for Chemistry 1925.

zucchini see ◊marrow.

Zuider Zee former sea inlet in Holland, cut off from the North Sea by the closing of a dyke in 1932, much of which has been reclaimed as land. The remaining lake is called the ◊IJsselmeer.

Zulu member of a group of S African peoples mainly from Natal, South Africa. The present homeland, Kwazulu, represents the nucleus of the once extensive and militaristic Zulu kingdom. The Zulu language, closely related to Xhosa, belongs to the Bantu branch of the Niger-Congo family.

Zululand region in Natal, South Africa, largely corresponding to the Black National State KwaZulu. It was formerly a province, annexed to Natal 1897.

Zurbarán Francisco de 1598–1664. Spanish painter, based in Seville. He painted religious subjects in a powerful, austere style, often focusing on a single figure in prayer.

Zurbarán used deep contrasts of light and shade to create an intense spirituality in his works and received many commissions from religious orders in Spain and South America. During the 1640s the softer, sweeter style of Murillo displaced Zurbarán's art in public favor in Seville, and in 1658 he moved to Madrid.

Zürich financial center and industrial city (machinery, electrical goods, textiles) on Lake Zürich; capital of Zürich canton and the largest city in Switzerland; population (1987) 840,000.

The university was refounded 1833.

Zweig Arnold 1887–1968. German novelist, playwright, and poet. He is remembered for his realistic novel of a Russian peasant in the German army *Der Streit um den Sergeanten Grischa/The Case of Sergeant Grischa* 1927.

Zweig Stefan 1881–1942. Austrian writer, author of plays, poems, and many biographies of writers (Balzac, Dickens) and historical figures (Marie Antoinette, Mary Stuart). He and his wife, exiles from the Nazis from 1934, despaired at what they saw as the end of civilization and culture and committed suicide in Brazil.

Zwingli *Swiss religious reformer Ulrich Zwingli, whose insistence on the authority of the Bible was later incorporated into Calvinist doctrine.*

Zwickau coal-mining and industrial town (vehicles, textiles) SW of Chemnitz in the state of Saxony, Federal Republic of Germany, on the river Mulde; population (1986) 121,000. It is the birthplace of the composer Robert Schumann.

Zwingli Ulrich 1484–1531. Swiss Protestant, born in St Gallen. He was ordained a Roman Catholic priest 1506, but by 1519 was a Reformer and led the Reformation in Switzerland with his insistence on the sole authority of the Scriptures. He was killed in a skirmish at Kappel during a war against the cantons that had not accepted the Reformation.

Zwolle capital of Overijssel province, the Netherlands; a market town with brewing, distilling, butter making, and other industries; population (1988) 91,000.

Zworykin Vladimir Kosma 1889–1982. Russian-born US electronics engineer, in the US from 1919. He invented a television camera tube and the ◊electron microscope.

zydeco style of dance music originating in Louisiana, similar to ◊Cajun but more heavily influenced by blues and West Indian music.

Zydeco is fast and bouncy, using instruments like accordions, saxophones, and washboards. It was widely popularized by the singer and accordion player Clifton Chenier (1925–1987).

zygote an ◊ovum (egg) after ◊fertilization but before it undergoes cleavage to begin embryonic development.